LANGENSCHEIDT'S STANDARD GERMAN DICTIONARY

English-German
German-English

by

PROF. E. KLATT, DR. D. ROY,
G. KLATT and H. MESSINGER

Enlarged and updated edition

LANGENSCHEIDT

NEW YORK · BERLIN · MUNICH · VIENNA · ZURICH

First Part

English-German

by

PROF. EDMUND KLATT

and

DR. DIETRICH ROY

Contents

———

Copyright 1884, 1911, 1929, 1951, © 1956, 1969, 1970, 1983

by Langenscheidt KG, Berlin and Munich

Printed in Germany

Preface

For a century now Langenscheidt's Taschenwörterbücher have been an indispensable tool of the language student in Germany. The English-German Taschenwörterbuch has been completely revised and reset six times.

The present enlarged and updated edition retains the long-established merits of the Taschenwörterbuch, while at the same time offering the very latest vocabulary of the eighties. Thousands of neologisms from all fields have been included in the dictionary, making an enlarged edition necessary.

The following brief excursion into a few of these areas gives some indication of the variety and scope of vocabulary covered by the many additions:

Pollution: *acid rain* (saurer Regen), *anti-pollution device* (Abgasentgiftungsanlage), *ecocidal* (umweltzerstörend), *ecocide* (Umweltzerstörung), *ecocrisis* (Umweltkrise)

Politics: *shuttle diplomacy* (Pendeldiplomatie), *urban guerilla* (Stadtguerilla), *nuke* (Atom-, Kernwaffe)

Fashion: *the beautiful people* (Schickeria), *drain-pipe trousers* (Röhrenhosen)

Technology: *digital telephone* (Tastentelefon), *light emitting diode* (Leuchtdiode)

Television: *chat show* (Talk-Show), *phone-in* (Sendung mit Zuschauer- od. Zuhörerbeteiligung)

Work: *time credit* (Zeitguthaben bei gleitender Arbeitszeit), *time debit* (Fehlzeit bei gleitender Arbeitszeit), *bleeper* (Piepser-, Funkrufempfänger), *mom-and-pop store* (Tante-Emma-Laden)

Traffic: *acceleration lane* (Beschleunigungsspur), *metermaid* (Politesse)

Music: *audiophile* (Hi-Fi-Fan), *deejay* (Diskjockey)

Similarly, careful consideration has been given to more general vocabulary such as *computer dating*, *character assassination*, *non-stick*, not forgetting slang and colloquialisms (cf. *aggro*, *dishy*). Among the very recent developments covered in detail in this dictionary are the revised film certificates (cf. p. 672).

The new Taschenwörterbuch has, needless to say, pre-served the time-honoured principles which secured its predecessor's reputation as a valuable source of information. The pronunciation of the headwords, given in the International Phonetic Alphabet, and the marking of word divisions make for easier use. American English continues to be well represented. Translations and additional explanations are consistently presented in systematic, readable and economical form; the wealth of information provided in the articles renders this Taschenwörterbuch a highly useful English-German reference work.

Among the nine appendices dealing with a variety of subjects there is an extensive new appendix on punctuation and capitalisation which deserves special mention as a thoroughly reliable and helpful guide on this particular aspect of the English language.

We trust that the English Taschenwörterbuch in this new enlarged edition will appeal to old and new users alike.

LANGENSCHEIDT

Vorwort

Seit 100 Jahren gehören die Taschenwörterbücher von Langenscheidt zum Handwerkszeug des Sprachenlernenden in Deutschland. Sechsmal wurde das englisch-deutsche Taschenwörterbuch vollständig neu bearbeitet, neu gesetzt und wesentlich erweitert.

Die vorliegende erweiterte Neuausgabe behält die millionenfach bewährte Grundstruktur des Wörterbuches bei – sie bietet aber jetzt dem Benutzer gleichzeitig den modernen Wortschatz der achtziger Jahre. Die aufgenommenen Neuwörter – es sind Tausende aus allen Lebensbereichen – machten wiederum eine Erweiterung dieses Standardwörterbuches notwendig.

Der folgende kleine Streifzug durch einige Fachgebiete gibt eine Vorstellung von der Vielgestaltigkeit dieses neuen Wortschatzes:

Umweltverschmutzung: *acid rain* (saurer Regen), *anti-pollution device* (Abgasentgiftungsanlage), *ecocidal* (umweltzerstörend), *ecocide* (Umweltzerstörung), *ecocrisis* (Umweltkrise)

Politik: *shuttle diplomacy* (Pendeldiplomatie), *urban guerilla* (Stadtguerilla), *nuke* (Atom-, Kernwaffe)

Mode: *the beautiful people* (Schickeria), *drain-pipe trousers* (Röhrenhosen)

Technik: *digital telephone* (Tastentelefon), *light emitting diode* (Leuchtdiode)

Fernsehen: *chat show* (Talk-Show), *phone-in* (Sendung mit Zuschauer- od. Zuhörerbeteiligung)

Arbeitswelt: *time credit* (Zeitguthaben bei gleitender Arbeitszeit), *time debit* (Fehlzeit bei gleitender Arbeitszeit), *bleeper* (Piepser, Funkrufempfänger), *mom-and-pop store* (Tante-Emma-Laden)

Straßenverkehr: *acceleration lane* (Beschleunigungsspur), *metermaid* (Politesse)

Musik: *audiophile* (Hi-Fi-Fan), *deejay* (Diskjockey)

Andere Beispiele mögen die Spannweite der im Bereich der Allgemeinsprache durchgeführten Neuwörter-Arbeit für dieses Wörterbuch zeigen: *computer dating, character assassination, non-stick.* Auch der Bereich des Slang und der Umgangssprache wurde bei den Neuaufnahmen nicht vernachlässigt (vgl. *aggro, dishy*). Neue Entwicklungen wie z. B. die veränderte Kennzeichnung der jugendfreien Filme wurden ausführlich dargestellt (vgl. S. 672).

Selbstverständlich wurden in der vorliegenden Neuausgabe die bewährten Grundsätze beibehalten, denen das englische Taschenwörterbuch seinen Ruf und seinen Nachschlagewert verdankt.

Die Angabe der Aussprache in Internationaler Lautschrift und die Markierung der Silbentrennungsmöglichkeiten erleichtern die Verwendung der englischen Stichwörter. Das amerikanische Englisch ist im Wörterverzeichnis nach wie vor stark vertreten. Alle Übersetzungen und Erläuterungen sind auf engstem Raum übersichtlich dargestellt; ihre Vielzahl macht das vorliegende Taschenwörterbuch zu einem englisch-deutschen Kompendium von hohem Informationswert.

Von den neun Anhängen mit verschiedenster Thematik sei vor allem der umfangreiche neue Anhang „Zeichensetzung und Großschreibung" erwähnt, der den Benutzer auf diesem Gebiet kaum jemals im Stich lassen dürfte.

Wir hoffen, daß das englische Tachenwörterbuch in seiner erweiterten Fassung noch zusätzliche Freunde gewinnen wird.

LANGENSCHEIDT

Guide to the Use of the Dictionary
Hinweise für den Benutzer

1. English Headwords. 1.1 The alphabetical order of the headwords has been observed throughout, including the irregular forms.

1.2 Centred dots or stress marks within a headword indicate syllabification,

e.g. **cul·ti·vat·ed** ... **cul·ti'va·tion**
1.3 In hyphenated compounds a hyphen coinciding with the end of a line is repeated at the beginning of the next.

1.4 The tilde (~, ~) is used to avoid repeating the headword. **1.41** If a headword constitutes the initial element of compounds which immediately follow, it is replaced by a boldfaced tilde (~),

e.g. **aft·er** ... **'~·birth** (= afterbirth) ...
1.42 The simple tilde (~) replaces the bold-faced word immediately preceding (which itself may have been formed with the aid of a tilde),

e.g. **dis·tance** ... *at a* ~ = at a distance
day ... **'~·light** ... *~-saving time* = daylight-saving time.
1.5 When the initial letter changes from small to capital or vice versa, the usual tilde is replaced by ⑨ or ⑨,

e.g. **foot...:** ... ⑨ **Guards** = Foot Guards.
2. Pronunciation. 2.1 The pronunciation of English headwords is given in square brackets by means of the symbols of the International Phonetic Association (see pp. 13 to 15).

2.2 To save space the tilde (~) has been made use of in many places within the phonetic transcription. It

1. Englisches Stichwort. 1.1 Das Wörterverzeichnis ist alphabetrich geordnet und verzeichnet auch die unregelmäßigen Formen an ihrer alphabetischen Stelle.

1.2 Der in den Stichwörtern auf Mitte stehende Punkt bzw. der Betonungsakzent zeigt an, wo das englische Wort getrennt werden kann:
cul·ti·vat·ed ... **cul·ti'va·tion**

1.3 Fällt bei einem mit Bindestrich zu schreibenden englischen Stichwort der Bindestrich auf das Zeilenende, so wird er am Anfang der folgenden Zeile wiederholt.

1.4 Um die Wiederholung des Stichworts zu vermeiden, wird die Tilde (~, ~) verwandt. **1.41** Folgen einem ausgerückten Stichwort weitere Zusammensetzungen mit diesem, so wird es durch die halbfette Tilde (~) ersetzt:
aft·er ... **'~·birth** (= afterbirth) ...

1.42 Die magere Tilde (~) ersetzt in Anwendungsbeispielen das unmittelbar vorangehende halbfette Stichwort, das auch selbst mit einer halbfetten Tilde gebildet sein kann:
dis·tance ... *at a* ~ = at a distance

day ... **'~·light** ... *~-saving time* = daylight-saving time.
1.5 Wenn sich der Anfangsbuchstabe eines Stichworts ändert (klein zu groß oder umgekehrt), steht statt der Tilde ⑨ bzw. ⑨:
foot...: ⑨ **Guards** = Foot Guards

2. Aussprache. 2.1 Die Aussprache des englischen Stichworts steht in eckigen Klammern und wird durch die Symbole der International Phonetic Association wiedergegeben. (Siehe Seite 13–15.)

2.2 Aus Gründen der Platzersparnis wird in der Lautschriftklammer oft die Tilde (~) verwandt. Sie ersetzt

replaces any part of the preceding complete transcription which remains unchanged,

  e.g. **as·so·ci·a·ble** [əˈsəuʃjəbl] ...
    as'so·ci·ate 1. [~ʃieit] ...
    2. [~ʃiit] ... **as·so·ci·a·tion**
    [~siˈeiʃən]

2.3 Words ending in one of the suffixes transcribed on p. 15 are given without transcription, unless they figure as headwords. For their stress marks see p. 14, paragraph C.

3. Subject Labels. The field of knowledge from which an English headword or some of its meanings are taken is indicated by symbols or labels, either in abbreviated form or written out in full. A figurative or abbreviated label placed between the headword and its phonetic transcription refers to all translations. A label preceding an individual translation refers to this translation only.

4. Usage Label. The indication of the level of usage by abbreviations such as F, *sl.*, *lit.*, *poet.*, refers to the English headword. Wherever possible the same level of usage between headword and translation has been aimed at.

5. Grammatical References.
5.1 In the appendix (pp. 663/664) the user will find a list of irregular verbs.
5.2 (*irr.*) following a verb refers the user to this list, where he will find the principal parts of this particular verb.

5.3 A reference such as (*irr. fall*) indicates that the compound verb is conjugated exactly like the primary verb as given in the list of irregular verbs.
5.4 An adjective marked with □ takes the regular adverbial form, i.e. by affixing ...ly to the adjective or by changing ...le into ...ly or ...y into ...ily.

5.5 (~*ally*) means that an adverb is formed by affixing ...ally to the adjective.

5.6 When there is only one adverb

---

den Teil der Lautschrift, der sich gegenüber der vorhergehenden Vollumschrift nicht verändert:

  as·so·ci·a·ble [əˈsəuʃjəbl] ... **as-'so·ci·ate** 1. [~ʃieit] ... 2. [~ʃiit] ...
  as·so·ci·a·tion [~siˈeiʃən] ...

2.3 Stichwörter mit einer der auf S. 15 umschriebenen Endungen erhalten keine Aussprachebezeichnung, es sei denn, sie seien ausgerückt. Zum Betonungsakzent siehe S. 14, Abschnitt C.

3. Sachgebiet. Das Sachgebiet, dem ein englisches Stichwort oder einige seiner Bedeutungen angehören, wird durch bildliche Abkürzungen oder ausgeschriebene Hinweise kenntlich gemacht. Steht die bildliche oder abgekürzte Sachgebietsbezeichnung vor der Lautschriftklammer , bezieht sie sich auf alle folgenden Übersetzungen. Steht sie innerhalb des Artikels vor einer Übersetzung, so gilt sie nur für diese.

4. Sprachebene. Die Kennzeichnung der Sprachebene durch Abkürzungen wie F, *sl.*, *lit.*, *poet.* etc. bezieht sich auf das englische Stichwort. Die deutsche Übersetzung wurde möglichst so gewählt, daß sie auf der gleichen Sprachebene wie das Stichwort liegt.

5. Grammatische Hinweise.
5.1 Eine Liste der unregelmäßigen Verben befindet sich im Anhang auf S. 663/664.
5.2 Der Hinweis (*irr.*) bei einem Verb zeigt an, daß es unregelmäßig konjugiert wird und daß seine Stammformen in dieser Liste aufgeführt sind.
5.3 Hinweise wie (*irr. fall*) zeigen an, daß das Stichwort ebenso konjugiert wird wie das in der Liste der unregelmäßigen Verben aufgeführte Grundverb *fall*.
5.4 Das Zeichen □ bei einem Adjektiv bedeutet, daß das Adverb regelmäßig, d. h. durch Anhängung von ...ly oder durch Verwandlung von ...le in ...ly oder ...y in ...ily gebildet wird.
5.5 Der Hinweis (~*ally*) bei einem Adjektiv bedeutet, daß das Adverb durch Anhängung von ...ally gebildet wird.
5.6 Bei Adjektiven, die auf ...ic und

for adjectives ending in both ...ic and ...ical, this is indicated in the following way:

his·tor·ic, his·tor·i·cal □,

i.e. historically is the adverb of both adjectives.

5.7 The indication of the parts of speech (noun, adjective, verb, etc.) has been omitted where it is obvious. In cases of doubt, however, the parts of speech have been indicated.

6. Translations.

6.1 Translations of a headword have been subdivided by Arabic numerals to distinguish the various parts of speech. Words of similar meanings have been subdivided by commas, those with distinct differences in meaning by semicolons.

6.2 Explanatory additions have been printed in italics; thus, for example, a direct object precedes a verb, a subject follows it in parentheses,

e.g. **a·bate** ... *v/t.* ... *Schmerz* lindern; ... *Preis* herabsetzen; ... *v/i.* ... sich legen (*Wind*); fallen (*Preis*) ...

6.3 Prepositions governing an English headword (verb, adjective, noun) are given in both languages,

e.g. **dis·sent** ... 2. (*from*) anderer Meinung sein (als), nicht übereinstimmen (mit); abweichen (von) ... **dis·qual·i·fy** ... unfähig *od.* untauglich machen *od.* erklären (*for* zu) ...

6.4 Where a German preposition may govern the dative or the accusative case, the case is given in parentheses,

e.g. **en·ter** ... eintreten in (*acc.*) ...

7. Illustrative phrases and their translations are given at the end of the respective part of speech (in verb articles at the end of *v/t* and *v/i.* respectively), e.g.

deal² ... **1.** Teil *m*; ... *a good* ~ ziemlich viel; *a great* ~ sehr viel; *give a square* ~ *to* gerecht werden (*dat.*); **2.** ...

...ical enden können, wird die Adverbbildung so gekennzeichnet:

his·tor·ic, his·tor·i·cal □,

d. h. historically ist das Adverb zu beiden Adjektivformen.

5.7 Die Kennzeichnung der Wortart (wie Substantiv, Adjektiv etc.) ist unterblieben, wenn sie aus der deutschen Übersetzung eindeutig hervorgeht. Wo Mißverständnisse möglich wären, wird die Wortart angegeben.

6. Deutsche Übersetzung.

6.1 Die Übersetzungen des englischen Stichworts sind durch arabische Ziffern nach Wortarten gegliedert. Innerhalb einer Wortart sind bedeutungsähnliche Wörter durch Komma, Bedeutungsunterschiede durch Semikolon getrennt.

6.2 Erläuternde Zusätze sind kursiv gegeben: bei Verben steht z. B. ein mögliches Objekt vor der Übersetzung, ein Subjekt in Klammern danach:

a·bate ... *v/t.* ... *Schmerz* lindern; ... *Preis* herabsetzen; ... *v/i.* ... sich legen (*Wind*); fallen (*Preis*) ...

6.3 Wird das englische Stichwort (Verb, Adjektiv oder Substantiv) von bestimmten Präpositionen regiert, so werden diese mit den deutschen Entsprechungen, der jeweiligen Bedeutung zugeordnet, angegeben:

dis·sent ... 2. (*from*) anderer Meinung sein (als), nicht übereinstimmen (mit); abweichen (von) ... **dis·qual·i·fy** ... unfähig *od.* untauglich machen *od.* erklären (*for* zu) ...

6.4 Bei deutschen Präpositionen, die den Dativ und den Akkusativ regieren können, wird der Fall in Klammern angegeben:

en·ter ... eintreten in (*acc.*) ...

7. Anwendungsbeispiele und ihre Übersetzungen sind am Ende der jeweiligen Wortart (bzw. bei Verbartikeln am Ende von *v/t.* oder *v/i.*) zusammengefaßt:

deal² ... **1.** Teil *m*; ... *a good* ~ ziemlich viel; *a great* ~ sehr viel; *give a square* ~ *to* gerecht werden (*dat.*); **2.** ...

8. Symbols — Bildliche Zeichen

~, ♀, ~, ♀ *s.* 1.4—1.5, 2.2.

F   familiär, *familiar;* Umgangssprache, *colloquial language.*

P   populär, ungebildet, *low colloquialism.*

V   vulgär, *vulgar.*

†   veraltet, *obsolete.*

~   selten, *rare, little used.*

♀   Pflanzenkunde, *botany.*

⊕   Handwerk, *handicraft;* Technik, *engineering.*

⚒   Bergbau, *mining.*

⚔   militärisch, *military term.*

⚓   Schiffahrt, *nautical term.*

✝   Handelswesen, *commercial term.*

☐   *s.* 5.4.

🚂   Eisenbahn, *railway, railroad.*

✈   Luftfahrt, *aviation.*

✉   Postwesen, *postal affairs.*

♪   Musik, *musical term.*

🏛   Architektur, *architecture.*

⚡   Elektrotechnik, *electrical engineering.*

⚖   Rechtswissenschaft, *jurisprudence.*

A   Mathematik, *mathematics.*

✓   Landwirtschaft, *agriculture.*

🜍   Chemie, *chemistry.*

⚕   Medizin, *medicine.*

9. Abbreviations — Abkürzungen

a.   *also,* auch.

abbr.   *abbreviation,* Abkürzung.

acc.   *accusative (case),* Akkusativ, 4. Fall.

adj.   *adjective,* Adjektiv, Eigen--schaftswort.

adv.   *adverb,* Adverb, Umstandswort.

allg.   allgemein, *commonly.*

Am.   *Americanism,* sprachliche Eigenheit aus dem oder (besonders) im amerikanischen Englisch.

anat.   *anatomy,* Anatomie, Körperbaulehre.

ast.   *astronomy,* Astronomie.

attr.   *attributively,* als Attribut od. Beifügung.

biol.   *biology,* Biologie.

b.s.   *bad sense,* abwertend.

bsd.   besonder(s), *particular(ly).*

cj.   *conjunction,* Konjunktion, Bindewort.

co.   *comical,* scherzhaft.

coll.   *collectively,* als Sammelwort.

comp.   *comparative,* Komparativ, Höherstufe.

contp.   *contemptuously,* verächtlich.

dat.   *dative (case),* Dativ, 3. Fall.

eccl.   *ecclesiastical,* kirchlich.

e-m ⎱
e-m ⎰   einem, *to a (an).*

e-n ⎱
e-n ⎰   einen, *a, an.*

engl.   englisch, *English.*

eng S.   in engerem Sinne, *specifically.*

e-r ⎱
e-r ⎰   einer, *of a (an), to a (an).*

e-s ⎱
e-s ⎰   eines, *of a (an).*

et. ⎱
et. ⎰   etwas, *something.*

etc.   *et cetera, and so on,* und so weiter.

f   *feminine,* weiblich.

fenc.   *fencing,* Fechtkunst.

fig.   *figuratively,* bildlich, im übertragenen Sinn.

fr.   französisch, *French.*

gen.   *genitive (case),* Genitiv, 2. Fall.

geogr.   *geography,* Geographie, Erdkunde.

geol.   *geology,* Geologie.

ger.   *gerund,* Gerundium.

Ggs.   Gegensatz, *antonym.*

gr.   *grammar,* Grammatik.

hist.   *history,* Geschichte.

hunt.   *hunting,* Jagd.

ichth.   *ichthyology,* Fischkunde.

inf.   *infinitive,* Infinitiv, Nennform.

int.   *interjection,* Interjektion, Ausruf.

ir.   irisch, *Irish.*

iro.   *ironically,* ironisch.

irr.   *irregular,* unregelmäßig (s. Hinweise für den Benutzer 5.2—5.3).

j., j-s, j-m, *j., j-s, j-m* jemand(es *of*; -em *to*) *somebody.*

konkr. konkret, *concretely.*

lit. literary, nur in der Schriftsprache vorkommend.

m masculine, männlich.

metall. metallurgy, Hüttenwesen.

meteor. meteorology, Wetterkunde.

min. mineralogy, Gesteinskunde.

m-n meinen, *my.*

mot. motoring, Kraftfahrwesen.

mount. mountaineering, Bergsteigerei.

m-r meiner, *of or to my.*

mst meistens, *mostly, usually.*

myth. mythology, Mythologie.

n neuter, sächlich.

npr. proper name, Eigenname.

od. oder, *or.*

opt. optics, Optik.

orn. ornithology, Vogelkunde.

o.s. oneself, sich.

P. Person, *person.*

paint. painting, Malerei.

parl. parliamentary term, parlamentarischer Ausdruck.

pharm. pharmacy, Arzneimittelwesen.

phls. philosophy, Philosophie.

phot. photography, Photographie.

phys. physics, Physik.

physiol. physiology, Physiologie.

pl. plural, Plural, Mehrzahl.

poet. poetry, Dichtkunst; *poetic,* dichterisch.

pol. politics, Politik.

p.p. past participle, Partizip Perfekt, Mittelwort der Vergangenheit.

p.pr. present participle, Partizip Präsens, Mittelwort der Gegenwart.

pred. predicatively, prädikativ, als Aussage gebraucht.

pret. preterit(e), Präteritum, Vergangenheit. [wort.

pron. pronoun, Pronomen, Für-

prov. provincialism, Provinzialismus.

prp. preposition, Präposition, Verhältniswort.

psych. psychology, Psychologie.

rhet. rhetoric, Rhetorik, Redekunst.

S. Sache, *thing.*

s. siehe, man sehe, *see, refer to.*

schott. schottisch, *Scots.*

s-e, *s-e* seine, *his, once's.*

sg. singular, Singular, Einzahl.

sl. slang, Slang.

s-m, *s-m* seinem, *to his, to one's.*

s-n, *s-n* seinen, *his, one's.*

s.o. someone, jemand.

s-r, *s-r* seiner } *of his,*

s-s, *s-s* seines } *of one's.*

s.th. something, etwas.

su. substantive, Hauptwort.

sup. superlative, Superlativ, höchste Steigerungsstufe.

surv. surveying, Landvermessung.

tel. telegraphy, Telegraphie.

teleph. telephony, Fernsprechwesen.

thea. theatre, Theater.

typ. typography, Buchdruck.

u. und, *and.*

unbet. unbetont, *unstressed.*

univ. university, Hochschulwesen.

v. von, vom, *of, by, from.*

v/aux. auxiliary verb, Hilfszeitwort.

vb. verb, Verb, Zeitwort.

vet. veterinary medicine, Tierheilkunde.

v/i. verb intransitive, intransitives Verb, nichtzielendes Zeitwort.

v/t. verb transitive, transitives Verb, zielendes Zeitwort.

weitS. in weiterem Sinne, *by extension.*

z. B. zum Beispiel, *for instance.*

zo. zoology, Zoologie.

zs. zusammen, *together.*

Zssg(n) Zusammensetzung(en), *compound word(s).*

Key to Pronunciation

A. Vokale und Diphthonge

[ɑ:] reines langes a, wie in Vater, kam, Schwan: *far* [fɑ:], *father* ['fɑ:ðə].

[ʌ] kommt im Deutschen nicht vor. Kurzes dunkles a, bei dem die Lippen nicht gerundet sind. Vorn und offen gebildet: *butter* ['bʌtə], *come* [kʌm], *colour* ['kʌlə], *blood* [blʌd], *flourish* ['flʌriʃ], *twopence* ['tʌpəns].

[æ] heller, ziemlich offener, nicht zu kurzer Laut. Raum zwischen Zunge und Gaumen noch größer als bei ä in Ähre: *fat* [fæt], *man* [mæn].

[ɛə] nicht zu offenes halblanges ä; im Englischen nur vor r, das als ein dem ä nachhallendes ə erscheint: *bare* [bɛə], *pair* [pɛə], *there* [ðɛə].

[ai] Bestandteile: helles, zwischen ɑ: und æ liegendes a und schwächeres offenes i. Die Zunge hebt sich halbwegs zur i-Stellung: *I* [ai], *lie* [lai], *dry* [drai].

[au] Bestandteile: helles, zwischen ɑ: und æ liegendes a und schwächeres offenes ü *house* [haus], *now* [nau].

[e] halboffenes kurzes e, etwas geschlossener als das e in Bett: *bed* [bed], *less* [les].

[ei] halboffenes e, nach i auslautend, indem die Zunge sich halbwegs zur i-Stellung hebt: *date* [deit], *play* [plei], *obey* [ə'bei].

[ə] flüchtiger Gleitlaut, ähnlich dem deutschen, flüchtig gesprochenen e in Gelage: *about* [ə'baut], *butter* ['bʌtə], *connect* [kə'nekt].

[əu] mit [ə] beginnend und in schwaches u auslautend; keine Rundung der Lippen, kein Heben der Zunge: *note* [nəut], *boat* [bəut], *below* [bi'ləu].

[i:] langes i, wie in lieb, Bibel, aber etwas offener einsetzend als im Deutschen; wird in Südengland doppellautig gesprochen, indem sich die Zunge allmählich zur i-Stellung hebt: *scene* [si:n], *sea* [si:], *feet* [fi:t], *ceiling* ['si:liŋ].

[i] kurzes i wie in bin, mit: *big* [big], *city* ['siti].

[iə] halboffenes halblanges i mit nachhallendem ə: *here* [hiə], *hear* [hiə], *inferior* [in'fiəriə].

[ɔ:] offener langer, zwischen a und o schwebender Laut: *fall* [fɔ:l], *nought* [nɔ:t], *or* [ɔ:], *before* [bi'fɔ:].

[ɔ] offener kurzer, zwischen a und o schwebender Laut, offener als das o in Motte: *god* [gɔd], *not* [nɔt], *wash* [wɔʃ], *hobby* ['hɔbi].

[ɔi] Bestandteile: offenes o und schwächeres offenes i. Die Zunge hebt sich halbwegs zur i-Stellung: *voice* [vɔis], *boy* [bɔi], *annoy* [ə'nɔi].

[ə:] im Deutschen fehlender Laut; offenes langes ö, etwa wie gedehnt gesprochens ö in öffnen, Mörder; kein Vorstülpen oder Runden der Lippen, kein Heben der Zunge: *word* [wə:d], *girl* [gə:l], *learn* [lə:n], *murmur* ['mə:mə].

[u:] langes u wie in Buch, doch ohne Lippenrundung; vielfach diphthongisch als halboffenes langes u mit nachhallendem geschlossenem u: *fool* [fu:l], *shoe* [ʃu:], *you* [ju:], *rule* [ru:l], *canoe* [kə'nu:].

[u] flüchtiges u: *put* [put], *look* [luk], *careful* ['kɛəful].

[uə] halboffenes halblanges u mit nachhallendem ə: *poor* [puə], *sure* [ʃuə], *allure* [ə'ljuə].

Ganz vereinzelt werden auch die folgenden französischen Nasallaute gebracht: [ã] wie in frz. *blanc*, [ɔ̃] wie in frz. *bonbon* und [ɛ̃] wie in frz. *vin*. Die **Länge eines Vokals** wird durch [ː] bezeichnet, z. B. *ask* [ɑːsk], *astir* [əˈstəː].

B. Konsonanten

[r] nur vor Vokalen gesprochen. Völlig verschieden vom deutschen Zungenspitzen- oder Zäpfchen-R. Die Zungenspitze bildet mit der oberen Zahnwulst eine Enge, durch die der Ausatmungsstrom mit Stimmton hindurchgetrieben wird, ohne den Laut zu rollen. Am Ende eines Wortes wird r nur bei Bindung mit dem Anlautvokal des folgenden Wortes gesprochen: *rose* [rəuz], *pride* [praid], *there is* [ðɛərˈiz].

[ʒ] stimmhaftes sch, wie g in Genie, j in Journal: *azure* [ˈæʒə], *jazz* [dʒæz], *jeep* [dʒiːp], *large* [lɑːdʒ].

[ʃ] stimmloses sch, wie im deutschen Schnee, rasch: *shake* [ʃeik], *washing* [ˈwɔʃiŋ], *lash* [læʃ].

[θ] im Deutschen nicht vorhandener stimmloser Lispellaut; durch Anlegen der Zunge an die oberen Schneidezähne hervorgebracht: *thin* [θin], *path* [pɑːθ], *method* [ˈmeθəd].

[ð] derselbe Laut stimmhaft, d.h. mit Stimmton: *there* [ðɛə], *breathe* [briːð], *father* [ˈfɑːðə].

[s] stimmloser Zischlaut, entsprechend dem deutschen ß in Spaß, reißen: *see* [siː], *hats* [hæts], *decide* [diˈsaid].

[z] stimmhafter Zischlaut wie im Deutschen sausen: *zeal* [ziːl], *rise* [raiz], *horizon* [həˈraizn].

[x] stimmloser, hinten im Mund gebildeter Reibelaut wie ch in ach: *loch* [lɔx].

[ŋ] wird wie der deutsche Nasenlaut in fangen, singen gebildet: *ring* [riŋ], *singer* [ˈsiŋə].

[ŋk] derselbe Laut mit nachfolgendem k wie im deutschen senken, Wink: *ink* [iŋk], *tinker* [ˈtiŋkə].

[w] flüchtiges, mit Lippe an Lippe gesprochenes w, aus der Mundstellung für u: gebildet: *will* [wil], *swear* [swɛə], *queen* [kwiːn].

[f] stimmloser Lippenlaut wie im Deutschen flott: *fat* [fæt], *tough* [tʌf], *effort* [ˈefət].

[v] stimmhafter Lippenlaut wie im Deutschen Vase, Ventil: *vein* [vein], *velvet* [ˈvelvit].

[j] flüchtiger zwischen j und i schwebender Laut: *onion* [ˈʌnjən], *yes* [jes], *filial* [ˈfiljəl].

C. Betonungsakzent

Die Betonung der englischen Wörter wird durch das Zeichen [ˈ] vor der zu betonenden Silbe angegeben, z. B. *onion* [ˈʌnjən]. Sind zwei Silben eines Wortes mit Betonungsakzent versehen, so sind beide gleichmäßig zu betonen, z. B. *upstairs* [ˈʌpˈstɛəz]; jedoch wird häufig, je nach der Stellung des Wortes im Satzverband und in nachdrucksvoller Sprache, nur eine der beiden Silben betont: z. B. *upstairs* in „the upstairs rooms" [ði ˈʌpstɛəz ˈrumz] und „on going upstairs" [ɔn ˈgəuiŋ ʌpˈstɛəz].

Bei zusammengesetzten Stichwörtern, deren Bestandteile als selbständige Stichwörter mit Aussprachebezeichnung im Wörterbuch gegeben sind, und bei Stichwörtern, die eine der unter D verzeichneten Endungen besitzen, wird der Betonungsakzent im Stichwort selbst gegeben. Die Betonung erfolgt auch im Stichwort, wenn nur ein Teil der Lautschrift gegeben wird und die Betonung nicht auf der ersten Silbe des durch eine Tilde ersetzten Lautschriftteils liegt, z. B. **adˈministratix** [~treitriks]. Liegt diese aber auf der ersten Silbe oder in dem gegebenen Lautschriftteil, dann erfolgt keine Betonungssetzung im Stichwort, sondern diese steht dann in der Klammer, z. B. **accurate** [ˈ~rit], **adamantine** [~ˈmæntain].

D. Endsilben ohne Lautschrift

Um Raum zu sparen, werden die häufigsten Endungen der englischen Stichwörter im folgenden einmal mit Lautschrift gegeben, dann aber im Wörterverzeichnis ohne Lautumschrift verzeichnet (sofern keine Ausnahmen vorliegen). Die nachstehenden Endungen sind auch dann nicht umschrieben, wenn ihnen ein Konsonant vorausgeht, der in der Lautschrift des vorhergehenden Wortes nicht gegeben war, im Englischen und Deutschen aber dasselbe Lautzeichen aufweist, z. B. -tation, -ring.

-ability [-əbiliti]
-able [-əbl]
-age [-idʒ]
-al [-əl]
-ally [-əli]
-an [-ən]
-ance [-əns]
-ancy [-ənsi]
-ant [-ənt]
-ar [-ə]
-ary [-əri]
-ation [-eiʃən]
-cious [-ʃəs]
-cy [-si]
-dom [-dəm]
-ed [-d; -t; -id]*
-edness [-dnis;
  -tnis; -idnis]*
-ee [-i:]
-en [-n]
-ence [-əns]

-ent [-ənt]
-er [-ə]
-ery [-əri]
-ess [-is]
-fication [-fikeiʃən]
-ial [-əl]
-ible [-əbl]
-ian [-jən]
-ic(s) [-ik(s)]
-ical [-ikəl]
-ily [-ili]
-iness [-inis]
-ing [-iŋ]
-ish [-iʃ]
-ism [-izəm]
-ist [-ist]
-istic [-istik]
-ite [-ait]
-ity [-iti]
-ive [-iv]

-ization [-aizeiʃən]
-ize [-aiz]
-izing [-aiziŋ]
-less [-lis]
-ly [-li]
-ment(s) [-mənt(s)]
-ness [-nis]
-oid [-ɔid]
-or [-ə]
-ous [-əs]
-ry [-ri]
-ship [-ʃip]
-(s)sion [-ʃən]
-sive [-siv]
-ties [-tiz]
-tion [-ʃən]
-tious [-ʃəs]
-trous [-trəs]
-try [-tri]
-y [-i]

* [-d] nach Vokalen und stimmhaften Konsonanten; [-t] nach stimmlosen Konsonanten; [-id] nach auslautendem d und t.

Über die Aussprache des amerikanischen Englisch vgl. Seite 16.

Das englische Alphabet

a [ei], b [bi:], c [si:], d [di:], e [i:], f [ef], g [dʒi:], h [eitʃ], i [ai], j [dʒei], k [kei], l [el], m [em], n [en], o [əu], p [pi:], q [kju:], r [ɑ:], s [es], t [ti:], u [ju:], v [vi:], w ['dʌblju:], x [eks], y [wai], z [zed].

American Pronunciation

Das amerikanische Englisch (AE) weist in Intonation, Rhythmus und Lautung gegenüber dem britischen Englisch (BE) hauptsächlich folgende Eigenheiten auf:

1. **Intonation:** Das AE zeigt größere Monotonie als das BE; das AE hat einfachere Satzmelodien.

2. **Rhythmus:** Wörter mit zwei oder mehr Silben nach der Hauptonsilbe [ˈ] haben im AE einen deutlichen Nebenton [ˌ], den die entsprechenden BE-Wörter nicht oder nur schwächer tragen, z. B. dictionary [AE ˈdikʃəˌnɛri = BE ˈdikʃənri], secretary [AE ˈsɛkrəˌtɛri = BE ˈsekrətri]; im AE werden kurze Tonvokale gedehnt (*American drawl*), z. B. capital [AE ˈkæːpətəl = BE ˈkæpitl]; im AE erfährt die unbetonte Silbe (nach einer betonten) eine Abschwächung, die u. a. anlautendes p, t, k zu b, d, g erweicht, z. B. property [AE ˈprɑbərti = BE ˈprɔpəti], united [AE juˈnaidid = BE juːˈnaitid].

3. Allgemein noch auffällige Merkmale der AE-Sprechweise im Vergleich zum BE sind die **Nasalierung** vor und nach nasalem Konsonant [m, n, ŋ] sowie die geschlossenere Aussprache von [-e] und [o-] als erster Bestandteil in Diphthongen, z. B. home [AE hoːm], take [AE teːk].

4. Geschriebenes r wird im Auslaut nach Vokal oder zwischen Vokal und Konsonant deutlich (retroflex) gesprochen, z. B. car [AE kɑːr = BE kɑː], care [AE kɛr = BE kɛə], border [AE ˈbɔːrdər = BE ˈbɔːdə].

5. Das o [BE ɔ] wird im AE etwa wie das dunkle **a** [AE ɑ] in „halten" ausgesprochen, z. B. dollar [AE ˈdɑlər = BE ˈdɔlə], college [AE ˈkɑliðʒ = BE ˈkɔlidʒ], lot [AE lɑt = BE lɔt], problem [AE ˈprɑbləm = BE ˈprɔbləm]; in zahlreichen Fällen besteht die [ɑ]- und [ɔ]-Aussprache nebeneinander, wenn auch nicht gleich üblich.

6. Das **a** [BE ɑː] wird im AE zu [æ] oder [æː] in Wörtern vom Typ pass [AE pæ(ː)s = BE pɑːs], answer [AE ˈæ(ː)nsər = BE ˈɑːnsə], dance [AE dæ(ː)ns = BE dɑːns], half [AE hæ(ː)f = BE hɑːf] sowie bei laugh [AE læ(ː)f = BE lɑːf].

7. Das u [BE juː] in Hauptonsilben im Inlaut wird im AE zu [uː], z. B. Tuesday [AE ˈtuːzdi = BE ˈtjuːzdi], student [AE ˈstuːdənt = BE ˈstjuːdənt], aber nicht in music [AE, BE = ˈmjuːzik], fuel [AE, BE = ˈfjuːəl].

8. Die Ableitungssilbe **-ile** (BE vorzugsweise [-ail]) wird im AE häufig zu [-əl] oder [-il] verkürzt, z. B. futile [AE ˈfjuːtəl = BE ˈfjuːtail], textile [AE ˈtekstil = BE ˈtekstail]; durchgehende [-əl]- oder [-il]-Lautung besteht nicht.

9. Die Endung **-ization** (BE meist [ai'zeiʃən]) wird im AE vorzugsweise [ə'zeiʃən] gesprochen, seltener [ai'zeiʃən]. Diesem Lautungsunterschied steht das Ausspracheverhältnis AE (bevorzugt) [ə] und BE (Standard) [i] nahe, z. B. editor [AE ˈedətər = BE ˈeditə], basket [AE ˈbæ(ː)skət = BE ˈbɑːskit].

A

a [ei; ə], *vor vokalischem Anlaut* **an** [æn; ən] *Artikel*: ein(e); der-, die-, dasselbe; per, pro, je; *they are of an age* sie sind gleichaltrig; *twice a week* zweimal wöchentlich *od.* in der Woche.

A 1 F ['ei 'wʌn] Ia, prima.

a·back [ə'bæk] rückwärts; *taken ~* überrascht, verblüfft, bestürzt.

ab·a·cus ['æbəkəs], *pl.* **ab·a·ci** ['~sai] Rechenbrett *n*; △ Säulendeckplatte *f*.

a·baft ⚓ [ə'bɑːft] **1.** *adv.* nach achtern zu; **2.** *prp.* achter.

a·ban·don [ə'bændən] auf-, preisgeben; im Stich lassen, verlassen; überlassen; *Sport*: aufgeben; *~ o.s. to* sich hingeben (*dat.*); **a'ban·doned** *adj.* verlassen; verworfen; **a'ban·don·ment** Auf-, Preisgabe *f*; Hingabe *f*; Unbeherrschtheit *f*.

a·base [ə'beis] erniedrigen; demütigen; **a'base·ment** Erniedrigung *f*; Demütigung *f*.

a·bash [ə'bæʃ] beschämen, verlegen machen; *~ed at* fassungslos über (*acc.*); **a'bash·ment** Beschämung *f*, Verlegenheit *f*.

a·bate [ə'beit] *v/t.* verringern, vermindern; *Schmerz* lindern; *Stolz* mäßigen; *Preis* herabsetzen; ⅔ aufheben; *Mißstand* abstellen; *v/i.* abnehmen, nachlassen; sich legen (*Wind*); fallen (*Preis*); **a'bate·ment** Verminderung *f*; *Preis-*, *Steuer-*Nachlaß *m*; Abschaffung *f*; Aufhebung *f*.

ab·at·tis ⚔ [ə'bætis] Verhau *m*, *n*.

ab·at·toir ['æbətwɑː] Schlachthaus *n*.

ab·ba·cy ['æbəsi] Abtwürde *f*; **'ab·bess** Äbtissin *f*; **ab·bey** ['æbi] Abtei *f*; **ab·bot** ['æbət] Abt *m*.

ab·bre·vi·ate [ə'briːvieit] (ab-, ver-) kürzen; **ab·bre·vi·a·tion** Abkürzung *f*.

ABC ['eibiː'siː] ABC *n*, Alphabet *n*; alphabetischer (Fahr)Plan *m*; *~ weapons* ABC-Waffen, atomare, biologische und chemische Waffen *f/pl.*

ab·di·cate ['æbdikeit] *v/i.* ab-

danken; *v/t. Amt* niederlegen, entsagen (*dat.*); *~ the throne* abdanken; **ab·di'ca·tion** Verzicht *m*; Abdankung *f*.

ab·do·men ['æbdəmen; ⚕ æb-'dəumen] Unterleib *m*, Bauch *m*; **ab·dom·i·nal** [æb'dɔminl] Unterleibs..., Bauch...

ab·duct [æb'dʌkt] entführen; **ab-'duc·tion** Entführung *f*.

a·be·ce·dar·i·an [eibiːsiː'deəriən] **1.** alphabetisch (geordnet); **2.** Abc-Schütze *m*.

a·bed [ə'bed] zu *od.* im Bett.

ab·er·ra·tion [æbə'reiʃən] Abweichung *f*; *fig.* Verirrung *f*; *ast. u. phys.* Aberration *f*.

a·bet [ə'bet] anstiften, aufhetzen; *mst aid and ~* ⅔ Vorschub leisten (*dat.*); **a'bet·ment** Anstiftung *f*, Aufhetzung *f*; Vorschub *m*; **a'bet·tor** Anstifter *m*; (Helfers)Helfer *m*.

a·bey·ance [ə'beiəns] Unentschiedenheit *f*; *in ~* ⅔ unentschieden, in der Schwebe; herrenlos.

ab·hor [əb'hɔː] verabscheuen; **ab·hor·rence** [əb'hɔrəns] Abscheu *m* (*of* vor *dat.*, gegen); *hold s.th. in ~* vor et. Abscheu haben; **ab'hor·rent** □ zuwider, verhaßt (*to dat.*); abstoßend; unvereinbar (*to*, *from* mit).

a·bide [ə'baid] (*irr.*) *v/i.* bleiben; *~ by* treu bleiben (*dat.*), festhalten an (*dat.*); *v/t.* erwarten; (v)ertragen, aushalten; *I cannot ~ him* ich kann ihn nicht ausstehen; **a'bid·ing** □ dauernd.

a·bil·i·ty [ə'biliti] Fähigkeit *f*; *to the best of one's ~* nach besten Kräften; *abilities pl.* geistige Anlagen *f/pl.*

ab·ject □ ['æbdʒekt] verworfen; gemein; **ab'jec·tion**, **ab'ject·ness** Verworfenheit *f*; Niedrigkeit *f*.

ab·jure [əb'dʒuə] abschwören; entsagen (*dat.*).

a·blaze [ə'bleiz] in Flammen; (*a. fig.*) lodernd.

a·ble □ ['eibl] fähig, tüchtig, geschickt; *be ~* imstande *od.* in der Lage sein, können; *~ to pay* zahlungsfähig; *~-bod·ied* ['~'bɔdid]

körperlich leistungsfähig, **kräftig**;
✕ tauglich; ~ *seaman* ⚓ Vollmatrose *m*.

ab·lu·tion [ə'bluːʃən] Waschung *f*.

ab·ne·gate ['æbnigeit] ab-, verleugnen; *Anspruch etc.* aufgeben; **ab·ne'ga·tion** Ableugnung *f*; *a.* self-~ Selbstverleugnung *f*; Verzicht *m*.

ab·nor·mal ☐ [æb'nɔːməl] ungewöhnlich, regelwidrig, abnorm; **ab'nor·mi·ty** Abnormität *f*.

a·board [ə'bɔːd] ⚓ an Bord (*gen.*); *all* ~! *Am.* 🚂, ✕ etc. einsteigen!

a·bode [ə'baud] **1.** *pret. u. p.p. von* abide; **2.** Aufenthalt *m*; Wohnung *f*, Wohnsitz *m*.

a·bol·ish [ə'bɔliʃ] abschaffen, aufheben; **a'bol·ish·ment**, **ab·o·li·tion** [æbəu'liʃən] Abschaffung *f*, Aufhebung *f*; **ab·o'li·tion·ist** Gegner *m* der Sklaverei.

A-bomb ['eibɔm] = atomic bomb.

a·bom·i·na·ble ☐ [ə'bɔminəbl] abscheulich; **a'bom·i·nate** [~neit] verabscheuen; **a·bom·i'na·tion** Abscheu *m* (*of* gegen); Greuel *m*.

ab·o·rig·i·nal [æbə'ridʒənl] **1.** ☐ eingeboren, einheimisch; Ur-...; **2.** Ureinwohner *m*; **ab·o'rig·i·nes** [~dʒiniːz] *pl.* Ureinwohner *m/pl.*, Urbevölkerung *f*.

a·bort [ə'bɔːt] 🞋 eine Fehl- *od.* Frühgeburt haben; *biol.* verkümmern; ~ *a mission* ✕, *Raumfahrt:* e-e Mission abbrechen; **a'bor·tion** 🞋 Fehl- *od.* Frühgeburt *f*; Abtreibung *f*; Mißgeburt *f* (*a. fig.*); *fig.* Fehlschlag *m*; *produce* ~ abtreiben; **a'bor·tive** [~tiv] ☐ vorzeitig; erfolglos, fehlgeschlagen; verkümmert.

a·bound [ə'baund] reichlich vorhanden sein; Überfluß haben (*in* an *dat.*); ~ *with* wimmeln von.

a·bout [ə'baut] **1.** *prp.* über (*acc.*); von; um ... herum; bei; im Begriff, dabei; *talk* ~ *business* über Geschäfte sprechen; *send s.o.* ~ *his business* j. wegschicken *od.* hinauswerfen *od.* kurz abfertigen; ~ *the house* irgendwo im Haus; *wander* ~ *the streets* in den Straßen umherwandern; *what are you* ~ was macht ihr da?; *I had no money* ~ *me* ich hatte kein Geld bei mir; *be* ~ *to do* im Begriff sein zu tun; **2.** *adv.* herum, umher; in der Nähe; auf den Beinen; etwa, ungefähr; ungefähr um, gegen; *travel* ~

umher- *od.* herumreisen; *it must be somewhere* ~ es muß hier in der Nähe sein; *a long way* ~ ein großer Umweg; *bring* ~ zustande bringen; *come* ~ zustande kommen; *be up and* ~ (wieder) auf den Beinen sein; *he is* ~ *my height* er hat etwa meine Größe; ~ *ten o'clock* gegen 10 Uhr; *right* ~! rechtsum!; ~ *turn!* kehrt!

a·bove [ə'bʌv] **1.** *prp.* über, oberhalb; *fig.* erhaben über; ~ *300* über 300; ~ *all* (things) vor allem; *be* ~ *s.o. in s.th.* j-m in e-r Sache überlegen sein; *it is* ~ *me* das ist mir zu hoch; **2.** *adv.* oben; darüber; *over and* ~ obendrein; **3.** *adj.* obig; oben-erwähnt; *the* ~ *points* die obenerwähnten Punkte; **4.** *das* Obige; **a'bove-'board** ehrlich, offen; **a'bove-'ground** am Leben.

ab·ra·ca·dab·ra [æbrəkə'dæbrə] Abrakadabra *n*; Kauderwelsch *n*.

ab·rade [ə'breid] abschaben, abschleifen, abreiben, abscheuern.

ab·ra·sion [ə'breiʒən] Abreiben *n*, Abschleifen *n*; Abnutzung *f*; (Haut)Abschürfung *f*; **ab'ra·sive** [~siv] ⊕ Schleifmittel *n*.

ab·re·act [æbri'ækt] abreagieren.

a·breast [ə'brest] nebeneinander; ~ *of od.* with auf der Höhe (*gen.*); *keep* ~ *of* Schritt halten mit.

a·bridge [ə'bridʒ] (ab-, ver)kürzen; *fig.* beschränken; **a'bridg(e)·ment** Ab-, Verkürzung *f*; Abriß *m*; Auszug *m*; gekürzte Ausgabe *f* e-s Buches.

a·broad [ə'brɔːd] im (ins) Ausland; überall(hin); draußen, im Freien; *there is a report* ~ es geht das Gerede *od.* Gerücht; *the thing has got* ~ die Sache ist ruchbar geworden; *all* ~ ganz im Irrtum.

ab·ro·gate ['æbrəugeit] abschaffen, aufheben; **ab·ro'ga·tion** Abschaffung *f*, Aufhebung *f*.

ab·rupt ☐ [ə'brʌpt] jäh; plötzlich, abrupt, unvermittelt; zs.-hanglos; schroff (*Benehmen*); **ab'rupt·ness** Steilheit *f* e-s Abhangs; Plötzlichkeit *f*; Zs.-hanglosigkeit *f*; Schroffheit *f*.

ab·scess 🞋 ['æbsis] Abszeß *m*, Geschwür *n*.

ab·scond [əb'skɔnd] sich heimlich davonmachen, flüchten.

ab·sence ['æbsəns] Abwesenheit *f*, Fehlen *n*; Mangel *m* (*of* an *dat.*);

~ *of mind* Geistesabwesenheit *f,* Zerstreutheit *f.*

ab·sent 1. □ ['æbsənt] abwesend; fehlend; *fig.* geistesabwesend, zerstreut; **2.** [æb'sent]: ~ *o.s.* fernbleiben *(from dat.)*; **ab·sen·tee** [æbsən'ti:] Abwesende *m, f;* dauernd im Ausland Lebende *m, f;* ~ *ballot bsd. Am.* Briefwahl *f;* ~ *voter bsd. Am.* Briefwähler *m;* **ab·sen·tee·ism** Absentismus *m (dauerndes Wohnen im Ausland); im Betrieb:* unerlaubtes Fernbleiben *n;* Drückebergerei *f;* **'ab·sent-'mind·ed** □ geistesabwesend, zerstreut; **'ab·sent-'mind·ed·ness** Geistesabwesenheit *f,* Zerstreutheit *f.*

ab·sinth ['æbsinθ] ♀ Wermut *m;* Absinth *m.*

ab·so·lute □ ['æbsəlu:t] absolut *(a. ♀, phys., gr.);* unum-, unbeschränkt; vollkommen; unvermischt; unbedingt; **'ab·so·lute·ness** Unumschränktheit *f etc.;* **ab·so'lu·tion** Lossprechung *f;* **'ab·so·lut·ism** Absolutismus *m,* unbeschränkte Regierung(sform)*f.*

ab·solve [əb'zɔlv] frei-, lossprechen; entbinden *(from* von), entheben *(from gen.).*

ab·sorb [əb'sɔ:b] absorbieren, aufsaugen; verschlucken; *fig.* fesseln, ganz in Anspruch nehmen *(Arbeit etc.); Wissen* sich aneignen; *Kaufkraft* abschöpfen; ~ed in vertieft in *(acc.);* **ab'sorb·ent** aufsaugend(es Mittel *n);* ~ *cotton wool* Verbandwatte *f.*

ab·sorp·tion [əb'sɔ:pʃən] Aufsaugung *f,* Absorption *f; fig.* Vertieftsein *n;* Abschöpfung *f der Kaufkraft.*

ab·stain [əb'stein] sich enthalten *(from gen.);* abstinent leben; ~ *(from voting)* parl. sich der Stimme enthalten; **ab'stain·er** *mst total* ~ Abstinenzler *m.*

ab·ste·mi·ous □ [æb'sti:mjəs] enthaltsam; mäßig; frugal.

ab·sten·tion [æb'stenʃən] Enthaltung *f (from* von); *parl.* Stimmenthaltung *f.*

ab·ster·gent [əb'stə:dʒənt] reinigend(es Mittel *n).*

ab·sti·nence ['æbstinəns] Enthaltsamkeit *f (from* von); *total* ~ Abstinenz *f vom Alkohol;* **'ab·sti·nent** □ enthaltsam.

ab·stract 1. □ ['æbstrækt] abstrakt; dunkel, schwer verständlich; **2.** [~] Abriß *m,* Auszug *m; a.* ~ *noun gr.* Abstraktum *n; in the* ~ rein theoretisch, rein begrifflich; **3.** [æb'strækt] *v/t.* abstrahieren; *Geist etc.* ablenken; absondern; entwenden; kurz zs.-fassen; **ab'stract·ed** □ (ab)gesondert; *fig.* zerstreut; **ab·strac·tion** [æb'strækʃən] Abstraktion *f;* (abstrakter) Begriff *m;* Entwendung *f; fig.* Zerstreutheit *f; Kunst:* abstrakte Komposition *f.*

ab·struse □ [æb'stru:s] *fig.* dunkel, schwerverständlich; tiefgründig; **ab'struse·ness** Dunkelheit *f etc.*

ab·surd □ [əb'sə:d] absurd, unsinnig, sinnwidrig; albern; lächerlich; abwegig; **ab'surd·ist** absurdistisch; **ab'surd·i·ty** Sinnwidrigkeit *f,* Albernheit *f etc.*

a·bun·dance [ə'bʌndəns] Überfluß *m;* Fülle *f (of* von, an *dat.);* Überschwang *m des Herzens;* **a'bun·dant** □ reichlich; ~ *in* reich an *(dat.);* **a'bun·dant·ly** vollauf.

a·buse 1. [ə'bju:s] Mißbrauch *m,* -stand *m;* Beschimpfung *f;* **2.** [~z] mißbrauchen; beschimpfen; † mißhandeln; **a'bu·sive** □ [~siv] mißbräuchlich; beleidigend, ausfallend; *Schimpf...; be* ~ schimpfen.

a·but [ə'bʌt] angrenzen, -stoßen *(on, upon, against* an *acc.);* **a'but·ment** ⚓ Strebepfeiler *m;* Widerlager *n e-r Brücke;* **a'but·ter** Anlieger *m.*

a·bysm [ə'bizəm] *poet.* = abyss; **a·bys·mal** □ [ə'bizməl] abgrundtief, bodenlos; **a·byss** [ə'bis] Abgrund *m,* Schlund *m;* Hölle *f.*

Ab·ys·sin·i·an [æbi'sinjən] abessinisch.

a·ca·cia ♀ [ə'keiʃə] Akazie *f.*

ac·a·dem·ic [ækə'demik] akademisch; Universitäts...; rein theoretisch; ~ *year* Studienjahr *n;* **ac·a·'dem·i·cal 1.** □ = *academic;* **2.** ~*s pl.* akademische Tracht *f;* **a·cad·e·mi·ci·an** [əkædə'miʃən] Akademiemitglied *n.*

a·cad·e·my [ə'kædəmi] Akademie *f.*

a·can·thus [ə'kænθəs] ♀ Bärenklau *m;* ⚓ Akanthusblatt *n.*

ac·cede [æk'si:d]: ~ *to e-m Verein* beitreten; *e-r Meinung etc.* zustimmen; *Amt* antreten; *Thron* besteigen.

ac·cel·er·ate [ək'seləreit] beschleunigen; *fig.* ankurbeln; **ac·cel·er'a-tion** Beschleunigung *f*; ~ *lane mot.* Beschleunigungsspur *f*; **ac'cel·er·a-tor** *mot.* Gaspedal *n.*

ac·cent 1. ['æksənt] Akzent *m*; Tonzeichen *n*; Betonung *f*; Ton *m*; Aussprache *f*; **2.** [æk'sent] *v/t.* akzentuieren; betonen (a. *fig.*).

ac·cen·tu·ate [æk'sentjueit] akzentuieren, betonen; **ac·cen·tu'a·tion** Betonung *f.*

ac·cept [ək'sept] *oft* ~ *of* annehmen; ✝ akzeptieren; übernehmen; hinnehmen; **ac·cept·a'bil·i·ty** Annehmbarkeit *f*; **ac'cept·a·ble** □ annehmbar; angenehm, erwünscht; **ac'cept·ance** Annahme *f*; Übernahme *f*; Hinnahme *f*; (freundliche) Aufnahme *f*; ✝ Akzept *n*; **ac·cep-ta·tion** [æksep'teiʃən] gebräuchlicher Sinn *m e-s Wortes*; **ac·cept·ed** □ [ək'septid] allgemein anerkannt; **ac'cept·er, ac'cept·or** Annehmer *m*; ✝ Akzeptant *m.*

ac·cess ['ækses] Zugang *m*, Zutritt *m* (to zu); *Wut-, Fieber- etc.* Anfall *m*; *Computer:* Zugriff *m*; easy of ~ zugänglich; ~ *road* Zufahrtsstraße *f*; **ac·ces·sa·ry** [ək'sesəri] Mitschuldige *m, f* (to an *dat.*), Helfershelfer(in); = accessory 2; **ac·ces·si·bil·i·ty** [~si'biliti] Zugänglichkeit *f*; **ac'ces·si·ble** □ [~səbl] zugänglich (to für); **ac'ces-sion** Gelangen *n* (to zu *e-r Würde*); Antritt *m* (to *e-s Amtes*); Eintritt *m* (to in *ein Alter*); Zuwachs *m*; ~ to the throne Thronbesteigung *f*; recent ~s *pl.* Neuanschaffungen *f/pl.*

ac·ces·so·ry [ək'sesəri] **1.** □ zusätzlich; nebensächlich; Neben...; **2.** Zubehörteil *n*; = accessary; accessories *pl.* Zubehör *n*; ~ **shoe** *phot.* Steckschuh *m.*

ac·ci·dence *gr.* ['æksidəns] Formenlehre *f.*

ac·ci·dent ['æksidənt] Zufall *m*; Un(glücks)fall *m*; Nebensache *f*; ~ *insurance* Unfallversicherung *f*; be killed in an ~ bei einem Unfall ums Leben kommen, tödlich verunglücken; by ~ zufällig; **ac·ci·den·tal** [æksi'dentl] **1.** □ zufällig; nebensächlich; ~ *death* Tod *m* durch Unfall; **2.** Zufällige *n*; Nebensache *f*; ♪ Versetzungszeichen *n.*

ac·claim [ə'kleim] mit Beifall od.

Jubel begrüßen (als).

ac·cla·ma·tion [æklə'meiʃən] *oft* ~s *pl.* lauter Beifall *m od.* Zuruf *m*; by ~ durch Zuruf.

ac·cli·mate *bsd. Am.* [ə'klaimit] □ acclimatize.

ac·cli·ma·ti·za·tion [əklaimətai-'zeiʃən] Akklimatisierung *f*; **ac'cli-ma·tize** (sich) akklimatisieren, (sich) eingewöhnen.

ac·cliv·i·ty [ə'kliviti] Steigung *f.*

ac·com·mo·date [ə'kɔmədeit] anpassen (to *dat.*; an *acc.*); unterbringen; *Streit* schlichten; *Streitende* versöhnen; *j-m* gefällig sein; versorgen (with mit); *j-m* aushelfen (with mit *Geld*); **ac'com·mo·dat-ing** □ gefällig, entgegenkommend; **ac·com·mo'da·tion** Anpassung *f*; Aushilfe *f*; Bequemlichkeit *f*; Unterbringung *f*, -kunft *f*; Beilegung *f*; Darlehe(n)n *n*; ~ *bill* ✝ Gefälligkeitswechsel *m*; ~ *ladder* ♣ Fallreep *n*; seating ~ Sitzgelegenheit *f*; ~ *train Am.* Personenzug *m.*

ac·com·pa·ni·ment [ə'kʌmpəni-mənt] Begleitung *f*; Begleiterscheinung *f*; **ac'com·pa·nist** ♪ Begleiter(in); **ac'com·pa·ny** begleiten; *accompanied with* verbunden mit.

ac·com·plice [ə'kɔmplis] Mitschuldige *m, f* (in an *dat.*); Komplice *m.*

ac·com·plish [ə'kɔmpliʃ] vollenden, zu Ende führen; zustande bringen; *Absicht etc.* ausführen; **ac'com-plished** vollendet, perfekt; kultiviert; **ac'com·plish·ment** Vollendung *f*; Ausführung *f*; Tat *f*; Leistung *f*; Meisterschaft *f*; mst ~s *pl.* Künste *f/pl.*, Talente *n/pl.*

ac·cord [ə'kɔ:d] **1.** □ Übereinstimmung *f*; Einklang *m*; ♪♪ Vergleich *m*; with one ~ einstimmig; of one's own ~ aus eigenem Antrieb; **2.** *v/i.* übereinstimmen (with mit); *v/t.* gewähren, geben, erweisen; **ac'cord-ance** Übereinstimmung *f*; in ~ with in Übereinstimmung mit, gemäß; **ac'cord·ant** □ (with, to) übereinstimmend (mit), gemäß (*dat.*); **ac-'cord·ing:** ~ to gemäß, laut, entsprechend (*dat.*); ~ as je nachdem (wie *od.* ob); **ac'cord·ing·ly** demgemäß; folglich.

ac·cor·di·on ♪ [ə'kɔ:djən] Handharmonika *f*, Akkordeon *n.*

ac·cost [ə'kɔst] *j.* bsd. *auf der Sraße*

ansprechen.
ac·cou·cheur [æku:'ʃɔ:] Geburtshelfer *m*; **ac·cou'cheuse** [‿z] Hebamme *f*.
ac·count [ə'kaunt] **1.** Rechnung *f*; Berechnung *f von Ausgaben*; Abrechnung *f*; Nota *f*; ✝ Konto *n*; Rechenschaft *f*; Bericht *m*, Darstellung *f*, Erzählung *f*; Geltung *f*; *current* ‿ Kontokorrent *n*; *payment on* ‿ Abschlag(s)zahlung *f*; *sale for the* ‿ Verkauf *m* auf Rechnung; *statement of* ‿ Kontoauszug *m*; *of no* ‿ ohne Bedeutung; *on no* ‿ auf keinen Fall; *on his* ‿ um seinetwillen; *on* ‿ *of wegen*; *have od. hold an* ‿ *with* ein Konto bei (*e-r Bank*) haben; *place to s.o.'s* ‿ j-m auf die Rechnung setzen; *take into* ‿, *take* ‿ *of* in Rechnung *od.* Betracht ziehen; *leave out of* ‿ außer acht lassen; *turn to* ‿ ausnutzen; *keep* ‿*s* die Bücher führen; *call to* ‿ zur Rechenschaft ziehen; *give od. render an* ‿ *of* Rechenschaft ablegen über (*acc.*); Bericht erstatten über (*acc.*); *et.* erklären; *give a good* ‿ *of o.s.* sich bewähren; *make (little)* ‿ *of* (wenig) Wert legen auf (*acc.*); **2.** *v/i.* ‿ *for* Rechenschaft ablegen über (*acc.*); (sich) erklären; *hunt.* zur Strecke bringen; *be much (little)* ‿*ed of* hoch (gering) geachtet sein; *v/t* ansehen als, halten für; ‿ *o.s. happy* sich glücklich schätzen; **ac·count·a'bil·i·ty** Verantwortlichkeit *f*; **ac'count·a·ble** ☐ verantwortlich; erklärlich; **ac-'count·an·cy** Rechnungswesen *n*; **ac'count·ant** Buchhalter *m*; *chartered* ‿, *Am.* certified public ‿ vereidigter Buchprüfer *m*; **ac'count·ing** Buchführung *f*.
ac·cou·tred [ə'ku:təd] ausgerüstet; **ac·cou·tre·ments** ✕[ə'ku:təmənts] *pl.* Ausrüstung *f* (*außer Uniform u. Waffen*).
ac·cred·it [ə'kredit] *Gesandten* beglaubigen, akkreditieren; bestätigen; anerkennen; ‿ *s.th. to s.o.*, ‿ *s.o. with s.th.* j-m *et.* zuschreiben.
ac·cre·tion [æ'kri:ʃən] Zuwachs *m*.
ac·crue [ə'kru:] erwachsen (*from aus*); zufallen; auflaufen (*Zinsen*).
ac·cu·mu·late [ə'kju:mjuleit] (sich) (an-, auf)häufen, ansammeln; **ac·cu·mu'la·tion** Anhäufung *f*, Ansammlung *f*; Haufe(n) *m*; **ac'cu·mu·la·tive** ☐ [‿lətiv] (sich) anhäufend; Anhäufungs...; **ac'cu-**

mu·lator ⚡[‿leitə] Akkumulator *m*.
ac·cu·ra·cy ['ækjurəsi] Genauigkeit *f*; Richtigkeit *f*; **ac·cu·rate** ☐ ['‿rit] genau; richtig; sorgfältig.
ac·curs·ed [ə'kɔ:sid], **ac·curst** [ə'kɔ:st] verflucht, verwünscht.
ac·cu·sa·tion [ækju:'zeiʃən] Anklage *f*, An-, Beschuldigung *f*; **ac·cu·sa·tive** [ə'kju:zətiv] *a.* ‿ *case gr.* Akkusativ *m*, 4. Fall *m*; **ac·cu·sa·to·ry** [ə'kju:zətəri] anklagend; **ac·cuse** [ə'kju:z] anklagen, beschuldigen (*of gen.*, *wegen*; *before*, *to bei*); *the* ‿*d* der (die) Angeklagte; **ac'cus·er** Kläger(in).
ac·cus·tom [ə'kʌstəm] gewöhnen (*to an acc.*); **ac'cus·tomed** gewohnt, üblich; gewöhnt (*to an acc.*, *zu inf.*); *be* ‿ *to doing* (*Am. a. to do*) *s.th.* et. zu tun pflegen.
ace [eis] As *n*; Eins *f auf Würfeln*; *fig.* As *n* (*erfolgreicher Flieger od. Rennfahrer*); ‿ *in the hole Am.* ⸀ Trumpf *m* in Reserve; *he was within an* ‿ *of dying* er wäre um ein Haar gestorben.
a·cer·bi·ty [ə'sɔ:biti] Herbheit *f*.
ac·e·tate ⚕ ['æsitit] Acetat *n*, essigsaures Salz *n*; ‿ *rayon* Acetatkunstseide *f*; ‿ *silk* Acetatseide *f*; **a·ce·tic** [ə'si:tik] essigsauer; ‿ *acid* Essigsäure *f*; **a·cet·i·fy** [ə'setifai] säuern; **ac·e·tone** ['æsitəun] Azeton *n*; **ac·e·tous** ['‿təs] sauer; Essig...; **a·cet·y·lene** [ə'setili:n] Azetylen *n*.
ache [eik] **1.** schmerzen, weh tun; Schmerzen haben; sich sehnen (*for nach*; *to do zu tun*); **2.** *anhaltende* Schmerzen *m/pl.*
a·chieve [ə'tʃi:v] ausführen; zustande bringen; leisten; erlangen; *Ziel* erreichen; *Erfolg* erzielen; **a'chieve·ment** Ausführung *f*, Vollendung *f*; *et.* ‿*s pl.* Leistung *f*, Errungenschaft *f*; Werk *n*.
ach·ing ['eikiŋ] ☐ schmerzhaft.
ach·ro·mat·ic [ækrəu'mætik] (‿*ally*) achromatisch (*farblos*).
ac·id ['æsid] **1.** sauer; ‿ *drops pl. Br.* saure Drops *m/pl.*; ‿ *rain* ⸀ saurer Regen *m*; **2.** Säure *f*; *sl.* LSD; '‿*head sl.* LSD-Süchtige *m, f*; **a·cid·i·fy** [ə'sidifai] säuern; **a'cid·i·ty** Säure *f*; **ac·i·do·sis** [æsi'dousis] Übersäuerung *f* des Blutes; '**ac·id-proof** säurefest; **a·cid·u·lant** [ə'sidjulənt] Säuremittel *n*; **a'cid·u·late** [‿leit] säuern; ‿*d drops pl.* saure Drops *m/pl.*; **a·cid·u·lous** [ə'sidjuləs] säuer-

lich.

ac·knowl·edge [ək'nɔlidʒ] anerkennen; zu-, eingestehen; ✝ bestätigen; sich erkenntlich zeigen für; **ac'knowl·edg(e)·ment** Anerkennung *f*; Eingeständnis *n*; *bsd.* ✝ Empfangsbestätigung *f*, -schein *m*.

ac·me ['ækmi] Gipfel *m*; 🔊 Krisis *f*.

ac·ne 🔊 ['ækni] Akne *f* (*Hautausschlag*).

ac·o·nite 🔊 ['ækənait] Eisenhut *m*.

a·corn 🔊 ['eikɔːn] Eichel *f*.

a·cous·tic, a·cous·ti·cal ☐ [ə'kuːstik(əl)] akustisch; Gehör...; **a'cous·tics** *mst sg*. Akustik *f*.

ac·quaint [ə'kweint] bekannt(*fig. a.* vertraut) machen; *j-m* mitteilen (*with s.th.* et.; *that* daß); *be* ~*ed with* kennen; *become* ~*ed with* kennenlernen; **ac'quaint·ance** Bekanntschaft *f* (*a. konkr.*); Kenntnis *f* (*with gen.*); Bekannte *m*, *f*.

ac·qui·esce [ækwi'es] (*in*) hinnehmen (*acc.*), dulden (*acc.*); einwilligen (in *acc.*); **ac·qui'es·cence** (*in*) Ergebung *f* (in *acc.*); Nachgeben *n*, Nachgiebigkeit *f* (gegenüber); Einwilligung *f* (in); **ac·qui'es·cent** ☐ ergeben; fügsam; nachgiebig.

ac·quire [ə'kwaiə] erwerben (*a. fig.*); ~*d taste* anerzogener Geschmack *m*; **ac'quire·ment** Erwerbung *f*; (erworbene) Fertigkeit *f*.

ac·qui·si·tion [ækwi'zifən] Erwerbung *f*; Erwerb *m*; Errungenschaft *f*; **ac·quis·i·tive** ☐ [ə'kwizitiv] auf Erwerb gerichtet; lernbegierig; **ac'quis·i·tive·ness** Gewinnsucht *f*.

ac·quit [ə'kwit] freisprechen (*of* von); ~ *o.s. of Pflicht* erfüllen; ~ *o.s. well* (*ill*) seine Sache gut (schlecht) machen; **ac'quit·tal** Freisprechung *f*; Erfüllung *f* *e-r Pflicht*; **ac'quittance** Tilgung *f*; Quittung *f*.

a·cre ['eikə] Acre *m* (4047 *qm*), Morgen *m*.

ac·rid ['ækrid] scharf, beißend (*a. fig.*).

ac·ri·mo·ni·ous ☐ [ækri'məunjəs] *fig.* scharf, beißend, bitter; **ac·ri·mo·ny** ['ækriməni] *fig.* Schärfe *f*, Bitterkeit *f*.

ac·ro·bat ['ækrəbæt] Akrobat *m*; **ac·ro·bat·ic** [ækrəu'bætik] (~*ally*) akrobatisch; **ac·ro'bat·ics** *pl*. Akrobatik *f*; ✈ Kunstflug *m*.

a·cross [ə'krɔs] 1. *adv.* hin-, her-

über; (quer) durch; im Durchmesser; drüben; kreuzweise, überkreuz; *come* ~ herüberkommen; *saw* ~ durchsägen; *a lake three miles* ~ ein 3 Meilen breiter See; *with arms* ~ mit verschränkten Armen; 2. *prp.* (quer) über (*acc.*); (mitten) durch; jenseits (*gen.*), über (*dat.*), auf der anderen Seite von; *run* ~ the road über die Straße laufen; ~ *the Channel* über dem Kanal, jenseits des Kanals; *come* ~, *run* ~ stoßen auf (*acc.*); *fig.* ~ *the board* linear; *a 5% wage increase* ~ *the board* eine lineare Lohnerhöhung von 5%.

act [ækt] 1. *v/i.* handeln; sich benehmen; wirken (*on, upon* auf *acc.*); fungieren (*as* als); funktionieren, gehen; *auf der Bühne* spielen; *fig.* Theater spielen, schauspielern, so tun als ob; ~ (*up)on s.o.'s advice* sich nach *j-s* Rat richten; *v/t.* Rolle spielen (*a. fig.*), *Stück* aufführen; 2. Handlung *f*, Tat *f*, Werk *n*; *thea.* Aufzug *m*, Akt *m*; *Zirkus*-Nummer *f*; Gesetz *n*, Beschluß *m*; Urkunde *f*, Vertrag *m*; ♀ *of God* höhere Gewalt *f*; ♀s *of the Apostles* Apostelgeschichte *f*; **'act·a·ble** bühnengerecht; **'act·ing** 1. Handeln *n*; *thea.* Spiel(en) *n*; 2. tätig, amtierend; stellvertretend; geschäftsführend; ~ *partner* ✝ tätiger Teilhaber *m*.

ac·tion ['ækfən] Handlung *f* (*a. thea.*); Tätigkeit *f*; Verrichtung *f*, Tat *f*; Wirkung *f*; 🏛 Klage *f*, Prozeß *m*; Gang *m* (*Maschine, Pferd*); Gefecht *n*; Vortragsweise *f*; *paint.* Stellung *f*, Haltung *f*; Mechanismus *m* (*Klavier etc.*); ~ *radius* Aktionsradius *m*; *bring an* ~ *against* klagen *od.* Klage erheben gegen; *killed in* ~ gefallen; *take* ~ Schritte unternehmen; **ac·tion·a·ble** ['~ʃnəbl] (ver)klagbar; strafbar.

ac·ti·vate ['æktiveit] aktivieren, in Betrieb setzen.

ac·tive ☐ ['æktiv] tätig; handelnd; rührig, geschäftig; wirksam; behend; aktiv; ✝ lebhaft; lebhaft; aktiv...; ~ *voice gr.* Tatform *f*, Aktiv *n*; **ac'tiv·i·ty** (*oft pl.*) Tätigkeit *f*; Betriebsamkeit *f*, Rührigkeit *f*; *bsd.* ✝ Lebhaftigkeit *f*; *in full* ~ in vollem Gange; *intense* ~ Hochbetrieb *m*.

ac·tor ['æktə] Schauspieler *m*; **actress** ['æktris] Schauspielerin *f*.

ac·tu·al □ ['æktʃuəl] wirklich, tatsächlich, eigentlich; gegenwärtig; **ac·tu·al·i·ty** [ˌ∼'æliti] Wirklichkeit *f*; **ac·tu·al·ly** ['æktʃuəli] tatsächlich; in Wirklichkeit; F eigentlich.

ac·tu·ar·y ['æktjuəri] Versicherungsstatistiker *m*.

ac·tu·ate ['æktjueit] in Gang bringen; *fig.* (an)treiben; **ac·tu'a·tion** Antrieb *m*; Anstoß *m*.

a·cu·men [ə'kju:men] Scharfsinn *m*.

ac·u·punc·ture ['ækjupʌŋktʃə] Akupunktur *f*.

a·cute □ [ə'kju:t] spitz; scharf (*Schmerz, Gehör etc.*); scharfsinnig; fein, klar; schrill (*Ton*); brennend (*Frage*); fühlbar; ♪ akut, heftig; **a'cute·ness** Schärfe *f*; Akutheit *f*; Scharfsinn *m*.

ad F [æd] = *advertisement*.

ad·age ['ædidʒ] Sprichwort *n*.

ad·a·mant ['ædəmənt] steinhart; *fig.* unerbittlich (to gegenüber); **ad·a·man·tine** [ˌ∼'mæntain] diamanten, Diamant...; *fig.* = *adamant*.

a·dapt [ə'dæpt] anpassen (to, for *dat.*); zurechtmachen; *Text* bearbeiten (*from* nach); ∼ed *from* frei nach; **a·dapt·a'bil·i·ty** Anpassungsfähigkeit *f*; **a'dapt·a·ble** anpassungsfähig; **ad·ap·ta·tion** [ædæp'teiʃən] Anpassung *f* (to an *acc.*); Bearbeitung *f*; **a·dap·ter** [ə'dæptə] *Radio:* Zwischenstecker *m*; **a'dap·tive** anpassungsfähig.

add [æd] *v/t.* hinzufügen, -zählen; erweitern; ∼ *up* zs.-zählen, addieren; ∼ *in* einschließen; *v/i.* hinzukommen; ∼ *up* F Sinn haben; ∼ *up to et.* ergeben; hinauskommen auf (*acc.*), *et.* bedeuten; ∼ *to* beitragen zu, vergrößern, vermehren; '**ad·ded** zusätzlich.

ad·den·dum [ə'dendəm], *pl.* **ad·'den·da** [ˌ∼də] Zusatz *m*; Nachtrag *m*.

ad·der ['ædə] Natter *f*.

ad·dict 1. [ə'dikt]: ∼ *o.s.* sich hin-, ergeben (*to dat.*); **2.** ['ædikt] (*opium etc.* ∼) (Opium- *etc.*) Süchtige *m*, *f*; **ad·dict·ed** [ə'diktid] ergeben (*to dat.*); süchtig (*to* nach), abhängig (*to* von).

add·ing ['ædiŋ] *attr.* Rechen...

ad·di·tion [ə'diʃən] Hinzufügen *n*; Zusatz *m*; An-, Ausbau *m* (*to* zu *od. gen.*); *Am.* parzelliertes Gelände *n*; ♀ Addition *f*; ∼ *to* Vermehrung *f* (*gen.*); *an* ∼ *to the family* Familienzuwachs *m*; *in* ∼ zu-, außerdem; *in* ∼ *to* außer, zu; **ad·'di·tion·al** □ zusätzlich, weiter; Zusatz...; Mehr...; Nach...

ad·di·tive ['æditiv] (Lebensmittel-) Zusatz *m*.

ad·dle ['ædl] **1.** faul (*Ei*); *fig.* hohl (*Verstand etc.*); **2.** verderben (*v/t. u. v/i.*); *Verstand* verwirren.

ad·dress [ə'dres] **1.** *Worte etc.* richten (*to* an *acc.*); sprechen zu; *j.* anreden (*as* als); *Brief* adressieren; *a.* ∼ *o.s. to* sich an *j.* wenden; ∼ *o.s. to s.th.* sich an et. machen; **2.** Adresse *f*, Anschrift *f*; Anrede *f*; *parl.* Ansprache *f*; Anstand *m*, Manieren *f/pl.*; Gewandtheit *f*; *give an* ∼ e-e Rede halten; *pay one's* ∼*es to a lady* e-r Dame den Hof machen; **ad·dress·ee** [ædre'si:] Adressat(in); **ad·dress tag** Kofferanhänger *m*.

ad·duce [ə'dju:s] *Beweis etc.* anführen, beibringen.

ad·e·noids ♪ ['ædinɔidz] *pl.* adenoide Wucherungen *f/pl.*, Polypen *m/pl.* (im Nasen-Rachenraum).

ad·ept ['ædept] **1.** erfahren; geschickt (*in* in *dat.*); **2.** Eingeweihte *m*, *f*; Kenner(in); *be an* ∼ *at* Meister sein in (*dat.*).

ad·e·qua·cy ['ædikwəsi] Angemessenheit *f*; **ad·e·quate** □ [ˌ∼kwit] angemessen, entsprechend; aus-, hinreichend.

ad·here [əd'hiə] (*to*) kleben, haften (an *dat.*); *fig.* festhalten (an *dat.*); sich an *e-e Regel etc.* halten; zu *j-m* halten; es halten mit; *e-r Partei etc.* angehören; **ad·'her·ence** (*to*) Anhaften *n* (an *dat.*); Festhalten *n* (an *dat.*); Befolgung *f* *e-r Regel etc.*; Anhänglichkeit *f* (an *acc.*); **ad·'her·ent 1.** anhaftend; **2.** Anhänger(in).

ad·he·sion [əd'hi:ʒən] *s. adherence*; *fig.* Einwilligung *f*; *phys.* Adhäsion *f*; *give one's* ∼ *to a plan* sich mit einem Plan einverstanden erklären.

ad·he·sive [əd'hi:siv] **1.** □ anklebend; klebrig; Klebe...; gummiert; ∼ *plaster*, ∼ *tape* Heftpflaster *n*; **2.** Klebstoff *m*.

a·dieu [ə'dju:] **1.** lebe wohl!; **2.** Lebewohl *n*; *make one's* ∼(*s*) Lebewohl sagen.

ad·i·pose ['ædipəus] Fett...; fett-
(halt)ig; ~ *tissue* Fettgewebe *n.*

ad·it ['ædit] Zugang *m*; ✕ Stollen *m.*

ad·ja·cen·cy [ə'dʒeisənsi] Angrenzen *n*; *adjacencies pl.* Umgebung *f*;
ad'ja·cent □ (to) anliegend (*dat.*),
anstoßend, angrenzend (an *acc.*),
benachbart (*dat.*).

ad·jec·ti·val □ [ædʒek'taivəl] adjek-
tivisch; **ad·jec·tive** ['ædʒiktiv] Adjektiv *n*, Eigenschaftswort *n.*

ad·join [ə'dʒɔin] angrenzen an
(*acc.*); **ad'join·ing** angrenzend,
benachbart, Neben...

ad·journ [ə'dʒəːn] aufschieben; (*v/i.*
sich) vertagen; *Sitzungsort* verlegen (to nach); **ad'journ·ment**
Aufschub *m*; Vertagung *f.*

ad·judge [ə'dʒʌdʒ] zuerkennen; 𝓼𝓽𝔃
entscheiden; als *et.* erklären; verurteilen (to zu).

ad·ju·di·cate [ə'dʒuːdikeit] *s. adjudge*; **ad·ju·di'ca·tion** Zuerkennung *f*; Entscheidung *f*, Urteil *n.*

ad·junct ['ædʒʌŋkt] Nebenumstand
m; Zusatz *m*; *gr.* Attribut *n.*

ad·ju·ra·tion [ædʒuə'reiʃən] Beschwörung *f*; **ad·jure** [ə'dʒuə] *j.*
beschwören, dringend bitten (to
inf. zu *inf.*).

ad·just [ə'dʒʌst] in Ordnung bringen, berichtigen; anpassen; *Streit*
schlichten; *Maße* eichen; *Mechanismus* einstellen; ~ *o.s.* to *fig.* sich
anpassen (*dat.*) *od.* an (*acc.*), sich
einfügen in (*acc.*); ~*ing screw* Stell-
schraube *f*; **ad'just·a·ble** □ ein-,
verstellbar; **ad'just·ment** Anordnung *f*; Berichtigung *f*; Einstellung
f; Einstellvorrichtung *f*; Schlichtung *f*; Eichung *f*; Justieren *n.*

ad·ju·tan·cy ✕ ['ædʒutənsi] Adju-
tantur *f*; **'ad·ju·tant** Adjutant *m.*

ad-lib F [æd'lib] improvisieren.

ad·man F ['ædmæn] Werbefach-
mann *m*; **ad·mass** ['ædmæs] *durch
Werbung beeinflußbares* Massen-
publikum *n.*

ad·min F ['ædmin] Verwaltung *f.*

ad·min·is·ter [əd'ministə] *v/t.* verwalten; *bsd. Sakramente u. fig.* darreichen, spenden; *Eid* abnehmen;
𝓼𝔃 verabfolgen; ~ *justice*, ~ *the law*
Recht sprechen; ~ *punishment*
strafen; *v/i.* beitragen (to zu);
ad·min·is'tra·tion Verwaltung *f*;
Handhabung *f*; Darreichung *f*;
Regierung *f*; *bsd. Am.* Amtsperiode
f e-s Präsidenten; ~ *of justice*
Rechtspflege *f*, Rechtsprechung *f*;
ad'min·is·tra·tive [‿trətiv] Ver-
waltungs...; ausführend; **ad'min-
is·tra·tor** [‿treitə] Verwalter *m*;
Nachlaß-, Vermögensverwalter *m*;
ad'min·is·tra·trix [‿treitriks] Ver-
walterin *f.*

ad·mi·ra·ble □ ['ædmərəbl] be-
wunderswert, (vor)trefflich.

ad·mi·ral ['ædmərəl] Admiral *m*;
♀ *of the Fleet* Großadmiral *m*;
'ad·mi·ral·ty Admiralität *f*; *First
Lord of the* ♀ *(britischer) Marine-
minister m.*

ad·mi·ra·tion [ædmə'reiʃən] Bewunderung *f*; Gegenstand *m* der
Bewunderung; *she was the* ~ *of all*
sie wurde von allen bewundert.

ad·mire [əd'maiə] bewundern; verehren; **ad'mir·er** Bewunderer *m*;
Verehrer(in).

ad·mis·si·bil·i·ty [ədmisə'biliti] Zu-
lässigkeit *f*; **ad'mis·si·ble** □ zulässig; zulassungsfähig; **ad'mission** Zulassung *f* (*into*, to zu), Aufnahme *f* (*into*, to in *acc.*); Ein-
tritt(sgeld *n*) *m*; Eingeständnis *n*
(*of gen.*; *that* daß).

ad·mit [əd'mit] *v/t.* (her)einlassen
(to, into in *acc.*), eintreten lassen;
aufnehmen (to in *acc.*), zulassen (to
zu); Raum haben für; zugeben;
~ *to the bar* 𝓼𝔃 *bsd. Am. j.* als
Rechtsanwalt zulassen; *v/i.*: ~ *of*
gestatten, zulassen; *it* ~*s of no excuse* es läßt sich nicht entschuldigen; **ad'mit·tance** Einlaß *m*,
Zutritt *m*; *no* ~*!* Zutritt verboten! **ad'mit·ted·ly** zugestandenermaßen. [mischung *f*, Zusatz *m.*]

ad·mix·ture [əd'mikstʃə] Bei-)

ad·mon·ish [əd'mɔniʃ] ermahnen
(to *inf.* zu *inf.*; *that* daß); warnen (*of,
against* vor *dat.*; *that* daß); **ad-
mo·ni·tion** [ædməu'niʃən] Ermahnung *f*; Warnung *f*; **ad·mon·i-
to·ry** □ [əd'mɔnitəri] ermahnend;
warnend; Warnungs...

a·do [ə'duː] Getue *n*, Aufheben *n*,
Lärm *m*; Mühe *f*; *without much* ~
mir nichts, dir nichts.

a·do·be [ə'dəubi] Luftziegel *m.*

ad·o·les·cence [ædəu'lesns] Ado-
leszenz *f*, Reifezeit *f*; **ad·o'les·cent**
1. jugendlich, heranwachsend; **2.**
Jugendliche *m*, *f.*

a·dopt [ə'dɔpt] adoptieren; *fig.* annehmen, sich zu eigen machen; ~ed *country* Wahlheimat *f*; a'dop·tion Adoption *f*; Annahme *f*; a'dop·tive Adoptiv...; a·dop·tive coun·try Wahlheimat *f*.

a·dor·a·ble ☐ [ə'dɔ:rəbl] ver- ehrungswürdig; ad·o·ra·tion [æ- dɔ:'reiʃən] Anbetung *f*; Verehrung *f*; a·dore [ə'dɔ:] anbeten (*a. fig.*); innig lieben; a'dor·er Anbeter (-in); Verehrer(in).

a·dorn [ə'dɔ:n] schmücken, zieren; a'dorn·ment Schmuck *m*; Ver- zierung *f*.

A·dri·at·ic [eidri'ætik] Adria *f*.

a·drift [ə'drift] ⚓ treibend; *fig.* aufs Geratewohl; *turn s.o.* ~ j. hinaus- werfen *od.* verjagen.

a·droit ☐ [ə'drɔit] gewandt; a'droit·ness Gewandtheit *f*.

ad·u·late ['ædjuleit] *j-m* schmei- cheln; ad·u'la·tion Schmeichelei *f*; 'ad·u·la·tor Schmeichler *m*; 'ad·u- la·to·ry schmeichlerisch.

a·dult [ə'dʌlt] 1. erwachsen; 2. Er- wachsene *m*, *f*; ~ *education* Er- wachsenenbildung *f*.

a·dul·ter·ant [ə'dʌltərənt] Ver- fälschungsmittel *n*; a'dul·ter·ate 1. [~reit] verfälschen; *fig.* ver- derben; 2. [~rit] verfälscht; ehe- brecherisch; a·dul·ter·a·tion [ədʌl- tə'reiʃən] Verfälschung *f*, Fäl- schung *f*; a'dul·ter·a·tor Ver- fälscher *m*; a'dul·ter·er Ehe- brecher *m*; a'dul·ter·ess Ehe- brecherin *f*; a'dul·ter·ous ☐ ehe- brecherisch; a'dul·ter·y Ehebruch *m*.

ad·um·brate ['ædʌmbreit] im Um- riß darstellen, skizzieren; an- deuten; ad·um'bra·tion Umriß *m*, Skizze *f*; Andeutung *f*.

ad·vance [əd'vɑ:ns] 1. *v/i.* vor- rücken, -gehen, -dringen; sich nähern; *im Rang* aufrücken; vor- ankommen; steigen (*Preis*); Fort- schritte machen; *v/t.* vorrücken, -schieben; vorverlegen; vorbrin- gen, äußern; vorausbezahlen; vor- schießen; (be)fördern; *Preis* er- höhen; beschleunigen; 2. Vor- rücken *n*; ✕ Vormarsch *m*; Be- förderung *f*; Fortschritt *m*; An- gebot *n*; Vorschuß *m*; Erhöhung *f* *des Preises etc.*; *in* ~ im voraus; *be in* ~ *of s.o.* j-m voraus sein; 3. Vor(aus)...; ad'vanced *adj.* vor-,

fortgeschritten; ~ *in years* in vor- gerücktem Alter; ~ *English* Eng- lisch für Fortgeschrittene; ad- 'vance·ment Beförderung *f*; För- derung *f*; Fortschritt *m*.

ad·van·tage [əd'vɑ:ntidʒ] Vorteil *m* (*a. beim Tennis*; *to* für); Überlegen- heit *f*; Gewinn *m*; *gain an* ~ *over s.o.* sich e-n Vorteil gegenüber j-m ver- schaffen; *take* ~ *of* ausnutzen; *j.* über- vorteilen; *to* ~ vorteilhaft; *you have the* ~ *of me iro.* ich habe nicht die Ehre, Sie zu kennen; ad·van·ta·geous ☐ [ædvən'teidʒəs] vorteilhaft, günstig.

ad·vent ['ædvənt] (Auf)Kommen *n*; ♀ *eccl.* Advent *m*; ad·ven·ti- tious ☐ [ædven'tiʃəs] zufällig; fremd; Neben...

ad·ven·ture [əd'ventʃə] 1. Aben- teuer *n*, Wagnis *n*; ✝ Spekula- tionsgeschäft *n*; 2. (sich) wagen; ad'ven·tu·r·er Abenteurer *m*; Spe- kulant *m*; ad'ven·tur·ess Aben- teu(r)erin *f*; ad'ven·tur·ous ☐ abenteuerlich; kühn, verwegen; abenteuer-, unternehmungslustig.

ad·verb ['ædvə:b] Adverb *n*; ad- ver·bi·al [əd'və:bjəl] ☐ adverbial; ~ *phrase* adverbiale Bestimmung *f*.

ad·ver·sar·y ['ædvəsəri] Gegner *m*, Widersacher *m*; ad·verse ☐ ['~və:s] widrig; gegnerisch, feind- lich; ungünstig, nachteilig (*to* für); ~ *to* gegen; ~ *balance of trade* un- günstige Handelsbilanz *f*; ad·ver- si·ty [əd'və:siti] Widerwärtigkeit *f*; Unglück *n*.

ad·vert [əd'və:t] hinweisen, sich be- ziehen (*to* auf *acc.*).

ad·ver·tise ['ædvətaiz] ankündigen; annoncieren, inserieren; Reklame machen (für); ~ *for* durch Inserat suchen; ad·ver·tise·ment [əd- 'və:tismənt] Ankündigung *f*, (Zei- tungs)Anzeige *f*, Annonce *f*, Inserat *n*; Reklame *f*; ad·ver- tis·er ['ædvətaizə] Anzeiger *m*, Anzeigenblatt *n*; Inserent *m*; 'ad·ver·tis·ing Werbung *f*, Re- klame *f*; ~ *agency* Werbeagentur *f*; ~ *campaign* Werbekampagne *f*; ~ *man- ager* Werbeleiter *m*.

ad·vice [əd'vais] Rat *m*; Ratschlag *m*; Ratschläge *m/pl.*; ✝ Avis *m*; Nach- richt *f*, Meldung *f*; *letter of* ~ Avis- brief *m*, Benachrichtigungsschreiben *n*; *on the* ~ *of* auf Anraten von; *take medical* ~ e-n Arzt zu Rate ziehen.

ad·vis·a·ble □ [əd'vaizəbl] ratsam; **ad'vise** v/t. et. (an)raten; j. beraten; j-m raten (to inf. zu inf.); † benachrichtigen (of von, that daß), avisieren (s.o. of s.th. j-m et.); v/i. (sich) beraten (with mit); ~ on zu et. raten; **ad'vised** □ wohlbedacht; **ad'vis·ed·ly** [~idli] mit Bedacht; **ad'vis·er** Ratgeber(in); **ad'vi·so·ry** [~əri] beratend; ⚥ Board Beratungsstelle f.

ad·vo·ca·cy ⊕ ['ædvəkəsi] (of) Eintreten n (für), Befürwortung f (gen.); **ad·vo·cate** 1. ['~kit] Advokat m, Anwalt m; fig. Verfechter m, Fürsprecher m; 2. ['~keit] verteidigen, verfechten, befürworten, vertreten.

adze ⊕ [ædz] Breitbeil n.

Ae·ge·an Sea [i:'dʒi:ən'si:] Ägäisches Meer n.

ae·gis ['i:dʒis] fig. Ägide f, Schutzherrschaft f.

Ae·o·li·an [i:'əuljən] äolisch; Äols...

ae·on ['i:ən] Äon m; fig. Ewigkeit f.

a·er·at·ed ['eiəreitid] kohlensauer.

a·e·ri·al ['eəriəl] 1. □ Luft...; Flieger...; gasförmig; ~ camera Luftbildgerät n; ~ survey Luftbildvermessung f; ~ view Luftaufnahme f; 2. Radio, Fernsehen: Antenne f.

a·er·ie ['eəri] Horst m (a. fig.).

a·er·o... ['eərəu] Luft...; **a·er·o·bat·ics** [~'bætiks] sg. Kunstfliegen n; **a·er·o·cab** ['eərəkæb] Am. F Lufttaxi n (Hubschrauber als Zubringer); **a·er·o·drome** ['~drəum] Flugplatz m, -hafen m; **a·er·o·gram** ['~græm] Funkspruch m; **a·er·o·lite** ['eərəulait] Meteorstein m; **a·er·o·naut** ['eərəno:t] Luftschiffer m; **a·er·o'nau·tic, a·er·o'nau·ti·cal** □ aeronautisch; Luftfahrt...; **a·er·o'nau·tics** mst sg. Luftfahrt f; **'a·er·o·plane** Flugzeug n; **a·er·o·sol** (can) ['~sɔl] Aerosolzerstäuber m; **a·er·o·space in·du·stry** Raumfahrtindustrie f; **a·er·o·stat** ['eərəustæt] Luftschiff n; Ballon m; **a·er·o'stat·ic** aerostatisch.

aes·thete ['i:sθi:t] Ästhet m, Schöngeist m; **aes·thet·ic, aes·thet·i·cal** □ [i:s'θetik(əl)] ästhetisch; **aes'thet·ics** sg. Ästhetik f.

a·far [ə'fa:] mst ~ off fern, weit (weg); from ~ von fern, weither.

af·fa·bil·i·ty [æfə'biliti] Leutselig-

keit f.

af·fa·ble □ ['æfəbl] leutselig.

af·fair [ə'feə] Geschäft n; Angelegenheit f, Sache f; F Sache f, Ding n; Liebschaft f; ~ of honour Ehrenhandel m.

af·fect [ə'fekt] (ein- od. sich aus-) wirken auf (acc.); beeinflussen; berühren, betreffen; rühren, ergreifen; die Gesundheit angreifen, in Mitleidenschaft ziehen; neigen zu, gern mögen, bevorzugen; vortäuschen, nachahmen; he ~s the freethinker er spielt den Freigeist; he ~s to sleep er tut so, als ob er schliefe; **af·fec·ta·tion** [æfek'teiʃən] Vorliebe f (of für); Ziererei f, Affektiertheit f; Verstellung f; **af·fect·ed** □ [ə'fektid] gerührt; befallen (von Krankheit); angegriffen (Augen etc.); geneigt, gesinnt (towards s.o. gegen j.); geziert, affektiert; erheuchelt; **af'fec·tion** Gemütsbewegung f, -zustand m; (Zu)Neigung f, Liebe f (for, towards zu); Erkrankung f; **af'fec·tion·ate** □ [~kʃnit] liebevoll, herzlich; yours ~ly Dein liebender (Briefschluß); **af'fec·tive** ergreifend; affektiv, Affekt...

af·fi·ance [ə'faiəns] 1. Vertrauen n (in in acc.); 2. verloben (to mit).

af·fi·da·vit [æfi'deivit] schriftliche beeidigte Erklärung f.

af·fil·i·ate [ə'filieit] als Mitglied aufnehmen; angliedern, anschließen (to dat. od. an acc.); verschmelzen (with mit); ⚥⁄⁄ die Vaterschaft e-s Kindes zuschreiben (on, to dat.); ~d company Tochtergesellschaft f; **af·fil·i·a·tion** Aufnahme f (als Mitglied etc.); Angliederung f.

af·fin·i·ty [ə'finiti] Verschwägerung f; fig. (geistige) Verwandtschaft f; 🜛 Affinität f.

af·firm [ə'fə:m] bejahen, behaupten; bestätigen; **af·fir·ma·tion** [æfə:'meiʃən] Behauptung f; Bestätigung f; **af·firm·a·tive** □ [ə'fə:mətiv] 1. bejahend; positiv; 2. su.: answer in the ~ bejahen.

af·fix 1. ['æfiks] Anhang m; 2. [ə'fiks] (to) anheften (an acc.); befestigen (an dat.); Siegel aufdrücken (auf acc.); beifügen (dat.); zufügen (zu).

af·flict [ə'flikt] betrüben; quälen; ~ed with geplagt von, leidend an (dat.); **af'flic·tion** Betrübnis f;

Leiden *n*; Pein *f.*

af·flu·ence [ˈæfluəns] Überfluß *m*; Reichtum *m*, Wohlstand *m*; **'af·flu·ent 1.** □ reich (fließend); reich (*in* an *dat.*); ~ **society** Wohlstandsgesellschaft *f*; **2.** Nebenfluß *m.*

af·flux [ˈæflʌks] Zufluß *m.*

af·ford [əˈfɔːd] gewähren; bieten; sich leisten; *I can* ~ *it* ich kann es mir leisten.

af·for·est [æˈfɔrist] aufforsten; **af·for·est'a·tion** Aufforstung *f.*

af·fran·chise [əˈfræntʃaiz] befreien.

af·fray [əˈfrei] Schlägerei *f.*

af·front [əˈfrʌnt] **1.** beleidigen; trotzen (*dat.*); **2.** Beleidigung *f*; *put an* ~ *upon, offer an* ~ *to j.* beleidigen.

a·fi·cio·na·do [əfisjəˈnɑːdəu] Fan *m*, Liebhaber *m.*

a·field [əˈfiːld] ins Feld; im Feld; (von zu Hause) weg; *far* ~ weit weg.

a·fire [əˈfaiə] in Flammen.

a·flame [əˈfleim] in Flammen; *fig.* glühend; *set s.th.* ~ et. in Brand stecken *od.* anzünden.

a·float [əˈfləut] ⚓ flott, schwimmend, auf See; in vollem Gange (*Geschäft etc.*); in Umlauf (*Gerücht*); von Wasser bedeckt; *keep* ~ sich über Wasser halten; *set* ~ flottmachen; *the rumour is* ~ das Gerücht geht um.

a·foot [əˈfut] im Gange; zu Fuß; auf den Beinen; in Bewegung.

a·fore ⚓ [əˈfɔː] *s. before*; **a·fore·men·tioned** [~menʃənd], **a·fore·named** [~neimd], **a·fore·said** vorerwähnt, vorgenannt; **a·fore·thought** vorbedacht.

a·fraid [əˈfreid] besorgt, bange; *be* ~ *of* sich fürchten *od.* Angst haben vor (*dat.*); *I am* ~ es tut mir leid; leider.

a·fresh [əˈfreʃ] von neuem.

Af·ri·can [ˈæfrikən] **1.** afrikanisch; **2.** Afrikaner(in); *bsd. Am. in Zssgn* Neger...; **Af·ri·can·der** [~ˈkændə] Kapholländer *m.*

Af·ri·kaans [æfriˈkɑːns] Kapholländisch *n*, Afrikaans *n.*

Af·ro [ˈæfrəu] **1.** afro...; **2.** Afro-Frisur *f.*

aft ⚓ [ɑːft] (nach) achtern *od.* hinten.

aft·er [ˈɑːftə] **1.** *adv.* hinterher; nachher, darauf; **2.** *prp. zeitlich:*

nach; *räumlich:* nach, hinter (... her); *Maß, Richtschnur:* nach, gemäß; ~ *all* nach alledem; schließlich (doch); im Grunde; immerhin; *be* ~ *s.o.* hinter j-m her sein, j. verfolgen; *time* ~ *time* immer wieder; ~ *having seen him* nachdem ich ihn gesehen hatte; **3.** *cj.* nachdem; **4.** *adj.* später; Nach...; ⚓ Achter...;

'**~·birth** ⚕ Nachgeburt *f*; '**~·care** ⚕ Nachbehandlung *f*; '**~·crop** Nachernte *f*; '**~·'din·ner** nach Tisch...; ~ *speech* Tischrede *f*; '**~·ef·fect** Nachwirkung *f*; '**~·glow** Abendrot *n*; '**~·hours** *pl.* Zeit *f* nach (Dienst)Schluß; **~·math** [ˈ~mæθ] *fig.* Nachwirkung(en *pl.*) *f*, Folgen *f*/*pl.*; '**~·'noon** Nachmittag *m*; *this* ~ heute nachmittag; '**~·pains** *pl.* ⚕ Nachwehen *pl.*

aft·ers F [ˈɑːftəz] *pl.* Nachtisch *m.* **aft·er...:** '**~·sales** serv·ice Kundendienst *m*; '**~·sea·son** Nachsaison *f*; '**~·shave** After-shave(-Lotion *f*) *n*; '**~·taste** Nachgeschmack *m*; '**~·-thought** nachträglicher Einfall *m*; '**~·treat·ment** Nachkur *f*; ~·**wards** [ˈ~wədz] nachher; hinterher; später; nachträglich.

a·gain [əˈɡən] wieder, abermals, noch einmal; wiederum; schon wieder; ferner, außerdem; dagegen; ~ *and* ~, *time and* ~ immer wieder; *as much* (*many*) ~ noch einmal soviel (so viele); *now and* ~ hin und wieder.

a·gainst [əˈɡenst] *räumlich:* gegen; *fig.* in Erwartung (*gen.*); *as* ~ verglichen mit; ~ *the wall* an der Wand; ~ *a background* vor *od.* auf e-m Hintergrund; *over* ~ gegenüber; *run* ~ *s.o.* j-m in den Weg laufen.

a·gape [əˈɡeip] gaffend, mit offenem Mund.

ag·ate [ˈæɡət] *min.* Achat *m*; *Am.* Murmel *f*; *Am. typ.* = *ruby.*

a·ga·ve ⚘ [əˈɡeivi] Agave *f.*

age [eidʒ] **1.** (Lebens)Alter *n*; Zeit (-alter *n*) *f*; Menschenalter *n*, Generation *f*; *oft* ~*s pl.* F Ewigkeit *f*; (*old*) ~ Greisenalter *n*; *at the* ~ *of* im Alter von; *in the* ~ *of Queen Anne* in der *od.* zur Zeit ...; *of* ~ mündig; *over* ~ zu alt; *under* ~ unmündig; *what is his* ~? wie alt ist er?; *when I was your* ~ als ich in deinem Alter war; *act od. be your* ~! sei kein Kindskopf!; *come of* ~ mündig werden; **2.** alt werden *od.*

machen; **'age-brack·et** Altersgrup-
pe *f*; **aged** [eidȝd] ... Jahre alt; ~
twenty 20 Jahre alt; **a·ged** ['~id] alt,
betagt, bejahrt; **'age-group** Alters-
gruppe *f*; **'age·less** zeitlos; **'age-
-lim·it** Altersgrenze *f*.

a·gen·cy ['eidȝənsi] Tätigkeit *f*,
Wirkung *f*; Vermittlung *f*; ✝ Agentur *f*, Büro *n*; Dienststelle *f*.

a·gen·da[ə'dȝendə] Tagesordnung *f*.

a·gent ['eidȝənt] Handelnde *m, f*;
Agent *m*; F (Handlungs)Reisende
m; wirkende Kraft *f*, Agens *n*.

age-old ['eidȝəuld] uralt.

age-worn['eidȝwɔːn] altersschwach.

ag·glom·er·ate [ə'glɔməreit] (sich)
zs.-ballen; (sich) (an)häufen; **ag-
glom·er'a·tion** Zs.-ballung *f*; Anhäufung *f*.

ag·glu·ti·nate 1. [ə'gluːtineit] zs.-,
an-, verkleben; ✻, *gr.* agglutinieren;
2. [~nit] zs.-geklebt, verbunden;
gr. agglutiniert; **ag·glu·ti·na·tion**
[~'neiʃən] Zs.-kleben *n*; ✻, *gr.* Ag-
glutination *f*; **ag·glu·ti·na·tive**
[~nətiv] zs.-klebend; agglutinie-
rend.

ag·gran·dize [ə'grændaiz] vergrößern; *im Range etc.* erhöhen; **ag-
'gran·dize·ment** [~dizmənt] Vergrößerung *f*; *fig.* Erhöhung *f*.

ag·gra·vate ['ægrəveit] erschweren;
verschlimmern, verschärfen; F ärgern; **ag·gra·va·tion** Erschwerung
f etc.; F Verärgerung *f*.

ag·gre·gate 1. ['ægrigeit] (sich)
anhäufen; vereinigen (to mit); F
sich insgesamt belaufen auf (*acc.*);
2. □ ['~git] gehäuft; gesamt; Gesamt...; 3. ['~git] Anhäufung *f*; Aggregat *n*; in the ~ im ganzen; **ag-
gre·ga·tion** [~'geiʃən] Anhäufung *f*.

ag·gres·sion [ə'greʃən] Angriff *m*,
Überfall *m*; **ag·gres·sive** □ [ə'gre-
siv] angreifend; aggressiv, streitlustig, -süchtig; ~ war Angriffskrieg
m; **ag'gres·sive·ness** Aggressivität *f*;
ag'gres·sor Angreifer *m*.

ag·grieve [ə'griːv] kränken.

ag·gro *sl.* ['ægrəu] Aggressivität *f*;
Aggression *f*; Ärger *m*.

a·ghast [ə'gɑːst] entsetzt, entsetzt, bestürzt (at über *acc.*).

ag·ile □ ['ædȝail] flink, behend.

a·gil·i·ty [ə'dȝiliti] Behendigkeit *f*.

ag·i·o ✝ ['ædȝəu] Agio *n*, Aufgeld *n*;
ag·i·o·tage ['ædȝətidȝ] Agiotage *f*,
Wechsel-, Börsengeschäft *n*.

ag·i·tate ['ædȝiteit] *v/t.* bewegen,
schütteln; *fig.* erregen; erörtern;
v/i. agitieren (for für); **ag·i'ta·tion**
Bewegung *f*, Erschütterung *f*; Aufregung *f*, Gärung *f*; Agitation *f*;
'ag·i·ta·tor Agitator *m*, Aufwiegler
m, Hetzredner *m*.

a·glow [ə'gləu] glutrot, glühend
(with von, vor *dat.*).

a·go [ə'gəu]: a year ~ vor einem
Jahre; it is a year ~ es ist ein Jahr
her; long ~ vor langer Zeit.

a·gog [ə'gɔg] erpicht; gespannt (for
auf *acc.*).

ag·o·nize ['ægənaiz] *v/t.* quälen; *v/i.*
(mit dem Tode *u. fig.*) ringen;
sich quälen; **'ag·o·niz·ing** □ qualvoll.

ag·o·ny ['ægəni] Qual *f*, Pein *f*;
Ringen *n*, Kampf *m*; Todesangst *f*;
a. ~ of death, mortal ~ Todeskampf
m; ~ column F Seufzerspalte *f*
(Zeitung).

a·grar·i·an [ə'grɛəriən] 1. Befürworter *m* der Landaufteilung; Agra-
rier *m*; 2. agrarisch; Agrar...

a·gree [ə'griː] *v/i.* übereinstimmen;
sich vertragen; einwilligen; (upon,
on) einig werden (über *acc.*), sich
einigen (auf *acc.*); übereinkommen,
vereinbaren (that daß); ~ with *j-m*
bekommen *od.* zuträglich sein; ~ to
zustimmen (*dat.*), eingehen auf
(*acc.*); einverstanden sein mit; ~ to
differ das Streiten aufgeben; *v/t.* ✝
Bücher etc. abstimmen; be ~d (sich)
einig sein (on über *acc.*; that darüber, daß); ~d! abgemacht!;
a·gree·a·ble □ [ə'griəbl] (to) angenehm (für); übereinstimmend (mit);
F einverstanden (mit); **a'gree·a-
ble·ness** Annehmlichkeit *f*; **a·gree-
ment** [ə'griːmənt] Übereinstimmung *f*; Einklang *m*; Vereinbarung
f, Überein-, Abkommen *n*; Vertrag
m; come to an ~ e-e Verständigung
erzielen; make an ~ ein Abkommen
treffen.

ag·ri·cul·tur·al[ægri'kʌltʃərəl]land-
wirtschaftlich; Ackerbau...; **ag·ri-
cul·ture** ['~tʃə] Ackerbau *m*, Landwirtschaft *f*; **ag·ri'cul·tur·ist**
[~tʃərist] Landwirt *m*.

a·ground ⚓ [ə'graund] gestrandet;
run ~ auflaufen, auf (den) Strand
setzen.

a·gue ['eigjuː] Wechselfieber *n*;
Schüttelfrost *m*; **'a·gu·ish** fieber-

haft, fieb(e)rig.

ah [ɑː] ah!, ach!

a·ha [ɑːˈhɑː] aha!

a·head [əˈhed] vorwärts; voraus; vorn; *straight* ~ geradeaus; ~ *of s.o.* j-m voraus; *go* ~ vorgehen, vorankommen; weitermachen; *go* ~*!* vorwärts!; los!; weiter!

a·hoi, a·hoy ⚓ [əˈhɔi] ho!, ahoi!

aid [eid] **1.** helfen (*dat.*; *in* bei *et.*); fördern; **2.** Hilfe *f*; *by* (*with*) *the* ~ *of* mit Hilfe von *od. gen.*; *in* ~ *of* zur Unterstützung *gen.*; ~*s and appliances* Hilfsmittel *n/pl.*

aide-de-camp ✕ [ˈeiddəˈkãːŋ] Adjutant *m.*

ai·grette [ˈeigret] Federbusch *m.*

ail [eil] *v/i.* kränkeln; *v/t.* schmerzen, weh(e) tun (*dat.*); *what* ~*s him?* was fehlt ihm?

ai·ler·on ✈ [ˈeilərɔn] Querruder *n.*

ail·ing [ˈeiliŋ] leidend, ˋkränklich; **'ail·ment** Leiden *n.*

aim [eim] **1.** *v/i.* zielen (*at* auf *acc.*); ~ *at fig.* abzielen auf, streben nach, bezwecken; ~ *to do bsd. Am.* beabsichtigen *od.* versuchen zu tun, tun wollen; *v/t. Geschütz, Schlag, Gewehr, etc.* richten (*at* auf *acc.*, gegen); **2.** Ziel *n*; *fig.* Zweck *m*, Absicht *f*; *Leistungs-*Soll *n*; *take* ~ zielen; **'aim·less** ☐ ziellos.

ain't F [eint] = *are not, am not, is not, have not, has not.*

air[1] [ɛə] **1.** Luft *f*; Luftzug *m*, Lüftchen *n*; *by* ~ auf dem Luftwege; *go by* ~ fliegen; *in the open* ~ im Freien; *castles in the* ~ Luftschlösser *n/pl.*; *be in the* ~ in der Luft liegen; ungewiß sein; *on the* ~ im Rundfunk *zu hören*; *go off the* ~ zu senden aufhören; ~ *supply* Luftzufuhr *f*; *take the* ~ frische Luft schöpfen; ✕ aufsteigen; **2.** (aus)lüften, an die Luft bringen; *Wäsche* trocknen; an die Öffentlichkeit bringen; erörtern; zur Schau tragen; ~ *o.s.* an die Luft gehen.

air[2] [~] Miene *f*; Aussehen *n*; *give o.s.* ~*s* vornehm tun; *with an* ~ mit Würde; ~*s and graces* Vornehmtuerei *f.*

air[3] ♩ [~] Weise *f*, Melodie *f*; Arie *f.*

air...: ‖ '~·bag *mot.* Luftsack *m*; '~·base Luftstützpunkt *m*; '~·bath Luftbad *n*; '~·bed Luftmatratze *f*; '~·bladder Schwimmblase *f*; '~·borne im

Flugzeug befördert; in der Luft (*Flugzeug*); ✕ Luftlande...; *we are* ~ wir fliegen; '~·brake Druckluftbremse *f*; '~·bus, ~ bus ✈ Airbus *m*; ~ car·go Luftfracht *f*; '~·cham·ber *biol.* Luftkammer *f*; ⊕ Windkessel *m*; '~·con·di·tioned mit Klimaanlage, klimatisiert; '~·con·di·tion·er Klimaanlage *f*; '~·con·di·tion·ing Klimaanlage *f*; '~·cooled luftgekühlt; '~·craft Luftfahrzeug(e *pl.*) *n*, Flugzeug(e *pl.*) *n*; ~ *carrier* Flugzeugträger *m*; '~·cush·ion Luftkissen *n*; '~-drop Abwerfen *n od.* Absetzen *n* aus der Luft; '~·ex·haust·er Entlüfter *m*; '~·field Flugplatz *m*; '~-force Luftwaffe *f*; '~·frame Flugzeugzelle *f*; ~ freight Luftfracht *f*; Luftfrachtgebühr *f*; '~·gun Luftgewehr *n*; ~ host·ess Stewardeß *f*, Flugbegleiterin *f.*

air·i·ness [ˈɛərinis] Luftigkeit *f*; Leicht(fert)igkeit *f.*

air·ing [ˈɛəriŋ] Lüften *n*; Spaziergang *m*, -fahrt *f*, -ritt *m*; *give s.th. an* ~ et. lüften; *the room needs an* ~ das Zimmer muß (durch)gelüftet werden; *take an* ~ frische Luft schöpfen.

air...: '~·jack·et Schwimmweste *f*; ⊕ Luftmantel *m*; '~·less ohne Luft (-zug); dumpf(ig); ~ let·ter *Am.* Luftpostleichtbrief *m*, Aerogramm *n*; Luftpostbrief *m*; '~·lift Luftbrücke *f* (*Versorgung auf dem Luftwege*); '~·line Luftverkehrslinie *f*, -gesellschaft *f*; '~·lin·er Verkehrsflugzeug *n*; '~·mail Luftpost *f*; '~man Flieger *m*; '~·me·chan·ic Bordmonteur *m*; '~·mind·ed flugbegeistert; '~·pas·sen·ger Fluggast *m*; ~ pho·to(·graph) Luftbild *n*; '~-pipe ⊕ Luftrohr *n*; '~·plane *bsd. Am.* Flugzeug *n*; '~·pock·et ✈ Luftloch *n*; '~·port Flughafen *m*; '~proof luftdicht; '~·pump Luftpumpe *f*; '~·raid ✕ Luftangriff *m*; ~ *precautions pl.* Luftschutz *m*; ~ *shelter* Luftschutzraum *m*; ~ scout ✕ Aufklärungsflugzeug *n*; '~·ship Luftschiff *n*; '~·sick luftkrank; '~·strip Start- u. Landestreifen *m*; ~ ter·mi·nal Flughafenabfertigungsgebäude *n*; '~·tight luftdicht; ~ *case sl.* todsicherer Fall *m*; '~·traf·fic con·trol·ler Fluglotse *m*; '~·tube Luftschlauch *m*; ~ um·brel·la ✕ Luftsicherung *f*, Deckung *f* durch die Luftwaffe; '~·way Flugstraße *f*;

Luftverkehrsgesellschaft *f*; '~·**wom-an** Fliegerin *f*; '~·**wor·thy** ⚔ lufttüchtig.

air·y □ ['ɛəri] luftig; leicht; lebhaft; leichtfertig.

aisle [ail] ⚓ Seitenschiff *n*; Gang *m zwischen Tischreihen etc.*; '~-**sit-ter** *Am.* F Theaterkritiker *m*.

aitch [eitʃ] *Name des englischen* h.

aitch·bone ['eitʃbəun] Lendenstück *n*.

a·jar [ə'dʒɑː] halb offen, angelehnt *(Tür)*; *fig.* im Zwiespalt.

a·kim·bo [ə'kimbəu] in die Seite gestemmt *(Arme)*.

a·kin [ə'kin] verwandt *(to* mit*)*.

al·a·bas·ter ['æləbɑːstə] 1. Alabaster *m*; 2. alabastern.

a·lack † [ə'læk] ach!, o weh!; ~-*a-day*! lieber Himmel!

a·lac·ri·ty [ə'lækriti] Munterkeit *f*; Bereitwilligkeit *f*, Eifer *m*.

a·larm [ə'lɑːm] 1. Alarm *m*, Warnung *f*; Alarmzeichen *n*; Angst *f*, Unruhe *f*; Wecker *m*; ~ *pistol* Schreckschußpistole *f*; *give (raise, ring, sound) the* ~ Alarm schlagen; 2. alarmieren; beunruhigen; **a'larm-bell** Sturmglocke *f*; **a'larm-clock** Wecker *m*; **a'larm-ist** 1. Bangemacher *m*; 2. beunruhigend.

a·lar·um [ə'lɛərəm] *obs. für* alarm*.*

a·las [ə'læs] ach!, o weh!, leider!

alb [ælb] Albe *f*, Chorhemd *n*.

Al·ba·ni·an [æl'beinjən] 1. albanisch; 2. Albanier(in).

al·ba·tross ['ælbətrɔs] Albatros *m*, Sturmvogel *m*.

al·be·it [ɔːl'biːit] obgleich, obwohl.

al·bi·no *biol.* [æl'biːnəu] Albino *m*.

al·bum ['ælbəm] Album *n*; Schallplattenalbum *n*.

al·bu·men, al·bu·min ⚗ ['ælbjumin] Eiweiß(stoff *m*) *n*; **al·bu·mi-nous** [æl'bjuːminəs] eiweißartig; eiweißhaltig.

al·chem·ic, al·chem·i·cal □ [æl-'kemik(əl)] alchimistisch; **al·che-mist** ['ælkimist] Alchimist *m*; '**al-che·my** Alchimie *f*.

al·co·hol ['ælkəhɔl] Alkohol *m*; **al-co'hol·ic** 1. alkoholisch; Alkohol...; 2. Alkoholiker(in); '**al·co·hol·ism** Alkoholvergiftung *f*; **al·co·hol·ize** ['~laiz] alkoholisieren.

al·cove ['ælkəuv] Alkoven *m*;

Nische *f*; (Garten)Laube *f*.

al·der ⚘ ['ɔːldə] Erle *f*; Erlen...

al·der·man ['ɔːldəmən] Ratsherr *m*; Stadtrat *m*; **al·der·man·ic** [~'mæ-nik] ratsherrlich; *fig.* würdevoll; **al·der·man·ship** ['~mənʃip] Ratsherrnamt *n*.

ale [eil] Ale *n (engl. Bier)*.

a·lee ⚓ [ə'liː] leewärts.

a·lem·bic ⚗ [ə'lembik] Destillierkolben *m*.

a·lert [ə'ləːt] 1. □ wachsam; munter; 2. Alarmbereitschaft *f*; (Flieger-) Alarm *m*; *on the* ~ auf der Hut; *in* Alarmbereitschaft; **a'lert·ness** Wachsamkeit *f*; Munterkeit *f*.

Al·ex·an·drine [ælig'zændrain] Alexandriner *m (12silbiger Vers)*.

al·fal·fa ⚘ [æl'fælfə] Luzerne *f*.

al·fres·co [æl'freskəu] im Freien; ~ *lunch* Mittagessen *n* im Freien.

al·ga ⚘ ['ælgə], *pl.* **al·gae** ['ældʒiː] Alge *f*.

al·ge·bra ⚗ ['ældʒibrə] Algebra *f*; **al·ge·bra·ic** [~'breiik] algebraisch.

a·li·as ['eiliæs] 1. alias, sonst (genannt); 2. angenommener Name *m*, Deckname *m*.

al·i·bi ['ælibai] Alibi *n*; *Am.* F Entschuldigung *f*; Ausrede *f*.

al·ien ['eiljən] 1. fremd, ausländisch; *fig.* fremd (*to dat.*); 2. Ausländer (-in); '**al·ien·a·ble** veräußerlich; **al·ien·ate** ['~eit] veräußern; *fig.* entfremden, abspenstig machen *(from dat.)*; **al·ien·a·tion** Veräußerung *f*; *fig.* Entfremdung *f*; ~ *of mind* Geistesgestörtheit *f*; '**al·ien-ist** Irrenarzt *m*, Psychiater *m*.

a·light[1] [ə'lait] brennend, in Flammen; erhellt.

a·light[2] [~] ab-, aussteigen; ⚔ niedergehen, landen; sich niederlassen *(on* auf *acc. od. dat.)*.

a·lign [ə'lain] (sich) (aus)richten *(with* nach*)*; *surv.* abstecken; ~ *o.s. with* sich anschließen an *(acc.)*; **a'lign·ment** Ausrichtung *f*; *surv.* Absteckung(slinie) *f*.

a·like [ə'laik] 1. *adj.* gleich, ähnlich; 2. *adv.* gleich; in gleicher Weise; ebenso.

al·i·ment ['ælimənt] Nahrung *f*; **al·i·men·ta·ry** [~'mentəri] nahrhaft; Nahrungs...; Ernährungs...; ~ *canal* Verdauungskanal *m*; **al·i-men'ta·tion** Ernährung *f*, Unterhalt *m*.

al·i·mo·ny ℔ ['ælimǝni] Unterhalt *m* (*bsd. für geschiedene Ehefrau*).

a·line(**·ment**) [ǝ'lain(mǝnt)] = *align* (*-ment*).

al·i·quant ∧ ['ælikwǝnt] nicht (*ohne Rest*) aufgehend; **al·i·quot** ['⁓kwɔt] (*ohne Rest*) aufgehend.

a·live [ǝ'laiv] lebend, lebendig; munter, lebhaft; in Kraft, wirksam, gültig; (*to*) bewußt (*gen.*), empfänglich (für), Anteil nehmend (an *acc.*); (*with*) voll (von), belebt (von), wimmelnd (von *od.* vor *dat.*); *be* ⁓ am Leben sein, leben; ⚡ Strom führen; *man* ⁓! F Menschenskind!; *keep* ⁓ aufrechterhalten; *look* ⁓! F beeil dich!, mach schnell!

al·ka·li ⚕ ['ælkǝlai] Alkali *n*, Laugensalz *n*; **al·ka·line** ['⁓lain] alkalisch.

all [ɔːl] **1.** *adj.* all; ganz; jede(r, -s); ⁓ *day* (*long*) den ganzen Tag; ⁓ *kind*(*s*) *of books* allerlei Bücher; *s. above, after*; *for* ⁓ *that* dessenungeachtet, trotzdem; **2.** alles; alle *pl.*; *my* ⁓ mein Alles; ⁓ *of them* sie alle; *not at* ⁓ durchaus nicht, überhaupt nicht; *for* ⁓ (*that*) *I care* meinetwegen; *for* ⁓ *i know* soviel ich weiß; *in* ⁓ zusammen, insgesamt; **3.** *adv.* ganz, gänzlich, völlig; ⁓ *at once* auf einmal, plötzlich; ⁓ *the better* desto besser; ⁓ *but* beinahe, fast; ⁓ *in Am.* F fertig, ganz erledigt; ⁓ *right* (alles) in Ordnung; fertig; ganz recht!; gut!, schön!

all-A·mer·i·can [ɔːlǝ'merikǝn] rein amerikanisch; die ganzen USA vertretend.

al·lay [ǝ'lei] beruhigen; mildern, lindern; *Durst* stillen.

al·le·ga·tion [æli'geiʃǝn] *unerwiesene* Behauptung *f*; Aussage *f*; Darstellung *f*; **al·lege** [ǝ'ledʒ] *Unerwiesenes* behaupten; angeben; **al·leged** angeblich, vermeintlich.

al·le·giance [ǝ'liːdʒǝns] Lehnspflicht *f*; Loyalität *f*; (Untertanen)Treue *f* (*to* zu); *oath of* ⁓ Treueid *m*, Untertaneneid *m*.

al·le·gor·ic, al·le·gor·i·cal □ [æli-'gɔrik(ǝl)] sinnbildlich, allegorisch; **al·le·go·rize** ['æligǝraiz] allegorisch darstellen; **'al·le·go·ry** Allegorie *f*.

al·le·lu·ia [æli'luːjǝ] Halleluja *n*.

al·ler·gic [ǝ'lǝːdʒik] (*a. fig.*) □ allergisch (*to* gegen); **al·ler·gy** ✿ ['ælǝdʒi] Allergie *f* (*Überempfindlichkeit*).

al·le·vi·ate [ǝ'liːvieit] erleichtern, lindern; **al·le·vi·a·tion** Erleichterung *f*, Linderung *f*.

al·ley ['æli] Allee *f*; Gäßchen *n*; *bsd. Am.* schmale Zufahrtstraße *f* zwischen der Rückseite zweier Häuserreihen; *s. back⁓*; Gang *m*; *s. blind 1, skittle-⁓*; *that is right down his* ⁓ F das ist etwas für ihn; das ist sein Fall; **'al·ley·way** *Am.* Gasse *f*, schmale Straße *f*.

All Fools' Day ['ɔːl'fuːlzdei] der 1. April.

al·li·ance [ǝ'laiǝns] Bündnis *n*, Bund *m*; Verwandtschaft *f*; *form an* ⁓ ein Bündnis schließen.

al·li·ga·tor *zo.* ['æligeitǝ] Alligator *m*.

all-in ['ɔːl'in] Gesamt..., alles inbegriffen.

al·lit·er·ate [ǝ'litǝreit] alliterieren; **al·lit·er·a·tion** Alliteration *f*, Stabreim *m*; **al·lit·er·a·tive** [⁓rǝtiv] □ alliterierend.

all...: '⁓-'mains ⚡ Allstrom...; '⁓-'met·al Ganzmetall...

al·lo·cate ['ælǝukeit] zuteilen; anweisen; **al·lo·ca·tion** Zuteilung *f*; Zahlungsanweisung *f*.

al·lo·cu·tion [ælǝu'kjuːʃǝn] feierliche Ansprache *f*.

al·lop·a·thist ✿ [ǝ'lɔpǝθist] Allopath *m*; **al'lop·a·thy** ✿ Allopathie *f*.

al·lot [ǝ'lɔt] an-, zuweisen, zuteilen; zugestehen; **al'lot·ment** Zu-, Verteilung *f*; Anteil *m*; Los *n im Leben*; Parzelle *f*; Schrebergarten *m*.

all-out ['ɔːl'aut] umfassend, total, Groß...; ⁓ *effort* Anstrengung *f* aller Kräfte.

al·low [ǝ'lau] erlauben; bewilligen, gewähren; einräumen; ermöglichen; ab-, anrechnen; vergüten; *be* ⁓*ed to* dürfen, die Erlaubnis haben zu; ⁓ *for* berücksichtigen, bedenken; in Betracht ziehen; *it* ⁓*s of no excuse* es läßt sich nicht entschuldigen; **al'low·a·ble** □ erlaubt, zulässig; **al'low·ance 1.** Erlaubnis *f*; Bewilligung *f*; Kost-, Taschengeld *n*, Zuschuß *m*; Rente *f*; Ration *f*; Abzug *m*, Rabatt *m*, Vergütung *f*; Ermäßigung *f*; Nachsicht *f*; ⊕ Toleranz *f*; *make* ⁓ *for* Nachsicht üben mit *j-m*; *et.*

berücksichtigen; 2. auf Rationen setzen; *Brot etc.* rationieren.

al·loy 1. ['æləi] Legierung *f*; [ə'ləi] *fig.* Beimischung *f*; 2. [ᴗ] legieren; *fig.* verunedeln; (ver)mischen.

all...: '**ᴗ-'pur·pose** Allzweck..., Universal...; '**ᴗ-'red** rein britisch; '**ᴗ-'round** allseitig; zu allem brauchbar; ✝ Pauschal...

All Saints' Day ['ɔ:l'seintsdei] Allerheiligen *n* (1. *November*).

All Souls' Day ['ɔ:l'səulzdei] Allerseelen *n* (2. *November*).

all...: '**ᴗ-'star** *Am. Sport u. thea.* aus den besten (Schau)Spielern bestehend; '**ᴗ-'time** unerreicht, beispiellos; ~ *high* Höchstleistung *f*, -stand *m*; ~ *low* Tiefststand *m*.

al·lude [ə'lu:d] anspielen (*to* auf *acc.*).

al·lure [ə'ljuə] (an-, ver)locken; **al'lure·ment** Verlockung *f*; Lockmittel *n*; Reiz *m*; **al'lur·ing** □ verlockend.

al·lu·sion [ə'lu:ʒən] Anspielung *f* (*to* auf *acc.*); **al'lu·sive** □ anspielend (*to* auf *acc.*); verblümt.

al·lu·vi·al [ə'lu:vjəl] alluvial, angeschwemmt; **al'lu·vi·on** [ᴗvjən] Anschwemmung *f*; **al'lu·vi·um** [ᴗvjəm] Schwemmland *n*, Alluvium *n*.

'**all-'weath·er** Allwetter...

al·ly 1. [ə'lai] (sich) vereinigen, -binden, -bünden (*to, with* mit); allied *to fig.* verwandt *od.* verbunden mit; 2. ['ælai] Verbündete *m, f*, Bundesgenosse *m; the Allies pl.* die Alliierten *pl.*

al·ma·nac ['ɔ:lmənæk] Almanach *m*.

al·might·i·ness [ɔ:l'maitinis] Allmacht *f*; **al'might·y** 1. □ allmächtig; F mächtig; 2. ♀ Allmächtige *m*.

al·mond ['ɑ:mənd] Mandel *f*.

al·mon·er ['ɑ:mənə] Krankenhausfürsorger(in); *hist.* Almosenpfleger *m*.

al·most ['ɔ:lməust] fast, beinahe.

alms [ɑ:mz] *sg. u. pl.* Almosen *n*; '**ᴗ-bag** Klingelbeutel *m*; '**ᴗ-house** Armenhaus *n*.

al·oe ♀ *u. pharm.* ['æləu] Aloe *f*.

a·loft [ə'lɔft] (hoch) (dr)oben; (nach) oben (♣ *in der od. die Takelung*).

a·lone [ə'ləun] allein; *let od.* leave *s.o.* ~ *j.* in Ruhe lassen; *let it* ~! laß das bleiben!; *let* ~ *...* abgesehen von *...*; geschweige denn *...*

a·long [ə'lɔŋ] 1. *adv.* weiter, vorwärts, her; mit, bei (sich); *all* ~ die ganze Zeit; ~ *with* zs. mit; *get* ~ *with* vorankommen mit, Fortschritte machen bei; auskommen mit; *get* ~ *with you!* F scher dich weg!; 2. *prp.* entlang, längs; ~ *here* in dieser Richtung; **a'long·shore** längs der Küste; **a'long'side** 1. ♣ *adv.* längsseits; Seite an Seite; 2. *prp. fig.* neben.

a·loof [ə'lu:f] fern; weitab; *keep* ~ (*from*) sich fernhalten (von); *stand* ~ für sich bleiben; **a'loof·ness** Sichfernhalten *n*; Zurückhaltung *f*.

a·loud [ə'laud] laut; hörbar.

alp [ælp] Alp(e) *f*; *ᴗs pl.* Alpen *pl.*

al·pac·a [æl'pækə] *zo.* Alpaka *n*; Alpakawolle *f*, -stoff *m*.

al·pen·stock ['ælpinstɔk] Bergstock *m*.

al·pha·bet ['ælfəbit] Alphabet *n*; **al·pha·bet·ic, al·pha·bet·i·cal** □ [ᴗ'betik(əl)] alphabetisch.

Al·pine ['ælpain] Alpen...; alpin; **al·pin·ist** ['ᴗpinist] Alpinist(in).

al·read·y [ɔ:l'redi] bereits, schon.

Al·sa·tian [æl'seiʃjən] 1. elsässisch; 2. Elsässer(in); *a.* ~ *dog* deutscher Schäferhund *m*.

al·so ['ɔ:lsəu] auch; ferner, außerdem; ~ *ran* Rennsport: ferner liefen; '**al·so-ran** siegloses Pferd *n*; *fig.* Versager *m*, Niete *f*.

al·tar ['ɔ:ltə] Altar *m*; '**ᴗ-piece** Altar(blatt *n*, -gemälde *n*) *m*.

al·ter ['ɔ:ltə] (sich) (ver)ändern; ab-, umändern; *Am.* F *Tier* kastrieren; '**al·ter·a·ble** veränderlich; **al·ter·'a·tion** Änderung *f* (*to an dat.*).

al·ter·cate ['ɔ:ltəkeit] zanken; **al·ter'ca·tion** Zank *m*, Streit *m*.

al·ter·nate 1. ['ɔ:ltəneit] abwechseln (lassen); *alternating current* ⚡ Wechselstrom *m*; 2. □ [ɔ:l'tə:nit] abwechselnd; Wechsel...; *on* ~ *days* einen Tag um den andern; 3. [ɔ:l'tə:nit] *Am.* Stellvertreter *m*; **al·ter·na·tion** [ɔ:ltə'neiʃən] Abwechslung *f*; Wechsel *m*; **al·ter·na·tive** [ɔ:l'tə:nətiv] 1. □ einander ausschließend; nur eine Möglichkeit lassend; ⊕ Ausweich...; 2. Alternative *f*; Wahl *f zwischen zwei Dingen*; Möglichkeit *f*; *I have no* ~ mir bleibt keine Wahl; **al·ter·na·tor** ⚡ ['ɔ:ltəneitə] Wechselstrommaschine *f*.

al·though [ɔːlˈðəu] obwohl, obgleich.

al·tim·e·ter [ˈæltimiːtə] Höhenmesser *m*.

al·ti·tude [ˈæltitjuːd] Höhe *f* (*bsd. bei Messungen*); ～ *flight* Höhenflug *m*.

al·to ♪ [ˈæltəu] Alt(stimme *f*) *m*.

al·to·geth·er [ɔːltəˈgeðə] **1.** im ganzen (genommen), alles in allem, insgesamt, gänzlich, ganz und gar; **2.** *in the* ～ F pudel-, splitternackt.

al·tru·ism [ˈæltruizəm] Altruismus *m*, Uneigennützigkeit *f*; **ˈal·tru·ist** Altruist(in); **al·tru·ˈis·tic** (～*ally*) altruistisch.

al·um ⚗ [ˈæləm] Alaun *m*; **a·lu·mi·na** [əˈljuːminə] Tonerde *f*; **al·u·min·i·um** [æljuˈminjəm] Aluminium *n*; ～ *acetate* essigsaure Tonerde *f*; **a·lu·mi·nous** [əˈljuːminəs] alaunartig, -haltig; **a·lu·mi·num** [əˈluːminəm] *Am. für* aluminium.

a·lum·na [əˈlʌmnə], *pl*. **a·ˈlum·nae** [～niː] *Am*. ehemalige Schülerin *f od*. Studentin *f*; **a·ˈlum·nus** [～nəs], *pl*. **a·ˈlum·ni** [～nai] *Am*. ehemaliger Schüler *m od*. Student *m*.

al·ve·o·lar [ælˈviələ] alveolar; *anat*. Zahn...; *gr*. am Zahndamm artikuliert.

al·ways [ˈɔːlweiz] immer, stets.

am [æm; əm] (*irr. be*) bin.

a·mal·gam [əˈmælgəm] Amalgam *n*; **a·ˈmal·gam·ate** [～meit] amalgam'ierⸯ; (sich) verschmelzen; **a·mal·gam·ˈa·tion** Amalgamierung *f*; Verschmelzung *f*; ✝ Fusion *f*.

a·man·u·en·sis [əmænjuˈensis], *pl*. **a·man·u·ˈen·ses** [～siːz] (Schreib-) Gehilfe *m*, Sekretär *m*.

am·a·ranth ♀ [ˈæmərænθ] Fuchsschwanz *m*.

a·mass [əˈmæs] an-, aufhäufen.

am·a·teur [ˈæmətəː] Amateur *m*; Liebhaber *m*; Dilettant *m*; **am·a·ˈteur·ish** dilettantisch.

am·a·tive [ˈæmətiv], **am·a·to·ry** [ˈ～təri] verliebt; Liebes...; erotisch.

a·maze [əˈmeiz] in Staunen setzen, überraschen, verblüffen; **a·ˈmazed** □ höchst erstaunt (*at* über *acc*.); **a·ˈmaze·ment** Staunen *n*, Verwunderung *f*, Verblüffung *f*; **a·ˈmaz·ing** □ erstaunlich, verblüffend.

Am·a·zon [ˈæməzən] Amazone *f*;

♀ Mannweib *n*; **Am·a·zo·ni·an** [～ˈzəunjən] amazonenhaft.

am·bas·sa·dor [æmˈbæsədə] Botschafter *m*, Gesandte *m*; **am·bas·sa·do·ri·al** [～ˈdɔːriəl] Botschafts..., Gesandtschafts...; **am·ˈbas·sa·dress** [～dris] Botschafterin *f*; Frau *f* e-s Botschafters.

am·ber [ˈæmbə] **1.** Bernstein *m*; Gelb *n*, gelbes Licht *n* (*Verkehrsampel*); **2.** bernsteinfarben; Bernstein...; **am·ber·gris** [ˈ～griːs] Ambra *f*.

am·bi·dex·trous □ [ˈæmbiˈdekstrəs] beidhändig, mit beiden Händen gleich geschickt; *fig*. hinterhältig.

am·bi·ent [ˈæmbiənt] umgebend, Umgebungs...

am·bi·gu·i·ty [æmbiˈgjuːiti] Zwei-, Vieldeutigkeit *f*, Doppelsinn *m*; **am·ˈbig·u·ous** [～gjuəs] □ zwei-, vieldeutig; doppelsinnig; zweifelhaft.

am·bit [ˈæmbit] Gebiet *n*, Bereich *m*.

am·bi·tion [æmˈbiʃən] Ehrgeiz *m*; Streben *n* (*of, for* nach); ～*s pl*. Bestrebungen *f/pl*.; **am·ˈbi·tious** □ ehrgeizig; begierig (*of, for* nach).

am·bi·va·lent [ˈæmbiˈveilənt] ambivalent, doppelwertig, zwiespältig.

am·ble [ˈæmbl] **1.** Paßgang *m*; **2.** im Paßgang gehen *od*. reiten; *fig*. (～ *up* daher)schlendern; **ˈam·bler** Paßgänger *m*, Zelter *m*.

am·bro·si·a [æmˈbrəuzjə] Ambrosia *f*, Götterspeise *f*; **am·ˈbro·si·al** □ ambrosisch; *fig*. köstlich.

am·bu·lance [ˈæmbjuləns] Krankenwagen *m*; *attr*. Sanitäts...; ～ *box* Verbandskasten *m*; ～ *station* Sanitätswache *f*, Unfallstation *f*; **ˈam·bu·lant** ambulant.

am·bu·la·to·ry [ˈæmbjulətəri]**1.**umherziehend, Wander...; zum Gehen geeignet; beweglich; **2.** Wandelhalle *f*, -gang *m*.

am·bus·cade [æmbəsˈkeid], **am·bush** [ˈæmbuʃ] **1.** Hinterhalt *m*; *be od. lie in* ～ *for s.o.* j-m auflauern; **2.** *v/t*. auflauern (*dat*.); aus dem Hinterhalt überfallen; *v/i*. im Hinterhalt liegen.

a·meer [əˈmiə] Emir *m*.

a·mel·io·rate [əˈmiːljəreit] verbessern; besser werden; **a·mel·io·ˈra·tion** Verbesserung *f*.

a·men ['ɑ:'men] Amen *n*.

a·me·na·ble □ [ə'mi:nəbl] unterworfen; zugänglich; verantwortlich (*alle: to dat.*).

a·mend [ə'mend] *v/t*. verbessern; 𝕥𝕥 berichtigen; *Gesetz* ergänzen, (ab)ändern; *v/i*. sich bessern; **a'mend·ment** Besserung *f*; 𝕥𝕥 Berichtigung *f*; *parl.* Zusatz-, Änderungsantrag *m*; *Am*. Zusatzartikel *m* zur Verfassung der USA; **a'mends** *pl*. Ersatz *m*; *make ~ for et*. ersetzen, wiedergutmachen.

a·men·i·ty [ə'mi:niti] Annehmlichkeit *f*; Anmut *f*; *amenities pl*. Höflichkeiten *f/pl*.; natürliche Vorzüge *m/pl*., Reize *m/pl*.

A·mer·i·can [ə'merikən] **1.** amerikanisch; *~ cloth* Wachstuch *n*; *~ Legion* Frontkämpferbund *m* der USA; *~ plan Am*. Hotelzimmervermietung *mit voller Verpflegung*; **2.** Amerikaner(in); **A'mer·i·can·ism** Amerikanismus *m*; **A·mer·i·can·i'za·tion** Amerikanisierung *f*; **A'mer·i·can·ize** (sich) amerikanisieren.

am·e·thyst *min*. ['æmiθist] Amethyst *m*.

a·mi·a·bil·i·ty [eimjə'biliti] Liebenswürdigkeit *f*; **'a·mi·a·ble** □ liebenswürdig, freundlich.

am·i·ca·ble □ ['æmikəbl] freundschaftlich; gütlich.

a·mid(st) [ə'mid(st)] inmitten (*gen*.); (mitten) unter; mitten in (*dat*.).

a·mid·ships ⚓ [ə'midʃips] mittschiffs.

a·miss [ə'mis] verkehrt; übel; ungelegen; *take ~* übelnehmen; *it would not be ~ (for him)* es würde (ihm) nicht schaden; *what is ~ with it?* was ist denn damit los?

am·i·ty ['æmiti] Freundschaft *f*.

am·me·ter ⚡ ['æmitə] Amperemeter *n*.

am·mo·ni·a [ə'məunjə] Ammoniak *n*; *liquid ~* Salmiakgeist *m*; **am'mo·ni·ac** [~niæk], **am·mo·ni·a·cal** [æmou'naiəkəl] ammoniakalisch; *s. sal*.

am·mon·ite ['æmənait] Ammonshorn *n*, Ammonit *m*.

am·mu·ni·tion ✕ [æmju'niʃən] Munition *f*.

am·ne·sia ✗ [æm'ni:zjə] Gedächtnisverlust *m*, Amnesie *f*.

am·nes·ty ['æmnisti] **1.** Amnestie *f*

(*Straferlaß*); **2.** begnadigen.

a·m(o)e·ba *zo*. [ə'mi:bə] Amöbe *f*.

a·mok [ə'mɔk] = *amuck*.

a·mong(st) [ə'mʌŋ(st)] (mitten) unter, zwischen; *from ~* aus ... hervor; *be ~* gehören zu; *they had two pounds ~ them* sie hatten zusammen ...

a·mor·al [ei'mɔrəl] amoralisch.

am·o·rous □ ['æmərəs] verliebt (*of in acc*.); Liebes...; **'am·o·rous·ness** Verliebtheit *f*.

a·mor·phous [ə'mɔ:fəs] *min*. amorph; *fig*. ungestalt; formlos.

am·or·ti·za·tion [əmɔ:ti'zeiʃən] Tilgung *f*, Amortisation *f*; **am'or·tize** [~taiz] amortisieren, tilgen.

a·mount [ə'maunt] **1.** *~ to* sich belaufen auf (*acc*.), betragen; hinauslaufen auf (*acc*.); **2.** Betrag *m*, (Gesamt)Summe *f*, Höhe *f* (*e~r Summe*); Menge *f*; Bedeutung *f*, Wert *m*; *to the ~ of* bis zur *od*. in Höhe von; im Betrage von.

a·mour [ə'muə] Liebschaft *f*; **~·pro·pre** ['æmuə'prɔpr] Selbstachtung *f*; Eitelkeit *f*.

amp ⚡, F [æmp] = *ampere*.

am·pere ⚡ ['æmpɛə] Ampere *n*.

am·phet·a·mine ⚗ [æm'fetəmi:n] Benzedrin *n*.

am·phib·i·an *zo*. [æm'fibiən] **1.** Amphibie *f*; **2.** = **am'phib·i·ous** □ Amphibien...; amphibisch.

am·phi·the·a·tre, *Am*. **am·phi·the·a·ter** ['æmfiθiətə] Amphitheater *n*.

am·ple □ ['æmpl] weit, groß; geräumig; reichlich, mehr als genug; genügend; ausführlich.

am·pli·fi·ca·tion [æmplifi'keiʃən] Erweiterung *f*; *rhet*. weitere Ausführung *f*; *phys*. Verstärkung *f*; **am·pli·fi·er** ['~faiə] *Radio*: Verstärker *m*; **'am·pli·fy** erweitern, ausdehnen; verstärken; weiter ausführen; ausführlich sprechen; *valve* Verstärkerröhre *f*; **am·pli·tude** ['~tju:d] Umfang *m*, Weite *f*, Fülle *f*; *phys*. Amplitude *f* (*Schwingungsweite*).

am·poule ['æmpu:l] Ampulle *f*.

am·pu·tate ⚕ ['æmpjuteit] amputieren, abnehmen; **am·pu'ta·tion** Amputation *f*.

a·muck [ə'mʌk]: *run ~* Amok laufen; *run ~ at od. on od. against* *fig.* herfallen über (*acc.*).

am·u·let ['æmjulit] Amulett *n.*

a·muse [ə'mju:z] amüsieren; unterhalten; belustigen, Spaß machen (*dat.*); **a'muse·ment** Unterhaltung *f;* Zeitvertreib *m;* Belustigung *f;* ~ arcade Spielhalle *f; for* ~ zum Vergnügen; **a'mus·ing** ☐ amüsant; unterhaltsam.

an [æn, ən] *Artikel: s. a.*

an·a·bap·tist [ænə'bæptist] Wiedertäufer *m.*

a·nach·ro·nism [ə'nækrənizəm] Anachronismus *m.*

an·a·con·da *zo.* [ænə'kəndə] Anakonda *f;* Riesenschlange *f.*

a·n(a)e·mi·a [ə'ni:mjə] Anämie *f,* Blutarmut *f;* **a'n(a)e·mic** blutarm.

an·(a)es·the·si·a [ænis'θi:zjə] Anästhesie *f,* Narkose *f;* **an·(a)es·thet·ic** [~'θetik] **1.** (~*ally*) betäubend, Narkose...; **2.** Betäubungsmittel *n;* **a'n(a)es·the·tist** Anästhesist *m,* Narkosearzt *m;* **a'n(a)es·the·tize** betäuben.

an·a·log·ic, an·a·log·i·cal ☐ [ænə-'lɔdʒik(əl)], **a·nal·o·gous** ☐ [ə'næləgəs] analog, ähnlich; **a'nal·o·gy** [~dʒi] Ähnlichkeit *f,* Analogie *f.*

an·a·lyse ['ænəlaiz] analysieren; zerlegen; *gr.* zergliedern; untersuchen; **a·nal·y·sis** [ə'næləsis], *pl.* **a'nal·y·ses** [~si:z] Analyse *f,* Zerlegung *f,* Zergliederung *f;* **an·a·lyst** ['ænəlist] Analytiker *m; public* ~ Gerichtschemiker *m.*

an·a·lyt·ic, an·a·lyt·i·cal ☐ [ænə-'litik(əl)] analytisch.

an·ar·chic, an·ar·chi·cal ☐ [æ'nɑː-kik(əl)] gesetzlos; zügellos; **an·ar·chism** ['ænəkizəm] Anarchismus *m;* **'an·arch·ist** Anarchist(in); **'an·arch·y** Anarchie *f,* Gesetzlosigkeit *f;* Zügellosigkeit *f.*

a·nath·e·ma [ə'næθimə] Kirchenbann *m;* **a'nath·e·ma·tize** in den Bann tun; (ver)fluchen.

an·a·tom·i·cal ☐ [ænə'tɔmikəl] anatomisch; **a·nat·o·mist** [ə'nætəmist] Anatom *m;* **a'nat·o·mize** zergliedern; **a'nat·o·my** Anatomie *f;* Zergliederung *f,* Analyse *f;* F Gerippe *n.*

an·ces·tor ['ænsistə] Stammvater *m,* Vorfahr *m,* Ahn *m;* **an·ces·tral** [~'sestrəl] angestammt; Stamm...; Ahnen...; **an·ces·tress** ['ænsistris] Stammutter *f,* Ahne *f;* **'an·ces·try** Abstammung *f;* Ahnen *m/pl.*

an·chor ⚓ *u. fig.* ['æŋkə] **1.** Anker *m; at* ~ vor Anker; **2.** *v/t.* verankern; *v/i.* ankern; vor Anker gehen; **'an·chor·age** Ankerplatz *m.*

an·cho·ret, an·cho·rite ['æŋkəret; '~rait] Einsiedler *m.*

an·chor·man ['æŋkəmən] *Am.* Moderator *m* e-r Nachrichtensendung.

an·cho·vy ['æntʃəvi] An(s)chovis *f,* Sardelle *f.*

an·cient ['einʃənt] **1.** alt, antik; uralt; **2.** *the* ~s *pl.* die Alten *pl.* (*Griechen und Römer*), die antiken Klassiker *pl.;* **'an·cient·ly** vorzeiten.

an·cil·lar·y [æn'siləri] untergeordnet (*to dat.*), Hilfs..., Neben...; ~ road Nebenstraße *f.*

and [ænd, ənd, F ən] und; *thousands* ~ *thousands* Tausende und aber Tausende; *there are flowers* ~ *flowers* es gibt mancherlei Blumen; *try* ~ *take it* versuche es zu nehmen.

and·i·ron ['ændaiən] Feuerbock *m.*

an·ec·do·tal [ænek'dəutl], **an·ec·dot·i·cal** [~'dɔtikəl] anekdotisch; **an·ec·dote** ['ænikdəut] Anekdote *f.*

an·e·mom·e·ter [æni'mɔmitə] Windmesser *m.*

a·nem·o·ne [ə'neməni] Anemone *f.*

an·er·oid ['ænərɔid] *a.* ~ *barometer* Aneroidbarometer *n.*

a·new [ə'nju:] von neuem.

an·gel ['eindʒəl] (*a. fig.*) Engel *m;* finanzkräftiger Hintermann *m;* **an·gel·ic, an·gel·i·cal** ☐ [æn'dʒelik(əl)] engelgleich, -haft.

an·ge·lus ['ændʒiləs] Angelus(gebet *n,* -läuten *n*) *m.*

an·ger ['æŋgə] **1.** Zorn *m,* Ärger *m* (*at über acc.*); **2.** erzürnen, ärgern.

an·gi·na ⚕ [æn'dʒainə] Angina *f,* Halsentzündung *f;* ~ *pectoris* Angina *f* pectoris.

an·gle ['æŋgl] **1.** Winkel *m,* Ecke *f;* *fig.* Gesichtswinkel *m,* Standpunkt *m;* ~-*dozer* Planierraupe *f;* ~-*iron* Winkeleisen *n;* ~-*parking mot.* Parken *n* quer zum Gehweg; *at right* ~*s* im rechten Winkel; **2.** angeln (*for* nach); **'an·gler** Angler(in).

An·gles ['æŋglz] *pl.* Angeln *pl.*

An·gli·can ['æŋglikən] **1.** anglikanisch, hochkirchlich; *Am. a.* englisch; **2.** Anglikaner(in).

An·gli·cism ['æŋglisizəm] englische Spracheigenheit f, Anglizismus m.

an·gling ['æŋglin] Angeln n.

An·glo-Sax·on ['æŋgləu'sæksən] **1.** Angelsachse m; **2.** angelsächsisch.

an·go·ra [æŋ'gɔːrə] Angorawolle f; ~ (cat) Angorakatze f.

an·gry ['æŋgri] zornig, böse (with s.o., at s.th. über, auf acc.); ärgerlich; 🌶 böse, schlimm.

an·guish ['æŋgwiʃ] Pein f, (Seelen-) Qual f, Schmerz m.

an·gu·lar □ ['æŋgjulə] wink(e)lig; Winkel...; fig. eckig; ~ point ⚚ Scheitelpunkt m; **an·gu·lar·i·ty** [~'læriti] Winkligkeit f; fig. Eckigkeit f.

an·i·line 🜚 ['ænili:n] Anilin n.

an·i·mad·ver·sion [ænimæd'vəːʃən] Verweis m, Tadel m; **an·i·madvert** [~'vəːt] tadeln, kritisieren, bekritteln (on, upon acc.).

an·i·mal ['æniməl] **1.** Tier n; **2.** animalisch; tierisch; Tier...; ~ home Tierheim n; ~ kingdom zo. Tierreich n; ~ lover Tierfreund m; ~ shelter Am. Tierheim n; ~ spirits pl. Lebensgeister m/pl.; **an·i·mal·cule** [~'mælkju:l] Tierchen n; **an·i·mal·ism** ['~məlizəm] Vertiertheit f, Sinnlichkeit f.

an·i·mate 1. ['ænimeit] beleben; beseelen; aufmuntern; **2.** ['~mit], mst **an·i·mat·ed** ['~meitid] belebt, lebend(ig); fig. lebhaft, munter.

an·i·ma·tion [æni'meiʃən] Leben n (und Treiben n), Lebhaftigkeit f, Munterkeit f.

an·i·mos·i·ty [æni'mɔsiti], a. **an·imus** ['æniməs] Feindseligkeit f.

an·ise ⚘ ['ænis] Anis m; **an·i·seed** ['~si:d] **1.** Anissamen m; **2.** Anis...

an·kle ['æŋkl] Fußknöchel m.

an·klet ['æŋklit] Fußkettchen n; Söckchen n.

an·nals ['ænlz] pl. Jahrbücher n/pl.; historischer Bericht m.

an·neal ⊕ [ə'niːl] Metall (aus-) glühen; härten (a. fig.).

an·nex 1. [ə'neks] anhängen, beifügen (to dat.); annektieren, sich aneignen; (sich) einverleiben; ~ to Bedingung etc. knüpfen an (acc.); **2.** ['æneks] Anhang m, Nachtrag m; Nebengebäude n; **an·nex·a'tion** Annexion f, Aneignung f; Einverleibung f.

an·ni·hi·late [ə'naiəleit] vernichten;

= annul; **an·ni·hi'la·tion** Vernichtung f; = annulment.

an·ni·ver·sa·ry [æni'vəːsəri] Jahrestag m; Jahresfeier f.

an·no·tate ['ænəuteit] mit Anmerkungen versehen; kommentieren (a. on acc.); **an·no'ta·tion** Kommentieren n; Anmerkung f.

an·nounce [ə'nauns] ankündigen, bekanntgeben, anzeigen; ansagen; (an)melden; **an'nounce·ment** Ankündigung f; Ansage f; Radio: Durchsage f; (An)Meldung f; Anzeige f; **an'nounc·er** Radio: Ansager m.

an·noy [ə'nɔi] ärgern; belästigen, stören; schikanieren; **an'noy·ance** Störung f; Plage f; Ärgernis n; **an'noyed** verdrießlich, ärgerlich (Person); **an'noy·ing** □ ärgerlich (Sache); lästig, störend.

an·nu·al [ə'njuəl] **1.** □ jährlich; Jahres...; bsd. ⚘ einjährig; ~ ring ⚘ Jahresring m; **2.** einjährige Pflanze f; Jahrbuch n.

an·nu·i·tant [ə'njuːitənt] Leibrentner m.

an·nu·i·ty [ə'njuːiti] (Jahres)Rente f, Jahreszahlung f; a. ~ bond ✝ Rentenbrief m; s. life.

an·nul [ə'nʌl] für ungültig erklären, aufheben, annullieren.

an·nu·lar □ ['ænjulə] ringförmig.

an·nul·ment [ə'nʌlmənt] Aufhebung f, Nichtigkeitserklärung f.

an·nun·ci·a·tion [ənʌnsi'eiʃən] Verkündigung f; **an'nun·ci·a·tor** Klappenkasten m e-r Klingelanlage etc. [sitiver Pol m]

an·ode ⚡ ['ænəud] Anode f, po-]

an·o·dyne ['ænəudain] schmerzstillend(es Mittel n).

a·noint [ə'nɔint] bsd. eccl. salben (a. fig.); einschmieren.

a·nom·a·lous □ [ə'nɔmələs] anomal, unregelmäßig, regelwidrig; **a'nom·a·ly** Anomalie f.

a·non [ə'nɔn] sogleich, sofort; bald; ever and ~ immer wieder.

an·o·nym·i·ty [ænə'nimiti] Anonymität f; **a·non·y·mous** □ [ə'nɔniməs] anonym, ungenannt.

a·noph·e·les zo. [ə'nɔfili:z] Fiebermücke f.

an·oth·er [ə'nʌðə] ein anderer; ein zweiter; noch ein; ~ ten years weitere zehn Jahre; tell us ~! F das glaubst du doch selbst nicht!

an·swer ['ɑːnsə] **1.** *v/t. et.* beantworten, *j-m* antworten; entsprechen (*dat.*); *Zweck* erfüllen; *dem Steuer* gehorchen; *e-r Vorladung* Folge leisten; ~ *the bell od. door* (die Haustür) aufmachen; *v/i.* antworten (*to s.o. j-m*; *to a question* auf e-e Frage); entsprechen (*to dat.*); Erfolg haben, anschlagen; sich lohnen; ~ *back* frech antworten *od.* widersprechen (*bsd. Kinder gegenüber Erwachsenen*); ~ *for* einstehen für, die Folgen tragen von; bürgen für; ~ *to the name of*... auf den Namen ... hören; **2.** Antwort *f* (*to* auf *acc.*); ℞ Lösung *f*; ⚡ Replik *f*; **'answer·a·ble** □ verantwortlich.

ant [ænt] Ameise *f*.

an't [ɑːnt] F = *are not, am not*; *sl. od. prov.* = *is not*.

an·tag·o·nism [æn'tægənizəm] Widerstreit *m* (*between* zwischen *dat.*); Widerstand *m*, Feindschaft *f* (*to* gegen); **an'tag·o·nist** Gegner(in); **an·tag·o'nis·tic** (~*ally*) widerstreitend (*to dat.*); gegnerisch, feindlich (*to* gegen); **an'tag·o·nize** ankämpfen gegen; sich *j-n* zum Feind machen.

ant·arc·tic [ænt'ɑːktik] antarktisch; Südpol...; *the* ♋ die Antarktis; ♋ *Circle* südlicher Polarkreis *m*.

an·te [ænti] *Pokerspiel:* **1.** Einsatz *m*; **2.** *mst* ~ *up v/t. u. v/i.* (ein)setzen; *v/i. fig.* sein Scherflein beitragen.

an·te·ced·ence [ænti'siːdəns] Vortritt *m*, -rang *m*; *ast.* Rückläufigkeit *f*; **an·te'ced·ent 1.** □ vorhergehend; früher (*to* als); **2.** Vorhergehende *n*; *gr.* Beziehungswort *n*; *his* ~*s pl.* sein Vorleben *n*.

an·te·cham·ber ['ænti∫eimbə] Vorzimmer *n*.

an·te·date ['ænti'deit] zurückdatieren; (*zeitlich*) vorangehen (*dat.*).

an·te·di·lu·vi·an ['æntidi'luːvjən] vorsintflutlich(er Mensch *m*).

an·te·lope *zo.* ['æntiləup] Antilope *f*.

an·te me·rid·i·em ['ænti mə'ridiəm] vormittags.

an·te·na·tal [ænti'neitl] *bsd. Br.* **1.** vor der Geburt, pränatal; **2.** Mutterschaftsvorsorgeuntersuchung *f*.

an·ten·na [æn'tenə], *pl.* **an'ten·nae** [~niː] *zo.* Fühler *m*; *Radio, Fernsehen:* Antenne *f*.

an·te·ri·or [æn'tiəriə] vorhergehend;

früher (*to* als); vorder.

an·te-room ['æntirum] Vorzimmer *n*.

an·them ['ænθəm] Hymne *f*.

an·ther ♀ ['ænθə] Staubbeutel *m*.

ant-hill ['ænthil] Ameisenhaufen *m*.

an·thol·o·gy [æn'θɔlədʒi] Anthologie *f*, Gedichtsammlung *f*.

an·thra·cite *min.* ['ænθrəsait] Anthrazit *m*, Glanzkohle *f*; **an·thrax** *vet.* ['ænθræks] Milzbrand *m*.

an·thro·poid ['ænθrəupɔid] **1.** menschenähnlich; **2.** Menschenaffe *m*; **an·thro·po·log·i·cal** [ænθrəpə'lɔdʒikəl] anthropologisch; **an·thro·pol·o·gist** [ænθrə'pɔlədʒist] Anthropologe *m*; **an·thro'pol·o·gy** [~dʒi] Anthropologie *f*, Menschenkunde *f*.

an·ti... ['ænti] *in Zssgn* Gegen...; gegen ... eingestellt; anti..., Anti...

an·ti-air·craft ['ænti'eəkrɑːft] Fliegerabwehr...; ~ *gun* Fliegerabwehrgeschütz *n*.

an·ti·bi·ot·ic ♣ ['æntibai'ɔtik] Antibiotikum *n*.

an·ti·bod·y ♣ ['æntibɔdi] Antikörper *m*, Abwehrstoff *m*.

an·tic ['æntik] Posse *f*; ~*s pl.* Mätzchen *n/pl.*; (tolle) Sprünge *m/pl.*

An·ti·christ ['æntikraist] Antichrist *m*.

an·tic·i·pate [æn'tisipeit] vorwegnehmen; zuvorkommen (*dat.*); voraussehen, ahnen; erwarten; im voraus verbrauchen; **an·tic·i'pa·tion** Vorwegnahme *f*; Zuvorkommen *n*; Voraussicht *f*; Erwartung *f*; Vorgefühl *n*; Vorfreude *f*; *payment by* ~ Vorauszahlung *f*; *in* ~ im voraus; **an'tic·i·pa·to·ry** [~peitəri] vorwegnehmend.

an·ti·cler·i·cal ['ænti'klerikəl] □ antiklerikal, kirchenfeindlich.

an·ti·cli·max *rhet. u. fig.* ['ænti'klaimæks] (Ab)Fallen *n*, Abstieg *m*.

an·ti·clock·wise ['ænti'klɔkwaiz] entgegen dem *od.* gegen den Uhrzeigersinn.

an·ti·cor·ro·sive a·gent ['æntikə-'rəusiv'eidʒənt] Rostschutzmittel *n*.

an·ti·cy·clone *meteor.* ['ænti'saikləun] Antizyklone *f*, Hoch(druckgebiet) *n*.

an·ti·daz·zle *mot.* ['ænti'dæzl] Blendschutz...; ~ *switch* Abblendumschalter *m*.

an·ti·dote ['æntidəut] Gegengift *n*, -mittel *n* (*against, for, to* gegen).

an·ti-fas·cist ['ænti'fæʃist] **1.** Antifaschist(in); **2.** antifaschistisch.

an·ti-freeze *mot.* ['æntifri:z] Gefrierschutzmittel *n*.

an·ti-fric·tion ['ænti'frikʃən] Reibungsschutz *m*; *attr.* ⊕ Gleit...

an·ti·ha·lo *phot.* ['ænti'heiləu] lichthoffrei.

an·ti-knock *mot.* ['ænti'nɔk] **1.** klopffest; **2.** Antiklopfmittel *n*.

an·ti·mo·ny *min.* ['æntiməni] Antimon *n*.

an·tip·a·thy [æn'tipəθi] Antipathie *f*, Abneigung *f* (*against, to* gegen).

an·tip·o·dal □ [æn'tipədl] antipodisch, genau entgegengesetzt; **an·ti·pode** *fig.* ['ᴗpəud] genaues Gegenteil *n*; **an'tip·o·des** [ᴗpədi:z] *pl.* einander gegenüberliegende Seiten *f/pl.* der Erde.

an·ti-pol·lu·tion de·vice ['æntipɔ-'lu:ʃəndi'vais] Abgasentgiftungsanlage *f*.

an·ti·quar·i·an [ænti'kwɛəriən] **1.** □ Altertums...; **2.** Altertumsforscher *m*; **an·ti·quar·y** ['ᴗkwəri] Altertumsforscher *m*; Antiquitätensammler *m*, -händler *m*; **an·ti·quat·ed** ['ᴗkweitid] veraltet, überlebt, altmodisch, antiquiert.

an·tique [æn'ti:k] **1.** □ antik, alt; altmodisch; **2.** Antike *f*; alter Kunstgegenstand *m*; **an·tiq·ui·ty** [ᴗ'tikwiti] Altertum *n*; *die* Antike; Vorzeit *f*; *antiquities pl.* Altertümer *n/pl.*; Antiquitäten *f/pl.*

an·ti-rust ['ænti'rʌst] Rostschutz *m*.

an·ti-Sem·ite ['ænti'si:mait] Antisemit(in); **an·ti-Se·mit·ic** ['ᴗsi'mitik] antisemitisch; **an·ti-Sem·i·tism** ['ᴗ'semitizəm] Antisemitismus *m*.

an·ti·sep·tic [ænti'septik] antiseptisch(es Mittel *n*).

an·ti-skid ['ænti'skid] *mot.* Gleitschutz...; rutschfest.

an·ti·so·cial [ænti'səuʃəl] gesellschaftsfeindlich.

an·ti·tank ✗ [ænti'tæŋk] Panzerabwehr...

an·tith·e·sis [æn'tiθisis], *pl.* **an'tith·e·ses** [ᴗθisi:z] Gegensatz *m*; **an·ti·thet·ic, an·ti·thet·i·cal** □ [ᴗ'θetik(əl)] gegensätzlich.

ant·ler ['æntlə] Sprosse *f am Geweih*; ᴗ*s pl.* Geweih *n*.

an·to·nym ['æntəunim] Wort *n* entgegengesetzter Bedeutung.

A num·ber 1 ['ei nʌmbə 'wʌn] *Am.*

F *s.* **A 1.**

a·nus ['einəs] After *m*.

an·vil ['ænvil] Amboß *m* (*a. fig.*).

anx·i·e·ty [æŋ'zaiəti] Angst *f*, Besorgnis *f*; *fig.* Sorge *f* (*for* um; *to inf.* zu *inf.*); 𝄢 Beklemmung *f*; ᴗ *dream* Angsttraum *m*.

anx·ious □ ['æŋkʃəs] ängstlich, besorgt (*about* um, wegen); bang; begierig, gespannt (*for* auf *acc.*; *to inf.* zu *inf.*); bemüht, bestrebt (*for* um; *to inf.* zu *inf.*); I am ᴗ *to see him* mir liegt daran, ihn zu sehen.

an·y ['eni] **1.** *pron.* (irgend)einer; einige *pl.*; (irgend)welcher; (irgend) etwas; jeder (beliebige); alle möglichen *pl.*; *not* ᴗ kein; **2.** *adv.* irgend (-wie); 'ᴗ·bod·y, 'ᴗ·one (irgend) jemand, irgendeiner; jeder; *not* ᴗ niemand; 'ᴗ·how irgendwie; jedenfalls; 'ᴗ·thing (irgend) etwas, alles; ᴗ *but* alles andere als; 'ᴗ·way = anyhow; ohnehin; 'ᴗ·where irgendwo(hin); überall.

a·or·ta 𝆃 [ei'ɔ:tə] Hauptschlagader *f*.

a·pace [ə'peis] schnell; rasch.

ap·a·nage ['æpənidʒ] *fig.* Attribut *n*, notwendige Begleiterscheinung *f*; Anhang *m*; Erbteil *m*.

a·part [ə'pa:t] einzeln; getrennt; für sich; beiseite; ᴗ *from* abgesehen von; *joking* ᴗ Spaß beiseite; *set* ᴗ *for* beiseite legen *od.* erübrigen für; bestimmen für.

a·part·heid *pol.* [ə'pa:theit] Apartheid *f*, Rassentrennung(spolitik) *f*.

a·part·ment [ə'pa:tmənt] Zimmer *n*; *Am.* Mietwohnung *f*; ᴗ*s pl.* Wohnung *f*; ᴗ *hotel Am.* Wohnhotel *n mit od. ohne Bedienung*; ᴗ *house Am.* Wohn-, Mietshaus *n*.

ap·a·thet·ic [æpə'θetik] (ᴗ*ally*) apathisch; 'ap·a·thy Apathie *f*; Gleichgültigkeit *f* (*to* gegen).

ape [eip] **1.** Affe *m*; *go* ᴗ *Am. sl.* durchdrehen, überschnappen; **2.** nachäffen.

a·peak ⚓ [ə'pi:k] senkrecht.

a·pe·ri·ent [ə'piəriənt] **1.** Abführmittel *n*; **2.** abführend.

ap·er·ture ['æpətjuə] Öffnung *f*.

a·pex ['eipeks], *pl.* oft **ap·i·ces** ['eipisi:z] Spitze *f*; *mst fig.* Gipfel *m*.

aph·o·rism ['æfərizəm] Aphorismus *m*, Maxime *f*; **aph·o'ris·tic** (ᴗ*ally*) aphoristisch.

a·pi·ar·y ['eipjəri] Bienenhaus *n*; **a·pi·cul·ture** ['eipikʌltʃə] Bienenzucht *f.*

a·piece [ə'piːs] (für) das Stück; je.

ap·ish □ ['eipiʃ] affig; äffisch.

a·plomb [ə'plɔm] selbstsicheres Auftreten *n.*

a·poc·a·lypse [ə'pɔkəlips] Offenbarung *f.*

A·poc·ry·pha [ə'pɔkrifə] *pl. Bibel:* Apokryphen *n/pl.*; **a'poc·ry·phal** apokryphisch; unecht; zweifelhaft.

ap·o·gee *ast.* ['æpəudʒiː] Erdferne *f,* Apogäum *n*; *fig.* Höhepunkt *m.*

a·pol·o·get·ic [əpɔlə'dʒetik] (~ally) verteidigend; rechtfertigend; entschuldigend; ~ *letter* Entschuldigungsbrief *m*; **a'pol·o·gist** Verteidiger(in); **a'pol·o·gize** sich entschuldigen (*for* wegen; *to* bei); **a'pol·o·gy** Entschuldigung *f*; Rechtfertigung *f*; Verteidigungsrede *f*; F Notbehelf *m*; *an* ~ *for a dinner* F ein armseliges Essen; *make an* ~ e-e Entschuldigung vorbringen.

ap·o·plec·tic, ap·o·plec·ti·cal □ [æpəu'plektik(əl)] apoplektisch, Schlag(fluß)...; **ap·o·plex·y** ['~pleksi] Schlag(fluß *m,* -anfall) *m.*

a·pos·ta·sy [ə'pɔstəsi] Abtrünnigkeit *f*; **a'pos·tate** [~stit] Apostat *m,* Abtrünnige *m*; **a'pos·ta·tize** [~stətaiz] abfallen (*from* von); abtrünnig werden (*from dat.*).

a·pos·tle [ə'pɔsl] Apostel *m*; **ap·os·tol·ic, ap·os·tol·i·cal** □ [æpəs'tɔlik(əl)] apostolisch.

a·pos·tro·phe [ə'pɔstrəfi] Anrede *f*; Apostroph *m*; **a'pos·tro·phize** anreden, sich wenden an (*acc.*).

a·poth·e·car·y † [ə'pɔθikəri] Apotheker *m.*

a·poth·e·o·sis [əpɔθi'əusis] Vergötterung *f*; Verherrlichung *f.*

ap·pal [ə'pɔːl] erschrecken; **ap'pall·ing** □ erschreckend, entsetzlich.

ap·pa·ra·tus [æpə'reitəs] Apparat(e *pl.*) *m,* Vorrichtung *f,* Gerät *n,* Anlage *f*; ~ *work* Geräteturnen *n.*

ap·par·el [ə'pærəl] **1.** Kleidung *f*; Gewand *n*; **2.** (be)kleiden.

ap·par·ent □ [ə'pærənt] augenscheinlich, offenbar; anscheinend; scheinbar; *s. heir*; **ap·pa·ri·tion** [æpə'riʃən] Erscheinung *f*; Gespenst *n.*

ap·peal [ə'piːl] **1.** ⚖ appellieren (*to an acc.*); sich berufen (*to auf e-n* *Zeugen*); dringend bitten (*to s.o. for s.th.* j. um et.); ~ *to* sich wenden an (*acc.*); ansprechen (*acc.*); wirken auf (*acc.*); Anklang finden bei, gefallen, zusagen (*dat.*); *s. country*; **2.** Appellation *f,* Berufung(sklage)*f*; *fig.* Appell *m,* dringende Bitte *f,* Aufruf *m* (*to an acc.*); Anrufung *f* (*to gen.*); Wirkung *f,* Anziehungskraft *f,* Reiz *m*; *court of* ~ Berufungsinstanz *f*; *lodge od. file an* ~ Berufung einlegen (*with* bei); *right of* ~ Einspruchsrecht *n*; ~ *for mercy* Gnadengesuch *n*; **ap'peal·er** Appellant(in); **ap'peal·ing** □ flehend; ansprechend.

ap·pear [ə'piə] erscheinen (*auch von Büchern u. vor Gericht*); sich zeigen; scheinen, den Anschein haben; *öffentlich* auftreten; **ap'pear·ance** Erscheinen *n,* Auftreten *n*; Äußere *n,* Erscheinung *f*; Anschein *m*; ~*s pl.* äußerer Schein *m*; *keep up od. save* ~*s* den Schein wahren; *make one's* ~ in Erscheinung treten, auftreten; *put in an* ~ (persönlich) erscheinen; *to od. by all* ~*s* allem Anschein nach.

ap·pease [ə'piːz] beruhigen, beschwichtigen, *Hunger etc.* stillen, *Leiden* mildern, *Streit* beilegen; **ap'pease·ment** Beruhigung *f*; Beschwichtigung(spolitik) *f*; ~ *policy* Beschwichtigungspolitik *f.*

ap·pel·lant [ə'pelənt] **1.** appellierend; **2.** Appellant(in), Berufungskläger(in); Beschwerdeführer(in); **ap'pel·late** [~lit] Berufungs...; **ap·pel·la·tion** [æpə'leiʃən] Benennung *f*; Name *m*; **ap·pel·la·tive** *gr.* [ə'pelətiv] *a.* ~ *name* Appellativum *n,* Gattungsname *m.*

ap·pel·lee [æpe'liː] Berufungsbeklagte *m, f.*

ap·pend [ə'pend] anhängen; hinzu-, beifügen; **ap'pend·age** Anhang *m*; Anhängsel *n*; Zubehör *n, m*; **ap·pen·dec·to·my** [~'dektəmi] Blinddarmoperation *f*; **ap·pen·di·ci·tis** [~di'saitis] Blinddarmentzündung *f*; **ap'pen·dix** [~diks], *pl. a.* **ap'pen·di·ces** [~disiːz] Anhang *m*; *a.* vermiform ~ *anat.* Wurmfortsatz *m.*

ap·per·tain [æpə'tein] (*to* zu)gehören (*dat.*); *fig.* gehören (zu) *j-m* zustehen.

ap·pe·tence, ap·pe·ten·cy ['æpitəns(i)] (*for, after, of*) Verlangen *n* (nach); Instinkt *m* (für).

ap·pe·tite [ˈæpitait] (*for*) Appetit *m* (auf *acc.*); *fig.* Verlangen *n*, Gelüst *n* (nach); Neigung *f*, Trieb *m* (zu); ~ **sup·pres·sant** [səˈpresənt] Appetitzügler *m.*

ap·pe·tiz·er [ˈæpitaizə] appetitanregendes Mittel *n*; **'ap·pe·tiz·ing** appetitanregend.

ap·plaud [əˈplɔːd] applaudieren, Beifall spenden (*dat.*); loben.

ap·plause [əˈplɔːz] Applaus *m*, Beifall *m.*

ap·ple [ˈæpl] Apfel *m*; *the* ~ *of s.o.'s eye fig.* j-s Augapfel *od.* Liebling; **'~-cart** Apfelkarren *m*; *upset s.o.'s* ~ F j-s Pläne über den Haufen werfen; **'~-jack** *Am.* Apfelschnaps *m*; **'~-'pie** gedeckter Apfelkuchen *m*; *in* ~ *order* F in schönster Ordnung; **'~-pol·ish** *sl.* sich lieb Kind machen bei (*j-m*); **'~'sauce** Apfelmus *n*; *Am. sl.* Schmus *m*; Quatsch *m.*

ap·pli·ance [əˈplaiəns] Vorrichtung *f*; Gerät *n*; Mittel *n.*

ap·pli·ca·bil·i·ty [æplikəˈbiliti] Anwendbarkeit *f*; **'ap·pli·ca·ble** anwendbar, zutreffend (*to* auf *acc.*); **'ap·pli·cant** Bittsteller(in); Bewerber(in) (*for* um); **ap·pli·ca·tion** (*to*) Auflegung *f*, Anlegen *n e-s Verbandes etc.* (auf *acc.*); Anwendung *f* (auf *acc.*), Verwendung *f* (für); Gebrauch *m* (für); Bedeutung *f* (für); Bitte *f*, Gesuch *n* (*for* um), Antrag *m* (auf *acc.*); Bewerbung *f* (um); Fleiß *m*; (*letter of*) ~ Bewerbungsschreiben *n*; *make an* ~ e-n Antrag stellen.

ap·ply [əˈplai] *v/t.* (*to*) an-, auflegen; anwenden (auf *acc.*); verwenden (für); gebrauchen (zu); *Gedanken etc.* richten (auf *acc.*); ~ *o.s.* sich verlegen auf (*acc.*); *v/i.* (*to*) passen, sich anwenden lassen, Anwendung finden (auf *acc.*); gelten, zutreffen (für); sich wenden an (*acc.*); sich befleißigen (*gen.*); ~ *for* sich bewerben um; nachsuchen um; *et.* beantragen; *applied sciences pl.* angewandte Naturwissenschaften *f/pl.*

ap·point [əˈpɔint] bestimmen; festsetzen; verabreden; ernennen, bestellen (*s.o. governor* j-n zum *...*); berufen (*to* auf *e-n Posten, in e-e Stellung*); *well* ~*ed* gut eingerichtet; **ap'point·ment** Festsetzung *f*, Bestimmung *f*; Stelldichein *n*; Verabredung *f*; Ernennung *f*, Bestel

lung *f*, Berufung *f*; Stelle *f*; ~*s pl.* Ausstattung *f*, Einrichtung *f*; ~ *book* Terminkalender *m*; *by* ~ nach Vereinbarung; *by special* ~ *to ...* Hoflieferant *m* des *...*

ap·por·tion [əˈpɔːʃən] ver-, zuteilen; **ap'por·tion·ment** *gleichmäßige* Ver-, Zuteilung *f.*

ap·po·site □ [ˈæpəuzit] (*to*) passend (für), angemessen (*dat.*); treffend; **'ap·po·site·ness** Angemessenheit *f.*

ap·po·si·tion [æpəuˈziʃən] Beifügung *f.*

ap·prais·al [əˈpreizəl] (Ab)Schätzung *f*; **ap'praise** abschätzen, taxieren; **ap'praise·ment** Schätzung *f*; Taxwert *m*; **ap'prais·er** Taxator *m.*

ap·pre·ci·a·ble □ [əˈpriːʃəbl] (ab-) schätzbar; merkbar; **ap'pre·ci·ate** [~ʃieit] *v/t.* schätzen; (hoch)schätzen; richtig einschätzen, würdigen, zu schätzen wissen; anerkennen; dankbar sein für; Gefallen finden an; aufwerten; *v/i.* im Werte steigen; **ap·pre·ci·a·tion** (Wert)Schätzung *f*, Würdigung *f*; Verständnis *n* (*of* für); Einsicht *f*; kritische Besprechung *f*; Dankbarkeit *f*; Aufwertung *f*; **ap·pre·ci·a·tive** □ [əˈpriːʃjətiv], **ap'pre·ci·a·to·ry** verständnisvoll (*of* für); *be* ~ *of* Verständnis haben für.

ap·pre·hend [æpriˈhend] ergreifen, festnehmen; fassen, begreifen; befürchten; **ap·pre·hen·si·ble** □ [~ˈhensəbl] begreiflich, faßlich; **appre'hen·sion** Ergreifung *f*, Festnahme *f*; Fassungskraft *f*; Auffassung *f*; Begriff *m*; Besorgnis *f*; **ap·pre'hen·sive** □ schnell begreifend (*of acc.*); ängstlich; besorgt (*of s.th., for s.o.* wegen, um; *that* daß).

ap·pren·tice [əˈprentis] **1.** Lehrling *m*; **2.** in die Lehre geben (*to* bei, zu); *be* ~*d to* in der Lehre sein bei; **ap'pren·tice·ship** Lehrzeit *f*; Lehre *f.*

ap·prise [əˈpraiz] in Kenntnis setzen, unterrichten (*of* von).

ap·pro ✝ [ˈæprəu]: *on* ~ zur Ansicht.

ap·proach [əˈprəutʃ] **1.** *v/i.* näherkommen, sich nähern, nahen; *fig.* nahekommen (*to dat.*); *v/t.* sich nähern (*dat.*), herankommen an (*acc.*), *fig.* nahekommen (*dat.*); herangehen *od.* -treten an (*acc.*) (*a. fig.*); sich wenden an (*s.o.* j.);

2. Annäherung *f*, Nahen *n*; *fig.* Herangehen *n*; Versuch *m*; Methode *f*, Weg *m*; Zutritt *m*; Zugang *m*, Auffahrt *f*; *easy (difficult) of* ~ leicht (schwer) zugänglich (*Sache*) *od.* zu erreichen (*Person*); *make* ~*es to s.o.* j-n zu gewinnen versuchen; **ap'proach·a·ble** zugänglich; erreichbar.

ap·pro·ba·tion [æprəu'beiʃən] Billigung *f*, Beifall *m*.

ap·pro·pri·ate 1. [ə'prəuprieit] sich aneignen; verwenden; *parl.* bewilligen (*to, for* zu, für); **2.** □ [~priit] (*to*) angemessen (*dat.*); passend, geeignet (für); entsprechend (*dat.*); eigen; **ap·pro·pri·a·tion** [~pri'eiʃən] Aneignung *f*; Verwendung *f*; ♀ *Committee parl.* Bewilligungsausschuß *m*.

ap·prov·a·ble [ə'pru:vəbl] löblich; **ap'prov·al** Billigung *f*, Beifall *m*; *on* ~ zur Ansicht; **ap'prove** *a.* ~ *of* billigen, gutheißen, anerkennen, genehmigen; (~ *o.s.* sich) erweisen (*as* als); **ap'proved** □ bewährt; **ap'prov·er** ⚖ Kronzeuge *m.*

ap·prox·i·mate 1. [ə'prɔksimeit] sich nähern; **2.** □ [~mit] annähernd; ungefähr; nahe (*to* bei, an *dat.*); **ap·prox·i·ma·tion** [~'meiʃən] Annäherung *f*; **ap'prox·i·ma·tive** □ [~mətiv] annähernd.

ap·pur·te·nance [ə'pə:tinəns] *mst* ~*s pl.* Zubehör *n*, *m.*

a·pri·cot ♀ ['eiprikɔt] Aprikose *f.*

A·pril ['eiprəl] April *m*; *make an* ~ *fool of s.o.* j. in den April schicken.

a·pron ['eiprən] Schürze *f*; Schurz (-fell *n*) *m*; 🗲 Hallenvorfeld *n*; *thea.* Vorbühne *f*; '~-string Schürzenband *n*; *be tied to one's wife's* (*mother's*) ~*s* unterm Pantoffel stehen (der Mutter am Rockzipfel hängen).

ap·ro·pos ['æprəpəu] angemessen; zur rechten Zeit; ~ *of* in bezug auf (*acc.*); gelegentlich (*gen.*).

apt □ [æpt] geeignet, passend; treffend (*Bemerkung etc.*); begabt; geschickt (*at* in *dat.*); *he is* ~ *to believe it* er wird es wahrscheinlich *od.* wohl glauben; ~ *to* geneigt zu; **ap·ti·tude** ['æptitju:d] Neigung *f* (*to* zu); Befähigung *f*, Eignung *f* (*to* für, zu); ~ *test* Eignungsprüfung *f*; '**apt·ness** = *aptitude.*

aq·ua·lung ['ækwəlʌŋ] Unterwasser-

Atmungsgerät *n.*

aq·ua·ma·rine *min.* [ækwəmə'ri:n] Aquamarin *m*; Aquamarinblau *n.*

aq·ua·plane ['ækwəplein] Gleitbrett *n zum Wellenreiten*; '**aq·ua·plan·ing** *bsd. Br.* Aquaplaning *n.*

aq·ua·relle [ækwə'rel] Aquarell (-malerei *f*) *n*; **aq·ua'rel·list** Aquarellmaler(in).

a·quar·i·um [ə'kwɛəriəm] Aquarium *n.*

A·quar·i·us *ast.* [ə'kwɛəriəs] Wassermann *m.*

a·quat·ic [ə'kwætik] **1.** Wasser...; ~ *sports pl.* Wassersport *m*; **2.** Wasserpflanze *f*; ~*s pl.* Wassersport *m.*

aq·ua·tint ['ækwətint] Aquatinta *f* (*Tuschmanier*).

aq·ue·duct ['ækwidʌkt] Aquädukt *m*, Wasserleitung *f*; **a·que·ous** □ ['eikwiəs] wässerig.

aq·ui·line ['ækwilain] Adler...; gebogen; ~ *nose* Adlernase *f.*

Ar·ab ['ærəb] Araber(in); Araber *m* (*Pferd*); *street* ♀ *sl.* Straßenjunge *m*; **ar·a·besque** [~'besk] **1.** Arabeske *f*; **2.** arabeskenhaft; **A·ra·bi·an** [ə'reibjən] **1.** arabisch; *The* ~ *Nights* Tausendundeine Nacht; **2.** Araber (-in); **Ar·a·bic** ['ærəbik] **1.** arabisch; *gum* ♀ Gummiarabikum *n*; **2.** Arabisch *n.*

ar·a·ble ['ærəbl] **1.** pflügbar; **2.** *a.* ~ *land* Ackerland *n.*

ar·bi·ter ['ɑ:bitə] Schiedsrichter *m*; *fig.* Gebieter *m*; **ar·bi·trage** ✝ [ɑ:bi'trɑ:ʒ] Arbitrage *f*; '**ar·bi·tral** **tri'bu·nal** Schiedsgericht *n*; **ar'bit·ra·ment** Schiedsspruch *m*; '**ar·bi·trar·i·ness** Willkür *f*; Eigenmächtigkeit *f*; '**ar·bi·trar·y** □ willkürlich; eigenmächtig; **ar·bi·trate** ['~treit] entscheiden, schlichten; **ar·bi'tra·tion** Schiedsgerichtsverfahren *n*; Schiedsspruch *m*; Entscheidung *f*; ~ *of exchange* ✝ Wechselarbitrage *f*; '**ar·bi·tra·tor** ⚖ Schiedsrichter *m*; '**ar·bi·tress** Schiedsrichterin *f*; *fig.* Gebieterin *f.*

ar·bor ['ɑ:bə] ⊕ Welle *f*, Spindel *f*; ♀ *Day Am.* Tag *m* des Baumes; **ar·bo·re·al** [ɑ:'bɔ:riəl], **ar'bo·re·ous** Baum...; **ar·bo·res·cent** □ [ɑ:bə'resnt] baumartig.

ar·bour ['ɑ:bə] Laube *f.*

ar·bu·tus ♀ [ɑ:'bju:təs] Erdbeerbaum *m.*

arc *ast.*, ♉ *etc.* [ɑ:k] (🗲 Licht-)

Bogen *m*; **ar·cade** [ɑːˈkeid] Arkade *f*; Bogen-, Laubengang *m*.

ar·ca·num [ɑːˈkeinəm], *pl.* **ar'ca·na** [_nə] Geheimnis *n*.

arch[1] [ɑːtʃ] **1.** *bsd.* △ Bogen *m*; Gewölbe *n*; Triumphbogen *m*; ~ *support* Senkfußeinlage *f*; **2.** (sich) wölben; überwölben.

arch[2] □ [_] schalkhaft, schelmisch; schlau.

arch[3] □ [_] erst; schlimmst; Haupt...; Erz...

ar·ch(a)e·o·log·i·cal [ɑːkiəˈlɔdʒikəl] □ archäologisch; **ar·ch(a)e·ol·o·gist** [_ˈɔlədʒist] Archäologe *m*; **ar·ch(a)e·ol·o·gy** Archäologie *f*, Altertumskunde *f*.

ar·cha·ic [ɑːˈkeiik] (_ally) altertümlich; **'ar·cha·ism** Archaismus *m*, veralteter Ausdruck *m*.   [*m*.]

arch·an·gel ['ɑːkeindʒəl] Erzengel]

arch·bish·op [ˈɑːtʃˈbiʃəp] Erzbischof *m*; **arch'bish·op·ric** [_rik] Erzbistum *n*.

arch·dea·con [ˈɑːtʃˈdiːkən] Archidiakon *m*.

arch·duch·ess [ˈɑːtʃˈdʌtʃis] Erzherzogin *f*; **'arch'duch·y** Erzherzogtum *n*; **arch'duke** Erzherzog *m*.

arch·er [ˈɑːtʃə] Bogenschütze *m*; **'arch·er·y** Bogenschießen *n*.

ar·che·type [ˈɑːkitaip] Urform *f*, -bild *n*, Archetyp *m*.

arch·fiend [ˈɑːtʃˈfiːnd] Erzfeind *m* (*der Teufel*).

ar·chi·e·pis·co·pal [ɑːkiiˈpiskəpəl] erzbischöflich.

ar·chi·pel·a·go [ɑːkiˈpeligəu] Archipel *m*; Inselmeer *n*; Inselgruppe *f*.

ar·chi·tect [ˈɑːkitekt] Architekt *m*, Baumeister(in), Erbauer(in); Urheber(in), Schöpfer(in); **ar·chi·tec·ton·ic** [_ˈtɔnik] (_ally) architektonisch; baulich; *fig.* aufbauend; **ar·chi'tec·tu·ral** [_tʃərəl] architektonisch; **'ar·chi·tec·ture** Architektur *f*; Baukunst *f*; Baustil *m*.

ar·chives [ˈɑːkaivz] *pl.* Archiv *n*.

arch·ness [ˈɑːtʃnis] Schalkhaftigkeit *f*, Schelmerei *f*.

arch·way [ˈɑːtʃwei] Triumphbogen *m*.

arc-lamp [ˈɑːklæmp], **'arc-light** ⚡ Bogenlampe *f*.

arc·tic [ˈɑːktik] **1.** arktisch, nördlich; Nord..., Polar...; *the* ♀ die Arktis; ♀ *Circle* Nördlicher Polarkreis *m*; ♀ *Ocean* Nördliches Eismeer *n*;

2. *Am.* wasserdichter, warmer Überschuh *m*.

ar·den·cy [ˈɑːdənsi] Hitze *f*, Glut *f*; Innigkeit *f*; **'ar·dent** □ *mst fig.* heiß, glühend; *fig.* feurig; eifrig; innig; ~ *spirits pl.* Spirituosen *pl.*

ar·do(u)r [ˈɑːdə] *fig.* Hitze *f*, Glut *f*; Eifer *m*.

ar·du·ous □ [ˈɑːdjuəs] schwierig, mühsam, anstrengend, beschwerlich.

are [ɑː] sind; seid.

a·re·a [ˈɛəriə] Areal *n*; (Boden-) Fläche *f*; Flächeninhalt *m*; Raum *m*, Gegend *f*; Gebiet *n*; Bereich *m*; Kellervorhof *m bei alten engl. Stadthäusern*; ~ *code Am. teleph.* Vorwählnummer *f*; *danger* ~ Gefahrenzone *f*; *goal* ~ *Fußball*: Torraum *m*; *penalty* ~ *Fußball*: Strafraum *m*; *prohibited* ~ Sperrzone *f*.

a·re·na [əˈriːnə] Arena *f*, Kampf-, Schauplatz *m* (*a. fig.*).

aren't F [ɑːnt] = *are not*.

a·rête *mount.* [æˈreit] Grat *m*, Gebirgskamm *m*.

ar·gent [ˈɑːdʒənt] silberfarben, silbern.

Ar·gen·tine [ˈɑːdʒəntain] **1.** argentinisch; **2.** Argentinier(in); *the* ~ Argentinien *n*.

ar·gil [ˈɑːdʒil] Ton(erde *f*) *m*; **ar·gil·la·ceous** [_ˈleiʃəs] tonig; Ton...

ar·gon 🜛 [ˈɑːgɔn] Argon *n*.

Ar·go·naut [ˈɑːgənɔːt] Argonaut *m*; *Am.* Goldsucher *m* in Kalifornien.

ar·gu·a·ble [ˈɑːgjuəbl] diskutabel; **ar·gue** [ˈɑːgjuː] *v/t.* erörtern; beweisen; begründen; ausführen, darlegen; vorbringen; einwenden; ~ *s.o. into j.* zu *et.* überreden; ~ *s.o. out of* j. von *et.* abbringen; *v/i.* streiten; Einwendungen machen.

ar·gu·ment [ˈɑːgjumənt] Argument *n*, Beweis(grund) *m*; Beweisführung *f*; Erörterung *f*; Thema *n*; Streit (-frage *f*) *m*; **ar·gu·men·ta·tion** [_men'teiʃən] Beweisführung *f*; **ar·gu·men·ta·tive** □ [_ˈmentətiv] beweiskräftig; streitlustig.

a·ri·a ♪ [ˈɑːriə] Arie *f*.

ar·id [ˈærid] dürr, trocken, öde (*a. fig.*); **a'rid·i·ty** Trockenheit *f*.

Ar·ies *ast.*ˈ[ˈɛəriːz] Widder *m*.

a·right [əˈrait] recht, richtig.

a·rise [əˈraiz] (*irr.*) *fig.* sich erheben; ent-, erstehen (*from* aus); **a·ris·en** [əˈrizn] *p.p. von* arise.

ar·is·toc·ra·cy [æris'tɔkrəsi] Aristo-
kratie *f* (*a. fig.*); **a·ris·to·crat**
['ˌtəkræt] Aristokrat(in); **a·ris·to-**
'**crat·ic**, **a·ris·to**'**crat·i·cal** □ ari-
stokratisch; vornehm.
a·rith·me·tic [ə'riθmətik] Arithme-
tik *f*, Rechnen *n*; **ar·ith·met·i·cal**
□ [æriθ'metikəl] arithmetisch.
ark [ɑːk] *Bibel*: Arche *f* (Noah); ♎ *of*
the Covenant Bundeslade *f*.
arm[1] [ɑːm] *allg.* Arm *m*; Armlehne *f*;
within ∼'s reach in Reichweite; *keep*
s.o at ∼'s length sich j. vom Leibe
halten; *infant in ∼s* Säugling *m*;
take s.o. to od. in one's ∼s j. in die
Arme nehmen.
arm[2] [∼] **1.** *mst ∼s pl.* Waffe *f*; *mst ∼s sg.*
Waffengattung *f*; *∼s pl.* Wappen *n*; *s.*
coat; *∼s race* Wettrüsten *n*; *∼s reduc-*
tion (*talks pl.*) Abrüstung(sgespräche
n/pl.) *f*; *be* (*all*) *up in ∼s* in vollem
Aufruhr sein; in Harnisch geraten;
entrüstet (und zum Streit bereit) sein
(*about* über); *take up ∼s* zu den Waffen
greifen; **2.** (sich) (be)waffnen; (aus-)
rüsten; ⊕ armieren; *zo.*, ⚓ bewehren.
ar·ma·da [ɑː'mɑːdə] Kriegsflotte *f*;
the (*Invincible*) ♎ die Armada (*1588*).
ar·ma·ment ['ɑːməmənt] (Kriegs-
aus)Rüstung *f*; Kriegsmacht *f*; ⚓
Bestückung *f*; *a. naval ∼* Kriegsflotte
f; *∼s industry* Rüstungsindustrie *f*; *∼*
race Wettrüsten *n*; **ar·ma·ture**
['ˌtjuə] Rüstung *f*; △, *phys.* Armatur
f; ⚡ Anker *m*; *zo.*, ⚓ Bewehrung *f*.
arm·chair ['ɑːm'tʃɛə] Lehnstuhl *m*,
Sessel *m*; *attr. ∼ politician* Bier-
bankpolitiker *m*.
armed [ɑːmd] bewaffnet; *∼ forces*
pl. Streitkräfte *f/pl.*
...-armed [ɑːmd] ...armig.
Ar·me·ni·an [ɑː'miːnjən] **1.** arme-
nisch; **2.** Armenier(in).
arm·ful ['ɑːmful] Armvoll *m*.
ar·mi·stice ['ɑːmistis] Waffenstillstand *m* (*a. fig.*).
arm·let ['ɑːmlit] Armspange *f*;
Armbinde *f* *als Abzeichen*.
ar·mo·ri·al [ɑː'mɔːriəl] Wappen...
ar·mo(u)r ['ɑːmə] **1.** ✠ Rüstung *f*,
(*a. fig.*, *zo.*) Panzer *m*; Taucheranzug *m*; ✠ *coll.* Panzerfahrzeuge
n/pl.; **2.** panzern; *∼ed car* Panzer-
wagen *m*; *∼ed division* Panzerdivi-
sion *f*; *∼ed turret* Panzerturm *m*;
'**∼-clad**, '**∼-plat·ed** gepanzert;
Panzer...; '**ar·mo(u)r·er** Waffen-
schmied *m*; ✠, ⚓ Waffenmeister *m*;

'**ar·mo(u)r·y** Rüstkammer *f* (*a. fig.*);
Zeughaus *n*; *Am.* Waffenfabrik *f*,
Rüstungsbetrieb *m*.
arm·pit ['ɑːmpit] Achselhöhle *f*;
'**arm·rest** Armlehne *f*.
ar·my ['ɑːmi] Heer *n*, Armee *f*; *fig.*
Menge *f*; *∼ chaplain* Militärgeist-
liche *m*; *s. service*; '**∼-corps** Armee-
korps *n*; '**∼-list** ✗ Rangliste *f*.
a·ro·ma [ə'rəumə] Aroma *n*; Duft
m; Würze *f*; **ar·o·mat·ic** [ærəu-
'mætik] (*∼ally*) aromatisch, würzig,
wohlriechend, -schmeckend.
a·rose [ə'rəuz] *pret. von arise.*
a·round [ə'raund] **1.** *adv.* rundher-
um; rundum; *Am.* F hier herum;
2. *prp.* um ... her(um); *bsd. Am.* F
ungefähr, etwa (*bei Zahlenangaben*).
a·rouse [ə'rauz] (auf)wecken; *fig.*
aufrütteln; erregen.
ar·rack ['ærək] Arrak *m*.
ar·raign [ə'rein] vor Gericht stellen,
anklagen; *fig.* rügen; **ar'raign-**
ment Anklage *f*.
ar·range [ə'reindʒ] *v/t.* (an)ordnen,
bsd. ♪ einrichten; *Tag* festsetzen;
Streit schlichten; arrangieren, veranstalten; abmachen, vereinbaren;
erledigen; *v/i.* Anordnungen *od.*
Vorkehrungen treffen (*for* für, zu);
sich verständigen; *∼ for s.th. to be*
there dafür sorgen, daß et. da ist;
ar'range·ment Anordnung *f*; Disposition *f*; ♪ Arrangement *n*;
Übereinkommen *n*; Abmachung *f*;
Vorkehrung *f*; *make one's ∼s* s-e
Dispositionen treffen.
ar·rant □ ['ærənt] völlig, ausgesprochen, komplett, heillos (*Unsinn*
etc.); Erz...; *∼ knave* Erzgauner *m*.
ar·ray [ə'rei] **1.** (Schlacht)Ordnung
f; *fig.* Aufgebot *n*; stattliche Reihe
f; *poet.* Kleid *n*; **2.** ordnen, aufstellen; aufbieten; kleiden, putzen.
ar·rear [ə'riə] Rückstand *m*; *∼s of*
rent rückständige Miete *f*; *be in ∼s*
im Rückstand sein; **ar'rear·age**
Restsumme *f*.
ar·rest [ə'rest] **1.** Verhaftung *f*,
Festnahme *f*; Haft *f*; Beschlagnahme *f*; Aufhalten *n*, Hemmung *f*;
under ∼ in Haft; **2.** verhaften; beschlagnahmen; an-, aufhalten, hemmen; *Aufmerksamkeit etc.* fesseln.
ar·riv·al [ə'raivəl] Ankunft *f*; Auftreten *n*; Ankömmling *m*; *∼s pl.*
angekommene Personen *f/pl.*; an-
kommende Züge *m/pl. od.* Schiffe

n/pl.; ✝ Zufuhren *f/pl.*; *attr.* An-
kunfts...; **ar'rive** (an)kommen, eintreffen; erscheinen; eintreten (*Ereignis*); ~ *at* erreichen (*acc.*); kommen zu.

ar·ro·gance ['ærəugəns] Anmaßung
f; Überheblichkeit *f*; Arroganz *f*;
'**ar·ro·gant** □ anmaßend; überheblich; arrogant; **ar·ro·gate** ['~-
geit] *mst* ~ *to o.s.* sich *et.* anmaßen,
et. für sich beanspruchen; in Anspruch nehmen (*to* für).

ar·row ['ærəu] Pfeil *m*; *surv.* Mar-
kierstab *m*; '**~·head** Pfeilspitze *f*;
'**~·root** ♀ Pfeilwurz(mehl *n*) *f*.

arse V [ɑːs] Arsch *m*.

ar·se·nal ['ɑːsinl] Zeughaus *n*, Arsenal *n*.

ar·se·nic ['ɑːsnik] Arsen(ik) *n*; **ar-
sen·i·cal** [ɑː'senikəl] arsen(ik)hal-
tig; Arsen(ik)...

ar·son ₰ [ˈɑːsn] Brandstiftung *f*.

art[1] [ɑːt] Kunst *f*; *engS.* Geschicklichkeit *f*; *fig.* List *f*, Verschlagen-
heit *f*; Kniff *m*; ~ *critic* Kunstkritiker
m; ~ *dealer* Kunsthändler *m*; ~*s pl.*
Geisteswissenschaften *f/pl.*; *Master of*
♀*s* (*abbr.* M. A.) Magister *m* der freien
Künste; *fine* ~*s die* schönen Künste;
liberal ~*s die* freien Künste; ~*s and
crafts* Kunstgewerbe *n*; *Faculty of* ♀*s*
philosophische Fakultät *f*; ~*s page
Zeitung*: Kulturseite *f*.

art[2] ✝ [~] *du* bist.

ar·te·ri·al [ɑː'tiəriəl] Pulsader...; ~
road Verkehrsader *f*; Hauptverkehrsstraße *f*; Ausfallstraße *f*; **ar·te·ri·o-
scle·ro·sis** [ɑː'tiəriəusklio'rəusis] Ar-
terienverkalkung *f*; **ar·ter·y** [ɑːtəri]
Arterie *f*, Schlag-, Pulsader *f*; *fig.*
Verkehrsader *f*.

Ar·te·sian well [ɑː'tiːzjən'wel] Ar-
tesischer Brunnen *m*.

art·ful □ ['ɑːtful] schlau, verschmitzt, listig.

art gal·ler·y ['ɑːt'gæləri] Kunst-
galerie *f*.

ar·thrit·ic ₰ [ɑː'θritik] gichtisch;
ar·thri·tis [ɑː'θraitis] Gelenkent-
zündung *f*.

ar·ti·choke ♀ ['ɑːtitʃəuk] Artischocke *f*.

ar·ti·cle ['ɑːtikl] **1.** Artikel *m* (*Abschnitt e-s Vertrages etc.*; *Aufsatz in
e-r Zeitung etc.*; *Handelsware*; *gr.
Geschlechtswort*); *fig.* Punkt *m*; ~ *of
clothing* Kleidungsstück *n*; ~*s of apprenticeship* Lehrvertrag *m*; ~*s of as-*

sociation Statuten *n/pl.* e-r Handeis-
gesellschaft; **2.** *v/t.* in die Lehre geben (*to* bei); förmlich anklagen (*for*
wegen); *Klage* vorbringen; ~*ed in der
Lehre* (*to* bei).

ar·tic·u·late 1. [ɑː'tikjuleit] deutlich
(aus)sprechen; *Knochen* zs.-fügen;
gliedern; **2.** □ [~lit] fähig, sich klar
auszudrücken; deutlich, klar; gegliedert; **ar'tic·u·lat·ed** [~leitid]
gegliedert; artikuliert; ~ *lorry mot.*
Sattelschlepper *m*; **ar·tic·u'la·tion**
Artikulation *f*, deutliche Aussprache
f; *anat.* Gelenkfügung *f*, -verbindung
f; Gliederung *f*.

ar·ti·fact ['ɑːtifækt] Kunstprodukt *n*;
von Menschenhand geschaffener
Gegenstand *m*.

ar·ti·fice ['ɑːtifis] Kunstgriff *m*, Kniff
m, List *f*; **ar'tif·i·cer** Handwerker *m*;
Urheber *m*; **ar·ti·fi·cial** □ [~'fiʃəl]
künstlich; Kunst...; ~ *insemination*
künstliche Befruchtung *f*; ~ *respiration* ₰ künstliche Beatmung *f*; ~ *silk*
Kunstseide *f*; ~ *person* ₰ juristische
Person *f*.

ar·til·ler·y [ɑː'tiləri] Artillerie *f*;
ar'til·ler·y·man [~mən] Artille-
rist *m*.

ar·ti·san [ɑːti'zæn] Handwerker *m*.

art·ist ['ɑːtist] Künstler(in), *bsd.*
Kunstmaler(in); **ar·tiste** [ɑː'tiːst]
Artist(in); Künstler(in), Sänger(in),
Tänzer(in); **ar·tis·tic**, **ar·tis·ti·cal**
□ [ɑː'tistik(əl)] künstlerisch;
Kunst...

art·less □ ['ɑːtlis] ungekünstelt,
schlicht; arglos; '**art·less·ness**
Schlichtheit *f*; Arglosigkeit *f*.

art·y ['ɑːti] künstlerisch aufgemacht; gewollt bohemienhaft.

Ar·y·an ['ɛəriən] **1.** arisch; **2.** Arier
(-in).

as [æz, əz] *adv. u. cj.* (eben)so;
während, als (*zeitlich*); da, weil;
(wenn) auch; (eben)so wie; wie;
(*in der Eigenschaft*) als; wie z. B.;
young ~ *I am* so jung ich auch bin;
such women ~ *knew him* jene Frauen,
die ihn kannten; ~ *heavy* ~ *lead* (so)
schwer wie Blei; ~ *if*, ~ *though* als
ob; ~ *for*, ~ *to was* ... betrifft, bezüglich (*gen.*); *so* ~ *to* um ... zu;
so ... *daß*; ~ *good* ~ so gut wie,
praktisch; *be* ~ *good* ~ *one's word*
sein Versprechen halten; ~ *long* ~
vorausgesetzt daß; solange (wie);
~ *much* gerade *od.* eben das;

I thought ~ *much* das dachte ich mir; ~ *from* (*Datum*) von ... an; ~ *per* laut (*gen.*); ~ *yet* bis jetzt; ~ *it were* gleichsam; ~ *well* ebenfalls, auch.

as·bes·tos [æz'bestɔs] Asbest *m.*

as·cend [ə'send] *v/i.* (auf-, empor-, hinauf)steigen; *zeitlich:* hinaufreichen, zurückgehen (*to* bis zu, bis auf, bis in *acc.*); *v/t.* be-, ersteigen; ~ *a river* e-n Fluß hinauffahren; ~ *the throne* den Thron besteigen; **as'cend·an·cy** (*over*) Überlegenheit *f*, Herrschaft *f* (über *acc.*); Einfluß *m* (auf *acc.*); **as'cend·ant 1.** aufsteigend; überlegen (*over dat.*); **2.** = *ascendancy; ast.* Aufgangspunkt *m;* Vorfahr *m; be in the* ~ *fig.* im Kommen sein; **as'cend·en·cy, as'cend·ent** = *ascendancy, ascendant.*

as·cen·sion [ə'senʃən] Aufsteigen *n* (*bsd. ast.*); *the* ♀ (Christi) Himmelfahrt *f;* ♀ *Day* Himmelfahrt(stag *m*) *f.*

as·cent [ə'sent] Aufstieg *m;* Besteigung *f;* Steigung *f;* Anstieg *m;* Aufgang *m.*

as·cer·tain [æsə'tein] ermitteln, feststellen; sich vergewissern; **as·cer'tain·a·ble** ☐ ermittelbar, feststellbar; **as·cer'tain·ment** Ermitt(e)lung *f*, Feststellung *f.*

as·cet·ic [ə'setik] **1.** (~ally) asketisch, mönchisch; **2.** Asket(in); **as'cet·i·cism** [~tisizəm] Askese *f.*

as·cor·bic ac·id [əs'kɔːbik'æsid] Ascorbinsäure *f*, Vitamin C *n.*

as·crib·a·ble [əs'kraibəbl] zuzuschreiben(d); **as'cribe** (*to*) zuschreiben, beimessen, beilegen (*dat.*), zurückführen (auf *acc.*).

a·sep·tic ⚕ [æ'septik] aseptisch(es Mittel *n*).

ash¹ [æʃ] ⚕ Esche *f;* Eschenholz *n.*

ash² [~], *mst* **ash·es** ['~ʃiz] *pl.* Asche *f; Ash Wednesday* Aschermittwoch *m.*

a·shamed [ə'ʃeimd] beschämt; *be od. feel* ~ *of* sich e-r Sache od. j-s schämen; *be* ~ *of o.s.* sich schämen.

ash-can *Am.* ['æʃkæn] Mülleimer *m.*

ash·en¹ ['æʃn] eschen, von Eschenholz.

ash·en² [~] Aschen...; aschgrau, aschfahl.

a·shore [ə'ʃɔː] am *oder* ans Ufer od. Land; *run* ~, *be driven* ~ stranden, auflaufen.

ash...: '~-**pan** Aschenkasten *m;* '~-**tray** Aschenbecher *m*, Ascher *m.*

ash...: '~-**tree** ⚕ Esche *f;* '~-**wood** Eschenholz *n.*

ash·y ['æʃi] aschig; Aschen...; aschgrau, -fahl.

A·si·at·ic [eiʃi'ætik] **1.** asiatisch; **2.** Asiat(in).

a·side [ə'said] **1.** beiseite (*a. thea*), auf die Seite; abseits; seitwärts; ~ *from Am.* abgesehen von; **2.** *thea.* Aparte *n.*

as·i·nine ['æsinain] Esels...; eselhaft, dumm.

ask [ɑːsk] *v/t. u. v/i.* fragen, sich erkundigen (*for* nach); bitten; einladen; verlangen, fordern; ~ *the price* nach dem Preis fragen; ~ (*s.o.*) *a question* (j-m) e-e Frage stellen; ~ (*him*) *his name* frage (ihn) nach seinem Namen; ~ *s.th. of s.o.* et. von j-m verlangen; *you are* ~*ing too much* Sie verlangen zuviel; ~ *s.o. for help* j. um Hilfe bitten; ~ *after s.o.* (*s.th.*) nach j-m (et.) fragen; ~ *s.o. to come* j. bitten zu kommen; ~ *s.o. to dinner* j. zum Essen einladen; ~ *s.o. in* j. hereinbitten; *he* ~*ed for it od. for trouble* er wollte es ja so haben; *to be had for the* ~*ing* umsonst zu haben.

a·skance [əs'kæns], **a'skant**, **askew** [əs'kjuː] von der Seite, seitwärts; *fig.* schief, scheel.

a·slant [ə'slɑːnt] schräg, schief.

a·sleep [ə'sliːp] schlafend; in den od. im Schlaf; eingeschlafen (*Glied*); *be* ~ schlafen; *fall* ~ einschlafen.

asp¹ *zo.* [æsp] Natter *f.*

asp² ⚕ [~] Espe *f.*

as·par·a·gus ⚕ [əs'pærəgəs] Spargel *m.*

as·pect ['æspekt] Aussehen *n*, Äußere *n;* Anblick *m;* Aussicht *f*, Lage *f;* Aspekt *m* (*a. gr.*), Seite *f*, Gesichtspunkt *m; the house has a southern* ~ das Haus liegt nach Süden.

as·pen ['æspən] Espe *f;* Espen...

as·per·gill, **as·per·gil·lum** *eccl.* ['æspədʒil, ~'dʒiləm] Weihwedel *m.*

as·per·i·ty [æs'periti] Rauheit *f;* Unebenheit *f; fig.* Schroffheit *f.*

as·perse [əs'pəːs] besprengen; *fig.* anschwärzen, schlechtmachen; **asper·sion** Besprengung *f; fig.* Verleumdung *f;* Anwurf *m.*

as·phalt ['æsfælt] **1.** Asphalt *m;*

2. asphaltieren.
as·pho·del ♀ ['æsfədel] Asphodill *m*; *poet.* Narzisse *f*.
as·phyx·i·a [æs'fiksiə] Erstickung(stod *m*) *f*; **as'phyx·i·ate** [‿eit] ersticken; **as·phyx·i'a·tion** Erstickung *f*.
as·pic ['æspik] Aspik *m*, Sülze *f*.
as·pi·dis·tra ♀ [æspi'distrə] Aspidistra *f*, Sternschild *n*.
as·pir·ant [əs'paiərənt] Bewerber (-in) (*to, after, for* um); ~ *officer* Offiziersanwärter *m*; **as·pi·rate** ['æspərit] **1.** *gr.* aspiriert; **2.** *gr.* Hauchlaut *m*; **3.** ['‿reit] *gr.* aspirieren; ⊕, ⚙ absaugen; **as·pi'ra·tion** Aspiration *f*; Bestrebung *f*; Trachten *n*, Sehnen *n*; ⊕, ⚙ Absaugung *f*; **as'pire** [əs'paiə] streben, trachten (*to, after, at* nach).
as·pi·rin *pharm.* ['æspərin] Aspirin *n*.
as·pir·ing □ [əs'paiəriŋ] hochstrebend.
ass[1] [æs] Esel *m*; *make an* ~ *of o.s.* sich lächerlich machen.
ass[2] *Am.* V [‿] Arsch *m*.
as·sail [ə'seil] angreifen, überfallen (*a. fig.*); befallen (*Zweifel etc.*); *fig.* bestürmen (*with* mit); *Aufgabe* in Angriff nehmen; ~ *s.o. with questions* j. mit Fragen bestürmen; **as'sail·a·ble** angreifbar; **as'sail·ant**, **as'sail·er** Angreifer(in), Gegner(in).
as·sas·sin [ə'sæsin] (Meuchel)Mörder *m*; **as'sas·si·nate** [‿neit] (hinterrücks) ermorden; **as·sas·si'na·tion** Ermordung *f*.
as·sault [ə'sɔːlt] **1.** Angriff *m* (*a. fig.*, *on, upon* auf *acc.*); ✗ Sturm *m*; ⚖ tätliche Bedrohung *f od.* Beleidigung *f*; *s. battery, indecent*; **2.** anfallen; ⚖ tätlich angreifen *od.* beleidigen; ✗ bestürmen (*a. fig.*).
as·say [ə'sei] **1.** (Erz-, Metall)Probe *f*; **2.** *v/t.* untersuchen; *v/i. Am.* Edelmetall enthalten.
as·sem·blage [ə'semblidʒ] Ver-, Ansammlung *f*; ⊕ Montage *f*; **as'sem·ble** (sich) versammeln; zs.-berufen; *Truppen* zs.-ziehen; ⊕ montieren; zs.-setzen, zs.-bauen; **as'sem·bler** ⊕ Monteur *m*; **as'sem·bly** Versammlung *f*; Zs.-kunft *f*; Gesellschaft *f*; ✗ Sammelsignal *n*; ⊕ Montage *f*; *a.* ~ *shop* Montagehalle *f*; ~ *hall* Aula *f*; Montagehalle *f*; ~ *line* Montage-,

Fließband *n*, (laufendes) Band *n*; ~ *man pol.* Abgeordnete *m*.
as·sent [ə'sent] **1.** Zustimmung *f*; Genehmigung *f*; **2.** (*to*) zustimmen (*dat.*), genehmigen; billigen.
as·sert [ə'sɔːt] behaupten, erklären; durchsetzen; geltend machen; ~ *s.th. to be true et.* für wahr erklären; **as'ser·tion** Behauptung *f*, Erklärung *f*; Geltendmachung *f*; **as'ser·tive** □ bestimmt, ausdrücklich; positiv; **as'ser·tor** Fürsprecher *m*.
as·sess [ə'ses] besteuern; zur Steuer veranlagen (*in, at* mit); *Steuer etc.* festsetzen (*at auf acc.*); **as'sess·a·ble** □ steuerpflichtig; **as'sess·ment** (Ein)Schätzung *f*; (Steuer)Veranlagung *f*; Steuer *f*; **as'ses·sor** Assessor *m*, Beisitzer *m*; Steuereinschätzer *m*.
as·set ['æset] ♣ Aktivposten *m*; *fig.* Gut *n*, Gewinn *m*; ~*s pl.* Vermögen *n*, Konkursmasse *f*; ♣ Aktiva *pl.*; ~*s pl. and liabilities pl.* Aktiva *pl.* und Passiva *pl.*
as·sev·er·ate [ə'sevəreit] beteuern; **as·sev·er'a·tion** Beteuerung *f*.
as·si·du·i·ty [æsi'djuːiti] Emsigkeit *f*; Fleiß *m*; *assiduities pl.* Aufmerksamkeiten *f/pl.*; **as·sid·u·ous** □ [ə'sidjuəs] emsig, fleißig; aufmerksam.
as·sign [ə'sain] **1.** an-, zuweisen, zuteilen; festsetzen, bestimmen; zuschreiben; *Grund* angeben; übertragen; **2.** ⚖ Rechtsnachfolger *m*; **as'sign·a·ble** □ bestimmbar; nachweisbar; übertragbar; **as·sig·na·tion** [æsig'neiʃən] Verabredung *f*, Stelldichein *n*; *s. assignment*; **as·sign·ee** [æsi'niː] = *assign 2*; Bevollmächtigte *m, f*; ⚖ Treuhänder *m*; ~ *in bankruptcy* Konkursverwalter *m*; **as·sign·ment** [ə'sainmənt] An-, Zuweisung *f*; *bsd. Am.* Auftrag *m*, Aufgabe *f*; Angabe *f* (*von Gründen*); ⚖ Übertragung *f*, Abtretung *f*; **as·sign·or** [æsi'nɔː] ⚖ Übertrager(in).
as·sim·i·late [ə'simileit] (*to, with dat.*) ähnlich *od.* gleich machen; (sich) angleichen; aufnehmen, absorbieren; sich aneignen; *physiol.* (sich) assimilieren; **as·sim·i'la·tion** Assimilation *f*, Angleichung *f*.
as·sist [ə'sist] *j-m* beistehen, helfen; *j. od. et.* unterstützen; ~ *at* bei-

wohnen (dat.), teilnehmen an (dat.);
as'sist·ance Beistand m; Hilfe f,
Unterstützung f; **as'sist·ant 1.** behilflich (to dat.); Hilfs...; **2.** Gehilfe m, Gehilfin f, Hilfskraft f,
Assistent(in).

as·size 🔊 [ə'saiz] (Schwur)Ge-
richtssitzung f; ~s pl. periodisches
Geschworenengericht n, Assisen
pl.

as·so·ci·a·ble [ə'səuʃjəbl] vereinbar
(with mit); **as'so·ci·ate 1.** [~ʃieit]
(sich) zugesellen (with dat.), (sich)
vereinigen; (sich) verbinden; Umgang haben (with mit); ~ in mit einbeziehen in (acc.); **2.** [~ʃiit] verbunden; beigeordnet; Mit...; **3.** [~-
ʃiit] Genosse m; Partner m; ✝ Gesellschafter m, Teilhaber m; außer-
ordentliches Mitglied n e-r wissen-
schaftlichen Gesellschaft etc.; **as-
so·ci·a·tion** [~si'eiʃən] Vereinigung f, Verbindung f, Bund m;
wissenschaftliche, Handels- etc. Gesellschaft f; Verband m, Verein m;
a. mutual ~ Genossenschaft f; Umgang m; (Ideen)Assoziation f; ~
football europäischer Fußball m.

as·so·nance ['æsəunəns] Assonanz f.

as·sort [ə'sɔ:t] v/t. sortieren, (passend) zs.-stellen, -bringen; ✝ assortieren; v/i. (with) übereinstimmen
(mit), passen (zu); ~ed toffees pl.
Bonbonmischung f; **as'sort·ment**
Sortieren n; ✝ Sortiment n, Auswahl f.

as·suage [ə'sweidʒ] v/t. lindern,
besänftigen, beschwichtigen; Hunger etc. stillen; **as'suage·ment**
Linderung f etc.

as·sume [ə'sju:m] annehmen, voraussetzen; Amt etc. übernehmen;
sich anmaßen; vorgeben; **as'sum-
ing** ☐ anmaßend; **as·sump·tion**
[ə'sʌmpʃən] Annahme f, Voraussetzung f; Übernahme f; Anmaßung f; ♀ (Day) eccl. Mariä Himmelfahrt f; on the ~ that in der Annahme, daß; **as'sump·tive** ☐ angenommen; anmaßend.

as·sur·ance [ə'ʃuərəns] Ver-, Zusicherung f; Zuversicht f; Sicherheit f, Gewißheit f; Selbstsicherheit f; b.s. Dreistigkeit f; (bsd. Lebens)Versicherung f; life ~ Lebensversicherung f; **as'sure** sichern; sicherstellen; Leben versichern; ~ s.o. of
s.th. j. e-r Sache versichern; j-m et.

ver- od. zusichern; ~ o.s. sich vergewissern; **as'sured 1.** (adv. **as'sur-
ed·ly** [~ridli]) sicher, gewiß; selbstsicher; b.s. dreist; **2.** Versicherte m, f;
as'sur·er [~rə] Versicherte m, f; a.
= **as'sur·or** [~rə] Versicherer m.

As·syr·i·an [ə'siriən] **1.** assyrisch;
2. Assyrer(in); Assyrisch n.

as·ter ♀ ['æstə] Aster f; **as·ter·isk**
typ. [~risk] Sternchen n (*).

as·ter·oid ast. ['æstərɔid] Asteroid
m, kleiner Planet m. [hinter.)

a·stern ⚓ [ə'stə:n] achteraus; of ~ʃ

asth·ma ['æsmə] Asthma n, Atem-
not f; **asth·mat·ic** [~'mætik] **1.** a.
asth'mat·i·cal ☐ asthmatisch;
Asthma...; **2.** Asthmatiker(in).

as·tig·mat·ic opt. [æstig'mætik]
(~ally) astigmatisch; **a'stig·ma-
tism** [~mətizəm] Astigmatismus m.

a·stir [ə'stə:] auf (den Beinen); in
Bewegung, rege.

as·ton·ish [əs'tɔniʃ] in Erstaunen
setzen; verwundern; befremden;
be ~ed erstaunt etc. sein (at über
acc.); **as'ton·ish·ing** ☐ erstaunlich;
as'ton·ish·ment Erstaunen n;
Staunen n; Verwunderung f.

as·tound [əs'taund] in Staunen
setzen; verblüffen.

as·tra·khan [æstrə'kæn] Astrachan
m, Krimmer m (Pelzart).

a·stray [əs'trei] vom (rechten) Wege
ab (a. fig.); irre; go ~ sich verlaufen,
irregehen.

a·stride [əs'traid] mit gespreizten
Beinen; rittlings (of auf dat.); ride ~
im Herrensitz reiten.

as·trin·gent ✗ ⚕ [əs'trindʒənt]
zusammenziehend(es Mittel n).

as·tro·dome ✈ ['æstrədəum] Kuppel f für astronomische Navigation.

as·trol·o·ger [əs'trɔlədʒə] Astro-
loge m, Sterndeuter m; **as·tro-
log·i·cal** ☐ [æstrə'bdʒikəl] astro-
logisch; **as·trol·o·gy** [əs'trɔlədʒi]
Astrologie f, Sterndeuterei f.

as·tro·naut ['æstrəunɔ:t] Astronaut
m, Raumfahrer m; **as·tro·nau·tics**
[æstrə'nɔ:tiks] mst sg. Astronautik f,
Raumfahrtwissenschaft f.

as·tron·o·mer [əs'trɔnəmə] Astro-
nom m; **as·tro·nom·i·cal** ☐
[æstrə'nɔmikəl] astronomisch; **as-
tron·o·my** [əs'trɔnəmi] Astronomie f, Sternkunde f; **as·tro·phys-
ics** [æstrəu'fiziks] sg. Astrophysik f.

as·tute ☐ [əs'tju:t] scharfsinnig;

schlau; **as'tute·ness** Scharfsinn *m*; Schlauheit *f*.

a·sun·der [ə'sʌndə] auseinander; entzwei.

a·sy·lum [ə'sailəm] Asyl *n*; Irrenanstalt *f*; Heim *n*.

a·sym·me·try [æ'simitri] Asymmetrie *f*, Ungleichmäßigkeit *f*.

at [æt; ət] *prp.* an; auf; aus; bei; für; in; mit; nach; über; um; von; vor; zu; ~ *the door* an *od.* vor der Tür; ~ *my expense* auf meine Kosten; ~ *a ball* auf e-m Ball; *run* ~ *s.o.* auf j. losstürzen; ~ *daybreak* bei Tagesanbruch; ~ *table* bei Tisch; ~ *a low price* zu einem niedrigen Preis; ~ *school* in der Schule; ~ *Stratford* in Stratford; ~ *peace* im Frieden; ~ *the age of* im Alter von; ~ *one blow* mit einem Schlag; ~ *five o'clock* um fünf Uhr; ~ *Christmas* zu Weihnachten.

at·a·vism *biol.* ['ætəvizəm] Atavismus *m*, Rückschlag *m*.

a·tax·y [ə'tæksi] Ataxie *f* (*Bewegungsstörung*).

ate [et] *pret. von eat 1.*

a·the·ism ['eiθiizəm] Atheismus *f*, Gottesleugnung *f*; **'a·the·ist** Atheist(in); **a·the'is·tic**, **a·the'is·ti·cal** ☐ atheistisch.

A·the·ni·an [ə'θi:njən] **1.** athenisch; **2.** Athener(in).

a·thirst [ə'θə:st] begierig (*for* nach).

ath·lete ['æθli:t] (*bsd.* Leicht)Athlet *m*, Sportler *m*; ~'s *foot* Fußpilz *m*; **ath·let·ic** [æθ'letik], **ath'let·i·cal** ☐ athletisch; *athletic heart* Sportherz *n*; **ath'let·ics** *pl.* (*bsd.* Leicht-) Athletik *f*.

at-home [ət'həum] Empfangstag *m*.

a·thwart [ə'θwɔ:t] **1.** *prp.* quer über; entgegen (*dat.*); **2.** *adv.* quer, ⚓ dwars; schräg; in die Quere.

a·tilt [ə'tilt] vorgebeugt; kippend.

a·tish·oo *co.* [ə'tiʃu:] hatschi!

At·lan·tic [ət'læntik] **1.** atlantisch; **2.** *a.* ~ *Ocean* Atlantik *m*.

at·las ['ætləs] Atlas *m* (*Buch*).

at·mos·phere ['ætməsfiə] Atmosphäre *f* (*a. fig.*); **at·mos·pher·ic**, **at·mos·pher·i·cal** ☐ [~'ferik(əl)] atmosphärisch; Luft...; **at·mos·'pher·ics** *pl. Radio:* atmosphärische Störungen *f/pl.*

at·oll *geogr.* ['ætɔl] Atoll *n*.

at·om ['ætəm] Atom *n* (*a. fig.*); ~ *bomb* Atombombe *f*; **a·tom·ic**

[ə'tɔmik] atomartig, Atom...; atomistisch; ~ *age* Atomzeitalter *n*; ~ *bomb* Atombombe *f*; ~ *energy* Atomenergie *f*; ~ *fission* Atomspaltung *f*; ~ *nucleus* Atomkern *m*; ~ *pile* Atombatterie *f*; ~ *power* Atomkraft *f*; ~ *research* Atomforschung *f*; ~ *waste* Atommüll *m*; ~ *weight* Atomgewicht *n*; **a'tom·ic-pow·ered** durch Atomkraft betrieben; **at·om·ize** ['ætəumaiz] in Atome auflösen; atomisieren; *Flüssigkeit* zerstäuben; **'at·om·iz·er** Zerstäuber *m* (*Gerät*); **at·o·my** ['ætəmi] Knirps *m*; *bsd. fig.* Skelett *n*, Gerippe *n*.

a·tone [ə'təun]: ~ *for* büßen für *et.*, *et.* sühnen; **a'tone·ment** Buße *f*; Sühne *f*; *the* ♀ *eccl.* das Sühneopfer Christi.

a·ton·ic [æ'tɔnik] atonisch, erschlafft; *gr.* unbetont; **at·o·ny** ['ætəni] Atonie *f*, Erschlaffung *f*.

a·top F [ə'tɔp] oben(auf); ~ *of* oben auf (*dat.*).

a·tro·cious [ə'trəuʃəs] scheußlich, gräßlich; **a·troc·i·ty** [ə'trɔsiti] Scheußlichkeit *f*, Gräßlichkeit *f*; Greuel(tat *f*) *m*, Grausamkeit *f*; F Verstoß *m*.

at·ro·phy ['ætrəfi] **1.** Atrophie *f*, Schwund *m*; **2.** atrophieren, verkümmern.

at·tach [ə'tætʃ] *v/t.* (*to*) anheften, -binden (an *acc.*), befestigen (an *dat.*); *Sinn* verknüpfen (mit *e-m Wort*); *Wert, Schuld, Namen, Wichtigkeit* beilegen (*dat.*); ⚖ *j.* verhaften; *et.* beschlagnahmen; ~ *o.s. to* sich anschließen an (*acc.*); ~ *value to* Wert legen auf, halten auf (*acc.*); *v/i.* ~ *to* anhaften (*dat.*), haften an (*dat.*), verbunden sein mit; **at·ta·ché** [ə'tæʃei] Attaché *m*; ~ *case* Aktentasche *f*; **at·tached** [ə'tætʃt]: ~ *to* gehörig zu; *j–m* zugetan, ergeben; ~ *house* Am. Reihenhaus *n*; **at'tach·ment** Befestigung *f*; (*to, for*) Bindung *f* (an *acc.*); Anhänglichkeit *f* (an *acc.*), Neigung *f* (zu); Anhängsel *n* (*to gen.*); ⊕ Zusatzeinrichtung *f*; ⚖ Verhaftung *f*; Beschlagnahme *f*.

at·tack [ə'tæk] **1.** angreifen (*a. fig.*); befallen (*Krankheit*); *Arbeit* in Angriff nehmen; **2.** Angriff *m* (*on auf acc.*; *a. fig.*); ✗ Anfall *m*; Inangriffnahme *f*; *heart* ~ Herzanfall *m*; **at·'tack·er** Angreifer *m*.

at·tain [ə'tein] v/t. *Ziel* erreichen, erlangen; erzielen; v/i. ~ *to* gelangen zu; erreichen; **at'tain·a·ble** erreichbar; **at'tain·der** ɫⁱₓ [ₓdə] Ehrverlust m; **at'tain·ment** Erreichung f; fig. Aneignung f; ~s pl. Kenntnisse f/pl., Fertigkeiten f/pl.

at·tar ['ætə]: ~ *of roses* Rosenöl n.

at·tem·per [ə'tempə] mildern, mäßigen; beruhigen; anpassen (to *dat.*).

at·tempt [ə'tempt] **1.** versuchen; ~ *the life of* ein Attentat verüben auf (*acc.*); **2.** Versuch m (to *inf.* zu *inf.*; *at* an *dat.*); Attentat n (on *od.* upon s.o.'s *life* auf j.).

at·tend [ə'tend] v/t. begleiten; bedienen; *Kranke* pflegen; *ärztlich* behandeln; j-m aufwarten; bei- wohnen (*dat.*); *Vorlesung etc.* besuchen; v/i. merken, achten, hören (to auf *acc.*); anwesend sein (*at* bei); ~ *on Kranke* pflegen; bedienen; ~ *to* erledigen; *are you being ~ed* to? werden Sie schon bedient?; **at·'tend·ance** Begleitung f; Aufwartung f, Bedienung f (*upon* bei); Pflege f; *ärztliche* Behandlung f; Dienerschaft f, Gefolge n; (*at*) Anwesenheit f (bei); Teilnahme (an *dat.*); Besuch m (*gen.*; *bsd. der Schule etc.*); Besucher(zahl f) m/pl., Publikum n, Zuhörerschaft f; *hours of* ~ Dienststunden f/pl.; *be in* ~ *zu Diensten stehen*; *dance* ~ F herumscharwenzeln (on um); **at'tend·ant 1.** begleitend (on, upon *acc.*); anwesend (*at* bei); diensttuend (on bei); **2.** Diener(in); Begleiter(in); Wärter(in); ⊕ Bedienungsmann m; Begleiterscheinung f (on, upon *gen.*); ~s pl. Dienerschaft f.

at·ten·tion [ə'tenʃən] Aufmerksamkeit f (*a. fig.*); ~! ✕ Achtung!; *s. call, give, pay*; **at'ten·tive** ☐ aufmerksam (to auf *acc.*; fig. gegen).

at·ten·u·ate [ə'tenjueit] dünn(er) machen, verdünnen; fig. vermindern, abschwächen.

at·test [ə'test] bezeugen (*a. fig.*); beglaubigen; bescheinigen; *bsd.* ✕ vereidigen; **at·tes·ta·tion** [ætes'teiʃən] Bezeugung f *etc.*; Zeugnis n; *bsd.* ✕ Vereidigung f; **at·test·er, at·test·or** [ə'testə] Zeuge m.

At·tic[1] ['ætik] attisch.

at·tic[2] [ₓ] Dachstube f, Mansarde f; ~s pl. Dachgeschoß n.

at·tire *lit.* [ə'taiə] **1.** kleiden; **2.** Ge-

wand n.

at·ti·tude ['ætitju:d] Stellung f, Haltung f; fig. Stellungnahme f, Einstellung f (to, towards zu); ✈ Fluglage f; *strike an* ~ eine Pose annehmen; ~ *of mind* Geisteshaltung f, Einstellung f; **at·ti·tu·di·nize** [ₓdinaiz] sich in Positur setzen; affektiert tun.

at·tor·ney [ə'tə:ni] Bevollmächtigte m, Stellvertreter m; *Am.* Rechtsanwalt m; *letter od. warrant of* ~ Vollmacht(erteilung) f; *power of* ~ erteilte Vollmacht f; 𝒜 *General* Oberstaats-, Kronanwalt m, *Am.* Justizminister m.

at·tract [ə'trækt] anziehen, *Aufmerksamkeit* auf sich ziehen, erregen; fig. (an)locken, reizen, fesseln; **at'trac·tion** [ₓkʃən] Anziehung(skraft) f; fig. Reiz m, Attraktion f; *thea.* Zugstück n, -nummer f; **at'trac·tive** ☐ *mst fig.* anziehend; hübsch, charmant; reizvoll, verlockend, einladend; *thea.* zugkräftig.

at·trib·ut·a·ble [ə'tribjutəbl] zuzuschreiben(d); **at·trib·ute** [ə'tribju:t] bemessen, zuschreiben; zurückführen (to auf *acc.*); **at·tri·bute** ['ætribju:t] Attribut n, Eigenschaft f; Merkmal n, (Kenn-) Zeichen n; *gr.* Attribut n, Beifügung f; **at·tri·bu·tion** Zuschreibung f; beigelegte Eigenschaft f; zuerkanntes Recht n; **at·trib·u·tive** *gr.* [ə'tribjutiv] **1.** ☐ attributiv; **2.** Attribut n.

at·tri·tion [ə'triʃən] Abrieb m; Abnutzung f, ⊕ Verschleiß m; Zermürbung f; *war of* ~ Zermürbungs-, Abnutzungskrieg m.

at·tune [ə'tju:n] ♪ stimmen; ~ *to fig.* abstimmen auf (*acc.*).

au·burn ['ɔːbən] gold-, nuß-, kastanienbraun.

auc·tion ['ɔːkʃən] **1.** Auktion f, Versteigerung f; *sell by* (*Am. at*) ~, *put up for* ~ versteigern, versteigern; *sale by* ~ Versteigerung f; **2.** *mst* ~ *off* versteigern; **auc·tion·eer** [ₓ'niə] Auktionator m.

au·da·cious ☐ [ɔː'deiʃəs] kühn, keck, verwegen; *b.s.* dreist, frech, unverschämt; **au·dac·i·ty** [ɔː'dæsiti] Kühnheit f; *b.s.* Dreistigkeit f, Frechheit f, Unverschämtheit f.

au·di·bil·i·ty [ɔːdi'biliti] Hörbar-

audible

keit *f*, Vernehmlichkeit *f*; **au·di·ble** ☐ [ˈɔːdəbl] hörbar, vernehmlich; Hör...

au·di·ence [ˈɔːdjəns] Publikum *n*, Zuhörerschaft *f*; Leserkreis *m*; Audienz *f*; Gehör *n*; **give ~ to** Gehör schenken (*dat.*).

au·di·o-fre·quen·cy [ˈɔːdiəuˈfriː-kwənsi] *Radio:* Tonfrequenz *f*.

au·di·on [ˈɔːdiən] *Radio:* Audion *n*, Verstärkerröhre *f*.

au·di·o·phile [ˈɔːdiəufail] Hi-Fi-Fan *m*; **au·di·o·typ·ist** [~ˈtaipist] Phonotypistin *f*; **au·di·o·vis·u·al aids** [~ˈvizjuəl eidz] *pl.* audiovisuelle Lehrmittel *n/pl.*

au·dit [ˈɔːdit] **1.** Rechnungsprüfung *f*; **2.** *Rechnungen* prüfen; **au'di·tion** Hörvermögen *n*; *thea.* Vorsprechen *n od.* -singen *n*; **'au·di·tor** *bsd. univ.* Hörer *m*; Rechnungs-, Buchprüfer *m*; **au·di·to·ri·um** [~ˈtɔːriəm] Auditorium *n*, Hörsaal *m*; *Am.* Festhalle *f* (*für Vorträge, Konzerte, Versammlungen etc.*); **au·di·to·ry** [ˈ~təri] **1.** (Ge)Hör...; **2.** Hörer(schaft *f*) *m/pl.*; = *auditorium*.

au·ger ⊕ [ˈɔːgə] großer Bohrer *m*.

aught [ɔːt] (irgend) etwas; *for ~ I care* meinetwegen; *for ~ I know* soviel ich weiß.

aug·ment [ɔːgˈment] *v/t.* vermehren, vergrößern; *v/i.* zunehmen; **aug·men·ta·tion** Vermehrung *f*, -größerung *f*, Zunahme *f*; Zusatz *m*.

au·gur [ˈɔːgə] **1.** Augur *m*; **2.** weissagen, prophezeien; **~ well** (*ill*) ein gutes (schlechtes) Zeichen sein (*for* für); **au·gu·ry** [ˈɔːgjuri] Prophezeiung *f*; An-, Vorzeichen *n*; Vorahnung *f*, Vorbedeutung *f*.

Au·gust 1. [ˈɔːgəst] *Monat* August *m*; **2.** ♀ ☐ [ɔːˈgʌst] erhaben, hehr; **Augus·tan** [ɔːˈgʌstən] augusteisch; klassisch.

auk *orn.* [ɔːk] Alk *m*.

auld lang syne *schott.* [ˈɔːldlæŋˈsain] die gute alte Zeit.

aunt [ɑːnt] Tante *f*; ♀ *Sally* volkstümliches Wurfspiel *n*; **aunt·ie**, **aunt·y** F [ˈ~ti] Tantchen *n*.

au pair [əuˈpɛə] Au-pair-Mädchen *n*.

au·ra [ˈɔːrə] Aura *f*, Atmosphäre *f*.

au·ral [ˈɔːrəl] Ohren...

au·re·ole *eccl.*, *ast.* [ˈɔːriəul] Aureole *f*.

au·ri·cle [ˈɔːrikl] äußeres Ohr *n*; Herzvorhof *m*; **au·ric·u·la** ♀ [əˈrikjulə] Aurikel *f*; **au·ric·u·lar** ☐ [ɔːˈrikjulə] das Ohr betreffend; Ohr(en)...; Hör...; **~ confession** *eccl.* Ohrenbeichte *f*; **~ witness** Ohrenzeuge *m*.

au·rif·er·ous [ɔːˈrifərəs] goldhaltig.

au·rist [ˈɔːrist] Ohrenarzt *m*.

au·rochs *zo.* [ˈɔːrɔks] Auerochs *m*, Ur *m*.

au·ro·ra [ɔːˈrɔːrə] Morgenröte *f*, -dämmerung *f*; ♀ Aurora *f* (*Göttin der Morgenröte*); **~ borealis** [bɔːriˈeilis] Nordlicht *n*; **au·ro·ral** die Morgenröte betreffend.

aus·cul·ta·tion ✚ [ɔːskəlˈteiʃən] Abhorchen *n*.

aus·pice [ˈɔːspis] Vorzeichen *n*; **~s** *pl.* Auspizien *pl.*, Schutz-, Schirmherrschaft *f*; **aus·pi·cious** ☐ [~ˈpiʃəs] günstig, glücklich.

Aus·sie F [ˈɔzi] **1.** Australier *m*; **2.** australisch.

aus·tere ☐ [ɔsˈtiə] streng; herb; hart, rauh; einfach; scharf (*Geschmack*); **aus·ter·i·ty** [~ˈteriti] Strenge *f*; Härte *f*; Einfachheit *f*; eingeschränkte Lebensweise *f*; **~ budget** Sparhaushalt *m*.

aus·tral [ˈɔːstrəl] südlich.

Aus·tra·lian [ɔsˈtreiljən] **1.** australisch; **2.** Australier(in).

Aus·tri·an [ˈɔstriən] **1.** österreichisch; **2.** Österreicher(in).

au·tar·ky [ˈɔːtɑːki] Autarkie *f* (*wirtschaftliche Unabhängigkeit*).

au·then·tic [ɔːˈθentik] (**~ally**) authentisch; zuverlässig; echt; **au·then·ti·cate** [~keit] beglaubigen; verbürgen; als echt erweisen; rechtsgültig machen; **au·then·ti·ca·tion** Legalisierung *f*, Beglaubigung *f*; **au·then·tic·i·ty** [~ˈsiti] Authentizität *f*; Glaubwürdigkeit *f*; Echtheit *f*.

au·thor [ˈɔːθə] Urheber(in); Autor (-in); Verfasser(in); Schriftsteller (-in); **au·thor·ess** Autorin *f*, Verfasserin *f*; Schriftstellerin *f*; **au·thor·i·tar·i·an** [ɔːθɔriˈtɛəriən] autoritär, Obrigkeits...; **au·thor·i·ta·tive** ☐ [~tətiv] maßgebend; gebieterisch; zuverlässig (*Bericht*); **au·thor·i·ty** Autorität *f*; (Amts-) Gewalt *f*, Vollmacht *f*, Ermächtigung *f*, Befugnis *f* (*for, to inf.* zu *inf.*); Einfluß *m* (*over* auf *acc.*); Ansehen *n* (*with* bei); Glaubwürdigkeit *f*; Zeugnis *n* e-r maßgebenden *Person etc.*; Gewährsmann *m*, Quelle *f*, Beleg *m*; Fachmann *m*, Autorität *f*; *mst pl.* Verwaltung *f*, Behörde *f*; on good ~ aus guter Quelle; on the ~ of auf *j-s* Zeugnis hin; I have it on the ~ of Mr. X ich habe es von Herrn X; **au·thor·i·za·tion** [ɔ:-θərai'zeiʃən] Bevollmächtigung *f*, Ermächtigung *f*; **'au·thor·ize** *j.* autorisieren, bevollmächtigen, ermächtigen, berechtigen; *et.* gutheißen, billigen; **'au·thor·ship** Urheberschaft *f*; Autorschaft *f*; Schriftstellerei *f*.

au·to ['ɔ:təu] Auto(mobil) *n*.

au·to... ['ɔ:təu] auto..., selbst...; Auto..., Selbst...

au·to·bi·og·ra·pher [ɔ:təubai'ɔgrəfə] Autobiograph(in); **au·to·bi·o·graph·ic**, **au·to·bi·o·graph·i·cal** ['.əu'græfik(əl)] autobiographisch; **au·to·bi·og·ra·phy** [ɔ'ɔgrəfi] Auto-, Selbstbiographie *f*.

au·to·bus ['ɔ:təubʌs] Autobus *m*.

au·to·cade *Am.* ['ɔ:təukeid] = motorcade.

au·toch·thon [ɔ:'tɔkθən] Autochthone *n* (*Ureinwohner*); **au·'toch·tho·nous** autochthon (*ureingesessen*).

au·to·cide ['ɔ:təusaid] tödlicher Autounfall *m*.

au·toc·ra·cy [ɔ:'tɔkrəsi] Autokratie *f*, unumschränkte Herrschaft *f*; **au·to·crat** ['ɔ:təukræt] Autokrat *m*, unumschränkter Herrscher *m*; **au·to'crat·ic**, **au·to'crat·i·cal** □ autokratisch, despotisch, unumschränkt.

au·tog·e·nous weld·ing ⊕ [ɔ:'tɔdʒənəs'weldiŋ] autogene Schweißung *f*.

au·to·gi·ro ✈ ['ɔ:təu'dʒaiərəu] Autogiro *n*, Tragschrauber *m*.

au·to·graph ['ɔ:təgrɑ:f] **1.** Autogramm *n* (*eigene Handschrift*); **2.** eigenhändig (unter)schreiben; ⊕ autographieren, umdrucken; **au·to·graph·ic** [ɔ:təu'græfik] (~ally) autographisch; **au·tog·ra·phy** [ɔ:'tɔgrəfi] Autographie *f*, Umdruck *m*.

au·to·mat ['ɔ:təmæt] Automaten-Restaurant *n*; **au·to·mate** ['~meit] automatisieren; **au·to·mat·ic** [~-'mætik] **1.** (~ally) automatisch, selbsttätig; unwillkürlich; ~ machine (Verkaufs)Automat *m*; ~ transmission *mot.*

Automatik *f*; **2.** *Am.* Selbstladepistole *f*, -gewehr *n*; **au·to'ma·tion** Automation *f*; **au·tom·a·ton** [ɔ:'tɔmətən], *pl. mst* **au'tom·a·ta** [~tə] *fig.* Roboter *m*.

au·to·mo·bile *bsd. Am.* ['ɔ:təməubi:l] Auto(mobil) *n*; **au·to·mo·tive** [ɔ:tə'məutiv] selbstfahrend; Kraftfahrzeug...

au·ton·o·mous [ɔ:'tɔnəməs] autonom (*sich selbst regierend*); **au'ton·o·my** Autonomie *f*, Selbständigkeit *f*.

au·to·pi·lot ['ɔ:təpailət] automatische Steuerung *f*.

au·top·sy ['ɔ:təpsi] Autopsie *f*, Obduktion *f*, Leichenöffnung *f*.

au·to·type ⊕ ['ɔ:təutaip] **1.** Faksimileabdruck *m*; **2.** autotypieren.

au·tumn ['ɔ:təm] Herbst *m*; **au·tum·nal** □ [ɔ:'tʌmnəl] herbstlich; Herbst...

aux·il·ia·ry [ɔ:g'ziljəri] **1.** helfend; Hilfs...; be ~ to helfen (*dat.*); **2.** *a.* ~ verb *gr.* Hilfszeitwort *n*; auxiliaries *pl.* Hilfstruppen *f/pl.*

a·vail [ə'veil] **1.** (*v/t. j-m*) nützen, helfen; ~ o.s. of sich e-r Sache bedienen, *et.* benutzen; **2.** Nutzen *m*; of no ~ nutzlos; of what ~ is it? was nützt es?; **a·vail·a'bil·i·ty** Benutzbar-, Verfügbar-, Gültigkeit *f*; **a'vail·a·ble** □ benutzbar; verfügbar; *pred.* erhältlich, vorhanden, zu haben; gültig (*Fahrkarte etc.*); make ~ zur Verfügung stellen.

av·a·lanche ['ævəlɑ:nʃ] Lawine *f*.

av·a·rice ['ævəris] Geiz *m*; Habsucht *f*; **av·a'ri·cious** □ geizig; habgierig.

a·vast! ⚓ [ə'vɑ:st] fest!

a·venge [ə'vendʒ] rächen, *et.* ahnden; ~ o.s., be ~d sich rächen (on, upon an *dat.*); avenging angel Racheengel *m*; **a'veng·er** Rächer (-in).

av·e·nue ['ævinju:] Allee *f*; Avenue *f*, Prachtstraße *f*; *fig.* Weg *m*, Straße *f*; ~s to success Wege zum Erfolg.

a·ver [ə'və:] als Tatsache hinstellen, behaupten; ⚖ beweisen.

av·er·age ['ævəridʒ] **1.** Durchschnitt *m*; general (particular) ~ ⚓ große (besondere od. partielle) Havarie *f*; on an ~ durchschnittlich; **2.** □ durchschnittlich; Durchschnitts...; **3.** durchschnittlich schätzen (at auf *acc.*); durchschnittlich betragen, erreichen, arbeiten, verlangen *etc.*

a·ver·ment [ə'vɔːmənt] Behauptung *f*; ⚖ Beweis(angebot *n*) *m.*

a·verse □ [ə'vɔːs] abgeneigt (*to, from dat.*); widerwillig; **a'verse·ness**, **a'ver·sion** Widerwille *m*, Abneigung *f* (*to, from, for* gegen); *he is my* ∼ er ist mir ein Greuel.

a·vert [ə'vɔːt] abwenden (*a. fig.*).

a·vi·ar·y ['eivjəri] Vogelhaus *n.*

a·vi·ate ⚹ ['eivieit] fliegen; **a·vi'a·tion** Fliegen *n*; Flugsport *m*, -wesen *n*; Luftfahrt *f*; ∼ *ground* Flugplatz *m*; ∼ *spirit* Flugbenzin *n*; **'a·vi·a·tor** Flieger *m.*

av·id □ ['ævid] gierig (*of* nach; *for* auf *acc.*); **a·vid·i·ty** [ə'viditi] Gier *f.*

a·vi·on·ics ⚹ [eivi'ɔniks] *sg.* Bordelektronik *f*, Avionik *f.*

av·o·ca·do ⚘ [ævəu'kaːdəu] Avocado *f.*

av·o·ca·tion [ævəu'keiʃən] Nebenbeschäftigung *f.*

a·void [ə'vɔid] (ver)meiden; entgehen (*dat.*); *j-m* ausweichen; *Pflicht* umgehen; ⚖ anfechten; aufheben, ungültig machen; **a·'void·a·ble** vermeidbar; **a'void·ance** Meiden *n*, Vermeidung *f*; ⚖ Anfechtung *f*; Aufhebung *f*; freie Stelle; ∼ *of taxation* Steuerhinterziehung *f.*

av·oir·du·pois † [ævədə'pɔiz] *a.* ∼ *weight* Handelsgewicht *n* (*das Pfund zu 16 Unzen*).

a·vouch [ə'vautʃ] verbürgen, bestätigen; = *avow.*

a·vow [ə'vau] bekennen, (ein)gestehen; anerkennen; **a'vow·al** Bekenntnis *n*, (Ein)Geständnis *n*; **a'vow·ed·ly** [∼idli] eingestandenermaßen.

a·wait [ə'weit] erwarten (*a. fig.*).

a·wake [ə'weik] **1.** wach, munter; ∼ *to* sich *e-r Sache* bewußt; *wide* ∼ hellwach, *fig.* schlau, auf der Hut; **2.** (*irr.*) *v/t. mst* **a'wak·en** (auf-, er-)wecken; ∼*n s.o. to s.th.* j-m *et.* zum Bewußtsein bringen; *v/i.* auf-, erwachen; gewahr werden (*to s.th. et.*).

a·ward [ə'wɔːd] **1.** Urteil *n*, Spruch *m*; Zuerkennung *f*; Belohnung *f*; Auszeichnung *f*, Preis *m*; **2.** zuerkennen; *Orden etc.* verleihen.

a·ware [ə'wɛə]: *be* ∼ wissen (*of* von

od. acc.; *that* daß), sich bewußt sein (*of gen.*; *that* daß); *become* ∼ *of et.* gewahr werden, merken, sich *e-r Sache* bewußt werden; **a'ware·ness** Bewußtsein *n.*

a·wash ⚓ [ə'wɔʃ] (im Wasser) treibend; unter der Wasseroberfläche.

a·way [ə'wei] weg, hinweg; fort, abwesend; *bei vb. auch* immer weiter, darauflos; *Sport.*: Auswärts...; *2 miles* ∼ 2 Meilen entfernt *od.* von hier; *water has boiled* ∼ Wasser ist verkocht; *explain* ∼ hinwegerklären; ∼ *back Am.* F (schon) damals, weit zurück; *right* ∼, *straight* ∼ sofort; *out and* ∼ bei weitem.

awe [ɔː] **1.** Ehrfurcht *f*, Scheu *f* (*of* vor *dat.*); **2.** Ehrfurcht *od.* Furcht einflößen (*dat.*); **'∼-in·spir·ing** Ehrfurcht einflößend; **∼·some** ['∼səm] ehrfurchtgebietend; **'∼-struck** von Ehrfurcht ergriffen.

aw·ful □ ['ɔːful] ehrfurchtgebietend; furchtbar; F schrecklich, kolossal; **aw·ful·ly** ['ɔːfli] F sehr, furchtbar, schrecklich; *I'm* ∼ *sorry* es tut mir furchtbar leid.

a·while [ə'wail] eine Weile.

awk·ward □ ['ɔːkwəd] ungeschickt, unbeholfen, linkisch; umständlich; unangenehm, peinlich; mißlich, fatal; dumm, ungünstig, unpraktisch; *an* ∼ *corner* eine dumme Ecke; **'awk·ward·ness** Ungeschicklichkeit *f*, Unbeholfenheit *f*; linkisches Wesen *n*; Unannehmlichkeit *f.*

awl [ɔːl] Ahle *f*, Pfriem *m.*

awn ⚘ [ɔːn] Granne *f.*

awn·ing ['ɔːniŋ] Wagendecke *f*, Plane *f*; Markise *f*; ⚓ Sonnensegel *n.*

a·woke [ə'wəuk] *pret. u. pp. von awake* 2.

a·wry [ə'rai] schief; *fig.* verkehrt; *go* ∼, *turn* ∼ schiefgehen (*Sache*).

ax(e) [æks] **1.** Axt *f*, Beil *n*; *apply the* ∼ F Streichungen *od.* Entlassungen vornehmen; *have an* ∼ *to grind* eigennützige Zwecke verfolgen; **2.** *v/t.* F *Ausgabe* zs.-streichen; *Beamte etc.* abbauen.

ax·i·om ['æksiəm] Axiom *n* (*Grundsatz*); **ax·i·o·mat·ic** [∼siəu'mætik] (∼*ally*) axiomatisch, unumstößlich.

ax·is ['æksis], *pl.* **ax·es** ['∼siːz] Achse *f* (*a. pol.*).

ax·le ⊕ ['æksl] (Rad)Achse *f*, Welle *f*.
ay(e) [ai] **1.** ja; **2.** Ja *n*; *parl.* Stimme *f* für; *the ~s have it* die Mehrheit ist dafür.
a·zal·ea ⚘ [ə'zeiljə] Azalee *f*.

az·i·muth *ast.* ['æziməθ] Scheitelkreis *m*, Azimut *m*, *n*.
a·zo·ic *geol.* [ə'zɔuik] azoisch (*keine Lebewesen enthaltend*).
az·ure ['æʒə] **1.** azurn, azurblau; **2.** Azur(blau *n*) *m*.

B

baa [ba:] **1.** blöken; **2.** Blöken *n*.
Ba·al ['beiəl] *Gott* Baal *m*; Abgott*m*, Götze *m*.
Bab·bitt ['bæbit] *Am.* Spieß(bürg)er *m*; ♀ *metal* ⊕ Lagerweißmetall *n*.
bab·ble ['bæbl] **1.** stammeln, lallen; (nach)plappern; *Geheimnis* ausplaudern; plätschern (*Bach*); **2.** Gestammel *n*; Geplapper *n*; Geschwätz *n*; '**bab·bler** Schwätzer(in).
babe [beib] *poet.* kleines Kind *n*; Naivling *m*.
Ba·bel ['beibəl] *Bibel:* Babel *n*; ♀ *fig.* (Stimmen)Gewirr *n*.
ba·boon *zo.* [bə'bu:n] Pavian *m*.
ba·by ['beibi] **1.** Säugling *m*, Baby *n*, kleines Kind *n*; *Am. sl.* Süße *f* (*Mädchen*); Kindchen *n*; *it's your* ~ F das ist dein Bier; *be left holding the* ~ F der Dumme sein; **2.** Kinder...; Zwerg...; klein; ~ **act:** *mst plead* (*play*) *the* ~ *Am.* Unreife *f* plädieren (spielen); ~ **boom** Geburtenboom *m*; ~ **car** Klein(st)wagen *m*; ~ **car·riage** *Am.* Kinderwagen *m*; '**~-farm·er** j., der Kinder gewerbsmäßig in Pflege nimmt; ~ **grand** ♪ Stutzflügel *m*; **ba·by·hood** ['~hud] Säuglingsalter *n*, frühe Kindheit *f*; '**ba·by·ish** □ kindlich; kindisch.
Bab·y·lo·ni·an [bæbi'ləunjən] **1.** babylonisch; **2.** Babylonier(in).
ba·by...: '~-**mind·er** Tagesmutter *f*; '~-**sit·ter** Babysitter *m*, Kinderhüter(in).
bac·cha·nal ['bækənl] = *bacchant*; '**bac·cha·nals** *pl.*, **bac·cha·na·li·a** [~'neiljə] *pl.* Bacchanal *n* (*wüstes Gelage*); **bac·cha'na·li·an** bacchantisch.
bac·chant ['bækənt] Bacchant(in); **bac·chante** [bə'kænti] Bacchantin *f*; **bac'chan·tic** bacchantisch.

bac·cy F ['bæki] Tabak *m*.
bach·e·lor ['bætʃələ] Junggeselle *m*; *univ.* Bakkalaureus *m*; ~ *girl* Junggesellin *f*; **bach·e·lor·hood** ['~hud] Junggesellenstand *m*, -leben *n*.
bac·il·la·ry [bə'siləri] Bazillen...; **ba'cil·lus** [~ləs], *pl.* **ba'cil·li** [~lai] Bazillus *m*.
back [bæk] **1.** Rücken *m* (*von Mensch od. Tier*); Rückenlehne *f*; Rücken *m*, Rückseite *f*; = *full--back; have s.o. at one's* ~ von j-m unterstützt werden; *behind s.o.'s* ~ hinter j-s Rücken; *put one's* ~ *into s.th.* sich in et. hineinknien; *put od. get od. set s.o.'s* ~ *up* j. in Wut bringen; *break s.o.'s* ~ j. überfordern; *break the* ~ *of s.th.* das Schlimmste von et. überstehen *od.* schaffen; *be on one's* ~ auf der Nase liegen; *with one's* ~ *to the wall* in Bedrängnis; *at the* ~ *of* hinter (*dat.*); *on the* ~ *of that* zu alledem; **2.** *adj.* Hinter..., Rück...; hinter; rückwärtig; entlegen; rückläufig; rückständig; **3.** *adv.* zurück; *go* ~ *from od. upon one's word* sein Wort nicht halten; **4.** *v/t.* mit *m* Rücken versehen; *a.* ~ *up* j-m den Rücken decken *od.* stärken, j-m beistehen, j-m helfen, j. unterstützen; hinten anstoßen *od.* grenzen an (*acc.*); zurückbewegen, -schieben, -drücken *etc.*; wetten *od.* setzen auf (*acc.*); auf der Rückseite beschreiben; ✝ indossieren; ~ *the sails* ⚓ die Segel backholen; ~ *water*, ~ *the oars* rückwärts rudern; ~ *up et.* befürworten; *v/i.* sich rückwärts bewegen, rückwärts fahren, zurückgehen *od.* -fahren; zurücktreten, abspringen (*out of* von *e-m Unternehmen*); ~ *down* F sich zurück-

ziehen (*from* von); ~ **al·ley** *Am.* finstere Seitengasse *f;* '~-'**bench·er** *pol.* Hinterbänkler *m;* '~-**bend** *Turnen:* Brücke *f;* '~-**bite** (*irr. bite*) verleumden; '~-**bone** Rückgrat *n* (*a. fig.*); *to the* ~ *fig.* bis auf die Knochen; '~-**break·ing** anstrengend; '~-**chat** (freche) Widerrede *f;* '~-**cloth** *thea. u. fig.* Hintergrund *m;* '~-**cou·pling** Rückkoppelung *f;* '~-**date** (zu)rückdatieren; ~*d* to rückwirkend ab; '~- -'**door** Hintertür *f* (*a. fig.*); '~-**drop** = *backcloth;* ~ **en·trance** Hintereingang *m;* '**back·er** Unterstützer(in); † Indossierer; Hintermann *m;* Wetter(in).

back...: '~-**field** *Sport:* Hinterfeld (-spieler *m*) *n;* '~-'**fire** *mot.* **1.** Frühzündung *f;* **2.** frühzünden; ~ **for·ma·tion** *gr.* Rückbildung *f;* ~ '**gam·mon** Puffspiel *n;* '~-**ground** Hintergrund *m;* Herkunft *f,* Milieu *n,* Bildung *f;* '~-'**hand 1.** Rückhand(schlag *m*) *f;* **2.** Rückhand...; '~-**hand·ed** rückhändig; *fig.* unerwartet; '~-**hand·er** *s. back-hand* **1**; unerwarteter Angriff *m.*

back·ing ['bækiŋ] Unterstützung *f.*

back...: '~-**lash** Rückschlag *m,* Gegenstoß *m;* white ~ weißer Gegenstoß *m gegen die Gleichberechtigung der Neger in den USA;* '~-**log** Rückstand *m* (of one); Reserve *f* (of an); ~ **num·ber** alte Nummer *f* (*e-r Zeitung*); *j. od. et.* Altmodisches *n;* '~-**pack** *Am.* Rucksack *m;* '~-'**pack·ing** Rucksacktourismus *m;* ~ **pay** Lohn-, Gehaltsnachzahlung *f;* '~-'**ped·al** rückwärtstreten (*Radfahrer*); ~*ling* brake Rücktrittbremse *f;* '~-**room** boy F Wissenschaftler *m mit Geheimauftrag;* ~ **seat** Rücksitz *m; take a* ~ sich im Hintergrund halten; *back- -seat driver* Besserwisser *m;* '~-'**side** Hinter-, Rückseite *f;* ∨ Hintern *m;* '~-**sight** (Visier)Kimme *f;* '~-**slap·per** *Am.* plump-vertraulicher Mensch *m;* '~-**slide** (*irr. slide*) rückfällig werden; '~-**slid·er** Rückfällige *m, f;* '~-**slid·ing** Rückfall *m;* '~-**stage** (*a. fig.*) hinter den Kulissen; in der Garderobe; '~-**stairs** Hintertreppe *f;* '~-**stitch 1.** Steppstich *m;* **2.** mit Steppstichen nähen; '~-**stop** *Am.* *Baseball:* Gitter *n hinter dem Fänger; Schießstand:* Kugelfang *m;* ~ **street** Seitenstraße *f;* '~-**street a'bor·tion·ist** Engelmacher(in); '~-**stroke**

Rückenschwimmen *n;* ~ **talk** *Am.* freche Antworten *f pl.;* ~ **to back** Rücken an Rücken (gebaut); nacheinander; ~ **to front** verkehrt herum, mit der Rückseite nach vorne; '~-**track** *Am.* F *fig.* e-n Rückzieher machen.

back·ward ['bækwəd] **1.** *adj.* rückwärts gerichtet; Rück(wärts)...; langsam; zurückgeblieben, rückständig; zurückhaltend; **2.** *adv. a.* '**back·wards** rückwärts, zurück; **back·ward'a·tion** † *Kursabschlag m;* '**back·ward·ness** Rückständigkeit *f;* Langsamkeit *f;* Widerstreben *n.*

back...: '~-**wa·ter** Stauwasser *n;* totes Wasser *n;* '~-**woods** *pl.* weit abgelegene Waldgebiete *n/pl.; fig.* Provinz *f;* '~-**woods·man** Hinterwäldler *m.*

ba·con ['beikən] Speck *m; save one's* ~ F mit heiler Haut davonkommen; *bring home the* ~ *sl.* es geschafft haben.

bac·te·ri·al □ [bæk'tiəriəl] bakteriell; Bakterien...; **bac·te·ri·o·log·i·cal** □ [~tiəriə'lɔdʒikəl] bakteriologisch; **bac·te·ri·ol·o·gist** [~tiəri-'ɔlədʒist] Bakteriologe *m;* **bac'te·ri·um** [~riəm], *pl.* **bac'te·ri·a** [~riə] Bakterie *f.*

bad □ [bæd] schlecht, böse; schlimm, arg; falsch (*Münze*); anstößig (*Wort etc.*); faul (*Schuld*); *not* (*too*) ~, *not so* ~, *not half* ~ F gar nicht übel; *things are not so* ~ die Sache ist halb so schlimm; *he is* ~*ly off* es geht ihm sehr schlecht; ~*ly wounded* schwerverwundet; *want* ~*ly* dringend brauchen; *in* ~ *with Am.* F in Ungnade bei; *s.* **worse**.

bade [bæd] *pret. von* bid V.

badge [bædʒ] Ab-, Kennzeichen *n.*

badg·er ['bædʒə] **1.** *zo.* Dachs *m;* **2.** hetzen, plagen, belästigen.

bad·lands *Am.* ['bædləndz] *pl.* Ödland *n,* unfruchtbares Land *n.*

bad·min·ton ['bædmintən] Federballspiel *n,* Badminton *n.*

bad·ness ['bædnis] schlechte Beschaffenheit *f;* Schlechtigkeit *f.*

bad-tem·pered ['bæd'tempəd] schlecht gelaunt, mürrisch.

baf·fle ['bæfl] *j.* verwirren, verblüffen; *Plan etc.* vereiteln, durchkreuzen; *they were* ~*d in their attempt* ihr Versuch wurde zunichte ge-

macht; *it* ⁓*s description* es spottet
jeder Beschreibung.
bag [bæg] **1.** Tasche *f*, Beutel *m*,
Sack *m*; Tüte *f*; *hunt.* Strecke *f*; ⁓*s*
pl. sl. Hosen *f/pl.*; *it's in the* ⁓ F das
haben wir sicher; ⁓ *and baggage*
mit Sack und Pack; ⁓*s of sl.* e-e
Menge; **2.** in e-n Beutel *etc.* tun,
einsacken; F stibitzen; *hunt.* zur
Strecke bringen; (sich) bauschen.
bag·a·telle [bægə'tel] Kleinigkeit *f*.
bag·gage ['bægidʒ] *Am.* (Reise-)
Gepäck *n*; ⚔ Troß *m*; *co.* kleines Biest
n, Fratz *m* (*Mädchen*); ⁓ **al·low·ance**
Freigepäck *n*; ⁓ **car** 🚋 *Am.* Gepäck-
wagen *m*; '⁓**-check** *Am.* Gepäckschein *m*; ⁓ (**re·**)**claim** Gepäckaus-
gabe *f am Flughafen*.
bag·ging ['bægiŋ] Sack-, Packlein-
wand *f*.
bag·gy ['bægi] ausgebeult (*Hose*);
sackartig; bauschig.
bag...: ⁓**man** ['bægmən] F Handlungsreisende *m*; '⁓**-pipes** *pl.* Dudelsack *m*; '⁓**-snatch·er** Handtaschen-
räuber *m*.
bah [bɑː] bah!, pah!
bail[1] [beil] **1.** Bürge *m*; Bürgschaft *f*;
Kaution *f*; *admit to* ⁓ 🏛 gegen
Bürgschaft freilassen; *be od. go od.
stand* ⁓ *for* bürgen für *j.*; **2.** bürgen
für; ⁓ *out j.* freibürgen; mit dem
Fallschirm abspringen.
bail[2] ⚓ [⁓] ausschöpfen.
bail[3] [⁓] *Kricket:* Querholz *n*.
bail[4] [⁓] Henkel *m e-s Eimers etc.*
bail·iff ['beilif] Gerichtsdiener *m*;
(Guts)Verwalter *m*; Amtmann *m*.
bail·ment 🏛 ['beilmənt] (vertragliche) Hinterlegung *f einer beweg-
lichen Sache*.
bail·or 🏛 ['beilə] Deponent *m*,
Hinterleger *m*.
bairn *schott.* [bɛən] Kind *n*.
bait [beit] **1.** Köder *m*; *fig.* Lockung *f*,
Reiz *m*; Rast *f*; *take the* ⁓ (*a. fig.*)
anbeißen; **2.** *v/t.* mit e-m Köder
versehen; *Pferde unterwegs* füttern;
hunt. hetzen; *fig.* quälen; reizen; *v/i.*
rasten, einkehren.
baize [beiz] (grüner) Fries *m*.
bake [beik] **1.** backen; braten; *Ziegel*
brennen; (aus)dörren; ⁓*d potatoes pl.*
Folien-, Ofenkartoffeln *f/pl.*; **2.** *Am.*
gesellige Zusammenkunft *f*.
ba·ke·lite ⊕ ['beikəlait] Bakelit *n*.
bak·er ['beikə] Bäcker *m*; ⁓*'s dozen*
dreizehn; '**bak·er·y** Bäckerei *f*;

'**bak·ing** *a.* ⁓ *hot* glühend heiß;
'**bak·ing-pow·der** Backpulver *n*.
bak·sheesh ['bækʃiːʃ] Bakschisch *n*
(*Trinkgeld im Orient*).
Ba·la·cla·va [bælə'klɑːvə]: ⁓ *helmet*
Hals *u. Ohren bedeckende* Woll-
mütze *f*.
bal·a·lai·ka ♪ [bælə'laikə] Balalaika *f*
(*dreieckige Gitarre*).
bal·ance ['bæləns] **1.** Waage *f*;
Gleich-, Übergewicht *n* (*a. fig.*);
Ausgeglichenheit *f*, Harmonie *f*; 🕐
Bilanz *f*, Saldo *m*, Überschuß *m*;
Restbetrag *m*; F Rest *m*, Überbleibsel *n*; *a.* ⁓ *wheel* Unruhe *f der Uhr*;
be od. hang in the ⁓ in der Schwebe
sein; *keep* (*lose*) *one's* ⁓ das Gleichgewicht halten (verlieren); *fig.* ruhig
bleiben (nervös werden); *throw s.o.
off his* ⁓ *fig.* j. aus der Fassung bringen; *turn the* ⁓ den Ausschlag geben; ⁓ *of payments* Zahlungsbilanz *f*;
⁓ *of power pol.* Kräftegleichgewicht *n*;
⁓ *of trade* (Außen)Handelsbilanz *f*; *s.
strike 2*; **2.** *v/t.* (ab-, er)wägen; im
Gleichgewicht halten; ins Gleichgewicht bringen, ausgleichen; 🕐 bi-
lanzieren, ausgleichen; saldieren, abschließen; *v/i.* balancieren; sich ausgleichen; '⁓**-sheet** 🕐 Bilanz *f*.
bal·co·ny ['bælkəni] Balkon *m* (*a.
thea.*); Rang *m*.
bald [bɔːld] kahl; *fig.* nackt; dürftig.
bal·da·chin ['bɔːldəkin] Baldachin
m.
bal·der·dash ['bɔːldədæʃ] Geschwätz *n*.
bald...: '⁓**-head**, '⁓**-pate** Kahlkopf
m; '⁓**-'head·ed** kahlköpfig; *go* ⁓
into blindlings hineinrennen in
(*acc.*); '**bald·ness** Kahlheit *f*.
bale[1] 🕐 [beil] Ballen *m*.
bale[2] ⚓ [⁓] ausschöpfen.
bale·fire ['beilfaiə] Signalfeuer *n*.
bale·ful □ ['beilful] verderblich;
unheilvoll.
balk [bɔːk] **1.** (Furchen)Rain *m*;
Balken *m*; Hemmnis *n*; **2.** *v/t.* (ver-)
hindern; enttäuschen; umgehen;
verpassen; stutzig machen; *v/i.*
stutzen, scheuen (*at* bei, *vor dat.*).
Bal·kan ['bɔːlkən] Balkan...; balka-
nisch.
ball[1] [bɔːl] **1.** Ball *m*; Kugel *f*;
(Hand-, Fuß)Ballen *m*; Knäuel *m*,
n; Kloß *m*; *Sport:* Wurf *m*; *Am.
Baseball:* falscher Wurf *m*; *start
(keep) the* ⁓ *rolling* die Sache *od.*

ball 56

das Gespräch in Gang bringen (halten); *have the ~ at one's feet* die beste Gelegenheit haben; *the ~ is with you* du bist dran; *play ~ Am.* F mitmachen; *be on the ~* auf Draht sein; 2. (sich) (zs.-)ballen; *~ed up Am. sl.* durcheinander.

ball² [~] Ball *m*, Tanzgesellschaft *f*; *open the ~ fig.* den Reigen eröffnen; *have a ~ fig.* sich köstlich amüsieren.

bal·lad ['bæləd] Ballade *f*; '**~-mon·ger** Bänkelsänger *m*.

ball-and-sock·et ['bɔːlən'sɔkit]: ~ *joint* ⊕ Kugelgelenk *n*.

bal·last ['bæləst] 1. ♨ Ballast *m* (*a. fig.*); ⚒ Schotter *m*, Bettung *f*; *mental ~* innerer Halt *m*; 2. mit Ballast beladen; ⚒ beschottern, betten.

ball...: '**~-'bear·ing**(*s pl.*) ⊕ Kugellager *n*; '**~-boy** *Tennis:* Balljunge *m*; '**~-car·tridge** scharfe Patrone *f*.

bal·let ['bælei] Ballett *n*.

bal·lis·tics [bə'listiks] *mst sg.* Ballistik *f*.

bal·loon [bə'luːn] 1. Ballon *m*; ~ *barrage* Ballonsperre *f*; ~ *tire mot.* Ballonreifen *m*; 2. im Ballon aufsteigen; sich bauschen; *sl. Ball* hoch in die Luft schießen; **bal·'loon·ist** Ballonfahrer *m*.

bal·lot ['bælət] 1. Wahlkugel *f*, -zettel *m*; (geheime) Wahl *f*; 2. (geheim) abstimmen; ~ *for* losen um; '**~-box** Wahlurne *f*.

ball...: '**~-(-point)** pen Kugelschreiber *m*; '**~-room** Ballsaal *m*; ~ *dancing* Gesellschaftstanz *m*.

balls V [bɔːlz] *pl.* Eier *n/pl.* (*Hoden*).

bal·ly·hoo F [bæli'huː] 1. Tamtam *n*, aufdringliche Reklame *f*; 2. marktschreierisch anpreisen.

bal·ly·rag F ['bæliræg] aufziehen; tyrannisieren.

balm [bɑːm] Balsam *m*; *fig.* Trost *m*. **balm·y** □ ['bɑːmi] balsamisch (*a. fig.*); mild.

ba·lo·ney *Am. sl.* [bə'ləuni] Quatsch *m*.

bal·sam ['bɔːlsəm] Balsam *m*; **bal·sam·ic** [~'sæmik] (~*ally*) balsamisch.

Bal·tic ['bɔːltik] 1. baltisch; ~ *Sea* = 2. Ostsee *f*.

bal·us·ter ['bæləstə] Geländersäule *f*. **bal·us·trade** [bæləs'treid] Balustrade *f*, Brüstung *f*; Geländer *n*.

bam·boo [bæm'buː] Bambus *m*.

bam·boo·zle F [bæm'buːzl] beschwindeln (*into ger.* zu *inf.*; *out of* um).

ban ['bæn] 1. Bann *m*; Achtung *f*, Acht *f*; (amtliches) Verbot *n*; 2. verbieten; ~ *s.o. from speaking* j-m verbieten zu sprechen.

ba·nal [bə'nɑːl] banal, abgedroschen.

ba·nan·a [bə'nɑːnə] ⚘ Banane *f*; ~ *split Am.* Eisbecher *m* mit Banane; **ba'na·nas** *sl.* bescheuert (*verrückt*).

band [bænd] 1. Band *n*; ⊕ Treibriemen *m*; Streifen *m*; Leiste *f*; Bande *f*; Trupp *m*; Gruppe *f*, Schar *f*; ♪ (Musik)Kapelle *f*, Band *f*; 2. zs.-binden; ~ *together* sich zs.-tun, *b.s.* sich zs.-rotten.

band·age ['bændidʒ] 1. Bandage *f*; Binde *f*; Verband *m*; *first-aid ~* Notverband *m*; 2. bandagieren; verbinden.

band-aid *Am.* ['bændeid] Heftpflaster *n*.

ban·dan·na [bæn'dɑːnə] buntes Halstuch *n*.

band·box ['bændbɔks] Hutschachtel *f*; *as if one came out of a ~* wie aus dem Ei geschält.

ban·dit ['bændit] Bandit *m*; '**ban·dit·ry** Banditentum *n*.

band·mas·ter ['bændmɑːstə] Kapellmeister *m*.

ban·do·leer [bændəu'liə] Patronengurt *m*.

bands·man ['bændzmən] Orchestermitglied *n*, Musiker *m*; '**band·stand** Musikpavillon *m*; **band wag·on** *Am.* Wagen *m* mit Musikkapelle; *jump on the ~ fig.* sich der erfolgversprechenden Sache anschließen.

ban·dy ['bændi] 1. *Ball etc.* hin und her werfen; *Worte* wechseln, *Blicke, Schläge etc.* tauschen; 2. krumm, gekrümmt; 3. Ochsenkarren *m*; '**~-leg·ged** O-beinig.

bane [bein] Ruin *m*; *the ~ of his life* der Fluch s-s Lebens; **bane·ful** □ ['beinful] verderblich.

bang [bæn] 1. bum(s)!, peng!; 2. gerade(swegs), genau; 3. Knall *m*; *go over with a ~ Am.* F ein Bombenerfolg sein; 4. dröhnend schlagen; knallen; F hauen; *Tür* zuschlagen; F knallen mit *et.*; *sl. Preise* drücken; '**bang·er** Knallkörper *m*; F Klapperkiste *f*; F (Brat)Würstchen *n*; ~*s pl. and mash* Würstchen *n/pl.* mit Kartoffelbrei.

ban·gle ['bæŋgl] Arm-, Fußring *m*.

bang-on F [bæŋ'ɔn] ganz genau (richtig).

bangs *Am.* [bæŋz] *pl.* Ponyfrisur *f*.

bang-up *Am. sl.* ['bæŋʌp] Klasse..., prima.

ban·ish ['bænɪʃ] verbannen; **'ban·ish·ment** Verbannung *f*.

ban·is·ter ['bænɪstə] Geländersäule *f*; **'ban·is·ters** *pl.* Treppengeländer *n*.

ban·jo ♪ ['bændʒəu] Banjo *n*.

bank [bæŋk] 1. Damm *m*, Ufer *n*; Böschung *f*; *Sand*-, *Wolken*- *etc.* Bank *f*; ✝ Bank(haus *n*) *f*; Spielbank *f*; ~ *of deposit* Depositenbank *f*; ~ *of issue* Notenbank *f*; 2. *v/t.* eindämmen; ✝ *Geld* auf die Bank legen; ✈ in die Kurve bringen; *v/i.* Bankgeschäfte machen; ein Bankkonto haben (*with* bei); ✈ in die Kurve gehen, in der Kurve liegen; ~ *on* sich verlassen auf (*acc.*); ~ *up* (sich) aufhäufen; **'bank·a·ble** bankfähig; **'bank-ac·count** Bankkonto *n*; **'bank-bill** Bankwechsel *m*; *Am. s. bank-note*; **'bank·er** Bankier *m*; *Roulette etc.*: Bankhalter *m*; **bank hol·i·day** gesetzlicher Feiertag *m*; **'bank·ing** 1. Bankgeschäft *n*; Bankwesen *n*; ✈ Schräglage *f*; 2. Bank...; **bank·ing charg·es** *pl.* Bankgebühren *f/pl.*; **'bank·ing-house** Bankhaus *n*; **'bank-note** Banknote *f*, Geldschein *m*; Kassenschein *m*; **'bank-rate** Diskontsatz *m*; **bank·rupt** ['~rʌpt] 1. Bankrotteur *m*; ~'s *estate* Konkursmasse *f*; 2. bankrott; *go* ~ Bankrott machen; ~ *in od. of e-r Eigenschaft* bar; 3. Bankrott machen; **bank·rupt·cy** ['~rəptsi] Bankrott *m*, Konkurs *m*; *declaration of* ~ Bankrotterklärung *f*; ~ *petition* Konkursantrag *m*.

ban·ner ['bænə] 1. Banner *n*; Fahne *f*; Transparent *n bei politischen Umzügen*; 2. *Am. in Zssgn* Haupt..., führend.

ban·nock *schott.* ['bænək] Haferbrot *m*.

banns [bænz] *pl.* Aufgebot *n* (*vor der Hochzeit*); *put up the* ~, *publish the* ~ *j-n* aufbieten.

ban·quet ['bæŋkwit] 1. Bankett *n*, Festmahl *n*, -essen *n*; 2. festlich bewirten; tafeln; ~*ing hall* Bankettsaal *m*; **'ban·quet·er** Bankettteilnehmer *m*.

ban·shee *schott.*, *ir.* [bæn'ʃi:] Todesfee *f*.

ban·tam ['bæntəm] Zwerghuhn *n*; *fig.* Zwerg *m*; ~ *weight Sport*: Bantamgewicht *n*.

ban·ter ['bæntə] 1. Neckerei *f*, Hänselei *f*; 2. necken, hänseln; **'ban·ter·er** Spötter(in), Spaßvogel *m*.

bap·tism ['bæptizəm] Taufe *f*; ~ *of fire* Feuertaufe *f*; **bap·tis·mal** [~'tizməl] Tauf...

bap·tist ['bæptist] Täufer *m*; **'bap·tis·ter·y** Taufkapelle *f*; **bap·tize** [~'taiz] taufen (*a. fig.*).

bar [ba:] 1. Stange *f*; Stab *m*; *metall.* Barren *m*; Riegel *m*; Tafel *f Schokolade*; Schranke *f*, Barriere *f*; Sandbank *f*; *fig.* Hindernis *n*; Streifen *m*, Band *n*; ✗ Spange *f*; ♪ Takt (-strich) *m*; (*Gerichts*)Schranke *f*; *fig.* Urteil *n*; Anwaltschaft *f*; Bar *f im Hotel etc.*; *horizontal* ~ Reck *n*; *parallel* ~*s pl.* Barren *m*; *be called to the* ~ ⚖ als Anwalt zugelassen werden; *prisoner at the* ~ Untersuchungsgefangene *m*, *f*; *stand at the* ~ vor Gericht stehen; *behind prison* ~*s* hinter Gittern; 2. verriegeln; (*ver*-, ab)sperren; verwehren; einsperren; aufhalten; (*ver*-)hindern (*from an dat.*); ausnehmen, absehen von; ~ *one* außer einem; ~ *out* aussperren.

barb [ba:b] *zo.* Bart(faden) *m*; Widerhaken *m*; Fahne *f der Feder*; **barbed** mit Widerhaken versehen; ~ *wire* Stacheldraht *m*.

bar·bar·i·an [ba:'beəriən] 1. fremd; barbarisch; grausam; 2. Barbar *m*; **bar·bar·ic** [~'bærik] (~*ally*) barbarisch; **bar·ba·rism** ['~bərizəm] Barbarismus *m*, Sprachwidrigkeit *f*; Unkultur *f*, Barbarei *f*; **bar·bar·i·ty** [~'bæriti] Barbarei *f*, Unmenschlichkeit *f*; **bar·ba·rize** ['~bəraiz] verrohen lassen; verderben; **'bar·ba·rous** □ barbarisch, unmenschlich, roh; grausam.

bar·be·cue ['ba:bikju:] 1. Grill *m*; Grillparty *f*; Grillfleisch *n*; 2. grillen, am Spieß braten.

bar·bel *ichth.* ['ba:bəl] Barbe *f*.

bar·bell ['ba:bel] *Sport*: Kugelhantel *f*.

bar·ber ['ba:bə] Barbier *m*; (Herren)Friseur *m*; ~ *shop* Friseurgeschäft *n*.

bar·bi·tu·rate [ba:'bitjuərət] Barbi-

turat *n*, Schlaf- *od.* Beruhigungsmittel *n.*

bard [ba:d] Barde *m*, Sänger *m.*

bare [beə] **1.** nackt, bloß; kahl; bar,
leer; arm, entblößt (*of* von); *the*
~ *idea* der bloße Gedanke; **2.** entblößen, zeigen; '~**back(ed)** unge-
sattelt; '~**faced** □ frech, schamlos;
'~**faced·ness** Frechheit *f*, Schamlosigkeit *f*; '~**foot** barfuß; '~**foot-
ed** barfüßig; barfuß; '~**head·ed**
barhäuptig; '**bare·ly** kaum, gerade,
knapp; '**bare·ness** Nacktheit *f*,
Blöße *f*; Dürftigkeit *f.*

bar·gain ['ba:gin] **1.** Geschäft *n*;
Handel *m*, Kauf *m* (*a. gekaufte
Sache*); Vertrag *m*, Abschluß *m*;
vorteilhafter Kauf *m*, Gelegenheitskauf *m*; ~ *price* Spottpreis *m*; *a
(dead)* ~ spottbillig; *it's a* ~! F abgemacht!; *into the* ~ noch dazu,
obendrein; *make od. strike a* ~
handelseinig werden, e-n Handel
abschließen; *drive a hard* ~ hart feilschen; **2.** handeln, feilschen (*about*
um), übereinkommen (*for* über *acc.*;
that daß); ~ *for* rechnen mit, gefaßt
sein auf (*acc.*); erwarten; ~ **basement** Sonderangebotsabteilung *f* im
Tiefgeschoß *e-s Kaufhauses*; '**bar-
gain·er** Handelnde *m*, *f*; **bar·gain
sale** Ausverkauf *m.*

barge [ba:dʒ] **1.** Flußboot *n*, Lastkahn *m*; ⚓ Barkasse *f*; Hausboot *n*;
2. F taumeln, torkeln; ~ *in* hereinplatzen; *fig.* sich *auf unwirsche Art*
einmischen; **bar'gee**, **barge·man**
['~mən] Kahnführer *m.*

bar·i·ron ['ba:aiən] Stabeisen *m.*
bar·i·tone ♪ ['bæritəun] Bariton *m.*
bar·i·um ⚗ ['bɛəriəm] Barium *n.*

bark[1] [ba:k] **1.** Borke *f*, Rinde *f*;
⊕ Lohe *f*; **2.** abrinden; *Haut* ab-
schürfen.

bark[2] [~] **1.** bellen, kläffen (*a. fig.*);
böllern (*Schußwaffe*); ~ *at* anbellen;
be ~*ing up the wrong tree* F auf dem
Holzweg sein; **2.** Bellen *n* (F *Husten*)
etc.

bark[3] [~] ⚓ = barque; *poet.* Barke *f.*
bar·keep·er ['ba:ki:pə] Barbesitzer
m; Barkellner *m.*
bark·er ['ba:kə] Kläffer *m* (*a. fig.*);
Kundenfänger *m.*
bar·ley ['ba:li] Gerste *f*; Graupe *f.*
barm [ba:m] Bärme *f*, Hefe *f.*
bar·maid ['ba:meid] Kellnerin *f*,
Bardame *f.*

bar·man ['ba:mən] *s.* bartender.
barm·y ['ba:mi] hefig; P verdreht.
barn [ba:n] Scheune *f*; *bsd. Am.*
(*Vieh*)Stall *m.*
bar·na·cle[1] ['ba:nəkl] *orn.* Bernikel-
gans *f*; *zo.* Entenmuschel *f*; *fig.*
Klette *f* (*nicht abzuschüttelnder
Mensch*).
bar·na·cle[2] [~] *vet.* Bremse *f*; ~*s pl.*
F Brille *f*, Kneifer *m.*
barn·storm *Am. pol.* ['ba:nstɔ:m]
herumreisen u. (Wahl)Reden halten; '**barn·yard** Hof *m zwischen
Bauernhaus u. Scheune.*
ba·rom·e·ter [bə'rɔmitə] Barometer *n*; **bar·o·met·ric**, **bar·o·
met·ri·cal** □ [bærəu'metrik(əl)]
barometrisch; Barometer...
bar·on ['bærən] Baron *m*, Freiherr
m; *coal* ~ Kohlenbaron *m*; '**bar·on-
ess** Baronin *f*; **bar·on·et** ['~nit]
Baronet *m*; **bar·on·et·cy** ['~nitsi]
Baronetswürde *f*; **ba·ro·ni·al** [bə-
'rəunjəl] freiherrlich; **bar·o·ny**
['bærəni] Baronie *f*; Baronswürde
f.
ba·roque [bə'rɔk] **1.** barock; **2.** Barock *n*, *m.*
barque ⚓ [ba:k] Bark *f.*
bar·rack ['bærək] **1.** *mst* ~*s pl.*
Kaserne *f*; Mietskaserne *f*; **2.** *sl.*
anpöbeln.
bar·rage ['bæra:ʒ] Staudamm *m*,
Talsperre *f*; *weitS.* Sperre *f*; ⚔
Sperrfeuer *n*; ~ *balloon* Sperrballon
m; *creeping* ~ ⚔ Feuerwalze *f.*
bar·rel ['bærəl] **1.** Faß *n*, Tonne *f*;
(*Gewehr*)Lauf *m*; (*Geschütz*)Rohr
n; ⊕ Trommel *f*; Walze *f*; Rumpf
m e-s Pferdes etc.; **2.** in Fässer
füllen; '**bar·relled** ...läufig (*Gewehr*); '**bar·rel·or·gan** ♪ Drehorgel *f.*
bar·ren □ ['bærən] unfruchtbar;
dürr, trocken (*alle a. fig.*); ✝ tot
(*Kapital*); '**bar·ren·ness** Unfruchtbarkeit *f.*
bar·ri·cade [bæri'keid] **1.** Barrikade *f*; **2.** verbarrikadieren, verrammeln; sperren.
bar·ri·er ['bæriə] Schranke *f* (*a.
fig.*); Barriere *f*, Sperre *f*; Schlagbaum *m*; Hindernis *n*; ~ *cream*
schmutzabweisende Hautcreme *f.*
bar·ring F ['ba:riŋ] ausgenommen,
abgesehen von; ~ *a miracle* es sei
kein Wunder geschieht.
bar·ris·ter ['bæristə] *a.* ~-*at-law*

bathos

(plädierender) Rechtsanwalt *m an*
den höheren Gerichtshöfen, Barrister *m.*

bar·row[1] ['bærəu] *s. hand-~, wheel-*
~; ~-man ['~mən] Straßenhändler
m.

bar·row[2] [~] Hügelgrab *n,* Tumulus *m.*

bar·tend·er ['bɑːtendə] Büfettier *m,*
Schankkellner *m.*

bar·ter ['bɑːtə] **1.** Tausch(handel)
m; ~ shop Tauschladen *m;* **2.** tauschen (*for* gegen); Tauschhandel
treiben; *b.s.* (ver)schachern; *~ away a.*
fig. verschachern.

bar·y·tone ♩ ['bæritəun] Bariton *m.*

ba·salt ['bæsɔːlt] Basalt *m;* **ba·sal-**
tic [bə'sɔːltik] basaltisch; Basalt...

base[1] □ [beis] gemein, niedrig;
unedel, unecht, falsch (*Metall etc.*).

base[2] [~] **1.** Basis *f,* Grundfläche *f,*
-linie *f,* -lage *f;* Fundament *n;* Fuß
m, Sockel *m;* ♙ Base *f;* Stützpunkt
m; Sport: Mal *n;* **2.** *fig.* gründen,
stützen, aufbauen (*on, upon* auf
acc.); ♚ landen; *~ o.s.* on sich
stützen auf (*acc.*); *be ~d* (*up*)*on* beruhen auf (*dat.*), sich stützen auf
(*acc.*).

base...: '*~*-**ball** Baseball *m;* '*~*-
board Fuß-, Scheuerleiste *f;* '*~*-
-born uneheliger Abkunft; unehelich; '*~*-**less** grundlos; '*~*-**line**
Grundlinie *f; surv.* Standlinie *f;*
'**base·ment** Fundament *n;* Keller-
geschoß *n.*

base·ness ['beisnis] Gemeinheit *f etc.*
(*s. base*[1]).

bash F [bæʃ] **1.** heftig schlagen; **2.**
heftiger Schlag *m; have a ~ at s.th.* et.
mal probieren.

bash·ful □ ['bæʃful] verschämt,
schüchtern.

bas·ic ['beisik] (*~ally*) grundlegend,
Grund...; ♙ basisch; ♀ *English* Basic
English *n* (*vereinfachtes Englisch*); *~*
iron Thomaseisen *n; ~ slag* Thomass-
schlacke *f;* '**bas·ics** *pl. das* Wesentliche.

basil ⚘ ['bæzl] Basilienkraut *n.*

ba·sil·i·ca ⚠ [bə'zilikə] Basilika *f.*

bas·i·lisk ['bæzilisk] **1.** Basilisk *m;*
2. Basilisken...

ba·sin ['beisn] *allg.* Becken *n; engS.*
Schüssel *f,* Schale *f;* Tal-, Wasser-,
Hafenbecken *n;* Innenhafen *m.*

ba·sis ['beisis], *pl.* **ba·ses** ['~siːz]
Basis *f,* Grundlage *f;* ✕, ⚓ Stütz-

punkt *m; take as ~* zugrunde legen.

bask [bɑːsk] sich sonnen (*a. fig.*);
sich wärmen.

bas·ket ['bɑːskit] Korb *m;* '*~*-**ball**
Korbball(spiel *n*) *m; ~ din·ner, ~*
sup·per *Am.* Picknick *n;* '**bas·ket-**
-work Korbgeflecht *n.*

bass[1] ♩ [beis] Baß *m.*

bass[2] *ichth.* [bæs] Barsch *m.*

bass[3] [~] Bast *m;* Bastmatte *f.*

bas·si·net [bæsi'net] Korbwiege *f,*
Stubenwagen *m.*

bas·soon ♩ [bə'suːn, ♩ bə'zuːn]
Fagott *m.*

bast [bæst] Bast *m.*

bas·tard ['bæstəd] **1.** □ unehelich;
unecht; Bastard...; **2.** Bastard *m;*
'**bas·tar·dy** uneheliche Geburt *f.*

baste[1] [beist] Braten (mit Fett) begießen; durchprügeln.

baste[2] [~] lose nähen, (an)heften.

bas·ti·na·do [bæsti'neidəu] **1.** Bastonade *f;* **2.** *j-m* die Bastonade geben.

bas·tion ✕ ['bæstiən] Bastion *f.*

bat[1] [bæt] Fledermaus *f; as blind*
as a ~ stockblind.

bat[2] [~] *Sport:* **1.** Schlagholz *n,*
Schläger *m;* Schläger *m* (*Spieler*);
off one's own ~ fig. selbständig;
2. (mit dem Schlagholz) schlagen;
am Schlagen sein; *~ for s.o.* für j-n
eintreten.

batch [bætʃ] Schub *m Brote;* Stoß *m*
Briefe etc.

bate [beit] verringern; *Preis* herun-
tersetzen; *with ~d breath* mit angehal-
tenem Atem, gespannt.

Bath[1] [bɑːθ]: *~ brick* Metallputzstein
m; ~ chair Rollstuhl *m.*

bath[2] [~] **1.** *pl.* **baths** [bɑːðz] Bad *n*
(*Wannen-, Licht-, Sonnenbad; Bade-*
wasser, -wanne, -zimmer, -ort); *~ foam*
Schaumbad *n;* **2.** *Kind* baden; *ein*
Bad nehmen.

bathe [beið] **1.** baden; **2.** Bad *n im*
Freien.

bath·house ['bɑːθhaus] Badeanstalt
f; Umkleidekabinen *f/pl.*

bath·ing ['beiðiŋ] Baden *n,* Bad *n;*
attr. Bade...; '*~*-**cap** Badekappe *f;*
'*~*-**cos·tume,** '*~*-**dress** Badeanzug
m; '*~*-**hut** Strandkorb *m;* '*~*-
-ma·chine Badekarren *m;* '*~*-**suit**
Badeanzug *m;* '*~*-**trunks** *pl.* Badehose *f.*

ba·thos *rhet.* ['beiθɔs] Abgleiten *n*
vom Erhabenen ins Niedrige; Niedergang *m;* Gemeinplatz *m.*

bath...: '**~·robe** *Am.* Bademantel *m*;
'**~-room** Badezimmer *n*; Toilette *f*;
'**~-sheet** Badelaken *n*; '**~-tow·el**
Badetuch *n*; '**~·tub** Badewanne *f*.

ba·tik ['bætik] Batik(druck) *m*.

ba·tiste [bæ'ti:st] Batist *m*.

bat·man ['bætmən] Offiziersbursche *m*.

ba·ton ['bætən] *Amts-, Kommando*-
Stab *m*; ♪ Taktstock *m*, Stab *m*;
(Polizei)Knüppel *m*.

bats·man ['bætsmən] *Kricket etc.*:
Schläger *m*.

bat·tal·ion [bə'tæljən] Bataillon *n*.

bat·ten ['bætn] **1.** Latte *f*; Leiste *f*;
2. (mit Latten) befestigen; sich
mästen (*on, upon* mit); ~ *down the
hatches* ♨ die Luken schalken.

bat·ter ['bætə] **1.** *Kricket*: Schläger
m; *Küche*: Rührteig *m*; **2.** heftig
schlagen, zerschlagen; ein-, ver-,
zerbeulen; arg mitnehmen; ✕
bombardieren; *fig.* herunter-, verreißen (*Kritiker etc.*); ~ *down* od.
in Tür einschlagen; '**bat·tered** zerschlagen, zertrümmert; abgenutzt;
mißhandelt; ~ *babies* mißhandelte
Kinder; ~ *wives* mißhandelte (Ehe-)
Frauen; '**bat·ter·ing** Belagerungs...,
Sturm...; ~ *ram* Sturmbock *m*; '**bat-
ter·y** ✕ Batterie *f*; ♨ Geschütz-
gruppe *f*; ∮ Batterie *f*, Akku *m*; *fig.*
Satz *m*; ⚖ Realinjurien *f/pl.*; *assault
and* ~ tätlicher Angriff *m*; ~*-operated*
mit Batteriebetrieb.

bat·tle ['bætl] **1.** Schlacht *f*, Gefecht *n* (*of* bei); ~ *royal* Massen-
schlägerei *f*; **2.** streiten (*for* um),
kämpfen (*against* gegen, *with* mit);
'**~-axe** Streitaxt *f*; F Xanthippe *f*.

bat·tle·dore ['bætldɔ:] Federball-
schläger *m*.

bat·tle·field ['bætli:ld], '**bat·tle-
-ground** Schlachtfeld *n*.

bat·tle·ment ['bætlmənt] Brustwehr *f*; ~*s pl.* Zinnen *f/pl.*

bat·tle·ship ✕ ['bætlʃip] Schlacht-
schiff *n*.

bat·tue [bæ'tu:] Treibjagd *f*.

bat·ty *sl.* ['bæti] nicht ganz bei
Trost.

bau·ble ['bɔ:bl] Spielzeug *n*, Tand
m.

baulk [bɔ:k] = *balk*.

baux·ite *min.* ['bɔ:ksait] Bauxit *m*.

Ba·var·i·an [bə'veəriən] **1.** bay(e)-
risch; **2.** Bayer(in).

baw·bee *schott.* [bɔ:'bi:] = *half-*

penny.

bawd [bɔ:d] Kupplerin *f*; '**bawd·y**
unzüchtig, obszön.

bawl [bɔ:l] brüllen; johlen, grölen;
j. anschreien; ~ *out* auf-, los-, *et.*
herausbrüllen; *Am. sl. j.* laut her-
unterputzen, anschnauzen.

bay[1] [bei] **1.** braun (*Pferd*); **2.** Braune
m, *f*.

bay[2] [~] Bai *f*, Bucht *f*; *geol.* Kar *n*;
~ *salt* Seesalz *n*.

bay[3] [~] ⚓ Joch *n*, Fach *n*; Erker *m*;
Abteilung *f*; Seitenbahnsteig *m*;
bomb ~ ✈ Bombenschacht *m*;
sick-~ ♨ Schiffslazarett *n*.

bay[4] ♀ [~] Lorbeer *m*.

bay[5] [~] **1.** bellen, anschlagen
(*Hund*); ~ *at* anbellen; **2.** *stand at* ~
sich verzweifelt wehren; *bring to* ~,
keep od. hold at ~ *Wild* stellen;
turn to ~ sich stellen (*a. fig.*).

bay·o·net ✕ ['beiənit] **1.** Bajonett *n*;
2. mit dem Bajonett niederstoßen;
'**~-catch** ⊕ Bajonettverschluß *m*.

bay·ou *Am. geogr.* ['baiu:] sumpfiger
Nebenarm *m, bsd. e-s Flusses.*

bay-win·dow ['bei'windəu] Erker-
fenster *n*; *Am. sl.* Vorbau *m* (*Bauch*).

ba·zaar [bə'za:] Basar *m*.

ba·zoo·ka ✕ [bə'zu:kə] Panzerfaust *f*.

be [bi:; bi] (*irr.*) a) sein; *there is* od.
are es gibt; *here's to you(r health)!*
auf Ihr Wohl!; *here you are again!*
da haben wir's wieder!; *as it were*
sozusagen; ~ *about* beschäftigt sein
mit; *im Begriff* sein; ~ *after s.o.*
hinter j-m her sein, j. verfolgen;
~ *at s.th. et.* vorhaben; ~ *off* fort
sein; *aus* sein; weggehen, aufbrechen; fortkommen; ausverkauft sein; ~ *off with you!* fort mit
dir!; ~ *on at s.o.* auf j-m herum-
hacken; ~ *on to s.th. et.* spitzkriegen;
b) *v/aux. mit p.pr. zum Ausdruck von
Unvollständigkeit u. Fortdauer:* ~
reading beim Lesen sein, gerade lesen; c) *v/aux. mit inf. zum Ausdruck
e-r Pflicht, Absicht, Möglichkeit: I am
to inform you* ich soll Ihnen mitteilen;
it is (not) to be seen es ist (nicht) zu
sehen; *if he were to die* wenn er
sterben sollte; d) *v/aux. mit p.p. zur
Bildung des Passivs:* werden; *I am
asked* ich werde gefragt.

beach [bi:tʃ] **1.** Strand *m*; **2.** ♨ auf den
Strand setzen *od.* ziehen; ~ **ball** Was-
serball *m*; '**~-comb·er** lange Welle *f*;
Strandgutjäger *m; fig.* Nichtstuer *m*;

'**~·head** ✗ Brückenkopf *m*.

bea·con ['biːkən] **1.** Feuerzeichen *n*, Signalfeuer *n*; Leuchtfeuer *n*, Leuchtturm *m*; ♎ Bake *f*; Blinklicht *n an Zebrastreifen*; *fig*. Fanal *n*; **2.** mit Baken versehen; *fig. j*. führen.

bead [biːd] **1.** *Glas-*, *Holz- etc*. Perle *f*; Tropfen *m*; *Visier*-Korn *n*; ~s *pl. a.* Rosenkranz *m*; **2.** *v/t*. mit Perlen besetzen; (wie Perlen) aufreihen; *v/i*. perlen; '**bead·ing** Perlstickerei *f*; △ Perlstab *m*.

bea·dle ['biːdl] Kirchendiener *m*.

beads·man, beads·wom·an['biːdzmən, '~wumən] Armenhäusler(in).

bead·y ['biːdi] perlartig; perlend; klein u. rund (*Augen*).

bea·gle ['biːgl] kleiner Spürhund *m*.

beak [biːk] Schnabel *m*; Tülle *f*; **beaked** schnabelförmig; spitz.

beak·er ['biːkə] Becher(glas *n*) *m*.

beam [biːm] Balken *m*; Weberbaum *m*; Pflugbaum *m*; Waagebalken *m*; ♎ Deck(s)balken *m*; *hunt*. Stange *f am Geweih*; (Licht-, Sonnen-) Strahl *m*; Glanz *m*; *Radio*: Leit-, Richtstrahl *m*; *be on* (*off*) ~ *fig. Person*: richtig- (daneben)liegen; **2.** (aus-) strahlen; '**~·'ends** *pl.*: *the ship is on her* ~ das Schiff hat starke Schlagseite; *on one's* ~ *fig.* (finanziell) am Ende.

bean [biːn] Bohne *f*; *Am. sl.* Birne *f* (*Kopf*); *full of* ~*s* F lebensprühend; *give s.o.* ~*s sl.* j-m Saures geben (*j. strafen, schelten*); '**~·feast**, **bean·o**[1] *sl.* ['biːnəu] Freudenfest *n*.

bear[1] [beə] **1.** Bär *m* (*fig. Tölpel*); ♈ *sl.* Baissier *m*; **2.** ♈ auf Baisse spekulieren; die Kurse drücken.

bear[2] [~] (*irr.*) *v/t.* tragen; hervorbringen, gebären; *Schwert, Namen* führen; *Liebe etc.* hegen; ertragen, dulden, leiden; zulassen; ~ *away* davon-, wegtragen; ~ *down* überwältigen; ~ *out* unterstützen, bestätigen; ~ *up* stützen, ermutigen; *v/i.* tragen; fruchtbar *od.* trächtig sein; leiden, dulden; ♎ (*mit adv.*) segeln; ~ *down upon* ♎ zusteuern auf (*acc.*); ~ *to the right* sich rechts halten; ~ *up* standhalten, fest bleiben; ~ (*up*)*on* einwirken auf (*acc.*); ~ *with* ertragen, Nachsicht haben mit; *bring to* ~ zur Anwendung bringen, einwirken lassen, *Druck etc.* ausüben (*on, upon* auf *acc.*); **bear-**

a·ble ['beərəbl] erträglich.

beard [biəd] **1.** Bart *m*; ⚜ Granne *f*; **2.** *j-m* entgegentreten, Trotz bieten; *j.* reizen; '**beard·ed** bärtig; '**beard·less** bartlos.

bear·er ['beərə] Träger(in); Überbringer(in); ♈ Inhaber(in), Vorzeiger(in) *e-s Wechsels*.

bear·ing ['beəriŋ] Tragen *n*; Ertragen *n*; Haltung *f*; Benehmen *n*; Beziehung *f*, Bezug *m* (*on* auf *acc.*); Tragweite *f*; Richtung *f*; ♎ Peilung *f*; ~*s pl.* Position *f*; ⊕ Lager *n*; Wappen *n*; *ball* ~*s pl.* ⊕ Kugellager *n*; *beyond all* ~ nicht zu ertragen; *in full* ~ gut tragend (*Baum*); *have no* ~ *on* nichts zu tun haben mit; *lose one's* ~*s* die Orientierung verlieren; *take one's* ~*s* sich orientieren.

bear·ish ['beəriʃ] bärenhaft; ♈ Baisse...

bear·skin ['beəskin] Bärenfell(mütze *f*) *n*.

beast [biːst] Vieh *n*, Tier *n*; *fig. a.* Bestie *f*, Biest *n*; **beast·li·ness** ['~linis] viehisches Wesen *n*; *fig.* Bestialität *f*, Brutalität *f*; '**beast·ly** viehisch, tierisch; bestialisch, brutal; F ekelhaft, scheußlich.

beat [biːt] **1.** (*irr.*) *v/t. wiederholt* schlagen; gegen *od.* mit *et.* schlagen; *a.* ~ *out Metall* schlagen, hämmern, schmieden; prügeln; besiegen, *Am.* F *j-m* zuvorkommen; übertreffen; *Am.* F beschummeln, betrügen; erschöpfen; F zu schwer *od.* viel sein für; *Pfad* treten; *hunt. Wild* treiben; *Revier* absuchen; ~ *it! Am. sl.* hau ab!; ~ *the band Am.* F wichtig *od.* großartig sein; ~ *one's brains* sich den Kopf zerbrechen; ~ *a retreat* zum Rückzug blasen; den Rückzug antreten; ~ *time* ♩ den Takt schlagen; ~ *one's way* sich durchschlagen; ~ *down* niederschlagen; ♈ drücken; ~ *up Eier etc.* schlagen; auftreiben; *v/i.* schlagen; ~ *about* (umher)suchen; ~ *about the bush* wie die Katze um den heißen Brei herumgehen; **2.** Schlag *m*; Trommel-, Takt-, Pulsschlag *m*; Runde *f od.* Revier *n e-s Schutzmanns etc.*; *Am.* sensationelle Erstmeldung *f e-r Zeitung*; *fig.* Sphäre *f*, Bereich *m*; *on the* ~ auf Streifendienst; = *beatnik*; **3.** F baff, verblüfft; *dead* ~ todmüde;

'**beat·en 1.** *p.p. von* beat 1; **2.** *adj.* (aus)getreten (*Weg*); '**beat·er** Schläger *m*; Stößel *m*; Ramme *f*; *hunt.* Treiber *m*.

be·a·tif·ic [biə'tifik] (glück)selig; seligmachend; ∼ *vision* Gottesvision *f*.

be·at·i·fi·ca·tion *eccl.* [bi:ætifi'keiʃən] Seligsprechung *f*; **be·at·i·fy** selig machen, beseligen; *eccl.* selig sprechen.

beat·ing ['bi:tiŋ] Schlagen *n*; Schläge *m*/*pl.*, Prügel *m*/*pl.*; *give s.o. a good* ∼ j-m e-e Tracht Prügel geben.

be·at·i·tude [bi:'ætitju:d] (Glück-)Seligkeit *f*.

beat·nik ['bi:tnik] Beatnik *m*, junger Antikonformist *m* und Bohemien *m*.

beau [bəu], *pl.* **beaux** [⌣z] Stutzer *m*; Anbeter *m*.

beau·teous *poet.* ['bju:tjəs] schön.

beau·ti·cian [bju:'tiʃən] Schönheitspfleger(in), Kosmetiker(in).

beau·ti·ful □ ['bju:təful] schön; *the* ∼ *people pl. bsd. Am.* die Schickeria.

beau·ti·fy ['bju:tifai] verschönern.

beau·ty ['bju:ti] Schönheit *f* (*a. schöne Frau*); Prachtstück *n*; *Sleeping* ♀ Dornröschen *n*; ∼ *parlo(u)r*, ∼ *shop* Schönheitssalon *m*; ∼ *sleep* Schlaf *m* vor Mitternacht; ∼ *spot* Schönheitspflästerchen *n*; schöner Fleck *m Erde*.

bea·ver ['bi:və] Biber *m*; Biberpelz *m*; Biber-, Kastorhut *m*.

be·bop ♪ *Am.* ['bi:bɔp] Bebop *m*.

be·calm [bi'ka:m] beruhigen, stillen; *be* ∼ *ed* ⚓ in e-e Flaute geraten.

be·came [bi'keim] *pret. von* become.

be·cause [bi'kɔz] weil, da; ∼ *of* wegen.

beck [bek] Wink *m*.

beck·on ['bekən] (*j-m* zu)winken.

be·cloud [bi'klaud] umwölken.

be·come [bi'kʌm] (*irr.*) *v/i.* werden (*of* aus); *v/t.* anstehen, (ge)ziemen (*dat.*); sich schicken für; kleiden (*Hut etc.*); **be'com·ing** □ passend; schicklich; kleidsam.

bed [bed] **1.** Bett *n* (*a. e-s Flusses etc.*); Lager *n e-s Tieres*; ✔ Beet *n*; ⊕ Bett(ung *f*) *n*, Unterlage *f*; Flöz *n*; *be brought to* ∼ *of* niederkommen mit; ∼ *and board* Tisch u. Bett *pl.* (*Ehe*); Unterkunft *f* u. Verpflegung *f*; *take to one's* ∼ das Bett hüten; *as you make your* ∼ *so you must lie on it* wie man sich bettet, so schläft man; ∼ *and breakfast* Übernachtung *f*

mit Frühstück; **2.** betten; *Pferd etc.* mit Streu versorgen; ✔ ∼ (*out* aus-) pflanzen.

be·daub [bi'dɔ:b] beschmieren.

be·dazzle [bi'dæzl] blenden; verblenden, -wirren.

bed...: '∼·**cham·ber** königliches Schlafgemach *n*; '∼·**clothes** *pl.* Bettzeug *n*.

bed·ding ['bediŋ] Bettzeug *n*; Streu *f*.

be·deck [bi'dek] zieren, schmücken.

be·dev·il [bi'devl] be-, verhexen; verhunzen; quälen; **be'dev·il·ment** Hexensabbat *m*.

be·dew [bi'dju:] betauen; *poet.* benetzen.

bed·fel·low ['bedfeləu] Schlafkamerad *m*.

be·dight † [bi'dait] schmücken, aufputzen.

be·dim [bi'dim] trüben.

be·diz·en [bi'daizn] herausputzen.

bed·lam ['bedləm] Tollhaus *n*; **bed·lam·ite** ['⌣mait] Tollhäusler (-in).

bed·lin·en ['bedlinin] Bettwäsche *f*.

Bed·ou·in ['beduin] **1.** Beduine *m*; **2.** Beduinen...

bed·pan ['bedpæn] Stechbecken *n*, Bettschüssel *f*.

be·drag·gle [bi'drægl] *Kleider etc.* beschmutzen, beschmuddeln.

bed...: '∼·**rid**(·**den**) bettlägerig; '∼·**rock** *geol.* Grundgebirge *n*; *fig.* Grundlage *f*; '∼·**room** Schlafzimmer *n*; '∼·**side**: *at the* ∼ am (Kranken)Bett; *good* ∼ *manner* gute Art, mit Kranken umzugehen; ∼ *lamp* Nachttischlampe *f*; ∼ *rug* Bettvorleger *m*; ∼ *table* Nachttisch *m*; '∼-'**sit·ter** F, '∼-'**sit·ting-room** Wohnschlafzimmer *n*; '∼-**sore** 🦯 wundgelegene Stelle *f*; '∼-**space** (An)Zahl *f* der Betten *in Klinik, Hotel etc.*; '∼-**spread** Tagesdecke *f*; '∼-**stead** Bettstelle *f*; '∼-**tick** Inlett *n*; '∼-**time** Schlafenszeit *f*; ∼ *reading* Bettlektüre *f*; ∼ *story* Gutenachtgeschichte *f*.

bee [bi:] Biene *f* (*a. fig.*); *Am.* nachbarliches Treffen *n*; Wettbewerb *m*; *have a* ∼ *in one's bonnet* F eine fixe Idee haben.

beech 🌳 [bi:tʃ] Buche *f*; '∼·**nut** Buchecker *f*.

beef [bi:f] **1.** Rind-, Ochsenfleisch *n*; F Muskelkraft *f*; **2.** *Am.* F nörgeln, sich beklagen; '∼·**eat·er** Tower-

wächter *m*; ~·**steak** [′bi:f′steik]
Beefsteak *n*; ′~·′**tea** klare Fleischbrühe *f*, Bouillon *f*; ′**beef·y**
fleischig; kräftig.

bee...: ′~·**hive** Bienenkorb *m*,
-stock *m*; ′~·**keep·er** Bienenzüchter
m; ′~·**keep·ing** Bienenzucht *f*;
′~·**line** kürzester Weg *m*; *make a ~
for schnurstracks losgehen auf
(acc.)*.

been [bi:n, bin] *p.p. von* be.

beer [biə] Bier *n*; ~ *on tap* Faßbier *n*,
Bier *n* vom Faß; *small ~* Dünnbier *n*;
F Kleinigkeit *f*; *he thinks no small ~ of
himself* er hält sich für wer weiß wen;
~ *can* Bierdose *f*; ′**beer·y** F bierselig.

bees·wax [′bi:zwæks] **1.** Bienenwachs *n*; **2.** mit Bienenwachs einreiben *od.* polieren.

beet ♥ [bi:t] Runkelrübe *f*, Bete *f*;
red ~ rote Rübe *f*; *white ~* Zuckerrübe *f*.

bee·tle[1] [′bi:tl] **1.** Ramme *f*; **2.** rammen, stampfen.

bee·tle[2] [~] Käfer *m*.

bee·tle[3] [~] **1.** überhängend; buschig
(*Brauen*); **2.** *v/i.* überhängen.

beet·root [′bi:tru:t] Runkelrübe *f*.

beet·sug·ar [′bi:tʃugə] Rübenzucker *m*.

beeves [bi:vz] *pl. von* beef.

be·fall [bi′fɔ:l] (*irr. fall*) *v/t.* zustoßen, widerfahren (*dat.*); *v/i.* sich
ereignen.

be·fit [bi′fit] sich schicken *od.* gehören für; passen (*dat.*); **be′fit·ting**
passend, schicklich.

be·fog [bi′fɔg] umnebeln.

be·fool [bi′fu:l] betören.

be·fore [bi′fɔ:] **1.** *adv. Raum:* vorn;
voran; *Zeit:* vorher, früher; schon
(früher); **2.** *cj.* bevor, ehe, bis;
3. *prp.* vor; *be ~ one's time* zu früh
kommen; *be ~ s.o.* vor j-m liegen;
fig. j-m vorliegen; ~ *long* binnen
kurzem, bald; ~ *now* schon früher;
the day ~ yesterday vorgestern; **be·
′fore·hand** vorher, zuvor; voraus;
im voraus.

be·foul [bi′faul] besudeln.

be·friend [bi′frend] *j-m* behilflich
sein; sich *j-s* annehmen.

beg [beg] *v/t. et.* erbetteln; erbitten
(*of* von); betteln *od.* bitten um *et.*;
j. bitten (*to do* zu tun); *v/i.* betteln;
bitten (*for s.th.* um et.; *of s.o.* j.);
betteln gehen; Männchen machen
(*Hund*); *I ~ to inform you* † ich

möchte Ihnen mitteilen; *go ~ging
fig.* keinen Interessenten finden.

be·gan [bi′gæn] *pret. von* begin.

be·get [bi′get] (*irr.*) (er)zeugen;
be′get·ter Erzeuger *m*.

beg·gar [′begə] **1.** Bettler(in);
F Kerl *m*; **2.** Bettel...; **3.** zum Bettler machen; *fig.* übertreffen; *it ~s all
description* es spottet jeder Beschreibung; ′**beg·gar·ly** arm(selig);
′**beg·gar·y** Bettelarmut *f*; *reduce
to ~* an den Bettelstab bringen.

be·gin [bi′gin] (*irr.*) beginnen, anfangen (*at* bei; mit); ~ (*up*)*on s.th.
et.* vornehmen; *to ~ with* um damit
zu beginnen, zunächst; **be′gin·ner**
Anfänger(in); **be′gin·ning** Beginn *m*, Anfang *m*; *from the ~* von
Anfang an.

be·gird [bi′gə:d] (*irr. gird*) umgürten; umschließen.

be·gone [bi′gɔn] fort!, pack dich!

be·go·ni·a ♥ [bi′gəunjə] Begonie *f*.

be·got, **be·got·ten** [bi′gɔt(n)] *pret.
u. p.p. von* beget.

be·grime [bi′graim] besudeln.

be·grudge [bi′grʌdʒ] *j-m et.* mißgönnen *od.* ungern geben.

be·guile [bi′gail] täuschen; betrügen (*of, out of* um); *Zeit* vertreiben, verkürzen; ~ *into* verlocken zu.

be·gun [bi′gʌn] *p.p. von* begin.

be·half [bi′hɑ:f]: *on od. in ~ of* im
Namen *od.* Auftrag von; *um ...
(gen.)* willen; seitens; für.

be·have [bi′heiv] sich benehmen,
auftreten; ~ *o.s.* sich anständig betragen; **be′hav·io(u)r** Benehmen
n, Betragen *n*; Auftreten *n*;
Verhalten *n* (*a. von Sachen*); *be on
one's good od. best ~* sich zs.-
nehmen; *put s.o. on his best ~* j-m
einschärfen, sich gut zu benehmen;
be′hav·io(u)r·al Verhaltens...; ~
psychology Verhaltenspsychologie *f*;
be′hav·io(u)r·ism *psych.* Behavioris-
mus *m*, Verhaltensforschung *f*.

be·head [bi′hed] enthaupten; **be·
′head·ing** Enthauptung *f*.

be·hest *poet.* [bi′hest] Geheiß *n*.

be·hind [bi′haind] **1.** *adv.* hinten; dahinter; hinterher; zurück; *be ~ with
s.th.* mit et. im Rückstand sein; **2.** *prp.*
hinter; *s. time*; **3.** F Hintern *m*; **be·
′hind·hand** zurück, im Rückstand.

be·hold [bi′həuld] **1.** (*irr. hold*) erblicken, anschauen; **2.** siehe (da)!;

be·hold·en verpflichtet, verbunden; **be'hold·er** Betrachter *m*, Zuschauer *m*.

be·hoof [bi'huːf]: *to* (*for, on*) (*the*) ~ *of* in *j-s* Interesse, um *j-s* willen.

be·hoove *Am.* [bi'huːv] = *behove.*

be·hove [bi'həuv]: *it* ~*s s.o. to inf.* es ist j-s Pflicht zu *inf.*

beige [beiʒ] **1.** Beige *f* (*Stoff*); **2.** beige(farben).

be·ing ['biːiŋ] Sein *n*; Dasein *n*; Wesen *n*; *in* ~ lebend; wirklich (vorhanden); *come into* ~ entstehen.

be·la·bo(u)r [bi'leibə] verbleuen.

be·laid [bi'leid] *pret. u. p.p. von belay.*

be·lat·ed [bi'leitid] verspätet.

be·lay [bi'lei] **1.** (*irr.*) ⚓ belegen; festmachen; *mount.* sichern; **2.** *mount.* Sicherung *f.*

belch [beltʃ] **1.** rülpsen; ausspeien; **2.** Rülpsen *n*; Ausbruch *m.*

bel·dam *contp.* ['beldəm] alte Hexe *f*, Vettel *f.*

be·lea·guer [bi'liːgə] belagern.

bel·fry ['belfri] Glockenstuhl *m*; Glockenturm *m.*

Bel·gian ['beldʒən] **1.** belgisch; **2.** Belgier(in).

be·lie [bi'lai] Lügen strafen; *Versprechen* nicht halten.

be·lief [bi'liːf] Glaube *m* (*in* an *acc.*; *that* daß); *the* ♀ das Apostolische Glaubensbekenntnis; *past all* ~ unglaublich; *to the best of my* ~ nach bestem Wissen u. Gewissen.

be·liev·a·ble [bi'liːvəbl] glaubhaft.

be·lieve [bi'liːv] glauben (*in* an *acc.*); ~ *in j-m* vertrauen; an *j. od. et.* glauben; viel halten von; **be'liev·er** Gläubige *m, f.*

be·like † [.] vielleicht.

Be·li·sha bea·con [bə'liːʃ[ə'biːkən] Blinklicht *n* an *Fußgängerüberwegen.*

be·lit·tle [bi'litl] *fig.* verkleinern.

bell[1] [bel] **1.** Glocke *f* (*a.* ⚘, ♠), Klingel *f*, Schelle *f*; ♪ Schalltrichter *m einer Trompete*; Taucherglocke *f*; **2.** *v/t.* ~ *the cat* der Katze die Schelle umhängen, die Gefahr auf sich nehmen.

bell[2] [bel] röhren (*Hirsch*).

bell·boy *Am.* ['belbɔi] Hotelpage *m.*

belle [bel] Schöne *f*, Schönheit *f.*

belles-let·tres ['bel'letr] *pl.* Belletristik *f*, schöne Literatur *f.*

bell...: '~-flow·er Glockenblume *f*; '~-found·er Glockengießer *m*;

'~-glass Glasglocke *f*; '~-hop *Am. sl.* Hotelpage *m.*

bel·li·cose ['belikəus] kriegslustig.

bel·lied ['belid] bauchig.

bel·lig·er·ent [bi'lidʒərənt] **1.** kriegführend; **2.** kriegführendes Land *n.*

bel·low ['beləu] **1.** brüllen; **2.** Gebrüll *n.*

bel·lows ['beləuz] *pl.* (*a pair of* ~ ein) Blasebalg *m*; *phot.* Balgen *m.*

bell...: '~-pull Klingelzug *m*; '~-push Klingelknopf *m*; '~-weth·er Leithammel *m* (*a. fig.*).

bel·ly ['beli] **1.** Bauch *m*; Magen *m*; ~ *landing* ⚓ Bauchlandung *f*; **2.** (sich) bauchen; (an)schwellen; ~ *but·ton* F (Bauch)Nabel *m*; '~-flop Bauchklatscher *m beim Schwimmen*; **bel·ly·ful** F ['.ful]: *one's* ~ (mehr als) genug, die Nase voll.

be·long [bi'lɔŋ] (an)gehören; ~ *to* gehören *dat. od.* zu; sich gehören für; *j-m* gebühren; **be'long·ings** *pl.* Habseligkeiten *f/pl.*, Habe *f*; F Angehörigen *pl.*

be·lov·ed [bi'lʌvd] **1.** geliebt; **2.** [*mst* ~vid] Geliebte *m, f.*

be·low [bi'ləu] **1.** *adv.* unten; *poet.* hienieden; **2.** *prp.* unter(halb); ~ *me fig.* unter meiner Würde.

belt [belt] **1.** Gürtel *m*; Gurt *m*; ✗ Koppel *n*; *fig.* Streifen *m*; Zone *f*, Bezirk *m*; ⊕ Treibriemen *m*; ⚓ Panzergürtel *m*; *hit below the* ~ unfair sein; **2.** umgürten; mit Streifen versehen; ~ *out Am.* F herausschmettern, loslegen (*singen*).

be·moan [bi'məun] betrauern, beklagen.

be·mused [bi'mjuːzd] verwirrt; gedankenverloren.

bench [bentʃ] Bank *f*; Richterbank *f*; Gerichtshof *m*; Arbeitstisch *m*, Werkbank *f*; *s. treasury*; **'bench·er** Vorstandsmitglied *n e-r Rechtsanwaltsinnung.*

bend [bend] **1.** Krümmung *f*, Biegung *f*, Bogen *m*, Kurve *f*; ⚓ Seemannsknoten *m*; **2.** (*irr.*) (sich) biegen, (sich) krümmen; *den Bogen* spannen; *Augen etc.* lenken, *Geist etc.* richten (*to, on* auf *acc.*); (sich) beugen (*a. fig.*); sich neigen (*to vor dat.*); ⚓ *Segel* anschlagen; *s. bent*[1] **1.**

be·neath [bi'niːθ] = *below.*

ben·e·dick ['benidik] junger Ehemann *m*; bekehrter Hagestolz *m.*

Ben·e·dic·tine [beni'diktin] Bene-

diktiner *m* (*Mönch*); [ˌtiːn] (*Likör*).
ben·e·dic·tion *eccl.* [beniˈdikʃən]
Segen *m*; Segnung *f*.
ben·e·fac·tion [beniˈfækʃən] Wohltat *f*; ˌs *pl.* Spenden *f/pl.*; **ben·e-**
fac·tor [ˈˌtə] Wohltäter *m*; **ben·e-**
fac·tress [ˈˌtris] Wohltäterin *f*.
ben·e·fice [ˈbenifis] Pfründe *f*;
be·nef·i·cence [biˈnefisəns] Wohltätigkeit *f*; **be·nef·i·cent** □ wohltätig.
ben·e·fi·cial □ [beniˈfiʃəl] wohl-
tuend; zuträglich, nützlich (*to*
dat.); ✴ nutznießend; ˌ *interest*
Nutzrecht *n*; **ben·e·fi·ci·ar·y** Nutz-
nießer *m*; Empfänger *m*; Pfründner
m.
ben·e·fit [ˈbenifit] **1.** Wohltat *f*;
Nutzen *m*, Vorteil *m*; Wohltätig-
keitsveranstaltung *f*; (Wohlfahrts-)
Unterstützung *f*; *for the* ˌ *of* zum
Besten, zugunsten (*gen.*); **2.** nützen;
begünstigen; Nutzen ziehen (*by*,
from, *of* von, aus, durch).
be·nev·o·lence [biˈnevələns] Wohlwollen *n*; Mildherzigkeit *f*; **be-**
nev·o·lent □ wohlwollend; gütig;
mildherzig; wohltätig; ˌ *society* Wohltätigkeitsverein *m*.
Ben·gal [beŋˈgɔːl] bengalisch; **Ben-**
gal·i [ˌli] **1.** Bengale *m*, Bengalin *f*;
Bengalisch *n*; **2.** bengalisch.
be·night·ed [biˈnaitid] von der
Nacht überfallen; *fig.* umnachtet,
unwissend.
be·nign □ [biˈnain] freundlich,
gütig; zuträglich; ✴ gutartig; **be-**
nig·nant □ [biˈnignənt] freundlich, gütig; zuträglich; **be·nig·ni-**
ty Freundlichkeit *f*, Güte *f*,
Milde *f*; Zuträglichkeit *f*.
bent[1] [bent] **1.** *pret. u. p.p. von*
bend 2; ˌ *on* versessen *od.* erpicht
auf (*acc.*); **2.** Hang *m*; Neigung *f*;
to the top of one's ˌ nach Herzenslust.
bent[2] ♀ [ˌ] Straußgras *n*; Grasland *n*.
be·numb [biˈnʌm] erstarren; lähmen.
ben·zene 🜍 [ˈbenziːn] Benzol *n*.
ben·zine 🜍 [ˈbenziːn] Benzin *n*.
be·queath [biˈkwiːð] vermachen.
be·quest [biˈkwest] Vermächtnis *n*.
be·rate [biˈreit] schelten.
be·reave [biˈriːv] (*irr.*) berauben; *be*
ˌd *of* durch den Tod *j-s* beraubt
sein; ˌd hinterblieben; *bereft of*

hope der Hoffnung beraubt; **be-**
reave·ment *schmerzlicher* Verlust
m; Trauerfall *m*.   [*bereave.*)
be·reft [biˈreft] *pret. u. p.p. von*)
be·ret [ˈberei] Baskenmütze *f*.
berg [bəːg] = *iceberg.*
Ber·lin [bəːˈlin]: ˌ *black* schwarzer
Eisenlack *m*; ˌ *wool* feine Strick-
wolle *f*.
ber·ry [ˈberi] Beere *f*.
berth [bəːθ] **1.** ⚓ Ankergrund *m*;
(Schlaf)Koje *f*; *fig.* (gute) Stelle *f*;
give s.o. a wide ˌ e-n großen Bogen
um j. machen; **2.** vor Anker legen;
j-m e-e Koje anweisen; unterbringen.
ber·yl *min.* [ˈberil] Beryll *m*.
be·seech [biˈsiːtʃ] (*irr.*) ersuchen;
dringend bitten; anflehen; um *et.*
bitten; **be·seech·ing** □ flehend;
be·seech·ing·ly flehentlich.
be·seem [biˈsiːm] sich ziemen für.
be·set [biˈset] (*irr.* set) umgeben;
bedrängen; verfolgen; ˌting sin
Gewohnheitssünde *f*.
be·side [biˈsaid] **1.** *s.* ˌs *1*; **2.** *prp.*
neben (*a. fig.*), (dicht) bei; weitab
von; verglichen mit; ˌ *o.s.* außer
sich (*with von Freude etc.*); ˌ *the*
purpose unzweckmäßig; ˌ *the*
question nicht zur Sache gehörig;
be·sides [ˌdz] **1.** *adv.* überdies,
außerdem; **2.** *prp. fig.* neben, abgesehen von, außer.
be·siege [biˈsiːdʒ] belagern; *fig.* bedrängen, bestürmen; **be·sieg·er**
Belagerer *m*.
be·slav·er [biˈslævə] begeifern; *fig.*
lobhudeln.
be·slob·ber [biˈslɔbə] abküssen.
be·smear [biˈsmiə] beschmieren.
be·smirch [biˈsməːtʃ] beschmutzen.
be·som [ˈbiːzəm] (Reisig)Besen *m*.
be·sot·ted [biˈsɔtid] vernarrt; betrunken.
be·sought [biˈsɔːt] *pret. u. p.p. von*
beseech.
be·spat·ter [biˈspætə] (be)spritzen;
fig. überhäufen; beschimpfen.
be·speak [biˈspiːk] (*irr.*) vorbestellen; (an)zeigen, verraten.
be·spoke [biˈspəuk] *pret. von be-*
speak; ˌ *tailor* Maßschneider *m*;
be·spo·ken *p.p. von bespeak.*
be·sprin·kle [biˈspriŋkl] besprengen.
best [best] **1.** *adj.* best; höchst;
größt, meist; ˌ *man* Brautführer *m*;
the ˌ *part of* der größte Teil (*gen.*);

all the ~! alles Gute!, viel Glück!;
s. seller; **2.** adv. am besten, aufs
beste; **3.** Beste m, f, n, Besten pl.;
Sunday ~ Sonntagsanzug m; for the
~ zum Besten; to the ~ of ... nach
bestem ...; have od. get the ~ of it am
besten dabei wegkommen; make
the ~ of tun, was man kann, mit;
make the ~ of a bad job gute Miene
zum bösen Spiel machen; I made
the ~ of my way to ... ich ging möglichst schnell nach ...; at ~ bestenfalls, im besten Falle; **4.** vb. F übervorteilen.

be·ste(a)d [bi'sted]: hard ~ hart bedrängt.

bes·tial □ ['bestjəl] tierisch, viehisch, bestialisch; **bes·ti·al·i·ty** [~-
ti'æliti] Bestialität f; **bes·tial·ize**
['~tjəlaiz] vertieren.

be·stir [bi'stə:]: ~ o.s. sich rühren.

be·stow [bi'stəu] geben, schenken,
verleihen (on, upon dat.); unterbringen; **be'stow·al**, **be'stow-
ment** Schenkung f, Verleihung f.

be·strew [bi'stru:] (irr. strew) bestreuen; verstreut liegen auf (dat.).

be·stride [bi'straid] (irr. stride) mit
gespreizten Beinen auf e-m Fleck,
über j-m stehen; reiten auf (dat.).

bet [bet] **1.** Wette f; **2.** (irr.) wetten;
you ~ F bestimmt, sicherlich; I ~
you a shilling ich wette mit dir um
'nen Taler.

be·take [bi'teik] (irr. take): ~ o.s. to
sich begeben nach; fig. seine Zuflucht nehmen zu.

be·think [bi'θiŋk] (irr. think): ~ o.s.
sich besinnen (of auf acc.); ~ o.s. to
inf. sich in den Kopf setzen zu inf.

be·tide [bi'taid] geschehen; j-m zustoßen; woe ~ him! wehe ihm!

be·times [bi'taimz] beizeiten.

be·to·ken [bi'təukən] ankündigen,
andeuten; anzeigen.

be·tray [bi'trei] verraten (a. fig.
offenbaren); verleiten; **be'tray·al**
Verrat m; ~ of trust Vertrauens-
bruch m; **be'tray·er** Verräter(in).

be·troth [bi'trəuð] verloben (to mit);
the ~ed das verlobte Paar; **be-
'troth·al** Verlobung f.

bet·ter[1] ['betə] **1.** adj. besser; he is ~ es
geht ihm besser; get ~ sich erholen; for
~ or (for) worse in Freud und Leid
(Trauungsformel); **2.** Besseres n; ~s pl.
Höherstehenden pl., Vorgesetzten pl.;
get the ~ of die Oberhand gewinnen

über (acc.); überwinden, besiegen;
j-m den Rang ablaufen; he is my ~ er
ist mir überlegen; **3.** adv. besser;
mehr; be ~ off besser daran sein; so
much the ~ desto besser; you had ~ go es
wäre besser, wenn du gingest; I know ~
ich weiß es besser; think ~ of it sich
eines Besseren besinnen; **4.** v/t. (ver-)
bessern; ~ o.s. sich im Lohn etc.
verbessern; v/i. besser werden, sich
verbessern.

bet·ter[2] [~] Wettende m, f.

bet·ter·ment ['betəmənt] Verbesserung f.

bet·ting ['betiŋ] Wetten n; ~ debt
Wettschuld f.

be·tween [bi'twi:n], poet. u. prov. a.
be·twixt [bi'twikst] **1.** adv. dazwischen; betwixt and ~ in der
Mitte; halb und halb; in ~ dazwischen; far ~ weit auseinander;
2. prp. zwischen, unter; ~ ourselves
unter uns; they had 5 shillings ~
them sie besaßen zusammen 5
Schilling; **be'tween-decks** ♤ Zwischendeck n.

bev·el ['bevəl] **1.** schräg, schief;
2. ⊕ Schrägung f; Schrägmaß n,
Schmiege f; **3.** v/t. abschrägen; v/i.
schräg verlaufen; '~-wheel ⊕ Kegelrad n.

bev·er·age ['bevəridʒ] Getränk n.

bev·y ['bevi] Schwarm m; Schar f.

be·wail [bi'weil] v/t. beklagen; v/i.
wehklagen.

be·ware [bi'wɛə] sich hüten, sich in
acht nehmen (of vor dat.); ~ of the dog!
Vorsicht, bissiger Hund!

be·wil·der [bi'wildə] irremachen;
verwirren, verblüffen; bestürzt
machen; **be'wil·der·ment** Verwirrung f; Bestürzung f.

be·witch F [bi'witʃ] bezaubern, b.s.
behexen; **be'witch·ment** Bezauberung f; Zauber m.

be·yond [bi'jɔnd] **1.** adv. darüber
hinaus; jenseits; **2.** prp. jenseits,
über (... hinaus); mehr od. weiter
als; außer; ~ endurance unerträglich; ~ measure über die Maßen;
~ dispute außer allem Zweifel; ~
words unsagbar; get ~ s.o. j-m über
den Kopf wachsen; go ~ one's depth
den Boden verlieren; it is ~ me es
geht über meinen Verstand.

bi... [bai] zwei...

bi·an·nu·al [bai'ænjuəl] halbjährlich.

bi·as ['baiəs] **1.** adj. u. adv. schief,

schräg; **2.** Neigung *f*, Hang *m*; Vorurteil *n*; *Schneiderei*: schräger Schnitt *m*; *cut on the* ~ diagonal geschnitten; **3.** (ungünstig) beeinflussen; ~*sed* voreingenommen, befangen.

bib [bib] Lätzchen *n*; Schürzenlatz *m*.

Bi·ble ['baibl] Bibel *f*.

bib·li·cal □ ['biblikəl] biblisch; Bibel...

bib·li·og·ra·pher [bibli'ɔgrəfə] Bibliograph *m*, Verfasser *m* e-r Bibliographie; **bib·li·o·graph·ic**, **bib·li·o·graph·i·cal** [⌣əu'græfik(ə)l] bibliographisch; **bib·li·og·ra·phy** [⌣'ɔgrəfi] Bibliographie *f*; **bib·li·o·ma·ni·a** [⌣əu'meinjə] Bücherleidenschaft *f*; **bib·li·o·ma·ni·ac** [⌣əu'meiniæk] Büchernarr *m*; **bib·li·o·phile** ['⌣əufail] Bücherfreund *m*, Bibliophile *m*.

bib·u·lous □ ['bibjuləs] saugfähig; trunksüchtig; feuchtfröhlich.

bi·car·bon·ate ⚗ [bai'kɑ:bənit] Bikarbonat *n*; ~ *of soda* doppeltkohlensaures Natron *n*.

bi·ceps ['baiseps] Bizeps *m* (*Muskel*); *fig.* Kraft *f*.

bick·er ['bikə] (sich) zanken; flackern (*Flamme*); plätschern (*Fluß, Regen*); prasseln (*Schläge*); **'bick·er·ing(s** *pl.*) Gezänk *n*.

bi·cy·cle ['baisikl] **1.** Fahrrad *n*; *folding* ~ Klapprad *n*; *ride a* ~ = **2.** radfahren, radeln.

bid [bid] **1.** (*irr.*) gebieten, befehlen; (*pret. u. p.p. bid*) *Versteigerung*: bieten; *Karten*: melden, reizen; *Gruß* entbieten; ~ *fair to inf.* scheinen zu; versprechen zu *inf.*; ~ *farewell* Lebewohl sagen; ~ *up Preis* hochtreiben; ~ *welcome* willkommen heißen; **2.** *Geld*-Gebot *n*, Angebot *n*; Versuch *m* (*to inf. zu inf.*); *to make a* ~ *for* sich bemühen um; *no* ~ *Karten*: ich passe; **'bid·den** *p.p. von* bid; **'bid·der** Bieter(in); *s.* high, low; **'bid·ding** Bieten *n*; Gebot *n*; Geheiß *n*; Einladung *f*.

bide [baid]: ~ *one's time* den rechten Augenblick abwarten.

bi·en·ni·al [bai'eniəl] zweijährig(e Pflanze *f*).

bier [biə] (Toten)Bahre *f*.

bi·fo·cals [bai'fəukəlz] *pl.* Zweistärkenbrille *f*.

bi·fur·cate ['baifə:keit] gabelförmig

teilen; sich gabeln; **bi·fur'ca·tion** Gabelung *f*.

big [big] groß; erwachsen; schwanger (*a. fig. with* mit); F wichtig; wichtigtuerisch; ♀ *Apple Spitzname für* New York City; ~ *bang* Urknall *m*; ♀ *Ben Uhrturm des Parlamentsgebäudes in London*; ~ *business* Großunternehmertum *n*; ~ *shot* F hohes Tier *n*; ~ *stick Am.* Macht(entfaltung) *f*; ~ *top* Zirkuszelt *n*, *a. fig.* Zirkus *m*; *the* ♀ *Three* die großen Drei; *talk* ~ den Mund (zu) voll nehmen.

big·a·mous ['bigəməs] bigamisch, in Doppelehe lebend; **'big·a·my** Bigamie *f*, Doppelehe *f*.

bight ⚓ [bait] Bucht *f*; Tauschleife *f*.

big·mouth F ['bigmauθ] Großmaul *n*.

big·ness ['bignis] Größe *f*.

big·ot ['bigət] blinder Anhänger *m* (*to gen.*); Frömmler(in); **'big·ot·ed** blindgläubig, bigott; *fig.* blind ergeben; **'big·ot·ry** Blindgläubigkeit *f*.

big·wig F *co.* ['bigwig] großes *od.* hohes Tier *n*.

bike F [baik] (Fahr)Rad *n*.

bi·lat·er·al □ [bai'lætərəl] zweiseitig.

bil·ber·y ♧ ['bilbəri] Heidelbeere *f*.

bile [bail] Galle *f* (*a. fig.*); ~-*stone* ⚕ Gallenstein *m*.

bilge [bildʒ] ⚓ Kielraum *m*, Bilge *f*, Kimm *f*; *sl.* Quatsch *m*, Mist *m*.

bi·lin·gual [bai'liŋwəl] zweisprachig.

bil·ious □ ['biljəs] Gallen..., gallig, biliös; *fig.* gallig, gereizt; ~ *colic* ⚕ Gallenkolik *f*.

bilk [bilk] betrügen, prellen.

bill¹ [bil] **1.** Schnabel *m*; Spitze *f am Anker, Zirkel*; Hippe *f*, Gartenmesser *n*; **2.** (sich) schnäbeln.

bill² [~] **1.** Rechnung *f*; Gesetzentwurf *m*, Vorlage *f*; Klage-, Rechtsschrift *f*; Schriftstück *n*; *a.* ~ *of exchange* Wechsel *m*; Zettel *m*, Schein *m*; Plakat *n*; *Am.* Banknote *f*; ~ *of fare* Speisekarte *f*; ~ *of health* Gesundheitspaß *m*; ~ *of lading* Seefrachtbrief *m*, Konnossement *n*; ~ *of sale* Sicherungsübereignung *f*; Kaufvertrag *m*; ♀ *of Rights englische* Freiheitsurkunde *f* (*1689*); *Am.* die ersten 10 Zusatzartikel zur Verfassung der USA; **2.** (durch Anschlag) ankündigen *od.*

bekanntmachen; in e-e Liste eintragen; auf die Rechnung setzen; *j-m* e-e Rechnung schicken; *Am.* buchen.

bill·board *Am.* [ˈbilbɔːd] Anschlagbrett *n*; Reklamefläche *f*.

bil·let [ˈbilit] **1.** ⚔ Quartier(zettel *m*) *n*; Unterkunft *f*; (Holz)Scheit *n*; **2.** ⚔ einquartieren (*on* bei, in *dat.*).

bill·fold *Am.* [ˈbilfəuld] Brieftasche *f für Papiergeld*.

bill·hook ⚔ [ˈbilhuk] Hippe *f*, Gartenmesser *n*.

bil·liard [ˈbiljəd] *in Zssgn* Billard...; '~**-cue** Queue *n*; '**bil·liards** *pl. od. sg.* Billard(spiel) *n*.

bil·lion [ˈbiljən] Milliarde *f*; *in England* †: Billion *f*.

bil·low [ˈbiləu] **1.** Welle *f*, Woge *f* (*a. fig.*); **2.** wogen; '**bil·low·y** wellig, wogend.

bill-stick·er [ˈbilstikə] Plakat-, Zettelankleber *m*.

bil·ly *Am.* [ˈbili] (Polizei-, Gummi-) Knüppel *m*; '~**-can** Kochtopf *m*; '~**-cock** F Melone *f* (*Hut*); '~**-goat** F Ziegenbock *m*.

bi·met·al·lism ♀ [baiˈmetəlizəm] Bimetallismus *m* (*Währung mit 2 Metallen*).   [motorig.\

bi·mo·tored [ˈbaiməutəd] zwei-⌡

bin [bin] Kasten *m*, Behälter *m*.

bi·na·ry [ˈbainəri] aus zwei (Einheiten) bestehend; ~ *fission biol.* Zellteilung *f*.

bin·au·ral [bainˈɔːrəl] beide Ohren betreffend; für beide Ohren; zweikanalig, stereo.

bind [baind] (*irr.*) *v/t.* binden; an-, um-, auf-, fest-, verbinden; verpflichten; *Handel* abschließen; *Rock*, *Saum* einfassen; *Rad* beschlagen; *Bücher* binden; *Sand etc.* fest *od.* hart machen; ~ *over* durch Bürgschaft verpflichten; *be bound up with fig.* eng verbunden sein mit; ~ *s.o. apprentice to* j. in die Lehre geben bei; *be bound up in fig.* nur leben für, aufgehen in (*dat.*); *s. bound*[1] [2]; *v/i.* binden; fest werden; '**bind·er** Binder *m*; Buchbinder *m*; Garbenbinder(in); Binde *f*, Band *n*; '**bind·ing 1.** bindend; verbindlich; **2.** Binden *n*; Einband *m*; *Schilauf:* Bindung *f*; *Schneiderei:* Einfaßband *n*, Einfassung *f*; '**bind·weed** ♀ Winde *f*; *lesser* ~ Ackerwinde *f*.

binge *sl.* [bindʒ] Sauferei *f*, Bierreise *f*.

bin·go [ˈbiŋgəu] (*Art*) Lottospiel *n*,

bin·na·cle ⚓ [ˈbinəkl] Kompaßhaus *n*.

bin·oc·u·lar 1. [baiˈnɔkjulə] für zwei Augen; **2.** [biˈnɔkjulə] *mst* ~*s pl.* Feldstecher *m*, Fern-, Opernglas *n*.

bi·o·chem·i·cal [ˈbaiəuˈkemikəl] biochemisch; '**bi·o·chem·ist** Biochemiker *m*; '**bi·o·chem·is·try** Biochemie *f*.

bi·og·ra·pher [baiˈɔgrəfə] Biograph (-in); **bi·o·graph·ic, bi·o·graph·i·cal** □ [~əuˈgræfik(əl)] biographisch; **bi·og·ra·phy** [~ˈɔgrəfi] Biographie *f*, Lebensbeschreibung *f*.

bi·o·log·ic, bi·o·log·i·cal □ [baiəuˈlɔdʒik(əl)] biologisch; **bi·ol·o·gist** [~ˈɔlədʒist] Biologe *m*; **bi·ol·o·gy** [~ˈɔlədʒi] Biologie *f*.

bi·par·ti·san [baipɑːtiˈzæn] Zweiparteien...

bi·par·tite [baiˈpɑːtait] zweiteilig; zweiseitig; doppelt ausgefertigt (*Dokumente*).

bi·ped [ˈbaiped] **1.** zweifüßig; **2.** Zweifüßer *m*.

bi·plane ✈ [ˈbaiplein] Doppeldecker *m*.

birch [bəːtʃ] **1.** ♀ Birke *f*; (Birken-) Rute *f*, **2.** Birken...; ~ *broom* Reisbesen *m*; **3.** mit der Rute züchtigen; '**birch·en** birken; Birken...

bird [bəːd] Vogel *m*; *kill two* ~*s with one stone* zwei Fliegen mit einer Klappe schlagen; *give the* ~ *Schauspieler* auszischen, -pfeifen; *a queer* ~ ein komischer Vogel (*Mensch*); *for the* ~*s für* die Katz; *tell a child about the* ~*s and the bees* ein Kind (sexuell) aufklären; '~**-call** Vogelruf *m*; '~**-fan·ci·er** Vogelliebhaber(in), -züchter(in), -händler(in); **bird·ie** [ˈbəːdi] Vögelchen *n*.

bird...: '~**-lime** Vogelleim *m*; ~ *sanc·tu·ar·y* Vogelschutzgebiet *n*; '~**-seed** Vogelfutter *n*; '**bird's-eye view** (Blick *m* aus der) Vogelperspektive *f*; allgemeiner Überblick *m*; '**bird's-nest 1.** Vogelnest *n*; **2.** Vogelnester ausnehmen; ~ *soup* Schwalbennestersuppe *f*.

bi·ro [ˈbaiərəu] Kugelschreiber *m*.

birth [bəːθ] Geburt *f*; Ursprung *m*; Entstehung *f*; Herkunft *f*; *new* ~ Wiedergeburt *f*; *bring to* ~ entstehen lassen, veranlassen; *come to*

～ entstehen, veranlaßt werden; *give* ～ *to* gebären, zur Welt bringen; *fig.* hervorbringen; '～**con·trol** Geburtenbeschränkung *f*, -regelung *f*; '～·**day** Geburtstag *m*; ～ *honours am offiziellen Geburtstag des britischen Monarchen verliehene Titel;* '～**mark** Muttermal *n*; '～**place** Geburtsort *m*, -haus *n*; '～**rate** Geburtenziffer *f*; '～**right** (Erst)Geburtsrecht *n*.

bis·cuit ['biskit] 1. Zwieback *m*; Keks *m* (*n*); Biskuit *n* (*Porzellan*); 2. hellbraun.

bi·sect ♀ [bai'sekt] halbieren; **bi-'sec·tion** Halbierung *f*.

bish·op ['biʃəp] Bischof *m*; Läufer *m im Schach*; **bish·op·ric** ['～rik] Bistum *n*.

bis·muth 🜍 ['bizməθ] Wismut *n*.

bi·son *zo.* ['baisn] Wisent *m*.

bis·sex·tile [bi'sekstail] 1. Schalt...; ～ *year* = 2. Schaltjahr *n*.

bit [bit] 1. Bißchen *n*, Stückchen *n*; (Pferde)Gebiß *n*; ⊕ (Zangen)Maul *n*; Bohrspitze *f*; Schlüsselbart *m*; *Computer:* Bit *n*; ～ *by* ～ allmählich; stückweise; *a* ～ *of a coward* ein wenig feige; *take the* ～ *between one's teeth* durchgehen (*Pferd*); *fig.* aufsässig werden; 2. aufzäumen; zügeln; 3. *pret. von* bite 2.

bitch [bitʃ] 1. Hündin *f*; ∨ Hure *f*; ～ *fox* Füchsin *f*; ～ *wolf* Wölfin *f*; 2. verpfuschen.

bite [bait] 1. Beißen *n*; Biß *m*; Bissen *m*, Happen *m*; Anbeißen *n*; ⊕ Fassen *n*, Haften *n*; 2. (*irr.*) beißen; brennen (*Pfeffer*); schneiden (*Kälte*); zerfressen (*Rost etc.*); (an-) beißen (*Fisch*); ⊕ fassen (*Anker, Schraube etc.*); *fig.* verletzen; ～ *at* schnappen nach; ～ *the dust fig.* ins Gras beißen (*sterben*); ～ *one's lips* sich auf die Lippen beißen; ～ *one's nails* Fingernägel kauen; '**bit·er** Beißer *m*; *the* ～ *bit* der betrogene Betrüger.

bit·ing □ ['baitiŋ] scharf, beißend.

bit·ten ['bitn] *p.p. von* bite 2; *be* ～ *fig.* hereingefallen sein; *once* ～ *twice shy* gebranntes Kind scheut das Feuer.

bit·ter ['bitə] 1. □ bitter; beißend, streng; *fig.* (v)erbittert; 2. *halbdunkles, herbes Bier.*

bit·tern *orn.* ['bitən] Rohrdommel *f*.

bit·ter·ness ['bitənis] Bitterkeit *f*, Verbitterung *f*.

bit·ters ['bitəz] *pl.* Bittere *m*,

Magenbitter *m*.

bi·tu·men ['bitjumin] Bitumen *n*, Asphalt *m*, Erdpech *n*; **bi·tu·mi-nous** [bi'tju:minəs] bituminös.

bi·valve *zo.* [bai'vælv] zweischalige Muschel *f*.

biv·ou·ac ['bivuæk] 1. Biwak *n*; 2. biwakieren.

biz F [biz] Geschäft *n*.

bi·zarre [bi'zɑ:] bizarr.

blab F [blæb] 1. *a.* '**blab·ber** Schwätzer(in); 2. (aus)schwatzen.

black [blæk] 1. □ schwarz; dunkel; finster, düster; ～ *cattle* Rind-, Hornvieh *n*; ～ *eye* blaues Auge *n*; *s. frost*; *in* ～ *and white* schwarz auf weiß; *beat s.o.* ～ *and blue* j. grün u. blau schlagen; ～ *in the face* dunkelrot (im Gesicht *vor Wut*); *look* ～ *at s.o.* j. böse anschauen; 2. schwärzen; wichsen; ～ *out* verdunkeln; 3. Schwarz *n* (*a. Kleidung*); Schwärze *f*; Schwarze *m*, *f* (*Neger*).

black...: ～·**a·moor** ['～əmuə] Neger *m*; '～·**ball** gegen *j.* stimmen; '～·**ber-ry** ♀ Brombeere *f*; *go* ～*ing* Brombeeren sammeln; '～·**bird** Amsel *f*; '～·**board** Wandtafel *f*; '～·**coat·ed:** ～ *worker* Büroangestellte *m*; '～·**cock** *orn.* Birkhahn *m*; '～·**cur·rant** schwarze Johannisbeere *f*; '**black-en** *v/t.* schwärzen, schwarz machen; *fig.* anschwärzen; *v/i.* schwarz werden.

black...: '～·**guard** ['blæɡɑ:d] 1. Lump *m*, Schuft *m*; 2. *a.* '～·**guard-ly** □ schuftig, niederträchtig; 3. *j.* (Lump) schimpfen; ～·**head** 🜍 ['blækhed] Mitesser *m*; ～ **ice** Glatteis *n*; '**black·ing** Schuhwichse *f*; '**black-ish** □ schwärzlich.

black...: '～·**jack** 1. *bsd. Am.* Totschläger *m* (*Instrument*); 2. niederknüppeln; ～·**lead** ['～'led] 1. Reißblei *n*; 2. mit Reißblei schwärzen; '～·**leg** Betrüger *m*; Streikbrecher *m*; '～·**let·ter** *typ.* Fraktur *f*; '～·**list** auf die schwarze Liste setzen; '～·**mail** 1. Erpressung(sgeld *n*) *f*; 2. Geld von *j-m* erpressen; '～·**mail-er** Erpresser *m*; ～ **mar·ket** schwarzer Markt *m*; ～ **mar·ket·eer** Schwarzhändler *m*, Schieber *m*; '**black·ness** Schwärze *f*.

black...: '～·**out** Verdunkelung *f*; Gedächtnisstörung *f*; *thea.* Verlöschen *n* der Lichter; *news* ～ Nachrichtensperre *f*; ～ **pud·ding** Blutwurst *f*; ～

sheep *fig.* schwarzes Schaf *n*; '**~- smith** Grobschmied *m*; '**~-tail** *zo. Am.* Kolumbischer Hirsch *m*; '**~- thorn** ♀ Schwarz-, Schlehdorn *m*; '**black·y** F Schwarze *m, f.*

blad·der ['blædə] (*bsd.* Harn-, Gallen-, Schwimm)Blase *f.*

blade [bleid] Blatt *n*, ♀ Halm *m*; *Säge-, Ruder-, Schulter- etc.* Blatt *n*; Propellerflügel *m*; Schneide *f*, Klinge *f eines Messers etc.*; '**~-bone** *anat.* Schulterblatt *n.*

blae·ber·ry ['bleibəri] Heidelbeere *f.*

blah F [blɑ:] leeres Gerede *n.*

blam·a·ble □ ['bleiməbl] tadelnswert; schuldhaft.

blame [bleim] 1. Tadel *m*; Schuld *f*; 2. tadeln; *be to ~ for* schuld sein an (*dat.*); *~ s.th. on s.o.* die Schuld für et. auf j. schieben.

blame·ful ['bleimful] tadelnswert; '**blame·less** □ untadelig; schuldlos; '**blame·less·ness** Makellosigkeit *f*; '**blame·wor·thy** tadelnswert.

blanch [blɑ:ntʃ] bleichen; erbleichen (lassen); *~ over* beschönigen.

blanc-mange [blə'mɔnʒ] *Küche:* Flammeri *m.*

bland □ [blænd] mild, sanft; '**blan·dish** schmeicheln (*dat.*), liebkosen; '**blan·dish·ment** Schmeichelei *f.*

blank [blæŋk] 1. □ blank; leer; unausgefüllt; unbeschrieben; ✝ Blanko...; verdutzt, verblüfft; *~ cartridge* ✕ Platzpatrone *f*; *fire ~* mit Platzpatronen schießen; 2. Weißes *n*; Leere *f*; leerer Raum *m*; Lücke *f*, freie Stelle *f*; unbeschriebenes Blatt *n*, leeres Formular *n*, Blankett *n*; Niete *f in der Lotterie*; Platzpatrone *f.*

blan·ket ['blæŋkit] 1. Wolldecke *f*; *engS.* (Bett-, Pferde)Decke *f*; *wet ~ fig.* Dämpfer *m*; Spielverderber *m*; Störenfried *m*; 2. mit e-r Wolldecke zudecken; F unterdrücken, vertuschen; 3. *Am.* umfassend, Gesamt..., Allgemein..., Pauschal...

blank·ness ['blæŋknis] Weiße *f*, Leere *f*; Verdutztheit *f*; **blank verse** *poet.* Blankvers *m.*

blare [bleə] schmettern (*Trompete*).

blar·ney ['blɑ:ni] 1. Schmus *m*, leeres Gerede *n*; Überredungskunst *f*; 2. *j.* einwickeln; schmeichelhaft reden.

bla·sé ['blɑ:zei] blasiert.

blas·pheme [blæs'fi:m] lästern (*against* über *acc.*); **blas'phem·er** Gotteslästerer *m*; **blas·phe·mous** □ ['blæsfiməs] blasphemisch, gotteslästerlich; '**blas·phe·my** Blasphemie *f*, Gotteslästerung *f.*

blast [blɑ:st] 1. Windstoß *m*; Ton *m e-s Blasinstruments*; ⊕ Gebläse (-luft *f*) *n*; Luftdruck *m e-r Explosion*; (Spreng)Ladung *f*; ♀ Mehltau *m*; *at full ~* mit Volldampf; *in (out of) ~* in (außer) Betrieb (*Hochofen*); *~ of a trumpet* Trompetenstoß *m*; 2. (in die Luft) sprengen; zerstören (*a. fig.*); *~ (it)!* verdammt!; '**blast·ed** verdammt, verflucht; '**blast·fur·nace** ⊕ Hochofen *m*; '**blast·ing** Sprengen *n*; '**blast-off** *Raumfahrt:* Raketenstart *m.*

bla·tant □ ['bleitənt] lärmend; marktschreierisch; *fig.* eklatant.

blath·er *Am.* ['blæðə] 1. Gewäsch *n*; 2. schwätzen.

blaze [bleiz] 1. Flamme(n *pl.*) *f*; Feuer *n*; heller Schein *m*; *fig.* Ausbruch *m*; *~s pl.* Hölle *f*, Teufel *m*; *go to ~s!* zum Teufel mit dir!; *like ~s* F wie ein Irrer; 2. *v/i.* brennen, flammen, lodern; leuchten; *~ away* F losschießen; *blazing scent* warme Fährte *f*; *v/t.* Baum markieren; *~ abroad* ausposaunen; *~ a trail* e-n Pfad markieren; *fig.* e-n Weg bahnen; '**blaz·er** Blazer *m.*

bla·zon ['bleizn] 1. Wappenkunde *f*; Wappen(schild) *n*; 2. *Wappen* beschreiben, malen; *fig.* schmücken; verherrlichen; (ver)künden; F ausposaunen; '**bla·zon·ry** Wappenkunde *f*; Zurschaustellung *f*; Schmuck *m.*

bleach [bli:tʃ] bleichen; '**bleach·er** Bleicher(in); *~s pl. Am.* nichtüberdachte Zuschauerplätze *m/pl. bei Sportveranstaltungen*; '**bleach·ing** Bleichen *n*; '**bleach·ing-pow·der** Bleichpulver *n.*

bleak □ [bli:k] öde, kahl; rauh; *fig.* trüb, freudlos, finster; '**bleak·ness** Öde *f*; Rauheit *f.*

blear [bliə] 1. trüb (*bsd. Auge*); 2. trüben; *~-eyed* ['bliəraid] triefäugig; '**blear·y** trüb.

bleat [bli:t] 1. Blöken *n*; 2. blöken.

bleb [bleb] Bläschen *n*, Pustel *f.*

bled [bled] *pret. u. p.p von* bleed.

bleed [bli:d] (*irr.*) *v/i.* bluten; *v/t.*

zur Ader lassen; *fig.* schröpfen;
'bleed·ing 1. Bluten *n*; Aderlaß
m; **2.** *sl.* verflixt.
bleep·er F ['bliːpə] Piepser *m*, Funkrufempfänger *m*.
blem·ish ['blemiʃ] **1.** Fehler *m*;
Makel *m*, Schande *f*; **2.** verunstalten; brandmarken.
blench [blentʃ] *v/i.* zurückschrek-
ken; *v/t.* die Augen schließen vor.
blend [blend] **1.** (sich) (ver)mischen;
Tee mischen; *Wein etc.* verschneiden; *fig.* (miteinander) verschmelzen; ineinander übergehen; **2.** Mischung *f*; ✝ Verschnitt *m*.
blende *min.* [blend] (Zink)Blende *f*.
bless [bles] segnen; preisen; be-
glücken (*with* mit); ~ me!, ~ my
soul! F meine Güte!, herrje!; ~
you! Gesundheit! (*beim Niesen*);
bless·ed □ [*p.p.* blest; *adj.* 'blesid]
glückselig; gesegnet; ~ *event* freu-
diges Ereignis *n*; **bless·ed·ness**
['blesidnis] Glückseligkeit *f*; *live in
single* ~ Junggeselle sein; **'blessing** Segen *m*; Segnung *f*; Wohltat *f*.
blest *poet.* [blest] *s. blessed.*
bleth·er ['bleðə] *s. blather.*
blew [bluː] *pret. von blow²* u. *blow³* 1.
blight [blait] **1.** ♨ Mehltau *m*;
fig. Gifthauch *m*; **2.** vernichten;
'blight·er *sl.* Ekel *n* (*Person*); Kerl
m, Bursche *m*.
Blight·y ✕ *sl.* ['blaiti] Heimat *f*;
a ~ *one* ein Heimatschuß *m*.
bli·mey V ['blaimi] verflucht!
blind [blaind] **1.** □ blind (*fig. to*
gegen); geheim; nicht erkennbar;
~ *alley* Sackgasse *f*; ~ *corner* un-
übersichtliche Straßenecke *f*; ~
flying ✈ Blindflug *m*; ~ *drunk* *sl.*
betrunken, blau; ~ *spot* blinder Fleck
m; toter Winkel *m*; *Radio:* Empfangs-
loch *n*; *turn one's* ~ *eye to s.th.* ein Auge
zudrücken bei et.; **2.** Blende *f*; (Fenster)Vorhang *m*, Jalousie *f*, Rouleau *n*;
Scheuklappe *f*; *Am.* Versteck *n*; Vorwand *m*; **3.** blenden, blind machen;
verblenden (*to* gegen); abblenden.
blind·fold ['blaindfəuld] **1.** blindlings; blind; mit verbundenen
Augen; **2.** *j-m* die Augen verbinden;
'blind·ly *fig.* blindlings; **'blind-
man's-'buff** Blindekuhspiel *n*;
'blind·ness Blindheit *f*; **'blind-
worm** *zo.* Blindschleiche *f*.
blink [bliŋk] **1.** Blinzeln *n*; Schimmer

m; ⚓ Blink *m*; *on the* ~ F defekt, nicht
in Ordnung; **2.** *v/i.* blinzeln; zwinkern; blinken; schimmern; *v/t.* ab-
sichtlich übersehen; blinzeln mit;
'blink·er Blinzler *m*; Scheuklappe *f*;
'blink·ing F verflixt.
blip [blip] *Radar:* Echozeichen *n*.
bliss [blis] Seligkeit *f*, Wonne *f*.
bliss·ful □ ['blisful] glückselig,
selig, wonnig; **'bliss·ful·ness**
Glückseligkeit *f*, Wonne *f*.
blis·ter ['blistə] **1.** Blase *f* (*auf der
Haut, im Lack*); Zugpflaster *n*;
2. Blasen bilden (*auf dat.*).
blithe □ [blaið], **~some** ['~səm]
mst poet. lustig, munter, fröhlich.
blith·er·ing *sl.* ['bliðəriŋ]: ~ *idiot*
Vollidiot *m*.
blitz [blits] **1.** Luftangriff *m*;
2. bombardieren.
bliz·zard ['blizəd] Schneesturm *m*.
bloat [bləut] aufblasen; aufschwellen; *Fische* räuchern; **~ed** aufgedunsen; *fig.* aufgeblasen; **'bloat·er**
Bückling *m*.
blob [blɔb] Tropfen *m*; Klümpchen
n.
block [blɔk] **1.** Block *m*; Klotz *m*;
(Häuser)Block *m*; ⊕ Block *m*,
Rolle *f*; Druckstock *m*; Verstopfung *f*, Stockung *f*; *the* ~ *der* Richt-
block; **2.** pressen, formen; verhindern, durchkreuzen; ~ *in* entwerfen, skizzieren; *mst* ~ *up* (ab-,
ver)sperren; *Hafen etc.* blockieren;
einschließen; **~ed** *account* Sperr-
konto *n*.
block·ade [blɔ'keid] **1.** Blockade *f*;
run the ~ die Blockade brechen;
2. blockieren; einschließen; **block-
'ade-run·ner** Blockadebrecher *m*.
block...: '~**·bust·er** *sl.* Luftmine *f*; F
Knüller *m*, Wucht *f*, tolle Sache *f*;
'~**·head** Dummkopf *m*; '~**·house**
Blockhaus *n*; ~ *let·ters pl.* Block-,
Druckschrift *f*; ~ *of flats* Wohnblock
m; '~**·sys·tem** 🚆 Block(signal)system
n.
bloke F [bləuk] Bursche *m*, Kerl *m*.
blond(e *f*) [blɔnd] **1.** blond; **2.**
Blondine *f*; *a. blonde-lace* ✝ Blonde
f, seidene Spitze *f*.
blood [blʌd] Blut *n*; *fig.* Blut *n*,
Temperament *n*; Geblüt *n*, Abstammung *f*; *in cold* ~ kalten Blutes,
kaltblütig; ~ *s. run* 1; '~**·and-'thunder** sensationell, dramatisch, aufregend; ~ *clot* ⚕ Blutgerinnsel *n*;

'**~cur·dling** haarsträubend, entsetzlich; ~ **do·nor** Blutspender(in).
blood·ed ['blʌdid] Vollblut...; ...-blütig.
blood...: '**~-guilt·i·ness** Blutschuld *f*; '**~-heat** Blutwärme *f*, Körpertemperatur *f*; '**~-horse** Vollblutpferd *n*; '**~-hound** Blut-, Schweißhund *m*; '**blood·i·ness** Blutgier *f*; '**blood·less** □ blutlos, -leer (*fig. bleich*; *kraft-*, *geistlos*); unblutig.
blood...: '**~-let·ting** Aderlaß *m*; '**~-poi·son·ing** ⚕ Blutvergiftung *f*; '**~-pres·sure** Blutdruck *m*; '**~-re·'la·tion** Blutsverwandte *m*, *f*; **~ sam·ple** ⚕ Blutprobe *f*; '**~-shed** Blutvergießen *n*; '**~-shot** blutunterlaufen; **~ sports** *pl. ‚blutige' Sportarten wie Fuchsjagd, Hahnenkampf etc.*; '**~-suck·er** Blutegel *m*; *fig.* Blutsauger *m*; '**~-thirst·y** blutdürstig; '**~-ves·sel** Blutgefäß *n*; '**blood·y** □ blutig; grausam; P verdammt; '**blood·y·'mind·ed** F stur; boshaft.
bloom [blu:m] **1.** Blüte *f*; *fig.* Blüte (-zeit) *f*; Reif *m*; Flaum *m auf Früchten*; *fig.* Schmelz *m*; *metall.* Luppe *f*; *be in* ~ blühen; **2.** (er-) blühen (*a. fig.*).
bloom·er ['blu:mə] *sl.* Schnitzer *m*; ~*s pl.* Schlüpfer *m*.
bloom·ing □ ['blu:miŋ] blühend; P verdammt, verflixt.
blos·som ['blɔsəm] **1.** *bsd. fruchtbildende* Blüte *f*; **2.** blühen; ~ *into* erblühen zu, sich entwickeln zu.
blot [blɔt] **1.** Klecks *m*, Fleck(en) *m*; *fig.* Makel *m*; **2.** beklecksen, beflecken (*a. fig.*); klecksen (*Feder*); (ab)löschen *mit Löschpapier*; *mst* ~ *out Schrift* ausstreichen, *fig.* auslöschen. [Klecks *m*.]
blotch [blɔtʃ] Pustel *f*; Fleck *m*;)
blot·ter ['blɔtə] Löscher *m*; *Am.* Protokollbuch *n bsd. der Polizei*.
blot·ting...: '**~-pad** Schreibunterlage *f*; '**~-pa·per** Löschpapier *n*.
blot·to *sl.* ['blɔtəu] besoffen.
blouse [blauz] Bluse *f*.
blow[1] [bləu] Schlag *m*, Stoß *m*; *at one* ~ mit einem Schlag; *come to* ~*s* handgemein werden.
blow[2] [~] (*irr.*) blühen.
blow[3] [~] **1.** (*irr.*) *v/i.* blasen; wehen; keuchen, schnaufen; geblasen *od.* geweht werden, fliegen; durchbrennen (*Sicherung*); ~ *over* vor-

überziehen, -gehen; *fig.* vergessen werden; ~ *up* explodieren, in die Luft fliegen; *v/t.* (*weg- etc.*)blasen, wehen; reißen; ertönen lassen; *Sicherung* durchbrennen lassen; *a.* ~ *up* (in die Luft) sprengen; *Geld* verpulvern, hinauswerfen; *sl. Chancen* vermasseln; ~ *one's nose* sich die Nase putzen, sich schneuzen; ~ *up Reifen* aufpumpen; *Photo* vergrößern; ~ *out one's brains* sich eine Kugel durch den Kopf jagen; *I'll be ~ed if ... sl.* zum Teufel, wenn ...; ~ *one's top* F in die Luft gehen; **2.** Blasen *n*, Wehen *n*; *get a* ~ F sich vom Wind durchblasen lassen; '**~-dry** *Haare* fönen; '**blow·er** Bläser *m*; Schieb(e)blech *n am Kamin*.
blow...: '**~-fly** Schmeißfliege *f*; '**~-hole** Luftloch *n*; '**~-lamp** (Benzin)Lötlampe *f*; Schweißbrenner *m*.
blown [bləun] *p.p von* **blow**[2] *u.* **blow**[3] *1.*
blow...: '**~-'out** *mot.* Reifenpanne *f*; '**~-pipe** Gebläsebrenner *m*; Schweißbrenner *m*; Blasrohr *n*; '**~-torch** *s.* *blowlamp*; '**~-up** Explosion *f*; F *fig.* Zornesausbruch *m*, Wutanfall *m*; F *fig.* Krach *m*, Streit *m*; *phot.* (Riesen)Vergrößerung *f*; '**blow·y** windig.
blowz·y ['blauzi] schlampig, ungepflegt u. mit grobem Teint.
blub·ber ['blʌbə] **1.** Walfischspeck *m*; **2.** heulen, weinen.
bludg·eon ['blʌdʒən] **1.** Knüppel *m*; **2.** niederknüppeln; prügeln.
blue [blu:] **1.** □ blau; F trüb, schwermütig; ~ *jokes pl.* unanständige Witze *m/pl.*; **2.** Blau *n*; *pol.* Konservative *m*, *f*; *out of the* ~ aus heiterem Himmel; **3.** blau färben, blauen.
blue...: '**~-ba·by** 🟎 Blue Baby *n* (*Kind n mit Blausucht durch angeborenen Herzfehler*); '**~-bell** 🟎 Sternhyazinthe *f*; Glockenblume *f*; '**~-ber·ry** 🟎 Blau-, Heidelbeere *f*; '**~-bird** *orn.* amerikanische Singdrossel *f*; '**~-book** *pol.* Blaubuch *n*; '**~-bot·tle** 🟎 Kornblume *f*; *zo.* Schmeißfliege *f*; '**~-jack·et** Blaujacke *f* (*Matrose*); '**~-jay** *orn.* Blauhäher *m*; ~ *jeans pl.* Blue jeans *pl.*; ~ *laws pl. Am.* strenge (puritanische) Gesetze *n/pl.*; '**blue·ness** Bläue *f*; '**blue-'pen·cil** zensieren, zs.-streichen; '**blueprint** Blaupause *f*; *fig.* Entwurf *m*; **blues** *pl.* Trübsinn *m*; ♪ Blues *m*; '**blue·stock·ing** *fig.* Blaustrumpf *m*.
bluff [blʌf] **1.** □ schroff; steil; derb,

gerade; **2.** Steilufer *n*; Bluff *m*, Irreführung *f*; **3.** bluffen, irreführen.

blu·ish ['bluːiʃ] bläulich.

blun·der ['blʌndə] **1.** Fehler *m*, Schnitzer *m*; **2.** einen Fehler *od.* Schnitzer machen; stolpern; stümpern; verpfuschen; ~ out F herausplatzen mit; **blun·der·buss** *hist.* ['blʌndəbʌs] Donnerbüchse *f*; **'blun·der·er**, **'blun·der·head** Stümper *m*.

blunt [blʌnt] **1.** □ stumpf (*a. fig.*); plump, grob, derb; **2.** abstumpfen; **'blunt·ness** Stumpfheit *f*; Grobheit *f*, Plumpheit *f*.

blur [bləː] **1.** Fleck(en) *m*; *fig.* Verschwommenheit *f*, Schleier *m*; **2.** *v/t.* beflecken; verwischen; *Sinn* trüben; ~red *bsd. phot.* verschleiert.

blurb [bləːb] Waschzettel *m*, Klappentext *m*.

blurt [bləːt]: ~ out herausplatzen mit.

blush [blʌʃ] **1.** (Scham)Röte *f*; Erröten *n*; flüchtiger Blick *m*; **2.** erröten (*at* über *acc.*); (sich) röten, rot werden; ~ to *inf.* sich schämen zu *inf.*; **'blush·er** Rouge *n*; **'blush·ing** □ schamhaft.

blus·ter ['blʌstə] **1.** Brausen *n*, Toben *n*, Getöse *n*; Prahlerei *f*; **2.** *v/i.* brausen, toben, tosen; prahlen; *v/t.* *a.* ~ out ausstoßen; **'blus·ter·er** Polterer *m*; Prahler *m*.

bo(h) [bəu] hu!, buh!

bo·a *zo.* ['bəuə] Boa *f*.

boar [bɔː] Eber *m*; *hunt.* Keiler *m*.

board [bɔːd] **1.** Brett *n*, Bohle *f*; Anschlagbrett *n*; Tafel *f*; Konferenztisch *m*; Ausschuß *m*, Komitee *n*, Kommission *f*; Gremium *n*; Behörde *f*, Amt *n*; Verpflegung *f*; Pappe *f*; the ~s *pl. thea.* die Bretter *n/pl.*; on ~ an Bord; on ~ a train *Am.* in e-m Zug; go by the ~s über Bord gehen, *fig.* ins Wasser fallen (*Plan etc.*); above ~ ehrlich, offen; sweep the ~ alles gewinnen; ~ of governors Kuratorium *n bsd. e-r Public School*; ♀ of Trade Handelsministerium *n*; ~ and lodging Unterkunft *f u.* Verpflegung *f*; **2.** *v/t.* dielen, verschalen; beköstigen; *a.* ~ out in Kost *od.* Pension geben; ♣ an Bord *e-s Schiffes* gehen; ♣ entern; *bsd. Am.* (*Fahr-, Flugzeug*) besteigen; einsteigen in (*acc.*); ~ up mit Brettern verschlagen

od. vernageln; *v/i.* in Kost sein (*with* bei); **'board·er** Kostgänger (-in); Internatsschüler(in).

board·ing ['bɔːdiŋ] Verschalung *f*; Verpflegung *f*; ♣ Entern *n*; *attr.* Kost...; **'~-axe** ♣ Enterbeil *n*; **'~-house** Pension *f*, Fremdenheim *n*; **'~-school** Internat(sschule *f*) *n*.

board...: ~ of di·rec·tors Aufsichts-, Verwaltungsrat *m*; **'~-room** Sitzungssaal *m*; **'~-walk** *bsd. Am.* Strandpromenade *f aus Holzplanken.*

boast [bəust] **1.** Prahlerei *f*; Stolz *m*; **2.** (*of, about*) sich rühmen (*gen.*), prahlen (mit); ~ *s.th.* sich (des Besitzes) e-r Sache rühmen, et. aufzuweisen haben; **'boast·er** Prahler(in); **boast·ful** □ ['~ful] prahlerisch.

boat [bəut] **1.** Boot *n*; Schiff *n*; burn one's ~s alle Brücken hinter sich abbrechen; take to the ~s in die Rettungsboote gehen; be in the same ~ in der gleichen Lage sein; *s.* sauce-~; **2.** in e-m Boot fahren; **'boat-hook** Bootshaken *m*; **'boat-house** Bootshaus *n*; **'boat·ing** Bootfahrt *f*; **'boat-race** Ruderregatta *f*; **boat-swain** ['bəusn] Bootsmann *m*; **'boat-train** Schiffszug *m*.

bob [bɔb] **1.** Bommel *f*, Quaste *f*; Pendellinse *f*; Ruck *m*; Knicks *m*; (Haar)Schopf *m*; *sl.* Schilling *m*; = ~bed hair; **2.** *v/t.* klopfen; stoßen; *Haar* stutzen; ~bed hair Bubikopf *m*; *v/i.* springen, tanzen; knicksen; ~ for schnappen nach.

bob·bin ['bɔbin] Spule *f* (*a. ⚡*); *Spitzen*-Klöppel *m*; Zugschnur *f*; **'~-lace** Klöppelspitze *f*.

bob·ble *Am.* F ['bɔbl] Schnitzer *m*, Fehler *m*.

bob·by *sl.* ['bɔbi] Polizist *m*; **'~-pin** Haarklemme *f*; **'~-socks** *pl.* Söckchen *n/pl.*; ~sox·er *Am.sl.* ['~sɔksə] Backfisch *m*.

bob·cat *zo.* ['bɔbkæt] Rotluchs *m*.

bob·o·link *orn.* ['bɔbəliŋk] Reisstärling *m*.

bob·sled ['bɔbsled], **bob·sleigh** ['bɔbslei] Bob(sleigh) *m* (*Mannschaftsrennschlitten*).

bob·tail ['bɔbteil] (*Pferd n od.* Hund *m* mit) Stutzschwanz *m*; the rag-tag and ~ Krethi u. Plethi *pl.*

bob·white *orn.* ['bɔb'wait] Virginische Wachtel *f*.

bode [bəud] prophezeien (*well* Gu-

tes *n, ill* Übles *n*).
bod·ice ['bɔdis] Leibchen *n*, Mieder *n*; Taille *f am Kleid*.
bod·i·ly ['bɔdili] **1.** *adj.* körperlich; ~ *injury* Körperverletzung *f*; **2.** *adv.* ganz u. gar; persönlich.
bod·kin ['bɔdkin] Ahle *f*; Durchziehnadel; Haarnadel *f*; *sit* ~ eingepfercht sitzen.
bod·y ['bɔdi] **1.** Körper *m*, Leib *m*; Rumpf *m*; Leichnam *m*; Person *f*; Körperschaft *f*; Hauptteil *m*; *mot.* Karosserie *f*; (Hut)Stumpen *m*; ✗ Truppenkörper *m*; *fig.* Masse *f*; *in a* ~ zusammen, geschlossen; **2.** ~ *forth* verkörpern; '~**guard** Leibwache *f*; ~ **o·do·(u)r** (*abbr. B.O.*) (unangenehmer) Körpergeruch *m*; ~ **snatch·er** Leichenräuber *m*; '~**work** *mot.* Karosserie *f*.
Boer ['bɔuə] **1.** Bure *m*; **2.** Buren..., burisch.
bof·fin *sl.* ['bɔfin] Wissenschaftler *m*, Experte *m*.
bog [bɔg] **1.** Sumpf *m*, Moor *n*; Morast *m*; **2.** im Schlamm versenken; *be od. get* ~*ged down* steckenbleiben.
bog·gle ['bɔgl] stutzen, schwanken, unschlüssig sein; pfuschen.
bog·gy ['bɔgi] sumpfig.
bo·gie ['bəugi] 🚋 Drehschemel *m*; *a. = bogy.*
bo·gus ['bəugəs] falsch, Schwindel...
bo·gy ['bəugi] Kobold *m*; Popanz *m*, Schreckgespenst *n*; *the* ~ (*man*) der Schwarze Mann.
Bo·he·mi·an [bəu'hi:mjən] **1.** böhmisch; **2.** Böhme *m*, Böhmin *f*; Zigeuner(in); *fig.* Bohemien *m*.
boil [bɔil] **1.** kochen, sieden (*a. fig.*); (sich) kondensieren; **2.** Sieden *n*; Beule *f*, Geschwür *n*; Furunkel *m*; '**boil·er** Sieder *m*; (Dampf-)Kessel *m*, Boiler *m*; ~ *suit* Overall *m*; '**boil·ing** siedend; Siede...
bois·ter·ous □ ['bɔistərəs] ungestüm; heftig, laut; lärmend; '**bois·ter·ous·ness** Ungestüm *n*.
bold □ [bəuld] kühn, keck; *b.s.* dreist; steil (*Küste*); deutlich; *typ.* fett; *make* (*so*) ~ (*as*) *to do* sich erkühnen zu tun; '**bold·ness** Kühnheit *f etc.*; *b.s.* Dreistigkeit *f*.
bole [bəul] starker Baumstamm *m*.
bo·ler·o [bə'lɛərəu] Bolero *m (Tanz)*; ['bɔlərəu] Bolero *m (Damenjacke)*.
boll 🌿 [bəul] Samenkapsel *f*.

bol·lard ['bɔləd] ⚓ Poller *m*; Verkehrsinsellampe *f*.
bo·lo·ney *sl.* [bə'ləuni] Quatsch *m*.
Bol·she·vism ['bɔlʃivizəm] Bolschewismus *m*; '**Bol·she·vist 1.** Bolschewist(in); **2.** bolschewistisch.
bol·ster ['bəulstə] **1.** Kopfkeil *m*; Unterlage *f* (*a.* ⊕); **2.** *mst* ~ *up* polstern; (unter)stützen.
bolt [bəult] **1.** Bolzen *m*; Tür-, Schloß- *etc.* Riegel *m*; Blitzstrahl *m*; Ausreißen *n*, Durchgehen *n*; ~ *upright* kerzengerade; **2.** *v/t.* verbolzen; verriegeln; F hinunterschlingen; *v/i.* eilen, stürzen; durchgehen (*Pferd u. fig.*); *Am. pol.* abtrünnig werden; sieben; '**bolt·er** Ausreißer(in), Durchgänger(in); Beutelsieb *n*.
bolt·hole ['bəulthəul] Schlupfloch *n*.
bomb [bɔm] **1.** *bsd.* ✗ Bombe *f*; ~ *alert* Bombenalarm *m*; ~ *disposal squad* Bombenräumkommando *n*; **2.** mit Bomben belegen, bombardieren; *bsd. Am.* F *im Examen* durchrasseln, -fallen; ~*ed out* ausgebombt; ~ *up Flugzeug* mit Bomben beladen.
bom·bard [bɔm'bɑ:d] beschießen; bombardieren (*a. fig. u. phys.*); **bom'bard·ment** Bombardement *n*; Beschießung *f*, Beschuß *m*.
bom·bast ['bɔmbæst] Bombast *m*, Schwulst *m*; **bom'bas·tic, bom'bas·ti·cal** □ bombastisch, schwülstig.
bomb-bay ['bɔmbei] Bombenschacht *m*.
bombed *sl.* [bɔmd] besoffen; high *durch Drogen.*
bomb·er ✈ ['bɔmə] Bomber *m*.
bomb...: '~**-proof 1.** bombensicher; **2.** Bunker *m*; '~**-shell** *fig.* Bombe *f*; '~**-sight** ✗ Bombenzielgerät *n*.
bo·nan·za *Am.* F [bəu'nænzə] **1.** *fig.* Goldgrube *f*; **2.** sehr einträglich; Groß...
bon·bon ['bɔnbɔn] Bonbon *m, n.*
bond [bɔnd] **1.** Band *n* (*a. fig.*); Fessel *f* (*a. fig.*); Bündnis *n*; Schuldschein *m*; ✝ Obligation *f*; *in* ~ ✝ unter Zollverschluß; **2.** verpfänden; ✝ unter Zollverschluß legen; ~*ed port* Zollhafen *m*; ~*ed warehouse* Zollspeicher *m*; '**bond·age** Leibeigenschaft *f*, Hörigkeit *f*; Knechtschaft *f* (*a. fig.*); '**bond-hold·er** Inhaber *m* von Obligationen; '**bond(s)·man** Leibeigene

m; '**bond(s)·wom·an** Leibeigene *f*, Hörige *f*.

bone [bəun] **1.** Knochen *m*, Bein *n*; Gräte *f*; ~s *pl. a.* Gebeine *n/pl.*; Kastagnetten *f/pl.*; Würfel *m/pl.*; ~ *of contention* Zankapfel *m*; *feel in one's* ~*s* in den Knochen spüren; sicher sein; *frozen to the* ~ durchgefroren; *have a* ~ *to pick with* F ein Hühnchen zu rupfen haben mit; *make no* ~*s about* F nicht lange fackeln mit; **2.** ausbeinen, entgräten; *a.* ~ *up* F büffeln, fest lernen; **3.** knöchern; Knochen...; **boned** ...knochig; '**bone-'dry** knochentrocken; '**bone--dust** Knochenmehl *n*; '**bone-head** *sl.* Dummkopf *m*; '**bone-'i·dle**, '**bone-'la·zy** *contp.* stinkfaul; '**bon·er** *Am. sl.* Schnitzer *m*, grober Fehler *m*; '**bone-set·ter** Heilgehilfe *m*; '**bone--shak·er** altes Fahrrad *n*; Klapperkasten *m*.

bon·fire ['bɔnfaiə] Freudenfeuer *n*; (Reisig-, Kartoffel- *etc.* Feuer *n*.

bon·kers *sl.* ['bɔŋkəz] verrückt.

bon·net ['bɔnit] **1.** Haube *f*, Schute(nhut *m*) *f*; Schottenmütze *f*; ⊕ (Motor)Haube *f*; *Schornstein- etc.* Kappe *f*, Haube *f*; ⚓ Bonnett *n*; **2.** mit e-r Mütze *etc.* bedecken.

bon·ny *bsd. schott.* ['bɔni] hübsch; drall; rosig; munter.

bo·nus ✝ ['bəunəs] Prämie *f*; Extradividende *f*; Gratifikation *f*; Gewinnanteil *m*; Zulage *f*.

bon·y ['bəuni] knöchern; Knochen ...; knochig; grätig.

boo [bu:] (nieder)brüllen, (aus)pfeifen.

boob *Am.* [bu:b] Simpel *m*, Dummkopf *m*.

boo·by ['bu:bi] Tölpel *m a. orn.* ; ~ *prize* Trostpreis *m*; ~ *hatch Am. sl.* Klapsmühle *f*; '~**-trap** Minenfalle *f*; grober Scherz *m*.

boog·ie-woog·ie ['bu:giwu'gi] Boogie-Woogie *m*.

boo·hoo F [bu:'hu:] plärren.

book [buk] **1.** Buch *n*; Heft *n*; Liste *f*; Block *m Fahrkarten etc.*; *the* ♀ die Bibel; *stand in the* ~*s at* ✝ zu Buche stehen mit; *be in s.o.'s good (bad)* ~*s fig.* bei j-m gut (schlecht) angeschrieben sein; *bring s.o. to* ~ von j-m Rechenschaft verlangen; **2.** buchen; einschreiben, -tragen; *Eintritts-, Fahr-*

karte lösen; *e-n Platz etc.* bestellen; *Gepäck* aufgeben; F *j.* vormerken; ~ *through* e-e durchgehende Fahrkarte lösen; '~**·bind--er** Buchbinder *m*; '~**·case** Bücherschrank *m*; '~**·end** Bücherstütze *f*; **book·ie** ['buki] F *Sport:* Buchmacher *m*; '**book·ing-clerk** Schalterbeamte *m*; '**book·ing-of·fice** Fahrkartenausgabe *f*, -schalter *m*; *thea.* Kasse *f*; '**book·ish** □ gelehrt; '**book--keep·er** Buchhalter *m*; '**book--keep·ing** Buchführung *f*; '**book·let** ['~lit] Büchlein *n*; Broschüre *f*.

book...: '~**-mak·er** Buchmacher *m*; '~**-mark(·er)** Lesezeichen *n*; '~**·mo·bile** *Am.* ['~mau'bi:l] Wanderbücherei *f*; '~**-plate** Exlibris *n*; '~**-sell·er** Buchhändler *m*; '~**·shop** Buchhandlung *f*; '~**·stall** Bücher(verkaufs)stand *m*; ~ **to·ken** Büchergutschein *m*; '~**·worm** Bücherwurm *m* (*a. fig.*).

boom¹ ⚓ [bu:m] Baum *m*; Ausleger *m*; Spiere *f*.

boom² [~] **1.** ✝ Aufschwung *m*, Hochkonjunktur *f*, Hausse *f*; Reklamerummel *m*; ~ *and bust* wirtschaftliches Hoch *n* und Tief *n*; **2.** in die Höhe treiben *od.* gehen; für *et.* Reklame machen.

boom³ [~] **1.** brummen; brausen; dröhnen; **2.** Donnern *n*.

boom·e·rang ['bu:məræŋ] Bumerang *m* (*a. fig.*).

boon¹ [bu:n] Gefallen *m*; Segen *m*, Wohltat *f*.

boon² [~] freundlich, munter; ~ *companion* Zechkumpan *m*.

boon·docks *Am. sl.* ['bu:ndɔks] *pl.* die Provinz.

boor *fig.* [buə] Bauer *m*, Lümmel *m*, Flegel *m*.

boor·ish □ ['buəriʃ] bäuerisch, lümmel-, flegelhaft; '**boor·ish·ness** flegelhaftes Wesen *n*.

boost [bu:st] heben; in die Höhe treiben; nachhelfen (*dat.*), Auftrieb geben (*dat.*); verstärken (*a.* ⚡); Reklame machen; ~ *business* die Wirtschaft ankurbeln; '**boost·er** Verstärkung *f*, Zusatz *m*; ~ *rocket* Startrakete *f*.

boot¹ [bu:t]: *to* ~ obendrein.

boot² [~] Stiefel *m*; Kofferraum *m*; *the* ~ *is on the other leg* es ist genau umgekehrt; *get the* ~ *sl.* rausfliegen (*entlassen werden*); *give s.o the* ~ *sl. j.* rausschmeißen *od.* -werfen (*entlas-*

sen); *put the* ~ *in sl.* kräftig zutreten; '~-**black** *Am.* = *shoeblack;* '**boot-ed** gestiefelt; **boot-ee** ['buːtiː] *Damen*-Halbstiefel *m.*

booth [buːð] (Markt-, Schau)Bude *f;* Wahlzelle *f; Am.* Fernsprechzelle *f.*

boot...: '~-jack Stiefelknecht *m;* '**~-lace** Schnürsenkel *m;* '**~-leg** *bsd. Am.* illegal (*hergestellt, transportiert, verkauft*); Geheim...; Schmuggel...; '**~-leg-ger** Alkoholschmuggler *m; weitS.* Schieber *m.*

boot-less *poet.* ['buːtlis] nutzlos.

boots [buːts] Hausdiener *m (Hotel).*

boot-tree ['buːttriː] Leisten *m.*

boo-ty ['buːti] Beute *f,* Raub *m.*

booze P [buːz] 1. saufen; 2. Sauferei *f;* '**booz-y** P besoffen.

bop [bɔp] = *bebop.* [Spiel *n.*⟩

bo-peep [bəu'piːp] Guck-guck-⟩

bo-rax ⚗ ['bɔːræks] Borax *m.*

bor-der ['bɔːdə] 1. Rand *m,* Bord *m,* Saum *m;* Grenze *f e-s Landes;* Einfassung *f;* Leiste *f;* (Schmal-)Beet *n,* Rabatte *f;* ~ *state* Randstaat *m;* 2. begrenzen, einfassen, besetzen; grenzen (*upon* an *acc.*); '**bor-der-er** Grenzbewohner *m;* '**bor-der-land** *mst fig.* Grenzgebiet *n;* '**bor-der-line** 1. Grenzlinie *f;* 2. zweifelhaft, an der Grenze, Grenz...

bore[1] [bɔː] 1. Bohrloch *n;* Bohrung *f e-r Feuerwaffe,* Seele *f;* Kaliber *n; et.* Langweiliges *od.* Stumpfsinniges; langweiliger Mensch *m;* 2. bohren; langweilen; belästigen, *j-m* lästig sein.

bore[2] [~] Springflut *f.*

bore[3] [~] *pret. von* bear[2].

bo-re-al ['bɔːriəl] nördlich, Nord...

bore-dom ['bɔːdəm] Langweiligkeit *f,* Langeweile *f,* Stumpfsinn *m.*

bor-er ['bɔːrə] Bohrer *m.*

bo-ric ac-id ⚗ ['bɔːrik'æsid] Borsäure *f.*

bor-ing ['bɔːriŋ] Bohr...; langweilig.

born [bɔːn] *p.p. von* bear[2] geboren.

borne [bɔːn] *p.p. von* bear[2] getragen.

bo-ron ⚗ ['bɔːrɔn] Bor *n.*

bor-ough ['bʌrə] Stadt *f od.* Stadtteil *m mit Parlamentsvertretung; Am. a.* Wahlbezirk *m* von New York City; *municipal* ~ Stadtgemeinde *f; parliamentary* ~ städtischer Wahlkreis *m.*

bor-row ['bɔrəu] borgen, aus-, entleihen; '**bor-row-er** Entleiher(in); Kreditnehmer(in); '**bor-row-ing** Anleihe *f; gr.* Lehnwort *n,* -form *f.*

Bor-stal ['bɔːstl] Besserungsanstalt *f;* ~ *training* Fürsorgeerziehung *f.*

bos-cage ['bɔskidʒ] Gebüsch *n.*

bosh F [bɔʃ] Blödsinn *m,* Quatsch *m.*

bos-om ['buzəm] Busen *m;* Brust *f; fig.* Schoß *m,* Herz *n,* Inneres *n;* ~-*friend* Busenfreund(in).

boss[1] [bɔs] 1. Buckel *m,* Knopf *m;* Schlußstein *m;* 2. bossieren, treiben.

boss[2] F [~] 1. Boß *m,* Chef *m;* (Partei)Bonze *m;* 2. leiten; *sl.* kommandieren.

boss-y ['bɔsi] gebuckelt; *Am.* F herrisch, tyrannisch.

Bos-ton ['bɔstən] *langsamer Walzer.*

bo-tan-ic, bo-tan-i-cal □ [bə'tænik(əl)] botanisch; Pflanzen...; **bot-a-nist** ['bɔtənist] Botaniker(in); **bot-a-nize** ['~naiz] botanisieren; '**bot-a-ny** Botanik *f.*

botch [bɔtʃ] 1. Flicken *m;* Flickwerk *n,* -wort *n;* 2. (zs.-)flicken; verpfuschen; '**botch-er** Flicker(in); *fig. contp.* (Flick)Schuster *m.*

both [bəuθ] beide(s); ~ *... and* sowohl ... als (auch); ~ *of them* alle beide.

both-er F ['bɔðə] 1. Plage *f;* 2. (sich) plagen, (sich) quälen, (sich) aufregen, (sich) beunruhigen, (sich) Sorgen machen; ~ *it!* zum Henker damit!; **both-er-a-tion** F Plage *f;* ~*!* zum Henker!; **both-er-some** ['~səm] ärgerlich, lästig.

bot-tle ['bɔtl] 1. Flasche *f;* Bund *n (Heu);* 2. auf Flaschen ziehen; ~ *up* ✕ einschließen; *fig.* Zorn *etc.* zurückhalten, unterdrücken; ~*d beer* Flaschenbier *n;* **bottling** *plant* (Flaschen)Abfüllanlage *f;* '~-**green** flaschengrün; '~-**neck** *fig.* Engpaß *m,* Enge *f;* Schwierigkeit *f;* '~-**nose** Schnapsnase *f.*

bot-tom ['bɔtəm] 1. Boden *m;* Grund *m;* Grundfläche *f,* Sohle *f,* Fuß *m,* Ende *n; Stuhl*-Sitz *m;* unterster Platz *m in e-r Reihe etc.;* hinterster Teil *m e-s Gartens etc.;* Ankergrund *m;* Schiffsboden *m;* F Hintern *m; fig.* Grund *m der Seele,* Wesen *n,* Kern *m; at the* ~ am untersten Ende, ganz unten; *fig. a. at* ~ im Grunde; *get to the* ~ *of a matter* e-r Sache auf den

Grund gehen *od.* kommen; *jealousy is at the ~ of it* Eifersucht steckt dahinter; *knock the ~ out of an argument* ein Argument entkräften; **2.** grundlegend, Grund...; letzt; **3.** mit e-m Boden versehen; gründen (*upon* auf *acc.*); ergründen; 'bot·tom·less bodenlos; 'bottom·ry ⚓ Bodmerei *f.*

bou·doir ['bu:dwɑ:] Boudoir *n.*

bough [bau] Ast *m*, Zweig *m.*

bought [bɔ:t] *pret. u. p.p. von* buy.

bouil·lon ['bu:jɔ̃:ŋ] Kraftbrühe *f*, Bouillon *f.*

boul·der ['bəuldə] Geröllblock *m*; Findlingsblock *m.*

bou·le·vard ['bu:lvɑ:] Boulevard *m.*

bounce [bauns] **1.** *plötzlicher* Sprung *m*; Auf-, Rückprall *m*; F Aufschneiderei *f*; Auftrieb *m*, Schwung *m*; **2.** (hoch)springen; hüpfen; schnellen; F platzen (*Scheck*); F aufschneiden; F auszanken; ~ *in* (*out*) hinein- (hinaus)stürmen; ~ *s.o. out of s.th.* j. aus et. hinausdrängen; **3.** bums!, plauz!; 'bouncer F Mordskerl *m*, -weib *n*, -ding *n*; *Am. sl.* Rausschmeißer *m*; unverschämte Lüge *f*; 'bounc·ing F Mords...; stramm, drall.

bound[1] [baund] **1.** *pret. u. p.p. von* bind; **2.** *adj.* verpflichtet; *be ~ to do* tun müssen, sicher tun werden; *I will be ~* ich bürge dafür; *s.* bind.

bound[2] [~] bestimmt, unterwegs (*for* nach).

bound[3] [~] **1.** Grenze *f*, Schranke *f*; *within the ~s of reason* in den Grenzen der Vernunft; *out of ~s* Zutritt verboten (*to* für); **2.** begrenzen; beschränken.

bound[4] [~] **1.** Sprung *m*; **2.** (hoch-) springen; an-, abprallen.

bound·a·ry ['baundəri] Grenze *f*; ~ *line* Grenzlinie *f.*

boun·den ['baundən]: *my ~ duty* meine Pflicht u. Schuldigkeit.

bound·less □ ['baundlis] end-, grenzenlos, unbegrenzt.

boun·te·ous □ ['bauntiəs], bounti·ful □ ['~tiful] freigebig; reichlich.

boun·ty ['baunti] Freigebigkeit *f*, Großmut *f*; *milde* Gabe *f*, Spende *f bsd. des Königs*; ✝ Prämie *f.*

bou·quet [bu:'kei] Bukett *n*; Strauß *m*; Blume *f des Weines.*

bour·bon ['bə:bən] Bourbon *m* (*amerikanischer Maiswhisky*).

bour·geois[1] ['buəʒwɑ:] **1.** Bourgeois *m*; Spießbürger *m*; **2.** bourgeois; spießbürgerlich.

bour·geois[2] *typ.* [bə:'dʒɔis] Borgis *f.*

bour·geoi·sie [buəʒwɑ:'zi:] Bourgeoisie *f.*

bourn(e) *poet.* [buən] Grenze *f.*

bout [baut] Mal *n*; *Fecht*-Gang *m*; *Tanz*-Tour *f*; *Krankheits*-Anfall *m*; Kraftprobe *f*; Gelage *n.*

bou·tique [bu:'ti:k] Modegeschäft*n.*

bo·vine ['bəuvain] rinderartig; träge, stur, dumm.

bov·ril ['bɔvril] Fleischextrakt *m.*

bov·ver *sl.* ['bɔvə] Schlägerei *f*; ~-*boots pl. schwere Stiefel, mit denen Rocker aufeinander eintreten.*

bow[1] [bau] **1.** Verbeugung *f*; **2.** *v/i.* sich beugen; sich verbeugen, sich verneigen (*to* vor *dat.*); ~*ing acquaintance* bloße Grußbekanntschaft *f*; *v/t.* biegen; *mst fig.* beugen; ~ *s.o. in* (*out*) j. mit tiefen Verbeugungen empfangen (hinausführen).

bow[2] ⚓ [~] Bug *m.*

bow[3] [bəu] **1.** Bogen *m*; Bügel *m*; *gebundene* Schleife *f*, Knoten *m*; **2.** ♪ den Bogen führen; geigen.

bowd·ler·ize ['baudləraiz] *Text* von anstößigen Stellen reinigen.

bow·els ['bauəlz] *pl.* Eingeweide *n*; *das* Innere; *fig.* Herz *n.*

bow·er ['bauə] Laube *f*; *poet.* (*Schlaf*)Gemach *n*; ⚓ Buganker *m.*

bow·ie-knife ['bəuinaif] langes Jagdmesser *n.*

bow·ing ♪ ['bəuiŋ] Bogenführung *f.*

bowl[1] [bəul] Schale *f*, Napf *m*, Schüssel *f*; Bowle *f*; *Pfeifen*-Kopf *m*; Höhlung *f e-s Löffels etc.*

bowl[2] [~] **1.** Kugel *f*; ~*s pl.* Bowlingspiel *n*; **2.** *v/t.* Ball etc. werfen; ~ *out* hinauswerfen; ~ *over* umwerfen (*a. fig.*); *v/i.* rollen; kegeln.

bow-legged ['bəulegd] O-beinig.

bowl·er ['bəulə] *Kricket*: Werfer *m*; *a.*~ *hat* Melone *f* (*steifer Filzhut*).

bowl-fire ⚡ ['bəulfaiə] Heizsonne *f.*

bow·line ⚓ ['bəulin] Bulin(e) *f.*

bowl·ing ['bəuliŋ] Bowling(spiel) *n*; ~ al·ley Kegelbahn *f*; ~ green Rasenplatz *m* zum Bowlingspiel.

bow...: ~·man ['bəumən] Bogenschütze *m*; '~-sprit ⚓ Bugspriet *n*; '~-string Bogensehne *f*; ~ tie Fliege *f*, Schleife *f* (*Querbinder*).

bow-wow! ['bau'wau] wauwau!

box¹ [bɔks] **1.** Buchsbaum *m*; Büchse *f*, Dose *f*; Schachtel *f*, Kiste *f*, Kasten *m*; Koffer *m*; ⊕ Gehäuse *n*; *thea.* Loge *f*; Häuschen *n*; Abteilung *f*; Bank *f der Geschworenen*; *a.* ~ *seat* Kutschbock *m*; Box *f im Pferdestall*; **2.** in Kästen *etc.* tun *od.* einschließen; *a.* ~ *up fig.* einpferchen.

box² [~] **1.** boxen; ~ *s.o.'s ear* j. ohrfeigen; **2.** ~ *on the ear* Ohrfeige *f*; '~-**calf** Boxkalf *n* (*Kalbleder*); '~-**car** *bsd. Am.* geschlossener Güterwagen *m*; '**box-er** Boxer *m*.

Box·ing-Day ['bɔksiŋdei] zweiter Weihnachtsfeiertag *m*.

box...: '~-**keep·er** Logenschließer (-in); '~-**num·ber** Chiffre *f* (*in Zeitungsanzeigen*); '~-**of·fice** Theaterkasse *f*.

boy [bɔi] **1.** Junge *m*, junger Mann *m*; Bursche *m* (*a. Diener*); **2.** Knaben...; jung, jugendlich; ~-**friend** Freund *m* (*eines Mädchens*); ~ *scout* Pfadfinder *m*.

boy·cott ['bɔikɔt] **1.** boykottieren; **2.** Boykott *m*.

boy·hood ['bɔihud] Knabenalter *n*, Kindheit *f*.

boy·ish □ ['bɔiiʃ] Knaben..., knaben-, jungenhaft; kindisch.

bra F [brɑ:] = *brassière.*

brace [breis] **1.** ⊕ Strebe *f*, Stütze *f*, Anker *m*; Stützbalken *m*; Bohrwinde *f*; Klammer *f*, *a. typ.* Akkolade *f*; *hunt.* Paar *n* (*Wild, Geflügel*); ⚓ Brasse *f*; ~s *pl.* Tragbänder *n/pl.*; Hosenträger *m/pl.*; **2.** stützen; versteifen; verankern; (an)spannen; ⚓ brassen; *fig.* stärken, erfrischen.

brace·let ['breislit] Armband *n*.

brac·ing ['breisiŋ] kräftigend, erfrischend (*Klima etc.*).

brack·en ♀ ['brækən] Farnkraut *n*.

brack·et ['brækit] **1.** ⚓ Kragstein *m*, Konsole *f*; Winkelstütze *f*; *typ.* Klammer *f*; *Leuchter-, Gas-Arm m*; ⚓ Klampe *f*; *lower income* ~ niedrige Einkommensstufe *f*; **2.** einklammern; *fig.* gleichstellen.

brack·ish ['brækiʃ] brackig, salzig.

bract ♀ [brækt] Deckblatt *n*.

brad [bræd] Drahtstift *m*.

brae *schott.* [brei] (Ab)Hang *m*.

brag [bræg] **1.** Prahlerei *f*; **2.** prahlen (*of, about* mit).

brag·gart ['brægət] **1.** Prahler *m*; **2.** □ prahlerisch.

Brahm·an ['brɑ:mən], *mst* **Brahmin** ['~min] **1.** Brahmane *m*; **2.** brahmanisch.

braid [breid] **1.** *Haar*-Flechte *f*; Borte *f*; Litze *f*; ✂ Tresse *f*; **2.** flechten; mit Borte *etc.* besetzen.

brail ⚓ [breil] Geitau *n*.

braille [breil] Blindenschrift *f*.

brain [brein] **1.** Gehirn *n*, Hirn *n*; ~s *pl. fig.* Kopf *m*, Köpfchen *n*, Verstand *m*; *have s.th. on the* ~ nur Gedanken für etwas haben; *pick od. suck s.o.'s* ~ F j-m die Würmer aus der Nase ziehen; j-s Ideen stehlen; *turn s.o.'s* ~ j. eingebildet machen; **2.** *j-m* den Schädel einschlagen; '~-**child** Geistesprodukt *n*; ~ **drain** Abwanderung *f* der Intelligenz; **brained** ...köpfig.

brain...: '~-**fag** geistige Erschöpfung *f*; '~-**fe·ver** Gehirnentzündung *f*; '~-**less** hirnlos; *fig.* unbesonnen; '~-**pan** Hirnschale *f*; '~-**storm·ing** Ideen-Konferenz *f*;

brain(s) trust *Am.* Expertenrat *m*, Beratergruppe *f* (*mst pol.*).

brain...: '~-**twist·er** Denkaufgabe *f*; harte Nuß *f*; '~-**wash** e-r Gehirnwäsche unterziehen; '~-**wash·ing** Gehirnwäsche *f*; '~-**wave** F Geistesblitz *m*, genialer Einfall *m*; '~-**work** Kopfarbeit *f*; '**brain·y** gescheit.

braise [breiz] *Küche:* schmoren, dünsten.

brake¹ [breik] Farnkraut *n*; Dickicht *n*, Unterholz *n*.

brake² [~] **1.** ⊕ Bremse *f* (*a. fig.*); Kremser *m*; Wagen *m zum Einfahren der Pferde*; ~ *fluid mot.* Bremsflüssigkeit *f*; ~ *pedal* Bremspedal *n*; **2.** bremsen; **brake(s)·man** 🚂 ['~(s)mən] Bremser *m*; *Am.* Schaffner *m*; '**brak·ing** Brems...; ~ *distance* Bremsweg *m*.

bram·ble ♀ ['bræmbl] Brombeerstrauch *m*; '**bram·bly** dornig.

bran [bræn] Kleie *f*.

branch [brɑ:ntʃ] **1.** Zweig *m*, Ast *m*; Arm *m*; Fach *n*; Dezernat *n*; Linie *f des Stammbaums*; Abkömmling *m*; Teil *m*; *a. local* ~ Zweigstelle *f*, Filiale *f*; Ortsgruppe *f*; *chief of* ~ Dezernent *m*; **2.** *a.* ~ *out* (sich) verzweigen; *a.* ~ *off* abzweigen; '**branch·ing** ⚡ Abzweigung *f*;

'**branch-line** 🚃 Nebenlinie *f*; **branch of·fice** Zweigstelle *f*, Filiale *f*; '**branch·y** zweigig.

brand [brænd] **1.** (Feuer)Brand *m*; ♀ Brand *m*; Brandzeichen *n*, -mal *n*; *a.* ⁓*ing iron* Brand-, Brenneisen *n*; Marke *f*; Sorte *f*; Fabrikzeichen *n*; *poet.* Schwert *n*; ⁓ *name* Markenname *m*; **2.** einbrennen; mit e-m Brandzeichen versehen; brandmarken.

bran·dish ['brændiʃ] schwingen.

bran(d)·new ['bræn(d)'nju:] nagelneu.

bran·dy ['brændi] Kognak *m*; Weinbrand *m*; Branntwein *m*; Schnaps *m*; '⁓**-ball** Kognakbohne *f*.

brant *orn.* [brænt] Wildgans *f*.

brash *contp.* [bræʃ] ungestüm; unverfroren; unüberlegt.

brass [brɑːs] Messing *n*; F (Kupfer-) Geld *n*; *fig.* Unverschämtheit *f*; *the* ⁓ ♪ die Blechbläser *m/pl.*; ⁓ *band* Blaskapelle *f*; ⁓ *hat* ✗ *sl.* Stabsoffizier *m*, hohes Tier *n*; ⁓ *knuckles pl. Am.* Schlagring *m*; ⁓ *tacks pl. sl.* die Hauptsache; *get down to* ⁓ *tacks* zur Sache kommen.

bras·sard ['bræsɑːd] Armbinde *f*.

bras·se·rie [brɑːsə'riː] Restaurant *n* (mit Bierausschank).

bras·sière ['bræsiə] Büstenhalter *m*.

bras·sy ['brɑːsi] messingartig; *fig.* unverschämt.

brat F [bræt] *contp.* Balg *m*, Range *f*.

bra·va·do [brə'vɑːdəu], *pl.* ⁓(e)**s** herausforderndes Benehmen *n*.

brave [breiv] **1.** □ brav, tapfer, mutig, kühn; großartig, prächtig; **2.** trotzen; mutig begegnen (*dat.*); **3.** indianischer Krieger *m*; '**brav·⁓ er·y** Tapferkeit *f*; Pracht *f*.

bra·vo ['brɑː'vəu] bravo!

brawl [brɔːl] **1.** Krakeel *m*, Krawall *m*; **2.** krakeelen, Krawall machen, lärmen, zanken; '**brawl·er** Krakeeler(in).

brawn [brɔːn] *Art* Sülze *f*; Muskeln *m/pl.*; *fig.* Muskelkraft *f*; '**brawn- i·ness** Muskelkraft *f*; '**brawn·y** muskulös.

bray¹ [brei] **1.** Eselsschrei *m*; Schmettern *n*, Dröhnen *n*; **2.** schreien (*Esel*); schmettern; dröhnen.

bray² [⁓] (zer)stoßen, kleinreiben.

braze ⊕ [breiz] hartlöten.

bra·zen □ ['breizn] **1.** bronzen; metallisch; *a.* ⁓**-faced** unverschämt; **2.** ⁓ *it out* es kaltschnäuzig durch-

stehen; '**bra·zen·ness** Unverschämtheit *f*.

bra·zier ['breizjə] Kupferschmied *m*; Kohlenpfanne *f*.

Bra·zil·ian [brə'ziljən] **1.** brasil(ian)isch; **2.** Brasil(an)er(in).

Bra·zil-nut [brə'zil'nʌt] Paranuß *f*.

breach [briːtʃ] **1.** Bruch *m*; *fig.* Verletzung *f*; ✗ Bresche *f*; ⁓ *of contract* Vertragsbruch *m*; ⁓ *of duty* Verletzung *f* der Amtspflicht; ⁓ *of peace* Friedensbruch *m*; **2.** eine Bresche schlagen in (*acc.*); durchbrechen.

bread [bred] Brot *n* (*a. Lebensunterhalt*); ⁓ *and butter* Butterbrot *n*; *take the* ⁓ *out of s.o.'s mouth* j-m sein Brot nehmen; *know which side one's* ⁓ *is buttered* s-n Vorteil (er)kennen; '⁓**-bas·ket** Brotkorb *m*; '⁓**-crumb 1.** Brotkrume *f*; **2.** panieren; '⁓**-fruit** ♀ Brotfrucht *f*; '⁓**-grains** *pl.* Brotgetreide *n*; '⁓**-line** Schlange *f* von Bedürftigen (*an die Lebensmittel verteilt werden*).

breadth [bredθ] Breite *f*, Weite *f*; Bahn *f* (*Stoff*); *fig.* Größe *f*; Großzügigkeit *f*.

bread-win·ner ['bredwinə] Ernährer *m* e-r *Familie*.

break [breik] **1.** Bruch *m*; Lücke *f*; Pause *f*, Unterbrechung *f*; Wechsel *m*, Umschwung *m*; *typ.* Absatz *m*; ✝ *Am.* (Preis)Rückgang *m*; Kremser *m*; Wagen *m zum Einfahren der Pferde*; Anbruch *m* (*of day des Tages*); *Billard:* Serie *f*; *a bad* ⁓ F e-e Dummheit *f*; Pech *n*; *a lucky* ⁓ Glück *n*; *give s.o. a* ⁓ F j-m e-e Chance geben; **2.** (*irr.*) *v/t.* (zer)brechen; unterbrechen; ∮ abausschalten; übertreten; abrichten; *Bank* sprengen; *Brief, Tür* erbrechen; zerschlagen; zerreißen; *Stück* abbrechen; *Vorrat* anbrechen; *Nachricht* schonend mitteilen; ∮ umbrechen; ruinieren; ⁓ *a leg! sl.* Hals- und Beinbruch!; ⁓ *down* niederbrechen, niederschlagen; ⁓ *in* einbrechen; abrichten, einfahren, zureiten; gewöhnen (*to an acc.*); ⁓ *up* entzwei-, zerbrechen; auflösen; entlassen; *Schule* schließen; *v/i.* (zer)brechen; bersten; sich brechen (*Wellen*); aus-, losbrechen; anbrechen; aufbrechen; hervorbrechen; umschlagen (*Wetter*); ⁓ *away* sich losreißen; abfallen; sich zerteilen; ~ down zs.-brechen; steckenbleiben; e-e Panne haben; versagen; durchfallen (*beim Examen*); ~ *into a run* sich in Lauf setzen; ~ *up* schließen (*Schule*); *s. a.* broken; '**break·a·ble** zerbrechlich; '**break·age** Zerbrechen *n*; Bruch *m*; Bruchstelle *f*; '**break-down** Zs.-bruch *m*; Maschinenschaden *m*; *mot.* Panne *f*; *nervous* ~ Nervenzusammenbruch *m*; ~ *lorry*, ~ *truck* Abschleppwagen *m*; ~ *service* Pannendienst *m*; '**break·er** Brecher(in) *etc.* (*s.* break 2); ~*s pl.* Brandung *f.*

break...: ~**fast** ['brekfəst] 1. Frühstück *n*; ~ *television* Fernsehen *n* am frühen Morgen; *have* ~ = 2. frühstücken; ~**neck** ['breiknek] halsbrecherisch; '~**out** Ausbruch *m*; '~**-through** ✗ Durchbruch *m*; '~'**up** Verfall *m*; Auflösung *f*; Schulschluß *m*; (Wetter)Umschlag *m*; '~**wa·ter** Wellenbrecher *m.*

bream *ichth.* [bri:m] Brassen *m.*

breast [brest] 1. Brust *f*; Busen *m*; Herz *n*; *make a clean* ~ *of s.th.* et. offen gestehen; 2. ankämpfen gegen; trotzen (*dat.*); '**breast·ed** ...brüstig.

breast...: '~**feed** Säugling stillen; '~**-pin** Busennadel *f*; '~**plate** Brustharnisch *m*; '~**stroke** Brustschwimmen *n*; '~**work** ✗ Brustwehr *f.*

breath [breθ] Atem *m*; Atemzug *m*; Hauch *m*; *bad* ~ übler Mundgeruch *m*; *under od. below one's* ~ flüsternd; *out of* ~ atemlos, außer Atem; *waste one's* ~ s-e Worte verschwenden.

breath·a·lys·er ['breθəlaizə] Alkoholtestgerät *n*, ‚Röhrchen' *n.*

breathe [bri:ð] atmen; Atem holen; *fig.* leben; *v/t.* (aus-, ein)atmen; hauchen; leise äußern; verschnaufen lassen; '**breath·er** Atemübung *f*; Atempause *f*; Strapaze *f.*

breath·ing ['bri:ðiŋ] 1. lebenstreu (*Porträt*); 2. Atmen *n*; Hauch *m*; '~**space**, ~**time** (Atem)Pause *f.*

breath·less □ ['breθlis] atemlos; '**breath·less·ness** Atemlosigkeit *f.*

breath-tak·ing ['breθteikiŋ] atemberaubend. [2.)

bred [bred] *pret. u. p.p. von* breed)

breech ⊕ [bri:tʃ] Verschluß *m am Gewehr od. Geschütz*; **breech·es** ['britʃiz] *pl.* Knie-, Reithosen *f/pl.*; F Hosen *f/pl.*; *she wears the* ~ sie

hat die Hosen an; '**breech·es-buoy** ⚓ Hosenboje *f*; **breech-load·er** ['bri:tʃləudə] Hinterlader *m.*

breed [bri:d] 1. Brut *f*, Zucht *f*; Rasse *f*; Herkunft *f*; Art *f*, Schlag *m*; 2. (*irr.*) *v/t.* erzeugen; auf-, erziehen; züchten; *v/i.* sich fortpflanzen; sich vermehren; '**breed·er** Erzeuger(in); Züchter(in); *phys.* Brutreaktor *m*; '**breed·ing** Erziehung *f*; Bildung *f*; Zucht *f von Tieren*; ~ *ground* Brutstätte *f.*

breeze¹ [bri:z] 1. Brise *f*, leichter Wind *m*; F Streit *m*; 2. ~ *in* F hereingeschneit kommen.

breeze² ⊕ [~] Kohlenlösche *f*; ~ *block* Leichtbaustein *m*; ~ *concrete* Leichtbeton *m.*

breez·y ['bri:zi] windig, luftig; frisch, flott, lebhaft.

Bren gun ✗ ['bren'gʌn] leichtes Maschinengewehr *n.*

brent-goose *orn.* ['brent'gu:s] Ringelgans *f.*

breth·ren *eccl.* ['breðrin] *pl.* Brüder *m/pl.*

breve [bri:v] Kürzezeichen *n* (*über Vokalen*).

bre·vet ✗ ['brevit] Brevet *n* (*höherer Rang ohne entsprechenden Sold*); ~ *rank* Titularrang *m*; ~ *major* Hauptmann *m im Rang e-s Majors.*

bre·vi·ar·y *eccl.* ['bri:vjəri] Brevier *n.*

brev·i·ty ['breviti] Kürze *f.*

brew [bru:] 1. *v/t. u. v/i.* brauen; zubereiten; *fig.* anzetteln; *v/i.* sich zs.-brauen, im Anzug sein (*Sturm, Gewitter*); 2. Gebräu *n*; '**brew·age** *lit.* Gebräu *n*; '**brew·er** Brauer *m*; '**brew·er·y** Brauerei *f.*

bri·ar ['braiə] = brier¹ *u.* brier².

brib·a·ble ['braibəbl] bestechlich; **bribe** 1. Bestechung(sgeld *n*, -sgeschenk *n*) *f*; 2. bestechen, verlocken (*to zu*); '**brib·er** Bestecher(in); '**brib·er·y** Bestechung *f.*

bric-a-brac ['brikəbræk] Nippsachen *f/pl.*

brick [brik] 1. Back-, Ziegelstein *m*; (Bau)Klotz *m*; *a regular* ~ F ein Prachtkerl *m*; *drop a* ~ F ins Fettnäpfchen treten; *make* ~*s without straw* et. Schwieriges versuchen; 2. mit Backsteinen mauern; '~**bat** Ziegelbrocken *m*; '~**kiln** Ziegelofen *m*; '~**lay·er** Maurer *m*; '~**works** *sg.* Ziegelei *f.*

brid·al ['braidl] **1.** □ bräutlich; Braut...; ~ *procession* Brautzug *m*; **2.** *mst poet.* Hochzeit *f*.

bride [braid] Braut *f* (*am Hochzeitstage, oft auch kurz vorher oder nachher*), Neuvermählte *f*; '~·**groom** Bräutigam *m*, Neuvermählte *m*; '**brides·maid** Brautjungfer *f*; **brides·man** ['~zmən] Brautführer *m*; **bride-to-**'be zukünftige Braut *f*.

bride·well ['braidwəl] Arbeitshaus *n*.

bridge[1] [bridʒ] **1.** Brücke *f* (*a.* ⚓); Steg *m* (*der Violine*); **2.** eine Brücke schlagen über (*acc.*); *fig.* überbrücken.

bridge[2] [~] Bridge *n* (*Kartenspiel*). **bridge...:** '~·**head** Brückenkopf *m*; '~·**work** Brücke *f* (*Zahnersatz*).

bri·dle ['braidl] **1.** Zaum *m*; Zügel *m*; **2.** *v/t.* (auf)zäumen; zügeln; *v/i. a.* ~ *up* den Kopf aufwerfen; '~·**path**, '~·**road** Reitweg *m*.

bri·doon [bri'duːn] Trense *f*.

brief [briːf] **1.** □ kurz, knapp, bündig; flüchtig; **2.** Auftrag *m* und schriftliche Instruktion *f* an den plädierenden Anwalt; *weitS.* Mandat *n*; *päpstliches* Breve *n*; ✝ Einsatzbesprechung *f*, Befehlsausgabe *f*; *hold a* ~ *for* einstehen für; *take a* ~ e-e Sache übernehmen; **3.** ⚖ Anwalt, *a.* ✗ beauftragen und informieren; '~·**bag**, '~·**case** Aktenmappe *f*; '**brief·ness** Kürze *f*.

bri·er[1] ♀ ['braiə] Dorn-, Hagebuttenstrauch *m*, wilde Rose *f*.

bri·er[2] [~] *a.* ~ *pipe* Bruyèrepfeife *f*.

brig ⚓ [brig] Brigg *f*.

bri·gade ✗ [bri'geid] **1.** Brigade *f*; **2.** zu einer Brigade vereinigen; **brig·a·dier** [brigə'diə] Brigadekommandeur *m*, -general *m*.

brig·and ['brigənd] Brigant *m*; '**brig·and·age** Brigantentum *n*; Räuberei *f*.

bright □ [brait] hell, leuchtend, glänzend, klar; blank; heiter; lebhaft; gescheit, klug, aufgeweckt; '**bright·en** *v/t.* auf-, erhellen; polieren; aufheitern; *v/i. a.* ~ *up* sich aufhellen; '**bright·ness** Helligkeit *f*; Glanz *m*, Helle *f*; Klarheit *f*; Heiterkeit *f*; Aufgewecktheit *f*; ~ *control Fernsehen*: Helligkeitsregler *m*.

brill *ichth.* [bril] Glattbutt *m*.

bril·liance, bril·lian·cy ['briljəns(i)] Glanz *m*; *fig.* Intelligenz *f*; '**bril-**

liant 1. □ glänzend, strahlend; prächtig; brillant; ausgezeichnet; hochbegabt; **2.** Brillant *m*.

brim [brim] **1.** Rand *m*; Krempe *f*; **2.** bis zum Rande füllen *od.* voll sein; ~ *over* überfließen (*a. fig.*), über den Rand treten; '~·'**ful**, '~-'**full** ganz voll; '~·**less** ohne Rand.

brim·stone ['brimstən] Schwefel *m*; ~ **but·ter·fly** *zo.* Zitronenfalter *m*.

brin·dle(d) ['brindl(d)] scheckig.

brine [brain] **1.** Salzwasser *n*, Sole *f*; *poet.* Meer *n*; **2.** (ein)salzen.

bring [briŋ] (*irr.*) bringen; tragen; *j.* veranlassen; *Klage* erheben; *Grund etc.* vorbringen; ~ *about*, ~ *to pass* zustande bringen, herbeiführen; ~ *along* mitbringen; ~ *down Preise* herabsetzen; ~ *down the house thea.* stürmischen Beifall ernten; ~ *forth* hervorbringen; gebären; ~ *forward* fördern; anführen; zitieren; ✝ übertragen; ~ *home to j.* überzeugen; *j-m et.* klarmachen *od.* nahebringen; ~ *in* (hin)einbringen; *Gewinn* bringen; ~ *in guilty* für schuldig erklären; ~ *off* zustande bringen; durchführen; ~ *on* herbeiführen; ~ *out* in die Gesellschaft einführen; herausbringen; veröffentlichen; vorbringen; ~ *round* wieder zu sich bringen; ~ *s.o. to do j.* dahin bringen, daß er tut; ~ *o.s. to do es* fertigbringen zu tun; ~ *to* ⚓ beidrehen; ~ *s.o. to himself* j. wieder zu sich bringen; ~ *under* unterwerfen; ~ *up* herauf-, *fig.* vorbringen; zur Sprache bringen; auf-, erziehen; erbrechen, ausspeien; innehalten lassen; *bsd.* ⚓ die Reise beenden.

bring·er ['briŋə] Überbringer(in).

brink [briŋk] Rand *m*; '~·**man·ship** Politik *f* des äußersten Risikos.

brin·y ['braini] salzig.

bri·quette [bri'ket] Brikett *n*.

brisk [brisk] **1.** □ lebhaft, munter, lebendig; frisch (drauflosgehend); rasch, flink; belebend, frisch; **2.** *mst* ~ *up* (sich) beleben.

bris·ket ['briskit] Bruststück *n* e-s Tieres. [keit *f*.]

brisk·ness ['brisknis] Lebhaftig-]

bris·tle ['brisl] **1.** Borste *f*; **2.** *oft* ~ *up* (sich) sträuben; hochfahren, zornig *od.* borstig werden (*with* vor *dat.*); ~ *with fig.* starren *od.* strotzen von; '**bris·tled**, '**bris·tly** gesträubt; borstig, struppig.

Bri·tan·nic ['bri'tænik] britannisch.

Brit·ish ['britiʃ] britisch; *the* ~ *pl.* die Briten *pl.*; '**Brit·ish·er** *bsd. Am.* Einwohner(in) Großbritanniens.

Brit·on *hist., poet.* ['britn] Brite *m.*

brit·tle ['britl] zerbrechlich, spröde; *fig.* reizbar; '**brit·tle·ness** Sprödigkeit *f etc.*

broach [brəutʃ] **1.** Bratspieß *m*; ⊕ Stecheisen *n*; Räumnadel *f*; **2.** Faß anzapfen, anstechen; vorbringen; *Thema* anschneiden.

broad □ [brɔ:d] breit; weit; hell (*Tag*); deutlich (*Wink etc.*); (zu) frei, derb (*Witz*); allgemein; weitherzig, liberal; breit (*Aussprache*); '~-**axe** ⊕ Breitbeil *n*, Zimmeraxt *f*; '~-'**brimmed** breitrandig; '~-**cast 1.** ✗ breitwürfig; *fig.* weitverbreitet; **2.** (*irr. cast*) *v/t.* ✗ breitwürfig säen; *fig.* weit verbreiten; *Radio:* senden, übertragen; *v/i.* senden; ~**ing station** Rundfunkstation *f*; ~**ing** Rundfunk(sendung *f*) *m*; '~-**cast·er** Rundfunksprecher(in); '~-**cloth** feiner Wollstoff *m*; '**broad·en** (sich) verbreitern; (sich) erweitern; '**broad**'**mind·ed** weitherzig, großzügig; '**broad·ness** Plumpheit *f*, Gemeinheit *f der Sprache*.

broad···: '~-**sheet** Flugblatt *n*; '~-**side** ⚓ Breitseite *f* (*a.* ✗ *u. fig.*); *a.* = *broadsheet*; '~-**sword** Pallasch *m.*

bro·cade [brəu'keid] Brokat *m*; **bro'cad·ed** brokaten, aus Brokat.

broc·co·li ♀ ['brɔkəli] Brokkoli *pl.*, Spargelkohl *m.*

bro·chure [brəu'ʃjuə] Broschüre *f.*

brogue [brəug] derber Schuh *m*; (*bsd.* irische) Mundart *f.*

broi·der ['brɔidə] = *embroider*.

broil [brɔil] **1.** Lärm *m*, Streit *m*; **2.** auf dem Rost braten; *fig.* in der Sonne braten; *fig.* kochen; ~**ing** glühend heiß; '**broil·er** Bratrost *m*; Brathühnchen *n.*

broke [brəuk] **1.** *pret. von break* 2; **2.** *sl.* pleite, ohne einen Pfennig.

bro·ken ['brəukən] *p.p. von break* 2; ~ *health* zerrüttete Gesundheit *f*; ~ *home* gestörte häusliche Verhältnisse *n/pl.*; ~ *stones pl.* Steinschlag *m*, Schotter *m*; ~ *time* Verdienstausfall *m*; *speak* ~ *English* gebrochen Englisch sprechen; '~-'**heart·ed** mit

gebrochenem Herzen; '**bro·ken·ly** gebrochen; mit Unterbrechungen; ruckweise; '**bro·ken-**'**wind·ed** *vet.* kurzatmig.

bro·ker ['brəukə] Zwangsversteigerer *m*; ✝ Makler *m*; Agent *m*; '**bro·ker·age** ✝ Maklergeschäft *n*; Maklergebühr *f.*

bro·king ✝ ['brəukiŋ] Maklergeschäft *n.*

bro·mide ['brəumaid] 🜛 Bromid *n*; *sl.* Binsenwahrheit *f*; **bro·mine** 🜛 ['~mi:n] Brom *n.*

bron·chi·al *anat.* ['brɔŋkjəl] Bronchial···; **bron·chi·tis** ✗ [brɔŋ-'kaitis] Bronchitis *f.*

bron·co ['brɔŋkəu] (halb)wildes Pferd *n*; ~-**bust·er** *sl.* ['~bʌstə] Zureiter *m.*

Bronx cheer *Am.* ['brɔŋks'tʃiə] *verächtliches* Zischen *n.*

bronze [brɔnz] **1.** Bronze *f*; **2.** bronzen, Bronze···; **3.** bronzieren; *fig.* bräunen; ♀ **Age** Bronzezeit *f.*

brooch [brəutʃ] Brosche *f*; Spange *f.*

brood [bru:d] **1.** Brut *f*; Schwarm *m*; *attr.* Zucht···, *z. B.* ~ *hen*, ~ *sow, etc.* Zuchthenne *f*, -sau *f etc.*; **2.** brüten (*a. fig.*); nachdenken; '**brood·er** *Am.* Brutkasten *m.*

brook[1] [bruk] Bach *m.*

brook[2] *rhet.* [~] *mst verneint:* *et.* vertragen; *the matter* ~*s no delay* die Sache gestattet keinen Aufschub.

brook·let ['bruklit] Bächlein *n.*

broom ♀ [bru:m] Ginster *m*; [brum] Besen *m*; ~**stick** ['brumstik] Besenstiel *m.*

broth [brɔθ] Fleisch-, Kraftbrühe *f.*

broth·el ['brɔθl] Bordell *n.*

broth·er ['brʌðə] Bruder *m*; ~(*s*) *and sister(s)* Geschwister *pl.*; '~-**hood** ['~hud] Bruderschaft *f*; '~-**-in-law** Schwager *m*; '**broth·er·ly** brüderlich.

brougham ['bru:əm] Brougham *m* (*zweisitziger Wagen*).

brought [brɔ:t] *pret. u. p.p. von bring*; ~-*in capital* Geschäftseinlage *f.*

brow [brau] (Augen)Braue *f*; Stirn *f*; Kante *f e-s Steilhanges*; Abhang *m*; Vorsprung *m*; '~-**beat** (*irr. beat*) einschüchtern; tyrannisieren.

brown [braun] **1.** braun; ~ *ale* mildes, dunkles Ale *n*; ~ *bread* Schwarzbrot *n*; ~ *paper* Packpapier *n*; *be in a* ~ *study* in

Gedanken versunken sein; 2. Braun *n*; **3.** (sich) bräunen; *~ed off sl.* gelangweilt; restlos bedient; **brown·ie** [ˈ~ni] Heinzelmännchen *n*; Pfadfinderin *f* (*8–11 Jahre alt*); **'brown·ish** bräunlich; **'brown·ness** Bräune *f* (*Farbe*); **'brown·stone** *Am.* **1.** rotbrauner Sandstein *m*; **2.** wohlhabend.

browse [brauz] **1.** Grasen *n*; *fig.* Schmökern *n*; **2.** grasen, weiden; *fig.* naschen (*on* von); schmökern.

Bru·in [ˈbruːin] Braun *m*, Petz *m* (*der Bär*).

bruise [bruːz] **1.** Quetschung *f*, blauer Fleck *m*; **2.** *v/t.* (zer)quetschen; *Malz* schroten; *v/i.* blaue Flecke bekommen; **'bruis·er** *sl.* Boxer *m*.

brunch [brʌntʃ] ausgedehntes, spätes Frühstück *n*.

bru·nette [bruːˈnet] **1.** Brünette *f*; **2.** brünett.

brunt [brʌnt] Hauptstoß *m*, (volle) Wucht *f*; *das Schwerste; bear the ~* die Hauptlast tragen.

brush [brʌʃ] **1.** Bürste *f*; großer Pinsel *m*; Rute *f des Fuchses*; *⚔* Strahlenbündel *n*; Scharmützel *n*; Unterholz *n*, Gestrüpp *n*; *give a ~* abbürsten; *have a ~ with s.o.* mit j-m aneinandergeraten; **2.** *v/t.* (ab-, aus)bürsten, abkehren; streifen (*leicht berühren*); *~ aside fig.* beiseite schieben; *~ away, ~ off et.* abbürsten; *~ down j.* abbürsten; *~ off j.* abblitzen lassen, abweisen; *~ up* wieder aufbürsten, *fig.* auffrischen; *v/i.* bürsten; *a. ~ away, ~ off* (davon)stürzen, (davon)eilen; *~ against s.o.* j. streifen; gegen j. laufen; *~ by od. past* vorbeisausen, -rennen (an *dat*); **'~·wood** Gestrüpp *n*, Unterholz *n*.

brusque □ [brusk] brüsk, barsch, schroff.

Brus·sels sprouts ♀ [ˈbrʌslˈsprauts] *pl.* Rosenkohl *m*.

bru·tal □ [ˈbruːtl] viehisch; brutal, roh, gemein; **bru·tal·i·ty** [~ˈtæliti] Brutalität *f*, Roheit *f*; **bru·tal·ize** [ˈ~təlaiz] zum Tier machen; brutal behandeln; **brute 1.** tierisch, viehisch; unvernünftig, dumm; gefühllos, roh; **2.** (unvernünftiges) Vieh *n* (*a. fig. roher Mensch*); F Untier *n*, Scheusal *n*; **'brut·ish** □ = *brute 1*; **'brut·ish·ness** Roheit *f*; Dummheit *f*.

bub·ble [ˈbʌbl] **1.** Blase *f*; *fig.* Sei-

fenblase *f*; Schwindel *m*; **2.** sieden; sprudeln; *~* **gum** Bubble-Gum *m*, Knallkaugummi *m*; **'bub·bly 1.** sprudelnd, schäumend; **2.** *co.* Schampus *m*, Sekt *m*.

buc·ca·neer [bʌkəˈniə] **1.** Seeräuber *m*; **2.** Seeräuberei treiben.

buck [bʌk] **1.** *zo.* (*bsd.* Reh)Bock *m*; Rammler *m* (*Hase*); Stutzer *m*; *Am. sl.* Dollar *m*; *pass the ~* F die Verantwortung von sich abschieben; **2.** bocken; *Am.* F dagegen sein; angehen gegen; *~ up* F sich zs.-reißen; sich beeilen; aufmuntern, in Schwung bringen.

bucket [ˈbʌkit] **1.** Eimer *m*, Kübel *m*; *a mere drop in the ~* ein Tropfen auf den heißen Stein; **2.** F *Pferd* abjagen; (dahin)rasen; *~·ful* [ˈ~ful] Eimervoll *m*; *~ seat mot.* Schalensitz *m*; **'~·shop** Winkelbörse *f*.

buck·le [ˈbʌkl] **1.** Schnalle *f*, Spange *f*; **2.** *v/t.* (an-, auf-, um-, zu)schnallen; *v/i.* ⊕ sich (ver)biegen; *~ to a task* sich ernsthaft an eine Aufgabe machen; **'buck·ler** Schild *m*.

buck·ram [ˈbʌkrəm] Steifleinen *n*; *fig.* Steifheit *f*.

buck...: '~·shot *hunt.* Rehposten *m*; **'~·skin** Wildleder *n*; Buckskin *m* (*Stoff*); **'~·wheat ♀** Buchweizen *m*.

bud [bʌd] **1.** Knospe *f*, Auge *n*; *fig.* Keim *m*; *Am.* Debütantin *f*; *in ~* in der Knospe; *nip in the ~ fig.* im Keim ersticken; **2.** *v/t.* okulieren; *v/i.* knospen, sprossen; *~ding lawyer etc.* angehender Jurist *m etc.*

Bud·dhism [ˈbudizəm] Buddhismus *m*; **'Bud·dhist** Buddhist(in).

bud·dy *Am.* F [ˈbʌdi] Kumpel *m*, Kamerad *m*.

budge [bʌdʒ] *v/i.* sich (von der Stelle) rühren; *v/t.* bewegen.

bud·ger·i·gar [ˈbʌdʒərigɑː] Wellensittich *m*.

budg·et [ˈbʌdʒit] Budget *n*, Staatshaushalt *m*, Haushaltsplan *m*; *mst fig.* Vorrat *m*, Menge *f*; *draft ~* Haushaltsplan *m*; *open the ~* das Budget vorlegen; **'budg·et·ar·y** Budget...

bud·gie F [ˈbʌdʒi] = *budgerigar*.

buff¹ [bʌf] **1.** Ochsenleder *n*; Lederfarbe *f*; *bloße Haut f; in (one's) ~ nackt*; **2.** lederfarben, blaßgelb.

buff² F [~] Fan *m*, ...narr *m*.

buf·fa·lo *zo.* [ˈbʌfələu], *pl.* **buf·fa-**

loes [ˈ‿z] Büffel *m*.
buff·er [ˈbʌfə] 🐟 Puffer *m*; *a*. ‿
stop Prellbock *m*; *old* ‿ *sl.* alter
Kauz *m*; ‿ *state* Pufferstaat *m*.
buf·fet[1] [ˈbʌfit] **1.** Puff *m*, Stoß *m*,
Schlag *m*; **2.** puffen, schlagen; ankämpfen gegen; kämpfen (*with
mit*).
buf·fet[2] [ˈbufei] Büfett *n*; Schank-
tisch *m*, Theke *f*; Tisch *m* mit
Speisen und Getränken; Erfrischungsraum *m*; ‿ *car* 🚃 Erfri-
schungswagen *m*.
buf·foon [bəˈfuːn] Possenreißer *m*;
buf'foon·er·y Possenreißerei *f*;
Possen *f/pl*.
bug [bʌg] *zo.* Wanze *f* (*sl. auch* Abhör-
gerät); *Am.* Käfer *m*, Insekt *n*; Bazillus
m; *Am. sl.* Defekt *m*, Fehler *m*; *big ‿ sl.*
hohes Tier *n*; ‿·**a·boo** [ˈ‿əbuː], ˈ‿·
bear Schreckbild *n*, Popanz *m*; ˈ**bug·
ger** ∨ Sodomit *m*; ∨ Scheißkerl *m*; ∨
Scheißding *n*; P Kerl *m*; *poor ‿!* armer
Kerl!; **bug·ging de·vice** Abhörgerät
n; ˈ**bug·gy** **1.** verwanzt; **2.** leichter
Einspänner *m*.
bu·gle[1] [ˈbjuːgl] Wald-, Signalhorn
n.
bu·gle[2] [‿] schwarze Glasperle *f*.
bu·gler ⚔ [ˈbjuːglə] Hornist *m*.
buhl [buːl] Einlege-, Boulearbeit *f*.
build [bild] **1.** (*irr.*) bauen; errichten; *fig.* bauen, sich verlassen (*on,
upon* auf *acc.*); ‿ *in* einbauen; ‿ *up*
ver-, zubauen; *be ‿ing* im Bau sein;
2. Bauart *f*; Schnitt *m*; ˈ**build·er**
Erbauer *m*, Baumeister *m*, -unter-
nehmer *m*; ˈ**build·ing** Erbauen *n*;
Bau *m*, Bauwerk *n*, Gebäude *n*; ‿
contractor Bauunternehmer *m*; ‿
craftsman Bauhandwerker *m*; ‿ *site*
Baustelle *f*; ‿ *society* Baugenossen-
schaft *f*; ‿ *trade* Baugewerbe *n*;
ˈ**build-up** Aufbau *m*; Reklame *f*.
built [bilt] **1.** *pret. u. p.p. von* build 1;
2. *adj.* ...gebaut; von ... Bau(art);
ˈ‿·ˈ**in** eingebaut, Einbau...; ˈ‿·ˈ**up**
a·re·a bebautes Gelände *n*.
bulb [bʌlb] ♣ Zwiebel *f*, Knolle *f*;
Kugel *f des Thermometers etc.*;
(Glüh)Birne *f*; ˈ**bulb·ous** ♣ knollig.
Bul·gar [ˈbʌlgɑː] Bulgare *m*, Bulga-
rin *f*; **Bul·gar·i·an** [‿ˈgɛəriən]
1. bulgarisch; **2.** Bulgare *m*, Bulga-
rin *f*.
bulge [bʌldʒ] **1.** (Aus)Bauchung *f*;
Anschwellung *f*; Beule *f*; Vorsprung *m*; **2.** sich (aus)bauchen;

(an-, auf)schwellen; hervorquellen.
bulk [bʌlk] Umfang *m*, Größe *f*;
Masse *f*; Hauptteil *m*, -masse *f*;
⚓ Ladung *f*; *in ‿* lose; *in großer
Menge*; ‿ *buying* Großeinkauf *m*; ‿
goods pl. lose Waren *f/pl.*; ˈ‿·**head**
⚓ Schott *n*; ˈ**bulk·i·ness** (großer)
Umfang *m*; ˈ**bulk·y** (sehr) umfangreich, dick; unhandlich; ⓥ sperrig.
bull[1] [bul] **1.** Bulle *m*, Stier *m*; ✝ *sl.*
Haussier *m*; *a ‿ in a china shop* ein
Elefant im Porzellanladen; *take the
‿ by the horns* den Stier bei den
Hörnern packen; ‿ *session Am. sl.*
Herrengesellschaft *f*; **2.** ✝ *sl.* auf
Hausse spekulieren; *die Kurse*
treiben.
bull[2] [‿] *päpstliche* Bulle *f*.
bull[3] [‿] Schnitzer *m*, grober Fehler
m; *oft Irish ‿* Quatsch *m*, Unsinn *m*.
bull-bait·ing [ˈbulbeitiŋ] Stier-
hetze *f*.
bull·dog [ˈbuldɔg] Bulldogge *f*;
F *univ.* Helfer *m* des *Proctor*.
bull·doze *Am.* F [ˈbuldəuz] terrorisieren; ˈ**bull·doz·er** Planierraupe *f*,
Bulldozer *m*.
bul·let [ˈbulit] Kugel *f*, Geschoß *n*
e-r Handfeuerwaffe.
bul·le·tin [ˈbulitin] Tagesbericht *m*;
Bekanntmachungsblatt *n*; ‿ *board
Am.* Schwarzes Brett *n* (*für Anschläge*).
bul·let-proof [ˈbulitpruːf] kugel-
sicher.
bull...: ˈ‿·**fight** Stierkampf *m*; ˈ‿·
finch *orn.* Dompfaff *m*; Hecke *f*;
ˈ‿·**frog** *zo.* Ochsenfrosch *m*.
bul·lion [ˈbuljən] Gold-, Silber-
barren *m*; ungemünztes Gold *n od.*
Silber *n*; Gold-, Silberlitze *f*.
bull·ock [ˈbulək] Ochse *m*.
bull·pen *Am.* [ˈbulpen] F *Unter-
suchungs*-Haftraum *m*; *Baseball*:
Platz *m* zum Üben u. Warmlaufen.
bull's-eye [ˈbulzai] ⚓ Bullauge *n*;
das Schwarze, Zentrum *n* *e-r
Schießscheibe*; Pfefferminzbonbon
m; ‿ *pane* Butzenscheibe *f*.
bull·shit *bsd. Am.* ∨ [ˈbulʃit] Scheiß-
dreck *m*; Quatsch *m*.
bully[1] [ˈbuli] **1.** brutaler Kerl *m*,
Kameradenschinder *m*; Maulheld
m; Tyrann *m*; Zuhälter *m*; **2.** lärmend, prahlerisch; *bsd. Am.* F prima (*a. int.*); **3.** einschüchtern; tyrannisieren, schikanieren, piesacken.
bul·ly[2] [‿] *a.* ‿ *beef* Rinderpökel-

fleisch *n*.
bul·rush ❦ ['bulrʌʃ] *große* Binse *f*.
bul·wark ['bulwək] *mst fig*. Bollwerk *n*; ⚓ Schanzkleid *n*.
bum[1] V [bʌm] Hintern *m*.
bum[2] *Am*. F [⌞] **1.** Nichtstuer *m*,
Vagabund *m*; *be od.* go on the ⁓ kaputt sein *od.* gehen; trampen; **2.**
nassauern, organisieren; **3.** armselig, schlecht.
bum·ble-bee ['bʌmblbi:] Hummel *f*.
bum·boat ['bʌmbəut] Proviant-
boot *n*.
bump [bʌmp] **1.** Schlag *m*, Stoß *m*;
Beule *f*; *fig*. Sinn *m*, Talent *n* (*of*
für, zu); **2.** stoßen; rumpeln, holpern (*Wagen*); *Wettrudern*: überholen; ⁓ *into s.o.* F j. anrempeln; ⁓
into s.th. F et. rammen, mit et. zs.-
stoßen; ⁓ *off* abmurksen, umlegen.
bump·er ['bʌmpə] volles Glas *n*
(*Wein*); F *et*. Riesiges *n*; *mot*. Stoß-
stange *f*; ⁓ *crop* Rekordernte *f*; ⁓ *house*
thea. volles Haus *n*; ⁓ *sticker* Auto-
aufkleber *m*.
bump·kin ['bʌmpkin] Tölpel *m*.
bump-start *mot*. ['bʌmpstɑ:t] **1.** Anschieben *n*; **2.** anschieben.
bump·tious ☐ F ['bʌmpʃəs] aufgeblasen; arrogant.
bump·y ['bʌmpi] holperig; ❦ böig.
bun [bʌn] Rosinenbrötchen *n*;
(Haar)Knoten *m*.
bu·na ['bu:nə] Buna *m* (*Kautschuk*).
bunch [bʌntʃ] **1.** Bund *n*, Bündel *n*;
Büschel *n*; Haufen *m* (*Menge*); ⁓ *of*
flowers Blumenstrauß *m*; ⁓ *of grapes*
Weintraube *f*; **2.** (zs.-)bündeln;
bauschen; '**bunch·y** büschelig;
bauschig.
bun·combe ['bʌŋkəm] Blödsinn *m*;
Mumpitz *m*.
bun·dle ['bʌndl] **1.** Bündel *n*, Bund
n; **2.** *v/t. a.* ⁓ *up* (zs.-)bündeln; ⁓
away, ⁓ *off* F wegjagen; *v/i.* ⁓ *off* sich
packen.
bung [bʌŋ] **1.** Spund *m*; **2.** (zu-)
spunden; ⁓*ed up* verstopft (*Nase*).
bun·ga·low ['bʌŋgələu] Bungalow
m (*einstöckiges Haus*).
bung-hole ['bʌŋhəul] Spundloch *n*.
bun·gle ['bʌŋgl] **1.** Pfuscherei *f*; **2.**
(ver)pfuschen; '**bun·gler** Pfuscher
(-in); '**bun·gling 1.** ☐ ungeschickt,
stümperhaft; **2.** Pfuscherei *f*.
bun·ion 𝖌 ['bʌnjən] entzündeter
Fußballen *m*.

bunk[1] *sl*. [bʌŋk] Geschwätz *n*,
Quatsch *m*.
bunk[2] [⌞] Schlafkoje *f*.
bunk·er ⚓ ['bʌŋkə] **1.** Bunker *m*
(*Kohlenbehälter*); **2.** bunkern; *be*
⁓*ed fig*. in e-e Klemme geraten.
bun·kum ['bʌŋkəm] = buncombe.
bun·ny ['bʌni] Kaninchen *n*; ⁓ (**girl**) F
Häschen *n*.
bun·sen ['bunsn]: ⁓ *burner* Bunsen-
brenner *m*.
bunt *Am*. [bʌnt] *Baseball*: Stopp-
ballschlag *m*.
bun·ting[1] *orn*. ['bʌntiŋ] Ammer *f*.
bun·ting[2] [⌞] Flaggen(tuch *n*) *f/pl*.
buoy ⚓ [bɔi] **1.** Boje *f*; **2.** *Fahr-*
wasser betonnen; *mst* ⁓ *up* schwimmend erhalten; *fig*. aufrechterhalten; emporheben.
buoy·an·cy ['bɔiənsi] Schwimm-,
fig. Spannkraft *f*; 🛩 *u. fig*. Auftrieb *m*; '**buoy·ant** ☐ schwimmfähig; hebend; *fig*. spannkräftig;
fig. heiter; ✝ steigend.
bur ❦ [bə:] Klette *f* (*a. fig*.).
Bur·ber·ry ['bə:bəri] *wasserdichter*
Stoff *od*. Mantel.
bur·bot *ichth*. ['bə:bət] Quappe *f*.
bur·den[1] ['bə:dn] **1.** Last *f*, Bürde *f*
(*on* für); ⚖ Auflage *f*; ⚓ Ladung *f*;
⚓ Tragfähigkeit *f*; **2.** beladen; belasten (*a. fig*.).
bur·den[2] [⌞] Kehrreim *m*, Refrain *m*.
bur·den·some ['bə:dnsəm] lästig;
drückend.   [(*Pflanze*).|
bur·dock ❦ ['bə:dɔk] Klette *f*⌋
bu·reau ['bjuərəu], *pl. a.* **bu·reaux**
['⌞z] Büro *n*, Geschäfts-, Amts-
zimmer *n*; Schreibpult *n*; *Am*.
Kommode *f*; **bu·reauc·ra·cy**
[⌞'rɔkrəsi] Bürokratie *f*; **bu·reau-**
crat ['bjuərəukræt] Bürokrat *m*;
bu·reau'crat·ic (⁓*ally*) bürokra-
tisch; **bu·reauc·ra·tize** [bjuə'rɔk-
rətaiz] bürokratisieren.
bu·rette ⚗ [bjuə'ret] Meßröhre *f*.
burg *Am*. F [bə:g] Stadt *f*.
bur·gee ⚓ ['bə:dʒi:] Stander *m*.
bur·geon *lit*. ['bə:dʒən] **1.** Knospe *f*;
Keim *m*; **2.** knospen, sprießen.
burg·er *Am*. F ['bə:gə] Hamburger *m*.
bur·gess ['bə:dʒis] stimmberechtig-
ter Bürger *m*; *hist*. Abgeordnete *m*.
burgh *schott*. ['bʌrə] Burgflecken *m*;
bur·gher *hist*. ['bə:gə] Bürger *m*
(*bsd. e-r holländischen od. deutschen*
Stadt).
bur·glar ['bə:glə] *nächtlicher* Ein-

brecher *m*; **bur·glar·i·ous** □ [bɔ:-'glɛəriəs] einbrecherisch; **bur·gla·ry** ['∪glɔri] *nächtlicher* Einbruch (-diebstahl) *m*; '**bur·gle** einbrechen (in *acc.*).

bur·go·mas·ter ['bɔ:gɔumɑːstə] Bürgermeister *m* (*e-r holländischen od. flämischen Stadt*). [*m* (*Wein*).]

bur·gun·dy ['bɔ:gəndi] Burgunder*m*.)

bur·i·al ['beriəl] Begräbnis *n*; '∪-**-ground** Begräbnisplatz *m*, Friedhof *m*; ∼ **serv·ice** Trauerfeier *f*.

bu·rin ⊕ ['bjuərin] Grabstichel *m*.

burke [bɔ:k] *et*. vertuschen.

burl [bɔ:l] Noppe *f im Tuch*.

bur·lap ['bɔ:læp] Sackleinwand *f*.

bur·lesque [bɔ:'lesk] **1.** burlesk, possenhaft; **2.** Burleske *f*, *n*, Posse*f*; **3.** burlesk behandeln; parodieren.

bur·ly ['bɔ:li] stämmig, kräftig.

Bur·mese [bɔ:'mi:z] **1.** birmanisch; **2.** Birmane *m*, Birmanin *f*; Birmanisch *n*.

burn [bɔ:n] **1.** Brandwunde *f*; Brandmal *n*; **2.** (*irr.*) *v/t. u. v/i.* (ver-, an)brennen; '**burn·er** Brenner *m*; '**burn·ing** □ brennend, glühend; heiß; Brenn...

bur·nish ['bɔ:niʃ] polieren, glätten; '**bur·nish·er** Polierer(in); Polierstahl *m*.

burnt [bɔ:nt] *pret. u. p.p. von burn* 2; ∼ *almond* gebrannte Mandel *f*; ∼ *offering* Brandopfer *n*.

burp *Am. sl.* [bɔ:p] **1.** Rülpser *m*; **2.** rülpsen, aufstoßen.

burr [bɔ:] **1.** Schwirrton *m* (*von Maschinen*); Zäpfchen-R *n*; **2.** (*das* R) guttural aussprechen; '∼-**drill** ✿ Drillbohrer *m*.

bur·ro F ['burəu] Packesel *m*.

bur·row ['bʌrəu] **1.** Höhle *f*, Bau *m*; **2.** (sich ein)graben; *fig.* sich vergraben; *in Geheimnisse* eindringen.

bur·sar ['bɔ:sə] Quästor *m* (*an Universitäten*); Stipendiat *m*.

bur·sa·ry ['bɔ:səri] Quästur *f*; Stipendium *n*.

burst [bɔ:st] **1.** Bersten *n*; Krach *m*; Riß *m*; Bruch *m*; Explosion *f*; *fig.* Ausbruch *m*, Anfall *m*; **2.** (*irr.*) *v/i.* bersten, platzen (a. *fig.*); zerspringen; brechen; ✿ aufspringen; aufgehen (*Geschwür*); explodieren; ∼ *from* sich losreißen von; ∼ *forth*, ∼ *out* hervorbrechen; ∼ *into flame* (*leaf*) aufflammen (-blühen); ∼ *into tears* in Tränen ausbrechen; ∼ *out*

laughing in Gelächter ausbrechen; ∼ *upon s.o.* sich j-m plötzlich zeigen; *v/t.* (zer)sprengen.

bur·then ⚓ ['bɔ:ðən] = *burden*.

bur·y ['beri] begraben, beerdigen; verbergen; vergraben; *be buried in thought* in Gedanken vertieft sein; '**bur·y·ing-ground** Begräbnisplatz *m*.

bus F [bʌs] **1.** (Omni)Bus *m*; *miss the* ∼ *sl.* den Anschluß verpassen; ∼ *boy Am.* Kellnerlehrling *m*, Pikkolo *m*; **2.** *v/t. u. v/i.* (*Kinder*) mit dem Bus (*in die Schule*) fahren.

bus·by 𝕏 ['bʌzbi] Bärenmütze *f*.

bush [buʃ] Busch *m*; Gebüsch *n*; ⊕ Buchse *f*; **bush·el** ['buʃl] Scheffel *m* (*36,35 Liter*); große Menge *f*; *hide one's light under a* ∼ sein Licht unter den Scheffel stellen; **bush league** *Am. Baseball:* untere Spielklasse *f*; '**bush·man** Buschmann *m*; '**bush-rang·er** Buschklepper *m*, Strauchdieb *m*.

bush·y ['buʃi] buschig.

busi·ness ['biznis] Geschäft *n* (*Unternehmen*); Beschäftigung *f*; Beruf *m*, Gewerbe *n*; Angelegenheit *f*, Sache *f*; Aufgabe *f*; ✝ Handel *m*; Geschäft(slokal) *n mit allem Zubehör*; ∼ *of the day* Tagesordnung *f*; ∼ *research* Konjunkturforschung *f*; *on* ∼ geschäftlich; *no admittance except on* ∼ Zutritt für Unbefugte verboten; *get down to* ∼ zur Sache kommen; *have no* ∼ *to inf.* nicht befugt sein zu *inf.*; *mind one's own* ∼ sich um seine eignen Angelegenheiten kümmern; *send s.o. about his* ∼ j. kurz abfertigen; *that's none of his* ∼ das geht ihn nichts an; ∼ *end* F wesentlicher Teil *m e-r Sache*; ∼ *hours pl.* Geschäftszeit *f*; '∼-**like** kaufmännisch, geschäftsmäßig; sachlich; '∼-**man** Geschäftsmann *m*; ∼ **tour**, ∼ **trip** Geschäftsreise *f*.

bus·ker ['bʌskə] Straßenmusikant *m*.

bus·kin ['bʌskin] Halbstiefel *m*; *Altertum:* Kothurn *m*.

bus·man ['bʌsmən] Busfahrer *m*; ∼*'s holiday* im Beruf verbrachter Urlaub *m*; '**bus·sing** *bsd. Am. Beförderung von Schülern mit Bussen in andere Schulen, um Rassenintegration zu erreichen*; '**bus-stop** Bushaltestelle *f*.

bust¹ [bʌst] Büste *f*.

bust² *Am.* F [∼] Bankrott *m*; Saufpartie *f*.

bus·tard *orn*. [ˈbʌstəd] Trappe *f*.

bus·tle [ˈbʌsl] **1.** Geschäftigkeit *f*; geschäftiges Treiben *n*, Getriebe *n*, Hast *f*; Turnüre *f*; **2.** *v/i*. sich tummeln; (umher)wirtschaften; hasten; *v/t*. hetzen, jagen (*a. fig*.); ˈbus·tler rühriger Mensch *m*; ˈbus·tling □ geschäftig, rührig.

bust-up F [ˈbʌstʌp] Zusammenbruch *m*; Krach *m* (*Streit*).

bus·y [ˈbizi] **1.** □ beschäftigt (*with* mit); geschäftig, emsig, fleißig, eifrig, tätig (*at* bei, an *dat*.); lebhaft; belebt, verkehrsreich; *teleph*. besetzt; *be* ~ (viel) zu tun haben; ~ *packing* mit Packen beschäftigt; **2.** (*mst* ~ *o.s*. sich) beschäftigen (*with, in, at, about, ger*. mit); ˈ~-bod·y G(e)schaftlhuber *m*; ˈbus·y·ness Geschäftigkeit *f*, Emsigkeit *f*.

but [bʌt, bət] **1.** *cj*. aber, jedoch, sondern; *a*. ~ *that* wenn nicht; indessen, nichtsdestoweniger; **2.** *prp*. außer; *the last* ~ *one* der vor- *od*. zweitletzte; *the next* ~ *one* der übernächste; ~ *for* wenn nicht … gewesen wäre; ohne; **3.** *nach Negation*: nur (die *od*. das) nicht; *there is no one* ~ *knows* es gibt niemand, der nicht wüßte; **4.** *adv*. nur; ~ *just* soeben, eben erst; ~ *now* erst jetzt; *all* ~ fast, nahe daran; *nothing* ~ nichts als; *I cannot* ~ *inf*. ich kann nicht umhin zu *inf*., ich kann nur *inf*.; **5.** Aber *n*, Einwendung *f*.

bu·tane [ˈbjuːtein] Butan *n*.

butch·er [ˈbutʃə] **1.** Schlächter *m*, Fleischer *m*, Metzger *m*; *fig*. Mörder *m*; **2.** (*fig*. ab-, hin)schlachten; ˈbutch·er·y Schlächterei *f* (*a. fig*.); Schlachthaus *n*; ~ *business* Metzgerhandwerk *n*.

but·ler [ˈbʌtlə] Butler *m*; Kellermeister *m*.

butt¹ [bʌt] **1.** Stoß *m* mit den Hörnern; *a.* ~ *end* dickes Ende *n* e-s *Baumes etc*.; Stummel *m*, Kippe *f*; Gewehr-Kolben *m*; ⊕ Balkenende *n*; Kugelfang *m*; *the* ~*s pl*. Schießstand *m*; *fig*. (End)Ziel *n*; *fig*. Zielscheibe *f*; **2.** (mit dem Kopf) stoßen; ~ *in* F herein-, hineinplatzen.

butt² [...] Stückfaß *n*.

butte *Am. geol*. [bjuːt] Restberg *m*.

but·ter [ˈbʌtə] **1.** Butter *f*; F Schöntuerei *f*, Schmeichelei *f*; *as if* ~ *would not melt in his mouth* als ob er

nicht bis drei zählen könnte; **2.** mit Butter bestreichen *od*. anrichten; ˈ~-cup Butterblume *f*, Hahnenfuß *m*; ˈ~-fin·gered ungeschickt im Gebrauch der Hände, tolpatschig; ˈ~-fin·gers *sg*. Tolpatsch *m*; ˈ~-fly Schmetterling *m* (*a. fig*.); *have butterflies in one's stomach* ein flaues Gefühl in der Magengegend haben; ˈ~-milk Buttermilch *f*; ˈbut·ter·y **1.** butter(art)ig; Butter…; **2.** Speisekammer *f*.

but·tock [ˈbʌtək], *mst* ˈbut·tocks *pl*. Hintern *m*.

but·ton [ˈbʌtn] **1.** Knopf *m*; ♀ Knospe *f*; ~*s sg*. F Hotelpage *m*; **2.** *oft* ~ *up Kleid* zuknöpfen; einknöpfen, *fig*. verschließen; Knöpfe nähen *od*. anbringen an; ˈ~-hole **1.** Knopfloch *n*; Knopflochsträußchen *n*; **2.** Knopflöcher nähen in; *j*. beim Knopf festhalten; ˈ~-hook Stiefelknöpfer *m*; ˈ~-wood ♀ Platane *f*.

but·tress [ˈbʌtris] **1.** Strebepfeiler *m*; *fig*. Stütze *f*; **2.** ~ *up* abstützen; *fig*. *Argument etc*. unterstützen.

bux·om [ˈbʌksəm] drall, stramm.

buy [bai] (*irr*.) *v/t*. (an-, ein)kaufen (*from* bei); *fig*. einbringen; erkaufen; *order to* ~ Kaufauftrag *m*; ˈbuy·er Käufer(in); Abnehmer(in); Einkäufer(in); ˈbuy·ing Kauf…

buzz [bʌz] **1.** Gesumm *n*; Gesurr(e) *n*; Geflüster *n*; ~ *saw Am*. Kreissäge *f*; **2.** *v/i*. summen; surren; ~ *about* herumschwirren, -eilen; *v/t*. *anderes Flugzeug durch Anfliegen* belästigen; F schmeißen.

buz·zard *orn*. [ˈbʌzəd] Bussard *m*.

buzz·er ⚡ [ˈbʌzə] Summer *m*; Sirene *f*.

by [bai] **1.** *prp*. Raum: bei; an, neben; Richtung: durch, über, via; an (*dat*.) entlang *od*. vorbei; Zeit: an, bei; spätestens bis, bis zu; Urheberschaft, Ursache: von, durch (*Passiv*); Mittel, Werkzeug: (ver)mittels, durch, mit; Art u. Weise: bei; Schwur: bei; Maß: um, bei; Richtschnur: gemäß, bei; North ~ East Nord zu Ost; side ~ side Seite an Seite; ~ day bei Tage; ~ now jetzt (schon); ~ the time (that) bis; a day ~ Shaw ein Stück von Shaw; ~ lamplight bei Lampenlicht; ~ the dozen dutzendweise; ~ far bei weitem; 50 feet ~ 20 fünfzig Fuß lang und zwanzig breit; ~ *half* um die Hälfte; ~ *o.s.* allein; für sich; aus eigner Kraft, aus sich; ~ *land* zu Lande; ~ *rail* per Bahn; *day* ~ *day* Tag für Tag; ~ *twos* zu zweien; **2.** *adv.* dabei; vorbei; beiseite; ~ *and* ~ nächstens, bald; nach und nach; ~ *the* ~ nebenbei bemerkt; *close* ~ dicht dabei; *go* ~ vorbeigehen; ~ *and large* im großen und ganzen; **3.** *adj.* Neben...; Seiten...

bye [bai] *Kricket*: Lauf, ohne den *Ball geschlagen zu haben*; *Tennis*: Überzählige *m*, *f*; *be od. draw a* ~ rasten (müssen).

bye-bye F ['bai'bai] Wiedersehen!; ['baibai] *Kindersprache*: Heia *f* (*Bett*).

by...: '~**-e·lec·tion** Nachwahl *f*; '~**gone 1.** vergangen, früher; **2.** ~*s pl.* Vergangene *n*; *let* ~*s be* ~*s* laß(t) die Vergangenheit ruhen;

'~**-law** Ortsstatut *n*; ~*s pl.* Satzung *f*, Statuten *n/pl.*; '~**-line** *Am.* Verfasserangabe *f zu e-m Artikel*; '~**-name** Bei-, Spitzname *m*; '~**-pass 1.** Umgehungsstraße *f*; **2.** umgehen, -fahren; *Verkehr* umleiten; '~**-path** Seitenpfad *m*; '~**-play** *thea.* Nebenhandlung *f*; stummes Spiel *n*; '~**-prod·uct** Nebenprodukt *n*.

byre ['baiə] Kuhstall *m*.

by-road ['bairəud] Seitenweg *m*, -straße *f*.

By·ron·ic [bai'rɔnik] (~*ally*) byronisch.

by...: '~**-stand·er** Zuschauer *m*; '~**-street** Neben-, Seitenstraße *f*; '~**-way** Seiten-, *b.s.* Schleichweg *m*; '~**-word** Sprichwort *n*; Inbegriff *m*; *be a* ~ *for* sprichwörtlich bekannt sein wegen.

By·zan·tine [bi'zæntain] **1.** byzantinisch; **2.** Byzantiner(in).

C

cab [kæb] **1.** Droschke *f*, Mietwagen *m*, Taxi *n*; 🚂 Führerstand *m*; **2.** ~ *it* F mit e-r Droschke *od.* e-m Taxi fahren.

ca·bal [kə'bæl] **1.** Kabale *f* (*Ränke*); Clique *f*; **2.** intrigieren.

cab·a·ret ['kæbərei] Kabarett *n*.

cab·bage ['kæbidʒ] Kohl(kopf) *m*; ~ *butterfly* Kohlweißling *m*; ~ *lettuce* Kopfsalat *m*.

cab·ba·lis·tic, cab·ba·lis·ti·cal □ [kæbə'listik(əl)] kabbalistisch.

cab·by F ['kæbi] Droschkenkutscher *m*, Taxifahrer *m*.

cab·in ['kæbin] **1.** Hütte *f*; ⚓ Kajüte *f*; Kabine *f*; Kammer *f*; **2.** einpferchen; '~**-boy** ⚓ Offiziersbursche *m*; Stewardhelfer *m*; ~ *class* ⚓ Kabinenklasse *f*, 2. Klasse *f*; ~ *cruis·er* ⚓ Kabinenkreuzer *m*.

cab·i·net ['kæbinit] Kabinett *n*, Ministerrat *m*; Schrank *m*, Vitrine *f*; (Radio)Gehäuse *n*; *phot.* Kabinettformat *n*; ♀ *Council* Kabinettssitzung *f*; '~**-mak·er** Kunsttischler *m*.

ca·ble ['keibl] **1.** ⚓ *u. tel.* Kabel *n*; ⚓ Trosse *f*, Ankertau *n*, -kette *f*; Telegramm *n*; *buried* ~ Erdkabel *n*; **2.** *tel.* telegraphieren, kabeln; '~**-car** Standseilbahn(wagen *m*) *f*; ~**gram** ['~græm] Kabeltelegramm *n*; ~ **re·lease** *phot.* Drahtauslöser *m*; '~**-stitched** mit Kreuzstichstickerei; ~ **tel·e·vi·sion** Kabelfernsehen *n*.

cab·man ['kæbmən] Droschkenkutscher *m*, Taxifahrer *m*.

ca·boo·dle *sl.* [kə'bu:dl]: *the whole* ~ der ganze Kram; die ganze Sippschaft.

ca·boose [kə'bu:s] ⚓ Kombüse *f*; *Am.* 🚂 Eisenbahnwagen *m am Güterzug.*

cab·ri·o·let *bsd. mot.* [kæbriə'lei] Kabriolett *n*, offener Wagen *m*.

cab-stand ['kæbstænd] (Kraft-) Droschkenhalteplatz *m*, Taxistand *m*.

ca'can·ny ⊕ [ka:'kæni] die Arbeitsleistung bremsen.

ca·ca·o [kə'ka:əu] Kakaobaum *m*; Kakaobohne *f*.

cache [kæʃ] **1.** unterirdisches Depot *n*; geheimes Lager *n*; **2.** verbergen.

cack·le ['kækl] **1.** Gegacker *n*, Geschnatter *n*; *fig.* Geschwätz *n*; **2.** gackern, schnattern; *fig.* schwatzen; '**cack·ler** gackerndes Huhn *n*; *fig.* Schwätzer(in).

ca·coph·o·ny [kæ'kɔfəni] Kakophonie *f* (*Mißklang*).

cac·tus ♀ ['kæktəs] Kaktus *m*.

cad F [kæd] Prolet *m*; übler Charakter *m*.

ca·das·tre [kə'dæstə] Grundbuch *n*.

ca·dav·er·ous □ [kə'dævərəs] leichenhaft; leichenblaß.

cad·die ['kædi] Golfjunge *m*, Caddie *m*.

cad·dis *zo.* ['kædis] Larve *f* der Köcherfliege.

cad·dish F □ ['kædiʃ] proletenhaft; gemein, schurkisch.

cad·dy ['kædi] Teebüchse *f*; = *caddie*.

ca·dence ['keidəns] ♪ Kadenz *f*; Tonfall *m*; Rhythmus *m*.

ca·det [kə'det] Kadett *m*; ~ corps Jugendkompanie *f* e-r *Schule*.

cadge [kædʒ] (er)betteln; schnorren; '**cadg·er** Schmarotzer *m*; Schnorrer *m*.

ca·di ['kɑːdi] Kadi *m* (*Richter im Orient*). [mium *n*.]
cad·mi·um ↑ ['kædmiəm] Kad-]
cad·re ['kɑːdə] Rahmen *m*; ✗ Kader *m*.

ca·du·cous ♀ *u. zo.* [kə'djuːkəs] abfallend.

cae·cum *anat.* ['siːkəm] Blinddarm *m*.

Cae·sar ['siːzə] Cäsar *m*; **Cae·sar·i·an** [siː'zɛəriən] cäsarisch.

cae·sar·e·an (**sec·tion**) ✗ [siː'zɛəriən 'sekʃən] Kaiserschnitt *m*.

cae·su·ra [siː'zjuərə] Zäsur *f*.

ca·fé ['kæfei] Café *n*; Restaurant *n*.

caf·e·te·ri·a [kæfi'tiəriə] Restaurant *n* mit Selbstbedienung.

caf·e·to·ri·um *Am.* [kæfi'tɔːriəm] Kantinen- und Festsaal *m*.

caf·fe·ine ['kæfiːn] Koffein *n*.

cage [keidʒ] **1.** Käfig *m* (*a. fig.*); Kriegsgefangenenlager *n*; ✗ Förderkorb *m*; **2.** einsperren.

cag·ey □ *bsd. Am.* F ['keidʒi] gerissen, raffiniert.

cairn [kɛən] Steinhaufen *m*.

cais·son [kə'suːn] ✗ Munitionswagen *m*; *Wasserbau*: Senkkasten*m*.

cai·tiff ['keitif] Lump *m*, Schurke *m*.

ca·jole [kə'dʒəul] *j-m* schöntun, schmeicheln; *j.* beschwatzen (*into* zu); **ca'jol·er** Schmeichler(in); **ca'jol·er·y** Schöntuerei *f*; Schmeichelei *f*.

cake [keik] **1.** Kuchen *m*; Stück *n* Seife *etc.*; ~*s and ale* Lustbarkeit *f*; *a piece of* ~ *sl.* ein Kinderspiel *n*; *like hot* ~*s* wie warme Semmeln; **2.** zs.-backen; überziehen (*with* mit).

cal·a·bash ['kæləbæʃ] Kalebasse *f* (*Flaschenkürbis*).

cal·a·mine *min.* ['kæləmain] Galmei *m*.

ca·lam·i·tous □ [kə'læmitəs] elend; katastrophal; **ca'lam·i·ty** Elend *n*, Unglück *n*, Unheil *n*; Katastrophe *f*; **ca'lam·i·ty-howl·er** Schwarzseher *m*; **ca'lam·i·ty-howl·ing** *bsd. Am.* Schwarzseherei *f*.

cal·car·e·ous [kæl'kɛəriəs] kalkartig, -reich, kalkig; Kalk...

cal·ce·o·la·ri·a ♀ [kælsiə'lɛəriə] Pantoffelblume *f*.

cal·ci·fi·ca·tion [kælsifi'keiʃən] Verkalkung *f*; **cal·ci·fy** ['~fai] (sich) verkalken; **cal·ci·na·tion** ↑ [kælsi'neiʃən] Kalzinierung *f*, Brennen *n*; **cal·cine** ↑ ['kælsain] kalzinieren, brennen; '**cal·cite** *min.* Kalzit *m*; **cal·ci·um** ↑ ['~siəm] Kalzium *n*; **cal·ci·um car·bide** ↑ Karbid *n*.

cal·cu·la·ble ['kælkjuləbl] berechenbar; **cal·cu·late** ['~leit] *v/t.* kalkulieren; be-, aus-, errechnen; ~*d* berechnet (*for auf acc.*); *v/i.* rechnen, vertrauen (*on, upon auf acc.*); F *Am.* vermuten; *calculating machine* Rechenmaschine *f*; **cal·cu·la·tion** Kalkulation *f*, Berechnung *f etc.*; '**cal·cu·la·tor** Kalkulator *m*; Rechner *m*; **cal·cu·lus** ['~ləs] ⚕ Differential- u. Integralrechnen *n*; ✗ Stein *m*.

cal·dron ['kɔːldrən] Kessel *m*.

cal·en·dar ['kælində] **1.** Kalender *m*; Liste *f*; **2.** registrieren.

cal·en·der ⊕ [~] **1.** Kalander *m*, Tuchpresse *f*; **2.** kalandern, pressen.

cal·ends ['kælindz]: *on the Greek* ~ am St. Nimmerleinstag.

calf [kɑːf], *pl.* **calves** [kɑːvz] Kalb *n* (*a. fig.*); *a.* ~-*leather* Kalbleder *n*; Lederband *m*; *anat.* Wade *f*; *in* ~, *with* ~ trächtig; ~ *love* F Jugendliebe *f*; '~-**skin** Kalbfell *n*.

cal·i·brate ⊕ [ˈkælibreit] kalibrieren; **cal·i·bre** [ˈ‿bə] Kaliber n (*Rohrweite*; *fig. Art*; *Gewicht*).

cal·i·co ✝ [ˈkælikəu] Kaliko m, (bedruckter) Kattun m.

Cal·i·for·nian [kæliˈfɔːnjən] **1.** kalifornisch; **2.** Kalifornier(in).

ca·liph [ˈkælif] Kalif m; **cal·iph·ate** [ˈ‿eit] Kalifat n.

calk [kɔːk] **1.** (durch)pausen; ⚓ kalfatern (*abdichten*); scharf beschlagen; **2.** Gleitschutzbeschlag m, Stollen m am Hufeisen; **calk·in** [ˈkælkin] s. calk 2.

call [kɔːl] **1.** Ruf m; *teleph.* Anruf m, Gespräch n; *fig.* Ruf m, Berufung f (to in *ein* Amt; auf *e-n* Lehrstuhl); Appell m; Signal n; *thea.* Hervorruf m; Lockruf m; (innere) Berufung f; Forderung f; F Anlaß m; *kurzer* Besuch m; Nachfrage f (for nach); Kündigung f v. *Geldern*; ~ money ✝ täglich kündbares Geld n; port of ~ Anlaufhafen m; on ~ ✝ auf Abruf; give s.o. a ~ *teleph.* j. anrufen; **2.** v/t. (herbei)rufen; (an)rufen; *Versammlung* (ein)berufen; *Am.* Baseball: Spiel abbrechen; *fig.* berufen (to in *ein* Amt); nennen; kommen lassen; wecken; *Aufmerksamkeit* lenken (to auf *acc.*); be ~ed heißen; ~ s.o. names j. beschimpfen *od.* beleidigen; ~ s.o. down *Am. sl.* j. anpfeifen; ~ forth hervorrufen; *Kraft* aufbieten; ~ in *Geld* kündigen, aufrufen; j. hinzuziehen; ~ out *Arbeiter* zum Streik auffordern; ~ over *Namen* verlesen; ~ up aufrufen; *teleph.* anrufen; v/i. rufen; *teleph.* (an)rufen; vorsprechen (at an *e-m* Ort; on s.o. bei j-m); ~ at a port e-n Hafen anlaufen; ~ for rufen nach; *thea.* herausrufen; *et.* fordern, verlangen; j. *od. et.* abholen; to be (left till) ~ed for postlagernd; ~ on e-n Besuch machen bei j-m; sich an j. wenden (for wegen); j. berufen, auffordern, aufrufen (to *inf.* zu *inf.*); ~ to j-m zurufen; ~ upon s. ~ on; **'call·a·ble** kündbar (*Geld*); **'call-box** Fernsprechzelle f; **'call·er** Rufer(in); Besucher(in); *teleph.* Anrufer(in); **'call-girl** Callgirl n (*Prostituierte*).

cal·li·graph·ic [kæliˈgræfik] (~ally) kalligraphisch; **cal·lig·ra·phy** [kəˈligrəfi] Kalligraphie f (*Schönschreibekunst*).

call-in [ˈkɔːlin] Sendung f mit Zuschauer- *od.* Zuhörerbeteiligung.

call·ing [ˈkɔːliŋ] Rufen n; Berufung f; Beruf m; ~ card *Am.* Visitenkarte f.

cal·li·pers [ˈkælipəz] *pl.* Tasterzirkel m.

cal·lis·then·ics [kælisˈθeniks] *mst sg.* Freiübungen f/pl.

call-of·fice [ˈkɔːlɔfis] Fernsprechstelle f.

cal·los·i·ty [kæˈlɔsiti] Verhärtung f, Schwiele f; *fig.* Dickfelligkeit f; Indifferenz f; **'cal·lous** ☐ schwielig; *fig.* dickfellig, herzlos; indifferent.

cal·low [ˈkæləu] nackt (*ungefiedert*); noch nicht flügge (*fig. unerfahren*).

call-up [ˈkɔːlʌp] Einberufung f.

cal·lus [ˈkæləs] Schwiele f.

calm [kɑːm] **1.** ☐ still, ruhig (*a. fig.*); **2.** Stille f, Ruhe f (*a. fig.*); ⚓ Windstille f, Flaute f; **3.** (~ down sich) beruhigen; besänftigen; **'calm·ness** Stille f; (Gemüts)Ruhe f.

Cal·or gas [ˈkæləˈgæs] Propangas n.

ca·lor·ic *phys.* [kəˈlɔrik] Wärme f; ~-engine Heißluftmaschine f; **cal·o·rie** *phys.* [ˈkæləri] Kalorie f, Wärmeeinheit f; **cal·o·rif·ic** [kæləˈrifik] Wärme erzeugend, erhitzend.

cal·trop ⚓ [ˈkæltrəp] Wegedistel f.

ca·lum·ni·ate [kəˈlʌmnieit] verleumden; **ca·lum·ni·a·tion** Verleumdung f; **ca·lum·ni·a·tor** Verleumder(in); **ca·lum·ni·ous** ☐ verleumderisch; **cal·um·ny** [ˈkæləmni] Verleumdung f.

Cal·va·ry [ˈkælvəri] Kalvarienberg m, Kreuzigungsgruppe f.

calve [kɑːv] kalben; **calves** [kɑːvz] *pl. von* calf.

Cal·vin·ism [ˈkælvinizəm] Kalvinismus m.

ca·lyp·so [kəˈlipsəu] Calypso m (*Tanz etc.*).

ca·lyx ⚓ *u. zo.* [ˈkeiliks], *pl.* **cal·y·ces** [ˈ‿lisiːz] Kelch m.

cam ⊕ [kæm] Nocken m, Daumen m; ~ gear Nockensteuerung f.

cam·ber ⊕ [ˈkæmbə] **1.** Wölbung f, Krümmung f; **2.** wölben.

cam·bric [ˈkeimbrik] Batist m.

came [keim] *pret. v.* come.

cam·el *zo. u.* ⚓ [ˈkæməl] Kamel n.

ca·mel·li·a ⚓ [kəˈmiːljə] Kamelie f.

cam·e·o [ˈkæmiəu] Kamee f.

cam·er·a [ˈkæmərə] Kamera f, Photoapparat m; in ~ ⚖ unter Ausschluß der Öffentlichkeit.

cami-knick·ers ['kæmi'nikəz] *pl.* Hemdhose *f.*

cam·i·on ['kæmiən] niedriger LKW *m.*

cam·o·mile ♀ ['kæməumail] Kamille *f*; ~ *tea* Kamillentee *m.*

cam·ou·flage ✗ ['kæmuflɑ:ʒ] **1.** Tarnung *f*; **2.** tarnen.

camp [kæmp] **1.** Lager *n*; ✗ Feldlager *n*; ~ *bed* Feldbett *n*; ~ *chair*, ~ *stool* Feldstuhl *m*; **2.** kampieren, lagern; ~ *out* zelten.

cam·paign [kæm'pein] **1.** Feldzug *m*; *pol. u. fig.* Kampagne *f*, Schlacht *f*; *election* ~ Wahlkampf *m*; **2.** einen Feldzug mitmachen *od.* unternehmen; **cam'paign·er** Feldzugsteilnehmer *m*; *old* ~ F alter Praktikus *m.*

camp·er ['kæmpə] Lager-, Zeltbewohner(in); Camper *m*; Wohnmobil *n.*

cam·phor ['kæmfə] Kampfer *m*; **cam·phor·at·ed** ['~reitid] Kampfer...

camp·ing ['kæmpiŋ] Camping *n*, Zelten *n.*

camp·site ['kæmpsait] Campingplatz *m.*

cam·pus *Am.* ['kæmpəs] Universitätsgelände *n.*

cam·shaft ⊕ ['kæmʃɑːft] Nockenwelle *f.*

can¹ [kæn] (*irr.*) *v/aux.* kann *etc.*

can² [~] **1.** Kanne *f*; *Am.* (Konserven)Büchse *f*; ~ *opener* Dosenöffner *m*; *carry the* ~ F die Schuld tragen; **2.** *Am.* in Büchsen konservieren, eindosen.

Ca·na·di·an [kə'neidjən] **1.** kanadisch; **2.** Kanadier(in).

ca·nal [kə'næl] Kanal *m*; *anat.* Gang *m*, Röhre *f*; ~*boat* Lastkahn *m*; **ca·nal·i·za·tion** [kænəlai'zeiʃən] Kanalisation *f*, Kanalbau *m*; **'ca·nal·ize** kanalisieren.

can·a·pé ['kænəpei] Appetithappen *m.*

ca·nard [kæ'nɑːd] (Zeitungs)Ente *f.*

ca·nar·y [kə'nɛəri] *a.* ~*-bird* Kanarienvogel *m.*

can·cel ['kænsəl] (durch)streichen; entwerten; absagen; ~ *out* (sich) aufheben; ⚖ sich heben; *be* ~*led* ausfallen; **can·cel'la·tion** Streichung *f*; Entwertung *f*; Aufhebung *f*; Absage *f*; ~ *charge*, ~ *fee* Rücktrittsgebühr *f.*

can·cer ['kænsə] ♐ Krebs *m*; ♋ *ast.* Krebs *m*; **'can·cer·ous** krebsartig.

can·de·la·bra [kændi'lɑːbrə], **can·de·la·brum** [~brəm] Kandelaber *m*, Leuchter *m.*

can·did ☐ ['kændid] aufrichtig; offen.

can·di·da·cy ['kændidəsi] Kandidatur *f*; **can·di·date** ['kændidit] Kandidat *m* (*for* für), Bewerber *m* (*for* um); **can·di·da·ture** ['~tʃə] Kandidatur *f.*

can·died ['kændid] kandiert; *fig.* schmeichelhaft.

can·dle ['kændl] Licht *n*, Kerze *f*; ~ *power* Lichtstärke *f*; *hold a* ~ *to fig.* herankommen an, den Vergleich aushalten mit; *not worth the* ~ nicht der Mühe wert; *burn the* ~ *at both ends* mit s-n Kräften Raubbau treiben; **'~light** Kerzenlicht *n*; **Can·dle·mas** *eccl.* ['~məs] Lichtmeß *f*; **'can·dle·stick** Leuchter *m.*

can·dour ['kændə] Unparteilichkeit *f*; Aufrichtigkeit *f*; Offenheit *f.*

can·dy ['kændi] **1.** Kandis(zucker) *m*; *Am.* Süßigkeiten *f pl.*, Bonbons *m pl.*; **2.** *v t.* kandieren; *v i.* kristallisieren; ~ **floss** Zuckerwatte *f.*

cane [kein] **1.** ♀ Rohr *n*; Peddigrohr *n*; (Rohr)Stock *m*; **2.** aus Rohr flechten; prügeln; ~ **sug·ar** Rohrzucker *m.*

ca·nine 1. ['keinain] Hunds..., Hunde...; **2.** ['kænain] *a.* ~ *tooth* Eckzahn *m.*

can·ing ['keiniŋ] Tracht *f* Prügel.

can·is·ter ['kænistə] Blechbüchse *f*; Kanister *m.*

can·ker ['kæŋkə] **1.** ♐ Krebs *m*; ♀ Brand *m*; *fig.* Krebsschaden *m*; **2.** anfressen; **'can·kered** *fig.* giftig (*bohaft*); **'can·ker·ous** krebsartig.

can·na·bis ['kænəbis] Hanf *m*; Haschisch *n.*

canned *Am.* [kænd] Büchsen..., eingemacht.

can·ner·y *Am.* ['kænəri] Konservenfabrik *f.*

can·ni·bal ['kænibəl] **1.** Kannibale *m*, Menschenfresser *m*; **2.** kannibalisch; Kannibalen...; **'can·ni·bal·ism** Kannibalismus *m*; **'can·ni·bal·ize** Auto *etc.* ausschlachten.

can·non ['kænən] **1.** ✗ Kanone *f*; Artillerie *f*; *Billard:* Karambolage *f*; **2.** karambolieren (*fig. against, with* mit); **can·non·ade** [~'neid]

Kanonade *f*; '**can·non-ball** Kanonenkugel *f*; '**can·non-fod·der** Kanonenfutter *n*.

can·not ['kænɔt] kann nicht.

can·ny □ *schott.* ['kæni] vorsichtig; sanft, ruhig.

ca·noe [kə'nu:] 1. Kanu *n*; Paddelboot *n*; 2. paddeln.

can·on ['kænən] Kanon *m* (*Regel*; *Richtschnur*; *Gesamtheit echter Schriften*; *Verzeichnis der Heiligen*; *Kettengesang*; *Schriftgrad*); Kanoniker *m*, Domherr *m*; ~ *law* kanonisches Recht *n*, Kirchenrecht *n*.

ca·ñon ['kænjən] = canyon.

can·on·ess ['kænɔnis] Stiftsdame *f*; **can·on·i·za·tion** [ˌnaiˈzeiʃən] Heiligsprechung *f*; '**can·on·ize** heiligsprechen; '**can·on·ry** Kanonikat *n*.

ca·noo·dle *sl.* [kə'nu:dl] knutschen.

can·o·py ['kænəpi] 1. Baldachin *m* (*a. fig.*); *fig.* Dach *n*; ⚓ Überdachung *f*; ✈ Kabinendach *n*; 2. (mit einem Baldachin) überdachen.

cant¹ [kænt] 1. Schrägung *f*; schräge Lage *f*; Stoß *m*, Ruck *m*; 2. (sich) auf die Seite legen *od.* werfen; kanten; ~ *over* umkippen.

cant² [ˍ] 1. Zunftsprache *f*, *besondere* Ausdrucksweise *f*; Gewäsch *n*; scheinheiliges Gerede *n*; Scheinheiligkeit *f*; thieves' ~ Diebessprache *f*; 2. zunftmäßig *od.* scheinheilig reden.

can't F [ka:nt] = cannot.

Can·tab F ['kæntæb] (Student *m*) von Cambridge.

can·ta·loup ♀ ['kæntəlu:p] Zuckermelone *f*.

can·tan·ker·ous F □ [kən'tæŋkərəs] zänkisch, mürrisch; rechthaberisch.

can·teen [kæn'ti:n] ✕ Feldflasche *f*; *Kasernen-, Betriebs- etc.* Kantine *f*; ✕ Kochgeschirr *n*; *Tafel*-Silberkasten *m*.

can·ter ['kæntə] 1. kurzer Galopp *m*, Kanter *m*; 2. in kurzem Galopp reiten, kantern.

can·ter·bur·y ['kæntəbəri] Notenständer *m*; ♀ *bell* ♀ Glockenblume *f*.

can·thar·i·des ✻ [kæn'θæridi:z] *pl.*, *mst sg.* Kanthariden *f/pl.* (*spanische Fliegen*).

can·ti·cle ['kæntikl] Lobgesang *m*; ♀s *pl. Bibel*: das Hohelied.

can·ti·le·ver ⚓ ['kæntili:və] Konsole *f*; freitragender Arm *m*;

~ **bridge** Auslegerbrücke *f*.

can·to ['kæntəu] Gesang *m* (*Abteilung e-s Gedichtes*).

can·ton 1. ['kæntən] Kanton *m*, Bezirk *m*; 2. ✕ [kən'tu:n] (sich) einquartieren; '**can·ton·ment** ✕ Quartier *n*, Ortsunterkunft *f*.

can·vas ['kænvəs] Segeltuch *n*; Zelt(e *pl.*) *n*; Zeltbahn *f*; *Wagen*-Plane *f*; Segel *n/pl.*; *paint.* Leinwand *f*, *weitS.* Gemälde *n*.

can·vass [ˍ] 1. (Stimmen)Werbung *f*; *Am. a.* Wahlnachprüfung *f*; 2. *v/t.* erörtern; *Wahlkreis od. Wähler* bearbeiten (*a. fig.*); *v/i.* (Stimmen, *a.* Kunden) werben; '**can·vass·er** Stimmen-, Kundenwerber(in); *Am. a.* Wahlprüfer *m*.

can·yon ['kænjən] Cañon *m*, Felsschlucht *f*.

caou·tchouc ['kautʃuk] Kautschuk *m*, *n*.

cap [kæp] 1. Kappe *f*; Mütze *f*; Haube *f*; *univ.* Barett *n*; ⊕, ⚑ *etc.* Kappe *f*, Haube *f*; ⊕ Aufsatz *m*; Zündhütchen *n*; ~ *and bells* Schellenkappe *f*; ~ *and gown* Barett *n* und Talar *m* (*akademische Tracht*); ~ *in hand fig.* demütig, unterwürfig; set one's ~ at *s.o.* nach j-m angeln (*Frau*); 2. mit einer Kappe *etc.* versehen; *fig.* krönen; F übertreffen, -trumpfen; die Mütze abnehmen (to *s.o.* vor j-m); be ~ped *Sport*: in die Nationalmannschaft berufen werden.

ca·pa·bil·i·ty [keipə'biliti] *körperliche od. geistige* Fähigkeit *f*; '**ca·pa·ble** □ fähig, imstande (of zu); tüchtig.

ca·pa·cious □ [kə'peiʃəs] geräumig, umfassend; **ca·pac·i·tate** [kə'pæsiteit] befähigen; **ca'pac·i·ty** 1. Inhalt *m*; Kapazität *f*, Aufnahme-, Ladefähigkeit *f*; *geistige* (*od.* ⊕ Leistungs)Fähigkeit *f* (for *ger.* zu *inf.*); *amtliche etc.* Stellung *f*; *disposing* ~ Geschäftsfähigkeit *f*; *full to* ~ voll besetzt; *legal* ~ Rechtsfähigkeit *f*; *in my* ~ *as* in meiner Eigenschaft als; 2. *attr.* Höchst...; zahlreich; *thea.* voll.

cap-à-pie [kæpə'pi:] von Kopf bis Fuß.

ca·par·i·son *lit.* [kə'pærisn] Schabracke *f*; *fig.* Putz *m*.

cape¹ [keip] Kap *n*, Vorgebirge *n*.

cape² [ˍ] Cape *n*, Umhang *m*.

caper[1] ⚘ ['keipə] Kaper *f*.

ca·per[2] [↲] **1.** Kapriole *f* (*a. fig.* = *toller Streich*), Luftsprung *m*; *cut* ↳*s* = **2.** Kapriolen *od.* Sprünge machen.

ca·pi·as ⚏ ['keipiæs]: *writ of* ↳ Haftbefehl *m*.

cap·il·lar·i·ty *phys.* [kæpi'læriti] Kapillarität *f*; **cap·il·lar·y** [kə'piləri] **1.** Kapillar...; haarfein; **2.** *anat.* Kapillargefäß *n*.

cap·i·tal ['kæpitl] **1.** ☐ Kapital...; todeswürdig, Tods...; verhängnisvoll; hauptsächlich, Haupt...; vortrefflich, F famos; ↳ *crime* Kapitalverbrechen *n*; ↳ *punishment* Todesstrafe *f*; **2.** Hauptstadt *f*; Kapital *n*; *a.* ↳ *letter typ.* Majuskel *f*, Großbuchstabe *m*; ⚠ Kapitell *n*; ↳ **as·sets** *pl.* Anlagevermögen *n*; ↳ **gains tax** Kapitalertragssteuer *f*; **cap·i·tal·ism** ['↳təlizəm] Kapitalismus *m*; **'cap·i·tal·ist** Kapitalist(in); **cap·i·tal'is·tic** kapitalistisch; **cap·i·tal·i·za·tion** [kəpitəlai'zeiʃən] Kapitalisierung *f*; **cap'i·tal·ize** kapitalisieren; groß schreiben.

cap·i·ta·tion [kæpi'teiʃən] *a.* ↳ *tax* Kopfsteuer *f*; Zahlung *f* pro Kopf.

Cap·i·tol ['kæpitl] Kapitol *n* (*Jupitertempel in Rom u. Sitz des Kongresses in Washington*).

ca·pit·u·late [kə'pitjuleit] kapitulieren (*to* vor *dat.*), sich ergeben; **ca·pit·u·la·tion** Kapitulation *f*, Übergabe *f*.

ca·pon ['keipən] Kapaun *m*.

ca·price [kə'pri:s] Kaprice *f*, Laune *f*; ♪ Capriccio *n*; **ca·pri·cious** ☐ [kə'priʃəs] kapriziös; launisch, launenhaft; **ca'pri·cious·ness** Launenhaftigkeit *f*.

Cap·ri·corn *ast.* ['kæprikɔ:n] Steinbock *m*.

cap·ri·ole ['kæpriəul] Kapriole *f* (*Luftsprung*).

cap·size ⚓ ['kæpsaiz] **1.** *v*/*i*. kentern; *fig.* sich überschlagen; *v*/*t*. zum Kentern bringen; **2.** Kentern *n*.

cap·stan ⚓ ['kæpstən] Gangspill *n*.

cap·su·lar ['kæpsjulə] kapselförmig; Kapsel...; **cap·sule** ♀ *u.* ⚕ ['kæpsju:l] Kapsel *f*.

cap·tain ['kæptin] Führer *m*; Heerführer *m*, Feldherr *m*; *Sport*: Spiel-, Mannschaftsführer *m*; ⚓ Kapitän *m*; ⚔ Hauptmann *m*; ↳ *of industry* Industriekapitän *m*; **cap·tain·cy,**

cap·tain·ship ['↳si, '↳ʃip] Führung *f*; Kapitäns-, Hauptmannsstelle *f*, -rang *m*.

cap·tion ['kæpʃən] **1.** Überschrift *f*; Titel *m*; *Film*: Untertitel *m*; **2.** *v*/*t*. *Am.* mit Überschrift *od.* Titel *etc.* versehen.

cap·tious ☐ ['kæpʃəs] krittelig; spitzfindig.

cap·ti·vate *fig.* ['kæptiveit] gefangennehmen, fesseln; **cap·ti'va·tion** Fesselung *f*; **'cap·tive 1.** gefangen, gefesselt; ↳ *balloon* Fesselballon *m*; **2.** Gefangene *m, f* (*a. fig.*); **cap·tiv·i·ty** [↳'tiviti] Gefangenschaft *f*.

cap·tor ['kæptə] Fänger *m*; ⚔ Kaper *m*; **cap·ture** ['↳tʃə] **1.** Eroberung *f*; Gefangennahme *f*; ⚔ Kapern *n*; **2.** (ein)fangen; gefangennehmen; erobern; erbeuten; ⚔ kapern, aufbringen.

Cap·u·chin *eccl.* ['kæpjuʃin] Kapuziner *m*.

car [kɑ:] Auto *n*, Wagen *m*; (Eisenbahn-, Straßenbahn)Wagen *m*; Ballonkorb *m*; Luftschiffgondel *f*; Kabine *f* e-s *Aufzugs*; ↳ *park* Parkplatz *m*; Parkhaus *n*; ↳ *pool* Fahrgemeinschaft *f*; Fahrbereitschaft *f*; ↳*port* überdachter Autoabstellplatz *m*.

car·a·cole ['kærəkəul] *Reitkunst*: **1.** Schwenkung *f*; **2.** schwenken.

ca·rafe [kə'ræf] Karaffe *f*.

car·a·mel ['kærəmel] Karamel *m*; Karamelle *f*.

car·a·pace *zo.* ['kærəpeis] Rückenschild *m*.

car·at ['kærət] Karat *n* (*Gewicht*).

car·a·van ['kærəvæn] Karawane *f*; Wohnwagen *m*; **car·a'van·se·rai** [↳sərai] Karawanserei *f*; **car·a·van site** Campingplatz *m* für Wohnwagen.

car·a·way ⚘ ['kærəwei] Kümmel *m*.

car·bide ⚗ ['kɑ:baid] Karbid *n*.

car·bine ['kɑ:bain] Karabiner *m*.

car·bo·hy·drate ⚗ ['kɑ:bəu'haidreit] Kohlehydrat *n*.

car·bol·ic ac·id ⚗ [kɑ:'bɔlik'æsid] Karbolsäure *f*.

car·bon ['kɑ:bən] ⚗ Kohlenstoff *m*; ⚡ Kohlestift *m*; *a.* ↳ *paper* Kohlepapier *n*; ↳ *copy* Durchschlag *m* von *Maschinenschrift*; ↳ *dioxide* Kohlendioxyd *n*; ↳ *monoxide* Kohlenmonoxyd *n*; **car·bo·na·ceous** [↳bəu'neiʃəs] kohlenstoffhaltig; **car·bon·ate** ['↳bənit] kohlensaures Salz

n; **car·bon·ic** [~'bɔnik] Kohlen...;
~ **acid** Kohlensäure *f*; **car·bon·if·er·ous** *geol.* [~bə'nifərəs] kohleführend (*Schicht*); **car·bon·i·za·tion** [~bənai'zeiʃən] Verkohlung *f*; **'car·bon·ize** verkohlen.

car·bo·run·dum [ka:bə'rʌndəm] Karborund *n* (*Schleifmittel*).

car·boy ['ka:bɔi] Säureballon *m*.

car·bun·cle ['ka:bʌŋkl] *min.* Karfunkel *m*; *s* Karbunkel *m*.

car·bu·ret 🜍 ['ka:bjuret] vergasen; **'car·bu·ret·ter**, *mst* **'car·bu·ret·tor** *mot.* Vergaser *m*.

car·case, *mst* **car·cass** ['ka:kəs] (Tier)Kadaver *m*; *Fleischerei:* Rumpf *m*; *fig.* Gerippe *n*.

car·ci·no·ma *s* [ka:si'nəumə] Karzinom *n*, Krebs *m*; **car·cin·o·gen·ic** [~nə'dʒenik] karzinogen, krebserregend.

card[1] ⊕ [ka:d] **1.** Wollkratze *f*, Karde *f*; **2.** *Wolle* karden, kämmen.

card[2] [~] Karte *f*; (Post-, Visiten-, Spiel)Karte *f*; *house of* ~s Kartenhaus *n*; *queer* ~ F komischer Kauz *m*; *have a* ~ *up one's sleeve et.* in petto haben.

car·dan ⊕ ['ka:dən]: ~ *joint* Kardangelenk *n*; ~ *shaft* Kardanwelle *f*.

card...: '~**board** Kartonpapier *n*; Pappe *f*; '~ *box* Pappkarton *m*.

car·di·ac *s* ['ka:diæk] **1.** Herz...; ~ *arrest* Herzstillstand *m*; ~ *stimulant* herzstärkendes Mittel; **2.** Herzmittel *n*.

car·di·gan ['ka:digən] Strickjacke *f*.

car·di·nal □ ['ka:dinl] **1.** Kardinal..., Haupt...; hochrot; ~ *number* Grundzahl *f*; **2.** Kardinal *m* (*a. orn.*); **car·di·nal·ate** ['~nəleit] Kardinalswürde *f*.

card...: '~**in·dex** Kartei *f*; '~**sharp·er** Falschspieler *m*.

care [kɛə] **1.** Sorge *f*; Sorgfalt *f*, Acht(samkeit) *f*; Obhut *f*, Pflege *f*; *medical* ~ ärztliche Behandlung *f*; ~ *of the mouth* Mundpflege *f*; ~ *of the nails* Nagelpflege *f*; ~ *of* (*abbr. c/o*) ... per Adresse, bei ...; *take* ~ sich in acht nehmen, achtgeben; *take* ~! *bsd. Am.* F mach's gut!; *take* ~ *of* aufpassen *od.* acht(geb)en auf (*acc.*); verantwortlich sein für; *with* ~! Vorsicht! (*Aufschrift*); **2.** Lust *od.* Interesse haben (*to inf.* zu *inf.*); ~ *for* sorgen für, sich kümmern um; *mst verneint:*

sich etwas machen aus, mögen; *I don't* ~ (*if I do*)! F meinetwegen!; *I don't* ~ *what he said* es ist mir egal, was er gesagt hat; *I couldn't* ~ *less* F es ist mir völlig schnuppe; *well* ~d-for gepflegt.

ca·reen ⚓ [kə'ri:n] kielholen.

ca·reer [kə'riə] **1.** Karriere *f*; Laufbahn *f*, Beruf *m*; Lauf *m*; ~ *diplomat* Berufsdiplomat *m*; **2.** rasen, rennen; **ca'reer·ist** Karrieremacher *m*, Streber *m*.

care·free ['kɛəfri:] sorgenfrei, sorglos.

care·ful □ ['kɛəful] besorgt (*for um*), achtsam (*of acc.*); sorgsam, vorsichtig; sorgfältig, gewissenhaft; *be* ~ *to inf.* darauf bedacht sein zu *inf.*; *nicht vergessen to inf.*; **'care·ful·ness** Sorgsamkeit *f*; Vorsicht *f*; Sorgfalt *f*.

care·less □ ['kɛəlis] sorglos; unbekümmert (*of um*); unsorgfältig, nachlässig; unachtsam; unbedacht, unbesonnen, leichtsinnig, unvorsichtig; **'care·less·ness** Sorglosigkeit *f*; Nachlässigkeit *f*.

ca·ress [kə'res] **1.** Liebkosung *f*; **2.** liebkosen; *fig.* schmeicheln.

care·tak·er ['kɛəteikə] Wärter(in); (Haus)Verwalter(in); ~ *government* geschäftsführende Regierung *f*.

care-worn ['kɛəwɔ:n] abgehärmt.

car·fare *Am.* ['ka:fɛə] Fahrgeld *n*.

car-ferry ['ka:feri] Autofährschiff *n*; *a. car-air-ferry* Autoluftfähre *f*.

car·go ⚓ ['ka:gəu] Ladung *f*, Fracht *f*; *mixed od. general* ~ Stückgut *n*; *shifting* ~ *lose* Ladung *f*.

car·i·bou *zo.* ['kæribu:] Karibu *m*.

car·i·ca·ture [kærikə'tjuə] **1.** Karikatur *f*; **2.** karikieren; **car·i·ca'tur·ist** Karikaturist *m*.

car·i·es *s* ['kɛərii:z] Karies *f*; Knochenfraß *m*; Zahnfäule *f*.

car·il·lon [kæ'riljən] Glockenspiel *n*.

car·i·ous ['kɛəriəs] kariös, angefault.

car·load ['ka:ləud] Wagenladung *f*; F Menge *f*.

car·man ['ka:mən] Fuhrmann *m*.

car·mine ['ka:main] Karmin(rot) *n*.

car·nage ['ka:nidʒ] Blutbad *n*; **'car·nal** □ fleischlich; sinnlich, geschlechtlich; **car·nal·i·ty** [~'næliti] Fleischeslust *f*; Sinnlichkeit *f*; **car·na·tion** [~'neiʃən] **1.** Fleischton *m*, Blaßrot *n*; ⚘ Nelke *f*; **2.** blaßrot.

car·ni·val ['ka:nivəl] Karneval *m*,

Fasching *m*.

car·ni·vore ['kɑːnivɔː] Fleischfresser *m*; **car·niv·o·rous** [ˌⁱniˈvərəs] fleischfressend.

car·ol ['kærəl] **1.** Weihnachtslied *n*; **2.** Weihnachtslieder singen.

ca·rot·id *anat.* [kəˈrɔtid] *a.* ⌣ *artery* Karotis *f* (*Halsschlagader*).

ca·rouse [kəˈrauz] **1.** *a.* **ca'rous·al** (Trink)Gelage *n*; **2.** zechen.

carp[1] [kɑːp] Karpfen *m*.

carp[2] [ˌⁱ] kritteln, nörgeln; ⌣ *at* kritteln an (*dat.*), bekritteln.

car·pen·ter ['kɑːpintə] **1.** Zimmermann *m*; **2.** zimmern; '**car·pen·try** Zimmerhandwerk *n*.

car·pet ['kɑːpit] **1.** Teppich *m* (*a. fig.*); *bring on the* ⌣ aufs Tapet bringen; ⌣ *dance* zwangloses Tänzchen *n*; **2.** mit e-m Teppich belegen; ⁼ zur Rede stellen; '⌣-**bag** Reisetasche *f*; '⌣-**bag·ger** politischer Abenteurer *m*; '**car·pet·ing** Teppichstoff *m*.

car·pet...: '⌣-'**knight** Salonlowe *m*; '⌣-**sweep·er** Teppichkehrmaschine *f*.

car·riage ['kæridʒ] Beförderung *f*. Transport *m*; Fracht *f*; Wagen *m* (*a.* ⊕); Kutsche *f*; ✕ Lafette *f*. Fuhr-, Frachtlohn *m*; KörperHaltung *f*, Gang *m*; Benehmen *n*; Aus-, Durchführung *f*; ⌣ *free,* ⌣ *paid* frachtfrei; **car·riage·a·ble** befahrbar (*Weg* .

car·riage...: ⌣-**drive** Anfahrt *f* (*vor e-m Hause* ; ⌣-**way** Fahrbahn *f*; *dual* ⌣ doppelte Fahrbahn *f*.

car·ri·er ['kæriə] Fuhrmann *m*; Spediteur *m*; Träger *m a.* ✠ = Keim ; Gepäckträger *m am Fahrrad*; '⌣-**bag** Trag e tasche *f*. '⌣-**pigeon** Brieftaube *f*.

car·ri·on ['kæriən] **1.** Aas *n*; Unrat *m*; **2.** Aas...

car·rot ['kærət] Mohrrübe *f*, Möhre *f*, Karotte *f*; '**car·rot·y** F rot (-blond).

car·ry ['kæri] **1.** *v/t. wohin* bringen, führen, tragen, fahren, befördern; (bei sich) haben; *Ansicht* durchsetzen; *Gewinn, Preis* davontragen; *Zahlen* übertragen; *Ernte, Zinsen* tragen; ⚓ *Segel* führen; *Mauer etc.* weiterführen; *Benehmen* fortsetzen; *Antrag, Kandidaten* durchbringen; ✕ *Festung etc.* erobern; *be carried* angenommen werden, durchgehen

(*Antrag*); durchkommen (*Kandidat*); ⌣ *the day* den Sieg davontragen; ⌣ *away* wegtragen; fortreißen (*a. fig.*); ⌣ *everything before one* alles mit sich fortreißen; ⌣ *forward od.* over ✝ vor-, übertragen; ⌣ *on* fortsetzen, weiterführen; *Geschäft, Prozeß etc.* betreiben, führen; ⌣ *out,* ⌣ *through* durchführen; ⌣ *out* ♂ *Strafe* vollstrecken; *v/i.* tragen; *weit etc.* tragen (*Gewehr*); ⌣ *on* F sich haben; weitermachen; ⌣ing *capacity* Tragfähigkeit *f*; **2.** Trag-, Schußweite *f*; '⌣-**cot** Babytragtasche *f*.

cart [kɑːt] **1.** Karren *m*; *bsd. in Zssgn:* Wagen *m*; ⌣ *grease* Wagenschmiere *f*; *put the* ⌣ *before the horse fig.* das Pferd beim Wagen aufzäumen; *in the* ⌣ *sl.* in der Patsche; **2.** karren, fahren; '**cart·age** Fahren *n*; Fuhrlohn *m*; Rollgeld *n*.

car·tel [kɑː tel] Kartell *n*, Zweckverband *m*; ✕ (Abkommen *n* über den Austausch *m* von Gefangenen.

cart·er [kɑːtə] Fuhrmann *m*.

car·ti·lage [kɑːtilidʒ] Knorpel *m*; **car·ti·lag·i·nous** [ˌⁱlædʒinəs] knorpelig.

cart·load [kɑːtləud] Fuhre *f*.

car·tog·ra·pher [kɑː tɔɡrəfə] Kartograph *m*; **car·tog·ra·phy** Kartographie *f*.

car·ton ['kɑːtən] Karton *m*; *a* ⌣ *of cigarettes* e-e Stange *f* Zigaretten.

car·toon [kɑː tuːn] **1.** *paint.* Karton *m*; ⊕ Musterzeichnung *f*; Karikatur *f*; Zeichentrickfilm *m*; **2.** karikieren; **car'toon·ist** Karikaturist *m*.

car·touche △ [kɑː tuːʃ] Kartusche *f*.

car·tridge ['kɑːtridʒ] Patrone *f*; Film Kassette *f*; '⌣-**pa·per** Zeichenpapier *n*.

cart·wheel ['kɑːtwiːl] Wagenrad *n*; *Am.* Silberdollar *m*; *turn* ⌣*s* radschlagen.

cart·wright ['kɑːtrait] Stellmacher *m*.

carve [kɑːv] *Fleisch* vorschneiden, zerlegen; (*in*) *Holz* schnitzen; (*in*) *Stein* meißeln; sich *e-n Weg* bahnen; '**carv·er** (Bild)Schnitzer *m*; Vorschneider *m*; Vorlegemesser *n*; ⌣*s pl.* Vorlegebesteck *n*; '**carv·ing** **1.** Schnitzerei *f*; **2.** Schnitz...; Vorlege...

car wash ['kɑːwɔʃ] Autowaschanlage *f*.

cas·cade [kæs'keid] Kaskade *f*
(*kleiner Wasserfall*).
case¹ [keis] **1.** Behälter *m*; Kiste *f*;
Futteral *n*, Etui *n*, Tasche *f*; Gehäuse *n*; Schachtel *f*; Scheide *f*;
Kapsel *f*; Fach *n*; Necessaire *n*;
Patronen-Hülse *f*; *typ.* Setzkasten
m; **2.** (ein)stecken; ver-, umkleiden
(with mit).
case² [~] Fall *m* (*a.* 🎖, ⚖); ⚕ *a.*
Kranke *m*, *f*; *Am.* F komischer
Kauz *m*; ⚖ *a.* Rechtsgrund *m*,
Schriftsatz *m*; Hauptargument *n*;
Sache *f*, Angelegenheit *f*; *a* ~ *for*
gewichtige Gründe für; *make out*
one's ~ seine Argumente vorbringen; *have a strong* ~ das Recht auf
seiner Seite haben; *as the* ~ *may be*
je nachdem; *in* ~ im Falle, falls, für
den Fall, daß; *in any* ~ jedenfalls.
case-book ['keisbuk] Patientenbuch *n*.
case-hard·en ⊕ ['keishɑ:dn] hart-
gießen; ~*ed fig.* hartgesotten.
case his·to·ry ['keishistəri] Vor-
geschichte *f*; Krankengeschichte *f*.
ca·se·in ⚗ ['keisi:in] Käsestoff *m*.
case·mate ⚔ ['keismeit] Kasematte *f*.
case·ment ['keismənt] Fenster-
flügel *m*; ~ *window* Flügelfenster *n*.
case-shot ⚔ ['keisʃɔt] Kartätsche *f*.
cash [kæʃ] **1.** Bargeld *n*, Kasse *f*;
~ *down, for* ~ gegen bar; *in* ~ bar,
netto Kasse; *be in (out of)* ~ bei
(nicht bei) Kasse sein; ~ *and carry*
Barzahlung *f* und Selbstabholung *f*
(im Großhandel); ~ *payment* Barzahlung *f*; ~ *on delivery* Lieferung *f*
gegen bar, (per) Nachnahme *f*; ~
price Kassenpreis *m*; ~ *register* Registrierkasse *f*; **2.** einkassieren, -lö-
sen; '~**book** Kassabuch *n*; '~-
cheque Barscheck *m*; ~ **desk** Kasse
f, Kassentisch *m*; ~ **dis·pens·er** Geld-
automat *m*; **cash·ier 1.** [kæ'ʃiə] Kas-
sierer(in); **2.** [kə'ʃiə] ⚔ kassieren (*entlassen*); **cash·less** ['kæʃlis] bargeldlos.
cash·mere [kæʃ'miə] Kaschmir *m*
(*feiner Wollstoff*).
cas·ing ['keisiŋ] Überzug *m*, Gehäuse *n*, Futteral *n*; ⚠ Verkleidung
f; ~ *paper* Packpapier *n*.
ca·si·no [kə'si:nəu] Kasino *n*.
cask [kɑ:sk] Faß *n*.
cas·ket ['kɑ:skit] Kassette *f*,
(Schmuck)Kästchen *n*; *Am.* Sarg *m*.
Cas·pi·an Sea ['kæspiən'si:] *das*
Kaspische Meer, *der* Kaspisee.

casque [kæsk] Helm *m*.
cas·sa·tion [kæ'seiʃən] Kassation *f*.
cas·sa·va ⚘ [kə'sɑ:və] Maniok-
strauch *m*.
cas·se·role ['kæsərəul] Kasserolle *f*,
Tiegel *m*.
cas·sette [kæ'set] Film-, Tonbandkas-
sette *f*; ~ **deck** Kassettendeck *n*.
cas·si·a ⚘ ['kæsiə] Kassia *f*; *Art*
Zimt *m*.
cas·sock ['kæsək] Soutane *f*, Prie-
sterrock *m*.
cas·so·war·y *orn.* ['kæsəweəri] Kasuar *m*; *New Holland* ~ Emu *m*.
cast [kɑ:st] **1.** Wurf *m*; Wurfweite
f; ⊕ Guß(form *f*) *m*; Abguß *m*,
-druck *m*; Schattierung *f*, Anflug
m; Form *f*, Art *f*, Zuschnitt *m*; ⚓
Auswerfen *n* von Senkblei, Netz
etc.; *thea.* (Rollen)Besetzung *f*; ✝
Aufrechnung *f*; **2.** (*irr.*) *v/t.* (ab-,
aus-, hin-, um-, weg)werfen; *zo.*
Haut *etc.* abwerfen; *Zähne etc.* verlieren; *Anker, fig. Blick, Licht,
Schatten etc.* werfen; verwerfen,
ausmustern; gestalten; *Metall* gießen; *a.* ~ *up* aus-, zs.-rechnen; *thea.
Rolle* besetzen; *Rolle* übertragen
(*to dat.*); *be* ~ *in costs* ⚖ zu den
Kosten verurteilt werden; *be* ~ *in a
lawsuit* ⚖ e-n Prozeß verlieren; ~
lots (for) losen (um); ~ *in one's lot
with s.o.* j-s Los teilen; ~ *one's skin*
sich häuten; ~ *s.th. in s.o.'s teeth*
j-m et. vorwerfen; ~ *away* wegwerfen; *be* ~ *away* ⚓ verschlagen werden; ~ *down* niederwerfen; *die Augen*
niederschlagen; *be* ~ *down* niedergeschlagen sein; ~ *up* aufwerfen;
erbrechen; ~ *up (accounts)* ✝ zs.-
rechnen; *v/i.* sich gießen lassen; ⊕
sich (ver)werfen; ~ *about for* sinnen
auf (*acc.*); sich *et.* überlegen; ~ *off*
⚓ loswerfen.
cas·ta·net [kæstə'net] Kastagnette *f*.
cast·a·way ['kɑ:stəwei] **1.** verworfen; ⚓ schiffbrüchig; **2.** Ver-
worfene *m*, *f*; Schiffbrüchige *m*, *f*
(*a. fig.*), Gestrandete *m*, *f*.
caste [kɑ:st] Kaste *f* (*a. fig.*); ~ *feeling* Kastengeist *m*.
cas·tel·lan ['kæstələn] Kastellan *m*;
cas·tel·lat·ed ['kæsteleitid] mit
Zinnen (versehen); burgenreich.
cast·er ['kɑ:stə] = *castor*².
cas·ti·gate ['kæstigeit] züchtigen;
fig. geißeln; **cas·ti·ga·tion** Züchtigung *f*; *fig.* Geißelung *f*.

cast·ing ['kɑːstiŋ] **1.** Wurf...; entscheidend (*Stimme*); **2.** Werfen *n* etc.; ~s *pl.* Gußwaren *f/pl.*

cast i·ron ['kɑːst'aiən] Gußeisen *n*; '**cast-'i·ron** gußeisern.

cas·tle ['kɑːsl] **1.** Burg *f*, Schloß *n*; *Schach*: Turm *m*; ~s *in the air*, ~s *in Spain* Luftschlösser *n/pl.*; **2.** *Schach*: rochieren.

cast-off ['kɑːst'ɔf] Verstoßene *m*, *f*; Abgelegte *n*.

cas·tor[1] *pharm.* ['kɑːstə]: ~ *oil* Rizinusöl *n*.

cas·tor[2] [~] Laufrolle *f* unter Möbeln; (Salz-, Zucker- etc.) Streuer *m*; ~ *sugar* Streuzucker *m*.

cas·trate [kæs'treit] kastrieren; **cas'tra·tion** Kastrierung *f*; Verstümmelung *f*.

cast steel ['kɑːst'stiːl] Gußstahl *m*; '**cast-'steel** aus Gußstahl.

cas·u·al □ ['kæʒjuəl] zufällig; gelegentlich; beiläufig; F lässig; ~ *labourer* Gelegenheitsarbeiter *m*; '**cas·u·al·ty** Unfall *m*; *casualties pl.* ✕ Verluste *m/pl.*

cas·u·ist ['kæzjuist] Kasuist *m*; '**cas·u·ist·ry** Kasuistik *f*.

cat [kæt] **1.** Katze *f*; *Am. sl.* Jazzfanatiker *m*; *wait for the ~ to jump*, *see which way the ~ jumps* sehen, wie der Hase läuft; *not room to swing a ~* kaum Platz zum Umdrehen; ~ *burglar* Fassadenkletterer *m*, Einsteigdieb *m*; **2.** P kotzen.

cat·a·clysm ['kætəklizəm] Sintflut *f*; Katastrophe *f*.

cat·a·comb ['kætəkuːm] Katakombe *f*.

cat·a·logue, *Am. a.* **cat·a·log** ['kætəlɔg] **1.** Katalog *m*; Liste *f*; (*Am. univ.* Vorlesungs)Verzeichnis *n*; **2.** katalogisieren.

ca·tal·y·sis ♈ [kə'tælisis], *pl.* **ca'tal·y·ses** [~siːz] Katalyse *f*; **cat·a·lyst** ['kætəlist] (*a. fig.*) Katalysator *m*.

cat·a·pult ['kætəpʌlt] Schleuder *f*; ✄ Katapult *m*, *n*.

cat·a·ract ['kætərækt] Katarakt *m*, Wasserfall *m*; ✖ grauer Star *m*.

ca·tarrh [kə'tɑː] Katarrh *m*; F *bsd.* Schnupfen *m*; **ca·tarrh·al** [kə'tɑːrəl] katarrhalisch; Schnupfen...

ca·tas·tro·phe [kə'tæstrəfi] Katastrophe *f*; **cat·a·stroph·ic** [kætə'strɔfik] (~*ally*) katastrophal.

ca·taw·ba *Am.* ♀ [kə'tɔːbə] Cataw-
ba-Rebe *f*.

cat·bird *zo.* ['kætbɔːd] Spottdrossel *f*.

cat bur·glar ['kætbɔːglə] Einsteigdieb *m*, Fassadenkletterer *m*.

cat·call ['kætkɔːl] **1.** *thea. etc.* (gellender) Pfiff *m*; **2.** auspfeifen.

catch [kætʃ] **1.** Fang *m*; Beute *f*, *fig.* Vorteil *m*; ♪ Rundgesang *m*; Kniff *m*; ⊕ Haken *m* (*a. fig. e-r Sache*), Griff *m*, Schnapper *m*, Klinke *f*; *s.* ~*word*; **2.** (*irr.*) *v/t.* fassen, *oft* F kriegen; fangen, ergreifen; abfassen, ertappen; *Blick etc.* auffangen, erhaschen; *Zug etc.* erreichen; bekommen, erhalten; sich *Krankheit* zuziehen, holen; angesteckt werden (von); *Feuer* fangen; *Atem* anhalten; *Schlag* versetzen, *mit e-m Schlag* treffen; *fig.* erfassen, verstehen; ~ *it* F es (*Prügel*, *Schelte*) kriegen; ~ *in the act* auf frischer Tat ertappen; ~ *me!* da kannst du lange warten!, das fällt mir nicht ein!; ~ (*a*) *cold* sich erkälten; ~ *s.o.'s eye* j-m ins Auge fallen; ~ *the Speaker's eye* (*im engl. Parlament*) das Wort erhalten; ~ *up* auffangen; F *j.* unterbrechen; einholen; *v/i.* sich verfangen, hängenbleiben; fassen, einschnappen (*Schloß etc.*); ~ *at* fassen *od.* greifen nach; ~ *on* F Anklang finden; *Am.* kapieren; ~ *up with j.* einholen; '~**all** *Am.* Platz *m od.* Behälter *m* für alles mögliche (*a. fig. u. attr.*); '~**-as-'catch-'can** *Sport*: Freistilringen *n*; '**catch·er** Fänger(in); '**catch·ing** packend; ♪ eingängig; ✿ ansteckend; '**catch-line** Schlagzeile *f*; '**catch·ment ba·sin** Einzugsgebiet *n e-s Stromes*; Staubecken *n*, -see *m*.

catch...: '~**-pen·ny** ✝ Lock..., Schleuder...; '~**-phrase** Schlagwort *n*; '~**pole** Büttel *m*; '~**word** Schlagwort *n*; *thea.*, *typ.* Stichwort *n*; '**catch·y** F *fig.* packend; verfänglich.

cat·e·chism ['kætikizəm] Katechismus *m*; **cat·e·chize** [~kaiz] katechisieren; **cat·e·chu·men** [~'kjuːmen] Konfirmand *m*.

cat·e·gor·i·cal □ [kæti'gɔrikəl] kategorisch; **cat·e·go·ry** ['~gəri] Kategorie *f*, Klasse *f*, Gruppe *f*.

ca·ter ['keitə]: ~ *for* Lebensmittel liefern für; *fig.* sorgen für; befriedigen; **'ca·ter·er** (Lebensmittel)Lieferant *m*; Gastwirt *m*; Hotelier *m*; **'ca·ter·ing** Verpflegung *f*.

cat·er·pil·lar ['kætəpilə] Raupe *f*.

cat·er·waul ['kætəwɔːl] miauen.

cat·fish ['kætfiʃ] Katzenfisch *m*, Wels *m*.

cat·gut ['kætgʌt] Darmsaite *f*.

ca·thar·sis [kə'θɑːsis] seelische Läuterung *f*; 𝒮 Abführen *n*; **ca'thar·tic** [∼tik] reinigend, läuternd.

ca·the·dral [kə'θiːdrəl] **1.** Dom *m*, Kathedrale *f*; **2.** Dom...

Cath·er·ine-wheel ['kæθərinwiːl] ⚙ Fensterrose *f*; *Feuerwerk:* Feuerrad *n*.

cath·e·ter 𝒮 ['kæθitə] Katheter *m*.

cath·ode ⚡ ['kæθəud] **1.** Kathode *f*; **2.** Kathoden...; **∼ ray** Kathodenstrahl *m*.

cath·o·lic ['kæθəlik] **1.** (∼ally) katholisch; **2.** Katholik(in); **ca·thol·i·cism** [kə'θɔlisizəm] Katholizismus *m*.

cat·kin ♀ ['kætkin] (Blüten)Kätzchen *n*.

cat·like ['kætlaik] katzenartig; **'cat·nap** Nickerchen *n*; **'cat·nip** ♀ Katzenminze *f*.

cat-o'-nine-tails ['kætə'nainteilz] neunschwänzige Katze *f* (*Peitsche*).

cat's...: ∼ **eye** Katzenauge *n*; **'∼-paw** *fig.* ['kætspɔː] (willenloses) Werkzeug *n*.

cat·suit ['kætsuːt] Overall *m*, einteiliger Hosenanzug *m*.

cat·tish *fig.* ['kætiʃ] falsch, hinterlistig, boshaft.

cat·tle ['kætl] Vieh *n*; **'∼-breed·ing** Viehzucht *f*; **∼-man** ['∼mən] Viehzüchter *m*; Viehknecht *m*; **'∼-plague** Rinderpest *f*; **'∼-rus·tler** *Am.* Viehdieb *m*; **'∼-show** Viehschau *f*, -ausstellung *f*.

cat·ty ['kæti] = *cattish*.

cat·walk ['kætwɔːk] Laufsteg *m*.

Cau·ca·sian [kɔː'keizjən] **1.** kaukasisch; **2.** Kaukasier(in).

cau·cus ['kɔːkəs] Wahlvorbereitung *f*, -ausschuß *m*; *contp.* Klüngel (-wirtschaft *f*) *m*; *Am. pol.* Parteitagung *f*.

cau·dal ['kɔːdl] Schwanz...; **cau·date** ['∼deit] geschwänzt. [2.)

caught [kɔːt] *pret. u. p.p von catch*)

caul·dron ['kɔːldrən] Kessel *m*.

cau·li·flow·er ♀ ['kɔliflauə] Blumenkohl *m*.

caulk ⚓ [kɔːk] kalfatern (*abdichten*); **'caulk·er** Kalfaterer *m*.

caus·al □ ['kɔːzəl] kausal, ursächlich; **cau·sal·i·ty** [∼'zæliti] Kausalität *f*, Ursächlichkeit *f*; **'caus·a·tive** verursachend (*of acc.*); **cause 1.** Ursache *f*, Grund *m*; 𝚫 Klage (-grund *m*) *f*; Prozeß *m*; Angelegenheit *f*, Sache *f*; *make common* ∼ *with* gemeinsame Sache machen mit; **2.** verursachen, veranlassen; **'cause·less** □ grundlos.

cause·way ['kɔːzwei], *a.* **cau·sey** ['∼zei] Damm *m im Sumpfgelände*.

caus·tic ['kɔːstik] **1.** Ätzmittel *n*; **2.** (∼ally) ätzend; *fig.* scharf, beißend.

cau·ter·i·za·tion 𝒮 [kɔːtərai'zeiʃən] Ausbrennen *n*; **'cau·ter·ize** (aus-) brennen, beizen; **'cau·ter·y** Brenneisen *n*.

cau·tion ['kɔːʃən] **1.** Vorsicht *f*; Warnung *f*; *tadelnde* Verwarnung *f*; 𝚫 Rechtsbelehrung *f*; F ulkige Nummer *f*; ∼ *money* Kaution *f*, Haftsumme *f*; **2.** warnen (*against* vor *dat.*); *tadelnd* verwarnen; 𝚫 belehren; **cau·tion·ar·y** ['∼ʃnəri] warnend.

cau·tious □ ['kɔːʃəs] behutsam, vorsichtig; **'cau·tious·ness** Behutsamkeit *f*, Vorsicht *f*.

cav·al·cade [kævəl'keid] Kavalkade *f*, Reiterzug *m*, -trupp *m*.

cav·a·lier [kævə'liə] **1.** Kavalier *m*; Reiter *m*; **2.** □ hochmütig.

cav·al·ry ⚔ ['kævəlri] Kavallerie *f*, Reiterei *f*.

cave [keiv] **1.** Höhle *f*; *attr.* Höhlen...; **2.** ∼ *in v/i.* einstürzen; klein beigeben; *v/t.* F einschlagen, -drücken.

ca·ve·at 𝚫 ['keiviæt] Einspruch *m*.

cave-dweller ['keivdwelə], **cave-man** ['∼mæn] Höhlenmensch *m*.

cav·en·dish ['kævəndiʃ] Plattentabak *m*.

cav·ern ['kævən] Höhle *f*; **'cav·ern·ous** voller Höhlen; *fig.* hohl.

cav·i·ar(e) ['kæviɑː] Kaviar *m*; ∼ *to the general* Kaviar fürs Volk.

cav·il ['kævil] **1.** Krittelei *f*; **2.** kritteln (*at, about* an *dat.*); **'cav·il·ler** Krittler(in).

cav·i·ty ['kæviti] Höhlung *f*, Höhle *f*; Loch *n*.

ca·vort *Am.* F [kə'vɔːt] sich aufbäumen, umherspringen.

ca·vy ['keivi] Meerschweinchen *n*.

caw [kɔ:] 1.krächzen; 2.Krächzen *n.*
cay·enne [kei'en] *a.* ~ *pepper* ['keien] Cayennepfeffer *m.*
cay·man *zo.* ['keimən] Kaiman *m.*
cease [si:s] *v/i.* *(from)* aufhören (mit), ablassen (von); *v/t.* aufhören mit, (⚔ *Feuer*) einstellen; '~-'**fire** ⚔ Feuereinstellung *f*, Waffenruhe *f*; '**cease·less** □ unaufhörlich.
ce·dar ♀ ['si:də] Zeder(nholz *n*) *f.*
cede [si:d] abtreten, überlassen.
ce·dil·la [si'dilə] Cedille *f.*
ceil [si:l] *Zimmer* mit e-r Decke versehen; *Decke* verschalen; '**ceil·ing** (Zimmer)Decke *f*; ⚔ Gipfelhöhe*f*; *fig.* Höchstgrenze *f*; ~ *lighting* Deckenbeleuchtung *f*; ~ *price* Höchstpreis *m.*
cel·an·dine ♀ ['seləndain] Schell-, Schöllkraut *n.* [(*Kunstseide*).]
cel·e·nese [selə'ni:z] Celanese *f*]
cel·e·brate ['selibreit] feiern(*fig.* = *rühmen*); *eccl.* zelebrieren; '**cel·e·brat·ed** gefeiert, berühmt (*for* wegen); **cel·e'bra·tion** Feier*f; eccl.* Zelebrierung *f; in* ~ *of* zur Feier (*gen.*); '**cel·e·bra·tor** Lobpreiser *m.*
ce·leb·ri·ty [si'lebriti] Berühmtheit *f.*
ce·ler·i·ty [si'leriti] Geschwindigkeit *f.*
cel·er·y ♀ ['seləri] Sellerie *m, f.*
ce·les·tial □ [si'lestjəl] himmlisch; Himmel(s)...
cel·i·ba·cy ['selibəsi] Zölibat *n, m*, Ehelosigkeit *f;* **cel·i·bate** ['~bit] 1. unverheiratet; 2. Junggeselle *m.*
cell [sel] *allg.* Zelle *f;* ⚡ Element *n.*
cel·lar ['selə] 1. Keller *m;* 2. einkellern; '**cel·lar·age** Keller(ei *f*) *m/pl.;* Kellermiete *f;* **cel·lar·et** [~'ret] Flaschenständer *m.*
...**celled** [seld] ...zellig.
cel·list ♪ ['tʃelist] Cellist(in) *f;* **cel·lo** ['~ləu] Cello *n.*
cel·lo·phane ['seləufein] Cellophan *n.*
cel·lu·lar ['seljulə] zellig; **cel·lule** ['~ju:l] kleine Zelle *f;* **cel·lu·loid** ['~juləid] Zelluloid *n;* **cel·lu·lose** ['~juləus] Zellstoff *m*, Zellulose *f.*
Celt [kelt] Kelte *m*, Keltin *f;* '**Celt·ic** keltisch.
ce·ment [si'ment] 1. Zement *m;* Kitt *m* (*a. fig.*); 2. zementieren; (ver)kitten (*a.fig.*); **ce·men·ta·tion** [si:men'teiʃən] Zementieren *n;* **ce-**

ment mix·er Betonmischmaschine *f.*
cem·e·ter·y ['semitri] Friedhof *m.*
cen·o·taph ['senəuta:f] Ehrengrabmal *n.*
cense [sens] beräuchern; '**cen·ser** Weihrauchfaß *n.*
cen·sor ['sensə] 1. Zensor *m;* 2. zensieren; **cen·so·ri·ous** □ [sen'sɔ:riəs] kritisch; kritt(e)lig, tadelsüchtig; **cen·sor·ship** ['~səʃip] *amtliche* Zensur *f;* Zensoramt *n.*
cen·sur·a·ble □ ['senʃərəbl] tadelnswert; '**cen·sure** 1. Tadel *m;* Verweis *m;* 2. tadeln.
cen·sus ['sensəs] Volkszählung *f;* '~-**pa·per** Erhebungsbogen *m.*
cent [sent] Hundert *n; Am.* Cent *m,* $^1/_{100}$ Dollar *m; per* ~ Prozent *n.*
cen·taur ['sentɔ:] Kentaur *m.*
cen·tau·ry ♀ ['sentɔ:ri] Flockenblume *f.*
cen·te·nar·i·an [senti'nɛəriən] 1. hundertjährig; 2. Hundertjährige *m, f;* **cen·te·nar·y** [sen'ti:nəri] *s.* centennial.
cen·ten·ni·al [sen'tenjəl] hundertjährig(es Jubiläum *n*).
cen·tes·i·mal □ [sen'tesiməl] hundertteilig.
cen·ti... ['senti]: '~-**grade** hundertgradig; *degrees* ~ Grad Celsius; ~ *thermometer* Celsiusthermometer *n;* '~-**gramme** Zentigramm *n;* '~-**me·tre** Zentimeter *n, m;* ~-**pede** *zo.* ['~pi:d] Hundertfüßer *m.*
cen·tral ['sentrəl] 1. □ zentral (gelegen); Zentral...; Mittel...; bedeutendst, Haupt...; ~ *heating* Zentralheizung *f;* ~ *locking mot.* Zentralverriegelung *f;* ♀ *Powers pl.* Mittelmächte *f/pl.;* ~ *office,* ⚡ ~ *station* Zentrale *f;* 2. *teleph.* Amt *n;* **cen·tral·i·za·tion** [~lai'zeiʃən] Zentralisation*f;* '**cen·tral·ize** zentralisieren.
cen·tre, *Am.* **cen·ter**['sentə] 1. Zentrum *n* (*a.* ⚔, *pol.*), Mittelpunkt *m,* Mitte *f;* ~ *forward Fußball:* Mittelstürmer *m;* ~ *half* Mittelläufer *m;* ~ *of gravity* Schwerpunkt *m;* 2. zentral; 3. (sich) konzentrieren; zentralisieren; zentrieren; '~-**bit** ⊕ Zentrumsbohrer *m;* '~-**board** Schwert *n e-s Segelboots.*
cen·tric, cen·tri·cal □ ['sentrik(əl)] zentrisch, zentral; **cen·trif·u·gal** □ [sen'trifjugəl] zentrifugal; **cen·'trip·e·tal** □ [~pitl] zentripetal.

cen·tu·ple ['sentjupl] **1.** ☐ hundertfältig; **2.** verhundertfachen.

cen·tu·ri·on [sen'tjuəriən] *Rom:* Zenturio *m.*

cen·tu·ry ['sentʃuri] Jahrhundert *n.*

ce·ram·ic [si'ræmik] keramisch; **ce'ram·ics** *pl.* Keramik *f,* Töpferkunst *f.*

ce·re·al ['siəriəl] **1.** Getreide...; **2.** *mst* ~s *pl.* Getreide(pflanze *f*) *n*; *bsd. Am.* (Frühstücks)Nahrung *f aus Weizen, Mais etc.*

cer·e·bel·lum *anat.* [seri'beləm] Zerebellum *n,* Kleinhirn *n.*

cer·e·bral *anat.* ['seribrəl] Gehirn...

ce·re·brum *anat.* ['seribrəm] Zerebrum *n,* Großhirn *n.*

cere·cloth ['siəklɔθ] Leichentuch *n.*

cer·e·mo·ni·al [seri'məunjəl] **1.** ☐ *a.* **cer·e'mo·ni·ous** ☐ zeremoniell; förmlich, formell, feierlich; **2.** Zeremoniell *n;* **cer·e·mo·ny** ['serimən i] Zeremonie *f;* Feierlichkeit *f;* Förmlichkeit(en *pl.*) *f; Master of Ceremonies* Zeremonienmeister *m;* Conférencier *m; stand on* ~ förmlich sein; *without* ~ ohne Umstände, ohne weiteres.

cert *sl.* [səːt] todsichere Sache *f.*

cer·tain ☐ ['səːtn] sicher, gewiß; zuverlässig; bestimmt (*festgesetzt*); gewisse(r, -s); *for* ~ bestimmt, mit Sicherheit; *make* ~ sich vergewissern; **'cer·tain·ly** sicherlich, selbstverständlich, bestimmt; **'cer·tain·ty** Sicherheit *f,* Gewißheit *f;* Zuverlässigkeit *f.*

cer·tes † ['səːtiz] sicherlich, gewißlich.

cer·ti·fi·a·ble ['səːtifaiəbl] nachweisbar; F unzurechnungsfähig.

cer·tif·i·cate 1. [sə'tifikit] Zeugnis *n,* Schein *m,* Bescheinigung *f;* ~ *of birth (death, marriage)* Geburts(Sterbe-, Heirats)urkunde *f;* ~ *of employment* Beschäftigungsnachweis *m,* Arbeitsbescheinigung *f; medical* ~ ärztliches Attest *n;* **2.** [sə'tifikeit] mit e-m Zeugnis versehen, bescheinigen; ~d staatlich anerkannt; **cer·ti·fi·ca·tion** [səːtifi'keiʃən] Bescheinigung *f;* **cer·ti·fy** ['~fai] *et.* bescheinigen; bezeugen; amtlich für geisteskrank erklären; *this is to* ~ hiermit wird bescheinigt; *certified cheque als gedeckt* bestätigter Scheck *m; s. accountant;* **cer·ti·tude** ['~tju:d] Gewißheit *f.*

ce·ru·le·an [si'ruːljən] azur-, tiefblau. [ken...]

cer·vi·cal [səː'vaikəl] Hals..., Nak-]

ces·sa·tion [se'seiʃən] Aufhören *n,* Einstellung *f.*

ces·sion ['seʃən] Abtretung *f,* Überlassung *f.*

cess·pit ['sespit], **cess·pool** ['sespuːl] Senkgrube *f.*

ce·ta·cean [si'teiʃən] **1.** Walfisch *m;* **2.** *a.* **ce'ta·ceous** Wal...

chafe [tʃeif] *v/t.* reiben; wundreiben; aufbringen, erzürnen; *v/i.* sich scheuern (*against* an *dat.*); sich wundreiben; toben, wüten.

chaff [tʃɑːf] **1.** Spreu *f;* Häcksel *n;* Plunder *m;* F Neckerei *f;* **2.** zu Häcksel schneiden; F necken; '~-cut·ter Häckselbank *f.*

chaf·fer ['tʃæfə] feilschen.

chaf·finch ['tʃæfintʃ] Buchfink *m.*

chaf·ing-dish ['tʃeifiŋdiʃ] Wärmeschüssel *f,* -pfanne *f.*

cha·grin ['ʃægrin] **1.** Ärger *m;* **2.** ärgern.

chain [tʃein] **1.** Kette *f;* Reihe *f; fig.* Fessel *f;* **2.** (an)ketten; *fig.* fesseln; ~ **re·ac·tion** Kettenreaktion *f;* '~-smoker Kettenraucher(in); '~-store Filialbetrieb *m.*

chair [tʃeə] **1.** Stuhl *m; Am. a.* elektrischer Stuhl *m;* Sitz *m; a. professorial* ~ Lehrstuhl *m;* Vorsitz *m;* ~! zur Ordnung!; *be in the* ~, *take the* ~ den Vorsitz führen; **2.** zum (zur) Vorsitzenden machen; im Triumph umhertragen; '~-lift Sessellift *m;* ~·man ['~mən] Vorsitzende *m;* Präsident *m;* '~-man·ship Vorsitz *m;* '~·per·son Vorsitzende *m, f;* '~·wom·an Vorsitzende *f,* Präsidentin *f.*

chaise [ʃeiz] Chaise *f,* Halbkutsche *f.*

chal·ice ['tʃælis] (Abendmahls-) Kelch *m.*

chalk [tʃɔːk] **1.** Kreide *f;* red ~ Rötel *m; by a long* ~ F bei weitem; **2.** mit Kreide (be)zeichnen; *mst* ~ *up* ankreiden; ~ *out* entwerfen; *fig. Weg* vorzeichnen; '**chalk·y** kreidig.

chal·lenge ['tʃælindʒ] **1.** Herausforderung *f,* Kampfansage *f;* Aufforderung *f;* ⚔ Anruf *m; bsd.* ♟ Ablehnung *f;* ~ *prize Sport:* Wanderpreis *m;* **2.** (*a. fig. Aufmerksamkeit etc.*) herausfordern; anrufen;

ablehnen (*bsd.* ⚓); anzweifeln; '**chal·leng·er** Herausforderer *m*.

cha·lyb·e·ate [kə'libiit] stahlhaltig.

cham·ber ['tʃeimbə] *parl.*, *zo.*, ⚓, ⊕ Kammer *f*; ∼s *pl*. Junggesellenwohnung *f*; Geschäftsräume *m/pl*.; ♀ *of Commerce* Handelskammer *f*; **cham·ber·lain** ['∼lin] Kämmerer *m*, Kammerdiener *m*; '∼·**maid** Zimmermädchen *n*; '∼·**mu·sic** Kammermusik *f*; '∼·**pot** Nachtgeschirr *n*.

cham·bray *Am.* ['ʃæmbrei] bunter Baumwollstoff *m*.

cha·me·le·on *zo.* [kə'mi:ljən] Chamäleon *n*.

cham·fer △ ['tʃæmfə] 1. Auskehlung *f*; 2. auskehlen.

cham·ois ['ʃæmwɑ:] 1. *zo.* Gemse *f*; *a.* ∼ *leather* Wildleder *n*; 2. chamois(farben) (*gelblichbraun*).

champ[1] [tʃæmp] (geräuschvoll) kauen, mampfen; *fig.* ungeduldig werden *od.* sein.

champ[2] F [∼] *s. champion* 1.

cham·pagne [ʃæm'pein] Champagner *m*, Sekt *m*.

cham·paign ['tʃæmpein] flaches Land *n*.

cham·pi·on ['tʃæmpjən] 1. Vorkämpfer *m*, Verfechter *m*, Verteidiger *m*; *Sport:* Meister *m*, Sieger *m*; 2. verteidigen; verfechten, kämpfen für; stützen; 3. großartig; '**cham·pi·on·ship** Meisterschaft *f*.

chance [tʃɑːns] 1. Zufall *m*; Schicksal *n*; Glück(sfall *m*) *n*; Chance *f*; Aussicht *f* (*of auf acc.*); (günstige) Gelegenheit *f*; Möglichkeit *f*; Wahrscheinlichkeit *f*; *by* ∼ zufällig; *take a* ∼, *take one's* ∼ es darauf ankommen lassen; *take no* ∼ nichts riskieren (wollen); 2. Zufalls..., zufällig; gelegentlich; 3. *v/i.* (zufällig) geschehen; sich ereignen; *I* ∼*d to be there* ich war zufällig da; ∼ *upon* stoßen auf (*acc.*); *v/t.* F wagen, es ankommen lassen auf (*acc.*).

chan·cel △ ['tʃɑːnsəl] hoher Chor *m*; '**chan·cel·ler·y** (Botschafts-, Konsulats)Kanzlei *f*; '**chan·cel·lor** Kanzler *m*; *s. exchequer*; '**chan·cel·lor·ship** Kanzleramt *n*.

chan·cer·y ['tʃɑːnsəri] Kanzleigericht *n*; *in* ∼ *fig.* in der Klemme.

chanc·y F ['tʃɑːnsi] gewagt.

chan·de·lier [ʃændi'liə] Lüster *m*.

chan·dler ['tʃɑːndlə] Krämer *m*, Händler *m*; '**chan·dler·y** Kramladen *m*; Krämerwaren *f/pl*.

change [tʃeindʒ] 1. Veränderung *f*, Wechsel *m*, Abwechslung *f*, Umstellung *f*; Tausch *m*; Wechselgeld *n*; Kleingeld *n*; ♀ Börse *f*; *for a* ∼ zur Abwechslung; *give* ∼ *for* herausgeben auf (*acc.*); 2. *v/t.* (ver)ändern; um-, verwandeln; (aus)wechseln, (aus-, ver)tauschen (*for gegen*); ∼ *over Industrie etc.* umstellen; *I've* ∼*d my mind* ich habe es mir anders überlegt; *v/i.* sich ändern, wechseln; sich umziehen; ∼ *into second gear mot.* in den 2. Gang schalten; *a.* ∼ *trains* umsteigen; **change·a'bil·i·ty** Veränderlichkeit *f*; '**change·a·ble** ☐ veränderlich; wankelmütig; launisch; '**change-gear** ⊕ Wechselgetriebe *n*; '**change·less** ☐ unveränderlich; **change·ling** ['∼liŋ] Wechselbalg *m*; '**change-'o·ver** Umstellung *f*; '**chang·ing** Wechsel *m*; Veränderung *f*; ✂ Wachablösung *f*.

chan·nel ['tʃænl] 1. Kanal *m*; Flußbett *n*; Rinne *f*; Furche *f*; Gosse *f*; *Radio, Fernsehen:* Kanal *m*, Programm *n*; *fig.* Weg *m*, Kanal *m*; *by the official* ∼s auf dem Dienstwege; 2. furchen; aushöhlen.

chant [tʃɑːnt] 1. Kirchengesang *m*; *fig.* Singsang *m*; 2. singen; **chan·ti·cleer** *poet.* [tʃænti'kliə] Hahn *m*; **chan·try** *eccl.* ['tʃɑːntri] Messe (-kapelle) *f*; **chan·ty** ['∼ti] Matrosenlied *n*, Shanty *n*.

cha·os ['keiɔs] Chaos *n*, Durcheinander *n*; **cha'ot·ic** (∼*ally*) chaotisch.

chap[1] [tʃæp] 1. Riß *m*, Sprung *m*; 2. rissig machen *od.* werden.

chap[2] [∼] Kinnbacken *m* (*bsd. von Tieren*).

chap[3] F [∼] Bursche *m*, Kerl *m*, Junge *m*; '∼-**book** Volksbuch *n*.

chap·el ['tʃæpəl] Kapelle *f*; Gottesdienst *m*; *typ.* Betrieb *m*, Betriebsversammlung *f*.

chap·er·on ['ʃæpərəun] 1. Anstandsdame *f*; 2. (als Anstandsdame) begleiten.

chap-fall·en ['tʃæpfɔːlən] entmutigt.

chap·lain ['tʃæplin] Kaplan *m*; '**chap·lain·cy** Kaplanstelle *f*.

chap·let ['tʃæplit] Kranz *m* (*aus Blumen etc.*); *eccl.* Rosenkranz *m*.
chap·man ['tʃæpmən] Hausierer *m*.
chap·py □ ['tʃæpi] rissig.
chap·ter ['tʃæptə] *Buch-, Dom-, Ordens*-Kapitel *n*; *Am.* Orts-, Untergruppe *f e-r Vereinigung*; *give* ~ *and verse* genaue Quellen *od.* Belegstellen angeben, genau zitieren.
char[1] *ichth.* [tʃɑ:] Saibling *m*, Rotforelle *f*.
char[2] [~] verkohlen.
char[3] [~] **1.** reinemachen, putzen; **2.** = charwoman.
char-à-banc ['ʃærəbæŋ] Gesellschaftswagen *m*, Kremser *m*.
char·ac·ter ['kærɪktə] Charakter *m*; Merkmal *n*; Schrift(zeichen *n*) *f*; (ausgeprägte) Sinnesart *f*; Art *f*, Beschaffenheit *f*; (ausgeprägte) Persönlichkeit *f*; Figur *f*, Gestalt *f*; F *a.* Original *n*; *thea., Roman*: Person *f*; Rang *m*, Würde *f*; Leumund *m*, (*bsd.* guter) Ruf *m*; Zeugnis *n e-s Angestellten*; ~ *assassination* Rufmord *m*; **char·ac·ter'is·tic 1.** (~*ally*) charakteristisch, kennzeichnend, bezeichnend (*of* für); **2.** Kennzeichen *n*, Merkmal *n*, Wesenszug *m*; **char·ac·ter·i·za·tion** [~rai'zeiʃən] Charakteristik *f*; **'char·ac·ter·ize** charakterisieren; kennzeichnen; schildern.
cha·rade [ʃə'rɑ:d] Scharade *f*, Silbenrätsel *n*.
char·coal ['tʃɑ:kəul] Holzkohle *f*; '~**-burn·er** Köhler *m*.
chard ♀ ['tʃɑ:d] Mangold *m*.
chare [tʃɛə] **1.** Hausarbeiten übernehmen, reinemachen (in *od.* bei); **2.** *mst* ~*s pl.* (tägliche) Hausarbeit *f*, -reinigung *f*.
charge [tʃɑ:dʒ] **1.** Ladung *f e-r Feuerwaffe*; *fig.* Last *f*, Belastung *f* (*on* für); Verwahrung *f*, Obhut *f*, Pflege *f*; Pflegebefohlene *m*, *f*, Schützling *m*; Mündel *m*, *f*, *n*; anvertrautes Gut *n*; Amt *n*, Stelle *f*; Auftrag *m*, Befehl *m*; ✗ Angriff *m*; Ermahnung *f*; *eccl.* Belehrung *f*; Beschuldigung *f*, Anklage *f*; ✗ Beschickung *f*; in Rechnung gestellter Betrag *m*, Preis *m*; Gebühr *f*; Forderung *f*; ~*s pl.* Kosten *pl.*, Spesen *pl.*; *be in* ~ *of* mit *et.* beauftragt sein; für *et.* sorgen; für *et.* verantwortlich sein; *et.* leiten; *be in the* ~ *of s.o.* in j-s Obhut sein; *take* ~ *of* die Verantwortung über-

nehmen für; sich kümmern um (*acc.*); *free of* ~ kostenlos; **2.** *v/t.* *Gewehr etc.* laden; beladen, belasten; beauftragen (*with* mit); *j-m et.* einschärfen, (an)befehlen, auferlegen; ermahnen; beschuldigen, anklagen (*with gen.*); zuschreiben, zur Last legen (*on, upon dat.*); *bsd.* fordern, verlangen (*s.o. a price* e-n Preis von j-m); *Preis, Ware* anberechnen, in Rechnung stellen (*to dat.*); ✗ beschicken; *mit der blanken Waffe* angreifen (*a. v/i.*); behaupten; ~ *s.o. with the duty of* ger. es j-m zur Pflicht machen zu *inf.*; **'charge·a·ble** □ zu belasten(d) (*with* mit); zur Last fallend, anzurechnen(d) (*to dat.*); zur Last zu legen(d) (*on dat.*); zahlbar; strafbar; **charge ac·count** Kundenkreditkonto *n*.
char·gé d'af·faires *pol.* ['ʃɑ:ʒeidæ'fɛə] Geschäftsträger *m*.
charg·er ['tʃɑ:dʒə] *poet.* Schlachtroß *n*; ✗ Dienstpferd *n*.
char·i·ot *poet. od. hist.* ['tʃæriət] Streit-, Triumphwagen *m*; **char·i·ot·eer** [~'tiə] Wagenlenker *m*.
char·i·ta·ble □ ['tʃæritəbl] wohltätig, mild(tätig); mild (*nachsichtig*); ~ *society* Wohltätigkeitsverein *m*; **'char·i·ta·ble·ness** Mildtätigkeit *f*; Milde *f*.
char·i·ty ['tʃæriti] Nächstenliebe *f*; Wohltätigkeit *f*; Güte *f*; Milde *f*, Nachsicht *f*; milde Gabe *f*; Wohlfahrtseinrichtung *f*; *sister of* ~ Barmherzige Schwester *f*; ~ *begins at home* die Nächstenliebe beginnt zu Hause; '~**-'child** Armenkind *n*; '~**-'school** Armenschule *f*.
cha·ri·va·ri ['ʃɑ:ri'vɑ:ri] Stimmengewirr *n*; Durcheinander *n*.
char·la·tan ['ʃɑ:lətən] Scharlatan *m*, Marktschreier *m*; **'char·la·tan·ry** Scharlatanerie *f*, Marktschreierei *f*.
char·lock ♀ ['tʃɑ:lɔk] Ackersenf *m*, Hederich *m*.
char·lotte ['ʃɑ:lət] *Küche:* Apfelpudding *m*.
charm [tʃɑ:m] **1.** Zauber *m*; *fig.* Reiz *m*; **2.** bezaubern; *fig.* entzücken; ~ *away etc.* weg- *etc.* zaubern; ~*ed a.* gefeit (*Leben*); **'charm·er** *fig.* Zauberin *f*, Schöne *f*; **'charm·ing** □ bezaubernd, reizend, entzückend.

char·nel-house ['tʃɑːnlhaus] Bein-, Leichenhaus *n.*

chart [tʃɑːt] **1.** ⚓ Seekarte *f;* Tabelle *f;* **2.** auf einer Karte einzeichnen, vermessen.

char·ter ['tʃɑːtə] **1.** Urkunde *f;* Freibrief *m (a. fig. = Vorrecht);* Patent *n;* ⚓ Schiffsmiete *f,* Frachtvertrag *m; mst ~-party* Chartepartie *f;* **2.** privilegieren, *j-m* e-n Freibrief ausstellen; chartern, mieten; *s. accountant;* ~ **mem·ber** *Am.* Gründungsmitglied *n.*

char·wom·an ['tʃɑːwumən] Putz-, Reinemachefrau *f.*

char·y □ ['tʃɛəri] *(of)* vorsichtig (in *dat.);* sparsam *od.* zurückhaltend (mit).

chase[1] [tʃeis] **1.** Jagd *f;* Verfolgung *f;* Jagdrevier *n;* gejagtes Wild *n (a. fig.) od.* Schiff *n; beasts of ~* jagdbares Wild *n; give ~ to* nachjagen *(dat.);* **2.** jagen, hetzen *(a. fig.);* Jagd machen auf *(acc.); j-m* nachjagen; vertreiben, verfolgen.

chase[2] [~] ziselieren.

chase[3] *typ.* [~] Setzrahmen *m.*

chas·er[1] ['tʃeisə] Jäger(in); Verfolger(in); ✠ Jagdflugzeug *n;* ⚓ Jagdgeschütz *n.*

chas·er[2] [~] Ziseleur *m.*

chasm ['kæzəm] Kluft *f,* Abgrund *m (a. fig.),* Spalt *m;* Lücke *f.*

chas·sis *mot.* ['ʃæsi], *pl.* **chas·sis** ['ʃæsiz] Fahrgestell *n.*

chaste □ [tʃeist] keusch, rein, unschuldig; schlicht *(Stil).*

chas·ten ['tʃeisn] züchtigen; reinigen, läutern; mäßigen.

chas·tise [tʃæs'taiz] züchtigen; **chas·tise·ment** ['~tizmənt] Züchtigung *f.*

chas·ti·ty ['tʃæstiti] Keuschheit *f; fig.* Reinheit *f.*

chas·u·ble *eccl.* ['tʃæzjubl] Meßgewand *n.*

chat [tʃæt] **1.** Geplauder *n,* Plauderei *f;* **2.** plaudern.

châ·teau ['ʃætəu] Schloß *n,* Landhaus *n in Frankreich.*

chat show ['tʃætʃəu] Talk-Show *f.*

chat·tels ['tʃætlz] *pl. mst goods and ~* Hab *n* und Gut *n;* Vermögen *n.*

chat·ter ['tʃætə] **1.** plappern, schwatzen; schnattern; klappern; **2.** Geplapper *n etc.;* '~**box** F Plaudertasche *f;* '**chat·ter·er** Schwätzer (-in).

chat·ty ['tʃæti] gesprächig.

chauf·feur ['ʃəufə] Chauffeur *m,* Fahrer *m;* **chauf·feuse** [~'fəːz] Chauffeurin *f.*

chau·vin·ism ['ʃəuvinizəm] Chauvinismus *m;* '**chau·vin·ist** Chauvinist(in); **chau·vin'is·tic** (~*ally*) chauvinistisch.

chaw *sl.* [tʃɔː] kauen; ~ *up Am. sl. mst fig.* fix und fertig machen *(vernichten);* '~-'**ba·con** Bauerntölpel *m.*

cheap □ [tʃiːp] billig; *fig. a.* gemein; *feel ~* F sich elend fühlen; sich schäbig vorkommen; *hold ~* niedrig einschätzen; *on the ~* F billig; *make o.s. ~* seinen guten Ruf ruinieren; ♀ *Jack* Hausierer *m;* '**cheap·en** (sich) verbilligen; *fig.* herabsetzen; '**cheap·skate** *Am. sl.* Knicker *m.*

cheat ['tʃiːt] **1.** Betrug *m,* Schwindel *m;* Betrüger(in); **2.** betrügen, prellen (*[out] of s.th.* um *et.);* '**cheat·ing** Betrügerei *f.*

check [tʃek] **1.** Schach(stellung *f) n;* Hemmnis *n,* Hindernis *n (on* für); ✕ Schlappe *f;* Zwang *m,* Aufsicht *f;* Kontrolle *f,* Untersuchung *f (on gen.);* Kontroll-, Garderobe-, Spielmarke *f; Am. Gepäck-*Schein *m; Am.* ✝ = cheque; *Am.* Rechnung *f im Restaurant;* karierter Stoff *m;* ~ *pattern* Karomuster *n; pass od. hand in one's ~s Am.* ✝ sterben, abkratzen; *keep s.o. in ~* j. in Schach halten; **2.** Schach bieten *(dat.); Am.* Scheck ausschreiben, einlösen; hemmen, aufhalten, *fig.* zügeln; kontrollieren; nach-, überprüfen; in der Garderobe abgeben; *bsd. Am.* stimmen *nach Kontrolle;* ~ *in Am.* in e-m Hotel absteigen; ~ *out v i.* ein Hotel verlassen; ausstempeln; *v t. Am.* überprüfen; ~ *one's baggage Am.* sein Gepäck aufgeben; ~ *up* genau prüfen, nachprüfen, -rechnen, -schlagen; '~-**book** *Am.* Scheckbuch *n;* **checked** kariert; '**check·er** Aufsichtsbeamte *m;* ~*s pl. Am.* Damespiel *n;* = chequer; '**check·er·board** *Am.* Damebrett *n;* '**check·ered** kariert; '**check-in count·er** Abfertigungsschalter *m;* '**check-in desk** Hotelrezeption *f;* Abfertigungsschalter *m;* '**check·ing** Hemmung *f;* Kontrolle *f; attr.* Kontroll...; '**check-in time** ✈ Eincheckzeit *f;* '**check·list** Kontroll-,

Checkliste f; '**check-mate 1.** Schachmatt n; **2.** matt setzen (mst fig.); '**check-out count·er** Kasse f e-s Supermarkts; '**check-point** Kontrollpunkt m; '**check·room** Am. Garderobe f; Gepäckaufbewahrung f; '**check-up** Am. scharfe Kontrolle f.

Ched·dar ['tʃedə] Cheddarkäse m.

cheek [tʃi:k] **1.** Backe f, Wange f; F Unverschämtheit f; ⊕ Backe f, Seitenteil n; s. jowl; **2.** F unverschämt werden gegen; '**cheek-bone** Backenknochen m; '**cheeked** ...wangig; '**cheek·y** F frech, dreist.

cheep [tʃi:p] piepen.

cheer [tʃiə] **1.** (engS. frohe) Stimmung f, Fröhlichkeit f; Hoch(ruf m) n; Beifall(sruf) m, Hurra n; Speisen f/pl., Mahl n; be of good ⁓ guter Dinge sein; three ⁓s! dreimal hoch!; **2.** v/t. a. ⁓ up aufheitern, trösten; mit Beifall begrüßen, j-m zujubeln; a. ⁓ on anspornen, ermutigen; v/i. hoch rufen; jauchzen, jubeln; a. ⁓ up Mut fassen; '**cheerful** ☐ heiter, fröhlich; '**cheer·fulness**, '**cheer·i·ness** Heiterkeit f; '**cheer·ing** Beifallsrufen n; cheeri·o ['⁓ri'əu] F mach's gut!, Tschüs!; prosit!; '**cheer·lead·er** Am. Sport: Einpeitscher m; '**cheer·less** ☐ freudlos; '**cheer·y** ☐ heiter, froh.

cheese [tʃi:z] Käse m; sl. das einzig Wahre; '**⁓-cake** Käsekuchen m; sl. Pin-up-Girl n; '**⁓-cloth** Seihtuch n; '**⁓·mon·ger** Käsehändler m; '**⁓-par·ing 1.** Käserinde f; fig. Knickerei f; **2.** knickerig.

chees·y ['tʃi:zi] käsig.

chee·tah zo. ['tʃi:tə] Jagdleopard m.

chef [ʃef] Küchenchef m.

chei·ro·man·cy ['kaiərəumænsi] Chiromantie f (Handlesekunst).

chem·i·cal ['kemikəl] **1.** ☐ chemisch; **2.** '**chem·i·cals** pl. Chemikalien pl.

che·mise [ʃə'mi:z] Frauen-Hemd n.

chem·ist ['kemist] Chemiker(in); Apotheker(in); Drogist(in); ⁓'s shop Apotheke f; Drogerie f; '**chem·is·try** Chemie f.

chem·i·ty·py ⊕ ['kemitaipi] Chemigraphie f.

chem·o·ther·a·py ⚕ [keməu'θerəpi] Chemotherapie f.

cheque ✝ [tʃek] Scheck m; not negotiable ⁓, crossed ⁓ Verrechnungsscheck m; ⁓ ac·count Girokonto n; '**⁓·book** Scheckbuch n.

chequer ['tʃekə] **1.** mst ⁓s pl. Karomuster n; **2.** karieren; '**chequered** kariert; fig. bunt.

cher·ish ['tʃeriʃ] hegen, pflegen; schätzen; festhalten an (dat.).

che·root [ʃə'ru:t] Stumpen m (Zigarre).

cher·ry ['tʃeri] **1.** Kirsche f; **2.** Kirsch...; kirschrot; ⁓ bran·dy Kirschlikör m.

cher·ub ['tʃerəb] Cherub m; **cheru·bic** [⁓'ru:bik] engelhaft.

cher·vil ⚘ ['tʃə:vil] Kerbel m.

chess [tʃes] Schach(spiel) n; '**⁓board** Schachbrett n; '**⁓·man** Schachfigur f.

chest [tʃest] Kiste f, Kasten m; Truhe f; anat. Brustkasten m; ⁓ of drawers Kommode f; ⁓ note Brustton m; get s.th. off one's ⁓ sich et. von der Seele schaffen; '**chest·ed** ...brüstig.

ches·ter·field ['tʃestəfi:ld] einreihiger Mantel m; Polstersofa n.

chest·nut ['tʃesnʌt] **1.** Kastanie f; Kastanienbraun n; F alter Witz m; **2.** kastanienbraun.

chest·y F ['tʃesti] tiefsitzend (Husten); vollbusig.

che·val-glass [ʃə'vælglɑ:s] Ankleidespiegel m.

chev·a·lier [ʃevə'liə] Ritter m.

chev·i·ot ['tʃeviət] Cheviot m (Tuchart).

chev·ron ✕ ['ʃevrən] Armwinkel m.

chev·y F ['tʃevi] **1.** Hetzjagd f; Barlaufspiel n; **2.** hetzen, jagen.

chew [tʃu:] kauen; sinnen (on, upon, over über acc.); ⁓ the fat od. rag sl. die Sache durchkauen; '**chewing-gum** Kaugummi m.

chi·cane [ʃi'kein] **1.** Schikane f; **2.** schikanieren; **chi'can·er·y** Schikane f; fig. Haarspalterei f.

chick [tʃik] s. chicken.

chick·a·dee Am. orn. ['tʃikədi:] Meise f.

chick·a·ree Am. zo. ['tʃikəri:] rotes Eichhörnchen n.

chick·en ['tʃikin] **1.** Hühnchen n, Küchlein n, Küken n; **2.** ⁓ out sl. e-n Rückzieher machen; '**⁓-farm·er** Geflügelzüchter m; '**⁓-feed** Am. Geflügelfutter n; sl. Pappenstiel m; '**⁓-heart·ed**, '**⁓-liv·ered** furchtsam,

feige; '~-**pox** ✼ Windpocken *f/pl.*; ~
run, *Am.* ~ **yard** Hühnerauslauf *m*;
'**chick-pea** ♦ Kichererbse *f*;
'**chick·weed** ♦ Vogelmiere *f*.
chic·o·ry ['tʃikəri] Zichorie *f*.
chid [tʃid] *pret. u. p.p.*, '**chid·den**
p.p. von chide.
chide *lit.* [tʃaid] *(irr.)* schelten.
chief [tʃiːf] **1.** ☐ oberst; Ober...,
Haupt...; hauptsächlich; ~ **clerk**
Bürovorsteher *m*; **2.** Oberhaupt *n*,
Haupt *n*, Chef *m*; Häuptling *m*;
...-**in**-~ Ober...; ~ **jus·tice** Oberrich-
ter *m*; *Am.* Vorsitzende *m e-s Bundes-
gerichts*; ♀ Vorsitzende *m des Supreme
Court*; **chief·tain** ['~tən] Häuptling
m; Anführer *m*.
chif·fon ['ʃifɔn] Chiffon *m* (*Seiden-
stoff*); **chif·fo·nier** [ʃifə'niə] Chif-
fonière *f* (*Schrank*).
chil·blain ['tʃilblein] Frostbeule *f*.
child [tʃaild], *pl.* **chil·dren** ['tʃil-
drən] Kind *n*; *be a good* ~ artig sein;
from a ~ von Kindheit an; *with* ~
schwanger; ~'*s play fig.* Kinderspiel
n; '~·**bed** Kindbett *n*; '~·**birth** Nie-
derkunft *f*; '**child·hood** Kindheit *f*;
second ~ Greisenalter *n*; '**child·ish**
☐ kindlich; *b.s.* kindisch; '**child-
ish·ness** Kindlichkeit *f*; *b.s.* kin-
disches Wesen *n*; '**child·less** kin-
derlos; '**child·like** *fig.* kindlich;
'**child·mind·er** Tagesmutter *f*;
chil·dren ['tʃildrən] *pl. von* child;
child wel·fare Jugendfürsorge *f*.
chil·i *Am.* ♦ ['tʃili] Paprika(schote *f*)
m.
Chil·i·an ['tʃiliən] **1.** Chilene *m*,
Chilenin *f*; **2.** chilenisch.
chill [tʃil] **1.** *lit.* eisig, frostig;
2. Frost *m*, Kälte *f* (*a. fig.*); ✼
Fieberfrost *m*; Erkältung *f*; *take
the* ~ *off a liquid* e-e Flüssigkeit anwärmen; **3.** *v/t.* erkalten lassen; erstarren lassen; (*bsd. fig.* ab)kühlen;
metall. abschrecken; ~*ed meat*
Kühlfleisch *n*; *v/i.* erkalten; erstarren; '**chill·ness**, '**chill·i·ness**
Kälte *f*; '**chill·y** kalt, frostig, kühl;
fröstelnd.
chime [tʃaim] **1.** Glockenspiel *n*;
Geläut *n*; *fig.* Einklang *m*; **2.** läuten;
fig. übereinstimmen, harmonieren;
~ *in* einfallen, -stimmen.
chi·me·ra [kai'miərə] Schimäre *f*,
Hirngespinst *n*; **chi·mer·i·cal** ☐
[~'merikəl] schimärisch, phantastisch.

chim·ney ['tʃimni] Schornstein *m*;
Kamin *m* (*a. mount.*); Rauchfang *m*;
(Lampen)Zylinder *m*; '~-**piece**
Kaminsims *m*; '~-**pot** Schornsteinkappe *f*; F *fig.* Angströhre *f*, Zylin-
der(hut) *m*; '~-**stalk** Schornstein-
kasten *m auf dem Dach*; Fabrik-
schornstein *m*; '~-**sweep**(·**er**)
Schornsteinfeger *m*.
chimp F [tʃimp] Schimpanse *m*.
chim·pan·zee *zo.* [tʃimpən'ziː]
Schimpanse *m*.
chin¹ [tʃin] **1.** Kinn *n*; *take it on the*
~ *Am.* F es standhaft ertragen; *keep
one's* ~ *up* F den Nacken steifhalten;
2. *Am.* e-n Klimmzug machen.
chin² *sl.* [~] schwatzen, quasseln.
chi·na ['tʃainə] Porzellan *n*; '♀·**man**
Chinese *m*.
chine [tʃain] Rückgrat *n*; *Küche:*
Kammstück *n*; Grat *m*, Kamm *m*.
Chi·nese ['tʃai'niːz] **1.** chinesisch;
2. Chinese(n *pl.*) *m*, Chinesin *f*;
Chinesisch *n*.
chink¹ [tʃiŋk] Ritz *m*, Ritze *f*, Spalt
m, Spalte *f*.
chink² [~] **1.** (*bsd. Geld-*)Klang *m*;
2. klimpern (*mit Geld*).
chintz [tʃints] Chintz *m*, Möbel-
kattun *m*.
chin·wag *sl.* ['tʃinwæg] Schwatz *m*.
chip [tʃip] **1.** Schnitzel *n*, Stückchen
n; Splitter *m*; Span *m*; angeschla-
gene Stelle *f in Glas etc.*; Spielmarke *f*; *Computer:* Chip *m*; *have a* ~
on one's shoulder aggressiv sein; ~*s pl.*
Pommes frites *pl.*; **2.** *v/t.* (ab)schnit-
zeln; an-, abschlagen; abschilfern (*a.
v/i.*); *v/i.* abbröckeln; ~ *in* F unterbrechen; sich einmischen; *Am.* F aushelfen; **chip·muck** ['~mʌk], **chip-
munk** ['~mʌŋk] nordamerikanisches
gestreiftes Eichhörnchen *n*; '**chip-
-pan** Friteuse *f*; '**chip·py** dürr; F
verkatert.
chi·rop·o·dist [ki'rɔpədist] Fuß-
pfleger(in); **chi·rop·o·dy** Fußpflege *f*; **chi·ro·prac·tor** ✼ [kai-
rəu'præktə] Chiropraktiker *m*.
chirp [tʃəːp] **1.** zirpen; zwitschern;
2. Gezirp *n*; '**chirp·y** F munter.
chirr [tʃəː] zirpen.
chir·rup ['tʃirəp] **1.** Zwitschern *n*;
2. zwitschern.
chis·el ['tʃizl] **1.** Meißel *m*; **2.** meißeln; F (be)mogeln; '**chis·el·er**
Nassauer *m*.
chit [tʃit] Kindchen *n*; *a* ~ *of a girl*

ein junges Ding *n.*
chit-chat ['tʃittʃæt] Geplauder *n.*
chiv·al·rous □ ['ʃivəlrəs] ritterlich;
'**chiv·al·ry** Ritterschaft *f,* Rittertum *n;* Ritterlichkeit *f.*
chive ♀ [tʃaiv] Schnittlauch *m.*
chiv·y F ['tʃivi] = *chevy.*
chlo·ral ♫ ['klɔːrəl] Chloral *n;*
chlo·ride ['‿aid] Chlorverbindung
f; ~ *of lime* Chlorkalk *m;* **chlo·rin·**
ate ['‿ineit] *Wasser* chloren; **chlo·**
rine ['‿iːn] Chlor *n;* **chlo·ro·form**
['klɔrəfɔːm] **1.** Chloroform *n;*
2. chloroformieren; **chlor·o·phyl(l)**
['‿əfil] Chlorophyll *n,* Blattgrün
n.   [ladeüberzug.]
choc-ice ['tʃɔkais] Eis *n* mit Schoko-]
chock ⊕ [tʃɔk] **1.** Keil *m;* **2.** fest-
keilen; '**‿-a-'block** verklemmt (*with*
mit); '**‿-'full** übervoll.
choc·o·late ['tʃɔkəlit] Schokolade *f;*
~ *cream* Praliné *n.*
choice [tʃɔis] **1.** Wahl *f;* Auswahl *f;*
have one's ~ die Wahl haben; *make*
od. take one's ~ s-e Wahl treffen;
multiple ~ Auswahlantwort(form) *f;*
2. □ auserlesen, vorzüglich; ausgesucht; ~ *fruit* Edelobst *n.*
choir ['kwaiə] (Kirchen-, Sänger-)
Chor *m;* '**‿-mas·ter** Chorleiter *m;* ~
stalls *pl.* Chorgestühl *n.*
choke [tʃəuk] **1.** *v/t.* (er)würgen,
(*a. v/i.*) ersticken (*a. fig.*); ⊕ würgen
(*verengen*); ⚡ (ab)drosseln; *mst* ~
up (ver)stopfen; *mst* ~ *down* hin-
unterwürgen; ~ *off* F abschütteln;
abbringen (*from* von); **2.** Erstik-
kungsanfall *m;* ⊕ Würgung *f; mot.*
Choke *m,* Starterklappe *f;* ~ *coil* ⚡
Drosselspule *f;* '**‿-bore** ⊕ (Flinte *f*
mit) Würgebohrung *f;* '**‿-damp** ⚒
Schwaden *m;* '**chok·er** *co.* steifer
Kragen *m;* Krawattenschal *m;* enge
Halskette *f;* '**chok·y** erstickend.
chol·er·a ⚕ ['kɔlərə] Cholera *f;*
'**chol·er·ic** cholerisch, jähzornig.
cho·les·te·rol [kə'lestərɔl] Cholesterin *n.*
choose [tʃuːz] (*irr.*) (aus)wählen;
~ *to inf.* vorziehen zu *inf.,* lieber
wollen; '**choos·y** wählerisch.
chop[1] [tʃɔp] **1.** Hieb *m* (*at* nach);
Kotelett *n;* ~*s pl.* Maul *n,* Rachen *m*
(*a. fig.*); ⊕ Backen *f/pl.;* ~*s and*
changes pl. Wechselfälle *m/pl.;*
2. *v/t.* hauen, hacken; *oft* ~ *up* zerhacken; austauschen; *v/i.* wechseln;
~ *about* umschlagen (*Wind u. fig.*);

~ *and change* schwanken.
chop[2] ✝ [~] Marke *f; first* ~ erste
Sorte *f; attr.* erster Güte.
chop-chop *sl.* ['tʃɔp'tʃɔp] schnell.
chop-house ['tʃɔphaus] Speisehaus
n; '**chop·per** Hackmesser *n;* F Hubschrauber *m;* '**chop·ping** Hack...;
'**chop·py** unstet; unruhig (*See*); böig
(*Wind*); = *chappy;* '**chop·stick** Eß-
stäbchen *n der Chinesen;* **chop-su·ey**
[~'suːi] Chop Suey *n* (*chinesisches Ge-*
richt).
cho·ral □ ['kɔːrəl] chormäßig;
Chor...; **cho·ral(e)** ♩ [kɔ'rɑːl]
Choral *m.*
chord [kɔːd] ♩, *poet. od. fig.* Saite *f;*
⚛ Sehne *f;* ♩ Akkord *m; anat.*
Strang *m,* Band *n.*
chore *bsd. Am.* [tʃɔː] = *chare* 2.
chor·e·og·ra·phy [kɔri'ɔgrəfi] Cho-
reographie *f.*
chor·ine ['kɔːriːn] *s. chorus-girl.*
chor·is·ter ['kɔristə] Chorist *m,*
Sängerknabe *m; Am. a.* Leiter *m*
des Kirchenchores.
cho·rus ['kɔːrəs] **1.** Chor *m;* Kehrreim *m;* **2.** im Chor singen *od.*
sprechen; '**‿-girl** Revuegirl *n.*
chose [tʃouz] *pret.,* '**cho·sen** *p.p.*
von choose.
chough *orn.* [tʃʌf] Dohle *f.*
chouse F [tʃaus] **1.** Prellerei *f;*
2. prellen.
chow *Am. sl.* [tʃau] Essen *n.*
chow·der *Am.* ['tʃaudə] *Mischgericht*
aus Fischen, Muscheln etc.
chrism ['krizəm] Salböl *n;* Ölung *f.*
Christ [kraist] Christus *m; for* ~'*s*
sake! Herrgott noch mal!
chris·ten ['krisn] taufen; **Chris·**
ten·dom ['‿dəm] Christenheit *f;*
'**chris·ten·ing** 1. Tauf...; 2. Taufe *f.*
Chris·tian ['kristjən] **1.** □ christlich; ~ *name* Vor-, Taufname *m;*
~ *Science* Christliche Wissenschaft *f,*
Szientismus *m;* **2.** Christ(in);
Chris·ti·an·i·ty [‿ti'æniti] Christentum *n;* **Chris·tian·ize** ['‿tjə-
naiz] zum Christentum bekehren.
Christ·mas ['krisməs] **1.** Weihnachten *n;* **2.** Weihnachts...; ~ *Day* erster
Weihnachtsfeiertag *m;* ~ *Eve* Heili-
ger Abend *m;* ~ **bo·nus** Weihnachts-
geld *n,* -gratifikation *f;* '**‿-box** Weih-
nachtsgeschenk *n* (*für Bedienstete*);
'**‿-tide** Weihnachtszeit *f;* '**‿-tree**
Weihnachtsbaum *m.*
chro·mat·ic *phys.,* ♩ [krəu'mætik]

(‿**ally**) chromatisch; Farben...; **chro'mat·ics** *pl. u. sg.* Farbenlehre *f.*

chrome ⚗ [krəum] Chrom *n* (*Farbe*); **chro·mi·um** ['‿jəm] Chrom *n* (*Metall*); **'chro·mi·um-** **-'plat·ed** verchromt; **chro·mo·** **lith·o·graph** ['‿əu'liθəugra:f] farbiger Steindruck *m.*

chron·ic ['krɔnik] (‿**ally**) chronisch (*mst ⚗*), dauernd; P ekelhaft; **chron·i·cle** ['‿l] **1.** Chronik *f*; **2.** aufzeichnen; **'chron·i·cler** Chronist *m.*

chron·o·log·i·cal □ [krɔnə'lɔdʒikəl] chronologisch; ‿**ly** in chronologischer Reihenfolge; **chro·nol·o·gy** [krə'nɔlədʒi] Zeitrechnung *f*; Zeitfolge *f.*

chro·nom·e·ter [krə'nɔmitə] Chronometer *n, m.*

chrys·a·lis ['krisəlis] *Insekten-Puppe f.*

chrys·an·the·mum ⚘ [kri'sænθəməm] Chrysantheme *f.*

chub *ichth.* [tʃʌb] Döbel *m*; **'chub·by** F rundlich; dick; pausbäckig; plump (*a. fig.*).

chuck¹ [tʃʌk] **1.** Glucken *n*; my ‿! mein Täubchen!; **2.** glucken; **3.** put, put! (*Lockruf für Hühner*).

chuck² F [‿] **1.** schmeißen, werfen; ‿ out 'rausschmeißen; ‿ under the *chin* unters Kinn fassen; ‿ it! *sl.* hör auf damit!; **2.** Hinauswurf *m.*

chuck³ ⊕ [‿] (Spann)Futter *n.*

chuck·er-out *sl.* ['tʃʌkər'aut] Rausschmeißer *m.*

chuck·le ['tʃʌkl] in sich hineinlachen.

chug [tʃʌg] tuckern (*Motor etc.*).

chum F [tʃʌm] **1.** (Stuben)Kamerad *m*; Busenfreund *m*; be great ‿s dicke Freunde sein; **2.** zs.-wohnen.

chump F [tʃʌmp] Holzklotz *m*; dickes Ende *n*; (Dumm)Kopf *m*; *off one's* ‿ P blödsinnig.

chunk F [tʃʌŋk] Klotz *m*, Runken *m*; **'chunk·y** klotzig, stämmig.

church [tʃə:tʃ] **1.** Kirche *f*; *attr.* Kirch(en)...; ♀ *of England* englische Staatskirche *f*; ‿ *rate* Kirchensteuer *f*; ‿ *service* Gottesdienst *m*; **2.** *be* ‿*ed* zum ersten Mal wieder in die Kirche gehen (*Wöchnerin*); **'‿** **-go·er** Kirchgänger(in); **'church·** **ing** Aussegnung *f e-r Wöchnerin*; **'church·man** Mitglied *n* der Kir-

che; **'church'ward·en** Kirchenvorsteher *m*; Tabakspfeife *f aus Ton*; **'church'yard** Kirchhof *m.*

churl [tʃə:l] Grobian *m*, Flegel *m*; Geizhals *m*, Knicker *m*; **'churl·ish** □ grob; roh, flegelhaft; knickerig.

churn [tʃə:n] **1.** Butterfaß *n*; Milchsammeleimer *m*; **2.** buttern; aufwühlen.

chute [ʃu:t] Stromschnelle *f*; Gleit-, Rutschbahn *f*; Fallschirm *m.*

chut·ney ['tʃʌtni] Chutney *n* (*Gewürz*).

chyle [kail] Chylus *m* (*Milchsaft*).

chyme [kaim] Chymus *m* (*Speisebrei*).

ci·ca·da *zo.* [si'ka:də] Zikade *f.*

cic·a·trice ['sikətris] Narbe *f*; **cic·a·** **tri·za·tion** [‿trai'zeiʃən] Vernarbung *f*; **'cic·a·trize** vernarben.

ci·ce·ro·ne [tʃitʃə'rəuni] Cicerone *m*, Fremdenführer *m.*

Cic·e·ro·ni·an [sisə'rəunjən] ciceron(ian)isch.

ci·der ['saidə] Apfelwein *m.*

ci·gar [si'ga:] Zigarre *f*; **ci'gar-case** Zigarrentasche *f*; **ci'gar-cut·ter** Zigarrenabschneider *m.*

cig·a·rette [sigə'ret] Zigarette *f*; **cig·** **a'rette-case** Zigarettenetui *n*; **cig·** **a'rette-end** Zigarettenstummel *m*; **cig·a'rette-hold·er** Zigarettenspitze *f.*

ci·gar-hold·er [si'ga:həuldə] Zigarrenspitze *f*; **ci'gar-tip** *abgeschnittene* Zigarrenspitze *f.*

cil·i·a ['siliə] *pl.* (Augen)Wimpern *f/pl.*; **cil·i·ar·y** ['siliəri] Wimper...

cinch *Am. sl.* [sintʃ] sichere Sache *f.*

cin·cho·na ⚘ [siŋ'kəunə] Chinarindenbaum *m.*   [*m.*]

cinc·ture ['siŋktʃə] Gürtel *m*, Gurt]

cin·der ['sində] Schlacke *f*; ‿*s pl.* Asche *f*; **Cin·der·el·la** [‿'relə] Aschenbrödel *n*; **'cin·der-track** *Sport:* Aschenbahn *f.*

cin·e·cam·er·a ['sinikæmərə] Filmkamera *f.*

cin·e-film ['sinifilm] Schmalfilm *m.*

cin·e·ma ['sinəmə] Kino *n*; Film *m* (*als Kunstform*); **cin·e·mat·o·** **graph** [‿'mætəgra:f] **1.** Filmprojektor *m*; *attr.* Kino...; **2.** (ver)filmen; **cin·e·mat·o·graph·ic** [‿mætə'græfik] (‿**ally**) kinematographisch.

cin·er·ar·y ['sinərəri] Aschen...

cin·na·bar ['sinəba:] Zinnober *m.*

cin·na·mon ['sinəmən] Zimt *m*,

Kaneel *m*; Zimtbraun *n*.

cinque [siŋk] Fünf *f auf Würfeln*;
~ **foil** ♧ Fingerkraut *n*.

ci·pher ['saifə] **1.** Ziffer *f*; Null *f*
(*a. fig.*); Geheimschrift *f*, Chiffre *f*;
in ~ chiffriert; **2.** chiffrieren; (aus-)
rechnen.

cir·ca ['sə:kə] um (*vor Jahreszahlen*).

cir·cle ['sə:kl] **1.** Kreis *m*; *Bekannt-*
ten-, *Gesellschafts-*, *Wirkungs-*Kreis
m; Kreislauf *m*; *thea.* Rang *m*;
Ring *m*, Reif *m*; **2.** Kreise ziehen;
(um)kreisen; *fig.* die Runde machen; **cir·clet** ['~klit] kleiner Kreis
m; Reif *m*.

circs F [sə:ks] = *circumstances*.

cir·cuit ['sə:kit] Kreislauf *m*; ⚡
Stromkreis *m*; Rundreise *f bsd. der*
Richter des High Court in der Pro-
vinz; Gerichtsbezirk *m*; ✈ Rund-
flug *m*; *integrated* ~ ⚡ integrierter
Schaltkreis *m*; *short* ~ ⚡ Kurzschluß
m; ~ *breaker* ⚡ Aus-, Selbstschalter
m; *make a* ~ *of* e-n Rundgang machen
durch; **cir·cu·i·tous** □ [sə:'kju:itəs]
weitschweifig; ~ *route* Umweg *m*.

cir·cu·lar ['sə:kjulə] **1.** □ kreisförmig, rund; Kreis...; Rund-
reise...; ~ *letter* Rundschreiben *n*;
~ *note* Kreditbrief *m*; ~ *railway*
Ringbahn *f*; ~ *saw* Kreissäge *f*; ~
skirt Glockenrock *m*; **2.** Rundschreiben *n*; Laufzettel *m*; '**cir·cu-**
lar·ize durch Rundschreiben benachrichtigen.

cir·cu·late ['sə:kjuleit] *v/i.* umlaufen, zirkulieren; *v/t.* in Umlauf setzen; verbreiten; ✞ *Wechsel* girieren;
'**cir·cu·lat·ing**: ~ *decimal* periodischer Dezimalbruch *m*; ~ *library*
Leihbücherei *f*; ~ *medium* Tausch-
mittel *n*; **cir·cu·la·tion** Zirkula-
tion *f*, Kreislauf *m*; *fig.* Umlauf *m*;
Verbreitung *f*; *Zeitungs-*Auflage *f*;
cir·cu·la·to·ry Kreislauf...

cir·cum... ['sə:kəm] (her)um; **cir-**
cum·cise ⚕, *eccl.* [~'saiz] beschneiden; **cir·cum·ci·sion** [~'siʒən]
Beschneidung *f*; **cir·cum·fer·ence**
[sə'kʌmfərəns] (Kreis)Umfang *m*;
Peripherie *f*; **cir·cum·flex** ['sə:-
kəmfleks] *gr.* Zirkumflex *m*; **cir-**
cum·ja·cent [~'dʒeisənt] umliegend; **cir·cum·lo·cu·tion** [~lə-
'kju:ʃən] Umständlichkeit *f*; Weitschweifigkeit *f*; **cir·cum·loc·u·to-**
ry [~'lɔkjutəri] weitschweifig; **cir-**
cum'nav·i·gate umsegeln; **cir-**

cum'nav·i·ga·tor (Welt)Umsegler
m; **cir·cum·scribe** ♧ [~'skraib]
umschreiben; *fig.* begrenzen; **cir-**
cum·scrip·tion ♧ [~'skripʃən]
Umschreibung *f*; *fig.* Begrenzung *f*;
Umschrift *f e-r Münze*; **cir·cum-**
spect □ ['~spekt] um-, vorsichtig;
cir·cum·spec·tion [~'spekʃən]
Um-, Vorsicht *f*; **cir·cum·stance**
['~stəns] Umstand *m*, Sachverhalt
m; Einzelheit *f*; Umständlichkeit *f*;
~*s pl.* Verhältnisse *n/pl.*; *in od.*
under the ~*s* unter diesen Umständen; '**cir·cum·stanced** *in e-r* ...
Lage; *poorly* ~ in ärmlichen Verhältnissen; **cir·cum·stan·tial** [~-
'stænʃəl] □ umständlich; ~ *evidence*
⚖ Indizienbeweis *m*; **cir·cum-**
stan·ti·al·i·ty ['~stænʃi'æliti] Umständlichkeit *f*; **cir·cum·vent** [~-
'vent] überlisten; vereiteln.

cir·cus ['sə:kəs] Zirkus *m*; (runder)
Platz *m* (*bsd. in Namen*).

cir·rho·sis ⚕ [si'rəusis] Zirrhose *f*.

cir·rus ['sirəs], *pl.* **cir·ri** ['~rai] Zir-
rus-, Federwolke *f*.

cis·sy ['sisi] = *sissy*.

cis·tern ['sistən] Zisterne *f*; Wasserbehälter *m*, -kasten *m*.

cit·a·del ['sitədl] Zitadelle *f*.

ci·ta·tion [sai'teiʃən] Vorladung *f*;
Anführung *f*, Zitat *n*; *Am. öffent-*
liche Ehrung *f*; **cite** zitieren; vorladen; anführen.

cit·i·zen ['sitizn] Bürger(in); Staatsangehörige *m*, *f*; Städter(in); ✕ Zivilist *m*; **cit·i·zen·ship** ['~ʃip] Bürgerrecht *n*; Staatsangehörigkeit *f*.

cit·ric ac·id ['sitrik'æsid] Zitronen-
säure *f*; **cit·ron** ['~rən] Zitrone *f*;
cit·rus ['~rəs] Zitrusfrucht *f*.

cit·y ['siti] **1.** Stadt *f*; *the* ♀ *London*:
die City, die Altstadt; das Ge-
schäftsviertel; **2.** städtisch, Stadt...;
♀ *article* Börsen-, Handelsbericht
m; ~ *editor Am.* Lokalredakteur *m*;
~ *hall Am.* Rathaus *n*; ~ *manager*
Am. Stadtdirektor *m*; ~ *state* Stadt-
staat *m*; ~'**fa·ther** *Am.* Stadtrat *m*;
~*s pl.* Stadtväter *m pl.*

civ·ic ['sivik] (staats)bürgerlich;
Bürger...; städtisch; ~ *rights pl.*
bürgerliche Ehrenrechte *n/pl.*; '**civ-**
ics *sg.* Staatsbürgerkunde *f*.

civ·il □ ['sivl] bürgerlich, Bürger...;
zivil, Zivil...; ⚖ zivilrechtlich; höflich; ~ *defence* Zivilverteidigung *f*,
Luftschutz *m*; ~ *war* Bürgerkrieg *m*;

♀ *Servant* Verwaltungsbeamte *m*; ~ *engineering* Hoch- und Tiefbau *m*; ~ *law* bürgerliches Recht *n*; ~ *rights pl.* Bürgerrechte *n/pl.*; ~ *rights activist* Bürgerrechtler *m*; ~ *rights movement* Bürgerrechtsbewegung *f*; ♀ *Service* Verwaltungs-, Staatsdienst *m*, öffentlicher Dienst *m*; **ci·vil·ian** ✗ [si'viljən] Zivilist *m*; ~ *population* Zivilbevölkerung *f*; **ci'vil·i·ty** Höflichkeit *f*; **civ·i·li·za·tion** [ˌlai'zeiʃən] Zivilisation *f*, Kultur *f*; **'civ·i·lize** zivilisieren; ~*d nation* Kulturnation *f*.

civ·vies *sl.* ['siviz] *pl.* Zivil(klamotten *f/pl.*) *n*; **'civ·vy street** *sl.* Zivilleben *n*.

clack [klæk] **1.** Geklapper *n*; *fig.* Geplapper *n*, Geschwätz *n*; ⊕ (Ventil-) Klappe *f*; **2.** klappern; *fig.* schwatzen.

clad *lit.* [klæd] *pret. u. p.p von clothe*; *hills* ~ *in verdure poet.* begrünte Hügel *m/pl.*

claim [kleim] **1.** Anspruch *m*; Anrecht *n* (*to* auf *acc.*); Forderung *f*; ⚖ Klagebegehren *n*; ✗ Mutung *f*; *bsd. Am.* selbstabgestecktes Stück Land *n* *zum Siedeln*; *lay* ~ *to* Anspruch erheben auf (*acc.*); *put in a* ~ *for* als Eigentum beanspruchen; **2.** beanspruchen, in Anspruch nehmen; fordern; behaupten; sich berufen auf (*acc.*); ~ *to be* sich ausgeben für; **'claim·a·ble** zu beanspruchen(d); **'claim·ant** Beansprucher *m*; ⚖ Kläger *m*.

clair·voy·ance [kleə'vɔiəns] Hellsichtigkeit *f* (*a. fig.*); **clair'voy·ant(e)** Hellseher(in).

clam *zo.* [klæm] Venusmuschel *f*.

cla·mant *lit.* ['kleimənt] lärmend, laut.

clam·ber ['klæmbə] klimmen, klettern.

clam·mi·ness ['klæminis] feuchte Kälte *f*; **'clam·my** □ feuchtkalt, klamm.

clam·or·ous □ ['klæmərəs] lärmend, schreiend; **'clam·our 1.** Geschrei *n*, Lärm *m*; Tumult *m*; **2.** schreien (*for* nach).

clamp[1] ⊕ [klæmp] **1.** Klammer *f*; Klampe *f*; **2.** verklammern; befestigen.

clamp[2] [ˌ] (Kartoffel- *etc.*)Miete *f*.

clan [klæn] Clan *m*, schottischer Stamm(verband) *m*; *fig.* Sippschaft *f*.

clan·des·tine □ [klæn'destin] heimlich; Geheim...

clang [klæŋ] **1.** Klang *m*, Geklirr *n*; **2.** schallen; klirren (lassen); **clang·or·ous** ['ˌgərəs] klirrend; gellend; **'clang·o(u)r** = *clang.*

clank [klæŋk] **1.** Gerassel *n*, Geklirr *n*; **2.** rasseln, klirren (mit).

clan·nish ['klæniʃ] Sippen...

clap [klæp] **1.** (Hände)Klatschen *n*; Schlag *m*, Klaps *m*; *sl.* Tripper *m*; **2.** klappen (mit); klatschen (*one's hands* in die Hände); *j-m* Beifall klatschen; *j-m auf die Schulter* klopfen; aufhalsen (*on dat.*); ~ *eyes on s.o.* j. erblicken, sehen; **'~·board** Schalbrett *n*; **'~·net** Schlagnetz *n* *zum Vogelfang*; **'clap·per** Klapper *f*; Klöppel *m* *e-r Glocke*; **'clap·trap 1.** Effekthascherei *f*; Klimbim *m*; **2.** auf Beifall berechnet.

clar·et ['klærət] roter Bordeaux *m*; *allg.* Rotwein *m*; Weinrot *n*; *sl.* Blut *n*.

clar·i·fi·ca·tion [klærifi'keiʃən] (Ab)Klärung *f*; **clar·i·fy** ['ˌfai] *v/t.* (ab)klären; *fig.* klären; *v/i.* sich klären.

clar·i·net [klæri'net], **clar·i·o·net** [ˌəˈnet] Klarinette *f*.

clar·i·on ['klæriən] lauter Ruf *m*.

clar·i·ty ['klæriti] Klarheit *f*.

clash [klæʃ] **1.** Geklirr *n*; Zs.-stoß *m*; Widerstreit *m*; **2.** klirren, rasseln (mit); zs.-stoßen; widerstreiten (*with dat.*).

clasp [klɑːsp] **1.** Haken *m*, Klammer *f*; Schnalle *f*; (*a. Ordens*)Spange *f*; Buch-Schloß *n*; *fig.* Umklammerung *f*; Umarmung *f*; Händedruck *m*; **2.** *v/t.* an-, zuhaken; umklammern; umfassen; ergreifen; *die Hände falten*; ~ *s.o.'s hand* j-m die Hand drücken; *v/i.* festhalten; **'~·knife** Klapp-, Taschenmesser *n*.

class [klɑːs] **1.** Klasse *f*; Stand *m*; (Unterrichts)Stunde *f*; Kursus *m*; *Am. univ.* Jahrgang *m*; *attr.* F Klasse...; erstklassig; **2.** (in Klassen) einteilen, einordnen, -reihen; ~ *with* gleichstellen mit; **'~·con·scious** klassenbewußt; **'~·fel·low** Klassenkamerad *m*, Mitschüler *m*.

clas·sic ['klæsik] **1.** Klassiker *m*; ~*s pl.* die alten Sprachen *f/pl.*; klassische Philologie *f*; Altphilologie *f*; **2.** = **'clas·si·cal** □ klassisch.

clas·si·fi·ca·tion [klæsifi'keiʃən]

Klassifizierung *f*, Einteilung *f*; Rubrik *f*; **clas·si·fied** ['⸍faid] in Klassen eingeteilt; *pol.* geheim; ~ **ads** *pl.* Kleinanzeigen *f/pl.*; **clas·si·fy** ['⸍fai] klassifizieren, (in Klassen) einteilen, einstufen.

class...: '~**mate** *s. class-fellow*; '~**room** Klassenzimmer *n*; '~ **strug·gle**, '~**war·fare** Klassenkampf *m*; '**class·y** F nobel, exklusiv.

clat·ter ['klætə] **1.** Geklapper *n*, Getrappel *n*; Geplapper *n*; **2.** klappern, rasseln (mit); plappern.

clause [klɔːz] Klausel *f*, Bestimmung *f*; *gr.* Satz *m*; *subordinate* ~ Nebensatz *m*.

claus·tral ['klɔːstrəl] klösterlich.

claus·tro·pho·bi·a *psych.* [klɔːstrə-'foubiə] Klaustrophobie *f*, Platzangst *f*.

clav·i·cle ['klævikl] Schlüsselbein *n*.

claw [klɔː] **1.** Klaue *f* (*a.* ⊕), Kralle *f*; Pfote *f*; *Krebs*-Schere *f*; **2.** (zer-)kratzen; (um)krallen; **clawed** mit (...) Klauen.

clay [klei] Ton *m*, Lehm *m*; *fig.* Erde *f*, Staub *m*; ~ *pigeon*, ~ *bird* Tontaube *f* *zum Übungsschießen*; **clay·ey** ['kleii] tonig.

clean [kliːn] **1.** *adj.* □ rein; sauber; *fig.* fehlerfrei; glatt (*Bruch*); geschickt; **2.** *adv.* rein, völlig; **3.** reinigen, säubern (*of* von); sich waschen lassen (*Stoff etc.*); *be* ~*ed out* F pleite sein; ~ *up* gründlich reinigen; aufräumen; '~**cut** klar umrissen; '**clean·er** Reiniger *m*; Putzfrau *f*; *mst* ~*s pl.* (chemische) Reinigung *f*; *send to the* ~*s* in die Reinigung geben, reinigen lassen; *take s.o. to the* ~*s* F j. schröpfen; '**clean·ing** Reinigung *f*; *attr.* Reinigungs...; ~ *woman* Reinemache-, Putzfrau *f*; **clean·li·ness** ['klenlinis] Reinlichkeit *f*; **clean·ly 1.** *adv.* ['kliːnli] rein *etc.*; **2.** *adj.* ['klenli] reinlich; **clean·ness** ['kliːnnis] Reinheit *f*; Sauberkeit *f*; **cleanse** [klenz] reinigen; säubern; '**cleans·er** Reinigungsmittel *n*; Reinigungsmilch *f od.* -creme *f*.

clean-shav·en ['kliːn'ʃeivən] glattrasiert.

clean-up ['kliːn'ʌp] Aufräumung *f*; *pol.* Säuberungsaktion *f*; *Am. sl.* Profit *m*.

clear [kliə] **1.** □ *mst* klar (*durchsichtig*; *deutlich*; *verständlich*; *scharf* [*Geist etc.*]; *sicher*, *gewiß*; *einwand-*

frei); *oft* hell, rein (*Ton*, *Licht etc.*); *fig.* rein (*from von* *Verdacht etc.*); frei (*unbehindert*; *of* von); ganz, voll; ✝ rein, netto; ~ *of* frei *od. fern od.* los von; *as* ~ *as day* sonnenklar; *get* ~ *of* loskommen von; **2.** *in the* ~ △ im Lichten; **3.** *v/t. a.* ~ *up* er-, aufhellen, *fig. a.* aufklären; klären; reinigen, säubern (*of*, *from* von); *Wald* lichten, roden; *a.* ~ *away*, ~ *off* wegräumen; *Hindernis* nehmen; *Rechnung* ins reine bringen, bezahlen; ✝ *s.* ~ *off*; ✝ (aus-)klarieren, verzollen; 🕰 lossprechen; befreien; rechtfertigen (*from* von); ✝ als Reingewinn erzielen; ~ *off* ✝ räumen; ~ *a port* aus einem Hafen auslaufen; ~ *a ship for action* ein Schiff klar zum Gefecht machen; ~ *one's throat* sich räuspern; *v/i. a.* ~ *up* sich aufhellen; *a.)* ~ *off* sich verziehen (*Wolken etc.*); ~ *out* F verschwinden; ~ *through e-n Ort* passieren; '**clear·ance** Aufklärung *f*; Freilegung *f*; Räumung *f*; ✝ Abrechnung *f*, ⚓, ✝ Verzollung *f*, Klarierung *f*; Zollschein *m*; ⊕ Spielraum *m*, lichter Raum *m*; ~ *sale* Räumungsausverkauf *m*; '**clear-'cut** ganz klar; '**clear·ing** Aufklärung *f* *etc. s. clear 3*; Rodung *f*, Lichtung *f*, Schneise *f*; ✝ Ab-, Verrechnung *f*; ~ *arrangement* Abrechnungsverkehr *m*; ~ *bank* Girobank *f*; ⚜ *House* Ab-, Verrechnungsstelle *f*; Abrechnungsbörse *f in London*; ~*hospital* Feldlazarett *n*; '**clear·ness** Klarheit *f*, Deutlichkeit *f*; Reinheit *f*.

cleat [kliːt] ⚓ Klampe *f*; Keil *m*; Pflock *m*.

cleav·age ['kliːvidʒ] Spaltung *f* (*a. fig.*); *min.* Spaltbarkeit *f*.

cleave[1] [kliːv] (*irr.*) (sich) spalten; *Wasser*, *Luft* (zer)teilen; *in a cleft stick* in der Klemme; *cleft palate* 🦴 Wolfsrachen *m*; *show the cloven hoof* sein wahres Gesicht zeigen.

cleave[2] [~] *fig.* festhalten (*to an dat.*); treu bleiben (*dat.*); ~ *together* zusammenhalten.

cleav·er ['kliːvə] Spaltende *m*; Hackmesser *n*.

cleek [kliːk] Haken *m*; Golfstock *m*.

clef ♪ [klef] Schlüssel *m*.

cleft [kleft] **1.** Spalte *f*; Sprung *m*; Riß *m*; **2.** *pret. u. p.p. von cleave*[1].

clem·a·tis ♧ ['klemətis] Waldrebe *f*,

Klematis *f.*

clem·en·cy ['klemǝnsi] Milde *f;* **'clem·ent** ☐ mild.

clench [klentʃ] *Lippen etc.* fest zs.-pressen; *Zähne* zs.-beißen; *Faust* ballen; festhalten; = *clinch.*

clere·sto·ry ⚠ ['kliǝstǝri] Lichtgaden *m e-r Kirche.*

cler·gy ['klǝ:dʒi] Geistlichkeit *f,* Klerus *m;* '∼·man, cler·ic ['klerik] Geistliche *m.*

cler·i·cal ['klerikǝl] **1.** ☐ geistlich; Schreib(er)...; ∼ *error* Schreibfehler *m;* ∼ *work* Büroarbeit *f;* **2.** Geistliche *m; pol.* Klerikale *m.*

cler·i·hew ['klerihju:] Clerihew *n (vierzeiliges witziges Gedicht).*

clerk [klɑ:k] (Büro)Schreiber *m,* Büroangestellte *m;* Sekretär *m;* ✝ kaufmännischer Angestellter *m,* Handlungsgehilfe *m,* Kommis *m; bsd. Am.* Verkäufer(in) *im Laden; eccl.* Küster *m.*

clev·er ☐ ['klevǝ] klug, gescheit; geschickt; ∼ **dick** F Besserwisser *m;* '**clev·er·ness** Geschicklichkeit *f;* Klugheit *f.*

clew [klu:] Knäuel *m, n; s. clue.*

cli·ché ['kli:ʃei] stehende Redensart *f,* übliche Phrase *f,* Schlagwort *n,* Klischee *n.*

click [klik] **1.** Klicken *n,* Knipsen *n,* Ticken *n,* Knacken *n;* ⊕ Sperrhaken *m,* -klinke *f;* **2.** klicken, ticken, knacken; zu-, einschnappen; tadellos klappen; *sl.* sich auf den ersten Blick ineinander verlieben; Glück haben.

cli·ent ['klaiǝnt] Klient(in); Kunde *m,* Kundin *f;* **cli·en·tèle** [kli:ã:n-'teil] Klientel *f,* Kundschaft *f.*

cliff [klif] Klippe *f;* Felsen *m;* (Steil)Abhang *m;* '∼·hang·er *bsd. Radio, Fernsehen:* Folge eines Mehrteilers, die im spannendsten Moment aufhört.

cli·mac·ter·ic [klai'mæktǝrik] **1.** (∼*ally*) klimakterisch; **2.** ♂ Klimakterium *n; fig.* Lebenswende *f,* Wendepunkt *m.*

cli·mate ['klaimit] Klima *n;* **cli·mat·ic** [∼'mætik] (∼*ally*) klimatisch.

cli·max ['klaimæks] **1.** Steigerung *f;* Gipfel *m,* Höhepunkt *m;* **2.** auf e-n Höhepunkt bringen; e-n Höhepunkt erreichen.

climb [klaim] **1.** (er)klettern, (er-)

klimmen, (er)steigen; **2.** Kletterei *f;* Kletterpartie *f;* '**climb·er** Kletterer *m,* Bergsteiger(in); *fig.* Streber(in); ♀ Kletterpflanze *f;* '**climb·ing** Klettern *n; attr.* Kletter...; '**climb·ing-i·ron** Steigeisen *n.*

clinch [klintʃ] **1.** ⊕ Vernietung *f; fig.* Festhalten *n; Boxen:* Umklammerung *f,* Clinch *m;* **2.** *v/t.* um-, vernieten; *Beweis* verstärken, *Handel* festmachen; entscheiden; *s. clench; v/i.* festhalten; '**clinch·er** ⊕ Krampe *f;* F treffende Antwort *f,* Trumpf *m.*

cling [kliŋ] (*irr.*) (*to*) festhalten (an *dat.*), sich (an)klammern (an *acc.*); sich (an)schmiegen (an *acc.*); *j-m* anhängen; sich heften *od.* hängen (an *acc.*); '**cling·ing** enganliegend (*Kleid*); anhänglich.

clin·ic ['klinik] Klinik *f;* klinisches Praktikum *n;* '**clin·i·cal** ☐ klinisch; ∼ *thermometer* Fieberthermometer *n.*

clink[1] *sl.* [kliŋk] Kittchen *n,* Gefängnis *n.*

clink[2] [∼] **1.** Klingen *n;* Geklirr *n;* **2.** klingen, klirren (lassen); klimpern mit; mit den Gläsern anstoßen; '**clink·er** Klinkerstein *m,* Schlacke *f; sl.* Prachtkerl *m,* -stück *n;* '**clin·ker-built** ⚓ klinkergebaut; '**clink·ing** *sl.* fabelhaft, F blendend.

clip[1] [klip] **1.** Schur *f;* at one ∼ *Am.* F auf einmal, auf e-n Schlag; **2.** ab-, aus-, beschneiden; *Schafe etc.* scheren; *Silben* verschlucken; *Fahrkarte* lochen; ∼ *s.o.'s ear sl.* j-m e-e knallen.

clip[2] [∼] **1.** (Büro-, Heft)Klammer *f;* Spange *f;* **2.** zs.-klammern.

clip·per ['klipǝ] Klipper *m;* ⚓ Schnellsegler *m;* schnelles Pferd *n; sl.* Prachtstück *n;* (*a. pair of*) ∼*s pl.* Haarschneide-, Schermaschine *f;* '**clip·pings** *pl.* Abfälle *m/pl.;* Schnitzel *n/pl.; Zeitungs- etc.* Ausschnitte *m/pl.*

clique [kli:k] Clique *f,* Sippschaft *f.*

clit·o·ris *anat.* ['klitǝris] Klitoris *f,* Kitzler *m.*

cloak [klǝuk] **1.** Umhang *m,* Mantel *m; fig.* Deckmantel *m;* **2.** *fig.* bemänteln, verhüllen; '∼·room Garderobe(nraum *m*) *f;* Toilette *f;* 🚻 Gepäckaufbewahrung *f.*

clob·ber *sl.* [ˈklɔbə] **1.** Klamotten *f/pl.*; **2.** (zs.-)schlagen; *fig.* besiegen.

clock [klɔk] **1.** *Schlag-, Wand-, Turm-*Uhr *f;* Zwickel *m* am *Strumpf; Sport sl.* Stoppuhr *f; put the ~ back fig.* die Uhr zurückdrehen; **2.** *v/t. Sport sl. Rennen* mit der Stoppuhr messen; *v/i. ~ in (out) Arbeitszeitkontrolle:* einstempeln (ausstempeln); '~**face** Zifferblatt *n;* **~ra·di·o** Radiowecker *m;* '~**wise** im Uhrzeigersinn; '~**work** Federwerk *n; ~ train* Eisenbahn *f* zum Aufziehen; *like ~* wie am Schnürchen.

clod [klɔd] Erdkloß *m;* Klumpen *m; a. ~-hopper* (Bauern)Tölpel *m.*

clog [klɔg] **1.** Klotz *m; fig.* Hindernis *n;* Holzschuh *m;* Überschuh *m;* **2.** belasten; *fig.* hemmen; (sich) verstopfen; '**clog·gy** klumpig.

clois·ter [ˈklɔistə] **1.** Kreuzgang *m;* Kloster *n;* **2.** (in ein Kloster) einschließen.

close 1. [kləuz] Schluß *m,* Ende *n;* Abschluß *m;* [kləus] Einfriedung *f,* Hof *m;* **2.** [kləuz] *v/t.* (ab-, ein-, ver-, zu)schließen; zumachen; beschließen; *~ down Betrieb* schließen, stillegen; *~ one's eyes* to die Augen schließen vor (*dat.*); *v/i.* (sich) schließen; abschließen; enden; zuheilen; handgemein werden (*with* mit); *~ in* hereinbrechen (*Nacht*); kürzer werden (*Tage*); *~ on (prp.)* sich schließen um, umschließen, umfassen; *~ up* ✗ aufschließen; *closing time Geschäfts-* etc. Schluß *m,* Feierabend *m;* Polizeistunde *f;* **3.** ☐ [kləus] geschlossen; verborgen; verschwiegen; knapp, eng; eng anliegend (*Kleid etc.*); begrenzt, geschlossen (*Gesellschaft*); nah, eng; bündig (*Stil etc.*); dicht; gedrängt (*Schrift etc.*); schwül, dumpf; knickerig; genau (*Aufmerksamkeit etc.*); eingehend (*Prüfung*); fest (*Griff*); fast gleich (*Wettkampf*); *~ by, ~ to* dicht bei *od.* daneben, ganz in der Nähe; *~ fight, ~ combat, ~ quarters pl.* Handgemenge *n,* Nahkampf *m; ~ prisoner* streng bewachter Gefangener *m; ~ season, ~ time hunt.* Schonzeit *f; sail ~ to the wind* ✗ hart am Wind segeln; *fig.* sich hart an der Grenze des Erlaubten bewegen; *a ~ shave* ein knappes Entrinnen; '~**cropped,** '~**cut** kurz geschnitten (*Haar,*

Gras etc.).

closed [kləuzd] geschlossen; *~ book fig.* Buch *n* mit sieben Siegeln; *~ cir·cuit* geschlossener Stromkreis *m;* **~cir·cuit tel·e·vi·sion** Fernsehüberwachungsanlage *f;* interne Fernsehanlage *f; ~ shop* Unternehmen *n* mit Gewerkschaftszwang.

close...: '~**ˈfist·ed** knickerig; '~**ˈfit·ting** eng anliegend; '~**ˈgrained** feinkörnig (*Holz*); '~**ˈhauled** ✗ hart am Wind; '~**ˈknit** eng (zs.-gewachsen) (*Familie, Gemeinschaft*); '~**ˈmeshed** engmaschig; '**close·ness** Genauigkeit *f,* Geschlossenheit *f* etc. (*s. close* 3).

clos·et [ˈklɔzit] **1.** *bsd. Am.* Abstell-, Vorratsraum *m;* (Wand)Schrank *m;* Kabinett *n,* Geheimzimmer *n; s. water-~;* **2.** *be ~ed with* mit *j-m* e-e geheime Beratung haben.

clos·ing [ˈkləuziŋ]: *~ date* Schlußtermin *m; ~ time* Ladenschluß *m;* Polizeistunde *f.*

close-up [ˈkləusʌp] *Film:* Groß-, Nahaufnahme *f.*

clo·sure [ˈkləuʒə] **1.** Verschluß *m; parl.* (Antrag *m* auf) Schluß *m e-r Debatte; apply the ~* Schluß der Debatte beantragen; die Debatte schließen; **2.** *Debatte etc.* schließen.

clot [klɔt] **1.** Klümpchen *n;* **2.** zu Klümpchen gerinnen (lassen).

cloth [klɔθ] Stoff *m,* Tuch *n;* Tischtuch *n;* Kleidung *f,* Tracht *f bsd. der Geistlichen; the ~* F der geistliche Stand *m; lay the ~* den Tisch decken; *bound in ~* in Leinen gebunden; *~ binding* Leinenband *m.*

clothe [kləuð] (*irr.*) (an-, be)kleiden; *fig.* be-, einkleiden.

clothes [kləuðz] *pl.* Kleider *n/pl.;* Kleidung *f;* Anzug *m;* Wäsche *f;* '~**-bas·ket** Waschkorb *m; ~ hang·er** Kleiderbügel *m; ~ horse** Wäscheständer *m;* '~**line** Wäscheleine *f;* '~**peg** Kleiderhaken *m;* Wäscheklammer *f;* '~**pin** *bsd. Am.* Wäscheklammer *f;* '~**press** Kleider-, Wäscheschrank *m.*

cloth·ier [ˈkləuðiə] Tuch-, Kleiderhändler *m.*

cloth·ing [ˈkləuðiŋ] Kleidung *f.*

cloud [klaud] **1.** Wolke *f* (*a. fig.*); dunkler Fleck *m,* Trübung *f;* Schatten *m; be under a ~* in Ungnade sein; *in the ~s* geistesabwesend; **2.** (sich) be-, umwölken, trüben (a. fig.); ~ed gewölkt (Bern-stein); geädert (Holz etc.); moiriert (Seide); '~-burst Wolkenbruch m; ~-'cuck·oo-land Wolkenkuckucks-heim n; 'cloud·less □ wolkenlos; 'cloud·y □ wolkig; Wolken...; trüb; unklar.

clough [klʌf] Schlucht f.

clout [klaut] **1.** F j-m e-e Kopfnuß geben; **2.** Flicken m, Lappen m; F Kopfnuß f.

clove[1] [kləuv] (Gewürz)Nelke f.

clove[2] [~] (Knoblauch)Zehe f.

clove[3] [~] pret. von cleave[1]; 'clo-ven **1.** p.p. von cleave[1]; **2.** adj. ge-spalten; Spalt...

clo·ver ♀ ['kləuvə] Klee m; live od. be in ~ im Wohlstand leben; '~-leaf Autobahn: Kleeblatt(kreu-zung f) n.

clown [klaun] Hanswurst m, Clown m; lit. Bauer m, Tölpel m; 'clown-ish □ bäurisch; plump; clownhaft.

cloy [klɔi] übersättigen, -laden; an-ekeln.

club [klʌb] **1.** Keule f; (Gummi-) Knüppel m; Klub m, Verein m; ~s pl. Karten: Treff n, Kreuz n, Eicheln f/pl.; **2.** v/t. mit e-r Keule od. dem Gewehrkolben schlagen; ~ together Geld zs.-legen; v/i. mst ~ together sich zs.-tun; 'club·a·ble klub-, gesellschafts-fähig; 'club-'foot Klumpfuß m; 'club-'house Klub-, Vereinshaus n; 'club-'law Faustrecht n.

cluck [klʌk] glucken (Henne).

clue fig. [klu:] Anhaltspunkt m, Fingerzeig m, Hinweis m.

clump [klʌmp] **1.** Klumpen m; (Baum)Gruppe f; mst ~ sole Dop-pelsohle f; **2.** trampeln; zs.-drängen; mit Doppelsohlen ver-sehen; in Gruppen pflanzen.

clum·si·ness ['klʌmzinis] Unbe-holfenheit f etc.; 'clum·sy □ unbe-holfen, ungeschickt, schwerfällig; plump.

clung [klʌŋ] pret. u. p.p. von cling.

clus·ter ['klʌstə] **1.** ♀ Traube f; Büschel m, n; Haufen m, Schwarm m, Gruppe f; **2.** büschelweise wachsen; (sich) zs.-drängen.

clutch[1] [klʌtʃ] **1.** Griff m; ⊕ Kupp-lung f; in his ~es in seinen Krallen; ~ pedal mot. Kupplungspedal n; **2.** (er)greifen, packen; greifen (at

nach).

clutch[2] [~] Gelege n, Brut f.

clut·ter ['klʌtə] **1.** Wirrwarr m, Durcheinander n; **2.** ~ up durch-einanderbringen, in Unordnung bringen; vollstopfen.

clys·ter ['klistə] Klistier n.

co... [kəu] Wortelement: mit, ge-meinsam, Ko...

coach [kəutʃ] **1.** Kutsche f; 🚌 Wagen m; Reisebus m; univ. Ein-pauker m; Sport: Trainer m; **2.** in e-r Kutsche fahren; (ein)pau-ken; trainieren; '~-man Kutscher m; '~-work mot. Karosserie f.

co·ad·ju·tor bsd. eccl. [kəu'ædʒutə] Gehilfe m, Koadjutor m.

co·ag·u·late [kəu'ægjuleit] gerinnen (lassen); **co·ag·u·la·tion** Gerinnen n.

coal [kəul] **1.** (Stein)Kohle f; coll. Kohlen pl.; carry ~s to Newcastle Eulen nach Athen tragen; haul od. call s.o. over the ~s fig. j-m die Hölle heiß machen; **2.** ⚓ (be-) kohlen; ~ing station Kohlenstation f; '~-bed Kohlenflöz m; '~-'dust Koh-lenstaub m.

co·a·lesce [kəuə'les] zs.-wachsen, sich vereinigen; **co·a·les·cence** Zs.-wachsen n; Vereinigung f.

coal...: '~-field Kohlenrevier n; '~-gas Leuchtgas n.

co·a·li·tion [kəuə'liʃən] Verbindung f; Bund m, Koalition f.

coal...: '~-mine, '~-pit Kohlen-grube f, -bergwerk n; '~-scut·tle Kohleneimer m.

coarse □ [kɔ:s] grob; fig. roh; un-geschliffen; 'coarse·ness Grob-, Derbheit f.

coast [kəust] **1.** Küste f; bsd. Am. Rodelbahn f, (Rodel)Abfahrt f; **2.** die Küste entlangfahren; im Freilauf fahren; rodeln; 'coast·al Küsten...

coast·er ['kəustə] Am. Rodel-schlitten m; ⚓ Küstenfahrer m; Untersetzer m für Gläser; ~ brake Am. Rücktrittbremse f.

coast-guard ['kəustgɑ:d] Küsten-wache f; 'coast·ing Küstenfahrt f; Rodeln n; ~ trade Küstenschiffahrt f; 'coast-line Küste(nlinie) f.

coat [kəut] **1.** Jackett n, Jacke f, Rock m; Mantel m; Haare n/pl., Pelz m, Gefieder n; Überzug m, Schicht f; Anstrich m; ~ of mail

Panzerhemd n; ~ of arms Wappen (-schild m) n; cut the ~ according to the cloth sich nach der Decke strecken; turn one's ~ sein Mäntelchen nach dem Wind hängen; **2.** bedecken; überziehen; anstreichen; '~-hang·er Kleiderbügel m; 'coat·ing Überzug m, Anstrich m; Bewurf m; Mantelstoff m.

coax [kəuks] schmeicheln (dat.); beschwatzen (into zu); ~ s.o. out of s.th. j-m et. abschwatzen.

cob [kɔb] kleines starkes Pferd n; männlicher Schwan m; Klumpen m; Am. Maiskolben m; = ~-nut.

co·balt min. [kəu'bɔːlt] Kobalt n.

cob·ble ['kɔbl] **1.** Kopf-, Pflasterstein m; ~s pl. = cob-coal; **2.** flikken; 'cob·bler Schuhmacher m; Stümper m; eisgekühltes Mischgetränk; 'cob·ble-stone Pflasterstein m.

cob...: '~-coal Nuß-, Stückkohle f; '~-loaf rundes Brot n; '~-nut Art Haselnuß f.

co·bra zo. ['kəubrə] Kobra f.

cob·web ['kɔbweb] Spinnwebe f.

co·caine pharm. [kə'kein] Kokain n.

coch·i·neal ['kɔtʃiniːl] Koschenille f.

cock [kɔk] **1.** Hahn m; Vogel-Männchen n; ⊕ Hahn m am Faß und Gewehr; Anführer m; kleiner Heuhaufen m; V Schwanz m, Penis m; **2.** oft ~ up aufrichten; die Ohren spitzen; Gewehrhahn spannen; den Hut aufs Ohr setzen; ~ one's eye (at s.o. j-m zu)zwinkern.

cock·ade [kɔ'keid] Kokarde f.

cock-a-doo·dle-doo ['kɔkəduːdl-'duː] Kikeriki n od. m.

cock-a-hoop ['kɔkə'huːp] frohlockend.

Cock·aigne [kɔ'kein] Schlaraffenland n.

cock-and-bull sto·ry ['kɔkənd-'bul'stɔːri] Räubergeschichte f.

cock·a·too [kɔkə'tuː] Kakadu m.

cock-a·trice ['kɔkətrais] Basilisk m (a. fig.).

cock·boat ⚓ ['kɔkbəut] Jolle f.

cock·chaf·er ['kɔktʃeifə] Maikäfer m.

cock-crow(·ing) ['kɔkkrəu(iŋ)] Hahnenschrei m; Tagesanbruch m.

cocked hat ['kɔkt'hæt] Zwei-, Dreispitz m; knock into a ~ zu Brei schlagen.

cock·er¹ ['kɔkə]: ~ up aufpäppeln.

cock·er² [~] Cockerspaniel m.

cock·er·el ['kɔkərəl] Hähnchen n.

cock...: '~-eyed sl. schieläugig; Am. blau (betrunken); '~-fight(·ing) Hahnenkampf m; '~-'horse Steckenpferd n.

cock·le¹ ⚘ ['kɔkl] Kornrade f.

cock·le² [~] **1.** zo. Herzmuschel f; Falte f; warm od. delight the ~s of one's heart dem Herzen wohltun; **2.** (sich) kräuseln, falten.

cock·ney ['kɔkni] waschechter Londoner m; 'cock·ney·ism Cockneyausdruck m.

cock·pit ['kɔkpit] Kampfplatz m für Hähne; ⚓ Raumdeck n; ✈ Führerraum m, Kanzel f.

cock·roach zo. ['kɔkrəutʃ] Schabe f.

cocks·comb ['kɔkskəum] Hahnenkamm m (a. ⚘); 'cock-'sure F absolut sicher; überheblich; 'cocktail Cocktail m (Mischgetränk; Früchte); 'cock-up: make a ~ of s.th. sl. et. verpfuschen; 'cock·y □ F selbstbewußt; naseweis; frech.

co·co ['kəukəu] Kokospalme f.

co·coa ['kəukəu] Kakao m.

co·co·nut ['kəukənʌt] Kokosnuß f.

co·coon [kə'kuːn] Kokon m der Seidenraupe.

cod ichth. [kɔd] Kabeljau m, Dorsch m; dried ~ Stockfisch m; cured ~ Klippfisch m.

cod·dle ['kɔdl] verhätscheln, verwöhnen; ~ up aufpäppeln.

code [kəud] **1.** Gesetzbuch n; (Ehren)Kodex m; Code m; Schlüssel m; **2.** tel. chiffrieren.

co·de·ine ⚕ ['kəudiːn] Kodein n.

co·dex ['kəudeks], pl. **co·di·ces** ['~disiːz] Kodex m, Handschrift f.

cod·fish ['kɔdfiʃ] = cod.

codg·er F ['kɔdʒə] komischer Kauz m.

co·di·ces ['kəudisiːz] pl. von codex.

cod·i·cil ['kɔdisil] Kodizill n; **cod-i·fi·ca·tion** Kodifikation f; **cod·i-fy** ['~fai] kodifizieren.

cod·ling ['kɔdliŋ] ⚘ Kochapfel m; ichth. junger Kabeljau m.

cod-liv·er oil ['kɔdlivər'ɔil] Lebertran m.

co·ed Am. F ['kəu'ed] Schülerin f e-r Koedukationsschule, allg. Studentin f.

co·ed·u·ca·tion ['kəuedjuːkeiʃən] Koedukation f (gemeinsamer Schulbesuch beider Geschlechter).

co·ef·fi·cient [kəui'fiʃənt] **1.** mitwirkend; **2.** Koeffizient *m*.

co·erce [kəuˈɜːs] zwingen; *et.* erzwingen; **coˈer·ci·ble** zu (er)zwingen(d); **coˈer·cion** [‿ʃən] Zwang *m*; Zwangsherrschaft *f*; *under* ‿ unter Zwang, in e-r Zwangslage; **coˈer·cive** [‿siv] ☐ Zwangs...

co·e·val ☐ [kəuˈiːvəl] gleichzeitig; gleichalterig.

co·ex·ist [ˈkəuigˈzist] gleichzeitig bestehen; **ˈco·exˈist·ence** Koexistenz *f*; Nebeneinander *n*; **ˈco·exˈist·ent** gleichzeitig (existierend).

cof·fee [ˈkɔfi] Kaffee *m*; **ˈ‿-bean** Kaffeebohne *f*; **ˈ‿-grounds** *pl.* Kaffeegrund *m*, -satz *m*; **ˈ‿-house** Kaffeehaus *n*; Café *n*; **ˈ‿-pot** Kaffeekanne *f*; **ˈ‿-room** Speisesaal *m* *e-s Hotels*; **ˈ‿-set** Kaffeeservice *n*; ‿ **shop** Kaffeegeschäft *n*; Kaffeestube *f*, kleines Restaurant *n*; ‿ **ta·ble** Couchtisch *m*.

cof·fer [ˈkɔfə] (Geld)Kasten *m*; △ Deckenkassette *f*; ‿**s** *pl.* Schatz (-kammer *f*) *m*, Tresor *m*; *a.* ‿**-dam** Senkkasten *m*, Caisson *m*.

cof·fin [ˈkɔfin] **1.** Sarg *m*; **2.** einsargen.

cog ⊕ [kɔg] Rad-Zahn *m*.

co·gen·cy [ˈkəudʒənsi] zwingende Kraft *f*; **ˈco·gent** ☐ zwingend.

cogged ⊕ [kɔgd] gezahnt, Zahn...

cog·i·tate [ˈkɔdʒiteit] *v/i.* nachdenken; *v/t.* (er)sinnen; **cog·iˈta·tion** Nachdenken *n*.

co·gnac [ˈkɔnjæk] Kognak *m*.

cog·nate [ˈkɔgneit] **1.** verwandt; **2.** Blutsverwandte *m, f*.

cog·ni·tion [kɔgˈniʃən] Erkenntnis *f*.

cog·ni·za·ble [ˈkɔgnizəbl] erkennbar; ⅔⅔ abzuurteilen(d); **ˈcog·ni·zance** Kenntnis *f*; Erkenntnis *f* (⅔⅔ *n*); Gerichtsbarkeit *f*, Zuständigkeit *f*; Abzeichen *n*; **ˈcog·ni·zant** Kenntnis habend (*of* von); zuständig.

cog·no·men [kɔgˈnəumen] Zuname *m*; Bei-, Spitzname *m*.

cog-wheel ⊕ [ˈkɔgwiːl] Zahnrad *n*.

co·hab·it [kəuˈhæbit] in wilder Ehe leben; **co·habˈi·ta·tion** wilde Ehe *f*.

co·heir [ˈkəuˈɛə] Miterbe *m*; **coheir·ess** [ˈkəuˈɛəris] Miterbin *f*.

co·here [kəuˈhiə] zs.-hängen; **coˈher·ence**, **coˈher·en·cy** Zs.-hang *m*; **coˈher·ent** ☐ zs.-hängend; klar, verständlich; **coˈher·er** *Radio*: Fritter *m*.

co·he·sion [kəuˈhiːʒən] Kohäsion *f*; **coˈhe·sive** [‿siv] (fest) zs.-hängend.

co·hort [ˈkəuhɔːt] Kohorte *f*; Schar *f*.

coif [kɔif] Haube *f*.

coif·feur [kwaːˈfɜː] Friseur *m*; **coif·fure** [‿ˈfjuə] **1.** Frisur *f*; **2.** frisieren.

coign of van·tage [kɔinəvˈvɑːntidʒ] guter Beobachtungsposten *m*.

coil [kɔil] **1.** *oft* ‿ *up* aufwickeln; (sich) zs.-rollen; sich winden; **2.** Rolle *f*, Spirale *f*; Wicklung *f*; ≠ Spule *f*; Windung *f*; ⊕ (Rohr-) Schlange *f*.

coin [kɔin] **1.** Münze *f*, Geldstück *n*; *pay s.o. back in his own* ‿ j-m mit gleicher Münze heimzahlen; **2.** prägen (*a. fig.*); münzen; *be* ‿*ing money* Geld wie Heu verdienen; **ˈcoin·age** Prägung *f*, Prägen *n* (*a. fig.*); Geld *n*, Münze *f*; Münzsystem *n*; **ˈcoin-box telˈe·phone** Münzfernsprecher *m*.

co·in·cide [kəuinˈsaid] zs.-treffen, -fallen; *fig.* übereinstimmen; **co·in·ci·dence** [kəuˈinsidəns] Zs.-treffen *n*, -fallen *n*; *fig.* Übereinstimmung *f*; *mere* ‿ bloßer Zufall *m*; **coˈin·ci·dent** ☐ zs.-fallend; *fig.* übereinstimmend.

coin·er [ˈkɔinə] Münzer *m*, Präger *m*; *bsd.* Falschmünzer *m*.

coir [ˈkɔiə] Kokosbast *m*.

coke [kəuk] **1.** Koks *m* (*a. sl.* = *Kokain*); *Am.* F Coca-Cola *f*; **2.** verkoken.

co·ker·nut [ˈkəukənʌt] = *coco-nut*.

col·an·der [ˈkʌləndə] *Küche:* Durchschlag *m*, Sieb *n*.

cold [kəuld] **1.** ☐ kalt (*a. fig.*); *throw* ‿ *water on* die Begeisterung für *et.* dämpfen; *give s.o. the* ‿ *shoulder* = ‿*-shoulder*; *have* ‿ *feet* F kalte Füße (*Angst*) haben; **2.** Kälte *f*, Frost *m*; Erkältung *f*; *oft* ‿ *in the head* Schnupfen *m*; *be left in the* ‿ vernachlässigt *od.* im Stich gelassen werden; **ˈ‿-ˈblood·ed** kaltblütig (*a. fig.*); **‿ cream** Feuchtigkeitscreme *f*; **ˈ‿-ˈheart·ed** kalt-, hartherzig; **ˈcold·ness** Kälte *f*.

cold...: **ˈ‿-ˈshoul·der** j-m die kalte Schulter zeigen, j. kühl behandeln, links liegen lassen; ‿ **steel** blanke Waffe *f*; **ˈ‿-ˈstor·age** Kühlhaus (-lagerung *f*) *n*; *attr.* Kühl(haus)...;

'⁓-'store kühl lagern; ⁓ **war** kalter Krieg *m*.

cole ♧ [kəul] *mst in Zssgn* Kohl *m*.
cole-seed ♧ ['kəulsi:d] Rübsamen *m*.
cole·slaw *Am.* ['kəulslɔ:] Krautsalat *m*.
col·ic ♂ ['kɔlik] Kolik *f*.
col·lab·o·rate [kə'læbəreit] zs.-arbeiten; **col·lab·o'ra·tion** Zs.-, Mitarbeit *f*; *in* ⁓ *with* gemeinsam mit; **col·lab·o'ra·tion·ist** *pol.* Kollaborateur *m*; **col'lab·o·ra·tor** Mitarbeiter *m*.
col·lapse [kə'læps] **1.** zs.-, einfallen; zs.-brechen; **2.** Zs.-bruch *m*; **col'laps·i·ble** zs.-klappbar; ⁓ *boat* Faltboot *n*.
col·lar ['kɔlə] **1.** Kragen *m*; Halsband *n*; Halskette *f*; Kum(me)t *n*; ⊕ Lager *n*, Pfanne *f*; **2.** beim Kragen packen; *Fleisch* zs.-rollen; '⁓-bone Schlüsselbein *n*; '⁓-stud Kragenknopf *m*.
col·late [kɔ'leit] *Texte etc.* vergleichen, kollationieren.
col·lat·er·al [kɔ'lætərəl] **1.** ☐ parallel laufend; Seiten..., Neben...; indirekt; **2.** Seitenverwandte *m, f*.
col·la·tion [kɔ'leiʃən] Vergleichung *f von Texten*; Imbiß *m*.
col·league ['kɔli:g] Kollege *m*, Kollegin *f*.
col·lect 1. ['kɔlekt] Kollekte *f* (*Altargebet*); **2.** [kə'lekt] *v/t.* (ein-, auf)sammeln; *Gedanken etc.* sammeln; *Geld* einziehen, einkassieren; abholen; ⁓ *one's wits* s-e Gedanken sammeln; ⁓*ing business* Inkassogeschäft *n*; *v/i.* sich (ver)sammeln; ⁓ **call** *Am. teleph.* R-Gespräch *n*; **col'lect·ed** ☐ *fig.* gefaßt; **col'lect·ed·ness** *fig.* Fassung *f*; **col'lec·tion** Sammlung *f*; Kollekte *f*; Einziehung *f*, Inkasso *n*; *forcible* ⁓ Zwangsbeitreibung *f*; **col'lec·tive** gesammelt; Sammel..., Kollektiv...; ⁓ *bargaining* Tarifverhandlungen *f/pl.*; **col'lec·tive·ly** insgesamt, im ganzen; gemeinschaftlich; **col'lec·tiv·ism** *pol.* Kollektivismus *m*; **col'lec·tiv·ize** in Gemeineigentum überführen, verstaatlichen; **col'lector** Sammler *m*; *Steuer*-Einnehmer *m*, Erheber *m*; 🚋 Fahrkartenabnehmer *m*; ⚡ Stromabnehmer *m*; ⁓*'s item* Sammler-, Liebhaberstück *n*.
col·leen *ir.* [kɔ'li:n] Mädchen *n*.

col·lege ['kɔlidʒ] College *n* (*Teil e-r Universität*); höhere Schule *f od.* Lehranstalt *f*; Hochschule *f*; Akademie *f*; Kollegium *n*; **col·le·gi·an** [kə'li:dʒjən] Student *m*; höherer Schüler *m*; **col'le·giate** [⁓dʒiit] Schul..., College...
col·lide [kə'laid] (*with*) kollidieren (mit); zs.-stoßen (mit); *fig.* widerstreiten (*dat.*).
col·lie ['kɔli] Collie *m*, schottischer Schäferhund *m*.
col·lier ['kɔliə] Bergmann *m*; ⚓ Kohlenschiff *n*; **col·lier·y** ['kɔljəri] Kohlenbergwerk *n*.
col·li·sion [kə'liʒən] Kollision *f*; Zs.-stoß *m*; *fig.* Widerstreit *m*.
col·lo·ca·tion [kɔləu'keiʃən] Anordnung *f*.
col·lo·di·on [kə'ləudjən] Kollodium *n*.
col·logue [kə'ləug] sich vertraulich besprechen.
col·lo·qui·al ☐ [kə'ləukwiəl] umgangssprachlich, familiär; **col'lo·qui·al·ism** Ausdruck *m* der Umgangssprache.
col·lo·quy ['kɔləkwi] Gespräch *n*.
col·lude [kə'lu:d] im heimlichen Einverständnis sein; **col'lu·sion** [⁓ʒən] heimliches Einverständnis *n*; ♊ Verdunkelung *f*.
col·ly·wob·bles F ['kɔliwɔblz]: *the* ⁓ ein flaues Gefühl in der Magengegend.
co·lon ['kəulən] *typ.* Kolon *n*, Doppelpunkt *m*; *anat.* Dickdarm *m*.
colo·nel ⚔ ['kə:nl] Oberst *m*; **'colo·nel·cy** Rang *m* e-s Obersten.
co·lo·ni·al [kə'ləunjəl] Kolonial...; **co'lo·ni·al·ism** *pol.* Kolonialismus *m*; **col·o·nist** ['kɔlənist] Kolonist *m*, Ansiedler *m*; **col·o·ni·za·tion** [kɔlənai'zeiʃən] Kolonisation *f*, Besiedelung *f*; **'col·o·nize** kolonisieren; (sich) ansiedeln; *Land* besiedeln.
col·on·nade [kɔlə'neid] Säulengang *m*, Kolonnade *f*.
col·o·ny ['kɔləni] Kolonie *f*; Siedlung *f*.
col·o·pho·ny [kɔ'lɔfəni] Kolophonium *n*, Geigenharz *n*.
Col·o·ra·do bee·tle [kɔlə'rɑ:dəu'bi:tl] Kartoffelkäfer *m*.
co·los·sal ☐ [kə'lɔsl] kolossal; **co'los·sus** [⁓səs] Koloß *m*, Riese *m*.
col·our, *Am.* **col·or** ['kʌlə] **1.** Farbe

f; Gesichts-, Hautfarbe *f*; *fig.* Färbung *f*; Anschein *m*; Vorwand *m*; ~s *pl.* ✖ Fahne *f*, Flagge *f*; *local* ~ Lokalkolorit *n*; **2.** *v/t.* färben; anstreichen; kolorieren; *fig.* beschönigen; *v/i.* sich färben; sich verfärben, erröten; **'col·o(u)r·a·ble** □ trügerisch; **col·o(u)r'a·tion** Färbung *f*; Farbgebung *f*.

col·o(u)r...: '~·bar Rassenschranke *f*; **'~·blind** farbenblind; **'col·o(u)red** gefärbt, farbig, bunt; ~ *film* Farbfilm *m*; ~ *pencil* Farbstift *m*; ~ (wo)man Farbige *m* (*f*); **'col·o(u)r·fast** farbecht; **col·o(u)r·ful** ['~·ful] farbenprächtig, -freudig, bunt; lebhaft; **'col·o(u)r·ing 1.** färbend; ~ *book* Malbuch *n*; ~ *matter* Farbstoff *m*; **2.** Färbung *f*; Farbgebung *f*, Ton *m*; *fig.* Beschönigung *f*; **'col·o(u)r·ist** Kolorist *m*; **'colo(u)r·less** □ farblos; **col·o(u)r line** *bsd. Am.* Rassenschranke *f*; **col·o(u)r scheme** Farbenzs.-stellung *f*; **col·o(u)r sup·ple·ment** Farbbeilage *f* e-r *Zeitung*; **col·o(u)r wash** farbige Tünche *f*.

colt [kəult] Hengstfüllen *n*; *fig.* Neuling *m*; **'colts·foot** ♀ Huflattich *m*.

col·um·bine ♀ ['kɔləmbain] Akelei *f*.

col·umn ['kɔləm] Säule *f*; Pfeiler *m*; *typ.* Spalte *f*; ✖ Kolonne *f*; **co·lum·nar** [kə'lʌmnə] säulenartig, -förmig; **col·um·nist** ['kɔləmnist] *Am.* Kolumnist *m* (*Journalist, für den stets e-e bestimmte Spalte reserviert ist*).

col·za ♀ ['kɔlzə] Raps *m*.

co·ma ['kəumə] ⚕ Koma *n*, tiefe Bewußtlosigkeit *f*; ♀ Schopf *m*, Haarbüschel *n*.

comb [kəum] **1.** Kamm *m* (*a. von Hahn u. Woge*); ⊕ Hechel *f*; *s. curry-~*; *s. honey-~*; **2.** *v/t.* kämmen; striegeln; *Flachs* hecheln; ~ *out* aus(aus)sieben; *v/i.* sich brechen (*Welle*).

com·bat ['kɔmbət] **1.** Kampf *m*, Streit *m*; *single ~* Zweikampf *m*; **2.** (be)kämpfen; **'com·bat·ant** Kämpfer *m*; **'com·bat·ive** □ streitbar, -süchtig; Kampf...

comb·er ['kəumə] ⊕ Krempelmaschine *f*; ♃ Schaumwelle *f*.

com·bin·a·ble [kəm'bainəbl] verbindungsfähig; **com·bi·na·tion** [kɔmbi'neiʃən] Verbindung *f* (*engS.* ⚛); Vereinigung *f*; Zs.-arbeit *f*;

mst ~s pl. Hemdhose *f*; Motorrad *n* mit Beiwagen; ~ *lock* Kombinationsschloß *n* (*mit Zahlen od. Buchstaben*); **com·bine 1.** [kəm'bain] (sich) verbinden *od.* -einigen; kombinieren; **2.** ['kɔmbain] ✝ Ring *m*, Interessengemeinschaft *f*; *a.* ~ *harvester* Mähdrescher *m*.

com·bus·ti·ble [kəm'bʌstəbl] **1.** brennbar; leicht entzündbar; **2.** ~s *pl.* Brennmaterial *n*; *mot.* Treibstoff *m*; **com·bus·tion** [~'bʌstʃən] Verbrennung *f*; ~ *engine* Verbrennungsmotor *m*.

come [kʌm] (*irr.*) kommen; *to* ~ künftig, kommend; *how* ~? F wieso denn?; ~ *about* sich zutragen; zustandekommen; ~ *across* auf *j. od. et.* stoßen; *j-m* zufällig begegnen; ~ *along* sich beeilen; mitkommen; ~ *at* erlangen, erreichen; *j-m od. der Wahrheit etc.* beikommen; ~ *by* vorbeikommen; zu *et.* kommen, *et.* bekommen; ~ *down* herunterkommen (*a. fig.*); zs.-stürzen; ~ *down upon s.o.* j. zurechtweisen; ~ *down upon s.o. for £ 10* von j-m £ 10 verlangen; ~ *down with* herausrücken mit *Geld*; *Am.* F erkranken an; ~ *for* abholen; ~ *in* hereinkommen; eintreten; ♃ einlaufen; aufkommen, Mode werden; zur Macht *od.* ins Amt *etc.* kommen; ~ *in!* herein!; ~ *in for* bekommen; ~ *off* davonkommen; gelingen; geraten (*Knopf*), ausfallen (*Haare etc.*); stattfinden; gelingen; ~ *on* herankommen; wachsen; vorankommen, Fortschritte machen; ~ *on!* komm her!; los!; vorwärts!; ~ *out* herauskommen; erscheinen; ausfallen; ~ *out right* stimmen (*Rechnung*); ~ *round* vorbeikommen (*bsd. zu Besuch*); wiederkehren; zu sich kommen; *fig.* einlenken; zustimmen; ~ *to adv.* dazukommen; = ~ *to o.s.*; ♃ beidrehen; *prp.* betragen, sich belaufen auf (*acc.*); ~ *to o.s. od. to one's senses* wieder zu sich kommen; ~ *to anchor* vor Anker gehen; ~ *to know* kennenlernen; ~ *up* herauf-, heraus-, herankommen; aufgehen, keimen; aufkommen; sich erheben (*Frage*); ~ *up against fig.* aufstehen gegen; ~ *up for* (*active*) *consideration* (ernsthaft) erwogen werden; ~ *up to* entsprechen (*dat.*); es *j-m* gleichtun; *Stand, Maß* errei-

chen; ~ *up with j.* einholen; ~ *upon*
stoßen auf (*acc.*); über *j.* kommen
(*Gefühl etc.*); überfallen; **~'at-**
-a·ble F erreichbar; zugänglich;
'~-back Wiederkehr *f*, Wieder-
hochkommen *n*, Comeback *n*; *Am.*
sl. schlagfertige Antwort *f*.
co·me·di·an [kə'miːdjən] Schau-
spieler(in); Komiker(in); Lustspiel-
dichter *m*.
com·e·dy ['kɔmidi] Komödie *f*,
Lustspiel *n*.
come·li·ness ['kʌmlinis] Anmut *f*;
'come·ly anmutig, hübsch.
com·er ['kʌmə] (An)Kommende
m, f.
co·mes·ti·ble [kə'mestibl] *mst* ~*s pl.*
Eßware(n *pl.*) *f*.
com·et ['kɔmit] Komet *m*.
com·fort ['kʌmfət] **1.** Bequemlichkeit *f*, Komfort *m*; Behaglichkeit *f*;
Trost *m*; *fig.* Beistand *m*; Labsal *n*,
Erquickung *f*; **2.** trösten; erquicken;
beleben; **'com·fort·a·ble** ☐ behaglich; angenehm; bequem, kom-
fortabel; tröstlich; *I am* ~ mir ist
behaglich, ich sitze *etc.* bequem;
'com·fort·er Tröster *m*; wollenes Halstuch *n*; Schnuller *m*; *Am.*
Steppdecke *f*; **'com·fort·less** ☐
unbehaglich; trostlos; **'com·fort**
sta·tion *Am.* Bedürfnisanstalt *f*.
com·frey ♣ ['kʌmfri] Schwarz-
wurz(el) *f*.
com·fy ☐ F ['kʌmfi] = *comfortable.*
com·ic ['kɔmik] (~*ally*) komisch;
Lustspiel...; *fig. mst* **'com·i·cal** ☐
lustig, drollig; ~ *journal,* ~ *paper*
Witzblatt *n*; **'com·ics** *pl.* Comics
pl. (*primitive Bildserien*).
Com·in·form ['kɔminfɔːm] *pol.*
Kominform *n*.
com·ing ['kʌmiŋ] **1.** kommend;
künftig; ~, *Sir!* sofort, der Herr!;
2. Kommen *n*, Ankunft *f*.
Com·in·tern *pol.* ['kɔmintəːn]
Komintern *f*.
com·i·ty ['kɔmiti] : ~ *of nations* gutes
Einvernehmen *n* der Nationen.
com·ma ['kɔmə] Komma *n*.
com·mand [kə'maːnd] **1.** Herrschaft *f*, Beherrschung *f* (*a. fig. e-r*
Sprache etc.); Befehl *m*; Königlicher Erlaß *m* (*mst Cmd.*); ✕ Kommando *n* (*in jedem Sinne*); *at od. by*
~ *of* auf Befehl (*gen.*); *have* ~ *of* beherrschen; *be* (*have*) *at* ~ zur Verfügung stehen (haben); *be in* ~ *of*

✕ befehligen; **2.** befehlen, gebieten; *Truppe, Schiff* befehligen, ✕
kommandieren; verfügen über
(*acc.*); beherrschen; ✕ bestreichen;
beherrschen (*überschauen*); **com-**
man·dant ✕ [kɔmən'dænt] Kommandant *m*, Befehlshaber *m e-r*
Festung; **com·man·deer** [~'diə] ✕
zum Militärdienst zwingen; requirieren; **com·mand·er** ✕ [kə-
'maːndə] Kommandeur *m*, Befehlshaber *m e-r Truppenabteilung*; ⚓
Fregattenkapitän *m*; *Ordens-Kom-*
tur *m*; **com'mand·er-in-'chief**
Oberbefehlshaber *m*; **com'mand-**
ing Herrscher...; beherrschend; *fig.*
hervorragend; ~ *point* strategischer
Punkt *m*; **com'mand·ment** Gebot *n*; **com·mand mod·ule** *Raum-*
fahrt: Kommandokapsel *f*; **com-**
'man·do ✕ [~dəu] Kommando
(*-truppe f*) *n*; **com'mand per-**
form·ance *thea.* Aufführung *f* auf
königlichen Wunsch.
com·mem·o·rate [kə'meməreit] gedenken (*gen.*), feiern; erinnern an
(*acc.*); **com·mem·o'ra·tion** Ge-
dächtnisfeier *f*; **com'mem·o·ra-**
tive ☐ [~rətiv] erinnernd (*of an*
acc.); Gedächtnis..., Erinnerungs...; ~ *issue Briefmarken etc.* Ge-
denkausgabe *f*.
com·mence [kə'mens] anfangen,
beginnen; ♊ anhängig machen;
com'mence·ment Anfang *m*, Beginn *m*; feierliche Verleihung *f*
akademischer Grade.
com·mend [kə'mend] empfehlen;
loben; anvertrauen; ~ *me to* ... F
da lobe ich mir ...; **com'mend·a-**
ble empfehlenswert; lobenswert;
com·men·da·tion [kɔmen'deiʃən]
Empfehlung *f*, Lob *n*; **com'mend-**
a·to·ry [~dətəri] empfehlend; Empfehlungs...
com·men·su·ra·ble ☐ [kə'menʃə-
rəbl] vergleichbar (*with, to* mit);
com'men·su·rate ☐ [~rit] (*with,*
to) angemessen (*dat.*), entsprechend
(*dat.*).
com·ment ['kɔmənt] **1.** Kommentar *m*; Erläuterung *f*; An-, Bemerkung *f*; Stellungnahme *f* (*on*
zu); Kritik *f*; **2.** (*upon*) erläutern,
kommentieren (*acc.*); sich auslassen
(über *acc.*); kritische Bemerkungen
machen (über *acc.*); **'com·men-**
tar·y Kommentar *m*; **com·men-**

communicate

ta·tor ['ˌteitə] Kommentator *m*; Erklärer *m*; *Radio*: Berichterstatter *m*.

com·merce ['kɔmə:s] Handel *m*; Verkehr *m*; Umgang *m*; *Chamber of ⚓ Handelskammer f*; **com·mer·cial** ⚓ [kə'mɔ:ʃəl] 1. kaufmännisch; Handels..., Geschäfts...; gewerbsmäßig; ~ *traveller* Handlungsreisende *m*; 2. P = ~ *traveller*; *bsd. Am. Radio*: kommerzielle Sendung *f*; **com'mer·cial·ism** Handelsgeist *m*; **com'mer·cial·ize** in den Handel bringen; ein Geschäft machen aus, kommerzialisieren; **com'mer·cial tel·e·vi·sion** kommerzielles Fernsehen *n*.

com·mie F ['kɔmi] Kommunist *m*.

com·min·gle [kɔ'miŋgl] zusammenmischen.

com·mis·er·ate [kə'mizəreit] bemitleiden; **com·mis·er·a·tion** [~'reiʃən] Mitleid *n* (*for* mit).

com·mis·sar *pol.* [kɔmi'sɑ:] Kommissar *m*.

com·mis·sar·i·at [kɔmi'sɛəriət] Kommissariat *n*; ✕ Intendantur *f*; **com·mis·sar·y** ['ˌsəri] Kommissar *m*; ✕ Intendanturbeamte *m*.

com·mis·sion [kə'miʃən] 1. Auftrag *m*; Übertragung *f von Macht etc.* (*to s.o.* auf j.); Begehung *f e-s Verbrechens*; Provision *f*; Kommission *f*, Ausschuß *m*; (Offiziers)Patent *n*; Bestallung *f*; ⚓ Bereitschaft *f*; ~ *sale* Kommissionsverkauf *m*; *on* ~ in Kommission; 2. beauftragen; bevollmächtigen; ✕ bestallen; ⚓ in Dienst stellen; **com·mis·sion·aire** [~'nɛə] Portier *m*; **com'mis·sion·er** Bevollmächtigte *m*, *f*; Beauftragte *m*, *f*; Kommissar *m*.

com·mit [kə'mit] anvertrauen; übergeben, (*parl.* e-r Kommission) überweisen; *Verbrechen etc.* begehen; bloßstellen; ~ (*o.s.* sich) festlegen (*to* auf *acc.*); (sich) verpflichten (*to* zu); ~ (*to prison*) in Untersuchungshaft nehmen; ~ *for trial* zur Aburteilung überweisen; **com'mit·ment** Überweisung *f* (*parl.* an eine Kommission); Verhängung *f* der Haft; Bindung *f*, Verpflichtung *f*; **com'mit·tal** = commitment; Verübung *f*, Begehung *f*; ~ *order* Haftanordnung *f*; **com'mit·tee** [~ti] Komitee *n*, Ausschuß *m*.

com·mode [kə'məud] Kommode *f*; Nachtstuhl *m*; **com'mo·di·ous** □ [~djəs] geräumig; **com·mod·i·ty** [kə'mɔditi] Ware *f* (*mst pl.*), Gebrauchsartikel *m*; ~ *value* Sachwert *m*.

com·mo·dore ⚓ ['kɔmədɔ:] Kommodore *m*, Geschwaderführer *m*.

com·mon ['kɔmən] 1. □ (all)gemein; gewöhnlich; gemeinschaftlich, gemeinsam; öffentlich; gemein (*niedrig*); *of* ~ *gender gr.* beiderlei Geschlechts; ~ *noun* Gattungsname *m*; ♀ *Council* Gemeinderat *m*; *Book of* ♀ *Prayer* das anglikanische Gebetbuch; ~ *weal* Gemeinwohl *n*; *in* ~ gemeinsam (*with* mit); *in* ~ *with fig.* genau wie; 2. Gemeindewiese *f*; **com·mon·al·ty** ['ˌnlti] *das* gemeine Volk; **'com·mon·er** Bürger *m*, Gemeine *m*, Nichtadlige *m*; Mitglied *n* des Unterhauses.

com·mon...: ~ *law* Gewohnheitsrecht *n*; ♀ **Mar·ket** Gemeinsamer Markt *m*; **'~·place** 1. Gemeinplatz *m*; 2. gewöhnlich, alltäglich; Alltags...; abgedroschen; '~-**room** Gemeinschaftsraum *m für Studenten, Lehrer od. Dozenten*.

com·mons ['kɔmənz] *pl. das* gemeine Volk; gemeinschaftliche Kost *f*; *short* ~ schmale Kost *f*; *mst House of* ♀ Unterhaus *n*.

com·mon...: ~ *sense* gesunder Menschenverstand *m*; '~·**wealth** Gemeinwesen *n*, Staat *m*; *bsd.* Republik *f*, Freistaat *m*; *the British* ♀ *das* Commonwealth; *the* ~ *of Australia* der Australische Staatenbund.

com·mo·tion [kə'məuʃən] Erschütterung *f*; Aufruhr *m*; Aufregung *f*; Aufsehen *n*.

com·mu·nal □ ['kɔmjunl] gemeinschaftlich; Gemeinschafts...; innerhalb der Gemeinde; Kommunal..., Gemeinde...; **com·mu·nal·ize** ['ˌnəlaiz] kommunalisieren; eingemeinden.

com·mune 1. [kə'mju:n] sich vertraulich besprechen, zu Rate gehen; 2. ['kɔmju:n] Gemeinde *f*, Kommune *f*.

com·mu·ni·ca·bil·i·ty [kəmju:nikə'biliti] Mitteilbarkeit *f*; **com'mu·ni·ca·ble** □ mitteilbar; **com'mu·ni·cant** Kommunikant(in); **com'mu·ni·cate** [~keit] *v/t.* mitteilen;

v/i. das Abendmahl nehmen, kommunizieren; in Verbindung stehen, sich in Verbindung setzen (*with* mit); **com·mu·ni'ca·tion** Mitteilung *f*; Verständigung *f*; Verbindung *f*; *be in ~ with* in Verbindung stehen mit; ~ *cord* 🚌 Notbremse *f*; **com'mu·ni·ca·tive** ☐ [~kətiv] mitteilsam, gesprächig; **com'mu·ni·ca·tor** [~keitə] Mitteilende *m*, *f*; *tel.* Zeichengeber *m*; 🚌 Notbremse *f*.

com·mun·ion [kəm'juːnjən] Gemeinschaft *f*; Kirchen-, Glaubensgemeinschaft *f*; *eccl.* Abendmahl *n*.

com·mu·ni·qué [kə'mjuːnikei] Kommuniqué *n*, amtliche Verlautbarung *f*.

com·mu·nism ['kɔmjunizəm] Kommunismus *m*; **'com·mu·nist 1.** Kommunist(in); **2.** = **com·mu·'nis·tic** (~ally) kommunistisch.

com·mu·ni·ty [kə'mjuːniti] Gemeinschaft *f*; Gemeinde *f*; Gemeinwesen *n*; *the ~* der Staat; *~ ownership* öffentliches Eigentum *n*; *~ service* Gemeinschaftsdienst *m*; *~ spirit* Gemeinschaftsgeist *m*; *~ of interests* Interessengemeinschaft *f*; *~ cen·tre* Gemeinschaftshaus *n*; *~ chest* *Am.* Wohlfahrtsfonds *m*.

com·mu·nize ['kɔmjunaiz] sozialisieren; kommunistisch machen.

com·mut·a·ble [kə'mjuːtəbl] ablösbar; umwandelbar; **com·mu·ta·tion** [kɔmjuː'teiʃən] Vertauschung *f*; Umwandlung *f* (*for, into* in *acc.*); Ablösung *f*; Strafmilderung *f*; *~ ticket* *Am.* Zeitkarte *f*; **com·mu·ta·tive** [kə'mjuːtətiv] wechselseitig; Tausch...; **com·mu·ta·tor** ⚡ ['kɔmjuːteitə] Stromwender *m*; **com·mute** [kə'mjuːt] (*for, into*) *Verpflichtung* ablösen (*durch*); *Strafe* (mildernd) umwandeln (in *acc.*); *Zahlung* umwandeln (in *acc.*); *Am.* pendeln, (täglich) hin- u. herfahren; **com·'mut·er** *Am.* Pendler *m*.

com·pact 1. ['kɔmpækt] Vertrag *m*; Kompaktpuder *m*; **2.** [kəm'pækt] dicht, fest; knapp, bündig; **3.** [~] fest verbinden; **com'pact·ness** Dichtigkeit *f*, Festigkeit *f*.

com·pan·ion [kəm'pænjən] Gefährte *m*, Gefährtin *f*; Kamerad(in); Gesellschafter(in); ⚓ Kompagnon *m*; ⚓ Kajütskappe *f*; Handbuch *n*;

~ in arms Waffenbruder *m*; **com·'pan·ion·a·ble** ☐ gesellig; **com·'pan·ion·ate** [~nit]: *~ marriage* Kameradschaftsehe *f*; **com'pan·ion·ship** Gesellschaft *f*; Genossenschaft *f*.

com·pa·ny ['kʌmpəni] Gesellschaft *f*; ✝ *u.* ✗ Kompanie *f*; Handelsgesellschaft *f*; Genossenschaft *f*, Innung *f*; ⚓ Mannschaft *f*; *thea.* Truppe *f*; *be good* (*bad*) *~* ein guter (schlechter) Gesellschafter sein; *bear s.o. ~* j-m Gesellschaft leisten; *have ~* Gäste haben; *keep ~ with* verkehren mit.

com·pa·ra·ble ☐ ['kɔmpərəbl] vergleichbar; **com·par·a·tive** [kəm'pærətiv] **1.** ☐ vergleichend; verhältnismäßig; *~ degree* = **2.** *gr.* Komparativ *m*; **com'par·a·tive·ly** ziemlich; vergleichsweise; **com·pare** [~'pɛə] **1.** *beyond ~, without ~, past ~* unvergleichlich; **2.** *v/t.* vergleichen (*with* mit); gleichstellen (*to* mit); *gr.* steigern; (*as*) *~d with* im Vergleich zu; *v/i.* sich vergleichen (lassen); **com·par·i·son** [~'pærisn] Vergleich *m*; *gr.* Steigerung *f*; *in ~ with* im Vergleich zu.

com·part·ment [kəm'pɑːtmənt] Abteilung *f*; ⚛ Fach *n*, Feld *n*; 🚌 (Wagen)Abteil *n*.

com·pass ['kʌmpəs] **1.** Bereich *m*; ♪ Umfang *m*; Kompaß *m*; (*oft pair of*) *~es pl.* Zirkel *m*; **2.** herumgehen um; einschließen; *Zweck* erreichen; planen; anstiften.

com·pas·sion [kəm'pæʃən] Mitleid *n*, -gefühl *n*; *have ~ on* Mitleid haben mit; **com'pas·sion·ate** ☐ [~nit] mitleidig; *on ~ grounds* aus Mitleid.

com·pat·i·bil·i·ty [kəmpætə'biliti] Vereinbarkeit *f*, Verträglichkeit *f*; **com'pat·i·ble** ☐ vereinbar, verträglich; schicklich, passend.

com·pa·tri·ot [kəm'pætriət] Landsmann *m*.

com·peer [kɔm'piə] (Standes)Genosse *m*, Genossin *f*.

com·pel [kəm'pel] *j.* zwingen, nötigen; *et.* erzwingen, zu *et.* zwingen.

com·pen·di·ous ☐ [kəm'pendiəs] kurz(gefaßt), gedrängt; **com'pen·di·ous·ness** Kürze *f*, Gedrängtheit *f*.

com·pen·di·um [kəm'pendiəm] Kompendium *n*, Abriß *m*.

com·pen·sate ['kɔmpenseit] v/t. j. entschädigen (*for* für; *with* mit; *by* durch); *et.* ersetzen; ausgleichen; ⊕ kompensieren; v/i. ～ *for* Ersatz leisten für, entschädigen für; *et.* ausgleichen, wettmachen; **com·pen·sa·tion** Ersatz *m*; Entschädigung *f*; Ausgleich(ung *f*) *m*; *Am.* Vergütung *f* (= *Gehalt*); ⊕ Kompensation *f*; **com·pen·sa·tive** [⹁sətiv], **com·pen·sa·to·ry** ausgleichend.

com·père ['kɔmpɛə] 1. Conférencier *m*; 2. ansagen (bei).

com·pete [kəm'piːt] sich (mit)bewerben (*for* um); konkurrieren (*with* mit); ～ *with s.o.* j-m Konkurrenz machen.

com·pe·tence, **com·pe·ten·cy** ['kɔmpitəns(i)] Kompetenz *f*, Befugnis *f*, Zuständigkeit *f*; Auskommen *n*; **'com·pe·tent** □ hinreichend; (leistungs)fähig; kompetent; fachkundig; berechtigt, zuständig.

com·pe·ti·tion [kɔmpi'tiʃən] Wettbewerb *m*, -streit *m*; ✝ Konkurrenz *f*; *rifle* ～ Preisschießen *n*; **com·pet·i·tive** □ [kəm'petitiv] wetteifernd; Konkurrenz...; **com'pet·i·tor** Mitbewerber(in); Konkurrent(in).

com·pi·la·tion [kɔmpi'leiʃən] Zs.-stellung *f*, Kompilation *f*; **com·pile** [kəm'pail] zs.-tragen, -stellen (*from* aus); sammeln.

com·pla·cence, **com·pla·cen·cy** [kəm'pleisns(i)] Selbstzufriedenheit *f*; **com'pla·cent** □ selbstzufrieden, selbstgefällig.

com·plain [kəm'plein] (sich be)klagen, sich beschweren (*about, of* über *acc.*; *that* daß; *to* bei); reklamieren; **com'plain·ant** Kläger(in); **com'plain·er** Klagende *m*; Beschwerdeführer(in); **com'plaint** Klage *f*, Beschwerde *f*; Reklamation *f*; ⚕ Leiden *n*.

com·plai·sance [kəm'pleizəns] Gefälligkeit *f*; Entgegenkommen *n*; Höflichkeit *f*; **com'plai·sant** □ gefällig; entgegenkommend; höflich.

com·ple·ment ['kɔmplimənt] 1. Ergänzung *f* (*a. gr.*); volle Anzahl *f* od. Stärke *f*; ♣ Komplement *n*; 2. ergänzen; **com·ple'men·tal**, **com·ple'men·ta·ry** ergänzend (*to acc.*); Ergänzungs...; Komplementär...

com·plete [kəm'pliːt] 1. □ voll-

ständig, ganz; völlig, vollkommen; 2. vervollständigen; -kommnen; ergänzen; vollenden, abschließen; **com'plete·ness** Vollständigkeit *f*; **com'ple·tion** Vervollständigung *f*; -kommnung *f*; Vollendung *f*, Abschluß *m*; Erfüllung *f*; Ergänzung *f*.

com·plex ['kɔmpleks] 1. □ zs.-gesetzt; *fig.* kompliziert, verwickelt; ～ *sentence gr.* Satzgefüge *n*; 2. Gesamtheit *f*, (*eng S. seelischer*) Komplex *m*; **com·plex·ion** [kəm'plekʃən] Aussehen *n*; Charakter *m*, Zug *m*; Gesichtsfarbe *f*, Teint *m*; **com'plex·i·ty** Kompliziert-, Verwickeltheit *f*; Verwick(e)lung *f*.

com·pli·ance [kəm'plaiəns] Einwilligung *f*; Willfährigkeit *f*; Einverständnis *n* (*with* mit); *in* ～ *with* gemäß; **com'pli·ant** □ willfährig; gefällig.

com·pli·cate ['kɔmplikeit] komplizieren, erschweren; **'com·pli·cat·ed** kompliziert, schwierig, verwickelt; **com·pli'ca·tion** Verwick(e)lung *f*; ⚕ Komplikation *f*.

com·plic·i·ty [kəm'plisiti] Mitschuld *f* (*in an dat.*).

com·pli·ment 1. ['kɔmplimənt] Kompliment *n*, Lob *n*; Schmeichelei *f*; Gruß *m*; 2. ['⹁ment] v/t. (*on*) beglückwünschen (zu); *j-m* Komplimente machen (über *acc.*); **com·pli'men·ta·ry** höflich; Höflichkeits...; ～ *dinner* Festessen *n*; ～ *ticket* Freikarte *f*.

com·ply [kəm'plai] sich fügen; nachkommen, entsprechen, willfahren (*with dat.*); einwilligen; ～ *with the rules* die Vorschriften befolgen.

com·po·nent [kəm'pəunənt] 1. Bestandteil *m*; 2. e-n Teil bildend; ～ *part* = ～ 1.

com·port [kəm'pɔːt] übereinstimmen (*with* mit); ～ *o.s.* sich betragen.

com·pose [kəm'pəuz] zs.-setzen; komponieren; verfassen; schriftstellern; zurechtlegen; ordnen; *Streit* beilegen; *Gemüt* beruhigen; *typ.* setzen; **com'posed**, *adv.* **com'pos·ed·ly** [⹁zidli] ruhig, gesetzt, gelassen; **com'pos·er** Komponist (-in); Verfasser(in); **com'pos·ing** 1. beruhigend; 2. Zs.-setzen *n*; Komponieren *n*; Dichten *n*; ～ *machine* Setzmaschine *f*; ～ *room*

Setzerei *f*; **com·pos·ite** ['kɔmpəzit]
1. zs.-gesetzt; **2.** *konkr.* Zs.-setzung
f; ⚘ Komposite *f*; **com·po'si·tion**
Zs.-setzung *f*; Abfassung *f*; ♪, ♫,
paint. Komposition *f*; (Schrift)Satz
m; (Schul)Aufsatz *m*; ♰ Vergleich
m; **com·pos·i·tor** [kəm'pɔzitə]
(Schrift)Setzer *m*; **com·post** ['kɔm-
pɔst] **1.** Kompost *m*; **2.** kompostie-
ren; **com·po·sure** [kəm'pəuʒə]
Fassung *f*, Gemütsruhe *f*, Gelassenheit *f*.

com·pote ['kɔmpɔt] Kompott *n*.
com·pound[1] **1.** ['kɔmpaund] zs.-
gesetzt; ∿ *fracture* ♰ komplizierter Bruch *m*; ∿ *interest* Zinseszinsen
m/pl.; **2.** [∿] Zs.-setzung *f*, Verbindung *f*; a. ∿ *word* gr. Kompositum
n; **3.** [kəm'paund] *v/t.* zs.-setzen;
Streit beilegen; *v/i.* sich einigen; ♰
sich vergleichen, akkordieren (*for*
über *acc.*).
com·pound[2] ['kɔmpaund] einge-
zäuntes Gelände *n*.

com·pre·hend [kɔmpri'hend] umfassen; begreifen, verstehen.
com·pre·hen·si·ble □ [kɔmpri'hen-
səbl] verständlich; **com·pre'hen-
sion** Verständnis *n*; Fassungskraft
f; Umfang *m*; **com·pre'hen·sive**
□ umfassend; ∿ *insurance* Vollkasko-
versicherung *f*; ∿ *school* Gesamtschu-
le *f*; **com·pre'hen·sive·ness** Umfassende *n*.

com·press 1. [kəm'pres] zs.-drücken,
-pressen; **2.** ['kɔmpres] ♰ Kom-
presse *f*; **com·pressed** [kəm'prest]
komprimiert; ∿ *air* Preß-, Druck-
luft *f*; **com'press·i·ble** kompri-
mierbar; **com·pres·sion** [∿'preʃən]
Zs.-drücken *n*; *phys.* Verdichtung *f*,
Kompression *f*; ⊕ Druck *m*; **com-
'pres·sor** [∿sə] ⊕ Kompressor *m*.
com·prise [kəm'praiz] umfassen,
einschließen, enthalten.
com·pro·mise ['kɔmprəmaiz]
1. Kompromiß *n*, *m*; Vergleich *m*;
2. *v/t. Streit* beilegen; bloßstellen,
kompromittieren; *v/i.* sich vergleichen, ein(en) Kompromiß
schließen (*on* über *acc.*).
comp·trol·ler [kən'trəulə] Rechnungsprüfer *m*.
com·pul·sion [kəm'pʌlʃən] Zwang
m; **com'pul·sive** [∿siv] zwanghaft;
com'pul·so·ry [∿səri] obligatorisch;
zwangsmäßig, Zwangs...; Pflicht...; ∿
military service Wehrpflicht *f*; ∿ *sub-*

ject Pflichtfach *n*.
com·punc·tion [kəm'pʌŋkʃən] Gewissensbisse *m/pl.*; Reue *f*; Bedenken *n*.
com·put·a·ble [kəm'pju:təbl] be-
rechen-, zählbar; **com·pu·ta·tion**
[kɔmpju:'teiʃən] Rechnung *f*; Berechnung *f*; **com·pu'ta·tor** =
computer; **com·pute** [kəm'pju:t]
(be-, er)rechnen; schätzen (*at* auf
acc.); **com'put·er** Computer *m*;
Elektronenrechner *m*; ∿-*controlled*
computergesteuert; ∿ *dating* Heirats-
vermittlung *f* mit Hilfe e-s Compu-
ters; ∿ *science* Informatik *f*.
com·rade ['kɔmrid] Kamerad *m*;
Genosse *m*; **'com·rade·ship** Kameradschaft *f*.
con[1] [kɔn] fleißig studieren, auswendig lernen.
con[2] ⚓ [∿] *Schiff* leiten, steuern.
con[3] [∿] *abbr.* = *contra* wider; *pro
and* ∿ für und wider; *the pros and*
∿s die Gründe für und wider.
con[4] *Am. sl.* [∿] **1.** *in Zssgn s. confidence man*; **2.** 'reinlegen (*betrügen*).
con·cat·e·nate [kɔn'kætineit] *mst
fig.* verketten; **con·cat·e'na·tion**
Verkettung *f* (*a. fig.*).
con·cave □ ['kɔn'keiv] konkav;
Hohl...; **con·cav·i·ty** [∿'kæviti]
Konkavität *f*; Höhlung *f*; Hohl-
rundung *f*.
con·ceal [kən'si:l] verhehlen; *fig.*
verhehlen, -heimlichen, -schwei-
gen, -bergen (*from s.o.* vor j-m);
con'ceal·ment Verbergung *f etc.*;
Verborgenheit *f*; a. *place of* ∿
Versteck *n*.
con·cede [kən'si:d] zugestehen; einräumen; gewähren; nachgeben;
con'ced·ed·ly zugestandenermaßen.
con·ceit [kən'si:t] Einbildung *f*,
Selbstüberschätzung *f*; spitzfindi-
ger Gedanke *m*; übertriebenes
sprachliches Bild *n*; *out of* ∿ *with*
unzufrieden mit; **con'ceit·ed** □
eingebildet, eitel, dünkelhaft; **con-
'ceit·ed·ness** Dünkel *m*.
con·ceiv·a·ble □ [kən'si:vəbl] denkbar; begreiflich; **con'ceive** *v/i.*
empfangen (*schwanger werden*); sich
denken (*of acc.*); *v/t. Kind* empfangen; sich (aus)denken, sich vorstellen; erdenken, ersinnen; *Abneigung* fassen; ∿*d in* ... ausgedrückt

in ... (*dat.*).

con·cen·trate [ˈkɔnsəntreit] **1.** (sich) zs.-ziehen, (sich) konzentrieren (*a. fig.*); verdichten; 🜍 sättigen; **2.** Konzentrat *n* (*angereicherter Stoff*); **con·cen'tra·tion** Konzentration *f*, Zs.-ziehung *f*, Zs.-fassung *f*; 🜍 Sättigung *f*; ~ *camp* Konzentrationslager *n*; **con'cen·tre**, **con-'cen·ter** [~tə] (sich) konzentrieren, (sich) vereinigen; **con'cen·tric** (~*ally*) konzentrisch.

con·cept [ˈkɔnsept] Begriff *m*, Vorstellung *f*; **con·cep·tion** [kən-'sepʃən] Begreifen *n*; Vorstellung *f*, Begriff *m*, Idee *f*; *biol.* Empfängnis *f*; **con·cep·tu·al** [kən'septjuəl] begrifflich.

con·cern [kən'sə:n] **1.** Angelegenheit *f*, Sache *f*, Anliegen *n*; Interesse *n* (*in* an *dat.*; *for* für); Unruhe *f*, Sorge *f*; Beziehung *f* (*with* zu); ✝ Geschäft *n*, (industrielles) Unternehmen *n*; F Ding *n*; **2.** betreffen, angehen, interessieren; ~ *o.s. with* sich befassen mit; ~ *o.s. about od. for* sich kümmern um; *be* ~*ed* in Betracht kommen; *be* ~*ed that* sich Sorgen darüber machen, daß; *I am* ~*ed to inf.* es kommt mir darauf an zu *inf.*; *be* ~*ed with* sich befassen mit, behandeln; **con'cerned** □ interessiert, beteiligt (*in* an *dat.*); bekümmert, betroffen (*at, about, for* um, wegen); *those* ~ die Beteiligten; **con'cern·ing** *prp.* betreffend, betreffs, in betreff, über, wegen, hinsichtlich.

con·cert 1. [ˈkɔnsət] Konzert *n*; [ˈ~sə:t] Einverständnis *n*; **2.** [kən-'sə:t] ein Einverständnis schaffen, verabreden; *Kräfte* zs.-fassen; **con-'cert·ed** gemeinsam, gemeinschaftlich; ♪ mehrstimmig; **con·cer·ti·na** ♪ [kɔnsə'ti:nə] *Art* Ziehharmonika *f*; **con·cer·to** ♪ [kən'ʃtə:təu] (Solo-) Konzert *n*.

con·ces·sion [kən'seʃən] Zugeständnis *n*; Erlaubnis *f*, Genehmigung *f*; zugewiesenes Land *n*; **con·ces·sion·aire** [~'nɛə] Konzessionär *m*.

con·ces·sive □ [kən'sesiv] einräumend.

conch [kɔŋk] *große* Seemuschel *f*.

con·cil·i·ate [kən'silieit] aus-, versöhnen; ausgleichen; in Einklang bringen; *Liebe etc.* gewinnen; **con-cil·i·a·tion** Aus-, Versöhnung *f*;

Ausgleich *m*; **con'cil·i·a·tor** Vermittler *m*; **con'cil·i·a·to·ry** [~ətəri] versöhnend, vermittelnd; ~ *proposal* Vorschlag *m* zur Güte.

con·cin·ni·ty [kən'siniti] Feinheit *f*, Eleganz *f des Stils*.

con·cise □ [kən'sais] kurz, bündig, knapp; **con'cise·ness** Kürze *f*.

con·clave [ˈkɔnkleiv] Konklave *n*.

con·clude [kən'klu:d] schließen, beschließen (*beendigen*; *das Ende bilden*); *Brief, Geschäft etc.* abschließen; folgern; beschließen, sich entscheiden (*to inf.* zu *inf.*); *to be* ~*d* Schluß folgt; **con'clud·ing** Schluß...

con·clu·sion [kən'klu:ʒən] Schluß *m*, Ende *n*; Abschluß *m e-s Vertrags etc.*; Schluß *m*, Folgerung *f*; Beschluß *m*; *in* ~ schließlich; *try* ~*s with* sich messen mit; **con'clu·sive** [~siv] □ beweiskräftig, schlüssig; überzeugend; endgültig.

con·coct [kən'kɔkt] zs.-brauen; *fig.* aussinnen, -hecken; **con'coc·tion** Zs.-brauen *n*; Gebräu *n*; *fig.* Erfindung *f*.

con·com·i·tance, con·com·i·tan·cy [kən'kɔmitəns(i)] Zs.-bestehen *n*, Gleichzeitigkeit *f*; **con'com·i·tant 1.** □ begleitend; **2.** begleitender Umstand *m*.

con·cord [ˈkɔŋkɔ:d] Eintracht *f*; Übereinstimmung *f* (*a. gr.*); ♪ Harmonie *f*, Zs.-klang *m*; **con-cord·ance** [kən'kɔ:dəns] Übereinstimmung *f*; *eccl.* Konkordanz *f*; **con'cord·ant** □ übereinstimmend; einstimmig; ♪ harmonisch; **con'cor·dat** *eccl.* [~dæt] Konkordat *n*.

con·course [ˈkɔŋkɔ:s] Zusammen-, Auflauf *m*; Menge *f*; *Am.* Bahnhofs-, Schalterhalle *f*.

con·crete 1. □ [ˈkɔnkri:t] konkret; Beton...; **2.** [~] Beton *m*; *phls.*, *gr.* Konkretum *n*; *in the* ~ im konkreten Falle; **3.** [kən'kri:t] *zu e-r Masse* verbinden; [ˈkɔnkri:t] betonieren; ~ *noun gr.* Konkretum *n*; **con·cre·tion** [kən'kri:ʃən] Zs.-wachsung *f*; Festwerden *n*, Verhärtung *f*.

con·cu·bi·nage [kɔn'kju:binidʒ] Konkubinat *n*; **con·cu·bine** [ˈkɔŋkjubain] Konkubine *f*.

con·cu·pis·cence [kən'kju:pisəns] Sinnenlust *f*, Begierde *f*; **con'cu·pis·cent** lüstern; sinnlich.

con·cur [kən'kəː] zs.-treffen, -wirken; übereinstimmen (*with* mit; *in* in *dat.*); mitwirken (*to* zu); **con·cur·rence** [ˌ'kʌrəns] Zusammentreffen *n*; Übereinstimmung *f*; Einverständnis *n*; Mitwirkung *f*; *in* ~ *with* gemeinschaftlich mit; **con'cur·rent** □ zs.-treffend *etc.* (*s. concur*); gleichzeitig.

con·cus·sion [kən'kʌʃən]: ~ *of the brain* Gehirnerschütterung *f*.

con·demn [kən'dem] verdammen; verurteilen (*to* zu) (*a. fig.*); (als untauglich) verwerfen; *Kranke* aufgeben; für verfallen erklären; beschlagnahmen; *his looks* ~ *him* s-e Augen verraten ihn; ~*ed cell* Zelle *f* für die zum Tode Verurteilten; **con'dem·na·ble** [ˌʌnəbl] verdammenswert, verwerflich; **con·dem·na·tion** [kɔndem'neiʃən] Verurteilung *f*; Verdammung *f*; Verwerfung *f*; **con'dem·na·to·ry** □ [kən'demnətəri] verurteilend.

con·den·sa·ble [kən'densəbl] verdichtbar; **con·den·sa·tion** [kɔnden'seiʃən] Verdichtung *f*; **con·dense** [kən'dens] (sich) verdichten; ⊕ kondensieren; abkürzen, zs.drängen; **con'dens·er** Verdichter *m*; ♪, ⊕ Kondensator *m*.

con·de·scend [kɔndi'send] sich herablassen; geruhen; **con·de'scend·ing** □ herablassend; **con·de'scen·sion** Herablassung *f*.

con·dign □ [kən'dain] angemessen; gehörig.

con·di·ment ['kɔndimənt] Würze *f*.

con·di·tion [kən'diʃən] **1.** Zustand *m*; Stand *m*, Stellung *f*; Bedingung *f*; Kondition *f*; Lage *f*; Befinden *n*; ~*s pl.* Verhältnisse *n/pl.*, Umstände *m/pl.*, Lage *f*; *on* ~ *that* unter der Bedingung, daß; *out of* ~ in schlechter Verfassung; **2.** bedingen; ausmachen, vereinbaren; in e-n bestimmten Zustand bringen, regulieren; **con'di·tion·al** □ bedingt (*on, upon* durch); Bedingungs...; Konditional...; ~ (*mood*) *gr.* Konditionalis *m*; **con·di·tion·al·i·ty** [ˌ'næliti] Bedingtheit *f*; **con'di·tion·al·ly** [ˌɔli] bedingungsweise; **con'di·tioned** bedingt; (*mst in Zssgn*) beschaffen; geartet; **con'di·tioned re·flex** *psych.* bedingter Reflex *m*.

con·dole [kən'dəul] kondolieren,

sein Beileid bezeigen (*with s.o.* j-m); **con'do·lence** Beileid *n*.

con·do·min·i·um ['kɔndə'miniəm] Kondominium *n* (*gemeinsame Herrschaft*); *Am.* Eigentumswohnung *f*, Haus *n* mit Eigentumswohnungen.

con·do·na·tion [kɔndəu'neiʃən] Verzeihung *f*; **con·done** [kən'dəun] *Vergehen* verzeihen.

con·dor *orn.* ['kɔndɔː] Kondor *m*.

con·duce [kən'djuːs] führen, dienen (*to* zu); **con'du·cive** dienlich, förderlich (*to dat.*).

con·duct 1. ['kɔndʌkt] Führung *f*, Leitung *f*; Verhalten *n*, Betragen *n*; Verwaltung *f*; **2.** [kən'dʌkt] führen, geleiten; durchführen; ♪ dirigieren; verwalten; *Tätigkeit* ausüben; *phys.* leiten; ~ *o.s.* (sich (auf)führen *od.* benehmen; **con·duct·i·bil·i·ty** [kəndʌkti'biliti] *phys.* Leitfähigkeit *f*; **con'duct·i·ble** [ˌtəbl] *phys.* leitfähig; leitend; **con'duct·ing** Leitungs...; **con'duc·tion** Leitung *f*; **con'duc·tive** □ [ˌtiv] *phys.* leitend; **con·duc·tiv·i·ty** [kɔndʌk'tiviti] *phys.* Leitfähigkeit *f*; **con·duc·tor** [kən'dʌktə] Führer *m*; Leiter *m* (*a. phys.*); Schaffner *m*; ♪ Dirigent *m*; ⚡ Leiter *m*; Blitzableiter *m*; **con'duc·tress** Schaffnerin *f*.

con·duit ['kɔndit] Leitungsröhre *f*; Kanal *m*; [ˌdjuit] ⚡ Isolierrohr *n*.

cone [kəun] Kegel *m*; ♀ Zapfen *m*.

co·ney ['kəuni] Kaninchen *n*.

con·fab F ['kɔnfæb] **1.** = **con·fab·u·late** [kən'fæbjuleit] plaudern; **2.** = **con·fab·u'la·tion** Geplauder *n*.

con·fec·tion [kən'fekʃən] *Schneiderei:* Konfektionsartikel *m*; Konfekt *n*; **con·fec·tion·er** [ˌ'fekʃnə] Konditor *m*; **con'fec·tion·er·y** Konfekt *n*; Konditorei *f*; *bsd. Am.* Süßwarengeschäft *n*.

con·fed·er·a·cy [kən'fedərəsi] Bündnis *n*, Bundesgenossenschaft *f*; Komplott *n*; *the* ♀ *Am.* die Konföderation *der 11 Südstaaten 1860 bis 1861*; **con'fed·er·ate 1.** [ˌrit] verbündet; **2.** [ˌrit] Bundesgenosse *m*, Verbündete *m*; Mitschuldige *m*; **3.** [ˌreit] (sich) verbünden; **con·fed·er'a·tion** Bund *m*, Bündnis *n*; Staatenbund *m*.

con·fer [kən'fəː] *v/t.* übertragen,

verleihen, erteilen; *Gunst* erweisen
(*alle*: *on dat.*); *v/i.* sich besprechen,
sich beraten, Rücksprache nehmen
(*with* mit; *about, upon* über *acc.*);
con·fer·ence ['kɔnfərəns] Konferenz *f*, Besprechung *f*, Beratung *f*;
Verhandlung *f*.

con·fess [kən'fes] bekennen, gestehen; beichten; *eccl. j-m* die
Beichte abnehmen; ~ *to* sich bekennen zu; **con'fess·ed·ly** [⸗sidli]
zugestandenermaßen; **con'fes·sion**
[⸗ʃən] Geständnis *n*; Bekenntnis
n; *eccl.* Beichte *f*; **con'fes·sion·al**
[⸗ʃənl] **1.** konfessionell; **2.** Beicht-
stuhl *m*; **con'fes·sor** [⸗sə] Be-
kenner *m*; *eccl.* Beichtvater *m*.

con·fet·ti [kən'feti:] *pl.* Konfetti *pl.*

con·fi·dant [kɔnfi'dænt] Vertraute
m; **con·fi'dante** [⸗] Vertraute *f*.

con·fide [kən'faid] anvertrauen (*to
s.o.* j-m); vertrauen, sich verlassen
(*in* auf *acc.*).

con·fi·dence ['kɔnfidəns] Vertrauen
n (*in* auf *acc.*); Zuversicht *f*; Zutrauen *n*; vertrauliche Mitteilung *f*;
~ **game** = *confidence trick*; ~ **man**
Schwindler *m*, Hochstapler *m*;
~ **trick** Bauernfängerei *f*; **'con·fi-
dent** □ vertrauend (*of* auf *acc.*);
vertrauensvoll; überzeugt, zuversichtlich; **con·fi·den·tial** □ [⸗
'denʃəl] vertraulich; vertraut; ~
clerk Privatsekretär *m*.

con·fig·u·ra·tion [kənfigju'reiʃən]
Gestalt(ung) *f*.

con·fine 1. ['kɔnfain] *mst* ~s *pl.*
Grenze *f*; **2.** [kən'fain] begrenzen;
ein-, beschränken (*to* auf *acc.*); einsperren; *be* ~*d to bed* das Bett hüten
müssen; *be* ~*d* (*of*) entbunden werden (von), niederkommen (mit);
con'fine·ment Einsperrung *f*;
Haft *f*; Beschränkung *f*; Entbindung *f*.

con·firm [kən'fə:m] (be)kräftigen;
bestätigen; aufrechterhalten; *eccl.*
konfirmieren, firmen; **con·fir·ma-
tion** [kɔnfə'meiʃən] Bestätigung *f*;
Konfirmation *f*, Firmung *f*; **con-
firm·a·tive** □ [kən'fə:mətiv], **con-
'firm·a·to·ry** [⸗təri] bestätigend;
con'firmed fest, bestimmt; chronisch (*bsd.* ♣); unheilbar.

con·fis·cate ['kɔnfiskeit] einziehen,
beschlagnahmen, konfiszieren; **con-
fis'ca·tion** Beschlagnahme *f*; **con-
'fis·ca·to·ry** [⸗kətəri] konfiszie-

rend.
con·fla·gra·tion [kɔnflə'greiʃən]
großer Brand *m*, Feuersbrunst *f*.
con·flict 1. ['kɔnflikt] Konflikt *m*;
Zs.-stoß *m*; Kampf *m*, Zwist *m*,
Streit *m*; *fig.* Widerstreit *m*; **2.** [kən-
'flikt] (*with*) sich im Konflikt befinden (mit); nicht übereinstimmen
(mit).
con·flu·ence ['kɔnfluəns], **con·flux**
['⸗flʌks] Zs.-fluß *m*; Zulauf *m*, Zs.-
strömen *n von Menschen*; **con-
flu·ent** ['⸗fluənt] **1.** zs.-fließend,
zs.-laufend; **2.** Zu-, Nebenfluß
m.
con·form [kən'fɔ:m] *v/t.* anpassen;
v/i. ~ *to* sich fügen in (*acc.*), sich
richten nach, sich anpassen an
(*acc.*); ~ *with* entsprechen (*dat.*);
con'form·a·ble □ (*to*) übereinstimmend (mit); entsprechend
(*dat.*); nachgiebig (*dat.*); **con·for-
ma·tion** [kɔnfɔ:'meiʃən] Bau *m*,
Gestalt *f*; **con·form·ist** [kən-
'fɔ:mist] Anhänger *m* der anglikanischen Staatskirche; **con'form-
i·ty** Übereinstimmung *f*; *in* ~ *with*
in Übereinstimmung *od.* übereinstimmend mit; gemäß.
con·found [kən'faund] vermengen;
verwechseln; *j.* verwirren; *et.* vereiteln; ~ *it!* F verdammt!; ~ *you!* F
zum Henker mit dir!; **con'founded** □ F verdammt.
con·fra·ter·ni·ty [kɔnfrə'tə:niti]
Brüderschaft *f*.
con·front [kən'frʌnt] gegenüberstellen (*with dat.*); entgegentreten
(*dat.*); entgegensehen (*dat.*); gegenüberstehen, gegenübertreten (*dat.*);
find o.s. ~*ed with* sich ... (*dat.*) gegenübersehen; **con·fron·ta·tion** [kɔn-
frʌn'teiʃən] Gegenüberstellung *f*.
con·fuse [kən'fju:z] vermischen (*a.
fig.*); verwechseln; verwirren, durcheinanderbringen; bestürzt machen;
con'fused □ verwirrt, bestürzt;
verworren; **con'fu·sion** [⸗ʒən] Verwirrung *f*; Bestürzung *f*; Verwechs-
lung *f*; Durcheinander *n*.
con·fut·a·ble [kən'fju:təbl] widerlegbar; **con·fu·ta·tion** [kɔnfju:-
'teiʃən] Widerlegung *f*; **con·fute**
[kən'fju:t] widerlegen.
con·gé ['kɔ̃:nʒei] Entlassung *f*; *give
s.o. his* ~ j. ohne weitere Umstände
entlassen.
con·geal [kən'dʒi:l] erstarren (las-

sen) (*a. fig.*); gefrieren (lassen); gerinnen (lassen); **con'geal·a·ble** gefrier-, gerinnbar.

con·ge·la·tion [kɔndʒi'leiʃən] Gefrieren *n*, Gerinnen *n*; Erstarren *n*.

con·gen·ial □ [kən'dʒiːnjəl] (geistes)verwandt, kongenial (*with dat.*); zusagend (*to dat.*); **con·ge·ni·al·i·ty** [ˌni'æliti] Geistesverwandtschaft *f*.

con·gen·i·tal [kən'dʒenitl] angeboren; **con'gen·i·tal·ly** [ˌtəli] von Geburt an.

con·ger (**eel**) *ichth.* ['kɔŋɡə(r'iːl)] Meeraal *m*.

con·gest [kən'dʒest] (*♂* mit Blut) überfüllen; **con'ges·tion** (Blut-) Andrang *m*, Stauung *f*, Überfüllung *f*; ~ *of population* Übervölkerung *f*; *traffic* ~ Verkehrsstockung *f*.

con·glom·er·ate 1. [kən'glɔmərit] zusammengeballt; **2.** [ˌ] Konglomerat *n*, (An)Häufung *f*; **3.** [ˌreit] (sich) zs.-ballen; **con·glom·er·'a·tion** Anhäufung *f*, Konglomerat *n*.

con·grat·u·late [kən'grætjuleit] beglückwünschen; gratulieren (*s.o. on od. upon s.th.* j-m zu et.); **con·grat·u·la·tion** Glückwunsch *m*; **con'grat·u·la·tor** Gratulant *m*; **con'grat·u·la·to·ry** Glückwunsch...

con·gre·gate ['kɔŋɡrigeit] (sich) (ver)sammeln; **con·gre'ga·tion** *eccl.* Gemeinde *f*; **con·gre'ga·tion·al** [ˌʃənl] kirchengemeindlich; *eccl.* unabhängig.

con·gress ['kɔŋgres] Kongreß *m*; ⚥ *Am. pol.* Kongreß *m* (*Senat u. Repräsentantenhaus*); **con·gression·al** [ˌ'greʃənl] Kongreß...; **'Con·gress·man**, **'Con·gress·wom·an** *Am. pol.* Mitglied *n* des Repräsentantenhauses.

con·gru·ence, **con·gru·en·cy** ['kɔŋgruəns(i)] = *congruity*; ⚥ Kongruenz *f*; **'con·gru·ent** = *congruous*; ⚥ kongruent; **con·gru·i·ty** [ˌ'gruːiti] Übereinstimmung *f*; Angemessenheit *f*, Geeignetheit *f*; Folgerichtigkeit *f*; **con·gru·ous** □ ['ˌgruəs] angemessen (*to* für); übereinstimmend (*to, mst with* mit); folgerichtig.

con·ic, **con·i·cal** □ ['kɔnik(əl)] konisch, kegelförmig; Kegel...; ~

section ⚥ Kegelschnitt *m*.

co·ni·fer ['kəunifə] Nadelholzbaum *m*; **co'nif·er·ous** zapfentragend.

con·jec·tur·al □ [kən'dʒektʃərəl] mutmaßlich; **con'jec·ture 1.** Mutmaßung *f*, Vermutung *f*; **2.** mutmaßen, vermuten.

con·join [kən'dʒɔin] (sich) verbinden; **con·joint** ['kɔndʒɔint] verbunden; **'con·joint·ly** gemeinschaftlich.

con·ju·gal □ ['kɔndʒugəl] ehelich; Ehe...; **con·ju·gate 1.** ['ˌgeit] *v/t.* konjugieren; *v/i. biol.* sich paaren (*Zellen*); **2.** ['ˌgit] ⚥ gepaart; **con·ju·ga·tion** [ˌ'geiʃən] Konjugation *f*.

con·junct □ [kən'dʒʌŋkt] verbunden; **con'junc·tion** Verbindung *f*; *ast., gr.* Konjunktion *f*; Zs.-treffen *n*; **con·junc·ti·va** *anat.* [kɔndʒʌŋk'taivə] Bindehaut *f*; **con'junc·tive** [kən'dʒʌŋktiv] verbindend; ~ *mood* Konjunktiv *m*; **con'junc·tive·ly** in Verbindung, zusammen; **con·junc·ti·vi·tis** *♂* [ˌ'vaitis] Bindehautentzündung *f*; **con'junc·ture** [ˌtʃə] Zs.-treffen *n* (*von Umständen*); Krise *f*.

con·ju·ra·tion [kɔndʒuə'reiʃən] Beschwörung *f*; **con·jure** [kən'dʒuə] *v/t.* beschwören, inständig bitten; ['kʌndʒə] *v/t.* beschwören, rufen; *et. wohin* zaubern; ~ *up* heraufbeschwören; *v/i.* zaubern; **'con·jur·er**, **'con·jur·or** Zauberer *m*, Zauberin *f*; Taschenspieler(in); **'con·jur·ing-trick** Zauberkunststück *n*.

conk F [kɔŋk] versagen, F streiken (*Mechanismus etc.*).

con·ker F ['kɔŋkə] (Roß)Kastanie *f*.

con man F ['kɔnmæn] = *confidence man.*

con·nate ['kɔneit] angeboren; ⚥ *u. anat.* verwachsen; **con·nat·u·ral** [kə'nætʃrəl] gleicher Natur (*to* wie); angeboren.

con·nect [kə'nekt] (sich) verbinden; *⚡* schalten; **con'nect·ed** □ verbunden; zs.-hängend (*Rede etc.*); *be* ~ *with* in Verbindung stehen mit *j-m*, beteiligt sein bei *od.* an et. (*dat.*); *be well* ~ gute Beziehungen haben; **con'nect·ing** Verbindungs-...; Binde...; Anschluß...; ~ *rod* Pleuelstange *f*; **con'nec·tion** *s. connexion*; **con'nec·tive** □ verbin-

dend; ⹀ *tissue anat.* Bindegewebe
n.

con·nex·ion [kə'nekʃən] Verbin-
dung *f*; ⚡ Schaltung *f*; Bahn- *etc.*
Verbindung *f*, Anschluß *m* (*a.* ⚡);
Zs.-hang *m*; Verwandtschaft *f*;
Verwandte *m*, *f*; Vereinigung *f von
Personen*; ✝ Kundschaft *f*; ⹀*s pl.*
(gute) Beziehungen *f*/*pl.*

conn·ing-tow·er ⚓ ['kɔniŋtauə]
Kommandoturm *m.*

con·niv·ance [kə'naivəns] still-
schweigende Duldung *f* (*at*, *in*, *with
gen.*); **con'nive**: ⹀ *at* ein Auge
zudrücken bei, *et.* stillschweigend
dulden.

con·nois·seur [kɔnə'sə:] (*of od. in
wine, etc.* Wein- *etc.*) Kenner(in).

con·no·ta·tion [kɔnəu'teiʃən] Be-
griffsinhalt *m*; (Neben)Bedeutung
f; **con'note** andeuten, (zugleich)
bedeuten.

con·nu·bi·al ☐ [kə'nju:bjəl] ehelich;
Ehe...; verheiratet.

con·quer ['kɔŋkə] erobern; *fig.* erringen; überwinden; (be)siegen;
'con·quer·or Eroberer *m*; Sieger
m; F Entscheidungsspiel *n.*

con·quest ['kɔŋkwest] Eroberung *f*;
Errungenschaft *f.*

con·san·guin·e·ous [kɔnsæŋ'gwi-
niəs] blutsverwandt; **con·san'guin-
i·ty** Blutsverwandtschaft *f.*

con·science ['kɔnʃəns] Gewissen *n*;
in all ⹀ *f* wahrhaftig, sicherlich;
have the ⹀ *to do* so unverschämt sein
zu tun; ⹀ *money* Reugeld *n*, freiwillige Zahlung *f*; **'con·science-
less** gewissenlos.

con·sci·en·tious ☐ [kɔnʃi'enʃəs]
gewissenhaft; Gewissens...; ⹀ *ob-
jector* Kriegsdienstverweigerer *m*
aus Gewissensgründen; **con·sci'en-
tious·ness** Gewissenhaftigkeit *f.*

con·scious ☐ ['kɔnʃəs] bewußt;
be ⹀ *of* sich bewußt sein (*gen.*;
that daß); **'con·scious·ness** Bewußtsein *n.*

con·script ✗ 1. [kən'skript] einberufen; 2. ['kɔnskript] einberufen,
eingezogen; 3. [⹀] Dienstpflichtige
m, Rekrut *m*; **con·scrip·tion** ✗
[kən'skripʃən] Einberufung *f*;
industrial ⹀ Arbeitsverpflichtung *f.*

con·se·crate ['kɔnsikreit] weihen,
einsegnen; heiligen; widmen; **con-
se'cra·tion** Weihung *f*, Einseg-
nung *f*; Heiligung *f*; **'con·se·cra-**

tor Weihende *m.*

con·sec·u·tive [kən'sekjutiv] aufeinanderfolgend; fortlaufend (*Nummer*); *gr.* konsekutiv; **con'sec·u-
tive·ly** nacheinander, fortlaufend.

con·sen·sus [kən'sensəs] allseitige
Zu- *od.* Übereinstimmung *f.*

con·sent [kən'sent] 1. (*to*) Zustimmung *f* (zu), Einwilligung *f* (in
acc.); *age of* ⹀ Mündigkeitsalter *n*;
with one ⹀ einstimmig; 2. (*to*) einwilligen (in *acc.*), zustimmen (*dat.*);
con·sen·tient [⹀'senʃənt] zustim-
mend.

con·se·quence ['kɔnsikwəns] Folge
f, Konsequenz *f*; Wirkung *f*, Einfluß *m* (*to* auf *acc.*); Bedeutung *f*
(*to* für); *in* ⹀ *of* infolge (*gen.*); **'con-
se·quent** 1. folgend; *be* ⹀ *on* die
Folge sein von; 2. Folge(rung) *f*,
Schluß *m*; **con·se·quen·tial** ☐
[⹀'kwenʃəl] (er)folgend (*on*, *upon*
aus); folgerecht; wichtigtuend; **con-
se·quent·ly** ['⹀kwəntli] folglich,
daher.

con·ser·va·tion [kɔnsə:'veiʃən] Erhaltung *f*; **con·ser'va·tion·ist** Umweltschützer *m*; **con·serv·a·tism**
[kən'sə:vətizm] Konservatismus *m*;
con·serv·a·tive ☐ 1. erhaltend (*of
acc.*); *pol.* konservativ; vorsichtig
(*Schätzung*); 2. Konservative *m*;
con·ser·va·toire [⹀twa:] ♪ Konservatorium *n*; **con·ser·va·tor** Konser-
vator *m*; **con·serv·a·to·ry** [⹀tri]
Treib-, Gewächshaus *n*; ♪ Konservatorium *n*; **con·serve** erhalten.

con·sid·er [kən'sidə] *v*/*t. geistig* betrachten; erwägen, bedenken; überlegen; beraten; *et.* in Betracht
ziehen; Rücksicht nehmen auf
(*acc.*); berücksichtigen; ansehen
als; halten für, erachten als; meinen,
glauben; *v*/*i.* überlegen; *all things*
⹀*ed* wenn man alles in Betracht
zieht; **con'sid·er·a·ble** ☐ ansehnlich, beträchtlich, erheblich; **con-
'sid·er·a·bly** bedeutend, ziemlich,
(sehr) viel; **con'sid·er·ate** [⹀rit] ☐
rücksichtsvoll; **con·sid·er·a·tion**
[⹀'reiʃən] Betrachtung *f*, Erwägung
f, Überlegung *f*; Rücksicht *f*; Berücksichtigung *f*; wichtiger Umstand *m*; Entschädigung *f*, Vergütung *f*; Entgelt *n*, Gegenleistung
f; ✝ Prämie *f*; *be under* ⹀ erwogen
werden; in Betracht kommen; *take
into* ⹀ in Erwägung *od.* Betracht

ziehen; *money is no* ~ *auf Geld* kommt es nicht an; *on no* ~ unter keinen Umständen; **con'sid·er·ing** □ **1.** *prp.* in Anbetracht (*gen.*); **2.** *adv.* F den Umständen entsprechend.

con·sign [kən'sain] übergeben, -liefern; anvertrauen; ✝ konsignieren; **con·sig·na·tion** [kɔnsai'nei∫ən], **con·sign·ment** [kən-'sainmənt] (Über)Sendung *f*; ✝ Konsignation *f*; **con·sign·ee** [kɔnsai'ni:] (Waren)Empfänger *m*; **con·sign·er**, **con·sign·or** [kən-'sainə] (Waren)Absender *m*; Verfrachter *m*.

con·sist [kən'sist] bestehen (*of* aus; *in* in *dat.*); in Einklang stehen (*with* mit); **con'sist·ence**, **con-'sist·en·cy** Festigkeit(sgrad *m*) *f*, Konsistenz *f*, Beschaffenheit *f*; Übereinstimmung *f*; Folgerichtigkeit *f*, Konsequenz *f*; **con'sist·ent** □ übereinstimmend, vereinbar (*with* mit); folgerichtig, konsequent; ~*ly a.* durchweg; **con'sis·to·ry** *eccl.* Konsistorium *n*.

con·sol·a·ble [kən'səuləbl] tröstbar, zu trösten(d); **con·so·la·tion** [kɔnsə-'lei∫ən] Trost *m*; ~ *goal Sport:* Ehrentor *n*; **con·sol·a·to·ry** [kən'sɔlətəri] tröstend, Trost...

con·sole 1. [kən'səul] trösten; **2.** ['kɔnsəul] Konsole *f*; ⌂ Krag-, Tragstein *m*; ~ *table* Wandtischchen *n*.

con·sol·er [kən'səulə] Tröster(in).

con·sol·i·date [kən'sɔlideit] festigen; *fig.* vereinigen; *Schuld* konsolidieren, fundieren; zs.-legen; ~*d annuities* = *consols*; ~*d Fund* konsolidierter Staatsfonds *m*; **con·sol·i'da-tion** Festigung *f*; Konsolidierung *f*; Vereinigung *f*; Zs.-legung *f*.

con·sols [kən'sɔlz] *pl.* Konsols *m/pl.*, konsolidierte Staatsanleihen *f/pl.*

con·som·mé [kən'sɔmei] klare Fleischbrühe *f*.

con·so·nance ['kɔnsənəns] Konsonanz *f*; Übereinstimmung *f*; **'con-so·nant 1.** □ ♪ konsonierend; übereinstimmend (*with*, *to* mit); **2.** *gr.* Konsonant *m*.

con·sort 1. ['kɔnsɔ:t] Gemahl(in); Geleitschiff *n*; **2.** [kən'sɔ:t] (*with*) sich gesellen (zu), umgehen (mit); passen (zu).

con·spec·tus [kən'spektəs] Über-

sicht *f*; Abriß *m*.

con·spic·u·ous □ [kən'spikjuəs] *deutlich* sichtbar; auffallend; *fig.* hervorragend; *be* ~ *by one's absence* durch Abwesenheit glänzen; *make o.s.* ~ sich auffällig benehmen.

con·spir·a·cy [kən'spirəsi] Verschwörung *f*; **con'spir·a·tor** [~tə] Verschwörer *m*; **con'spir·a·tress** Verschwörerin *f*; **con·spire** [kən-'spaiə] sich verschwören; zs.-wirken.

con·sta·ble ['kʌnstəbl] Polizist *m*, Schutzmann *m*; **con'stab·u·lar·y** [kən'stæbjuləri] Polizei(truppe) *f*.

con·stan·cy ['kɔnstənsi] Standhaftigkeit *f*; Beständigkeit *f*; Unveränderlichkeit *f*; Bestand *m*, Dauer *f*; **'con·stant 1.** □ konstant, beständig, fest; unveränderlich, gleich; bleibend; fortwährend, dauernd; treu, getreu; **2.** ♉ Konstante *f*.

con·stel·la·tion *ast.* [kɔnstə'lei∫ən] Sternbild *n*.

con·ster·na·tion [kɔnstə:'nei∫ən] Bestürzung *f*.

con·sti·pate ⚕ ['kɔnstipeit] verstopfen; **con·sti'pa·tion** ⚕ Verstopfung *f*.

con·stit·u·en·cy [kən'stitjuensi] Wählerschaft *f*; Wahlkreis *m*; F Kunden-, Abonnentenkreis *m*; **con'stit·u·ent 1.** wesentlich; Grund..., Bestand...; konstituierend; **2.** wesentlicher Bestandteil *m*; Wähler *m*; Vollmachtgeber *m* (*a.* ✝).

con·sti·tute ['kɔnstitju:t] ein-, errichten; einsetzen, ernennen; zs.-setzen; bilden, ausmachen; ~ *s.o. judge* j. als Richter einsetzen, *fig.* zum Richter machen; **con·sti-'tu·tion** Ein-, Errichtung *f*; Bildung *f*, Zs.-setzung *f*; Konstitution *f*, Körperbau *m*; Verfassung *f*, Konstitution *f*, Satzung *f*; **con·sti'tu-tion·al** [~∫ənl] **1.** □ konstitutionell; körperlich bedingt; natürlich; verfassungsmäßig; ~ *law* Verfassungsrecht *n*; **2.** F Spaziergang *m bsd. zur Verdauung*; **con·sti'tu·tion·al-ist** [~∫nəlist] Anhänger(in) der konstitutionellen Regierungsform; **con·sti·tu·tive** □ ['kɔnstitju:tiv] wesentlich.

con·strain [kən'strein] zwingen; *et.* erzwingen; **con·straint** [~'streint] Zwang *m*; ⚖ Nötigung *f*.

con·strict [kənˈstrikt] zs.-ziehen, -schnüren; verengen; **conˈstric·tion** Zs.-ziehung *f etc.*; **conˈstric·tor** *anat.* Schließmuskel *m; zo. a.* boa ⌔ Riesenschlange *f*, Boa *f*.

con·strin·gent [kənˈstrindʒənt] zs.-ziehend.

con·struct [kənˈstrʌkt] konstruieren, bauen, errichten; *fig.* bilden, erdenken; **conˈstruc·tion** Konstruktion *f*; Bau *m*, Gebäude *n*; Auslegung *f*; Sinn *m;* ⌔ site Baustelle *f; under* ⌔ im Bau; **conˈstruc·tive** aufbauend, schöpferisch, konstruktiv, positiv; Bau...; Konstruktions...; gefolgert, angenommen; **conˈstruc·tor** Erbauer *m*, Konstrukteur *m*.

con·strue [kənˈstruː] *gr.* konstruieren; auslegen, auffassen; Wort für Wort übersetzen.

con·sue·tu·di·nar·y [kɔnswiˈtjuːdinəri] gewohnheitsmäßig; Gewohnheits...

con·sul [ˈkɔnsəl] Konsul *m;* ⌔ *general* Generalkonsul *m;* **con·su·lar** [ˈkɔnsjulə] konsularisch; Konsular...; **con·su·late** [ˈ⌔lit] Konsulat *n (a. Gebäude);* ⌔ *general* Generalkonsulat *n;* **con·sul·ship** [ˈkɔnsəlʃip] Konsulat *n*.

con·sult [kənˈsʌlt] *v/t.* konsultieren, um Rat fragen, zu Rate ziehen; befragen; in *e-m Buch* nachschlagen; berücksichtigen; ⌔*ing engineer* technischer Berater *m;* ⌔*ing physician* fachärztlicher Berater *m; v/i.* sich beraten; **conˈsult·ant** (ärztliche *etc.*) Autorität *f;* **con·sul·ta·tion** [kɔnsəlˈteiʃən] Konsultation *f*, Beratung *f;* Rücksprache *f;* Konferenz *f;* ⌔ *hour* Sprechstunde *f;* **conˈsult·a·tive** [kənˈsʌltətiv] beratend.

con·sum·a·ble [kənˈsjuːməbl] verzehrbar; **conˈsume** *v/t.* verzehren *(a. fig.);* verbrauchen; vergeuden; zerstören; *v/i.* sich verzehren; **conˈsum·er** Konsument *m*, Verbraucher *m;* Abnehmer *m;* ⌔ *association* Verbraucherverband *m;* ⌔ *demand* Verbrauchernachfrage *f;* ⌔ *goods pl.* Verbrauchsgüter *n/pl.*

con·sum·mate 1. □ [kənˈsʌmit] vollendet; **2.** [ˈkɔnsəmeit] vollenden, vervollständigen; *Ehe* vollziehen; **con·sum·ma·tion** [⌔ˈmeiʃən] Vollendung *f;* Vollziehung *f;* Ende *n; fig.* Ziel *n*.

con·sump·tion [kənˈsʌmpʃən] Verbrauch *m*, Konsum *m;* 𝒮 Auszehrung *f*, Schwindsucht *f;* **conˈsump·tive** □ verzehrend; schwindsüchtig.

con·tact 1. [ˈkɔntækt] Berührung *f;* Fühlung(nahme) *f;* ⚡ Kontakt *m; make (break)* ⌔ den Kontakt herstellen (unterbrechen); **2.** [kənˈtækt] Fühlung nehmen mit; ⌔ **lens·es** [ˈkɔntæktˈlensiz] *pl.* Haft-, Kontaktschalen *f/pl.;* ⌔ **print** *phot.* Kontaktabzug *m*.

con·ta·gion 𝒮 [kənˈteidʒən] Ansteckung *f;* Verseuchung *f;* Seuche *f (a. fig.);* **conˈta·gious** □ ansteckend; verseuchend.

con·tain [kənˈtein] (ent)halten, (um)fassen; ✕ *den Feind* festhalten; *fig.* in Schach halten; ⌔ *o.s.* an sich halten, sich mäßigen; **conˈtain·er** Behälter *m;* Container *m;* **conˈtain·ment** Festhalten *n etc.; pol.* Eindämmung *f*.

con·tam·i·nate [kənˈtæmineit] verunreinigen; *fig.* anstecken, vergiften; verseuchen; **con·tam·iˈna·tion** Verunreinigung *f etc.,* (radioaktive) Verseuchung *f; gr.* Kontamination *f*.

con·temn *lit.* [kənˈtem] verachten.

con·tem·plate [ˈkɔntempleit] *fig.* betrachten; beabsichtigen; **con·temˈpla·tion** Betrachtung *f;* Nachsinnen *n; have in* ⌔ beabsichtigen; **ˈcon·tem·pla·tive** □ nachdenklich; beschaulich.

con·tem·po·ra·ne·ous □ [kɔntempəˈreinjəs] gleichzeitig; ⌔ *performance* 𝒯 Erfüllung *f* Zug um Zug; **conˈtem·po·rar·y 1.** zeitgenössisch; gleichzeitig; **2.** Zeitgenosse *m*, Zeitgenossin *f;* Altersgenosse *m*, Altersgenossin *f*.

con·tempt [kənˈtempt] Verachtung *f;* Verächtlichkeit *f;* ⌔ *of court* Mißachtung *f* des Gerichts; Nichterscheinen *n* vor Gericht; *hold in* ⌔ verachten; *in* ⌔ *of* in Mißachtung *(gen.);* **conˈtempt·i·ble** □ verächtlich; zu verachten(d); **conˈtemp·tu·ous** □ [⌔tjuəs] geringschätzig *(of gegen);* verachtungsvoll; verächtlich.

con·tend [kənˈtend] *v/i.* streiten, ringen *(for* um); *v/t.* behaupten.

con·tent [kənˈtent] **1.** zufrieden; *parl.* einverstanden; *not* ⌔ dagegen;

2. befriedigen, zufriedenstellen; ~ o.s. sich begnügen (with mit); **3.** Zufriedenheit f; to one's heart's ~ nach Herzenslust; ['kontent] Umfang m; innerer Gehalt m; ~s pl. Inhalt m; table of ~s Inhaltsverzeichnis n; **con·tent·ed** □ [kən'tentid] zufrieden.

con·ten·tion [kən'tenʃən] (Wort-) Streit m; Wetteifer m; Behauptung f; **con'ten·tious** □ streitsüchtig; streitig.

con·tent·ment [kən'tentmənt] Zufriedenheit f, Genügsamkeit f.

con·test 1. ['kontest] Streit m; Wettkampf m, -bewerb m; **2.** [kən'test] (be)streiten; anfechten; um et. streiten; ~ a borough sich um das Mandat e-s Wahlkreises bewerben; ~ s.o.'s right to do s.th. j-m das Recht streitig machen, et. zu tun; **con'test·a·ble** bestreit-, anfechtbar, streitig; **con'test·ant** streitende Partei f; Herausforderer m; **con'test·ed** umstritten.

con·text ['kontekst] Zusammenhang m, Kontext m; **con·tex·tu·al** □ [kən'tekstjuəl] dem Zs.-hang entsprechend; aus dem Zs.-hang sich ergebend; **con'tex·ture** [⁓tʃə] Gewebe n, Bau m, Struktur f.

con·ti·gu·i·ty [konti'gju:iti] Berührung f; Nähe f; **con·tig·u·ous** □ [kən'tigjuəs] anstoßend (to an acc.); benachbart.

con·ti·nence ['kontinəns] Enthaltsamkeit f; Mäßigung f; **'con·ti·nent 1.** □ enthaltsam; mäßig; **2.** Kontinent m, Erdteil m; Festland n; **con·ti·nen·tal** [⁓'nentl] **1.** □ kontinental; Kontinental...; ~ quilt Federbett n; **2.** Kontinentaleuropäer(in).

con·tin·gen·cy [kən'tindʒənsi] Zufälligkeit f; Zufall m; Möglichkeit f; unvorhergesehener Fall m; **con-'tin·gen·cies** pl. unvorhergesehene Ausgaben f/pl.; **con'tin·gent 1.** □ zufällig; unter Umständen möglich (to bei), eventuell; ~ on abhängig von; **2.** ⚔ Truppen-Kontingent n.

con·tin·u·al □ [kən'tinjuəl] fortwährend, unaufhörlich, dauernd, ständig; **con'tin·u·ance** Fortdauer f, Dauer f; Bleiben n; Anhalten n; **con·tin·u'a·tion** Fortsetzung f; Fortdauer f; ✝ Prolongation f; ~ school Fortbildungsschule f; **con-**

'tin·ue [⁓nju:] v/t. fortsetzen; fortführen, verlängern; beibehalten; ~ reading weiter lesen; to be ~d Fortsetzung folgt; v/i. sich fortsetzen, fortdauern; (ver)bleiben, beharren; fortfahren; ~ (in) a business ein Geschäft fortführen; **con·ti·nu·i·ty** [konti'nju:iti] Kontinuität f; Stetigkeit f; Film: Drehbuch n; Radio: verbindende Worte n/pl.; ~ girl Skriptgirl n; **con·tin·u·ous** □ [kən-'tinjuəs] ununterbrochen, fortlaufend, durchgehend; ~ current ⚡ Gleichstrom m.

con·tort [kən'tɔ:t] verdrehen; verzerren; **con'tor·tion** Verdrehung f; Verzerrung f; **con'tor·tion·ist** [⁓ʃnist] Schlangenmensch m.

con·tour ['kontuə] Umriß m, Kontur f; ~ line surv. Höhenschichtlinie f; ~ map Höhenlinienkarte f.

con·tra ['kontrə] wider; per ~ ✝ als Gegenleistung.

con·tra·band ['kontrəbænd] **1.** Schmuggel...; **2.** Schmuggelware f; Schleichhandel m; Konterbande f.

con·tra·cep·tion [kontrə'sepʃən] Empfängnisverhütung f; **con·tra-'cep·tive** empfängnisverhütend(es Mittel n).

con·tract 1. [kən'trækt] v/t. zs.-ziehen; Gewohnheit annehmen; Krankheit sich zuziehen; Schulden machen; Heirat etc. (ab)schließen; v/i. sich zs.-ziehen, einschrumpfen; e-n Vertrag schließen (for auf acc.); sich vertraglich verpflichten (to zu); ~ for (aus)bedingen; ~ing party vertragschließende Partei f; **2.** ['kontrækt] Kontrakt m, Vertrag m; by ~ vertraglich; under ~ im Auftrag gegeben (Bau); **con·tract·ed** □ [kən-'træktid] zs.-gezogen etc.; fig. beschränkt; ~ form gr. Kurzform f; **con·tract·i'bil·i·ty** Zs.-ziehbarkeit f; **con'tract·i·ble** zs.-ziehbar; **con'trac·tile** [⁓tail] zs.-ziehend; zs.-ziehbar; ⚡ einziehbar (Fahrwerk); **con'trac·tion** Zs.-ziehung f; gr. Kurzform f; **con'trac·tor** Unternehmer m (for e-s Baues etc.); Lieferant m; anat. Schließmuskel m; **con'trac·tu·al** □ [⁓tjuəl] vertraglich, vertragsmäßig; Vertrags...

con·tra·dict [kontrə'dikt] widersprechen (dat.); **con·tra'dic·tion** Widerspruch m; **con·tra'dic·tious** □ zum Widerspruch neigend;

streitsüchtig; con·tra'dic·to·ry [~-
təri] □ (sich) widersprechend.
con·tra·dis·tinc·tion [kɔntrədis-
'tiŋkʃən] Gegensatz *m*; con·tra-
dis'tin·guish [~gwiʃ] unterscheiden.
con·tral·to ♪ [kən'træltəu] 1. Alt
(-stimme *f*) *m*; Altistin *f*; 2. Alt...
con·trap·tion *sl.* [kən'træpʃən] (ko-
misches) Ding(s) *n*, Apparat *m*.
con·tra·ri·e·ty [kɔntrə'raiəti] Widerspruch *m*; Widrigkeit *f des Wetters
etc.*; con·tra·ri·ly ['~trərili] entgegen, zuwider; 'con·tra·ri·ness
Gegensätzlichkeit *f*; Widerstand *m*,
-spenstigkeit *f*; con·tra·ri·wise
['~waiz] entgegengesetzt; umgekehrt; 'con·tra·ry 1. entgegengesetzt (*a. adv.*); ungünstig, widrig;
F [kən'treəri] widerspenstig, eigensinnig; ~ to *prp.* zuwider (*dat.*),
gegen (*acc.*); entgegen (*dat.*);
2. Gegenteil *n*; on the ~ im Gegenteil; to the ~ dagegen.
con·trast 1. ['kɔntraːst] Kontrast *m*,
Gegensatz *m*; in ~ to im Gegensatz
zu; by ~ als Gegensatz (hierzu);
2. [kən'traːst] *v/t.* gegenüberstellen;
(*with dat.*); vergleichen; sich abheben von; *v/i.* sich unterscheiden,
abstechen (*with von*).
con·tra·vene [kɔntrə'viːn] zuwiderhandeln (*dat.*); übertreten; im
Widerspruch stehen zu; bestreiten;
con·tra·ven·tion [~'venʃən] Zuwiderhandlung *f*; Übertretung *f*;
Verstoß *m* (*of gegen*).
con·trib·ute [kən'tribjuːt] *v/t.* beitragen, beisteuern; einbringen; *v/i.*
beitragen, mitwirken (*to an dat.*,
bei); con·tri·bu·tion [kɔntri'bjuː-
ʃən] Mitwirkung *f*; Beitrag *m*; eingebrachtes Gut *n*; Einlage *f*; ✕
Kontribution *f*, Kriegssteuer *f*;
con·trib·u·tor [kən'tribjutə] Bei-
tragende *m*; Mitarbeiter(in) (*to a
newspaper* an e-r Zeitung); con-
'trib·u·to·ry beitragend (*to* zu).
con·trite □ ['kɔntrait] zerknirscht,
reuevoll; con·tri·tion [kən'triʃən]
Zerknirschung *f*.
con·triv·ance [kən'traivəns] Erfindung *f*; Plan *m*; Vorrichtung *f*;
Kunstgriff *m*; Scharfsinn *m*, Findigkeit *f*; con'trive *v/t.* ersinnen;
ausdenken; planen; zuwegebrin-
gen; *v/i.* fertig werden, auskommen;
es möglich machen, es fertigbrin-

gen (*to inf.* zu *inf.*); con'triv·er
Erfinder(in); erfinderischer Kopf
m; *she is a good* ~ sie ist eine gute
Hausfrau.
con·trol [kən'trəul] 1. Kontrolle *f*,
Aufsicht *f*; Überwachung *f*; Beherrschung *f*; Befehl *m*; Zwang *m*;
Macht *f*, Gewalt *f*, Herrschaft *f*;
(Nach)Prüfung *f*; Zwangsbewirt-
schaftung *f*, -wirtschaft *f*; ⚡ Ver-
fügungsgewalt *f*; Kontrollvorrich-
tung *f*, Regler *m*, Steuerung *f*; *attr.*
Kontroll...; ~ surfaces *pl.* ✈ Leit-
werk *n*; *foreign* ~ Überfremdung *f*;
remote od. distant ~ Fernsteuerung
f; ~ board ⊕ Schaltbrett *n*; ~ column ✈ Steuerknüppel *m*; ~ desk
Steuer-, Schaltpult *n*; *Fernsehen:* Re-
giepult *n*; ~ knob Bedienungsknopf *m*;
~ panel *mot.* Armaturenbrett *n*; ~
tower ✈ Kontrollturm *m*, Tower *m*; ~
valve *Radio:* Steuerröhre *f*; *be in* ~ die
Aufsicht führen (*of über acc.*); *put s.o.
in* ~ j-m die Aufsicht übertragen (*of
über acc.*); 2. kontrollieren; einschränken; beaufsichtigen; überwachen; beherrschen; (nach)prüfen;
Waren bewirtschaften; ⊕ regeln; ✈
steuern; ~ling interest maßgebliche
Beteiligung *f an e-m Unternehmen*;
con'trol·la·ble kontrollierbar; lenkbar; con'trol·ler Kontrolleur *m*,
Aufseher *m*; Leiter *m*, Geschäftsführer *m*; Rechnungsprüfer *m*.
con·tro·ver·sial □ [kɔntrə've:ʃəl]
umstritten; streitsüchtig; polemisch; con·tro·ver·sy ['~və:si]
Streit *m*; Streitfrage *f*; con·tro-
vert ['~və:t] bestreiten; *j-m* widersprechen; con·tro'vert·i·ble □
bestreitbar.
con·tu·ma·cious □ [kɔntju'meiʃəs]
widerspenstig; ⚖ ungehorsam;
con·tu·ma·cy ['kɔntjuməsi] Widerspenstigkeit *f*; ⚖ absichtliches
Nichterscheinen *n*.
con·tu·me·li·ous □ [kɔntju:'miːljəs]
frech, beleidigend; con·tu·me·ly
['kɔntju:mli] Beschimpfung *f*;
Schmach *f*.
con·tuse ⚕ [kən'tjuːz] quetschen;
con'tu·sion [~ʒən] Quetschung *f*.
co·nun·drum [kə'nʌndrəm] Scherz-
rätsel *n*.
con·ur·ba·tion [kɔnə:'beiʃən] Ballungsraum *m*, Gruppe *f* zs.-ge-
wachsener Städte.
con·va·lesce [kɔnvə'les] genesen;

con·va·les·cence Genesung *f*;
con·va·les·cent 1. ☐ genesend;
Genesungs...; **2.** Genesende *m*, *f*.
con·vec·tion *phys.* [kən'vekʃən]
Fortpflanzung *f*, Übertragung *f*;
con'vec·tor Konvektor *m* (*Heizkörper*).
con·vene [kən'viːn] (sich) versammeln; zs.-rufen; *Versammlung*
(ein)berufen; ⚖ vorladen.
con·ven·ience [kən'viːnjəns] Bequemlichkeit *f*, Annehmlichkeit *f*;
Angemessenheit *f*; Vorteil *m*; Klosett *n*; *at your earliest ~ möglichst
bald; make a ~ of s.o.* j. ausnutzen;
marriage of ~ Vernunftehe *f*; **con-
'ven·ient** ☐ bequem, angenehm;
passend (*to, for* für); brauchbar.
con·vent ['kɔnvənt] (*bsd.* Nonnen-)
Kloster *n*; **con·ven·ti·cle** [kən-
'ventikl] Versammlung *f*; Konven-
tikel *n* (*bsd. v. non-conformists*);
con'ven·tion Versammlung *f*;
Konvent *m*; Konvention *f*, Übereinkommen *n*, Vertrag *m*; Herkommen *n*; **con'ven·tion·al** [~ʃənl] vertraglich; herkömmlich, konventio-
nell; *~ weapons pl.* konventionelle
Waffen *f/pl.*; **con'ven·tion·al·ism**
[~ʃnəlizəm] Festhalten *n* am Her-
kömmlichen; *das* Herkömmliche;
con·ven·tion·al·i·ty [~ʃə'næliti]
Herkömmlichkeit *f*; **con'ven·tu·al**
[~tjuəl] ☐ Kloster..., klösterlich.
con·verge [kən'vɜːdʒ] konvergieren,
zs.-laufen (lassen); **con'ver·gence**,
con'ver·gen·cy Konvergenz *f*;
con'ver·gent, con'verg·ing kon-
vergierend.
con·vers·a·ble [kən'vɜːsəbl] umgänglich; gesprächig; **con'ver·sant**
(*with*) vertraut (mit); bewandert (in
dat.); **con·ver·sa·tion** [~və'seiʃən]
Gespräch *n*, Unterhaltung *f*; **con-
ver'sa·tion·al** [~ʃənl] Unterhal-
tungs...; gesprächig; umgangssprachlich; **con·verse 1.** ☐ ['kɔn-
vɜːs] umgekehrt; **2.** [~] Gespräch *n*;
vertrauter Umgang *m*; Å·, *phls.*
Kehrsatz *m*; Umkehrung *f*; **3.** [kən-
'vɜːs] sich unterhalten (*with* mit);
con'ver·sion Um-, Verwandlung *f*;
⊕, ⚡ Umformung *f*; *phls.* Umkehrung *f*; *eccl.* Bekehrung *f* (*to* zu);
pol. Meinungswechsel *m*, Übertritt
m; ✝ Konvertierung *f*; Umstellung
f e-r Währung, e-s Betriebs etc.
con·vert 1. ['kɔnvɜːt] Bekehrte *m*,

f, Konvertit *m*; **2.** [kən'vɜːt] (sich)
um- *od.* verwandeln; ⊕, ⚡ umfor-
men; *eccl.* bekehren; verwenden
(*to* zu); *e-n Satz* umkehren; ✝
konvertieren; *Betrieb, Währung etc.*
umstellen; große Wohnung in
kleinere Wohnungen umbauen, aufteilen; **con'vert·er** Bekehrer(in);
⊕, ⚡ Umformer *m*; **con·vert·i-
bil·i·ty** [~ə'biliti] Umwandelbarkeit
f; ✝ Konvertierbarkeit *f*; **con-
'vert·i·ble 1.** ☐ um-, verwandelbar;
✝ konvertierbar; **2.** *mot.* Kabrio
(-lett) *n*.
con·vex ☐ ['kɔn'veks] konvex; **con-
'vex·i·ty** Konvexheit *f*.
con·vey [kən'vei] befördern, bringen, schaffen, tragen; übermitteln;
vermitteln, mitteilen; *phys.* leiten;
ausdrücken; sagen; ⚖ übertragen;
con'vey·ance Transport *m*, Beförderung *f*; Spedition *f*; Übermittlung *f*; Transportmittel *n*;
Fuhrwerk *n*; ⚖ Übertragung *f*;
⚡ Leitung *f*; *public ~* öffentliches
Verkehrsmittel *n*; **con'vey·anc·er**
Notar *m für Übertragungen von
Grundeigentum*; **con'vey·or** ⊕ *a. ~
belt* Förderband *n*.
con·vict 1. ['kɔnvikt] Zuchthäusler
m, Sträfling *m*; **2.** [kən'vikt] überführen (*of gen.*); ⚖ für schuldig erklären (*of gen.*); **con'vic·tion** ⚖
Überführung *f*, Schuldigerklärung
f, Verurteilung *f*; Überzeugung *f*
(*of* von); *previous ~* Vorstrafe *f*.
con·vince [kən'vins] überzeugen (*of*
von); **con'vinc·ing** überzeugend.
con·viv·i·al [kən'viviəl] Fest...; festlich; gesellig; **con·viv·i·al·i·ty** [~-
'æliti] Geselligkeit *f*; festliche
Stimmung *f*.
con·vo·ca·tion [kɔnvəu'keiʃən] Einberufung *f*; Versammlung *f*.
con·voke [kɔn'vəuk] einberufen.
con·vo·lu·tion [kɔnvə'luːʃən] Zs.-
wicklung *f*; Windung *f*.
con·vol·vu·lus ♀ [kən'vɔlvjuləs]
Winde *f*.
con·voy ['kɔnvɔi] **1.** Geleit *n*; Ge-
leitzug *m*; (Geleit)Schutz *m*; **2.** geleiten.
con·vulse *fig.* [kən'vʌls] erschüttern;
be ~d with laughter sich biegen vor
Lachen; **con'vul·sion** Zuckung *f*,
Krampf *m*; *~s of laughter* Lachkrampf *m*; **con'vul·sive** ☐ krampfhaft, -artig; konvulsiv.

co·ny ['kəuni] Kaninchen *n*.

coo [ku:] girren, gurren.

cook [kuk] **1.** Koch *m*; Köchin *f*; **2.** kochen; *fig.* zs.-brauen; sich kochen lassen; F *Bericht etc.* zurechtstutzen, frisieren; '~·**book** *Am.* Kochbuch *n*; '**cook·er** Kocher *m*; Kochapfel *m*, -birne *f*; F Erfinder *m*; ~ *hood* Abzugshaube *f über dem Herd*; '**cook·er·y** Kochen *n*; Kochkunst *f*; ~ *book* Kochbuch *n*; '**cook·house** Lagerküche *f*; ♣ Kombüse *f*; **cook·ie** *Am.* ['~i] Plätzchen *n*; '**cook·ing** Kochen *n*; Küche *f* (*Kochweise*); **cook·y** ['~i] = *cookie*.

cool [ku:l] **1.** □ kühl (*a. Gefühl*), frisch; *fig.* kaltblütig, gelassen; *b. s.* unverfroren; *a* ~ *thousand pounds* F die Kleinigkeit von tausend Pfund; **2.** Kühle *f*; **3.** (sich) abkühlen; *let him* ~ *his heels* laß ihn warten; '**cool·er** (Wein)Kühler *m*; *sl.* Gefängnis(zelle *f*) *n*; '**cool-'head·ed** mit kühlem Kopf, besonnen.

coo·lie ['ku:li] Lastträger *m*, Kuli *m*.

cool·ing ⊕ ['ku:liŋ] Kühlung *f*; *attr.* Kühl...; '**cool·ness** Kühle *f*, Kälte *f* (*a. fig.*); Kaltblütigkeit *f*.

coomb [ku:m] Talmulde *f*.

coon *Am.* F [ku:n] *zo.* Waschbär *m*; Neger *m*; (schlauer) Bursche *m*; *a gone* ~ ein hoffnungsloser Fall *m*; ~ *song* Negerlied *n*.

coop [ku:p] **1.** Hühnerkorb *m*; **2.** ~ *up od.* in einsperren.

co-op F ['kəuɔp] = *co-operative* (*store*) Konsum *m*.

coop·er ['ku:pə] Böttcher *m*; Küfer *m*; '**coop·er·age** Böttcherei *f*.

co-op·er·ate [kəu'ɔpəreit] mitwirken; zs.-arbeiten; **co-op·er'a·tion** Mitwirkung *f*; Zs.-arbeit *f*; **co-'op·er·a·tive** [~rətiv] **1.** zs.-wirkend; genossenschaftlich; ~ *society* Konsumverein *m*; ~ *store* Konsum(vereinsladen) *m*; **2.** = ~ *store*; **co-'op·er·a·tor** [~reitə] Mitarbeiter *m*; Konsumvereinsmitglied *n*.

co-opt [kəu'ɔpt] hinzuwählen; **co-op'ta·tion** Zuwahl *f*.

co-or·di·nate 1. □ [kəu'ɔ:dinit] gleich-, beigeordnet; **2.** [~neit] koordinieren, gleichordnen, ~schalten; aufeinander einstellen *od.* abstimmen; **co-or·di'na·tion** Gleichordnung *f*, -stellung *f*, -schaltung *f*.

coot [ku:t] Wasserhuhn *n*; F Tölpel *m*; **coot·ie** ✕ *sl.* ['~i] (Kleider-)

Laus *f*.

cop *sl.* [kɔp] **1.** erwischen; ~ *it es* kriegen; **2.** Polyp *m* (*Polizist*); Gefangennahme *f*.

co·pal ['kəupəl] Kopal(harz *n*) *m*.

co·part·ner ['kəu'pɑ:tnə] Teilhaber *m*; '**co·part·ner·ship** Genossenschaft *f*; Teilhaberschaft *f*; Gewinnbeteiligung *f* der Arbeitnehmer.

cope¹ [kəup] **1.** Chorrock *m*; *fig.* Decke *f*; Gewölbe *n des Himmels*; **2.** decken, überwölben.

cope² [~]: ~ *with* sich messen mit, fertig werden mit.

Co·per·ni·can [kəu'pə:nikən] kopernikanisch.

cope·stone ['kəupstəun] *mst fig.* Schlußstein *m*.

cop·i·er ['kɔpiə] Kopiergerät *n*.

co-pi·lot [kəu'pailət] Kopilot *m*.

cop·ing ⌂ ['kəupiŋ] (Mauer-) Kappe *f*; '~·**stone** *fig.* Krönung *f*.

co·pi·ous □ ['kəupjəs] reich(lich); weitschweifig; '**co·pi·ous·ness** Fülle *f*; Weitläufigkeit *f*.

cop·per¹ ['kɔpə] **1.** Kupfer *n*; Kupfermünze *f*; Kupfergeld *n*; Kupfergeschirr *n*; **2.** kupfern; Kupfer...; **3.** verkupfern.

cop·per² *sl.* [~] Polyp *m* (*Polizist*).

cop·per·as ⚗ ['kɔpərəs] Vitriol *n*.

cop·per...: ~ *beech* ⍋ Blutbuche *f*; '~·**plate** Kupferstich(platte *f*) *m*; *like* ~ wie gestochen (*Schrift*); '~·**smith** Kupferschmied *m*.

cop·pice ['kɔpis], **copse** [kɔps] Unterholz *n*, Dickicht *n*.

cop·u·late *zo.* ['kɔpjuleit] sich paaren; **cop·u'la·tion** Paarung *f*; **cop·u·la·tive** ['~lətiv] **1.** verbindend; **2.** *gr.* Kopula *f*, Bindewort *n*.

cop·y ['kɔpi] **1.** Kopie *f*, Nachbildung *f*; Abschrift *f*; Durchschlag *m*; Vorlage *f*; Muster *n*; Exemplar *n e-s Buches*; Zeitungsnummer *f*; druckfertiges Manuskript *n*; Zeitungsstoff *m*; *fair od. clean* ~ Reinschrift *f*; *rough od. foul* ~ Entwurf *m*, Konzept *n*; **2.** kopieren; abschreiben; nachbilden, nachahmen; ~ *fair* ins reine schreiben; ~*ing stand phot.* Kopierrahmen *m*; '~·**book** (Schön)Schreibheft *n*; '~·**cat** F *contp.* Nachäffer *m*; *ped.* Abschreiber *m*; ~ *desk* Redaktionstisch *m*; ~ **ed·i·tor** Redakteur *m*; '~·**hold** Lehnbesitz *m*; Lehngut *n*; '**cop·y-**

ing-ink Kopiertinte *f*; **'cop·y·ing-**
-press Kopierpresse *f*; **'cop·y·ist**
Abschreiber *m*; Nachahmer *m*; **'cop-**
y·right Verlags-, Urheberrecht *n*,
Copyright *n*; *attr.* verlags-, urheber-
rechtlich; **cop·y writ·er** Werbe-
texter *m*.

co·quet [kɔ'ket] kokettieren; **co-**
quet·ry ['ˌkitri] Gefallsucht *f*; **co-**
quette [ˌ'ket] Kokette *f*; **co'quet-**
tish □ kokett.

cor·a·cle ['kɔrəkl] Boot *n* aus über-
zogenem Weidengeflecht.

cor·al ['kɔrəl] 1. Koralle *f*; Kinder-
klapper *f* mit Beißkoralle; 2. *a.*
cor·al·line ['ˌlain] Korallen...;
korallenartig, -rot.

cor·bel △ ['kɔːbəl] Kragstein *m*.

cord [kɔːd] 1. Schnur *f*, Strick *m*,
Seil *n*; Kabel *n*; Klafter *f Holz*; *fig.*
Fessel *f*; *anat.* Strang *m*, Band *n*;
= *corduroy*; 2. (zu)schnüren, binden; **'cord·ed** gerippt (*Stoff*);
'cord·age Tauwerk *n*.

cor·dial ['kɔːdjəl] 1. □ herzlich,
aufrichtig; herzstärkend; 2. Herz-
stärkung *f*; (Magen)Likör *m*; **cor-**
dial·i·ty [ˌdi'æliti] Herzlichkeit *f*.

cord-mak·er ['kɔːdmeikə] Seiler *m*.

cor·don ['kɔːdn] 1. △ Mauerkranz
m; ✗ Kordon *m*, Postenkette *f*;
Polizeikordon *m*; Ordensband *n*;
2. ~ *off* abriegeln, -sperren (*Polizei*).

cor·do·van ['kɔːdəvən] Korduan
(-leder *n*) *m*.

cor·du·roy ['kɔːdərɔi] Kord(samt) *m*
(*gerippter Stoff*); ~s *pl.* Kordhosen
f/pl.; ~ *road* Knüppeldamm *m*.

core [kɔː] 1. ✿ Kernhaus *n*; *fig.* Innerste *n*; Herz *n*; Kern *m*; Eiter-
pfropf *m* e-s *Geschwürs*; ~ *time* Ar-
beitszeit: Kernzeit *f*; 2. entkernen;
'cor·er Fruchtentkerner *m*.

co·re·li·gion·ist ['kəuri'lidʒənist]
Glaubensgenosse *m*, Glaubens-
genossin *f*.

Co·rin·thi·an [kə'rinθiən] korin-
thisch.

cork [kɔːk] 1. Kork *m*; 2. (ver-)
korken, *fig. a.* ~ *up* verschließen;
'cork·age Ver-, Entkorken *n*;
Korkengeld *n*; **'corked** korkig,
nach dem Kork schmeckend;
'cork·er *sl.* Prachtkerl *m*; *prima od.*
pfundige Sache *f*; *das* Entscheidende; **'cork·ing** *Am.* F fabelhaft,
prima.

cork...: **'~·jack·et** Schwimmweste *f*;

'~·screw 1. Kork(en)zieher *m*; **'~-**
-tree ✿ Korkeiche *f*; **'cork·y** korkig; F lebhaft.

cor·mo·rant *orn.* ['kɔːmərənt]
Scharbe *f*, Kormoran *m*.

corn[1] [kɔːn] 1. Korn *n*; Getreide *n*;
a. Indian ~ *Am.* Mais *m*; *Am. in
Zssgn* ~ *bread* Maisbrot *f*; 2. einpökeln; ~ed *beef* Corned Beef *n*,
Büchsenfleisch *n*.

corn[2] 𝄋 [ˌ] Hühnerauge *n*.

corn...: **'~·chan·dler** Korn-, Samenhändler *m*; **'~·cob** *Am.* Maiskolben *m*.

cor·ne·a *anat.* ['kɔːniə] Hornhaut *f*
des Auges.

cor·nel ✿ ['kɔːnəl] Kornelkirsche *f*.

cor·nel·ian *min.* [kɔː'niːljən] Kar-
neol *m*.

cor·ne·ous ['kɔːniəs] hornartig.

cor·ner ['kɔːnə] 1. Ecke *f*, Winkel *m*;
Kurve *f*; *fig.* Enge *f*, Klemme *f*; ✝
spekulativer Aufkauf *m*; ✝ (Aufkäufer)Ring *m*; ~ *kick* Eckball *m*;
2. in die Ecke (*fig.* Enge) treiben;
✝ aufkaufen; **'cor·nered** ...eckig.

corner...: **'~·house** Eckhaus *n*;
'~·stone Eck-, *fig.* Grundstein *m*.

cor·net ['kɔːnit] ♩ (kleines) Horn *n*;
*Spitz-*Tüte *f*; Schwesternhaube *f*.

corn...: **'~·ex·change** Getreide-
börse *f*; **'~·field** Korn-, *Am.* Mais-
feld *n*; ~ *flakes* *pl.* Corn-flakes *pl.*;
'~·flour = *corn-starch*; **'~·flow·er**
Kornblume *f*.

cor·nice ['kɔːnis] △ Karnies *n*, Gesims *n*; Schnee-Wächte *f*.

Cor·nish ['kɔːniʃ] kornisch; aus
Cornwall.

corn...: **'~·juice** *Am. sl.* Mais-
schnaps *m*; ~ *pone* *Am.* Maisbrot *n*;
'~·pop·py ✿ Klatschmohn *m*; **'~-**
-stalk Getreidehalm *m*; *Am.* Mais-
stengel *m*; **'~·starch** *Am.* Mais-
mehl *n*.

cor·nu·co·pi·a *poet.* [kɔːnju'kəupjə]
Füllhorn *n*.

corn·y ['kɔːni] kornreich; körnig;
sl. abgedroschen, altmodisch; *bsd.
Am.* ♩ schmalzig (*sehr sentimental*).

co·rol·la ✿ [kə'rɔlə] Blumenkrone *f*;
cor'ol·la·ry Folgesatz *m*; *fig.*
Folge *f*.

co·ro·na [kə'rəunə], *pl.* **co'ro·nae**
[ˌniː] *ast.* Korona *f*; △ Kranzleiste
f; **co'ro·nal** *anat.* Scheitel...,
Stirn...; **cor·o·nar·y** 𝄋 ['kɔrənəri]

1. Herzkranz...; ᴗ *thrombosis* Herzinfarkt *m*; 2. F Herzinfarkt *m*; **cor·o·na·tion** [kɔre'neiʃən] Krönung *f*; **'cor·o·ner** Leichenbeschauer *m* u. Untersuchungsrichter *m*; **cor·o·net** ['ᴗnit] Adelskrone *f*.
cor·po·ral ['kɔːpərəl] 1. □ körperlich; 2. ✖ Korporal *m*; Unteroffizier *m*; **cor·po·rate** ['ᴗrit] □ vereinigt; körperschaftlich; gemeinsam, Gemeinschafts...; ᴗ *body* juristische Person *f*; **cor·po·ra·tion** [ᴗ'reiʃən] Korporation *f*, Körperschaft *f*, Zunft *f*; Stadtverwaltung *f*; *Am.* Aktiengesellschaft *f*; F Schmerbauch *m*; ᴗ *tax* Körperschaftssteuer *f*; **cor·po·ra·tive** ['ᴗrətiv] korporativ; **cor·po·re·al** □ [ᴗ'pɔːriəl] körperlich; materiell; **cor·po·re·i·ty** [ᴗpə-'riːiti] Körperlichkeit *f*.
corps [kɔː], *pl.* **corps** [kɔːz] Korps *n*.
corpse [kɔːps] Leichnam *m*.
cor·pu·lence, **cor·pu·len·cy** ['kɔː-pjuləns(i)] Beleibtheit *f*, Korpulenz *f*; **'cor·pu·lent** beleibt, korpulent.
cor·pus ['kɔːpəs], *pl.* **cor·po·ra** ['ᴗpərə] Körper *m*; Sammlung *f von Gesetzen etc.*; ♀ *Christi* ['kristi] *Day* Fronleichnamstag *m*; **cor·pus·cle** ['kɔːpʌsl] Teilchen *n*, Korpuskel *n*.
cor·ral *bsd. Am.* [kɔː'rɑːl] 1. Umzäunung *f*, Pferch *m* (*a.fig.*); Wagenburg *f*; 2. zs.-pferchen, *fig.* einsperren; e-e Wagenburg bilden.
cor·rect [kə'rekt] 1. *adj.* □ korrekt, richtig; *be* ᴗ richtig sein, stimmen; 2. *v/t.* korrigieren, berichtigen, verbessern; zurechtweisen; strafen; *Mißbrauch* abstellen; ♒ mildern; **cor'rec·tion** Berichtigung *f*, Verbesserung *f*; Verweis *m*; Strafe *f*; ♒ Milderung *f*; Korrektur *f*; *house of* ᴗ Besserungsanstalt *f*, Zuchthaus *n*; *I speak under* ᴗ ich lasse mich gern korrigieren; **cor'rect·i·tude** [ᴗtitjuːd] Korrektheit *f*; **cor'rec·tive** 1. verbessernd; ♒ mildernd; 2. Besserungsmittel *n*; **cor'rec·tor** Verbesserer *m*, Berichtiger *m*; *typ.* Korrektor *m*; Milderungsmittel *n*.
cor·re·late ['kɔrileit] 1. in Wechselbeziehung stehen *od.* bringen; 2. Korrelat *n*; **cor·re'la·tion** Wechselbeziehung *f*; **cor·rel·a·tive** □ [ᴗ'relətiv] in Wechselbeziehung (stehend).

cor·re·spond [kɔris'pɔnd] (*with, to*) entsprechen (*dat.*), übereinstimmen (*mit*); in Briefwechsel stehen, korrespondieren (*with mit*); **cor·re'spond·ence** Übereinstimmung *f*; Briefwechsel *m*, Korrespondenz *f*; Briefe *m/pl.*; Verbindung *f*; **cor·re'spond·ent** 1. □ entsprechend; 2. Briefschreiber(in); Korrespondent(in); Geschäftsfreund *m*; *my* ᴗ*s* Leute, mit denen ich im Briefwechsel stehe; **cor·re'spond·ing** entsprechend; korrespondierend (*Akademiemitglied*).
cor·ri·dor ['kɔridɔː] Korridor *m*; Gang *m*, Flur *m*; ᴗ *train* D-Zug *m*.
cor·ri·gi·ble □ ['kɔridʒəbl] verbesserlich, zu verbessern(d).
cor·rob·o·rant [kə'rɔbərənt] 1. stärkend; bestätigend; 2. Stärkungsmittel *n*; Bestätigung *f*; **cor'rob·o·rate** [ᴗreit] stärken; bestätigen; **cor·rob·o'ra·tion** Bestätigung *f*; **cor'rob·o·ra·tive** [ᴗrətiv] bestätigend.
cor·rode [kə'rəud] zerfressen, angreifen, korrodieren, wegätzen; **cor'ro·dent** 1. ätzend; 2. Ätzmittel *n*; **cor'ro·sion** [ᴗʒən] Ätzen *n*, Zerfressen *n*; ⊕ Korrosion *f*; Rost *m*; **cor'ro·sive** [ᴗsiv] 1. □ zerfressend, ätzend; *fig.* nagend; 2. Ätzmittel *n*; **cor'ro·sive·ness** ätzende Schärfe *f*.
cor·ru·gate ['kɔrugeit] runzeln; ⊕ riefen; ᴗ*d cardboard* Wellpappe *f*; ᴗ*d iron* Wellblech *n*.
cor·rupt [kə'rʌpt] 1. □ verdorben, faul; verderbt (*a. Text etc.*); bestechlich, bestochen; ᴗ *practices pl. pol.* Bestechungsmanöver *n/pl.*; 2. *v/t.* verderben; bestechen; anstecken; *v/i.* (ver)faulen, verderben; **cor'rupt·er** Verderber(in); Bestecher(in); **cor·rupt·i·bil·i·ty** [ᴗtə'biliti] Verderbbarkeit *f*; Bestechlichkeit *f*; **cor'rupt·i·ble** □ verderblich; bestechlich; **cor'rup·tion** Verderbnis *f*, Verdorbenheit *f* (*a. fig.*); Fäulnis *f*; Verderbtheit *f e-s Textes*; Bestechung *f*; **cor'rup·tive** □ verderbend.
cor·sage [kɔː'sɑːʒ] Taille *f*, Mieder *n*; *Am.* Ansteckblume(n *pl.*) *f*.
cor·sair [kɔː'sɛə] Seeräuber(schiff *n*) *m*, Korsar *m*.
corse [kɔːs] *poet.* = *corpse*.
cors(e)·let ['kɔːslit] Brustschild *m*.

cor·set ['kɔːsit] Korsett *n*; '**cor-set·ed** geschnürt.

cor·tège [kɔːˈteiʒ] Gefolge *n*; Pro-zession *f*.

cor·tex ♀, *zo.*, *anat.* ['kɔːteks], *pl.* **cor·ti·ces** ['˷tisiːz] Rinde *f*.

cor·ti·cal ['kɔːtikəl] rindig; *fig.* äußerlich.

co·run·dum *min.* [kəˈrʌndəm] Ko-rund *m*.

cor·us·cate ['kɔrəskeit] (auf)blitzen, funkeln.

cor·vette ⚓ [kɔːˈvet] Korvette *f*.

cor·vine ['kɔːvain] raben-, krähen-artig; Raben...; Krähen...

cosh *sl.* [kɔʃ] **1.** Knüppel *m*, Tot-schläger *m*; **2.** mit einem Knüppel schlagen; '**˷·boy** *sl.* jugendlicher Straßenräuber *m*.

cosh·er ['kɔʃə] (ver)hätscheln.

co·sig·na·to·ry ['kəu'signətəri] **1.** mitunterzeichnend; **2.** Mitunter-zeichner *m*.

co·sine ⚹ ['kəusain] Kosinus *m*.

co·si·ness ['kəuzinis] Behaglich-keit *f*.

cos·met·ic [kɔzˈmetik] **1.** kos-metisch, verschönernd; **2.** Schön-heitsmittel *n*; Kosmetik *f*; **cos·me-ti·cian** [kɔzmeˈtiʃən] Kosmetiker (-in).

cos·mic, cos·mi·cal □ ['kɔzmik(əl)] kosmisch; Welt(en)...; *cosmic rays pl.* kosmische Strahlung *f*.

cos·mo·naut ['kɔzmənɔːt] Welt-raumfahrer *m*, Kosmonaut *m*.

cos·mo·pol·i·tan [kɔzməuˈpɔlitən], **cos·mop·o·lite** ['˷'mɔpəlait] **1.** kos-mopolitisch; **2.** Weltbürger(in).

cos·mos ['kɔzmɔs] Kosmos *m*, Uni-versum *n*.

Cos·sack ['kɔsæk] Kosak *m*.

cos·set ['kɔsit] **1.** Nesthäkchen *n*; **2.** (ver)hätscheln.

cost [kɔst] **1.** Preis *m*; Kosten *pl.*; Schaden *m*, Nachteil *m*; ˷s *pl.* Ge-richtskosten *pl.*; Spesen *pl.*; *first od. prime ˷* Anschaffungskosten *pl.*; *˷ of living* Lebenshaltungskosten *pl.*; *at all ˷s* um jeden Preis; *to my ˷* zu meinem Schaden; *as I know to my ˷* wie ich aus eigner Erfahrung weiß; **2.** *(irr.)* kosten; ✝ die Selbst-kosten *e-r Ware etc.* berechnen; *˷ dearly* teuer zu stehen kommen.

co·star ['kəustɑː] **1.** e-r der Haupt-darsteller; **2.** e-e der Hauptrollen spielen; *˷ring* in e-r der Hauptrollen.

cos·ter F ['kɔstə] = '˷·mon·ger Höker(in) mit Handwagen.

cost·ing ['kɔstiŋ] Kostenberech-nung *f*; Herstellungskosten *pl.*

cos·tive □ ['kɔstiv] hartleibig.

cost·li·ness ['kɔstlinis] Kostspielig-keit *f*; Kostbarkeit *f*; '**cost·ly** kostbar; kostspielig, teuer.

cost-price ✝ ['kɔstprais] Selbst-kosten-, Einkaufspreis *m*.

cos·tume ['kɔstjuːm] Kostüm *n*; Kleidung *f*; Tracht *f*; **cos'tum·i·er** [˷miə] Kostümier *m*; Kostüm-verleiher *m*.

co·sy ['kəuzi] **1.** □ behaglich, ge-mütlich; **2.** = *tea-cosy.*

cot [kɔt] Feldbett *n*; ⚓ Hänge-matte *f* mit Rahmen; Kinderbett *n*.

cote [kəut] Stall *m*, Schuppen *m*.

co·te·rie ['kəutəri] Klüngel *m*, Clique *f*; Zirkel *m*, Kreis *m*, Gruppe *f*.

cot·tage ['kɔtidʒ] Hütte *f*; kleines Landhaus *n*, Sommerhaus *n*; ˷ *cheese* Hüttenkäse *m*; ˷ *industry* Heimindu-strie *f*; ˷ *piano* Pianino *n*; '**cot·tag·er** Häusler *m*; Hüttenbewohner *m*; *Am.* Sommergast *m*.

cot·ter ⊕ ['kɔtə] Querkeil *m*; Splint *m*.

cot·ton ['kɔtn] **1.** Baumwolle *f*; ✝ Kattun *m*; *Näh*-Garn *n*; **2.** baum-wollen; Baumwoll...; ˷ *bud* Watte-stäbchen *n*; ˷ *candy Am.* Zuckerwatte *f*; ˷ *wool* Watte *f*; **3.** F sich vertragen, sympathisieren *(with mit)*; sich an-schließen *(to s.o.* an j.); ˷ *on (to s.th.)* F (et.) kapieren; ˷ *to s.th.* sich befreun-den mit et.; ˷ *up* sich anfreunden *(with, to* mit *j-m)*; '**˷-grass** Wollgras *n*; '**˷-seed** ♀ Baumwollsamen *m*; '**˷-wood** ♀ *e-e* amerikanische Pappel *f*; '**cot·ton·y** baumwollartig.

cot·y·le·don ♀ [kɔtiˈliːdən] Keim-blatt *n*.

couch [kautʃ] **1.** Lager *n*; Couch *f*, Sofa *n*, Liege *f*; Schicht *f*; **2.** *v/t.* Lanze einlegen; *Meinung etc.* aus-drücken; *Schriftsatz etc.* abfassen; *den Star stechen; v/i.* sich (nieder-) legen; versteckt liegen; kauern; '**˷-grass** ♀ Quecke *f*.

cou·gar *zo.* ['kuːgə] Kugar *m*, Puma *m*.

cough [kɔf] **1.** Husten *m*; **2.** (aus-) husten; ˷ *down* durch Husten zum Schweigen bringen; ˷ *up* aushusten; *sl.* herausrücken mit; ˷ **drop** Hu-

counterpane

stenbonbon *m, n;* ~ **mix·ture** Hustensaft *m.*
could [kud] *pret. von can.*
couldn't ['kudnt] = *could not.*
cou·lee *Am.* ['ku:li] (trockenes) Bachbett *n.*
coul·ter ['kəultə] Pflugeisen *n.*
coun·cil ['kaunsl] Rat(sversammlung *f) m;* ~ **house** stadteigenes Haus *n* mit niedriger Miete; **coun·ci**(l)**·lor** ['~silə] Ratsmitglied *n,* Ratsherr *m,* Stadtrat *m.*
coun·sel ['kaunsəl] **1.** Beratung *f;* Rat(schlag) *m;* ⚖ Anwalt *m;* ~ *for the defence* Verteidiger *m;* ~ *for the prosecution* Anklagevertreter *m; keep one's (own)* ~ s-e Gedanken für sich behalten; *take* ~ *with sich* Rat holen bei; **2.** *j.* beraten; *j-m* raten *(to zu);* zu *et.* raten; **coun·se**(l)**·lor** ['~slə] Ratgeber(in); Anwalt *m; s. counci(l)lor.*
count[1] [kaunt] **1.** Rechnung *f;* Zahl *f;* ⚖ Anklagepunkt *m; Boxen:* Auszählen *n; a.* ~*-out parl.* Vertagung *f* wegen Beschlußunfähigkeit; Berücksichtigung *f,* Notiz *f; lose* ~ die Übersicht verlieren *(of* über *acc.); take no* ~ *of what s.o. says* sich nicht darum kümmern, was j. sagt; **2.** *v/t.* zählen; rechnen; mit(ein)rechnen; *fig.* schätzen, halten für; *be* ~*ed out Boxen:* ausgezählt werden; *v/i.* zählen; rechnen *(fig. on, upon* auf *acc.);* gelten *(for* little wenig).
count[2] [~] *nichtbritischer* Graf *m.*
count·a·ble ['kauntəbl] zählbar.
count-down ['kauntdaun] Startvorbereitungen *f/pl.,* Countdown *m (beim Raketenstart).*
coun·te·nance ['kauntinəns] **1.** Gesicht(sausdruck *m) n,* Miene *f;* Fassung *f,* (Gemüts)Ruhe *f;* Ermutigung *f,* Unterstützung *f; put s.o. out of* ~ j. aus der Fassung bringen; **2.** begünstigen, unterstützen; gutheißen.
count·er[1] ['kauntə] Zähler *m,* Zählapparat *m;* Spielmarke *f,* Zahlpfennig *m;* Laden-, Zahltisch *m;* Schalter *m.*
count·er[2] [~] **1.** *(to dat.)* entgegen; zuwider; Gegen...; **2.** Gegenschlag *m (to gegen);* **3.** Gegenmaßnahmen treffen; *Boxen:* kontern.
coun·ter·act [kauntə'rækt] zuwiderhandeln *(dat.);* **coun·ter'ac·tion** Gegenwirkung *f;* Widerstand *m.*

coun·ter-at·tack ['kauntərətæk] Gegenangriff *m.*
coun·ter·bal·ance 1. ['kauntəbæləns] Gegengewicht *n;* **2.** [~'bæləns] das Gegengewicht halten *(dat.),* aufwiegen; ⚖ ausgleichen, ausbalancieren.
coun·ter·blast ['kauntəblɑːst] kräftige Entgegnung *f.*
coun·ter·charge ['kauntətʃɑːdʒ] Gegenklage *f.*
coun·ter·check ['kauntətʃek] Gegenstoß *m;* Hindernis *n.*
coun·ter·claim ⚖ ['kauntəkleim] Gegenforderung *f.*
coun·ter·clock·wise ['kauntə'klɔkwaiz] entgegen dem Uhrzeigersinn.
coun·ter·cur·rent ['kauntə'kʌrənt] Gegenstrom *m.*
coun·ter·es·pi·o·nage ['kauntərespiə'nɑːʒ] Spionageabwehr *f.*
coun·ter·feit ['kauntəfit] **1.** □ nachgemacht; falsch, unecht; verstellt; **2.** Nachahmung *f;* Nachdruck *m;* Fälschung *f;* Falschgeld *n;* **3.** nachmachen; nachdrucken; fälschen; heucheln; sich verstellen; **'coun·ter·feit·er** Nachahmer(in); Fälscher(in); Falschmünzer *m;* Nachdrucker *m;* Heuchler(in).
coun·ter·foil ['kauntəfɔil] Kontrollblatt *n,* -abschnitt *m.*
coun·ter·fort △ ['kauntəfɔːt] Strebepfeiler *m.*
coun·ter·in·tel·li·gence ✕ ['kauntərin'telidʒəns] Gegenspionage *f.*
coun·ter·ir·ri·tant ❧ [kauntər'iritənt] Gegen(reiz)mittel *n.*
coun·ter·jump·er F ['kauntədʒʌmpə] Ladenschwengel *m.*
coun·ter·mand [kauntə'mɑːnd] **1.** Gegenbefehl *m;* Widerruf *m;* **2.** widerrufen; abbestellen.
coun·ter·march ['kauntəmɑːtʃ] **1.** Rückmarsch *m;* **2.** zurückmarschieren.
coun·ter·mark ['kauntəmɑːk] Gegenzeichen *n.*
coun·ter·mine 1. ['kauntəmain] Gegenmine *f;* **2.** [~'main] Gegenminen legen (gegen) *(a. fig.).*
coun·ter·move ['kauntəmuːv] *fig.* Gegenzug *m,* -maßnahme *f.*
coun·ter·or·der ['kauntərɔːdə] Gegenbefehl *m.*
coun·ter·pane ['kauntəpein] Bett-, Steppdecke *f.*

coun·ter·part ['kauntəpɑːt] Gegenstück n; Duplikat n.

coun·ter·point ♪ ['kauntəpɔint] Kontrapunkt m.

coun·ter·poise ['kauntəpɔiz] 1. Gegengewicht n; 2. das Gleichgewicht halten (dat.) (a. fig.), ausbalancieren.

coun·ter·pro·duc·tive ['kauntəprə-'dʌktiv] widersinnig; destruktiv.

coun·ter·rev·o·lu·tion ['kauntərevəluːʃən] Konter-, Gegenrevolution f.

coun·ter·scarp ✕ ['kauntəskɑːp] äußere Grabenböschung f.

coun·ter·shaft ⊕ ['kauntəʃɑːft] Vorgelegewelle f.

coun·ter·sign ['kauntəsain] 1. Gegenzeichen n; ✕ Losung(swort n) f; 2. gegenzeichnen.

coun·ter·sink ⊕ ['kauntəsiŋk] (aus-) fräsen; Schraubenkopf etc. versenken.

coun·ter·stroke ['kauntəstrəuk] Gegenstoß m.

coun·ter·ten·or ♪ ['kauntə'tenə] Altstimme f; Falsettstimme f.

coun·ter·vail ['kauntəveil] aufwiegen; ersetzen.

coun·ter·weight ['kauntəweit] Gegengewicht n (to gegen).

count·ess ['kauntis] Gräfin f.

count·ing-house ['kauntiŋhaus] Kontor n.

count·less ['kauntlis] zahllos.

coun·tri·fied ['kʌntrifaid] ländlich; bäurisch.

coun·try ['kʌntri] 1. Land n; Gegend f; Heimatland n; appeal od. go to the ~ Neuwahlen ausschreiben; 2. Land..., ländlich; Lands...; ~ **club** Klubhaus n auf dem Land; '~-**dance** englischer Volks-, Reihentanz m; ~ **gen·tle·man** Landedelmann m; Gutsherr m; '~-**house** Landhaus n, -sitz m; '~-**man** Landmann m (Bauer); Landsmann m; '~-**side** Land n im Gegensatz zur Stadt; Gegend f; Land(bevölkerung f) n; '~-**wom·an** Landfrau f; Landsmännin f.

coun·ty ['kaunti] Grafschaft f, Kreis m; ~ **coun·cil** Grafschaftsrat m; ~ **seat** Am. = ~ **town** Kreisstadt f.

coup [kuː] Schlag m, Streich m; ~ **d'état** Staatsstreich m.

cou·pé ['kuːpei] mot. Coupé n.

cou·ple ['kʌpl] 1. Paar n; Koppel f;

a ~ of zwei; F ein paar; 2. (ver-) koppeln; ⊕ kuppeln; Radio: koppeln; (sich) ehelich verbinden; (sich) paaren; ~ back rückkoppeln; '**cou·pler** Radio: Koppler m; '**cou·ple-skat·ing** Sport: Paarlaufen n; **cou·plet** ['kʌplit] Verspaar n.

cou·pling ⊕ ['kʌpliŋ] Kupplung f; Radio: Kopplung f; attr. Kupplungs..., Kopplungs...

cou·pon ['kuːpɔn] Coupon m; Abschnitt m; Bezugschein m; Rabattmarke f; Abonnement(karte f) n; Rundreiseheft n.

cour·age ['kʌridʒ] Mut m, Tapferkeit f; take od. muster up od. pluck up ~ Mut fassen; **cou·ra·geous** □ [kə'reidʒəs] mutig, beherzt, tapfer.

cour·gette [kuə'ʒet] Zucchini f.

cour·i·er ['kuriə] Kurier m, (Eil-) Bote m; Reiseleiter(in).

course [kɔːs] 1. Lauf m, Gang m; Weg m; ♣ Kurs m; ♣ Fahrt f; Richtung f; Lebensbahn f; Gewohnheit f; Wettrennen n; Rennbahn f; Gang m (Speisen); Lehrgang m, Kursus m; univ. Vorlesung f; Ordnung f, Folge f; Verfahren n; ♰ (Geld)Kurs m; in due ~ zur gegebenen od. rechten Zeit; of ~ natürlich, selbstverständlich; matter of ~ Selbstverständlichkeit f; ~ of exchange Wechselkurs m; stay the ~ durchhalten; 2. v/t. hetzen; jagen; v/i. rennen.

cours·er poet. ['kɔːsə] Renner m, schnelles Pferd n.

cours·ing ['kɔːsiŋ] Hetzjagd f.

court [kɔːt] 1. Hof(raum) m; Hof m e-s Fürsten; Hofgesellschaft f; Hof m, Aufwartung f; Gericht(shof m) n; at ~ bei Hofe; pay (one's) ~ j-m den Hof machen; 2. den Hof machen, huldigen (dat.); werben um j.; Unheil heraufbeschwören; '~-**card** Bildkarte f beim Kartenspiel; ~ **cir·cu·lar** Hofnachrichten f/pl.; '~-**day** Gerichtstag m; **cour·te·ous** □ ['kɔːtjəs] höflich, artig; **cour·te·san**, a. **cour·te·zan** [kɔːti'zæn] Kurtisane f; **cour·te·sy** ['kɔːtisi] Höflichkeit f; Gefälligkeit f; ~ **call** Anstandsbesuch m; ~ **light** mot. Innenleuchte f; **court-guide** ['kɔːtgaid] Verzeichnis n der hoffähigen Personen; **court-house** ['kɔːthaus] Gerichtsgebäude n; Am. a.

Amtshaus *n e-s Kreises*; **cour·ti·er** ['kɔːtjə] Höfling *m*; **'court·li·ness** feiner Ton *m*, Höflichkeit *f*; **'court·ly** höfisch; Hof...; höflich, artig.

court...: **'⁓·'mar·tial** ⚔ **1.** Kriegsgericht *n*; **2.** vor ein Kriegsgericht stellen; **'⁓·'plas·ter** Heftpflaster *n*; **'⁓·room** Gerichtssaal *m*; **'⁓·ship** Werbung *f*; **'⁓·yard** Hof *m*.

cous·in ['kʌzn] Vetter *m*, Cousin *m*; Base *f*, Cousine *f*; **first** ⁓, ⁓ **german** leiblicher Vetter *m*; **cous·in·hood** ['⁓hud], **'cous·in·ship** Vetter(n)-schaft *f*; **'cous·in·ly** vetterlich.

cove¹ [kəuv] **1.** Bucht *f*; *fig.* Obdach *n*; ⚛ Wölbung *f*; **2.** überwölben.

cove² P [⁓] Kerl *m*.

cov·e·nant ['kʌvənənt] **1.** ⚖ Vertrag *m*; *Bibel*: Bund *m*; **2.** *v/t.* geloben; (aus)bedingen; *v/i.* übereinkommen (*with s.o. for s.th.* mit j-m um et.).

Cov·en·try ['kɔvəntri]: *send s.o. to* ⁓ j. gesellschaftlich boykottieren.

cov·er ['kʌvə] **1.** Decke *f*; Deckel *m*; Umschlag *m*; Futteral *n*; Hülle *f*; Deckung *f*; Schutz *m*; Dickicht *n*; Deckmantel *m*; Decke *f*, Mantel *m* (*Bereifung*); Gedeck *n*; *a.* ⁓ *address* Deckadresse *f*; ⁓ *charge* Kosten *pl.* für das Gedeck; *under separate* ⁓ gesondert, mit getrennter Post; **2.** (be-, zu)decken; einschlagen, -wickeln (*with* in *acc.*); verbergen, verdecken; schützen; durchlaufen, zurücklegen; ✗ decken; *mit Schuß-waffe* zielen nach; *Gelände* bestreichen (*Geschütz*); umfassen, einschließen; *fig.* erfassen; *Zeitung*: berichten über (*acc.*), behandeln; ⁓ed *button* bezogener Knopf *m*; ⁓ed *court Tennis*: Halle *f*; ⁓ed *wire* umsponnener Draht *m*; **'cov·er·age** Berichterstattung *f* (*of* über *acc.*); **'cov·er girl** Titelbildschönheit *f*; **'cov·er·ing 1.** Decke *f*; Futteral *n*; *Bett-*Bezug *m*; Überzug *m*; Bekleidung *f*; Bedachung *f*; *floor* ⁓ Fußbodenbelag *m*; **cov·er·let** ['⁓lit] Bettdecke *f*; **cov·er sto·ry** Titelgeschichte *f*.

cov·ert 1. ['kʌvət] ☐ heimlich, versteckt; ⚖ verheiratet; **2.** ['kʌvə] Schutz *m*; Versteck *n*; Dickicht *n*.

cov·er-up ['kʌvərʌp] Vertuschung(s-manöver *n*) *f*.

cov·et ['kʌvit] heftig begehren, sich

gelüsten lassen nach; **'cov·et·ous** ☐ (be)gierig, lüstern (*of* nach); habsüchtig; **'cov·et·ous·ness** Gier *f*; Habsucht *f*.

cov·ey ['kʌvi] Volk *n Feldhühner*.

cov·ing ⚛ ['kəuviŋ] Überhang *m*, Vorsprung *m*.

cow¹ [kau] Kuh *f*.

cow² [⁓] einschüchtern, ducken.

cow·ard ['kauəd] **1.** ☐ feig; **2.** Feigling *m*; **cow·ard·ice** ['⁓dis], **'cow·ard·li·ness** Feigheit *f*; **'cow·ard·ly** feig(e).

cow·boy ['kaubɔi] Cowboy *m* (*berittener Rinderhirt*); **'cow-catch·er** ⚙ *Am.* Schienenräumer *m*.

cow·er ['kauə] (nieder)kauern; *fig.* sich ducken (*from* vor *dat.*).

cow·herd ['kauhɔːd] Kuh-, Rinderhirt *m*; **'cow·hide 1.** Kuhhaut *f*; Kuh-, Rindsleder *n*; Ochsenziemer *m*; **2.** peitschen; **'cow-house** Kuhstall *m*.

cowl [kaul] Mönchskutte *f*; Kapuze *f*; Schornsteinkappe *f*.

cow...: **'⁓·man** Melker *m*; *Am.* Viehzüchter *m*; **'⁓·'pars·ley** ♣ Wiesenkerbel *m*; **'⁓·'pars·nip** ♣ Bärenklau *m*; **'⁓·pox** Kuhpocken *f/pl.*; **'⁓·punch·er** *Am.* F Rinderhirt *m*.

cow·rie ['kauri] Kauri(muschel) *f*.

cow...: **'⁓·shed** Kuhstall *m*; **'⁓·slip** ♣ Schlüsselblume *f*. [steuern]

cox F [kɔks] **1.** = coxswain; **2.**

cox·comb ['kɔkskəum] Narr *m*; Narrenkappe *f*; **cox'comb·i·cal** ☐ närrisch.

cox·swain ['kɔkswein, ⚓ 'kɔksn] Bootsführer *m*, Steuermann *m*.

coy [kɔi] ☐ schüchtern; spröde; **'coy·ness** Sprödigkeit *f*.

coy·ote zo. ['kɔiəut] Steppenwolf *m*.

coy·pu zo. ['kɔipuː] Nutria *f*, Biberratte *f*.

coz·en *lit.* ['kʌzn] prellen; **'coz·en·age** Prellerei *f*.

co·zy ['kəuzi] = cosy.

crab¹ [kræb] Krabbe *f*, Taschenkrebs *m*; *ast.* Krebs *m*; ⊕ Winde *f*; Laufkatze *f*; *catch a* ⁓ e-n Krebs fangen (*mit dem Ruder im Wasser steckenbleiben*).

crab² [⁓] **1.** ♣ Holzapfel *m*; F Querkopf *m*; Meckerer *m*; Tadel *m*; **2.** meckern über; **'crab·bed** ☐ verdrießlich; herb; verworren, kraus.

crab-louse ['kræblaus] Filzlaus *f*.

crack [kræk] **1.** Knall *m*, Krach *m*;

Riß *m*, Sprung *m*; F derber Schlag *m*; *Sport sl.* Kanone *f*; Versuch *m*; Witz *m*; *in a ~* im Nu; *have a ~ at s.th.* et. versuchen, e-n Versuch mit et. machen; **2.** F erstklassig; **3.** krach!; **4.** *v/t.* (ver)sprengen; knallen mit *et.*; *Nuß* (auf)knacken; *Ei* aufschlagen; ⚛ *Öl* kracken, spalten; *~ a bottle* e-r Flasche den Hals brechen; *~ a joke* e-n Witz reißen; *~ up* F groß herausstellen; *v/i.* platzen, springen, bersten, rissig werden; e-n Sprung bekommen; knallen; umschlagen (*Stimme*); *~ down on sl.* scharf vorgehen gegen; *~ a crib sl.* in ein Haus einbrechen; *get ~ing* mit der Arbeit anfangen; **'~-brained** verrückt; **'~-down** *sl.* Razzia *f*, Blitzmaßnahme(n *pl.*) *f*; **'cracked** rissig, geborsten; F verrückt; **'cracker** Knallbonbon *m*; Schwärmer *m*; Lüge *f*; *Am.* Keks *m*; Kräcker *m*; Zwieback *m*; Zs.-bruch *m*; **'cracker-bar·rel** *Am.* F *attr.* Biertisch...; **'crack·er-jack** *Am.* F prima (*Sache od. Person*); **'crack·ers** F verrückt; **'crack-jaw** Zungenbrecher *m*; **crack·le** ['krækl] knattern, knistern; **'crack·ling** braune Kruste *f* des Schweinebratens; Geknister *n*; **crack·nel** ['~nl] Brezel *f*; **'crack-pot** F **1.** Spinner *m* (*verrückter Kerl*); **2.** verrückt; **'cracks·man** *sl.* Einbrecher *m*; **'crack-up** Zs.-stoß *m*; ✈ Bruchlandung *f*; **'crack·y** = *cracked*.

cra·dle ['kreidl] **1.** Wiege *f* (*a. fig.*); Kindheit *f*; ⚓ Stapelschlitten *m*; *teleph.* Gabel *f*; **2.** (ein)wiegen.

craft [krɑːft] Handwerk *n*, Gewerbe *n* (*a. coll.* = *Handwerker*); Fahrzeug *n*, *coll.* Fahrzeuge *n/pl.*, *bsd.* Schiffe *n/pl.*; Gerissenheit *f*, Raffinesse *f*; *the gentle ~* die edle Kunst des Angelns; **'craft·i·ness** Verschmitztheit *f*; **'crafts·man** (Kunst)Handwerker *m*; **'craftsman·ship** handwerkliches Können *n*; **'craft·y** □ gerissen, raffiniert.

crag [kræg] Klippe *f*, Felsspitze *f*; **'crag·gy** felsig; uneben; **'cragsman** Felsgeher *m*, Kletterer *m*.

crake *orn.* [kreik] Schnarre *f*.

cram [kræm] **1.** (voll)stopfen; *Geflügel* mästen, nudeln; (sich) mit Speisen vollstopfen; (ein)pauken; **2.** Einpauken *n*; **'~-'full** vollgestopft; **'cram·mer** Einpauker *m*.

cramp [kræmp] **1.** Krampf *m*; ⊕ Klammer *f*, Krampe *f*; *fig.* Fessel *f*; **2.** ⊕ verklammern; einengen, *fig.* hemmen; **'cramped** verkrampft; krampfhaft; eng, beengt; schwer leserlich; **'cramp-frame** ⊕ Schraubzwinge *f*; **'cramp-i·ron** Eisenklammer *f*.

cram·pon ['kræmpən] Steigeisen *n*.

cran·ber·ry ♧ ['krænbəri] Preiselbeere *f*.

crane [krein] **1.** Kranich *m*; ⊕ Kran *m*; **2.** (den Hals) vorstrecken, sich (aus)recken; ⊕ hochwinden; *~ at* zaudern vor (*dat.*); **'crane·fly** *zo.* Schnake *f*; **'crane's-bill** ♧ Storchschnabel *m*.

cra·ni·um *anat.* ['kreinjəm] Schädel *m*.

crank [kræŋk] **1.** ⊕ verdreht, verbogen; wacklig; ⚓ rank; munter; **2.** Kurbel *f*; Schwengel *m*; Wortspiel *n*; Schrulle *f*, Laune *f*; komischer Kauz *m*, Fanatiker *m*; *starting ~ mot.* Andrehkurbel *f*; *fresh air ~* Frischluftfanatiker *m*; **3.** *v/t. ~ off Film* kurbeln; *~ up mot.* ankurbeln (*a. v/i.*); **'~-case** Kurbelgehäuse *n*; **'crank·i·ness** Verschrobenheit *f*; **'crank-shaft** ⊕ Kurbelwelle *f*; **'crank·y** wacklig; launisch; verschroben, verdreht.

cran·nied ['krænid] rissig; **'cran·ny** Riß *m*, Ritze *f*, Spalt *m*.

crape [kreip] **1.** Krepp *m*, Flor *m*; **2.** kräuseln.

craps *Am.* [kræps] *pl. ein Würfelspiel.*

crap·u·lence ['kræpjuləns] Trunkenheit *f*; F Katzenjammer *m*.

crash[1] [kræʃ] **1.** Krach *m* (*a.* ✝); ✈ Absturz *m*; **2.** krachen; *in od.* auf *et.* fahren, fliegen, fallen, stürzen *etc.*; einstürzen; ✈ abstürzen, Bruch machen; **3.** *Am.* F blitzschnell ausgeführt; *~ course* Intensivkurs *m*; *~ diet* radikale Abmagerungskur *f*.

crash[2] [~] grober Drillich *m*.

crash...: **'~-dive** ⚓ **1.** Schnelltauchen *n*; **2.** schnelltauchen; **'~-hel·met** Sturzhelm *m*; **'~-land** ✈ bruchlanden; **'~-land·ing** ✈ Bruchlandung *f*.

crass *lit.* [kræs] derb, kraß.

crate [kreit] Lattenkiste *f für Porzellan, Fahrräder etc.*; *sl.* Kiste *f* (*Flugzeug*).

cra·ter [ˈkreitə] Krater *m*; (Granat-
etc.)Trichter *m*.
cra·vat [krəˈvæt] Krawatte *f*.
crave [kreiv] *v/t.* dringend bitten
od. flehen um; *v/i.* sich sehnen (*for
nach*).
cra·ven [ˈkreivən] **1.** feig; **2.** Feigling *m*.
crav·ing [ˈkreiviŋ] heftige Begierde
f, Sehnsucht *f* (*for* nach).
craw [krɔ:] Kropf *m der Vögel*.
craw·fish [ˈkrɔ:fiʃ] **1.** Krebs *m*;
2. *Am.* F kneifen, sich drücken.
crawl [krɔ:l] **1.** Kriechen *n*; Kraul
m; **2.** kriechen; schleichen; wimmeln (*with* von); kribbeln; *Schwimmen*: kraulen; *it makes one's flesh ~*
man bekommt e-e Gänsehaut da-
von; ˈ**crawl·er** *fig.* Kriecher(in);
Gewürm *n*; Laus *f*; Raupenschlep-
per *m*; ~*s pl.* Krabbelanzug *m*.
cray·fish [ˈkreifiʃ] Flußkrebs *m*.
cray·on [ˈkreiən] **1.** Zeichenstift *m*,
bsd. Farb-, Pastellstift *m*; Pastell
(-gemälde) *n*; *blue* ~, *red* ~ Blau-,
Rotstift *m*; **2.** zeichnen, skizzieren.
craze [kreiz] Verrücktheit *f* (*for*
nach); übertriebene Begeisterung *f*,
Fimmel *m* (*for* für); *be the* ~ Mode
sein; ˈ**crazed** verrückt (*with* vor
dat.); ˈ**cra·zi·ness** Verrücktheit *f*;
ˈ**cra·zy** ☐ verrückt (*for, about*
nach; *with* vor *dat.*); wahnsinnig;
wild begeistert; baufällig; zs.-
gestückelt, Flicken...; *Mosaik*...
creak [kri:k] **1.** Knarren *n*; **2.** knarren; ˈ**creak·y** ☐ knarrend.
cream [kri:m] **1.** Rahm *m*, Sahne *f*;
Creme(speise) *f*; *fig.* Creme *f*, Auslese *f*; *das Beste*; *cold* ~ Cold Cream
n; ~ *of tartar* gereinigter Weinstein
m; **2.** abrahmen; *fig.* den Rahm
abschöpfen von *et.*; mit Sahne vermengen; ˈ**cream·er·y** Molkerei *f*;
Milchgeschäft *n*; ˈ**cream·y** sahnig.
crease [kri:s] **1.** Falte *f*, Kniff *m*;
Bügelfalte *f*; Eselsohr *n* (*Buch*);
Kricket: (Mal)Linie *f*; **2.** (sich)
falten, (sich) kniffen.
cre·ate [kri:ˈeit] (er)schaffen; *thea.*
kreieren, gestalten; verursachen,
hervorrufen; erzeugen; ernennen,
machen zu; **cre·ˈa·tion** Schöpfung
f; Ernennung *f*; **cre·ˈa·tive** schaffend, schöpferisch; **cre·ˈa·tor**
Schöpfer *m*; **cre·ˈa·tress** Schöpfe-
rin *f*; **crea·ture** [ˈkri:tʃə] Geschöpf *n*,
Wesen *n*; Kreatur *f* (*a. contp.*); ~

comforts pl. die leiblichen Genüsse
m/*pl.*
crèche [kreiʃ] Kinderhort *m*.
cre·dence [ˈkri:dəns] Glaube *m*;
give ~ *to* Glauben schenken (*dat.*);
letter of ~ Empfehlungsschreiben *n*;
cre·den·tials [kriˈdenʃəlz] *pl.* Be-
glaubigungsschreiben *n*; schriftliche Unterlagen *f*/*pl.*
cred·i·bil·i·ty [krediˈbiliti] Glaubwürdigkeit *f*; **cred·i·ble** ☐ [ˈkre-
dəbl] glaubwürdig; glaubhaft.
cred·it [ˈkredit] **1.** Glaube *m*; Ruf *m*,
Ansehen *n*; Glaubwürdigkeit *f*;
Guthaben *n*; ✝ Kredit *n*; ✝ Borg
m, Kredit *m*; Einfluß *m*; Verdienst
n, Ehre *f*; *Am. Schule:* (Anrech-
nungs)Punkt *m*; ~ *balance* Guthaben
n; ~ *card* Kreditkarte *f*; ~ *note* ✝
Gutschriftsanzeige *f*; ~ *rating* Kredit-
würdigkeit *f*; *do s.o.* ~ j-m Ehre machen; *get* ~ *for s.th.* et. angerechnet
bekommen; *give s.o.* ~ *for s.th.* j-m et.
hoch *od.* als Verdienst anrechnen; *put
od. place od. pass to s.o.'s* ~ j-m gut-
schreiben; **2.** *j-m* glauben; *j-m* trau-
en; ✝ *Summe* kreditieren, gutschrei-
ben; ~ *s.o. with s.th.* j-m et. zutrauen;
ˈ**cred·it·a·ble** ☐ achtbar; ehrenvoll
(*to* für); ˈ**cred·i·tor** Gläubiger *m*.
cred·it...: ~ squeeze ✝ Kredit-
restriktionen *f*/*pl.*; ~ **ti·tles** *pl.* die
Namen *von Regisseur, Produzent etc.
im Vorspann e-s Films.*
cre·du·li·ty [kriˈdju:liti] Leichtgläubigkeit *f*; **cred·u·lous** ☐
[ˈkredjuləs] leichtgläubig.
creed [kri:d] Glaubensbekenntnis *n*.
creek [kri:k] Bucht *f*; *Am.* Bach *m*.
creel [kri:l] Fischkorb *m* aus Weidengeflecht.
creep [kri:p] **1.** (*irr.*) kriechen; *fig.*
(sich ein)schleichen; kribbeln; *it
makes my flesh* ~ ich bekomme e-e
Gänsehaut davon; **2.** Kriechen *n*;
~*s pl.* Schauder *m*, Gruseln *n*; *it
gave me the* ~*s* es überlief mich kalt;
ˈ**creep·er** Kriecher(in); Kriechtier
n; ♀ Schling-, Kletterpflanze *f*;
ˈ**creep·y** kriechend; fröstelnd; gruselig.
creese [kri:s] Kris *m* (*malaiischer
Dolch*).
cre·mate [kriˈmeit] *Leichen* verbrennen; **cre·ˈma·tion** (Leichen-)
Verbrennung *f*; **crem·a·to·ri·um**
[kreməˈtɔ:riəm], *bsd. Am.* **cre·ma-
to·ry** [ˈ~təri] Krematorium *n*.

cren·el·(l)at·ed ['krenileitid] mit Zinnen *od.* Schießscharten (versehen).

cre·ole ['kri:əul] **1.** Kreole *m*, Kreolin *f*; **2.** kreolisch.

cre·o·sote ⚗ ['kriəsəut] Kreosot *n*.

crêpe [kreip] Krepp *m*; ~ **pa·per** Kreppapier *n*; ~ **rub·ber** Kreppgummi *m*.

crep·i·tate ['krepiteit] knistern; rasseln; **crep·i·ta·tion** Knistern *n*; Knirschen *n*; Rasseln *n*.

crept [krept] *pret. u. p.p von* creep.

cre·pus·cu·lar [kri'pʌskjulə] dämmerig; Dämmerungs...

cres·cen·do ♪ [kri'ʃendəu] Krescendo *n* (*a. fig.*).

cres·cent ['kresnt] **1.** zunehmend; halbmondförmig; **2.** Halbmond *m* (*a. halbmondförmig gebaute Häuserreihe*); Hörnchen *n* (*Gebäck*); ♀ City Am. New Orleans.

cress ♣ [kres] Kresse *f*.

cres·set ['kresit] Leuchtfeuer *n*.

crest [krest] Kamm *m des Hahnes, e-r Woge*; Schopf *m der Vögel*; Mähne *f*; Federbusch *m*; Helm (-busch, -schmuck) *m*; Berg-Kamm *m*, Gipfel *m*; *Heraldik*: Helmzier *f*; *family* ~ Familienwappen *n*; '**crest·ed** mit einem Kamm *etc.*; ~ *lark* Haubenlerche *f*; ~ *note-paper* Briefpapier *n* mit Familienwappen; '**crest·fall·en** niedergeschlagen.

cre·ta·ceous [kri'teiʃəs] kreidig.

cre·tin ['kretin] Kretin *m*; '**cre·tin·ous** kretinhaft. [(*Gewebe*).\

cre·tonne [kre'tɔn] Kretonne *f, m*)

cre·vasse [kri'væs] (Gletscher-) Spalte *f*; *Am.* Deichbruch *m*.

crev·ice ['krevis] Riß *m*, Spalte *f*.

crew¹ [kru:] Schar *f, b.s.* Bande *f*; Gruppe *f von Arbeitern*; ⚓, ✈ Mannschaft *f*, Besatzung *f*.

crew² [~] *pret. von* crow 2.

crew cut ['kru:kʌt] Bürstenhaarschnitt *m*.

crew·el ⚓ ['kru:il] Stickwolle *f*.

crib [krib] **1.** Krippe *f*; Kinderbettstelle *f*; F *Schule*: Klatsche *f*; F Plagiat *n*; *bsd. Am.* Behälter *m für Mais etc.*; *crack a* ~ *sl.* in ein Haus einbrechen; **2.** einsperren; F mausen; F abschreiben; '**crib·bage** Cribbage(karten)spiel *n*; **crib·ble** ['~bl] grobes Sieb *n*; **crib·bit·er** ['kribbaitə] Krippensetzer *m*.

crick [krik] **1.** Krampf *m*; ~ *in the* neck steifer Hals *m*; **2.** verrenken.

crick·et¹ *zo.* ['krikit] Grille *f*, Heimchen *n*.

crick·et² [~] **1.** Kricket *n*; *not* ~ F nicht fair; **2.** Kricket spielen; '**crick·et·er** Kricketspieler *m*.

cri·er ['kraiə] Schreier(in); Ausrufer *m*.

crime [kraim] Verbrechen *n*.

Cri·me·an War [krai'miən'wɔ:] Krimkrieg *m*.

crim·i·nal ['kriminl] **1.** verbrecherisch; Kriminal..., Straf...; **2.** Verbrecher(in); **crim·i·nal·i·ty** [~'næliti] Strafbarkeit *f*; Verbrechertum *n*; **crim·i·nate** *lit.* ['~neit] beschuldigen, anklagen; **crim·i·na·tion** *lit.* Beschuldigung *f*, Anklage *f*.

crimp¹ ⚓, ✕ [krimp] **1.** Werber *m*; **2.** anwerben, pressen.

crimp² [~] **1.** kräuseln; **2.** ~ *cut* Krüllschnitt *m* (*Tabak*).

crim·son ['krimzn] **1.** karmesin; **2.** Karmesin(rot) *n*; **3.** *v/t.* karmesinrot färben; *v/i.* rot werden.

cringe [krindʒ] **1.** sich ducken; *fig.* (zu Kreuze) kriechen (*to vor dat.*); **2.** *fig.* Kriecherei *f*.

crin·kle ['kriŋkl] **1.** Windung *f*; Falte *f*; **2.** (sich) winden; (sich) falten; *Haar* kräuseln.

crin·o·line ['krinəli:n] Reifrock *m*.

crip·ple ['kripl] **1.** Krüppel *m*; Lahme *m, f*; **2.** verkrüppeln; *fig.* lähmen.

cri·sis ['kraisis] *pl.* **cri·ses** ['~si:z] Krisis *f*, Krise *f*, Wende-, Höhepunkt *m*.

crisp [krisp] **1.** kraus; knusperig; frisch (*Luft*); klar (*Kontur, Ton*); lebendig (*Stil*); steif (*Papier*); **2.** (sich) kräuseln; knusperig machen *od.* werden, braun rösten; **3.** *a. potato* ~*s pl.* Kartoffelchips *pl.*

criss·cross ['kriskrɔs] **1.** Kreuzzeichen *n*; Gewirr *n von Linien*; **2.** kreuz und quer (laufend); **3.** (durch)kreuzen.

cri·te·ri·on [krai'tiəriən] *pl.* **cri·te·ri·a** [~ə] Kennzeichen *n*, Prüfstein *m*, Kriterium *n*, Maßstab *m*.

crit·ic ['kritik] Kritiker(in); Kunstrichter(in); Krittler(in); '**crit·i·cal** ☐ kritisch; bedenklich; *be* ~ *of* kritisch gegenüberstehen (*dat.*); *in* ~ *condition* ✚ in Lebensgefahr; **crit·i·cism** ['~sizəm] Kritik *f* (*of* an *dat.*); **crit·i·cize** ['~saiz] kritisieren; beurteilen; tadeln; **cri·tique** [kri'tiːk] kritischer Essay *m*; *die* Kritik.

croak [krəuk] **1.** krächzen; quaken; *fig.* unken; F abkratzen (*sterben*); *sl.* abmurksen (*töten*); **2.** Krächzen *n*; Quaken *n*; '**croak·er** *fig.* Schwarzseher *m*, Unke *f*; '**croak·y** □ krächzend.

Cro·at ['krəuət] Kroat(in).

cro·chet ['krəuʃei] **1.** Häkelei *f*; **2.** häkeln.

crock [krɔk] **1.** irdener Topf *m*; Topfscherbe *f*; F Klepper *m* (*altes Pferd*); F Ruine *f* (*kranker Mensch*); F Klapperkasten *m*, alter Schlitten *m* (*Auto*); **2.** *mst* ~ *up sl.* zs.-brechen; '**crock·er·y** Töpferware *f*; Geschirr *n*.

croc·o·dile ['krɔkədail] *zo.* Krokodil *n*; F Zweierreihe *f* von Schulmädchen; ~ *tears pl. fig.* Krokodilstränen *f pl.*

cro·cus ⚘ ['krəukəs] Krokus *m.*

Croe·sus *fig.* ['kriːsəs] Krösus *m* (*Reicher*).

croft ['krɔft] kleines, eingefriedetes Feld *n*; kleiner Bauernhof *m*; '**croft·er** Kleinbauer *m.*

crom·lech ['krɔmlek] Kromlech *m*, druidischer Steinkreis *m.*

crone F [krəun] altes Weib *n.*

cro·ny F ['krəuni] Spezi *m*, Kumpan *m*, alter Freund *m.*

crook [kruk] **1.** Krümmung *f*; Haken *m* (*a. fig.*); Hirtenstab *m*; Krummstab *m*; *sl.* Schieber *m*, Gauner *m*; *on the* ~ auf krummen Wegen; **2.** (sich) krümmen; (sich) (ver)biegen; **crook·ed** [~kt] krumm, gekrümmt; ['~kid] □ *fig.* krumm, bucklig; unehrlich; F ergaunert.

croon [kruːn] summen; schmalzig singen; '**croon·er** sentimentaler Schlagersänger *m*, Schnulzensänger *m.*

crop [krɔp] **1.** Kropf *m*; Peitschenstiel *m*; Reitpeitsche *f*; Ernte *f*, Getreide *n*, Feldfrucht *f*; (Ernte-)Ertrag *m*, *fig.* Ausbeute *f*; kurzer Haarschnitt *m*; Menge *f*; **2.** (ab-, be)schneiden; stutzen; (ab)ernten; (ab)weiden; *Acker* bebauen; (Frucht) tragen; ~ *up* auftauchen; '**~-dust·ing** Sprühen *n* des Getreides *zur Schädlingsbekämpfung*; '**~-eared** stutzohrig; ~ **fail·ure** Miß-

ernte *f*; '**crop·per** Stutzende *m etc.* (*s. crop* 2); Kropftaube *f*; F schwerer Sturz *m*; (Frucht)Träger *m*; *Am. sl.* Pächter *m*; *come a* ~ F stürzen; *fig.* Pech haben.

cro·quet ['krəukei] **1.** Krocket(spiel) *n*; **2.** krockieren.

cro·quette [krɔ'ket] *Küche*: Krokette *f.*

cro·sier ['krəuʒə] Bischofsstab *m.*

cross [krɔs] **1.** Kreuz *n* (*fig. Leiden*); (Ordens)Kreuz *n*; Kreuzung *f von Rassen*; *sl.* Unehrlichkeit *f*; **2.** □ sich kreuzend; quer (liegend, laufend *etc.*); F ärgerlich, verdrießlich, böse (*with, at* auf *acc.*); entgegengesetzt; wechselseitig; Kreuz..., Quer...; widerwärtig; *sl.* unehrlich; **3.** *v/t.* kreuzen, durchstreichen; *fig.* durchkreuzen; überqueren, über (*acc.*) gehen, fahren, setzen; in den Weg kommen (*dat.*); *fig.* in die Quere kommen (*dat.*); ~ *o.s.* sich bekreuzigen; ~ *out Wort* ausstreichen; *keep one's fingers* ~*ed* den Daumen halten; *v/i.* sich kreuzen; ~ *over* hinübergehen; '**~-bar** *Fußball*: Torlatte *f*; '**~-beam** Querbalken *m*; '**~-bench** *parl.* Bank *f* der Parteilosen; '**~-bones** *pl.* zwei gekreuzte Knochen *m/pl. unter e-m Totenkopf*; **~-bow** ['krɔsbəu] Armbrust *f*; '**~-breed** (Rassen)Kreuzung *f*, Mischrasse *f*; Mischling *m*; '**~-'bun** Kreuzbrötchen *n*; '**~-'check** überprüfen; die Gegenprobe machen; '**~-'coun·try** querfeldein; Gelände...; Überland...; ~ *skiing* (Ski)Langlauf *m*; '**~-cut saw** Schrotsäge *f*; '**~-ex·am·i'na·tion** Kreuzverhör *n*; '**~-ex'amine** ins Kreuzverhör nehmen; '**~-eyed** schielend; '**~-fer·ti·li'za·tion** ⚘ Kreuzbefruchtung *f*; *fig.* gegenseitige Befruchtung *f*; ~ **fire** Kreuzfeuer *n* (*a. fig.*); '**~-grained** gegen die Faser (geschnitten); *fig.* widerhaarig; '**cross·ing** (Weg-, Schienen)Kreuzung *f*; Übergang *m*; Überfahrt *f*; Hindernis *n*; '**cross-legged** mit übereinandergeschlagenen Beinen; '**cross·ness** Verdrießlichkeit *f.*

cross...: '**~-patch** F übellauniger Person *f*; ~ **pur·pos·es** *pl.* Widerspruch *m*; *be at* ~ einander mißverstehen; das Entgegengesetzte wollen; ~ **ref·er·ence** Querverweis *m*; '**~-road** Querstraße *f*; '**~-**

-roads *pl. od. sg.* (Straßen)Kreuzung *f; fig.* Scheideweg *m;* '~-'**section** Querschnitt *m;* '~-**stitch** Kreuzstich *m;* '~-**talk** witziges Wortgefecht *n; teleph.* Nebensprechen *n;* '~-**walk** *Am.* Fußgängerüberweg *m;* '~-**wind** Seitenwind *m;* '~-**wise** kreuzweise; '~-**word puz·zle** Kreuzworträtsel *n.*

crotch [krɔtʃ] Haken *m;* Gabel(ung) *f;* **crotch·et** ['~it] Haken *m;* ♪ Viertelnote *f;* wunderlicher Einfall *m;* '**crotch·et·y** F wunderlich.

cro·ton ♀ ['krəutən] Kroton *m.*

crouch [krautʃ] **1.** sich ducken (*to* vor *dat.*) (*a. fig.*); **2.** Hockstellung *f.*

croup[1] [kru:p] Kruppe *f des Pferdes.*

croup[2] ♣ [~] Krup(p) *m* (*Kinderkrankheit*).

crou·pi·er ['kru:pia] Croupier *m.*

crow [krəu] **1.** Krähe *f;* Krähen *n; eat* ~ *Am.* F zu Kreuze kriechen; *have a* ~ *to pick with* ein Hühnchen zu rupfen haben mit; *in a* ~ *line, as the* ~ *flies* schnurgerade, (in der) Luftlinie; **2.** (*irr.*) krähen; *fig.* triumphieren (*over* über *acc.*); '~-**bar** Brecheisen *n,* -stange *f.*

crowd [kraud] **1.** Haufen *m,* Menge *f;* Masse *f* (*a. gemeines Volk*); Gedränge *n;* F Gesellschaft *f,* Bande *f,* Truppe *f;* **2.** (sich)drängen; (über-) füllen, vollstopfen (*with* mit); wimmeln; bedrängen; eilen; ~ *out* verdrängen; ~ *on sail* ♣ alle Segel beisetzen; '**crowd·ed** übervölkert, -füllt, -laufen.

crow·foot ♀ ['krəufut] Hahnenfuß *m.*

crown [kraun] **1.** *mst* Krone *f* (*des Königs; Ehre, Ruhm; Vollendung; Fünfschillingstück; e-s Zahnes*); Kranz *m;* Gipfel *m;* Scheitel *m;* Kopf *m e-s Hutes;* **2.** krönen (*king* zum König; *a. fig.*); Zahn überkronen; *to* ~ *all* zu guter Letzt, zu allem Überfluß; '**crown·ing** *fig.* höchst; letzt; '**crown-jew·els** *pl.* Kronjuwelen *n/pl.,* -schatz *m.*

crow's... [krəuz:] '~-**feet** *pl.* Krähenfüße *m/pl.* (*Fältchen um die Augen*); '~-**nest** ♣ Krähennest *n* (*Mastkorb*).

cru·cial □ ['kru:ʃəl] entscheidend; kritisch; **cru·ci·ble** ['kru:sibl] Schmelztiegel *m; fig.* Feuerprobe *f;* **cru·ci·fix** ['~fiks] Kruzifix *n;* **cru·ci·fix·ion** [~'fikʃən] Kreuzi-

gung *f;* '**cru·ci·form** kreuzförmig; **cru·ci·fy** ['~fai] kreuzigen (*a. fig.*).

crude □ [kru:d] roh (*unbearbeitet; ungekocht; unreif; unverdaut; unfein*); Roh... (*oil, steel etc.*); grell (*Licht etc.*); '**crude·ness, cru·di·ty** ['~diti] roher Zustand *m;* Roheit *f;* Unreife *f* (*a. fig.*).

cru·el □ ['kruəl] grausam; hart; *fig.* blutig; '**cru·el·ty** Grausamkeit *f.*

cru·et ['kru:it] (Essig-, Öl)Fläschchen *n;* '~-**stand** Gewürzständer *m.*

cruise ♣ [kru:z] **1.** Kreuz-, Vergnügungsfahrt *f;* **2.** kreuzen; *cruising speed* Reisegeschwindigkeit *f;* ~ *mis·sile* ✗ Marschflugkörper *m;* '**cruis·er** ♣ Kreuzer *m;* Jacht *f;* Segler *m; Am.* Funkstreifenwagen *m;* ~ *weight Boxen:* Halbschwergewicht *n.*

crumb [krʌm] **1.** Krume *f,* Brosame *f;* Brocken *m* (*a. fig.*); **2.** *Fleisch* panieren; = **crum·ble** ['~bl] (zer)krümeln, (-)bröckeln; *fig.* zugrunde gehen; '**crum·bling,** '**crum·bly** bröckelig; **crumb·y** ['krʌmi] krumig.

crum·my *sl.* ['krʌmi] mies (*wertlos, schlecht*); *feel* ~ sich mies fühlen.

crump *sl.* [krʌmp] Krachen *n;* ✗ dicker Brocken *m.*

crum·pet ['krʌmpit] lockerer Teekuchen *m; sl.* Birne *f* (*Kopf*); *be off one's* ~ e-e weiche Birne haben.

crum·ple ['krʌmpl] *v/t.* zerknüllen, -knittern; *fig.* vernichten; *v/i.* zerknüllt werden; sich knüllen.

crunch [krʌntʃ] (zer)kauen; zermalmen; knirschen.

crup·per ['krʌpə] Schwanzriemen *m;* Kruppe *f.*

cru·ral *anat.* ['kruərəl] Schenkel...

cru·sade [kru:'seid] **1.** Kreuzzug *m* (*a. fig.*); **2.** e-n Kreuzzug unternehmen; **cru·sad·er** Kreuzfahrer *m.*

crush [krʌʃ] **1.** Druck *m;* Gedränge *n;* F große Gesellschaft *f;* (Frucht-) Saft *m; have a* ~ *sl.* verknallt sein (*on* in); **2.** *v/t.* (zer)quetschen, (-)drücken; zermalmen; *fig.* vernichten; *Flasche* leeren; ~ *out fig.* zertreten; *v/i.* zs.-gequetscht werden; sich drängen; *Am. sl.* flirten; ~ **barri·er** Absperrgitter *n;* '**crush·er** Brechmaschine *f;* F *et.* Überwältigendes *n,* Schlag *m;* '**crush--room** *thea.* Foyer *n.*

crust [krʌst] **1.** Kruste *f*, Rinde *f*; *Am. sl.* Frechheit *f*; **2.** ver-, überkrusten; verharschen.

crus·ta·cean *zo.* [krʌsˈteiʃ(ə)n] Krusten-, Krebstier *n*.

crust·ed [ˈkrʌstid] abgelagert (*Wein*); eingewurzelt (*Sitte*); ~ snow Harsch(schnee) *m*; **'crust·y** □ krustig; mürrisch.

crutch [krʌtʃ] Krücke *f*; **crutched** an Krücken gehend; Krück...

crux [krʌks] *fig.* Kreuz *n*, Haken *m*, harte Nuß *f*.

cry [krai] **1.** Schrei *m*; Geschrei *n*; Ruf *m*; Weinen *n*; Gebell *n*; *a far* ~ *from* ... *to* ein weiter Weg von ... bis; *fig.* ein großer Unterschied zwischen ... und; *within* ~ (*of*) in Rufweite (von); **2.** schreien; (aus-) rufen; weinen; ~ *for* verlangen nach; ~ *off* plötzlich absagen; ~ *out* aufschreien; sich beschweren (*against* über *acc.*); ~ *up* rühmen; *Preise* hochtreiben; **'~-ba·by** kleiner Schreihals *m*; Heulsuse *f*; **'cry·ing** *fig.* himmelschreiend; dringend.

crypt [kript] Krypta *f*, Gruft *f*; **'cryp·tic** verborgen, geheim; **crypto-** [ˈ~təu] *Wortelement*: verborgen, geheim, verkappt.

crys·tal [ˈkristl] **1.** Kristall *m*; Kristall(glas) *n*; *bsd. Am.* Uhrglas *n*; **2.** kristallen; kristallklar; ~ *ball* Kristallkugel *f* *e-s Hellsehers*; **'~-clear** sonnenklar; **'~-gaz·ing** Hellsehen *n*; **crys·tal·line** [ˈ~təlain] kristallen; Kristall...; **crys·tal·li·za·tion** Kristallisation *f*; **'crys·tal·lize** kristallisieren; ~d kandiert (*Frucht*).

cub [kʌb] **1.** Junge *n von Bären etc.*; Bengel *m*, Flegel *m*; Anfänger *m*; **2.** (Junge) werfen; **'cub·bing** Jagd *f* auf Jungfüchse.

cu·bage [ˈkjuːbidʒ] Kubikinhalt *m*.

cub·by-hole [ˈkʌbihəul] behagliches Kämmerchen *n*.

cube Ⱥ [kjuːb] **1.** Würfel *m*, Kubus *m*; Kubikzahl *f*; **2.** in die dritte Potenz erheben; ~ *root* Kubikwurzel *f*; **'cu·bic**, **'cu·bi·cal** □ würfelförmig; kubisch; Kubik...

cu·bi·cle [ˈkjuːbikl] Schlafkammer *f*.

cu·bit [ˈkjuːbit] Elle *f* (*Maß*).

cub·hood [ˈkʌbhud] Flegeljahre *n/pl.*

cuck·old [ˈkʌkəuld] **1.** Hahnrei *m*; **2.** zum Hahnrei machen.

cuck·oo [ˈkukuː] **1.** Kuckuck *m*;

2. *sl.* plemplem (*verrückt*).

cu·cum·ber [ˈkjuːkʌmbə] Gurke *f*; *as cool as a* ~ *fig.* eiskalt, gelassen.

cu·cur·bit [kjuˈkəːbit] Kürbis *m*.

cud [kʌd] wiedergekäutes Futter *n*; *chew the* ~ wiederkäuen; *fig.* überlegen.

cud·dle [ˈkʌdl] **1.** F Liebkosung *f*; **2.** *v/t.* (ver)hätscheln; *v/i.* sich zs.-kuscheln.

cudg·el [ˈkʌdʒəl] **1.** Knüttel *m*; *take up the* ~*s for* Partei ergreifen für; **2.** (ver)prügeln; ~ *one's brains* sich den Kopf zerbrechen (*about* über *acc.*; *for* um).

cue [kjuː] *Billard-*Queue *n*; *bsd. thea.* Stichwort *n*; Wink *m*; *take the* ~ *from s.o.* sich nach j-m richten.

cuff [kʌf] **1.** (Faust)Schlag *m*; **2.** knuffen, schlagen.

cuff² [~] Manschette *f*; Handschelle *f*; (Ärmel-, *Am. a.* Hosen)Aufschlag *m*; **'~-links** *pl.* Manschettenknöpfe *m/pl.*

cui·rass [kwiˈræs] Küraß *m*.

cui·sine [kwiˈziːn] Küche *f* (*Art zu kochen*).

cul-de-sac [ˈkuldəˈsæk] Sackgasse *f*.

cu·li·nar·y [ˈkʌlinəri] kulinarisch.

cull *lit.* [kʌl] auslesen, -suchen; pflücken.

cul·len·der [ˈkʌlində] = *colander*.

culm [kʌlm] Kohlengrus *m*.

cul·mi·nate [ˈkʌlmineit] *ast.* kulminieren; *fig.* gipfeln, den Höhepunkt erreichen; **cul·mi·na·tion** *ast.* Kulmination *f*; *fig.* Höhepunkt *m*.

cu·lottes [kjuːˈlɔts] *pl.* Hosenrock *m*.

cul·pa·bil·i·ty [kʌlpəˈbiliti] Strafbarkeit *f*; **'cul·pa·ble** □ tadelnswert; strafbar; schuldhaft.

cul·prit [ˈkʌlprit] Angeklagte *m, f*; Schuldige *m, f*, Missetäter(in).

cult [kʌlt] Kult(us) *m*.

cul·ti·va·ble [ˈkʌltivəbl] kulturfähig; ⚹ anbaufähig.

cul·ti·vate [ˈkʌltiveit] kultivieren; urbar machen; an-, bebauen; *fig.* ausbilden; *Fertigkeit* üben, betreiben; *Geschmack etc.* pflegen; **'cul·ti·vat·ed** *fig.* gepflegt, kultiviert, gebildet; **cul·ti·va·tion** (An-, Acker)Bau *m*; Ausbildung *f*; Übung *f* *e-r Kunst etc.*; Pflege *f*, Zucht *f*; **'cul·ti·va·tor** Landwirt *m*; Züchter *m*; Kultivator *m* (*Maschine*).

cul·tur·al □ [ˈkʌltʃərəl] kulturell; Kultur...

cul·ture ['kʌltʃə] Kultur *f*; Pflege *f*; Zucht *f*; '**cul·tured** kultiviert; gebildet; '**cul·ture-me·di·um** *biol.* künstlicher Nährboden *m*; '**cul-ture-pearl** Zuchtperle *f*.

cul·vert ['kʌlvət] Abzugskanal *m*.

cum·ber ['kʌmbə] überladen; belasten; **⁓some** ['⁓səm], **cum·brous** ⧠ ['⁓brəs] beschwerlich, lästig; schwerfällig; ⧓ sperrig, Sperr...

cum·in ⚘ ['kʌmin] Kümmel *m*.

cu·mu·la·tive ⧠ ['kju:mjulətiv] (an-, auf)häufend; kumulativ; Zusatz...; sich steigernd; **cu·mu·lus** ['⁓ləs], *pl.* **cu·mu·li** ['⁓lai] Haufenwolke *f*, Kumulus *m*.

cu·ne·i·form ['kju:niifɔ:m]⟍ keilförmig; Keil(schrift)...

cun·ning ['kʌniŋ] 1. ⧠ schlau, listig, verschmitzt; scheit; *Am.* reizend; 2. List *f*, Schlauheit *f*.

cunt ∨ [kʌnt] Fotze *f* (*Vagina*).

cup [kʌp] 1. Becher *m*, Schale *f*, Tasse *f* (*a. als Maß*); Kelch *m* (*a.* ⚘ *u. fig.*); *Sport*: Pokal *m*; 2. schröpfen; *die Hand* wölben; **⁓board** ['kʌbəd] (Speise-, Silber- *etc.*) Schrank *m*; **⁓ love** *fig.* Liebe *f* aus Berechnung; **⁓ fi·nal** *Sport*: Pokalendspiel *n*; **⁓ful** ['⁓ful] Tasse *f* (*als Maß*).

Cu·pid ['kju:pid] Cupido *m*, Amor *m*.

cu·pid·i·ty [kju:'piditi] Habgier *f*.

cu·po·la ['kju:pələ] Kuppel *f*; ✕, ⚓ Panzerturm *m*.

cup·ping-glass ⚕ ['kʌpiŋglɑ:s] Schröpfkopf *m*.

cu·pre·ous *min.* ['kju:priəs] kupfern;
cu·pric ['⁓prik] Kupfer...

cup-tie ['kʌptai] *Sport*: Pokalspiel *n*.

cur [kə:] Köter *m*; Schurke *m*, Halunke *m*.

cur·a·bil·i·ty [kjuərə'biliti] Heilbarkeit *f*; '**cur·a·ble** heilbar.

cur·a·çao [kjuərə'səu] Curaçao *m* (*Likör*).

cu·ra·cy ['kjuərəsi] Unterpfarre *f*;
cu·rate ['⁓rit] Hilfsgeistliche *m*, Unterpfarrer *m*; **cu·ra·tor** ['⁓'reitə] Kurator *m*.

curb [kə:b] 1. Kinnkette *f*; Kandare *f*; *fig.* Zaum, Zügel *m*; *a.* **⁓stone** steinerne Einfassung *f*; *bsd.* Bordschwelle *f*, Randstein *m*; 2. an die Kandare nehmen; *fig.* zügeln, im Zaume halten; '**⁓-'mar·ket** *Am. Börse*: Freiverkehr *m*;

'**⁓-roof** Mansardendach *n*.

curd [kə:d] 1. Quark *m*; 2. *mst* **cur·dle** ['⁓dl] gerinnen (lassen).

cure [kjuə] 1. Kur *f*; Heilmittel *n*; **⁓ of souls** Seelsorge *f*; 2. heilen; einlegen, pökeln; räuchern; *Heu* trocknen; '**⁓-all** Allheilmittel *n*.

cur·few ['kə:fju:] Abendglocke *f*; -läuten *n*; *pol.* Ausgehverbot *n*.

cu·ri·a *eccl.* ['kjuəriə] Kurie *f*.

cu·rie *phys.* ['kjuəri] Curie *n* (*Maßeinheit der Radioaktivität*).

cu·ri·o ['kjuəriəu] Rarität *f*; **cu·ri·os·i·ty** [⁓'ɔsiti] Neugier *f*; Rarität *f*, Seltenheit *f*; Seltsamkeit *f*; '**cu·ri·ous** ⧠ neugierig; genau; seltsam, merkwürdig.

curl [kə:l] 1. *Haar-*Locke *f*; Kräuselung *f*, **⁓-paper** Lockenwickel *m aus Papier*; 2. (sich) kräuseln; (sich) locken; (sich) ringeln; '**curl·er** Lockenwickel *m*.

cur·lew *orn.* ['kə:lju:] Brachvogel *m*.

curl·ing ['kə:liŋ] *Sport*: Eiskegeln *n*; '**⁓-i·ron**, '**⁓-tongs** *pl.* Brenneisen *n*, -schere *f*; '**curl·y** gekräuselt; lockig; Locken...

cur·mudg·eon [kə:'mʌdʒən] Geizhals *m*, Knicker *m*.

cur·rant ['kʌrənt] Johannisbeere *f*; *a.* **⁓ dried** ⚘ Korinthe *f*.

cur·ren·cy ['kʌrənsi] Umlauf *m*, Verbreitung *f*; ✝ Lauffrist *f*; Kurs *m*, Währung *f*; *fig.* Geltung *f*; '**cur·rent** 1. ⧠ umlaufend; ✝ kursierend, gangbar (*Geld*); allgemein (bekannt); laufend (*Monat, Jahr*); gegenwärtig; **⁓ events** *pl.* Tagesereignisse *n/pl.*; **⁓ account** ✝ Girokonto *n*; 2. Strom *m* (*a.* ⚡); Strömung *f* (*a. fig.*); *Luft-*Zug *m*; **⁓ impulse** ⚡ Stromstoß *m*; **⁓ junction** elektrischer Anschluß *m*.

cur·ric·u·lum [kə'rikjuləm], *pl.* **cur·ric·u·la** [⁓lə] Lehr-, Stundenplan *m*; Pensum *n*; **⁓ vi·tae** ['vaiti:] Lebenslauf *m*.

cur·ri·er ['kʌriə] Lederzurichter *m*.

cur·rish ⧠ ['kə:riʃ] *fig.* hündisch; bissig.

cur·ry¹ ['kʌri] 1. Curry *m*, *n*; **⁓-powder** Currypulver *n* (*Gewürz*); 2. mit Curry würzen.

cur·ry² [⁓] *Leder* zurichten; *Pferd* striegeln; *j.* durchprügeln; **⁓ favour with** sich einzuschmeicheln versuchen bei; '**⁓-comb** Striegel *m*.

curse [kəːs] **1.** Fluch *m*; **2.** (ver-)fluchen; strafen (*with* mit); **curs·ed** □ ['kəːsid] verflucht.

cur·sive ['kəːsiv] Kursiv...; Schreib-...

cur·so·ry □ ['kəːsəri] flüchtig, oberflächlich; kursorisch.

curt □ [kəːt] kurz, knapp; barsch.

cur·tail [kəːˈteil] beschneiden (*a. fig.*); *fig.* beschränken; kürzen (*of* um); **cur'tail·ment** Kürzung *f.*

cur·tain ['kəːtn] **1.** Vorhang *m*; Gardine *f*; *fig.* Schleier *m*; ✗ Zwischenwall *m*; *draw a ~ over s.th. fig.* et. begraben; **2.** verhängen, verschleiern; *~ off* durch e-n Vorhang abtrennen; '*~-call thea.* Hervorruf *m* (*e-s Schauspielers*); '*~-fire* ✗ Sperrfeuer *n*; '*~-lec·ture* F Gardinenpredigt *f*; '*~-rais·er thea. u. fig.* Vorspiel *n.*

curt·s(e)y ['kəːtsi] **1.** Knicks *m*; *drop a ~* e-n Knicks machen; **2.** knicksen (*to* vor).

cur·va·ture ['kəːvətʃə] Krümmung *f*; *~ of the spine* Rückgratverkrümmung *f.*

curve [kəːv] **1.** Kurve *f*; Krümmung *f*; *Am. Baseball:* Effetball *m*; **2.** (sich) krümmen; (sich) biegen.

cush·ion ['kuʃən] **1.** Kissen *n*; Polster *n*; *Billard*-Bande *f*; **2.** mit Kissen versehen; polstern; *fig.* unterdrücken; ⊕ abfedern.

cush·y *sl.* ['kuʃi] leicht, bequem.

cusp [kʌsp] Spitze *f*; Scheitelpunkt *m*; Horn *n des Mondes.*

cus·pi·dor *Am.* ['kʌspidɔː] Spucknapf *m*; Speitüte *f.*

cuss *Am.* F [kʌs] **1.** Nichtsnutz *m*, *co.* Kerl *m*; **2.** fluchen; **cuss·ed** ['kʌsid] verflucht; widerborstig.

cus·tard ['kʌstəd] Eierspeise *f*; '*~-pow·der* Puddingpulver *n.*

cus·to·di·an [kʌsˈtəudjən] Hüter *m*; Verwalter *m*; Treuhänder *m*; **cus·to·dy** ['kʌtədi] Haft *f*; (Ob)Hut *f*; Betreuung *f*; Verwaltung *f*; Schutz *m.*

cus·tom ['kʌstəm] Gewohnheit *f*, Brauch *m*; Sitte *f*; ⚖ Gewohnheitsrecht *n*; ☨ Kundschaft *f*; *~s pl.* Zoll *m*; '**cus·tom·ar·y** □ gewöhnlich, üblich; '**cus·tom·er** Kunde *m*, Kundin *f*; F Bursche *m*; '**cus·tom·-house** Zollamt *n*; *~ officer* Zollbeamte *m*; '**cus·tom·-'made** *Am.* nach Maß gearbeitet; '**cus·toms**

clear·ance Zollabfertigung *f*; **customs du·ty** Zoll(gebühr *f*) *m.*

cut [kʌt] **1.** Schnitt *m*; Hieb *m*; Stich *m*; (Schnitt)Wunde *f*; Ab-, Einschnitt *m*; Durchstich *m*; Graben *m*; Beschneidung *f*; Kürzung *f*; Abstrich *m*; Ausschnitt *m*; *mst short-cut* Wegabkürzung *f*; *Holz-*Schnitt *m*; *Kupfer-*Stich *m*; *Kleider-*Schnitt *m*; Schnitte *f*, Scheibe *f von Braten etc.*; *fig.* Schneiden *n* (*Nichtkennenwollen*); ⚡ (Strom-) Sperre *f*; *iro.* Stück(chen) *n* (*verletzende Handlung*); *Karten-*Abheben *n*; *cold ~s pl.* Küche: kalter Aufschnitt *m*; *give s.o. the ~* (direct) F j. schneiden; **2.** (*irr.*) *v/t.* schneiden; schnitzen; gravieren; ab-, an-, auf-, aus-, be-, durch-, zer-, zuschneiden; ⚓ kappen; *Karten* abheben; F sich drücken von; *j. beim Begegnen* schneiden; *~ one's finger* sich in den Finger schneiden; *~ teeth* zahnen; *~ a figure* F eine Figur machen; *~ and come again* in Hülle und Fülle; *~ it fine* F es knapp machen, keinen (*zeitlichen*) Spielraum lassen; *~ short* j. unterbrechen; *to ~ a long story short* um es kurz zu sagen; *~ and run* F auskneifen; *~ back* einschränken; *~ down* fällen; *Getreide* mähen; *Umfang* beschneiden; *Preis* drücken; *~ off* abschneiden (*a. fig.*); *teleph.* trennen; *~ out* ausschneiden; *Am. Vieh* aussondern *aus der Herde*; *fig. j.* ausstechen; aufhören mit, einstellen; ⚡ ausschalten; *Radio:* abstellen; *be ~ out for* das Zeug zu e-r Sache haben; *have one's work ~ out* (for one) genug zu tun haben; *~ it out!* *sl.* hör auf!; *~ up* zer-, aufschneiden; zerlegen; *fig.* heruntermachen, -reißen; *v/i.* *~ in* sich einschieben; **3.** geschnitten *etc.*; *sl.* betrunken; *~ flowers pl.* Schnittblumen *f/pl.*; *~ glass* geschliffenes Glas *n*, Kristall *n*; *~ and dry od.* dried fix und fertig.

cu·ta·ne·ous [kjuːˈteinjəs] Haut...

cut·a·way ['kʌtəwei] *a.* *~ coat* Cut (-away) *m.*

cut·back ['kʌtbæk] Kürzung *f*; *Film:* Rückblende *f.*

cute □ F [kjuːt] klug, schlau; *Am.* F reizend, nett.

cu·ti·cle *anat.*, ⚘ ['kjuːtikl] Oberhaut *f*; ⌇ *scissors pl.* Hautschere *f*.

cut-in ['kʌtin] *Film*: Zwischentitel *m*.

cut·lass ['kʌtləs] ⚓ Entermesser *n*; Hirschfänger *m*.

cut·ler ['kʌtlə] Messerschmied *m*; '**cut·ler·y** Messerschmiedearbeit *f*; Messerschmiedewaren *f/pl.*; Stahlwaren *f/pl.*; Besteck(e *pl.*) *n*.

cut·let ['kʌtlit] Kotelett *n*; Schnitzel *n*.

cut...: '**~-off** *Am.* Abkürzung *f* (*Straße, Weg*) (*a. attr.*); '**~-out** *mot.* Auspuffklappe *f*; ⚡ Sicherung *f*; Ausschalter *m*; *Am.* Ausschneidebogen *m*, -bild *n*; '**~-price** verbilligt, *im Preis* herabgesetzt; '**~-purse** Taschendieb *m*; '**~-rate** *im Preis* ermäßigt; '**cut·ter** Schneidende *m, f*; Schnitzer *m*; Zuschneider(in); *Film*: Cutter *m*, Schnittmeister *m*; ⚒ Hauer *m*; ⊕ Schneidezeug *n*, -maschine *f*; ⚓ Kutter *m*; *Am.* leichter Schlitten *m*; '**cut-throat 1.** Halsabschneider *m*; Meuchelmörder *m*; **2.** halsabschneiderisch; mörderisch; '**cut·ting 1.** □ schneidend; scharf; ⊕ Schneid..., Fräs...; ⌇ *edge* Schneide *f*; ⌇ *nippers pl.* Kneifzange *f*; **2.** Schneiden *n*; 🔬 *etc.* Einschnitt *m*, Durchstich *m*; ♀ Steckling *m*; *Zeitungs*-Ausschnitt *m*; ⌇*s pl.* Schnipsel *n/pl.*; ⊕ Schneidspäne *m/pl.*

cut·tle *ichth.* ['kʌtl] = ⌇*-fish*; '**~-bone** Schale *f* des Tintenfischs; '**~-fish** Tintenfisch *m*.

cy·a·nide ⚗ ['saiənaid] Zyan *n*; ⌇ *of potassium* Zyankali *n*.

cy·ber·net·ics [saibə:'netiks] *sg.* Kybernetik *f*.

cyc·la·men ♀ ['sikləmən] Alpenveilchen *n*.

cy·cle ['saikl] **1.** Zyklus *m*; Kreis(-lauf) *m*; Periode *f*; ⊕ Arbeitsgang *m*; ⚡ Konjunkturzyklus *m*; Fahrrad *n*; *four*-⌇ *engine mot.* Viertaktmotor *m*; **2.** radfahren; '**cy·clic,** '**cy·cli·cal** □ zyklisch; ⚡ konjunkturell; Konjunktur...; **cy·cling** ['saikliŋ] **1.** Radfahren *n*; **2.** Rad...; '**cy·clist** Radfahrer(in).

cy·clone ['saikləun] Zyklon *m*, Wirbelsturm *m*; **cy·clon·ic** [⌇'klɔnik] wirbelsturmartig.

cy·clo·pae·di·a [saiklou'pi:djə] Konversationslexikon *n*.

Cy·clo·pean [sai'kləupjən] zyklopisch, riesig.

cy·clo·style ['saikləustail] Vervielfältigungsapparat *m*; **cy·clo·tron** *phys.* ['saiklɔtrɔn] Zyklotron *n*.

cyg·net ['signit] junger Schwan *m*.

cyl·in·der ['silində] Zylinder *m*, Walze *f*; Trommel *f*; **cy'lin·dric, cy'lin·dri·cal** □ [⌇'drik(əl)] zylindrisch.

cym·bal ♪ ['simbl] Zimbel *f*, Becken *n*.

cyn·ic ['sinik] **1.** *a.* '**cyn·i·cal** □ zynisch, spöttisch; **2.** Zyniker *m*, Spötter *m*; **cyn·i·cism** ['⌇sizəm] Zynismus *m*.

cy·no·sure *fig.* ['sinəzjuə] Gegenstand *m* der Bewunderung, Mittelpunkt *m* des Interesses.

cy·press ♀ ['saipris] Zypresse *f*.

Cyp·ri·an ['sipriən], **Cyp·ri·ot** ['sipriət] **1.** Zypriot(in); **2.** zyprisch.

cyst [sist] Blase *f*; 🔬 Sackgeschwulst *f*, Zyste *f*; '**cyst·ic** Blasen...; **cys·ti·tis** 🔬 [sis'taitis] Blasenentzündung *f*.

Czar [zɑ:] Zar *m*.

Czech [tʃek] **1.** Tscheche *m*, Tschechin *f*; **2.** tschechisch.

Czech·o·Slo·vak ['tʃekəu'sləuvæk] **1.** tschechoslowakisch; **2.** Tschechoslowake *m*, Tschechoslowakin *f*.

D

'd F = *had*; *would*.

dab [dæb] **1.** Klaps *m*; Betupfen *n*; Tupfen *m*, Klecks *m*; *ichth.* Butt *m*; Kenner *m*; *be a* ⌇ (*hand*) *at s.th.* sich auf et. verstehen; **2.** klapsen; (be-)tupfen; *Farbe etc.* auftragen; *typ.* abklatschen, klischieren.

dab·ble ['dæbl] bespritzen; plätschern; (hinein)pfuschen (*in* in *acc.*); sich ein wenig befassen (*in* mit); '**dab·bler** Amateur(in); Pfuscher(in).

dace *ichth.* [deis] *Art* Weißfisch *m.*

dac·tyl *poet.* ['dæktil] Daktylus *m* (*Versfuß*).

dad F [dæd], **dad·dy** F ['ˏdi] Papa *m*, Vati *m.*

dad·dy-long·legs F *zo.* ['dædi'lɔŋlegz] Schnake *f.*

daf·fo·dil ⚲ ['dæfədil] gelbe Narzisse *f*, Osterglocke *f.*

daft F [dɑːft] blöde, doof.

dag·ger ['dægə] Dolch *m*; *be at* ⸾s *drawn* auf Kriegsfuß stehen; *look* ⸾s *at s.o. j.* mit Blicken durchbohren.

dag·gle ['dægl] beschmuddeln.

da·go *Am. sl.* ['deigəu] *contp.* = Spanier, Portugiese, Italiener.

dahl·ia ⚲ ['deiljə] Dahlie *f.*

Dail Eir·eann [dail'ɛərən] Abgeordnetenkammer *f des irischen Parlaments.*

dai·ly ['deili] 1. täglich; ⸾ *dozen* F Morgengymnastik *f*; 2. Tageszeitung *f*; Tag(es)mädchen *n.*

dain·ti·ness ['deintinis] Leckerhaftigkeit *f*; Verwöhntheit *f*; Zartheit *f*, Feinheit *f*; '**dain·ty** ☐ 1. lecker, delikat; zart, fein; wählerisch, verwöhnt; 2. Leckerbissen *m*; Delikatesse *f.*

dair·y ['dɛəri] Molkerei *f*, Milchwirtschaft *f*; Milchgeschäft *n*; ⸾ **cat·tle** Milchvieh *n*; '⸾**-farm** Meierei *f*; Molkerei *f* und Käserei *f*; '⸾**·maid** Milch-, Kuhmagd *f*; '⸾**-man** Milchhändler *m.*

da·is ['deiis] Estrade *f.*

dai·sy ['deizi] 1. Gänseblümchen *n*; *push up the daisies* F die Radieschen von unten wachsen sehen (*tot sein*); 2. F reizend, lieb.

dale [deil] Tal *n.*

dal·li·ance ['dæliəns] Trödelei *f*; Schäkerei *f*; '**dal·ly** schäkern; vertrödeln.

dam[1] [dæm] Mutter *f* von Tieren.

dam[2] [⸾] 1. Deich *m*, Damm *m*; Wehr *n*; Talsperre *f*; 2. (ab)dämmen (*a. fig.*); ⸾ *in* eindeichen.

dam·age ['dæmidʒ] 1. Schaden *m*; ⸾s *pl.* ⚖ Schadenersatz *m*; 2. (be-) schädigen; '**dam·age·a·ble** leicht zu beschädigen(d).

dam·a·scene ['dæməsiːn] 1. damas-

zenisch, Damaszener...; 2. damaszieren; **dam·ask** ['dæməsk] 1. Damast *m*; Damaszenerstahl *m*; Rosenrot *n*; 2. damasten; rosenrot; 3. *Stahl* damaszieren; *Stoff* damastartig weben.

dame [deim] Dame *f* (*bsd. als Titel*); *sl.* Frau *f*, Mädchen *n.*

damn [dæm] 1. verdammen; verurteilen; *thea.* ablehnen; ⸾ *it!* verwünscht!, verdammt!; 2. Fluch *m*; *fig.* Pfifferling *m*; *I don't care a* ⸾*!* ich schere mich den Teufel darum!; **dam·na·ble** ☐ ['dæmnəbl] verdammenswert; abscheulich; **dam·'na·tion** Verdammnis *f*, Verdammung *f*; **dam·na·to·ry** ☐ ['ˏnətəri] verdammend; **damned** [dæmd] *adj. u. adv.* verdammt (*a.* = *sehr*); **damn·ing** ['dæmiŋ] schwer belastend.

Dam·o·cles ['dæməkliːz]: *sword of* ⸾ Damoklesschwert *n.*

damp [dæmp] 1. feucht, dunstig; 2. Feuchtigkeit *f*, Dunst *m*; *fig.* Gedrücktheit *f*, Lähmung *f*; ✗ Schwaden *m*; *cast a* ⸾ *over* e-n Schatten werfen auf (*acc.*); ⸾ *course* Isolierschicht *f*; 3. *a.* '**damp·en** an-, befeuchten; *Feuer, Eifer etc.* dämpfen; *fig.* niederdrücken; '**damp·er** Dämpfer *m* (*♩ u. fig.*); Ofenklappe *f*; '**damp·ish** etwas feucht; '**damp·proof** feuchtigkeitsbeständig.

dam·sel † ['dæmzəl] junges Mädchen *n.*

dam·son ⚲ ['dæmzən] Damaszenerpflaume *f*; ⸾ *cheese* Pflaumenmus *n.*

dance [dɑːns] 1. Tanz *m*; Ball *m*; *lead s.o. a* ⸾ j-m Scherereien machen; 2. tanzen (lassen); aufwallen; '⸾**-band** Tanzkapelle *f*; '⸾**-hall** Ballsaal *m*; '⸾**-hos·tess** Taxigirl *n*; '**danc·er** Tänzer(in).

danc·ing ['dɑːnsiŋ] Tanzen *n*; *attr.* Tanz...; '⸾**-girl** Tänzerin *f*; '⸾**-les·son** Tanzstunde *f*; '⸾**-room** Tanzsaal *m.*

dan·de·li·on ⚲ ['dændilaiən] Löwenzahn *m.*

dan·der *sl.* ['dændə] gereizte Stimmung *f*; *get s.o.'s* ⸾ *up* j. auf die Palme bringen.

dan·dle ['dændl] *Kind auf den Armen od. Knien* wiegen.

dan·druff ['dændrʌf] Kopfschuppen *f/pl.*

dan·dy ['dændi] 1. Dandy *m*, Stutzer

m; F prima Sache *f*; **2.** *bsd. Am.* F Klasse, prima, erstklassig; **dan-dy·ish** ['⁓diiʃ] stutzerhaft; **'dan-dy·ism** stutzerhaftes Wesen *n*.
Dane [dein] Däne *m*, Dänin *f*.
dan·ger ['deindʒə] Gefahr *f*; '**⁓-list:** *be on the* ⁓ F in Lebensgefahr sein; ⁓ **mon·ey** Gefahrenzulage *f*; **'dan-ger·ous** ☐ gefährlich; **'dan·ger--sig·nal** 🚩 Notsignal *n*.
dan·gle ['dæŋgl] baumeln (lassen); schlenkern (mit); *fig.* schwanken; ⁓ *about, after, round s.o.* j-m nach-laufen; **'dan·gler** Schürzenjäger *m*.
Dan·ish ['deiniʃ] dänisch.
dank [dæŋk] dunstig, feucht.
Da·nu·bi·an [dæ'nju:bjən] Donau...
daph·ne ['dæfni] ♣ Seidelbast *m*; Lorbeer *m*.
dap·per ☐ F ['dæpə] nett, fein; behend, gewandt.
dap·ple ['dæpl] sprenkeln, scheckig machen; **'dap·pled** scheckig; ge-sprenkelt; **'dap·ple-'grey** Apfel-schimmel *m*.
dare [dɛə] *v/i.* es wagen, sich (ge-) trauen, sich unterstehen; *I* ⁓ *say* ich darf wohl sagen; freilich; das glaube ich wohl; *v/t. et.* wagen; *j.* herausfordern; j-m trotzen; '**⁓--dev·il** Draufgänger *m*, Wagehals *m*; **'dar·ing** ☐ **1.** verwegen, kühn; **2.** Verwegenheit *f*, Kühnheit *f*.
dark [dɑːk] **1.** ☐ *mst* dunkel, finster; brünett; schwer verständlich; ge-heim(nisvoll); trüb(selig); **2.** Dun-kel(heit *f*) *n*; *before (after)* ⁓ vor (nach) Einbruch der Dunkelheit; *leap in the* ⁓ Sprung *m* ins Unge-wisse; ♀ **A·ges** *pl.* das frühe Mittel-alter; **'dark·en** (sich) verdunkeln; (sich) verfinstern; *fig.* verdüstern; verwirren; *never* ⁓ *s.o.'s door* nie mehr j-s Schwelle betreten; **dark horse** Außenseiter *m*; *fig.* unbe-schriebenes Blatt *n*; **'dark·ish** schwärzlich; **dark·ling** ['⁓liŋ] dun-kel (werdend); **'dark·ness** Dunkel-heit *f*, Finsternis *f*; **'dark·room** Dunkelkammer *f*; **dark·some** ['⁓-səm] *poet.* = *dark* 1; **'dark·y** F Schwarze *m*, *f* (*Neger*).
dar·ling ['dɑːliŋ] **1.** Liebling *m*; **2.** Lieblings...; geliebt.
darn[1] *sl.* [dɑːn] = **damn**.
darn[2] [⁓] **1.** Stopfnaht *f*; Stopfstelle *f*; **2.** stopfen; ausbessern; **'darn·er** Stopfpilz *m*.

darn·ing ['dɑːniŋ] Stopferei *f*; '**⁓--cot·ton** Stopfgarn *n*; '**⁓-nee·dle** Stopfnadel *f*.
dart [dɑːt] **1.** Wurfspieß *m*, -pfeil *m*, -speer *m*; Satz *m*, Sprung *m*; ⁓*s pl.* Wurfpfeilspiel *n*; **2.** *v/t.* werfen, schleudern; *v/i. fig.* schießen, (sich) stürzen (*at* auf *acc.*). [nismus *m*.｜
Dar·win·ism ['dɑːwinizəm] Darwi-｝
dash [dæʃ] **1.** Schlag *m*, (Zs.-)Stoß *m*; Klatschen *n*; *fig.* Schwung *m*; Vorstoß *m*, Ansturm *m* (*for* auf *acc.*); *fig.* Anflug *m*; Prise *f Salz etc.*; Schuß *m Rum etc.*; Feder-Strich *m* (*a. ʃ, tel.*); *typ.* Gedanken-strich *m*; *cut a* ⁓ eine gute Figur machen; *at a* ⁓ schnell; **2.** *v/t.* schlagen, werfen, schleudern; *mst* ⁓ *to pieces* zerschmettern; *Hoffnung* vernichten; (be)spritzen; vermen-gen; verwirren; ⁓ *down*, ⁓ *off Brief etc.* hinhauen; ⁓ *it! sl.* verdammt!; *v/i.* stoßen, schlagen; stürzen; stürmen; jagen; rasen; ⁓ *off* davon-jagen; ⁓ *through* durchbrechen, -waten; ⁓ *up* heranjagen; '**⁓-board** *mot.* Armaturenbrett *n*; Spritzbrett *n* (*am Pferdewagen*); **'dash·er** F ele-gante Erscheinung *f*; **'dash·ing** ☐ schneidig, forsch; F flott, fesch.
das·tard ['dæstəd] heimtückischer Kerl *m*; **'das·tard·ly** heimtückisch; feig.
da·ta ['deitə] *pl., Am. a. sg.* An-gaben *f/pl.*; Tatsachen *f/pl.*; Unter-lagen *f/pl.*; Daten *n/pl.*; *personal* ⁓ Personalangaben *f/pl.*; ⁓ **print·er** Datenschreiber *m*; ⁓ **pro·cess·ing** Datenverarbeitung *f*; ⁓ **trans·mis-sion** Datenübertragung *f*.
date[1] [deit] Dattel *f*.
date[2] [⁓] **1.** Datum *n*; Zeit *f*; ✉, ✝ Termin *m*; *bsd. Am.* F Verabredung *f*; Freund(in); *make a* ⁓ sich ver-abreden; *out of* ⁓ veraltet, unmo-dern; *to* ⁓ bis heute; *up to* ⁓ zeit-gemäß, modern; auf der Höhe (der Zeit); **2.** datieren; *bsd. Am.* F sich verabreden; ⁓ *back to*, ⁓ *from* her-rühren von, stammen aus, zurück-gehen auf; '**⁓-block** Abreißkalender *m*; **'dat·ed** altmodisch, veraltet, überholt; **'date·less** ohne Datum; **'date-line** Datumsgrenze *f*; **'date--stamp** Datums-, Poststempel *m*.
da·tive ['deitiv] *a.* ⁓ *case* Dativ *m*.
da·tum ['deitəm] Angabe *f*; Einzel-heit *f*; gegebene Größe *f od.* Tat-

sache *f*.

daub [dɔ:b] **1.** Schmiererei *f*, Sudelei *f*; **2.** (be)schmieren; *paint*. sudeln; **daub·(st)er** ['ˏ(st)ə] Sudler *m*, Farbenkleckser *m*.

daugh·ter ['dɔ:tə] Tochter *f*; ˏ *company* Tochtergesellschaft *f*; **ˏ-in-law** ['dɔ:tərinlɔ:] Schwiegertochter *f*; **'daugh·ter·ly** töchterlich.

daunt [dɔ:nt] entmutigen, schrekken; *nothing* ˏ*ed* unerschrocken; **'ˏ·less** furchtlos, unerschrocken.

dau·phin ['dɔ:fin] Dauphin *m* (*ältester Sohn des französischen Königs*).

dav·en·port ['dævnpɔ:t] Schreibschrank *m*, Sekretär *m*; Doppelbettcouch *f*, Wiener Bank *f*.

dav·it ⚓ ['dævit] Davit *m*, Bootskran *m*.

da·vy[1] ⚒ ['deivi] *a.* ˏ-*lamp* Sicherheitslampe *f*.

da·vy[2] *sl.* [ˏ] Eid *m*; *take one's* ˏ schwören.

daw *orn.* [dɔ:] Dohle *f*.

daw·dle F ['dɔ:dl] (ver)trödeln; bummeln; **'daw·dler** F Tagedieb *m*; *fig.* Schlafmütze *f*.

dawn [dɔ:n] **1.** Morgendämmerung *f*; *fig.* Anfang *m*, Anbruch *m*, Erwachen *n*; **2.** dämmern, tagen; *it* ˏ*ed upon him* es wurde ihm langsam klar.

day [dei] Tag *m*; *oft* ˏ*s pl.* (*bsd.* Lebens)Zeit *f*; Zeiten *pl.*; ˏ *off* (dienst)freier Tag *m*; *carry od. win the* ˏ den Sieg davontragen; *the other* ˏ neulich; *this* ˏ *week* heute in acht Tagen; *heute vor acht Tagen*; *let's call it a* ˏ machen wir Schluß für heute!; *have a nice* ˏ *Am.* mach's gut!; *pass the time of* ˏ *with s.o.* j-m guten Tag sagen; **'ˏ-book** ♰ Journal *n*; **'ˏ-boy** Tagesschüler *m*, Externe *m*; **'ˏ-break** Tagesanbruch *m*; **'ˏ-care cen·ter** *Am.* Kindertagesstätte *f*; **'ˏ-dream 1.** Wachtraum *m*; **2.** (mit offenen Augen) träumen; **'ˏ-fly** Eintagsfliege *f*; **'ˏ-'la·bo(u)r·er** Tagelöhner *m*; **'ˏ-light** Tageslicht *n*; ˏ-*saving time* Sommerzeit *f*; *beat the living* ˏ*s out of s.o.* j. grün und blau schlagen; **'ˏ-long** den ganzen Tag (dauernd); **'ˏ-'nur·se·ry** Kindergarten *m*; **'ˏ-star** Morgenstern *m*; **'ˏ-time** Tageszeit *f*; **'ˏ-to-'day** täglich; dauernd.

daze [deiz] verwirren; betäuben;

dazed benommen.

daz·zle ['dæzl] blenden; ⚓ tarnen.

D-Day ['di:dei] Tag *m* der Invasion (*6. 6. 1944*).

dea·con ['di:kən] Diakon(us) *m*; **'dea·con·ess** Diakonissin *f*; **'dea·con·ry** Diakonat *n*.

dead [ded] **1.** tot, gestorben; unempfindlich (*to* für); öde; still (*Wasser*, ⚓); matt (*Farben*, *Gold etc.*); blind (*Fenster etc.*); glanzlos (*Augen*); erloschen (*Feuer*); schal (*Getränk*); tief (*Schlaf*); totliegend (*Kapital etc.*); ⚡ stromlos; völlig, gänzlich; genau; ˏ *bargain* spottbillige Ware *f*; *at a* ˏ *bargain* zu e-m Spottpreis; ˏ *calm* Wind-, *fig.* Totenstille *f*; ˏ *centre* genaue Mitte *f*; ˏ *centre*, ˏ *point* toter Punkt *m*; ˏ *heat* totes Rennen *n*; ˏ *letter fig.* toter Buchstabe *m* (*nicht mehr beachtetes Gesetz*); unzustellbarer Brief *m*; ˏ *load* Leer-, Eigengewicht *n*; ˏ *loss* Totalverlust *m*; F Versager *m*; ˏ *march* Trauermarsch *m*; ˏ *set* entschlossener Angriff *m*; *a* ˏ *shot* ein Meisterschütze *m*; ˏ *wall* blinde Mauer *f*; ˏ *water* stehendes Wasser *n*; Kielwasser *n*; ˏ *weight* totes Gewicht *n*; *fig.* schwere Last *f*; ˏ *wood* Reisig *n*; *Am.* Plunder *m*; *play* ˏ sich totstellen; **2.** *adv.* gänzlich, völlig, total; durchaus; genau, (haar)scharf; ˏ *against* gerade *od.* ganz und gar (ent)gegen; ˏ *asleep* in tiefem Schlaf; ˏ *drunk* total betrunken; ˏ *sure* todsicher; ˏ *tired* todmüde; **3.** *the* ˏ der Tote; die Toten *pl.*; Totenstille *f*; *in the* ˏ *of winter* im tiefsten Winter; *in the* ˏ *of night* mitten in der Nacht; **'ˏ-a'live** halbtot; zum Sterben langweilig; **'ˏ-'beat 1.** todmüde; **2.** *Am. sl.* Schnorrer *m*, Herumtreiber *m*; **'dead·en** abstumpfen (*to* gegen); *fig.* (er)töten; (ab)schwächen; dämpfen; ⊕ mattieren.

dead...: ˏ *end* Sackgasse *f* (*a. fig.*); **'ˏ-end** ohne Ausgang; *fig.* ausweglos, zu nichts führend; ˏ *kids pl.* Straßenkinder *n/pl.*; ˏ *street* Sackgasse *f*; **'ˏ-head** blinder Passagier *m*; Freikarteninhaber *m*; **'ˏ-line** *Am.* Sperrlinie *f* im *Gefängnis*; Schlußtermin *m*; Stichtag *m*; **'ˏ-lock** Stillstand *m*, Stockung *f*; *fig.* toter Punkt *m*; **'dead·ly** tödlich; ˏ *pale* totenblaß; ˏ *enemy* Todfeind *m*; ˏ *sin* Todsünde *f*; **'dead·ness**

Erstarrung *f*; Unempfindlichkeit *f* (*to* gegen); Schalheit *f*, Mattheit *f*; ✝ Flaute *f*.

dead...: '~-'net·tle Taubnessel *f*; '~-'pan *Am. sl.* ausdruckslos (*Gesicht*).

deaf □ [def] taub (*to* gegen, für); ~ *and dumb* taubstumm; *turn a* ~ *ear* sich taub stellen (*to* gegen); ~ **aid** F Hörgerät *n*; '**deaf·en** taub machen; betäuben; '**deaf-'mute** Taubstumme *m*, *f*; '**deaf·ness** Taubheit *f*.

deal[1] [di:l] Brett *n*, Diele *f*; Fichtenholz *n*.

deal[2] [~] **1.** Teil *m*; Menge *f*; Kartengeben *n*; F Geschäft *n*; *Am. mst b. s.* Abmachung *f*; *a good* ~ ziemlich viel; *a great* ~ sehr viel; *give a square* ~ *to* gerecht werden (*dat.*); **2.** (*irr.*) *v/t.* (aus-, ver-, zu-) teilen; *Karten* geben; *e-n Schlag* versetzen (*at* s.o. j-m); *v/i.* handeln (*in* mit *e-r Ware*); verfahren; verkehren; ~ *with* sich befassen mit, behandeln; *have* ~*t with* s.o. fertig sein mit j-m; '**deal·er** Händler *m* (*in* mit *e-r Ware*); Kartengeber *m*; *plain* ~ ehrlicher Mensch *m*; *sharp* ~ gerissener Kerl *m*; '**deal·ing** *mst* ~*s pl.* Handlungsweise *f*; Verfahren *n*; Umgang *m*, (*bsd.* Geschäfts)Verkehr *m*.

dealt [delt] *pret. u. p.p. von* deal[2] 2.

dean [di:n] Dekan *m*; '**dean·er·y** Dekanat *n*.

dear [diə] **1.** □ teuer; lieb; **2.** Liebling *m*; herziges Geschöpf *n*; **3.** F *o(h)* ~*!*, ~ *me!* du meine Güte!; ach herrje!; '**dear·ness** Teuerkeit *f*, Wert *m*; **dearth** [də:θ] Teuerung *f*; Mangel *m*; **dear·y** F ['diəri] Liebling *m*, Schatz *m*.

death [deθ] Tod *m*; ~*s pl.* Todesfälle *m/pl.*; ~ *penalty* Todesstrafe *f*; *tired to* ~ todmüde; '~-**bed** Sterbebett *n*; '~-**blow** Todesstreich *m*, -stoß *m*; '~-**du·ty** Erbschaftssteuer *f*; ~ **grant** Sterbegeld *n*; '~-**less** unsterblich; '~-**like** totenähnlich; '**death·ly** tödlich; '**death-rate** Sterblichkeitsziffer *f*; '**death-roll** ✗ Gefallenenliste *f*; **death row** Todeszellen *f/pl.*; '**death's-head** Totenkopf *m*; '**death-trap** Todesstrecke *f*, -kurve *f etc.*; *fig.* Mausefalle *f*; '**death-war·rant** Todesurteil *n*.

dé·bâ·cle [dei'bɑ:kl] Zs.-bruch *m*, Katastrophe *f*.

de·bar [di'bɑ:] ausschließen (*from* von); *j.* hindern (*from an dat.*); *et.* verhindern. [schiffung *f*.\
de·bar·ka·tion [di:bɑ:'keiʃən] Aus-/
de·base [di'beis] verschlechtern; erniedrigen; verfälschen; **de'base·ment** Verschlechterung *f etc.*

de·bat·a·ble □ [di'beitəbl] strittig; umstritten; **de'bate 1.** Erörterung *f*, Debatte *f*; **2.** debattieren; erörtern; beraten; überlegen ([*on*] s.th. etwas, *with* o.s. bei sich); **de'bat·er** Diskussionsredner *m*; geschickter Disputant *m*.

de·bauch [di'bɔ:tʃ] **1.** Ausschweifung *f*; **2.** verderben; verführen; **deb·au·chee** [debɔ:'tʃi:] Wüstling *m*; **de·bauch·er·y** [di'bɔ:tʃəri] Ausschweifung *f*.

de·ben·ture [di'bentʃə] Schuldschein *m*; Rückzollschein *m*.

de·bil·i·tate [di'biliteit] schwächen; entkräften; **de·bil·i'ta·tion** Schwächung *f*; **de'bil·i·ty** Schwäche *f*.

deb·it ✝ ['debit] **1.** Debet *n*, Schuld *f*; *to one's* ~ zu j-s Lasten; **2.** *j.* belasten; *Summe* zu Lasten schreiben (*against od. to* s.o. j-m).

deb·o·nair [debə'nɛə] heiter, fröhlich.

de·bouch [di'bautʃ] hervorbrechen, -kommen; sich ergießen.

de·bris ['deibri:] Trümmer *n/pl.*, Schutt *m*.

debt [det] Schuld *f*; *active* ~ ausstehende Forderung *f*; ~ *collector* Schuldeneintreiber *m*; *owe* s.o. *a* ~ *of gratitude* j-m Dank schulden; *pay the* ~ *of nature*, *pay one's* ~ *to nature* der Natur s-n Tribut entrichten (*sterben*); '**debt·or** Schuldner(in).

de·bug [di:'bʌg] ⊕ den Defekt od. Fehler beheben bei; *sl. Raum* entwanzen (*Abhörgeräte entfernen*).

de·bunk F ['di:'bʌŋk] *fig.* vom Podest stoßen, den Nimbus nehmen (*dat.*).

de·bus [di:'bʌs] abladen; aussteigen (lassen).

dé·but ['deibu:] Debüt *n*; **dé·bu·tante** ['debju:tɑ:nt] Debütantin *f*.

dec·ade ['dekəid] Dekade *f*; Jahrzehnt *n*.

de·ca·dence ['dekədəns] Dekadenz *f*, Verfall *m*; **de·ca·dent** verfallend, morsch, dekadent.

de·caf·fei·nat·ed [di:'kæfineitid] koffeinfrei (*Kaffee*).

dec·a·log(ue) ['dekələg] Dekalog *m*, *die* Zehn Gebote *n/pl.*

de·camp [di'kæmp] aufbrechen; ausreißen, sich aus dem Staube machen; **de'camp·ment** Aufbruch *m*.

de·cant [di'kænt] abgießen; umfüllen; **de'cant·er** Karaffe *f*.

de·cap [di:'kæp] *Bombe etc.* entschärfen.

de·cap·i·tate [di'kæpiteit] enthaupten; *Am.* absägen (*entlassen*); **de·cap·i'ta·tion** Enthauptung *f*.

de·car·bon·ize *mot.* [di:'ka:bənaiz] von Verbrennungsrückständen säubern.

de·car·tel·i·za·tion [di:ka:təlai-'zaiʃən] Entflechtung *f von Kartellen.*

de·cath·lon [di'kæθlɔn] *Sport*: Zehnkampf *m*.

de·cay [di'kei] **1.** Verfall *m*; Fäulnis *f*; Verwesung *f*; **2.** verfallen; *fig.* schwinden; (ver)faulen; verwesen; ⁓ed *with age* altersschwach.

de·cease *bsd.* ⚹⚹ [di'si:s] **1.** Ableben *n*; **2.** sterben; *the* ⁓d der (die) Verstorbene.

de·ceit [di'si:t] Täuschung *f*; Betrug *m*; **de'ceit·ful** ⚊ [⁓ful] (be-) trügerisch; hinterlistig; **de'ceit·ful·ness** Hinterlist *f*.

de·ceiv·a·ble [di'si:vəbl] leicht zu betrügen(d); **de'ceive** betrügen; täuschen; verleiten (*into* zu); *be* ⁓d sich täuschen; **de'ceiv·er** Betrüger(in).

de·cel·er·ate [di:'seləreit] (sich) verlangsamen; **de·cel·er'a·tion** Verlangsamung *f*; ⁓ *lane mot.* Verzögerungsspur *f*.

De·cem·ber [di'sembə] Dezember *m*.

de·cen·cy ['di:snsi] Anstand *m*; '**de·cen·cies** *pl.* Anstandsformen *f/pl.*

de·cen·ni·al [di'senjəl] zehnjährig; **de'cen·ni·um** [⁓jəm] Dezennium*n*, Jahrzehnt *n*.

de·cent ⚊ ['di:snt] anständig, ordentlich; F annehmbar, nett.

de·cen·tral·i·za·tion [di:sentrəlai-'zeiʃən] Dezentralisierung *f*; **de·'cen·tral·ize** dezentralisieren.

de·cep·tion [di'sepʃən] Täuschung *f*, Betrug *m*; Trugbild *n*; **de'cep·tive** ⚊ täuschend, (be)trügerisch.

dec·i·bel *phys.* ['desibel] Dezibel *n*.

de·cide [di'said] (sich) entscheiden

(*in favour of, on, upon* für); bestimmen; zu dem Schluß kommen; beschließen; sich entschließen; **de·'cid·ed** ⚊ entschieden; bestimmt; entschlossen; **de'cid·er** *Sport*: Entscheidungskampf *m*.

de·cid·u·ous ♀, *zo.* ⚊ [di'sidjuəs] *jährlich* ab-, ausfallend; ⁓ *tree* Laubbaum *m*.

dec·i·mal ['desiməl] **1.** Dezimal...; ⁓ *point* Komma *n* (*in England*: Punkt *m*) *im Dezimalbruch*; ⁓ *system* Dezimalsystem *n*; *go* ⁓ das Dezimalsystem einführen; **2.** Dezimalbruch *m*; **dec·i·mate** ['⁓meit] dezimieren; **dec·i'ma·tion** Dezimierung *f*.

de·ci·pher [di'saifə] entziffern; entschlüsseln; **de'ci·pher·a·ble**[⁓rəbl] entzifferbar; **de'ci·pher·ment** Entzifferung *f*.

de·ci·sion [di'siʒən] Entscheidung*f*; ⚹⚹ Urteil *n*; Beschluß *m*; Entschluß *m*; Entschlossenheit *f*; *take a* ⁓ e-e Entscheidung treffen; e-n Entschluß fassen; **de·ci·sive** ⚊ [di-'saisiv] entscheidend; ausschlaggebend; entschieden.

de·civ·i·lize [di:'sivilaiz] entzivilisieren.

deck [dek] **1.** ⚓ Deck *n*, Verdeck *n*; *bsd. Am. ein* Spiel *n* Karten; *on* ⁓ auf Deck; *Am.* F bereit, auf dem Posten; **2.** *lit.* zieren, schmücken; ⚓ mit e-m Deck versehen; '⁓-chair Liegestuhl *m*; '⁓-hand ⚓ Matrose *m*.

deck·le-edged ['dekl'edʒd] mit Büttenrand (*Papier*).

de·claim [di'kleim] deklamieren; eifern (*against* gegen).

dec·la·ma·tion [deklə'meiʃən] Deklamation *f*; öffentliche Rede *f*; **de·clam·a·to·ry** [di'klæmətəri] deklamatorisch.

de·clar·a·ble [di'kleərəbl] steuer-, zollpflichtig; **dec·la·ra·tion** [deklə'reiʃən] Erklärung *f*; Zollerklärung *f*; *make a* ⁓ e-e Erklärung abgeben; **de·clar·a·to·ry** [di'kleərətəri] erklärend; ausdrücklich; **de·'clare** *v/t.* erklären, kundtun; behaupten; *Zollpflichtiges* deklarieren; ⁓ *o.s.* sich erklären; ⁓ *off* rückgängig machen; *v/i.* sich erklären, sich aussprechen; *well, I* ⁓! F na aber!; **de'clared** ⚊ ausgesprochen, erklärt.

de·class·i·fy ['di:'klæsifai] die Geheimhaltungspflicht aufheben für, *Information* freigeben.

de·clen·sion [di'klenʃən] Abfall *m* (*Neigung*); Verfall *m*; *gr.* Deklination *f*.

de·clin·a·ble [di'klainəbl] deklinierbar; **dec·li·na·tion** [dekli'neiʃən] Neigung *f*; Abweichung *f*; *ast.*, *phys.* Deklination *f*; **de·cline** [di'klain] **1.** Abnahme *f*; *fig.* Niedergang *m*; Verfall *m*; ⚕ Abzehrung *f*; **2.** *v/t.* neigen, biegen; *gr.* deklinieren; ablehnen; *v/i.* sich neigen; abnehmen; verfallen.

de·cliv·i·ty [di'kliviti] Abhang *m*; **de·cliv·i·tous** abschüssig.

de·clutch *mot.* ['di:'klʌtʃ] auskuppeln.

de·coct [di'kɔkt] absied:n; **de·coction** Abkochung *f*; *bsd. pharm.* Dekokt *n*.

de·code *tel.* ['di:'kəud] entschlüsseln.

dé·colle·té(e) [dei'kɔltei] dekolletiert.

de·col·o(u)r·ize [di:'kʌləraiz] entfärben, bleichen.

de·com·pose [di:kəm'pəuz] zerlegen; (sich) zersetzen; verwesen; **de·com·po·si·tion** [di:kɔmpə'ziʃən] Zerlegung *f etc.*

de·con·tam·i·nate ['di:kən'tæmineit] entgiften; **'de·con·tam·i'na·tion** Entgiftung *f*; ~ squad Entgiftungstrupp *m*.

de·con·trol ['di:kən'trəul] **1.** die Zwangswirtschaft aufheben; *Waren, Handel* freigeben; **2.** Aufhebung *f* der Zwangswirtschaft.

dé·cor *thea.* ['deikɔ:] Bühnenbild *n*, Ausstattung *f*.

dec·o·rate ['dekəreit] (ver)zieren; schmücken; *mit e-m Orden* dekorieren; **dec·o'ra·tion** Verzierung *f*; Schmuck *m*; Orden(sauszeichnung *f*) *m*; ⚓ *Day Am.* Heldengedenktag *m*; **dec·o·ra·tive** ['dekərətiv] Zier..., Schmuck...; **dec·o·ra·tor** ['ˌreitə] Dekorateur *m*, Maler *m*, Anstreicher *m*.

dec·o·rous ☐ ['dekərəs] anständig.

de·cor·ti·cate [di'kɔ:tikeit] entrinden; abschälen.

de·co·rum [di'kɔ:rəm] Anstand *m*.

de·coy [di'kɔi] **1.** Entenfang *m*, -falle *f*; *a.* ~ *bird*, ~ *duck* Lockvogel *m* (*a. fig.*); Köder *m*; **2.** ködern, locken.

de·crease 1. ['di:kri:s] Abnahme *f*; *on the* ~ im Abnehmen (begriffen); **2.** [di:'kri:s] (sich) vermindern; abnehmen, zurückgehen.

de·cree [di'kri:] **1.** Dekret *n*, Verordnung *f*, Erlaß *m*; ⚖ Entscheid *m*; Ratschluß *m Gottes*; Fügung *f des Schicksals*; **2.** beschließen; verordnen, verfügen; ~ **ni·si** ⚖ [ˌ~ 'naisai] vorläufiges Scheidungsurteil *n*. [nahme *f*.)

dec·re·ment ['dekrimənt] Ab-)

de·crep·it [di'krepit] altersschwach; **de'crep·i·tude** [ˌtju:d] Altersschwäche *f*.

de·cres·cent [di'kresnt] abnehmend (*Mond*).

de·cry [di'krai] in Verruf bringen; heruntermachen.

dec·u·ple ['dekjupl] **1.** zehnfach; **2.** Zehnfache *n*; **3.** verzehnfachen.

ded·i·cate ['dedikeit] widmen; (ein)weihen; **ded·i'ca·tion** Widmung *f*; Zueignung *f*; Hingabe *f*; Einweihung *f*; **'ded·i·ca·tor** Widmende *m*, *f*; **ded·i·ca·to·ry** ['ˌ~kətəri] Widmungs..., Zueignungs...

de·duce [di'dju:s] ab-, herleiten; folgern; **de'duc·i·ble** herleitbar.

de·duct [di'dʌkt] abziehen; **de'duc·tion** Abzug *m*; ✝ Rabat *m*; Schlußfolgerung *f*; **de'duc·tive** folgernd, deduktiv.

deed [di:d] **1.** Tat *f*; Helden-, Großtat *f*; Urkunde *f*, Dokument *n*; **2.** *Am.* urkundlich übertragen (*to* auf *acc.*).

dee·jay ⊦ ['di:dʒei] Diskjockey *m*.

deem [di:m] *v/t.* halten für; *v/i.* denken, urteilen (*of* über *acc.*).

deep [di:p] **1.** ☐ tief; gründlich; schlau; scharfsinnig; innig; vertieft (*in* in *acc.*); dunkel (*a. fig.*); verborgen; ~ *hit Boxen*: Tiefschlag *m*; *in* ~ *water(s) fig.* in Schwierigkeiten; **2.** Tiefe *f*; *poet.* Meer *n*; '~·'**breathing** Atemübungen *f pl.*; '**deep·en** (sich) vertiefen; dunkler machen *od.* werden (*Farben*); (sich) verstärken (*Kummer etc.*).

deep...: '~·'**freeze 1.** tiefkühlen; **2.** Tiefkühlfach *n*, -truhe *f*; '~·'**fro·zen** tiefgefroren, Tiefkühl...; '~·'**fry** fritieren; ~*ing pan* Friteuse *f*; '~·'**laid** sorgfältig geplant u. geheimgehalten; '**deep·ness** Tiefe *f*.

deep...: '~·'**root·ed** tiefwurzelnd; '~·'**sea** Tiefsee...; '~·'**seat·ed** tiefsitzend, tief eingewurzelt; '~-set tiefliegend (*Augen*).

deer [diə] Rotwild *n*; Hirsch *m*; Reh *n*; '~-lick Salzlecke *f*; '~-shot Rehposten *m*; '~-skin Hirsch-, Rehleder *n*; '~-stalk·er Pirschjäger *m*; '~-stalk·ing Pirsch(jagd)*f*.

de-es·ca·late ✕ [di:'eskəleit] deeskalieren; **de-es·ca'la·tion** Deeskalation *f*.

de·face [di'feis] entstellen, verunstalten; ausstreichen; **de'face·ment** Entstellung *f etc.*

de fac·to [di:'fæktəu] tatsächlich, De-facto-...; de facto.

de·fal·ca·tion [di:fæl'keiʃən] Unterschlagung *f*, Veruntreuung *f*; *das* unterschlagene Geld.

def·a·ma·tion [defə'meiʃən] Verleumdung *f*; **de·fam·a·to·ry** [di'fæmətəri] verleumderisch; Schmäh...; **de·fame** [di'feim] verleumden; verunglimpfen; **de-'fam·er** Verleumder(in).

de·fault [di'fɔːlt] **1.** Nichterscheinen *n vor Gericht*; Säumigkeit *f im Zahlen*; Verzug *m*; *judgement by ~* ᵗᵗₜ Versäumnisurteil *n*; *in ~ of which* in Ermangelung dessen; widrigenfalls; *make ~* nicht erscheinen; nicht zahlen; **2.** s-n Verbindlichkeiten nicht nachkommen; im Verzug sein (*with* mit); ᵗᵗₜ wegen Nichterscheinens verurteilen; **de-'fault·er** zum Termin Nichterscheinende *m, f*; säumiger Zahler *m*; ✕ Delinquent *m*.   [rung *f*.\

de·fea·sance [di'fi:zəns] Annullie-\
de·feat [di'fi:t] **1.** Niederlage *f*; Besiegung *f*; Vereitelung *f*; **2.** ✕ schlagen, besiegen; vereiteln, vernichten; *parl.* zu Fall bringen; **de'feat·ist** Defätist *m*.

def·e·cate ['defikeit] den Darm entleeren, Stuhlgang haben.

de·fect [di'fekt] Mangel *m*; Fehler *m*; **de'fec·tion** Abfall *m* (*from* von); Treubruch *m*; **de'fec·tive** □ mangelhaft; unvollständig (*a. gr.*); schadhaft, fehlerhaft; ermangelnd (*in gen.*); **de'fec·tor** *pol.* Überläufer *m*.

de·fence, *Am.* **de·fense** [di'fens] Verteidigung *f*; Schutzmaßnahme *f*; *~ mechanism* Abwehrmechanismus *m od.* -maßnahme *f*; *~ spending* ✕ Verteidigungsausgaben *f pl.*; *witness for the ~* Entlastungszeuge *m*; **de'fence-less** schutzlos, wehrlos; ✕ unver-

teidigt.

de·fend [di'fend] verteidigen (*against* gegen); schützen (*from* vor *dat.*); **de'fen·dant** ᵗᵗₜ Beklagte *m, f*; **de'fend·er** Verteidiger(in).

de·fen·si·ble [di'fensəbl] zu verteidigen(d), haltbar; vertretbar; **de'fen·sive 1.** □ verteidigend; Verteidigungs...; Schutz...; **2.** Defensive *f*; *be on the ~* sich in der Defensive befinden; *act od. stand on the ~* sich defensiv verhalten.

de·fer[1] [di'fə:] auf-, verschieben; *Am.* ✕ zurückstellen; *~red payment, payment on ~red terms* Ratenzahlung *f*.

de·fer[2] [~] (*to*) sich fügen (in *acc.*); sich beugen (vor *dat.*); nachgeben (*dat.*); **def·er·ence** ['defərəns] Ehrerbietung *f*; Nachgiebigkeit *f*; *in ~ to, out of ~ to* aus Rücksicht gegen; **def·er·en·tial** □ [~'renʃəl] ehrerbietig.

de·fer·ment [di'fə:mənt] Aufschub *m*; *Am.* ✕ Zurückstellung *f*.

de·fi·ance [di'faiəns] Herausforderung *f*; *bid ~ to* Trotz bieten (*dat.*); *in ~ of j-m* zum Hohn; **de'fi·ant** □ herausfordernd; trotzig.

de·fi·cien·cy [di'fiʃənsi] Unzulänglichkeit *f*; Mangel *m*; = *deficit*; **de'fi·cient** mangelhaft; unzureichend; *be ~ in* Mangel haben an (*dat.*).   [betrag *m*.\

def·i·cit ['defisit] Defizit *n*, Fehl-\
de·fi·er [di'faiə] Herausforderer *m*; Verächter *m*.

de·file[1] **1.** ['di:fail] Engpaß *m*, Hohlweg *m*; **2.** [di'fail] defilieren, vorbeiziehen.

de·file[2] [di'fail] beschmutzen, verunreinigen; beflecken, schänden; entweihen; **de'file·ment** Befleckung *f etc.*

de·fin·a·ble [di'fainəbl] bestimm-, erklär-, definierbar; **de'fine** definieren; erklären; genau bestimmen; **def·i·nite** ['definit] □ bestimmt; deutlich; genau; **def·i-'ni·tion** Definition *f*; (Begriffs-) Bestimmung *f*; Erklärung *f*; *opt.* Schärfe *f*; **de·fin·i·tive** [di-'finitiv] bestimmt; entscheidend; endgültig.

de·flate [di'fleit] Luft ablassen aus *Ballon etc.*; die Inflation beseitigen; **de'fla·tion** Entleerung *f*; Deflation *f e-r Währung*; **de'fla·tion-a·ry** Deflations...

de·flect [di'flekt] ablenken; abweichen; **de·flec·tion, mst de·flex·ion** [di'flekʃən] Ablenkung *f*; Abweichung *f*.

de·flow·er [di:'flauə] entjungfern; *fig.* schänden.

de·fo·li·ate [di:'fəulieit] sich entlauben.

de·form [di'fɔːm] entstellen, verunstalten; ‿ed verwachsen; **de·for·ma·tion** [diːfɔː'meiʃən] Entstellung *f*; Abformung *f* **de·form·i·ty** [di'fɔːmiti] Häßlichkeit *f*; Auswuchs *m* (*a. fig.*); Mißgestalt *f*.

de·fraud [di'frɔːd] betrügen (*of* um).

de·fray [di'frei] *Kosten* tragen *od.* bestreiten.

de·freez·er *mot.* [di:'friːzə] Frostschutzscheibe *f*.

de·frost ['diː'frɔst] entfrosten, ab-, auftauen; **de'frost·er** Entfroster *m*; **de'frost·ing** Entfrosten *n*; ‿ *rear window mot.* heizbare Heckscheibe *f*.

deft □ [deft] gewandt, flink.

de·funct [di'fʌŋkt] 1. verstorben; *fig.* veraltet; 2. Verstorbene *m, f*.

de·fy [di'fai] herausfordern; trotzen, sich widersetzen (*dat.*); mißachten.

de·gen·er·a·cy [di'dʒenərəsi] Entartung *f*; Verkommenheit *f*; **de'gen·er·ate** 1. [‿reit] aus-, entarten; 2. □ [‿rit] entartet; **de·gen·er·a·tion** [‿'reiʃən] Entartung *f*; **de'gen·er·a·tive** [‿rətiv] Entartungs...

deg·ra·da·tion [degrə'deiʃən] Degradierung *f*; Absetzung *f*; **de·grade** [di'greid] *v/t.* degradieren; absetzen; herabwürdigen; erniedrigen; demütigen; *fig.* verringern; *v/i.* entarten.

de·gree [di'griː] Grad *m* (*a. geogr., gr., ⯑, phys., univ.*); Verwandtschaftsgrad *m*; *fig.* Stufe *f*, Schritt *m* (*to* zu); Rang *m*, Stand *m*; *by* ‿s allmählich, nach u. nach; *in no* ‿ in keiner Weise; *in some* ‿ einigermaßen; *to a* ‿ F außerordentlich, ziemlich; *take one's* ‿ sein Abschlußexamen machen.

de·hu·man·ize [di:'hjuːmənaiz] entmenschlichen.

de·hy·drate [di:'haidreit] austrocknen; **de'hy·drat·ed** Trocken...; ‿ *eggs pl.* Trockenei *n*; ‿ *potatoes pl.* Trockenkartoffeln *f/pl.*; ‿ *vegetables pl.* Trockengemüse *n*.

de·ice 🛪 ['di:'ais] enteisen; **de'ic·er** Enteisungsanlage *f*.

de·i·fi·ca·tion [di:ifi'keiʃən] Vergötterung *f*; Vergöttlichung *f*; **de·i·fy** ['di:ifai] vergöttern; vergöttlichen.

deign [dein] geruhen; gewähren.

de·ism ['di:izəm] Deismus *m*; **de·ist** Deist(in); **de'is·tic, de'is·ti·cal** □ deistisch.

de·i·ty ['di:iti] Gottheit *f*.

de·ject [di'dʒekt] entmutigen; **de·'ject·ed** □ niedergeschlagen; **de·'ject·ed·ness, de'jec·tion** Niedergeschlagenheit *f*.

de ju·re [di:'dʒuəri] rechtmäßig, De-jure-...; de jure.

dek·ko *sl.* ['dekəu] kurzer Blick *m*; *have a* ‿ mal schauen.

de·lay [di'lei] 1. Aufschub *m*, Verzug *m*; Verzögerung *f*, Verspätung *f*; 2. *v/t.* aufschieben; verzögern; aufhalten; hinhalten; *v/i.* zögern; Zeit verlieren; ‿ing *tactics pl.* Verzögerungstaktik *f*; **de'layed-'ac·tion** Verzögerungs...

de·le *typ.* ['di:li:] 1. Tilgungszeichen *n*; 2. tilgen.

de·lec·ta·ble *oft iro.* □ [di'lektəbl] ergötzlich; **de·lec·ta·tion** [di:lek·'teiʃən] Ergötzung *f*.

del·e·ga·cy ['deligəsi] Abordnung *f*; **del·e·gate** 1. ['‿geit] delegieren; abordnen; übertragen (*to s.o.* j-m); 2. ['‿git] Abgeordnete *m, f*, Delegierte *m, f*; Referent *m*; **del·e·ga·tion** [‿'geiʃən] Abordnung *f*; *Am. parl.* die Kongreßabgeordneten *m/pl.* e-s Staates; Überweisung *f*.

de·lete [di'li:t] streichen, tilgen; **del·e·te·ri·ous** □ [deli'tiəriəs] schädlich; **de·le·tion** [di'li:ʃən] Streichung *f*.

delf(t) [delf(t)] Delfter Steingut *n*.

de·lib·er·ate 1. [di'libəreit] *v/t.* überlegen, erwägen; *v/i.* nachdenken; beraten (*on* über *acc.*); 2. □ [‿rit] bedachtsam, besonnen; wohlüberlegt; bewußt, absichtlich, vorsätzlich; **de'lib·er·ate·ness** Bedachtsamkeit *f*; **de·lib·er·a·tion** [‿'reiʃən] Überlegung *f*; Beratung *f*; Bedächtigkeit *f*; **de'lib·er·a·tive** □ [‿rətiv] überlegend; beratend.

del·i·ca·cy ['delikəsi] Wohlgeschmack *m*; Leckerbissen *m*; Feinheit *f*, Zartheit *f* (*a. fig.*); Schwächlichkeit *f*; Mißlichkeit *f*; Zartgefühl *n*, Feinfühligkeit *f*; **del·i·cate** ['ˏkit] ⎕ schmackhaft; lecker; zart (*a. fig.*); fein; schwach; mißlich, heikel; empfindlich; zartfühlend, feinfühlig; wählerisch, verwöhnt; **del·i·ca·tes·sen** [delikə-'tesn] Feinkost(geschäft *n*) *f*.

de·li·cious [di'liʃəs] köstlich.

de·light [di'lait] **1.** Lust *f*, Freude *f*, Wonne *f*, Entzücken *n*; take ⁓ in sich ein Vergnügen aus *et.* machen; **2.** entzücken; (sich) erfreuen (*in* an *dat.*); ⁓ *to inf.* Freude daran finden zu *inf.*; **de'light·ful** ⎕ [ˏful] reizend, entzückend.

de·lim·it [di:'limit], **de·lim·i·tate** [di'limiteit] abgrenzen; **de·lim·i·'ta·tion** Abgrenzung *f*.

de·lin·e·ate [di'linieit] entwerfen; zeichnen; schildern; **de·lin·e·'a·tion** Entwurf *m*; Schilderung *f*; **de'lin·e·a·tor** Schilderer *m*.

de·lin·quen·cy [di'liŋkwənsi] Vergehen *n*; Kriminalität *f*; Pflichtvergessenheit *f*; **de'lin·quent 1.** straffällig; pflichtvergessen; **2.** Verbrecher(in).

del·i·quesce [deli'kwes] zergehen.

de·lir·i·ous ⎕ [di'liriəs] irre, wahnsinnig; rasend (*with* vor *dat.*); **de·'lir·i·ous·ness** Wahnsinn *m*; **de·'lir·i·um** [ˏəm] Delirium *n*, Fieberwahn *m*; Verzückung *f*; ⁓ tremens [ˏəm 'tri:menz] Säuferwahnsinn *m*.

de·liv·er [di'livə] befreien, retten (*from* von, aus); *a.* ⁓ up über-, ausliefern; *Botschaft* ausrichten; *Meinung* äußern; *Rede etc.* vortragen, halten; ✗ entbinden (*of* von); *Waren etc.* abgeben, liefern; ⍟ zustellen, austragen; *Schlag* führen; *Ball* werfen; **de'liv·er·a·ble** zu (über)liefern(d); **de'liv·er·ance** Befreiung *f*; (Meinungs)Äußerung *f*, Ausführung *f*; **de'liv·er·er** Befreier(in); Überbringer(in); **de·'liv·er·y** ✗ Entbindung *f*; Lieferung *f*, Ablieferung *f*; ⍟ Austragen *n*, Zustellung *f*; Übergabe *f e-r Urkunde*; Vortrag *m*; *Kricket:* Wurf *m*; special ⁓ Zustellung *f* durch Eilboten; on ⁓ of bei Lieferung von; **de·liv·er·y charge** Zustellgebühr *f*; **de'liv·er·y-note** Lieferschein *m*; **de·liv·er·y room** ✗ Entbindungssaal *m*, -zimmer *n*; **de'liv·er·y-truck**, **de'liv·er·y-van** Lieferwagen *m*.

dell [del] kleines Tal *n*.

de·louse ['di:'laus] entlausen; **de·'lous·ing cen·tre** Entlausungsanstalt *f*.

del·ta ['deltə] Delta *n*.

de·lude [di'lu:d] täuschen; verleiten (*into* zu).

del·uge ['delju:dʒ] **1.** Überschwemmung *f*; *fig.* Flut *f*; ♀ Sintflut *f*; **2.** überfluten, -schwemmen (*with* mit).

de·lu·sion [di'lu:ʒən] Täuschung *f*, Verblendung *f*; Wahn *m*; **de'lu·sive** [ˏsiv] ⎕, **de'lu·so·ry** [ˏsəri] (be)trügerisch; täuschend.

delve [delv] graben; suchen, forschen.

dem·a·gog·ic, **dem·a·gog·i·cal** [demə'gɔgik(əl)] demagogisch; **dem·a·gogue** ['ˏgɔg] Demagoge *m*; **'dem·a·gog·y** Demagogie *f*.

de·mand [di'mɑ:nd] **1.** Verlangen *n*; Forderung *f* (*on* an *acc.*); Bedarf *m* (*for* an *dat.*); ✝ Nachfrage *f* (*for* nach); ♃ Rechtsanspruch *m* (*on* an *acc.*); in ⁓ begehrt, gesucht, gefragt; on ⁓ auf Verlangen; **2.** verlangen, fordern (*of* von); erfordern; ♃ beanspruchen; fragen (nach); ⁓ note Zahlungsaufforderung *f*.

de·mar·cate ['di:mɑ:keit] abgrenzen; **de·mar'ca·tion** Abgrenzung *f*; *mst* line of ⁓ Demarkations-, Grenzlinie *f*.

dé·marche *pol.* ['deimɑ:ʃ] Démarche *f*, diplomatischer Schritt *m*.

de·mean¹ [di'mi:n] *mst* ⁓ o.s. sich erniedrigen.

de·mean² [ˏ] ⁓ o.s. sich benehmen; **de'mean·o(u)r** Benehmen *n*.

de·ment·ed [di'mentid] wahnsinnig.

de·mer·it [di:'merit] Unwürdigkeit *f*; Mangel *m*, Fehler *m*, Nachteil *m*.

de·mesne [di'mein] (Land-, Grund-) Besitz *m*; Domäne *f*; *fig.* Gebiet *n*.

demi... ['demi] Halb..., halb...

dem·i·god ['demigɔd] Halbgott *m*; **'dem·i·john** große Korbflasche *f*, Glasballon *m*.

de·mil·i·ta·ri·za·tion ['di:militərai-'zeiʃən] Entmilitarisierung *f*; **'de·mil·i·ta·rize** entmilitarisieren.

dem·i·mon·daine ['demimɔn'dein] Halbweltdame *f*; **dem·i·monde** ['ˏˏmɔ:nd] Halbwelt *f*.

de·mise [di'maiz] **1.** Ableben *n*; *Besitz*-Übertragung *f*; **2.** übertragen; vermachen.

de·mist *mot.* [di:'mist] *Scheiben* beschlagfrei machen; **de'mist·er** Entfroster *m*.

demo F ['deməu] Demonstration *f*.

de·mob *sl.* [di:'mɔb] = *demobilize*; **de·mo·bi·li·za·tion** ['di:məubilai-'zeiʃən] Demobilisierung *f*; **de'mo·bi·lize** demobilisieren.

de·moc·ra·cy [di'mɔkrəsi] Demokratie *f*; **dem·o·crat** ['deməkræt] Demokrat(in); **dem·o'crat·ic, dem·o'crat·i·cal** □ demokratisch; **de·moc·ra·tize** [di'mɔkrətaiz] demokratisieren.

dé·mo·dé [dei'məudei] altmodisch.

de·mog·ra·phy [di:'mɔgrəfi] Demographie *f*.

de·mol·ish [di'mɔliʃ] nieder-, abreißen; *fig.* zerstören; herunterreißen; F verputzen (*essen*); **dem·o·li·tion** [demə'liʃən] Niederreißen *n*; Abbruch *m*; Zerstörung *f*.

de·mon ['di:mən] Dämon *m*, böser Geist *m*; *he is a ⁓ for work* F er ist von der Arbeit besessen; **de·mo·ni·ac** [di'məuniæk] **1.** *a.* **de·mo·ni·a·cal** □ [di:məu'naiəkəl] dämonisch; teuflisch; **2.** Besessene *m*, *f*; **de·mon·ic** [di:'mɔnik] dämonisch; übernatürlich.

de·mon·stra·ble □ ['demənstrəbl] nachweislich; **dem·on·strate** ['⁓streit] demonstrieren, zeigen, vorführen, anschaulich darstellen, dartun; beweisen (*from* aus); **dem·on·'stra·tion** Demonstration *f*; anschauliche Darstellung *f*; Beweis *m*; Äußerung *f*, Bezeigung *f* *von Gefühlen*; *pol.* Kundgebung *f*; ✗ Scheinmanöver *n*; ⁓ *car mot.* Vorführwagen *m*; **de·mon·stra·tive** [di-'mɔnstrətiv] **1.** □ anschaulich darstellend *od.* zeigend (*of acc.*); überzeugend; demonstrativ; *gr.* hinweisend; ausdrucksvoll; auffällig, überschwenglich; **2.** *gr.* hinweisendes Fürwort *n*; **dem·on·stra·tor** ['demənstreitə] Erklärer *m*; *anat.* Prosektor *m*; *pol.* Demonstrant *m*.

de·mor·al·i·za·tion [dimɔrəlai-'zeiʃən] Sittenverfall *m*; **de'mor·al·ize** demoralisieren; entmutigen.

de·mote *Am.* [di:'məut] degradieren; *Schule*: zurückversetzen; **de·'mo·tion** Degradierung *f etc.*

de·mur [di'mə:] **1.** Einwendung *f*, Widerrede *f*; **2.** Einwendungen erheben (*to* gegen).

de·mure □ [di'mjuə] ernst, gesetzt; zimperlich; prüde; **de'mure·ness** Gesetztheit *f*; Zimperlichkeit *f*.

de·mur·rage ⚓, 🚋 [di'mʌridʒ] Überliegezeit *f*; Liegegeld *n*; **de·'mur·rer** ⚖ Einwand *m*.

den [den] Höhle *f*; Grube *f*; *sl.* Bude *f*.

de·na·tion·al·ize [di:'næʃnəlaiz] reprivatisieren, entstaatlichen.

de·na·ture 🜂 [di:'neitʃə] denaturieren.

de·na·zi·fi·ca·tion ['di:na:tsifi'keiʃən] Entnazifizierung *f*; **de'na·zi·fy** [⁓fai] entnazifizieren.

de·ni·a·ble [di'naiəbl] abzuleugnen(d); **de'ni·al** Leugnen *n*; Verleugnung *f*; Verneinung *f*; abschlägige Antwort *f*.

de·ni·er¹ [di'naiə] Verneiner(in), Leugner(in); Verweigerer(in).

de·nier² ['deniei] Denier *n* (*Feinheitsmaß für Seide und Chemiefasern*).

den·i·grate ['denigreit] (*fig.* an-) schwärzen.

den·im ['denim] Baumwolldrillich *m*.

den·i·zen ['denizn] Bewohner *m*.

de·nom·i·nate [di'nɔmineit] (be-) nennen; **de·nom·i'na·tion** Benennung *f*; Klasse *f*; Sekte *f*; Konfession *f*; Nennwert *m*; **de·nom·i·na·tion·al** [⁓'neiʃənl] Sekten..., konfessionell; ⁓ *school* Bekenntnisschule *f*; **de'nom·i·na·tive** [⁓nə-tiv] benennend; **de'nom·i·na·tor** ⚕ [⁓neitə] Nenner *m*; *common ⁓* gemeinsamer Nenner *m* (*a. fig.*).

de·no·ta·tion [di:nəu'teiʃən] Bezeichnung *f*; Bedeutung *f*; **de·no·ta·tive** [di'nəutətiv] bezeichnend; bedeutend (*of acc.*); **de'note** bezeichnen; bedeuten.

de·nounce [di'nauns] anzeigen, denunzieren; brandmarken, anprangern; *Vertrag* kündigen; **de·'nounce·ment** öffentliche Anklage *f*; Brandmarkung *f*.

dense □ [dens] dicht, dick (*Nebel*); gedrängt; beschränkt, schwer von Begriff; **'dense·ness** Dichtigkeit *f*; *fig.* Beschränktheit *f*; **'den·si·ty** Dichtigkeit *f*; *phys.* Dichte *f*.

dent [dent] **1.** Beule *f*, Einbeulung *f*; **2.** ver-, einbeulen.

den·tal ['dentl] **1.** Zahn...; ⁓ *floss* Zahnseide *f*; ⁓ *surgeon* Zahnarzt *m*; **2.** Dentallaut *m*; **den·tate** ['⁓teit] 🜊

gezähnt; **den·ti·frice** ['ⁿtifris] Zahn-
pulver *n*, -paste *f*; '**den·tist** Zahnarzt
m; '**den·tist·ry** Zahnheilkunde *f*;
den'ti·tion Zahnen *n*; **den·ture**
['ⁿtʃə] (künstliches) Gebiß *n*.

den·u·da·tion [di:nju:'deiʃən] Ent-
blößung *f*; geol. Abtragung *f*; **de-**
nude [di'nju:d] (*of*) entblößen
(*gen.*); *fig.* berauben (*gen.*).

de·nun·ci·a·tion [dinʌnsi'eiʃən] Anzeige *f*, Denunziation *f*; Kündigung
f; **de'nun·ci·a·tor** Denunziant *m*;
de'nun·ci·a·to·ry [ⁿətəri] denun-
zierend; brandmarkend.

de·ny [di'nai] verneinen, leugnen;
verleugnen; bestreiten; verweigern,
versagen, abschlagen; *j.* abweisen;
~ *o.s. s.th.* sich et. versagen; ~ *o.s.*
(*to a visitor*) sich verleugnen lassen.

de·o·dor·ant [di'əudərənt] desodorierendes Mittel *n*; **de'o·dor·ize**
geruchlos machen, desodorieren;
de'o·dor·iz·er desodorierendes
Mittel *n*; Lufttreiniger *m*.

de·part [di'pa:t] *v/i.* abreisen, abfahren, absegeln (*for* nach); F scheiden (*from* von); abstehen, (ab-)
weichen, abgehen (*from* von); verscheiden; *the* ~*ed der od.* die Verstorbene; die Verstorbenen *pl.*; *v/t.*
~ *this life* aus diesem Leben scheiden; **de'part·ment** Abteilung *f*;
Bezirk *m*, Ressort *n*; ✝ Branche *f*;
Am. Ministerium *n*; ♀ *of Education*
and Science, *Am.* ♀ *of Education* Unterrichtsministerium *n*; ♀ *of the Environ-*
ment Umweltschutzministerium *n*;
State ♀ Außenministerium *n*; ~ *store*
Kauf-, Warenhaus *n*; **de·part·men-**
tal [di:pa:t'mentl] Abteilungs...;
Fach...; **de·par·ture** [di'pa:tʃə] Abreise *f*, 🚂, ⚓ Abfahrt *f*; Weggang *m*;
Abweichung *f*, Abwendung *f* (*from*
von); *a new* ~ eine neue Richtung *f*,
ein neuer Weg *m*, et. Neues *n*; ~
lounge Abflughalle *f*; ~ *platform* Ab-
fahrtsbahnsteig *m*.

de·pend [di'pend] abhängen (*on*,
upon von); angewiesen sein, sich
verlassen (*on*, *upon* auf *acc.*); ⚖
schweben; *it* ~*s* F es kommt (ganz)
darauf an; **de'pend·a·ble** zuverlässig; **de'pend·ant** Abhängige *m*,
f, Diener *m*, Anhänger *m*;
(Familien)Angehörige *m*, *f*; **de-**
'**pend·ence** Abhängigkeit *f* (*upon*
von); Bedingtheit *f* (*on* durch);
Vertrauen *n* (*on* auf *acc.*); **de-**

'**pend·en·cy** Schutzgebiet *n*; **de-**
'**pend·ent 1.** ☐ (*on*) abhängig (von);
angewiesen (auf *acc.*); bedingt
(durch); bauend (auf *acc.*); **2.** *s.*
dependant.

de·pict [di'pikt] darstellen; schildern.

de·pil·a·to·ry [de'pilətəri] **1.** ent-
haarend; **2.** Enthaarungsmittel *n*.

de·plane [di:'plein] aus dem Flugzeug aussteigen.

de·plete [di'pli:t] (ent)leeren; *fig.* erschöpfen; **de'ple·tion** Entleerung
f etc.; **de'ple·tive** entleerend.

de·plor·a·ble ☐ [di'plɔ:rəbl] beklagenswert; kläglich; jämmerlich;
de'plore beklagen, bedauern.

de·ploy ✗ [di'plɔi] (sich) entwickeln, ausschwärmen; **de'ploy-**
ment Aufmarsch *m*, Entwickeln *n*
von Truppen.

de·po·nent [di'pəunənt] ⚖ vereidigter Zeuge *m*; *gr.* Deponens *n*.

de·pop·u·late [di:'pɔpjuleit] (sich)
entvölkern; **de·pop·u'la·tion** Ent-
völkerung *f*.

de·port [di'pɔ:t] *Ausländer* abschieben; verbannen; ~ *o.s.* sich
benehmen; **de·por·ta·tion** [di:-
pɔ:'teiʃən] Deportation *f*, Verbannung *f*; **de·port'ee** Deportierte
m, *f*; **de·port·ment** [di'pɔ:tmənt]
Verhalten *n*, Benehmen *n*.

de·pos·a·ble [di'pəuzəbl] absetzbar;
de'pose absetzen; ⚖ (eidlich) aussagen (*to s.th.* et., *that* daß).

de·pos·it [di'pɔzit] **1.** *geol.* Ablagerung *f* (*a.* ⚗), Lager *n*; ⛏ Niederschlag *m*; ✝ Depot *n*; *Bank*-Einlage
f; Pfand *n*; ✝ Anzahlung *f*; Hinterlegung *f*; *attr.* Depositen...; ~ *account*
Sparkonto *n*; **2.** (nieder-, ab-, hin)le-
gen; *Geld* einzahlen; hinterlegen, de-
ponieren; (sich) absetzen *od.* -lagern;
de'pos·i·ta·ry Verwahrer *m*; **dep·o-**
si·tion [depə'ziʃən] Ablagerung *f*;
eidliche Zeugenaussage *f*; Absetzung
f (*from* von); *eccl.* Kreuzesabnahme *f*;
de·pos·i·tor [di'pɔzitə] Hinterleger
m, Einzahler *m*; **de'pos·i·to·ry** Verwahrungsort *m*; Niederlage *f*; *fig.*
Fundgrube *f*.

de·pot ['depəu] Depot *n*; Niederlage *f*; Lager(haus) *n*; Sammelplatz
m; *Am.* Bahnhof *m*.

dep·ra·va·tion [deprə'veiʃən] =
depravity; **de·prave** [di'preiv] *sitt-*
lich verderben; **de'praved** *sittlich*

de·prav·i·ty [di'præviti] Verderbtheit f.

dep·re·cate ['diprikeit] mißbilligen; ablehnen; verurteilen; **dep·re·ca·tion** Mißbilligung f; Ablehnung f; **dep·re·ca·to·ry** ['˷kətəri] mißbilligend; ablehnend.

de·pre·ci·ate [di'pri:ʃieit] herabsetzen; *fig.* geringschätzen; im Wert *od.* Preis herabsetzen *od.* (*v/i.*) sinken, entwerten; **de·pre·ci·a·tion** Herabsetzung f; Geringschätzung f; Entwertung f; ✝ Abschreibung f; **de'pre·ci·a·to·ry** [˷ʃjətəri] herabsetzend, geringschätzig.

dep·re·da·tion [depri'deiʃən] Plünderung f; ˷s pl. Verheerungen f/pl.; **'dep·re·da·tor** Plünderer m; **dep·re·da·to·ry** [di'predətəri] verheerend.

de·press [di'pres] niederdrücken; *den Handel* drücken, *Preise* senken, drücken; *Stimme* senken; *fig.* bedrücken; **de'pres·sant** ⚕ Beruhigungsmittel n; **de'pressed** *fig.* niedergeschlagen; **de'press·ing** bedrückend, deprimierend; **de·pres·sion** [di'preʃən] Depression f; Senkung f; Niedergeschlagenheit f; ✝ Flaute f, Wirtschaftskrise f; ⚙ Abspannung f; Schwäche f; ⊕, *phys., ast.* Sinken n; *geogr.* Senke f; *meteor.* Tief n.

dep·ri·va·tion [depri'veiʃən] Beraubung f; *eccl.* Amtsenthebung f; Verlust m; **de·prive** [di'praiv] berauben; ˷ s.o. of s.th. j-m et. nehmen *od.* entziehen; ausschließen (*of* von); *eccl.* absetzen; **de'prived** arm, unterprivilegiert.

depth [depθ] Tiefe f (*a. fig.*); *attr.* Tiefen...; ˷ bomb, ˷ charge Unterwasserbombe f; *in* ˷ gründlich, eingehend; ˷ of field *od.* focus *phot.* Schärfentiefe f, Tiefenschärfe f; *go beyond one's* ˷ den Boden unter den Füßen verlieren; *be out of one's* ˷ *fig.* unsicher sein, schwimmen.

dep·u·ta·tion [depju:'teiʃən] Abordnung f; **de·pute** [di'pju:t] abordnen, deputieren; **dep·u·tize** ['depjutaiz] abordnen; ˷ for j. vertreten; **'dep·u·ty 1.** Abgeordnete m, f; ⚖ Stellvertreter m, Beauftragte m, f; **2.** Vize...; Stellvertreter m des ...

de·rac·i·nate [di'ræsineit] entwurzeln.

de·rail 🚃 [di'reil] *v/i.* entgleisen; *v/t.* zum Entgleisen bringen; **de'rail·ment** Entgleisung f.

de·range [di'reindʒ] in Unordnung bringen; stören; zerrütten; (*mentally*) ˷d geistesgestört; *a* ˷d stomach e-e Magenverstimmung f; **de'range·ment** Unordnung f; Zerrüttung f; Geistesgestörtheit f.

de·rate [di:'reit] die Steuern herabsetzen (für j.).

de·ra·tion [di:'ræʃən] freigeben, die Rationierung von ... aufheben.

Der·by ['dɑ:bi] *Sport:* Derby ⟨-rennen⟩ n; **'der·by** *Am.* Melone f (*steifer Hut*).

der·e·lict ['derilikt] **1.** verlassen, herrenlos; *bsd. Am.* nachlässig, säumig; **2.** herrenloses Gut n; Wrack n; **der·e'lic·tion** Aufgeben n; Verlassen n; Vernachlässigung f; ˷ of duty Pflichtvergessenheit f.

de·ride [di'raid] verlachen, verspotten; **de'rid·er** Spötter(in).

de ri·gueur [dəri'gə:] unerläßlich.

de·ri·sion [di'riʒən] Verspottung f; Hohn m; Spott m; Gespött n; **de·ri·sive** □ [di'raisiv], **de'ri·so·ry** [˷səri] spöttisch; lächerlich (klein).

de·riv·a·ble □ [di'raivəbl] her-, ableitbar; **der·i·va·tion** [deri'veiʃən] Ableitung f; Herkunft f, Ursprung m; **de·riv·a·tive** [di'rivətiv] **1.** □ abgeleitet; **2.** Ableitung f (*Wort etc.*); **de·rive** [di'raiv] ab-, herleiten (*from* von); *Nutzen etc.* ziehen (*from* aus); ˷ from, be ˷d from stammen von *od.* aus.

der·ma·ti·tis [də:mə'taitis] Dermatitis f, Hautentzündung f.

der·ma·tol·o·gist [də:mə'tɔlədʒist] Hautarzt m, Dermatologe m; **der·ma'tol·o·gy** Dermatologie f.

der·o·gate ['derəugeit] Abbruch tun (*from dat.*), schmälern (*from acc.*); **der·o'ga·tion** Beeinträchtigung f (*from gen.*); Herabwürdigung f; **de·rog·a·to·ry** □ [di'rɔgətəri] (*to*) beeinträchtigend (*acc.*); nachteilig (*dat.*, für); herabwürdigend (*acc.*).

der·rick ['derik] ⊕ Drehkran m; ⚓ Ladebaum m; ⚒ Bohrturm m.

der·ring-do ['deriŋ'du:] Verwegenheit f.

derv [də:v] Dieseltreibstoff m.

der·vish ['də:viʃ] Derwisch m.

de·sal·i·nate ['di:'sælineit] *Meerwas-*

ser entsalzen; **de·sal·i'na·tion** Entsalzung *f*; ~ *plant* Entsalzungsanlage *f*.

de·scale ['di:'skeil] den Kesselstein entfernen von.

des·cant [dis'kænt] sich verbreiten *od.* auslassen (*upon* über *ein Thema*).

de·scend [di'send] herab-, hinabsteigen, -fließen, herabkommen; absteigen; ✗ einfahren; fallen, sinken; ⚡ niedergehen; ~ (*up*)*on* herfallen über (*acc.*); einfallen in (*acc.*); hereinbrechen über (*acc.*); ~ *to* durch Erbschaft zufallen (*dat.*); sich hergeben zu *et. Niedrigem*; ~ *from*, *be* ~*ed from* abstammen von; **de'scend·ant** Nachkomme *m*, Abkömmling *m*.

de·scent [di'sent] Herabsteigen *n*; Abstieg *m*; *Fallschirm*-Absprung *m*; ✗ Einfahrt *f*; Fallen *n*, Sinken *n*; Gefälle *n*; *feindlicher* Einfall *m*, Landung *f*; Abstammung *f*, Geschlecht *n*; Abhang *m*; ⚏ Heimfall *m* *e-r Erbschaft etc*; *line of* ~ *Skilauf*: Fallinie *f*.

de·scrib·a·ble [dis'kraibəbl] zu beschreiben(d); **de'scribe** beschreiben, schildern.

de·scrip·tion [di'skripʃən] Beschreibung *f*, Schilderung *f*; F Art *f*; **de'scrip·tive** ☐ beschreibend; darstellend; schildernd.

de·scry [dis'krai] sehen, erspähen; wahrnehmen.

des·e·crate ['desikreit] entweihen, schänden; **des·e'cra·tion** Entweihung *f*, Schändung *f*.

de·seg·re·gate *Am.* ['di:'segrigeit] die Rassenschranke (zwischen Weißen und Negern) aufheben in; **'de·seg·re'ga·tion** Aufhebung *f* der Rassentrennung.

de·sen·si·tize ['di:'sensitaiz] ⚛ desensibilisieren; *phot.* lichtunempfindlich machen.

des·ert¹ ['dezət] **1.** verlassen; wüst, öde; Wüsten...; **2.** Wüste *f*.

de·sert² [di'zə:t] *v/t.* verlassen; *fig.* :m Stich lassen; untreu werden (*dat.*); *v/i.* ausreißen; desertieren.

de·sert³ [di'zə:t] *mst* ~*s pl.* Verdienst *n*; verdienter Lohn *m*, verdiente Strafe *f*.

de·sert·er [di'zə:tə] Fahnenflüchtige *m*, Deserteur *m*; **de'ser·tion** Verlassen *n*; ⚏ böswilliges Verlassen *n*; Fahnenflucht *f*; Einsamkeit *f*.

de·serve [di'zə:v] verdienen; sich verdient machen (*of* um); **de'serv·ed·ly** [~vidli] nach Verdienst; **de'serv·ing** verdienend (*of acc.*), würdig (*of gen.*); verdienstvoll.

des·ha·bille ['dezæbi:l] = *dishabille*.

des·ic·cate ['desikeit] (aus)trocknen; **des·ic'ca·tion** Austrocknung *f*; **'des·ic·ca·tor** Trockenapparat *m*.

de·sid·er·ate [di'zidəreit] bedürfen (*gen.*); wünschen; erfordern; **de·sid·er·a·tum** [~'reitəm] Erwünschte *n*; Bedürfnis *n*; Erfordernis *n*.

de·sign [di'zain] **1.** Plan *m*; Entwurf *m*, Riß *m*; *b. s.* Anschlag *m*; Vorhaben *n*, Absicht *f*; Zeichnung *f*, Muster *n*; ⊕ Konstruktion *f*, Ausführung *f*; *by* ~ mit Absicht; *with the* ~ in der Absicht; *protection of* ~*s*, *copyright in* ~*s* Musterschutz *m*; **2.** ersinnen; zeichnen, entwerfen (*a. fig.*); planen; beabsichtigen; bestimmen (*for* zu); ~*ed to inf.* dazu bestimmt *od.* darauf abgestellt zu *inf.*

des·ig·nate 1. ['dezigneit] bezeichnen (*as* als); ernennen, bestimmen (*for* zu); **2.** ['~nit] *nachgestellt* vorläufig ernannt, designiert; **des·ig·na·tion** [~'neiʃən] Bezeichnung *f*; Bestimmung *f*, Ernennung *f*.

de·sign·ed·ly [di'zainidli] absichtlich; **de'sign·er** (Muster)Zeichner (-in); Konstrukteur *m*; *fig.* Ränkeschmied *m*; **de'sign·ing** ränkevoll.

de·sir·a·bil·i·ty [dizaiərə'biliti] Erwünschtheit *f*; **de'sir·a·ble** ☐ wünschenswert; angenehm; **de·sire** [di'zaiə] **1.** Wunsch *m*; Verlangen *n* (*for* nach; *to inf.* zu *inf.*); *at s.o.'s* ~ auf j-s Wunsch *etc.*; **2.** verlangen, wünschen; *what do you* ~ *me to do?* was soll ich tun?; **de·sir·ous** ☐ [di-'zaiərəs] begierig (*of* nach; *to do* zu tun).

de·sist [di'zist] abstehen, ablassen (*from* von).

desk [desk] Pult *n*; Schreibtisch *m*; ~ *pad* Schreibtischunterlage *f*.

des·o·late 1. ['desəleit] verwüsten, -heeren; **2.** ☐ ['~lit] einsam, verlassen; öde; trostlos; **des·o·la·tion** [~'leiʃən] Verwüstung *f*; Einöde *f*; Verlassenheit *f*.

de·spair [dis'pɛə] **1.** Verzweiflung *f*; **2.** verzweifeln (*of* an *dat.*); **de'spair·ing** ☐ verzweifelt.

des·patch [dis'pætʃ] = dispatch.

des·per·a·do [despə'rɑːdəu] Desperado *m*, Bandit *m*.

des·per·ate □ ['despərit] adj. u. adv. verzweifelt; zu allem fähig; hoffnungslos; F schrecklich; **des·per·a·tion** [ˌ'reiʃən] Verzweiflung *f*; Raserei *f*.

des·pi·ca·ble □ ['despikəbl] verächtlich; jämmerlich.

de·spise [dis'paiz] verachten; verschmähen.

de·spite [dis'pait] 1. Verachtung *f*; Trotz *m*; Bosheit *f*, Tücke *f*; in ~ of j-m zum Trotz, trotz; 2. prp. a. ~ of trotz, ungeachtet; **de·spite·ful** □ poet. [ˌful] boshaft; tückisch.

de·spoil [dis'poil] berauben (of gen.), plündern; **de·spoil·ment** Beraubung *f*, Plünderung *f*.

de·spond [dis'pond] verzagen, verzweifeln (of an dat.); **de·spond·en·cy** Verzagtheit *f*; **de·spond·ent** □, **de·spond·ing** □ verzagt, kleinmütig, mutlos.

des·pot ['despot] Despot *m*, Tyrann *m*; **des·pot·ic** (ˌally) despotisch; **des·pot·ism** ['ˌpətizəm] Despotismus *m*.

des·qua·ma·tion [deskwə'meiʃən] Abschuppung *f* der Haut.

des·sert [di'zəːt] Nachtisch *m*, Dessert *n*; Am. (Süß)Speise *f*; ~ powder Puddingpulver *n*; **des·sert-spoon** Dessertlöffel *m*.

des·ti·na·tion [desti'neiʃən] Bestimmung(sort *m*) *f*; Ziel *n*; **des·tine** ['ˌtin] bestimmen (to, for zu); be ˌd to do tun sollen; **des·ti·ny** Schicksal *n*; Los *n*; höhere Fügung *f*.

des·ti·tute □ ['destitjuːt] mittellos, notleidend; entblößt (of von); **des·ti·tu·tion** Mangel *m* (of an dat.); bittere Not *f*.

de·stroy [dis'troi] zerstören, vernichten; töten; unschädlich machen; ˌing angel Würgeengel *m*; **de·stroy·er** Zerstörer(in), Vernichter(in); ♣ Zerstörer *m*.

de·struct·i·bil·i·ty [distrʌkti'biliti] Zerstörbarkeit *f*; **de·struct·i·ble** [ˌtəbl] zerstörbar; **de·struc·tion** Zerstörung *f*, Vernichtung *f*; Tötung *f*; Untergang *m*; **de·struc·tive** □ zerstörend; vernichtend (of, to acc.); zerstörerisch; rein negativ, destruktiv; **de·struc·tive·ness** zerstörende Gewalt *f*; Zerstörungswut

f; **de·struc·tor** (Müll)Verbrennungsofen *m*.

des·ue·tude [di'sjuːitjuːd] Ungebräuchlichkeit *f*; fall into ~ außer Gebrauch kommen.

des·ul·to·ri·ness ['desəltərinis] Planlosigkeit *f*, Sprunghaftigkeit *f*; Oberflächlichkeit *f*; **des·ul·to·ry** □ unstet, sprunghaft; planlos; oberflächlich.

de·tach [di'tætʃ] losmachen, (los-) trennen, (ab)lösen; absondern; ✕ (ab)kommandieren; **de·tach·a·ble** abnehm-, abtrenn-, ablösbar; **de·tached** einzeln; freistehend (Haus); unbeeinflußt, objektiv (Urteil); unbeschwert (Gemütsart); **de·tach·ment** Loslösung *f*; Trennung *f*; Absonderung *f*; ✕ Abteilung *f*; Objektivität *f*; Unbeschwertheit *f*.

de·tail ['diːteil] 1. Einzelheit *f*; genaue od. eingehende Darstellung *f* od. Schilderung *f*; ✕ Kommando *n* (Abteilung); ~s pl. (nähere) Einzelheiten *f/pl.*, Nähere *n*; in ~ ausführlich; go into ~s auf die Einzelheiten eingehen; 2. genau od. eingehend darstellen od. schildern od. erzählen; ✕ abkommandieren; **de·tailed** eingehend, ausführlich.

de·tain [di'tein] zurück-, auf-, abhalten; ♯♯ vorenthalten; j. in Haft behalten; **de·tain·ee** Häftling *m*; **de·tain·er** Vorenthaltung *f*; ♯♯ Haftverlängerungsbefehl *m*.

de·tect [di'tekt] entdecken; (auf-) finden; **de·tect·a·ble** entdeckbar; **de·tec·tion** Ent-, Aufdeckung *f*; **de·tec·tive** 1. Detektiv..., Kriminal...; ~ force Kriminalpolizei *f*; ~ story, ~ novel Kriminalroman *m*; 2. Geheimpolizist *m*, Detektiv *m*; **de·tec·tor** Aufdecker *m*; Anzeigevorrichtung *f*; Radio: Detektor *m*.

de·tent ⊕ [di'tent] Sperrklinke *f*.

dé·tente pol. [dei'tãːt] Entspannung *f*.

de·ten·tion [di'tenʃən] Vorenthaltung *f*; Zurück-, Abhaltung *f*; Haft *f*; Schule: Arrest *m*.

de·ter [di'təː] abschrecken (from von).

de·ter·gent [di'təːdʒənt] 1. reinigend; 2. Reinigungsmittel *n*.

de·te·ri·o·rate [di'tiəriəreit] (sich) verschlechtern; an Wert verlieren; entarten; **de·te·ri·o·ra·tion** Verschlechterung *f*; Entartung *f*.

deviser

de·ter·ment [di'tə:mənt] Abschrekkungsmittel *n*.

de·ter·mi·na·ble □ [di'tə:minəbl] bestimmbar; **de'ter·mi·nant 1.** bestimmend; **2.** Bestimmende *n*; **de'ter·mi·nate** □ [∠nit] bestimmt; entschieden; festgesetzt; **de·ter·mi·na·tion** [∠'neiʃən] Bestimmung *f*; Entschlossenheit *f*, Bestimmtheit *f*; Entscheidung *f*; Entschluß *m*; **de'ter·mi·na·tive** [∠nətiv] bestimmend; einschränkend; entscheidend; **de'ter·mine** *v/t.* bestimmen; entscheiden; veranlassen (*to inf.* zu *inf.*); *bsd.* ⚖ *Strafe* festsetzen; beendigen; *be* ∠*d* entschlossen sein; *v/i.* sich entschließen (*on zu et.*; *to inf.*, *on ger.* zu *inf.*); **de'ter·mined** entschlossen; **de'ter·min·er** *gr.* Bestimmungswort *n*.

de·ter·rent [di'terənt] **1.** abschreckend; **2.** Abschreckungsmittel *n*; *nuclear* ∼ *pol.* atomare Abschreckung *f*.

de·test [di'test] verabscheuen; **de'test·a·ble** □ abscheulich; **de·tes·ta·tion** [di:tes'teiʃən] Verabscheuung *f*; Abscheu *m* (*of vor dat.*); *he is my* ∼ er ist mir ein Greuel.

de·throne [di'θrəun] entthronen; **de'throne·ment** Entthronung *f*.

det·o·nate ['detəuneit] detonieren, explodieren (lassen); **'det·o·nat·ing** Knall..., Zünd...; ∼ *cap* Zündhütchen *n*; **det·o'na·tion** Detonation *f*; Explosion *f*; Knall *m*; **'det·o·na·tor** 🚊 Knallsignal *n*; ⚔ Zünder *m*; Sprengkapsel *f*.

de·tour ['di:tuə], **dé·tour** ['deituə] Umweg *m*; Umleitung *f*.

de·tract [di'trækt]: ∼ *from s.th. et.* beeinträchtigen, schmälern; **de'trac·tion** Verleumdung *f*; Herabsetzung *f*; **de'trac·tive** verleumderisch; **de'trac·tor** Verleumder *m*.

de·train [di:'trein] *v/t. Truppen* ausladen; *v/i.* aussteigen.

de·trib·al·i·za·tion [di:traibəlai'zeiʃən] Auflösung *f* des Stammesverbands; **de'trib·al·ize** aus dem Stammesverband herauslösen.

det·ri·ment ['detrimənt] Nachteil *m*, Schaden *m* (*to für*); **det·ri·men·tal** □ [∠'mentl] schädlich, nachteilig (*to für*).

de·tri·tus *geol.* [di'traitəs] Geröll *n*.

de·tune [di:'tju:n] *Radio:* verstimmen.

deuce [dju:s] Zwei *f im Spiel*; *Tennis:* Einstand *m*; F Teufel *m*; *the* ∼! zum Teufel!; *(the)* ∼ *a one* nicht einer; **deu·ced** F [dju:st] verteufelt.

de·val·u·ate ['di:'væljueit] abwerten; **de·val·u·a·tion** [di:vælju'eiʃən] Abwertung *f*; **de·val·ue** ['di:'vælju:] abwerten.

dev·as·tate ['devəsteit] verwüsten, verheeren; **'dev·as·tat·ing** verheerend; vernichtend (*Kritik*); anwerfend (*Aussehen, Charme etc.*); **dev·as·ta·tion** Verwüstung *f*, Verheerung *f*.

de·vel·op [di'veləp] (sich) entwickeln; (sich) entfalten; (sich) erweitern; *phot.* entwickeln; *Baugelände* erschließen; ausbauen; *Am.* (sich) zeigen, bekannt werden; **de'vel·op·er** *phot.* Entwickler *m*; **de'vel·op·ing** *phot.* Entwickeln *n*; *attr.* Entwicklungs...; **de'vel·op·ment** Entwicklung *f*, Entfaltung *f*; Erweiterung *f*; Ausbau *m*.

de·vi·ate ['di:vieit] abweichen (*from von*); **de·vi·a·tion** Abweichung *f*; Ablenkung *f der Magnetnadel*; **de·vi·a·tion·ism** *pol.* Abweichen *n* von der Parteilinie; **de·vi·a·tion·ist** *pol.* Abweichler *m*.

de·vice [di'vais] Plan *m*; Einfall *m*; Kunstgriff *m*, Kniff *m*; Erfindung *f*; Vorrichtung *f*; Muster *n*; Wappenbild *n*, Wahlspruch *m*; *leave s.o. to his own* ∼*s* j. sich selbst überlassen.

dev·il ['devl] **1.** Teufel *m* (*a. fig.*); Teufelskerl *m*; ⚖ Hilfsanwalt *m*; *fig.* Handlanger *m*; Laufbursche *m*; ⊕ Wolf *m*; *Küche:* gepfeffertes Gericht *n*; *the* ∼! zum Teufel!; *between the* ∼ *and the deep sea* in der Klemme; **2.** *v/t.* stark gepfeffert braten; ⊕ *im Wolf* zerkleinern; *Am.* plagen, quälen; *v/i.* als Hilfsanwalt arbeiten; **'dev·il·ish** □ teuflisch; F verteufelt; **'dev·il·may-·care** sorglos; verwegen; **'dev·il·ment** Teufelei *f*, Unfug *m*, Dummheiten *f/pl.*; **'dev·il·(t)ry** Teufelei *f*; Teufelskunst *f*.

de·vi·ous □ ['di:vjəs] abgelegen; abwegig (*a. fig.*); unredlich; ∼ *step* Fehltritt *m*.

de·vis·a·ble [di'vaizəbl] erdenkbar; **de'vise** **1.** ⚖ Vermachen *n*; Vermächtnis *n*; **2.** erdenken, ersinnen; ⚖ vermachen; **dev·i·see** ⚖ [devi'zi:] Vermächtnisnehmer *m*; **de-**

vis·er [di'vaizə] Erfinder(in); **de·vi·sor** i̯t͡s [devi'zɔ:] Erblasser *m*.

de·vi·tal·ize [di:'vaitəlaiz] die Lebenskraft nehmen (*dat*.); entkräften.

de·void [di'vɔid] (*of*) bar (*gen*.), ohne, ...los.

dev·o·lu·tion [di:və'lu:ʃən] i̯t͡s Heimfall *m*; *parl*. Überweisung *f*; Verlauf *m*; *biol*. Entartung *f*; **de·volve** [di'vɔlv] (*upon, to*) *v/t*. abwälzen (auf *acc*.); *j-m* übertragen; *v/i*. übergehen (auf *acc*.); zufallen (*dat*.).

de·vote [di'vout] weihen, widmen; hingeben; **de'vot·ed** □ ergeben; zärtlich; **dev·o·tee** [devou'ti:] Verehrer(in); Frömmler(in); **de·votion** [di'vouʃən] Ergebenheit *f* (*to s.o.* für j.); Hingabe *f*, Hingebung *f* (*an acc*.); Frömmigkeit *f*; ⁓*s pl*. Andacht *f*; **de'vo·tion·al** □ [⁓ʃənl] andächtig, fromm.

de·vour [di'vauə] verschlingen (*a. fig*.); ⁓*ed with* verzehrt von *Neugier etc*.; **de'vour·ing** □ verzehrend.

de·vout □ [di'vaut] andächtig, fromm; innig; **de'vout·ness** Frömmigkeit *f etc*.

dew [dju:] 1. Tau *m*; 2. tauen; '⁓-drop Tautropfen *m*; '⁓-lap Wamme *f e-s Rindes*; '**dew-pond** Tau(sammel)teich *m*; '**dew·y** tauig, betaut; taufrisch.

dex·ter ['dekstə] recht, rechts (-seitig).

dex·ter·i·ty [deks'teriti] Gewandtheit *f*; **dex·ter·ous** □ ['⁓tərəs] gewandt, flink, geschickt.

di·a·be·tes [daiə'bi:ti:z] Zuckerkrankheit *f*, Diabetes *m*; **di·a·bet·ic** [⁓'betik] 1. Diabetiker(in), Zuckerkranke *m*, *f*; 2. diabetisch, zuckerkrank; Diabetiker...

di·a·bol·ic, di·a·bol·i·cal □ [daiə-'bɔlik(əl)] teuflisch.

di·a·dem ['daiədem] Diadem *n*.

di·ag·nose ['daiəgnəuz] diagnostizieren, erkennen; **di·ag'no·sis** [⁓sis], *pl*. **di·ag'no·ses** [⁓si:z] Diagnose *f*.

di·ag·o·nal [dai'ægənl] 1. □ diagonal; 2. Diagonale *f*; Diagonal *m*, schräggeripptes Gewebe *n*.

di·a·gram ['daiəgræm] Diagramm *n*; graphische Darstellung *f*; Schema *n*, Plan *m*; **di·a·grammat·ic** [daiəgrə'mætik] (⁓*ally*) schematisch.

di·al ['daiəl] 1. Sonnenuhr *f*; Zifferblatt *n*; Skala *f*; *teleph*. Wähl(er)scheibe *f*; *Radio*: Skalenscheibe *f*; ⁓ *light* Skalenbeleuchtung *f*; 2. *teleph*. wählen.

di·a·lect ['daiəlekt] Mundart *f*, Dialekt *m*; **di·a'lec·tic, di·a'lec·ti·cal** □ dialektisch; **di·a'lec·tic(s)** *sg*. Dialektik *f*.

di·a·logue, *Am. a.* **di·a·log** ['daiə-lɔg] Dialog *m*, Gespräch *n*; ⁓ *track Film*: Sprechband *n*.

di·al...: '⁓-sys·tem *teleph*. Wählsystem *n*; '⁓-tone *teleph*. Amtszeichen *n*. [messer *m*.\

di·am·e·ter [dai'æmitə] Durch-\
di·a·met·ri·cal □ [daiə'metrikəl] diametrisch; diametral *od*. genau entgegengesetzt.

di·a·mond ['daiəmənd] 1. Diamant *m*; Rhombus *m*; *Am. Baseball*: Spielfeld *n*; *Karten*: Karo *m*; ⁓ *cut* ⁓ *Wurst wider Wurst*; *he is a rough* ⁓ er hat e-e rauhe Schale, aber e-n guten Kern; 2. Diamant(en)...; Karo...; kariert; rautenförmig; '⁓-'cut·ter Diamantenschleifer *m*; ⁓ **wed·ding** diamantene Hochzeit *f*.

di·a·pa·son ♪ [daiə'peisn] Zs.-klang *m*; Tonfülle *f*; Mensur *f der Orgel*; Stimm-Umfang *m* (*a. fig*.).

di·a·per ['daiəpə] 1. rautenförmig gemusterte Leinwand *f*; *Am*. Windel *f*; 2. *Stoff* rautenförmig mustern; *Am. Baby* trockenlegen.

di·aph·a·nous [dai'æfənəs] durchscheinend.

di·a·phragm ['daiəfræm] Zwerchfell *n*; ⊕ Scheidewand *f*; *opt*. Blende *f*; *teleph*. Membran(e) *f*.

di·a·rist ['daiərist] Tagebuchschreiber(in); '**di·a·rize** Tagebuch führen.

di·ar·rhoea 𝄞 [daiə'riə] Durchfall *m*.

di·a·ry ['daiəri] Tagebuch *n*; Taschenkalender *m*.

Di·as·po·ra [dai'æspərə] Diaspora *f*, (christliche *od*. jüdische) religiöse Minderheit *f*.

di·a·ther·my 𝄞 ['daiəθə:mi] Diathermie *f*.

di·a·tribe ['daiətraib] Schmähschrift *f*; Schmähung *f*.

dib·ble ['dibl] 1. Pflanz-, Setzstock *m*; 2. *Pflanzen* stecken.

dibs *sl*. [dibz] *pl*. Moneten *pl*.

dice [dais] 1. *pl. von die*[2] Würfel *m/pl*.;

no ⸃ *Am.* F nichts zu machen; 2.
würfeln; in Würfel schneiden; '⸝~
-box Würfelbecher *m*; '**dic·er** Wür-
felspieler(in); **dic·ey** F ['daisi] prekär,
heikel.

di·chot·o·my [dai'kɔtəmi] (Zwei)Tei-
lung *f*, Dichotomie *f*.

dick¹ *Am. sl.* [dik] Detektiv *m*, Kri-
minalbeamte *m*.

dick² *sl.* [⸝~] Erklärung *f*; *take one's* ~
schwören.

dick·ens F ['dikinz] Teufel *m*.

dick·er *Am.* ['dikə] (ver)schachern,
feilschen.

dick·(e)y ['diki] **1.** *sl.* schlecht,
schlimm, mau; **2.** F Notsitz *m*;
Hemdenbrust *f*; *a.* ~**-bird** Piep-
vögelchen *n*.

dic·tate **1.** ['dikteit] Diktat *n*, Vorschrift *f*; Gebot *n*; **2.** [dik'teit] diktieren; *fig.* vorschreiben; **dic'tation** Diktat *n* (*Diktieren*; *Nieder-
schrift*); = *dictate* 1; **dic'ta·tor**
Diktator *m*; **dic·ta·to·ri·al** □ [diktə-
tə'tɔːriəl] diktatorisch; **dic·ta·tor-
ship** [dik'teitəʃip] Diktatur *f*.

dic·tion ['dikʃən] Ausdruck(sweise
f) *m*, Diktion *f*, Stil *m*; **dic·tion-
ar·y** ['⸝~ri] Wörterbuch *n*.

dict·um ['diktəm], *pl.* **dic·ta** ['⸝~tə]
(Aus)Spruch *m*; geflügeltes Wort *n*.

did [did] *pret. von* do.

di·dac·tic [di'dæktik] (~*ally*) didak-
tisch, (be)lehrend; Lehr...

did·dle *sl.* ['didl] übers Ohr hauen,
betrügen.

didn't ['didnt] = *did not; s. do.*

die¹ [dai] (*p.pr. dying*) sterben, umkommen (*of an dat., from* vor *dat.*);
untergehen; absterben; F schmachten, sich sehnen (*for* nach; *to inf.*
danach, zu *inf.*); ~ *away* ersterben,
sich legen (*Wind*); verklingen (*Ton*);
sich verlieren (*Farbe*); verlöschen
(*Licht*); ~ *down* ersterben; (dahin-)
schwinden; erlöschen; ~ *off* absterben; ~ *out* aussterben; ~ *hard*
ein zähes Leben haben; nicht tot zu
kriegen sein; *never say* ~! nur nicht
verzweifeln!

die² [⸝~], *pl.* **dice** [dais] Würfel *m*;
pl. **dies** [daiz] ⊕ Preßform *f*, Gesenk *n*; *Münz*-Stempel *m*; Kubus
m; *lower* ~ Matrize *f*; *upper* ~ Pa-
trize *f*; *as straight as a* ~ kerzengerade; *the* ~ *is cast* die Würfel sind
gefallen.

die...: '~**-a'way** schmachtend; '~

-cast·ing ⊕ Spritzguß *m*; '~**-hard**
Unentwegte *m*, Reaktionär *m*.

di·e·lec·tric [daii'lektrik] dielek-
trisch.

Die·sel en·gine ['diːzl'endʒin] Dieselmotor *m*.

die-sink·er ['daisiŋkə] Stempel-
schneider *m*; Werkzeugmacher *m*.

die-stock ⊕ ['daistɔk] Schneid-
kluppe *f*.

di·et¹ ['daiət] **1.** Diät *f*; Nahrung *f*,
Ernährung *f*, Kost *f*; *be* (*put*) *on a* ~
diät leben (müssen); **2.** *v/t.* Diät vorschreiben (*dat.*); beköstigen; *v/i.* diät
leben.

di·et² [⸝~] Reichstag *m* (*hist.*); Parlament *n* in bestimmten Ländern.

di·e·tar·y ['daiətəri] **1.** Diätregel *f*;
Ration *f*; **2.** diätetisch; **di·e·tet·ics**
[daii'tetiks] *sg.* Diätkunde *f*; **di·e·ti-
cian, di·e·ti·tian** [⸝~'tiʃən] Diätspe-
zialist *m*.

dif·fer ['difə] sich unterscheiden;
andrer Meinung sein (*with, from*
als); abweichen (*from* von); *they
agreed to* ~ sie gaben es auf, einander zu überzeugen; **dif·fer·ence**
['difrəns] Unterschied *m*, Verschiedenheit *f*; Ⱥ *u.* ✝ Differenz *f*; Meinungsverschiedenheit *f*; Streit(igkeit *f*) *m*; *split the* ~ auf halbem
Wege einander entgegenkommen;
'**dif·fer·ent** □ verschieden (*from, to*
von); anders, andere(r, -s) (*from* als);
dif·fer·en·ti·a [difə'renʃiə] charakteristisches Merkmal *n*; **dif·fer'ential** [⸝~əl] **1.** unterscheidend; Differential...; ~ *calculus* Differentialrech-
nung *f*; **2.** *mot.* Differential-, Aus-
gleichsgetriebe *n*; **dif·fer'en·ti·ate**
[⸝~ʃieit] (sich) unterscheiden; **dif-
fer·en·ti'a·tion** Differenzierung
f.

dif·fi·cult □ ['difikəlt] schwierig
(*a. Charakter etc.*); schwer; beschwerlich; '**dif·fi·cul·ty** Schwierigkeit *f*; *difficulties pl. a.* Verlegenheit *f* (*for um*).

dif·fi·dence ['difidəns] Mangel *m* an
Selbstvertrauen, Schüchternheit *f*;
'**dif·fi·dent** □ ohne Selbstvertrau-
en, schüchtern.

dif·fract *phys.* [di'frækt] *Licht* beugen.

dif·frac·tion *phys.* [di'frækʃən] Dif-
fraktion *f*, Beugung *f*.

dif·fuse 1. [di'fjuːz] *fig.* verbreiten;
⚕ (sich) durchdringen; **2.** □ [⸝~s]

weitverbreitet, zerstreut, diffus (*bsd. Licht*); weitschweifig, breit; **dif'fused** [~zd] zerstreut (*Licht*); **dif'fu·sion** [~ʒən] Verbreitung *f*; ⚛, *phys.* Durchdringung *f*; **dif'fu·sive** □ [~siv] sich verbreitend; weitschweifig.

dig [dig] **1.** (*irr.*) (um-, aus)graben; wühlen (in *dat.*); F stoßen, puffen; ~ *for* graben nach; ~ *in* (sich) eingraben, schuften; ~ *into* sich vergraben in (*acc.*); ~ *up* ausgraben; **2.** Ausgrabungsstelle *f*, Grabung *f*; F Stoß *m*, Puff *m*; ~s *pl.* F Bude *f*, Einzelzimmer *n*.

di·gest 1. [di'dʒest] ordnen; verdauen (*a. fig. = überdenken*); *verwinden*); *v/i.* verdaut werden; **2.** ['daidʒest] Abriß *m*, Übersicht *f*; Auslese *f*, -wahl *f*; ⅀ Gesetzessammlung *f*; **di·gest·i·bil·i·ty** [didʒesti'biliti] Verdaulichkeit *f*; **di·'gest·i·ble** verdaulich; **di·'ges·tion** Verdauung *f*; **di·'ges·tive** Verdauungsmittel *n*.

dig·ger ['digə] (*bsd.* Gold)Gräber *m*; *sl.* Australier *m*; **dig·gings** F ['~giŋz] *pl.* Bude *f* (*Wohnung*); *Am.* Goldmine(*n pl.*) *f*.

dig·it ['didʒit] Finger(breite *f*) *m*; ∦ Ziffer *f*; Stelle *f*; **'dig·it·al** Finger...; Ziffer...; ~ *telephone* Tastentelefon *n*.

dig·ni·fied ['dignifaid] würdevoll; würdig; **dig·ni·fy** ['~fai] Würde verleihen (*dat.*); (be)ehren; *fig.* adeln; hochtrabend benennen.

dig·ni·tar·y *bsd. eccl.* ['dignitəri] Würdenträger *m*; **'dig·ni·ty** Würde *f*; *stand* (*up*)*on one's* ~ formell sein.

di·graph *gr.* ['daigrɑːf] Digraph *m* (*2 Buchstaben, die e-n Laut bilden*).

di·gress [dai'gres] abschweifen; **di·'gres·sion** Abschweifung *f*; **di·'gres·sive** □ abschweifend.

dike[1] [daik] **1.** Deich *m*; Damm *m*; Graben *m*; **2.** eindeichen; eindämmen.

dike[2] *sl.* [~] Lesbe *f*, Lesbierin *f*.

di·lap·i·date [di'læpideit] verfallen (lassen); **di'lap·i·dat·ed** verfallen, baufällig; schäbig; **di·lap·i'da·tion** Verfall *m*; Baufälligkeit *f*.

di·lat·a·bil·i·ty *phys.* [daileitə'biliti] (Aus)Dehnungsvermögen *n*; **di·'lat·a·ble** (aus)dehnbar; **dil·a'ta·tion** Ausdehnung *f*, Erweiterung *f*;

di'late (sich) ausdehnen; *Augen, Nüstern* weit öffnen; ~ *upon* sich weitläufig über *et.* verbreiten; **di·'la·tion** = *dilatation*; **dil·a·to·ri·ness** ['dilətərinis] Saumseligkeit *f*; **'dil·a·to·ry** □ aufschiebend, hinhaltend, saumselig.

di·lem·ma [di'lemə] Dilemma *n*; *fig.* Verlegenheit *f*, Klemme *f*.

dil·et·tan·te, *pl.* **dil·et·tan·ti** [dili-'tænti, *pl.* ~'tænti:] Dilettant(in).

dil·i·gence ['dilidʒəns] Fleiß *m*; **'dil·i·gent** □ fleißig, emsig.

dill ♧ [dil] Dill *m*.

dil·ly-dal·ly F ['dilidæli] (die Zeit ver)trödeln.

dil·u·ent ['diljuənt] verdünnend(es Mittel *n*); **di·lute** [dai'ljuːt] **1.** (mit Wasser) verdünnen; *fig.* verwässern; **2.** verdünnt; *fig.* verwässert; **di·'lu·tion** Verdünnung *f*; *fig.* Verwässerung *f*.

di·lu·vi·al [dai'luːvjəl], **di·'lu·vi·an** *geol.* diluvial.

dim [dim] **1.** □ trüb; dunkel; matt; F schwer von Begriff; **2.** (sich) verdunkeln; *mot., Film:* abblenden; (sich) trüben, matt werden.

dime *Am.* [daim] Zehncentstück *n*; ~ *novel* Groschenroman *m*; ~ *store* Einheitspreisgeschäft *n*.

di·men·sion [di'menʃən] Dimension *f*, Abmessung *f*; ~s *pl. a.* Ausmaß *n*.

di·min·ish [di'miniʃ] (sich) vermindern *od.* -ringern *od.* -jüngen; abnehmen; **dim·i·nu·tion** [dimi-'njuːʃən] Verminderung *f*; Abnahme *f* (*in an dat.*); △ Verjüngung *f*; **di·min·u·tive** [~njutiv] **1.** □ *gr.* verkleinernd; winzig; **2.** Verkleinerungsform *f*, Diminutiv *n*.

dim·mer ['dimə] Abblendvorrichtung *f*.

dim·ness ['dimnis] Dunkelheit *f*; Mattheit *f*.

dim·ple ['dimpl] **1.** Grübchen *n*; **2.** Grübchen bekommen; (sich) kräuseln; **'dim·pled** mit Grübchen.

din [din] **1.** Getöse *n*, Lärm *m*; **2.** (durch Lärm) betäuben; lärmen; dröhnen; ~ *s.th. into s.o.*('*s ears*) j-m dauernd et. (vor)predigen.

dine [dain] (zu Mittag) essen; bewirten; (Mittagsgäste) fassen (*Saal*); ~ *out* zum Essen ausgehen; **'din·er** Speisende *m*, *f*; (Mittags)Gast *m*;

🍴 *bsd. Am.* Speisewagen *m;* **'din·er·'out** *j.,* der (oft) auswärts ißt; **di·nette** [dai'net] Eßnische *f in der Küche.*

ding [diŋ] klingen; beständig wiederholen; **~-dong** [' ~'dɔŋ] **1.** bim bam; **2.** Klingklang *m;* **3.** unentschieden *(Rennen);* heiß *(Kampf).*

din·gey, din·ghy ['diŋgi] Dingi *n (kleines Boot);* **rubber ~** Schlauchboot *n.*

din·gle ['diŋgl] Waldschlucht *f.*

din·gus *Am. sl.* ['diŋgəs] Dingsbums *n.*

din·gy ☐ ['dindʒi] schmutzig; schmierig; schmuddelig; schäbig.

din·ing... ['dainiŋ]: '**~-'al·cove** Eßnische *f;* '**~-car 🍴** Speisewagen *m;* '**~-room** Eß-, Speisezimmer *n;* **~ table** Eßtisch *m.*

dink·ey *Am.* ['diŋki] *kleine* Rangierlok *f.*

dink·y F ['diŋki] niedlich; nett.

din·ner ['dinə] Hauptmahlzeit *f (Mittag- oder Abendessen);* Festessen *n;* '**~-jack·et** Smoking *m;* '**~-pail** *Am.* Essenträger *m (Gerät);* '**~-par·ty** Tischgesellschaft *f;* '**~-serv·ice,** '**~-set** Tafelgeschirr *n.*

di·no·saur *zo.* ['dainəusɔ:] Dinosaurier *m.*

dint [dint] **1.** Strieme *f,* Beule *f;* **by ~ of** kraft, vermöge *(gen.);* **2.** ver-, einbeulen.

di·o·ce·san *eccl.* [dai'ɔsisən] **1.** Diözesan...; **2.** Diözesanbischof *m;* **di·o·cese** ['daiəsis] Diözese *f.*

di·ode ⚡ ['daiəud] Diode *f; light- -emitting ~* Leuchtdiode *f.*

di·op·tric *opt.* [dai'ɔptrik] **1.** dioptrisch; **2.** Dioptrie *f (Lichtbrechungseinheit).*

di·ox·ide ⚗ [dai'ɔksaid] Dioxyd *n.*

dip [dip] **1.** *v/t.* (ein)tauchen; senken, ⚓ *Flagge* dippen; *Stoff* (auf)färben; schöpfen *(out of, from aus); mot.* abblenden; *v/i.* (unter)tauchen, untersinken; sich neigen; sich senken; *geol.* einfallen; **~ into in den** *Geldbeutel* greifen; e-n flüchtigen Blick werfen in *(acc.);* **2.** Eintauchen *n;* Desinfektionsbad *n für Schafe;* F kurzes Bad *n;* Senkung *f,* Neigung *f;* Dippen *n der Flagge; have a ~, take a ~* kurz baden gehen.

diph·the·ri·a [dif'θiəriə] Diphtherie *f.*

diph·thong ['difθɔŋ] Diphthong *m,*

Doppellaut *m.*

di·plo·ma [di'pləumə] Diplom *n;* **di·plo·ma·cy** Diplomatie *f;* Verhandlungsgeschick *n;* **di·plo·maed** [~məd] diplomiert; Diplom...; **dip·lo·mat** ['dipləmæt] Diplomat(in); **dip·lo·mat·ic, dip·lo·mat·i·cal** ☐ diplomatisch; **dip·lo·mat·ics** *sg.* Diplomatik *f;* **di·plo·ma·tist** [di-'pləumətist] Diplomat(in).

dip·per ['dipə] Schöpfkelle *f; Am. Big ♀ ast. der* Große Bär; '**dip·py** *sl.* verrückt.

dip·so·ma·ni·a [dipsəu'meinjə] Trunksucht *f;* **dip·so'ma·ni·ac** [~niæk] Trunksüchtige *m, f.*

dip-stick ['dipstik] *(bsd. mot.* Öl-) Meßstab *m.*

dip-switch *mot.* ['dipswitʃ] Abblendschalter *m.*

dire ['daiə] gräßlich, schrecklich.

di·rect [di'rekt] **1.** ☐ direkt; gerade; unmittelbar; offen, aufrichtig; deutlich; glatt, genau; **~ current** Gleichstrom *m;* **~** *dial(l)ing teleph.* Durchwahl *f;* **~ hit** Volltreffer *m;* **~ speech** direkte Rede *f;* **~ tax** direkte Steuer *f;* **~ train** durchgehender Zug *m;* **2.** *adv.* geradeswegs; **= ~ly 1;** **3.** richten *(to, towards, at* nach, auf *acc.,* gegen); lenken, steuern; leiten, führen, anordnen; *j.* anweisen; *j.* weisen *(to* nach; an *j.); Brief* adressieren; **~ to** zuleiten *(dat.);* **di'rec·tion** Richtung *f;* Gegend *f;* Lenkung *f;* Leitung *f,* Führung *f;* Anordnung *f;* Anweisung *f;* Adresse *f;* Direktion *f,* Vorstand *m;* **di'rec·tion·al** [~ʃənl] *Radio:* Peil..., Richt...; **di'rec·tion- -find·er** *Radio:* (Funk)Peiler *m;* Peil(funk)empfänger *m;* **di'rec·tion- -find·ing** *Radio:* Funkortung *f; attr.* (Funk)Peil...; **~ set** Peilgerät *n;* **~ station** Funkpeilstelle *f;* **di'rec·tion in·di·ca·tor** *mot.* Fahrtrichtungsanzeiger *m;* 🔑 Kursweiser *m;* **di'rec·tive** richtungweisend; leitend; anweisend; **di'rect·ly 1.** *adv.* unmittelbar; sofort, gleich; **2.** *cj.* sobald (als); **di'rect·ness** gerade Richtung *f; fig.* Geradheit *f.*

di·rec·tor [di'rektə] Direktor *m; Film:* Regisseur *m;* Mitglied *n des* Aufsichtsrats; *board of* **~s** Aufsichtsrat *m;* **di'rec·to·rate** [~rit] Direktorium *n,* Direktion *f; a.* **di- 'rec·tor·ship** Direktorat *n;* **di'rec- to·ry** Adreßbuch *n; telephone ~**

Telefonbuch; ~ enquiries pl., Am. ~ assistance Telefonauskunft f.

di·rec·tress [di'rektris] Vorsteherin f, Direktorin f.

dire·ful □ ['daiəful] schrecklich.

dirge [də:dʒ] Grabgesang m; Klage (-lied n) f.

dir·i·gi·ble ['diridʒəbl] **1.** lenkbar; **2.** lenkbares Luftschiff n.

dirk [də:k] **1.** Dolchmesser n; **2.** erdolchen.

dirt [də:t] Schmutz m; fig. contp. Dreck m; (lockere) Erde f; treat s.o. like ~ j. wie den letzten Dreck behandeln; fling od. throw ~ at s.o. j. mit Schmutz bewerfen; '~-**cheap** F spottbillig; ~ **road** Am. unbefestigte Straße f; '~-**track** Sport: Aschenbahn f; '**dirt·y 1.** □ schmutzig (a. fig.); **2.** beschmutzen; besudeln.

dis·a·bil·i·ty [disə'biliti] Unvermögen n; (Dienst-, Rechts)Unfähigkeit f.

dis·a·ble [dis'eibl] (bsd. dienst-, kampf)unfähig od. unbrauchbar machen; **dis'a·bled** dienst-, kampfunfähig; invalide, körperbehindert; kriegsversehrt, -beschädigt; **dis'a·ble·ment** Invalidität f; Kampfunfähigkeit f.

dis·a·buse [disə'bju:z] e-s Bessern belehren (of über acc.).

dis·ac·cord [disə'kɔ:d] nicht übereinstimmen (with mit).

dis·ac·cus·tom ['disə'kʌstəm]: ~ s.o. to s.th. j-m et. abgewöhnen.

dis·ad·van·tage [disəd'va:ntidʒ] Nachteil m; Schaden m; sell to ~ mit Verlust verkaufen; **dis·ad·van·ta·geous** □ [disædva:n'teidʒəs] nachteilig, ungünstig.

dis·af·fect·ed □ [disə'fektid] (to, towards) abgeneigt (gegen); unzufrieden (mit); **dis·af'fec·tion** Abneigung f; Unzufriedenheit f.

dis·af·firm [disə'fə:m] umstoßen.

dis·af·for·est [disə'fɔrist] abholzen.

dis·a·gree [disə'gri:] nicht übereinstimmen, nicht einverstanden sein (with mit); uneinig sein (on über acc.); Antrag etc. ablehnen (to, with acc.); nicht bekommen (with s.o. j-m); **dis·a·gree·a·ble** □ [~'griəbl] unangenehm (a. fig.); **dis·a·gree·ment** [~'gri:mənt] Verschiedenheit f; Unstimmigkeit f; Meinungsverschiedenheit f; Verstimmung f.

dis·al·low ['disə'lau] nicht erlauben; ablehnen; nicht gelten lassen.

dis·ap·pear [disə'piə] verschwinden; **dis·ap·pear·ance** [~'piərəns] Verschwinden n.

dis·ap·point [disə'pɔint] enttäuschen; vereiteln; j. im Stich lassen; **dis·ap'point·ment** Enttäuschung f; Vereitelung f; ~ in love unglückliche Liebe f.

dis·ap·pro·ba·tion [disæprəu'beiʃən] Mißbilligung f.

dis·ap·prov·al [disə'pru:vl] Mißbilligung f; **dis·ap'prove** mißbilligen (of et.).

dis·arm [dis'a:m] v/t. entwaffnen (a. fig.); v/i. abrüsten; **dis'ar·ma·ment** Entwaffnung f; Abrüstung f.

dis·ar·range ['disə'reindʒ] in Unordnung bringen, verwirren; **dis·ar'range·ment** Verwirrung f, Unordnung f.

dis·ar·ray ['disə'rei] **1.** Unordnung f; **2.** in Unordnung bringen.

dis·as·sem·bly ⊕ [disə'sembli] Auseinandernehmen n.

dis·as·ter [di'za:stə] Unglück(sfall m) n, Unheil n, Katastrophe f; ~ relief Katastrophenhilfe f; **dis'as·trous** □ unheilvoll, unglücklich; verheerend, katastrophal.

dis·a·vow ['disə'vau] (ab)leugnen; nicht gutheißen; **dis·a'vow·al** Ableugnung f; Nichtanerkennung f.

dis·band [dis'bænd] Truppen entlassen; (sich) auflösen; **dis'band·ment** Auflösung f.

dis·bar [dis'ba:] vom Anwaltsamt ausschließen.

dis·be·lief ['disbi'li:f] Unglaube m, Zweifel m (in an dat.); **dis·be·lieve** ['disbi'li:v] nicht glauben, bezweifeln; '**dis·be'liev·er** Ungläubige m, f, Zweifler(in).

dis·bud [dis'bʌd] überschüssige Knospen entfernen von.

dis·bur·den [dis'bə:dn] entlasten; befreien (of von e-r Last); Herz erleichtern; entladen (a. fig.).

dis·burse [dis'bə:s] auszahlen; verauslagen; **dis'burse·ment** Auszahlung f; Verauslagung f.

disc [disk] = disk.

dis·card 1. [dis'ka:d] Karten weglegen, abwerfen; Kleid, Vorurteil etc. ablegen; aufgeben; entlassen; **2.** ['diska:d] Karten: Abwerfen n; bsd. Am. Abfall(haufen) m.

dis·cern [di'sə:n] unterscheiden; erkennen; wahrnehmen; beurteilen; **dis'cern·i·ble** □ unterscheidbar; erkennbar; sichtbar; **dis'cern·ing** **1.** □ kritisch, scharfsichtig; **2.** Einsicht *f*; Scharfblick *m*; **dis'cern·ment** Einsicht *f*; Scharfsinn *m*.

dis·charge [dis'tʃɑ:dʒ] **1.** *v/t.* ent-, ab-, ausladen; ⚓ löschen; ⚡ entladen; entlasten, entbinden; abfeuern; verwalten, *Amt* versehen; *Pflicht etc.* erfüllen; *Zorn etc.* auslassen; ausströmen lassen; *Schuld* abtragen, tilgen; *Rechnung* quittieren; *Wechsel* einlösen; entlassen, abdanken; freisprechen; *v/i.* sich entladen; sich ergießen; eitern; **2.** Entladung *f* (*a.* ⚡); ⚓ Löschen *n*; Abfeuern *n*; Salve *f*; Ausströmen *n*; Ausfluß *m*, Eiter(ung *f*) *m*; Entlassung *f*; Entlastung *f*; Bezahlung *f*; Quittung *f*; Verwaltung *f*; Erfüllung *f* e-r *Pflicht*; **dis'charg·er** Entlader *m* (*a. phys.*).

dis·ci·ple [di'saipl] Schüler *m*; Jünger *m*; **dis'ci·ple·ship** Jüngerschaft *f*.

dis·ci·pli·nar·i·an [disipli'neəriən] strenger Lehrer *m od.* Vorgesetzter *m*; *he is a poor* ～ er kann keine Disziplin halten; **'dis·ci·pli·nar·y** erzieherisch; disziplinar, Disziplinar...; **'dis·ci·pline 1.** Disziplin *f*, Zucht *f*; Erziehung *f*; (Studien-) Fach *n*, Wissenschaft *f*; Züchtigung *f*; **2.** an Disziplin gewöhnen; erziehen; schulen; strafen.

dis·claim [dis'kleim] (ab)leugnen; ablehnen; verzichten auf (*acc.*); **dis'claim·er** Verzicht(leistung *f*) *m*; Dementi *n*.

dis·close [dis'kləuz] aufdecken; erschließen, offenbaren, eröffnen, enthüllen; **dis'clo·sure** [～ʒə] Enthüllung *f etc.*

dis·col·o(u)r [dis'kʌlə] (sich) verfärben; **dis·col·o(u)r'a·tion** Verfärbung *f*.

dis·com·fit [dis'kʌmfit] *in die Flucht* schlagen; vereiteln; aus der Fassung bringen; **dis'com·fi·ture** [～tʃə] Niederlage *f*; Verwirrung *f*; Vereitelung *f*.

dis·com·fort [dis'kʌmfət] **1.** Unbehagen *n*; **2.** *j-m* Unbehagen verursachen.

dis·com·pose [diskəm'pəuz] beunruhigen; **dis·com'po·sure** [～ʒə]

Beunruhigung *f*, Erregung *f*.

dis·con·cert [diskən'sə:t] aus der Fassung bringen; vereiteln.

dis·con·nect ['diskə'nekt] trennen (*from, with* von); ⊕ abstellen; auskuppeln; ⚡ Netzstecker ziehen; **'dis·con'nect·ed** □ zs.-hanglos; **'dis·con'nec·tion** Trennung *f*; ⊕ Auskuppelung *f etc.*

dis·con·so·late □ ['dis'kɔnsəlit] untröstlich.

dis·con·tent ['diskən'tent] **1.** ⚔ = ～ed; **2.** Unzufriedenheit *f*; **'dis·con'tent·ed** □ mißvergnügt, unzufrieden.

dis·con·tin·u·ance [diskən'tinjuəns] Unterbrechung *f*; Aufhören *n*, Aufgabe *f*; **'dis·con'tin·ue** [～nju:] aufgeben, aufhören mit; *Zeitung* abbestellen; **'dis·con'tin·u·ous** □ [～njuəs] unzusammenhängend, mit Unterbrechungen, unterbrochen.

dis·cord ['diskɔ:d], **dis'cord·ance** Uneinigkeit *f*; ♪ Mißklang *m*; **dis'cord·ant** □ verschieden, abweichend (*to, from, with* von); uneinig; ♪ mißtönend, -klingend.

dis·co·theque ['diskəutek] Diskothek *f*.

dis·count ['diskaunt] **1.** ✝ Diskont *m*, Skonto *m*; Abzug *m* (*a. fig.*), Rabatt *m*; ～ *store* Discountladen *m*; *at a* ～ unter Pari; *fig.* nicht gefragt; **2.** ✝ diskontieren; abrechnen, abziehen (*a. fig.*); *fig.* absehen von; *Nachricht* mit Vorsicht aufnehmen; beeinträchtigen; **dis'count·a·ble** diskontierbar; **dis'coun·te·nance** [～tinəns] (offen) mißbilligen; entmutigen.

dis·cour·age [dis'kʌridʒ] entmutigen; *j.* abschrecken (*from* von); abschrecken von *et.*; **dis'cour·age·ment** Entmutigung *f*; Schwierigkeit *f*.

dis·course [dis'kɔ:s] **1.** Rede *f*; Abhandlung *f*; Predigt *f*; **2.** (*on, upon, about*) reden, sprechen (über *acc.*); e-n Vortrag halten (über *acc.*), *et.* abhandeln.

dis·cour·te·ous □ [dis'kə:tjəs] unhöflich; **dis'cour·te·sy** [～tisi] Unhöflichkeit *f*.

dis·cov·er [dis'kʌvə] entdecken; ausfindig machen; **dis'cov·er·a·ble** □ entdeckbar, auffindbar; ersichtlich; **dis'cov·er·er** Entdecker(in); **dis'cov·er·y** Entdeckung *f*.

dis·cred·it [dis'kredit] **1.** schlechter

Ruf *m*, Mißkredit *m*; Unglaubwürdigkeit *f*; **2.** nicht glauben; diskreditieren, in Mißkredit bringen; **dis'cred·it·a·ble** □ entehrend, schimpflich (*to* für).

dis·creet □ [dis'kri:t] besonnen, vorsichtig; klug; verschwiegen; diskret, taktvoll.

dis·crep·an·cy [dis'krepənsi] Verschiedenheit *f*, Widerspruch *m*, Diskrepanz *f*; Unstimmigkeit *f*; Zwiespalt *m*.

dis·crete □ [dis'kri:t] abgesondert, getrennt.

dis·cre·tion [dis'kreʃən] Besonnenheit *f*, Klugheit *f*; Diskretion *f*, Takt(gefühl *n*) *m*; Verschwiegenheit *f*; Verfügungsfreiheit *f*, Belieben *n*; *banker's* ～ Bankgeheimnis *n*; *at one's* ～ nach *od.* in j-s Belieben; *age od. years of* ～ Strafmündigkeit *f* (*14 Jahre*); *surrender at* ～ sich auf Gnade und Ungnade ergeben; **dis'cre·tion·ar·y** [～ʃnəri] willkürlich; unumschränkt.

dis·crim·i·nate [dis'krimineit] unterscheiden; ～ *against* benachteiligen; **dis'crim·i·nat·ing** □ unterscheidend; scharfsinnig; urteilsfähig; **dis·crim·i'na·tion** Unterscheidung *f*; unterschiedliche (*bsd.* nachteilige) Behandlung *f*; Urteilskraft *f*; *reverse* ～ Bevorzugung *f* von Farbigen auf Kosten der Weißen; **dis'crim·i·na·tive** [～nətiv] □ diskriminierend; **dis'crim·i·na·to·ry law** Ausnahmegesetz *n*.

dis·cur·sive □ [dis'kə:siv] weitschweifig; sprunghaft, abschweifend; *phls.* schließend; Urteils...

dis·cus ['diskəs] *Sport*: Diskus *m*.

dis·cuss [dis'kʌs] diskutieren, erörtern, besprechen; untersuchen; *co.* Essen *od.* Getränk sich zu Gemüte führen; **dis'cuss·i·ble** diskutabel; **dis'cus·sion** Diskussion *f*, Erörterung *f*, Aussprache *f*.

dis·dain [dis'dein] **1.** Geringschätzung *f*, Verachtung *f*; **2.** geringschätzen, verachten; verschmähen; **dis'dain·ful** □ [～ful] verachtend (*of acc.*); geringschätzig.

dis·ease [di'zi:z] Krankheit *f*; Leiden *n*; **dis'eased** krank.

dis·em·bark ['disim'ba:k] ausschiffen, landen, an Land gehen; **disem·bar·ka·tion** [disəmba:'keiʃən] Ausschiffung *f*.

dis·em·bar·rass ['disim'bærəs] frei-, losmachen (*of* von).

dis·em·bod·y [disim'bɔdi] entkörpern; *Truppen* auflösen.

dis·em·bogue [disim'bəug] (sich) ergießen. [weiden.]

dis·em·bow·el [disim'bauəl] aus-

dis·em·broil [disim'brɔil] entwirren.

dis·en·chant ['disin'tʃɑ:nt] desillusionieren, ernüchtern.

dis·en·cum·ber ['disin'kʌmbə] entlasten, freimachen (*of, from,* von).

dis·en·gage ['disin'geidʒ] (sich) freimachen, (sich) lösen; ⊕ loskuppeln; ausschalten; **'dis·en'gaged** frei; **'dis·en'gage·ment** Freimachung *f*; Ungebundenheit *f*; Entlobung *f*.

dis·en·tan·gle ['disin'tæŋgl] entwirren; *fig.* freimachen (*from* von); **'dis·en'tan·gle·ment** Entwirrung *f*.

dis·en·tomb [disin'tu:m] ausgraben.

dis·e·qui·lib·ri·um ['disekwi'libriəm] Unausgeglichenheit *f*.

dis·es·tab·lish ['disis'tæbliʃ] *Kirche* entstaatlichen; **dis·es'tab·lishment** Entstaatlichung *f*.

dis·fa·vo(u)r ['dis'feivə] **1.** Mißfallen *n*, Ungnade *f*, Unwillen *m*; **2.** nicht mögen; ungnädig behandeln; mißbilligen.

dis·fig·ure [dis'figə] entstellen, verunstalten; **dis'fig·ure·ment** Entstellung *f*.

dis·fran·chise ['dis'fræntʃaiz] *j-m* das Wahlrecht *od.* e-r *Stadt* die bürgerlichen Freiheiten nehmen; **disfran·chise·ment** [dis'fræntʃizmənt] Entziehung *f* des Wahl- *od.* Bürgerrechts.

dis·frock [dis'frɔk] *j-m* das Priesteramt entziehen.

dis·gorge [dis'gɔ:dʒ] ausspeien; von sich geben; wieder herausgeben; *a.* ～ *o.s.* sich ergießen.

dis·grace [dis'greis] **1.** Ungnade *f*; Schande *f*; **2.** in Ungnade fallen lassen; *j.* entehren, schänden; *be* ～*d* in Ungnade fallen; **dis'grace·ful** □ [～ful] schimpflich; schändlich.

dis·grun·tled [dis'grʌntld] verdrossen (*at* über *acc.*).

dis·guise [dis'gaiz] **1.** verkleiden; *Stimme* verstellen; verhehlen; **2.** Verkleidung *f*; Verstellung *f*; Maske *f*; *blessing in* ～ Glück im Unglück.

dis·gust [dis'gʌst] **1.** (*at, for*) Ekel *m*, Abscheu *m*, *f* (vor *dat.*); Widerwille *m* (gegen); **2.** anekeln; ~ed *with* angewidert durch; **dis'gusting** □ ekelhaft, widerwärtig.

dish [diʃ] **1.** Schüssel *f*, Platte *f*; Gericht *n* (*Speise*); *the* ~es *pl.* das Geschirr; *standing* ~ *fig.* ständiges Thema *n*; **2.** anrichten; *mst* ~ *up* auftischen (*a. fig.*); *sl. j.* erledigen; hereinlegen; *et.* vermasseln.

dis·ha·bille [disæ'biːl] Negligé *n*; *in* ~ nachlässig gekleidet; im Negligé.

dis·har·mo·ny [dis'hɑːməni] Mißklang *m*, Disharmonie *f*.

dish-cloth ['diʃklɔθ] Geschirrspültuch *n*.

dis·heart·en [dis'hɑːtn] entmutigen.

di·shev·el(l)ed [di'ʃevəld] zerzaust (*Haar*); *fig.* liederlich.

dis·hon·est □ [dis'ɔnist] unehrlich, unredlich; **dis'hon·est·y** Unredlichkeit *f*.

dis·hon·o(u)r [dis'ɔnə] **1.** Unehre *f*, Schande *f*; **2.** entehren; schänden; Schande machen (*dat.*); *Wechsel* nicht honorieren; **dis'hon·o(u)r·a·ble** □ entehrend, schimpflich; ehrlos; ~ *discharge* ✗ unehrenhafte Entlassung *f*.

dish...: '~**pan** *Am.* Spülschüssel *f*; '~**rag** *Am.* = *dish-cloth*; '~**washer** Tellerwäscher *m*; Geschirrspülmaschine *f*; '~**wa·ter** Spülwasser *n*.

dish·y F ['diʃi] attraktiv, (sexuell) anziehend.

dis·il·lu·sion [disi'luːʒən] **1.** Ernüchterung *f*, Enttäuschung *f*; **2.** ernüchtern, enttäuschen; **dis·il'lu·sion·ment** = *disillusion* 1.

dis·in·cen·tive [disin'sentiv] Entmutigung *f*.

dis·in·cli·na·tion [disinkli'neiʃən] Abneigung *f* (*for, to* gegen); **dis·in·cline** ['~'klain] abgeneigt machen; '**dis·in'clined** abgeneigt (*for, to* gegen).

dis·in·fect [disin'fekt] desinfizieren; **dis·in'fect·ant** Desinfektionsmittel *n*; **dis·in'fec·tion** Desinfektion *f*.

dis·in·fla·tion [disin'fleiʃən] Rückgang *m* der Inflation.

dis·in·gen·u·ous □ [disin'dʒenjuəs] unaufrichtig; falsch.

dis·in·her·it ['disin'herit] enterben; **dis·in'her·it·ance** Enterbung *f*.

dis·in·te·grate [dis'intigreit] (sich) (in seine Bestandteile) auflösen; (sich) zersetzen; aufschließen; **dis·in·te'gra·tion** Auflösung *f etc.*

dis·in·ter ['disin'tə:] wieder ausgraben.

dis·in·ter·est·ed □ [dis'intristid] uneigennützig, selbstlos.

dis·join [dis'dʒɔin] trennen; **dis·joint** [~'dʒɔint] in Unordnung bringen; (ab)trennen; auseinandernehmen; **dis'joint·ed** unzusammenhängend (*Rede*).

dis·junc·tion [dis'dʒʌŋkʃən] Trennung *f*; **dis'junc·tive** □ [~tiv] trennend; *gr.* disjunktiv.

disk [disk] Scheibe *f*; Platte *f*; Schallplatte *f*; ~ **brake** *mot.* Scheibenbremse *f*; ~ **clutch** *mot.* Scheibenkupplung *f*; '~**har·row** Scheibenegge *f*; ~ **jock·ey** *sl.* Ansager *m* e-r Schallplattensendung.

dis·like [dis'laik] **1.** Abneigung *f*; Widerwille *m* (*for, of, to* gegen); **2.** nicht mögen, nicht lieben, nicht leiden können; ~d unbeliebt.

dis·lo·cate ['disləukeit] aus den Fugen bringen; verrücken; verrenken; verlagern; *fig.* verwirren; **dis·lo'ca·tion** Verrenkung *f*; Verlagerung *f*; Verlegung *f* (*bsd.* ✗); *geol.* Verwerfung *f*; *fig.* Verwirrung *f*.

dis·lodge [dis'lɔdʒ] vertreiben, verjagen; umquartieren.

dis·loy·al □ ['dis'lɔiəl] treulos; '**dis'loy·al·ty** Treulosigkeit *f*.

dis·mal ['dizməl] **1.** □ *fig.* trüb (-selig), traurig, düster; öde; trostlos, elend; schaurig; **2.** *the* ~s *pl.* F der Trübsinn.

dis·man·tle [dis'mæntl] abbrechen, niederreißen; *Festung* schleifen; ⚓ abtakeln; *Haus* (aus)räumen; *Mechanismus etc.* auseinandernehmen; *Industriewerk* demontieren; **dis'man·tling** Demontage *f*.

dis·mast ⚓ [dis'mɑːst] entmasten.

dis·may [dis'mei] **1.** Furcht *f*, Schrecken *m*, Bestürzung *f*; **2.** *v/t.* erschrecken.

dis·mem·ber [dis'membə] zergliedern, zerstückeln; **dis'mem·ber·ment** Zergliederung *f*, -stückelung *f*.

dis·miss [dis'mis] *v/t.* entlassen, wegschicken; abtun (*as* als); ablehnen; *Thema etc.* fallen lassen; 🔨 abweisen; *be* ~ed *the service* aus dem Dienst entlassen werden; *v/i.*

✗ wegtreten; **dis'miss·al** Entlassung *f*; Aufgabe *f*; ⚖ Abweisung *f*.

dis·mount ['dis'maunt] *v/t.* vom Pferde werfen; *Geschütz* demontieren; ⊕ abmontieren, auseinandernehmen; *v/i.* absteigen.

dis·o·be·di·ence [disə'bi:djəns] Ungehorsam *m*; **dis·o'be·di·ent** □ ungehorsam (*to* gegen); **'dis·o'bey** nicht gehorchen (*dat.*), ungehorsam sein (gegen).

dis·o·blige ['disə'blaidʒ] ungefällig sein gegen; kränken; **'dis·o'bliging** □ ungefällig; unhöflich; **'dis·o'blig·ing·ness** Ungefälligkeit *f*.

dis·or·der [dis'ɔ:də] 1. Unordnung *f*; Aufruhr *m*, Unruhe *f*; ♣ Störung *f*, Krankheit *f*; *mental* ~ Geistesstörung *f*; 2. in Unordnung bringen; stören; zerrütten; **dis'ordered** □ unordentlich; verdorben (*Magen*); zerrüttet; **dis'or·der·ly** unordentlich; ordnungswidrig; unruhig, aufrührerisch; liederlich.

dis·or·gan·i·za·tion [disɔ:gənai'zeiʃən] Auflösung *f*, Zerrüttung *f*; **dis'or·gan·ize** zerrütten; in Unordnung bringen.

dis·or·i·en·tate [dis'ɔ:rienteit] irremachen; *he was* ~*d* er hatte die Orientierung verloren.

dis·own [dis'əun] nicht anerkennen, verleugnen; ablehnen.

dis·par·age [dis'pæridʒ] verächtlich machen, verunglimpfen, herabsetzen; **dis'par·age·ment** Herabsetzung *f*, Verunglimpfung *f*; Schande *f*; **dis'par·ag·ing** □ verächtlich.

dis·pa·rate ['dispərit] 1. □ ungleichartig, (ganz) verschieden; 2. ~*s pl.* unvereinbare Dinge *n/pl.*; **dis'par·i·ty** [dis'pæriti] Ungleichheit *f*.

dis·part [dis'pɑ:t] (sich) trennen; (sich) spalten; ⊕ kalibrieren.

dis·pas·sion·ate □ [dis'pæʃnit] leidenschaftslos; gelassen; unparteiisch.

dis·patch [dis'pætʃ] 1. (schnelle) Erledigung *f*; (schnelle) Absendung *f*, Abfertigung *f*; Versand *m*; Eile *f*; Depesche *f*; *mentioned in* ~*es* im Kriegsbericht rühmend erwähnt; *happy* ~ Harakiri *n*; 2. (schnell) abmachen, erledigen (*a.* ~ *töten*); abfertigen; absenden; **dis'patch-box** Dokumententasche *f*; **dis'patch-goods** *pl.* Eilgut *n*; **dis-**

patch note ⚓ Begleitschein *m*; **dis'patch-rid·er** ✗ Meldereiter *m*, -fahrer *m*.

dis·pel [dis'pel] vertreiben, zerstreuen (*a. fig.*).

dis·pen·sa·ble [dis'pensəbl] erläßlich; entbehrlich; **dis'pen·sa·ry** Apotheke *f*; Ambulanz *f für Unbemittelte*; **dis·pen·sa·tion** [dispen-'seiʃən] Austeilung *f*; Dispensation *f*, Befreiung *f* (*with* von); *göttliche* Fügung *f*.

dis·pense [dis'pens] *v/t.* austeilen, spenden; *Recht* sprechen; *Arzneien* nach Vorschrift bereiten und ausgeben; ~ *from* befreien *od.* entbinden von; *e-r Arbeit etc.* entheben; *v/i.* ~ *with et.* unnötig machen; fertig werden ohne, verzichten auf (*acc.*); **dis'pens·er** Austeiler(in); Apotheker(in).

dis·per·sal [dis'pə:səl] = *dispersion*; **dis'perse** (sich) zerstreuen; verstreuen, -breiten; auseinandergehen; **dis'per·sion** Zerstreuung *f* (*a. opt.*); Streuung *f*; Verbreitung *f*; ≳ *eccl.* Diaspora *f*.

dis·pir·it [di'spirit] entmutigen; **dis'pir·it·ed** □ mutlos.

dis·place [dis'pleis] verrücken, verschieben; absetzen; ersetzen; verdrängen; ~*d person* Verschleppte *m*, *f*; **dis'place·ment** Verrückung *f etc.*; Ersatz *m*; (*bsd.* Wasser)Verdrängung *f*.

dis·play [dis'plei] 1. Entfaltung *f*; Aufwand *m*; Schaustellung *f*; (Schaufenster)Auslage *f*; Prunk *m*; 2. entfalten, an den Tag legen; zur Schau stellen; ausstellen, -breiten; zeigen; hervorheben; ~ **case** Vitrine *f*, Schaukasten *m*; ~ **stand** Verkaufsständer *m*.

dis·please [dis'pli:z] *j-m* mißfallen; *fig.* verletzen; **dis'pleased** □ ungehalten (*at, with* über *acc.*); **dis'pleas·ing** □ mißfällig, unangenehm; **dis'pleas·ure** [~'pleʒə] Mißfallen *n*, -vergnügen *n*; Verdruß *m* (*at, over* über *acc.*).

dis·port [dis'pɔ:t]: ~ *o.s.* sich (lustig) tummeln, herumtollen.

dis·pos·a·ble [dis'pəuzəbl] verfügbar; **dis'pos·al** Anordnung *f*; Verfügung(srecht *n*) *f* (*of* über *acc.*); Beseitigung *f*; Veräußerung *f*, Verkauf *m*; Übergabe *f*; *at one's* ~ zu j-s Verfügung; **dis'pose** *v/t.* (an-)

ordnen, einrichten, verteilen; geneigt machen, veranlassen (*for zu*
et., *to inf.* zu *inf.*); *v/i.* ~ *of* verfügen
über (*acc.*); erledigen; verwenden;
gebrauchen; veräußern; vermachen;
unterbringen, versorgen; beseitigen;
verzehren; **dis'posed** □ geneigt
(*for*, *to* zu); ...gesinnt; *well* (*ill*) ~
towards s.o. j-m wohl-(übel)gesinnt;
dis·po·si·tion [͵po'ziʃən] Disposition *f*; Anordnung *f*; *fig.* Neigung
f, Hang *m*; Sinnesart *f*; Verfügung *f* (*of* über *acc.*); *make* ~*s*
Anordnungen treffen.
dis·pos·sess ['dispə'zes] (*of*) vertreiben (aus); berauben (*gen.*); *j.*
enteignen; *fig.* freimachen (von);
dis·pos·ses·sion [~'seʃən] Vertreibung *f etc.*
dis·praise [dis'preiz] 1. Tadel *m*;
2. tadeln; geringschätzen.
dis·proof ['dis'pruːf] Widerlegung *f*.
dis·pro·por·tion [disprə'pɔːʃən]
Mißverhältnis *n*; **dis·pro'por-**
tion·ate □ [~ʃnit] unverhältnismäßig, unproportioniert, ungleichmäßig; **dis·pro'por·tion·ate·ness**
Mißverhältnis *n*; **'dis·pro'por-**
tioned [~ʃənd] = *disproportionate*.
dis·prove [dis'pruːv] widerlegen.
dis·pu·ta·ble [dis'pjuːtəbl] strittig,
fraglich; **dis'pu·tant** Disputant *m*;
dis·pu'ta·tion Disputation *f*; **dis-**
pu'ta·tious □ streitsüchtig; **dis-**
'pute 1. Streit(igkeit *f*) *m*; Auseinandersetzung *f*; Rechtsstreit *m*;
in ~ streitig; *beyond* (*all*) ~, *past* ~
unstreitig, zweifellos; 2. *v/t.* bestreiten, anfechten, in Zweifel
ziehen; streiten um, streitig machen; *v/i.* streiten (*about* um).
dis·qual·i·fi·ca·tion [diskwɔlifi-
'keiʃən] Unfähig-, Untauglich-
keit(serklärung) *f*; *Sport:* Ausschluß *m*, Disqualifikation *f*; Nachteil *m*; **dis'qual·i·fy** [~fai] unfähig *od.* untauglich machen *od.*
erklären (*for* zu); *Sport:* ausschließen, disqualifizieren.
dis·qui·et [dis'kwaiət] 1. Unruhe *f*,
Sorge *f*; 2. beunruhigen; **dis'qui·et-**
ing beunruhigend; **dis·qui·e·tude**
[~'kwaiitjuːd] Unruhe *f*.
dis·qui·si·tion [diskwi'ziʃən] Untersuchung *f*; Abhandlung *f* (*on* über
acc.).
dis·re·gard ['disri'gɑːd] 1. Nicht-
(be)achtung *f*, Mißachtung *f*; 2. un-

beachtet lassen; mißachten, nicht
beachten.
dis·rel·ish [dis'reliʃ] 1. Ekel *m*;
Widerwille *m* (*for* gegen); 2. Wider-
willen haben gegen.
dis·re·pair ['disri'peə] Baufälligkeit *f*; *fall into* ~ in Verfall geraten.
dis·rep·u·ta·ble □ [dis'repjutəbl]
schimpflich; verrufen; **dis·re·pute**
['͵ri'pjuːt] übler Ruf *m*; Schande *f*.
dis·re·spect ['disris'pekt] Nichtachtung *f*; Respektlosigkeit *f*;
dis·re'spect·ful [~ful] □ respektlos; unhöflich.   [kleiden.]
dis·robe ['dis'rəub] (sich) ent-]
dis·root [dis'ruːt] entwurzeln.
dis·rupt [dis'rʌpt] zerreißen; spalten; **dis'rup·tion** Zerbrechen *n*;
Spaltung *f*, Zusammenbruch *m*; **dis-**
'rup·tive störend.
dis·sat·is·fac·tion ['dissætis'fækʃən]
Unzufriedenheit *f*; **dis·sat·is·fac-**
to·ry ['͵'fæktəri] unbefriedigend;
'dis'sat·is·fied [~faid] unzufrieden;
'dis'sat·is·fy [~fai] nicht befriedigen; unzufrieden machen; *j-m* mißfallen.
dis·sect [di'sekt] zerlegen; *anat.* se-
zieren; *fig.* zergliedern; **dis'sec-**
tion Zerlegung *f*; *anat.* Sektion *f*;
fig. Zergliederung *f*.
dis·sem·ble [di'sembl] *v/t.* verhehlen, verbergen; nicht beachten;
v/i. sich verstellen, heucheln.
dis·sem·i·nate [di'semineit] ausstreuen; verbreiten; **dis·sem·i'na-**
tion Ausstreuung *f etc.*
dis·sen·sion [di'senʃən] Zwietracht
f, Streit *m*, Uneinigkeit *f*.
dis·sent [di'sent] 1. abweichende
Meinung *f*; Nichtzugehörigkeit
f zur Landeskirche; 2. (*from*)
anderer Meinung sein (als), nicht
übereinstimmen (mit); abweichen
(von); nicht der Landeskirche angehören; **dis'sent·er** Andersdenkende *m*, *f*; Dissenter *m*, nicht der
Landeskirche Angehörende *m*, *f*;
dis'sen·tient [~ʃiənt] 1. anders-
denkend; 2. Andersdenkende *m*,
f.
dis·ser·ta·tion [disə'teiʃən] Abhandlung *f*, Dissertation *f* (*on* über
acc.).
dis·serv·ice ['dis'sɔːvis]   (*to*)
schlechter Dienst *m* (an *dat.*);
Nachteil *m* (für).
dis·sev·er [dis'sevə] (zer)teilen, tren-

nen; **dis'sev·er·ance, dis'sev·er·ment** Trennung f.
dis·si·dence ['disidəns] Uneinigkeit f; **'dis·si·dent 1.** uneinig; **2.** Andersdenkende m, f; Dissident(in) (bes. pol., eccl.).
dis·sim·i·lar □ ['di'similə] unähnlich (to, from dat.); verschieden (to von); **dis·si·lar·i·ty** [‿'læriti] Unähnlichkeit f; Verschiedenheit f (to von).
dis·sim·u·late [di'simjuleit] = dissemble; **dis·sim·u·la·tion** Verstellung f, Heuchelei f.
dis·si·pate ['disipeit] (sich) zerstreuen; verschwenden; ein ausschweifendes Leben führen; **'dis·si·pat·ed** ausschweifend, zügellos; **dis·si'pa·tion** Zerstreuung f; Verschwendung f; ausschweifendes Leben n.
dis·so·ci·ate [di'səuʃieit] trennen; zersetzen; ‿ o.s. sich distanzieren, abrücken (from von); **dis·so·ci·a·tion** [‿si'eiʃən] Trennung f etc.; psych. Bewußtseinsspaltung f.
dis·sol·u·bil·i·ty [disɔlju'biliti] Auflösbarkeit f; Trennbarkeit f; **dis·'sol·u·ble** [‿jubl] (auf)lösbar; trennbar.
dis·so·lute □ ['disəlu:t] liederlich, ausschweifend; **dis·so'lu·tion** Auflösung f; Zerstörung f; Tod m.
dis·solv·a·ble [di'zɔlvəbl] (auf)lösbar; **dis'solve 1.** v/t. auflösen (a. fig.); lösen; schmelzen; v/i. sich auflösen; fig. vergehen; **2.** Am. Film: langsames Überblenden n; **dis'solv·ent 1.** (auf)lösend; zersetzend; **2.** Lösungsmittel n.
dis·so·nance ['disənəns] ♪ Mißklang m; Uneinigkeit f; **'dis·so·nant** ♪ mißtönend; fig. abweichend (from, to von).
dis·suade [di'sweid] j-m abraten (from von); **dis'sua·sion** [‿ʒən] Abraten n; **dis'sua·sive** [‿siv] □ abratend.
dis·taff ['distɑ:f] Spinnrocken m; fig. das Reich der Frau; ‿ side weibliche Linie f e-r Familie.
dis·tance ['distəns] **1.** Abstand m, Entfernung f (örtlich, zeitlich, fig.); Ferne f; Strecke f; Zurückhaltung f; at a ‿ von weitem; in e-r gewissen Entfernung; weit weg; in the ‿ in der Ferne; a great ‿ away weit weg; striking ‿ Wirkungsweite f;

keep one's ‿ Abstand halten; keep s.o. at a ‿ j-m gegenüber reserviert sein; **2.** hinter sich lassen (a. fig.); **'dis·tant** □ entfernt; fern; zurückhaltend; Fern...; ‿ control Fernsteuerung f; ‿ relative entfernter Verwandter m.
dis·taste ['dis'teist] Widerwille m (for vor od. gegen); fig. Abneigung f (for gegen); **dis'taste·ful** □ [‿ful] widerwärtig; ärgerlich.
dis·tem·per¹ ['dis'tempə] **1.** Temperamalerei f, -farbe f; **2.** mit Temperafarben (an)malen; streichen.
dis·tem·per² [‿] Krankheit f (bsd. von Tieren); (Hunde)Staupe f; politische Unruhe f; **dis'tem·pered** zerrüttet; krank.
dis·tend [dis'tend] (sich) ausdehnen; (auf)blähen; (sich) weiten; **dis'ten·sion** Ausdehnung f.
dis·tich ['distik] Distichon n (Verspaar).
dis·til(l) [dis'til] herabtröpfeln (lassen); ♣ destillieren (a. fig.), ausziehen; Branntwein brennen; **dis·til·late** ['‿lit] Destillat n; **dis·til·la·tion** [‿'leiʃən] Destillierung f; **dis'till·er** Branntweinbrenner m, Destillateur m; **dis'till·er·y** Branntweinbrennerei f.
dis·tinct □ [dis'tiŋkt] verschieden; getrennt; deutlich, klar; **dis'tinc·tion** Unterscheidung f; Unterschied m; Auszeichnung f; Rang m, Würde f; Absonderung f; das Individuelle; draw a ‿ between e-n Unterschied machen zwischen; have the ‿ of ger. den Vorzug haben zu inf.; **dis'tinc·tive** □ unterscheidend, besonder; apart; kennzeichnend, bezeichnend (of für); **dis'tinct·ness** Verschiedenheit f; Deutlichkeit f.
dis·tin·guish [dis'tiŋgwiʃ] unterscheiden; auszeichnen; **dis'tin·guish·a·ble** unterscheidbar; **dis·'tin·guished** berühmt, ausgezeichnet, hervorragend; vornehm.
dis·tort [dis'tɔ:t] verdrehen (a. fig.), verzerren, -ziehen; ‿ing mirror Zerrspiegel m; **dis'tor·tion** (Wort-) Verdrehung f; Verzerrung f.
dis·tract [dis'trækt] ablenken, zerstreuen; beunruhigen; verwirren; verrückt machen; **dis'tract·ed** □ verwirrt; von Sinnen, außer sich

(*with* vor *dat.*); **dis'tract·ing** □ wahnsinnig machend; **dis'traction** Zerstreutheit *f*; Verwirrung *f*; Raserei *f*, Wahnsinn *m*; Zerstreuung *f*.

dis·train [dis'trein] pfänden (*on*, *upon acc.*); **dis'train·a·ble** pfändbar; **dis·traint** [ˏ'treint] Pfändung *f*.

dis·traught [dis'trɔːt] verstört, verwirrt, bestürzt.

dis·tress [dis'tres] **1.** Qual *f*; Elend *n*, Not *f*, Bedrängnis *f*; Erschöpfung *f*; = *distraint*; ⁓ *rocket* ⚓ Notsignal *n*; **2.** in Not bringen; quälen; erschöpfen; **dis'tressed** notleidend; bedrängt; bekümmert (*for* um); ⁓ *area* Notstandsgebiet *n*; **dis'tress·ful** □ [ˏful] *lit.* qualvoll; gequält, unglücklich; **dis'tressing** □ qualvoll; erschütternd.

dis·trib·ut·a·ble [dis'tribjutəbl] verteilbar; **dis'trib·ute** [ˏjuːt] verteilen (*among* unter *acc.*, *to* an *acc.*); *Ware* vertreiben; einteilen; verbreiten; *typ. Schrift* ablegen; **distri'bu·tion** Verteilung *f*; *Waren*-Vertrieb *m*; *Film*-Verleih *m*; Verbreitung *f*; Einteilung *f*; **dis'tribu·tive** aus-, zu-, verteilend; *gr.* distributiv; **dis'trib·u·tive·ly** im einzelnen, gesondert; **dis'trib·u·tor** Verteiler *m* (*bsd.* ⊕); ✝ Vertreiber *m*, Vertriebsstelle *f*; *Film*-Verleiher *m*.

dis·trict ['distrikt] Distrikt *m*, Bezirk *m*, Kreis *m*; Landstrich *m*, Gegend *f*; ⁓ *council* Bezirksregierung *f*; ⁓ *court Am.* Bezirksgericht *n*; ⁓ *manager* Bezirksleiter *m*.

dis·trust [dis'trʌst] **1.** Mißtrauen *n*, Argwohn *m* (*of* gegen); **2.** mißtrauen (*dat.*); **dis'trust·ful** □ [ˏful] mißtrauisch; ⁓ (*of o.s.*) schüchtern.

dis·turb [dis'tɜːb] beunruhigen; stören; verwirren; **dis'turb·ance** Störung *f*; Unruhe *f*; Aufruhr *m*; ⁓ *of the peace* ⚖ öffentliche Ruhestörung *f*; **dis'turbed** geistig gestört; verhaltensgestört; **dis'turb·er** Störenfried *m*, Unruhestifter *m*.

dis·un·ion ['dis'juːnjən] Trennung *f*; Uneinigkeit *f*; **dis·u·nite** [ˏ'nait] (sich) trennen; (sich) entzweien; **disu·ni·ty** [dis'juːniti] Uneinigkeit *f*.

dis·use 1. ['dis'juːs] Nichtgebrauch *m*; *fall into* ⁓ außer Gebrauch

kommen; **2.** ['dis'juːz] nicht mehr gebrauchen.

di·syl·lab·ic ['disi'læbik] (ˏ*ally*) zweisilbig; **di·syl·la·ble** [di'siləbl] zweisilbiges Wort *n*.

ditch [ditʃ] **1.** Graben *m*; *die in the last* ⁓ bis zum letzten Blutstropfen kämpfen; **2.** *v/t.* mit Gräben versehen; in den Graben fahren; *v/i.* graben, Gräben machen *od.* ausbessern; *Am. sl.* im Stich lassen; notlanden auf dem Wasser; **'ditcher** Grabbagger *m*.

dith·er F ['diðə] bibbern (*zittern*); zaudern, schwanken.

dith·y·ramb ['diθiræmb] Dithyrambe *f*; begeistertes Lob *n*.

dit·to ['ditəu] dito, desgleichen; (*suit of*) ⁓s Anzug *m* aus gleichem Stoff.

dit·ty ['diti] Liedchen *n*.

di·ur·nal □ [dai'ə:nl] täglich.

di·va·gate *fig.* ['daivəgeit] abschweifen.

di·va·ga·tion [daivə'geiʃən] Abschweifung *f*.

di·van [di'væn] Diwan *m*; ⁓**-bed** [*oft* 'daivænbed] Bettcouch *f*, Liege *f*.

di·var·i·cate [dai'værikeit] sich gabeln; abzweigen.

dive [daiv] **1.** (unter)tauchen; *vom Sprungbrett* springen; ✖ e-n Sturzflug machen; F sich ducken; stürzen; ⁓ *into* tief eindringen in (*acc.*); *in* (*acc.*) hineinlangen; **2.** *Schwimmen:* Springen *n*; (Kopf)Sprung *m* (*a. fig.*); Sturzflug *m*; Kellerlokal *n*; *Am.* F Kaschemme *f*; '⁓**-bomb** im Sturzflug bombardieren; **'div·er** Taucher *m*; Kunstspringer(in).

di·verge [dai'və:dʒ] divergieren, auseinanderlaufen; abweichen; **di'ver·gence**, **di'ver·gen·cy** Divergenz *f*; Abweichung *f*; **di'ver·gent** □ divergierend; (voneinander) abweichend.

di·vers ['daivə:z] mehrere.

di·verse □ [dai'və:s] *dem Wesen nach* verschieden; ungleich(artig); mannigfaltig; **di·ver·si·fi·ca·tion** [ˏfi'keiʃən] Veränderung *f*, Abwechslung *f*; **di'ver·si·fy** [ˏfai] verschieden machen; Abwechslung bringen in (*acc.*); **di·ver·sion** [dai'və:ʃən] Ablenkung *f*; Ablenkungsmanöver *n*; Zerstreuung *f*, Zeitvertreib *m*; Umleitung *f*; **di'ver·sion·a·ry** ✖ Ablenkungs...;

di'ver·si·ty [‿siti] Verschiedenheit *f*; Mannigfaltigkeit *f*.

di·vert [dai'və:t] ablenken; *j*. zerstreuen; unterhalten; *Verkehr* umleiten.

di·vest [dai'vest] entkleiden; *fig*. berauben; ‿ *o.s. of* verzichten auf (*acc*.); di'vest·ment Entkleidung *f*; Beraubung *f*.

di·vide [di'vaid] 1. *v/t. oft* ‿ *up* teilen; trennen; verteilen (*among* unter *acc*.); einteilen; entzweien; ⚕ dividieren (*by* durch); ‿ *the house parl*. das Haus abstimmen lassen; *v/i.* sich teilen *etc*.; ⚕ teilbar sein (*by* durch); aufgehen (*into* in); *parl*. abstimmen; 2. Wasserscheide *f*; div·i·dend ['dividend] † Dividende *f*, Gewinnanteil *m*; ⚕ Dividend *m*; 'div·i·dend-war·rant † Dividendenschein *m*; di·vid·er [di-'vaidə] *Am. mot*. Mittelstreifen *m*; ‿s *pl*. Stechzirkel *m*; di'vid·ing Trennungs...; ‿ *ridge* Wasserscheide *f*.

div·i·na·tion [divi'neiʃən] Weissagung *f*; Ahnung *f*; di·vine [di'vain] 1. □ göttlich (*a. fig*.); ‿ *service* Gottesdienst *m*; 2. Geistliche *m*; 3. weissagen; ahnen; di'vin·er Wahrsager(in); Rutengänger(in).

div·ing ['daiviŋ] *Schwimmen*: Kunstspringen *n*; *attr*. Taucher...; '‿-bell Taucherglocke *f*; '‿-board Sprungbrett *n*; '‿-dress, '‿-suit Taucheranzug *m*.

di·vin·ing-rod [di'vaininŋrɔd] Wünschelrute *f*; di·vin·i·ty [di'viniti] Gottheit *f*; Göttlichkeit *f*; Theologie *f*.

di·vis·i·bil·i·ty [divizi'biliti] Teilbarkeit *f*; di'vis·i·ble □ [‿zəbl] teilbar; di'vi·sion [‿ʒən] (Ein-, Ver)Teilung *f*; Spaltung *f*, Uneinigkeit *f*; Trennung(slinie) *f*; Teil *m*, Abteilung *f*; Bezirk *m*; ✕, ⚕ Division *f*; *parl*. Hammelsprung *m*; ‿ *bell* Abstimmungsglocke *f*; ‿ *of* labo(u)r Arbeitsteilung *f*; di'vi·sion·al [‿ʒənl] (Ab)Teilungs...; ✕ Divisions...; di·vi·sive [di'vaisiv] auf Trennung abzielend; di'vi·sor ⚕ [‿zə] Teiler *m*, Divisor *m*.

di·vorce [di'vɔːs] 1. (Ehe)Scheidung *f*; *fig*. Scheidung *f*, Trennung *f*; 2. *Ehe* scheiden (*a. fig*.); sich scheiden lassen von; di·vor·cee [di:-

vɔ:'si:] Geschiedene *m*, *f*; di·vorc·er [di'vɔ:sə] der die Ehescheidung veranlassende Teil.

di·vulge [dai'vʌldʒ] ausplaudern; verbreiten, bekanntmachen.

dix·ie ✕ *sl*. ['diksi] Kochgeschirr *n*; Feldkessel *m*; ♀ *Am*. die Südstaaten *pl*.; ♀*crat Am. pol. opponierender* Südstaatendemokrat *m*.

diz·zi·ness ['dizinis] Schwindel *m*; 'diz·zy 1. □ schwind(e)lig (*Person*); Schwindel erregend (*Sache*); verwirrt; ‿ *spell* Schwindelanfall *m*; 2. schwindelig machen.

do [du:] (*irr*.) (*s. a.* done) 1. *v/t.* tun, machen; an-, verfertigen; ausführen, vollbringen; *Strecke* zurücklegen; (fertig)machen; verrichten; (zu)bereiten, kochen; ‿*en Gefallen etc.* erweisen; *Rolle, Stück* spielen; F übers Ohr hauen, prellen; ‿ *London* F London besichtigen; ‿ *s.o.* F j. versorgen, beköstigen; *what is to be done?* was ist zu tun *od*. zu machen?; ‿ *the polite, etc.* den Höflichen *etc*. spielen; *have done reading* fertig sein mit Lesen; ‿ *a room* ein Zimmer aufräumen; ‿ (*over*) *again* noch einmal machen; ‿ *down* F unterkriegen; ‿ *in* F um die Ecke bringen; ‿ *into* übersetzen, -tragen in; ‿ *out* ausfegen; ‿ *over* mit *Farbe etc.* überstreichen, -ziehen; ‿ *up* zs.-legen; instandsetzen, reparieren, renovieren; einpacken; F kaputt machen (*gänzlich ermüden*); 2. *v/i.* tun, handeln; sich benehmen; sich befinden; dem Zweck entsprechen, genügen; tauglich sein, passen; *that will* ‿ das genügt; *that won't* ‿ das geht nicht; das reicht nicht; *how* ‿ *you* ‿? guten Tag!, Wie geht's?; ‿ *well* s-e Sache gut machen; gute Geschäfte machen; gut fahren; ‿ *badly* schlechte Geschäfte machen; *have done!* hör auf!; ‿ *away with* abschaffen; ‿ *for j-m* den Haushalt führen; ‿ *with* auskommen mit; *I could* ‿ *with ...* ich könnte ... brauchen *od*. vertragen; *have done with* fertig sein mit, erledigt haben; ‿ *without* fertig werden ohne, entbehren können, verzichten auf (*acc*.); 3. *v/aux. Frage:* ‿ *you know him* kennen Sie ihn?; *Verneinung mit* not: *I* ‿ *not know him* ich kenne ihn nicht; *emphatisch*, *verstärkend:* I ~ *feel better* ich fühle mich wirklich besser; ~ *come and see me* besuche mich doch einmal; ~ *be quick* beeile dich doch; *für ein vorausgegangenes Verb:* ~ *you like London* — I *do* gefällt Ihnen London? — Ja; *you write better than* I ~ Sie schreiben besser als ich; I *take a bath every day.* — So ~ I ich nehme täglich ein Bad. — Ich auch; **4.** F Schwindel *m;* große Sache *f,* Fest *n,* Party *f.*

doc F [dɔk] = *doctor.*

doc·ile ['dəusail] gelehrig; fügsam; **do·cil·i·ty** [~'siliti] Gelehrigkeit *f;* Fügsamkeit *f.*

dock[1] [dɔk] stutzen; *fig.* kürzen (of um).

dock[2] ⚘ [~] Ampfer *m.*

dock[3] [~] **1.** ⚓ Dock *n;* Hafenbecken *n; bsd. Am.* Kai *m,* Pier *m, f;* ⚒ Anklagebank *f; dry ~, graving ~* Trockendock *n; floating ~* Schwimmdock *n; wet ~* Schleusenhafen *m;* **2.** ⚓ docken; *Raumfahrt:* ankoppeln; '~**dues** *pl.* Dock-, Hafengebühren *f/pl.;* '**dock·er** Dock-, Hafenarbeiter *m.*

dock·et ['dɔkit] **1.** Aktenschwanz *m;* Inhaltsvermerk *m;* Bestellschein *m;* Etikett *n;* Adreßzettel *m;* Gerichtskalender *m;* **2.** mit Aktenschwanz *etc.* versehen.

dock·yard ['dɔkjɑːd] Werft *f.*

doc·tor ['dɔktə] **1.** Doktor *m;* Arzt *m;* ~'s *certificate* ärztliche Bescheinigung *f,* ärztliches Attest *n;* **2.** F verarzten; zurechtflicken; (*a.* ~ *up* zurecht)doktern (*fälschen*); **doc·tor·ate** ['~rit] Doktorwürde *f.*

doc·tri·naire [dɔktri'nɛə] **1.** Doktrinär *m,* Prinzipienreiter *m;* **2.** doktrinär, schulmeisterlich; **doc·tri·nal** ☐ [~'trainl] die Lehre betreffend, lehrmäßig; **doc·trine** ['~trin] Lehre *f,* Doktrin *f;* Dogma *n.*

doc·u·ment 1. ['dɔkjumənt] Dokument *n,* Urkunde *f,* Schriftstück *n; travel ~s pl.* Reiseunterlagen *f/pl.;* **2.** ['~ment] beurkunden; mit Urkunden versehen *od.* belegen, dokumentieren; **doc·u·men·ta·ry 1.** ☐ urkundlich; ~ *film* = **2.** Kultur-, Dokumentarfilm *m;* **doc·u·men·ta·tion** Benutzung *f* von Urkunden.

dod·der ['dɔdə] **1.** ⚘ Flachsseide *f;* **2.** schlottern, schwanken.

dodge [dɔdʒ] **1.** Sprung *m* zur Seite;

Schlich *m,* Kniff *m,* Winkelzug *m;* **2.** *v/t.* ausweichen (*dat.*); zum besten haben; *v/i.* ausweichen, zur Seite springen; sich drücken vor; Winkelzüge machen; schlüpfen; **dod·gem** F ['dɔdʒəm] Autoskooter *m auf dem Jahrmarkt;* '**dodg·er** Schieber(in); *Am.* Hand-, Reklamezettel *m; Am.* Maisbrot *n,* -kuchen *m;* **dodg·y** F ['dɔdʒi] vertrackt; riskant; nicht einwandfrei.

do·do *orn.* ['dəudəu] Dodo *m* (*ausgestorben*).

doe [dəu] Hindin *f;* Reh *n;* Häsin *f.*

do·er ['duːə] Täter(in), Handelnde *m, f.*

does [dʌz] *er, sie, es* tut (*s.* do).

doe·skin ['dəuskin] Rehleder *n;* Doeskin *n* (*Gewebe*).

doesn't F ['dʌznt] = *does not* (*s.* do).

dog [dɔg] **1.** Hund *m;* Rüde *m* (*männlicher Hund od. Fuchs*); ⊕ Feuerbock *m;* Haken *m,* Klammer *f;* Klaue *f;* ⚒ Förderwagen *m;* F Kerl *m; Am.* F Angabe *f* (*Prahlerei*); *go to the ~s* vor die Hunde gehen, auf den Hund kommen; **2.** sich an *j-s* Fersen heften, *j-m* nachspüren; '~-**bis·cuit** Hundekuchen *m;* '~-**cart** leichter Jagdwagen *m;* '~-**cheap** spottbillig; '~-**col·lar** Hundehalsband *n;* F *hoher, steifer Kragen e-s Geistlichen;* '~-**days** *pl.* Hundstage *m/pl.*

doge [dəudʒ] Doge *m.*

dog...: '~-**eared** = *dog's-eared;* '~-**fight** F Luftkampf *m;* '~-**fish** *zo.* Hundshai *m.*

dog·ged ☐ ['dɔgid] verbissen.

dog·ger·el ['dɔgərəl] *a.* ~ *rhymes pl.* Knüttelverse *m/pl.*

dog·gie ['dɔgi] = *doggy;* '~-**bag** *Restaurant:* Beutel *zum Mitnehmen von Essensresten.*

dog·gish ['dɔgiʃ] hündisch; knurrig; **dog·go** *sl.* ['dɔgəu]: *lie ~* sich nicht rühren; '**dog·gy 1.** Hündchen *n;* **2.** hundefreundlich; Hunde...; *Am.* F äußerlich aufgemacht; '**dog--Lat·in** Küchenlatein *n;* '~-**like** hündisch. [Kälbchen *n.*\

do·gie *Am.* ['dəugi] *mutterloses*\

dog·ma ['dɔgmə] Dogma *n,* Lehr-, Glaubenssatz *m;* Glaubenslehre *f;* **dog·mat·ic, dog·mat·i·cal** ☐ [~'mætik(əl)] dogmatisch, lehrhaft; bestimmt; selbstherrlich; **dog·mat·ics** *sg.* Dogmatik *f;* **dog·ma-**

tism ['ˌmətizəm] Bestimmtheit *f*, Selbstherrlichkeit *f*; Dogmatismus *m*; '**dog·ma·tist** Dogmatiker *m*; dreister Behaupter *m*; **dog·ma·tize** ['ˌmətaiz] seine Meinung als maßgeblich hinstellen.

dog's-bod·y *sl.* ['dɔgzbɔdi] Sklave *m*, Arbeitstier *n*, Kuli *m*; '**dog's--ear** Eselsohr *n im Buch*; '**dog's--eared** mit Eselsohren.

dog...: 'ˌ~'**tired** hundemüde; 'ˌ~-**tooth** △ Zahnornament *n*; 'ˌ~-**trot** leichter Trab *m*; 'ˌ~-**watch** ⚓ Spaltwache *f*, Plattfuß *m*; 'ˌ~-**wood** ♀ Hartriegel *m*.

doi·ly ['dɔili] Tellerdeckchen *n*.

do·ing ['duːiŋ] **1.** *p.pr. von* **do 1**; *nothing* ~ nichts zu machen; ✝ kein Geschäft; **2.** Tun *n*, Tat *f*; ~s *pl.* Dinge *n/pl.*, Begebenheiten *f/pl.*; Treiben *n*; Betragen *n*.

doit [dɔit] Deut *m*, Heller *m*.

do-it-your·self ['duːitjɔ:'self] **1.** Do-it-yourself *n*, Selbstanfertigen *n*; **2.** Bastler..., Hobby...

dol·drums ['dɔldrəmz] *pl.* Niedergeschlagenheit *f*; ⚓ Kalmen(zone *f*) *f/pl.*

dole [dəul] **1.** (milde) Spende *f*; F Arbeitslosenunterstützung *f*; *be od. go on the* ~ stempeln gehen; **2.** *mst* ~ *out* verteilen.

dole·ful □ ['dəulful] trübselig, traurig; '**dole·ful·ness** Traurigkeit *f*, Trübseligkeit *f*; Kummer *m*.

doll [dɔl] **1.** Puppe *f (a. fig.)*; **2.** ~ *up* F sich aufdonnern.

dol·lar ['dɔlə] Dollar *m*.

dol·lop F ['dɔləp] Klumpen *m*.

doll·y ['dɔli] Püppchen *n*; Transportkarren *m*; Kamerawagen *m*.

dol·o·mite *min.* ['dɔləmait] Dolomit *m*.

dol·o(u)r *mst poet., co.* ['dəulə] Leid *m*, Schmerz *m*; **dol·o·rous** ['dɔlərəs] schmerzhaft; trübselig, traurig.

dol·phin *ichth.* ['dɔlfin] Delphin *m*.

dolt [dəult] Tölpel *m*; '**dolt·ish** □ tölpelhaft.

do·main [dəu'mein] Domäne *f*; *fig.* Gebiet *n*, Bereich *m*.

dome [dəum] Dom *m*; Kuppel *f*; ⊕ Deckel *m*; **domed** gewölbt.

Domes·day Book ['duːmzdei'buk] Reichsgrundbuch *n Englands*.

do·mes·tic [dəu'mestik] **1.** (~*ally*) häuslich; Haus..., Privat...; in-

ländisch; einheimisch; Innen...; zahm; ~ *animal* Haustier *n*; ~ *appliance* Haushaltsgerät *n*; ~ *bliss* häusliches Glück *n*; ~ *coal* Hausbrandkohle *f*; ~ *flight* Inlandsflug *m*; ~ *science* Hauswirtschaftskunde *f*; **2.** *a.* ~ *servant* Hausangestellte *f*; ~s *pl.* Haushaltsartikel *m/pl.*; **do·mes·ti·cate** [ˌkeit] häuslich *od.* heimisch machen; zähmen; **do·mes·ti·ca·tion** Eingewöhnung *f*; Zähmung *f*; **do·mes·tic·i·ty** [ˌ'tisiti] Häuslichkeit *f*.

dom·i·cile ['dɔmisail] **1.** *bsd.* ⚖ Wohnsitz *m*; Zahlungsort *m*; **2.** ✝ *Wechsel* domizilieren; '**dom·i·ciled** ansässig, wohnhaft; **dom·i·cil·i·ar·y** [ˌ'siljəri] Haus...; ~ *visit* Haussuchung *f*; ✞ Hausbesuch *m*.

dom·i·nance ['dɔminəns] Herrschaft *f*; '**dom·i·nant 1.** (vor-)herrschend; emporragend; **2.** ♪ Dominante *f*; **dom·i·nate** ['ˌneit] (be)herrschen; **dom·i·na·tion** Herrschaft *f*; '**dom·i·na·tor** Herrscher *m*; **dom·i·neer** [dɔmi'niə] (despotisch) herrschen; ~ *over* tyrannisieren; **dom·i'neer·ing** □ tyrannisch, herrisch; überheblich.

do·min·i·cal [də'minikəl] Sonntags...; ~ *prayer* Vaterunser *n*.

Do·min·i·can [də'minikən] Dominikaner *m*.

do·min·ion [də'minjən] Herrschaft *f*; *oft* ~s *pl.* Gebiet *n (a. fig.)*; 2 Dominion *n (im Brit. Commonwealth)*.

dom·i·no ['dɔminəu] Domino *m*; Maskenkostüm *n*; **dom·i·noes** ['ˌz] *pl.* Domino(spiel) *n*.

don¹ *univ.* [dɔn] Universitätslehrer *m*.

don² [ˌ] *Kleidungsstück* anziehen.

do·nate *Am.* [dəu'neit] schenken; spenden; **do·na·tion**, **don·a·tive** ['ˌnətiv] Schenkung *f*, Stiftung *f*; Gabe *f*.

done [dʌn] **1.** *p.p. von* **do**; *be* ~ *oft* geschehen; **2.** *adj.* abgemacht; *a.* ~ *up* erschöpft; fertig; *well* ~ gar gekocht; durchgebraten; *he is* ~ *for* es ist aus mit ihm; **3.** *int.* abgemacht!

do·nee ⚖ [dəu'niː] Beschenkte *m*, *f*.

don·jon ['dɔndʒən] Bergfried *m*.

don·key ['dɔŋki] Esel *m*; *attr.* Hilfs...; 'ˌ~-**en·gine** Hilfsmotor *m*; Rangierlokomotive; 'ˌ~-**work** Idiotenarbeit *f*.

don·na ['dɔnə] Dame *f*, Frau *f*; Donna *f*.

do·nor ['dəunə] Schenker *m*, (Blut-) Spender *m*; Geber *m*.

do-noth·ing F ['du:nʌθiŋ] **1.** Faulenzer(in); **2.** faul.

don't [dəunt] **1.** = do not; ~! nicht (doch)!; **2.** Verbot *m*.

doo·dle ['du:dl] **1.** gekritzelte Figur *f*; **2.** Männchen malen, kritzeln.

doom [du:m] **1.** *mst b. s.* Schicksal *n*, Verhängnis *n*; Jüngstes Gericht *n*; **2.** verurteilen, verdammen; **dooms·day** ['du:mzdei] Jüngster Tag *m*.

door [dɔ:] Tür *f*, Tor *n*; next ~ (to) nebenan; *fig.* nicht weit (von); two ~s off zwei Häuser weiter; (with)in ~s zu Hause; out of ~s im Freien, draußen; show s.o. the ~ j-m die Tür weisen; turn out of ~s hinauswerfen; lay s.th. to od. at s.o.'s ~ j-m et. zur Last legen; '~-bell Türklingel *f*; '~-case, '~-frame Türrahmen *m*; '~--han·dle Türgriff *m*; '~-keep·er, '~·man Pförtner *m*, Portier *m*; '~-mat Fußabstreifer *m*; '~-nail Türnagel *m*; dead as a ~ mausetot; '~-post Türpfosten *m*; '~-plate Türschild *n*; '~-step Haustürstufe *f*; Türschwelle *f*; '~·way Türöffnung *f*, -eingang *m*; Torweg *m*; '~·yard *Am.* Vorhof *m*, -garten *m*.

dope [dəup] **1.** Schmiere *f*; *bsd.* 🐎 Lack *m*, Firnis *m*; Nervenreizmittel *n*; Rauschgift *n*; *Am. sl.* Geheimtip *m*, -information(en *pl.*) *f*; Tölpel *m*, Depp *m*; Schwindel *m*; **2.** lackieren, firnissen; *Sport:* dopen, künstlich anreizen, aufpulvern; *Am. sl.* herauskriegen, -tüfteln; **'dope·y** *Am. sl.* doof, belämmert.

Dor·ic ['dɔrik] dorisch; ~ order dorische Säulenordnung *f*.

dorm F [dɔ:m] = dormitory.

dor·mant ['dɔ:mənt] *mst fig.* schlafend, ruhend; latent; unbenutzt, tot; ~ partner stiller Teilhaber *m*.

dor·mer(-win·dow) ['dɔ:mə('windəu)] Dachfenster *n*.

dor·mi·to·ry ['dɔ:mitri] Schlafsaal *m*; *bsd. Am.* Studentenwohnheim *n*; ~ **town** Schlafstadt *f*.

dor·mouse ['dɔ:maus], *pl.* **dormice** ['dɔ:mais] Haselmaus *f*.

dor·sal ⬜ ['dɔ:səl] dorsal, am Rükken; Rücken...

do·ry ⚓ ['dɔ:ri] Dory *n*, flaches Boot *n*.

dose [dəus] **1.** Dosis *f*, Portion *f*; **2.** *a.* ~ with eine Dosis geben (*dat.*); Wein etc. verfälschen.

doss *sl.* [dɔs] **1.** Klappe *f*, Flohkiste *f* in e-r Penne; **2.** ~ (down) pennen, sich hinhauen; **'doss·er** *sl.* Penner *m*.

doss-house *sl.* ['dɔshaus] Penne *f* (Herberge).

dos·si·er ['dɔsiei] Dossier *m*, *n*, Akten(bündel *n*) *f/pl.*

dost † [dʌst, dəst] *du* tust (s. do).

dot [dɔt] **1.** Punkt *m*, Tüpfelchen *n*; Fleck *m*; Knirps *m*; on the ~ mit dem Glockenschlag; **2.** punktieren, tüpfeln; *a.* ~ about *fig.* verstreuen; hier und da hinsetzen od. -stellen; über e-e Fläche verstreut sein; ~ted with übersät mit.

dot·age ['dəutidʒ] Altersschwachsinn *m*; Affenliebe *f*; **do·tard** ['dəutəd] kindischer Greis *m*; alter Narr *m*; **dote** [dəut] kindisch sein, faseln; vernarrt sein (on, upon in acc.).

doth † [dʌθ, dəθ] er, sie, es tut (s. do).

dot·ing ['dəutiŋ] ⬜ kindisch; vernarrt (on in acc.).

dot·ty *sl.* ['dɔti] verdreht, verrückt.

dou·ble ⬜ ['dʌbl] **1.** doppelt; gepaart; zu zweien; gekrümmt; zweideutig; falsch; gefüllt (Blume); **2.** Doppelte *n*; Doppelgänger(in); Ebenbild *n*; Haken *m* e-s Flußlaufs, Hasen; Tennis: Doppel(spiel) *n*; 🎯 Laufschritt *m*; Winkelzug *m*; **3.** *v/t.* verdoppeln; *a.* ~ up zs.-legen, -falten; die Faust ballen; um et. herumgehen, et. umfahren, -segeln; ~d up zs.-gekrümmt; be ~d up with sich biegen od. krümmen vor Schmerzen etc. *v/i.* sich verdoppeln; *a.* ~ back e-n Haken schlagen (Hase); 🎯 Laufschritt machen; Karten: Kontra geben; ~ up sich krümmen od. biegen; sich falten od. rollen lassen; '~-bar·relled doppelläufig, Doppel... (Gewehr); *fig.* zweideutig; ~ name Doppelname *m*; '~-'bass 🎵 Kontrabaß *m*; '~-bed·ded mit Doppelbett od. zwei Betten; '~--'bend S-Kurve *f*; '~-'breast·ed zweireihig (Jackett); '~-'check noch einmal (nach-, über)prüfen; '~-

-'**cross** *sl. Partner* betrügen; '~- -'**deal·er** *m*, Betrüger *m*; '~-'**deal·ing** Doppelzüngigkeit *f*; '~-'**deck·er** Doppeldecker *m* (*Autobus, Schiff*), *Am.* F doppeltes Sandwich *n*; '~-'**dyed** *fig.* eingefleischt; '~-'**edged** zweischneidig (*a. fig.*); '~-'**en·try** ✝ doppelte Buchführung *f*; '~-'**faced** unaufrichtig; '~-'**feature** *Am.* Doppelprogramm *n im Kino*; '~-'**glaz·ing** (Fenster *n* mit) Doppelverglasung *f*; '~-'**head·er** *Am. Baseball*: Doppelspiel *n*; '~-'**joint·ed** mit Gummigelenken; '~-'**line** ⊞ Doppelgleis *n*; '**dou·ble·ness** Doppelte *n*; *fig.* Zweideutigkeit *f*, Falschheit *f*; '**dou·ble·**-'**park** *Am.* in zweiter Reihe parken; '**dou·ble**-'**quick** ✕ (im) Geschwindschritt *m*.

dou·blet ['dʌblit] Dublette *f*; Doppel-, Nebenform *f*, -stück *n*; *hist.* Wams *n*, Jacke *f*; ~s *pl.* Pasch *m beim Würfeln*.

dou·ble...: ~ **take** F Spätzündung *f*; '~-**talk** doppelzüngiges Gerede *n*; '~--**time** *sl.* übers Ohr hauen; '~-'**track** zweigleisig.

doub·ling ['dʌbliŋ] Verdoppelung *f*; Falte *f*; Umsegelung *f*; '**doub·ly** doppelt.

doubt [daut] **1.** *v/i.* zweifeln; Bedenken tragen; *v/t.* bezweifeln; mißtrauen (*dat.*); **2.** Zweifel *m*; Ungewißheit *f*; Bedenken *n*; no ~ ohne Zweifel, zweifellos; '**doubt·er** Zweifler(in); **doubt·ful** □ ['~ful] zweifelhaft (*unschlüssig; ungewiß*; *verdächtig*); be ~ im Zweifel sein; '**doubt·ful·ness** Zweifelhaftigkeit *f*; '**doubt·less** ohne Zweifel, zweifellos.

douche [duːʃ] **1.** Dusche *f*; ⚕ Irrigator *m*; **2.** duschen; spülen.

dough [dəu] Teig *m*; *sl.* Moneten *pl.*; '~-**boy** *Am.* F Landser *m*; '~-**nut** Krapfen *m*, (Berliner) Pfannkuchen *m*. [herzt.]

dough·ty *co.* ['dauti] mannhaft, be-] **dough·y** ['dəui] teigig (*a. fig.*); klitschig, nicht durchgebacken.

dour *schott.* ['duə] starr; stur; streng.

douse [daus] *s.* **dowse**.

dove [dʌv] Taube *f*; *fig.* Täubchen *n*; '~-**col·o(u)red** taubengrau; ~-**cot(e)** ['~kɔt] Taubenschlag *m*; '~-**tail** ⊕ **1.** Schwalbenschwanz *m*; **2.** *v/t.* verschwalben; *v/i. fig.* genau zs.-passen.

dow·a·ger ['dauədʒə] Witwe *f* (*von Stande*).

dow·dy F ['daudi] **1.** unelegant (gekleidet); schlampig; **2.** Schlampe *f*.

dow·el ⊕ ['dauəl] Dübel *m*, Holzpflock *m*.

dow·er ['dauə] **1.** Wittum *n*; *mst fig.* Mitgift *f*; **2.** ausstatten.

down¹ [daun] Daune *f*; Flaum *m*.

down² [~] = *dune*; ~s *pl.* kahles Hügelland *n*, Höhenrücken *m*.

down³ [~] **1.** *adv.* nieder; her-, hinunter, -ab; abwärts; unten; ~ *and out fig.* erledigt, kaputt; be ~ gefallen sein (*Preis*); be ~ upon F über *j-n* herfallen; streng sein mit; ~ *in the country* auf dem Lande; ~ *under* F in Australien; **2.** *prp.* her-, hinab, her-, hinunter; ~ *the river* flußabwärts; ~ (*the*) *wind* mit dem Wind; **3.** *int.* nieder!; **4.** *adj.* ~ *train* Zug *m* von London nach außerhalb; **5.** F *v/t.* niederwerfen; herunterholen; ~ *tools* die Arbeit niederlegen; **6.** *s. up* 4; '~-**and-**'**out** Pennbruder *m*, Penner *m*; '~-**cast** niedergeschlagen; '~-**draft**, '~-**draught** Fallstrom *m*, Abwind *m*; '~-'**East·er** *Am.* Neuengländer *m bsd. aus Maine*; '~-'**fall** Fall *m*, Sturz *m*; Verfall *m*; '~-**grade** niedriger einstufen; '~-'**heart·ed** niedergeschlagen; gedrückt; '~-'**hill** **1.** bergab; **2.** abschüssig; ~ **payment** Anzahlung *f*; '~-'**pour** Regenguß *m*; ⊕ Kolbenniedergang *m*; '~-'**right** □ **1.** *adv.* geradezu, durchaus, völlig; **2.** *adj.* offen, ehrlich; plump (*Benehmen*); richtig, glatt (*Lüge, Unsinn etc.*); '~-'**right·ness** Geradheit *f*, Offenheit *f*.

Down's syn·drome ⚕ ['dauns 'sindrəum] Down-Syndrom *n*, Mongolismus *m*.

down...: '~'**stairs 1.** unten *im Hause*; die Treppe hinunter, nach unten; **2.** unten befindlich, untere(r, -s); '~-'**stream** stromabwärts (gelegen *od.* gerichtet); '~-**stroke** Grundstrich *m beim Schreiben*; ⊕ Kolbenniedergang *m*; ~-**to-**'**earth** nüchtern, realistisch; '~-'**town** *bsd. Am.* Hauptgeschäftsviertel *n*; '~-'**trod·den** unterdrückt; ~-**ward** ['~wəd] **1.** sich senkend, abschüssig (*a. fig.*); **2.** *a.* ~s abwärts; '~-'**wash** ✈ Abwind *m*.

down·y ['dauni] flaumig; *sl.* gerissen (*schlau*).

dow·ry ['dauəri] Mitgift *f* (*a. fig.*).

dowse ['dauz] **1.** gießen über (*acc.*);

begießen; auslöschen; **2.** mit der Wünschelrute suchen; '**dows·er** Rutengänger(in); '**dows·ing-rod** Wünschelrute f.

doze [dəuz] **1.** schlummern, (~ *away* ver)dösen; **2.** Schläfchen n.

doz·en ['dʌzn] Dutzend n; *talk nineteen to the* ~ wie ein Wasserfall reden.

doz·y ['dəuzi] schläfrig; F schwer von Begriff.

drab [dræb] **1.** gelblichgrau; *fig.* eintönig; **2.** Gelblichgrau n; graugelber Stoff m; *fig.* Eintönigkeit f; Schlampe f; Hure f, Dirne f.

drachm [dræm] Drachme f (*Gewicht*); = **drach·ma** ['drækmə] Drachme f (*Münze*).

draff [dræf] Bodensatz m; Abhub m.

draft [drɑːft] **1.** Entwurf m, Konzept n, Skizze f; ✝ Tratte f; Abhebung f; ✖ (Sonder)Kommando n; Einberufung f; = **draught**; ~ *agreement* Vertragsentwurf m; **2.** entwerfen; aufsetzen, abfassen; ✖ abkommandieren; *Am.* einziehen, einberufen; **draft'ee** ✖ *Am.* Dienstpflichtige m; '**drafts·man** (technischer) Zeichner m; Verfasser m, Entwerfer m.

drag [dræg] **1.** Schleppnetz n; Schleife f *für Lasten*; Egge f; Hemmschuh m (*a. fig.*); Blockwagen m *für Holz etc.*; *von e-m Mann getragene* Frauenkleidung f; **2.** *v/t.* schleppen, schleifen, ziehen, zerren; ⚓ eggen; *Rad* hemmen; = dredge 2; ~ *along* mitschleppen; ~ *out Leben* hinschleppen; ~ *one's feet* sich Zeit lassen, es nicht eilig haben; ~ *up a child* ein Kind lieblos u. ohne Erziehung aufwachsen lassen; *v/i.* (sich) schleppen, schleifen; (mit einem Schleppnetz) fischen (*for* nach); ✝ flau gehen; ~ **art·ist** *männlicher Entertainer, der in Frauenkleidern auftritt.*

drag·gle ['drægl] durch den Schmutz ziehen; '**~-tail** Schlampe f.

drag·o·man ['drægəumən] Dolmetscher m, Dragoman m.

drag·on ['drægən] Drache m; '**~-fly** Wasserjungfer f, Libelle f.

dra·goon [drə'guːn] **1.** Dragoner m; *fig.* Rohling m; **2.** zwingen (*into ger.* zu *inf.*).

drain [drein] **1.** Abfluß m, Abzug(s-

graben m, -rohr n) m; Rinne f; F Schluck m, Tropfen m; Inanspruchnahme f (*on gen.*); ~s pl. Kanalisation f; **2.** *v/t.* entwässern, drainieren, trockenlegen; *Glas* leeren; *a.* ~ *off* abziehen, -leiten; verzehren; berauben (*of gen.*); *v/i.* ablaufen; '**drain·age** Abfluß m; Kanalisation f; Entwässerung(sanlage) f; '**drain·ing 1.** Abzugs...; **2.** Trockenlegung f; ~s pl. Abzugsröhren f/pl.; '**drain·ing-board** Ablaufbrett n; '**drain-pipe** Abflußrohr n; ~ *trousers* pl. F Röhrenhose(n pl.) f.

drake [dreik] Enterich m.

dram [dræm] Drachme f (*Gewicht*); Schluck m; Schnaps m.

dra·ma ['drɑːmə] Drama n, Schauspiel n; **dra·mat·ic** [drə'mætik] (~ally) dramatisch; Theater...; **dra-'mat·ics** *mst sg.* Theater n; **dram-a·tist** ['dræmətist] Dramatiker m; **dram·a·tis per·so·nae** ['drɑːmətis pɔː'səunai] pl. *die* Personen f/pl. der Handlung; **dram·a·tize** ['dræmə-taiz] dramatisieren; **dram·a·tur·gy** ['~təːdʒi] Dramaturgie f.

drank [dræŋk] *pret. von* drink 2.

drape [dreip] drapieren, behängen; in Falten ordnen; '**drap·er** Tuchhändler m; '**dra·per·y** Tuchhandel m; Tuchwaren f/pl.; Draperie f; Faltenwurf m.

dras·tic ['dræstik] (~ally) drastisch.

draught [drɑːft] Zug m (*Ziehen*; *Fischzug*; *Zugluft*; *Schluck*); ⚓ Tiefgang m; ~s pl. Damespiel n; *s. draft*; ~ *beer* Faßbier n; *at a* ~ auf einen Zug; '**~-board** Damebrett n; '**~-horse** Zugpferd n; '**draughts-man** Damestein m; = draftsman; '**draught·y** zugig.

draw [drɔː] **1.** (*irr.*) ziehen; an-, auf-, ein-, zuziehen; sich zs.-ziehen; in die Länge ziehen, dehnen; nach sich ziehen; herausziehen, -locken; entnehmen; *Geld* abheben; *Ware etc.* beziehen; anlocken, anziehen; abzapfen; ausfischen; *Geflügel* ausnehmen; *Zinsen* bringen; zeichnen; entwerfen; *Urkunde* abfassen; *Kampf etc.* unentschieden lassen; unentschieden spielen; ⚓ Tiefgang von ... haben; *e-n Seufzer* ausstoßen; *Luft* schöpfen; ~ *away* wegnehmen, entwenden; ~ *down* senken; ~ *forth* hervorziehen; ~ *near* heranrücken, sich nähern; ~ *on her-*

beiführen, veranlassen; ~ out in die
Länge ziehen; *j.* ausholen; ~ up aufsetzen, ab-, verfassen; entwerfen;
Truppen etc. aufstellen; vorfahren;
halten; ~ (up)on ✝ (e-n Wechsel)
ziehen auf (*acc.*); *fig.* in Anspruch
nehmen, angreifen; **2.** Zug *m* (*Zie-
hen*); *Lotterie*: Ziehung *f*; Los *n*;
Sport: unentschiedenes Spiel *n*; F
Zugkraft *f*, -stück *n*, -artikel *m*; F
Anzapfung *f*; '~-**back** Beeinträchtigung *f* (*from gen.*); Nachteil *m*,
Schattenseite *f*; Hindernis *n*; ✝
Rückzoll *m*; *Am.* Rückzahlung *f*;
'~-**bridge** Zugbrücke *f*; **draw'ee** ✝
Bezogene *m*; Trassat *m*; '**draw·er**
Ziehende *m*; Zeichner *m*; ✝ Aus-
steller *m*, Trassant *m*; [*mst* drɔ:]
Schublade *f*; (*pair of*) ~*s pl.* Unterhose *f*; Schlüpfer *m*; *mst* chest of ~s
Kommode *f*.
draw·ing ['drɔ:iŋ] Ziehen *n*; Zeichnen *n*; Ziehung *f* (*Lotterie*); Zeichnung *f*; ✝ Trassierung *f*; out of ~
verzeichnet; ~ *instruments pl.* Reiß-
zeug *n*; '~-**ac'count** Girokonto *n*;
'~-**board** Zeichen-, Reißbrett *n*;
'~-**pen** Reißfeder *f*; '~-**pin** Reiß-
zwecke *f*; '~-**room** Gesellschaftszimmer *n*, Salon *m*; *bei Hofe*: großer
Empfang *m*.
drawl [drɔ:l] **1.** *a.* ~ out gedehnt *od.*
schleppend sprechen; **2.** gedehnte
Sprechweise *f*.
drawn [drɔ:n] **1.** *p.p. von draw 1*;
2. *adj.* unentschieden; verzerrt.
draw-well ['drɔ:wel] Ziehbrunnen
m.
dray [drei] *a.* ~-**cart** Roll-, *bsd.* Bier-
wagen *m*; '~-**man** Roll-, Bierkut-
scher *m.*
dread [dred] **1.** Furcht *f*; Schrecken
m; **2.** (sich) fürchten (vor), Angst
haben (vor); **dread·ful** □ ['~ful]
1. schrecklich; furchtbar; schauerlich; **2.** *penny* ~ billiger Schauerroman *m*; **dread·nought** ['~nɔ:t]
dicker Flaus(ch) *m*; ⚓ Schlacht-
schiff *n.*
dream [dri:m] **1.** Traum *m*; **2.** (*irr.*)
träumen (*of* von); ~ *away* verträu-
men; '**dream·er** Träumer(in);
'**dream-land** Traumwelt *f*;
'**dream-like** traumhaft; '**dream-
-read·er** Traumdeuter(in); **dreamt**
[dremt] *pret. u. p.p von dream 2*;
'**dream·y** □ träumerisch; verträumt; traumhaft.

drear *poet.* [driə] = *dreary.*
drear·i·ness ['driərinis] Traurigkeit
f; Öde *f*; '**drear·y** □ traurig; öde;
düster; langweilig.
dredge[1] [dredʒ] **1.** Schleppnetz *n*;
Bagger(maschine *f*) *m*; **2.** *a.* ~ up, ~
out (mit dem Schleppnetz) fischen;
(aus)baggern.
dredge[2] [~] (be)streuen.
dredg·er[1] ['dredʒə] Schleppnetz-
fischer *m*; Bagger(maschine *f*) *m.*
dredg·er[2] [~] (Mehl)Streubüchse *f.*
dregs [dregz] *pl.* Bodensatz *m*, Hefe
f; Abschaum *m*; *drink od. drain to
the* ~ bis zur Neige leeren.
drench [drentʃ] **1.** Arzneitrank *m*;
(Regen)Guß *m*; **2.** *e-m Tier* Arznei
einflößen; durchnässen, *fig.* baden;
'**drench·er** F (Regen)Guß *m.*
dress [dres] **1.** (Damen)Kleid *n*;
Kleidung *f*; *fig.* Gewand *n*; *full* ~
Gala *f*; **2.** an-, ein-, zurichten; ⚔
(sich) richten; zurechtmachen; (sich)
anziehen *od.* ankleiden; putzen; dekorieren; *Wunde* verbinden; *Wein-
stock* beschneiden; frisieren; ✐ düngen; ~ *s.o. down* j. ausschimpfen; j.
durchprügeln; ~ *it thea.* Kostüm-
probe abhalten; ~ *up* sich herausputzen; sich verkleiden; '~-'**cir·cle**
thea. erster Rang *m*; '~-'**coat** Frack
m; '**dress·er** Anrichter(in); An-
kleider(in); Assistenzarzt *m*; Dekorateur *m*; Anrichte *f*; *Am.* Frisierkommode *f*; Küchenschrank *m.*
dress·ing ['dresiŋ] An-, Zurichten
n; Ankleiden *n*; Behandeln *n e-r
Wunde*; Verband *m*; Appretur *f*;
Küche: Zutat *f*; ✐ Dünger *m*;
Tracht *f* Prügel; ~s *pl.* Verband-
zeug *n*; '~-*down* Standpauke *f*; '~-
-**case** Reisenecessaire *n*; Verbandskasten *m*; '~-**glass** Toilettenspiegel
m; '~-**gown** Morgenrock *m*; '~-
-**jack·et** Frisiermantel *m*; ~ *room*
Umkleidezimmer *n*; Garderobe *f*;
'~-**ta·ble** Frisierkommode *f.*
dress...: '~-**mak·er** (Damen)Schnei-
derin *f*; '~-**pa·rade** Modenschau *f*;
⚔ Parade *f* in Galauniform; ~ *re-
hears·al* Generalprobe *f*; '~-**shield**
Schweißblatt *n*; '~-'**shirt** Frack-
hemd *n*; '~-'**suit** Frackanzug *m*;
'**dress·y** F putzsüchtig; geschnie-
gelt; modisch.
drew [dru:] *pret. von draw 1.*
drib·ble ['dribl] tröpfeln, träufeln
(lassen); geifern, sabbern; *Fußball*:

dribbeln.
drib·let ['driblit] Kleinigkeit *f.*
dribs and drabs F ['dribzən'dræbz]
pl.: in ~ kleckerweise.
dried [draid] Dörr...; Trocken...; ~
fruit Dörrobst *n.*
dri·er ['draiə] Trockner *m*, Trockenapparat *m*; Trockenmittel *n.*
drift [drift] **1.** (Dahin)Treiben *n*;
♨ Drift *f*, Abtrift *f*; *fig.* Lauf *m*;
fig. Hang *m*, Neigung *f*; Zweck *m*;
Inhalt *m*, Sinn *m*; Gestöber *n*
(*Schnee*); Guß *m* (*Regen*); (Schnee-,
Sand)Wehe *f*; *geol.* Geschiebe *n*; ✕
Strecke *f*; **2.** *v/t.* (zs.-)treiben,
(zs.-)wehen; *v/i.* getrieben werden,
(dahin)treiben; sich anhäufen;
'**drift·er** Mensch *m* ohne Ziele;
'**drift-ice** Treibeis *n*; '**drift-net**
Treibnetz *n*; '**drift-wood** Treibholz
n.
drill¹ [dril] **1.** Drillbohrer *m*; Furche *f*; ✔ Drill-, Sämaschine *f*; ✕
Exerzieren *n*, Übung *f*, Drill *m* (*a.
fig.*); ~ *ground* Exerzierplatz *m*;
2. drillen, bohren; ✕ (ein)exerzie-
ren (*a. fig.*); einüben; ✔ in Rillen
säen.
drill², **drill·ing** [dril, '~iŋ] Drillich
m.
drink [driŋk] **1.** Trank *m*, Trunk *m*;
(geistiges)Getränk *n*; *in* ~ betrunken;
2. (*irr.*) trinken; ~ *s.o.'s health* auf
j-s Wohl *od.* Gesundheit trinken;
~ *away* vertrinken; ~ *in* einsaugen;
~ *to* trinken auf (*acc.*); ~ *off od. out
od.up* austrinken; aufsaugen; '**drink-
a·ble** trinkbar; '**drink·er** Trinker
m; Säufer *m.*
drink·ing ['driŋkiŋ] Trinken *n*,
Zechen *n*; '~-**bout** Trinkgelage *n*;
'~-**foun·tain** Trinkbrunnen *m*; '~-
-**song** Trinklied *n*; '~-**wa·ter**
Trinkwasser *n.*
drip [drip] **1.** Tröpfeln *n*; Traufe *f*; F
✚ Tropf *m* (*Infusionsapparat, Infusion*); F Person: Flasche *f*, Waschlappen *m*; *be on the* ~ F ✚ am Tropf
hängen; **2.** tröpfeln (lassen); triefen;
~*ping wet* triefnaß; '~-'**dry shirt** bü-
gelfreies Hemd *n*; '**drip·ping** Bra-
tenfett *n*; ~*s pl.* herabtröpfelnde Flüssigkeit *f*; ~ *pan* Fettpfanne *f.*
drive [draiv] **1.** (Spazier)Fahrt *f*;
Auffahrt *f*, Fahrweg *m*; *Tennis etc.*:
Treibschlag *m*, Flachball *m*; *mot.*
Antrieb *m*; *fig.* (Auf)Trieb *m*,
Schwung *m*; Drang *m* (*for* nach);

Unternehmen *n*, Bewegung *f*, Feldzug *m*, Rummel *m*, Treiben *n*;
Treibjagd *f*; *Am.* Sammelaktion *f*;
2. (*irr.*) *v/t.* (an-, ein)treiben; *Geschäft* betreiben; fahren, lenken;
zwingen (*to, into* zu); *oft* ~ *away*
vertreiben; *v/i.* treiben (*a.* ♨ *u.
hunt.*); *im Wagen* fahren; eilen,
jagen; ~ *at s.th.* hinzielen auf et.;
et. wollen; ~ *on* weiterfahren; ~ *up*
to vorfahren bei.
drive-in *Am.* ['draivin] **1.** *mst attr.*
Auto...; ~ *cinema* Autokino *n*;
2. Autokino *n*; Autorestaurant *n.*
driv·el ['drivl] **1.** geifern; faseln;
2. Geifer *m*; Faselei *f.*
driv·en ['drivn] *p.p. von* drive 2.
driv·er ['draivə] Treiber *m*; Fahrer
m, Chauffeur *m*; 🚂 Führer *m*;
† Kutscher *m*; ⊕ Mitnehmer *m*;
Treibrad *n*; '**drive·way** *Am.* Fahrweg *m*; Einfahrt *f.*
driv·ing ['draiviŋ] Treiben *n etc.*; *attr.*
Treib...; Antriebs...; Fahr...; '~-**belt**
Treibriemen *m*; ~ *force* treibende
Kraft *f*; '~-**gear** Triebwerk *n*; ~ *in-
struc·tor* Fahrlehrer *m*; ~ *li·cence*
Führerschein *m*; ~ *mir·ror* Rückspiegel *m*; ~ *school* Fahrschule *f*; '~-
-**wheel** Treibrad *n.*
driz·zle ['drizl] **1.** Sprühregen *m*;
2. sprühen, nieseln; '**drizz·ly** regnerisch.
droll [drəul] (*adv.* drolly) drollig;
'**droll·er·y** Drolligkeit *f.*
drom·e·dar·y *zo.* ['drʌmədəri] Dromedar *n.*
drone¹ [drəun] **1.** *zo.* Drohne *f*; *fig.*
Faulenzer *m*; **2.** faulenzen.
drone² [~] **1.** Summen *n*, Dröhnen
n; ♩ Baßpfeife *f*; **2.** summen;
dröhnen.
drool [dru:l] **1.** sabbern; **2.** *Am.* F
dummes Geschwätz *n.*
droop [dru:p] *v/t.* sinken lassen; *v/i.*
schlaff (herab)hängen; den Kopf
hängen lassen; (ver)welken; schwinden; '**droop·ing** ⬜ matt; mutlos.
drop [drop] **1.** Tropfen *m*; Drops *m*,
Fruchtbonbon *m*; Sinken *n*, Fall *m*;
Falltür *f*; *thea.* Vorhang *m*; *get od.
have the* ~ *on Am.* überlegen sein
(*dat.*), zuvorkommen (*dat.*); ~ *light*
Hängelicht *n*; *in* ~*s*, ~ *by* ~ tropfen-
weise (*a. fig.*); **2.** *v/t.* tropfen lassen; herunterlassen; *Anker* (aus-)
werfen; *Bomben* abwerfen; *Brief*
einwerfen; *Tränen etc.* vergießen;

Gegenstand, Wort, Thema etc. fallen lassen; *Fahrgast* absetzen; *Gesicht, Stimme* senken; *Knicks* machen; ~ s.o. *a few lines* j-m ein paar Zeilen schreiben; ~ *it!* F laß das!; *v/i.* tröpfeln, lecken (*Faß*);(herab)fallen;aufhören; um-, hinsinken; sterben; ~ *behind* zurückbleiben; ~ *in* unerwartet kommen *od.* vorsprechen (*at, on, upon* bei); ~ *off* allmählich fortgehen; einschlafen; abfallen; ~ *out* aus-, wegfallen; nicht mehr mitmachen; sich wegstehlen; ~ **ac·tion pen·cil** Druckbleistift *m*; **drop·let** ['drɔplit] Tröpfchen *n*; **'drop-out** Aussteiger *m*; Studienabbrecher *m*; **'drop·ping** Tröpfeln *n*; ~s *pl.* Mist *m*; **'drop-scene** *thea.* Vorhang *m*; Schluß(szene *f) m*.

drop·si·cal □ ['drɔpsikəl] wassersüchtig; **'drop·sy** Wassersucht *f*.

dross [drɔs] Schlacke *f*; Unrat *m*.

drought [draut], **drouth** [drauθ] Trockenheit*f*, Dürre*f*; **'drought·y, 'drouth·y** trocken, dürr.

drove [drəuv] **1.** Trift *f Rinder*; Herde *f* (*a. fig.*); **2.** *pret. von* drive 2; **'dro·ver** Viehtreiber *m*, -händler *m*.

drown [draun] *v/t.* ertränken; überschwemmen;*fig.* übertäuben; übertönen; ersticken; *be ~ed* ertrinken; *v/i.* ertrinken.

drowse [drauz] schlummern, schläfrig sein *od.* machen; **'drow·si·ness** Schläfrigkeit *f*; **'drow·sy** schläfrig; einschläfernd.

drub [drʌb] (ver)prügeln; trommeln auf (*dat.*); **'drub·bing** Tracht *f* Prügel.

drudge [drʌdʒ] **1.** *fig.* Sklave *m*, Packesel *m*, Kuli *m*; **2.** sich (ab-) placken; **'drudg·er·y** Plackerei *f*.

drug [drʌg] **1.** Droge *f*, Arznei (-mittel *n*) *f*, Medikament *n*; Rauschgift *n*; ~ *on the market* unverkäufliche Ware *f*; ~ *abuse* Drogenmißbrauch *m*; **2.** mit (schädlichen) Zutaten versetzen; viel Arznei eingeben (*dat.*); Rauschgifte *od.* Schlafmittel geben (*dat.*) *od.* nehmen; **'drug·gist** Drogist *m*; Apotheker *m*; **drug push·er** Dealer *m*; **'drug·store** *Am.* Drugstore *m*; **drug traf·fic(k·ing** Drogenhandel *m*.

dru·id *hist.* ['dru:id] Druide *m*.

drum [drʌm] **1.** Trommel *f* (*a.* ⊕); *anat.* Trommelhöhle *f*; **2.** trommeln; **'~·fire** ⚔ Trommelfeuer *n*; **'~·head** Trommelfell *n*; ~ *court--martial* ⚔ Standgericht *n*; **'~- -'ma·jor** ⚔ Tambourmajor *m*; **'drum·mer** Trommler *m*; *bsd. Am.* F Handlungsreisende *m*, Vertreter *m*; **'drum-stick** Trommelstock *m*; Unterschenkel *m von Geflügel*.

drunk [drʌŋk] **1.** *p.p von* drink 2; **2.** *pred.* (be)trunken; *get ~* sich betrinken; **drunk·ard** ['~əd] Trinker *m*, Trunkenbold *m*; **'drunk·en** *attr.* (be)trunken; trunksüchtig; ~ *driving* Trunkenheit *f* am Steuer; **'drunk·en·ness** Trunkenheit *f*; Trunksucht *f*.

drupe ⚘ [dru:p] Steinfrucht *f*.

dry [drai] **1.** □ *allg.* trocken; dürr; uninteressant, nüchtern; kühl; derb (*Witz*); herb (*Wein*); nicht milchend (*Kuh*); F durstig; F antialkoholisch; ~ *cell* Trockenelement *n*; ~ *goods pl.* F *Am.* Kurzwaren *f/pl.*; **2.** *Am.* F Alkoholgegner *m*; **3.** (ab-) trocknen; dörren; ~ *up* austrocknen; verdunsten; ~ *up!* F sei still!

dry·ad ['draiəd] Waldnymphe *f*.

dry...: ~ **bat·ter·y** Trockenbatterie *f*; ~ **bulb ther·mom·e·ter** *das trockene Thermometer e-s Psychrometers*; ~ **cell** ⚡ Trockenelement *n*; **'~-'clean** chemisch reinigen; **'~- -'clean·ing** chemische Reinigung *f*.

dry·er ['draiə] = drier.

dry...: ~ **goods** *pl. Am.* Textilien *pl.*; ~ **mount·ing** *phot.* Trockenklebung *f*; **'~-'nurse 1.** Kinderfrau *f*; **2.** bemuttern; betreuen; **'~-'rot** Trockenfäule *f*; *fig.* Verfall *m*; **'~-'shod** trockenen Fußes; **'~-'wall·ing** Trockenmauern *n*.

du·al □ ['dju:əl] zweifach, doppelt; Doppel...; ~ *income family* Doppelverdiener *m pl.*; **'du·al·ism** Dualismus *m*.

dub [dʌb] zum Ritter schlagen; titulieren; ernennen zu; *Leder* (ein-) fetten; *Film etc.* synchronisieren; **'dub·bing** Lederfett *n*.

du·bi·e·ty [dju:'baiəti] Fragwürdigkeit *f*; zweifelhafte Sache *f*.

du·bi·ous □ ['dju:bjəs] zweifelhaft; *be ~* im Zweifel sein (*of, about, over* über *acc.*); **'du·bi·ous·ness** Ungewißheit *f*.

du·cal ['dju:kəl] herzoglich.

duc·at ['dʌkət] Dukaten *m*.

duch·ess ['dʌtʃis] Herzogin *f*.

duch·y ['dʌtʃi] Herzogtum *n*.
duck[1] [dʌk] Ente *f*; *Am. sl.* Kerl *m*.
duck[2] [˯] **1.** Verbeugung *f*; Neigen *n* des Kopfes; Ducken *n*; **2.** (unter-)tauchen; (sich) ducken; *Am. j-m* ausweichen, F sich verziehen.
duck[3] F [˯] Liebling *m*, Püppchen *n*.
duck[4] [˯] (Segel)Leinen *n*.
duck...: '˯**bill** *zo*. Schnabeltier *n*; '˯**boards** *pl*. Lattenrost *m*.
duck·ling ['dʌkliŋ] Entchen *n*.
duck·weed ♀ ['dʌkwiːd] Wasserlinse *f*.
duck·y F ['dʌki] **1.** = *duck*[3]; **2.** lieb, nett.
duct [dʌkt] Gang *m*; Röhre *f*.
duc·tile □ ['dʌktail] dehnbar; fügsam; geschmeidig; **duc·til·i·ty** [˯'tiliti] Dehnbarkeit *f*.
dud *sl*. [dʌd] **1.** Blindgänger *m*; *fig*. Versager *m*; ˯s *pl*. Lumpen *m/pl*. (*Kleider*); **2.** verfehlt; falsch.
dude *Am*. [djuːd] Geck *m*; ˯ **ranch** Vergnügungsfarm *f* für Feriengäste aus der Großstadt.
dudg·eon ['dʌdʒən] Groll *m*; *in high* ˯ kochend vor Wut.
due [djuː] **1.** schuldig; gebührend; angemessen; gehörig; fällig; *in* ˯ *time* zur rechten *od*. gegebenen Zeit; *the train is* ˯ *at* ... der Zug ist fällig *od*. kommt an um ...; *in* ˯ *course* zu seiner Zeit; *be* ˯ *to j-m* gebühren; zu verdanken sein; herrühren *od*. kommen von; *be* ˯ *to inf*. sollen; müssen; *Am*. im Begriff sein zu; *fall* ˯ ✝ fällig werden; ˯ *date* Fälligkeitstermin *m*; **2.** *adv*. ⚓ gerade; ˯ *east* genau nach Osten; **3.** Gebührende *n*, Schuldigkeit *f*; Recht *n*, Anspruch *m*; Lohn *m*; *mst* ˯s *pl*. Abgabe(n *pl*.) *f*, Gebühr(en *pl*.) *f*; (Mitglieds)Beitrag *m*.
du·el ['djuːəl] **1.** Duell *n*, Zweikampf *m*; **2.** sich duellieren; '**du·el·list** Duellant *m*.
du·et(·to) [djuː'et(əu)] Duett *n*.
duf·fel ['dʌfəl] Düffel *m*, grober Wollstoff *m*; ˯**bag** Matchbeutel *m*, -sack *m*; ˯ **coat** Dufflecoat *m*.
duff·er F ['dʌfə] Dummkopf *m*.
duf·fle ['dʌfəl] = *duffel*.
dug [dʌg] **1.** *pret. u. p.p. von dig*; **2.** Zitze *f*; '˯**out** ✕ Unterstand *m*; Einbaum *m*; *sl*. wiedereingestellter Offizier *m*; *Am*. *Baseball*: überdachte Spielerbank *f*.
duke [djuːk] Herzog *m*; '**duke·dom**

Herzogtum *n*; Herzogswürde *f*.
dul·cet ['dʌlsit] wohlklingend, lieblich; '**dul·ci·mer** ♪ ['˯simə] Hackbrett *n*, Zimbel *f*.
dull [dʌl] **1.** □ dumm; träg, schwerfällig; stumpfsinnig; matt (*Auge, Farbe etc*.); schwach (*Gehör*); langweilig, fad(e); teilnahmslos; stumpf; dumpf (*Schmerz, Kopf*); trüb (z.B. *Wetter*); flau (*Handel*); ⚓ windstill; **2.** stumpf machen; *fig*. abstumpfen; (sich) trüben; **dull·ard** ['˯əd] Dummkopf *m*; '**dull·ness** Stumpfsinn *m*; Dummheit *f*; Schwerfälligkeit *f*; Mattheit *f*; Langweiligkeit *f*; Teilnahmslosigkeit *f*; Trübheit *f*; Flauheit *f*.
du·ly ['djuːli] *s. due*; gehörig; ordnungsgemäß; richtig; pünktlich.
dumb □ [dʌm] stumm; sprachlos *vor Staunen etc*.; *Am*. F doof, blöd; *deaf and* ˯ taubstumm; *s. show* 2; *strike* ˯ die Sprache verschlagen; '˯**bell** Hantel *f*; *Am. sl*. Dussel *m*; ˯'**found** F zum Schweigen bringen; ˯*ed* sprachlos; '**dumb·ness** Stummheit *f*; '**dumb-'wait·er** Drehtisch *m*; *Am*. Speiseaufzug *m*.
dum·my ['dʌmi] Attrappe *f*; *fig*. Kulisse *f*; Schein *m*, Schwindel *m*; *fig*. Strohmann *m*; Statist *m*; (Kleider)Puppe *f*; Schnuller *m*; *attr*. Schein...; Schwindel...; ˯ *whist* Whist *n* mit Strohmann.
dump [dʌmp] **1.** auskippen; *Schutt etc*. abladen; *Last* abwerfen (*a. fig*.); *Waren* zu Schleuderpreisen ausführen; hinplumpsen; **2.** Klumpen *m*; Plumps *m*; Abfall-, Schutthaufen *m*; Schuttabladestelle *f*; ✕ Munitionslager *n*; = ˯*ing*; '**dump·ing** ✝ Schleuderausfuhr *f*, Dumping *n*; '**dump·ing-ground** (Schutt)Abladeplatz *m*; '**dumpling** Kloß *m*; F Dickerchen *n*, Mops *m*; '**dumps** F *pl*.: (down) *in the* ˯ niedergeschlagen, verdrießlich; '**dump·y** untersetzt.
dun[1] [dʌn] **1.** fahl(braun); falb; **2.** Falbe *m* (*Pferd*).
dun[2] [˯] **1.** ungestümer Mahner *m od*. Gläubiger *m*; **2.** mahnen, drängen; ˯*ning letter* Mahnbrief *m*.
dunce [dʌns], **dun·der·head** ['dʌndəhed] Dummkopf *m*.
dune [djuːn] Düne *f*; ˯ **bug·gy** *mot*. Strandbuggy *m*.
dung [dʌŋ] **1.** Mist *m*, Dung *m*;

2. düngen.

dun·ga·rees [dʌŋgə'riːz] *pl.* Overall *m aus grobem Kattun.*

dun·geon ['dʌndʒən] Kerker *m,* Verlies *n.*

dung·hill ['dʌŋhil] Misthaufen *m.*

dunk [dʌŋk] (ein)tunken.

du·o ['djuːəu] Duett *n.*

du·o·dec·i·mal [djuːəu'desiməl] zwölfteilig; Duodezimal...; **du·o·'dec·i·mo** [‿məu] *typ.* Duodez *n; fig.* Knirps *m.*

du·o·de·nal *anat.* [djuːəu'diːnl] Zwölffingerdarm...; **du·o'de·num** [‿nəm] Zwölffingerdarm *m.*

dupe [djuːp] **1.** Gimpel *m,* Angeführte *m, f;* **2.** anführen, täuschen; **'dup·er·y** Prellerei *f.*

du·plex ['djuːpleks] **1.** Doppel...; *tel.* Gegensprech..., Duplex...; **2.** *Am.* Zweifamilienhaus *n; ‿ apartment Am.* Maison(n)ette *f (zweistöckige Wohnung).*

du·pli·cate 1. ['djuːplikit] doppelt; **2.** ['‿kit] Duplikat *n,* Doppel *n; in ‿* doppelt; **3.** ['‿keit] verdoppeln; doppelt ausfertigen; **du·pli·ca·tion** Verdoppelung *f;* **du·pli·ca·tor** Vervielfältigungsapparat *m;* **du·plic·i·ty** [djuː'plisiti] Zweiheit *f;* Doppelzüngigkeit *f.*

du·ra·bil·i·ty [djuərə'biliti] Dauerhaftigkeit *f;* **'du·ra·ble** □ dauerhaft; **'dur·ance †** Haft *f;* **du·ra·tion** [‿'reiʃən] Dauer *f.*

du·ress ʒʒ [djuə'res] Zwang *m,* Nötigung *f;* Freiheitsberaubung *f.*

du·ring ['djuəriŋ] *prp.* während.

durst [dɜːst] *pret. von* dare.

dusk [dʌsk] Halbdunkel *n,* (Abend-) Dämmerung *f;* **'dusk·y** □ dämmerig, düster (*a. fig.*); dunkel; schwärzlich.

dust [dʌst] **1.** Staub *m;* **2.** abstauben; bestreuen; **'‿bin** Mülleimer *m; ‿ liner* Müllbeutel *m;* **'‿bowl** *Am.* Sandstaub- *u.* Dürregebiet *n im Westen der USA;* **'‿cart** Müllwagen *m;* **'‿cloak, '‿coat** Staubmantel *m;* **'dust·er** Staublappen *m,* -wedel *m; Am.* Staubmantel *m;* **'dust·i·ness** Staubigkeit *f;* **'dust·ing** *sl.* Tracht *f* Prügel; **'dust-'jack·et** *Am.* Schutzumschlag *m e-s Buches;* **'dust·man** Müllabfuhrmann *m;* Sandmann *m;* **'dust·pan** Müllschaufel *f;* **dust trap** Staubfänger *m;* **'dust-'up** Lärm *m,* Tumult *m;* **'dust·y** □ staubig.

Dutch [dʌtʃ] **1.** holländisch; *hist. u. Am. sl.* deutsch; **go ‿ (with s.o.)** (mit j-m) die Kosten teilen; **2.** Holländisch *n; the ‿ pl.* die Holländer *pl.; double ‿* Kauderwelsch *n;* **‿ auc·tion** (Auktion *f* mit) Abschlag *m;* **‿ cour·age** angetrunkener Mut *m;* **'‿man** Holländer *m; hist. u. Am. sl.* Deutsche *m;* **'‿wom·an** Holländerin *f.*

du·te·ous ['djuːtjəs] = *dutiful;* **du·ti·a·ble** ['‿tjəbl] zoll-, steuerpflichtig; **du·ti·ful** □ ['‿tiful] pflichtbewußt; gehorsam; ehrerbietig.

du·ty ['djuːti] Pflicht *f,* Schuldigkeit *f* (**to** gegenüber *dat.*); Ehrerbietung *f;* Abgabe *f,* Zoll *m;* Dienst *m; on ‿* im Dienst; **off ‿** dienstfrei; **‿ call** Anstandsbesuch *m; in ‿ bound* pflichtschuldig; **do ‿ for** vertreten; *fig.* dienen als; **'‿-'free** zollfrei.

dwarf [dwɔːf] **1.** Zwerg *m;* **2.** in der Entwicklung hindern; klein erscheinen lassen; verkleinern; **‿ed** verkümmert; **'dwarf·ish** □ zwerghaft; **'dwarf·ish·ness** Winzigkeit *f.*

dwell [dwel] (*irr.*) wohnen; verweilen (**on, upon** bei); **‿ (up)on** bestehen auf; **'dwell·er** Bewohner *m;* **'dwell·ing** Wohnung *f;* **'dwelling-house** Wohnhaus *n;* **'dwelling-place** Wohnsitz *m.*

dwelt [dwelt] *pret. u. p.p. von* dwell.

dwin·dle ['dwindl] (dahin)schwinden, abnehmen; zs.-schrumpfen; **'dwin·dling** Schwund *m.*

dye [dai] **1.** Farbe *f; of deepest ‿ fig.* schlimmster Art; **2.** färben; **'dy·er** Färber *m;* **'dye-stuff** Färbemittel *n;* Farbstoff *m;* **'dye-works** *pl.,* oft sg. Färberei *f.*

dy·ing □ ['daiiŋ] (*s.* die[1]) **1.** sterbend; Sterbe...; **lie ‿** im Sterben liegen; **2.** Sterben *n etc.*

dyke [daik] = *dike[1] u.[2].*

dy·nam·ic [dai'næmik] **1.** *a.* **dy·'nam·i·cal** □ dynamisch, kraftgeladen; **2.** Triebkraft *f;* **dy'nam·ics** *mst sg.* Dynamik *f;* **dy·na·mite** ['dainəmait] **1.** Dynamit *n;* **2.** mit Dynamit sprengen; **'dy·na·mit·er** Sprengstoffattentäter *m;* **dy·na·mo** ['‿məu] Dynamomaschine *f.*

dy·nas·tic [di'næstik] (‿ally) dynastisch; **dy·nas·ty** ['dinəsti] Dynastie *f,* Herrscherhaus *n.*

dyne *phys.* [dain] Dyn *n (Krafteinheit).*

dys·en·ter·y ⚕ ['disntri] Ruhr *f*.
dys·lex·i·a [dis'leksiə] Dyslexie *f*,
Buchstabenblindheit *f*; **dys'lex·ic**
1. buchstabenblind; 2. an Dyslexie
Leidende *m*, *f*.

dys·pep·sia ⚕ [dis'pepsiə] Verdauungsstörung *f*; **dys'pep·tic** [⌣tik]
1. (⌣*ally*) an Verdauungsstörung
leidend, magenkrank; 2. Magen-
kranke *m*, *f*.

E

each [i:tʃ] jede(r, -s); ⌣ *other* einander, sich; *they cost a shilling* ⌣
sie kosten je einen Schilling.
ea·ger □ ['i:gə] (be)gierig (*about*,
after, *for* auf *acc*., nach), gespannt;
fig. eifrig; heftig (*Begierde*); **'ea-**
ger·ness Begierde *f*; Eifer *m*.
ea·gle ['i:gl] Adler *m*; Zehndollar-
stück *n*; '⌣-'**eyed** scharfsichtig;
ea·glet ['⌣lit] junger Adler *m*.
ea·gre ['eigə] Springflut *f*.
ear[1] [iə] Ähre *f*.
ear[2] [⌣] Ohr *n*, Gehör *n*; Öhr *n*,
Henkel *m*; *be all* ⌣*s* ganz Ohr sein;
fall on deaf ⌣*s fig.* auf taube Ohren
stoßen; *keep an* ⌣ *to the ground bsd.*
Am. aufpassen, was die Leute sagen
od. denken; *up to the* ⌣*s fig.* bis über
die Ohren *in Arbeit*; *play by* ⌣ nach
dem Gehör spielen; *set by the* ⌣*s*
gegeneinander aufhetzen; ⌣**ache**
['iəreik] Ohrenschmerz(en *pl*.) *m*; ⌣-
deaf·en·ing ['⌣defniŋ] ohrenbetäu-
bend; '⌣-**drum** Trommelfell *n*.
earl [ə:l] *britischer* Graf *m*; ♀ *Marshal*
Oberzeremonienmeister *m*; **'earl-**
dom Grafenstand *m*.
ear·li·ness ['ə:linis] Frühzeitigkeit *f*.
ear·lobe ['iələub] Ohrläppchen *n*.
ear·ly ['ə:li] früh(zeitig); Früh...; *An-*
fangs...; erst; bald(ig); ⌣ *bird fig.*
Frühaufsteher *m*; *the* ⌣ *bird catches*
the worm Morgenstund hat Gold im
Mund; ⌣ *closing* früher Ladenschluß
m; *it's* ⌣ *closing* (*day*) *today* heute
haben die Geschäfte nachmittags zu;
⌣ *life Jugendzeit f*; ⌣ *warning system* ⚔
Frühwarnsystem *n*; *as* ⌣ *as* schon in
(*dat*.); *earlier on* früher.
ear·mark ['iəma:k] 1. Ohren-
zeichen *n bei Tieren*; *fig.* Kennzeichen *n*; 2. an den Ohren zeichnen; *fig.* (kenn)zeichnen; *für e-n*
Zweck bereitlegen, bestimmen.

ear·muffs ['iəmʌfs] *pl*. Ohrenschüt-
zer *m pl*.
earn [ə:n] verdienen; erwerben;
einbringen (*for dat*.); ⌣*ed income*
Arbeitseinkommen *n*.
ear·nest[1] ['ə:nist] *a*. ⌣-*money* Hand-
geld *n*, Anzahlung *f*; Pfand *n*; *fig*.
Vorgeschmack *m*, Probe *f*; Beweis *m*.
ear·nest[2] [⌣] 1. □ ernst; eifrig;
ernstlich; aufrichtig; ernstgemeint;
2. Ernst *m*; *be in* ⌣ es ernst meinen;
'ear·nest·ness Ernst(lichkeit *f*) *m*;
Eifer *m*.
earn·ings ['ə:niŋz] *pl*. Verdienst *m*,
Lohn *m*, Einkommen *n*; *gross* ⌣ *pl*.
Bruttoeinkommen *n*.
ear...: '⌣-**phones** *pl*. *Radio:* Kopfhörer *m*; '⌣-**piece** *teleph*. Hörmuschel *f*; '⌣-**pierc·ing** ohrenzerreißend; '⌣-**plug** Wattepfropf *m*;
'⌣-**ring** Ohrring *m*; '⌣-**shot** Hörweite
f; '⌣-**split·ting** ohrenzerreißend.
earth [ə:θ] 1. Erde *f*; Land *n*;
Boden *m*; *Fuchs- etc*. Bau *m*; *a*.
⌣-*connection Radio:* Erdung *f*, Erdschluß *m*; 2. *v/t*. ⚡ erden; ⌣ *up*
mit Erde bedecken, anhäufeln;
'earth·en irden; **'earth·en·ware**
1. Töpferware *f*, Steingut *n*;
2. irden; **'earth·ing** ⚡ Erdung *f*;
'earth·li·ness *das* Irdische; Weltlichkeit *f*; **'earth·ly** irdisch; F
denkbar; *no* ⌣ ... gar kein ...;
'earth·quake Erdbeben *n*; **'earth-**
worm Regenwurm *m*; *fig*. Erden-
wurm *m*; **'earth·y** erdig; irdisch;
fig. sinnlich, roh.
ear...: '⌣-**trum·pet** Hörrohr *n*;
'⌣-**wax** Ohrenschmalz *n*; '⌣-**wig**
Ohrwurm *m*.
ease [i:z] 1. Gemütlichkeit *f*, Bequemlichkeit *f*, Behagen *n*; Ruhe *f*;
Gemächlichkeit *f*; Erleichterung *f*;
Ungezwungenheit *f*; Leichtigkeit *f*;

at ~ bequem, behaglich, zwanglos, ungezwungen; *be od. feel at one's* ~ sich wohlfühlen; *ill at* ~ unbehaglich; *stand at* ~*!* ✗ rührt euch!; *take one's* ~ es sich bequem machen; *with* ~ mit Leichtigkeit; *live at* ~ in guten Verhältnissen leben; **2.** erleichtern; *Schmerz* lindern; beruhigen; bequem(er) machen; lockern, *Tau etc.* nachlassen; befreien (*of* von); sich entspannen (*Lage*); ~ *nature* ein Bedürfnis verrichten, sich erleichtern; **ease·ful** □ ['~ful] behaglich; beruhigend; müßig.

ea·sel ['i:zl] Staffelei *f*.

eas·i·ly ['i:zili] leicht, mit Leichtigkeit; sicher, bei weitem; **'eas·i·ness** Bequemlichkeit *f*, Gemächlichkeit *f*; Leichtigkeit *f*; Ungezwungenheit *f*; ~ *of belief* Leichtgläubigkeit *f*.

east [i:st] **1.** Ost(en *m*); Orient *m*; *the* ☌ *Am.* die Oststaaten *pl. der USA*; **2.** Ost...; östlich; ostwärts; **'~-bound** in Richtung Osten fahrend.

East·er ['i:stə] Ostern *n od. pl.*; *attr.* Oster...; ~ *egg* Osterei *n*.

east·er·ly ['i:stəli] östlich; Ost...; nach Osten; **east·ern** ['~tən] = *easterly*; orientalisch; **'east·ern·er** Ostländer(in); Orientale *m*, Orientalin *f*; ☌ *Am.* Oststaatler(in); **east·ern·most** ['~məust] östlichst.

East In·di·a·man ⚓ *hist.* [i:st-'indjəmən] Ostindienfahrer *m* (*Schiff*).

east·ing ⚓ ['i:stiŋ] zurückgelegter östlicher Kurs *m*; Ostrichtung *f*.

east·ward(s) ['i:stwəd(z)] ostwärts.

eas·y ['i:zi] **1.** □ leicht; bequem, behaglich; frei von Schmerzen; unbesorgt, ruhig; willig; ungezwungen; bequem (*Kleid*); ✝ flau, lustlos; *in* ~ *circumstances* wohlhabend; *on* ~ *street* in guten Verhältnissen; *on* ~ *terms* ✝ zu günstigen Bedingungen; *make o.s.* ~ es sich bequem machen; *take it* ~ sich Zeit lassen; es sich leicht machen; *take it* ~*!* nur keine Aufregung!; sachte!; **2.** kurze Pause *f*; **'~-'chair** Lehnstuhl *m*, Klubsessel *m*; **'~-go·ing** *fig.* bequem, lässig; leichtlebig.

eat [i:t] **1.** (*irr.*) *v/t.* essen; fressen; zerfressen; verzehren; ~ *up* aufessen; auffressen; verzehren (*a. fig.*); *v/i.*

essen; schmecken; ~ *out* im Restaurant essen; **2.** ~*s pl. Am. sl.* Essen *n*, Eßwaren *f pl.*; **'eat·a·ble** eßbar; **'eat·a·bles** *pl.* Eßwaren *f pl.*; **'eat·en** *p.p. von eat* 1; **'eat·er** Esser(in); *be a great* (*poor*) ~ ein starker (schwacher) Esser sein; **'eat·ing** Essen *n*; **eat·ing ap·ple** Speiseapfel *m*; **'eat·ing--house** Speisehaus *n*.

eau-de-Co·logne ['əudəkə'ləun] Kölnischwasser *n*.

eaves [i:vz] *pl.* Dachvorsprung *m*, Dachüberstand *m*; Traufe *f*; **'~-drop** (er)lauschen; horchen; **'~-drop·per** Horcher(in).

ebb [eb] **1.** Ebbe *f*; *fig.* Abnahme *f*; Verfall *m*; *at a low* ~ heruntergekommen; **2.** verebben; *fig.* abnehmen, sinken; **'~-'tide** Ebbe *f* (*a. fig.*).

eb·on *poet.* ['ebən] aus Ebenholz; schwarz wie Ebenholz; **eb·on·ite** ['~nait] Hartgummi *m*; **'eb·on·y** Ebenholz *n*.

e·bri·e·ty [i:'braiəti] Trunkenheit *f*.

e·bul·li·ent [i'bʌljənt] überschäumend, -schwenglich; *fig.* sprudelnd (*with* vor); **eb·ul·li·tion** [ebə'liʃən] Überschäumen *n*; Aufbrausen *n*.

ec·cen·tric [ik'sentrik] **1.** *a.* ec'cen·tri·cal □ exzentrisch; *fig.* überspannt; **2.** ⊕ Exzentrik *f*; Sonderling *m*; **ec·cen·tric·i·ty** [eksen-'trisiti] Exzentrizität *f*; *fig.* Überspanntheit *f*.

ec·cle·si·as·tic [ikli:zi'æstik] Geistliche *m*; **ec·cle·si·as·ti·cal** □ geistlich, kirchlich.

ech·e·lon ✗ ['eʃəlɔn] **1.** Staffel(aufstellung) *f*; **2.** staffeln.

e·chi·nus *zo.* [e'kainəs] Seeigel *m*.

ech·o ['ekəu] **1.** Echo *n*; **2.** widerhallen; *Ton* zurückwerfen; *fig.* echoen, nachsprechen; **'~-sound·er** Echolot *n*.

e·clat ['eiklɑ:] Eklat *m*; allgemeiner Beifall *m*; glänzender Erfolg *m*.

ec·lec·tic [ek'lektik] **1.** eklektisch, auswählend; **2.** Eklektiker *m*; **ec-'lec·ti·cism** [~sizəm] Eklektizismus *m*.

e·clipse [i'klips] **1.** Verfinsterung *f*; Verdunkelung *f* (*a. fig.*); Finsternis *f* (*a. fig.*); *in* ~ im Sinken; **2.** (sich) verfinstern, verdunkeln (*a. fig.*); **e·clip·tic** *ast.* [~tik] Ekliptik *f*, Sonnenbahn *f*.

ec·logue ['eklɔg] Ekloge *f*, Hirtengedicht *n*.

e·co·cid·al [i:kəu'saidl] umweltzerstörend; **e·co·cide** ['ˌsaid] Umweltzerstörung *f*; '**e·co·cri·sis** Umweltkrise *f*.

e·col·o·gist [i:'kɔlədʒist] Umweltschutzexperte *m*; **e'col·o·gy** Ökologie *f*; ˌ *movement* Umweltschutzbewegung *f*.

e·co·nom·ic [i:kə'nɔmik], **e·co-'nom·i·cal** □ ökonomisch, haushälterisch; (volks- *etc.*) wirtschaftlich; sparsam; Wirtschafts...; *economic aid* Wirtschaftshilfe *f*; *economic growth* Wirtschaftswachstum *n*; *economic summit* Wirtschaftsgipfel *m*; **e·co'nom·ics** *sg.* Nationalökonomie *f*, Volkswirtschaft(slehre) *f*; **e·con-o·mist** [i:'kɔnəmist] Haushälter *m*; Volkswirt *m*; **e'con·o·mize** sparsam wirtschaften mit; (ein)sparen (*in*, *on* an *dat.*, *with* mit); **e'con·o·my** Haushaltung *f*, Wirtschaft *f*; Wirtschaftlichkeit *f*, Sparsamkeit *f*; Einsparung *f*; System *n*; *economies pl.* Ersparnisse *f pl.*; Sparmaßnahmen *f/pl.*; *political* ˌ Volkswirtschaft(slehre) *f*; ˌ *class Touristik:* Touristenklasse *f*; ˌ *drive* Sparmaßnahmen *f pl.*, -aktion *f*; ˌ *size* Sparpackung *f*.

e·co·sys·tem ['ikəusistəm] Ökosystem *n*.

ec·sta·size ['ekstəsaiz] außer sich bringen (*od. v/i.* geraten), verzücken; '**ec·sta·sy** Ekstase *f*, Verzückung *f*; *go into* ˌ in Verzückung geraten; **ec·stat·ic** [eks'tætik] (ˌ*ally*) verzückt; ˌ *fit* Verzückung *f*.

e·cu·men·i·cal [i:kju:'menikl] ökumenisch.

ec·ze·ma ⚕ ['eksimə] Ekzem *n*, Ausschlag *m*.

e·da·cious [i'deiʃəs] gefräßig.

ed·dy ['edi] **1.** Wirbel *m*, Strudel *m*; **2.** wirbeln, strudeln.

e·den·tate *zo.* [i:'denteit] zahnlos.

edge [edʒ] **1.** Schneide *f*, Schärfe *f*; Rand *m*; (scharfe) Kante *f*; Tisch-Ecke *f*; Rand *m*, Saum *m*; Grat *m*; *Buch*-Schnitt *m*; Schärfe *f*, Heftigkeit *f*; *be on* ˌ nervös sein; *have the* ˌ *on s.o. sl.* j-m über sein; *put an* ˌ *on* schärfen; *put on* ˌ hochkantig legen; *set s.o.'s teeth on* ˌ j-m auf die Nerven gehen; **2.** schärfen; (um)säumen, einfassen; (sich) schieben *od.* drängen; rücken;

edged scharf; ...schneidig; ...kantig.

edge...: 'ˌ·less stumpf; 'ˌ·tool Schneidewerkzeug *n*; 'ˌ·ways, ˌ·wise ['ˌwaiz] seitwärts; von der Seite; *get a word in* ˌ zu Wort kommen.

edg·ing ['edʒiŋ] Schärfen *n*; Rand *m*, Borte *f*, Einfassung *f*, Besatz *m*; 'ˌ·shears *pl.* Grasschere *f*.

edg·y ['edʒi] scharf; F kratzbürstig, nervös.

ed·i·ble ['edibl] eßbar; '**ed·i·bles** *pl.* Eßwaren *f/pl.*

e·dict ['i:dikt] Edikt *n*, Verordnung *f*.

ed·i·fi·ca·tion *fig.* [edifi'keiʃən] Erbauung *f*; **ed·i·fice** ['ˌfis] Gebäude *n* (*a. fig.*); **ed·i·fy** *fig.* ['ˌfai] erbauen; '**ed·i·fy·ing** □ erbaulich.

ed·it ['edit] *Text* herausgeben, redigieren; *Zeitung* als Herausgeber leiten; '**ed·it·ing ta·ble** *Film:* Schneidetisch *m*; **e·di·tion** [i'diʃən] Ausgabe *f e-s Buches*; Auflage *f*; **ed·i·tor** ['editə] Herausgeber *m*; Schriftleiter *m*, Chefredakteur *m*; *letters pl. to the* ˌ Leserbriefe *m/pl.*; **ed·i·to·ri·al** [ˌ'tɔ:riəl] **1.** Redaktions...; ˌ *office* Redaktion *f (Büro)*; ˌ *staff* Redaktion *f (Personal)*; **2.** Leitartikel *m*; **ed·i·torship** ['ˌtəʃip] Schriftleitung *f*, Redaktion *f*; Amt *n* e-s Herausgebers.

ed·u·cate ['edju:keit] erziehen; unterrichten, (aus)bilden; **ed·u'ca-tion** Erziehung *f*; Ausbildung *f*; Bildung *f*; Erziehungs-, Schulwesen *n*; *Ministry of* ♀ Unterrichtsministerium *n*; **ed·u·ca·tion·al** □ [ˌ'keiʃənl], **ed·u·ca·tive** ['ˌkətiv] erzieherisch; Erziehungs...; Bildungs...; erziehlich; *educational film* Lehrfilm *m*; *educational policy* Bildungspolitik *f*; **ed·u·ca·tion·(al)-ist** [ˌ'keiʃn(ə)list] Pädagoge *m*, Schulmann *m*; '**ed·u·ca·tor** Erzieher *m*.

e·duce [i'dju:s] entwickeln; *fig.* ableiten; 🔥 darstellen.

e·duc·tion [i'dʌkʃən] Entwicklung *f*; Ableitung *f*; ⊕ Abzug *m*; **e'duc-tion-pipe** Abzugsröhre *f*.

eel [i:l] Aal *m*.

e'en [i:n] = *even*.

e'er [ɛə] = *ever*.

ee·rie, ee·ry ['iəri] unheimlich.

ef·face [i'feis] auslöschen; *fig.* tilgen; *fig.* in den Schatten stellen;

ef·face·a·ble auslöschbar; **ef'face-
ment** Auslöschung *f*; Tilgung *f*.
ef·fect [i'fekt] **1.** Wirkung *f*; Folge *f*;
Inhalt *m*; Eindruck *m*, Effekt *m*;
ᵗᵗₐ Rechtswirksamkeit *f*; ⊕ Effekt
m, Leistung *f*; ⁓s *pl.* Effekten *pl.*;
Habseligkeiten *f/pl.*; ✝ Guthaben
n; *bring to* ⁓, *carry into* ⁓ verwirklichen, bewerkstelligen; *take* ⁓, *be
of* ⁓ Wirkung haben (*on* auf *acc.*); in
Kraft treten; *of no* ⁓ vergeblich;
in ⁓ in der Tat; in Kraft; *to the* ⁓
des Inhalts; *to this* ⁓ in diesem
Sinn; **2.** bewirken, ausführen; *be
⁓ed* erfolgen; **ef'fec·tive 1.** ⬚ wir-
kend; (ᵗᵗₐ rechts)wirksam; effekt-,
wirkungs-, eindrucksvoll; ✗, ⚓
dienst-, kampffähig; wirklich vorhanden; ⊕ nutzbar; ⁓ *capacity* ⊕
Nutzleistung *f*; ⁓ *date* Tag *m* des
Inkrafttretens; ⊕ nutzbar; **2.** ✗
mst ⁓s *pl.* Effektivbestand *m*; **ef-
'fec·tive·ness** Wirksamkeit *f*; **ef-
'fec·tu·al** [⁓tʃuəl] wirksam, kräftig;
ef'fec·tu·ate [⁓tjueit] bewerkstelligen.
ef·fem·i·na·cy [i'feminəsi] Verweichlichung *f*; **ef'fem·i·nate**
[⁓nit] ⬚ verweichlicht; weibisch.
ef·fer·vesce [efə'ves] (auf)brausen,
(auf)schäumen; *fig.* überschäumen;
ef·fer'ves·cence Aufbrausen *n* etc.;
ef·fer'ves·cent sprudelnd, schäumend; ⁓ *powder* Brausepulver *n*.
ef·fete [e'fiːt] verbraucht; entkräftet.
ef·fi·ca·cious ⬚ [efi'keiʃəs] wirksam; **ef·fi·ca·cy** [⁓kəsi] Wirksamkeit *f*, Kraft *f*.
ef·fi·cien·cy [i'fiʃənsi] Leistungsfähigkeit *f*, Tüchtigkeit *f*; ⊕ Wir-
kungsgrad *m*; (Nutz)Leistung *f*;
Wirksamkeit *f*; ⁓ *expert* Rationali-
sierungsfachmann *m*; **ef'fi·cient** ⬚
wirksam; leistungsfähig, tüchtig.
ef·fi·gy ['efidʒi] Bild(nis) *n*; *burn s.o.
in* ⁓ j. in effigie *od.* im Bild verbrennen.
ef·flo·resce [eflɔː'res] ⚘ (auf)blühen
(*a. fig.*); ⚗ beschlagen, auswittern;
ef·flo'res·cence Blütezeit *f*; ⚗ Beschlag *m*; **ef·flo'res·cent** beschla-
gend, auswitternd.
ef·flu·ence ['efluəns] Ausfließen *n*,
Ausfluß *m*; **'ef·flu·ent 1.** ausflie-
ßend; **2.** Ausfluß *m*.
ef·flux ['eflʌks] Ausströmen *n*; Ausfluß *m*.

ef·fort ['efət] Anstrengung *f*, Bemühung *f* (*at* um); Mühe *f*; F
Leistung *f*; **'ef·fort·less** ⬚ mühelos.
ef·fron·ter·y [i'frʌntəri] Frechheit
f, Unverschämtheit *f*.
ef·ful·gence [e'fʌldʒəns] Glanz *m*;
ef'ful·gent ⬚ strahlend, glänzend.
ef·fuse [e'fjuːz] aus-, vergießen;
ef·fu·sion [i'fjuːʒən] Ausgießung
f; Erguß *m* (*a. fig.*); **ef'fu·sive** ⬚
[⁓siv] überschwenglich; **ef'fu·sive-
ness** Überschwenglichkeit *f*.
eft *zo.* [eft] Sumpfeidechse *f*.
egg[1] [eg] *mst* ⁓ *on* drängen, auf-,
anreizen, anstacheln.
egg[2] [⁓] Ei *n*; *in the* ⁓ im Anfangs-
stadium; *bad* ⁓ F schlechter Kerl *m*;
put all one's ⁓s *in one basket* alles
auf eine Karte setzen; *as sure as* ⁓s
is ⁓s F todsicher; '⁓-**cup** Eier-
becher *m*; '⁓-**flip** Eierflip *m*; '⁓-
head Intellektuelle *m*; '⁓-**nog** =
egg-flip; '⁓-**plant** ⚘ Aubergine *f*,
Eierfrucht *f*; '⁓-**shell** Eierschale *f*;
'⁓-**whisk** Schneebesen *m*.
eg·lan·tine ⚘ ['egləntain] Hecken-
rose *f*.
e·go ['egəu] *das* Ich; **e·go·cen·tric**
[⁓'sentrik] egozentrisch; **'e·go·ism**
Egoismus *m*, Selbstsucht *f*; **'e·go·ist**
Egoist(in); **e·go'is·tic**, **e·go'is·ti·cal**
⬚ egoistisch, selbstsüchtig; **e·go-
tism** ['⁓tizəm] Selbstgefälligkeit *f*,
Eigendünkel *m*; **'e·go·tist** Egotist *m*,
selbstgefälliger Mensch *m*; **e·go'tis-
tic**, **e·go'tis·ti·cal** ⬚ nur von sich
redend; selbstgefällig.
e·gre·gious *iro.* ⬚ [i'griːdʒəs] großartig; ungeheuer, unerhört.
e·gress ['iːgres] Ausgang *m*; Ausfluß *m*; *fig.* Ausweg *m*.
e·gret ['iːgret] *orn.* kleiner weißer
Reiher *m*; Federbusch *m*.
E·gyp·tian [i'dʒipʃən] **1.** ägyptisch;
2. Ägypter(in).
eh [ei] wie?; nicht wahr?; ei!; sieh
da!
ei·der ['aidə] *a.* ⁓-**duck** *orn.* Eider-
ente *f*; ⁓ *down* Eiderdaunen *f/pl.*;
Daunendecke *f*.
eight [eit] **1.** acht; **2.** Acht *f*; ⚓
Achter *m*; *behind the* ⁓ *ball Am.* in
der (die) Klemme; **eight·een**
['ei'tiːn] achtzehn; **'eight'eenth**
[⁓θ] achtzehnt; **'eight·fold** achtfach; **eighth** [eitθ] **1.** achte(r, -s);
2. Achtel *n*; **'eighth·ly** achtens;

eight-'hour day Achtstundentag *m*; **eight·i·eth** [ˈ⌣iiθ] achtzigste(r, -s); '**eight·some**[⌣səm] schottischer Tanz *m für 8 Tänzer*; '**eight·y** achtzig.

eis·tedd·fod [ais'teðvɔd] wallisisches Sängerfest *n*, Eisteddfod *n*.

ei·ther [ˈaiðə] **1.** *adj. u. pron.* einer *von beiden*; beide; jeder *von zweien*; **2.** *cj.* ⌣ ... *or* entweder ... oder; *not* (...) ⌣ auch nicht.

e·jac·u·late [i'dʒækjuleit] *Worte* ausstoßen; **e·jac·u'la·tion** Ausruf *m*; Stoßgebet *n*; Ausstoßen *n*.

e·ject [iːˈdʒekt] ausstoßen; vertreiben *(from von)*; ausweisen; *e-s Amtes* entsetzen; **e'jec·tion** Ausstoßung *f*, Vertreibung *f*; Ausweisung *f*; **e'ject·ment** 🕮 Vertreibung *f*; **e'jec·tor** ⊕ Auswerfer *m*; ⌣-seat 🖾 Schleudersitz *m*.

eke [iːk]: ⌣ *out* ergänzen; verlängern *(with durch)*; sich mit *et.* durchhelfen; ⌣ *out a miserable existence* sich kümmerlich durchschlagen.

el *Am.* F [el] = *elevated railroad.*

e·lab·o·rate 1. ☐ [i'læbərit] sorg-fältig ausgearbeitet; kunstvoll; vollendet; kompliziert; reich verziert; **2.** [⌣reit] sorgfältig ausarbeiten; herausarbeiten; **e'lab·o·rate·ness** [⌣ritnis], **e·lab·o·ra'tion** [⌣'reiʃən] sorgfältige Ausarbeitung *f*.

e·lapse [i'læps] verfließen, -streichen.

e·las·tic [i'læstik] **1.** (⌣ally) elastisch, dehnbar *(a. fig.)*; geschmeidig; spannkräftig; **2.** Gummiband *n*; **e·las·tic·i·ty** [elæs'tisiti] Elastizität *f*, Dehnbarkeit *f*; *fig.* Spannkraft *f*.

e·late [i'leit] (er)heben, ermutigen, froh erregen; stolz machen; **e'lat·ed** in gehobener Stimmung, freudig erregt *(at über acc.; with durch)*; **e'la·tion** gehobene Stimmung *f*.

el·bow ['elbəu] **1.** Ellbogen *m*; Krümmung *f*, Biegung *f*; ⊕ Knie *n*, Winkel *m*; *at one's* ⌣ nahe, bei der Hand; *out at* ⌣s am Ellbogen zerrissen; *fig.* heruntergekommen; **2.** mit dem Ellbogen (weg)stoßen; ⌣ *one's way through* sich durchdrängen; ⌣ *out* verdrängen; '⌣- -'chair Lehnstuhl *m*; '⌣-grease F Armschmalz *n (Kraftanstrengung)*; '⌣-room Spielraum *m*.

eld·er¹ ['eldə] **1.** älter; ⌣ *statesman* Politiker *m mst im Ruhestand*, der

(inoffiziell) als Berater tätig ist; *fig.* großer alter Mann *m e-r Berufsgruppe*; **2.** der *od.* die Ältere; (Kirchen)Älteste *m*; *my* ⌣s *pl.* ältere Leute als ich.

el·der² 🖾 [⌣] Holunder *m*; '⌣·ber·ry Holunderbeere *f*.

eld·er·ly ['eldəli] ältlich; älter.

eld·est ['eldist] ältest; *the* ⌣ *born* der Erstgeborene.

e·lect [i'lekt] **1.** (aus)gewählt; *eccl.* auserwählt; *bride* ⌣ Verlobte *f*; **2.** (aus-, er)wählen; (er)wählen; *eccl.* auserwählen; vorziehen, sich entschließen *(to do zu tun)*; **3.** *the* ⌣ *pl. eccl.* die Auserwählten *pl.*; **e'lec·tion** Wahl *f*; ⌣ *address*, ⌣ *speech* Wahlrede *f*; **e·lec·tion·eer** [⌣ʃəˈniə] Wahlpropaganda machen; **e·lec·tion'eer·ing** Wahlpropaganda *f*; **e'lec·tive 1.** ☐ wählend; gewählt; Wahl...; *Am.* fakultativ; **2.** *Am.* Wahlfach *n*; **e'lec·tive·ly** durch Wahl; **e'lec·tor** Wähler *m*; *Am.* Wahlmann *m*; *hist.* Kurfürst *m*; **e'lec·tor·al** Wähler..., Wähler...; kurfürstlich; ⌣ *address* Wahlrede *f*; ⌣ *campaign* Wahlkampf *m*, -kampagne *f*; ⌣ *college Am.* Wahlmänner *m pl.*; ⌣ *roll* Wählerliste *f*; **e'lec·tor·ate** [⌣tərit] Wähler(schaft *f) m pl.*; Kurwürde *f*; Kurfürstentum *n*; **e'lec·tress** *hist.* Kurfürstin *f*; Wählerin *f*.

e·lec·tric [i'lektrik], **e'lec·tri·cal** ☐ elektrisch; Elektro...; *fig.* elektrisierend, faszinierend; **e'lec·tri·cal en·gi·neer** Elektrotechniker *m*.

e·lec·tric...: ⌣ *blue* stahlblau; ⌣ *chair* elektrischer Stuhl *m für Hinrichtungen*; ⌣ *eel* Zitteraal *m*; ⌣ *eye* Photozelle *f*; ⌣ *fence* Elektrozaun *m*.

e·lec·tri·cian [ilek'triʃən] Elektriker *m*, Elektrotechniker *m*; **e·lec'tric·i·ty** [⌣siti] Elektrizität *f*; **e·lec·tri·fi'ca·tion** Elektrifizierung *f*; **e'lec·tri·fy** [⌣fai], **e'lec·trize** elektrifizieren; elektrisieren *(a. fig.)*; begeistern.

e·lec·tro [i'lektrəu] Elektro...; **e·'lec·tro·cute** [⌣trəkjuːt] auf dem elektrischen Stuhl hinrichten; durch elektrischen Strom töten; **e·lec·tro'cu·tion** Hinrichtung *f od.* Tod *m* durch elektrischen Strom; **e'lec·trode** [⌣trəud] Elektrode *f*; **e'lec·tro·dy'nam·ics** *mst sg.* Elektrodynamik *f*; **e·lec·tro·lier** [⌣'liə] elektrischer Kronleuchter *m*; **e'lec·tro·lyse** [⌣laiz] elektrisch zersetzen; **e·lec·trol·y·sis** [ilek-'trɔlisis] Elektrolyse *f*; **e·lec·tro·lyte** [i'lektrəulait] Elektrolyt *m*; **e·lec·tro·lyt·ic** [ˌ'litik] elektrolytisch; **e'lec·tro'mag·net** Elektromagnet *m*; **e'lec·tro'met·al·lur·gy** Elektrometallurgie *f*; **e'lec·tro'mo·tive** elektromotorisch; **e·'lec·tro'mo·tor** Elektromotor *m*.

e·lec·tron [i'lektrɔn] Elektron *n*; *attr.* Elektronen...; **e·lec'tron·ic** Elektronen...; ˌ *data processing* elektronische Datenverarbeitung *f*; **e·lec'tron·ics** *sg.* Elektronenphysik *f*, Elektronik *f*.

e·lec·tro·plate [i'lektrəupleit] **1.** galvanisch versilbern; **2.** galvanisch versilberte Gegenstände *m/pl.*; **e'lec·tro·type** galvanischer Druck *m*; Elektrotype *f*.

el·ee·mos·y·nar·y [elii:'mɔsinəri] Almosen..., Wohltätigkeits...

el·e·gance ['eligəns] Eleganz *f*, Vornehmheit *f*, Gepflegtheit *f*, Anmut *f*; **'el·e·gant** ☐ elegant, vornehm, gepflegt; anmutig; geschmackvoll; *Am.* erstklassig.

el·e·gi·ac [eli'dʒaiək] **1.** elegisch; **2.** elegischer Vers *m*.

el·e·gy ['elidʒi] Elegie *f* (*Klagelied*).

el·e·ment ['elimənt] Element *n*, Urstoff *m*; (Grund)Bestandteil *m*; (Lebens)Element *n*; ⚡ Element *n*; Umstand *m*; Naturkraft *f*; *fig.* Körnchen *n*; ˌs *pl.* Anfangsgründe *m/pl.*; **el·e·men·tal** [ˌ'mentl] ☐ elementar; gewaltig; wesentlich; **el·e'men·ta·ry** ☐ elementar, einfach; Anfangs...; ˌ *school* Volks-, Grundschule *f*; *elementaries pl.* Anfangsgründe *m/pl.*, Elemente *n/pl.*

el·e·phant ['elifənt] Elefant *m*; *white* ˌ nutzloses Wertstück *n*; **el·e·phan·tine** [ˌ'fæntain] Elefanten...; elefantenhaft; plump.

el·e·vate ['eliveit] erhöhen; *fig.* erheben; **'el·e·vat·ed 1.** hoch, erhaben; F angeheitert; ˌ *railroad* = **2.** *Am.* F Hochbahn *f*; **el·e'va·tion** Erhebung *f*, Erhöhung *f* (*a. fig.*); Höhe *f*; Erhabenheit *f*; Hoheit *f*; *ast.* Höhe *f*; ⊕ Aufriß *m*; **'el·e·va·tor** ⊕ Hebe-, Förderwerk *n*, Aufzug *m*; *Am.* Fahrstuhl *m*; ✈ Höhenruder *n*; (*grain*) ˌ *Am.* Getreidespeicher *m*; *bucket* ˌ ⊕ Becherwerk *n*; ˌ *shaft Am.* Aufzug-

schacht *m*.

e·lev·en [i'levn] **1.** elf; **2.** Elf *f*; ˌ'plus **ex·am·i·na·tion** Aufnahmeprüfung *f* in die höhere Schule; **e'lev·en·ses** F [ˌziz] kleiner Imbiß *m um ca. 11 Uhr*, zweites Frühstück *n*; **e'lev·enth** [ˌθ] elfte(r, -s); *at the* ˌ *hour* in letzter Minute.

elf [elf], *pl.* **elves** [elvz] Elf(e *f*) *m*, Kobold *m*; Zwerg *m*; **elf·in** ['ˌin] elfisch; Elfen...; **'elf·ish** elfengleich; boshaft.

e·lic·it [i'lisit] hervorlocken, herausholen.

e·lide *gr.* [i'laid] elidieren, auslassen.

el·i·gi·bil·i·ty [elidʒə'biliti] Eignung *f*; Vorzug *m*; **'el·i·gi·ble** ☐ geeignet, annehmbar; passend; akzeptabel, in Frage kommend; (teilnahme)berechtigt.

e·lim·i·nate [i'limineit] aussondern, ausscheiden (*bsd.* 🜨, ♈, ♃); ausmerzen; **e·lim·i'na·tion** Aussonderung *f*; Ausscheidung *f*.

e·li·sion *gr.* [i'liʒən] Elision *f*, Auslassung *f*.

é·lite [ei'li:t] Elite *f*, Auslese *f*; Oberschicht *f*.

é·lit·ist [ei'li:tist] elitär.

e·lix·ir [i'liksə] Elixier *n*.

E·liz·a·be·than [ilizə'bi:θən] **1.** elisabethanisch; **2.** Elisabethaner(in).

elk *zo.* [elk] Elch *m*.

ell *hist.* [el] Elle *f*.

el·lipse ⅄ [i'lips] Ellipse *f*; **el'lipsis** [ˌsis], *pl.* **el'lip·ses** *gr.* [ˌsi:z], Ellipse *f*, Auslassung *f*; **el'lip·tic**, **el'lip·ti·cal** ☐ [ˌtik(ə)l] elliptisch.

elm ♀ [elm] Ulme *f*, Rüster *f*.

el·o·cu·tion [elə'kju:ʃən] Vortrag(s-kunst *f*, -sweise *f*) *m*; **el·o'cu·tion·ar·y** [ˌʃnəri] rednerisch; **el·o'cu·tion·ist** Vortragskünstler *m*; Sprecherzieher *m*.

e·lon·gate ['i:lɔŋgeit] verlängern; **e·lon'ga·tion** Verlängerung *f*; *ast.* Elongation *f*, Winkelabstand *m*.

e·lope [i'ləup] (dem Gatten) entlaufen, durchgehen; **e'lope·ment** Entlaufen *n*.

el·o·quence ['eləukwəns] Beredsamkeit *f*; **'el·o·quent** ☐ beredt, redegewandt.

else [els] sonst, andere(r, -s), weiter; *all* ˌ alles andere; *anyone* ˌ irgendein anderer; *what* ˌ? was sonst?; *or* ˌ oder aber; **'else'where** anderswo(hin).

e·lu·ci·date [iˈluːsideit] aufklären, erläutern; **e·lu·ci'da·tion** Aufklärung *f*, Erläuterung *f*; **e'lu·ci·da·to·ry** aufklärend, erläuternd.

e·lude [iˈluːd] geschickt umgehen; ausweichen, sich entziehen *(dat.)*.

e·lu·sion [iˈluːʒən] Umgehung *f*; Ausflucht *f*; Ausweichen *n*; **e'lu·sive** [∼siv] nicht zu fassen(d); **e'lu·sive·ness** (listiges) Ausweichen *n*; **e'lu·so·ry** trügerisch.

elves [elvz] *pl. von* elf.

E·lys·ian [iˈliziən] elysisch, himmlisch; **E'lys·ium** [∼iəm] Elysium *n*.

em [em] *typ.* Geviert *n*.

e·ma·ci·ate [iˈmeiʃieit] abzehren, ausmergeln; **e·ma·ci·a·tion** [imeisiˈeiʃən] Abzehrung *f*.

em·a·nate [ˈeməneit] ausströmen; ausgehen *(from* von*)*; **em·a'na·tion** Ausströmung *f*; *fig.* Ausstrahlung *f*; *phys.* Emanation *f*.

e·man·ci·pate [iˈmænsipeit] emanzipieren, befreien; **e·man·ci'pa·tion** Emanzipation *f*, Befreiung *f*; **e'man·ci·pa·tor** Befreier *m*.

e·mas·cu·late 1. [iˈmæskjuleit] entmannen; verweichlichen; *Text* verstümmeln; 2. [∼lit] entmannt; weibisch; **e·mas·cu·la·tion** [∼ˈleiʃən] Entmannung *f*; Verweichlichung *f*; *Text*-Verstümmelung *f*.

em·balm [imˈbɑːm] (ein)balsamieren; vor Vergessenheit bewahren; *be ∼ed in* fortleben in *(dat.)*; **em·'balm·ment** Einbalsamierung *f*.

em·bank [imˈbæŋk] eindämmen; **em'bank·ment** Eindämmung *f*; Deich *m*; (Bahn)Damm *m*; Uferstraße *f*, Kai *m*.

em·bar·go [emˈbɑːgəu] 1. Embargo *n*; (Hafen-, Handels)Sperre *f*, Beschlagnahme *f*; 2. *Hafen, Handel* sperren; *Schiff etc.* beschlagnahmen.

em·bark [imˈbɑːk] (sich) einschiffen, verladen *(for* nach*)*; *Geld* anlegen; sich einlassen *(in, on, upon* in, auf *acc.)*; **em·bar·ka·tion** [embɑːˈkeiʃən] Einschiffung *f*, Verladung *f*.

em·bar·rass [imˈbærəs] (be)hindern; verwirren, in Verlegenheit bringen; in e-e unangenehme Lage bringen; erschweren, verwickeln; *∼ed* verlegen, betreten; in (Geld-)Verlegenheit; **em'bar·rass·ing** □ unangenehm; unbequem; peinlich;

em'bar·rass·ment (Geld)Verlegenheit *f*; Verwirrung *f*; Schwierigkeit *f*.

em·bas·sy [ˈembəsi] Botschaft *f*; Gesandtschaft *f*.

em·bat·tle [imˈbætl] in Schlachtordnung aufstellen; mit Zinnen versehen.

em·bed [imˈbed] (ein)betten, lagern.

em·bel·lish [imˈbeliʃ] verschönern; *Geschichte* ausschmücken; **em'bel·lish·ment** Verschönerung *f*; Schmuck *m*; Ausschmückung *f*.

em·ber·days [ˈembədeiz] *pl.* Quatember *m (die vier Fastenzeiten)*.

em·bers [ˈembəz] *pl.* glühende Asche *f*; *fig.* Funken *m/pl.*

em·bez·zle [imˈbezl] veruntreuen, unterschlagen; **em'bez·zle·ment** Veruntreuung *f*, Unterschlagung *f*; **em'bez·zler** Veruntreuer *m*.

em·bit·ter [imˈbitə] verbittern; verschlimmern; erbittern.

em·bla·zon [imˈbleizən] mit e-m Wappenbild bemalen; *fig.* verherrlichen; **em'bla·zon·ry** Wappenmalerei *f*.

em·blem [ˈembləm] Sinnbild *n*, Emblem *n*, Symbol *n*; Wahrzeichen *n*; **em·blem·at·ic**, **em·blem·at·i·cal** □ [embliˈmætik(əl)] sinnbildlich, symbolisch.

em·bod·i·ment [imˈbɔdimənt] Verkörperung *f*; **em'bod·y** verkörpern; vereinigen; *Land* einverleiben *(in dat.)*.

em·bold·en [imˈbəuldən] ermutigen.

em·bo·lism [ˈembəlizəm] Embolie *f*.

em·bos·om [imˈbuzəm] ins Herz schließen; *∼ed with* umgeben von.

em·boss [imˈbɔs] bossieren; *mit dem Hammer* treiben; **em'bossed** getrieben, erhaben gearbeitet; *∼ note-paper* geprägtes Briefpapier *n*.

em·bow·el [imˈbauəl] ausweiden.

em·brace [imˈbreis] 1. (sich) umarmen; umschließen; umfassen, einschließen; *Gelegenheit, Beruf* ergreifen; *Angebot* annehmen; in sich aufnehmen; 2. Umarmung *f*.

em·bra·sure [imˈbreiʒə] Leibung *f*; Schießscharte *f*.

em·bro·cate [ˈembrəukeit] einreiben; **em·bro'ca·tion** Einreibung *f*, Liniment *n*.

em·broi·der [imˈbrɔidə] sticken; *fig.* ausschmücken; **em'broi·der·y**

Stickerei *f*; *fig.* Ausschmückung *f*.

em·broil [im'brɔil] (in Streit) verwickeln; verwirren; **em'broil-
ment** Verwirrung *f*.

em·bry·o ['embriəu] Embryo *m*,
Fruchtkeim *m*; *in* ~ im Werden;
em·bry·on·ic [~'ɔnik] embryonal,
(noch) unentwickelt (*a. fig.*).

em·bus [im'bʌs] (auf Kraftfahr-
zeuge) verladen *od.* steigen.

em·cee F [em'si:] Conférencier *m*.

e·mend [i:'mend] *Text* verbessern,
korrigieren; **e·men·da·tion** Verbesserung *f*; **'e·men·da·tor** (Text-)
Verbesserer *m*; **e'mend·a·to·ry**
[~dətəri] verbessernd.

em·er·ald ['emərəld] **1.** Smaragd *m*;
2. smaragdgrün.

e·merge [i'mə:dʒ] auftauchen (*a.
fig.*); zum Vorschein kommen; her-
vorgehen (als; *from* aus); sich erheben (*into* zu); sich ergeben *od.*
zeigen; **e'mer·gence** Auftauchen *n*.

e·mer·gen·cy [i'mə:dʒənsi] uner-
wartetes Ereignis *n*; Notfall *m*;
dringende Not *f*; ~ **brake** Notbremse *f*; ~ **call** Notruf *m*; ~ **decree** Notverordnung *f*; ~ **ex·it** Not-
ausgang *m*; ~ **land·ing** ✈ Notlandung *f*; ~ **man** *Sport*: Ersatzmann *m*; ~ **num·ber** Notruf(nummer *f*) *m*; ~ **serv·ice** Notdienst *m*.

e·mer·gent [i'mə:dʒənt] auftau-
chend, entstehend; ~ *countries pl.*
junge Staaten *m/pl.*, Entwicklungs-
länder *n/pl.*

e·mer·sion [i'mə:ʃən] Auftauchen
n; *ast.* Austritt *m*.

em·er·y ['eməri] Schmirgel *m*;
~ **board** Sandblattnagelfeile *f*; **'~
-cloth** Schmirgelleinen *n*; **'~·pa·per**
Schmirgelpapier *n*.

e·met·ic [i'metik] **1.** erbrechener-
regend; Brech...; **2.** Brechmittel *n*.

em·i·grant ['emigrənt] **1.** aus-
wandernd; **2.** Auswanderer *m*; **em·
i·grate** ['~greit] auswandern; **em·
i'gra·tion** Auswanderung *f*; **em·
i·gra·to·ry** ['~greitəri] Auswande-
rungs...

em·i·nence ['eminəns] Anhöhe *f*;
Auszeichnung *f*, Ruhm *m*; hohe
Stellung *f*; ♗ Eminenz *f* (*Titel*);
'em·i·nent □ *fig.* ausgezeichnet
(*in, for* durch), bedeutend, hervorragend; **'em·i·nent·ly** in hohem
Maße, ganz besonders.

e·mir [e'miə] Emir *m*; **e·mir·ate**

[e'miərit] Emirat *n*.

em·is·sar·y ['emisəri] Sendbote *m*,
Emissär *m*; **e·mis·sion** [i'miʃən]
Aussenden *n*; *phys.* Ausströmen *n*;
fig. Ausfluß *m*; ✝ Emission *f*.

e·mit [i'mit] von sich geben; aussenden, -strömen; ✝ ausgeben, in
Umlauf setzen.

e·mol·u·ment [i'mɔljumənt] Vergütung *f*; ~*s pl.* Einkünfte *pl.*, Be-
züge *pl.*

e·mo·tion [i'məuʃən] (Gemüts-)
Bewegung *f*; Gefühl(sregung *f*) *n*;
Erregung *f*; Rührung *f*; **e'mo-
tion·al** [~ʃənl] □ gefühlsmäßig;
Gefühls...; gefühlvoll, gefühls-
betont, emotional; **e·mo·tion·al·
i·ty** [~ʃə'næliti] gefühlvolles Wesen *n*; **e'mo·tion·less** gefühllos,
kühl; **e'mo·tive** gefühlsmäßig.

em·pan·el [im'pænl] in die (*bsd.*
Geschworenen)Liste eintragen.

em·pa·thy *psych.* ['empəθi] Ein-
fühlung(svermögen *n*) *f*.

em·per·or ['empərə] Kaiser *m*.

em·pha·sis ['emfəsis], *pl.* **em·pha-
ses** ['~si:z] Nachdruck *m*, Betonung
f, Ton *m*; **em·pha·size** ['~saiz]
nachdrücklich betonen; hervorheben; **em·phat·ic** [im'fætik]
(~*ally*) nachdrücklich; ausgesprochen; *be* ~ *that* betonen, daß.

em·pire ['empaiə] (Kaiser)Reich *n*;
Herrschaft *f*; *the British* ♗ das britische Weltreich.

em·pir·ic [em'pirik] **1.** Empiriker
m; Quacksalber *m*; **2.** *mst* **em'pir-
i·cal** □ erfahrungsmäßig, em-
pirisch; quacksalberisch; **em'pir-
i·cism** [~sizəm] Empirismus *m*;
em'pir·i·cist Empiriker *m*.

em·place·ment ⚔ [im'pleismənt]
Instellungbringen *n*; Geschütz-
stand *m*.

em·plane [im'plein] in ein Flugzeug
steigen *od.* verladen.

em·ploy [im'plɔi] **1.** beschäftigen,
anstellen; an-, verwenden, gebrauchen; **2.** Dienst (*e pl.*) *m*, Beschäftigung *f*; *in the* ~ *of* angestellt
bei; **em·ploy·é** *m*, **em·ploy·ée** *f*
[ɔm'plɔiei], **em·ploy·ee** [emplɔi'i:]
Angestellte *m, f*; Arbeitnehmer(in);
em·ploy·er [im'plɔiə] Arbeitgeber
m, Dienstherr *m*; ✝ Auftraggeber
m; **em·ploy·ment** Beschäftigung *f*;
Geschäft *n*; Beruf *m*, (An)Stellung
f, Arbeit *f*; ~ *agency* Stellenvermitt-

lungsbüro *n*; *place of* ~ Arbeits-stätte *f*; ♀ *Exchange* Arbeitsamt *n*.
em·po·ri·um [em'pɔ:riəm] Handels-, Umschlagplatz *m*; Warenhaus *n*; Laden *m*.
em·pow·er [im'pauə] ermächtigen; befähigen.
em·press ['empris] Kaiserin *f*.
emp·ti·ness ['emptinis] Leere *f*, Leerheit *f*; Hohlheit *f*; **'emp·ty 1.** □ leer; *fig*: hohl; F hungrig; **2.** (sich) (aus-, ent)leeren; sich ergießen; **3.** leerer Behälter *m*; *empties pl.* ⚓ Leergut *n*; **'emp·ty-'hand·ed** mit leeren Händen.
em·pur·ple [im'pə:pl] purpurrot färben.
e·mu *orn.* ['i:mju:] Emu *m*, Kasuar *m*.
em·u·late ['emjuleit] wetteifern mit; nacheifern, es gleichtun (*dat.*); **em·u'la·tion** Wetteifer *m*; **em·u·la·tive** ['~lətiv] nacheifernd (*of dat.*); **em·u·la·tor** ['~leitə] Nacheiferer *m*; **'em·u·lous** □ (*of*) nacheifernd (*dat.*); eifersüchtig (auf *acc.*).
e·mul·sion ⚗ [i'mʌlʃən] Emulsion *f*.
en·a·ble [i'neibl] befähigen, in den Stand setzen, es *j-m* ermöglichen (*to inf.* zu *inf.*); ermächtigen.
en·act [i'nækt] verfügen, verordnen; *Gesetz* erlassen; *thea.* spielen; *be* ~*ed* sich abspielen; **en'act·ment** gesetzliche Verfügung *f*; Erlassen *n* *e-s Gesetzes*.
en·am·el [i'næməl] **1.** Email(le *f*) *n*, (*bsd.* Zahn)Schmelz *m*; Glasur *f*; **2.** emaillieren; glasieren; *poet.* (bunt) schmücken.
en·am·o(u)r [i'næmə] verliebt machen; *be* ~*ed of* verliebt sein in (*acc.*).
en·cage [in'keidʒ] einsperren.
en·camp ✕ [in'kæmp] (sich) lagern, das Lager aufschlagen; **en'camp·ment** Lager(n) *n*.
en·case [in'keis] einschließen; umgeben; (um)hüllen; **en'case·ment** Gehäuse *n*; Hülle *f*.
en·cash·ment ⚓ [in'kæʃmənt] Inkasso *n*, Einkassierung *f*.
en·caus·tic [en'kɔ:stik] **1.** enkaustisch; **2.** Enkaustik *f* (*antike Maltechnik*).
en·ceph·a·li·tis 𝆏 [enkefə'laitis] Gehirnentzündung *f*, Enzephalitis *f*.
en·chain [in'tʃein] anketten; fes-

seln.
en·chant [in'tʃɑ:nt] bezaubern; *fig.* entzücken; **en'chant·er** Zauberer *m*; **en'chant·ing** bezaubernd; **en'chant·ment** Ver-, Bezauberung *f*; Zauber *m*; **en'chant·ress** Zauberin *f*.
en·chase [in'tʃeis] ziselieren; *Edelstein* fassen; *fig.* schmücken.
en·ci·pher [in'saifə] verschlüsseln, chiffrieren.
en·cir·cle [in'sə:kl] einkreisen; umfassen, -geben; **en'cir·cle·ment** Umfassung *f*; *pol.* Einkreisung *f*.
en·close [in'kləuz] einzäunen; einfassen; einschließen; beilegen, beifügen; **en'clo·sure** [~ʒə] Einzäunung *f*; eingehegtes Grundstück *n*; Bei-, Anlage *f zu e-m Brief*.
en·code [in'kəud] = *encipher*.
en·co·mi·ast [en'kəumiæst] Lobredner *m*; **en'co·mi·um** [~mjəm] Lobrede *f*.
en·com·pass [in'kʌmpəs] umgeben.
en·core [ɔŋ'kɔ:] **1.** noch einmal!; da capo!; **2.** *v/i.* da capo rufen; *v/t.* nochmals verlangen; *j.* um *e-e* Zugabe bitten; **3.** Dakaporuf *m*; Wiederholung *f*; Zugabe *f*.
en·coun·ter [in'kauntə] **1.** Zs.-treffen *n*; Begegnung *f*; Gefecht *n*; **2.** (plötzlich) begegnen (*dat.*), treffen; entgegentreten (*dat.*); *auf Schwierigkeiten etc.* stoßen, mit *j-m* zs.-stoßen.
en·cour·age [in'kʌridʒ] ermutigen, unterstützen, fördern; **en'cour·age·ment** Ermutigung *f*; Unterstützung *f*, Förderung *f*; **en'cour·ag·er** Förderer *m*.
en·croach [in'krəutʃ] eingreifen, -dringen (*on, upon* in *acc.*); beeinträchtigen (*on acc.*); ~ *upon s.o.'s kindness* *j-s* Güte mißbrauchen; **en'croach·ment** Ein-, Übergriff *m* (*on, upon* in, auf *acc.*).
en·crust [in'krʌst] (sich) überkrusten; ⊕ inkrustieren.
en·cum·ber [in'kʌmbə] belasten; beladen; beschweren; (be)hindern, versperren; **en'cum·brance** Last *f*; *fig.* Hindernis *n*; Hypothekenschuld *f*; Schuldenlast *f*; *without* ~ ohne (Familien)Anhang.
en·cyc·li·cal *eccl.* [en'siklikəl] (päpstliche) Enzyklika *f*.
en·cy·clo·p(a)e·di·a [ensaikləu'pi:djə] Enzyklopädie *f*, Konversationslexikon *n*; **en·cy·clo·p(a)e·dic**

enzyklopädisch.

end [end] **1.** Ende *n*; Ziel *n*, (End-)
Zweck *m*; Folge *f*; Endchen *n*; be
at an ~ zu Ende sein; no ~ of unendlich viel(e), unzählige, sehr groß
etc.; have s.th. at one's fingers' ~s
et. beherrschen; in the ~ am Ende,
auf die Dauer; on ~ aufrecht; hintereinander; ununterbrochen; stand
on ~ zu Berge stehen; to the ~ that
damit; to no ~ vergebens; to this ~
zu dem Zweck; come to an ~ zu
Ende gehen; go off the deep ~ fig. in
die Luft gehen; make an ~ of, put
an ~ to e-r Sache ein Ende machen;
make both ~s meet (mit dem Geld)
gerade auskommen, sich nach der
Decke strecken; **2.** enden, been-
d(ig)en.

en·dan·ger [in'deindʒə] gefährden.
en·dear [in'diə] teuer machen; en-
'**dear·ing** reizend; zärtlich; **en-**
'**dear·ment** Liebkosung *f*, Zärtlichkeit *f*.
en·deav·o(u)r [in'devə] **1.** Bestreben
n, Bemühen *n*, Bemühung *f*, Anstrengung *f*; **2.** sich bemühen, bestrebt sein (after nach).
en·dem·ic [en'demik] **1.** *a.* **en-**
'**dem·i·cal** □ endemisch; einheimisch; **2.** endemische Krankheit *f*.
end·ing ['endiŋ] Ende *n*; Schluß *m*;
gr. Endung *f*.
en·dive ['endiv] Endivie *f*.
end·less □ ['endlis] endlos, unendlich; ⊕ ohne Ende.
end-of-term [endəv'tə:m] Semester-
abschluß...; ~ *exam* Semesterab-
schlußprüfung *f*.
en·dorse [in'dɔ:s] † indossieren,
girieren, überweisen; mit e-m Vermerk (on auf der Rückseite e-r Urkunde) versehen; gutheißen; bei-
pflichten (dat.); endorsing ink
Stempelfarbe *f*; **en·dor·see** [en-
dɔ:'si:] Indossat *m*; **en·dorse·ment**
[in'dɔ:smənt] Aufschrift *f*; Bestätigung *f*; † Indossament *n*, Giro *n*;
en'dors·er Indossant *m*, Girant *m*.
en·do·sperm ['endəuspə:m] En-
dosperm *n*, Nährgewebe *n* des
Samens.
en·dow [in'dau] ausstatten, begaben; Kirche etc. dotieren; **en'dow-**
ment Ausstattung *f*, Stiftung *f*,
Dotation *f*; Begabung *f*; ~ policy Lebensversicherung *f* mit Rentenwahl-
recht.

en·due mst fig. [in'dju:] bekleiden,
versehen, ausstatten (with mit).
en·dur·a·ble [in'djuərəbl] erträglich; **en'dur·ance** Dauer *f*; Ertragen *n*, Aushalten *n*; Ausdauer *f*;
Geduld *f*; past ~ unerträglich; ~
flight Dauerflug *m*; ~ run Dauerlauf
m; **en'dure** (aus)dauern; aushalten;
ertragen; **en'dur·ing** dauernd,
dauerhaft.
end·way(s) ['endwei(z)], **end·wise**
['~waiz] mit dem Ende nach vorn;
gerade, aufrecht.
en·e·ma ⚕ ['enimə] Einlauf *m*;
Klistierspritze *f*.
en·e·my ['enimi] **1.** Feind *m*; the
♀ der Teufel, der böse Feind;
2. feindlich.
en·er·get·ic [enə'dʒetik] (~ally) energisch, tatkräftig; wirksam; '**en·er-**
gize ⚡ erregen; '**en·er·gy** Energie
f, Kraft *f* (a. phys.); Willens-, Tatkraft *f*; Wirksamkeit *f*; Nachdruck
m; ~ crisis Energiekrise *f*; '**en·er·gy-**
-sav·ing energiesparend.
en·er·vate ['enə:veit] entnerven,
schwächen; **en·er'va·tion** Ent-
nervung *f*, Schwächung *f*; Schwäche *f*.
en·fee·ble [in'fi:bl] schwächen; **en-**
'**fee·ble·ment** Schwächung *f*.
en·feoff [in'fef] belehnen; **en'feoff·**
ment Belehnung *f*; Lehnsbrief *m*.
en·fi·lade ✗ [enfi'leid] **1.** Längs-
bestreichung *f*; **2.** bestreichen.
en·fold [in'fəuld] einhüllen; umfassen.
en·force [in'fɔ:s] erzwingen (upon
s.o. von j-m); durchsetzen (upon
s.o. bei j-m); aufzwingen (upon s.o.
j-m); bestehen auf (dat.); zur Geltung bringen, durchführen; **en-**
'**force·a·ble** erzwingbar; vollstreck-
bar; **en'force·ment** Erzwingung *f*;
Geltendmachung *f*; Durchführung *f*.
en·fran·chise [in'fræntʃaiz] das
Wahlrecht verleihen (dat.); Sklaven
befreien; **en'fran·chise·ment** [~
tʃizmənt] Verleihung *f* des Wahl-
rechts; Freilassung *f*.
en·gage [in'geidʒ] v/t. ein-, anstellen; verpflichten; mieten; in
Anspruch nehmen; ✗ angreifen;
be ~d verlobt sein (to mit); beschäftigt sein (in mit); besetzt sein; ~ the
clutch einkuppeln; v/i. sich verpflichten, versprechen, garantieren;

sich beschäftigen (*in* mit); ✂ angreifen; ⊕ greifen (*Zahnräder*); **engaged sig·nal** *od.* **tone** *teleph.* Besetztzeichen *n*; **en'gage·ment** Verpflichtung *f*; Verlobung *f*; Verabredung *f*; Stellung *f*, Beschäftigung *f*;
✂ Gefecht *n*, Kampf *m*; ⊕ Einrücken
n e-s Ganges etc.; **en·gage·ment ring**
Verlobungsring *m*.
en·gag·ing *fig.* □ [in'geidʒiŋ] gewinnend, einnehmend.
en·gen·der *fig.* [in'dʒendə] erzeugen, hervorbringen, -rufen.
en·gine ['endʒin] Maschine *f*, Motor
m; ⛟ Lokomotive *f*; Feuerspritze *f*;
fig. Mittel *n*, Werkzeug *n*; **'engined** ...motorig; **'en·gine-driv·er**
Lokomotivführer *m*.
en·gi·neer [endʒi'niə] **1.** Ingenieur
m, Techniker *m*; Maschinenbauer
m; ✂ Pionier *m*; ⚓ Maschinist *m*;
Am. Lokomotivführer *m*; **2.** Ingenieur sein; bauen; F deichseln; **en-
gi'neer·ing** Maschinenbau *m*; In-
genieurwesen *n*; F Manipulation *f*;
attr. technisch; Ingenieur...
en·gine...: **'~-fit·ter** Maschinen-
schlosser *m*; **'~·man** Maschinist *m*;
Lokomotivführer *m*.
en·gird [in'gə:d] (*irr. gird*) umgürten; *fig.* umgeben.
Eng·lish ['iŋgliʃ] **1.** englisch; **2.**
Englisch *n*; the ~ *pl.* die Engländer
pl.; *in plain* ~ *fig.* unverblümt; *the
Queen's* (*King's*) ~ korrektes Englisch *n*; **'~·man** Engländer *m*;
'~·wom·an Engländerin *f*.
en·gorge [in'gɔ:dʒ] gierig verschlingen; überfüllen.
en·graft [in'grɑ:ft] pfropfen; *fig.*
einprägen (*in dat.*); (ein)pfropfen
(*into in acc.*); aufpfropfen (*on dat.*).
en·grain [in'grein] tief färben; *fig.*
(unauslöschlich) einprägen; **en-
'grained** eingefleischt, unverbesserlich; eingewurzelt.
en·grave [in'greiv] gravieren, stechen; einmeißeln; *fig.* einprägen;
en'grav·er Graveur *m*, Stecher *m*;
~ *on copper* Kupferstecher *m*; **en-
'grav·ing** Gravieren *n etc.*; (Kup-
fer-, Stahl)Stich *m*; Holzschnitt
m.
en·gross [in'grəus] an sich ziehen;
ganz in Anspruch nehmen; ins
reine schreiben; *Unterhaltung* völlig
an sich reißen; ~*ed in* vertieft in,
beschäftigt mit; ~*ing* fesselnd; ~*ing*

hand Kanzleischrift *f*; **en'gross-
ment** Anhäufung *f von Besitz*; Inanspruchnahme *f* (*of, with* durch);
Urkunde *f*.
en·gulf [in'gʌlf] *fig.* verschlingen
(*Abgrund*); (in e-n Abgrund) stürzen.
en·hance [in'hɑ:ns] steigern, vergrößern, erhöhen; **en'hance·ment**
Steigerung *f*, Vergrößerung *f*, Erhöhung *f*.
e·nig·ma [i'nigmə] Rätsel *n*; **e·nig-
mat·ic, e·nig·mat·i·cal** □ [enig-
'mætik(əl)] rätselhaft.
en·join [in'dʒɔin] auferlegen, an-
befehlen (*on, upon s.o.* j-m).
en·joy [in'dʒɔi] sich erfreuen an
(*dat.*), sich freuen über (*acc.*); Gefallen finden an (*dat.*), Freude haben an (*dat.*); genießen; *did you* ~
it? hat es Ihnen gefallen?; ~ *o.s.*
sich gut unterhalten *od.* amüsieren;
I ~ *my dinner* es schmeckt mir; **en-
'joy·a·ble** genußreich, erfreulich;
angenehm; **en'joy·ment** Genuß *m*,
Vergnügen *n*, Freude *f*.
en·kin·dle [in'kindl] entzünden,
entflammen (*a. fig.*).
en·lace [in'leis] umschlingen.
en·large [in'lɑ:dʒ] *v/t.* erweitern,
ausdehnen; vergrößern (*a. phot.*);
v/i. sich erweitern *etc.*; sich verbreiten (*on, upon* über *acc.*); **en-
'large·ment** Erweiterung *f*, Ausdehnung *f*; Vergrößerung *f*; **en-
'larg·er** *phot.* Vergrößerungsge-
rät *n*.
en·light·en [in'laitn] *fig.* erleuchten;
j. aufklären, belehren; **en'light·en-
ment** Aufklärung *f*.
en·list [in'list] *v/t. Soldaten* anwerben; gewinnen (*in* für); ~*ed man*
✂ Soldat *m*; *v/i.* sich anwerben
lassen, sich freiwillig melden; ~ *in*
eintreten für; **en'list·ment** ✂ (An-)
Werbung *f*; *fig.* Gewinnung *f*.
en·liv·en [in'laivn] beleben; *fig.* ankurbeln.
en·mesh [in'meʃ] umgarnen.
en·mi·ty ['enmiti] Feindschaft *f*.
en·no·ble [i'nəubl] adeln (*a. fig.*);
veredeln.
e·nor·mi·ty [i'nɔ:miti] Ungeheuer-
lichkeit *f*; **e'nor·mous** □ ungeheuer, gewaltig, riesig.
e·nough [i'nʌf] genug; *sure* ~! freilich!, gewiß!; *well* ~ recht wohl;
ziemlich gut; *be kind* ~ *to inf.* so

freundlich sein zu *inf.*

en·plane [in'plein] = *emplane.*

en·quire [in'kwaiə] = *inquire.*

en·rage [in'reidʒ] wütend machen; **en'raged** wütend (*at* über *acc.*).

en·rap·ture [in'ræptʃə] entzücken.

en·rich [in'ritʃ] bereichern; anreichern; verzieren; **en'rich·ment** Bereicherung *f;* Verzierung *f.*

en·rol(l) [in'rəul] *in e-e* Liste eintragen; ✕ anwerben; *in e-n* Verein *etc.* aufnehmen; protokollieren; aufzeichnen; ~ (*o.s.*) sich einschreiben lassen; sich anwerben lassen; **en'rol(l)·ment** Eintragung *f etc.;* Verzeichnis *n;* Stärke *f,* Schüler-, Studenten-, Teilnehmerzahl *f.*

en route [ã:n'ru:t] unterwegs.

en·san·guined [in'sæŋgwind] blutbefleckt.

en·sconce [in'skɔns] verbergen; *mst* ~ *o.s.* F es sich bequem machen.

en·sem·ble [ã:n'sã:mbl] Gesamteindruck *m;* *thea.,* ♪ Ensemble *n;* *Kleider:* Komplet *n,* Ensemble *n.*

en·shrine [in'ʃrain] einschließen, (als Heiligtum) verwahren.

en·shroud [in'ʃraud] einhüllen.

en·sign ['ensain] Fahne *f,* Flagge *f;* Abzeichen *n;* ⚓ *Am.* ['ensn] Leutnant *m* zur See.

en·si·lage ['ensilidʒ] **1.** Silospeicherung *f,* -futter *n;* **2.** = **en·sile** [in'sail] in e-m Silo einlagern.

en·slave [in'sleiv] zum Sklaven machen (*to gen.*); versklaven, knechten; **en'slave·ment** Versklavung *f,* Knechtung *f;* **en'slav·er** Unterjocher *m* (*bsd. fig.*).

en·snare [in'snɛə] in e-r Schlinge fangen; *fig.* verführen.

en·sue [in'sju:] folgen, sich ergeben (*from, on* aus); (nach)folgen.

en·sure [in'ʃuə] sichern, sicherstellen (*against, from* gegen); garantieren.   [lengebälk *n.*╲

en·tab·la·ture ⚠ [en'tæblətʃə] Säu-╱

en·tail [in'teil] **1.** zur Folge haben, mit sich bringen; als unveräußerliches Gut vererben; **2.** (Übertragung *f* als) unveräußerliches Gut *n.*

en·tan·gle [in'tæŋgl] (in ein Netz *etc.*) verwickeln (*a. fig.*); *fig.* verstricken; verworren machen; **en·'tan·gle·ment** Verwicklung *f;* ✕ *Draht*-Verhau *m.*

en·tente [ã:n'tã:nt] Bündnis *n.*

en·ter ['entə] *v/t.* (ein)treten in

(*acc.*); betreten; einsteigen, -fahren *etc.* in (*acc.*); eindringen in (*acc.*); in *die Debatte* eingreifen; hineinbringen; einschreiben, eintragen, ✝ buchen; *Protest* einbringen; einstellen, aufnehmen; melden; *Tier* abrichten; *it* ~*ed his head* es kam ihm in den Sinn; ~ *s.o. at school* j. zur Schule anmelden; ~ *up* ✝ buchen; *v/i.* eintreten; sich einschreiben; *Sport:* melden, nennen (*for* zu); aufgenommen werden; ~ *Macbeth thea.* Macbeth tritt auf; ~ *into* hineingehen, hereinkommen *etc.* in (*acc.*); *Unterhaltung etc.* anfangen; *fig.* eingehen auf *e-n Vorschlag; fig.* Bündnis *etc.* eingehen; *Thema* anschneiden; ~ (*up*)*on* betreten; eintreten in *ein Amt, Lebensjahr;* sich einlassen auf *ein Unternehmen, Thema etc.;* 🕮 Besitz *e-r Sache* antreten.

en·ter·ic 𝕤 [en'terik] Darm...; **en·ter·i·tis** [ˌentə'raitis] Darmkatarrh *m.*

en·ter·prise ['entəpraiz] Unternehmung *f,* -nehmen *n;* Betrieb *m;* Unternehmertum *n;* Unternehmungsgeist *m,* -lust *f; private* ~ freie Wirtschaft *f;* **'en·ter·pris·ing** ☐ unternehmend; unternehmungslustig; kühn.

en·ter·tain [entə'tein] unterhalten; bewirten; in Erwägung ziehen; *Meinung etc.* hegen; eingehen auf (*acc.*); *they* ~ *a great deal* sie geben oft Gesellschaften; ~ *s.o. to supper* j. zum Abendessen einladen; **en·ter'tain·er** Gastgeber *m,* Wirt *m;* Unterhaltungskünstler *m;* **en·ter·'tain·ing** ☐ unterhaltend, amüsant; **en·ter'tain·ment** Unterhaltung *f;* Aufnahme *f,* Bewirtung *f;* Fest *n,* Gesellschaft *f;* ~ *tax* Vergnügungssteuer *f.*

en·thral(l) [in'θrɔ:l] *fig.* bezaubern, fesseln.

en·throne [in'θrəun] auf den Thron setzen; **en'throne·ment, en·thron·i·za·tion** [enθrəunai'zeiʃən] Einsetzung *f* (als Herrscher).

en·thuse F [in'θju:z]: ~ *over* schwärmen von, sich begeistern für.

en·thu·si·asm [in'θju:ziæzəm] Begeisterung *f;* **en'thu·si·ast** [ˌæst] Schwärmer(in) (*for, of* für); **en·thu·si·as·tic** (ˌally) begeistert (*at, about* von).

en·tice [in'tais] (ver)locken; **en·**

'tice·ment Verlockung *f*, Reiz *m*; en'tic·er Verführer(in); en'tic·ing □ verführerisch, verlockend.

en·tire □ [in'taiǝ] ganz, unversehrt; vollständig; ungeteilt, voll; vollzählig; nicht kastriert (*Pferd etc.*); en'tire·ly völlig, durchaus; lediglich; en'tire·ness Vollständigkeit *f*; Unversehrtheit *f*; en'tire·ty Gesamtheit *f*.

en·ti·tle [in'taitl] betiteln; berechtigen (*to* zu); be ~d *to* Anspruch haben auf (*acc.*).

en·ti·ty ['entiti] Wesen(heit *f*) *n*; Dasein *n*; legal ~ juristische Person *f*.

en·tomb [in'tu:m] begraben; en·'tomb·ment Begräbnis *n*.

en·to·mol·o·gy *zo.* [entǝ'mɔlǝdʒi] Insektenkunde *f*.

entr'acte *thea.* ['ɔntrækt] Zwischenspiel *n*.

en·trails ['entreilz] *pl.* Eingeweide *n/pl.*; Innere *n*.

en·train ✕ [in'trein] in e-n Eisenbahnzug verladen *od.* steigen.

en·trance¹ ['entrǝns] Ein-, Zutritt *m*; Einfahrt *f*, Eingang *m*, Einzug *m*; Antritt *m* (*into od. upon office des Amtes*); Eintrittsgeld *n*; *thea.* Auftritt *m*; Einlaß *m*; Eingang *m*, *Hafen*-Einfahrt *f*.

en·trance² [in'trɑːns] entzücken, hinreißen.

en·trance... ['entrǝns]: ~ ex·am·i·na·tion Aufnahmeprüfung *f*; ~ fee, ~ mon·ey Eintritt(sgeld *n*) *m*.

en·trant ['entrǝnt] (neu) Eintretende *m*; *Sport:* Teilnehmer *m*.

en·trap [in'træp] (ein)fangen; bestricken; verleiten (*into*, *to* zu).

en·treat [in'triːt] (inständig) bitten, ersuchen; *et.* erbitten (*of* von); en·'treat·y (dringende) Bitte *f*, Gesuch *n*.

en·trée ['ɔntrei] Zutritt *m*; Entrée *n*, Zwischengericht *n*.

en·trench [in'trentʃ] ✕ verschanzen; *fig.* einwurzeln; en'trench·ment Verschanzung *f*.

en·tre·pre·neur [ɔntrǝprǝ'nǝː] Unternehmer *m*; en·tre·pre·neur·i·al [~'nǝːriǝl] Unternehmer...

en·trust [in'trʌst] anvertrauen (*s.th. to s.o.* j.-m *et.*); betrauen (*s.o. with s.th.* j. mit et.).

en·try ['entri] Eintritt *m*; Eingang *m*, Einzug *m*; ⚖ Besitzantritt *m* (*on*, upon gen.*); Eintragung *f*, Notiz *f*; Zolldeklaration *f*; *gebuchter* Posten *m*; Eingang *m von Geldern etc.*; *Sport:* Nennung(sliste) *f*, Meldung *f*; Eingang(stür *f etc.*) *m*; ~ permit Einreisegenehmigung *f*; ~ visa Einreisevisum *n*; make an ~ of *s.th. et.* buchen; *book-keeping by double (single)* ~ doppelte (einfache) Buchführung *f*; '~·phone Sprechanlage *f*.

en·twine [in'twain], en·twist [in'twist] (um)winden; verflechten.

e·nu·mer·ate [i'njuːmǝreit] aufzählen; e·nu·mer'a·tion Aufzählung *f*.

e·nun·ci·ate [i'nʌnsieit] verkünden; *Lehrsatz etc.* aufstellen; aussprechen; e·nun·ci'a·tion Aufstellung *f*; Aussprache *f*; Ausdrucksweise *f*.

en·vel·op [in'velǝp] einhüllen; einwickeln; umhüllen, -geben; ~ einkreisen; en·ve·lope ['envǝlǝup], *Am. a.* en·vel·op [in'velǝp] Briefumschlag *m*; (Ballon)Hülle *f*; en·vel·op·ment [in'velǝpmǝnt] Umhüllung *f*.

en·ven·om [in'venǝm] vergiften; *fig. a.* verschärfen.

en·vi·a·ble □ ['enviǝbl] beneidenswert; 'en·vi·er Neider(in); 'en·vi·ous □ neidisch (*of auf acc.*).

en·vi·ron [in'vaiǝrǝn] umringen, umgeben; en'vi·ron·ment Umgebung *f e-r Person*; en·vi·ron·men·tal [~'mentl] Umwelt...; en·vi·ron·'men·tal·ist [~'tǝlist] Umweltschützer *m*; en·vi·rons ['environz] *pl.* Umgebung *f e-r Stadt*.

en·vis·age [in'vizidʒ] *e-r Gefahr* ins Auge sehen; *Ziel* ins Auge fassen; sich *et.* vorstellen, betrachten.

en·vi·sion [in'viʒǝn] sich *et.* vorstellen.

en·voy¹ ['envɔi] Gesandte *m*; Bote *m*.

en·voy² [~] Schlußstrophe *f*.

en·vy ['envi] **1.** Neid *m* (*of s.o. auf* j.; *of od. at s.th.* über, auf et.); *his car is the ~ of his friends* um s-n Wagen beneiden ihn s-e Freunde; **2.** beneiden (*s.o. s.th.* j. um et.).

en·wrap [in'ræp] einwickeln, -hüllen.

en·zyme *biol.* ['enzaim] Enzym *n*.

e·on ['iːǝn] = aeon.

ep·au·let(te) ['epǝulet] Epaulette *f*, Achsel-, Schulterstück *n*.

e·pergne [i'pəːn] Tafelaufsatz *m*.

e·phem·er·a *zo*. [i'femərə], **e'phem·er·on** [‿rən] *pl. a.* **e'phem·er·a** [‿rə] Eintagsfliege *f*; **e'phem·er·al** kurzlebig; vergänglich.

ep·ic ['epik] **1.** □ episch; **2.** Epos *n*.

ep·i·cure ['epikjuə] Feinschmecker *m*, Genießer *m*, Epikureer *m*; **ep·i·cu·re·an** [‿'riːən] **1.** genußsüchtig, epikureisch; **2.** = *epicure*.

ep·i·dem·ic . [epi'demik] **1.** (*‿ally*) epidemisch, seuchenartig; *‿ disease* = **2.** Seuche *f*, Epidemie *f*.

ep·i·der·mis *anat.* [epi'dəːmis] Oberhaut *f*.

ep·i·di·a·scope [epi'daiəskəup] Epidiaskop *n*, Bildwerfer *m*.

ep·i·gram ['epigræm] Epigramm *n*; **ep·i·gram·mat·ic**, **ep·i·gram·mat·i·cal** □ [‿grə'mætik(əl)] epigrammatisch.

ep·i·lep·sy 𝄞 ['epilepsi] Epilepsie *f*; **ep·i'lep·tic** 𝄞 **1.** epileptisch; **2.** Epileptiker(in).

ep·i·logue ['epiləg] Nachwort *n*.

E·piph·a·ny [i'pifəni] Dreikönigsfest *n*, -tag *m*.

e·pis·co·pa·cy [i'piskəpəsi] bischöfliche Verfassung *f*; **e'pis·co·pal** bischöflich; **e·pis·co·pa·li·an** [‿kəu'peiljən] Anhänger *m* der Episkopalkirche; **e'pis·co·pate** [‿kəupit] Episkopat *n*, Bischofswürde *f*; Bistum *n*.

ep·i·sode ['episəud] Episode *f*; Ereignis *n*; **ep·i·sod·ic**, **ep·i·sod·i·cal** □ [‿'sɔdik(əl)] episodisch.

e·pis·tle [i'pisl] Epistel *f*, Sendschreiben *n*; **e'pis·to·lar·y** [‿tələri] brieflich; Brief...

ep·i·taph ['epitɑːf] Grabschrift *f*.

ep·i·thet ['epiθet] Beiwort *n*; Beiname *m*; Attribut *n*; Epitheton *n*.

e·pit·o·me [i'pitəmi] Auszug *m*, Abriß *m*; Inhaltsangabe *f*; **e'pit·o·mize** e-n Auszug machen *od.* geben von; (zs.-)drängen.

ep·och ['iːpɔk] Epoche *f*; '‿**mak·ing** epochemachend.

ep·o·xy [i'pɔksi] Epoxyd *n*.

Ep·som salts ['epsəm'sɔːlts] *pl.* Bittersalz *n*.

eq·ua·bil·i·ty [ekwə'biliti] Gleichförmigkeit *f*; Gleichmut *m*; **'eq·ua·ble** □ gleichförmig, -mäßig; *fig.* gleichmütig.

e·qual ['iːkwəl] **1.** □ gleich, gleichmäßig, -förmig; gleichberechtigt;

angemessen; ebenbürtig; ‿ *to* fähig zu; gewachsen (*dat.*); ‿ *opportunities pl.* Chancengleichheit *f*; ‿ *rights pl.* Gleichberechtigung *f*; **2.** Gleiche *m*; *my ‿s pl.* meinesgleichen; **3.** gleichen, gleichkommen (*dat.*); *not to be ‿ed* seinesgleichen nicht haben; **e·qual·i·ty** [iː'kwɔliti] Gleichheit *f*; Gleichberechtigung *f*; **e·qual·i·za·tion** [iːkwəlai'zeiʃən] Gleichmachung *f*; Ausgleich *m*; **'e·qual·ize** *v/t.* gleichmachen (*to, with dat.*); *v/i.* *Sport:* ausgleichen; **'e·qual·iz·er** *Sport:* Ausgleich(stor *n*) *m*.

e·qua·nim·i·ty [ekwə'nimiti] Gleichmut *m*.

e·quate [i'kweit] gleichsetzen, -stellen (*to, with dat.*); **e'qua·tion** Ausgleich *m*; 🜨 Gleichung *f*; **e'qua·tor** Äquator *m*; **e·qua·to·ri·al** □ [ekwə'tɔːriəl] äquatorial.

eq·uer·ry [i'kweri] Stallmeister *m*.

e·ques·tri·an [i'kwestriən] **1.** Reit..., Reiter...; **2.** (Kunst)Reiter *m*.

e·qui·dis·tant ['iːkwi'distənt] gleich weit entfernt.

e·qui·lat·er·al □ ['iːkwi'lætərəl] gleichseitig.

e·qui·li·brate [iːkwi'laibreit] *v/t.* ins Gleichgewicht bringen; im Gleichgewicht halten; *v/i.* im Gleichgewicht sein; **e·quil·i·brist** [iː'kwilibrist] Seiltänzer *m*; **e·qui·lib·ri·um** [‿əm] Gleichgewicht *n*; Ausgleich *m*.

e·quine *zo.* ['iːkwain] pferdeartig; Pferde...

e·qui·noc·tial [iːkwi'nɔkʃəl] Äquinoktial...; **e·qui·nox** ['‿nɔks] Tag-undnachtgleiche *f*.

e·quip [i'kwip] ausrüsten; ausstatten; einrichten; **eq·ui·page** ['ekwipidʒ] Ausrüstung *f*; Equipage *f*, Kutsche *f*; **e·quip·ment** [i'kwipmənt] Ausrüstung *f*, -stattung *f*; Einrichtung *f*; Gerätschaften *f/pl.*; *fig.* Rüstzeug *n*.

e·qui·poise ['ekwipɔiz] **1.** Gleichgewicht *n*; Gegengewicht *n*; **2.** aufwiegen; im Gleichgewicht halten.

eq·ui·ta·ble □ ['ekwitəbl] billig, gerecht; **'eq·ui·ty** Billigkeit *f*; 🜨 Billigkeitsrecht *n*; *equities pl.* Aktien *f/pl.*

e·quiv·a·lence [i'kwivələns] Gleichwertigkeit *f*; **e'quiv·a·lent 1.** gleichwertig; gleichbedeutend (*to* mit); **2.** Äquivalent *n*, Gegenwert *m*;

Gegenstück *n*, *genaue* Entsprechung *f*.

e·quiv·o·cal □ [i'kwivəkəl] zweideutig, zweifelhaft; **e'quiv·o·cal·ness** Zweideutigkeit *f*; **e'quiv·o·cate** [‿keit] zweideutig reden; **e·quiv·o'ca·tion** Zweideutigkeit *f*; Wortverdrehung *f*.

eq·ui·voque, eq·ui·voke ['ekwivəuk] Wortspiel *n*; Zweideutigkeit *f*.

e·ra ['iərə] Ära *f*, Zeitrechnung *f*; Zeitalter *n*.

e·rad·i·cate [i'rædikeit] ausrotten; **e·rad·i'ca·tion** Ausrottung *f*.

e·rase [i'reiz] auskratzen; ausradieren, -streichen; auslöschen (*a. fig.*); **e'ras·er** Radiermesser *n*, -gummi *m*; **e'ra·sure** [‿ʒə] Ausradieren *n*; radierte Stelle *f*.

ere *poet.* [ɛə] **1.** *cj.* ehe, bevor; **2.** *prp.* vor; ~ *this* schon früher; ~ *long* bald; ~ *now* vormals.

e·rect [i'rekt] **1.** □ aufrecht; zu Berge stehend (*Haare*); **2.** aufrichten; *Denkmal etc.* errichten; *Theorie etc.* aufstellen; **e'rect·ing** Montage *f*; **e'rec·tion** Auf-, Errichtung *f*; Gebäude *n*; **e'rect·ness** Geradheit *f*, aufrechte Haltung *f*; **e'rec·tor** Errichter *m*, Erbauer *m*.

er·e·mite ['erimait] Einsiedler *m*; **er·e·mit·ic** [‿'mitik] einsiedlerisch.

erg *phys.* [ə:g] Erg *n* (*Arbeitseinheit*).

er·go·nom·ics [ə:gəu'nɔmiks] *sg.* Ergonomie *f*, Arbeitswissenschaft *f*.

er·got ♀ ['ɔ:gɔt] Mutterkorn *n*.

er·mine ['ə:min] *zo.* Hermelin *n*; Hermelin(pelz) *m*; *fig.* Richterwürde *f*.

e·rode [i'rəud] zer-, wegfressen; erodieren.

e·rog·e·nous [i'rɔdʒinəs] erogen.

e·ro·sion [i'rəuʒən] Zerfressung *f*, ✗, *geol.* Erosion *f*; **e'ro·sive** [‿siv] zerfressend.

e·rot·ic [i'rɔtik] **1.** erotisch; **2.** erotisches Gedicht *n*; **e'rot·i·cism** [‿sizəm] Erotik *f*.

err [ə:] (sich) irren; fehlen, sündigen.

er·rand ['erənd] Botengang *m*, Auftrag *m*; *fool's* ~ Metzgergang *m*, vergebliches Bemühen *n*; *go (on)* ~s Botengänge machen; '~**boy** Laufbursche *m*.

er·rant □ ['erənt] irrend; *s. knight-*~; **'er·rant·ry** Umherschweifen *n*;

Irrfahrt *f e-s Ritters*.

er·rat·ic [i'rætik] (‿*ally*) wandernd; regellos; unberechenbar; ~ *fever* Wechselfieber *n*; **er·ra·tum** [e'rɑ:təm], *pl.* **er'ra·ta** [‿tə] Druckfehler *m*.

er·ro·ne·ous □ [i'rəunjəs] irrig.

er·ror ['erə] Irrtum *m*, Fehler *m*; ~ *of judgement* Fehlschluß *m*; ~ *rate* Fehlerquote *f*; ~s *excepted* Irrtümer vorbehalten.

Erse [ə:s] **1.** gälisch; irisch; **2.** Gälisch *n*; Irisch *n*.

erst·while ['ə:stwail] früher, ehedem; ehemalig.

e·ruc·ta·tion [i:rʌk'teiʃən] Aufstoßen *n*, Rülpsen *n*; Ausbruch *m*.

er·u·dite □ ['eru:dait] gelehrt; **er·u·di·tion** [‿'diʃən] Gelehrsamkeit *f*.

e·rupt [i'rʌpt] ausbrechen (*Vulkan*); durchbrechen (*Zähne*); **e'rup·tion** Ausbruch *m e-s Vulkans* (*a. fig.*); ✗ Hautausschlag *m*; **e'rup·tive** ausbrechend; eruptiv; Eruptiv...

er·y·sip·e·las ✗ [eri'sipiləs] Erysipel *n*, (Wund)Rose *f*.

es·ca·late ✗ *u. fig.* ['eskəleit] *v/t.* eskalieren, steigern; *v/i.* sich steigern; in die Höhe schnellen (*Preise etc.*); **es·ca·la·tion** Eskalation *f*, Steigerung *f*.

es·ca·la·tor ['eskəleitə] Rolltreppe *f*.

es·ca·lope ['eskələup] Schnitzel *n*.

es·ca·pade [eskə'peid] toller Streich *m*, Eskapade *f*; *fig.* Seitensprung *m*; **es·cape** [is'keip] **1.** *v/t.* entschlüpfen, entgehen (*dat.*); umgehen; *j-m* entfallen; *v/i.* entkommen, entrinnen (*from dat.*); ausbrechen; entweichen (*Gas etc.*); **2.** Entrinnen *n*, Flucht *f*; Rettung *f*; Entweichen *n*; (Mittel *n* der) Entspannung *f*; *attr.* Abfluß...; Auslaß...; ~ *artist* Entfesselungskünstler *m*; ~ *hatch* Notluke *f*, -ausstieg *m*; *have a narrow* ~ mit knapper Not davon- od. entkommen; **es·ca·pee** [eskei'pi:] Ausbrecher *m*, Flüchtling *m*; **es·cape·ment** ⊕ [is'keipmənt] Hemmung *f an der Uhr*; **es'cap·ism** Eskapismus *m*, Wirklichkeitsflucht *f*; **es'cap·ist 1.** j., der die Wirklichkeit flieht; **2.** Illusions...

es·carp [is'kɑ:p] **1.** *a.* **es'carp·ment** Böschung *f*, Abdachung *f*; **2.** böschen, abdachen.

es·cheat ⚖ [is'tʃi:t] **1.** Heimfall *m*

an den Staat etc.; **2.** *v/i.* heimfallen; *v/t.* konfiszieren.

es·chew [is'tʃu:] scheuen, (ver-)meiden.

es·cort 1. ['eskɔːt] Eskorte *f*; Geleit *n* (*a. fig.*); Begleitung *f*; **2.** [is'kɔːt] eskortieren, geleiten.

es·cri·toire [eskri:'twaː] Schreibpult *n*.

es·cu·lent ['eskjulənt] **1.** eßbar; **2.** Nahrungsmittel *n*.

es·cutch·eon [is'kʌtʃən] Wappenschild *m*, *n*; Namensschild *n*.

Es·ki·mo ['eskiməu] Eskimo *m*.

e·soph·a·gus [i:'sɔfəgəs] = *oesophagus*.

es·o·ter·ic [esəu'terik] esoterisch, nur für Eingeweihte.

es·pal·ier ✗ [is'pæljə] Spalier *n*; Spalierbaum *m*.

es·pe·cial [is'peʃəl] besonder; vorzüglich; **es·pe·cial·ly** besonders.

Es·pe·ran·to [espə'ræntəu] Esperanto *n*.

es·pi·al [is'paiəl] Spähen *n*.

es·pi·o·nage [espiə'naːʒ] Spionage *f*.

es·pla·nade [esplə'neid] Esplanade *f*; Promenade *f*.

es·pous·al [is'pauzəl] Eintreten *n* (*of* für); **es'pouse** heiraten; sich *e-r Sache* annehmen.

es·pres·so [es'presəu] Espresso *m* (*Kaffee*); **~ bar**, **~ ca·fé** Espresso (-bar *f*) *n*.

es·py [is'pai] erspähen, erblicken.

es·quire [is'kwaiə] Landedelmann *m*, Gutsbesitzer *m*; *auf Briefen*: *John Smith Esq.* Herrn John Smith.

es·say 1. [e'sei] versuchen; probieren; **2.** ['esei] Versuch *m* (*at* mit), Probe *f*; Aufsatz *m*, kurze Abhandlung *f*, Essay *m*; **'es·say·ist** Essayist *m*.

es·sence ['esns] Geist *m*, Wesen *n* *e-r Sache*; Extrakt *m*, Essenz *f*;

es·sen·tial [i'senʃəl] **1.** □ (*to*) wesentlich (für); wichtig (für); **~ likeness** Wesensgleichheit *f*; **~ oil** ätherisches Öl *n*; **2.** *das* Wesentliche, Hauptsache *f*; Grundzug *m*; **es·'sen·tial·ly** im Grunde genommen.

es·tab·lish [is'tæbliʃ] festsetzen; errichten, gründen; einrichten, -führen; *Beamten etc.* einsetzen; *Kinder* versorgen; nachweisen; **~ o.s.** sich niederlassen *od.* etablieren; **~ed Church** Staatskirche *f*; **~ed merchant** selbständiger Kaufmann *m*;

es·tab·lish·ment Festsetzung *f*; Gründung *f*; Er-, Einrichtung *f*; (*bsd. großer*) Haushalt *m*; Anstalt *f*; Firma *f*; *das* Establishment, *die* herrschenden Kreise *m/pl.*; ✗, ⚓ *Mannschafts*-Bestand *m*; *military* **~** stehendes Heer *n*.

es·tate [is'teit] Grundstück *n*; Landsitz *m*; Grundbesitz *m*, Gut *n*; Besitz *m*, Vermögen *n*; (Konkurs-) Masse *f*, Nachlaß *m*; Stand *m*, Klasse *f*; *family* **~** Familienbesitz *m*; *personal* **~** bewegliches Eigentum *n*; *real* **~** Liegenschaften *f/pl.*; *housing* **~** Wohnsiedlung *f*; *industrial* **~** Industriegebiet *n*; **~a·gent** Grundstücks-, Häusermakler *m*; **~car** Kombiwagen *m*; **~ du·ty** Nachlaßsteuer *f*.

es·teem [is'ti:m] **1.** Achtung *f*, Ansehen *n* (*with* bei); **2.** (hoch)achten, (hoch)schätzen; erachten für.

es·ter ⚗ ['estə] Ester *m*.

es·thet·ic [i:s'θetik] = *aesthetic*.

Es·tho·ni·an [es'təunjən] **1.** Este *m*, Estin *f*; Estländisch *n*; **2.** estnisch.

es·ti·ma·ble ['estiməbl] achtens-, schätzenswert.

es·ti·mate 1. ['estimeit] (ab)schätzen; veranschlagen (*at* auf *acc.*); **2.** ['~mit] Schätzung *f*; (Vor)Anschlag *m*, Überschlag *m*; *the* **~s** *pl. parl. der* Haushaltsplan, *das* Budget; **es·ti·ma·tion** [~'meiʃən] Schätzung *f*; Urteil *n*, Meinung *f*; Achtung *f*; **'es·ti·ma·tor** Abschätzer *m*.

es·trade [es'traːd] Estrade *f*, erhöhter Platz *m*.

es·trange [is'treindʒ] entfremden (*from* s.o. j-m); **~d couple** getrennt lebendes Ehepaar *n*; **es'trange·ment** Entfremdung *f*.

es·tro·gen *biol.* ['estrədʒen] Östrogen *n*.

es·tu·ar·y ['estjuəri] Trichtermündung *f*.

et·cet·er·as [it'setrəz] *pl.* Kleinigkeiten *f/pl.*

etch [etʃ] ätzen, radieren; **'etch·ing** Radierung *f*; Kupferstich *m*.

e·ter·nal □ [i:'təːnl] immerwährend, unaufhörlich, ewig; **e'ter·nal·ize** [~nəlaiz] verewigen; **e'ter·ni·ty** Ewigkeit *f*; **e'ter·nize** [~naiz] verewigen.

e·ther ['i:θə] Äther *m* (*a.* ⚗); **e·the·re·al** □ [i:'θiəriəl] ätherisch (*a. fig.*); **'e·ther·ize** mit Äther betäuben, narkotisieren.

eth·i·cal □ [ˈeθikəl] sittlich, ethisch; **ˈeth·ics** *mst sg.* Sittenlehre *f,* Ethik *f.*

E·thi·o·pi·an [iːθiˈəupjən] **1.** äthiopisch; **2.** Äthiopier(in).

eth·nic [ˈeθnik] ethnisch, völkisch; ~ *joke* Witz *m* auf Kosten e-r bestimmten Volksgruppe.

eth·nog·ra·phy [eθˈnɔgrəfi] Ethnographie *f,* (beschreibende) Völkerkunde *f;* **eth·ˈnol·o·gy** [ˌləˈdʒi] Ethnologie *f,* (vergleichende) Völkerkunde *f.*

eth·yl ⚗ [ˈeθil]; ⚗ ˈiːθail] Äthyl *n;* **eth·yl·ene** [ˈeθiliːn] Äthylen *n,* Kohlenwasserstoffgas *n.*

e·ti·o·late [ˈiːtiəuleit] etiolieren, *durch Lichtmangel* bleichen, vergeilen; *fig.* schwächen.

e·ti·ol·o·gy ⚗ [iːtiˈɔlədʒi] Ätiologie *f,* Ursachenforschung *f.*

et·i·quette [ˈetiket] Etikette *f.*

E·ton crop [ˈiːtnˈkrɔp] Herrenschnitt *m (Damenfrisur).*

E·trus·can [iˈtrʌskən] **1.** etruskisch; **2.** Etrusker(in); Etruskisch *n.*

et·y·mo·log·i·cal □ [etiməˈlɔdʒikl] etymologisch; **et·y·mol·o·gy** [ˌˈmɔlədʒi] Etymologie *f,* Wortableitung *f.*

eu·ca·lyp·tus ♣ [juːkəˈliptəs] Eukalyptus *m.*

Eu·cha·rist [ˈjuːkərist] Abendmahl *n.*

Eu·clid ⚗ [ˈjuːklid] euklidische Geometrie *f.*

eu·gen·ic [juːˈdʒenik] (~*ally*) eugenisch; **eu·ˈgen·ics** *sg.* Eugenik *f,* Erbgesundheitslehre *f.*

eu·lo·gist [ˈjuːlədʒist] Lobredner *m;* **eu·lo·gize** [ˈˌdʒaiz] loben; **eu·lo·gy** [ˈˌdʒi] Lob(rede *f*) *n.*

eu·nuch [ˈjuːnək] Eunuch *m.*

eu·phe·mism [ˈjuːfimizəm] Euphemismus *m,* beschönigender Ausdruck *m;* **eu·ˈphe·mis·tic, eu·phe·ˈmis·ti·cal** □ beschönigend.

eu·phon·ic, eu·phon·i·cal □ [juː-ˈfɔnik(əl)] wohlklingend; **eu·pho·ny** [ˈjuːfəni] Wohlklang *m.*

eu·phor·ia [juːˈfɔːriə] Euphorie *f,* Wohlbefinden *n.*

eu·phu·ism [ˈjuːfjuːizəm] gezierte Ausdrucksweise *f,* Schwulst *m.*

Eur·a·sian [juəˈreiʒən] **1.** Eurasier (-in); **2.** eurasisch.

eu·re·ka [juəˈriːkə] heureka (*ich*

---

even

hab's gefunden).

Eu·ro·cheque [ˈjuərətʃek] Euroscheck *m;* **Eu·ro·ˈcom·mu·nism** Eurokommunismus *m;* **Eu·ro·ˈcrat** [ˈˌkræt] Eurokrat *m.*

Eu·ro·pe·an [juərəˈpiːən] **1.** europäisch; ~ *Commission* Europäische Kommission *f;* ~ *Community* Europäische Gemeinschaft *f;* ~ *Court of Justice* Europäischer Gerichtshof *m;* ~ *Parliament* Europaparlament *n;* **2.** Europäer(in).

Eu·ro·pol·i·tics [ˈjuərəpɔlitiks] *sg. od. pl.* Europapolitik *f.*

Eu·ro·vi·sion [juərəˈviʒən] europäische Fernsehringsendung *f,* Eurovision *f.*

eu·tha·na·si·a [juːθəˈneizjə] Euthanasie *f (leichter Tod;* Sterbehilfe).

e·vac·u·ate [iˈvækjueit] entleeren; evakuieren; *Land etc.* räumen; *Bewohner* aussiedeln; ⚗ abführen; **e·vac·u·a·tion** Entleerung *f;* Evakuierung *f;* **e·vac·u·ˈee** Evakuierte *m, f.*

e·vade [iˈveid] (geschickt) ausweichen (*dat.*); umgehen, sich drücken um.

e·val·u·ate *bsd.* ⚗ [iˈvæljueit] zahlenmäßig bestimmen, auswerten; berechnen; **e·val·u·a·tion** Auswertung *f;* Berechnung *f.*

ev·a·nesce [iːvəˈnes] (ver)schwinden; **ev·a·ˈnes·cence** (Dahin-) Schwinden *n;* **ev·a·ˈnes·cent** □ (ver)schwindend.

e·van·gel·ic, e·van·gel·i·cal □ [iːvænˈdʒelik(əl)] evangelisch; **e·van·ge·list** [iˈvændʒilist] Evangelist *m;* **e·ˈvan·ge·lize** *j-m* das Evangelium predigen; bekehren.

e·vap·o·rate [iˈvæpəreit] verdampfen (lassen); *fig.* verschwinden, sich verflüchtigen; ~*ed milk* Kondensmilch *f;* **e·vap·o·ˈra·tion** Verdunstung *f,* Verdampfung *f.*

e·va·sion [iˈveiʒən] Umgehung *f;* Ausflucht *f;* **e·ˈva·sive** □ [ˌsiv] ausweichend (*of dat.*); *be* ~ *fig.* ausweichen.

eve [iːv] Vorabend *m;* Vortag *m; poet.* Abend *m; on the* ~ *of* unmittelbar vor (*dat.*), am Vorabend (*gen.*).

e·ven[1] [ˈiːvən] **1.** *adj.* □ eben, gerade, gleich; gleichmäßig, -förmig; ausgeglichen; ruhig; glatt; gerade

(*Zahl*); unparteiisch; *make* ~ *with the ground* dem Boden gleichmachen; *be* ~ *with s.o.* mit j-m quitt sein; *get* ~ *with s.o.* *fig.* mit j-m abrechnen; *odd or* ~ gerade oder ungerade; *of* ~ *date* ✝ gleichen Datums; *break* ~ F ohne Gewinn u. Verlust abschließen; **2.** *adv.* gerade, eben; selbst, sogar, auch; *vor comp.* noch; *not* ~ nicht einmal; ~ *though*, ~ *if* selbst wenn, wenn auch; **3.** ebnen, glätten; gleichstellen (*to dat.*).

e·ven² *poet.* [~] Abend *m*.

e·ven·hand·ed ['iːvən'hændid] unparteiisch.

eve·ning ['iːvniŋ] Abend *m*; ~ *class* Abendkurs *m*; ~ *dress* Gesellschaftsanzug *m*, Frack *m*, Smoking *m*; Abendkleid *n*.

e·ven·ness ['iːvənnis] Ebenheit *f*; Geradheit *f*; Gleichmäßigkeit *f*; Unparteilichkeit *f*; Seelenruhe *f*.

e·ven·song ['iːvənsɔŋ] Abendgottesdienst *m*.

e·vent [i'vent] Ereignis *n*, Vorfall *m*, Begebenheit *f*; *fig.* Ausgang *m*; sportliche Veranstaltung *f*; (Programm)Nummer *f*; *athletic* ~s *pl.* Leichtathletikwettkämpfe *m/pl.*; *table of* ~s Festprogramm *n*; *at all* ~s auf alle Fälle; *in any* ~ sowieso; *in the* ~ *of* im Falle (*gen.*).

e·ven-tem·pered ['iːvəntempəd] ausgeglichen; gelassen.

e·vent·ful [i'ventful] ereignisreich.

e·ven·tide *poet.* ['iːvəntaid] Abend *m*.

e·ven·tu·al □ [i'ventʃuəl] etwaig, möglich; schließlich; ~*ly* am Ende; schließlich, endlich; **e·ven·tu·al·i·ty** [~tju'æliti] Möglichkeit *f*; **e'ven·tu·ate** [~tjueit] endigen; die Folge sein.

ev·er ['evə] je, jemals; immer, immer wieder; ~ *so* noch so (sehr); *as soon as* ~ *I can* sobald ich nur irgend kann; ~ *after*, ~ *since* von der Zeit an; ~ *and anon* von Zeit zu Zeit; *for* ~, *for* ~ *and* ~, *for* ~ *and a day* für immer, auf ewig; *liberty for* ~! es lebe die Freiheit!; ~ *so much* F recht viel; *for* ~ *so much* um alles in der Welt; *I wonder who* ~ ich möchte wissen, wer nur ...; *the best* ~ F der beste, den es je gegeben hat; *yours* ~ stets Dein ...

(*Briefschluß*); '~·glade *Am.* sumpfiges Grasland *n*; '~·green **1.** immergrün; **2.** immergrüne Pflanze *f*; ~'last·ing **1.** □ ewig; dauerhaft **2.** Ewigkeit *f*; ♀ Immortelle *f*; '~·more immerfort; stets.

ev·er·y ['evri] jede(r, -s); alle(s); ~ *bit as much* genau so viel; ~ *now and then* dann und wann; ~ *one of them* jeder von ihnen, alle ausnahmslos; ~ *other day* einen Tag um den andern; jeden zweiten Tag; ~ *twenty years* alle zwanzig Jahre; *her* ~ *movement* jede ihrer Bewegungen; '~·bod·y jeder(mann); '~·day Alltags...; '~·one jeder (-mann); '~·thing alles; '~·way in jeder Hinsicht; '~·where überall.

e·vict [i'vikt] exmittieren; ausweisen; **e'vic·tion** Exmittierung *f*; Ausweisung *f*; ~ *order* Räumungsbefehl *m*.

ev·i·dence ['evidəns] **1.** Beweis (-stück *n*, -material *n*) *m*, Befund *m*; ✞ Zeugnis *n*; Zeuge *m*; *in* ~ als Beweis; deutlich sichtbar, zu sehen; *furnish* ~ *of*, *be* ~ *of et.* beweisen; *give* ~, *bear* ~ Zeugnis ablegen (*of* von; *for* für; *against* gegen); **2.** beweisen; zeigen; **'ev·i·dent** □ augenscheinlich, offenbar, -sichtlich, klar; **ev·i·den·tial** □ [~'denʃəl] als Beweis dienend.

e·vil ['iːvl] **1.** □ übel, schlimm; schlecht; *moralisch mst* böse; *the* ~ *eye* der böse Blick; *the* ♀ *One* der Böse (*Teufel*); **2.** Übel *n*, Böse *n*; '~-'do·er Übeltäter(in); '~-'minded übelgesinnt, boshaft.

e·vince [i'vins] zeigen, bekunden.

e·vis·cer·ate [i'visəreit] ausweiden.

ev·o·ca·tion [evəu'keiʃən] (Geister-) Beschwörung *f*; **e·voc·a·tive** [i'vɔkətiv] beschwörend, wachrufend.

e·voke [i'vəuk] (herauf)beschwören, wachrufen; hervorrufen.

ev·o·lu·tion [iːvə'luːʃən] Entwicklung *f*; ♈ Wurzelziehen *n*; ✕ Entfaltung *f* e-r Formation; **ev·o·'lu·tion·a·ry** [~ʃnəri] Entwicklungs..., Evolutions...

e·volve [i'vɔlv] (sich) entfalten, (sich) entwickeln; herausarbeiten.

ewe [juː] Mutterschaf *n*.

ew·er ['juːə] Wasserkanne *f*, -krug *m*.

ex [eks] **1.** ✝ *ab Fabrik etc.*; *Börse:* ohne; aus; **2.** *vor su.* ehemalig, frü-

her; *ex-minister* Ex-Minister *m.*
ex·ac·er·bate [eks'æsɔ:beit] verschlimmern; verschärfen; erbittern.
ex·act [ig'zækt] **1.** □ genau; pünktlich; tatsächlich; **2.** *Zahlung* eintreiben; fordern; **ex'act·ing** streng, genau; anspruchsvoll; **ex'ac·tion** Eintreibung *f*; (ungebührliche) Forderung *f*; Erpressung *f*; **ex-'act·i·tude** [‿titju:d] Genauigkeit *f*; Pünktlichkeit *f*; **ex'act·ly** genau; *Antwort:* ganz recht; *not* ‿ nicht gerade; **ex'act·ness** = *exactitude.*
ex·ag·ger·ate [ig'zædʒɔreit] übertreiben; **ex·ag·ger'a·tion** Übertreibung *f.*
ex·alt [ig'zɔ:lt] erhöhen, erheben; verherrlichen, in den höchsten Tönen loben; **ex·al·ta·tion** [egzɔ:l-'teiʃɔn] Erhöhung *f*, Erhebung *f*; Höhe *f*; Verzücktheit *f*; **ex·alt·ed** [ig'zɔ:ltid] erhaben, hoch; verzückt.
ex·am *Schul-sl.* [ig'zæm] Examen *n.*
ex·am·i·na·tion [igzæmi'neiʃɔn] Examen *n*, Prüfung *f*; Untersuchung *f*; Vernehmung *f*; **ex'am·ine** untersuchen (*a.* ‿ *into s.th.* et.); prüfen, examinieren; verhören; **ex·am·i'nee** Prüfling *m*; **ex'am·in·er** Prüfer *m*; Untersucher *m*; **ex-'am·in·ing** *bod·y* Prüfungsausschuß *m.*
ex·am·ple [ig'zɑ:mpl] Beispiel *n*; Vorbild *n*, Muster *n*; *beyond* ‿ beispiellos; *for* ‿ zum Beispiel; *make an* ‿ *of* ein Exempel statuieren an *j-m*; *set an* ‿ ein Beispiel geben.
ex·as·per·ate [ig'zɑ:spɔreit] erbittern; (ver)ärgern; (auf)reizen; verschlimmern; **ex·as·per'a·tion** Erbitterung *f*, Ärger *m* (*of* über *acc.*).
ex·ca·vate ['ekskɔveit] ausgraben, -heben, -schachten; **ex·ca'va·tion** Ausgrabung *f etc.*; Höhle *f*; '**ex-ca·va·tor** Trockenbagger *m*; Erdarbeiter *m.*
ex·ceed [ik'si:d] überschreiten, hinausgehen über (*acc.*); übertreffen (*in* an, in *dat.*); zu weit gehen; **ex'ceed·ing** übermäßig; **ex'ceeding·ly** außerordentlich, überaus.
ex·cel [ik'sel] *v/t.* übertreffen; *v/i.* sich auszeichnen (*in*, *at* in *dat.*); **ex·cel·lence** ['eksɔlɔns] Vortrefflichkeit *f*; hervorragende Leistung *f*; Vorzug *m*; '**Ex·cel·len·cy** Exzellenz *f* (*Titel*); '**ex·cel·lent** □

vortrefflich, ausgezeichnet, hervorragend.
ex·cept [ik'sept] **1.** ausnehmen, -schließen; Einwendungen machen; *present company* ‿*ed* die Anwesenden ausgenommen; **2.** *cj.* außer, es sei denn, daß; **3.** *prp.* ausgenommen, außer; ‿ *for* abgesehen von; **ex'cept·ing** *prp.* ausgenommen; **ex'cep·tion** Ausnahme *f*; Einwendung *f* (*to* gegen); *take* ‿ *to* Anstoß nehmen an (*dat.*); **ex'ception·a·ble** [‿ʃnɔbl] anstößig; **ex-'cep·tion·al** außergewöhnlich; **ex-'cep·tion·al·ly** ausnahmsweise.
ex·cerpt **1.** [ek'sɔ:pt] *Schriftstelle* ausziehen, exzerpieren (*from* aus); **2.** ['eksɔ:pt] Auszug *m*, Exzerpt *n* (*from* aus).
ex·cess [ik'ses] Übermaß *n*; Überschuß *m*; Unmäßigkeit *f*, Ausschweifung *f*, Exzeß *m*; *attr.* Mehr...; *in* ‿ *of* mehr als; *carry to* ‿ *et.* übertreiben; ‿ *charge* zusätzliche Gebühr *f*; ‿ *fare* Zuschlag *m*; ‿ *luggage* Übergewicht *n* (*Gepäck*); ‿ *postage* Nachgebühr *f*; ‿ *profit* Mehrgewinn *m*; **ex'ces·sive** □ übermäßig, übertrieben.
ex·change [iks'tʃeindʒ] **1.** (aus-, ein-, um)tauschen (*for* gegen); (aus-, um)wechseln; wert sein (*for acc.*); **2.** (Aus-, Um)Tausch *m*; (*bsd.* Geld)Wechsel *m*; *a. bill of* ‿ Wechsel *m*; *a.* ☿ Börse *f*; Fernsprechamt *n*; *a. foreign* ‿*s pl.* Devisen *f/pl.*; *in* ‿ *for* (als Entgelt) für, gegen; *account of* ‿ Wechselkonto *n*; ‿ *control* Devisenbewirtschaftung *f*; ‿ *list* Kurszettel *m*; *par of* ‿ Wechselpari *n*; (*rate of*) ‿ Wechselkurs *m*; ‿ *student* Austauschstudent(in); **ex'change·a·ble** austauschbar (*for* gegen); ‿ *value* Tauschwert *m.*
ex·cheq·uer [iks'tʃekɔ] Schatzamt *n*; Staatskasse *f*; *Chancellor of the* ☿ *britischer* Schatzkanzler *m*, Finanzminister *m*; ‿ *bond* Schatzanweisung *f.*
ex·cise¹ [ek'saiz] **1.** indirekte Steuer *f*, Verbrauchssteuer *f*; **2.** besteuern.
ex·cise² [‿] (her)ausschneiden; **exci·sion** [ek'siʒɔn] Ausschneidung *f.*
ex·cit·a·bil·i·ty [iksaitɔ'biliti] Reizbarkeit *f*; **ex'cit·a·ble** reizbar; **ex·cit·ant** ['eksitɔnt] Reizmittel *n*; **ex·ci·ta·tion** [‿'teiʃɔn] An-, Er-

regung *f*; Reizung *f*; **ex·cite** [ik-
'sait] erregen; anregen; reizen; ~d
aufgeregt; *get* ~d sich aufregen;
ex'cite·ment Auf-, Erregung *f*;
Anreizung *f*; **ex'cit·er** Erreger *m*;
Reizmittel *n*; **ex'cit·ing** aufregend;
erregend; spannend.

ex·claim [iks'kleim] ausrufen; eifern
(*against* gegen).

ex·cla·ma·tion [eksklə'meiʃən] Aus-
ruf(ung *f*) *m*; ~s *pl.* Geschrei *n*;
note of ~, *point of* ~, ~ *mark* Ausrufezeichen *n*; **ex·clam·a·to·ry** □
[~'klæmətəri] Ausrufe...; eifernd.

ex·clude [iks'klu:d] ausschließen.

ex·clu·sion [iks'klu:ʒən] Ausschlie-
ßung *f*, Ausschluß *m*; *to the* ~ *of*
unter Ausschluß (*gen.*); **ex'clu-
sive** □ [~siv] ausschließend (*of
acc.*); ausschließlich; sich abschlie-
ßend, exklusiv; ~ *of* ohne; *be mutually*
~ einander ausschließen.

ex·cog·i·tate [eks'kɔdʒiteit] ausdenken, -hecken; **ex·cog·i·ta·tion**
Ausdenken *n*, Erfindung *f*.

ex·com·mu·ni·cate [ekskə'mju:ni-
keit] exkommunizieren; **'ex·com-
mu·ni'ca·tion** Kirchenbann *m*,
Exkommunikation *f*.

ex·con·vict ['eks'kɔnvikt] ehemaliger Häftling *m*.

ex·co·ri·ate [eks'kɔ:rieit] die Haut
abziehen (*dat.*); *Haut* wund reiben;
fig. heftig kritisieren.

ex·cre·ment ['ekskrimənt] Exkre-
ment *n*, Kot *m*.

ex·cres·cence [iks'kresns] Auswuchs *m*; **ex'cres·cent** auswach-
send; überflüssig.

ex·crete [eks'kri:t] absondern, ausscheiden; **ex'cre·tion** Absonderung *f etc.*; **ex'cre·tive**, **ex'cre-
to·ry** [~təri] Absonderungs... *etc.*

ex·cru·ci·ate [iks'kru:ʃieit] martern,
quälen; **ex'cru·ci·at·ing** □ qualvoll.

ex·cul·pate ['ekskʌlpeit] entschuldigen; rechtfertigen; freisprechen
(*from* von); **ex·cul'pa·tion** Entschuldigung *f etc.*

ex·cur·sion [iks'kə:ʃən] Ausflug *m*;
Abstecher *m*; ~ *train* Sonderzug *m*;
ex'cur·sion·ist [~ʃnist] Ausflügler *m*.

ex·cur·sive □ [eks'kə:siv] abschweifend.

ex·cus·a·ble □ [iks'kju:zəbl] ent-
schuldbar; **ex'cuse 1.** entschuldi-

gen; ~ *s.o. s.th.* j-m et. erlassen;
be ~*d from s.th.* et. erlassen bekommen; ~ *me* entschuldigen Sie bitte;
2. [iks'kju:s] Entschuldigung *f*.

ex·di·rec·to·ry [eksdi'rektəri] nicht
im Telefonbuch stehend.

ex·e·at ['eksiæt] *Schule etc.*: Urlaub
m.

ex·e·cra·ble □ ['eksikrəbl] abscheulich; **ex·e·crate** ['~kreit] ver-
wünschen; verabscheuen; **ex·e-
'cra·tion** Verwünschung *f*; Abscheu *m*.

ex·e·cu·tant ♪ [ig'zekjutənt] Vortragende *m*, *f*; **ex·e·cute** ['eksi-
kju:t] ausführen, vollziehen; ♪ vortragen; hinrichten; ♫ vollziehen,
rechtsgültig machen; *Testament*
vollstrecken; **ex·e·cu·tion** Aus-,
Durchführung *f*, Vollziehung *f*;
Ausfertigung *f e-r Urkunde*; Vollstreckung *f e-s Testaments*; Zwangs-
vollstreckung *f*; Hinrichtung *f*;
♪ Vortrag *m*; Technik *f*; *a man of* ~
ein tatkräftiger Mensch *m*; *take
out an* ~ *against j.* auspfänden
lassen; *do* ~ Wirkung tun; *put od.
carry a plan into* ~ e-n Plan ausführen *od.* verwirklichen; **ex·e-
cu·tion·er** [~'kju:ʃnə] Scharfrichter *m*; **ex·ec·u·tive** [ig'zekjutiv]
1. □ ausübend, vollziehend; ~
committee Vorstand *m*; ~ *editor*
Chefredakteur *m*; ~ *suite* Vorstands-
etage *f*; **2.** vollziehende Gewalt *f*,
Exekutive *f*; Organ(e *pl.*) *n e-s Verbandes etc.*; *Am.* Staats-Präsident *m*;
♰ leitender Angestellter *m*; Geschäftsführer *m*; **ex'ec·u·tor** (Testaments)Vollstrecker *m*; **ex'ec·u·to·ry**
vollziehend; Ausführungs...; ♫ Voll-
streckungs...; **ex'ec·u·trix** [~triks]
(Testaments)Vollstreckerin *f*.

ex·e·ge·sis [eksi'dʒi:sis] Exegese *f*,
Auslegung *f bsd. der Bibel.*

ex·em·plar [ig'zemplə] Muster *n*;
ex'em·pla·ri·ness Musterhaftig-
keit *f*; **ex'em·pla·ry** vorbildlich;
Muster...; exemplarisch.

ex·em·pli·fi·ca·tion [igzemplifi-
'keiʃən] Erläuterung *f durch Beispiele*; Veranschaulichung *f*; ♫ Abschrift *f*; **ex'em·pli·fy** [~fai] durch
Beispiele belegen; veranschaulichen; ♫ e-e beglaubigte Abschrift
machen von.

ex·empt [ig'zempt] **1.** befreit, frei
(*from* von); bevorrechtet; **2.** aus-

                   expansible

nehmen, befreien (*from* von); **ex-'emp·tion** Befreiung *f*, Freiheit *f* (*from* von).

ex·e·quies ['eksikwiz] *pl.* Leichenbegängnis *n*.

ex·er·cise ['eksəsaiz] **1.** Übung *f*; Ausübung *f e-r Kunst*; körperliche Bewegung *f*, Leibesübung *f*; Übungsarbeit *f*; *take* ⁓ sich Bewegung machen; ⁓*s pl. Am.* Feierlichkeit(en *pl.*) *f*; ✂ Manöver *n*; **2.** *v/t. Körper etc.* üben; *Macht etc.* ausüben; Bewegung machen (*dat.*); exerzieren; beunruhigen; *v/i.* üben; sich Bewegung machen; ⁓ **book** (Schul)Heft *n*; **'ex·er·cis·er** Trainingsgerät *n*.

ex·ert [ig'zəːt] anwenden; *Einfluß etc.* ausüben; ⁓ *o.s.* sich anstrengen *od.* bemühen; **ex'er·tion** Ausübung *f*; Anstrengung *f*, Bemühung *f*.

ex·e·unt *thea.* ['eksiʌnt] (sie gehen) ab.   [blättern.]

ex·fo·li·ate [eks'fəulieit] (sich) ab-]

ex·ha·la·tion [ekshə'leiʃən] Ausdünstung *f*, -atmung *f*; Dunst *m*; Ausbruch *m*; **ex·hale** [⁓'heil] ausdünsten, -atmen; *Leben etc.* aushauchen; *Gefühlen* Luft machen.

ex·haust [ig'zɔːst] **1.** erschöpfen (*a. fig.*); entleeren (*of gen.*); *Luft* auspumpen; **2.** ⊕ Abgas *n*, -dampf *m*; Auspuff *m*; ⁓ **box** Auspufftopf *m*; ⁓ *fumes pl.* Abgase *n/pl.*; ⁓ *pipe* Auspuffrohr *n*; **ex'haust·ed** erschöpft (*a. fig.*); vergriffen (*Auflage*); **ex-'haust·i·ble** erschöpflich; **ex'hausting** ⊕ anstrengend, mühselig; ⊕ Auspump...; **ex'haus·tion** [⁓tʃən] Erschöpfung *f*; **ex'haus·tive** □ = *exhausting*; erschöpfend.

ex·hib·it [ig'zibit] **1.** ausstellen; zeigen, darlegen, an den Tag legen, aufweisen; vorführen; ⚖ vorlegen; **2.** Ausstellungsstück *n*; Eingabe *f*; Beweisstück *n*; *on* ⁓ ausgestellt; **exhi·bi·tion** [eksi'biʃən] Ausstellung *f*; Darlegung *f*; Zurschaustellung *f*, Vorführung *f*; Stipendium *n*; *make an* ⁓ *of o.s.* sich zum Gespött machen; *on* ⁓ ausgestellt; **ex·hi'bition·er** [⁓ʃnə] Stipendiat *m*; **ex·hi'bi·tion·ism** *psych.* Exhibitionismus *m*; **ex·hi'bi·tion·ist** Exhibitionist *m*.

ex·hil·a·rate [ig'ziləreit] erheitern; **ex·hil·a'ra·tion** Erheiterung *f*.

ex·hort [ig'zɔːt] ermahnen; **ex·hor-**

ta·tion [egzɔː'teiʃən] Ermahnung *f*.

ex·hu·ma·tion [ekshjuː'meiʃən] Exhumierung *f*; **ex'hume** *Leiche* exhumieren.

ex·i·gence, ex·i·gen·cy ['eksidʒəns (-i)] dringende Not *f*, kritische Lage *f*; Erfordernis *n*; **'ex·i·gent** dringlich; anspruchsvoll; *be* ⁓ *of* erfordern.

ex·ig·u·ous [eg'zigjuəs] klein, dürftig, gering.

ex·ile ['eksail] **1.** Verbannung *f*, Exil *n*; Verbannte *m*, *f*; **2.** verbannen (*from* aus, von).

ex·ist [ig'zist] existieren, dasein, vorhanden sein; leben; bestehen; **ex'ist·ence** Existenz *f*, Dasein *n*, Vorhandensein *n*; Leben *n*; *be in* ⁓ existieren, bestehen; *in* ⁓ = **ex'istent** vorhanden; lebend; **ex·is·tential·ism** *phls.* [egzis'tenʃəlizəm] Existenzphilosophie *f*.

ex·it ['eksit] **1.** Abgang *m*; Tod *m*; Ausgang *m*; *make one's* ⁓ abtreten; ⁓ *permit* Ausreisegenehmigung *f*; ⁓ *visa* Ausreisevisum *n*; **2.** *thea.* (geht) ab.

ex·o·dus ['eksədəs] Auszug *m aus Ägypten*; *fig.* Aus-, Abwanderung *f*, Massenflucht *f*; ♀ Exodus *m*, Zweites Buch *n* Mose.

ex of·fi·ci·o [eksə'fiʃiəu] amtlich; von Amts wegen.

ex·on·er·ate [ig'zɔnəreit] *fig.* entlasten, entbinden, befreien (*from* von); rechtfertigen; **ex·on·er'a·tion** Entlastung *f*, Befreiung *f*.

ex·or·bi·tance, ex·or·bi·tan·cy [ig'zɔːbitəns(i)] Übermaß *n*; **ex'or·bitant** □ maßlos, übermäßig.

ex·or·cism ['eksɔːsizəm] Geisterbeschwörung *f*; **'ex·or·cist** Geisterbeschwörer *m*; **ex·or·cize** ['⁓saiz] *Geister* beschwören, bannen, austreiben (*from* aus); befreien (*of* von).

ex·ot·ic [ig'zɔtik] ausländisch; exotisch; fremdländisch.

ex·pand [iks'pænd] (sich) ausbreiten; (sich) ausdehnen; (sich) erweitern (*into* zu); größer machen *od.* werden; *Abkürzungen* (voll) ausschreiben; freundlich *od.* heiter werden; **ex'pand·er** Expander *m*; **ex·panse** [iks'pæns] Ausdehnung *f*, Weite *f*; Breite *f*; weite Fläche *f*; **ex·pan·si·bil·i·ty** [⁓sə'biliti] Ausdehnbarkeit *f*; **ex'pan·si·ble** ausdehnbar; **ex'pan·sion** Ausdehnung *f*; *pol.* Expansion *f*; Weite *f*, Raum *m*; **ex'pan·sive** ☐ Expansions...; ausdehnungsfähig; ausgedehnt, weit; *fig.* mitteilsam; **ex'pan·sive·ness** Ausdehnungsfähigkeit *f*; Weite *f*, Breite *f*; Mitteilsamkeit *f*.

ex·pa·ti·ate [eks'peiʃieit] sich weitläufig auslassen (*on* über *acc.*); **ex·pa·ti·a·tion** weitläufige Erörterung *f*; Gerede *n*.

ex·pa·tri·ate [eks'pætrieit] **1.** ausbürgern; ∼ *o.s.* auswandern; **2.** im Ausland Lebende *m*, *f*; **ex·pa·tri·'a·tion** Ausbürgerung *f*.

ex·pect [iks'pekt] erwarten (*of*, *from et.* von *j-m*); F annehmen, denken, vermuten, glauben; **ex'pect·an·cy** Erwartung *f*; Anwartschaft *f*; **ex·'pect·ant 1.** erwartend (*of acc.*); be ∼ ein Kind erwarten; ∼ *mother* werdende Mutter *f*; **2.** Anwärter *m*; **ex·pec·ta·tion** [ekspek'teiʃən] Erwartung *f*; Aussicht *f*; Wahrscheinlichkeit *f*; *contrary to* ∼ wider Erwarten; *beyond* ∼ über Erwarten; *on od. in* ∼ *of* in Erwartung (*gen.*); ∼ *of life* Lebenserwartung *f*; **ex·'pect·ing** = expectant.

ex·pec·to·rate [eks'pektəreit] aushusten, -werfen (*Schleim etc.*); **ex·pec·to'ra·tion** Auswurf *m*.

ex·pe·di·ence, ex·pe·di·en·cy [iks-'piːdjəns(i)] Zweckmäßigkeit *f etc.*; *schlaue* Berechnung *f*; **ex'pe·di·ent 1.** ☐ zweckmäßig, ratsam; nützlich; berechnend; **2.** (Hilfs)Mittel *n*; (Not)Behelf *m*; **ex·pe·dite** ['ekspidait] beschleunigen; (be)fördern; ausführen; **ex·pe·di·tion** [∼'diʃən] Eile *f*; ✗ Feldzug *m*; (Forschungs-) Reise *f*, Fahrt *f*, Expedition *f*; Unternehmung *f*; **ex·pe'di·tion·ar·y** [∼ʃnəri] Expeditions...; **ex·pe'di·tious** ☐ schnell, geschwind, eilig, flink.

ex·pel [iks'pel] (hin)ausstoßen; vertreiben, -jagen (*from* von, aus); ausschließen; ∼ *from school* von der Schule verweisen.

ex·pend [iks'pend] *Geld* ausgeben; *Mühe, Zeit* auf-, verwenden (*on, in* auf *acc.*); verbrauchen; **ex'pend·a·ble** verwend-, verbrauchbar; Verbrauchs...; **ex'pend·i·ture** [∼ditʃə] Verausgabung *f*, Ausgabe *f*; Aufwand *m* (*of* an); Verbrauch *m*; Aufwendungen *f|pl.*, Ausgaben *f|pl.*;

ex·pense [iks'pens] Ausgabe *f*; (Kosten)Aufwand *m*; Kosten *pl.*; ∼*s pl.* Unkosten *pl.*, Auslagen *f|pl.*; *at my* ∼ auf meine Kosten; *at the* ∼ *of* auf Kosten (*gen.*); *at any* ∼ um jeden Preis; *at great* ∼ mit großen Kosten; *go to the* ∼ *of* Geld ausgeben für; *put s.o. to great* ∼ j. viel Geld kosten, j-m große Unkosten verursachen; **ex'pense ac·count** Spesenrechnung *f*; **ex'pen·sive** ☐ kostspielig, teuer.

ex·pe·ri·ence [iks'piəriəns] **1.** Erfahrung *f*; Erlebnis *n*; **2.** erfahren, erleben; *Verlust etc.* erleiden; **ex·'pe·ri·enced** erfahren, erprobt.

ex·per·i·ment 1. [iks'perimənt] Versuch *m*, Experiment *n*; **2.** [∼ment] experimentieren, Versuche anstellen (*on, with* mit); **ex·pe·ri·men·tal** ☐ [eksperi'mentl] Experimental...; Versuchs...; erfahrungsmäßig; **ex·per·i·men·ta·tion** Experimentieren *n*; **ex·per·i·ment·er** [iks'perimentə] Experimentierer (-in).

ex·pert ['ekspəːt] **1.** ☐ [*pred.* eks'pəːt] erfahren, geschickt (*at, in* in *dat.*); (sach)kundig, fachmännisch, Fach...; Sachverständigen...; ∼ *advice* Rat *m* e-s Fachmanns; ∼ *opinion* (Sachverständigen)Gutachten *n*; **2.** Fachmann *m*; Sachverständige *m*, *f* (*at, in* in *dat.*); Sachbearbeiter(in); Experte *m*; **ex·per·tise** [∼'tiːz] (Sachverständigen)Gutachten *n*; Sachkenntnis *f*; **'ex·pert·ness** Erfahrenheit *f*.

ex·pi·a·ble ['ekspiəbl] sühnbar; **ex·pi·ate** ['∼pieit] büßen; sühnen; **ex·pi'a·tion** Sühnung *f*; Sühne *f*; **ex·pi·a·to·ry** ['∼piətəri] sühnend (*of acc.*); Sühn...

ex·pi·ra·tion [ekspaiə'reiʃən] Ausatmung *f*; Ablauf *m*, Ende *n*; *at the time of* ∼ ✝ zur Verfallzeit; **ex·pir·a·to·ry** [iks'paiərətəri] Ausatmungs...; **ex'pire** ausatmen; sterben, verscheiden; ablaufen (*Zeit, Vertrag etc.*); ✝ verfallen, fällig werden; erlöschen (*Feuer, Anspruch etc.*); **ex'pi·ry** Ablauf *m*.

ex·plain [iks'plein] *v/t.* erklären, erläutern; verständlich machen; *Gründe* auseinandersetzen; *v/i.* e-e Erklärung abgeben; ∼ *away* wegdiskutieren; **ex'plain·a·ble** erklärbar.

ex·pla·na·tion [eksplə'neiʃən] Erklärung *f*; Erläuterung *f*; **ex·plan·a·to·ry** □ [iks'plænətəri] erklärend.

ex·ple·tive [eks'pli:tiv] **1.** □ ausfüllend; **2.** Füll-, Flickwort *n*; Fluch *m*; Lückenbüßer *m*.

ex·pli·ca·ble ['eksplikəbl] erklärlich; **ex·pli·cate** ['⌣keit] erklären; *Begriff* entwickeln.

ex·plic·it □ [iks'plisit] ausdrücklich, deutlich; bestimmt; *fig.* offen.

ex·plode [iks'pləud] explodieren (lassen); ausbrechen; platzen (*with* vor); *Theorie* widerlegen; über den Haufen werfen; bloßstellen; **ex-'plod·ed view** ⊕ Darstellung *f* in auseinandergezogener Anordnung.

ex·ploit 1. [iks'plɔit] ausbeuten, -nutzen; **2.** ['eksplɔit] Heldentat *f*; **ex·ploi'ta·tion** Ausbeutung *f*, Ausnutzung *f*; Auswertung *f*; *a.* ⌣ *of soil* Raubbau *m*.

ex·plo·ra·tion [eksplɔ:'reiʃən] Erforschung *f*; **ex·plor·a·to·ry** [⌣rətəri] Erforschungs...; **ex·plore** [iks'plɔ:] erforschen; untersuchen; **ex'plor·er** (Er)Forscher *m*; Forschungsreisende *m*.

ex·plo·sion [iks'pləuʒən] Explosion *f*; Ausbruch *m*; **ex'plo·sive** [⌣siv] **1.** □ explosiv; Knall...; **2.** Sprengstoff *m*; *gr.* Verschlußlaut *m*.

ex·po·nent [eks'pəunənt] Ⱥ Exponent *m*; Erklärer *m*; Vertreter *m*.

ex·port 1. [eks'pɔ:t] ausführen, exportieren; **2.** ['ekspɔ:t] Ausfuhr (-artikel *m*) *f*, Export *m*; ⌣*s pl.* Gesamtausfuhr *f*; Exportgüter *n*/*pl.*; **ex'port·a·ble** ausführbar; **ex·por·'ta·tion** Ausfuhr *f*, Export *m*; **ex-'port·er** Exporteur *m*.

ex·po·sé [eks'pəuzei] Exposé *n*.

ex·pose [iks'pəuz] aussetzen; *phot.* belichten; ausstellen; enthüllen, entlarven; bloßstellen; **ex·po·si-tion** [ekspəu'ziʃən] Ausstellung *f*; Darstellung *f*, Erklärung *f*; **ex-'pos·i·tor** Ausleger *m*, Erklärer *m*.

ex·pos·tu·late [iks'pɔstjuleit] protestieren; ⌣ *with s.o.* j-m Vorhaltungen machen; **ex·pos·tu'la·tion** Vorhaltung *f*; **ex'pos·tu·la·to·ry** [⌣lətəri] mahnend.

ex·po·sure [iks'pəuʒə] Aussetzen *n*; Ausgesetztsein *n*; Aufdeckung *f*; Enthüllung *f*, Entlarvung *f*; *phot.* Belichtung *f*; Bild *n*; Lage *f* e-s Hauses; ⌣ *meter* Belichtungs-

messer *m*; *death from* ⌣ Tod *m* durch Erfrieren.   [legen.)

ex·pound [iks'paund] erklären, aus-)

ex·press [iks'pres] **1.** □ ausdrücklich, deutlich; Expreß..., Eil...; ⌣ *company Am.* Transportfirma *f*; ⌣ *highway* Schnell(verkehrs)straße *f*; ⌣ *parcel* Eilpaket *n*; **2.** Eilbote *m*; *a.* ⌣ *train* Schnellzug *m*; *by* ⌣ = **3.** *adv.* durch Eilboten; als Eilgut; **4.** *Gedanken etc.* äußern, ausdrücken, zum Ausdruck bringen; bezeigen, an den Tag legen; auspressen; *be* ⌣*ed* zum Ausdruck kommen; **ex'press·i·ble** ausdrückbar; **ex·pres·sion** [⌣'preʃən] Ausdruck *m* (*Sprache*, *Gesicht*, ♪, *paint.*, Ⱥ); **ex'pres·sion·ism** *Kunst:* Expressionismus *m*; **ex'pres·sion·less** ausdruckslos; **ex'pres·sive** □ ausdrückend (*of acc.*); ausdrucksvoll; **ex'press·ly** ausdrücklich, eigens; **ex'press·way** *Am.* Autobahn *f*.

ex·pro·pri·ate [eks'prəuprieit] enteignen (*s.th. et.*; *s.o.* j.; *s.o. from s.th.* j-m et.); **ex·pro·pri'a·tion** Enteignung *f*.

ex·pul·sion [iks'pʌlʃən] Vertreibung *f*; **ex'pul·sive** (aus)treibend.

ex·punge [eks'pʌndʒ] tilgen, streichen.

ex·pur·gate ['ekspə:geit] *von Anstößigem* reinigen, säubern; *Anstößiges* ausmerzen; **ex·pur'ga·tion** Reinigung *f etc.*; **ex'pur·ga·to·ry** [⌣gətəri] reinigend *etc.*

ex·qui·site □ ['ekskwizit] auserlesen, vorzüglich, köstlich; fein (*Gehör etc.*); heftig, scharf, groß; **'ex·qui·site·ness** Vorzüglichkeit *f*; Feinheit *f*; Feinfühligkeit *f*; Heftigkeit *f*.

ex·serv·ice·man ✕ ['eks'sə:vismən] ehemaliger (Front)Soldat *m*.

ex·tant [eks'tænt] (noch) vorhanden.

ex·tem·po·ra·ne·ous □ [ekstempə-'reinjəs], **ex·tem·po·rar·y** [iks-'tempərəri], **ex·tem·po·re** [eks-'tempəri] aus dem Stegreif (vorgetragen); **ex·tem·po·rize** [iks-'tempəraiz] aus dem Stegreif reden, vortragen; **ex'tem·po·riz·er** Stegreifredner *m*, -dichter *m*, -spieler *m*, Improvisateur *m*.

ex·tend [iks'tend] *v*/*t.* ausdehnen; *Hand etc.* ausstrecken; *Gebiet etc.* erweitern; *Frist etc.* verlängern; *Linie, Draht* ziehen; fortsetzen; *fig.* ausbauen; *Kurzschrift* übertragen;

Gunst etc. erweisen, *Hilfe* gewähren, *Einladung* aussprechen; ✗ (aus)schwärmen lassen; *Sport:* alles herausholen aus; *he was fully ~ed* er gab sein Letztes her; *~ed order* Schützenlinie *f*; *v*/*i.* sich erstrecken, reichen (*to* bis); **ex'tend·ed** ausgedehnt, ausgestreckt, verlängert.

ex·ten·si·bil·i·ty [ikstensə'biliti] Ausdehnbarkeit *f*; **ex'ten·si·ble** ausdehnbar; **ex'ten·sion** Ausdehnung *f*; Erweiterung *f* (*a. gr.*); Verlängerung *f*; Aus-, Anbau *m*; *teleph.* Nebenanschluß *m*; *~ cord* ✗ Verlängerungsschnur *f*; *~ ladder* Ausziehleiter *f*; *University* ♀ Volkshochschule *f*; **ex'ten·sive** □ ausgedehnt, umfassend; **ex'ten·sive·ness** Ausdehnung *f*, Umfang *m*, Weite *f.*

ex·tent [iks'tent] Ausdehnung *f*, Weite *f*, Größe *f*, Umfang *m*; Grad *m*, Maß *n*; *to the ~ of* bis zum Betrage von; *to a certain ~* gewissermaßen, bis zu e-m gewissen Grade; *to a great ~* in hohem Maße; *to some ~* einigermaßen; *to that ~* so weit; *grant ~ for* stunden.

ex·ten·u·ate [eks'tenjueit] abschwächen, mildern, beschönigen; **ex·ten·u'a·tion** Abschwächung *f etc.*

ex·te·ri·or [eks'tiəriə] **1.** □ äußerlich; Außen...; außerhalb (*to gen.*); **2.** Äußere *n*; *Film:* Außenaufnahme *f.*

ex·ter·mi·nate [iks'təmineit] ausrotten, vertilgen; **ex·ter·mi'na·tion** Ausrottung *f*; **ex'ter·mi·na·tor** Vertilger *m.*

ex·ter·nal [eks'tə:nl] **1.** □ äußere (-r, -s), äußerlich; außerhalb (*to gen.*) befindlich; Außen...; **2.** *~s pl.* Äußere *n*; *fig.* Äußerlichkeiten *f*/*pl.*

ex·ter·ri·to·ri·al ['eksteri'tɔ:riəl] exterritorial, den Landesgesetzen nicht unterworfen.

ex·tinct [iks'tiŋkt] erloschen (*a. fig.*); ausgestorben; **ex'tinc·tion** (Aus-, Er)Löschen *n* (*a. fig.*); Aussterben *n.*

ex·tin·guish [iks'tiŋgwiʃ] auslöschen, zum Erlöschen bringen; *fig.* in den Schatten stellen; vernichten; *Amt* abschaffen; *Schuld* löschen; *Gegner* zum Schweigen bringen; **ex'tin·guish·er** = *fire-~.*

ex·tir·pate ['ekstə:peit] ausrotten; ⚕ ausschneiden; **ex·tir'pa·tion** Ausrottung *f*; ⚕ Extirpation *f.*

ex·tol [iks'təul] erheben, preisen; *~ s.o. to the skies fig.* j. in den Himmel heben.

ex·tort [iks'tɔ:t] erpressen (*from* von); abnötigen (*from dat.*); **ex'tor·tion** Erpressung *f*; **ex'tor·tion·ate** [-ʃnit] erpresserisch; **ex'tor·tion·er** Erpresser *m*; Wucherer *m.*

ex·tra ['ekstrə] **1.** Extra...; außer...; Neben...; zusätzlich; besondere(r, -s), Sonder...; *~ pay* Zulage *f*; *~ time Sport:* Verlängerung *f*; **2.** *adv.* besonders; außerdem; **3.** *et.* Zusätzliches *n*; Zuschlag *m*; Extrablatt *n*; *thea., Film:* Statist(in).

ex·tract 1. ['ekstrækt] Auszug *m* (*a.* ⚕); Ausschnitt *m*; Extrakt *m*; **2.** [iks'trækt] (heraus)ziehen; *Text,* ⚕ ausziehen; ⚕ *Wurzel* ziehen; *Geständnis, Geld etc.* herauslocken; ab-, herleiten (*from* von); **ex'trac·tion** (Heraus)Ziehen *n*; Herkunft *f.*

ex·tra·cur·ric·u·lar ['ekstrəkə'rikjulə] außerhalb des Lehrplans.

ex·tra·dit·a·ble ['ekstrədaitəbl] auslieferbar; **'ex·tra·dite** *Verbrecher* ausliefern (lassen); **ex·tra·di·tion** [-'diʃən] Auslieferung *f.*

ex·tra...: '~·ju'di·cial außergerichtlich; **'~·mar·i·tal** außerehelich; **'~·mu·ral** außerhalb der Mauern *od.* der Universität; *~ student* Gasthörer (-in).

ex·tra·ne·ous [eks'treinjəs] unwesentlich (*to* für); fremd.

ex·traor·di·nar·y [iks'trɔ:dnri] außerordentlich, -gewöhnlich; besonder, Sonder..., Extra...; ungewöhnlich; *envoy ~* bevollmächtigter Gesandter *m.*

ex·trap·o·late [ek'stræpəuleit] extrapolieren.

ex·tra·sen·so·ry per·cep·tion *psych.* ['ekstrə'sensəri pə'sepʃən] anomale Fähigkeit *f* der Sinneswahrnehmung.

ex·tra·ter·res·tri·al ['ekstrəti'restriəl] außerirdisch.

ex·tra·ter·ri·to·ri·al ['ekstrəteri'tɔ:riəl] = *exterritorial.*

ex·trav·a·gance [iks'trævigəns] Übertriebenheit *f*; Überspanntheit *f*; Verstiegenheit *f*; Verschwendung *f*, Extravaganz *f*; **ex'trav·a·gant** □ übertrieben, -spannt; verstiegen; verschwenderisch, extravagant; **ex·trav·a·gan·za** *thea.*

[ekstrævəˈgænzə] Ausstattungs-
stück *n*.

ex·treme [iksˈtriːm] **1.** ⎕ äußerst;
größt, höchst; sehr groß *od*. hoch;
sehr streng; außergewöhnlich; ~
unction eccl. letzte Ölung *f*; **2.** Äußerste *n*; Extrem *n*; *der* höchste
Grad; äußerste Maßnahme *f*; *go
to* ~*s* äußerste Maßnahmen ergreifen; *in the* ~ äußerst; **ex'trem·
ist** Radikale *m*; **ex·trem·i·ty** [~-
ˈtremiti] Äußerste *n*; äußerste Verlegenheit *f*; höchste Not *f*; äußerste
Maßnahme *f*; **ex'trem·i·ties** [~z]
pl. Gliedmaßen *pl*.

ex·tri·cate [ˈekstrikeit] herauswinden, -ziehen; befreien; ⌒ entwickeln; **ex·tri'ca·tion** Befreiung
f; Entwicklung *f*.

ex·trin·sic [eksˈtrinsik] (~*ally*) äußerlich, nicht gehörend (*to* zu).

ex·tro·vert [ˈekstrəuvəːt] extraver-
tierter Typ *m*, nur auf die Außenwelt eingestellter Mensch *m*.

ex·trude [eksˈtruːd] ausstoßen; verdrängen.

ex·u·ber·ance [igˈzjuːbərəns] Überfluß *m*, Fülle *f*; Überschwenglichkeit *f*; **ex'u·ber·ant** reichlich; üppig (wuchernd); übermäßig; überschwenglich.

ex·u·da·tion [eksjuːˈdeiʃən] Aus-
schwitzung *f*; **ex·ude** [igˈzjuːd]
ausschwitzen; absondern.

ex·ult [igˈzʌlt] frohlocken (*at od. in*

s.th. uber *et*.); triumphieren (*over
s.o.* über j.); **ex'ult·ant** frohlok-
kend; **ex·ul·ta·tion** [egzʌlˈteiʃən]
Frohlocken *n*.

eye [ai] **1.** Auge *n* (*a. fig. u.* ❀);
Blick *m*; Öhr *n*; Öse *f*; *have an* ~
for Sinn haben für; *my* ~*s! sl.* au
Backe!; *it's all my* ~*! sl.* Quatsch!;
make ~*s at s.o.* j-m verliebte Blicke
zuwerfen; *up to the* ~*s in work* bis
über die Ohren in Arbeit; *mind
your* ~*!* (sei) vorsichtig!; *with an* ~ *to*
mit Rücksicht auf (*acc*.); mit der
Absicht zu; **2.** ansehen, betrachten,
beäugen; *mit Erstaunen etc.* mustern; '~**·ball** Augapfel *m*; '~-
brow Augenbraue *f*; '~**·catch·er**
Blickfang *m*; **eyed** [aid] …äugig.

eye…: '~**·glass** Augenglas *n*; Oku-
lar *n*; (*pair of*) ~*es pl*. Kneifer *m*,
Zwicker *m*; Brille *f*; '~**·hole** Augen-
höhle *f*; Guckloch *n*; '~**·lash**
Augenwimper *f*; **eye·let** [ˈ~lit]
Schnürloch *n*; Guckloch *n*; Öse *f*.

eye…: '~**·lid** Augenlid *n*; '~**·o·pen·
er** überraschende Aufklärung *f*;
'~**·piece** *opt*. Okular *n*; '~**·shad·
ow** Lidschatten *m*; '~**·shot** Sehweite
f; '~**·sight** Augen(licht *n*) *pl*., Gesicht
n; Sehkraft *f*; '~**·sore** *fig*. Dorn *m* im
Auge; unschöner Anblick *m*; '~-
·tooth Augenzahn *m*; '~**·wash** *sl*.
Schwindel *m*, Betrug *m*; '~**·'wit·ness**
Augenzeuge *m*, -zeugin *f*.

ey·rie, ey·ry [ˈaiəri] = *aerie*.

F

Fa·bian [ˈfeibjən] vorsichtig, zögernd; ~ *policy* Verzögerungs-
politik *f*.

fa·ble [ˈfeibl] Fabel *f*; Mythen *f/pl*.,
Legenden *f/pl*.; Unwahrheit *f*, Lüge
f.

fab·ric [ˈfæbrik] Bau *m*, Gebäude *n*;
Gefüge *n*, Struktur *f*; Gewebe *n*,
Stoff *m*; **fab·ri·cate** [ˈ~keit] fabrizieren (*mst fig*.: *erdichten*; *fälschen*);
fab·ri·ca·tion Fabrikation *f*; Erfindung *f*, Fälschung *f*; '**fab·ri·ca·
tor** Verfertiger *m*; Erfinder *m von*
Lügen; Fälscher *m*.

fab·u·list [ˈfæbjulist] Fabeldichter
m; '**fab·u·lous** ⎕ legendär; sagen-,
fabelhaft.

fa·çade ⚠ [fəˈsɑːd] Fassade *f*.

face [feis] **1.** Gesicht *n*; Miene *f*;
Anblick *m*; *fig*. Stirn *f*, Unverschämtheit *f*; Oberfläche *f*, Fläche
f; Vorderseite *f*; rechte Seite *f von*
Tuch; Zifferblatt *n*; *in* (*the*) ~ *of*
angesichts (*gen*.); trotz (*gen*.); ~ *to* ~
with Auge in Auge mit; *save one's* ~
das Gesicht wahren; *lose* ~ das Gesicht verlieren; *on the* ~ *of it* auf
den ersten Blick; *set one's* ~ *against*

sich gegen *et*. stemmen; **2.** *v/t*. ins Gesicht sehen (*dat*.), ansehen; gegenüberliegen, gegenüberstehen (*dat*.); unter die Augen treten (*dat*.); ins Auge sehen (*dat*.); (hinaus)gehen auf (*acc*.) (*Fenster etc*.); die Stirn bieten (*dat*.); *Kleid etc*. einfassen, besetzen (*with* mit); *Wand* bekleiden; *be ~d with* sich ... (*dat*.) gegenübersehen; *v/i*. *~ about* sich umdrehen; *left ~!* ✕ links um!; *about ~!* kehrt!; *~ card Karten*: Bildkarte *f*; '*~-cloth* Waschlappen *m*; **faced** mit e-m ... Gesicht; '**face-down** *Am*. Machtprobe *f*; '**face-less** *fig*. anonym, undefinierbar; '**face-lift-ing** *Kosmetik*: Gesichtsstraffung *f*; *fig*. Verschönerung *f*; '**fac-er** Schlag *m* ins Gesicht; plötzliche Schwierigkeit *f*.

fac-et ⊕ ['fæsit] Facette *f*; '**fac-et-ed** facettiert.

fa-ce-tious □ [fə'si:ʃəs] witzig, drollig, spaßhaft.

face val-ue ['feis'vælju:] ✝ Nennwert *m*; *fig*. das Äußere; *take s.th. at its ~* et. für bare Münze nehmen.

fa-ci-a ['feiʃə] = *fascia*.

fa-cial ['feiʃəl] **1.** Gesichts...; **2.** Gesichtsmassage *f*.

fac-ile ['fæsail] leicht; gewandt; gefällig; nachgiebig; **fa-cil-i-tate** [fə'siliteit] erleichtern, fördern; **fa-cil-i-ta-tion** Erleichterung *f*, Förderung *f*; **fa-cil-i-ty** Leichtigkeit *f*; Gewandtheit *f*; *facilities pl*. Möglichkeiten *f/pl*.; Gelegenheiten *f/pl*.; Einrichtungen *f/pl*.; Anlagen *f/pl*.

fac-ing ['feisiŋ] ⊕ Verkleidung *f*; ✕ Wendung *f*; *~s pl*. Besatz *m*.

fac-sim-i-le [fæk'simili] Faksimile *n*, treue Nachbildung *f*.

fact [fækt] Tatsache *f*; Wirklichkeit *f*; Wahrheit *f*; Tat *f*; *~s pl*. (*of the case*) Tatbestand *m*; *after* (*before*) *the ~* nach (vor) begangener Tat; *in* (*point of*) *~*, *as a matter of ~* in der Tat, tatsächlich; *know for a ~* bestimmt wissen; '*~-find-ing* zur Feststellung des Sachverhalts (dienend).

fac-tion ['fækʃən] Splitterpartei *f*; Clique *f*, Klüngel *m*; Uneinigkeit *f*; '**fac-tion-ist** Parteigänger *m*.

fac-tious □ ['fækʃəs] parteisüchtig; aufrührerisch; '**fac-tious-ness** Parteisucht *f*.

fac-ti-tious □ [fæk'tiʃəs] nachgemacht, künstlich.

fac-tor ['fæktə] 🝓 Faktor *m*; *fig*. Umstand *m*, Moment *n*, Faktor *m*; Agent *m*, Vertreter *m*; Verwalter *m*; '**fac-to-ry** Fabrik *f*.

fac-to-tum [fæk'təutəm] Faktotum *n*, Mädchen *n* für alles.

facts of life [fæktsəv'laif] *pl*.: *tell s.o. about the ~* j. sexuell aufklären.

fac-tu-al ['fæktʃuəl] Tatsachen...; sachlich.

fac-ul-ty ['fækəlti] Fähigkeit *f*; Kraft *f*; *fig*. Gabe *f*; Gewandtheit *f*; 🝓 Vorrecht *n*; *univ*. Fakultät *f*.

fad F [fæd] Liebhaberei *f*, Steckenpferd *n*; Laune *f*, Mode *f*; '**fad-dish**, '**fad-dy** launisch; schrullig; '**fad-dist** Fex *m*; Sonderling *m*.

fade [feid] (ver)welken (lassen); verblassen; verschießen; schwinden; verklingen; *Radio*: schwinden; *~ away*, *~ out* dahinschwinden; *~ in* einblenden; *~ out* ausblenden; '**fade-less** licht-, farbecht; '**fad-ing 1.** □ vergänglich; **2.** *Radio*: (Ton)Schwund *m*, Fading *n*.

fae-ces *physiol*. ['fi:si:z] *pl*. Kot *m*.

faer-ie, **faer-y** ['feiəri] Feen-, Märchenland *n*.

fag F [fæg] **1.** Plackerei *f*; Erschöpfung *f*; *Schüler*, *der e-m älteren Dienste leisten muß*; *fig*. Packesel *m*; *sl*. Zigarette *f*; **2.** *v/i*. sich placken; *e-m älteren Schüler Dienste leisten*; *v/t*. erschöpfen, mürbe machen; '*~-'end* F (letzter, schäbiger) Rest *m*; Stummel *m*, Kippe *f*.

fag-ot, **fag-got** ['fægət] Reisigbündel *n*; ⊕ Bündel *n* Stahlstäbe; Frikadelle *f*; *Am*. F Schwule *m*.

Fahr-en-heit ['færənhait]: *~ thermometer* Fahrenheitthermometer *n*.

fail [feil] **1.** *v/i*. versagen, mißlingen, fehlschlagen; versiegen (*Quelle*); stocken, versagen (*Stimme*); nachlassen, abnehmen, schwächer werden (*Kraft etc*.); unterlassen; ermangeln (*in gen*.); bankrott machen; durchfallen (*Kandidat*); *he ~ed to do od*. *in doing* es mißlang ihm zu tun; *he cannot ~ to inf*. er muß (einfach) *inf*.; *v/t*. im Stich lassen, verlassen; verfehlen, versäumen; durchfallen lassen; *his heart ~ed him* ihm sank der Mut; **2.** *su*.: *without ~* unfehlbar, ganz gewiß; '**fail-ing 1.** Mangel *m*,

Fehler m, Schwäche f; **2.** prp. in Ermangelung (gen.); ~ which widrigenfalls; **fail·ure** ['~jə] Fehlen n, Ausbleiben n; Fehlschlag(en n) m; Mißlingen n; Mißerfolg m; Versagen n; Verfall m; Zs.-bruch m; Versäumnis n; Bankrott m; Versager m (Person).

fain poet. [fein] gern.

faint [feint] **1.** □ schwach, matt; zaghaft; undeutlich; **2.** schwach werden; in Ohnmacht fallen, ohnmächtig werden (with vor); **3.** Ohnmacht f; '~-'heart·ed □ verzagt; '~-'heart·ed·ness Kleinmut m; 'faint·ness Schwäche f, Mattigkeit f.

fair¹ [fɛə] **1.** adj. gerecht, ehrlich, anständig, fair; recht u. billig; ganz gut, ordentlich; schön (Wetter), günstig (Wind); reichlich, beträchtlich; blond, hellhäutig; freundlich, höflich; sauber, in Reinschrift; schön (Frau); ~ name guter Name; the ~ sex das schöne Geschlecht; **2.** adv. gerecht, ehrlich, anständig, fair; in Reinschrift; direkt; write s.th. out ~ et. ins reine schreiben; ~ in the face mitten ins Gesicht.

fair² [~] (Jahr)Markt m, Messe f; '~·ground Rummelplatz m.

fair-haired ['fɛə'heəd] blond.

fair·ly ['fɛəli] s. fair¹; erträglich, leidlich; ziemlich; völlig, gänzlich; 'fair·ness Schönheit f; Blondheit f; Gerechtigkeit f; Redlichkeit f; Billigkeit f; 'fair-'spo·ken höflich; 'fair·way ⚓ Fahrwasser n; 'fair-weath·er friend Freund m im Glück.

fair·y ['fɛəri] **1.** feenhaft; Feen...; Zauber...; **2.** Fee f; Zauberin f; Elf(e f) m; 'Fair·y·land Feen-, Märchenland n; 'fair·y·like feenhaft; 'fair·y·tale Märchen n.

faith [feiθ] Glaube(n) m; Vertrauen n; Treue f, Redlichkeit f; gegebenes Wort n; have ~ in s.th. an et. glauben; in good ~ in gutem Glauben; '~-cure = faith-healing; **faith·ful** □ ['~ful] treu; gewissenhaft, ehrlich; zuverlässig; wahrheitsgetreu; the ~ pl. die Gläubigen pl.; yours ~ly ... Ihr ergebener ...; hochachtungsvoll ...; 'faith·ful·ness Treue f; Ehrlichkeit f; 'faith-heal·ing Gesundbeten n; 'faith·less □ treulos; ungläubig; 'faith·less·ness Treu-

losigkeit f.

fake sl. [feik] **1.** Schwindel m; Fälschung f; Am. a. 'fak·er Schwindler m; **2.** a. ~ up zurechtmachen, fälschen.

fal·con ['fɔːlkən] Falke m; 'fal·con·er Falkner m; 'fal·con·ry Falkenbeize f; Falknerei f.

fall [fɔːl] **1.** Fall(en n) m; Sturz m; Verfall m; Einsturz m; (Blätter-, Schnee- etc.) Fall m; bsd. Am. Herbst m; Sinken n der Preise etc., Kurssturz m, Baisse f; Fällen n von Holz; Gefälle n; mst ~s pl. Wasserfall m; Senkung f, Abhang m; ⚓ Fall n; the ♀ (of Man) der Sündenfall m; have a ~ fallen, stürzen; **2.** (irr.) fallen; ab-, einfallen; abnehmen; sinken (Mut etc.); heruntergehen (Preise); fig. (herab-) stürzen; sich legen (Wind); (mit Prädikatsnomen) werden; in e-n Zustand verfallen; geworfen werden (Tiere); münden (into in acc.); his countenance fell er machte ein langes Gesicht; ~ asleep einschlafen; ~ away schwinden; abfallen; ~ back zurückweichen; ~ back (up)on zurückkommen auf (acc.); ~ behind zurückbleiben (in mit); ~ between two stools sich zwischen zwei Stühle setzen; ~ down niederfallen; einstürzen; F Pech haben; ~ due fällig werden; ~ for F hereinfallen auf (acc.), auf den Leim gehen; ~ from abfallen von; ~ ill od. sick krank werden; ~ in einfallen; ⚔ (sich) formieren, antreten; ablaufen (Pacht etc.); fällig werden (Schuld etc.); ~ in with stoßen auf (acc.); übereinstimmen mit e-r Ansicht; ~ in love with sich verlieben in (acc.); ~ into verfallen in; geraten in (acc.); ~ into line with übereinstimmen mit, sich j-m anschließen; ~ off abfallen (a. fig., from von); nachlassen; ~ on (prp.) über j. herfallen; ~ out zanken; sich zerstreiten (with mit); sich zutragen; ⚔ wegtreten; ~ short knapp werden (of an dat.); ~ short of nicht erreichen, zurückbleiben hinter (dat.); ~ to zufallen (Tür); zugreifen (beim Essen); anfangen, sich machen an (acc.); ~ under unter e-e Zahl etc. fallen.

fal·la·cious □ [fə'leiʃəs] trügerisch; irreführend; irrig.

fal·la·cy ['fæləsi] Trugschluß *m*; Irrtum *m*; Täuschung *f*.

fall·en ['fɔːlən] *p.p. von fall 2.*

fall guy *Am. sl.* ['fɔːl'gai] *der* Lackierte, *der* Dumme.

fal·li·bil·i·ty [fæli'biliti] Fehlbarkeit *f*; **fal·li·ble** □ ['fæləbl] fehlbar.

fall·ing ['fɔːliŋ] Fallen *n*; ~ off Abfall *m*; Abnahme *f*; ~ sick·ness Fallsucht *f*; ~ star Sternschnuppe *f*.

fall·out ['fɔːlaut] Fallout *m*, radioaktiver Niederschlag *m*.

fal·low ['fæləu] **1.** *zo.* falb; ⚡brach (-liegend); **2.** Brachland *n*; '~-deer *zo.* Damwild *n*; '**fal·low·ness** Brachliegen *n*.

false ⸍ [fɔːls] falsch, unwahr; unrichtig; treulos (*to* gegen); unecht; Fehl...; ~ imprisonment Freiheitsberaubung *f*; ~ key Nachschlüssel *m*; play s.o. ~ falsches Spiel mit j-m treiben; **false·hood** ['~hud] Falschheit *f*; Unwahrheit *f*, Lüge *f*; '**false·ness** Falschheit *f der Gesinnung*; Verrat *m*; **false teeth** [fɔːls 'tiːθ] *künstliches* Gebiß *n*.

fal·set·to ♪ [fɔːl'setəu] Fistelstimme *f*, Falsett *n*.

fal·si·fi·ca·tion ['fɔːlsifi'keiʃən] Verfälschung *f*; Fälschung *f*; **fal·si·fi·er** ['~faiə] Fälscher(in); **fal·si·fy** ['~fai] (ver)fälschen; als falsch nachweisen; **fal·si·ty** ['~ti] Falschheit *f*, Unrichtigkeit *f*.

fal·ter ['fɔːltə] schwanken; *fig.* stocken (*Ton, Stimme*); stammeln; *fig.* zaudern.

fame [feim] Ruf *m*, Ruhm *m*; **famed** berühmt (*for* wegen).

fa·mil·iar [fə'miljə] **1.** □ vertraut (*to dat.*); intim; bekannt (*with* mit); gewohnt; ungezwungen, vertraulich, familiär; be ~ with gut kennen; **2.** Vertraute *m*; **fa·mil·i·ar·i·ty** [~li'æriti] Vertrautheit *f*; *familiarities pl.* (plumpe) Vertraulichkeit *f*; **fa·mil·iar·i·za·tion** [~ljərai'zeiʃən] Gewöhnung *f* (*with* an *acc.*); **fa·mil·iar·ize** vertraut machen, bekannt machen.

fam·i·ly ['fæmili] **1.** Familie *f*; **2.** Familien..., Haus...; *in the* ~ *way* F in anderen Umständen; ~ *allowance* Kinderzulage *f*; ~ *doctor* Hausarzt *m*; ~ *man* Hausvater *m*; ~ *planning* Familienplanung *f*; ~

~ *tree* Stammbaum *m*.

fam·ine ['fæmin] Hungersnot *f*; Mangel *m* (*of* an *dat.*); Not *f*.

fam·ish ['fæmiʃ] aushungern; verhungern (lassen); darben.

fa·mous □ ['feiməs] berühmt (*for* wegen); F famos, ausgezeichnet.

fan¹ [fæn] **1.** Fächer *m*; Ventilator *m*; ⚓ (Schrauben)Flügel *m*; **2.** (an-) fächeln; an-, *fig.* entfachen; ~ *out* ⚔ ausschwärmen.

fan² F [~] *Sport- etc.* Fanatiker *m*, Liebhaber *m*, Fan *m*; *Radio*: Bastler *m*; ...narr *m*, ...fex *m*.

fa·nat·ic [fə'nætik] **1.** *a.* **fa·nat·i·cal** □ fanatisch; **2.** Fanatiker(in), Eiferer *m*; **fa·nat·i·cism** [~sizəm] Fanatismus *m*.

fan belt *mot.* ['fænbelt] Keilriemen *m*.

fan·ci·er ['fænsiə] *Vogel- etc.* Liebhaber(in); Züchter(in).

fan·ci·ful □ ['fænsiful] phantastisch; '**fan·ci·ful·ness** Phantasterei *f*.

fan·cy ['fænsi] **1.** *spielerische* Phantasie *f*; Einbildung(skraft) *f*; Schrulle *f*; Neigung *f*, Vorliebe *f*; Liebhaberei *f*; *the* ~ die (*Sport-, Tier- etc.*)Liebhaberwelt *f*; *take a* ~ *to* Gefallen finden an (*dat.*), e-e Neigung fassen zu; **2.** Phantasie...; Liebhaber...; Luxus...; Mode...; ~ *apron* Tändelschürze *f*; ~ *articles pl.* Modeartikel *m/pl.*; ~ *dress* Maskenkostüm *n*; ~*-dress ball* Maskenball *m*; ~ *fair* Art Wohltätigkeitsbasar *m*; ~ *goods pl.* Galanteriewaren *f/pl.*; ~ *man sl.* Zuhälter *m*; ~ *price* Liebhaberpreis *m*, Phantasiepreis *m*; **3.** sich einbilden, sich vorstellen; Gefallen finden an (*dat.*), gern haben; (aus Liebhaberei) züchten; *just* ~! denken Sie nur!; '~-**'free** frei und ungebunden; '~-**work** feine Handarbeit *f*, Stickerei *f*.

fane *poet.* [fein] Tempel *m*.

fan·fare ['fænfeə] Fanfare *f*; Tusch *m*; **fan·fa·ron·ade** [~færə'naːd] Großsprecherei *f*, Prahlerei *f*.

fang [fæŋ] Fangzahn *m*; Giftzahn *m*; Zahnwurzel *f*; ⊕ Klaue *f*; Dorn *m*.

fan·ner ⊕ ['fænə] Gebläse *n*.

fan·tail *zo.* ['fænteil] Pfauentaube *f*.

fan·ta·sia ♪ [fæn'teizjə] Phantasie *f*; **fan·tas·tic** [~'tæstik] (~*ally*) phantastisch; **fan·ta·sy** ['~təsi] Phantasie *f*, Einbildung *f*, Hirngespinst *n*.

fastness

far [fɑ:] *adj.* fern, entfernt; weit; *adv.* fern; weit; (sehr) viel; ⁓ *better* weit *od.* viel besser; ⁓ *the best* weitaus der beste; *as* ⁓ *as* bis; *by* ⁓ bei weitem; ⁓ *from ger.* weit davon entfernt zu *inf.*; *in so* ⁓ *as* insofern als; ⁓ *and near*, ⁓ *and wide* weit u. breit; ⁓-a·way ['fɑːrəwei] weit entfernt, fern.

farce *thea.* [fɑːs] Posse *f*, Farce *f*, Schwank *m*; **far·ci·cal** □ ['⁓sikəl] possenhaft.

fare [feə] **1.** Fahrgeld *n*; Fahrgast *m*; Verpflegung *f*, Kost *f*; **2.** *j-m* (er)gehen; *gut* leben; *how did you* ⁓? wie ist es Ihnen ergangen?; ⁓ *well!* lebe(n Sie) wohl!; ⁓ *stage* Teilstrecke *f*; ⁓ *'well* **1.** lebe(n Sie) wohl!; **2.** Abschied *m*, Lebewohl *n*; **3.** Abschieds...; ⁓ *party* Abschiedsfeier *f*.

far... [fɑ:]: '⁓-'**fetched** *fig.* weithergeholt, gesucht; '⁓-'**flung** weit (ausgedehnt); *fig.* weitgespannt; ⁓ **gone** F fertig (*todkrank, betrunken etc.*).

far·i·na·ceous [færi'neiʃəs] mehlig; stärkehaltig.

farm [fɑːm] **1.** Bauernhof *m*, -gut *n*, Gehöft *n*, Farm *f*; Züchterei *f*; *chicken* ⁓ Hühnerfarm *f*; **2.** pachten; *a.* ⁓ *out* verpachten, *Land* bewirtschaften, bebauen; *Kinder* in (bezahlte) Pflege nehmen; '**farm·er** Landwirt *m*, Bauer *m*; Pächter *m*; '**farm·hand** Landarbeiter(in); '**farm-house** Bauern-, Gutshaus *n*; '**farm·ing 1.** Acker...; landwirtschaftlich; *Land*...; **2.** Landwirtschaft *f*; **farm·stead** ['⁓sted] Bauernhof *m*, Gehöft *n*; '**farm·yard** Wirtschaftshof *m* e-s *Bauernguts*.

far·o ['fɛərəu] Pharo *n* (*Kartenspiel*).

far-off ['fɑːr'ɔ:f] entfernt, fern, abgelegen.

far-out *sl.* [fɑːr'aut] toll, super.

far·ra·go [fə'rɑːgəu] Mischmasch *m*.

far-reach·ing ['fɑː'riːtʃiŋ] weitreichend.

far·ri·er ['færiə] Hufschmied *m*.

far·row ['færəu] **1.** Wurf *m* Ferkel; **2.** (Ferkel) werfen, ferkeln.

far-see·ing ['fɑː'siːiŋ], '**far-'sight-ed** *fig.* weitblickend.

fart V [fɑːt] **1.** Furz *m*; **2.** furzen.

far·ther ['fɑːðə], **far·thest** ['⁓ðist]

comp. u. sup. von far.

far·thing ['fɑːðiŋ] Farthing *m* (¹/₄ *Penny*; *abgeschafft seit 1961*); *not worth a* ⁓ keinen (roten) Heller wert.

fas·ci·a *mot.* ['feiʃə] Armaturenbrett *n*.

fas·ci·nate ['fæsineit] bezaubern, faszinieren; **fas·ci'na·tion** Bezauberung *f*; Zauber *m*, Reiz *m*, Faszination *f*.

fas·cine [fæ'siːn] Faschine *f* (*Reisigbündel*).

Fas·cism *pol.* ['fæʃizəm] Faschismus *m*; '**Fas·cist** Faschist(in); **fa'scis·tic** (⁓ally) faschistisch.

fash·ion ['fæʃən] **1.** Mode *f*; Art *f*, Weise *f*; feine Lebensart *f*; Form *f*; Schnitt *m*; *rank and* ⁓ *die* vornehme Welt; *in* (*out of*) ⁓ (un)modern; *set the* ⁓ tonangebend sein; **2.** gestalten, formen; *Kleid* machen; **fash·ion·a·ble** □ ['fæʃnəbl] Mode-...; modern, elegant; fein; '**fash·ion·a·ble·ness** Modernität *f*, *das* Moderne, Eleganz *f*; '**fash·ion-·pa'rade** Mode(n)schau *f*; '**fash·ion-plate** Modebild *n*.

fast¹ [fɑːst] fest (*a. Schlaf etc.*); schnell; *phot.* lichtstark; treu (*Freund*); waschecht (*Farbe*); leichtlebig, flott; ⁓ *to light* lichtecht; ⁓ *breeder phys.* schneller Brüter *m*; ⁓ *food* Schnellgerichte *n/pl.*; ⁓ *train* Schnellzug *m*; *my watch is* ⁓ meine Uhr geht vor.

fast² [⁓] **1.** Fasten *n*; **2.** fasten.

fast...: '⁓**back** *mot.* (Wagen *m* mit) Fließheck *n*; '⁓**day** Fasttag *m*.

fas·ten ['fɑːsn] *v t.* befestigen (*to* an *dat.*); anheften, -hängen (*to* an *acc.*); festmachen; fest zumachen; zubinden; *Augen etc.* heften (*on, upon* auf *acc.*); *v/i.* schließen (*Tür*); ⁓ *upon fig.* sich heften *od.* klammern an (*acc.*); '**fas·ten·er** Befestiger *m*; Verschluß *m*; Musterklammer *f*; *a.* '**fas·ten·ing** Schließe *f*; *patent* ⁓ Druckknopf *m* am *Kleid*.

fast-food re·stau·rant ['fɑːstfuːd 'restərɔ:n] Schnellgaststätte *f*.

fas·tid·i·ous □ [fəs'tidiəs] anspruchsvoll, heikel, eigen (*im Essen*), wählerisch, verwöhnt; **fas-'tid·i·ous·ness** wählerisches Wesen *n*, Verwöhntheit *f*.

fast·ness ['fɑːstnis] Festigkeit *f*; Schnelligkeit *f*; Leichtlebigkeit *f*;

✕ Feste *f*, fester Platz *m*.
fat [fæt] **1.** ☐ fett (*a. Boden*); dick; fettig; **2.** Fett *n*; *live on the ~ of the land* in Saus und Braus leben; *the ~ is in the fire* der Teufel ist los; **3.** fett machen *od.* werden; mästen.

fa·tal ☐ ['feitl] verhängnisvoll (*to* für); Schicksals...; tödlich; ~ *accident* tödlicher Unfall *m*; **fa·tal·ism** ['~təlizm] Fatalismus *m* (*Glaube an ein vorherbestimmtes Schicksal*); **'fa·tal·ist** Fatalist(in); **fa·tal·i·ty** [fə'tæliti] Verhängnis *n*; *das* Verhängnisvolle; Tödlichkeit *f*; Unglücks-, Todesfall *m*.

fate [feit] Schicksal *n*; Verhängnis *n*; Verderben *n*; *the ~s pl.* die Parzen *f/pl.*; **'fat·ed** vom Schicksal verhängt; dem Schicksal verfallen; **fate·ful** ☐ ['~ful] verhängnisvoll, schicksalhaft.

fa·ther ['fɑːðə] **1.** Vater *m*; **2.** der Urheber sein von; die Vater- *od.* Urheberschaft von ... anerkennen; die Vaterschaft von (*Kind*) *od.* Urheberschaft von (*et.*) *j-m* zuschreiben; *to ~ an article on* s.o. *j.* als Autor e-s Artikels hinstellen; **fa·ther·hood** ['~hud] Vaterschaft *f*; **'fa·ther-in-law** Schwiegervater *m*; **'fa·ther·land** Vaterland *n*; **'fa·ther·less** vaterlos; **'fa·ther·ly** väterlich.

fath·om ['fæðəm] **1.** Klafter *f* (*Maß*); ♣ Faden *m*; **2.** sondieren; ♣ loten; *fig.* ergründen; **'fath·om·less** unergründlich.

fa·tigue [fə'tiːg] **1.** Ermüdung *f*; Strapaze *f*; ✕ Arbeitsdienst *m*; *~s pl.* ✕ Arbeitsanzug *m*; **2.** ermüden; strapazieren; **fa'tigue--par·ty** ✕ Arbeitskommando *n*.

fat·ling ['fætliŋ] junges Mastvieh *n*; **'fat·ness** Fettigkeit *f*; Fettheit *f*; **'fat·ten** fett machen *od.* werden; mästen; *Boden* düngen; **'fat·ty 1.** fettig; Fett...; ~ *degeneration* Verfettung *f*; **2.** F Dickerchen *n*.

fa·tu·i·ty [fə'tjuːiti] Albernheit *f*; **fat·u·ous** ☐ ['fætjuəs] albern.

fau·cet *bsd. Am.* ['fɔːsit] (Zapf-) Hahn *m*.

faugh [fɔː] pfui!

fault [fɔːlt] Fehler *m* (*a. Tennis*); Defekt *m* (*a.* ✼, ⊕); ⊕ Störung *f*; Vergehen *n*, Versehen *n*; Schuld *f*; *geol.* Verwerfung *f*; *find ~ with et.*

auszusetzen haben an (*dat.*); *be at ~* auf falscher Fährte sein; *to a ~ fig.* übermäßig, zu (sehr); **'~-find·er** Besserwisser *m*, Nörgler *m*; **'~-find·ing 1.** krittelnd, nörgelnd; **2.** Nörgelei *f*, Krittelei *f*; **'fault·i·ness** Fehlerhaftigkeit *f*; **'fault·less** ☐ fehlerfrei, tadellos; **'faults·man** *teleph.* Störungssucher *m*; **'fault·y** ☐ fehlerhaft, mangelhaft.

faun [fɔːn] Faun *m*.

faun·a ['fɔːnə] Fauna *f*, Tierwelt *f*.

fa·vo(u)r ['feivə] **1.** Gunst(bezeigung) *f*; Gefallen *m*; Begünstigung *f*; Bandschleife *f als Abzeichen*; *in ~ of zugunsten von od. dat.; I am (not) in ~ of it* ich bin (nicht) dafür; *under ~ of night* unter dem Schutz der Nacht; *do s.o. a ~* j-m e-n Gefallen tun; **2.** begünstigen; beehren (*with* mit); *j-m* nachgeraten, -schlagen; **fa·vo(u)r·a·ble** ☐ ['~vərəbl] (*to*) günstig (für); gewogen (*dat.*); vorteilhaft (für); **'fa·vo(u)r·a·ble·ness** Gunst *f*; **fa·vo(u)red** ['~vəd] begünstigt; *most-~ nation clause* Meistbegünstigungsklausel *f*; **fa·vo(u)r·ite** ['~vərit] **1.** Lieblings-...; **2.** Günstling *m*; Liebling *m*; *Sport:* Favorit *m*; **'fa·vo(u)r·it·ism** Günstlingswirtschaft *f*; Favoritentum *n*.

fawn[1] [fɔːn] **1.** *zo.* (Dam)Kitz *n*; Rehbraun *n*; **2.** (Kitze) setzen.

fawn[2] [~] schwänzeln (*Hund*); *fig.* kriechen (*upon* vor *dat.*); **'fawn·er** Kriecher *m*; **'fawn·ing** kriecherisch.

fay *poet.* [fei] Fee *f*.

faze *bsd. Am.* F [feiz] *j.* durcheinanderbringen.

fe·al·ty ['fiːəlti] (Lehns)Treue *f*.

fear [fiə] **1.** Furcht *f* (*of* vor *dat.*); Befürchtung *f*; Grund *m* zur Furcht; *through od. from ~ of* aus Angst vor (*dat.*); *for ~ of doing* um nicht zu tun; *in ~ of one's life* um sein Leben besorgt; **2.** (be)fürchten; scheuen; sich fürchten (vor *dat.*); Angst haben; **fear·ful** ☐ ['~ful] furchtsam (*of* vor *dat.*); furchtbar; *be ~ that* Angst haben, daß; **'fear·ful·ness** Furchtsamkeit *f*; Furchtbarkeit *f*; **'fear·less** ☐ furchtlos (*of* vor *dat.*); **'fear·less·ness** Furchtlosigkeit *f*.

fea·si·bil·i·ty [fiːzə'biliti] Durchführbarkeit *f*; **'fea·si·ble** durch-, ausführbar.

feast [fi:st] **1.** Fest *n*; Feiertag *m*; Festmahl *n*, Schmaus *m*; **2.** *v/t.* festlich bewirten; ~ one's eyes on seine Augen weiden an (*dat.*); *v/i.* sich ergötzen (*upon* an *dat.*); schmausen (*on* von).

feat [fi:t] (Helden)Tat *f*; Kunststück *n*; Leistung *f*.

feath·er ['feðə] **1.** Feder *f*; *a.* ~*s pl.* Gefieder *n*; show the white ~ F sich feige zeigen; that is a ~ in his cap er kann sich et. darauf zugute tun; in high ~ in gehobener Stimmung; **2.** mit Federn versehen *od.* schmücken; ⚓ die Riemen platt werfen; ~ one's nest sich warm betten; '~-bed **1.** (*Feder*)Unterbett *n*; **2.** verwöhnen, verpäppeln; *j-m* das Leben leicht machen (*z. B.* durch Subventionen*); '~-brained, '~-head·ed unbesonnen; albern; 'feath·ered be-, gefiedert; 'feath·er-edge ⊕ scharfe Kante *f*; 'feath·er·ing Gefieder *n*; Federbesatz *m*; 'feath·er·stitch Stickerei: Grätenstich *m*; 'feath·er-weight Boxen: Federgewicht *n*; 'feath·er·y federig; federleicht.

fea·ture ['fi:tʃə] **1.** (Gesichts-, Grund-, Haupt-, Charakter)Zug *m*; Gesichtsteil *m*; (charakteristisches) Merkmal *n*, Besonderheit *f*; Hauptfilm *m*; *Radio:* Feature *n*; *Am.* Bericht *m*, Artikel *m*; ~*s pl.* Gesicht *n*; Gepräge *n*; Charakter *m*; **2.** kennzeichnen; sich auszeichnen durch; groß aufziehen; *Film:* (in der Hauptrolle) darstellen, gestalten; die Hauptrolle spielen in (*dat.*); a film featuring N. N. ein Film mit N. N. in der Hauptrolle; ~ film Haupt-, Spielfilm *m*; 'fea·ture·less ohne besondere Züge; eintönig.

feb·ri·fuge ['febrifju:dʒ] Fiebermittel *n*.

fe·brile ['fi:brail] fieberhaft.

Feb·ru·ar·y ['februəri] Februar *m*.

feck·less ['feklis] unfähig.

fe·cun·date ['fi:kəndeit] befruchten; **fe·cun'da·tion** Befruchtung *f*; **fe·cun·di·ty** [fi'kʌnditi] Fruchtbarkeit *f*.

fed [fed] *pret. u. p.p. von* feed 2.

Fed *Am.* F [fed] = Federal Reserve Board.

fed·er·al ['fedərəl] Bundes...; ℒ Reserve Board *Am.* Zentralbankrat *m*;

'fed·er·al·ism Föderalismus *m*; 'fed·er·al·ist Föderalist *m*; 'fed·er·al·ize (sich) verbünden; (sich) zu einem Staatenbund vereinigen; **fed·er·ate 1.** ['~reit] (sich) zu einem Bunde vereinigen; **2.** ['~rit] verbündet; Bundes...; **fed·er·a·tion** [~'reiʃən] (Staaten)Bund *m*, Föderation *f*; beruflicher etc. Verband *m*; **fed·er·a·tive** ['~rətiv] föderativ.

fee [fi:] **1.** Gebühr *f*; Schulgeld *n*; Honorar *n*; Gehalt *n*; Trinkgeld *n*; Entgelt *n*; Lohn *m*; Lehen *n*; Besitz *m*; ~ simple Eigengut *n*; **2.** bezahlen; honorieren; *j-m* ein Trinkgeld geben.

fee·ble □ ['fi:bl] schwach; '~-mind·ed geistesschwach; 'fee·ble·ness Schwäche *f*.

feed [fi:d] **1.** Futter *n*; Nahrung *f*; F Mahlzeit *f*; Futterration *f*, Fütterung *f*; ⊕ Vorschub *m*; ⊕ Zuführung *f*, Speisung *f*, (*a.* ✕) Ladung *f*; *attr.* Speise...; **2.** (*irr.*) *v/t.* füttern; speisen, (er)nähren; Auge weiden (*with* an *dat.*); Hoffnung etc. nähren; als Nahrung dienen (*dat.*); Maschine speisen; Material etc. zuführen; ~ o.s. selbst *od.* alleine essen; ~ off *od.* down abweiden; ~ up mästen; be fed up with et. *od. j.* satt haben; well fed wohlgenährt; *v/i.* fressen; essen, leben, sich nähren (*upon* von); '~back **1.** *Radio:* Rückkoppelung *f*; **2.** rückkoppeln; 'feed·er Fütterer *m*; *Am.* Viehmäster *m*; Esser(in); Fresser(in); Saugflasche *f*; (Kinder)Lätzchen *n*; ⊕ Zuführungsvorrichtung *f*, Speiseleitung *f*; Zuflußgraben *m*; 'feed·er line 🚂 Zubringerlinie *f*; 'feed·er road Zubringer(straße *f*) *m*; 'feed·ing Fütterung *f*; Mästung *f*; Fressen *n*, Essen *n*; *attr.* Futter...; ⊕ Speise...; high ~ Wohlleben *n*; ~ crane 🚂 Wasserkran *m*; 'feed·ing-bottle Saugflasche *f*; 'feed·ing-stuff Futtermittel *n*.

feel [fi:l] **1.** (*irr.*) *v/t.* fühlen; befühlen; empfinden, spüren; glauben; halten für; ✕ erkunden; *v/i.* fühlen, empfinden; sich fühlen (*P.*); sich anfühlen (*S.*); ~ bad about s.th. et. bedauern; ~ cold frieren; I ~ like doing ich habe Lust zu tun, ich möchte am liebsten tun; ~ for mit *j-m* fühlen; nach et. fühlen;

2. Gefühl(ssinn *m*) *n*; Empfindung *f*; '**feel·er** Fühler *m* (*a. fig.*); *zo.* Fühlhorn *n*; ⚒ Kundschafter *m*; '**feel·ing 1.** ☐ fühlend; gefühlvoll; mitfühlend; tief empfunden, lebhaft; **2.** Gefühl *n*; Meinung *f*; Erregung *f*; good ⁓ Entgegenkommen *n*.

feet [fiːt] *pl. von* foot.

feign [fein] heucheln; ⁓ *illness* Krankheit vortäuschen; ⁓ *to do* vorgeben zu tun; ⁓ *o.s. mad* sich wahnsinnig stellen; **feigned** vorgeblich; Schein...; **feign·ed·ly** ['⁓idli] zum Schein.

feint [feint] **1.** Verstellung *f*; Finte *f* (*a.* ⚔); **2.** ein Täuschungsmanöver machen.

feld·spar *min.* ['feldspaː] Feldspat *m*.

fe·lic·i·tate [fi'lisiteit] beglückwünschen (*on* zu); **fe·lic·i'ta·tion** Glückwunsch *m*; **fe'lic·i·tous** ☐ glücklich (gewählt), treffend; **fe·'lic·i·ty** Glück(seligkeit *f*) *n*; glücklicher Einfall *m*.

fe·line ['fiːlain] katzenartig, Katzen...

fell¹ [fel] **1.** *pret. von* fall 2; **2.** niederschlagen; fällen; umsäumen.

fell² *poet.* [⁓] grausam, grimmig.

fell³ [⁓] Fell *n*; (Haar)Schopf *m*.

fel·loe ['feləu] (Rad)Felge *f*.

fel·low ['feləu] Gefährte *m*, Gefährtin *f*, Kamerad(in); Gleiche *m*, *f u. n*; Gegenstück *n*; *univ.* Fellow *m*, Mitglied *n e-s College*; F Kerl *m*, Bursche *m*, Mensch *m*; *attr.* Mit...; Neben...; *a* ⁓ F eine(r), man; *old* ⁓ F alter Junge *m*; *the* ⁓ *of a glove* der andere Handschuh; *be* ⁓*s* zs.-gehören; *he has not his* ⁓ er hat nicht seinesgleichen; '⁓-'**be·ings** *pl.* Mitmenschen *m/pl.*; '⁓-'**cit·i·zen** Mitbürger *m*; '⁓-'**coun·try·man** Landsmann *m*; '⁓-'**crea·ture** Mitgeschöpf *n*; Mitmensch *m*; '⁓-'**feel·ing** Mitgefühl *n*; '⁓-'**pas·sen·ger** Mitreisende *m*, *f*; '⁓-**ship** Gemeinschaft *f*; Gesellschaft *f*; *a.* good ⁓ Kameradschaft *f*; Mitgliedschaft *f*; *univ.* Stelle *f od.* Einkommen *n e-s* Fellows; ⁓ **sol·dier** (Kriegs-)Kamerad *m*; '⁓-'**stu·dent** Studienkamerad *m*; '⁓-'**trav·el·ler** Mitreisende *m*, *f*; *pol.* Mitläufer *m*.

fel·ly ['feli] (Rad)Felge *f*.

fel·on ['felən] ⚖ Verbrecher *m*; ⚕ Nagelgeschwür *n*; **fe·lo·ni·ous** ☐

[fi'ləunjəs] verbrecherisch; mit böser Absicht; **fel·o·ny** ⚖ ['feləni] Kapitalverbrechen *n*.

fel·spar ['felspaː] = *feldspar*.

felt¹ [felt] *pret. u. p.p. von* feel 1.

felt² [⁓] **1.** Filz *m*; **2.** (be)filzen; (sich) verfilzen; ⁓**tip(ped) pen** ['⁓tip(t) pen] Filzstift *m*.

fe·male ['fiːmeil] **1.** weiblich; ⁓ *child* Mädchen *n*; ⁓ *screw* Schraubenmutter *f*; **2.** Weib *n*; Weibchen *n* *von Tieren*.

fem·i·nine ☐ ['feminin] weiblich (*a. gr.*); *contp.* weibisch; **fem·i·'nin·i·ty** Weiblichkeit *f*; weibliches *od. contp.* weibisches Wesen *n*; '**fem·i·nism** Frauenrechtlertum *n*; '**fem·i·nist** Frauenrechtler(in); **fem·i·nize** ['⁓naiz] weiblich (*contp.* weibisch) machen *od.* werden.

fe·mur *anat.* ['fiːmə] Oberschenkelknochen *m*.

fen [fen] Fenn *n*, Moor *n*; Marsch *f*.

fence [fens] **1.** Einzäunung *f*, Hecke *f*, Zaun *m*, Staket *n*; Hürde *f*; Fechtkunst *f*; *sl.* Hehler(nest *n*) *m*; *sit on the* ⁓ abwarten; **2.** *v/t. a.* ⁓ *in* einhegen, ein-, umzäunen; schützen (*from* vor *dat.*); *v/i.* fechten; *fig.* ausweichen (*with dat.*); *Sport:* e-e Hürde nehmen; *sl.* hehlen; '**fence·less** offen; schutzlos.

fenc·ing ['fensiŋ] Einhegung *f*, -fried(ig)ung *f*; Zaunmaterial *n*; Fechten *n*; *attr.* Fecht...; '⁓-**foil** Florett *n*; '⁓-**mas·ter** Fechtmeister *m*.

fend [fend]: ⁓ *off* abwehren; ⁓ *for* sorgen für; '**fend·er** Schutzvorrichtung *f*; Schutzblech *n*; Kamingitter *n*, -vorsetzer *m*; Stoßfänger *m*, Puffer *m*; ⚓ Fender *m*.

Fe·ni·an ['fiːnjən] **1.** fenisch; **2.** Fenier *m* (*Mitglied e-r irischen Unabhängigkeitspartei in USA*).

fen·nel ♣ ['fenl] Fenchel *m*.

fen·ny ['feni] moorig; Moor...

feoff [fef] Leh(e)n *n*; **feoff·ee** [fe'fiː] Belehnte *m*; '**feoff·ment** Belehnung *f*; **feof·for** [fe'fɔː] Lehnsherr *m*.

fer·ment 1. ['fəːmənt] Gärung(smittel *n*) *f*; Ferment *n*; **2.** [fəː-'ment] gären; in Gärung bringen (*a. fig.*); **fer'ment·a·ble** gärungsfähig; **fer·men'ta·tion** Gärung *f* (*a. fig.*); Unruhe *f*; **fer'ment·a-**

tive [ˌtɔtiv] Gärung erregend.

fern ♃ [fɔːn] Farn(kraut *n*) *m*.

fe·ro·cious □ [fɔˈrəuʃɔs] wild; grausam; **fe·roc·i·ty** [fɔˈrɔsiti] Wildheit *f*; Grausamkeit *f*.

fer·ret [ˈferit] **1.** *zo.* Frettchen *n*; *fig.* Spürhund *m*; **2.** *hunt.* frettieren; (umher)stöbern; ~ *out* aufstöbern; herausjagen; aufspüren.

fer·ric ⚗ [ˈferik] Eisen...; **fer·rif·er·ous** [feˈrifɔrɔs], **fer·ru·gi·nous** [feˈruːdʒinɔs] eisenhaltig; **fer·ro·-con·crete** ⊕ [ˈferɔuˈkɔŋkriːt] Eisenbeton *m*; **fer·rous** ⚗ [ˈferɔs] Eisen...

fer·rule [ˈferuːl] Zwinge *f*.

fer·ry [ˈferi] **1.** Fähre *f*; **2.** übersetzen; '~**·boat** Fährboot *n*, Fähre *f*; '**fer·ry·man** Fährmann *m*.

fer·tile □ [ˈfɔːtail] fruchtbar; reich (*of*, in an *dat.*) (*a. fig.*); **fer·til·i·ty** [fɔːˈtiliti] Fruchtbarkeit *f* (*a. fig.*); **fer·ti·li·za·tion** [ˌai'zeiʃɔn] Befruchtung *f*; (künstliche) Düngung *f*; '**fer·ti·lize** fruchtbar machen; *bsd. biol.* befruchten; düngen; '**fer·ti·liz·er** Düngemittel *n*, (Kunst-)Dünger *m*.

fer·ule [ˈferuːl] Lineal *n* *zur Züchtigung*; *fig.* Rute *f*.

fer·ven·cy [ˈfɔːvɔnsi] *mst fig.* Glut *f*; Inbrunst *f*; '**fer·vent** □ heiß; *fig.* inbrünstig, glühend.

fer·vid □ [ˈfɔːvid] = *fervent*.

fer·vo(u)r [ˈfɔːvɔ] Glut *f*; Inbrunst *f*.

fes·tal □ [ˈfestl] festlich.

fes·ter [ˈfestɔ] **1.** eitern (lassen); verfaulen; **2.** Geschwür *n*.

fes·ti·val [ˈfestɔvɔl] Fest *n*; Feier *f*; Festspiele *n/pl.*; **fes·tive** □ [ˈ~tiv] festlich; **fes'tiv·i·ty** Festlichkeit *f*; festliche Stimmung *f*.

fes·toon [fesˈtuːn] **1.** Girlande *f*; **2.** mit Girlanden schmücken.

fetch [fetʃ] holen; *Preis* erzielen, bringen; F reizen, fesseln; F *Schlag* versetzen; *Seufzer* ausstoßen; ~ *and carry for s.o.* j-s Diener sein; ~ *up* *Verlust* einholen; ausspeien; zum Stehen kommen; '**fetch·ing** F □ bezaubernd, reizend.

fête [feit] **1.** Fest(lichkeit *f*) *n*; *a.* ~*-day* Namenstag *m*; **2.** feiern.

fet·id □ [ˈfetid] stinkend.

fe·tish [ˈfiːtiʃ] Fetisch *m* (*a. fig.*).

fet·lock [ˈfetlɔk] Köte *f*, Fesse (-gelenk *n*) *f* *des Pferdes*.

fet·ter [ˈfetɔ] **1.** Fessel *f*; **2.** fesseln; *fig.* zügeln.

fet·tle [ˈfetl] Form *f*, Verfassung *f*; *in fine* ~ in Form.

feud [fjuːd] Fehde *f*; Leh(e)n *n*; **feu·dal** □ [ˈ~dl] lehnbar; Lehns...; **feu·dal·ism** [ˈ~dɔlizɔm] Lehnswesen *n*, Feudalismus *m*; **feu·dal·i·ty** [ˌ~ˈdæliti] Lehnbarkeit *f*; Lehnsverfassung *f*; **feu·da·to·ry** [ˈ~dɔtɔri] **1.** lehnspflichtig; **2.** Lehnsmann *m*.

fe·ver [ˈfiːvɔ] Fieber *n*; *fig.* Erregung *f*; '**fe·vered** *bsd. fig.* fiebernd; '**fe·ver·ish** □ fieberig; *fig.* fieberhaft, aufgeregt.

few [fjuː] wenige; *a* ~ einige, ein paar; *quite a* ~, *a good* ~ e-e ganze Menge; *the* ~ die Minderheit.

fi·an·cé(e *f*) [fiˈãːnsei] Verlobte *m*, *f*.

fi·as·co [fiˈæskɔu] Reinfall *m*, Mißerfolg *m*, Fiasko *n*.

fi·at [ˈfaiæt] Machtspruch *m*, Befehl *m*; ~ *money Am.* Papiergeld *n* (*ohne Deckung*).

fib F [fib] **1.** Flunkerei *f*, Schwindelei *f*; **2.** schwindeln, flunkern; '**fib·ber** Flunkerer *m*.

fi·bre [ˈfaibɔ] Fiber *f*, Faser *f*; Struktur *f*; Charakter(eigenschaft *f*) *m*; '~**·board** Hartfaserplatte *f*; '~**·glass** Glaswolle *f*; **fi·brin** [ˈ~brin] Fibrin *n*, Blutfaserstoff *m*; '**fi·brous** □ faserig; ~ *material* Spinnstoff *m*.

fib·u·la *anat.* [ˈfibjulɔ] Wadenbein *n*.

fick·le [ˈfikl] wankelmütig; unbeständig; '**fick·le·ness** Wankelmut *m*; Unbeständigkeit *f*.

fic·tion [ˈfikʃɔn] Erdichtung *f*; ♃ Fiktion *f*; Roman-, Unterhaltungsliteratur *f*, erzählende Literatur *f*; **fic·tion·al** □ [ˈ~ʃɔnl] erdichtet; Roman...

fic·ti·tious □ [fikˈtiʃɔs] unecht; erdichtet, erfunden, fiktiv; (nur) angenommen; Roman...; '**fic·tive** unecht, erfunden.

fid·dle [ˈfidl] **1.** Geige *f*, Fiedel *f*; **2.** *v/i.* fiedeln; tändeln; *v/t. sl.* *Steuererklärung etc.* frisieren; ~ *away* vergeuden; '**fid·dle·de·dee** [ˈ~diˈdiː] Unsinn *m*; **fid·dle·fad·dle** F [ˈ~fædl] **1.** Lappalie *f*; ~*!* Unsinn!; **2.** vertrödeln; '**fid·dler** Geiger(in); Spielmann *m*; *sl.* Steuerhinterzieher *m*; '**fid·dle·stick** Geigenbogen *m*; ~*s!* dummes Zeug!; '**fid·dling** läppisch, trivial.

fi·del·i·ty [fi'deliti] Treue *f* (*to* zu, gegen); Genauigkeit *f*.

fidg·et F ['fidʒit] **1.** *oft* ~s *pl.* nervöse Unruhe *f*; Zappelphilipp *m*; *have the* ~s kein Sitzfleisch haben; **2.** nervös machen *od.* sein; (um-her)zappeln; '**fidg·et·y** nervös, un-ruhig, kribbelig.

fi·du·ci·ar·y [fi'dju:ʃjəri] **1.** anver-traut; Vertrauens...; ✝ ungedeckt; **2.** Verwahrer *m*, Treuhänder *m*.

fie [fai] pfui!

fief [fi:f] Leh(e)n *n*.

field [fi:ld] **1.** Feld *n*; Wiese *f*; Schlachtfeld *n*; Spielfeld *n*, Spiel-platz *m*; Arbeitsfeld *n*, Gebiet *n*; Bereich *m*; *Sport*: Feld *n*, Teilneh-mer *m*/*pl.*; Besetzung *f*; *hold the* ~ das Feld behaupten; *take the* ~ ins Feld rücken; **2.** *Kricket*: Ball fan-gen u. zurückgeben; Fänger sein; '~-**day** ✕ Felddienstübung *f*; Parade *f*; *fig.* großer Tag *m*; *Am.* (Schul)Sportfest *n*; *Am.* Ex-kursionstag *m*; '**field·er** *Kricket*: Fänger *m*.

field...: ~ **e·vents** *pl.* Sprung- u. Wurfwettkämpfe *m*/*pl.*; '~-**fare** Wacholderdrossel *f*; '~-**glass·es** *pl.* Feldstecher *m*; '~-**gun** ✕ Feld-geschütz *n*; '~-**hos·pi·tal** ✕ Feld-lazarett *n*; '~-**mar·shal** Feld-marschall *m*; '~-**of·fi·cer** Stabs-offizier *m*; '~-**sports** *pl.* Jagen *n* u. Fischen *n*; '~-**work** praktische Arbeit *f*; Außendienst *m*.

fiend [fi:nd] böser Feind *m*, Teufel *m*; Unhold *m*; *Frischluft- etc.* Fa-natiker *m*; '**fiend·ish** ☐ teuflisch, boshaft.

fierce ☐ [fiəs] wild; grimmig; hitzig; heftig; '**fierce·ness** Wild-heit *f*; Grimm *m*; Ungestüm *n*.

fi·er·i·ness ['faiərinis] Hitze *f*, Feuer *n*; '**fi·er·y** ☐ feurig, glühend; hitzig; feuergefährlich; Feuer...

fife [faif] **1.** Querpfeife *f*; **2.** auf der Querpfeife blasen; '**fif·er** Pfeifer *m*.

fif·teen ['fif'ti:n] fünfzehn; '**fif-'teenth** [~θ] fünfzehnte(r, -s); **fifth** [fifθ] **1.** fünfte(r, -s); **2.** Fünf-tel *n*; **fifth col·umn** *pol.* Fünfte Kolonne *f*; '**fifth·ly** fünftens; **fif·ti·eth** ['~tiiθ] **1.** fünfzigste(r, -s); **2.** Fünfzigstel *n*; '**fif·ty** fünfzig; '**fif·ty-'fif·ty** F zu gleichen Teilen, halb und halb; *go* ~ halbe halbe machen.

fig[1] [fig] Feige *f*; *a* ~ *for* ...! zum Teufel mit ...!; *I don't care a* ~ *for him* ich mache mir gar nichts aus ihm.

fig[2] [~] **1.** F Zustand *m*, Form *f*; *in full* ~ in vollem Wichs; **2.** ~ *out* F herausputzen.

fight [fait] **1.** Kampf *m*; Faust-kampf *m*; Schlägerei *f*; Kampflust *f*, -geist *m*; Gefecht *n*; *make a* ~ *for* kämpfen für *od.* um; *put up a good* ~ sich wacker schlagen; *show* ~ sich zur Wehr setzen; **2.** (*irr.*) *v*/*t.* bekämpfen, sich schlagen mit, kämpfen mit *od.* gegen; verfechten; erkämpfen; ✕ (im Kampf) führen; ~ *off* abwehren; ~ *one's way* sich durchschlagen; *v*/*i.* sich schlagen, kämpfen, fechten; ~ *against s.th.* et. bekämpfen, gegen et. an-kämpfen; ~ *back* zurückschlagen; ~ *shy of j-m* aus dem Wege gehen; '**fight·er** Kämpfer *m*, Fechter *m*, Streiter *m*; ✕ Jagdflugzeug *n*; ~ *pilot* Jagdflieger *m*; '**fight·ing** Kampf *m*, Gefecht *n*; *attr.* Kampf-...; ~ *chance* Erfolgschance *f bei großer Anstrengung*.

fig·ment ['figmənt] reine Erfin-dung *f*.

fig-tree ['figtri:] Feigenbaum *m*.

fig·u·rant(e *f*) ['figjurənt; (~'rɑ:nt)] Ballettänzer(in); Statist(in).

fig·u·ra·tion [figju'reiʃən] Gestal-tung *f*; **fig·ur·a·tive** ☐ ['~rətiv] bildlich, figürlich, übertragen; bil-derreich.

fig·ure ['figə] **1.** Figur *f* (*a.* ⚥), Ge-stalt *f*; Zahl *f*, Ziffer *f*; Preis *m*; ~ *of speech* Redefigur *f*, bildlicher Ausdruck *m*; *what's the* ~? was kostet es?; *at a high* ~ zu e-m hohen Preis; *be good at* ~s gut im Rechnen sein; **2.** *v*/*t.* abbilden, darstellen; *a.* ~ *to o.s.* sich et. vorstellen; mit Zahlen bezeichnen; ~ *up od. out* berechnen; ~ *out* sich *et.* ausmalen *od.* ausdenken; verstehen; *v*/*i.* er-scheinen, e-e Rolle spielen (*as* als); ~ *on Am. et.* überdenken, rechnen auf *od.* mit; ~ *out at* sich beziffern auf (*acc.*); '~-**head** ⚓ Galionsfigur *f*; *fig.* Aushängeschild *n*; '~-**skat-ing** Eiskunstlauf *m*.

fig·u·rine ['figjuri:n] Statuette *f*.

fil·a·ment ['filəmənt] Faden *m*, Faser *f*; ⚜ Staubfaden *m*; ⚡ Glüh-, Heizfaden *m*.

fil·a·ture ['filətʃə] Seidenspinnerei *f.*
fil·bert ♀ ['filbə:t] Haselnuß *f.*
filch [filtʃ] stibitzen *(from dat.)*.
file¹ [fail] **1.** Akte *f*, Ordner *m*;
Reihe *f*; ✕ Rotte *f*; *on* ~ bei den
Akten; aktenkundig; **2.** *v/t.* aufreihen; *Briefe etc.* einordnen; zu
den Akten nehmen, ablegen; *Klage
etc.* einreichen; *v/i.* ✕ hintereinander marschieren; ~ *in* (*out*) hintereinander hereinkommen (hinausgehen).
file² [⌐] **1.** Feile *f*; **2.** feilen.
fil·i·al [⌐] ['filjəl] kindlich, Kindes...;
fil·i·a·tion [fili'eiʃən] Kindschaft *f*;
Abstammung *f*; Abzweigung *f*,
Zweig *m.*
fil·i·bus·ter ['filibʌstə] **1.** *Am.* Ob-
struktion(spolitiker *m*) *f*; **2.** *Am.*
Obstruktion treiben.
fil·i·gree ['filigri:] Filigran(arbeit *f*)
n.
fil·ing cab·i·net ['failiŋkæbinit] Ak-
tenschrank *m.*
fil·ings ['failiŋz] *pl.* Feilspäne *m/pl.*
fill [fil] **1.** (sich) füllen; voll werden;
an-, aus-, erfüllen; (voll)stopfen;
Zahn plombieren; *Stelle etc.* bekleiden, einnehmen, ausfüllen, innehaben; *Am.* Auftrag ausführen;
~ *in Lücke, Scheck etc.* ausfüllen;
einsetzen; ~ *out* sich füllen; stärker
werden; ~ *up* ausfüllen; zuschütten;
sich füllen; **2.** Fülle *f*, Genüge *f*;
Füllung *f*; *eat* (*drink*) *one's* ~ sich
satt essen (trinken) *(of an dat.)*.
fill·er ['filə] Füller *m*; Trichter *m.*
fil·let ['filit] **1.** Haarband *n*; Lenden-
braten *m*, Filet *n*; Roulade *f*; Band
n, Leiste *f* (*bsd.* △); *tel.* Papierstreifen *m*; **2.** mit e-m Haarband
etc. schmücken.
fill·ing ['filiŋ] Füllung *f*; ~ **sta·tion**
Am. Tankstelle *f.*
fil·lip ['filip] **1.** Schnippchen *n mit
dem Finger*; Nasenstüber *m*; Anregung *f*; **2.** einen Nasenstüber
geben *(dat.)*; antreiben.
fil·ly ['fili] (Stuten)Füllen *n*; *fig.*
wilde Hummel *f.*
film [film] Häutchen *n*; Schicht *f*,
Überzug *m*; Membran(e) *f*; *Zahn-
etc.* Belag *m*; *phot. u. thea.* Film *m*;
Trübung *f des Auges*; Nebel-
schleier *m*; Fädchen *n*; *take od.*
shoot a ~ e-n Film drehen; **2.** (sich)
mit einem Häutchen überziehen;
verschleiern; (ver)filmen; **'film·y** □

häutig; trüb; hauchdünn.
fil·ter ['filtə] **1.** Filter *m*; **2.** filtrieren;
durchsickern; ~ *in mot.* sich einord-
nen; **'fil·ter·ing** Filtrier...; **'fil·ter
tip** Filtermundstück *n e-r Zigarette.*
filth [filθ] Schmutz *m*; *bsd. fig.* Unflat *m*; **'filth·y** □ schmutzig; unflätig.   [tion Filtrierung *f.*\
fil·trate ['filtreit] filtrieren; **fil'tra-**⌐
fin [fin] Flosse *f* (*sl. Hand*); 🐟
Steuerflosse *f*; *mot.* Kühlrippe *f.*
fi·nal ['fainl] **1.** □ letzt, endlich;
schließlich; End...; endgültig, entscheidend; *gr.* Absichts...; **2.** *a.* ~*s*
pl. Schlußprüfung *f*; *Sport*: Schluß-
runde *f*; **fi·na·le** [fi'nɑ:li] Finale *n*,
Schluß(satz *m*, -szene *f*) *m*; **fi·nal-**
ist ['fainəlist] *Sport*: Schlußrunden-
teilnehmer *m*; **fi·nal·i·ty** [⌐'næliti]
Endgültigkeit *f*; **fi·nal·ize** ['⌐nəlaiz]
abschließen; endgültige Form ge-
ben *(dat.)*; **fi·nal whis·tle** *Sport*:
Schluß-, Abpfiff *m.*
fi·nance [fai'næns] **1.** Finanzwesen
n; ~*s pl.* Finanzen *pl.*, Vermögens-
lage *f*; **2.** *v/t.* finanzieren; *v/i.* Geld-
geschäfte machen; **fi'nan·cial** □
[⌐ʃəl] finanziell; ~ *year* Rechnungs-,
Geschäftsjahr *n*; **fi'nan·cier** [⌐siə]
Finanzier *m*; Geldgeber *m.*
finch *orn.* [fintʃ] Fink *m.*
find [faind] **1.** *(irr.)* finden; (an)tref-
fen; auf-, herausfinden; ⚖ *schuldig
etc.* befinden, erklären, stellen, stellen; versorgen (*in* mit); ~ *o.s.* sich
(be)finden; seine Fähigkeiten erkennen; *all found* freie Station; ~
out herausfinden; ertappen; *I cannot* ~ *it in my heart* ich kann es nicht
übers Herz bringen; **2.** Fund *m*;
'find·er Finder(in); *opt.* Sucher *m*;
'find·ing Entdeckung *f*; *a.* ~*s pl.*
Befund *m*; ⚖ Wahrspruch *m*, Urteil *n.*
fine¹ □ [fain] **1.** schön; fein; verfeinert; rein; spitz, dünn, scharf;
geziert; vornehm; *you are a* ~ *fellow!*
iro. du bist mir ein sauberer Kerl!;
~ *arts pl.* schöne Künste *f/pl.*; **2.** *adv.*
gut, bestens; *cut* ~ *Preis, Zeit* zu
knapp berechnen; **3.** *meteor.* Schön-
wetter *n*; **4.** (sich) klären (*bsd. Bier*);
~ *away*, ~ *down*, ~ *off* abschleifen;
zuspitzen.
fine² [⌐] **1.** Geldstrafe *f*; Abstands-
summe *f*; *in* ~ kurzum; **2.** zu e-r
Geldstrafe verurteilen; ~ *s.o. 5 sh.*
j. zu 5 Schilling Geldstrafe verur-

teilen.

fine-draw ['fain'drɔː] kunststopfen.

fine·ness ['fainnis] Feinheit *f etc.*
(*s. fine¹*); Feingehalt *m*; Reinheit
f.

fin·er·y ['fainəri] Glanz *m*; Putz *m*,
Staat *m*; ⊕ Frischofen *m.*

fi·nesse [fi'nes] Finesse *f*, Schlauheit *f*, Spitzfindigkeit *f.*

fin·ger ['fiŋgə] **1.** Finger *m*; *have a ~
in the pie* die Hand im Spiel haben;
s. end 1; **2.** befingern, betasten,
(herum)fingern an (*dat.*); ♪ mit
Fingersatz versehen; spielen; üben;
'**~-al·pha·bet** Fingeralphabet *n*;
'**~-board** ♪ Griffbrett *n*; '**~-bowl**
Fingerschale *f*; '**fin·gered** ...finge-
rig; '**fin·ger·ing** Betasten *n*; ♪ Fingersatz *m*; Strumpfwolle *f.*

fin·ger...: '**~-lan·guage** Zeichen-
sprache *f*; '**~-mark** Fingerabdruck
m; '**~-nail** Fingernagel *m*; '**~-plate**
Türschoner *m*; '**~-post** Wegweiser
m; '**~-print 1.** Fingerabdruck *m*;
2. *j-s* Fingerabdruck nehmen; '**~-
-stall** Fingerling *m.*

fin·i·cal □ ['finikəl], **fin·ick·ing**
['~iŋ], '**fin·ick·y** geziert; wählerisch;
knifflig; pedantisch.

fin·ish ['finiʃ] **1.** *v/t.* beenden, vollenden; fertigstellen; abschließen; *a.
~ off, ~ up* vervollkommnen; ⊕ fer-
tig(bearbeit)en; ⊕ appretieren; aufhören mit; erledigen; *~ed goods pl.*
Fertigwaren *f/pl.*; *~ing line Sport:*
Ziel(linie *f*) *n*; *~ing touch* letzter
Schliff *m*; *v/i.* enden, aufhören; *have
~ed* fertig sein; **2.** Vollendung *f*, letzte
Hand *f*; Schluß *m*; Entscheidung *f*;
⊕ Appretur *f*; *Sport:* Ziel *n*; '**fin-
ish·er** Fertigsteller *m*; ⊕ Appretierer
m; entscheidender Schlag *m.*

fi·nite □ ['fainait] endlich, begrenzt;
~ verb gr. Verbum *n* finitum; '**fi-
nite·ness** Endlichkeit *f.*

fink *Am. sl.* [fiŋk] Streikbrecher *m.*

Finn [fin] Finne *m*, Finnin *f.*

Finn·ish ['finiʃ] **1.** finnisch; **2.** Finnisch *n.*

fin·ny ['fini] mit Flossen (versehen).

fiord [fjɔːd] Fjord *m.*

fir [fəː] (Weiß)Tanne *f*; *Scotch ~*
Föhre *f*, Kiefer *f*; '**~-cone** Tannen-
zapfen *m.*

fire ['faiə] **1.** Feuer *n*, Brand *m*; Glanz
m; Glut *f*, Heftigkeit *f*; *on ~* in Feuer,
in Brand, in Flammen; *come under ~
from s.o. fig.* in j-s Schußlinie geraten;

lay a ~ ein Feuer anlegen; *set ~ to* in
Brand stecken, anzünden; **2.** *v/t.* an-,
entzünden; *fig.* anfeuern; *a. ~ off*
abfeuern; *Ziegel etc.* brennen; röten;
F rausschmeißen (*entlassen*); *~*
anfeuern, -heizen; *v/i.* Feuer fangen
(*a. fig.*); feuern (*at, upon* auf *acc*); sich
röten; *~ away!* F schieß los!; *~ up*
auffahren (*at über acc.*); '**~-a·larm**
Feuermelder *m*; '**~-arms** *pl.* Schuß-,
Feuerwaffen *f/pl.*; '**~-ball** Meteor *m*;
Feuerball *m e-r Atomexplosion*; '**~-
-bomb** Brandbombe *f*; '**~-box** ⊕
Feuerbüchse *f*; '**~-brand** Feuer-
brand *m; fig.* Aufwiegler *m*; '**~-break**
Schneise *f*; Brandmauer *f*; '**~-brick**
feuerfester Stein *m*; '**~-bri·gade**
Feuerwehr *f*; '**~-bug** *Am.* F Brandstifter *m*; '**~-clay** feuerfester Ton *m*;
'**~-con·trol** ⚔ Feuerleitung *f*; '**~-
crack·er** Frosch *m* (*Feuerwerkskör-
per*); '**~-damp** ⚒ schlagendes Wetter *n*; '**~-de·part·ment** *Am.* Feuerwehr *f*; '**~-dog** Feuerbock *m*; '**~-door**
Feuerschutztür *f*; '**~-drill** Feuerlösch-
übung *f*; '**~-eat·er** Raufbold *m*,
Kampfhahn *m*; '**~-en·gine** ⊕
(Feuer)Spritze *f*; '**~-es·cape** Ret-
tungsgerät *n*, -tuch *n*, -leiter *f*; Nott-
treppe *f*; '**~-ex·tin·guish·er** Feuer-
löscher *m*; '**~-fight·er** Brandschüt-
zer *m*, Feuerwehrmann *m bsd. bei
Waldbränden u. im Krieg*; '**~-fly**
Leuchtkäfer *m*; '**~-guard** Kamingitter *n*; Brandwache *f*; '**~-in·sur·ance**
Feuerversicherung *f*; '**~-i·rons** *pl.*
Kamingerät *n*; '**~-light·er** Kohlen-
anzünder *m*; '**~-man** Feuerwehrmann *m*; Heizer *m*; '**~-of·fice** Feuer-
versicherungsanstalt *f*; '**~-place**
Feuerstelle *f*; Feuerherd *m*; Kamin
m; '**~-pow·er** ⚔ Feuerkraft *f*;
'**~-plug** Hydrant *m*; '**~-proof** feuerfest; '**~-rais·ing** Brandstiftung *f*;
'**~-screen** Ofenschirm *m*; '**~-side 1.**
Kamin *m*; Häuslichkeit *f*; **2.** häuslich; '**~-sta·tion** Feuerwache *f*;
'**~-wood** Brennholz *n*; '**~-work(s** *pl.*
fig.) Feuerwerk *n.*

fir·ing ['faiəriŋ] Heizung *f*; Feuerung *f*; ⚔ Feuern *n*; '**~-line** vorderster Graben *m*; '**~-par·ty**,
squad ⚔ Exekutionskommando *n.*

fir·kin ['fəːkin] Viertelfaß *n*; (*But-
ter- etc.*)Fäßchen *n.*

firm [fəːm] **1.** □ fest; derb; standhaft; entschlossen; **2.** Firma *f.*

fir·ma·ment ['fəːməmənt] Firma-

fix

ment *n*, Himmelsgewölbe *n*.
firm·ness ['fə:mnis] Festigkeit *f*,
Entschlossenheit *f*.
first [fə:st] **1.** *adj.* erste(r, -s); beste(r,
-s); *at ~ hand* aus erster Hand, direkt;
at ~ sight auf den ersten Blick; *~ strike*
※ Erstangriff *m*; **2.** *adv.* erstens;
zuerst; *at ~* zuerst, anfangs; *~ of all* an
erster Stelle; *zu allererst; ~ and last*
alles in allem; **3.** Erste *m, f u. n; ~ of
exchange* ✝ Primawechsel *m; from the
~* von Anfang an; *go ~* vorangehen; 🚗
erster Klasse fahren; *~ aid* 🏥 Erste
Hilfe *f*; '*~-'aid box* Verbandkasten
m; '*~-'aid post* Unfallstation *f*;
'*~-born* erstgeboren; *~ class* 1.
Klasse *f (e-s Verkehrsmittels)*; '*~-
-'class* erstklassig, prima; '*~-fruits*
pl. Erstlinge *m/pl.*; Erstlingswerk *n*;
'*~-'hand* aus erster Hand, direkt;
'**first·ly** erstlich; erstens.
first...: *~ name* Vorname *m*; Beiname
m; ~ pa·pers pl. Am. vorläufige Ein-
bürgerungspapiere *n/pl.*; '*~-'rate* ersten Ranges; *= first-class*; '*~-time*
vot·er *pol.* Erstwähler(in).
firth [fə:θ] Förde *f*; (Flut)Mündung *f*.
fis·cal ['fiskəl] fiskalisch; Finanz...
fish [fiʃ] **1.** Fisch *m*; *coll.* Fische
m/pl.; 🚃 (Schienen)Lasche *f*; F
Kerl *m; odd ~ komischer Kauz m;
have other ~ to fry* Wichtigeres zu
tun haben; *a pretty kettle of ~* ein
hübsches Durcheinander *n*; **2.**
fischen; angeln; haschen *(for nach)*;
🚃 verlaschen; *~ out* herausholen; *~
in troubled waters* im trüben fischen;
'*~-bone* Gräte *f*; '*~-cake* Fischfrika-
delle *f*.
fish·er ['fiʃə], **fish·er·man** ['~mən]
Fischer *m*; '**fish·er·y** Fischerei *f*.
fish...: '*~-eye lens phot.* Fischauge *n*,
extremes Weitwinkelobjektiv *n; ~
fin·ger Fischstäbchen *n*; *~-hatch-*
er·y ['fiʃhætʃəri] Fischzuchtanstalt *f*.
fish-hook ['fiʃhuk] Angelhaken *m*.
fish·ing ['fiʃiŋ] Fischen *n*, Angeln *n*;
'*~-boat* Fischerboot *n*; '*~-line* An-
gelschnur *f*; '*~-rod* Angelrute *f*;
'*~-tack·le* Angelgerät *n*.
fish...: '*~-liv·er oil* Lebertran *m*;
'*~-mon·ger* Fischhändler *m; ~ stick*
Am. Fischstäbchen *n*; '*~-wife* Fisch-
weib *n*; '**fish·y** fisch(art)ig; fisch-
reich; trüb *(Auge)*; F verdächtig, faul.
fis·sile ['fisail] spaltbar.
fis·sion ['fiʃən] Spaltung *f; s. atomic*; **fis·sure** ['fiʃə] **1.** Spalt *m*, Riß *m*;

2. spalten.
fist [fist] Faust *f*; F Klaue *f (Hand;
Handschrift)*; **fist·i·cuffs** ['~ikʌfs]
pl. Faustschläge *m/pl.*
fis·tu·la ['fistjulə] Fistel *f*.
fit¹ [fit] **1.** □ geeignet, passend *(for
für)*; schicklich, tauglich; fähig;
Sport: in (guter) Form, auf der
Höhe, fit; bereit *(to zu)*; *it is not ~*
es ziemt sich nicht; *~ as a fiddle*
quietschvergnügt; kerngesund; **2.**
v/t. passen für *od. dat.*; anpassen,
passend machen; befähigen; geeignet machen *(for, to für, zu)*; ⊕
a. ~ in einpassen; *a. ~ on* anprobieren; versehen, ausstatten *(with
mit)*; *~ out* ausrüsten; *~ up* einrichten, ausstatten; montieren; *v/i.*
passen; sich eignen; sich schicken
od. gehören; sitzen *(Kleid)*; **3.** Sitz
m e-s Kleides; it is a bad ~ es sitzt
schlecht.
fit² [~] Anfall *m*; Ausbruch *m e-r
Krankheit;* Anwandlung *f; by ~s
and starts* ruckweise; dann und
wann; *give s.o. a ~* j. hochbringen;
j-m e-n Schock versetzen.
fitch·ew *zo.* ['fitʃu:] Iltis *m*.
fit·ful □ ['fitful] ruck-, krampfartig;
fig. unstet, unregelmäßig, launenhaft; '**fit·ment** Einrichtungsgegen-
stand *m; ~s pl.* Einrichtung *f*; '**fitness** Schicklichkeit *f*; Tauglichkeit *f*,
Eignung *f; ~ trail Am.* Trimmpfad *m*;
'**fit-out** Ausstattung *f*; '**fit·ted** ausgestattet *(with mit); ~ carpet* Teppichboden *m; ~ cupboard* Einbauschrank
m; ~ sheet Spannbettuch *n*; '**fit·ter**
Monteur *m*; Einrichter *m*; Installateur *m*; Zuschneider *m*; '**fit·ting 1.** □
passend, geeignet, angemessen;
schicklich; **2.** Montage *f*; Anprobe *f*;
~s pl. Einrichtung *f e-s Hauses etc.*;
Armaturen *f/pl.*; Beleuchtungskörper *m pl.*; '**fit-up** F provisorische
Bühne *f; a. ~ company* Wanderbühne
f.
five [faiv] **1.** fünf; **2.** Fünf *f; ~s sg.*
Wandball(spiel *n) m*; '**five·fold**
fünffach; **fiv·er** F ['~və] Fünf-
pfundnote *f*.
fix [fiks] **1.** befestigen, anheften;
phot. etc., j. mit den Augen fixieren;
Augen etc. heften, richten *(on auf
acc.)*; fesseln; fest werden lassen;
aufstellen, unterbringen; bestimmen, festsetzen; anberaumen; *bsd.
Am.* F (her)richten, *Bett etc.* ma-

chen; ~ o.s. sich niederlassen; ~ up in Ordnung bringen, arrangieren; unterbringen; v/i. fest werden; ~ on sich entschließen für; **2.** F Klemme f, Patsche f, Verlegenheit f; **fix'a-tion** Fixierung f; **fix·a·tive** ['~ətiv], **fix·a·ture** ['~ətʃə] Fixiermittel n; **fixed** fest (a. ⚓); bestimmt (Summe etc.); starr (Blick); **fixed i·de·a** psych. fixe Idee f; **'fixed--'in·ter·est** festverzinslich; **fix·ed·ly** ['fiksidli] bestimmt; ständig; starr; **'fix·ed·ness** Festigkeit f (a. fig.); **fixed star** Fixstern m; **'fix·er** phot. Fixierbad n; **'fix·ing** Befestigen n etc.; ~s pl. Am. Zubehör n, Extraausrüstung f, -sachen f/pl.; Garnierung f; **'fix·i·ty** Festigkeit f; **fix·ture** ['~tʃə] fest angebrachtes Zubehörteil n, feste Anlage f; Inventarstück n (a. fig. Person); Sport: zeitlich festgesetzte Veranstaltung f; ~s pl. Einrichtungsstücke n/pl., festes Inventar n, Zubehör n; lighting ~ Beleuchtungskörper m.

fizz [fiz] **1.** zischen, sprudeln; **2.** Zischen n; F Schampus m (Sekt); **fizzle** ['fizl] **1.** zischen, sprühen; mst ~ out verpuffen; mißglücken; **2.** Zischen n; Fiasko n, Pleite f; **'fiz·zy** sprudelnd, mit Kohlensäure (versetzt).

flab·ber·gast F ['flæbəgɑ:st] verblüffen; be ~ed baff od. platt sein.

flab·by ☐ ['flæbi] schlaff, schlapp.

flac·cid ☐ ['flæksid] schlaff, schlapp.

flag¹ [flæg] **1.** Flagge f; Fahne f; Fähnchen n; black ~ Seeräuberflagge f; ~ of convenience billige Flagge f; **2.** beflaggen; durch Flaggen signalisieren.

flag² [~] **1.** Fliese f; **2.** mit Fliesen belegen.

flag³ ♀ [~] Schwertlilie f.

flag⁴ [~] ermatten; mutlos werden.

flag-cap·tain ⚓ ['flæg'kæptin] Kommandant m e-s Flaggschiffs.

flag-day ['flægdei] Opfertag m; Am. Flag Day Tag m des Sternenbanners (14. Juni).

flag·el·lant ['flædʒilənt] Flagellant m; **flag·el·late** ['~dʒeleit] geißeln; **flag·el·la·tion** Geißelung f.

flag·eo·let ♪ [flædʒəu'let] Flageolett n.

fla·gi·tious ☐ [flə'dʒiʃəs] abscheulich, schändlich, kriminell.

flag·on ['flægən] (Deckel)Kanne f;

Bocksbeutel m.

flag·post ['flægpəust] Fahnenstange f.

fla·grant ☐ ['fleigrənt] abscheulich; berüchtigt; offenkundig.

flag...: '~·ship Flaggschiff n; '~·staff Fahnenstange f, -mast m; ⚓ Flaggenstock m; '~·stone (Stein-) Fliese f.

flail ✗ [fleil] Dreschflegel m.

flair [flɛə] Spürsinn m, feine Nase f.

flake [fleik] **1.** Flocke f; Schicht f; **2.** (sich) flocken; abblättern; **'flak·y** flockig, schuppig.

flam F [flæm] Schwindel m, fauler Zauber m.

flam·beau ['flæmbəu] Fackel f.

flam·boy·ant [flæm'bɔiənt] farbenprächtig; pompös; auffallend.

flame [fleim] **1.** Flamme f, Feuer n; fig. Hitze f, Leidenschaft f; Geliebte m, f; **2.** flammen, lodern (a. fig.); ~ out, ~ up aufflammen; **'flam·ing** flammend, glühend, zündend (a. fig.).

fla·min·go orn. [flə'miŋgəu] Flamingo m.

flam·ma·ble (bsd. Am.) ['flæməbl] feuergefährlich.

flan [flæn] Obstkuchen m.

flange ⊕ [flændʒ] Flansch m.

flank [flæŋk] **1.** Flanke f; Weiche f der Tiere; **2.** flankieren.

flan·nel ['flænl] Flanell m; Waschlappen m; **flan·nel·ette** [~'et] Baumwollflanell m; **'flan·nels** pl. Flanellunterwäsche f, -anzug m, -hose f.

flap [flæp] **1.** (Ohr)Läppchen n; Rockschoß m; Hut-Krempe f; Klappe f; Lasche f; Klaps m; (Flügel)Schlag m; F nervöse Aufregung f; be (get) in a ~ aus dem Häuschen sein (geraten); **2.** v t. klatschen(d schlagen), klapsen (mit); v i. lose herabhängen; flattern; **'flap·jack** Pfannkuchen m; **'flap·per** Flosse f; Fliegenklatsche f; Klapper f; sl. Backfisch m; = flap 1.

flare [flɛə] **1.** flackern; sich nach außen erweitern, sich bauschen; ~ up aufflammen; fig. aufbrausen; **2.** flackerndes Licht n; Lichtsignal n, Leuchtkugel f; '~-'up Aufflackern n; fig. Aufbrausen n.

flash [flæʃ] **1.** aufgedonnert; unecht, falsch; Gauner...; **2.** Blitz m; fig. Aufblitzen n, Auflodern n; bsd.

flexor

Am. Zeitung: kurze Meldung *f*; *in a* ~ im Nu, sofort; ~ *of* wit Geistesblitz *m*; ~ *in the pan* Schlag *m* ins Wasser; **3.** blitzen; aufblitzen, auflodern (lassen); *Licht, Blick etc.* werfen; flitzen; funken, telegraphieren; *it* ~*ed on me* mir kam plötzlich der Gedanke; '~**-back** *Film:* Rückblende *f*; '~**-bulb** *phot.* Blitzlicht(lampe *f*) *n*; '~**-cube** *phot.* Blitzwürfel *m*.

flash·er ['flæʃə] *mot.* Lichthupe *f*; F Exhibitionist *m*.

flash...: '~**-gun** *phot.* Blitzgerät *n*; '~**-light** *phot.* Blitzlicht *n*; Blinklicht *n*; *bsd. Am.* Taschenlampe *f*; '~**-point** Flammpunkt *m*; '**flash·y** □ auffallend; aufdringlich, grell.

flask [flɑːsk] Taschen-, Reiseflasche *f*; ⚗ Kolben *m*.

flat [flæt] **1.** □ flach, platt; schal, matt; ♯ flau; klar; glatt (*Lüge etc.*); ♪ um e-n Halbton erniedrigt (*Note*); *Börse*: ohne Zinsenberechnung; ~ *price* Einheitspreis *m*; *fall* ~ danebengehen; *sing* ~ zu tief singen; **2.** Fläche *f*, Ebene *f*; Flachland *n*; Untiefe *f*; flache Seite *f e-s Schwertes*; (Etagen-, Miet)Wohnung *f*; ⚓ Prahm *m*; ♪ B *n*; F Schwachkopf *m*, Simpel *m*; *mot. sl.* Plattfuß *m* (*luftleerer Reifen*); '~**-boat** ⚓ Prahm *m*; '~**-foot** Plattfuß *m*; *Am. sl.* Polyp *m* (*Polizist*); '~**-'foot·ed** plattfüßig; *Am.* F geradeheraus, kompromißlos; '~**-i·ron** Bügeleisen *n*; **flat·let** ['~lit] kleine Wohnung *f*; '**flat·ness** Flachheit *f*; *fig.* Plattheit *f*; ♯ Flauheit *f*; **flat out** F **1.** *adv.* auf Hochtouren; *work* ~ mit Volldampf arbeiten; **2.** *adj.* abgeschlafft (*total erschöpft*); '**flat·ten** (sich) ab-, verflachen; ~ *out* flach *od.* eben werden; *Flugzeug* abfangen.

flat·ter ['flætə] schmeicheln (*dat.*); '**flat·ter·er** Schmeichler(in); '**flat·ter·ing** schmeichelhaft; '**flat·ter·y** Schmeichelei *f*.

flat·u·lence, flat·u·len·cy ['flætjuləns(i)] Blähung *f*; Aufgeblähtheit *f*; '**flat·u·lent** □ blähend; aufgebläht.

flaunt [flɔːnt] prunken (mit); offen zeigen; prangen.

flau·tist ['flɔːtist] Flötist(in).

fla·vo(u)r ['fleivə] **1.** Geschmack *m*; Aroma *n*; Blume *f des Weines*; *fig.* Beigeschmack *m*; Würze *f*; **2.** würzen; '**fla·vo(u)red** mit ...ge-schmack; '**fla·vo(u)r·ing** Gewürz *n*; '**fla·vo(u)r·less** geschmacklos, fad.

flaw [flɔː] **1.** Sprung *m*, Riß *m*; Fleck *m*; (⚙ Form-, ⊕ Fabrikations)Fehler *m*; Makel *m*, Defekt *m*; ⚓ Bö *f*; **2.** zerbrechen; *fig.* beschädigen; '**flaw·less** □ ohne Sprünge *etc.*; fehler-, makellos.

flax ⚘ [flæks] Flachs *m*, Lein *m*; '**flax·en**, '**flax·y** flachsen; flachsfarben, -blond.

flay [flei] die Haut abziehen (*dat.*), schinden; *fig. j-m* das Fell über die Ohren ziehen; '**flay·er** Schinder *m*.

flea [fliː] Floh *m*; '~**-bane** ⚘ Flohkraut *n*; '~**-bite** Flohstich *m*; *fig.* Bagatelle *f*, kleine Unannehmlichkeit *f*; '~**-pit** F Flohkino *n*.

fleck [flek] **1.** Fleck *m*; **2.** sprenkeln.

flec·tion ['flekʃən] *s.* flexion.

fled [fled] *pret. u. p.p. von* flee.

fledge [fledʒ] *v/i.* flügge werden; *v/t.* befiedern; **fledg(e)·ling** ['~liŋ] Küken *n* (*a. fig.*); Grünschnabel *m*.

flee [fliː] (*irr.*) fliehen (*from* von; vor *dat.*); *a.* ~ *from* meiden.

fleece [fliːs] **1.** Vlies *n*; Schäfchenwolke *f*; **2.** scheren; prellen, schröpfen (*of* um); '**fleec·y** wollig, flockig.

fleer [fliə] **1.** Hohn(lachen *n*) *m*; **2.** höhnen, hohnlachen (*at* über *acc.*).

fleet [fliːt] **1.** □ *poet.* schnell; flüchtig; **2.** Flotte *f*; (Wagen)Park *m*; ♀ *Street* die (Londoner) Presse *f*; **3.** dahineilen; fliehen; '**fleet·ing** □ flüchtig, vergänglich.

Flem·ing ['flemiŋ] Flame *m*, Flamin *f*; '**Flem·ish 1.** flämisch; **2.** Flämisch *n*.

flesh [fleʃ] **1.** (Muskel)Fleisch *n*; Fruchtfleisch *n*; *fig.* Fleisch(eslust *f*) *n*; *make s.o.'s* ~ *creep* j. gruselig machen; **2.** Blut kosten lassen (*a. fig.*); '~**-brush** Frottierbürste *f*; '**flesh·ings** *pl.* fleischfarbenes Trikot *n*; '**flesh·ly** fleischlich; sinnlich; irdisch; '**flesh·y** fleischig; fett.

flew [fluː] *pret. von* fly[1] **2.**

flex ⚡ [fleks] Litze *f*; Kabel *n*; **flex·i·bil·i·ty** [~ə'biliti] Biegsamkeit *f* (*a. fig.*); '**flex·i·ble** □ biegsam; lenksam; anpassungsfähig, flexibel; ~ *working hours pl.* gleitende Arbeitszeit *f*; **flex·ion** ['flekʃən] Biegung *f*; *gr.* Flexion *f*, Beugung *f*; **flex·or**

['ʌksə] Beugemuskel *m*; **flex·ure** ['flekʃə] Biegung *f*, Krümmung *f*.

fib·ber·ti·gib·bet ['flibəti'dʒibit] Klatschbase *f*; Irrwisch *m*.

flick [flik] **1.** schnippen; schnellen (*at nach*); **2.** leichter Hieb *m* od. Schlag *m*.

flick·er ['flikə] **1.** flackern; flattern; flimmern; **2.** Flackern *n etc.*; *Am.* Buntspecht *m*.

flick-knife ['fliknaif] Schnappmesser *n*.

fli·er ['flaiə] *s.* flyer.

flight [flait] Flucht *f*; Flug *m* (*a. fig.*); Schwarm *m*; ✈, ✗ Kette *f*; *a.* ~ of stairs Treppe(nflucht) *f*; put to ~ in die Flucht schlagen; take (to) ~ die Flucht ergreifen; ~ bag Schultertasche *f*; '~com-'mand·er Flugkapitän *m*; '~deck ⚓ Flugdeck *n*; ~ en·gi·neer Bordmechaniker *m*; '~lieu'ten·ant Fliegerhauptmann *m*; ~ re·cord·er Flugschreiber *m*; 'flight·y □ flüchtig, fahrig; leichtsinnig; flatterhaft.

flim·sy ['flimzi] **1.** dünn, locker; nichtig, schwach; fadenscheinig (*Entschuldigung*); **2.** Durchschlagpapier *n*; *sl.* Banknote *f*; Telegramm *n*.

flinch [flintʃ] zurückweichen, -schrecken (*from vor dat.*); zucken.

fling [fliŋ] **1.** Wurf *m*; Schlag *m des Pferdes*; *fig.* Hieb *m* (*at gegen*); have one's ~ sich austoben; have a ~ at sich versuchen in (*dat.*); sich lustig machen über (*acc.*), *j.* verhöhnen; **2.** (*irr.*) *v/i.* eilen, stürzen; ausschlagen (*Pferd*); *a.* ~ out *fig.* toben; *v/t.* werfen, schleudern; ~ o.s. sich stürzen; ~ away wegwerfen; verschleudern; fahren lassen; ~ forth herausschleudern, ausstoßen; ~ open aufreißen.

flint [flint] Kiesel *m*; Feuerstein *m*; 'flint·y kieselhaltig; *fig.* hart.

flip [flip] **1.** Klaps *m*; Ruck *m*; ✗ *sl.* Vergnügungsflug *m*, Spritztour *f*; Flip *m* (*alkoholisches Heißgetränk*); **2.** schnippen; knipsen; klapsen; (umher)flitzen.

flip-flap ['flipflæp] Purzelbaum *m*; Luftschaukel *f*.

flip-flop ['flipflɔp] Gummilatsche *f*.

flip·pan·cy ['flipənsi] Leichtfertigkeit *f etc.*; 'flip·pant □ leichtfertig; schnippisch; frivol.

flip·per ['flipə] Flosse *f e-r Schildkröte etc.*; Schwimmflosse *f*.

flip side F ['flipsaid] B-Seite *f* einer Single.

flirt [flə:t] **1.** Ruck *m*; Kokette *f*; Weiberheld *m*, Filou *m*; **2.** flirten, kokettieren; = flip 2; **flir'ta·tion** Liebelei *f*, Flirt(en *n*) *m*; **flir'ta·tious** kokett.

flit [flit] huschen, flitzen; wandern; umziehen.

flitch [flitʃ] Speckseite *f*.

flit·ter ['flitə] flattern.

fliv·ver *Am.* F ['flivə] **1.** Nuckelpinne *f* (*billiges Auto*); **2.** mißlingen.

float [fləut] **1.** Schwimmer *m an Angel, Netz u.* ⊕; Floß *n*; *thea.* Rampenlicht *n*; Plattformwagen *m*; Fest(zugs)wagen *m*; **2.** *v/t.* überfluten (*mst fig.*); flößen; tragen (*Wasser*); *Schiff* flott machen, *fig.* in Gang bringen; ✝ gründen; verbreiten; *v/i.* obenauf schwimmen, treiben; schweben; umlaufen; 'float·a·ble schwimmfähig, flößbar; 'float·age Schwimmkraft *f*; **float'a·tion** *s.* flotation; 'float·ing schwimmend, treibend; schwebend (*Schuld*); ~ bridge Schiffbrücke *f*; ~ capital Umlaufskapital *n*; ~ ice Treibeis *n*; ~ kidney Wanderniere *f*; ~ light Feuerschiff *n*; ~ rate flexibler Wechselkurs *m*; ~ voter *pol.* Wechselwähler *m*; 'float-plane Schwimmerflugzeug *n*.

flock[1] [flɔk] **1.** Herde *f* (*a. fig.*); Schar *f*, Haufe(n) *m*; Flug *m Vögel*; **2.** sich scharen; zs.-strömen.

flock[2] [~] (*bsd.* Woll)Flocke *f*.

floe [fləu] schwimmendes Eisfeld *n*; Eisscholle *f*.

flog [flɔg] peitschen; prügeln; ~ a dead horse seine Mühe verschwenden, sich umsonst anstrengen; 'flog·ging Prügeln *n*; Prügelstrafe *f*.

flood [flʌd] **1.** *a.* ~-tide Flut *f*; Überschwemmung *f*; Hochwasser *n*; the ♀ die Sintflut; **2.** überfluten, -schwemmen; '~-dis·as·ter Hochwasserkatastrophe *f*; '~-gate Schleusentor *n*; '~-light **1.** Scheinwerfer-, Flutlicht *n*; **2.** (mit Scheinwerfern) anstrahlen.

floor [flɔ:] **1.** (Fuß)Boden *m*; Stockwerk *n*; ✗ Tenne *f*; *parl.* Sitzungssaal *m*; *sl.* Börse *f*; ~ leader *Am.* Fraktionsvorsitzende *m*; ~ price

Mindestpreis *m*; ∼ show *Tanz-* etc.
Darbietung(en *pl.*) *f* in *Nachtklubs etc.*; *hold the* ∼ *parl.* e-e Rede halten; *be kept on the* ∼ zur Debatte stehen; *take the* ∼ das Wort ergreifen; **2.** mit e-m Boden versehen, dielen; zu Boden schlagen; verblüffen; **'∼-cloth** Aufwisch-, Putzlappen *m*; **'floor·er** zu Boden werfender Schlag *m*; **'floor·ing** Dielung *f*; Fußboden(belag) *m*; **'floor-lamp** Stehlampe *f*; **floor man·ag·er** *Kaufhaus*: Abteilungsleiter; *Fernsehen*: Aufnahmeleiter *m*; **floor show** Varieté-Darbietungen *f/pl.* im *Nachtklub od. Restaurant*; **'floor-walk·er** *Am.* Aufsicht *f* im *Kaufhaus*; **'floor-wax** Bohnerwachs *n*.

floo·zy *Am. sl.* [ˈfluːzi] Flittchen *n*.

flop F [flɔp] **1.** (mit den Flügeln) schlagen; (hin)plumpsen (lassen); baumeln; *Krempe* herunterschlagen; *sl.* versagen; **2.** Plumps *m*; Reinfall *m*; Versager *m*; ∼ *house Am. sl.* Penne *f*; **3.** plumps; **'flop·py** schlapp; schludrig.

flo·ra [ˈflɔːrə] Flora *f*, Pflanzenwelt *f*; **'flo·ral** Blüten...; Blumen...; ∼ *design* Blumenmuster *n*.

flo·res·cence[flɔːˈresns]Blüte(zeit)*f*.

flor·id □ [ˈflɔrid] blühend; *fig.* blumig; überladen; **'flor·id·ness** lebhafte Farbe *f*; blumiger Stil *m*; Überladenheit *f*.

flor·in [ˈflɔrin] Gulden *m*; Zweischillingstück *n*.

flo·rist [ˈflɔrist] Blumenhändler *m*, -züchter *m*.

floss [flɔs] Kokonseide *f*; ∼ *silk* Florettseide *f*; **'floss·y** florettseiden.

flo·ta·tion [fləuˈteiʃən] Schwimmen *n*; Schweben *n*; Ingangbringen *n*; ✝ Gründung *f*.

flo·til·la ⚓ [fləuˈtilə] Flottille *f*.

flot·sam ⚓ [ˈflɔtsəm] (treibendes) Wrackgut *n*.

flounce¹ [flauns] **1.** Volant *m*, Falbel *f*; **2.** mit Falbeln *etc.* besetzen.

flounce² [∼] stürzen, stürmen; plumpsen; hopsen; zappeln.

floun·der¹ *ichth.* [ˈflaundə] Flunder *f*.

floun·der² [∼] sich (ab)mühen, sich quälen; sich mühsam bewegen.

flour [ˈflauə] **1.** feines Mehl *n*; **2.** mit Mehl bestreuen.

flour·ish [ˈflʌriʃ] **1.** Schnörkel *m*; *Rede*-Floskel *f*; Schwingen *n*; ♪ Verzierung *f*; Trompetenstoß *m*, Tusch *m*; **2.** *v/i.* blühen, gedeihen; seine Blütezeit haben; leben; Schnörkel *etc.* machen; *v/t. Schwert etc.* schwingen; *Fahne* schwenken.

flout [flaut] *v/t.* verspotten; ignorieren; *v/i.* spotten (*at* über *acc.*).

flow [fləu] **1.** Fluß *m*; Erguß *m*; Schwall *m*; Überfluß *m*; Flut *f*; ∼ *of spirits* heitere Laune *f*; **2.** fließen, fluten, strömen; überfließen (*with* von); wallen (*Haar etc.*); hereinkommen, steigen (*Flut*); ∼ *from* herrühren von; ∼ **chart** *Datenverarbeitung*: Flußdiagramm *n*.

flow·er [ˈflauə] **1.** Blume *f*; Blüte *f* (*fig. Auslese*); Zierde *f*; *say it with* ∼*s* durch die Blume sprechen; **2.** blühen; **flow·er·et** [ˈ∼rit] Blümchen *n*; (Blumenkohl)Röschen *n*; **'flow·er·i·ness** Blumenreichtum *m* (*a. fig.*); **'flow·er-pot** Blumentopf *m*; **'flow·er·y** blumig.

flown [fləun] *p.p. v. fly¹* 2.

flu F [fluː] = *influenza*.

flub·dub *Am. sl.* [ˈflʌbdʌb] Geschwätz *n*.

fluc·tu·ate [ˈflʌktjueit] schwanken; fluktuieren; **fluc·tu'a·tion** Schwanken *n*; ∼*s pl.* Schwankungen *f/pl.*

flue [fluː] Kaminrohr *n*; Heizrohr *n*; (Feuerungs)Zug *m*; Rauchfang *m*; Staubflocke(n *pl.*) *f*; = *flu.*

flu·en·cy [ˈfluːənsi] Fluß *m der Rede*, Geläufigkeit *f*; **'flu·ent** □ fließend; geläufig (*Rede*).

fluff [flʌf] **1.** Flaum *m*; Staub-, Federflocke *f*; *fig.* Schnitzer *m*, Fehler *m*; **2.** *Kissen* aufschütteln; *Federn* aufplustern (*Vogel*); **'fluff·y** flaumig; locker, flockig; *sl.* angeheitert.

flu·id [ˈfluːid] **1.** flüssig; *fig.* nicht fixiert; **2.** *konkr.* Flüssigkeit *f*; **flu'id·i·ty** Flüssigkeit *f* (*Zustand*).

fluke [fluːk] Ankerschaufel *f*; F Dusel *m* (*Glück*).

flume [fluːm] Kanal *m*.

flum·mer·y[ˈflʌməri] *Küche*: Flammeri *m*; fades Geschwätz *n*.

flum·mox F [ˈflʌməks] verblüffen, verwirren.

flung [flʌŋ] *pret. u. p.p. von fling* 2.

flunk *Am.* F [flʌŋk] durchfallen *im Examen*, durchfallen lassen; sich drücken.

flunk·(e)y ['flʌŋki] Lakai *m*; Be-
dientenseele *f*; '**flunk·ey·ism** La-
kaienwesen *n*.
flu·o·res·cence *phys.* [fluə'resns]
Fluoreszenz *f*; **flu·or'es·cent** flu-
oreszierend; ~ *lamp* Leuchtstoff-
lampe *f*.
flur·ry ['flʌri] **1.** Nervosität *f*, Un-
wirschheit *f*; Bö *f*; (Schnee)Schauer
m; **2.** nervös *od.* unwirsch machen.
flush [flʌʃ] **1.** ⊕ in gleicher Ebene;
reichlich; (über)voll; **2.** Erröten *n*;
Übermut *m*, Rausch *m*; Fülle *f*;
Wachstum *n*; *fig.* Blüte *f*; Spülung
f; *Karten*: Flöte *f*; **3.** über-, durch-
fluten; (aus)spülen; strömen; sprießen (lassen); erröten (lassen); übermütig machen; aufjagen.
flus·ter ['flʌstə] **1.** Aufregung *f*;
2. *v/t.* durcheinanderbringen, aufregen, nervös machen; *v/i.* aufgeregt *od.* nervös sein.
flute [fluːt] **1.** ♪ Flöte *f*; △ *Säulen-*
Auskehlung f; Plisse- etc. Falte *f*;
2. (auf der) Flöte spielen; *fig.* flöten;
auskehlen, riefeln; fälteln; '**flut·ist**
Flötist(in).
flut·ter ['flʌtə] **1.** Flattern *n*; Erregung *f*, Unruhe *f*; F Spekulation
f; *have a ~* sein Glück (*im Spiel etc.*)
probieren; **2.** *v/t.* flattern lassen;
aufregen; *v/i.* flattern; zittern; sich
unruhig hin- u. herbewegen.
flux [flʌks] *fig.* Fluß *m*, Strom *m*;
♣ Ausfluß *m*; beständiger Wechsel
m; ~ *and reflux* Flut *f* und Ebbe *f*.
fly¹ [flai] **1.** Fliege *f*; Flug *m*; *Am.*
Baseball: hochgeschlagener Ball *m*;
Droschke *f*; Unruh *f der Uhr*; *flies*
pl. thea. Soffitten *f/pl.*; **2.** (*irr.*)
fliegen (lassen); eilen, entfliehen
(*Zeit*); eilen, stürzen; *Flugzeug*
fliegen; *Flagge* hissen; = *flee*; ~
the Channel über den Kanal fliegen;
~ *high* hoch hinauswollen; ~ *at* herfallen über (*acc.*); ~ *in the face of*
sich nicht scheren um; trotzen
(*dat.*); ~ *into a passion od. rage* in
Zorn geraten; ~ *off* davonfliegen;
~ *blind od. on instruments* blindfliegen; ~ *out at* ausfällig werden
gegen; ~ *open* auffliegen (*Tür*);
send s.o. ~ing j. fortjagen.
fly² *sl.* [⏑] auf Draht; mit allen
Wassern gewaschen.
fly...: '**~-blow 1.** Fliegenschmutz *m*;
2. Eier ablegen (auf); *fig.* beschmutzen; '**~-blown** fliegen-

beschmutzt; *fig.* schmutzig; wenig
vertrauenerweckend; '**~-catch·er**
Fliegenfänger *m*; *orn.* Fliegen-
schnäpper *m*.
fly·er ['flaiə] Flieger *m* (*bsd.* ✈);
Renner *m*; Sprung *m* mit Anlauf;
Flüchtling *m*; *take a ~ Am.* F Vermögen riskieren; ~*s pl.* △ Frei-
treppe *f*.
fly-flap ['flaiflæp] Fliegenklatsche *f*.
fly·ing ['flaiiŋ] fliegend; schnell;
Flug...; ~ *boat* Flugboot *n*; ~ *but-*
tress △ Strebebogen *m*; ~ *deck*
Landedeck *n*; ~ *field* Flugplatz *m*;
~ *jump* Sprung *m* mit Anlauf; ~
machine Flugzeug *n*; ~ *school*
Fliegerschule *f*; ~ *squad* Überfallkommando *n*; ~ *start* fliegender
Start *m*; ~ *visit* flüchtiger Besuch *m*;
'**~-of-fi·cer** Oberleutnant *m* der
RAF.
fly...: '**~-leaf** *typ.* Vorsatzblatt *n*;
'**~-o·ver** (Straßen)Überführung *f*;
✈ = '**~-past** Luftparade *f*;
'**~-sheet** *Camping etc.*: Überzelt *n*;
'**~-weight** *Boxen*: Fliegengewicht *n*;
'**~-wheel** Schwungrad *n*.
foal [fəul] **1.** Fohlen *n*; *in ~, with ~*
trächtig **2.** fohlen.
foam [fəum] **1.** Schaum *m*; **2.** schäumen; '**~-rub·ber** Schaumgummi *n*,
m; '**foam·y** schaumig.
fob¹ [fɔb] Uhrtasche *f in der Hose*;
Chatelaine *f* (*Uhranhänger*).
fob² [⏑]: ~ *off fig. j.* abspeisen (*with*
mit); *et.* aufschwatzen (*on dat.*).
fo·cal ['fəukəl] den Brennpunkt betreffend, fokal; ~ *length*, ~ *distance*
phot. Brennweite *f*; ~*-plane shutter*
phot. Schlitzverschluß *m*.
fo'c'sle ['fəuksl] = forecastle.
fo·cus ['fəukəs] **1.** *pl. a.* **fo·ci**
['fəusai] Brennpunkt *m*; *fig. a.*
Herd *m*, Mittel-, Schwerpunkt *m*;
2. (sich) im Brennpunkt vereinigen;
opt. einstellen (*a. fig.*); *Aufmerk-*
samkeit konzentrieren (*on, upon*
auf *acc.*); '**fo·cus·(s)ing screen**
phot. Mattscheibe *f*.
fod·der ['fɔdə] **1.** (Trocken)Futter
n; **2.** füttern.
foe *poet.* [fəu] Feind *m*, Gegner *m*;
'**~-man** † Feind *m*.
foe·tus ♣ ['fiːtəs] Fötus *m*, Leibes-
frucht *f*.
fog [fɔg] **1.** (dichter) Nebel *m*; *fig.*
Umnebelung *f*; *phot.* Schleier *m*;
2. *mst fig.* umnebeln; *phot.* ver-

schleiern; '~-**bank** Nebelbank *f*;
'~-**bound** ⚓ durch Nebel behindert.

fo·gey F ['fəugi]: *old* ~ komischer
alter Kauz *m*.

fog·gy □ ['fɔgi] neb(e)lig; *fig*. nebelhaft; '**fog-horn** Nebelhorn *n*;
'**fog-sig·nal** 🚩 Nebelsignal *n*.

fo·gy *Am*. ['fəugi] = *fogey*.

foi·ble *fig*. ['fɔibl] Schwäche *f*,
schwache Seite *f*.

foil¹ [fɔil] Folie *f*; Spiegelbelag *m*;
fig. Hintergrund *m*.

foil² [~] **1.** vereiteln; durchkreuzen;
j-m e-n Strich durch die Rechnung
machen; **2.** *fenc*. Florett *n*.

foist [fɔist]: ~ *s.th*. (*off*) *on s.o.* j-m
et. andrehen *od*. aufschwatzen.

fold¹ [fəuld] **1.** Schafhürde *f*; *fig*.
Herde *f*; **2.** einpferchen.

fold² [~] **1.** Falte *f*; Falz *m*, Kniff *m*,
Bruch *m*; **2.** ...fach, ...fältig; **3.** *v/t*.
falten; falzen; kniffen; *Arme*
kreuzen; *a*. ~ *up* einwickeln; ~
down umkniffen; ~ *in one's arms* in
die Arme schließen; ~ *up* zs.-legen;
v/i. sich falten; sich zs.-klappen
lassen; *Am*. F eingehen; ~ *up* F
zusammenbrechen; Schluß ma-
chen; '**fold·er** Mappe *f*, Schnellhefter *m*; Faltprospekt *m*.

fold·ing ['fəuldiŋ] zs.-legbar; Klapp-
...; '~-**bed** Feldbett *n*; '~-**boat**
Faltboot *n*; '~-**door**(*s pl*.) Flügeltür
f; '~-**screen** spanische Wand *f*;
'~-**seat** Klappsitz *m*.

fo·li·age ['fəuliidʒ] Laub(werk) *n*.

fo·li·o ['fəuliəu] Folio *n*; Foliant *m*;
Mappe *f*.

folk [fəuk] *pl*. Leute *pl*.; ~*s pl*. F *m-e*
etc. Leute *pl*. (*Angehörige*); '~-**dance**
Volkstanz *m*; ~·**lore** ['~lɔ:] Volks-
kunde *f*, -sagen *f/pl*.; Folklore *f*; ~
mu·sic Folklore *f*; '~-**song** Volkslied
n.

fol·low ['fɔləu] folgen (*dat*.); folgen
auf (*acc*.); be-, nach-, verfolgen;
s-m Vergnügen, Beruf etc. nachgehen; *to* ~ hinterher, als Nachspeise; *it* ~*s that* es folgt daraus,
daß; ~ *out* weiter verfolgen; ~ *the
sea* Seemann sein; ~ *up* (weiter-)
verfolgen; '**fol·low·er** Nachfolger
(-in); Verfolger(in); Anhänger(in),
Gefolgsmann *m*, Jünger *m*; F Verehrer *m* (*e-s Dienstmädchens*);
'**fol·low·ing 1.** Anhängerschaft *f*,
Gefolge *n*; *the* ~ das Folgende;

2. ~ *wind* Rückenwind *m*; '**fol·low-
-up** weitere Verfolgung *f* *e-r* Sache;
🩺 Nachbehandlung *f*.

fol·ly ['fɔli] Torheit *f*; Narrheit *f*.

fo·ment [fəu'ment] 🩺 bähen; *j-m*
warme Umschläge machen; *Unruhe* stiften *od*. schüren; **fo·men-
'ta·tion** Bähung *f*; warmer Umschlag *m*; Anstiftung *f*; **fo'ment·er**
fig. Anstifter *m*.

fond □ [fɔnd] zärtlich; vernarrt
(*of* in *acc*.); töricht, kühn (*Hoffnung etc*.); *be* ~ *of* gern haben,
lieben; *be* ~ *of dancing* gern tanzen.

fon·dant ['fɔndənt] Fondant *m*.

fon·dle ['fɔndl] liebkosen; streicheln; (ver)hätscheln.

fond·ness ['fɔndnis] Zärtlichkeit *f*;
Vorliebe *f* (*for* für).

font *eccl*. [fɔnt] Taufstein *m*.

food [fu:d] Speise *f*, Nahrung *f*
(*a. fig*.); Essen *n*, Beköstigung *f*;
Futter *n*; Lebensmittel *n/pl*., Eßwaren *f/pl*.; ~ **hall** Lebensmittelab-
teilung *f*; '~-**stuff** Nahrungsmittel *n*.

fool¹ [fu:l] **1.** Narr *m*, Tor *m*,
Dummkopf *m*; Betrogene *m*;
Hanswurst *m*; *make a* ~ *of s.o.* j.
zum besten haben; *make a* ~ *of
o.s.* sich lächerlich machen; *I am
a* ~ *to him* gegen ihn bin ich ein
Waisenknabe; ~*'s paradise* Schlaraffenland *n*; **2.** *Am*. F närrisch,
dumm; **3.** *v/t*. narren, aufziehen;
zum Narren halten; prellen (*out of*
um *et*.); verleiten (*into ger.* zu *inf*.);
~ *away* F vertrödeln; *v/i*. Spaß
machen, albern; (herum)spielen;
~ *about* herumalbern; ~ (*a*)*round*
bsd. Am. Zeit vertrödeln.

fool² [~] Fruchtcreme *f*.

fool·er·y ['fu:ləri] Torheit *f*; '**fool-
hard·y** □ tollkühn; '**fool·ish** □
töricht, albern, dumm; '**fool·ish-
ness** Torheit *f*; '**fool-proof** ⊕
narrensicher; kinderleicht; **fool-
scap** ['fu:lskæp] Kanzleipapier *n*;
fool's-cap ['fu:lzkæp] Narrenkappe *f*.

foot [fut] **1.** *pl*. **feet** [fi:t] Fuß *m*;
Fußende *n*; ✕ Infanterie *f*; Fuß *m*
(= *12 Zoll*); Füßling *m am Strumpf*;
on ~ zu Fuß; im Gange; *be on one's
feet* auf den Beinen sein; *fig*. keine
Hilfe brauchen, auf eigenen Füßen
stehen; *put one's* ~ *down* fest auftreten; *I have put my* ~ *into it* F ich
bin ins Fettnäpfchen getreten; *set*

on ~ in Gang bringen; set ~ on
betreten; **2.** v/t. Füß(ling)e anstrik-
ken an (acc.); mst ~ up Rechnung
addieren; ~ the bill F die Zeche bezahlen; v/i. ~ it zu Fuß gehen; tanzen; '**foot·age** Gesamtlänge f (in
Fuß).

foot...: '**~-and-'mouth dis·ease**
Maul- und Klauenseuche f; '**~·ball**
Fußball(spiel n) m; '**~·board**
Trittbrett n; '**~·boy** Hotel- etc.
Page m; '**~·brake** Fußbremse f;
'**~·bridge** Steg m.

foot·ed ['futid] ...füßig; '**foot·er** F
Fußball(spiel n) m.

foot...: '**~·fall** Tritt m, Schritt m;
'**~·gear** Schuhwerk n; ⚥ **Guards**
pl. ✕ Gardeinfanterie f; '**~·hills**
pl. Vorgebirge n; '**~·hold** fester
Stand m; fig. Halt m.

foot·ing ['futiŋ] Halt m, Stand m;
Grundlage f, Basis f; Stellung f;
fester Fuß m; Verhältnis n; ✕ Zustand m; Endsumme f; be on a
friendly ~ with s.o. ein gutes Verhältnis zu j-m haben; upon the
same ~ as auf gleichem Fuße mit;
get a ~ festen Fuß fassen; lose
one's ~ ausgleiten.

foo·tle F ['fu:tl] **1.** albern (sein);
2. Albernheit f; Spielerei f.

foot·lights thea. ['futlaits] pl.
Rampenlicht(er pl.) n; Bühne f.

foot·ling ['fu:tliŋ] läppisch, unbedeutend.

foot...: '**~·loose** ungebunden, unbeschwert; ~ and fancy-free frei und
ungebunden; '**~·man** Diener m, Lakai m; '**~·mark** Fußspur f; '**~·note**
1. Fußnote f; **2.** mit Fußnoten versehen; '**~·pad** Straßenräuber m; '**~-
-pas·sen·ger** Fußgänger(in); '**~-
-path** Fußpfad m; '**~·print** Fußstapfe f, -spur f; '**~·race** Wettlauf m;
'**~·rule** Zollstock m.

foot·sie ['futsi] play ~ F fußeln.

foot...: '**~·slog** sl. latschen; '**~·sore**
fußkrank; '**~·stalk** ♀ Stengel m, Stiel
m; '**~·step** Fußstapfe f, Spur f; Tritt
m, Schritt m; '**~·stool** Fußbank f;
'**~·wear** = foot-gear; '**~·work** Sport:
Beinarbeit f.

fop [fɔp] Geck m, Fatzke m; '**fop-
per·y** Ziererei f, Afferei f; '**foppish** □ geckenhaft, affig.

for [fɔ:; fə; f] **1.** prp. mst für; Son-
derfälle: a) Zweck, Ziel, Richtung:
zu; nach; come ~ dinner zum Essen

kommen; the train ~ London der
Zug nach London; it is ~ you to
decide es ist an dir zu entscheiden;
b) Wunsch, Erwartung: warten,
hoffen etc. auf (acc.); sich sehnen etc.
nach; c) Grund, Anlaß: aus, vor
(dat.), wegen; were it not ~ that
wenn das nicht wäre; he is a fool ~
doing that er ist töricht, daß er das
tut; d) Zeitdauer: ~ three days drei
Tage (lang); auf drei Tage; seit
drei Tagen; e) Entfernung: I walked
~ a mile ich ging eine Meile (weit);
f) Austausch: (an)statt; g) in der
Eigenschaft als; I ~ one ich zum Beispiel; ~ sure! sicher!, gewiß!;
h) nach adj. vor acc. u. inf.: it is
good ~ us to be here es ist gut, daß
wir hier sind; the snow was too deep
~ them to go on der Schnee war zu
tief, als daß sie weiter gekonnt
hätten; **2.** cj. denn.

for·age ['fɔridʒ] **1.** F(o)urage f,
Futter n; **2.** (nach Futter) suchen.

for·as·much [fərəz'mʌtʃ]: ~ as weil,
da, insofern als.

for·ay ['fɔrei] räuberischer Einfall m.

for·bade [fə'bæd] pret. von forbid.

for·bear[1] ['fɔ:bɛə] Vorfahr m.

for·bear[2] [fɔ:'bɛə] (irr.) v/t. unterlassen; v/i. sich enthalten (from
gen.); Geduld haben; **for'bear-
ance** Unterlassung f; Geduld f,
Nachsicht f.

for·bid [fə'bid] (irr.) verbieten (s.o.
s.th. j-m et.); hindern; God ~! Gott
behüte!; **for'bid·den** p.p. von forbid; ~ fruit verbotene Frucht f;
for'bid·ding □ abstoßend.

for·bore, for·borne [fɔ:'bɔ:(n)]
pret. u. p.p. von forbear[2].

force [fɔ:s] **1.** mst Kraft f, Stärke f,
Gewalt f; Nachdruck m; Gültig-
keit f; Zwang m; Bedeutung f;
Heer n, Truppe f; Streitmacht f;
the ~ die Polizei; armed ~s pl.
Streitkräfte f/pl.; by ~ gewaltsam;
come (put) in ~ in Kraft treten
(setzen); **2.** zwingen, nötigen; erzwingen (upon von); aufzwingen,
-drängen (upon dat.); forcieren, beschleunigen; Worten, e-r Frau Gewalt antun; Schritt beschleunigen;
Tür etc. aufbrechen; erstürmen;
Früchte künstlich reif machen;
~ back zurücktreiben; ~ down ✈
zum Landen zwingen; ~ s.o.'s hand
j. zwingen; ~ on antreiben; ~ open

forge

aufbrechen; **forced** (*adv.* **forced·ly** ['ͺidli]) er-, gezwungen; ~ *loan* Zwangsanleihe *f*; ~ *landing* Notlandung *f*; ~ *march* Eilmarsch *m*; ~ *sale* Zwangsversteigerung *f*; '**force·feed** zwangsernähren; **forceful** ☐ ['ͺful] kräftig, wirkungsvoll; eindringlich; '**force·meat** *Küche*: gehacktes Füllsel *n*. **for·ceps** ⚥ ['fɔːseps] *sg. u. pl.* Zange *f*.

force-pump ['fɔːspʌmp] Druckpumpe *f*.

forc·er ⊕ ['fɔːsə] Kolben *m*.

for·ci·ble ☐ ['fɔːsəbl] gewaltsam; Zwangs...; eindringlich; wirksam.

forc·ing-house ['fɔːsiŋhaus] Treibhaus *n*.

ford [fɔːd] **1.** Furt *f*; **2.** durchwaten; '**ford·a·ble** durchwatbar.

fore [fɔː] **1.** *adv.* vorn; ~ *and aft* ⚓ vorn und hinten; **2.** Vorderteil *m*, *n*; *to the* ~ greifbar, verfügbar, vorhanden; zur Hand; *bring* (*come*) *to the* ~ zum Vorschein bringen (kommen); **3.** *adj.* vorder; Vorder...; '~·**arm**[1] Vorderarm *m*; ~'**arm**[2] (sich) wappnen; ~'**bode** vorhersagen; ahnen; ~'**bod·ing** (böses) Vorzeichen *n*; Ahnung *f*; '~·**cast** **1.** (*bsd.* Wetter)Vorhersage *f*; **2.** (*irr. cast*) vorhersehen; voraussagen; '~·**cas·tle** ⚓ ['fəuksl] Vorderdeck *n*; Logis *n*; ~'**close** [fɔːˈkləuz] ausschließen (*of* von); *Hypothek* für verfallen erklären; ~'**clo·sure** [ͺ3ə] Verfallserklärung *f*; '~·**court** Vorhof *m*; ~'**date** vorausdatieren; ~'**doom** im voraus verurteilen *od.* bestimmen; '~·**father** Vorfahr *m*; '~·**fin·ger** Zeigefinger *m*; '~·**foot** Vorderfuß *m*; '~·**front** Vorderseite *f*; vorderste Reihe *f*; ~'**go** (*irr. go*) vorangehen; ~*ing* vorhergehend; ~'**gone** von vornherein feststehend; ~ *conclusion* Selbstverständlichkeit *f*, ausgemachte Sache *f*; '~·**ground** Vordergrund *m*; '~·**hand** Vorhand *f*; ~·**head** ['fɔrid] Stirn *f*.

for·eign ['fɔrin] fremd; ausländisch; auswärtig; ~ *body* Fremdkörper *m*; ~ *affairs pl. pol.* Außenpolitik *f*, auswärtige Angelegenheiten *f*|*pl.*; ~ *aid* Auslandshilfe *f*; ~-*born* im Ausland geboren; ~ *exchange* Devisen *pl.*; '**for·eign·er** Ausländer(in), Fremde *m, f*; '**for·eign·ness** Fremdheit *f*.

for·eign...: ⚥ **Of·fice** Außenministerium *n*; ~ **pol·i·cy** Außenpolitik *f*; ⚥ **Sec·re·tar·y** Außenminister *m*; ~ **trade** Außenhandel *m*.

fore...: ~'**judge** im voraus (ver)urteilen; ~'**know** (*irr. know*) vorherwissen; '~·**knowl·edge** Vorherwissen *n*, -sehen *n*; ~·**land** ['fɔːlənd] Vorgebirge *n*; '~·**leg** Vorderbein *n*; '~·**lock** Stirnhaar *n*; *take time by the* ~ die Gelegenheit beim Schopfe ergreifen; '~·**man** ⚒ Obmann *m*; Vorarbeiter *m*, (Werk-) Meister *m*; ⚒ Steiger *m*; '~·**mast** ⚓ Fockmast *m*; '~·**most** **1.** *adj.* vorderst, erst; **2.** *adv.* zuerst; '~·**name** Vorname *m*; '~·**noon** Vormittag *m*.

fo·ren·sic [fəˈrensik] gerichtlich; Gerichts...; ~ *science* Gerichtskriminalistik *f*.

fore...: '~·**or·dain** vorherbestimmen; '~·**paw** Vorderpfote *f*; '~·**play** (sexuelles) Vorspiel *n*; '~·**run·ner** Vorläufer *m*, -bote *m*; ~·**sail** ⚓ ['ͺseil; ⚓ '~sl] Focksegel *n*; ~'**see** (*irr. see*) vorhersehen; ~'**see·a·ble** vorauszusehen(d); absehbar (*Zeit*); ~'**shad·ow** ankündigen; '~·**shore** (Küsten)Vorland *n*, Strand *m*; ~'**short·en** in der Verkürzung zeichnen; '~·**sight** Voraussicht *f*; Vorsorge *f*; Korn *n am Gewehr*; '~·**skin** Vorhaut *f*.

for·est ['fɔrist] **1.** Wald *m* (*a. fig.*), Forst *m*; **2.** beforsten.

fore·stall [fɔːˈstɔːl] *et.* vereiteln; *j-m* zuvorkommen.

for·est·er ['fɔristə] Förster *m*; Waldarbeiter *m*; '**for·est·ry** Forstwirtschaft *f*; Waldgebiet *n*.

fore...: ~'**taste** Vorgeschmack *m*; ~'**tell** (*irr. tell*) voraus-, vorhersagen; vorbedeuten; '~·**thought** Vorbedacht *m*. [ständig.\ ]

for·ev·er [fəˈrevə] für immer;/

fore...: ~'**warn** vorher warnen; '~·**wom·an** Aufseherin *f*; Vorarbeiterin *f*; '~·**word** Vorwort *n*.

for·feit ['fɔːfit] **1.** verwirkt; **2.** Verwirkung *f*; Strafe *f*, Buße *f*; Pfand *n*; ✝ *u. Sport*: Reugeld *n*; ~*s pl.* Pfänderspiel *n*; **3.** verwirken; einbüßen; '**for·feit·a·ble** verwirkbar; **for·fei·ture** ['ͺtʃə] Verwirkung *f*; Verlust *m*.

for·gath·er [fɔːˈgæðə] zs.-kommen.

for·gave [fəˈgeiv] *pret. von* forgive.

forge[1] [fɔːdʒ] **1.** Schmiede *f*;

2. schmieden (*fig. ersinnen*); *Urkunde etc.* fälschen.

forge² [⌄] *mst* ~ *ahead* sich vor-(wärts)arbeiten.

forg·er ['fɔ:dʒə] Schmied *m*; Fälscher *m*; **'forg·er·y** Fälschung *f*.

for·get [fə'get] (*irr.*) vergessen; vernachlässigen; *I* ~ F ich habe vergessen, ich weiß nicht mehr; **for-'get·ful** □ [⌄ful] vergeßlich; **for-'get·ful·ness** Vergeßlichkeit *f*; **for-'get-me-not** ♀ Vergißmeinnicht *n*.

for·give [fə'giv] (*irr.*) vergeben, verzeihen; *Schuld* erlassen; **for'giv·en** *p.p. von forgive*; **for'give·ness** Verzeihung *f*, -gebung *f*; **for'giv·ing** □ versöhnlich; nachsichtig, mild.

for·go [fɔ:'gəu] (*irr. go*) verzichten auf (*acc.*); aufgeben.

for·got [fə'gɔt], **for'got·ten** [⌄tn] *pret. u. p.p. von forget*.

fork [fɔ:k] **1.** Gabel *f*; Gabelung *f*; **2.** (sich) gabeln; ~ *out* F *Geld* herausrücken; **forked** gabelförmig; gegabelt; **'fork-lift** Gabelstapler *m*.

for·lorn [fə'lɔ:n] verloren, verlassen; hoffnungslos; hilflos; ~ *hope* aussichtsloses Unternehmen *n*; ✗ verlorener Posten *m*, Himmelfahrtskommando *n*.

form [fɔ:m] **1.** Form *f*; Gestalt *f*; Formalität *f*; Formular *n*; (Schul-)Bank *f*; (Schul)Klasse *f*; Form *f*, Kondition *f*; geistige Verfassung *f*; *in* (*good*) ~ *Sport:* in (guter) Form *od.* Verfassung; *good* (*bad*) ~ gutes (schlechtes) Benehmen *n*; **2.** (sich) formen, (sich) bilden; gestalten; entwerfen, erdenken; ✗ (sich) aufstellen, formieren; vereinbaren (*into* zu); *Bündnis* schließen; sich *e-e Meinung* bilden.

for·mal □ ['fɔ:məl] formal; förmlich; formell; äußerlich, scheinbar; **'for·mal·ism** Formalismus *m*; **'for·mal·ist** Formenmensch *m*; **for·mal·i·ty** [fɔ:'mæliti] Förmlichkeit *f*, Formalität *f*; **for·mal·ize** ['fɔ:məlaiz] in die richtige Form bringen.

for·mat ['fɔ:mæt] Format *n* (*e-s Buches*).

for·ma·tion [fɔ:'meiʃən] Bildung *f*, Gestaltung *f*; *bsd.* ✗ *u. geol.* Formation *f*; ~ *flying* ✈ Fliegen *n* im Verband; **form·a·tive** ['fɔ:mətiv] formend, bildend; gestaltend; ~ *years pl.* Entwicklungsjahre *n/pl.*

form·er¹ ⊕ ['fɔ:mə] Former *m* (*a. fig.*).

for·mer² [⌄] vorig, früher; ehemalig; vorhererwähnt; erstere(r, -s), jene(r, -s); **'for·mer·ly** ehemals, früher, einst.

for·mic ['fɔ:mik]: ~ *acid* Ameisensäure *f*.

for·mi·da·ble □ ['fɔ:midəbl] furchtbar, schrecklich; ungeheuer.

form·less □ ['fɔ:mlis] formlos.

For·mo·san [fɔ:'məusən] aus Formosa, Formosa...

for·mu·la ['fɔ:mjulə], *pl. mst* **for·mu·lae** [⌄li:] Formel *f*; ✞ Rezept *n*; **for·mu·lar·y** ['⌄ləri] **1.** formelhaft; **2.** Formelbuch *n*; **for·mu·late** ['⌄leit] formulieren; **for·mu·'la·tion** Formulierung *f*.

for·ni·cate ['fɔ:nikeit] außerehelichen Geschlechtsverkehr haben, Unzucht treiben; **for·ni'ca·tion** Unzucht *f*.

for·rad·er F ['fɔrədə] (weiter) vorwärts.

for·sake [fə'seik] (*irr.*) aufgeben; verlassen; **for'sak·en** *p.p. von forsake*; **for·sook** [⌄'suk] *pret. von forsake*.

for·sooth *iro.* [fə'su:θ] wahrlich.

for·swear [fɔ:'sweə] (*irr. swear*) abschwören; ~ *o.s.* falsch schwören; **for'sworn** meineidig.

fort ✗ [fɔ:t] Fort *n*, Festung(swerk *n*) *f*.

forte *fig.* [fɔ:t] Stärke *f*, starke Seite *f*.

forth [fɔ:θ] *räumlich:* vor(wärts), voran, vorauf; hinaus, hervor; *in Zeit, Ordnung etc.:* vorwärts, weiter, fort(an); *from this day* ~ von heute an; ~'**com·ing** herauskommend, erscheinend; bereit; bevorstehend; F entgegenkommend; *be* ~ zum Vorschein kommen, erscheinen; '~**right** gerade; geradeheraus; '~**with** sogleich.

for·ti·eth ['fɔ:tiiθ] **1.** vierzigste(r, -s); **2.** Vierzigstel *n*.

for·ti·fi·ca·tion [fɔ:tifi'keiʃən] Befestigung *f*; ✗ Festungswerk *n*; **for·ti·fy** [⌄'fai] ✗ befestigen; *fig.* (ver)stärken; **for·ti·tude** ['⌄tju:d] Seelenstärke *f*; Tapferkeit *f*, Mut *m*.

fort·night ['fɔ:tnait] vierzehn Tage; *this day* ~ heute in 14 Tagen; *this* ~ seit 14 Tagen; **'fort·night·ly** vierzehntägig, alle 14 Tage (erscheinend).

for·tress ['fɔːtris] Festung *f*.

for·tu·i·tous □ [fɔː'tjuːitəs] zufällig; **for'tu·i·tous·ness, for'tu·i·ty** Zufälligkeit *f*, Zufall *m*.

for·tu·nate ['fɔːtʃnit] glücklich; **'for·tu·nate·ly** glücklicherweise, zum Glück.

for·tune ['fɔːtʃən] Glück *n*; (zukünftiges) Schicksal *n*; Zufall *m*; Vermögen *n*; ♀ Fortuna *f*; *good* ~ Glück *n*; *bad* ~, *ill* ~ Unglück *n*; *marry a* ~ e-e reiche Partie machen; *tell* ~*s* wahrsagen; '~**-hunt·er** Mitgiftjäger *m*; '~**-tel·ler** Wahrsager(in).

for·ty ['fɔːti] **1.** vierzig; ~*-niner Am.* F *kalifornischer* Goldsucher *m von 1849*; ~ *winks pl.* F Nickerchen *n*; **2.** Vierzig *f*; *the forties* die vierziger Jahre (*e-s Jahrhunderts*); die Vierziger(jahre) (*Alter*).

fo·rum ['fɔːrəm] Forum *n*; Gericht *n*.

for·ward ['fɔːwəd] **1.** *adj.* vorder; bereit(willig); fortschrittlich; vorschnell; vorwitzig, keck; frühzeitig; vorgerückt; ✝ Zeit..., Termin...; ~ *planning* Vorausplanung *f*; **2.** *adv.* vorwärts; nach vorn; ✝ auf Ziel; *from this time* ~ von jetzt an; **3.** *Fußball*: Stürmer *m*; **4.** (be)fördern, beschleunigen; (ab-, ver)senden; *please* ~ ☜ bitte nachsenden; '**for·ward·er** Spediteur *m*.

for·ward·ing ['fɔːwədiŋ] Versand *m*; Spedition *f*; ~ **ad·dress** Nachsendeadresse *f*; ~ **a·gent** Spediteur *m*.

for·ward·ness ['fɔːwədnis] Bereitwilligkeit *f*; Frühreife *f*; Voreiligkeit *f*; Keckheit *f*; **for·wards** ['fɔːwədz] vorwärts.

fosse [fɔs] ✂ Graben *m*; *anat.* Höhlung *f*, Grube *f*.

fos·sil ['fɔsl] **1.** fossil, versteinert; *fig.* rückständig; **2.** Fossil *n* (*a. fig.*).

fos·ter ['fɔstə] **1.** *fig.* nähren, pflegen; begünstigen; ~ *up* aufziehen; **2.** Pflege...; '**fos·ter·age** Pflege *f*; '**fos·ter-child** Pflegekind *n*; '**fos·ter·ling** ['-liŋ] Pflegekind *n*, Schützling *m*.

fought [fɔːt] *pret. u. p.p. von* fight **2.**

foul [faul] **1.** □ widerwärtig, ekelhaft; schmutzig(*fig. = zotig, gemein*); verschmutzt (*Garten, Gewehr etc.*); schimpfend, Schimpf...; schändlich; unehrlich; falsch, regelwidrig (*Spiel*); ♣ unklar; faul, verdorben (*Wasser etc.*); übelriechend (*Atem*

etc.); schlecht (*Wetter*); widrig (*Wind*); ruchlos (*Tat*); ~ *tongue* böse Zunge *f*, loses Maul *n*; *fall* ~ *of* mit dem Gesetz in Konflikt kommen; ♣ zs.-stoßen mit; **2.** Zs.-stoß *m*; *Sport*: Foul *n*, Regelverstoß *m*; *through fair and* ~ durch dick u. dünn; **3.** be-, verschmutzen; schmutzig werden; (sich) verwickeln, hemmen, (ver)sperren; ♣ ansegeln; ~**-mouthed** ['~mauðd], '~**-spo·ken** schmutzige Reden führend.

found¹ [faund] *pret. u. p.p. von* find *1*.

found² [~] (be)gründen (*a. fig.*); stiften.

found³ ⊕ [~] schmelzen, gießen.

foun·da·tion [faun'deiʃən] Gründung *f*; Stiftung *f*; Fundament *n*; Grund-, Unterlage *f* (*a. fig.*); ~ **cream** Make-up-Unterlage *f*; ~ **gar·ment** Mieder *n*; ~**-stone** Grundstein *m*.

found·er¹ ['faundə] (Be)Gründer(in), Stifter(in); ~ *member* Gründungsmitglied *n*.

found·er² ⊕ [~] Schmelzer *m*, Gießer *m*.

found·er³ [~] *v/i.* ♣, *fig.* scheitern, untergehen; lahmen (*Pferd*); zs.-fallen; *v/t.* zum Scheitern bringen; lahm machen, zuschanden reiten.

found·ling ['faundliŋ] Findling *m*, Findelkind *n*; ~ **hos·pi·tal** Findelhaus *n*.

found·ress ['faundris] Gründerin *f*.

found·ry ⊕ ['faundri] Gießerei *f*.

fount [faunt] *poet.* Quell(e *f*) *m*; *typ.* [*a.* fɔnt] Schriftguß *m*, -satz *m*.

foun·tain ['fauntin] Quelle *f*; Springbrunnen *m*; ⊕ *Flüssigkeits*-Behälter *m*; '~**-head** Urquell *m* (*a. fig.*); '~**-pen** Füllfederhalter *m*, Füller *m*.

four [fɔː] **1.** vier; **2.** Vier *f*; *Sport*: Vierer *m*; '~**-eyes** *sg. iro.* Brillenträger *m*; '~**-flush·er** *Am. sl.* Blender *m*; Hochstapler *m*; '~**-fold** vierfach; '~**-in-'hand** Vierspänner *m*; '~**-letter word** unanständiges Wort *n*; '~**-part** ♪ vierstimmig; '~**-pence** vier Pence; '~**-ply** vierfach (*Sperrholz, Wolle*); '~**-post·er** Himmelbett *n*; '~**-score** achtzig; ~**-some** ['fɔːsəm] *Golf*: Viererspiel *n*; '~**-square** viereckig; *fig.* unerschütterlich, fest (*to gegen*); '~**-stroke** *mot.* Viertakt...

four·teen [ˈfɔːˈtiːn] vierzehn; **'four-'teenth** [.θ] **1.** vierzehnte(r, -s); **2.** Vierzehntel n; **fourth** [fɔːθ] **1.** vierte(r, -s); **2.** Viertel n; **'fourth·ly** viertens; **'four-'wheel-er** Droschke f.

fowl [faul] **1.** Geflügel n; Huhn n; Vogel m; **2.** Vögel fangen od. schießen; **'fowl·er** Vogelsteller m, -jäger m.

fowl·ing [ˈfauliŋ] Vogelfang m, -jagd f; **'~-piece** Vogelflinte f.

fowl-run [ˈfaulrʌn] Hühnerhof m, Auslauf m.

fox [fɔks] **1.** Fuchs m; **2.** überlisten; **'~-brush** Fuchsschwanz m; **'~--earth** Fuchsbau m; **foxed** stockfleckig.

fox...: **'~-glove** ♀ Fingerhut m; **'~-hole** ✕ Schützenloch n; **'~-hound** Hund m zur Fuchsjagd; **'~-hunt** Fuchsjagd f; **'~-'ter·ri·er** zo. Foxterrier m; **'~-trot** Foxtrott m (Tanz); **'fox·y** fuchsartig; schlau; fuchsig, fuchsrot; stockfleckig.

foy·er thea. [ˈfɔiei] Foyer n, Wandelhalle f. [takel m.]

fra·cas [ˈfrækɑː], pl. ~ [ˈ~z] Spek-]

frac·tion [ˈfrækʃən] ⚕ Bruch m; Bruchstück n, -teil m; ~ line Bruchstrich m; **frac·tion·al** [ˈ~ʃənl] □ gebrochen (Zahl); Bruch...

frac·tious [ˈfrækʃəs] reizbar, zanksüchtig, unleidlich.

frac·ture [ˈfræktʃə] **1.** (bsd. Knochen)Bruch m; **2.** brechen.

frag·ile [ˈfrædʒail] zerbrechlich; fig. gebrechlich; **fra·gil·i·ty** [.ˈdʒiliti] Zer-, Gebrechlichkeit f.

frag·ment [ˈfrægmənt] Bruchstück n, Fragment n; **'frag·men·tar·y** □ bruchstückhaft, fragmentarisch; in Bruchstücken (vorhanden).

fra·grance [ˈfreigrəns] Wohlgeruch m, Duft m; **'fra·grant** □ wohlriechend, duftend.

frail[1] [freil] Binsen-, Feigenkorb m.

frail[2] □ [.] ge-, zerbrechlich; bsd. moralisch schwach; **'frail·ty** fig. Schwachheit f; Schwäche f.

frame [freim] **1.** Rahmen m; Gerippe n; (Brillen)Gestell n; Körper m; (An)Ordnung f, System n; ⚓ Spant n; phot. (Einzel)Bild n (e-s Films); ✿ Frühbeetkasten m; ~ of mind (Gemüts)Verfassung f; **2.** bilden, formen, bauen, machen; entwerfen; (ein)rahmen; sich entwik-

keln, zu werden versprechen; a. ~ up sl. j. mit Absicht fälschlich beschuldigen; ~ **aer·i·al** Rahmenantenne f; ~ **house** Holzhaus n; **'fram·er** Gestalter m; Rahmenmacher m; **'frame-up** bsd. Am. F abgekartetes Spiel n; **'frame·work** ⊕ Geripp n; ⚙ Fachwerk n; Rahmen m; fig. Bau m; System n.

franc [fræŋk] Franc m; Franken m.

fran·chise ⚕ [ˈfræntʃaiz] Wahlrecht n; Bürgerrecht n; bsd. Am. Konzession f.

Fran·cis·can eccl. [frænˈsiskən] Franziskaner m.

Fran·co- [ˈfræŋkəu] in Zssgn französisch.

fran·gi·ble [ˈfrændʒibl] zerbrechlich.

Frank[1] [fræŋk] Franke m.

frank[2] [.] **1.** □ frei(mütig), offen; **2.** Brief maschinell frankieren.

frank·furt·er [ˈfræŋkfətə] Frankfurter Würstchen n.

frank·in·cense [ˈfræŋkinsens] Weihrauch m.

frank·ing-ma·chine [ˈfræŋkiŋmə-ʃiːn] Frankiermaschine f.

frank·ness [ˈfræŋknis] Freimut m, Offenheit f.

fran·tic [ˈfræntik] (~ally) wahnsinnig, rasend (with vor); wütend; verzweifelt.

fra·ter·nal □ [frəˈtəːnl] brüderlich; **fra·ter·ni·ty** Brüderlichkeit f; Brüderschaft f; univ. Am. Verbindung f; **frat·er·ni·za·tion** [frætənaiˈzei-ʃən] Verbrüderung f; **'frat·er·nize** sich verbrüdern.

frat·ri·cide [ˈfreitrisaid] Brudermord m; Brudermörder m.

fraud [frɔːd] Betrug m; F Schwindel m; F Schwindler(in); **fraud·u·lence** [ˈ~julens] Betrügerei f; **'fraud·u·lent** □ betrügerisch.

fraught poet. [frɔːt] beladen; voll (with von).

fray[1] [frei] (sich) abnutzen; (sich) durchscheuern; ausfransen.

fray[2] [.] Schlägerei f, Streit m.

fraz·zle bsd. Am. F [ˈfræzl] **1.** Fetzen m/pl.; beat to a ~ in Fetzen hauen; **2.** zerfetzen.

freak [friːk] **1.** Einfall m, Laune f; sl. Exzentriker m, Fanatiker m, ...narr m; film ~ Kinonarr m; ~ of nature Laune f der Natur; Monstrum n; **2.** ~ out sl. ausflippen; **'freak·ish** □ lau-

nenhaft; abnorm.
freck·le ['frekl] **1.** Sommersprosse *f*;
fig. Fleckchen *n*; **2.** sommersprossig
machen *od.* werden; (sich) sprenkeln; **freck·led** ['⁓ld] sommersprossig.
free [fri:] **1.** ☐ *allg.* frei (*from*, *of* von)
(*unabhängig*; *unbehindert*; *unge-
zwungen*; *unbeschäftigt*; *offen*); kostenlos, unentgeltlich; freigebig (*of*
mit); reichlich; freiwillig; lose; ⁓ *of
debt* schuldenfrei; *he is* ⁓ *to inf.*
es steht ihm frei zu *inf.*; ⁓ *and
easy* zwanglos; sorglos; *have a* ⁓
hand freie Hand haben; *give od.
allow s.o. a* ⁓ *hand* j-m freie Hand
lassen; *have one's hands* ⁓ *fig.* ungebunden sein; *make* ⁓ *with et.* ohne
zu fragen benutzen; sich Freiheiten
erlauben gegen *j.*; *make* ⁓ *of* zur
Verfügung stellen; *make s.o.* ⁓ *of
the city* j. zum Ehrenbürger machen; *set* ⁓ freilassen; **2.** befreien
(*from*, *of* von); freilassen; *et.* freimachen; **⁓·boot·er** ['⁓bu:tə] Freibeuter *m*; **'free·dom** Freiheit *f etc.*
(*s. free 1*); Freisein *n* (*from* von);
Leichtigkeit *f der Auffassung etc.*;
freie Benutzung *f*; ⁓ *of the city* Eh-
renbürgerrecht *n*; ⁓ *of movement*
Freizügigkeit *f*; ⁓ *of speech* Redefreiheit *f*.
free...: ⁓ **en·ter·prise** freie Wirtschaft *f*; ⁓ **fight** allgemeine Schlägerei *f*; **'⁓-for-all** allgemeines Geschrei *n*; = *free fight*; **'⁓-'hand·ed**
freigebig, großzügig; **'⁓-hold** 🏛
freier Grundbesitz *m*; **'⁓-hold·er**
Grundeigentümer *m*; ⁓ **kick** *Sport:*
Freistoß *m*; ⁓ **la·bo(u)r** nichtorga-
nisierte Arbeiter *m/pl.*; **'⁓-'lance
1.** freier Journalist *m*; **2.** als freier
Journalist arbeiten; **'⁓-'list** Liste *f*
der zollfreien Waren *od.* der Frei-
kartenempfänger; ⁓ **liv·er** Schlemmer *m*; **'⁓-man** freier Mann *m*;
Vollbürger *m*; **'⁓-ma·son** Freimaurer *m*; **'⁓-ma·son·ry** Freimaurerei
f; ⁓ **port** Freihafen *m*; ⁓ **speech**
Redefreiheit *f*; **'⁓-'spo·ken** freimütig; ⁓ **state** Freistaat *m*; **'⁓-
-stone** Sandstein *m*; **'⁓-'think·er**
Freidenker(in); **'⁓-'think·ing**, **'⁓-
-thought 1.** Freidenkerei *f*; **2.** frei-
denkerisch; ⁓ **trade** Freihandel *m*;
'⁓-'trad·er Verfechter *m* des Frei-
handels; **'⁓-way** *Am.* Autobahn *f*; **'⁓-
-'wheel 1.** Freilauf *m*; **2.** im Freilauf

fahren.
freeze [fri:z] **1.** (*irr.*) *v/i.* (ge)frieren;
erstarren; ⁓ *to death* erfrieren; *v/t.*
gefrieren lassen; *Kapital* einfrieren;
Löhne, Preise stoppen; ⁓ *out sl. j.*
kaltstellen; **2.** Frostperiode *f*; Einfrieren *n*; *wage-*⁓ Lohnstopp *m*;
'⁓-dry gefriertrocknen; **'freez·er**
Eismaschine *f*; Gefrierautomat *m*,
-truhe *f*; 🚗 Kühlwagen *m*; **'freez·ing**
☐ eisig; ⁓ *compartment* Tiefkühlfach
n; ⁓ *mixture phys.* Kältemischung *f*; ⁓
point Gefrierpunkt *m*.
freight [freit] **1.** Fracht *f*; Fracht-
geld *n*; *attr. Am.* Güter...; ⁓ *out*
(*home*) Hin- (Rück)fracht *f*; **2.** be-,
verfrachten; beladen; **'freight·age**
= *freight 1*; **'freight-car** 🚗 *Am.*
Güterwagen *m*; **'freight·er** ⚓
Frachter *m*; ✈ Transportflugzeug
n; **freight train** *Am.* Güterzug *m*.
French [frentʃ] **1.** französisch; ⁓
beans pl. grüne Bohnen *f pl.*; ⁓ *dressing* Salatsoße *f aus Essig, Öl, Senf u.
Gewürzen*; ⁓ *fried potatoes pl., Am.* ⁓
fries pl. Pommes frites *pl.*; ⁓ *kiss*
Zungenkuß *m*; *take* ⁓ *leave* heimlich
weggehen; ⁓ *letter* F Kondom *n*; ⁓
windows pl. zweiflügelige Terrassen-,
Balkon-, Verandatür *f*; **2.** Französisch *n*; *the* ⁓ *pl.* die Franzosen *pl.*; ⁓
horn ♪ Horn *n*; **'⁓-man** Franzose *m*;
'⁓-wom·an Französin *f*.
fren·zied ['frenzid] wahnsinnig;
'fren·zy Wahnsinn *m*; Raserei *f*.
fre·quen·cy ['fri:kwənsi] Häufig-
keit *f*; ⚡ Frequenz *f*; ⁓ **mod·u·la·
tion** ⚡ Frequenzmodulation *f*; **fre·
quent 1.** ☐ ['⁓kwənt] häufig;
2. [fri'kwent] (oft) besuchen; **fre·
quen·ta·tion** [fri:kwen'teiʃən] häufiger Besuch *m*; Verkehr *m* (*of* in
dat.); **fre·quent·er** [fri'kwentə]
regelmäßige Besucher(in), Stammgast *m*.
fres·co ['freskəu], *pl.* **fres·co(e)s**
['⁓z] Fresko(gemälde) *n*.
fresh [freʃ] **1.** ☐ *allg.* frisch (*noch
unverändert*; *gesund*; *munter*; *spannkräftig*; *kühl*; *ungesalzen*); neu; unerfahren; *Am. sl.* pampig, frech;
break ⁓ *ground fig.* Neuland betreten; ⁓ *water* Süßwasser *n*; **2.** *Morgen-*
Kühle *f*; Hochwasser *n*; **'fresh·en**
frisch machen *od.* werden; auffrischen; **fresh·et** ['⁓it] *fig.* Flut *f*;
'fresh-fro·zen tiefgekühlt; **'fresh·
man** *univ.* Student *m* im ersten

Jahr; '**fresh·ness** Frische *f*; Neuheit *f*, Unerfahrenheit *f*; '**freshwa·ter** Süßwasser...; ~ *college Am.* drittrangiges College *n*.

fret[1] [fret] **1.** Aufregung *f*; Ärger *m*, Verdruß *m*; **2.** zerfressen; (sich) ärgern; (sich) grämen; *Loch* fressen; *Wasser* kräuseln; ~ *away*, ~ *out* aufreiben, verzehren.

fret[2] [~] **1.** △ gebrochener Stab *m*; **2.** gittern; *fig.* bunt machen.

fret[3] [~] ♪ Bund *m*, Griffleiste *f*.

fret·ful □ ['fretful] ärgerlich, verdrießlich, mürrisch; unzufrieden.

fret-saw ['fretsɔ:] Laubsäge *f*.

fret·work ['fretwɔ:k] (geschnitztes) Gitterwerk *n*; Laubsägearbeit *f*.

Freud·i·an ['frɔidjən] Freudsch; ~ *slip psych.* Freudsche Fehlleistung *f*.

fri·a·bil·i·ty [fraiə'biliti] Bröckligkeit *f*; '**fri·a·ble** bröcklig; zerreibbar.

fri·ar [fraiə] (Bettel)Mönch *m*; '**friar·y** Mönchskloster *n*.

frib·ble ['fribl] **1.** (ver)gammeln, (ver)trödeln; **2.** Tagedieb *m*.

fric·as·see [frikə'si:] **1.** Frikassee *n*; **2.** frikassieren.

fric·tion ['frikʃən] Reibung *f* (*a. fig.*); *attr.* = **fric·tion·al** ['~ʃənl] Reibungs...

Fri·day ['fraidi] Freitag *m*.

fridge F [fridʒ] Kühlschrank *m*.

fried egg [fraid'eg] Spiegelei *n*.

friend [frend] Freund(in); Bekannte *m*, *f*; ♀ Quäker(in); *his* ~*s pl.* oft seine Bekannten *pl.*; *make* ~*s with* sich anfreunden mit; '**friend·less** freundlos; '**friend·li·ness** Freundlichkeit *f*; '**friend·ly** freundschaftlich; freundlich (*a. fig.*); befreundet; ♀ *Society* Versicherungsverein *m* auf Gegenseitigkeit; '**friend·ship** Freundschaft *f*.

frieze [fri:z] Fries *m* (*Stoff u.* △).

frig·ate ♣ ['frigit] Fregatte *f*.

frig(e) F [fridʒ] = *fridge*.

fright [frait] Schreck(en) *m*, Furcht *f*; *fig.* Schreckbild *n*, Vogelscheuche *f*; '**fright·en** erschrecken, in Schrecken versetzen; *be* ~*ed of* F Angst haben vor (*dat.*); **fright·ful** □ ['~ful] schrecklich; '**fright·fulness** Schrecklichkeit *f*.

frig·id □ ['fridʒid] kalt, frostig (*a. fig.*); *psych.* frigid; **fri'gid·i·ty** Kälte *f*, Frostigkeit *f*; *psych.* Frigidität *f*.

frill [fril] **1.** Krause *f*, Rüsche *f*; *put on* ~*s* F *fig.* vornehm tun; **2.** kräuseln.

fringe [frindʒ] **1.** Franse *f*; Rand *m*; *a.* ~*s pl.* Ponyfrisur *f*; ~ *benefits pl.* zusätzliche Sozialleistungen *f pl. des Arbeitgebers*; ~ *event* Randveranstaltung *f*; ~ *group* Randgruppe *f*; **2.** mit Fransen besetzen, (um)säumen.

frip·per·y ['fripəri] **1.** Flitterkram *m*, Plunder *m*; **2.** wertlos; Flitter...

Fri·sian ['friziən] **1.** friesisch; **2.** Friese *m*, Friesin *f*; das Friesische.

frisk [frisk] **1.** Hüpfen *n*, Springen *n*; Luftsprung *m*; **2.** hüpfen; *nach Waffen etc.* durchsuchen; '**frisk·iness** Munterkeit *f*; '**frisk·y** □ hüpfend; munter, lustig.

frith [friθ] = *firth*.

frit·ter ['fritə] **1.** Pfannkuchen *m*, Krapfen *m*; **2.** ~ *away* verzetteln.

fri·vol ['frivəl] leichtsinnig sein; *Zeit* verplempern; **fri·vol·i·ty** [~'vɔliti] Leichtfertigkeit *f*, Frivolität *f*; **friv·o·lous** □ ['~vələs] nichtig; leichtfertig, leichtsinnig, frivol.

frizz [friz] (sich) kräuseln; *Küche:* brutzeln; **friz·zle** ['~l] *a.* ~ *up* (sich) kräuseln; knusperig braten; brutzeln; '**friz·z(l)y** kraus, gekräuselt.

fro [frou]: *to and* ~ hin und her, auf und ab.

frock [frɔk] *Mönchs*-Kutte *f*; *Frauen*-Kleid *n*; (Kinder)Röckchen *n*; Kittel *m*; '~-'coat Gehrock *m*.

frog [frɔg] Frosch *m*; Schnurverschluß *m e-s Mantels*; ♥ Herzstück *n e-r Weiche*; ✗ Säbeltasche *f*; '~man Froschmann *m*, Kampfschwimmer *m*; '~-march *Gefangenen* an Armen u. Beinen wegtragen.

frol·ic ['frɔlik] **1.** Fröhlichkeit *f*; lustiger Streich *m*, Scherz *m*; Lustbarkeit *f*; **2.** scherzen, spaßen; **frolic·some** □ ['~səm] lustig, fröhlich.

from [frɔm, frəm] von; aus, von ... her; von (... an); seit; (entfernt) von; aus, vor, wegen; nach, gemäß; *defend* ~ schützen vor (*dat.*); *draw* ~ *nature* nach der Natur zeichnen; *hide* ~ verbergen vor (*dat.*); ~ *above* von oben herab; ~ *amidst* mitten aus; ~ *before* aus der Zeit vor.

frond ♣ [frɔnd] (Farn-, Palm-) Wedel *m*.

front [frʌnt] **1.** Stirn *f*; Vorderseite *f*; ✗ Front *f*; Hemdbrust *f*; Strandpromenade *f*; Kühnheit *f*, Frechheit *f*; *poet.* Stirn *f*, Gesicht *n*; *in ~* vorne; *in ~ of räumlich* vor; *come to the ~ fig.* sich zeigen, hervortreten; **2.** Vorder...; **3.** *a. ~ on, ~ towards* die Front haben nach; gegenüberstehen, -liegen (*dat.*); gegenübertreten (*dat.*); '**front·age △** Vorderfront *f*; '**fron·tal 1.** Stirn...; Front...; Vorder...; **2. △** Fassade *f*; **front bench** *pol.* vorderste Sitzbänke *f/pl.* im Parlament, *für führende Mitglieder der Regierung u. der Opposition*; **front bench·er** führendes Fraktionsmitglied *n*; **front door** Haustür *f*; **fron·tier** ['⌣tiə] **1.** Grenz...; **2.** Grenze *f* (*bsd. hist. Am.* Grenze zum Wilden *Westen*); '**fron·tiers·man** Grenzbewohner *m*; *fig.* Pionier *m*; **fron·tis·piece** ['⌣tispi:s] **△** Vorderseite *f*; *typ.* Titelbild *n*; **front·let** ['frʌntlit] Stirnbinde *f*; **front line** Front(linie) *f*; *be in the ~* (*a. fig.*) an vorderster Front stehen; **front man** *fig.* Aushängeschild *n*; '**front-page** *Zeitung:* Titelseite *f*; '**front-'wheel drive** *mot.* Vorderradantrieb *m*.

frost [frɔst] **1.** Frost *m*; *a.* hoar *~*, white *~* Reif *m*; F Reinfall *m*; *black ~* trockener Frost *m*; **2.** (mit Zucker) bestreuen; glasieren; mattieren; durch Frost beschädigen; *~ed glass* Milchglas *n*; '**~-bite** Erfrierung *f e-s Körperteils*; '**frost·bit·ten** erfroren (*Körperteil*); '**frost-bound** gefroren (*Boden*); '**frost·ed** glasiert (*Kuchen*); erfroren (*Pflanzen etc.*); *~ glass* Mattglas *n*; '**frost·i·ness** Frost *m*, Kälte *f* (*a. fig.*); '**frost·ing** Zuckerguß *m*; '**frost·y** ☐ frostig, eisig (*a. fig.*); bereift (*fig. ergraut*).

froth [frɔθ] **1.** Schaum *m*; *fig.* Schaumschlägerei *f*; **2.** schäumen; zu Schaum schlagen; '**froth·i·ness** das Schaumige; *fig.* Seichtheit *f*; '**froth·y** ☐ schaumig; *fig.* seicht; schaumschlägerisch.

fro·ward † ['frəuəd] eigensinnig, widerspenstig.

frown [fraun] **1.** Stirnrunzeln *n*; finsterer Blick *m*; **2.** *v/t. ~ down* durch finstere Blicke einschüchtern; *v/i.* die Stirn runzeln; finster blicken; *~ at, ~ (up)on* finster ansehen; ablehnen, mißbilligen.

frowst F [fraust] Mief *m* (*schlechte Luft*); '**frowst·y** ☐, **frowz·y** ['frauzi] moderig, muffig; schlampig; schmutzig.

froze [frəuz] *pret. von freeze* 1; '**fro·zen 1.** *p.p. von freeze* 1; **2.** *adj.* (eis-) kalt; eingefroren (*Kapital etc.*); *~ assets pl.* festliegendes Kapital *n*; *~ meat* Gefrierfleisch *n*.

fruc·ti·fi·ca·tion [frʌktifi'keiʃən] Befruchtung *f*; **fruc·ti·fy** ['⌣fai] *v/t.* befruchten; *v/i.* Früchte bringen (*a. fig.*).

fru·gal ☐ ['fru:gəl] genügsam, mäßig; sparsam; einfach, frugal; **fru·gal·i·ty** [⌣'gæliti] Mäßigkeit *f*; Sparsamkeit *f*.

fruit [fru:t] **1.** Frucht *f* (*fig. = Erfolg*); *coll.* Früchte *f/pl.*, Obst *n*; **2.** Frucht tragen; '**fruit·age** (Frucht-) Tragen *n*; **frui·ta·ri·an** [fru:'teəriən] Rohköstler(in); '**fruit-cake** englischer Kuchen *m*; '**fruit·er·er** Fruchtträger *m* (*Baum*); '**fruit·er·er** Obsthändler *m*; **fruit·ful** ☐ ['⌣ful] fruchtbar (*a. fig.*); ergiebig; '**fruit·ful·ness** Fruchtbarkeit *f* (*a. fig.*); **fru·i·tion** [fru:'iʃən] (Voll-) Genuß *m*; Erfüllung *f*, Verwirklichung *f*; **fruit knife** Obstmesser *n*; '**fruit·less** ☐ unfruchtbar; *fig.* fruchtlos, vergeblich; '**fruit-ma·chine** F Spielautomat *m*; **fruit sal·ad** Obstsalat *m*; '**fruit·y** fruchtig; F deftig, saftig, derb.

frump [frʌmp] *fig.* Vogelscheuche *f*; '**frump·ish**, '**frump·y** altmodisch.

frus·trate [frʌs'treit] vereiteln; enttäuschen; **frus'tra·tion** Vereitelung *f*; Enttäuschung *f*; *psych.* Frustration *f*.

fry [frai] **1.** Gebratene *n*; **2.** Fischbrut *f*; *small ~* F junges Gemüse *n* (*Kinder*); kleine Leute *pl.*; **3.** braten, backen; *s. egg; fried potatoes pl.* Bratkartoffeln *f/pl.*; '**fry·ing-pan** Bratpfanne *f*; *get out of the ~ into the fire* vom Regen in die Traufe kommen.

fuch·sia ♀ ['fju:ʃə] Fuchsia *f*.

fuck V [fʌk] **1.** ficken; **2.** *int.* verdammte Scheiße!

fud·dle ['fʌdl] **1.** (sich) berauschen; **2.** Rausch *m*.

fudge F [fʌdʒ] **1.** zurechtpfuschen; schwindeln; **2.** Fälschung *f*; letzte Meldung *f*; Weichkaramelle *f*; *~!* Schwindel!; Unsinn!

fuel [ˈfjuəl] **1.** Brennmaterial *n*; Betriebs-, *mot.* Kraftstoff *m*; ~ *ga(u)ge mot.* Benzinuhr *f*; ~ *oil* Heizöl *n*; **2.** mit Brennstoff versehen; *mot.* tanken.

fug [fʌg] **1.** Mief *m*; Staubflocken *f/pl.*; **2.** ein Stubenhocker sein.

fu·ga·cious [fjuːˈgeiʃəs] flüchtig, vergänglich.

fu·gi·tive [ˈfjuːdʒitiv] **1.** flüchtig (*a. fig.*); **2.** Flüchtling *m*.

fu·gle·man [ˈfjuːglmæn] (An-, Wort)Führer *m*.

fugue ♩ [fjuːg] Fuge *f*.

ful·crum [ˈfʌlkrəm] Drehpunkt *m*.

ful·fil(l) [fulˈfil] erfüllen; vollziehen; **ful'fill·er** Vollbringer(in); **ful-ˈfil(l)·ment** Erfüllung *f*.

ful·gent *poet.* [ˈfʌldʒənt] glänzend.

full[1] [ful] **1.** □ *allg.* voll; Voll...; vollständig, völlig; reif; reichlich; ausführlich; *at ~ length* ausführlich; *of ~ age* volljährig; ~ *stop gr.* Punkt *m*; ~ *up* besetzt; *house ~ thea.* ausverkauft; **2.** *adv.* völlig, ganz; genau, gerade; recht, sehr; **3.** Fülle *f*; Ganze *n*; Höhepunkt *m*; *in ~* völlig, gänzlich; ausführlich; *pay in ~* voll bezahlen; *to the ~* vollständig, bis ins kleinste.

full[2] ⊕ [~] walken.

full...: '~-'back *Fußball:* Verteidiger *m*; '~-'blood·ed vollblütig, kräftig; reinrassig; '~-'blown voll erblüht; '~-'bod·ied schwer (*Wein*); ~ *dress* Gesellschaftsanzug *m*; '~-dress formell, Gala...; *Am.* ausführlich; ~ *debate* wichtige Debatte *f*; ~ *rehearsal thea.* Generalprobe *f*.

full·er ⊕ [ˈfulə] Walker *m*.

full...: '~-'fledged *orn.* flügge; voll ausgewachsen, fertig; '~-'grown ausgewachsen.

full-ing-mill ⊕ [ˈfuliŋmil] Walkmühle *f*.

full-length [ˈfulˈleŋθ] in Lebensgröße.

ful(l)·ness [ˈfulnis] Fülle *f*.

full...: '~-'page ganzseitig; '~-'scale in Lebensgröße, im Maßstab 1 : 1; total, regelrecht; vollständig; '~-'time vollbeschäftigt; hauptberuflich (tätig); ganztägig.

ful·ly [ˈfuli] voll, völlig, gänzlich; ~ *two hours* ganze zwei Stunden; '~-'fash·ioned mit Paßform (*Damenstrümpfe etc.*); '~-'fledged flügge (*Vogel, a. fig.*); vollausgebildet, -entwickelt.

ful·mar *orn.* [ˈfulmə] Fulmar *m*, Eissturmvogel *m*.

ful·mi·nate *fig.* [ˈfʌlmineit] losdonnern, wettern (*against* gegen); **ful·mi'na·tion** Drohung *f*; Wettern *n*.

ful·some □ [ˈfulsəm] widerlich.

fum·ble [ˈfʌmbl] herumtappen, -tasten, -fummeln; '**fum·bler** Tolpatsch *m*.

fume [fjuːm] **1.** Dunst *m*, Dampf *m*; Rauch *m*, Qualm *m*; *in a ~* wütend, aufgebracht; **2.** rauchen, dunsten, dampfen; wütend sein.

fu·mi·gate [ˈfjuːmigeit] (aus)räuchern, desinfizieren; **fu·mi'ga·tion** (Aus)Räucherung *f*, Desinfektion *f*.

fum·ing □ [ˈfjuːmiŋ] aufgebracht, wütend.

fun [fʌn] Scherz *m*, Spaß *m*; *have ~* sich amüsieren; *make ~ of* sich lustig machen über (*acc.*).

func·tion [ˈfʌŋkʃən] **1.** Funktion *f*; Beruf *m*; Tätigkeit *f*, Wirksamkeit *f*; *physiol.*, ⚕ Funktion *f*; Aufgabe *f*; Feierlichkeit *f*; **2.** funktionieren, arbeiten; **func·tion·al** □ [ˈ~ʃənl] amtlich; ⚕ funktionell; sachlich; **func·tion·ar·y** [ˈ~ʃnəri] Beamte *m*; Funktionär *m*.

fund [fʌnd] **1.** Fonds *m*, Kapital *n*; ~*s pl.* Staatsschulden *f/pl.*, -papiere *n/pl.*; Geld(er *n/pl.*, -mittel *n/pl.*) *n*; Vorrat *m*, Schatz *m*; *in ~s* be Geld; **2.** *Schuld* fundieren; *Geld* anlegen.

fun·da·men·tal [fʌndəˈmentl] **1.** □ grundlegend, -sätzlich; Grund...; **2.** ~*s pl.* Grundlage *f*, -züge *m/pl.*, -begriffe *m/pl.*, -tatsachen *f/pl.*

fu·ner·al [ˈfjuːnərəl] **1.** Beerdigung *f*, Bestattung *f*; **2.** Begräbnis..., Trauer..., Leichen...; ~ *pile* Scheiterhaufen *m*; **fu·ne·re·al** □ [~-ˈniəriəl] Trauer...; düster, traurig.

fun·fair [ˈfʌnfεə] Rummelplatz *m*.

fun·gous [ˈfʌŋgəs] pilz-, schwammartig; **fun·gus** [ˈ~gəs], *pl. mst* **fun·gi** [ˈ~gai] ⚘ Schwamm *m*, Pilz *m*; ⚘ Wucherung *f*.

fu·nic·u·lar [fjuːˈnikjulə] **1.** Seil...; **2.** *a.* ~ *railway* (Draht)Seilbahn *f*.

funk F [fʌŋk] **1.** Mordsangst *f*; Angsthase *m*; **2.** Angst haben; sich drücken (vor); '**funk·y** F feig(e).

fun·nel [ˈfʌnl] Trichter *m*; Rauchfang *m*; ⚓, 🚂 Schornstein *m*.

fun·nies *Am.* [ˈfʌniz] *pl.* = *comics.*

fun·ny ☐ ['fʌni] spaßig, komisch; sonderbar; '**~-bone** Musikantenknochen *m*.

fur [fə:] **1.** Pelz *m*; Belag *m der Zunge*; Kesselstein *m*; **~s** *pl*. Pelzwaren *f/pl*.; *make the* **~** *fly* ein großes Theater machen; **2.** mit Pelz kleiden *od*. besetzen *od*. füttern; Kesselstein ansetzen; **~red** belegt (*Zunge*).

fur·be·low ['fə:biləu] Falbel *f*.

fur·bish ['fə:biʃ] putzen, polieren.

fur·ca·tion [fə:'keiʃən] Gabelung *f*.

fur coat ['fə:'kəut] Pelzmantel *m*.

fu·ri·ous ☐ ['fjuəriəs] wütend; wild, rasend.

furl [fə:l] *Segel* festmachen; *Schirm* einrollen; *Fächer* zs.-klappen; *Vorhang* aufziehen.

fur·long ['fə:lɔŋ] Achtelmeile *f*.

fur·lough ['fə:ləu] **1.** Urlaub *m*; **2.** beurlauben (*bsd.* ✕).

fur·nace ['fə:nis] Schmelz-, Hochofen *m*; (Heiz)Kessel *m*; Feuerung *f*.

fur·nish ['fə:niʃ] versehen, ausstatten (*with* mit); *et*. liefern; *Zimmer* möblieren, einrichten; '**fur·nish·er** Lieferant *m*; Möbelhändler *m*; '**fur·nish·ings** *pl*. Einrichtung(sgegenstände *m/pl*.) *f*.

fur·ni·ture ['fə:nitʃə] Möbel *n/pl*., Mobiliar *n*, Einrichtung *f*; Ausstattung *f*; ⊕ Zubehör *n*.

fu·ro·re [fjuə'rɔ:ri] Furore *n*; Begeisterung *f*; Aufregung *f*.

fur·ri·er ['fʌriə] Kürschner *m*; '**fur·ri·er·y** Kürschnerei *f*.

fur·row ['fʌrəu] **1.** Furche *f*; Nut *f*; **2.** furchen; auskehlen.

fur·ry ['fə:ri] pelzig; Pelz...

fur·ther ['fə:ðə] **1.** *adj. u. adv.* ferner, weiter; **2.** fördern; '**fur·therance** Förderung *f*, Unterstützung *f*; '**fur·ther·er** Förderer *m*, Förderin *f*; '**fur·ther'more** ferner, überdies, außerdem; '**fur·ther·most** weitest, entferntest; am weitesten.

fur·thest ['fə:ðist] *s*. *furthermost*;

at (*the*) **~** spätestens.

fur·tive ☐ ['fə:tiv] verstohlen.

fu·ry ['fjuəri] Raserei *f*, Wut *f*; Furie *f*.

furze ♀ [fə:z] Stechginster *m*.

fuse [fju:z] **1.** schmelzen; verschmelzen; *als Folge e-s Kurzschlusses* ausgehen (*Licht*); ✕ mit Zünder versehen; **2.** ⚡ (Schmelz-) Sicherung *f*; ✕ Zünder *m*; *time-*~ Zeitzünder *m*.

fu·se·lage ['fju:zila:ʒ] (Flugzeug-) Rumpf *m*.

fu·si·bil·i·ty [fju:zə'biliti] Schmelzbarkeit *f*; **fu·si·ble** ['fju:zəbl] schmelzbar.

fu·sil·ier ✕ [fju:zi'liə] Füsilier *m*.

fu·sil·lade [fju:zi'leid] Gewehrfeuer *n*.

fu·sion ['fju:ʒən] Schmelzen *n*; Verschmelzung *f*; **~ bomb** ✕ Wasserstoffbombe *f*.

fuss F [fʌs] **1.** Lärm *m*; Wesen *n*, Getue *n*; Aufregung *f*; *make a* **~** *about* viel Aufhebens über (*acc.*); *make a* **~** *of s.o.* viel Wesens um j. machen; **2.** viel Aufhebens machen (*about* um, von); hasten; nervös machen, belästigen; '**~·pot** F Umstandskrämer *m*; '**fuss·y** ☐ F *unnötig* geschäftig, viel Aufhebens machend.

fus·tian ✝ ['fʌstiən] Barchent *m*; *fig*. Schwulst *m*.

fust·i·ness ['fʌstinis] Modergeruch *m*; '**fust·y** ☐ muffig; *fig*. verstaubt.

fu·tile ☐ ['fju:tail] unnütz; wirkungs-, nutzlos; **fu·til·i·ty** [~'tiliti] Nichtigkeit *f*, Nutzlosigkeit *f*.

fu·ture ['fju:tʃə] **1.** (zu)künftig; **~** *tense gr*. Futur *n*; **2.** Zukunft *f*; **~s** *pl*. ✝ Termingeschäfte *n/pl*.; '**fu·tur·ism** *paint*. Futurismus *m*; **fu·tu·ri·ty** [fju:'tjuəriti] Zukunft *f*; zukünftiges Ereignis *n*.

fuzz [fʌz] **1.** feiner Flaum *m*; Fussel *f*; *the* **~** *sl*. die Bullen *m/pl*.; die Polizei *f*; **2.** fusseln, (zer)fasern; '**fuzz·y** ☐ fusselig, faserig; kraus; verschwommen, trüb.

G

gab F [gæb] Geschwätz *n*; *the gift of the* ~ ein gutes Mundwerk *n*.

gab·ar·dine ['gæbədi:n] Gabardine *m* (*Wollstoff*).

gab·ble ['gæbl] **1.** Geschnatter *n*, Geschwätz *n*; **2.** schnattern, schwatzen; '**gab·bler** Schwätzer (-in); '**gab·by** F geschwätzig.

gab·er·dine ['gæbədi:n] Kaftan *m*; = *gabardine*.

ga·ble ['geibl] Giebel *m*; '**ga·bled** mit Giebel(n); Giebel...

ga·by ['geibi] Trottel *m*.

gad F [gæd]: ~ *about* sich herumtreiben; ⚲ wuchern; '**gad·a·bout** F Herumtreiber *m*, Nichtstuer *m*.

gad·fly *zo.* ['gædflai] Bremse *f*.

gadg·et *sl.* ['gædʒit] Dings *n*, Apparat *m*; Kniff *m*, Pfiff *m*; '**gadg·et·ry** *mst contp.* Apparate *m pl.*, technisches Zubehör.

Gael·ic ['geilik] Gälisch *n*.

gaff [gæf] Fischhaken *m*; ⚓ Gaffel *f*; *sl.* Tingeltangel *n*, *m*; *blow the* ~ *sl.* alles verraten.

gaffe F [gæf] Dummheit *f* (*Fehler*).

gaf·fer F ['gæfə] Alte *m*; Vorarbeiter *m*.

gag [gæg] **1.** Knebel *m* (*a. fig.*); *parl.* Schluß *m* der Debatte; *thea.* Improvisation *f*; Witz *m*, Trick *m*; Gag *m*; **2.** knebeln; *thea.* improvisieren; *fig.* mundtot machen.

ga·ga *sl.* ['ga:ga:] senil, verblödet; verrückt.

gage[1] [geidʒ] **1.** Pfand *n*; Fehdehandschuh *m*; **2.** zum Pfand geben.

gage[2] [⌣] = *gauge*.

gag·gle ['gægl] Schar *f* Gänse; *fig.* Herde *f*.

gai·e·ty ['geiəti] Fröhlichkeit *f*; Lustbarkeit *f*; Heiterkeit *f*.

gai·ly ['geili] *adv. von gay.*

gain [gein] **1.** Gewinn *m* (*bsd.* ✝ ~*s pl.*); **2.** *v/t.* gewinnen; erreichen; bekommen; *v/i.* vorgehen (*Uhr*); ~ *on* Vorteil erlangen über (*acc.*); ~ *in* zunehmen an (*dat.*); '**gain·er** Gewinner(in); **gain·ful** □ ['⌣ful] einträglich; ~ *employment* Erwerbstätigkeit *f*; ~*ly occupied* erwerbstätig; '**gain·ings** *pl.* Gewinn *m*, Verdienst *m*.

gain·say *lit.* [gein'sei] (*irr. say*) widersprechen (*dat.*); leugnen.

gainst *poet.* [geinst] = *against*.

gait [geit] Gang(art *f*) *m*; Haltung *f*; Schritt *m*.

gai·ter ['geitə] Gamasche *f*.

gal *Am. sl.* [gæl] Mädel *n*.

ga·la ['gɑ:lə] Fest(lichkeit *f*) *n*.

ga·lac·tic *ast.* [gə'læktik] Milchstraßen...

gal·an·tine ['gælənti:n] Galantine *f* (*Geflügelsülze*).

gal·ax·y ['gæləksi] *ast.* Milchstraße *f*; *fig.* (glänzende) Schar *f*.

gale [geil] Sturm *m* (*a. fig.*); steife Brise *f*.

ga·le·na *min.* [gə'li:nə] Galenit *m*, Bleiglanz *m*.

gall[1] [gɔ:l] Galle *f* (*a. fig.*); *bsd. Am. sl.* Frechheit *f*.

gall[2] ⚲ [⌣] Gallapfel *m*.

gall[3] [⌣] **1.** wundgeriebene Stelle *f*, Wolf *m*; *fig.* Pein *f*; **2.** wundreiben; peinigen; reizen, ärgern.

gal·lant ['gælənt] **1.** □ stattlich; tapfer; galant; ritterlich; **2.** Kavalier *m*; *b.s.* Galan *m*, Stutzer *m*; **3.** galant sein; '**gal·lant·ry** Tapferkeit *f*; Galanterie *f*; Liebelei *f*.

gal·leon ⚓ ['gæliən] Galeone *f*.

gal·ler·y ['gæləri] Galerie *f*; Empore *f*; ✕ Stollen *m*; *play to the* ~ den Beifall der Menge suchen.

gal·ley ['gæli] ⚓ Galeere *f*; ⚓ Kombüse *f*; *typ.* Schiff *n*; ~ *proof* Korrekturfahne *f*; '~**-slave** Galeerensklave *m*.

Gal·lic ['gælik] gallisch; *co.* französisch; **Gal·li·can** ['⌣kən] gallikanisch; **gal·li·cism** ['⌣sizəm] Gallizismus *m*, französische Spracheigenheit *f*.

gal·li·vant [gæli'vænt] sich herumtreiben.

gall·nut ['gɔ:lnʌt] Gallapfel *m*.

gal·lon ['gælən] Gallone *f* (*4,54 Liter, Am. 3,78 Liter*).

gal·lop ['gæləp] **1.** Galopp *m*; **2.** galoppieren (lassen).

gal·lows ['gæləuz] *sg.* Galgen *m*; '~**-bird** Galgenvogel *m*.

Gal·lup poll ['gæləp'pəul] Meinungsumfrage *f*.

ga·lore [gə'lɔ:] in Menge.

ga·losh [gə'lɔʃ] Galosche *f*, Überschuh *m*, Gummischuh *m*.

ga·lumph [gə'lʌmf] (einher)stolzieren.

gal·van·ic [gæl'vænik] (~*ally*) galvanisch; **gal·va·nism** ['gælvə-nizəm] Galvanismus *m*; '**gal·va·nize** galvanisieren; anfeuern, stimulieren (*into* zu); **gal·va·no·plas·tic** [ˌnəu'plæstik] galvanoplastisch.

gam·bit ['gæmbit] *Schach*: Gambit *n*; *fig*. Einleitung *f*.

gam·ble ['gæmbl] (um Geld) spielen; **2.** F Glücksspiel *n* (*mst fig*.); '**gam·bler** Spieler(in); '**gam·bling-den**, '**gam·bling-house** Spielhölle *f*. [gutt *n*.]

gam·boge [gæm'bu:ʒ] Gummi-J

gam·bol ['gæmbəl] **1.** Luftsprung *m*; **2.** (fröhlich) hüpfen, tanzen.

game¹ [geim] **1.** Spiel *n*; Scherz *m*; *b.s.* Schlich *m*; Wild *n*; *beat s.o. at his own ~* j. mit s-n eigenen Waffen schlagen; *play the ~* sich an die Spielregeln halten; *fig*. anständig handeln; *be off one's ~* nicht in Form sein; *make ~ of s.o.* sich über j. lustig machen; **2.** F entschlossen; bereit; *die ~* furchtlos in den Tod gehen; **3.** spielen.

game² [ˌ] lahm; verkrüppelt.

game...: '**~-cock** Kampfhahn *m*; '**~·keep·er** Wildhüter *m*; '**~-laws** *pl*. Jagdgesetze *n/pl*.; '**~·li·cence** Jagdschein *m*; '**games-mas·ter** Turnlehrer *m*; **game·ster** ['ˌstə] Spieler(in); '**gam·ing-house** Spielkasino *n*.

gam·ma rays *phys.* ['gæmə'reiz] *pl.* Gammastrahlen *m/pl*.

gam·mon ['gæmən] (geräucherter) Schinken *m*; F Unsinn *m*, Quatsch *m*.

gam·my F ['gæmi] = *game²*.

gamp *co.* [gæmp] Regenschirm *m*.

gam·ut ['gæmət] ♪ Tonleiter *f*; *fig*. Skala *f*.

gam·y ['geimi] nach Wild schmeckend; wildreich.

gan·der ['gændə] Gänserich *m*.

gang [gæŋ] **1.** Abteilung *f*, Trupp *m*; Rotte *f*; *b.s.* Bande *f*; **2.** *~ up* sich zs.-rotten *od*. -tun (*against*, *on* gegen); '**~-board** ♆ Laufplanke *f*; **gang·er** ['gæŋə] Rottenführer *m*.

gan·gli·on ['gæŋliən] *anat.* Ganglion *n*, Nervenknoten *m*; *fig*. Knotenpunkt *m*.

gang-plank ♆ ['gæŋplæŋk] Laufplanke *f*.

gan·grene ⚕ ['gæŋgri:n] Gangrän *f*, Brand *m*.

gang·ster *Am.* ['gæŋstə] Gangster *m*, Verbrecher *m*.

gang·way ['gæŋwei] (Durch)Gang *m*; ♆ Fallreep *n*; ♆ Laufplanke *f*.

gan·net *orn.* ['gænit] Tölpel *m*.

gan·try ['gæntri] ⎈ Signalbrücke *f*; ♆ Verladebrücke *f*; Gerüst *n*.

gaol [dʒeil], '**~-bird**, '**gaol·er** *s. jail etc.*

gap [gæp] Lücke *f*; *fig*. Kluft *f*; Spalte *f*; Riß *m*.

gape [geip] **1.** gähnen; klaffen; *~ at* angaffen, -starren; **2.** *the ~s pl.* Schnabelsperre *f*.

ga·rage ['gæra:dʒ] **1.** Garage *f*; Autowerkstatt *f*; **2.** *Auto* einstellen.

garb [ga:b] **1.** Gewand *n*, Tracht *f*; **2.** kleiden.

gar·bage ['ga:bidʒ] Abfall *m*; Schund *m*; *~ can Am.*, *~ pail* Mülleimer *m*; *~ collector Am.* Müllabfuhrmann *m*.

gar·ble ['ga:bl] verstümmeln; zustutzen; entstellen.

gar·den ['ga:dn] **1.** Garten *m*; *lead s.o. up the ~ path* j. an der Nase herumführen; **2.** Gartenbau treiben; im Garten arbeiten; '**gar·den·er** Gärtner(in).

gar·de·nia ♀ [ga:'di:njə] Gardenie *f*.

gar·den·ing ['ga:dniŋ] Gartenarbeit *f*; Gärtnerei *f*; '**gar·den-par·ty** Gartenfest *n*.

gar·gan·tu·an [ga:'gæntjuən] gewaltig, ungeheuer.

gar·gle ['ga:gl] **1.** gurgeln; **2.** Gurgelwasser *n*.

gar·goyle ⚠ ['ga:gɔil] Wasserspeier *m*.

gar·ish ☐ ['gɛəriʃ] grell, auffallend.

gar·land ['ga:lənd] **1.** Kranz *m*; Girlande *f*; **2.** bekränzen.

gar·lic ♀ ['ga:lik] Knoblauch *m*.

gar·ment ['ga:mənt] Kleidungsstück *n*; Gewand *n*.

gar·ner ['ga:nə] **1.** Kornspeicher *m*; *fig*. Speicher *m*; **2.** aufspeichern.

gar·net *min.* ['ga:nit] Granat *m*.

gar·nish ['ga:niʃ] garnieren; zieren, schmücken; '**gar·nish·ing** Garnierung *f*.

gar·ret ['gærit] Dachstube *f*.

gar·ri·son ⚔ ['gærisn] **1.** Besatzung *f*; Garnison *f*; **2.** mit einer Besatzung *od*. Garnison belegen; in Garnison legen.

gar·ru·li·ty [gæ'ru:liti] Schwatzhaftigkeit *f*; **gar·ru·lous** ☐ ['gæruləs] schwatzhaft, geschwätzig.

gar·ter ['gɑːtə] Strumpfband n; Am. Socken-, Strumpfhalter m; Order of the ♀ Hosenbandorden m.

gas [gæs] **1.** Gas n; F leeres Gerede n; Am. = gasoline; step on the ~ Gas geben; **2.** vergasen; F faseln; '~-**bag** ⚓ Gaszelle f; F Schwätzer m; '~-**brack·et** Gasarm m; '~-**burn·er** Gasbrenner m; '~-**cham·ber** Gaskammer f; '~-**cook·er** Gasherd m; '~-**en·gine** Gasmotor m; **gas·e·ous** ['geizjəs] gasförmig.

gas...: '~-**fire** Gasofen m; '~-**fit·ter** Installateur m, Rohrleger m; '~-**fit·tings** pl. Gasinstallation f.

gash [gæʃ] **1.** klaffende Wunde f; Hieb m; Riß m; **2.** tief (ein)schneiden in (acc.). [Dichtung f.]

gas·ket ['gæskit] ⚓ Seising n; ⊕

gas...: '~-**light** Gaslicht n, Gasbeleuchtung f; '~-**mask** Gasmaske f; '~-**me·ter** Gasuhr f; **gas·o·lene, gas·o·line** Am. mot. ['gæsəuliːn] Benzin n; **gas·om·e·ter** [gæ'sɔmitə] Gasometer m, Gasbehälter m; '**gas-oven** Gasbackofen m, Gasherd m.

gasp [gɑːsp] **1.** Keuchen n; schwerer Atemzug m; **2.** keuchen; a. ~ for breath nach Luft schnappen.

gas-pok·er ['gæs'pəukə] Gasanzünder m; '**gas-'proof** gassicher; '**gas-range** Gasherd m; '**gas-ring** Gasbrenner m, -kocher m; **gassed** gasvergiftet; **gas sta·tion** Am. Tankstelle f; '**gas-stove** Gasofen m, Gasherd m; '**gas·sy** Gas...; geschwätzig; '**gas-tar** Steinkohlenteer m.

gas·tric ♂ ['gæstrik] gastrisch; Magen...; **gas·tri·tis** [gæs'traitis] Magenentzündung f, Gastritis f.

gas·tron·o·my [gæs'trɔnəmi] Gastronomie f, Kochkunst f.

gas-works ['gæswəːks] mst sg. Gaswerk n, -anstalt f. [Pistole f.]

gat Am. sl. [gæt] Revolver m,|

gate [geit] Tor n; Pforte f; Gatter n; fig. Weg m; Sport: Besucher(zahl f) m/pl.; ⚡ ~-money; Sperre f; '~-crash·er sl. ungebetener Gast m; '~-**house** Pförtnerhaus n; '~-**keep·er** Pförtner m; '~-**leg(ged) ta·ble** Klapptisch m; '~-**man** ⚡ Schrankenwärter m; '~-**mon·ey** Sport: Eintrittsgeld n; '~-**post** Tür-, Torpfosten m; between you and me and the ~ im Vertrauen (gesagt); '~-**way** Torweg m, Einfahrt f; fig. Weg m, Tor n.

gath·er ['gæðə] **1.** v/t. (ein-, ver-) sammeln; ernten; pflücken; schließen (from aus); zs.-ziehen; Schneiderei: einhalten, ankrausen; s. information; ~ speed schneller werden; v/i. sich (ver)sammeln; sich vergrößern; a. ~ to a head ♂ u. fig. reifen; **2.** ~s pl. (Kräusel)Falten f/pl.; '**gath·er·ing** Versammlung f; Zs.-kunft f; ♂ Geschwür n.

gauche [gəuʃ] linkisch; taktlos; **gau·che·rie** ['~əriː] linkisches od. taktloses Benehmen n.

gaud·y ['gɔːdi] **1.** ☐ grell, protzig; **2.** univ. jährliches Festmahl n.

gauge [geidʒ] **1.** (Normal)Maß n; Maßstab m; Lehre f; ⚡ Spurweite f; ⊕ Querschnitt m; ✝ Maschengröße f bei Strümpfen; Meßgerät n; **2.** eichen; (aus)messen; fig. abschätzen; '**gaug·er** Eichmeister m.

Gaul [gɔːl] Gallier m; co. Franzose m.

gaunt ☐ [gɔːnt] hager; finster.

gaunt·let[1] ['gɔːntlit] Stulp-, fig. Fehdehandschuh m; throw down (pick up, take up) the ~ den Fehdehandschuh hinwerfen (aufnehmen).

gaunt·let[2] [~]: run the ~ Spießruten laufen.

gauze [gɔːz] Gaze f; silk ~ Seidenflor m; '**gauz·y** gazeartig.

gave [geiv] pret. von give 1 u. 2.

gav·el Am. ['gævl] Hammer m des Versammlungsleiters od. Auktionators.

gawk F [gɔːk] Tölpel m; Schlaks m; '**gawk·y** tölpisch; schlaksig.

gay ☐ [gei] lustig, heiter; bunt, lebhaft, glänzend; ausschweifend; F schwul, homosexuell; Am. sl. frech; **gay·e·ty** ['geiəti] = gaiety.

gaze [geiz] **1.** starrer od. aufmerksamer Blick m; **2.** starren; ~ at, ~ on aufmerksam anblicken; anstarren, -staunen; '**gaz·er** Gaffer(in).

ga·zelle zo. [gə'zel] Gazelle f.

ga·zette [gə'zet] **1.** (offizielle) Zeitung f; der Staatsanzeiger; **2.** amtlich bekanntgeben; **gaz·et·teer** [gæzi'tiə] geographisches Lexikon n.

gear [giə] **1.** ⊕ Getriebe n; mot. Gang m; Mechanismus m; Gerät n, Zeug n; Ausrüstung f; in ~ mit eingelegtem Gang; in Betrieb; in Ordnung; out of ~ ohne Gang, im Leerlauf; außer Betrieb; nicht in Ordnung; *landing-*⤸ ✈ Fahrgestell *n*; *steering-*⤸ ⚓ Ruderanlage *f*; *mot.* Lenkgetriebe *n*; *hunting-*⤸ Jagdausrüstung *f*; **2.** einschalten; ⊕ greifen; *fig.* abstimmen (*to* auf *acc.*); ⤸ *up* (*down*) über- (unter)setzen; '⤸*-box* Getriebe(gehäuse) *n*; '**gear·ing** (Zahnrad)Getriebe *n*; Übersetzung *f*; '**gear-le·ver,** *bsd.* *Am.* '**gear-shift** Schalthebel *m.*

gee [dʒiː] **1.** *Kindersprache:* Hottehü *n* (*Pferd*); **2.** *Fuhrmannsruf:* hü! hott!; *Am.* so was!; Donnerwetter!

geese [giːs] *pl. von* goose.

Gei·ger ['gaigə]: ⤸ *counter* Geigerzähler *m.*

gei·sha ['geiʃə] Geisha *f.*

gel·a·tin(e) [dʒelə'tiːn] Gelatine *f*; **ge·lat·i·nize** [dʒi'lætinaiz] gelatinieren; **ge'lat·i·nous** gallertartig.

geld [geld] (*irr.*) *Tier* verschneiden; '**geld·ing** Wallach *m.*

gel·ig·nite ['dʒelignait] Gelatinedynamit *n.*

gelt [gelt] *pret. u. p.p. von* geld.

gem [dʒem] **1.** Edelstein *m*; Gemme *f*; *fig.* Glanzstück *n*; **2.** mit Edelsteinen besetzen *od.* schmücken.

Gem·i·ni *ast.* ['dʒeminai] *pl.* Zwillinge *m/pl.*

gen *sl.* [dʒen] Information *f.*

gen·darme ['ʒɑ̃ːndɑːm] Gendarm *m*, Landjäger *m.*

gen·der *gr.* ['dʒendə] Geschlecht *n.*

gene *biol.* [dʒiːn] Gen *n.*

gen·e·a·log·i·cal □ [dʒiːnjə'lɔdʒikəl] genealogisch; Stamm...; ⤸ *tree* Stammbaum *m*; **gen·e·al·o·gy** [dʒiːni'ælədʒi] Genealogie *f*; Stammbaum *m.*

gen·er·a ['dʒenərə] *pl. von* genus.

gen·er·al ['dʒenərəl] **1.** □ allgemein; gewöhnlich; Haupt..., General...; ⤸ *an(a)esthetic* ✄ Vollnarkose *f*; ♀ *Assembly* Generalversammlung *f*; ⤸ *election* allgemeine Wahlen *f/pl.*; ⤸ *staff* ✕ Generalstab *m*; ⤸ *store* Gemischtwarenhandlung *f*; *as a* ⤸ *rule,* *in* ⤸ im allgemeinen; ⤸ *knowledge* Allgemeinwissen *n*; **2.** ✕ General *m*; Feldherr *m*; F *a.* ⤸ *servant* Mädchen *n* für alles; **gen·er·al·i·ty** [⤸'ræliti] Allgemeinheit *f*; *die* große Masse; **gen·er·al·i·za·tion** [⤸rəlai'zeiʃən] Verallgemeinerung *f*; '**gen·er·al·ize** verallgemeinern; '**gen·er·al·ly** im allgemeinen, überhaupt; gewöhnlich; **gen·er·al-'pur·pose** Mehrzweck...,

Universal...; '**gen·er·al·ship** Generalsrang *m*; Feldherrnkunst *f*; Leitung *f.*

gen·er·ate ['dʒenəreit] erzeugen (*a. fig.*); '**gen·er·at·ing sta·tion** Kraftwerk *n*; **gen·er·a·tion** (Er-)Zeugung *f*; Generation *f*, Geschlecht *n*; Menschenalter *n*; **gen·er·a·tive** ['⤸rətiv] zeugend; Zeugungs...; fruchtbar; **gen·er·a·tor** ['⤸reitə] Erzeuger *m*; ⊕ Generator *m*; *bsd. Am. mot.* Lichtmaschine *f.*

ge·ner·ic [dʒi'nerik] Gattungs...

gen·er·os·i·ty [dʒenə'rɔsiti] Großmut *f*; Großzügigkeit *f*, Freigebigkeit *f*; '**gen·er·ous** □ großmütig; großzügig, freigebig; reichlich; kräftig, voll (*Wein etc.*).

gen·e·sis ['dʒenisis] Entstehung(s-geschichte) *f*; ⸳ *Bibel:* Genesis *f*, Erstes Buch *n* Mose; **ge·net·ic** [dʒi'netik] (⤸*ally*) genetisch; Entstehungs...; ⤸ *engineering biol.* Genmanipulation *f*; **ge'net·ics** *pl.* Vererbungslehre *f.*

gen·ial □ ['dʒiːnjəl] freundlich; mild (*Klima*); anregend; gemütlich (*Person*); heiter; **ge·ni·al·i·ty** [⤸ni-'æliti] Freundlichkeit *f.*

ge·nie ['dʒiːni] Dschinn *m*, Geist *m* (*in arabischen Märchen*).

ge·ni·i ['dʒiːniai] *pl. von* genius.

gen·i·tals ['dʒenitlz] *pl.* Geschlechtsteile *m/pl.* [Genitiv *m.*\
gen·i·tive *gr.* ['dʒenitiv] *a.* ⤸ *case*]
gen·ius ['dʒiːnjəs], *pl.* **ge·ni·i** ['⤸niai] Genius *m*, (Schutz)Geist *m*; *pl.* **gen·ius·es** ['⤸njəsiz] Genie *n*; Geist *m* (*inneres Wesen*).

genned up *sl.* [dʒend'ʌp] gut informiert (*about* über *acc.*).

gen·o·cide ['dʒenəusaid] Völker-, Rassenmord *m.*

Gen·o·ese [dʒenəu'iːz] **1.** Genuese *m*, Genuesin *f*; **2.** genuesisch.

genre [ʒɑ̃ːŋr] Genre *n*, Stil *m*, Art *f*; ⤸*-painting* Genremalerei *f.*

gent F [dʒent] Herr *m.*

gen·teel □ V *od. iro.* [dʒen'tiːl] vornehm; fein, elegant.

gen·tian ♀ ['dʒenʃiən] Enzian *m.*

gen·tile ['dʒentail] **1.** heidnisch, nichtjüdisch; **2.** Heide *m*, Heidin *f*, Nichtjude *m.*

gen·til·i·ty *mst iro.* [dʒen'tiliti] Vornehmheit *f.*

gen·tle □ ['dʒentl] sanft, mild; fromm; zahm (*Tier*); leise, sacht;

lind (*Lüftchen*); ruhig fließend (*Fluß*); geneigt (*Leser*); vornehm; '~·folk(s *pl.*) *die* Vornehmen *pl.*; '~·man Herr *m*; Gentleman *m*; *gentlemen!* meine Herren!; '~·man·like, '~·man·ly gebildet; vornehm; '~·man's a·gree·ment Gentleman's Agreement *n*, Kavaliersabkommen *n*; 'gen·tle·ness Milde *f*, Güte *f*; Sanftheit *f*, -mut *f*; 'gen·tle·wom·an Dame *f* von Stand.

gen·try ['dʒentri] niederer Adel *m*; gebildete Stände *m/pl.*; *contp.* Leute *pl.*

gen·u·flec·tion, gen·u·flex·ion [dʒenju:'flekʃən] Kniebeugung *f*.

gen·u·ine □ ['dʒenjuin] echt, wahr; wirklich; aufrichtig, ehrlich.

ge·nus ['dʒi:nəs], *pl.* **gen·er·a** ['dʒenərə] Geschlecht *n*, Gattung *f*.

ge·o·cen·tric [dʒi:əu'sentrik] geozentrisch, mit der Erde als Mittelpunkt.

ge·od·e·sy [dʒi:'ɔdisi] Geodäsie *f*.

ge·og·ra·pher [dʒi'ɔgrəfə] Geograph *m*; **ge·o·graph·ic, ge·o·graph·i·cal** □ [ˌ~ə'græfik(əl)] geographisch; **ge·og·ra·phy** [ˌ'ɔgrəfi] Geographie *f*, Erdkunde *f*.

ge·o·log·ic, ge·o·log·i·cal □ [dʒiə'lɔdʒik(əl)] geologisch; **ge·ol·o·gist** [ˌ'ɔlədʒist] Geologe *m*; **ge·ol·o·gy** [ˌ'ɔlədʒist] Geologie *f*.

ge·om·e·ter [dʒi'ɔmitə] Geometer *m*; **ge·o·met·ric, ge·o·met·ri·cal** □ [dʒiə'metrik(əl)] geometrisch; *geometrical progression* geometrische Reihe *f*; **ge·om·e·try** [ˌ'ɔmitri] Geometrie *f*.

ge·o·phys·ics [dʒi:əu'fiziks] *sg.* Geophysik *f*.

ge·o·pol·i·tics [dʒi:əu'pɔlitiks] *sg.* Geopolitik *f*.

geor·gette [dʒɔ:'dʒet] Georgette *m*, Seidenkrepp *m*.

ge·ra·ni·um ♀ [dʒi'reinjəm] Geranie *f*.

ger·i·at·rics ⚘ [dʒeri'ætriks] *pl.* Geriatrie *f*, Lehre *f* von den Alterskrankheiten.

germ [dʒə:m] **1.** Keim *m*; **2.** keimen.

Ger·man[1] ['dʒə:mən] **1.** deutsch; **2.** Deutsche *m*, *f*; Deutsch *n*.

ger·man[2] [ˌ]: *brother etc.* ~ leiblicher Bruder *m etc.*; **ger·mane** [dʒə:'mein] (*to*) verwandt (mit); entsprechend (*dat.*), passend (zu),

gehörig (zu).

Ger·man·ic [dʒə:'mænik] germanisch; **Ger·man·ism** ['dʒə:mənizəm] deutsche Spracheigenheit *f*, Germanismus *m*.

germ-car·ri·er ['dʒə:mkæriə] Bazillenträger *m*.

ger·mi·cide ['dʒə:misaid] keimtötende Substanz *f*.

ger·mi·nal ['dʒə:minl] Keim...; **ger·mi·nate** ['~neit] keimen (lassen); **ger·mi·na·tion** Keimen *n*.

germ...: '~-proof keimsicher, -frei; ~ war·fare ⚔ biologische Kriegführung *f*.

ger·on·tol·o·gy ⚘ [dʒerɔn'tɔlədʒi] Gerontologie *f*, Lehre *f* von den Altersvorgängen.

ger·ry·man·der *pol.* ['dʒerimændə] (Wahl)Schiebung *f*.

ger·und *gr.* ['dʒerənd] Gerundium *n*.

ges·ta·tion [dʒes'teiʃən] Trächtigkeit *f bei Tieren*; Schwangerschaft *f*.

ges·tic·u·late [dʒes'tikjuleit] gestikulieren, Gebärden machen; **ges·tic·u·la·tion** Gebärden *f/pl.*, Gestikulieren *n*.

ges·ture ['dʒestʃə] Geste *f*, Gebärde *f*.

get [get] (*irr.*) **1.** *v/t.* erhalten, bekommen, F kriegen; sich verschaffen; besorgen; holen; bringen; erwerben; verdienen; veranlassen; bewegen; ergreifen, fassen; machen, (veran)lassen; *have got* haben; *you have got to obey* F Sie haben zu gehorchen; ~ *one's hair cut* sich die Haare schneiden lassen; ~ *me the book!* besorge mir das Buch!; ~ *by heart* auswendig lernen; ~ *with child* schwängern; ~ *away* wegbringen; ~ *down* hinunterbringen, -schlucken; aufschreiben; ~ *in* hineinbringen; *Wort, Schlag* anbringen; ~ *s.o. in* j. kommen lassen; ~ *off Kleid* ausziehen; *Ware* loswerden; ~ *on* anziehen; ~ *out* herausbringen, -locken; ~ *over* hinüberbringen; *et.* hinter sich bringen; ~ *through* durchbringen; ~ *up* aufstehen lassen; organisieren; aufmachen; einrichten, herrichten, ausstatten; ~ *up steam* Dampf aufmachen. **2.** *v/i.* gelangen, geraten, kommen; sich begeben, gehen; werden; ~ *ready* sich fertig machen; ~ *about* auf den Beinen sein; herumkommen; die Runde machen (*Gerücht etc.*); ~

abroad unter die Leute kommen; bekannt werden; ~ *ahead* vorwärtskommen; ~ *along* fort-, weiterkommen; ~ *along with* mit *j-m* auskommen; ~ *around to* s.*th.* zu et. kommen, Zeit finden für et.; ~ *at* (heran-) kommen an (*acc.*); zu *et.* kommen; ~ *away* weg-, davonkommen; sich fortmachen; ~ *away with* s.*th.* sich et. (ungestraft) leisten können; ~ *by* vorbei-, durchkommen; ~ *down to* sich auseinandersetzen mit; F herangehen an (*acc.*); gelangen zu; ~ *in* einsteigen; ~ *into* hineinkommen *od.* geraten in (*acc.*); ~ *off* davonkommen, entwischen; aus-, absteigen; ⚓ loskommen; ~ *off with* s.*o.* j. kennenlernen; ~ *on* gelangen auf (*acc.*); vorwärtskommen; aufsitzen, -steigen; ~ *over* hinwegkommen über (*acc.*); ~ *through* durchkommen (*a. teleph.*); ~ *to hear od.* know *od.* learn erfahren; ~ *up* aufstehen; hinaufsteigen; steigen (*Preise etc.*); **get-at-·a·ble** [get'ætəbl] zugänglich; erreichbar; **get-a·way** ['getəwei] *Sport:* Ablauf *m*; Entkommen *n*; ~ *car* Fluchtwagen *m*; *make one's* ~ sich aus dem Staub machen; **'get·ter** Zeuger *m* (*von Pferden*); Gewinner *m*; **'get·ting** Gewinn *m*, Erwerb *m*; **'get-to·geth·er** F Treffen *n*; **'get-up** Aufmachung *f*; *Am.* F Unternehmungsgeist *m*.

gew·gaw ['gju:gɔ:] Spielerei *f*; ~*s pl.* Kinkerlitzchen *n/pl.*

gey·ser ['gaizə] *geogr.* Geysir *m*; ['gi:zə] Boiler *m*, Warmwasserbereiter *m*; (Gas)Badeofen *m*.

ghast·li·ness ['ga:stlinis] schreckliches Aussehen *n*; Grausigkeit *f*; **'ghast·ly** gräßlich, grausig; schrecklich, schauderhaft; (toten)bleich; gespenstisch.

gher·kin ['gə:kin] Gewürzgurke *f*.

ghet·to ['getəu] Getto *n*, Judenviertel *n*.

ghost [gəust] Geist *m*, Gespenst *n*; Schatten *m*, Spur *f*; = ~ *writer*; **'ghost·like** geisterhaft; **'ghost·ly** geisterhaft; *eccl.* geistlich; **ghost writ·er** Ghostwriter *m* (*j.*, *der für e-n anderen schreibt*).

ghoul [gu:l] Ghul *m* (*Dämon*); *fig.* Unhold *m*.

gi·ant ['dʒaiənt] **1.** riesig; **2.** Riese *m*; **'gi·ant·ess** Riesin *f*.

gib·ber ['dʒibə] kauderwelschen,

schnattern; **gib·ber·ish** ['~riʃ] Kauderwelsch *n*, Geschnatter *n*.

gib·bet ['dʒibit] **1.** Galgen *m*; ⊕ Kranbalken *m*; **2.** aufhängen; *fig.* anprangern.

gib·bon *zo.* ['gibən] Gibbon *m*.

gib·bos·i·ty [gi'bɔsiti] Höcker *m*; Buckel *m*; **'gib·bous** buck(e)lig; gewölbt; dreiviertelvoll (*Mond*).

gibe [dʒaib] **1.** verspotten, aufziehen (*a. at* s.*o.* j-n); **2.** Spott *m*, Stichelei *f*.

gib·lets ['dʒiblits] *pl.* Gänseklein *n*.

gid·di·ness ['gidinis] Schwindel(gefühl *n*) *m*; Unbeständigkeit *f*; *fig.* Unbesonnenheit *f*, Leichtsinn *m*; **'gid·dy** ☐ schwind(e)lig; schwindelerregend; *fig.* unbesonnen, leichtfertig, gedankenlos; unbeständig; albern.

gift [gift] **1.** Gabe *f*; Geschenk *n*; Talent *n*; Verleihungsrecht *n*; Schenkung *f*; ~ *box* Geschenkpackung *f*; *s. horse*; **2.** (be)schenken; **'gift·ed** begabt.

gig [gig] Gig *n* (*Einspänner*); ⚓ Gig *n*.

gi·gan·tic [dʒai'gæntik] (~*ally*) riesenhaft, riesig, gigantisch.

gig·gle ['gigl] **1.** kichern; **2.** Gekicher *n*.

gig·o·lo ['ʒigələu] Gigolo *m*, Eintänzer *m*.

gild [gild] (*irr.*) vergolden; verschönern; ~ *the pill fig.* die bittere Pille versüßen; ~*ed youth* Jeunesse *f* dorée; **'gild·er** Vergolder *m*; **'gild·ing** Vergoldung *f*.

gill¹ [dʒil] Viertelpinte *f*.

gill² [gil] *ichth.* Kieme *f*; *fig.* Doppelkinn *n*; ♀ *Pilz*-Lamelle *f*.

gill³ [dʒil] Mädchen *n*.

gil·lie ['gili] (Jagd)Helfer *m*, Junge *m*.

gilt [gilt] **1.** *pret. u. p.p. von* gild; **2.** Vergoldung *f*; ~*s pl.* F mündelsichere Wertpapiere *n/pl.*; **'~-edged** mit Goldschnitt; ✝ mündelsicher; ✝ *sl.* hochfein, prima.

gim·bal ['dʒimbəl] *mst* ~*s pl.* Kardanaufhängung *f*.

gim·crack ['dʒimkræk] **1.** Spielerei *f*, Kinkerlitzchen *n*; **2.** wertlos.

gim·let ⊕ ['gimlit] Handbohrer *m*.

gim·mick *Am. sl.* ['gimik] Trick *m*, Dreh *m*.

gin¹ [dʒin] Gin *m* (*Wacholderschnaps*).

gin² [ˌ] **1.** Falle f, Schlinge f; ⊕ Entkörnungsmaschine f; **2.** mit e-r Schlinge fangen; ⊕ entkörnen.

gin·ger ['dʒindʒə] **1.** Ingwer m; Lebhaftigkeit f, Kraft f, Schwung m, Energie f; **2.** ～ up ankurbeln, in Schwung bringen; **3.** hellrot, rötlich-gelb; ～ **ale** Ingwer-Limonade f; '～**bread** Leb-, Pfefferkuchen m; ～ **group** pol. Scharfmacher m/pl.; '**gin·ger·ly** adj. u. adv. zimperlich; sacht, behutsam; '**gin·ger-nut** Pfeffernuß f.

ging·ham ['giŋəm] Gingham m (Baumwollstoff).

gip·sy ['dʒipsi] Zigeuner(in).

gi·raffe zo. [dʒi'rɑːf] Giraffe f.

gird¹ [gəːd] **1.** Spott m, Stichelei f; **2.** höhnen, sticheln (at über acc.).

gird² [ˌ] (irr.) (um)gürten; umgeben.

gird·er ⊕ ['gəːdə] Tragbalken m; Träger m.

gir·dle ['gəːdl] **1.** Gurt m, Gürtel m; Hüfthalter m, -gürtel m; **2.** umgürten.

girl [gəːl] Mädchen n; ～-friend Freundin f; ～ **Fri·day** Büro: Mädchen n für alles; ♀ **Guide** Pfadfinderin f; **girl·hood** ['～hud] Mädchenzeit f; Mädchenjahre n/pl.; **girl·ie** ['～i] (kleines) Mädchen n; '**girl·ish** ☐ mädchenhaft; '**girl·ish·ness** Mädchenhaftigkeit f; **girl scout** Am. Pfadfinderin f; '**girl·y** Am. F mit spärlich bekleideten Mädchen (Magazin, Varieté etc.).

Giro ['dʒaiərəu]: the ～ der Postscheckdienst (in England).

girt [gəːt] **1.** pret. u. p.p. von gird²; **2.** ⊕ Umfang m.

girth [gəːθ] (Sattel)Gurt m; Umfang m.

gist [dʒist] das Wesentliche.

git sl. [git] = get.

give [giv] **1.** (irr.) v/t. geben; ab-, übergeben; her-, hingeben; überlassen; Lied etc. zum besten geben, vortragen; schenken; gewähren; Seufzer etc. von sich geben; Resultat ergeben; ～ attention to achtgeben auf (acc.); ～ battle e-e Schlacht liefern; ～ birth to zur Welt bringen; ～ chase to verfolgen; ～ credit to Glauben schenken (dat.); ～ ear to Gehör schenken (dat.); ～ one's mind to sich (dat.) widmen; ～ it to s.o. es j-m geben (prügeln; die Meinung sagen); ～ away weggeben,

verschenken; F verraten; ～ away the bride Brautvater sein; ～ back zurückgeben; ～ forth von sich geben; herausgeben; ～ in eingeben, -reichen; ～ out ausgeben; verteilen; bekanntmachen; Duft etc. ausströmen; ～ over übergeben; aufgeben; ～ up Geschäft, Recht, Kranke aufgeben; j. ausliefern; ～ o.s. up sich ergeben (to dat.); **2.** v/i. mst ～ in nachgeben; weichen; ～ into, ～ (up)on hinausgehen auf (acc.) (Fenster etc.); ～ out zu Ende gehen, aufhören, versiegen; versagen; ～ over aufhören; **3.** Nachgeben n; Elastizität f; ～ **and take** ['givən'teik] (Meinungs)Austausch m; Geben und Nehmen n; Kompromiß m, n; ～-**a·way** ['～əwei] Preisgabe f; ～ show, ～ program Radio, Fernsehen: öffentliches Preisraten n; '**giv·en** p.p. von give 1 u. 2; ～ to ergeben (dat.); ～ ... wenn man ... als gegeben ansieht; '**giv·er** Geber(in); ～ of a bill Wechselaussteller m.

giz·zard orn. ['gizəd] Muskelmagen m; it sticks in my ～ es ist mir zuwider.

gla·cé ['glæsei] glasiert; kandiert.

gla·ci·al ☐ ['gleisjəl] eisig; Eis...; Gletscher...; ～ era Eiszeit f; **gla·ci·a·tion** geol. [glæsi'eiʃən] Vereisung f, Vergletscherung f; **gla·cier** ['glæsjə] Gletscher m; **gla·cis** ['glæsis] Glacis n.

glad ☐ [glæd] froh, erfreut (of, at über acc.); erfreulich, Freuden...; give s.o. the ～ eye F j-m schöne Augen machen; ～ rags pl. sl. Sonntagsstaat m; '**glad·den** ['～dn] erfreuen.

glade [gleid] Lichtung f; Am. sumpfige Niederung f.

glad·i·a·tor ['glædieitə] Gladiator m.

glad·i·o·lus ♀ [glædi'əuləs] Gladiole f.

glad·ly ['glædli] gerne, mit Freuden; '**glad·ness** Freude f, Fröhlichkeit f; **glad·some** ['～səm] freudig, fröhlich.

Glad·stone ['glædstən] a. ～ bag Handkoffer m.

glair [glɛə] **1.** Eiweiß n; **2.** mit Eiweiß überziehen.

glam·or·ize ['glæməraiz] glanzvoll(er) erscheinen lassen; (übertrieben) verherrlichen; '**glam·or·ous** strahlend (schön), bezaubernd; **glam·our** ['～mə] **1.** Zauber m, Glanz

glory

m, Reiz *m*; ~ *girl* Reklameschönheit *f*;
2. bezaubern.

glance [glɑːns] 1. Schimmer *m*,
Blitz *m*; flüchtiger Blick *m*; 2. hin-
weggleiten (*over* über *acc.*); blitzen;
glänzen; ~ *at* flüchtig ansehen; anspielen auf (*acc.*); *mst* ~ *off* abprallen; ~ *over* flüchtig überblicken.

gland *anat.*, ⚕ [glænd] Drüse *f*;
glan·dered *vet.* [ˈ~dəd] rotzig;
glan·ders *vet.* [ˈ~dəz] *sg.* Rotz
(-krankheit *f*) *m*; **glan·du·lar**
[ˈ~djulə] Drüsen...

glare [glɛə] 1. grelles Licht *n*; wilder, starrer Blick *m*; 2. grell leuchten; wild blicken; (*at* an)starren;
glar·ing □ [ˈ~riŋ] grell (leuchtend); *fig.* grell hervortretend,
kraß.

glass [glɑːs] 1. Glas *n*; Spiegel *m*;
Opernglas *n*; Fernglas *n*; Barometer *n*; (*a pair of*) ~es *pl.* (eine) Brille
f; 2. gläsern; Glas...; 3. verglasen;
'~-blow·er Glasbläser *m*; '~-case
Vitrine *f*; Schaukasten *m*; '~-cut-
ter Glasschleifer *m*; Glaserdia-
mant *m*; **glass-ful** [ˈ~ful] Glas(voll)
n; '**glass-house** Treibhaus *n*; ⚔ *sl.*
Bau *m*; '**glass·i·ness** *das* Glasige,
Spiegelglätte *f*; '**glass·ware** Glas
(-waren *f/pl.*) *n*; '**glass·y** gläsern;
glasig.

glau·co·ma 🌿 [glɔːˈkəumə] Glau-
kom *n*, grüner Star *m*; '**glau·cous**
graugrün.

glaze [gleiz] 1. Glasur *f*; 2. *v/t.* verglasen; glasieren; polieren; *v/i.*
trübe *od.* glasig werden (*Auge*); ~d
paper Glanzpapier *n*; ~d(-*in*) *veranda*
Glasveranda *f*; **gla·zier** [ˈ~jə] Glaser *m*; '**glaz·ing** Verglasung *f*;
Glasur *f*; '**glaz·y** glasiert; blank;
glasig.

gleam [gliːm] 1. Schimmer *m*,
Schein *m*; 2. schimmern, scheinen.

glean [gliːn] *v/t.* nachlesen, sammeln; *v/i.* Ähren lesen; '**glean·er**
Ährenleser(in); *fig.* Sammler(in);
'**glean·ings** *pl.* Nachlese *f*.

glebe [gliːb] Pfarrland *n*; *poet.*
(Erd)Scholle *f*.

glee [gliː] Fröhlichkeit *f*; mehrstimmiges Lied *n*, Rundgesang *m*; ~
club Gesangverein *m*; **glee·ful** □
[ˈ~ful] fröhlich.

glen [glen] Bergschlucht *f*.

glib □ [glib] *fig.* glatt, *bsd.* zungenfertig; '**glib·ness** Zungenfertig-

keit *f*.

glide [glaid] 1. Gleiten *n*; 🛩 Gleitflug *m*; *gr.* Gleitlaut *m*; 2. (dahin-)
gleiten (lassen); e-n Gleitflug
machen; '**glid·er** Segelflugzeug *n*;
~ *pilot* Segelflieger *m*; '**glid·ing**
Gleit-, Segelflug *m*.

glim·mer [ˈglimə] 1. Schimmer *m*;
min. Glimmer *m*; 2. schimmern.

glimpse [glimps] 1. flüchtiger Blick
m (*of* auf *acc.*); Schimmer *m*; flüchtiger Eindruck *m*; 2. *v/t.* flüchtig
erblicken; *v/i.* ~ *at* e-n flüchtigen
Blick werfen auf (*acc.*).

glint [glint] 1. blitzen, glitzern,
schimmern; 2. Lichtschein *m*.

glis·sade *mount.* [gliˈsɑːd] 1. abfahren; rutschen; 2. Abfahrt *f*.

glis·ten [ˈglisn], **glis·ter** † [ˈglistə],
glit·ter [ˈglitə] glitzern, glänzen,
funkeln; gleißen; '**glit·ter·ing** glänzend, verlockend; ~ *personality*
blendende Erscheinung *f*.

gloam·ing [ˈgləumiŋ] (Abend-)
Dämmerung *f*.

gloat [gləut]: ~ (*up*)*on*, ~ *over* sich
weiden an (*dat.*), sich hämisch
freuen über (*acc.*).

glob·al [ˈgləubəl] global, (welt)um-
fassend; Welt..., Gesamt...; **globe**
Kugel *f*; Erdkugel *f*, -ball *m*; Globe
bus *m*; '**globe-fish** *ichth.* Kugel-
fisch *m*; '**globe-trot·ter** Welten-
bummler(in); **glo·bose** [ˈ~bəus],
glob·u·lar □ [ˈglɔbjulə] kugelförmig; **glo·bos·i·ty** [gləuˈbɔsiti] Ku-
gelform *f*; **glob·ule** [ˈglɔbjuːl] Kügelchen *n*.

gloom [gluːm] 1. Düsterkeit *f*, Dunkelheit *f*; Schwermut *f*; Trübsinn
m; 2. *v/i.* verdrießlich *od.* schwermütig *od.* trüb sein *od.* blicken; *v/t.*
verdunkeln, verdüstern; '**gloom·i-
ness** Düsternis *f*; Schwermut *f*;
'**gloom·y** □ dunkel, düster;
schwermütig; verdrießlich.

Glo·ri·a *eccl.* [ˈglɔːriə] Gloria *n*.
glo·ri·fi·ca·tion [glɔːrifiˈkeiʃən] Verherrlichung *f*; **glo·ri·fy** [ˈ~fai] verherrlichen, verklären; F verschönern, verbessern; '**glo·ri·ous** □
herrlich, köstlich, prächtig; wunderbar; glorreich.

glo·ry [ˈglɔːri] 1. Ruhm *m*; Glorie *f*,
Herrlichkeit *f*, Pracht *f*; Glorien-
schein *m*; Glanzpunkt *m*; 2. (*in*)
frohlocken (über *acc.*); stolz sein
(auf *acc.*).

gloss[1] [glɔs] **1.** Glosse *f*, (erläuternde) Bemerkung *f*; **2.** glossieren; Glossen machen (zu).

gloss[2] [◡] **1.** Glanz *m*; **2.** Glanz geben (*dat.*); ◡ *over* beschönigen.

glos·sa·ry [ˈglɔsəri] Glossar *n*, Wörterbuch *n*.

gloss·i·ness [ˈglɔsinis] Glanz *m*; **ˈgloss·y** □ glänzend, blank; ◡ *periodical* Illustrierte *f*, bsd. Modejournal *n*.

glot·tis *anat.* [ˈglɔtis] Stimmritze *f*.

glove [glʌv] Handschuh *m*; ◡ *compartment mot.* Handschuhfach *n*; *s. hand* 1; **ˈglov·er** Handschuhmacher *m*.

glow [gləu] **1.** Glühen *n*; Glut *f*; **2.** glühen.

glow·er [ˈglauə] finster blicken.

glow-worm [ˈgləuwə:m] Glühwurm *m*.

gloze [gləuz]: ◡ *over* beschönigen.

glu·cose [ˈgluːkəus] Traubenzucker *m*.

glue [gluː] **1.** Leim *m*; **2.** leimen; *fig.* (an)drücken, heften (*to* an, auf *acc.*); **ˈglue·y** klebrig, leimig.

glum □ [glʌm] mürrisch, verdrießlich.

glut [glʌt] **1.** Überfüllung *f*; Übersättigung *f*; Überfülle *f*; **2.** überfüllen; (über)sättigen.

glu·ten [ˈgluːtən] Gluten *n*, Kleber *m*; **glu·ti·nous** □ [ˈ◡tinəs] leimig, klebrig.

glut·ton [ˈglʌtn] Schlemmer *m*; Unersättliche *m* (*of, for, at* in *dat.*); *zo.* Vielfraß *m*; **ˈglut·ton·ous** □ gefräßig; **ˈglut·ton·y** Gefräßigkeit *f*.

glyc·er·in [ˈglisərin], **glyc·er·ine** [◡ˈriːn] Glyzerin *n*.

G-man *Am.* F [ˈdʒiːmæn] FBI-Agent *m*.

gnarl [nɑːl] Knorren *m*, Ast *m*; **gnarled**, *a.* **ˈgnarl·y** knorrig.

gnash [næʃ] knirschen (mit).

gnat [næt] (Stech)Mücke *f*.

gnaw [nɔː] (zer)nagen; (zer)fressen; **ˈgnaw·er** Nagetier *n*.

gnome [nəum] Erdgeist *m*, Gnom *m*; [ˈnəumiː] Sinnspruch *m*, Gnome *f*; **gnom·ish** [ˈnəumiʃ] gnomenhaft.

go [gəu] **1.** (*irr.*) *allg.* gehen (*s. a. going, gone*); fahren, reisen, werden; reichen, führen (*to* nach); wenden, appellieren (*to* an *acc.*); funktionieren, arbeiten, gehen; kommen, gestellt werden; passen, gehen; *in*

e-m bestimmten Zustand sein; (über-)gehen (*to* an *acc.*), zuteil werden (*to dat.*); nötig sein (*to* für), dienen; *ungestraft etc.* ausgehen; weg-, abgehen, verkauft werden; ausgegeben werden (*Geld*); aufgegeben werden; nachlassen (*Augenlicht*); umgehen (*Gerücht etc.*); angenommen werden (*Geld*); kaputtgehen, brechen; *mst im p.p.* sterben; verlaufen; lauten; *ein bestimmtes Geräusch* machen; *in der Verlaufsform u. mit nachfolgendem inf. zur Bildung des Futurs:* werden; ◡ *bad* verderben; *s. mad*; *s. sick*; *the dog must* ◡ der Hund muß weg; *the story* ◡*es* man erzählt sich; *here* ◡*es*! *sl.* los!; ◡ *it sl.* sich daranmachen, drauflosgehen; ◡ *it*! *sl.* feste!; *as men, etc.* ◡ wie Männer *etc.* nun einmal sind; *let* ◡ fahren lassen, loslassen; ◡ *shares* teilen; ◡ *to see*, ◡ *and see* besuchen; *just* ◡ *and try*! versuch's doch mal!; ◡ *about* umher-, umgehen; herangehen an *e-e Arbeit*; ◡ *abroad* auf Reisen gehen; ruchbar werden; ◡ *ahead* vorwärtsgehen; ◡ *at* losgehen auf (*acc.*); ◡ *back* zurückgehen; ◡ *back from*, F *on Versprechen etc.* rückgängig machen; ◡ *behind* untersuchen, nachprüfen; ◡ *between* vermitteln (zwischen); ◡ *by* vergehen; vorübergehen; sich richten nach; ◡ *by the name of* ... unter dem Namen ... gehen; ◡ *down* (hin)untergehen; erliegen (*before dat.*); Glauben finden (*with* bei); ◡ *for* gehen nach, holen; gelten für; j. angreifen; ◡ *for a walk, etc.* e-n Spaziergang *etc.* machen; ◡ *in* hineingehen; ◡ *in for* sich widmen (*dat.*), sich befassen mit; sich verlegen auf (*acc.*); ◡ *in for an examination* e-e Prüfung machen; ◡ *into Rechnen:* gehen in (*acc.*); *e-r Frage etc.* auf den Grund gehen; ◡ *off* weggehen; abgehen (*Zug, Waren*); losgehen (*Schuß etc.*); vergehen; sich verschlechtern; einschlafen; sterben; ◡ *on* vor sich gehen; vorwärts- *od.* weitergehen; fortfahren; ◡ *on*! weiter!; ◡ *out* ausgehen; abgehen, abtreten; ◡ *over* übergehen *zu e-r Partei*; durchgehen, -sehen, prüfen; ◡ *through* durchgehen; ausführen; durchmachen; ◡ *through with Aufgabe etc.* durchführen; ◡ *to an j.* gehen *od.*

fallen; sich belaufen auf (*acc.*); ~
up hinaufgehen; steigen; entstehen
(*Gebäude*); *in Flammen* aufgehen,
in die Luft fliegen; *zur Universität*
gehen; ~ *with* passen zu; ~ *without*
sich behelfen ohne; entbehren; **2.** F
Gang *m*; Mode *f*; Schwung *m*,
Schmiß *m*, Schneid *m*; Begeisterung *f*; (*unangenehme*) Geschichte
f; Schluck *m*; Happen *m*; ✗ Anfall
m; Versuch *m*; *little* ~ *univ. sl.* Vor-
examen *n*; *great* ~ Hauptexamen *n*;
on the ~ auf den Beinen, in Bewegung; im Gange; *it is no* ~ es geht
nicht; *is it a* ~? abgemacht?; *in one*
~ auf Anhieb; *have a* ~ *at s.th.* et.
in Angriff nehmen, et. versuchen.
goad [gəud] **1.** Stachelstock *m*; *fig.*
Stachel *m*; Ansporn *m*; **2.** *fig.* anstacheln.
go·a·head F ['gəuəhed] **1.** zielstrebig, rührig; unternehmungslustig; fortschrittlich; **2.** *bsd. Am.* F
Unternehmungsgeist *m*, -lust *f*;
Erlaubnis *f* zum Weitermachen.
goal [gəul] Mal *n*; Ziel *n* (*a. fig.*);
Fußball: Tor *n*; **goal·ie** F ['gəuli] =
'**goal·keep·er** *Fußball*: Torwart *m*;
goal kick *Fußball*: Abstoß *m*; '**goal-
mouth** *Sport*: Torraum *m*; *in the* ~
(unmittelbar) vor dem Tor.
goat [gəut] *zo.* Ziege *f*, Geiß *f*; *get
s.o.'s* ~ *sl.* j. hochbringen (*ärgern*);
separate the sheep from the ~*s fig.*
die Schafe von den Böcken scheiden; *play the giddy* ~ sich närrisch
benehmen; **goat'ee** Spitzbart *m*;
'**goat·ish** ziegenartig; bockig; geil;
'**goat·skin** Ziegenleder *n*.
gob [gɔb] V Schleimklumpen *m*;
Maul *n*; *Am.* F Blaujacke *f* (*Matrose*); **gob·bet** ['gɔbit] Bissen *m*.
gob·ble ['gɔbl] *gierig* verschlingen;
kollern *wie ein Truthahn*; **gob·ble-
dy·gook** *Am. sl.* ['gɔbldiguk] Amts-,
Berufsjargon *m*, Geschwafel *n*;
'**gob·bler** Vielfraß *m*; Truthahn *m*.
go-be·tween ['gəubitwi:n] Ver-
mittler(in).
gob·let ['gɔblit] Kelchglas *n*; Pokal
m.   [*m.*]
gob·lin ['gɔblin] Kobold *m*, Gnom⌡
go-by ['gəubai]: *give s.o. the* ~ j. unbeachtet lassen, j. ignorieren.
go-cart ['gəukɑːt] Laufgestell *n für
Kinder*; Sportwagen *m für Kinder*.
god, *eccl.* ♀ [gɔd] Gott *m*; *fig.* Abgott *m*; *the gods pl. thea.* der

Olymp; '**god·child** Patenkind *n*;
'**god·dess** Göttin *f*; '**god·fa·ther**
Pate *m*; '**god·fear·ing** gottesfürchtig; '**god·for·sak·en** gottverlassen;
'**god·head** Gottheit *f*; '**god·less** gottlos; '**god·like** gottähnlich; göttlich,
erhaben; '**god·li·ness** Frömmigkeit
f; '**god·ly** gottesfürchtig; fromm;
'**god·moth·er** Patin *f*; '**god·par·ent**
Pate *m*, Patin *f*; '**god·send** Geschenk
n des Himmels, Gottesgabe *f*; '**god-
'speed: bid** *od.* **wish s.o.** ~ j-m glück-
liche Reise wünschen; j-m guten Erfolg wünschen.
go·er ['gəuə] Geher(in), Läufer(in).
gof·fer ['gəufə] kräuseln, plissieren.
go-get·ter *Am.* F ['gəu'getə] Draufgänger *m*, Allerweltskerl *m*.
gog·gle ['gɔgl] **1.** glotzen; **2.** ~*s pl.*
Schutzbrille *f*; '~**box** *sl.* Glotze *f*
(*Fernsehgerät*); '~**eyed** glotzäugig.
go·ing ['gəuiŋ] **1.** gehen; im Gange
(*befindlich*); vorhanden; *be* ~ *to*
inf. im Begriff sein zu *inf.*, gleich
od. bald *tun* wollen *od.* werden;
keep ~ in Gang halten; *set* ~ in
Gang bringen; *a* ~ *concern* ein gut-
gehendes Geschäft *n*; ~, ~, *gone!*
zum ersten, zum zweiten, zum
dritten!; **2.** Gehen *n*, Gang *m*; Vorwärtskommen *n*; Straßenzustand
m; Geschwindigkeit *f*, Leistung *f*;
'**go·ings-'on** F *pl.* Vorgänge *m*/*pl.*;
Treiben *n*.
goi·tre ✗ ['gɔitə] Kropf *m*; **goi-
trous** ['gɔitrəs] Kropf...; mit
Kropf (behaftet).
go-kart *mot.* ['gəukɑːt] Go-Kart *m*
(*Kleinstrennwagen*).
gold [gəuld] **1.** Gold *n*; **2.** golden;
'~**bear·ing** goldhaltig; '~**brick**
1. *fig.* Talmi *n*, Schwindel *m*; **2.** sich
drücken; '~**dig·ger** *Am.* Gold-
gräber *m*; *sl.* Männerausbeuterin *f*;
'**gold·en** *mst fig.* golden, goldgelb;
'**gold·en-rod** ♀ Goldrute *f*.
gold····: '~**finch** *orn.* Stieglitz *m*;
'~**fish** *ichth.* Goldfisch *m*; '~**mine**
Goldbergwerk *n*; *fig.* Goldgrube *f*;
~ **plate** goldenes Tafelgeschirr *n*;
'~**'plat·ed** vergoldet; '~**rush** Gold-
rausch *m*; '~**smith** Goldschmied *m*.
golf [gɔlf] **1.** Golf(spiel) *n*; **2.** Golf
spielen; '~**ball** Golfball *m*; Schreib-
kopf *m* e-r *Schreibmaschine*; ~ *typewriter* Kugelkopfschreibmaschine *f*;
'~**club** Golfschläger *m*; Golfklub *m*;
'~**course** = *golf-links*; '**golf·er**

Golfspieler(in); **'golf-links** pl. Golf-platz m.

gol·li·wog(g) ['gɔliwɔg] Neger-puppe f; fig. Popanz m.

go·losh [gə'lɔʃ] Galosche f, Über-schuh m.

gon·do·la ⚓, ✈ ['gɔndələ] Gondel f; **gon·do·lier** [ˌ∼'liə] Gondoliere m.

gone [gɔn] **1.** p.p. von go; **2.** adj. fort; dahin; F futsch; vergangen; tot; F hoffnungslos; be ∼!, get you ∼! mach, daß du wegkommst!; ∼ on s.o. sl. in j. verknallt; **'gon·er** sl. er-ledigter Mensch m.

gong [gɔŋ] Gong m.

good [gud] **1.** allg. gut; lieb, brav (Kind); gültig (Gesetz); ✝ zah-lungsfähig; gründlich, gehörig; the ∼ Samaritan der Barmherzige Sama-riter; ∼ at geschickt in (dat.); in ∼ earnest in vollem Ernst; **2.** Gute n; Wohl n, Beste n; ∼s pl. Waren f/pl.; Güter n pl.; that's no ∼ das nützt nichts; it is no ∼ talking es ist un-nütz zu reden; for ∼ endgültig, für immer; piece of ∼s F Frauenzimmer n, Stück n; ∼s pl. in process Halb-fabrikate n pl.; **∼-bye,** Am. a. **∼-by 1.** [gud'bai] Lebewohl n; **2.** ['gud-'bai] Auf Wiedersehen!; Lebe-wohl!; **'∼-for-'noth·ing 1.** nichts-nutzig; **2.** Taugenichts m; ♀ **Fri-day** Karfreitag m; **'∼'hu·mo(u)red** gutmütig; guter Laune, gutgelaunt; **'good·li·ness** Anmut f; **'good--'look·ing** gutaussehend, hübsch; **'good·ly** anmutig, hübsch; fig. an-sehnlich; tüchtig; **good·man** ✝ (Haus)Vater m; Ehemann m; **'good-'na·tured** gutmütig; **'good-ness** Güte f (gute Beschaffenheit; Freundlichkeit); das Beste; in Aus-rufen: mein Gott!, du meine Güte!; s. gracious; **goods train** Güterzug m; **'good·wife** Hausfrau f; **'good-'will** Wohlwollen n; freundliche Einstellung f (towards zu); ✝ Kundschaft f; ✝ Firmenwert m.

good·y¹ ['gudi] Bonbon m.

good·y² [ˌ∼], a. **'good·y-'good·y 1.** prüde; scheinheilig; **2.** Schein-heilige m, f.

goo·ey F ['guːi] klebrig; pappig.

goof F [guːf] **1.** Trottel m; Schnitzer m; **2.** ∼ (up) vermasseln, verpatzen; **'goof·y** sl. doof, blöde.

goon Am. sl. [guːn] gedungener Raufbold m bsd. für Streik; Dumm-kopf m.

goose [guːs], pl. **geese** [giːs] Gans f (a. fig.); cook s.o.'s ∼ j-m e-n Strich durch die Rechnung machen; pl. **'goos·es** Bügeleisen n.

goose·ber·ry ['guzbəri] Stachel-beere f; play ∼ F Anstandswauwau spielen.

goose...: **'∼-flesh** Gänsehaut f; **'∼-herd** Gänsehirt(in); ∼ **pim·ples** pl. Am. = goose-flesh; **'∼-step** Parade-schritt m; **'goos·ey, 'goos·ie** F Gänschen n.

go·pher bsd. Am. ['gəufə] Erdeich-hörnchen n; eine Ratte f.

Gor·di·an ['gɔːdjən] gordisch; ∼ knot gordischer Knoten m.

gore¹ [gɔː] (geronnenes) Blut n.

gore² [∼] **1.** Keil m, Zwickel m im Kleid etc.; **2.** durchbohren, auf-spießen.

gorge [gɔːdʒ] **1.** Kehle f, Schlund m; enge (Fels)Schlucht f; my ∼ rises mir wird übel (at bei, von); **2.** (ver-)schlingen; (sich) vollstopfen.

gor·geous □ ['gɔːdʒəs] prächtig, glänzend; **'gor·geous·ness** Pracht f.

go·ril·la zo. [gə'rilə] Gorilla m.

gor·mand·ize ['gɔːməndaiz] schlem-men, fressen, prassen.

gorm·less F ['gɔːmlis] stupid, be-griffsstutzig.

gorse ♀ [gɔːs] Stechginster m.

gor·y □ ['gɔːri] blutig.

gosh P [gɔʃ] (bei) Gott!, Mensch!

gos·hawk orn. ['gɔshɔːk] Hühner-habicht m.

gos·ling ['gɔzliŋ] Gänschen n.

go-slow ['gəu'sləu] Bummelstreik m.

gos·pel ['gɔspəl] Evangelium n (a. fig.); **'gos·pel·(l)er** Wanderpredi-ger m.

gos·sa·mer ['gɔsəmə] Altweiber-sommer m; feine Gaze f.

gos·sip ['gɔsip] **1.** Geschwätz n, Klatsch m; Plauderei f; Klatschbase f; ∼ column Klatschspalte f; **2.** schwat-zen, klatschen.

got [gɔt] pret. u. p.p. von get.

Goth [gɔθ] hist. Gote m; fig. Barbar m, Wandale m; **'Goth·ic** gotisch; fig. wandalisch, barbarisch.

got·ten Am. ['gɔtn] p.p. von get.

gouge [gaudʒ] **1.** ⊕ Hohlmeißel m; **2.** mst ∼ out ausmeißeln; Am. F betrügen.

gou·lash ['guːlæʃ] Gulasch m, n.

gourd ♀ ['guəd] Kürbis m.

gour·mand ['guəmənd] 1. gefräßig;
2. Vielfraß *m*.
gour·met ['guəmei] Feinschmecker
m; ~ *restaurant* Schlemmerlokal *n*.
gout ♂ [gaut] Gicht *f*; **'gout·y** □
gichtisch; gichtkrank; Gicht...
gov·ern ['gʌvən]*v/t*. regieren (*a.gr.*),
verwalten; beherrschen (*a. fig.*);
lenken, leiten; *v/i*. herrschen; ~*ing*
body konkr. Leitung *f*; **'gov·ern·ess**
Erzieherin *f*, Gouvernante *f*; **'gov·
ern·ment** Regierung *f*; Leitung *f*;
Herrschaft *f* (*of* über *acc.*); Re-
gierung(sform) *f*; Verwaltung *f*;
Ministerium *n*; Statthalterschaft *f*;
attr. Staats...; ~ *spokesman* Regie-
rungssprecher *m*; **gov·ern·men·tal**
[~'mentl] Regierungs...; **'gov·er·nor**
Gouverneur *m*; Direktor *m*, Präsident *m*, Leiter *m*; Kurator *m*; F Alte
m (*Vater*; *Chef*); *Anrede*: mein Herr!;
⊕ Regulator *m*; **gov·er·nor gen·er·
al** Generalgouverneur *m*; **'gov·er·
nor·ship** Gouverneursamt *n*.
gown [gaun] 1. (Frauen)Kleid *n*;
Robe *f*, Talar *m*; 2. kleiden;
'gowns·man Student *m*; ✗ Zivilist *m*.
grab F [græb] 1. grapsen (*at* nach);
an sich reißen, packen, schnappen;
2. plötzlicher Griff *m*, Graps *m*; ⊕
Greifer *m*; ~*bag Am.* Glückstopf
m; **'grab·ber** Habsüchtige *m*, Raffke
m; Straßenräuber *m*.
grace [greis] 1. Gnade *f*; Gunst *f*;
(Gnaden)Frist *f*, Aufschub *m*;
Grazie *f*, Anmut *f*; Anstand *m*;
Zier(de) *f*; ~*s pl.* Reize *m/pl.*; ♪
Verzierungen *f/pl.*; ♫*s pl.* die Gra-
zien *f/pl.*; *act of* ~ Gnadenakt *m*;
with (*a*) *good* (*bad*) ~ bereit-
(wider)willig; *Your* ♫ Euer Gnaden;
good ~*s pl.* Gunst *f*; *period of* ~
Karenzzeit *f*; *s. say* 1; 2. zieren,
schmücken; begünstigen, auszeichnen; **grace·ful** □ ['~ful] anmutig,
graziös; höflich; taktvoll; **'grace-
ful·ness** Grazie *f*, Anmut *f*;
'grace·less □ gottlos; schamlos;
reizlos.
gra·cious □ ['greiʃəs] gnädig, gütig,
huldvoll; *good* ~*!*, *goodness* ~*!*, ~
me! ach du meine Güte!; **'gra·
cious·ness** Gnade *f*.
grack·le *orn.* ['grækl] *ein* Star
m.
gra·da·tion [grə'deiʃən] Stufengang
m, Abstufung *f*; *gr.* Ablaut *m*.

grade [greid] 1. Grad *m*, Rang *m*;
Stufe *f*; Qualität *f*; *bsd. Am.* =
gradient; *Am. Schule*: Klasse *f*,
Note *f*; *make the* ~ *Am.* F Erfolg
haben; ~ *crossing Am.* schienengleicher Bahnübergang *m*; ~(*d*)
school Am. Grundschule *f*; 2. abstufen; einteilen; 💼 *etc.* planieren;
Vieh (auf)kreuzen.
gra·di·ent ['greidjənt] 💼 *etc.* Steigung *f*, Neigung *f*.
grad·u·al □ ['grædʒuəl] stufen-
weise (fortschreitend), allmählich;
'grad·u·al·ly nach u. nach; allmählich; **grad·u·ate** 1. ['~djueit]
graduieren: mit Gradeinteilung
versehen; (sich) abstufen; die Abschlußprüfung machen; promovieren; 2. ['~dʒuit] Absolvent(in) *e-r*
Universität etc., Graduierte *m*, *f*;
grad·u·a·tion [~dju'eiʃən] Gradeinteilung *f*; Abschlußprüfung *f*;
Promotion *f*.
graft[1] [gra:ft] 1. ✗ Pfropfreis *n*;
2. ✗ pfropfen (*in, upon* auf *acc.*);
fig., ♂ verpflanzen.
graft[2] *Am.* [~] 1. Bestechung *f*,
Korruption *f*, Schiebung(en *pl.*) *f*,
Schmiergeld(er *pl.*) *n*; 2. F Kor-
ruptionsgelder einschieben; **'graft-
er** F *bsd. pol.* Schieber *m*.
gra·ham ['greiəm]: ~ *bread* Gra-
ham-, Weizenschrotbrot *n*.
Grail [greil] *Sage*: Gral *m*.
grain [grein] Korn *n*; Samenkorn *n*;
Getreide *n*; Körnchen *n* (*a. fig.*);
Gefüge *n*, Struktur *f*; Maserung *f*
(*Holz*); Strich *m des Tuches*; *fig.*
Natur *f*; Gran *n* (*kleines Gewicht*);
in ~ echt, gründlich; *dyed in the* ~
in der Wolle gefärbt; *against the* ~
gegen den Strich (*a. fig.*); **grained**
in der Wolle gefärbt; gemasert.
gram [græm] = *gramme*.
gra·mer·cy † [grə'mə:si] tausend
Dank!
gram·i·na·ceous [greimi'neiʃəs],
gra·min·e·ous [grei'miniəs] gras-
artig; Gras...
gram·ma·logue ['græməlɔg] *Kurzschrift*: Sigel *n*, Kürzel *n*.
gram·mar ['græmə] Grammatik
f; **gram·mar·i·an** [grə'mɛəriən]
Grammatiker *m*; **'gram·mar-
-school** höhere Schule *f*, Gymnasium *n*; *Am. a.* Mittelschule *f*;
gram·mat·i·cal □ [grə'mætikəl]
grammati(kali)sch.

gramme [græm] Gramm *n.*

gram·o·phone ['græməfəun] Grammophon *n*; ~ *record* Schallplatte *f.*

gran·a·ry ['grænəri] Kornspeicher *m.*

grand ▢ [grænd] **1.** *fig.* großartig; erhaben; groß; Groß..., Haupt...; ♀ *Duchess* Großherzogin *f*; ♀ *Duke* Großherzog *m*; ♂ *Old Party Am.* Republikanische Partei *f*; ~ *stand* (Haupt)Tribüne *f*; **2.** *a.* ~ *piano ♪* Flügel *m*; *Am. sl.* tausend Dollar *m/pl.*; *miniature* ~ Stutzflügel *m*; **gran·dad** F ['grændæd] Opa *m*; **gran·dam(e)** ['~dæm] Mütterchen *n*; '**grand·child** Enkel(in); '**grand·daugh·ter** Enkelin *f*; **gran·dee** [græn'di:] *spanischer* Grande *m*; vornehmer Herr *m*; **gran·deur** ['grændʒə] Größe *f*, Hoheit *f*; Erhabenheit *f*, Würde *f*; '**grand·fa·ther** Großvater *m*; ~*'s clock* hohe Standuhr *f.*

gran·dil·o·quence[græn'diləkwəns] Redeschwulst *m*; **gran·dil·o·quent** ▢ hochtrabend, schwülstig.

gran·di·ose ▢ ['grændiəus] grandios, großartig; pompös.

grand·moth·er ['grændmʌðə], F **grand·ma** ['grænmɑ:] Großmutter *f*; **Grand Na·tion·al** *größtes englisches Pferderennen*; '**grand·ness** = *grandeur.*

grand...: ~**·pa** ['grænpɑ:] = *grandfather*; '~**·par·ents** *pl.* Großeltern *pl.*; ~**·sire** ['~saiə] † *od. v. Tieren:* Großvater *m*; Ahnherr *m*; '~**·son** Enkel *m*; '~**·stand** Haupttribüne *f.*

grange [greindʒ] Farm *f*; kleiner Gutshof *m*; *Am. Name für* Farmerorganisation *f*; '**grang·er** Farmer *m.*

gran·ite ['grænit] Granit *m*; **gran·it·ic** [~'nitik] granitartig; Granit...

gran·ny F ['græni] Oma *f* (*Großmutter*).

grant [grɑ:nt] **1.** Gewährung *f*; Unterstützung *f*, Zuschuß *m*; Stipendium *n*; ⚖ Übertragung *f*; **2.** gewähren; bewilligen; verleihen; zugestehen; ⚖ übertragen; *take for* ~*ed* für selbstverständlich halten; ~*ing this* (*to*) *be so* angenommen, dies wäre so; *God* ~ *...!* Gott gebe ...!; **gran'tee** ⚖ Begünstigte *m*; **grant-in-aid** ['grɑ:ntin'eid] Zuschuß *m*, Beihilfe *f*; **grant·or** ⚖

[~'tɔ:] Verleiher *m.*

gran·u·lar ['grænjulə]körnig;**gran·u·late** ['~leit] (sich) körnen; '**gran·u·lat·ed** körnig, gekörnt; ~ *sugar* Kristallzucker *m*; **gran·u'la·tion** Körnung *f*; **gran·ule** ['~ju:l] Körnchen *n*; **gran·u·lous** ['~juləs] körnig.

grape [greip] Weinbeere *f*, -traube *f*; '~**·fruit** ♀ Pampelmuse *f*; '~**·shot** ✕ Kartätsche *f*; '~**·sug·ar** Traubenzucker *m*; '~**·vine** Rebe *f*; *a.* ~ *telegraph* unterirdisches Nachrichtensystem *n*, Flüsterparolen *f/pl.*; *hear s.th. through the* ~ et. gerüchtweise erfahren.

graph [græf] graphische Darstellung *f*; '**graph·ic,** '**graph·i·cal** ▢ graphisch; Schreib...; anschaulich; *graphic arts pl.* Graphik *f*; **graph·ite** *min.* ['~fait] Graphit *m*; **graph·ol·o·gy** [~'fɔlədʒi] Graphologie *f* (*Handschriftendeutung*); **graph pa·per** Millimeterpapier *n.*

grap·nel ⚓ ['græpnəl] Enterhaken *m*; Dreganker *m.*

grap·ple ['græpl] **1.** ⚓ Enterhaken *m*; ⊕ Greifer *m*; **2.** entern; packen, fassen; ringen; ~ *with* kämpfen mit; in Angriff nehmen.

grasp [grɑ:sp] **1.** Griff *m*; Bereich *m*; Beherrschung *f*; Fassungskraft *f*; Begriff *m*; **2.** *v/t.* (er)greifen, packen; begreifen; *v/i.* greifen, streben (*at* nach); '**grasp·ing** ▢ habsüchtig.

grass [grɑ:s] **1.** Gras *n*; Rasen *m*; *sl.* Marihuana *n*; *at* ~ *auf der* Weide; *fig.* im Urlaub; *send to* ~ = **2.** auf die Weide treiben; '~**·hop·per** Heuschrecke *f*; '~**·plot** Rasenplatz *m*; ~**·roots** *pl. Am. die* landwirtschaftlichen Bezirke *m/pl.*; *die* Landbevölkerung; Grundlage *f*, Quelle *f*; *pol.* Basis *f*; ~ *snake* Ringelnatter *f*; '~**·wid·ow(·er)** Strohwitwe(r *m*) *f*; '**grass·y** grasig, grasreich; grasbewachsen.

grate[1] [greit] (Kamin)Gitter *n*; (Feuer)Rost *m*; *fig.* Herd *m.*

grate[2] [~] *v/t.* raspeln, (zer)reiben; *mit den Zähnen* knirschen; *v/i.* knirschen, knarren; ~ (*up*)*on fig. das Ohr etc.* verletzen.

grate·ful ▢ ['greitful] dankbar; *von Dingen:* angenehm, willkommen.

grat·er ['greitə] Reibeisen *n.*

grat·i·fi·ca·tion [grætifi'keiʃən] Befriedigung *f*; Freude *f*; Genuß *m*; **grat·i·fy** [' ͜ fai] erfreuen; befriedigen; '**grat·i·fy·ing** erfreulich.

grat·ing ['greitiŋ] **1.** □ schrill, unangenehm; **2.** Gitter(werk) *n*.

gra·tis ['greitis] umsonst.

grat·i·tude ['grætitjuːd] Dankbarkeit *f*.

gra·tu·i·tous □ [grə'tjuːitəs] unentgeltlich; freiwillig; mutwillig; grundlos; **gra·tu·i·ty** Abfindung *f*; Gratifikation *f*; Trinkgeld *n*.

gra·va·men 🏛 [grə'veimen] (Haupt)Beschwerdepunkt *m*; *das* Belastende.

grave[1] □ [greiv] ernst; (ge)wichtig; gemessen; gesetzt; feierlich; ~ *accent gr.* Gravis *m*.

grave[2] [͜] **1.** Grab *n*; **2.** *(irr.) mst fig.* (ein)graben; '**~-dig·ger** Totengräber *m*.

grav·el ['grævəl] **1.** Kies *m*; 🪨 Harngrieß *m*; **2.** mit Kies bedecken; F in Verlegenheit bringen; verblüffen; **grav·el·ly** ['grævli] kiesig.

grav·en ['greivən] *p.p von* grave[2] **2.**

grav·er ⊕ ['greivə] Grabstichel *m*.

grave...: '**~-side**: *at his* ~ an seinem Grabe; '**~-stone** Grabstein *m*; '**~-yard** Kirchhof *m*.

grav·ing dock ⚓ ['greiviŋ'dɔk] Trockendock *n*, Kalfaterdock *n*.

grav·i·tate ['græviteit] (hin)neigen (*towards* zu, nach); **grav·i·ta·tion** Schwerkraft *f*; *fig.* Hang *m*; **grav·i·ta·tion·al** [͜ ʃənl] Schwerkraft..., Anziehungs...; ~ *force* Schwerkraft *f*; ~ *pull* Anziehungskraft *f*.

grav·i·ty ['græviti] Schwere *f*; Wichtigkeit *f*; Ernst *m*; Feierlichkeit *f*; Schwerkraft *f*; *centre of* ~ Schwerpunkt *m*; *specific* ~ spezifisches Gewicht *n*.

gra·vy ['greivi] Fleischsaft *m*, Bratensoße *f*; '**~-boat** Saucière *f*, Soßenschüssel *f*.

gray *bsd. Am.* [grei] grau; F nicht ganz legal; **gray·ish** *bsd. Am.* [' ͜ iʃ] gräulich.

graze [greiz] **1.** (ab)weiden; (ab-) grasen; streifen, schrammen; **2.** Schramme *f*.

gra·zier ['greizjə] Viehmäster *m*.

grease 1. [griːz] (ein)fetten, (be-) schmieren; ~ *s.o.'s palm fig.* j. schmieren; **2.** [griːs] Fett *n*; Schmiere *f*; '**~-cup** ⊕ Schmier-

büchse *f*; '**~-gun** *mot.* Schmierpresse *f*; '**~-proof** fettdicht; ~ *paper* Pergamentpapier *n*; **greas·er** *Am. sl.* ['griːzə] *Schimpfwort für* Mexikaner *m*.

greas·y □ ['griːzi] fettig; schmierig.

great □ [greit] **1.** *allg.* groß (*nach Ausdehnung, Dauer, Zahl, Grad*; *fig.* = *tüchtig*; *geschickt*; *eifrig*; *großmütig*; *bedeutend*; *vornehm*; *mächtig*); Groß...; F großartig; Ur...; *s. deal*[2] *1, many*; **2.** *the* ~ *pl.* die Großen *m/pl.*, die Vornehmen *m/pl.*; ~*s pl.* Abschlußexamen *n* für B.A. in Oxford; '**~-coat** (Winter)Mantel *m*; '**~-'grand·child** Urenkel(in); '**~-'grand·fa·ther** Urgroßvater *m*; '**great·ly** sehr; '**great·ness** Größe *f*; Stärke *f*.

Gre·cian ['griːʃən] griechisch.

greed [griːd], '**greed·i·ness** Gier(igkeit) *f*; '**greed·y** □ (be)gierig (*of, for* nach); habgierig; gefräßig.

Greek [griːk] **1.** griechisch; **2.** Grieche *m*, Griechin *f*; Griechisch *n*; *that is* ~ *to me* das sind mir böhmische Dörfer.

green [griːn] **1.** □ grün (*a.* = *unreif*; F *unerfahren*); frisch (*Fisch etc.*); (⊕ fabrik)neu; Grün...; **2.** Grün *n*; Jugend(kraft) *f*; Rasen *m*; Wiese *f*; ~*s pl.* frisches Gemüse *n*; '**~-back** *Am.* Dollarnote *f*; **green·er·y** [' ͜ nəri] Grün *n*, Laub *n*.

green...: ~ **fin·gers** *pl.* gärtnerische Begabung *f*; '**~-gage** 🌳 Reineclaude *f*; '**~-gro·cer** Gemüsehändler(in); '**~-gro·cer·y** Gemüsehandlung *f*; '**~-horn** Grünschnabel *m*; '**~-house** Gewächshaus *n*; '**green·ish** grünlich.

Green·land·er ['griːnləndə] Grönländer(in); **Green·land·man** [' ͜ ləndmən] Grönlandfahrer *m*.

green light ['griːn'lait] grünes Licht *n* (F *fig.* = *Genehmigung*); '**green·ness** Grün *n*; Frische *f*; Unreife *f*.

green...: '**~-room** *thea.* Künstlergarderobe *f*; '**~-sick·ness** 🪨 Bleichsucht *f*; ~**sward** [' ͜ swɔːd] Rasen *m*.

Green·wich ['grinidʒ]: ~ *time* Greenwicher Zeit *f*.

green·wood ['griːnwud] (belaubter) Wald *m*.

greet [griːt] (be)grüßen; '**greet·ing** Begrüßung *f*; Gruß *m*; ~*s card* Glückwunschkarte *f*.

gre·gar·i·ous [gri'gɛəriəs] in Herden lebend; gesellig.

gre·nade ✕ [gri'neid] (Hand-, Gewehr)Granate *f*; **gren·a·dier** [grenə'diə] Grenadier *m*.

grew [gru:] *pret. von grow.*

grey [grei] **1.** □ grau; ♀ *Friar* Franziskaner *m*; **2.** Grau *n*; Grauschimmel *m*; **3.** grau machen *od.* werden; ~ **a·re·a** Grauzone *f*; '~**beard** Graubart *m*, alter Mann *m*.

grey...: '~**head·ed** *fig.* altgedient; '~**hound** Windhund *m*; '**grey·ish** gräulich; **grey mat·ter** *anat.* graue Substanz *f*; *fig.* Grips *m*, Verstand *m*.

grid [grid] *bsd. Radio:* Gitter *n*; *Linien-, Eisenbahn-, Strom-* etc. Netz *n*; *Am. Fußball:* Spielfeld *n*.

grid·dle ['gridl] Backblech *n*.

grid·i·ron ['gridaiən] (Brat)Rost *m*.

grief [gri:f] Gram *m*, Kummer *m*.

griev·ance ['gri:vəns] Beschwerde *f*; Miß-, Übelstand *m*; **grieve** kränken, *j-m* weh tun; sich grämen; '**griev·ous** □ kränkend, schmerzlich; drückend; schlimm; '**griev·ous·ness** *das* Schmerzliche; Druck *m*.

grif·fin ['grifin] *Sage:* Greif *m*.

grig [grig] kleiner Aal *m*; Grille *f*.

grill [gril] **1.** grillen; braten (*a. fig.*); *sl. j.* weichmachen; **2.** Bratrost *m*, Grill *m*; Rostbraten *m*; *a.* ~**room** Grillroom *m*.

grim □ [grim] grimmig; schrecklich; hart; finster, düster; ~ *facts pl. die* unerbittlichen Tatsachen *f*/*pl.*; ~ *humour* Galgenhumor *m*.

gri·mace [gri'meis] **1.** Grimasse *f*; **2.** Grimassen machen.

grime [graim] **1.** Schmutz *m*; Ruß *m*; **2.** beschmutzen; '**grim·y** □ schmutzig; rußig. [(*at* über *acc.*).]

grin [grin] Grinsen *n*; **2.** grinsen)

grind [graind] **1.** (*irr.*) *v*/*t.* (zer)reiben; mahlen; wetzen; schleifen; *Leierkasten etc.* drehen; leiern; *fig.* schinden; *sl.* (ein)pauken; mit *den* Zähnen knirschen; ~ *out* herunterleiern; *v*/*i.* sich mahlen lassen; sich schinden; *sl.* büffeln; **2.** Schinderei *f*; '**grind·er** Schleifer *m*; Backenzahn *m*; Mahlwerk *n*; Leiermann *m*; *sl.* Einpauker *m*; '**grind·ing** Mahl...; Schleif...; '**grind·stone** Schleif-, Mühlstein *m*; *keep s.o.'s nose to the* ~ *j.* (dauernd) schinden.

grip [grip] **1.** packen, fassen (*a. fig.*); greifen; **2.** Griff *m*; Gewalt *f*; Herr-

schaft *f* (*of* über *acc.*); ⊕ Greifer *m*; *Am.* = *gripsack; get to* ~*s with* sich auseinandersetzen mit.

gripe [graip] **1.** Griff *m*; Gewalt *f*; ~*s pl.* F Bauchgrimmen *n*; *bsd. Am.* Beschwerden *f*/*pl.* **2.** *v*/*t.* (er)greifen, packen; drücken, zwicken; *v*/*i. bsd. Am.* F meckern.

grip·ping ['gripiŋ] fesselnd, spannend.

grip·sack *Am.* ['gripsæk] Handtasche *f*, -köfferchen *n*.

gris·ly ['grizli] gräßlich, schrecklich.

grist [grist] Mahlgut *n*; *bring* ~ *to the mill fig.* Gewinn bringen; *all is* ~ *that comes to his mill* er weiß mit allem et. anzufangen. [knorpelig.)

gris·tle ['grisl] Knorpel *m*; '**gris·tly**)

grit [grit] **1.** Schrot(mehl) *n*; Kies *m*; Sand(stein) *m*; *fig.* Mumm *m*; **2.** knirschen (mit); '**grit·ty** sandig.

griz·zle F ['grizl] quengeln; '**griz·zled** = *grizzly 1*; '**griz·zly 1.** grau (-haarig); ~ *bear* = **2.** Graubär *m*.

groan [grəun] **1.** Stöhnen *n*, Seufzen *n*; Ächzen *n*; Murren *n*; **2.** seufzen, stöhnen (*for* nach).

groat [grəut]: *not worth a* ~ keinen Heller wert.   [Grütze *f*.)

groats [grəuts] *pl.* (*bsd. Hafer-*))

gro·cer ['grəusə] Lebensmittelhändler *m*; **gro·cer·ies** ['~riz] *pl.* Lebensmittel *n*/*pl.*; '**gro·cer·y** Lebensmittelgeschäft *n*.

gro·ce·ri·a *Am.* [grəusi'tiəriə] Selbstbedienungsladen *m*.

grog [grɔg] Grog *m*; '**grog·gy** betrunken; taumelig; wack(e)lig.

groin [grɔin] **1.** *anat.* Leisten (-gegend *f*) *f*/*pl.*; △ Grat *m*, Rippe *f*; **2.** mit Kreuzgewölbe bauen.

groom [grum] **1.** Reit-, Stallknecht *m*; = *bridegroom*; **2.** *Pferde* pflegen; *Am. pol. Kandidat* lancieren; *well* ~*ed* gepflegt; elegant; **grooms·man** ['~zmən] Brautführer *m*.

groove [gru:v] **1.** Rinne *f*, Furche *f*, Nut *f*; Rille *f*; *fig.* Gewohnheit *f*, Schablone *f*; ~*s pl.* Züge *m*/*pl.* im Gewehr; *in the* ~ *fig.* im richtigen Fahrwasser; **2.** nuten, falzen; riefeln; '**groov·y** *Am.* toll, einfach phantastisch.

grope [grəup] (be)tasten; tappen; ~ *one's way* sich vorwärtstasten.

gross [grəus] **1.** □ dick; grob; derb; roh; üppig (*Wachstum*); dick, feist (*Person*); unanständig; ungeheuer-

lich; ✝ Brutto...; ⏜ *national product*
✝ Bruttosozialprodukt *n*; 2. Gros *n*
(*12 Dutzend*); *in the* ⏜ im ganzen, in
Bausch und Bogen; '**gross·ness**
Dichtheit *f*; Grobheit *f*; Derbheit *f*,
Roheit *f*.

gro·tesque □ [grəʊ'tesk] grotesk.

grot·to ['grɔtəʊ], *pl.* '**grot·to(e)s**
Grotte *f*.

grouch *Am.* F [grautʃ] 1. quengeln,
meckern; 2. Meckerei *f*; schlechte
Laune *f*; Meckerer *m*; '**grouch·y**
queng(e)lig.

ground[1] [graʊnd] *pret. u. p.p. von*
grind 1; ⏜ *glass* Mattglas *n*; *phot.*
Mattscheibe *f*.

ground[2] [⏜] 1. *mst* Grund *m*, Boden
m; Gebiet *n*; *Spiel- etc.* Platz *m*;
Jagd-Revier *n*; *paint.* Grundierung
f; *Beweg- etc.* Grund *m*; ♀ Erde *f*,
Erdschluß *m*; ⏜*s pl.* Grundstück *n*,
Park(s *pl.*) *m*, Gärten *m*/*pl.*; *Kaffee*-
Satz *m*; Anfangsgründe *m*/*pl.*; *on
the* ⏜(s) *of* auf Grund (*gen.*); *on the*
⏜(s) *that* mit der Begründung, daß;
fall to the ⏜ hinfallen; *fig.* ins Wasser fallen; *give* ⏜ zurückweichen;
stand od. hold od. keep one's ⏜ sich
behaupten; 2. niederlegen; (be-)
gründen; *j-m* die Anfangsgründe
beibringen; ⊕ grundieren; ♀ erden; ⚓ auflaufen (lassen); *be* ⏜*ed*
🗲 Startverbot bekommen; *well* ⏜*ed*
mit guter Grundlage; '**ground·age**
⚓ Hafengebühr *f*, Ankergeld *n*.

ground...: '⏜**·con·nex·ion** ♀ Erdung
f; ⏜ **crew** = *ground-staff*; ⏜ **floor**
Erdgeschoß *n*; ⏜ **forc·es** *pl.* ✕ Bodentruppen *f*/*pl.*; '⏜**'hog** *zo.* *bsd. Am.*
Murmeltier *n*; '⏜**·less** □ grundlos;
ground·ling *thea.* ['⏜liŋ] Gründling
m, Parterrezuschauer *m*.

ground...: '⏜**·nut** Erdnuß *f*; '⏜**'plan**
Grundriß *m*; '⏜**'rent** Grundpacht *f*.

ground·sel ⚘ ['graʊnsl] Kreuzkraut
n.

ground·sheet ['graʊndʃiːt] *Camping
etc.*: Unterlegplane *f*.

grounds·man ['graʊndzmən] *Sport:*
Platzwart *m*.

ground...: ⏜ **speed** ⚓ Geschwindigkeit *f* über Grund; '⏜**·staff** 🗲 Bodenpersonal *n*; ⏜ **swell** Dünung *f*; '⏜**-to-'air mis·sile** ✕ Boden-Luft-Rakete *f*; '⏜**·wire** ♀ Erdleitung *f*; '⏜**work** Grundlage *f*, Fundament *n*.

group [gruːp] 1. Gruppe *f*; Truppe *f*;
⏜ *dynamics v̱.* Gruppendynamik *f*;

2. (sich) gruppieren.

grouse[1] *orn.* [graus] Schottisches
Mohrhuhn *n*.

grouse[2] F [⏜] meckern, nörgeln.

grove [grəʊv] Wäldchen *n*, Hain *m*;
Gehölz *n*.

grov·el ['grɔvl] *mst fig.* kriechen;
'**grov·el·(l)er** Kriecher(in); '**grov·el·(l)ing** 1. kriechend; kriecherisch
niedrig; 2. Kriecherei *f*.

grow [grəʊ] (*irr.*) *v*/*i.* wachsen;
werden; ⏜ *out of* herauswachsen
aus; entwachsen (*dat.*); *et.* überwinden; kommen von, entstehen
aus; ⏜ (*up*)*on s.o.* j-m ans Herz
wachsen; ⏜ *up* heranwachsen, erwachsen werden; *v*/*t.* anpflanzen,
-bauen, ziehen; *Bart* wachsen lassen; '**grow·er** Bauer *m*, Züchter *m*.

growl [graul] 1. Knurren *n*, Brummen *n*; 2. knurren, brummen;
'**growl·er** *fig.* Brummbär *m*; *Am.
sl.* Bierkrug *m*.

grown [grəʊn] 1. *p.p. von* grow;
2. *adj.* erwachsen; bewachsen; '⏜**-up** 1. erwachsen; 2. Erwachsene
m, *f*; **growth** [grəʊθ] Wachstum *n*;
(An)wachsen *n*; Entwicklung *f*;
Wuchs *m*; Gewächs *n*, Erzeugnis *n*;
of one's own ⏜ selbstgezogen.

groyne [grɔin] Buhne *f*.

grub [grʌb] 1. Raupe *f*, Larve *f*,
Made *f*; *contp.* Prolet *m*; *sl.* Futter
n; 2. graben (*for nach*); sich abmühen; *sl.* futtern (*essen*); ⏜ *up* ausjäten, ausroden; *mst* ⏜ *out* aufstöbern, ausgraben; '**grub·by** schmierig, schmutzig; madig.

grudge [grʌdʒ] 1. Groll *m*; *bear s.o. a* ⏜
einen Groll gegen j. hegen; 2. mißgönnen, neiden; ungern geben *od.*
tun *etc.*; ⏜ *no pains* keine Mühe
scheuen; '**grudg·er** Neider *m*;
'**grudg·ing·ly** widerwillig, ungern.

gru·el ['gruəl] Haferschleim *m*; *get
od. have one's* ⏜ *sl.* sein Fett kriegen;
'**gru·el·(l)ing** zermürbend.

grue·some □ ['gruːsəm] grausig,
schauerlich.

gruff [grʌf], '**gruff·y** grob, schroff,
barsch; mürrisch; rauh.

grum·ble ['grʌmbl] murren, brummen, nörgeln (*at über acc.*); (g)rollen (*Donner*); '**grum·bler** *fig.*
Brummbär *m*. [knurrig.]

grump·y □ F ['grʌmpi] brummig,[

Grun·dy·ism ['grʌndiizəm] Engstirnigkeit *f*, engstirniger Konformismus *m*.

grunt [grʌnt] **1.** Grunzen *n*, Grunz-, Knurrlaut *m*; **2.** grunzen; **'grunt·er** Schwein *n*.

guar·an·tee [gærən'ti:] **1.** Bürgschaftsempfänger *m*; Bürge *m*; = *guaranty*; **2.** bürgen für, garantieren; **guar·an·tor** [‿'tɔ:] Bürge *m*; **'guar·an·ty** Bürgschaft *f*, Garantie *f*; Gewähr(leistung) *f*.

guard [gɑ:d] **1.** Wacht *f*; ✗ Wache *f*; Wächter *m*, Wärter *m*; 🚋 Schaffner *m*; Schutz(vorrichtung *f*) *m*; ‿s *pl*. ✗ Garde *f*; *be on (off) one's* ‿ (nicht) auf der Hut sein; *mount* ‿ ✗ auf Wache ziehen; *relieve* ‿ ✗ die Wache ablösen; **2.** *v/t*. bewachen, (be)schützen (*from* vor *dat*.; *against* gegen); (be)hüten; *v/i*. sich hüten (*against* vor *dat*.); **'‿-boat** ⚓ Wachboot *n*; **'guard·ed** □ behutsam, vorsichtig; **'guard·house** Wachlokal *n*; Arrestlokal *n*; **'guard·i·an** Hüter *m*, Wächter *m*; ⚖ Vormund *m*; *attr*. Schutz...; ‿ *angel* Schutzengel *m*; ‿ *of the poor* Armenpfleger(in); **'guard·i·an·ship** Obhut *f*; Vormundschaft *f*; **'guard·rail** Schutzgeländer *n*; **guards·man** ✗ ['gɑ:dzmən] Gardist *m*.

gudg·eon ['gʌdʒən] *ichth*. Gründling *m*; *fig*. Einfaltspinsel *m*; ⊕ Bolzen *m*. [**2.** belohnen.]

guer·don *lit*. ['gə:dən] **1.** Lohn *m*;]

gue(r)·ril·la [gə'rilə] Partisan *m*, Guerillakämpfer *m*; ‿ *war* Kleinkrieg *m*.

guess [ges] **1.** Vermutung *f*; *at a* ‿ schätzungsweise; **2.** *v/t*. vermuten; (er)raten; *v/i*. mutmaßen, raten (*at acc*.); *bsd. Am*. denken, meinen, annehmen; **'guess·work** Mutmaßung *f*.

guest [gest] Gast *m*; *paying* ‿ zahlender Gast *m*; **'‿-house** (Hotel-) Pension *f*, Fremdenheim *n*; **'‿-room** Gast-, Fremdenzimmer *n*.

guf·faw [gʌ'fɔ:] **1.** schallendes Gelächter *n*; **2.** laut (los)lachen.

guid·a·ble ['gaidəbl] lenksam; **guid·ance** ['‿dəns] Führung *f*, (An-) Leitung *f*; Orientierung *f*.

guide [gaid] **1.** Führer *m*; *s*. ‿-*book*; ⊕ Führung *f*; *attr*. Führungs..., Leit...; **2.** leiten, führen, steuern, lenken; ‿*d missile* ✗ Fernlenkgeschoß *n*, Rakete *f*; *guiding principle*

Leitgedanke *m*; bestimmendes Prinzip *n*; **'‿-book** Reiseführer *m*; ‿ *dog* Blindenhund *m*; **'‿-lines** *pl*. Richtlinien *f/pl*.; **'‿-post** Wegweiser *m*; **'‿-rope** ✈ Schleppseil *n*.

gui·don ✗ ['gaidən] Standarte *f*.

guild [gild] Gilde *f*, Zunft *f*, Innung *f*; **'guild·er** Gulden *m*; **'Guild·hall** Rathaus *n* (*London*).

guile [gail] (Arg)List *f*; **guile·ful** □ ['‿ful] arglistig; **'guile·less** □ arglos; **'guile·less·ness** Arglosigkeit *f*.

guil·lo·tine [gilə'ti:n] **1.** Guillotine *f*, Fallbeil *n*; ⊕ Papierschneidemaschine *f*; *pol*. Befristung *f* der Debatte; **2.** hinrichten.

guilt [gilt] Schuld *f*; Strafbarkeit *f*; **'guilt·i·ness** Schuld *f*; **'guilt·less** □ schuldlos (*of* an *dat*.); unkundig (*of gen*.); **'guilt·y** □ schuldig; strafbar; *plead* ‿ sich schuldig bekennen.

guin·ea ['gini] Guinee *f* (*21 Schilling*); **'‿-fowl** Perlhuhn *n*; **'‿-pig** Meerschweinchen *n*; *fig*. Versuchskaninchen *n*.

guise [gaiz] *bsd. angenommene* Erscheinung *f*, Gestalt *f*, Maske *f*; Vorwand *m*.

gui·tar ♪ [gi'tɑ:] Gitarre *f*.

gulch *Am*. [gʌlf] tiefe Schlucht *f*.

gulf [gʌlf] Meerbusen *m*, Golf *m*; Abgrund *m*, Kluft *f* (*a. fig*.); Strudel *m*.

gull[1] *orn*. [gʌl] Möwe *f*.

gull[2] [‿] **1.** Trottel *m*, Tölpel *m*; **2.** übertölpeln; verleiten (*into* zu).

gul·let ['gʌlit] Speiseröhre *f*; Gurgel *f*, Schlund *m*.

gul·li·bil·i·ty [gʌli'biliti] Leichtgläubigkeit *f*; **gul·li·ble** □ ['‿ləbl] leichtgläubig.

gul·ly ['gʌli] Schlucht *f* *e-s* Gießbachs; Abzugskanal *m*; Gully *m*, Sinkkasten *m*.

gulp [gʌlp] **1.** Schluck *m*; Schlucken *n*; **2.** (gierig) schlucken.

gum[1] [gʌm] *a*. ‿*s* *pl*. Zahnfleisch *n*.

gum[2] [‿] **1.** Gummi *n*; Klebstoff *m*; Kaugummi *m*; ‿*s* *pl*. *Am*. Gummischuhe *m/pl*.; **2.** gummieren; zukleben. [geschwür *n*.]

gum·boil 💊 ['gʌmbɔil] Zahn-]

gum·my ['gʌmi] gummiartig; klebrig.

gump·tion F ['gʌmpʃən] Grips *m*, Köpfchen *n*; Schwung *m*, Mumm *m*.

gun [gʌn] **1.** Gewehr *n*; Flinte *f*; Büchse *f*; Geschütz *n*, Kanone *f*; *bsd. Am.* Revolver *m*, Pistole *f*; Schütze *m*; *big od. great* ~ F hohes Tier *n* (*wichtige Person*); *stick to one's* ~ festbleiben, nicht nachgeben; **2.** *Am.* auf die Jagd gehen; '~**boat** ⚓ Kanonenboot *n*; '~**carriage** ✗ Lafette *f*; '~**cot·ton** Schießbaumwolle *f*; '~**li·cence** Waffenschein *m*; '~**man** *bsd. Am.* Gangster *m*, Bandit *m*; '~**met·al** Rotguß *m*; '**gun·ner** ✗, ⚓ Kanonier *m*; ✗ Bordschütze *m*; '**gunner·y** ✗ Geschützwesen *n*; Ballistik *f*.

gun·ny ['gʌni] Sackleinwand *f*.

gun...: '~**pow·der** Schießpulver *n*; ♀ *Plot hist.* Pulververschwörung *f* (*1605*); '~**room** ⚓ Kadettenmesse *f*; '~**run·ning** Waffenschmuggel *m*; '~**shot** Schußweite *f*; Schuß *m*; '~**shy** schußscheu; '~**smith** Büchsenmacher *m*; '~**tur·ret** Geschützturm *m*.   [Dollbord *n*.\
gun·wale ⚓ ['gʌnl] Schandeckel *m*;}

gur·gle ['gɜːgl] **1.** Gluckern *n*; **2.** gurgeln, gluckern, glucksen.

gush [gʌʃ] **1.** Guß *m*; *fig.* Erguß *m*; **2.** (sich) ergießen, schießen (*from* aus); *fig.* schwärmen; '**gush·er** *fig.* Schwärmer(in); Ölquelle *f*; '**gushing** □ überschwenglich, überspannt; '**gush·y** überschwenglich, schwärmerisch.

gus·set ['gʌsit] *Schneiderei:* Zwickel *m*.

gust [gʌst] Windstoß *m*, Bö *f*; Ausbruch *m*, Sturm *m der Leidenschaft*.

gus·ta·to·ry ['gʌstətəri] Geschmacks...

gus·to ['gʌstəu] Geschmack *m* (*for* an *dat.*); Vergnügen *n*.

gus·ty □ ['gʌsti] stürmisch.

gut [gʌt] **1.** Darm *m*; ♪ Darmsaite *f*; ~*s* *pl.* F Eingeweide *n/pl.*, Bauch *m*; *das Innere*; Durchschlagskraft *f*; Mut *m*; **2.** *Fisch* ausnehmen; *fig.* plündern, ausrauben; ausbrennen; '**gut·less** F feige, ohne Mumm; '**guts·y** F drauf-

gängerisch.

gut·ta·per·cha ['gʌtə'pɜːtʃə] Guttapercha *f*.

gut·ter ['gʌtə] **1.** Dachrinne *f*; Gosse *f* (*a. fig.*), Rinnstein *m*; **2.** *v/t.* furchen; auskehlen; *v/i.* rinnen, triefen, tropfen; ~ **press** Schmutzpresse *f*; '~**snipe** Straßenjunge *m*.

gut·tur·al ['gʌtərəl] **1.** □ Kehl...; kehlig; guttural; **2.** *gr.* Kehllaut *m*.

guy¹ [gai] **1.** F Vogelscheuche *f*; *bsd. Am.* F Kerl *m*, Kumpel *m*; **2.** verulken.

guy² [~] Halteseil *n*; ⚓ Gei *f*.

guz·zle ['gʌzl] saufen; fressen.

gym F [dʒim] = *gymnasium, gymnastics.*

gym·kha·na [dʒim'kɑːnə] *Geschicklichkeitswettkampf*, *Sportfest*.

gym·na·si·um [dʒim'neizjəm] Turnhalle *f*; **gym·nast** ['~næst] Turner(in); **gym'nas·tic** **1.** (~*ally*) gymnastisch; Turn...; ~ *competition* Wetturnen *n*; **2.** ~*s* *pl.* Turnen *n*, Gymnastik *f*; '**gym-shoes** *pl.* F Turnschuhe *m/pl.*

gyn·ae·col·o·gist [gaini'kɔlədʒist] Gynäkologe *m*, Frauenarzt *m*; **gyn·ae'col·o·gy** Gynäkologie *f*.

gyp [dʒip] Studentendiener *m in Cambridge u. Durham*; Gauner *m*; Gaunerei *f*; *give s.o.* ~ j-m das Leben sauer machen.

gyp·se·ous ['dʒipsiəs] gipsartig.

gyp·sum *min.* ['dʒipsəm] Gips *m*.

gyp·sy *bsd. Am.* ['dʒipsi] = *gipsy.*

gy·rate [dʒaiə'reit] kreisen; wirbeln; **gy'ra·tion** Kreisbewegung *f*; **gy·ra·to·ry** ['~rətəri] Kreis...; Wirbel...

gy·ro·com·pass *phys.* ['dʒaiərəu-'kʌmpəs] Kreiselkompaß *m*; **gy·ro·scope** ['gaiərəskəup] Gyroskop *n* (*Kreiselvorrichtung*); **gy·ro'scop·ic** **sta·bi·liz·er** [gaiərəs'kɔpik'steibilaizə], **gy·ro'sta·bi·liz·er** Schiffskreisel *m*, Stabilisator *m*.

gyve *poet.* [dʒaiv] **1.** ~*s* *pl.* Fesseln *f/pl.*; **2.** fesseln.

H

h [eitʃ]: *drop one's h's* ohne H od.
ha [haː] ha! [ungebildet sprechen.]
ha·be·as cor·pus ⚖ ['heibjəs-'kɔːpəs] a. writ of ~ Vorführungsbefehl m.
hab·er·dash·er ['hæbədæʃə] Kurzwarenhändler m; Am. Herrenartikelhändler m; **'hab·er·dash·er·y** Kurzwaren(geschäft n) f/pl.; Am. Herrenartikel m/pl.
ha·bil·i·ments [hə'bilimənts] pl. Gewand n; Kleider n/pl.
hab·it ['hæbit] **1.** (An)Gewohnheit f; Verfassung f; Kleid(ung f) n; fall od. get into bad ~s schlechte Gewohnheiten annehmen; get out of a ~ e-e Gewohnheit ablegen; get into the ~ of smoking sich das Rauchen angewöhnen; be in the ~ of ger. pflegen zu inf.; **2.** (an)kleiden; **'hab·it·a·ble** bewohnbar; **hab·i·tat** ♀, zo. ['~tæt] Vorkommen n, Stand-, Fundort m, Heimat f; **hab·i'ta·tion** Wohnen n; Wohnung f.
ha·bit·u·al □ [hə'bitjuəl] gewohnt, gewöhnlich; Gewohnheits...; **ha·'bit·u·ate** [~eit] gewöhnen (to an acc.); **hab·i·tude** f ['hæbitjuːd] Gewohnheit f; **ha·bit·u·é** [hə'bitjuei] Gewohnheit f; ständiger Besucher m, Stammgast m.
hack¹ [hæk] **1.** Hieb m; Einkerbung f; Fußball: Tritt m; **2.** (zer)hacken; Fußball: j. vor das Schienbein treten; ~ing cough kurzer, trockener Husten m.
hack² [~] **1.** Mietpferd n; Arbeitsgaul m (a. fig.); a. ~ writer literarischer Tagelöhner m; Schreiberling m; **2.** Miet(s)...; fig. abgedroschen; **3.** abnutzen.
hack·le ['hækl] **1.** ⊕ Hechel f; orn. Nackenfeder(n pl.) f; get s.o.'s ~s up fig. j. in Wut bringen; **2.** hecheln; zerhacken.
hack·ney ['hækni] (Kutsch)Gaul m; Klepper m; ~ car·riage, ~ coach Mietsdroschke f; **'hack·neyed** fig. abgedroschen.
hack-saw ⊕ ['hæksɔː] Metallsäge f.
had [hæd, həd] pret. u. p.p. von have.
had·dock ichth. ['hædək] Schellfisch m. [welt f.]
Ha·des ['heidiːz] Hades m, Unter-

h(a)e·mal ['hiːməl] Blut...
h(a)em·a·tite min. ['hemətait] Roteisenerz n.
h(a)e·mo... ['hiːməu] Blut...
h(a)e·mo·glo·bin ♣ [hiːməu'gləubin] Hämoglobin n, roter Blutfarbstoff m; **h(a)e·mo·phil·i·a** [~'filiə] Bluterkrankheit f.
h(a)em·or·rhage ['heməridʒ] Blutsturz m; **h(a)em·or·rhoids** ['~rɔidz] pl. Hämorrhoiden f/pl.
haft [hɑːft] Heft n, Stiel m.
hag [hæg] (mst fig. alte) Hexe f.
hag·gard □ ['hægəd] wild, verstört; hager; abgehärmt.
hag·gis ['hægis] schottisches Gericht aus Schafinnereien.
hag·gle ['hægl] feilschen, schachern.
hag·i·ol·o·gy [hægi'ɔlədʒi] Heiligenleben n/pl. u. -legenden f/pl.
hag·rid·den ['hægridn] (vom Alpdruck) gequält.
hah [hɑː] haha!
ha-ha [hɑː'hɑː] (in e-m Graben versenkter) Grenzzaun m.
hail¹ [heil] **1.** Hagel m; **2.** v/i. hageln; v/t. niederhageln lassen.
hail² [~] **1.** anrufen; (be)grüßen; ~ from stammen aus; **2.** Anruf m; ~! Heil!; within ~ in Rufweite; be ~-fellow-well-met with allzu vertraut sein mit j-m.
hail·stone ['heilstəun] Hagelkorn n; **'hail·storm** Hagelschauer m; fig. Schauer m, Flut f.
hair [hɛə] Haar n; keep your ~ on! sl. immer mit der Ruhe!; not turn a ~ ganz gelassen bleiben; ~'s breadth = **'~-breadth** Haaresbreite f; by od. within ~ um Haaresbreite; **'~-cut** Haarschnitt m; **'~-do** Am. Frisur f; **'~-dress·er** (bsd. Damen)Friseur m; **'~-dri·er** Haartrockner m, Fön m; **haired** behaart; **'hair·i·ness** Haarigkeit f, Behaartheit f.
hair...: **'~·less** ohne Haare, kahl; **'~·line** Haaransatz m; Schrift: Haarstrich m; **'~·piece** Haarteil n; Toupet n; **'~·pin** Haarnadel f; ~ bend Haarnadelkurve f; **'~-rais·ing** haarsträubend; **~ re·stor·er** Haarwuchsmittel n; **'~-shirt** härenes Hemd n; **'~-split·ting** Haarspalterei f; **'~-spring** ⊕ Unruhfeder f; **'hair·y**

haarig.
ha·la·tion *phot.* [hə'leiʃən] Lichthof
m.

hal·berd ⚔ ['hælbə:d] Hellebarde *f.*
hal·cy·on ['hælsiən] **1.** Eisvogel *m*;
2. still, ruhig, friedlich.
hale [heil] gesund, frisch, rüstig;
∼ *and hearty* gesund und munter.
half [hɑ:f] **1.** halb; ∼ *a crown* eine
halbe Krone; *a pound and a* ∼
anderthalb Pfund; *not* ∼ *sl.* nicht
wenig, gehörig, gar nicht schlecht;
2. *pl.* **halves** [hɑ:vz] Hälfte *f*;
Schule: Halbjahr *n*; ⚫ Partei *f*;
too clever by ∼ viel zu gescheit; *by*
halves nur halb; *go halves* teilen;
'∼-'**back** *Fußball:* Läufer *m*;
'∼-'**baked** *fig.* unfertig; unaus-
gegoren; '∼-**bind·ing** Halbfranzband *m*; '∼-**blood** Halbblut *n*;
'∼-'**bound** in Halbfranz gebunden;
'∼-'**bred** Halbblut...; '∼-**breed**
Halbblut *n*; '∼-**calf** Halbfranzband
m; '∼-**caste** Halbblut *n*; '∼-'**crown**
halbe Krone *f* (2¹/₂ *Schilling*);
'∼-'**heart·ed** ☐ lustlos, halbherzig,
lau; '∼-'**hol·i·day** halber Feiertag
m; freier Nachmittag *m*; '∼-'**hour**
1. halbe Stunde *f*; **2.** halbstündig,
-stündlich; '∼-'**hour·ly** halbstünd-
lich; '∼-'**length** Brustbild *n*;
'∼-**life** (**pe·ri·od**) *phys.* Halbwerts-
zeit *f*; '∼-'**mast:** (*at*) ∼ halbmast;
'∼-'**moon** Halbmond *m*; '∼-
-'**mourn·ing** Halbtrauer *f*; '∼-
-'**pay** Halbsold *m*: ∼**pen·ny**
['heipni] halber Penny *m* (=
¹/₂ p = £ 0.00¹/₂); ∼**seas-o·ver** F
['hɑ:fsi:z'əuvə] angesäuselt; '∼-
'**time** *Sport:* Halbzeit *f*; '∼-**tone**
proc·ess ⊕ Rasterverfahren *n*;
'∼-**track** Halbkettenantrieb *m*,
-fahrzeug *n*; '∼-'**way** auf halbem Wege, halbwegs; ∼ *house*
Zwischenstation *f*; *fig.* Mittel-
ding *n*; '∼-'**wit** Schwachkopf
m; '∼-'**wit·ted** einfältig, idiotisch.
hal·i·but *ichth.* ['hælibət] Heilbutt
m.
hal·i·to·sis [hæli'təusis] übler Mundgeruch *m.*
hall [hɔ:l] Halle *f*; Saal *m*; Vorsaal
m, -raum *m*; Flur *m*, Diele *f*;
Herren-, Gutshaus *n*; *univ.* Speisesaal *m*; Mahlzeit *f*; ∼ *of residence*
(Studenten)Wohnheim *n.*
hal·le·lu·jah [hæli'lu:jə] Hallelu-
ja(h) *n.*

hall...: '∼-**mark 1.** Feingehalts-
stempel *m*; *fig.* Stempel *m* (der
Echtheit), Zeichen *n*; **2.** (ab)stem-
peln; '∼-'**stand** Flurgarderobe *f.*
hal·lo(a) [hə'ləu] hallo!, he!
hal·loo [hə'lu:] **1.** hallo!; **2.** Hallo *n*;
3. *v/i.* (hallo) rufen; *v/t.* anfeuern.
hal·low ['hæləu] heiligen, weihen;
Hal·low·mas ['∼mæs] Allerheili-
gen(fest) *n.*
hal·lu·ci·na·tion [həlu:si'neiʃən]
Halluzination *f*, Sinnestäuschung *f.*
hall·way ['hɔ:lwei] Diele *f*, Flur *m.*
ha·lo ['heiləu] *ast.* Hof *m*; Heiligenschein *m.*
halt [hɔ:lt] **1.** Halt *m*; Stillstand *m*;
🚃 Haltestelle *f*; **2.** (an)halten; *mst*
fig. hinken; schwanken, zögern;
stocken; **3.** lahm.
hal·ter ['hɔ:ltə] Halfter *m*, *n*;
Strick *m* (*zum Hängen*).
halve [hɑ:v] halbieren; **halves** [∼z]
pl. von *half* 2.
hal·yard ⚓ ['hæljəd] Fall *n.*
ham [hæm] Schenkel *m*; Schinken
m; *sl.* Funkamateur *m*; *a.* ∼ *actor*
sl. Schmierenkomödiant *m.*
ham·burg·er *Am.* ['hæmbə:gə] Frikadelle *f*; Hamburger *m*, mit Frikadelle belegtes Brötchen *n*; Rinder-
hack *n.*
ham-fist·ed ['hæm'fistid], **ham-**
-hand·ed ['∼hændid] ungeschickt
(mit den Händen).
ham·let ['hæmlit] Weiler *m*, Dörf-
chen *n.*
ham·mer ['hæmə] **1.** Hammer *m*;
∼ *and tongs* F wild darauflos; **2.** hämmern; behämmern; schlagen; *Bör-*
se: für zahlungsunfähig erklären;
∼ *at* eifrig arbeiten an (*dat.*); ∼ *out*
zurechtschmieden, herausarbeiten.
ham·mock ['hæmək] Hängematte *f*;
∼ *chair* Liegestuhl *m.*
ham·per ['hæmpə] **1.** Packkorb *m*;
Geschenk-, Freßkorb *m*; **2.** verstricken, verwickeln; behindern;
hemmen.
ham·ster *zo.* ['hæmstə] Hamster *m.*
ham·string ['hæmstriŋ] **1.** *anat.*
Kniesehne *f*; **2.** die Kniesehnen
zerschneiden (*dat.*); *fig.* lähmen.
hand [hænd] **1.** Hand *f* (*fig. = Obhut,*
Besitz, Gewalt; Wirksamkeit; Ge-
schicklichkeit; Einfluß); Handschrift *f*; Unterschrift *f*; Hand-
breit *f*; Seite *f*; *zo.* Vorderfuß *m*;
(Uhr)Zeiger *m*; Hilfe *f*; Mann *m*,

Arbeiter *m*, Matrose *m*; Kenner *m*;
F Kerl *m*; *Karten:* Handkarten *f/pl.*,
Blatt *n*; Spieler *m*; *at* ~ bei der
Hand; nahe bevorstehend; *be at* ~
zur Verfügung stehen; *at first* ~ aus
erster Hand; *at s.o.'s* ~*s* von seiten
j-s; *a good* (*poor*) ~ *at* (un)geschickt
in (*dat.*); ~ *and glove* ein Herz und
eine Seele; *bear a* ~ (schnelle) Hilfe
leisten, zugreifen; *by* ~ von Hand;
durch Boten (*nicht per Post*);
change ~*s* den Besitzer wechseln;
get out of ~ außer Kontrolle geraten;
have a ~ *in* beteiligt sein an (*dat.*);
in ~ in der Hand; unter Kontrolle;
in Arbeit; zur Verfügung; vorliegend; ✝ bar; *lay* ~*s on* Hand an
j. legen; *lend a* ~ (mit) anfassen,
helfen; *off* ~ aus dem Handgelenk
od. Stegreif; auf der Stelle; ~*s off!*
Hände weg!; *on* ~ in Händen; ✝
vorrätig, auf Lager; *bsd. Am.* zur
Stelle, bereit; *on one's* ~*s* auf dem
Halse; *on all* ~*s* auf *od.* von allen
Seiten; *on the one* ~ einerseits; *on
the other* ~ andererseits; *have one's*
~ *out* aus der Übung sein; *out of* ~
sogleich; ~ *over fist* spielend; *take
a* ~ *at* bei e-m Spiel mitspielen; *to
(one's)* ~ zur Hand, bereit; ~ *to* ~
Mann gegen Mann; *come to* ~ sich
bieten; einlaufen (*Briefe*); *you can
feed him out of your* ~ *fig.* er frißt
aus der Hand; *get the upper* ~ *of*
die Oberhand gewinnen über (*acc.*);
put one's ~ *to* Hand legen an (*acc.*);
he can turn his ~ *to anything* er ist zu
allem zu gebrauchen; ~*s up!* Hände
hoch!; *s.* high 1; **2.** (~ *about, etc.*
herum- *etc.*) reichen; aushändigen,
übergeben; ~ *down* der Nachwelt
überliefern; vererben; ~ *in* ein-
händigen, abgeben; *Gesuch* einreichen; hineinhelfen; ~ *out* heraus-
helfen; ~ *over* aushändigen; '~**-bag**
Handtasche *f*; '~**-bar·row** Hand-
karre *f*; Trage *f*; '~**·bill** Flugblatt *n*,
Hand-, Reklamezettel *m*; '~**·book**
Handbuch *n*; '~**-brake** ⊕ Hand-
bremse *f*; '~**·cart** Handwagen *m*;
'~**·clap** Klatschen *n*; '~**·cuff** **1.**
Handschelle *f*; **2.** *j-m* Handschellen
anlegen; '**hand·ed** ...händig; mit
... Händen; F Plage *f*; F Sorgenkind *n*;
'**hand-glass** Handspiegel *m*; Lese-
lupe *f*; '**hand·gun** Faustfeuerwaffe *f*.
hand·i·cap ['hændikæp] **1.** Handikap

n; Vorgaberennen *n*, -spiel *n*; (Extra)Belastung *f* (*a. fig.*); **2.** (extra)
belasten; behindern; *fig. a.* beeinträchtigen; '**hand·i·capped 1.** *the* ~
pl. die Behinderten *pl.*; **2.** behindert.
hand·i·craft ['hændikrɑːft] Handwerk *n*; Handfertigkeit *f*; '**hand·i-
crafts·man** Handwerker *m*; '**hand-
i·ness** Gewandtheit *f*; Handlich-
keit *f*; '**hand·i·work** Handarbeit *f*;
Werk *n*, Schöpfung *f*.
hand·ker·chief ['hæŋkətʃif] Taschentuch *n*; *dünnes* Halstuch *n*.
han·dle ['hændl] **1.** Griff *m*; Stiel *m*;
Kurbel *f*; Henkel *m*; Schwengel *m*
der Pumpe etc.; *fig.* Handhabe *f*; F
Titel *m*; *fly off the* ~ F platzen vor
Wut; **2.** anfassen; handhaben; behandeln; umgehen mit; '~**-bar**
Lenkstange *f e-s Fahrrades*; *dropped* ~
Fahrrad: Rennlenker *m*.
hand...: '~**·loom** Handwebstuhl *m*;
'~**-lug·gage** Handgepäck *n*; '~**-
-'made** von Hand gemacht; ~
paper handgeschöpftes Bütten-
papier *n*; '~**-maid**(**·en**) *fig.* Magd *f*;
'~**-me-downs** *Am.* F *pl.* fertige *od.*
getragene Kleider *n/pl.*; '~**-or·gan**
Drehorgel *f*; '~**-out** F Almosen *n*;
Presseerklärung *f*; '~**-rail** Geländer *n*; '~**·saw** Handsäge *f*,
Fuchsschwanz *m*; **hand·sel** ['hæn-
səl] Neujahrsgeschenk *n*; Hand-
geld *n*; Vorgeschmack *m*; **hand·
shake** ['hændʃeik] Händedruck *m*;
hand·some □ ['hænsəm] ansehnlich, stattlich; schön, hübsch; anständig, nobel.
hand...: '~**·work** Handarbeit *f*
(*keine Maschinenarbeit*); '~**·writ-
ing** Handschrift *f*; '**hand·y** □ geschickt; handlich; zur Hand, nahe;
~ *man* Gelegenheitsarbeiter *m*;
Faktotum *n*.
hang [hæŋ] **1.** (*irr.*) *v/t.* hängen;
auf-, einhängen; verhängen (*with*
mit); (*pret. u. p.p. mst* ~*ed*) (er-)
hängen; hängen lassen; *Tapete* ankleben; *I'll be* ~*ed if* ... F ich lasse
mich hängen, wenn ...; ~ *it!* F hol's
der Henker!; ~ *fire* auf sich warten
lassen; ~ *out* (hin)aushängen; ~ *up*
aufhängen; an den Nagel hängen;
fig. verschieben; *v/i.* hängen (*on*
an *dat.*); schweben; sich neigen;
~ *about* herumlungern; sich an *j.*
hängen; ~ *back* sich zurückhalten,
zögern; ~ *on* sich klammern an

(*acc.*); *fig.* hängen an (*dat.*); ~ *up* den (Telefon)Hörer auflegen; ~ *by a hair*, ~ *by a single thread fig.* an einem Haar hängen; *let things go* ~ F sich um nichts kümmern; **2.** Hang *m*; Fall *m e-r Gardine etc.*; F Wesen *n*; *get the* ~ *of s.th.* F den Dreh von et. rauskriegen; *I don't care a* ~ *sl.* es ist mir Wurst.

hang·ar ['hæŋə] Flugzeughalle *f*.

hang·dog ['hæŋdɔg] **1.** Galgenstrick *m*; **2.** Armesünder...

hang·er ['hæŋə] Aufhänger *m*; Hirschfänger *m*; Waldhang *m*; Kesselhaken *m*; '~-'on *contp. fig.* Klette *f*, Schmarotzer *m*.

hang-glid·ing ['hæŋglaidiŋ] Drachenfliegen *n*.

hang·ing ['hæŋiŋ] Hänge...; ~ *committee Kunst:* Hängekommission *f*; '**hang·ings** *pl. Wand- etc.* Behang *m*; Tapeten *f/pl.*

hang·man ['hæŋmən] Henker *m*.

hang-nail 🎗 ['hæŋneil] Niednagel *m*.

hang·out F ['hæŋˈaut] Aufenthaltsort *m*, Treffpunkt *m*; Bumslokal *n*.

hang·over ['hæŋəuvə] *sl.* Katzenjammer *m*, Kater *m*; *Am.* Überbleibsel *n*.

hang·up *sl.* ['hæŋʌp] Komplex *m*, Hemmung *f*.

hank [hæŋk] Docke *f*, Strähne *f*.

han·ker ['hæŋkə] sich sehnen, verlangen (*after, for* nach); '**han·ker·ing** Verlangen *n*.

han·kie, han·ky F ['hæŋki] Taschentuch *n*.

han·ky-pan·ky F ['hæŋki'pæŋki] Hokuspokus *m*; Gaunerei *f*.

Han·o·ve·ri·an [hænəu'viəriən] **1.** hannover(i)sch; **2.** Hannoveraner (-in).

Han·sard ['hænsɑ:d] amtlicher Parlamentsbericht *m*.

Hanse [hæns]: *the* ~ *hist.* die Hanse; **Han·se·at·ic** [hænsi'ætik] hanseatisch.

han·sel ['hænsəl] = *handsel*.

han·som ['hænsəm] *a.* ~-*cab* zweirädrige Droschke *f*.

hap 🎗 [hæp] Zufall *m*; Glück *n*; **hap'haz·ard 1.** Zufall *m*; *at* ~ aufs Geratewohl; **2.** zufällig; wahllos; '**hap·less** ☐ unglücklich; '**hap·ly** † zufällig, vielleicht.

ha'p'orth F ['heipəθ] = *halfpennyworth.*

hap·pen ['hæpən] sich ereignen, geschehen, vorkommen; *he* ~*ed to be at home* er war zufällig zu Hause; ~ *on*, ~ *upon* zufällig treffen auf (*acc.*); ~ *in Am.* F hereingeschneit kommen; '**hap·pen·ing** Ereignis *n*.

hap·pi·ly ['hæpili] glücklicherweise.

hap·pi·ness ['hæpinis] Glück(seligkeit *f*) *n*; Gewandtheit *f im Ausdruck.*

hap·py ☐ ['hæpi] *allg.* glücklich; glückselig; geschickt, treffend (*Ausdruck*); F angeheitert; '~-**go-'luck·y** F unbekümmert.

ha·rangue [hə'ræŋ] **1.** Ansprache *f*, Rede *f*; **2.** *v/t.* feierlich anreden; *v/i.* eine Ansprache halten.

har·ass ['hærəs] fortwährend belästigen, quälen, beunruhigen; '**har·ass·ment** Schikanierung *f*, fortwährende Belästigung *f*.

har·bin·ger ['hɑ:bindʒə] **1.** Vorbote *m*; **2.** ankündigen.

har·bo(u)r ['hɑ:bə] **1.** Hafen *m*; Zufluchtsort *m*; **2.** (be)herbergen; Unterschlupf gewähren (*dat.*); *Rachegedanken etc.* hegen; ankern; '**har·bo(u)r·age** Herberge *f*; Zuflucht *f*; **har·bo(u)r dues** ⚓ *pl.* Hafengebühren *f/pl.*

hard [hɑ:d] **1.** *adj. allg.* hart; schwer, schwierig; kräftig; schwer (zu ertragen), mühselig; streng; abgehärtet, ausdauernd; fleißig; heftig; *gr.* als Verschlußlaut ausgesprochen (*c u. g*); *bsd. Am.* hochprozentig (*von Alkohol*); *the* ~ *facts pl.* die nackten Tatsachen *f/pl.*; ~ *of hearing* schwerhörig; ~ *to deal with* schwer zu behandeln(d), schwierig; *be* ~ (*up*)*on s.o.* j-m hart zusetzen; mit j-m streng sein; *give s.o. a* ~ *time* j-m das Leben schwer machen; **2.** *adv.* heftig, stark; fleißig, tüchtig; mit Mühe, mühselig, schwer; ~ *by* nahe bei; ~ *up* in Not *od.* Verlegenheit (*for* um); *be* ~ *put to it* es sich sauer werden lassen; *ride* ~ scharf reiten; **3.** F Zwangsarbeit *f*; ~*s pl.* Nöte *f/pl.*; ~ *and fast* starr (*Regel*); '~-**back** Buch *n* mit festem Einband; '~-'**bit·ten** verbissen; '~-**board** Preßspanplatte(n *pl.*) *f*; '~-'**boiled** hartgesotten, kaltschnäuzig; *bsd. Am.* gerissen; ~ **cash** Bargeld *n*; klingende Münze *f*; ~ **core** Schotter *m*; *fig.* harter Kern *m*; '~-**cov·er** = *hardback*; ~ **cur·ren·cy** harte Währung *f*; ~ **drinks** *pl.* harte Getränke *n/pl.* (*stark alkoholisch*); '~·'**fist·ed** geizig; ~ **hat** Schutzhelm *m*; *fig.* Bauarbeiter *m*; Melone *f* (*Hut*); *fig.* Reaktionär *m*; '~·'**head-ed** nüchtern *od.* praktisch denkend; '~·'**heart·ed** □ hartherzig.

har·di·hood ['hɑ:dihud] Kühnheit *f*; '**har·di·ness** Widerstandsfähigkeit *f*, Härte *f*; ⚔ Kühnheit *f*.

hard·ly ['hɑ:dli] kaum; streng; mit Mühe; **hard line** *pol.* harter Kurs *m*; ~**s** *pl.* F Pech *n*; **hard-'lin·er** *pol.* Verfechter *m* e-s harten Kurses; '**hard-'mouthed** hartmäulig (*Pferd*); '**hard·ness** Härte *f* (*a. fig.*); Strenge *f*; Schwierigkeit *f*; Not *f*.

hard...: '~·**pan** *Am.* harter Boden *m*, *fig.* Grundlage *f*; ~ **sell** aggressive Verkaufsmethode *f*; '~·'**set** in Not; starr; '~·**shell** hartschalig; *fig.* starr; '**hard·ship** Ungemach *n*; Mühsal *f*; Bedrängnis *f*, Not *f*; Härte *f*; **hard shoul·der** *mot.* Standspur *f*; '**hard-ware** Eisenwaren *f/pl.*; *Computer*: Hardware *f*, Maschinenausrüstung *f*; '**hard·wood** Hartholz(baum *m*) *n*; '**hard-work·ing** fleißig.

har·dy □ ['hɑ:di] mutig, kühn; widerstandsfähig, hart; abgehärtet; winterfest (*Pflanze*).

hare [hɛə] Hase *m*; ~ **and hounds** Schnitzeljagd *f*; '~·**bell** Glockenblume *f*; '~·**brained** zerfahren, gedankenlos; '~·**lip** 𝄌 Hasenscharte *f*.

ha·rem ['hɛərəm] Harem *m*.

har·i·cot ['hærikəu] Hammelragout *n*; *a.* ~ **bean** weiße Bohne *f*.

hark [hɑ:k] horchen (*to auf acc.*); ~! horch!; ~ **back** *hunt.* auf der Fährte zurückgehen; *fig.* zurückkommen (*to auf acc.*); '**hark·en** = hearken.

har·lot ['hɑ:lət] Hure *f*; '**har·lot·ry** Hurerei *f*.

harm [hɑ:m] **1.** Schaden *m*; Unrecht *n*, Böse *n*; *out of* ~'*s way* in Sicherheit; **2.** beschädigen, verletzen; schaden, Leid zufügen (*dat.*); '**harm·ful** □ ['~ful] schädlich; '**harm·less** □ arg-, harmlos; unschädlich.

har·mon·ic [hɑ:'mɔnik] (~*ally*) harmonisch; **har'mon·i·ca** ♪ [~kə] Mundharmonika *f*; **har·mo·ni·ous** □ [hɑ:'məunjəs] harmonisch (*a. fig.*); **har·monize** ['hɑ:mənaiz] *v/t.* harmonisieren, in Einklang bringen; *v/i.* harmonieren, übereinstimmen; '**har·mo·ny** Harmonie *f*, Übereinstimmung *f*.

har·ness ['hɑ:nis] **1.** Harnisch *m*; *Zug*-Geschirr *n*; *die in* ~ in den Sielen sterben; **2.** anschirren; bändigen; *Wasserkraft* nutzbar machen.

harp ♪ [hɑ:p] **1.** Harfe *f*; **2.** (auf der) Harfe spielen; ~ (*up*)*on* herumreiten auf (*dat.*); *be always* ~*ing on the same string* immer die alte Leier anstimmen; '**harp·er**, '**harp·ist** Harfenist(in); Harfner(in).

har·poon [hɑ:'pu:n] **1.** Harpune *f*; **2.** harpunieren.

harp·si·chord ♪ ['hɑ:psikɔ:d] Cembalo *n*.

har·py ['hɑ:pi] *Sage*: Harpyie *f*; *fig.* Blutsauger *m*.

har·ri·dan ['hæridən] alte Vettel *f*.

har·ri·er *hunt.* ['hæriə] Hasenhund *m*.

har·row 🖈 ['hærəu] **1.** Egge *f*; **2.** eggen; *fig.* quälen, martern; ~*ing* erschütternd.

har·ry ['hæri] plündern, verheeren, quälen, martern.

harsh □ [hɑ:ʃ] rauh; herb; grell (*Ton, Farbe etc.*); hart, streng; schroff; barsch; '**harsh·ness** Rauheit *f*; Herbheit *f*; Strenge *f*.

hart *zo.* [hɑ:t] Hirsch *m*; **harts-horn** 🍄 ['hɑ:tshɔ:n] Hirschhorn *n*.

har·um-scar·um F ['hɛərəm'skɛərəm] **1.** zerfahren, fahrig; leichtsinnig; wild; **2.** Springinsfeld *m*; Wirrkopf *m*.

har·vest ['hɑ:vist] **1.** Ernte(zeit) *f*; Ertrag *m*; ~ *festival*, ~ *thanksgiving* Erntedankfest *n*; **2.** ernten; *Ernte* einbringen; '**har·vest·er** Schnitter(in); Mähmaschine *f*; '**har·vest-'home** Erntefest *n*.

has [hæz, həz] *er, sie, es* hat; '~-**been** F Ehemalige *m*, *f*, *n*; Gestrige *m*, *f*, *n*.

hash¹ [hæʃ] **1.** gehacktes Fleisch *n*; *Am.* F Essen *n*, Fraß *m*; *fig.* Mischmasch *m*; *make a* ~ *of* F *et.* verpfuschen; *settle s.o.'s* ~ F es j-m besorgen; **2.** (zer)hacken.

hash² F [~] Hasch(isch) *n*.

hash·ish ['hæʃiːʃ] Haschisch *n*.

hasp [haːsp] 1. Haspe *f*; Spange *f*; 2. zuhaken.

has·sle F ['hæsl] Auseinandersetzung *f*; *fig.* Theater *n*, Zirkus *m*.

has·sock ['hæsək] Grasbüschel *n*, -polster *n*; *eccl.* Kniekissen *n*.

hast † [hæst] *du* hast.

haste [heist] Eile *f*; Hast *f*; *make* ~ (sich be)eilen; *more* ~ *less speed*, *make* ~ *slowly* Eile mit Weile; **has·ten** ['heisn] (sich be)eilen, *j.* an-treiben; *et.* beschleunigen; **hast·i-ness** ['heistinis] Hastigkeit *f*, Über-eilung *f*; Hitze *f*, Eifer *m*; '**hast·y** □ eilig, hastig; voreilig; hitzig, heftig.

hat [hæt] Hut *m*; *my* ~! *sl.* na, ich danke!; *hang up one's* ~ F sich häuslich niederlassen; *talk through one's* ~ phantasieren, Unsinn reden.

hatch[1] [hætʃ] 1. Brut *f*, Hecke *f*; Halbtür *f*; ⚓, ✠ Luke *f*; Durch-reiche *f*; *under* ~*es* unter Deck; 2. (aus)brüten (*a. fig.*); aushecken.

hatch[2] [~] schraffieren.

hatch·back *mot.* ['hætʃbæk] (Wagen *m* mit) Heckklappe *f*.

hatch·er·y ['hætʃəri] Brutplatz *m* *bsd. für Fische.*

hatch·et ['hætʃit] Beil *n*; *bury the* ~ das Kriegsbeil begraben; '~-face scharfgeschnittenes Gesicht *n*.

hatch·way ⚓ ['hætʃwei] Luke *f*.

hate [heit] 1. *poet.* Haß *m* (*to, to-wards* gegen, auf *acc.*); 2. hassen; nicht mögen; F bedauern; **hate·ful** □ ['~ful] verhaßt; hassenswert; ab-scheulich; '**hat·er** Hasser(in).

hath † [hæθ] er, sie, es hat.

ha·tred ['heitrid] Haß *m*, Groll *m* (*of* gegen).

hat·ter ['hætə] Hutmacher *m*; *as mad as a* ~ völlig verrückt.

haugh·ti·ness ['hɔːtinis] Stolz *m*; Hochmut *m*; '**haugh·ty** □ stolz; hochmütig.

haul [hɔːl] 1. Ziehen *n*; (Fisch)Zug *m*; Fang *m*, Beute *f*; *Am.* Transportweg *m*; *long* ~ (*a. fig.*) weiter Weg *m*; Durststrecke *f*; 2. ziehen (*at* an *dat.*); ⚓ holen; schleppen; transportieren; ✠ fördern; umspringen (*Wind*); ⚓ abdrehen; ~ *down one's flag* die Flagge streichen; *fig.* sich geschlagen geben; '**haul·age** Schleppen *n*; Transport (-kosten *pl.*) *m*; ✠ Förderung *f*; **haul·ier** ['~jə] Transportunterneh-

mer *m*.

haulm [hɔːm] *Pflanzen*-Stengel *m*; *Bohnen- etc.* Stroh *n*.

haunch [hɔːntʃ] Hüfte *f*; Keule *f* *von Wild.*

haunt [hɔːnt] 1. Aufenthaltsort *m*; Schlupfwinkel *m*; 2. oft besuchen; heimsuchen; verfolgen; plagen, be-unruhigen; spuken in (*dat.*); *the house is* ~*ed* in dem Hause spukt es; '**haunt·er** häufige Besucher(in), Stammgast *m*.

haut·boy ♩ ['əubɔi] Oboe *f*.

hau·teur [əu'təː] Hochmut *m*.

Ha·van·a [hə'vænə] *a.* ~ *cigar* Havanna(zigarre) *f*.

have [hæv, həv] 1. (*irr.*) *v/t.* haben, besitzen; bekommen; *Mahlzeit* ein-nehmen; lassen; ~ *to do* tun müssen; *I* ~ *my hair cut* ich lasse mir das Haar schneiden; *he had his leg broken* er brach sich das Bein; *I would* ~ *you know* ich möchte, daß Sie wissen; *he will* ~ *it that ...* er behauptet, daß ...; *I had as well ...* es wäre ebenso gut, wenn ich ...; *I had better* (*best*) *go* es wäre besser (am besten), wenn ich ginge; *I had rather go* ich möchte lieber gehen; *let s.o.* ~ *it* es j-m besorgen; ~ *about one* bei *od.* an sich haben; ~ *at him!* auf ihn!; ~ *on* anhaben; *fig.* vorhaben; ~ *it out with* sich ausein-andersetzen mit; ~ *s.o. up* F j. 'ran-kriegen (*verklagen*; *for* wegen); 2. *v/aux.* haben; sein; ~ *come* ge-kommen sein; 3. Besitzende *m*; F Schwindel *m*, Betrug *m*.

ha·ven ['heivn] Hafen *m* (*a. fig.*); Zufluchtsort *m*.

have-not ['hævnɔt] Habenichts *m*.

haven't ['hævnt] = *have not*.

hav·er·sack ['hævəsæk] ✗ Brot-beutel *m*; Rucksack *m*.

hav·ing ['hæviŋ] *oft* ~*s pl.* Habe *f*, Besitz *m*.

hav·oc ['hævək] Verwüstung *f*, Ver-heerung *f*; *make* ~ *of*, *play* ~ *with od. among* verwüsten, verheeren; übel zurichten.

haw[1] ♣ [hɔː] Hagebutte *f*.

haw[2] [~] 1. sich räuspern; stottern; 2. Räuspern *n*.

Ha·wai·ian [haː'waiiən] 1. ha-waiisch; 2. Hawaiier(in).

haw·finch *orn.* ['hɔːfintʃ] Kern-beißer *m*.

haw-haw ['hɔː'hɔː] laut lachen.

hawk[1] [hɔːk] **1.** *orn.* Habicht *m* (*a. fig.*); Falke *m*; **2.** Jagd machen (*at* auf *acc.*).

hawk[2] [↲] sich räuspern.

hawk[3] [↲] verhökern, hausieren mit; **hawk·er** ['hɔːkə] Hausierer *m*, Straßenhändler *m*.

hawk-eyed ['hɔːkaid] scharfäugig; '**hawk·ing** Falkenbeize *f*.

hawse ⚓ [hɔːz] *a.* ~-**hole** Klüse *f*.

haw·ser ⚓ ['hɔːzə] Kabeltau *n*, Trosse *f*.

haw·thorn ♀ ['hɔːθɔːn] Hagedorn *m*.

hay [hei] **1.** Heu *n*; **make** ~ **of** durcheinanderwerfen; **2.** heuen; '~-**box** *a.* ~ **cooker** Kochkiste *f*; '~-**cock** Heuhaufen *m*; '~-**fe·ver** ⚕ Heuschnupfen *m*; '~-**loft** Heuboden *m*; '~-**mak·er** *sl.* K.-o.-Schlag *m*; '~-**rick** = *haycock*; '~-**seed** *bsd. Am.* F Bauerntölpel *m*; '~-**stack** = *haycock*; '~-**wire**: go ~ drunter u. drüber gehen, durcheinandergeraten; überschnappen.

haz·ard ['hæzəd] **1.** Zufall *m*; Gefahr *f*, Wagnis *n*; Hasard(spiel) *n*; **run a** ~ et. riskieren; **2.** wagen, aufs Spiel setzen; '**haz·ard·ous** □ gewagt, gefährlich.

haze[1] [heiz] Dunst *m*; *fig.* Unklarheit *f*, Verwirrtheit *f*.

haze[2] ⚓ *u. Am.* [↲] schinden; schurigeln.

ha·zel ['heizl] **1.** ♀ Hasel(staude) *f*; **2.** nußbraun; '~-**nut** Haselnuß *f*.

ha·zy □ ['heizi] dunstig, diesig; *fig.* nebelhaft, verschwommen; unklar; **be** ~ im unklaren sein.

H-bomb ⚔ ['eitʃbɔm] H-Bombe *f*, Wasserstoffbombe *f*.

he [hiː; hi] **1.** er; ~ **who** derjenige, welcher; wer; **2.** *in Zssgn*: ...männchen *n*; ...bock *m*, ...hahn *m*.

head [hed] **1.** *allg.* Kopf *m* (*fig.* Verstand, Geist, Wille); Haupt *n*; *nach Zahlwort:* Mann *m* (*pl.*), Stück *n* (*pl.*); *fig.* Haupt *n*, Führer *m*; Leiter(in), Vorsteher(in); Chef *m*; Direktor *m*; Häuptling *m*; *Nagel-, Noten-, Seiten-, Kohl-* etc. Kopf *m*; Kopfende *n* e-s *Bettes, Tisches etc.*; Kopfseite *f* e-r *Münze*; Spitze *f* e-s *Berges, Geschwürs, Zuges etc.*; Schaum *m auf Bier*; *Baum-*Krone *f*; Quelle *f*; *Schiffs-*Vorderteil *n*; Vorgebirge *n*; Kopf(haar *n*) *m*; Geweih *n*; Höhe *f*, Krisis *f* e-r *Krankheit*; Hauptpunkt *m*; Abschnitt *m*, Kapitel *n*; Rubrik *f*; Posten *m in Rechnungen*; Überschrift *f*; ~ **and shoulders above the rest** allen haushoch überlegen; **bring to a** ~ zur Entscheidung *od.* zum Klappen bringen; **come to a** ~ aufbrechen, eitern (*Geschwür*); sich zuspitzen, zur Entscheidung kommen (*Lage etc.*); **gather** ~ überhandnehmen; zu Kräften kommen; **get it into one's** ~ **that** ... es sich in den Kopf setzen, daß; **keep one's** ~ den Kopf nicht verlieren; ~(s) **or tail(s)?** Zahl oder Wappen?; ~ **over heels** Hals über Kopf; **over** ~ **and ears bis** über die Ohren; **I can't make** ~ **or tail of it** ich kann daraus nicht klug werden; **take the** ~ die Führung übernehmen; **2.** erst; voranstehen; Ober...; Haupt...; **3.** *v/t.* (an)führen; an der Spitze von *et.* stehen, leiten; vorausgehen (*dat.*); mit e-m Kopf versehen; *Kapitel* überschreiben; *Fußball:* köpfen; **be** ~**ed in e-r Richtung bewegen;** ~ **off** ablenken; *v/i.* ⚓ Kurs halten, zusteuern (*for* auf *acc.*); *Am.* entspringen (*Fluß*); '**head-ache** Kopfweh *n*, -schmerz(en *pl.*) *m* (*a. fig.*); '**head·ach·y** an Kopfweh leidend; Kopfweh verursachend; '**head·band** Stirnband *n*; '**head-boy** Schulsprecher *m*; '**head-dress** Kopfputz *m*, -schmuck *m*; Frisur *f*; '**head·ed** ...köpfig; '**head·er** △ Bindestein *m*; F Kopfsprung *m*; '**head-gear** Kopfbedeckung *f*; Zaumzeug *n*; '**head-girl** Schulsprecherin *f*; '**head-hunt·er** Kopfjäger *m*; '**head·i·ness** Ungestüm *n*; Starrsinn *m*; berauschende Wirkung *f*; '**head·ing** Titelkopf *m*, Rubrik *f*; Überschrift *f*, Titel *m*; Briefkopf *m*; *Sport:* Kopfball *m*; '**head·land** Vorgebirge *n*; '**head·less** kopflos (*a. fig.*); ohne Führer.

head...: '~-**light** *mot.* Scheinwerfer (-licht *n*) *m*; '~-**line** Überschrift *f*; Schlagzeile *f*; ~**s** *pl. Radio:* das Wichtigste in Kürze; **he hits the** ~**s** F er liefert Schlagzeilen; '~-**long 1.** *adj.* ungestüm; unbesonnen, übereilt; **2.** *adv.* kopfüber; '~-**man** Vorsteher *m*; Häuptling *m*; Vorarbeiter *m*; '~-**mas·ter** Direktor *m* e-r *Schule*; '~-**mis·tress** Direktorin *f*; '~-**most** vorderst; '~-**'on**

heat-flash

mit dem Kopf(ende) voran; Frontal...; ~ collision Frontalzusammenstoß *m*; '~-phone *Radio*: Kopfhörer *m*; '~-piece Helm *m*; F Grips *m*, Verstand *m*; *typ.* Titelvignette *f*; '~'quar·ters *pl.* ✕ Hauptquartier *n*; Zentral(stell)e *f*; '~-rest Kopfstütze *f*; ~ re·straint *mot.* Kopfstütze *f*; '~-room lichte Höhe *f*; '~-set *Radio*: Kopfhörer *m/pl.*; 'head·ship Direktorenstelle *f*; 'head·shrink·er *iro.* Psychiater *m*; 'heads·man Scharfrichter *m*.

head...: ~ start *Sport*: Vorsprung *m*; '~·stone Grabstein *m*; '~·strong halsstarrig; '~·wa·ters *pl.* Quellgebiet *n*; '~·way Fortschritt(e *pl.*) *m*; make ~ vorwärtskommen, Fortschritte machen; '~·wind Gegenwind *m*; '~·word Stichwort *n e-s Wörterbuchs*; '~·work Kopfarbeit *f*; 'head·y □ ungestüm; voreilig; heftig; zu Kopf steigend (*Getränk*).

heal [hi:l] heilen (*of* von); ~ up zuheilen; '~-all Allheilmittel *n*; 'heal·er Heilpraktiker *m*; Heilmittel *n*; *time is a great ~* die Zeit heilt alle Wunden; 'heal·ing 1. □ Heil...; heilsam; heilend; 2. Heilung *f*.

health [helθ] Gesundheit *f* (*a. beim Zutrinken*); *Ministry of* ♀ Gesundheitsministerium *n*; ~ food(s *pl.*) Reformkost *f*; ~ shop, *Am.* ~ store Reformhaus *n*; health·ful □ ['~ful] gesund; heilsam; health haz·ard Gesundheitsrisiko *n*; 'health·i·ness Gesundheit *f*; 'health-re·sort Kurort *m*; health serv·ice Gesundheitsdienst *m*; 'health·y □ gesund.

heap [hi:p] 1. Haufe(n) *m*; F Menge *f*, Masse *f*; *all of a ~* auf einen Schlag; *struck od. knocked all of a ~* sprachlos; 2. *a.* ~ up (auf)häufen; überhäufen.

hear [hiə] (*irr.*) hören; erfahren; an-, zuhören; erhören; *Zeugen* verhören; *Lektion* abhören; ~ *s.o. out* j. ausreden lassen; heard [hə:d] *pret. u. p.p. von hear*; hear·er ['hiərə] Hörer *m*, Zuhörer(in); 'hear·ing Gehör *n*; Audienz *f*; ☆ Verhör *n*; öffentliche Informationssitzung *f*, Anhörung *f*; Hörweite *f*; ~ *aid* Hörgerät *n*; hark·en ['ha:kən] horchen; hören (*to auf acc.*); hear·say ['hiəsei] Hörensagen *n*.

hearse [hə:s] Leichenwagen *m*.

heart [ha:t] *allg.* Herz *n* (*fig. = Mut, Erbarmen etc.*); Innere *n*; Wesentlichste *n*, Kern *m*; *Karten*: Herz *n*, Coeur *n*; *a. dear ~* Liebling *m*, Schatz *m*; ~ *and soul* mit Leib und Seele; *change of ~* Gesinnungswandel *m*; *at ~* im Inneren *od.* Herzen; *I have a matter at ~ et.* liegt mir am Herzen; *by ~* auswendig; *for one's ~* ums Leben gern; *in good ~* in gutem Zustand (*Boden*); *in his ~* (*of ~s*) im Grunde seines Herzens; *out of ~* mutlos; in schlechtem Zustand; *speak from one's ~* frisch von der Leber weg sprechen; *cross my ~* Hand aufs Herz!; *cut to the ~* aufs tiefste verletzen; *with all my ~* von ganzem Herzen; *lose ~* den Mut verlieren; *take ~* sich ein Herz fassen; *take od. lay to ~* sich *et.* zu Herzen nehmen; '~·ache Kummer *m*; '~-beat Herzschlag *m*; '~-break *herzeleid n*; '~-break·ing □ herzzerbrechend, -zerreißend; '~-bro·ken gebrochenen Herzens; '~-burn Sodbrennen *n*; '~-burn·ing Groll *m*, Neid *m*; '~-com·plaint, '~-dis·ease Herzleiden *n*; 'heart·ed ...herzig; 'heart·en ermutigen, ermuntern; 'heart-fail·ure Herzversagen *n*; 'heart·felt innig, tief empfunden.

hearth [ha:θ] Herd *m* (*a. fig.*); '~-rug Kaminvorleger *m*; '~-stone Kaminplatte *f*.

heart·i·ness ['ha:tinis] Herzlichkeit *f*; Herzhaftigkeit *f etc.* (*s. hearty*); 'heart·less □ herzlos; 'heart-rend·ing herzzerreißend.

heart...: '~'s-ease ♣ Stiefmütterchen *n*; '~-sick *fig.* krank im Herzen; verzagt; '~-strings *pl. fig.* Herz *n*, innerste Gefühle *n/pl.*; '~-throb F Schwarm *m*; ~ trans·plant Herzverpflanzung *f*; '~-whole nicht verliebt, frei; aufrichtig, herzlich; 'heart·y 1. □ herzlich; aufrichtig; gesund; kräftig, herzhaft; ~ *eater* tüchtiger Esser *m*; 2. ⚓ Matrose *m*; *univ.* Sportler *m*.

heat [hi:t] 1. *allg.* Hitze *f*; Wärme *f* (*bsd. phys.*); Eifer *m*; Zorn *m*; *Sport*: Gang *m*, einzelner Lauf *m*; Läufigkeit *f von Tieren*; *dead ~* totes *od.* unentschiedenes Rennen *n*; 2. heizen; (sich) erhitzen *od.* erwärmen (*a. fig.*); heiß werden; 'heat·ed □ hitzig; 'heat·er ⊕ Erhitzer *m*; Ofen *m*; 'heat-flash

Hitzestrahlung f e-r Atombomben-
explosion.

heath [hi:θ] Heide f; ⚘ Heidekraut
n; '~-cock Birkhahn m.

hea·then ['hi:ðən] **1.** Heide m, Heidin f; **2.** heidnisch; '**hea·then·dom**
Heidentum n; '**hea·then·ish** □ mst
fig. heidnisch; roh; '**hea·then·ism**
Heidentum n; Roheit f.

heath·er ⚘ ['heðə] Heide f; Heidekraut n; '~-**bell** ⚘ Glockenheide f.

heat·ing ['hi:tiŋ] Heizung f; attr.
Heiz...; ~ battery Heizbatterie f; ~
pad Heizkissen n.

heat...: ~ **light·ning** Am. Wetterleuchten n; '~-**re·sist·ant** hitzebe-
ständig; '~-**stroke** Hitzschlag m; ~
treat·ment ⚕ Wärmebehandlung f;
'~-**val·ue** Heizwert m; '~-**wave** Hit-
zewelle f.

heave [hi:v] **1.** Heben n; Schwellen n
der Brust etc.; Übelkeit f; **2.** (irr.)
v/t. heben, hieven; schwellen;
Seufzer ausstoßen; ~ the anchor den
Anker lichten; ~ down ⚓ kielholen;
~ out auswerfen; v/i. sich heben und
senken, wogen, schwellen (Brust,
Wellen); sich übergeben wollen; ~
for breath keuchen; ~ in sight ⚓ in
Sicht kommen; ~ to ⚓ beidrehen.

heav·en ['hevn] Himmel m; ~s pl.
der sichtbare Himmel; move ~ and
earth Himmel u. Hölle in Bewegung setzen; '**heav·en·ly** himmlisch (a. fig.); **heav·en·ward(s)**
['~wəd(z)] himmelwärts.

heav·er ['hi:və] Hebebaum m; Ab-
lader m.

heav·i·ness ['hevinis] Schwere f,
Gewicht n, Druck m (a. fig.);
Schwerfälligkeit f; Schwermut f.

heav·y □ ['hevi] allg. schwer;
schwermütig; schwerfällig; schläfrig; trüb; drückend; heftig (Regen
etc.); schwer (Speise); unwegsam,
schmierig (Straße); ⚔ schwer(bewaffnet); Schwer...; ~ **cur·rent** ⚡
Starkstrom m; '~'**du·ty** strapazierfähig; Hochleistungs...; '~-'**go·ing**
schwierig, anstrengend; '~-'**hand·ed**
ungeschickt; '~-'**heart·ed** niedergeschlagen; '~-'**lad·en** schwerbeladen;
fig. bedrückt; '~-**weight** Boxen:
Schwergewicht n.

heb·dom·a·dal □ [heb'dɔmədl]
wöchentlich. [bräisch.⎱
He·bra·ic [hi'breiik] (~ally) he-⎰
He·brew ['hi:bru:] **1.** hebräisch;

2. Hebräer m; Hebräisch n.

hec·a·tomb ['hekətu:m] Hekatombe
f (Massenopfer).

heck·le ['hekl] durch Zwischenfra-
gen in die Enge treiben; '**heck·ler**
Zwischenrufer m, Störenfried m.

hec·tic ⚕ ['hektik] **1.** hektisch (aus-
zehrend; schwindsüchtig; sl. fieberhaft erregt); **2.** hektische Röte f;
mst ~ fever hektisches Fieber n.

hec·tor ['hektə] v/t. einschüchtern,
anmaßend behandeln; v/i. großtun,
prahlen, renommieren.

hedge [hedʒ] **1.** Hecke f; fig. Mauer
f; **2.** v/t. einhegen, einzäunen; umgeben; ~ off abzäunen; ~ up sperren;
~ a bet auf beide Möglichkeiten
wetten; v/i. sich decken; sich nicht
festlegen, ausweichen; '~-**hog** zo.
Igel m; Am. Stachelschwein n;
'~-**hop** sl. ✈ tieffliegen; '~-**row**
Hecke f; '~-**spar·row** orn. Hecken-
braunelle f.

heed [hi:d] **1.** Beachtung f, Aufmerksamkeit f; take ~ of, give od.
pay ~ to achtgeben auf (acc.), beachten; **2.** beachten, achten auf
(acc.); '**heed·ful** □ ['~ful] achtsam
(of auf acc.); '**heed·less** □ unachtsam; unbekümmert (of um).

hee-haw ['hi:'hɔ:] **1.** Iah n (Eselsschrei); fig. Gewieher n; **2.** iahen;
fig. wiehern (laut lachen).

heel¹ ⚓ [hi:l] (sich) auf die Seite
legen, überholen, krängen.

heel² [~] **1.** Ferse f; Hacken m,
Absatz m; letzter Teil m, Ende n;
bsd. Am. sl. Lump m; ~s pl. F Hin-
terfüße m/pl. e-s Tiers; at od. on od.
upon s.o.'s ~s j-m auf den Fersen
folgen; down at ~ mit schiefgetre-
tenen Absätzen; fig. abgerissen,
schäbig; schlampig; take to one's ~s,
show a clean pair of ~s Fersengeld
geben, die Beine in die Hand nehmen; lay s.o. by the ~s j. einsperren;
come to ~ bei Fuß gehen (Hund);
gehorchen; **2.** mit e-m Absatz etc.
versehen; a. ~ out Fußball: aus-
fersen; **heeled** Am. F finanzstark;
'**heel·er** Am. sl. pol. Befehlsemp-
fänger m.

heel-tap ['hi:ltæp] Neige f im Glas;
no ~! ausgetrunken!

heft [heft] **1.** Gewicht n; Am. F
Hauptteil m; **2.** (hoch-, an)heben;
'**heft·y** F stramm, kräftig.

he·gem·o·ny pol. [hi:'gemɔni] He-

henceforward

gemonie *f*, Vorherrschaft *f*.

he·goat ['hi:gəut] Ziegenbock *m*.

heif·er ['hefə] Färse *f* (*junge Kuh*).

heigh [hei] hei!, he(da)!; **~ho**
['~'həu] ach (jeh)!

height [hait] Höhe *f*; Anhöhe *f*;
Höhepunkt *m*, höchster Grad *m*;
what is your ~? wie groß sind Sie?;
'**height·en** erhöhen (*a. fig.*), höher
machen; vergrößern.

hei·nous □ ['heinəs] abscheulich;
verrucht; '**hei·nous·ness** Ver-
ruchtheit *f*.

heir [ɛə] Erbe *m*; **be ~ to et.** erben;
~ apparent, **~ at law** rechtmäßiger
Erbe *m*; **~ presumptive** mutmaß-
licher Erbe *m*; '**heir·dom** Erbfolge
f; Erbschaft *f*; '**heir·ess** Erbin *f*;
'**heir·less** ohne Erben; **heir·loom**
['~lu:m] Erbstück *n*.

held [held] *pret. u. p.p. von* hold 2.

hel·i·bus *Am.* F ['helibʌs] Hubschrauber *m als Zubringer zum Flugplatz*.

hel·i·cal ['helikəl] spiralen-, schnek-
kenförmig.

hel·i·cop·ter ['helikɔptə] Hubschrauber *m*.

he·li·o... ['hi:liəu] Sonnen..., Helio...;
he·li·o·graph ['~əugrɑ:f] Helio-
graph *m*; Spiegeltelegraph *m*;
Lichtdruck *m*; **he·li·o·trope** ['hel-
jətrəup] ⚘ Heliotrop *n*, Sonnenwende *f*.

hel·i·pad ['helipæd] Hubschrauber-
landeplatz *m*.

hel·i·port ['helipɔ:t] Hubschrauber-
landeplatz *m*.

he·li·um ⚗ ['hi:ljəm] Helium *n*.

he·lix ['hi:liks], *pl. mst* **hel·i·ces**
['helisi:z] Schneckenlinie *f*; *zo.*, ⚗
Schnecke *f*; *anat.* Ohrleiste *f*.

hell [hel] Hölle *f*; *attr.* Höllen...;
like ~ höllisch; oh **~!** verdammt!;
go to ~ zur Hölle fahren; **what the
~ ...?** F was zum Teufel ...?; **a ~ of**
a noise ein Höllenlärm *m*; **raise ~**
Krach machen; **ride ~ for leather**
wie der Teufel reiten; '**~·'bent** *Am.*
sl. unweigerlich entschlossen; '**~·**
·cat *fig.* Hexe *f*.

hel·le·bore ⚘ ['helibɔ:] Nieswurz *f*.

Hel·lene ['heli:n] Hellene *m*, Grieche *m*; **Hel·len·ic** [he'li:nik] helle-
nisch, griechisch.

hell·ish □ ['heliʃ] höllisch.

hel·lo [he'ləu] hallo!

helm ⚓ [helm] (Steuer)Ruder *n*

(*a. fig.*).

hel·met ['helmit] Helm *m*; '**hel-
met·ed** behelmt.

helms·man ⚓ ['helmzmən] Steuermann *m*.

hel·ot *hist.* ['helət] Helot *m*; *fig.*
Sklave *m*.

help [help] **1.** *allg.* Hilfe *f*, Beistand
m; (Hilfs)Mittel *n*; (Dienst)Mäd-
chen *n*; **by the ~ of** mit Hilfe (*gen.*);
2. *v/t.* helfen (*dat.*); abhelfen (*dat.*);
unterlassen; *bei Tisch* geben, rei-
chen (*s.th. et.*; *s.o. to s.th.* j-m et.);
~ o.s. sich bedienen, zulangen; **~**
o.s. to s.th. sich et. nehmen; **I could**
not ~ laughing ich konnte nicht umhin zu lachen; **that cannot be ~ed** da
läßt sich nichts ändern; *v/i.* helfen,
dienen (*to* zu); '**help·er** Helfer(in),
Gehilfe *m*, Gehilfin *f*; **help·ful** □
['~ful] behilflich, hilfreich; nützlich; '**help·ing** (Essens)Portion *f*;
'**help·less** □ hilflos; '**help·less-
ness** Hilflosigkeit *f*; '**help·mate**,
help·meet ['~mi:t] Gehilfe *m*, Gehilfin *f*; Gattin *f*.

helter-skel·ter ['heltə'skeltə] hol-
terdiepolter.

helve [helv] Stiel *m*, Griff *m*.

Hel·ve·tian [hel'vi:ʃjən] **1.** helve-
tisch; Schweizer...; **2.** Helvetier(in).

hem¹ [hem] **1.** *Kleider*-Saum *m*;
2. säumen; **~ in** einschließen.

hem² [~] **1.** sich räuspern; **2.** hm!

he·man *sl.* ['hi:mæn] richtiger
Mann *m*.

hem·i·sphere ['hemisfiə] Halb-
kugel *f*, Hemisphäre *f*.

hem·line ['hemlain] Saum *m e-s*
Kleides; **lower (raise) the ~** das
Kleid *etc.* länger (kürzer) machen.

hem·lock ⚘ ['hemlɔk] Schierling *m*;
'**~-tree** Schierlingstanne *f*.

he·mo... ['hi:məu] *s.* haemo...

hemp [hemp] Hanf *m*; '**hemp·en**
hanfen, hänfen; Hanf...

hem·stitch ['hemstitʃ] **1.** Hohlsaum *m*; **2.** mit Hohlsaum verzieren.

hen [hen] Huhn *n*, Henne *f*; *Vogel*-
Weibchen *n*; **~'s egg** Hühnerei *n*.

hen·bane ['henbein] Bilsenkraut *n*.

hence [hens] *oft from* **~** von hinnen,
weg; hieraus, hiervon; daher, deshalb; von jetzt an; **~!** fort!, hinweg!; **a year ~** heute übers Jahr;
'**~'forth**, '**~'for·ward** von nun an,
fortan.

hench·man *pol.* [ˈhentʃmən] Gefolgsmann *m*, Handlanger *m*.

hen...: '∼-coop Hühnerstall *m*; '∼- -'par·ty F Damengesellschaft *f*, Kaffeekränzchen *n*; '∼·pecked unter dem Pantoffel (stehend); '∼- -roost Hühnerstange *f*.

hep *Am. sl.* [hep]: *be* ∼ *to* kennen, eingeweiht sein in.

he·pat·ic *anat.* [hiˈpætik] Leber...

hep·cat *Am. sl.* [ˈhepkæt] Eingeweihte *m*, *f*; Jazzfanatiker(in).

hep·ta... [ˈheptə] Sieben...; **hep·ta·gon** [ˈ∼gən] Siebeneck *n*.

her [hɔː, hə] sie, ihr; ihr(e).

her·ald [ˈherəld] **1.** Herold *m*; **2.** (sich) ankündigen; ∼ *in* einführen; **he·ral·dic** [heˈrældik] (∼*ally*) heraldisch; **her·ald·ry** [ˈherəldri] Wappenkunde *f*, Heraldik *f*.

herb [hɔːb] Kraut *n*; **her·ba·ceous** [∼ˈbeiʃəs] krautartig; **'herb·age** Gras *n*; Weide *f*; ⚖ Weiderecht *n*; **'herb·al 1.** Kräuter...; **2.** Kräuterbuch *n*; **'herb·al·ist** Pflanzenkenner *m*, -sammler *m*; **her·bar·i·um** [∼ˈbeəriəm] Herbarium *n*; **her·biv·o·rous** [∼ˈbivərəs] pflanzenfressend; **her·bo·rize** [ˈ∼bəraiz] botanisieren.

Her·cu·le·an [hɔːkjuˈliːən] herkulisch, Herkules...

herd [hɔːd] **1.** (*bsd.* Rinder)Herde *f* (*a. fig.*); **2.** *v/t.* Vieh hüten; ∼ *together* zs.-pferchen; *v/i. a.* ∼ *together* in e-r Herde leben; zs.-hausen; **'herd·er**, **'herds·man** Hirt *m*.

here [hiə] hier; hierher; ∼'*s to* ...! auf das Wohl von ...!

here·a·bout(s) [ˈhiərəbaut(s)] hierherum; **here·aft·er** [hiərˈɑːftə] **1.** künftig; **2.** Zukunft *f*; *das* künftige Leben; **'here'by** hierdurch, hiermit.

he·red·i·ta·ble [hiˈreditəbl] vererbbar; **her·e·dit·a·ment** ⚖ [heriˈditəmənt] Erbgut *n*; **he·red·i·tar·y** [hiˈreditəri] erblich; Erb...; **he'red·i·ty** Erblichkeit *f*.

here·in [ˈhiərˈin] hierin; **here·of** [hiərˈɔv] hiervon.

her·e·sy [ˈherəsi] Ketzerei *f*.

her·e·tic [ˈherətik] **1.** Ketzer(in); **2.** = **he·ret·i·cal** □ [hiˈretikəl] ketzerisch.

here·to·fore [ˈhiətuˈfɔː] bis jetzt; ehemals; **here·up·on** [ˈhiərəˈpɔn]

hierauf, darauf; 'here'with hiermit.

her·it·a·ble [ˈheritəbl] erbfähig; erblich; 'her·it·age Erbschaft *f*.

her·maph·ro·dite [hɔːˈmæfrədait] Zwitter *m*, Hermaphrodit *m*.

her·met·ic, **her·met·i·cal** □ [hɔː-ˈmetik(əl)] hermetisch, luftdicht.

her·mit [ˈhɔːmit] Einsiedler *m*; 'her·mit·age Einsiedelei *f*.

her·ni·a ⚕ [ˈhɔːnjə] Bruch *m*; 'her·ni·al Bruch...

he·ro [ˈhiərəu], *pl.* **he·roes** [ˈ∼rəuz] Held *m*; **he·ro·ic** [hiˈrəuik], **he'ro·i·cal** heroisch; heldenmütig, -haft; Helden...

her·o·in *pharm.* [ˈherəuin] Heroin *n*.

her·o·ine [ˈherəuin] Heldin *f*; 'her·o·ism Heldenmut *m*, -tum *n*.

her·on *orn.* [ˈherən] Reiher *m*; 'her·on·ry Reiherhorst *m*.

her·ring *ichth.* [ˈheriŋ] Hering *m*; 'her·ring-bone Heringsgräte *f*; Fischgrätenmuster *n*; Fischgrätenstich *m*.

hers [hɔːz] der (die, das) ihrige; ihr.

her·self [hɔːˈself] (sie, ihr) selbst; sich.

Hertz·i·an ⚡ [ˈhɔːtsiən]: ∼ *waves* Hertzsche Wellen *f/pl.*

he's [ˈhiːz] = *he is*; *he has*.

hes·i·tance, **hes·i·tan·cy** [ˈhezitəns(i)] Zaudern *n*, Unschlüssigkeit *f*; **hes·i·tate** [ˈ∼teit] zögern, zaudern, unschlüssig sein (*about*, *over* über *acc.*); Bedenken tragen (*to inf.* zu *inf.*); **hes·i'ta·tion** Zögern *n*, Zaudern *n*; Unschlüssigkeit *f*; Bedenken *n*.

Hes·sian [ˈhesiən] **1.** hessisch; **2.** Hesse *m*, Hessin *f*; ♀ Rupfen *m*, Sackleinwand *f*.

het·er·o·dox [ˈhetərəudɔks] heterodox, irrgläubig; 'het·er·o·dox·y Irrlehre *f*; **het·er·o·dyne** [ˈ∼dain] *Radio*: Überlagerungs...; **het·er·o·ge·ne·i·ty** [∼dʒiˈniːiti] Anders-, Ungleichartigkeit *f*; **het·er·o·ge·ne·ous** □ [ˈ∼rəuˈdʒiːnjəs] ungleichartig, heterogen.

het up F [hetˈʌp] aufgeregt.

hew [hjuː] (*irr.*) hauen, hacken; ⊕ behauen; 'hew·er Hauer *m*; ✗ Häuer *m*; **hewn** [hjuːn] *p.p. von* hew.

hex·a... [ˈheksə] Sechs...; **hex·a·gon** [ˈ∼gən] Sechseck *n*; **hex·ag·o·nal**

□ [hek'sægǝnl] sechseckig; **hex-am·e·ter** [hek'sæmitǝ] Hexameter *m.*

hey [hei] ei!; hei!; heda!

hey·day ['heidei] **1.** heisa!; oho!; **2.** *fig.* Höhepunkt *m*; Vollkraft *f*, Blüte *f*; Sturm *m der Leidenschaft.*

hi [hai] he!, heda!; hallo!

hi·a·tus [hai'eitǝs] Lücke *f*, Spalt *m*, Kluft *f*; *gr.* Hiatus *m.*

hi·ber·nate ['haibǝneit] überwintern; Winterschlaf halten; **hi·ber-'na·tion** Winterschlaf *m.*

hi·bis·cus ♀ [hi'biskǝs] Eibisch *m.*

hic·cup, *a.* **hic·cough** ['hikʌp] **1.** Schlucken *m*, Schluckauf *m*; **2.** schlucken; den Schluckauf haben.   [Bauern...\
hick F [hik] Bauer(ntölpel) *m*; *attr.*∫
hick·o·ry ['hikǝri] Hickorynußbaum *m.*

hid [hid] *pret. von hide*²; **hid·den** ['hidn] *p.p. von hide*².

hide¹ [haid] **1.** Haut *f*, Fell *n*; **2.** F durchprügeln.

hide² [⌣] *(irr.)* (sich) verbergen, verstecken *(from s.o.* vor j-m); verheimlichen; **'hide-and-'seek** Versteckspiel *n*; *play (at)* ⌣ Versteck(en) spielen; **'hide·a·way** F Versteck *n.*

hide·bound *fig.* ['haidbaund] engherzig, -stirnig, stur.

hid·e·ous □ ['hidiǝs] häßlich; abscheulich, scheußlich; schrecklich, gräßlich; **'hid·e·ous·ness** Scheußlichkeit *f.*

hide·out ['haidaut] Versteck *n.*

hid·ing¹ F ['haidiŋ] Tracht *f* Prügel.

hid·ing² [⌣] Verbergen *n*; *in* ⌣ verborgen; versteckt; flüchtig; **'⌣-place** Versteck *n*; Schlupfwinkel *m.*

hie *poet.* [hai] *(p.pr. hying)* eilen.

hi·er·arch·y ['haiǝraːki] Hierarchie *f*; Priesterherrschaft *f*; Rangordnung *f.*

hi·er·o·glyph ['haiǝrɔuglif] Hieroglyphe *f*; **hi·er·o'glyph·ic,** *a.* **hi·er·o'glyph·i·cal** □ hieroglyphisch; **hi·er·o'glyph·ics** *pl.* Hieroglyphen *f/pl. (Bilderschrift*; *fig. Gekritzel).*

hi-fi *Am.* ['hai'fai] = *high fidelity.*

hig·gle·dy-pig·gle·dy ['higldi'pigldi] wirr durcheinander, kunterbunt.

high [hai] **1.** *adj.* □ *(s. a.* ⌣*ly)* allg. hoch; vornehm; erhaben; gut, edel *(Charakter)*; stolz; anmaßend;

hochtrabend; angegangen *(Fleisch)*; extrem; groß, stark, heftig; üppig, flott *(Leben)*; Hoch...; Ober...; ⌣ *and dry* auf dem trocknen; *be on one's* ⌣ *horse, ride the* ⌣ *horse* auf dem hohen Roß sitzen; *with a* ⌣ *hand* arrogant, anmaßend; *in* ⌣ *spirits* in gehobener Stimmung, guter Laune; *a* ⌣ *Tory* ein Erzkonservativer *m*; ⌣ *colo(u)r,* ⌣ *complexion* rote Gesichtsfarbe *f*; ⌣ *life* die vornehme Welt; ⌣ *words* *pl.* heftige Worte *n/pl.*; ⌣ *time* höchste Zeit; **2.** *meteor.* Hoch *n*; *Am.* F = *high school*; ⌣ *and low* hoch und niedrig; *on* ⌣ in die *od.* der Höhe; **3.** *adv.* hoch; sehr, mächtig; **'⌣-ball** *Am.* Whisky *m* mit Soda; **'⌣-born** hochgeboren; **'⌣-bred** vornehm erzogen; **'⌣-brow** F **1.** Intellektuelle *m, f*, geistig Anspruchsvolle *m, f*; **2.** betont intellektuell; **'⌣-chair** Kinderhochstuhl *m*; ♀ **Church** anglikanische Hochkirche *f*; **'⌣-class** hochwertig; **'⌣-'col·o(u)red** von lebhafter Farbe; ♀ **Com·mis·sion·er** Hochkommissar *m*; **'⌣-ex'plo·sive** hochbrisant; Brisanz...; Spreng...; **⌣-fa·lu·tin(g)** ['⌣fǝ'luːtin, '⌣fǝ'luːtiŋ] **1.** Schwulst *m*; **2.** schwülstig; **'⌣-fi'del·i·ty** mit höchster Wiedergabetreue, Hi-Fi; **'⌣-fli·er** = *highflyer*; **'⌣-flown** überschwenglich; **'⌣-fly·er** ehrgeiziger Mensch *m*; **'⌣-grade** erstklassig; **'⌣-'hand·ed** anmaßend, willkürlich; **'⌣-'hat** *sl.* **1.** Snob *m*; **2.** von oben herab behandeln; **'⌣-'heeled** mit hohen Absätzen; **'⌣-land·er** Hochländer(in); **'⌣-lands** *pl.* Hochland *n*; **'⌣-'lev·el** auf hoher Ebene *(Konferenz etc.)*; **'⌣-light** hervorheben; **'⌣-lights** *pl. fig.* Höhepunkte *m/pl.*; ⌣ *liv·ing* Wohlleben *n*; **'high·ly** hoch; höchlich; sehr; *speak* ⌣ *of s.o.* j. loben; ⌣ *descended* hochgeboren; **'high-'mind·ed** hochgesinnt; **'high-'necked** hochgeschlossen *(Kleid)*; **'high·ness** Höhe *f*; *fig., Titel:* Hoheit *f.*

high...: '⌣-'pitched schrill *(Ton)*; steil *(Dach)*; '⌣-'pow·er: ⌣ *station* Großkraftwerk *n*; ⌣ *radio station* Großfunkstation *f*; '⌣-'pow·ered mächtig, einflußreich *(Person)*; '⌣-'priced teuer; '⌣-'rank·ing von hohem Rang; ⌣ *officer* hoher Offizier *m*; '⌣-'rise: ⌣ *flats pl.* Hochhaus *n*; ⌣ *road* Landstraße *f*;

~**school** höhere Schule *f*; '~-'**spir·it-ed** lebhaft, kühn; ~ **street** Hauptstraße *f*; '~-'**strung** überempfindlich.

hight *poet. od. co.* [hait] genannt.

high...: ~ **tea** frühes Abendessen *n mit Tee u. Fleisch etc.*; ~ **time** höchste Zeit; '~-'**toned** erhaben; vornehm; ~ **wa·ter** Hochwasser *n*; '~-'**way** Landstraße *f*; *fig.* Weg *m*; ~ **code** Straßenverkehrsordnung *f*; '~-'**way·man** Straßenräuber *m*.

hi·jack ['haidʒæk] *Flugzeug etc.* entführen; '**hi·jack·er** Gauner *m*, Dieb *m*; (*Flugzeug- etc.*) Entführer *m*; Luftpirat *m*.

hike F [haik] **1.** wandern; **2.** Wanderung *f*; *bsd. Am.* F Anstieg *m*, Erhöhung *f* (*Preis etc.*); '**hik·er** Wanderer *m*.

hi·lar·i·ous □ [hi'lɛəriəs] ausgelassen.

hi·lar·i·ty [hi'læriti] Ausgelassenheit *f*.

Hil·a·ry ['hiləri] : ~ **term** 📖 im Januar beginnender Termin; *univ.* Frühjahrssemester *n*.

hill [hil] Hügel *m*, Berg *m*; ~-**bil·ly** *Am.* F ['~bili] Hinterwäldler *m*; ~ **climb** *mot.* Bergrennen *n*; **hill·ock** ['hilək] kleiner Hügel *m*; '**hill·side** Hang *m*; '**hill-top** Bergspitze *f*; '**hill·y** hügelig.

hilt [hilt] Griff *m* (*bsd. am Degen*); *up to the* ~ bis ans Heft; *fig.* völlig, restlos.

him [him] ihn; ihm; den, dem (-jenigen).

him·self [him'self] (er, ihm, ihn, sich) selbst; sich; *of* ~ von selbst; *by* ~ allein, für sich.

hind[1] [haind] Hirschkuh *f*, Hindin *f*.

hind[2] [~] Hinter...; ~ **leg** Hinterbein *n*; ~ **wheels** *pl.* Hinterräder *n/pl.*

hind·er[1] ['haində] *adj.* hintere(r, -s); Hinter...

hin·der[2] ['hində] *v/t.* hindern (*from an dat.*); hemmen, aufhalten.

hind·most ['haindməust] hinterst, letzt.

hind·quar·ters ['haindkwɔːtəz] *pl.* Hinterteil *n e-s Tieres.*

hin·drance ['hindrəns] Hinderung *f*; Hindernis *n* (*to* für).

hind·sight ['haindsait] : *with* ~ im nachhinein.

Hin·du, *a.* **Hin·doo** ['hin'duː] Hindu *m*.

Hin·du·sta·ni [hindu'stɑːni] hindostanisch.

hinge [hindʒ] **1.** Türangel *f*; Scharnier *n*; *fig.* Angelpunkt *m*; *off the* ~**s** *fig.* aus den Angeln *od.* Fugen; **2.** ~ *upon fig.* abhängen von.

hin·ny ['hini] Maulesel *m*.

hint [hint] **1.** Hinweis *m*, Wink *m*; Anspielung *f*; **2.** andeuten; anspielen (*at auf acc.*); zu verstehen geben.

hin·ter·land ['hintəlænd] Hinterland *n*.

hip[1] [hip] Hüfte *f*; *attr.* Hüft...

hip[2] ♀ [~] Hagebutte *f*.

hip[3] [~] : ~, ~, *hurra(h)!* hipp, hipp, hurra!

hip...: '~-**bath** Sitzbad *n*; '~-**flask** Flachmann *m* (*Reiseflasche*).

hip·po F ['hipəu] = *hippopotamus.*

hip-pock·et ['hippɔkit] Gesäßtasche *f*.

hip·po·pot·a·mus [hipə'pɔtəməs], *pl. a.* **hip·po'pot·a·mi** [~mai] Nil-, Flußpferd *n*.

hip·py ['hipi] *Art beatnik.*

hip-roof △ ['hipruːf] Walmdach *n*.

hip-shot ['hipʃɔt] lendenlahm.

hire ['haiə] **1.** Miete *f*, Entgelt *m*, *n*, Lohn *m*; *on* ~ mietweise; *zu vermieten*; **2.** mieten; *j.* anstellen; ~ *out* vermieten; '~-**charge** Leihgebühr *f*; **hire·ling** *contp.* ['~liŋ] **1.** Mietling *m*; **2.** feil, käuflich; '**hire-** -'**pur·chase** Teilzahlungskauf *m*; *by* ~ auf Raten.

hir·sute ['həːsjuːt] haarig; zottig; struppig; rauh.

his [hiz] sein, seine; der, die, das seinige.

hiss [his] **1.** Zischen *n*; Gezisch *n*; **2.** *v/i.* zischen; zischeln; *v/t. a.* ~ *off* auszischen, -pfeifen.

hist [s:t] st!; still!

his·to·ri·an [his'tɔːriən] Geschichtsschreiber *m*, Historiker *m*; **his·tor·ic, his·tor·i·cal** □ [~'tɔrik(əl)] historisch, geschichtlich; Geschichts...; **his·to·ri·og·ra·pher** [~tɔːri'ɔgrəfə] Geschichtsschreiber *m*; **his·to·ry** ['~təri] Geschichte *f*; Werdegang *m*; Vergangenheit *f*; *make* ~ Geschichte machen.

his·tri·on·ic [histri'ɔnik] Schauspieler...; schauspielerisch.

hit [hit] **1.** Schlag *m*, Stoß *m*; *fig.* (Seiten)Hieb *m*; Glücksfall *m*; Treffer *m*; *thea.*, ♪ Schlager *m*;

2. (*irr.*) schlagen, stoßen; *Ziel, Ton, Ausdruck etc.* treffen; treffen *od.* stoßen auf (*acc.*); *Am.* F ankommen in (*dat.*), erreichen; ~ *s.o. a blow* j-m e-n Schlag versetzen; ~ *at* schlagen nach; ~ *or miss* aufs Geratewohl; ~ *off* F treffend darstellen; ~ *it off with* F sich vertragen mit; ~ *out* um sich schlagen; ~ (*up*)*on* (zufällig) kommen *od.* stoßen *od.* verfallen auf (*acc.*); *he* ~ *his head against a tree* er stieß mit dem Kopf gegen einen Baum; '~-and-'run driv·er *mot.* flüchtiger Fahrer *m.*

hitch [hitʃ] **1.** Ruck *m*; ⚓ Stich *m*, Knoten *m*; *fig.* Haken *m*, Hindernis *n*, Störung *f*; **2.** rücken; (sich) festmachen, -haken; hängenbleiben (*on an dat.*); rutschen; ~ *up Hosen* hochziehen; *Kinn etc.* aufwerfen; '~-hike f per Anhalter fahren.

hith·er *lit.* ['hiðə] hierher; **hith·er·to** ['~'tu:] bisher; **hith·er·ward(s)** ['~wəd(z)] = *hither*.

hit...: ~ **list** F (*a. fig.*) Abschußliste *f*; '~-man *sl.* ['hitmæn] Killer *m.*

hive [haiv] **1.** Bienenstock *m*, -korb *m*; Bienenschwarm *m*; *fig.* Schwarm *m*; ~*s pl.* ☆ Nesselausschlag *m*; **2.** *v/t.* Bienen in e-n Stock bringen; ~ *up* aufspeichern; *v/i.* zs.-wohnen.

ho [həu] holla!; heda!; halt!

hoar [hɔ:] (alters)grau.

hoard [hɔ:d] **1.** Vorrat *m*, Schatz *m*; **2.** *a.* ~ *up* horten, aufhäufen, sammeln; '**hoard·er** Hamsterer *m.*

hoard·ing ['hɔ:diŋ] Bauzaun *m*; Reklamefläche *f.*

hoar·frost ['hɔ:'frɔst] (Rauh)Reif *m.*

hoar·i·ness ['hɔ:rinis] Grauheit *f.*

hoarse ☐ [hɔ:s] heiser, rauh; '**hoarse·ness** Heiserkeit *f.*

hoar·y ['hɔ:ri] (alters)grau.

hoax [həuks] **1.** Täuschung *f*, Betrug *m*; Falschmeldung *f*; Schwindel *m*, Manöver *n*; **2.** anführen, foppen, zum besten haben.

hob[1] [hɔb] Kamineinsatz *m*; Zielpflock *m bei Wurfspielen.*

hob[2] [~] = *hobgoblin*; *raise* ~ *bsd. Am.* F die Hölle loslassen, Krach schlagen.

hob·ble ['hɔbl] **1.** Hinken *n*, Humpeln *n*; F Klemme *f*, Patsche *f*; **2.** *v/i.* humpeln, hinken (*a. fig.*); *v/t.* an den Füßen fesseln.

hob·ble·de·hoy F ['hɔbldi'hɔi] linkischer Bursche *m*, F Schlaks *m.*

hob·by *fig.* ['hɔbi] Steckenpferd *n*, Hobby *n*, Lieblingsbeschäftigung *f*; '~-horse Steckenpferd *n*; Schaukelpferd *n*; Karussellpferd *n.*

hob·gob·lin ['hɔbgɔblin] Kobold *m.*

hob·nail ['hɔbneil] Sohlennagel *m.*

hob·nob ['hɔbnɔb] freundschaftlich verkehren; plaudern; *zs.* eins trinken.

ho·bo *Am. sl.* ['həubəu] Landstreicher *m*, Tippelbruder *m.*

Hob·son's choice *fig.* ['hɔbsnz 'tʃɔis] keine Wahl *f.*

hock[1] [hɔk] **1.** *zo.* Hachse *f*; Sprunggelenk *n*; **2.** lähmen.

hock[2] [~] Rheinwein *m.*

hock[3] *sl.* [~] **1.** Pfand *n*; Loch *n*, Gefängnis *n*; **2.** verpfänden; '~-shop Pfandleihe *f.*

hock·ey ['hɔki] *Sport:* Hockey *n.*

ho·cus ['həukəs] betrügen; narkotisieren; *e-m Getränk* ein Betäubungsmittel zusetzen; ~**po·cus** ['~'pəukəs] Hokuspokus *m.*

hod [hɔd] Mörteltrog *m.*

hodge-podge ['hɔdʒpɔdʒ] = *hotchpotch.*

hod·man ['hɔdmən] Handlanger *m.*

hoe ⚶ [həu] **1.** Hacke *f*; **2.** hacken.

hog [hɔg] **1.** Schwein *n*; *fig.* Schwein(ehund *m*) *n*; *go the whole* ~ *sl.* aufs Ganze gehen; **2.** *v/t.* Mähne stutzen; F gierig an sich reißen; *v/i. mot.* drauflos rasen; **hogged** stark gekrümmt; '**hog·gish** ☐ schweinisch; gefräßig; '**hog·gish·ness** Schweinerei *f*; Gefräßigkeit *f.*

hog·ma·nay *schott.* ['hɔgmənei] Silvester *m.*

hogs·head ['hɔgzhed] Oxhoft *n* (*etwa 240 Liter*); großes Faß *n*; '**hog·skin** Schweinsleder *n*; '**hog·wash** Schweinetrank *m*; F Gewäsch *n.*

hoi(c)k [hɔik] *Flugzeug* hochreißen.

hoi pol·loi [hɔi'pɔlɔi] *pl.* die große Masse.

hoist [hɔist] **1.** Aufzug *m*; **2.** hochziehen; *Flagge* hissen.

hoi·ty-toi·ty F ['hɔiti'tɔiti] **1.** arrogant, anmaßend; **2.** holla!

ho·kum *Am. sl.* ['həukəm] Effekthascherei *f*; Kitsch *m*; Humbug *m.*

hold [həuld] **1.** Halten *n*; Halt *m*, Griff *m*; Gewalt *f*, Einfluß *m*; ⚓ Lade-, Frachtraum *m*; *catch, get, lay, take, seize* ~ *of* fassen, ergreifen; Besitz ergreifen von, sich

aneignen; *have a* ~ *of od. on* beherrschen; *keep* ~ *of* festhalten; **2.** (*irr.*)
v/t. allg. halten; festhalten; enthalten, fassen; auf-, zurück-, anhalten; *im Gedächtnis* behalten;
Versammlung etc. abhalten; (inne-)
haben, besitzen; *Ansicht* vertreten;
Gedanken etc. hegen; halten für,
schätzen; glauben; behaupten; ᵗᵗₛ
entscheiden (*that* daß); ~ *a job
down* F fest in e-r Stellung sitzen; ~
one's ground, ~ *one's own* sich behaupten, standhalten; ~ *the line*
teleph. am Apparat bleiben; ~ *water*
wasserdicht sein; *fig.* stichhaltig
sein; ~ *off* zurück-, abhalten; ✄ abfangen; ~ *on et.* (an s-m Platz fest-)
halten; ~ *out* ausstrecken; darbie-
ten; ~ *over* aufschieben; ~ *up* hoch-
halten; aufrechthalten; (unter-)
stützen; *dem Spott etc.* preisgeben;
aufhalten; (räuberisch) überfallen;
3. (*irr.*) *v/i.* (fest)halten; gelten; sich
bewähren; standhalten, sich halten;
~ *forth* Reden halten, sich auslassen
(*on* über *acc.*); ~ *good od. true* gelten; sich bestätigen; ~ *hard!* F
warte(t) mal!; halt!; ~ *in* innehalten; an sich halten; ~ *off* sich fernhalten; ~ *on* ausharren; fortdauern;
sich festhalten; *teleph.* am Apparat
bleiben; ~ *on!* F warte(t) mal!; halt!;
~ *to* festhalten an (*dat.*); ~ *up* sich
(aufrecht) halten; '**hold·all** Reisetasche *f;* '**hold·er** Haltende *m;*
Pächter *m;* Halter *m* (*Gerät*); In-
haber(in) (*bsd.* ✝); ~ *of shares* Ak-
tienbesitzer *m;* '**hold·fast** Klammer *f;* Haken *m;* Zwinge *f;* '**hold·
ing** Halten *n;* Halt *m;* Pachtgut *n;*
Besitz *m; small* ~ Kleingrundbesitz
m; ~ *company* Dachgesellschaft *f;*
'**hold·o·ver** *Am.* Überbleibsel *n,*
Rest *m;* '**hold·up** bewaffneter
Raubüberfall *m;* Stauung *f,* Stok-
kung *f.*

hole [həul] **1.** Loch *n* (*a. fig.*); Höhle
f; F *fig.* Klemme *f;* *pick* ~*s in* bekritteln; **2.** aushöhlen; durchlöchern; *Ball* in ein Loch spielen;
'**hole-and-'cor·ner** heimlich, hin-
tenherum (geschehen).

hol·i·day ['hɔlədi] Feiertag *m;* freier
Tag *m;* ~*s pl.* Ferien *pl.,* Urlaub *m;*
'~**mak·er** Ferienreisende *m,* *f,*
Urlauber(in).

ho·li·ness ['həulinis] Heiligkeit *f.*

hol·la ['hɔlə] **1.** hallo; **2.** hallo rufen.

hol·land ['hɔlənd] *a.* brown ~ unge-
bleichte Leinwand *f;* ♀s *sg.* Wacholderschnaps *m.*

hol·ler *Am.* F ['hɔlə] **1.** laut rufen;
2. Krach *m.*

hol·lo(a) ['hɔləu] = holla.

hol·low ['hɔləu] **1.** ☐ hohl; leer;
falsch; **2.** F *adv. a. all* ~ völlig;
3. Höhle *f,* (Aus)Höhlung *f;* *Land-
Senke *f;* ⊕ Rinne *f;* **4.** aushöhlen;
'**hol·low·ness** Hohlheit *f;* *fig.*
Falschheit *f.*

hol·ly ♣ ['hɔli] Stechpalme *f.*

hol·ly·hock ♣ ['hɔlihɔk] Stockrose *f.*

holm [həum] Holm *m,* Werder *m;*
'~'**oak** ♣ Steineiche *f.*

hol·o·caust ['hɔləkɔːst] Massenver-
nichtung *f;* Brandopfer *n.*

hol·ster ['həulstə] Pistolentasche *f.*

ho·ly ['həuli] **1.** heilig; ♀ *Thursday*
Gründonnerstag *m;* ~ *water* Weih-
wasser *n;* ♀ *Week* Karwoche *f;*
2. ~ *of holies* Bibel: *das* Allerheiligste; '~**stone** ⚓ Scheuerstein *m.*

hom·age ['hɔmidʒ] Huldigung *f;* *do
od. pay od.* render ~ huldigen (*to
dat.*).

home [həum] **1.** Heim *n;* Haus *n,*
Wohnung *f;* Heimat *f;* Mal *n,* Ziel
n; at ~ zu Hause, daheim; *make
o.s. at* ~ es sich bequem machen; *be
not at* ~ *to anyone* niemanden empfangen; **2.** *adj.* heimisch, häuslich;
inländisch; wirkungsvoll, tüchtig
(*Schlag etc.*); treffend (*Wahrheit*); ♀
Office Innenministerium *n;* ♀ *Rule*
Selbstregierung *f;* ♀ *Secretary* In-
nenminister *m;* ~ *trade* Binnen-
handel *m;* **3.** *adv.* heim, nach Hause;
an die richtige Stelle; gründlich; *be
~ (wieder) zu Hause sein; bring od.
drive s.th.* ~ *to s.o.* j-m et. klarmachen; j-m et. nachweisen; *come
~ heimkommen; come* ~ *to s.o. fig.
j-n nahe berühren; that comes* ~ *to
you das geht auf Sie; hit od. strike* ~
fig. ins Schwarze treffen; **4.** heimkehren; ~ *af·fairs pl. pol.* innere
Angelegenheiten *f pl.;* '~'**brewed**
selbstgebraut; '~**com·ing** Heimkehr *f;* ♀ **Coun·ties** *pl. die* Graf-
schaften *f pl.* um London; ~ **e·co-
'nom·ics** *mst sg. Am.* Hauswirt-
schaftslehre *f;* '~**felt** tief empfunden; '~'**grown** einheimisch; ~ **help**
Haushaltshilfe *f;* '**home·less** heimat-
los; '**home·like** anheimelnd, gemütlich; '**home·li·ness** Hausbackenheit

f; Anspruchslosigkeit *f*; *Am.* Reizlosigkeit *f*; '**home·ly** ☐ *fig.* anheimelnd, häuslich; hausbacken; einfach, schlicht; anspruchslos; *Am.* reizlos.

home...: '∼-'**made** selbstgemacht, Hausmacher...; '∼-'**mak·er** Hausfrau *f* (u. Mutter *f*); '∼-'**sick**: *be* ∼ Heimweh haben; '∼-'**sick·ness** Heimweh *n*; '∼-'**spun 1.** selbstgesponnen; *fig.* hausbacken; **2.** rauher Wollstoff *m*; '∼-'**stead** Heimstätte *f*; Gehöft *n*, Anwesen *n*; ∼ **team** *Sport:* Gastgeber *m/pl.*; ∼ **truth** unangenehme Wahrheit *f*; ∼-**ward(s)** ['∼wəd(z)] heimwärts (gerichtet), Heim...; '∼-'**work** Hausaufgabe(n *pl.*) *f*, Schularbeiten *f/pl.*; *do one's* ∼ Hausaufgaben machen; *fig.* sich gründlich vorbereiten.

hom·i·cide ['hɔmisaid] Totschlag *m*; Mord *m*; Totschläger(in).

hom·i·ly ['hɔmili] (Lehr)Predigt *f*.

hom·ing ['həumiŋ] Heimkehr *f*; ∼ *instinct* Heimkehrvermögen *n*; ∼ *pigeon* Brieftaube *f*.

hom·i·ny ['hɔmini] Maisbrei *m*.

ho·mo F ['həuməu] Homo *m*.

ho·m(o)e·o·path ['həumjəupæθ] Homöopath(in); **ho·m(o)e·o'path·ic** (∼*ally*) homöopathisch; **ho·m(o)e·op·a·thist** [∼mi'ɔpəθist] Homöopath *m*; **ho·m(o)e'op·a·thy** Homöopathie *f*.

ho·mo·ge·ne·i·ty [həuməudʒe'niːiti] Gleichartigkeit *f*; **ho·mo·ge·ne·ous** ☐ [∼'dʒiːnjəs] homogen, gleichartig; **ho·mog·en·ized** [hɔ'mɔdʒənaizd] homogenisiert; **hom·o·graph** ['hɔməugrɑːf] Homograph *n* (*Wort mit gleicher Schreibung aber anderer Bedeutung*); **ho·mol·o·gous** [hɔ'mɔləgəs] homolog; **ho'mol·o·gy** [∼dʒi] Übereinstimmung *f*; **hom·o·nym** ['hɔmənim] Homonym *n* (*Wort mit gleicher Lautung aber anderer Bedeutung*); **hom·o·phone** ['∼fəun] = *homonym*; **ho·mo·sex·u·al** ['həuməu'seksjuəl] homosexuell.

hom·y F ['həumi] = *homelike*.

hone ⊕ [həun] **1.** Abziehstein *m*; **2.** *Rasiermesser* abziehen.

hon·est ☐ ['ɔnist] ehrlich, rechtschaffen; aufrichtig; echt; '**hon·es·ty** Rechtschaffenheit *f*, Ehrlichkeit *f etc.*

hon·ey ['hʌni] Honig *m*; F Liebling *m*, Süße *f*; '**hon·ey·bee** (Honig-)

Biene *f*; '**hon·ey·comb 1.** (Honig-)Wabe *f*; **2.** durchlöchern; unterminieren; **hon·eyed** ['hʌnid] honigsüß; '**hon·ey·moon 1.** Flitterwochen *f/pl.*; Hochzeitsreise *f*; **2.** die Flitterwochen verleben; '**hon·ey·suck·le** ♦ Geißblatt *n*.

honk *mot.* [hɔŋk] **1.** Hupenton *m*; **2.** hupen, tuten.

honk·y-tonk *Am. sl.* ['hɔŋkitɔŋk] Bumslokal *n*, übles Nachtlokal *n*.

hon·o·rar·i·um [ɔnə'rɛəriəm] Honorar *n*; **hon·or·ar·y** ['ɔnərəri] Ehren...; ehrenamtlich.

hon·o(u)r ['ɔnə] **1.** Ehre *f*; Achtung *f*; Würde *f*; *fig.* Zierde *f*; ∼*s pl.* Auszeichnungen *f/pl.*; ∼*s degree* Honours-Grad *m*; *Your* ♀ Euer Gnaden; *in* ∼ *of s.o.* j-m zu Ehren; *do the* ∼*s of the house* die Honneurs machen; **2.** ehren; beehren; ✝ honorieren, einlösen.

hon·o(u)r·a·ble ☐ ['ɔnərəbl] ehrenvoll; redlich; ehrbar; ehrenwert; ∼ *discharge* ⚔ ehrenhafte Entlassung *f*; *Right* ♀ Sehr Ehrenwert; *receive* ∼ *mention* lobend erwähnt werden; '**hon·o(u)r·a·ble·ness** Ehrenhaftigkeit *f*.

hooch *sl.* [huːtʃ] Fusel *m*.

hood [hud] Kapuze *f*; *mot.* Verdeck *n*; *Am.* (Motor)Haube *f*; ⊕ Kappe *f*; *univ.* Talarüberwurf *m*; '**hood·ed** mit e-r Kapuze *od.* Kappe; *fig.* verhüllt.

hood·lum *Am.* F ['huːdləm] Strolch *m*; Raufbold *m*; Rowdy *m*.

hoo·doo *bsd. Am.* ['huːduː] **1.** Unglücksbringer *m*; Pech *n* (*Unglück*); **2.** Unglück bringen.

hood·wink ['hudwiŋk] täuschen.

hoo·ey *Am. sl.* ['huːi] Quatsch *m*.

hoof [huːf], *pl.* **hoofs** *od.* **hooves** [huːvz] Huf *m*; Klaue *f*; '∼-**beat** Hufschlag *m*; **hoofed** [huːft] gehuft, ...hufig.

hook [huk] **1.** (*bsd. Angel*)Haken *m*; Sichel *f*; ∼*s and eyes* Haken und Ösen; *by* ∼ *or by crook* mit allen Mitteln; ∼, *line, and sinker* F mit allem Drum und Dran; **2.** *v/t.* (zu-, fest)haken; fangen, angeln (*a. fig.*); *sl.* klauen; ∼ *it sl.* abhauen; ∼ *up* anhaken; *v/i. a.* ∼ *on* sich festhaken.

hook·a(h) ['hukə] Wasserpfeife *f*.

hooked [hukt] hakenförmig; *sl.* süchtig; '**hook·er** ⚓ Huker *m*; *Am. sl.* Nutte *f*; '**hook·ey** = *hooky*; '**hook-**

hooky

-up Bündnis *n*, Übereinkommen *n*; *Radio*: Ringsendung *f*; '**hook·y** 1. hakig; 2. *play* ~ *Am. sl.* (die Schule *etc.*) schwänzen.

hoo·li·gan ['huːligən] Rowdy *m*.

hoop [huːp] 1. *Faß- etc.* Reif(en) *m*; ⊕ Ring *m*; Reifrock *m*; 2. *Fässer* binden, mit Reifen belegen; '**hoop·er** Küfer *m*, Böttcher *m*.

hoop·ing-cough ['huːpiŋkɔf] Keuchhusten *m*.

hoo·poe *orn.* ['huːpuː] Wiedehopf *m*.

hoot [huːt] 1. Schrei *m*; Geheul *n*; Getute *n*; 2. *v/i.* heulen; johlen; tuten; *mot.* hupen; *v/t. a.* ~ *at*, ~ *out*, ~ *away* auspfeifen, -zischen; '**hoot·er** Schreier *m*; Sirene *f*, Dampfpfeife *f*; *mot.* Hupe *f*.

Hoov·er ['huːvə] 1. Staubsauger *m*; 2. (mit e-m Staubsauger) saugen *od.* reinigen.

hop¹ [hɔp] 1. ♀ Hopfen *m*; ~s *pl.* Hopfen(früchte *f/pl.*) *m*; ~*-picker* Hopfenpflücker *m*; 2. *v/t.* Bier *etc.* hopfen; *v/i.* Hopfen pflücken.

hop² [~] 1. Hopser *m*, Sprung *m*; ⚚ Etappe *f*; F (*zwanglose*) Tanzveranstaltung *f*, Tanzerei *f*; 2. hüpfen, springen (über *acc.*); ~ *it sl.* verduften; ~ *off* ⚚ starten.

hope [həup] 1. Hoffnung *f* (*of auf acc.*); *of great* ~s vielversprechend; 2. hoffen (*for auf acc.*); ~ *in* vertrauen auf (*acc.*); ~ *against* ~ verzweifelt hoffen; '**hope·ful** □ ['~ful] hoffnungsvoll; *be* ~ *that* die Hoffnung haben, daß; '**hope·ful·ly** *bsd. Am.* hoffentlich; '**hope·less** □ hoffnungslos; verzweifelt.

hop-o'-my-thumb ['hɔpəmi'θʌm] Knirps *m*, Dreikäsehoch *m*.

hop·per ['hɔpə] ⊕ Mühlentrichter *m*; Floh *m*; Känguruh *n*.

horde [hɔːd] Horde *f*.

ho·ri·zon [hə'raizn] Horizont *m*; **hor·i·zon·tal** □ [hɔri'zɔntl] horizontal, waag(e)recht; Horizont...

hor·mone ['hɔːməun] Hormon *n*.

horn [hɔːn] Horn *n der Tiere, des Mondes*; *zo.* Fühlhorn *n*; Trinkhorn *n*; Schalltrichter *m*; *mot.* Hupe *f*; *draw in one's* ~s *fig.* sich (*von e-m Unternehmen*) zurückziehen, kein Interesse mehr zeigen; (*stag's*) ~s *pl.* Geweih *n*; ~ *of plenty* Füllhorn *n*; '**~-beam** ♀ Hainbuche *f*; **~·blende** ['~blend] *min.* Horn-

blende *f*; **horned** ['~id, *in Zssgn* hɔːnd] gehörnt; Horn...

hor·net *zo.* ['hɔːnit] Hornisse *f*.

horn·less ['hɔːnlis] hornlos; '**horn-pipe** *a. sailor's* ~ *ein* (Seemanns-) Tanz *m*; '**horn·rimmed**: ~ *spectacles pl.* Hornbrille *f*; **horn·swog-gle** *Am. sl.* ['~swɔgl] *j.* (he)reinlegen; '**horn·y** □ hornig; schwielig; *sl.* geil (*Mann*).

ho·rol·o·gy [hɔ'rɔlədʒi] Uhrmacherkunst *f*; **hor·o·scope** ['hɔrəskəup] Horoskop *n*; *cast a* ~ das Horoskop stellen.

hor·ren·dous [hɔ'rendəs] entsetzlich.

hor·ri·ble □ ['hɔrəbl] entsetzlich; scheußlich; **hor·rid** □ ['hɔrid] gräßlich, abscheulich; schrecklich; **hor·rif·ic** [hɔ'rifik] entsetzlich; **hor·ri·fy** ['~fai] erschrecken; entsetzen; **hor·ror** ['hɔrə] Entsetzen *n*, Schauder *m*, Abscheu *f*, *m* (*of vor dat.*); Schrecken *m*; Greuel *m*; *chamber of* ~s Schreckenskammer *f*; ~ *fiction* (*film*) Gruselroman *m* (*-film m*); '**hor·ror-strick·en** starr vor Entsetzen.

horse [hɔːs] 1. Pferd *n*, Roß *n*, Gaul *m*; *coll.* Reiterei *f*; ⊕ Bock *m*, Gestell *n*; *look a gift* ~ *in the mouth fig.* e-m geschenkten Gaul ins Maul schauen; *a* ~ *of another colo(u)r et.* ganz anderes; (*straight*) *from the* ~'s *mouth* aus erster Hand; 2. bespannen; beritten machen; *j.* auf den Rücken nehmen; '**~·back**: *on* ~ zu Pferd; *go on* ~ reiten; '**~-bean** ♀ Pferdebohne *f*; '**~-box** Pferdetransportwagen *m*; '**~-break·er** Zureiter *m*; ~ *chest·nut* ♀ Roßkastanie *f*; '**~-col·lar** Kum(me)t *n*; '**~-deal·er** Pferdehändler *m*; '**~-flesh** Pferdefleisch *n*; *coll.* Pferde *n/pl.*; '**~-fly** *zo.* Bremse *f*; ♀ **Guards** *pl. englisches* Garde-Kavallerie-Regiment *n*; '**~-hair** Roßhaar *n*; '**~-laugh** F wieherndes Lachen *n*; '**~-man** Reiter *m*; '**~-man·ship** Reitkunst *f*; ~ *op·er·a Am.* drittklassiger Wildwestfilm *m*; '**~-play** grober Scherz *m*; '**~-pond** Pferdeschwemme *f*, -tränke *f*; '**~-pow·er** Pferdestärke *f*; '**~-race** Pferderennen *n*; '**~-rad·ish** ♀ Meerrettich *m*; '**~-sense** gesunder Menschenverstand *m*; '**~-shoe** Hufeisen *n*; '**~-whip** Reitgerte *f*; '**~-wom·an** Reiterin *f*.

housemaster

hors·y [ˈhɔːsi] pferdenärrisch; Pferde..., Reit..., Jockei...

hor·ta·tive □ [ˈhɔːtətiv], **hor·ta·to·ry** [ˈ⁓təri] ermahnend.

hor·ti·cul·tur·al [hɔːtiˈkʌltʃərəl] Gartenbau...; ˈhor·ti·culˈture Gartenbau m; hor·tiˈculˈtur·ist Gartenkünstler m.

ho·san·na [həuˈzænə] Hosianna n, Loblied n.

hose [həuz] 1. Schlauch m; Strumpfhose f; coll. Strümpfe m/pl.; 2. mit e-m Schlauch (be)sprengen od. waschen.

ho·sier [ˈhəuziə] Strumpfwarenhändler m; ˈho·sier·y Strumpfwaren f/pl.; Strumpffabrik f.

hos·pice [ˈhɔspis] Hospiz n.

hos·pi·ta·ble □ [ˈhɔspitəbl] gastfrei, gast(freund)lich; aufgeschlossen (to dat.).

hos·pi·tal [ˈhɔspitl] Hospital n, Krankenhaus n; ✕ Lazarett n; **hos·pi·tal·i·ty** [⁓ˈtæliti] Gastfreundschaft f, Gastlichkeit f; **hos·pi·tal·ize** [ˈ⁓təlaiz] ins Krankenhaus einliefern; stationär behandeln; ˈhos·pi·tal-train ✕ Lazarettzug m.

host¹ [həust] Wirt m (a. zo., ♀); Gastgeber m; Gastwirt m; Fernsehen: Showmaster m; reckon without one's ⁓ die Rechnung ohne den Wirt machen.

host² [⁓] fig. Heer n (große Menge), Unzahl f; Schwarm m; Lord of ⁓s Bibel: Herr m der Heerscharen; he is a ⁓ in himself er leistet so viel wie hundert andere zusammen.

Host³ eccl. [⁓] Hostie f.

hos·tage [ˈhɔstidʒ] Geisel m, f.

hos·tel [ˈhɔstəl] Herberge f; univ. Studenten(wohn)heim n; ˈhos·tel-(l)er Herbergsbenützer m; ˈhos·tel·ry [ˈ⁓ri] Gasthaus n, Herberge f.

host·ess [ˈhəustis] Wirtin f; Gastgeberin f; = air ⁓.

hos·tile [ˈhɔstail] feindlich (gesinnt); **hos·til·i·ty** [⁓ˈtiliti] Feindseligkeit f (to gegen).

hos·tler [ˈɔslə] Stallknecht m.

hot [hɔt] 1. □ heiß; scharf; beißend; hitzig, heftig; eifrig; warm (Speise, Fährte); Am. sl. falsch (Scheck); gestohlen; radioaktiv; ⁓ air F leeres Geschwätz n; go like ⁓ cakes wie warme Semmeln weggehen; ⁓ line pol. heißer Draht m; ⁓ spot pol. Kri-

senherd m; ⁓ stuff sl. toller Kerl m; tolle od. heikle Sache f; get into ⁓ water in des Teufels Küche kommen; 2. mst ⁓ up F heiß machen; ˈhot·bed Mistbeet n; fig. Pflanz-, Brutstätte f; ˈhot--ˈblood·ed heißblütig.

hotch·potch F [ˈhɔtʃpɔtʃ] Mischmasch m; Gemüsesuppe f.

hot dog F [ˈhɔtˈdɔg] heißes Würstchen n.

ho·tel [həuˈtel] Hotel n.

hot...: ˈ⁓·foot 1. eiligst; 2. F eilen; ˈ⁓·head Hitzkopf m; ˈ⁓·house Treibhaus n; ˈhot·ness Hitze f; Schärfe f.

hot...: ˈ⁓·plate Heiz-, Kochplatte f; ˈ⁓·pot Irish Stew n; ˈ⁓·press Papier heiß pressen; Stoff dekatieren; ⁓ rod mot. Am. sl. frisiertes altes Auto n; ⁓ shoe phot. Blitz-Mittenkontakt m; ˈ⁓·spur Heißsporn m, Hitzkopf m; ⁓·ˈwa·ter bot·tle Wärmflasche f.

hough [hɔk] = hock¹.

hound [haund] 1. Jagdhund m, bsd. Spürhund m; fig. Hund m, Schurke m; 2. jagen, hetzen (at, on auf acc.).

hour [ˈauə] Stunde f; Zeit f, Uhr f; ⁓s pl. Dienst(stunden f/pl.) m; eccl. Stundengebete n/pl.; s. eleventh; ˈ⁓·glass Sanduhr f; ˈ⁓--hand Stundenzeiger m; ˈhour·ly stündlich; ständig.

house 1. [haus], pl. **hous·es** [ˈhauziz] allg. Haus n (a. ✝, parl., thea.); the ⁊ das Unterhaus n; die Börse f; ⁓ and home Haus und Hof; keep ⁓ den Haushalt führen; on the ⁓ auf Kosten des Wirts, umsonst; put one's ⁓ in order fig. sein Haus bestellen; 2. [hauz] v/t. einen, unterbringen; v/i. hausen; **⁓·a·gent** [ˈhauseidʒənt] Häusermakler m; ⁓ ar·rest Hausarrest m; ˈ⁓·boat Hausboot n; ˈ⁓·break·er Einbrecher m bei Tage; Abbrucharbeiter m; ˈ⁓·flag ⚓ Reedereiflagge f; ˈ⁓·fly Stubenfliege f; ˈ⁓·hold Haushalt m; attr. Haushalts...; Haus-...; King's ⁓ königliche Hofhaltung f; ⁓ troops pl. Gardetruppen f pl.; ⁓ word fester od. geläufiger Begriff m; ˈ⁓--hold·er Haushaltsvorstand m, Hausherr m; ˈ⁓·hunt·ing F Wohnungssuche f; ˈ⁓·hus·band Hausmann m; ˈ⁓·keep·er Haushälterin f; ˈ⁓·keep·ing 1. Haushaltung f; 2. häuslich; ˈ⁓·less obdachlos; ˈ⁓·maid Hausangestellte f; ˈ⁓·mas·ter Internatsleiter

m; ~ **of cards** Kartenhaus *n* (*a. fig.*);
♀ **of God** Gotteshaus *n*; '~**paint·er** Anstreicher *m*; '~**phy·si·cian** Krankenhausarzt *m*; '~**proud:** be ~ übertrieben ordentlich sein; e-n Putzfimmel haben; '~**room** Platz *m* im Haus; *give s.o.* ~ j. in sein Haus aufnehmen; '~**-to-'house** Haus...; ~ **collection** Haussammlung *f*; '~**top** Dach *n*; *proclaim from the* ~s öffentlich verkünden; '~**-train·ed** stubenrein (*Tier*); '~**-warm·ing** Einzugsfeier *f*; ~**wife** ['~waif] Hausfrau *f*; ['hʌzif] Nähtäschchen *n*; ~**wife·ly** ['hauswaifli] hausfraulich; Haushaltungs-...; ~**wif·er·y** ['~wifəri] Haushaltung *f*; '~**work** Haus(halts)arbeiten *f pl*.; '~**wreck·er** *Am.* Abbruchunternehmer *m*.

hous·ing[1] ['hauziŋ] Unterbringung *f*; Wohnung *f*; ~ **conditions** *pl.* Wohnverhältnisse *n pl*.; ~ **estate** Wohnsiedlung *f*; ~ **scheme** Wohnungsbauprojekt *n*; ~ **shortage** Wohnungsnot *f*; ~ **subsidy** Wohngeld *n*.

hous·ing[2] [~] Schabracke *f*.

hove [houv] *pret. u. p.p. von* heave 2.

hov·el ['hovəl] Schuppen *m*; Hütte *f*.

hov·er ['hovə] schweben; lungern; *fig.* schwanken, ~**ing** *accent* schwebender Akzent *m*; '~**craft** Luftkissenfahrzeug *n*.

how [hau] wie; ~ **do you do?** Guten Tag!; ~ **large a room!** was für ein großes Zimmer!; ~ **about** ...? wie steht's mit ...?; ~**-be·it** † F ['~'bi:it] nichtsdestoweniger; ~**-d'ye-do** *sl.* ['~djə'du:] unangenehme Geschichte *f*, Bescherung *f*; ~'**ev·er**, *a.* **how-e'er** [~'ɛə] **1.** *adv.* wie auch (immer); *bei adj. u. adv.:* wenn auch noch so ..., so ... auch; F wie eigentlich?; **2.** *conj.* jedoch, gleichwohl, doch.

how·itz·er ⚔ ['hauitsə] Haubitze *f*.

howl [haul] **1.** heulen, brüllen; **2.** Heulen *n*, Geheul *n*; *Radio:* Pfeifen *n*; '**howl·er** Heuler *m*; *sl.* grober Fehler *m*; '**howl·ing 1.** heulend; F fürchterlich; **2.** Heulen *n*.

how·so·ev·er [hausəu'evə] wie(sehr) auch immer.

hoy [hoi] **1.** holla!; **2.** ⚓ Leichter *m* (*kleines Küstenfahrzeug*).

hoy·den ['hoidn] Wildfang *m*, Range *f* (*Mädchen*).

hub [hʌb] (Rad)Nabe *f*; *fig.* Mittel-,

Angelpunkt *m*.

hub·ble-bub·ble ['hʌblbʌbl] Geblubber *n*; *Art* Wasserpfeife *f*.

hub·bub ['hʌbʌb] Tumult *m*, Lärm *m*.

hub(·by) F ['hʌb(i)] Männchen *n* (*Ehemann*).

hu·bris ['hju:bris] Hybris *f*, Selbstüberhebung *f*.

huck·a·back ['hʌkəbæk] Drell *m*.

huck·le ['hʌkl] Hüfte *f*; '~**-ber·ry** ♀ amerikanische Heidelbeere *f*; '~**-bone** Fußknöchel *m*; Hüftknochen *m*.

huck·ster ['hʌkstə] **1.** Höker(in); **2.** (ver)hökern, schachern (mit).

hud·dle ['hʌdl] **1.** *a.* ~ **together** (sich) zs.-drängen, zs.-pressen; ~ (*o.s.*) up sich zs.-kauern; **2.** Gewirr *n*, Wirrwarr *m*, Gehudel *n*; *go into a* ~ F Kriegsrat halten.

hue[1] [hju:] Farbe *f*, Färbung *f*.

hue[2] [~]: ~ **and cry** Zetergeschrei *n*; Hetze *f*.

huff [hʌf] **1.** üble Laune *f*; **2.** *v/t.* grob anfahren; beleidigen; *e-n Damstein* pusten; *v i.* wütend werden; schmollen; '**huff·ish** ▱ übelnehmerisch; '**huff·i·ness**, '**huffish·ness** Übelnehmerei *f*; Übellaunigkeit *f*; '**huff·y** ▱ übelnehmerisch; F eingeschnappt.

hug [hʌg] **1.** Umarmung *f*; **2.** an sich drücken, umarmen; umklammern; *fig.* festhalten an (*dat.*), hegen; sich dicht am *Lande od. Wege* halten; ~ *o.s.* sich beglückwünschen (on zu).

huge ▱ [hju:dʒ] ungeheuer, riesig; '**huge·ness** ungeheure Größe *f*.

hug·ger-mug·ger F ['hʌgəmʌgə] **1.** unordentlich; heimlich; **2.** *v/t.* verheimlichen; *v i.* Heimlichkeiten haben; **3.** Kuddelmuddel *m*.

Hu·gue·not *hist.* ['hju:gənɔt] Hugenotte *m*, Hugenottin *f*.

hu·la ['hu:lə] Hula(-Hula) *m* (*hawaiischer Tanz*).

hulk ⚓ [hʌlk] Hulk *m, f*, (*abgetakeltes*) altes Schiff *n*; *fig.* Klotz *m*; '**hulk·ing** ungeschlacht, klobig.

hull [hʌl] **1.** ♀ Schale *f*; Hülse *f*; ⚓ Rumpf *m*; ~ **down** weit entfernt; **2.** enthülsen; schälen; ⚓ in den Schiffsrumpf treffen.

hul·la·ba·loo [hʌləbə'lu:] Spektakel *m*, Lärm *m*.

hul·lo ['hʌ'ləu] hallo (*bsd. teleph.*).
hum [hʌm] **1.** Summen *n*; Brumme(l)n *n*; Gesumm *n*; **2.** hm!;
3. summen; brumme(l)n; *sl.*
stinken; ~ *and haw* verlegen stottern, sich verlegen räuspern; *make
things* ~ F Schwung in die Sache
bringen.
hu·man ['hju:mən] **1.** □ menschlich; ~*ly* nach menschlichem Ermessen; ~*ly possible* menschenmöglich; ~*ly speaking* nach menschlichen Begriffen; ~ *rights pl.* Menschenrechte *n/pl.*; **2.** F Mensch *m*;
hu·mane □ [hju:'mein] human,
menschenfreundlich; ~ *killer*
Schlachtmaske *f*; ~ *learning* humanistische Bildung *f*; **hu·man·ism**
['hju:mənizəm] Humanismus *m*;
'**hu·man·ist** Humanist *m*; **hu·man·i·tar·i·an** [hju:mæni'tɛəriən] **1.** Menschenfreund *m*; **2.** menschenfreundlich; **hu'man·i·ty** menschliche Natur *f*; Menschheit *f*; Menschlichkeit
f, Menschenliebe *f*, Humanität *f*; *the
humanities pl.* die antiken Sprachen
und Literaturen *f/pl.*; die Geisteswissenschaften *f/pl.*; **hu·man·i·za·tion** [hju:mənai'zeiʃən] Humanisierung *f*; '**hu·man·ize** menschlich *od.*
gesittet machen *od.* werden; **hu·man·kind** ['hju:mən'kaind] das
Menschengeschlecht, die Menschheit.
hum·ble ['hʌmbl] **1.** □ demütig;
bescheiden; niedrig, gering; *my* ~
self meine Wenigkeit *f*; *your* ~
servant Ihr ergebenster Diener *m*;
eat ~ *pie* zu Kreuze kriechen, sich
demütigen; **2.** erniedrigen; demütigen.
hum·ble-bee ['hʌmblbi:] Hummel *f*.
hum·ble·ness ['hʌmblnis] Demut *f*;
Bescheidenheit *f*.
hum·bug ['hʌmbʌg] **1.** Schwindel
m; Unsinn *m*, Humbug *m*; Schwindler *m*; Pfefferminzbonbon *n*;
2. prellen, (be)schwindeln.
hum·ding·er *Am. sl.* [hʌm'diŋə]
Mordskerl *m*; Mordssache *f*.
hum·drum ['hʌmdrʌm] **1.** eintönig,
langweilig; fad; **2.** Alltagseinerlei *n*,
Eintönigkeit *f*.
hu·mer·al *anat.* ['hju:mərəl] Schulter...
hu·mid ['hju:mid] feucht, naß;
hu'mid·i·ty Feuchtigkeit *f*.

hu·mil·i·ate [hju:'milieit] erniedrigen, demütigen; **hu·mil·i'a·tion**
Erniedrigung *f*, Demütigung *f*.
hu·mil·i·ty [hju:'militi] Demut *f*.
hum·mer ['hʌmə] Summer *m* (*bsd.
teleph.*); *sl.* Betriebmacher *m*.
hum·ming F ['hʌmiŋ] mächtig, gewaltig; '~**-bird** *orn.* Kolibri *m*;
'~**-top** Brummkreisel *m*.
hum·mock ['hʌmək] Erd-, Eis-
Buckel *m*; Hügel *m*.
hu·mor·ist ['hju:mərist] Humorist *m*; Spaßmacher *m*, -vogel *m*.
hu·mor·ous □ ['hju:mərəs] humoristisch, humorvoll; spaßig;
'**hu·mor·ous·ness** Humor *m*; das
Spaßige.
hu·mo(u)r ['hju:mə] **1.** Humor *m*;
das Spaßige; Stimmung *f*, Laune *f*;
Körpersaft *m*; *out of* ~ schlecht
gelaunt; **2.** *j-m* s-n Willen lassen;
eingehen auf (*acc.*); '**hu·mo(u)r·less** humorlos; **hu·mo(u)r·some**
□ ['~səm] launisch.
hump [hʌmp] **1.** Höcker *m*, Buckel
m; *sl.* üble Laune *f*; *give s.o. the* ~ *j.*
verdrießen; **2.** krümmen; ärgern,
verdrießen; ~ *o.s. Am. sl.* sich
dranhalten; '**hump·back**, '**hump·backed** *s.* hunchback.
humph [mm; hʌmf] hm! (*zum Ausdruck des Zweifels od. der Verachtung*).
Hum·phrey ['hʌmfri]: *dine with
Duke* ~ kein Mittagessen haben.
hump·ty-dump·ty F ['hʌmpti-
'dʌmpti] Dickerchen *n*, Stöpsel *m*.
hump·y ['hʌmpi] bucklig.
hu·mus ['hju:məs] Humus *m*.
hunch [hʌntʃ] **1.** *s.* hump; großes
Stück *n*, Runken *m*; *Am.* F Ahnung
f, Verdacht *m*; **2.** *a.* ~ *out*, ~ *up*
krümmen; '**hunch·back** Bucklige
m, *f*; '**hunch·backed** bucklig.
hun·dred ['hʌndrəd] **1.** hundert;
2. Hundert *n*; Hundertschaft *f*;
Bezirk *m*; **hun·dred·fold** ['~fəuld]
hundertfältig; **hun·dredth** ['~θ]
1. hundertste; **2.** Hundertstel *n*;
'**hun·dred·weight** englischer Zentner *m* (*50,8 kg*).
hung [hʌŋ] **1.** *pret. u. p.p. von* hang **1**;
2. *adj.* abgehangen (*Fleisch*).
Hun·gar·i·an [hʌŋ'gɛəriən] **1.** ungarisch; **2.** Ungar(in); Ungarisch *n*.
hun·ger ['hʌŋgə] **1.** Hunger *m* (*a.
fig.*; *for* nach); **2.** *v/i.* hungern (*for,
after* nach); *v/t.* durch Hunger

zwingen (*into* zu); ～ **strike** Hungerstreik *m*; *go on* (*a*) ～ in den Hungerstreik treten.

hun·gry □ ['hʌŋgri] hungrig (*for* nach); mager (*Boden*); ～ **work** Arbeit, die hungrig macht.

hunk F [hʌŋk] dickes Stück *n*, Runken *m*; '**bun·kers** *pl*. Hinterbacken *f/pl*.

hunks F [hʌŋks] Geizhals *m*.

hunt [hʌnt] **1.** Jagd *f* (*for* auf *acc.*, *fig.* nach); Jagd(revier *n*) *f*; Jagd (-gesellschaft) *f*; **2.** *v/t.* jagen; *Revier* bejagen; *Hund* hetzen; ～ **out** *od.* **up** aufstöbern, -spüren; *v/i.* jagen; Jagd machen (*for*, *after* auf *acc.*); '**hunter** Jäger *m*; Jagdpferd *n*; '**hunt·ing 1.** Jagen *n*; Verfolgung *f*; **2.** Jagd...; '**hunt·ing-box** Jagdhütte *f*; '**hunt·ing-ground** Jagdrevier *n*; '**hunt·ress** Jägerin *f*; '**hunts·man** Jäger *m*; Rüdemann *m* (*Meutenführer*).

hur·dle ['hə:dl] Hürde *f* (*a. fig.*); Faschine *f*; '**hur·dler** Hürdenläufer *m*; '**hur·dle-race** Hürdenrennen *n*, -lauf *m*.

hur·dy-gur·dy ['hə:digə:di] Leierkasten *m*.

hurl [hə:l] **1.** Schleudern *n*; **2.** schleudern; *Worte* ausstoßen.

hurl·y-burl·y ['hə:libə:li] Tumult *m*, Aufruhr *m*, Wirrwarr *m*.

hur·ra(h) [hu'rɑ:], **hur·ray** [～'rei] hurra!

hur·ri·cane ['hʌrikən] Hurrikan *m*, Wirbelsturm *m*, Orkan *m*; ～ **lamp** Sturmlaterne *f*.

hur·ried □ ['hʌrid] eilig; übereilt.

hur·ry ['hʌri] **1.** (große) Eile *f*, Hast *f*; *in a* ～ in Eile; *be in a* ～ es eilig haben; *is there any* ～? ist es eilig?; *not ... in a* ～ F nicht so bald, nicht so leicht; **2.** *v/t.* (an)treiben; drängen; hetzen; *et.* beschleunigen; eilig schicken *od.* bringen; ～ *on*, ～ *up* antreiben; beschleunigen; *v/i.* eilen, hasten; *a.* ～ *up* sich beeilen; ～ *over s.th.* et. eilig erledigen; '～'**scur·ry 1.** Unruhe *f*, wilde Hast *f*; **2.** in wilder Hast.

hurt [hə:t] **1.** Verletzung *f*; Schaden *m*; **2.** (*irr.*) *v/t.* (*a. fig.*) verletzen; weh tun (*dat.*); schaden (*dat.*); beschädigen; *v/i.* weh tun, schmerzen; F Schaden nehmen; **hurt·ful** □ ['～ful] schädlich (*to* für).

hur·tle ['hə:tl] sausen; fegen; (p)rasseln.

hus·band ['hʌzbənd] **1.** Ehemann *m*, Gatte *m*; **2.** haushalten mit; verwalten; '**hus·band·man** Landwirt *m*; '**hus·band·ry** Landwirtschaft *f*, Ackerbau *m*; *good etc.* ～ gutes *etc.* Wirtschaften *n*.

hush [hʌʃ] **1.** still; **2.** Stille *f*; **3.** *v/t.* zum Schweigen bringen; beruhigen; *Stimme* dämpfen; ～ **up** vertuschen; *v/i.* still sein; '～-'**hush** streng geheim; '～-**mon·ey** Schweigegeld *n*.

husk [hʌsk] **1.** ♀ Hülse *f*, Schote *f*; Schale *f* (*a. fig.*); **2.** enthülsen; '**husk·i·ness** Heiserkeit *f*, Rauheit *f*.

husk·y¹ ['hʌski] **1.** □ hülsig; trocken; rauh, heiser; F stramm, stämmig, kräftig; **2.** F stämmiger Kerl *m*.

hus·ky² [～] Eskimo *m*; Eskimohund *m*.

hus·sar ✕ [hu'zɑ:] Husar *m*.

hus·sy ['hʌsi] Flittchen *n*; Range *f*.

hus·tings ['hʌstiŋz] *pl*. Wahlkampf *m*.

hus·tle ['hʌsl] **1.** *v/t.* im *Gedränge* stoßen; drängen, treiben; *v/i.* (sich) drängen; eilen; mit Hochdruck arbeiten, sich dranhalten; **2.** (Hoch-) Betrieb *m*; Getriebe *n*; ～ *and bustle* Gedränge *n* und Gehetze *n*; '**hus·tler** rühriger Mensch *m*.

hut [hʌt] **1.** Hütte *f*; ✕ Baracke *f*; **2.** in Hütten *od.* Baracken unterbringen *od.* hausen.

hutch [hʌtʃ] Kasten *m*; *bsd.* Kaninchen-Stall *m* (*a. fig.*); Trog *m*.

hut·ment ✕ ['hʌtmənt] *a.* ～ *camp* Barackenunterkunft *f*, -lager *n*.

huz·za [hu'zɑ:] hussa!, hurra!

huz·zy ['hʌzi] = **hussy**.

hy·a·cinth ♀ ['haiəsinθ] Hyazinthe *f*.

hy·ae·na *zo.* [hai'i:nə] Hyäne *f*.

hy·brid ['haibrid] **1.** Bastard *m*, Mischling *m*; Kreuzung *f*; **2.** Bastard...; Zwitter...; '**hy·brid·ism** Bastardierung *f*, Kreuzung *f*; **hy·'brid·i·ty** Bastardnatur *f*; '**hy·brid·ize** bastardieren, kreuzen.

hy·dra ['haidrə] Hydra *f* (*vielköpfige Seeschlange der griechischen Mythologie*). [tensie *f.*]

hy·dran·gea ♀ [hai'dreindʒə] Hor-

hy·drant ['haidrənt] Hydrant *m*.

hy·drate ⚗ ['haidreit] **1.** Hydrat *n*; **2.** mit Wasser verbinden.

hy·drau·lic [hai'drɔ:lik] **1.** (～*ally*)

hydraulisch; 2. ␣s *sg.* Hydraulik *f.*
hy·dro ['haidrəu] Wasserkuranstalt *f.*
hy·dro... ['haidrəu] Wasser...; '␣-
'**car·bon** Kohlenwasserstoff *m*;
'␣'**chlo·ric ac·id** Salzsäure *f*;
'␣·**dy'nam·ics** *sg.* Hydrodynamik
f; '␣-e'**lec·tric** hydroelektrisch; ␣
generating station Wasserkraftwerk
n; '␣·**foil** Tragflächenboot *n*; **hy·
dro·gen** ⚛ ['haidridʒən] Wasserstoff
m; **hy·dro·gen·at·ed** [hai'drɔdʒin-
eitid] hydriert; **hy·dro·gen bomb**
Wasserstoffbombe *f*; **hy·drog·e·
nous** [hai'drɔdʒinəs] wasserstoffhal-
tig; **hy'drog·ra·phy** [␣grəfi] Hydro-
graphie *f*; **hy·dro·path·ic** ['haidrəu-
'pæθik] 1. hydropathisch; 2. *a.* ␣
establishment (Kalt)Wasserheilan-
stalt *f*; **hy·drop·a·thy** [hai'drɔpəθi]
Wasserheilkunde *f*, -kur *f*.
hy·dro...: ␣·**pho·bi·a** ['haidrəu-
'fəubjə] Wasserscheu *f*; Tollwut
f; '␣·**plane** (Motor)Gleitboot *n*,
Rennboot *n*; Wasserflugzeug *n*;
␣·**po·nics** [␣'pɔnics] *sg.* Wasser-
kultur *f*; ␣'**stat·ic** 1. hydrostatisch;
␣ *press* hydraulische Presse *f*; 2. ␣s
sg. Hydrostatik *f.*
hy·e·na *zo.* [hai'i:nə] Hyäne *f.*
hy·giene ['haidʒi:n] Hygiene *f*;
hy'gien·ic (␣*ally*) hygienisch; ␣s
sg. = *hygiene.*
hy·grom·e·ter [hai'grɔmitə] Feuch-
tigkeitsmesser *m.*
Hy·men ['haimen] Hymen *m* (*Gott
der Ehe*); **hy·me·ne·al** [␣'ni:əl]
hochzeitlich.
hymn [him] 1. Hymne *f*; Kirchen-
lied *n*; 2. preisen; lobsingen (*dat.*);
hym·nal ['␣nəl] 1. hymnisch;
2. *a.* '**hymn-book** Gesangbuch *n.*
hy·per·bo·la ⅄ [hai'pə:bələ] Hyperbel *f*; **hy'per·bo·le** *rhet.* [␣bəli]
Übertreibung *f*, Hyperbel *f*; **hy-
per·bol·ic** ⅄ [␣'bɔlik] hyper-
bolisch; **hy·per'bol·i·cal** □ *rhet.*
übertreibend; **hy·per·crit·i·cal** □
['␣'kritikəl] hyperkritisch, allzu
scharf; '**hy·per'mar·ket** Verbrau-

chermarkt *m*; **hy'per·tro·phy** [␣-
trəufi] übermäßiges Wachstum *n*,
Hypertrophie *f.*
hy·phen ['haifən] 1. Bindestrich *m*;
2. mit Bindestrich schreiben *od.*
verbinden; **hy·phen·at·ed** ['␣eitid]
mit Bindestrich geschrieben; ␣
Americans pl. Bindestrich-, Halb-
Amerikaner *m/pl.* (*z. B. German-
Americans*).
hyp·no·sis [hip'nəusis], *pl.* **hyp-
'no·ses** [␣si:z] Hypnose *f.*
hyp·not·ic [hip'nɔtik] 1. (␣*ally*) einschläfernd; 2. Schlafmittel *n*; **hyp-
no·tism** ['␣nətizəm] Hypnotismus
m; '**hyp·no·tist** Hypnotiseur *m*;
hyp·no·tize ['␣taiz] hypnotisieren.
hy·po *phot.* ['haipəu] Fixiersalz *n.*
hy·po·chon·dri·a [haipəu'kɔndriə]
Schwermut *f*, Hypochondrie *f*;
hy·po'chon·dri·ac [␣driæk] 1. hypochondrisch; 2. Hypochonder *m*;
hy·poc·ri·sy [hi'pɔkrəsi] Heuchelei
f; **hyp·o·crite** ['hipəkrit] Heuchler
(-in); Scheinheilige *m*, *f*; **hyp·o-
crit·i·cal** □ [hipəu'kritikəl] heuchlerisch; **hy·po·der·mic** ⚕ [haipəu-
'dɔ:mik] 1. subkutan, unter der *od.*
die Haut; ␣ *injection* = 2. Einspritzung *f* unter die Haut; **hy-
pot·e·nuse** ⅄ [hai'pɔtinju:z] Hypotenuse *f*; **hy'poth·e·car·y** [␣-
θikəri] pfandrechtlich, hypothe-
karisch; **hy'poth·e·cate** [␣'θikeit]
verpfänden; **hy·po·ther·mi·a** [hai-
pəu'θə:miə] Unterkühlung *f*; **hy-
poth·e·sis** [␣'pɔθisis], *pl.* **hy·poth·e-
ses** [␣'pɔθisi:z] Hypothese *f*; **hy·po-
thet·ic, hy·po·thet·i·cal** □ [haipəu-
'θetik(əl)] hypothetisch.
hys·sop ♣ ['hisəp] Ysop *m.*
hys·ter·ec·to·my ⚕ [histə'rektəmi]
Hysterektomie *f.*
hys·te·ri·a ⚕ [his'tiəriə] Hysterie *f*;
hys·ter·ic, *mst* **hys·ter·i·cal** □
[his'terik(əl)] hysterisch; **hys'ter·
ics** *pl.* hysterischer Anfall *m*, hyste-
rische Anfälle *m/pl.*; *go into* ␣
hysterisch werden.

I [ai] ich.

i·am·bic [ai'æmbik] **1.** iambisch; **2.** *a.* **i'am·bus** [‿bəs] Jambus *m*.

i·bex *zo.* ['aibeks] Steinbock *m*.

i·bi·dem [i'baidem] ebenda.

ice [ais] **1.** Eis *n*; (Speise)Eis *n*; *cut no* ‿ F nicht von Belang sein; nicht ziehen; *skate on thin* ‿ *fig.* sich aufs Glatteis begeben; **2.** gefrieren lassen; *a.* ‿ *up* vereisen; *Kuchen* mit Zuckerguß überziehen; in Eis kühlen; '‿**age** Eiszeit *f*; ‿**axe** Eispickel *m*; ‿**bag** ✗ Eisbeutel *m*; **ice·berg** ['‿bəːg] Eisberg *m* (*a. fig.*).

ice...: '‿**boat** Eisjacht *f*, Segelschlitten *m*; '‿**field** (polare) Eisdecke *f*; '‿**floe** Eisscholle *f*; '‿**free** eisfrei; '‿**hock·ey** Eishockey *n*; '‿**house** Eiskeller *m*.

Ice·land·er ['aisləndə] Isländer(in).

Ice·lan·dic [‿'lændik] Isländisch *n*.

ice...: '‿**lol·ly** Eis *n* am Stiel; '‿**pack** Packeis *m*; ✗ Eisumschlag *m*; '‿**rink** Eisbahn *f*; '‿**show** Eisrevue *f*; '‿**skate** Schlittschuhlaufen *n*.

ich·thy·ol·o·gy [ikθi'ɔlədʒi] Fischkunde *f*.

i·ci·cle ['aisikl] Eiszapfen *m*.

i·ci·ness ['aisinis] eisige Kälte *f*.

ic·ing ['aisiŋ] Zuckerguß *m*; Vereisung *f*; ‿ **sug·ar** Puderzucker *m*.

i·con ['aikɔn] Ikone *f*.

i·con·o·clast [ai'kɔnəuklæst] Bilderstürmer *m*.

i·cy ⃞ ['aisi] eisig (*a. fig.*); vereist.

I'd [aid] = *I had*; *I would*.

i·de·a [ai'diə] Idee *f*; Begriff *m*, Vorstellung *f*; Gedanke *m*; Meinung *f*; Ahnung *f*; Plan *m*; *form an* ‿ *of* sich e-e Vorstellung machen von; **i'de·al 1.** ⃞ ideell, eingebildet; Gedanken..., Ideen...; vorbildlich, ideal; **2.** Musterbild *n*, Ideal *n*; **i'de·al·ism** Idealismus *m*; **i'de·al·ist** Idealist(in); **i·de·al'is·tic** (‿ally) idealistisch; **i'de·al·ize** [‿laiz] idealisieren.

i·den·ti·cal ⃞ [ai'dentikəl] iden-

tisch, gleich(bedeutend); **i'den·ti·cal·ness** = *identity*; **i·den·ti·fi·'ca·tion** Identifizierung *f*; Ausweis *m*; ‿ *card* = *identity card*; ‿ *mark mot.* Kennzeichen *n*; **i'den·ti·fy** [‿fai] identifizieren; gleichsetzen (*with* mit *od. dat.*); (die Persönlichkeit *j-s*, die Gleichheit *od.* Art *e-r Sache*) feststellen; ausweisen; erkennen; **i'den·ti·kit** [‿kit] Phantombild *m*; **i'den·ti·ty** Identität *f*; Persönlichkeit *f*, Eigenart *f*; ‿ *card* Personalausweis *m*, Kennkarte *f*; ‿ *disc* ✗ Erkennungsmarke *f*.

id·e·o·gram ['idiəugræm], **'id·e·o·graph** ['‿grɑːf] *gr.* Schriftzeichen *n*, Ideogramm *n*.

id·e·o·log·i·cal ⃞ [aidiə'lɔdʒikl] ideologisch; **id·e·ol·o·gy** [‿'ɔlədʒi] Ideologie *f*; Begriffslehre *f*.

ides [aidz] *pl. die* Iden *pl.*

id·i·o·cy ['idiəsi] Schwach-, Blödsinn *m*.

id·i·om ['idiəm] Idiom *n*; Mundart *f*; Spracheigentümlichkeit *f*; idiomatische Wendung *f*, Redewendung *f*; **id·i·o·mat·ic** [‿'mætik] (‿ally) idiomatisch; spracheigentümlich.

id·i·o·syn·cra·sy [idiə'siŋkrəsi] Idiosynkrasie *f*; persönliche Eigenart *f*.

id·i·ot ['idiət] Idiot(in), Schwach-, Blödsinnige *m*, *f*; **id·i·ot·ic** [idi-'ɔtik] (‿ally) blödsinnig; idiotisch.

i·dle ['aidl] **1.** ⃞ müßig; untätig; unbenutzt; träg, faul; unnütz, zwecklos; nichtig, eitel; tot (*Kapital*); ‿ *hours pl.* Mußestunden *f/pl.*; **2.** *v/t. mst* ‿ *away* vertrödeln, müßig hinbringen; *v/i.* faulenzen; ⊕ leerlaufen; **'i·dle·ness** Muße *f*; Trägheit *f*; Nichtigkeit *f*; **'i·dler** Müßiggänger(in).

i·dol ['aidl] Idol *n*, Götzenbild *n*; *fig.* Abgott *m*; **i·dol·a·ter** [ai'dɔlətə] Götzendiener *m*; blinder Verehrer *m*; **i'dol·a·tress** Götzendienerin *f etc.*; **i'dol·a·trous** ⃞ abgöttisch; **i'dol·a·try** Abgötterei *f*, Götzendienst *m*; Vergötterung *f*; **i·dol·ize** ['aidəulaiz] vergöttern.

i·dyll ['idil] Idyll(e *f*) *n*; **i·dyl·lic** [ai'dilik] (‿ally) idyllisch.

if [if] **1.** wenn, falls; ob; **2.** Wenn *n*; **'if·fy** *Am.* F zweifelhaft.

imaginable

ig·loo ['iglu:] Iɡlu *m*, Schneehütte *f*.

ig·ne·ous ['igniəs] feurig.

ig·nit·a·ble [ig'naitəbl] entzündbar; **ig'nite** (sich) entzünden; zünden; ⚡ erhitzen; **ig·ni·tion** [ig'niʃən] Entzündung *f*; *mot.* Zündung *f*; ⚡ Erhitzung *f*; ∿ **key** *mot.* Zündschlüssel *m*.

ig·no·ble □ [ig'nəubl] unedel; niedrig, gemein.

ig·no·min·i·ous □ [ignəu'miniəs] schändlich, schimpflich; **ig·no·min·y** ['ignəmini] Schmach *f*, Schande *f*.

ig·no·ra·mus F [ignə'reiməs] Ignorant(in); Nichtskönner(in); **'ig·no·rance** Unwissenheit *f*; Unkenntnis *f*; **'ig·no·rant** unwissend; unkundig (*of gen.*); **ig·nore** [ig'nɔ:] ignorieren, nicht beachten, übersehen; ⚖ verwerfen.

i·gua·na *zo.* [i'gwɑ:nə] Leguan *m*.

i·kon ['aikɔn] = *icon.*

i·lex ♀ ['aileks] Stechpalme *f*.

Il·i·ad ['iliəd] Ilias *f Homers.*

ill [il] **1.** *adj. u. adv.* übel, böse; schlimm, schlecht; krank; *adv.* schwerlich, mit Mühe, kaum; **fall** ∿, **be taken** ∿ krank werden; *s. ease*; **2.** Übel *n*; Übles *n*, Böses *n*. **I'll** [ail] = *I will.*

ill...: '∿-'ad'vised schlecht beraten; unbesonnen, unklug; '∿-af'fect·ed übelgesinnt (*to dat.*); '∿-'bred ungebildet, ungezogen, unhöflich; ∿ **breed·ing** schlechtes Benehmen *n*; '∿-con'di·tioned in schlechtem Zustand; bösartig; '∿-dis-'posed übelgesinnt (*to dat.*).

il·le·gal □ [i'li:gəl] ungesetzlich, illegal; **il·le·gal·i·ty** [ili:'gæliti] Ungesetzlichkeit *f*.

il·leg·i·ble □ [i'ledʒəbl] unleserlich.

il·le·git·i·ma·cy [ili'dʒitiməsi] Unrechtmäßigkeit *f*; Unehelichkeit *f*; **il·le'git·i·mate** □ [∿mit] illegitim; unrechtmäßig; unlogisch; unehelich.

ill...: '∿-'fat·ed unglücklich; '∿--'fa·vo(u)red häßlich; '∿-'got·ten unrechtmäßig erworben; '∿-'hu·mo(u)red übellaunig.

il·lib·er·al □ [i'libərəl] engstirnig; intolerant; knauserig; **il·lib·er·al·i·ty** [∿'ræliti] Engstirnigkeit *f etc.*

il·lic·it □ [i'lisit] unerlaubt; ∿ **trade** Schwarzhandel *m*.

il·lim·it·a·ble □ [i'limitəbl] unbegrenzbar, grenzenlos.

il·lit·er·a·cy [i'litərəsi] Unbildung *f*; Analphabetentum *n*; **il'lit·er·ate** [∿rit] **1.** ungelehrt, ungebildet; **2.** Analphabet(in).

ill...: '∿-'judged unklug, unvernünftig; '∿-'man·nered ungezogen; mit schlechten Umgangsformen; '∿-'na·tured □ boshaft, bösartig.

ill·ness ['ilnis] Krankheit *f*.

il·log·i·cal □ [i'lɔdʒikəl] unlogisch.

ill...: ∿-o·mened ['il'əumend] von schlechten Vorzeichen begleitet; Unglücks...; '∿-'starred unglücklich; '∿-'tem·pered schlecht gelaunt; '∿-'timed ungelegen, zur Unzeit (geschehend *etc.*); '∿-'treat mißhandeln.

il·lume *poet.* [i'lju:m] erleuchten (*a. fig.*).

il·lu·mi·nant [i'lju:minənt] **1.** (er-)leuchtend; **2.** Beleuchtungskörper *m*; **il'lu·mi·nate** [∿neit] be-, erleuchten (*a. fig.*); erläutern; aufklären; *festlich* illuminieren; bunt ausmalen; ∿d *advertising* Lichtreklame *f*; **il'lu·mi·nat·ing** Leucht...; *fig.* aufschlußreich; **il·lu·mi·na·tion** Erleuchtung *f*; Illumination *f*; Erläuterung *f*; Aufklärung *f*; **il'lu·mi·na·tive** [∿nətiv] erleuchtend; Leucht...; **il-'lu·mi·na·tor** Erleuchter *m*; **il'lu·mine** = *illuminate.*

ill-use ['il'ju:z] mißhandeln.

il·lu·sion [i'lu:ʒən] Illusion *f*, Täuschung *f*, Einbildung *f*; **il'lu·sive** □ [∿siv], **il'lu·so·ry** □ [∿səri] illusorisch, täuschend.

il·lus·trate ['iləstreit] illustrieren; erläutern; veranschaulichen; bebildern; **il·lus'tra·tion** Erläuterung *f*; Illustration *f*; **'il·lus·tra·tive** □ erläuternd; *be* ∿ *of* erläutern; **'il·lus·tra·tor** Erläuterer *m*; Illustrator *m*.

il·lus·tri·ous □ [i'lʌstriəs] berühmt.

ill will ['il'wil] Feindschaft *f*.

I'm [aim] = *I am.*

im·age ['imidʒ] **1.** Bild *n* (*a. rhet.*); Standbild *n*; Ebenbild *n*; Vorstellung *f*; **2.** abbilden; widerspiegeln; anschaulich schildern; **'im·age·ry** Bilder *n/pl.*; Bildersprache *f*, Metaphorik *f*.

im·ag·i·na·ble □ [i'mædʒinəbl]

denkbar; im·ag·i·nar·y eingebildet, imaginär; im·ag·i·na·tion [ˌˈneiʃən] *schöpferische* Einbildung (-skraft) *f*, Phantasie *f*, Vorstellungskraft *f*, Ideenreichtum *m*; im·ag·i·na·tive □ [ˌnətiv] Einbildungs...; ideen-, einfallsreich; schöpferisch; im·ag·ine sich *et.* einbilden, sich *et.* vorstellen, sich *et.* denken.

im·bal·ance [im'bæləns] Unausgeglichenheit *f* (*bsd. der Zahlungsbilanz*).

im·be·cile □ ['imbisi:l] 1. schwachsinnig; 2. Schwachsinnige *m, f*; im·be·cil·i·ty [ˌ'siliti] Schwachsinn *m*.

im·bed [im'bed] = *embed*.

im·bibe [im'baib] einsaugen; *fig.* sich zu eigen machen.

im·bro·glio [im'brəuliəu] Verwirrung *f*.

im·brue [im'bru:] beflecken, benetzen (*in, with* mit).

im·bue [im'bju:] (durch)tränken; tief färben; *fig.* erfüllen.

im·i·ta·ble ['imitəbl] nachahmbar; im·i·tate ['ˌteit] nachahmen; nachbilden; ⊕ imitieren; im·i'ta·tion Nachahmung *f*; ⊕ Imitation *f*; *attr.* künstlich, Kunst...; ~ *leather* Kunstleder *n*; im·i·ta·tive □ ['ˌtə-tiv] nachahmend (*of acc.*); ~ *word* lautmalendes Wort *n*; im·i·ta·tor ['ˌteitə] Nachahmer *m*.

im·mac·u·late □ [i'mækjulit] unbefleckt, rein; fehlerlos.

im·ma·nent ['imənənt] immanent, innewohnend.

im·ma·te·ri·al □ [imə'tiəriəl] unkörperlich; unwesentlich (*to* für).

im·ma·ture [imə'tjuə] unreif, unentwickelt; im·ma'tu·ri·ty Unreife *f*.

im·meas·ur·a·ble □ [i'meʒərəbl] unermeßlich.

im·me·di·ate □ [i'mi:djət] unmittelbar; unverzüglich, sofortig; im'me·di·ate·ly 1. *adv.* sofort; 2. *cj.* gleich nachdem.

im·me·mo·ri·al □ [imi'mɔ:riəl] un(vor)denklich; *from time* ~ seit unvordenklichen Zeiten.

im·mense □ [i'mens] unermeßlich; ungeheuer, gewaltig; *sl.* fabelhaft; im'men·si·ty Unermeßlichkeit *f*.

im·merse [i'mə:s] (ein-, unter-) tauchen; ~ *o.s. in fig.* sich versenken

od. vertiefen in (*acc.*); ~*d in* vertieft in *ein Buch*; verwickelt in *Schulden etc.*; im'mer·sion (Ein-, Unter-) Tauchen *n*; Einsinken *n*; *fig.* Versenkung *f*; ~ *heater* Heizspirale *f e-s Boilers*; Tauchsieder *m*.

im·mi·grant ['imigrənt] Einwanderer *m*; im·mi·grate ['ˌgreit] *v/i.* einwandern; *v/t.* ansiedeln (*into* in *dat.*); im·mi'gra·tion Einwanderung *f*.

im·mi·nence ['iminəns] Bevorstehen *n*, Drohen *n*; 'im·mi·nent □ bevorstehend, drohend.

im·mit·i·ga·ble □ [i'mitigəbl] nicht zu besänftigen(d); unerbittlich.

im·mo·bile [i'məubail] unbeweglich; im·mo·bil·i·ty [ˌ'biliti] Unbeweglichkeit *f*; im'mo·bi·lize [ˌbilaiz] unbeweglich machen; festlegen; *Geld* aus dem Verkehr ziehen.

im·mod·er·ate □ [i'mɔdərit] übermäßig, maßlos; im'mod·er·ate·ness Maßlosigkeit *f*.

im·mod·est □ [i'mɔdist] unbescheiden; unanständig; im'mod·es·ty Unbescheidenheit *f*; Unanständigkeit *f*.

im·mo·late ['iməuleit] opfern; im·mo'la·tion Opferung *f*, Opfer *n*.

im·mor·al □ [i'mɔrəl] unmoralisch, unsittlich; im·mo·ral·i·ty [imə'ræliti] Unsittlichkeit *f*.

im·mor·tal [i'mɔ:tl] 1. □ unsterblich; 2. Unsterbliche *m, f*; im·mor·tal·i·ty [ˌ'tæliti] Unsterblichkeit *f*; im'mor·tal·ize [ˌtəlaiz] unsterblich machen.

im·mov·a·ble [i'mu:vəbl] 1. □ unbeweglich; unerschütterlich; 2. ~*s pl.* Immobilien *pl.*

im·mune [i'mju:n] ⚕ *u. fig.* (*from*) immun, gefeit (gegen); unempfänglich (für); frei (von); im'mu·ni·ty Immunität *f*, Freiheit *f* (*from* von *Steuern etc.*); Unempfänglichkeit *f* (*from* für); Vorrecht *n*; im·mu·nize ['ˌnaiz] immunisieren.

im·mure [i'mjuə] einkerkern.

im·mu·ta·bil·i·ty [imju:tə'biliti] Unveränderlichkeit *f*; im'mu·ta·ble □ unveränderlich.

imp [imp] Teufelchen *n*; Kobold *m*; Schelm *m*, Schlingel *m*.

im·pact ['impækt] (Zs.-)Stoß *m*; Anprall *m*; Einwirkung *f*; *Geschoß*-Aufschlag *m*.

im·pair [im'pɛə] schwächen; (ver-) mindern; beeinträchtigen.

im·pale [im'peil] pfählen; aufspießen.

im·pal·pa·ble □ [im'pælpəbl] unfühlbar; *fig.* unfaßbar; sehr fein.

im·pan·el [im'pænl] = *empanel.*

im·part [im'pɑːt] verleihen; weitergeben; vermitteln; mitteilen.

im·par·tial □ [im'pɑːʃəl] unparteiisch; **im·par·ti·al·i·ty** ['ˌʃiˈæliti] Unparteilichkeit *f*, Objektivität *f*.

im·pass·a·ble □ [im'pɑːsəbl] ungangbar, unpassierbar.

im·passe [æm'pɑːs] Sackgasse *f (a. fig.)*; *fig.* toter Punkt *m*.

im·pas·si·ble □ [im'pæsibl] unempfindlich, gefühllos (*to* gegen).

im·pas·sion [im'pæʃən] leidenschaftlich bewegen *od.* erregen; **im'pas·sioned** leidenschaftlich.

im·pas·sive □ [im'pæsiv] unempfindlich; teilnahmslos; heiter; **im·'pas·sive·ness** Unempfindlichkeit *f*.

im·pa·tience [im'peiʃəns] Ungeduld *f*; Unduldsamkeit *f*; **im'pa·tient** □ ungeduldig (*at, of* über *acc.*); **be** ~ *of s.th.* et. nicht ertragen können; ~ *for* begierig nach.

im·peach [im'piːtʃ] anklagen, beschuldigen (*of, with gen.*); zur Verantwortung ziehen; anfechten, anzweifeln; **im'peach·a·ble** anklagbar; anfechtbar; **im'peach·ment** Anzweiflung *f*; Anfechtung *f*; öffentliche Anklage *f*.

im·pec·ca·bil·i·ty [impekə'biliti] Sündlosigkeit *f*; Makellosigkeit *f*; **im'pec·ca·ble** □ sündlos; makellos, einwandfrei.

im·pe·cu·ni·ous [impi'kjuːnjəs] ohne Geld, mittellos.

im·pede [im'piːd] (ver)hindern.

im·ped·i·ment [im'pedimənt] Hindernis *n (to* für); ~ *in one's speech* Sprachfehler *m*; **im·ped·i·men·ta** ✕ [ˌ'mentə] *pl.* Gepäck *n*, Troß *m*.

im·pel [im'pel] (an)treiben; **im·'pel·lent 1.** treibend; **2.** Triebkraft *f*.

im·pend [im'pend] hängen, schweben (*over* über *dat.*); bevorstehen, drohen; **im'pend·ence** drohende Nähe *f*; **im'pend·ent**, **im'pend·ing** nahe (bevorstehend); drohend.

im·pen·e·tra·bil·i·ty [impenitrə'biliti] Undurchdringlichkeit *f (a. fig.)*;

im·pen·e·tra·ble □ undurchdringlich (*to, by* für); *fig.* unergründlich; *fig.* unzugänglich (*to dat.*).

im·pen·i·tence [im'penitəns] Unbußfertigkeit *f*, Verstocktheit *f*; **im'pen·i·tent** □ unbußfertig, verstockt.

im·per·a·tive [im'perətiv] **1.** □ notwendig, dringend, unbedingt erforderlich; befehlend; gebieterisch; *gr.* imperativisch; ~ *mood* = **2.** *gr.* Imperativ *m*.

im·per·cep·ti·ble □ [impə'septəbl] unmerklich.

im·per·fect [im'pəːfikt] **1.** □ unvollkommen; unvollständig; unvollendet; ~ *tense* = **2.** *gr.* Imperfekt *n*; **im·per·fec·tion** [ˌpə'fekʃən] Unvollkommenheit *f*; *fig.* Schwäche *f*.

im·pe·ri·al [im'piəriəl] **1.** □ kaiserlich; Kaiser..., Reichs...; gebietend; großartig; **2.** Fliege *f (Bart*); Imperialpapier *n*; **im'pe·ri·al·ism** Imperialismus *m*, Weltmachtpolitik *f*; **im'pe·ri·al·ist** Imperialist *m*, Anhänger *m* der Weltmachtpolitik; **im·pe·ri·al'is·tic** imperialistisch.

im·per·il [im'peril] gefährden.

im·pe·ri·ous □ [im'piəriəs] gebieterisch; anmaßend; dringend.

im·per·ish·a·ble □ [im'periʃəbl] unvergänglich.

im·per·ma·nent [im'pəːmənənt] unbeständig.

im·per·me·a·ble □ [im'pəːmjəbl] undurchdringlich, -lässig.

im·per·son·al □ [im'pəːsnl] unpersönlich; **im·per·son·al·i·ty** [ˌsə'næliti] Unpersönlichkeit *f*.

im·per·son·ate [im'pəːsəneit] verkörpern; *thea.* darstellen; **im·per·son'a·tion** Verkörperung *f*; *thea.* Darstellung *f*.

im·per·ti·nence [im'pəːtinəns] Impertinenz *f*, Unverschämtheit *f*, Ungehörigkeit *f*; Nebensächlichkeit *f*; **im'per·ti·nent** □ impertinent, unverschämt; ungezogen, frech; ungehörig; ♫♫ nicht zur Sache gehörig; nebensächlich.

im·per·turb·a·bil·i·ty ['impəːtəːbə-'biliti] Unerschütterlichkeit *f*; **im·per'turb·a·ble** □ unerschütterlich.

im·per·vi·ous □ [im'pəːvjəs] unzugänglich (*to* für) (*a. fig.*); undurchlässig.

im·pe·ti·go ♫ [impi'taigəu] Impetigo *m*, Blasengrind *m*.

im·pet·u·os·i·ty [impetju'ɔsiti] Ungestüm *m*, *n*; **im'pet·u·ous** □ ungestüm, heftig; **im·pe·tus** ['impitəs] Antrieb *m*, Anstoß *m* (*a. fig.*).

im·pi·e·ty [im'paiəti] Gottlosigkeit *f*; Mangel *m* an Ehrfurcht.

im·pinge [im'pindʒ] (ver)stoßen (*on, upon, against* gegen); ~ *on* übergreifen auf (*acc.*); **im'pinge·ment** Stoß *m*, Anprall *m* (*on, upon* gegen); *fig.* Verstoß *m* (gegen).

im·pi·ous □ ['impiəs] gottlos; pietätlos; frevelhaft. [misch.\
imp·ish □ ['impiʃ] boshaft; schel-/
im·pla·ca·bil·i·ty [implækə'biliti] Unversöhnlichkeit *f*; **im'pla·ca·ble** □ unversöhnlich, unerbittlich.

im·plant [im'plɑːnt] *mst fig.* einpflanzen (*in in acc.*).

im·plau·si·ble [im'plɔːzəbl] unglaubwürdig.

im·ple·ment 1. ['implimənt] Werkzeug *n*; Gerät *n*; **2.** ['~ment] bewerkstelligen; ausführen; verwirklichen; **im·ple·men'ta·tion** [~men-'teiʃən] Ausführung *f*; Verwirklichung *f*.

im·pli·cate ['implikeit] verwickeln, hineinziehen (*in in acc.*); mit einbegreifen, in sich schließen; **im·pli'ca·tion** Verwick(e)lung *f*; *still-schweigende* Folgerung *f*; *what are the* ~*s?* was soll damit gesagt werden?

im·plic·it □ [im'plisit] (stillschweigend) mit eingeschlossen *od.* sich ergebend; unausgesprochen; verblümt; unbedingt, blind (*Glaube etc.*); **im'plic·it·ly** implizite, stillschweigend; unbedingt.

im·plied □ [im'plaid] (stillschweigend) mit inbegriffen; angedeutet.

im·plore [im'plɔː] (an-, er)flehen; flehentlich bitten; **im'plor·ing** □ [~riŋ] flehentlich.

im·ply [im'plai] einschließen, enthalten, in sich schließen; besagen, bedeuten; andeuten; unterstellen; *do you* ~ *that...?* wollen Sie damit sagen, daß ...?

im·po·lite □ [impə'lait] unhöflich.

im·pol·i·tic □ [im'pɔlitik] unpolitisch, unklug.

im·pon·der·a·ble [im'pɔndərəbl] **1.** unwägbar; **2.** ~*s pl.* unwägbare Dinge *n/pl.*, Imponderabilien *n/pl.*

im·port 1. ['impɔːt] Bedeutung *f*,

Sinn *m*; Wichtigkeit *f*; ✝ Einfuhr *f*; ~*s pl.* Einfuhrwaren *f pl.*; ~ *duty* Einfuhrzoll *m*; **2.** [im'pɔːt] *Waren* einführen; bedeuten; besagen; *j.* betreffen, für *j.* wichtig sein; **im'por·tance** Wichtigkeit *f*; Bedeutung *f*; Einfluß *m*; **im'por·tant** □ wichtig; bedeutend; wichtigtuerisch; **im·por·ta·tion** [~'teiʃən] Einfuhr *f*; Einfuhrwaren *f pl.*; **im'port·er** Importeur *m*.

im·por·tu·nate □ [im'pɔːtjunit] lästig, zudringlich; **im'por·tune** [~tjuːn] dringend bitten, bestürmen; belästigen; **im·por'tu·ni·ty** Zudringlichkeit *f*.

im·pose [im'pəuz] *v/t.* auf(er)legen, aufbürden, aufdrängen (*on, upon dat.*); *v/i.* ~ *upon j-m* imponieren; *j.* täuschen; *j-s Güte etc.* mißbrauchen; **im'pos·ing** □ imponierend, eindrucksvoll; **im·po·si·tion** [impə'ziʃən] Auflegung *f der Hände*; Beilegung *f e-s Namens*; Auflage *f*, Steuer *f*; *Schule:* Strafarbeit *f*; Betrügerei *f*.

im·pos·si·bil·i·ty [impɔsə'biliti] Unmöglichkeit *f*; **im'pos·si·ble** □ unmöglich.

im·post ['impəust] Abgabe *f*, Steuer *f*; **im·pos·tor** [im'pɔstə] Betrüger *m*; **im'pos·ture** [~tʃə] Betrug *m*.

im·po·tence ['impətəns] Unfähigkeit *f*; Machtlosigkeit *f*; *physiol.* Impotenz *f*; **im'po·tent** unvermögend, machtlos, schwach; impotent.

im·pound [im'paund] beschlagnahmen; *Vieh* einpferchen.

im·pov·er·ish [im'pɔvəriʃ] arm machen; *Boden* auslaugen.

im·prac·ti·ca·bil·i·ty [impræktikə-'biliti] Undurchführbarkeit *f*; Unwegsamkeit *f*; **im'prac·ti·ca·ble** □ undurchführbar; unwegsam.

im·prac·ti·cal [im'præktikəl] unpraktisch; theoretisch; unnütz.

im·pre·cate ['imprikeit] *Böses* herabwünschen (*upon* auf *acc.*); **im·pre'ca·tion** Verwünschung *f*; **im·pre·ca·to·ry** ['~keitəri] Verwünschungs...

im·preg·na·bil·i·ty [impregnə'biliti] Unüberwindlichkeit *f*; **im'preg·na·ble** □ uneinnehmbar; unüberwindlich; **im·preg·nate 1.** ['~neit] schwängern; ⚲ befruchten; 🜨 sättigen, tränken (*a. fig.*); *fig.* durchdringen; ⊕ imprägnieren; **2.** [im-'pregnit] geschwängert; durchtränkt; **im·preg·na·tion** [₍neiʃən] Schwängerung *f*; Befruchtung *f*; Sättigung *f*; Imprägnierung *f*.

im·pre·sa·ri·o [impre'saːriəu] Impresario *m*, Manager *m*.

im·pre·scrip·ti·ble [impris'kriptəbl] unverjährbar; unveräußerlich.

im·press 1. ['impres] (Ab-, Ein-) Druck *m*; *fig.* Stempel *m*; **2.** [im-'pres] eindrücken, prägen (*on s.th. od. s.th. with* auf *acc.*); *Kraft etc.* übertragen (*on, upon* auf *acc.*); *Gedanken etc.* aufzwingen, einprägen (*on dat.*); Eindruck machen auf *j.*, beeindrucken; *j-m* imponieren; ₍ *s.o. with s.th.* j. mit et. erfüllen; ⚓ *Matrosen* (zum Dienst) pressen; **im-'press·i·ble** eindrucksfähig; **im-'pres·sion** [₍ʃən] Eindruck *m* (*a. fig.*); *typ.* Abdruck *m*, Abzug *m*; Auflage *f*; *be under the* ₍ *that* den Eindruck haben, daß; **im'pres·sion·a·ble** [₍ʃnəbl] empfänglich, leicht zu beeindrucken(d), eindrucksfähig; **im'pres·sion·ism** Impressionismus *m*; **im'pres·sion·ist** Impressionist *m*; **im'pres·sion·is·tic** impressionistisch; **im'pres·sive** □ [₍siv] eindrucksvoll; **im-'press·ment** ⚓ Pressen *n*.

im·print 1. [im'print] aufdrücken, prägen (*on* auf *acc.*); *fig.* einprägen (*on, in dat.*); **2.** ['imprint] Eindruck *m*; Stempel *m* (*a. fig.*); *typ.* Druckvermerk *m*.

im·pris·on [im'prizn] ins Gefängnis werfen, einsperren, -kerkern; **im-'pris·on·ment** Einkerkerung *f*; Haft *f*; Gefängnis(strafe *f*) *n*.

im·prob·a·bil·i·ty [imprɔbə'biliti] Unwahrscheinlichkeit *f*; **im'prob·a·ble** □ unwahrscheinlich.

im·pro·bi·ty [im'prəubiti] Unredlichkeit *f*, Unehrlichkeit *f*.

im·promp·tu [im'prɔmptjuː] **1.** ♩ Impromptu *n*; **2.** aus dem Stegreif.

im·prop·er □ [im'prɔpə] ungeeignet, unpassend; unzutreffend, falsch; unanständig; ₍ *fraction* ₳ unechter Bruch *m*; **im·pro·pri·e·ty** [imprə'praiəti] Ungeeignetheit *f*; Ungehörigkeit *f*; Unrichtigkeit *f*; Unanständigkeit *f*.

im·prov·a·ble □ [im'pruːvəbl] verbesserungsfähig; anbaufähig(*Land*).

im·prove [im'pruːv] *v/t.* verbessern; veredeln; *Gelegenheit etc.* aus-, benutzen; *v/i.* sich (ver)bessern, Fortschritte machen; ₍ *upon* vervollkommnen; **im'prove·ment** Verbesserung *f*, Vervollkommnung *f*; (Nutz)Anwendung *f*; Ausnutzung *f*; Fortschritt *m* (*on, upon* gegenüber *dat.*); **im'prov·er** Verbesserer *m*; Volontär *m*.

im·prov·i·dence [im'prɔvidəns] Unbedachtsamkeit *f*; **im'prov·i·dent** □ unbedachtsam; leichtsinnig.

im·pro·vi·sa·tion [imprəvai'zeiʃən] Improvisation *f*; **im·pro·vise** ['₍vaiz] improvisieren; '**im·pro·vised** behelfsmäßig; Behelfs...

im·pru·dence [im'pruːdəns] Unklugheit *f*; **im'pru·dent** □ unklug.

im·pu·dence ['impjudəns] Unverschämtheit *f*, Frechheit *f*; '**im·pu·dent** □ unverschämt, frech.

im·pugn [im'pjuːn] anfechten, bestreiten, bezweifeln; **im'pugn·a·ble** anfechtbar.

im·pulse ['impʌls], **im'pul·sion** Impuls *m*, (An)Stoß *m*; *fig.* (An-) Trieb *m*; **im'pul·sive** □ (an)treibend; *fig.* impulsiv, leicht erregbar; rasch (handelnd); **im'pul·sive·ness** Impulsivität *f*.

im·pu·ni·ty [im'pjuːniti] Straflosigkeit *f*; *with* ₍ ungestraft.

im·pure □ [im'pjuə] unrein (*a. fig.*); unkeusch; **im'pu·ri·ty** [₍riti] Unreinheit *f*; Unkeuschheit *f*.

im·put·a·ble [im'pjuːtəbl] zuzuschreiben(d), beizumessen(d); **im·pu·ta·tion** [₍'teiʃən] Beschuldigung *f*; **im'pute** zurechnen, beimessen; zur Last legen.

in [in] **1.** *prp. allg.* in (*dat.*); *engS.*: (₍ *the morning, a wound* ₍ *the head,* ₍ *number,* ₍ *size,* ₍ *itself, professor* ₍ *the university*) an (*dat.*); (₍ *a field,* ₍ *the street,* ₍ *the country,* ₍ *search of, blind* ₍ *one eye,* ₍ *English*) auf (*dat.*); (₍ *this manner, trust* ₍ *s.o.*) auf (*acc.*); (*bust* ₍ *marble, coat* ₍ *velvet*) aus; (₍ *Shakespeare,* ₍ *the daytime,* ₍ *crossing the road*) bei; (*engaged* ₍ *reading, written* ₍ *pencil, a word,* ₍ *a few words*) mit; (₍ *my opinion,* ₍ *all probability*) nach; (*rejoice* ₍ *s.th.*) über (*acc.*); (₍ *the circumstances,* ₍ *the reign of,* ₍ *ten*) unter (*dat.*); (*cry out* ₍ *alarm*) vor (*dat.*); (*grouped* ₍ *tens, speak* ₍ *reply,* ₍ *s.o.'s defence,*

~ *excuse*, ~ *honour of*) zu; ~ *1969* (im Jahr) 1969; *two days* ~ *three* an zwei von drei Tagen; *there is nothing* ~ *it* es ist nichts daran; F es kommt nichts dabei heraus; *it is not* ~ *her* es liegt ihr nicht; *he hasn't it* ~ *him* er hat nicht das Zeug dazu; ~ *that* ... insofern als, weil; *bei Zeitwörtern der Bewegung u. Veränderung*: in (*acc.*); **2.** *adv.* drin(nen); herein; hinein; *bei Zeitwörtern oft* ein...; *be* ~ drin(nen) sein (*im Zimmer, Haus*); d(a)ran sein (*an der Macht, am Spiel*); *be* ~ *for et.* zu erwarten haben, dran sein bei; *e-e Prüfung etc.* vor sich haben; *be well* ~ *with* F sich gut mit *j-m* stehen; **3.** *adj.* hereinkommend; Innen...; F in, in Mode; **4.** *su.*: *the* ~s *pl. parl.* die Regierungspartei; *the* ~s *and outs pl.* alle Winkel u. Ecken *pl.*; alle Einzelheiten *f/pl.*

in·a·bil·i·ty [inə'biliti] Unfähigkeit *f*, Unvermögen *n*.

in·ac·ces·si·bil·i·ty ['inæksesə'biliti] Unzugänglichkeit *f*; **in·ac'ces·si·ble** □ unzugänglich.

in·ac·cu·ra·cy [in'ækjurəsi] Ungenauigkeit *f*; **in·ac·cu·rate** □ [‿rit] ungenau; unrichtig.

in·ac·tion [in'ækʃən] Untätigkeit *f*.

in·ac·tive □ [in'æktiv] untätig, ✞ lustlos; ♔ unwirksam; **in·ac'tiv·i·ty** Untätig-, Lustlosigkeit *f*.

in·ad·e·qua·cy [in'ædikwəsi] Unangemessenheit *f*; Unzulänglichkeit *f*; **in'ad·e·quate** □ [‿kwit] unangemessen; unzulänglich.

in·ad·mis·si·bil·i·ty ['inədmisə'biliti] Unzulässigkeit *f*; **in·ad'mis·si·ble** □ unzulässig.

in·ad·vert·ence, **in·ad·vert·en·cy** [inəd'və:təns(i)] Unachtsamkeit *f*; Versehen *n*; **in·ad'vert·ent** □ unachtsam; unbeabsichtigt, versehentlich; ‿ly *a.* aus Versehen.

in·ad·vis·a·ble □ [inəd'vaizəbl] nicht ratsam, nicht empfehlenswert.

in·al·ien·a·ble □ [in'eiljənəbl] unveräußerlich.

in·al·ter·a·ble □ [in'ɔ:ltərəbl] unveränderlich.

in·am·o·ra·ta *f* [inæmə'rɑːtə] Geliebte *f*; **in·am·o'ra·to** *m* [‿təu] Geliebte *m*, Liebhaber *m*.

in·ane □ [i'nein] *mst fig.* leer; geistlos; albern; fad; unsinnig.

in·an·i·mate □ [in'ænimit] unbe-

seelt, leblos; *fig.* unbelebt; geistlos, langweilig.

in·a·ni·tion ♫ [inə'niʃən] Entkräftung *f*.

in·an·i·ty [i'næniti] Leere *f*; Geistlosigkeit *f etc.* (*s. inane*).

in·ap·pli·ca·bil·i·ty ['inæplikə'biliti] Unanwendbarkeit *f*; **in'ap·pli·ca·ble** unanwendbar (*to* auf *acc.*); nicht zu- *od.* betreffend.

in·ap·po·site □ [in'æpəzit] unpassend.

in·ap·pre·ci·a·ble □ [inə'pri:ʃəbl] unmerklich; unbedeutend.

in·ap·pre·hen·si·ble □ [inæpri-'hensəbl] unbegreiflich, unfaßbar.

in·ap·proach·a·ble [inə'prəutʃəbl] unnahbar, unzugänglich.

in·ap·pro·pri·ate □ [inə'prəupriit] unangebracht, unpassend.

in·apt □ [in'æpt] ungeeignet, untauglich; ungeschickt; unpassend; **in'apt·i·tude** [‿titjuːd], **in'apt·ness** Ungeeignetheit *f*; Ungeschicktheit *f etc.*

in·ar·tic·u·late □ [inɑː'tikjulit] undeutlich; schwer zu verstehen(d); undeutlich sprechend; *zo.* ungegliedert; **in·ar'tic·u·late·ness** Undeutlichkeit *f der Aussprache.*

in·as·much [inəz'mʌtʃ]: ~ *as* da, weil; insofern als.

in·at·ten·tion [inə'tenʃən] Unaufmerksamkeit *f*; **in·at'ten·tive** □ [‿tiv] unaufmerksam (*to* gegen).

in·au·di·ble □ [in'ɔ:dəbl] unhörbar.

in·au·gu·ral [i'nɔ:gjurəl] **1.** Antritts...; ~ *lecture* Antrittsvorlesung *f*; **2.** Antrittsrede *f*; **in'au·gu·rate** [‿reit] (feierlich) einführen, einweihen; beginnen; **in·au·gu'ra·tion** Einführung *f*, Einweihung *f*; ♀ *Day Am.* Amtseinführung *f* des neugewählten Präsidenten der USA.

in·aus·pi·cious □ [inɔːs'piʃəs] ungünstig, unheilvoll.

in·board ⚓ ['inbɔːd] (b)innenbords.

in·born ['in'bɔːn] angeboren.

in·bred ['in'bred] angeboren; durch Inzucht erzeugt.

in·breed·ing ['in'briːdiŋ] Inzucht *f*.

in·cal·cu·la·ble □ [in'kælkjuləbl] unberechenbar; unzählig.

in·can·des·cence ['inkæn'desns] Weißglühen *n*, -glut *f*; **'in·can·'des·cent** weißglühend; ~ *light* Glühlicht *n*; ~ *mantle* Glühstrumpf *m.*

in·can·ta·tion [inkæn'teiʃən] Beschwörung *f;* Zauberformel *f.*

in·ca·pa·bil·i·ty [inkeipə'biliti] Unfähigkeit *f,* Untüchtigkeit *f;* Untauglichkeit *f;* **in'ca·pa·ble** □ unfähig, ungeeignet *(of* zu); hilflos *(Betrunkener);* **in·ca·pac·i·tate** [inkə'pæsiteit] unfähig machen *(for, from* zu); außer Gefecht setzen; (ver)hindern; **in·ca'pac·i·ty** Unfähigkeit *f (for* für, zu).

in·car·cer·ate [in'kɑːsəreit] einkerkern; **in·car·cer'a·tion** Einkerkerung *f.*

in·car·nate 1. [in'kɑːnit] fleischgeworden; *fig.* verkörpert; **2.** ['inkɑː-neit] Fleisch werden lassen; *fig.* verkörpern; **in·car'na·tion** Fleischwerdung *f; fig.* Verkörperung *f.*

in·case [in'keis] = *encase.*

in·cau·tious □ [in'kɔːʃəs] unvorsichtig; **in'cau·tious·ness** Unvorsichtigkeit *f.*

in·cen·di·ar·y [in'sendjəri] **1.** brandstifterisch; *fig.* aufwieglerisch; ~ *(bomb)* Brandbombe *f;* **2.** Brandstifter *m;* Aufwiegler *m.*

in·cense[1] ['insens] **1.** Weihrauch *m;* **2.** beweihräuchern; durchduften.

in·cense[2] [in'sens] in Wut bringen, aufbringen *(with* über *acc.).*

in·cen·tive [in'sentiv] **1.** anreizend; **2.** Antrieb *m,* Anreiz *m.*

in·cep·tion [in'sepʃən] Anfang *m;* **in'cep·tive** [~tiv] Anfangs...; *gr.* inchoativ *(den Anfang e-r Handlung bezeichnend).*

in·cer·ti·tude [in'səːtitjuːd] Ungewißheit *f.*

in·ces·sant □ [in'sesnt] unaufhörlich; ohne Unterbrechung.

in·cest ['insest] Blutschande *f,* Inzest *m;* **in·ces·tu·ous** □ [in'sestjuəs] blutschänderisch.

inch [intʃ] Zoll *m (2,54 cm); fig.* bißchen; ~es *pl. a.* Körper-Größe *f; by* ~es knapp; allmählich; *every* ~ ganz (u. gar); **inched** ...zöllig.

in·cho·a·tive ['inkəueitiv] anfangend; *gr.* inchoativ.

in·ci·dence ['insidəns] Vorkommen *n,* Auftreten *n;* Wirkung *f,* Einfluß *m; angle of* ~ Einfallswinkel *m;* **'in·ci·dent 1.** zs.-hängend *(to* mit); vorkommend *(to* bei), eigen *(to dat.);* **2.** Zufall *m,* Vorfall *m,* Zwischenfall *m;* Ereignis *n;* Nebenumstand *m;*

thea. Zwischenhandlung *f;* **in·ci·den·tal** □ [~'dentl] zufällig, gelegentlich; Neben..., Zwischen...; *be* ~ *to* gehören zu; ~*ly* nebenbei.

in·cin·er·ate [in'sinəreit] *Leiche* einäschern; *Müll* verbrennen; **in·cin·er'a·tion** Einäscherung *f;* **in·'cin·er·a·tor** Verbrennungsofen *m.*

in·cip·i·en·cy [in'sipiənsi] Anfang *m;* **in'cip·i·ent** anfangend; Anfangs...

in·cise [in'saiz] einschneiden; einritzen; **in·ci·sion** [~'siʒən] Einschnitt *m;* 𝕤 Schnitt *m;* **in·ci·sive** □ [~'saisiv] (ein)schneidend, scharf; treffend; **in·ci·sor** [~'saizə] Schneidezahn *m.*

in·ci·ta·tion [insai'teiʃən] = *incitement;* **in'cite** ansporren, anregen, anstacheln; anstiften; **in'cite·ment** Anstiftung *f;* Anregung *f;* Ansporn *m,* Antrieb *m.*

in·ci·vil·i·ty [insi'viliti] Unhöflichkeit *f.*

in·clem·en·cy [in'klemənsi] Unfreundlichkeit *f,* Rauheit *f des Wetters;* **in'clem·ent** unfreundlich, rauh.

in·cli·na·tion [inkli'neiʃən] Neigung *f (a. fig.);* **in·cline** [~'klain] **1.** *v/i.* sich neigen *(a. fig., Tag etc.);* geneigt sein; ~ *to fig.* zu *et.* neigen; dazu neigen, zu *inf.;* *v/t.* neigen; geneigt machen; ~*d plane* schiefe Ebene *f;* **2.** Neigung *f,* Abhang *m.*

in·close [in'kləuz], **in'clos·ure** [~ʒə] = *enclose, enclosure.*

in·clude [in'kluːd] einschließen; enthalten; mit einbeziehen.

in·clu·sion [in'kluːʒən] Einschließung *f,* Einschluß *m;* **in'clu·sive** [~siv] einschließlich; alles inbegriffen; *be* ~ *of* einschließen; ~ *terms pl.* Pauschalpreis *m.*

in·cog [in'kɔg], **in'cog·ni·to** [~'nitəu] **1.** inkognito, unerkannt; anonym; **2.** Inkognito *n.*

in·co·her·ence, in·co·her·en·cy [inkəu'hiərəns(i)] Zs.-hangslosigkeit *f;* Unvereinbarkeit *f;* Inkonsequenz *f;* **in·co'her·ent** □ unzs.-hängend; inkonsequent.

in·com·bus·ti·ble □ [inkəm'bʌs-təbl] unverbrennbar.

in·come ['inkʌm] Einkommen *n;* **'in·com·er** Ankömmling *m;* 𝕤 Nachfolger *m;* Eindringling *m;* **income-tax** ['inkəmtæks] Einkommensteuer *f*.

in·com·ing ['inʌmin] **1.** Eintritt *m*; **~s** *pl*. Einkünfte *pl*.; **2.** hereinkommend; neu eintretend.

in·com·men·su·ra·bil·i·ty ['inkəmenʃərə'biliti] Unmeßbarkeit *f*; **in·com'men·su·ra·ble** □ unmeßbar; unvergleichbar; **in·com'men·su·rate** [~rit] in keinem Verhältnis stehend (*with, to* zu); = *incommensurable*.

in·com·mode [inkə'məud] belästigen; stören; **in·com'mo·di·ous** □ [~djəs] unbequem, lästig.

in·com·mu·ni·ca·ble [inkə'mju:nikəbl] □ nicht mitteilbar; **in·com·mu·ni·ca·do** *bsd. Am.* [~'ka:dəu] ohne Verbindung mit der Außenwelt; **in·com'mu·ni·ca·tive** □ [~kətiv] nicht mitteilsam, verschlossen.

in·com·mut·a·ble □ [inkə'mju:təbl] unwandelbar.

in·com·pa·ra·ble □ [in'kɔmpərəbl] unvergleichlich.

in·com·pat·i·bil·i·ty ['inkəmpætə-'biliti] Unvereinbarkeit *f*; Unverträglichkeit *f*; **in·com'pat·i·ble** □ unvereinbar; unverträglich (*Mensch*).

in·com·pe·tence, in·com·pe·ten·cy [in'kɔmpitəns(i)] Unfähigkeit *f*; Unzulänglichkeit *f*; Inkompetenz *f*; Unzuständigkeit *f*; **in'com·pe·tent** □ untauglich, unfähig; unzuständig, unbefugt.

in·com·plete □ [inkəm'pli:t] unvollständig; unvollkommen.

in·com·pre·hen·si·bil·i·ty [inkəmprihensə'biliti] Unbegreiflichkeit *f*; **in·com·pre'hen·si·ble** □ unbegreiflich; **in·com·pre'hen·sion** Nichtverstehen *n*.

in·com·press·i·ble [inkəm'presəbl] nicht zusammendrückbar.

in·con·ceiv·a·ble □ [inkən'si:vəbl] unbegreiflich, unfaßbar.

in·con·clu·sive □ [inkən'klu:siv] nicht überzeugend; ergebnislos; **in·con'clu·sive·ness** Mangel *m* an Beweiskraft.

in·con·gru·i·ty [inkɔŋ'gru:iti] Nichtübereinstimmung *f*; Unangemessenheit *f*; Mißverhältnis *n*; **in'con·gru·ous** □ [~gruəs] nicht übereinstimmend (*with* mit); unangebracht, unpassend; widersinnig, widerspruchsvoll.

in·con·se·quence [in'kɔnsikwəns] Folgewidrigkeit *f*, Inkonsequenz *f*; **in'con·se·quent** □ folgewidrig, inkonsequent; **in·con·se·quen·tial** [~'kwenʃəl] unbedeutend; = *inconsequent*.

in·con·sid·er·a·ble □ [inkən'sidərəbl] unbedeutend; **in·con'sid·er·ate** □ [~rit] unüberlegt, unbesonnen; rücksichtslos (*towards* gegen); **in·con'sid·er·ate·ness** Unüberlegtheit *f*; Rücksichtslosigkeit *f*.

in·con·sist·en·cy [inkən'sistənsi] Unvereinbarkeit *f*; Inkonsequenz *f* (*gen.*); Unstimmigkeit *f*; **in·con'sist·ent** □ unvereinbar; widerspruchsvoll; ungereimt; inkonsequent.

in·con·sol·a·ble □ [inkən'səuləbl] untröstlich.

in·con·spic·u·ous □ [inkən'spikjuəs] unauffällig, unscheinbar.

in·con·stan·cy [in'kɔnstənsi] Unbeständigkeit *f*; **in'con·stant** □ unbeständig; veränderlich.

in·con·test·a·ble □ [inkən'testəbl] unbestreitbar, unstreitig.

in·con·ti·nence [in'kɔntinəns] Unenthaltsamkeit *f*; Ausschweifung *f*; **~ of urine** ✗ Harnfluß *m*; **in'con·ti·nent** □ unenthaltsam; ausschweifend; **~ly** unverzüglich, sofort.

in·con·tro·vert·i·ble □ ['inkəntrə-'və:təbl] unbestreitbar.

in·con·ven·ience [inkən'vi:njəns] **1.** Unbequemlichkeit *f*; Unannehmlichkeit *f*; **2.** belästigen, *j-m* lästig fallen; **in·con'ven·ient** □ unbequem; ungelegen; lästig (*to* für *od. dat.*).

in·con·vert·i·bil·i·ty ['inkənvə:tə-'biliti] Unverwandelbarkeit *f*; ✝ Nichtkonvertierbarkeit *f*; **in·con'vert·i·ble** □ unverwandelbar; ✝ nicht umsetzbar, nicht konvertierbar.

in·con·vin·ci·ble □ [inkən'vinsəbl] nicht zu überzeugen(d).

in·cor·po·rate 1. [in'kɔ:pəreit] einverleiben (*into dat.*); (sich) vereinigen, (sich) verbinden; (ver-) mischen; *als Mitglied* aufnehmen; eingemeinden; ✝ als Körperschaft eintragen; **2.** [in'kɔ:pərit] einverleibt; vereinigt; **in'cor·po·rat·ed** [~reitid] (amtlich) eingetragen; **~**

bank Aktienbank *f*; **in·cor·po'ration** Einverleibung *f*; Verbindung *f*;
Vermischung *f etc.*

in·cor·po·re·al □ [inkɔ:'pɔ:riəl] unkörperlich, nicht stofflich.

in·cor·rect ⊡ [inkə'rekt] unrichtig;
fehlerhaft; falsch; ungehörig; **in-
cor'rect·ness** Unrichtigkeit *f*;
Fehlerhaftigkeit *f*.

in·cor·ri·gi·bil·i·ty [inkɔridʒə'biliti]
Unverbesserlichkeit *f*; **in'cor·ri-
gi·ble** □ unverbesserlich.

in·cor·rupt·i·bil·i·ty ['inkərʌptə-
'biliti] Unverderblichkeit *f*; Unbe-
stechlichkeit *f*; **in·cor'rupt·i·ble** □
unverderblich; unvergänglich; un-
bestechlich.

in·crease 1. [in'kri:s] *v/i.* wachsen,
zunehmen (*in an dat.*); sich verstärken *od.* vergrößern *od.* vermehren; *v/t.* vermehren, vergrößern; verstärken, erhöhen;
2. ['inkri:s] Zunahme *f*; Wachstum
n, Vergrößerung *f etc.*; Anwachsen
n; Zuwachs *m*; **in'creas·ing·ly** zunehmend, immer (*mit folgendem
comp.*); ~ *difficult* immer schwieri-
ger.

in·cred·i·bil·i·ty [inkredi'biliti] Un-
glaublichkeit *f*; **in'cred·i·ble** □
[⌣dəbl] unglaublich.

in·cre·du·li·ty [inkri'dju:liti] Unglaube *m*; **in·cred·u·lous** □ [in-
'kredjuləs] ungläubig, skeptisch.

in·cre·ment ['inkrimənt] Zuwachs
m, Zunahme *f*; Steigerungsbetrag
m; Wertzuwachs *m*.

in·crim·i·nate [in'krimineit] beschuldigen; belasten; **in'crim·i-
na·to·ry** [⌣nətəri] belastend.

in·crust [in'krʌst] = *encrust*; **in-
crus'ta·tion** Bekrustung *f*; Kruste
f, Ablagerung *f*; ⊕ Verkleidung *f*,
Belag *m*; Kesselstein *m*.

in·cu·bate ['inkjubeit] (aus)brüten;
in·cu'ba·tion Brüten *n*; *biol.*, ⚕
Entwicklungszeit *f*; **'in·cu·ba·tor**
Brutapparat *m*; **in·cu·bus** ['iŋ-
kjubəs] Alp(druck) *m*.

in·cul·cate ['inkʌlkeit] einschärfen
(*upon dat.*); **in·cul'ca·tion** Ein-
schärfung *f*.

in·cul·pate ['inkʌlpeit] beschuldigen; anklagen; **in·cul'pa·tion** Beschuldigung *f*, Tadel *m*; **in'cul-
pa·to·ry** [⌣pətəri] tadelnd, be-
schuldigend; Anklage...

in'cum·ben·cy [in'kʌmbənsi] Ob-

liegenheit *f*; Amtszeit *f*; *eccl.*
Pfründenbesitz *m*; **in'cum·bent
1.** aufliegend; obliegend; *be* ~ *on
s.o.* j-m obliegen; **2.** *eccl.* Pfründen-
inhaber *m*.

in·cu·nab·u·la [inkju:'næbjulə] *pl.*
Inkunabeln *f/pl.*, Wiegendrucke
m/pl.

in·cur [in'kə:] sich *et.* zuziehen; sich
e-r Gefahr etc. aussetzen; *Schulden*
machen; *Verpflichtung* eingehen;
Verlust erleiden.

in·cur·a·bil·i·ty [inkjuərə'biliti] Un-
heilbarkeit *f*; **in'cur·a·ble 1.** □
unheilbar; **2.** Unheilbare *m, f*.

in·cu·ri·ous □ [in'kjuəriəs] gleichgültig, uninteressiert.

in·cur·sion [in'kə:ʃən] *feindlicher*
Einfall *m*, Raubzug *m*; *fig.* Eingriff *m*.

in·cur·va·tion [inkə:'veiʃən] Krümmung *f*; **'in'curve** einwärts krümmen, biegen.

in·debt·ed [in'detid] verschuldet;
fig. (zu Dank) verpflichtet; **in-
'debt·ed·ness** Verschuldung *f*;
Verpflichtung *f*; Schulden *f/pl.*

in·de·cen·cy [in'di:snsi] Unanständigkeit *f*; **in'de·cent** □ unanständig; ungebührlich; ⚡ unzüchtig.

in·de·ci·pher·a·ble □ [indi'saifərəbl]
unentzifferbar.

in·de·ci·sion [indi'siʒən] Unentschlossenheit *f*; **in·de·ci·sive** □
[⌣'saisiv] nicht entscheidend; unentschieden, schwankend; unbestimmt.

in·de·clin·a·ble *gr.* [indi'klainəbl]
undeklinierbar.

in·dec·o·rous □ [in'dekərəs] unpassend; ungehörig; **in'dec·o-
rous·ness** = **in·de·co·rum** [indi-
'kɔ:rəm] Ungehörigkeit *f*.

in·deed [in'di:d] in der Tat, tatsächlich; wirklich; allerdings; so?;
nicht möglich!

in·de·fat·i·ga·ble □ [indi'fætigəbl]
unermüdlich.

in·de·fea·si·ble □ [indi'fi:zəbl] unverletzlich; unveräußerlich.

in·de·fect·i·ble □ [indi'fektəbl] unvergänglich; unfehlbar.

in·de·fen·si·ble □ [indi'fensəbl] unhaltbar.

in·de·fin·a·ble □ [indi'fainəbl] unbestimmbar, undefinierbar.

in·def·i·nite □ [in'definit] unbestimmt (*a. gr.*); unbeschränkt;

ungenau.

in·del·i·ble ☐ [in'delibl] unauslöschbar, untilgbar; ~ **ink** Kopiertinte *f*; ~ **pencil** Tintenstift *m*.

in·del·i·ca·cy [in'delikəsi] Unfeinheit *f*; Taktlosigkeit *f*; **in'del·i·cate** ☐ [~kit] unfein; taktlos.

in·dem·ni·fi·ca·tion [indemnifi-'keiʃən] Entschädigung *f*; **in'demni·fy** [~fai] sicherstellen (*from*, *against* gegen); *j-m* Straflosigkeit zusichern; entschädigen; **in'demni·ty** Sicherstellung *f*; Straflosigkeit *f*; Entschädigung *f*, Schadenersatz *m*.

in·dent 1. [in'dent] einkerben, auszacken; eindrücken; *Zeile* einrücken; ⚄ *Vertrag* mit Doppel ausfertigen; ✝ bestellen (*upon s.o. for s.th.* et. bei j-m); ~ed *coastline* zerklüftete Küste *f*; **2.** ['indent] Einschnitt *m*, Kerbe *f*; Vertiefung *f*; ✝ Auslandsauftrag *m*; ✂ Requisition *f*; = *indenture*; **in·den·ta·tion** Zähnung *f*; Einschnitt *m*, Auszackung *f*; **in'den·tion** *typ.* Einzug *m*; **in'den·ture** [~tʃə] **1.** Vertrag *m*, Kontrakt *m*; Lehrbrief *m*; (amtliche) Liste *f*; **2.** vertraglich verpflichten.

in·de·pend·ence, in·de·pend·en·cy [indi'pendəns(i)] Unabhängigkeit *f*; Selbständigkeit *f*; hinreichendes Auskommen *n*, Vermögen *n*; *Independence Day Am.* Unabhängigkeitstag *m* (4. *Juli*); **in·de'pendent** ☐ **1.** unabhängig (*of* von); selbständig; ~ *means* eigenes Vermögen *n*; **2.** *pol.* Unabhängige *m*.

in-depth ['indepθ] gründlich.

in·de·scrib·a·ble ☐ [indis'kraibəbl] unbeschreiblich.

in·de·struct·i·ble ☐ [indis'trʌktəbl] unzerstörbar.

in·de·ter·mi·na·ble ☐ [indi'tə:-minəbl] unbestimmbar; **in·de'termi·nate** ☐ [~nit] unbestimmt; **in·de'ter·mi·nate·ness, in·de·ter·mi·na·tion**['~'neiʃən]Unbestimmtheit *f*.

in·dex ['indeks] **1.** *pl. a.* **in·di·ces** ['indisiːz] Zeiger *m*, Anzeiger *m*; Anzeichen *n*; Zeigefinger *m*; Index *m*, (Inhalts-, Namen-, Sach)Verzeichnis *n*; *eccl.* Verzeichnis *n* der verbotenen Bücher; ⚹ Exponent *m*, Kennziffer *f*; *a.* ~ *number* Richtzahl *f*; **2.** *Buch* mit e-m Index

versehen; ~ **card** Karteikarte *f*; ~ **fin·ger** Zeigefinger *m*; '~'**linked** dem Lebenshaltungsindex angeglichen; dynamisch.

In·di·a·man ['indjəmən] ⚓ (Ost-) Indienfahrer *m* (*Schiff*).

In·di·an ['indjən] **1.** indisch; indianisch; **2.** Inder(in); *a. Red* ~ Indianer(in); ~ **club** *Turnen*: Keule *f*; ~ **corn** Mais *m*; ~ **file**: *in* ~ im Gänsemarsch; ~ **giv·er** *Am.* F *j.*, *der ein Gegengeschenk erwartet bz.* *ein Geschenk zurückverlangt*; ~ **ink** chinesische Tusche *f*; ~ **pud·ding** *Am.* Maismehlpudding *m*; ~ **sum·mer** Altweiber-, Nachsommer *m*.

India...: ~ **paper** Dünndruckpapier *n*; '2'**rub·ber** Radiergummi *m*.

in·di·cate ['indikeit] (an)zeigen; hinweisen auf (*acc.*); andeuten; angezeigt erscheinen lassen; **in·di-'ca·tion** Anzeige *f*; Anzeichen *n*; Andeutung *f*; **in·dic·a·tive** ☐ [in'dikətiv] anzeigend (*of acc.*); ~ *mood gr.* Indikativ *m*; **in·di·ca·tor** ['~keitə] Anzeiger *m*; ⊕ Indikator *m*; *tel.* Zeigerapparat *m*; **in'di·ca·to·ry** [~kətəri] (an)zeigend (*of acc.*); Anzeige...

in·di·ces ['indisiːz] *pl. von* index.

in·dict [in'dait] anklagen (*for, on charge of* wegen); **in'dict·a·ble** (an)klagbar; **in'dict·er** Ankläger *m*; **in'dict·ment** Anklage *f*.

in·dif·fer·ence [in'difrəns] Gleichgültigkeit *f* (*to, towards* gegen); **in'dif·fer·ent** ☐ gleichgültig (*to* gegen); unparteiisch; leidlich, mittelmäßig; (nur) mäßig; unwesentlich; unbedeutend.

in·di·gence ['indidʒəns] Armut *f*.

in·di·gene ['indidʒiːn] Eingeborene *m*, *f*; **in'dig·e·nous** [~dʒinəs] eingeboren, einheimisch (*to* in *dat.*).

in·di·gent ☐ ['indidʒənt] arm.

in·di·gest·ed [indi'dʒestid] unverdaut; **in·di'gest·i·ble** ☐ unverdaulich; **in·di'ges·tion** Verdauungsstörung *f*, Magenverstimmung *f*.

in·dig·nant ☐ [in'dignənt] entrüstet, empört, ungehalten (*at* über *acc.*); unwillig; **in·dig'na·tion** Entrüstung *f*; Unwille *m* (*with* über *acc.*); ~ *meeting* Protestversammlung *f*; **in'dig·ni·ty** [~niti] unwürdige Behandlung *f*, Demütigung *f*; Beschimpfung *f*.

in·di·go ['indigəu] Indigo *m*; ~ *blue* indigoblau.

in·di·rect □ [indi'rekt] mittelbar, indirekt; nicht direkt; *gr. a.* abhängig.

in·dis·cern·i·ble [indi'sə:nəbl] nicht wahrnehmbar, unmerklich.

in·dis·ci·pline [in'disiplin] Disziplinlosigkeit *f*.

in·dis·creet □ [indis'kri:t] unbesonnen; unachtsam; indiskret, taktlos; **in·dis·cre·tion** [~'kreʃən] Unachtsamkeit *f*; Unbesonnenheit *f*; Indiskretion *f*, Taktlosigkeit *f*.

in·dis·crim·i·nate □ [indis'kriminit] unterschieds-, wahllos; = **in·dis'crim·i·nat·ing** □ [~neitiŋ], **in·dis'crim·i·na·tive** [~nətiv] keinen Unterschied machend; *fig.* blind; **in·dis·crim·i·na·tion** ['~'neiʃən] Wahllosigkeit *f*.

in·dis·pen·sa·ble □ [indis'pensəbl] unentbehrlich, unerläßlich (*Sache*); unabkömmlich (*Person*).

in·dis·pose [indis'pəuz] abgeneigt machen (*towards*, *from* gegen); untauglich machen (*for s.th.*, *to inf.* für et., zu *inf.*); **in·dis'posed** unpäßlich; (*to*) abgeneigt (gegen), nicht aufgelegt (zu); **in·dis·po·si·tion** [indispə'ziʃən] Abneigung *f* (*to* gegen); Unpäßlichkeit *f*.

in·dis·pu·ta·ble □ ['indis'pju:təbl] unbestreitbar, unstreitig.

in·dis·so·lu·bil·i·ty ['indisɔlju'biliti] Unauflösbarkeit *f* (*a. fig.*); **in·dis·so·lu·ble** □ [~'sɔljubl] unauflösbar; *fig.* unlöslich; untrennbar.

in·dis·tinct □ [indis'tiŋkt] undeutlich; unklar; **in·dis'tinct·ness** Undeutlichkeit *f*; Unklarheit *f*.

in·dis·tin·guish·a·ble □ [indis-'tiŋgwiʃəbl] ununterscheidbar.

in·dite [in'dait] *Gedicht etc.* ab-, verfassen; *Schrift* aufsetzen.

in·di·vid·u·al [indi'vidjuəl] **1.** □ persönlich, individuell, charakteristisch; besonder, eigentümlich; Privat...; einzeln; Einzel...; **2.** Individuum *n*, Einzelne *m*; **in·di'vid·u·al·ism** Individualismus *m*; **in·di·'vid·u·al·ist** Individualist *m*; **in·di·vid·u·al·i·ty** [~'æliti] Individualität *f*; Einzelpersönlichkeit *f*; **in·di'vid·u·al·ize** [~əlaiz] individualisieren.

in·di·vis·i·bil·i·ty ['indivizi'biliti]

Unteilbarkeit *f*; **in·di'vis·i·ble** □ unteilbar.

In·do... ['indəu] Indo...

in·doc·ile [in'dəusail] ungelehrig; unfügsam; **in·do·cil·i·ty** [~'siliti] Ungelehrigkeit *f*.

in·doc·tri·nate [in'dɔktrineit] unterweisen, schulen; durchdringen (*with* mit).

In·do-Eu·ro·pe·an ['indəujuərə-'pi:ən] Indogermanisch *n*.

in·do·lence ['indələns] Trägheit *f*, Indolenz *f*; '**in·do·lent** □ indolent, träge, lässig; *ℱ* schmerzlos.

in·dom·i·ta·ble □ [in'dɔmitəbl] unbezähmbar.

in·door ['indɔ:] im Hause (befindlich); Haus..., Zimmer..., *Sport*: Hallen...; ~ *aerial* Zimmerantenne *f*; ~ *game* Hallenspiel *n*; ~ *plant* Zimmerpflanze *f*; ~ *swimming-bath* Hallenbad *n*; '**in'doors** zu Hause; im *od.* ins Haus.

in·dorse [in'dɔ:s], **in'dorse·ment**, *etc.* = endorse, *etc.*

in·du·bi·ta·ble □ [in'dju:bitəbl] unzweifelhaft, zweifellos.

in·duce [in'dju:s] veranlassen, *j.* bewegen, dazu bringen, *et.* herbeiführen; *ℱ* induzieren; ~*d current ℱ* Induktionsstrom *m*; **in'duce·ment** Anlaß *m*, Antrieb *m*, Anreiz *m*.

in·duct *eccl.* [in'dʌkt] einführen; **in'duct·ance** *ℱ* Induktivität *f*; ~ *coil* Drosselspule *f*; **in'duc·tion** Einführung *f*, Einsetzung *f* in *Amt*, *Pfründe*; *phys.*, *phls.* Induktion *f*; **in'duc·tive** □ *phys.*, *phls.* induktiv; Induktions...

in·due [in'dju:] = endue.

in·dulge [in'dʌldʒ] nachsichtig sein gegen *j.*, *j-m* nachgeben (*in* in *dat.*); *s-n* *Wünschen etc.* nachgeben, frönen; ~ *with j.* erfreuen mit; ~ (*o.s.*) *in s.th.* sich et. erlauben *od.* gönnen; sich *e-r Sache* hin- *od.* ergeben, *e-r Sache* frönen; **in'dul·gence** Nachsicht *f*; Nachgiebigkeit *f* (*of*, *in* gegenüber *dat.*); Sichgehenlassen *n*, Zügellosigkeit *f*; Vergünstigung *f*; Stundung *f*; *eccl.* Ablaß *m*; **in'dul·gent** □ nachsichtig, schonend.

in·du·rate ['indjuəreit] (sich) (ver-) härten; **in·du'ra·tion** Verhärtung *f*.

in·dus·tri·al [in'dʌstriəl] **1.** □ gewerbetreibend, gewerblich; industriell; Gewerbe...; Industrie...;

~ *action* Arbeitskampf(maßnahmen
f|*pl.*) *m*; ~ *area* Industriebezirk *m*; ~
disease Berufskrankheit *f*; ~ *espionage*
Werkspionage *f*; ~ *estate* Industriegebiet *n* e-r *Stadt*; ~ *school* Gewerbeschule *f*; ~ *tribunal* Arbeitsgericht *n*;
2. = **in'dus·tri·al·ist** Industrielle *m*;
in'dus·tri·al·ize [⌐laiz] industrialisieren; **in'dus·tri·ous** ☐ fleißig, arbeitsam.

in·dus·try ['indəstri] Fleiß *m*, Betriebsamkeit *f*, Emsigkeit *f*; Gewerbe *n*; Industrie *f*; *heavy industries pl.* Schwerindustrie *f*.

in·dwell ['in'dwel] (*irr. dwell*) (be-)
wohnen; *fig.* innewohnen (*dat.*).

in·e·bri·ate 1. [i'ni:brieit] betrunken
machen; **2.** [⌐briit] betrunken;
3. [⌐briit] Trunkenbold *m*; **in·e·
bri'a·tion, in·e·bri·e·ty** [⌐'braiəti]
Trunkenheit *f*.

in·ed·i·ble [in'edibl] ungenießbar.

in·ed·it·ed [in'editid] unveröffentlicht.

in·ef·fa·ble ☐ [in'efəbl] unaussprechlich.

in·ef·face·a·ble ☐ [ini'feisəbl] unauslöschlich.

in·ef·fec·tive [ini'fektiv], **in·ef'fec·
tu·al** ☐ [⌐tʃuəl] unwirksam, fruchtlos; (*bsd.* ✕ dienst)unfähig.

in·ef·fi·ca·cious ☐ [inefi'keiʃəs] unwirksam; **in'ef·fi·ca·cy** [⌐kəsi] Unwirksamkeit *f*, Fruchtlosigkeit *f*.

in·ef·fi·cien·cy [ini'fiʃənsi] (Leistungs)Unfähigkeit *f*; Wirkungslosigkeit *f*; **in·ef'fi·cient** ☐ unwirksam, wirkungslos; (leistungs-)
unfähig.

in·el·e·gance [in'eligəns] Unfeinheit *f*, Geschmacklosigkeit *f*; **in·
'el·e·gant** ☐ unelegant, geschmacklos.

in·el·i·gi·bil·i·ty [inelidʒə'biliti] Unwählbarkeit *f*; Ungeeignetheit *f*;
in'el·i·gi·ble ☐ nicht wählbar; ungeeignet; *bsd.* ✕ untauglich.

in·e·luc·ta·ble ☐ [ini'lʌktəbl] unentrinnbar.

in·ept ☐ [i'nept] unpassend; abwegig; albern; **in'ept·i·tude** [⌐titju:d], **in'ept·ness** Ungeeignetheit *f*; Abwegigkeit *f*; Albernheit
f.

in·e·qual·i·ty [ini:'kwɔliti] Ungleichheit *f*; Ungleichmäßigkeit *f*; Unebenheit *f*.

in·eq·ui·ta·ble ☐ [in'ekwitəbl] un

gerecht, unbillig; **in'eq·ui·ty** Unbilligkeit *f*, Ungerechtigkeit *f*.

in·e·rad·i·ca·ble ☐ [ini'rædikəbl]
unausrottbar.

in·ert ☐ [i'nə:t] träge; **in·er·tia**
[i'nə:ʃiə], **in'ert·ness** Trägheit *f*.

in·es·cap·a·ble [inis'keipəbl] unentrinnbar; unvermeidlich.

in·es·sen·tial ['ini'senʃəl] unwesentlich (*to* für).

in·es·ti·ma·ble ☐ [in'estiməbl] unschätzbar.

in·ev·i·ta·ble ☐ [in'evitəbl] unvermeidlich, nicht zu umgehen(d);
in'ev·i·ta·ble·ness Unvermeidlichkeit *f*; **in'ev·i·ta·bly** unweigerlich.

in·ex·act ☐ [inig'zækt] ungenau;
in·ex'act·i·tude [⌐titju:d], **in·ex·
'act·ness** Ungenauigkeit *f*.

in·ex·cus·a·ble ☐ [iniks'kju:zəbl]
unentschuldbar.

in·ex·haust·i·bil·i·ty ['inigzɔ:stə
'biliti] Unerschöpflichkeit *f*; **in·
ex'haust·i·ble** ☐ unerschöpflich;
unermüdlich.

in·ex·o·ra·bil·i·ty [ineksərə'biliti]
Unerbittlichkeit *f*; **in'ex·o·ra·ble**
☐ unerbittlich.

in·ex·pe·di·en·cy [iniks'pi:djənsi]
Unzweckmäßigkeit *f*; **in·ex'pe·
di·ent** ☐ unzweckmäßig, unpassend.

in·ex·pen·sive ☐ [iniks'pensiv]
nicht teuer, billig, preiswert.

in·ex·pe·ri·ence [ineks'piəriəns] Unerfahrenheit *f*; **in·ex'pe·ri·enced**
unerfahren.

in·ex·pert ☐ [in'ekspə:t] unerfahren,
ungeübt.

in·ex·pi·a·ble ☐ [in'ekspiəbl] unsühnbar; unversöhnlich (*Haß etc.*).

in·ex·pli·ca·ble ☐ [in'eksplikəbl]
unerklärlich.

in·ex·press·i·ble ☐ [iniks'presəbl]
unaussprechlich.

in·ex·pres·sive ☐ [iniks'presiv] ausdruckslos; **in·ex'pres·sive·ness**
Ausdruckslosigkeit *f*.

in·ex·tin·guish·a·ble ☐ [iniks'tiŋgwiʃəbl] unauslöschlich.

in·ex·tri·ca·ble ☐ [in'ekstrikəbl]
unentwirrbar.

in·fal·li·bil·i·ty [infælə'biliti] Unfehlbarkeit *f*; **in'fal·li·ble** ☐ unfehlbar; untrüglich, sicher.

in·fa·mous ☐ ['infəməs] ehrlos;
schändlich, gemein; verrufen; **'in·
fa·my** Ehrlosigkeit *f*; Schande *f*;

Niedertracht *f.*

in·fan·cy ['infənsi] Kindheit *f*; ⚏ Minderjährigkeit *f*; *in its ~ in den* Anfängen; **in·fant** ['infənt] **1.** Säugling *m*; (kleines) Kind *n*; Minderjährige *m*, *f*; ~ *school* Kindergarten *m*; **2.** kindlich, jugendlich, jung.

in·fan·ta [in'fæntə] Infantin *f*; **in-'fan·te** [~ti] Infant *m.*

in·fan·ti·cide [in'fæntisaid] Kindesmord *m*; Kindesmörder(in); **infan·tile** ['infəntail] kindlich; Kindes..., Kinder...; *b. s.* kindisch; ~ *paralysis* Kinderlähmung *f*; **infan·tine** ['~tain] = *infantile.*

in·fan·try ⚔ ['infəntri] Infanterie *f*; **'in·fan·try·man** Infanterist *m.*

in·fat·u·ate [in'fætjueit] betören, verblenden; ~*d* vernarrt (*with* in *acc.*); **in·fat·u'a·tion** Betörung *f*; Vernarrtheit *f* (*for* in *acc.*).

in·fect [in'fekt] anstecken (*a. fig.*); infizieren, verseuchen, verpesten; *become* ~*ed* sich anstecken; **in-'fec·tion** Infektion *f*, Ansteckung *f*; **in'fec·tious** □, **in'fec·tive** [~tiv] ansteckend; Ansteckungs...

in·fe·lic·i·tous [infi'lisitəs] unglücklich; ungeschickt; **in·fe'lic·i·ty** Unglück *n*, Elend *n*; ungeschickter Ausdruck *m.*

in·fer [in'fə:] folgern, schließen (*from* aus); **in'fer·a·ble** zu folgern(d), ableitbar; **in·fer·ence** ['infərəns] Folgerung *f*, Schluß *m*; **in·fer·en·tial** □ [~'renʃəl] folgernd; gefolgert; **in·fer'en·tial·ly** durch Folgerung.

in·fe·ri·or [in'fiəriə] **1.** untere(r, -s); untergeordnet, niedriger; geringer; schwächer (*sämtlich*: to als); unterlegen (*to* dat.); minderwertig; **2.** Untere *m*, *f*, Geringere *m*, *f*; Untergebene *m*, *f*; **in·fe·ri·or·i·ty** [~ri'ɔriti] geringerer Wert *m* od. Stand *m*; Unterlegenheit *f*; Minderwertigkeit *f*; ~ *complex* Minderwertigkeitskomplex *m.*

in·fer·nal □ [in'fə:nl] höllisch; Höllen...; F entsetzlich; ~ *machine* Höllenmaschine *f*; **in'fer·no** [~nəu] Inferno *n*, Hölle *f.*

in·fer·tile [in'fə:tail] unfruchtbar; **in·fer·til·i·ty** [~'tiliti] Unfruchtbarkeit *f.*

in·fest [in'fest] heimsuchen; verseuchen, plagen; *fig.* überschwem-

men; **in·fes'ta·tion** Heimsuchung *f*; Verseuchung *f.*

in·fi·del ['infidəl] **1.** ungläubig; **2.** Ungläubige *m*; **in·fi·del·i·ty** [~'deliti] Unglaube *m*; Untreue *f* (*to* gegen).

in·field ['infi:ld] *Sport*: inneres Spielfeld *n*, Innenfeld *n*; Innenfeldspieler *m.*

in·fight·ing ['infaitiŋ] *Boxen*: Nahkampf *m*; *fig.* interne Streitereien *f/pl.* od. Machtkämpfe *m/pl.*

in·fil·trate ['infiltreit] *v/t.* durchdringen; durchtränken; durchsickern lassen; *v/i.* durchsickern, eindringen; **in·fil'tra·tion** Infiltration *f*; Durchsickern *n.*

in·fi·nite □ ['infinit] unendlich, endlos, unbegrenzt; ungeheuer; zahllos; **in·fin·i·tes·i·mal** [~'tesiməl] winzig, unendlich klein; **in'fin·i·tive** *gr. a.* ~ *mood* Infinitiv *m*, Grund-, Nennform *f*; **in'fin·i·tude** [~tju:d], **in'fin·i·ty** Unendlichkeit *f*; unendliche Größe *f* od. Menge *f.*

in·firm □ [in'fə:m] kraftlos, schwach; gebrechlich; ~ *of purpose* unentschlossen; **in'fir·ma·ry** Krankenhaus *n*; (Kranken)Revier *n*; **in-'fir·mi·ty** Schwäche *f* (*a. fig.*); Gebrechen *n.*

in·fix [in'fiks] hineintreiben; einfügen (*in* in *acc.*); *fig.* einprägen.

in·flame [in'fleim] entflammen (*mst fig.*); (sich) entzünden (*a. fig. u.* 🎇).

in·flam·ma·bil·i·ty [inflæmə'biliti] Entzündlichkeit *f*; **in'flam·ma·ble 1.** □ entzündlich; feuergefährlich; **2.** ~*s pl.* leicht entzündbare Stoffe *m/pl.*; **in·flam·ma·tion** [inflə-'meiʃən] Entzündung *f*; **in·flam·ma·to·ry** [in'flæmətəri] entzündlich; aufrührerisch; hetzerisch; Hetz...

in·flate [in'fleit] aufblasen, aufblähen (*a. fig.*); **in'flat·ed** schwülstig; **in'fla·tion** Aufblähung *f*; 🕈 Inflation *f*; *fig.* Aufgeblasenheit *f*; **in'fla·tion·ar·y** 🕈 [~'ʃnəri] inflationistisch; Inflations...; ~ *spiral* Lohn-Preis-Spirale *f.*

in·flect [in'flekt] biegen; *gr.* flektieren; **in'flec·tion** = *inflexion.*

in·flex·i·bil·i·ty [infleksə'biliti] Unbiegsamkeit *f*; *fig.* Unbeugsamkeit *f*; **in'flex·i·ble** □ unbiegsam; *fig.* unbeugsam; **in'flex·ion** [~ʃən] Biegung *f*; *gr.* Flexion *f*, Beugung *f*; Modulation *f der Stimme.*

in·flict [in'flikt] auferlegen; zufügen; aufzwingen; *Hieb* versetzen (*alle*: *on, upon s.o.* j-m); *Strafe* verhängen (*on* über *acc.*); **in'flic·tion** Auferlegung *f etc.*; Heimsuchung *f*, Plage *f.*

in-flight ['inflait] während des Fluges.

in·flo·res·cence ♀ [inflɔ:'resns] Aufblühen *n*; Blütenstand *m.*

in·flow ['infləu] = *influx.*

in·flu·ence ['influəns] **1.** Einfluß *m* (*with* bei, *on, upon* auf *acc.*); (Ein-) Wirkung *f* (*on, upon* auf *acc.*); **2.** einwirken auf (*acc.*); beeinflussen; **in·flu·en·tial** □ [ˌ~'enʃəl] einflußreich.

in·flu·en·za ✚ [influ'enzə] Grippe *f.*

in·flux ['inflʌks] Einströmen *n*; *fig.* Zufluß *m*, (Zu)Strom *m.*

in·fo F ['infəu] Info *f* (*Information*).

in·fold [in'fəuld] = *enfold.*

in·form [in'fɔ:m] *v/t.* benachrichtigen, in Kenntnis setzen, unterrichten (*of* von, *about* über *acc.*); mitteilen (*s.o. of s.th.* j-m et.*); *well* ~ed gut unterrichtet; *keep s.o.* ~ed j. auf dem laufenden halten; *v/i.* anzeigen, denunzieren (*against s.o.* j.); **in'for·mal** □ formlos, zwanglos; formwidrig; **in·for·mal·i·ty** [ˌ~'mæliti] Formlosigkeit *f etc.*; Formfehler *m*; **in'form·ant** [ˌ~mənt] (Informations)Quelle *f*; Gewährsmann *m*; = *informer*; **in·for·ma·tion** [infə'meiʃən] Auskunft *f*; Nachricht *f*, Information *f*; Unterweisung *f*; Kenntnis *f*; 🕸️ Anklage *f*; ~ *science* Informatik *f*; *gather* ~ Erkundigungen einziehen (*about* über *acc.*); **in·form·a·tive** [in'fɔ:mətiv] informatorisch; lehrreich; mitteilsam; **in'form·er** *a.* *common* ~ Denunziant *m*; Spitzel *m.*

in·fra F ['infrə] unten; *see* ~ siehe unten (*in Büchern*).

in·frac·tion [in'frækʃən] Verletzung *f*, Übertretung *f.*

in·fra...: ~ *dig* F ['infrə'dig] unter j-s Würde; '~'**red** *phys.* infrarot; '~ **struc·ture** Infrastruktur *f*, Unterbau *m.*

in·fre·quen·cy [in'fri:kwənsi] Seltenheit *f*; **in'fre·quent** □ selten.

in·fringe [in'frindʒ] *a.* ~ *upon Vertrag etc.* verletzen; *Gesetz* über-

treten; **in'fringe·ment** Übertretung *f*; Verletzung *f.*

in·fu·ri·ate [in'fjuərieit] wütend machen.

in·fuse [in'fju:z] einflößen, eingeben (*into dat.*); ✚, *pharm.* einweichen; *Tee etc.* aufgießen; **in'fu·sion** [ˌ~ʒən] Aufguß *m*; *fig.* Einflößung *f*; **in·fu·so·ri·a** *zo.* [ˌ~'zɔ:riə] *pl.* Infusorien *n/pl.*; **in·fu'so·ri·al** Infusorien...

in·gath·er·ing ['ingæðəriŋ] Einernten *n*; Sammeln *n.*

in·gen·ious □ [in'dʒi:njəs] geistreich; sinnreich; erfinderisch; raffiniert; **in·ge·nu·i·ty** [indʒi'nju:iti] Scharfsinn *m*; *das Sinnreiche*; **in·gen·u·ous** □ [in'dʒenjuəs] aufrichtig, offen, freimütig; unbefangen.

in·gle ['iŋgl] Kamin(feuer *n*) *m*; '~·**nook** Kaminecke *f.*

in·glo·ri·ous □ [in'glɔ:riəs] ruhmlos; unrühmlich, schimpflich.

in·go·ing ['ingəuiŋ] **1.** Hineingehen *n*; Antritt *m*; **2.** (hin)eingehend; (neu) eintretend (*Mieter etc.*).

in·got ['iŋgət] Gold- *etc.* Barren *m*; '~-**steel** Flußstahl *m.*

in·grain [in'grein] in der Wolle gefärbt; *fig. a.* ~ed eingewurzelt; *von Personen*: eingefleischt.

in·gra·ti·ate [in'greiʃieit]: ~ *o.s.* sich beliebt machen (*with* bei); **in·grat·i·tude** [in'grætitju:d] Undankbarkeit *f.*

in·gre·di·ent [in'gri:djənt] Bestandteil *m*; Zutat *f.*

in·gress ['ingres] Eintritt *m*; Zutritt *m.*

in·grow·ing ['ingrəuiŋ] nach innen wachsend, eingewachsen.

in·gui·nal *anat.* ['iŋgwinl] Leisten...

in·gur·gi·tate [in'gɔ:dʒiteit] hinunterschlingen, -schlucken.

in·hab·it [in'hæbit] bewohnen; **in·'hab·it·a·ble** bewohnbar; **in'hab·it·an·cy** Aufenthalt *m*; **in'hab·it·ant** Bewohner(in), Einwohner(in).

in·ha·la·tion [inhə'leiʃən] Einatmung *f*; ✚ Inhalation *f*; **in·hale** [in'heil] einatmen; ✚ inhalieren; **in'hal·er** ✚ Inhalationsapparat *m.*

in·har·mo·ni·ous □ [inhɑ:'məunjəs] unharmonisch.

in·here [in'hiə] anhaften, innewohnen (*in* in *dat.*); **in'her·ence**, **in'her·en·cy** [ˌ~rəns(i)] Anhaften *n*,

Innewohnen *n*; in'her·ent ☐ anhaftend; innewohnend, angeboren, eigen (*in dat.*).

in·her·it [in'herit] (er)erben; in-'her·it·a·ble ☐ erblich, vererbbar; in'her·it·ance Erbteil *n*, Erbe *n*; Erbschaft *f*; *biol.* Vererbung *f*; in-'her·i·tor Erbe *m*; in'her·i·tress, in'her·i·trix [‿triks] Erbin *f*.

in·hib·it [in'hibit] (ver)hindern; hemmen; verbieten (*s.o. from s.th.* j-m et.); zurückhalten; in·hi·bition [‿'biʃən] Hemmung *f*; Verbot *n*; in'hib·i·to·ry [‿təri] hemmend; verbietend; Hemmungs...

in·hos·pi·ta·ble ☐ [in'hɔspitəbl] ungastlich, unwirtlich; in·hos·pi·tal·i·ty [‿'tæliti] Ungastlich-, Unwirtlichkeit *f*.

in·hu·man ☐ [in'hju:mən] unmenschlich; in·hu·mane [‿'mein] unmenschlich, grausam; in·human·i·ty [‿'mæniti] Unmenschlichkeit *f*.

in·hu·ma·tion [inhju:'meiʃən] Beerdigung *f*.

in·hume [in'hju:m] beerdigen.

in·im·i·cal ☐ [i'nimikəl] feindlich; schädlich.

in·im·i·ta·ble ☐ [i'nimitəbl] unnachahmlich.

in·iq·ui·tous ☐ [i'nikwitəs] ungerecht; frevelhaft; in'iq·ui·ty Ungerechtigkeit *f*; Schlechtigkeit *f*.

in·i·tial [i'niʃəl] 1. ☐ Anfangs...; anfänglich; ‿ *payment* Anzahlung *f*; ‿ *salary* Anfangsgehalt *n*; 2. Anfangsbuchstabe *m*; 3. mit den Anfangsbuchstaben *e-s Namens* versehen; in·i·ti·ate 1. [i'niʃiit] eingeweiht (*in* in *acc.*); Eingeweihte *m*; 2. [‿ʃieit] beginnen; anbahnen; *pol.* zuerst beantragen; einführen, einweihen (*into* in *acc.*); in·i·ti·a·tion Einleitung *f*; Einführung *f*, Einweihung *f*; *bsd. Am.* ‿ *fee* Aufnahmegebühr *f* (*Vereinigung*); in'i·ti·a·tive [‿ətiv] 1. einleitend; 2. Initiative *f*; einleitender Schritt *m*; Entschlußkraft *f*; Unternehmungsgeist *m*; Volksbegehren *n*; *on one's own* ‿ aus eigener Initiative; *take the* ‿ die Initiative ergreifen; in'i·ti·a·tor [‿eitə] Initiator *m*, Anreger *m*, Urheber *m*; in'i·ti·a·to·ry [‿ətəri] einleitend, -weihend.

in·ject [in'dʒekt] einspritzen (*into* in *acc.*); ausspritzen (*with* mit); in-'jec·tion Einspritzung *f*; ⚕ Injek-

tion *f*.

in·ju·di·cious ☐ [indʒu:'diʃəs] unverständig, unklug, unüberlegt.

in·junc·tion [in'dʒʌŋkʃən] gerichtliche Verfügung *f*; ausdrücklicher Befehl *m*.

in·jure ['indʒə] (be)schädigen; schaden, Unrecht tun (*dat.*); verletzen; beleidigen, kränken; in·ju·ri·ous ☐ [in'dʒuəriəs] schädlich, nachteilig; ungerecht; beleidigend; in·ju·ry ['indʒəri] Unrecht *n*; Schaden *m*; Verletzung *f*; Beleidigung *f*, Kränkung *f*; Schädigung *f*.

in·jus·tice [in'dʒʌstis] Ungerechtigkeit *f*; Unrecht *n*.

ink [iŋk] 1. Tinte *f*; *mst printer's* ‿ Druckerschwärze *f*; *attr.* Tinten...; 2. (mit Tinte) schwärzen; beklecksen; ‿ *in* od. *over* nach-, ausziehen.

ink·ling ['iŋkliŋ] Andeutung *f*; dunkle od. leise Ahnung *f*.

ink...: '‿·pad Stempelkissen *n*; '‿·pen·cil Tintenstift *m*; '‿·pot Tintenfaß *n*; '‿·stand Schreibzeug *n*; 'ink·y tintig; Tinten...; tintenschwarz; tintenfleckig.

in·laid ['inleid] eingelegt; Einlege...; ‿ *floor* Parkettfußboden *m*.

in·land 1. ['inlənd] binnenländisch, inländisch; Binnen...; im Inland gelegen; ♞ *Revenue* Steuereinnahmen *f/pl.*; 2. [‿] Innere *n* des Landes, Binnenland *n*; 3. [in'lænd] landeinwärts; in·land·er ['inləndə] Binnenländer(in).

in-law ['inlɔ:] angeheiratete Verwandte *m*, *f*.

in·lay 1. [in'lei] (*irr.* lay) einlegen; 2. ['inlei] Einlage *f*; Einlegearbeit *f*.

in·let ['inlet] Meeresarm *m*, Bucht *f*; ⊕ Einlaß *m*, -gang *m*.

in·mate ['inmeit] Insasse *m*, Insassin *f*, Bewohner(in); Hausgenosse *m*, Hausgenossin *f*.

in·most ['inməust] innerst.

inn [in] Gasthof *m*, -haus *n*, Wirtshaus *n*; ♞ *pl.* of *Court* die vier Rechtsschulen *f/pl.* in *London.*

in·nards F ['inədz] *pl.* Eingeweide *n*, Innereien *f/pl.*

in·nate ☐ ['i'neit] angeboren.

in·ner ['inə] inner, inwendig; geheim; ‿ *tube* Schlauch *m e-s Reifens*; *the* ‿ *man* die Seele, das Innere; *co.* der Magen; in·ner·most ['‿məust] innerst; geheimst.

in·ner·vate ['inə:veit] Nervenkraft

zuführen (dat.), kräftigen.

in·nings ['iniŋz] sg. Sport: Dransein n; have one's ~ am Spiel sein; fig. an der Macht sein.

inn·keep·er ['inki:pə] Gastwirt(in).

in·no·cence ['inəsns] Unschuld f; Harmlosigkeit f; Einfalt f; **in·no·cent** ['~snt] **1.** □ unschuldig (of an dat.); harmlos (arglos; unschädlich); ~ of F ohne; **2.** Unschuldige m; Einfältige m; Idiot m.

in·noc·u·ous □ [i'nɔkjuəs] unschädlich, harmlos.

in·nom·i·nate [i'nɔminit] namenlos, unbenannt.

in·no·vate ['inəuveit] Neuerungen machen; **in·no·va·tion** Neuerung f; **'in·no·va·tor** [~tə] Neuerer m.

in·nox·ious □ [i'nɔkʃəs] unschädlich.

in·nu·en·do [inju:'endəu] Andeutung f, Anspielung f, Wink m.

in·nu·mer·a·ble □ [i'nju:mərəbl] unzählbar, unzählig.

in·nu·tri·tious [inju:'triʃəs] nicht nahrhaft, ohne Nährwert.

in·ob·serv·ance [inəb'zə:vəns] (of) Unachtsamkeit f (gegen); Nichtbeachtung f (gen.).

in·oc·cu·pa·tion ['inɔkju'peiʃən] Beschäftigungslosigkeit f.

in·oc·u·late [i'nɔkjuleit] ✻ u. fig. j. impfen (with mit, for gegen); et. einimpfen (on, into dat.); ✗ okulieren; **in·oc·u·la·tion** (Ein)Impfung f; Okulieren n.

in·o·dor·ous [in'əudərəs] geruchlos.

in·of·fen·sive □ [inə'fensiv] harmlos, gutartig; **in·of'fen·sive·ness** Harmlosigkeit f.

in·of·fi·cial [inə'fiʃəl] nichtamtlich, inoffiziell.

in·op·er·a·ble ✻ [in'ɔpərəbl] inoperabel (Tumor).

in·op·er·a·tive [in'ɔpərətiv] unwirksam.

in·op·por·tune □ [in'ɔpətju:n] unangebracht, zur Unzeit.

in·or·di·nate □ [i'nɔ:dinit] regellos; übermäßig; zügellos.

in·or·gan·ic [inɔ:'gænik] unorganisch.

in·pa·tient ['inpeiʃənt] Krankenhauspatient m, stationärer Patient m.

in·put ['input] Input m, a. n; Energiezufuhr f; Einsatz m; ⊕, bsd. ⚡ Eingangsenergie f.

in·quest ⚖ ['inkwest] Unter-

suchung f (on über acc.); coroner's ~ Gerichtsverhandlung f zur Feststellung der Todesursache.

in·qui·e·tude [in'kwaiitju:d] Unruhe f.

in·quire [in'kwaiə] fragen, sich erkundigen (about, after, for nach; of bei j-m); ~ into untersuchen, erforschen; **in'quir·er** Fragende m, f, Frager(in); Untersucher(in); **in'quir·ing** □ forschend; **in'quir·y** Erkundigung f, An-, Nachfrage f; Untersuchung f, Nachforschung f; Ermittlung f; make inquiries Erkundigungen einziehen (of bei j-m; on, about über acc.); **in'quir·y-of·fice** Auskunft(sbüro n) f.

in·qui·si·tion [inkwi'ziʃən] Untersuchung f (a. ⚖); ♀ hist. Inquisition f; **in'quis·i·tive** □ [~tiv] neugierig; wißbegierig; **in'quis·i·tive·ness** Neugier f; Wißbegierde f; **in'quis·i·tor** Untersucher m; hist. Inquisitor m; **in·quis·i·to·ri·al** □ [~'tɔ:riəl] inquisitorisch, forschend; aufdringlich fragend; neugierig.

in·road ['inrəud] feindlicher Einfall m; Ein-, Übergriff m (in, on in, auf acc.).

in·rush ['inrʌʃ] Zustrom m.

in·sa·lu·bri·ous [insə'lu:briəs] ungesund.

in·sane □ [in'sein] geisteskrank, wahnsinnig; verrückt, unsinnig; ~ asylum Irrenanstalt f; **in·san·i·tar·y** □ [in'sænitəri] ungesund, unhygienisch; **in'san·i·ty** Wahnsinn m.

in·sa·ti·a·bil·i·ty [inseiʃjə'biliti] Unersättlichkeit f; **in'sa·ti·a·ble** □, **in'sa·ti·ate** [~ʃiit] unersättlich (of nach).

in·scribe [in'skraib] ein-, aufschreiben; beschreiben (with mit); beschriften; ✝ eintragen; ♣ einzeichnen; fig. einprägen (in, on dat.); Buch zueignen (to dat.); ~d stock pl. Namensaktien f/pl.

in·scrip·tion [in'skripʃən] In-, Aufschrift f; ✝ Eintragung f.

in·scru·ta·bil·i·ty [inskru:tə'biliti] Unerforschlichkeit f; **in'scru·ta·ble** □ unerforschlich, unergründlich.

in·sect ['insekt] Insekt n; **in'sec·ti·cide** [~tisaid] Insektengift n; **in·sec·tiv·o·rous** [~'tivərəs] insektenfressend.

in·se·cure ☐ [insi'kjuə] unsicher;
in·se'cu·ri·ty [⌣riti] Unsicherheit *f*;
Ungewißheit *f*.
in·sem·i·nate *biol.* [in'semineit] befruchten; *fig.* einpflanzen, einprägen; **in·sem·i'na·tion** Befruchtung *f*.
in·sen·sate [in'senseit] empfindungs-, gefühllos; unvernünftig;
in·sen·si·bil·i·ty [⌣sə'biliti] Unempfindlichkeit *f*; Bewußtlosigkeit *f*; Gleichgültigkeit *f* (*of, to* gegen); **in'sen·si·ble** ☐ unempfindlich (*of, to* für); bewußtlos; unmerklich; gleichgültig; ⌣ *of od. to s.th.* sich e-r Sache nicht bewußt;
in'sen·si·tive [⌣sitiv] unempfindlich (*to* gegen).
in·sen·ti·ent [in'senʃənt] empfindungslos.
in·sep·a·ra·bil·i·ty [insepərə'biliti]
Untrennbarkeit *f etc.*; **in'sep·a·ra·ble** ☐ untrennbar; unzertrennlich.
in·sert 1. [in'sə:t] einsetzen,-führen, -schalten, -fügen; (hinein)stecken;
Münze einwerfen; *in e-e Zeitung*
einrücken, inserieren; 2. ['insə:t]
Bei-, Einlage *f*; **in'ser·tion** Einsetzung *f*, -fügung *f*, -tragung *f*;
Einwurf *m e-r Münze*; Anzeige *f*,
Inserat *n*.
in·set ['inset] Einsatz *m*, -lage *f*;
Nebenbild *n*.
in·shore ⚓ ['in'ʃɔ:] an *od.* nahe der
Küste (befindlich); Küsten...
in·side ['in'said] 1. Innenseite *f*;
Innere *n* (F *Magen*); turn ⌣ *out* umkrempeln; auf den Kopf stellen;
2. *adj.* inner, inwendig; Innen...; ⌣
information Einblick *m in interne
Dinge*; ⌣ *lane Sport*: Innenbahn *f*; ⌣
left Fußball: Halblinke *m*; ⌣ *right*
Halbrechte *m*; 3. *adv.* im Innern; ⌣ *of*
F innerhalb; 4. *prp.* innerhalb; **'in-'sid·er** Eingeweihte *m*, *f*.
in·sid·i·ous ☐ [in'sidiəs] heimtückisch.
in·sight ['insait] Einsicht *f*; ⌣ *into*
fig. Einblick *m* in (*acc.*).
in·sig·ni·a [in'signiə] *pl.* Abzeichen
n/pl., Insignien *pl.*
in·sig·nif·i·cance, *a.* **in·sig·nif·i-can·cy** [insig'nifikəns(i)] Bedeutungslosigkeit *f*; **in·sig'nif·i·cant**
bedeutungslos; unbedeutend.
in·sin·cere ☐ [insin'siə] unaufrichtig, falsch; **in·sin·cer·i·ty** [⌣'seriti]

Unaufrichtigkeit *f*, Falschheit *f*.
in·sin·u·ate [in'sinjueit] unbemerkt
hineinbringen; zu verstehen geben;
andeuten; durchblicken lassen; ⌣
o.s. into sich einschleichen in (*acc.*);
in'sin·u·at·ing ☐ einschmeichelnd;
in·sin·u·a·tion Einschmeichelung
f; Anspielung *f*, Andeutung *f*;
Wink *m*.
in·sip·id ☐ [in'sipid] geschmacklos,
fad, schal; **in·si'pid·i·ty** Geschmacklosigkeit *f*; Fadheit *f*,
Schalheit *f*.
in·sist [in'sist]: ⌣ *on*, ⌣ *upon* bestehen *od.* beharren auf (*dat.*); dringen auf (*acc.*); Gewicht legen auf
(*acc.*), halten auf (*acc.*); *et.* betonen;
⌣ *that* darauf bestehen, daß; **in-'sist·ence** Bestehen *n* (*on, upon* auf
dat.); Beharrlichkeit *f*; *at his* ⌣ auf
sein Drängen hin; **in'sist·ent** ☐
beharrend (*on, upon* auf *dat.*); beharrlich; eindringlich.
in·so·bri·e·ty [insəu'braiəti] Unmäßigkeit *f*.
in(·)so(·)far as [insə'fɑːrəz] insofern
als.
in·so·la·tion [insəu'leiʃən] Sonnenbestrahlung *f*; Sonnenstich *m*.
in·sole ['insəul] Brandsohle *f*; Einlegesohle *f*.
in·so·lence ['insələns] Unverschämtheit *f*; **'in·so·lent** ☐ unverschämt,
frech.
in·sol·u·bil·i·ty [insɔlju'biliti] Unlöslichkeit *f*; **in'sol·u·ble** ☐ [⌣jubl]
unlöslich; unlösbar.
in·sol·ven·cy [in'sɔlvənsi] Zahlungsunfähigkeit *f*; **in'sol·vent** 1. zahlungsunfähig; 2. zahlungsunfähiger
Schuldner *m*.
in·som·ni·a [in'sɔmniə] Schlaflosigkeit *f*.
in·so·much [insəu'mʌtʃ]: ⌣ *that*
dermaßen *od.* so sehr, daß.
in·spect [in'spekt] untersuchen,
prüfen, nachsehen, inspizieren; **in-'spec·tion** Prüfung *f*, Untersuchung *f*; Inspektion *f*; *for* ⌣ ⚕ zur
Ansicht; **in'spec·tor** Aufsichtsbeamte *m*; (Polizei)Inspektor *m*;
in'spec·tor·ate [⌣tərit] Aufsichtsbehörde *f*.
in·spi·ra·tion [inspə'reiʃən] Einatmung *f*; Eingebung *f*, Erleuchtung; Inspiration *f*; Begeisterung *f*;
in·spire [in'spaiə] einatmen; *Leben*
einhauchen (*into, in dat.*); *fig.* ein-

geben (*s.th. in s.o., s.o. with s.th.* j-m et.), erfüllen; *j.* begeistern; **in-spir·it** [in'spirit] beleben; anfeuern.

in·spis·ate [in'spiseit] eindicken, eindampfen.

in·sta·bil·i·ty [instə'biliti] Unstetig-keit *f*; *bsd. fig.* Unbeständigkeit *f*.

in·stall [in'stɔ:l] einsetzen (*in* in *ein Amt*); (sich) niederlassen; ⊕ instal-lieren, einbauen, einrichten; **in-stal·la·tion** [instə'leiʃən] Einset-zung *f*, Bestallung *f*; ⊕ Installation *f*, Einrichtung *f*; ☆ *etc.* Anlage *f*.

in·stal(l)·ment [in'stɔ:lmənt] Rate *f*; Abschlagszahlung *f*; (Teil)Liefe-rung *f*, Faszikel m (*e-s Buchs*); Fort-setzung *f*; *by* ⁓s ratenweise; in Fort-setzungen; *payment by* ⁓s Raten-zahlung *f*; ⁓ **plan** Teilzahlungs-system *n*.

in·stance ['instəns] **1.** dringende Bitte *f*, Ersuchen *n*; Beispiel *n*; (be-sonderer) Fall *m*; ☆ Instanz *f*; *for* ⁓ zum Beispiel; *in the first* ⁓ erstens; *at the* ⁓ *of* auf Veranlassung (*gen.*); **2.** *als Beispiel* anführen.

in·stant □ ['instənt] **1.** dringend; unmittelbar, sofortig; gegenwärtig, laufend; ⁓ *coffee* Pulverkaffee *m*; *on the 10th* ⁓ am 10. dieses Monats; **2.** Augenblick *m*; *in an* ⁓, *on the* ⁓ im Augenblick; augenblicklich; *the* ⁓ *you call* sobald du rufst; **in·stan-ta·ne·ous** □ [⁓'teinjəs] augenblick-lich, sofortig; gleichzeitig; Augen-blicks...; Moment...; '**in·stant·ly** sogleich, sofort.

in·state [in'steit] einsetzen (*in* in *acc.*).

in·stead [in'sted] statt dessen, dafür; ⁓ *of* anstatt, statt; an Stelle von; ⁓ *of going* statt zu gehen.

in·step ['instep] Spann *m*, Rist *m*; *be high in the* ⁓ F die Nase hoch tragen.

in·sti·gate ['instigeit] anstiften; auf-hetzen; **in·sti'ga·tion** Anstiftung *f*; *at the* ⁓ *of* auf Betreiben *gen.*; '**in·sti·ga·tor** Anstifter *m*, Hetzer *m*.

in·stil(l) [in'stil] einträufeln; *fig.* einflößen (*into dat.*); **in·stil'la·tion**, **in'stil(l)·ment** Einträufeln *n*; Ein-flößung *f*.

in·stinct 1. ['instiŋkt] Instinkt *m*, (Natur)Trieb *m*; **2.** [in'stiŋkt] er-füllt; ⁓ *with life* voller Leben; **in-'stinc·tive** □ instinkt-, triebmäßig;

unwillkürlich, instinktiv.

in·sti·tute ['institju:t] **1.** (gelehrte) Gesellschaft *f*, Institut *n* (*a. das Gebäude*); **2.** *et.* einsetzen, stiften, gründen, einrichten; an-, verord-nen; *j.* einsetzen (*to, into* in *ein Amt*); **in·sti'tu·tion** Einsetzung *f*, Einrichtung *f*; An-, Verordnung *f*; Gesetz *n*, Satzung *f*; Institut(ion *f*) *n*; Gesellschaft *f*; Anstalt *f*; **in·sti-'tu·tion·al** [⁓ʃənl] Instituts..., An-stalts...; ⁓ *care* Anstaltsfürsorge *f*; **in·sti'tu·tion·al·ize** [⁓ʃnəlaiz] in-stitutionalisieren; F in eine Anstalt schicken.

in·struct [in'strʌkt] unterrichten, informieren; belehren, unterwei-sen; *j.* anweisen; **in'struc·tion** Vorschrift *f*, Instruktion *f*; Unter-weisung *f*, Belehrung *f*; Merkblatt *n*; Auftrag *m*; **in'struc·tion·al** [⁓ʃənl] Lehr...; ⁓ *film* Lehrfilm *m*; **in'struc·tive** □ belehrend; lehr-reich; **in'struc·tor** Lehrer *m*; Aus-bilder *m*; *Am. univ.* Dozent *m*; **in-'struc·tress** Lehrerin *f*.

in·stru·ment ['instrumənt] Instru-ment *n* (*a.* ♪), Werkzeug *n* (*a. fig.*); Handlanger *m*; ☆ Urkunde *f*; ⁓ *board*, ⁓ *panel mot.*, ✈ Armaturen-brett *n*; *fly on* ⁓*s* ✈ blindfliegen; **in·stru·men·tal** □ [instru'mentl] als Werkzeug dienend; dienlich, be-hilflich, förderlich; ♪ Instrumental-...; *be* ⁓ *to* zu *e-m Zweck* beitragen; *be* ⁓ *in* zu *e-r Tätigkeit* beitragen; **in-stru'men·tal·ist** ♪ [⁓təlist] Instru-mentalist(in); **in·stru·men·tal·i·ty** [⁓'tæliti] Mitwirkung *f*, Mittel *n*.

in·sub·or·di·nate [insə'bɔ:dnit] auf-sässig; **in·sub·or·di·na·tion** ['⁓di-'neiʃən] Auflehnung *f*.

in·sub·stan·tial [insəb'stænʃəl] un-wirklich.

in·suf·fer·a·ble □ [in'sʌfərəbl] un-erträglich, unausstehlich (*arro-gant*).

in·suf·fi·cien·cy [insə'fiʃənsi] Un-zulänglichkeit *f*; **in·suf'fi·cient** □ unzulänglich, ungenügend.

in·su·lar □ ['insjulə] insular, In-sel...; *fig.* beschränkt, engstirnig; **in·su·lar·i·ty** [⁓'læriti] insulare Lage *f*; *fig.* insulare Beschränkt-heit *f*; **in·su·late** ['⁓leit] zur Insel machen; isolieren (*a.* ♪); '**in·su-lat·ing** Isolier...; ⁓ *tape* Isolierband *n*; **in·su'la·tion** Absonderung *f*;

Isolierung *f (a. phys.)*; 'in·su·la·tor
⚡ Isolator *m*.

in·su·lin ⚡ ['insjulin] Insulin *n*.

in·sult 1. ['insʌlt] Beleidigung *f*;
Beschimpfung *f*; 2. [in'sʌlt] beleidigen, beschimpfen.

in·su·per·a·bil·i·ty [insjuːpərə'bil-
iti] Unüberwindlichkeit *f*; in'su-
per·a·ble □ unüberwindlich.

in·sup·port·a·ble □ [insə'pɔːtəbl]
unerträglich, unausstehlich.

in·sup·press·i·ble [insə'presəbl] ununterdrückbar.

in·sur·ance [in'ʃuərəns] Versicherung *f*; *attr.* Versicherungs...; ~
coverage Versicherungsschutz *m*; ~
fraud Versicherungsbetrug *m*; ~ per-
formances *pl.* Versicherungsleistun-
gen *f pl.*; ~ pol·i·cy Versicherungs-
police *f*, -schein *m*; in'sur·ant Ver-
sicherungsnehmer *m*; in'sure versichern; in'sured *der od. die* Versicherte; in'sur·er *der* Versicherer.

in·sur·gent [in'səːdʒənt] 1. aufrührerisch; 2. Aufrührer *m*.

in·sur·mount·a·ble □ [insəː'maun-
təbl] unübersteigbar; *fig.* unüberwindlich.

in·sur·rec·tion [insə'rekʃən] Aufstand *m*, Empörung *f*; in·sur'rec-
tion·al [~ʃənl] aufständisch; in-
sur'rec·tion·ist [~ʃnist] Aufstän-
dische *m*.

in·sus·cep·ti·ble [insə'septəbl] unempfänglich (*of, to* für).

in·tact [in'tækt] unberührt; unversehrt; intakt; unangetastet.

in·take ['inteik] *Wasser- etc.* Einlaß
m; (Neu)Aufnahme *f*, Zustrom *m*,
-fluß *m*; Neuland *n*.

in·tan·gi·bil·i·ty [intændʒə'biliti]
Unfühlbarkeit *f*; in'tan·gi·ble □
unfühlbar; unfaßbar (*a. fig.*); unantastbar.

in·te·ger ['intidʒə] Ⱥ ganze Zahl *f*;
das Ganze; in·te·gral ['~grəl] 1. □
ganz, vollständig; wesentlich; Ⱥ
Integral...; 2. Ⱥ Integral *n*; in·te-
grant ['~grənt] integrierend; in-
te·grate ['~greit] ergänzen; zs.-
tun; einfügen (*into, in* in *acc.*); in-
tegrieren; ~d circuit ⚡ integrierter
Schaltkreis *m*; in·te'gra·tion *mst pol.*
Integration *f*; Eingliederung *f*; in-
teg·ri·ty [in'tegriti] Vollständigkeit
f; Unversehrtheit *f*; Redlichkeit *f*,
Integrität *f*.

in·teg·u·ment [in'tegjumənt] Hülle

f, Decke *f (a.* ⚘, *anat.).*

in·tel·lect ['intilekt] Verstand *m*;
konkr. die Intelligenz; in·tel'lec-
tu·al [~tjuəl] 1. □ intellektuell;
Verstandes..., geistig; verständig,
vernünftig; 2. Intellektuelle *m*,
f; in·tel·lec·tu·al·i·ty ['~tjuˈæliti]
Verstandeskraft *f*.

in·tel·li·gence [in'telidʒəns] Intelligenz *f*; Verstand *m*; Einsicht *f*,
Verständnis *n*; Nachricht *f*, Auskunft *f*; ~ department Nachrichtendienst *m*; in'tel·li·genc·er Nach-
richtenagent *m*; Spion *m*.

in·tel·li·gent □ [in'telidʒənt] intelligent; klug, gescheit; in·tel·li-
gent·si·a [~'dʒentsiə] Intelligenz *f*,
die Gebildeten *pl.*; in·tel·li·gi·bil-
i·ty [~dʒə'biliti] Verständlichkeit *f*;
in'tel·li·gi·ble □ verständlich (*to*
für).

in·tem·per·ance [in'tempərəns] Unmäßigkeit *f*; Trunksucht *f*; in-
'tem·per·ate □ [~rit] unmäßig;
zügellos; unbeherrscht; trunksüchtig.

in·tend [in'tend] beabsichtigen, wollen; meinen (*sagen wollen; by* mit);
~ *for* bestimmen für *od.* zu; in-
'tend·ant Verwalter *m*; in'tend·ed
1. absichtlich; verlobt; ~ husband
Verlobte *m*; 2. F *der od. die* Zukünftige *od.* Verlobte.

in·tense □ [in'tens] intensiv; angespannt, angestrengt; stark, heftig; lebhaft (*Farbe*); eindringlich,
leidenschaftlich; in'tense·ness In-
tensität *f*; Anstrengung *f*, Anspannung *f*; Stärke *f*, Heftigkeit *f*; Lebhaftigkeit *f*.

in·ten·si·fi·ca·tion [intensifi'keiʃən]
Verstärkung *f (a. phot.);* in'ten·si-
fy [~fai] (sich) verstärken *od.*
steigern.

in·ten·sion [in'tenʃən] Anstrengung
f; Verstärkung *f*; Stärke *f*; in'ten-
si·ty = *intenseness;* in'ten·sive □
= *intense;* verstärkend; Verstär-
kungs...; ~ *care unit* ⚡ Intensivstation
f.

in·tent [in'tent] 1. □ gespannt; bedacht, erpicht (*on auf acc.*); beschäftigt (*on* mit); aufmerksam;
2. Absicht *f*, Vorhaben *n*; *to all* ~s
and purposes in jeder Hinsicht;
durchaus; *with* ~ *to kill* in der Absicht zu töten; in'ten·tion Absicht
f; Zweck *m*; in'ten·tion·al □

[‿ʃənl] absichtlich; **in'ten·tioned** ...gesinnt; *well-*‿ wohlmeinend; **in'tent·ness** gespannte Aufmerksamkeit *f*; Eifer *m*.

in·ter [in'tə:] beerdigen, begraben.

in·ter... ['intə] zwischen; Zwischen-...; gegenseitig, einander.

in·ter·act 1. ['intərækt] *thea.* Zwischenakt *m*; **2.** [‿'ækt] sich gegenseitig beeinflussen; **in·ter'ac·tion** Wechselwirkung *f*.

in·ter·breed ['intə:bri:d] (*irr.* breed) (sich) kreuzen (*Tiere etc.*).

in·ter·ca·lar·y [in'tə:kələri] eingeschaltet; Schalt...; **in'ter·ca·late** [‿leit] einschalten; **in·ter·ca'la·tion** Einschaltung *f*.

in·ter·cede [intə:'si:d] sich verwenden, Fürbitte einlegen (*with* bei); **in·ter'ced·er** Fürsprecher(in).

in·ter·cept [intə:'sept] ab-, auffangen; *Nachricht* abhören; hemmen, aufhalten; unterbrechen, abschneiden; **in·ter'cep·tion** Abfangen *n etc.*; **in·ter'cep·tor** Geruchsverschluß *m in Abflußrohren*; ✕ Abfangjäger *m*.

in·ter·ces·sion [intə:'seʃən] Verwendung *f*, Fürbitte *f*; **in·ter·ces·sor** [‿'sesə] Vermittler *m*, Fürsprecher *m*; **in·ter'ces·so·ry** fürsprechend.

in·ter·change 1. [intə:'tʃeindʒ] *v/t.* austauschen, -wechseln; *v/i.* abwechseln; **2.** ['‿tʃeindʒ] Austausch *m*; Abwechs(e)lung *f*; **in·ter'change·a·ble** austauschbar.

in·ter·com ✍, ⚓ F ['intə:kɔm] (Bord)Sprechanlage *f*.

in·ter·com·mu·ni·cate [intə:kə'mju:nikeit] miteinander in Verbindung stehen; **'in·ter·com·mu·ni'ca·tion** gegenseitige Verbindung *f od.* Verständigung *f*; ‿ *system* = *intercom*; **in·ter·com'mun·ion** [‿njən] wechselseitiger Verkehr *m*.

in·ter·con·nect ['intə:kə'nekt] untereinander verbinden.

in·ter·con·ti·nen·tal ['intə:kɔnti'nentl] interkontinental, von Kontinent zu Kontinent (reichend).

in·ter·course ['intə:kɔ:s] Verkehr *m*, Umgang *m*.

in·ter·de·nom·i·na·tion·al [intədi-nɔmi'neiʃənl] interkonfessionell.

in·ter·de·pend·ence [intə:di'pendəns] gegenseitige Abhängigkeit *f*; **in·ter·de'pend·ent** voneinander abhängig.

in·ter·dict 1. [intə:'dikt] untersagen, verbieten (*s.th.* to *s.o.* j-m et.; *s.o.* from doing j-m zu tun); **2.** ['intə:-dikt], **in·ter'dic·tion** Verbot *n*; Interdikt *n*.

in·ter·est ['intrist] **1.** Interesse *n*; Anziehungskraft *f*; Bedeutung *f*; Nutzen *m*; ♥ Anteil *m*, Beteiligung *f*, Kapital *n*; Zins(en *pl.*) *m*; ‿*s pl.* Interessenten *m/pl.*, Kreise *m/pl.*; in the ‿ of zum Nutzen; für; be of ‿ to von Interesse sein für; take an ‿ in sich interessieren für; return a blow with ‿ noch heftiger zurückschlagen; banking ‿*s pl.* Bankkreise *m/pl.*; **2.** allg. interessieren; anziehen; angehen; j-s Teilnahme erregen (*for s.o.* für j.); be ‿ed in beteiligt sein *od.* Interesse haben an (*dat.*); ‿ *o.s.* in sich interessieren für; **'in·ter·est·ed** □ interessiert; beteiligt; eigennützig; **'in·ter·est-free** zinslos; **'in·ter·est·ing** □ interessant, fesselnd, anziehend.

in·ter·face ['intə:feis] Berührungspunkt(e *pl.*) *m*, Wechselbeziehung (-en *pl.*) *f*.

in·ter·fere [intə'fiə] sich einmengen *od.* -mischen (*with* in *acc.*); einschreiten; vermitteln (*in* bei, in *dat.*); stören (*with acc.*); aufeinandertreffen; **in·ter'fer·ence** Einmischung *f*, Eingreifen *n*; Beeinträchtigung *f*; *phys.* Interferenz *f*, Störung *f*.

in·ter·flow [intə'fləu] ineinanderfließen.

in·ter·fuse [intə'fju:z] (sich) vermischen.

in·ter·im ['intərim] **1.** Zwischenzeit *f*; in the ‿ einstweilen; **2.** vorläufig; Interims...; ‿ *report* Zwischenbericht *m*.

in·te·ri·or [in'tiəriə] **1.** □ inner; innerlich; Innen...; binnenländisch; ‿ *decorator* Innenarchitekt *m*; Maler *m*, Tapezierer *m*; **2.** Innere *n* e-*r Sache*; Binnenland *n*; *paint.* Interieur *n*; *phot.* Innenaufnahme *f*; *pol.* innere Angelegenheiten *f/pl.*; *Department of the* ♀ *Am.* Innenministerium *n*.

in·ter·ja·cent [intə:'dʒeisənt] dazwischenliegend.

in·ter·ject [intə:'dʒekt] einschieben, -werfen; **in·ter'jec·tion** Interjektion *f*, Ausruf *m*; **in·ter'jec·tion·al**

□ [˛ʃənl] eingeschoben (*Wort etc.*).
in·ter·lace [intə:'leis] *v/t.* durch-
flechten, -weben; *v/i.* sich kreuzen.
in·ter·lard [intə:'la:d] *fig.* spicken.
in·ter·leave [intə:'li:v] *Buch mit
Papier* durchschießen.
in·ter·line [intə:'lain] zwischen die
Zeilen schreiben; *typ.* durchschießen; **in·ter·lin·e·ar** [˛'liniə]
zwischenzeilig, interlinear; **in·ter-
lin·e·a·tion** ['˛lini'eiʃən] Zwischen-
schreiben *n*; Zwischengeschrie-
bene *n*.
in·ter·link [intə:'liŋk] miteinander
verbinden.
in·ter·lock [intə:'lɔk] ineinandergreifen; -haken; miteinander verbinden.
in·ter·lo·cu·tion [intə:ləu'kju:ʃən]
Unterredung *f*; **in·ter·loc·u·tor**
[˛'lɔkjutə] Gesprächspartner *m*;
in·ter'loc·u·to·ry in Gesprächs-
form; 𝕛𝕥 Zwischen...
in·ter·lope [intə:'ləup] sich eindrängen; 🕇 wilden Handel treiben;
'in·ter·lop·er Eindringling *m*; 🕇
wilder Händler *m*.
in·ter·lude ['intə:lu:d] Zwischenspiel *n*; Zwischenzeit *f*; ˛*s of bright
weather* zeitweilig schön.
in·ter·mar·riage [intə:'mæridʒ]
Mischehe *f*; **'in·ter'mar·ry** unter-
einander heiraten.
in·ter·med·dle [intə:'medl] sich einmischen (*with, in* in *acc.*); **in·ter-
'med·dler** Eindringling *m*; Unberufene *m, f*.
in·ter·me·di·ar·y [intə:'mi:djəri]
1. dazwischen befindlich; vermittelnd; **2.** Vermittler *m*; 🕇
Zwischenhändler *m*; **in·ter·me-
di·ate** □ [˛'mi:djət] in der Mitte
liegend; Mittel..., Zwischen...; ˛
landing 🛪 Zwischenlandung *f*; ˛-
-range ballistic missile* Mittelstrek-
kenrakete *f*; ˛ *school Am.* Mittelschule *f*; ˛ *stage* Zwischenstadium
n; ˛ *trade* Zwischenhandel *m*.
in·ter·ment [in'tə:mənt] Beerdigung *f*.
in·ter·mez·zo [intə:'metsəu] Inter-
mezzo *n*, Zwischenspiel *n*.
in·ter·mi·na·ble □ [in'tə:minəbl]
endlos, unendlich.
in·ter·min·gle [intə:'miŋgl] (sich)
vermischen.
in·ter·mis·sion [intə:'miʃən] Aussetzen *n*, Unterbrechung *f*; Pause *f*.

in·ter·mit [intə:'mit] unterbrechen,
(*a. v/i.*) aussetzen; **in·ter'mit·tent
1.** □ aussetzend; ˛ *fever* = **2.** 🥼
Wechselfieber *n*; **in·ter'mit·tent-
ly** sprunghaft, ruckweise.
in·ter·mix [intə:'miks] (sich) vermischen; **in·ter'mix·ture** [˛tʃə]
Mischung *f*; Beimischung *f*.
in·tern¹ [in'tə:n] internieren.
in·tern² ['intə:n] Assistenzarzt *m*.
in·ter·nal □ [in'tə:nl] inner(lich);
inländisch; ˛**-com'bus·tion engine** Verbrennungsmotor *m*; ˛ **rev-
e·nue** *Am.* Steueraufkommen *n*.
in·ter·na·tion·al [intə:'næʃənl] **1.** □
international; ˛ *date line* Datumsgrenze *f*; ˛ *departures pl.* Auslands-
flüge *m/pl.*; ˛ *flight* Auslandsflug *m*; ˛
law Völkerrecht *n*; ♀ *Monetary Fund*
Internationaler Währungsfonds *m*; ˛
player Sport: Nationalspieler(in);
2. *pol.* ♀ Internationale *f*; **in·ter·na-
tion·al·i·ty** [˛'næliti] Internationali-
tät *f*; **in·ter'na·tion·al·ize** [˛nəlaiz]
für international erklären.
in·terne ['intə:n] = *intern²*.
in·ter·ne·cine *war* [intə:'ni:sain-
'wɔ:] gegenseitiger Vernichtungs-
krieg *m*.
in·tern·ee [intə:'ni:] Internierte *m, f*;
in'tern·ment Internierung *f*; ˛
camp Internierungslager *n*.
in·ter·pel·late [in'tə:peleit] inter-
pellieren, um Aufschluß ersuchen;
in·ter·pel'la·tion Anfrage *f*, Interpellation *f*.
in·ter·phone ['intə:fəun] Hausteler-
phon *n*; 🕿 *Am.* Bordsprechanlage *f*.
in·ter·plan·e·ta·ry [intə:'plænitəri]
interplanetarisch. [wirkung *f.*╲
in·ter·play ['intə:plei] Wechsel-╱
in·ter·po·late [in'tə:pəuleit] einschieben; **in·ter·po'la·tion** Einschaltung *f*, Einschub *m*.
in·ter·pose [intə:'pəuz] *v/t. Veto*
einlegen; *Wort* einwerfen; *v/i.* da-
zwischentreten, einschreiten; vermitteln; **in·ter·po·si·tion** [intə:pə-
'ziʃən] Eingreifen *n*; Vermittlung *f*.
in·ter·pret [in'tə:prit] auslegen, erklären, interpretieren; dolmetschen;
darstellen, wiedergeben; **in·ter-
pre'ta·tion** Auslegung *f*; Interpretation *f*; Darstellung *f*; **in'ter-
pre·ta·tive** [˛tətiv] auslegend (*of
acc.*); **in'ter·pret·er** Ausleger(in);
Dolmetscher(in); Interpret(in).
in·ter·ra·cial [intə:'reiʃəl] zwischen

den Rassen, interrassisch.

in·ter·reg·num [intəˈregnəm] Interregnum *n*, Zwischenregierung *f*; Pause *f*.

in·ter·re·la·tion [ˈintəːriˈleiʃən] Wechselbeziehung *f*.

in·ter·ro·gate [inˈterəugeit] (be-, aus)fragen; verhören; **in·ter·ro·ga·tion** (Be-, Aus)Fragen *n*, Verhör(en) *n*; Frage *f*; *note od. mark od. point of* ~ Fragezeichen *n*; **in·ter·rog·a·tive** [intəˈrɔgətiv] 1. □ fragend; Frage...; 2. *gr.* Fragewort *n*; **in·ter·ˈrog·a·to·ry** [~təri] 1. fragend; 2. Frage *f*; Verhör *n*.

in·ter·rupt [intəˈrʌpt] unterbrechen; **in·ter·ˈrupt·ed·ly** mit Unterbrechungen; **in·ter·ˈrupt·er** ≠ Unterbrecher *m*; **in·ter·ˈrup·tion** Unterbrechung *f*.

in·ter·sect [intəːˈsekt] durchschneiden; (sich) schneiden; **in·ter·ˈsec·tion** Durchschnitt *m*; Schnittpunkt *m*; ⚙ Kreuzung *f*.

in·ter·space [ˈintəːˈspeis] Zwischenraum *m*.

in·ter·sperse [intəːˈspəːs] einstreuen; untermengen, durchsetzen (*with* mit).

in·ter·state *Am.* [ˈintəːˈsteit] zwischenstaatlich.

in·ter·stel·lar [intəˈstelə] interstellar, zwischen den Sternen.

in·ter·stice [inˈtəːstis] Zwischenraum *m*; Lücke *f*, Riß *m*, Spalt *m*; **in·ter·sti·tial** [~ˈstiʃəl] in Zwischenräumen; Zwischen...

in·ter·tri·bal [intəːˈtraibəl] zwischen den Stämmen.

in·ter·twine [intəːˈtwain], **in·ter·twist** [~ˈtwist] (sich) verflechten.

in·ter·ur·ban [intərˈəːbən] zwischen Städten, zwischenstädtisch.

in·ter·val [ˈintəvəl] Zwischenraum *m*; (*a.* Zeit)Abstand *m*; Zwischenzeit *f*, Pause *f*; ♪ Intervall *n*.

in·ter·vene [intəːˈviːn] dazwischenkommen, -treten; sich einmischen; einschreiten; intervenieren; vermitteln, dazwischenliegen; **in·ter·ven·tion** [~ˈvenʃən] Dazwischenkommen *n*; Einmischung *f*; Intervention *f*; Vermitt(e)lung *f*; Dazwischenliegen *n*.

in·ter·view [ˈintəvjuː] 1. Zusammenkunft *f*, Unterredung *f*; *bsd. Zeitung:* Interview *n*, Befragung *f*; 2. interviewen; **in·ter·view·ee** [~ˈiː] Interviewte *m*; Kandidat *m*; **ˈin·ter·view·er** Interviewer *m*.

in·ter·weave [intəːˈwiːv] (*irr. weave*) verweben (*a. fig.*).

in·tes·ta·cy ⚖ [inˈtestəsi] Fehlen *n* e-s Testaments; **in·tes·tate** ⚖ [~tit] 1. ohne Testament; 2. ohne Testament Verstorbene *m, f*.

in·tes·ti·nal *anat.* [inˈtestinl] Eingeweide..., Darm...; **in·tes·tine** 1. inner; einheimisch; 2. Darm *m*; ~s *pl.* Eingeweide *n/pl.*

in·ti·ma·cy [ˈintiməsi] Intimität *f*, Vertraulichkeit *f*; vertrauter Umgang *m*; **in·ti·mate** 1. [ˈ~meit] bekanntgeben; mitteilen; zu verstehen geben; 2. □ [ˈ~mit] vertraut, intim; innig, eng; 3. [ˈ~mit] Vertraute *m, f*; **in·ti·ma·tion** [~ˈmeiʃən] Andeutung *f*, Wink *m*; Ankündigung *f*, Anzeige *f*.

in·tim·i·date [inˈtimideit] einschüchtern; **in·tim·i·da·tion** Einschüchterung *f*.

in·to [ˈintu, *vor Konsonant* ˈintə] *prp.* in (*acc.*), in ... hinein.

in·tol·er·a·ble □ [inˈtɔlərəbl] unerträglich, unausstehlich; **in·ˈtol·er·ance** Unduldsamkeit *f*, Intoleranz *f*; **in·ˈtol·er·ant** □ unduldsam, intolerant.

in·to·na·tion [intəuˈneiʃən] Anstimmung *f*; ♪ Tongebung *f*; *gr.* Intonation *f*, Tonfall *m*; **in·to·nate** [ˈ~neit], **in·ˈtone** anstimmen; *mit besonderem Tonfall* aussprechen.

in·tox·i·cant [inˈtɔksikənt] 1. berauschend; 2. berauschendes Getränk *n*; **in·ˈtox·i·cate** [~keit] berauschen (*a. fig.*); **in·tox·i·ca·tion** Berauschung *f*; Rausch *m* (*a. fig.*).

in·trac·ta·bil·i·ty [intræktəˈbiliti] Widerspenstigkeit *f*; **in·ˈtrac·ta·ble** □ unlenksam, störrisch; schwer zu bändigen(d).

in·tra·mu·ral [ˈintrəˈmjuərəl] innerhalb der Mauern (vorkommend *etc.*).

in·tran·si·gent [inˈtrænsidʒənt] unversöhnlich.

in·tran·si·tive [inˈtrænsitiv] 1. □ intransitiv; 2. Intransitivum *n*.

in·tra·state *Am.* [intrəˈsteit] innerstaatlich.

in·tra·u·te·rine ⚕ [intrəˈjuːtərain] intrauterin; ~ *device* (Intrauterin)Spirale *f*.

in·tra·ve·nous ♃ [intrə'viːnəs] intravenös.

in·trench [in'trentʃ], **in'trench·ment** = *entrench etc.*

in·tre·pid ☐ [in'trepid] unerschrocken; **in·tre·pid·i·ty** [intri'piditi] Unerschrockenheit *f.*

in·tri·ca·cy ['intrikəsi] Komplizertheit *f;* Schwierigkeit *f;* Knifflichkeit *f;* **in·tri·cate** ☐ ['⌣kit] verwickelt; kompliziert; verzwickt; schwierig.

in·trigue [in'triːg] **1.** Ränkespiel *n,* Intrige *f;* (Liebes)Verhältnis *n;* **2.** *v/i.* Ränke schmieden, intrigieren; ein (Liebes)Verhältnis haben; *v/t.* interessieren; neugierig machen; **in'tri·guer** Intrigant(in).

in·trin·sic, **in·trin·si·cal** ☐ [in'trinsik(əl)] inner(lich); wirklich, wahr.

in·tro·duce [intrə'djuːs] einführen (*a. fig.*); bekannt machen (*to* mit), *Leute* vorstellen; *Buch etc.* einleiten; *Thema* zur Sprache bringen; **in·tro·duc·tion** [⌣'dʌkʃən] Einführung *f;* Einleitung *f,* Vorrede *f;* Vorstellung *f,* Bekanntmachen *n; letter of ⌣* Empfehlungsschreiben *n;* **in·tro'duc·to·ry** [⌣təri] einleitend, einführend.

in·tro·spect [intrəu'spekt] sich (innerlich) prüfen; **in·tro'spec·tion** Selbstprüfung *f;* Selbstbetrachtung *f,* Introspektion *f;* **in·tro'spec·tive** ☐ [⌣tiv] beschaulich; introspektiv.

in·tro·vert 1. [intrəu'vəːt] einwärts kehren; **2.** ['intrəuvəːt] introvertierter *od.* nach innen gekehrter Mensch *m.*

in·trude [in'truːd] hineinzwängen; eindringen; (sich) eindrängen (*into* in *acc.*); (sich) aufdrängen (*upon* s.o. j-m); stören (*upon acc.*); **in'trud·er** Eindringling *m;* Störenfried *m; a. ⌣ aircraft* Störflugzeug *n.*

in·tru·sion [in'truːʒən] Eindringen *n;* Auf-, Zudringlichkeit *f.*

in·tru·sive ☐ [in'truːsiv] zudringlich.

in·trust [in'trʌst] = *entrust.*

in·tu·it [in'tjuːit] intuitiv wissen.

in·tu·i·tion [intjuːˈiʃən] unmittelbare Erkenntnis *f,* Intuition *f;* **in'tu·i·tive** ☐ [⌣tiv] intuitiv, unmittelbar erkennend.

in·un·date ['inʌndeit] überschwemmen; **in·un'da·tion** Über

schwemmung *f.*

in·ure [i'njuə] gewöhnen (*to* an *acc.*); **in'ure·ment** Gewöhnung *f.*

in·u·til·i·ty [inju:'tiliti] Nutzlosigkeit *f.*

in·vade [in'veid] eindringen in, einfallen in (*acc.*), *Land* überfallen; *fig.* befallen; *Recht* verletzen; **in'vad·er** Angreifer *m;* Eindringling *m.*

in·val·id[1] ['invəliːd] **1.** dienstunfähig; kränklich, gebrechlich; **2.** Kranke *m;* ✕, ⚓ Invalide *m;* **3.** zum Invaliden machen *od.* werden; ✕, ⚓ als dienstunfähig entlassen.

in·val·id[2] [in'vælid] (rechts)ungültig; nichtig; **in·val·i·date** [in'vælideit] entkräften; ♃ ungültig machen; **in·val·i'da·tion** Entkräftung *f;* Ungültigmachen *n;* **in·va·lid·ity** [invə'liditi] Invalidität *f;* Ungültigkeit *f.*

in·val·u·a·ble ☐ [in'væljuəbl] unschätzbar.

in·var·i·a·ble ☐ [in'vɛəriəbl] unveränderlich; beständig; **in'var·ia·bly** ausnahmslos, immer, stets.

in·va·sion [in'veiʒən] Einfall *m,* Angriff *m,* Invasion *f;* Überfall *m;* ♃ Eingriff *m* (*of* in *acc.*); ♃ Anfall *m;* **in'va·sive** [⌣siv] angreifend; Angriffs...; eingreifend (*of* in *acc.*); zudringlich.

in·vec·tive [in'vektiv] Schmähung *f,* Schimpfrede *f,* -wort *n.*

in·veigh [in'vei] schimpfen (*against* über, auf *acc.*), herziehen (*against* über *acc.*).

in·vei·gle [in'viːgl] verleiten, (ver-) locken (*into* zu); **in'vei·gle·ment** Lockung *f.*

in·vent [in'vent] erfinden; ersinnen, erdichten; **in'ven·tion** Erfindung (-sgabe) *f;* Erdichtung *f,* Lüge *f;* **in'ven·tive** ☐ [⌣tiv] erfinderisch; **in'ven·tive·ness** Erfindungsgabe *f;* **in'ven·tor** Erfinder(in); **in·ven·to·ry** ['invəntri] **1.** Inventar *n;* Inventur *f;* **2.** inventarisieren.

in·verse ☐ ['invəːs] umgekehrt; **in'ver·sion** Umkehrung *f; gr.* Inversion *f.*

in·vert 1. [in'vəːt] umkehren; umstellen; *⌣ed commas pl.* Anführungszeichen *n/pl.; ⌣ed flight* ✈ Rückenflug *m;* **2.** ['invəːt] Homosexuelle *m;* Lesbierin *f.*

in·ver·te·brate [in'vəːtibrit] **1.** wir

bellos; *fig.* rückgrat-, haltlos; **2.** wirbelloses Tier *n*; *fig.* rückgratloser Mensch *m*.

in·vest [in'vest] *v/t.* investieren, anlegen (*in* in *dat.*); bekleiden; ausstatten (*with* mit); umgeben (*with* von); ✕ belagern; *v/i.* ~ *in* F kaufen, sich zulegen.

in·ves·ti·gate [in'vestigeit] erforschen; untersuchen; nachforschen; *investigating committee* Untersuchungsausschuß *m*; **in·ves·ti·ga·tion** Erforschung *f*; Untersuchung *f*; Nachforschung *f*; **in·ves·ti·ga·tor** [~geitə] Untersuchende *m, f*.

in·ves·ti·ture [in'vestitʃə] Amtseinführung *f*; **in·vest·ment** Kapitalanlage *f*, Investition *f*; ✕ Einschließung *f*; Amtseinführung *f*; **in'vest·or** Geldgeber *m*.

in·vet·er·a·cy [in'vetərəsi] Unausrottbarkeit *f*, Hartnäckigkeit *f*; **in'vet·er·ate** □ [~rit] eingewurzelt, unausrottbar (*Sache*); eingefleischt (*Person*); hartnäckig.

in·vid·i·ous □ [in'vidiəs] verhaßt, hassenswert; beneidenswert.

in·vig·i·late [in'vidʒileit] die Aufsicht führen (*bei Prüfungen*); **in'vig·i·la·tor** Aufsichtführende *m, f*.

in·vig·or·ate [in'vigəreit] kräftigen, stärken, beleben; **in·vig·or·a·tion** Kräftigung *f*, Stärkung *f*.

in·vin·ci·bil·i·ty [invinsi'biliti] Unüberwindlichkeit *f*; **in'vin·ci·ble** □ unbesiegbar; unüberwindlich.

in·vi·o·la·bil·i·ty [invaiələ'biliti] Unverletzlichkeit *f*; **in'vi·o·la·ble** □ unverletzlich; unverbrüchlich; **in'vi·o·late** [~lit] unverletzt.

in·vis·i·bil·i·ty [invizə'biliti] Unsichtbarkeit *f*; **in'vis·i·ble** □ unsichtbar; ~ *earnings* ✝ unsichtbare Einkünfte *pl.*; ~ *ink* Geheimtinte *f*; ~ *mending* Kunststopfen *n*.

in·vi·ta·tion [invi'teiʃən] Einladung *f*, Aufforderung *f*; **in·vite** [in'vait] einladen; auffordern; herausfordern; (an)locken; *et.* erbitten; **in'vit·ing** einladend, verlockend.

in·vo·ca·tion [invəu'keiʃən] Anrufung *f*; **in·voc·a·to·ry** [in'vɔkətəri] anrufend.

in·voice ✝ ['invɔis] **1.** Faktura *f*, Warenrechnung *f*; **2.** fakturieren, in Rechnung stellen.

in·voke [in'vəuk] *Gott, j-s Rat etc.* anrufen; *Geist* herauf-, *Rache etc.*

herabbeschwören.

in·vol·un·tar·y □ [in'vɔləntəri] unfreiwillig; unwillkürlich.

in·vo·lute ['invəlu:t] eingerollt; verwickelt; **in·vo'lu·tion** Einrollung *f*; Verwicklung *f*; ⅋ Potenzierung *f*.

in·volve [in'vɔlv] verwickeln, hineinziehen; in sich schließen, enthalten; nach sich ziehen, mit sich bringen; **in'volved** verwickelt, kompliziert; **in'volve·ment** Verwicklung *f*; (*bsd.* Geld)Schwierigkeit *f*.

in·vul·ner·a·bil·i·ty [invʌlnərə'biliti] Unverwundbarkeit *f*; **in'vulner·a·ble** □ unverwundbar; *fig.* unanfechtbar.

in·ward ['inwəd] **1.** inner(lich) (*a. fig.*); nach innen gehend; **2.** *adv.* = *inwards*; **3.** *fig.* Innere *n*; ~*s pl.* Eingeweide *n/pl.*; **'in·ward·ly** innerlich (*a. fig.*); **'in·ward·ness** Innere *n*; Innerlichkeit *f*; **in·wards** ['~z] einwärts; nach innen.

i·od·ic ⚗ [ai'odik] Jod...; **i·o·dide** ['aiədaid] Jodid *n*; **i·o·dine** ['~di:n] Jod *n*.

i·o·do·form ⚗ [ai'ɔdəfɔ:m] Jodoform *n*.

i·on *phys.* ['aiən] Ion *n*.

I·o·ni·an [ai'əunjən] **1.** ionisch; **2.** Jonier(in).

I·on·ic [ai'ɔnik] ionisch.

i·on·ic² *phys.* [~] Ionen...; **i·on·ize** *phys.* ['aiənaiz] ionisieren.

i·o·ta [ai'əutə] Jota *n*; Körnchen *n*.

I O U ['aiəu'ju:] (= *I owe you*) Schuldschein *m*.

ip·so fac·to ['ipsəu'fæktəu] gerade durch diese Tatsache.

I·ra·ni·an [ai'reinjən] **1.** iranisch; **2.** Iranier(in).

i·ras·ci·bil·i·ty [iræsi'biliti] Reizbarkeit *f*, Jähzorn *m*; **i'ras·ci·ble** □ [~sibl] reizbar, jähzornig.

i·rate [ai'reit] zornig, wütend.

ire *poet.* ['aiə] Zorn *m*.

ire·ful □ ['aiəful] zornig, wütend.

ir·i·des·cence [iri'desns] Schillern *n* in Regenbogenfarben; **ir·i'des·cent** schillernd, irisierend.

i·rid·i·um [ai'ridiəm] Iridium *n* (*Metall*).

i·ris ['aiəris] *anat.* Regenbogenhaut *f*, Iris *f*; ♣ Schwertlilie *f*; ~ *diaphragm phot.* Irisblende *f*.

I·rish ['aiərif] **1.** irisch, irländisch; **2.** Irisch *n*; *the* ~ *pl.* die Iren *pl.*;

'**I·rish·ism** irische Spracheigenheit *f*; '**I·rish·man** Irländer *m*, Ire *m*; '**I·rish·wom·an** Irländerin *f*, Irin *f*.

irk [ə:k] verdrießen.

irk·some □ ['ɔ:ksəm] lästig, ermüdend.

i·ron ['aiən] **1.** Eisen *n* (*a. fig. u. als Werkzeug od. Waffe*); *a.* flat-~ Bügeleisen *n*; ~s *pl.* Fesseln *f/pl.*; *strike while the ~ is hot fig.* das Eisen schmieden, solange es heiß ist; **2.** eisern (*fig. fest, hart, unerschütterlich*); Eisen...; **3.** plätten, bügeln; in Eisen legen; mit Eisen beschlagen; '~·bound eisenbeschlagen; felsig; unbeugsam, hart; '~·clad **1.** gepanzert; **2.** Panzerschiff *n*; ~ cur·tain *pol.* eiserner Vorhang *m*; '**i·ron·er** Bügler(in); '**i·ron-found·ry** Eisengießerei *f*; '**i·ron-'heart·ed** *fig.* hartherzig.

i·ron·ic, i·ron·i·cal □ [ai'rɔnik(əl)] ironisch, spöttisch.

i·ron·ing ['aiəniŋ] **1.** Bügeln *n*, Plätten *n*; **2.** *in Zssgn* Plätt..., Bügel...; ~·board Bügelbrett *n*.

i·ron...: ~ lung 𝕩 eiserne Lunge *f*; '~·mas·ter Eisenhüttenbesitzer *m*; '~·mon·ger Eisenwarenhändler *m*; '~·mon·ger·y Eisenwarenhandlung *f*; Eisenwaren *f/pl.*; '~·mould Rostfleck *m*; '2-sides *pl.* Reiterei *f* Cromwells; '~·work schmiedeeiserne Arbeit *f*; '~·works ⊕ *mst sg.* Eisenhütte *f*.

i·ro·ny¹ ['aiəni] eisenartig, -haltig.

i·ro·ny² ['aiərəni] Ironie *f*.

ir·ra·di·ance, ir·ra·di·an·cy [i'reidjəns(i)] Strahlen(glanz *m*) *n*; Erleuchtung *f* (*a. fig.*); **ir'ra·di·ant** strahlend (*with vor Freude etc.*).

ir·ra·di·ate [i'reidieit] bestrahlen (*a.* 𝕩); *fig.* aufklären; strahlen machen (*with vor Freude etc.*); **irra·di'a·tion** Strahlen *n*; *phys.* Bestrahlung *f*; *fig.* Erleuchtung *f*.

ir·ra·tion·al □ [i'ræʃənl] unvernünftig; vernunftwidrig; ⅍ irrational; **ir·ra·tion·al·i·ty** [~'næliti] Unvernunft *f*; Vernunftwidrigkeit *f*.

ir·re·claim·a·ble □ [iri'kleiməbl] unverbesserlich.

ir·rec·og·niz·a·ble □ [i'rekəgnaizəbl] nicht (wieder)erkennbar.

ir·rec·on·cil·a·ble □ [i'rekənsailəbl] unversöhnlich; *von Dingen:*

unvereinbar.

ir·re·cov·er·a·ble □ [iri'kʌvərəbl] unersetzlich; unwiederbringlich (verloren).

ir·re·deem·a·ble □ [iri'di:məbl] nicht rückkaufbar; nicht tilgbar, unkündbar (*Rente etc.*); nicht einlösbar (*Papiergeld*); unersetzlich; unverbesserlich.

ir·re·duc·i·ble [iri'dju:səbl] nicht reduzierbar; absolut, äußerst; nicht verwandelbar (*into in acc., to zu*).

ir·ref·ra·ga·bil·i·ty [irefrəgə'biliti] Unwiderlegbarkeit *f etc.*; **ir'refra·ga·ble** □ unwiderlegbar, unumstößlich.

ir·ref·u·ta·ble □ [i'refjutəbl] unwiderleglich, unwiderlegbar.

ir·reg·u·lar [i'regjulə] **1.** □ unregelmäßig, regelwidrig, irregulär; unordentlich; ungleichmäßig; **2.** ~s *pl.* Freischärler *m/pl.*; **ir·reg·u·lar·i·ty** [~'læriti] Unregelmäßigkeit *f etc.*

ir·rel·a·tive [i'relətiv] ohne Beziehung (*to auf acc., zu*).

ir·rel·e·vance, ir·rel·e·van·cy [i'relivəns(i)] Belanglosigkeit *f*, Unerheblichkeit *f*; **ir'rel·e·vant** □ nicht zur Sache gehörig; unzutreffend; unerheblich, belanglos (*to für*).

ir·re·li·gion [iri'lidʒən] Unglaube *m*; Irreligiosität *f*; **ir·re'li·gious** □ gottlos; irreligiös.

ir·re·me·di·a·ble □ [iri'mi:djəbl] unheilbar; unersetzlich.

ir·re·mis·si·ble □ [iri'misəbl] unerläßlich, unverzeihlich.

ir·re·mov·a·ble □ [iri'mu:vəbl] nicht entfernbar; unabsetzbar.

ir·rep·a·ra·ble □ [i'repərəbl] nicht wieder gutzumachen(d).

ir·re·place·a·ble [iri'pleisəbl] unersetzlich.

ir·re·press·i·ble □ [iri'presəbl] ununterdrückbar; unbezähmbar.

ir·re·proach·a·ble □ [iri'prəutʃəbl] einwandfrei, untadelig; **ir·re-'proach·a·ble·ness** Untadel(haft)igkeit *f*.

ir·re·sist·i·bil·i·ty ['irizistə'biliti] Unwiderstehlichkeit *f*; **ir·re'sisti·ble** □ unwiderstehlich.

ir·res·o·lute □ [i'rezəlu:t] unentschlossen, unschlüssig; **ir'res·olute·ness, ir·res·o'lu·tion** Unentschlossenheit *f*.

ir·re·solv·a·ble [iri'zɔlvəbl] unlöslich; nicht auflösbar.

ir·re·spec·tive □ [iri'spektiv] (of) rücksichtslos (gegen); ohne Rücksicht (auf acc.); unabhängig (von).

ir·re·spon·si·bil·i·ty ['irispɔnsə'biliti] Unverantwortlichkeit f; **ir·re·'spon·si·ble** □ unverantwortlich; verantwortungslos.

ir·re·triev·a·ble □ [iri'tri:vəbl] unwiederbringlich, unersetzlich; nicht wieder gutzumachen(d).

ir·rev·er·ence [i'revərəns] Respektlosigkeit f; **ir'rev·er·ent** □ respekt-, ehrfurchtslos.

ir·re·vers·i·ble □ [iri'və:səbl] nicht umkehrbar; unwiderruflich.

ir·rev·o·ca·bil·i·ty [irevəkə'biliti] Unwiderruflichkeit f; Unabänderlichkeit f; **ir'rev·o·ca·ble** □ unwiderruflich; unabänderlich, endgültig (Urteil etc.).

ir·ri·gate ['irigeit] bewässern; berieseln; ⚕ spülen; **ir·ri·ga·tion** Bewässerung f; Berieselung f etc.

ir·ri·ta·bil·i·ty [iritə'biliti] Reizbarkeit f; **'ir·ri·ta·ble** □ reizbar; **'irri·tant 1.** aufreizend; **2.** Reizmittel n; **ir·ri·tate** ['⌣teit] reizen; ärgern; **'ir·ri·tat·ing** □ aufreizend; ärgerlich (Sache); **ir·ri'ta·tion** Reizung f; Gereiztheit f, Ärger m.

ir·rup·tion [i'rʌpʃən] Einbruch m (mst fig.); feindlicher Einfall m; **ir'rup·tive** [⌣tiv] (her)einbrechend.

is [iz] er, sie, es ist (s. be).

i·sin·glass ['aiziŋglɑ:s] Fischleim m; Hausenblase f.

Is·lam ['izlɑ:m] Islam m.

is·land ['ailənd] Insel f (a. fig.); Verkehrsinsel f; **'is·land·er** Inselbewohner(in).

isle [ail] poet. od. in festen Zssgn Insel f; **is·let** ['ailit] Inselchen n.

ism mst contp. ['izəm] Ismus m, Theorie f, System n.

isn't ['iznt] = is not.

i·so... ['aisəu] in Zssgn gleich..., iso...

i·so·bar meteor. ['aisəubɑ:] Isobare f, Linie f gleichen Luftdrucks.

i·so·late ['aisəleit] absondern; isolieren; **'i·so·lat·ed** abgeschieden; **i·so·la·tion** Isolierung f, Absonderung f; ~ ward Isolierstation f; **i·so'la·tion·ist** Am. pol. [⌣ʃnist] Isolationist m.

i·so·met·rics [aisəu'metriks] pl. isometrische Übungen f/pl.

i·sos·ce·les △ [ai'sɔsili:z] gleichschenk(e)lig (Dreieck).

i·so·therm meteor. ['aisəuθə:m] Isotherme f, Linie f gleicher Temperatur.

i·so·tope ⚛ ['aisəutəup] Isotop n.

i·so·type ['aisəutaip] statistisches Schaubild n od. Diagramm n.

Is·ra·el·ite ['izriəlait] Israelit(in); **'Is·ra·el·it·ish** israelitisch.

is·sue ['iʃu] **1.** Herauskommen n, -fließen n; Abfluß m, Abgang m (von Blut); Ausgang m, -weg m; (Fluß)Mündung f; mst ⚕ Nachkommen(schaft f) m/pl.; fig. Ausgang m, Ergebnis n; ⚖ Streitfrage f; Ausgabe f von Material etc., † Emission f von Banknoten; Erlaß m von Befehlen; Ausgabe f, Exemplar n; Nummer f e-r Zeitung; ~ in fact Tatsachenfrage f; ~ in law Rechtsfrage f; force an ~ e-e Entscheidung erzwingen; join (the) ~ (die) Verhandlungen aufnehmen (on über acc.); join ~ with s.o. anderer Meinung sein als j.; be at ~ uneinig sein; point at ~ strittiger Punkt m; **2.** v/i. herauskommen, -fließen; ausgehen, herkommen, entspringen (from von, aus); endigen (in in acc.); v/t. aussenden; von sich geben; Material etc. ausgeben, † Banknoten emittieren; Befehl erlassen; Buch herausgeben; j. beliefern (with mit); **'is·sue·less** ohne Nachkommen.

isth·mus ['isməs] Landenge f, Isthmus m.

it [it] **1.** es; nach prp. da... (z. B. by it dadurch; for it dafür); how is ~ with ...? wie steht es mit ...? s. lord **2**; foot **2**; go ~ F es wagen; go ~! sl. los (doch)!, feste! we had a very good time of ~ wir haben uns sehr gut amüsiert; **2.** das gewisse Etwas.

I·tal·ian [i'tæljən] **1.** italienisch; **2.** Italiener(in); Italienisch n.

i·tal·ics typ. [i'tæliks] pl. Kursivschrift f; **i'tal·i·cize** [⌣saiz] in Kursive drucken.

itch [itʃ] **1.** ⚕ Krätze f; Jucken n; dringendes Verlangen n (for nach; to inf. zu inf.); **2.** jucken (fig. begierig sein); I ~ es juckt mich; be ~ing to inf. darauf brennen zu inf.; have an ~ing palm raffgierig sein; **'itch·ing** Jucken n; fig. Gelüste n;

'itch·y krätzig.
i·tem ['aitəm] 1. desgleichen; 2. Einzelheit f, Punkt m; (Rechnungs-) Posten m; (Zeitungs)Artikel m; 3. notieren; i·tem·ize ['∼maiz] einzeln angeben od. aufführen.
it·er·ate ['itəreit] wiederholen; it·er'a·tion Wiederholung f; it·er·a·tive □ ['itərətiv] (sich) wiederholend.
i·tin·er·ant □ [i'tinərənt] reisend; umherziehend; Reise..., Wander...; i·tin·er·ar·y [ai'tinərəri] 1. Reiseroute f, -plan m; Reisebericht m; 2. Reise...; i·tin·er·ate [i'tinəreit]

(umher)reisen.
its [its] sein(er); dessen, deren.
it's F [its] = it is, it has.
it·self [it'self] (es) selbst; sich; of ∼ von selbst; in ∼ in sich, an sich; by ∼ für sich allein, besonders.
I've F [aiv] = I have.
i·vied ['aivid] mit Efeu bedeckt.
i·vo·ry ['aivəri] 1. Elfenbein n; ivories pl. F Klaviertasten f pl.; tickle the ivories F iro. Klavier spielen; 2. elfenbeinern; Elfenbein...; ∼ tower fig. Elfenbeinturm m.
i·vy ♀ ['aivi] Efeu m; ♀ League Eliteuniversitäten im Osten der USA.

J

J [dʒei]: ∼ pen breite (Schreib-) Feder f.
jab F [dʒæb] 1. stechen; stoßen; 2. Stich m, Stoß m; Boxen: linke Gerade f; F Spritze f, Injektion f.
jab·ber ['dʒæbə] 1. plappern; quasseln; 2. Geplapper n.
jab·ot ['ʒæbəu] Spitzenbesatz m, Jabot n.
Jack¹ [dʒæk] Hans m; ∼ Frost der Winter; ∼ and Gill Hans und Grete; before one could say ∼ Robinson eh man sich's versah.
jack² [∼] 1. Hebevorrichtung f, bsd. Wagenheber m; Malkugel f beim Bowlsspiel; ⚓ Gösch f, kleine Flagge f; Karten: Bube m; 2. a. ∼ up aufbocken.
jack·al ['dʒækɔ:l] zo. Schakal m; fig. Handlanger m.
jack·a·napes ['dʒækəneips] Geck m, Affe m; Naseweis m; Schlingel m; 'jack·ass Esel m; fig. Dummkopf m; 'jack·boots pl. Reiterstiefel m/pl.; hohe Wasserstiefel m/pl.; 'jack·daw orn. Dohle f.
jack·et ['dʒækit] Jacke f; ⊕ Mantel m; Schutzumschlag m e-s Buches; dust s.o.'s ∼ F j-m die Jacke voll hauen; potatoes in their ∼s Pellkartoffeln f/pl.
jack...: '∼-in-of·fice Bürokrat m; '∼-in-the-box Schachtelmännchen n; ♀ Ketch der Henker; '∼-knife

(großes) Klappmesser n; '∼-of-'all-trades Hansdampf m in allen Gassen; '∼-of-'all-work Faktotum n; ∼-o'-lan·tern ['dʒækəulæntən] Irrlicht n; Kürbislaterne f; '∼-plane Schrupphobel m; '∼-pot Poker: Einsatz m; hit the ∼ Am. F großes Glück haben; ∼ pud·ding Hanswurst m; ∼ tar Teerjacke f (Matrose); '∼-tow·el Rollhandtuch n.
Jac·o·bin hist. ['dʒækəubin] Jakobiner m; Jac·o·bite hist. ['∼bait] Jakobit m.
jade¹ [dʒeid] 1. (Schind)Mähre f; Klepper m; contp. Frauenzimmer n, Weib n; 2. ermüden, abhetzen.
jade² min. [∼] Jade m, Nephrit m.
jag [dʒæg] 1. Zacken m; sl. Sauferei f, Sauftour f; 2. zacken; 'jag·ged □, 'jag·gy zackig; gekerbt; bsd. Am. sl. jagged voll (betrunken).
jag·uar zo. ['dʒægjuə] Jaguar m.
jail [dʒeil] 1. Gefängnis n; Kerker m; 2. ins Gefängnis werfen, einsperren; '∼-bird Galgenvogel m; '∼-break Ausbruch m aus dem Gefängnis.
jail·er ['dʒeilə] Gefängniswärter m, Kerkermeister m.
ja·lop·(p)y bsd. Am. F mot., 🏎 [dʒə'lɔpi] Karre f, Kiste f.
jam¹ [dʒæm] Marmelade f.
jam² [∼] 1.Gedränge n; ⊕ Hemmung f; Radio: Störung f; traffic ∼ Ver-

kehrsstockung *f*; *be in a ~ sl.* in der Klemme sein; *~ session* improvisiertes Zusammenspielen *n* von Jazzmusikern; **2.** (sich) (fest-, ver-) klemmen; (zs.-)pressen; *Durchgang* versperren; *Radio*: stören; ⊕ stokken; blockieren; *~ the brakes* mit aller Kraft bremsen.

Ja·mai·ca [dʒəˈmeikə] *a. ~ rum* Jamaika-Rum *m*.

jamb [dʒæm] (Tür)Pfosten *m*.

jam·bo·ree [dʒæmbəˈriː] (*bsd.* Pfadfinder)Treffen *n*; *sl.* Lustbarkeit *f*.

jam-jar [ˈdʒæmdʒɑː] Marmeladenglas *n*.

jam·my *sl.* [ˈdʒæmi] Glücks...; *~ fellow* Glückspilz *m* (*Person*).

jam-packed F [ˈdʒæmˈpækt] proppenvoll.

jan·gle [ˈdʒæŋgl] **1.** schrillen (lassen); laut streiten, keifen; **2.** Mißklang *m*; **ˈjan·gling** mißtönend, schrill.

jan·i·tor [ˈdʒænitə] Portier *m*, Pförtner *m*; *Am.* Hausmeister *m*.

Jan·u·ar·y [ˈdʒænjuəri] Januar *m*.

Jap F [dʒæp] Japaner *m*.

ja·pan [dʒəˈpæn] **1.** Japanlack *m*; Lackmalerei *f*, -arbeit *f*; **2.** *auf japanische Weise* lackieren.

Jap·a·nese [dʒæpəˈniːz] **1.** japanisch; **2.** Japaner(in); Japanisch *n*; *the ~ pl.* die Japaner *pl.*

ja·pan·ner [dʒəˈpænə] Lackierer *m*.

jar[1] [dʒɑː] Krug *m*; Topf *m*; Glas *n*.

jar[2] [ˌ] **1.** Knarren *n*, Mißton *m*; Streit *m*; mißliche Lage *f*; **2.** knarren, schnarren (lassen); unangenehm berühren, beleidigen (*upon acc.*); erzittern (lassen); streiten; *~ with* widerstreiten (*dat.*); nicht harmonieren.

jar·gon [ˈdʒɑːgən] Kauderwelsch *n*; Berufs-, Fachsprache *f*, Jargon *m*.

jas·min(e) ♀ [ˈdʒæsmin] Jasmin *m*.

jas·per *min.* [ˈdʒæspə] Jaspis *m*.

jaun·dice [ˈdʒɔːndis] 🐝 Gelbsucht *f*; *fig.* Scheelsucht *f*, Neid *m*; **ˈjaundiced** gelbsüchtig; *fig.* neidisch.

jaunt [dʒɔːnt] **1.** Ausflug *m*, Spritztour *f*; **2.** e-n Ausflug machen; **ˈjaun·ti·ness** munteres Wesen *n*; **ˈjaunt·ing-car** zweirädriger Pferdewagen *m*; **ˈjaun·ty** ☐ munter; flott; forsch; keck.

Jav·a·nese [dʒɑːvəˈniːz] **1.** javanisch; **2.** Javaner(in); Javanisch *n*; *the ~ pl.* die Javaner *pl.*

jave·lin [ˈdʒævlin] Wurfspieß *m*; *Sport*: Speer *m*; *throwing the ~* Speerwerfen *n*.

jaw [dʒɔː] **1.** Kinnbacken *m*, Kiefer *m*; P Getratsch *n*; *~s pl.* Rachen *m*; Maul *n*; *Tal-* etc. Enge *f*, Schlund *m*; ⊕ Backen *f/pl.* e-r *Zange* etc.; F Moralpredigt *f*; **2.** *v/i.* schwatzen; *v/t.* P anschnauzen; e-e Moralpredigt halten (*dat.*); **ˈ~-bone** Kieferknochen *m*; **ˈ~-break·er** F Zungenbrecher *m*.

jay [dʒei] *orn.* Eichelhäher *m*; F Quasselpeter *m*; **ˈ~-walk·er** achtlos die Straße überquerender Fußgänger *m*.

jazz [dʒæz] **1.** Jazz *m*; **2.** F grell, schreiend; **3.** Jazz spielen *od.* tanzen; *~ up* Leben bringen in (*acc.*); **ˈ~-band** Jazzkapelle *f*; **ˈjaz·zy** = *jazz* 2.

jeal·ous ☐ [ˈdʒeləs] (*of*) eifersüchtig (auf *acc.*); besorgt (um), eifrig bedacht (auf *acc.*); neidisch (auf *acc.*); **ˈjeal·ous·y** Eifersucht *f*; Eifersüchtelei *f*; Besorgtheit *f*; Neid *m*.

jean [dʒiːn] Köper *m*; *~s pl.* Arbeitsanzug *m*; Jeans *pl.*, Niethose *f*.

jeep [dʒiːp] Jeep *m*, kleines Mehrzweckfahrzeug *n*.

jeer [dʒiə] **1.** Spott *m*, Spötterei *f*; **2.** *v/i.* höhnen, spotten (*at* über *acc.*); *v/t. j.* verhöhnen; **ˈjeer·er** Spötter(in); **ˈjeer·ing** ☐ spöttisch.

je·june ☐ [dʒiˈdʒuːn] nüchtern, fad, trocken; dürr (*Boden*).

jell F [dʒel] gelieren; zum Gelieren bringen; *fig.* feste Form geben (*dat.*).

jel·ly [ˈdʒeli] **1.** Gallert(e *f*) *n*; Gelee *n*; **2.** zu Gallert etc. machen *od.* werden, gelieren; **~ ba·by** = **bean** Geleebonbon *m*, *n*; **ˈ~-fish** *zo.* Qualle *f*.

jem·my [ˈdʒemi] Brecheisen *n*.

jen·ny ⊕ [ˈdʒeni] Laufkran *m*; = *spinning-~*.

jeop·ard·ize [ˈdʒepədaiz] aufs Spiel setzen, gefährden; **ˈjeop·ard·y** Gefahr *f*. [springmaus *f*.\

jer·bo·a *zo.* [dʒəˈbəuə] Wüsten-⌐

jer·e·mi·ad [dʒeriˈmaiəd] Klagelied *n*, Jeremiade *f*.

jerk [dʒəːk] **1.** Ruck *m*, Stoß *m*; (Muskel)Zuckung *f*, (-)Krampf *m*; *by ~s* ruckweise; *put a ~ in it sl.* tüchtig 'rangehen; *physical ~s pl.* F Turnen *n*; **2.** rucken *od.* zerren (an *dat.*); ziehen; schnellen; schleudern; *mit adv. od. prp.* reißen; *Fleisch* an der Luft trocknen.

jer·kin ['dʒɔːkin] (Leder)Wams *n.*

jerk·wa·ter *Am.* ['dʒɔːkwɔːtə] **1.** Nebenbahn *f;* **2.** F klein, unbedeutend; **'jerk·y 1.** ☐ ruck-, sprungartig; hoppelig, holperig; **2.** *Am. luftgetrocknetes* Rindfleisch *n.*

jer·ry *sl.* ['dʒeri] ✕ ⚲ deutscher Soldat *m;* Nachttopf *m;* '**~-build·er** Bauschwindler *m;* '**~-build·ing** unsolide Bauart *f;* '**~-built** unsolide gebaut; **~** *house* Bruchbude *f;* '**~-can** Benzin-, Wasserkanister *m.*

jer·sey ['dʒɔːzi] Wollpullover *m;* wollenes Unterhemd *n;* ⚲ *zo.* Jerseyrind *n.*   **[***m.***\]**

jes·sa·mine ♀ ['dʒesəmin] Jasmin *J*

jest [dʒest] **1.** Scherz *m,* Spaß *m;* **2.** scherzen, spaßen; '**jest·er** Spaßmacher *m;* Hofnarr *m.*

Jes·u·it ['dʒezjuit] Jesuit *m;* **Jes·u-'it·ic, Jes·u·'it·i·cal** ☐ jesuitisch.

jet¹ *min.* [dʒet] Jett *n,* Pechkohle *f.*

jet² [~] **1.** (Wasser-, Gas)Strahl *m;* Strahlrohr *n;* ⊕ Düse *f;* Düsenflugzeug *n;* Düsenmotor *m;* **~** *age* Düsenzeitalter *n;* **~** *propulsion* Düsenantrieb *m;* **~** *set* Jet-set *m;* **~-setter** Angehörige *m, f* des Jet-set; **2.** hervorsprudeln.

jet-black ['dʒet'blæk] pechschwarz.

jet...: **~** **en·gine** Düsenmotor *m;* **~** **fight·er** ✕ Düsenjäger *m;* '**~-lag** Schwierigkeiten *f/pl.* mit der Zeitumstellung *nach langen Flugreisen;* '**~-plane** Düsenflugzeug *n;* '**~-pow-ered** mit Düsenantrieb.

jet·sam ['dʒetsəm] über Bord geworfene Ladung *f;* Strandgut *n;* *flotsam and* **~** *fig.* (menschliches) Strandgut *n.*

jet·ti·son ['dʒetisn] **1.** Überbordwerfen *n,* Notwurf *m;* **2.** über Bord werfen; '**jet·ti·son·a·ble** abwerfbar, Abwurf...

jet·ty ⊕ ['dʒeti] Mole *f;* Pier *m, f.*

Jew [dʒuː] Jude *m; attr.* Juden...; **~'s** *harp* ♪ Maultrommel *f.*

jew·el ['dʒuːəl] **1.** Juwel *n, m* (*a. fig.*), Kleinod *n;* **2.** mit Juwelen schmücken; *Uhr* mit Steinen auslegen; '**jew·el(l)er** Juwelier *m;* '**jew·el·ry, 'jew·el·ler·y** Juwelen *n/pl.,* Schmuck *m.*

Jew·ess ['dʒuːis] Jüdin *f;* '**Jew·ish** jüdisch; **Jew·ry** ['dʒuəri] Judentum

n, die Juden *pl.*

jib [dʒib] **1.** ⚓ Klüver *m;* ⊕ Kranbalken *m; the cut of his* **~** seine äußere Erscheinung; **2.** scheuen, bocken (*Pferd*); *fig.* nicht mehr wollen; **~** *at* keine Lust haben zu; '**jib·ber** scheuendes Pferd *n;* '**jib-'boom** ⚓ Klüverbaum *m;* **~** *door* Tapetentür *f.*   [= *gibe.\]*

jibe [dʒaib] *Am.* F übereinstimmen;*J*

jif·fy F ['dʒifi] Augenblick *m; in a* **~** im Handumdrehen, im Nu, sofort.

jig [dʒig] **1.** Gigue *f* (*Tanz*); ⊕ Einspannvorrichtung *f;* **2.** Gigue tanzen; auf- und abschnellen.

jig·ger ['dʒigə] Floh *m;* Milbe *f; Am.* Meßglas *n für Cocktails.*

jig·gered F ['dʒigəd]: *I'm* **~** *if ...* verdammt will ich sein, wenn ...

jig·gle F ['dʒigl] *v/t.* (leicht) rütteln; *v/i.* wackeln, wippen.

jig-saw ['dʒigsɔː] Laubsäge(maschine) *f;* **~** *puz·zle* Zusammensetz-, Puzzlespiel *n.*

jill [dʒil] = *gill³.*

jilt [dʒilt] **1.** Kokette *f;* **2.** *Liebhaber* versetzen.

Jim *Am. sl.* [dʒim]: **~** *Crow* Nigger *m;* Rassentrennung *f.*

jim-jams *sl.* ['dʒimdʒæmz] *pl.* Säuferwahnsinn *m;* Tatterich *m;* Gruseln *n.*

jim·my ['dʒimi] Brecheisen *n.*

jin·gle ['dʒiŋgl] **1.** Geklingel *n;* Wortgeklingel *n;* **2.** klingeln *od.* klimpern (mit).

jin·go ['dʒiŋgəu] Chauvinist *m,* Hurrapatriot *m; by* **~***! sl.* Donnerwetter!; '**jin·go·ism** Chauvinismus *m.*

jinks [dʒiŋks] *pl.: mst high* **~** Ausgelassenheit *f.*

jinn [dʒin] = *genie.*

jinx *sl.* [dʒiŋks] Unglücksbringer *m.*

jit·ney *Am. sl.* ['dʒitni] 5-Cent-Stück *n;* billiger Omnibus *m.*

jit·ter F ['dʒitə] **1.** zittern, bibbern; tanzen; **2.** **~***s pl. sl.* Nervosität *f; have the* **~***s* nervös sein, den Tatterich haben; **~-bug** ['~bʌg] **1.** *fig.* Nervenbündel *n;* Swingenthusiast (-in) *m;* **2.** wild tanzen; '**jit·ter·y** *sl.* ängstlich, nervös.

jiu-jit·su [dʒuː'dʒitsuː] Jiu-Jitsu *n.*

jive *Am. sl.* [dʒaiv] *heiße* Jazzmusik *f;* Jazzjargon *m.*

Job¹ [dʒəub]: **~***'s comforter* schlechter Tröster *m;* **~***'s post* Hiobsbotschaft *f*.

job² [dʒɔb] **1.** (Stück *n*) Arbeit *f*; Sache *f*, Aufgabe *f*; Beruf *m*; Beschäftigung *f*, Stellung *f*, Posten *m*; ✝ Partieware *f*; *contp*. Schiebung *f*; *typ*. Akzidenzarbeit *f*; *by the ~* stückweise; im Akkord; *make a good ~ of it* s-e Sache ordentlich machen; *a bad ~* eine aussichtslose Sache *od*. Lage; *on the ~ training* Ausbildung *f* am Arbeitsplatz; *~ lot* Gelegenheitskauf *m*, Ramschware *f*; *~ printer* Akzidenzdrucker *m*; *~ work* Akkordarbeit *f*; **2.** *v/t*. Pferd *etc.* (ver-) mieten; ✝ vermitteln; *Amt* mißbrauchen; *v/i*. Gelegenheitsarbeit machen; im Akkord arbeiten; Maklergeschäfte machen; Amtsmißbrauch treiben.

job·ber ['dʒɔbə] Gelegenheits-, Akkordarbeiter *m*; Makler *m*; Aktienhändler *m*; Schieber *m*; '**job·ber·y** Amtsmißbrauch *m*; *a piece of ~* e-e Schiebung *f*; '**job·bing** Akkordarbeit *f*; Börsenwucher *m*; *jobbery*; '**job-hunt·ing** ⊢ Arbeitssuche *f*; '**job·less** arbeitslos; **job mar·ket** Arbeitsmarkt *m*; **job se·cu·ri·ty** Sicherheit *f* des Arbeitsplatzes.

jock·ey ['dʒɔki] **1.** Jockei *m*; **2.** prellen, (be)gaunern.

jock·strap ['dʒɔkstræp] *Sport*: Suspensorium *n*.

jo·cose □ [dʒəu'kəus] scherzhaft, lustig; **jo'cose·ness** Scherzhaftigkeit *f*.

joc·u·lar ['dʒɔkjulə] scherzhaft; **joc·u·lar·i·ty** [~'læriti] Scherzhaftigkeit *f*.

joc·und □ ['dʒɔkənd] lustig, fröhlich, heiter.   [hose *f*\

Jodh·purs ['dʒɔdpuəz] *pl*. Reit-∫

Joe [dʒəu]: *~ Miller* fader Witz *m*, Kalauer *m*.

jog [dʒɔg] **1.** Stoß(en *n*) *m*; Rütteln *n*; Trott *m*; **2.** *v/t*. (an)stoßen, (auf-) rütteln; stoßen an (*acc*.); *v/i. mst ~ along, ~ on* dahinschlendern, -trotten; zuckeln.

jog·ging ['dʒɔgiŋ] Trimm-Trab *m*, Trablaufen *n*.

jog·gle ['dʒɔgl] **1.** rütteln, (sich) schütteln; ⊕ verzahnen, verschränken; **2.** Rütteln *n*; ⊕ Falz *m*, Nut *f*; Fuge *f*.

jog-trot ['dʒɔg'trɔt] Trott *m*; *fig*. Schlendrian *m*.

john¹ *Am*. ⊢ [dʒɔn] Klo *n*.

John² [~]: *~ Bull* John Bull *m* (*der Engländer*); *~ Hancock Am*. Friedrich Wilhelm *m* (*Unterschrift*).

join [dʒɔin] **1.** *v/t*. verbinden, zs.-fügen (*to* mit); ⊕ fügen; sich vereinigen mit, sich gesellen zu, stoßen zu, treffen, eintreten in (*acc*.); *~ battle* den Kampf beginnen; *~ company* sich anschließen (*with dat*.); *~ hands* die Hände falten; sich die Hände reichen (*a. fig*.); *v/i*. sich verbinden, sich vereinigen; angrenzen, anstoßen; *~ in* sich e-r Sache anschließen, sich beteiligen an (*dat*.), mitmachen bei; mit einstimmen in (*acc*.); *~ up* Soldat werden; *I ~ with you* ich halte es mit Ihnen; **2.** Verbindung(sstelle) *f*; Naht *f*; Fuge *f*.

join·er ['dʒɔinə] Schreiner *m*, Tischler *m*; '**join·er·y** Schreiner-, Tischlerhandwerk *n*, -arbeit *f*.

joint [dʒɔint] **1.** Verbindung *f*, Fuge *f*; Scharnier *n*; Gewinde *n*; *anat*. Gelenk *n*; ♀ Knoten *m*; Braten *m*, Keule *f*; *Am. sl*. Bumslokal *n*, Spelunke *f*; *put out of ~* verrenken; *out of ~ fig*. aus den Fugen; **2.** □ verbunden, vereint; gemeinsam; Mit...; *~ heir* Miterbe *m*; *~ ownership* Miteigentum *n*; *~ production* Koproduktion *f*; *~ venture* Gemeinschaftsunternehmen *n*; **3.** zs.-fügen; ⊕ aneinanderpassen; zergliedern, zerlegen; '**joint·ed** gegliedert; mit Gelenken; *~ doll* Gliederpuppe *f*;

joint stock Aktienkapital *n*; '**joint- -stock com·pa·ny** Aktiengesellschaft *f*; **join·ture** ⚖ ['~tʃə] Wittum *n*.

joist [dʒɔist] Querbalken *m*; Profilträger *m*.

joke [dʒəuk] **1.** Scherz *m*, Spaß *m*, Witz *m*; *practical ~* Streich *m*, Schabernack *m*; **2.** *v/i*. scherzen, spaßen; schäkern; *v/t*. necken, aufziehen (*about* mit); '**jok·er** Spaßvogel *m*, -macher *m*; *Karten*: Joker *m*; *Am*. versteckte Klausel *f*; '**jok·y** ⏄ scherzhaft, spaßig.

jol·li·fi·ca·tion ⏄ [dʒɔlifi'keiʃən] Lustbarkeit *f*; '**jol·li·ness**, '**jol·li·ty** Lustigkeit *f*.

jol·ly ['dʒɔli] **1.** □ lustig, fröhlich, vergnügt, fidel; ⊢ nett, famos; **2.** ⊢ *adv*. sehr, riesig, mächtig; **3.** ⊢ *j-m* um den Bart gehen.

jol·ly-boat ⚓ ['dʒɔlibəut] Jolle *f*.

Jol·ly Rog·er [ˈdʒɔliˈrɔdʒə] Totenkopf-, Piratenflagge *f.*
jolt [dʒəult] **1.** stoßen, rütteln; holpern; **2.** Stoß *m*; Rütteln *n*; ˈjolt·y rüttelnd; holperig.
Jon·a·than [ˈdʒɔnəθən]: *Brother* ◠ Bruder *m* Jonathan (*Amerikaner*).
jon·quil ⚥ [ˈdʒɔŋkwil] *e-e* Narzisse *f.*
jo·rum [ˈdʒɔːrəm] großer Humpen *m*; Punsch *m.*
josh *Am. sl.* [dʒɔʃ] **1.** Ulk *m*; **2.** aufziehen, auf die Schippe nehmen.
joss [dʒɔs] chinesisches Idol *n*; ˈ◠-house chinesischer Tempel *m*; ˈ◠-stick Räucherstäbchen *n.*
jos·tle [ˈdʒɔsl] **1.** anrennen; (an-)stoßen; (an)rempeln; **2.** Stoß *m*; Zs.-Stoß *m.*
jot [dʒɔt] **1.** Fünkchen *n*, Körnchen *n*; **2.** ◠ *down* notieren; ˈjot·ter Notizbuch *n*, -block *m*; ˈjot·tings *pl.* Notizen *f pl.*
joule [dʒuːl] Joule *n.*
jour·nal [ˈdʒəːnl] Journal *n* (*a.* ✝, ⚓); Tagebuch *n*; Zeitung *f*; Zeitschrift *f*; ⊕ Wellenzapfen *m*; **jour·nal·ese** F [ˈ◠nəˈliːz] Zeitungsstil *m*; ˈjour·nal·ism Zeitungswesen *n*, Journalismus *m*; ˈjour·nal·ist Journalist (-in); **jour·nal·is·tic** (◠*ally*) journalistisch; ˈjour·nal·ize ✝ (in das Journal) eintragen.
jour·ney [ˈdʒəːni] **1.** Reise *f*; Fahrt *f*, Tour *f*; **2.** reisen, wandern; ˈ◠-man Geselle *m*; ˈ◠-work Tagelöhnerarbeit *f.*
joust [dʒaust] **1.** Turnier *n*; **2.** turnieren.　　　　　　　　　[Gott!]
Jove [dʒəuv] Jupiter *m*; *by* ◠*!* bei⎪
jo·vi·al ☐ [ˈdʒəuvjəl] heiter, lustig; gemütlich; **jo·vi·al·i·ty** [◠viˈæliti] Heiterkeit *f*, Frohsinn *m.*
jowl [dʒaul] Backe *f*; *cheek by* ◠ dicht nebeneinander.
joy [dʒɔi] Freude *f*; Fröhlichkeit *f*; **joy·ful** ☐ [ˈ◠ful] freudig; erfreut; fröhlich; ˈjoy·ful·ness Fröhlichkeit *f*; ˈjoy·less ☐ freudlos; unerfreulich; ˈjoy·ous ☐ freudig, fröhlich; ˈjoy·ride *sl.* Spritztour *f od.* Vergnügungsfahrt *f mit e-m gestohlenen Wagen*; ˈjoy-stick ✈ *sl.* Steuerknüppel *m.*
ju·bi·lant [ˈdʒuːbilənt] jubilierend, frohlockend; **ju·bi·late** [ˈ◠leit] jubeln; **ju·bi·la·tion** Jubel *m*; **ju·bi·lee** [ˈ◠liː] Jubiläum *n.*

Ju·da·ism [ˈdʒuːdeiizəm] Judentum *n.*
Ju·das [ˈdʒuːdəs] *fig.* Judas *m*, Verräter *m*; *a.* ☽-*hole* Guckloch *n.*
judge [dʒʌdʒ] **1.** Richter *m*; Schiedsrichter *m*; Beurteiler(in), Kenner (-in), Sachverständige *m*, *f*; **2.** *v/i.* urteilen (*from*, *by* nach; *of* über *acc.*); *v/t.* richten; aburteilen; beurteilen (*by* nach); ansehen als; entscheiden.
judg(e)·ment [ˈdʒʌdʒmənt] Urteil *n*; Urteilsspruch *m*; Urteilskraft *f*, -vermögen *n*; Einsicht *f*; Ansicht *f*, Meinung *f*; *göttliches* (Straf)Gericht *n*; *in my* ◠ meiner Meinung nach; *pronounce* ◠ für Recht erkennen; *sit in* ◠ zu Gericht sitzen; *come to* ◠ zur Einsicht kommen; *Day of* ☽, ☽-*Day* Jüngster Tag *m*, Jüngstes Gericht *n.*
judge·ship [ˈdʒʌdʒʃip] Richteramt *n.*
ju·di·ca·ture [ˈdʒuːdikətʃə] Gerichtshof *m*; Rechtspflege *f*; Richteramt *n*; Richter *m/pl.*
ju·di·cial ☐ [dʒuːˈdiʃəl] gerichtlich; Gerichts...; richterlich; kritisch; unparteiisch; ◠ *murder* Justizmord *m*; ◠ *system* Gerichtswesen *n.*
ju·di·ci·a·ry [dʒuːˈdiʃiəri] *die* Richterschaft *f.*
ju·di·cious ☐ [dʒuːˈdiʃəs] verständig, klug; **ju·di·cious·ness** Einsicht *f.*
ju·do [ˈdʒuːdəu] *Sport:* Judo *n.*
jug [dʒʌg] **1.** Krug *m*, Kanne *f*; *sl.* Loch *n* (*Gefängnis*); **2.** dämpfen; *sl.* einlochen; ◠*ged hare* Hasenpfeffer *m.*

Jug·ger·naut *fig.* [ˈdʒʌgənɔːt] Moloch *m*, Götze *m*; Popanz *m.*
jug·gins F [ˈdʒʌginz] Trottel *m.*
jug·gle [ˈdʒʌgl] **1.** Trick *m*; Schwindel *m*; **2.** jonglieren (*a. fig.*), Kunststücke machen; *fig.* frisieren, verfälschen; betrügen (*out of* um); ˈjug·gler Jongleur *m*; Taschenspieler(in); ˈjug·gler·y Jonglieren *n*; Taschenspielerei *f*; Betrügerei *f.*
Ju·go·slav [ˈjuːgəuˈslɑːv] **1.** Jugoslawe *m*, Jugoslawin *f*; **2.** jugoslawisch.

jug·u·lar *anat.* [ˈdʒʌgjulə] Kehl...; ◠ *vein* Halsader *f*; **ju·gu·late** *fig.* [ˈ◠leit] abwürgen.
juice [dʒuːs] Saft *m*; *mot. sl.* Sprit *m*, Gas *n*; ⚡ *sl.* Strom *m*; ˈjuic·i·ness Saftigkeit *f*; ˈjuic·y ☐ saftig; F

interessant; pikant.
ju·jube ['dʒuːdʒuːb] ♃ Brustbeere *f*; *pharm.* Brustbonbon *m*, *n*.
ju·jut·su [dʒuː'dʒutsuː] Jiu-Jitsu *n*.
juke-box *Am.* F ['dʒuːkbɔks] Musikautomat *m*.
ju·lep ['dʒuːlep] *süßes* (Arznei)Getränk *n*; *bsd. Am. alkoholisches* Eisgetränk *n*.
Ju·ly [dʒuː'lai] Juli *m*.
jum·ble ['dʒʌmbl] **1.** Durcheinander *n*; **2.** *v/t. a.* ~ up durcheinanderwerfen; *v/i.* durcheinanderlaufen; '~-sale Wohltätigkeitsbasar *m*.
jum·bo ['dʒʌmbəu], *a.* ~ jet Jumbo(-Jet) *m*; '~-sized Riesen...
jump [dʒʌmp] **1.** Sprung *m*; sprunghafter Anstieg *m*; ~s *pl.* nervöses Zs.-Fahren *n*; high (long) ~ Hoch-(Weit)Sprung *m*; get (have) the ~ on *Am.* F zuvorkommen; give a ~ e-n Satz machen; zs.-fahren; **2.** *v/i.* springen; stoßen; ~ at sich *begierig* stürzen auf (*acc.*); ~ to conclusions übereilte Schlüsse ziehen; ~ on, ~ upon sich auf *j.* stürzen; *fig. j-m* aufs Dach steigen; *v/t.* hinwegspringen *od.* -setzen über (*acc.*); überspringen; springen lassen; mit Gewalt (weg-) nehmen; ~ the gun *Sport:* e-n Fehlstart verursachen; *fig.* verfrüht handeln *od.* reagieren; ~ the lights bei Rot über die Kreuzung fahren; ~ the queue sich vordrängen; '**jump·er** Springer *m*; Jumper *m*; Matrosenbluse *f*; '**jump·ing-'off** Absprung *m*; '**jump-seat** 🚗, *mot.* Klappsitz *m*; '**jump-suit** Overall *m*; '**jump·y** nervös; nervös machend.
junc·tion ['dʒʌŋkʃən] Verbindung *f*; Kreuzung *f*; ⚡ Knotenpunkt *m*; ~ box ⚡ Abzweigdose *f*; **junc·ture** ['~tʃə] Verbindungspunkt *m*, -stelle *f*; (kritischer) Zeitpunkt *m*; at this ~ bei diesem Stand der Dinge.
June [dʒuːn] Juni *m*.
jun·gle ['dʒʌŋgl] Dschungel *m*.
jun·ior ['dʒuːnjə] **1.** jünger (to als); Unter...; *Am. univ.* der Unterstufe (angehörend); ~ high school *Am.* Schule mit Klasse 7, 8, 9; ~ partner jüngerer Teilhaber *m*, Associé *m*; **2.** Jüngere *m*, *f an Jahren od. im Amt*; Junior *m*; *Am.* (Ober)Schüler *m od.* Student *m* im 3. Jahr; F Kleine *m*; he is my ~ by four years, he is four years my ~ er ist vier

Jahre jünger als ich; **jun·ior·i·ty** [dʒuːni'ɔriti] geringeres Alter *n od.* Dienstalter *n*.
ju·ni·per ♃ ['dʒuːnipə] Wacholder *m*.
junk¹ ⚓ [dʒʌŋk] Dschunke *f*.
junk² [~] F Talmi *n*, Plunder *m*, alter Kram *m*; *contp.* Schund *m*, Mist *m*; *sl.* Rauschgift *n*; ~ mail *Am.* Reklamesendung(en *pl.*) *f*.
jun·ket ['dʒʌŋkit] **1.** Sauermilch-, Quarkspeise *f*; *Am.* Party *f*; Picknick *n*; Festessen *n*; Vergnügungsfahrt *f*; **2.** feiern.
junk·ie, junk·y *sl.* ['dʒʌŋki] Drogensüchtige *m*, *f*.
junk·yard ['dʒʌŋkjɑːd] Schrottplatz *m*.
jun·ta ['dʒʌntə] (spanische) Junta *f*; **jun·to** ['~təu] Clique *f*.
ju·rid·i·cal □ [dʒuə'ridikəl] rechtlich, gerichtlich; Rechts...
ju·ris·dic·tion [dʒuəris'dikʃən] Rechtsprechung *f*; Gerichtsbarkeit *f*; Gerichtsbezirk *m*; **ju·rispru·dence** ['~pruːdəns] Rechtswissenschaft *f*; '**ju·ris·pru·dent** Rechtsgelehrte *m*, Jurist *m*.
ju·rist ['dʒuərist] Jurist *m*.
ju·ror 🏛 ['dʒuərə] Geschworene *m*.
ju·ry 🏛 ['dʒuəri] Geschworenengericht *n*; Preisgericht *n*, Jury *f*; '**ju·ry-box** Geschworenenbank *f*; '**ju·ry·man** Geschworene *m*.
ju·ry-mast ⚓ ['dʒuərimɑːst] Notmast *m*.
just [dʒʌst] **1.** *adj.* □ gerecht; rechtschaffen; richtig, wahr; genau; gehörig, recht (*Maß etc.*); ganz; **2.** *adv.* gerade, genau; (so)eben, gerade; gerade noch; nur; ~ now eben jetzt, gerade jetzt; ~ over (below) ... knapp über (unter) ...; but ~ eben erst; ~ let me see! laß mal sehen!; it's ~ splendid! es ist einfach glänzend!
jus·tice ['dʒʌstis] Gerechtigkeit *f*, Billigkeit *f*; Richter *m*; Recht *n*; Rechtswesen *n*; Rechtsverfahren *n*; ♀ of the Peace Friedensrichter *m*; court of ~ Gericht(shof *m*) *n*; do ~ to s.o. j-m Gerechtigkeit widerfahren lassen; do o.s. ~ sein wahres Können zeigen; '**jus·tice·ship** Richteramt *n*.
jus·ti·fi·a·bil·i·ty [dʒʌstifaiə'biliti] Entschuldbarkeit *f*; '**jus·ti·fi·a·ble**

□ zu rechtfertigen(d).
jus·ti·fi·ca·tion [dʒʌstifi'keiʃən]
Rechtfertigung *f;* **jus·ti·fi·ca·to·ry**
['⁓təri] rechtfertigend.
jus·ti·fi·er *typ.* ['dʒʌstifaiə] Justie-
rer *m;* '**jus·ti·fy** rechtfertigen; *typ.*
justieren.
just·ly ['dʒʌstli] mit Recht.
just·ness ['dʒʌstnis] Gerechtigkeit *f*
etc. (s. just 1).
jut [dʒʌt] **1.** *a.* ⁓ *out* hervor-, heraus-
ragen, -stehen; vorspringen; **2.** Vorsprung *m.*
Jute¹ [dʒuːt] Jüte *m,* Jütin *f.*

jute² ⚲ [⁓] Jute *f.*
ju·ve·nes·cence [dʒuːvi'nesns] Verjüngung *f;* Jugend *f;* **ju·ve'nes-**
cent jugendlich; **ju·ve·nile** ['⁓nail]
1. jung, jugendlich; Jugend...; ⁓
Court Jugendgericht *n;* ⁓ *delin-*
quency Jugendkriminalität *f;* ⁓ *delin-*
quent jugendlicher Straftäter *m;* **2.**
junger Mensch *m;* **ju·ve·nil·i·ty** [⁓-
'niliti] Jugendlichkeit *f;* Kinderei *f.*
jux·ta·pose [dʒʌkstə'pəuz] nebenein-
anderstellen, vergleichen; **jux·ta-**
po·si·tion [⁓pə'ziʃən] Nebeneinan-
derstellung *f.*

K

Ka(f)·fir ['kæfə] Kaffer *m;* ⁓*s pl.* ⚲
sl. Südafrikanische Bergwerks-
aktien *f/pl.*
kale [keil] *(bsd.* Kraus-, Grün)Kohl
m; Am. sl. Moos *n (Geld).*
ka·lei·do·scope *opt.* [kə'leidəskəup]
Kaleidoskop *n.*
kal·ends ['kælendz] = *calends.*
kan·ga·roo [kæŋgə'ruː] Känguruh *n.*
ka·o·lin *min.* ['keiəlin] Kaolin *n.*
ka·pok ['keipɔk] Kapok *m.*
ka·put *sl.* [kæ'puːt] kaputt, erledigt.
ka·yak ['kaiæk] Kajak *m, n;* Paddelboot *n.*
keck [kek] würgen; sich ekeln *(at*
vor).
kedge ⚓ [kedʒ] **1.** Warpanker *m;*
2. warpen, verholen.
ked·ge·ree [kedʒə'riː] Reisgericht *n*
mit Fisch und Eiern.
keel ⚓ [kiːl] **1.** Kiel *m; on an even* ⁓
gleichlastig; *fig.* gleichmäßig; **2.** ⁓
over kieloben legen *od.* liegen; umschlagen; kentern; '**keel·age** ⚓
Kielgeld *n;* **keeled** ⚲ gekielt; **keel-**
-haul ⚓ ['⁓hɔːl] kielholen; **keel·son**
⚓ ['kelsn] Kielschwein *n (Kiel-*
verstärkung).
keen¹ □ [kiːn] scharf *(fig.* Kälte,
*Blick, Verstand, Kampf, Kritik,
Verhör etc.);* eifrig, begierig; stark‚
groß *(Appetit etc.);* ⁓ *on* F scharf *od.*
erpicht auf *acc.;* be ⁓ *on hunting* ein
leidenschaftlicher Jäger sein.
keen² *ir.* [⁓] Totenklage *f.*

keen-edged ['kiːnedʒd] scharfge-
schliffen; '**keen·ness** Schärfe *f;*
Heftigkeit *f;* Scharfsinn *m,* Feinheit *f.*
keep [kiːp] **1.** *Lebens*-Unterhalt *m;*
hist. Bergfried *m; for* ⁓*s* F für immer, endgültig; zum Behalten;
2. *(irr.) v/t. allg.* halten; behalten;
unterhalten *(ernähren); in e-m Zu-*
stand (er)halten; *Versprechen, Ge-*
setz, Regel, Feiertag, Richtung, Ver-
abredung etc. einhalten; *Fest* (ab-)
halten, feiern; *Konto* unterhalten;
Buch, Ware etc. führen; *Bett etc.*
hüten; fest-, aufhalten; (bei)behal-
ten; (auf)bewahren; (be)hüten *(from*
vor *dat.);* ⁓ *s.o. company* j-m Gesellschaft leisten; ⁓ *company with*
verkehren mit; ⁓ *silence* Schweigen
bewahren; ⁓ *one's temper* sich beherrschen; ⁓ *time* richtig gehen
(Uhr); ♩, ✗ Takt, Schritt halten;
⁓ *watch* aufpassen; ⁓ *s.o. waiting*
j. warten lassen; ⁓ *away* fernhalten;
⁓ *down* niederhalten; *Preise* niedrig
halten; ⁓ *s.o. from* j. abhalten von;
⁓ *s.th. from s.o.* j-m et. vorenthalten;
⁓ *in* drinbehalten; *Gefühl etc.* zurückhalten; *Schüler* nachsitzen lassen; *Feuer* unterhalten; ⁓ *in money*
mit Geld versehen; ⁓ *in view* im
Auge behalten; ⁓ *off* abhalten; ⁓ *on*
(bei)behalten; *Kleid* anbehalten,
Hut aufbehalten; ⁓ *out* nicht her-
einlassen, ausschließen; ⁓ *up* auf-

rechterhalten; *Mut* bewahren; in Ordnung halten; hindern, zu Bett zu gehen; aufbleiben lassen; *Gespräch* in Gang halten; ~ *it up* (es) durchhalten; **3.** *irr. v/i.* sich halten, bleiben; F sich aufhalten; sich halten (*Früchte etc.*); *mit Partizip*: ~ *doing* immer wieder tun; fortwährend tun; weiter tun; ~ *away* sich fernhalten; ~ *clear of* sich frei halten von; ~ *from* sich fernhalten von; ~ *in* with sich gut stehen mit *j-m*; ~ *off* sich fernhalten (von); ~ *on* fortfahren, weitermachen; ~ *on talking* fortfahren zu sprechen, weitersprechen; ~ *on at s.o.* j-m ständig zusetzen; ~ *to* sich halten an (*acc.*), bleiben bei, beibehalten; ~ *up* sich aufrecht(er)halten; ~ *up with* Schritt halten mit; ~ *up with the Joneses* es den Nachbarn gleichtun.

keep·er ['ki:pə] Wärter *m*, Wächter *m*; Aufseher *m*; Verwalter *m*; Inhaber *m*; **'keep·ing** Verwahrung *f*, Aufsicht *f*; Obhut *f*; Gewahrsam *m*; Unterhalt *m*; *be in* (*out of*) ~ *with* (nicht) übereinstimmen mit; **keepsake** ['~seik] Andenken *n* (*Geschenk etc.*).

keg [keg] Fäßchen *n*.

kelp ♃ [kelp] *ein* Seetang *m*.

kel·son ⚓ ['kelsn] = keelson.

ken [ken] Gesichtskreis *m*.

ken·nel¹ ['kenl] Gosse *f*, Rinnstein *m*.

ken·nel² [~] Hundehütte *f*, -zwinger *m*.

kept [kept] *pret. u. p.p. von* keep 2.

kerb [kə:b], '~·**stone** = curb etc.

ker·chief ['kə:tʃif] (Kopf-, Hals-) Tuch *n*; **'ker·chiefed** verschleiert.

kerf [kə:f] (Ein)Schnitt *m*.

ker·nel ['kə:nl] Kern *m* (*a. fig.*); Hafer-, Mais- *etc.* -korn *n*.

ker·o·sene ['kerəsi:n] Kerosin *n* (*Brennöl*).

kes·trel *orn.* ['kestrəl] Turmfalke *m*.

ketch ⚓ [ketʃ] Ketsch *f* (*Küstensegler*).

ketch·up ['ketʃəp] (Tomaten)Ketchup *m*.

ket·tle ['ketl] Kessel *m*; '~·**drum** ♪ (Kessel)Pauke *f*.

key [ki:] **1.** Schlüssel *m* (*a. fig.*); Schlußstein *m*; ⊕ Keil *m*, Splint *m*; Schraubenschlüssel *m*; Taste *f an Klavier, Schreibmaschine etc.*; Klappe *f e-r Flöte etc.*; ♪ Taste *f*, Druckknopf *m*; ♪ Tonart *f*; *fig.* Ton *m*; **2.** ~ *up* ♪ stimmen; erhöhen; *fig.* in erhöhte Spannung versetzen; '~·**board** Klaviatur *f*, Tastatur *f*; ~*s pl.* F Tasteninstrumente *n/pl.*; ~ *operator typ.* Maschinensetzer *m*; '~·**bu·gle** ♪ Klappenhorn *n*; '~·**hole** Schlüsselloch *n*; ~ **in·dus·try** Schlüsselindustrie *f*; '~·**man** Schlüsselfigur *f*; '~·**mon·ey** Ablösung *f* (*für e-e Wohnung*); '~·**note** Grundton *m*; ~ **punch** Kartenlocher *m*; ~ **sig·na·ture** ♪ Tonartbezeichnung *f*; '~·**stone** Schlußstein *m*; *fig.* Grundlage *f*.

khak·i ['ka:ki] **1.** khaki-, staubfarben; **2.** Khaki (*Farbe*) *n*, (*Stoff*) *m*.

khan¹ [ka:n] Khan *m*, *orientalischer Herrscher m*.

khan² [~] Karawanserei *f*.

kibe [kaib] (offene) Frostbeule *f*.

kib·itz·er *Am.* F ['kibitsə] Kiebitz *m*; Besserwisser *m*.

ki·bosh *sl.* ['kaibɒʃ] Unsinn *m*; *put the* ~ *on s.o.* es j-m besorgen.

kick [kik] **1.** (Fuß)Tritt *m*; Stoß *m*; Rückschlag *m des Gewehres*; Elan *m*, Schwung *m*; F Nervenkitzel *m*; *fig.* Feuer *n*, Kraft *f*, Prozente *n/pl.*; Fußballspieler *m*; *more* ~*s than halfpence* mehr Prügel als Lob; *get the* ~ *sl.* rausfliegen; *get a* ~ *out of* F Spaß finden an (*dat.*); *do s.th. for* ~*s* F et. aus Spaß *od.* Jux machen; *it's got a* ~ *to it* das hat's in sich; **2.** *v/t.* (mit dem Fuß) stoßen *od.* treten; F *Verehrer* abblitzen lassen; *Fußball:* schießen; ~ *the bucket sl.* ins Gras beißen; ~ *downstairs* die Treppe hinunterwerfen; ~ *one's heels* F sich die Beine in den Leib stehen (*warten müssen*); ~ *s.o. around* F j. schlecht behandeln, j. schikanieren; ~ *out* F hinauswerfen; ~ *up a row od. fuss od. dust* F Radau machen; *v/i.* (hinten) ausschlagen; stoßen (*Gewehr*); sich auflehnen *od.* sträuben (*against, at gegen*); ~ *in with Am. sl.* Geld reinbuttern; ~ *off Fußball:* anstoßen; ~ *over F* Fußball: Anstoß *m*; '**kick·shaw** Leckerei *f*; Kinkerlitzchen *n*; '**kick-start·er** Kickstarter *m* (*am Motorrad*); '**kick·up** *sl.* Radau *m*, Krach *m*.

'**kick·back** *bsd. Am.* F Rückzahlung *f*; '**kick·er** Schläger *m* (*Pferd*); Fußballspieler *m*; '**kick-'off** Fußball:

kid [kid] **1.** Zicklein *n*; Ziegenleder *n*; *sl.* Kind *n*; **2.** *sl.* foppen, (an-) pflaumen, (ver)kohlen; 'kid·dy *sl.* Kind *n*; **kid glove** Glacéhandschuh *m* (*a. fig.*); 'kid-glove sanft, zart.

kid·nap ['kidnæp] *bsd. Kinder* entführen; 'kid-nap·(p)er Kindesentführer *m*, Kidnapper *m*.

kid·ney ['kidni] *anat.* Niere *f*; F Art *f*, Schlag *m*; ∼ *bean* ♀ weiße Bohne *f*; ∼ **ma·chine** ⚙ künstliche Niere *f*.

kike *Am. sl. contp.* [kaik] Jude *m*.

kill [kil] **1.** töten (*a. fig.*), umbringen; schlachten; *fig.* vernichten, morden; erdrücken; *parl.* zu Fall bringen; *fig.* überwältigen; ∼ *off* abschlachten; ∼ *time* die Zeit totschlagen; **2.** Tötung *f*; Jagdbeute *f*; 'kill·er Totschläger *m*; Vernichtungsmittel *n*; 'kill·ing **1.** ▢ mörderisch; unwiderstehlich; F urkomisch; **2.** *Am.* F *finanzieller* Volltreffer *m*; 'kill-joy Spaßverderber *m*.

kiln [kiln, ⊕ kil] Brenn-, Darrofen *m*; '∼-dry darren, dörren.

kil·o·cy·cle *phys.* ['kiləusaikl] Kilohertz *n*; **kil·o·gram, kil·o·gramme** ['∼græm] Kilogramm *n*; **kil·o·me·ter, kil·o·me·tre** ['kiləumi:tə] Kilometer *n*; **ki·lo·watt** ⚡ ['kiləuwɔt] Kilowatt *n*.

kilt [kilt] **1.** Kilt *m*, Schottenrock *m*; **2.** aufschürzen, plissieren.

ki·mo·no [ki'məunəu] Kimono *m*; kimonoartiger Morgenrock *m*.

kin [kin] **1.** (Bluts)Verwandtschaft *f*; Sippe *f*; *the next of* ∼ die nächsten Verwandten; **2.** verwandt (*to* mit).

kind [kaind] **1.** ▢ gütig, freundlich (*to* zu, gegen); **2.** Art *f*, Sorte *f*; Gattung *f*, Geschlecht *n*; Art und Weise *f*; Natur *f*; *people of all* ∼s allerhand Leute; *different in* ∼ artverschieden; *pay in* ∼ in Waren (*fig.* mit gleicher Münze) zahlen; *I* ∼ *of expected it* F ich habe es beinahe *od.* so ziemlich erwartet.

kin·der·gar·ten ['kindəga:tn] Kindergarten *m*; ∼ *teacher* Kindergärtnerin *f*.

kind-heart·ed ['kaind'ha:tid] gütig, gutherzig.

kin·dle ['kindl] anzünden; (sich) entzünden (*a. fig.*).

kind·li·ness ['kaindlinis] Freundlichkeit *f*, Güte *f*.

kin·dling ['kindliŋ] *a.* ∼*s pl.* Holz *n* zum Anfeuern.

kind·ly ['kaindli] *adj.* freundlich (*a. adv.*); günstig (*Klima etc.*).

kind·ness ['kaindnis] Güte *f*, Freundlichkeit *f*; Gefälligkeit *f*.

kin·dred ['kindrid] **1.** verwandt, gleichartig; **2.** Verwandtschaft *f*.

kine † [kain] *pl. von* cow[1].

ki·ne·ma ['kinimə] = *cinema.*

kin·e·mat·o·graph [kaini'mætəugra:f] = *cinematograph.*

ki·net·ic [kai'netik] bewegend; kinetisch; **ki'net·ics** *sg.* Kinetik *f*.

king [kiŋ] König *m* (*a. fig. u. Schach, Kartenspiel*); *fig.* Magnat *m*; ∼'*s evil* ⚕ Skrofulose *f*; *turn* ∼'*s evidence* gegen seine Komplizen aussagen; 'king·bird *orn.* Königsvogel *m*; 'king·craft Herrscherkunst *f*; 'king·cup ♀ Butterblume *f*; Sumpfdotterblume *f*; 'king·dom Königreich *n*; *bsd.* ♀, *zo.* Reich *n*, Gebiet *n*; *eccl.* Reich *n Gottes*; ∼ *come* F das Jenseits; 'king·fish·er Eisvogel *m*; **king·let** ['∼lit] Duodezfürst *m*; 'king·like königlich; 'king·li·ness das Königliche, königliches Wesen *n*; 'king·ly königlich; 'king·pin Achszapfen *m*; *fig.* Hauptperson *f*; 'king·post ⚙ Giebelbalken *m*; 'king·ship Königtum *n*; Königswürde *f*; 'king-size F überlang, übergroß.

kink [kiŋk] **1.** Schleife *f im Tau etc.*; Knoten *m*; *fig.* Schrulle *f*, Fimmel *m*; *Am.* Betriebsfehler *m*; *have a* ∼ F e-n Vogel haben; **2.** (sich) verfitzen; knicken; 'kink·y kraus (*Haar*); verrückt, ausgefallen.

kins·folk ['kinzfəuk] Verwandten *pl.*; 'kin·ship Verwandtschaft *f*; 'kins·man Verwandte *m*; 'kins·wom·an Verwandte *f*.

ki·osk ['ki:ɔsk] Kiosk *m*; Telefonzelle *f*.

kip F [kip] **1.** Schlaf *m*; **2.** pennen.

kip·per ['kipə] **1.** Räucherhering *m*, Bückling *m*; *sl.* Mensch *m*, Kerl *m*; **2.** Fische leicht räuchern.

kirk [kə:k] (schottische) Kirche *f*.

kir·tle † ['kə:tl] kurzer Frauenrock *m*; Wams *n*.

kiss [kis] **1.** Kuß *m*; *fig.* leichte Berührung *f*; **2.** (sich) küssen; ∼ *the book* die Bibel küssen *beim Schwören*; ∼ *the dust* im Staub kriechen

(*sich unterwerfen*); ins Gras beißen;
'~-**proof** kußfest.

kit [kit] Ausrüstung *f* (*a.* ⚔ *u.*
Sport); Handwerkszeug *n*, Werkzeug *n*; *do-it-yourself* ~ Bausatz *m*,
-kasten *m*; '~-**bag** ⚔ Tornister *m*;
⚓ Seesack *m*; Reisetasche *f*.

kitch·en ['kitʃin] Küche *f*; '**kitch-en·er** Küchenherd *m*; **kitch·en-ette** [~'net] Kochnische *f*.

kitch·en...: '~-'**gar·den** Gemüsegarten *m*; '~-**maid** Küchenmädchen *n*; '~**range** Kochherd *m*; ~
scales *pl.* Küchenwaage *f*; ~ **sink**
Spüle *f*; ~ *drama* realistisches Sozialdrama *n*.

kite [kait] *orn.* Gabelweihe *f*;
Papier-Drachen *m*; *fig.* Versuchsballon *m*; ✝ *sl.* Kellerwechsel *m*;
~ *balloon* ⚔ Fesselballon *m*; *fly a* ~
e-n Drachen *od. fig.* Versuchsballon steigen lassen.

kith [kiθ]: ~ *and kin* Freunde und
Verwandte *pl.*

kit·ten ['kitn] **1.** Kätzchen *n*;
2. Junge werfen (*Katze*); **kit·ten-ish** ['kitniʃ] kätzchenhaft.

kit·tle *fig.* ['kitl] kitz(e)lig, heikel.

kit·ty¹ ['kiti] Kätzchen *n*.

kit·ty² [~] (gemeinsame) Kasse *f*.

ki·wi *orn.* ['ki:wi:] Kiwi *m*.

Klan *Am.* [klæn] Ku-Klux-Klan *m*;
Klansman ['klænzmən] Mitglied *n*
des Ku-Klux-Klan.

klax·on *mot.* ['klæksn] Hupe *f*.

klep·to·ma·ni·a [kleptəu'meinjə]
Kleptomanie *f* (*krankhafter Stehltrieb*); **klep·to'ma·ni·ac** [~niæk]
Kleptomane *m*, Kleptomanin *f*.

knack [næk] Kunstgriff *m*, Kniff *m*,
Dreh *m*; Geschicklichkeit *f*.

knack·er ['nækə] Abdecker *m*,
Schinder *m*; Abbruchunternehmer
m; '**knack·ered** *sl.* total geschafft;
'**knack·er·y** Abdeckerei *f*.

knag [næg] Knorren *m*.

knap·sack ['næpsæk] Tornister *m*;
Rucksack *m*.

knar [nɑ:] Knorren *m*.

knave [neiv] Schurke *m*; *Karten*:
Bube *m*; '**knav·er·y** Gaunerei *f*,
Schurkenstreich *m*; '**knav·ish** ☐
schurkisch.

knead [ni:d] kneten; massieren.

knee [ni:] **1.** Knie *n*; ⊕ Kniestück *n*;
bring s.o. to his ~s j. auf die Knie
zwingen; *on the* ~s *of the gods* noch
ungewiß, im Schoße der Götter;

2. *Hose* am Knie ausbeulen; '~-**breech·es** *pl.* Kniehose(n *pl.*) *f*;
'~-**cap** Kniescheibe *f*; Knieschützer *m*; '~-'**deep** bis an die Knie
(reichend); '~-**joint** Kniegelenk *n*;
kneel [ni:l] (*irr.*) knien (*to* vor
dat.); '**kneel·er** Kniende *m*, *f*;
'**knee-pan** Kniescheibe *f*.

knell [nel] Totenglocke *f*.

knelt [nelt] *pret. u. p.p. von* kneel.

knew [nju:] *pret. von* know 1.

knick·er·bock·ers ['nikəbɔkəz] *pl.*
Knickerbocker *pl.*, Kniehosen *f/pl.*;
'**knick·ers** F *pl.* *Damen*-Schlüpfer
m; = *knickerbockers*.

knick·knack ['niknæk] Spielerei *f*,
Nippsache *f*; ~s *pl.* Kinkerlitzchen
n/pl.

knife [naif] **1.** *pl.* **knives** [naivz]
Messer *n*; *get one's* ~ *into s.o. fig.*
j. gefressen haben, j-m übelwollen;
2. schneiden; (er)stechen; '~-**grind·er** Scherenschleifer *m*.

knight [nait] **1.** Ritter *m*; *Springer*
m im Schach; **2.** zum Ritter schlagen,
adeln; **knight-er·rant** ['~'erənt]
fahrender Ritter *m*; **knight·hood**
['~hud] Rittertum *n*; Ritterschaft *f*;
'**knight·li·ness** Ritterlichkeit *f*;
'**knight·ly** ritterlich.

knit [nit] (*irr.*) stricken; (ver)knüpfen; (sich) eng verbinden; ~ *the*
brows die Stirn runzeln; '**knit·ter**
Stricker(in); = *knitting-machine*;
'**knit·ting** 1. Stricken *n*; Strickzeug
n; **2.** Strick...; '**knit·ting-ma-chine** Strickmaschine *f*; '**knitting-nee·dle** Stricknadel *f*; '**knit-wear** Strickkleidung *f*, Strick-,
Wirkwaren *f/pl.*

knives [naivz] *pl. von* knife.

knob [nɔb] Knopf *m*; Buckel *m*;
Brocken *m Kohle etc.*; '**knobbed**,
'**knob·by** mit einem Knopf *etc.*;
knorrig; '**knob-stick** Knotenstock
m; Streikbrecher *m*.

knock [nɔk] **1.** Schlag *m*; Anklopfen
n; *mot.* Klopfen *n*; **2.** *v/i.* klopfen
(*a. mot.*); pochen; stoßen; schlagen;
~ *about* F sich herumtreiben; ~ *off*
sl. abhauen; Schluß *od.* Feierabend
machen; ~ *under* sich ergeben; *v/t.*
klopfen, stoßen, schlagen; *Am. sl.*
bekritteln, schlechtmachen; ~ *about*
herumstoßen, übel zurichten; ~
down niederschlagen; zu Boden
werfen; *Auktion*: zuschlagen; ⊕
auseinandernehmen; *be* ~*ed down*

überfahren werden; ~ *off* abschlagen; aufhören mit; F zs.-hauen (*schnell erledigen*); *Summe* abziehen; ~ *out Boxen*: k.o. schlagen; ~ *up* (durch Klopfen) wecken; erschöpfen; ~·a·bout [ˈ~əbaut] **1.** lärmend; unstet; Strapazier... (*Kleidung*); *thea.* Clown..., Radau...; **2.** Radaustück *n*; 'ˣ~-'**down** niederschmetternd; äußerst(*Preis*); '**knock·er** Klopfende *m*; Türklopfer *m*; *Am. sl.* Kritikaster *m*; ~s *pl. sl.* Titten *f pl.*; '**knock-**'**kneed** X-beinig; *fig.* hinkend; '**knock-out** *Boxen*: Knockout *m*, K.o. *m*; *sl.* tolle Sache *f od.* Person *f.*

knoll[1] [nəul] kleiner Erdhügel *m.*

knoll[2] [~] (*bsd.* zu Grabe) läuten.

knot [nɔt] **1.** Knoten *m*; Knorren *m*, Ast(knoten) *m*; ⚓ Knoten *m*, Seemeile *f*; ⚘ Knospe *f*; Schleife *f*, (Achsel)Band *n*; Schwierigkeit *f*; **2.** (ver)knoten, (ver)knüpfen (*a. fig.*); *Stirn* runzeln; verwickeln; '**knot·hole** Astloch *n*; '**knot·ti·ness** das Knotige; Schwierigkeit *f*; '**knot·ty** knotig, knorrig; *fig.* verwickelt; '**knot·work** Knüpfarbeit*f.*

knout [naut] **1.** Knute *f*; **2.** *j-m* die Knute geben.

know [nəu] **1.** (*irr.*) wissen; kennen; erkennen; erfahren; ~ *French* Französisch können; *come to* ~ erfahren; *get to* ~ kennenlernen; ~ *one's business,* ~ *the ropes,* ~ *a thing or two,* ~ *what's what* sich auskennen, Erfahrung haben; *do you* ~ *how to play chess?* können Sie Schach spielen?; *you ought to* ~ *better than to do that* Sie sollten so klug sein, das nicht zu tun; *I don't* ~ *one from the other* ich kann

den einen nicht vom andern unterscheiden; *you* ~ *am Ende des Satzes:* nämlich; **2.** *be in the* ~ F Bescheid wissen (*of* über *acc.*), im Bilde sein; '**know·a·ble** (er)kennbar; '**know-all 1.** allwissend; **2.** Alleswisser *m*; '**know-how** praktische Erfahrung *f*; Know-how *n*; '**know·ing 1.** ☐ erfahren; klug; schlau; verständnisvoll; wissentlich; F schick; **2.** Wissen *n*; '**know·ing·ly** wissentlich; bewußt, absichtlich; **knowl·edge** [ˈnɔlidʒ] Kenntnis(se *f/pl.*) *f*; Wissen *n*; *to my* ~ meines Wissens; '**knowl·edge·a·ble** F gut informiert; kenntnisreich, klug; aufgeschlossen; **known** [nəun] *p.p. von* know 1; *come to be* ~ bekannt werden; *make* ~ bekanntmachen; *make o.s.* ~ sich bekannt machen, sich vorstellen.

knuck·le [ˈnʌkl] **1.** *a.* '~-**bone** Knöchel *m*; Kniestück *n vom Kalb etc.*; **2.** ~ *down,* ~ *under* nachgeben; '~-**dust·er** Schlagring *m.*

ko·a·la *zo.* [kəuˈɑːlə] Koala *m.*

kook *Am. sl.* [kuk] Spinner *m.*

Ko·ran [kɔˈrɑːn] Koran *m.*

Ko·re·an [kəˈriən] **1.** Koreaner(in); **2.** koreanisch.

kosh·er [ˈkəuʃə] **1.** koscher (*Speisen*); F rechtmäßig, in Ordnung; **2.** koscheres Essen *n.*

ko·tow [ˈkəuˈtau] **1.** Kotau *m* (*demütige Ehrenerweisung*); **2.** Kotau machen, *fig.* kriechen (*to* vor *dat.*).

Krem·lin [ˈkremlin] *der* Kreml.

ku·dos *co.* [ˈkjuːdɔs] Ruhm *m.*

Ku-Klux-Klan *Am.* [ˈkjuːˈklʌks-ˈklæn] Ku-Klux-Klan *m* (*Geheimbund in den USA*).

L

la ♪ [lɑː] la *n* (*Solmisationssilbe*).

lab F [læb] = laboratory.

la·bel [ˈleibl] **1.** Zettel *m*, Etikett *n*; Aufschrift *f*; Schildchen *n*; Bezeichnung *f*; ⚘ Kranzleiste *f*; **2.** etikettieren, beschriften; ✝ mit Preis auszeichnen; *fig.* abstempeln

(*as* als).

la·bi·al [ˈleibjəl] **1.** Lippen..., labial; **2.** Lippenlaut *m*, Labial *m.*

lab·o·ra·to·ry [ləˈbɔrətəri] Laboratorium *n*; ~ *assistant* Laborant(in).

la·bo·ri·ous ☐ [ləˈbɔːriəs] mühsam, -selig; anstrengend; arbeitsam;

schwerfällig (*Stil*).
la·bo(u)r ['leibə] **1.** Arbeit *f*; Mühe *f*, Anstrengung *f*; (Geburts')Wehen *f/pl.*; Arbeiter *m/pl.*, Arbeitskräfte *f/pl.*; Arbeiterschaft *f*; *Ministry of* ⳠArbeitsministerium *n*; *hard* ⳠZwangsarbeit *f*; **2.** Arbeiter...; Arbeits...; **3.** *v/i.* arbeiten; sich abmühen; sich mühsam (vorwärts-) bewegen; Ⳡ *under* leiden unter (*dat.*), zu kämpfen haben mit; Ⳡ *under a delusion* sich e-r Täuschung hingeben; *v t.* ausarbeiten; ausführlich eingehen auf (*acc.*); Ⳡ **camp** Arbeitslager *n*; Ⳡ**Day** Tag *m* der Arbeit; Ⳡ **dis·pute** Arbeitskonflikt *m*; **'labo(u)red** schwerfällig, steif (*Stil*); mühsam (*Atem etc.*); **'la·bo(u)r·er** ungelernter Arbeiter *m*; **La·bo(u)r Ex·change** Arbeitsamt *n*; **la·bo(u)r force** Belegschaft *f*; **'la·bo(u)r·ing** arbeitend; Arbeits...; Ⳡ *breath* schwerer Atem *m*; **la·bo(u)r·ite** ['Ⳡrait] Mitglied *n od.* Anhänger *m* der Labour Party; **La·bour Par·ty** *pol.* Labour Party *f*; **'la·bo(u)r-sav·ing** arbeitssparend; **la·bor un·ion** *Am.* Gewerkschaft *f*.
Lab·ra·dor ['læbrədɔ:]: Ⳡ *dog* *zo.* Neufundländer *m*.
la·bur·num ♀ [lə'bə:nəm] Goldregen *m*.
lab·y·rinth ['læbərinθ] Labyrinth *n*; **lab·y'rin·thi·an** [ⳠΘiən], *mst* **lab·y'rin·thine** [Ⳡθain] labyrinthisch.
lac [læk] (Gummi)Lack *m*; Lak *n*; *a* Ⳡ *of rupees* 100 000 Rupien.
lace [leis] **1.** Spitze *f*; Borte *f*, Tresse *f*; Schnur *f*; Schnürband *n*; **2.** (zu)schnüren; mit Spitze *etc.* besetzen; *Schnur* durch-, einziehen; *Getränk* mischen, versetzen (*with mit Spirituosen*); Ⳡ (*into*) *s.o.* j. verprügeln.
lac·er·ate 1. ['læsəreit] auf-, zerreißen, zerfleischen; *fig.* quälen; **2.** ['Ⳡrit] zerrissen; **lac·er·a·tion** [Ⳡ'reiʃən] Zerreißen *n*; Riß *m*.
lach·es ⳠⳠ ['leitʃiz] Fahrlässigkeit *f*, Versäumnis *n*.
lach·ry·mal ['lækriməl] Tränen...; **lach·ry·mose** ['Ⳡməus] weinerlich; tränenreich.
lack [læk] **1.** Fehlen *n*, Mangel *m*; **2.** *v/t.* ermangeln (*gen.*); *he* Ⳡ*s money* es fehlt ihm an Geld; *v/i.* *be* Ⳡ*ing* fehlen, mangeln; *he is* Ⳡ*ing in courage* es fehlt ihm an Mut.

lack·a·dai·si·cal ☐ [lækə'deizikəl] gelangweilt, gleichgültig, uninteressiert.
lack·ey ['læki] **1.** Lakai *m* (*a. fig.*); **2.** *j-s* Lakai sein.
lack·ing ['lækiŋ] *s. lack 1.*
lack·land ['læklænd] **1.** ohne Land; besitzlos; **2.** Habenichts *m*; **lack·lus·tre**, *Am.* **lack·lus·ter** ['Ⳡlʌstə] glanzlos, matt.
la·con·ic [lə'kɔnik] (Ⳡ*ally*) lakonisch, wortkarg, kurz u. prägnant.
lac·quer ['lækə] **1.** Lack *m*; **2.** lakkieren; Ⳡ*ed* Lack...
lac·quey ['læki] = **lackey.**
la·crosse [lə'krɔs] *Sport:* Lacrosse *n* (*Ballspiel*).
lac·ta·tion [læk'teiʃən] Säugen *n*, Stillen *n*.
lac·tic ['læktik] Milch...; Ⳡ *acid* Milchsäure *f*.
la·cu·na [lə'kju:nə] Lücke *f*.
lac·y ['leisi] spitzenartig; Spitzen...
lad [læd] Bursche *m*, Junge *m*.
lad·der ['lædə] **1.** Leiter *f* (*a. fig.*); ⚓ Strickleiter *f*, *a.* Treppe *f*; Laufmasche *f im Strumpf*; **2.** e-e Laufmasche bekommen; **'Ⳡ-proof** maschenfest (*Strumpf etc.*).
lad·die ['lædi] Bürschlein *n*.
lade [leid] (*irr.*) = *load*; **'lad·en 1.** *p.p. von lade*; **2.** *adj.* beladen.
la-di-da ['lɑ:di'dɑ:] **1.** Fatzke *m*, Affe *m*; **2.** affig, geckenhaft.
la·ding ['leidiŋ] Ladung *f*, Fracht *f*.
la·dle ['leidl] **1.** Schöpflöffel *m*, Kelle *f*; **2.** Ⳡ *out Suppe* austeilen; *fig.* ver-, austeilen.
la·dy ['leidi] Dame *f*; Lady *f*, Herrin *f*; *Ladies sg.* Damentoilette *f*; *Ladies and Gentlemen!* meine Damen u. Herren!; ⳠⲢ *Day* Mariä Verkündigung *f* (*25. März*); Ⳡ *doctor* Ärztin *f*; Ⳡ*'s maid* Zofe *f*; Ⳡ*'s od. ladies' man* Weiberheld *m*; **'Ⳡ-bird** Marienkäfer *m*; **'Ⳡ-in-'wait·ing** Hofdame *f*; **'Ⳡ-kill·er** Herzensbrecher *m*; **'Ⳡ-like** damenhaft; *contp.* weibisch; **'Ⳡ-love** Geliebte *f*; Ⳡ *of the bed·cham·ber* Hofdame *f*; **'Ⳡ-ship:** *her* Ⳡ die gnädige Frau; *Your* Ⲣ gnädige Frau, Euer Gnaden.
lag¹ [læg] **1.** zögern; *a.* Ⳡ *behind* zurückbleiben; **2.** Verzögerung *f*.
lag² *sl.* [Ⳡ] **1.** Zuchthäusler *m*; **2.** ins Zuchthaus bringen.
lag³ [Ⳡ] *Wasserrohr etc.* isolieren.

landslide

la·ger (beer) [ˈlɑːɡə(ˈbiə)] Lagerbier *n*; ⁓ *and lime Lagerbier mit e-m Schuß Limonensirup*.

lag·gard [ˈlæɡəd] Nachzügler *m*; Trödler *m*, Bummler *m*.

la·goon [ləˈɡuːn] Lagune *f*.

la·ic [ˈleiik] 1. *a.* **ˈla·i·cal** □ weltlich; Laien...; 2. Laie *m*; **la·i·cize** [ˈ⁓saiz] verweltlichen.

laid [leid] *pret. u. p.p. von lay*[1] 2; ⁓ *up* bettlägerig (*with* infolge).

lain [lein] *p.p. von lie*[2] 2.

lair [lɛə] Lager *n* e-s *wilden Tieres*.

laird *schott.* [lɛəd] Gutsherr *m*.

la·i·ty [ˈleiiti] Laien *m*/*pl.*

lake[1] [leik] See *m*.

lake[2] [⁓] rote Pigmentfarbe *f*.

lake-dwel·lings [ˈleikdweliŋz] *pl.* Pfahlbauten *m*/*pl.*

lam *sl.* [læm] abhauen, verduften; ⁓ *into s.o.* j. verdreschen, j. vermöbeln.

la·ma [ˈlɑːmə] Lama *m*, buddhistischer Mönch *m*; **ˈla·ma·se·ry** [ˈ⁓səri] Lamakloster *n*.

lamb [læm] 1. Lamm *n*; Lammfleisch *n*; 2. lammen.

lam·baste *sl.* [læmˈbeist] vermöbeln; zs.-stauchen (*abkanzeln*).

lam·bent [ˈlæmbənt] leckend; züngelnd (*Flamme*); funkelnd, sprühend.

lamb·kin [ˈlæmkin] Lämmchen *n*; **ˈlamb·like** lammfromm; **ˈlamb·skin** Lammfell *n*.

lame [leim] 1. □ lahm (*a. fig. = mangelhaft*); 2.lähmen; **ˈlame·ness** Lahmheit *f*.

la·ment [ləˈment] 1. Wehklage *f*; 2. (be)klagen; trauern (*for* um); **lam·en·ta·ble** □ [ˈlæməntəbl] beklagenswert; kläglich, jämmerlich; **lam·en·ta·tion** Wehklage *f*.

lam·i·na [ˈlæminə], *pl.* **lam·i·nae** [ˈ⁓niː] Plättchen *n*; ⁓, ⚘ Lamelle *f*; **ˈlam·i·nar** in Plättchen; **lam·i·nate** [ˈ⁓neit] auswalzen; aufspalten; schichten; belegen; ⁓*d glass* Verbundglas *n*.

lamp [læmp] Lampe *f*; *fig.* Leuchte *f*; **ˈ⁓·black** Ruß *m*; **ˈ⁓·chim·ney** Lampenzylinder *m*; **ˈ⁓·light** Lampenlicht *n*; **ˈ⁓·light·er** Laternenanzünder *m*; **ˈ⁓·oil** Petroleum *n*.

lam·poon [læmˈpuːn] 1. Schmähschrift *f*; 2. schmähen.

lamp-post [ˈlæmppəust] Laternenpfahl *m*.

lam·prey *ichth.* [ˈlæmpri] Neunauge *n*.

lamp·shade [ˈlæmpʃeid] Lampenschirm *m*.

lance [lɑːns] 1. Lanze *f*; Speer *m*; 2. aufschneiden (*a.* ✳); **ˈ⁓·cor·po·ral** ⚔ Gefreite *m*; **lan·ce·o·late** ⚘ [ˈlænsiəlit] lanzettförmig; **lanc·er** ⚔ [ˈlɑːnsə] Ulan *m*; ⁓*s pl.* Lanciers *m*/*pl.* (*englischer Tanz*).

lan·cet [ˈlɑːnsit] Lanzette *f*; ⁓ **arch** △ Spitzbogen *m*; ⁓ **win·dow** Spitzbogenfenster *n*.

land [lænd] 1. *das* feste Land; Land *n*; Grund und Boden *m*; Gut *n*, Grundstück *n*; *by* ⁓ auf dem Landweg; ⁓*s pl.* Ländereien *f*/*pl.*; *see how the* ⁓ *lies* sehen, wie die Sache steht *od.* wie der Hase läuft; 2. landen; ⚓ löschen; *Hieb* anbringen, versetzen; *Preis* gewinnen; **ˈ⁓-a·gent** Grundstücksmakler *m*; Gutsverwalter *m*.

lan·dau [ˈlændɔː] Landauer *m* (*Pferdewagen*).

land·ed [ˈlændid] Grund besitzend; Land..., Grund...; ⁓ *gentry* Landadel *m*.

land...: **ˈ⁓·fall** ⚓ Landkennung *f*; **ˈ⁓·forc·es** *pl.* Landstreitkräfte *f*/*pl.*; **ˈ⁓·grab·ber** Landraffer *m*; **ˈ⁓·hold·er** Grundbesitzer(in).

land·ing [ˈlændiŋ] Landung *f*; Treppenabsatz *m*; Anlegestelle *f*; **ˈ⁓·craft** ⚓, ⚔ Landungsboot *n*; **ˈ⁓·field** ✈ Landebahn *f*; **ˈ⁓·gear** ✈ Fahrgestell *n*; **ˈ⁓·net** Hamen *m*; **ˈ⁓·par·ty** ⚔ Landungstrupp *m*; **ˈ⁓·stage** ⚓ Landungsbrücke *f*; **ˈ⁓·strip** = *landing-field*.

land·la·dy [ˈlænleidi] Vermieterin *f*, Wirtin *f*. [besitz.]

land·less [ˈlændlis] ohne Grund-|

land...: **ˈ⁓·locked** landumschlossen; **ˈ⁓·lop·er** Landstreicher *m*; **ˈ⁓·lord** [ˈlænlɔːd] Vermieter *m*, Wirt *m*; Haus-, Grundbesitzer *m*; **⁓·lub·ber** ⚓ *contp.* [ˈlændlʌbə] Landratte *f*; **ˈ⁓·mark** *bsd.* ⚓ Landmarke *f*; Grenz-, Markstein *m* (*a. fig.*); Wendepunkt *m*; Wahrzeichen *n*; **ˈ⁓·own·er** Grundbesitzer(in); **ˈ⁓·plane** Landflugzeug *n*; **⁓·scape** [ˈlænskeip] Landschaft *f*; Landschaftsmalerei *f*; ⁓ *gardener* Gartenarchitekt *m*; ⁓ *gardening* Gartenarchitektur *f*; **⁓·slide** [ˈlændslaid] Erdrutsch *m* (*a. pol.*); *a Democratic* ⁓ *ein*

Erdrutsch zugunsten der Demokraten; '~·**slip** *konkr.* Erdrutsch *m*; ~**s·man** ⚓ ['~zmən] Landratte *f*; '~·**-sur·vey·or** Landmesser *m*; '~·**tax** Grundsteuer *f*; ~·**ward** ['~wəd] landwärts (gelegen).

lane [lein] Feldweg *m*; Gasse *f*; Spalier *n*; *mot.* Fahrbahn *f*, Spur *f*.

lang syne *schott.* ['læŋ'sain] längst vergangen(e Zeit *f*).

lan·guage ['læŋgwidʒ] Sprache *f*; Worte *n/pl.*; *bad* ~ häßliche Worte *n pl.*; *strong* ~ Kraftausdrücke *m pl.*; ~ **lab·o·ra·to·ry** Sprachlabor *n*.

lan·guid ☐ ['læŋgwid] matt, schlaff; teilnahmslos; träg (*Strom etc.*); ⚕ flau; '**lan·guid·ness** Mattigkeit *f*; Flauheit *f*.

lan·guish ['læŋgwiʃ] matt werden; schmachten (*for* nach); dahinsiechen; ⚕ darniederliegen; '**lan·guish·ing** ☐ schmachtend; ⚕ flau.

lan·guor ['læŋgə] Mattigkeit *f*; Schlaffheit *f*; Schmachten *n*; Stille *f*; '**lan·guor·ous** ☐ matt; schlaff; drückend.

lank ☐ [læŋk] schmächtig, dünn; schlaff (*Börse*); schlicht, glatt (*Haar*); '**lank·y** ☐ schlaksig.

lan·o·lin ['lænəuli:n] Lanolin *n*, Wollfett *n*.

lan·tern ['læntən] Laterne *f* (*a.* △); *dark* ~ Blendlaterne *f*; '~**-jawed** hohlwangig; '~**-slide** Dia(positiv) *n*, Lichtbild *n*; ~ *lecture* Lichtbildervortrag *m*.

lan·yard ⚓ ['lænjəd] Taljereep *n*.

lap¹ [læp] 1. Schoß *m* (*a. fig.*); ⊕ übergreifende Kante *f*; Vorstoß *m*; *Garn*-Windung *f*; *Sport:* Runde *f*; ~ *of hono(u)r Sport:* Ehrenrunde *f*; 2. übereinanderlegen, umschlagen; (ein)hüllen (*in* in *acc.*).

lap² [~] 1. Lecken *n*; Schluck *m*; Anschlagen *n*, Plätschern *n von Wellen*; 2. (auf)lecken; schlürfen; verschlingen; plätschern (gegen) (*Wellen*).

lap-dog ['læpdɔg] Schoßhund *m*.

la·pel [lə'pel] Aufschlag *m am Rock.*

lap·i·dar·y ['læpidəri] 1. Stein...; Lapidar...; 2. Steinschneider *m*.

lap·is laz·u·li [læpis'læzjulai] Lapislazuli *m*, Lasurstein *m*.

lapse [læps] 1. Dahingleiten *n*; Verlauf *m der Zeit*; Verfallen *n* (*into* in *acc.*); ⚖ Verfall *m*; Fehltritt *m*, Versehen *n*; 2. fallen, gleiten; ver-

fließen (*Zeit*); *moralisch* fallen; verfallen (*into* in *acc.*); fehlen; ⚖ verfallen; erlöschen.

lap-strap ⚞ ['læpstræp] Beckengurt *m*.

lap·wing *orn.* ['læpwiŋ] Kiebitz *m*.

lar·ce·ny ⚖ ['lɑ:səni] Diebstahl *m*.

larch ♧ [lɑ:tʃ] Lärche *f*.

lard [lɑ:d] 1. (Schweine)Schmalz *n*; 2. spicken (*a. fig.*); '**lard·er** Speisekammer *f*; '**lard·ing-nee·dle**, '**lard·ing-pin** Spicknadel *f*.

large ☐ [lɑ:dʒ] groß; weit, umfassend; reichlich; weitherzig; flott, schwungvoll; *at* ~ auf freiem Fuße; ausführlich; in seiner *od.* ihrer Gesamtheit, im allgemeinen; wahllos; *talk at* ~ in den Tag hineinreden; *in* ~ im großen; '**large·ly** zum großen Teil, weitgehend; großzügig, reichlich; '**large·ness** Größe *f* (*a. fig.*); Weite *f*; '**large-'mind·ed** weitherzig; '**large-'scale** Groß-...; '**large-'sized** groß(formatig).

lar·gess(e) † [lɑ:'dʒes] Freigebigkeit *f*; Schenkung *f*.

lar·go ♪ ['lɑ:gəu] 1. Largo *n*; 2. largo, sehr langsam.

lar·i·at *Am.* ['læriət] Lasso *n*, *m*.

lark¹ *orn.* [lɑ:k] Lerche *f*.

lark² [~] 1. Streich *m*, Jux *m*; 2. tolle Streiche machen; **larksome** ['səm] = *larky*.

lark·spur ♧ ['lɑ:kspə:] Rittersporn *m*.

lark·y F ['lɑ:ki] zu Streichen aufgelegt; scherzhaft.

lar·va *zo.* ['lɑ:və], *pl.* **lar·vae** ['~vi:] Larve *f*, Puppe *f*; **lar·val** ['~vəl] Larven...

lar·yn·gi·tis ⚕ [lærin'dʒaitis] Kehlkopfentzündung *f*; **lar·ynx** ['læriŋks] Kehlkopf *m*.

las·civ·ious ☐ [lə'siviəs] lüstern.

la·ser ['leizə] Laser *m*; ~ *beam* Laserstrahl *m*.

lash [læʃ] 1. Peitschenschnur *f*; (Peitschen)Hieb *m*; Geißel *f*, Rute *f*; Wimper *f*; *the* ~ Auspeitschen *n*; die Prügelstrafe; 2. peitschen; peitschen gegen *et.* (*Wogen etc.*); *fig.* geißeln; schlagen (*at* nach); anbinden (*to* an *acc.*); ~ *out* um sich schlagen; ausschlagen (*Pferd*); *fig.* losbrechen; '**lash·er** Wehr *n*; '**lashing** Prügel *pl.*; ~*s pl.* F Unmenge *f*.

lass [læs] Mädchen *n*; Liebste *f*; **las·sie** ['læsi] Mädelchen *n*.

las·si·tude ['læsitjuːd] Mattigkeit *f*, Abgespanntheit *f*, Desinteresse *n*.

las·so ['læsəu] **1.** Lasso *n*, *m*; **2.** mit dem Lasso fangen.

last[1] [lɑːst] **1.** *adj.* letzt; vorig; äußerst, höchst; geringst; ～ *but one* vorletzt; ～ *night* gestern abend; **2.** Letzte *m*; Ende *n*; *my* ～ mein letzter Brief *m*; mein Jüngster *m*; *at* ～ zuletzt; schließlich, endlich; *at long* ～ zu guter Letzt; *breathe one's* ～ den letzten Atemzug tun; **3.** *adv.* zuletzt; ～, *but not least* nicht zuletzt.

last[2] [～] dauern, währen; halten (*Farbe etc.*); ausreichen (*Vorräte etc.*); ausdauern (*bei Rennen etc.*).

last[3] [～] *Schuhmacher*-Leisten *m*; *stick to one's* ～ bei s-m Leisten bleiben.

last-ditch [lɑːstˈditʃ] allerletzt; ～ *attempt* allerletzter (verzweifelter) Versuch *m*.

last·ing ['lɑːstiŋ] **1.** □ dauerhaft; beständig; **2.** dauerhafter Stoff *m*.

last·ly ['lɑːstli] zuletzt, schließlich.

latch [lætʃ] **1.** Klinke *f*, Drücker *m*; Schnapp-, Druckschloß *n*; *on the* ～ (nur) eingeklinkt; **2.** ein-, zuklinken, zugehen (*Tür*); '～**-key** Hausschlüssel *m*.

late [leit] spät; zu spät, verspätet; (kürzlich) verstorben, selig; ehemalig; jüngst; *at* (*the*) ～*st* spätestens; *as* ～ *as yesterday* erst *od.* noch gestern; *of* ～ letzthin, neulich; *of* ～ *years* seit einigen Jahren; ～*r on* später; *be* ～ (zu) spät kommen; 🚂 Verspätung haben; *keep* ～ *hours* spät aufbleiben; spät heimkommen; '～**-com·er** Nachzügler *m*.

la·teen ⚓ [ləˈtiːn]: ～ *sail* Lateinsegel *n*.

late·ly ['leitli] in letzter Zeit, vor kurzem, unlängst, letzthin, neulich, kürzlich.

la·ten·cy ['leitənsi] Verborgenheit *f*, Gebundenheit *f*, Latenz *f*.

late·ness ['leitnis] Verspätung *f*; späte Zeit *f*.

la·tent □ ['leitənt] verborgen, gebunden (*Wärme etc.*), latent.

lat·er·al □ ['lætərəl] seitlich; Seiten... [*des Gummibaums.*\

la·tex ⚕ ['leiteks] Milchsaft *n bsd.*\

lath [lɑːθ] **1.** Latte *f*; **2.** belatten.

lathe [leið] Drehbank *f*; Lade *f* am *Webstuhl.*

lath·er ['lɑːðə, 'læðə] **1.** (*bsd.* Seifen)Schaum *m*; **2.** *v/t.* einseifen; P verdreschen; *v/i.* schäumen.

Lat·in ['lætin] **1.** lateinisch; **2.** Latein *n*; ～ **A·mer·i·ca** Lateinamerika *n*; '**Lat·in·ism** Latinismus *m*; '**Lat·in·ize** latinisieren; ins Lateinische übersetzen.

lat·i·tude ['lætitjuːd] Breite *f* (*a. geogr., ast.*); *fig.* Umfang *m*, Weite *f*; Spielraum *m*; ～*s pl.* Breiten *pl.* (*Gegenden*); **lat·i·tu·di·nal** [～dinl] Breiten...; **lat·i·tu·di·nar·i·an** ['～di'neəriən] **1.** frei(sinnig); **2.** Freidenker *m*.

la·trine [ləˈtriːn] Latrine *f*.

lat·ter ['lætə] neuer; *der*, *die*, *das* letztere; *poet.* später, Spät...; ～ *end* Ende *n*; '～**-day** aus neuester Zeit; ～ *saints eccl. die* Heiligen *pl.* der letzten Tage (*Mormonen*); '**lat·ter·ly** neuerdings.

lat·tice ['lætis] **1.** *a.* ～**-work** Gitter *n*; **2.** (ver)gittern.

Lat·vi·an ['lætviən] **1.** lettisch; **2.** Lette *m*, Lettin *f*; Lettisch *n*.

laud [lɔːd] loben, preisen; '**laud·a·ble** □ lobenswert, löblich; **lau'da·tion** Lob *n*; **laud·a·to·ry** □ ['～dətəri] lobend, preisend (*of acc.*).

laugh [lɑːf] **1.** Gelächter *n*, Lachen *n*; *have a* ～ lachen; *raise a* ～ Gelächter erregen; **2.** lachen (*at über acc.*); ～ *at s.o.* j. auslachen; ～ *off* lachend hinweggehen über (*acc.*); ～ *out of j.* durch Lachen abbringen von; *you will* ～ *on the wrong side od. on the other side of your mouth od. face* dir wird das Lachen noch vergehen; *he* ～*s best who* ～*s last* wer zuletzt lacht, lacht am besten; *s. sleeve*; '**laugh·a·ble** □ lächerlich; '**laugh·er** Lacher(in); '**laugh·ing 1.** Lachen *n*; **2.** □ lachend; *it is no* ～ *matter* es ist nicht zum Lachen; '**laugh·ing-gas** Lachgas *n*; '**laugh·ing-stock** Gegenstand *m* des Gelächters; **laugh·ter** ['～tə] Gelächter *n*, Lachen *n*.

launch [lɔːntʃ] **1.** ⚓ Stapellauf *m*; Barkasse *f*; Ausflugsdampfer *m*; **2.** *v/t.* vom Stapel lassen; *Boot* aussetzen; schleudern (*a. fig.*); *Schläge* versetzen; *Rakete* starten, abschießen; *fig.* in Gang bringen; lancieren; *v/i.* ～ *out* loslegen; ～ (*out*) *into* sich stürzen in (*acc.*); sich ergehen in (*dat.*); '**launch·ing-**

-pad (Raketen)Abschußrampe *f*;
launch·ing site (Raketen)Abschußbasis *f*; **'launch·ing-tube** ⚓,
✗ Torpedorohr *n*.
laun·der ['lɔːndə] waschen (u. bügeln); sich waschen (lassen); **launder·ette** [lɔːndə'ret] Selbstbedienungswaschsalon *m*.
laun·dress ['lɔːndris] Wäscherin *f*;
'laun·dry Waschanstalt *f*; Wäsche
f; **'laun·dry-man** Wäscher *m*;
(Aus)Fahrer *m* einer Wäscherei.
lau·re·ate ['lɔːriit] **1.** lorbeergekrönt; **2.** the ♀, the Poet ♀ der Hofdichter.
lau·rel ♀ ['lɔrəl] Lorbeer *m*; win ~s
fig. Lorbeeren ernten; **'lau·relled**
lorbeerumkränzt.
lav F [læv] Klo *n*.
la·va ['lɑːvə] Lava *f*.
lav·a·to·ry ['lævətəri] Waschraum *m*;
Toilette *f*; *public* ~ Bedürfnisanstalt *f*;
~ *attendant* Toilettenfrau *f*.
lave *mst poet.* [leiv] (sich) waschen,
baden; bespülen.
lav·en·der ♀ ['lævində] Lavendel *m*.
lav·ish ['læviʃ] **1.** □ freigebig, verschwenderisch (*of* mit; *in* in *dat.*);
2. verschwenden; **'lav·ish·ness**
Verschwendung *f*.
law [lɔː] Gesetz *n*; Vorschrift *f*, (*bsd.*
Spiel)Regel *f*; ⁊⁊ Gesetze *n/pl.*,
Recht *n*; Rechtswissenschaft *f*; Juristenberuf *m*; Gericht(sverfahren)
n; *at* ~ gesetzlich; *be a* ~ *unto o.s.*
sich über Konventionen hinwegsetzen; *go to* ~ vor Gericht gehen;
have the ~ *of s.o.* j. gerichtlich belangen; *...-in-law* Schwieger...;
necessity knows no ~ Not kennt kein
Gebot; *lay down the* ~ den Ton angeben; *practise* ~ als Rechtsanwalt
praktizieren; **'~-a·bid·ing** ⁊⁊ gesetzestreu, friedlich; **'~-break·er**
Gesetzesübertreter *m*; **'~court**
Gericht(shof *m*) *n*); **law·ful** □
['lɔːful] gesetzlich; rechtmäßig; gültig (*Urkunde etc.*); **'law·giv·er**
Gesetzgeber *m*; **'law·less** □ gesetzlos; ungesetzlich; zügellos; **'lawmak·er** Gesetzgeber *m*.
lawn¹ [lɔːn] Batist *m*.
lawn² [~] Rasen(platz) *m*; **'~-mower** Rasenmäher *m*; **'~-sprin·kler**
Rasensprenger *m*; **'~-'ten·nis**
(Lawn-)Tennis *n*.
law...: ~ **school** juristische Fakultät *f*;
~suit ['lɔːsjuːt] Prozeß *m*; **law·yer**

['~jə] Jurist *m*; (Rechts)Anwalt *m*.
lax □ [læks] lax; locker; lose,
schlaff (*a. fig.*); lasch, lässig; **lax·ative** ['~ətiv] **1.** abführend; **2.** Abführmittel *n*; **'lax·i·ty, lax·ness**
Laxheit *f etc.*
lay¹ [lei] *pret. von* lie² 2.
lay² [~] Ballade *f*; *poet.* Lied *n*.
lay³ [~] weltlich; Laien...; ~ *preacher*
Laienprediger *m*.
lay⁴ [~] **1.** Lage *f*, Richtung *f*; *sl.*
Unternehmen *n*, Beschäftigung *f*;
2. (*irr.*) *v/t.* legen; nieder-, umlegen; *Geister* bannen; stellen,
setzen; *Tisch* decken; löschen,
dämpfen, stillen; besänftigen; vorlegen; *Summe* wetten; *Wette* eingehen; ~ *aside* beiseite legen; aufgeben; ~ *bare* bloßlegen, aufdecken;
~ *before s.o.* j-m vorlegen; ~ *by* beiseite legen; ~ *down* niederlegen;
Hoffnung aufgeben; *Weg etc.* bauen;
Grundsatz festlegen, aufstellen; ~
s.o. (*fast*) *by the heels* j. dingfest
machen; ~ *in* einlagern, sich eindecken mit; ~ *low* niederwerfen; ~
off ablegen; (zeitweilig) entlassen;
Am. sl. aufhören mit *et. od. j.*; ~ *on*
Farbe auftragen; *Steuer* auferlegen;
Schläge versetzen; *Wasserleitung*
legen; ~ *it on* (*thick*) *fig.* (dick) auftragen; ~ *open* darlegen; ~ (*o.s.*)
open to s.th. (sich) e-r Sache aussetzen; ~ *out* ausbreiten, -legen;
Garten, Geld etc. (gut) anlegen; ~
o.s. out sich einrichten (*for* für); ~
s.o. under an obligation od. a necessity j. zwingen; ~ *up Geld, Vorräte*
hinlegen, aufbewahren; *Kenntnisse*
sammeln; *Land* brachliegen lassen;
⚓ auflegen; *be laid up* ans Bett gefesselt sein; ~ *with* belegen mit; *v/i.*
(Eier) legen; *a.* ~ *a wager* wetten; ~
about one um sich schlagen; ~
into s.o. sl. j. verdreschen; ~ (*it*) *on*
F zuschlagen.
lay·a·bout *sl.* ['leiəbaut] Strolch *m*,
Stromer *m*; **'lay-by** Park-, Rastplatz *m an e-r Fernstraße*.
lay·er 1. ['leiə] Leger *m*; Lage *f*,
Schicht *f*; ✓ Ableger *m*; **2.** ✓
['leə] absenken.
lay·ette [lei'et] Babyausstattung *f*.
lay-fig·ure ['lei'figə] Gliederpuppe *f*.
lay·man ['leimən] Laie *m*.
lay...: **'~-off** Arbeitsunterbrechung
f; **'~-out** Anlage *f*; Entwurf *m*;

Aufmachung f.
laz·a·ret, *mst* **laz·a·ret·to** [læzə-'ret(əu)] Aussätzigenspital *n*.
laze F [leiz] faulenzen, bummeln; '**laz·i·ness** Faulheit *f*; '**la·zy** träg, faul; '**la·zy-bones** Faulpelz *m*.
lea *poet*. [li:] Au(e) *f*, Flur *f*.
leach [li:tʃ] auslaugen; durchsickern lassen.
lead¹ [led] 1. Blei *n*; ⚓ Lot *n*, Senkblei *n*; *typ*. Durchschuß *m*; ~s *pl*. Bleiplatten *f/pl*.; Bleidach *n*; ~ *pencil* Bleistift *m*; *swing the* ~ *sl*. sich drücken; 2. verbleien; *typ*. durchschießen.
lead² [li:d] 1. Führung *f*, Leitung *f*; Beispiel *n*; Vorsprung *m*; *thea*. Hauptrolle *f*; Hauptdarsteller(in); *Karten*: Vorhand *f*; ⚡ Leitung *f*; *Hunde*-Leine *f*; Mühlkanal *m*; *it's my* ~ *Karten*: ich spiele aus; *take the* ~ die Leitung übernehmen; vorangehen; ~ *story Zeitung*: Hauptartikel *m*; 2. (*irr*.) *v/t*. (an)führen, leiten; dazu bringen, bewegen (*to zu*); *Karte* ausspielen; ~ *on* (*ver*)locken; *v/i*. vorangehen; Anführer sein; ~ *off* den Anfang machen; *Sport*: anspielen; ~ *up to* überleiten zu.
lead·en ['ledn] bleiern (*a. fig*.); Blei...
lead·er ['li:də] (An)Führer(in), Leiter(in); ⚖ erster Anwalt *m*; Erste *m*; Leitpferd *n*; Leitartikel *m*; *Film*: Startband *n*; ♀ Leit-, Haupttrieb *m*; *anat*. Sehne *f*; **lead·er·ette** [~'ret] *kurzer Leitartikel m*; '**lead·er·ship** Führerschaft *f*; Führungsqualitäten *f/pl*.
lead-in ⚡ ['li:din] Antennenzuleitung *f*.
lead·ing ['li:diŋ] 1. leitend; Leit...; Haupt...; ~ *article* Leitartikel *m*; ✝ Lockartikel *m*, Schlager *m*; ~ *case* ⚖ Präzedenzfall *m*; ~ *man thea*. Hauptdarsteller *m*, erster Liebhaber *m*; ~ *lady* Hauptdarstellerin *f*, erste Liebhaberin *f*; ~ *question* Suggestivfrage *f*; 2. Leitung *f*, Führung *f*; '~-strings *pl*. Gängelband *n*.
lead... [led]: ~ **poi·son·ing** Bleivergiftung *f*; '~-works *mst sg*. Bleihütte *f*.
leaf [li:f], *pl*. **leaves** [li:vz] Blatt *n*; *Tür*- *etc*. Flügel *m*; *Tisch*-Klappe *f*, Platte *f*; *in* ~ belaubt; *come into* ~ ausschlagen, Blätter bekommen; '**leaf·age** Laub(werk) *n*; '**leaf-bud**

Blattknospe *f*; '**leaf·less** blätterlos; **leaf·let** ['~lit] Blättchen *n*; Flug-, Merk-, Faltblatt *n*; Prospekt *m*; '**leaf·y** belaubt; Laub...
league¹ [li:g] 1. Liga *f* (*a. hist. u. Sport*); Bund *m*; ♀ *of Nations* Völkerbund *m*; 2. (sich) verbünden.
league² *mst poet*. [~] Meile *f* (*4,8 km*).
leak [li:k] 1. Leck *n*, Loch *n*; 2. leck sein, lecken; tropfen (*Wasserhahn*); ~ *out* auslaufen; *fig*. durchsickern; '**leak·age** Lecken *n*; ✝ Leckage *f*; *fig*. Verlust *m*; Durchsickern *n*; '**leak·y** leck; undicht.
lean¹ [li:n] 1. mager; 2. mageres Fleisch *n*.
lean² [~] 1. (*irr*.) (sich) (an)lehnen (*against an acc*.); (sich) stützen (*on, upon auf acc*.); (sich) (hin)neigen (*to zu*); 2. (*fig. a.* '**lean·ing**) Neigung *f*.
lean·ness ['li:nnis] Magerkeit *f*.
leant [lent] *pret. u. p.p. von lean²* 1.
lean-to ['li:ntu:] Anbau *m*.
leap [li:p] 1. Sprung *m*; *by* ~s (*and bounds*) sprunghaft, rapide; 2. (*irr*.) *v/i*. springen, hüpfen; *fig*. hervorschießen; *he* ~*t at the opportunity* er stürzte sich auf die Gelegenheit; *v/t*. überspringen; '~-frog 1. Bockspringen *n*; 2. bockspringen; **leapt** [lept] *pret. u. p.p. von leap* 2; '**leap-year** Schaltjahr *n*.
learn [lə:n] (*irr*.) lernen; erfahren, hören; V beibringen; ~ *from* ersehen aus; **learn·ed** □ ['~nid] gelehrt; '**learn·er** Anfänger(in); '**learn·ing** Lernen *n*; Gelehrsamkeit *f*; **learnt** [lə:nt] *pret. u. p.p. von learn*.
lease [li:s] 1. Verpachtung *f*, -mietung *f*; Pacht *f*, Miete *f*; Pacht-, Mietvertrag *m*; *let* (*out*) *on* ~ verpachten; *a new* ~ *of life* neues Leben *n*; 2. (ver)pachten, (-)mieten; '~-hold 1. Pacht(ung) *f*; 2. Pacht...; '~-hold·er Pächter *m*.
leash [li:ʃ] 1. Koppelleine *f*, Koppel *f* (= *3 Hunde etc.*); *hold in* ~ *fig*. im Zaum halten; *strain at the* ~ *fig*. kaum zu halten sein; 2. koppeln.
least [li:st] 1. *adj*. kleinst, geringst; wenigst, mindest; 2. *adv. a.* ~ *of all* am wenigsten; *at* (*the*) ~ wenigstens; zum mindesten; *at the very* ~ allermindestens; *not in the* ~ nicht im geringsten; *to say the* ~ gelinde

gesagt.

leath·er ['leðə] **1.** Leder n (*fig. Haut*); F Leder(ball m) n; ~s pl. Lederhosen f/pl.; Ledergamaschen f/pl.; **2.** ledern; Leder...; **3.** mit Leder beziehen; versohlen (*prügeln*); **leath·er·ette** [~'ret] Kunstleder n; **leath·ern** ['leðən] ledern; 'leath·er·neck ⚔ *Am. sl.* Ledernacken m, Marineinfanterist m; 'leath·er·y ledern, zäh.

leave [li:v] **1.** Erlaubnis f; a. ~ of absence Urlaub m; Abschied m; by your ~ mit Verlaub; take one's ~ Abschied nehmen, (weg)gehen; take ~ of sich verabschieden von; take ~ of one's senses den Verstand verlieren; **2.** (*irr.*) v/t. (ver)lassen; hinterlassen (*vermachen*); zurück-, hinterlassen; übriglassen; überlassen, anheimstellen; be left (übrig)bleiben; ~ it at that es dabei bewenden lassen; s. call; ~ behind j. hinter sich lassen; *Spur etc.* hinterlassen; et. stehen od. liegen lassen; zurücklassen; ~ off aufhören (mit); *Gewohnheit* aufgeben; *Kleid* ablegen; ~ s.o. to himself od. to his own devices j. sich selbst überlassen; ~ s.o. od. s.th. alone in od. et. in Ruhe lassen; be (nicely) left F (schön) in der Patsche sitzen; ~ go od. s.th. et. loslassen; v/i. ablassen; weggehen; abgehen, abreisen (for nach).

leav·en ['levn] **1.** Sauerteig m (a. *fig.*), Hefe f; **2.** säuern; *fig.* durchsetzen; 'leav·en·ing Gärungsmittel n.

leaves [li:vz] pl. von leaf; oft Laub n.

leav·ings ['li:viŋz] pl. Überbleibsel n/pl., (Speise)Reste m/pl.

lech·er ['letʃə] Wüstling m; 'lech·er·ous wollüstig; 'lech·er·y Wollust f. [Chorpult n.]

lec·tern eccl. ['lektə:n] Lese-,)

lec·ture ['lektʃə] **1.** Vorlesung f, Vortrag m (on über acc.; to vor dat.); Strafpredigt f; s. curtain; read s.o. a ~ j. abkanzeln; ~ room Hörsaal m; Vortragsraum m; **2.** v/i. Vorlesungen od. Vorträge halten, lesen (on über acc.); v/t. abkanzeln; 'lec·tur·er Vortragende m; univ. Dozent(in); eccl. Hilfsprediger m; 'lec·ture·ship Dozentur f; Hilfspredigeramt n.

led [led] pret. u. p.p. von lead² 2.

ledge [ledʒ] Leiste f; Sims m, n; Riff n.

ledg·er ['ledʒə] ✝ Hauptbuch n; ⊕ Querbalken m am Gerüst; a. ~ line ♪ Hilfslinie f.

lee ⚓ [li:] Lee(seite) f.

leech [li:tʃ] zo. Blutegel m; *fig.* Blutsauger m.

leek 🜨 [li:k] Lauch m, Porree m.

leer [liə] **1.** (lüsterner od. finsterer) Seitenblick m; **2.** schielen (at nach); 'leer·y □ *sl.* argwöhnisch.

lees [li:z] pl. Bodensatz m, Hefe f.

lee·ward ⚓ ['li:wəd] leewärts.

lee·way ⚓ ['li:wei] Abtrift f; make ~ abtreiben; *fig.* zurückbleiben; make up ~ *fig.* Versäumtes nachholen.

left¹ [left] pret. u. p.p. von leave 2.

left² [~] **1.** adj. linke(r, -s); **2.** adv. links; **3.** Linke f; '~-hand linke(r, -s); mit der linken Hand; ~ drive mot. Linkssteuerung f; '~-'hand·ed □ linkshändig; *fig.* linkisch; zur linken Hand (*Ehe*); fragwürdig (*Kompliment*); ⊕ linksgängig.

left·ist pol. ['leftist] **1.** linksgerichtet; **2.** Linksgerichtete m, f.

left...: '~-'lug·gage lock·er (Gepäck)Schließfach n; '~-'lug·gage office Gepäckaufbewahrung(sstelle) f; '~-o·vers pl. Speisereste m/pl.

left-wing ['left'wiŋ] pol. Links..., des linken Flügels.

left·y F pol. ['lefti] Linke m, f.

leg [leg] Bein n; *Hammel- etc.* Keule f; (Stiefel)Schaft m; ♫ Schenkel m; Etappe f, Teilstrecke f bsd. e-r *Flugreise*; give s.o. a ~ up j-m (hin)aufhelfen; *fig.* j-m unter die Arme greifen; be on one's last ~s F auf dem letzten Loch pfeifen; pull s.o.'s ~ j. auf den Arm nehmen (*hänseln*); not have a ~ to stand on *fig.* der od. jeglicher Grundlage entbehren.

leg·a·cy ['legəsi] Vermächtnis n; '~-hunt·er Erbschleicher(in).

le·gal □ ['li:gəl] gesetzlich, legal; rechtsgültig; rechtlich, juristisch; Rechts...; ~ aid Rechtshilfe f; ~ capacity Geschäftsfähigkeit f; ~ costs pl. Gerichtskosten pl.; ~ dispute Rechtsstreit m; ~ entity juristische Person f; ~ remedy Rechtsmittel n; ~ status Rechtsstellung f; s. tender; **le·gal·i·ty** [li:'gæliti] Gesetzlichkeit f, Legalität f; **le·gal·i·za·tion** [li:gəlai'zeiʃən] Legalisierung f; 'le·gal·ize legalisieren, rechtskräftig machen; beurkunden.

leg·ate ['legit] *päpstlicher* Legat *m*.

leg·a·tee ɻ̃ [legə'ti:] Vermächtnisnehmer *m*, Erbe *m*.

le·ga·tion [li'geiʃən] Gesandtschaft *f*.

leg-bail ['leg'beil]: *give* ~ Fersengeld geben.

leg·end ['ledʒənd] Legende *f*, Sage *f*; Inschrift *f*; Text *m zu e-r Illustration*; **'leg·end·ar·y** legendär, sagenhaft.

leg·er·de·main ['ledʒədə'mein] Taschenspielerei *f*, Kunststück *n*.

legged [legd] ...beinig; **'leg·gings** *pl.* Gamaschen *f/pl.*; **'leg·gy** langbeinig.

leg·horn [le'gɔ:n] italienischer Strohhut *m*; Leghorn *n* (*Hühnerrasse*).

leg·i·bil·i·ty [ledʒi'biliti] Leserlichkeit *f*; **leg·i·ble** ['ledʒəbl] □ leserlich.

le·gion ['li:dʒən] Legion *f* (*a. fig.*); **'le·gion·ar·y 1.** Legions...; **2.** Legionär *m*.

leg·is·late ['ledʒisleit] Gesetze geben *od.* erlassen; **leg·is'la·tion** Gesetzgebung *f*; **leg·is·la·tive** □ ['~lətiv] gesetzgebend; Gesetzgebungs...; **leg·is·la·tor** ['~leitə] Gesetzgeber *m*; **leg·is·la·ture** ['~leitʃə] Legislatur *f*, Gesetzgebung *f*; gesetzgebende Körperschaft *f*.

le·git·i·ma·cy [li'dʒitiməsi] Rechtmäßigkeit *f*, Legitimität *f*; Ehelichkeit *f*; **le'git·i·mate 1.** □ [~mit] legitim, rechtmäßig; berechtigt, zu rechtfertigen(d); ehelich; **2.** [~meit] legitimieren, für rechtmäßig erklären, rechtfertigen; **le·git·i'ma·tion** Legitimierung *f*; Legitimation *f*, Ausweis *m*; **le'git·i·ma·tize** [~mətaiz], **le'git·i·mize** = *legitimate 2*.

leg-room ['legrum] Beinfreiheit *f*.

leg·ume ['legju:m] Hülsenfrucht *f*; **le'gu·mi·nous** [~minəs] Hülsenfrucht...

lei·sure ['leʒə] **1.** Muße *f*, Freizeit *f*; *be at* ~ Muße haben; *at your* ~ wenn es Ihnen paßt; **2.** müßig; Muße...; ~ **ac·tiv·i·ties** *pl.* Freizeitbeschäftigung(en *pl.*) *f*; **'lei·sured** unbeschäftigt; *the* ~ *classes* die begüterten Klassen; **'lei·sure·ly** *adj. u. adv.* gemächlich; **lei·sure wear** Freizeitkleidung *f*.

lem·on ['lemən] Zitrone *f*; Zitronenbaum *m*; **lem·on·ade** [~-'neid] Zitronenlimonade *f*; **'lem·on-'squash** Zitronenwasser *n*; **'lem·on-squeez·er** Zitronenpresse *f*.

lend [lend] (*irr.*) (ver-, aus)leihen; *Hilfe* leisten, gewähren, ~ *a hand* helfen; ~ *o.s. to* sich hergeben zu (*Person*); sich eignen zu *od.* für (*Sache*); ~*ing library* Leihbücherei *f*; **'lend·er** (Ver)Leiher(in); **'Lend-'Lease Act** Leih-Pacht-Gesetz *n* (*1941*).

length [leŋθ] Länge *f*; Strecke *f*; (Zeit)Dauer *f*; *at* ~ endlich, zuletzt; *at(great)*~(sehr)ausführlich; *go all* ~*s* aufs Ganze gehen; *go (to) great* ~*s* sehr weit gehen; *he goes the* ~ *of saying* er geht so weit zu sagen; **'length·en**(sich)verlängern, (sich) ausdehnen; **'length·ways**, **'length·wise** der Länge nach, längs; **'length·y** □ sehr lang; weitschweifig.

le·ni·ence, **le·ni·en·cy** ['li:njəns(i)] = *lenity*; **'le·ni·ent** □ mild, nachsichtig; **'len·i·tive** ﴾ **1.** lindernd; **2.** linderndes Mittel *n*; **len·i·ty** ['leniti] Milde *f*, Nachsicht *f*.

lens [lenz] *Glas*-Linse *f*; *phot.* Objektiv *n*; ~ *system phot.* Optik *f*.

lent¹ [lent] *pret. u. p.p. von lend*.

Lent² [~] Fasten *pl.*, Fastenzeit *f*.

Lent·en ['lentən] Fasten..., fastenmäßig.

len·tic·u·lar □ [len'tikjulə] linsenförmig; Linsen...

len·til ♀ ['lentil] Linse *f*.

Leo *ast.* ['li:əu] Löwe *m*.

leop·ard ['lepəd] Leopard *m*.

le·o·tard ['li:əuta:d] Gymnastikanzug *m*.

lep·er ['lepə] Aussätzige *m, f*.

lep·re·chaun *ir.* ['leprəkɔ:n] Kobold *m*.

lep·ro·sy ﴾ ['leprəsi] Aussatz *m*, Lepra *f*; **'lep·rous** aussätzig.

Les·bian ['lezbiən] Lesbierin *f*; **'Les·bian·ism** weibliche Homosexualität *f*.

lese-maj·es·ty ɻ̃ ['li:z'mædʒisti] Majestätsbeleidigung *f*; Hochverrat *m*.

le·sion ['li:ʒən] Verletzung *f*, Wunde *f*.

less [les] *adj. u. adv.* kleiner, geringer; weniger (*a.* 𝔸); *prp.* 𝔸 minus; ✝ abzüglich; *no ~ than* ebenso gut wie; *no ~ a p. than* kein Geringerer als; *none the ~* dennoch, trotzdem, nichtsdestoweniger.

...less [lis] ...los, un...

les·see [le'si:] Pächter *m*, Mieter *m*.

less·en ['lesn] *v/t.* vermindern, verringern, verkleinern, schmälern (*a. fig.*); *v/i.* kleiner werden, abnehmen.

less·er ['lesə] kleiner; geringer.

les·son ['lesn] Lektion *f*; Aufgabe *f*; (Unterrichts)Stunde *f*; Lehre *f*; *eccl.* Lesung *f*; *~s pl.* Unterricht *m*; *teach s.o. a ~* j-m e-e Lektion erteilen; *j-m e-e Lehre sein*.

les·sor [le'sɔ:] Verpächter *m*, -mieter *m*.

lest [lest] damit nicht, daß nicht; aus Furcht, daß.

let¹ [let] (*irr.*) *v/t.* lassen, zulassen, gestatten; vermieten, verpachten; *~ alone* nicht anrühren; zufrieden *od.* in Ruhe lassen; *adv.* geschweige denn; *~ be* in Ruhe lassen; *~ down j.* im Stich lassen, versetzen; *~ s.o. down gently* j. glimpflich behandeln; *~ drive at s.o.* auf j. losschlagen *od.* losfeuern; *~ fly* loslassen; *fig.* vom Stapel lassen; *~ go* loslassen; *Anker* fallen lassen; *~ it go at that* es dabei bewenden lassen; *~ o.s. in for* sich auf *et.* einlassen; *~ into* einweihen in (*acc.*), wissen lassen; *~ loose* loslassen; *~ off* abschießen; *Witz* loslassen; *j.* laufen lassen; *s. steam*; *~ out* hinauslassen; ausplaudern; vermieten; *Arbeit* vergeben; *v/i.* sich vermieten (*at, for* für); *~ on* F es verraten, plaudern; *~ out at* treten, schlagen; *fig.* ausfällig werden gegenüber *j-m*; *~ up* aufhören.

let² [~] *a. ~ ball Tennis*: Netzball *m*; *without ~ or hindrance* unbehindert.

let·down F ['letdaun] Enttäuschung *f*.

le·thal ☐ ['li:θəl] tödlich; Todes...

le·thar·gic, le·thar·gi·cal ☐ [le'θɑ:dʒik(əl)] lethargisch (*a. fig.*).

leth·ar·gy ['leθədʒi] Lethargie *f*; Schlafsucht *f*; *fig.* Teilnahmslosigkeit *f*.

Le·the ['li:θi:] Lethe *f* (*Fluß des Vergessens im Hades*).

let·ter ['letə] **1.** Buchstabe *m*; Type *f*; Brief *m*; buchstäblicher Sinn *m*; *~s pl.* Literatur *f*, Wissenschaft *f*;

by ~ brieflich; *man of ~s* Literat *m*; *to the ~* buchstäblich; **2.** mit Buchstaben versehen, zeichnen; *Buch* betiteln; '*~-bal·ance* Briefwaage *f*; '*~-box* Briefkasten *m*; '*~-card* Kartenbrief *m*; '*~-car·ri·er Am.* Briefträger *m*; '*~-case* Brieftasche *f*; '*~-cov·er* Briefumschlag *m*; '*let·tered* (literarisch) gebildet; '*let·ter-file* Briefordner *m*; '*let·ter-found·er* Schriftgießer *m*; *let·ter·gram* ['~græm] Brieftelegramm *n*; '*let·ter·head* (gedruckter) Briefkopf *m*; Kopfpapier *n*; '*let·ter·ing* Beschriftung *f*.

let·ter...: '*~-less* ungebildet; '*~-o·pen·er* Brieföffner *m*; '*~-'per·fect theat.* rollensicher; '*~-press typ.* Druck *m*, Text *m*; *~ printing* Hoch-, Buchdruck *m*; '*~-press* Kopierpresse *f*; '*~-weight* Briefbeschwerer *m*.

let·tuce ⚕ ['letis] (Kopf)Salat *m*.

let·up F ['letʌp] Nachlassen *n*; Unterbrechung *f*.

leu·co... ['lju:kəu] weiß; **leu·co·cyte** ['~sait] weißes Blutkörperchen *n*, Leukozyte *f*; **leu·k(a)e·mi·a** ⚕ [lju:'ki:miə] Leukämie *f*.

le·vant¹ [li'vænt] durchbrennen.

le·vant² [~] Levante *f*; **le·vant·ine** ['levəntain] **1.** Levantiner(in); **2.** levantinisch.

lev·ee¹ *hist.* ['levi] Lever *n*, Morgenempfang *m*.

lev·ee² *Am.* [~] Ufer-, Schutzdamm *m*.

lev·el ['levl] **1.** waagerecht, eben, gleich; ausgeglichen; *my ~ best* mein möglichstes; *~ crossing* ⚑ schienengleicher Übergang *m*; *~ stress gr.* schwebende Betonung *f*; *~ teaspoon* gestrichener Teelöffel *m*; **2.** ebene Fläche *f*; (gleiche) Höhe *f*, Niveau *n*, Stufe *f*; Stand *m*; Ebene *f*; *fig.* Richtschnur *f*, Maßstab *m*; Wasserwaage *f*, Libelle *f*; *~ of the sea* Meeresspiegel *m*; *on a ~ with* in *od.* auf gleicher Höhe mit (*a. fig.*); *dead ~* gerade Ebene *f*; *fig.* Eintönigkeit *f*; *on the ~* F offen, aufrichtig, fair; **3.** *v/t.* gleichmachen, ebnen; *surv.* nivellieren; *fig.* anpassen; richten, zielen mit (*at* auf *acc.*, nach); *~ with the ground* dem Boden gleichmachen; *~ down* erniedrigen; *~ up* erhöhen; *v/i. ~ at*, *against* zielen auf (*acc.*); *~ off* heruntergehen (*Preis*); '*~-'head·ed* ver-

nünftig; 'lev·el·(l)er *surv.* Nivellierer
m; *fig.* Gleichmacher *m*; 'lev·el-
(l)ing Nivellier...
le·ver ['li:və] 1. Hebel *m*; Hebe-
stange *f*; 2. (mit e-m Hebel) bewegen, hebeln; 'le·ver·age Hebel-
kraft *f*.
lev·er·et ['levərit] Häschen *n*. [*f*.\
le·ver-watch ['li:vəwɔtʃ] Ankeruhr╎
le·vi·a·than [li'vaiəθən] Leviathan
m; Ungetüm *n*.
lev·i·tate ['leviteit] *Spiritismus*:
schweben (lassen).
Le·vite ['li:vait] *Bibel*: Levit *m*.
lev·i·ty ['leviti] Leichtfertigkeit *f*.
lev·y ['levi] 1. Erhebung *f von Steu-*
ern; ✕ Aushebung *f*; Aufgebot *n*;
capital ~ Kapitalabgabe *f*; 2. *Steu-*
ern erheben, auferlegen; *Truppen*
ausheben; *Krieg* führen (on, *against*
gegen); beschlagnahmen; *Beschlag-*
nahme durchführen.
lewd □ [lu:d] liederlich, unzüchtig;
'lewd·ness Unzüchtigkeit *f*.
lex·i·cal □ ['leksikəl] lexikalisch.
lex·i·cog·ra·pher [leksi'kɔgrəfə] Lexikograph *m*, Verfasser *m* e-s
Wörterbuchs; lex·i·co·graph·i·cal
□ [‿kəu'græfikəl] lexikographisch;
lex·i·cog·ra·phy [‿'kɔgrəfi] Lexi-
kographie *f*; lex·i·con ['‿kən] *bsd.*
griechisches od. hebräisches Wörterbuch *n*.
li·a·bil·i·ty [laiə'biliti] Verantwortlichkeit *f*; ⚖ Haftpflicht *f*; Verpflichtung *f*; Unterworfensein *n*;
fig. Hang *m*, Neigung *f*; *liabilities*
pl. Verbindlichkeiten *f|pl.*, ✝ Pas-
siva *pl.*
li·a·ble □ ['laiəbl] verantwortlich
(*for* für); ⚖ haftpflichtig; verpflichtet (*to* zu); unterliegend, ausgesetzt (*to dat.*); in Gefahr (*to inf.*
zu inf.); neigend (*to* zu); *be* ~ *to*
neigen *od.* geneigt sein zu; leicht
et. tun können; ~ *to duty* zollpflichtig; ~ *to punishment* straffällig, -bar.
li·aise F [li'eiz] Verbindung aufnehmen (*with* mit); als Verbindungs-
mann fungieren.
li·ai·son [li:'eizɔ̃:ŋ] Liebschaft *f*,
Liaison *f*; [li:'eizən] ✕ Verbindung
f; Zs.-arbeit *f*; ~ *officer* Verbin-
dungsoffizier *m*.
li·ar ['laiə] Lügner(in).
li·ba·tion [lai'beiʃən] Trankopfer *n*.
li·bel ['laibəl] 1. Schmähschrift *f*;
Verleumdung *f*; Hohn *m* (on auf

acc.); ⚖ Klageschrift *f*; 2. schmähen; verunglimpfen; ⚖ schriftlich
klagen gegen; 'li·bel·(l)ous □ verleumderisch; Schmäh...
lib·er·al ['libərəl] 1. □ liberal (*a.*
pol.), freigebig, großzügig (*of* mit);
reichlich; unbefangen; frei; frei-
sinnig; 2. Liberale *m*; 'lib·er·al-
ism Liberalismus *m*; lib·er·al·i·ty
[‿'ræliti] Freigebigkeit *f*; Frei-
sinnigkeit *f*; Vorurteilslosigkeit *f*.
lib·er·ate ['libəreit] befreien (*from*
von); *Sklaven* freilassen; lib·er'a-
tion Befreiung *f*; 'lib·er·a·tor Befreier *m*.
lib·er·tine ['libə:tain] 1. Wüstling
m; 2. liederlich; lib·er·tin·ism
['libətinizəm] Liederlichkeit *f*, Zügellosigkeit *f*.
lib·er·ty ['libəti] Freiheit *f*; Vorrecht *n*; *take liberties* sich Freiheiten erlauben; *be at* ~ frei sein;
be at ~ *to do* tun dürfen; ~ *of con-*
science Gewissensfreiheit *f*; ~ *of*
speech Redefreiheit *f*; ~ *of the press*
Pressefreiheit *f*.
li·bid·i·nous □ [li'bidinəs] wollüstig, unzüchtig; libidinös.
Li·bra *ast.* ['librə] Waage *f*.
li·brar·i·an [lai'breəriən] Bibliothe-
kar(in); li·brar·y ['laibrəri] Büche-
rei *f*, Bibliothek *f*.
li·bret·to ♪ [li'bretəu] Libretto *n*,
Text(buch *n*) *m*.
lice [lais] *pl. von* louse.
li·cence ['laisəns] Lizenz *f*; Erlaubnis *f*, Genehmigung *f*; Konzession
f; (*bsd. dichterische*) Freiheit *f*; Zügellosigkeit *f*; *driving* ~ Führerschein
m; ~ *plate mot.* Nummernschild *n*.
li·cense [‿] 1. *bsd. Am.* = licence;
2. lizenzieren, berechtigen, konzes-
sionieren, *et.* genehmigen; *Buch etc.*
zensieren; (*fully*) *licensed* mit (voller)
Schankerlaubnis; *licensing hours pl.*
Ausschankstunden *f|pl.*; li·cen·see
[‿'si:] Lizenznehmer *m*, Konzes-
sionsinhaber *m*; li·cense plate *Am.*
= licence plate; 'li·cens·er Lizenzge-
ber *m*; Zensor *m*.
li·cen·ti·ate *univ.* [lai'senʃiit] Lizen-
tiat *m*.
li·cen·tious □ [lai'senʃəs] unzüchtig; ausschweifend.
li·chen ♀ *u.* ⚕ ['laiken] Flechte *f*.
lich-gate ['litʃgeit] = lychgate.
lick [lik] 1. Lecken *n*; *Am.* Salzlecke *f*; *sl.* Schlag *m*; F Tempo *n*;

2. lecken; belecken; F verdreschen; übertreffen, schlagen; ~ the dust im Staub kriechen; fallen; geschlagen werden; ~ into shape zurechtbiegen, -stutzen, in die richtige Form bringen; '**lick·er** Lecker m; ⊕ Öler m; '**lick·er·ish** lecker (-haft); lüstern (after nach); '**lick·ing** Lecken n; F Dresche f; '**lick·spit·tle** Speichellecker m.

lic·o·rice ♀ ['likəris] Lakritze f.

lid [lid] Deckel m (sl. Hut);(Augen-) Lid n; put the ~ on it F das Maß vollmachen.

li·do ['li:dəu] Strandbad n.

lie¹ [lai] **1.** Lüge f; give s.o. the ~ j. Lügen strafen; tell a ~ lügen; white ~ Notlüge f; **2.** lügen.

lie² [~] **1.** Lage f; the ~ of the land die Lage der Dinge, die Sachlage; **2.** (irr.) liegen; ⚖ zulässig sein; ~ by still-, brachliegen; ~ down sich niederlegen; take it lying down nicht mucken, es über sich ergehen lassen; as far as in me ~s nach Kräften, soweit es in meinen Kräften steht; ~ in (adv.) in den Wochen liegen; länger liegen bleiben; (prp.) liegen in od. an (dat.); ~ in wait for j-m auflauern; ~ over ♰ nicht zur Verfallzeit bezahlt werden; aufgeschoben werden; ~ to ⚓ beiliegen; ~ under e-r Sache unterworfen sein, unterliegen (dat.); unter Verdacht etc. stehen; ~ up ruhen; das Bett hüten; it ~s with you es liegt bei dir; let sleeping dogs ~ fig. daran rühren wir lieber nicht.

lie-a·bed ['laiəbed] Langschläfer (-in); **lie-'down** Nickerchen n, Schläfchen n.

lief lit. [li:f] gern; '**lief·er** lieber.

liege hist. [li:dʒ] **1.** lehnspflichtig; **2.** a. ~man Lehnsmann m; a. ~ lord Lehnsherr m.

lie-in [lai'in]: have a ~ sich gründlich ausschlafen.

li·en ⚖ ['liən] Pfandrecht n.

lieu [lju:]: in ~ of (an)statt.

lieu·ten·an·cy [lef'tenənsi, ⚓ le-'tenənsi] Leutnantsstelle f; Statthalterschaft f; die Leutnants m/pl.

lieu·ten·ant [lef'tenənt, ⚓ le-'tenənt] Leutnant m; Statthalter m; Stellvertreter m; '**~·colo·nel** Oberstleutnant m; '**~·com'mand·er** Korvettenkapitän m; '**~·'gen·**

er·al Generalleutnant m; '**~·'gov·er·nor** Vizegouverneur m.

life [laif], pl. **lives** [laivz] Leben n; Menschenleben n; Lebensbeschreibung f; ~ and limb Leib u. Leben; for ~ auf Lebenszeit, lebenslänglich; for one's ~, for dear ~ ums (liebe) Leben; to the ~ naturgetreu (Bild); ~ sentence lebenslängliche Zuchthausstrafe f; have the time of one's ~ die schönste Zeit seines Lebens haben; '**~·an·nu·i·ty** Leibrente f; '**~·as·sur·ance**Lebensversicherung f; '**~·belt** Rettungsgürtel m; '**~·blood** Herzblut n; '**~·boat** Rettungsboot n; '**~·buoy** Rettungsboje f; ~ **ex·pect·an·cy** Lebenserwartung f; '**~·giv·ing** lebenspendend; '**~·guard** Leibwache f; Rettungsschwimmer m, Bademeister m am Strand; '**~·'in·ter·est** lebenslängliche Nutznießung f (in aus); '**~·jack·et** ⚓ Schwimmweste f; '**life·less** ☐ leblos; kraftlos, matt (a. fig.); '**life·less·ness** Leblosigkeit f etc.; '**life·like** lebenswahr, naturgetreu; '**life·line** Rettungsleine f; '**life·long** lebenslänglich; '**life-pre·serv·er** Am. Schwimmgürtel m; Bleistock m, Totschläger m.

lif·er sl. ['laifə] lebenslängliche Zuchthausstrafe f.

life...: '**~·sav·er** Australien: Rettungsschwimmer m; '**~·size(d)** lebensgroß; '**~·span** Lebensdauer f; Lebenserwartung f; '**~·strings** pl. Lebensfaden m; '**~·time** Lebenszeit f; '**~·work** Lebenswerk n.

lift [lift] **1.** Heben n, ⊕ Hub m; phys., ✈ Auftrieb m; fig. Erhebung f; Aufzug m, Fahrstuhl m; give s.o. a ~ j-m helfen; j. (im Auto) mitnehmen; **2.** v/t. (a. fig. Maßnahme etc.) auf)heben; hoch-, anheben; oft ~ up Augen, Stimme etc. erheben (a. fig.); beseitigen; abnehmen; sl. klauen, stehlen; v/i. sich heben; '**~·at·tend·ant**, '**~·boy** Fahrstuhlführer m; '**lift·er** der, die, das Hebende; Dieb m; '**lift·ing** ⊕ Hebe...; Hub...; ~ power ✈ Auftrieb m; '**lift-off** Start m, Abheben n (Hubschrauber, Rakete).

lig·a·ment anat. ['ligəmənt] Band n.

lig·a·ture ['ligətʃuə] **1.** Binde f; ✚ Verband m; ♪, typ. Ligatur f; **2.** (ab)binden.

light¹ [lait] **1.** Licht n (a. fig.);

Fenster *n*; Aspekt *m*, Gesichtspunkt *m*; Feuer *n*; Glanz *m*; *fig.* Leuchte *f*; ‿*s pl.* Fähigkeiten *f/pl.*; *a box of* ‿*s* eine Schachtel Streichhölzer; *in the* ‿ *of* im Lichte (*gen.*), angesichts (*gen.*); *bring* (*come*) *to* ‿ an den Tag bringen (kommen); *will you give me a* ‿ darf ich Sie um Feuer bitten; *put a* ‿ *to* anzünden; *see the* ‿ das Licht der Welt erblicken; *fig.* verstehen, begreifen; 2. licht, hell; blond; ‿ *ale* helles, leichtes Ale *n*; 3. (*irr.*) *v t. oft* ‿ *up* be-, erleuchten; anzünden; *j-m* leuchten; *v i. mst* ‿ *up* aufleuchten; ‿ *out Am. sl.* schnell losziehen, abhauen.

light² [‿] 1. ☐ *adj. u. adv.* leicht (*a. Speisen, Stoffe, Regen, Truppen, Gang, Münzen, Charakter, Kenntnisse etc.*); ‿ *current* ⚡ Schwachstrom *m*; ‿ *reading* Unterhaltungslektüre *f*; *make* ‿ *of et.* leicht *od.* auf die leichte Schulter nehmen; 2. *su.* = *lights*; 3. ‿ *on*, ‿ *upon* stoßen auf (*acc.*), geraten an (*acc.*); zufällig kommen zu; sich niederlassen auf (*dat.*) (*Vogel*); fallen auf (*acc.*).

light-col·o(u)red ['laitkʌləd] hell (*Kleid etc.*).

light·en¹ ['laitn] erleuchten, erhellen; sich erhellen; blitzen.

light·en² [‿] leichter machen *od.* werden, (sich) erleichtern (*a. fig.*).

light·er¹ ['laitə] Anzünder *m*; (Taschen)Feuerzeug *n*.

light·er² ⚓ [‿] L(e)ichter *m* (*leichtes Entladungsschiff*).

light...: '‿**-fin·gered** geschickt; langfingerig, diebisch; '‿**-foot·ed** leichtfüßig; flink; '‿**-hand·ed** e-e leichte Hand habend; mit leichter Hand (gemacht); *fig.* geschickt in der Menschenführung; '‿**-hand·ed·ness** Geschick *n*, leichte Hand *f*; '‿**-head·ed** wirr im Kopfe; leichtsinnig; '‿-**-heart·ed** ☐ leichtherzig; fröhlich; ‿**-heav·y·weight** *Sport*: 1. Halbschwergewichts...; Leichtschwergewichts...; 2. Halbschwergewichtler *m*; Leichtschwergewichtler *m*; '‿**house** Leuchtturm *m*.

light·ing ['laitiŋ] Beleuchtung *f*; Anzünden *n*; ‿ *up* Aufblenden *n*.

light·ly ['laitli] *adv.* leicht; leichtsinnig, -fertig; heiter; **light me·ter** *phot.* Belichtungsmesser *m*; **light--mid·dle·weight** *Sport*: 1. Halbmittelgewichts...; 2. Halbmittelge-

wichtler *m*; '**light·mind·ed** leichtsinnig; '**light·ness** Leichtigkeit *f*; Leichtsinn *m*, -fertigkeit *f*.

light·ning ['laitniŋ] Blitz *m*; *like* ‿, *with* ‿ *speed* blitzschnell; '‿-**ar-**'**rest·er** Blitzschutzsicherung *f*; ‿ *bug Am.* Leuchtkäfer *m*; '‿-**con-duc·tor,** '‿-**rod** Blitzableiter *m*.

light pen ['laitpen] *Computer*: Lichtgriffel *m*.

lights [laits] *pl.* Lunge *f von Tieren.*

light·ship ['laitʃip] Feuerschiff *n*.

light·some ['laitsəm] anmutig; lustig, fröhlich; leichtfertig.

light·weight ['laitweit] *Sport*: Leichtgewicht *n*.

light-'wel·ter·weight *Sport*: 1. Halbweltergewichts...; 2. Halbweltergewichtler *m*.

lig·ne·ous ['ligniəs] holzig; holzartig; **lig·nite** ['lignait] Braunkohle *f*.

lik·a·ble ['laikəbl] liebenswert, sympathisch, angenehm.

like [laik] 1. *adj. u. adv.* gleich; ähnlich; wie; ‿ *a man* wie ein Mann; *such* ‿ dergleichen; *feel* ‿ F sich aufgelegt fühlen zu *et.*, Lust haben auf *et.*; *s.* look; *something* ‿ ... so etwa ...; ‿ *that* so; *what is he* ‿? wie sieht er aus?; wie ist er?; *that's more* ‿ *it* das läßt sich eher hören; 2. Gleiche *m*, *f*, *n*; ‿*s pl.* Neigungen *f/pl.*; *his* ‿ seinesgleichen; *the* ‿ der-, desgleichen; *the* ‿(*s*) *of* F eine(r) wie, solche wie; 3. gut leiden können, mögen, gern haben; ‿ *best* am liebsten haben; *how do you* ‿ *London?* wie gefällt Ihnen London?, wie finden Sie London?; *I should* ‿ *to know* ich möchte wissen.

like·a·ble ['laikəbl] = likable.

like·li·hood ['laiklihud] Wahrscheinlichkeit *f*; '**like·ly** wahrscheinlich; geeignet, richtig; aussichtsreich; *as* ‿ *as not* sehr wahrscheinlich; *he is* ‿ *to die* er wird wahrscheinlich sterben.

like-mind·ed ['laik'maindid] gleichgesinnt; '**lik·en** vergleichen (*to* mit); '**like·ness** Ähnlichkeit *f*; Abbild *n*; Gestalt *f*; *have one's* ‿ *taken* sich malen *od.* photographieren lassen; '**like·wise** gleich-, ebenfalls.

lik·ing ['laikiŋ] (*for*) Neigung *f* (für, zu), Gefallen *n* (an *dat.*); *to s.o.'s* ‿ nach j-s Geschmack.

li·lac ['lailək] **1.** lila; **2.** ♀ spanischer Flieder m.

Lil·li·pu·tian [lili'pju:ʃjən] **1.** Liliputaner m; **2.** winzig, liliputanerhaft.

lilt [lilt] **1.** trällern; **2.** rhythmische Weise f; Schwung m.

lil·y ♀ ['lili] Lilie f; ~ **of the valley** Maiglöckchen n; '~-'liv·ered feige; '~-white schneeweiß.

limb[1] [lim] Körper-Glied n; ♀ Ast m; F Range f; **out on a** ~ **F** in e-r gefährlichen Lage.

limb[2] ast., ♀ [~] Rand m.

limbed [limd] ...gliederig.

lim·ber[1] ['limbə] **1.** ✕ Protze f; **2.** mst ~ **up** aufprotzen.

lim·ber[2] [~] **1.** biegsam, geschmeidig; **2.** ~ **up** (sich) geschmeidig machen, (sich) lockern.

lim·bo ['limbəu] Vorhölle f; sl. Gefängnis n; Rumpelkammer f; fig. Vergessenheit f.

lime[1] [laim] **1.** Kalk m; Vogelleim m; **2.** mit Kalk düngen; Rute leimen (a. fig.).

lime[2] ♀ [~] Linde f.

lime[3] ♀ [~] Limone f; '~-juice Limonensaft m.

lime...: '~-kiln Kalkofen m; '~-light Kalklicht n; Bühnenlicht n; fig. Mittelpunkt m des öffentlichen Interesses.

lim·er·ick ['limərik] Limerick m (absurdes Gedicht).

lime...: '~-stone Kalkstein m; '~-tree ♀ Linde(nbaum m) f; '~-twig Leimrute f.

lim·it ['limit] **1.** Grenze f; in (off) ~s Zutritt gestattet (verboten) (to für); that is the ~! F das ist der Gipfel!; das ist (doch) die Höhe!; **go the** ~ Am. F bis zum Äußersten gehen; **2.** begrenzen; beschränken (to auf acc.); **lim·i'ta·tion** Begrenzung f, Beschränkung f; fig. Grenze f; ₺ Verjährung f; 'lim·it·ed **1.** beschränkt, begrenzt (to auf acc.); ~ (liability) company Gesellschaft f mit beschränkter Haftung; ~ in time befristet; **2.** Schnellzug m, -bus m mit Platzkarten; 'lim·it·less □ grenzen-, schrankenlos.

limn † [lim] (ab)malen; schildern.

lim·ou·sine ['limu:zi:n] Limousine f mit Trennwand zwischen Fahrer u. Passagieren.

limp[1] [limp] **1.** hinken (a. fig.),

humpeln; sich mühsam bewegen; **2.** Hinken n.

limp[2] [~] schlaff; weich.

lim·pet ['limpit] zo. Napfschnecke f; fig. j. der sein Amt nicht abgeben will; fig. Klette f; ~ **mine** ⚓, ✕ Haftmine f.

lim·pid □ ['limpid] klar, durchsichtig, hell, rein; 'lim·pid·ness Klarheit f, Reinheit f.

lim·y ['laimi] kalkig.

lin·age ['lainidʒ] Zeilenzahl f; Zeilenhonorar n.

linch·pin ['lintʃpin] Vorstecker m am Wagenrad.

lin·den ♀ ['lindən] Linde f.

line[1] [lain] **1.** Linie f; Reihe f; Zeile f; Vers m; Strich m; Falte f, Furche f; (Menschen)Schlange f; Folge f; Verkehrsgesellschaft f; (Eisenbahn-, Autobus-, Schiffahrts)Linie f; Strecke f; teleph. Leitung f; Branche f, Fach n, Sparte f; Leine f, Schnur f; Äquator m; Grenze f; Richtung f; fig. Richtschnur f; Maßnahme f, Methode f; ✝ Ware f, Artikel m, Sorte f; ✕ Linie(ntruppe) f; Front f; ~s pl. Richtlinien f/pl., Grundsätze m/pl.; Grundlage f; Trau- etc. Schein m; thea. Rolle f; ~ **of battle** Gefechtslinie f; ~ **of business** Geschäftszweig m, Fach n; ~ **of conduct** Lebensweise f; ship of the ~ Linienschiff n; hard ~s hartes Los n, Pech n; **all down the** ~ auf der ganzen Linie; **in** ~ **with** in Übereinstimmung mit; that is not in my ~ das schlägt nicht in mein Fach; **stand in** ~ Schlange stehen; **fall into** ~ **with** s.o. sich j-m anschließen; **draw the** ~ fig. nicht mehr mitmachen; **party** ~ pol. Parteilinie f; **party** ~, **shared** ~ teleph. Gemeinschaftsanschluß m; **toe the** ~ pol. sich der (Partei)Disziplin beugen; **hold the** ~ tel. am Apparat bleiben; **2.** v/t. liniieren; fig. furchen; aufstellen; Weg etc. umsäumen, einfassen; ~ **the streets** die Straßen säumen; ~ **out** entwerfen; ~ **through** durchstreichen; v/i. ~ **up** sich aufod. anstellen.

line[2] [~] Kleid etc. füttern; sich die Taschen etc. füllen.

lin·e·age ['liniidʒ] Abstammung f; Familie f; Stammbaum m; **lin·e·al** □ ['~əl] gerade, direkt (Nach-

komme etc.); **lin·e·a·ment** ['ɹ̩əmənt] (Gesichts)Zug *m*; **lin·e·ar** ['ɹ̩ə] linear, geradlinig; Längen...

line·man ['lainmən] Telegraphenarbeiter *m*, Störungssucher *m*; *Am.* = *linesman*.

lin·en ['linin] 1. Leinen *n*, Leinwand *f*; Wäsche *f*; *wash one's dirty* ~ *in public fig.* s-e schmutzige Wäsche vor allen Leuten waschen; 2. leinen; ~ **bas·ket** Wäschekorb *m*; '~-**clos·et**, '~-**cup·board** Wäscheschrank *m*; '~-**drap·er** Weißwarenhändler *m*, Wäschegeschäft *n.*

lin·er ['lainə] Linienschiff *n*, Passagierdampfer *m*; Verkehrsflugzeug *n*; Zeilenschinder *m*; **lines·man** ['lainzmən] *Sport:* Linienrichter *m*; '**line-up** Reihe *f*; Verbindung *f*; *Sport:* Aufstellung *f.*

ling[1] *ichth.* [liŋ] Leng(fisch) *m.*

ling[2] ♀ [ɹ̩] Heidekraut *n.*

lin·ger ['liŋgə] zögern, säumen; (ver)weilen; sich aufhalten (*over, upon* bei); sich hinziehen (*Krankheit*); dahinsiechen (*Kranker*); nachklingen (*Ton*); ~ *at*, ~ *about* sich herumdrücken an *od.* bei (*dat.*).

lin·ge·rie ['læ̃:nʒəri:] Damenunterwäsche *f.*

lin·ger·ing ['liŋgəriŋ] □ zögernd; bleibend; schleichend (*Krankheit etc.*); in Resten vorhanden.

lin·go ['liŋgəu] Kauderwelsch *n.*

lin·gua fran·ca ['liŋgwə'fræŋkə] Verkehrssprache *f.*

lin·gual ['liŋgwəl] Zungen...

lin·guist ['liŋgwist] Linguist(in); Sprachenkenner(in); **lin'guis·tic** (~*ally*) sprachwissenschaftlich, linguistisch; **lin'guis·tics** *sg.* Sprachwissenschaft *f*, Linguistik *f.*

lin·i·ment ♣ ['linimənt] Liniment *n*, Einreibemittel *n.*

lin·ing ['lainiŋ] Futter *n e-s Kleides*; Besatz *m*; *fig.* Saum *m*; Verkleidung *f e-r Wand etc.*; *every cloud has a silver* ~ jedes Unglück hat auch sein Gutes.

link[1] [liŋk] 1. *Ketten*-Glied *n*, Gelenk *n*; Manschettenknopf *m*; *fig.* Bindeglied *n*, Band *n*; 2. (sich) verketten, (sich) verbinden.

link[2] *hist.* [ɹ̩] Fackel *f.*

link·man ['liŋkmən] Fackelträger*m.*

links [liŋks] *pl.* Dünen *f/pl.*; *a. golf-*~ Golfplatz *m.*

link·up ['liŋkʌp] Zusammenschluß *m*; *Raumfahrt:* Kopplung *f.*

lin·net *orn.* ['linit] Hänfling *m.*

li·no ['lainəu] = *linoleum*; '~-**cut** Linolschnitt *m.*

li·no·leum [li'nəuljəm] Linoleum *n.*

lin·o·type *typ.* ['lainəutaip] Linotype *f*, Zeilensetz- und -gießmaschine *f.*

lin·seed ['linsi:d] Leinsamen *m*; ~ *oil* Leinöl *n.*

lin·sey-wool·sey ['linzi'wulzi] Halbwollzeug *n.*

lint ♣ [lint] Scharpie *f.*

lin·tel △ ['lintl] Oberschwelle *f*; Fnotensturz *m.*

li·on ['laiən] Löwe *m* (*a. ast. u. fig.*); *fig.* Größe *f*, Berühmtheit *f*; *the* ~*'s share* der Löwenanteil; '**li·on·ess** Löwin *f*; '**li·on-heart·ed** tapfer; '~-**hunt·er** *fig.* Prominentenjäger (-in); '**li·on·ize** *j.* als Zelebrität herumreichen, *j.* feiern.

lip [lip] Lippe *f* (*a.* ♀); Rand *m e-r Tasse, Wunde*; *sl.* Unverschämtheit *f*; *curl one's* ~ die Lippen verächtlich schürzen; *none of your* ~! keine Unverschämtheiten!; '~-**read** von den Lippen ablesen; '~-**serv·ice** Lippendienst *m*; '~-**stick** Lippenstift *m.*

liq·ue·fac·tion [likwi'fækʃən] Verflüssigung *f*; **liq·ue·fi·a·ble** ['~faiəbl] schmelzbar; '**liq·ue·fy** (sich) verflüssigen; schmelzen; **liq·ues·cent** [li'kwesnt] sich (leicht) verflüssigend.

li·queur [li'kjuə] Likör *m.*

liq·uid ['likwid] 1. □ flüssig, fließend; ♣ liquid; klar (*Augen, Luft etc.*); 2. Flüssigkeit *f*; *gr.* Liquida *f.*

liq·ui·date ['likwideit] ♣ liquidieren; *Schulden* tilgen; **liq·ui·da·tion** Abwicklung *f*, Liquidation *f*; '**liq·ui·da·tor** Liquidator *m*; '**liq·uid·iz·er** Mixer *m*, Mixgerät *n*; Entsafter *m.*

liq·uor ['likə] 1. Flüssigkeit *f*; Alkohol *m*, alkoholisches Getränk *n*; *in* ~, *the worse for* ~ betrunken; 2. *a.* ~ *up sl.* einen heben.

liq·uo·rice ♀ ['likəris] Lakritze *f.*

li·ra ['liərə], *pl.* **li·re** ['~ri] Lira *f* (*italienische Währungseinheit*).

lisp [lisp] 1. Lispeln *n*; 2. lispeln.

lis·som(e) ['lisəm] geschmeidig, wendig.

list[1] [list] 1. Liste *f*, Verzeichnis *n*;

Rand *m*, Leiste *f*; Webkante *f*;
2. *v/t.* (in e-e Liste) eintragen; verzeichnen, aufführen; katalogisieren;
v/i. sich *als Soldat* anwerben lassen.
list² ⚓ [~] 1. Schlagseite *f*; 2. Schlagseite haben.
list·ed ['listid] unter Denkmalsschutz
(stehend).
list·en ['lisn] (*to*) hören, horchen
(auf *acc.*); anhören (*acc.*); zuhören
(*dat.*); lauschen (*dat.*); folgen (*dat.*);
~ *in teleph.*, *Radio*: (mit)hören; ~ *in
to Radio*: hören; '**lis·ten·er** Horcher(in), (Zu)Hörer(in).
lis·ten·ing ['lisniŋ] Horch...; ~ *apparatus* Horchgerät *n*; '~-**post**
Horchposten *m*.
list·less □ ['listlis] gleichgültig;
lust-, teilnahmslos; '**list·less·ness**
Lustlosigkeit *f*.
lists [lists] *pl.* Schranken *f/pl.*,
Kampfplatz *m*; *enter the* ~*s fig.* in
die Schranken treten.
lit [lit] 1. *pret. u. p.p. von light¹* 3;
2. ~ *up sl.* beschwipst.
lit·a·ny *eccl.* ['litəni] Litanei *f*.
li·ter *Am.* ['liːtə] = *litre*.
lit·er·a·cy ['litərəsi] Fähigkeit *f* zu
lesen u. zu schreiben; '**lit·er·al** 1. □
Buchstaben...; buchstäblich; am
Buchstaben klebend; wörtlich; *fig.*
nüchtern, prosaisch; 2. *a.* ~ *error*
Druckfehler *m*; '**lit·er·al·ism**, '**lit·er·al·ness** Buchstabenglaube *m*.
lit·er·ar·y □ ['litərəri] literarisch;
Literatur...; Schrift..., Buch...; ~
man Schriftsteller *m*; literarisch Interessierte *m*; **lit·er·ate** ['~rit]
1. des Lesens u. Schreibens kundig;
gebildet; literarisch; 2. Gebildete
m; **lit·e·ra·ti** [litə'raːtiː] *pl.* Literaten *m/pl.*, *die Gelehrten m/pl.*; **lit·e'ra·tim** [~tim] buchstäblich; **lit·er·a·ture** ['litəritʃə] Literatur *f*,
Schrifttum *n*.
lithe(·some) ['laið(səm)] geschmeidig, wendig.
lith·o·graph ['liθəugraːf] 1. Lithographie *f*, Steindruck *m* (*Bild od.
Druck*); 2. lithographieren; **li·thog·ra·pher** [li'θɔgrəfə] Lithograph *m*; **lith·o·graph·ic** [liθəu-'græfik] (~*ally*) lithographisch; **li·thog·ra·phy** [li'θɔgrəfi] Lithographie *f*, Steindruck *m*.
Lith·u·a·ni·an [liθju:'einjən] 1. litauisch; 2. Litauer(in); Litauisch *n*.
lit·i·gant ⚖ ['litigənt] 1. streitend;

2. (streitende) Partei *f*; **lit·i·gate**
['~geit] prozessieren *od.* streiten
(um); **lit·i·ga·tion** Prozeß *m*; **li·ti·gious** □ [li'tidʒəs] streitsüchtig;
⚖ streitig, strittig.
lit·mus 🜍 ['litməs] Lackmus *m*;
'~-**pa·per** Lackmuspapier *n*.
li·to·tes *rhet.* ['laitəutiːz] Litotes *f*
(*Bejahung durch doppelte Verneinung*).
li·tre ['liːtə] Liter *n, m.*
lit·ter ['litə] 1. Sänfte *f*; Tragbahre
f; Streu *f*; Abfall *m*; Wust *m*; Unordnung *f*; Wurf *m junger Tiere*;
2. *Junge* werfen; ~ *down e-m Tier*
streuen; ver-, bestreuen; ~ *up
Zimmer* in Unordnung bringen;
'~-**bas·ket**, '~-**bin** Abfallkorb *m*; '~-**bug** F *j.*, *der Abfall auf der Straße
wegwirft.*
lit·tle ['litl] 1. *adj.* klein; kurz (*Zeit*);
gering(fügig); wenig; kleinlich; *a* ~
one ein Kleines (*Kind*); *a* ~ *house*
ein Häuschen; *my* ~ *Mary* F mein
Magen; *his* ~ *ways* seine komische
Art; ~ *people* Heinzelmännchen
n/pl.; 2. *adv.* wenig; *a* ~ *red*
schwachrot; 3. Wenige *n*, Kleinigkeit *f*; ~ *by* ~, *by* ~ *and* ~ nach und
nach; *for a* ~ für ein Weilchen; *not
a* ~ nicht wenig; '~-**go** F *univ.* Vorexamen *n*; '**lit·tle·ness** Kleinheit
f; Geringfügigkeit *f*; Kleinlichkeit *f*.
lit·to·ral ['litərəl] 1. Küsten...;
2. Küstengebiet *n*.
lit·ur·gy *eccl.* ['litə:dʒi] Liturgie *f*.
liv·a·ble ['livəbl] F wohnlich (*Haus
etc.*); erträglich (*Leben*); *mst* ~-*with*
F umgänglich (*Person*).
live 1. [liv] *allg.* leben; wohnen;
fortleben, -dauern, bestehen; sich
(er)nähren, leben (on von); *Leben*
führen; ~ *to see* erleben; ~ *s.th.
down et.* durch guten Lebenswandel vergessen machen; ~ *in* (out) im
(außer) Hause wohnen (*Hausangestellte*); ~ *through* durchmachen,
-stehen, überleben; ~ *up to s-m Ruf*
gerecht werden, *s-n Grundsätzen*
gemäß leben; *Versprechen* halten; ~
and learn man lernt nie aus;
~ *and let* ~ leben u. leben lassen;
2. [laiv] lebendig; richtig; aktuell;
glühend, brennend (*Kohle etc.*); ✕
scharf (*Munition*); ⚡ stromführend;
Radio: Direkt...; Original...; ~ *wire*
fig. energiegeladener Mensch *m*; ~
broadcast Direktübertragung *f*;

live·a·ble ['livəbl] s. livable; **lived**
...lebig; **live·li·hood** ['laivlihud]
Unterhalt m; '**live·li·ness** Lebhaftigkeit f; **live·long** ['livlɔŋ]: the
~ day poet. den lieben langen Tag;
live·ly ['laivli] lebhaft; lebendig;
aufregend; schnell; bewegt; make
things ~ for s.o. j. in Atem halten,
j-m einheizen.
liv·en ['laivn] mst ~ up F sich beleben, munter werden.
liv·er[1] ['livə] Lebende m; fast ~
Lebemann m; good ~ Schlemmer m.
liv·er[2] [~] Leber f; '**liv·er·ish** F
leberleidend; mürrisch.
liv·er·y[1] ['livəri] = liverish.
liv·er·y[2] [~] Livree f; (Amts)Tracht
f; fig. Kleid n; = ~-stable; ~ compa·ny (Handels)Zunft f der City
of London; '~·man Zunftmitglied
n der City of London; '~-sta·ble
Mietstall m.
lives [laivz] pl. von life; '**live-stock**
Vieh(bestand m) n; '**live-weight**
Lebendgewicht n.
liv·id ['livid] bläulich; fahl; wütend,
wild; **li'vid·i·ty** Fahlheit f.
liv·ing ['liviŋ] 1. □ lebend(ig); the ~
image of das genaue Ebenbild gen.;
the ~ theatre die Bühne, das Theater (im Ggs. zu Film u. Fernsehen);
the ~ pl. die Lebenden pl.; in ~
memory seit Menschengedenken;
2. Leben n; Wohnen n; Lebensweise f; Lebensunterhalt m; eccl.
Pfründe f; '~-room Wohnzimmer
n; '~-space Lebensraum m.
Li·vo·ni·an [li'vəunjən] 1. livländisch; 2. Livländer(in).
liz·ard ['lizəd] Eidechse f.
Liz·zie Am. co. ['lizi] billiges kleines
Auto n; alte Kiste f.
lla·ma ['lɑːmə] Lama(wolle f) n.
Lloyd's [lɔidz] Lloyd's (Gemeinschaft f von Seeversicherern in London); A 1 at ~ erstklassig.
lo † [ləu] siehe!
loach ichth. [ləutʃ] Schmerle f.
load [ləud] 1. Last f (a. fig.); Ladung f; ⊕ (Arbeits)Belastung f,
Leistung f; ~s of F e-e Menge;
2. Güter, Gewehr, Kamera etc.
laden; beladen; beschweren (a.
fig.); fig. überhäufen (with mit); den
Magen überladen; ~ test Belastungsprobe f; ~ed bleibeschwert (Stock);
~ed dice pl. falsche Würfel m/pl.;
~ed question Fangfrage f; ~ the dice

against s.o. fig. j. ins Unrecht setzen;
j-s Chancen verringern; zu j-s Ungunsten sprechen; '**load·er** (Ver-)
Lader m; (Gewehr)Lader m; '**load·
ing** 1. Lade...; 2. Laden n; Ladung f,
Fracht f; '**load-line** ⚓ Ladelinie f;
'**load·stone** Magnet(eisenstein) m.
loaf[1] [ləuf], pl. **loaves** [ləuvz] Brot
Laib m; Zucker-Hut m; Fleisch-,
Fisch-Kloß m; sl. Kopf m, Verstand
m; use your ~ streng deinen Grips
an.
loaf[2] [~] herumlungern, bummeln;
'**loaf·er** Müßiggänger m, Faulenzer
m, Bummler m.
loaf-sug·ar ['ləufʃugə] Würfelzucker m.
loam [ləum] Lehm m, Mutterboden
m, Ackerkrume f; '**loam·y** lehmig.
loan [ləun] 1. Anleihe f, Darlehen
n; Leihen n; Leihgabe f; on ~ leihweise; ask for the ~ of s.th. et. leihweise erbitten; put out to ~ verleihen; 2. bsd. Am. ausleihen; '~
word gr. Lehnwort n.
loath [ləuθ] abgeneigt; be ~ for
s.o. to do s.th. dagegen sein, daß j.
et. tut; nothing ~ durchaus nicht
abgeneigt.
loathe [ləuð] sich ekeln vor (dat.);
verabscheuen; nicht mögen; '**loathing** Ekel m; Abscheu m; **loathsome** □ ['~səm] ekelhaft; verhaßt;
'**loath·some·ness** Ekelhaftigkeit f.
loaves [ləuvz] pl. von loaf[1].
lob [lɔb] Tennis: 1. Hochschlag m;
2. Ball hochschlagen.
lob·by ['lɔbi] 1. Vorhalle f, Vestibül
n; parl. Wandelgang m; thea. Foyer
n; parl. Lobby f, Interessenvertreter m/pl.; 2. v/i. parl. s-n Einfluß
geltend machen; v/t. Gesetz etc. mit
Hilfe der Lobby durchbringen;
'**lob·by·ist** parl. Lobbyist m, Interessenvertreter m.
lobe anat., ♀ [ləub] Lappen m; ~ of
the ear Ohrläppchen n.
lo·be·lia ♀ [ləu'biːljə] Lobelie f.
lob·ster ['lɔbstə] Hummer m.
lo·cal □ ['ləukəl] 1. örtlich; Orts...;
lokal; am Ort befindlich; s. branch;
~ an(a)esthetic örtliche Betäubung f; ~
call teleph. Ortsgespräch n; ~ colour
Lokalkolorit n; ~ elections pl. Kommunalwahlen f/pl.; ~ government Gemeindeverwaltung f; 2. Zeitung: Lokalnachricht f; a. ~ train 🚆 Vorortzug
m; F Wirtshaus n (am Ort); ~s pl.

locale

Ortsbewohner *m/pl.*; **lo·cale** [ləu-'kɑːl] Schauplatz *m e-s Ereignisses*; **lo·cal·ism** ['‿kəlizəm] Lokalpatriotismus *m*; Provinzialismus *m*; **lo·cal·i·ty** ['‿kælìti] Örtlichkeit *f*; Lage *f*; **lo·cal·ize** ['‿kəlaiz] lokalisieren.

lo·cate [ləu'keit] *v/t.* versetzen, -legen, unterbringen; ausfindig machen; *Am.* an-, festlegen; *be ‿d gelegen sein*; wohnen; *v/i.* sich niederlassen; **lo'ca·tion** Standort *m*; Lage *f*; Niederlassung *f*; 🎬 Vermietung *f*; *Am.* Anweisung *f* von Land; angewiesenes Land *n*; Ort *m*; Eingeborenenviertel *n bsd. in Südafrika*; *Film:* Gelände *n* für Außenaufnahmen; *on ‿ auf Außenaufnahme.*

loch *schott.* [lɔx] See *m*; Bucht *f.*

lock¹ [lɔk] **1.** *Tür-, Gewehr- etc.* Schloß *n*; Schleuse(nkammer) *f*; ⊕ Sperrvorrichtung *f*; Gedränge *n*, Stauung *f von Wagen*; ‿, *stock and barrel* völlig, gänzlich, mit allem Drum u. Dran; **2.** (ver)schließen *(a. fig.)*, absperren; *ein Schloß haben*, sich verschließen lassen; ⊕ blockieren, sperren, greifen; umschließen, umfassen, ineinander verschlingen; *‿ s.th. away et.* wegschließen; *‿ s.o. in j.* einsperren; *‿ s.o. out j.* aussperren; *‿ up* wegschließen; abschließen; einsperren; *in e-e Irrenanstalt* einliefern; *Geld* fest anlegen.

lock² [‿] Locke *f*; Wolldecke *f*; *‿s pl. co.* Haare *n/pl.*

lock·age ['lɔkidʒ] Schleusengeld *n*; Schleusen(anlage *f*) *f/pl.*; **'lock·er** Schrank *m*, Kasten *m*; *go to Davy Jones's ‿* ertrinken; **lock·et** ['lɔkit] Medaillon *n.*

lock...: **'‿-gates** *pl.* Schleusentore *n/pl.*; **'‿-jaw** Kaumuskelkrampf *m*; **'‿-keep·er** Schleusenwärter *m*; **'‿-nut** ⊕ Gegenmutter *f*; **'‿-out** Aussperrung *f von Arbeitern*; **'‿-smith** Schlosser *m*; **'‿-stich** Steppstich *m*; **'‿-up 1.** Haftzelle *f*; ✝ zinslose (Kapital)Anlage *f*; **2.** verschließbar.

lo·co *Am. sl.* ['ləukəu] verrückt.

lo·co·mo·tion [ləukə'məuʃən] Fortbewegung(sfähigkeit) *f*; **lo·co·mo·tive** ['‿tiv] **1.** (sich) fortbewegend; beweglich; **2.** *a. ‿ engine* Lokomotive *f.*

lo·cust ['ləukəst] Heuschrecke *f*; *a.*

‿-tree 🌿 unechte Akazie *f.*

lo·cu·tion [ləu'kjuːʃən] Ausdruck *m*, Redensart *f.*

lode ⚒ [ləud] Erzgang *m*; **'‿-star** Leitstern *m (a. fig.)*; Polarstern *m*; **'‿-stone** Magnet(eisenstein) *m.*

lodge [lɔdʒ] **1.** *(bsd.* Jagd)Hütte *f*, Häuschen *n*; (Forst-, Park-, Pförtner)Haus *n*; Portierloge *f*; *Freimaurer-Loge f*; **2.** *v/t.* beherbergen, *(bsd.* als Mieter) aufnehmen; unterbringen; *Geld* hinterlegen; *Klage* einreichen; *Kugel* hineinschießen, *Hieb* versetzen; *Korn* umlegen; *v/i.* *(bsd.* zur Miete) wohnen; logieren; steckenbleiben; **'lodge·ment** = lodgment; **'lodg·er** (Unter)Mieter (-in); **'lodg·ing** Unterkunft *f*; *‿s pl.* möbliertes Zimmer *n*; Wohnung *f*; **'lodg·ing-house** Fremdenheim *n*; **'lodg·ment** 🎬 Einreichung *f*; Deponierung *f*; Anhäufung *f.*

lo·ess ['ləuis] Löß *m.*

loft [lɔft] (Dach)Boden *m*; Empore *f*, Chor *m*, *n*; **'loft·i·ness** Höhe *f*, Erhabenheit *f (a. fig.)*; Hochmut *m*; **'loft·y** □ sehr hoch; erhaben; stolz, hochmütig.

log [lɔg] Klotz *m*; Block *m*; *gefällter* Baumstamm *m*; ⚓ Log *n*; = *log-book.*

lo·gan·ber·ry 🌿 ['ləugənbəri] Loganbeere *f (Kreuzung zwischen Brombeere u. Himbeere).*

log·a·rithm 🅰 ['lɔgəriθm] Logarithmus *m.*

log...: **'‿-book** ⚓ Log-, *mot.* Fahrten-, ✈ Bordbuch *n*; *‿ cab·in* Blockhaus *n*; **logged** (mit Wasser) vollgesogen; **log·ger** ['lɔgə] Holzfäller *m*; **'log·ger·head:** *be at ‿s* sich in den Haaren liegen.

log·gia ['lɔdʒə] Loggia *f.*

log·ging ['lɔgiŋ] Holzfällen *n*; *‿ camp* Holzfällerlager *n*; **log house**, **log hut** Blockhaus *n.*

log·ic ['lɔdʒik] Logik *f*; **'log·i·cal** □ logisch; **lo·gi·cian** [ləu'dʒiʃən] Logiker *m.*

lo·gis·tics ⚔ [ləu'dʒistiks] *oft sg.* Logistik *f (Nachschubwesen).*

log·roll *bsd. pol.* [lɔgrəul] (sich gegenseitig) in die Tasche arbeiten; **'log·roll·ing** *pol.* Kuhhandel *m*; *Sport:* Baumstammtreten *n.*

log·wood ['lɔgwud] Kampescheholz *n.*

loin [lɔin] Lende *f*; *Fleischerei:*

Lenden-, Nierenstück *n*; *gird up one's* ⁓*s* s-e Lenden gürten, sich reisefertig machen; '⁓-**cloth** Lendenschurz *m*.

loi·ter ['lɔitə] trödeln, bummeln; (herum)lungern; schlendern; ⁓ *away* vertrödeln; '**loi·ter·er** Trödler(in), Bummler(in); Faulenzer (-in).

loll [lɔl] (sich) lehnen, (sich) hinstrecken, (sich) rekeln; ⁓ *about* herumlungern; ⁓ *out* heraushängen (lassen) (*Zunge*).

lol·li·pop F ['lɔlipɔp] Lutscher *m* (*Bonbon am Stiel*); ⁓ **man**, ⁓ **woman** F Schülerlotse *m*, -lotsin *f*.

lol·lop F ['lɔləp] latschen.

lol·ly ['lɔli] F = lollipop; *sl.* Mäuse *f pl.* (*Geld*).

Lom·bard ['lɔmbəd] Lombarde *m*; ⁓ *Street* Londoner Geldmarkt.

Lon·don·er ['lʌndənə] Londoner *m*.

lone [ləun] einsam; ⁓ *wolf* = '**lon·er** Einzelgänger *m*; **lone·li·ness** ['⁓linis] Einsamkeit *f*; '**lone·ly** □, **lone·some** □ ['⁓səm] einsam.

long[1] [lɔŋ] 1. Länge *f*; *before* ⁓ binnen kurzem; *for* ⁓ lange; *take* ⁓ lange brauchen *od.* dauern; *the* ⁓ *and the short of it* die ganze Geschichte; 2. *adj.* lang; langfristig; langsam; *at* ⁓ *date* ⁊ langfristig; *in the* ⁓ *run* am Ende; *auf die Dauer; be* ⁓ lange dauern *od.* brauchen; *take* ⁓ *views* weit vorausblicken; 3. *adv.* lang; lange; *as* ⁓ *ago as 1900* schon 1900; *so* ⁓! bis dann! (*auf Wiedersehen*); ⁓*er* länger; mehr; *no* ⁓*er ago than* erst (nach) ...

long[2] [⁓] sich sehnen (*for* nach).

long...: '⁓**boat** ⚓ Großboot *n*; ⁓-**bow** ['⁓bəu] *hist.* Langbogen *m*; *draw the* ⁓ *fig.* aufschneiden, übertreiben; '⁓-'**dated** langfristig; '⁓-'**dis·tance** Fern...; Weit...; ⁓ *flight* Langstreckenflug *m*; ⁓ *race* Langstreckenlauf *m*; '⁓-**drawn**-'**out**, *a.* '⁓-'**drawn** in die Länge gezogen; lang(atmig); **lon·gev·i·ty** [lɔn'dʒeviti] Langlebigkeit *f*; langes Leben *n*; **long firm** Schwindelfirma *f*; '**long·hair** F konservativer Musiker *m*, Gegner *m* der Swingmusik; Intellektuelle *m*, *f*; '**long-haired** F betont intellektuell; '**long·hand** *gewöhnliche* Schreibschrift *f*; '**long-'head·ed** *fig.* schlau, klug.

long·ing ['lɔŋiŋ] 1. □ sehnsüchtig; 2. Sehnsucht *f*; Verlangen *n*.

long·ish ['lɔŋiʃ] länglich, ziemlich lang.

lon·gi·tude *geogr.* ['lɔndʒitju:d] Länge *f*; **lon·gi·tu·di·nal** □ [⁓dinl] Längen...; *der Länge nach.*

long...: ⁓ **johns** *pl.* F lange Unterhose *f*; ⁓ **jump** *Sport:* Weitsprung *m*; '⁓-'**lived** langlebig; '⁓'**range** weittragend; *auf lange Sicht;* ⚔ Fernkampf...; ⚒ Langstrecken...; ⁓ **run:** *in the* ⁓ langfristig (gesehen), auf die Dauer; '⁓-**shore·man** Hafenarbeiter *m*; '⁓-**shot** *Film:* Fernaufnahme *f*; '⁓-'**sight·ed** weitsichtig, -blickend; '⁓-'**stand·ing** seit langer Zeit bestehend, alt; '⁓-'**suf·fer·ing** 1. langmütig; 2. Langmut *f*; '⁓-'**term** langfristig, Langzeit...; ⁓ *memory* Langzeitgedächtnis *n*; ⁓ *waves pl.* ⚡ Langwellen *f pl.*; '⁓-**ways** der Länge nach; '⁓-**wind·ed** □ langatmig.

loo[1] [lu:] Lu *n* (*ein Kartenspiel*).

loo[2] F [⁓] Klo *n* (*Toilette*).

loo·fah ♣ ['lu:fɑ:] Luffaschwamm *m*.

look [luk] 1. Blick *m*; *oft* ⁓*s pl.* Aussehen *n*; *new* ⁓ neueste Mode *f*; *have a* ⁓ *at s.th.* sich et. ansehen; *I don't like the* ⁓ *of it* es gefällt mir nicht; 2. *v/i.* sehen, blicken (*at, on* auf *acc.*, nach); zusehen, daß *od. wie* ...; nachsehen, *wer etc.* ...; *krank etc.* aussehen; *nach e-r Richtung liegen; it* ⁓*s like rain* es sieht nach Regen aus; *he* ⁓*s like winning* es sieht so aus, als ob er gewinnt; ⁓ *about* sich umsehen (*for* nach); ⁓ *after* sehen nach, sich kümmern um; versorgen; nachsehen, -blicken; ⁓ *at* ansehen; *not much to* ⁓ *at* nicht sehr ansehnlich; ⁓ *down on* verachten; ⁓ *for* erwarten; suchen; ⁓ *forward to* sich freuen auf (*acc.*); ⁓ *in als Besucher* herein-, hineinschauen (*on* bei); ⁓ *into* prüfen; erforschen; ⁓ *on* zuschauen; betrachten (*as* als); gelegen sein zu, liegen zu, gehen auf (*Zimmer*); ⁓ *out* sich vorsehen, aufpassen; ⁓ *out for* sich umsehen nach; sich in acht nehmen vor (*dat.*); ⁓ *over s.th.* et. genau ansehen *od.* inspizieren; et. durchsehen; et. übersehen; ⁓ *round* sich umsehen; ⁓ *through* durchsehen; durchlesen; heausblicken aus; ⁓ *to* im Auge haben, achtgeben auf (*acc.*); sich verlassen auf (*acc.*); ⁓ *to*

s.o. to inf. von j-m erwarten, daß er ...; ~ **up** aufblicken; steigen (*Aktien*), sich bessern; ~ (*up*)on *fig.* ansehen, betrachten (*as* als), halten (*as* für); *v/t.* ~ **s.o. in the face** j-m ins Gesicht sehen; ~ **one's age** so alt aussehen, wie man ist; ~ **disdain** verächtlich blicken; ~ **over** *et.* durchsehen; *j.* mustern; ~ **up** *et.* nachschlagen; F *j.* aufsuchen.

look·a·like *Am.* ['lukəlaik] Doppelgänger *m*.

look·er-on ['lukər'ɔn] Zuschauer (-in).

look-in ['luk'in] kurzer Besuch *m*; F Chance *f*.

look·ing-glass ['lukiŋglɑːs] Spiegel *m*.

look-out ['luk'aut] Ausguck *m*; Ausblick *m*, -sicht *f* (*a. fig.*); **be on the** ~ Ausschau halten; auf der Hut sein; *that is my* ~ das ist meine Sache; **'look-o·ver** Durchsicht *f*; **give s.th.** *a* ~ e-n prüfenden Blick auf et. werfen.

loom[1] [luːm] Webstuhl *m*.

loom[2] [~] undeutlich zu sehen sein, sich abzeichnen; ~ *large fig.* von großer Bedeutung sein *od.* scheinen.

loon[1] *schott.* [luːn] Lümmel *m*; Bursche *m*; Dummkopf *m*.

loon[2] *orn.* [~] Taucher *m*.

loon·y *sl.* ['luːni] 1. verrückt, bekloppt; 2. Verrückte *m*, *f*; ~ **bin** *sl.* Klapsmühle *f*.

loop [luːp] 1. Schlinge *f*, Schleife *f*, Schlaufe *f*, Öse *f*; ~ *aerial Radio*: Rahmenantenne *f*; 2. *v/t.* in Schleifen legen; schlingen; ~ *a Kleid, Haar* aufstecken; ~ **the** ~ ✈ e-n Looping drehen; *v/i.* e-e Schleife machen; sich winden; **'~-hole** Guckloch *n*; Schlupfloch *n* (*a. fig.*); ✗ Schießscharte *f*; Sehschlitz *m*; **'~-line** ⬤ *u. tel.* Schleife *f*.

loose [luːs] 1. ☐ *allg.* lose, locker; schlaff; weit; frei; unzs.-hängend; ungenau, nachlässig; liederlich; ~ **connection** ⚡ Wackelkontakt *m*; *at a* ~ **end** beschäftigungslos; *play fast and* ~ **with** Schindluder treiben mit; ~ **is not to say so too genau nehmen mit;** 2. *v/t. Knoten, Zunge, Schuß* lösen; *a.* ~ **off** aufbinden; *Griff* lockern; ~ **one's hold on s.th. et.** loslassen *od.* fahren lassen; *v/i.* schießen; 3. **give** (*a*) ~ **to** freien Lauf lassen (*dat.*); **'~-leaf** Loseblatt...; ~ **book,** ~

ledger Loseblattbuch *n*; **loos·en** ['luːsn] (sich) lösen, (sich) lockern; **'loose·ness** Lockerheit *f*; Ungenauigkeit *f*; Liederlichkeit *f*; ✛ Durchfall *m*.

loot [luːt] 1. plündern; erbeuten; 2. Beute *f*.

lop[1] [lɔp] *Baum* beschneiden; stutzen; *mst* ~ **away,** ~ **off** abhauen.

lop[2] [~] schlaff herunterhängen (lassen).

lope [ləup] 1. (daher)trotten; 2. Trott *m*, Lauf *m*.

lop...: '**~-ears** *pl.* Hängeohren *n/pl.*; '**~-'sid·ed** schief; einseitig.

lo·qua·cious [ləu'kweiʃəs] geschwätzig; **lo·quac·i·ty** [ləu'kwæsiti] Schwatzhaftigkeit *f*.

lo·ran ⚓ ['lɔːrən] Loran *n*, Fernbereichs-Navigationssystem *n*.

lord [lɔːd] 1. Herr *m*; Gebieter *m*; Magnat *m*; Lord *m*; **the** ♀ **der Herr** (*Gott*); *my* ~ Mylord, Euer Gnaden; **the** ♀**'s Prayer** das Vaterunser; **the** ♀**'s Supper** das Abendmahl; (*House of*) ♀**s** *pl.* Oberhaus *n*; 2. ~ **it** den Herrn spielen; ~ **it over** herrschen über (*acc.*); **'lord·li·ness** Würde *f*; *b.s.* Hochmut *m*; **'lord·ling** Herrchen *n*; **'lord·ly** vornehm, edel; großartig; hochmütig, arrogant; **Lord May·or** Oberbürgermeister *m*; **'lord·ship** Lordschaft *f*, Herrlichkeit *f* (*Titel*).

lore [lɔː] Lehre *f*, Kunde *f*.

lor·gnette [lɔː'njet] Stielbrille *f*.

lor·ry ['lɔri] Last(kraft)wagen *m*, Lkw *m*; ⬤ Lore *f*, Lori *f*.

lose [luːz] (*irr.*) *v/t.* verlieren; einbüßen; vergeuden; *Zug, Gelegenheit* verpassen, versäumen; *j.* um *et.* bringen; *Leiden etc.* loswerden; *Gewicht* abnehmen; ~ **o.s.** sich verlieren; sich verirren; ~ **sight of** aus den Augen verlieren; *v/i.* verlieren, Verlust(e) haben; nachgehen (*Uhr*); **'los·er** Verlierer(in); **come off** *a* ~ den kürzeren ziehen; **'los·ing** 1. verlustbringend; Verlust...; 2. ~**s** *pl.* Verluste *m/pl.* im Spiel.

loss [lɔs] Verlust *m*; Schaden *m*; *at a* ~ in Verlegenheit; außerstande (**to** *inf.* zu *inf.*); *be at a* ~ **for words** keine Worte finden; *be at a* ~ **what to say** nicht wissen, was man sagen soll; **'~-lead·er** ✝ Zugartikel *m*, Schlager *m*.

lost [lɔst] *pret. u. p.p. von* **lose**; **be** ~ verlorengehen; verschwunden sein;

fig. versunken sein; *this won't be* ~ *on me* das werde ich mir merken; *be* ~ *upon s.o.* keinen Eindruck machen auf j.; *get* ~ hau ab!, verdufte!; '~-'**prop·er·ty of·fice** Fundbüro *n*.

lot [lɔt] **1.** Los *n*; *fig.* Schicksal *n*; Anteil *m*; **✝** Partie *f*; Posten *m*; F Menge *f*, Haufen *m*, Masse *f*; Bauplatz *m*, Parzelle *f*, Stück *n* Land; *Am. Film:* Ateliergelände *n*; *a* ~ *of people* F eine Menge Leute; *draw* ~*s* losen *(for* um*); fall to s.o.'s* ~ j-m zufallen; *throw in one's* ~ *with* sich auf Gedeih und Verderb verbinden mit; *he is feeling a* ~ *better* F er fühlt sich sehr viel wohler; **2.** durch das Los verteilen; zuteilen.

loth [louθ] = *loath.*

lo·tion ['louʃən] (Haut-, Schönheits)Wasser *n*, Emulsion *f*.

lot·ter·y ['lɔtəri] Lotterie *f*.

lo·tus ♀ ['loutəs] Lotos *m (a. Frucht der Sage);* '~-**eater** Lotosesser *m*; Träumer *m*, Genußmensch *m*.

loud ☐ [laud] laut *(a. adv.)*; schreiend; grell; '~-'**hail·er** ⚓ Megaphon *n*; '~·**mouth** Großmaul *n*; '**loud·ness** Lautheit *f*; Lärm *m*; Auffallende *n; Radio:* Lautstärke *f*; '**loud-** -'**speak·er** Lautsprecher *m*.

lough *irisch* [lɔk] See *m*; Bucht *f*.

lounge [laundʒ] **1.** sich rekeln; faulenzen, herumlungern; **2.** Bummel *m*; Wohnzimmer *n*, -diele *f*; Gesellschaftsraum *m e-s Hotels; thea.* Foyer *n*; Chaiselongue *f*; '~-'**chair** Klubsessel *m*; '~-**liz·ard** *sl.* Salonlöwe *m*; Gigolo *m*; '**loung·er** Faulenzer(in); '**lounge-**'**suit** Straßenanzug *m*; **lounge suite** Couchgarnitur *f*.

lour ['lauə] finster blicken *od.* aussehen; die Stirn runzeln; **lour·ing** ☐ ['~riŋ] trüb, finster.

louse [laus], *pl.* **lice** [lais] Laus *f*; **2.** [lauz] lausen; **lous·y** ['lauzi] verlaust; lausig; Lause...; ~ *with money sl.* stinkreich.

lout [laut] Tölpel *m*, Lümmel *m*; '**lout·ish** tölpelhaft.

lou·vre, *Am.* **lou·ver** ['lu:və] Jalousie *f*.

lov·a·ble ☐ ['lʌvəbl] liebenswürdig, -wert.

love [lʌv] **1.** Liebe *f (of, a. for, to, towards* zu*);* Liebschaft *f*, Angebetete *f*; Liebling *m (als Anrede);* F goldi-

ges Ding *n (Person od. Sache);* liebe Grüße *m/pl.;* ♀ Liebesgott *m;* ~*s pl.* Amoretten *f/pl.; Sport:* nichts, null; *attr.* Liebes...; *a* ~ *of a book* F ein allerliebstes Buch; *for the* ~ *of God* um Gottes willen; *play for* ~ um nichts spielen; *four* (*to*) ~ vier zu null; *give od. send one's* ~ *to s.o.* j. freundlichst grüßen lassen; *in* ~ *with* verliebt in (*acc.*); *fall in* ~ *with* sich verlieben in; *make* ~ *to* werben um; *neither for* ~ *nor money* weder für Geld noch für gute Worte; **2.** lieben; gern haben; ~ *to do* gern tun; '~-**af·fair** Liebschaft *f*; '~- -**bird** Sperlingspapagei *m*; '~-**child** Kind *n* der Liebe; '**love·less** lieblos; '**love-let·ter** Liebesbrief *m*; '**love·li·ness** Lieblichkeit *f*; '**love·lock** Schmachtlocke *f*; **love-lorn** ['~lɔ:n] unglücklich verliebt; '**love·ly** lieblich; entzückend, reizend; '**love-mak·ing** Lieben *n*; Liebeswerben *n*; '**love-match** Liebesheirat *f*; '**love-phil·tre,** '**love- -po·tion** Liebestrank *m*; '**lov·er** Liebhaber *m; fig.* Verehrer(in), Liebhaber(in); ~*s pl.* Liebende *pl.*; *pair of* ~*s* Liebespaar *n*; '**love-set** *Sport:* Nullpartie *f*; '**love·sick** liebeskrank; '**love-to·ken** Liebespfand *n*.

lov·ing ☐ ['lʌviŋ] liebevoll; '~- -'**kind·ness** (Herzens)Güte *f*.

low¹ (☐ ✎) [lou] **1.** niedrig; tief; seicht; gering; kärglich; leise; *fig.* niedergeschlagen; schwach (✸ *Puls etc.*); gemein, erbärmlich, schlecht; ~*est bid* Mindestgebot *n; in a* ~ *voice* leise; *be brought* ~ gedemütigt werden; *lay* ~ niederwerfen; *lie* ~ ausgestreckt liegen; sich verborgen halten; **2.** *meteor.* Tief(druckgebiet) *n; bsd. Am.* Tiefstand *m*, -punkt *m*.

low² [~] **1.** brüllen, muhen *(Rind);* **2.** Brüllen *n*.

low...: '~-'**born** von niedriger Geburt; '~-'**bred** ungebildet, ohne Manieren; '~-**brow 1.** geistig anspruchslos, spießig; **2.** Spießer *m*, Banause *m*; '~-'**browed** mit niederem Eingang, düster *(Gebäude etc.);* = *low-brow 1*; ~ **co·me·di·an** *mst fig.* Hanswurst *m*; ~ **com·e·dy** Posse *f*, Schwank *m*; '~-'**cost** preiswert, billig; ~ **coun·try** Tiefland *n*; '~-**down 1.** F niederträchtig, gemein; **2.** *sl. die* eigentliche Wahrheit *f*, *die*

Hintergründe *m/pl.*

low·er¹ ['ləuə] **1.** niedriger *etc.* (*s. low¹*); nieder(e), unter(e); Unter...; ~ *case typ.* Kleinbuchstaben *m/pl.* **2.** *v/t.* nieder-, herab-, herunterlassen; senken; *die Augen* niederschlagen; erniedrigen; abschwächen; *Preise* herunter-, herabsetzen; ~ *one's voice* leiser sprechen; *v/i.* fallen, sinken.

low·er² ['ləuə] *s. lour.*

low·er·most ['ləuəməust] niedrigst; am niedrigsten; **low-'in·come** einkommensschwach; **low-'key** unaufdringlich, verhalten; *phot.* in dunklen Tönen gehalten; **'low·land** Tiefland *n*; **'low·land·er** Tieflandbewohner (-in); **Low Lat·in** *gr.* Vulgärlatein *n*; **'low·li·ness** Demut *f*; Niedrigkeit *f*; **'low·ly** *adj. u. adv.* niedrig, tief; gering; demütig, bescheiden, gering; **'low-'necked** tief ausgeschnitten (*Kleid*); **'low·ness** Niedrigkeit *f*; Kärglichkeit *f*; ♪ Tiefe *f*; ~ *of spirits* Niedergeschlagenheit *f*; **'low-'noise** rauscharm; **low pres·sure** ⊕ Nieder-, Unterdruck *m*; *meteor.* Tiefdruck *m*; **'low-'spir·it·ed** niedergeschlagen; **low wa·ter** Niedrigwasser *n*; tiefste Ebbe *f*; *in* ~ *fig.* knapp bei Kasse.

loy·al □ ['lɔiəl] loyal, treu; **'loy·al·ist** Regierungstreue *m*; **'loy·al·ty** Treue *f*, Loyalität *f*.

loz·enge ['lɔzind3] Raute *f*; *pharm.* Pastille *f*; Tablette *f*; (Brust)Bonbon *m, n*.

£.s.d. F ['eles'di:] Geld *n*.

lub·ber ['lʌbə] Tölpel *m*, Stoffel *m*; **'lub·ber·ly** plump, tölpelhaft.

lu·bri·cant ['lu:brikənt] Schmiermittel *n*; **lu·bri·cate** ['~keit] schmieren; **lu·bri·ca·tion** Schmieren *n*, ⊕ Ölung *f*; **'lu·bri·ca·tor** ⊕ Schmierbüchse *f*; **lu·bric·i·ty** [~siti] ⊕ Schmierfähigkeit *f*; *fig.* Schlüpfrigkeit *f*.

lu·cerne ♣ ['lu:'sə:n] Luzerne *f*.

lu·cid □ ['lu:sid] *mst poet.* leuchtend, hell; klar, deutlich; ~ *interval* ♣ lichter Augenblick *m*; **lu'cid·i·ty**, **'lu·cid·ness** Klarheit *f*.

Lu·ci·fer ['lu:sifə] Satan *m*, Luzifer *m*; Morgenstern *m*.

luck [lʌk] Glück(sfall *m*) *n*; Geschick *n*; *good* ~ Glück *n*; *bad* ~, *hard* ~, *ill* ~ Unglück *n*, Pech *n*; *be down on one's* ~ F Pech haben;

worse ~ unglücklicherweise; **'luck·i·ly** glücklicherweise, zum Glück; **'luck·i·ness** Glück *n*; **'luck·less** unglücklich; **'luck·y** □ glücklich; glückbringend; Glücks...; *be* ~ Glück haben; **'luck·y-bag**, **'luck·y-dip** Glücksbeutel *m*.

lu·cra·tive □ ['lu:krətiv] einträglich, lukrativ; **lu·cre** ['lu:kə] Gewinn(sucht *f*) *m*.

lu·cu·bra·tion [lu:kju:'breiʃən] mühsames Studium *n*; *mst* ~*s pl.* gelehrte Arbeit *f*.

lu·di·crous □ ['lu:dikrəs] lächerlich, albern.

lu·do ['lu:dəu] *Spiel:* Mensch, ärgere dich nicht.

luff ⚓ [lʌf] **1.** Luv *f*; Luvseite *f*; **2.** *a.* ~ *up* anluven.

lug¹ [lʌg] **1.** zerren, schleppen; ~ *in fig.* an den Haaren herbeiziehen; **2.** Henkel *m*, Öhr *n*.

lug² [~] = *lugsail*.

luge [lu:3] **1.** Rodelschlitten *m*; **2.** rodeln.

lug·gage ['lʌgid3] Gepäck *n*; **'~-car·ri·er** Gepäckträger *m am Fahrrad*; **'~-of·fice** Gepäckschalter *m*; **'~-rack** Gepäcknetz *n*; **'~-tick·et** Gepäckschein *m*; **'~-van** 🚃 Gepäck-, Packwagen *m*.

lug·ger ⚓ ['lʌgə] Logger *m*, Lugger *m*.

lug·sail ⚓ ['lʌgseil, ⚓ 'lʌgsl] Lugger-, Sturmsegel *n*.

lu·gu·bri·ous □ [lu:'gu:briəs] traurig, kläglich, düster, finster.

luke·warm ['lu:kwɔ:m] lau (*a. fig.*); **'luke·warm·ness** Lauheit *f*.

lull [lʌl] **1.** *v/t.* einlullen; beruhigen; *v/i.* sich beruhigen; sich legen (*Wind*); **2.** Ruhepause *f*.

lull·a·by ['lʌləbai] Wiegenlied *n*.

lum·ba·go ⚕ [lʌm'beigəu] Hexenschuß *m*, Lumbago *f*.

lum·ber ['lʌmbə] **1.** Bau-, Nutzholz *n*; Gerümpel *n*, Plunder *m*; **2.** *v/t. a.* ~ *up* vollstopfen; *v/i.* rumpeln, poltern; sich (dahin)schleppen; **'lum·ber·er**, **'lum·ber·man** Holzfäller *m*, -arbeiter *m*; **'lum·ber·ing** schwerfällig; **'lum·ber·jack** Holzfäller *m*; **'lum·ber·mill** Sägewerk *n*; **'lum·ber·room** Rumpelkammer *f*; **'lum·ber·yard** Holzplatz *m*, -lager *n*.

lu·mi·nar·y ['lu:minəri] Himmelskörper *m*; Leuchtkörper *m*; *fig.*

Leuchte *f*, Koryphäe *m*, *f*; **lu·mi·nos·i·ty** [ˌɭuˈnɔsiti] Helle *f*, Glanz *m*; **'lu·mi·nous** □ leuchtend; Licht...; *fig.* lichtvoll; klar; ˷ *dial* Leuchtzifferblatt *n*; ˷ *paint* Leuchtfarbe *f*.

lump [lʌmp] **1.** Klumpen *m*; *fig.* Klotz *m*; Beule *f*; Stück *n* Zucker *etc.*; in the ˷ in Bausch und Bogen; ˷ *sugar* Würfelzucker *m*; ˷ *sum* Pauschalsumme *f*; *have a* ˷ *in the throat fig.* e-n Kloß im Hals haben; **2.** *v/t.* zs.-stecken, -werfen, -fassen (*into, in* zu); *fig.* hinnehmen; *if you don't like it you can* ˷ *it* du mußt dich damit abfinden; ˷ *together* in einen Topf werfen; *v/i.* Klumpen bilden; **'lump·ish** schwerfällig; dumm; **'lump·y** □ klumpig; unruhig (*Wasser*).

lu·na·cy [ˈluːnəsi] Irr-, Wahnsinn *m*.
lu·nar [ˈluːnə] Mond...; ˷ *caustic* ⚕ Höllenstein *m*; ˷ **mod·ule** Mondfähre *f*.
lu·na·tic [ˈluːnətik] **1.** irr-, wahnsinnig; **2.** Irre *m*, *f*; Wahnsinnige *m*, *f*; Geistesgestörte *m*, *f*; ˷ **a·sy·lum** Irrenhaus *n*, -anstalt *f*; ˷ **fringe** *die* Extremen *pl.*, *die* Hundertfünfzigprozentigen *pl.*
lunch [lʌntʃ] **1.** Lunch *m*, Mittagessen *n*; zweites Frühstück *n*; *packed* ˷ Lunchpaket *n*; **2.** zu Mittag essen; *j-m ein* Mittagessen geben; **lunch·eon** [ˈlʌtʃən] = *lunch* 1; ˷ *meat* Frühstücksfleisch *n*; ˷ *voucher* Essensgutschein *m*; **'lunch-hour** Mittagszeit *f*, -pause *f*.
lu·nettes [luːˈnets] *pl.* Taucherbrille *f*.
lung [lʌŋ] Lunge(nflügel *m*) *f*; *the* ˷*s pl. die* Lunge *f*.
lunge [lʌndʒ] **1.** *fenc.* Ausfall *m*; **2.** *v/i.* ausfallen (*at* gegen); (dahin-) stürmen; *v/t.* stoßen.
lung·er *sl.* [ˈlʌŋə] Lungenkranke *m*, *f*; **'lung-pow·er** Stimmkraft *f*.
lu·pin(e) ♀ [ˈluːpin] Lupine *f*.
lurch[1] [lɔːtʃ] **1.** ⚓ Überholen *n*; *fig.* Taumeln *n*; **2.** ⚓ überholen, schlingern; *fig.* taumeln, torkeln.
lurch[2] [ˌ]: *leave in the* ˷ im Stich lassen.
lurch·er [ˈlɔːtʃə] Spürhund *m*.
lure [ljuə] **1.** Köder *m*; *fig.* Lockung *f*; **2.** ködern, (an)locken.
lu·rid [ˈljuərid] gespenstisch, un

heimlich; düster, finster.
lurk [lɔːk] lauern; versteckt liegen; **'lurk·ing-place** Schlupfwinkel *m*.
lus·cious □ [ˈlʌʃəs] köstlich; üppig; sehr süß; *b.s.* süßlich, widerlich; **'lus·cious·ness** Süße *f*; Üppigkeit *f*.
lush [lʌʃ] üppig, saftig (*Pflanze*).
lust *lit.* [lʌst] **1.** (sinnliche) Begierde *f*; Wollust *f*; *fig.* Gier *f*, Sucht *f*; **2.** *I* ˷ es gelüstet mich (*after, for* nach); **lust·ful** □ [ˈˌful] lüstern.
lust·i·ness [ˈlʌstinis] Rüstigkeit *f*.
lus·tre [ˈlʌstə] Glanz *m*; Lüster *m*, Kronleuchter *m*; **'lus·tre·less** glanzlos.
lus·trous □ [ˈlʌstrəs] glänzend.
lust·y □ [ˈlʌsti] rüstig; *fig.* lebhaft; kräftig.
lu·ta·nist [ˈluːtənist] Lautenspieler (-in), Lautenist(in).
lute[1] ♪ [luːt] Laute *f*.
lute[2] [ˌ] **1.** Kitt *m*; **2.** verkitten.
Lu·ther·an [ˈluːθərən] **1.** lutherisch; **2.** Lutheraner(in); **'Lu·ther·an·ism** Luthertum *n*.
lut·ist [ˈluːtist] = *lutanist*.
lux·ate [ˈlʌkseit] verrenken.
lux·u·ri·ance [lʌɡˈzjuəriəns] Üppigkeit *f*; **lux'u·ri·ant** □ üppig; **lux·'u·ri·ate** [ˌrieit] schwelgen (*fig. in* in *dat.*); **lux'u·ri·ous** □ luxuriös, üppig, verschwenderisch; F feudal; **lux·'u·ri·ous·ness** Verschwendung *f*; **lux·u·ry** [ˈlʌkʃəri] Luxus *m*, Üppigkeit *f*; Luxusartikel *m*; Genußmittel *n*.
ly·ce·um [laiˈsiəm] Vortragsraum *m*; *bsd. Am.* Volkshochschule *f*.
lych-gate [ˈlitʃɡeit] überdachtes Friedhofstor *n*.
lye [lai] Lauge *f*.
ly·ing [ˈlaiiŋ] **1.** *p.pr. von lie[1]* 2 *u. lie[2]* 2; **2.** *adj.* lügnerisch; **'˷-in** Wochenbett *n*; ˷ *hospital* Entbindungsanstalt *f*, -heim *n*.
lymph [limf] 🞧 Lymphe *f*; *poet.* Quellwasser *n*; **lym·phat·ic** [ˌˈfætik] **1.** (˷*ally*) lymphatisch, Lymph...; *fig.* schwerfällig, langsam; **2.** Lymphgefäß *n*.
lynch [lintʃ] lynchen; **'˷-law** Lynchjustiz *f*.
lynx *zo.* [liŋks] Luchs *m*; **'˷-eyed** *fig.* luchsäugig, mit Luchsaugen.
lyre [laiə] Lyra *f*, Leier *f*; **'˷-bird** *orn.* Leierschwanz *m*.
lyr·ic [ˈlirik] **1.** lyrisch; liedhaft;

2. lyrisches Gedicht *n*; ⁓s *pl.* (Lied-) Text *m* (*bsd. e-s Musicals*); Lyrik *f*; **'lyr·i·cal** ☐ lyrisch, gefühlvoll;

schwärmerisch, begeistert.
ly·sol *pharm.* ['laisɔl] Lysol *n*.

M

ma F [mɑ:] Mama *f.*
ma'am [mæm] Majestät *f* (*Anrede für die Königin*); Hoheit *f* (*Anrede für Prinzessinnen*); [məm] F gnä' Frau *f* (*von Dienstboten verwendete Anrede*).
mac F [mæk] = *mackintosh.*
ma·ca·bre [mə'kɑ:br] grausig, makaber; *danse* ⁓ Totentanz *m.*
mac·ad·am [mə'kædəm] Schotter (-straße *f*) *m*; **mac·ad·am·ize** makadamisieren, beschottern.
mac·a·ro·ni [mækə'rəuni] Makkaroni *pl.*
mac·a·roon [mækə'ru:n] Makrone *f.*
mace¹ [meis] *hist.* Streitkolben *m*; Amtsstab *m.*
mace² [⁓] Muskatblüte *f.*
Mac·e·do·ni·an [mæsi'dəunjən] **1.** Mazedonier(in); **2.** mazedonisch.
mac·er·ate ['mæsəreit] *durch Flüssigkeit* erweichen; auslaugen, ausmergeln; kasteien; **mac·er'a·tion** Einweichung *f etc.*
Mach *phys.* [mæk]: ⁓ *number* Machsche Zahl *f*, Machzahl *f*; ⁓ *two* Mach 2 (*doppelte Schallgeschwindigkeit*).
ma·che·te [mə'tʃeiti] Machete *m, f*, Buschmesser *n.*
Mach·i·a·vel·li·an [mækiə'veliən] machiavellistisch.
mach·i·na·tion [mæki'neiʃən] Anschlag *m*; ⁓s *pl.* Machenschaften *f/pl.*, Ränke *pl.*; **mach·i·na·tor** ['⁓tə] Ränkeschmied *m*; **ma·chine** [mə'ʃi:n] **1.** Maschine *f*; Maschinerie *f*, Mechanismus *m* (*fig. Organisation*); **2.** maschinell herstellen *od.* (be)arbeiten; **ma'chine-gun** ⚔ Maschinengewehr *n*; **ma'chine-made** maschinell hergestellt; **ma'chin·er·y** Maschinen *f/pl.*; Maschinerie *f*, Mechanismus *m*; **ma'chine-shop** Maschinenhalle *f*; **ma'chine-tool** Werkzeugmaschine

f; **ma'chine-wash·a·ble** waschmaschinenfest; **ma'chin·ist** Maschinist *m*; Maschinennäherin *f.*
mack F [mæk] = *mackintosh.*
mack·er·el *ichth.* ['mækrəl] Makrele *f.*
mack·i·naw *Am.* ['mækinɔ:] Stutzer *m* (*Kleidungsstück*).
mac(k)·in·tosh ['mækintɔʃ] Regenmantel *m.*
mac·ro... ['mækrəu] groß..., lang...; **⁓·bi·ot·ic** [⁓bai'ɔtik] makrobiotisch; **⁓·bi'ot·ics** *sg.* Makrobiotik *f*; **⁓·cosm** ['⁓kɔzəm] Makrokosmos *m.*
mad ☐ [mæd] wahnsinnig, verrückt (*with* vor); *bsd. von Tieren*: toll; *fig.* toll, wild (*on, about, after,* for nach; *at, about* über *acc.*); F wütend, böse; *go* ⁓ verrückt werden; *drive* ⁓ verrückt machen.
mad·am ['mædəm] gnädige Frau *f*, gnädiges Fräulein *n* (*Anrede*); *she's a bit of a* ⁓ F sie kommandiert e-n gerne herum.
Ma·dame ['mædəm] Frau *f* (*vor dem Namen e-r verheirateten Ausländerin*).
mad·cap ['mædkæp] **1.** toll; **2.** Tollkopf *m*; Wildfang *m*; **mad·den** ['mædn] toll *od.* rasend machen; *it is* ⁓*ing* es ist zum Verrücktwerden.
mad·der ♀, ⊕ ['mædə] Krapp *m.*
made [meid] *pret. u. p.p. von make* 1.
made(-)to(-)meas·ure ['meidtə'meʒə] maßgeschneidert.
made-up ['meid'⁓p] zurechtgemacht; erfunden; fertig; ⁓ *clothes pl.* Konfektion *f*; ⁓ *of* bestehend aus.
mad·house ['mædhaus] Toll-, Irrenhaus *n*; **'mad·man** Wahnsinnige *m*, Irre *m*, Verrückte *m*; **'mad·ness** Wahnsinn *m*; *vet.* Tollwut *f*; Tollheit *f*; *Am.* Wut *f* (*at* über *acc.*).

ma·don·na [mə'dɔnə] Madonna *f*, Madonnendarstellung *f*; ～ **li·ly** ♀ weiße Lilie *f*.   [gal *n*.\
mad·ri·gal ♪ ['mædrigəl] Madri-\
mad·wom·an ['mædwumən] Wahnsinnige *f*.
mael·strom ['meilstrəum] Mahlstrom *m* (*Strudel*).
ma·es·tro [mɑː'estrəu] Maestro *m*, Meister *m*.
maf·fick ['mæfik] wild *od.* lärmend feiern.
mag·a·zine [mægə'ziːn] Magazin *n*; Vorratsraum *m*; ⚔ Munitionslager *n*; Patronenbehälter *m*; Zeitschrift *f*.
mag·da·len ['mægdəlin] reuige Sünderin *f*.
ma·gen·ta ⚗ [mə'dʒentə] Magenta (-rot) *n* (*Färbemittel*).
mag·got ['mægət] Made *f*; *fig.* Grille *f*; **'mag·got·y** madig; grillenhaft.
Ma·gi ['meidʒai] *pl. die drei* Weisen *m/pl.* aus dem Morgenlande.
mag·ic ['mædʒik] **1.** *a.* **'mag·i·cal** ☐ magisch; zauberhaft; Zauber...; **2.** Magie *f*, Zauberei *f*; *fig.* Zauber *m*; **ma·gi·cian** [mə'dʒiʃən] Zauberer *m*, Magier *m*; **mag·ic lantern** Laterna magica *f*.
mag·is·te·ri·al ☐ [mædʒis'tiəriəl] obrigkeitlich; behördlich; maßgebend, autoritativ; *b. s.* herrisch; **mag·is·tra·cy** ['ɹtrəsi] Richteramt *n*; die Richter *m/pl.*; **mag·is·trate** ['ɹtreit] (Polizei-, Friedens)Richter *m*.
mag·na·nim·i·ty [mægnə'nimiti] Großmut *f*; **mag·nan·i·mous** ☐ [ɹ'næniməs] großmütig.
mag·nate ['mægneit] Magnat *m*.
mag·ne·sia ⚗ [mæg'niːʃə] Magnesia *f*; **mag·ne·si·um** ⚗ [ɹzjəm] Magnesium *n*.
mag·net ['mægnit] Magnet *m*; **mag·net·ic** [ɹ'netik] (ɹally) magnetisch; ～ field Magnetfeld *n*; ～ pole Magnetpol *m*; ～ tape Tonband *n*; **mag·net·ism** ['ɹnitizəm] Magnetismus *m*; *fig.* Anziehungskraft *f* e-r Person; **mag·net·i·za·tion** [ɹnitai-'zeiʃən] Magnetisierung *f*; **'mag·net·ize** magnetisieren; **'mag·net·iz·er** Magnetiseur *m*; **mag·ne·to** [mæg'niːtəu] *mot.* Magnetzünder *m*.
mag·nif·i·cat *eccl.* [mæg'nifikæt] Magnifikat *n*; *fig.* Lobgesang *m*.

mag·nif·i·cence [mæg'nifisns] Pracht *f*, Herrlichkeit *f*; **mag·nif·i·cent** prächtig, prachtvoll, herrlich; **mag·ni·fi·er** ['ɹfaiə] Vergrößerungsglas *n*; **'mag·ni·fy** vergrößern (*a. fig.*); ～*ing glass* Vergrößerungsglas *n*, Lupe *f*; **mag·nil·o·quence** [mæg'niləukwəns] Großsprecherei *f*; **mag·nil·o·quent** großsprecherisch; **mag·ni·tude** ['ɹtjuːd] Größe *f*; Wichtigkeit *f*; *star of the first* ～ Stern *m* erster Größe.
mag·no·lia ♀ [mæg'nəuljə] Magnolie *f*.
mag·pie *orn.* ['mægpai] Elster *f*; *fig.* Klatschbase *f*.
Magyar ['mægjɑː] **1.** Madjar(in); **2.** madjarisch.
mahl·stick *paint.* ['mɔːlstik] Malstock *m*.
ma·hog·a·ny [mə'hɔgəni] Mahagoni(holz) *n*.
maid [meid] *lit.* Mädchen *n*; † Jungfrau *f*; (Dienst)Mädchen *n*; *old* ～ alte Jungfer *f*; ～ *of hono(u)r* Ehren-, Hofdame *f*; *Am.* erste Brautjungfer *f*.
maid·en ['meidn] **1.** *prov. od. co.* = *maid*; **2.** jungfräulich; unverheiratet; *fig.* Jungfern..., Erstlings...; ～ *name* Mädchenname *m* e-r *Frau*; ～ *speech* Jungfernrede *f*; **'ɹhair** ♀ Frauenhaar *n*; **'ɹhead** Jungfräulichkeit *f*; **'ɹhood** Mädchenjahre *n/pl.*; **'ɹlike**, **'maiden·ly** jungfräulich, mädchenhaft; **maid·en voy·age** ⚓ Jungfernfahrt *f*; ✈ Jungfernflug *m*.
maid-of-all-work ['meidəv'ɔːlwəːk] Mädchen *n* für alles; **'maidserv·ant** Dienstmädchen *n*.
mail[1] *hist.* [meil] (Ketten)Panzer *m*.
mail[2] [ɹ] **1.** Post(dienst *m*) *f*; Post (-sendung) *f*; **2.** *bsd. Am.* aufgeben, mit der Post schicken; ～*ing list* Adressenkartei *f*; **'mail·a·ble** *Am.* postversandfähig.
mail...: **'ɹbag** Briefträger-, Posttasche *f*; Postsack *m*; **'ɹbox** *bsd. Am.* Briefkasten *m*; ～ **car·ri·er** *Am.* Briefträger *m*; **'ɹcoach** Postkutsche *f*; **'ɹman** *bsd. Am.* Briefträger *m*; **'ɹor·der cat·a·log(ue)** Versandhauskatalog *m*; **'ɹor·der firm**, *bsd. Am.* **'ɹor·der house** Versandhaus *n*; **'ɹtrain** Postzug *m*.
maim [meim] verstümmeln.

main [mein] **1.** Haupt..., hauptsächlich; ~ *chance* materieller Vorteil *m*; ~ *station teleph.* Haupt-
anschluß *m*; *by* ~ *force* mit voller
Kraft; ~ *plane unit* ✈ Tragwerk *n*;
2. Hauptrohr *n*, -leitung *f*; Wasserleitung *f*; *poet.* Meer *n*; ~*s pl.* ⚡
(Strom)Netz *n*; ~*s adapter* Netzteil *n*
e-s Batteriegeräts; ~*s aerial* Netz-
antenne *f*; ~*s operated* mit Netzbe-
trieb; ~*s set* Netzempfänger *m*; *in the*
~ in der Hauptsache, im wesent-
lichen; *s. might* 1; '~·**land** Festland *n*;
'**main·ly** hauptsächlich.

main...: ~·**mast** ['~mɑ:st, ⚓ '~məst]
Großmast *m*; ~·**sail** ['~seil, ⚓ '~sl]
Großsegel *n*; '~·**spring** Uhrfeder
f; *fig.* Haupttriebfeder *f*; '~·**stay**
⚓ Großstag *n*; *fig.* Hauptstütze
f; '~·**stream** *fig.* Hauptströmung *f*,
-richtung *f*; ⩣ **Street** *Am.* Hauptstra-
ße *f*; Kleinstadtbewohner *m*|*pl.*

main·tain [mein'tein] (aufrecht)er-
halten; beibehalten; *Meinung etc.*
(unter)stützen; *Familie, Gespräch,
Briefwechsel, Weg etc.* unterhalten;
Stellung, Preis etc. behaupten; ~
that behaupten, daß; **main'tain-
a·ble** haltbar; **main'tain·er** Ver-
sorger(in); Verfechter(in).

main·te·nance ['meintənəns] Erhaltung *f*; Unterhalt *m*; Behau-
tung *f*; Instandhaltung *f*; ~ *costs pl.*
Unterhaltskosten *pl.*

main·top ⚓ ['meintɔp] Großmars
m.

mai·son·(n)ette [meizə'net] Einfamilienhaus *n*; zweistöckige Miets-
wohnung *f.*

maize ⚘ [meiz] Mais *m.*

ma·jes·tic [mə'dʒestik] (~*ally*) majestätisch; **maj·es·ty** ['mædʒisti]
Majestät *f*; Würde *f*, Hoheit *f.*

ma·jor ['meidʒə] **1.** größer; be-
deutend(er), wichtig(er); mündig,
volljährig; ♩ Dur *n*; A ~ A-Dur *n*;
~ *third* große Terz *f*; ~ *key* Dur-
Tonart *f*; ~ *league Am.* Baseball:
Oberliga *f* **2.** Major *m*; Mündige *m*,
f, Volljährige *m*, *f*; *hinter Eigennamen*: der Ältere; *phls.* Obersatz
m; *Am. univ.* Hauptfach *n*; **3.** *Am.*
als Hauptfach studieren, sich spezialisieren *auf e-m Gebiet*; '~-'**gen-
er·al** Generalmajor *m*; **ma·jor·i·ty**
[mə'dʒɔriti] Mehrheit *f*, Majorität
f; Mehrzahl *f*; Mündigkeit *f*, Voll-
jährigkeit *f*; Majorsstelle *f*, -rang *m*;

~ *decision* Mehrheitsbeschluß *m*; ~
rule Mehrheitsregierung *f*; *join the* ~
sich zu seinen Vätern versammeln;
win by a large ~ mit großer Mehrheit
gewinnen; **ma·jor road** Vorfahrts-
straße *f.*

make [meik] **1.** (*irr.*) *v*/*t. allg.*
machen; herstellen, anfertigen,
fabrizieren; schaffen; bilden; hervorbringen; (er)bauen; ergeben;
(veran)lassen; machen *od.* ernennen
zu; gewinnen, verdienen; sich erweisen als, abgeben; *Regel* aufstellen; *Verlust* (er)leiden; *Freundschaft,
Frieden* schließen; *e-e Rede* halten; ~
believe tun so tun als ob, vorgeben
zu; ~ *the best of it* das Beste daraus
machen, es möglichst gut aus-
nützen; sich damit abfinden; ~
capital out of Kapital schlagen
aus; ~ *do with* sich behelfen mit,
auskommen mit; ~ *good ein Unrecht etc.* wieder gutmachen; *et.* ersetzen; *Wort* halten; wahr machen;
glücklich bewerkstelligen; ~ *it* F es
schaffen; ~ (*the*) *land* ⚓ Land sichten; ~ *or mar s.o.* j-s Glück oder Unglück sein; *do you* ~ *one of us?* machen Sie mit?; ~ *port* ⚓ den Hafen
anlaufen; ~ *shift* sich behelfen; ~ *way*
vorwärtskommen; ~ *way for* vor *j-m*
zurücktreten (*a. fig.*); ~ *into* verarbeiten zu; ~ *out* ausfindig machen; ausmachen, erkennen; verstehen; entziffern; beweisen; zu
erkennen geben; hinstellen als;
Rechnung etc. ausstellen, ausfertigen; vervollständigen; ~ *over* übertragen; ~ *up* ergänzen; vervollständigen; *zs.*-setzen, -stellen, -brin-
gen *etc.*; bilden, ausmachen; ✝ ausgleichen; *Streit* beilegen; verfertigen; zurechtmachen, schminken;
erfinden; = ~ *up for* (*v*/*i.*); ~ *up
one's mind* sich schlüssig werden,
sich entschließen (*to inf.* zu *inf.*);
sich abfinden (*to, for* mit *et.*); **2.** (*irr.*)
v/*i.* sich *in e-r Richtung* bewegen;
eintreten (*Flut*); ~ *as if* sich stellen
als ob; ~ *after* nachjagen (*dat.*);
~ *against* schaden (*dat.*); sprechen
gegen; ~ *at* auf *j.* losgehen; ~ *away*
sich davonmachen; ~ *away with*
beseitigen; umbringen; *Geld* ver-
tun; ~ *for* zugehen auf (*acc.*); sich
aufmachen *od.* begeben nach;
sprechen für, fördern; ~ *off* sich
fortmachen, verschwinden; ~ *up*

sich zurechtmachen, sich schminken; ⌵ *up for* nach-, aufholen; wieder gutmachen; für *et.* entschädigen; *Verlust* wieder einholen; ⌵ *up to s.o.* sich an j. heranmachen; sich mit j-m versöhnen; **3.** Mach-, Bauart *f;* Bau *m des Körpers;* Form *f,* Fasson *f,* Schnitt *m;* Fabrikat *n,* Erzeugnis *n;* Marke *f,* Typ *m;* ⚡ Schließen *n e-s Stromkreises; of poor* ⌵ minderwertig; *on the* ⌵ *sl.* auf Profit *od.* s-n Vorteil aus; '⌵-be·lieve **1.** Spiegelfechterei *f;* Schein *m,* Vorwand *m,* Verstellung *f;* **2.** vorgeblich, scheinbar; 'mak·er Hersteller *m,* Erzeuger *m;* ⌵ Schöpfer *m (Gott).*

make...: '⌵-·shift **1.** Notbehelf *m;* **2.** behelfsmäßig; Behelfs..., Not...; '⌵-up Umbruch *m,* typographische Anordnung *f; fig.* Beschaffenheit *f,* Charakter *m,* Natur *f;* Schminke *f,* Make-up *n;* '⌵-weight Zugabe *f zum Gewicht; fig.* Lückenbüßer *m.*

mak·ing ['meikiŋ] Machen *n etc.;* Herstellung *f;* ⌵s *pl.* ⚡ Verdienst *m; in the* ⌵ im Werden; *that was the* ⌵ *of him* das machte ihn zu dem, was er ist; *have the* ⌵*s of* das Zeug haben zu.

mal·a·chite *min.* ['mæləkait] Malachit *m.*

mal·ad·just·ed *psych.* ['mælə-'dʒʌstid] s-r Umwelt entfremdet, schlecht angepaßt; 'mal·ad'just·ment mangelhafte Anpassung *f.*

mal·ad·min·is·tra·tion ['mæləd-minis'treiʃən] schlechte Verwaltung *f,* Mißwirtschaft *f.*

mal·a·droit ['mælə'drɔit] ungeschickt.

mal·a·dy ['mælədi] Krankheit *f.*

ma·laise [mæ'leiz] Unbehagen *n,* Unwohlsein *n.*

mal·a·prop·ism ['mæləprɔpizəm] Wortverwechslung *f;* **mal·a·pro·pos** ['⌵'æprəpəu] **1.** *adj.* ungelegen; **2.** *adv.* zur unrechten Zeit; **3.** *et.* Unangebrachtes *n.*

ma·lar·i·a ⚕ [mə'lɛəriə] Malaria *f,* Sumpffieber *n;* **ma·lar·i·al** malariaverseucht; Malaria...

Ma·lay [mə'lei] **1.** Malaie *m,* Malaiin *f;* **2.** malaiisch.

mal·con·tent ['mælkəntent] **1.** unzufrieden; **2.** Unzufriedene *m, f.*

male [meil] **1.** männlich; ⌵ *chauvinism* Männlichkeitswahn *m;* ⌵ *child* Knabe

m; ⌵ *model* Dressman *m;* ⌵ *nurse* Krankenpfleger *m;* ⌵ *screw* Schraube(nspindel) *f;* **2.** Mann *m;* Männchen *n der Tiere.*

mal·e·dic·tion [mæli'dikʃən] Fluch *m,* Verwünschung *f.* [täter *m.*\

mal·e·fac·tor ['mælifæktə] Übel-|

ma·lef·i·cence [mə'lefisns] Schädlichkeit *f;* **ma'lef·i·cent** schädlich.

ma·lev·o·lence [mə'levələns] Böswilligkeit *f;* **ma'lev·o·lent** böswillig *(to* gegen).

mal·for·ma·tion ['mælfɔ:'meiʃən] Mißbildung *f.*

mal·func·tion [mæl'fʌŋkʃən] **1.** ⚕ Funktionsstörung *f;* ⊕ Defekt *m;* **2.** defekt sein.

mal·ice ['mælis] Bosheit *f;* Groll *m;* ⚖ böse Absicht *f; bear s.o.* ⌵ e-n Groll *od.* Rachegefühle gegen j. hegen; *with* ⌵ *aforethought* ⚖ vorsätzlich.

ma·li·cious ⌐ [mə'liʃəs] boshaft, heimtückisch; ⚖ böswillig; **ma'li·cious·ness** Bosheit *f.*

ma·lign [mə'lain] **1.** ⌐ schädlich; ⚕ bösartig; **2.** verleumden, beschimpfen; **ma·lig·nan·cy** [mə-'lignənsi] Bosheit *f;* ⚕ Bösartigkeit *f;* **ma'lig·nant** ⌐ **1.** boshaft, böswillig; ⚕ bösartig; **2.** Übelgesinnte *m;* **ma'lig·ni·ty** Bosheit *f;* Schadenfreude *f; bsd.* ⚕ Bösartigkeit *f.*

ma·lin·ger [mə'liŋgə] simulieren; **ma'lin·ger·er** Simulant *m.*

mall [mɔ:l] Promenade *f;* Mittelstreifen *m e-r Autobahn; Am.* Einkaufszentrum *n.*

mal·lard *orn.* ['mæləd] Stockente *f.*

mal·le·a·ble ['mæliəbl] hämmerbar, verformbar; *fig.* geschmeidig, anpassungsfähig.

mal·let ['mælit] Holzhammer *m,* Schlegel *m; Sport:* Schlagholz *n.*

mal·low ♀ ['mæləu] Malve *f.*

malm·sey ['mɑ:mzi] Malvasier (-wein) *m.*

mal·nu·tri·tion ['mælnju:'triʃən] Unterernährung *f.*

mal·o·dor·ous ⌐ [mæ'ləudərəs] übelriechend.

mal·prac·tice ['mæl'præktis] Übeltat *f;* ⚕ falsche Behandlung *f;* ⚖ Amtsmißbrauch *m.*

malt [mɔ:lt] **1.** Malz *n;* ⌵ *liquor* gegorener Malztrank *m, bsd.* Bier *n;* **2.** malzen; zu Malz machen; mit Malz versetzen.

Mal·tese [ˈmɔːlˈtiːz] **1.** maltesisch; **2.** Malteser(in).

mal·treat [mælˈtriːt] schlecht behandeln; mißhandeln; **malˈtreat·ment** Mißhandlung f.

malt·ster [ˈmɔːltstə] Mälzer m.

mal·ver·sa·tion [mælvɔːˈseiʃən] Veruntreuung f; Amtsmißbrauch m.

ma·ma, mam·ma [məˈmɑː] Mama f.

mam·mal [ˈmæməl] Säugetier n; **mam·ma·li·an** [məˈmeiljən] Säugetier...

mam·mon [ˈmæmən] Mammon m.

mam·moth [ˈmæməθ] **1.** zo. Mammut n; **2.** riesig, ungeheuer.

mam·my F [ˈmæmi] Mami f; Am. farbiges Kindermädchen n.

man [mæn, in Zssgn ... mən] **1.** pl. **men** [men] Mann m (a. ✕); Mensch(en pl.) m; Menschheit f; Diener m; Untertan m; Schach: Figur f; Damestein m; attr. männlich; to a ⌣, to the last ⌣ bis auf den letzten Mann; ⌣ on leave ✕ Urlauber m; be one's own ⌣ sein eigener Herr sein; **2.** ✕, ⚓ bemannen, besetzen; ⌣ o.s. sich ermannen.

man·a·cle [ˈmænəkl] **1.** Handfessel f; **2.** fesseln.

man·age [ˈmænidʒ] v/t. handhaben; behandeln; Geschäft etc. verwalten, führen, leiten; Menschen, Tiere leiten, lenken; j. herumbringen; mit j-m fertig werden; et. fertigbringen, möglich machen; ⌣ to inf. es fertigbringen zu inf.; v/i. die Aufsicht haben, die Geschäfte führen; es schaffen; auskommen, sich behelfen (with mit; without ohne); **ˈman·age·a·ble** ☐ handlich; lenksam; **ˈman·age·ment** Handhabung f; Verwaltung f, Leitung f, Direktion f, Geschäftsführung f; geschickte Behandlung f; Kunst (-griff m) f; **ˈman·ag·er** Verwalter m, Leiter m, Vorsteher m, Direktor m, Regisseur m, Unternehmer m, Impresario m, Manager m; departmental ⌣ Abteilungsleiter m; good (bad) ⌣ guter (schlechter) Haushälter m; sales ⌣ Verkaufsleiter m; **ˈman·ag·er·ess** Leiterin f, Vorsteherin f, Direktorin f; **man·a·ge·ri·al** ☐ [ˌ⌣əˈdʒiəriəl] geschäftsführend, leitend, Direktions...

man·ag·ing [ˈmænidʒiŋ] geschäftsführend; Betriebs...; sparsam; ⌣ clerk Geschäftsführer m, Prokurist m.

man-at-arms [ˈmænətˈɑːmz] Gewappnete m.

Man·ches·ter [ˈmæntʃistə] ⌣ goods pl. Baumwollwaren f/pl.

Man·chu [mænˈtʃuː], **Man·chu·ri·an** [ˌ⌣ˈtʃuəriən] **1.** mandschurisch; **2.** Mandschu m; das Mandschurische.

man·da·mus ✟ [mænˈdeiməs] Befehl m e-s höheren Gerichtes an ein niederes.

man·da·rin [ˈmændərin] Mandarin m; das Mandarinische (chines. Gebildetensprache); a. ˈman·da·rine ✿ Mandarine f.

man·da·tar·y ✟ [ˈmændətəri] Mandatar m (Bevollmächtigter); **man·date** [ˈ⌣deit] **1.** Mandat n; Befehl m; Auftrag m; Vollmacht f; **2.** unter ein Mandat stellen; **manˈda·tor** Mandant m (Vollmachterteiler); **man·da·to·ry** [ˈ⌣dətəri] **1.** befehlend; Am. obligatorisch; **2.** Mandatar(staat) m.

man·di·ble anat. [ˈmændibl] Kinnbacken m, Kiefer m.

man·do·lin ♪ [ˈmændəlin] Mandoline f.

man·drag·o·ra [mænˈdrægərə], **man·drake** ✿ [ˈ⌣dreik] Alraun(e f) m.

man·drel ⊕ [ˈmændril] Dorn m.

man·drill zo. [ˌ⌣] Mandrill m.

mane [mein] Mähne f; **maned** mit einer Mähne.

man-eat·er [ˈmæniːtə] Menschenfresser m.

ma·nes [ˈmɑːneiz] pl. Manen pl. (Geister der Toten). [vre.⌣]

ma·neu·ver [məˈnuːvə] = manoeu-⌣

man·ful ☐ [ˈmænful] mannhaft; **ˈman·ful·ness** Mannhaftigkeit f.

man·ga·nese ⚗ [ˈmæŋgəˈniːz] Mangan n; **man·gan·ic** [ˌ⌣ˈgænik] manganhaltig; Mangan...

mange vet. [meindʒ] Räude f.

man·gel(-wur·zel) [ˈmæŋgl(ˈwəːzl)] = mangold.

man·ger [ˈmeindʒə] Krippe f; dog in the ⌣ F Neidhammel m.

man·gle[1] [ˈmæŋgl] **1.** Wringmaschine f; Wäschemangel f; **2.** mange(l)n; wringen.

man·gle[2] [ˌ⌣] zerstückeln, zerfleischen; *fig.* verstümmeln; **'man-gler** Fleischwolf *m.*

man·go ⚥ ['mæŋgəu] Mango-pflaume *f;* -baum *m.*

man·gold ⚥ ['mæŋgəld] Mangold *m.*

man·grove ⚥ ['mæŋgrəuv] Mangrove *f.*

man·gy ['meindʒi] räudig; schäbig.

man...: '⁓-han·dle durch Menschenkraft bewegen; *sl.* rauh anpacken *od.* behandeln; **'⁓-hat·er** Menschenfeind(in); **'⁓·hole** ⊕ Mann-, Einsteigloch *n;* **'⁓·hood** Mannesalter *n;* Männlichkeit *f;* Männer *m'pl.;* Menschentum *n;* **'⁓-'hour** Arbeitsstunde *f* pro Mann.

ma·ni·a ['meinjə] Wahnsinn *m;* Sucht *f,* Manie *f; in Zssgn:* ...sucht *f;* ...trieb *m;* ...narrheit *f;* **ma·ni·ac** ['⁓niæk] **1.** Wahnsinnige *m;* **2.** *a.* **ma·ni·a·cal** ⊏ [məˈnaiəkəl] wahnsinnig.

man·ic-de·pres·sive *psych.* ['mænikdiˈpresiv] **1.** manisch-depressiv; **2.** Manisch-Depressive *m, f.*

man·i·cure ['mænikjuə] **1.** Maniküre *f;* **2.** manikürien; **'⁓-case** Maniküreetui *n;* **man·i·cur·ist** ['⁓rist] Maniküre *f (Person).*

man·i·fest ['mænifest] **1.** ⬚ offenbar, -kundig, augenscheinlich; **2.** ⚓ Ladungsverzeichnis *n;* **3.** *v/t.* offenbaren; zeigen, kundtun; *v/i.* e-e Kundgebung veranstalten; **man·i·fes'ta·tion** Offenbarung *f;* Kundgebung *f;* **man·i·fes·to** [⁓təu] Manifest *n (öffentliche Erklärung).*

mani·fold ⬚ ['mænifəuld] **1.** mannigfaltig; zahlreich; **2.** vervielfältigen; **3.** ⊕ Rohrverzweigung *f; intake* ⁓ *mot.* Einlaßkrümmer *m;* ⁓ **writ·er** Vervielfältigungsgerät *n.*

man·i·kin ['mænikin] Männlein *n;* Gliederpuppe *f.*

Ma·nil·(l)a [məˈnilə] *a.* ⁓ *cheroot* Manilazigarre *f; a.* ⁓ *hemp* Manilahanf *m;* ⁓ *paper* Packpapier *n.*

ma·nip·u·late [məˈnipjuleit] (geschickt) handhaben *od.* behandeln; zurechtmachen; **ma·nip·u'la·tion** Manipulation *f,* Handhabung *f,* Behandlung *f,* Verfahren *n;* (künstliche) Beeinflussung *f;* Kniff *m;* **ma'nip·u·la·tive** [⁓lətiv] Handhabungs...; **ma'nip·u·la·tor** [⁓-leitə] Handhaber *m; phys.* Manipu-

lator *m.*

man·kind [mænˈkaind] Menschheit *f;* ['⁓] Männerwelt *f;* **'man-like** = *manly; mannish;* **'man·li-ness** Männlich-, Mannhaftigkeit *f;* **'man·ly** männlich; mannhaft; **'man-'made** künstlich; von Menschen geschaffen; ⁓ *fibre, Am.* ⁓ *fiber* Kunst-, Chemiefaser *f.*

man·na ['mænə] Manna *n, f.*

man·ne·quin ['mænikin] Mannequin *n, m,* Vorführdame *f;* ⁓ *parade* Modenschau *f.*

man·ner ['mænə] (Art *f* u.) Weise *f;* Art *f,* Gattung *f; paint. etc.* Manier *f,* Stil *m;* ⁓s *pl.* Manieren *f pl.;* Umgangsformen *f/pl.;* Benehmen *n; no* ⁓ *of doubt* gar kein Zweifel; *in a* ⁓ gewissermaßen; *in such a* ⁓ *that* derartig, daß; **'man·nered** ...gesittet, ...geartet; manieriert, gekünstelt; **'man·ner·ism** Manieriertheit *f,* Künstelei *f;* Manierismus *m;* **'man·ner·li·ness** Manierlichkeit *f,* gute Lebensart *f;* **'man·ner·ly** gesittet, manierlich.

man·nish ['mæniʃ] männlich *(Frau).*

ma·noeu·vra·ble, *Am. a.* **ma·neu·ver·a·ble** [məˈnuːvrəbl] manövrierfähig; **ma'noeu·vre,** *Am. a.* **ma-'neu·ver** [⁓və] **1.** Manöver *n (a. fig.);* ⁓s *pl.* F *fig.* Mätzchen *pl.;* **2.** manövrieren (lassen).

man-of-war ['mænəvˈwɔː] Kriegsschiff *n.*

ma·nom·e·ter *phys.,* ⊕ [məˈnɔmitə] Manometer *n,* Druckmesser *m.*

man·or ['mænə] (Ritter)Gut *n; lord of the* ⁓ Gutsherr *m;* **'⁓-house** Herrschaftshaus *n,* Herrensitz *m;* Schloß *n;* **ma·no·ri·al** [məˈnɔːriəl] herrschaftlich; Ritterguts...

man·pow·er ['mænpauə] Menschenpotential *n;* Arbeitskräfte *f/pl.*

manse *schott.* [mæns] Pfarrhaus *n.*

man·serv·ant ['mænsəːvənt] Diener *m.*

man·sion ['mænʃən] herrschaftliches Wohnhaus *n;* ⁓s *pl.* Häuserblock *m.*

man·slaugh·ter ['mænslɔːtə] Totschlag *m,* fahrlässige Tötung *f.*

man·tel·piece ['mæntlpiːs], **'man-tel·shelf** Kaminsims *m,* -platte *f.*

man·til·la [mænˈtilə] Mantille *f.*

man·tle ['mæntl] **1.** Mantel *m (a. anat.,* 🜨, *zo.); fig.* Schleier *m,* Hülle *f; a. incandescent* ⁓ Glüh-

strumpf *m*; **2.** *v. t.* verhüllen; *fig.*
bemänteln; ~ *on* überziehen; *v. i.*
sich röten (*Gesicht*); ~ *with* sich
überziehen mit.
man·trap ['mæntræp] Fußangel *f.*
man·u·al ['mænjuəl] **1.** ⬚ Hand...;
mit der Hand (gemacht); ~*ly operated*
handgesteuert; ~ *exercises pl.* ✗ Grif-
feüben *n*; ~ *training* Werkunterricht
m; **2.** Handbuch *n*, Leitfaden *m*;
Manual *n der Orgel*; *instruction* ~
Bedienungsanleitung(en *pl.*) *f.*
man·u·fac·to·ry [mænju'fæktəri]
Fabrik *f.*
man·u·fac·ture [mænju'fæktʃə] **1.**
Fabrikation *f*, Herstellung *f*; Fabrikat *n*; **2.** fabrizieren, herstellen;
verarbeiten (*into* zu); *fig.* erfinden;
~*d goods pl.* Fabrik-, Fertig-,
Manufakturwaren *f pl.*; **man·u-**
'fac·tur·er Fabrikant *m*, Hersteller *m*; **man·u'fac·tur·ing** Fabrik...; Gewerbe...; Industrie...
ma·nure [mə'njuə] **1.** Dünger *m*;
2. düngen.
man·u·script ['mænjuskript] **1.** Manuskript *n*; Handschrift *f*; **2.** hand-
schriftlich.
Manx [mæŋks] **1.** von der Insel
Man; **2.** *die* Bewohner *m pl.* der
Insel Man.
man·y ['meni] **1.** viele; ~ *a* man-
che(*r*, -*s*); ~ *a one* manch eine(*r*, -*s*);
as ~ *as* nicht weniger als; *one too* ~
einer zuviel; überflüssig; *be one*
too ~ *for s.o.* j-m überlegen sein;
2. Menge *f*; *a great* ~, *a good* ~ e-e
ziemliche Menge, ziemlich viele,
sehr viele; '~'**sid·ed** vielseitig.
map [mæp] **1.** (Land-, *a.* Himmels-)
Karte *f*; *off the* ~ F nicht vorhanden
od. da, erledigt; *on the* ~ F noch
vorhanden, da; **2.** aufzeichnen, eintragen; kartographisch erfassen;
~ *out* planen; einteilen.
ma·ple ⚲ ['meipl] Ahorn *m.*
map·per ['mæpə] Kartograph *m.*
ma·quis ['mæki:] *der* Maquis, *die*
französische Widerstandsbewegung.
mar [mɑ:] beeinträchtigen; stören,
verderben.
mar·a·bou *orn.* ['mærəbu:] Marabu
m.
mar·a·schi·no [mærə'ski:nəu] Ma-
raschino(likör) *m.*
Mar·a·thon ['mærəθ(l)ən] *a.* ~ *race*
Langstrecken-, Marathonlauf *m.*
ma·raud [mə'rɔ:d] plündern; **ma-**

'**raud·er** Plünderer *m*, Marodeur *m.*
mar·ble ['mɑ:bl] **1.** Marmor *m*;
Marmorbildwerk *n*; Murmel *f*; **2.**
marmorn; *fig.* hart; **3.** marmorie-
ren.
mar·cel [mɑ:'sel] **1.** *a.* ~ *wave*
Ondulationswelle *f*; **2.** ondulieren.
March[1] [mɑ:tʃ] März *m.*
march[2] [~] **1.** Marsch *m*; Fortschritt *m*; Gang *m der Ereignisse*
etc.; ~ *past* ✗ Vorbei-, Parade-
marsch *m*; *steal a* ~ *on s.o.* j-m
zuvorkommen; **2.** marschieren (lassen), ziehen; gehen, schreiten; *fig.*
vorwärtsschreiten; ~ *off* ✗ *Ge-*
fangene abführen; ~ *past* vorbeimarschieren.
march[3] [~] **1.** *mst* ~*es pl. hist.* Mark
f, Grenzgebiet *n*; **2.** grenzen (*with*
an *acc.*).
march·ing ['mɑ:tʃiŋ] Marsch...;
~ *order* Marschausrüstung *f*; ~
orders pl. Marschbefehl *m*; *in*
heavy ~ *order* feldmarschmäßig.
mar·chion·ess ['mɑ:ʃənis] Mar-
quise *f.*
march·pane ['mɑ:tʃpein] Marzipan
n, *m.*
mare [mɛə] Stute *f*; ~'*s nest fig.*
Schwindel *m*; (Zeitungs)Ente *f.*
mar·ga·rine [mɑ:dʒə'ri:n], F *a.*
marge [mɑ:dʒ] Margarine *f.*
mar·gin ['mɑ:dʒin] Rand *m*;
Grenze *f*; Spielraum *m*; *a.* ~ *of*
profit Verdienst-, Gewinn-, Han-
delsspanne *f*, Marge *f*; *safety* ~ Si-
cherheitsfaktor *m*; '**mar·gin·al** ☐
am Rande (befindlich); Rand...; ~
note Randbemerkung *f.*
mar·grave ['mɑ:greiv] Markgraf
m; **mar·gra·vine** ['~grəvi:n] Mark-
gräfin *f.*
mar·gue·rite ⚲ [mɑ:gə'ri:t] Gänseblümchen *n*; Marguerite *f.*
Ma·ri·a [mə'raiə]: *Black* ~ F grüne
Minna *f.*
mar·i·gold ⚲ ['mærigəuld] Dotter-
blume *f.*
mar·i·jua·na [mæri'hwɑ:nə] Marihuana *n* (*Rauschgift*).
ma·ri·nade [mæri'neid] **1.** Marinade
f; marinierter Fisch *m*; **2.** = **ma-**
ri·nate ['~neit] marinieren.
ma·rine [mə'ri:n] **1.** See..., Marine...; Schiffs...; **2.** Marineinfanterist *m*; Marine *f*; *paint.* Seestück *n*; *tell that to the* ~*s!* mach
das einem anderen weis!; **mar·i-**

ner *poet. od.* ⚓ ['mærinə] Seemann *m.* [nette *f.*]

mar·i·o·nette [mæriə'net] Mario-

mar·i·tal ['mæritl] ehelich, Ehe..., Gatten...; ~ *status* Familienstand *m.*

mar·i·time ['mæritaim] an der See liegend *od.* lebend, See...; Küsten-...; Schiffahrt(s)...; ~ *power* Seemacht *f.*

mar·jo·ram ⚘ ['mɑːdʒərəm] Majoran *m.*

mark¹ [mɑːk] Mark *f* (*Geldstück*).

mark² [~] **1.** Marke *f*, Merkmal *n*, Zeichen *n*; ⚓ Preiszettel *m*, Auszeichnung *f an Waren*; Fabrik-, Schutzmarke *f*; (Brand)Mal *n*; Narbe *f*; Kratzer *m*, Fleck(en) *m*; Zeichen *n*, Kreuz *n* (*als Unterschrift*); Norm *f*, Standard *m*; *Schule*: Zensur *f*, Note *f*, Punkt *m*; *Sport*: Startlinie *f*; Ziel *n*; *vet.* Kennung *f*; *a man of* ~ ein Mann von Bedeutung; *up to the* ~ *fig.* auf der Höhe; den Erwartungen entsprechend; *hit the* ~ ins Schwarze treffen; *miss the* ~ vorbeischießen; *beside the* ~, *wide of the* ~ den Kern der Sache verfehlend; unrichtig; **2.** *v/t.* (be)zeichnen; *Waren* auszeichnen; *Stand e-s Spiels* anschreiben; kundtun; kennzeichnen, markieren; beachten, aufpassen auf (*acc.*); sich *et.* merken; ~ *down* (im Preis) herabsetzen; *j.* vormerken; ~ *off* abtrennen; ~ *out* bezeichnen; abstecken; vormerken; ~ *time* ✕ auf der Stelle treten (*a. fig.*); **3.** *v/i.* achtgeben; ~! Achtung!; **marked** auffallend; merklich; ausgeprägt, markant; **mark·ed·ly** ['mɑːkidli] ausgesprochen; '**mark·er** *Billard*: Markör *m*; Lesezeichen *n.*

mar·ket ['mɑːkit] **1.** Markt *m*; Marktplatz *m*; Handel *m*; Absatz *m von Waren*; *in the* ~ am Markt; *come into the* ~ auf den Markt kommen, zum Verkauf angeboten werden; *play the* ~ *Am. sl.* an der Börse spekulieren; **2.** *v/t.* auf den Markt bringen, verkaufen; *v/i.* auf den Markt gehen; einkaufen; '**mar·ket·a·ble** ⚓ marktfähig, -gängig, verkäuflich; **mar·ket·eer** [~'tiə]: *black* ~ Schwarzhändler *m*; '**mar·ket-gar·den** (Gemüse)Gärtnerei *f*;

'**mar·ket·ing** Marketing *n*, Absatzpolitik *f*; Marktbesuch *m*; '**mar·ket-place** Marktplatz *m*; **mar·ket re·search** Marktforschung *f*; '**mar·ket-town** Markt(flecken) *m*; '**mar·ket-value** Markt-, Kurswert *m.*

mark·ing ['mɑːkiŋ] Bezeichnung *f*, Markierung *f*; Musterung *f*, Zeichnung *f*; '~-ink Wäschetinte *f.*

marks·man ['mɑːksmən] (guter) Schütze *m*; '**marks·man·ship** Schießkunst *f.*

marl [mɑːl] **1.** *min.* Mergel *m*; **2.** ✗ mergeln.

mar·ma·lade ['mɑːməleid] Orangenmarmelade *f.*

mar·mo·re·al *poet. u. rhet.* [mɑː'mɔːriəl] marmorn.

mar·mot *zo.* ['mɑːmət] Murmeltier *n.*

ma·roon¹ [mə'ruːn] kastanienbraun.

ma·roon² [~] *auf e-r einsamen Insel* aussetzen.

ma·roon³ [~] Leuchtrakete *f.*

mar·plot ['mɑːplɔt] Störenfried *m.*

marque ⚓ [mɑːk]: *letter(s pl.) of* ~ Kaperbrief *m.*

mar·quee [mɑː'kiː] (großes) Zelt *n.*

mar·quess, *mst* **mar·quis** ['mɑːkwis] Marquis *m* (*englischer Adelstitel*).

mar·que·try ['mɑːkitri] Einlegearbeit *f.*

mar·riage ['mæridʒ] Heirat *f*, Ehe *f*; Ehestand *m*; Hochzeit *f*; *civil* ~ standesamtliche Trauung *f*; *by* ~ angeheiratet; *related by* ~ verschwägert; *take in* ~ zum Mann (zur Frau) nehmen; '**mar·riage·a·ble** heiratsfähig. **mar·riage...:** ~ **ar·ti·cles** *pl.* Ehevertrag *m*; ~ **cer·e·mo·ny** Trauung *f*; ~ **guid·ance** Eheberatung *f*; ~ **lines** *pl.* Trauschein *m*; ~ **por·tion** Mitgift *f.*

mar·ried ['mærid] verheiratet; ehelich; Ehe...; ~ *couple* Ehepaar *n.*

mar·row ['mærəu] Mark *n*; *fig.* Kern *m*, Beste *n*; *vegetable* ~ ⚘ Markkürbis *m*; '~-bone Markknochen *m*; ~s *pl. co.* Knie *n pl.*; '**mar·row·y** markig.

mar·ry ['mæri] *v/t.* heiraten; verheiraten (*a. fig.*), vermählen (*to* mit); *eccl.* trauen; *v/i. a. get married* (sich verheiraten.

marsh [mɑːʃ] **1.** Sumpf *m*, Morast *m*, Marsch *f*; **2.** Sumpf...; ~ *fever*

Sumpffieber *n*; ~ *gas* Sumpfgas *n*.
mar·shal ['mɑːʃəl] **1.** Marschall *m*;
hist. Hofmarschall *m*; Zeremonienmeister *m*, Festordner *m*; *Am.* Be-
zirkspolizeichef *m*; Leiter *m* der
Feuerwehr; **2.** ordnen; führen; zs.-
stellen; **mar·shal·ling-yard** ['~ʃ-
liŋjɑːd] Verschiebebahnhof *m*;
'**mar·shal·ship** Marschallamt *n*.
marsh mal·low ['mɑːʃmælou] ❦
Eibisch *m*, Althee *f*; *Art* türkischer
Honig *m*; **marsh mar·i·gold**
Sumpfdotterblume *f*; '**marsh·y**
sumpfig.
mar·su·pi·al *zo.* [mɑːˈsjuːpjəl] **1.**
Beutel...; Beuteltier...; **2.** Beuteltier *n*.
mart [mɑːt] Markt *m*; Auktions-
raum *m*.
mar·ten *zo.* ['mɑːtin] Marder *m*.
mar·tial ~ ['mɑːʃəl] kriegerisch;
Kriegs...; ~ *law* Kriegs-, Stand-
recht *n*; *state of* ~ *law* Belagerungs-
zustand *m*; ~ *music* Militärmusik *f*.
Mar·tian ['mɑːʃjən] **1.** Marsbewoh-
ner *m*; **2.** Mars...
mar·tin[1] ['mɑːtin] Mauerschwalbe *f*.
Mar·tin[2] [~]: *St.* ~'s *summer* Alt-
weibersommer *m*.
mar·ti·net [mɑːtiˈnet] Zuchtmeister
m; Leuteschinder *m*.
mar·ti·ni [mɑːˈtiːni] Martini *m*
(*Cocktail*).
Mar·tin·mas ['mɑːtinməs] Martins-
tag *m* (*11. November*).
mar·tyr ['mɑːtə] **1.** Märtyrer(in);
2. zum Märtyrer machen; (zu Tode)
martern; '**mar·tyr·dom** Märtyrer-
tum *n*; '**mar·tyr·ize** quälen; opfern.
mar·vel ['mɑːvəl] **1.** Wunder *n*;
2. sich wundern (*at* über *acc.*).
mar·vel·(l)ous ['mɑːvələs] wunderbar, erstaunlich; '**mar·vel·**
(l)ous·ness das Wunderbare.
Marx·ian ['mɑːksjən] **1.** Marxist *m*;
2. marxistisch; '**Marx·ism** Marxis-
mus *m*; '**Marx·ist** = *Marxian*.
mar·zi·pan [mɑːziˈpæn] Marzipan
n, *m*.
mas·ca·ra [mæsˈkɑːrə] Wimpern-
tusche *f*.
mas·cot ['mæskət] Maskottchen *n*,
Talisman *m*, Glücksbringer(in);
radiator ~ *mot.* Kühlerfigur *f*.
mas·cu·line ['mæskjulin] **1.** ~
männlich; mannhaft; **2.** *gr.* Maskulinum *n*.

mash [mæʃ] **1.** Gemisch *n*; *Brauerei*:
Maische *f*; ✔ Mengfutter *n*;
2. mischen; zerdrücken, -quet-
schen; (ein)maischen; *sl. j-m* den
Kopf verdrehen; ~*ed potatoes pl.*
Kartoffelbrei *m*; *be* ~*ed on sl.* verschossen (*verliebt*) sein in (*acc.*);
'**mash·er** Maischapparat *m*; *sl.*
Geck *m*; Schwerenöter *m*, Schürzenjäger *m*.
mash·ie ['mæʃi] Mashie *m* (*Golfschläger*).
mask [mɑːsk] **1.** Maske *f*; Larve *f*;
s. masque; **2.** maskieren; *fig.* verbergen, verdecken; tarnen; **masked**
maskiert; Masken...; ~ *ball* Maskenball *m*; '**mask·er** Maske *f*
(*Person*).
ma·so·chism *psych.* ['mæzəukizəm]
Masochismus *m*.
ma·son ['meisn] Steinmetz *m*; Maurer *m*; Freimaurer *m*; **ma·son·ic**
[məˈsɔnik] freimaurerisch; **ma·**
son·ry ['meisnri] Mauerwerk *n*.
masque [mɑːsk] Maskenspiel *n*;
mas·quer·ade[mæskəˈreid]**1.** Maskenball *m*; Verkleidung *f*, Maskerade *f*; **2.** *fig.* sich maskieren.
mass[1] *eccl.* [mæs] Messe *f*; *High* ~
Hochamt *n*; *Low* ~ stille Messe *f*.
mass[2] [~] **1.** Masse *f*; Menge *f*; *the*
~*es pl.* die breite Masse; *in the* ~
im ganzen; **2.** (sich) (an)häufen;
(sich) (an)sammeln.
mas·sa·cre ['mæsəkə] **1.** Blutbad *n*,
Gemetzel *n*; **2.** niedermetzeln.
mas·sage ['mæsɑːʒ] **1.** Massage *f*;
~ (*suction*) *roller* Punktroller *m*;
2. massieren.
mass com·mu·ni·ca·tions ['mæs-
kəmjuːniˈkeiʃənz] *pl.* = *mass media*.
mas·seur [mæˈsə:] Masseur *m*;
mas·seuse [mæˈsəːz] Masseuse *f*.
mas·sif ['mæsiːf] (Gebirgs)Massiv *n*.
mas·sive ['mæsiv] massiv;
schwer; gediegen; mächtig; '**mas·**
sive·ness *das* Massive, *das* Schwere;
Gediegenheit *f*.
mass...: ~ me·di·a *pl.* Massen-
medien *n pl.*; ~ **meet·ing** Massenversammlung *f*, -veranstaltung *f*;
'**~-pro·duce** serienmäßig herstellen; ~ **pro·duc·tion** Massen-,
Serienproduktion *f*; ~ **so·ci·e·ty**
Massengesellschaft *f*.
mas·sy ['mæsi] massig; schwer;
derb. [masten.|
mast[1] ⚓ [mɑːst] **1.** Mast *m*; **2.** be-|

mast[2] [˽] Mast(futter *n*) *f.*
mas·ter[1] ['mɑːstə] **1.** Meister *m in
Handwerk, Kunst etc. u. fig.*; Herr *m
(a. fig.)*; Gebieter *m*; Lehrer *m*;
Kapitän *m e-s Handelsschiffs*; *Anrede*: (junger) Herr *m*; *univ.* Rektor
m e-s College; ⸱ *of Arts* Magister *m*
Artium; ⸱ *of Ceremonies* Conférencier *m*; *be one's own* ˽ sein eigener
Herr sein; **2.** Meister...; *fig.* leitend,
führend; Haupt...; **3.** Herr sein *od.*
werden über (*acc.*); *Sprache etc.*
meistern, beherrschen.
mas·ter[2] ⚓ [˽] ...master *m; three-*˽
Dreimaster *m.*
mas·ter-at-arms ⚓ ['mɑːstərət-
'ɑːmz] Schiffsprofos *m*; **mas·ter
build·er** Baumeister *m*; **mas·ter
cop·y** Original *n*; **mas·ter·ful** □
['˽ful] herrisch, gebieterisch; meisterhaft; '**mas·ter·key** Hauptschlüssel *m*; '**mas·ter·less** herrenlos,
unbändig; '**mas·ter·ly** meisterhaft.
mas·ter...: '˽**mind** *fig.* der Kopf sein
von; '˽**piece** Meisterstück *n*; '˽**-ship**
Meisterschaft *f*; Herrschaft *f*; Vor-
steher-, Lehramt *n*; '˽**stroke** Mei-
ster-, Glanzstück *n*; '**mas·ter·y**
Herrschaft *f*, Gewalt *f*; Vorrang *m*;
Oberhand *f*; Meisterschaft *f*; Beherrschung *f e-r Sprache etc.*
mast-head ['mɑːsthed] Mars *m*,
Mastkorb *m.*
mas·tic ['mæstik] Mastix(harz *n*)
m.
mas·ti·cate ['mæstikeit] kauen;
mas·ti·ca·tion Kauen *n.*
mas·tiff ['mæstif] englische Dogge *f.*
mas·to·don *zo.* ['mæstədɔn] Masto-
don *n.*
mas·toid 🜨 ['mæstɔid] Warzenfort-
satz *m hinter der Ohrmuschel.*
mat[1] [mæt] **1.** Matte *f*; Deckchen *n*;
Unterlage *f*; **2.** mit Matten belegen;
fig. bedecken; (sich) verflechten;
(sich) verfilzen.
mat[2] ⊕ [˽] mattiert, matt.
match[1] [mætʃ] Streichholz *n.*
match[2] [˽] **1.** der *od.* die *od.* das
Gleiche *od.* Passende; Partie *f*;
Wettspiel *n*, -kampf *m*; Heirat *f*;
be a ˽ *for j-m* gewachsen sein;
meet one's ˽ seinen Meister finden;
2. *v/t.* passend machen, anpassen;
vergleichen (*with* mit); passen zu,
entsprechen (*dat.*); *et.* Gleiches *od.*
Passendes finden *od.* geben zu; es
aufnehmen mit; *well* ˽*ed* zs.-pas-

send; *v/i.* zs.-passen; ˽ *with* passen
zu; *to* ˽ dazu passend.
match-box ['mætʃbɔks] Streich-
holzschachtel *f.*
match·et ['mætʃet] = *machete.*
match·less □ ['mætʃlis] unvergleichlich, ohnegleichen; '**match-
mak·er** Ehestifter(in).
match·wood ['mætʃwud] Kleinholz
n, Splitter *m/pl.*
mate[1] [meit] *Schach*: matt (setzen).
mate[2] [˽] **1.** Gefährte *m*, Gefährtin *f*,
Genosse *m*, Genossin *f*, Kamerad
(-in); Gatte *m*, Gattin *f*; Männchen
n, Weibchen *n von Tieren*; Gehilfe
m, Gehilfin *f*; ⚓ Maat *m*; **2.** (sich)
verheiraten; *zo.* (sich) paaren;
'**mate·less** ohne Gefährten.
ma·ter *sl.* ['meitə] Mutter *f.*
ma·te·ri·al [mə'tiəriəl] **1.** □ materiell; stofflich; körperlich; materialistisch; wesentlich (*to* für); **2.** Material *n*, Stoff *m*; *coll. od.* ˽*s pl.* Ma-
terialien *n/pl.*; Bestandteile *m/pl.*;
working ˽ Werkstoff *m*; *writing* ˽*s
pl.* Schreibzeug *n*; **ma·te·ri·al·ism**
Materialismus *m*; **ma·te·ri·al·ist**
Materialist(in); **ma·te·ri·al·is·tic**
(˽*ally*) materialistisch; **ma·te·ri-
al·i·ty** [˽ri'æliti] Stofflichkeit *f etc.*;
ma·te·ri·al·i·za·tion [˽riəlai'zei-
ʃən] Materialisierung *f*; **ma·te·ri-
al·ize** (sich) materialisieren; (sich)
verkörperlichen; (sich) verwirklichen.
ma·ter·nal □ [mə'təːnl] mütterlich;
Mutter...; mütterlicherseits; **ma-
'ter·ni·ty** [˽niti] Mutterschaft *f*;
Mütterlichkeit *f*; *mst* ˽ *hospital* Entbindungsanstalt *f*; ˽ *benefit* Mutter-
schaftsgeld *n*; ˽ *dress* Umstandskleid
n; ˽ *leave* Mutterschaftsurlaub *m*; ˽
ward Entbindungsstation *f (e-r Klinik).*
mat·ey ['meiti] vertraulich, kamerad-
schaftlich.
math *Am.* F [mæθ] = *maths.*
math·e·mat·i·cal □ [mæθi'mætikəl]
mathematisch; **math·e·ma·ti·cian**
[˽mə'tiʃən] Mathematiker *m*; **math-
e·mat·ics** [˽'mætiks] *mst sg.* Mathematik *f.*
maths F [mæθs] Mathe *f (Mathematik).*
mat·ie ['meiti] Matjeshering *m.*
mat·in ['mætin] **1.** *poet.* Morgen...,
früh; **2.** ˽*s pl. eccl.* Morgengebet *n*;
poet. Morgenlied *n der Vögel.*

mat·i·née ['mætinei] Nachmittags-vorstellung f; Matinee f.

mat·ing ['meitiŋ] Paarung f; ~ season Paarungszeit f.

ma·tri·arch ['meitriɑːk] Stammes-mutter f; '**ma·tri·ar·chy** Matriar-chat n, Mutterrecht n; **ma·tri·cide** ['~said] Muttermord m; Mutter-mörder(in).

ma·tric·u·late [mə'trikjuleit] (sich) immatrikulieren (lassen); **ma·tric·u'la·tion** Immatrikulation f.

mat·ri·mo·ni·al □ [mætri'məunjəl] ehelich; Ehe...; **mat·ri·mo·ny** ['~məni] Ehe(stand m) f.

ma·trix ['meitriks] fig. Nährboden m; geol. Mutterboden m; Grund-masse f, umgebendes Gestein n; ⊕ a. ['mætriks] Matrize f, Gieß-form f.

ma·tron ['meitrən] Matrone f, ver-heiratete Frau f; Hausmutter f e-s Internats etc.; Oberin f in e-m Kran-kenhaus etc.; '**ma·tron·ize** bemut-tern; '**ma·tron·ly** matronenhaft; fig. gesetzt.

mat·ter ['mætə] 1. Materie f, Stoff m; ⚕ Eiter m; Gegenstand m; In-halt m; Ursache f; Sache f, An-gelegenheit f, Geschäft n; typ. Satz m; ~s pl. die Umstände m/pl., die Lage f; postal ~ Postsachen f/pl.; printed ~ Drucksache f; in the ~ of hinsichtlich (gen.); what's the ~? was gibt es?; was ist los?; what's the ~ with you? was fehlt Ihnen?; no ~ es hat nichts zu sagen; no ~ who gleichgültig wer; ~ of course Selbst-verständlichkeit f; as a ~ of course selbstverständlich; for that ~, for the ~ of that was dies betrifft; ~ of fact Tatsache f; as a ~ of fact tat-sächlich, in der Tat; in Wirklich-keit; ~ in hand vorliegende Sache f; that is a hanging ~ das kann dich etc. den Hals kosten; no laughing ~ nichts zum Lachen; 2. von Bedeu-tung sein, darauf ankommen (to für); ins Gewicht fallen; they ~ auf sie kommt es an; it does not ~ es macht nichts; '~-of-'course selbst-verständlich; '~-of-'fact tatsäch-lich; sachlich, nüchtern.

mat·ting ['mætiŋ] Mattenstoff m; -belag m.

mat·tock ['mætək] (Breit)Hacke f.

mat·tress ['mætris] Matratze f.

ma·ture [mə'tjuə] 1. □ reif; reiflich (Überlegungen etc.); † fällig (Wech-sel); 2. reifen; zur Reife bringen; † fällig werden; **ma'tu·ri·ty** Reife f; † Fälligkeit f; Verfall(frist f) m.

ma·tu·ti·nal □ [mætju·'tainl] mor-gendlich; Morgen...

maud·lin □ ['mɔːdlin] sentimental, rührselig.

maul [mɔːl] schwer beschädigen; mißhandeln; fig. heruntermachen; ~ about roh umgehen mit.

maul·stick paint. ['mɔːlstik] Mal-stock m.

maun·der ['mɔːndə] ziellos han-deln, gammeln; faseln.

Maun·dy Thurs·day ['mɔːndi-'θəːzdi] Gründonnerstag m.

mau·so·le·um [mɔːsə'liəm] Mauso-leum n.

mauve [məuv] 1. Malvenfarbe f; 2. hellviolett.

mav·er·ick Am. ['mævərik] herren-loses Vieh n ohne Brandzeichen; pol. u. fig. Einzelgänger m.

maw [mɔː] Tier-Magen m; Rachen m.

mawk·ish □ ['mɔːkiʃ] rührselig, sentimental; '**mawk·ish·ness** Rührseligkeit f, Sentimentalität f.

maw·worm ['mɔːwəːm] Spulwurm m.

max·il·lar·y [mæk'siləri] Kiefer...

max·im ['mæksim] Maxime f, Grundsatz m; '**max·i·mal** maximal; '**max·i·mize** †, ⊕ maximieren; **max·i·mum** ['~məm] 1. Maximum n, Höchstmaß n, -stand m, -betrag m; 2. Höchst..., Maximal...; ~ wages pl. Spitzenlohn m.

May¹ [mei] Mai m; ♀ ♣ Weißdorn-blüte f. [darf.]

may² [~] v/aux. (irr.) mag, kann,]

may·be ['meibiː] vielleicht.

may-bee·tle zo. ['meibiːtl], '**may--bug** Maikäfer m.

may·day ['meidei] internationales Funk-Notsignal.

May Day ['meidei] der 1. Mai.

may·fly zo. ['meiflai] Eintagsfliege f.

may·hap † ['meihæp] vielleicht.

may·hem ['meihem] Am., ⚕ schwe-re Körperverletzung f od. Verstüm-melung f; Chaos n, Verwüstung f.

may·on·naise [meiə'neiz] Mayon-naise f.

may·or [mɛə] Bürgermeister m; '**may·or·al** bürgermeisterlich;

'**may·or·al·ty** Bürgermeisteramt *n*, -würde *f*; '**may·or·ess** Bürgermeisterin *f*.

may·pole ['meipəul] Maibaum *m*.

maze [meiz] Irrgarten *m*, Labyrinth *n*; *fig. a.* Wirrnis *f*; *be* ⁓*d*, *be in a* ⁓ bestürzt *od.* verlegen sein; '**ma·zy** ☐ labyrinthisch; wirr, verworren.

Mc·Coy *Am. sl.* [mə'kɔi]: *the real* ⁓ der wahre Jakob, das Richtige.

me [mi:, mi] mich; mir; F ich.

mead¹ [mi:d] Met *m*.

mead² *poet.* [⁓] = *meadow*.

mead·ow ['medəu] Wiese *f*; '⁓-'**saffron** ♣ Herbstzeitlose *f*; '**mead·ow·y** wiesenartig, -reich.

mea·ger, mea·gre ☐ ['mi:gə] mager, dürr (*a. fig.*); dürftig; '**mea·ger·ness**, '**mea·gre·ness** Magerkeit *f*; Dürre *f*; Dürftigkeit *f*.

meal¹ [mi:l] Mahl *n*; Mahlzeit *f*; ⁓*s pl. on wheels* Essen *n* auf Rädern.

meal² [⁓] *grobes* Mehl *n*; **meal·ies** ['⁓iz] *pl. Süd-Afrika:* Mais *m*.

meal·time ['mi:ltaim] Essenszeit *f*.

meal·y ['mi:li] mehlig; '⁓-'**mouthed** duckmäuserig; zimperlich.

mean¹ ☐ [mi:n] gemein, niedrig, gering; armselig; niederträchtig; schäbig; knauserig; kleinlich.

mean² [⁓] **1.** mittel, mittler, mittelmäßig; Durchschnitts...; *in the* ⁓ *time* = ⁓*time*; **2.** Mitte *f*; Mittelmäßigkeit *f*; ⅍ Mittel *n*; ⁓*s pl.* (Geld)Mittel *n/pl.*, Vermögen *n*; (Vermögens)Verhältnisse *n/pl.*; (*a. sg.*) Mittel *n*, Weg *m zu e-m Zweck*, Möglichkeit *f*; *by all* ⁓*s* jedenfalls; ganz gewiß; *by no* ⁓*s* keineswegs; *by this* ⁓*s* hierdurch; *by* ⁓*s of* mit Hilfe (*gen.*), durch; *by some* ⁓*s or other* auf irgendeine Weise; ⁓*s test* Bedürftigkeitsüberprüfung *f*.

mean³ [⁓] (*irr.*) meinen; (ge)denken, beabsichtigen, vorhaben; bestimmen (*for zu*); sagen wollen (*by mit*); bedeuten, heißen; ⁓ *well* (*ill*) es gut (schlecht) meinen (*by, a. to mit*).

me·an·der [mi'ændə] **1.** Windung *f*, Krümmung *f*; ⁓*s pl. a.* Schlängelweg *m*; **2.** sich schlängeln.

mean·ing ['mi:niŋ] **1.** ☐ bedeutsam; *well* ⁓ wohlmeinend, -wollend; **2.** Sinn *m*, Bedeutung *f*; ⚓ Absicht *f*; '**mean·ing·less** bedeutungslos; sinnlos; ausdruckslos (*Züge*).

mean·ness ['mi:nnis] Gemeinheit *f*, Niedrigkeit *f etc.* (*s. mean¹*).

meant [ment] *pret. u. p.p. von mean³*.

mean·time ['mi:n'taim], **meanwhile** ['mi:n'wail] mittlerweile, inzwischen, unterdessen.

mea·sles ['mi:zlz] *pl.* ✻ Masern *pl.*; *vet.* Finnen *f/pl.*; *German* ⁓ Röteln *pl.*; '**mea·sly** finnig; fleckig; *sl.* armselig.

meas·ur·a·ble ☐ ['meʒərəbl] meßbar.

meas·ure ['meʒə] **1.** Maß *n*; ♪ Takt *m*; Maßnahme *f*, -regel *f*; ⁓ *of capacity* Hohlmaß *n*; *beyond* ⁓ über alle Maßen; *in some* ⁓ gewissermaßen; *in a great* ⁓ großenteils; *made to* ⁓ nach Maß gemacht; *for good* ⁓ gut gemessen; *set* ⁓*s to* Grenzen setzen (*dat.*); *take s.o.'s* ⁓ j. taxieren, j. abschätzen; *take* ⁓*s* Maßnahmen ergreifen; **2.** messen; ab-, aus-, vermessen; *j-m* Maß nehmen (*for zu*); ⁓ *up* *Am.* heranreichen (*to an*); '**mea·sure·less** ☐ unermeßlich; '**meas·ure·ment** (Ab)Messung *f*; Maß *n*; ⚓ Tonnengehalt *m*.

meas·ur·ing ['meʒəriŋ] messend; Meß...

meat [mi:t] Fleisch *n* (*a. von Früchten*); † *od. prov.* Speise *f*; *fig.* (innerer) Gehalt *m*; *butcher's* ⁓ Schlachtfleisch *n*; *cold* ⁓ kalter Braten *m*; *fresh* ⁓ Frischfleisch *n*; *preserved* ⁓ Fleischkonserve *f*; *roast* ⁓ Braten *m*; '⁓-**ball** Fleischklößchen *n*; '⁓-**fly** *zo.* Schmeißfliege *f*; ⁓ **loaf** Hackbraten *m*; ⁓ **pie** Fleischpastete *f*; '⁓-**safe** Fliegen-, Speiseschrank *m*; ⁓ **tea** = *high tea*; '**meat·y** fleischig; *fig.* gehaltvoll.

mec·ca·no [mi'ka:nəu] Stabilbaukasten *m*.

me·chan·ic [mi'kænik] Handwerker *m*; Mechaniker *m*; **me'chan·i·cal** ☐ mechanisch; Maschinen...; ⁓ *engineering* Maschinenbau(kunde*f*) *m*; **mech·a·ni·cian** [mekə'niʃən] Mechaniker *m*; Monteur *m*; **me·chan·ics** [mi'kæniks] *mst sg.* Mechanik *f*.

mech·a·nism ['mekənizəm] Mechanismus *m*; '**mech·a·nize** mechanisieren; ✕ motorisieren.

med·al ['medl] Medaille *f*, Denkmünze *f*; Orden *m*, Auszeichnung *f*;

'med·al(l)ed medaillengeschmückt;
me·dal·lion [mi'dæljən] Medaillon
n; Schaumünze *f*; med·al·(l)ist
['medlist] Medaillenschneider *m*;
Münzkenner *m*; Medaillenträger
(-in).

med·dle ['medl] (*with, in*) sich einmischen (in *acc.*); sich abgeben
(mit); 'med·dler Eindringling *m*,
Unberufene *m*; med·dle·some
['⁓səm] ⁓ zudringlich; vorwitzig.

me·di·a¹ ['mi:djə] *pl. von medium.*

me·di·a² [⁓] *pl.* Medien *n pl.*

me·di·ae·val [medi'i:vəl] = medie-
val.

me·di·al ⬚ ['mi:djəl], 'me·di·an
Mittel..., in der Mitte (stehend *od.*
befindlich).

me·di·an strip *Am.* ['mi:djən'strip]
Mittelstreifen *m* (*der Autobahn etc.*).

me·di·ate 1. ⬚ ['mi:diit] mittelbar;
2. ['mi:dieit] vermitteln; me·di'a-
tion Vermittlung *f*; 'me·di·a·tor
Vermittler *m*; *eccl.* Mittler *m*; me-
di·a·to·ri·al ⬚ [⁓ə'tɔ:riəl], me-
di·a·to·ry ['⁓ətəri] vermittelnd;
Mittler...; me·di·a·trix ['⁓eitriks]
Vermittlerin *f*.

med·ic F ['medik] Mediziner(in)(*Medizinstudent, a. Arzt*).

Med·ic·aid *Am.* ['medikeid] Gesund-
heitsfürsorge *f* für Arme und Ar-
beitsunfähige.

med·i·cal ⬚ ['medikəl] medizinisch,
ärztlich; ⁓ board Gesundheits-
behörde *f*; ⁓ certificate Kranken-
schein *m*, Attest *n*; ⁓ evidence ärztliches Gutachten *n*; ⁓ jurisprudence
Gerichtsmedizin *f*; ⁓ man Arzt *m*,
Mediziner *m*; ⁓ officer Amtsarzt *m*;
⁓ specialist Facharzt *m*; ⁓ student
Medizinstudent *m*; ⁓ Superintendent Chefarzt *m*; ⁓ ward innere Abteilung *f e-s Krankenhauses*; me-
'dic·a·ment Heilmittel *n*.

Med·i·care *Am.* ['medikεə] Gesund-
heitsfürsorge *f bsd. für ältere Bürger.*

med·i·cate ['medikeit] medizinisch
behandeln; mit Arzneistoff versetzen; med·i'ca·tion Beimischung
f von Arzneistoffen; medizinische
Behandlung *f*; med·i·ca·tive ['⁓-
kətiv] heilend.

me·dic·i·nal ⬚ [me'disinl] medizinisch; heilend, heilsam; als Arznei
(dienend).

med·i·cine ['medsin] Medizin *f*;
Arznei *f*; Heilkunde *f*; '⁓-ball

Sport: Medizinball *m*; '⁓-chest
Hausapotheke *f*; '⁓-man Medizinmann *m*.

med·i·co F *co.* ['medikəu] Medikus
m (*Arzt*).

me·di·e·val ⬚ [medi'i:vəl] mittel-
alterlich.

me·di·o·cre [mi:di'əukə] mittelmäßig; me·di·oc·ri·ty [⁓'ɔkriti]
Mittelmäßigkeit *f*; kleiner Geist *m*.

med·i·tate ['mediteit] *v/i.* nachdenken (on über *acc.*), überlegen;
v/t. sinnen auf (*acc.*); erwägen;
planen; med·i'ta·tion Nachdenken *n*, -sinnen *n*; *innere* Betrachtung *f*; med·i·ta·tive ⬚ ['⁓tə-
tiv] nachdenklich, meditativ.

Med·i·ter·ra·ne·an [meditə'reinjən]
Mittelmeer *n*.

me·di·um ['mi:djəm] 1. *pl. a.* me-
di·a ['⁓djə] Mitte *f*; Mittelweg *m*;
Mittel *n*; Vermittlung *f*; vermit-
telnder Stoff *m*; *phys. u.* Spiritis-
mus: Medium *n*; *biol.* Nährboden
m; *Lebens*-Element *n*; 2. mittel,
mittlere(r, -s); *Zensur*: genügend;
Mittel..., Durchschnitts...; '⁓-
-'sized mittelgroß; ⁓ wave *Radio*:
Mittelwelle *f*.

med·lar ⚘ ['medlə] Mispel *f*.

med·ley ['medli] Gemisch *n*; *contp.*
Mischmasch *m*; ♪ Potpourri *n*.

me·dul·la [me'dʌlə] Mark *n*; med-
'ul·lar·y Mark...; markig.

me·du·sa *zo.* [mi'dju:zə] Meduse *f*,
Qualle *f*.

meed *poet.* [mi:d] Lohn *m*.

meek ⬚ [mi:k] sanft(mütig); demütig; bescheiden; 'meek·ness
Sanftmut *f*; Demut *f*.

meer·schaum ['miəʃəm] Meer-
schaum(pfeife *f*) *m*.

meet¹ [mi:t] passend; schicklich.

meet² [⁓] 1. (*irr.*) *v/t.* treffen; begegnen (*dat.*); kennenlernen; abholen *vom Bahnhof etc.*; stoßen auf
den Gegner; *e-r* Meinung *etc.* entgegenkommen; *Wunsch, Nach-
frage* befriedigen, *e-m Wunsch* gerecht werden, *e-r Verpflichtung*
nachkommen; *der Not* steuern; ⁓
s.o. half-way *fig.* j-m auf halbem
Weg entgegenkommen; come *od.*
go *od.* run to ⁓ *s.o.* j-m entgegenkommen *od.* -gehen *od.* -laufen;
they are well met sie passen zueinander; ⁓ one's death den Tod
finden; ⁓ the eye (ear) zu sehen

(hören) sein; ~ *s.o.'s eye* j-s Blick erwidern; *v/i.* sich treffen, einander begegnen; feindlich zs.-stoßen, handgemein werden; sich versammeln; ~ *with* stoßen auf (*acc.*); erfahren, erleiden, betroffen werden von; ~ *with an accident* verunglücken; *make both ends* ~ mit seinen Einkünften auskommen, sich einrichten; **2.** *Sport*: (Zs.-) Treffen *n*.

meet·ing ['mi:tiŋ] Begegnung *f*; (Zs.-)Treffen *n*, Zs.-kunft *f*, Versammlung *f*; Sitzung *f*, Tagung *f*; '~-house Versammlungshaus *n*; Andachtshaus *n*, Kirche *f bsd. der Quäker*; '~-place Sammelplatz *m*.

meg·a·cy·cle ≠ ['megəsaikl] Megahertz *n*; **meg·a·fog** ['~fɔg] sehr lautes Nebelsignal *n*; **meg·a·lith** ['~liθ] Megalith *m*, großer Steinblock *m*; **meg·a·lo·ma·ni·a** ['~ləu-'meinjə] Größenwahn *m*; **meg·a·lop·o·lis** [~'lɔpəlis] Großstadt *f*; Ballungsraum *m*; **meg·a·phone** ['~fəun] Megaphon *n*, Sprachrohr *n*; **meg·a·ton** ['~tʌn] Megatonne *f* (*Sprengwirkung von 1 Million t Trinitrotuluol*).

me·grim ['mi:grim] Migräne *f*; Grille *f*, Schrulle *f*; ~*s pl.* Schwermut *f*.

mel·an·chol·ic [melən'kɔlik] melancholisch; **mel·an·chol·y** ['~kəli] **1.** Melancholie *f*, Schwermut *f*; **2.** melancholisch; schwermütig; düster.   [Gemisch *n*.]

mé·lange [mei'lɑ̃:nʒ] Mischung *f*,]

mê·lée ['melei] Handgemenge *n*; Tumult *m*.

mel·io·rate ['mi:ljəreit] (sich) verbessern.

mel·lif·lu·ent [me'lifluənt], *mst* **mel'lif·lu·ous** honigsüß.

mel·low ['meləu] **1.** □ mürbe, reif, weich; *fig.* gereift (*Urteil etc.*); mild; *fig.* weich, sanft, zart (*Ton, Farbe, Licht*); *sl.* angeheitert; **2.** reifen (lassen); weich machen *od.* werden; (sich) mildern; '**mellow·ness** Reife *f*, Mürbheit *f*; Milde *f*; Sanftheit *f*, Weichheit *f*.

me·lo·di·ous □ [mi'ləudjəs] melodisch, wohlklingend; **me'lo·di·ous·ness** Wohlklang *m*; **mel·o·dist** ['melədist] Liederkomponist *m*, -sänger *m*; '**mel·o·dize** melodisch machen; *Lied etc.* vertonen; **mel·o-**

dra·ma ['melədrɑːmə] Melodrama *n*; Volksstück *n*; **me·lo·dra'mat·ic** melodramatisch; **mel·o·dy** ['melədi] Melodie *f*; Lied *n*.

mel·on ♀ ['melən] Melone *f*.

melt [melt] (zer)schmelzen, zergehen (lassen); *fig.* zerfließen; *Gefühl* erweichen; ~ *away* dahinschmelzen; *fig.* (dahin)schwinden; ~ *down* einschmelzen; ~ *into tears* in Tränen zerfließen.

melt·ing □ ['meltiŋ] schmelzend; Schmelz...; *fig.* weich; schmachtend; '~-point Schmelzpunkt *m*; '~-pot Schmelztiegel *m* (*a. fig.*).

mem·ber ['membə] Mitglied *n*; *parl.* Abgeordnete *m*, *f*; Glied *n*; *make a* ~ eingliedern (*of in acc.*); '**mem·ber·ship** Mitgliedschaft *f*; Mitgliederzahl *f*; ~ *card* Mitgliedsausweis *m*; ~ *fee* Mitgliedsbeitrag *m*.

mem·brane ['membrein] Membran(e) *f*, Häutchen *n*; **mem'bra·nous**, **mem'bra·ne·ous** [~jəs] häutig.

me·men·to [mi'mentəu] Erinnerungszeichen *n*, Andenken *n*.

mem·o ['meməu] = *memorandum*.

mem·oir ['memwɑ:] Denkschrift *f*; ~*s pl.* Memoiren *n/pl.*; Lebenserinnerungen *f/pl.*

mem·o·ra·ble □ ['memərəbl] denkwürdig.

mem·o·ran·dum [memə'rændəm] Notiz *f*; *pol.* Note *f*, Memorandum *n*; Schriftsatz *m* (*mst innerbetriebliche*) Mitteilung *f*.

me·mo·ri·al [mi'mɔ:riəl] **1.** Gedächtnis..., Gedenk...; ♀ *Day Am.* Gefallenengedenktag *m* (*30. Mai*); **2.** Denkmal *n*; Denkschrift *f*; Eingabe *f*; Gesuch *n*; **me'mo·ri·al·ist** Bittsteller(in); **me'mo·ri·al·ize** ein Gesuch einreichen bei.

mem·o·rize ['meməraiz] auswendig lernen, memorieren.

mem·o·ry ['meməri] Gedächtnis *n*; Erinnerung(svermögen *n*) *f*; Andenken *n*; *Computer*: Speicher *m*; *commit to* ~ dem Gedächtnis einprägen; *beyond* (*within*) *the* ~ *of man* vor (seit) Menschengedenken; *in* ~ *of* zum Andenken an (*acc.*).

men [men] *pl. von man*; Männer *m/pl.*; Menschen *m/pl.*; Mannschaft *f*.

men·ace ['menəs] **1.** (be)drohen; **2.** Gefahr *f*; Drohung *f*.

me·nag·er·ie [mi'nædʒəri] Menagerie *f.*

mend [mend] **1.** *v/t.* (ver)bessern; ausbessern, flicken; besser machen; *den Schritt* beschleunigen; ~ *the fire* (Kohlen *etc.*) nachlegen; ~ *one's ways* sich *moralisch* bessern; *v/i.* sich bessern; genesen; **2.** Flicken *m*; *on the* ~ auf dem Wege der Besserung.

men·da·cious ☐ [men'deiʃəs] lügnerisch, verlogen; **men·dac·i·ty** [~'dæsiti] Verlogenheit *f*; Unwahrheit *f.*

mend·er ['mendə] Ausbesserer *m.*

men·di·can·cy ['mendikənsi] Bettelei *f*; **'men·di·cant 1.** bettelnd; Bettel...; **2.** Bettler *m*; Bettelmönch *m*; **men'dic·i·ty** [~siti] Bettelei *f.*

men·folk F ['menfəuk] *die* Männer *pl.*

men·hir ['menhiə] Druidenstein *m.*

me·ni·al *contp.* ['mi:njəl] **1.** ☐ knechtisch, niedrig; **2.** Knecht *m*; Lakai *m.*

men·in·gi·tis ⚕ [menin'dʒaitis] Hirnhautentzündung *f*, Meningitis *f.*

men·o·pause ['menəupɔ:z] Wechseljahre *pl*, Menopause *f.*

men·ses ['mensi:z] *pl.* (*s. menstruation*) Menses *pl.* ; **men·stru·al** ['~struəl] monatlich; Menstruations...; **'men·stru·ate** menstruieren, die Regel haben; **men·stru'a·tion** Menstruation *f*, monatliche Regel *f*, Periode *f.*

men·su·ra·ble ['menʃurəbl] meßbar; **men·su·ra·tion** [~sjuə'reiʃən] Meßkunst *f.*

men·tal ☐ ['mentl] geistig; Geistes-...; seelisch; ~ *arithmetic* Kopfrechnen *n*; ~ *home*, ~ *hospital* Nervenheilanstalt *f*; ~*ly handicapped* geistig behindert; ~*ly ill* geisteskrank; **men·tal·i·ty** [~'tæliti] Mentalität *f*, Geisteshaltung *f*, Denkart *f.*

men·thol *pharm.* ['menθɔl] Menthol *n.*

men·tion ['menʃən] **1.** Erwähnung *f*; **2.** erwähnen; *don't* ~ *it!* bitte!; *not to* ~ ..., *without* ~*ing* ... ganz zu schweigen von ...; **men·tion·a·ble** ['~ʃnəbl] erwähnenswert.

men·tor ['mentɔ:] Mentor *m.*

men·u ['menju:] Speisenfolge *f*, Menü *n*; Speisekarte *f.*

Meph·is·to·phe·le·an [mefistə'fi:l-

jən] mephistophelisch, teuflisch.

mer·can·tile ['mə:kəntail] kaufmännisch; Handels...; ~ *marine* Handelsmarine *f.*

mer·ce·nar·y ['mə:sinəri] **1.** ☐ feil, käuflich; gedungen; gewinnsüchtig; **2.** ⚔ Söldner *m.*

mer·cer ['mə:sə] Seidenwaren-, Stoffhändler *m*; **'mer·cer·y** Seidenwaren *f/pl.*, Stoffe *m/pl.*; Stoffgeschäft *n.*

mer·cer·ize ['mə:səraiz] *Baumwolle* merzerisieren (*veredeln*).

mer·chan·dise ['mə:tʃəndaiz] Ware(n *pl.*) *f.*

mer·chant ['mə:tʃənt] **1.** Kaufmann *m*; *Am.* Kleinhändler *m*, Händler *m*; **2.** Handels..., Kaufmanns...; *law* ~ Handelsrecht *n*; **'mer·chant·a·ble** marktfähig; **mer·chant bank** Handelsbank *f*; **'mer·chant·man**, **merchant ship** Handelsschiff *n*; **merchant na·vy** Handelsmarine *f.*

mer·ci·ful ☐ ['mə:siful] barmherzig; gnädig (*Gott, Strafe*); **'merci·ful·ness** Barmherzigkeit *f*, Gnade *f.*

mer·ci·less ☐ ['mə:silis] unbarmherzig, erbarmungslos; **'merci·less·ness** Erbarmungslosigkeit *f.*

mer·cu·ri·al [mə:'kjuəriəl] Merkur...; ⚕ Quecksilber...; *fig.* quecksilbrig; unbeständig, launisch.

Mer·cu·ry ['mə:kjuri] Merkur *m*; *fig.* Bote *m*; ♀ ⚕ Quecksilber *n*; ♀ *poisoning* Quecksilbervergiftung *f.*

mer·cy ['mə:si] Barmherzigkeit *f*; Gnade *f*; *be at s.o.'s* ~ in j-s Gewalt sein; *at the* ~ *of the waves* den Wellen preisgegeben; *have* ~ *upon* sich erbarmen (*gen.*); *it is a* ~ *that* ... es ist ein wahrer Segen, daß ...; ~ *killing* Gnadentod *m.*

mere¹ [miə] Teich *m*, Weiher *m.*

mere² [~] rein, lauter; bloß; ~(*st*) *nonsense* rein(st)er Unsinn *m*; ~ *words pl.* bloße Worte *n/pl.*; **'mere·ly** nur, rein, bloß, lediglich, allein.

mer·e·tri·cious ☐ [meri'triʃəs] hurerisch; *fig.* aufdringlich; kitschig.

merge [mə:dʒ] *v/t.* (*in*) verschmelzen (mit); einverleiben (*dat.*); *v/i.* (*in*) verschmelzen (mit), aufgehen (in *dat.*); *Am. mot.* sich (in den Verkehr) einfädeln; **'merg·er** Verschmelzung *f*; ✝ Fusion *f.*

me·rid·i·an [məˈridiən] **1.** mittägig; Mittags...; *fig.* höchst; **2.** *geogr.* Meridian *m*; Mittag *m*; *fig.* Gipfel *m*; **me'rid·i·o·nal** □ mittägig, südlich.

me·ringue [məˈræŋ] Baiser *n*, Meringe *f*.

me·ri·no [məˈriːnəu] Merinoschaf *n*; Merinowolle *f*; Merino *m* (*Stoff*).

mer·it [ˈmerit] **1.** Verdienst *n*; Wert *m*; Vorzug *m*; Bedeutung *f*; ⁓*s pl.* bsd. ⚖ Hauptpunkte *m/pl.*, Wesen *n* *e-r* Sache; *on the* ⁓*s of the case* nach wesentlichen Gesichtspunkten; *on its (own)* ⁓*s* für sich allein, an sich; *make a* ⁓ *of* als Verdienst ansehen; **2.** *fig.* verdienen; **mer·i·to·ri·ous** □ [⁓ˈtɔːriəs] verdienstvoll, lobenswert.

mer·maid [ˈmɜːmeid] Seejungfer *f*, Nixe *f*; **mer·man** [ˈ⁓mæn] Wassermann *m*; Triton *m*.

mer·ri·ment [ˈmerimənt] Lustigkeit *f*; Belustigung *f*, Lustbarkeit *f*. **mer·ry** □ [ˈmeri] lustig, fröhlich; scherzhaft, ergötzlich; *make* ⁓ vergnügt *od.* lustig sein; **⁓-an·drew** [ˈ⁓ændruː] Hanswurst *m*; '**⁓-go-round** Karussell *n*; '**⁓-mak·ing** Lustbarkeit *f*, Fest *n*; '**⁓·thought** Gabelbein *n e-s* Huhns.

me·sa *geogr.* [ˈmeisə] Tafelberg *m*, kleines Plateau *n*.

mé·sal·li·ance [meˈzæliəns] Mesalliance *f*, Mißheirat *f*.

me·seems † [miˈsiːmz] es scheint mir.

mes·en·ter·y *anat.* [ˈmesəntəri] Gekröse *n*.

mesh [meʃ] **1.** Masche *f*; *fig. oft* ⁓*es pl.* Netz *n*; *be in* ⁓ ⊕ (ineinander-) greifen; **2.** in *e-m* Netz fangen; ⊕ (ineinander)greifen; **meshed** ...-maschig; '**mesh-work** Netzwerk *n*; Gespinst *n*.

mes·mer·ism [ˈmezmərizəm] Mesmerismus *m*; '**mes·mer·ize** magnetisieren.

mess[1] [mes] **1.** Wirrwarr *m*; Unordnung *f*, Durcheinander *n*; Schmutz *m*; F Manscherei *f*, P Schweinerei *f*; F Schlamassel *m*; Klemme *f*; *look a* ⁓ F scheußlich aussehen; *make a* ⁓ *of* verpfuschen, P versauen; **2.** *v/t. a.* ⁓ *up* in Unordnung bringen; verpfuschen, verderben; *v/i.* ⁓ *about* herummanschen, -murksen. **mess**[2] [⁓] **1.** Gericht *n*, Portion *f*; ⚔

Kasino *n*, Messe *f*; ⚓ Back *f*; **2.** zusammen speisen.

mes·sage [ˈmesidʒ] Botschaft *f*, Sendung *f*; Meldung *f*, Mitteilung *f*; *get the* ⁓ F (es) kapieren; *go on a* ⁓ e-e Besorgung machen; *take a* ⁓ et. ausrichten.

mes·sen·ger [ˈmesindʒə] Bote *m*; ⁓ *boy* Botenjunge *m*, Kurier *m*.

Mes·si·ah *eccl.* [miˈsaiə] Messias *m*.

Mes·sieurs, *mst* **Messrs.** [ˈmesəz] (die) Herren *m/pl.*; Firma *f*.

mess·ing al·low·ance ⚔ [ˈmesiŋ-əˈlauəns] Verpflegungsgeld *n*.

mess...: '**⁓-jacket** ⚔ kurze Uniformjacke *f*; '**⁓·mate** ⚔, ⚓ Tischgenosse *m*; '**⁓-room** Kasino *n*; '**⁓-tin** Kochgeschirr *n*.

mes·suage ⚖ [ˈmeswidʒ] Anwesen *n*.

mess-up F [ˈmesʌp] Durcheinander *n*; Mißverständnis *n*.

mess·y [ˈmesi] unordentlich, schlampig; schmutzig.

met [met] *pret. u. p.p. von* meet[2] **1.**

met·a·bol·ic [metəˈbɔlik] Stoffwechsel...; **me·tab·o·lism** *physiol.* [meˈtæbəlizəm] Stoffwechsel *m*.

met·age [ˈmiːtidʒ] Meß-, Wägegeld *n*.

met·al [ˈmetl] **1.** Metall *n*; *Wegebau:* Beschotterung *f*, Schotter *m*; ⁓*s pl.* F Schienen *f/pl.*, Geleise *n*; **2.** beschottern; **me·tal·lic** [miˈtælik] (⁓*ally*) metallisch; Metall...; **met·al·lif·er·ous** [metəˈlifərəs] metallhaltig; **met·al·line** [ˈ⁓lain] metallen; '**met·al·lize** metallisieren; **met·al·log·ra·phy** [⁓ˈlɔgrəfi] Metallographie *f*; **met·al·loid** [ˈ⁓lɔid] **1.** metallartig; **2.** Nichtmetall *n*; **met·al·lur·gic, met·al·lur·gi·cal** □ [⁓ˈlɜːdʒik(əl)] metallurgisch; **met·al·lur·gy** [meˈtælədʒi] Metallurgie *f*, Hüttenkunde *f*.

met·a·mor·phose [metəˈmɔːfəuz] verwandeln, umgestalten; **met·a·'mor·pho·sis** [⁓fəsis], *pl.* **met·a·'mor·pho·ses** [⁓fəsiːz] Verwandlung *f*, Metamorphose *f*.

met·a·phor [ˈmetəfə] Metapher *f*, bildlicher Ausdruck *m*; **met·a·phor·ic**, *mst* **met·a·phor·i·cal** □ [⁓ˈfɔrik(əl)] bildlich, übertragen, metaphorisch.

met·a·phys·ic [metəˈfizik] **1.** *mst* **met·a·'phys·i·cal** □ metaphysisch; **2. met·a·'phys·ics** *oft sg.* Meta-

mete

physik *f.*
mete [miːt] messen; *mst* ~ *out* zumessen.
me·te·or ['miːtjə] Meteor *m*, *n* (*a. fig.*); **me·te·or·ic** [miːti'ɔrik] meteorisch; Meteor...; **me·te·or·ite** ['miːtjərait] Meteorstein *m*, Meteorit *m*; **me·te·or·o·log·i·cal** □ [miːtjərə'lɔdʒikəl] meteorologisch; **me·te·or·ol·o·gist** [~'rɔlədʒist] Meteorologe *m*; **me·te·or·ol·o·gy** Meteorologie *f*, Wetterkunde *f*.
me·ter ['miːtə] Messer *m*, Meßinstrument *n*, Zähler *m*; '~·maid *Am.* F Politesse *f*.
me·thinks † [mi'θiŋks] (*pret. methought*) mich dünkt.
meth·od ['meθəd] Methode *f*; Art u. Weise *f*; Verfahren *n*; Ordnung *f*, System *n*; **me·thod·ic**, *mst* **me·thod·i·cal** □ [mi'θɔdik(əl)] methodisch; **Meth·od·ism** *eccl.* ['meθə-dizəm] Methodismus *m*; '**Meth·od·ist** *eccl.* Methodist *m*; '**meth·od·ize** methodisch ordnen.
me·thought † [mi'θɔːt] *pret. von methinks.*
meth·yl 🜍 ['meθil] Methyl *n*, **meth·yl·at·ed spir·it** ['meθileitid-'spirit] vergällter Spiritus *m*; **meth·yl·ene** ['meθiliːn] Methylen *n*.
me·tic·u·lous □ [mi'tikjuləs] peinlich genau, äußerst gewissenhaft.
me·tre ['miːtə] Versmaß *n*, Metrum *n*; Meter *n*, *m*.
met·ric ['metrik] (~*ally*) metrisch; ~ *system* Dezimalsystem *n*; '**met·ri·cal** □ metrisch; Vers...; messend; Maß...; '**met·rics** *pl. u. sg.* Metrik *f*, Verslehre *f*.
Met·ro F ['metrəu] Metro *f*, Stadtbahn *f*, U-Bahn *f*; '~·land F *die* Außenbezirke *m/pl.*, *die* Vororte *m/pl. Londons.*
me·trop·o·lis [mi'trɔpəlis] Hauptstadt *f*, Metropole *f*; **met·ro·pol·i·tan** [metrə'pɔlitən] 1. hauptstädtisch; ~ *Railway* Stadtbahn *f*; 2. Erzbischof *m*; Metropolit *m*.
met·tle ['metl] Feuereifer *m*, Mut *m*; *be on one's* ~ sein Bestes tun; *put s.o. on his* ~ j. ansporren, sein möglichstes zu leisten; *a horse full of* ~ ein feuriges Pferd *n*; '**met·tled**, **met·tle·some** ['~səm] hitzig, feurig, mutig.
mew[1] *orn.* [mjuː] Möwe *f.*
mew[2] [~] 1. Miau *n*; 2. miauen.

mew[3] [~] *mst* ~ *up* einsperren, einschließen.
mewl [mjuːl] wimmern, F mauzen.
mews [mjuːz] *hist.* königlicher Marstall *m*; Stallung *f*; *daraus entstandene* Garagen *f/pl. od.* Wohnhäuser *n/pl.*
Mex·i·can ['meksikən] 1. mexikanisch; 2. Mexikaner(in).
mez·za·nine ['metsəniːn] Zwischenstock *m*, Mezzanin *f.*
mi·aow [miːˈau] 1. Miau *n*; 2. miauen.
mi·as·ma [mi'æzmə], *pl. a.* **mi·as·ma·ta** [~tə] schädliche Ausdünstung *f*; Ansteckungsstoff *m*; **mi·as·mal** □ miasmatisch.
miaul [mi'ɔːl] miauen; mauzen.
mi·ca *min.* ['maikə] Glimmer *m*; **mi·ca·ce·ous** [~'keiʃəs] glimmerartig; Glimmer...
mice [mais] *pl. von* mouse.
Mich·ael·mas ['miklməs] Michaelis(tag *m*) *n* (*29. September*).
mick·ey ['miki] P Betäubungspille *f*; *take the* ~ *out of s.o.* F j. veräppeln, j. auf den Arm nehmen.
mi·cro... ['maikrəu] klein..., Klein...
mi·crobe ['maikrəub] Mikrobe *f*, Bakterie *f*; **mi·cro·bi·al** [~bjəl] mikrobisch.
mi·cro·cosm ['maikrəukɔzəm] Mikrokosmos *m*; **mi·cro·fiche** ['~fiːʃ] Mikrofiche *m*; **mi·cro·film** ['~film] 1. Mikrofilm *m*; 2. auf Mikrofilm aufnehmen.
mi·crom·e·ter [mai'krɔmitə] Mikrometer *n*, *m*; **mi·cro·or·gan·ism** [maikrəu'ɔːgənizəm] Mikroorganismus *m*; **mi·cro·phone** ['maikrəfəun] Mikrophon *n*; **mi·cro·proces·sor** [~'prəusesə] Mikroprozessor *m*; **mi·cro·scope** ['~skəup] Mikroskop *n*; **mi·cro·scop·ic**, **mi·cro·scop·i·cal** □ [~s'kɔpik(əl)] mikroskopisch; Mikroskop...; winzig; äußerst genau *od.* fein; **mi·cro·wave** 𝄞 ['maikrəuweiv] Mikrowelle *f*, Dezimeterwelle *f*; ~ *oven* Mikrowellenherd *m.*
mid [mid] *s.* middle 2; Mitt...; *poet.* = amid inmitten *etc.*; in ~ *air* mitten in der Luft; in ~ *winter* mitten im Winter; '~·day 1. Mittag *m*; 2. mittägig; Mittags...
mid·den ['midn] Misthaufen *m*; Müllgrube *f.*
mid·dle ['midl] 1. Mitte *f*; Hüften

f|pl.; ⁓*s pl.* ✝ Mittelsorte *f*; **2.** mittlere(r, -s); Mittel...; ♀ *Ages pl.* Mittelalter *n*; ⁓ **America** *Am.* die amerikanischen Mittelklassen *pl.*; ⁓ *class(es pl.)* Mittelstand *m*; '⁓-'**aged** von mittlerem Alter; '⁓-'**class** Mittelstands...; ⁓ **dis·tance** *paint.* Mittelgrund *m*; ♀ **King·dom** *das* Reich der Mitte; ⁓ **life** die mittleren Lebensjahre *n pl.*; '⁓-**man** Mittelsmann *m*; ✝ Zwischenhändler *m*; '⁓-**most** mittelste(r, -s); ⁓ **name** 2. Vorname *m*; '⁓-**of-the-**'**road** *pol.* Extreme meidend, gemäßigt; '⁓-'**sized** mittelgroß; '⁓-**weight** *Boxen*: Mittelgewicht *n*.

mid·dling ['midliŋ] **1.** *adj.* mittelmäßig; leidlich; Mittel...; Durchschnitts...; **2.** *adv. a.* ⁓*ly* ziemlich, leidlich; **3.** ⁓*s pl.* ✝ Mittelsorte *f*.

mid·dy F ['midi] = *midshipman*.

midge [midʒ] Mücke *f*; **midg·et** ['midʒit] Zwerg *m*, Knirps *m*.

mid·land ['midlənd] **1.** binnenländisch; **2.** *the* ♀*s pl.* Mittelengland *n*; '**mid**-'**morn·ing** **break** große (Vormittags)Pause *f*; '**mid**-**most** mittelste(r, -s); '**mid·night** **1.** Mitternacht *f*; **2.** mitternächtlich; Mitternachts...; **mid·riff** ['⁓rif] Zwerchfell *n*; '**mid·ship·man** Seekadett *m*; Leutnant *m* zur See; *Am.* Oberfähnrich *m* zur See; '**mid·ships** ⚓ mittschiffs; **midst** [midst] **1.** Mitte *f*; *in the* ⁓ *of* inmitten *(gen.)*; *in our* ⁓ (mitten) unter uns; **2.** *prp. poet. s. amidst* inmitten *etc.*; '**mid·stream** **1.** Strom-, Flußmitte *f*; **2.** *adv.* in der Flußmitte; '**mid·sum·mer** Sommersonnenwende *f*; Hochsommer *m*; ♀ *Day* Johannistag *m*; '**mid**'**way 1.** halber Weg *m*; *Am.* Schaubudenstraße *f*, Rummelplatz *m*; **2.** *adj.* in der Mitte befindlich; **3.** *adv.* auf halbem Wege; '**mid·wife** Hebamme *f*; **mid·wife·ry** ['⁓wifəri] Geburtshilfe *f*; '**mid**-'**win·ter** Wintersonnenwende *f*; Mitte *f* des Winters.

mien *lit.* [mi:n] Miene *f*.

miff F [mif] Verstimmung *f*.

might [mait] **1.** Macht *f*, Gewalt *f*, Kraft *f*; *with* ⁓ *and main* mit aller Gewalt; **2.** *pret. von may*; **might·i·ness** ['⁓tinis] Macht *f*, Gewalt *f*; '**might·y** □ **1.** *adj.* mächtig, gewaltig; F riesig; **2.** F *adv.* sehr, mächtig.

mi·gnon·ette ♀ [minjə'net] Reseda *f*.

mi·graine ['mi:grein] Migräne *f*.

mi·grant ['maigrənt] **1.** = *migratory*; **2.** *a.* ⁓ *bird* Zugvogel *m*.

mi·grate [mai'greit] (fort)ziehen; (aus)wandern; **mi·gra·tion** Wanderung *f*; Zug *m*; **mi·gra·to·ry** ['⁓grətəri] wandernd; Zug...; nomadisch.

mike *sl.* [maik] Mikrophon *n*.

mil [mil] Tausend *n*; $^1/_{1000}$ Zoll *m*.

mil·age ['mailidʒ] = *mileage*.

Mil·an·ese [milə'ni:z] **1.** mailändisch; **2.** Mailänder(in).

milch [miltʃ] milchgebend, melkbar; Milch...; ⁓ *cow* Milchkuh *f*.

mild □ [maild] mild, sanft; gelind; *to put it* ⁓*ly* gelinde gesagt.

mil·dew ['mildju:] **1.** Mehltau *m*, Brand *m* im Getreide; Moder-, Stockflecke *m|pl.*; **2.** mit Mehltau überziehen, brandig machen *od.* werden.

mild·ness ['maildnis] Milde *f*.

mile [mail] Meile *f* (1609,33 *m*).

mile·age ['mailidʒ] Laufzeit *f in* Meilen, Meilenstand *m* e-s Autos; Kilometergeld *n*.

mil·er ['mailə] *Sport*: Meilenläufer *m*.

mile·stone ['mailstəun] Meilenstein *m* (a. fig.).

mil·foil ♀ ['milfɔil] Schafgarbe *f*.

mi·lieu ['mi:ljə:] Umwelt *f*, Milieu *n*.

mil·i·tan·cy ['militənsi] Kriegszustand *m*; '**mil·i·tant** □ streitend, kriegführend; kämpferisch, militant, aggressiv; **mil·i·ta·rism** ['⁓tərizəm] Militarismus *m*; '**mil·i·ta·rist** Militarist *m*; '**mil·i·tar·y 1.** □ militärisch; Kriegs...; ⁓ *college* Kriegsschule *f*; ♀ *Government* Militärregierung *f*; ⁓ *map* Generalstabskarte *f*; ⁓ *service* Militär-, Wehrdienst *m*; **2.** *das* Militär *n*; **mil·i·tate** ['⁓teit]: ⁓ *in favour of (against)* sprechen für (gegen); **mi·li·tia** [mi-'liʃə] Miliz *f*, Land-, Bürgerwehr *f*; **mi·li·tia·man** Milizsoldat *m*.

milk [milk] **1.** Milch *f*; *the* ⁓ *of human kindness* die Milch der frommen Denkungsart; *it's no use crying over spilt* ⁓ geschehen ist geschehen; ⁓ *and water fig.* Gewäsch *n*; **2.** *v/t.* melken; *fig.* schröpfen; ⚡ *u. tel.* anzapfen; *v/i.* Milch geben;

'milk-and-'wa·ter weichlich; empfindsam; 'milk-bar Milchbar f; 'milk-churn Milchkanne f; 'milk·er Melker(in); Milchkuh f; milk float Milchwagen m; 'milking-ma'chine Melkmaschine f.

milk...: '~·maid Milch-, Kuhmagd f; '~·man Milchmann m; '~·pow·der Milchpulver n, Trockenmilch f; '~ -'shake Milchmischgetränk n; '~ sop Weichling m; '~·tooth Milchzahn m; '~·weed ♀ Wolfsmilch f; '~ -white milchweiß; 'milk·y milchig; Milch...; fig. weichlich; ♀ Way Milchstraße f.

mill¹ [mil] 1. Mühle f; Fabrik f; Spinnerei f; Prägewerk n; sl. Keilerei f; go through the ~ fig. e-e harte Schule durchmachen; 2. mahlen; ⊕ fräsen; Geld prägen; Münze rändeln; Tuch walken; Ei quirlen; (rund)herumlaufen; sl. durchwalken.

mill² Am. [~] ein tausendstel Dollar m (= ¹/₁₀ cent).

mill-board ['milbɔːd] starker Pappdeckel m; 'mill·dam Mühlwehr n.

mil·le·nar·i·an [mili'nɛəriən], mil·len·ni·al [mi'leniəl] tausendjährig; mil·le·nar·y ['~nəri] 1. aus 1000 (Jahren) bestehend; 2. Jahrtausend (-feier f) n; mil'len·ni·um [~niəm] Jahrtausend n; das Tausendjährige Reich Christi.

mil·le·pede zo. ['milipiːd] Tausendfüßer m.

mill·er ['milə] Müller m; ⊕ Fräsmaschine f.

mil·les·i·mal [mi'lesiməl] tausendste(r, -s); tausendfach.

mil·let ♀ ['milit] Hirse f.

mill...: '~·girl Fabrik-, bsd. Spinnereiarbeiterin f; '~·hand Fabrikarbeiter m.

mil·li·ard ['miljaːd] Milliarde f.

mil·li·gram ['miligræm] Milligramm n.

mil·li·me·tre ['milimiːtə] Millimeter n.

mil·li·ner ['milinə] Putzmacherin f, Modistin f; 'mil·li·ner·y Modewaren(geschäft n) pl.

mill·ing ['miliŋ] Mahlen n etc.; ~ cutter ⊕ Fräser m; ~ machine Fräsmaschine f; ~ product Mühlen-, Walzprodukt n.

mil·lion ['miljən] Million f; mil·lion·aire [~'nɛə] Millionär(in);

mil·lionth ['miljənθ] 1. millionste (-r, -s); 2. Millionstel n.

mill...: '~·pond Mühlteich m; '~·race Mühlgerinne n; '~·stone Mühlstein m; see through a ~ F das Gras wachsen hören; '~·wheel Mühlrad n; '~·wright Mühlenbauer m.

mi·lord [mi'lɔːd] Lord m; reicher Engländer m.

milt¹ [milt] Milch f der Fische.

milt² ⚓ [~] Milz f.

milt·er ichth. ['miltə] Milch(n)er m.

mime [maim] 1. Mime m; 2. mimen, spielen.

mim·e·o·graph ['mimiəgraːf] 1. Vervielfältigungsgerät n; 2. vervielfältigen.

mi·met·ic [mi'metik] nachahmend.

mim·ic ['mimik] 1. mimisch, nachahmend; nachgeahmt, Schein...; 2. Mime m, Schauspieler m; 3. nachahmen, nachäffen; 'mim·ic·ry (possenhafte) Nachahmung f; zo. Angleichung f, Mimikry f.

mi·mo·sa ♀ [mi'məuzə] Mimose f.

min·a·ret ['minəret] Minarett n.

min·a·to·ry ['minətəri] drohend.

mince [mins] 1. v/t. zerhacken, kleinschneiden; he does not ~ matters er nimmt kein Blatt vor den Mund; ~ one's words geziert sprechen; v/i. sich zieren; 2. a. ~d meat Hackfleisch n; '~·meat Pastetenfüllung f (Rosinen, Talg, Zucker, Zitrone etc.) e-s mince-pie; make ~ of in Stücke reißen; '~·pie (mit mincemeat gefüllte) Pastete f; 'minc·er Fleischwolf m.

minc·ing □ ['minsiŋ] affektiert; geziert; '~·ma·chine = mincer.

mind [maind] 1. Sinn m, Gemüt n; Geist m, Verstand m; Meinung f; Absicht f; Neigung f, Lust f, Wille m; Gedächtnis n; Achtsamkeit f, Sorge f; to my ~ meiner Ansicht nach, meines Erachtens; nach meinem Sinn; ~'s eye geistiges Auge n; out of one's ~, not in one's right ~ von Sinnen; since time out of ~ seit unvordenklichen Zeiten; change one's ~ sich anders besinnen; bear s.th. in ~ (immer) an et. denken; blow s.o.'s ~ P fig. j. umwerfen; have (half) a ~ to (beinahe) Lust haben zu; have s.th. on one's ~ et. auf dem Herzen haben; have in ~ im Sinne haben; (not) know one's own ~

(nicht) wissen, was man will; *make up one's* ⌒ sich entschließen; *make up one's* ⌒ *to s.th.* sich mit et. abfinden; *put s.o. in* ⌒ *of* j. erinnern an (*acc.*); *speak one's* ⌒ offen s-e Meinung sagen; **2.** merken *od.* achten auf (*acc.*); beachten; sich kümmern um; etwas (einzuwenden) haben gegen, *et.* nicht mögen; ⌒! gib acht!; *never* ⌒! mach dir nichts daraus!; macht nichts!; ⌒ *the step!* Achtung, Stufe!; *I don't* ⌒ (*it*) ich habe nichts dagegen; *do you* ⌒ *if I smoke?* stört es Sie, wenn ich rauche?; *would you* ⌒ *taking off your hat?* würden Sie so freundlich sein, den Hut abzunehmen?; ⌒ *your own business!* kümmern Sie sich um Ihre Angelegenheiten; **'mind-bend·ing, 'mind--blow·ing** F bewußtseinsverändernd, -erweiternd; P irre; **'mind--bog·gling** F unvorstellbar; **'mind-ed** gesonnen, gewillt; ...gesinnt; **'mind·er** Wärter *m*; **mind·ful** ['⌒ful] (*of*) eingedenk (*gen.*); achtsam (auf *acc.*); **'mind·ful·ness** Achtsamkeit *f*; **'mind·less** ◻ geistlos, unvernünftig; achtlos; unbekümmert (*of* um), ungeachtet (*of gen.*); **'mind--read·er** Gedankenleser *m*.

mine¹ [main] **1.** der (die, das) meinige; mein; **2.** die Mein(ig)en *pl.*

mine² [⌒] **1.** Bergwerk *n*, Grube *f*; *fig.* Fundgrube *f*; ✕ Mine *f*; **2.** *v/i.* graben, minieren; *v/t.* graben; ✕ fördern; ✕ unterminieren; ✕ verminen; ⌒ **de·tec·tor** ✕ Minensuchgerät *n*; **'⌒·field** ✕ Minenfeld *n*; ✕ Grubengelände *n*; **'⌒·lay·er** ⚓, ✕ Minenleger *m*; **'min·er** Bergmann *m*; *bsd.* ✕ Minierer *m*; ⚓ Minenleger *m*; ⌒s' **association** Knappschaft *f*.

min·er·al ['minərəl] **1.** Mineral *n*; ⌒s *pl.*, ⌒ *water* Mineralwasser *n*; **2.** mineralisch; **'min·er·al·ize** vererzen; versteinern; **min·er·al·o·gist** [⌒'rælədʒist] Mineraloge *m*; **min·er·al·o·gy** Mineralogie *f*.

mine·sweep·er ⚓ ['mainswi:pə] Minensucher *m*.

min·gle ['miŋgl] mischen; vermischen; sich mischen *od.* mengen (*with* unter).

min·gy F ['mindʒi] knickerig.

min·i·a·ture ['minjətʃə] **1.** Miniatur(gemälde *n*) *f*; **2.** in Miniatur; Miniatur...; Klein...; ⌒ *camera* Kleinbildkamera *f*.

min·i·bus ['minibʌs] Klein-, Mini-

bus *m*.

min·i·kin ['minikin] **1.** winzig; geziert; **2.** Knirps *m*.

min·im ['minim] ♩ halbe Note *f*; Tropfen *m* (*kleinste Flüssigkeitsmenge*); Knirps *m*; **'min·i·mize** möglichst klein machen; *fig.* verringern, bagatellisieren; **min·i·mum** ['⌒məm] **1.** Minimum *n*; Mindestmaß *n*, -stand *m*, -betrag *m*; **2.** Minimal..., Mindest...

min·ing ['mainiŋ] **1.** Berg(bau)...; Gruben...; ⚒ Montan...; ✕, ⚓ Minen...; **2.** Bergbau *m*.

min·ion ['minjən] Günstling *m*; *fig.* Lakai *m*; *typ.* Kolonelschrift *f*; ⌒s *of the law* das Auge des Gesetzes.

min·i·skirt ['miniskə:t] Minirock *m*.

min·is·ter ['ministə] **1.** Diener *m*; *fig.* Werkzeug *n*; Geistliche *m*, Pfarrer *m*; *pol.* Minister *m*; Gesandte *m*; **2.** *v/t.* darreichen, spenden; *v/i.* dienen, aufwarten; dienen, behilflich sein (*to s.th.* e-r Sache); Gottesdienst halten; **min·is·te·ri·al** ◻ [⌒'tiəriəl] *pol.* ministeriell, Ministerial...; Regierungs...; *eccl.* geistlich.

min·is·trant ['ministrənt] **1.** dienend; **2.** *eccl.* Ministrant *m*; **min·is'tra·tion** Dienst *m*, Amt *n* (*bsd. eccl.*); **'min·is·try** geistliches Amt *n*; *pol.* Ministerium *n*; Regierung *f*, Kabinett *n*.   [Feh *n* (*Pelz*).]

min·i·ver ['minivə] Grauwerk *n*,╯

mink *zo.* [miŋk] Nerz *m*.

min·now *ichth.* ['minəu] Elritze *f*.

mi·nor ['mainə] **1.** kleiner, geringer, weniger bedeutend; Unter...; ♩ Moll...; A ⌒ a-Moll *n*; ⌒ *third* kleine Terz *f*; ⌒ *key* Moll-Tonart *f*; **2.** Minderjährige *m*, *f*; *nach Eigennamen:* der Jüngere; *phls.* Untersatz *m*; *Am. univ.* Nebenfach *n*; **mi·nor·i·ty** [mai'nɔriti] Minderheit *f*; Unmündigkeit *f*; ⌒ *government* Minderheitsregierung *f*.

min·ster ['minstə] Münster *n*.

min·strel ['minstrəl] Spielmann *m*, Minnesänger *m*; ⌒s *pl.* Negersänger *m/pl.*; **min·strel·sy** ['⌒si] Spielmannsdichtung *f*; Spielleute *pl.*

mint¹ ♀ [mint] Minze *f*; ⌒ *sauce* (saure) Minzsoße *f*.

mint² [⌒] **1.** Münze *f*, Münzstätte *f*; *fig.* Gold-, Fundgrube *f*; *a* ⌒ *of money* e-e Menge Geld; **2.** einwandfrei, unbeschädigt (*Buch etc.*);

3. münzen, prägen; **'mint·age** Prägung *f*; geprägtes Geld *n*; Münzgebühr *f*.

min·u·et ♪ [minju'et] Menuett *n*.

mi·nus ['mainəs] **1.** *prp.* weniger; F ohne; **2.** *adj.* negativ; **2.** Minus (-zeichen) *n*; Mangel *m*.

mi·nute¹ [mai'nju:t] ☐ sehr klein, winzig; unbedeutend; sehr genau, sorgfältig.

min·ute² ['minit] **1.** Minute *f*; *fig.* Augenblick *m*; kurzer Entwurf *m*; Notiz *f*; ∽s *pl.* Protokoll *n*; *in a* ∽ gleich, sofort; *just a* ∽! Moment mal!; *to the* ∽ auf die Minute; *the* ∽ *(that)* sobald; **2.** protokollieren; entwerfen; aufzeichnen; **'min·ute-hand** Minutenzeiger *m*.

min·ute·ly¹ ['minitli] *adv.* jede Minute.

mi·nute·ly² [mai'nju:tli] peinlich genau; **mi'nute·ness** Kleinheit *f*; Genauigkeit *f*.

mi·nu·ti·a [mai'nju:ʃiə], *pl.* **mi'nu·ti·ae** [∽ʃii:] Einzelheit *f*.

minx [miŋks] dreistes Mädchen *n*, Racker *m*.

mir·a·cle ['mirəkl] Wunder *n*; *to a* ∽ wundervoll; ∽ *play* Mirakel(spiel) *n*; **mi·rac·u·lous** ☐ [mi'rækjuləs] wunderbar; übernatürlich; **mi'rac·u·lous·ness** *das* Wunderbare.

mi·rage ['mira:ʒ] Luftspiegelung *f*, Fata Morgana *f (a. fig.)*.

mire ['maiə] **1.** Sumpf *m*, Kot *m*, Schlamm *m*, Dreck *m*; *be in the* ∽ in der Patsche sitzen; *drag s.o. through the* ∽ j. in den Schmutz ziehen; **2.** mit Schlamm *od.* Schmutz bedecken; *fig.* j. in Schwierigkeiten bringen; *his car was* ∽*d* sein Auto blieb im Schlamm stecken.

mirk [mə:k] dunkel, düster.

mir·ror ['mirə] **1.** Spiegel *m*; **2.** (wider)spiegeln *(a. fig.)*.

mirth [mə:θ] Fröhlichkeit *f*, Freude *f*; **mirth·ful** ☐ ['∽ful] fröhlich; **'mirth·less** ☐ freudlos.

mir·y ['maiəri] kotig.

mis... [mis] miß..., übel, falsch.

mis·ad·ven·ture ['misəd'ventʃə] Mißgeschick *n*, Unfall *m*.

mis·al·li·ance ['misə'laiəns] Mißheirat *f*, Mesalliance *f*.

mis·an·thrope ['mizənθrəup] Menschenfeind *m*; **mis·an·throp·ic**, **mis·an·throp·i·cal** ☐ [∽'θrɔpi-

k(əl)] menschenfeindlich; **mis·an·thro·pist** [mi'zænθrəpist] Menschenfeind *m*; **mis'an·thro·py** Menschenhaß *m*.

mis·ap·pli·ca·tion ['misæpli'keiʃən] falsche Anwendung *f*, Mißbrauch *m*; **mis·ap·ply** ['∽ə'plai] falsch anwenden, mißbrauchen.

mis·ap·pre·hend ['misæpri'hend] mißverstehen; **'mis·ap·pre'hen·sion** Mißverständnis *n*.

mis·ap·pro·pri·ate ['misə'prəuprieit] sich *et.* widerrechtlich aneignen, unterschlagen, veruntreuen; **'mis·ap·pro·pri'a·tion** widerrechtliche Aneignung *f*, Unterschlagung *f*, Veruntreuung *f*.

mis·be·come ['misbi'kʌm] sich nicht schicken für; **'mis·be'com·ing** unschicklich.

mis·be·got(·ten) ['misbigɔt(n)] unehelich gezeugt; scheußlich.

mis·be·have ['misbi'heiv] sich schlecht benehmen; **'mis·be'hav·io(u)r** [∽jə] schlechtes Benehmen *n*.

mis·be·lief ['misbi'li:f] Irrglaube *m*; **mis·be·lieve** ['∽'li:v] irrgläubig sein; **'mis·be'liev·er** Irrgläubige *m*, *f*.

mis·cal·cu·late ['mis'kælkjuleit] falsch (be)rechnen; sich verrechnen; **'mis·cal·cu'la·tion** falsche (Be)Rechnung *f*; Rechenfehler *m*.

mis·call ['mis'kɔ:l] fälschlich nennen.

mis·car·riage [mis'kæridʒ] Mißlingen *n*; Verlust *m von Briefen*; Fehlgeburt *f*; ∽ *of justice* Fehlspruch *m*; **mis'car·ry** mißlingen, fehlschlagen; verlorengehen *(Brief)*; fehlgebären.

mis·cast *thea.* [mis'ka:st] *(irr. cast)* *e-m Schauspieler* die falsche Rolle geben; *Stück* fehlbesetzen.

mis·ce·ge·na·tion [misidʒi'neiʃən] Rassenmischung *f*.

mis·cel·la·ne·ous ☐ [misi'leinjəs] ge-, vermischt; vielseitig; **mis·cel'la·ne·ous·ness** Gemischtheit *f*; Mannigfaltigkeit *f*.

mis·cel·la·ny [mi'seləni] Gemisch *n*; Sammelband *m*; **mis'cel·la·nies** *pl.* vermischte Schriften *f/pl.*

mis·chance [mis'tʃa:ns] unglücklicher Zufall; Unfall *m*.

mis·chief ['mistʃif] Schaden *m*, Unheil *n*; Unfug *m*, Mutwille *m*, Übermut *m*; F Racker *m*, Schelm *m*

(*Kind*); *make* ~ *between* Unfrieden stiften zwischen; *get into* ~ Unfug treiben; *what etc. the* ~ *...?* was *etc.* zum Teufel *...?*; '~-mak·er Unheilstifter(in).

mis·chie·vous ☐ ['mistʃivəs] schädlich; schadenfroh; mutwillig; 'mis·chie·vous·ness Schädlichkeit *f*; Schadenfreude *f*; Mutwille *m*.

mis·con·ceive ['miskən'siːv] falsch auffassen *od.* verstehen; **mis·con·cep·tion** ['~sepʃən] falsche Auffassung *f*, Mißverständnis *n*.

mis·con·duct 1. [mis'kɔndʌkt] schlechtes Benehmen *n*; Fehltritt *m*, Ehebruch *m*; schlechte Verwaltung *f*; **2.** ['~kən'dʌkt] schlecht verwal*r*en; ~ *o.s.* sich schlecht benehmen; e-n Fehltritt begehen.

mis·con·struc·tion ['miskən'strʌkʃən] Mißdeutung *f*; **mis·con·strue** ['~'struː] mißdeuten.

mis·count ['mis'kaunt] **1.** falsch rechnen *od.* zählen; sich verrechnen; **2.** falsche Rechnung *f od.* Zählung *f*.

mis·cre·ant ['miskriənt] **1.** Schurke *m*; **2.** abscheulich, gemein.

mis·cre·a·ted ['miskri'eitid] monströs, unförmig.

mis·date [mis'deit] **1.** falsches Datum *n*; **2.** falsch datieren.

mis·deal ['mis'diːl] (*irr. deal*) Karten: vergeben. [tat *f.*]

mis·deed ['mis'diːd] Un-, Misse-]

mis·de·mean·ant ⚖ [misdi'miːnənt] Übeltäter *m*; **mis·de'mean·o(u)r** ⚖ [~nə] Vergehen *n*.

mis·di·rect ['misdi'rekt] irreleiten; an die falsche Adresse richten; 'mis·di'rec·tion Irreleitung *f*; falsche Adressierung *f*.

mis·do·ing ['mis'duːiŋ] *mst* ~s *pl.* Vergehen *n*.

mise-en-scène *thea.* ['miːzãːn'sein] Inszenierung *f*.

mi·ser ['maizə] Geizhals *m*.

mis·er·a·ble ☐ ['mizərəbl] elend; unglücklich, erbärmlich; 'mis·er·a·ble·ness Elend *n*.

mi·ser·ly ['maizəli] geizig, filzig.

mis·er·y ['mizəri] Elend *n*, Not *f*; Trübsal *f*, Jammer *m*; Leid *n*; F Elendsgestalt *f*.

mis·fea·sance ⚖ [mis'fiːzəns] Mißbrauch *m* der Amtsgewalt.

mis·fire ['mis'faiə] **1.** Versager *m* beim Schießen; *mot.* Fehlzündung *f*;

2. versagen; fehlzünden; *fig.* danebengehen.

mis·fit ['misfit] schlecht passendes Stück *n* (*Kleid, Stiefel etc.*); Einzelgänger *m*, Eigenbrötler *m*.

mis·for·tune [mis'fɔːtʃən] Unglück (-sfall *m*) *n*; Mißgeschick *n*.

mis·give [mis'giv] (*irr. give*) Böses ahnen lassen; *my heart misgave me* mir ahnte Böses; **mis'giv·ing** böse Ahnung *f*, Befürchtung *f*.

mis·gov·ern ['mis'gʌvən] schlecht regieren; 'mis'gov·ern·ment schlechte Regierung *f*.

mis·guide ['mis'gaid] irreleiten; 'mis'guid·ed irre-, fehlgeleitet.

mis·han·dle ['mis'hændl] mißhandeln; falsch handhaben.

mis·hap ['mishæp] Unfall *m*; Unglück *n*; Mißgeschick *n*; Panne *f*.

mis·hear [mis'hiə] (*irr. hear*) sich verhören; falsch hören.

mish·mash ['miʃmæʃ] Mischmasch *m*.

mis·in·form ['misin'fɔːm] falsch unterrichten; 'mis·in·for'ma·tion falscher Bericht *m*, falsche Auskunft *f*.

mis·in·ter·pret ['misin'təːprit] mißdeuten, falsch auslegen; 'mis·in·ter·pre'ta·tion falsche Auslegung *f*.

mis·judge ['mis'dʒʌdʒ] falsch (be-) urteilen *od.* einschätzen; sich verschätzen (in); 'mis'judg(e)·ment falsche Beurteilung *f*; falsches Urteil *n*.

mis·lay [mis'lei] (*irr. lay*) verlegen.

mis·lead [mis'liːd] (*irr. lead*) irreführen; verleiten; **mis'lead·ing** irreführend.

mis·man·age ['mis'mænidʒ] schlecht verwalten; 'mis'man·age·ment schlechte Verwaltung *f*; Mißwirtschaft *f*.

mis·name ['mis'neim] beschimpfen; fälschlich nennen.

mis·no·mer ['mis'nəumə] falsche Benennung *f od.* Bezeichnung *f*.

mi·sog·a·mist [mi'sɔgəmist] Ehefeind *m*.

mi·sog·y·nist [mai'sɔdʒinist] Weiberfeind *m*; **mi'sog·y·ny** Weiberhaß *m*.

mis·place ['mis'pleis] falsch stellen, verstellen; verlegen; übel anbringen.

mis·print 1. [mis'print] verdrucken;

mispronounce

2. ['mis'print] Druckfehler *m*.

mis·pro·nounce ['misprə'nauns] falsch aussprechen; **mis·pro·nun·ci·a·tion** ['prənʌnsi'eiʃən] falsche Aussprache *f*.

mis·quo·ta·tion ['miskwəu'teiʃən] falsches Zitat *n*; **'mis'quote** falsch anführen *od*. zitieren.

mis·read ['mis'ri:d] (*irr. read*) falsch lesen *od*. deuten.

mis·rep·re·sent ['misrepri'zent] falsch darstellen, verdrehen; **'mis·rep·re·sen'ta·tion** falsche Darstellung *f*, Verdrehung *f*.

mis·rule ['mis'ru:l] **1.** Unordnung *f*; Tumult *m*; schlechte Regierung *f*; **2.** schlecht regieren.

miss[1] [mis] *mst* ♀ Fräulein *n*; junges Mädchen *n*, Backfisch *m*.

miss[2] [] **1.** Verlust *m*; Fehlschuß *m*, -stoß *m*, -wurf *m*, -schlag *m*; **2.** *v/t*. (ver)missen; *Weg*, *Ziel* verfehlen; *Gelegenheit etc.* verpassen, sich entgehen lassen; auslassen; übersehen, -hören; versäumen; *fire* versagen; *one's footing* ausgleiten; *one's hold* fehlgreifen; *out* auslassen; *v/i.* fehlen (*nicht treffen*); fehlgehen; *out on s.th.* et. verpassen.

mis·sal *eccl.* ['misəl] Meßbuch *n*.

mis·shap·en ['mis'ʃeipən] verunstaltet; mißgestaltet.

mis·sile ['misail] (Wurf)Geschoß *n*; Rakete *f*; *site* ✕ Raketenstellung *f*; *intercontinental ballistic* Interkontinentalrakete *f*.

miss·ing ['misiŋ] fehlend, abwesend; *bsd.* ✕ vermißt; verschollen; *be* fehlen, vermißt werden.

mis·sion ['miʃən] Sendung *f*; Auftrag *m*; Berufung *f*, Lebensziel *n*; Gesandtschaft *f*; *eccl.*, *pol.* Mission *f*; **mis·sion·ar·y** ['miʃnəri] **1.** Missionar *m*; **2.** Missions...

mis·sis F ['misiz] Frau *f*.

mis·sive ['misiv] Sendschreiben *n*.

mis·spell ['mis'spel] (*irr. spell*) falsch buchstabieren *od*. schreiben.

mis·spend ['mis'spend] (*irr. spend*) falsch verwenden, vergeuden.

mis·state ['mis'steit] falsch angeben; **'mis'state·ment** falsche Angabe *f*.

mis·sus F ['misəz] Frau *f*.

miss·y F ['misi] kleines Fräulein *n*.

mist [mist] **1.** Nebel *m*; *in a* irre, verdutzt; **2.** (um)nebeln; sich trü-

ben; beschlagen.

mis·tak·a·ble [mis'teikəbl] leicht mißzuverstehend *od*. zu verkennend; **mis'take 1.** (*irr. take*) *v/t.* sich irren in (*dat.*), verkennen; falsch auffassen, mißverstehen; verwechseln (*for* mit), fälschlich halten (*for* für); *be* *n* sich irren; *v/i.* ⚒ sich irren; **2.** Irrtum *m*; Versehen *n*; Fehler *m*; *by* aus Versehen; *and no* F ganz gewiß; **mis'tak·en** □ irrig, falsch (verstanden); *identity* Personenverwechslung *f*.

mis·ter ['mistə] (*abbr.* **Mr.**) Herr *m*.

mis·time ['mis'taim] zur unrechten Zeit tun *od*. sagen; **'mis'timed** unzeitig.

mist·i·ness ['mistinis] Nebligkeit *f*; *fig.* Unklarheit *f*.

mis·tle·toe ♀ ['misltəu] Mistel *f*.

mis·trans·late ['mistræns'leit] falsch übersetzen; **'mis·trans'la·tion** falsche Übersetzung *f*.

mis·tress ['mistris] Herrin *f*; Hausfrau *f*; Lehrerin *f*; Geliebte *f*, Mätresse *f*; Meisterin *f in e-r Kunst etc.*

mis·tri·al ⚖ ['mis'traiəl] ungültiges Verfahren *n*.

mis·trust ['mis'trʌst] **1.** mißtrauen (*dat.*); **2.** Mißtrauen *n*; **'mis'trust·ful** □ [ful] mißtrauisch.

mist·y □ ['misti] neb(e)lig; *fig.* unklar.

mis·un·der·stand ['misʌndə'stænd] (*irr. stand*) mißverstehen; **'mis·un·der'stand·ing** Mißverständnis *n*.

mis·us·age [mis'ju:zidʒ] Mißbrauch *m*; Mißhandlung *f*.

mis·use 1. ['mis'ju:z] mißbrauchen; mißhandeln; **2.** [''ju:s] Mißbrauch *m*.

mite[1] *zo*. [mait] Milbe *f*.

mite[2] [] Heller *m*; Scherflein *n*; *a* (*of a child*) ein Wurm *m* (von Kind).

mit·i·gate ['mitigeit] mildern, lindern (*a. fig.*); **mit·i'ga·tion** Milderung *f*, Linderung *f*.

mi·tre, **mi·ter** ['maitə] **1.** Mitra *f*, Bischofsmütze *f*, -würde *f*; ⊕ Gehrung *f*; **2.** mit der Bischofswürde bekleiden; ⊕ auf Gehrung verbinden; **'mi·tre-wheel** ⊕ Kegelrad *n*.

mitt [mit] Baseball-Handschuh *m*;

F Boxhandschuh *m*; = *mitten*.

mit·ten ['mitn] Fausthandschuh *m*; Halbhandschuh *m* (*ohne Finger*); *Am. sl.* Tatze *f* (*Hand*); *get the* ~ F einen Korb bekommen.

mix [miks] **1.** (sich) (ver)mischen, mengen; ~ *in society* in der Gesellschaft verkehren; ~*ed* gemischt (*fig.* *zweifelhaft*); ~*ed marriage* Mischehe *f*; ~*ed pickles pl.* Mixed Pickles *pl.* (*Essiggemüse*); ~*ed up* verwirrt, konfus, durcheinander; ~ *up* vermengen; verwechseln; *be* ~*ed up with* in *e-e Angelegenheit* verwickelt sein; ~ *with* verkehren mit; **2.** (back- *od.* kochfertige) Mischung *f*; **'mix·er** Mischer *m*; (Bar)Mixer *m*; *Radio:* Toningenieur *m*; *Küche:* Mixer *m*; *good* (*bad*) ~ (wenig) umgänglicher Mensch *m*; **mix·ture** ['~tʃə] Mischung *f*, Gemisch *n* (*a. fig.*), Mixtur *f*; **'mix-'up** Durcheinander *n*.

miz·en, miz·zen ⚓ ['mizn] Besan *m*; *attr.* Besan..., Kreuz...

miz·zle F ['mizl] nieseln; jammern, klagen; verwirren.

mne·mon·ic [niː'mɔnik] **1.** (~*ally*) mnemotechnisch; Gedächtnis...; **2. mne'mon·ics** *pl.* Gedächtniskunst *f*.

mo *co. od.* V [məu] = *moment*.

moan [məun] **1.** Stöhnen *n*; **2.** stöhnen.

moat [məut] Burg-, Stadtgraben *m*; **'moat·ed** von e-m Wassergraben umgeben.

mob [mɔb] **1.** Pöbel *m*, Mob *m*; Pöbelhaufen *m*; **2.** anpöbeln; **'mob·bish** pöbelhaft.

mob·cap ['mɔbkæp] Morgenhaube *f*.

mo·bile ['məubail] **1.** beweglich; ⚔ mobil; ~ *home mot.* Wohnmobil *n*; **2.** Mobile *n*; **mo·bil·i·ty** [~'biliti] Beweglichkeit *f*; **mo·bi·li·za·tion** ⚔ [~bilai'zeiʃən] Mobilmachung *f*; **'mo·bi·lize** ⚔ mobil machen.

mob-law ['mɔblɔː] Lynchjustiz *f*.

mob·oc·ra·cy [mɔ'bɔkrəsi] Pöbelherrschaft *f*; **mob·ster** ['mɔbstə] Bandenmitglied *n*.

moc·ca·sin ['mɔkəsin] weiches Leder *n*; Mokassin *m* (*Schuh*).

mo·cha ['mɔkə] Mokka(kaffee) *m*.

mock [mɔk] **1.** Hohn *m*, Spott *m*; **2.** Schein..., falsch, nachgemacht; ~ *fight* Scheingefecht *n*; **3.** *v/t.* verhöhnen, verspotten; nachmachen;

täuschen; vereiteln; *v/i.* spotten (*at* über *acc.*); **'mock·er** Spötter(in); **'mock·er·y** Spötterei *f*, Gespött *n*; Hohn *m*; Äfferei *f*; **'mock-he'ro·ic** komisch-heroisch; **'mock·ing 1.** Gespött *n*; Hohn *m*; **2.** □ spöttisch; **'mock·ing-bird** Spottdrossel *f*.

mock...: '~-king Schattenkönig *m*; **'~-'tur·tle soup** falsche Schildkrötensuppe *f*; **'~-up** Nachbildung *f*, Modell *n*.

mod·al □ ['məudl] *bsd. gr.* modal; **mo·dal·i·ty** [~'dæliti] Modalität *f*.

mode [məud] (Art *f* u.) Weise *f*; (Erscheinungs)Form *f*; Sitte *f*, Mode *f*; *gr.* Modus *m*.

mod·el ['mɔdl] **1.** Modell *n*; Muster *n*; *fig.* Vorbild *n*; Vorführdame *f*; *attr.* Muster..., musterhaft, vorbildlich; *act as a* ~ Modell stehen (*to dat.*); ~ *aircraft* Flug(zeug)modell *n*; **2.** modellieren; abformen; *fig.* modeln, bilden (*after, on, upon* nach); **mod·el·(l)er** ['mɔdlə] Modellierer *m*.

mod·er·ate 1. □ ['mɔdərit] mäßig; gemäßigt, mittelmäßig; **2.** ['~reit] (sich) mäßigen, mildern; **mod·er·ate·ness** ['mɔdəritnis] Mäßigkeit *f*; Mittelmäßigkeit *f*; **mod·er·a·tion** [~'reiʃən] Mäßigung *f*; Mäßigkeit *f*; *in* ~ mit Maß; Ǫs *pl. univ.* erste öffentliche Prüfung *f* *in Oxford*; **'mod·er·a·tor** Mittelsmann *m*; *univ.* Examinator *m*; *phys.* Moderator *m*; Diskussionsleiter *m*.

mod·ern ['mɔdən] **1.** modern, neu (-zeitlich); ~ *languages pl.* neuere Sprachen *f/pl.*; **2.** the ~s *pl.* die Modernen *pl.*; **'mod·ern·ism** moderne (Geistes)Richtung *f*; **'mod·ern·ist** Modernist *m*, Anhänger *m* der Moderne; **mod·ern'is·tic** modernistisch; **mo·der·ni·ty** [mɔ'dəːniti] Modernität *f*; **mod·ern·ize** ['mɔdənaiz] (sich) modernisieren.

mod·est □ ['mɔdist] bescheiden; anständig; anspruchslos; mäßig; **'mod·es·ty** Bescheidenheit *f*.

mod·i·cum ['mɔdikəm] geringe Menge *f*, Wenige *n*, Quentchen *n*.

mod·i·fi·a·ble ['mɔdifaiəbl] änderungsfähig; **mod·i·fi·ca·tion** [~fi-'keiʃən] Ab-, Veränderung *f*; Einschränkung *f*; **mod·i·fy** ['~fai] modifizieren, (ab)ändern; *gr.* umlauten; näher bestimmen; einschränken, mildern.

mod·ish ['məudiʃ] modisch, modern.

mo·diste [məu'di:st] Modistin *f*; Damenschneiderin *f*.

mod·u·late ['mɔdjuleit] modulieren; einstellen; *Radio:* (aus)steuern; **mod·u·la·tion** Modulation *f*; '**mod·u·la·tor** Regler *m*; ~ of *tonality Film:* Tonblende *f*; **mod·ule** ['~dju:l] Modul *m* (*a.* △); Maßeinheit *f*; *s. lunar* ~; **mod·u·lus** *phys.* ['~djuləs] Modul *m*.

Mo·gul [məu'gʌl]: *the Great od. Grand* ~ der Großmogul.

mo·hair ['məuhɛə] Angorahaar *n*; Mohair(stoff) *m*.

Mo·ham·med·an [məu'hæmidən] 1. Mohammedaner(in); 2. mohammedanisch.

moi·e·ty ['mɔiəti] Hälfte *f*; Teil *m*.

moil [mɔil] sich schinden.

moire [mwɑ:] Moiré *m*, Wasserglanz *m auf Stoffen*; Moiréstoff *m*.

moi·ré ['mwɑ:rei] geflammt (*Stoff*).

moist [mɔist] feucht, naß; **mois·ten** ['mɔisn] *v/t.* an-, befeuchten; *v/i.* feucht werden; **moist·ness** ['mɔistnis], **mois·ture** ['~tʃə] Feuchtigkeit *f*; **mois·tur·ize** ['~tʃəraiz] (*Luft*) befeuchten; (*Haut*) eincremen; '**moist·ur·iz·ing cream** Feuchtigkeitscreme *f*.

moke *sl.* [məuk] Esel *m*.

mo·lar ['məulə] *a.* ~ *tooth* Backenzahn *m*. [Sirup *m*.\

mo·las·ses [məu'læsiz] Melasse *f*;\

mold [məuld], '**mold·board** *etc. s. mould etc.*

mole[1] *zo.* [məul] Maulwurf *m*.

mole[2] [~] Muttermal *n*.

mole[3] [~] Mole *f*, Hafendamm *m*.

mo·lec·u·lar [məu'lekjulə] Molekular...; **mol·e·cule** *phys.* ['mɔlikju:l] Molekül *n*.

mole·hill ['məulhil] Maulwurfshaufen *m*; *make a mountain out of a* ~ *aus e-r Mücke e-n Elefanten machen*; '**mole·skin** Maulwurfsfell *n*; Moleskin *m*, Englischleder *n*.

mo·lest [məu'lest] belästigen; **mo·les·ta·tion** [~'teiʃən] Belästigung *f*.

moll F [mɔl] Gangsterbraut *f*; Nutte *f* (*Prostituierte*).

mol·li·fy ['mɔlifai] besänftigen.

mol·lusc *zo.* ['mɔləsk] Molluske *f*, Weichtier *n*; **mol·lus·cous** [mɔ-'lʌskəs] molluskenartig, -haft; '**mol·lusk** = *mollusc.*

mol·ly·cod·dle ['mɔlikɔdl] 1. Weichling *m*, Muttersöhnchen *n*; 2. verzärteln.

mo·loch ['məulɔk] Moloch *m*.

mol·ten ['məultən] geschmolzen.

mo·lyb·den·um ⚗ [mɔ'libdinəm] Molybdän *n*.

mom *Am.* [mɔm] Mama *f*, Mami *f*; ~*-and-pop store Am.* Tante-Emma-Laden *m*.

mo·ment ['məumənt] Augenblick *m*, Moment *m*; Bedeutung *f*; = ~*um; at od. for the* ~ augenblicklich; *to the* ~ pünktlich; genau; '**mo·men·tar·y** ☐ augenblicklich, vorübergehend; stet, ständig (*Angst etc.*); '**mo·ment·ly** *adv.* jeden Augenblick; **mo·men·tous** ☐ [məu-'mentəs] (ge)wichtig, bedeutend; **mo·men·tum** *phys.* [~təm] Moment *n*, Impuls *m*; Triebkraft *f*; *fig.* Wucht *f*, Schwung *m*.

mon·a·chism ['mɔnəkizəm] Mönchtum *n*.

mon·ad *phls.* ['mɔnæd] Monade *f*.

mon·arch ['mɔnək] Monarch(in), Herrscher(in); **mo·nar·chic, mo·nar·chi·cal** ☐ [mɔ'nɑ:kik(əl)] monarchisch; '**mon·arch·ism** ['mɔnəkizəm] Monarchismus *m*; '**mon·arch·ist** Monarchist *m*; '**mon·arch·y** Monarchie *f*.

mon·as·ter·y ['mɔnəstəri] (Mönchs-) Kloster *n*; **mo·nas·tic, mo·nas·ti·cal** [mə'næstik(əl)] klösterlich; Mönchs...; **mo·nas·ti·cism** [~sizəm] Mönchtum *n*, mönchisches Leben *n*.

mon·au·ral [mɔn'ɔ:rəl] monaural, nicht stereophon.

Mon·day ['mʌndi] Montag *m*.

mon·e·tar·y ['mʌnitəri] Geld...; ~ *reform* Währungsreform *f*.

mon·ey ['mʌni] Geld *n*; *ready* ~ Bargeld *n*; *out of* ~ nicht bei Kasse; ~ *down in bar*; *get one's* ~*'s worth et. für sein Geld bekommen*; *marry* ~ *sich reich verheiraten*; *make* ~ Geld verdienen (*by an dat.*, bei); '~**-box** Sparbüchse *f*; '~**-chang·er** (Geld-) Wechsler *m*; **mon·eyed** ['mʌnid] vermögend; in Geld bestehend.

mon·ey...: '~-grub·ber Geldraffer *m*; '~**-lend·er** Geldverleiher *m*; '~**-mar·ket** Geldmarkt *m*; ~ **mat·ters** *pl.* Geldangelegenheiten *f pl.*; '~**-or·der** Postanweisung *f*; '~**-spin·ner** F (gute) Einnahmequelle *f*.

mon·ger ['mʌŋgə] ...händler *m*, ...krämer *m*.

Mon·gol ['mɔŋgɔl], **Mon·go·lian** [⌣'gəuljən] **1.** mongolisch; **2.** Mongole *m*, Mongolin *f*.

mon·grel ['mʌŋgrəl] **1.** Mischling *m*, Bastard *m*; **2.** Bastard...

mo·ni·tion [məu'niʃən] Mahnung *f*, Warnung *f*; **mon·i·tor** ['mɔnitə] Ermahner *m*; (Klassen)Ordner *m*; ⚓ *Art* Panzerschiff *n*, Monitor *m*; *Radio*: Überwacher *m* der Auslandssendungen; Monitor *m*, Kontrollschirm *m*; **'mon·i·tor·ing:** ⌣ *device* Überwachungsanlage *f*; **'mon·i·to·ry** ermahnend; warnend; Mahn...

monk [mʌŋk] Mönch *m*; **'monk·er·y** *bsd. contp.* Mönchswesen *n*, Mönchtum *n*.

mon·key ['mʌŋki] **1.** Affe *m* (*a. fig.*); ⊕ Rammblock *m*; *sl.* 500 Pfund Sterling; ⌣'s *allowance sl.* mehr Schläge als Brot; *put s.o.'s* ⌣ *up* F j. auf die Palme bringen; ⌣ *business Am sl.* fauler Zauber *m*; **2.** F (herum)albern; ⌣ *about with* herummurksen an (*dat.*); **'⌣-en·gine** Rammaschine *f*; **'⌣-jack·et** ⚓ Munkijacke *f*, Bordjackett *n*. **'⌣-nut** ♀ Erdnuß *f*; **'⌣-puz·zle** ♀ Schuppentanne *f*; **'⌣-wrench** ⊕ Engländer *m* (*Schraubenschlüssel*); *throw a* ⌣ *in s.th. Am. sl. et.* über den Haufen werfen.

monk·hood ['mʌŋkhud] Mönchswesen *n*, Mönchtum *n*; **'monk·ish** *mst contp.* mönchisch.

mon·o ['mɔnəu] **1.** mono; **2.** F Mono(schall)platte *f*.

mono... ['mɔnəu] ein(fach)...; **mo·no·chrome** *paint.* ['mɔnəkrəum] **1.** monochrom; **2.** monochrome Malerei *f*; **mon·o·cle** ['mɔnɔkl] Monokel *n*; **mo·no·cot·y·le·don** ♀ ['mɔnəukɔti'li:dən] Einkeimblättrige *f*; **mo·noc·u·lar** [mɔ'nɔkjulə] einäugig; für ein Auge; **mo'nog·a·my** [⌣gəmi] Einehe *f*, Monogamie *f*; **mon·o·gram** ['mɔnəgræm] Monogramm *n*; **mon·o·graph** ['⌣grɑːf] Monographie *f*; **mon·o·lith** ['mɔnəuliθ] Monolith *m*; **mon·o·lith·ic** [mɔnəu'liθik] monolithisch; *fig.* gigantisch; **mon·o·logue** ['mɔnəlɔg] Monolog *m*, Selbstgespräch *n*; **mon·o·ma·ni·a** ['mɔnəu'meinjə] fixe Idee *f*, Monomanie *f*;

'mon·o'ma·ni·ac [⌣niæk] Monomane *m*, von e-r fixen Idee Besessener *m*; **mon·o·plane** ✈ ['mɔnəuplein] Eindecker *m*; **mo·nop·o·list** [mə'nɔpəlist] Monopolist *m*; **mo'nop·o·lize** [⌣laiz] monopolisieren; *fig.* an sich reißen; **mo'nop·o·ly** Monopol *n* (*of* auf *acc.*); **mon·o·syl·lab·ic** ['mɔnəusi'læbik] (⌣*ally*) einsilbig; **mon·o·syl·la·ble** ['mɔnəsiləbl] einsilbiges Wort *n*; **mon·o·the·ism** ['mɔnəuθi:izəm] Monotheismus *m* (*Glaube an e-n einzigen Gott*); **mon·o·tone** ['mɔnətəun] **1.** gleichbleibender Ton *m*; *in* ⌣ eintönig; **2.** herleiern; **mo·not·o·nous** □ [mə'nɔtnəs] monoton, eintönig, -förmig; **mo'not·o·ny** Monotonie *f*; Eintönigkeit *f*, -förmigkeit *f*; **Mon·o·type** *typ.* ['mɔnəutaip] Monotype *f* (*Setzmaschine für Einzelbuchstaben*); **mon·ox·ide** ['mɔ'nɔksaid] Monoxyd *n*.

mon·sieur [mə'sjɔː] Monsieur *m*, Herr *m*.

mon·soon [mɔn'suːn] Monsun *m*.

mon·ster ['mɔnstə] Ungeheuer *n* (*a. fig.*); Monstrum *n*, Mißbildung *f*; *attr.* Riesen... [Monstranz *f*.\]

mon·strance *eccl.* ['mɔnstrəns]\

mon·stros·i·ty [mɔns'trɔsiti] Ungeheuer(lichkeit *f*) *n*; **'mon·strous** □ ungeheuer(lich); gräßlich.

mon·tage [mɔn'tɑːʒ] *Film-, Photo*-Montage *f*.

month [mʌnθ] Monat *m*; *this day* ⌣ heute in e-m Monat; **'month·ly 1.** monatlich; ⌣ *season ticket* Monatskarte *f*; **2.** Monatsschrift *f*.

mon·u·ment ['mɔnjumənt] Denkmal *n*; **mon·u·men·tal** □ [⌣'mentl] monumental; Denkmal...; Gedächtnis..., Gedenk...; großartig; riesig.

moo [muː] **1.** muhen; **2.** Muhen *n*.

mooch F [muːtʃ]: ⌣ *about* herumlungern; herumlatschen.

mood¹ *gr.* [muːd] Modus *m*.

mood² [⌣] Stimmung *f*, Laune *f*.

mood·i·ness ['muːdinis] üble Laune *f*; **'mood·y** □ launisch; schwermütig; übellaunig.

moon [muːn] **1.** Mond *m*; *poet.* Monat *m*; *be over the* ⌣ überglücklich sein; *cry for the* ⌣ nach den Sternen greifen; *promise s.o.* ⌣ j-m das Blaue vom Himmel (herunter) versprechen; *once in a blue* ⌣ F alle Jubeljahre einmal; **2.** *mst* ⌣ *about* F herumdösen;

'moon·beam Mondstrahl *m*; **'moon·less** mondlos; **'moon·light** Mondlicht *n*, -schein *m*; **'moon·light·ing** Nebenbeschäftigung *f*; Schwarzarbeit *f*; **'moon·lit** mondhell.

moon...: '~·shine Schwindel *m*, Unsinn *m*; geschmuggelter *od.* schwarz gebrannter Alkohol *m*; '~·shin·er *Am.* F Schwarzbrenner *m*; Alkoholschmuggler *m*; '~·struck mondsüchtig; **'moon·y** □ Mond...; mondförmig; mondhell; F träumerisch, dösig; *sl.* beschwipst.

Moor¹ [muə] Maure *m*; Mohr *m*.

moor² [~] Ödland *n*, *bsd.* Heideland *n*; † *od. prov.* Moor *n*, Sumpf *m*.

moor³ ⚓ [~] festmachen, (sich) vertäuen; **moor·age** ['muəridʒ] Ankerplatz *m*.

moor·fowl ['muəfaul], **'moor·game** ['~geim] Moorhuhn *n*.

moor·ing-mast ['muəriŋmɑːst] Ankermast *m für Luftschiffe.*

moo·rings ⚓ ['muəriŋz] *pl.* Vertäuungen *f/pl.*; Ankerplatz *m*.

Moor·ish ['muəriʃ] maurisch.

moor·land ['muələnd] Heidemoor *n*.

moose *zo.* [muːs] *a.* ~-deer amerikanischer Elch *m*.

moot [muːt] **1.** ~ case, ~ point Streitpunkt *m*; **2.** diskutieren.

mop [mɔp] **1.** Mop *m*; (Haar)Wust *m*, (Haar)Schopf *m*; **2.** auf-, abwischen; ~ up Feuchtigkeit auf-, abtrocknen; *sl.* wegschnappen; *sl.* aufräumen mit; ~ the floor with s.o. *j.* in Grund u. Boden schlagen.

mope [məup] **1.** Trübsalbläser(in); the ~s *pl.* Trübsinn *m*, das heulende Elend; **2.** *v/i.* Trübsal blasen, den Kopf hängen lassen.

mo·ped ['məuped] Moped *n*.

mop·ing □ ['məupiŋ], **'mop·ish** □ kopfhängerisch, niedergeschlagen; verdrießlich.

mo·raine *geol.* [mɔ'rein] Moräne *f*.

mor·al ['mɔrəl] **1.** □ Moral...; moralisch, sittlich (gut); **2.** Moral *f*, Nutzanwendung *f*; ~s *pl.* Moral *f*, sittliches Verhalten *n*, Sitten *f/pl.*; **mo·rale** [mɔ'rɑːl] *bsd.* ✠ Moral *f*, Selbstzucht *f*, innerer Halt *m*; (Arbeits-, Kampf)Geist *m*; **mor·al·ist** ['mɔrəlist] Moralist *m*, Sittenlehrer *m*; **mo·ral·i·ty** [mɔ'ræliti] Sittenlehre *f*; Sittlichkeit *f*, Moral *f*; *contp.* Sittenpredigt *f*; *hist. thea.*

Moralität *f*; **mor·al·ize** ['mɔrəlaiz] *v/i.* moralisieren (*upon* über *acc.*); *v/t.* moralisch machen.

mo·rass [mə'ræs] Morast *m*, Sumpf *m*.

mor·bid □ ['mɔːbid] krankhaft; **mor'bid·i·ty**, **'mor·bid·ness** Krankhaftigkeit *f*; Krankheitsziffer *f*.

mor·dant ['mɔːdənt] **1.** beißend; **2.** Beize *f*, Beizmittel *n*.

more [mɔː] **1.** *adj.* mehr; **2.** *adv.* mehr; noch (dazu); wieder; once ~ noch einmal; two ~ noch zwei; so much ~, all the ~ um so mehr; no ~ nicht mehr; ~ and ~ immer mehr; **3.** Mehr *n*.

mo·rel ♀ [mɔ'rel] Morchel *f*.

mo·rel·lo ♀ [mə'reləu] *a.* ~ cherry Morelle *f*, schwarze Sauerweichsel *f*.

more·o·ver [mɔː'rəuvə] außerdem, überdies, weiter, ferner.

Mo·resque [mɔ'resk] **1.** maurisch; **2.** Arabeske *f*.

mor·ga·nat·ic [mɔːgə'nætik] (~ally) morganatisch, zur linken Hand (getraut). [Archiv *n.*]

morgue [mɔːg] Leichenhaus *n*;]

mor·i·bund ['mɔribʌnd] im Sterben (liegend), dem Tode geweiht.

Mor·mon ['mɔːmən] Mormone *m*, Mormonin *f*.

morn *poet.* [mɔːn] Morgen *m*.

morn·ing ['mɔːniŋ] **1.** Morgen *m*; Vormittag *m*; in the ~, during the ~ am Morgen, morgens; this ~ heute morgen; tomorrow ~ morgen früh; **2.** früh; Morgen...; ~ coat Cut (-away) *m*; ~ dress Besuchsanzug *m*; Stresemann *m*; '~-'glo·ry ♀ Prunkwinde *f*; ~ per·form·ance Matinee *f*.

Mo·roc·can [mə'rɔkən] marokkanisch.

mo·roc·co [mə'rɔkəu] *a.* ~ leather Maroquin *m*, Saffian *m*.

mo·ron ['mɔːrɔn] Schwachsinnige *m*, *f*.

mo·rose □ [mə'rəus] mürrisch; **mo'rose·ness** Grämlichkeit *f*.

mor·pheme *gr.* ['mɔːfiːm] Morphem *n*.

mor·phi·a ['mɔːfjə], **mor·phine** ['mɔːfiːn] Morphium *n*.

mor·pho·log·i·cal *biol.*, *gr.* [mɔːfə'lɔdʒikl] morphologisch, Form...; **mor·phol·o·gy** [~'fɔlədʒi] Morphologie *f*, Formenlehre *f*.

motor

mor·row ['mɔrəu] *mst poet.* Morgen *n*, folgende Tag *m*; the ~ of der Tag *od.* die Zeit nach.

Morse [mɔːs] *a.* ~ code Morsealphabet *n*.

mor·sel ['mɔːsəl] Bissen *m*; Bißchen *n*, Stückchen *n*.

mor·tal ['mɔːtl] **1.** □ sterblich; tödlich; Tod(es)...; menschlich; F fürchterlich, gewaltig; F (zum Sterben) langweilig; **2.** Sterbliche *m*, *f*; **mor·tal·i·ty** [mɔː'tæliti] Sterblichkeit *f*; Sterblichkeitsziffer *f*.

mor·tar ['mɔːtə] **1.** Mörser *m* (*a.* ✕); Mörtel *m*; **2.** mörteln, mit Mörtel verbinden; '~-board Mörtelbrett *n*; *univ.* Barett *n*.

mort·gage ['mɔːgidʒ] **1.** Verpfändung *f*; Pfandgut *n*, Hypothek *f*; *a.* ~-deed Pfandbrief *m*; **2.** verpfänden; **mort·ga·gee** [mɔːgə'dʒiː] Hypothekengläubiger *m*; **mort·ga·gor** [~'dʒɔː] Hypothekenschuldner *m*.

mor·tice ['mɔːtis] = **mortise**.

mor·ti·cian *Am.* [mɔː'tiʃən] Leichenbestatter *m*.

mor·ti·fi·ca·tion [mɔːtifi'keiʃən] ✚ kalter Brand *m*; Kasteiung *f*; Demütigung *f*; Kränkung *f*; Ärger *m*. **mor·ti·fy** ['mɔːtifai] *v/t.* ertöten; kasteien; demütigen; ärgern, kränken; *v/i.* ✚ brandig werden.

mor·tise ⊕ ['mɔːtis] **1.** Zapfenloch *n*, Nut *f*; **2.** mit e-m Zapfen versehen; verzapfen.

mor·tu·ar·y ['mɔːtjuəri] **1.** Leichen...; Begräbnis...; **2.** Leichenhalle *f*.

mo·sa·ic¹ [məu'zeiik] Mosaik *n*.

Mo·sa·ic² [~] mosaisch.

mo·selle [məu'zel] Moselwein *m*.

Mos·lem ['mɔzlem] **1.** muselmanisch; **2.** Moslem *m*, Muselman *m*.

mosque [mɔsk] Moschee *f*.

mos·qui·to *zo.* [məs'kiːtəu], *pl.* **mos'qui·toes** [~z] Stechmücke *f*, Moskito *m*; **mos'qui·to-craft** ⚓ Schnellboot *n*; **mos'qui·to-net** Moskitonetz *n*.

moss [mɔs] ♣ Moos *n*; (Torf-) Moor *n*; '**moss·i·ness** *das* Moosige; Moosüberzug *m*; '**moss·y** moosig; bemoost.

most [məust] **1.** *adj.* □ meist; größt; for the ~ part meistens; **2.** *adv.* meist, am meisten; höchst, äußerst; **3.** das meiste; die meisten; Höchste *n*, Äußerste *n*; at (the) ~ höchstens; make the ~ of möglichst ausnutzen; möglichst gut darstellen. [*des sup.*] ...**most** [məust, məst] *Bezeichnung*┘ **most·ly** ['məustli] meistens, größtenteils, hauptsächlich.

mote [məut] (Sonnen)Stäubchen *n*; the ~ in another's eye der Splitter im Auge des anderen.

mo·tel [məu'tel] Motel *n*.

mo·tet ♪ [məu'tet] Motette *f*.

moth [mɔθ] Motte *f*; '~-ball Mottenkugel *f*; in ~s *fig.* eingemottet; '~-eat·en mottenzerfressen.

moth·er ['mʌðə] **1.** Mutter *f*; **2.** hervorbringen; bemuttern; ~ coun·try Vaterland *n*; Mutterland *n*; **moth·er·hood** ['~hud] Mutterschaft *f*; '**moth·er-in-law** Schwiegermutter *f*; '**moth·er·less** mutterlos; '**moth·er·li·ness** Mütterlichkeit *f*; '**moth·er·ly** mütterlich; '**moth·er-of-'pearl** Perlmutter *f*; **Moth·er's Day** Muttertag *m*; **moth·er ship** Mutterschiff *n*; **moth·er tongue** Muttersprache *f*.

moth-proof ['mɔθpruːf] **1.** mottensicher, -echt; **2.** mottensicher machen; '**moth·y** vermottet.

mo·tif [məu'tiːf] (Leit)Motiv *n*.

mo·tion ['məuʃən] **1.** Bewegung *f*, Gang *m* (*a.* ⊕); *parl.* Antrag *m*; ✚ Stuhlgang *m*; bring forward a ~ e-n Antrag stellen; agree upon a ~ e-n Antrag annehmen; go through the ~s et. nachlässig *od.* unaufrichtig tun; set in ~ in Gang bringen; **2.** *v/t.* durch Gebärden auffordern *od.* andeuten; *j.* wohin winken; *v/i.* winken; '**mo·tion·less** bewegungs, reglos; **mo·tion of no con·fi·dence** *parl.* Mißtrauensantrag *m*; **mo·tion pic·ture** Film *m*; **mo·tion stud·y** Arbeitsstudie *f*.

mo·ti·vate ['məutiveit] motivieren, begründen; **mo·ti·va·tion** Motivierung *f*.

mo·tive ['məutiv] **1.** Bewegungs...; bewegend; ~ power Antriebskraft *f*; **2.** Beweggrund *m*, Motiv *n*; **3.** veranlassen; '**mo·tive·less** grundlos. **mo·tiv·i·ty** [məu'tiviti] Bewegungskraft *f*.

mot·ley ['mɔtli] (bunt)scheckig.

mo·tor ['məutə] **1.** Motor *m*; treibende Kraft *f*; Automobil *n*; ✚ Muskel *m*; **2.** motorisch, bewegend; Motor...; Kraft...; Auto...; ~ nerve motorischer Nerv *m*; **3.** (im) Auto

fahren; '~-as·sist·ed mit Hilfsmotor; '~-bi·cy·cle, '~-bike =
motor·cycle; '~-boat Motorboot *n*;
'~-'bus Autobus *m*; ~·cade *Am.*
['~keid] Autokolonne *f*; '~-car Au-
to(mobil) *n*, (Kraft)Wagen *m*;
'~-coach Reisebus *m*; '~-cy·cle
Motorrad *n*; '~-cy·clist Motorrad-
fahrer *m*; mo·to·ri·al [mou'tɔ:riəl]
bewegend, Bewegungs..., motorisch; mo·tor·ing ['məutəriŋ] Au-
tofahren *n*; 'mo·tor·ist Auto-,
Kraftfahrer(in); mo·tor·i·za·tion
[~rai'zeifən] Motorisierung *f*; 'mo-
tor·ize motorisieren; 'mo·tor-
-launch Motorbarkasse *f*; 'mo·tor-
less motorlos.
mo·tor...: '~·man Wagenführer *m*;
'~-plough Motorpflug *m*; '~-road,
'~·way Autobahn *f*.
mot·tle ['mɔtl] flecken, sprenkeln;
'mot·tled gefleckt, gesprenkelt.
mot·to ['mɔtəu], *pl.* mot·toes ['~z]
Wahl-, Sinnspruch *m*, Motto *n*.
mo(u)ld¹ [məuld] Damm-, Garten-
erde *f*; Schimmel *m*, Moder *m*.
mo(u)ld² [~] 1. (Guß)Form *f* (*a.
fig.*); Schablone *f*; Abdruck *m*; Art
f, Schlag *m*; 2. formen; gießen (*on,
upon* nach *e-m Muster*).
mo(u)ld-board ['məuldbɔ:d] Form-
brett *n der Maurer*.
mo(u)ld·er¹ ['məuldə] Former(in),
Bildner(in).
mo(u)ld·er² ['məuldə] *a.* ~ *away* zer-
bröckeln, zerfallen.
mo(u)ld·i·ness ['məuldinis] *das*
Schimm(e)lige, Moder *m*.
mo(u)ld·ing ['məuldiŋ] Formen *n*;
△ Gesims *n*; Fries *m*; *attr.* Form...;
Modellier...
mo(u)ld·y ['məuldi] schimm(e)lig,
dumpfig, mod(e)rig.
moult [məult] 1. Mauser *f*; 2. (*fig.*
sich) mausern; haaren.
mound [maund] Erdwall *m*; *burial-*~
Grabhügel *m*.
mount [maunt] 1. Berg *m* (*poet.
außer in geogr. Eigennamen*); Karton
m, Papier *n zum Aufziehen von Bil-
dern*; Reitpferd *n*; 2. *v/i.* (empor-)
steigen; aufsteigen (*Reiter*); *mst* ~
up anwachsen; *v/t.* be-, ersteigen;
Pferd besteigen, reiten; beritten
machen; montieren; ⊕ beschlagen;
Zeichnung etc. aufziehen, -kleben;
Edelstein fassen; *thea.* in Szene setzen; ~ed beritten; *s.* guard 1.

moun·tain ['mauntin] 1. Berg *m*; ~s
pl. Gebirge *n*; *make a* ~ *out of a molehill* aus einer Mücke einen Elefanten
machen; 2. Berg..., Gebirgs...; ~ ash
♣ Eberesche *f*; ~ chain Bergkette *f*; ~
dew F schottischer Whisky *m*;
moun·tain·eer [~ti'niə] Bergbe-
wohner(in); Bergsteiger(in); mountain'eer·ing Bergsteigen *n*, Alpinis-
mus *m*; 'moun·tain·ous bergig, gebirgig; berghoch; moun·tain range
Gebirgskette *f*; moun·tain sickness Berg-, Höhenkrankheit *f*.
moun·te·bank ['mauntibæŋk]
Marktschreier *m*, Scharlatan *m*.
mount·ing ⊕ ['mauntiŋ] Montage
f; Beschlag *m*.
mourn [mɔ:n] (be)trauern; 'mourner Leidtragende *m*, *f*; ~'s bench
Am. = *anxious bench*; mourn-
ful □ ['~ful] Trauer...; traurig;
'mourn·ful·ness Traurigkeit *f*.
mourn·ing ['mɔ:niŋ] 1. □ trauernd;
Trauer...; 2. Trauer *f*; Trauerkleidung *f*; *national day of* ~ Staats-
trauertag *m*; '~-band Trauerflor *m*;
'~-bor·der, '~-edge Trauerrand *m*;
'~-pa·per Briefpapier *n* mit Trauerrand.
mouse 1. [maus], *pl.* mice [mais]
Maus *f*; 2. [mauz] mausen; mous-
er ['mauzə] Mäusefänger *m*;
'mouse-trap Mausefalle *f*.
mousse [mu:s] gefrorene Schaum-
speise *f*. [*m*.]
mous·tache [məs'ta:ʃ] Schnurrbart/
mous·y ['mausi] schüchtern, furchtsam (*bsd. Frau*); unscheinbar;
braungrau u. glanzlos (*Haar*).
mouth 1. [mauθ], *pl.* mouths
[mauðz] Mund *m*; Maul *n*; Mündung *f e-s Flusses, e-r Flasche etc.*;
Mundstück *n e-s Horns etc.*; Loch *n*,
Öffnung *f e-s Ofens, Sackes etc.*; Grimasse *f*; *by word of* ~ mündlich; *down
in the* ~ niedergeschlagen; *laugh on the
wrong side of one's* ~ jammern; enttäuscht sein; *keep one's* ~ *shut* den
Mund halten, schweigen; 2. [mauð]
mit vollem Munde aussprechen; laut
und affektiert reden; in den Mund
nehmen; mouth·ful ['mauθful]
Mundvoll *m*, Happen *m*.
mouth...: '~-or·gan Mundharmonika *f*; '~-piece Mundstück *n*; ⊕
Schalltrichter *m*, Sprechmuschel *f*;
fig. Sprachrohr *n*; '~-wash Mundwasser *n*; '~-wa·ter·ing leckeraus-

sehend, -riechend.

mov(e)·a·ble ['mu:vəbl] **1.** beweglich; **2.** ~s pl. Mobilien pl.; '**mov(e)-a·ble·ness** Beweglichkeit f.

move [mu:v] **1.** v/t. allg. bewegen; in Bewegung setzen; (weg)rücken; antreiben; Leidenschaft erregen; seelisch rühren, ergreifen; Antrag einbringen, beantragen; ~ on zum Weitergehen veranlassen; ~ heaven and earth Himmel und Hölle in Bewegung setzen; v/i. sich (fort-) bewegen; sich regen; sich rühren; aufbrechen, abmarschieren; Schach etc.: ziehen; a. ~ house (um)ziehen (die Wohnung wechseln); ~ for s.th. et. beantragen; ~ in einziehen; ~ on weitergehen; ~ out ausziehen; **2.** Bewegung f; Schach etc.: Zug m; fig. Schritt m, Maßnahme f; on the ~ in Bewegung; get a ~ on F sich beeilen; make a ~ sich (von der Stelle) rühren; die Tafel aufheben; '**move-ment** Bewegung f; ♪ Tempo n; ♪ Satz m; ⊕ (Geh)Werk n; ✠ Stuhlgang m; '**mov·er** Bewegende m, n; Anreger(in), Urheber(in); Antragsteller(in); Triebkraft f.

mov·ie F ['mu:vi] Film...; Kino...; ~s pl. Film m; Kino n.

mov·ing □ ['mu:viŋ] bewegend; beweglich; fig. rührend; ~ staircase Rolltreppe f.   [Heuboden m.\

mow[1] [mau] Heu-, Strohhaufen m;\
mow[2] [məu] (irr.) mähen; '**mow·er** Mäher(in), Schnitter(in); Mähmaschine f; '**mow·ing** Mähen n; Mahd f; '**mow·ing-ma·chine** Mähmaschine f; **mown** p.p. von mow[2].

much [mʌtʃ] adj. viel; adv. sehr; weit, bei weitem; fast; as ~ more, as ~ again noch einmal soviel; as ~ as soviel wie; not so ~ as nicht einmal; nothing ~ nichts Bedeutendes; ~ less geschweige denn; ~ as I would like so gern ich möchte; I thought as ~ das dachte ich mir; make ~ of verstehen; Bedeutung beimessen; viel Wesens machen von; I am not ~ af a dancer ich bin kein großer Tänzer; (not) up to ~ (nicht) viel wert; this od. that ~ soviel; '**much·ness** F Menge f; much of a ~ so ziemlich dasselbe.

mu·ci·lage ['mju:silidʒ] (Pflanzen-) Schleim m; ✝ Klebstoff m; **mu·ci·lag·i·nous** [~'lædʒinəs] schlei-

mig; klebrig.

muck [mʌk] **1.** Mist m (F a. fig.); F Dreck m (a. fig.); make a ~ of s.th. et. schmutzig machen; et. verpfuschen; **2.** düngen; mst ~ up beschmutzen; ~ s.th. up et. in Unordnung bringen; et. verpfuschen; ~ about sl. herumtrödeln; '**muck·er** sl. schwerer Sturz m; come od. go a ~ bsd. fig. reinfallen; **muck-rake** ['~reik] **1.** Mistgabel; = ~r; **2.** im Schmutz wühlen; '**muck·rak·er** Am. Korruptionsschnüffler m, Skandalmacher m; '**muck·y** schmutzig, dreckig.

mu·cous [physiol.] ['mju:kəs] schleimig; ~ membrane Schleimhaut f.

mu·cus ['mju:kəs] (Nasen)Schleim m.

mud [mʌd] Schlamm m; Kot m; Schmutz m; Lehm m; '**mud-bath** Moorbad n; '**mud·di·ness** Schlammigkeit f; **mud·dle** ['mʌdl] **1.** v/t. verwirren, in Unordnung bringen; a. ~ up, ~ together verwechseln, durcheinanderbringen; F benebeln; v/i. stümpern; ~ through F sich durchwursteln; **2.** Verwirrung f; Wirrwarr m; F Wurstelei f; get into a ~ in Schwierigkeiten geraten; '**mud·dle-head·ed** wirrköpfig; '**mud·dy 1.** □ schlammig; trüb (Wasser etc.); schmutzig; verworren; **2.** trüben; beschmutzen.

mud...: '~**guard** Kotflügel m; '~**lark** F Dreckspatz m; '~**sling·ing** F Beschmutzung f, Verleumdung f.

muff[1] [mʌf] **1.** F Tolpatsch m; Stümper m; Stümperei f; **2.** (ver-) pfuschen; verpatzen; Ball entschlüpfen lassen.

muff[2] [~] Muff m.

muf·fin ['mʌfin] Muffin n (heißes Teegebäck); **muf·fin·eer** [~'niə] Salz-, Zuckerstreuer m.

muf·fle ['mʌfl] **1.** ⊕ Muffel f; **2.** oft ~ up ein-, umhüllen; Stimme etc. dämpfen; Ruder umwickeln; '**muf·fler** Halstuch n; Boxhandschuh m; ♪ Dämpfer m; mot. Auspufftopf m.

muf·ti ['mʌfti] Mufti m; bsd. ✗ Zivilkleidung f; in ~ in Zivil.

mug [mʌg] **1.** Krug m; Becher m; sl. Schnauze f, Fresse f, Visage f; Trottel m; Büffler m, Streber m; a ~'s game ein undankbares Geschäft n; **2.** überfallen und berauben; '**mug·ging** Raubüberfall m auf der

Straße; **mug up** *et.* ochsen.

mug·gy ['mʌgi] schwül.

mug·wort ♀ ['mʌgwəːt] Beifuß *m.*

mug·wump *Am. iro.* ['mʌgwʌmp] großes Tier *n* (*Person*); *pol.* Unabhängige *m.*

mu·lat·to [mju:'lætəu] Mulatte *m,* Mulattin *f.*

mul·ber·ry ['mʌlbəri] Maulbeere *f.*

mulch [mʌltʃ] 1. Torfmull *m;* 2. mit Torfmull abdecken.

mulct [mʌlkt] 1. ♀ Geldstrafe *f;* 2. mit e-r Geldstrafe belegen; bestrafen (*in* mit); berauben (*of gen.*).

mule [mju:l] Maultier *n,* -esel *m;* Bastard *m;* sturer Kerl *m;* flache Pantolette *f;* = '∼**-jenny** Mule-(spinn)maschine *f;* **mu·le·teer** [⌣li'tiə] Maultiertreiber *m;* '**mule·-track** Saumpfad *m.*

mul·ish □ ['mju:liʃ] störrisch.

mull[1] ✝ [mʌl] Mull *m.*

mull[2] F [⌣]: ∼ *over* hin und her überlegen.

mulled [mʌld]: ∼ *ale* Warmbier *n;* ∼ *wine* Glühwein *m.*

mul·le·(i)n ♀ ['mʌlin] Wollkraut *n,* Königskerze *f.*

mul·let *ichth.* ['mʌlit] Meeräsche *f.*

mul·li·gan *Am.* F ['mʌligən] Eintopf *m aus Resten;* **mul·li·ga·taw·ny** [mʌligə'tɔ:ni] *a.* ∼ *soup* Currysuppe *f.*

mul·li·grubs *sl.* ['mʌligrʌbz] *pl.* Bauchweh *n;* miese Laune *f.*

mul·lion △ ['mʌliən] 1. Fensterpfosten *m;* 2. durch Pfosten abteilen.

mul·ti·far·i·ous □ [mʌlti'feəriəs] mannigfaltig; **mul·ti·form** ['⌣fɔːm] vielförmig; **mul·ti·lat·er·al** □ ['⌣'lætərəl] vielseitig; **mul·ti·mil·lion·aire** ['⌣miljə'nɛə] Multimillionär *m;* **mul·ti·na·tion·al** [⌣'næʃənl] multinationaler Konzern *m;* **mul·ti·ple** ['mʌltipl] 1. vielfach, mannigfaltig; ∼ *firm,* ∼ *shop* Firma *f* mit Zweigniederlassungen (in verschiedenen Orten); ∼ *switchboard* ⚡ Vielfachumschalter *m;* 2. Vielfache *n;* **mul·ti·plex** ['⌣pleks] vielfach; **mul·ti·pli·cand** ⚹ [⌣pli'kænd] Multiplikand(us) *m;* **mul·ti·pli·ca·tion** [⌣pli'keiʃən] Vervielfältigung *f,* Vermehrung *f;* Multiplikation *f; compound (simple)* ∼ Großes (Kleines) Einmaleins *n;* ∼ *table* Einmaleins *n;* **mul·ti·plic·i·ty** [⌣'plisiti] Vielfältigkeit *f;* Menge *f;* **mul·ti·pli·er** [⌣-

'plaiə] Multiplikator *m;* Vermehrer (-in); **mul·ti·ply** ['⌣plai] (sich) vervielfältigen; multiplizieren; sich vermehren; **mul·ti·pur·pose** ['⌣'pəː-pəs] Mehrzweck...; **mul·ti·ra·cial** ['⌣'reiʃəl] Vielvölker...; **mul·ti·tude** ['⌣tju:d] Vielheit *f,* Menge *f; der* große Haufe, Pöbel *m;* **mul·ti·tu·di·nous** [⌣'tju:dinəs] □ zahlreich; vielfach.

mum[1] [mʌm] 1. still; 2. st!, still!; 3. Mummenschanz treiben; maskiert herumlaufen.

mum[2] F [⌣] Mama *f.*

mum·ble ['mʌmbl] murmeln; mummeln (*mühsam essen*).

Mum·bo Jum·bo ['mʌmbəu'dʒʌm-bəu] Idol *n;* Hokuspokus *m.*

mum·mer *contp.* ['mʌmə] Komödiant *m;* '**mum·mer·y** *contp.* Mummenschanz *m,* Maskerade *f;* Hokuspokus *m.*

mum·mied ['mʌmid] mumienhaft.

mum·mi·fi·ca·tion [mʌmifi'keiʃən] Mumifizierung *f;* **mum·mi·fy** ['⌣fai] mumifizieren; als Mumie aufbewahren.

mum·my[1] ['mʌmi] Mumie *f; beat to a* ∼ F zu Brei schlagen.

mum·my[2] F [⌣] Mami *f,* Mutti *f.*

mump [mʌmp] betteln; schmollen; '**mump·ish** verdrießlich; **mumps** [mʌmps] *sg.* ♨ Ziegenpeter *m,* Mumps *m;* üble Laune *f.*

munch [mʌntʃ] mit vollen Backen kauen, mampfen.

mun·dane □ ['mʌndein] weltlich; Welt...; irdisch.

mu·nic·i·pal □ [mju:'nisipl] städtisch, Gemeinde..., Stadt...; **mu·nic·i·pal·i·ty** [⌣'pæliti] Stadtbezirk *m; konkr.* Stadtverwaltung *f.*

mu·nif·i·cence [mju:'nifisns] Freigebigkeit *f;* **mu'nif·i·cent** □ freigebig.

mu·ni·ments ['mju:nimənts] *pl.* Urkunden *f/pl.*

mu·ni·tion [mju:'niʃən] 1. Munitions...; 2. ∼*s pl.* Kriegsmaterial *n,* Munition *f.*

mu·ral ['mjuərəl] 1. Mauer...; 2. Wandgemälde *n.*

mur·der ['məːdə] 1. Mord *m; get away with (blue)* ∼ sich alles erlauben können; 2. (er)morden; *fig.* verhunzen; '**mur·der·er** Mörder *m;* '**mur·der·ess** Mörderin *f;* '**mur·der·ous** □ mörderisch; *fig.* blutig.

mure [mjuə] *mst* ~ *up* einsperren.
mu·ri·at·ic ac·id ⚗ [mjuəri'ætik-
'æsid] Salzsäure *f*.
murk·y □ ['mə:ki] dunkel, trübe.
mur·mur ['mə:mə] **1.** Gemurmel *n*;
Rauschen *n*; Murren *n*; **2.** murmeln; murren (*against*, *at* über
acc.); '**mur·mur·ous** □ murmelnd.
mur·phy *sl.* ['mə:fi] Kartoffel *f*.
mur·rain ['mʌrin] Viehseuche *f*,
Maul- und Klauenseuche *f*.
mus·ca·dine ['mʌskədin], **mus·cat**
['ˌkət], **mus·ca·tel** [ˌkə'tel] Mus-
katellerwein *m*, -traube *f*.
mus·cle ['mʌsl] **1.** Muskel *m*;
2. ~ *in Am. sl.* sich rücksichtslos
eindrängen; '~-bound mit Muskelkater; *be* ~ Muskelkater haben;
mus·cu·lar □ ['ˌkjulə] Muskel...;
muskulös.
Muse[1] [mju:z] Muse *f*.
muse[2] [ˌ] (nach)sinnen, grübeln
(*on*, *upon* über *acc.*); '**mus·er**
Träumer(in).
mu·se·um [mju:'ziəm] Museum *n*.
mush [mʌʃ] Brei *m*, Mus *n*; *Am.*
Polenta *f*, Maisbrei *m*.
mush·room ['mʌʃrum] **1.** Pilz *m*,
bsd. Champignon *m*; *fig.* Empor-
kömmling *m*; **2.** Pilz...; *fig.* plötzlich
emporgeschossen; **3.** rasch wachsen, zunehmen; ~ *up* in die Höhe
schießen; ~ *out* sich rasch ausbreiten; *go* ~*ing* Pilze sammeln.
mu·sic ['mju:zik] Musik *f* (*a. fig.*),
Tonkunst *f*; Musikstück *n*; Noten
f/pl.; *set to* ~ vertonen; *face the* ~ F
die Sache ausbaden; '**mu·si·cal**
1. □ musikalisch; Musik...; wohlklingend; ~ *box* Spieldose *f*; ~
clock Spieluhr *f*; ~ *instrument* Mu-
sikinstrument *n*; **2.** *a.* ~ *comedy*
Musical *n* (*musikalisches Lustspiel*).
mu·sic...: '~-book Notenheft *n*;
'~-box *Am.* Spieldose *f*; '~-hall
Varieté(theater) *n*.
mu·si·cian [mju:'ziʃən] Musiker
(-in); Musikant(in); *be a good* ~
gut spielen; musikalisch sein.
mu·si·col·o·gy [mju:zi'kɔlədʒi] Mu-
sikwissenschaft *f*.
mu·sic...: '~-pa·per Notenpapier *n*;
'~-stand Notenständer *m*, -pult *n*;
'~-stool Klavierstuhl *m*.
musk [mʌsk] Moschus *m*, Bisam *m*;
♀ Bisampflanze *f*; = '~-deer *zo.*
Moschustier *n*.
mus·ket ['mʌskit] Muskete *f*,

Flinte *f*; **mus·ket·eer** *hist.* [ˌ'tiə]
Musketier *m*; **mus·ket·ry** ✕ ['ˌri]
Schießunterricht *m*.
musk...: '~-rat *zo.* Bisamratte *f*;
'~-rose ♀ Moschusrose *f*; '**musk·y**
nach Moschus riechend; Moschus...
Mus·lim ['mʌslim] *s.* Moslem.
mus·lin ✝ ['mʌzlin] Musselin *m*.
mus·quash ['mʌskwɔʃ] Bisamratte
f; Bisampelz *m*.
muss *bsd. Am.* F [mʌs] **1.** Durcheinander *n*; **2.** in Unordnung bringen.
mus·sel ['mʌsl] (Mies)Muschel *f*.
Mus·sul·man ['mʌslmən] **1.** Musel-
man(n) *m*; **2.** muselmanisch.
must[1] [mʌst, məst] **1.** *v/aux. (irr.)*
muß(te) *etc.*; *I* ~ *not* ich darf nicht;
2. Muß *n*, zwingende Notwendigkeit *f*; *this book is a* ~ dieses Buch
muß man lesen.
must[2] [mʌst] Most *m*.
must[3] [ˌ] Schimmel *m*, Moder *m*.
mus·tache *Am.* [məs'ta:ʃ], **mus-
ta·chio** *Am.* [məs'ta:ʃiːəu] *s.* moustache.
mus·tang ['mʌstæŋ] Mustang *m*
(*halbwildes Pferd*).
mus·tard ['mʌstəd] Senf *m*; ~ *gas*
✕ Senfgas *n*, Gelbkreuz *n*; ~ *plaster* ✚ Senfpflaster *n*.
mus·ter ['mʌstə] **1.** ✕ Musterung *f*,
Parade *f*; *mst* ~ *roll* ✕ Stammrolle *f*;
fig. Heerschau *f*, Aufgebot *n*; *pass* ~
fig. durchgehen, Zustimmung finden; **2.** *v/t.* ✕ mustern; aufbieten,
-bringen, zs.-bringen (*fig. mst* ~ *up*);
~ *in* einstellen; *v/i.* sich sammeln.
mus·ti·ness ['mʌstinis] Modrig-,
Muffigkeit *f*; '**mus·ty** modrig,
muffig.
mu·ta·bil·i·ty [mju:tə'biliti] Veränderlichkeit *f*; Wankelmütigkeit *f*;
'**mu·ta·ble** □ veränderlich; wankelmütig; **mu·ta·tion** [ˌ'teiʃən]
Veränderung *f*; *gr.* Umlaut *m*.
mute [mju:t] **1.** □ stumm; **2.** Stum-
me *m*; Statist *m*; ♪ Dämpfer *m*; *gr.*
Verschlußlaut *m*; **3.** *bsd.* ♪ dämpfen.
mu·ti·late ['mju:tileit] verstümmeln
(*a. fig.*); **mu·ti·la·tion** Verstümmelung *f*.
mu·ti·neer [mju:ti'niə] Meuterer *m*;
'**mu·ti·nous** □ meuterisch; '**mu-
ti·ny 1.** Meuterei *f*; **2.** meutern.
mutt *sl.* [mʌt] Dussel *m*.
mut·ter ['mʌtə] **1.** Gemurmel *n*;
2. murmeln; murren.

mut·ton ['mʌtn] Hammelfleisch *n*; *leg of* ~ Hammelkeule *f*; ~ **chop** Hammelkotelett *n*; ~s *pl.* Koteletten *pl.* (*Backenbart*).

mu·tu·al ☐ ['mjuːtʃuəl] gegenseitig, wechselseitig; gemeinsam; *by* ~ *consent* in gegenseitigem Einvernehmen; ~ *insurance* Versicherung *f* auf Gegenseitigkeit; **mu·tu·al·i·ty** [ˌtjuˈæliti] Gegenseitigkeit *f*.

muz·zle ['mʌzl] 1. Maul *n*, Schnauze *f*; Mündung *f* e-r *Feuerwaffe*; Maulkorb *m*; 2. e-n Maulkorb anlegen (*dat.*); *fig.* den Mund stopfen (*dat.*); knebeln; '~-**load·er** ✕ Vorderlader *m*.

muz·zy ☐ ['mʌzi] stumpfsinnig; wirr, duselig.

my [mai] mein.

my·al·gi·a ✗ [mai'ældʒiə] Muskelrheumatismus *m*.

my·col·o·gy [mai'kɔlədʒi] Pilzkunde *f*, Mykologie *f*.

my·ope ✗ ['maiəup] Kurzsichtige *m*, *f*; **my·o·pi·a** [mai'əupjə] Kurzsichtigkeit *f*; **my·op·ic** [ˌ'ɔpik] 1. (~*ally*) kurzsichtig; 2. Kurzsichtige *m*, *f*.

myr·i·ad ['miriəd] 1. Myriade *f*; Unzahl *f*; 2. unzählig, zahllos.

myr·mi·don ['məːmidən] *contp.* Helfershelfer *m*; Scherge *m*.

myrrh ✗ [məː] Myrrhe *f*.

myr·tle ✗ ['məːtl] Myrte *f*.

my·self [mai'self] ich selbst; mir; mich.

mys·te·ri·ous ☐ [mis'tiəriəs] geheimnisvoll, rätselhaft, mysteriös; **mys'te·ri·ous·ness** *das* Geheimnisvolle.

mys·ter·y ['mistəri] Mysterium *n*; Geheimnis *n*, Rätsel *n*; Geheimlehre *f*; *a.* ~ *play* hist. Mysterienspiel *n*; ~ **mod·el** *mot.* Erlkönig *m*; '~-**ship** U-Bootfalle *f*.

mys·tic ['mistik] 1. *a.* 'mys·ti·cal ☐ mystisch, geheimnisvoll; sinnbildlich; 2. Mystiker *m*; **mys·ti·cism** [ˌsizəm] Mystizismus *m*; **mys·ti·fi·ca·tion** [ˌfiˈkeiʃən] Irreführung *f*; **mys·ti·fy** ['ˌfai] mystifizieren, täuschen, hinters Licht führen; verblüffen.

mys·tique [mis'tiːk] Nimbus *m*; Geheimwissenschaft *f*.

myth [miθ] Mythe *f*, Mythos *m*, Sage *f*; **myth·ic, myth·i·cal** ☐ ['ˌik(ə)l] mythisch.

myth·o·log·ic, myth·o·log·i·cal ☐ [miθə'lɔdʒik(əl)] mythologisch; **my·thol·o·gy** [miˈθɔlədʒi] Mythologie *f*, Sagenkunde *f*.

myx·o·ma·to·sis [miksəumə'təusis] Myxomatose *f* (*Viruskrankheit der Kaninchen*).

N

nab *sl.* [næb] schnappen, erwischen.

na·bob ['neibɔb] Nabob *m*, Krösus *m* (*sehr reicher Mann*).

na·celle ✗ [næ'sel] Motorgehäuse *n*; Motorgondel *f* e-s *Luftschiffes*.

na·cre ['neikə] Perlmutter *f*; **na·cre·ous** ['ˌkriəs] perlmutterartig; Perlmutter...

na·dir ['neidiə] *ast.* Nadir *m* (*Fußpunkt*); *fig.* tiefster Stand *m*.

nag[1] F [næg] *kleiner* Klepper *m*.

nag[2] [ˌ] nörgeln, quengeln; bekritteln; quälen; '**nag·ging** 1. Meckerei *f*, Nörgelei *f*; 2. nörglerisch; *fig.* nagend.

Nai·ad ['naiæd] Najade *f* (*Quell-*

nymphe).

nail [neil] 1. (Finger-, Zehen)Nagel *m*; ⊕ Nagel *m*; *zo.* Kralle *f*, Klaue *f*; *fight tooth and* ~ bis zum Äußersten kämpfen; *on the* ~ sofort; *hit the* (*right*) ~ *on the head* den Nagel auf den Kopf treffen; *as hard as* ~*s* eisern, unbarmherzig; fit, in Form; 2. (an-, fest)nageln; *Augen etc.* heften (*to* auf *acc.*); F abfassen; ~ *down* an-, fest-, zunageln; ~ *s.o. down to fig.* j. festnageln auf (*acc.*); ~ *to the counter et.* als Lüge entlarven; '~-**brush** Nagelbürste *f*; '~-**file** Nagelfeile *f*; '**nail·ing** *sl. oft* ~ *good* fabelhaft; '**nail·scis·sors** *pl.* Nagelschere

f; **'nail·var·nish** Nagellack *m*.
nain·sook ['neinsuk] feines Baumwollgewebe *n*.
na·ïve ☐ [nɑ:'i:v], **na·ive** ☐ [neiv], unbefangen; ungekünstelt; **na·ïve·te** [nɑ:'i:vtei], **na·ive·ty** ['neivti] Naivität *f*.
na·ked ☐ ['neikid] nackt, bloß; kahl; *fig.* unverhüllt; *poet.* schutzlos; ausgesetzt; *the* ⌣ *eye* das bloße Auge; **'na·ked·ness** Nacktheit *f*, Blöße *f etc*.
nam·by-pam·by ['næmbi'pæmbi] **1.** abgeschmackt, fad; **2.** Fadheit *f*.
name [neim] **1.** Name *m*; Ruf *m*; bloßes Wort *n*; *of od. by the* ⌣ *of* ... namens ..., ... mit Namen; *call s.o.* ⌣*s j.* beschimpfen; *not have a penny to one's* ⌣ keinen Pfennig besitzen; *know s.o. by* ⌣ *j.* dem Namen nach kennen; **2.** (be)nennen; erwähnen; ernennen; **'⌣-day** Namenstag *m*; **'⌣-drop·ping** *Wichtigtuerei durch Erwähnung von Prominenten, die man angeblich kennt;* **'name·less** ☐ namenlos; unbekannt; unbeschreiblich; **'name·ly** (*abbr. viz.*) nämlich; **'name·part** Titelrolle *f*; **'name·plate** Namen-, Tür-, Firmenschild *n*; **'name·sake** Namensvetter *m*.
nan·cy *sl.* ['nænsi] Weichling *m*; Homosexuelle *m*.
nan·keen [næŋ'ki:n] Nanking *m* (*Stoff*); ⌣*s pl.* Nankinghose *f*.
nan·ny ['næni] Kindermädchen *n*; **'⌣-goat** Ziege *f*.
nap¹ [næp] *Tuch*-Noppe *f*; Haar (-seite *f*) *n des Tuches*.
nap² [⌣] **1.** Schläfchen *n*; *have od. take a* ⌣ ein Nickerchen machen; **2.** schlummern; *catch s.o.* ⌣*ping* j-n überrumpeln.
nap³ [⌣]: *go* ⌣ *Karten*: alles auf e-e Karte setzen.
na·palm ['neipɑ:m]: ⌣ *bomb* ✕ Napalmbombe *f*.
nape [neip] *mst* ⌣ *of the neck* Genick *n*.
naph·tha ⚗ ['næfθə] Naphtha *n*, *f*.
nap·kin ['næpkin] Serviette *f*; Windel *f*; Monatsbinde *f*; **'⌣-ring** Serviettenring *m*.
Na·po·le·on·ic [nəpəuli'ɔnik] napoleonisch.
na·poo(h) *sl.* [nɑ:'pu:] aus; futsch, alles alle.
nap·py F ['næpi] Windel *f*.
nar·cis·sism *psych.* [nɑ:'sisizm] Narzißmus *m*; **nar·ciss·us** ⚘

[⌣'sisəs] Narzisse *f*.
nar·co·sis ⚕ [nɑ:'kəusis] Narkose *f*.
nar·cot·ic [nɑ:'kɔtik] **1.** (⌣*ally*) narkotisch; **2.** Betäubungsmittel *n*; ⌣*s squad* Rauschgiftdezernat *n*; **nar·co·tize** ['nɑ:kətaiz] narkotisieren.
nard [nɑ:d] Narde(nsalbe) *f*.
nark¹ *sl.* [nɑ:k] Polizeispitzel *m*.
nark² F [⌣] verärgern.
nar·rate [næ'reit] erzählen; **nar'ra·tion** Erzählung *f*; **nar·ra·tive** ['nærətiv] **1.** ☐ erzählend; **2.** Erzählung *f*; **nar·ra·tor** [næ'reitə] Erzähler *m*.
nar·row ['nærəu] **1.** ☐ eng, schmal, beschränkt; knapp (*Mehrheit, Entkommen*); engherzig; *s. escape*; **2.** ⌣*s pl.* Engpaß *m*; Meerenge *f*; **3.** *v/t.* verengen; beschränken; ein-, beengen; *Maschen* abnehmen; *v/i.* sich verengen; **'⌣-'chest·ed** eng-, schmalbrüstig; **'⌣-gauge** 🚂 schmalspurig; **'⌣-'mind·ed** ☐ engherzig; **'nar·row·ness** Enge *f*; Beschränktheit *f* (*a. fig.*); Engherzigkeit *f*.
nar·whal *zo.* ['nɑ:wəl] See-Einhorn *n*.
nar·y *Am.* ['nɛəri] kein.
na·sal ['neizəl] **1.** ☐ nasal; Nasen...; näselnd; **2.** Nasallaut *m*; **na·sal·i·ty** [⌣'zæliti] Nasalität *f*; **na·sal·ize** ['⌣zəlaiz] durch die Nase sprechen, näseln; *gr.* nasalieren.
nas·cent ['næsnt] werdend, entstehend, wachsend.
nas·ti·ness ['nɑ:stinis] Schmutz *m*; Unflätigkeit *f*.
nas·tur·tium ⚘ [nəs'tə:ʃəm] Kapuzinerkresse *f*.
nas·ty ['nɑ:sti] ☐ schmutzig; garstig; eklig; widerlich, häßlich; unflätig; ungemütlich.
na·tal ['neitl] Geburts...; **na·tal·i·ty** [nə'tæliti] Geburtenziffer *f*.
na·ta·tion [nə'teiʃən] Schwimmen *n*; **na·ta·to·ri·al** [nætə'tɔ:riəl] Schwimm...
na·tion ['neiʃən] Nation *f*, Volk *n*; *member* ⌣ Mitgliedstaat *m*.
na·tion·al ['næʃənl] **1.** ☐ national; Volks..., Staats...; ⌣ *champion* Landesmeister *m*; **2.** Staatsangehörige *m*, *f*; **na·tion·al·ism** ['næʃnəlizəm] Nationalismus *m*; **'na·tion·al·ist 1.** Nationalist(in); **2.** = **na·tion·al'is·tic** nationalistisch; **na·tion·al·i·ty** [næʃə'næliti] Nationalität *f*; Nationalcharakter *m*; Nationalgefühl *n*;

Staatsangehörigkeit *f;* **na·tion·al·i-za·tion** [næʃnəlai'zeiʃən] Verstaatlichung *f;* **'na·tion·al·ize** naturalisieren, einbürgern; verstaatlichen; zu e-r Nation machen.

na·tion·hood ['neiʃənhud] nationale Selbständigkeit *f;* **na·tion-wide** ['⏜waid] die ganze Nation umfassend.

na·tive ['neitiv] **1.** □ angeboren, natürlich; heimatlich, Heimat...; Landes...; eingeboren; einheimisch (to in *dat.*); gediegen (*Metall*); ⏜ *land* Vaterland *n;* ⏜ *language* Muttersprache *f;* ⏜ *speaker* Muttersprachler *m;* **2.** Eingeborene *m, f;* Einheimische *m, f;* einheimisches Tier *n;* einheimische Pflanze *f;* (*bsd.* gezüchtete) britische Auster *f; a ⏜ of Ireland* ein gebürtiger Ire *m;* '⏜-born (im Lande) geboren, einheimisch.

na·tiv·i·ty [nə'tiviti] Geburt *f;* Nativität *f,* Horoskop *n;* ♀ **Play** Krippenspiel *n.*

na·tron ♫ ['neitrən] Natron *n.*

nat·ter F ['nætə] plaudern.

nat·ty □ ['næti] schmuck, nett, fein; flink, geschickt.

na·tu·ral ['nætʃrəl] **1.** □ natürlich; *engS.* angeboren; ungezwungen; unehelich (*Kind*); ⏜ *disaster* Naturkatastrophe *f;* ⏜ *gas* Erdgas *n;* ⏜ *history* Naturgeschichte *f;* ⏜ *note* ♪ Note *f* ohne Vorzeichen; ⏜ *philosopher* Naturforscher *m;* ⏜ *philosophy* Physik *f,* Naturlehre *f;* ⏜ *resources pl.* Bodenschätze *m pl.;* ⏜ *science* Naturkunde *f;* **2.** Idiot(in); ♪ Auflösungszeichen *n;* **'nat·u·ral·ism** Naturalismus *m;* **'nat·u·ral·ist** Naturalist *m;* Naturforscher *m,* -freund *m;* Tierhändler *m;* Präparator *m;* **nat·u·ral·i·za·tion** [⏜lai'zeiʃən] Naturalisierung *f;* **'nat·u·ral·ize** naturalisieren, einbürgern; ♀, *zo.* eingewöhnen; **'nat·u·ral·ness** Natürlichkeit *f;* **na·tu·ral se·lec·tion** *biol.* natürliche Zuchtwahl *f.*

na·ture ['neitʃə] Natur *f; engS.* Beschaffenheit *f;* Art *f;* Wesen(sart *f) n;* ⏜ *reserve* Naturschutzgebiet *n;* ⏜ *study Schule:* Naturkunde *f;* ⏜ *trail* Naturlehrpfad *m; by ⏜* von Natur (aus); **'na·tured** ...geartet, ...artig.

na·tur·ism ['neitʃərizəm] Freikörperkultur *f;* **'na·tur·ist** FKK-Anhänger(in).

naught [nɔːt] Null *f;* † nichts; *bring* (*come*) *to ⏜* zunichte machen (wer-

den); *set at ⏜* für nichts achten; **naugh·ti·ness** ['⏜tinis] Ungezogenheit *f,* Unartigkeit *f;* **'naugh·ty** □ unartig, ungezogen; ungehörig; unanständig.

nau·se·a ['nɔːsjə] Seekrankheit *f;* Übelkeit *f; fig.* Ekel *m;* **nau·se·ate** ['nɔːsieit] *v/i.* Ekel empfinden (*at* vor *dat.*); *v/t.* verabscheuen; *be ⏜d* sich ekeln; **nau·seous** □ ['nɔːsjəs] ekelhaft.

nau·ti·cal □ ['nɔːtikəl] nautisch; See..., Schiffs...; ⏜ *mile* Seemeile *f.*

naut·i·lus *zo.* ['nɔːtiləs] Nautilus *m,* Perlboot *n* (*Seetier*).

na·val □ ['neivəl] See..., Schiffs..., Marine...; ⏜ *architect* Schiffsbauingenieur *m;* ⏜ *base* Flottenstützpunkt *m;* ⏜ *staff* Admiralstab *m.*

nave¹ ⚛ [neiv] (Kirchen)Schiff *n.*

nave² [⏜] Rad-Nabe *f.*

na·vel ['neivəl] Nabel *m; fig.* Mitte *f;* ⏜ *or·ange* Navelorange *f.*

nav·i·ga·ble □ ['nævigəbl] schiff-, fahrbar; lenkbar (*Luftschiff*); **nav·i·gate** ['⏜geit] *v/i.* schiffen, (zu Schiff) fahren; *v/t. See etc.* befahren; *Schiff etc.* steuern; **nav·i·ga·tion** Schiffahrt *f;* Navigation *f* (*Schiffsführung*); **'nav·i·ga·tor** Seefahrer *m;* Steuermann *m;* Luftschiffer *m.*

nav·vy ['nævi] Erdarbeiter *m.*

na·vy ['neivi] Marine *f,* Kriegsflotte *f;* '⏜-'blue marineblau.

nay [nei] **1.** † *od. prov.* nein; nein vielmehr; **2.** Nein *n bei* Abstimmung.

Naz·a·rene [næzə'riːn] Nazarener *m.*

naze [neiz] Landzunge *f.*

Na·zi ['nɑːtsi] **1.** Nazi *m;* **2.** Nazi..., nazistisch.

neap [niːp] *a.* ⏜-*tide* Nippflut *f;* **'neaped:** *be ⏜* ⚓ bei Ebbe auf Grund kommen.

Ne·a·pol·i·tan [niə'pɔlitən] **1.** neapolitanisch; **2.** Neapolitaner(in).

near [niə] **1.** *adj.* nahe; gerade (*Weg*); nahe verwandt; vertraut; genau (*z.B. Übersetzung*); knapp (*Entkommen etc.*); knauserig; link vom Reiter *etc.;* ⏜ *at hand* dicht dabei; ⏜ *miss* Beinahezusammenstoß *m; a ⏜ thing* ein knappes Entkommen; **2.** *adv.* nahe; **3.** *prp.* nahe (*dat.*), nahe bei *od.* an; **4.** sich nähern (*dat.*); **near·by** ['⏜bai] in der Nähe (gelegen); nah; **'near·ly** nahe; fast, beinahe; genau; *not ⏜* bei weitem nicht;

'**near·ness** Nähe *f*; nahe Verwandtschaft *f*; Genauigkeit *f*; '**near-
-'sight·ed** kurzsichtig.
neat[1] □ [ni:t] nett, geschmackvoll;
zierlich, niedlich; geschickt; ordentlich; sorgfältig; sauber; rein, unverdünnt; pur (*Whisky etc.*); treffend,
bündig (*Stil*).
neat[2] ⚡ [~] Rind(vieh) *n*.
neat·ness ['ni:tnis] Nettigkeit *f*;
Sauberkeit *f*; Zierlichkeit *f*.
neat...: '**~'s-foot oil** Klauenfett *n*;
'**~'s-leath·er** Rindsleder *n*; '**~'s-
-tongue** Rinderzunge *f*.
neb·u·la *ast.* ['nebjulə] Nebel(fleck)
m; '**neb·u·lar** Nebel(fleck)..., Ne-
bular...; **neb·u·los·i·ty** [~'lɔsiti]
Nebligkeit *f*; Nebel *m*; '**neb·u·lous**
□ neblig; nebelhaft (*a. fig.*).
ne·ces·sa·ri·ly ['nesisərili] notwendigerweise, unbedingt; '**nec·es·
sar·y** □ **1.** notwendig; unvermeidlich; gezwungen; **2.** *mst necessaries*
pl. Bedürfnisse *n/pl.*; ✝ Bedarfsar-
tikel *m/pl.*; **ne·ces·si·tate** [ni'sesi-
teit] *et.* erfordern, notwendig machen; zwingen; **ne'ces·si·tous** bedürftig; **ne'ces·si·ty** Notwendigkeit
f; Bedürfnis *n*; Zwang *m*; *mst necessities pl.* Not *f*, Armut *f*; *of ~*
notgedrungen; *the bare necessities (of
life)* das Nötigste zum Leben.
neck [nek] **1.** Hals *m*; Nacken *m*,
Genick *n*; Halsstück *n vom Hammel*; *Flaschen- etc.* Hals *m*; Ausschnitt *m* (*Kleid*); *break the ~ of a
task* das Schwierigste e-r Aufgabe
hinter sich bringen; *~ and ~* Kopf
an Kopf; Seite an Seite; *~ and crop*
F mit Haut und Haaren; *~ or nothing* F alles oder nichts; *auf Leben
und Tod*; *be up to one's ~ in s.th.* bis
über die Ohren in et. stecken; *get it in
the ~ sl.* eins aufs Dach bekommen;
stick one's ~ out einiges riskieren
(*et. tun od. sagen, was unangenehme
Folgen haben könnte*); **2.** *sl.* sich abknutschen; '**~·band** Halsbund *m*; '**~-
cloth** Krawattenschal *m*; **neck·er·
chief** ['nekətʃif] Halstuch *n*; **neck·
lace** ['~lis], **neck·let** ['~lit] Halskette
f; '**neck·line** (Hals)Ausschnitt *m* (*e-s
Kleides*); '**neck·tie** Krawatte *f*;
'**neck·wear** ✝ Krawatten und Kragen *pl.*
ne·crol·o·gy [ne'krɔlədʒi] Toten-
register *n*; Nachruf *m*; **nec·ro·
man·cy** ['nekrəumænsi] Nekro-

mantie *f*, Schwarze Kunst *f*, Zauberei *f*.
nec·tar ['nektə] Nektar *m*; **nec·tar·
ine** ['~rin] *e-e Pfirsichsorte.*
née [nei] *bei Frauennamen*: geborene.
need [ni:d] **1.** Not *f*; Notwendigkeit
f; Bedürfnis *n* (*for nach*); Mangel
m; Bedarf *m* (*of an dat.*); *one's own
~s pl.* Eigenbedarf *m*; *if ~ be* nöti-
genfalls; *be od. stand in ~ of* brauchen, benötigen; **2.** nötig haben,
brauchen, benötigen; bedürfen
(*gen.*); müssen; *need·ful* ['~ful]
1. □ notwendig; **2.** F *das Nötige*
(*bsd. Geld*); '**need·i·ness** Dürftigkeit *f*, Armut *f*.
nee·dle ['ni:dl] **1.** Nadel *f*; Zeiger *m*;
2. (*mit e-r Nadel*) nähen; *bsd. Am.*
irritieren; anstacheln; F *Getränk
durch Alkoholzusatz schärfen*; *~
one's way through* sich durchschlängeln durch; '**~·case** Nadelbüchse *f*;
'**~·gun** Zündnadelgewehr *n*.
need·less ⌐ ['ni:dlis] unnötig;
'**need·less·ly** unnötig(erweise);
'**need·less·ness** Unnötigkeit *f*.
nee·dle...: '**~·wom·an** Näherin *f*;
'**~·work** Handarbeit *f*.
needs [ni:dz] notwendigerweise,
notgedrungen, durchaus; '**need·y**
⌐ bedürftig, arm, notleidend.
ne'er [nɛə] = *never*; **~-do-well**
['~du:wel] Tunichtgut *m*.
ne·far·i·ous ⌐ [ni'fɛəriəs] ruchlos,
schändlich.
ne·gate [ni'geit] verneinen; **ne'ga·
tion** Verneinung *f*; Nichts *n*; **neg·
a·tive** ['negətiv] **1.** ⌐ negativ; verneinend; **2.** Verneinung *f*; *phot.*
Negativ *n*; **3.** *a. answer in the ~* verneinen, negieren; ablehnen; widerlegen; unwirksam machen.
neg·lect [ni'glekt] **1.** Vernachlässigung *f*; Nachlässigkeit *f*; Verwahr-
losung *f*; **2.** vernachlässigen; *eine
Gelegenheit* versäumen; **neg'lect·
ful** ⌐ [~ful] nachlässig; achtlos (*of
auf acc.*).
nég·li·gé, neg·li·gee ['negli:ʒei] Negligé *n* (*Hauskleidung*; *Morgenman-
tel*).
neg·li·gence ['neglidʒəns] Nach-,
🕱 Fahrlässigkeit *f*; '**neg·li·gent** ⌐
nach-, fahrlässig; *~ of* gleichgültig
gegen.
neg·li·gi·ble ['neglidʒəbl] nebensächlich; geringfügig, unbedeutend.
ne·go·ti·a·bil·i·ty [nigəuʃjə'biliti]

Verkäuflichkeit *f*; **ne·go·ti·a·ble** ☐ verkäuflich, umsetzbar; börsenfähig; begebbar (*Wechsel*); zu nehmen(d) (*Hindernis*); passierbar (*Straße*); *not* ⁓ nur zur Verrechnung; *not* ⁓ nur zur Verrechnung; **ne·go·ti·ate** [⁓ʃieit] *v*/*t*. verhandeln (über *acc.*); zustande bringen; *Hindernis, Kurve* nehmen; bewältigen; *Wechsel* begeben; *v*/*i*. unterhandeln; **ne·go·ti·at·ing:** ⁓ *table* Verhandlungstisch *m*; **ne·go·ti·a·tion** Begebung *f e-s Wechsels, e-r Anleihe*; Unterhandlung *f*; Bewältigung *f*; *under* ⁓ zur Verhandlung stehend; **ne·go·ti·a·tor** Unterhändler *m*.

ne·gress ['niːgris] Negerin *f*; **ne·gro** ['niːgrəu], *pl.* **ne·groes** ['⁓z] Neger *m*; **ne·groid** ['niːgrɔid] negroid, negerähnlich.

ne·gus ['niːgəs] Glühwein *m*.

neigh [nei] 1. Wiehern *n*; 2. wiehern.

neigh·bo(u)r ['neibə] 1. Nachbar(in); Nächste *m, f*; 2. angrenzen an (*acc.*); **neigh·bo(u)r·hood** ['⁓hud] Nachbarschaft *f*; Umgebung *f*; *in the* ⁓ *of* in der Umgebung von; *fig.* F *um* ... *herum*; **neigh·bo(u)r·ing** benachbart, angrenzend; ⁓ *state* Anlieger-, Nachbarstaat *m*; **neigh·bo(u)r·li·ness** gutnachbarliches Verhalten *n*; **neigh·bo(u)r·ly** nachbarlich, freundlich.

nei·ther ['naiðə] 1. *adj. od. pron.* keiner (von beiden); 2. *adv.* ⁓ ... *nor* ... weder ... noch ...; *not* ... ⁓ auch nicht.

nem·e·sis ['nemisis] Nemesis *f*, strafende Gerechtigkeit *f*.

ne·o·lith·ic [niːəu'liθik] jungsteinzeitlich, neolithisch.

ne·ol·o·gism [niː'ɔlədʒizəm] Neologismus *m*, Wortneubildung *f*.

ne·on ['niːən] Neon *n*; ⁓ *light* Neonlicht *n*; ⁓ *sign* Leuchtreklame *f*.

neph·ew ['nevjuː] Neffe *m*.

ne·phri·tis [ne'fraitis] Nierenentzündung *f*.

nep·o·tism ['nepətizəm] Nepotismus *m*, Vetternwirtschaft *f*.

Nep·tune ['neptjuːn] Neptun *m* (*Meergott; Planet*).

Ne·re·id ['niəriid] Nereide *f*.

nerve [nɔːv] 1. Nerv *m*; Sehne *f*; *Blatt*-Rippe *f*; Kraft *f*, Mut *m*; Dreistigkeit *f*; *be all* ⁓*s* ein Nervenbündel sein; *get on s.o.'s* ⁓*s* j-m auf die

Nerven gehen; *have the* ⁓ *to do s.th.* es wagen, et. zu tun; *lose one's* ⁓ den Mut *od.* die Nerven verlieren; 2. kräftigen; ermutigen (*for* zu); '⁓-cell Nervenzelle *f*; '⁓-cen·tre, *Am.* '⁓-cen·ter Nervenzentrum *n*; **nerved** ♀ gerippt; ...nervig; **nerve·less** ☐ kraftlos; **nerve·rack·ing** nervenaufreibend.

nerv·ine ♣ ['nɔːviːn] 1. nervenstärkend; 2. nervenstärkendes Mittel *n*.

nerv·ous ☐ ['nɔːvəs] Nerven...; nervig, kräftig; nervös, reizbar; ängstlich; aufgeregt; ⁓ *breakdown* Nervenzusammenbruch *m*; ⁓ *system* Nervensystem *n*; **nerv·ous·ness** Nervosität *f*.

nerv·y *sl.* ['nɔːvi] dreist; auf die Nerven gehend; nervös.

nes·ci·ence ['nesiəns] Unwissenheit *f*; **nes·ci·ent** unwissend (*of* in *dat.*).

ness [nes] Vorgebirge *n*.

nest [nest] 1. Nest *n* (*a. fig.*); Schlupfwinkel *m*; Satz *m* ineinanderpassender *Dinge*; 2. nisten; **nest·ed** eingenistet; **nest-egg** Nestei *n*; *fig.* Spar-, Notgroschen *m*; **nest·er** nistender Vogel *m*; Siedler *m*; **nes·tle** ['nesl] *v*/*i*. nisten; sich einnisten; sich (an-) schmiegen (*to an acc.*); *v*/*t*. schmiegen; **nest·ling** ['nestliŋ] Nestling *m*.

net¹ [net] 1. Netz *n* (*a. fig.*); Tüll *m*, Musselin *m*; ⁓ *curtains pl.* Stores *m pl.*; 2. mit e-m Netz fangen *od.* umgeben (*a. fig.*).

net² [⁓] 1. netto, rein; Rein...; 2. netto einbringen.

net·ball ['netbɔːl] Netzball *m*; *Art* Korbball(spiel *n*) *m*.

neth·er ['neðə] nieder; Unter...; '⁓-most (zu)unterst.

net·ting ['netiŋ] Netzstricken *n*, Filetarbeit *f*; Netzwerk *n*.

net·tle ['netl] 1. ♀ Nessel *f*; 2. ✎ mit Nesseln brennen; *fig.* ärgern; '⁓-rash ♣ Nesselfieber *n*.

net·work ['netwɔːk] (Straßen-, Kanal- *etc.*)Netz *n*; *Radio:* Sendergruppe *f*.

neu·ral ♣ ['njuərəl] Nerven...

neu·ral·gia ♣ [njuə'rældʒə] Nervenschmerz *m*, Neuralgie *f*; **neu·ras·the·ni·a** ♣ [njuərəs'θiːnjə] Neurasthenie *f*, Nervenschwäche *f*; **neu·ras·then·ic** [⁓'θenik] 1. neurasthenisch; **2.** Neurastheniker(in); **neu·ri·tis** ☞ [nju͡ə'raitis] Nervenentzündung *f*; **neu·rol·o·gist** [ˌ-'rɔlədʒist] Neurologe *m*; **neu'rol·o·gy** Neurologie *f*; **neu·ro·path·ic** ☞ [ˌ-rəu'pæθik] **1.** nervenleidend; **2.** Nervenleidende *m*; **neu·ro·sis** ☞ [ˌ-'rəusis] Neurose *f*; **neu·rot·ic** [ˌ-'rɔtik] **1.** neurotisch; Nerven...; **2.** Neurotiker(in); Nervenmittel *n*. **neu·ter** ['nju:tə] **1.** geschlechtslos; *gr.* sächlich; intransitiv; **2.** geschlechtsloses Tier *n*; *gr.* Neutrum *n*.

neu·tral ['nju:trəl] **1.** □ neutral (*a.* ⚡); unparteiisch, parteilos, unbeteiligt; **2.** Neutrale *m*, *f*; Null (-punkt *m*) *f*; Leerlauf(stellung *f*) *m*; **neu·tral·i·ty** [ˌ-'træliti] Neutralität *f*; **neu·tral·i·za·tion** [ˌ-trəlai-'zeiʃən] Neutralisierung *f* (*a.* ⚡); **'neu·tral·ize** neutralisieren (*a.* ⚡); unwirksam machen.

neu·tron *phys.* ['nju:trɔn] Neutron *n*; ~ bomb ✗ Neutronenbombe *f*.

né·vé *mount.* ['nevei] Firn(feld *n*) *m*.

nev·er ['nevə] nie(mals); durchaus nicht, gar nicht; ~ so (auch) noch so; on the ~-~ *sl.* auf Stottern (*Raten*); the Ω-Ω (*Land*) der (australische) Busch; **'nev·er'more** nimmermehr, nie wieder; **nev·er·the·less** [ˌˌðə'les] nichtsdestoweniger.

new [nju:] neu (*a. adv.*); frisch; modern; unerfahren; **'~·born 1.** neugeboren; **2.** Neugeborene *n*; **'new-'com·er** Ankömmling *m*, Fremde *m*; Neuling *m*; **New England·er** Neuengländer(in); **new·fan·gled** ['ˌfæŋgld] neuerungssüchtig; neu(modisch); **new look** neue Mode *f*; neues Äußeres *n*; **'new·ly** neulich, kürzlich, jüngst; neu; **'newly-weds** *pl. die* Neuvermählten *pl.*; **'new·ness** Neuheit *f*; Unerfahrenheit *f*.

news [nju:z] *sg.* Neuigkeit(en *pl.*) *f*, Nachricht(en *pl.*) *f*; *what's the ~?* was gibt's Neues?; *break the* (*bad*) ~ *to s.o.* j-m die (*schlechte*) Nachricht (schonend) beibringen; *he is much in the ~* F alle Zeitungen schreiben über ihn; **'~·a·gen·cy** Nachrichtenbüro *n*; **'~·a·gent** Zeitungshändler *m*; **'~·boy** Zeitungsausträger *m*; **'~·butch·er** *Am. sl.* Zeitungsverkäufer *m*; **'~·cast** *Radio:* Nachrichten *pl.*; **'~·cast·er** *bsd. Am.* Nachrichten-

sprecher *m*; ~ **cin·e·ma** Aktualitätenkino *n*; ~ **con·fer·ence** Pressekonferenz *f*; **'~·flash** (eingeblendete) Kurzmeldung *f*; **'~·let·ter** Rundschreiben *n*; ~ **mag·a·zine** Nachrichtenmagazin *n*; **'~·mon·ger** Neuigkeitskrämer *m*; **'~·pa·per 1.** Zeitung *f*; **2.** Zeitungs...; **'~·print** Zeitungspapier *n*; **'~·read·er** *Br.* Nachrichtensprecher *m*; **'~·reel** *Film:* Wochenschau *f*; **'~·room** Zeitschriftenlesesaal *m*; *Am. Zeitung:* Redaktionsabteilung *f für Nachrichten*; **'~·stall**, *Am.* **'~·stand** Zeitungsstand *m*; **'~·ven·dor** Zeitungsverkäufer *m*; **news·y** ['nju:zi] F voller Nachrichten.

newt *zo.* [nju:t] Wassermolch *m*.

New World ['nju:'wɔ:ld] *die* Neue Welt (*Amerika*); **'new-world** neuweltlich.

new year ['nju:'jə:] Neujahr *n*; ~*'s day* Neujahrstag *m*; ~*'s eve* Silvester(abend *m*) *n*; ~*'s gift* Neujahrsgeschenk *n*.

next [nekst] **1.** *adj.* nächst; nächst (-folgend); ~ *but one der* übernächste; ~ *door* nebenan; ~ *door to fig.* (schon) beinahe; *the* ~ *of kin der* (*pl. die*) nächste(n) Verwandte(n) *od.* Angehörige(n); ~ *to* nächst (*dat.*); ~ *to nothing* fast gar nichts; *what* ~? was denn noch?; **2.** *adv.* zunächst; gleich darauf; dann; demnächst, nächstens.

nex·us ['neksəs] Verknüpfung *f*, Zusammenhang *m*.

nib [nib] (Schreib)Feder *f aus Stahl od. Gold*.

nib·ble ['nibl] *v/t.* knabbern an (*dat.*); benagen, anknabbern; *v/i.* ~ *at* nagen *od.* knabbern an (*dat.*); *fig.* (herum)kritteln an (*dat.*); *fig.* spielen mit.

nib·lick ['niblik] *ein* Golfschläger *m*.

nice □ [nais] fein (*Beobachtung, Sinn; Urteil; Unterschied; Waage etc.*); wählerisch (*about in dat.*); peinlich (genau); heikel; nett; niedlich; hübsch, schön; ~ *and warm* hübsch warm; **'nice·ly** F (sehr) gut; **'nice·ness** Feinheit *f*; Genauigkeit *f*; Nettigkeit *f*; **nice·ty** ['ˌsiti] Feinheit *f*, Schärfe *f*; Genauigkeit *f*; Spitzfindigkeit *f*; *to a* ~ bis aufs Haar; *stand upon niceties* es allzu genau nehmen.

niche [nitʃ] Nische *f*; *fig. der rechte*

Platz.

Nick¹ [nik]: *Old* ~ der Teufel.

nick² [~] **1.** Kerbe *f*; *sl.* Kittchen *n*; *in the (very)* ~ *of time* gerade zur rechten Zeit; **2.** (ein)kerben; *sl.* schnappen (*erwischen*).

nick·el ['nikl] **1.** *min.* Nickel *m* (*Am. a. Fünfcentstück*); ~*in-the-slot machine Am.* Warenautomat *m*; **2.** vernickeln.

nick·el·o·de·on *Am.* [nikl'əudjən] Kintopp *n*; Musikautomat *m*.

nick-nack ['niknæk] = *knickknack.*

nick·name ['nikneim] **1.** Spitzname *m*; **2.** e-n Spitznamen geben (*dat.*).

nic·o·tine ['nikəti:n] Nikotin *n*.

nid-nod ['nidnɔd] nicken.

niece [ni:s] Nichte *f*.

niff *sl.* [nif] Mief *m*, Gestank *m*.

niffed F [nift] eingeschnappt (*beleidigt*).

niff·y *sl.* ['nifi] stinkend.

nif·ty *Am.* ['nifti] **1.** elegant; sauber (*hervorragend*); *sl.* stinkend; **2.** treffende Bemerkung *f*.

nig·gard ['nigəd] **1.** Knicker *m*, Geizhals *m*; **2.** □ karg, geizig; **'nig·gard·li·ness** Knickerei *f*, Geiz *m*; **'nig·gard·ly** *adj. u. adv.* geizig, knauserig; karg.

nig·ger F *mst contp.* ['nigə] Nigger *m* (*Neger*); *that's the* ~ *in the woodpile Am. sl.* da liegt der Hund begraben.

nig·gle ['nigl] (s-e Zeit für Kleinigkeiten ver)trödeln; **'nig·gling** kleinlich; peinlich genau.

nigh † *od. prov.* [nai] = *near.*

night [nait] Nacht *f*; Abend *m*; *by* ~, *in the* ~, *at* ~ nachts, bei Nacht; ~ *out* freier Abend *m*; *make a* ~ *of it* die Nacht durchmachen; **'~-bell** Nachtglocke *f*; **'~-bird** Nacht(raub)vogel *m*; *fig.* Nachtschwärmer *m*; **'~-cap** Nachtmütze *f*; Schlummertrunk *m*; **'~-club** Nachtlokal *n*; **'~-dress** Damennachthemd *n*; **'~-fall** Einbruch *m* der Nacht; **'~-gown** = *night-dress*; **night-in-gale** *orn.* ['~ɪŋgeil] Nachtigall *f*; **'night·ly** Nacht..., nächtlich; jede Nacht.

night...: '~-mare Alptraum *m*, Alpdruck *m*; böser Traum *m*; **'~-school** Abendschule *f*; **'~-shade** ♀ Nachtschatten *m*; *deadly* ~ Tollkirsche *f*; ~ *shift* Nachtschicht *f*; **'~-shirt** (Herren)Nachthemd *n*; **'~-spot** *Am.* Nachtlokal *n*; **'~-stop** Auf-

enthalt *m* mit Übernachtung; **'~-stop** e-n Nachtaufenthalt haben; **'~-time** Nacht(zeit) *f*; **'~-walk·er** Nacht-, Schlafwandler(in); **'~-watch** Nachtwache *f*; **'~-'watch-man** Nachtwächter *m*; **'~-work** Nachtarbeit *f*; **'night·y** F Damen- *od.* Kindernachthemd *n*.

ni·hil·ism ['naiilizəm] Nihilismus *m*; **'ni·hil·ist** Nihilist(in).

nil [nil] *bsd. Sport*: nichts, null.

nim·ble □ ['nimbl] flink, behend, gewandt; **'nim·ble·ness** Behendigkeit *f*; **'nim·ble-'wit·ted** schlagfertig.

nim·bus ['nimbəs] Nimbus *m*, Heiligenschein *m*; Regenwolke *f*.

nim·i·ny-pim·i·ny ['nimini'pimini] zimperlich, geziert.

Nim·rod ['nimrɔd] Nimrod *m* (*großer Jäger*).

nin·com·poop F ['ninkəmpu:p] Einfaltspinsel *m*, Trottel *m*.

nine [nain] **1.** neun; ~ *days' wonder* Tagesgespräch *n*; **2.** Neun *f*; *dressed up to the* ~*s* F aufgedonnert; **'~-fold** neunfach; **'~-pins** *pl.* Kegel *m*/*pl.*; Kegelspiel *n*; **nine·teen** ['~'ti:n] neunzehn; *talk* ~ *to the dozen* unaufhörlich reden; **'nine·teenth** neunzehnte(r, -s); **nine·tieth** ['~tiiθ] **1.** neunzigste(r, -s); **2.** Neunzigstel *n*; **'nine·ty** neunzig.

nin·ny F ['nini] Dummkopf *m*.

ninth [nainθ] **1.** neunte(r, -s); **2.** Neuntel *n*; ♪ None *f*; **'ninth·ly** neuntens.

nip¹ [nip] **1.** Kniff *m*, Kneifen *n*; ♀ Frostbrand *m*; scharfer Frost *m*; **2.** kneifen, zwicken; schneiden (*Kälte*); *durch* Frost beschädigen, vernichten; *sl.* flitzen, huschen, eilen; ~ *in the bud* im Keim ersticken.

nip² [~] **1.** Schlückchen *n*; **2.** nippen.

nip·per ['nipə] F Bengel *m*, Stift *m*; Krebsschere *f*; (*a pair of*) ~*s pl.* (eine) (Kneif)Zange *f*; (ein) Kneifer *m*.

nip·ple ['nipl] Brustwarze *f*; Saughütchen *n*; ⊕ Nippel *m*.

nip·py F ['nipi] **1.** bitter kalt; behende, flink; **2.** Kellnerin *f*.

nir·va·na [niə'va:nə] Nirwana *n*.

Ni·sei *Am.* ['ni'sei] (*a. pl.*) Japaner *m*, geboren in den *USA*.

Nis·sen hut ['nisn'hʌt] Nissenhütte

f, Wellblechbaracke *f*.

nit [nit] Niß *f* (*Ei der Laus etc.*); '~-
-**pick·ing** F pingelig, kleinlich.

ni·trate ⚗ ['naitreit] Nitrat *n*, sal-
petersaures Salz *n*.

ni·tre, ni·ter ⚗ ['naitə] Salpeter *m*.

ni·tric ac·id ⚗ ['naitrik'æsid] Sal-
petersäure *f*.

ni·tro·chalk ['nautrəu'tʃɔːk] *ein*
Rasendünger *m*.

ni·tro·gen ⚗ ['naitrədʒən] Stick-
stoff *m*; **ni·trog·e·nous** [~'trɔdʒi-
nəs] stickstoffhaltig.

ni·tro·glyc·er·ine ⚗ ['naitrəuglisə-
'riːn] Nitroglyzerin *n*.

ni·trous ⚗ ['naitrəs] salpetrig.

nit·ty-grit·ty P ['niti'griti]: *get down to
the* ~ zum problematischen Teil der
Sache kommen.

nit·wit F ['nitwit] Schwachkopf *m*;
'**nit·wit·ted** F schwachsinnig.

nix [niks] Nix *m*; **nix·ie** ['~i] Nixe *f*.

no [nəu] **1.** *adj.* kein; *in* ~ *time* im Nu;
~-*claims bonus* Schadenfreiheitsra-
batt *m od.* -prämie *f*; ~ *man's land*
Niemandsland *n*; ~ *one* keiner, niemand; **2.** *adv.* nein; *beim comp.* nicht;
3. Nein *n*; noes *pl.* Stimmen *f/pl.*
dagegen.

nob¹ *sl.* [nɔb] Dez *m* (*Kopf*); ⊕
Knopf *m*.

nob² *sl.* [~] feiner Pinkel *m*.

nob·ble *sl.* ['nɔbl] *j.* (he)rumkriegen;
et. mopsen (*stehlen*).

nob·by *sl.* ['nɔbi] nobel, schick,
schnieke.

No·bel Prize [nəu'bel'praiz] Nobelpreis *m*; *Nobel Peace Prize* Friedens-
nobelpreis *m*; ~ *winner* Nobelpreis-
träger(in).

no·bil·i·ar·y [nəu'biliəri] Adels...

no·bil·i·ty [nəu'biliti] Adel *m* (*a.
fig.*); Würde *f*.

no·ble ['nəubl] **1.** □ adlig; edel, vornehm; prächtig; vortrefflich; Edel-
... (*Gas, Metall etc.*); **2.** Adlige *m*, *f*;
'~·**man** Edelmann *m*, Adlige *m*;
'~-'**mind·ed** edelgesinnt; '**no·ble·
ness** Adel *m*; Würde *f*; '**no·ble·
wom·an** Edelfrau *f*.

no·bod·y ['nəubədi] **1.** niemand;
2. unbedeutende Persönlichkeit *f*.

nock [nɔk] Kerbe *f*.

noc·tur·nal [nɔk'təːnl] Nacht...

noc·turne ['nɔktəːn] Nachtszene *f*;
♪ Notturno *n*.

nod [nɔd] **1.** *v/i.* nicken; schlafen;
sich neigen; ~*ding acquaintance*

oberflächliche Bekanntschaft *f*; ~ *off*
einnicken; *v/t. Haupt* neigen; ~ *out
j.* hinauswinken; **2.** Nicken *n*;
Wink *m*.

nod·dle F ['nɔdl] Birne *f* (*Kopf*).

node [nəud] Knoten *m* (*a.* ♀ *u. ast.*);
♂ Überbein *n*.

nod·u·lar ['nɔdjulə] knotenartig.

nod·ule ['nɔdjuːl] Knötchen *n*.

No·el [nəu'el] Weihnacht *f*.

nog [nɔg] Holznagel *m*; Holzblock
m; **nog·gin** ['nɔgin] kleiner (hölzerner) Krug *m*; '**nog·ging** 🏗 Riegel-
mauer *f*.

no·how F ['nəuhau] in keiner Weise;
nicht in Ordnung.

noil [nɔil] *Tuchmacherei:* Kämm-
ling *m*, Kurzwolle *f*.

noise [nɔiz] **1.** Lärm *m*; Geräusch *n*;
Geschrei *n*, Aufsehen *n*; *big* ~ *bsd.
Am.* F großes Tier (*Person*) *n*; ~
abatement Lärmbekämpfung *f*; ~ *level*
Geräusch-, Lärmpegel *m*; **2.** ~ *abroad*
in der Öffentlichkeit bekanntmachen; ausschreien.

noise·less □ ['nɔizlis] geräuschlos;
'**noise·less·ness** Geräuschlosig-
keit *f*.

nois·i·ness ['nɔizinis] Geräusch *n*,
Getöse *n*.

noi·some ['nɔisəm] schädlich, ungesund; widerlich; '**noi·some·ness**
Schädlichkeit *f*; Ekelhaftigkeit *f*.

nois·y □ ['nɔizi] geräuschvoll, lärmend; aufdringlich (*Farbe*).

no·mad ['nəuməd] Nomade *m*, No-
madin *f*; **no·mad·ic** [~'mædik]
(~*ally*) nomadisch; **no·mad·ize**
['~mədaiz] nomadisieren.

nom de plume ['nɔ̃ːmdə'pluːm]
Pseudonym *n*, Schriftstellername *m*.

no·men·cla·ture [nəu'menklətʃə]
Nomenklatur *f*; *systematische* Benennung *f*; Fachsprache *f*; Namens-
verzeichnis *n*.

nom·i·nal □ ['nɔminl] nominell;
(nur) dem Namen nach (vorhanden); namentlich; Namen...; ~
value Nennwert *m*; **nom·i·nate**
['~neit] ernennen; zur Wahl vorschlagen; **nom·i'na·tion** Ernennung *f*; Vorschlagsrecht *n*; *in* ~
vorgeschlagen; **nom·i·na·tive** *gr.*
['~nətiv] *a.* ~ *case* Nominativ *m*;
nom·i·na·tor ['~neitə] Ernenner
m; **nom·i·nee** [~'niː] *zu e-m Amt
etc.* Vorgeschlagener *m*, Kandidat
(-in).

non [nɔn] *in Zssgn*: nicht, un..., Nicht...

non·ac·cept·ance [ˈnɔnəkˈseptəns] Nichtannahme *f*.

non·age [ˈnəunidʒ] Minderjährigkeit *f*.

non·a·ge·nar·i·an [nəunədʒiˈnɛəriən] Neunzigjährige *m*, *f*.

non·ag·gres·sion [ˈnɔnəˈgreʃən]: ~ *pact* Nichtangriffspakt *m*.

non·al·co·hol·ic [ˈnɔnælkəˈhɔlik] alkoholfrei.

non·a·lign·ment *pol.* [nɔnəˈlainmənt] Blockfreiheit *f*.

non·ap·pear·ance 🏛 [ˈnɔnəˈpiərəns] Nichterscheinen *n*.

non·at·tend·ance 🏛 [ˈnɔnəˈtendəns] Ausbleiben *n*, Nichterscheinen *n*.

nonce [nɔns]: *for the* ~ nur für diesen Fall; ~ *word* Ad-hoc-Bildung *f* (*für einen besonderen Fall geprägtes Wort*).

non·cha·lance [ˈnɔnʃələns] Lässigkeit *f*; **'non·cha·lant** □ lässig.

non·com ⚔ F [nɔnˈkɔm] Unteroffizier *m*.

non·com·mis·sioned [ˈnɔnkəˈmiʃənd] nicht bevollmächtigt; ohne Bestallung; ~ *officer* ⚔ Unteroffizier *m*.

non·com·mit·tal [ˈnɔnkəˈmitl] unverbindlich, nichtssagend.

non·com·pli·ance [ˈnɔnkəmˈplaiəns] Zuwiderhandlung *f*, Verstoß *m* (*with o.*)

non com·pos men·tis 🏛 [nɔnˈkɔmpɔsˈmentis] unzurechnungsfähig.

non·con·duc·tor ⚡ [ˈnɔnkəndʌktə] Nichtleiter *m*.

non·con·form·ist [ˈnɔnkənˈfɔːmist] Dissident(in), Freikirchler(in); **non·con·form·i·ty** Mangel *m* an Übereinstimmung; *eccl.* Dissidententum *n*.

non·con·ten·tious 🏛 [ˈnɔnkənˈtenʃəs] nicht strittig.

non·de·liv·er·y [ˈnɔndiˈlivəri] Nichtauslieferung *f*, Nichterfüllung *f*.

non·de·nom·i·na·tion·al school [ˈnɔndinəmiˈneiʃənlˈskuːl] Simultanschule *f*.

non·de·script [ˈnɔndiskript] **1.** unbestimmbar; schwer zu beschreibend; **2.** schwer zu beschreibende Person *f*.

none [nʌn] **1.** keine(r, -s); nichts; **2.** keinesfalls, gar nicht; ~ *the less*

nichtsdestoweniger.

non·en·ti·ty [nɔˈnentiti] Nichtsein *n*; Unding *n*; Nichts *n*; *fig.* Null *f*.

non·es·sen·tial [ˈnɔniˈsenʃəl] **1.** unwesentlich; **2.** Unwesentlichkeit *f*.

non·ex·ist·ence [ˈnɔnigˈzistəns] Nicht(da)sein *n*; **'non·ex·ist·ent** nicht vorhanden, nicht existierend.

non·fic·tion [ˈnɔnˈfikʃən] Sachbücher *n/pl.*

non·ha·la·tion *phot.* [ˈnɔnhəˈleiʃən] lichthoffrei.

non·in·ter·fer·ence [ˈnɔnintəˈfiərəns], **non·in·ter·ven·tion** [ˈnɔnintəˈvenʃen] Nichteinmischung *f*.

non·i·ron [ˈnɔnˈaiən] bügelfrei.

non·lad·der·ing [ˈnɔnˈlædəriŋ] maschenfest.

non·mem·ber [ˈnɔnˈmembə] Nichtmitglied *n*.

non·ob·serv·ance [ˈnɔnəbˈzəːvəns] Nichtbeobachtung *f*.

non·pa·reil [nɔnpəˈrel] Unvergleichliche *m*, *f*, *n*; *typ.* Nonpareille (-schrift) *f*.

non·par·ti·san [nɔnˈpɑːtizæn] überparteilich.

non·par·ty *pol.* [ˈnɔnˈpɑːti] parteilos.

non·pay·ment [ˈnɔnˈpeimənt] Nichtzahlung *f*.

non·per·form·ance 🏛 [ˈnɔnpəˈfɔːməns] Nichterfüllung *f*.

non·plus [ˈnɔnˈplʌs] **1.** Verlegenheit *f*; *at a* ~ ratlos; **2.** in Verlegenheit bringen; ~*sed* ratlos, verdutzt.

non·pro·lif·er·a·tion [ˈnɔnprəulifəˈreiʃən] Nichtweiterverbreitung *f* (*von Atomwaffen*); ~ *treaty* Atomsperrvertrag *m*.

non·res·i·dent [ˈnɔnˈrezidənt] nicht am Platze wohnend.

non·sense [ˈnɔnsəns] Unsinn *m*; **non·sen·si·cal** □ [~ˈsensikəl] unsinnig, albern.

non·skid [ˈnɔnˈskid] rutschfest, -sicher (*Reifen etc.*).

non·smok·er [ˈnɔnˈsməukə] Nichtraucher *m*.

non·start·er *fig.* [ˈnɔnˈstɑːtə] *Mensch*: Blindgänger *m*; *Idee, Plan*: totgeborenes Kind *n*, Rohrkrepierer *m*.

non·stick [ˈnɔnˈstik] mit Antihaftbeschichtung (*Pfanne*).

non·stop [ˈnɔnˈstɔp] 🚂 durchgehend; ✈ ohne Zwischenlandung; Ohnehalt...; Nonstop...

non·such [ˈnʌnsʌtʃ] Unvergleichliche *m*, *f*, *n*.

non·suit ⚖ ['nɔn'sju:t] Abweisung *f* einer Klage.

non-U F ['nɔnju:] unkultiviert.

non-un·ion [nɔn'ju:njən] nicht organisiert (*Arbeiter*).

noo·dle¹ F ['nu:dl] Dummkopf *m*.

noo·dle² [‿] Nudel *f*.

nook [nuk] Ecke *f*, Winkel *m*.

noon [nu:n] **1.** Mittag *m*; **2.** mittägig; Mittags...; '**‿·day**, '**‿·tide** = noon.

noose [nu:s] **1.** Schlinge *f*; **2.** (mit der Schlinge) fangen; schlingen.

nope *Am.* F [nəup] nein!

nor [nɔ:] *nach neither*: noch; *am Satzanfang*: auch nicht; ‿ *do I* ich auch nicht.

Nor·folk jack·et ['nɔ:fək'dʒækit] Herrenjackett *n* mit Gürtel.

norm [nɔ:m] Norm *f*; Regel *f*; Muster *n*; Maßstab *m*; '**nor·mal** □ **1.** normal, regelrecht, üblich; ⅋ senkrecht; ‿ *school* Pädagogische Hochschule *f*; **2.** Normalstand *m*; ⅋ Senkrechte *f*; '**nor·mal·ize** normalisieren; normen.

Nor·man ['nɔ:mən] **1.** Normanne *m*; **2.** normannisch.

Norse [nɔ:s] **1.** norwegisch; **2.** Norwegisch *n*; '**Norse·man** Nordländer *m*; Norweger *m*.

north [nɔ:θ] **1.** Nord(en) *m*; **2.** nördlich; Nord...; '**‿·bound** in Richtung Norden fahrend; '**‿·east 1.** Nordost *m*; **2.** *a.* **‿·'east·ern** nordöstlich; **north·er·ly** ['‿ðəli] nördlich; **north·ern** ['‿ðən] nördlich; Nord...; '**north·ern·er** Nordländer(in); ⚥ *Am.* Nordstaatler *m*; '**north·ern·most** nördlichst; **north·ing** ⚓ ['‿θiŋ] Weg *m*, *ast.* Distanz *f* nach Nord; '**North·man** Nordländer *m*, Skandinavier *m*; Wikinger *m*; **north·ward(·ly)** ['‿wəd(li)] *adj. u. adv.*, **north·wards** ['‿wədz] *adv.* nördlich; nordwärts.

north...: '‿·'west 1. Nordwest *m*; **2.** *a.* **'‿·'west·ern**, '**‿·'west·er·ly** nordwestlich.

Nor·we·gian [nɔ:'wi:dʒən] **1.** norwegisch; **2.** Norweger(in).

nose [nəuz] **1.** Nase *f*; Spitze *f*; Mündung *f* *e-s Rohres*; Schnauze *f*, Tülle *f*; *cut off one's ‿ to spite one's face* sich ins eigene Fleisch schneiden; *pay through the ‿* sich übervorteilen lassen, zuviel bezahlen; *poke od. push od. thrust one's ‿ into*

s.th. s-e Nase in et. (hinein)stecken; *turn one's ‿ up at* die Nase rümpfen über; *put s.o.'s ‿ out of joint* j-m e-n Strich durch die Rechnung machen; *j-m die Freundin etc.* ausspannen; **2.** *v/t. a.* ‿ *out* riechen, wittern; ‿ *one's way* vorsichtig fahren; *v/i.* schnüffeln (*after, for* nach); '**‿·bag** Futterbeutel *m*; '**‿·band** Nasenriemen *m*; '**‿·cone** Raketenspitze *f*; **nosed** ...nasig.

nose...: '‿·dive ✈ Sturzflug *m*; '**‿·gay** Blumenstrauß *m*; '**‿·heav·y** ✈ kopflastig; '**‿·o·ver** ✈ Überschlagen *n beim Landen*; '**‿·ring** Nasenring *m*.

nos·ing ⌂ ['nəuziŋ] Ausladung *f*, Kante *f*.

nos·tal·gi·a [nɔs'tældʒiə] Heimweh *n*; Nostalgie *f*, Sehnsucht *f* (*nach et. Vergangenem*); **nos'tal·gic** [‿dʒik] Heimweh...; heimwehkrank; nostalgisch, wehmütig.

nos·tril ['nɔstril] Nasenloch *n*, Nüster *f*.

nos·trum ['nɔstrəm] Geheimmittel *n*; Patentlösung *f*.

nos·y ['nəuzi] **1.** duftend; *b. s.* muffig; F neugierig; ⚥ *Parker* = **2.** neugieriger Kerl *m*.

not [nɔt] nicht.

no·ta·bil·i·ty [nəutə'biliti] wichtige Persönlichkeit *f*; hervorragende Eigenschaft *f*; '**no·ta·ble 1.** □ bemerkenswert; namhaft; bedeutend; angesehen; hausfraulich tüchtig, fleißig; **2.** angesehene Person *f*, Standesperson *f*; '**no·ta·bly** ganz besonders.

no·tar·i·al □ [nəu'tɛəriəl] Notariats-...; notariell (beglaubigt); **no·ta·ry** ['nəutəri] *oft public* ‿ Notar *m*.

no·ta·tion [nəu'teiʃən] Bezeichnung *f* (*bsd.* ⅋ *u.* ♪); Zeichensystem *n*.

notch [nɔtʃ] **1.** Kerbe *f*, Einschnitt *m*; ⊕ Nut(e) *f*; *Am.* Engpaß *m*, Hohlweg *m*; **2.** einkerben; nuten.

note [nəut] **1.** Zeichen *n*, Merkmal *n*; Brandmal *n*; (Satz)Zeichen *n*; Notiz *f*, Aufzeichnung *f*; Anmerkung *f*; Briefchen *n*; (*bsd.* Schuld-) Schein *m*, Zettel *m*; ♪, *pol.*, ✝ Note *f*; ♪ Taste *f*; Ton *m*; Klang *m*; Bedeutung *f*, Ruf *m*; Beachtung *f*; *take ‿s of* sich Notizen machen über (*acc.*); *strike the right ‿* den rechten Ton treffen; *strike od. sound a false ‿* sich im Ton vergreifen; **2.** be(ob)achten; besonders erwähnen; merken, zur Kenntnis nehmen; *a.* ~ *down* notieren, aufschreiben; mit Anmerkungen versehen; *Wechsel* protestieren; '~**book** Notizbuch *n*; Heft *n*; '**not·ed** bekannt, berühmt; berüchtigt (*for* wegen); ~*ly* deutlich; besonders; '**note·pa·per** Briefpapier *n*; '**note·wor·thy** bemerkens-, beachtenswert.

noth·ing ['nʌθiŋ] **1.** nichts; Nichts *n*; Null *f*; *for* ~ umsonst; *good for* ~ untauglich; *bring* (*come*) *to* ~ zunichte machen (werden); *go for* ~ umsonst sein (*Mühe etc.*); *make* ~ *of* sich nichts machen aus; *I can make* ~ *of it* ich kann damit nichts anfangen; *think* ~ *of et.* als normal betrachten; **2.** *adv.* durchaus nicht; '**noth·ing·ness** Nichts *n*; Nichtigkeit *f*.

no·tice ['nəutis] **1.** Notiz *f*, Nachricht *f*, Anzeige *f*; Bekanntmachung *f*; Kenntnis *f*; Kündigung *f*; Warnung *f*; Aufmerksamkeit *f*, Beachtung *f*, Notiz *f*; (Buch-)Besprechung *f*; *at short* ~ kurzfristig; *give* ~ *that* bekanntgeben, daß, *give a week's* ~ j-m acht Tage vorher kündigen; *take* ~ *of* Notiz nehmen von, Beachtung schenken (*dat.*); *until further* ~ bis auf weiteres; *without* ~ fristlos; ~ *of departure* Abmeldung *f*; **2.** bemerken, beobachten; feststellen; beachten; erwähnen; F mit Aufmerksamkeit behandeln; *Buch* besprechen; '**no·tice·a·ble** □ wahrnehmbar; bemerkenswert; beachtlich; '**no·tice·board** Anschlagbrett *n*; Schwarzes Brett *n*.

no·ti·fi·a·ble ['nəutifaiəbl] meldepflichtig; **no·ti·fi·ca·tion** [~fi'keiʃən] Anzeige *f*; Meldung *f*; Bekanntmachung *f*; Ankündigung *f*. **no·ti·fy** ['nəutifai] *et.* anzeigen, melden; bekanntmachen; *j.* benachrichtigen.

no·tion ['nəuʃən] Begriff *m*, Vorstellung *f*, Idee *f*; Meinung *f*, Ansicht *f*; Absicht *f*; ~*s pl. Am.* Kurzwaren *f/pl.*; *kleine* Gebrauchsartikel *m/pl.*; *have no* ~ *of* keine Ahnung haben von; '**no·tion·al** □ begrifflich; nur in der Vorstellung vorhanden; grillenhaft; ausgefallen. **no·to·ri·e·ty** [nəutə'raiəti] Allbekanntheit *f*; allbekannte Sache *f*

od. Person *f*; **no·to·ri·ous** □ [~'tɔ:riəs] all-, stadt-, weltbekannt; notorisch; *b. s.* berüchtigt (*for* wegen). **not·with·stand·ing** [nɔtwiθ'stændiŋ] **1.** *prp.* ungeachtet, trotz (*gen.*); **2.** *adv.* trotzdem, dennoch; **3.** *cj.* ~ *that* obgleich.

nou·gat ['nu:gɑ:] Nougat *m*.

nought *bsd.* Å [nɔ:t] Null *f*, Nichts *n*; *come to* ~ zunichte werden, fehlschlagen.

noun *gr.* [naun] Substantiv *n*, Hauptwort *n*.

nour·ish ['nʌriʃ] (er)nähren; *fig.* nähren, hegen; '**nour·ish·ing** nahrhaft; '**nour·ish·ment** Ernährung *f*, Nahrung(smittel *n*) *f*.

nous [naus] Vernunft *f*; gesunder Menschenverstand *m*.

nov·el ['nɔvəl] **1.** neu; ungewöhnlich; **2.** Roman *m*; *short* ~ = **nov·el·ette** [nɔvə'let] kurzer Roman *m*; '**nov·el·ist** Romanschriftsteller(in), Romancier *m*; '**nov·el·ty** ['nɔvəlti] Neuheit *f*.

No·vem·ber [nəu'vembə] November *m*.

nov·ice ['nɔvis] Neuling *m*, Anfänger *m*; *eccl.* Novize *m, f*.

no·vi·ci·ate, no·vi·ti·ate [nəu'viʃiit] Lehr(lings)zeit *f*; Noviziat *n*.

now [nau] **1.** nun, jetzt; eben; nun (aber); *by* ~ mittlerweile, jetzt; *just* ~ soeben; *before* ~ schon früher; ~ *and again*, ~ *and then* dann u. wann, hin u. wieder, manchmal; **2.** *cj. a.* ~ *that* nun da; **3.** Jetzt *n*.

now·a·day ['nauədei] heutig; **now·a·days** ['~z] heutzutage.

no·way(s) F ['nəuwei(z)] keineswegs.

no·where ['nəuweə] nirgends.

no·wise ['nəuwaiz] keineswegs; in keiner Weise.

nox·ious □ ['nɔkʃəs] schädlich.

noz·zle ['nɔzl] ⊕ Düse *f*; Tülle *f*.

nu·ance [nju:'ɑ̃:ns] Nuance *f*, Schattierung *f*.

nub [nʌb] Knubbe(n *m*) *f*; *Am.* F springende Punkt *m in e-r Sache*.

nu·bile ['nju:bail] heiratsfähig.

nu·cle·ar ['nju:kliə] Kern..., Nuklear..., Atom...; ~ *deterrent* nukleares Abschreckungsmittel *n*; ~ *disintegration* Kernzerfall *m*; ~ *energy*, ~ *power* Kernkraft *f*, -energie *f*; ~ *physics sg.* Kernphysik *f*; ~ *pile* Atomsäule *f*; ~ *power plant* Kernkraftwerk *n*; ~ *research* (Atom)Kernforschung *f*; ~

submarine Atom-U-Boot *n*; ⁓ *warfare* Atomkrieg *m*; ⁓ *warhead* Atomsprengkopf *m*; **nu·cle·on** *phys.* [ˈ⌣kliɔn] Nukleon *n*; **nu·cle·us** [ˈ⌣kliəs], *pl. a.* **nu·cle·i** [ˈ⌣kliai] Kern *m*.

nude [njuːd] **1.** nackt; **2.** nackter Körper *m*; *paint.* Akt *m*; *study from the* ⌣ Aktstudie *f*.

nudge F [nʌdʒ] **1.** *j.* heimlich anstoßen; **2.** Rippenstoß *m*.

nud·ism [ˈnjuːdizəm] Freikörper-, Nacktkultur *f*; **nud·ist** Anhänger (-in) der Freikörperkultur; ⌣ *camp*, ⌣ *colony* FKK-Platz *m*; **nu·di·ty** Nacktheit *f*; nackte Figur *f*.

nu·ga·to·ry [ˈnjuːgətəri] albern, kindisch; unwirksam.

nug·get [ˈnʌgit] (*bsd.* Gold)Klumpen *m*.

nui·sance [ˈnjuːsns] Mißstand *m*; Ärgernis *n*; Unfug *m*; *fig.* Last *f*, Plage *f* (*a. Person*); Quälgeist *m*; *what a* ⌣! wie ärgerlich!; *commit no* ⌣! dieser Ort darf nicht verunreinigt werden!; *make o.s. od. be a* ⌣ lästig fallen.

nuke *Am. sl.* [nuːk] Atom-, Kernwaffe *f*; Atom-, Kernkraftwerk *n*.

null [nʌl] *rtš u. fig.* nichtig; nichtssagend (*Gesicht*); ⌣ *and void* null u. nichtig; **nul·li·fi·ca·tion** [nʌlifiˈkeiʃən] Ungültigkeitserklärung *f*; **nul·li·fy** [ˈ⌣fai] zunichte machen; aufheben, ungültig machen; **nul·li·ty** Nichtigkeit *f*, Ungültigkeit *f*; Nichts *n*; *fig.* Null *f*.

numb [nʌm] **1.** starr (*with* vor *Kälte etc.*); taub (*empfindungslos*); **2.** starr *od.* taub machen; ⌣*ed* erstarrt.

num·ber [ˈnʌmbə] **1.** Nummer *f*; Zahl *f* (*a. gr.*); Anzahl *f*; Heft *n*, Lieferung *f*, Nummer *f e-s Werkes*; ⌣*s pl. poet.* Verse *m/pl.*; ♪ Weise(n *pl.*) *f*; *without* ⌣ zahllos; *in* ⌣ an der Zahl; **2.** zählen; numerieren; ⌣ *among*, ⌣ *in*, ⌣ *with* rechnen zu *od.* unter (*acc.*); **num·ber·less** zahllos; **num·ber one** F die eigene Person *f*, das liebe Ich; *look after* ⌣ den eigenen Vorteil wahren; **num·ber-plate** *mot.* Nummernschild *n*.

numb·ness [ˈnʌmnis] Erstarrung *f*, Betäubung *f*; Starr-, Taubheit *f*.

nu·mer·a·ble [ˈnjuːmərəbl] zählbar; **nu·mer·al 1.** Zahl...; **2.** Zahlzeichen *n*, Ziffer *f*; Zahlwort *n*;

nu·mer·a·tion Zählen *n*; Zählung *f*; Numerierung *f*; **nu·mer·a·tor** Å Zähler *m e-s Bruches*.

nu·mer·i·cal □ [njuːˈmerikəl] numerisch, zahlenmäßig; Zahl...

nu·mer·ous □ [ˈnjuːmərəs] zahlreich; **nu·mer·ous·ness** große Zahl *f*.

nu·mis·mat·ic [njuːmizˈmætik] (⌣*ally*) numismatisch; Münz...; **nu·mis'mat·ics** *mst sg.* Numismatik *f*, Münzkunde *f*; **nu'mis·ma·tist** [⌣mətist] Numismatiker *m*.

num·skull F [ˈnʌmskʌl] Dummkopf *m*.   [meise *f*.\

nun [nʌn] Nonne *f*; *orn.* Blau-\

nun·ci·a·ture *eccl.* [ˈnʌnʃjətʃə] Nuntiatur *f*; **nun·ci·o** *eccl.* [ˈ⌣ʃiəu] Nuntius *m*.

nun·ner·y [ˈnʌnəri] Nonnenkloster *n*.

nup·tial [ˈnʌpʃəl] **1.** Hochzeits..., Ehe..., Braut...; **2.** ⌣*s pl.* Hochzeit *f*.

nurse [nɔːs] **1.** Kindermädchen *n*, Säuglingsschwester *f*; *a.* wet ⌣, Amme *f*; (Kranken)Pflegerin *f*, (Kranken)Schwester *f*; *at* ⌣ in Pflege; *put out to* ⌣ in Pflege geben; **2.** stillen, nähren, säugen; auf-, großziehen; pflegen, warten; hätscheln, liebkosen; ⌣ *a cold* e-e Erkältung auskurieren; **⌣-maid** Kindermädchen *n*.

nurs·er·y [ˈnɔːsri] Kinderzimmer *n*; ♪ Baumschule *f*; *fig.* Pflegestätte *f*; ⌣ *school* Kindergarten *m*; **⌣·man** Kunstgärtner *m*; **⌣-rhymes** *pl.* Kinderlieder *n/pl.*, -reime *m/pl.*; ⌣ *slopes pl. Ski:* Idiotenhügel *m/pl.*

nurs·ing [ˈnɔːsiŋ] Still-n; (Kranken)Pflege *f*; **⌣-bot·tle** Saugflasche *f*; **⌣-home** Privatklinik *f*.

nurs·ling [ˈnɔːsliŋ] Säugling *m*, Pflegling *m*; Liebling *m*; Hätschelkind *n*.

nur·ture [ˈnɔːtʃə] **1.** Pflege *f*; Erziehung *f*; **2.** *a.* ⌣ *up* aufziehen; *fig.* nähren.

nut [nʌt] **1.** Nuß *f*; ⊕ (Schrauben-) Mutter *f*; *sl.* Birne *f* (*Kopf*); Verrückte *m*; ⌣*s pl.* Nußkohle *f*; *that is* ⌣*s to od. for him sl.* das ist was für ihn; *be* ⌣*s on sl.* verrückt sein nach; *drive* ⌣*s sl.* verrückt machen; *go* ⌣*s sl.* verrückt werden; **2.** *go* ⌣*ting* in die Nüsse gehen.

nu·ta·tion *ast.* [njuːˈteiʃən] Schwanken *n der Erdachse*.

nut·crack·er [ˈnʌtkrækə], *mst (a*

pair of) ~s *pl.* (ein) Nußknacker *m*; **'nut-gall** Gallapfel *m*; **nut-meg** ['~meg] Muskatnuß *f*.

nu-tri-a ['nju:triə] Nutria(fell *n*) *f*.

nu-tri-ent ['nju:triənt] **1.** Ernährungs...; **2.** Nährstoff *m*; **'nu-tri-ment** Nahrung *f*, Futter *n*.

nu-tri-tion [nju:'triʃən] Ernährung *f*; Nahrung *f*; **nu-tri-tion-al** [~'tri-ʃənl] Ernährungs...; ~ *science* Ernährungswissenschaft *f*; **nu'tri-tious** □ nährend, nahrhaft; Ernährungs...; **nu'tri-tious-ness** Nahrhaftigkeit *f*.

nu-tri-tive □ ['nju:tritiv] = *nutritious*.

nut-shell ['nʌtʃel] Nußschale *f*; *in a* ~ *in* aller Kürze; **'nut-ting** *s*. *nut* 2; **nut-ty** ['nʌti] nußreich; nußartig; *sl.* verrückt (*on* nach).

nuz-zle ['nʌzl] mit der Schnauze wühlen *od.* stoßen; *a.* ~ *o.s.* sich (an)schmiegen.

ny-lon ['nailɔn] Nylon *n* (*Kunstfaser*); ~s *pl.* Nylonstrümpfe *m/pl.*

nymph [nimf] Nymphe *f*.

O

o [əu] **1.** oh!; ach!; **2.** (*in Telephonnummern*) Null *f*.

oaf [əuf] Dummkopf *m*; Tölpel *m*; **'oaf-ish** dumm.

oak [əuk] **1.** *su.* Eiche *f*; Eichentür *f*; *s. sport*; **2.** *adj.* eichen; '~**ap-ple**, '~**gall** Gallapfel *m*; **'oak-en** *adj.* eichen.

oa-kum ['əukəm] Werg *n*.

oar [ɔ:] **1.** Ruder *n*, Riemen *m*; F Ruderer *m*; *pull a good* ~ ein guter Ruderer sein; *put in one's* ~ F sich einmischen; *rest on one's* ~s ausspannen, sich ausruhen; **2.** rudern; **oared** [ɔ:d] mit Rudern; ...rud(e)-rig; **oars-man** ['ɔ:zmən] Ruderer *m*; **'oars-man-ship** Gewandtheit *f* im Rudern; **'oars-wom-an** Ruderin *f*.

o-a-sis [əu'eisis], *pl.* **o'a-ses** [~si:z] Oase *f* (*a. fig.*).

oast [əust] Hopfendarre *f*.

oat [əut] *mst* ~s *pl.* Hafer *m*; *feel one's* ~s *Am.* F groß sich in Form sein; sich wichtig vorkommen; *sow one's wild* ~s sich austoben; **'oat-en** Hafer...

oath [əuθ], *pl.* **oaths** [əuðz] Eid *m*; Schwur *m*; *b. s.* Fluch *m*; *administer od. tender an* ~ *to s.o., put s.o. to od. on his* ~ j. schwören lassen; *bind by* ~ eidlich verpflichten; *on* ~ eidlich, unter Eid; *take od. make od. swear an* ~ e-n Eid leisten *od.* ablegen, schwören (*on, to* auf *acc.*).

oat-meal ['əutmi:l] Haferflocken

f/pl.; -mehl *n*.

ob-du-ra-cy ['ɔbdjurəsi] Verstocktheit *f*; **ob-du-rate** □ ['~rit] verstockt.

o-be-di-ence [ə'bi:djəns] Gehorsam *m*; *in* ~ *to* gemäß (*dat.*), gehorchend (*dat.*); **o'be-di-ent** □ gehorsam.

o-bei-sance [əu'beisəns] Ehrerbietung *f*; Verbeugung *f*; *do od. make od. pay* ~ huldigen.

ob-e-lisk ['ɔbilisk] Obelisk *m*; *typ.* Kreuz(zeichen) *n*.

o-bese □ [əu'bi:s] fettleibig; **o'bese-ness, o'bes-i-ty** Fettleibigkeit *f*.

o-bey [ə'bei] gehorchen (*dat.*); *Befehl etc.* befolgen, Folge leisten (*dat.*).

ob-fus-cate *fig.* ['ɔbfʌskeit] verwirren; verdunkeln.

o-bit-u-ar-y [ə'bitjuəri] **1.** Totenliste *f*; Todesanzeige *f*; Nachruf *m*; **2.** Todes...; ~ *notice* Todesanzeige *f*.

ob-ject 1. ['ɔbdʒikt] Gegenstand *m*; Ziel *n*, *fig.* Zweck *m*; *gr.* Objekt *n*; komische *od.* erbärmliche Sache *f od.* Person *f*; *what an* ~ *you look!* wie komisch du aussiehst!; *salary no* ~ Gehalt Nebensache; **2.** [əb'dʒekt] *v/t.* einwenden (*to* gegen); *v/i. et.* dagegen haben (*to ger.* daß); Einspruch erheben, protestieren (*to* gegen); ~**glass** *opt.* ['ɔbdʒiktgla:s] Objektiv *n*.

ob-jec-tion [əb'dʒekʃən] Einwand *m*; *there is no* ~ (*to it*) es ist nichts (dagegen) einzuwenden; **ob'jec-**

tion·a·ble □ [~ʃnəbl] nicht einwandfrei; unangenehm.
ob·jec·tive [ɔbˈdʒektiv] **1.** □ objektiv, sachlich; **2.** (✕ Operations-)
Ziel n; opt. Objektiv n; a. ~ case gr.
Objektsfall m; **obˈjec·tive·ness,**
ob·jecˈtiv·i·ty Objektivität f, Sachlichkeit f.
obˈject...: 'ˈ~·lens opt. Objektiv n;
'~·less □ gegenstandslos, zwecklos;
'~·les·son Anschauungsunterricht
m; fig. praktisches Beispiel n; **'~·**
teach·ing Anschauungsunterricht
m; **ob·jec·tor** [əbˈdʒektə] Gegner
m; s. conscientious.
ob·jur·gate [ˈɔbdʒɔːgeit] schelten;
ob·jurˈga·tion Tadel m; **obˈjur·**
ga·to·ry [~gətəri] scheltend.
ob·late □ [ˈɔbleit] (an den Polen)
abgeplattet; **'ob·late·ness** Ab-
plattung f.
ob·la·tion [əuˈbleiʃen] Opfer(gabe f)
n.
ob·li·gate fig. [ˈɔbligeit] binden, verpflichten; **ob·liˈga·tion** Verpflichtung f, Verbindlichkeit f; Schuld-
verschreibung f, Obligation f; be
under (an) ~ to s.o. j-m zu Dank
verpflichtet sein; be under ~ to inf.
die Verpflichtung haben, zu inf.;
ob·lig·a·to·ry □ [ˈ~gətəri] ver-
pflichtend; verbindlich (on für).
o·blige [əˈblaidʒ] v/t. (zu Dank) verpflichten; nötigen, zwingen; ~ s.o.
j-m e-n Gefallen tun; ~ the company
with die Gesellschaft mit e-m Lied
etc. erfreuen; be ~d müssen; much
~d sehr verbunden; danke bestens;
v/i. ~ with a song etc. F ein Lied etc.
zum besten geben; please ~ with
an early reply um baldige Antwort
wird gebeten; **ob·li·gee** [ɔbliˈdʒiː]
Gläubiger m; **o·blig·ing** □
[əˈblaidʒiŋ] verbindlich, hilfsbereit,
gefällig; **oˈblig·ing·ness** Zuvor-
kommenheit f; **ob·li·gor** [ɔbliˈgɔː]
Schuldner m.
ob·lique □ [əˈbliːk] schief, schräg;
mittelbar, versteckt; unaufrichtig;
gr. abhängig (Rede); ~ case abhän-
giger Fall m; **obˈlique·ness, ob-**
liqˈui·ty [əˈblikwiti] Schiefheit f;
schiefe Richtung f; Verirrung f.
ob·lit·er·ate [əˈblitəreit] auslöschen,
tilgen (a. fig.); Schrift ausstreichen;
Briefmarken entwerten; **ob·lit·er·**
'a·tion Auslöschen n; Tilgung f,
Vernichtung f.

25 TW E I

ob·liv·i·on [əˈbliviən] Vergessen n;
Vergessenheit f; pol. Amnestie f;
fall od. sink into ~ in Vergessenheit
geraten; **obˈliv·i·ous** □ be ~ of et.
vergessen; be ~ to et. nicht beachten.
ob·long [ˈɔblɔŋ] **1.** länglich; rechteckig; **2.** Rechteck n.
ob·lo·quy [ˈɔbləkwi] Schmähung f;
Vorwurf m; Schande f.
ob·nox·ious □ [əbˈnɔkʃəs] anstößig;
widerwärtig, verhaßt; **obˈnox·**
ious·ness Anstößigkeit f; Ver-
haßtheit f.
o·boe ♩ [ˈəubəu] Oboe f.
ob·scene □ [ɔbˈsiːn] obszön, unanständig, unzüchtig; zotig; **ob-**
ˈscen·i·ty [~niti] Obszönität f, Unanständigkeit f; Zote f.
ob·scu·ra·tion [ɔbskjuəˈreiʃən] Verdunkelung f; **ob·scure** [əbˈskjuə]
1. □ dunkel (a. fig.); unbekannt,
unbedeutend; verborgen; **2.** verdunkeln; verdecken; verbergen;
obˈscu·ri·ty Dunkelheit f (a. fig.);
Unbekanntheit f; Niedrigkeit f der
Geburt.
ob·se·quies [ˈɔbsikwiz] pl. Leichenbegängnis n, Trauerfeier f.
ob·se·qui·ous □ [əbˈsiːkwiəs] unterwürfig (to gegen); knechtisch; **ob-**
ˈse·qui·ous·ness Unterwürfigkeit f.
ob·serv·a·ble □ [əbˈzəːvəbl] be-
merkbar; bemerkenswert; **obˈserv-**
ance Befolgung f, Einhaltung f
von Gesetzen etc.; Brauch m, Sitte f;
eccl. Observanz f; **obˈserv·ant** □
beobachtend (of acc.); achtsam,
aufmerksam (of auf acc.); be ~ of the
rules die Regeln beachten; **ob·ser-**
va·tion [ɔbzəˈveiʃən] Beobachtung
f; Bemerkung f; attr. Beobach-
tungs...; Aussichts...; ~ car 🚃 Aus-
sichtswagen m; ~ platform Aus-
sichtsterrasse f; ~ ward 🚑 Beobach-
tungsstation f; **obˈserv·a·to·ry** [əb-
ˈzɔːvətri] Observatorium n, Stern-
warte f; Wetterwarte f; **obˈserve** v/t.
beobachten; fig. beachten; Regel etc.
ein-, innehalten; acht(geb)en auf
(acc.); bemerken (wahrnehmen; sagen); v/i. sich äußern (on über acc.);
obˈserv·er Beobachter(in).
ob·sess [əbˈses] heimsuchen, quälen;
~ed by od. with besessen von; **ob-**
ses·sion [əbˈseʃən] Besessenheit f,
fixe Idee f.   [dian m.]
ob·sid·i·an min. [ɔbˈsidiən] Obsi-]
ob·so·les·cence [ɔbsəuˈlesns] Ver-

alten *n*; **ob·so'les·cent** veraltend.
ob·so·lete [ˈɔbsəliːt] veraltet; altmodisch; *biol.* zurückgeblieben.
ob·sta·cle [ˈɔbstəkl] Hindernis *n*; ~ **race** Hindernisrennen *n*.
ob·stet·ric [ɔbˈstetrik], **ob'stet·ri·cal** ⚕ Entbindungs..., geburtshilflich; **ob·ste·tri·cian** [⌐ˈtriʃən] Geburtshelfer *m*; **ob'stet·rics** [⌐triks] *mst sg.* Geburtshilfe *f*.
ob·sti·na·cy [ˈɔbstinəsi] Hartnäckigkeit *f*; Starr-, Eigensinn *m*; **ob·sti·nate** □ [⌐nit] halsstarrig; eigensinnig; hartnäckig (*fig. Krankheit*).
ob·strep·er·ous □ [əbˈstrepərəs] lärmend; ungebärdig.
ob·struct [əbˈstrʌkt] *v/t.* verstopfen, versperren; hindern; *v/i.* Obstruktion treiben; **ob'struc·tion** Verstopfung *f*; Hemmung *f*; *parl.* Obstruktion *f*; Hindernis *n*; **ob'struc·tive** □ [⌐tiv] hinderlich (*of* für).
ob·tain [əbˈtein] *v/t.* erlangen, erhalten, erreichen, bekommen; *Preis* erzielen; *v/i.* sich erhalten (haben), bestehen; **ob'tain·a·ble** erlangbar; ✝ erhältlich; **ob'tain·ment** Erlangung *f*.
ob·trude [əbˈtruːd] (sich) aufdrängen (*on dat.*); **ob'tru·sion** [⌐ʒən] Aufdrängen *n*; Aufdringlichkeit *f*; **ob'tru·sive** □ [⌐siv] aufdringlich.
ob·tu·rate [ˈɔbtjuəreit] verstopfen, abdichten; **ob·tu·ra·tor** Abdichtung(smittel *n*) *f*.
ob·tuse □ [əbˈtjuːs] stumpf (*a.* ⋀ *Winkel*); *fig.* stumpf(sinnig); schwerfällig; **ob'tuse·ness** Stumpfheit *f* (*a. fig.*).
ob·verse [ˈɔbvəːs] Vorderseite *f*; Bildseite *f* *e-r Münze*; *fig.* Gegenstück *n*.
ob·vi·ate *fig.* [ˈɔbvieit] begegnen, vorbeugen (*dat.*); aus dem Weg räumen.
ob·vi·ous □ [ˈɔbviəs] offensichtlich, augenfällig, einleuchtend, klar; **ob·vi·ous·ness** Offensichtlichkeit *f*.
oc·ca·sion [əˈkeiʒən] **1.** Gelegenheit *f*; Anlaß *m*; Grund *m*; Veranlassung *f*; F (*festliches*) Ereignis *n*; *on* ~ gelegentlich; *on the* ~ *of* anläßlich (*gen.*); *rise to the* ~ sich der Lage gewachsen zeigen; **2.** verursachen, veranlassen; **oc'ca·sion·al** □ [⌐ʒənl] gelegentlich; Gelegenheits...; zufällig; **oc'ca·sion·al·ly** [⌐ʒnəli] gele-

gentlich, ab u. zu, dann u. wann, manchmal.
oc·ci·dent *poet. u. rhet.* [ˈɔksidənt] Westen *m*; Abendland *n*; Okzident *m*; **oc·ci·den·tal** □ [⌐ˈdentl] abendländisch, westlich.
oc·cult □ [ɔˈkʌlt] geheim, verborgen; magisch, okkult; **oc·cul'ta·tion** *ast.* Verfinsterung *f*; **oc·cult·ism** [ˈɔkəltizəm] Geheimwissenschaft *f*, Okkultismus *m*; **'oc·cult·ist** Okkultist(in); **oc·cult·ness** [ɔˈkʌltnis] Verborgenheit *f*.
oc·cu·pan·cy [ˈɔkjupənsi] Besitz (-ergreifung *f*) *m*; Einzug *m* (*of in e-e Wohnung*); **'oc·cu·pant** Besitzergreifer(in); Inhaber(in); Bewohner(in); **oc·cu'pa·tion** Besitz(ergreifung *f*) *m*; ⚔ Besetzung *f*; Beruf *m*; Beschäftigung *f*; Zeitvertreib *m*; **oc·cu'pa·tion·al** [⌐ʃənl] Berufs...; ~ *disease* Berufskrankheit *f*; ~ *hazard* Berufsrisiko *n*; ~ *therapy* Beschäftigungstherapie *f*; **oc·cu·pi·er** [ˈɔkjupaiə] *s. occupant*; **oc·cu·py** [ˈ⌐pai] einnehmen, in Besitz nehmen; ⚔ besetzen; besitzen; *Amt* bekleiden, innehaben; *Raum* einnehmen; *Wohnung* beziehen; bewohnen; *Zeit in Anspruch nehmen; beschäftigen; ~ o.s. od. be occupied with od. in* sich beschäftigen mit, arbeiten an (*dat.*).
oc·cur [əˈkəː] vorkommen; sich finden; sich ereignen, geschehen; *it ~red to me* es fiel mir ein; **oc·cur·rence** [əˈkʌrəns] Vorkommen *n*; Vorfall *m*, Ereignis *n*, Geschehnis *n*.
o·cean [ˈəuʃən] Ozean *m*, Meer *n*; ~ *liner* Ozeandampfer *m*; ~ *yacht* Hochseejacht *f*; ~s *of time* F massenhaft Zeit; **'~-go·ing** Übersee...; seetüchtig; **o·ce·an·ic** [əuʃiˈænik] Meeres..., See...
o·chre *min.* [ˈəukə] Ocker *m*.
o'clock [əˈklɔk] Uhr (*bei Zeitangaben*); *five* ~ fünf Uhr.
oc·ta·gon [ˈɔktəgən] Achteck *n*; **oc·tag·o·nal** [ɔkˈtægənl] achteckig.
oc·tane 🜛 [ˈɔktein] Oktan *n*; ~ *rating mot.* Oktanzahl *f*.
oc·tave ♩ [ˈɔktiv] Oktave *f*; **oc·ta·vo** [ɔkˈteivəu] Oktav(format *n*, -band *m*) *n*; **oc·tet(te)** [ɔkˈtet] ♩ Oktett *n*; *die beiden Quartette e-s Sonetts.*
Oc·to·ber [ɔkˈtəubə] Oktober *m*.
oc·to·ge·nar·i·an [ɔktəudʒiˈnɛəriən] **1.** achtzigjährig; **2.** Achtzigjährige *m*, *f*.

oc·to·pus *zo.* [ˈɔktəpəs] Polyp *m* (*a. fig.*).

oc·to·roon [ɔktəˈruːn] Achtelneger (-in).

oc·u·lar □ [ˈɔkjulə] Augen...; ~ *demonstration*, ~ *proof* sichtbarer Beweis *m*; **'oc·u·list** Augenarzt *m*.

odd □ [ɔd] ungerade (*Zahl*); einzeln (*Handschuh etc.*), vereinzelt; und einige *od.* etwas darüber; überzählig; gelegentlich, Gelegenheits...; seltsam, sonderbar, merkwürdig, komisch; *40* ~ einige 40; *12 pounds* ~ über 12 Pfund; ~ *jobs pl.* Gelegenheitsarbeiten *f/pl.*; *at* ~ *times* dann und wann; ~ *man out* Übriggebliebene *m*, Überzählige *m*; Außenseiter *m*; *s.* odds; **'~·ball** *Am.* F komischer Kauz; **'odd·i·ty** Seltsamkeit *f*; F Original *n* (*Person*); **'odd·ly:** ~ *enough* seltsamerweise; **'odd·ments** *pl.* Überbleibsel *n/pl.*, Reste *m pl.*; Krimskrams *m*; ✝ Einzelstücke *n/pl.*; **odds** [ɔdz] *pl. oft sg.* (Gewinn)Chancen *f/pl.*; Wahrscheinlichkeit *f*; Vorteil *m*; Vorgabe *f*, Handikap *n*; Verschiedenheit *f*; Unterschied *m*; Streit *m*; *the* ~ *are against you* du bist im Nachteil; *the* ~ *are 3 to 1 in his favour* die Chancen stehen 3 : 1 für ihn; *the* ~ *are that* es ist sehr wahrscheinlich, daß; *be at* ~ *with s.o.* mit j-m im Streit sein; nicht übereinstimmen mit j-m; ~ *and ends* Reste *m/pl.*, Krimskrams *m*; *it makes no* ~ es spielt keine Rolle, es macht nichts aus; *what's the* ~? was tut's?

ode [əud] Ode *f* (*Gedicht*).

o·di·ous □ [ˈəudjəs] verhaßt, abscheulich; widerlich, ekelhaft; **o·di·um** [ˈəudjəm] Haß *m*; Vorwurf *m*; Schande *f*; Odium *n*.

o·dom·e·ter *mot.* [oˈdɔmitə] Kilometerzähler *m*.

o·don·to·lo·gy 🦷 [ɔdɔnˈtɔlədʒi] Zahnheilkunde *f*.

o·dor·if·er·ous □ [əudəˈrifərəs], **'o·dor·ous** □ wohlriechend, duftend.

o·do(u)r [ˈəudə] Geruch *m*; Wohlgeruch *m*, Duft *m*; *fig.* Ruf *m*; **'o·dor·less** geruchlos. [(*a. fig.*).\
O·dys·sey [ˈɔdisi] Odyssee *f Homers*)
oe·col·o·gy [iːˈkɔlədʒi] *s.* ecology.
oec·u·men·i·cal *eccl.* □ [iːkjuˈmenikəl] ökumenisch.
oe·de·ma 🩺 [iːˈdiːmə] Ödem *n*.
o'er [əuə] = *over.*

oe·soph·a·gus *anat.* [iːˈsɔfəgəs] Speiseröhre *f.*

of [ɔv, *schwache Formen* əv, v] *prp. allg.* von; *Bezeichnung des Genitivs*; *Ort:* bei (*the battle of Quebec*); *räumlicher Abstand:* von (*north of*); *Herkunft:* von, aus (*of good family*); *Trennung, Befreiung:* von (*rid* ~, *cure* ~ *s.th.*); *gen.* (*robbed* ~ *one's purse*); um (*cheat* ~ *s.th.*); *Teil:* von, *gen.* (*the best* ~ *my friends*); *Stoff:* aus, von (*a dress* ~ *silk*); *Eigenschaft:* von, mit (*a man* ~ *honour*, ~ *means*); *Urheber, Art u. Weise:* von; ~ *o.s.* von selbst; *Ursache, Grund:* von, an (*dat.*) (*die* ~); aus (~ *charity*); vor (*dat.*) (*afraid* ~); auf (*acc.*) (*proud* ~); über (*acc.*) (*ashamed* ~); nach (*smell* ~ *roses*); *Beziehung:* hinsichtlich, in betreff (*quick* ~ *eye*): *Ziel:* nach (*desirous* ~); *Thema:* von, über (*acc.*) (*speak* ~ *s.th.*); an (*acc.*) (*think* ~ *s.th.*); *deutsch unausgedrückt:* *Apposition* (*the city* ~ *London*); *Maß* (*a glass* ~ *wine*); *this world* ~ *ours* diese unsere Welt; ~ *an evening* F abends.

off [ɔːf, ɔf] **1.** *adv. mst in Zssg mit vb:* weg, ab; herunter; aus (*vorbei*); *Raum:* weg (*3 miles* ~); *Zeit:* hin (*3 months* ~); ~ *and on* ab u. an, ab u. zu; hin u. her; *be* ~ fort sein, weg sein; *engS.*: (weg)gehen, (ab-)fahren; weg müssen; zu sein (*Hahn etc.*); aus sein; ausverkauft sein; *be* ~ *with s.o.* mit j-m auseinander sein; *right* ~, *straight* ~ sofort; *have one's shoes etc.* ~ seine *od.* die Schuhe *etc.* aus(gezogen) haben; *well etc.* ~ gut *etc.* daran; **2.** *prp.* von ... (weg, ab, herunter); frei von, ohne; abseits von, unweit (*gen.*), neben; ⚓ auf der Höhe von; *a street* ~ *the Strand* e-e Nebenstraße des Strand; *be* ~ *duty* (dienst)frei haben; *be* ~ *smoking* das Rauchen aufgegeben haben; ~ *the point* nicht zur Sache gehörend; *be* ~ *one's feed sl.* keinen Hunger haben; ~ *one's head sl.* verrückt; **3.** *adj.* entfernt(er); abseits liegend; Seiten..., Neben...; ab(-), los(gegangen); *bei Pferd, Wagen:* rechte(r, -s); arbeits-, dienstfrei; ab, unwohl; nicht frisch; *Kricket:* abseitig; ~ *chance* schwache Möglichkeit *f*; ~ *shade* ✝ Fehlfarbe *f*; **4.** *int.* weg!, fort!, raus!

of·fal [ˈɔfəl] Abfall *m*; Schund *m*;

~s *pl. Fleischerei*: Innereien *f/pl.*

off...: ~'**beat** F ['ɔf'biːt] ungewöhnlich, ausgefallen; '~**-chance:** *on the* ~ auf die entfernte Möglichkeit hin, auf gut Glück; ~'**col·o(u)r** unwohl; *be od. feel* ~ sich unwohl fühlen; unanständig (*Witz etc.*); '~**-day** schlechter Tag; *this is an* ~ *for me* heute geht mir alles schief.

of·fence [ə'fens] Angriff *m*; Beleidigung *f*, Kränkung *f*; Ärgernis *n*, Verstoß *m*; Vergehen *n*; *no* ~! nichts für ungut!; *give* ~ Anstoß *od.* Ärgernis erregen; *take* ~ Anstoß nehmen (*at an dat.*).

of·fend [ə'fend] *v/t.* beleidigen, verletzen; ärgern; *v/i.* verstoßen, sich vergehen (*against gegen*); **of'fend·er** Übel-, Missetäter(in); Straffällige *m, f*; *first* ~ noch nicht Vorbestrafte *m, f*.

of·fense [ə'fens] = *offence*.

of·fen·sive [ə'fensiv] **1.** □ anstößig; widerlich, ekelhaft; Offensiv..., Angriffs...; ~ *weapon* Angriffswaffe *f*; **2.** Offensive *f*.

of·fer ['ɔfə] **1.** Angebot *n*, Anerbieten *n*; ~ *of marriage* Heiratsantrag *m*; *on* ~ zu verkaufen, verkäuflich; **2.** *v/t.* anbieten; *Preis, Möglichkeit etc.* bieten; *Gebet, Opfer* darbringen; *versuchen*; *zeigen*; *Widerstand* leisten; *v/i.* sich bieten; '**of·fer·ing** Opfer *n*; Anerbieten *n*, Angebot *n*; Antrag *m*.

of·fer·to·ry *eccl.* ['ɔfətəri] Kollekte *f*.

off-face ['ɔːf'feis] randlos (*Damenhut*).

off-hand ['ɔːf'hænd] aus dem Handgelenk *od.* Stegreif, unvorbereitet; ungezwungen, frei, lässig.

of·fice ['ɔfis] Büro *n*, Kontor *n*; Geschäftsstelle *f*; Ministerium *n*; Amt *n*, Pflicht *f*; ~s *pl.* Hilfe *f*; ~s *pl.* Nebenräume *m/pl. e-s Hauses*; *booking* ~ Schalter *m*; *box* ~ (Theater-, *etc.*) Kasse *f*; *Divine* ♀ Gottesdienst *m*; '~**-bear·er** Amtsträger *m*; '~**-block** Bürohaus *n*; '~**-boy** Laufbursche *m*; '~**-hours** *pl.* Dienststunden *f pl.*; Geschäftszeiten *f pl.*

of·fi·cer ['ɔfisə] Beamte *m*; ⚔ Offizier *m*; '**of·fi·cered:** ~ *by* geführt *od.* befehligt von; **of·fice sup·plies** Bürobedarf *m.*

of·fi·cial □ [ə'fiʃəl] **1.** offiziell, amtlich; Amts...; ⚙ = *official*; **2.** Beamte *m*; Sachbearbeiter *m*; **of'fi-**

cial·dom Beamtentum *n*; Bürokratismus *m*; **of·fi·cial·ese** [~'liːz] Amts-, Behördensprache *f*; **of'fi·cial·ism** = *officialdom*.

of·fi·ci·ate [ə'fiʃieit] amtieren.

of·fic·i·nal [ɔfi'sainl] offizinell, als Arznei (anerkannt).

of·fi·cious □ [ə'fiʃəs] aufdringlich, übereifrig; offiziös, halbamtlich.

off·ing ⚓ ['ɔfiŋ] offene See *f*, Seeraum *m*; *in the* ~ *fig.* in (Aus)Sicht; '**off·ish** F reserviert, steif.

off...: ~'**key** ♪ falsch; '~**-li·cence** Schankrecht *n* über die Straße; '~**-peak:** ~ *charges pl.* verbilligter Tarif *m*; ~ *hours pl.* verkehrsschwache Stunden *f pl.*; '~**-print** Sonderdruck *m*; ~'**put·ting** unangenehm, störend, wenig einladend; unsympathisch (*Person, Wesen*); '~**scourings** *pl.*, '~**-scum** Kehricht *m*; Abschaum *m*; '~**-sea·son** Nebensaison *f*; '~**-set 1.** ⚖ Absatz *m e-r Mauer etc.*; ⊕ Biegung *f e-s Rohrs*; *typ.* Offsetdruck *m*; *s. offshoot*; *s. set-off*; **2.** ausgleichen; '~**-shoot** Sproß *m*; Ausläufer *m*; '~**-shore** küstennah; ablandig (*Wind etc.*); ~ *purchases pl. pol.* Off-shore-Käufe ~ *m pl.*; '~**-side** *Sport*: abseits; '~**-spring** Abkömmling *m*; Nachkommenschaft *f*; Ergebnis *n*; ~'**stage** hinter den Kulissen; ~**-the-'cuff** aus dem Handgelenk *od.* Stegreif; ~**-the-'peg** von der Stange; '~**-the-'rec·ord** inoffiziell, vertraulich (*Mitteilung*); '~**-time** Freizeit *f*, freie Zeit *f*; ~**-'white** gebrochen weiß.

oft *poet.* [ɔft] oft.

of·ten ['ɔfn] oft(mals), häufig; *as* ~ *as* jedesmal wenn; *as* ~ *as not, more* ~ *than not* sehr oft *od.* häufig; *every so* ~ von Zeit zu Zeit; '**of·ten·times**, '**oft-times** † oft.

o·gee ⚙ ['əudʒiː] S-Bogen *m*; Kehlleiste *f*.

o·gi·val ['əu'dʒaivəl] Spitzbogen...; '**o·give** ⚙ Spitzbogen *m*; Gratrippe *f e-s Gewölbes*.

o·gle ['əugl] liebäugeln (mit).

o·gre ['əugə] Menschenfresser *m* (*im Märchen*); **o·gress** ['əugris] Menschenfresserin *f*.

oh [əu] oh!; ach! [*Widerstands*).

ohm ⚡ [əum] Ohm *n* (*Einheit des*]

o·ho [əu'həu] aha!; haha!

oil [ɔil] **1.** Öl *n*; Erdöl *n*, Petroleum *n*; *burn the midnight* ~ bis spät in die Nacht hinein arbeiten; *smell of* ～ nach Schweiß riechen (*Werk*); *pour* ～ *on the flame(s)* Öl ins Feuer gießen; *pour* ～ *on the (troubled) waters* Öl auf die Wogen gießen; *strike* ～ Erdöl finden; *fig.* plötzlich reich werden; *paint in* ～*s in* Öl malen; **2.** ölen; schmieren (*a. fig.*); ～ *s.o.'s palm* j. schmieren; **'～-burn·er** Schiff *n* mit Dieselantrieb; Dieselmotor *m*; Ölofen *m*; **'～-cake** Ölkuchen *m* (*Viehfutter*); **'～-can** Ölkännchen *n*; **'～-change** *mot.* Ölwechsel *m*; **'～-cloth** Linoleum *n*; Wachstuch *n*; **'～-col·o(u)r** Ölfarbe *f*; **'～-dip·stick** *mot.* Ölmeßstab *m*; **'oil·er** = *oil-can*; *oil-tanker*; **'oil-field** Ölfeld *n*; **oil glut** Ölschwemme *f*; **'oil·i·ness** Öligkeit *f* (*a. fig.*); Fettigkeit *f*; Schmierigkeit *f*; **'oil-lev·el** *mot.* Ölstand *m*; **'oil-man** Ölmann *m*, -händler *m*; Ölproduzent *m*; Farbenhändler *m*; **'oil-paint·ing** Ölmalerei *f*; Ölgemälde *n*; **'oil-pa·per** Ölpapier *n*; **'oil-rig** Bohrinsel *f*; **'oil--skin** Ölleinwand *f*; ～*s pl.* Ölzeug *n*; **oil slick** Ölteppich *m*; **'oil-tank·er** Öltanker *m*; Tankwagen *m*; **'oil-well** Ölquelle *f*; **'oil·y** □ ölig (*a. fig.*); fettig, schmierig; *fig.* aalglatt.

oint·ment ['ɔintmənt] Salbe *f*.

O.K., **o·kay** ['əu'kei] **1.** richtig, stimmt!; gut, in Ordnung; **2.** annehmen, gutheißen.

old [əuld] alt; altbekannt; althergebracht; erfahren; F oll; *sl.* (*zur Verstärkung*) toll; *the* ～ die Alten; *young and* ～ jung und alt; ～ *age* das Alter; *the* ～ *man* der Alte (*Vater, Gatte, Kapitän*); ～ *man als Anrede*: alter Freund, mein Lieber; *the* ～ *woman* die Alte (*Gattin*); *the* ～ *country* die alte Heimat; *an* ～ *boy* ein ehemaliger Schüler; *a high* ～ *time sl.* e.-e tolle Zeit; *the* ～ *one, the* ～ *gentleman*, ～ *Harry od. Scratch* der Teufel; *days of* ～ alte Zeiten; **'～-age** Alters...; ～ *pension* Pension *f*; Rente *f*; ～ *pensioner* Rentner(in); **'～--'clothes·man** Trödler *m*; **'old·en** † *od. poet.* alt, früher; *in the* ～ *days in* alten *od.* früheren Zeiten.

old...: '～-'fash·ioned 1. altmodisch; altväterlich; altklug (*Kind*); mißbilligend (*Blick*); **2.** *Am.* ein Cocktail *mit Whisky*; **'～-'fo·g(e)y·ish** altmodisch, verknöchert; ⚥ **Glo·ry** Sternenbanner *n*; **'old·ish** ältlich;

'old-'maid·ish pingelig; umständlich; altjüngferlich; **old·ster** ['～stə] alter Knabe *m*; **'old-time** alt(ertümlich); **'old-'tim·er** alter Hase *m*; **old wives' tale** Ammenmärchen *n*; **'old-'wom·an·ish** altweiberhaft; **'old-world** altmodisch, altertümlich; altweltlich.

o·le·ag·i·nous [əuli'ædʒinəs] ölig; Öl...

o·le·an·der ♀ [əuli'ændə] Oleander *m*.

ol·fac·to·ry *anat.* [ɔl'fæktəri] Geruchs...

ol·i·garch·y ['ɔligɑ:ki] Oligarchie *f*.

ol·ive ['ɔliv] ♀ Olive *f*; Olivgrün *n*; **'～-branch** Ölzweig *m*; **'～-tree** Ölbaum *m*.

O·lym·pi·ad [əu'limpiæd] Olympiade *f*; **O'lym·pi·an** [～piən] olympisch, göttlich; **O'lym·pic games** *pl.* Olympische Spiele *n/pl.*

om·buds·man ['ɔmbudzmən] Ombudsmann *m*.

om·e·let, om·e·lette ['ɔmlit] Eierkuchen *m*, Omelett *n*.

o·men ['əumen] Omen *n*, Vorzeichen *n*, Vorbedeutung *f*.

om·i·nous □ ['ɔminəs] unheilvoll; ～ *of disaster* unheilverkündend.

o·mis·si·ble [əu'misibl] auszulassen(d); **o·mis·sion** [ə'miʃən] Unterlassung *f*; Aus-, Weglassung *f* (*from aus*); *sin of* ～ Unterlassungssünde *f*.

o·mit [əu'mit] unterlassen, versäumen (*a. to inf.* zu *inf.*); auslassen, übergehen.

om·ni·bus ['ɔmnibəs] **1.** † Omnibus *m*; **2.** allumfassend; Sammel...; ～ *volume* Sammelband *m*.

om·nip·o·tence [ɔm'nipətəns] Allmacht *f*; **om'nip·o·tent** □ allmächtig.

om·ni·pres·ence ['ɔmni'prezəns] Allgegenwart *f*; **'om·ni'pres·ent** □ allgegenwärtig.

om·nis·cience [ɔm'nisiəns] Allwissenheit *f*; **om'nis·cient** □ allwissend. —

om·niv·o·rous [ɔm'nivərəs] alles fressend *od. fig.* verschlingend.

on [ɔn] **1.** *prp. mst* auf; *engS.* festgemacht *od. unmittelbar* an (～ *the wall, chain, Thames*); beschäftigt mit, an (*be* ～ *the Stock Exchange*); *Richtung, Ziel*: auf ... (los), nach ... (hin) (*march* ～ *London*); *Grund*: auf ...

(hin) (~ *his authority*); *Zeit*: an (~ *Friday*, ~ *the 1st of April*); (gleich) nach, bei (~ *his arrival*); *Thema*: über (*acc.*) (*talk* ~ *a subject*); *siehe die mit on verbundenen Wörter*; get ~ *a train bsd. Am.* in e-n Zug einsteigen; *turn one's back* ~ *s.o.* j-m den Rücken kehren; ~ *these conditions* unter diesen Bedingungen; ~ *this model* nach diesem Muster; ~ *hearing it* als ich *etc.* es hörte; **2.** *adv.* darauf; *bsd. Kleidung*: auf (*keep one's hat* ~), an (*have a coat* ~); voran, -aus, -wärts; weiter (*and so* ~); ~ *and* ~ immer weiter; ~ *to* ... auf (*acc.*) ... hinauf *od.* hinaus; *from that day* ~ von dem Tage an; *be* ~ (mit) dabei sein; im Gange sein, vor sich gehen; *thea.* gegeben werden; *what is* ~ *tonight?* Was gibt es heute abend?; d(a)ran (*an der Reihe*) sein; auf sein (*Hahn etc.*); an sein (*Licht, Wasser etc.*); *be a bit* ~ *sl.* e-n Schwips haben (*angetrunken sein*); **3.** *int.* drauf!, ran!

once [wʌns] **1.** *adv.* einmal; einst (-mals); *at* ~ (so)gleich, sofort; zugleich, auf einmal; *all at* ~ auf einmal; ~ *again* noch einmal; ~ *for all* ein für allemal; *for* ~ für diesmal (*ausnahmsweise*); ~ *in a while* dann u. wann; *this* ~ dieses eine Mal; ~ *more* noch einmal; *im Märchen*: ~ *upon a time there was* ... es war einmal ...; **2.** *cj.* a. ~ *that* sobald, wenn erst einmal.

once-o·ver *Am.* F ['wʌnsəuvə] *kurze Musterung* f.

on·com·ing ['ɔnkʌmiŋ] **1.** kommend, (heran)nahend; entgegenkommend; ~ *traffic* Gegenverkehr m; **2.** Nahen n, Kommen n.

one [wʌn] **1.** adj. einzig; eine(r), ein; eins; man; *his* ~ *care* seine einzige Sorge; ~ *day* eines Tages; ~ *of these days* dieser Tage; ~ *Mr. Miller* ein gewisser Herr Miller; *s. any, every, no; take* ~'*s walk* s-n Spaziergang machen; *a large dog and a little* ~ ein großer Hund und ein kleiner; *for* ~ *thing* auf alle Fälle; ~ *and the same* ein und derselbe *etc.*); **2.** Einer m, Eins f; *the little* ~s pl. die Kleinen n/pl., die Kinder n/pl.; ~ *another* einander; *at* ~ einig; ~ *by* ~, ~ *after another* einzeln, einer nach dem andern; *it is all* ~ (*to me*) es ist (mir) ganz einerlei; *I for* ~ ich

für meinen Teil; ~ *with another* im Durchschnitt; '~-**armed** einarmig; ~ *bandit* Spielautomat m; '~-'**eyed** einäugig; *fig.* beschränkt; '~-'**horse** einspännig; *fig. sl.* armselig, zweitrangig; ~ *town* Nest n; '~-**i'dea'd** in e-e einzige Idee verrannt; '**one-ness** Einheit f; Identität f; Einigkeit f; '**one-night stand** einmaliger Auftritt m.

on·er·ous □ ['ɔnərəs] lästig, beschwerlich.

one...: ~'**self** (man) selbst, sich; *by* ~ aus eigener Kraft, von selbst; allein; '~-'**sid·ed** □ einseitig; '~-**time** einstig; '~-'**track** eingleisig; *have a* ~ *mind* immer nur dasselbe im Kopf haben, monoman sein; **one-'up-man·ship** *die Kunst, allen anderen ständig um eine Nasenlänge voraus zu sein*; '**one-way street** Einbahnstraße f.

on·fall ['ɔnfɔːl] Angriff m.

on·go·ings ['ɔngəuiŋz] pl. Vorgänge m/pl.

on·ion ['ʌnjən] Zwiebel f; *off one's* ~ *sl.* übergeschnappt.

on·look·er ['ɔnlukə] Zuschauer(in).

on·ly ['əunli] **1.** adj. einzig; **2.** adv. nur; bloß; erst; ~ *yesterday* erst gestern; ~ *just* eben erst, gerade, kaum; ~ *think!* denken Sie nur!; **3.** cj. ~ (*that*) nur daß.

on·o·mat·o·poe·ia [ɔnəumætəu-'piːə] Lautmalerei f.

on·rush ['ɔnrʌʃ] Ansturm m.

on·set ['ɔnset], **on·slaught** ['ɔnslɔːt] Angriff m; *bsd. fig.* Anfall m; Anfang m.

on·shore [ɔn'ʃɔː] landwärts; in Küstennähe; an Land.

on·to ['ɔntu, 'ɔntə] auf (*acc.*).

on·tol·o·gy *phls.* [ɔn'tɔlədʒi] Ontologie f, Seinslehre f.

o·nus *fig.* ['əunəs] (*ohne pl.*) Last f.

on·ward ['ɔnwəd] **1.** adj. vorwärts-, fortschreitend; **2.** a. ~s adv. vorwärts, weiter.

on·yx *min.* ['ɔniks] Onyx m.

oo·dles *sl.* ['uːdlz] pl. Unmengen f/pl. (of von).

oof *sl.* [uːf] Moneten pl. (Geld).

oomph *sl.* [uːmf] *das (gewisse) Etwas*; Verve f; Sex Appeal m.

ooze [uːz] **1.** Schlamm m; Schlick m; ⊕ Lohbrühe f; **2.** (durch)sickern (lassen); ausströmen, ausschwitzen; ~ *away* schwinden.

oo·zy □ ['uːzi] schlammig; feucht.
o·pac·i·ty [əu'pæsiti] Undurchsichtigkeit *f*; *fig.* Stumpfheit *f*.
o·pal *min.* ['əupəl] Opal *m*; **o·pales·cent** [␣'lesnt] opalisierend.
o·paque □ [əu'peik] undurchsichtig; *fig.* dunkel; stumpf(sinnig).
ope *poet.* [əup] = *open*.
o·pen ['əupən] **1.** □ *allg.* offen; geöffnet, auf; frei (*Feld etc.*); öffentlich; offenstehend, unentschieden; aufrichtig, freimütig; ausgesetzt, zugänglich (*to dat.*); nicht abgeschlossen (*Konto*); aufgeschlossen (*to gegenüber*); mild, frostfrei (*Wetter*); *with ␣ arms* begeistert, herzlich; *with ␣ hands* großzügig; *the ␣ door* die Politik der offenen Tür; *keep ␣ house* ein gastfreies *od.* offenes Haus haben; *lay o.s. ␣ to* sich (*dat.*) aussetzen; *␣ letter* offener Brief *m*; *␣ season* Jagd-, Fischzeit *f*; **2.** *in the ␣* (*air*) im Freien; *come out into the ␣ fig.* an die Öffentlichkeit treten; **3.** *v/t.* öffnen, aufmachen; *Buch* aufschlagen; eröffnen (*zugänglich machen*; *beginnen*; *mitteilen*); *Verhandlungen etc.* anknüpfen; *Konto* eröffnen; *␣ up* Land erschließen; (*Brunnen*) bohren; (*Straße*) bauen; *v/i.* sich öffnen, sich auftun, aufgehen; aufmachen, öffnen, geöffnet sein (*Laden etc.*); anfangen, beginnen; *␣ into* führen in (*acc.*) (*Tür etc.*); *␣ on* to hinausgehen auf (*acc.*) (*Fenster etc.*); *␣ out* sich ausbreiten; **␣·'ac·cess li·brar·y** Freihandbibliothek *f*; **'␣·'air** im Freien (stattfindend), Freilicht...; Frei(luft)...; **'␣·-'armed** herzlich, warm; **'␣·'end·ed** *fig.* offen, (*bsd.* zeitlich) unbegrenzt; **o·pen·er** ['əupnə] (Er)Öffner(in); (Dosen)Öffner *m*; **'o·pen-'eyed** wach; mit offenen Augen; aufmerksam; überrascht; **'o·pen-'hand·ed** freigebig, großzügig; **'o·pen-'heart·ed** offen(herzig), aufrichtig; **o·pen·ing** ['əupniŋ] **1.** Öffnung *f* (*a. konkr.*); Eröffnung *f*; Gelegenheit *f*, Aussicht *f*; **2.** Eröffnungs...; *␣ night* Eröffnungsvorstellung *f*; *␣ time bsd.* Lokal: Öffnungszeit *f*; **'o·pen-'mind·ed** *fig.* aufgeschlossen; **'o·pen-'mouthed** gierig; verdutzt; **o·pen·ness** ['əupnnis] Offenheit *f*; Milde *f des Wetters*.
open...: *␣ or·der* ⚔ geöffnete Ordnung *f*; **'␣·'plan of·fice** Großraum-

büro *n*; *␣ shop* Betrieb *m* ohne Gewerkschaftszwang; ♀ **U·ni·ver·si·ty** Fern(seh)universität *f*, *deren Kurse auch ohne entsprechenden Schulabschluß belegt werden können*; *␣ vow·el* offener Vokal *m*; *␣ work* Durchbruchsarbeit *f*.
op·er·a ['ɔpərə] Oper *f*.
op·e·ra·ble ['ɔpərəbl] ♣ operierbar; durchführbar, praktikabel.
opera...: **'␣·cloak** Theatermantel *m*; **'␣·glass(es** *pl.*) Opernglas *n*; **'␣·hat** Klapphut *m*; **'␣·house** Opernhaus *n*.
op·er·ate ['ɔpəreit] *v/t.* (ein)wirken; ✝, ♣, ⚒ operieren; *bsd. Am.* in Gang bringen; ⊕ handhaben, bedienen; *Unternehmen* leiten; *v/i.* sich auswirken; *be operating* in Betrieb sein, funktionieren, arbeiten; **op·er·at·ic** [␣'rætik] opernhaft; *␣ singer* Opernsänger(in); **op·er·at·ing** ['ɔpəreitiŋ] Operations...; *␣ expenses pl.* Betriebsunkosten *pl.*; *␣ instructions pl.* Bedienungsvorschriften *f/pl.*; *␣ theatre* Operationssaal *m mit Zuschauergalerie*; **op·er·a·tion** Wirkung *f*; Wirksamkeit *f*; Tätigkeit *f*; ✝ Transaktion *f*; ♣, ⚒, ✝ Operation *f*; *be in ␣* in Kraft sein; *come into ␣* in Kraft treten; **op·er·a·tion·al** [␣'fənl] Betriebs..., Arbeits...; Operations...; einsatzfähig; **op·er·a·tive** ['ɔpərətiv] **1.** □ wirksam, tätig; praktisch; ♣ operativ; **2.** Arbeiter *m*; **op·er·a·tor** [␣'reitə] Wirkende *m*, *f*, *n*; ♣ Operateur *m*; *Film:* Vorführer *m*; Telephonist(in); ⊕ Maschinist *m*; ✝ Spekulant *m*; Unternehmer *m*.
op·er·et·ta [ɔpə'retə] Operette *f*.
oph·thal·mi·a ♣ [ɔf'θælmiə] Augenentzündung *f*; **oph'thal·mic** Augen...; augenkrank; *␣ hospital* Augenklinik *f*.
o·pi·ate *pharm.* ['əupiit] **1.** Schlafmittel *n*; **2.** einschläfernd.
o·pine [əu'pain] meinen; **o·pin·ion** [ə'pinjən] Meinung *f*; Ansicht *f*; Stellungnahme *f*; Gutachten *n*; (gute) Meinung *f*; *the (public) ␣* die öffentliche Meinung; *counsel's ␣* Rechtsgutachten *n*; *␣ poll* Meinungsumfrage *f*; *I am of the ␣ that* ich bin der Meinung, daß; *in my ␣* meines Erachtens; **o'pin·ion·at·ed** [␣eitid] starr-, eigensinnig.
o·pi·um *pharm.* ['əupjəm] Opium *n*.
o·pos·sum *zo.* [ə'pɔsəm] Opossum

n, Beutelratte *f*.

op·po·nent [ə'pəunənt] **1.** Gegner *m*; **2.** gegnerisch.

op·por·tune □ ['ɔpətjuːn] günstig; passend; rechtzeitig; **'op·por·tun·ism** Opportunismus *m*; **'op·por·tun·ist** Opportunist(in); **op·por·'tu·ni·ty** (günstige) Gelegenheit *f*, Möglichkeit *f*.

op·pose [ə'pəuz] entgegen-, gegenüberstellen; bekämpfen; sich widersetzen (*dat.*); entgegentreten (*dat.*); **op'posed** entgegengesetzt; feindlich; *be* ~ *to* gegen ... sein; **op·po·site** ['ɔpəzit] **1.** □ gegenüberliegend ([*to*] *s.th. dat.*); entgegengesetzt; ~ *number* Gegenspieler(in); Kollege *m*, Kollegin *f*; **2.** *prp. u. adv.* gegenüber; **3.** Gegenteil *n*, -satz *m*; **op·po·si·tion** Gegenüberstehen *n*; Widerstand *m*; (*to* gegen) Gegensatz *m*; Widerspruch *m*, -streit *m*; † Konkurrenz *f*; *parl. u. ast.* Opposition *f*.

op·press [ə'pres] be-, unter-, niederdrücken; **op·pres·sion** [ə'preʃən] Unterdrückung *f*; Druck *m*; Bedrängnis *f*, Not *f*; Bedrücktheit *f*; **op'pres·sive** □ [~siv] (be)drückend; gewaltsam; **op'pres·sive·ness** Druck *m*; Schwüle *f*; **op'pres·sor** Unterdrücker *m*.

op·pro·bri·ous [ə'prəubriəs] schimpfend, schmähend; **op·pro·bri·um** [~briəm] Schimpf *m*; Schande *f*.

op·pugn [ɔ'pjuːn] bestreiten.

opt [ɔpt] optieren (*for* für); **op·ta·tive** *gr.* ['ɔptətiv] Wunschform *f*, Optativ *m*.

op·tic ['ɔptik] Augen..., Seh...; = **'op·ti·cal** □ optisch; **op'ti·cian** [~ʃən] Optiker *m*; **'op·tics** *sg.* Optik *f*.

op·ti·mism ['ɔptimizəm] Optimismus *m*; **'op·ti·mist** Optimist(in); **op·ti'mis·tic** (~*ally*) optimistisch; **'op·ti·mize** optimieren.

op·ti·mum ['ɔptiməm] **1.** Optimum *n*, *das* Beste; **2.** optimal, günstigst, best.

op·tion ['ɔpʃən] Wahl *f*; Wahlfreiheit *f*; † Vorkaufsrecht *n*, Option *f*; **op·tion·al** □ ['ɔpʃənl] freigestellt, wahlfrei.

op·u·lence ['ɔpjuləns] Reichtum *m*; **'op·u·lent** □ (sehr) reich; üppig, verschwenderisch, opulent.

o·pus ['əupəs] Werk *n*, Opus *n*; *magnum* ~ Hauptwerk *n*.

or [ɔː] oder; *either* ... ~ entweder ... oder; ~ *else* sonst, wo nicht; *two* ~ *three* zwei bis drei; ~ *so* (*nachgestellt*) ungefähr, etwa.

or·a·cle ['ɔrəkl] Orakel *n*; *work the* ~ F hinter den Kulissen arbeiten; **o·rac·u·lar** [ɔ'rækjulə] orakelhaft (*fig. rätselhaft, dunkel*); Orakel...

o·ral □ ['ɔːrəl] mündlich; Mund...

o·rang ['ɔːrəŋ] = *orang-outang*.

or·ange ['ɔrindʒ] **1.** Orange *f*, Apfelsine *f*; Orangenbaum *m*; Orangefarbe *f*; **2.** orange(farben); **or·ange·ade** ['~eid] Orangenlimonade *f*; **or·ange·ry** ['~əri] Orangerie *f*.

o·rang-ou·tang *zo.* ['ɔːrəŋ'uːtæŋ] Orang-Utan *m*.

o·ra·tion [ɔ'reiʃən] *förmliche* Rede *f*; **or·a·tor** ['ɔrətə] Redner *m*; **or·a·tor·i·cal** □ [~'tɔrikəl] rednerisch; **or·a·to·ri·o** ♪ [~'tɔːriəu] Oratorium *n*; **or·a·to·ry** ['~təri] Redekunst *f*, Beredsamkeit *f*, Rhetorik *f*; *eccl.* Kapelle *f*.

orb [ɔːb] Ball *m*; *fig.* Himmelskörper *m*; *poet.* Augapfel *m*; **or·bic·u·lar** □ [ɔː'bikjulə] kugelförmig, rund; **or·bit** ['ɔːbit] **1.** Planetenbahn *f*; Kreis-, Umlaufbahn *f*; Auge(n-höhle *f*) *n*; **2.** sich in e-r Umlaufbahn bewegen.

or·chard ['ɔːtʃəd] Obstgarten *m*.

or·ches·tra ♪ ['ɔːkistrə] Orchester *n*; ~ *pit thea.* Orchesterraum *m*; **or·ches·tral** [ɔː'kestrəl] Orchester...; **or·ches·trate** ♪ ['ɔːkistreit] instrumentieren.

or·chid ⚘ ['ɔːkid] Orchidee *f*; **or·chis** ⚘ ['ɔːkis] Knabenkraut *n*.

or·dain [ɔː'dein] an ~, verordnen; bestimmen; *Priester* ordinieren.

or·deal [ɔː'diːl] Gottesurteil *n*; *fig.* Feuerprobe *f*, schwere Prüfung *f*.

or·der ['ɔːdə] **1.** Ordnung *f*; Anordnung *f*; Reihenfolge *f*; Befehl *m*; Regel *f*, Vorschrift *f*; † Order *f*, Bestellung *f*, Auftrag *m*; Zahlungsanweisung *f*; Klasse *f*, Stand *m*, Rang *m*; Orden *m* (*a. eccl.*); *by* ~ im Auftrag; ~ *of the day* Tagesordnung *f*; ✕ Tagesbefehl *m*; *take (holy)* ~*s* in den geistlichen Stand treten; *put in* ~ in Ordnung bringen; *in* ~ *to* ... um zu ...; *in* ~ *that* damit; *on the* ~*s of* auf Befehl von; *on* ~ † bestellt; *make to* ~ auf Bestellung anfertigen;

rise to ~ zur Geschäftsordnung sprechen; *standing* ~*s pl. parl.* Geschäftsordnung *f*; **2.** (an)ordnen, einrichten; verordnen; befehlen; ✝ bestellen, kommen lassen; beordern, schicken; ~ *arms!* Gewehr ab!; ~ *about* herumkommandieren; ~ *down* (*up*) herunter- (herauf)kommen lassen; '~-**book** ✝ Auftragsbuch *n*; '**or·dered** geordnet; ordentlich; **or·der form** Bestellschein *m*; '**or·der·li·ness** Regelmäßigkeit *f*; Ordnung *f*; Ordentlichkeit *f*; '**order·ly 1.** ordentlich; ruhig, gesittet; methodisch; ⚔ diensttuend, Ordonnanz...; ~ *officer* Ordonnanzoffizier *m*, Offizier *m* vom Dienst; ~ *room* Geschäftszimmer *n*; **2.** ⚔ Ordonnanz *f*; Bursche *m*; Krankenpfleger *m*.

or·di·nal ['ɔ:dinl] **1.** Ordnungs...; **2.** *a.* ~ *number* Ordnungszahl *f*.

or·di·nance ['ɔ:dinəns] Verordnung *f*; vorgeschriebener Brauch *m*.

or·di·nar·y ['ɔ:dnri] **1.** ☐ gewöhnlich, üblich; ~ *debts pl.* ✝ Buchschulden *f/pl.*; ~ *seaman* Leichtmatrose *m*; *s. share*; **2.** *das* Gewöhnliche; Gasthaus *n*; Tagesgericht *n*; ordentlicher Richter *m*; *in* ~ ordentlich; Leib..., Hof...

or·di·nate ↳ ['ɔ:dnit] Ordinate *f*.

or·di·na·tion [ɔ:di'neiʃən] Ordination *f*, (Priester)Weihe *f*.

ord·nance ⚔, ⚓ ['ɔ:dnəns] Artillerie *f*, Geschütze *n/pl.*; Feldzeugwesen *n*; ~ *map* Generalstabskarte*f*; ~ *survey* amtliche Landesvermessung *f*; ~-*survey map* Meßtischblatt *n*.

or·dure ['ɔ:djuə] Kot *m*, Schmutz *m*.

ore [ɔ:] Erz *n*; *poet.* Metall *n*.

or·gan ['ɔ:gən] ♪ Orgel *f*; Organ *n* (*Körperteil*); *fig.* Werkzeug; *Stimme*; *Partei- etc. Blatt*).

or·gan·die, or·gan·dy ['ɔ:gəndi] Organdy *m* (*Baumwollgewebe*).

or·gan-grind·er ['ɔ:gəngraində] Leierkastenmann *m*; **or·gan·ic** [ɔ:'gænik] (~*ally*) organisch; **organ·ism** ['ɔ:gənizəm] Organismus *m*; '**or·gan·ist** Organist *m*; **or·gan·i·za·tion** [~nai'zeiʃən] Organisation *f*; Einrichtung *f*; Bau *m*; Verein(igung *f*) *m*; '**or·gan·ize** organisieren, einrichten; '**organ·iz·er** Organisator(in).

or·gasm ['ɔ:gæzəm] Orgasmus *m*.

or·gy ['ɔ:dʒi] Orgie *f*.

o·ri·el ⚙ ['ɔ:riəl] Erker *m*.

o·ri·ent 1. ['ɔ:riənt] aufgehend; östlich; glänzend (*Perle*); **2.** [~] Osten *m*; Orient *m*, Morgenland *n*; **3.** ['~ent] orientieren; **o·ri·en·tal** [~'entl] **1.** ☐ östlich; orientalisch; morgenländisch; **2.** Orientale *m*, Orientalin *f*; **o·ri·en·tate** ['ɔ:rienteit] orientieren; **o·ri·en'ta·tion** Orientierung *f*.   [nung *f*.\

or·i·fice ['ɔrifis] Mündung *f*, Öff-ʃ **or·i·gin** ['ɔridʒin] Ursprung *m*; Anfang *m*; Herkunft *f*.

o·rig·i·nal [ə'ridʒənl] **1.** ☐ ursprünglich; originell; Ur...; Original...; ✝ *Stamm*...; *s. share*; ~ *capital* Stammkapital *n*; ~ *sin* Erbsünde *f*; **2.** Original *n* (*a. Person*), Urbild *n*, -schrift *f*; **o·rig·i·nal·i·ty** [~'næliti] Originalität *f*; **o·rig·i·nal·ly** [ə'ridʒnəli] originell; ursprünglich, zuerst, anfangs, anfänglich.

o·rig·i·nate [ə'ridʒineit] *v/t.* hervorbringen, schaffen, ins Leben rufen; *v/i.* entstehen (*from, in s.th.* aus et.; *with, from s.o.* bei j-m, durch j.); **o·rig·i'na·tion** Schaffung *f*, Veranlassung *f*; Entstehung *f*; Ursprung *m*; **o'rig·i·na·tive** ☐ [~tiv] schöpferisch; **o'rig·i·na·tor** Urheber *m*.

o·ri·ole *orn.* ['ɔ:riəul] Goldamsel *f*.

o·ri·son ['ɔrizən] Gebet *n*.

or·mo·lu ['ɔ:məulu:] Malergold *m*.

or·na·ment 1. ['ɔ:nəmənt] Verzierung *f*, Ornament *n*; *fig.* Zierde*f*; **2.** ['~ment] verzieren; schmücken; **or·na'men·tal** ☐ ornamental, zierend; schmückend; Zier...; **or·na·men'ta·tion** Ausschmückung *f*, Verzierung *f*.

or·nate ☐ [ɔ:'neit] reich verziert; überladen.

or·ni·tho·log·i·cal ☐ [ɔ:niθə'lɔdʒikl] ornithologisch; **or·ni·thol·o·gist** [~'θɔlədʒist] Ornithologe *m*; **or·ni·'thol·o·gy** Ornithologie *f*, Vogelkunde *f*.

o·ro·tund ['ɔrəutʌnd] volltönend; bombastisch.

or·phan ['ɔ:fən] **1.** Waise(nkind *n*) *f*; **2.** *a.* ~*ed* verwaist; '**or·phan·age** Waisenhaus *n*.

or·rer·y ['ɔrəri] Planetarium *n*.

or·tho·dox ☐ ['ɔ:θədɔks] orthodox; rechtgläubig; üblich; anerkannt; '**or·tho·dox·y** Rechtgläubigkeit *f*.

or·tho·graph·ic, or·tho·graph·i·cal □ [ɔːθəuˈgræfik(əl)] orthographisch; **or·thog·ra·phy** [ɔːˈθɔgrəfi] Rechtschreibung f, Orthographie f.

or·tho·pae·dic [ɔːθəuˈpiːdik] (~ally) orthopädisch; **or·tho'pae·dist** Orthopäde m; '**or·tho·pae·dy** Orthopädie f.

or·to·lan orn. [ˈɔːtələn] Ortolan m, Gartenammer f.

Os·car [ˈɔskə] Oscar m (amerikanischer Filmpreis).

os·cil·late [ˈɔsileit] schwingen; fig. schwanken; **os·cil'la·tion** Schwingung f; **os·cil·la·to·ry** [ˈ~lətəri] schwingend; **os·cil·lo·graph** [ɔˈsiləugrɑːf] Oszillograph m.

os·cu·late co. [ˈɔskjuleit] (sich) küssen; sich berühren (mit).

o·sier ♦ [ˈəuʒə] Korbweide f.

os·mo·sis phys. [ɔzˈməusis] Osmose f.

os·prey [ˈɔspri] Seeadler m; ♱ Reiherfeder f.

os·se·ous [ˈɔsiəs] Knochen...; knochig; **os·si·fi·ca·tion** [ɔsifiˈkeiʃən] Verknöcherung f; **os·si·fy** [ˈ~fai] verknöchern; **os·su·ar·y** [ˈɔsjuəri] Beinhaus n.

os·ten·si·ble □ [ɔsˈtensəbl] vor-, angeblich; scheinbar.

os·ten·ta·tion [ɔstenˈteiʃən] Zurschaustellung f; Protzerei f; **os·ten·'ta·tious** □ ostentativ, prahlend, prahlerisch, großtuerisch.

os·te·ol·o·gy anat. [ɔstiˈɔlədʒi] Osteologie f, Knochenlehre f; **os·te·o·path** [ˈɔstiəpæθ] Osteopath m.

ost·ler [ˈɔslə] Stallknecht m.

os·tra·cism [ˈɔstrəsizəm] Scherbengericht n; Verbannung f, Ächtung f; **os·tra·cize** [ˈ~saiz] verbannen; ächten.

os·trich orn. [ˈɔstritʃ] Strauß m.

oth·er [ˈʌðə] andere(r, -s) (than, from als); the ~ day neulich; the ~ morning neulich morgens; every ~ day einen Tag um den andern; each ~ einander; somebody or ~ irgendeiner, einer oder der andere; '~·wise anders; sonst.

o·ti·ose □ [ˈəuʃiəus] müßig; zwecklos.

ot·ter zo. [ˈɔtə] Otter m; Otterpelz m.

Ot·to·man [ˈɔtəumən] **1.** ottomanisch, türkisch; **2.** ♀ Ottomane f (Sofa).

ought [ɔːt] **1.** = aught; **2.** v/aux.

(irr.) sollte; I ~ to do it ich sollte es eigentlich tun; you ~ to have done it Sie hätten es tun sollen.

ounce[1] [auns] Unze f (= 28,35 g); by the ~ nach (dem) Gewicht.

ounce[2] zo. [~] Schneeleopard m.

our [ˈauə] unser; **ours** [ˈauəz] **1.** der (die, das) unsrige; unsere(r, -s); pred. unser; **2.** die Unsrigen; **our·'selves** wir selbst; uns (selbst).

oust [aust] verdrängen, vertreiben, hinauswerfen; e-s Amtes entheben.

out [aut] **1.** adv. aus; hinaus, heraus; draußen; außerhalb; (bis) zu Ende (z.B. hear ~); be ~ nicht zu Hause sein; ausgeliehen sein; aus der Mode sein; streiken (Arbeiter); aus (= zu Ende) sein; aus der Übung sein; heraus sein (Blüte, neues Buch, Geheimnis, verrenktes Glied etc.); draußen od. F 'raus sein (nicht mehr an der Macht od. am Spiel); ungenau od. nicht richtig sein; im Irrtum sein; be ~ for s.th. od. to do s.th. sl. auf et. aus sein; darauf aus sein, et. zu tun; she is not ~ yet sie ist noch nicht in die Gesellschaft eingeführt; be ~ with böse sein mit; ~ and ~ durch u. durch; ~ and about wieder auf den Beinen; ~ and away bei weitem; s. elbow; have it ~ with s.o. sich mit j-m aussprechen; sich zs.-raufen; voyage ~ Ausreise f; way ~ Ausgang m; her day ~ ihr freier Tag; ~ with him! hinaus mit ihm!; **2.** typ. Auslassung f, Leiche f; Am. F Ausweg m; the ~s pl. parl. die Opposition; Sport: die nicht am Schlag befindliche Partei; **3.** auswärtig (Wettspiel); ♱ übernormal, Über... (Größe); **4.** prp. ~ of aus, aus ... heraus; außerhalb; außer; aus, von; nicht gemäß, zuwider; s. date, drawing, laugh, money; **5.** F 'rausschmeißen; Boxen: niederschlagen.

out...: ~-and-~ [ˈautndˈaut] absolut, völlig, Erz...; '~-and-'out·er Extremist m, Radikale m; '~·back **1.** entlegen, dünn besiedelt; **2.** die entlegenen Gebiete n/pl. Australiens; ~'bal·ance schwerer wiegen als; ~'bid (irr. bid) überbieten; '~·board Außenbord...; ~'brave an Kühnheit übertreffen; Trotz bieten (dat.); ~'break Ausbruch m; '~·build·ing Nebengebäude n; '~·burst Ausbruch m; '~·cast **1.** ausgestoßen; **2.** Ausgestoßene m, f;

'**~·caste** Kastenlose *m*, *f*, Ausgestoßene *m*, *f*; **~'class** *Sport: j-m* weit
überlegen sein; *be* **~ed** deklassiert
werden; '**~·come** Ergebnis *n*, Folge
f; '**~·crop** Zutagetreten *n*; *geol.*
Schichtenkopf *m*; '**~·cry** Aufschrei
m, Schrei *m* der Entrüstung; **~**-
-'**dat·ed** (zeitlich) überholt; **~'distance** überholen, hinter sich lassen;
~'do (*irr. do*) übertreffen, -bieten;
'**~·door** *adj.*, '**~'doors** *adv.* Außen...; draußen, außer dem Hause
(*a. parl.*); im Freien; *outdoor dress*
Straßenkleidung *f*.
out·er ['autə] äußer, Außen...; **~**
garments pl. Oberbekleidung *f*; '**~**-
most äußerst.
out...: **~'face** Trotz bieten (*dat.*);
außer Fassung bringen; '**~·fall**
Ausfluß *m*, Mündung *f*; '**~·fit** Ausrüstung *f*, Ausstattung *f*; *Am.* Haufen *m*, Trupp *m*, (Arbeits)Gruppe *f*;
'**~·fit·ter** Ausrüstungslieferant *m*;
Herrenausstatter *m*; **~'flank** ✕
überflügeln; '**~·flow** Ausfluß *m*;
~'gen·er·al überlisten; **~'go 1.** (*irr.
go*) schneller gehen als; *fig.* übertreffen; **2.** ['**~**] Ausgaben *f/pl.*; **~'going 1.** weg-, abgehend; **2.** Ausgehen
n; **~s** *pl.* Ausgaben *f/pl.*; **~'grow**
(*irr. grow*) *j-m* über den Kopf
wachsen; herauswachsen aus; *fig.*
entwachsen (*dat.*); '**~·growth**
Schößling *m*; Auswuchs *m*; (natürliche) Folge *f*; Erzeugnis *n*; '**~**-
house Nebengebäude *n*; Schuppen
m; *Am.* Außenabort *m*.
out·ing ['autiŋ] Ausflug *m*, Tour *f*;
Rudern u. Pferderennen: Training *n*.
out...: **~'land·ish** ausländisch;
fremdartig; seltsam (anmutend);
unkultiviert; **~'last** überdauern;
'**~·law 1.** Geächtete *m*, *f*, Verfemte
m, *f*; **2.** ächten; '**~·law·ry** Achtung
f; Verbrechertum *n*; '**~·lay** *Geld-*
Auslage(n *pl.*) *f*; '**~·let** Auslaß *m*;
Ausgang *m*; Aus-, Abfluß *m*; *fig.*
Ventil *n*; ⚡ Absatzgebiet *n*; ⚡
Steckdose *f*; '**~·line 1.** Umriß *m*;
Überblick *m*; Plan *m*, Skizze *f*; Abriß *m*, **~s** *pl.* Grundzüge *m/pl.*;
2. umreißen; skizzieren; **~d** scharf
abgehoben; **~'live** überleben; '**~**-
look Aussicht *f*, Ausblick *m* (*a. fig.*);
Auffassung *f*; Weltanschauung *f*;
Standpunkt *m*; *pol.* Zielsetzung *f*;
'**~·ly·ing** entlegen; **~·ma'noeu·vre**
ausmanövrieren; '**~'march** schnel-

ler marschieren als; **~'match** weit
übertreffen; **~'mod·ed** unmodern,
überholt, veraltet; '**~·most** äußerst;
~'num·ber an Zahl übertreffen;
'**~-of-'door(s)** = *outdoor(s)*; '**~-of-
-the-'way** entlegen; *fig.* ausgefallen; '**~-of-'work pay** Erwerbs-
losenunterstützung *f*; **~'pace** überholen; '**~-pa·tient** ambulant Be-
handelte *m*, *f*; **~'play** schlagen;
'**~-post** Vorposten *m*; '**~·pour·ing**
Erguß *m* (*a. fig.*); '**~·put** Produktion *f*, Ertrag *m*; (Produktions-)
Leistung *f*; Ausbeute *f*; Ausstoß *m*;
Computer: Datenausgabe *f*.
out·rage ['autreidʒ] **1.** Gewalttätigkeit *f*; Gewalttat *f* (*on* gegen);
Attentat *n* (*on* auf *acc.*); gröbliche
Beleidigung *f* (*on gen.*); **2.** gröblich
beleidigen *od.* verletzen; Gewalt antun (*dat.*), schänden; **out'ra·geous**
□ abscheulich; heftig; empörend;
beschimpfend; zügellos.
out...: **~'range** an Reichweite übertreffen; **~'rank** in den Schatten
stellen, übertreffen.
ou·tré ['u:trei] outriert, ausgefallen.
out...: **~'reach** weiter reichen als;
'**~-re·lief** Hauspflege *f für Arme*;
~'ride (*irr. ride*) schneller reiten
als; ⚓ *Sturm* abreiten; '**~·rid·er**
Vorreiter *m*; '**~·rig·ger** ⚓ Ausleger
(-boot *n*) *m*; **~'right** [*adj.* 'autrait,
adv. aut'rait] gerade heraus; gänzlich, völlig, glatt; auf der Stelle;
~'ri·val übertreffen, -bieten; **~'run**
(*irr. run*) schneller laufen als; hinausgehen über (*acc.*); '**~·run·ner**
Vorreiter *m*; Beipferd *n*; '**~·set** Anfang *m*; Aufbruch *m zur Reise*;
~'shine (*irr. shine*) überstrahlen;
'**~·side 1.** Äußere *n*; Außenseite *f*;
fig. das Äußerste; *at the* **~** höchstens; **2.** äußer; Außen...; außen-
stehend; äußerst (*Preis*); **~** *right*
Sport: Rechtsaußen *m*; **~** *left* Links-
außen *m*; **3.** (dr)außen; nach (dr)au-
ßen; **~** *of* = **4.** *prp.* außerhalb; über
... hinaus; '**~'sid·er** Außenseiter *m*,
-stehende *m*; '**~·size** ⚡ Übergröße
f; '**~·skirts** *pl.* Außenbezirke *m/pl.*,
Peripherie *f*; *(Stadt)Rand m*;
~'smart *Am.* F übervorteilen;
~'spoken □ freimütig; **~'spread**
ausgestreckt, ausgebreitet; **~'standing** hervorragend (*a. fig.*); hervorstehend, auffallend; ausstehend
(*Schuld*); offenstehend (*Frage*);

~'**stay** länger bleiben als; ~ *one's welcome* länger als erwünscht bleiben; ~'**stretched** = *outspread*; ~-'**strip** überholen (*a. fig.*); aus dem Felde schlagen, überflügeln; '~-**turn** Ertrag *m*; ~'**vie** sich gegenseitig zu überbieten suchen; ~'**vote** überstimmen.

out·ward ['autwəd] **1.** äußer, äußerlich; nach (dr)außen gerichtet; **2.** *adv. mst* '**out·wards** auswärts, nach (dr)außen; '**out·ward·ly** äußerlich; an der Oberfläche; '**out·ward·ness** Äußerlichkeit *f*; äußere Form *f*.

out...: ~'**wear** (*irr. wear*) überdauern; abnutzen; erschöpfen; ~-'**weigh** überwiegen; ~'**wit** überlisten; '~-**work** ✕ Außenwerk *n*; ⊕ Heimarbeit *f*; '~-**work·er** Heimarbeiter(in); '~-**worn** erschöpft; *fig.* abgegriffen; überholt.

ou·zel *orn.* ['uːzl] Drossel *f*.

o·val ['əuvəl] **1.** oval; **2.** Oval *n*.

o·va·ry ['əuvəri] *anat.* Eierstock *m*; ♀ Fruchtknoten *m*.

o·va·tion [əu'veiʃən] Ovation *f*, Huldigung *f*.

ov·en ['ʌvn] Backofen *m*; '~-**bird** *orn. Am.* Goldkopf-Waldsänger *m*; ~ **cloth** Topflappen *m*; ~ **read·y** bratfertig.

o·ver ['əuvə] **1.** *adv.* über; hin-, herüber; drüben; vorbei, vorüber; allzusehr; übermäßig; darüber, mehr; von Anfang bis zu Ende; noch einmal; ~ *and above* neben, zusätzlich zu; (*all*) ~ *again* noch einmal (von vorn); ~ *against* gegenüber (*dat.*); *all* ~ über und über; ganz u. gar; ~ *and* ~ *again* immer wieder; *fifty times* ~ fünfzigmal hintereinander; *get s.th.* ~ (*and done*) *with* et. hinter sich bringen; *read* ~ durchlesen; **2.** *prp.* über; *all* ~ *the town* durch die ganze *od.* in der ganzen Stadt; ~ *night* über Nacht; ~ *a glass of wine* bei e-m Glas Wein; ~ *the way* gegenüber.

o·ver...: '~'**act** übertreiben; '~-**all 1.** Arbeitsanzug *m*, -kittel *m*; Overall *m*; Kittel(schürze *f*) *m*; ~*s pl.* Überziehhosen *f/pl.*; **2.** allumfassend, gesamt, Gesamt...; ~'**arch** überwölben; ~'**awe** einschüchtern; ~'**bal·ance 1.** Übergewicht *n*, Mehr *n*; **2.** umkippen, das Gleichgewicht verlieren; überwiegen; ~-'**bear** (*irr. bear*) überwältigen; ~-

'**bear·ing** ☐ anmaßend; ~'**bid** (*irr. bid*) überbieten; '~-'**blown** am Verblühen; '~-**board** ⚓ über Bord; '~-'**brim** überfließen; ~'**bur·den** überladen; '~-**cast 1.** bewölkt; *fig.* traurig; **2.** Bewölkung *f*; '~-'**charge 1.** überladen; überfordern; **2.** Überladung *f*; Überforderung *f*; ~'**cloud** be-, überwölken, trüben; '~-**coat** Mantel *m*; ~'**come** (*irr. come*) überwinden, -wältigen; besiegen; '~-'**con·fi·dent** ☐ allzu vertrauend (*of auf acc.*); zu selbstsicher; vermessen; ~'**crowd** überfüllen; ~'**do** (*irr. do*) zu viel tun; übertreiben, zu weit treiben; zu sehr kochen *od.* braten; überanstrengen; ~-**done** [~'dʌn] übertrieben; überanstrengt; ['~'dʌn] übergar; '~-**draft** ♦ überzogener Betrag *m*; '~-'**draw** (*irr. draw*) übertreiben; ♦ *Konto* überziehen; ~'**dress** (sich) zu sehr herausputzen; '~-**drive** *mot.* Overdrive *m*, Schnellgang *m*; ~'**due** fällig; 📷, ♦ überfällig; '~-'**eat** (*irr. eat*): ~ *o.s.* sich überessen; '~-'**es·ti·mate** überschätzen; '~-'**ex·pose** *phot.* überbelichten; '~-'**ex·po·sure** *phot.* Überbelichtung *f*; '~-**fa·tigue 1.** übermüden; **2.** Übermüdung *f*; '~-'**feed** (*irr. feed*) überfüttern; ~**flow 1.** [~'fləu] *v t.* überfluten; *v i.* überfließen; **2.** ['~fləu] Überfluß *m*; Überschwemmung *f*; Überfüllung *f*; '~-**freight** Überfracht *f*; '~-**ground** über der Erde (befindlich); '~-'**grow** (*irr. grow*) überwuchern; zu sehr wachsen; '~-**growth** übermäßiges Wachstum *n*; '~-**hand** *Sport*: Überhand...; Hand-über-Hand-...; ~**hang 1.** ['~'hæŋ] (*irr. hang*) *v/t.* über (*acc.*) hängen; *v/i.* überhängen; *fig.* drohen; **2.** ['~-hæŋ] Überhang *m*; '~'**haul** überholen (*gründlich nachsehen*; *einholen*); ~**head 1.** [~'hed] *adv.* (dr)oben; **2.** ['~hed] *adj.* ♦ allgemein (*Unkosten*); ~ *railway* Hochbahn *f*; ~ *wire* ⚡ Oberleitung *f*; **3.** ['~hed]: ~*s pl.* ♦ allgemeine Unkosten *pl.*; ~'**hear** (*irr. hear*) be-, erlauschen; zufällig hören; '~-**heat** überhitzen; ~-**in'dulge** zu nachsichtig sein mit; *e-m Laster, e-r Leidenschaft* (übermäßig) frönen; (allzusehr) schwelgen in (*dat.*); '~-**issue** zu viel *Banknoten etc.* ausgeben;

'~**joyed** hocherfreut, entzückt; '~**kill** ⚔ Overkill *n*; gefährliches Übermaß *n*; '~**land** Überland...; ~**lap** *v/t.* übergreifen auf (*acc.*); überragen; überschneiden; *v/i.* ineinandergreifen, überlappen; ~**lay 1.** [~'lei] (*irr. lay*) belegen; ⊕ überlagern; **2.** ['~lei] Auflage *f*; Deckchen *n*; ~ *mattress* Auflagematratze *f*; '~**leaf** umseitig; '~**leap** (*irr. leap*) springen über (*acc.*); ~ *o.s. fig.* über das Ziel hinausschießen; ~**load 1.** [~'ləud] überladen; **2.** ['~ləud] Überbelastung *f*; ~**look** *Fehler etc.* übersehen; überblicken; beaufsichtigen; hinwegsehen über (*acc.*); '~**lord** Ober(lehns)herr *m*.

o·ver·ly ['əuvəli] übermäßig; allzu (-sehr).

o·ver...: '~**man·tel** Kaminaufsatz *m*; ~'**mas·ter** überwältigen; ~'**match** *j-m* weit überlegen sein; '~'**much** zu viel; '~'**night 1.** am Vorabend; über Nacht; **2.** Nacht...; nächtlich; Übernachtungs...; ~ *bag* Reisetasche *f*; ~ *stop* Aufenthalt *m* für eine Nacht; '~**pass** Überführung *f*; '~'**pay** (*irr. pay*) zu viel bezahlen; ~'**peo·pled** übervölkert; ~'**play** hochspielen, übertreiben; ~ *one's hand Karten*: sich überreizen; *fig.* sich übernehmen, es übertreiben; '~**plus** Überschuß *m*; ~'**pow·er** überwältigen; '~'**print** überdrucken; '~·**pro'duc·tion** Überproduktion *f*; '~'**rate** überschätzen; ~'**reach** übervorteilen; ~ *o.s.* sich übernehmen; ~·**re'act** übertrieben reagieren (*to auf acc.*); ~'**ride** (*irr. ride*) *fig.* sich hinwegsetzen über (*acc.*); umstoßen; ~'**rid·ing** ausschlaggebend; ~'**rule** überstimmen; ⚖ verwerfen; ~'**run** (*irr. run*) überrennen; überziehen; überlaufen; bedecken; *Zeit* überschreiten; *typ.* umbrechen; '~'**sea 1.** *a.* ~s überseeisch; Übersee...; ~s *aid* Entwicklungshilfe *f*; **2.** ~s *in od.* nach Übersee; '~'**see** (*irr. see*) beaufsichtigen; '~·**se·er** Aufseher *m*; ~'**set** (*irr. set*) umstoßen; *fig.* zerrütten; '~'**sew** (*irr. sew*) überwendlich nähen; ~'**shad·ow** überschatten, verdunkeln; '~**shoe** Überschuh *m*; '~'**shoot** (*irr. shoot*) über *ein Ziel* hinausschießen; ~ *o.s.* zu weit gehen; '~'**shot** oberschlächtig (*Wasserrad*); '~**sight** Versehen *n*; '~·**sim·pli·fi'ca·tion** allzu große Vereinfachung *f*; '~'**sleep** (*irr. sleep*) *a.* ~ *o.s.*

verschlafen; '~·**sleeve** Ärmelschoner *m*; '~·**spill** (*bsd.* Bevölkerungs)Überschuß *m*; ~'**staffed** übersetzt; '~·'**state** übertreiben; '~·'**state·ment** Übertreibung *f*; '~'**step** überschreiten; '~'**stock** überfüllen; ~'**strain 1.** ['~'strein] (sich) überanstrengen; *fig.* übertreiben; **2.** ['~strein] Überanstrengung *f*; ~'**strung** ['~'strʌŋ] überreizt; [~strʌŋ] kreuzsaitig (*Klavier*); '~·**sub'scribe** *Anleihe* überzeichnen; '~·**sup'ply** Überangebot *n*.

o·vert ['əuvə:t] offen(kundig).

over...: '~'**take** (*irr. take*) einholen; *et.* auf-, nachholen; *j.* überraschen; '~'**tax** zu hoch besteuern; *fig.* überschätzen; übermäßig in Anspruch nehmen; ~'**throw 1.** [~'θrəu] (*irr. throw*) (um)stürzen (*a. fig.*); vernichten, besiegen; **2.** ['~θrəu] Sturz *m*; Vernichtung *f*; ⚔ Niederlage *f*; '~·**time** Überstunden *f/pl.*; '~'**tire** übermüden; '~·**tone** ♪ Oberton *m*; *fig.* Unter-, Zwischenton *m*; '~'**top** überragen; '~'**trump** übertrumpfen.

over·ture ['əuvətjuə] ♪ Ouvertüre *f*, Vorspiel *n*; Vorschlag *m*, Antrag *m*.

o·ver...: ~'**turn 1.** ['~tə:n] Umsturz *m*; **2.** [~'tə:n] umstürzen, -werfen; kentern (lassen); '~'**val·ue** zu hoch einschätzen; überschätzen; ~·'**ween·ing** eingebildet; ~'**weight 1.** ['~weit] Übergewicht *n*; **2.** ['~'weit] überladen, -lasten; ~'**whelm** überhäufen, -schütten (*a. fig.*); überwältigen (*a. fig.*); erdrücken; '~'**wise** ☐ überklug; ~'**work 1.** ['~'wə:k] übermäßige Arbeit *f*; Überarbeitung *f*; **2.** [~'wə:k] (*irr. work*) sich überarbeiten; schinden, überanstrengen; '~'**wrought** überarbeitet; überreizt.

o·vi·duct ⚕ ['əuvidʌkt] Eileiter *m*; o·vi·form ['~fɔ:m] eiförmig; o'vip·a·rous *zo.* [~pərəs] eierlegend; o·vule *biol.* ['əuvju:l] Ovulum *n*, kleines Ei *n*; o·vum *biol.* ['əuvəm], *pl.* o·va ['əuvə] Ovum *n*, Ei(zelle *f*) *n*.

owe [əu] *Geld, Dank etc.* schulden, schuldig sein; verdanken; *Sport*: vorgeben; ~ *s.o. a grudge* Groll gegen j. hegen.

ow·ing ['əuiŋ] schuldig; ~ *to* infolge (*gen.*), wegen (*gen.*), dank (*dat.*); *be* ~ *to* herkommen von, zu verdanken *od.* zuzuschreiben sein

(*dat.*).
owl *orn.* [aul] Eule *f;* **owl·et** ['aulit] (junge) Eule *f;* '**owl·ish** ☐ eulenhaft, -artig.
own [əun] **1.** eigen; wirklich, richtig; einzig, innig geliebt; *my ~ self* ich selbst; *~ brother to s.o.* j-s rechter Bruder; *she makes her ~ clothes* sie näht ihre Kleider selbst; **2.** *my ~* mein Eigentum *n;* meine Angehörigen *pl.; a house of one's ~* ein eigenes Haus *n; come into one's ~* zu s-m Recht kommen; *get one's ~ back* F sich rächen; sich sein Recht holen; *hold one's ~* standhalten; sich behaupten; *on one's ~* F selbständig; von sich aus, auf eigene Faust; allein; **3.** besitzen; zugeben, zugestehen; anerkennen; sich bekennen (*to* zu); *~ up* (*to*) F bekennen.
own·er ['əunə] Eigentümer(in), Inhaber(in); '*~·***driv·er** Herrenfahrer *m;* '*~·***less** herrenlos; '*~·***oc·cu·pied** vom Eigentümer bewohnt (*Haus*); '**own·er·ship** Eigentum(srecht) *n,* Besitz(recht *n*) *m.*
ox [ɔks], *pl.* **ox·en** ['ɔksən] Ochs *m,* Ochse *m;* Rind *n.*
ox·al·ic ac·id ⚗ [ɔk'sælik'æsid] Oxal-, Kleesäure *f.*
Ox·bridge ['ɔksbridʒ] (die Universitäten *f*/*pl.*) Oxford und Cambridge.
ox-cart ['ɔkskɑːt] Ochsenkarren *m;* **ox·en** ['ɔksən] *pl. von ox;* '**ox-eye** ♀ Gänseblümchen *n.*
Ox·ford shoes ['ɔksfəd'ʃuːz] *pl.* Halbschuhe *m*/*pl.*
ox·i·da·tion ⚗ [ɔksi'deiʃən] Oxydation *f,* Oxydierung *f;* **ox·ide** ['ɔksaid] Oxyd *n;* **ox·i·dize** ['ɔksidaiz] oxydieren.
ox·lip ♀ ['ɔkslip] hohe Schlüsselblume *f.*
Ox·o·ni·an [ɔk'səunjən] **1.** Oxforder, Oxford...; **2.** Student *m od.* Absolvent *m* der Universität Oxford.
ox·tail soup ['ɔksteil'suːp] Ochsenschwanzsuppe *f.*
ox·y·a·cet·y·lene [ɔksiə'setiliːn] Azetylensauerstoff *m; ~ torch* Schweißbrenner *m.*
ox·y·gen ⚗ ['ɔksidʒən] Sauerstoff *m;* **ox·y·gen·ate** [ɔk'sidʒineit] mit Sauerstoff versetzen *od.* behandeln.
ox·y·hy·dro·gen ⚗ ['ɔksi'haidridʒən] Knallgas *n.*
o·yer ⚖ ['ɔiə] Verhör *n.*
o·yez [əu'jes] hört (zu)!; Ruhe!
oys·ter ['ɔistə] Auster *f; attr.* Austern...; '*~-***bed** Austernbank *f.*
o·zone ⚗ ['əuzəun] Ozon *n; ~ lay·er* Ozonschicht *f;* **o·zon·ic** [əu'zɔnik] ozonhaltig; Ozon...

P

P [piː]: *mind one's Ps and Qs* sich sehr in acht nehmen.
pa F [pɑː] Papa *m.*
pab·u·lum ['pæbjuləm] Nahrung *f.*
pace [peis] **1.** Schritt *m* (*a. als Maß*); Gang(art *f*) *m;* Paßgang *m;* Geschwindigkeit *f,* Tempo *n; keep ~ with* Schritt halten *od.* mitkommen mit; *put s.o. through his ~s* j. auf Herz u. Nieren prüfen; *set the ~* das Tempo bestimmen, Schrittmacher sein; **2.** *v*/*t.* abschreiten; *Sport:* Schrittmacher sein für; *v*/*i.* (einher)schreiten; (im) Paß gehen; **paced 1.** ... schreitend; **2.** *Sport:* mit Schrittmachern; '**pace-mak-er** *Sport:* Schrittmacher *m;* '**pac·er** Schrittmacher *m;* ⚕ Herzschrittmacher *m;* '**pac·er** Schreitende *m;* Fußgänger *m;* = *pace-maker.*
pach·y·derm *zo.* ['pækidəːm] Dickhäuter *m.*
pa·cif·ic [pə'sifik] **1.** (*~ally*) friedlich; *the ♀ Ocean* = **2.** *the ♀* der Pazifik, der Pazifische *od.* Stille Ozean; **pac·i·fi·ca·tion** [pæsifi'keiʃən] Befriedung *f;* Beruhigung *f.*
pac·i·fi·er ['pæsifaiə] Friedensstifter *m; Am.* Schnuller *m;* '**pac·i·fism** Pazifismus *m;* '**pac·i·fist** Pazifist(in).
pac·i·fy ['pæsifai] besänftigen, beruhigen; *Land* befrieden.
pack [pæk] **1.** Pack *m, n;* Packen *m;*

Paket *n*; Ballen *m*; Spiel *n Karten*; Meute *f Hunde*, Rudel *n Wölfe*; Rotte *f*, Bande *f*; Packung *f (a. ✈)*; *a.* ⁓ice Packeis *n*; *a* ⁓ *of nonsense* lauter Unsinn *m*; **2.** *v/t.* packen; *oft* ⁓ *up* zs.-, verpacken; einpacken (*a.* ✈); *a.* ⁓ *off* fortjagen; parteiisch zs.-setzen; *Am.* F (bei sich) tragen (*als Gepäck, Ausrüstung*); bepacken, vollstopfen; ⊕ dichten; *v/i. a.* ⁓ *up* packen; sich packen (lassen) (*Ware*); *send s.o.* ⁓*ing* j. fortjagen; ⁓ *up* F aufhören; **'pack·age** Pack *m*, Ballen *m*; *bsd. Am.* Paket *n*; Pakkung *f*; Frachtstück *n*; Verpakkung *f*; Verhandlungspaket *n*; ⁓ *deal* Pauschalangebot *n*; ⁓ *tour* Pauschalreise *f*; **'pack-an·i·mal** Tragtier *n*; **'pack·er** Packer(in); *Am.* Konservenfabrikant *m*; **pack·et** ['pækit] Paket *n*; Päckchen *n*; Pakkung *f*, Schachtel *f*; *a.* ⁓*-boat* Postschiff *n*, Paketboot *n*; *catch a* ⁓ *sl.* schwer verwundet werden; **'pack-horse** Packpferd *n*; Saumtier *n*; *fig.* Packesel *m*.

pack·ing ['pækiŋ] Packen *n*; Verpackung *f*; Packmaterial *n*; ⊕ Dichtung *f*; *attr.* Pack...; **'⁓-box** 🞨 Stopfbüchse *f*; ⁓ *house Am.* (*bsd.* Fleisch)Konservenfabrik *f*.

pack·thread ['pækθred] Bindfaden *m*, Packzwirn *m*.

pact [pækt] Vertrag *m*, Pakt *m*.

pad¹ *sl.* [pæd] *a.* ⁓ *it*, ⁓ *along* tippeln.

pad² [⁓] **1.** Polster *n*; *Sport:* Beinschutz *m*; Schreibblock *m*; Stempelkissen *n*; *hunt.* Pfote *f*; (Abschuß)Rampe *f*; **2.** (aus)polstern; wattieren; ⁓ *out fig.* auffüllen; ⁓*ded cell* Gummizelle *f*; **'pad·ding** Auspolstern *n*; Polsterung *f*, Wattierung *f*; *fig.* Lückenbüßer *m*.

pad·dle ['pædl] **1.** Paddel(ruder) *n*; ⚓ (Rad)Schaufel *f*; **2.** rudern, *bsd.* paddeln; planschen; *paddling pool* Planschbecken *n*; ⁓ *one's own canoe* sich selbst durchschlagen; **'⁓-box** ⚓ Radkasten *m*; **'⁓-steam·er** ⚓ Raddampfer *m*; **'⁓-wheel** Schaufelrad *n*.

pad·dock ['pædək] (Pferde)Koppel *f*; *Sport:* Sattelplatz *m*.

pad·dy¹ ✝ ['pædi] Reis *m* in Hülsen.

pad·dy² F [⁓] Wutanfall *m*.

pad·dy wag·on *Am.* P ['pædiwægən] Gefangenenwagen *m*, „Grüne Minna“ *f*.

pad·lock ['pædlɔk] Vorhängeschloß *n*.

pad·re F 🞨 ['pɑ:dri] Kaplan *m*, Geistliche *m*.

pae·an ['pi:ən] Dank-, Lob-, Freudengesang *m*.

paed·er·as·ty ['pedəræsti] Päderastie *f*, Knabenliebe *f*.

pae·di·a·tri·cian [pi:diə'triʃən] Kinderarzt *m*; **pae·di·at·rics** [⁓'ætriks] *sg.* Kinderheilkunde *f*.

pa·gan ['peigən] **1.** heidnisch; **2.** Heide *m*, Heidin *f*; **'pa·gan·ism** Heidentum *n*.

page¹ [peidʒ] **1.** Page *m*; Edelknabe *m*; junger Diener *m*; Hotelpage *m*; *Am.* Amtsdiener *m*; **2.** *Am.* (durch e-n Pagen) holen lassen.

page² [⁓] **1.** *Buch*-Seite *f*; *fig.* Blatt *n*; **2.** paginieren.

pag·eant ['pædʒənt] historisches Schau- *od.* Festspiel *n*; festlicher Umzug *m*; **'pag·eant·ry** Prunk *m*, Gepränge *n*.

pag·i·nate ['pædʒineit] *s. page²* 2; **pag·i'na·tion** Paginierung *f*.

pa·go·da [pə'gəudə] Pagode *f*.

paid [peid] *pret. u. p.p. von pay* 2.

pail [peil] Eimer *m*.

pail·lasse ['pæliæs] Strohsack *m*.

pain [pein] **1.** Pein *f*, Schmerz *m*; Kummer *m*; Strafe *f*; ⁓*s pl.* Leiden *n/pl.*; Mühe *f*; Wehen *f/pl.*; *on od. under* ⁓ *of death* bei Todesstrafe; *be in* ⁓ leiden; *be a* ⁓ *in the neck* F e-m auf den Wecker gehen; *be at* ⁓*s, take* ⁓*s* sich Mühe geben; **2.** *j-m* weh tun, *j.* schmerzen; **pain·ful** ☐ ['⁓ful] schmerzhaft, schmerzlich; peinlich; mühevoll; **'pain-kill·er** schmerzstillendes Mittel *n*; **'pain·less** ☐ schmerzlos; **'pains-tak·ing 1.** ☐ arbeitsam; sorgfältig; **2.** Sorgfalt *f*.

paint [peint] **1.** Farbe *f*; Schminke *f*; Anstrich *m*; *wet* ⁓*!* frisch gestrichen!; **2.** (be)malen; anstreichen; (sich) schminken; *fig.* malen, schildern; ⁓ *out* übermalen; **'⁓-box** Malkasten *m*; **'⁓-brush** Malerpinsel *m*.

paint·er¹ ['peintə] Maler(in).

paint·er² ⚓ [⁓] Fangleine *f*.

paint·ing ['peintiŋ] Malen *n*; Malerei *f*; Gemälde *n*.

paint·work ['peintwɔ:k] *Auto:* Lack *m*; Anstrich *m*.

pair [pɛə] **1.** Paar *n*; Gespann *n*; Partner *m*; Gegenstück *n*; *a* ⁓ *of* *scissors* eine Schere *f; in ~s* paarweise; **2.** (sich) paaren; zs.-passen; *a. ~ off* paarweise weggehen; *~ off with* F heiraten.

pa·ja·mas [pə'dʒɑːməz] = *pyjamas*.

Pa·kis·ta·ni [pɑːkis'tɑːni] **1.** Pakistaner(in); **2.** pakistanisch.

pal *sl.* [pæl] **1.** Kamerad *m*, Kumpel *m*; **2.** *~ up with s.o.* sich mit j-m anfreunden.

pal·ace ['pælis] Palast *m*.

pal·ae·o- ['pæliəu] Alt..., Früh..., Ur..., Vor...; **pal·ae·o·lith·ic** [~əu-'liθik] altsteinzeitlich; **pal·ae·on·tol·o·gy** [~ɔn'tɔlədʒi] Paläontologie *f*.

pal·at·a·ble □ ['pælətəbl] schmackhaft (*a. fig.*); **'pal·at·a·ble·ness** Schmackhaftigkeit *f*.

pal·a·tal ['pælətl] **1.** Gaumen...; **2.** *gr.* Gaumenlaut *m*, Palatal *m*.

pal·ate ['pælit] Gaumen *m*; Geschmack *m* (*a. fig.*).

pa·la·tial □ [pə'leiʃəl] palastartig.

pa·lat·i·nate [pə'lætinit] Pfalzgrafschaft *f; the ♀ die Pfalz.

pal·a·tine ['pælətain] pfälzisch; Pfalz...; *Count ♀* Pfalzgraf *m*.

pa·lav·er [pə'lɑːvə] **1.** Unterredung *f*; Geschwätz *n*, Palaver *n*; *sl.* Geschäft *n*; **2.** (be)schwatzen; schmeicheln (*dat.*).

pale[1] [peil] **1.** □ blaß, bleich; fahl; *~ ale* helles, starkes Ale *n*; **2.** *v t.* bleich machen, bleichen; *v i.* bleich werden, (er)bleichen.

pale[2] [~] Pfahl *m*; *die Grenzen* (*des Erlaubten*).

pale-face ['peilfeis] Bleichgesicht *n*.

pale·ness ['peilnis] Blässe *f*.

pa·le·o- ['pæliəu] *s. palaeo-*.

pal·ette *paint.* ['pælit] Palette *f*; **'~-knife** Streichmesser *n*.

pal·frey ['pɔːlfri] Zelter *m*.

pal·imp·sest ['pælimpsest] Palimpsest *m, n* (*zweimal beschriebenes Pergament*).

pal·ing ['peiliŋ] Pfahlzaun *m*.

pal·i·sade [pæli'seid] **1.** Palisade *f*; Staket *n; ~s pl. Am.* Steilufer *n*; **2.** umpfählen.

pall[1] [pɔːl] **1.** Bahrtuch *n; fig.* Decke *f*, Wolke *f*; **2.** einhüllen.

pall[2] [~] schal werden, den Reiz verlieren (*upon s.o.* für j.).

pal·la·di·um [pə'leidjəm] Palladium *n*; Hort *m*, Schutz *m*.

pall·bear·er ['pɔːlbɛərə] Sargträger *m*.

pal·let ['pælit] Strohsack *m*.

pal·liasse ['pæliæs] = *paillasse*.

pal·li·ate ['pælieit] bemänteln; beschönigen; lindern; **pal·li·a·tion** Bemäntelung *f*; Beschönigung *f*; Linderung *f*; **pal·li·a·tive** ['~ətiv] **1.** bemäntelnd; lindernd; **2.** Linderungsmittel *n; fig.* Bemäntelung *f*.

pal·lid □ ['pælid] blaß; **'pal·lid·ness, pal·lor** ['pælə] Blässe *f*.

pal·ly F ['pæli] freundlich, gesellig; *be ~ with s.o.* mit j-m gut Freund sein.

palm [pɑːm] **1.** Handfläche *f*; Handbreite *f* (*als Maß*); Schaufel *f des Ankers, Hirschgeweihes*; ♀ Palme *f* (*fig. Sieg*); *have an itching ~* bestechlich sein; **2.** betasten; in der Hand verbergen; *~ s.th. off upon s.o.* j-m et. andrehen; **pal·mer** ['pɑːmə] Pilger *m*; **'palm·ist** Handleser(in); **'palm·is·try** Handlesekunst *f*; **'palm-oil** Palmöl *n; co.* Schmiergeld(er *pl.*) *n*; **Palm Sunday** Palmsonntag *m*; **'palm-tree** Palme *f*; **'palm·y** glücklich, blühend.

pal·pa·ble ['pælpəbl] □ fühlbar; *fig.* handgreiflich, klar, eindeutig, augenfällig.

pal·pi·tate ['pælpiteit] schlagen, pochen (*Herz*); zittern; **pal·pi·ta·tion** Herzklopfen *n*.

pal·sy ['pɔːlzi] **1.** Lähmung *f; fig.* Ohnmacht *f*; **2.** *fig.* lähmen.

pal·ter ['pɔːltə] sein Spiel treiben (*with* mit).

pal·tri·ness ['pɔːltrinis] Erbärmlichkeit *f*; **'pal·try** □ erbärmlich; armselig; schäbig; wertlos.

pam·pas ['pæmpəz] *pl.* die Pampas *pl.*

pam·per ['pæmpə] verzärteln.

pam·phlet ['pæmflit] Flugschrift *f*, Broschüre *f*; **pam·phlet·eer** [~'tiə] Pamphletist *m*.

pan [pæn] **1.** Pfanne *f*; Tiegel *m*; **2.** *v/t. Gold etc.* waschen; *Kamera* schwenken; *Am.* F heruntermachen (*scharf kritisieren*); *v/i.* schwenken (*Kamera*); *~ out* sich bezahlt machen.

pan... [~] all..., gesamt...; All...; Gesamt...; pan..., Pan...

pan·a·ce·a [pænə'siə] Allheilmittel *n*.

pan·cake ['pænkeik] Pfannkuchen *m; ~ landing* ✈ Bumslandung *f*.

pan·cre·as ✗ ['pæŋkriəs] Bauch-

speicheldrüse *f.*
pan·da ['pændə] Panda *m (Bärenart)*;
~ **car** Streifenwagen *m.*
pan·de·mo·ni·um *fig.* [pændi'məun-jəm] Hölle(nlärm *m) f.*
pan·der ['pændə] **1.** Vorschub leisten (*to dat.*); kuppeln; **2.** Kuppler (-in).
pane [pein] (Fenster)Scheibe *f;* ⊕ Fach *n,* Feld *n.*
pan·e·gyr·ic [pæni'dʒirik] Lobrede *f;* **pan·e·gyr·ist** Lobredner *m.*
pan·el ['pænl] **1.** ⚠ Fach *n,* Feld *n;* Füllung *f e-r Tür etc.; paint.* Holztafel *f;* Einsatz *m am Kleid;* ⚙ Geschworenenliste *f; die* Geschworenen *m/pl.;* Ausschuß *m;* Diskussionsteilnehmer *m/pl.,* -redner *m/pl.;* Verzeichnis *n* der Kassenärzte; **2.** täfeln; in Felder einteilen; ~ **dis·cus·sion** Podiumsdiskussion *f;* '~**doc·tor** Kassenarzt *m;* '**pan·el·ist** Diskussionsteilnehmer *m;* '**pan·el·(l)ing** Täfelung *f.*
pang [pæŋ] plötzlicher Schmerz *m,* Weh *n; fig.* Angst *f,* Qual *f;* ~*s pl. of hunger* nagender Hunger *m.*
pan·go·lin *zo.* [pæŋ'gəulin] Schuppentier *n.*
pan·han·dle ['pænhændl] **1.** Pfannenstiel *m; Am.* schmaler Fortsatz *m e-s Staatsgebiets;* **2.** *Am.* F betteln; '**pan·han·dler** *Am.* F Bettler *m.*
pan·ic ['pænik] **1.** panisch; **2.** Panik *f,* panischer Schrecken *m;* ~ *buying* Angstkäufe *m/pl.;* **3.** *pret. u. p.p.* '**pan·icked** Angst bekommen; '**pan·ick·y** F beunruhigend; unruhig (*at* über *acc.*); '**pan·ic·-mon·ger** Bangemacher(in); '**pan·ic-strick·en** von panischer Angst erfüllt.
pan·nier ['pæniə] (Trag)Korb *m.*
pan·ni·kin ['pænikin] Kännchen *n;* Pfännchen *n.*
pan·o·ply ['pænəpli] volle Rüstung *f; fig.* Anordnung *f,* Reihe *f.*
pan·o·ra·ma [pænə'rɑːmə] Panorama *n,* Rundblick *m;* **pan·o·ram·ic** [~'ræmik] (~*ally*) panoramahaft; umfassend.
pan·sy ['pænzi] ♀ Stiefmütterchen *n; a.* ~**-boy** Weichling *m;* Homosexuelle *m.*
pant [pænt] *v/i.* schnappen (*for breath* nach Luft); keuchen, schnaufen; klopfen (*Herz*); ver-

langen, lechzen (*for, after* nach); *v/t.* ~ *out* (hervor)keuchen.
pan·ta·loon [pæntə'luːn] Hanswurst *m;* ~*s pl. co. od. Am. für pants.*
pan·tech·ni·con [pæn'teknikən] *a.* ~ *van* Möbelwagen *m.*
pan·the·ism ['pænθiizm] Pantheismus *m;* **pan·the·is·tic** (~*ally*) pantheistisch.
pan·ther *zo.* ['pænθə] Panther *m.*
pant·ies F ['pæntiz] *pl.* Damenschlüpfer *m;* Kinderhöschen *n.*
pan·tile ['pæntail] Dachpfanne *f.*
pan·to F ['pæntəu] = *pantomime.*
pan·to·graph ⊕ ['pæntəugrɑːf] Storchschnabel *m.*
pan·to·mime ['pæntəmaim] Pantomime *f;* revueartiges Märchenspiel *n;* **pan·to·mim·ic** [~'mimik] (~*ally*) pantomimisch.
pan·try ['pæntri] Speise-, Vorratskammer *f;* Geschirr- und Wäschekammer *f.*
pants [pænts] *pl.* Hose *f; Am.* Herrenhose *f;* ⚡ lange Unterhose *f.*
pant(s) suit ['pæntsuːt] *Am.* Hosenanzug *m.*
pan·ty ['pænti]: ~ **gir·dle** Miederhöschen *n;* ~ **hose** *bsd. Am.* Strumpfhose *f.*
pap [pæp] Brei *m.*
pa·pa [pə'pɑː] Papa *m.*
pa·pa·cy ['peipəsi] Papsttum *m.*
pa·pal ☐ ['peipəl] päpstlich.
pa·per ['peipə] **1.** Papier *n;* Zeitung *f;* Prüfungsaufgabe *f;* Vortrag *m,* Aufsatz *m; a.* ~ *money* Papiergeld *n;* ~*s pl.* (Ausweis)Papiere *n/pl.; send in one's* ~*s* zurücktreten; **2.** tapezieren; '~**-back** Taschenbuch *n,* Paperback *n;* ~ **bag** (Papier)Tüte *f;* '~**-chase** Schnitzeljagd *f;* '~**-clip** Büroklammer *f;* ~ **cred·it** ⚡ Wechselkredit *m;* ~ **cup** Pappbecher *m;* '~**-fast·en·er** Musterklammer *f;* '~**-hang·er** Tapezierer *m;* '~**-hang·ings** *pl.* Tapeten *f/pl.;* ~ **knife** Brieföffner *m;* '~**-mill** Papierfabrik *f;* ~ **plate** Pappteller *m;* ~ **tape** Lochstreifen *m;* '~**·thin** hauchdünn; '~**-weight** Briefbeschwerer *m;* '**pa·per·y** papierartig, -dünn.
pa·pier mâ·ché ['pæpjei'mɑːʃei] Papiermaché *n.* [Katholik *m.*]
pa·pist *contp.* ['peipist] Papist *m,*]
pap·py ['pæpi] breiig.
pap·ri·ka ['pæprikə] Paprika *m.*
pa·py·rus [pə'paiərəs] Papyrus *m.*

par [pɑ:] ⴕ Nennwert *m*, Pari *n*; *above* (*below*) ∼ über (unter) Pari; *at* ∼ zum Nennwert; *be on a* ∼ *with* gleich, ebenbürtig sein (*dat.*).

par·a F ['pærə] Fallschirmjäger *m*.

par·a·ble ['pærəbl] Parabel *f*, Gleichnis *n*.

pa·rab·o·la A [pə'ræbələ] Parabel *f*; **par·a·bol·ic, par·a·bol·i·cal** □ [pærə'bɔlik(əl)] in Gleichnissen; A parabolisch.

par·a·chute ['pærəʃuːt] Fallschirm *m*; '**par·a·chut·ist** Fallschirmspringer(in).

pa·rade [pə'reid] **1.** ⚔ (Truppen-) Parade *f*; Appell *m*; *eccl.* Prozession *f*; Zurschaustellung *f*; Promenade *f*; (Um)Zug *m*; Modenschau *f*; *programme* ∼ *Radio*: Programmvorschau *f*; *make a* ∼ *of s.th.* et. zur Schau stellen; **2.** ⚔ antreten (lassen); vorbeimarschieren (lassen); zur Schau stellen; **pa'rade-ground** ⚔ Exerzier-, Paradeplatz *m*.

par·a·digm *gr.* ['pærədaim] Paradigma *n*, (Muster)Beispiel *n*.

par·a·dise ['pærədais] Paradies *n*.

par·a·dis·i·ac [pærə'disiæk] paradiesisch.

par·a·dox ['pærədɔks] Paradox(on) *n*; **par·a'dox·i·cal** □ paradox, widersinnig.

par·af·fin ⚗ ['pærəfin] Paraffin *n*.

par·a·gon ['pærəgən] Vorbild *n*; Muster *n*; Ausbund *m*.

par·a·graph ['pærəgrɑːf] Absatz *m*, Abschnitt *m*; Paragraph(zeichen *n*) *m*; kurze Zeitungsnotiz *f*.

par·a·keet *orn.* ['pærəkiːt] Sittich *m*.

par·al·lel ['pærəlel] **1.** parallel, gleichlaufend; *fig.* entsprechend; **2.** Parallele *f* (*a. fig.*); Breitengrad *m*; Gegenstück *n*; Vergleich *m*; *without* (*a*) ∼ ohnegleichen; **3.** vergleichen; entsprechen; gleichen; parallel laufen (mit); ∼ **bars** *pl. Sport*: Barren *m*; '**par·al·lel·ism** Parallelismus *m*; **par·al'lel·o·gram** A [̩ləugræm] Parallelogramm *n*.

par·a·lyse ['pærəlaiz] lähmen; *fig.* unwirksam machen; **pa·ral·y·sis** ﬡ [pə'rælisis] Paralyse *f*, Lähmung *f*; **par·a·lyt·ic** [pærə'litik] **1.** (∼*ally*) paralytisch; gelähmt; **2.** Gelähmte *m*, *f*.

par·a·mil·i·tar·y ['pærə'militəri] halbmilitärisch.

par·a·mount ['pærəmaunt] oberst,

höchst, hervorragend, überragend; größer, höher stehend (*to* als).

par·a·mour *rhet.* ['pærəmuə] Geliebte *m*, *f*; Buhle *m*, *f*.

par·a·noi·a ﬡ [pærə'nɔiə] Verfolgungswahn *m*; **par·a·noi·ac** [∼'nɔiæk] **1.** paranoisch; **2.** Paranoiker *m*; **par·a·noid** ['∼nɔid] paranoid.

par·a·pet ['pærəpit] ⚔ Brustwehr *f*; Brüstung *f*; Geländer *n*.

par·a·pher·na·li·a [pærəfə'neiljə] *pl.* Ausrüstung *f*; Zubehör *n*, *m*; Drum u. Dran *n*.

par·a·phrase ['pærəfreiz] **1.** Paraphrase *f*, Umschreibung *f*; **2.** paraphrasieren, umschreiben.

par·a·ple·gi·a ﬡ [pærə'pliːdʒə] Querschnitt(s)lähmung *f*; **par·a'ple·gic 1.** querschnitt(s)gelähmt; **2.** Querschnitt(s)gelähmte *m*.

par·a·site ['pærəsait] Parasit *m*, Schmarotzer *m*; **par·a·sit·ic, par·a·sit·i·cal** □ [∼'sitik(əl)] schmarotzerhaft, parasitisch.

par·a·sol [pærə'sɔl] Sonnenschirm *m*.

par·a·troop·er ['pærətruːpə] ⚔ Fallschirmjäger *m*; '**par·a·troops** *pl.* Luftlandetruppen *f*/*pl.*

par·a·ty·phoid ﬡ ['pærə'taifɔid] Paratyphus *m*. [braten, schmoren.]

par·boil ['pɑːbɔil] ankochen; *fig.*⌡

par·cel ['pɑːsl] **1.** Paket *n*, Päckchen *n*; ⴕ Partie *f*; *contp.* Haufe(n) *m*; (Land)Parzelle *f*; **2.** ∼ *out* (in Stücke) teilen, *Land* parzellieren; ∼ **post** Paketpost *f*.

parch [pɑːtʃ] rösten, (aus)dörren; ∼*ing heat* sengende Hitze *f*.

parch·ment ['pɑːtʃmənt] Pergament *n*.

pard *sl.* [pɑːd] Partner *m*.

par·don ['pɑːdn] **1.** Verzeihung *f*; ⚖ Begnadigung *f*; *eccl.* Ablaß *m*; *I beg your* ∼ (ich bitte um) Verzeihung!; *wie bitte?*; **2.** verzeihen (*s.o.* j-m; *s.th.* et.); *j.* begnadigen; '**par·don·a·ble** □ verzeihlich; '**par·don·er** *hist.* Ablaßkrämer *m*.

pare [pɛə] *Fingernägel etc.* (be-) schneiden; *Äpfel etc.* schälen; ∼ *away*, ∼ *down fig.* beschneiden.

par·ent ['pɛərənt] **1.** Vater *m*, Mutter *f*; Elternteil *m*; Ursache *f*; ∼*s pl.* Eltern *pl.*; ∼*-teacher association* Elternbeirat *m*; ∼*-teacher meeting* Elternabend *m*; **2.** *fig.* Mutter...; Stamm...; Ursprungs...; '**par·ent-**

age Herkunft *f*; Elternschaft *f*; **pa·ren·tal** ☐ [pəˈrentl] elterlich.
pa·ren·the·sis [pəˈrenθisis], *pl.* **pa·'ren·the·ses** [‿siːz] Parenthese *f*, Einschaltung *f*; *typ.* (runde) Klammer *f*; **par·en·the·tic, par·en·thet·i·cal** ☐ [pærənˈθetik(əl)] eingeschaltet, beiläufig.
par·ent·hood [ˈpɛərənthud] Elternschaft *f*; **'par·ent·less** elternlos.
pa·ri·ah [ˈpæriə] Paria *m*, Rechtlose *m, f*.
pa·ri·e·tal [pəˈraiitl] Wand...; ‿ *bone anat.* Scheitelbein *n*.
par·ing [ˈpɛəriŋ] Schälen *n*, Abschneiden *n*; ‿s *pl.* Schalen *f/pl.*, Schnipsel *m/pl.*; '‿-knife ⊕ Schälmesser *n*; Schustermesser *n*.
par·ish [ˈpæriʃ] 1. Kirchspiel *n*, Gemeinde *f*; go on the ‿ der Gemeinde zur Last fallen; 2. Pfarr...; Gemeinde...; ‿ clerk Küster *m*; ‿ council Gemeinderat *m*; ‿ register Kirchenbuch *n*; **pa·rish·ion·er** [pəˈriʃənə] Pfarrkind *n*, Gemeindeglied *n*.
Pa·ri·sian [pəˈrizjən] 1. *adj.* Pariser; 2. Pariser(in).
par·i·ty [ˈpæriti] Gleichheit *f*; *Börse:* Parität *f*.
park [paːk] 1. Park *m* (*a.* ✕), Anlagen *f/pl.*; Naturschutzgebiet *n*; *mst car‿* Parkplatz *m*; ‿ keeper Parkwächter *m*; 2. *mot.* parken, abstellen.
par·ka [ˈpaːkə] Anorak *m*, Schneehemd *n*.
park·ing *mot.* [ˈpaːkiŋ] Parken *n*; ‿ fee Parkgebühr *f*; ‿ lot Parkplatz *m*; ‿ me·ter Parkuhr *f*; ‿ space Parkplatz *m*, -lücke *f*; ‿ tick·et Strafzettel *m für unerlaubtes Parken*.
par·ky *sl.* [ˈpaːki] kalt; frisch.
par·lance [ˈpaːləns] Ausdrucksweise *f*, Sprache *f*.
par·ley [ˈpaːli] 1. Unterhandlung *f*, Konferenz *f*; 2. *v/i.* unterhandeln; sich besprechen; *v/t.* parlieren (*sprechen*).
par·lia·ment [ˈpaːləmənt] Parlament *n*; **par·lia·men·tar·i·an** [‿menˈtɛəriən] Parlamentarier(in); **par·lia·men·ta·ry** ☐ [‿ˈmentəri] parlamentarisch; Parlaments...
par·lo(u)r [ˈpaːlə] Wohnzimmer *n*; Empfangs-, Sprechzimmer *n*; *beauty* ‿ *bsd. Am.* Schönheitssalon *m*; ‿ car 🚃 *Am.* Salonwagen *m*; '‿-maid Stubenmädchen *n*.

pa·ro·chi·al ☐ [pəˈrəukjəl] parochial; Pfarr...; Gemeinde...; *fig.* engstirnig, beschränkt; ‿ *politics pi.* Kirchturmpolitik *f*.
par·o·dist [ˈpærədist] Parodist(in); **'par·o·dy** 1. Parodie *f*; 2. parodieren.
pa·role [pəˈrəul] 1. ✕ Parole *f*, Kennwort *n*; Ehrenwort *n*; put on ‿ = 3; 2. ♪♪ mündlich; 3. ♪♪ *bsd. Am.* bedingt freilassen.
par·ox·ysm [ˈpærəksizəm] Paroxysmus *m*, Anfall *m*.
par·quet [ˈpaːkei] Parkett(fußboden *m*) *n*; *Am. thea.* Parkett *n*; **par·quet·ed** [ˈpaːkitid] Parkett...; '**par·quet·ry** Parkett(ierung *f*) *n*.
par·ri·cide [ˈpærisaid] Vater-, Muttermörder(in); Vater-, Muttermord *m*.
par·rot [ˈpærət] 1. *orn.* Papagei *m* (*a. fig.*); 2. wie ein Papagei (nach-)plappern.
par·ry *fenc.* [ˈpæri] 1. Parade *f*; 2. abwehren, parieren (*a. fig.*).
parse [paːz] grammatisch zerlegen, analysieren.
Par·see [paːˈsiː] Parse *m*, Parsin *f*.
par·si·mo·ni·ous ☐ [paːsiˈməunjəs] sparsam, karg; *b.s.* knauserig; **par·si·mo·ni·ous·ness, par·si·mo·ny** [ˈ‿məni] Sparsamkeit *f*; Knauserigkeit *f*.
pars·ley ♣ [ˈpaːsli] Petersilie *f*.
pars·nip ♣ [ˈpaːsnip] Pastinake *f*.
par·son [ˈpaːsn] Pfarrer *m*, Pastor *m*; Geistliche *m*; '**par·son·age** Pfarrei *f*; Pfarrhaus *n*; **par·son's nose** F Bürzel *m von gebratenem od. gekochtem Geflügel*.
part [paːt] 1. Teil *m, n*; Stück *n*; Anteil *m* (of, in an *dat.*); Seite *f*, Partei *f*; Pflicht *f*, Amt *n*; Rolle *f* (*thea. u. fig.*); Lieferung *f* e–s *Buches*; ♩ Einzel-Stimme *f*; Körperteil *m*; † geistige Anlagen *f/pl.*; ‿s *pl.* Gegend *f*; ‿ of speech *gr.* Wortart *f*; ‿ and parcel of untrennbar von; *a man of* ‿s ein fähiger Mensch *m*; *have neither* ‿ *nor lot in* nicht das geringste zu tun haben mit; *in foreign* ‿s im Ausland; *play a* ‿ *fig.* schauspielern; *take* ‿ *in s.th.* an e-r Sache teilnehmen; *take in good* (*bad*) ‿ gut (übel) aufnehmen; *for my* (*own*) ‿, was mich betrifft; meinerseits; *for the most* ‿ meistenteils; *in* ‿ teilweise; Abschlags...; *do one's* ‿ das

Seinige tun; *on the* ~ *of* von seiten
(*gen.*); *on my* ~ meinerseits; **2.** *adv.*
teils, zum Teil; **3.** *v/t.* (zer)teilen;
trennen; *Haar* scheiteln; ~ *company*
sich trennen (*with* von); *v/i.* sich
trennen; scheiden (*from* von); ~
with sich trennen von; aufgeben.
par·take [pɑːˈteik] (*irr. take*) teilnehmen, -haben (*in od. of s.th.* an
e-r Sache); ~ *of* mitessen *od.* -trinken
von; *Mahlzeit* einnehmen; grenzen
an (*acc.*); etwas an sich haben von;
par'tak·er Teilnehmer(in), -haber
(-in) (*of* an *dat.*).
par·terre [pɑːˈteə] Ziergarten *m*;
thea. Parterre *n*.
Par·thian [ˈpɑːθjən] parthisch.
par·tial □ [ˈpɑːʃl] Teil...; teilweise;
partiell; parteiisch; eingenommen
(*to* von, für); **par·ti·al·i·ty** [pɑːʃi-
ˈæliti] Parteilichkeit *f*; Vorliebe *f*
(*to, for* für).
par·tic·i·pant [pɑːˈtisipənt] Teil-
nehmer(in); **par'tic·i·pate** [~peit]
teilhaben *od.* -nehmen (*in* an *dat.*);
par·tic·i'pa·tion Teilnahme *f*;
par·ti·cip·i·al □ [~ˈsipiəl] *gr.* par-
tizipial; **par·ti·ci·ple** [ˈ~sipl] *gr.*
Partizip(ium) *n*, Mittelwort *n*.
par·ti·cle [ˈpɑːtikl] Teilchen *n*; *fig.*
Fünkchen *n*; *gr.* Partikel *f*; ~ **phys·ics**
sg. Elementarteilchen-, Hochener-
giephysik *f*.
par·ti·col·oured [ˈpɑːtikʌləd] bunt.
par·tic·u·lar [pəˈtikjulə] **1.** □ *mst*
besonder; einzeln; Sonder...; sonderbar; genau, ausführlich; genau,
eigen; wählerisch (*in, about,* as to
in *dat.*); **2.** Einzelheit *f*; einzelner
Punkt *m*, Umstand *m*; ~*s pl.* nähere
Umstände *m/pl., das* Nähere; *in* ~
insbesondere; **par·tic·u·lar·i·ty**
[~ˈlæriti] Besonderheit *f*; Ausführ-
lichkeit *f*; Eigenheit *f*; **par'tic·u-
lar·ize** [~ləraiz] einzeln *od.* ausführlich angeben; **par'tic·u·lar·ly**
besonders.
part·ing [ˈpɑːtiŋ] **1.** Trennung *f*;
Teilung *f*; Abschied *m*; *Haar*-
Scheitel *m*; ~ *of the ways bsd. fig.*
Scheideweg *m*; **2.** Abschieds...,
Scheide...
par·ti·san [pɑːtiˈzæn] **1.** Parteigän-
ger(in); ✕ Partisan *m*; **2.** Partei...;
par·ti'san·ship Parteigängertum *n*.
par·ti·tion [pɑːˈtiʃən] **1.** Teilung *f*;
Scheidewand *f*; Verschlag *m*, Fach
n; ~ *wall* Zwischenwand *f*, -mauer *f*;

2. teilen; ~ *off* abteilen, -trennen.
par·ti·tive □ [ˈpɑːtitiv] partitiv.
part·ly [ˈpɑːtli] teilweise, zum Teil.
part·ner [ˈpɑːtnə] **1.** Partner(in),
Gefährte *m*, Gefährtin *f*; Tänzer
(-in); ✝ Kompagnon *m*, Teilhaber
(-in); Gatte *m*, Gattin *f*; **2.** zs.-
bringen; sich zs.-tun mit, zs.-
arbeiten mit; **'part·ner·ship** Teilhaberschaft *f*; ✝ Handelsgesellschaft *f*; Partnerschaft *f*; *enter into*
~ *with* sich assoziieren mit.
part...: **'~-own·er** Miteigentümer
(-in); **'~-pay·ment** Teilzahlung *f*.
par·tridge *orn.* [ˈpɑːtridʒ] Reb-
huhn *n*.
part...: **'~-song** mehrstimmiges
Lied *n*; **'~-time 1.** *adj.* Teilzeit...,
Halbtags...; ~ *job* Teilzeitbeschäfti-
gung *f*; **2.** *adv.* halbtags.
par·ty [ˈpɑːti] Partei *f* (*pol.*, ½*ts*);
Parteisystem *n*; ✕ Trupp *m*, Kommando *n*; Party *f*, Gesellschaft *f*;
Gruppe *f*; Teilnehmer *m*, Beteiligte
m; *co.* Type *f*, Individuum *n*;
s. line[1] **1**; ~ **lin·er** Linientreue *m*.
par·ve·nu [ˈpɑːvənjuː] Empor-
kömmling *m*, Parvenü *m*.
pas·chal [ˈpɑːskəl] Passah..., Oster...
pa·sha [ˈpɑːʃə] Pascha *m*.
pass [pɑːs] **1.** Paß *m*, Ausweis *m*;
Passierschein *m*; Bestehen *n* e-s
Examens; *univ.* gewöhnlicher Grad
m; Zustand *m*, (kritische) Lage *f*;
Fußball: Paß *m*; Bestreichung *f*,
Strich *m*; *fenc.* Ausfall *m*, Stoß *m*;
sl. Annäherungsversuch *m*; (Gebirgs)Paß *m*, Durchgang *m*; *Karten:*
Passen *n*; *free* ~ Freikarte *f*; *hold the*
~ *fig.* die Stellung halten; **2.** *v/i.*
passieren, vorgehen, geschehen;
hingenommen werden, hingehen;
Karten: passen; gehen, kommen,
fahren; vorbeigehen, -kommen,
-fahren; vorübergehen, vergehen
(*Zeit*); sich verwandeln; angenommen werden (*Banknoten*); bekannt
sein; vergehen; aussterben; *a.* ~
away sterben; verscheiden; durchkommen (*Gesetz*; *Prüfling*); ~ *for*
gelten als; ~ *off* vonstatten gehen;
~ *out* F ohnmächtig werden; *come to*
~ geschehen; *bring to* ~ bewirken;
3. *v/t.* vorbeigehen, -kommen,
-fahren an (*dat.*); passieren; kommen *od.* fahren durch; verbringen;
reichen, geben; *Bemerkung* machen,
von sich geben; *Banknoten* in Um-

lauf bringen; *Gesetz* durchbringen,
annehmen; *Prüfling* durchkommen
lassen; *Prüfung* bestehen; (hinaus-)
gehen über (*acc.*); *Urteil* abgeben;
Meinung äußcrn; bewegen; streichen mit; *Ball* zuspielen; *Truppen*
vorbeimarschieren lassen; ⁓ *s.o.*
(*s.th.*) *by* j. (et.) übergehen; ⁓ *off* ablenken von; ⁓ *s.o.* (*s.th.*) *off as* j. (et.)
ausgeben als; ⁓ *over* übergehen,
übersehen; *it* ⁓*es my comprehension*
es geht über m-n Verstand; ⁓ *one's*
hand across one's forehead mit der
Hand über die Stirn streichen; ⁓
s.th. round s.th. et. um et. legen; ⁓
water Wasser lassen; ⁓ *one's word*
sein Ehrenwort geben; '**pass·a·ble**
passierbar; gangbar, gültig (*Geld*);
□ erträglich, leidlich, passabel.

pas·sage ['pæsidʒ] Durchgang *m*,
-fahrt *f*; Überfahrt *f*; (See-, Flug-)
Reise *f*; Durchreise *f*; Korridor *m*,
Flur *m*, Gang *m*; Weg *m*; Annahme
f e-s Gesetzes; ♩ Passage *f*; Text-
Stelle *f*; ⁓*s pl*. Beziehungen *f/pl.*;
⁓ *of od. at arms* Waffengang *m*; *bird*
of ⁓ Zugvogel *m*; '⁓·**way** Durchgang *m*; Korridor *m*.

pass-book ✝ ['pɑːsbuk] Sparbuch
n.

pas·sé(e) ['pɑːsei] vergangen, veraltet; verblüht; passé.

pas·sen·ger ['pæsindʒə] Passagier *m*,
Fahr-, Fluggast *m*, Reisende *m, f*; ⁓
train Personenzug *m.*

passe-par·tout ['pæspɑːtuː] Passepartout *n* (*Hauptschlüssel*); *phot.*
Wechselrahmen).

pass·er-by, *pl.* **pass·ers-by** ['pɑː-
sə(z)'bai] Vorübergehende *m, f*,
Passant(in).

pas·sim ['pæsim] passim, an vielen
Stellen *e-s Buchs.*

pass·ing ['pɑːsiŋ] 1. Vorbei-, Vorübergehen *n*; Dahinschwinden *n*;
Annahme *f e-s Gesetzes*; Hin-
scheiden *n*; *in* ⁓ beiläufig; 2. vorübergehend, flüchtig; '⁓**-bell** Totenglocke *f.*

pas·sion ['pæʃən] Leidenschaft *f*
(*Gemütserregung; heftige Liebe;
Liebhaberei*); (Gefühls)Ausbruch*m*;
Zorn *m*; ♀ Leiden *n* (Christi), Passion *f*; *be in a* ⁓ zornig sein; *in* ⁓ 𝔤𝔥
im Affekt; ♀ *Week* Karwoche *f*;
Woche *f* vor der Karwoche; **pas-
sion·ate** □ ['⁓ʃənit] leidenschaftlich; '**pas·sion-flow·er** ♣ Pas-

sionsblume *f*; '**pas·sion·less** □
leidenschaftslos; '**pas·sion-play**
Passionsspiel *n.*

pas·sive □ ['pæsiv] passiv (*a. gr.*);
teilnahmslos; untätig; '**pas·sive-
ness**, **pas'siv·i·ty** Passivität *f*;
Teilnahmslosigkeit *f.*

pass-key ['pɑːskiː] Hauptschlüssel
m, Nachschlüssel *m*, Drücker *m.*

Pass·o·ver ['pɑːsəuvə] Passah(fest)
n; Osterlamm *n.*

pass·port ['pɑːspɔːt] (Reise)Paß *m.*

pass·word ✕ ['pɑːswəːd] Losung *f.*

past [pɑːst] 1. *adj.* vergangen; letzt;
gr. Vergangenheits...; ⁓ *master*
Altmeister *m*; *for some time* ⁓ seit
einiger Zeit; 2. *adv.* vorbei; *rush* ⁓
vorbeieilen; 3. *prp.* nach, über;
über ... (*acc.*) hinaus; an (*dat.*) vorbei; *half* ⁓ *two* halb drei; *it is* ⁓
comprehension es geht über alle Begriffe; ⁓ *cure* unheilbar; ⁓ *endurance*
unerträglich; ⁓ *hope* hoffnungslos;
I would not put it ⁓ *her* das traue ich ihr
glatt zu; 4. Vergangenheit *f.*

paste [peist] 1. Teig *m*; Kleister *m*;
Paste *f*; unechter Stein *m*; 2. kleistern, kleben; bekleben; '⁓·**board**
Pappe *f*; *sl.* Karte *f*; *attr.* Papp...;
aus Pappe.

pas·tel [pæs'tel] ♀ Färberwaid *m*;
paint. Pastellstift *m*; Pastell(bild) *n*;
pas·tel·(l)ist ['⁓təlist] Pastellmaler
(-in).

pas·tern *vet.* ['pæstəːn] Fessel *f.*

paste-up ['peistʌp] Photomontage*f*;
Zs.-stellung *f.*

pas·teur·ize ['pæstəraiz] pasteurisieren, keimfrei machen.

pas·tille ['pæstəl] Pastille *f.*

pas·time ['pɑːstaim] Zeitvertreib *m*,
Kurzweil *f.*

pas·tor ['pɑːstə] Pastor *m*; Seel-
sorger *m*; '**pas·to·ral 1.** □ Hirten-
...; pastoral; ⁓ *staff* Krummstab *m*;
2. Hirtengedicht *n*; Pastorale *n, f*;
paint. Idyll *n*; *eccl.* Hirtenbrief
m.

pas·try ['peistri] Tortengebäck *n*,
Konditorwaren *f/pl.*; Pasteten *f/pl.*;
'⁓-**cook** Pastetenbäcker *m*, Konditor *m.*

pas·tur·age ['pɑːstjuridʒ] Weiden *n*;
Weide(land *n*) *f.*

pas·ture ['pɑːstʃə] 1. Weide(gras *n*) *f*;
Futter *n*; ⁓ *ground* Weideland *n*;
2. *v/t.* weiden (*a. v/i.*); abweiden.

past·y 1. ['peisti] teigig; bleich;

2. ['pæsti] (Fleisch)Pastete *f*.
pat [pæt] **1.** leichter Schlag *m*, Klaps *m*; Portion *f Butter*; **2.** tätscheln; klopfen; leicht schlagen; **3.** gelegen, gerade recht; bereit, bei der Hand; *stand* ~ festbleiben; *have od. know s.th.* (*off*) ~ et. aus dem Effeff können.
patch [pætʃ] **1.** Fleck *m*; Flicken *m*; Stück *n* Land; Stelle *f*; ✚ Pflaster *n*; ✚ Augenklappe *f*; *Nebel*-Feld *n*; Schönheitspflästerchen *n*; *strike a bad* ~ e-e Pechsträhne haben; ~ *pocket* aufgesetzte Tasche *f*; **2.** flicken; ~ *up* zs.-flicken; *fig.* zs.-stoppeln.
patch·work ['pætʃwɔːk] Flickwerk *n*; **'patch·y** voller Flicken; *fig.* zs.-gestoppelt; ungleichmäßig.
pate F [peit] Schädel *m*.
pat·ent ['peitənt, 'pætənt] **1.** offenkundig; patentiert; Patent...; *letters* ~ ['pætənt] *pl.* Freibrief *m*; ~ *article* Markenartikel *m*; ~ *leather* Lackleder *n*; **2.** Patent *n*; Privileg(ium) *n*, Freibrief *m*; ~ *pending* ⚙ Patent angemeldet; ~ *agent* Patentanwalt *m*; ~ *office* Patentamt *n*; **3.** patentieren (lassen); **pat·ent·ee** [peitən'tiː] Patentinhaber *m*.
pa·ter·nal □ [pə'tɜːnl] väterlich; **pa'ter·ni·ty** Vaterschaft *f*.
path [pɑːθ], *pl.* **paths** [pɑːðz] Pfad *m*; Weg *m*; *Sport*: Bahn *f*; *cross s.o.'s* ~ j-m über den Weg laufen.
pa·thet·ic [pə'θetik] (~*ally*) rührend, ergreifend; bemitleidenswert.
path·less ['pɑːθlis] unwegsam.
path·o·log·i·cal □ [pæθə'lɔdʒikəl] pathologisch; **pa·thol·o·gist** [pə'θɔlədʒist] Pathologe *m*; **pa'thol·o·gy** Krankheitslehre *f*, Pathologie *f*.
pa·thos ['peiθɔs] Pathos *n*.
path·way ['pɑːθwei] Pfad *m*, Weg *m*.
path·y *Am.* ✚ *contp.* ['pæθi] Behandlung(sart) *f*.
pa·tience ['peiʃəns] Geduld *f*; Ausdauer *f*; Patience *f* (*Kartenspiel*); *be out of* ~ *with*, *have no* ~ *with* es nicht (mehr) aushalten können mit; **'pa·tient 1.** □ geduldig; *be* ~ *of* ertragen; *fig.* zulassen; **2.** Patient (-in), Kranke *m*, *f*.
pa·ti·o *Am.* ['pætiəu] Innenhof *m*, Patio *m*.
pa·tri·arch ['peitriɑːk] Patriarch *m*; **pa·tri'ar·chal** □ patriarchalisch.
pa·tri·cian [pə'triʃən] **1.** patrizisch; **2.** Patrizier(in).

pat·ri·cide ['pætrisaid] Vatermord *m*; Vatermörder *m*.
pat·ri·mo·ny ['pætriməni] väterliches Erbteil *n*.
pa·tri·ot ['pætriət] Patriot(in); **pa·tri·ot·eer** [‿ə'tiə] Hurrapatriot *m*; **pa·tri·ot·ic** [‿'ɔtik] (~*ally*) patriotisch; **pa·tri·ot·ism** ['‿ətizəm] Patriotismus *m*, Vaterlandsliebe *f*.
pa·trol ✗ [pə'trəul] **1.** Patrouille *f*, Streife *f*; Spähtrupp *m*; ~ *wagon Am.* Polizeigefangenenwagen *m*; **2.** (ab)patrouillieren; **~·man** [pə'trəulmæn] patrouillierender Polizist *m*; Pannenhelfer *m* e-s *Automobilclubs*.
pa·tron ['peitrən] Patron *m*, Schutzherr *m*; Schutzheilige *m*, *f*; Gönner *m*; Kunde *m*; **pa·tron·age** ['pætrənidʒ] Gönnerschaft *f*; Kundschaft *f*; Schutz *m*; Patronatsrecht *n*; gönnerhaftes Wesen *n*; **pa·tron·ess** ['peitrənis] Patronin *f* etc. (*s. patron*); **pa·tron·ize** ['pætrənaiz] beschützen; begünstigen; Kunde sein bei; gönnerhaft behandeln; **'pa·tron·iz·er** Beschützer(in), Gönner(in).
pat·ter ['pætə] **1.** *v/i.* platschen; trappeln; *v/t.* (her)plappern; **2.** Platschen *n*; Getrappel *n*; Geplapper *n*; Jargon *m*, Rotwelsch *n*.
pat·tern ['pætən] **1.** Muster *n* (*a. fig.*); Modell *n*; Schablone *f*; Schnittmuster *n*; *fig.* Form *f*; Vorbild *n*; *by* ~ *post* als Muster ohne Wert; **2.** formen (*after*, *on* nach); mustern; **'~-mak·er** ⊕ Modellbauer *m*.
pat·ty ['pæti] Pastetchen *n*.
pau·ci·ty ['pɔːsiti] Wenigkeit *f*.
Paul·ine ['pɔːlain] paulinisch.
paunch [pɔːntʃ] Wanst *m*; **'paunch·y** dickbauchig.
pau·per ['pɔːpə] **1.** Arme *m*, *f*, Fürsorgeempfänger(in); **2.** Armen...; **'pau·per·ism** Massenarmut *f*; **'pau·per·ize** arm machen.
pause [pɔːz] **1.** Pause *f*, Unterbrechung *f*; ♪ Fermate *f*; *give* ~ *to s.o.* j-m zu denken geben; **2.** pausieren, innehalten; stehen bleiben; verweilen (*upon* bei).
pave [peiv] pflastern; *fig. Weg* bahnen; **'pave·ment** Bürgersteig *m*, Gehweg *m*; Pflaster *n*; ~ *artist* Pflastermaler *m*; ~ *café* Straßencafé *n*.
pa·vil·ion [pə'viljən] Pavillon *m*;

Zelt *n*; Gartenhaus *n*.
pav·ing-stone ['peiviŋstɔun] Pflasterstein *m*.
paw [pɔ:] **1.** Pfote *f*, Tatze *f*; **2.** *v/t.*
mit den Pfoten berühren *od.* schla-
gen; F befingern; rauh behandeln;
v/i. scharren.
pawn[1] [pɔ:n] Bauer *m im Schach*;
fig. (willenloses) Werkzeug *n*.
pawn[2] [◡] **1.** Pfand *n*; *in ◡, at ◡* verpfändet; **2.** verpfänden, versetzen;
'◡·**bro·ker** Pfandleiher *m*; **pawn'ee**
Pfandinhaber(in); '**pawn·er** Verpfänder *m*; '**pawn·shop** Leihhaus
n; '**pawn-tick·et** Pfandschein *m*.
pay [pei] **1.** Bezahlung *f*; Sold *m*,
Lohn *m*; *fig.* Belohnung *f*; **2.** *(irr.)*
v/t. (be)zahlen; (be)lohnen; sich
lohnen *für j.*; *Ehre etc.* erweisen;
Besuch abstatten; ◡ *attention od.*
heed to achtgeben auf *(acc.)*; ◡
away, ◡ *out* ♩ *Tau* ablaufen lassen;
◡ *down* bar bezahlen; ◡ *off j.* bezahlen u. entlassen; *j.* voll auszahlen;
◡ *s.o. out for s.th.* j-m et. heimzahlen; ◡ *up* voll bezahlen; ◡ *one's way*
ohne Verlust arbeiten; *put paid to*
s.th. F et. erledigen; *v/i.* zahlen;
sich lohnen *od.* rentieren; sich bezahlt machen; ◡ *for* (für) *et.* bezahlen; (für) *et.* büßen; '**pay·a·ble**
zahlbar; fällig; ✂, ✝ rentabel;
'**pay-as-you-'earn** Lohnsteuerabzug *m*; '**pay-bed** Privatbett *n in e-r*
Klinik; '**pay-day** Zahltag *m*; **pay**
dirt *Am.* goldhaltige Erde *f*; **pay'ee**
✝ Zahlungsempfänger *m*; Wechsel-
nehmer *m*; '**pay-en·ve·lope** Lohntüte *f*; '**pay·er** Zahler *m*; ✝ Trassat
m, Bezogene *m*; **pay freeze** Lohnstopp *m*; '**pay·ing** lohnend, rentabel;
Zahl(ungs)..., Kassen...; ◡ *concern*
lohnendes Geschäft *n*; **pay·ing-'in**
slip Einzahlungsschein *m*; '**pay-**
-load Nutzlast *f*; '**pay·mas·ter** ✂,
♩ Zahlmeister *m*; '**pay·ment** (Be-)
Zahlung *f*; Lohn *m*, Sold *m*; Belohnung *f*; *additional* ◡ Nachzahlung *f*; *on*
◡ *of* gegen Zahlung von.
pay...: '◡-**off** Abrechnung *f (a. fig.)*;
Am. F Gipfelpunkt *m*; '◡-**of·fice**
Lohnbüro *n*; '◡-**pack·et** Lohntüte
f; '◡-**roll** Lohnliste *f*; '◡-**station**
Am. öffentlicher Fernsprecher *m*.
pea ♀ [pi:] Erbse *f*.
peace [pi:s] Friede(n) *m*, Ruhe *f*; *the*
(King's) ◡ Landfrieden *m*; *be at* ◡ *in*
Frieden leben; *break the* ◡ die

öffentliche Ruhe stören; *keep the* ◡
Ruhe halten; '**peace·a·ble** ☐ fried-
fertig, -liebend, friedlich; '**peace-**
-break·er Ruhestörer *m*; **Peace**
Corps Friedenstruppe *f*; **peace·ful**
☐ ['◡ful] friedlich; ruhig, ungestört.
peace...: '◡-**keep·ing force** Friedenstruppe *f*; '◡-**mak·er** Friedens-
stifter(in); ◡ **move·ment** Friedens-
bewegung *f*; '◡-**of·fer·ing** Versöh-
nungsgeschenk *n*; versöhnliche Geste *f*, Friedenszeichen *n*; ◡ **set·tle-**
ment Friedensregelung *f*.
peach[1] [pi:tʃ] ♀ Pfirsich(baum) *m*;
sl. süßer Käfer *m*; *fig.* Gedicht *n*.
peach[2] *sl.* [◡]: ◡ *(up)on Mittäter* ver-
pfeifen; *Schule:* verpetzen.
pea-chick ['pi:tʃik] junger Pfau *m*.
peach·y ['pi:tʃi] pfirsichähnlich,
-farben; *sl.* famos, toll.
pea·cock ['pi:kɔk] Pfau(hahn) *m*;
Pfauenauge *n (Schmetterling)*; '**pea-**
fowl Pfau *m*; '**pea'hen** Pfau-
henne *f*.
pea-jack·et ♩ ['pi:dʒækit] Bord-
jacke *f*.
peak [pi:k] **1.** Spitze *f*; Gipfel *m*;
Mützen-Schirm *m*; *attr.* Spitzen...,
Höchst...; ◡ *hour* Hauptverkehrs-,
Stoßzeit *f*; ◡ *load* Spitzenbelastung
f; ◡ *power etc.* Spitzenleistung *f etc.*;
◡ *season* Haupt-, Hochsaison *f*; **2.** F
spitz aussehen, kränkeln; **peaked**
[pi:kt] spitz; ◡ *cap* Schirmmütze *f*;
'**peak·y** spitz(ig); F spitz (aussehend)
(Gesicht).
peal [pi:l] **1.** Geläut *n*; Glockenspiel *n*; Dröhnen *n*; ◡*s pl. of laughter*
schallendes Gelächter *n*; **2.** *v/t.* erschallen lassen; laut verkünden;
v/i. erschallen; dröhnen, krachen.
pea·nut ['pinʌt] Erdnuß *f*; *fig.*
Kleinigkeit *f*.
pear ♀ [peə] Birne *f*.
pearl [pə:l] **1.** Perle *f (a. fig.)*; *typ.*
Perlschrift *f*; *attr.* Perl(en)...;
2. tropfen, perlen; nach Perl-
muscheln tauchen; '**pearl·y** perlen-
artig; perlenreich.
pear-tree ['peətri:] Birnbaum *m*.
peas·ant ['pezənt] **1.** Bauer *m*;
2. bäuerlich; '**peas·ant·ry** Land-
volk *n*.
pease [pi:z] Erbse(n *pl.*) *f*.
pea-shoot·er ['pi:ʃu:tə] Blasrohr *n*.
pea soup ['pi:'su:p] Erbsensuppe *f*;
'**pea-'soup·er** F dicker, gelber
Nebel *m*.

peat [pi:t] Torf *m*; '**~-bog** Torf-moor *n*.

peb·ble ['pebl] Kiesel(stein) *m*; *Art* Achat *m*; '**peb·bly** kieselig.

pe·can ♀ [pi'kæn] Pekanhickory *m*.

pec·ca·ble ['pekəbl] sündhaft.

peck¹ [pek] Viertelscheffel *m* (9,087 Liter); *fig.* Menge *f*.

peck² [∼] picken, hacken (*at* nach); **~** *at one's food* im Essen umher-stochern; '**peck·er** *sl.* Zinken *m* (*Nase*); *keep one's* **~** *up* nicht den Mut verlieren; '**peck·ish** F hungrig.

pec·to·ral ['pektərəl] 1. Brust...; 2. Brustschild *n*; Brustmittel *n*.

pec·tin ['pektin] Pektin *n*.

pec·u·late ['pekjuleit] unterschlagen; **pec·u·la·tion** Unterschlagung *f*; '**pec·u·la·tor** Veruntreuer *m*.

pe·cul·iar □ [pi'kju:ljə] eigen(tümlich); besonder; seltsam, merkwürdig; **pe·cu·li·ar·i·ty** [∼li'æriti] Eigenheit *f*; Eigentümlichkeit *f*.

pe·cu·ni·ar·y [pi'kju:njəri] geldlich; Geld...; pekuniär.

ped·a·gog·ic, ped·a·gog·i·cal □ [pedə'gɔdʒik(əl)] pädagogisch; Erziehungs...; **ped·a'gog·ics** *mst sg.* Pädagogik *f*; **ped·a·gogue** ['∼gɔg] Pädagoge *m*; Lehrer *m*, Schulmann *m*; **ped·a·go·gy** ['∼gɔdʒi] Pädagogik *f*.

ped·al ['pedl] 1. Pedal *n*; 2. Fuß...; 3. *Radfahren:* fahren, treten; '**~-bin** Treteimer *m*.

ped·ant ['pedənt] Pedant(in); **pe·dan·tic** [pi'dæntik] (*~ally*) pedantisch; **ped·ant·ry** ['pedəntri] Pedanterie *f*.

ped·dle ['pedl] hausieren (mit); tändeln, spielen; '**ped·dling** geringfügig; '**ped·dler** *Am.* = *pedlar*.

ped·es·tal ['pedistl] Sockel *m* (*a. fig.*); Säulenfuß *m*; **pe·des·tri·an** [pi'destriən] 1. Fuß...; zu Fuß; prosaisch, nüchtern; 2. Fußgänger (-in); **~** *crossing* Fußgängerüberweg *m*.

ped·i·cab ['pedikæb] Fahrrad-rikscha *f*.

ped·i·cure ['pedikjuə] Fußpflege *f*; Fußpfleger(in); **ped·i·cur·ist** ['∼kjuərist] Fußpfleger(in).

ped·i·gree ['pedigri:] 1. Stammbaum *m*; 2. **~d** mit Stammbaum; reinrassig.

ped·i·ment ⚠ ['pedimənt] (Zier-) Giebel *m*.

ped·lar ['pedlə] Hausierer *m*; '**ped-lar·y** Hausierware *f*.

pe·dom·e·ter [pi'dɔmitə] Schrittmesser *m*.

pee F pinkeln; *go for a* **~** pinkeln gehen.

peek [pi:k] 1. spähen, gucken, lugen; 2. flüchtiger Blick *m*; **peek·a·boo** ['pi:kəbu:] Guck-Guck-Spiel *n*.

peel [pi:l] 1. *Zitronen- etc.* Schale *f*; Rinde *f*; 2. *a.* **~** *off v/t.* (ab)schälen; *Kleid* abstreifen; *v/i.* sich (ab-) schälen; *sl.* sich entblättern (*auskleiden*).

peel·er *sl.* † ['pi:lə] Polyp *m* (*Polizist*).

peel·ing ['pi:liŋ] *lose* Schale *f*.

peep¹ [pi:p] 1. Piepen *n*; 2. piepen.

peep² [∼] 1. verstohlener Blick *m*; Anbruch *m des Tages*; 2. (verstohlen) gucken, lugen; *a.* **~** *out* (her-vor)gucken (*a. fig.*); **~** *at* angucken; '**peep·er** Gucker *m* (*sl. Auge*); '**peep-hole** Guckloch *n*; '**peep·ing Tom** Voyeur *m*; '**peep-show** Peep--Show *f*.

peer¹ [piə] spähen, lugen; prüfend blicken, **~** *at* an-, begucken.

peer² [∼] Gleiche *m*; Pair *m*, Mitglied *n* des Hochadels; '**peer·age** Pairswürde *f*; Pairs *m/pl.*; '**peer·ess** Gemahlin *f* e-s Pairs; '**peer·less** □ unvergleichlich.

peeved F [pi:vd] eingeschnappt.

pee·vish □ ['pi:viʃ] verdrießlich, grämlich, mürrisch; '**pee·vish·ness** Verdrießlichkeit *f*.

pee·wit ['pi:wit] = *pewit*.

peg [peg] 1. Stöpsel *m*, Dübel *m*, Pflock *m*; *Kleider*-Haken *m*; ♪ Wirbel *m*; *Wäsche*-Klammer *f*; *fig.* Aufhänger *m*; (Zelt)Hering *m*; Whisky *m* mit Soda; *take s.o. down a* **~** *or two* j. demütigen; *be a round* **~** *in a square hole* an der falschen Stelle stehen; 2. festpflöcken; *a.* **~** *out Grenze* abstecken; *Löhne, Preise* festlegen, halten; **~** *away,* **~** *along* F darauflosarbeiten; **~** *out sl.* abkratzen.

peg-top ['pegtɔp] Kreisel *m*.

peign·oir ['peinwa:] Frisiermantel *m*, Morgenrock *m* e-r Dame.

pe·jo·ra·tive ['pi:dʒərətiv, pi'dʒɔrə-tiv] verschlechternd, herabsetzend.

peke F [pi:k] = *pekinese*.

pe·kin·ese [pi:ki'ni:z] Pekinese *m* (*Hund*).

pelf *contp.* [pelf] Mammon *m*.

penny

pel·i·can *orn.* ['pelikən] Pelikan *m*; ～ **cross·ing** *mit* Ampeln *gesicherter Fußgängerüberweg.*
pel·let ['pelit] Kügelchen *n*; Pille *f*; Schrotkorn *n*.
pel·li·cle ['pelikl] Häutchen *n*.
pell-mell ['pel'mel] **1.** durcheinander; **2.** Durcheinander *n*.
pel·lu·cid [pe'lju:sid] durchsichtig.
Pel·o·pon·ne·sian [peləpə'ni:ʃən] peloponnesisch.
pelt¹ [pelt] Fell *n*; ✝ *rohe* Haut *f*.
pelt² [～] **1.** *v/t. mit Steinen etc.* bewerfen, bombardieren; *v/i.* niederprasseln (*Regen*); **2.** Wurf *m*, Schlag *m*; Prasseln *n*; *at full* ～ *in* voller Geschwindigkeit.
pelt·ry ['peltri] Rohpelze *m/pl.*, Rauchwaren *f/pl.*
pel·vis *anat.* ['pelvis] Becken *n*.
pem·mi·can ['pemikən] Pemmikan *m* (*Dörrfleisch*).
pen¹ [pen] **1.** (Schreib)Feder *f*; Federhalter *m*; **2.** schreiben, abfassen.
pen² [～] **1.** Hürde *f*; ⚓ U-Boot-Bunker *m*; *a. play-*～ (Kinder)Ställchen *n*, Laufgitter *n*; **2.** (*irr.*) *oft* ～ *up*, ～ *in* einpferchen.
pe·nal ['pi:nl] Straf...; strafbar; ～ *code* Strafgesetzbuch *n*; ～ *servitude* Zuchthausstrafe *f*; **pe·nal·ize** ['pi:nəlaiz] mit Strafe belegen; *fig.* belasten; *e-m Spieler* e-n Strafpunkt geben; **pen·al·ty** ['penlti] Strafe *f*, Buße *f*; *Sport*: Strafpunkt *m*; ～ *area Fußball*: Strafraum *m*; ～ *goal Fußball*: Elfmetertor *n*; ～ *kick* Strafstoß *m*; ～ *spot Fußball*: Elfmeterpunkt *m*; *under* ～ *of* bei Strafe von.
pen·ance ['penəns] Buße *f*.
pen...: '～**-and-**'**ink** draw·ing Federzeichnung *f*.
pence [pens] *pl. von* penny.
pen·chant ['pã:ʃã] Neigung *f*, Hang *m*, Vorliebe *f*.
pen·cil ['pensl] **1.** Bleistift *m*; **2.** zeichnen; (mit Bleistift) anzeichnen *od.* anstreichen; *die Augenbrauen* nachziehen; '～**-case** Federmäppchen *n*; '～**-sharp·en·er** Bleistiftspitzer *m*.
pend·ant ['pendənt] Anhänger *m* (*Schmuckstück*); Wimpel *m*; Gegenstück *n*, Pendant *n*.
pend·ent [～] hängend; schwebend.
pend·ing ['pendin] **1.** ⚖ schwebend, noch unentschieden; **2.** *prp.* während; bis zu.

pen·du·lous ['pendjuləs] frei hängend; pendelnd; **pen·du·lum** ['～ləm] Pendel *n*.
pen·e·tra·bil·i·ty [penitrə'biliti] Durchdringbarkeit *f*; '**pen·e·tra·ble** ☐ durchdringbar; **pen·e·tra·li·a** [～'treiljə] Innerste *n*, Allerheiligste *n*; **pen·e·trate** ['～treit] *v/t.* durchdringen (*with* mit); ergründen; durchschauen; eindringen in (*acc.*); *v/i.* eindringen; vordringen (*to* bis zu); **pen·e'tra·tion** Durch-, Eindringen *n*; Scharfsinn *m*; **pen·e·tra·tive** ☐ ['～trətiv] durchdringend (*a. fig.*); eindringlich; scharfsinnig; ～ *effect* Durchschlagskraft *f*.
pen-friend ['penfrend] Brieffreund (-in).
pen·guin *orn.* ['peŋgwin] Pinguin *m*.
pen·hold·er ['penhəuldə] Federhalter *m*.
pen·i·cil·lin *pharm.* [peni'silin] Penicillin *n*.
pen·in·su·la [pi'ninsjulə] Halbinsel *f*; **pen'in·su·lar** Halbinsel...; halbinselförmig.
pe·nis ['pi:nis] Penis *m*.
pen·i·tence ['penitəns] Bußfertigkeit *f*, Buße *f*, Reue *f*; '**pen·i·tent 1.** ☐ reuig, bußfertig; **2.** Bußfertige *m*, *f*; Büßer(in); **pen·i·ten·tial** ☐ [～'tenʃəl] bußfertig; Buß...; **pen·i·ten·tia·ry** [～'tenʃəri] Besserungsanstalt *f*; *Am.* Zuchthaus *n*.
pen·knife ['pennaif] Taschenmesser *n*.
pen·man ['penmən] Schönschreiber *m*; Schriftsteller *m*; *he is a poor* ～ *s-e* Schrift ist schlecht; '**pen·man·ship** Schreibkunst *f*; Stil *m*.
pen-name ['penneim] Schriftstellername *m*, Pseudonym *n*.
pen·nant ['penənt] ⚓ Wimpel *m*; *bsd. Am.* Siegerwimpel *m*; *fig.* Meisterschaft *f* (*Sport*).
pen·ni·less ☐ ['penilis] ohne Geld, mittellos, ganz arm.
pen·non ['penən] ✗ Lanzen-Fähnlein *n*; Wimpel *m*.
pen·ny ['peni], *pl. bei Zssgn* **pence** [pens] (englischer) Penny *m* (～ *1 p = £ 0.01*); *Am.* Centstück *n*; Kleinigkeit *f*; *oft* Groschen *m*; *a pretty* ～ *e-e* hübsche Summe *f*; *in for a* ～, *in for a pound* wer A sagt, muß auch B sagen; *turn an honest* ～ sich auf ehrliche Weise durchschlagen; ～ *wise and pound foolish*

im Kleinen sparsam, im Großen verschwenderisch; '~-a-'lin·er Zeilenschinder m; '~-'dread·ful Groschenroman m; Revolverblatt n; ~ **pinch·er** Geizhals m; '~-**weight** *englisches* Pennygewicht n (1¹/₂ *Gramm*); ~**worth** ['penəθ] Pennywert m, für einen Penny; a ~ *of tobacco* für einen Penny Tabak.

pen...: ~ **pal** = *pen-friend*; '~--**push·er** F *contp.* Schreiberling m.

pen·sion ['penʃən] **1.** Pension f, Rente f, Ruhegehalt n; ['pã:ŋsiɔ̃:ŋ] Pension f, Fremdenheim n; **2.** *oft* ~ *off* pensionieren; '**pen·sion·ar·y**, '**pen·sion·er** Ruhegehaltsempfänger(in), Pensionär(in); *contp.* Mietling m; **pen·sion scheme** Rentenversicherung f.

pen·sive □ ['pensiv] gedankenvoll; nachdenklich; ernst; '**pen·sive·ness** Nachdenklichkeit f; Ernst m.

pent [pent] *pret. u. p.p. von* pen² 2.

pen·ta·gon ['pentəgən] Fünfeck n; *the* ♀ *das* Pentagon (*amerikanisches Verteidigungsministerium*); **pen·tag·o·nal** [~'tægənl] fünfeckig.

pen·tath·lon [pen'tæθlən] *Sport:* Fünfkampf m.

Pen·te·cost ['pentikɔst] Pfingsten n *od. pl.*; **pen·te'cos·tal** pfingstlich; Pfingst...

pent·house ['penthaus] Wetter-, Schutzdach n; Dachwohnung f *auf e-m Hochhaus.*

pent-up ['pent'ʌp] aufgestaut (*Zorn etc.*); ~ *feelings* aufgestaute Gefühle n/pl.

pe·nul·ti·mate [pi'nʌltimit] vorletzt.

pe·num·bra [pi'nʌmbrə] Halbschatten m.

pe·nu·ri·ous □ [pi'njuəriəs] geizig; karg; **pe'nu·ri·ous·ness** Geiz m; Kargheit f.

pen·u·ry ['penjuri] Armut f; Mangel m.

pe·o·ny ♀ ['piəni] Pfingstrose f.

peo·ple ['pi:pl] **1.** a) *coll.* die Leute pl., man; Volk n; *my* ~ m-e Angehörigen pl., m-e Familie f; b) Volk n, Nation f; *the* ~*s pl. of Asia* die Völker n/pl. Asiens; **2.** bevölkern.

pep *sl.* [pep] **1.** Schmiß m; Schwung m; **2.** ~ *up* aufmöbeln.

pep·per ['pepə] **1.** Pfeffer m; **2.** pfeffern; '~-**box** Pfefferstreuer m; '~-**corn** Pfefferkorn n; '~-**mint** ♀ Pfefferminze f; Pfefferminz(bon-

bon) n; ~ **pot** Pfefferstreuer m; '**pep·per·y** □ pfefferig; *fig.* hitzig.

pep...: ~ **pill** Aufputschtablette f; ~ **talk** aufmunternde Worte n/pl.

pep·tic ['peptik]: ~ *ulcer* Magengeschwür n.

per [pə:, pə] per, durch, für; laut; je.

per·ad·ven·ture *rhet.* [pərəd'ventʃə] **1.** vielleicht, etwa; **2.** Vielleicht n; *beyond* ~, *without* ~ ohne Zweifel.

per·am·bu·late [pə'ræmbjuleit] (durch)wandern; *Grenzen etc.* be-, abgehen; bereisen; **per·am·bu'la·tion** Durchwanderung f; Besichtigungsreise f; **per·am·bu·la·tor** ['præmbjuleitə] Kinderwagen m.

per·cale [pə'keil] Perkal m (*Baumwollgewebe*).

per cap·i·ta [pə'kæpitə] pro Kopf; ~ *income* Pro-Kopf-Einkommen n.

per·ceive [pə'si:v] (be)merken, wahrnehmen; empfinden; erkennen.

per cent, *a.* **per·cent** [pə'sent] Prozent n; **per'cent·age** Prozent-, Hundertsatz m; Prozente n/pl.; *fig.* Teil m.

per·cep·ti·ble □ [pə'septəbl] wahrnehmbar; **per'cep·tion** Wahrnehmung(svermögen n) f; Erkenntnis f; Auffassung(skraft) f; **per'cep·tive** □ [~tiv] wahrnehmend; Wahrnehmungs...; **per'cep·tive·ness, per·cep'tiv·i·ty** Wahrnehmungsvermögen n.

perch¹ *ichth.* [pə:tʃ] Barsch m.

perch² [~] **1.** Rute f (*Längenmaß* = 5,029 *m*); (Sitz)Stange f für Vögel; F *fig.* Thron m; **2.** (sich) setzen; sitzen; ~*ed fig.* thronend, hoch *auf et.* gelegen.

per·chance [pə'tʃɑ:ns] zufällig; vielleicht.

per·cip·i·ent [pə'sipiənt] **1.** wahrnehmend; **2.** Wahrnehmende m.

per·co·late ['pə:kəleit] durchtropfen, -sickern (lassen); '**per·co·la·tor** Perkolator m, Kaffeemaschine f.

per·cus·sion [pə:'kʌʃən] Schlag m; Erschütterung f; *∮* Beklopfen n; ~ *cap* Zündhütchen n; ~ *instruments pl. ∮* Schlagzeug n; **per'cus·sive** [~siv] Schlag...

per·di·tion [pə:'diʃən] Verderben n.

per·e·gri·nate ['perigrineit] (durch-)wandern; **per·e·gri'na·tion** Wanderschaft f; Wanderung f.

per·emp·to·ri·ness [pəˈremptərinis] Bestimmtheit *f*; *b.s.* rechthaberische Art *f*; **per'emp·to·ry** □ bestimmt, entschieden; zwingend; *b.s.* rechthaberisch.

per·en·ni·al [pəˈrenjəl] **1.** □ dauernd; immerwährend; ⚲ perennierend; **2.** ⚲ perennierende Pflanze *f*.

per·fect 1. [ˈpəːfikt] □ vollkommen (*a. moralisch*); vollendet, perfekt; gänzlich, völlig; ⁓ *pitch ♩* absolutes Gehör; **2.** [⁓] *a.* ⁓ *tense gr.* Perfekt *n*; **3.** [pəˈfekt] vervollkommnen; vollenden; **per'fec·tion** Vervollkommnung *f*, Vollendung *f*, Perfektion *f*; Vollkommenheit *f*; *fig.* Gipfel *m*; **per'fec·tion·ist** Perfektionist(in) (*a. phls.*).

per·fid·i·ous □ [pəːˈfidiəs] treulos (*to* gegen), verräterisch; **per'fid·i·ous·ness**, **'per·fi·dy** Treulosigkeit *f*, Falschheit *f*.

per·fo·rate [ˈpəːfəreit] durchbohren, durchlöchern; lochen; **per·fo·'ra·tion** Durchbohrung *f*, Durchlöcherung *f*; Lochung *f*; Loch *n*; **'per·fo·ra·tor** Locher *m* (*Gerät*).

per·force [pəˈfɔːs] notgedrungen.

per·form [pəˈfɔːm] verrichten, leisten; durch-, ausführen, vollziehen; *Pflicht etc.* erfüllen; *thea.*, *♩* aufführen, spielen (*a. v/i.*), vortragen; **per'form·ance** Verrichtung *f*; Erfüllung *f*; *thea.* Aufführung *f*, Vorstellung *f*; Vortrag *m*; ⊕ Leistung *f* (*a. fig.*); Werk *n*, Tat *f*; **per'form·er** Vollzieher(in); Schauspieler(in); Darsteller(in); Künstler(in); **per·'form·ing** dressiert (*Tier*).

per·fume 1. [ˈpəːfjuːm] Wohlgeruch *m*, Duft *m*; Parfüm *n*; **2.** [pəˈfjuːm] durchduften; parfümieren; **per'fum·er** Parfümeur *m*; **per'fum·er·y** Parfümerie *f* (*Geschäft*); Parfümeriewaren *f/pl.*

per·func·to·ry □ [pəˈfʌŋktəri] nachlässig; mechanisch, schablonenhaft; oberflächlich; interesselos.

per·haps [pəˈhæps, præps] vielleicht.

per·i·gee *ast.* [ˈperidʒiː] Erdnähe *f*.

per·il [ˈperil] **1.** Gefahr *f*; *at my* ⁓ auf meine Gefahr; **2.** gefährden; **'per·il·ous** □ gefährlich.

pe·ri·od [ˈpiəriəd] Periode *f*; Zeitabschnitt *m*, -raum *m*, -dauer *f*; *gr.* Punkt *m*; Periode *f*, langer Satz *m*; (Unterrichts)Stunde *f*; ⁓*s pl.* ♂

Periode *f*; ⁓ *furniture* Stilmöbel *n/pl.*; **per·i·od·ic** [⁓ˈɔdik] periodisch; **pe·ri'od·i·cal 1.** □ periodisch; **2.** Zeitschrift *f*.

per·i·pa·tet·ic [peripəˈtetik] (⁓*ally*) (umher)wandernd.

pe·riph·er·y [pəˈrifəri] Peripherie *f*.

pe·riph·ra·sis [pəˈrifrəsis], *pl.* **pe·'riph·ra·ses** [⁓siːz] Umschreibung *f*; **per·i·phras·tic** [periˈfræstik] (⁓*ally*) umschreibend.

per·i·scope ⚓, ✗ [ˈperiskəup] Periskop *n*, Sehrohr *n*.

per·ish [ˈperiʃ] umkommen, zugrunde gehen; kaputt machen; *be* ⁓*ed with* umkommen vor *Kälte etc.*; **'per·ish·a·ble 1.** □ vergänglich; leicht verderblich (*Eßwaren etc.*); **2.** ⁓*s pl.* leicht verderbliche Waren *f/pl.*; **'per·ish·ing** □ vernichtend, tödlich; F scheußlich.

per·i·style [ˈperistail] Säulengang *m*.

per·i·wig [ˈperiwig] Perücke *f*.

per·i·win·kle[1] ⚲ [ˈperiwiŋkl] Immergrün *n*. [schnecke *f.*ǀ

per·i·win·kle[2] *zo.* [⁓] (eßbare) Ufer-ǀ

per·jure [ˈpəːdʒə]: ⁓ *o.s.* falsch schwören; **'per·jured** meineidig; **'per·jur·er** Meineidige *m*; **'per·ju·ry** Meineid *m*.

perk[1] F [pəːk] = *percolate*.

perk[2] F [⁓] **1.** *mst* ⁓ *up v/i.* selbstbewußt auftreten, die Nase hoch tragen; sich recken; sich wieder erholen; zu Kräften *od.* in Stimmung kommen; *v/t.* recken, aufrichten; **2.** = ⁓*y*; **perk·i·ness** [ˈ⁓inis] Keckheit *f*.

perks F [pəːks] *pl.* = *perquisites*.

perk·y □ [ˈpəːki] keck, dreist; flott, forsch.

perm F [pəːm] **1.** Dauerwelle *f*; **2.** *j-m* Dauerwellen machen.

per·ma·frost [ˈpəːməfrɔst] Dauerfrostboden *m*.

per·ma·nence [ˈpəːmənəns] Dauer *f*, Ständigkeit *f*; **'per·ma·nen·cy** *s. permanence*; etwas Bleibendes *n*; Dauerstellung *f*; **'per·ma·nent** □ dauernd, bleibend, ständig, anhaltend; dauerhaft; fest, Dauer... (*Stellung*); ⁓ *wave* Dauerwelle *f*; ⁓ *way* 🚉 Bahnkörper *m*.

per·me·a·bil·i·ty [pəːmjəˈbiliti] Durchdringbarkeit *f*; **'per·me·a·ble** □ durchdringbar, durchlässig (*to* für); **per·me·ate** [ˈ⁓mieit] *v/t.* durchdringen; *v/i.* eindringen (*into* in *acc.*); sich verbreiten (*among* unter *dat.*).

per·mis·si·ble ☐ [pə'misəbl] zulässig; **per·mis·sion** [pə'miʃən] Erlaubnis *f*, Genehmigung *f*; **per'mis·sive** ☐ [‿siv] gestattend; ⚓ fakultativ; ‿ *society* tabufreie Gesellschaft *f*.

per·mit 1. [pə'mit] *a*. ‿ *of* erlauben, gestatten; *weather* ‿*ting* bei günstiger Witterung; **2.** ['pəːmit] Erlaubnis *f*, Genehmigung *f*; Erlaubnis-, Passierschein *m*.

per·ni·cious ☐ [pəː'niʃəs] verderblich; ☞ perniziös, bösartig.

per·nick·et·y F [pə'nikiti] umständlich, pedantisch; heikel.

per·o·ra·tion [perə'reiʃən] Redeschluß *m*.

per·ox·ide ⚗ [pə'rɔksaid]: ‿ *of hydrogen* Wasserstoffsuperoxyd *n*.

per·pen·dic·u·lar [pəːpən'dikjulə] **1.** ☐ senkrecht; aufrecht; steil; ‿ *style* △ englische Spätgotik *f*; **2.** Senkrechte *f*; Perpendikel *n*, *m*.

per·pe·trate ['pəːpitreit] *Verbrechen etc.* begehen, verüben; F *Witz etc.* verbrechen; **per·pe'tra·tion** Verübung *f*; '**per·pe·tra·tor** Täter *m*.

per·pet·u·al ☐ [pə'petʃuəl] fortwährend, ewig; lebenslänglich; **per'pet·u·ate** [‿eit] verewigen; **per·pet·u'a·tion** Verewigung *f*; **per·pe·tu·i·ty** [pəːpi'tjuːiti] Ewigkeit *f*; lebenslängliche Rente *f*; *in* ‿ auf ewig.

per·plex [pə'pleks] verwirren, verblüffen; verkomplizieren; **per'plexed** ☐ verwirrt, bestürzt, verdutzt; kompliziert; **per'plex·i·ty** Verwirrung *f*; Verlegenheit *f*; Verworrenheit *f*.

per·qui·sites ['pəːkwizits] *pl.* Nebenverdienst *m*, Sporteln *f/pl.*

per·se·cute ['pəːsikjuːt] verfolgen; drangsalieren; **per·se'cu·tion** Verfolgung *f*; Drangsalierung *f*; ‿ *mania* Verfolgungswahn *m*; **per·se·cu·tor** ['‿tə] Verfolger *m*.

per·se·ver·ance [pəːsi'viərəns] Beharrlichkeit *f*, Ausdauer *f*; **per·se·vere** [‿'viə] beharren (*in* bei); aushalten (*with* bei); festhalten (*in* an *dat.*); **per·se'ver·ing** ☐ beharrlich, standhaft.

Per·sian ['pəːʃən] **1.** persisch; **2.** Perser(in); Persisch *n*.

per·sim·mon ♀ [pəː'simən] Dattel-

pflaume *f*, Persimone *f*.

per·sist [pə'sist] beharren, bestehen (*in auf dat.*); fortdauern, anhalten; (bestehen) bleiben; **per'sist·ence, per'sist·en·cy** Beharrlichkeit *f*; Fortdauer *f*; **per'sist·ent** ☐ beharrlich; hartnäckig.

per·son ['pəːsn] Person *f* (*a. gr.*); Persönlichkeit *f*; *thea.* Rolle *f*; Körper *m*; *in* ‿ in eigener Person, persönlich; ‿*-to*-‿ *call teleph.* Voranmeldungsgespräch *n*; '**per·son·a·ble** ansehnlich; '**per·son·age** Persönlichkeit *f*; *thea.* Charakter *m*; '**per·son·al 1.** ☐ persönlich (*a. gr.*); Personal...; Privat...; eigen; ‿ *property od. estate* ⚓ *s. personalty*; **2.** *Zeitung*: Familienanzeige *f*, Persönliches *n*; **per·son·al·i·ty** [pəːsə'næliti] Persönlichkeit *f*; *personalities pl.* persönliche Bemerkungen *f pl.*; ‿ *clash psych.* Persönlichkeitskonflikt *m*; **per·son·al·ty** ['pəːsnlti] ⚓ persönliches *od.* bewegliches Eigentum *n*; **per·son·ate** ['‿səneit] vor-, darstellen; sich ausgeben für; **per·son'a·tion** Vor-, Darstellung *f*; Verkörperung *f*; **per·son·i·fi·ca·tion** [pəːsɔnifi'keiʃən] Verkörperung *f*; **per·son·i·fy** [pəː'sɔnifai] personifizieren; verkörpern; **per·son·nel** [pəːsə'nel] Personal *n*; Belegschaft *f*.

per·spec·tive [pə'spektiv] **1.** ☐ perspektivisch; **2.** Perspektive *f*; Ausblick *m*, Fernsicht *f*.

per·spex ['pəːspeks] Plexiglas *n*.

per·spi·ca·cious ☐ [pəːspi'keiʃəs] scharfsichtig, -sinnig; **per·spi·cac·i·ty** [‿'kæsiti] Scharfblick *m*, -sinn *m*; **per·spi·cu·i·ty** [‿'kjuiti] Klarheit *f*, Deutlichkeit *f*; **per·spic·u·ous** [pəː'spikjuəs] ☐ klar, deutlich.

per·spi·ra·tion [pəːspə'reiʃən] Schwitzen *n*; Schweiß *m*; **per·spire** [pəs'paiə] (aus)schwitzen.

per·suade [pə'sweid] überreden, bereden (*to inf., into ger.* zu *inf.*); überzeugen (*of* von; *that* daß); **per'suad·er** *sl.* Überredungsmittel *n*.

per·sua·sion [pə'sweiʒən] Überredung *f*; Überzeugung *f*; Glaube *m*; F *co.* Gattung *f*; *powers pl. of* ‿ Überredungskünste *f pl.*

per·sua·sive ☐ [pə'sweisiv] überredend, -zeugend; **per'sua·sive·ness** Überzeugungskraft *f*.

pert ☐ [pəːt] keck, vorlaut, naseweis.

per·tain [pəː'tein] (*to*) gehören (*dat.*

od. zu); sich für *j.* gehören (*geziemen*); betreffen (*acc.*).
per·ti·na·cious □ [pə:tiˈneiʃəs] hartnäckig, zäh; **per·ti·nac·i·ty** [~ˈnæsiti] Hartnäckig-, Zähigkeit *f.*
per·ti·nence, per·ti·nen·cy [ˈpə:tinəns(i)] Sachdienlichkeit *f*, Gemäßheit *f*; ˈ**per·ti·nent** □ sachdienlich, -gemäß; zur Sache gehörig; *be ~ to* Bezug haben auf (*acc.*).
pert·ness [ˈpə:tnis] Keckheit *f.*
per·turb [pəˈtə:b] beunruhigen; stören; **per·tur·ba·tion** [pə:tə:ˈbeiʃən] Beunruhigung *f*; Störung *f.*
pe·ruke [pəˈru:k] Perücke *f.*
pe·rus·al [pəˈru:zəl] sorgfältiges Durchlesen *n*, Durchsicht *f*; Prüfung *f*; **peˈruse** sorgfältig durchlesen; *fig.* durchgehen, prüfen.
Pe·ru·vi·an [pəˈru:vjən] **1.** peruanisch; *~ bark* ⚘ Chinarinde *f*; **2.** Peruaner(in).
per·vade [pə:ˈveid] durchdringen, -ziehen, erfüllen; **perˈva·sion** [~ʒən] Durchdringung *f*; **perˈva·sive** [~siv] durchdringend.
per·verse □ [pəˈvə:s] verkehrt; ⚕ pervers; eigensinnig, bockig; vertrackt (*Sache*); **perˈverse·ness** = *perversity*; **perˈver·sion** Verdrehung *f*; Abkehr *f vom Guten etc.*; **perˈver·si·ty** Verkehrtheit *f*; ⚕ Perversität *f*; Verderbtheit *f*; Eigensinn *m*; **perˈver·sive** verderblich (*of* für).
per·vert 1. [pəˈvə:t] verdrehen; verführen; **2.** [ˈpə:və:t] ⚕ perverser Mensch *m*; **perˈvert·er** [pəˈvə:tə] Verdreher(in); Verführer(in).
per·vi·ous [ˈpə:vjəs] zugänglich (*a. fig.*); durchlässig (*to* für).
pes·ky □ *sl.* [ˈpeski] verflixt.
pes·sa·ry [ˈpesəri] Scheidenzäpfchen *n*; Pessar *n*, Mutterring *m.*
pes·si·mism [ˈpesimizəm] Pessimismus *m*; ˈ**pes·si·mist** Pessimist(in), Schwarzseher(in); **pes·siˈmis·tic** (*~ally*) pessimistisch.
pest [pest] *fig.* Pest *f*; Plage *f*; Schädling *m*; *~* **con·trol** Schädlingsbekämpfung *f*; ˈ**pes·ter** belästigen; plagen; quälen.
pest·i·cide [ˈpestisaid] Schädlingsbekämpfungsmittel *n*; **pesˈtif·er·ous** □ [~fərəs] krankheitserregend; verderblich; **pes·ti·lence** [ˈ~ləns] Seuche *f*, *bsd.* Pest *f*; ˈ**pes·ti·lent** gefährlich; *co.* verdammt; **pes·ti·len·tial** □ [~ˈlenʃəl] pestartig; verderbenbringend; verdammt.
pes·tle [ˈpesl] **1.** Mörserkeule *f*, Stößel *m*; **2.** zerstoßen.
pet¹ [pet] Ärger *m*, üble Laune *f*; *in a ~* übelgelaunt.
pet² [~] **1.** zahmes Tier *n*; Liebling *m*, Schoßkind *n*; **2.** Lieblings...; zahm; *~ dog* Schoßhund *m*; *~ name* Kosename *m*; *it is my ~ aversion* es ist mir ein Greuel; **3.** (ver)hätscheln; F knutschen; *petting party* Knutscherei *f.*
pet·al ⚘ [ˈpetl] Blumenblatt *n.*
pe·tard [peˈtɑ:d] Schwärmer *m* (*Feuerwerk*).
pe·ter [ˈpi:tə]: *~ out* zu Ende gehen; im Sande verlaufen.
pet·i·ole ⚘ [ˈpetiəul] (Blatt)Stiel *m.*
pet·it [ˈpeti] klein, geringfügig; **pe·tite** [pəˈti:t] klein, zierlich (*Frau*).
pe·ti·tion [piˈtiʃən] **1.** Bitte *f*; Bittschrift *f*, Eingabe *f*, Gesuch *n*; *~ in bankruptcy* ⚖ Konkursantrag *m*; *~ for divorce* ⚖ Scheidungsklage *f*; **2.** bitten, ersuchen (*for* um; *to inf.* zu *inf.*); eine Bittschrift *etc.* einreichen (*s.o.* an j.; *for* um); **peˈti·tion·er** [~ʃnə] Bittsteller(in).
pet·rel *orn.* [ˈpetrəl] Sturmvogel *m.*
pet·ri·fac·tion *geol.* [petriˈfækʃən] Versteinerung *f.*
pet·ri·fy [ˈpetrifai] versteinern.
pet·rol *mot.* [ˈpetrəl] Benzin *n*; Treibstoff *m*; *~ bomb* Molotowcocktail *m*; *~ coupon* Benzingutschein *m*; *~ engine* Benzinmotor *m*; *~ station* Tankstelle *f*; *~ tank* Benzintank *m.*
pe·tro·le·um [piˈtrəuljəm] Petroleum *n*, Erdöl *n*; *~ jelly* Vaseline *f.*
pe·trol·o·gy *geol.* [peˈtrɔlədʒi] Gesteinskunde *f.*
pet·ti·coat [ˈpetikəut] Unterrock *m*; *~ government contp.* Weiberregiment *n.*
pet·ti·fog·ger [ˈpetifɔgə] Winkeladvokat *m*; ˈ**pet·ti·fog·ging** kleinlich, pedantisch.
pet·ti·ness [ˈpetinis] Geringfügigkeit *f.*
pet·tish □ [ˈpetiʃ] launisch, verdrießlich; ˈ**pet·tish·ness** Verdrießlichkeit *f.*
pet·ty □ [ˈpeti] klein, geringfügig; Klein...; *~ bourgeois* Kleinbürger *m*; kleinbürgerlich; *~ bourgeoisie* Klein-

bürgertum *n*; ⌐ *cash* ✝ kleine Summen *f/pl.*; ⌐ *officer* ♗ Maat *m*; ⌐ *sessions pl.* ⚖ Bagatellgericht *n*.

pet·u·lance ['petjuləns] *s. pettishness*; **'pet·u·lant** *s. pettish*.

pew [pju:] Kirchensitz *m*; -stuhl *m*.

pe·wit *orn.* ['pi:wit] Lachmöwe *f*; Kiebitz *m*.

pew·ter ['pju:tə] Zinn *n*; Zinngefäße *n/pl.*; '**pew·ter·er** Zinngießer *m*.

pha·e·ton *hist.* ['feitn] Phaethon *m* (*Wagen*).

pha·lanx ['fælæŋks] Phalanx *f*.

phan·tasm ['fæntæzəm] Trugbild *n*; **phan·tas·ma·go·ri·a** [⸜mə-'gɔːriə] Gaukelbild *n*, Phantasmagorie *f*.

phan·tom ['fæntəm] **1.** Phantom *n*, Trugbild *n*; Gespenst *n*; Hirngespinst *n*; **2.** Gespenster...

Phar·i·sa·ic, Phar·i·sa·i·cal □ [ˌfæri'seiik(əl)] pharisäisch, scheinheilig.

Phar·i·see ['færisi:] Pharisäer *m*.

phar·ma·ceu·ti·cal □ [fɑːmə'sju:-tikəl] pharmazeutisch; **phar·ma·'ceu·tics** *sg.* Pharmazeutik *f*, Arzneimittelkunde *f*; **phar·ma·cist** ['⸜sist] Pharmazeut *m*, Apotheker *m*; **phar·ma·col·o·gy** [⸜'kɔlədʒi] Arzneimittellehre *f*; '**phar·ma·cy** Pharmazie *f*; Apotheke *f*.

phar·ynx *anat.* ['færiŋks] Rachenhöhle *f*.

phase [feiz] Phase *f*, (Entwicklungs)Stufe *f*, Stadium *n*; **phased** in Phasen.

pheas·ant *orn.* ['feznt] Fasan *m*; '**pheas·ant·ry** Fasanerie *f*.

phe·nom·e·nal □ [fi'nɔminl] phänomenal; außergewöhnlich; **phe·'nom·e·non** [⸜nən], *pl.* **phe'nom·e·na** [⸜nə] Phänomen *n*, Erscheinung *f*; *fig.* Wunder *n*.

phew [fju:] puh!

phi·al ['faiəl] Phiole *f*, Fläschchen *n*.

Phi Be·ta Kap·pa *Am.* ['fai 'bi:tə 'kæpə] *e-e* Studentenverbindung *f*.

phi·lan·der [fi'lændə] flirten; **phi·'lan·der·er** Schürzenjäger *m*.

phil·an·throp·ic [filən'θrɔpik] (⸜*al-ly*) menschenfreundlich; **phi·lan·thro·pist** [fi'lænθrəpist] Menschenfreund(in); **phi'lan·thro·py** Menschenliebe *f*.

phi·lat·e·list [fi'lætəlist] Briefmarkensammler(in); **phi'lat·e·ly** Briefmarkensammeln *n*; Philatelie *f*.

phi·lip·pic [fi'lipik] Philippika *f*, Standpauke *f*, Strafpredigt *f*.

Phi·lis·tine ['filistain] Philister *m* (*a. fig.*).

phil·o·log·i·cal □ [filə'lɔdʒikəl] sprachwissenschaftlich, philologisch; **phi·lol·o·gist** [fi'lɔlədʒist] Philologe *m*, Philologin *f*; Sprachforscher(in); **phi'lol·o·gy** Philologie *f*, Sprachwissenschaft *f*.

phi·los·o·pher [fi'lɔsəfə] Philosoph *m*; ⸜*s'* stone Stein *m* der Weisen; **phil·o·soph·ic, phil·o·soph·i·cal** [filə'sɔfik(əl)] philosophisch; **phi·los·o·phize** [fi'lɔsəfaiz] philosophieren; **phi'los·o·phy** Philosophie *f*.

phil·tre, phil·ter ['filtə] Liebestrank *m*.

phiz F *co.* [fiz] Visage *f*, Gesicht *n*.

phle·bi·tis ☞ [fli'baitis] Venenentzündung *f*.

phlegm [flem] Schleim *m*; Phlegma *n*; **phleg·mat·ic** [fleg'mætik] (⸜*ally*) phlegmatisch.

pho·bi·a ['fəubiə] Phobie *f* (*Angst*).

phoe·be *orn.* ['fi:bi] Tyrannvogel *m*.

Phoe·ni·cian [fi'niʃən] **1.** phönizisch; **2.** Phönizier(in).

phoe·nix *myth.* ['fi:niks] Phönix *m*.

phone[1] F [fəun] **1.** Telefon *n*; **2.** telefonieren.

phone[2] [⸜] (Einzel)Laut *m*.

phone-in ['fəunin] Sendung *f* mit Zuschauer- *od.* Zuhörerbeteiligung.

pho·neme ['fəuni:m] Phonem *n*; **pho'nem·ic** phonemisch.

pho·net·ic [fəu'netik] (⸜*ally*) phonetisch; ⸜ *spelling* phonetische Schreibung *f* (*z. B.* thru *für* through); ⸜ *transcription* Lautschrift *f*; **pho·ne·ti·cian** [ˌfəuni'tiʃən] Phonetiker *m*; **pho·net·ics** [⸜'netiks] *sg.* Phonetik *f*, Laut(bildungs)lehre *f*.

pho·ney *sl.* ['fəuni] unecht; falsch; Schein...

pho·no·graph *Am.* ['fəunəgrɑːf] Plattenspieler *m*; Grammophon *n*.

pho·nol·o·gy [fəu'nɔlədʒi] Phonologie *f*, Lautlehre *f*.

pho·ny *Am. sl.* ['fəuni] **1.** Fälschung *f*; Schwindler *m*; **2.** = phoney.

phos·phate ⚗ ['fɔsfeit] Phosphat *n*.

phos·pho·resce [fɔsfə'res] phosphoreszieren; **phos·pho·'res·cent** phosphoreszierend; **phos·phor·ic** ⚗ [⸜'fɔrik] Phosphor...; **phos-**

pho·rous ⌢ ['ˌfərəs] phosphorig; phos·pho·rus ⌢ ['ˌfərəs] Phosphor m.

pho·to F ['foutəu] Photo n; 'ˌ·cop·i·er Photokopiergerät n; 'ˌ·cop·y Photokopie f; photokopieren; ˌ·en'grav·ing Lichtdruck(verfahren n) m; 'ˌ--'fin·ish Am. Entscheidung f durch Zielphotographie; 'ˌ·flash Blitzlicht n, -lampe f; ˌ·gen·ic [fəutəu'dʒenik] photogen; ˌ·gram·me·try [ˌ'græmitri] Meßbildverfahren n.

pho·to·graph ['foutəgrɑːf] 1. Photographie f, Lichtbild n, Aufnahme f; take a ˌ e-e Aufnahme machen; 2. photographieren; pho·tog·ra·pher [fə'tɒgrəfə] Photograph(in); pho·to·graph·ic [fəutə'græfik] (ˌally) photographisch; ˌ library Bildarchiv n; Photothek f; ˌ print Lichtpause f; pho·tog·ra·phy [fə'tɒgrəfi] Photographie f.

pho·to·gra·vure [fəutəgrə'vjuə] Lichtkupferätzung f, Kupfertiefdruck m; pho·tom·e·ter [ˌ'tɒmitə] Belichtungsmesser m; pho·to-play ['ˌtəplei] Filmdrama n; pho·to·sen·si·tive ['ˌtəusensətiv] lichtempfindlich; pho·to·stat ['ˌtəustæt] Photokopiergerät n; Photokopie f; pho·to·te·leg·ra·phy [ˌtəti'legrəfi] Bildtelegraphie f; pho·to·type ['ˌtəutaip] Lichtpause f.

phrase [freiz] 1. (Rede)Wendung f, Redensart f; Ausdruck m; Schlagwort n; ♪ Satz m; 2. ausdrücken; formulieren; 'ˌ·book Sprachführer m; 'ˌ·mon·ger Phrasendrescher m; phra·se·ol·o·gy [ˌi'ɒlədʒi] Ausdrucksweise f; Phraseologie f; 'phras·ing Formulierung f.

phre·net·ic [fri'netik] (ˌally) toll, rasend, frenetisch.

phre·nol·o·gy [fri'nɒlədʒi] Schädellehre f.

phthis·i·cal ✶ ['θaisikəl] schwindsüchtig; phthi·sis ['ˌsis] Schwindsucht f.

phut sl. [fʌt]: go ˌ futschgehen.

phys·ic F ['fizik] 1. Arznei f; 2. j. verarzten; 'phys·i·cal □ physisch; körperlich; physikalisch; ˌ condition Gesundheitszustand m; ˌ culture Körperpflege f; ˌ education, ˌ training Leibeserziehung f; phy·si·cian [fi'ziʃən] Arzt m; phys·i·cist ['ˌsist] Physiker m; phys·ics ['fiziks] sg. Physik f.

phys·i·og·no·my [fizi'ɒnəmi] Physiognomie f; Gesichtsausdruck m; phys·i·o·log·i·cal [ˌə'lɒdʒikəl] physiologisch; phys·i·ol·o·gist [ˌ'ɒlədʒist] Physiologe m; phys·i·ol·o·gy Physiologie f.

phys·i·o·ther·a·py [fiziəu'θerəpi] Physiotherapie f.

phy·sique [fi'ziːk] Körperbau m.

pi·an·ist ['piənist] Pianist(in), Klavierspieler(in).

pi·a·no¹ ♪ ['pjɑːnəu] piano.

pi·an·o² ['pjænəu] a. pi·an·o·for·te [ˌ'fɔːti] Klavier n; grand piano Flügel m.

pi·az·za [pi'ætsə] Piazza f, (Markt-)Platz m; Am. große Veranda f.

pi·broch ['piːbrɒk] Dudelsackvariationen f/pl.

pic·a·resque [pikə'resk] pikaresk; ˌ novel Schelmenroman m.

pic·a·yune Am. [pikə'juːn] 1. mst fig. Pfennig m; Null f; Lappalie f; 2. unbedeutend, schäbig.

pic·ca·lil·li [pikə'lili] Piccalilli pl. (scharf eingemachtes, kleingeschnittenes Mischgemüse).

pic·ca·nin·ny co. ['pikənini] 1. bsd. Neger-Kind n, Gör n; 2. kindlich.

pick [pik] 1. Auswahl f, -lese f; das Beste; = pickaxe; 2. auf-, wegnehmen; (Blumen, Früchte) pflücken; in den Zähnen stochern; in der Nase bohren; Knochen abnagen; Schloß knacken; Streit suchen; auswählen, -suchen; (auf)picken; im Essen herumstochern; ˌ s.o.'s pocket j-m die Tasche ausräumen; ˌ one's way vorsichtig gehen; ˌ one's words sich gewählt od. vorsichtig ausdrücken; ˌ at herumnörgeln an (dat.); ˌ off abnehmen, -machen; abschießen; ˌ on verfallen auf, auswählen; ˌ out auswählen; herausfinden, -suchen, ausfindig machen; Melodie nach Gehör spielen; ˌ over Früchte etc. auslesen; ˌ up aufreißen, -brechen; aufnehmen, -heben; sich e-e Fremdsprache aneignen; aufgreifen; auflesen; erfassen; auffangen, -schnappen; j. (im Auto) mitnehmen; j. abholen; Täter ergreifen; Gesundheit wiedererlangen; gesund werden, sich erholen ˌ o.s. up wieder hochkommen; ˌ up speed auf Touren kommen; ˌ up with kennenlernen; ˌ-a-back

['ˌəbæk] huckepack; '~·axe Spitz-hacke *f*; 'pick·er Pflücker(in), Leser(in); Zupfer(in); Pflück-maschine *f*.

pick·er·el *ichth.* ['pikərəl] junger Hecht *m*.

pick·et ['pikit] 1. Pfahl *m*; Pflock *m*; ⚔ Feldwache *f*; Streikposten *m*; 2. *v/t.* einpfählen; an e-n Pfahl binden; ⚔ als Feldwache auf-stellen; mit Streikposten besetzen; *v/i.* Streikposten stehen.

pick·ing ['pikiŋ] Picken *n*, Pflücken *n etc.* (*s. pick*); Abfall *m*; *mst* ~s *pl.* (unehrlicher) Nebengewinn *m*.

pick·le ['pikl] 1. Pökel *m*, Salzlake *f*; Eingepökelte *n*, Pickles *pl.*; F Wild-fang *m*; F mißliche Lage *f*; *s. mix*; 2. (ein)pökeln; ~d herring Salz-hering *m*.

pick...: '~·lock Dietrich *m*; Ein-brecher *m*; '~·me-up F (Magen-) Stärkung *f*; '~·pock·et Taschen-dieb *m*; '~·up Ansteigen *n*; Ton-abnehmer *m am Plattenspieler*; *a.* ~ *in prices* ✝ Hausse *f*; Klein-lieferwagen *m*; Pritschenwagen *m*; Beschleunigung *f*; *sl.* Straßen-bekanntschaft *f*; ~ *dinner* Essen *n* aus (Fleisch)Resten; 'pick·y F wäh-lerisch.

pic·nic ['piknik] 1. Picknick *n*; *fig.* Kinderspiel *n*; 2. picknicken.

pic·to·ri·al [pik'tɔːriəl] 1. □ Maler-...; malerisch; illustriert; ~ *ad-vertising* Bildreklame *f*; 2. Illu-strierte *f*.

pic·ture ['piktʃə] 1. Bild *n*, Gemälde *n*; Ebenbild *n*; Verkörperung *f*; *et.* Bildschönes *n*; ~s *pl.* F Kino *n*; *put s.o. in the* ~ j. ins Bild setzen, j. in-formieren; 2. malen; schildern; illustrieren; sich *et.* vorstellen *od.* ausmalen; '~·book Bilderbuch *n*; ~ *ed·i·tor* Bildredakteur *m*; '~·gal·ler·y Gemäldegalerie *f*; '~·go·er Ki-nobesucher(in); ~ *post·card* An-sichtskarte *f*; ~ *res·o·lu·tion Fern-sehen*: Bildauflösung *f*.

pic·tur·esque □ [piktʃə'resk] male-risch; pic·tur'esque·ness *das* Male-rische.

pidg·in ['pidʒin]: ~ *English* Pidgin-Englisch *n*; *that's not my* ~ F das geht mich nichts an.

pie¹ [pai] Pastete *f*, Obsttorte *f*, -kuchen *m*; *typ.* Zwiebelfische *m/pl.*; *s. finger 1.*

pie² *orn.* [~] Elster *f*.

pie·bald ['paibɔːld] gescheckt; buntscheckig.

piece [piːs] 1. Stück *n* (*a. Teil, Kunstwerk, Münze*); Geschütz *n*; Gewehr *n*; Teil *n* *e-s Services*; (*Schach- etc.*)Figur *f*; *a* ~ *of advice* ein Rat *m*; *a* ~ *of news* e-e Neuigkeit; ~ *by* ~ eines nach dem anderen; *of a* ~ gleichmäßig; *be of a* ~ *with* im Einklang stehen mit; *give s.o. a* ~ *of one's mind* j-m gründ-lich die Meinung sagen; *take to* ~s zerlegen; 2. *a.* ~ *up* flicken, aus-bessern; ~ *together* zs.-stellen, -setzen, -stücken, -flicken; ~ *out* ausfüllen; '~·goods *pl.* Meter-ware *f*; '~·meal stückweise; '~·work Akkordarbeit *f*.

pied [paid] scheckig, bunt.

pie-eyed ['pai'aid] besoffen.

pie·plant *Am.* ['paiplɑːnt] Rha-barber *m*.

pier [piə] Pfeiler *m*; Wellenbrecher *m*; Pier *m, f*, Hafendamm *m*, Mole *f*, Landungsbrücke *f*; 'pier·age ⚓ Kaigeld *n*.

pierce [piəs] *v/t.* durchbohren; Ohr durchdringen; eindringen *in Geheimnisse etc.*; *v/i.* eindringen (*a. fig.*); 'pierc·ing □ durchdrin-gend (*a. fig.*).

pier-glass ['piəglɑːs] Pfeilerspiegel *m*.

pi·e·tism ['paiətizəm] Pietismus *m*.

pi·e·ty ['paiəti] Frömmigkeit *f*; Pietät *f*.

pif·fle *sl.* ['pifl] 1. Quatsch *m*; Kitsch *m*; 2. quatschen.

pig [pig] 1. Ferkel *n*; Schwein *n*; *metall.* Roheisenbarren *m*, Massel *f*, Mulde *f*; *buy a* ~ *in a poke* die Katze im Sack kaufen; 2. ferkeln; F zs.-gepfercht leben.

pi·geon ['pidʒin] Taube *f*; *sl.* Gimpel *m*; '~·'breast·ed hühner-brüstig; '~·hole 1. *Brief- etc.* Fach *n*; 2. in ein Fach legen, aufheben; einordnen; (vorläufig) beiseite-legen; 'pi·geon·ry Taubenschlag *m*.

pig·ger·y ['pigəri] Schweinezucht *f*.

pig·gish □ ['pigiʃ] schweinisch.

pig·gy ['pigi] 1. Schweinchen *n*; ~ *bank* Sparschwein *n*; 2. gierig.

pig·head·ed ['pig'hedid] dick-köpfig.

pig-i·ron ['pigaiən] Roheisen *n*.

pig·let ['piglit] Ferkel *n*, Schweinchen *n*.
pig·ment ['pigmənt] Pigment *n*.
pig·my ['pigmi] = *pygmy*.
pig...: '∼·nut Erdnuß *f*; '∼·skin Schweinsleder *n*; ∼·sty ['∼stai] Schweinestall *m*, Koben *m*; '∼·tail (Haar)Zopf *m*; '∼·wash Schweinetrank *m*.
pike [paik] ✕ Pike *f*; Spitze *f*; *ichth.* Hecht *m*; Schlagbaum *m*; gebührenpflichtige Straße *f*; '**pik·er** *Am. sl.* Geizhals *m*; *fig.* kleiner Mann *m*; '**pike·staff**: *as plain as a ∼* sonnenklar.
pil·chard *ichth.* ['piltʃəd] Sardine *f*.
pile[1] [pail] **1.** Haufen *m*; Stoß *m*, Stapel *m*; Scheiterhaufen *m*; großes Gebäude *n*; ⚡ Batterie *f*; *atomic ∼* Atommeiler *m*, Reaktor *m*; **2.** *oft ∼ up, ∼ on* auf-, anhäufen, aufschichten; (auf)stapeln, auftürmen.
pile[2] [∼] Pfahl *m*.
pile[3] [∼] Haar *n*; Noppe *f*; Flor *m* des Samtes.
pile-driv·er ⊕ ['paildraivə] Ramme *f*; '**pile-dwell·ing** Pfahlbau *m*.
piles ✻ [pailz] *pl.* Hämorrhoiden *f/pl.*
pile-up F ['pailʌp] Massenkarambolage *f*.
pil·fer ['pilfə] stehlen, klauen.
pil·grim ['pilgrim] Pilger *m*, Wallfahrer *m*; ♀ *Fathers pl.* Pilgerväter *m/pl. (puritanische Einwanderer nach Amerika)*; '**pil·grim·age** Pilgerfahrt *f*.
pill [pil] Pille *f*, Tablette *f*.
pil·lage ['pilidʒ] **1.** Plünderung *f*; **2.** plündern.
pil·lar ['pilə] Pfeiler *m*, Ständer *m*; Säule *f (a. fig.)*; '∼·box Briefkasten *m*; '**pil·lared** mit Pfeilern; säulenförmig.
pil·lion ['piljən] Sattelkissen *n*; *mot.* Soziussitz *m*; *ride ∼* auf dem Soziussitz (mit)fahren.
pil·lo·ry ['piləri] **1.** Pranger *m*; *in the ∼* am Pranger; **2.** an den Pranger stellen; *fig.* anprangern.
pil·low ['piləu] **1.** (Kopf)Kissen *n*; ⊕ (Zapfen)Lager *n*; **2.** betten, stützen (*on* auf *acc.*); '∼·case, '∼·slip (Kissen)Bezug *m*.
pi·lot ['pailət] **1.** ⚓ Lotse *m*; ✈ Pilot *m*, Flugzeugführer *m*; *fig.* Führer *m*; ∼ *instructor* Fluglehrer *m*; ∼ *officer* Fliegerleutnant *m*; ∼

pupil Flugschüler *m*; **2.** Versuchs...; ∼ *plant* Versuchsanlage *f*; ∼ *project* Versuchs-, Testprojekt *n*; **3.** lotsen, steuern; '**pi·lot·age** Lotsen(geld) *n*; Führung(skunst) *f*; '**pi·lot-bal'loon** Versuchsballon *m*; '**pi·lot-light** Zündflamme *f e-s Gasgeräts.*
pi·men·to [pi'mentəu] Piment *m, n*, Nelkenpfeffer *m*.
pimp [pimp] **1.** Kuppler(in), Zuhälter *m*; **2.** kuppeln.
pim·ple ['pimpl] Pickel *m*, Pustel *f*; '**pim·pled**, '**pim·ply** pickelig, finnig.
pin [pin] **1.** (Steck)Nadel *f*; (Krawatten-, Hut- *etc.*)Nadel *f*; Bolzen *m*; Pflock *m*; Kegel *m*; Reißnagel *m*; ♩ Wirbel *m*; ∼*s pl. sl.* Stelzen *f/pl. (Beine)*; **2.** (an)heften; befestigen; *a. ∼ down sl. fig.* festnageln, fassen; *∼ one's hopes on* seine Hoffnung setzen auf (*acc.*).
pin·a·fore ['pinəfɔ:] Lätzchen *n*; Kinder-, Frauenschürze *f*.
pin·ball ma·chine *f* ['pinbɔ:lməʃi:n] Flipper *m (Spielautomat)*.
pin·cers ['pinsəz] *pl. (a pair of ∼* eine) Kneifzange *f*.
pinch [pintʃ] **1.** Kniff *m*; Prise *f (Tabak etc.)*; Druck *m*, Not *f*; *at a ∼* notfalls; **2.** *v/t.* kneifen, zwicken, klemmen; F klauen (*stehlen*); *sl.* kassieren, festnehmen; *be ∼ed for money* knapp bei Kasse sein; *v/i.* drücken; in Not sein; knausern; '**pinched** zs.-gedrückt, schmal; *fig.* zs.-geschnurrt; dünn.
pinch·beck ['pintʃbek] **1.** ⊕ Tombak *m*; Talmi *n (a. fig.)*; **2.** Talmi...
pinch-hit *Am.* ['pintʃhit] *(irr. hit)* einspringen (*for* für *j.*).
pin·cush·ion ['pinkuʃən] Nadelkissen *n*.
pine[1] ♀ [pain] Kiefer *f*, Föhre *f*.
pine[2] [∼] sich abhärmen; sich sehnen, schmachten (*for, after* nach); *∼ away* sich verzehren.
pine...: '∼·ap·ple ♀ Ananas *f*; '∼·cone Kiefernzapfen *m*; '**pin·er·y** Treibhaus *n* für Ananas; Kiefernpflanzung *f*; '∼·**tree** = *pine*[1].
pin-feath·er ['pinfeðə] Stoppelfeder *f*.
ping [piŋ] schwirren, pfeifen.
ping-pong ['piŋpɔŋ] Tischtennis *n*.
pin·ion ['pinjən] **1.** Flügelspitze *f*; *poet.* Schwinge *f*; *a. ∼-feather* Schwungfeder *f*; ⊕ Ritzel *n (An-*

triebsrad); **2.** die Flügel beschneiden (*dat.*); *fig.* fesseln.

pink¹ [piŋk] **1.** ♀ Nelke *f*; Blaßrot *n*, Rosa *n*; Gipfel *m*, höchster Grad *m*; *in the* ~ *sl.* in bester Verfassung; **2.** rosa(farben).

pink² [~] durchstechen; auszacken; ~*ing shears pl.* Zickzackschere *f*.

pink³ *mot.* [~] klopfen, klingeln.

pink·ish ['piŋkiʃ] blaßrosa.

pin·nace ⚓ ['pinis] Pinasse *f*.

pin·na·cle ['pinəkl] ⚔ Zinne *f*, Spitztürmchen *n*; (Berg)Spitze *f*; *fig.* Gipfel *m*.

pin·nate ♀ ['pineit] gefiedert.

pi·noc(h)·le *Am.* ['pi:nʌkl] Binokel *n* (*Kartenspiel*).

pin...: '~·**point** genau lokalisieren; *fig.* genau bestimmen; '~·**prick** *fig.* Nadelstich *m*; '~·**stripe** Nadelstreifen *m* (*Stoff*).

pint [paint] Pinte *f* (*0,57 od. Am. 0,47 Liter*).

pin-up ['pinʌp] Pin-up-girl *n*.

pi·o·neer [paiə'niə] **1.** Pionier *m* (*a.* ✗), Bahnbrecher *m*, Vorkämpfer *m*; **2.** *Weg* bahnen; den Weg bahnen (für).

pi·ous ☐ ['paiəs] fromm, religiös; pflichtgetreu.

pip¹ [pip] *vet.* Pips *m*; *sl.* miese Laune *f*; *have the* ~ nicht auf dem Damm sein; *it gives me the* ~ es geht mir auf die Nerven.

pip² [~] Obstkern *m*; Auge *n auf Würfeln etc.*; ✗ Stern *m* (*Rangabzeichen*).

pip³ *sl.* [~] zunichte machen; durchfallen (lassen); abknallen; ~ *out* eingehen (*sterben*).

pip⁴ [~] Ton *m* (*Zeitzeichen etc.*).

pipe [paip] **1.** Rohr *n*, Röhre *f*; ♪ (Orgel)Pfeife *f*, Flöte *f*; ⚓ Bootsmannspfeife *f*, -pfiff *m*; Lied *n e-s Vogels*; Luftröhre *f*; (Tabaks)Pfeife *f*; Pipe *f* (*Weinfaß* = *470 l*); **2.** pfeifen; quieken; durch Röhren leiten; mit Röhren versehen; *Schneiderei:* paspeln; ~*d music contp.* Musikberieselung *f in Supermärkten etc.*; ~ *one's eye* F weinen; ~ *down* F den Mund halten; ~ *up* F loslegen; '~·**clay** 1. Pfeifenton *m*; **2.** mit Pfeifenton weißen; ~·**dream** Luftschloß *n*; '~·**-lay·er** Rohrleger *m*; *Am. pol.* Drahtzieher *m*; '~·**line** Ölleitung *f*, Pipeline *f*; '**pip·er** Pfeifer *m*; *pay the* ~ F die Zeche bezahlen.

pip·ing ['paipiŋ] **1.** pfeifend; schrill (*Stimme*); fröhlich (*Zeit*); ~ *hot* siedend heiß; **2.** Rohrnetz *n*, -system *n*; *coll.* Rohr *n*; *Schneiderei:* Paspel *m*, *f*, Biese *f*; Zuckerguß *m*.

pip·pin ♀ ['pipin] Pippinapfel *m*.

pip-squeak *sl.* ['pipskwi:k] Knülch *m*, Würstchen *n*.

pi·quan·cy ['pi:kənsi] Pikantheit *f*; '**pi·quant** ☐ pikant.

pique [pi:k] **1.** Groll *m*; **2.** *Zorn od.* Neugier reizen; ~ *o.s. upon* sich etwas zugute tun auf (*acc.*).

pi·ra·cy ['paiərəsi] Seeräuberei *f*; Raubdruck *m von Büchern*; **pi·rate** ['~rit] **1.** Seeräuber(schiff *n*) *m*; Raubdrucker *m*; *wireless* ~, *radio* ~, ~ *listener* Schwarzhörer(in); ~ *station Radio:* Schwarz-, Piratensender *m*; **2.** unerlaubt nachdrucken; **pi·rat·i·cal** ☐ [pai'rætikl] (see)räuberisch.

Pis·ces *ast.* ['paisi:z] Fische *m/pl.*

pis·ci·cul·ture ['pisikʌltʃə] Fischzucht *f*.

pish [piʃ] pfui!; pah!

piss V [pis] **1.** Pisse *f*; **2.** (be)pissen; ~ *off!* verdufte!; *be* ~*ed off* die Nase voll haben; **pissed** V besoffen.

pis·ta·chi·o [pi'sta:ʃiəu] Pistazie *f*.

pis·til ♀ ['pistil] Stempel *m*, Griffel *m*; **pis·til·late** ['~lit] mit Stempel(n), weiblich.

pis·tol ['pistl] Pistole *f*.

pis·ton ⊕ ['pistən] Kolben *m*; '~·**rod** Kolbenstange *f*; '~·**stroke** Kolbenhub *m*.

pit [pit] **1.** Grube *f* (*a.* ✗, *anat.*); ✗ Miete *f*; *thea.* Parterre *n*; Pockennarbe *f*; (Tier)Falle *f*; *Autorennen:* Box *f*; *Am. Börse:* Maklerstand *m*; *the* ~ die Hölle; **2.** mit Narben bedecken; ~ *against s-e Kraft etc.* messen mit; ~*ted with smallpox* pockennarbig.

pit-a-pat ['pitə'pæt] ticktack.

pitch¹ [pitʃ] **1.** Pech *n*; **2.** (ver-) pichen; ⚓ teeren.

pitch² [~] **1.** Stand(platz) *m e-s Straßenhändlers etc.*; ♪ Tonhöhe *f*; Grad *m*, Stufe *f*; Steigung *f*, Neigung *f e-s Daches*; *Kricket:* Feld zwischen den Dreistäben; Wurf *m*; ⚓ Stampfen *n*; **2.** *v/t.* werfen; schleudern; *Heu etc.* aufladen; feststecken; *Zelt etc.* aufschlagen, aufstellen; ♪ *Grundton* angeben; ♪ stimmen (*a. fig.*); ~*ed battle*

regelrechte *od.* offene (Feld-)
Schlacht *f*; ~ one's hopes too high
s-e Hoffnungen zu hoch stecken;
v/i. ✗ (sich) lagern; fallen; ⚓
stampfen; ~ *upon* verfallen auf
(*acc.*); ~ *into* F herfallen über (*acc.*).
pitch...: '~-and-'toss Kopf oder
Schrift (*Spiel*); **'~-'black, '~-
-'dark** pechschwarz.
pitch·er ['pitʃə] (Ball)Werfer *m*;
Krug *m.*
pitch·fork ['pitʃfɔːk] **1.** Heu-, Mistgabel *f*; ♪ Stimmgabel *f*; **2.** mit der
Heugabel werfen; zwängen, drän-
gen (*into in e-e Lage*).
pitch-pine ♧ ['pitʃpain] Pechkiefer *f.*
pitch·y ['pitʃi] pechartig.
pit-coal ⚒ ['pitkəul] Steinkohle *f.*
pit·e·ous □ *rhet.* ['pitiəs] traurig;
kläglich.
pit·fall ['pitfɔːl] Fallgrube *f*, Falle *f.*
pith [piθ] Mark *n*; *fig.* Kern *m*; Kraft
f; Gewicht *n*; ~ **hel·met** Tropenhelm
m.
pith·y □ ['piθi] markig, kernig;
prägnant, inhaltsreich.
pit·i·a·ble □ ['pitiəbl] erbärmlich.
pit·i·ful □ ['pitiful] mitleidig; mit-
leiderregend; erbärmlich, jämmerlich, kläglich (*a. contp.*).
pit·i·less □ ['pitilis] unbarmherzig.
pit·man ['pitmən] Bergmann *m.*
pit·tance ['pitəns] Hungerlohn *m*;
(kleines) Bißchen.
pi·tu·i·tar·y [pi'tjuːitəri] Schleim...;
~ *gland* Hypophyse *f.*
pit·y ['piti] **1.** Mitleid *n* (*on* mit);
for ~'s *sake!* um Gottes willen!;
it is a ~ es ist schade; *it is a thousand
pities* es ist jammerschade; **2.** bemitleiden; *I* ~ *him* er tut mir leid.
piv·ot ['pivət] **1.** ⊕ Zapfen *m*;
(Tür)Angel *f*; *fig.* Dreh-, Angelpunkt *m*; ✗ Flügelmann *m*; **2.** sich
drehen (*on, upon* um); **piv·o·tal**
['~tl] den Angelpunkt bildend;
Kardinal...
pix·ie ['piksi] Elf *m*, Kobold *m*; Elfe *f.*
pix·i·lat·ed *Am.* F ['piksəleitid] verdreht; irritiert.
pix·y ['piksi] = *pixie.*
pla·ca·bil·i·ty [plækə'biliti] Ver-
söhnlichkeit *f*; **'pla·ca·ble** □ versöhnlich.
pla·card ['plækɑːd] **1.** Plakat *n*, Anschlag *m*; **2.** anschlagen; mit An-
schlagzetteln bekleben.
pla·cate [plə'keit] versöhnlich stim-

men.
place [pleis] **1.** Platz *m*; Ort *m*;
Stadt *f*; Stelle *f*; Stätte *f*; Stellung *f*;
Rang *m*; Aufgabe *f*; Anwesen *n*,
Haus *n*, Wohnung *f*; ~ *of delivery*
Erfüllungsort *m*; ~ *of employment*
Arbeitsplatz *m*; *give* ~ *to j-m* Platz
machen; *in* (*out of*) ~ (nicht) am
rechten Ort; *fig.* (fehl) am Platz; *in*
~ *of* anstatt (*gen.*); *in his* ~ an seiner
Stelle; *in the first* ~ an erster Stelle;
zunächst (einmal); **2.** stellen, legen,
setzen; *j.* anstellen; ✗ Posten aufstellen; *Geld* anlegen; *Person* unterbringen (*identifizieren*); *Bestellung*
aufgeben, *Auftrag* erteilen; *be* ~*d
Sport*: sich placieren; ~ **mat** Platzdeckchen *n*, Set *n*; **'~-name** Orts-
name *m*; **'plac·er** Leger(in); Ord-
ner(in); Preisträger(in).
plac·id □ ['plæsid] mild, sanft;
ruhig; **pla'cid·i·ty** Sanftheit *f*;
Ruhe *f.*   [*Damenrock*]
plack·et ['plækit] Schlitz *m am*
pla·gi·a·rism ['pleidʒiərizəm] Plagiat *n*; **'pla·gi·a·rist** Plagiator *m*,
Abschreiber *m*; **'pla·gi·a·rize** abschreiben, plagiieren.
plague [pleig] **1.** Plage *f*; Seuche *f*;
Pest *f*; **2.** plagen, quälen; **'~-spot**
mst fig. Pestbeule *f.*
pla·guy ['pleigi] widerwärtig, F verwünscht, verdammt.
plaice *ichth.* [pleis] Scholle *f.*
plaid [plæd] *schottisches* Plaid
(-tuch) *n.*
plain [plein] **1.** □ flach, eben; klar,
offenbar; deutlich; rein (*Wahrheit*);
einfach, schlicht; unscheinbar (*Gesicht*); offen, ehrlich; unumwunden;
einfarbig; ~ *chocolate* bittere Schokolade *f*; ~ *fare* Hausmannskost *f*; ~
knitting Rechtsstrickerei *f*; ~ *paper*
unliniertes Papier; ~ *sewing* Weiß-
näherei *f*; **2.** *adv.* klar, deutlich; **3.**
Ebene *f*, Fläche *f*; *bsd. Am. attr.*
Prärie...; **'~-clothes** *Am.* Geheimpolizist *m*; ~ **deal·ing** ehrliche Handlungsweise *f*; **'plain·ness** Einfachheit *f*, Offenheit *f*; Klarheit *f*; **plain
sail·ing** *fig.* einfache *od.* klare Sache
f.
plains·man ['pleinzmən] Flach-
landbewohner *m*; *Am.* Prärie-
bewohner *m.*
plaint ⚖ [pleint] Klage(schrift) *f*;
plain·tiff ['~tif] ⚖ Kläger(in);
'plain·tive □ traurig, klagend.

plait

plait [plæt] 1. *Haar- etc.* Flechte *f*; Zopf *m*; = *pleat* 1; 2. flechten; = *pleat* 2.

plan [plæn] 1. Plan *m*; Entwurf *m*; (Grund)Riß *m*; 2. e-n Plan entwerfen von *od.* zu; *fig.* planen, vorhaben; ~ned economy Planwirtschaft *f*; ~ning board Planungsamt *n*.

plane[1] [plein] 1. flach, eben; 2. ⅄ Ebene *f*, Fläche *f*; ⚔ Tragfläche *f*; Flugzeug *n*; *fig.* Stufe *f*; ⊕ Hobel *m*; *elevating (depressing)* ~*s pl.* ⚔ Höhen- (Flächen)steuer *n*; 3. ebnen, glätten; (ab)hobeln; ⚔ fliegen; gleiten.

plane[2] ⚘ [~] *a.* ~-tree Platane *f.*

plan·et *ast.* ['plænit] Planet *m.*

plane-ta·ble *surv.* ['pleinteibl] Meßtisch *m.*

plan·e·tar·i·um [plæni'tɛəriəm] Planetarium *n*; **plan·e·tar·y** ['~təri] planetarisch; Planeten...; *fig.* umherirrend.

pla·nim·e·try ⅄ [plæ'nimitri] Planimetrie *f.*

plan·ish ⊕ ['plæniʃ] glätten; polieren.

plank [plæŋk] 1. Planke *f*, Bohle *f*, Diele *f*, Brett *n*; *Am. parl.* Programmpunkt *m*; 2. dielen; verschalen; ~ *down od. out sl., Am.* F *Geld* auf den Tisch legen; ~ **bed** Pritsche *f im Gefängnis*; **'plank·ing** Verschalung *f*; Planken *f/pl.*

plank·ton *biol.* ['plæŋktɔn] Plankton *n.*

plant [plɑːnt] 1. Pflanze *f*; (Betriebs)Anlage *f*; Betriebsmaterial *n*; Fabrik *f*, Werk *n*; *sl.* Falle *f*; Schwindel *m*; 2. (an-, ein)pflanzen (*a. fig.*); ~ *o.s.* sich aufpflanzen, (auf)stellen, (auf)setzen; anlegen, errichten, gründen; ansiedeln; *sl. Schlag* verpassen; *Land* bepflanzen; *Land* besiedeln; ~ *s.o. on s.th. sl.* j-m et. andrehen.

plan·tain[1] ⚘ ['plæntin] Wegerich *m.*

plan·tain[2] ⚘ [~] Pisang *m*; Banane *f.*

plan·ta·tion [plæn'teiʃən] Pflanzung *f*; Plantage *f*; Ansiedlung *f*; **plant·er** ['plɑːntə] Pflanzer *m*; Pflanzmaschine *f*; **'plant-louse** Blattlaus *f.*

plaque [plɑːk] (Schmuck)Platte *f*; Agraffe *f*, Schnalle *f*; Gedenktafel *f*; *dental* ~ Zahnbelag *m.*

plash [plæʃ] 1. Platschen *n*; Pfütze *f*; 2. platsch!; 3. platschen, plätschern.

plash·y ['plæʃi] pfützig; sumpfig; feucht.

plas·ma *biol.* ['plæzmə] Plasma *n.*

plas·ter ['plɑːstə] 1. *pharm.* Pflaster *n*; ⊕ Mörtel *m*, Putz *m*; *mst* ~ of *Paris* Gips *m*; Gipsmörtel *m*, Stuck *m*; ~ cast Gipsabdruck *m*, -abguß *m*; ⚘ Gipsverband *m*; 2. bepflastern; (über)tünchen, gipsen; bedecken; **'plas·ter·er** Stukkateur *m*; **'plaster·ing** Verputz *m*; Stuck *m*; Gipsen *n.*

plas·tic ['plæstik] 1. (~ally) plastisch; Plastik...; formbar; ~ art Bildhauerkunst *f*; 2. Plastik(material) *n*, Kunststoff *m*; **plas·ti·cine** ['~tisi:n] Plastilin *n*; **plas·tic·i·ty** [~'tisiti] Plastizität *f*, Formbarkeit *f*; **'plastics** = *plastic* 2.

plat [plæt] *s. plait*; *s. plot*[1].

plate [pleit] 1. *allg.* Platte *f* (*a. phot., typ.*); *Bild*-Tafel *f*; *Namen-*, *Tür*-Schild *n*; *Kupfer- etc.* Stich *m*; Silber(geschirr, -besteck) *n*; (Eß-) Teller *m*; Preis *m bei Rennen*; *Am. Baseball*: (Schlag)Mal *n*; *a. dental* ~ Gaumenplatte *f*; *Radio*: Anode *f* e-r *Röhre*; ⊕ Grobblech *n*; 2. plattieren, versilbern; ⚒, ⚓ panzern.

pla·teau *geogr.* ['plætəu] Hochebene *f*, Plateau *n.*

plate-bas·ket ['pleitbɑːskit] Besteckkorb *m*; **plate·ful** ['~ful] Teller(voll) *m.*

plate...: **'~-glass** Spiegelglas *n*; **'~-lay·er** 🚃 Streckenarbeiter *m.*

plat·en ['plætən] *typ.* Drucktiegel *m*; (Schreibmaschinen)Walze *f.*

plat·er ['pleitə] ⊕ Plattierer *m*; *Sport*: minderwertiges Rennpferd *n.*

plat·form ['plætfɔːm] Plattform *f*; *geogr.* Hochebene *f*; 🚃 Bahnsteig *m*; *Am. bsd.* Plattform *f* am Wagenende; Podium *n*, Rednerbühne *f*; *pol.* Parteiprogramm *n*; *bsd. Am. pol.* Aktionsprogramm *n im Wahlkampf.*

plat·i·num *min.* ['plætinəm] Platin *n.*

plat·i·tude *fig.* ['plætitjuːd] Plattheit *f.*

pla·toon ⚒ [plə'tuːn] Zug *m.*

plat·ter ['plætə] Servierplatte *f.*

plau·dit ['plɔːdit] *mst* ~*s pl.* Beifallklatschen *n.*

plau·si·bil·i·ty [plɔːzə'biliti] Glaubwürdigkeit *f*; Einnehmende *n.*

plau·si·ble ☐ ['plɔːzəbl] glaubhaft, einleuchtend, plausibel; einnehmend.

play [plei] **1.** Spiel *n*; *thea.* Schauspiel *n*, (Theater)Stück *n*; Spielerei *f*; ⊕ Spiel *n*, Gang *m*; Spielraum *m* (*a. fig.*); *fair* (*foul*) ~ (un)ehrliches Spiel *n*; ~ *on words* Wortspiel *n*; *bring into* ~ in Gang *od.* zur Anwendung bringen; *make great* ~ *with groß* angeben mit; **2.** *v/i.* spielen (*a. fig.*); mitspielen; tändeln; ⊕ laufen; ~ *fast and loose with* Schindluder treiben mit; ~ *at cards* Karten spielen; ~ *for time* Zeit zu gewinnen suchen; ~ *up* loslegen; ~ *upon* einwirken auf (*acc.*); *v/t.* spielen (gegen); *thea.* spielen, darstellen; ~ *down fig.* herunterspielen; ~ *off fig.* ausspielen (*against each other* gegeneinander); ~*ed out* erledigt, abgetan; '~·**act·ing** Theaterspielen *n*; *fig.* Schauspielern *n*, Verstellung *f*; '~·**back** Playback *n* e-r *Tonaufnahme*; '~·**bill** Theaterzettel *m*; '~·**book** *thea.* Textbuch *n*; '~·-**boy** Playboy *m*; '**play·er** Spieler (-in); Schauspieler(in); '**play·er·-pi·an·o** elektrisches Klavier *n*; '**play·fel·low** Spielkamerad(in); **play·ful** □ ['~ful] spielerisch, scherzhaft; '**play·ful·ness** Mutwille *m*.

play...: '~·**go·er** Theaterbesucher (-in); '~·**ground** Spiel-, Tummelplatz *m*; Schulhof *m*; '~·**house** Schauspielhaus *n*; *Am.* Miniaturhaus *n für Kinder*.

play·ing...: '~·**card** Spielkarte *f*; '~-**field** Sport-, Spielplatz *m*.

play...: '~·**mate** *s. playfellow*; '~·**off** *Sport:* Entscheidungsspiel *n*; '~·**pen** Laufställchen *n*; '~·**thing** Spielzeug *n* (*a. fig.*); '~·**wright** Bühnenautor *m*, Dramatiker *m*.

pla·za ['plɑːzə] (Markt)Platz *m in Spanien*.

plea [pliː] ⅔⅔ Einrede *f*; Ausrede *f*, Vorwand *m*; Befürwortung *f*; Gesuch *n*; Bitte *f*; *make a* ~ Einspruch erheben; *on the* ~ *of od. that* unter dem Vorwand (*gen.*) *od.* daß.

plead [pliːd] *v/i.* vor Gericht reden, plädieren; ~ *for* für *j.* sprechen, bitten; sich einsetzen für; *s. guilty*; *v/t. Sache* vertreten, verteidigen; als Beweis anführen, geltend machen; sich entschuldigen mit; '**plead·a·ble** rechtsgültig; triftig; '**plead·er** ⅔⅔ Sachwalter *m*; Verteidiger *m*; '**plead·ing** ⅔⅔ Schrift-

satz *m*; ~*s pl.* Prozeßakten *f/pl.*; Verhandlung(en *pl.*) *f*.

pleas·ant □ ['pleznt] angenehm; vergnüglich; nett; erfreulich; freundlich; '**pleas·ant·ness** Annehmlichkeit *f*; '**pleas·ant·ry** Lustigkeit *f*; Scherz *m*, Spaß *m*.

please [pliːz] *v/i.* gefallen; belieben; *if you* ~ *iro.* stellen Sie sich vor; ~ *come in!* bitte, treten Sie ein!; *v/t. j-m* gefallen, angenehm sein; befriedigen; zufriedenstellen; ~ *yourself* tun Sie, was Ihnen gefällt; *be* ~*d to do* sich freuen, *et.* zu tun; *et.* gerne tun; *be* ~*d with* mit Vergnügen haben an (*dat.*); **pleased** erfreut, zufrieden.

pleas·ing □ ['pliːzɪŋ] angenehm, gefällig.

pleas·ur·a·ble □ ['pleʒərəbl] angenehm, vergnüglich.

pleas·ure ['pleʒə] **1.** Vergnügen *n*, Freude *f*; Belieben *n*; *attr.* Vergnügungs...; *at* ~ nach Belieben; *give s.o.* ~ *j-m* Vergnügen *od.* Freude machen; *take* ~ *in* Vergnügen finden an (*dat.*); **2.** (sich) erfreuen; '~·**ground** (Vergnügungs)Park *m*.

pleat [pliːt] **1.** Plisseefalte *f*; **2.** fälteln, plissieren.

ple·be·ian [pliˈbiːən] **1.** plebejisch; **2.** Plebejer(in).

pleb·i·scite ['plebisit] Volksentscheid *m*.

pledge [pledʒ] **1.** Pfand *n*; Zutrinken *n*; Gelübde *n*, Gelöbnis *n*, Versprechen *n*; *put in* ~ verpfänden; *take out of* ~ *Pfand* auslösen; **2.** verpfänden; *j-m* zutrinken; *he* ~*d himself* er gelobte; **pledg'ee** Pfandnehmer *m*; '**pledg·er** Verpfänder *m*.

Ple·iad ['plaiəd], *pl.* **Ple·ia·des** ['~diːz] Siebengestirn *n*.

ple·na·ry ['pliːnəri] vollständig; Voll...

plen·i·po·ten·ti·ar·y [plenipəu'tenʃəri] **1.** bevollmächtigt; **2.** Bevollmächtigte *m*.

plen·i·tude ['plenitjuːd] Fülle *f*.

plen·te·ous □ *poet.* ['plentjəs] voll, reichlich; '**plen·te·ous·ness** Fülle *f*.

plen·ti·ful □ ['plentiful] reichlich.

plen·ty ['plenti] **1.** Fülle *f*, Überfluß *m*; ~ *of* viel, eine Menge, reichlich; *horn of* ~ Füllhorn *n*; **2.** F reichlich.

ple·o·nasm ['pliːənæzəm] Pleonasmus *m*.

pleth·o·ra ['pleθərə] Blutandrang *m*;

ple·thor·ic [ple'θɔrik] (~ally) vollblütig; *fig.* dick.

pleu·ri·sy ♂ ['pluərisi] Brustfellentzündung *f*.

pli·a·bil·i·ty [plaiə'biliti] Biegsamkeit *f*.

pli·a·ble □ ['plaiəbl] biegsam; *fig.* geschmeidig, nachgiebig.

pli·an·cy ['plaiənsi] Biegsamkeit *f*.

pli·ant □ ['plaiənt] = *pliable.*

pli·ers ['plaiəz] *pl.* (*a pair of* ~ eine) (Draht-, Kombi)Zange *f*.

plight[1] [plait] **1.** *Ehre, Wort* verpfänden; verloben; **2.** Gelöbnis *n*.

plight[2] [plait] Zustand *m*, (Not)Lage *f*.

plim·soll ['plimsɔl] Turnschuh *m*.

plinth △ [plinθ] Säulenplatte *f*.

plod [plɔd] *a.* ~ *along,* ~ *on* sich dahinschleppen; sich plagen, schuften; **'plod·ding** □ arbeitsam; schwerfällig.

plonk F [plɔŋk] billiger Wein *m*.

plop [plɔp] **1.** plumps!; **2.** Plumps *m*; **3.** plumpsen.

plot[1] [plɔt] Stück(chen) *n*, Fleckchen *n Land*; Platz *m*; Parzelle *f*.

plot[2] [~] **1.** Plan *m*; Komplott *n*, Verschwörung *f*, Anschlag *m*; Intrige *f*; Handlung *f e-s Dramas etc.*; **2.** *v/t. a.* ~ *down* aufzeichnen; *in e-e Landkarte etc.* einzeichnen, -tragen; *b.s.* planen, anzetteln; *v/i.* sich verschwören, intrigieren; **'plot·ter** Anstifter(in); Verschwörer(in).

plough [plau] **1.** Pflug *m*; ⊕ Falzhobel *m*; *univ. sl.* Durchfall *m*; *the* ♀ *ast.* der Große Wagen; **2.** pflügen; furchen (*a. fig.*); ~ *back Gewinn* wieder in das Geschäft stecken; *be* ~*ed univ. sl.* durchfallen; **'~·man** Pflüger *m*; ~*'s lunch kaltes Mittagessen, mst aus Brot, Käse u. Bier bestehend;* **'~·share** Pflugschar *f*.

plov·er ['plʌvə] *orn.* Regenpfeifer *m*; Strandläufer *m*; F Kiebitz *m*.

plow [plau], **'plow·man** *bsd. Am.* = *plough etc.*

ploy F [plɔi] Masche *f*, Tour *f* (*List*).

pluck [plʌk] **1.** Mut *m*, Schneid *m*; Innereien *f/pl.*; Zug *m*, Ruck *m*; **2.** pflücken; *Vogel* rupfen; zerren, zupfen; reißen (*from* von); *sl. j.* rupfen, ausplündern; *univ. sl.* durchfallen lassen; ~ *at* zerren an; ~ *up courage* Mut fassen.

pluck·y F □ ['plʌki] mutig, schneidig.

plug [plʌg] **1.** Pflock *m*; Dübel *m*; Stöpsel *m*; ∮ Stecker *m*; Zahn-Plombe *f*; Priem *m* (*Tabak*); Klosettspülvorrichtung *f*; *Feuer*-Hydrant *m*; *Am. Radio:* Reklamehinweis *m*; alter Gaul *m*; ~ *socket* Steckdose *f*; **2.** *v/t.* zu-, verstopfen; *Zahn* plombieren; stöpseln; *sl. j-m* eins auswischen; *Am.* F *im Rundfunk etc.* Reklame machen für *et.*; ~ *in* ∮ einstöpseln; *v/i. sl.* schuften; **'plug-'ug·ly** *Am. sl.* Schläger *m* (*Person*).

plum [plʌm] Pflaume *f*, Zwetsch(g)e *f*; Rosine *f* (*a. fig.* = *das Beste*); *sl.* £ 100 000.

plum·age ['plu:midʒ] Gefieder *n*.

plumb [plʌm] **1.** lotrecht; gerade; richtig; **2.** (Blei)Lot *n*; Senkblei *n*; **3.** *v/t.* lotrecht machen; loten; (*a. fig.*) sondieren; F Rohre legen in (*dat.*); *v/i.* F als Rohrleger arbeiten; **plum·ba·go** [~'beigəu] Graphit *m*; **plumb·er** ['plʌmə] Klempner *m*, Installateur *m*; **plum·bic** ['plʌmbik] 🜍 Blei...; **plumb·ing** ['~miŋ] Klempnerarbeit *f*; Rohrleitungen *f/pl.*; **'plumb-line** ⊕ Lotleine *f*, Senkschnur *f*; **'plumb-rule** Lot-, Senkwaage *f*.

plume [plu:m] **1.** *Schmuck*-Feder *f*; Federbusch *m*; **2.** *die Federn* putzen; mit Federn schmücken; ~ *o.s. on* sich brüsten mit.

plum·met ['plʌmit] (Blei)Lot *n*; Senkblei *n*.

plum·my F ['plʌmi] prima.

plump[1] [plʌmp] **1.** drall, prall, mollig, dick; **2.** prall machen *od.* werden.

plump[2] [~] **1.** (schwer) fallen, (hin-) plumpsen (lassen); *parl.* seine Stimme ungeteilt geben (*for dat.*); **2.** Plumps *m*; **3.** F *adv.* plumps; geradewegs; rundweg; **4.** F □ glatt, offen (*Absage etc.*), plump (*Lüge*).

plump·er ['plʌmpə] *parl.* ungeteilte Wahlstimme *f*; *sl.* plumpe Lüge *f*.

plump·ness ['plʌmpnis] Prallheit *f*, Beleibtheit *f*; F Offenheit *f e-r Antwort etc.*

plum-pud·ding ['plʌm'pudiŋ] Plumpudding *m.* [artig]

plum·y ['plu:mi] gefiedert; feder-]

plun·der ['plʌndə] **1.** Plünderung *f*; Raub *m*, Beute *f*; **2.** plündern; **'plun·der·er** Plünderer *m*; Räuber *m*.

plunge [plʌndʒ] **1.** (Unter)Tauchen *n*; Sturz *m*; (Kopf)Sprung *m*; Ausschlagen *n e-s Pferdes etc.*; *make od. take the* ~ den entscheidenden Schritt tun; **2.** *v/t.* tauchen, stürzen (*into in acc.*); *Schwert etc.* stoßen; *v/i.* (unter)tauchen; sich stürzen (*into in acc.*); ausschlagen (*Pferd*); ⚓ stampfen.

plung·er [ˈplʌndʒə] (Pumpen)Kolben *m*; *sl.* Spekulant *m*.

plunk [plʌŋk] *v/t. Saite* zupfen; *et.* hinplumpsen lassen, hinwerfen; *v/i.* (hin)plumpsen, fallen.

plu·per·fect *gr.* [ˈpluːˈpəːfikt] Plusquamperfekt(um) *n.*

plu·ral *gr.* [ˈpluərəl] Mehrzahl *f*, Plural *m*; **plu·ral·i·ty** [~ˈræliti] Vielheit *f*, Mehrheit *f*; Mehrzahl *f*; ~ *of wives* Vielweiberei *f.*

plus [plʌs] **1.** *prp.* plus, und; **2.** *adj.* positiv; **3.** Plus *n*; Mehr *n*; ~-**fours** F [ˈ~ˈfɔːz] *pl.* Golfhose(n *pl.*) *f*; Knickerbocker *pl.*

plush [plʌʃ] Plüsch *m.*

plush·y [ˈplʌʃi] plüschartig; *sl.* feudal, luxuriös.

plu·to·ra·cy [pluːˈtɔkrəsi] Plutokratie *f* (*Geldherrschaft*); **plu·to·crat** [ˈ~təukræt] Plutokrat *m.*

plu·to·ni·um ⚛ [pluːˈtəunjəm] Plutonium *n.*

plu·vi·al [ˈpluːviəl], **plu·vi·ous** regnerisch; Regen...; **plu·vi·om·e·ter** [~ˈɔmitə] Regenmesser *m.*

ply [plai] **1.** Lage *f Tuch od. Holz*; Strähne *f*; *fig.* Neigung *f*, Gewohnheit *f*; **2.** *v/t.* fleißig anwenden, handhaben; *j-m* zusetzen (*mit Fragen etc.*), *j.* überhäufen; ~ *a trade* ein Gewerbe betreiben; *v/i.* regelmäßig fahren *od.* verkehren.

ply-wood [ˈplaiwud] Sperrholz *n.*

pneu·mat·ic [njuːˈmætik] **1.** (~*ally*) Luft...; pneumatisch; ~ *hammer* Preßlufthammer *m*; ~ *tire* Luftreifen *m*; **2.** Luftreifen *m.*

pneu·mo·ni·a ✚ [njuːˈməunjə] Lungenentzündung *f.*

poach¹ [pəutʃ] wildern.

poach² [~] *a.* ~ *up* Erde zertreten, aufwühlen.

poach³ [~]: ~*ed eggs pl.* verlorene Eier *m/pl.*

poach·er [ˈpəutʃə] Wilddieb *m.*

PO Box [piːˈəubɔks] Postfach *n.*

po·chette [pɔˈʃet] Handtäschchen *n.*

pock ✚ [pɔk] Pocke *f*, Blatter *f.*

pock·et [ˈpɔkit] **1.** Tasche *f*; *geol.* Nest *n*; Sack *m Wolle, Hopfen*; ✚ Luft-Loch *n*; **2.** einstecken (*a. fig.*); *Am. pol. Gesetzesvorlage* nicht unterschreiben, Veto einlegen gegen (*v. Präsidenten*); *Gefühl* unterdrücken; **3.** Taschen...; ~ *lighter* Taschenfeuerzeug *n*; ~ *lamp* Taschenlampe *f*; ˈ~·**book** Notizbuch *n*; Brieftasche *f*; *Am.* Geldbeutel *m*; Damenhandtasche *f*; ~ **cal·cu·la·tor** Taschenrechner *m*; ~ **e·di·tion** Taschenausgabe *f e-s Buches.*

pod [pɔd] **1.** ✿ Hülse *f*, Schale *f*, Schote *f*; *sl.* Bauch *m*; **2.** Schoten ansetzen; *Erbsen etc.* enthülsen.

po·dag·ra ✚ [ˈpɔdəgrə] Podagra *n* (*Fußgicht*).

podg·y F [ˈpɔdʒi] quabbelig.

po·di·um [ˈpəudiəm] Podium *n.*

po·em [ˈpəuim] Gedicht *n.*

po·e·sy [ˈpəuizi] Poesie *f.*

po·et [ˈpəuit] Dichter *m*; **po·et·as·ter** [~ˈtæstə] Dichterling *m*; ˈ**po·et·ess** Dichterin *f*; **po·et·ic, po·et·i·cal** □ [pəuˈetikəl] poetisch, dichterisch; **po·et·ics** *pl.* Poetik *f*; **po·et·ize** [ˈ~itaiz] dichten; in Verse bringen; ˈ**po·et·ry** Dichtkunst *f*, Poesie *f*; Dichtung *f*, *coll.* Dichtungen *f/pl.*, Gedichte *n/pl.*

poign·an·cy [ˈpɔinənsi] Schärfe *f*; *fig.* Eindringlichkeit *f*; ˈ**poign·ant** □ scharf, beißend; *fig.* eindringlich.

point [pɔint] **1.** Spitze *f*; Pointe *f e-s Witzes etc.*; Landspitze *f*, -vorsprung *m*; *s.* ~-*lace*; Radiernadel *f*; *gr.*, ⚛, *phys. etc.* Punkt *m*; Fleck *m*, Stelle *f*; Stehen *n des Jagdhundes*; (Geweih)Ende *n*; ⚡ Kontakt *m*; ⚓ Kompaßstrich *m*; Auge *n auf Karten*, *Würfeln*; Grad *m* (*a. ast.*), Stufe *f*; (springender) Punkt *m*, Frage *f*, Sache *f*; Zweck *m*, Sinn *m*; Wirksamkeit *f*, Gewicht *n*; Anliegen *n*; Kernfrage *f*, -punkt *m*; *fig. hervorstechende* Eigenschaft *f*; ~*s pl.* ⚑ Weichen *f/pl.*; ~ *of view* Stand-, Gesichtspunkt *m*; *the* ~ *is that ...* die Sache ist die, daß ...; *there is no* ~ *in ger.* es hat keinen Zweck, zu *inf.*; *make a* ~ *of s.th.* auf et. achten; *make the* ~ *that* die Feststellung machen, daß; *stretch a* ~ fünf gerade sein lassen; *in* ~ *of* in Hinsicht auf (*acc.*); *in* ~ *of fact* tatsächlich; *off od. beyond the* ~ nicht zur Sache (gehörig); *differ on many* ~*s* in vielen

Punkten abweichen; *he was on the ~ of coming* er war im Begriff *od.* nahe daran zu kommen; *win on ~s Boxen*: nach Punkten siegen; *to the ~* zur Sache (gehörig); *stick to the ~* bei der Sache bleiben; **2.** *v/t.* (zu)spitzen; richten, stellen; *oft ~ out* (auf-)zeigen, hinweisen auf (*acc.*); ausführen; punktieren; *~ at Waffe etc.* richten auf (*acc.*); *v/i.* stehen (*Jagdhund*); *~ at* zeigen *od.* weisen auf (*acc.*); *~* to nach *e-r* Richtung weisen; '*~*-'**blank** gerade; Kernschuß...; unumwunden; rundweg; *~ shot* Fleckschuß *m*; '*~*-**du·ty** (*bsd.* Verkehrs)Postendienst *m*; '**point·ed** ☐ spitz; *fig.* scharf, beißend; '**point·ed·ness** Spitze *f*; Schärfe *f*; '**point·er** Zeiger *m*; Zeigestock *m*; Vorsteh-, Hühnerhund *m*; F Tip *m*; '**point·'lace** genähte Spitzen *f/pl.*; '**point·less** stumpf; witzlos; zwecklos, sinnlos; '**point-po'lice·man** Verkehrspolizist *m*; '**points·man** ⚑ Weichensteller *m*; Verkehrspolizist *m*; '**point-to-'point race** Geländejagdrennen *n*.

poise [pɔiz] **1.** Gleichgewicht *n*; Schwebe *f*; Haltung *f*; Gelassenheit *f*; **2.** *v/t.* im Gleichgewicht halten; ins Gleichgewicht bringen; *Kopf etc.* besonders tragen, halten; *be ~d = v/i.* schweben.

poison ['pɔizn] **1.** Gift *n*; *~-pen letter verleumderischer od. obszöner anonymer Brief*; **2.** vergiften; '**poi·son·er** Vergifter(in); Giftmischer(in); '**poison·ous** ☐ giftig (*a. fig.*); Gift...; F ekelhaft.

poke [pəuk] **1.** Stoß *m*, Puff *m*; **2.** *v/t.* stoßen; *a. ~ up Feuer* schüren; stecken; *~ fun at* sich über *j.* lustig machen; *v/i.* stoßen (*at* nach); stochern; stöbern (*into in dat.*).

pok·er¹ ['pəukə] Feuerhaken *m*.

po·ker² [⌣] Poker(spiel) *n*; *~ face fig.* Pokergesicht *n*.

pok·er-work ['pəukəwəːk] Brandmalerei *f*.

pok·y ['pəuki] klein, eng, winzig; schäbig; erbärmlich.

po·lar ['pəulə] polar; Polar...; *~ bear* Eisbär *m*; **po·lar·i·ty** [pəu'læriti] Polarität *f*; **po·lar·i·za·tion** *phys.* [⌣lərai'zeiʃən] Polarisation *f*; *~ filter phot.* Pol(arisations)filter *m*; '**po·lar·ize** *phys.* polarisieren.

Pole¹ [pəul] Pole *m*, Polin *f*.

pole² [⌣] Pol *m* (*geogr.*, *ast.*, *phys.*, *fig.*).

pole³ [⌣] **1.** Stange *f*, Mast *m*; Pfosten *m*, Pfahl *m*; Deichsel *f*; (Meß-) Rute *f* (*5,029 Meter*); (Sprung-)Stab *m*; **2.** *Bohnen etc.* stängen; staken; '*~*-**ax(e)** ⚔ Streitaxt *f*; ⚓ Enterbeil *n*; Schlachtbeil *n*; '*~*-**cat** *zo.* Iltis *m*; *Am.* Skunk *m*; *~* **jump** = *pole vault.*

po·lem·ic [pɔ'lemik] **1.** *a.* po'lem·i·cal ☐ polemisch; feindselig; Streit...; **2.** Polemiker *m*; po'lem·ics *pl.* Polemik *f*.

pole-star ['pəulstɑː] Polarstern *m*; *fig.* Leitstern *m*.

pole-vault ['pəulvɔːlt] Stabhochsprung *m*.

po·lice [pə'liːs] **1.** Polizei *f*; *two ~* zwei Polizisten *m/pl.*; *~ dossier* polizeiliches Führungszeugnis *n*; *~ force* Polizei *f*, -streitkräfte *f pl.*; *~ record* Vorstrafen *f/pl.*; **2.** überwachen; po'lice·man Polizist *m*; po-'lice-of·fice Polizeipräsidium *n*; po-'lice-of·fi·cer Polizeibeamte *m*, Polizist *m*; po'lice-sta·tion Polizeiwache *f*; po'lice-sur'veil·lance Polizeiaufsicht *f*; po'lice-trap Autofalle *f*; po'lice·wom·an Polizistin *f*, Polizeibeamtin *f*.

pol·i·cy¹ ['pɔlisi] Politik *f*; (Welt-)Klugheit *f*; geschicktes Verhalten *n*.

pol·i·cy² [⌣] Police *f*; *Am.* Zahlenlotto *n*.

po·li·o·my·e·li·tis ['pəuliəu(maiə-'laitis)] spinale Kinderlähmung *f*.

Pol·ish¹ ['pəuliʃ] polnisch.

pol·ish² ['pɔliʃ] **1.** Politur *f*; Schuhcreme *f*; *fig.* Umgangsformen *f/pl.*, Schliff *m*; **2.** *v/t.* polieren, glätten; bohnern; *fig.* verfeinern; *~ off* verputzen (*essen*); hinhauen (*schnell erledigen*); *~ up* aufpolieren, auffrischen; *v/i.* glänzend werden; '**pol·ish·ing 1.** Politur *f*; **2.** Glanz..., Putz...

po·lite ☐ [pə'lait] artig, höflich; fein; po'lite·ness Höflichkeit *f*.

pol·i·tic ☐ ['pɔlitik] politisch; schlau, weltklug; *body ~* Staatskörper *m*; **po·lit·i·cal** ☐ [pə'litikəl] politisch; staatlich; Staats...; *~ science* Politologie *f*; *~-login f*; **pol·i·ti·cian** [pɔli'tiʃən] Staatsmann *m*, Politiker *m*; *contp.* Intrigant *m*; **pol·i·tics** ['⌣tiks] *sg.*

od. pl. Staatswissenschaft *f*, Politik *f*; politische Überzeugung *f*.

pol·i·ty ['pɔliti] Verfassung *f*; Regierung(sform) *f*; Staatswesen *n*.

pol·ka ['pɔlkə] Polka *f*; ~ **dot** *Am.* Punktmuster *n auf Stoff.*

poll[1] [pəul] **1.** Wählerliste *f*; Stimmenzählung *f*; Abstimmung *f*; Wahl *f*; Stimmenzahl *f*; Umfrage *f*; *co.* Kopf *m*; *go to the* ~*s* zur Wahl gehen; **2.** *v/t.* Stimmen erhalten; = *pollard* 2; *v/i.* wählen; ~ *for* stimmen für.

poll[2] [pɔl] Papagei *m*.

pol·lard ['pɔləd] **1.** gekappter Baum *m*; hornloses Tier *n*; Kleie(nmehl *n*) *f*; **2.** kappen, stutzen.

poll-book ['pəulbuk] Wählerliste *f*.

pol·len ⚕ ['pɔlin] Blütenstaub *m*; **pol·li·na·tion** [pɔli'neiʃən] Bestäubung *f*.

poll·ing...: '~**-booth** Wahlzelle *f*; '~**-dis·trict** Wahlbezirk *m*; '~**-place** Wahlort *m*; '~**-sta·tion** Wahllokal *n*.

poll·ster ['pəulstə] Meinungsforscher *m*.

poll-tax ['pəultæks] Kopfsteuer *f*.

pol·lut·ant [pə'lu:tənt] Schadstoff *m*.

pol·lute [pə'lu:t] beschmutzen, beflecken (*a. fig.*); entweihen; **pol·lution** Verunreinigung *f*; Umweltverschmutzung *f*; Befleckung *f*; Entweihung *f*.

po·lo ['pəuləu] *Sport:* Polo *n*; ~ **neck** Rollkragen(pullover) *m*.

po·lo·ny [pə'ləuni] grobe Zervelatwurst *f*.

pol·troon [pɔl'tru:n] Feigling *m*; **pol'troon·er·y** Feigheit *f*.

po·lyg·a·my [pɔ'ligəmi] Vielweiberei *f*; **pol·y·glot** ['~glɔt] vielsprachig; **pol·y·gon** ['~gən] Vieleck *n*; **po'lyg·o·nal** [~gənl] vieleckig; **pol·y·phon·ic** ♩ [~'fɔnik] polyphon; **pol·yp** *zo.* ['pɔlip], **pol·y·pus** ✱ ['~pəs] Polyp *m*; **pol·y·sty·rene** [pɔli'staiəri:n] Styropor *n*; **pol·y·syl·lab·ic** ['~si'læbik] vielsilbig; **pol·y·syl·la·ble** ['~siləbl] vielsilbiges Wort *n*; **pol·y·tech·nic** [~'teknik] polytechnisch(e Schule *f*); **pol·y·the·ism** ['~θi:izəm] Polytheismus *m*, Vielgötterei *f*; **pol·y·thene** ['~θi:n] Polyäthylen *n*; ~ *bag* Plastiktüte *f*.

po·made [pə'mɑ:d] Pomade *f*.

po·man·der [pəu'mændə] Duftkugel *f*.

pome·gran·ate ⚕ ['pɔmgrænit] Granatapfel *m*.

Pom·er·a·nian [pɔmə'reinjən] **1.** pommer(i)sch; **2.** Pommer(in); *a.* ~ *dog* Spitz *m*.

pom·mel ['pʌml] **1.** *Degen-, Sattel-, Turm-*Knopf *m*, Knauf *m*; **2.** knuffen, schlagen.

pomp [pɔmp] Pomp *m*, Gepränge *n*.

pompom ['pɔmpɔm] (Flak-) Schnellfeuergeschütz *n*.

pom·pos·i·ty [pɔm'pɔsiti] Prunk *m*; Pomphaftigkeit *f*; '**pomp·ous** ☐ prunkvoll; hochtrabend; pompös.

ponce *sl.* [pɔns] Zuhälter *m*; *contp.* Schwule *m*; weibischer Kerl *m*.

pon·cho ['pɔntʃəu] Poncho *m*, (Regen)Umhang *m*.

pond [pɔnd] Teich *m*, Weiher *m*.

pon·der ['pɔndə] *v/t.* erwägen, überlegen; *v/i.* nachdenken (*on, over* über *acc.*); **pon·der·a·bil·i·ty** [~rə'biliti] Wägbarkeit *f*; '**pon·der·a·ble** wägbar; **pon·der·os·i·ty** [~'rɔsiti] Schwere *f*, Gewichtigkeit *f*, Schwerfälligkeit *f*; '**pon·der·ous** ☐ schwer, gewichtig; schwerfällig; '**pon·der·ous·ness** = *ponderosity*.

pone [pəun] Maisbrot *n*.

pong *sl.* [pɔŋ] Gestank *m*, unangenehmer Geruch *m*.

pon·iard ['pɔnjəd] Dolch *m*.

pon·tiff ['pɔntif] Hohepriester *m*; Papst *m*; **pon'tif·i·cal** ☐ oberpriesterlich; päpstlich; **pon'tif·i·cate** [~kit] Pontifikat *n*.

pon·toon ⚓ [pɔn'tu:n] Ponton *m*; **pon'toon-bridge** Schiffsbrücke *f*.

po·ny ['pəuni] Pony *n*, Pferdchen *n*; *sl.* £ 25; '~**-en·gine** 🚂 Rangierlokomotive *f*; '~**-tail** Pferdeschwanz *m* (*Frisur*).

pooch *Am. sl.* [pu:tʃ] Köter *m*.

poo·dle ['pu:dl] Pudel *m*.

poof *sl.* [pu:f], *a.* **poof·ter** ['~tə] Schwule *m*.

pooh [pu:] pah!

pooh-pooh [pu:'pu:] geringschätzig behandeln.

pool[1] [pu:l] Teich *m*, Tümpel *m*; Pfütze *f*, Lache *f*; (Schwimm)Becken *n*.

pool[2] [~] **1.** (Spiel)Einsatz *m*; *Billard:* Poulespiel *n*; ✝ Ring *m*, Kartell *n*; gemeinsame Kasse *f*; ~ *room* Billardzimmer *n*; *Am.* Wettannahmestelle *f*; **2.** ✝ zu einem Ring vereinigen; *Gelder* zs.-legen.

pools [puːlz] Toto *m, a. n.*

poop ⚓ [puːp] **1.** Heck *n*; Achterhütte *f*; **2.** *das Schiff* von hinten treffen (*Woge*).

poor □ [puə] arm; armselig, gering; dürftig, dürr, mager (*Boden*); schlecht (*Ernte*); unruhig, schlecht (*Nacht etc.*); the ∼ die Armen *pl.*; ∼ *me!* ich Armer!; ∼ *health* schwache Gesundheit *f*; '∼-box Armenkasse *f*; '∼-house Armenhaus *n*; '∼-law ⚖ Armenrecht *n*; 'poor·ly **1.** *adj. pred.* unpäßlich; **2.** *adv.* dürftig; *he is* ∼ *off* es geht ihm schlecht; 'poor·ness Armut *f*; Armseligkeit *f*, Dürftigkeit *f*; 'poor-rate Armensteuer *f*; 'poor·'spir·it·ed verzagt, feig.

pop[1] [pɔp] **1.** Puff *m*, Knall *m*; F Sprudel *m*; Schampus *m* (*Sekt*); *in* ∼ *sl.* verpfändet; **2.** *v/t.* knallen lassen; *Am.* *Mais* rösten; schnell *wohin* tun, stecken, gießen; ∼ *the question to a lady* e-r Dame e-n Heiratsantrag machen; *v/i.* puffen, knallen; *mit adv.* huschen; ∼ *in* hereinplatzen; **3.** plötzlich; **4.** puff!

pop[2] F [∼] **1.** populär, beliebt; **2.** Schlager *m*; volkstümliche Musik *f*.

pop[3] *Am.* F [pɔp] Papa *m*, Papi *m*.

pop-corn *bsd. Am.* ['pɔpkɔːn] Puffmais *m*.

pope [pəup] Papst *m*; 'pope·dom Papsttum *n*; 'pop·er·y *contp.* Papismus *m*.

pop-eyed ['pɔpaid] glotzäugig.

pop·gun ['pɔpgʌn] Knallbüchse *f*.

pop·in·jay ['pɔpindʒei] Geck *m*.

pop·ish □ ['pəupiʃ] papistisch.

pop·lar ♀ ['pɔplə] Pappel *f*.

pop·lin ['pɔplin] Popelin *m*.

pop·per F ['pɔpə] Druckknopf *m*.

pop·pet ['pɔpit] ⚓ Schlittenständer *m*; ⊕ *Drehbank*-Docke *f*; *s.* puppet.

pop·py ♀ ['pɔpi] Mohn *m*; '∼-cock *Am.* F Quatsch *m*.

pop·u·lace ['pɔpjuləs] Pöbel *m*.

pop·u·lar □ ['pɔpjulə] volkstümlich, populär; beliebt; Volks...; ∼ *front* Volksfront *f*; **pop·u·lar·i·ty** [∼'læriti] Popularität *f*, Volkstümlichkeit *f*, Beliebtheit *f*; **pop·u·lar·ize** ['∼ləraiz] popularisieren; volkstümlich machen; gemeinverständlich darstellen; 'pop·u·lar·ly im

Volk(smund).

pop·u·late ['pɔpjuleit] bevölkern; **pop·u·la·tion** Bevölkerung *f*; Einwohnerzahl *f*; ∼ *explosion* Bevölkerungsexplosion *f*.

pop·u·lous □ ['pɔpjuləs] volkreich, dicht besiedelt.

por·ce·lain ['pɔːslin] Porzellan *n*.

porch [pɔːtʃ] Vorhalle *f*, Portal *n*; überdachter Hauseingang *m*; *Am.* Veranda *f*. [chelschwein *n*.\

por·cu·pine *zo.* ['pɔːkjupain] Stai

pore[1] [pɔː] Pore *f*.

pore[2] [∼] eifrig studieren (*over acc.*); grübeln, brüten (*over, on, upon* über *dat.*).

pork [pɔːk] Schweinefleisch *n*; '∼-bar·rel *Am. sl. politisch berechnete Geldzuwendung f der Regierung*; '∼-butch·er Schweinemetzger *m*; 'pork·er (Mast-) Schwein *n*; 'pork·y **1.** F fett, dick; **2.** *Am.* F = porcupine.

por·nog·ra·phy [pɔː'nɔgrəfi] Pornographie *f*, Schmutzliteratur *f*.

po·ros·i·ty [pɔː'rɔsiti], **po·rous·ness** ['pɔːrəsnis] Porosität *f*.

po·rous □ ['pɔːrəs] porös.

por·phy·ry *min.* ['pɔːfiri] Porphyr *m*.

por·poise *ichth.* ['pɔːpəs] Meerschwein *n*, Tümmler *m*.

por·ridge ['pɔridʒ] Porridge *m, n*, Hafer(flocken)brei *m*; **por·rin·ger** ['pɔrindʒə] Suppennapf *m*.

port[1] [pɔːt] Hafen *m*; ∼ *of call* Anlaufhafen *m*; ∼ *of destination* Bestimmungshafen *m*; ∼ *of trans-shipment* Umschlaghafen *m*.

port[2] ⚓ [∼] (Pfort-, Lade)Luke *f*.

port[3] [∼] ✕ *das Gewehr* schräg vor der Brust halten; **2.** Haltung *f*, Benehmen *n*.

port[4] ⚓ [∼] **1.** Backbord *n*; **2.** *das Steuer* links halten.

port[5] [∼] Portwein *m*.

port·a·ble ['pɔːtəbl] tragbar; ∼ *radio set* Kofferradio *n*; ∼ *typewriter* Reiseschreibmaschine *f*.

por·tage ['pɔːtidʒ] (*bsd.* Trage-) Transport *m*; *s.* porterage.

por·tal ['pɔːtl] Portal *n*, Haupttor *n*; *fig.* Pforte *f*; '**por·tal-to-'por·tal pay** Lohn *m* für die Zeit zu und von der Arbeitsstätte (*innerhalb der Fabrik etc.*).

port·cul·lis ✕ [pɔːt'kʌlis] Fallgatter *n*.

por·tend [pɔː'tend] vorbedeuten.

por·tent ['pɔːtent] (*bsd.* üble) Vorbedeutung *f*; Vorzeichen *n*; Wunder *n*; **por'ten·tous** □ [‿təs] unheilvoll; wunderbar; unheimlich (*a. co.*).

por·ter¹ ['pɔːtə] Pförtner *m*.

por·ter² [‿] (Gepäck- *etc.*) Träger *m*; Porterbier *n*; **'por·ter·age** Tragen *n*; Trägerlohn *m*; Zustellungsgebühr *f*; **'por·ter-house** Bier-, Speisehaus *n*; *a.* ‿ *steak bsd. gutes Beefsteak n.*

port·fire ['pɔːtfaiə] Lunte *f*.

port·fo·li·o [pɔːt'fəuljəu] (Akten-) Mappe *f*; (Minister)Portefeuille *n*.

port-hole ⚓ ['pɔːthəul] = *port².*

por·ti·co ⚠ ['pɔːtikəu] Säulenhalle *f*.

por·tière [pɔːtiɛə] Portière *f*, Türvorhang *m*.

por·tion ['pɔːʃən] **1.** Teil *m*; Anteil *m*; Portion *f Essen*; Erbteil *n*; Heiratsgut *n*, Aussteuer *f*; Los *n*, Schicksal *n*; **2.** teilen; ausstatten; **'por·tion·less** ohne Aussteuer.

port·li·ness ['pɔːtlinis] Stattlichkeit *f*, Würde *f*; **'port·ly** stattlich.

port·man·teau [pɔːt'mæntəu] Handkoffer *m*; † Mantelsack *m*; ‿ *word gr.* Schachtelwort *n*.

por·trait ['pɔːtrit] Porträt *n*, Bildnis *n*; **'por·trait·ist** Porträtmaler *m*; **por·trai·ture** [‿tʃə] = *portrait*; Porträtmalerei *f*.

por·tray [pɔː'trei] (ab)malen, porträtieren; schildern; **por'tray·al** Porträtieren *n*; Schilderung *f*.

Por·tu·guese [pɔːtju'giːz] **1.** portugiesisch; **2.** Portugiese *m*, Portugiesin *f*; Portugiesisch *n*.

pose [pəuz] **1.** Pose *f*; **2.** (sich) in Positur stellen; auftreten, sich hinstellen (*as* als); *Frage* aufwerfen; **'pos·er** schwierige Frage *f*; Poseur *m*.

posh *sl.* [pɔʃ] schick, pikfein, erstklassig.

po·si·tion [pə'ziʃən] Lage *f*, Stellung *f* (*a. fig.*); Rang *m*; Stand *m*; *fig.* Standpunkt *m*; ✕, *ast.*, ⚓ Position *f*; ‿ *light* Positionslicht *n*; *be in a* ‿ *to do* in der Lage sein zu tun.

pos·i·tive ['pɔzətiv] **1.** □ bestimmt, ausdrücklich; positiv; feststehend, sicher; vollkommen; unbedingt; ⚕, *phls., phys., phot.,* ∮ positiv; überzeugt, sicher; rechthaberisch, eigensinnig; **2.** *das* Bestimmte; Positiv (*gr. m*; *phot. n*); **'pos·i·tive·ness** Bestimmtheit *f etc.*

pos·se ['pɔsi] (Polizei- *etc.*)Aufgebot *n*; Haufen *m*, Schar *f*.

pos·sess [pə'zes] besitzen; beherrschen; *fig.* erfüllen (*with* mit); ‿*ed* besessen; ‿*ed of* im Besitz *e-r Sache*; ‿*o.s. of et.* in Besitz nehmen, sich *e-r Sache* bemächtigen; **pos·ses·sion** [pə'zeʃən] Besitz *m*; *fig.* Besessenheit *f*; ‿*s pl.* Besitz(tum *n*) *m*; Besitzungen *f/pl.*; Habe *f*, Eigentum *n*; *in* ‿ *of* im Besitz *e-r Sache*; **pos'ses·sive** *gr.* [‿siv] **1.** □ besitzanzeigend; ‿ *case* Genitiv *m*; **2.** besitzanzeigendes Fürwort *n*; Genitiv *m*; **pos'ses·sor** Besitzer *m*; **'pos·ses·so·ry** Besitz...

pos·set ['pɔsit] heiße Milch *f* mit Bier *od.* Wein.

pos·si·bil·i·ty [pɔsə'biliti] Möglichkeit *f*; **'pos·si·ble** □ **1.** möglich; **2.** *Sport*: Höchstleistung *f*; **'pos·si·bly** möglicherweise, vielleicht; *if I* ‿ *can* wenn ich irgend kann; *how can I* ‿ *do it?* wie kann ich es nur *od.* bloß machen?; *I cannot* ‿ *do it* ich kann es unmöglich tun.

pos·sum F ['pɔsəm] = *opossum*; *play* ‿ krank spielen.

post¹ [pəust] **1.** Pfosten *m*, Pfahl *m*; **2.** *mst* ‿ *up* Plakat anschlagen.

post² [‿] **1.** ✕, ✝ Posten *m*; ✕ Standort *m*; Stelle *f*, Amt *n*, Posten *m*; ✡ Post *f* (*Postamt, -zustellung, -sendung*); Briefpapier *n*; *at one's* ‿ ✕ auf (s-m) Posten; *by* ‿ mit der Post; **2.** *v/t. Soldaten etc.* aufstellen, postieren; ✝ eintragen, verbuchen; *oft* ‿ *up* ✝ *die Bücher* in Ordnung bringen; zur Post geben; per Post senden; *keep s.o.* ‿*ed up* j. auf dem laufenden halten; *v/i.* (dahin)eilen.

post³ ✕ [‿] Signal *n*; *last* ‿ Zapfenstreich *m*.

post·age ['pəustidʒ] Porto *n*, Postgebühr *f*; ‿ *due* Nachgebühr *f*; ‿ **stamp** Briefmarke *f*.

post·al □ ['pəustəl] **1.** postalisch; Post...; ‿ *order* Postanweisung *f*; ♀ *Union* Weltpostverein *m*; **2.** *a.* ‿ *card Am.* Postkarte *f*.

post...: **'‿·card** Postkarte *f*; **'‿·code** Postleitzahl *f*.

post·date ['pəust'deit] vorausdatieren.

post·er ['pəustə] Plakat *n*, Anschlag *m*; *a. bill-*‿ Plakatankleber *m*.

poste res·tante ['pəust 'restãːnt] **1.** postlagernd; **2.** Schalter *m* für postlagernde Sendungen.

pos·te·ri·or F [pɔs'tiəriə] **1.** □ später (*to* als); hinter; Hinter...; **2.** *a.* ~s *pl.* Hintern *m*.

pos·ter·i·ty [pɔs'teriti] Nachwelt *f*; Nachkommenschaft *f*.

pos·tern ['pəustəːn] Hintertür *f*.

post-free ['pəust'friː] portofrei.

post-grad·u·ate ['pəust'grædjuit] **1.** nach beendigter Studienzeit; **2.** Graduierte *m*, *der s-e Studien fortsetzt*; Doktorand(in).

post-haste ['pəust'heist] eilig(st).

post·hu·mous □ ['pɔstjuməs] nachgeboren; hinterlassen; post(h)um.

pos·til·(l)ion [pəs'tiljən] Postillion *m*.

post...: '~·man Briefträger *m*, Postbote *m*; '~·mark **1.** Poststempel *m*; **2.** abstempeln; '~·mas·ter Postamtsvorsteher *m*; ♀ *General* Postminister *m*.

post me·rid·i·em ['pəust məˈridiem] nachmittägig; Nachmittags...; **post-mor·tem** ['~'mɔːtem] **1.** nach dem Tode; **2.** *a.* ~ *examination* Autopsie *f*.

post...: '~-of·fice, *mst* ~ of·fice Postamt *n*; *Am. ein Kußspiel*; *general* ~ Hauptpost(amt *n*) *f*; ~ *box* Post(schließ)fach *n*; ~ *engineer* Fernmeldetechniker *m*; ~ *order* Postanweisung *f*; ~ *savings-bank* Postsparkasse *f*; '~-**paid** franko.

post·pone [pəust'pəun] ver-, aufschieben; *j. od. et.* unterordnen; **post'pone·ment** Aufschub *m*.

post·pran·di·al □ *co.* [pəust'prændiəl] nach Tisch (stattfindend).

post·script ['pəusskript] Nachschrift *f*, Postskriptum *n*.

pos·tu·lant ['pɔstjulənt] Bewerber *m*, Antragsteller *m*; **pos·tu·late 1.** ['~lit] Postulat *n*, Forderung *f*; **2.** ['~leit] fordern; (als gegeben) voraussetzen; **pos·tu·la·tion** Gesuch *n*; Annahme *f*.

pos·ture ['pɔstʃə] **1.** Stellung *f*, Haltung *f des Körpers*; **2.** *v/t.* zurechtstellen; *v/i.* sich zurechtstellen; posieren.

post-war ['pəust'wɔː] Nachkriegs...

po·sy ['pəuzi] Motto *n*, Sinnspruch *m*; Blumenstrauß *m*.

pot [pɔt] **1.** Topf *m*; Tiegel *m*; F *Sport:* Silberpokal *m*; *Am. sl.* Marihuana *n*; *a* ~ *of money* F ein Sackvoll *m* Geld; *big* ~ F hohes Tier *n*;

2. in e-n Topf tun; *Pflanze* eintopfen; *Fleisch* einlegen; F schießen, erlegen.

po·ta·ble ['pəutəbl] trinkbar.

pot·ash ⛤ ['pɔtæʃ] Pottasche *f*.

po·tas·si·um ⛤ [pə'tæsjəm] Kalium *n*.

po·ta·tion [pəu'teiʃən] *mst* ~s *pl.* Trinken *n*, Zecherei *f*; Trunk *m*.

po·ta·to [pə'teitəu], *pl.* **po'ta·toes** [~z] Kartoffel *f*; ~ **bee·tle** *zo.* Kartoffelkäfer *m*; ~ **chips** *pl. Am.* (Kartoffel)Chips *pl.*; ~ **mash·er** Kartoffelstampfer *m*.

pot...: '~-**bel·ly** Schmerbauch *m*; '~-**boil·er** Brotarbeit *f*; Routinewerk *n*; '~-**boy** Bierkellner *m*.

po·ten·cy ['pəutənsi] Macht *f*; Stärke *f*; '**po·tent** □ mächtig; stark; überzeugend; **po·ten·tate** ['~teit] Machthaber *m*, Potentat *m*; **po·ten·tial** [pəu'tenʃəl] **1.** potentiell; möglich; in der Anlage vorhanden; *phys.* gebunden; **2.** *a.* ~ *mood gr.* Potentialis *m*, Möglichkeitsform *f*; ⚡ Spannung *f*; Leistungsfähigkeit *f*, Potential *n*, Kraftvorrat *m*; **po·ten·ti·al·i·ty** [~ʃi'æliti] Potentialität *f*; (Entwicklungs)Möglichkeit *f*.

poth·er ['pɔðə] **1.** Aufregung *f*; Lärm *m*; **2.** (sich) aufregen.

pot...: '~-**herb** Küchenkraut *n*; '~-**hole** *mot.* Schlagloch *n*; *geol.* Gletschertopf *m*; '~-**hol·er** Höhlenforscher *m*; '~-**hook** Kesselhaken *m*; Schörkel *m*; ~s *pl.* Gekritzel *n*; '~-**house** Kneipe *f*.

po·tion ['pəuʃən] (Arznei- *etc.*) Trank *m*.

pot-luck ['pɔt'lʌk]: *take* ~ vorliebnehmen mit dem, was es gibt.

pot·tage ['pɔtidʒ] dicke Suppe *f*.

pot·ter[1] ['pɔtə]: ~ *about* herumwerkeln, -hantieren; ~ *away* vertrödeln.

pot·ter[2] [~] Töpfer *m*; ~'*s wheel* Töpferscheibe *f*; '**pot·ter·y** Töpferei *f*; Töpferware(n *pl.*) *f*.

pot·ty *sl.* ['pɔti] lächerlich, unbedeutend; verrückt.

pouch [pautʃ] **1.** Tasche *f*; Beutel *m* (*a. zo.*); Tabaksbeutel *m*; Patronentasche *f*; **2.** einstecken; (sich) beuteln; **pouched** Beutel...

poul·ter·er ['pəultərə] Geflügelhändler *m*.

poul·tice ⚕ ['pəultis] Breiumschlag

prate

m, Packung *f*.

poul·try ['pɔultri] Geflügel *n*.

pounce [pauns] **1.** Stoß *m*, Sprung *m*; **2.** (herab)stoßen (*Raubvogel*), sich stürzen (*on, upon* auf *acc*.).

pound[1] [paund] Pfund *n* (*abbr. lb.* = *453,6 g*); ~ (*sterling*) Pfund Sterling (*abbr. £ = 100 pence*).

pound[2] [~] **1.** Pfandstall *m*; Tierasyl *n*; **2.** einpferchen.

pound[3] [~] (zer)stoßen; stampfen; donnern; hämmern, schlagen; *sl. Börse*: drücken; ~ *away* drauflosarbeiten.

pound·age ['paundidʒ] Provision *f od.* Prozentsatz *m* per Pfund.

pound·er ['paundə] ...pfünder *m*.

pour [pɔː] *v/t.* gießen, schütten; ~ *out* Getränk eingießen; *fig. sein Herz* ausschütten; *v/i.* sich ergießen, strömen; ~ *with rain* in Strömen gießen; *it never rains but it* ~*s fig.* ein Unglück kommt selten allein.

pout [paut] **1.** Schmollen *n*; **2.** *v/t. Lippen* aufwerfen; *v/i.* schmollen; hervorstehen (*Lippen*); '**pout·er** *zo.* Kropftaube *f*.

pov·er·ty ['pɔvəti] Armut *f*; ~ **line** Existenzminimum *n*; '~**-strick·en** verarmt; arm(selig), dürftig.

pow·der ['paudə] **1.** Pulver *n*; Staub *m*; Puder *m*; **2.** pulverisieren; (sich) pudern; bepudern, bestreuen; '~**-box** Puderdose *f*; ~ **keg** *fig.* Pulverfaß *n*; '~**-puff** Puderquaste *f*; ~ **room** Damentoilette *f*; '**pow·der·y** pulverig; überpulvert.

pow·er ['pauə] Kraft *f* (*a.* ⊕, *ƒ*), Vermögen *n*; Fähigkeit *f*; Macht *f*, Gewalt *f*; 🜨 Vollmacht *f*; ⫪ Potenz *f*; F Masse *f*; *in* ~ an der Macht, im Amt; '~**-cur·rent** Starkstrom *m*; ~ **cut** Stromausfall *m*, -sperre *f*; '~**-dive** 🜨 Vollgassturzflug *m*; ~ **fail·ure** Stromausfall *m*; **pow·er·ful** ['~ful] ☐ mächtig, kräftig; einflußreich; wirksam; '**pow·er·house** = *power-station*; '**pow·er·less** machtlos, kraftlos; **pow·er line** *ƒ* Starkstromleitung *f*; **pow·er plant** = *power-station*; **pow·er point** *ƒ* Steckdose *f*; **pow·er pol·i·tics** *sg. od. pl.* Machtpolitik *f*; **pow·er saw** Motorsäge *f*; '**pow·er·sta·tion** Kraftwerk *n*; **pow·er steer·ing** *mot.* Servolenkung *f*; **pow·er strug·gle** Machtkampf *m*.

pow·wow ['pauwau] Medizinmann *m*; *Am.* lärmende Versammlung *f*; F Palaver *n*.

pox V [pɔks] Syphilis *f*.

pra(a)m ⚓ [prɑːm] Prahm *m*.

prac·ti·ca·bil·i·ty [præktikə'biliti] Durchführbarkeit *f*; '**prac·ti·ca·ble** ☐ tunlich, durch-, ausführbar; gangbar (*Weg*); brauchbar; '**prac·ti·cal** ☐ praktisch; erfahren, geschickt; tatsächlich, wirklich; eigentlich; sachlich; ~ *joke* Schabernack *m*, Streich *m*; ~ *chemistry* angewandte Chemie *f*; **prac·ti·cal·i·ty** ['~kæliti] *das* Praktische; Sachlichkeit *f*; **prac·ti·cal·ly** ['~kəli] praktisch, so gut wie.

prac·tice ['præktis] **1.** Praxis *f* (*a. des Arztes u. Anwalts*); Übung *f*; Gewohnheit *f*; Brauch *m*; Praktik *f*; *out of* ~ außer Übung; *put into* ~ in die Praxis umsetzen; *sharp* ~ unsaubere Geschäfte *n/pl.*; **2.** *Am.* = *practise*; ~ **am·mu·ni·tion** 🜨 Übungsmunition *f*.

prac·tise [~] *v/t.* in die Praxis umsetzen; *Beruf* ausüben; *Geschäft etc.* betreiben; *et.* auf *e-m Instrument* üben; *j.* schulen; *v/i.* (sich) üben, Übungen machen; *Sport*: trainieren; *ƒ* üben; praktizieren; ~ *upon j-s Schwäche* ausnutzen; '**prac·tised** geübt (*Person*).

prac·ti·tion·er [præk'tiʃnə] Praktiker *m*; Rechtsanwalt *m*; *a. general* ~ praktischer Arzt *m*.

prae·tor ['priːtə] *römischer* Prätor *m*.

prag·mat·ic [præg'mætik] (~*ally*) pragmatisch, praktisch, sachlich; geschäftig; vorwitzig; rechthaberisch.

prai·rie *Am.* ['prɛəri] Grasebene *f*; Prärie *f*; ~ *schooner Am.* Planwagen *m der Kolonialzeit*.

praise [preiz] **1.** Preis *m*, Lob *n*; **2.** loben, preisen.

praise·wor·thy ['preizwə:ði] ☐ lobenswert.

pram F [præm] Kinderwagen *m*.

prance [prɑːns] sich bäumen; tänzeln (*Pferd*); paradieren; einherstolzieren.

pran·di·al ☐ ['prændiəl] auf die Mahlzeit bezüglich; Tafel..., Tisch...

prank [præŋk] **1.** Possen *m*, Streich *m*; **2.** ~ *out* (heraus)putzen.

prate [preit] **1.** Geschwätz *n*;

2. schwatzen, plappern; **'prat·er** Schwätzer(in).
prat·tle ['prætl] = *prate*.
prawn *zo.* [prɔ:n] Steingarnele *f*.
pray [prei] *v/i.* beten (to zu; for um; für); bitten (*for* um); *v/t. j.* inständig bitten, ersuchen (*for* um); *et.* erbitten; ~ *tell* me bitte sagen Sie mir.
prayer [prɛə] Gebet *n*; Bitte *f*; *oft* ~*s pl.* Andacht *f*; *Lord's* ~ Vaterunser *n*; *Book of Common* ♀ Gebetbuch *n* der anglikanischen Kirche; '~-**book** Gebetbuch *n*.
pre... [pri:, pri] vor(her)...; Vor...; früher.
preach [pri:tʃ] predigen, *Predigt* halten; **'preach·er** Prediger(in); **'preach·ing** Predigen *n*; Lehre *f*; **'preach·ment** Salbaderei *f*.
pre·am·ble [pri:'æmbl] Einleitung *f*, Präambel *f*.
preb·end *eccl.* ['prebənd] Präbende *f*, Pfründe *f*; **'pre·ben·dar·y** Pfründner *m*; Domherr *m*.
pre·car·i·ous □ [pri'kɛəriəs] unsicher, prekär; **pre'car·i·ous·ness** Unsicherheit *f*.
pre·cau·tion [pri'kɔ:ʃən] Vorsicht(smaßregel) *f*; **pre'cau·tion·ar·y** [~ʃnəri] vorbeugend; Warnungs..., Vorsichts...
pre·cede [pri:'si:d] voraus-, vorangehen (*dat.*); *fig.* vorgehen (*dat.*); einführen, -leiten; **pre'ced·ence** Vorhergehen *n*; Vortritt *m*, Vorrang *m*; **prec·e·dent** ['presidənt] Präzedenzfall *m*; **pre·ced·ing** [pri:'si:diŋ] vorhergehend.
pre·cen·tor *eccl.* [pri:'sentə] Vorsänger *m*, Kantor *m*.
pre·cept ['pri:sept] Vorschrift *f*, Regel *f*; 🕮 Verordnung *f*; **pre·cep·tor** [pri'septə] Lehrer *m*; **pre·'cep·tress** [~tris] Lehrerin *f*.
pre·cinct ['pri:siŋkt] Bezirk *m*; *bsd. Am.* Wahlbezirk *m*, -kreis *m*; ~*s pl.* Nachbarschaft *f*, Umgebung *f*; Bereich *m*; Grenze *f*; *pedestrian* ~ Fußgängerzone *f*.
pre·cious ['preʃəs] 1. □ kostbar (*a. iro.*); edel (*Steine etc.*); geschraubt, affektiert (*Sprache*); F arg, beträchtlich, schön; 2. F *adv.* recht, äußerst; **'pre·cious·ness** Kostbarkeit *f*.
prec·i·pice ['presipis] Abgrund *m*;

pre·cip·i·tance, pre·cip·i·tan·cy [pri'sipitəns(i)] Hast *f*, Übereilung *f*; **pre'cip·i·tate** 1. [~teit] (herab)stürzen; 🜍 fällen; beschleunigen; überstürzen; 2. [~tit] □ hastig, voreilig; übereilt, schleunig; 3. 🜍 [~tit] Niederschlag *m*; **pre·cip·i·ta·tion** [~'teiʃən] Sturz *m*; Hast *f*; 🜍 Niederschlag(en *n*)*m*; **pre'cip·i·tous** □ steil, jäh, abschüssig.
pré·cis ['preisi:] gedrängte Übersicht *f*, Zs.-fassung *f*.
pre·cise □ [pri'sais] genau; pedantisch; ~*ly!* ganz recht!; **pre'cise·ness** Genauigkeit *f*.
pre·ci·sion [pri'siʒən] Genauigkeit *f*; Präzision *f*; *attr.* Präzisions...
pre·clude [pri'klu:d] ausschließen; vorbeugen (*dat.*); ~ *s.o. from ger. j.* daran hindern, zu *inf.*
pre·co·cious □ [pri'kəuʃəs] frühreif; altklug; **pre'co·cious·ness, pre·coc·i·ty** [pri'kɔsiti] Frühreife *f*.
pre·con·ceive [pri:kən'si:v] vorher ausdenken; ~*d* vorgefaßt(*Meinung*).
pre·con·cep·tion ['pri:kən'sepʃən] vorgefaßte Meinung *f*.
pre·con·cert·ed ['pri:kən'sə:tid] verabredet; *b. s.* abgekartet.
pre·cur·sor [pri:'kə:sə] Vorläufer *m*, Vorbote *m*; **pre'cur·so·ry** vorausgehend; vorbereitend.
pre·date ['pri:'deit] vordatieren.
pred·a·to·ry ['predətəri] räuberisch.
pre·de·cease ['pri:di'si:s] früher sterben als.
pre·de·ces·sor ['pri:disesə] Vorgänger *m*.
pre·des·ti·nate [pri:'destineit] vorherbestimmen; **pre·des·ti'na·tion** Vorherbestimmung *f*; *eccl.* Gnadenwahl *f*, Prädestination *f*; **pre'destined** auserkoren.
pre·de·ter·mine ['pri:di'tə:min] vorher festsetzen; vorherbestimmen.
pred·i·ca·ble ['predikəbl] aussagbar.
pre·dic·a·ment [pri'dikəmənt] *phls.* Kategorie *f*; (mißliche) Lage *f*.
pred·i·cate 1. [~keit] behaupten; aussagen; 2. ['~kit] *gr.* Prädikat *n*, Satzaussage *f*; **pred·i·ca·tion** [~'keiʃən] Aussage *f*; **pred·i·ca·tive** [pri'dikətiv] □ aussagend; *gr.* prädikativ.
pre·dict [pri'dikt] vorhersagen; **pre·dic·tion** [~'dikʃən] Prophezeiung *f*, Vorhersage *f*.

pre·di·lec·tion [pri:di'lekʃən] Vorliebe *f* (*for* für).

pre·dis·pose ['pri:dis'pəuz] vorher geneigt *od.* empfänglich machen (*to* für); **pre·dis·po·si·tion** ['⁓dispə'ziʃən] Geneigtheit *f*; *bsd.* ⚕ Anfälligkeit *f* (*to* für).

pre·dom·i·nance [pri'dɔminəns] Vorherrschen *n*, Vorherrschaft *f*; Übergewicht*n*; Vormacht(stellung) *f*; **pre'dom·i·nant** vorherrschend, über-, vorwiegend; **pre-'dom·i·nate** [⁓neit] die Oberhand haben (*over* über *acc.*); vorherrschen.

pre·em·i·nence [pri:'eminəns] Hervorragen *n*; Vorrang *m*; **pre-'em·i·nent** ☐ hervorragend.

pre·emp·tion [pri:'empʃən] Vorkauf(srecht *n*) *m*; **pre-'emp·tive** [⁓tiv] Vorkaufs...; präventiv; ⁓ *first strike* ⚔ Präventivangriff *m*.

preen [pri:n] *das Gefieder* putzen; ⁓ *o.s. on fig.* sich et. einbilden auf (*acc.*).

pre·en·gage [pri:in'geidʒ] vorher verpflichten *od.* bestellen; **pre·en·'gage·ment** frühere Verpflichtung *f*.

pre·ex·ist ['pri:ig'zist] vorher dasein; **'pre·ex'ist·ence** früheres Vorhandensein *n*; **'pre·ex·ist·ent** vorher vorhanden.

pre·fab ['pri:fæb] **1.** zs.-setzbar; Fertig...; **2.** Fertighaus *n*; **'pre-'fab·ri·cate** [⁓rikeit] vorfabrizieren.

pref·ace ['prefis] **1.** Vorrede *f*, -wort *n*, Einleitung *f*; **2.** einleiten.

pref·a·to·ry ☐ ['prefətəri] einleitend.

pre·fect ['pri:fekt] Präfekt *m*; *Schule*: Vertrauensschüler *m*.

pre·fer [pri'fə:] vorziehen; *Gesuch etc.* vorbringen; *Klage* einreichen (*to* bei); befördern; *s. share 1*; *I should* ⁓ *you not to go* es wäre mir lieber, wenn du nicht gingst; **pref·er·a·ble** ☐ ['prefərəbl] (*to*) vorzuziehen(d) (*dat.*); vorzüglicher (als); **'pref·er·a·bly** vorzugsweise; lieber; besser; **'pref·er·ence** Vorliebe *f*; *bsd.* ✝ Vorzug *m*; *Zoll*: Meistbegünstigung *f*; *s. share 1*; **pref·er·en·tial** ☐ [⁓'renʃəl] bevorzugt; Vorzugs...; **pref·er'en·tial·ly** vorzugsweise; **pre·fer·ment** [pri-'fə:mənt] Beförderung *f*; höheres

Amt *n*.

pre·fix 1. ['pri:fiks] Präfix *n*, Vorsilbe *f*; **2.** [pri:'fiks] vorsetzen; vorausgehen lassen.

preg·nan·cy ['pregnənsi] Schwangerschaft *f*; *fig.* Fruchtbarkeit *f*; Bedeutungsreichtum *m*; **'preg·nant** ☐ schwanger; trächtig (*Tier*); *fig.* fruchtbar, inhaltvoll.

pre·heat ⊕ ['pri:'hi:t] vorwärmen.

pre·hen·sile [pri'hensail] Greif...

pre·his·tor·ic ['pri:his'tɔrik] vorgeschichtlich.

pre·ig·ni·tion *mot.* ['pri:ig'niʃən] Frühzündung *f*.

pre·judge ['pri:'dʒʌdʒ] vorher (ver-) urteilen.

prej·u·dice ['predʒudis] **1.** Voreingenommenheit *f*; Vorurteil *n*; vorgefaßte Meinung *f*; Schaden *m*; *without* ⁓ *to* unbeschadet (*gen.*); **2.** einnehmen; benachteiligen; *e-r Sache* Abbruch tun; ⁓*d* (vor)eingenommen.

prej·u·di·cial ☐ [predʒu'diʃəl] nachteilig, schädlich (*to* für).

prel·a·cy ['preləsi] Prälaten(würde *f*) *m*/*pl.*

prel·ate ['prelit] Prälat *m*.

pre·lec·tion [pri'lekʃən] Vorlesung *f*; **pre'lec·tor** Vorleser *m*.

pre·lim ℉ [pri'lim] Vorexamen *n*.

pre·lim·i·nar·y [pri'liminəri] **1.** ☐ vorläufig; einleitend; Vor...; **2.** Einleitung *f*; **pre'lim·i·na·ries** [⁓riz] *pl.* Vorbereitungen *f*/*pl.*, Vorverhandlungen *f pl.*

prel·ude ['prelju:d] **1.** ♪ Vorspiel *n*; Einleitung *f*; **2.** ♪ präludieren; einleiten.

pre·mar·i·tal [pri:'mæritl] vorehelich.

pre·ma·ture ☐ [premə'tjuə] *fig.* frühreif; vorzeitig; vorschnell; verfrüht; ⁓ *delivery* Frühgeburt *f*; **pre·ma'ture·ness, pre·ma'tu·ri·ty** [⁓riti] *fig.* Frühreife *f*; Vorzeitigkeit *f*; Voreiligkeit *f*.

pre·med·i·tate [pri:'mediteit] vorher überlegen; ⁓*d murder* ⚖ vorsätzlicher Mord *m*; **pre·med·i-'ta·tion** Vorbedacht *m*.

pre·mi·er ['premjə] **1.** erst; **2.** Premierminister *m*.

prem·ière ['premiɛə] Uraufführung *f*.

pre·mi·er·ship ['premjəʃip] Amt *n* *od.* Würde *f* des Premierministers.

prem·ise 1. ['premis] Prämisse *f*, Vordersatz *m*; ~s *pl.* (Gebäude *n*/*pl.* mit) Grundstück *n*, Anwesen *n*; Lokal *n*; *licensed* ~s *pl.* Schankstätte *f*; *on the* ~s an Ort und Stelle, im Hause *od.* Lokal; 2. **pre·mise** [pri-'maiz] vorausschicken.

pre·mi·um ['pri:mjəm] Prämie *f*, Preis *m*; Anzahlung *f*; ✝ Agio *n*; Versicherungsprämie *f*; Lehrgeld *n*; Anzahlung *f auf Mieten*; Super(benzin) *n*; *at a* ~ über pari; sehr gesucht.

pre·mo·ni·tion [pri:mə'niʃən] Warnung *f*; (Vor)Ahnung *f*; **pre·mon·i·to·ry** □ [pri'mɔnitəri] warnend.

pre·na·tal ['pri:'neitl] vor der Geburt (eintretend).

pre·oc·cu·pan·cy *fig.* [pri:'ɔkju-pənsi] Vertieftsein *n* (*in* in *acc.*); **pre·oc·cu·pa·tion** [~'peiʃən] vorherige Besitznahme *f*; Vorurteil *n*; Haupttätigkeit *f*; Beschäftigtsein *n* (*with* mit); **pre'oc·cu·pied** [~paid] in Gedanken verloren; **pre'oc·cu·py** [~pai] vorher in Besitz nehmen; ausschließlich beschäftigen; in Anspruch nehmen.

pre·or·dain ['pri:ɔ:'dein] vorher bestimmen.   [*paratory school.*\
prep F [prep] = *preparation*, *pre-*/
pre·paid ['pri:'peid] vorausbezahlt; frankiert.

prep·a·ra·tion [prepə'reiʃən] Vorbereitung *f*; Zubereitung *f*; **pre·par·a·tive** [pri'pærətiv] Vorbereitung *f*; **pre'par·a·to·ry** [~tətri] □ vorbereitend, Vorbereitungs...; ~ *school* Vorschule *f*; ~ *to* vor (*dat.*).

pre·pare [pri'pɛə] *v/t.* vorbereiten; zurechtmachen, herrichten; *Speise etc.* (zu)bereiten; (aus)rüsten; *v/i.* sich vorbereiten; sich anschicken; **pre'pared** □ bereit; ~ *for* gefaßt auf (*acc.*); **pre'pared·ness** Bereitschaft *f*; Gefaßtsein *n* (*for* auf *acc.*).

pre·pay ['pri:'pei] (*irr. pay*) vorausbezahlen; frankieren; **'pre'pay·ment** Vorausbezahlung *f*; Frankierung *f*.

pre·pense □ [pri'pens] vorbedacht; *with malice* ~ in böswilliger Absicht.

pre·pon·der·ance [pri'pɔndərəns] Übergewicht *n*; **pre'pon·der·ant** □ überwiegend; **pre'pon·der·ate** [~reit] überwiegen.

prep·o·si·tion *gr.* [prepə'ziʃən] Präposition *f*, Verhältniswort *n*; **prep-**

o·si·tion·al □ [~ʃənl] präpositional.

pre·pos·sess [pri:pə'zes] günstig stimmen, einnehmen; **pre·pos-'sess·ing** □ einnehmend, anziehend; **pre·pos·ses·sion** [~'zeʃən] Voreingenommenheit *f*; Vorurteil *n*.

pre·pos·ter·ous [pri'pɔstərəs] widersinnig, albern; grotesk.

pre·puce *anat.* ['pri:pju:s] Vorhaut *f*.

pre·re·cord·ed [pri:ri'kɔ:did] bespielt (*Musik-*, *Videokassette*).

pre·req·ui·site ['pri:'rekwizit] Vorbedingung *f*, Voraussetzung *f*.

pre·rog·a·tive [pri'rɔgətiv] Vorrecht *n*, Prärogativ *n*.

pres·age ['presidʒ] 1. Vorbedeutung *f*; Ahnung *f*; 2. vorbedeuten; ahnen; prophezeien.

pres·by·ter ['prezbitə] Kirchenälteste *m*; **Pres·by·te·ri·an** [~'tiə-riən] 1. presbyterianisch; 2. Presbyterianer(in); **pres·by·ter·y** *eccl.* ['~təri] Presbyterium *n*; *katholisches* Pfarrhaus *n*.

pre·sci·ence ['presiəns] Vorherwissen *n*, Voraussicht *f*; **'pre·sci·ent** vorherwissend.

pre·scribe [pris'kraib] *v/t.* vorschreiben; ⚕ verschreiben, verordnen; *v/i.* etwas verschreiben (*for dat.*); ⚖ verjähren.

pre·script ['pri:skript] Vorschrift *f*; **pre·scrip·tion** [pris'kripʃən] Vorschrift *f*, Verordnung *f*; ⚕ Rezept *n*; ⚖ Verjährung *f*; ~ *charge* Rezeptgebühr *f*; **pre'scrip·tive** □ [~tiv] Verjährungs...; verjährt.

pres·ence ['prezns] Gegenwart *f*; Anwesenheit *f*; Vorhandensein *n*; (äußere) Erscheinung *f*; (Geister-) Erscheinung *f*; ~ *of mind* Geistesgegenwart *f*; **'~-cham·ber** Audienzzimmer *n*.

pres·ent[1] ['preznt] 1. □ gegenwärtig; anwesend, vorhanden; jetzig; heutig; laufend (*Jahr etc.*); vorliegend (*Fall etc.*); ~ *tense gr.* Präsens *n*; ~ *company* die Anwesenden *pl.*; ~ *value* Gegenwartswert *m*; ~! hier!; 2. Gegenwart *f*; *gr. a.* Präsens *n*; *by the* ~ ✝, *by these* ~s ⚖ hiermit, -durch; *at* ~ jetzt; *for the* ~ für jetzt, einstweilen.

pre·sent[2] [pri'zent] (dar)bieten; darstellen, zeigen; *j.* vorstellen; *Wechsel* vorzeigen; *Kandidaten* vorschlagen; ⚔ präsentieren; (über)reichen;

verleihen; vorlegen; *et.* schenken; *j.* beschenken (*with* mit); ~ *o.s.* sich einfinden; sich melden; ~ one's *compliments to s.o.* sich j-m empfehlen.

pres·ent³ ['preznt] Geschenk *n*; *make s.o. a ~ of s.th.* j-m et. zum Geschenk machen.

pre·sent·a·ble [pri'zentəbl] präsentabel; *is this suit ~?* kann man sich mit diesem Anzug sehen lassen?

pres·en·ta·tion [prezən'teiʃən] Dar-, Vorstellung *f*; Vorschlag(srecht *n*) *m*; Ein-, Überreichung *f*; Schenkung *f*; Vorzeigung *f e-s Wechsels*; ~ *copy* Frei- od. Widmungsexemplar *n*.

pres·ent·day ['prezentdei] gegenwärtig, modern, Gegenwarts...

pre·sen·ti·ment [pri'zentimənt] Vorgefühl *n*, Ahnung *f*.

pres·ent·ly ['prezntli] sogleich, bald (darauf), alsbald; *Am.* zur Zeit.

pre·sent·ment [pri'zentmənt] *s.* presentation; ⚖ Anklage *f* von Amts wegen; *thea.* Vorstellung *f*.

pres·er·va·tion [prezə:'veiʃən] Bewahrung *f*, Erhaltung *f*; *in good ~* gut erhalten; **pre·serv·a·tive** [pri-'zə:vətiv] **1.** bewahrend; **2.** Schutz-, Konservierungsmittel *n*.

pre·serve [pri'zə:v] **1.** bewahren, behüten (*from* vor *dat.*); erhalten, konservieren; *Obst etc.* einmachen; *Wild* hegen; (bei)behalten; **2.** *hunt.* *oft ~s pl.* Gehege *n* (*a. fig.*); *fig.* Reich *n*; *mst ~s pl.* Eingemachte *n*; **pre'serv·er** Bewahrer(in), Retter (-in); Erhalter(in); *hunt.* Heger *m*; Konservierungsmittel *n*; Einkochapparat *m*.

pre·side [pri'zaid] präsidieren, den Vorsitz führen (*over* bei); ~ *over an assembly* e-e Versammlung leiten.

pres·i·den·cy ['prezidənsi] Vorsitz *m*; Oberaufsicht *f*; Präsidentschaft *f*; **pres·i·dent** Präsident *m*, Vorsitzende *m*; *Am.* ✝ Direktor *m*; **pres·i·den·tial** [~'denʃəl] Präsidenten...

press [pres] **1.** Druck *m der Hand*; (Wein- *etc.*)Presse *f*; *die* Presse (*Zeitungen*); Druckerei *f*; Verlag *m*; Druck(en *n*) *m*; *a.* printing-~ Druckerpresse *f*; Menge *f*; *fig.* Druck *m*, Last *f*, Andrang *m*; Schrank *m*; ~ *of sail* ⚓ Segelpreß *m*; **2.** *v/t.*

pressen (*a.* ✂), drücken; auspressen; bügeln; (be)drängen; drängen; dringen auf (*acc.*); *fig.* *Rat etc.* aufdrängen (*on dat.*); belasten, lasten auf (*dat.*); ~ *the button* auf den Knopf drücken; ~ *the point that* besonders betonen, daß; *be ~ed for time* es eilig haben; *v/i.* drücken; (sich) drängen; ~ *for* sich eifrig bemühen um; ~ *on* vorwärtsdrängen, weitereilen; ~ (*up*)*on* eindringen auf (*acc.*); in *j.* dringen; **'~-a·gen·cy** Nachrichtenbüro *n*; ~ **a·gent** Reklameagent *m*; ~ **bar·on** Pressezar *m*; **'~-but·ton** Druckknopf *m*; **'~-cor·rec·tor** *typ.* Korrektor *m*; **'~-cut·ting** Zeitungsausschnitt *m*; **'press·er** Presser *m*; Drucker *m*; **'press·gal·le·ry** Pressetribüne *f*; **'press·gang:** ~ *s.o. into doing s.th.* F j. zu et. zwingen od. drängen; **'press·ing 1.** ☐ pressend; dringend; Preß...; **2.** Plattenpressung *f*; **press lord** Pressezar *m*; **'press·man** Mann *m* der Presse; **'press·mark** Bibliotheksnummer *f* *e-s Buches*; **'press·stud** Druckknopf *m*; **'press·up** *Sport:* Liegestütz *m*; **pres·sure** ['preʃə] Druck *m* (*a. fig.*); Drang *m*; Drangsal *f*; **pres·sure cook·er** Dampfkochtopf *m*; **pres·sure e·qual·i·za·tion** Druckausgleich *m*; **'pres·sure-ga(u)ge** ⊕ Druckmesser *m*; **'pres·sure-group** *pol.* Interessengruppe *f*; **pres·sur·ize** ['~raiz] unter Druck setzen; **'press·work** *typ.* Druckarbeit *f*.

pres·ti·dig·i·ta·tion ['prestididʒi'teiʃən] Taschenspielerei *f*.

pres·tige [pres'ti:ʒ] Prestige *n*, Ansehen *n*, Geltung *f*; **pres·ti·gious** [~'tidʒəs] renommiert.

pres·to ['prestəu] schnell.

pre·stressed ['pri:'strest]: ~ *concrete* Spannbeton *m*.

pre·sum·a·ble ☐ [pri'zju:məbl] mutmaßlich, vermutlich; **pre'sume** *v/t.* *als wahr* annehmen; vermuten, mutmaßen; voraussetzen; *v/i.* vermuten; sich erdreisten, wagen (*to inf.* zu *inf.*); anmaßend sein; ~ (*up*)*on* pochen auf, ausnutzen, mißbrauchen; **pre'sum·ed·ly** [~idli] mutmaßlich; **pre'sum·ing** anmaßend.

pre·sump·tion [pri'zʌmpʃən] Mutmaßung *f*; Wahrscheinlichkeit *f*; Anmaßung *f*, Dünkel *m*; Voraussetzung *f*; **pre'sump·tive** [~tiv]

mutmaßlich; **pre'sump·tu·ous** □
[~tjuəs] überheblich; vermessen.

pre·sup·pose [pri:sə'pəuz] voraussetzen; **pre·sup·po·si·tion** [pri:-sʌpə'ziʃən] Voraussetzung f.

pre·tense, *Am.* **pre·tense** [pri'tens]
Vortäuschung f; Vorwand m;
Schein m, Verstellung f; *false* ~
Vorspiegelung f falscher Tatsachen; *make* ~ vorgeben, den Anschein erwecken.

pre·tend [pri'tend] vorgeben; vortäuschen; heucheln; Anspruch
erheben (*to* auf *acc.*); ~ *to be ill*
so tun, als ob man krank sei; **pre-'tend·ed** □ angeblich; **pre'tend·er**
Beansprucher m; (Thron)Bewerber
m, Prätendent m; Heuchler m,
Schauspieler m.

pre·ten·sion [pri'tenʃən] Anspruch
m (*to* auf *acc.*); Anmaßung f.

pre·ten·tious [pri'tenʃəs] anmaßend; **pre'ten·tious·ness** Anmaßung f.

pret·er·it(e) gr. ['pretərit] Präteritum n, Vergangenheit(sform) f.

pre·ter·mis·sion [pri:tə'miʃən]
Übergehung f; Unterlassung f.

pre·ter·nat·u·ral □ [pri:tə'nætʃrəl]
außergewöhnlich, abnorm.

pre·text ['pri:tekst] Vorwand m.

pret·ti·fy ['pritifai] verniedlichen.

pret·ti·ness ['pritinis] Niedlichkeit
f; Geziertheit f des Ausdrucks.

pret·ty ['priti] **1.** □ hübsch, niedlich; nett; F beträchtlich, schön; *a*
~ *penny* F e-e hübsche Summe, e-e
Menge Geld; *my* ~! mein Herzchen!; **2.** *adv.* ziemlich; ganz schön.

pre·vail [pri'veil] die Oberhand
haben *od.* gewinnen (*over, against*
über *acc.*); sich durchsetzen; (vor-)
herrschen; maßgebend *od.* ausschlaggebend sein; ~ (*up*)*on s.o.*
to do j. dazu bewegen, *et.* zu tun;
pre'vail·ing (vor)herrschend.

prev·a·lence ['prevələns] Vorherrschen n, Verbreitung f; **'prev·a·lent** vorherrschend, weit verbreitet.

pre·var·i·cate [pri'værikeit] Ausflüchte machen; **pre·var·i'ca·tion**
Ausflucht f.

pre·vent [pri'vent] *et.* verhüten,
verhindern, *e-r Sache* vorbeugen;
j. hindern (*from* an *dat.*); *j.* abhalten (*from* von); **pre'vent·a·ble**
verhütbar; **pre'vent·a·tive** [~-

tətiv] = *preventive*; **pre'ven·tion**
Verhinderung f; Verhütung f;
pre'ven·tive 1. □ vorbeugend (*of*
dat.); ~ *detention* Sicherheitsverwahrung f; ~ *medicine* Präventivmedizin f; **2.** Schutzmittel n *of*
gegen).

pre·view ['pri:vju:] Vorschau f;
Vorbesichtigung f *e-r Ausstellung*;
thea., Film: Probeaufführung f.

pre·vi·ous ['pri:vjəs] vorhergehend; früher; Vor...; F voreilig;
~ *conviction* Vorstrafe f; ~ *to* vor
(*dat.*); **'pre·vi·ous·ly** vorher, früher.

pre·vi·sion [pri:'viʒən] Voraussicht f.

pre·war ['pri:'wɔ:] Vorkriegs...

prey [prei] **1.** Raub m, Beute f;
beast (bird) of ~ Raubtier n (-vogel
m); *be a* ~ *to* geplagt werden von;
2. Beute machen; ~ *on,* ~ *upon*
rauben, plündern; fressen; *fig.*
nagen an (*dat.*).

price [prais] **1.** Preis m; Lohn m;
at any ~ um jeden Preis; **2.** mit
Preisen versehen; die Preise festsetzen (für); (ab)schätzen; ~ *s.o. out of*
the market j. durch niedrige Preise
vom Markt verdrängen; **'price·less**
unschätzbar; unbezahlbar; **price**
range Preisklasse f; **price tag, price**
tick·et Preisschild n; **'pric·ey** F (ganz
schön) teuer.

prick [prik] Stich m *e-s Insekts etc.*;
Stachel m (*a. fig.*); **2.** *v/t.* (durch-)
stechen; prickeln auf *od.* in (*dat.*);
a. ~ *out* (aus)stechen, lochen,
Muster punktieren; ~ *out* 🎯 (aus-)
pflanzen; ~ *up one's ears* die Ohren
spitzen; *v/i.* stechen; prickeln; ~ *up*
sich aufrichten, sich recken; **'prick-er** Pfriem m; **prick·le** ['~l] Stachel
m, Dorn m; **'prick·ly** stachelig;
~ *heat* 🎯 Hitzpickel m/pl.; ~ *pear* 🎯
Feigendistel f (*ein Kaktus*).

pric·y ['praisi] = *pricey*.

pride [praid] **1.** Stolz m; Genugtuung f; Hochmut m; Blüte f, Höhe
f *der Saison etc.*; ~ *of place* Ehrenplatz m; Standesdünkel m; *take (a)*
~ *in* stolz sein auf (*acc.*); **2.** ~ *o.s.*
(*up*)*on* sich brüsten mit; sich etwas
einbilden, stolz sein (auf *acc.*), sich
rühmen (*gen.*).

priest [pri:st] Priester m, Geistliche
m; **'~·craft** Pfaffenlist f; **'priest·ess**
Priesterin f; **priest·hood** ['~hud]

Priesteramt *n*; Priesterschaft *f*; **'priest·ly** priesterlich; **'priest--rid·den** von Priestern beherrscht.

prig [prig] Tugendbold *m*, selbstgerechter Mensch *m*; Pedant *m*; **'prig·gish** □ selbstgerecht, -gefällig.

prim □ [prim] steif; spröde, zimperlich.

pri·ma·cy ['praiməsi] Vorrang *m*; **pri·mal** ['praiməl] erst, ursprünglich; wichtigst, Haupt...; **pri·ma·ri·ly** ['‿rili] in erster Linie; **'pri·ma·ry** □ **1.** ursprünglich; frühest; hauptsächlich; Ur..., Anfangs..., Grund..., Haupt...; Elementar...; höchst (*Wichtigkeit*); ✗, ✗ Primär...; **2.** *a.* ‿ *meeting Am.* Wahlversammlung *f*; *Am.* (*oft pl.*) Vorwahl *f zur Präsidentenwahl*; *s.* share; **'pri·ma·ry school** Volks-, Grundschule *f*; **pri·mate** *eccl.* ['‿mit] Primas *m*.

prime [praim] **1.** □ erste(r, -s); Haupt...; vorzüglich(st); erstklassig, prima; ‿ *cost* Gestehungs-, Selbstkosten *pl.*; ‿ *rate* Eckzins *m*; ♀ *Minister* Premierminister *m*; ‿ *number* Primzahl *f*; ‿ *time* Hauptsendezeit *f*; **2.** *fig.* Blüte(zeit) *f*; Vollkraft *f*; *das Beste*, Kern *m*; höchste Vollkommenheit *f*; **3.** *v/t.* vorbereiten; *Pumpe* anlassen; F vollaufen lassen; *paint.* grundieren.

prim·er[1] ['praimə] Fibel *f*, Elementarbuch *n*; *typ.* ['primə]: *great* ‿ Tertia(schrift) *f*; *long* ‿ Korpus *f*.

prim·er[2] ['praimə] Grundierer *m*; Zündvorrichtung *f*.

pri·me·val [prai'mi:vəl] uranfänglich; Ur...

prim·ing ['praimiŋ] *paint.* Grundierung *f*; ✗ Zündung *f*; Zündmasse *f*; *attr.* Zünd...; Pulver...

prim·i·tive ['primitiv] **1.** □ erst, ursprünglich; Stamm...; Grund...; einfach, primitiv; **2.** *gr.* Stammwort *n*; **'prim·i·tive·ness** Ursprünglichkeit *f*; Primitivität *f*.

prim·ness ['primnis] Steifheit *f*; Sprödigkeit *f*; Zimperlichkeit *f*.

pri·mo·gen·i·ture [praiməu'dʒenitʃə] Erstgeburt(srecht *n*) *f*.

pri·mor·di·al □ [prai'mɔ:djəl] uranfänglich.

prim·rose ♀ ['primrəuz] Primel *f*; ‿ *path od. way fig.* Rosenpfad *m des Vergnügens; take the* ‿ *path das*

Leben genießen.

prince [prins] Fürst *m*; Prinz *m*; ♀ **Con·sort** Prinzgemahl *m*; **'prince·ly** fürstlich; königlich; **prin·cess** [prin'ses, *vor npr.* 'prinses] Fürstin *f*; Prinzessin *f*.

prin·ci·pal ['prinsəpəl] **1.** □ erst, hauptsächlich(st); Haupt...; *gr.* ‿ *parts pl.* Stammformen *f/pl. des vb.*; **2.** Hauptperson *f*; Vorsteher *m*; *bsd. Am.* (Schul)Direktor *m*, Rektor *m*; ✝ Prinzipal *m*, Chef *m*; Auftraggeber *m*; Hauptschuldige *m*; Kapital *n*; **prin·ci·pal·i·ty** [prinsi'pæliti] Fürstentum *n*.

prin·ci·ple ['prinsəpl] Prinzip *n*, Grundsatz *m*; Grund *m*, Ursprung *m*; ♠ (Grund)Bestandteil *m*; *in* ‿ im Prinzip; *on* ‿ grundsätzlich, aus Prinzip.

prink F [priŋk] (sich) putzen.

print [print] **1.** Druck *m*; (Fuß-) Spur *f*; (Finger- *etc.*)Abdruck *m*; bedruckter Kattun *m*, Druckstoff *m*; Stich *m*; *phot.* Abzug *m*; *Am.* Zeitungsdrucksache *f*; *out of* ‿ vergriffen; *in cold* ‿ schwarz auf weiß; **2.** *v/t.* drucken; ab-, auf-, bedrucken; *print.* kopieren; *fig.* einprägen (*on dat.*); ‿*ed form* Vordruck *m*; *v/i.* drucken; in Druckbuchstaben schreiben; **'print·er** (Buch)Drucker *m*; ‿*'s devil* Setzerjunge *m*; ‿*'s flower* Vignette *f*; ‿*'s ink* Druckerschwärze *f*.

print·ing ['printiŋ] Druck *m*; Drucken *n*; *phot.* Abziehen *n*, Kopieren *n*; **'‿-frame** *phot.* Kopierrahmen *m*; **'‿-ink** Druckerschwärze *f*; **'‿-of·fice** (Buch-) Druckerei *f*; **'‿-press** Druckerpresse *f*.

print-out ['printaut] *Computer:* Ausdruck *m*, Printout *m*.

pri·or ['praiə] **1.** früher, älter (*to* als); **2.** *adv.* ‿ *to* vor (*dat.*); **3.** *eccl.* Prior *m*; **'pri·or·ess** *eccl.* Priorin *f*; **pri·or·i·ty** [‿'ɔriti] Priorität *f*; Vorrang *m*, Vorzugsrecht *n*; Vorfahrtsrecht *n* (*to, over* vor *dat.*); *give s.th.* ‿ *et.* vorrangig behandeln; *s.* share 1; **pri·o·ry** *eccl.* ['‿əri] Priorei *f*.

prism ['prizəm] Prisma *n*; ‿ *binoculars pl.* Prismen(fern)glas *n*; **pris·mat·ic** [‿'mætik] (‿*ally*) prismatisch.

pris·on ['prizn] **1.** Gefängnis *n*; **2.** *poet.* einkerkern; **'pris·on·er** Ge-

fangene *m, f*, Häftling *m*; ₰₰ Angeklagte *m, f*; *be a* ~ *to fig.* gefesselt sein an (*acc.*); *take s.o.* ~]. gefangennehmen; ~*'s bars*, ~*'s base* Barlauf(spiel *n*) *m*.   [etepetete.\
pris·sy *Am.* F ['prisi] zimperlich,]
pris·tine ['pristain] ursprünglich, urtümlich; unverdorben.
prith·ee † ['priði:] bitte.
pri·va·cy ['praivəsi] Zurückgezogenheit *f*; Privatleben *n*; Heimlichkeit *f*; Geheimhaltung *f*.
pri·vate ['praivit] **1.** □ privat; Privat...; eigen, persönlich; ohne (Regierungs)Amt *od.* Rang; nichtöffentlich; außeramtlich; vertraulich; geheim; ~ *company* offene Handelsgesellschaft *f*; ~ *lessons pl.* Privatunterricht *m*; ~ *member* Parlamentsmitglied *n* ohne Regierungsamt; ~ *theatre* Liebhabertheater *n*; ~ *view* Besichtigung *f* durch geladene Gäste; *at* ~ *sale* unter der Hand; **2.** ✗ (gewöhnlicher) Soldat *m*; ~*s pl.*, *mst* ~ *parts pl.* Geschlechtsteile *m/pl.*; *in* ~ privatim; im geheimen.
pri·va·teer ⚓ [praivə'tiə] Freibeuter *m*, Kaperschiff *n*; Kaperer *m*; **pri·va'teer·ing** Kaperei *f*; *attr.* Kaper...
pri·va·tion [prai'veiʃən] Mangel *m*, Entbehrung *f*.
pri·va·tive □ ['privətiv] beraubend; verneinend (*a. gr.*).
priv·et ♀ ['privit] Liguster *m*.
priv·i·lege ['privilidʒ] **1.** Privileg *n*, Vorrecht *n*; **2.** privilegieren, bevorrecht(ig)en.
priv·i·ty ₰₰ ['priviti] Mitwisserschaft *f*; Interessengemeinschaft *f*.
priv·y ['privi] **1.** □ ~ *to* eingeweiht in (*acc.*); ₰₰ mitbeteiligt an (*dat.*); ♀ *Council* Staatsrat *m*; ♀ *Councillor* Geheimer Rat *m*; ~ *parts pl.* Geschlechtsteile *m/pl.*; ~ *purse* Privatschatulle *f*; ♀ *Seal* Geheimsiegel *n*; *Lord* ♀ *Seal* Geheimsiegelbewahrer *m*; **2.** ₰₰ Mitinteressent *m* (*to an dat.*); Abtritt *m*, Latrine *f*.
prize[1] [praiz] **1.** Preis *m*, Prämie *f*; ⚓ Beute *f*, Prise *f*; (Lotterie)Gewinn *m*; Vorteil *m*; *first* ~ *Lotterie*: *das Große Los*; **2.** preisgekrönt, Preis...; ⚓ Prisen...; ~ *competition* Preisausschreiben *n*; **3.** (hoch-)schätzen; ⚓ aufbringen, kapern.
prize[2] [~] **1.** *a.* ~ *open* aufbrechen (*öffnen*); **2.** Hebel *m*.

prize...: '~**fight·er** Berufsboxer *m*; '~**-list** Gewinnliste *f*; '~**·man** = *prize-winner*; '~**-ring** *Boxen*: Ring *m*; '~**-winner** Preisträger *m*.
pro[1] [prəu] für; *s. con*[3].
pro[2] F [~] Profi *m*; Professionelle *m*; Nutte *f*.
prob·a·bil·i·ty [prɔbə'biliti] Wahrscheinlichkeit *f*; '**prob·a·ble** □ wahrscheinlich.
pro·bate ₰₰ ['prəubit] gerichtliche Testamentsbestätigung *f*.
pro·ba·tion [prə'beiʃən] Probe *f*, Probezeit *f*, *bsd.* ₰₰ Bewährungsfrist *f*; ~ *bedingte Strafaussetzung f*; ~ *officer* Bewährungshelfer *m*; *on* ~ auf Probe; ₰₰ mit Bewährungsfrist; **pro'ba·tion·ar·y**: ~ *period* ₰₰ Bewährungsfrist *f*; **pro'ba·tion·er** Probeanwärter(in); Lernschwester *f*; ₰₰ Verurteilte *m, f* mit Bewährungsfrist.
pro·ba·tive ₰₰ ['prəubətiv]: ~ *force* Beweiskraft *f*.
probe [prəub] **1.** ✿ Sonde *f*; *fig.* Untersuchung *f*; *lunar* ~ Mondsonde *f*; **2.** *a.* ~ *into* sondieren; untersuchen; '~**-scis·sors** *pl.* Wundschere *f*.
prob·i·ty ['prəubiti] Redlichkeit *f*.
prob·lem ['prɔbləm] Problem *n*; schwierige Frage *f*; ⅍ Aufgabe *f*; ~ *child* Sorgenkind *n*; *do a* ~ e-e Aufgabe lösen; **prob·lem·at·ic, prob·lem·at·i·cal** □ [~'mætik (-əl)] problematisch, zweifelhaft.
pro·bos·cis [prəu'bɔsis] Rüssel *m*.
pro·ce·dur·al [prə'si:dʒərəl] Verfahrens...; **pro'ce·dure** Verfahren *n*; Handlungsweise *f*; Vorgehen *n*.
pro·ceed [prə'si:d] weitergehen (*a. fig.*); fortfahren (*with* mit, in *dat.*); vor sich gehen; vorgehen (*handeln*; ₰₰ *against* gegen); *univ.* promovieren; ~ *from* von *od.* aus *et.* kommen; ausgehen von; ~ *on one's journey* s-e Reise fortsetzen; ~ *to* zu *et.* schreiten *od.* übergehen; **pro'ceed·ing** Vorgehen *n*, Verfahren *n*; Handlung *f*; ~*s pl.* ₰₰ Verfahren *n*; Verhandlungen *f/pl.*, (Tätigkeits-) Bericht *m* e-r Körperschaft *etc.*; *take* ~*s against* gerichtlich vorgehen gegen; **pro·ceeds** ['prəusi:dz] *pl.* Einnahmen *f/pl.*, Ertrag *m*, Gewinn *m* (*from* aus).
proc·ess ['prəuses] **1.** Fortschreiten *n*, -gang *m*; Vorgang *m*; Verlauf

m der Zeit; ꝗ̃, ⚛ Prozeß *m*, Verfahren *n*; Arbeitsgang *m*; *anat.*, ⚕ Fortsatz *m*; *in* ~ im Gange; *in* ~ *of construction* im Bau (befindlich); **2.** gerichtlich belangen; ⊕ behandeln, bearbeiten; ~ *into* verarbeiten zu; ~*ed cheese* Käsezubereitung *f*; **'pro·cess·ing** ⊕ Veredelung *f*, Verarbeitung *f*; **pro·ces·sion** [prə'seʃən] Prozession *f*, Umzug *m*; **pro'ces·sion·ar·y** [~ʃnəri] Prozessions...

pro·claim [prə'kleim] proklamieren, öffentlich verkünden; erklären; ausrufen; verraten (als).

proc·la·ma·tion [prɔklə'meiʃən] Proklamation *f*, Verkündung *f*; Bekanntmachung *f*; Erklärung *f*.

pro·cliv·i·ty [prə'kliviti] Neigung *f*; Anlage *f* (*to* zu).

pro·con·sul [prəu'kɔnsəl] Prokonsul *m*.

pro·cras·ti·nate [prəu'kræstineit] zaudern; **pro·cras·ti'na·tion** Zaudern *n*.

pro·cre·ate ['prəukrieit] (er)zeugen; **pro·cre'a·tion** Zeugung *f*; **'pro·cre·a·tive** zeugungsfähig; Zeugungs...

proc·tor ['prɔktə] ꝗ̃ Anwalt *m*, Sachwalter *m*; *univ.* Proktor *m*, Disziplinarbeamte *m*.

pro·cum·bent [prəu'kʌmbənt] (nieder)liegend.

pro·cur·a·ble [prə'kjuərəbl] beschaffbar, erhältlich.

proc·u·ra·tion[prɔkjuə'reiʃən] Stellvertretung *f*; Vollmacht *f*; ✝ Prokura *f*; *per* Prokura *f*; **'proc·u·ra·tor** Bevollmächtigte *m*.

pro·cure [prə'kjuə] *v/t.* beschaffen; verschaffen, besorgen (*s.o. s.th., s.th. for s.o.* j-m et.); *v/i.* kuppeln; **pro'cure·ment** Beschaffung *f*; Vermittlung *f*; **pro'cur·er** Beschaffer(in); Kuppler(in); **pro'cur·ess** Kupplerin *f*.

prod [prɔd] **1.** Stich *m*; Stoß *m*; *fig.* Ansporn *m*; **2.** stechen; stoßen; *fig.* anstacheln.

prod·i·gal □ ['prɔdigəl] **1.** verschwenderisch (*of* mit); *the* ~ *son* der verlorene Sohn; **2.** Verschwender(in); **prod·i·gal·i·ty** [~'gæliti] Verschwendung *f*.

pro·di·gious □ [prə'didʒəs] erstaunlich, ungeheuer; wunderbar; **prod·i·gy** ['prɔdidʒi] Wunder *n* (*a.*

fig.); Ungeheuer *n*; *oft infant* ~ Wunderkind *n*.

prod·uce¹ ['prɔdjuːs] (Natur)Erzeugnis(se *pl.*) *n*, Produkt *n*, Ertrag *m*.

pro·duce² [prə'djuːs] vorbringen, -führen, -legen, -zeigen; *Zeugen etc.* beibringen; hervorbringen, -holen, -ziehen; *Waren, Früchte etc.* produzieren, erzeugen; herstellen; *Zinsen etc.* (ein)bringen; ⚥ verlängern; *Film etc.* herausbringen; **pro'duc·er** Erzeuger *m*, Hersteller *m*; *Film*: Produzent *m*, Produktionsleiter *m*; *thea.* Regisseur *m*; *Radio*: Spiel-, Sendeleiter *m*; (Gas)Generator *m*; **pro'duc·i·ble** erzeugbar; vorführbar; **pro'duc·ing** Produktions...; Herstellungs...

prod·uct ['prɔdʌkt] Produkt *n* (*a.* ⚥), Erzeugnis *n*; **pro·duc·tion** [prə'dʌkʃən] Hervorbringung *f*; Vorlegung *f*, Beibringung *f*; Produktion *f*, Erzeugung *f*; *thea.* Inszenierung *f*; Erzeugnis *n*, Produkt *n*; ~ *line* Fließband *n*; **pro'duc·tive** □ hervorbringend (*of acc.*); schöpferisch; produktiv, erzeugend; schaffend; ertragreich, ergiebig; fruchtbar; **pro'duc·tive·ness, pro·duc·tiv·i·ty** [prɔdʌk-'tiviti] Produktivität *f*.

prof *Am.* F [prɔf] Professor *m*.

prof·a·na·tion [prɔfə'neiʃən] Entweihung *f*; **pro·fane** [prə'fein] **1.** □ profan; weltlich; uneingeweiht; gottlos, lästerlich; **2.** entweihen, profanieren; **pro·fan·i·ty** [~'fæniti] Gott-, Ruchlosigkeit *f*; Fluchen *n*.

pro·fess [prə'fes] bekennen, erklären; sich bekennen zu; *Reue etc.* bekunden; *Beruf* ausüben, betreiben; lehren; **pro'fessed** □ erklärt, ausgesprochen; an-, vorgeblich; Berufs...; **pro'fess·ed·ly** [~sidli] erklärtermaßen.

pro·fes·sion [prə'feʃən] Bekenntnis *n*; Erklärung *f*; Beruf *m*, Stand *m*; **pro'fes·sion·al** [~ʃənl] **1.** □ Berufs..., beruflich; Amts...; berufsmäßig; freiberuflich; ~ *men pl.* Akademiker *m/pl.* **2.** Fachmann *m*; Berufskünstler *m*, -spieler *m etc.*, *bsd. Sport*: Profi *m*, Professional *m*; **pro'fes·sion·al·ism** [~ʃnəlizm] *Sport*: Berufsspielertum *n*.

pro·fes·sor [prə'fesə] Professor *m*; **pro'fes·sor·ship** Professur *f*.

prof·fer ['prɔfə] 1. anbieten; 2. Anerbieten *n.*

pro·fi·cien·cy [prə'fiʃənsi] Tüchtigkeit *f;* **pro'fi·cient 1.** □ tüchtig; geübt, bewandert (*in, at* in *dat.*); 2. Meister *m* (*in* in *dat.*).

pro·file ['prəufail] Profil *n,* Seitenansicht *f;* △ Profil *n,* Durchschnitt *m; fig.* Querschnitt *m;* Kurzbiographie *f.*

prof·it ['prɔfit] 1. Vorteil *m,* Nutzen *m,* Gewinn *m,* Profit *m,* Ertrag *m;* 2. *v/t.* j-m Nutzen bringen; *v/i.* ⁓ *by* Nutzen ziehen aus; profitieren von; *Gelegenheit* aus-, benutzen; **prof·it·a'bil·i·ty** Rentabilität *f;* '**prof·it·a·ble** □ nützlich, vorteilhaft, einträglich, gewinnbringend; '**prof·it·a·ble·ness** Nützlichkeit *f;* Einträglichkeit *f;* **prof·it·eer** [⁓'tiə] 1. Schiebergeschäfte machen; 2. Profitmacher *m,* Schieber *m; war* ⁓ Kriegsgewinnler *m;* **prof·it'eer·ing** Schiebergeschäfte *n/pl.;* '**prof·it·less** □ nutzlos; nichts einbringend; **prof·it mar·gin** Gewinnspanne *f;* **prof·it-shar·ing** ['⁓ʃɛəriŋ] Gewinnbeteiligung *f.*

prof·li·ga·cy ['prɔfligəsi] Liederlichkeit *f;* Verschwendung *f;* **prof·li·gate** ['⁓git] 1. □ verworfen; liederlich; verschwenderisch; 2. liederlicher Mensch *m.*

pro·found □ [prə'faund] tief; tiefgründig, gründlich; *fig.* dunkel; **pro'found·ness, pro·fun·di·ty** [⁓'fʌnditi] Tiefe *f* (*a. fig.*).

pro·fuse □ [prə'fju:s] verschwenderisch (*in, of* mit); übermäßig, -reich; reich(haltig); **pro'fuse·ness, pro·fu·sion** [⁓'fju:ʒən] Verschwendung *f; fig.* Überfluß *m.*

prog *sl. univ.* [prɔg] Proktor *m.*

pro·gen·i·tor [prəu'dʒenitə] Vorfahr *m,* Ahn *m;* **pro'gen·i·tress** [⁓tris] Ahne *f;* **prog·e·ny** ['prɔdʒini] Nachkommen(schaft *f*) *m/pl.;* Brut *f; fig.* Produkt *n.*

prog·no·sis ♬ [prɔg'nəusis], *pl.* **prog·no·ses** [⁓si:z] Prognose *f.*

prog·nos·tic [prɔg'nɔstik] 1. voraussagend (*of acc.*); 2. Vorzeichen *n;* **prog'nos·ti·cate** [⁓keit] voraus-, vorhersagen; **prog·nos·ti·ca·tion** Vorhersage *f.*

pro·gram, *mst* **pro·gramme** ['prəugræm] 1. Programm *n; Radio: a.* Sendung *f;* 2. programmieren; '**pro-**

gram·er, *mst* '**pro·gram·mer** *Computer:* Programmierer *m.*

prog·ress[1] ['prəugres] Fortschreiten *n;* Vorrücken *n* (*a.* ✗.); Fortgang *m,* Lauf *m;* Weiterentwicklung *f;* Fortschritt(e *pl.*) *m;* Rundreise *f e-s Fürsten; in* ⁓ im Gang.

pro·gress[2] [prə'gres] fortschreiten, vorankommen, Fortschritte machen; **pro'gres·sion** [⁓ʃən] Fortschreiten *n;* ♬ Progression *f;* **pro'gres·sion·ist** [⁓ʃnist], **pro'gress·ist** [⁓sist] *pol.* Fortschrittler *m;* **pro'gres·sive 1.** □ fortschreitend; zunehmend; progressiv; *pol.* fortschrittlich; ⁓ *form gr.* Verlaufsform *f;* 2. *pol.* Fortschrittler *m.*

pro·hib·it [prə'hibit] verbieten (*s.th. et.;* s.o. *from ger.* j-m zu *inf.*); verhindern; **pro·hi·bi·tion** [prəui-'biʃən] Verbot *n;* Prohibition *f,* Alkoholverbot *n;* **pro·hi'bi·tion·ist** [⁓ʃnist] Schutzzöllner *m; bsd. Am.* Alkoholgegner *m;* **pro·hib·i·tive** □ [prə'hibitiv] verbietend; Prohibitiv...; unerschwinglich (*Preis*); ⁓ *duty* Sperrzoll *m.*

proj·ect ['prɔdʒekt] Projekt *n;* Vorhaben *n,* Plan *m.*

pro·ject [prə'dʒekt] *v/t.* planen, entwerfen, projektieren; werfen, schleudern; ♬ projizieren; ⁓ *o.s. into* sich versetzen in (*acc.*); *v/i.* vorspringen; **pro·jec·tile 1.** ['prɔdʒiktail] Projektil *n,* Geschoß *n;* 2. [prəu'dʒektail] Wurf...; **pro·jec·tion** [prə'dʒekʃən] Werfen *n,* Wurf *m;* Entwurf *m;* Vortreiben *n;* Fortsatz *m,* Vorsprung *m;* ♬, *ast., phot.* Projektion *f;* Widerspiegelung *f* (*a. fig.*); ⁓ *room Film:* Vorführraum *m;* **pro'jec·tion·ist** [⁓ʃnist] Filmvorführer *m;* **pro'jec·tor** Plänemacher *m;* ✝ Gründer *m; opt.* Projektionsapparat *m,* Bildwerfer *m,* Projektor *m.*

pro·le·tar·i·an [prəuli'tɛəriən] 1. proletarisch; 2. Proletarier(in); **pro·le'tar·i·at,** *mst* **pro·le'tar·i·ate** [⁓riət] Proletariat *n.*

pro·lif·e·rate [prəu'lifəreit] sich stark vermehren *od.* ausbreiten; *einfache Lebewesen:* sich fortpflanzen; wuchern; **pro·lif·er'a·tion** starke Vermehrung *f od.* Ausbreitung *f;* Fortpflanzung *f;* Wuchern *n.*

pro·lif·ic [prəu'lifik] (⁓*ally*) fruchtbar; *fig.* reich (*of, in* an *dat.*).

pro·lix □ ['prəuliks] weitschweifig; **pro'lix·i·ty** Weitschweifigkeit f.
pro·logue, Am. a. **pro·log** ['prəuləg] Prolog m; Einleitung f; ~ to fig. Auftakt m od. Vorspiel n zu.
pro·long [prəu'ləŋ] verlängern; † prolongieren; **pro·lon·ga·tion** [~gei∫ən] Verlängerung f.
prom F [prəm] = promenade concert.
prom·e·nade [prəmi'naːd] 1. Promenade f; Spaziergang m; Spazierweg m; 2. promenieren (auf, in dat.); spazierenführen; ~ **con·cert** Promenadenkonzert n.
prom·i·nence ['prəminəns] Hervorragen n (a. fig.); konkr. Erhebung f, Vorsprung m; Berühmtheit f; **'prom·i·nent** □ hervorragend (a. fig.); fig. prominent.
prom·is·cu·i·ty [prəmis'kjuːiti] Verworrenheit f; Durcheinander n; Wahllosigkeit f; Promiskuität f; **pro·mis·cu·ous** □ [prə'miskjuəs] unordentlich, verworren; gemeinsam; unterschiedslos.
prom·ise ['prəmis] 1. Versprechen n; Verheißung f; fig. Aussicht f (of auf acc.); of great ~ vielversprechend; 2. v/t. versprechen; I ~ you F ich versichere Ihnen; v/i. Hoffnungen erwecken; **'prom·is·ing** □ vielversprechend, verheißungsvoll; **prom·is·so·ry** ['~sə-ri] versprechend; ~ note † Eigen-, Solawechsel m.
prom·on·to·ry ['prəməntri] Vorgebirge n.
pro·mote [prə'məut] et. fördern; j. befördern; bsd. Am. Schule: versetzen; parl. unterstützen; † gründen; bsd. Am. Verkauf durch Werbung steigern; **pro'mot·er** Förderer m; † Gründer m; Veranstalter m von Boxkämpfen etc.; **pro·'mo·tion** Förderung f; Beförderung f; † Gründung f; ~ prospects pl. Aufstiegschancen f/pl.
prompt [prəmpt] 1. □ schnell; bereit(willig); unverzüglich, prompt, umgehend, sofortig; pünktlich; 2. adv. pünktlich; 3. j. (an)treiben, bewegen (to zu); et. veranlassen; Gedanken eingeben; j-m vorsagen, einhelfen, thea. soufflieren; 4. † Ziel n; thea. Stichwort n; '**~-box** thea. Souffleurkasten m; '**prompt·er** Anreger(in); Eingeber(in); thea.

Souffleur m, Souffleuse f; **prompti·tude** ['~titjuːd], **'prompt·ness** Schnelligkeit f; Bereitschaft f.
pro·mul·gate ['prəməlgeit] verkünden, verbreiten; **pro·mul'ga·tion** Bekanntmachung f, Verbreitung f.
prone □ [prəun] mit dem Gesicht nach unten (liegend); hingestreckt; vornüber geneigt; abschüssig; ~ to fig. geneigt od. neigend zu; anfällig für; **'prone·ness** Neigung f (to zu).
prong [prəŋ] Zinke f e-r Gabel; Spitze f; Heu-, Mistgabel f; **pronged** zinkig, zackig.
pro·nom·i·nal □ gr. [prəu'nəminl] pronominal.
pro·noun gr. ['prəunaun] Fürwort n, Pronomen n.
pro·nounce [prə'nauns] v/t. aussprechen; verkünden; behaupten; erklären für; v/i. sich erklären (on über acc.); **pro'nounced** □ [adv. ~idli] ausgesprochen; entschieden; **pro'nounce·ment** Erklärung f.
pro·nounc·ing [prə'naunsiŋ] Aussprache... [gleich.]
pron·to Am. F ['prəntəu] sofort,]
pro·nun·ci·a·tion [prənʌnsi'ei∫ən] Aussprache f.
proof [pruːf] 1. Beweis m; Probe f, Versuch m; typ. Korrekturbogen m; typ., phot. Probeabzug m; ⚗ Normalstärke f alkoholischer Getränke; in ~ of zum od. als Beweis (gen.); 2. fest (against, to gegen); sicher; undurchlässig; in Zssgn: ...fest, ...dicht, ...sicher; fig. gefeit (against gegen); 3. undurchlässig machen, wasserdicht machen, imprägnieren; '**~-read** Korrektur lesen; '**~-read·er** typ. Korrektor m; '**~-sheet** typ. Korrekturbogen m; '**~-spir·it** ⚗ Normalweingeist m.
prop [prəp] 1. Stütze f (a. fig.); Stützbalken m; ⚒ pit-~s pl. Grubenhölzer n/pl.; 2. a. ~ up (unter)stützen.
prop·a·gan·da [prəpə'gændə] Propaganda f; **prop·a'gan·dist** Propagandist(in); **prop·a·gate** ['~geit] (sich) fortpflanzen; fig. aus-, verbreiten; **prop·a'ga·tion** Fortpflanzung f; Verbreitung f; '**prop·a·ga·tor** Fortpflanzer m; Verbreiter m.
pro·pel [prə'pel] (vorwärts-, an-) treiben; **pro'pel·lant** Treibstoff m; **pro'pel·lent** treibende Kraft f;

Treibstoff *m*; **pro'pel·ler** Propeller *m*, (Schiffs-, Luft)Schraube *f*; ~ shaft Kardanwelle *f*; **pro'pel·ling** Trieb...; ~ pencil Drehbleistift *m*.

pro·pen·si·ty [prə'pensiti] Hang *m*, Neigung (to, for zu).

prop·er □ ['prɔpə] eigen; (oft nach dem su.) eigentlich; eigentümlich (to dat.); passend, geeignet (for für); angemessen; genau; anständig; ordentlich; F richtig; ~ name Eigenname *m*; **'prop·er·ty** Eigentum *n*, Besitztum *n*; Vermögen *n*; Eigenschaft *f*; ⚖ Eigentumsrecht *n*; properties pl. thea. Requisiten *n/pl.*; **'prop·er·ty-man** thea. Requisiteur *m*; **'prop·er·ty-tax** Vermögenssteuer *f*.

proph·e·cy ['prɔfisi] Prophezeiung *f*; **proph·e·sy** ['~sai] prophezeien; weissagen; voraussagen.

proph·et ['prɔfit] Prophet *m*; Vorkämpfer *m*; **'proph·et·ess** Prophetin *f*; **pro·phet·ic**, **pro·phet·i·cal** □ [prə'fetik(əl)] prophetisch.

pro·phy·lac·tic ⚕ [prɔfi'læktik] (~ally) vorbeugend(es Mittel *n*).

pro·pin·qui·ty [prə'piŋkwiti] Nähe *f*; nahe Verwandtschaft *f*.

pro·pi·ti·ate [prə'piʃieit] günstig stimmen; versöhnen; **pro·pi·ti·a·tion** Versöhnung *f*; Sühne *f*; **pro'pi·ti·a·tor** [~ʃieitə] Versöhner *m*; **pro'pi·ti·a·to·ry** □ [~ʃiətəri] versöhnend; Sühn(e)...

pro·pi·tious □ [prə'piʃəs] gnädig; günstig; **pro'pi·tious·ness** Gnade *f*; Gunst *f* (a. des Klimas).

pro·po·nent [prə'pəunənt] Verfechter *m*, Befürworter *m*.

pro·por·tion [prə'pɔ:ʃən] 1. Verhältnis *n*; Gleichmaß *n*; ⚖, ⚗ Proportion *f*; Anteil *m*; Teil *m*; ~s pl. (Aus)Maße *n/pl.*; 2. in ein Verhältnis bringen (to zu); **pro'por·tion·al** 1. □ proportional, verhältnismäßig; s. proportionate; 2. ⚖ Proportionale *f*; **pro'por·tion·ate** □ [~ʃnit] angemessen; im richtigen Verhältnis (stehend) (to zu); **pro'por·tioned** ...proportioniert.

pro·pos·al [prə'pəuzəl] Vorschlag *m*, (a. Heirats)Antrag *m*; Angebot *n*; Plan *m*; **pro'pose** *v/t.* vorschlagen; e-n Toast ausbringen auf (acc.); ~ to o.s. sich vornehmen; ~ a motion e-n Antrag einbringen; *v/i.* beabsichtigen; e-n Heiratsantrag machen

(to *j-m*); **pro'pos·er** Antragsteller (-in); **pro·po·si·tion** [prɔpə'ziʃən] Vorschlag *m*, Antrag *m*; Behauptung *f*; phls., ⚖ (Lehr)Satz *m*; Frage *f*, Problem *n*; sl. Geschäft *n*; Sache *f*.

pro·pound [prə'paund] Frage etc. vorlegen; vorschlagen.

pro·pri·e·tar·y [prə'praiətəri] 1. e-m Besitzer gehörig; gesetzlich geschützt (bsd. Arzneimittel); Besitz(er)...; ~ name Markenbezeichnung *f*; 2. Eigentümer *m/pl.*; **pro'pri·e·tor** Eigentümer *m*, Besitzer *m*; **pro'pri·e·tress** Eigentümerin *f*, Besitzerin *f*; **pro'pri·e·ty** Richtigkeit *f*; Schicklichkeit *f*; the proprieties pl. die Anstandsformen *f/pl.*

props F thea. [prɔps] pl. Requisiten *n/pl.*

pro·pul·sion ⊕ [prə'pʌlʃən] Antrieb *m*; **pro'pul·sive** [~siv] (vorwärts)treibend; Trieb...

pro·rate Am. [prəu'reit] anteilmäßig verteilen.

pro·ro·ga·tion parl. [prəurə'geiʃən] Vertagung *f*; **pro·rogue** parl. [prə'rəug] (sich) vertagen.

pro·sa·ic [prəu'zeiik] (~ally) fig. prosaisch, nüchtern, trocken.

pro·scribe [prəus'kraib] ächten.

pro·scrip·tion [prəus'kripʃən] Ächtung *f*; Acht *f*; Verbannung *f*.

prose [prəuz] 1. Prosa *f*; 2. prosaisch; Prosa...; 3. langweilig erzählen.

pros·e·cute ['prɔsikju:t] e-n Plan etc. verfolgen; Gewerbe etc. betreiben; ⚖ gerichtlich verfolgen, belangen; verklagen (for wegen); **pros·e·cu·tion** Verfolgung *f* e-s Plans etc.; Fortsetzung *f*; Betreiben *n* e-s Gewerbes etc.; ⚖ gerichtliche Verfolgung *f*; witness for the ~ Belastungszeuge *m*; **'pros·e·cu·tor** ⚖ Kläger *m*; Anklagevertreter *m*; public ~ Staatsanwalt *m*.

pros·e·lyte eccl. ['prɔsilait] Proselyt(in); **pros·e·lyt·ism** ['~litizəm] Proselytentum *n*; Bekehrungseifer *m*; **'pros·e·lyt·ize** (v/t. j. zum) Proselyten machen.

pros·er ['prəuzə] langweiliger Erzähler *m*.

pros·o·dy ['prɔsədi] Verslehre *f*.

pros·pect 1. ['prɔspekt] Aussicht *f* (a. fig.); Anblick *m*, Ansicht *f*; ✝ bsd. Am. Interessent *m*, möglicher

Kunde *m*; have in ~ in Aussicht haben; hold out a ~ of *s.th.* et. in Aussicht stellen; **2.** [prəs'pekt] ⚒ schürfen (for nach); bohren (for nach Öl); **pro'spec·tive** □ vorausblickend; voraussichtlich; ~ buyer Kauflustige *m*; **pros'pec·tor** ⚒ Prospektor *m*, Schürfer *m*; Gold-, Ölsucher *m*; **pro'spec·tus** [~təs] (Werbe)Prospekt *m*.

pros·per ['prɔspə] *v/i.* Erfolg haben, gedeihen, florieren, blühen; *v/t.* begünstigen, segnen; **pros·per·i·ty** [~'periti] Gedeihen *n*; Wohlfahrt *f*, -stand *m*; Glück *n*; *fig.* Blüte *f*; **pros·per·ous** □ ['~pərəs] glücklich, gedeihlich; wohlhabend; *fig.* blühend; günstig (*Wind etc.*).

pros·tate ['prɔsteit], *a.* ~ gland Prostata *f*, Vorsteherdrüse *f*.

pros·ti·tute ['prɔstitju:t] **1.** Prostituierte *f*, Dirne *f*; **2.** zur Dirne machen; (öffentlich der Schande) preisgeben, feilbieten (*a. fig.*); **pros·ti·tu·tion** Prostitution *f*, gewerbsmäßige Unzucht *f*; Dirnenwesen *n*; *fig.* Entehrung *f*, Schändung *f*.

pros·trate 1. ['prɔstreit] hingestreckt; erschöpft; daniederliegend; demütig; gebrochen; **2.** [prɔs'treit] niederwerfen; *fig.* niederschmettern; entkräften; **pros·tra·tion** Niederwerfung *f*; Fußfall *m*; *fig.* Demütigung *f*; Entkräftung *f*.

pros·y □ *fig.* ['prəuzi] prosaisch; langweilig.

pro·tag·o·nist [prəu'tægənist] *thea.* Träger(in) der Handlung; Hauptfigur *f*; *fig.* Vorkämpfer(in).

pro·tect [prə'tekt] schützen (*from* vor *dat.*); beschützen; ✝ *Wechsel* einlösen; **pro'tec·tion** Schutz *m*; Wirtschaftsschutz *m*, Schutzzoll *m*; **pro'tec·tion·ist 1.** Schutzzöllner *m*; **2.** protektionistisch; **pro'tec·tive** schützend; Schutz...; ~ custody Schutzhaft *f*; ~ duty Schutzzoll *m*; **pro'tec·tor** Schützer *m* (*a. Vorrichtung*); Schutz-, Schirmherr *m*; *hist.* Protektor *m*; **pro'tec·tor·ate** [~tərit] Protektorat *n*; **pro'tec·to·ry** Fürsorgeanstalt *f*; **pro'tec·tress** Beschützerin *f*, Schutz-, Schirmherrin *f*.

pro·té·gé ['prəuteʒei] Protégé *m*, Schützling *m*. [(*Eiweißstoff*).)

pro·te·in ⚗ ['prəuti:n] Protein *n*)

pro·test 1. ['prəutest] Protest *m*; Ein-, Widerspruch *m*; in ~ against aus Protest gegen; enter *od.* make a ~ Einspruch erheben; **2.** [prə'test] *v/t.* beteuern; *Wechsel* protestieren; reklamieren; *v/i.* protestieren, sich verwahren, Einspruch erheben (*against* gegen).

Prot·es·tant ['prɔtistənt] **1.** protestantisch; **2.** Protestant(in); **'Prot·es·tant·ism** Protestantismus *m*.

prot·es·ta·tion [prəutes'teiʃən] Beteuerung *f*; Verwahrung *f*.

pro·to·col ['prəutəkɔl] **1.** Protokoll *n*; **2.** protokollieren.

pro·ton *phys.* ['prəutɔn] Proton *n* (*positiv geladenes Elementarteilchen*).

pro·to·plasm *biol.* ['prəutəuplæzəm] Protoplasma *n*.

pro·to·type ['prəutəutaip] Urbild *n*; Prototyp *m*, Modell *n*.

pro·tract [prə'trækt] in die Länge *od.* hinziehen; **pro'trac·tion** Hinziehen *n*; Hinausschieben *n*; **pro'trac·tor** ⟁ Winkelmesser *m*.

pro·trude [prə'tru:d] (sich) (her-) vorstrecken; (her)vorstehen, -treten; **pro'tru·sion** [~ʒən] Vorstrecken *n*; (Her)Vorstehen *n*, -treten *n*.

pro·tu·ber·ance [prə'tju:bərəns] Hervortreten *n*; Auswuchs *m*, Höcker *m*; **pro'tu·ber·ant** hervorstehend.

proud □ [praud] stolz (*of* auf *acc.*; to *inf.* zu *inf.*); ~ flesh 🌶 wildes Fleisch *n*; do s.o. ~ F j-m große Ehre erweisen.

prov·a·ble □ ['pru:vəbl] be-, nachweisbar; **prove** *v/t.* beweisen; er-, nachweisen; prüfen; erproben; erleben, erfahren; *v/i.* sich herausstellen (als), sich erweisen (als); ausfallen; ~ true (*false*) sich (nicht) bestätigen, sich als richtig (falsch) herausstellen; he has ~d to be the heir es hat sich herausgestellt, daß er der Erbe ist; **prov·en** ['~vən] erwiesen; bewährt.

prov·e·nance ['prɔvinəns] Herkunft *f* e-r Sache.

prov·en·der ['prɔvində] *Vieh*-Futter *n* (F *co. a. von Menschen*).

prov·erb ['prɔvə:b] Sprichwort *n*; be a ~ sprichwörtlich *od. b.s.* berüchtigt sein (*for* wegen); **pro·ver·bi·al** □ [prə'və:bjəl] sprichwörtlich.

provide

pro·vide [prə'vaid] *v/t.* besorgen, beschaffen, liefern; bereitstellen; *j.* versehen, versorgen, ausstatten (*with* mit); ⚖ vorsehen, festsetzen; ~d *school* Gemeindeschule *f*; *v/i.* sorgen (*for* für); vorsorgen (*against* gegen; *for* für); ~ *for Maßnahmen etc.* vorsehen; *Gelder etc.* bereitstellen; ~d (*that*) vorausgesetzt, daß; sofern.

prov·i·dence ['prɔvidəns] Vorsehung *f*; Voraussicht *f*; Vorsorge *f*; '**prov·i·dent** □ vorausblickend; vorsorglich; haushälterisch; **prov·i·den·tial** □ [~'denʃəl] durch die *göttliche* Vorsehung bewirkt; glücklich.

pro·vid·er [prə'vaidə] Ernährer *m der Familie*; Lieferant *m*.

prov·ince ['prɔvins] Provinz *f*; *fig.* Gebiet *n*, Fach *n*; Amt *n*, Aufgabe *f*.

pro·vin·cial [prə'vinʃəl] **1.** provinziell; Provinz...; ländlich, kleinstädtisch; **2.** Provinzbewohner(in); *contp.* Provinzler(in); **pro'vin·cial·ism** Provinzialismus *m*; Provinzlertum *n*.

pro·vi·sion [prə'viʒən] **1.** Beschaffung *f*, Bereitstellung *f*; Vorsorge *f*; ⚖ Bestimmung *f*; Vorkehrung *f*, Maßnahme *f*; Vorrat *m*, Lager *n*; ~s *pl.* Proviant *m*, Lebensmittel *n/pl.*; make ~ *for* Vorkehrungen treffen für, sorgen für; ~ *merchant* Lebensmittelhändler *m*; **2.** verproviantieren; **pro'vi·sion·al** [~ʒənl] □ vorläufig, provisorisch.

pro·vi·so [prə'vaizəu] Vorbehalt *m*; Klausel *f*; **pro'vi·so·ry** [~zəri] provisorisch.

Pro·vo ['prɔvəu] Mitglied *n* der provisorischen irisch-republikanischen Armee.

prov·o·ca·tion [prɔvə'keiʃən] Herausforderung *f*; **pro·voc·a·tive** [prə'vɔkətiv] **1.** herausfordernd; (auf)reizend (*of* zu); **2.** Reiz(mittel *n*) *m*.

pro·voke [prə'vəuk] auf-, anreizen; herausfordern, provozieren; hervorrufen; **pro'vok·ing** □ herausfordernd; empörend.

prov·ost ['prɔvəst] Leiter *m e-s College*; *schott.* Bürgermeister *m*; ✕ [prə'vəu] ~ *marshal* Kommandeur *m* der Militärpolizei.

prow ⚓ [prau] Bug *m*, Schiffsschnabel *m*.

prow·ess ['prauis] Tapferkeit *f*.

prowl [praul] **1.** *v/i.* umherstreifen; *v/t.* durchstreifen; **2.** Umherstreifen *n*; ~ *car Am.* Streifenwagen *m der Polizei.*

prox·i·mate □ ['prɔksimit] nächst, unmittelbar; **prox'im·i·ty** Nähe *f*; **prox·i·mo** ['~məu] ✝ (des) nächsten Monats.

prox·y ['prɔksi] Stellvertreter *m*; Stellvertretung *f*; Vollmacht *f*; *by* ~ in Vertretung. [Zimperliese *f*.\]

prude [pru:d] Prüde *f*, Spröde *f*,\

pru·dence ['pru:dəns] Klugheit *f*, Vorsicht *f*; '**pru·dent** □ klug, vorsichtig; **pru·den·tial** □ [~'denʃəl] klug; Klugheits...; vorsichtig.

prud·er·y ['pru:dəri] Prüderie *f*, Sprödigkeit *f*, Zimperlichkeit *f*; '**prud·ish** □ prüde, zimperlich.

prune¹ [pru:n] Backpflaume *f*.

prune² [~] *Baum* beschneiden (*a. fig.*); *a.* ~ *away*, ~ *off* wegschneiden.

prun·ing...: '~**hook**, '~**knife** Gartenmesser *n*; '~**saw** Baumsäge *f*.

pru·ri·ence, pru·ri·en·cy ['pruəriəns(i)] Lüsternheit *f*, Laszivität *f*; '**pru·ri·ent** □ geil (*a.* ⚥), lüstern, lasziv.

Prus·sian ['prʌʃən] **1.** preußisch; ~ *blue* Preußisch-, Berlinerblau *n*; **2.** Preuße *m*, Preußin *f*.

prus·sic ac·id 🜍 ['prʌsik'æsid] Blausäure *f*.

pry¹ [prai] **1.** ~ *open* aufbrechen; ~ *up* hochheben; **2.** Hebelbewegung *f*.

pry² [~] neugierig gucken; ~ *into* s-e Nase stecken in (*acc.*); '**pry·ing** □ neugierig.

psalm [sɑ:m] Psalm *m*; '**psalm·ist** Psalmist *m*; **psal·mo·dy** ['sælmədi] Psalmengesang *m*.

Psal·ter ['sɔ:ltə] Psalter *m*.

pse·phol·o·gy [pse'fɔlədʒi] Analyse *f* von Wahlergebnissen *od.* -trends.

pseu·do... ['psju:dəu] Pseudo..., falsch; **pseu·do·nym** ['~dənim] Pseudonym *n*, Deckname *m*; **pseu·don·y·mous** □ [~'dɔniməs] pseudonym.

pshaw [pʃɔ:] pah!

pso·ri·a·sis 🜊 [psɔ'raiəsis] Schuppenflechte *f*.

psy·che ['saiki] Psyche *f*, Seele *f*; Mentalität *f*.

psy·chi·a·trist [sai'kaiətrist] Psychiater *m*; **psy'chi·a·try** Psychiatrie *f*.

psy·chic, psy·chi·cal □ ['saikik(əl)]

puffy

psychisch, seelisch; **'psy·chics** *sg.* Seelenforschung *f*, -kunde *f*.

psy·cho-a·nal·y·sis [saikəuə'næləsis] Psychoanalyse *f*; **psy·cho-ana·lyst** [‿'ænəlist] Psychoanalytiker (-in).

psy·cho·log·i·cal ☐ [saikə'lɔdʒikəl] psychologisch; **psy·chol·o·gist** [sai'kɔlədʒist] Psychologe *m*, Psychologin *f*; **psy'chol·o·gy** Psychologie *f* (*Seelenkunde*).

psy·cho·path ['saikəupæθ] Psychopath(in).

psy·cho·sis [sai'kəusis] Psychose *f*, Seelenstörung *f*.

psy·cho·ther·a·py ['saikəu'θerəpi] Psychotherapie *f*.

pto·maine ⚗ ['təumein] Ptomain *n* (*Leichengift*).

pub F [pʌb] Kneipe *f*, Wirtschaft *f*.

pu·ber·ty ['pju:bəti] Geschlechtsreife *f*, Pubertät *f*.

pu·bes·cence [pju:'besns] Geschlechtsreife *f*; **pu'bes·cent** geschlechtsreif werdend; ⚘ flaumhaarig.

pub·lic ['pʌblik] **1.** ☐ öffentlich; staatlich, Staats...; allbekannt; ‿ *address system* öffentliche Lautsprecheranlage *f*; ‿ *holiday* gesetzlicher Feiertag *m*; ‿ *man* Mann *m* der Öffentlichkeit; ‿ *spirit* Gemeinsinn *m*; *s. utility*; *works*; **2.** *sg. u. pl.* Publikum *n*; Öffentlichkeit *f*, Welt *f*, Leute *pl.*; Leserschaft *f*; F Kneipe *f*; *in* ‿ öffentlich; **pub·li·can** ['‿kən] Gastwirt *m*; *hist.* Zöllner *m*; **pub·li·ca·tion** [‿'keiʃən] Bekanntmachung *f*; Veröffentlichung *f e-s Werkes*; Verlagswerk *n*; *monthly* ‿ Monatsschrift *f*; **pub·lic house** Wirtshaus *n*; **pub·li·cist** ['‿sist] Publizist *m*, Tagesschriftsteller *m*; **pub·lic·i·ty** [‿'lisiti] Öffentlichkeit *f*; Reklame *f*, Propaganda *f*, Werbung *f*; Publicity *f*; ‿ *agent* Werbe-, Reklameagent *m*; **pub·li·cize** ['‿saiz] bekanntmachen; werben für.

pub·lic...: ‿ **li·bra·ry** Volksbücherei *f*; '‿-'**pri·vate** gemischtwirtschaftlich; ‿ **re·la·tions** *pl.* Verhältnis *n* zur Öffentlichkeit; Öffentlichkeitsarbeit *f*, Public Relations *pl.*; ‿ **school** Public School *f*, Internatsschule *f*; '‿-'**spir·it·ed** ☐ sozial gesinnt.

pub·lish ['pʌbliʃ] bekanntmachen, veröffentlichen; *Buch etc.* herausgeben, verlegen; **'pub·lish·er** Herausgeber *m*, Verleger *m*; *Am.* Besitzer *m* eines Zeitungsverlags; ‿*s pl.* Verlag(sanstalt *f*) *m*; **'pub·lish·ing** Herausgabe *f*; Verlag *m*; *attr.* Verlags...; ‿ *house* Verlag *m*.

puce [pju:s] braunrot.

puck [pʌk] Puck *m*, Kobold *m*; *Eishockey*: Puck *m*, Scheibe *f*.

puck·a ['pʌkə] echt; solide.

puck·er ['pʌkə] **1.** Bausch *m*; Falte *f*; **2.** *a.* ‿ *up* falten; Falten werfen; runzeln.

puck·ish ☐ ['pʌkiʃ] koboldhaft.

pud·ding ['pudiŋ] Pudding *m*; Süßspeise *f*; Auflauf *m*; Wurst *f*; *black* ‿ Blutwurst *f*; '‿-face Mondgesicht *n*.

pud·dle ['pʌdl] **1.** Pfütze *f*; ⊕ Lehmschlag *m*; **2.** *v/t.* ⊕ mit Lehmschlag dichtmachen; *Stahl* puddeln; zementieren; *v/i.* man(t)schen; **'pud·dler** ⊕ Puddler *m*; **'pud·dling-fur·nace** ⊕ Puddelofen *m*.

pu·den·cy ['pju:dənsi] Verschämtheit *f*; **pu·den·da** [pju:'dendə] *pl.* Schamgegend *f* (*äußere Geschlechtsteile, bsd. e-r Frau*); **'pu·dent** verschämt.

pudg·y F ['pʌdʒi] dicklich.

pueb·lo [pu'ebləu] Pueblo *m*, Dorf *n*.

pu·er·ile ☐ ['pjuərail] knabenhaft, kindisch; **pu·er·il·i·ty** [‿'riliti] Knabenhaftigkeit *f*; Kinderei *f*.

puff [pʌf] **1.** Hauch *m*; Windstoß *m*; Zug *m beim Rauchen*; (*Dampf-*, *Rauch*)Wölkchen *n*; *Bäckerei*: Windbeutel *m*; Puffe *f* (*als Besatz etc.*); Puderquaste *f*; (*aufdringliche*) Reklame *f*; **2.** *v/t.* (*von sich*) blasen, pusten; *a.* ‿ *at Pfeife etc.* paffen; *oft* ‿ *out*, ‿ *up* aufblasen, -blähen (*a. fig.*); außer Atem bringen; anpreisen; ‿ *up Preise* hochtreiben; ‿*ed up fig.* aufgeblasen, eingebildet; ‿*ed eyes pl.* geschwollene Augen *n/pl.*; ‿*ed sleeve* Puffärmel *m*; *v/i.* puffen; pusten, keuchen; '‿-box Puderdose *f*; **'puff·er** Marktschreier *m*; Preistreiber *m*; **'puff·er·y** Marktschreierei *f*; **'puffi·ness** Dickheit *f*; **'puff·ing** Marktschreierei *f*; Preistreiberei *f*; **puff paste** Blätterteig *m*; **'puff·y** böig (*Wind*); kurzatmig; geschwollen; dick; bauschig (*Ärmel*).

pug [pʌg], '**~-dog** Mops *m*.
pu·gil·ism ['pjuːdʒilizəm] Faustkampf *m*; '**pu·gil·ist** Boxer *m*.
pug·na·cious [pʌg'neiʃəs] kämpferisch; kampflustig; streitsüchtig;
pug·nac·i·ty [~'næsiti] Kampflust *f*; Streitsucht *f*.
pug-nose ['pʌgnəuz] Stupsnase *f*.
puis·ne ⚸ ['pjuːni] jünger *an Rang*; Unter...
pu·is·sant ['pjuːisnt] mächtig, einflußreich.
puke [pjuːk] (sich) erbrechen.
pule [pjuːl] piepsen; wimmern.
pull [pul] **1.** Zug *m*; Ruck *m*; Anziehung(skraft) *f*; *typ.* Abzug *m*; Ruderfahrt *f*, -partie *f*; Griff *m*, Schwengel *m*; Vorteil *m* (*of* über *acc.*); *sl.* heimlicher Einfluß *m* (*with* auf *acc.*), Beziehungen *f/pl.* (*with* zu); ~ *at the bottle sl.* Zug *m* aus der Flasche; ~ *fastener* Reißverschluß *m*; **2.** *v/t.* ziehen; zerren; rupfen; reißen; zupfen; ziehen *etc.* an (*dat.*); *Obst* pflücken; *Rennsport:* *Pferd* zügeln, pullen; *typ. Fahne* abziehen; ⚓ rudern; ~ *one's weight* sein volles Teil leisten; sich ins Zeug legen; ~ *about* hin- u. herzerren; ~ *down* ab-, niederreißen; ~ *in Ausgaben* kürzen; *sl.* festnehmen; ~ *off* schaffen, zustande bringen; ~ *round* wiederherstellen; ~ *through j.* durchbringen; ~ *o.s. together sich* zs.-nehmen; ~ *up Wagen* anhalten; *v/i.* ziehen (*at an dat.*); zerren, reißen; ⚓ rudern, pullen; fahren, sich bewegen; ~ *in* einfahren (*Zug*); ~ *out* her-, hinausfahren; ausscheren; ~ *round* sich erholen; ~ *through* sich erholen; durchkommen; ~ *together* zs.arbeiten; ~ *up* (an)halten; vorfahren; bremsen; ~ *up with*, ~ *up to* einholen; '**pull·er** Zieher *m*, Reißer *m*; Schlager *m*, Zugartikel *m*.
pul·let ['pulit] Hühnchen *n*.
pul·ley ⊕ ['puli] Rolle *f*, Flasche *f*; Riemenscheibe *f*; *a.* set *of* ~s Flaschenzug *m*.
pull-in ['pulin] = *pull-up*.
Pull·man car ⚏ ['pulmən'kaː] Pullmanwagen *m* (*Salon- u. Schlafwagen*).
pull...: '**~-out** Zeitschriftenbeilage *f*; ✕ (Truppen)Abzug *m*; '**~-o·ver** Pullover *m*; '**~-up** Halteplatz *m*, Raststätte *f*.

pul·mo·nar·y *anat.* ['pʌlmənəri] Lungen...
pulp [pʌlp] **1.** Brei *m*; *Frucht-, Zahn*-Mark *n*; ⊕ Papierbrei *m*, Pulpe *f*; *a.* ~ *magazine Am.* Schundillustrierte *f*; **2.** breiig machen *od.* werden; *Papier* einstampfen.
pul·pit ['pulpit] Kanzel *f*.
pulp·y □ ['pʌlpi] breiig; fleischig.
pul·sate [pʌl'seit] pulsieren; pochen, schlagen; **pul·sa·tile** ♪ ['~sətail] Schlag...; **pul·sa·tion** [~'seiʃən] Pulsieren *n etc.*; Pulsschlag *m*.
pulse[1] [pʌls] **1.** Puls(schlag) *m*; **2.** pulsieren; pochen, schlagen.
pulse[2] [~] Hülsenfrüchte *f/pl.*
pul·ver·i·za·tion [pʌlvərai'zeiʃən] Pulverisierung *f etc.*; '**pul·ver·ize** *v/t.* pulverisieren, zu Staub machen; *fig.* zermalmen; *v/i.* zu Staub werden; '**pul·ver·iz·er** Zerstäuber *m*.
pu·ma *zo.* ['pjuːmə] Puma *m*. [*m.*]
pum·ice ['pʌmis], *a.* ~-stone Bimsstein *m*. [bearbeiten.]
pum·mel ['pʌml] mit den Fäusten
pump[1] [pʌmp] **1.** Pumpe *f*; *attr.* Pumpen...; **2.** pumpen; *F j.* ausholen, -horchen; *sl. j.* auspumpen (*erschöpfen*).
pump[2] [~] Pumps *m* (*Damenschuh*).
pump·kin ♣ ['pʌmpkin] Kürbis *m*.
pump-room ['pʌmprum] Trinkhalle *f in Badeorten*.
pun [pʌn] **1.** Wortspiel *n*; **2.** ein Wortspiel machen.
Punch[1] [pʌntʃ] Hanswurst *m*, Kasperle *n*, *m*; ~ *and Judy show* ['dʒuːdi] Kasperletheater *n*; *be as pleased as* ~ F sich freuen wie ein Schneekönig.
punch[2] [~] ⊕ Punze(n *m*) *f*, Locheisen *n*, Locher *m*; Dorn *m*; Lochzange *f*; **2.** punzen, durchbohren, -schlagen; lochen; ~(ed) *card* Lochkarte *f*.
punch[3] [~] **1.** (Faust)Schlag *m*; F Schlagkraft *f*; *fig.* Energie *f*, Schwung *m*; **2.** knuffen, puffen; *Am. Vieh* treiben, hüten.
punch[4] [~] Punsch *m*.
punch-drunk ['pʌntʃdrʌŋk] *Boxen:* von vielen Schlägen benommen; *fig.* F ganz benommen.
pun·cheon ['pʌntʃən] Stützpfosten *m*; Puncheon *n* (*Faß von ca. 320 l*).
punch·er ['pʌntʃə] Locheisen *n*, Locher *m*; F Schläger *m*; *Am.*

Cowboy *m*; **'punch·ing-ball** Punchingball *m der Boxer*; **punch line** Pointe *f e-s Witzes*; **'punch-up** F Schlägerei *f*.

punc·til·i·o [pʌŋk'tiliəu] heikler *od.* kitzliger Punkt *m*; = *punctiliousness*; **punc·til·i·ous** [.'tiliəs] peinlich (genau), spitzfindig; förmlich; **punc'til·i·ous·ness** peinliche Genauigkeit *f*; Förmlichkeit *f*.

punc·tu·al □ ['pʌŋktjuəl] pünktlich; **punc·tu·al·i·ty** [.'æliti] Pünktlichkeit *f*.

punc·tu·ate ['pʌŋktjueit] (inter-) punktieren; *fig.* unterbrechen; **punc·tu·a·tion** Interpunktion *f*.

punc·ture ['pʌŋktʃə] 1. Punktur *f*, Stich *m*; *mot. etc.* Reifenpanne *f*; 2. (durch)stechen; platzen *(Reifen)*.

pun·dit ['pʌndit] Pandit *m*, gelehrter Brahmane *m*; F gelehrtes Haus *n*; Koryphäe *m*, *f*.

pun·gen·cy ['pʌndʒənsi] Schärfe *f* (*a. fig.*); **'pun·gent** stechend, beißend, scharf.

pun·ish ['pʌniʃ] (be)strafen; *j-m* hart zusetzen; *e-r Speise* tüchtig zusprechen; **'pun·ish·a·ble** □ strafbar; **'pun·ish·er** Bestrafer(in); **'pun·ish·ment** Strafe *f*, Bestrafung *f*; Schaden *m*. [Straf...]

pu·ni·tive ['pju:nitiv] strafend;)

punk[1] *Am.* [pʌŋk] 1. Zunderholz *n*; Zündmasse *f*; F Mist *m*, Käse *m*; 2. *sl.* miserabel, nichts wert.

punk[2] [pʌŋk] Anhänger *m* des *punk rock* (*der auch durch schockierende Kleidung auffällt*); ~ **rock** *s. Art pop music mit gesucht schockierender Wirkung*.

pun·ster ['pʌnstə] Wortspielmacher *m*. [kahn *m*; 2. staken.)

punt[1] ⚓ [pʌnt] 1. Punt *n*, Stak-)

punt[2] [.] *Spiel*: setzen.

pu·ny □ ['pju:ni] winzig; schwächlich.

pup [pʌp] 1. = *puppy*; 2. (Junge) werfen.

pu·pa *zo.* ['pju:pə] Puppe *f*.

pu·pil ['pju:pl] *anat.* Pupille *f*; Schüler(in), Zögling *m*; Mündel *n*; **pu·pil·(l)age** ['~pilidʒ] Schüler-, Lehrjahre *n/pl.*; Unmündigkeit *f*.

pup·pet ['pʌpit] Marionette *f* (*a. fig.*); **'~-show** Marionettentheater *n*, Puppenspiel *n*.

pup·py ['pʌpi] Welpe *m*, junger Hund *m*; *fig.* Laffe *m*, Schnösel *m*.

pur·blind ['pə:blaind] halbblind; *fig.* kurzsichtig.

pur·chase ['pə:tʃəs] 1. (An-, Ein-) Kauf *m*; Erwerb(ung *f*) *m*; Anschaffung *f*; ⊕ Hebevorrichtung *f*; Halt *m*; *fig.* Ansatzpunkt *m*; *make* ~s Einkäufe machen; *at twenty years'* ~ zum Zwanzigfachen des Jahresertrags; *his life is not worth an hour's* ~ er hat keine Stunde mehr zu leben; 2. kaufen; erwerben; *fig.* erkaufen; anschaffen; ⊕ aufwinden; **'pur·chas·er** Käufer(in); Abnehmer(in).

pure □ [pjuə] *allg.* rein; *engS.* lauter; echt; gediegen; theoretisch (*Physik etc.*); **'~-bred** *Am.* reinrassig; **pu·rée** ['pjuərei] pürierte Gemüsesuppe *f*; Pürée *n*; **'pure·ness** Reinheit *f*.

pur·ga·tion [pə:'geiʃən] *mst fig.* Reinigung *f*; ☞ Abführen *n*; **pur·ga·tive** ☞ ['~gətiv] 1. abführend; 2. Abführmittel *n*; **'pur·ga·to·ry** *eccl.* Fegefeuer *n*.

purge [pə:dʒ] 1. ☞ Abführmittel *n*; *pol.* Säuberung(saktion) *f*; 2. *mst fig.* reinigen (*of, from* von); *pol.* säubern; läutern; ☞ abführen.

pu·ri·fi·ca·tion [pjuərifi'keiʃən] Reinigung *f*; **pu·ri·fi·er** ['~faiə] Reiniger *m* (*bsd. Gerät*); **pu·ri·fy** ['~fai] reinigen (*of, from* von); ⊕ *u. fig.* läutern.

Pu·ri·tan ['pjuəritən] 1. Puritaner (-in); 2. puritanisch; **pu·ri·tan·ic** [.'tænik] (.ally) puritanisch; **Pu·ri·tan·ism** ['~tənizəm] Puritanismus *m*.

pu·ri·ty ['pjuəriti] Reinheit *f* (*a. fig.*).

purl[1] [pə:l] Golddraht *m*; Zäckchen (-borte *f*) *n*; Häkelkante *f*.

purl[2] [.] 1. Murmeln *n des Baches*; 2. murmeln.

purl·er F ['pə:lə] schwerer Sturz *m*; *come a* ~ der Länge nach hinfallen.

pur·lieus ['pə:lju:z] *pl.* Umgebung *f*.

pur·loin [pə:'lɔin] entwenden; **pur·'loin·er** Dieb *m*.

pur·ple ['pə:pl] 1. purpurn, purpurrot; ~ *passage* Glanzstelle *f*; 2. Purpur *m*; 3. (sich) purpurn färben; **'pur·plish** purpurartig.

pur·port ['pə:pət] 1. Sinn *m*; Inhalt *m*; 2. besagen; beabsichtigen; vorgeben.

pur·pose ['pə:pəs] 1. Vorsatz *m*; Absicht *f*, Zweck *m*; Wirkung *f*;

Entschlußkraft *f; for the* ~ *of* um zu; *on* ~ absichtlich; *to the* ~ zur Sache (gehörig), zweckdienlich; *to no* ~ vergebens, umsonst, sinn-, zwecklos; **2.** vorhaben, beabsichtigen, bezwecken; ~-'**built** zweckmäßig *od.* für einen bestimmten Zweck gebaut; **pur·pose·ful** ☐ ['~ful] zweckmäßig; absichtlich; zielbewußt; '**pur·pose·less** ☐ zwecklos; ziellos; '**pur·pose·ly** *adv.* vorsätzlich.

purr [pə:] **1.** schnurren (*Katze*); brummen (*Motor*); **2.** Schnurren *n*, Brummen *n*.

purse [pə:s] **1.** Geldbeutel *m*, Börse *f*, Portemonnaie *n*; Geld *n*; Fonds *m*; Geldpreis *m*; *public* ~ Staatssäckel *m*; **2.** *oft* ~ *up* Mund spitzen; *Stirn* runzeln; *Augen* zs.-kneifen; '~-**proud** protzig; '**purs·er** ⚓ Proviant-, Zahlmeister *m*; '**purse--strings:** *hold the* ~ das Geld verwalten.

pur·si·ness ['pə:sinis] Kurzatmigkeit *f*.

purs·lane ⚘ ['pə:slin] Portulak *m*.

pur·su·ance [pə'sju:əns] Verfolgung *f*; *in* ~ *of* zufolge (*dat.*), im Verfolg (*gen.*); **pur'su·ant** ☐ : ~ *to* zufolge, gemäß, entsprechend.

pur·sue [pə'sju:] *v/t.* verfolgen (*a. fig.*); streben nach; *e-m Beruf etc.* nachgehen; fortsetzen; *v/i.* fortfahren; ~ *after j.* verfolgen; **pur-'su·er** Verfolger(in); **pur·suit** [pə-'sju:t] Verfolgung *f*; Streben *n* (*of* nach); *mst* ~*s pl.* Beschäftigung *f*, Studien *n/pl.*, Arbeiten *f/pl.*; ~ *plane* Jagdflugzeug *n*; **pur·sui-vant** ['pə:sivənt] Unterherold *m*; Gefolgsmann *m*.

pur·sy[1] ['pə:si] kurzatmig; fett, dick.

pur·sy[2] [~] zusammengekniffen (*Mund etc.*); faltig; protzig.

pu·ru·lent ☐ ['pjuərulənt] eitrig.

pur·vey [pə:'vei] *v/t. Lebensmittel* liefern; *v/i.* ~ *for* beliefern, versorgen; **pur'vey·ance** Lieferung *f*; **pur'vey·or** Lieferant *m*; *bsd.* Lebensmittelhändler *m*.

pur·view ['pə:vju:] Wirkungskreis *m*, Bereich *m*; Gesichtskreis *m*.

pus [pʌs] Eiter *m*.

push [puʃ] **1.** (An-, Vor)Stoß *m*; Schub *m*; Druck *m*; Notfall *m*; Energie *f*; Unternehmungsgeist *m*;

Elan *m*, Schwung *m*; Anstrengung *f*; *at a* ~ im Notfall; *when it comes to the* ~ wenn es darauf ankommt; *get the* ~ *sl.* 'rausfliegen; *give s.o. the* ~ *sl. j.* 'rausschmeißen; **2.** *v/t.* stoßen, treiben; schieben; drängen; *Knopf* drücken; *fig.* drängen, antreiben; *a.* ~ *through* durchführen; *Anspruch etc.* zur Geltung bringen, durchdrücken; vorwärtsbringen; fördern; ~ *s.th. on s.o.* j-m et. aufdrängen; ~ *one's way* sich durchod. vordrängen; *be* ~*ed for time* (*money*) in Zeit- (Geld)not sein; *v/i.* stoßen; schieben; (sich) drängen; ~ *along*, ~ *on*, ~ *forward* weitermachen, -gehen, -fahren *etc.*; ~ *off* abstoßen (*Boot*); F sich auf den Weg machen; '~-**ball** Push-, Stoßball *m*; '~-**bike** Fahrrad *n*; '~-**button** ⚡ Druckknopf *m*; '~-**chair** (Kinder)Sportwagen *m*; '**push·er** Streber(in); Flugzeug *n* mit Druckschraube; *Am.* 🚂 Hilfslokomotive *f*; **push·ful** ☐ ['~ful], '**push·ing** ☐ rührig, strebsam; *b.s.* zudringlich; '**push-off** Anfang *m*; '**push-o·ver** *bsd. Am.* Kinderspiel *n*; leicht zu beeinflussender Mensch *m*; '**push--up** *bsd. Am.* Liegestütz *m*; '**push·y** penetrant, aufdringlich; aggressiv.

pu·sil·la·nim·i·ty [pju:silə'nimiti] Kleinmut *m*; **pu·sil·lan·i·mous** ☐ [~'læniməs] kleinmütig.

puss [pus] Kätzchen *n*, Katze *f* (*a. fig.* = *Mädchen*); '**puss·y** ⚘ (Weiden)Kätzchen *n*; *a.* ~-*cat* Mieze *f*, Kätzchen *n*; '**puss·y·foot** *Am.* F **1.** Leisetreter *m*, Schleicher *m*; **2.** F leisetreten, sich zurückhalten.

pus·tule ⚘ ['pʌstju:l] Pustel *f*.

put [put] (*irr.*) **1.** *v/t.* setzen, legen, stellen, stecken, tun, machen (*on* auf *acc.*, *to* an *acc.*); *fig. j.* wohin setzen; *den Fall* setzen; *Frage* stellen, vorlegen; werfen, schleudern; ausdrücken, sagen; (ab)schätzen (*at* auf *acc.*); ~ *about Gerücht etc.* verbreiten; ⚓ wenden; *j.* in Verlegenheit bringen; ~ *across sl.* drehen, schaukeln; schmackhaft machen; weismachen; ~ *away* weglegen, -stecken; auf die Seite legen; F in e-e Anstalt bringen; *sl.* verputzen; aufgeben; ~ *back* zurückstellen, -schieben; *Uhr* zurückstellen; *fig.* zurückwerfen; ~ *by*

Geld zurücklegen; beiseite schieben; ~ *down* niederlegen, -setzen, -werfen, ~ -schlagen; absetzen, aussteigen lassen; niederschreiben; *j.* notieren, vormerken (*for* für); zuschreiben (*to dat.*), schieben (*to auf acc.*); schätzen (*at auf acc.*), ansehen (*as, for* als); zum Schweigen bringen; unterdrücken; demütigen; *Vorräte* einlagern; ~ *forth Kräfte* aufbieten; *Knospen etc.* treiben; aufbieten; ~ *forward e-e Meinung etc.* vorbringen; *als Kandidat etc.* vorschlagen, aufstellen; *Uhrzeiger* vorstellen; ~ *o.s. forward* sich hervortun; ~ *in* hinein-, hereinst(r)ecken; *Anspruch* erheben, geltend machen; *Gesuch* einreichen; *Urkunde* vorlegen; einsetzen, anstellen; *gutes Wort* einlegen; *Bemerkung* einwerfen; *Schlag* anbringen; F *Zeit* verbringen; ~ *in an hour's work* e-e Stunde arbeiten; ~ *off* auf-, verschieben; vertrösten, abspeisen; ablenken, abbringen; hindern; *fig.* ablegen; ~ *on Kleid* anziehen; *Hut* aufsetzen; *Charakter etc.* annehmen; hinzufügen; ✝ aufschlagen (*to auf e-n Preis*); an-, einschalten; vergrößern, verstärken; *Uhr* vorstellen; *Ersatzmann, Sonderzug etc.* einsetzen; *he is* ~*ting it on* er gibt an; ~ *it on thick* dick auftragen; ~ *on airs* sich aufspielen; ~ *on weight* zunehmen; ~ *out* ausmachen, (-)löschen; verrenken; (her)ausstrecken; hinauswerfen; aus der Fassung bringen, durcheinanderbringen, verwirren; *j-m* Ungelegenheiten bereiten; *Kraft* aufbieten; *Arbeit* vergeben, außer Haus geben; *Geld* ausleihen; produzieren; ~ *out of action* außer Gefecht *od.* Betrieb setzen; ~ *over e-m Film etc.* zum Erfolg verhelfen; ~ *o.s. over* Anklang finden; ~ *right* in Ordnung bringen; ~ *through teleph.* verbinden (*to* mit); F durchführen; ~ *s.o. through it* F j. durch die Mühle drehen (*gründlich prüfen*); ~ *to* hinzufügen; *be* (*hard*) ~ *to it* Schwierigkeiten haben; ~ *to expense j-m* Unkosten machen; ~ *to death* hinrichten; ~ *to the rack od.* torture auf die Folter spannen; ~ *together* zs.-setzen; zs.-zählen; ~ *up* aufstellen *etc.*; errichten, bauen; *Hände* er-, hochheben;

Fahne, Segel hissen; *Haar* hochstecken; *Waren* anbieten; *Miete* erhöhen; verpacken; *Widerstand* leisten; *Kampf* liefern; (als Kandidaten) vorschlagen; *Geld* beisteuern; wegpacken; *Wild* aufjagen; *Gäste* unterbringen; *Bekanntmachung* anschlagen; *Eheaufgebot* verkünden; ~ *s.o. up to s.th.* j. über et. informieren; j. zu et. anregen *od.* anstiften; **2.** *v/i.*: ~ *off,* ~ *out,* ~ *to sea* ⚓ auslaufen; ~ *in* ⚓ einlaufen; ~ *up at* einkehren, absteigen in (*dat.*); ~ *up for* sich bewerben um; sich als Kandidat aufstellen lassen für; ~ *up with* sich gefallen lassen; sich abfinden mit, hinnehmen.

pu·ta·tive [ˈpjuːtɔtiv] vermeintlich; mutmaßlich.

put·log ⊕ [ˈpʌtlɔg] Gerüsthebel *m.*

put-on F [ˈputɔn] Mache *f* (*Schau, Täuschung*); *Am.* Spaß *m*; 2. gemacht (*vorgetäuscht*).

pu·tre·fac·tion [pjuːtriˈfækʃən] Fäulnis *f*; **pu·tre·fac·tive** [~tiv] Fäulnis erregend; faulig.

pu·tre·fy [ˈpjuːtrifai] (ver)faulen.

pu·tres·cence [pjuːˈtresns] Fäulnis *f*; **pu·tres·cent** faulend.

pu·trid □ [ˈpjuːtrid] faul, verdorben; *sl.* scheußlich, saumäßig; **pu·trid·i·ty** Fäulnis *f.*

putt [pʌt] *Golf*: **1.** putten, leicht schlagen; **2.** Putten *n*, leichter Schlag *m.*

put·tee [ˈpʌti] Wickelgamasche *f.*

putt·er [ˈpʌtə] *Golf*: Putter *m.*

put·ty [ˈpʌti] **1.** *a. glaziers'* ~ Glaserkitt *m*; *a. plasterers'* ~ Kalkkitt *m*; *a. jewellers'* ~ Zinnasche *f*; **2.** kitten.

put-up job [ˈputˈʌpˈdʒɔb] abgekartetes Spiel *n.*

puz·zle [ˈpʌzl] **1.** schwierige Aufgabe *f*, Rätsel *n*; Verlegenheit *f*, Verwirrung *f*; Puzzle-, Geduldspiel *n*; **2.** *v/t.* verwirren, irre machen, in Verlegenheit bringen; *j-m* Kopfzerbrechen machen; ~ *out* austüfteln; ~ *one's brains* = *v/i.* sich den Kopf zerbrechen (*over über acc.*); ˈ~-head·ed konfus; ˈpuz·zler schwierige Frage *f.*

pyg·m(a)e·an [pigˈmiːən] pygmäisch, zwerghaft; **pyg·my** [ˈpigmi] Pygmäe *m*; *fig.* Zwerg *m*; *attr.* Zwerg...; zwerghaft.

py·ja·mas [pə'dʒɑːməz] *pl.* Schlafanzug *m*, Pyjama *m*.

py·lon ['pailən] Hochspannungsmast *m*.

py·lo·rus *anat.* [pai'lɔːrəs] Pförtner *m*.

py·or·rh(o)e·a 𝕄 [paiə'riə] Paradentose *f*.

pyr·a·mid ['pirəmid] Pyramide *f*; **py·ram·i·dal** □ [pi'ræmidl] pyramidal.

pyre ['paiə] Scheiterhaufen *m*.

py·ri·tes [pai'raitiːz]: *copper* ~ Kupferkies *m*; *iron* ~ Pyrit *m*, Eisenkies *m*.

py·ro... ['paiərəu] Feuer..., Brand-..., Wärme..., Glut...; **py·rog·ra·phy** [pai'rɔgrəfi] Brandmalerei *f*; **py·ro·tech·nic, py·ro·tech·ni·cal** [pairəu'teknik(əl)] pyrotechnisch, Feuerwerks...; **py·ro'tech·nics** *pl.* Feuerwerkerei *f*; *fig.* Feuerwerk *n*; **py·ro'tech·nist** Feuerwerker *m*.

Pyr·rhic vic·to·ry ['pirik'viktəri] Pyrrhussieg *m*.

Py·thag·o·re·an [paiθægə'riːən] 1. pythagoreisch; 2. Pythagoreer *m*.

Pyth·i·an ['piθiən] pythisch.

py·thon ['paiθən] Python-, Riesenschlange *f*.

pyx [piks] *eccl.* Monstranz *f*; Büchse *f* mit Probemünzen.

Q

Q-boat ⚓ ['kjuːbəut] U-Bootfalle *f*.

quack¹ [kwæk] 1. Quaken *n*; 2. quaken.

quack² [~] 1. Scharlatan *m*; Quacksalber *m*; Kurpfuscher *m*; Marktschreier *m*; 2. quacksalberisch; Quacksalber...; 3. quacksalbern (an *dat.*); **quack·er·y** ['~əri] Quacksalberei *f*; Marktschreierei *f*.

quad [kwɔd] = *quadrangle, quadrat, quadruplet.*

quad·ra·ge·nar·i·an [kwɔdrədʒi-'neəriən] 1. vierzigjährig; 2. Vierzigjährige *m, f.*

quad·ran·gle ['kwɔdræŋgl] Viereck *n*; Innenhof *m e-s College.*

quad·rant ['kwɔdrənt] Quadrant*m*; *bsd.* ⚓ Viertelkreis *m*.

quad·ra·phon·ic [kwɔdrə'fɔnik] quadrophon.

quad·rat *typ.* ['kwɔdræt] (großer) Ausschluß*m*; **quad·rat·ic** ⚓ [kwə-'drætik] 1. quadratisch; 2. quadratische Gleichung *f*; **quad·ra·ture** ['kwɔdrətʃə] Quadratur *f*.

quad·ren·ni·al □ [kwɔ'drenjəl] vierjährig; vierjährlich.

quad·ri·lat·er·al ⚓ [kwɔdri'lætərəl] 1. vierseitig; 2. Viereck *n*.

qua·drille [kwə'dril] Quadrille *f*.

quad·ri·par·tite [kwɔdri'pɑːtait] vierteilig; Vierer...

quad·ru·ped ['kwɔdruped] 1. Vierfüßer *m*; 2. *a.* **quad·ru·pe·dal** [kwɔ'druːpidl] vierfüßig; **quad·ru·ple** ['kwɔdrupl] 1. □ vierfach; *a.* ~ *to*, ~ *of* viermal so groß wie; 2. Vierfache *n*; 3. (sich) vervierfachen; **quad·ru·plet** ['~plit] Vierling *m*; **quad·ru·pli·cate** 1. [kwɔ'druːplikit] vierfach(e Ausfertigung *f*); 2. [~keit] vervierfachen.

quaff [kwɑːf] zechen; ~ *off* in langen Zügen trinken.

quag [kwæg] = ~*mire*; **'quag·gy** sumpfig, moorig; **quag·mire** ['~maiə] Sumpf(land *n*) *m*, Moor *n*.

quail¹ *orn.* [kweil] Wachtel *f*.

quail² [~] verzagen; beben.

quaint □ [kweint] anheimelnd; malerisch; putzig; seltsam, wunderlich; **'quaint·ness** Seltsamkeit*f*.

quake [kweik] 1. beben, zittern (*with, for* vor *dat.*); 2. Erdbeben *n*. **Quak·er** ['kweikə] Quäker *m*.

qual·i·fi·ca·tion [kwɔlifi'keiʃən] (erforderliche) Befähigung *f*; Einschränkung *f*; *gr.* nähere Bestimmung *f*; **qual·i·fied** ['~faid] befähigt; geeignet; eingeschränkt; bedingt; **qual·i·fy** ['~fai] *v/t.* befähigen; (be)nennen; *gr.* näher bestimmen; einschränken, mäßigen; mildern; *Getränk* verdünnen; *v/i.* seine Befähigung nachweisen; sich qualifizieren; *qualifying exami-*

nation Eignungsprüfung *f*; **qual·i·ta·tive** □ ['ˌtətiv] qualitativ; **'qual·i·ty** Eigenschaft *f*, Beschaffenheit *f*; Qualität *f*, Güte *f*; Fähigkeit *f*, Talent *n*; vornehmer Stand *m*.

qualm [kwɑ:m] Übelkeit(sanfall *m*) *f*; Zweifel *m*; Bedenken *n*; **'qualm·ish** □ übel, unwohl.

quan·da·ry ['kwɔndəri] verzwickte Lage *f*, Verlegenheit *f*.

quan·go ['kwæŋgəu] *in Großbritannien*: unabhängige Kommission, unabhängiger Ausschuß.

quan·ti·ta·tive □ ['kwɔntitətiv] quantitativ; **'quan·ti·ty** Quantität *f*, Menge *f*; Anzahl *f*; großer Teil *m*; *Å* Größe *f*; (Silben)Zeitmaß *n*; ~ *surveyor* Bausachverständige *m*.

quan·tum ['kwɔntəm] Menge *f*, Größe *f*, Quantum *n*; Anteil *m*; ~ *theory phys.* Quantentheorie *f*.

quar·an·tine ['kwɔrənti:n] **1.** Quarantäne *f*; **2.** unter Quarantäne stellen.

quar·rel ['kwɔrəl] **1.** Zank *m*, Streit *m*; **2.** (sich) zanken, streiten; **quar·rel·some** ['ˌsəm] □ zänkisch; streitsüchtig.

quar·ry¹ ['kwɔri] **1.** Steinbruch *m*; *fig.* Fundgrube *f*; **2.** *Steine* brechen; *fig.* zs.-tragen; stöbern (*for* nach).

quar·ry² [~] (Jagd)Beute *f*.

quar·ry·man ['kwɔrimən] Steinbrucharbeiter *m*.

quart [kwɔ:t] Quart *n* (*1,136 l*); *fenc.* [kɑ:t] Quart(e) *f*.

quar·ter ['kwɔ:tə] **1.** Viertel *n*, vierter Teil *m*; *bsd.* Viertelstunde *f*; Vierteljahr *n*, Quartal *n*; Viertelzentner *m*; *Am.* 25 Cent; Keule *f*, Viertel *n* *e-s geschlachteten Tieres*; Mondviertel *n*; Stadtviertel *n*, -teil *m*; *♆* Achterschiff *n*; (Himmels-)Richtung *f*, Gegend *f*; *♆* Posten *m*; *⚔* Gnade *f*, Pardon *m*; *fig.* Schonung *f*, Nachsicht *f*; *fig.* Stelle *f*, Seite *f*; ~*s pl.* Quartier *n* (*a.* ⚔), Unterkunft *f*; *fig.* Kreise *m/pl.*; *live in close* ~*s* beengt wohnen; *at close* ~*s* dicht aufeinander; *come to close* ~*s* handgemein werden; **2.** vierteln, vierteilen; beherbergen; ⚔ einquartieren; **'~·back** *Am. Sport:* wichtigster Spieler der Angriffsformation; **'~·deck** Achterdeck *n*; Offiziere *m/pl.*; **'quar·ter·ly 1.** vierteljährlich; Vierteljahrs...; **2.** Vierteljahrsschrift *f*; **'quar·ter·mas·ter** ⚔

Quartiermeister *m*; **quar·tern** ['~tən] Viertel(pinte *f*) *n*; Vierpfundbrot *n*; **'quar·ter·staff** Stange *f* *als Waffe*.

quar·tet(te) ♪ [kwɔ:'tet] Quartett *n*.

quar·to ['kwɔ:təu] Quart(format) *n*.

quartz *min.* [kwɔ:ts] Quarz *m*; **quartz·ite** ['~ait] Quarzit *m*.

quash ⚖ [kwɔʃ] aufheben, verwerfen; unterdrücken.

qua·si ['kwɑ:zi:] gleichsam, sozusagen; Quasi..., Schein...

qua·ter·na·ry [kwə'tə:nəri] aus vier bestehend; *geol.* Quartär...

quat·rain ['kwɔtrein] Vierzeiler *m*.

qua·ver ['kweivə] **1.** Zittern *n*; ♪ Triller *m*; ♪ Achtelnote *f*; **2.** mit zitternder Stimme sprechen *od.* singen; trillern; **'qua·ver·y** zitternd.

quay [ki:] Kai *m*; Uferstraße *f*; **quay·age** ['~idʒ] Kaigeld *n*.

quea·si·ness ['kwi:zinis] Empfindlichkeit *f*; Übelkeit *f*; Ekel *m*; **'quea·sy** □ empfindlich (*Magen, Gewissen*); heikel, mäkelig; ekelhaft; *I feel* ~ mir ist übel.

queen [kwi:n] **1.** Königin *f*; *Schach etc.*: Dame *f*; *sl.* Schwule *m*, Homo *m*; ~ *bee* Bienenkönigin *f*; ~'*s metal* Weißmetall *n*; ~'*s ware* gelbes Steingut *n*; **2.** *Schach*: in e-e Dame verwandeln *od.* verwandelt werden; ~ *it* die Dame spielen; **'queen·like, 'queen·ly** wie eine Königin, königlich.

queer [kwiə] **1.** sonderbar, seltsam; wunderlich; komisch, unwohl; homosexuell; **2.** ~ *s.o.'s pitch sl.* j-m e-n Strich durch die Rechnung machen; **3.** Homosexuelle *m*.

quell *rhet.* [kwel] bezwingen; unterdrücken.

quench [kwentʃ] *fig. Durst etc.* löschen, stillen, kühlen; *Aufruhr* unterdrücken; *rhet.* (aus)löschen; **'quench·er** F Trunk *m*, Schluck *m*; **'quench·less** □ unauslöschlich.

que·rist ['kwiərist] Fragesteller (-in).

quern [kwə:n] Handmühle *f*.

quer·u·lous □ ['kweruləs] quengelig, mürrisch, verdrossen.

que·ry ['kwiəri] **1.** (*mst abbr.* qu.) bitte!, sage mir; **2.** Frage(zeichen *n*) *f*; **3.** (be)fragen; (be-, an)zweifeln.

quest [kwest] **1.** Suche(n *n*) *f*,

Nachforschen *n*; *in* ~ *of* auf der Suche nach; **2.** suchen, forschen.

ques·tion ['kwestʃən] **1.** Frage *f*; Problem *n*; Untersuchung *f*; Streitfrage *f*; Zweifel *m*; Sache *f*, Angelegenheit *f*; ~*! parl.* zur Sache!; *beyond (all)* ~ ohne Frage, fraglos; *in* ~ fraglich; *come into* ~ in Frage kommen; *call in* ~ anzweifeln; *beg the* ~ die in Frage gestellte Sache als erwiesen ansehen; *the* ~ *is* ... es handelt sich darum ...; *that is out of the* ~ das steht außer *od.* kommt nicht in Frage; *there is no* ~ *of od.* of *ger.* es ist nicht die Rede von *od.* davon, daß; **2.** befragen; bezweifeln; verhören; '**ques·tion·a·ble** □ fraglich, zweifelhaft; bedenklich, fragwürdig; '**ques·tion·a·ble·ness** Zweifelhaftigkeit *f*; Fragwürdigkeit *f*; '**ques·tion·er** Fragende *m*, *f*, Fragesteller(in); **ques·tion mark** Fragezeichen *n*; **ques·tion mas·ter** Moderator *m e-s Quiz*; **ques·tion·naire** [kwestiə'nɛə] Fragebogen *m*; **ques·tion time** *parl.* Fragestunde *f*.

queue [kju:] **1.** Reihe *f von Personen od. Wagen*, Schlange *f*; Zopf *m*; **2.** *mst* ~ *up* (in e-r Reihe) anstehen, Schlange stehen; '~-**jump·er** j., der sich vordrängelt; *mot.* Kolonnenspringer *m*.

quib·ble ['kwibl] **1.** Wortspiel *n*; Spitzfindigkeit *f*; Ausflucht *f*; **2.** *fig.* ausweichen; witzeln; '**quib·bler** Wortklauber *m*, Sophist *m*.

quick [kwik] **1.** schnell, rasch; voreilig; lebhaft; gescheit; beweglich; lebendig; scharf (*Gehör etc.*); ~ *march* ✕ Eil-, Geschwindmarsch *m*; **2.** lebendes Fleisch *n*; *the* ~ *pl.* die Lebenden *m/pl.*; *to the* ~ (bis) ins Fleisch; *fig.* (bis) ins Herz, tief; *cut s.o. to the* ~ j. aufs empfindlichste kränken; **3.** *s.* ~/*y*; '~-**change ac·tor** Verwandlungskünstler *m*; '**quick·en** *v/t.* beleben; beschleunigen; *v/i.* aufleben; sich regen; '**quick-fir·ing** ✕ Schnellfeuer...; '**quick-fro·zen** tiefgekühlt; **quick·ie** F ['~i] *auf die Schnelle gemachte Sache*; *have a* ~ *mst* auf die Schnelle einen trinken; '**quick·lime** ungelöschter Kalk *m*; '**quick·ly** schnell, rasch; '**quick-match** Zündschnur *f*; '**quick-mo·tion pic·ture** *Film*: Zeitrafferaufnahme *f*; '**quick·ness** Lebhaftigkeit *f*; Schnelligkeit *f*; Vor-

eiligkeit *f*; Schärfe *f des Verstandes etc.*

quick...: '~-**sand** Treibsand *m*; '~-**set** ⚷ Setzling *m*; Hagedorn *m*; *a.* ~ *hedge* lebende Hecke *f*; '~-'**sight·ed** scharfsichtig; '~-'**sil·ver** *min.* Quecksilber *n*; '~-**step** Quickstep *m* (*Tanzschritt*); ✕ Geschwindschritt *m*; '~-'**tem·pered** leicht erregbar, hitzig; '~-'**wit·ted** schlagfertig.

quid[1] [kwid] Priem *m* (*Kautabak*).

quid[2] *sl.* [~] Pfund Sterling.

quid·di·ty *phls.* ['kwiditi] Wesen *n e-r Sache*; Spitzfindigkeit *f*.

quid pro quo ['kwid prəu 'kwəu] Gegenleistung *f*; Äquivalent *n*.

qui·es·cence [kwai'esns] Ruhe *f*, Stille *f*; **qui·es·cent** □ ruhend; *fig.* ruhig, still.

qui·et ['kwaiət] **1.** □ ruhig, still; **2.** Ruhe *f*; *on the* ~ (*sl.: on the q.t.* ['kju:'ti:]) unter der Hand, im stillen; im Vertrauen; **3.** *a.* ~ *down* (sich) beruhigen; '**qui·et·en** = *quiet 3*; '**qui·et·ism** ['kwaiitizəm] *eccl.* Quietismus *m*; '**qui·et·ist** Quietist *m*; **qui·et·ness** ['kwaiətnis], **qui·e·tude** ['kwaiitju:d] Ruhe *f*, Stille *f*.

qui·e·tus [kwai'i:təs] Endquittung *f*; Ende *n*, Tod *m*; Todesstoß *m*.

quill [kwil] **1.** Federkiel *m*; *fig.* Feder *f*; Stachel *m des Igels etc.*; **2.** rund fälteln; '~-**driv·er** Federfuchser *m*; '**quill·ing** Krause *f*, Rüsche *f*; '**quill-pen** Gänsefeder *f zum Schreiben*.

quilt [kwilt] **1.** Steppdecke *f*; **2.** steppen; '**quilt·ing** Steppen *n*; gesteppte Arbeit *f*; Pikee *m*.

quince ⚘ [kwins] Quitte *f*.

qui·nine *pharm.* [kwi'ni:n, *bsd. Am.* 'kwainain] Chinin *n*.

quin·qua·ge·nar·i·an [kwiŋkwədʒi'nɛəriən] **1.** fünfzigjährig; **2.** Fünfzigjährige *m*, *f*.

quin·quen·ni·al □ [kwiŋ'kweniəl] fünfjährig; fünfjährlich.

quins F [kwinz] *pl.* Fünflinge *pl.*

quin·sy 🡒 ['kwinzi] Mandelentzündung *f*.

quin·tal ['kwintl] (Doppel)Zentner *m*.

quint·es·sence [kwin'tesns] Quintessenz *f*, Kern *m*, Inbegriff *m*.

quin·tu·ple ['kwintjupl] **1.** fünffach; **2.** (sich) verfünffachen; **quin-**

tu·plets [ˈ‿plits] *pl.* Fünflinge *pl.*

quip [kwip] Stich(elei *f*) *m*; Witz (-wort *n*) *m*; Spitzfindigkeit *f*.

quire [ˈkwaiə] Buch *n* Papier; *Buchbinderei:* Lage *f*.

quirk [kwəːk] Spitzfindigkeit *f*; Witz(elei *f*) *m*; Kniff *m*; Schnörkel *m*; ♠ Hohlkehle *f*.

quis·ling [ˈkwizliŋ] Quisling *m*, Kollaborateur *m*.

quit [kwit] **1.** *v/t.* verlassen; aufgeben, verzichten auf (*acc.*); *Am.* aufhören; vergelten; *Schuld* tilgen; *v/i.* ausziehen (*Mieter*); weggehen; aufhören; **2.** quitt; frei (*of* von), los.

quite [kwait] ganz, gänzlich; recht; durchaus; ~ a *lot* e-e ziemliche *od.* ganze Menge; ~ (so)!, ~ that! ganz recht!, genau!; ~ the thing F große Mode *f*; genau das Richtige.

quits [kwits] quitt (*with* mit); cry ~ genug haben.

quit·tance [ˈkwitəns] Quittung *f*.

quit·ter *Am.* F [ˈkwitə] Drückeberger *m*.

quiv·er[1] [ˈkwivə] **1.** Zittern *n*, Beben *n*; **2.** zittern, beben.

quiv·er[2] [‿] Köcher *m*.

quix·ot·ic [kwikˈsɔtik] donquichotisch, weltfremd, überspannt.

quiz [kwiz] **1.** Prüfung *f*, Test *m*; Quiz *n*, Frage- u. Antwortspiel *n*; belustigter Blick *m*; **2.** (aus)fragen, prüfen; necken, foppen; anstarren, beäugen; ˈquiz·zi·cal ☐ spöttisch; komisch.

quod *sl.* [kwɔd] Loch *n* (*Gefängnis*).

quoin [kɔin] Ecke *f*; *typ.* Keil *m*.

quoit [kɔit] Wurfring *m*; ~s *pl.* Wurfringspiel *n*.

quon·dam [ˈkwɔndæm] ehemalig.

quon·set *Am.* [ˈkwɔnsit] *a.* ~ hut Wellblechbaracke *f*.

quo·rum *parl.* [ˈkwɔːrəm] beschlußfähige Mitgliederzahl *f*; *have a* ~, *form a* ~ beschlußfähig sein.

quo·ta [ˈkwəutə] Quote *f*, Anteil *m*, Kontingent *n*.

quot·a·ble [ˈkwəutəbl] zitierbar.

quo·ta·tion [kwəuˈteiʃən] Anführung *f*, Zitat *n*; ✝ Preisnotierung *f*; Kostenvoranschlag *m*; *familiar* ~s *pl.* geflügelte Worte *n/pl.*; **quoˈta·tion-marks** *pl.* Anführungszeichen *n/pl.*

quote [kwəut] anführen, zitieren; angeben; ✝ berechnen, notieren (*at* mit).   [ich, sagte er.]

quoth ✝ [kwəuθ]: ~ *I*, ~ he sagte

quo·tid·i·an [kwɔˈtidiən] (all)täglich.

quo·tient ♠ [ˈkwəuʃənt] Quotient *m*.

R

r [ɑː]: *the three R's* (= *reading, writing, arithmetic*) Lesen *n*, Schreiben *n* u. Rechnen *n*.

rab·bet ⊕ [ˈræbit] **1.** Falz *m*, Fuge *f*, Nut *f*; **2.** (ein)falzen, (ein)fügen, fugen.

rab·bi [ˈræbai] Rabbiner *m*.

rab·bit [ˈræbit] Kaninchen *n*; ˈ~-fe·ver Hasenpest *f*.

rab·ble [ˈræbl] Pöbel(haufen) *m*; ˈ~-rous·er Demagoge *m*; ˈ~-rous·ing aufwieglerisch, demagogisch.

rab·id ☐ [ˈræbid] tollwütig (*Tier*); *fig.* wild, rasend, wütend; **ˈrab·id·ness** Tollheit *f*.

ra·bies *vet.* [ˈreibiːz] Tollwut *f*.

rac·coon [rəˈkuːn] = racoon.

race[1] [reis] Geschlecht *n*, Stamm *m*; Volk *n*; Rasse *f*, Schlag *m*.

race[2] [‿] Rennen *n/pl.*; Lauf *m* (*a. fig.*); Wettlauf *m*, -rennen *n*; Strömung *f*, Strom *m*; ~s *pl.* Pferderennen *n*; **2.** rennen; *weitS.* rasen; um die Wette laufen (mit); rasen mit; *Gesetz* durchpeitschen; *Motor im Leerlauf* hochjagen; ˈ~-course Rennbahn *f*, -strecke *f*.

race-ha·tred [ˈreisˈheitrid] Rassenhaß *m*.

race-horse [ˈreishɔːs] Rennpferd *n*.

rac·er [ˈreisə] Rennpferd *n*; Rennboot *n*; Rennwagen *m*.

ra·cial [ˈreiʃəl] Rassen...; ~ *discrimination* Rassendiskriminierung *f*; ~ *equality* Rassengleichheit *f*; ~ *segregation* Rassentrennung *f*; ˈra·cial-

ism Rassenbewußtsein *n*, -haß *m*.

rac·i·ness ['reisinis] Lebhaftigkeit *f*; Urwüchsigkeit *f*.

rac·ing ['reisiŋ] Rennsport *m*; *attr.* Renn...; ~ *car* Rennwagen *m*.

ra·cism ['reisizəm] Rassismus *m*; **'ra·cist** Rassist *m*.

rack¹ [ræk] **1.** Gerüst *n*, Gestell *n*; Kleiderständer *m*; Gepäcknetz *n*; Raufe *f*, Futtergestell *n*; ⊕ Zahnstange *f*; Folter(bank) *f*; **2.** recken, strecken; foltern, martern, quälen (*a. fig.*); ausnutzen; auf *od.* in das Gestell *etc.* tun; ~ *one's brains* sich den Kopf zermartern.

rack² [~] **1.** ziehende Wolkenmasse *f*; **2.** ziehen (*Wolken*).

rack³ [~]: *go to ~ and ruin* ganz und gar zugrunde gehen.

rack⁴ [~] *a.* ~ *off Wein* abfüllen.

rack·et¹ ['rækit] *Tennis etc.*: Schläger *m*, Rakett *n*; ~*s pl.* Rakettspiel *n*.

rack·et² [~] **1.** Lärm *m*, Krach *m*; *fig.* Getriebe *n*, Trubel *m*; *Am.* F Schwindel(geschäft *n*) *m*; Strapaze *f*, Nervenprobe *f*; *stand the* ~ es durchstehen; die Folgen tragen; **2.** lärmen; sich amüsieren; **rack·et·eer** *bsd. Am. sl.* [~'tiə] Erpresser *m*; **rack·et'eer·ing** *bsd. Am.* Erpresserwesen *n*; **'rack·et·y** ausgelassen.

rack-rail·way ['rækreilwei] Zahnradbahn *f*.

rack-rent ['rækrent] **1.** Wuchermiete *f*, -pacht *f*; **2.** *j-m e-e* Wuchermiete abverlangen.

ra·coon *zo.* [rə'ku:n] Waschbär *m*.

rac·y ['reisi] kraftvoll, lebendig; stark; würzig (*Geruch etc.*); urwüchsig.

ra·dar ['reidə] Radar(gerät) *n*; ~ **scan·ner** Radarsuchgerät *n*.

rad·dle ['rædl] **1.** Rötel *m*; **2.** rot bemalen.

ra·di·al □ ['reidjəl] radial, strahlenförmig; ~ *engine* Sternmotor *m*; ~ *tyre*, *Am.* ~ *tire* Gürtelreifen *m*.

ra·di·ance, ra·di·an·cy ['reidjəns(i)] Strahlen *n*; **'ra·di·ant** □ strahlend, leuchtend (*a. fig.*); Strahlungs...

ra·di·ate ['reidieit] (aus)strahlen; strahlenförmig ausgehen; **2.** ['~it] strahl(enförm)ig; Strahl(en)...; **ra·di·a·tion** (Aus)Strahlung *f*; **ra·di·a·tor** ['~eitə] Heizkörper *m*; *mot.* Kühler *m*.

rad·i·cal ['rædikəl] **1.** □ Wurzel...,

Stamm..., Grund...; grundlegend; gründlich; eingewurzelt; radikal (*a. pol.*); ~ *sign* Ⱥ Wurzelzeichen *n*; **2.** *gr.* Wurzelbuchstabe *m*, -wort *n*; ⌒ℝ Grundstoff *m*; *bsd. pol.* Radikale *m*; **'rad·i·cal·ism** Radikalismus *m*.

ra·di·o ['reidiəu] **1.** Radio *n*, Rundfunk *m*; Funkspruch *m*; Rundfunk-, Radiogerät *n*; Funkgerät *n*; ~*-car* Funkstreifenwagen *m*; ~ *drama*, ~ *play* Hörspiel *n*; ~ *engineering* Funktechnik *f*; ~ *operator* Funker *m*; ~ *set* Radiogerät *n*; **2.** funken; (drahtlos) senden; **'~'ac·tive** radioaktiv; ~ *waste* radioaktiver Müll *m*, Atom-Müll *m*; **'~·ac'tiv·i·ty** Radioaktivität *f*; ~ **con·tact** Funkkontakt *m*; **ra·di·o·gram** ['~græm] Funktelegramm *n*; Röntgenaufnahme *f*; = **ra·di·o·gram·o·phone** ['~'græməfəun] Musiktruhe *f*, Radiogerät *n* mit Plattenspieler; **ra·di·o·graph** ['~gra:f] **1.** Röntgenbild *n*; **2.** ein Röntgenbild machen von; **ra·di·og·ra·pher** [reidi'ɔgrəfə] Röntgenassistent *m*; **ra·di·og·ra·phy** Röntgenographie *f*; **'ra·di·o·lo'ca·tion** Funkortung *f*; **ra·di·ol·o·gist** [reidi'ɔlədʒist] Röntgenologe *m*; **ra·di·ol·o·gy** *phys.* [reidi'ɔlədʒi] Strahlenlehre *f*; -forschung *f*, -kunde *f*; Röntgenologie *f*; **ra·di·o·tel·e·gram** ['reidiəu'teligræm] Funktelegramm *n*; **'ra·di·o·'ther·a·py** Strahlen-, Röntgentherapie *f*.

rad·ish ♀ ['rædiʃ] Rettich *m*; *a. red ~* Radieschen *n*.

ra·di·um ['reidjəm] Radium *n*.

ra·di·us ['reidjəs], *pl.* **ra·di·i** ['~diai] Radius *m*; Ⱥ Halbmesser *m*; *anat.*, *a.* ⊕ Speiche *f*; ♀ Strahl *m*; *fig.* Umkreis *m*.

raff·ish ['ræfiʃ] liederlich.

raf·fle ['ræfl] **1.** Tombola *f*, Verlosung *f*; **2.** verlosen.

raft [ra:ft] **1.** Floß *n*; **2.** flößen; **'raft·er** ⊕ (Dach)Sparren *m*; **'rafts·man** Flößer *m*.

rag¹ [ræg] Lumpen *m*; Fetzen *m*; Lappen *m*; *contp.* Käseblatt *n*.

rag² *sl.* [~] **1.** Unfug treiben (mit); *j.* aufziehen; *j.* beschimpfen; herumtollen, Radau machen; **2.** Unfug *m*; Radau *m*.

rag·a·muf·fin ['rægəmʌfin] Lumpenkerl *m*; Gassenjunge *m*.

rag...: **'~-and-'bone man** Lumpensammler *m*; **'~-bag** Lumpensack *m*;

'∼-**book** unzerreißbares Bilderbuch *n.*

rage [reidȝ] **1.** Wut *f*, Zorn *m*; Sucht *f*, Gier *f* (*for* nach); Manie *f*; Begeisterung *f*, Ekstase *f*; *it is all the* ∼ es ist allgemein Mode, alles ist wild danach; **2.** wüten, rasen, toben.

rag-fair ['rægfɛə] Trödelmarkt *m.*

rag-ged □ ['rægid] rauh; zottig; zackig; unregelmäßig; zerlumpt.

rag-man ['rægmən] Lumpensammler *m.*

ra-gout ['rægu:] Ragout *n.*

rag...: '∼-**tag** *mst* ∼ *and bobtail* Pack *n*, Pöbel *m*; Krethi u. Plethi *pl.*; '∼-**time** ♩ Ragtime *m* (*Jazzstil*).

raid [reid] **1.** (feindlicher) Überfall *m*, Streifzug *m*; (Luft)Angriff *m*; Razzia *f*; **2.** einbrechen in *acc.*; e-n Überfall machen auf *acc.*; überfallen; plündern; '**raid-er** Stoßtruppteilnehmer *m.*

rail[1] [reil] **1.** *a.* ∼s *pl.* Geländer *n*; Stange *f*; 🚂 Schiene *f*; *fig.* Eisenbahn *f*; ∼ *strike* Eisenbahnerstreik *m*; *off the* ∼s entgleist; *fig.* in Unordnung; *by* ∼ per Bahn; **2.** *a.* ∼ *in*, ∼ *off* mit e-m Geländer umgeben. [*acc.*).\
rail[2] [∼] schimpfen (*at, against* auf)\
rail[3] *orn.* [∼] Ralle *f.*

rail-car ['reilkɑ:] Triebwagen *m.*

rail-ing ['reiliŋ] *a.* ∼s *pl.* Geländer *n*, Gitter *n*; Reling *f*; Staket *n.*

rail-lery ['reiləri] Spötterei *f.*

rail-road *Am.* ['reilrəud] **1.** Eisenbahn *f*; **2.** *Gesetz, Maßnahme* durchpeitschen.

rail-way ['reilwei] Eisenbahn *f*; ∼-**car-riage** Eisenbahnwagen *m*; '∼-**man** Eisenbahner *m.*

rai-ment *rhet.* ['reimənt] Kleidung *f.*

rain [rein] **1.** Regen *m*; **2.** regnen; ∼**bow** ['∼bəu] Regenbogen *m*; '∼-**coat** *Am.* Regenmantel *m*; '∼-**drop** Regentropfen *m*; '∼-**fall** Niederschlagsmenge *f*; Regenschauer *m*; ∼-**ga(u)ge** ['∼geidȝ] Regenmesser *m*; '∼-**proof 1.** regen-, wasserdicht; **2.** Regenmantel *m*; '**rain-y** □ regnerisch; Regen...; *a* ∼ *day fig.* Notzeiten *f*/*pl.*

raise [reiz] *oft* ∼ *up* heben; auf-, erheben; auf-, errichten; erhöhen (*a. fig.*); *Geld* aufbringen; *Anleihe* aufnehmen; *Heer* aufstellen; *Steuern, Stimme, Geschrei, Anspruch, Einwand, Frage etc.* erheben; verur-

sachen, hervorrufen; erwecken, erregen, in Bewegung setzen; anstiften, aufwiegeln; *Tiere* züchten; *Pflanzen* ziehen; *Getreide* (an)bauen; *Geister* beschwören; *Belagerung* aufheben; '**rais-er** Züchter *m*; Gründer *m.*

rai-sin ['reizn] Rosine *f.*

ra-ja(h) ['rɑ:dȝə] Radscha *m* (*indischer Fürst*).

rake[1] [reik] **1.** Rechen *m*, Harke *f*; **2.** *v/t.* (glatt-, zs.-)harken; *mst* ∼ *together* zs.-scharren; *a.* ∼ *up*, ∼ *over fig.* durchstöbern; ✕, ⚓ beharken, (mit Feuer) bestreichen; überblicken; ∼ *off*, ∼ *away* wegräumen; *v/i.* harken, herumstöbern (*for* nach); '∼-**off** *Am. sl.* Schwindelprofit *m.*

rake[2] ⚓ [∼] **1.** Hang *m*; **2.** überhängen (lassen).

rake[3] [∼] Wüstling *m*; Lebemann *m.*

rak-ish ['reikiʃ] **1.** flott, schnittig; **2.** □ liederlich, ausschweifend; verwegen; salopp.

ral-ly[1] ['ræli] **1.** Sammeln *n*; Tagung *f*, Treffen *n*; Massenversammlung *f*; Erholung *f*; *Tennis:* Ballwechsel *m*; *mot.* Rallye *f*, Sternfahrt *f*; **2.** (sich ver)sammeln; sich erholen.

ral-ly[2] [∼] *j.* aufziehen, necken.

ram [ræm] **1.** *zo., ast.* Widder *m*; ✕, *hist.* Sturmbock *m*; ⊕, ⚓ Ramme *f*; **2.** (fest)rammen; ⚓ rammen; ∼ *up* verrammeln.

ram-ble ['ræmbl] **1.** Streifzug *m*; **2.** umherstreifen; abschweifen; '**ram-bler** Wanderer *m*; 🌹 Kletterrose *f*; '**ram-bling** **1.** □ umherschweifend; abschweifend, unstet; weitläufig; unzusammenhängend; **2.** Umherschweifen *n.*

ram-i-fi-ca-tion [ræmifi'keiʃən] Verzweigung *f*; **ram-i-fy** ['∼fai] (sich) verzweigen.

ram-jet ['ræmdȝet] *a.* ∼ *engine* Staustrahltriebwerk *n.*

ram-mer ⊕ ['ræmə] Ramme *f.*

ramp[1] *sl.* [ræmp] Schwindel(manöver *n*) *m*; Geldschneiderei *f.*

ramp[2] [∼] **1.** Rampe *f*; **2.** sich zum Sprunge erheben; toben; **ram-page** *co.* [ræm'peidȝ] **1.** toben, tollen; **2.** *be on the* ∼ sich austoben; **ramp-an-cy** ['∼pənsi] Wuchern *n*; Zügellosigkeit *f*; '**ramp-ant** □ wuchernd; *fig.* zügellos; *Heraldik u.* 🛡 steigend.

ram·part ['ræmpɑːt] Wall *m* (*a. fig.*).

ram·rod ['ræmrɔd] Ladestock *m*.

ram·shack·le ['ræmʃækl] baufällig, wackelig, klapperig.

ran [ræn] *pret. von* run 1.

ranch [rɑːntʃ] Ranch *f*, Viehfarm *f*; **'ranch·er**, **'ranch·man** Rancher *m*, Viehzüchter *m*; Farmer *m*.

ran·cid □ ['rænsid] ranzig; **ran-'cid·i·ty**, **'ran·cid·ness** Ranzigkeit *f*.

ran·cor·ous □ ['ræŋkərəs] voller Groll, boshaft.

ran·co(u)r ['ræŋkə] Groll *m*, Haß *m*.

ran·dom ['rændəm] **1.** at ~ aufs Geratewohl, blindlings; **2.** ziel-, wahllos; zufällig; ~ *sample* Stichprobe *f von Waren*; ~ *shot* Schuß *m* ins Blaue.

rand·y F ['rændi] geil.

rang [ræŋ] *pret. von* ring² 2.

range [reindʒ] **1.** Reihe *f*; (Berg-) Kette *f*; ✝ Kollektion *f*; Sortiment *n*; Herd *m*; Raum *m*; Umfang *m*, Bereich *m*; Spielraum *m*; Reichweite *f*; Schuß-, Tragweite *f*; (ausgedehnte) Fläche *f*; Weide- od. Jagdgebiet *n*; *take the* ~ die Entfernung schätzen; **2.** *v/t.* (ein)reihen, ordnen; *ein Gebiet etc.* durchstreifen, -laufen; ⚓ längs *et.* fahren; *v/i.* in e-r Reihe *od.* Linie stehen; sich (auf)stellen; (umher)streifen; sich erstrecken, reichen; e-e Reichweite haben (*over* von); ~ *along* entlang fahren; **'~-find·er** Entfernungsmesser *m*; **'rang·er** Förster *m*; Aufseher *m* e-s Parks; ✗ Nahkampfspezialist *m*; **'rang·y** ausgedehnt; gebirgig; schlank.

rank¹ [ræŋk] **1.** Reihe *f*, Linie *f*; ✗ Glied *n*; Klasse *f*; Rang *m*, Stand *m*; the ~s *pl.*, the ~ *and file* die Mannschaften *f/pl.*; *fig.* die große Masse; *join the* ~s in das Heer eintreten; *rise from the* ~s von der Pike auf dienen; **2.** *v/t.* (ein)reihen, ordnen; rechnen (*with* zu); *v/i.* sich reihen, sich ordnen; gehören, sich rechnen, gerechnet werden (*with* zu); *among* unter *acc.*); e-e Stelle einnehmen, rangieren (*above* über *dat.*; *next to* hinter *dat.*); ~ *as* gelten als.

rank² [~] üppig, geil (*Pflanze*); fett (*Boden*); ranzig, stinkend; verderbt; *b.s.* kraß.

rank·er ['ræŋkə] aus dem Mannschaftsstand hervorgegangener Of-

fizier *m*.

ran·kle *fig.* ['ræŋkl] nagen, fressen.

rank·ness ['ræŋknis] Üppigkeit *f des Wachstums*; Ranzigkeit *f*.

ran·sack ['rænsæk] durchwühlen, -stöbern, -suchen; ausrauben.

ran·som ['rænsəm] **1.** Lösegeld *n*; Auslösung *f*; *eccl.* Erlösung *f*; **2.** loskaufen, auslösen; erlösen.

rant [rænt] **1.** Wortschwall *m*, Schwulst *m*; **2.** Phrasen dreschen; mit Pathos vortragen; **'rant·er** Phrasendrescher *m*.

ra·nun·cu·lus ♀ [rə'nʌŋkjuləs] Ranunkel *f*, Hahnenfuß *m*.

rap¹ [ræp] **1.** Klaps *m*; Klopfen *n*; **2.** schlagen, klopfen (*at* an *acc.*); ~ *s.o.'s fingers od. knuckles fig.* j-m auf die Finger klopfen; ~ *out* herauspoltern.

rap² *fig.* [~] Heller *m*, Deut *m*.

ra·pa·cious □ [rə'peiʃəs] raubgierig; Raub...; habgierig; **ra·pac·i·ty** [rə'pæsiti] Raub-, Habgier *f*.

rape¹ [reip] **1.** Raub *m*; Entführung *f*; ⚖ Notzucht *f*, Vergewaltigung *f*; ~ *and murder* Lustmord *m*; **2.** rauben; vergewaltigen.

rape² ♀ [~] Raps *m*; **'~-oil** Raps-, Rüböl *n*; **'~-seed** Rübsamen *m*.

rap·id ['ræpid] **1.** □ schnell, rasch, reißend, rapid(e); Schnell...; steil, jäh; *phot.* lichtstark (*Objektiv*); hochempfindlich (*Film*); ~ *fire* Schnellfeuer *n*; **2.** ~s *pl.* Stromschnelle(n *pl.*) *f*; **ra·pid·i·ty** [rə'piditi] Schnelligkeit *f*.

ra·pi·er *fenc.* ['reipjə] Rapier *n*.

rap·ine *rhet.* ['ræpain] Raub *m*.

rap·ist ['reipist] Vergewaltiger *m*.

rap·proche·ment *pol.* [ræ'prɔʃmãːŋ] Wiederannäherung *f*.

rapt [ræpt] *fig.* hingerissen, entzückt (*with* vor *dat.*); versunken (*in* in *acc.*).

rap·ture ['ræptʃə] *a.* ~s *pl.* Entzücken *n*; Begeisterung *f*; Taumel *m*; *in* ~s entzückt; *go into* ~s in Entzücken geraten; **'rap·tur·ous** □ entzückt; leidenschaftlich.

rare¹ □ [rɛə] selten (*a. fig. ungewöhnlich*; *hervorragend*; *köstlich*); vereinzelt; *phys. etc.* dünn.

rare² [~] halbgar, blutig (*Fleisch*).

rare·bit ['rɛəbit]: *Welsh* ~ geröstete Käseschnitte *f*.

rar·e·fac·tion *phys.* [rɛəri'fækʃən] Verdünnung *f*; **rar·e·fy** ['~fai]

(sich) verdünnen; verfeinern;
'**rare·ness**, '**rar·i·ty** Seltenheit *f*;
Dünnheit *f*; Kostbarkeit *f*.
ras·cal ['rɑːskəl] Schuft *m*, Schurke
m; Schelm *m*; **ras·cal·i·ty** [⌣'kæliti]
Schurkerei *f*; **ras·cal·ly** *adj. u. adv.*
['⌣kəli] schuftig; erbärmlich.
rash¹ □ [ræʃ] hastig, vorschnell;
unbesonnen; waghalsig.
rash² ⚕ [⌣] Hautausschlag *m*.
rash·er ['ræʃə] Speckschnitte *f*.
rash·ness ['ræʃnis] Voreiligkeit *f*;
Unbesonnenheit *f*.
rasp [rɑːsp] 1. Raspel *f*; 2. raspeln;
j-m weh(e) tun; kratzen; krächzen.
rasp·ber·ry ❦ ['rɑːzbəri] Himbeere *f*.   [eisen *n*.⎫
rasp·er ['rɑːspə] Raspler *m*; Kratz-⎬
rasp·ing ['rɑːspiŋ] Raspeln *n*; ⌣*s pl*.
Raspelspäne *m/pl*.
rat [ræt] 1. *zo.* Ratte *f*; *pol.* Überläufer *m*; *sl.* Streikbrecher *m*; *smell
a* ⌣ Lunte *od.* den Braten riechen;
⌣*s! sl.* quatsch!; 2. Ratten fangen;
pol. überlaufen.
rat·a·ble □ ['reitəbl] steuerpflichtig.
ratch ⊕ [rætʃ] Sperrstange *f*; Uhr-
macherei: Auslösung *f*.
ratch·et ⊕ ['rætʃit] Sperrklinke *f*;
'⌣**-wheel** Sperrad *n*.
rate¹ [reit] 1. Verhältnis *n*, Maß *n*,
Satz *m*; Rate *f*; Preis *m*, Gebühr *f*;
Taxe *f*; (Gemeinde)Abgabe *f*,
Steuer *f*; Grad *m*, Rang *m*; *bsd.* ⚓
Klasse *f*; Geschwindigkeit *f*, Gang
m; *at the* ⌣ *of* im Verhältnis von;
zum Satz von; mit einer Geschwindigkeit von; *at a cheap* ⌣ ✝ zu
billigem Preis; *at any* ⌣ auf jeden
Fall; ⌣ *of exchange* (Umrechnungs-)
Kurs *m*; ⌣ *of interest* Zinsfuß *m*; ⌣
of taxation Steuersatz *m*; 2. (ein-)
schätzen, taxieren (*at* auf *acc.*); besteuern.
rate² [⌣] *v/t.* ausschelten (*for, about
wegen*); *v/i.* schelten (*at* auf, *über
acc.*).
rate-pay·er ['reitpeiə] (Gemeinde-)
Steuerzahler *m*.
rath·er ['rɑːðə] eher, lieber; vielmehr; besser gesagt; ziemlich; ⌣!
[*a.* 'rɑː'ðə:] F na gewiß!, und ob!;
I had od. would ⌣ *do* ich möchte
lieber tun; *I* ⌣ *expected it* ich habe
es eigentlich erwartet.
rat·i·fi·ca·tion [rætifi'keiʃən] Bestätigung *f*; **rat·i·fy** ['⌣fai] bestätigen,
ratifizieren.

rat·ing¹ ['reitiŋ] Schätzung *f*;
Steuersatz *m*; ⚓ Dienstgrad *m*; ⚓
(Segel)Klasse *f*; Matrose *m*; *Fernsehen*: Einschaltquote *f*.
rat·ing² [⌣] Schelte(n *n*) *f*.
ra·tio ['reiʃiəu] Verhältnis *n*.
ra·tion ['ræʃən] 1. Ration *f*; Zuteilung *f*; ⌣ *card* (*book*) Lebens-
mittelkarte(n *pl*.) *f*; 2. rationieren;
einschränken.
ra·tion·al □ ['ræʃənl] vernunftge-
mäß; vernünftig, rational (*a.* Ⱥ);
ra·tion·al·ism ['ræʃnəlizəm] Ratio-
nalismus *m*; '**ra·tion·al·ist** Ratio-
nalist *m*; **ra·tion·al·i·ty** [ræʃə'næ-
liti] Vernunft(mäßigkeit) *f*; **ra·tion-
al·i·za·tion** [ræʃnəlai'zeiʃən] Ra-
tionalisierung *f*; wirtschaftliche
Vereinfachung *f*; '**ra·tion·al·ize**
rationalisieren; wirtschaftlich vereinfachen.
rat race ['rætreis] sinnlose Hetze *f*;
rücksichtsloses Aufstiegsstreben *n*;
Prestigesucht *f*.
rat-tat ['ræt'tæt] Pochen *n*.
rat·ten ['rætn] *v/t.* sabotieren; *v/i.*
Sabotage treiben; '**rat·ten·ing**
Sabotage *f*.
rat·tle ['rætl] 1. Gerassel *n*; Geklapper *n*; Geplauder *n*, Geplapper *n*;
Klapper *f*, Rassel *f*; (Todes)Rö-
cheln *n*; 2. *v/i.* rasseln, rattern;
klappern; plappern; röcheln; *v/t.*
rasseln mit; jagen; erschüttern; F
nervös machen; ⌣ *off od.* out her-
(unter)rasseln, -schnurren; '⌣-
-**brain**, '⌣-**pate** Hohl-, Wirrkopf
m; '⌣-**brained**, '⌣-**pat·ed** hohl-,
wirrköpfig; '**rat·tler** Lärmmacher
m; Schwätzer *m*; *sl.* Mordskerl *m*,
-ding *n*; *Am.* F = '**rat·tle·snake**
Klapperschlange *f*; '**rat·tle·trap**
1. klapperig; 2. Klapperkasten *m*
(*Fahrzeug*).
rat·tling □ ['rætliŋ] rasselnd; F lebhaft, schneidig; *adv.* sehr, äußerst;
at a ⌣ *pace* in rasendem Tempo.
rat·ty *sl.* ['ræti] nervös, gereizt.
rau·cous □ ['rɔːkəs] heiser, rauh.
rav·age ['rævidʒ] 1. Verwüstung *f*;
2. *v/t.* verwüsten, verheeren; *v/i.*
Verheerungen anrichten.
rave [reiv] rasen, toben; phantasieren; schwärmen (*about, of* von).
rav·el ['rævəl] *v/t.* verwickeln; *a.* ⌣
out entflechten, auftrennen; *v/i. a.* ⌣
out ausfasern, aufgehen.
ra·ven¹ ['reivn] Rabe *m*.

rav·en² ['rævn] **1.** *s. ravin*; **2.** rauben; gierig sein; verschlingen; **rav·en·ous** □ ['rævənəs] gefräßig; heißhungrig; **'rav·en·ous·ness** Raubgier *f*; Gefräßigkeit *f*; Heißhunger *m*.

rav·in *rhet.* ['rævin] Raubgier *f*; Beute *f*.

ra·vine [rə'viːn] Schlucht *f*; Hohlweg *m*.

rav·ings ['reiviŋz] *pl.* Delirien *n/pl.*; irres Gerede *n*.

rav·ish ['ræviʃ] entzücken, hinreißen; vergewaltigen; *rhet.* rauben, entreißen; **'rav·ish·er** Schänder *m*; **'rav·ish·ing** □ hinreißend; entzückend; **'rav·ish·ment** Schändung *f*; Entzücken *n*.

raw □ [rɔː] **1.** roh (*ungekocht; unbearbeitet*); Roh...; wund; rauh (*Wetter*); ungeübt, unerfahren; ~ material Rohmaterial *n*; *he got a* ~ *deal sl.* man hat ihm übel mitgespielt; **2.** wunde *od.* empfindliche Stelle *f* (*bsd. fig.*); **'~-boned** hager, knochig; **'~-hide** Rohleder *n*; **'raw·ness** Roheit *f*; Rauhigkeit *f*; Unerfahrenheit *f*.

ray¹ [rei] **1.** Strahl *m* (*a.* ♀); *fig.* Schimmer *m*; **2.** ausstrahlen.

ray² *ichth.* [~] Rochen *m*.

ray·less ['reilis] strahlenlos.

ray·on ['reiɔn] Kunstseide *f*.

raze [reiz] *Haus etc.* abreißen; *Festung* schleifen; ~ *to the ground* dem Erdboden gleichmachen.

ra·zor ['reizə] Rasiermesser *n*, -apparat *m*; **'~-blade** Rasierklinge *f*; **'~-edge** *fig. des Messers* Schneide *f*, kritische Lage *f*; **'~-strop** Streichriemen *m*.

razz *Am. sl.* [ræz] aufziehen.

raz·zi·a ['ræziə] Beute-, Raubzug *m*.

raz·zle-daz·zle *sl.* ['ræzldæzl] Durcheinander *n*; Schwindel *m*; Tamtam *m*; Sauftour *f*.

re ♯♭, ♮ [riː] betrifft, bezüglich.

re... [~] wieder...; zurück...; neu...; um...

reach [riːtʃ] **1.** Ausstrecken *n*; Griff *m*; Reichweite *f*; Fassungskraft *f*, Horizont *m*; Flußabschnitt *m*, -strecke *f*; *beyond* ~, *out of* ~ unerreichbar; *within easy* ~ leicht erreichbar; **2.** *v/i. a.* ~ *out* (mit der Hand) reichen, langen, greifen; reichen, sich erstrecken (*to* bis); *v/t.* (hin-, her)reichen, (-)langen;

oft ~ *out* ausstrecken; erreichen.

reach-me-downs F ['riːtʃmi'daunz] *pl.* Kleider *n/pl.* von der Stange.

re·act [riː'ækt] reagieren (*to* auf *acc.*); (ein)wirken (*on, upon* auf *acc.*); sich auflehnen (*against* gegen).

re·ac·tion [ri'ækʃən] Reaktion *f* (*to* auf *acc.*), Rückwirkung *f* (*upon* auf *acc.*); *pol.* Rückschritt *m*; **re'ac·tion·ar·y** *bsd. pol.* [~ʃnəri] **1.** reaktionär; **2.** Reaktionär *m*.

re·ac·tive □ [ri:'æktiv] rück-, gegenwirkend; **re'ac·tor** *phys.* Reaktor *m*, Umwandlungsanlage *f*.

read 1. [riːd] (*irr.*) *v/t.* lesen (*a. fig.*); deuten; (an)zeigen (*Thermometer etc.*); ~ *off* ablesen; ~ *out* laut (vor-) lesen; *zu Ende lesen*; ~ *to s.o.* j-m vorlesen; *v/i.* lesen; studieren; sich *gut etc. lesen; so u. so lauten*; **2.** [red] *pret. u. p.p. von* 1; **3.** [red] *adj.* belesen, bewandert (*in in dat.*).

read·a·ble □ ['riːdəbl] lesbar; leserlich; lesenswert.

re·ad·dress ['riːə'dres] umadressieren.

read·er ['riːdə] Leser(in); Vorleser (-in); *typ.* Korrektor *m*; *univ.* Dozent *m* (*in* für); Lesebuch *n*; **'read·er·ship** Vorleseramt *n*; *univ.* Dozentenstelle *f*.

read·i·ly ['redili] *adv.* bereit, gleich, leicht; gern; **'read·i·ness** Bereitschaft *f*; Bereitwilligkeit *f*; Schnelligkeit *f*; Raschheit *f*; Fertigkeit *f*; ~ *of mind od. wit* Geistesgegenwart *f*.

read·ing ['riːdiŋ] Lesen *n*; Lesung *f* (*a. parl.*); Stand *m* des Thermometers *etc.*; Belesenheit *f*; Lektüre *f*; Lesart *f*, Version *f*; Auffassung *f*; *attr.* Lese...; ~ *mat·ter* Lesestoff *m*, Lektüre *f*; **'~-room** Lesesaal *m*, -zimmer *n*.

re·ad·just ['riːə'dʒʌst] wieder in Ordnung bringen; wieder anpassen; *pol. etc.* neu orientieren; **'re·ad·'just·ment** Wiederanpassung *f*; Neuordnung *f*.

re·ad·mis·sion ['riːəd'miʃən] Wiederzulassung *f*.

re·ad·mit ['riːəd'mit] wieder zulassen; **'re·ad'mit·tance** Wiederzulassung *f*.

read·y ['redi] **1.** *adj.* □ bereit, fertig; bereitwillig, geneigt; schnell bei der Hand; im Begriff (*to inf.* zu *inf.*);

schnell; gewandt (*at,* in in *dat.*); bequem, leicht; gleich zur Hand, nahe; ✝ bar; ⚓ klar; ~ *reckoner* Rechentabelle *f;* ~ *for action* gefechtsbereit; ~ *for take-off* ✈ startbereit; ~ *for use* gebrauchsfertig; ~ *to serve* tafelfertig; *make od. get* ~ (sich) fertig machen; **2.** *adv.* fertig; *readier* schneller; *readiest* am schnellsten; **3.** *su. at the* ~ schußfertig; '~-'**made** fertig, Konfektions... (*Kleidung*); *fig.* schematisch, alltäglich; '~-to-'**wear** Konfektions...

re·af·firm ['ri:ə'fə:m] nochmals versichern.

re·a·gent ⚗ [ri:'eidʒənt] Reagens *n.*

re·al □ [riəl] wirklich, tatsächlich, real; echt; ~ **es·tate** Grundbesitz *m,* Immobilien *f/pl.*

re·a·lign ['ri:ə'lain] politisch neuordnen; '**re·a·lign·ment** politische Neuordnung *f.*

re·a·lism ['riəlizəm] Realismus *m;* '**re·al·ist 1.** Realist *m;* **2.** = **re·al·'is·tic** (~*ally*) realistisch; sachlich; wirklichkeitsnah; **re·al·i·ty** [ri'æliti] Wirklichkeit *f;* **re·al·iz·a·ble** □ ['riəlaizəbl] zu verwirklichen(d); verwertbar; **re·al·i'za·tion** Verwirklichung *f;* Vergegenwärtigung *f,* Erkenntnis *f;* ✝ Verwertung *f,* Realisierung *f;* '**re·al·ize** merken, sich klarmachen, sich im klaren sein über *acc.,* erkennen, sich vergegenwärtigen; verwirklichen, in die Tat umsetzen; ✝ realisieren, zu Geld machen; *Gewinn* erzielen; '**re·al·ly** wirklich, in der Tat.

realm [relm] Königreich *n; fig.* Reich *n; Peer of the* ~ Mitglied *n* des Oberhauses.

re·al·tor *Am.* ['riəltə] Grundstücksmakler *m;* '**re·al·ty** 🏠 Grundeigentum *n.*

ream[1] [ri:m] Ries *n* (*Papier*).

ream[2] ⊕ [~] *Loch* erweitern; ⊕ *mst* ~ *out* nachbohren; '**ream·er** Reibahle *f.*

re·an·i·mate ['ri:'ænimeit] wiederbeleben; '**re·an·i'ma·tion** Wiederbelebung *f.*

reap [ri:p] *Korn* schneiden; *Feld* mähen; *fig.* ernten; '**reap·er** Schnitter(in); Mähmaschine *f;* '**reap·ing** Ernten *n;* '**reap·ing--hook** Sichel *f;* '**reap·ing-ma·chine** Mähmaschine *f.*

re·ap·pear ['ri:ə'piə] wieder erscheinen; '**re·ap'pear·ance** Wiedererscheinen *n.*

re·ap·pli·ca·tion ['ri:æpli'keiʃən] wiederholte Anwendung *f.*

re·ap·point ['ri:ə'pɔint] wiederanstellen, -ernennen.

re·ap·prais·al ['ri:ə'preizəl] Neubeurteilung *f.*

rear[1] [riə] *v/t.* auf-, großziehen; züchten; *rhet.* errichten; *v/i.* sich aufrichten.

rear[2] [~] **1.** Rück-, Hinterseite *f;* Hintergrund *m; mot.,* ⚓ Heck *n;* ✕ Nachhut *f;* hinterer Teil *m; at the* ~ *of, in* (the) ~ *of* hinter (*dat.*); *from the* ~ von hinten; **2.** Hinter..., Rück..., Nach...; ~-*end collision* mot. Auffahrunfall *m;* ~-*view mirror* mot. Rückspiegel *m;* ~ *wheel drive* mot. Hinterradantrieb *m;* ~ *window* mot. Heckscheibe *f;* '~-'**ad·mi·ral** ⚓ Konteradmiral *m;* ~ **ex·it** Hinterausgang *m;* '~-**guard** ✕ Nachhut *f;* '~-**lamp** *mot.* Schlußlicht *n.*

re·arm ['ri:'ɑ:m] aufrüsten; '**re--'ar·ma·ment** Aufrüstung *f.*

rear·most ['riəməust] hinterst.

re·ar·range ['ri:ə'reindʒ] neu ordnen.

rear·ward ['riəwəd] **1.** *adj.* rückwärtig; **2.** *adv. a.* ~*s* rückwärts.

re·as·cend ['ri:ə'send] wieder aufsteigen.

rea·son ['ri:zn] **1.** Vernunft *f;* Verstand *m;* Recht *n,* Billigkeit *f;* Ursache *f,* Grund *m; by* ~ *of* wegen; *for this* ~ aus diesem Grund; *listen to* ~ Vernunft annehmen; *it stands to* ~ *that* ... es leuchtet ein, daß; **2.** *v/i.* logisch *od.* vernünftig denken; schließen; urteilen; argumentieren; *v/t. a.* ~ *out* durchdenken; ~ *away* wegdisputieren; ~ *s.o. into* (*out of*) *s.th.* j-m et. ein- (aus)reden; ~*ed* (wohl)durchdacht; '**rea·son·a·ble** □ vernünftig; billig; mäßig; angemessen; leidlich; '**rea·son·a·bly** ziemlich, leidlich; '**rea·son·er** Denker(in); '**rea·son·ing** Urteilen *n;* Schluß *m;* Beweisführung *f; attr.* Denk..., Urteils...

re·as·sem·ble ['ri:ə'sembl] (sich) wieder versammeln.

re·as·sert ['ri:ə'sə:t] wieder behaupten.

re·as·sur·ance [ri:ə'ʃuərəns] wiederholte Versicherung *f;* Beruhigung *f*; **re·as'sure** wieder versichern; (wieder) beruhigen.

re·a·wak·en [ri:ə'weikən] wieder erwecken; wieder erwachen.

re·bap·tize ['ri:bæp'taiz] wiedertaufen.

re·bate¹ † ['ri:beit] Rabatt *m*, Abzug *m*; Rückzahlung *f*.

re·bate² ⊕ ['ræbit] 1. Falz *m*, Nut *f*; 2. (ein)falzen.

reb·el 1. ['rebl] Rebell *m*; Empörer *m*, Aufrührer *m*; 2. [~] aufrührerisch, rebellisch; *fig.* aufsässig, widerspenstig; 3. [ri'bel] rebellieren, sich empören, sich auflehnen; **re'bel·lion** [~jən] Aufruhr *m*, -lehnung *f*, Rebellion *f*, Empörung *f*; **re'bel·lious** = *rebel 2*.

re·birth ['ri:'bə:θ] Wiedergeburt *f*.

re·bound [ri'baund] 1. zurückprallen; 2. Rückprall *m*, -schlag *m*.

re·buff [ri'bʌf] 1. Zurück-, Abweisung *f*; 2. zurück-, abweisen.

re·build ['ri:'bild] (*irr. build*) wieder (auf)bauen.

re·buke [ri'bju:k] 1. Tadel *m*, Rüge *f*; 2. tadeln, rügen.

re·bus ['ri:bəs] Rebus *m*, *n*, Bilderrätsel *n*.

re·but [ri'bʌt] zurückweisen; widerlegen; **re'but·tal** Zurückweisung *f*.

re·cal·ci·trant [ri'kælsitrənt] widerspenstig.

re·call [ri'kɔ:l] 1. Zurückrufung *f*; Abberufung *f*; Widerruf *m*; (Rück-) Erinnerung *f*; total ~ absolutes Gedächtnis *n*; beyond ~, past ~ unwiderruflich; 2. zurückrufen (*fig. to s.o.'s mind* j-m ins Gedächtnis); abberufen; *Ware* abrufen; (sich) erinnern an (*acc.*); *Gefühl* wieder wachrufen; widerrufen; † *Kapital etc.* kündigen; ~ *that* daran erinnern, daß; *until* ~ed bis auf Widerruf.

re·cant [ri'kænt] (als irrig) widerrufen; **re·can·ta·tion** [ri:kæn'teiʃən] Widerruf(ung *f*) *m*.

re·cap¹ F ['ri:kæp] = *recapitulate*; *recapitulation*.

re·cap² *Am.* ['ri:'kæp] *Reifen* besohlen.

re·ca·pit·u·late [ri:kə'pitjuleit] kurz wiederholen, zs.-fassen; **'re·ca·pit·u'la·tion** kurze Wiederholung *f*.

re·cap·ture ['ri:'kæptʃə] 1. Wiedererlangung *f*, -ergreifung *f*; *fig.* Wiederhervorholen *n*; 2. wiedererlangen; wieder ergreifen; zurück-

erobern.

re·cast ['ri:'kɑ:st] 1. (*irr. cast*) ⊕ umgießen; umformen, neu gestalten; neu berechnen; *thea.* neu besetzen; 2. Umformung *f etc.*

re·cede [ri:'si:d] zurücktreten, -weichen; † zurückgehen; *receding* fliehend (*Kinn, Stirn*).

re·ceipt [ri'si:t] 1. Empfang *m e-s Briefes etc.*; Eingang *m von Waren*; † Empfangsschein *m*, Quittung *f*; (Koch)Rezept *n*; ~s *pl.* Einnahmen *f/pl.*; 2. quittieren.

re·ceiv·a·ble [ri'si:vəbl] annehmbar; † noch zu fordern(d), ausstehend; **re'ceive** *v/t.* Besuch, Radio etc. empfangen, erhalten, bekommen; *Eid etc.* abnehmen; *als Gast etc.* aufnehmen; annehmen, anerkennen; *v/i.* empfangen; **re'ceived** anerkannt; allgemein üblich; **re'ceiv·er** Empfänger *m* (*a. tel. u. Radio*); *teleph.* Hörer *m*; *a. ~ of stolen goods* Hehler *m*; *Steuer- etc.* Einnehmer *m*; *a. official ~* ⚖ Masseverwalter *m*; *phys.*, 🔬 Rezipient *m*; **re'ceiv·er·ship** ⚖ Konkursverwaltung *f*; **re'ceiv·ing** Annahme *f*; *Radio*: Empfang *m*; Hehlerei *f*; ~ *set* Rundfunkempfänger *m*.

re·cen·cy ['ri:snsi] Neuheit *f*.

re·cen·sion [ri'senʃən] Durchsicht *f*, Prüfung *f e-s Textes*.

re·cent □ ['ri:snt] neu; frisch; modern; jüngst; *in ~ years* in den letzten Jahren; **'re·cent·ly** neulich, kürzlich, vor kurzem, unlängst; **'re·cent·ness** Neuheit *f*.

re·cep·ta·cle [ri'septəkl] Behälter *m*; *a. floral ~* 🌿 Fruchtboden *m*.

re·cep·tion [ri'sepʃən] Aufnahme *f* (*a. fig.*), (*a. Radio*)Empfang *m*; Annahme *f*; **re'cep·tion·ist** Empfangsdame *f*, -herr *m*; **re'cep·tion--room** Gesellschaftszimmer *n*.

re·cep·tive □ [ri'septiv] empfänglich, aufnahmefähig (*of* für); **re·cep'tiv·i·ty** Empfänglichkeit *f*.

re·cess [ri'ses] 1. Unterbrechung *f*, Pause *f*; *bsd. parl.* Ferien *pl.*; (entlegener) Winkel *m*; Nische *f*, Vertiefung *f*; ~ *es pl. fig.* Tiefe(n *pl.*) *f*; 2. zurücksetzen; ausbuchten.

re·ces·sion [ri'seʃən] Zurückziehen *n*, -treten *n*; † Konjunkturrückgang *m*, rückläufige Bewegung *f*; **re'ces·sion·al** [~ʃənl] 1. *eccl.* Schluß...; *parl.* Ferien...; 2. *eccl.*

Schlußgesang *m*; re'ces·sive [ˌsiv] zurücktretend; rezessiv.

re·chris·ten ['ri:'krisn] umtaufen.

re·cid·i·vist [ri'sidivist] Rückfällige *m*.

rec·ipe ['resipi] Rezept *n*; ~ **book** Kochbuch *n*.

re·cip·i·ent [ri'sipiənt] Empfänger (-in).

re·cip·ro·cal [ri'siprəkəl] **1.** wechsel-, gegenseitig; ⚕, *gr.*, *phls.* reziprok; **2.** ⚕ reziproker Wert *m*; re-'cip·ro·cate [ˌkeit] *v/i.* sich revanchieren, sich erkenntlich zeigen; ⊕ sich hin- und herbewegen; *reciprocating engine* Kolbenmotor *m*; *v/t.* *Glückwünsche etc.* austauschen, erwidern; **re·cip·ro'ca·tion** Hinundherbewegung *f*; Wechselwirkung *f*; Austausch *m*, Erwiderung *f*; **rec·i·proc·i·ty** [resi'prɔsiti] Gegenseitigkeit *f*.

re·cit·al [ri'saitl] Bericht *m*; Erzählung *f*; ⚖ Darlegung *f* des Sachverhalts; ♪ (Solo)Vortrag *m*, Konzert *n*; **rec·i·ta·tion** [resi'teiʃən] Hersagen *n*; Vortrag *m*, Rezitation *f*; **rec·i·ta·tive** ♪ [ˌtə'ti:v] **1.** rezitativartig; **2.** Rezitativ *n* (*Sprechgesang*); **re·cite** [ri'sait] vortragen, rezitieren; deklamieren; aufsagen; berichten; **re'cit·er** Vortragskünstler(in); Vortragsbuch *n*.

reck *poet.* [rek] sich kümmern (*of* um), fragen (*of* nach).

reck·less □ ['reklis] unbekümmert (*of* um); rücksichtslos; leichtsinnig, sorglos; '**reck·less·ness** Unbekümmertheit *f*; Rücksichtslosigkeit *f*; Leichtsinn *m*.

reck·on ['rekən] *v/t.* rechnen, zählen; *a.* ~ *for*, ~ *as* schätzen, halten für, ansehen als; ~ *up* zs.-rechnen, -zählen; *v/i.* rechnen; meinen, denken, vermuten; ~ (*up*)*on* rechnen, sich verlassen auf (*acc.*); ~ *with* rechnen mit *Tatsachen etc.*; **reck·on·er** ['rekən] Rechner(in); '**reck·on·ing** Rechnen *n*; (Ab)Rechnung *f*; Berechnung *f*; *be out in od. of one's* ~ *fig.* sich verrechnen *od.* verrechnet haben.

re·claim [ri'kleim] wiedergewinnen; *j.* bessern; bekehren; zähmen; zivilisieren; *Land* urbar machen; ⊕ aus Altmaterial gewinnen; zurückfordern; **re'claim·a·ble** verbesserungsfähig.

rec·la·ma·tion [reklə'meiʃən] Besserung *f*; Urbarmachung *f*; Zurückforderung *f*; Einspruch *m*.

re·cline [ri'klain] (sich) (zurück-) lehnen; ~ *upon fig.* sich stützen auf (*acc.*); **re·clin·ing chair** Lehnstuhl *m*.

re·cluse [ri'klu:s] **1.** zurückgezogen, einsiedlerisch; **2.** Einsiedler(in).

rec·og·ni·tion [rekəg'niʃən] Anerkennung *f*; (Wieder)Erkennen *n*; **rec·og·niz·a·ble** □ ['ˌnaizəbl] erkennbar; **re·cog·ni·zance** ⚖ [ri'kɔgnizəns] schriftliche Verpflichtung *f*; Kaution *f*; **rec·og·nize** ['rekəgnaiz] anerkennen; (wieder-) erkennen; *auf der Straße* grüßen.

re·coil [ri'kɔil] **1.** zurückprallen; **2.** Rückstoß *m*, -lauf *m*.

rec·ol·lect[1] [rekə'lekt] sich erinnern (*gen.*) *od.* an (*acc.*).

re·col·lect[2] [ri:kə'lekt] wieder sammeln; ~ *o.s.* sich fassen.

rec·ol·lec·tion [rekə'lekʃən] Erinnerung *f* (*of an acc.*); Gedächtnis *n*.

re·com·mence ['ri:kə'mens] wieder beginnen.

rec·om·mend [rekə'mend] empfehlen; **rec·om'mend·a·ble** empfehlenswert; **rec·om·men'da·tion** Empfehlung *f*; Vorschlag *m*; **rec·om'mend·a·to·ry** [ˌdətəri] empfehlend; Empfehlungs…

re·com·mis·sion ['ri:kə'miʃən] wieder an- *od.* einstellen.

re·com·mit ['ri:kə'mit] *parl. an e-n Ausschuß* zurückverweisen; ~ *to prison* wieder verhaften.

rec·om·pense ['rekəmpens] **1.** Belohnung *f*, Vergeltung *f*; Entgelt *n*, Ersatz *m*; **2.** *j. od. et.* belohnen, *et.* vergelten; *j.* entschädigen; *et.* ersetzen, wiedergutmachen.

re·com·pose ['ri:kəm'pəuz] neu zs.-setzen; wieder beruhigen.

rec·on·cil·a·ble □ ['rekənsailəbl] versöhnbar; vereinbar; '**rec·on·cile** versöhnen; in Einklang bringen (*with*, *to* mit); *Streit* schlichten; ~ *o.s. to* sich aussöhnen mit; sich abfinden mit; '**rec·on·cil·er** Versöhner(in); **rec·on·cil·i·a·tion** [ˌsili'eiʃən] Versöhnung *f*; Aussöhnung *f*.

re·con·dite □ *fig.* [ri'kɔndait] tief, dunkel; entlegen, ausgefallen.

re·con·di·tion ['ri:kən'diʃən] wieder herrichten; ⊕ überholen.

re·con·nais·sance ['ri'kɔnisəns] ✕ Aufklärung *f*, Erkundung *f*; *fig.* Übersicht *f*; ~ **car** ✕ Panzerspähwagen *m*; ~ **flight** ✕ Aufklärungsflug *m*.

rec·on·noi·ter, rec·on·noi·tre ✕ [rekə'nɔitə] erkunden, auskundschaften.

re·con·quer ['ri:'kɔŋkə] wiedererobern; 're·con·quest [~kwest] Wiedereroberung *f*.

re·con·sid·er ['ri:kən'sidə] wieder erwägen; 're·con·sid·er'a·tion nochmalige Erwägung *f*.

re·con·sti·tute ['ri:'kɔnstitju:t] wiederherstellen; 're·con·sti'tu·tion Wiederherstellung *f*.

re·con·struct ['ri:kəns'trʌkt] wiederaufbauen; *fig.* rekonstruieren; 're·con'struc·tion Wiederaufbau *m*, -herstellung *f*.

re·con·ver·sion ['ri:kən'və:ʃən] Umstellung *f auf Friedensproduktion*; 're·con'vert umstellen.

rec·ord[1] ['rekɔ:d] Aufzeichnung *f*; ⚖ Protokoll *n*; Akte *f*; schriftlicher Bericht *m*; Urkunde *f* (*a. fig.*); persönliche Vergangenheit *f*, Ruf *m*, Leumund *m* (*bsd. pol.*); Verzeichnis *n*; Wiedergabe *f*; Schallplatte *f*; *Sport:* Rekord *m*, Höchstleistung *f*; ~ **time** Rekordzeit *f*; *it is on* ~ es steht fest; *place on* ~ schriftlich niederlegen; *beat od. break the* ~ den Rekord brechen; *set up od. establish a* ~ e-n Rekord aufstellen; ♌ *Office* Staatsarchiv *n*; *off the* ~ inoffiziell.

re·cord[2] [ri'kɔ:d] auf-, verzeichnen, eintragen; festhalten; *by* ~*ed delivery* ✉ per Einschreiben; **re'cord·er** Registrator *m*; Stadtrichter *m*; Aufnahme-, *bsd.* Tonbandgerät *n*; ♪ Blockflöte *f*; **re'cord·ing** *Radio:* Aufzeichnung *f*, Aufnahme *f*; 'rec·ord-play·er Plattenspieler *m*.

re·count[1] [ri'kaunt] (eingehend) erzählen.

re·count[2] ['ri:'kaunt] **1.** nachzählen; **2.** Nachzählung *f*.

re·coup [ri'ku:p] *j.* schadlos halten (für); *et.* wieder einbringen.

re·course [ri'kɔ:s] Zuflucht *f*; *have* ~ *to* s-e Zuflucht nehmen zu.

re·cov·er[1] [ri'kʌvə] *v/t.* wiedererlangen, -finden, -gewinnen; wiedererobern; wieder einbringen, wiedergutmachen; *Schulden etc.*

eintreiben; *be* ~*ed* wiederhergestellt sein (*Kranker*); *v/i.* sich erholen; wieder zu sich kommen; *a.* ~ *o.s.* sich fangen; ⚖ (*in one's suit* s-n Prozeß) gewinnen.

re·cov·er[2] ['ri:'kʌvə] wiederbedekken; *Schirm etc.* neu beziehen.

re·cov·er·a·ble [ri'kʌvərəbl] wiedererlangbar; eintreibbar; wiederherstellbar; **re'cov·er·y** Wiedererlangung *f*; Wiederherstellung *f*; Genesung *f*, Erholung *f*; ~ **vehicle** Abschleppwagen *m*.

rec·re·ant ['rekriənt] **1.** □ feig; abtrünnig; **2.** Feigling *m*; Abtrünnige *m*.

rec·re·ate ['rekrieit] *v/t.* auf-, erfrischen; erquicken; erheitern; *v/i. a.* ~ *o.s.* sich erholen; **rec·re'a·tion** Erholung *f*; Erholungspause *f*; Erheiterung *f*; ~ **centre**, *Am.* ~ **center** Freizeitzentrum *n*; ~ **ground** Sport-, Spielplatz *m*; 'rec·re·a·tive erquickend; erheiternd.

re·crim·i·nate [ri'krimineit] Gegenbeschuldigungen vorbringen; **re·crim·i'na·tion** Gegenbeschuldigung *f*; Gegenklage *f*.

re·cross ['ri:'krɔs] wieder überqueren.

re·cru·desce [ri:kru:'des] wieder aufbrechen (*Wunde*); wieder ausbrechen (*Krankheit*); **re·cru'descence** Wiederauf-, Wiederausbrechen *n*.

re·cruit [ri'kru:t] **1.** Rekrut *m*; *fig.* Neuling *m*; **2.** *v/t.* erneuern, ergänzen; rekrutieren; *Rekruten* ausheben, einziehen, anwerben; *Gesundheit* wiederherstellen; *v/i.* sich erholen; ✕ Rekruten ausheben, werben; **re'cruit·ment** Rekrutierung *f*; Erholung *f*.

rec·tan·gle ['rektæŋgl] Rechteck *n*; **rec'tan·gu·lar** □ [~gjulə] rechteckig, -winklig.

rec·ti·fi·a·ble ['rektifaiəbl] zu berichtigen(d); **rec·ti·fi·ca·tion** [~fi-'keiʃən] Berichtigung *f*; Verbesserung *f*; ♒, ♓ Rektifikation *f*; **rec·ti·fi·er** ['~faiə] Berichtiger *m*; ♓ *etc.* Rektifizierer *m*; *Radio:* Gleichrichter *m*; **rec·ti·fy** ['~fai] berichtigen; verbessern; ♒, ♓ rektifizieren; *⚡, Radio:* gleichrichten; **rec·ti·lin·e·al** [rekti'linjəl], **rec·ti·lin·e·ar** □ [~njə] geradlinig; **rec·ti·tude** ['rektitju:d] Geradheit *f*; Redlichkeit *f*, Aufrichtigkeit *f*.

rec·tor ['rektə] Pfarrer *m*; *univ*. Rektor *m*; (Schul)Direktor *m*; **rec·tor·ate** ['ˌrit], **'rec·tor·ship** Rektorat *n*; **'rec·to·ry** Pfarre *f*; Pfarrhaus *n*.

rec·tum *anat*. ['rektəm] Mastdarm *m*.

re·cum·bent □ [ri'kʌmbənt] lehnend, liegend; ruhend.

re·cu·per·ate [ri'kju:pəreit] sich erholen; **re·cu·per'a·tion** Erholung *f*; **re'cu·per·a·tive** [ˌrətiv] wiederherstellend.

re·cur [ri'kə:] *in Gedanken od. Worten* zurückkehren (*to* zu), -kommen (*to* auf *acc*.); wiederkehren, -kommen, sich wieder einstellen (*Gedanke etc*.); (periodisch) wiederkehren; ~ *to s.o.* (periodisch) wiederkehren; ~ *to s.o.'s mind* j-m wieder ins Gedächtnis kommen, j-m wieder einfallen; ~*ring decimal* periodischer Dezimalbruch *m*; **re·cur·rence** [ri'kʌrəns] Wieder-, Rückkehr *f*; ~ *to* Zurückkommen *n* auf (*acc*.); **re'cur·rent** □ wiederkehrend; *anat*. rückläufig; ~ *fever* Rückfallfieber *m*.

re·curve [ri:'kə:v] (sich) zurückbiegen.

rec·u·sant ['rekjuzənt] widerspenstig.

re·cy·cle [ri:'saikl] wieder verwerten; **re'cy·cling** Wiederverwertung *f*, Recycling *n*.

red [red] **1.** rot (*engS. pol*.); ♀ *Cross* Rotes Kreuz *n*; ~ *currant* Johannisbeere *f*; ~ *deer* Rotwild *n*; ~ *ensign* britische Handelsflagge *f*; ~ *heat* Rotglut *f*; ~ *herring* Bückling *m*; *draw a ~ herring across the trail* e-n Ablenkungsversuch machen; ~ *lead* Mennige *f*; *paint the town ~ sl.* auf die Pauke hauen; **2.** Rot *n*; *bsd. pol*. Rote *m*; *bsd. Am*. F roter Heller *m*; *see ~ rot sehen*, wild werden; *be in the ~ Am*. F in Schulden stecken.

re·dact [ri'dækt] abfassen; herausgeben; **re'dac·tion** Redaktion *f*, Fassung *f*; Neuausgabe *f*.

red·breast ['redbrest] *a. robin ~* Rotkehlchen *n*; **'Red·brick** die Provinzuniversitäten *f/pl*.; **'red·cap** Militärpolizist *m*; *Am*. Gepäckträger *m*; **red·den** ['redn] (sich) röten; erröten; **'red·dish** rötlich; **red·dle** ['ˌl] Rötel *m*.

re·dec·o·rate ['ri:'dekəreit] *Zimmer* renovieren (lassen); **'re·dec·o'ra·tion** Renovierung *f*.

re·deem [ri'di:m] zurück-, loskaufen; aus-, ablösen; *Pfand, Versprechen* einlösen; ✝ amortisieren; büßen, wiedergutmachen; *Zeit* wieder einbringen; ersetzen, entschädigen für; erlösen; bewahren (*from* vor *dat*.); **re'deem·a·ble** ablösbar; tilgbar; ✝ kündbar; wiedergutzumachen(d); wiedererlangbar; **Re'deem·er** Erlöser *m*, Heiland *m*.

re·de·liv·er ['ri:di'livə] wieder ab-, ausliefern; wieder befreien.

re·demp·tion [ri'dempʃən] Rückkauf *m*; Auslösung *f*; ✝ Amortisation *f*; Wiedergutmachung *f*; Erlösung *f*; **re'demp·tion·er** *hist*. Amerikaeinwanderer *m*, der s-e Überfahrt abdiente; **re'demp·tive** erlösend.

re·de·ploy ['ri:di'plɔi] umgruppieren.

re·de·vel·op ['ri:di'veləp] *Haus, Stadtteil* sanieren; **'re·de'vel·op·ment** Sanierung *f e-s Hauses od. Stadtteils*.

red...: '~**faced** mit rotem Kopf; '~**haired** rothaarig; '~'**hand·ed:** *catch s.o. ~* j. auf frischer Tat ertappen; '~**head** Rotschopf *m*; Hitzkopf *m*; '~'**head·ed** rothaarig; '~'**hot** rotglühend; *fig*. hitzig.

re·dif·fu·sion ['ri:di'fju:ʒən] Übernahme *f* e-s Radio- *od*. Fernsehprogramms.

Red In·di·an [re'dindjən] Indianer (-in).

red·in·te·grate [re'dintigreit] wiederherstellen, erneuern; **red·in·te·'gra·tion** Wiederherstellung *f*.

re·di·rect [ri:di'rekt] *Brief* umadressieren, nachsenden.

re·dis·count [ri:'diskaunt] **1.** rediskontieren; **2.** Rediskont(ierung *f*) *m*.   [entdecken.]

re·dis·cov·er ['ri:dis'kʌvə] wieder-/

re·dis·trib·ute ['ri:dis'tribju:t] neu verteilen.

red-let·ter day ['red'letə'dei] Fest-, *fig*. Freuden-, Glückstag *m*.

red-light dis·trict ['redlait'distrikt] Bordellviertel *n*.

red·ness ['rednis] Röte *f*.

re·do ['ri:'du] (*irr. do*) neu machen.

red·o·lence ['redəuləns] Duft *m*; **'red·o·lent** duftend (*of* nach); *be* ~ *of fig.* gemahnen an.

re·dou·ble [riː'dʌbl] (sich) verdoppeln.

re·doubt ⚔ [riː'daut] Redoute *f*; **re'doubt·a·ble** *rhet.* fürchterlich.

re·dound [riː'daund]: ~ *to* beitragen, gereichen, führen zu; ~ (*up*)*on* zurückfallen auf (*acc.*).

re·draft ['riː'drɑːft] 1. neuer Entwurf *m*; † Rückwechsel *m*; 2. neu entwerfen.

re·dress [riː'dres] 1. Abhilfe *f*; Wiedergutmachung *f*; ⚖ Entschädigung *f*; *legal* ~ Rechtshilfe *f*; 2. abhelfen (*dat.*); wiedergutmachen.

red...: '~·**skin** Rothaut *f* (*Indianer*); '~·**start** *orn.* Rotschwänzchen *n*; ~ **tape**, ~-**tap·ism** ['~'teipizəm] Bürokratismus *m*, Amtsschimmel *m*; '~-'**tap·ist** Bürokrat *m*, Aktenmensch *m*.

re·duce [riː'djuːs] *fig.* zurückführen, bringen (*to* auf, *in acc.*, zu); verwandeln (*to in acc.*); verringern, -mindern; verkleinern; einschränken; *Preise* herabsetzen; *fig.* herunterbringen; bezwingen; zwingen (*to* zu); ♉, ⚕ reduzieren; ⚗ einrenken; † *Konten* abstimmen; F *e-e* Abmagerungskur machen; ~ *to writing* schriftlich niederlegen; **re'duc·i·ble** zurückführbar, reduzierbar (*to* auf *acc.*); **re·duc·tion** [riː'dʌkʃən] Reduktion *f*; *fig.* Zurückführung *f*; Verwandlung *f*; Herabsetzung *f*, (Preis)Nachlaß *m*, Rabatt *m*; Verminderung *f*; Verkleinerung *f e-s Bildes etc.*; Bezwingung *f*; ⚗ Einrenkung *f*.

re·dun·dance, **re·dun·dan·cy** [riː'dʌndəns(i)] Überfülle *f*, Überfluß *m*; Arbeitslosigkeit *f*; **re'dun·dant** □ überflüssig, -zählig; arbeitslos; übermäßig; üppig; weitschweifig.

re·du·pli·cate [riː'djuːplikeit] verdoppeln; wiederholen; **re·du·pli-'ca·tion** Verdoppelung *f*.

red·wood ['redwud] Rotholz *n*, Redwood *n*.

re·dye ['riː'dai] (wieder)auffärben.

re·ech·o [riː'ekəu] widerhallen.

reed [riːd] Ried *n*, Schilfrohr *n*; Rohrflöte *f*; *the* ~*s pl.* ♪ die Rohrblattinstrumente *n/pl.*

re·ed·it ['riː'edit] neu herausgeben.

re·ed·u·ca·tion ['riːedjuˈkeiʃən] Umschulung *f*, Umerziehung *f*.

reed·y ['riːdi] schilfreich; lang aufgeschossen; schrill; piepsend (*Stimme*).

reef[1] [riːf] (Felsen)Riff *n*.

reef[2] ⚓ [~] 1. Reff *n*; 2. reffen.

reef·er[1] ['riːfə] Seemannsjacke *f*.

reef·er[2] *Am. sl.* [~] Marihuana-Zigarette *f*.

reek [riːk] 1. Rauch *m*, Dampf *m*; Dunst *m*; 2. rauchen, dampfen (*with* von); dunsten, *unangenehm* riechen (*of* nach); '**reek·y** rauchig; dunstig.

reel [riːl] 1. Haspel *f*; (Garn-, Film)Rolle *f*, Spule *f*; *schottischer Tanz*; 2. *v/t.* haspeln; wickeln, spulen; ~ *off* abhaspeln, herunterleiern; *v/i.* wirbeln; schwanken; taumeln.

re·e·lect ['riːi'lekt] wiederwählen; '**re·e'lec·tion** Wiederwahl *f*.

re·el·i·gi·ble ['riː'elidʒəbl] wiederwählbar.

re·en·act ['riːi'nækt] wieder in Kraft setzen; *thea.* neu inszenieren; wiederholen.

re·en·force ['riːin'fɔːs] *etc.* = *reinforce etc.*

re·en·gage ['riːin'geidʒ] *j.* wieder ein-, anstellen.

re·en·list ⚔ ['riːin'list] wieder eintreten, weiter dienen.

re·en·ter ['riː'entə] wieder eintreten (*in acc.*); '**re·'ent·er·ing**, **re·en·trant** [riː'entrənt] einspringend (*Winkel*); '**re·'en·try** *Raumfahrt:* Wiedereintritt *m* in die Erdatmosphäre.

re·es·tab·lish ['riːis'tæbliʃ] wiederherstellen; '**re·es'tab·lish·ment** Wiederherstellung *f*.

reeve[1] ⚓ [riːv] einscheren.

reeve[2] [~] Vogt *m*, Statthalter *m*; Aufseher *m*.

re·ex·am·i·na·tion ['riːigzæmi'neiʃən] nochmalige Prüfung *f*; '**re-·ex'am·ine** nochmals prüfen.

re·ex·change ['riːiks'tʃeindʒ] Rücktausch *m*; † Rückwechsel *m*.

re·fec·tion [riˈfekʃən] Erfrischung *f*; **re'fec·to·ry** [~təri] Refektorium *n*, Speisesaal *m*.

re·fer [riˈfəː]: ~ *to* verweisen, überweisen an (*acc.*); sich beziehen, anspielen auf (*acc.*); sprechen von, erwähnen (*acc.*); gelten für (*od.*

dat.); befragen (*acc.*), nachschlagen in (*dat.*); zurückführen auf (*acc.*), zuschreiben (*dat.*); **re·fer·a·ble:** ~ *to* zu beziehen(d) auf (*acc.*); zuzuschreiben(d) (*dat.*); **ref·er·ee** [refə-'ri:] Schiedsrichter *m*; *Boxen*: Ringrichter *m*; *parl. etc.* Referent *m*, Sachbearbeiter *m*; **ref·er·ence** ['refrəns] Referenz *f*, Empfehlung *f*, Zeugnis *n*; Bezugnahme *f*, Verweisung *f* (*to* auf *acc.*); Anspielung *f*; Beziehung *f*; Auskunft(geber *m*) *f*; *in od. with* ~ *to* in betreff, hinsichtlich (*gen.*), in bezug auf (*acc.*); *terms pl. of* ~ Richtlinien *f/pl.*; Zuständigkeitsbereich *m*; *work of* ~, ~ *book* Nachschlagewerk *n*; ~ *library* Handbibliothek *f*; ~ *number* Aktenzeichen *n*; *make* ~ *to* erwähnen; eingehen auf (*acc.*). **ref·er·en·dum** [refə'rendəm] Volksentscheid *m*.

re·fill ['ri:fil] 1. Nachfüllung *f*; Ersatzfüllung *f*, -mine *f*, -batterie *f*; 2. (sich) wieder füllen, auffüllen.

re·fine [ri'fain] verfeinern, veredeln (*a.* ⊕ *u. fig.*); ⊕ raffinieren, (*a. fig.*) läutern; *v/i.* sich verfeinern *od.* veredeln *od.* läutern; klügeln, tüfteln (*on, upon* an *dat.*); ~ (*up*)*on et.* verfeinern, verbessern; **re·fine·ment** Verfeinerung *f*, Veredlung *f*; Läuterung *f*; Feinheit *f*, Bildung *f*; Klügelei *f*, Spitzfindigkeit *f*; **re·'fin·er** Verfeinerer *m*; ⊕ Raffinateur *m*; Klügler(in); **re·'fin·er·y** ⊕ Raffinerie *f*; *metall.* (Eisen)Hütte *f*.

re·fit ⚓ ['ri:'fit] 1. *v/t.* ausbessern; neu ausrüsten; *v/i.* ausgebessert werden; 2. Ausbesserung *f*.

re·flect [ri'flekt] *v/t.* zurückwerfen, reflektieren; zurückstrahlen, widerspiegeln (*a. fig.*); zum Ausdruck bringen; *v/i.* ~ (*up*)*on* nachdenken über (*acc.*); überlegen (*acc.*); sich abfällig äußern über (*acc.*); ein schlechtes Licht werfen auf (*acc.*); **re·'flec·tion** Rückstrahlung *f*, Reflexion *f*, (Wider)Spiegelung *f*; Reflex *m*; Spiegelbild *n*; Überlegung *f*; Gedanke *m*; abfällige Bemerkung *f*; Makel *m*; **re·'flec·tive** □ reflektierend; nachdenklich; **re·'flec·tor** Reflektor *m*; Scheinwerfer *m*; Rückstrahler *m*.

re·flex ['ri:fleks] 1. zurückgebogen; Reflex...; 2. Widerschein *m*, (*a. physiol.*) Reflex *m*; ~ **ac·tion** Reflex

(-bewegung *f*) *m*; ~ **cam·er·a** Spiegelreflexkamera *f*; **re·flex·ion** [ri-'flekʃən] = *reflection*; **re·flex·ive** □ [ri'fleksiv] zurückwirkend; *gr.* reflexiv, rückbezüglich.

ref·lu·ent ['refluənt] zurückflutend.

re·flux ['ri:flʌks] Rückfluß *m*; Ebbe *f*.   [Aufforstung *f.*|

re·for·est·a·tion ['ri:fɔris'teiʃən]|

re·form[1] [ri'fɔ:m] 1. Verbesserung *f*, Reform *f*; 2. verbessern, reformieren; (sich) bessern.

re·form[2] ['ri:'fɔ:m] (sich) neu bilden; ✗ sich wieder formieren.

ref·or·ma·tion [refə'meiʃən] Umgestaltung *f*; Besserung *f*; 2 *eccl.* Reformation *f*; **re·form·a·to·ry** [ri'fɔ:mətəri] 1. bessernd; 2. Besserungsanstalt *f*; *eccl.* reformiert; **re·'form·er** Reformator *m*; **re·'form·ist** reformistisch.

re·found ['ri:'faund] umgießen.

re·fract [ri'frækt] *Strahlen* brechen; ~*ing telescope* Refraktor *m*; **re·'frac·tion** Strahlenbrechung *f*; **re·'frac·tive** *opt.* Brechungs...; **re·'frac·tor** *opt.* Refraktor *m*; **re·'frac·to·ri·ness** Widerspenstigkeit *f*; Hartnäckigkeit *f*; ⚒ Strengflüssigkeit *f*; **re·'frac·to·ry** 1. □ widerspenstig; aufsässig; hartnäckig; ⊕ feuerfest; ⚒ strengflüssig; 2. ⊕ feuerfester Baustoff *m*.

re·frain[1] [ri'frein] sich enthalten (*from gen.*), unterlassen (*from acc.*).

re·frain[2] [~] Kehrreim *m*, Refrain *m*.

re·fran·gi·ble *phys.* [ri'frændʒəbl] brechbar.

re·fresh [ri'freʃ] (sich) erfrischen; auffrischen; **re·'fresh·er** F Erfrischung *f*; *fig.* Auffrischung *f*; ⚖ Nachschuß *m*; ~ *course* Auffrischungs-, Fortbildungskurs *m*; **re·'fresh·ment** Erfrischung *f*, Erquickung *f*; ~ *room* Erfrischungsraum *m*.

re·frig·er·ant [ri'fridʒərənt] 1. kühlend; 2. Kühlmittel *n*, -trank *m*; **re·'frig·er·ate** [~reit] kühlen; **re·'frig·er·at·ing** Kühl...; Eis...; **re·frig·er·a·tion** Abkühlung *f*; **re·'frig·er·a·tor** Kühlschrank *m*, -raum *m*; ~ *lorry* Kühlwagen *m*.

re·fu·el ['ri:'fjuəl] tanken.

ref·uge ['refju:dʒ] Zuflucht(sstätte) *f*; *a.* street-~ Verkehrsinsel *f*;

mount. (Schutz)Hütte *f*; *take ~ in* s-e Zuflucht nehmen zu; **ref·u·gee** [‿'dʒi:] Flüchtling *m*; *~ camp* Flüchtlingslager *n*.

re·ful·gence [ri'fʌldʒəns] Glanz *m*; **re'ful·gent** □ strahlend.

re·fund 1. [ri:'fʌnd] zurückzahlen; **2.** ['ri:fʌnd] Rückzahlung *f*.

re·fur·bish ['ri:'fə:biʃ] aufpolieren.

re·fur·nish ['ri:'fə:niʃ] neu möblieren.

re·fus·al [ri'fju:zəl] abschlägige Antwort *f*; Weigerung *f*; Verweigerung *f*; Vorkaufsrecht *n* (*of auf acc.*).

re·fuse[1] [ri'fju:z] *v/t.* abschlagen, verweigern; ab-, zurückweisen, ablehnen; scheuen vor (*dat.*); *v/i.* sich weigern; scheuen (*Pferd*).

ref·use[2] ['refju:s] Ausschuß *m*; Abfall *m*, Müll *m*; *fig.* Auswurf *m*.

ref·u·ta·ble □ ['refjutəbl] widerlegbar; **ref·uta·tion** [refju:'teiʃən] Widerlegung *f*; **re·fute** [ri'fju:t] widerlegen.

re·gain [ri'gein] wiedergewinnen.

re·gal □ ['ri:gəl] königlich; Königs...

re·gale [ri'geil] *v/t.* festlich bewirten; erfreuen; *v/i.* schwelgen (*on in dat.*).

re·ga·li·a [ri'geiljə] *pl.* (Krönungs-) Insignien *pl.*

re·gard [ri'gɑ:d] **1.** *fester* Blick *m*; (Hoch)Achtung *f*, Rücksicht *f*; Beziehung *f*; *~s pl.* Grüße *m/pl.*, Empfehlungen *f/pl.*; *have ~ to* Rücksicht nehmen auf (*acc.*); berücksichtigen; sich beziehen auf (*acc.*); *with ~ to* in Hinsicht auf (*acc.*); *with kind ~s* mit herzlichen Grüßen; **2.** ansehen (*as als*); (be)achten; betrachten; betreffen; *as ~s ...* was ... anbetrifft; **re'gard·ful** □ [‿ful] rücksichtsvoll (*of gegen*); **re'gard·ing** hinsichtlich, betreffs (*gen.*); **re'gard·less** □ unbekümmert, sorglos; achtlos; *~ of* ohne Rücksicht auf (*acc.*); unbeschadet (*gen.*).

re·gat·ta [ri'gætə] Regatta *f*.

re·gen·cy ['ri:dʒənsi] Regentschaft *f*.

re·gen·er·ate 1. [ri'dʒenəreit] (sich) erneuern; (sich) regenerieren; (sich) neu bilden; (sich) bessern; **2.** [‿rit] wiedergeboren; **re·gen·er·a·tion** [‿'reiʃən] Erneuerung *f*, *bsd. biol.* Neubildung *f*; *fig.* Wiedergeburt *f*; **re'gen·er·a·tive** [‿rətiv] *Radio:* Rückkopplungs...

re·gent ['ri:dʒənt] **1.** herrschend; **2.** Regent *m*; **'re·gent·ship** Regentschaft *f*.

reg·i·cide ['redʒisaid] Königsmord *m*; Königsmörder *m*.

ré·gime, re·gime [rei'ʒi:m] Regime *n*, Regierungsform *f*; herrschendes System *n*; = *regimen.*

reg·i·men ['redʒimen] Diätvorschriften *f/pl.*; Therapie *f*; *gr.* Rektion *f*; = *régime.*

reg·i·ment ['redʒimənt] **1.** ✕ Regiment *n*; *fig.* Schar *f*; **2.** ['‿ment] reglementieren; organisieren; **reg·i·men·tal** [‿'mentl] ✕ Regiments-...; **reg·i·men·tal·ly** [‿'mentəli] regimentsweise; **reg·i'men·tals** ✕ *pl.* Uniform *f*; **reg·i·men'ta·tion** Reglementierung *f*; Organisierung *f*.

re·gion ['ri:dʒən] Gegend *f*, Gebiet *n*, Region *f*; *fig.* Bereich *m*; **re·gion·al** ['‿dʒənl] **1.** □ örtlich; Orts...; *Radio:* *~ station* = **2.** Regionalsender *m*.

reg·is·ter ['redʒistə] **1.** Register *n*, Verzeichnis *n*; ⊕ Schieber *m*, Ventil *n*; ♪ Register *n*; Stimmumfang *m*; Zählwerk *n*; *cash ~* Registrierkasse *f*; *parish ~* Kirchenbuch *n*; **2.** registrieren *od.* eintragen (lassen); (an)zeigen, auf-, verzeichnen; *Sendung* einschreiben (lassen), *Gepäck* aufgeben, sich *polizeilich* melden; **'reg·is·tered** eingetragen; eingeschrieben (*Brief*); gesetzlich geschützt; *~ design* Gebrauchsmuster *n*.

reg·is·trar [redʒis'trɑ:] Registrator *m*; Standesbeamte *m*; **reg·is·tra·tion** [‿'treiʃən] Registrierung *f*, Eintragung *f*; *~ fee* Anmeldegebühr *f*; **'reg·is·try** Eintragung *f*; Registratur *f*; Register *n*; *~ office* Standesamt *n*; *servants' ~* Stellenvermittlungsbüro *n*.

reg·nant ['regnənt] regierend.

re·gress ['ri:gres] Rückkehr *f*; *fig.* Rückgang *m*; **re·gres·sion** [ri'greʃən] Rückkehr *f*; *fig.* Rückgang *m*; *psych.* Regression *f*; **re'gres·sive** □ [‿siv] rückläufig; rückwirkend.

re·gret [ri'gret] **1.** Bedauern *n* (*at über acc.*); Schmerz *m*, Trauer *f* (*for um*); **2.** bedauern; bereuen; nachtrauern (*dat.*); *schmerzlich* vermissen; **re'gret·ful** □ [‿ful] bedauernd; ~*ly* mit Bedauern; **re-'gret·ta·ble** □ bedauerlich.

re·group ['ri:'gru:p] umgruppieren; **re'group·ment** Umgruppierung *f*.

reg·u·lar ['regjulə] **1.** □ regelmäßig; regelrecht, richtig; ordentlich; pünktlich; ✗ regulär; *eccl.* Ordens...; **2.** *eccl.* Ordensgeistliche *m*; ✗ aktiver Soldat *m*; F Stammgast *m*, -kunde *m*; ~ (**gas**) *Am.* Normal(benzin) *n*; **reg·u·lar·i·ty** [~-'læriti] Regelmäßigkeit *f*; Richtigkeit *f*, Ordnung *f*.

reg·u·late ['regjuleit] regeln, ordnen; regulieren, stellen; **'reg·u·lat·ing** ⊕ Regulier..., Stell...; **reg·u'la·tion 1.** Regulierung *f*; Vorschrift *f*, Bestimmung *f*; Verordnung *f*; Regel *f*; *contrary to* ~*s* ordnungswidrig; **2.** vorschriftsmäßig; ✗ Kommiß...; **reg·u·la·tive** □ ['~lətiv] regelnd; **reg·u·la·tor** ['~leitə] Regulierer *m*, Ordner *m*; ⊕ Regulator *m* (*a.* Uhr).

re·gur·gi·tate [ri:'gə:dʒiteit] *v/t.* wieder ausströmen; *Essen* erbrechen; *v/i.* zurückfließen.

re·ha·bil·i·tate [ri:ə'biliteit] *Haus* renovieren; *Stadtviertel* sanieren; *ins Berufsleben* wiedereingliedern; rehabilitieren; **'re·ha·bil·i'ta·tion** Sanierung *f*; Wiedereingliederung *f*; Rehabilitierung *f*.

re·hash *fig.* ['ri:'hæʃ] **1.** wieder durchkauen *od.* aufwärmen; **2.** Aufguß *m*.

re·hears·al [ri'hə:səl] *thea.*, ♪ Probe *f*; Wiederholung *f*; **re'hearse** *thea.* proben, einstudieren; wiederholen; aufsagen.

re·heat [ri:'hi:t] wieder erhitzen.

reign [rein] **1.** Regierung *f*; *fig.* Herrschaft *f*; **2.** herrschen, regieren.

re·im·burse [ri:im'bə:s] *j.* entschädigen; *Kosten* (wieder)erstatten; ✝ decken; **re·im'burse·ment** Wiedererstattung *f*; Deckung *f*; Entschädigung *f*.

rein [rein] **1.** Zügel *m*; *give* ~ *to* die Zügel schießen lassen (*dat.*); **2.** ~ *in*, ~ *up*, ~ *back* zügeln.

rein·deer *zo.* ['reindiə] Ren(tier) *n*.

re·in·force [ri:in'fɔ:s] **1.** verstärken; ~*d concrete* ⊕ Stahlbeton *m*; **2.** ⊕ Verstärkung *f*; **re·in'force·ment** Verstärkung *f*; Armierung *f* (*Beton*); ~*s pl.* ✗ Verstärkungen *f/pl.*

re·in·stall ['ri:in'stɔ:l] wieder einsetzen; **'re·in'stal(l)·ment** Wiedereinsetzung *f*.

re·in·state ['ri:in'steit] wieder einsetzen; wieder instandsetzen; **'re·in'state·ment** Wiedereinsetzung*f*; Wiederinstandsetzung *f*.

re·in·sur·ance ['ri:n'ʃuərəns] Rückversicherung *f*; **re·in·sure** ['~'ʃuə] rückversichern.

re·in·vest ['ri:in'vest] wieder investieren *od.* anlegen.

re·is·sue ['ri:'isju:] **1.** wieder ausgeben; **2.** Wiederausgabe *f*.

re·it·er·ate [ri:'itəreit] (dauernd) wiederholen; **re·it·er'a·tion** Wiederholung *f*.

re·ject [ri'dʒekt] ver-, wegwerfen; *als wertlos* ausscheiden; ablehnen, ausschlagen; zurückweisen; **re-'jec·tion** Verwerfung *f*; Ablehnung *f*; Zurückweisung *f*; Ausscheidung *f*; ~*s pl.* Ausschußwaren *f/pl.*; **re·jec·tor cir·cuit** *Radio:* Sperrkreis *m*.

re·jig ['ri:'dʒig] *Fabrik* maschinell neu ausstatten.

re·joice [ri'dʒɔis] *v/t.* erfreuen; *rejoiced at od. by* erfreut über (*acc.*); *v/i.* sich freuen (*at*, *in* über *acc.*); **re'joic·ing 1.** □ freudig; **2.** *oft* ~*s pl.* Freude *f*; Freudenfest *n*.

re·join¹ ['ri:'dʒɔin] (sich) wieder vereinigen (*to*, *with* mit); wieder zurückkehren zu; *j.* wieder treffen.

re·join² [ri'dʒɔin] erwidern; **re-'join·der** Erwiderung *f*.

re·ju·ve·nate [ri'dʒu:vineit] verjüngen; **re·ju·ve'na·tion** Verjüngung *f*.

re·kin·dle ['ri:'kindl] (sich) wieder entzünden.

re·lapse [ri'læps] **1.** Rückfall *m*; **2.** zurückfallen, rückfällig werden.

re·late [ri'leit] *v/t.* berichten, erzählen; in Verbindung bringen (*to*, *with* mit); *v/i.* sich beziehen (*to* auf *acc.*), betreffen (*to acc.*); **re'lat·ed** verwandt (*to* mit); **re'lat·er** Erzähler(in).

re·la·tion [ri'leiʃən] Bericht *m*; Erzählung *f*; Beziehung *f* (*with* zu); Verhältnis *n* (*to* zu *j-m*); Verwandtschaft *f*; Verwandte *m*, *f*; *in* ~ *to* in bezug auf (*acc.*); **re'la·tion·ship** Verwandtschaft *f*; Beziehung *f*.

rel·a·tive ['relətiv] **1.** □ sich beziehend, bezüglich (*to gen.*); *gr.*

relativ; bezüglich; verhältnismäßig; entsprechend; jeweilig; **2.** *gr.* Relativpronomen *n*; Verwandte *m, f*; **'rel·a·tive·ly** relativ, verhältnismäßig; **rel·a'tiv·i·ty** Relativität *f*; *theory of* ~ *phys.* Relativitätstheorie *f*.

re·lax [ri'læks] *v/t.* lockern; mildern; nachlassen in *e-r Bemühung etc.*; entspannen; *v/i.* nachlassen; ausspannen, -ruhen, sich entspannen; milder *od.* freundlicher werden; **re·lax'a·tion** Lockerung *f*; Nachlassen *n*; Entspannung *f*, Erholung *f*; **re'laxed** entspannt; zwanglos.

re·lay[1] [ri'lei] **1.** frisches Gespann *n*; Ablösung(smannschaft) *f*; ['ri:'lei] *⚡* Relais *n*; *Radio*: Übertragung *f*; ~ *race Sport*: Staffellauf *m*; ~ *team Sport*: Staffel *f*; **2.** *Radio*: übertragen.

re·lay[2] ['ri:'lei] *(irr. lay) Kabel etc.* neu verlegen.

re·lease [ri'li:s] **1.** Freilassung *f*; *fig.* Befreiung *f*; Freigabe *f*; *Film*: oft *first* ~ Uraufführung *f*; *⚖* Verzichtleistung *f*; *⊕*, *phot.* Auslöser *m*; *press* ~ Pressemitteilung *f*; **2.** frei-, loslassen, erlösen *(from* von); freigeben, entlassen; *Recht* aufgeben; übertragen; *Film* uraufführen; *⊕* auslösen.

rel·e·gate ['religeit] verbannen; verweisen *(to an acc.*); *be* ~*d Sport*: absteigen; **rel·e'ga·tion** Verbannung *f*; Verweisung *f*; *Sport*: Abstieg *m*; *danger of* ~ *Sport*: Abstiegsgefahr *f*.

re·lent [ri'lent] sich erweichen lassen; **re'lent·less** □ unbarmherzig.

rel·e·vance, rel·e·van·cy ['relivəns(i)] Erheblichkeit *f*; Bedeutung *f (to* für); **'rel·e·vant** sachdienlich; zutreffend; wichtig, erheblich *(to* für); entsprechend *(to dat.*).

re·li·a·bil·i·ty [rilaiə'biliti] Zuverlässigkeit *f*; **re'li·a·ble** □ zuverlässig.

re·li·ance [ri'laiəns] Vertrauen *n*, Zutrauen *n*; Verlaß *m* (on auf *acc.*); *fig.* Stütze *f*; **re'li·ant** vertrauensvoll.

rel·ic ['relik] Überrest *m*, -bleibsel *n*; Reliquie *f*; **rel·ict** ['relikt] Witwe *f*.

re·lief [ri'li:f] Erleichterung *f*; Trost *m*; (angenehme) Unterbrechung *f*; Unterstützung *f*; *✗* Ablösung *f*; *✗*

Entsatz *m*; Beistand *m*; Hilfe *f*; *⚖* Abhilfe *f*; *△ etc.* Relief *n*, erhabene Arbeit *f*; *be on* ~ Unterstützung beziehen; *poor* ~ Armenpflege *f*; ~ *work* Hilfswerk *n*; ~ *works pl.* Notstandsarbeiten *f/pl.*; *stand out in* ~ *against* sich abheben gegen.

re·lieve [ri'li:v] erleichtern; mildern, lindern; *Arme etc.* unterstützen; *✗* ablösen; *✗* entsetzen; *⚖* (ab)helfen *(dat.*); befreien *(of* von); entheben *(of gen.*); hervortreten lassen; (angenehm) unterbrechen; ~ *nature,* ~ *o.s.* s-e Notdurft verrichten.

re·lie·vo [ri'li:vəu] Relief *n*.

re·li·gion [ri'lidʒən] Religion *f*; Ordensleben *n*; *fig.* Ehrensache *f*

re·li·gious □ [ri'lidʒəs] Religions...; religiös; fromm; *eccl.* Ordens...; gewissenhaft; **re'li·gious·ness** Religiosität *f*.

re·lin·quish [ri'liŋkwiʃ] aufgeben; verzichten auf *(acc.*); *et.* loslassen; **re'lin·quish·ment** Aufgeben *n*; Verzicht *m* (of auf *acc.*).

rel·i·quar·y ['relikwəri] Reliquienschrein *m*.

rel·ish ['reliʃ] **1.** Geschmack *m*; Beigeschmack *m*; *fig.* Kostprobe *f*; Würze *f*; Behagen *n*, Genuß *m*; **2.** *v/t.* gern essen; Geschmack finden an *(dat.*); schmackhaft machen; *did you* ~ *your dinner?* hat Ihnen das Essen geschmeckt?; *v/i.* schmecken *(of* nach).

re·load ['ri:'ləud] wieder laden.

re·lo·cate ['ri:'ləu'keit] *Betrieb, Werk* verlegen; **'re·lo'ca·tion** Umsiedlung *f*.

re·luc·tance [ri'lʌktəns] Widerstreben *n*; *bsd. phys.* Widerstand *m*; **re'luc·tant** □ widerstrebend, -willig; zögernd; *be* ~ *to do* sich sträuben zu tun, ungern tun.

re·ly [ri'lai] ~ *(up)on* sich verlassen auf *(acc.*), bauen *od.* vertrauen auf *(acc.*).

re·main [ri'mein] **1.** (ver)bleiben; zurück-, übrigbleiben; **2.** ~*s pl.* Überbleibsel *n/pl.*, -reste *m/pl.*; sterbliche Reste *m/pl.*; **re'main·der** [~də] Rest *m*; *Buchhandel*: Restauflage *f*, Remittenden *pl.*; *⚖* Anwartschaft *f*; **re'main·ing** übrig, restlich.

re·make 1. (*irr. make*) ['ri:'meik] *bsd. Film* neu machen; **2.** ['ri:meik] Neuverfilmung *f*.

re·mand[ri'mɑ:nd] **1.**(ᵼᵼ in die Untersuchungshaft) zurückschicken; **2.** (Zurücksendung *f* in die) Untersuchungshaft *f*; *be on ~* sich in Untersuchungshaft befinden; *prisoner on ~* Untersuchungsgefangene *m*, *f*; *~* **home** Jugendstrafanstalt *f*.

re·mark [ri'mɑ:k] **1.** Beachtung *f*; Bemerkung *f*; *pass a ~* e-e Bemerkung machen; **2.** *v/t.* bemerken (*beobachten*; *äußern*); *v/i.* e-e Bemerkung machen, sich äußern(*upon* über *acc.*); **re'mark·a·ble** □ bemerkenswert; ungewöhnlich; **re·'mark·a·ble·ness** Merkwürdigkeit *f*.

re·mar·riage ['ri:'mæridʒ] Wiederverheiratung *f*; **'re'mar·ry** (sich) wieder verheiraten; wieder heiraten.

re·me·di·a·ble □ [ri'mi:djəbl] heil-, abstellbar; **re·me·di·al** □ [ri'mi:djəl] heilend; abhelfend; *~ teaching* Förderunterricht *m für Lernschwache*.

rem·e·dy ['remidi] **1.** (Heil-, Hilfs-, Gegen-, Rechts)Mittel *n*; (Ab-) Hilfe *f*; **2.** heilen; abhelfen (*dat.*).

re·mem·ber [ri'membə] sich erinnern an (*acc.*); denken an (*acc.*); beherzigen; *im Brief:* j. empfehlen; j. bedenken (*mit e-m Geschenk*); *~ me to him!* grüßen Sie ihn von mir!; **re'mem·brance** Erinnerung *f*; Gedächtnis *n*; Andenken *n*; *~s pl.* Empfehlungen *f/pl.*, Grüße *m/pl.*

re·mil·i·ta·rize ['ri:'militəraiz] remilitarisieren.

re·mind [ri'maind] erinnern (*of an acc.*); *~ me to answer that letter* erinnere mich daran, den Brief zu beantworten; **re'mind·er** Mahnung *f*; Wink *m*.

rem·i·nisce [remi'nis] in Erinnerungen schwelgen; **rem·i·nis·cence** [-'nisns] Erinnerung *f*; **rem·i·nis·cent** □ (sich) erinnernd (*of an acc.*); Erinnerungs...; *be ~ of* erinnern an (*acc.*).

re·miss □ [ri'mis] schlaff, (nach-) lässig; **re'mis·si·ble** (er)läßlich; **re'mis·sion** Vergebung *f von Sünden*; Erlassung *f von Schulden*;

Nachlassen *n*, Abnahme *f*; *~ of fees* Gebührenerlaß *m*; **re'miss·ness** (Nach)Lässigkeit *f*.

re·mit [ri'mit] *v/t.* Sünden vergeben; *Schuld etc.* erlassen; nachlassen in (*dat.*); abstehen von; überweisen; ᵼᵼ zurückverweisen; übersenden; *v/i.* nachlassen; **re·'mit·tance** Geld)Sendung *f*; Überweisung *f*; † Wechselsendung *f*, Rimesse *f*; **re·mit'tee** Empfänger *m*; **re'mit·tent** nachlassend, remittierend(es Fieber *n*); **re'mit·ter** (Geld)Sender *m*, † Remittent *m*.

rem·nant ['remnənt] Überrest *m*; (Stoff)Rest *m*; *~ sale* Resteverkauf *m*.

re·mod·el ['ri:'mɔdl] umbilden.

re·mon·strance [ri'mɔnstrəns] Vorstellung *f*, Einwendung *f*; **re'mon·strant** Einsprucherhebende *m*; **re·mon·strate** ['remənstreit] Vorstellungen machen (*on* über *acc.*; *with s.o.* j-m); einwenden (*that* daß).

re·morse [ri'mɔ:s] Gewissensbisse *m/pl.*; **re'morse·ful** □ [~ful] reuevoll; **re'morse·less** □ hart(herzig), unbarmherzig.

re·mote □ [ri'məut] fern, entfernt, entlegen, abgelegen; *~ control* Fernsteuerung *f*; **re'mote·ness** Entfernung *f*, Ferne *f*, Entlegenheit *f*.

re·mount 1. [ri:'maunt] *v/t.* wieder besteigen; ✕ mit frischen Pferden versehen; neu rahmen; *v/i.* wieder aufsteigen; **2.** ['ri:maunt] frisches Reitpferd *n*; ✕ Remonte *f*.

re·mov·a·ble [ri'mu:vəbl] abnehmbar; abstellbar (*Übel*); absetzbar; **re'mov·al** [~vəl] Entfernen *n*; Wegräumen *n*; Beseitigung *f*; Umzug *m*; Entlassung *f* (*from office aus dem Amt*); *~ service* Möbelspedition *f*; *~ van* Möbelwagen *m*; **re'move 1.** *v/t.* entfernen; wegräumen, -rücken; weg-, abnehmen; beseitigen; entlassen (*from office aus dem Dienst*); *v/i.* (aus-, um-, ver)ziehen; **2.** Entfernung *f*, Abstand *m*; Stufe *f*, Grad *m*; *Schule:* Versetzung *f*; *be a ~ of e-r Klasse*; *get one's ~* versetzt werden; **re'mov·er** (Möbel)Spediteur *m*.

re·mu·ner·ate [ri'mju:nəreit] (be-) lohnen; entschädigen; **re·mu·ner·**

'a·tion Be-, Entlohnung *f*; re-'mu·ner·a·tive □ [⏜rətiv] lohnend.

Ren·ais·sance [ri'neisəns] Renaissance *f*.

re·nal *anat.* ['ri:nl] Nieren...

re·name ['ri:'neim] umbenennen; neu benennen.

re·nas·cence [ri'næsns] Wiedergeburt *f*; Renaissance *f*; re'nas·cent wieder wachsend.

rend [rend] (*irr.*) (zer)reißen.

ren·der ['rendə] wieder-, zurückgeben; *Dienst, Gehorsam etc.* leisten; *Aufmerksamkeit, Ehre etc.* erweisen; *Dank* abstatten; übersetzen (*into* in *acc.*); ♪ vortragen; *künstlerisch* wiedergeben; darstellen, interpretieren; *Grund* angeben; ✝ *Rechnung* überreichen; übergeben; machen (zu); *Fett* auslassen; 'ren·der·ing Wiedergabe *f*; Interpretation *f*; Übersetzung *f etc.*

ren·dez·vous ['rɔndivu:] Treffpunkt *m*; Stelldichein *n*.

ren·di·tion [ren'diʃən] Wiedergabe *f*.

ren·e·gade ['renigeid] Renegat(in), Abtrünnige *m, f*.

re·new [ri'nju:] erneuern; re'new·al Erneuerung *f*.

ren·net ['renit] Lab *n*.

re·nom·i·nate [ri:'nɔmineit] wieder (als Kandidaten) aufstellen.

re·nounce [ri'nauns] *v/t.* entsagen (*dat.*); verzichten auf (*acc.*); verleugnen; *v/i. Karten:* nicht bedienen.

ren·o·vate ['renəuveit] erneuern, renovieren; ren·o'va·tion Erneuerung *f*, Renovierung *f*; 'ren·o·va·tor (Er)Neuerer *m*.

re·nown [ri'naun] Ruhm *m*, Ansehen *n*; re'nowned berühmt, namhaft.

rent[1] [rent] **1.** *pret. u. p.p. von* rend; **2.** Riß *m*; Spalte *f*.

rent[2] [⏜] **1.** Miete *f*; Pacht *f*; **2.** (ver-) mieten, (ver)pachten; vermietet werden; '*rent·a·ble* (ver)mietbar; 'rent-a-'car (serv·ice) Autoverleih *m*; 'rent·al (Einkommen *n* aus) Miete *f od.* Pacht *f*; ⏜ *value* Miet-, Pachtwert *m*; 'rent-charge Erbzins *m*; 'rent·er Mieter *m*, Pächter *m*; Filmverleih(er) *m*; 'rent-'free miet-, pachtfrei; rent tri·bu·nal Mieterschiedsgericht *n*.

re·nun·ci·a·tion [rinʌnsi'eiʃən] Entsagung *f*; Verzicht *m* (*of* auf *acc.*).

re·o·pen ['ri:'əupən] *v/t.* wieder (er)öffnen; *v/i.* (sich) wieder öffnen; wieder beginnen.

re·or·ga·ni·za·tion ['ri:ɔgənai'zeiʃən] Neugestaltung *f*; ✝ Sanierung *f*; 're·or·gan·ize reorganisieren, neugestalten; ✝ sanieren.

rep[1] [rep] Rips *m* (*Stoff*).

rep[2] *sl.* [⏜] Wüstling *m*.

rep[3] F [⏜] Repertoiretheater *n*.

re·pack ['ri:'pæk] umpacken.

re·paint ['ri:'peint] neu anstreichen.

re·pair[1] [ri'pɛə] **1.** Ausbesserung *f*, Reparatur *f*; ⏜*s pl.* Instandsetzungsarbeiten *f/pl.*; ⏜ *shop* Reparaturwerkstatt *f*; *in good* ⏜ in gutem baulichen Zustand, gut erhalten; *out of* ⏜ baufällig; **2.** reparieren, ausbessern; erneuern; wiedergutmachen.

re·pair[2] [⏜]: ⏜ *to* sich begeben nach.

rep·a·ra·ble ['repərəbl] wiedergutzumachen(d); rep·a'ra·tion Ersatz *m*; Entschädigung *f*; *pol.* Wiedergutmachungsleistung *f*; *pol. make* ⏜*s pol.* Reparationen leisten.

rep·ar·tee [repɑ:'ti:] schlagfertige Antwort *f*; Schlagfertigkeit *f*; *be good at* ⏜ schlagfertig sein.

re·par·ti·tion ['ri:pɑ:'tiʃən] (Neu-) Verteilung *f*.

re·pass ['ri:'pɑ:s] *v/i.* zurückgehen; *v/t.* wieder vorbeigehen an (*dat.*).

re·past [ri'pɑ:st] Mahl(zeit *f*) *n*.

re·pa·tri·ate **1.** [ri:'pætrieit] in die Heimat zurückführen; **2.** [⏜it] Heimkehrer *m*; re·pa·tri·a·tion ['⏜'eiʃən] Rückführung *f* in die Heimat.

re·pay (*irr.* pay) [ri:'pei] *et.* zurückzahlen; *fig.* erwidern; *et.* vergelten, lohnen; *j.* entschädigen; ['ri:'pei] nochmals (be)zahlen; re'pay·a·ble rückzahlbar; re'pay·ment Rückzahlung *f*.

re·peal [ri'pi:l] **1.** Aufhebung *f von Gesetzen*; **2.** aufheben, widerrufen.

re·peat [ri'pi:t] **1.** *v/t.* wiederholen; her-, aufsagen; nachliefern; ⏜ *an order for s.th. et.* nachbestellen; *v/i.* sich wiederholen; repetieren (*Uhr, Gewehr*); aufstoßen (*Essen*); **2.** Wiederholung *f*; *oft* ⏜ *order* Nachbestellung *f*; ♪ Wiederholungszeichen *n*; re'peat·ed □ wiederholt; re·'peat·er Wiederholer(in); periodischer Dezimalbruch *m*; Repetieruhr *f*, -gewehr *n*; *tel.* Übertrager *m*.

re·pel [ri'pel] zurückstoßen, -treiben, -weisen; *fig.* abstoßen; **re·'pel·lent** zurück-, abstoßend.

re·pent [ri'pent] *a.* ~ *of* bereuen.

re·pent·ance [ri'pentəns] Reue *f*; **re'pent·ant** reuig.

re·peo·ple ['ri:'pi:pl] wiederbevölkern.

re·per·cus·sion [ri:pə:'kʌʃən] Rückprall *m*; *fig.* Rückwirkung *f*; Widerhall *m*.

rep·er·toire *thea. etc.* ['repətwa:] Repertoire *n*.

rep·er·to·ry ['repətəri] *thea.* Repertoire *n*; *fig.* Fundgrube *f*.

rep·e·ti·tion [repi'tiʃən] Wiederholung *f*; Aufsagen *n*; Stück *n* zum Aufsagen; Nachbildung *f*; ~ *order* † Nachbestellung *f*.

re·pine [ri'pain] unzufrieden sein, murren (*at* über *acc.*); **re'pin·ing** □ mürrisch, unzufrieden.

re·place [ri'pleis] wieder hinstellen *od.* einsetzen; ersetzen; an *j-s* Stelle treten; **re'place·ment** Ersatz *m*; Vertretung *f*.

re·plant ['ri:'pla:nt] umpflanzen.

re·play ['ri:plei] *Sport:* Wiederholungsspiel *n*; *Fernsehen:* Wiederholung *f e-r Spielszene* (in Zeitlupe).

re·plen·ish [ri'pleniʃ] wieder auffüllen; **re'plen·ish·ment** Auffüllung *f*; Ergänzung *f*.

re·plete [ri'pli:t] angefüllt, voll (*with* von); **re'ple·tion** Überfülle *f*.

rep·li·ca ['replikə] *paint. etc.* Nachbildung *f*, Kopie *f*; *fig.* Ab-, Ebenbild *n*.

rep·li·ca·tion [repli'keiʃən] ⟂ Replik *f*; Echo *n*; Nachbildung *f*.

re·ply [ri'plai] **1.** antworten, erwidern (*to auf acc.*); **2.** Antwort *f*, Erwiderung *f*; ~ *postcard* Postkarte *f* mit Rückantwort.

re·port [ri'pɔ:t] **1.** Bericht *m* (*on* über *acc.*); Gerücht *n*; *guter* Ruf *m*; Knall *m*; *school* ~ (Schul)Zeugnis *n*; **2.** *v/t.* berichten (über *acc.*), melden; anzeigen; *v/i.* Bericht erstatten, berichten (*on, upon* über *acc.*); *sich melden* (*to* bei); **re·port·ed speech** *gr.* indirekte Rede; **re'port·er** Berichterstatter(in), Reporter(in).

re·pose [ri'pəuz] **1.** *allg.* Ruhe *f* (*a. fig.*); **2.** *v/t.* ausruhen; *v/t.* (aus-) ruhen lassen; *j-m* Ruhe gewähren; ~ *trust etc. in* Vertrauen *etc.* setzen auf (*acc.*); *v/i. a.* ~ *o.s.* (sich) aus-

ruhen; ruhen, schlafen; beruhen (*on auf dat.*); **re·pos·i·to·ry** [ri'pɔzitəri] Verwahrungsort *m*; Niederlage *f*; Warenlager *n*; *fig.* Fundgrube *f*.

rep·re·hend [repri'hend] tadeln; **rep·re'hen·si·ble** □ [~səbl] tadelnswert; **rep·re'hen·sion** Verweis *m*.

rep·re·sent [repri'zent] darstellen; verkörpern; *thea. Stück* aufführen; schildern; bezeichnen (*as* als); angeben (*that daß*); *j-m et.* vorhalten; *j. od. j-s Sache* vertreten; **rep·re·sen'ta·tion** Darstellung *f*; Schilderung *f*; *thea.* Aufführung *f*; Vorstellung *f*, Begriff *m*; ⟂, *pol.* Vertretung *f*; **rep·re'sent·a·tive** □ [~tətiv] **1.** dar-, vorstellend (*of acc.*); vorbildlich, Muster...; (stell)vertretend; repräsentativ; typisch, bezeichnend (*of* für); ~ *government* parlamentarische Regierung *f*; **2.** Vertreter(in); *House of 2s Am. parl.* Repräsentantenhaus *n*.

re·press [ri'pres] unterdrücken; *psych.* verdrängen; **re'pres·sion** Unterdrückung *f*; Verdrängung *f*; Hemmung *f*; **re'pres·sive** □ unterdrückend.

re·prieve [ri'pri:v] **1.** (Gnaden-) Frist *f*; Aufschub *m*; **2.** *j-m* Aufschub *od.* e-e Gnadenfrist gewähren.

rep·ri·mand ['reprima:nd] **1.** Verweis *m*; **2.** *j-m* e-n Verweis geben.

re·print ['ri:print] **1.** neu drucken; **2.** Neudruck *m*.

re·pris·al [ri'praizəl] Wiedervergeltung, Repressalie *f*.

re·proach [ri'prəutʃ] **1.** Vorwurf *m*; Schande *f*; **2.** vorwerfen (*s.o. with s.th. j-m et.*); *j-m* Vorwürfe machen; ein Vorwurf sein für; **re'proach·ful** □ [~ful] vorwurfsvoll.

rep·ro·bate ['reprəubeit] **1.** verkommen, verderbt; **2.** verkommenes Subjekt *n*; **3.** mißbilligen; verdammen; **rep·ro'ba·tion** Mißbilligung *f*; Verurteilung *f*.

re·pro·cess [ri:'prəuses] *Kernbrennstoffe* wiederaufbereiten; ~*ing plant* Wiederaufbereitungsanlage *f*.

re·pro·duce [ri:prə'dju:s] wiedererzeugen; (sich) fortpflanzen; *Glied* neu bilden; *bildlich etc.* wiedergeben, nachbilden, reproduzieren; **re·pro·duc·tion** [~'dʌkʃən] Wiedererzeugung *f* (*a. physiol.*); Fortpflanzung *f*; Nachbildung *f*, Reproduktion *f*; **re·pro'duc·tive** □ sich vermehrend; Fortpflanzungs...

re·proof[1] [ri'pru:f] Vorwurf *m*, Tadel *m*; Verweis *m*.

re·proof[2] ['ri:'pru:f] *Regenmantel etc.* neu imprägnieren.

re·prov·al [ri'pru:vəl] Tadel *m*, Rüge *f*; **re'prove** tadeln, rügen.

rep·tile ['reptail] **1.** Reptil *n*, Kriechtier *n*; *fig.* Kriecher(in); **2.** kriechend.

re·pub·lic [ri'pʌblik] Republik *f*; **re'pub·li·can 1.** republikanisch; **2.** Republikaner(in); **re'pub·li·can·ism** republikanische Gesinnung *f od.* Regierungsform *f*.

re·pub·li·ca·tion ['ri:pʌbli'keiʃən] Wiederveröffentlichung *f*; Neuausgabe *f*.

re·pub·lish ['ri:'pʌbliʃ] wieder veröffentlichen.

re·pu·di·ate [ri'pju:dieit] nicht anerkennen; *als unberechtigt* verwerfen, ab-, zurückweisen; verstoßen; **re·pu·di'a·tion** Verwerfung *f*, Zurückweisung *f*; Nichtanerkennung *f*; Verstoßung *f*.

re·pug·nance [ri'pʌgnəns] Abneigung *f*, Widerwille *m* (*to* gegen); **re'pug·nant** □ abstoßend; widerwärtig.

re·pulse [ri'pʌls] **1.** Zurücktreiben *n*; *fig.* Zurückweisung *f*; **2.** zurücktreiben; *fig.* zurückweisen; **re'pul·sion** *phys.* Abstoßung *f*; *fig.* Widerwille *m*; Abneigung *f*; **re'pul·sive** □ *phys. u. fig.* abstoßend; widerwärtig.

re·pur·chase [ri'pə:tʃəs] **1.** Rückkauf *m*; **2.** zurückkaufen.

rep·u·ta·ble □ ['repjutəbl] achtbar; ehrbar, anständig; **rep·u·ta·tion** [repju:'teiʃən] (*bsd.* guter) Ruf *m*, Ansehen *n*; **re·pute** [ri'pju:t] **1.** Ruf *m*, Ansehen *n*; *by* ~ dem Rufe nach; **2.** halten für; *be* ~*d to be od. as* gelten für; *be well* (*ill*) ~*d* in gutem (schlechtem) Ruf stehen; **re'put·ed** vermeintlich; angeblich; landesüblich (*Maß etc.*); **re'put·ed·ly** angeblich.

re·quest [ri'kwest] **1.** Gesuch *n*, Bitte *f*; Ersuchen *n*; † Nachfrage *f*; *at s.o.'s* ~ auf j-s Bitte; *by* ~, *on* ~ auf Wunsch; *in* (*great*) ~ (sehr) gesucht, begehrt; ~ *stop* Bedarfshaltestelle *f*;

(*musical*) ~ *programme* Wunschkonzert *n*; **2.** um *et.* bitten *od.* ersuchen; *j.* bitten (*to inf.* zu *inf.*); *et.* erbitten.

re·qui·em ['rekwiem] Totenmesse *f*, Requiem *n*.

re·quire [ri'kwaiə] *et.* verlangen, fordern (*of* von *j-m*); brauchen, erfordern; ~ (*of*) *s.o. to inf.* j. auffordern zu *inf.*; **re'quired** erforderlich; **re'quire·ment** (*fig.* An)Forderung *f*; Erfordernis *n*.

req·ui·site ['rekwizit] **1.** erforderlich; **2.** Erfordernis *n*; Gebrauchsartikel *m*; *toilet* ~*s pl.* Toilettenartikel *m/pl.*; **req·ui'si·tion 1.** Ersuchen *n*; ⚔ Requisition *f*; **2.** verlangen; ⚔ requirieren, beschlagnahmen; in Anspruch nehmen.

re·quit·al [ri'kwaitl] Vergeltung *f*.

re·quite [ri'kwait] *et. j-m* vergelten; *et.* erwidern.

re·read ['ri:'ri:d] (*irr. read*) nochmals (durch)lesen.

re·re·lease ['ri:ri'li:s] Wiederauflage *f* *e-r Schallplatte.*

re·run 1. (*irr. run*) ['ri:'rʌn] *Film* wiederaufführen; *Fernsehsendung* wiederholen; **2.** ['ri:'rʌn] Wiederaufführung *f*; Wiederholung *f*.

re·sale ['ri:seil] Wiederverkauf *m*; ~ *price* Wiederverkaufspreis *m*.

re·scind [ri'sind] aufheben; zurücktreten von.

re·scis·sion [ri'siʒən] Aufhebung *f*.

re·script ['ri:skript] Erlaß *m*.

res·cue ['reskju:] **1.** Rettung *f*; (⚖ gewaltsame) Befreiung *f*; ~ *operation* Rettungs-, Bergungsaktion *f*; **2.** retten; (⚖ gewaltsam) befreien; **'res·cu·er** Befreier(in); Retter(in).

re·search [ri'sə:tʃ] Forschung *f*; Untersuchung *f*; Nachforschung *f*; ~ *assignment* Forschungsauftrag *m*; **re'search·er** Forscher *m*.

re·seat ['ri:'si:t] (sich) wieder setzen; mit neuen Sitzen versehen.

re·se·da ['residə] Reseda(grün) *n*.

re·sell ['ri:'sel] (*irr. sell*) wieder verkaufen; **'re'sell·er** Wiederverkäufer *m*.

re·sem·blance [ri'zembləns] Ähnlichkeit *f* (*to* mit); *bear* ~ *to* Ähnlichkeit haben mit; **re'sem·ble** [~bl] gleichen, ähneln, ähnlich sein (*dat.*).

re·sent [ri'zent] sich ärgern über (*acc.*); übelnehmen; **re'sent·ful** □

[~ful] empfindlich; grollend; ~ of
ärgerlich über od. auf (acc.); **re-
'sent·ment** Ärger m; Verstimmung
f; Empfindlichkeit f, Groll m, Unwille m.
res·er·va·tion [rezə'veiʃən] Vorbehalt m; Am. Indianerreservation f;
Vorbestellung f, Reservierung f von
Zimmern etc.
re·serve [ri'zəːv] **1.** Vorrat m; ✝
Rücklage f; Reserve f (a. fig., ✕);
Zurückhaltung f, Verschlossenheit
f; Vorsicht f; Vorbehalt m; Sport:
Ersatzmann m; Reservat n, Schutzgebiet n; in ~ in Reserve, vorrätig;
with certain ~s mit gewissen Ein-
schränkungen; **2.** aufbewahren,
-sparen, reservieren; vorbehalten;
zurückstellen, -legen; Platz belegen, vormerken, vorbestellen; **re-
'served** □ fig. zurückhaltend, reserviert.
re·serv·ist ✕ [ri'zəːvist] Reservist
m.
res·er·voir ['rezəvwɑː] Behälter m
für Wasser etc.; Sammel-, Stau-
becken n; fig. Reservoir n.
re·set ['riː'set] (irr. set) wieder einfassen; typ. neu setzen.
re·set·tle ['riː'setl] neuordnen; um-
siedeln; **'re'set·tle·ment** Neuordnung f; Umsiedlung f.
re·ship ['riː'ʃip] wieder verschiffen.
re·shuf·fle ['riː'ʃʌfl] **1.** umgruppieren; umbilden; **2.** Umgruppierung
f etc.
re·side [ri'zaid] wohnen; (orts)an-
sässig sein; ~ in innewohnen (dat.);
liegen in (dat.); **res·i·dence** ['rezi-
dəns] Wohnen n; Ortsansässigkeit f;
(Wohn)Sitz m; Residenz f; (herrschaftliches) Wohnhaus n; ~ permit
Aufenthaltsgenehmigung f; **'res·i-
dent 1.** wohnhaft; ortsansässig; im
Dienstgebäude wohnend (Lehrer
etc.); **2.** Ortsansässige m, Einwohner m; Ministerresident m (Gesandter); **res·i·den·tial** [~'denʃəl]
Wohn...; herrschaftlich.
re·sid·u·al [ri'zidjuəl] übrigblei-
bend; **re'sid·u·ar·y** restlich, übrig
(-geblieben); **res·i·due** ['rezidjuː]
Rest m; Rückstand m; ⚖ Reinn-
nachlaß m; **re·sid·u·um** [ri'zid-
juəm] bsd. 🜍 Rückstand m; Bodensatz m (a. fig.); ⚖ Rest m.
re·sign [ri'zain] v/t. aufgeben, verzichten auf (acc.); Amt niederlegen;

überlassen; ~ o.s. to sich ergeben in
(acc.), sich abfinden mit; v/i. vom
Amt zurücktreten; resignieren;
res·ig·na·tion [rezig'neiʃən] Amts-
niederlegung f, Rücktritt m; Ergebung f; Entlassungsgesuch n;
re·signed □ [ri'zaind] ergeben, re-
signiert.
re·sil·i·ence [ri'ziliəns] Elastizität f,
fig. Spannkraft f; **re'sil·i·ent** elastisch, fig. spannkräftig.
res·in ['rezin] **1.** Harz n; **2.** harzen;
'res·in·ous harzig.
re·sist [ri'zist] widerstehen (dat.);
sich widersetzen (dat.); **re'sist-
ance** Widerstand m (a. phys., ⚡;
to gegen); line of least ~ Weg m des
geringsten Widerstands; attr. Widerstands...; **re'sist·ant** wider-
stehend; widerstandsfähig; **re'sis-
tor** ⚡ Widerstand m.
re·sit 1. ['riːsit] Wiederholungsprü-
fung f; **2.** ['~'sit] (irr. sit) v/t. Prüfung
wiederholen; v/i. die Prüfung wiederholen.
re·sole ['riː'səul] neu besohlen.
res·o·lute □ ['rezəluːt] entschlossen;
'res·o·lute·ness Entschlossenheit f.
res·o·lu·tion [rezə'luːʃən] phys., ♪,
♩ Auflösung f; fig. Lösung f; Entschluß m; Entschlossenheit f; parl.
Resolution f, Beschluß(fassung f)
m; Entschließung f; **re·solv·a·ble**
[ri'zɔlvəbl] auflösbar.
re·solve [ri'zɔlv] **1.** v/t. auflösen (into in acc.; a. 🜍, ⚡, ♩); fig. Frage
etc. lösen; Zweifel etc. beheben;
entscheiden; the House ~s itself into
a committee parl. das Haus konsti-
tuiert sich als Ausschuß; v/i. a. ~
o.s. sich auflösen; beschließen; ~
(up)on sich entschließen zu; **2.** Entschluß m; Beschluß m; lit. Entschlossenheit f; **re'solved** □ entschlossen.
res·o·nance ['reznəns] Resonanz f;
Nach-, Widerhall m; **'res·o·nant**
□ nach-, widerhallend; volltönend.
re·sorp·tion physiol. [ri'sɔːpʃən]
Aufsaugung f, Resorption f.
re·sort [ri'zɔːt] **1.** Zuflucht f; Besuch m, Zustrom m; Aufenthalt(s-
ort m); Erholungsort m; health ~
Kurort m; seaside ~ Seebad n;
summer ~ Sommerfrische f; in the
last ~ letzten Endes; **2.** ~ to sich begeben zu od. nach; Ort oft besuchen; seine Zuflucht nehmen zu;

zurückgreifen auf (acc.).

re·sound [ri'zaund] widerhallen (lassen) (with von).

re·source [ri'sɔːs] natürlicher Reichtum m; Hilfsquelle f, -mittel n; Mittel n, Zuflucht f; Fähigkeit f, sich zu helfen; Findigkeit f; Zeitvertreib m, Entspannung f, Unterhaltung f; **re'source·ful** □ (‿ful) reich an Hilfsquellen; findig; **re'source·ful·ness** Reichtum m; Findigkeit f.

re·spect [ris'pekt] **1.** Rücksicht f (to, of auf acc.); Hinsicht f, Beziehung f; Achtung f, Ehrerbietung f (for vor dat.); ‿s pl. Empfehlungen f/pl.; with ‿ to in bezug auf (acc.), was ... anbetrifft; in ‿ of in Anbetracht (gen.); pay one's ‿s on s.o. j-m seine Aufwartung machen; **2.** v/t. hochachten; achten, Rücksicht nehmen auf (acc.); betreffen; **re·spect·a-'bil·i·ty** Achtbarkeit f; Ehrbarkeit f; Ansehnlichkeit f; ♱ Solidität f; respectabilities pl. Anstandsregeln f/pl.; **re'spect·a·ble** □ achtbar; ehrbar; ansehnlich; achtenswert; anständig; bsd. ♱ solid; **re'spectful** □ (‿ful) respektvoll; ehrerbietig, höflich; Yours ‿ly hochachtungsvoll; **re'spect·ful·ness** Ehrerbietung f; **re'spect·ing** in betreff, hinsichtlich (gen.); **re'spective** □ jedem einzeln zukommend; jeweilig; we went to our ‿ places wir gingen jeder an seinen Platz; **re'spec·tive·ly** beziehungsweise, je.

res·pi·ra·tion [respə'reiʃən] Atmung f; Atemzug m.

res·pi·ra·tor ['respəreitə] Atemfilter m; Gasmaske f; ♣ Atemgerät n; **re·spir·a·to·ry** [ris'paiərətəri] Atmungs...

re·spire [ris'paiə] atmen; aufatmen.

res·pite ['respait] **1.** ⚖ Frist f; Aufschub m; Stundung f; **2.** Urteilsvollstreckung aufschieben; j-m e-e Frist gewähren.

re·splend·ence, **re·splend·en·cy** [ris'plendəns(i)] Glanz m; fig. Pracht f; **re'splend·ent** □ glänzend.

re·spond [ri'spɔnd] bsd. feierlich antworten, erwidern; ‿ to reagieren auf (acc.), empfänglich sein für; **re'spond·ent 1.** ⚖ beklagt; ‿ to empfänglich für; **2.** ⚖ Beklagte m, f.

re·sponse [ris'pɔns] Antwort f, Erwiderung f; fig. Widerhall m, Reaktion f (to auf acc.).

re·spon·si·bil·i·ty [rispɔnsə'biliti] Verantwortlichkeit f, Verantwortung f (for, of für); Vertrauenswürdigkeit f, ♱ Zahlungsfähigkeit f; **re'spon·si·ble** verantwortlich; verantwortungsvoll (Amt); haftbar; vertrauenswürdig, ♱ zahlungsfähig; be ‿ for a. et. verschulden; schuld sein an (dat.); **re'spon·sive** □ antwortend; Antwort...; verständnisvoll; empfänglich (to für).

rest¹ [rest] **1.** Ruhe f; Rast f; Schlaf m; fig. Tod m; Auflage f, Stütze f; ♩ Pause f; at ‿ in Ruhe, ruhig; **2.** v/i. ruhen; rasten; schlafen; (sich) lehnen, sich stützen (on auf acc.); ‿ (up)on fig. beruhen auf (dat.); it ‿s with you es obliegt Ihnen; v/t. (aus)ruhen (lassen); stützen (on, upon auf acc.).

rest² [‿] **1.** Rest m; das übrige, die übrigen; ♱ Reserve(fonds m) f; for the ‿ im übrigen; **2.** in e-m Zustand bleiben; ‿ assured sei versichert.

re·state ['riː'steit] neu formulieren.

re·stau·rant ['restərɔ̃ːŋ] Restaurant n, Gaststätte f; '‿-car Speisewagen m.

rest-cure ⚕ ['restkjuə] Liegekur f.

rest·ful ['restful] ruhig, geruhsam.

rest-home ['resthəum] Altenheim n.

rest·ing-place ['restiŋpleis] Ruheplatz m, -stätte f.

res·ti·tu·tion [resti'tjuːʃən] Wiederherstellung f; Rückerstattung f; make ‿ Ersatz leisten (of für).

res·tive □ ['restiv] widerspenstig, störrisch; **'res·tive·ness** Widerspenstigkeit f.

rest·less ['restlis] ruhelos; rastlos; unruhig; **'rest·less·ness** Ruhelosigkeit f; Rastlosigkeit f; Unruhe f.

re·stock ['riː'stɔk] Vorrat wieder auffüllen.

res·to·ra·tion [restə'reiʃən] Wiederherstellung f; Wiedereinsetzung f (to in ein Amt); Rekonstruktion f, Nachbildung f; **re·stor·a·tive** [ris'tɔrətiv] stärkend(es Mittel n).

re·store [ris'tɔː] wiederherstellen; wiedereinsetzen (to in acc.); wiedergeben, ersetzen; ‿ s.o. to liberty j-m die Freiheit schenken; ‿ to health od. life wieder gesund od. lebendig machen; **re·stor·er** Wiederhersteller(in); *hair* ~ Haarwuchsmittel *n*.

re·strain [ris'trein] zurückhalten (*from* von); in Schranken halten; unterdrücken; einsperren; **re'strained** beherrscht; **re·straint** [~'treint] Zurückhaltung *f* (*a. fig.*); Beschränkung *f*, Zwang *m*; Zwangshaft *f*.

re·strict [ris'trikt] be-, einschränken; **re'stric·tion** Be-, Einschränkung *f* (*of, on gen.*); Vorbehalt *m*; Restriktion *f*; **re'stric·tive** □ be-, einschränkend.

rest room *Am.* ['restrum] Toilette *f*.

re·struc·ture ['ri:'strʌktʃə] umstrukturieren.

re·sult [ri'zʌlt] **1.** Ergebnis *n*, Folge *f*, Resultat *n*; **2.** folgen, sich ergeben (*from* aus); ~ *in* hinauslaufen auf (*acc.*), enden in (*dat.*), zur Folge haben; **re'sult·ant 1.** sich ergebend; **2.** ⊕ Resultante *f*.

ré·su·mé ['rezju:mei] Resümee *n*, Zs.-fassung *f*.

re·sume [ri'zju:m] wiedernehmen, -erlangen, -aufnehmen, -anfangen; zs.-fassen; fortfahren; **re·sump·tion** [ri'zʌmpʃən] Zurücknahme *f*; Wiederaufnahme *f*.

re·sur·face ['ri:'sə:fis] *v/t.* Straße mit neuem Belag versehen; *v/i.* wieder auftauchen (*U-Boot*).

re·sur·gence [ri'sə:dʒəns] Wiederemporkommen *n*; **re'sur·gent** sich wiedererhebend, wieder aufkommend.

res·ur·rect [rezə'rekt] wiedererwekken; wiederaufleben lassen; F ausgraben; **res·ur'rec·tion** (Wieder-) Auferstehung *f*; Wiederaufleben *n*; **res·ur'rec·tion·ist** [~ʃnist], **res·ur'rec·tion-man** [~ʃənmən] Leichenräuber *m*.

re·sus·ci·tate [ri'sʌsiteit] *v/t.* wiedererwecken, -beleben; *v/i.* wieder auflösen; **re·sus·ci'ta·tion** Wiedererweckung *f*.

re·tail 1. ['ri:teil] Einzelhandel *m*, Detailgeschäft *n*; *by* ~ im Einzelverkauf; ~ *price* Einzelhandelspreis *m*; **2.** [~] Einzelhandels..., Detail...; **3.** [~] *adv. s. by* ~; **4.** [ri:'teil] *v/t.* im kleinen verkaufen; haarklein (weiter)erzählen; *v/i.* verkauft werden (*at* zu); ~ **book·sell·er** Sortimentsbuchhändler *m*; **re'tail·er** Einzelhändler *m*.

re·tain [ri'tein] behalten (*a. im Gedächtnis*); bewahren; zurück-, festhalten; *Brauch etc.* beibehalten; *Anwalt* nehmen; **re'tain·er** *hist.* Gefolgsmann *m*; *old* ~ altes Faktotum *n*; **re'tain·ing fee** Vorschuß *m für e-n Anwalt*.

re·take ['ri:'teik] (*irr. take*) wiedernehmen.

re·tal·i·ate [ri'tælieit] *v/t. Unrecht* vergelten; sich rächen, Vergeltung üben (*on, upon an dat.*); **re'tal·i·a·tion** Vergeltung *f*; **re'tal·i·a·to·ry** [~ətəri] Vergeltungs...

re·tard [ri'ta:d] verzögern; aufhalten; verspäten; ~ed *ignition mot.* Spätzündung *f*; *mentally* ~ed geistig zurückgeblieben; **re·tar·da·tion** [ri:ta:'deiʃən] Verzögerung *f*, -spätung *f*.

retch [retʃ] würgen (*beim Erbrechen*).

re·tell ['ri:'tel] (*irr. tell*) nochmals erzählen, nacherzählen.

re·ten·tion [ri'tenʃən] Zurück-, Behalten *n*; ♂ Verhaltung *f*; Beibehaltung *f von Sitten*; **re'ten·tive** □ zurück-, behaltend (*of acc.*); gut (*Gedächtnis*).

re·think ['ri:'θiŋk] (*irr. think*) neu (durchdenken)

ret·i·cence ['retisəns] Verschwiegenheit *f* (*of in dat.*); **'ret·i·cent** verschwiegen; schweigsam; zurückhaltend.

ret·i·cle ['retikl] Fadenkreuz *n*.

re·tic·u·late □ [ri'tikjulit], **re'tic·u·lat·ed** □ [~leitid] netzartig; Netz...; **ret·i·cule** ['retikju:l] Damenhandtasche *f*; = *reticle*.

ret·i·na *anat.* ['retinə] Netzhaut *f*.

ret·i·nue ['retinju:] Gefolge *n*.

re·tire [ri'taiə] *v/t.* zurückziehen; in den Ruhestand versetzen, pensionieren; *v/i.* sich zurückziehen; zurück-, abtreten; in den Ruhestand treten; *a.* ~ *to bed* zu Bett gehen; **re'tired** □ zurückgezogen; im Ruhestand (lebend); entlegen (*Ort*); ~ *pay* Pension *f*, Ruhegehalt *n*; **re'tire·ment** Sichzurückziehen *n*; Aus-, Rücktritt *m*; Ruhestand *m*; Zurückgezogenheit *f*; *early* ~ vorzeitiger Ruhestand *m*; **re'tir·ing** □ zurückhaltend; schüchtern; ~ *pension* Ruhegehalt *n*.

re·tort [ri'tɔ:t] **1.** Erwiderung *f*; schlagfertige Antwort *f*; ⚗ Retorte *f*; **2.** *v/t. Beleidigung etc.* zurückgeben (*on, upon dat.*); *v/i.* (scharf *od.* treffend) erwidern.

re·touch ['ri:'tʌtʃ] *et.* überarbeiten; *phot.* retuschieren.

re·trace [ri'treis] zurückverfolgen; ~ one's steps zurückgehen.

re·tract [ri'trækt] (sich) zurückziehen; ⊕ einziehen; widerrufen, zurücknehmen; **re'tract·a·ble** einziehbar (⚔ *Fahrgestell*); **re'trac·'ta·tion** Widerruf *m*; Zurücknahme *f*; **re'trac·tion** Zurückziehen *n*.

re·train ['ri:'trein] umschulen.

re·trans·late ['ri:trænsˈleit] (zu-) rückübersetzen; **'re·trans'la·tion** Rückübersetzung *f*.

re·tread ['ri:'tred] 1. *Reifen* runderneuern; 2. runderneuerter Reifen *m*.

re·treat [ri'tri:t] 1. Rückzug *m*; Zurückgezogenheit *f*; Zuflucht(sort *m*) *f*; Schlupfwinkel *m*; ⚔ Zapfenstreich *m*; beat a ~ *fig.* es aufgeben; 2. sich zurückziehen; *fig.* zurücktreten.

re·trench [ri'trentʃ] *v/t.* einschränken; kürzen, beschneiden; *Wort etc.* streichen; ⚔ verschanzen; *v/i.* sich einschränken; **re'trench·ment** Kürzung *f*; Einschränkung *f*; ⚔ (innere) Verteidigungsstellung *f*.

re·tri·al ⚖ ['ri:'traiəl] Wiederaufnahme(verfahren *n*) *f*.

ret·ri·bu·tion [retri'bju:ʃən] Vergeltung *f*; **re·trib·u·tive** □ [ri-'tribjutiv] vergeltend; Vergeltungs...

re·triev·a·ble [ri'tri:vəbl] ersetzlich; **re'triev·al** Wiedergewinnung *f*; beyond ~, past ~ unwiederbringlich (verloren).

re·trieve [ri'tri:v] wiederbekommen; wiederherstellen; wiedergutmachen; *hunt.* apportieren; **re'triev·er** *hunt.* Apportierhund *m*.

ret·ro... ['retrəu] (zu)rück...; ~'active rückwirkend; ~'cede zurückgehen; wieder abtreten; ~'ces·sion Zurückweichen *n*; Wiederabtretung *f*; ~'gra'da·tion *ast.* rückläufige Bewegung *f*; Zurückgehen *n*; *fig.* Niedergang *m*; '~'grade 1. rückläufig; 2. zurückgehen (*a. fig.*).

ret·ro·gres·sion [retrəu'greʃən] Rück-, Niedergang *m*; **ret·ro·spect** ['~spekt] Rückblick *m*; in ~ rückschauend; **ret·ro'spec·tion**

Rückblick *m*; Erinnerung *f*; **ret·ro'spec·tive** □ zurückblickend; rückwirkend; ~ view Rückblick *m*.

re·trous·sé [rə'tru:sei]: ~ nose Stupsnase *f*.

re·try ⚖ ['ri:'trai] *Prozeß* wiederaufnehmen; neu verhandeln gegen *j*.

re·turn [ri'tə:n] 1. Rückkehr *f*; Wiederkehr *f*; *parl.* Wiederwahl *f*; oft ~s *pl.* Gewinn *m*, Ertrag *m*; (Kapital)Umsatz *m*; ⚕ Rückfall *m*; Rückgabe *f*, -zahlung *f*; Vergeltung *f*; Erwiderung *f*; Gegenleistung *f*; Dank *m*; amtlicher Bericht *m*; (Bank)Ausweis *m*; Steuererklärung *f*; △ Seitenflügel *m*; F Rückfahrkarte *f*; ~s *pl.* statistische Aufstellungen *f/pl.*; many happy ~s of the day herzliche Glückwünsche zum heutigen Tage; election ~s *pl.* Wahlergebnis *n*; in ~ dafür; in ~ for (als Gegenleistung) für; by ~ (of post) postwendend; ~ match Rückspiel *n*; ~ ticket Rückfahrkarte *f*; ~ visit Gegenbesuch *m*; *attr.* Rück...; 2. *v/i.* zurückkehren; wiederkehren; ~ to *fig.* zurückkehren zu *e-m Thema etc.*; zurückfallen in *e-e Gewohnheit etc.*; *j-m* wieder zufallen; *v/t.* zurückgeben; zurücktun (to in *acc.*); zurückzahlen; zurücksenden; *Dank* abstatten; *Rede, Schlag, Gruß, Liebe etc.* erwidern; ⚖ *Urteil* aussprechen; *amtlich* berichten, melden, angeben; ins Parlament wählen; *Gewinn* abwerfen; *Karte* nachspielen; ~ guilty ⚖ schuldig sprechen; **re'turn·a·ble** zurückzugeben(d); **re'turn·er** Zurücksendende *m*, -zahlende *m*; **re'turn·ing-of·fi·cer** Wahlkommissar *m*.

re·u·ni·fi·ca·tion *pol.* ['ri:ju:nifi-'keiʃən] Wiedervereinigung *f*.

re·un·ion ['ri:'ju:njən] Wiedervereinigung *f*; Treffen *n*, Zs.-kunft *f*; **re·u·nite** ['ri:ju:'nait] (sich) wieder vereinigen.

rev *mot.* F [rev] 1. Umdrehung *f*; 2. (sich) drehen; ~ up auf Touren kommen *od.* bringen.

re·val·or·i·za·tion ['ri:vælərai-'zeiʃən], **re·val·u·a·tion** ['ri:vælju-'eiʃən] Auf-, Neuwertung *f*; **re'val·or·ize** [~əraiz], **re·val·ue** ['ri:-'vælju:] aufwerten, neu bewerten.

revoke

re·vamp ⊕ ['riː'væmp] vorschuhen; *Am.* F aufmöbeln; erneuern.

re·veal [ri'viːl] enthüllen; offenbaren; zeigen; **re'veal·ing** aufschlußreich.

re·veil·le ⚔ [ri'væli] Reveille *f.*

rev·el ['revl] **1.** Lustbarkeit *f;* lärmende Festlichkeit *f;* Gelage *n;* Rummel *m;* **2.** ausgelassen sein; schwelgen (*in* in *dat.*); sich ergötzen (*in* an *dat.*).

rev·e·la·tion [revi'leiʃən] Enthüllung *f;* Offenbarung *f.*

rev·el·(l)er ['revlə] Feiernde *m, f;* (Nacht)Schwärmer *m;* Zechbruder *m;* 'rev·el·ry laute Lustbarkeit *f,* Rummel *m,* Orgie *f.*

re·venge [ri'vendʒ] **1.** Rache *f,* Vergeltung *f;* Revanche *f bei Spielen;* **2.** *et., a. j.* rächen (*on, upon* an *dat.*); ~ *o.s.* on, be ~d on sich rächen an (*dat.*); **re'venge·ful** □ [~ful] rachsüchtig; **re'venge·ful·ness** Rachsucht *f;* **re'veng·er** Rächer(in).

rev·e·nue ['revinjuː] Einkommen *n;* ~s *pl.* Einkünfte *pl.;* ~ board, ~ office Finanzamt *n;* ~ cutter Zollkutter *m;* ~ officer Zollbeamte *m;* ~ stamp Banderole *f.*

re·ver·ber·ate [ri'vəːbəreit] *v/t.* zurückwerfen, -strahlen; *v/i.* zurückstrahlen; widerhallen; **re·ver·ber·'a·tion** Zurückwerfen *n;* Widerhall(en *n*) *m;* **re'ver·ber·a·tor** Scheinwerfer *m.*

re·vere [ri'viə] (ver)ehren; **rev·er·ence** ['revərəns] **1.** Verehrung *f;* Ehrfurcht *f; Your* ♁ † *od. co.* Euer Ehrwürden; **2.** (ver)ehren; 'rev·er·end **1.** ehrwürdig; *Right* ♁ hochwürdig; **2.** Geistliche *m.*

rev·er·ent □ ['revərənt], **rev·er·en·tial** □ [~'renʃəl] ehrerbietig, ehrfurchtsvoll.

rev·er·ie ['revəri] Träumerei *f.*

re·ver·sal [ri'vəːsəl] Umkehrung *f;* Umschwung *m;* ♁ Umstoßung *f;* ⊕ Umsteuerung *f;* **re'verse 1.** Gegenteil *n;* Rück-, Kehrseite *f;* Schlappe *f;* Rückschlag *m; in* ~ im umgekehrten Sinne; ⚔ im Rücken; **2.** □ umgekehrt; Rück(wärts)...; ~ (*gear*) *mot.* Rückwärtsgang *m;* ~ *side* linke *Stoff*-Seite *f;* **3.** umkehren, umdrehen; *Urteil etc.* umstoßen; ⊕ umsteuern; **re'vers·i·ble** umkehrbar; umsteuerbar; doppelseitig (*Stoff, Mantel*); **re'vers-**

ing ⊕ Umsteuerungs...

re·ver·sion [ri'vəːʃən] Umkehrung *f;* Rückkehr *f;* ♁ Heimfall *m;* Anwartschaft *f* (*of* auf *acc.*); *biol.* Rückartung *f;* **re'ver·sion·ar·y** ♁ [~ʃnəri] anwartschaftlich; **re'ver·sion·er** ♁ [~ʃnə] Anwärter *m.*

re·vert [ri'vəːt] umkehren; zurückkommen, -gehen (*to* auf *acc.*); *fig.* zurückfallen (*to* in *acc.*); *biol.* zurückarten (*to* zu); ♁ heimfallen; *Blick* wenden.

rev·er·y ['reveri] = *reverie.*

re·vet·ment ⊕ [ri'vetmənt] Verkleidung *f,* Futtermauer *f.*

re·view [ri'vjuː] **1.** Nachprüfung *f;* ⚔, ⚓ Parade *f,* Truppen-, Flottenschau *f;* Rückblick *m;* Überblick *m;* Besprechung *f,* Rezension *f e-s Buches;* Zeitschrift *f; pass s.th. in* ~ et. Revue passieren lassen; *year under* ~ Berichtsjahr *n;* **2.** *v/t.* wieder durchsehen; (über-, nach-) prüfen; zurückblicken auf (*acc.*); überblicken; ⚔, ⚓ besichtigen; *kritisch* besprechen, rezensieren; *v/i.* Rezensionen schreiben; **re'view·er** Rezensent *m;* ~'s *copy* Rezensionsexemplar *n.*

re·vile [ri'vail] schmähen, beschimpfen (*for* wegen).

re·vis·al [ri'vaizl] Revision *f.*

re·vise [ri'vaiz] **1.** *Buch etc.* überarbeiten, durchsehen; überprüfen, revidieren; **2.** *typ.* Korrekturabzug *m;* = *revision;* **re'vis·er** Bearbeiter *m;* *typ.* Korrektor *m.*

re·vi·sion [ri'viʒən] Revision *f,* nochmalige Durchsicht *f;* Überarbeitung *f.*

re·vis·it ['riː'vizit] wieder besuchen.

re·vi·so·ry [ri'vaizəri] Revisions...

re·vi·tal·ize ['riː'vaitəlaiz] neu beleben.

re·viv·al [ri'vaivəl] Wiederbelebung *f;* Wiederaufleben *n,* -aufblühen *n,* neue Blüte *f;* Erneuerung *f; fig.* Erweckung *f;* **re'vive** *v/t.* wiederbeleben, wieder aufleben lassen; erneuern, wieder einführen; *v/i.* wieder aufleben, -blühen; **re'viv·er** Wiederbeleber(in); Auffrischung(smittel *n*) *f;* **re·viv·i·fy** [riː'vivifai] wiederbeleben.

rev·o·ca·ble □ ['revəkəbl] widerruflich; **rev·o·ca·tion** [~'keiʃən] Widerruf *m;* Aufhebung *f.*

re·voke [ri'vəuk] *v/t.* widerrufen,

zurücknehmen, einziehen v/i. *Karten*: nicht bedienen.

re·volt [ri'vəult] **1.** Revolte *f*, Empörung *f*, Aufruhr *m*, -stand *m*; **2.** v/i. sich empören (a. *fig.*); abfallen (*from* von); v/t. *fig.* empören, abstoßen; **re'volt·ing** abstoßend.

rev·o·lu·tion [revə'lu:ʃən] Umwälzung *f*, Umdrehung *f*; *pol.* Revolution *f*; ~s *per minute mot.* Drehzahl *f*; **rev·o'lu·tion·ary** [~ʃnəri] **1.** revolutionär; umwälzend; **2.** *a.* **rev·o'lu·tion·ist** Revolutionär(in); **rev·o'lu·tion·ize** revolutionieren; aufwiegeln; umgestalten; umwälzen.

re·volve [ri'vɔlv] v/i. sich drehen (*about*, *round* um); v/t. umdrehen; *fig.* erwägen; **re'volv·er** Revolver *m*; **re'volv·ing** sich drehend; Dreh-... (*-tür*, *-bleistift*, *-bühne*).

re·vue *thea.* [ri'vju:] Revue *f*; Kabarett *n*.

re·vul·sion [ri'vʌlʃən] *fig.* Umschwung *m*; ⚕ Ableitung *f*; **re'vul·sive** ⚕ [~siv] **1.** □ ableitend; **2.** ableitendes Mittel *n*.

re·ward [ri'wɔ:d] **1.** Belohnung *f*; Lohn *m*; Vergeltung *f*; **2.** belohnen; vergelten.

re·word ['ri:'wɔ:d] neu formulieren.

re·write ['ri:'rait] (*irr. write*) nochmals *od.* neu schreiben, umschreiben.

rhap·so·dist ['ræpsədist] Rhapsode *m*; **'rhap·so·dize** begeistert reden; **'rhap·so·dy** Rhapsodie *f*; *fig.* Schwärmerei *f*; Wortschwall *m*.

rhe·o·stat ⚡ ['ri:əustæt] Rheostat *m*, Regelwiderstand *m*.

rhet·o·ric ['retərik] Rhetorik *f*; **rhe·tor·i·cal** □ [ri'tɔrikəl] rhetorisch; **rhet·o·ri·cian** [retə'riʃən] guter Redner *m*; *contp.* Phrasendrescher *m*.

rheu·mat·ic ⚕ [ru:'mætik] **1.** (~*ally*) rheumatisch; ~ *fever* Gelenkrheumatismus *m*; **2.** Rheumatiker (-in); ~s F *pl.* = **rheu·ma·tism** ⚕ ['ru:mətizəm] Rheumatismus *m*.

rhi·no¹ *sl.* ['rainəu] Moneten *pl.*

rhi·no² F [~] = **rhi·noc·er·os** *zo.* [rai'nɔsərəs] Rhinozeros *n*, Nashorn *n*.

rhomb, rhom·bus ⚮ ['rɔm(bəs)] Rhombus *m*, Raute *f*.

rhu·barb ♗ ['ru:bɑ:b] Rhabarber *m*.

rhyme [raim] **1.** Reim *m* (*to* auf *acc.*); Vers *m*; *without* ~ *or reason* ohne Sinn u. Verstand; **2.** (sich) reimen; **'rhyme·less** □ reimlos; **'rhym·er, rhyme·ster** ['~stə] Verseschmied *m*.

rhythm ['riðəm] Rhythmus *m*; **rhyth·mic, rhyth·mi·cal** □ ['riðmik(əl)] rhythmisch.

Ri·al·to *Am.* [ri'æltəu] Theaterviertel *n* e-r Stadt.

rib [rib] **1.** Rippe *f*; **2.** *Stoff etc.* rippen; *Am. sl.* aufziehen, necken.

rib·ald ['ribəld] **1.** lästerlich; unflätig; **2.** Lästermaul *n*; Zotenreißer *m*; **'rib·ald·ry** Zoten *f/pl.*; derbe Späße *m/pl.*

rib·and ⊕ ['ribənd] Band *n*.

ribbed [ribd] ...rippig.

rib·bon ['ribən] Band *n*; Ordensband *n*; Farbband *n der Schreibmaschine*; Streifen *m*; ~s *pl.* Fetzen *m/pl.*; Zügel *m/pl.*; ~ *building*, ~ *development* Bebauung *f* entlang e-r Ausfallstraße; **'rib·boned** bebändert; streifig.

rib cage ['ribkeidʒ] Brustkorb *m*.

rice [rais] Reis *m*; ~ *pudding* Milchreis *m*.

rich □ [ritʃ] reich (*in* an *dat.*); reichlich; prächtig, kostbar; ergiebig, fruchtbar; voll (*Ton*); fett, schwer (*Speise*); kräftig (*Wein*, *Geruch*); satt (*Farbe*); F prächtig, köstlich (*Scherz etc.*); *mot.* fett (*Gemisch*); the ~ *pl.* die Reichen *pl.*; **rich·es** ['~iz] *pl.* Reichtum *m*, Reichtümer *m/pl.*; **'rich·ness** Reichtum *m*; Fülle *f*.

rick¹ ✓ [rik] **1.** (Heu)Schober *m*; **2.** in Schobern aufsetzen.

rick² [~] = **wrick**.

rick·ets ⚕ ['rikits] *sg. od. pl.* Rachitis *f*; **'rick·et·y** rachitisch; gebrechlich, wackelig.

rick·shaw ['rikʃɔ:] Rikscha *f*.

rid [rid] (*irr.*) befreien, frei machen (*of* von); *get* ~ *of* loswerden; **'rid·dance** Befreiung *f*; *he is a good* ~ es ist gut, daß man ihn los ist.

rid·den ['ridn] *p.p. von* ride 2; *in Zssgn*: bedrückt *od.* geplagt von ...

rid·dle¹ ['ridl] **1.** Rätsel *n*; **2.** enträtseln; ~ *me* rate mal.

rid·dle² [~] **1.** grobes Sieb *n*; **2.** sieben; durchlöchern.

rid·dling □ ['ridliŋ] rätselhaft.

ride [raid] **1.** Ritt *m*; Fahrt *f*; Reitweg *m*; Schneise *f*; *go for a* ~ ausfahren; -reiten; **2.** (*irr.*) *v/i.* reiten; rittlings sitzen; *bsd. auf dem Fahrrad od. mit e-m öffentlichen Verkehrsmittel* fahren; getragen werden, treiben, *fig.* schweben; ruhen; liegen; ⚓ *at anchor* vor Anker liegen; ～ *for a fall* wild drauflosreiten; *fig.* ins Unglück rennen; *v/t.* *ein Pferd etc.* reiten; rittlings sitzen auf (*dat.*); *Land etc.* durchreiten; reiten lassen; ～ *s.o. down* j. niederreiten; j. einholen; ～ (*on*) *a bicycle* radfahren; ～ *out* ⚓ *Sturm* gut überstehen (*a. fig.*); '**rid·er** Reiter(in); Fahrende *m*; Beiblatt *n*; Anhängsel *n*, (Zusatz)Klausel *f*; ⊕ Laufgewicht *n*, Reiter *m*.

ridge [ridʒ] **1.** (Gebirgs)Kamm *m*, Grat *m*; △ First *m*; ✗ Rain *m*; **2.** (sich) furchen; '**～-pole** Firstbalken *m*, -stange *f*.

rid·i·cule ['ridikjuːl] **1.** Hohn *m*, Spott *m*; *hold s.o. up to* ～ j. der Lächerlichkeit preisgeben; **2.** lächerlich machen; bespötteln; **ri-**'**dic·u·lous** [～juləs] lächerlich; **ri-**'**dic·u·lous·ness** Lächerlichkeit *f*.

rid·ing ['raidiŋ] **1.** Reiten *n*; **2.** Reit...; '**～-breech·es** *pl.* Reithose *f*; '**～-hab·it** Reitkleid *n*.

rife ＿ [raif] häufig; vorherrschend; ～ *with* voll von.

riff-raff ['rifræf] Gesindel *n*, Pöbel *m*.

ri·fle[1] ['raifl] (aus)plündern.

ri·fle[2] [～] **1.** *gezogenes* Gewehr *n*, Büchse *f*; ～*s pl.* ✗ Schützen *m/pl.*; **2.** *Gewehrlauf* ziehen; '**～·man** ✗ Jäger *m*; Schütze *m*; '**～·range** Schießstand *m*; Schußweite *f*.

ri·fling ⊕ ['raifliŋ] Züge *m/pl.* im Gewehr.

rift [rift] Riß *m*, Sprung *m*; Spalte *f*.

rig[1] [rig] **1.** *Markt etc.* manipulieren; **2.** Schwindelmanöver *n*.

rig[2] [～] **1.** ⚓ Takelung *f*, Takelage *f*; F Aufmachung *f*, -zug *m*, Kluft *f*; **2.** auftakeln; ～ *s.o. out* j. versorgen *od.* ausrüsten (*with* mit); j. herausputzen, herrichten, kleiden; ～ *s.th. up et.* (behelfsmäßig) zs.-bauen; et. zs.-basteln; '**rig·ger** ⚓ Takler *m*; ✈ Monteur *m*; '**rigging** ⚓ Takelage *f*; ✈ Verspannung *f*.

right [rait] **1.** ＿ recht; richtig; gesund, wohl; recht (*Ggs. left*); ～ *angle* ⅄ rechter Winkel *m*; *be* ～

recht *od.* richtig sein; recht haben; *be* ～ *to inf.* recht daran tun *zu inf.*; *all* ～*!* alles in Ordnung!; *ganz* recht!, sehr wohl!; *on the* ～ *side of 50* noch nicht 50 Jahre alt; *get s.th.* ～ et. in Ordnung bringen; et. richtig verstehen; *put od.* set ～ *in* Ordnung bringen; richtigstellen, berichtigen; **2.** *adv.* recht, richtig; (nach) rechts; gerade; direkt; stracks; ganz (und gar); *in Titeln*: hoch, sehr; ⚔ recht (*sehr*); ～ *away* schnurstracks; sogleich; los!; ～ *on* geradeaus, -zu; **3.** Recht *n*, Anspruch *m* (*to auf acc., of ger.* darauf *zu inf.*); Rechte *f* (*Hand*; *Seite*, *a. parl.*); *Boxen*: Rechte *m*; *the* ～*s of man* die Menschenrechte *n/pl.*; *in* ～ *of his mother* von seiten s-r Mutter; *in one's own* ～ aus eigenem Recht; *the* ～*s and wrongs pl.* der wahre Sachverhalt; *by* ～(*s*) von Rechts wegen; *by* ～ *of* kraft, auf Grund (*gen.*); *set od. put to* ～*s* wieder in Ordnung bringen; *on od. to the* ～ rechts; **4.** *j-m* Rechte verschaffen; *et.* in Ordnung bringen; ⚓ (sich) aufrichten; '**～-an·gled** ⅄ ['～æŋgld] rechtwinklig; '**～-down** regelrecht, ausgemacht; wirklich; '**right·eous** □ ['～ʃəs] gerecht, rechtschaffen; '**right·eous·ness** Rechtschaffenheit *f*; '**right·ful** □ ['～ful] recht(mäßig); gerecht; '**right-hand** recht (*Handschuh*, *Seite*); '**right-'hand·ed** rechtshändig; ⊕ rechtsläufig; '**right·ist** *pol.* Rechte *m*; **2.** rechtsgerichtet; '**right·ly** richtig; mit Recht; '**right-'mind·ed** rechtschaffen; '**right·ness** Richtigkeit *f*; Rechtlichkeit *f*; **right of way** Wegerecht *n*; Vorfahrt(srecht *n*) *f*; **right wing** *Sport*: Rechtsaußen *m*; *pol.* rechter Flügel *m*; '**right- -wing** *pol.* rechtsorientiert, -stehend; **right-'wing·er** *pol.* Rechte *m*; *Sport*: Rechtsaußen *m*.

rig·id □ ['ridʒid] starr; *fig. a.* streng, hart, unbeugsam; **ri'gid·i·ty** Starrheit *f*; Strenge *f*, Härte *f*.

rig·ma·role ['rigmərəul] Geschwätz *n*, Salbaderei *f*.

rig·or ['raigɔː] Fieberfrost *m*; ～ *mortis* ['mɔːtis] Leichenstarre *f*; **rig·or·ous** □ ['rigərəs] streng, rigoros.

rig·o(u)r ['rigə] Strenge *f*, Härte *f*; ～*s pl.* Unbilden *pl. des Klimas etc.*

rile 478

rile F [rail] ärgern, wurmen.

rill *poet.* [ril] Bächlein *n*.

rim [rim] **1.** Felge *f*; Radkranz *m*; Rand *m*; **2.** rändern; einfassen.

rime[1] [raim] Reim *m*.

rime[2] *poet.* [ᴗ] Rauhreif *m*; '**rim·y** bereift.

rind [raind] Rinde *f*, Schale *f*; *Speck*-Schwarte *f*.

ring[1] [rin] **1.** Ring *m* (*a. Boxring, Manege, Kartell*); Kreis *m*; Buchmacher(stand *m*) *m/pl.*; *make* ᴗ*s round s.o.* F viel schneller sein als j.; **2.** beringen; mit e-m (Nasen)Ring versehen; *mst* ᴗ *in,* ᴗ *round,* ᴗ *about* umringen.

ring[2] [ᴗ] **1.** Klang *m*; Geläut(e) *n*; Klingeln *n*; Rufzeichen *n*; Anruf *m*; *give s.o. a* ᴗ j. anrufen; **2.** (*irr.*) *v/i.* läuten; klingen (*Münze, Stimme, Ohr etc.*); *oft* ᴗ *out* erschallen (*with von*); ᴗ *again* widerhallen; ᴗ *off teleph.* das Gespräch beenden, den Hörer auflegen; *the bell* ᴗ*s* es klingelt; *v/t.* klingen lassen; läuten; ᴗ *the bell* klingeln; F Erfolg haben; ᴗ *a bell* F an et. erinnern; ᴗ *s.o. up* j. *od.* bei j-m anrufen; '**ᴗ-bind·er** Ringbuch *n*; '**ring·er** Glöckner *m*; '**ring·ing** □ klingend; laut; '**ring·lead·er** Rädelsführer *m*; **ring·let** ['ᴗlit] (Ringel-) Locke *f*; **ring road** Ringstraße *f*; '**ring·worm** ⚕ Ringelflechte *f*.

rink [rink] (*a.* künstliche) Eisbahn *f*; Rollschuhbahn *f*.

rinse [rins] **1.** *oft* ᴗ *out* (aus)spülen; **2.** = '**rins·ing** Spülen *n*; Spülung *f*; ᴗ*s pl.* Spülicht *n*.

ri·ot ['raiət] **1.** Krawall *m*, Tumult *m*; Aufruhr *m*; Orgie *f* (*a. fig.*); *fig.* Bombenerfolg *m*; *run* ᴗ durchgehen; (sich aus)toben; **2.** Krawall machen, in Aufruhr sein; toben; schwelgen (*in in dat.*); '**ri·ot·er** Aufrührer(in); Randalierer *m*; '**ri·ot·ous** □ aufrührerisch; lärmend; liederlich (*Leben*); **ri·ot shield** Schutzschild *m der Polizei*; **ri·ot squad** Bereitschaftspolizei *f*, Überfallkommando *n*.

rip[1] [rip] **1.** Riß *m*; **2.** *v/t.* Naht etc. (auf)trennen; (zer)reißen; ᴗ *up* aufschlitzen, -reißen; *v/i.* reißen; (dahin)rasen.

rip[2] F [ᴗ] Schindmähre *f*; Taugenichts *m*.

ri·par·i·an [rai'pɛəriən] **1.** Ufer...;
2. (Ufer)Anlieger *m*.

rip·cord ['ripkɔːd] Reißleine *f am Fallschirm*.

ripe □ [raip] reif; '**rip·en** reifen; '**ripe·ness** Reife *f*.

rip-off P ['ripɔf] Wucher *m*, Nepp *m*; Schwindel *m*.

ri·poste [ri'pəust] **1.** *fenc.* Gegenstoß *m*, -hieb *m* (*a. fig.*); **2.** erwidern.

rip·per ['ripə] Trennmesser *n*, -säge *f*, -maschine *f*; *sl.* Prachtkerl *m*; -stück *n*; '**rip·ping** □ *sl.* fabelhaft, blendend, glänzend.

rip·ple ['ripl] **1.** kleine Welle *f*; Kräuselung *f*; Geriesel *n*; **2.** (sich) kräuseln; rieseln.

rise [raiz] **1.** (An-, Auf)Steigen *n*; Anwachsen *n*; Anschwellen *n des Wassers, der Stimme*; (Preis-, Gehalts)Erhöhung *f*; *fig.* Aufstieg *m*; ☀ Aufgang *m der Sonne*; Steigung *f*, Anhöhe *f*; Erhöhung *f* (*a. fig.*); Zuwachs *m*; Ursprung *m*, Anfang *m*; *give* ᴗ *to* verursachen, hervorrufen; *take* (*one's*) ᴗ entstehen; entspringen; **2.** (*irr.*) sich erheben, aufstehen; aufbrechen, die Sitzung schließen; in die Höhe gehen, steigen; aufsteigen (*a. fig., Erinnerung etc.*) (*on, upon* vor *j-s Geist etc.*); auferstehen; aufgehen (*Sonne, Samen*); anschwellen, wachsen; sich empören (*against, on* gegen); entspringen (*Fluß*); ᴗ *to such* e-r *Lage* gewachsen zeigen; ᴗ *to the bait* nach dem Köder schnappen; **ris·en** ['rizn] *p.p. von* rise 2; '**ris·er** Aufstehende *m*; Steigung *f* e-r *Stufe*; *early* ᴗ Frühaufsteher(in).

ris·i·bil·i·ty [rizi'biliti] Neigung *f* zu lachen; **ris·i·ble** □ ['ᴗibl] Lach...; zum Lachen aufgelegt.

ris·ing ['raizin] **1.** (Auf)Steigen *n*; Steigung *f*; *ast.* Aufgang *m*; Aufbruch *m* e-r *Versammlung*; Aufstand *m*; **2.** heranwachsend (*Generation*).

risk [risk] **1.** Gefahr *f*, Wagnis *n*; ✝ Risiko *n*; *at the* ᴗ *of ger.* auf die Gefahr hin, zu *inf.*; *run the* ᴗ das Risiko eingehen, Gefahr laufen; **2.** wagen, riskieren, aufs Spiel setzen; '**risk·y** □ gefährlich, gewagt.

ris·sole ['risəul] *Küche:* Frikadelle *f*.

rite [rait] Ritus *m*, *feierlicher* Brauch *m*; **rit·u·al** ['ritʃuəl] **1.** □ rituell, feierlich; **2.** Ritual *n.*

ri·val ['raivǝl] **1.** Nebenbuhler(in); Rivale *m*, Rivalin *f*; **2.** rivalisierend; ✝ Konkurrenz...; **3.** wetteifern *od.* rivalisieren (mit); '**ri·val·ry** Rivalität *f*; Wetteifer *m.*

rive [raiv] (*irr.*) (sich) spalten.

riv·en ['rivn] *p.p. von* rive.

riv·er ['rivǝ] Fluß *m*; Strom *m* (*a. fig.*); *sell s.o.* down the ~ *fig.* j. verraten; '**~-horse** Flußpferd *n*; '**~-po·lice** Wasserschutzpolizei *f*; '**~-side** (Fluß)Ufer *n*; *attr.* am Wasser (gelegen).

riv·et ['rivit] **1.** ⊕ Niet(e *f*) *m*; **2.** (ver)nieten; *fig.* heften (to an *acc.*; on, upon auf *acc.*); fesseln.

riv·u·let ['rivjulit] Bach *m*, Flüßchen *n.*

roach *ichth.* [rǝutʃ] Plötze *f.*

road [rǝud] Straße *f* (*a. fig.*), Weg *m*; *Am.* = railroad; *mst* ~s *pl.* ⚓ Reede *f*; *on the* ~ unterwegs; *take the* ~ aufbrechen; *main* ~ Haupt(verkehrs)straße *f*; '**~-bed** Straßenunterbau *m*; 🚉 Bahnkörper *m*; '**~-block** Straßensperre *f*; '**~-hog** *mot.* Verkehrsrowdy *m*; '**~-man** Straßenarbeiter *m*; ~ **map** Straßen-, Autokarte *f*; '**~-mend·er** Straßenarbeiter *m*; '**~-race** Straßenrennen *n*; '**~-sense** *mot.* Fahrverstand *m*; '**~-side** Straßenrand *m*; '**~-stead** ⚓ Reede *f*; **road·ster** ['~stǝ] Roadster *m*, offener Sportwagen *m*; '**road·way** Fahrbahn *f*; **road works** *pl.* Straßenarbeiten *f/pl.*; Baustelle *f auf e-r* Straße; '**road·wor·thi·ness** Verkehrssicherheit *f e-s* Autos; '**road·wor·thy** verkehrssicher (*Auto*).

roam [rǝum] *v/i.* umherstreifen, wandern; *v/t.* durchstreifen; '**roam·er** Herumtreiber(in); Wanderer *m.*

roan [rǝun] **1.** rötlichgrau; **2.** Rotschimmel *m*; ⊕ Schafleder *n.*

roar [rɔː] **1.** brüllen (*a. fig. überlaut sprechen, lachen*); brausen, tosen, donnern; **2.** Gebrüll *n*; Brausen *n*; Krachen *n*, Getöse *n*; brüllendes Gelächter *n*; **roar·ing** ['~riŋ] **1.** = roar 2; **2.** ☐ brüllend; lärmend; stürmisch; schwunghaft; *be in* ~ *health* vor Gesundheit strotzen.

roast [rǝust] **1.** rösten, braten; backen; *sl. j.* verkohlen (*hänseln*); **2.** geröstet; gebraten; ~ *beef* Rinderbraten *m*; ~ *meat* Braten *m*; **3.**

rule the ~ das Regiment führen; '**roast·er** Röster *m*; Kaffeeröstmaschine *f*; Spanferkel *n*; '**roasting-jack** Bratenwender *m.*

rob [rɔb] (be)rauben; (aus)plündern; '**rob·ber** Räuber *m*; '**rob·ber·y** Raub(überfall) *m*; Räuberei *f.*

robe [rǝub] **1.** (Amts)Robe *f*, Talar *m*; Staatskleid *n*; *poet.* Gewand *n*; Kleid *n*; *Am.* Morgenrock *m*; ~s *pl.* Amtstracht *f*; *gentlemen of the* ~ Juristen *m/pl.*; **2.** kleiden; *j–m* die Robe *etc.* anlegen; *fig.* schmücken.

rob·in *orn.* ['rɔbin] Rotkehlchen *n.*

ro·bot ['rǝubɔt] **1.** Roboter *m*; Automat *m*; automatisches Verkehrszeichen *n*; **2.** automatisch, mechanisch.

ro·bust ☐ [rǝu'bʌst] robust, derb, kräftig; widerstandsfähig; **ro·bust·ness** Robustheit *f*, Derbheit *f*, Kraft *f.*

rock¹ [rɔk] Fels(en) *m*; Klippe *f*; Gestein *n*; Zuckerstange *f*; *get down to* ~ *bottom* der Sache auf den Grund gehen; ~ *crystal* Bergkristall *m*; ~ *salt* Steinsalz *n.*

rock² [~] *v/t.* schaukeln; (ein)wiegen; rütteln; *fig.* erschüttern; ~ *s.o. to sleep* j. in den Schlaf wiegen; *v/i.* schaukeln, (sch)wanken.

rock³ ♪ [~] Rock *m.*

rock-bot·tom F ['rɔk'bɔtǝm] allerniedrigst (*Preis*).

rock·er ['rɔkǝ] *Wiegen- etc.* Kufe *f*; *Am.* Schaukelstuhl *m*; Rocker *m*, Halbstarke *m.*

rock·er·y ['rɔkǝri] Steingarten *m.*

rock·et¹ ['rɔkit] **1.** Rakete *f*; ~-*launching site* Raketenabschußbasis *f*; ~ *plane* Raketenflugzeug *n*; ~ *propulsion* Raketenantrieb *m*; **2.** F in die Höhe schießen (*Preise*).

rock·et² ♣ [~] Rauke *f*, Senfkohl *m*; Nachtviole *f.*

rock·et-pow·ered ['rɔkitpauǝd] mit Raketenantrieb; **rock·et·ry** ['~ri] Raketentechnik *f.*

rock...: '**~-fall** Steinschlag *m*; '**~-gar·den** Steingarten *m.*

rock·ing... ['rɔkiŋ]: '**~-chair** Schaukelstuhl *m*; '**~-horse** Schaukelpferd *n.*

rock·y ['rɔki] felsig; Felsen...; F wackelig.

ro·co·co [rǝu'kǝukǝu] Rokoko *n.*

rod [rɔd] Rute *f*; Stab *m*; ⊕ Stange *f*; Meßrute *f* (= $5^1/_2$ *yards*); *Am. sl.*

Pistole *f; have a ~ in pickle for s.o.* mit j-m noch ein Hühnchen zu rupfen haben.

rode [rəud] *pret. von ride 2.*

ro·dent ['rəudənt] Nagetier *n.*

ro·de·o *Am.* [rəu'deiəu] Rodeo *m;* Zusammentreiben *n von Vieh;* Cowboy-Turnier *n.*

rod·o·mon·tade [rɔdəmɔn'teid] Aufschneiderei *f,* Prahlerei *f.*

roe[1] [rəu] *a. hard ~* Rogen *m; soft ~* Milch *f.*

roe[2] [~] Reh *n;* '~·buck Rehbock *m.*

ro·ga·tion *eccl.* [rəu'geiʃən] (Für-) Bitte *f; ~ Sunday* Sonntag Rogate *m.*

rogue [rəug] Schurke *m;* Schelm *m,* Spitzbube *m; ~s' gallery* Verbrecheralbum *n;* '**ro·guer·y** Schurkerei *f;* Schelmerei *f;* '**ro·guish** □ schurkisch; schelmisch.

roist·er ['rɔistə] krakeelen; '**roist·er·er** Krakeeler *m.*

role, rôle *thea.* [rəul] Rolle *f (a. fig.).*

roll [rəul] **1.** Rolle *f;* ⊕ Walze *f;* Brötchen *n,* Semmel *f;* Rolle *f,* Verzeichnis *n,* Liste *f;* Urkunde *f;* (Donner)Rollen *n;* (Trommel)Wirbel *m;* ♧ Schlingern *n;* **2.** *v/t.* rollen; wälzen; walzen; strecken; *Zigarette* drehen; rollend (aus-) sprechen; *~ up* aufrollen; einwickeln; *~ed gold* Walzgold *n,* Dublee *n; v/i.* rollen *(a. Donner etc.);* sich wälzen; *bsd. ast.* sich drehen; wirbeln *(Trommel);* ♧ schlingern; *be ~ing in money* im Geld schwimmen; *~ up* vorfahren *(Wagen);* aufkreuzen; *~ bar mot.* Überrollbügel *m;* '~·call Namensaufruf *m;* ✕ Appell *m;* '**roll·er** Rolle *f,* Walze *f;* Sturzwelle *f; mst ~ bandage* Rollbinde *f; ~ coaster Am.* Achterbahn *f; ~ skate* Rollschuh *m; ~ towel* Rollhandtuch *n;* '**roll-film** *phot.* Rollfilm *m.*

rol·lick·ing ['rɔlikiŋ] ausgelassen, übermütig.

roll·ing ['rəuliŋ] **1.** rollend; Roll...; Walz...; well(enförm)ig; **2.** Rollen *n,* Walzen *n; ~ mill* ⊕ Walzwerk *n; ~ pin* Nudelholz *n; ~ press typ.* Rotationspresse *f;* '~·stock ♒ rollendes Material *n.*

roll-neck ['rəulnek] Rollkragen *m.*

roll-on ['rəulɔn] *a. ~ belt* Gummischlüpfer *m,* Hüftformer *m;* Deoroller *m.*

roll-top desk ['rəultɔp'desk] Rollpult *n.*

ro·ly-po·ly ['rəuli'pəuli] **1.** Rollkuchen *m;* **2.** rund und dick.

Ro·man ['rəumən] **1.** römisch; **2.** Römer(in); *mst* ♀ *typ.* Antiqua (-schrift) *f; ~·'Cath·o·lic eccl.* **1.** (römisch-)katholisch; **2.** Katholik(in).

ro·mance[1] [rəu'mæns] **1.** (Ritter-, Vers)Roman *m;* Abenteuer-, Liebesroman *m;* Romanze *f (a. fig.); fig.* Märchen *n;* Romantik *f;* **2.** *fig.* aufschneiden.

Ro·mance[2] [rəu'mæns]: *~ languages pl.* romanische Sprachen *f/pl.*

ro·manc·er [rəu'mænsə] Romanschreiber *m;* Aufschneider *m.*

Ro·man·esque [rəumə'nesk] romanisch(er Baustil *m*).

Ro·man·ic [rəu'mænik] romanisch; *bsd. ~ peoples pl.* Romanen *m/pl.*

ro·man·tic [rəu'mæntik] **1.** *(~ally)* romantisch; **2.** = **ro·man·ti·cist** [~tisist] Romantiker *m;* **ro·man·ti·cism** Romantik *f.*

Ro·ma·ny ['rəumǝni] **1.** Zigeuner(in); Zigeunersprache *f;* **2.** Zigeuner...

Rom·ish *mst contp.* ['rəumiʃ] römisch(-katholisch).

romp [rɔmp] **1.** Range *f,* Wildfang *m;* Balgerei *f;* **2.** sich balgen, toben, tollen; '**romp·er(s** *pl.*) Spielanzug *m e-s Kindes.*

ron·do ♪ ['rɔndəu] Rondo *n.*

rood [ruːd] Kruzifix *n;* Viertelmorgen *m (10,117 Ar);* '~·loft △ Chorbühne *f.*

roof [ruːf] **1.** Dach *n; ~ of the mouth* Gaumen *m;* **2.** *a. ~ over* überdachen; '**roof·ing 1.** Bedachung *f;* Dachwerk *n;* **2.** Dach...; *~ felt* Dachpappe *f;* **roof rack** *Auto:* Dachgepäckträger *m;* '**roof-tree** Firstbalken *m.*

rook[1] [ruk] **1.** *orn.* Saatkrähe *f; fig.* Bauernfänger *m;* **2.** betrügen.

rook[2] [~] *Schach:* Turm *m.*

rook·er·y ['rukəri] Krähenhorst *m; fig.* Brutstätte *f;* Nistplatz *m.*

rook·ie *sl.* ['ruki] ✕ Rekrut *m; fig.* Neuling *m,* Anfänger *m.*

room [rum] Raum *m;* Platz *m;* Zimmer *n;* Spielraum *m,* Möglichkeit *f; ~s pl.* Wohnung *f; in my ~* an meiner Stelle; *make ~* Platz machen; *...roomed* ...zimmerig; '**room·er** *bsd. Am.* Untermieter *m;*

roughen

'**room·ing-house** *bsd. Am.* Miets-, Logierhaus *n*; '**room-mate** Stubenkamerad *m*; '**room·y** □ geräumig.

roost [ru:st] **1.** Schlafplatz *m e-s Vogels*; Hühnerstange *f*; Hühnerstall *m*; *rule the* ~ F *fig.* Herr im Haus sein; **2.** sich (zum Schlaf) niederhocken; *fig.* übernachten; '**roost·er** Haushahn *m*.

root¹ [ru:t] **1.** Wurzel *f* (*a. fig., anat.,* ₳, *gr.*); ~ *and branch* völlig, mit Stumpf u. Stiel; *take od. strike* ~ Wurzel fassen *od.* schlagen; ~ *idea* Grundgedanke *m*; **2.** (ein)wurzeln; ~ *out* ausrotten; '**root·ed** eingewurzelt; wurzelnd (*in* in *dat.*).

root² [~] *v/t. a.* ~ *up* auf-, umwühlen); ~ *out od. up* ausgraben, aufstöbern; *v/i.* wühlen; ~ *for Am. sl.* Stimmung machen für *j.*; '**root·er** *Am. sl.* Schreier *m*, Fanatiker *m* für *et.*

root·let ['ru:tlit] Wurzelfaser *f*.

rope [rəʊp] **1.** Tau *n*, Seil *n*; Strang *m*, Strick *m* (*bsd. zum Hängen*); Schnur *f Perlen etc.*; *on the* ~ am Seil, angeseilt; *be at the end of one's* ~ F mit s-m Latein zu Ende sein; *know the* ~*s* sich auskennen; *learn the* ~*s* sich einarbeiten; *show s.o. the* ~*s* j-m zeigen, wie der Laden läuft; **2.** *v t.* mit e-m Seil befestigen; *mst* ~ *in*, ~ *off*, ~ *out* absperren; *mount.* anseilen; ~ *down* abseilen; *v i.* Fäden ziehen (*Sirup etc.*); '~**-danc·er** Seiltänzer(in); '~**-lad·der** Strickleiter *f*; '~**-mak·er** Seiler *m*; '**rop·er·y** Seilerei *f*; '**rope-walk** Seilerbahn *f*; '**rope-way** Seilbahn *f*.

rop·i·ness ['rəʊpinis] Klebrigkeit *f*. **rop·y** ['rəʊpi] klebrig, zähflüssig.

ro·sa·ry ['rəʊzəri] *eccl.* Rosenkranz *m*; Rosengarten *m*, -beet *n*.

rose¹ [rəʊz] ♀ Rose *f*; (Gießkannen)Brause *f*; Rosenrot *n*.

rose² [~] *pret. von rise* 2.

rose...: '~**-bud** Rosenknospe *f*; *Am.* hübsches Mädchen *n*; Debütantin *f*; '~**-col·o(u)red** rosarot (*a. fig.*); rosig.

ro·se·ate ['rəʊziit] rosig.

rose·hip ♀ ['rəʊzhip] Hagebutte *f*.

rose·mar·y ♀ ['rəʊzməri] Rosmarin *m*.

ro·se·ry ['rəʊzəri] Rosenbeet *n*.

ro·sette [rəʊ'zet] Rosette *f*.

rose...: ~ **win·dow** (Fenster)Rosette *f*; '~**wood** Rosenholz *n*.

ros·in ['rɔzin] **1.** (Geigen)Harz *n*, Kolophonium *n*; **2.** harzen.

ros·ter ['rəʊstə] Dienstplan *m*; Diensttabelle *f*.

ros·trum['rɔstrəm]Rednertribüne *f*.

ros·y □ ['rəʊzi] rosig.

rot [rɔt] **1.** Fäulnis *f*, Fäule *f*; *sl.* Quatsch *m*; **2.** *v/t.* faulen lassen; *sl. Plan etc.* vermurksen; Quatsch machen mit *j-m*; *v/i.* verfaulen, vermodern.

ro·ta ['rəʊtə] = roster.

ro·ta·ry ['rəʊtəri] drehend; Rotations...; ~ *press typ.* Rotations-(druck)presse *f*; ~ *pump* Kreiselpumpe *f*; **ro·tate** [rəʊ'teit] (sich) drehen, rotieren, (ab)wechseln; **ro'ta·tion** Umdrehung *f*; Kreislauf *m*; Abwechs(e)lung *f*; ~ *of crops* ✔ Fruchtfolge *f*, -wechsel *m*; **ro·ta·to·ry** ['~tətəri] *s. rotary*; abwechselnd.

rote [rəʊt]: *by* ~ auswendig.

ro·tor ['rəʊtə] ⊕ Rotor *m*; ✈ Läufer *m*; ✈ Rotor *m*, Drehflügel *m des Hubschraubers.*

rot·ten □ ['rɔtn] verfault, faul(ig); verderbt, verdorben; modrig; morsch (*alle a. fig.*); *sl.* saumäßig, dreckig; '**rot·ten·ness** Fäulnis *f*; Morschheit *f*.

rot·ter *sl.* ['rɔtə] Schweinehund *m*.

ro·tund □ [rəʊ'tʌnd] rund; voll (*Stimme*); hochtrabend; **ro'tun·da** ∆ [~də] Rundbau *m*; **ro'tun·di·ty** Rundheit *f*.

rouge [ru:ʒ] **1.** Rouge *n*; Silberputzmittel *n*; **2.** Rouge auflegen (auf).

rough [rʌf] **1.** □ rauh; roh; grob (*alle a. fig.*); holperig; stürmisch; *fig.* ungehobelt; herb (*Wein etc.*); ungefähr (*Schätzung*); ~ *and ready* grob(gearbeitet); (Not)Behelfs...; *fig.* grobschlächtig; ~ *copy* roher Entwurf *m*; ~ *draft* Rohfassung *f*; *cut up* ~ F massiv werden; **2.** Rauhe *n*, Grobe *n*; Lümmel *m*, Strolch *m*; **3.** (an-, auf)rauhen; *Hufeisen* schärfen; ~ *it* sich mühsam durchschlagen; '**rough·age** grobe Nahrung *f*, Grobfutter *n*; '**rough-and-'read·y** grob; provisorisch; Behelfs... (*gerade ausreichend für den Zweck*); '**rough-and-'tum·ble 1.** wild, unordentlich; heftig; **2.** Schlägerei *f*; '**rough-cast 1.** ∆ Rauhputz *m*; **2.** unfertig; **3.** ∆ berappen; roh entwerfen; '**rough·en** rauh machen *od.* werden.

rough...: '∼-'**hewn** roh behauen; flüchtig; ungehobelt; '∼-**house** *sl.* **1.** Radau *m*; Keilerei *f*; **2.** rauhbeinig gegen *j.* sein; Radau machen; '∼-**neck** *Am. sl.* Rabauke *m*; '**roughness** Rauheit *f*; Roheit *f*; Grobheit *f*; '**rough-rid·er** Zureiter *m*; verwegener Reiter *m*; '**rough·shod:** *ride* ∼ *over* rücksichtslos behandeln.

rou·lette [ru:'let] Roulett *n*.

Rou·ma·nian [ru:'meinjən] = *Rumanian.*

round [raund] **1.** □ rund (*a. Zahl, Summe*); voll (*Stimme etc.*); flott, scharf (*Gangart*); abgerundet (*Stil*); unverblümt (*Antwort etc.*); derb (*Fluch etc.*); ∼ *game* Gesellschaftsspiel *n*; ∼ *hand* Rundschrift *f*; ∼ *table* Konferenztisch *m*; ∼ *trip* Rundreise *f*, Hin- und Rückfahrt *f*; **2.** *adv.* rund-, ringsum(her); *a.* ∼ *about* in der Runde; *all* ∼ ringsum; *fig.* durch die Bank, ohne Unterschied; *all the year* ∼ das ganze Jahr hindurch; *10 inches* ∼ 10 Zoll im Umfang; **3.** *prp.* um ... herum; *go* ∼ *the house* im Haus herumgehen; ∼ *about 2 o'clock* etwa um 2 Uhr; **4.** Rund *n*, Kreis *m*; Rundgang *m*, Runde *f*; Kreislauf *m*; (Leiter-)Sprosse *f*; ♪ Rundgesang *m*, Kanon *m*; Rundtanz *m*; ✗ Ronde *f*; Lage *f* Bier *etc.*; ✗, *a. fig.* Lach-, Beifalls-Salve *f*; *100* ∼*s* ✗ 100 Schuß; **5.** *v/t.* runden; herumgehen, -fahren *od.* -segeln um; umfahren, -schiffen; ∼ *off* abrunden; ∼ *up* einkreisen; *j.* stellen; *Vieh* zs.-treiben; *v/i.* sich runden; sich umdrehen.

round·a·bout ['raundəbaut] **1.** umschweifig; umwegig; **2.** Umweg *m*; Umschweife *pl.*; Karussell *n*; Kreisverkehr *m*.

roun·del ['raundl] Rondell *n*; **roun·de·ly** ['∼dilei] Rundgesang *m*.

round·ers ['raundəz] *pl.* Schlagballspiel *n*; '**round·head** *hist.* Rundkopf *m*, Puritaner *m*; '**round·ish** rundlich; '**round·ness** Rundheit *f*; Rundung *f*; Unverblümtheit *f e-r Antwort etc.*; **round rob·in** *von mehreren Leuten unterschriebene* Petition *f*, Denkschrift *f*; **rounds-man** ✝ ['∼zmən] Austräger *m*; '**round-ta·ble con·fer·ence** Konferenz *f* am runden Tisch; '**round-the-clock** ununterbrochen, 24-stündig; '**round-**

-up Einkreisung *f*; Razzia *f*; Zs.-fassung *f*; Zs.-treiben *n*.

roup *vet.* [ru:p] Darre *f der Hühner.*

rouse [rauz] *v/t. a.* ∼ *up* wecken; ermuntern, aufrütteln; *Wild* aufjagen; (auf)reizen; ∼ *o.s.* sich aufraffen; *v/i.* aufwachen; '**rous·ing** brausend (*Beifall etc.*).

roust·a·bout *Am.* ['raustə'baut] ungelernter (*mst* Hafen)Arbeiter *m*.

rout[1] [raut] Rotte *f*; ✝ große Gesellschaft *f*.

rout[2] [∼] **1.** wilde Flucht *f*; Vernichtung *f*; *put to* ∼ = **2.** vernichtend schlagen.

rout[3] [∼] = *root*[2].

route [ru:t, ✗ *a.* raut] Weg *m*; (Reise)Route *f*; Strecke *f*; ✗ Marschroute *f*; *en* ∼ unterwegs; '∼-**march** Übungsmarsch *m*.

rou·tine [ru:'ti:n] **1.** Routine *f*; Schablone *f*; **2.** schablonenmäßig; üblich, laufend.

roux [ru:] Mehlschwitze *f*, Einbrenne *f*.

rove [rəuv] umherstreifen, umherwandern; '**rov·er** Wanderer *m*; Herumstreicher *m*; Seeräuber *m*; älterer Pfadfinder *m*.

row[1] [rəu] Reihe *f*; Häuser-, *thea.* Sitzreihe *f*; ∼ *house Am.* Reihenhaus *n*; *a hard* ∼ *to hoe* e-e schwierige Sache *f*.

row[2] [∼] **1.** rudern; **2.** Ruderfahrt *f*, -partie *f*.

row[3] F [rau] **1.** Spektakel *m*; Krawall *m*, Krach *m*; Schlägerei *f*; *what's the* ∼*?* was ist denn los?; **2.** ausschimpfen; zanken (*with* mit).

row·an ♥ ['rauən] Eberesche *f*; '∼-**ber·ry** Vogelbeere *f*.

row-boat ['rəubəut] Ruderboot *n*.

row·dy ['raudi] **1.** Raufbold *m*, Strolch *m*, Rowdy *m*; **2.** gewalttätig; flegelhaft.

row·el ['rauəl] **1.** Spornrädchen *n*; **2.** spornen.

row·er ['rəuə] Ruderer(in *f*) *m*.

row·ing-boat ['rəuiŋbəut] Ruderboot *n*.

row·lock ['rɔlək] Ruderklampe *f*.

roy·al ['rɔiəl] **1.** □ königlich; prächtig; ∼ *stag* Kapitalhirsch *m*; **2.** ⚓ Oberbramsegel *n*; '**roy·al·ism** Königstreue *f*; '**roy·al·ist** **1.** Royalist *m*, Königstreue *m*; **2.** königstreu; '**roy·al·ty** Königtum *n*, -reich *n*, Königswürde *f*; königliche Persönlichkeit *f*; königliches Vorrecht *n*; vom König verliehenes Verfügungsrecht *n*; Ertragsanteil *m*, Tantieme *f* *e-s Autors etc.*

rub [rʌb] **1.** Reiben *n*; Schwierigkeit *f*; *fig.* Hieb *m*, Stich *m*; Unannehmlichkeit *f*; *there is the ~* das ist der Haken; **2.** *v/t.* reiben; (ab-)wischen, scheuern; (wund)scheuern; schleifen; *~ down* abreiben; *Pferd* striegeln; *~ in* einreiben; *fig.* betonen, herumreiten auf; *~ off* abreiben; abschleifen; *~ out* auslöschen; -radieren; *~ up* auffrischen; *Farbe etc.* verreiben; *v/i.* sich reiben (*against, on* an *dat.*); *~ along, ~ on, ~ through fig.* sich durchschlagen.

rub·ber [ˈrʌbə] Gummi *n*, *m*; Kautschuk *m*; Radiergummi *m*; Masseur *m*; Wischtuch *n*; ⊕ Polierkissen *n*, -tuch *n*; *Bridge*, *Whist*: Robber *m*; *~s pl.* Gummi-, Überschuhe *m/pl.*; *attr.* Gummi...; *~ check Am. sl.* geplatzter Scheck *m*; *~ solution* Gummilösung *f*; *ˈ~·neck Am. sl.* **1.** Gaffer(in); **2.** sich den Hals verrenken; mithören; *~ pants pl.* Gummihöschen *n für Babys*; *~ stamp* Gummistempel *m*; *Am.* F *fig.* Nachbeter *m*; *ˈ~-ˈstamp* automatisch gutheißen.

rub·bish [ˈrʌbiʃ] Schutt *m*; Abfall *m*; Kehricht *m*; *fig.* Schund *m*; Unsinn *m*; *~ bin* Abfalleimer *m*; *~ chute* Müllschlucker *m*; *ˈrub·bish·y fig.* wertlos; unsinnig.

rub·ble [ˈrʌbl] Schutt *m*.

rube *Am. sl.* [ruːb] Bauernlümmel *m*.

ru·be·fa·cient 🏥 [ruːbiˈfeiʃjənt] hautrötend.

ru·bi·cund [ˈruːbikənd] rötlich, rot.

ru·bric [ˈruːbrik] Rubrik *f*; *eccl.* liturgische Vorschrift *f*; **ru·bri·cate** [ˈ~keit] rot bezeichnen.

ru·by [ˈruːbi] **1.** *min.* Rubin *m*; Rubinrot *n*; *typ.* Pariser Schrift *f*; **2.** rubinrot.

ruck [rʌk] *Rennsport*: *the ~* das Feld; *the (common) ~ fig.* der Haufe(n) *m*.

ruck(·le) [ˈrʌk(l)] *a. ~ up* (sich) falten *od.* zerknittern.

ruck·sack [ˈruksæk] Rucksack *m*.

ruc·tion *sl.* [ˈrʌkʃən] Krawall *m*, Krach *m*.

rud·der ⚓ [ˈrʌdə] (Steuer)Ruder *n*; 𝒦 Seitenruder *n*.

rud·di·ness [ˈrʌdinis] Röte *f*;

rud·dy rot, rötlich; frisch (*Gesichtsfarbe*); rotbäckig; *sl.* verflixt.

rude ☐ [ruːd] unhöflich; unanständig; grob, heftig, unsanft; ungebildet; einfach, kunstlos; robust; roh; **ˈrude·ness** Unhöflichkeit *f*, Unanständigkeit *f etc.*

ru·di·ment *biol.* [ˈruːdimənt] Ansatz *m* (*of* zu *e-m Organ*; *a. fig.*); *~s pl.* Anfangsgründe *m/pl.*; **ru·di·men·ta·ry** [~ˈmentəri] rudimentär.

rue[1] 🌿 [ruː] Raute *f*.

rue[2] [~] bereuen, beklagen.

rue·ful ☐ [ˈruːful] reuig; traurig, kläglich; **ˈrue·ful·ness** Traurigkeit *f*, Gram *m*.

ruff[1] [rʌf] (Hals-, Papier)Krause *f*.

ruff[2] [~] *Whist*: **1.** Trumpfen *n*; **2.** trumpfen.

ruf·fi·an [ˈrʌfjən] Rohling *m*; Raufbold *m*; Schurke *m*; **ˈruf·fi·an·ly** roh, wüst.

ruf·fle [ˈrʌfl] **1.** Rüsche *f*, Krause *f*; Kräuseln *n des Wassers*; *fig.* Unruhe *f*; *~ collar* Rüschenkragen *m*; **2.** *v/t.* kräuseln; zerwühlen, -drücken, -zausen; *fig.* aus der Ruhe bringen; *gute Laune etc.* stören; *v/i.* die Ruhe verlieren.

rug [rʌg] (Woll-, Reise)Decke *f*; Vorleger *m*, Brücke *f* (*kleiner Teppich*).

Rug·by [ˈrʌgbi] *a. ~ football* Rugby *n* (*Ballspiel*).

rug·ged ☐ [ˈrʌgid] rauh (*a. fig.*); uneben; zackig; zerklüftet; gefurcht (*Gesicht*); **ˈrug·ged·ness** Rauheit *f etc.*

rug·ger F [ˈrʌgə] = *Rugby*.

ru·in [ˈruːin] **1.** Ruin *m*, Zs.-bruch *m*; Untergang *m*; Verfall *m*; *mst ~s pl.* Ruine(n *pl.*) *f*; *lay in ~s* in Trümmer legen; **2.** ruinieren; zugrunde richten; zerstören; verderben; **ru·in·a·tion** Zerstörung *f*; F Verderben *n*, Untergang *m*; **ˈru·in·ous** ☐ ruinenhaft, verfallen; baufällig; verderblich, ruinös.

rule [ruːl] **1.** Regel *f*; *eccl.* Ordensregel *f*; Vorschrift *f*; ⚖ Verfügung *f*; *a. standing ~* Satzung *f*; Herrschaft *f*; Lineal *n*; ⊕ Zollstock *m*; *as a ~* in der Regel; *~(s) of court* Prozeßordnung *f*; *~(s) of the road* Straßenverkehrsordnung *f*; *~ of three* ♣ Regeldetri *f*; *~ of thumb* Faustregel *f*; *make it a ~* es sich zur Regel machen; *work to ~* genau nach Vorschrift arbeiten (*als Streik-mittel*); **2.** *v/t.* regeln; leiten; *a.* ~ *over* beherrschen; entscheiden, verfügen; *Papier* liniieren; ~ *out* ausschließen; *v/i.* herrschen, regieren; ✝ stehen, notieren (*Preise*); **'rul·er** Herrscher(in); Lineal *n*; **'rul·ing 1.** *bsd.* ⚖ Verfügung *f*; **2.** ~ *price* ✝ Tagespreis *m.*

rum¹ [rʌm] Rum *m*; *Am.* Alkohol *m.*

rum² *sl.* □ [~] ulkig, komisch.

Ru·ma·nian [ru:'meinjən] **1.** rumänisch; **2.** Rumäne *m*, Rumänin *f*; Rumänisch *n.*

rum·ble¹ ['rʌmbl] **1.** Rumpeln *n*; Poltern *n*; (G)Rollen *n*; *Am. a.* ~-*seat mot.* Notsitz *m*; *Am.* F Fehde *f* zwischen Gangsterbanden; **2.** rumpeln, rasseln, poltern; grollen (*Donner*).

rum·ble² *sl.* [~] *et.* rauskriegen.

rum·bus·tious F [rʌm'bʌstiəs] ausgelassen, laut und fröhlich, wild.

ru·mi·nant ['ru:minənt] **1.** wiederkäuend; **2.** Wiederkäuer *m*; **ru·mi·nate** ['~neit] wiederkäuen; *fig.* nachsinnen; **ru·mi·na·tion** Wiederkäuen *n*; Nachdenken *n.*

rum·mage ['rʌmidʒ] **1.** Durchsuchung *f*; Ramsch *m*, Ausschuß *m*, Restwaren *f/pl.*; ~ *sale* Wohltätigkeitsbazar *m*; **2.** *v/t.* (durch)suchen, (-)stöbern, (-)wühlen; *v/i.* wühlen.

rum·mer ['rʌmə] Römer *m* (*Trinkglas*).

rum·my¹ *sl.* □ ['rʌmi] = *rum²*.

rum·my² [~] Rommé *n* (*Kartenspiel*).

ru·mo(u)r ['ru:mə] **1.** Gerücht *n*; **2.** (als Gerücht) verbreiten; *it is* ~*ed* es geht das Gerücht; **'~-monger** Gerüchteverbreiter *m.*

rump *anat.* [rʌmp] Steiß *m*; *orn.* Bürzel *m*; Rumpf *m*, Rest *m.*

rum·ple ['rʌmpl] zerknittern, zerknüllen; *Haar* zerwühlen, (zer)zausen; **'rum·pled** zerknittert, zerzaust.

rump·steak ['rʌmpsteik] *Küche:* Rumpsteak *n.*

rum·pus F ['rʌmpəs] Krawall *m.*

rum-run·ner *Am.* ['rʌmrʌnə] Alkoholschmuggler *m.*

run [rʌn] **1.** (*irr.*) *v/i. allg.* laufen (*Mensch, Tier*; *a. Kerze, Gefäß, Augen etc.*; = fließen; verfließen; verkehren [*Zug etc.*]; im Gang sein; ⚖ in Kraft sein; *thea.* gegeben werden; sich erstrecken; eitern); rennen (*Mensch, Tier*); eilen; zerlaufen (*Farbe etc.*); umlaufen, -gehen (*Gerücht etc.*); lauten (*Text*); gehen (*Melodie*); sich stellen (*Preis*); ~ *across s.o.* j-m in die Arme laufen; ~ *after* hinter *j-m* herlaufen *od.* -sein; ~ *away* davonlaufen, durchgehen (*a. fig.*); ~ *down* hinunterlaufen; ablaufen (*Uhr etc.*); *fig.* herunterkommen; ~ *dry* aus-, vertrocknen; ~ *for* laufen nach, sich bemühen um; *parl.* kandidieren für; ~ *high* hochgehen; ~ *in* hineinlaufen; *that* ~*s in the blood* (*family*) das liegt im Blut (in der Familie); ~ *into* laufen *od.* rennen in (*acc.*); ~ *into* geraten *od.* (sich) stürzen in (*acc.*); werden zu; ~ *into s.o.* j-m in die Arme laufen; ~ *low* zur Neige gehen; ~ *mad* verrückt werden; ~ *off* weglaufen; ~ *on* fortlaufen, fortgesetzt werden; fortfahren; weiterreden; ~ *out* (hin-)auslaufen; zu Ende gehen; *I have* ~ *out of tobacco* der Tabak ist mir ausgegangen; ~ *over* hinüberlaufen; überlaufen (*Gefäß*); ~ *short* knapp werden, zu Ende gehen; ~ *through* laufen durch; durchmachen, durcheleben; durchlesen, -gehen; *Vermögen* durchbringen; ~ *to* sich belaufen auf (*acc.*); sich entwickeln zu; F sich *et.* leisten; reichen *od.* langen zu (*Geldmittel*); ~ *up* hinauflaufen; emporschießen; ~ *up to* sich belaufen auf (*acc.*); ~ (*up*)*on* losgehen auf (*acc.*); sich beschäftigen mit, betreffen; ~ *with* triefen von; in *Tränen* schwimmen; **2.** (*irr.*) *v/t. Strecke* durchlaufen; *Rennen* austragen; *Weg* einschlagen; laufen lassen; *Züge etc.* verkehren lassen; *Augen, Hand etc.* gleiten lassen; *Nadel etc.* stecken, stoßen; (vorwärts)treiben; transportieren, fahren, bringen; *Flut* ergießen; *Gold etc.* führen (*Fluß*); *Eisen etc.* schmelzen; *Kugeln* gießen; *Geschäft* betreiben, leiten; *hunt.* verfolgen, hetzen; um die Wette rennen mit; *Waren* schmuggeln; lose nähen, heften; ~ *the blockade* die Blockade brechen; ~ *down* niederrennen, -segeln; abhetzen; *j.* einholen; zur Strecke bringen; *fig.* schlecht machen; herunterwirtschaften; *be* ~ *down* abgearbeitet *od.* erschöpft sein; ~ *errands* Botengänge machen; ~ *hard*

j. bedrängen; ~ *in mot.* einfahren; F einbuchten; ~ *into* hineinstoßen in *(acc.)*; hinreißen *od.* bringen zu; fahren an *(acc.)*; ~ *off* ablaufen lassen; ~ *out* hinausstoßen, -schieben, -jagen; ~ *over j.* überfahren; *Text* überfliegen; ~ *s.o. through j.* durchbohren; ~ *up Fahne etc.* aufziehen; *Preis* hochtreiben; *Neubau* hochziehen; *Rechnung etc.* auflaufen lassen; **3.** Laufen *n*, Rennen *n*, Lauf *m* (*bsd. im Sport*); Verlauf *m*, Gang *m*, Fortgang *m*; Fahrt *f e-s Schiffes*; Reise *f*, Ausflug *m*; ✝ Andrang *m*; ✝ stürmische Nachfrage *f* (*on, upon* nach); *Am.* kleiner Wasserlauf *m*; *bsd. Am.* Laufmasche *f*; ♪ Lauf *m*; *Vieh-*Trift *f*; *Mühle:* Mahlgang *m*; freie Benutzung *f*; Art *f*, Schlag *m*; ✝ Sorte *f*; the *common* ~ die übliche Art, die große Masse; *have a* ~ *of* 20 *nights thea.* 20mal nacheinander gegeben werden; *have the* ~ *of s.th. et.* frei zur Verfügung haben; *be in the* ~ *od.* ~*ning bei e-r Wahl* in Frage kommen; *in the long* ~ auf die Dauer, am Ende; *in the short* ~ fürs nächste; *on the* ~ auf den Beinen; auf der Flucht.   [(Sport)Wagen *m*.⎫
run·a·bout *mot.* [ˈrʌnəbaut] kleiner ⎬
run·a·way [ˈrʌnəwei] **1.** Ausreißer *m*; Durchgänger *m* (*Pferd*); **2.** entlaufen, -kommen; **3.** flüchtig.
run-down 1. [rʌnˈdaun] heruntergekommen (*Haus etc.*); abgespannt (*Person*); leer (*Batterie*); **2.** F [ˈrʌndaun] (ausführlicher) Bericht *m*.
rune [ruːn] Rune *f*.
rung[1] [rʌŋ] *p.p. von* ring[2] **2.**
rung[2] [~] (Leiter)Sprosse *f* (*a. fig.*).
run·ic [ˈruːnik] runisch; Runen...
run-in [ˈrʌnˈin] *Sport:* Einlauf *m*; F Krach *m*, Zs.-stoß *m* (*Streit*).
run·let [ˈrʌnlit], **run·nel** [ˈrʌnl] Rinnsal *n*; Rinnstein *m*.
run·ner [ˈrʌnə] Renner *m*, Läufer *m*; Bote *m*; ⚒ Meldegänger *m*; (Schlitten)Kufe *f*; Schieber *m am Schirm*; ♀ Ausläufer *m*; gun-~ Waffenschmuggler *m*; ˈ~-ˈup *Sport:* Zweitbeste *m*.
run·ning [ˈrʌniŋ] **1.** laufend; fließend (*Wasser*); *two days* ~ zwei Tage nacheinander; ~ *hand* Kurrentschrift *f*; ~ *start* fliegender Start *m*; ~ *stitch* Stielstich *m*; **2.** Laufen *n*, Rennen *m*; ˈ~-**board**

mot., ⚓ *etc.* Trittbrett *n*; ~ **mate** *Am.* Vizepräsidentschaftskandidat *m*; ~s *pl. Am. Präsidentschaftskandidat und (sein) Vizepräsidentschaftskandidat.*
run-of-the-mill *contp.* [rʌnəvðə- ˈmil] mittelmäßig, Durchschnitts...
runt [rʌnt] *zo.* Zwergrind *n*; *fig.* Zwerg *m.*
run-up [ˈrʌnʌp] *Sport:* kurzer Probelauf *m*, Anlauf *m*; *fig.* Vorbereitung(szeit) *f.*
run·way [ˈrʌnwei] ✈ Rollbahn *f*; *hunt.* Wechsel *m*; Holzrutsche *f*; ~ watching Ansitzjagd *f.*
ru·pee [ruːˈpiː] Rupie *f.*
rup·ture [ˈrʌptʃə] **1.** Bruch *m* (*a.* ⚕); **2.** brechen; sprengen.
ru·ral □ [ˈruərəl] ländlich; Land...; ˈ**ru·ral·ize** verländlichen.
ruse [ruːz] List *f*, Kniff *m.*
rush[1] ♀ [rʌʃ] Binse *f*; *fig. mit Verneinung:* Pfifferling *m*, Deut *m.*
rush[2] [~] **1.** Jagen *n*, Hetzen *n*, Stürmen *n*; (An)Sturm *m*; Andrang *m*; Hochbetrieb *m*; ✝ stürmische Nachfrage *f (for* nach); *Wasser- etc.* Flut *f*; ⚡ (Strom)Stoß *m*; ~ *hour(s pl.)* Hauptverkehrszeit *f*; ~ *order* ✝ eiliger Auftrag *m*; **2.** *v/i.* stürzen, jagen, hetzen, stürmen, schießen, sausen, eilen; ~ *at* sich stürzen auf *(acc.)*; ~ *into extremes* ins Extrem verfallen; ~ *into print* et. überstürzt veröffentlichen; *v/t.* jagen, hetzen; drängen; ⚔ *u. fig.* stürmen; *Arbeit etc.* herunterhasten; *sl. j.* neppen (£ 5 um fünf Pfund); ~ *s.o. off his feet j.* überfahren; ~ *through parl.* durchpeitschen; ˈ**rush·ing** □ stürmisch.   [Binsen...]
rush·y [ˈrʌʃi] binsenbestanden;⎦
rusk [rʌsk] *Art* Zwieback *m.*
rus·set [ˈrʌsit] **1.** rostbraun; **2.** Rostbraun *n*; grober Stoff *m.*
Rus·sia (**leath·er**) [ˈrʌʃə(ˈleðə)] Juchten(leder) *n*; ˈ**Rus·sian 1.** russisch; **2.** Russe *m*, Russin *f*; Russisch *n.*
rust [rʌst] **1.** Rost *m*; **2.** (ver-, ein-) rosten (lassen) (*a. fig.*).
rus·tic [ˈrʌstik] **1.** (~*ally*) ländlich (*a. fig.*); Land...; *fig.* bäurisch; roh (gearbeitet); **2.** Landmann *m*; **rus·ti·cate** [ˈ~keit] *v/t.* zeitweilig von der Universität verweisen; *v/i.* auf dem Lande leben; **rus·ti·ca·tion** Landleben *n*; *univ.* zeitweilige Verweisung *f*; **rus·tic·i·ty** [~ˈtisiti]

Ländlichkeit *f*; bäurisches Wesen *n*.

rus·tle ['rʌsl] **1.** rascheln (mit *od.* in *dat.*); rauschen; *Am.* F sich ran-halten; *Vieh* stehlen; ~ *up* auf-treiben; **2.** Rascheln *n*.

rust...: '~**·less** rostfrei; '~-'**proof**, '~-**re'sist·ant** rostbeständig; '**rusty** rostig; eingerostet (*a. fig.*); ver-schossen (*Stoff*); rostfarben.

rut¹ *hunt.* [rʌt] **1.** Brunft *f*; **2.** brunf-ten.

rut² [~] Wagenspur *f*; *bsd. fig.* aus-gefahrenes Geleise *n*.

ruth·less □ ['ruːθlis] unbarmherzig; rücksichts-, skrupellos; '**ruth·less-ness** Unbarmherzigkeit *f*; Rück-sichts-, Skrupellosigkeit *f*.

rut·ted ['rʌtid] ausgefahren (*Weg*).

rut·ting *hunt.* ['rʌtiŋ] brunftig; Brunft...; ~ *season* Brunftzeit *f*.

rut·ty ['rʌti] ausgefahren (*Weg*).

rye ♃ [rai] Roggen *m*.

S

sab·bath ['sæbəθ] Sabbat *m*.

sab·bat·i·cal □ [sə'bætikəl] Sab-bat...; ~ *year univ.* Ferienjahr *n e-s Professors*.

sa·ble ['seibl] **1.** Zobel(pelz) *m*; Schwarz *n*; **2.** *lit.* schwarz; düster.

sab·o·tage ['sæbətɑːʒ] **1.** Sabotage *f*; **2.** sabotieren.

sa·bre ['seibə] **1.** Säbel *m*; **2.** mit dem Säbel niedermachen.

sac *anat., zo.* [sæk] Sack *m*, Beutel *m*.

sac·cha·rin ♃ ['sækərin] Sacharin *n*; Süßstoff *m*; **sac·cha·rine** ['~-rain] Zucker...; Süßstoff...; *fig.* zuckersüß; süßlich.

sac·er·do·tal □ [sæsə'dəutl] prie-sterlich; Priester...

sack¹ [sæk] **1.** Sack *m*; *Am.* Tüte *f*; Sackkleid *n*; Sakko *m*; *give* (*get*) *the* ~ F entlassen (werden); den Lauf-paß geben (bekommen); *hit the* ~ F sich in die Falle hauen; **2.** einsacken; F *j.* rausschmeißen; *j-m* den Laufpaß geben.

sack² [~] **1.** Plünderung *f*; **2.** plün-dern.

sack³ [~] heller Südwein *m*.

sack·cloth ['sækklɔːθ], '**sack·ing** Sackleinwand *f*.

sac·ra·ment *eccl.* ['sækrəmənt] Sa-krament *n*; **sac·ra·men·tal** □ [~'mentl] sakramental.

sa·cred □ ['seikrid] heilig; geistlich (*Dichtung, Musik*); '**sa·cred·ness** Heiligkeit *f*.

sac·ri·fice ['sækrifais] **1.** Opfer *n*; *at a* ~ ✝ mit Verlust; **2.** opfern; ✝ mit Verlust verkaufen.

sac·ri·fi·cial [sækri'fiʃəl] Opfer...; ✝ Schleuder...

sac·ri·lege ['sækrilidʒ] Kirchenraub *m*, -schändung *f*; Sakrileg *n*; **sac-ri·le·gious** □ [~'lidʒəs] sakrile-gisch, frevelhaft.

sa·crist, **sac·ris·tan** *eccl.* ['sæk-rist(ən)] Sakristan *m*, Kirchen-diener *m*.

sac·ris·ty *eccl.* ['sækristi] Sakristei *f*.

sad □ [sæd] traurig, betrübt; jäm-merlich, kläglich; schlimm, arg; dunkel, düster (*Farbe*).

sad·den ['sædn] (sich) betrüben.

sad·dle ['sædl] **1.** Sattel *m*; *break to the* ~ einreiten; **2.** satteln; *fig.* be-lasten; aufbürden (*upon dat.*); '~-**backed** hohlrückig (*Pferd*); '~-**bag** Satteltasche *f*; '~-**cloth** Sattel-decke *f*; '**sad·dler** Sattler *m*; '**sad-dler·y** Sattlerei *f*; Sattelzeug *n*.

sad·ism ['seidizəm] Sadismus *m*; '**sad·ist** Sadist *m*; **sa·dis·tic** [sæ-'distik] (~*ally*) sadistisch.

sad·ness ['sædnis] Traurigkeit *f*, Trauer *f*, Schwermut *f*.

sa·fa·ri [sə'fɑːri] Safari *f*.

safe [seif] **1.** □ *allg.* sicher; heil, un-versehrt; gefahrlos; außer Gefahr; zuverlässig; *to be on the* ~ *side* um ganz sicher zu gehen; **2.** Safe *m*, Geldschrank *m*; Speiseschrank *m*; ~ *deposit* Stahlkammer *f*; '~-**blow-er** *Am.* Geldschrankknacker *m*; ~ **con·duct** freies Geleit *n*; Geleit-brief *m*; '~-**guard 1.** Schutz *m*, Sicherung *f*; **2.** sichern; schützen (*against* vor *dat.*); ~*ing duty* Schutz-

zoll m; 'safe·ness Sicherheit f.
safe·ty ['seifti] Sicherheit f; ~ belt
mot. Sicherheitsgurt m; ~ cur·tain
thea. eiserner Vorhang m; ~ is·land
Verkehrsinsel f; '~-lock Sicher-
heitsschloß n; '~-pin Sicherheits-
nadel f; ~ ra·zor Rasierapparat m; ~
valve Sicherheitsventil n.
saf·fron ['sæfrən] 1. Safran m;
Safrangelb n; 2. safrangelb.
sag [sæg] 1. durchsacken; ⊕ durch-
hängen; ♨ (ab)sacken (a. fig.);
2. Durchsacken n etc.; ⊕ Durch-
hang m.
sa·ga ['sɑːgə] Saga f (Erzählung).
sa·ga·cious □ [sə'geiʃəs] scharfsinnig, klug.
sa·gac·i·ty [sə'gæsiti] Scharfsinn m.
sag·a·more ['sægəmɔː] Indianer-
häuptling m.
sage¹ [seidʒ] 1. □ klug, weise;
2. Weise m.
sage² ♣ [~] Salbei f.
sage·brush ♣ ['seidʒbrʌʃ] nord-
amerikanischer Beifuß m.
Sa·git·tar·i·us ast. [sædʒi'tɛəriəs]
Schütze m.
sa·go ['seigəu] Sago m.
sa·hib ['sɑːhib] Herr m, Sahib m.
said [sed] pret. u. p.p. von say 1.
sail [seil] 1. Segel n; Fahrt f; Wind-
mühlenflügel m; (Segel)Schiff(e pl.)
n; set ~ in See stechen; 2. v/i. (ab-)
segeln, fahren (for nach); fig.
schweben; v/t. befahren; Schiff
führen; '~-boat Segelboot n;
'~-cloth Segeltuch n; 'sail·er
Segler m (Schiff); 'sail·ing-ship,
'sail·ing-ves·sel Segelschiff n;
'sail·or Seemann m, Matrose m;
~'s knot Schifferknoten m; be a good
(bad) ~ (nicht) seefest sein; 'sail-
-plane Segelflugzeug n.
saint [seint] 1. Heilige m, f; [vor npr.
snt] Sankt...; 2. heiligsprechen;
'saint·ed heilig; selig (verstorben);
'saint·li·ness Heiligkeit f; 'saintly adj. heilig, fromm.
saith † od. poet. [seθ] 3. sg. Präsens
von say.
sake [seik]: for the ~ of um ... (gen.)
willen; for my ~ meinetwegen, mir
zuliebe; for God's ~ um Gottes
willen.
sal ♑ [sæl] Salz n; ~ ammoniac
Salmiak m; ~ volatile Riechsalz n.
sal·a·ble ['seiləbl] verkäuflich.
sa·la·cious □ [sə'leiʃəs] geil; zotig.

sal·ad ['sæləd] Salat m; ~ dress·ing
Salatsoße f.
sal·a·man·der ['sæləmændə] zo.
Salamander m; Schüreisen n.
sa·la·mi [sə'lɑːmiː] Salami(wurst) f.
sal·a·ried ['sælərid] besoldet; Gehalts...; 'sal·a·ry 1. Besoldung f;
Gehalt n; 2. besolden; 'sal·a·ry-
earn·er Gehaltsempfänger m.
sale [seil] Verkauf m; Absatz m;
Ausverkauf m; Auktion f; for ~, on
~ zum Verkauf, zu verkaufen(d),
verkäuflich; by private ~ unter der
Hand; 'sale·a·ble verkäuflich,
gangbar.
sales... [seilz]: ~ clerk Am. Verkäu-
fer(in); ~ com·mis·sion Verkaufs-
provision f; '~-man Verkäufer m;
'~-man·ship Geschäftstüchtigkeit f;
~ re·sist·ance Kaufunlust f; '~-
wom·an Verkäuferin f.
sa·li·ence ['seiljəns] Vorspringen n;
Vorsprung m; 'sa·li·ent 1. □ vorspringend; fig. hervorragend, -tre-
tend; Haupt...; 2. vorstehende
Ecke f, Vorsprung m; ⚔ (Front)Keil
m.
sa·line 1. ['seilain] salzig; Salz...;
2. [sə'lain] Saline f; ⚗ Salzlösung f.
sa·li·va physiol. [sə'laivə] Speichel
m; sal·i·var·y ['sælivəri] Speichel...; sal·i'va·tion Speichelfluß
m.
sal·low¹ ♣ ['sæləu] Salweide f.
sal·low² [~] blaß; gelblich; 'sal-
low·ness Blässe f; gelbliche Farbe f.
sal·ly ['sæli] 1. ⚔ Ausbruch m;
witziger Einfall m; 2. ⚔ a. ~ out
ausbrechen; ~ forth, ~ out sich aufmachen.
sal·ma·gun·di [sælmə'gʌndi] Ragout n; fig. Mischmasch m.
salm·on ['sæmən] 1. Lachs m,
Salm m; Lachsfarbe f; 2. lachs-
farben.
sal·on ['sælɔ̃ːŋ] literarischer Salon
m; Kunstausstellung f.
sa·loon [sə'luːn] Salon m; (Gesellschafts)Saal m; erste Klasse f auf
Schiffen; Am. Kneipe f; = sa-
'loon-car ⚒ Salonwagen m; mot.
Limousine f.
salt [sɔːlt] 1. Salz n (a. fig.); fig.
Würze f; old ~ alter Seebär m; with
a grain of ~ cum grano salis, mit
Vorbehalt; 2. salzig; gesalzen (a.
fig.); Salz...; Pökel...; 3. (ein)salzen,
pökeln; '~-cel·lar Salzfäßchen n;

'**salt·ed** gesalzen; *sl.* gewiegt, gerieben; '**salt·free** salzlos; **salt·pe·tre** ['‿pi:tə] Salpeter *m*; '**salt·wa·ter** Salzwasser...; '**salt·works** *sg.* Salzwerk *n*, Saline *f*; '**salt·y** salzig; pikant.

sa·lu·bri·ous □ [sə'lu:briəs] heilsam, gesund; **sa·lu·bri·ty** [sə'lu:-briti], **sal·u·tar·i·ness** ['sæljutərinis] Heilsamkeit *f*, Bekömmlichkeit *f*; **sal·u·tar·y** □ ['sæljutəri] = *salubrious.*

sal·u·ta·tion [sælju:'teiʃən] Gruß *m*, Begrüßung *f*; Anrede *f*; **sa·lu·ta·to·ry** [sə'lju:tətəri] grüßend; Begrüßungs...; **sa·lute** [sə'lu:t] 1. Gruß *m*; *co.* Kuß *m*; ✕ Salut *m*; 2. (be)grüßen; ✕ salutieren.

sal·vage ['sælvidʒ] 1. Bergung *f*; Bergungsgut *n*; Bergegeld *n*; 2. bergen.

sal·va·tion [sæl'veiʃən] Erlösung *f*; (Seelen)Heil *n*; *fig.* Rettung *f*; ♀ *Army* Heilsarmee *f*; **sal·va·tion·ist** Mitglied *n* der Heilsarmee.

salve[1] [sælv] retten, bergen.

salve[2] [sɑːv] 1. Salbe *f*; *fig.* Balsam *m*; 2. *mst fig.* (ein)salben; beruhigen.

sal·ver ['sælvə] Präsentierteller *m*.

sal·vo ['sælvəu] Vorbehalt *m*; *pl.* **sal·voes** ['‿z] ✕ Salve *f* (*fig. Beifall*); ～ *release* ♓ Massenabwurf *m*; **sal·vor** ♎ ['‿və] Berger *m*.

Sa·mar·i·tan [sə'mæritn] 1. samaritisch; 2. Samariter(in).

same [seim]: *the* ～ der-, die-, dasselbe; *all the* ～ gleichwohl, dennoch, trotzdem; *it is all the* ～ *to me* es ist mir (ganz) gleich *od.* einerlei; '**same·ness** Gleichheit *f*; Identität *f*; Eintönigkeit *f*.

Sa·mo·an [sə'məuən] 1. samoanisch; 2. Samoaner(in).

samp *Am.* [sæmp] grobgemahlener Mais *m*.

sam·ple ['sɑːmpl] 1. *bsd.* ✝ Probe *f*, Muster *n*; Exemplar *n*; 2. eine Probe zeigen *od.* nehmen von; bemustern; (aus)probieren; '**sam·pler** Sticktuch *n*; '**sam·pling** Kostprobe *f*.

san·a·tive ['sænətiv] heilend, heilsam; **san·a·to·ri·um** [‿'tɔ:riəm] (*bsd.* Lungen)Sanatorium *n*; Luftkurort *m*; **san·a·to·ry** ['‿təri] heilsam.

sanc·ti·fi·ca·tion [sæŋktifi'keiʃən] Heiligung *f*; Weihung *f*; **sanc·ti·fy** ['‿fai] heiligen; weihen; **sanc·ti·mo·ni·ous** □ [‿'məunjəs] scheinheilig; **sanc·tion** ['sæŋkʃən] 1. Sanktion *f*; Bestätigung *f*; Genehmigung *f*; Zwangsmaßnahme *f*; 2. bestätigen, gutheißen, genehmigen; **sanc·ti·ty** ['‿titi] Heiligkeit *f*; **sanc·tu·ar·y** ['‿tjuəri] Heiligtum *n*; *das Allerheiligste*; Asyl *n*, Freistätte *f*; **sanc·tum** ['‿təm] Heiligtum *n*; F Privatgemach *n*.

sand [sænd] 1. Sand *m*; ～s *pl.* Sand (-massen *f/pl.*) *m*; Sandwüste *f*; Sandbank *f*; *his* ～s *are running out* s-e Tage sind gezählt; 2. mit Sand bestreuen.

san·dal[1] ['sændl] Sandale *f*.

san·dal[2] [‿], '**‿·wood** Sandelholz *n*.

sand...: '**‿·bag** Sandsack *m*; '**‿·bank** Sandbank *f*; '**‿·blast** ⊕ Sandstrahlgebläse *n*; '**‿·boy**: *as jolly as a* ～ kreuzfidel; '**‿·glass** Sanduhr *f*; '**‿·hill** Sanddüne *f*; '**‿·pa·per** 1. Sand-, Schmirgelpapier *n*; 2. (ab)schmirgeln; '**‿·pip·er** *orn.* Flußuferläufer *m*; '**‿·pit** Sandkasten *m*; '**‿·shoes** Strandschuhe *m/pl.*; '**‿·stone** Sandstein *m*.

sand·wich ['sænwidʒ] 1. Sandwich *n*; 2. *a.* ～ *in* einlemmen, -klemmen; ～ *course* Ausbildung, *in der sich Theorie und Praxis abwechseln*; '**‿·man** Plakatträger *m*.

sand·y ['sændi] sandig; Sand...; sandfarben; strohblond (*Haar*).

sane [sein] geistig gesund *od.* normal; vernünftig (*Antwort etc.*).

San·for·ize ['sænfəraiz] *Stoff* sanforisieren (*gegen Einlaufen behandeln*).

sang [sæŋ] *pret. von* sing.

san·gui·nar·y □ ['sæŋgwinəri] blutdürstig; blutig; **san·guine** ['‿gwin] sanguinisch, leichtblütig; zuversichtlich; vollblütig; **san·guin·e·ous** [‿'gwiniəs] Blut...; *s. sanguine.*

san·i·tar·i·an [sæni'teəriən] Gesundheitsapostel *m*; **san·i·ta·ri·um** [sæni'teəriəm] *Am. für sanatorium*; **san·i·tar·y** □ ['‿təri] Gesundheits...; gesundheitlich; ⊕ Sanitär...; ～ *towel* Damenbinde *f*.

san·i·ta·tion [sæni'teiʃən] Sanierung *f*; Gesundheitspflege *f*; sanitäre Einrichtung *f od.* Anlage *f*; '**san·i·ty** geistige Gesundheit *f*; gesunder Verstand *m*.

sank [sæŋk] *pret. von* sink *1.*
sans *lit.* [sænz] ohne.
San·skrit ['sænskrit] Sanskrit *n.*
San·ta Claus [sæntə'klɔːz] Weih-
nachtsmann *m*, St. Nikolaus *m.*
sap[1] [sæp] ♀ Saft *m*; *fig.* Lebenskraft *f*, Mark *n*; *sl.* Trottel *m.*
sap[2] [◠] *1.* ✕ Sappe*f*; Laufgraben*m*;
Büffler *m*; Büffelei *f*; *2. v/i.* sap-
pieren; *sl.* ochsen, büffeln; *v/t.*
untergraben (*a. fig.*); unterminieren, schwächen.
sap·id ['sæpid] schmackhaft; **sa-
pid·i·ty** [sə'piditi] Schmackhaftigkeit *f.*
sa·pi·ence *mst iro.* ['seipjəns] Weisheit *f*; '**sa·pi·ent** *mst iro.* □ weise.
sap·less ['sæplis] saft-, kraftlos.
sap·ling ['sæpliŋ] junger Baum *m*;
fig. Grünschnabel *m.*
sap·o·na·ceous ⌢ *od. co.* [sæpəu-
'neiʃəs] seifig.   [Pionier *m.*]
sap·per ✕ ['sæpə] Sappeur *m*;⌋
sap·phire *min.* ['sæfaiə] Saphir *m.*
sap·pi·ness ['sæpinis] Saftigkeit *f.*
sap·py ['sæpi] saftig; *fig.* kraftvoll;
sl. trottelhaft.
Sar·a·cen ['særəsn] Sarazene *m.*
sar·casm ['sɑːkæzəm] bitterer Spott
m, Sarkasmus *m*; **sar·cas·tic, sar-
cas·ti·cal** □ [sɑː'kæstik(əl)] beißend, bissig, sarkastisch.
sar·coph·a·gus, *pl.* **sar·coph·a·gi**
[sɑː'kɔfəgəs, ◡gai] Sarkophag *m.*
sar·dine *ichth.* [sɑː'diːn] Sardine *f.*
Sar·din·i·an [sɑː'dinjən] 1. sardi-
nisch; 2. Sardinier(in).
sar·don·ic [sɑː'dɔnik] (◡*ally*) sardo-
nisch, verächtlich, zynisch.
sark·y F ['sɑːki] = *sarcastic.*
sar·to·ri·al [sɑː'tɔːriəl] Schneider…;
Kleider…
sash[1] [sæʃ] Fensterrahmen *m e-s*
Schiebefensters.
sash[2] [◠] Schärpe *f.*
sash-window ['sæʃwindəu] Schie-
befenster *n.*
sas·sa·fras ♀ ['sæsəfræs] Sassafras
(-baum) *m.*
sat [sæt] *pret. u. p.p. von* sit.
Sa·tan ['seitən] Satan *m.*
sa·tan·ic [sə'tænik] (◡*ally*) satanisch,
teuflisch.
satch·el ['sætʃəl] Schulmappe *f.*
sate [seit] = *satiate.*
sa·teen [sæ'tiːn] Satin *m.*
sat·el·lite ['sætəlait] (*a.* künstlicher)
Satellit *m*, Trabant *m*; Satelliten-

staat *m*; ~ **town** Trabantenstadt *f*; ~
trans·mis·sion Satellitenübertra-
gung *f.*
sa·ti·ate ['seiʃieit] (über)sättigen,
sa·ti'a·tion Sättigung *f*; **sa·ti·e·ty**
[sə'taiəti] Sattheit *f*; Überdruß *m.*
sat·in ['sætin] Seidensatin *m*, Atlas
m (Stoff); **sat·i·net(te)** [◡'net]
Halbatlas *m.*
sat·ire ['sætaiə] Satire *f*; **sa·tir·ic,
sa·tir·i·cal** □ [sə'tirik(əl)] satirisch;
sat·i·rist ['sætərist] Satiriker *m*;
'**sat·i·rize** verspotten.
sat·is·fac·tion [sætis'fækʃən] Befriedigung *f*; Genugtuung *f*, Satisfaktion *f*; Zufriedenheit *f*; Sühne *f*;
Gewißheit *f.*
sat·is·fac·to·ri·ness [sætis'fæktəri-
nis] *das* Befriedigende; **sat·is'fac-
to·ry** □ befriedigend, zufrieden-
stellend.
sat·is·fied □ ['sætisfaid] zufrieden;
überzeugt (*that* daß); **sat·is·fy**
['◡fai] *allg.* befriedigen; *e-r Bedingung etc., j-m* genügen; zufriedenstellen; überzeugen (*of* von);
Zweifel beheben.
sa·trap ['sætrəp] Satrap *m.*
sat·u·rate ⌢ *u. fig.* ['sætʃəreit] sättigen; **sat·u'ra·tion** Sättigung *f*; ~
point Sättigungspunkt *m.*
Sat·ur·day ['sætədi] Sonnabend *m*,
Samstag *m.*
Sat·urn ['sætən] Saturn *m*; **sat·ur-
nine** ['◡nain] melancholisch.
sat·yr ['sætə] Satyr *m.*
sauce [sɔːs] **1.** (*oft kalte*) Soße *f*;
Am. Kompott *n*; *fig.* Würze *f*;
F Frechheit *f*; **2.** würzen; F frech
werden zu *j-m*; '**~-boat** Soßenschüssel *f*; '**~-pan** Kochtopf *m*;
Kasserolle *f*; '**sauc·er** Untertasse *f*;
Untersatz *m e-s Blumentopfs.*
sau·ci·ness F ['sɔːsinis] Frechheit
f.
sau·cy □ F ['sɔːsi] keck, frech; dreist,
unverschämt.
sau·na ['sɔːnə] Sauna *f.*
saun·ter ['sɔːntə] **1.** Schlendern *n*;
Bummel *m*; **2.** (umher)schlendern;
bummeln; '**saun·ter·er** Bummler
(-in).
sau·ri·an *zo.* ['sɔːriən] Saurier *m.*
sau·sage ['sɔsidʒ] Wurst *f.*
sau·té ['sɔutei] sauté, sautiert (*in
wenig Fett schnell gebraten*).
sav·age ['sævidʒ] **1.** □ wild; roh,
grausam; unbebaut, wüst; F wü-

tend; **2.** Wilde *m*; *fig.* Barbar *m*;
3. anfallen (*Tier*); **'sav·age·ness**,
'sav·age·ry Wildheit *f*; Barbarei *f*.
sa·van·na(h) [sə'vænə] Savanne *f*.
sav·ant ['sævənt] Gelehrte *m*.
save [seiv] **1.** *v/t.* retten; *Schiff etc.*
bergen; erlösen; erhalten; bewahren (*from* vor *dat.*); (er)sparen;
schonen; *v/i.* sparen; sparsam
leben; **2.** *prp. u. cj.* außer, ausgenommen; ~ *for* bis auf (*acc.*); ~
that nur daß.
sav·e·loy ['sævilɔi] Zervelatwurst *f*.
sav·er ['seivə] Retter(in); Sparer(in);
sparsames Gerät *n*.
sav·ing ['seiviŋ] **1.** ☐ sparsam; ⁂
~ *clause* Vorbehalt(sklausel *f*) *m*;
2. Rettung *f*; ~*s pl.* Ersparnisse *f/pl.*
sav·ings... ['seivinz]: ~ **ac·count**
Sparkonto *n*; **'~-bank** Sparkasse *f*;
'~-de·pos·it Spareinlage *f*.
sav·io(u)r ['seivjə] Retter *m*, Erlöser *m*; *Saviour* Heiland *m*.
sa·vo(u)r ['seivə] **1.** Geschmack *m*;
fig. Beigeschmack *m*; **2.** ~ *of*
schmecken, riechen (*of* nach); *v/t.*
fig. schmecken *od.* riechen nach;
auskosten; **sa·vo(u)r·i·ness** ['~rinis] Wohlgeschmack *m*; Wohlgeruch *m*; **'sa·vo(u)r·less** geschmack-, geruchlos.
sa·vo(u)r·y[1] ☐ ['seivəri] schmackhaft; appetitlich; wohlriechend;
pikant(e Vor- *od.* Nachspeise *f*).
sa·vo(u)r·y[2] ♀ [~] Bohnenkraut *n*.
sa·voy [sə'vɔi] Wirsingkohl *m*.
sav·vy *sl.* ['sævi] **1.** kapieren;
2. Grips *m* (*Verstand*).
saw[1] [sɔ:] *pret. von* see.
saw[2] [~] Spruch *m*, Redensart *f*.
saw[3] [~] **1.** Säge *f*; **2.** (*irr.*) sägen;
'~-dust Sägespäne *m/pl.*; **'~-horse**
Sägebock *m*; **'~-mill** Sägewerk *n*;
sawn [sɔːn] *p.p. von* saw[3] 2; **saw·yer** ['~jə] Säger *m*.
Sax·on ['sæksn] **1.** sächsisch; germanisch; **2.** Sachse *m*, Sächsin *f*.
sax·o·phone ♪ ['sæksəfoun] Saxophon *n*; **sax·o·phon·ist** [~'sɔfənist]
Saxophonist *m*.
say [sei] **1.** (*irr.*) sagen; hersagen;
berichten; ~ *grace* das Tischgebet
sprechen; ~ *mass* die Messe lesen;
that is to ~ das heißt; *do you* ~ *so?*
meinen Sie wirklich?; *you don't* ~
so! was Sie nicht sagen!; *I* ~ sag(en
Sie) mal; ich muß schon sagen;
unübersetzt am Anfang der Rede; *he*

is said to be ... es heißt, daß er... *ist*,
er soll ... sein; *no sooner said than
done* gesagt, getan; **2.** Rede *f*, Wort
n; *it is my* ~ *now* jetzt ist die Reihe
zu reden an mir; *let him have his* ~
laßt ihn zu Wort kommen; *have a
od. some (no)* ~ *in s.th.* etwas (nichts)
zu sagen haben bei et.; **'say·ing**
Rede *f*; Redensart *f*, Ausspruch *m*;
it goes without ~ es versteht sich
von selbst.
scab [skæb] Schorf *m*; Räude *f*; *sl.*
Streikbrecher *m*.
scab·bard['skæbəd] *Säbel*-Scheide*f*.
scab·by ☐ ['skæbi] schorfig; räudig.
sca·bi·es ⚕ ['skeibii:z] Krätze *f*.
sca·bi·ous ♀ ['skeibjəs] Skabiose *f*.
sca·brous ['skeibrəs] heikel; anstößig.
scaf·fold ['skæfəld] (Bau)Gerüst *n*;
Schafott *n*; **'scaf·fold·ing** (Bau)Gerüst *n*; Rüstmaterial *n*.
scald [skɔ:ld] **1.** Verbrühung *f*;
2. verbrühen; *a.* ~ *out* auskochen;
Milch abkochen.
scale[1] [skeil] **1.** Schuppe *f*; Kesselstein *m*; Zahnstein *m*; *remove the* ~*s
from s.o.'s eyes j-m* die Augen öffnen; **2.** *v/t.* abschuppen, -lösen,
-schaben; ⊕ *Kesselstein* abklopfen;
Zähne vom Zahnstein reinigen; *v/i.*
oft ~ *off* sich (ab)schuppen, abblättern.
scale[2] [~] **1.** Waagschale *f*; (*a pair of*)
~*s pl.* (eine) Waage *f*; ~*s pl. ast.*
Waage *f*; **2.** wiegen.
scale[3] [~] **1.** Stufenleiter *f*; ♪ Tonleiter *f*; Skala *f*; Gradeinteilung *f*;
Maßstab *m*; *fig.* Ausmaß *n*; ~ *model*
maßstabgetreues Modell *n*; *on a large*
~ im großen; **2.** ersteigen, erklimmen;
~ *up* (*down*) maßstabgetreu vergrößern (verkleinern).
scaled [skeild] schuppig.
scale·less ['skeillis] schuppenlos.
scal·ing-lad·der ['skeiliŋlædə] ⚔
Sturmleiter *f*; Feuerleiter *f*.
scal·lion ♀ ['skæljən] Schalotte *f*.
scal·lop ['skɔləp] **1.** *zo.* Kammmuschel *f*; Ausbogung *f*; ⊕ Langette *f*; **2.** ausbogen; langettieren.
scalp [skælp] **1.** Kopfhaut *f*; Skalp
m; **2.** skalpieren.
scal·pel ⚕ ['skælpəl] Skalpell *n*.
scal·y ['skeili] schuppig; voll Kesselstein.
scamp [skæmp] **1.** Taugenichts *m*;
2. pfuschen; **'scamp·er 1.** (umher-)

tollen; hetzen; **2.** *fig.* Hetzjagd *f*; Galopp(tour *f*) *m*.

scan [skæn] *v/t.* *Verse* skandieren; absuchen; *fig.* überfliegen; *Fernsehen:* abtasten; *v/i.* sich skandieren lassen.

scan·dal ['skændl] Skandal *m*; Ärgernis *n*; Schande *f*; Klatsch *m*; **'scan·dal·ize** *j-m* Ärgernis geben; *be* ~*d at* od. *by* Anstoß nehmen an (*dat.*); **'scan·dal·mon·ger** Klatschbase *f*; **scan·dal·ous** □ ['~dələs] skandalös, Ärgernis erregend, anstößig; schimpflich; klatschhaft; **'scan·dal·ous·ness** Anstößigkeit *f* etc.

Scan·di·na·vi·an [skændi'neivjən] **1.** skandinavisch; **2.** Skandinavier (-in).

scant *lit.* [skænt] **1.** knapp, kärglich; **2.** knausern mit, sparen an. **scant·i·ness** ['skæntinis] Knappheit *f*; Kärglichkeit *f*. **scant·ling** ['skæntliŋ] Sparren *m*; kleines Brett *n*. **scant·y** □ ['skænti] knapp; spärlich; kärglich, dürftig.

scape·goat ['skeipgout] Sündenbock *m*, Prügelknabe *m*. **scape·grace** ['skeipgreis] Taugenichts *m*.

scap·u·lar ['skæpjulə] **1.** *anat.* Schulterblatt...; **2.** *eccl.* Skapulier *n*.

scar[1] [skɑ:] **1.** Narbe *f*; Schramme *f*; *fig.* (Schand)Fleck *m*, Makel *m*; **2.** *v/t.* schrammen; *v/i.* vernarben. **scar**[2] [skɑ:] Klippe *f*; Steilhang *m*. **scar·ab** *zo.* ['skærəb] Skarabäus *m*; (Mist)Käfer *m*.

scarce [skɛəs] knapp; rar; selten; Mangel...; *make o.s.* ~ F sich rar machen; **'scarce·ly** kaum; fast nicht; **'scar·ci·ty** Mangel *m*; Knappheit *f* (*of an dat.*); Teuerung *f*.

scare [skɛə] **1.** er-, aufschrecken; *a.* ~ *away* verscheuchen; ~*d* verstört; ängstlich; **2.** Panik *f*; '~**·crow** Vogelscheuche *f* (*a. fig.*); Schreckbild *n*; '~**·head** *Am.* große, sensationelle Schlagzeile *f*; '~**·mon·ger** Miesmacher(in).

scarf[1] [skɑ:f], *pl. a.* **scarves** [skɑ:vz] Schal *m*; Halstuch *n*; Kopftuch *n*; Krawatte *f*; ✂ Schärpe *f*. **scarf**[2] ⊕ [~] **1.** Laschung *f*, Lasche *f*; **2.** (ver)laschen. **scarf...:** '~**·pin** Krawattennadel *f*;

'~**·skin** Oberhaut *f*.

scar·i·fi·ca·tion [skɛərifi'keiʃən] ♣ Einritzung *f*; Verriß *m* (*heftige Kritik*); **scar·i·fy** ['~fai] (ein)ritzen; *fig.* herunter-, verreißen (*Kritiker*); ⚕ lockern.

scar·la·ti·na ♣ [skɑ:lə'ti:nə] Scharlach *m*.

scar·let ['skɑ:lit] **1.** Scharlach(rot *n*, -tuch *n*) *m*; **2.** scharlachrot; ~ *fever* ♣ Scharlach *m*; ~ *runner* ♀ Feuerbohne *f*.

scarp [skɑ:p] **1.** abböschen; ~*ed* steil; **2.** Böschung *f*. **scarred** [skɑ:d] narbig. **scarves** [skɑ:vz] *pl. von* scarf[1]. **scar·y** F ['skɛəri] erschreckend.

scath·ing *fig.* ['skeiðiŋ] vernichtend; verletzend.

scat·ter ['skætə] (sich) zerstreuen; ausstreuen; (sich) verbreiten; bestreuen; ~*ed* verstreut; '~**·brain** Wirrkopf *m*; '~**·brained** wirr, konfus.

scav·enge ['skævindʒ] (die Straßen) kehren; **'scav·en·ger** Straßenkehrer *m*.

sce·nar·i·o [si'nɑ:riəu] *Film:* Drehbuch *n*; **sce·nar·ist** ['si:nərist] Drehbuchautor(in).

scene [si:n] Szene *f*; Auftritt *m e-s Dramas* (*a. fig.*); Bühne(nbild *n*) *f*; Schauplatz *m*; ~*s pl.* Kulissen *f/pl.*; '~**·paint·er** Bühnenmaler *m*; **scen·er·y** ['~əri] Szenerie *f*; Bühnenausstattung *f*; Landschaft *f*. **sce·nic, sce·ni·cal** □ ['si:nik(əl)] szenisch, Bühnen...; landschaftlich; *scenic railway* Miniaturbahn *f*; *scenic road* landschaftlich schöne Strecke *f*.

scent [sent] **1.** (Wohl)Geruch *m*; Duft *m*; Parfüm *n*; *hunt.* Witterung(svermögen *n*) *f*; *hunt.* Fährte *f*; **2.** wittern; durchduften; parfümieren; **'scent·ed** wohlriechend; **'scent·less** geruchlos.

scep·tic ['skeptik] Skeptiker(in), Zweifler(in); **'scep·ti·cal** □ skeptisch (*about* mit Bezug auf *acc.*), zweiflerisch, zweifelnd; **scep·ti·cism** ['~sizəm] Skeptizismus *m*. **scep·tre** ['septə] Zepter *n*.

sched·ule ['ʃedju:l, *Am.* 'skedʒu:l] **1.** Verzeichnis *n*; Tabelle *f*; ⚥ Anhang *m*; *bsd. Am.* Fahrplan *m*; *on* ~ fahrplanmäßig; **2.** auf-, verzeichnen; festsetzen; ⚥ anhängen (*to dat.*); ~*d for* vorgesehen für;

sched·uled flight ✈ Linienflug *m*.
scheme [ski:m] **1.** Schema *n*; Zs.-stellung *f*; Plan *m*, Entwurf *m*; **2.** *v/t.* planen; *v/i.* Pläne machen; *b.s.* Ränke schmieden; **'schem·er** Plänemacher *m*; Intrigant *m*.
schism ['sizəm] Schisma *n*, Kirchenspaltung *f*; *fig.* Riß *m*; **schis-mat·ic** [siz'mætik] **1.** *a.* **schis'mat-i·cal** □ schismatisch; **2.** Abtrünnige *m*, Schismatiker *m*.
schist *min.* [ʃist] Schiefer *m*.
schi·zo·phre·nia *psych.* [skitsəu-'fri:njə] Schizophrenie *f*.
schol·ar ['skɔlə] Gelehrte *m*; *univ.* Stipendiat *m*; † Schüler(in); *he is an apt ~ er* hat e-e gute Auffassungsgabe; **'schol·ar·ly** *adj.* gelehrtenhaft; gelehrt; wissenschaftlich; **'schol·ar·ship** Gelehrsamkeit *f*; Wissenschaftlichkeit *f*; *univ.* Stipendium *n*.
scho·las·tic [skə'læstik] **1.** (*~ally*) scholastisch; schulmäßig; Schul...; **2.** Scholastiker *m*; **scho·las·ti·cism** [skə'læstisizəm] Scholastik *f*.
school¹ [sku:l] = **shoal**¹ **1.**
school² [~] **1.** Schule *f* (*a. fig.*); *univ.* Fakultät *f*; Disziplin *f*; Hochschule *f*; *at ~ auf* od. in der Schule; *put to ~* einschulen; **2.** schulen, erziehen; **'~·boy** Schüler *m*; **'~·fel-low** Mitschüler(in); **'~·girl** Schülerin *f*; **'~·house** Schulhaus *n*; **'school·ing** (Schul)Ausbildung *f*; Schulgeld *n*.
school...: **'~·leav·er** Schulabgänger (-in); **'~·leav·ing age** Schulentlassungsalter *n*; **'~·man** Scholastiker *m*; **'~·mas·ter** Lehrer *m* (*bsd. e-r höheren Schule*); **'~·mate** Mitschüler(in); **'~·mis·tress** Lehrerin *f* (*bsd. e-r höheren Schule*); **'~·teach·er** (*bsd.* Volks-schul)Lehrer(in).
schoon·er ['sku:nə] ♺ Schoner *m*; *Am.* großes Bierglas *n*; = *prairie-~*.
sci·at·i·ca ✻ [sai'ætikə] Ischias *f*.
sci·ence ['saiəns] Wissenschaft *f*; Naturwissenschaft(en *pl.*) *f*; Technik *f*; **~ fic·tion** Science-fiction *f*.
sci·en·tif·ic [saiən'tifik] (*~ally*) (*engS.* natur)wissenschaftlich; *Sport:* kunstgerecht.
sci·en·tist ['saiəntist] (*bsd.* Natur-) Wissenschaftler *m*.
sci-fi F ['saifai] = *science fiction*.
scim·i·tar ['simitə] Krummsäbel *m*.

scin·til·late ['sintileit] funkeln; **scin·til'la·tion** Funkeln *n*.
sci·on ['saiən] ✱ Pfropfreis *n*; *fig.* Sprößling *m*.
scis·sion ['siʒən] Spalten *n*, Schnitt *m*; **scis·sors** ['sizəz] *pl.* (*a pair of ~* eine) Schere *f*.
scle·ro·sis ✻ [sklia'rəusis] Sklerose *f*.
scoff [skɔf] **1.** Spott *m*; **2.** höhnen, spotten (*at über acc.*); **'scoff·er** Spötter(in).
scold [skəuld] **1.** zänkisches Weib *n*; **2.** (aus)schelten, schimpfen; **'scold-ing** Schelte(n *n*) *f*.
scol·lop ['skɔləp] = *scallop*.
sconce¹ [skɔns] Wandleuchter *m*; Klavierleuchter *m*.
sconce² *univ. sl.* [~] *zu e-r Strafe* verdonnern.
scon(e) [skɔn] Brötchen *n aus Rührteig*.
scoop [sku:p] **1.** Schaufel *f*, Schippe *f*; Schöpfeimer *m*, -kelle *f*; ✻ Spatel *m*; F Coup *m*, gutes Geschäft *n*; F Exklusivmeldung *f*; **2.** *mst ~ out* (aus)schaufeln; aushöhlen; *sl.* Gewinn scheffeln.
scoot·er ['sku:tə] (Kinder)Roller *m*; Motorroller *m*; Schnellboot *n*.
scope [skəup] Bereich *m*; *geistiger* Gesichtskreis *m*, Reichweite *f*; Umfang *m*; Gebiet *n*; Spielraum *m*; *have free ~* freie Hand haben.
scorch [skɔ:tʃ] *v/t.* versengen, -brennen; *v/t.* F (dahin)rasen; **'scorch·er** F sengend heißer Tag *m*; wilder Fahrer *m*, Raser *m*.
score [skɔ:] **1.** Kerbe *f*; Zeche *f*, Rechnung *f*; 20 Stück; *Sport:* Punktzahl *f*; (Tor)Stand *m*; Grund *m*, Ursache *f*; ♪ Partitur *f*, *weitS.* Musik *f*; *sl.* schlagfertige Entgegnung *f*; *~s* of eine Menge (von), viele; *four ~* achtzig; *run up ~s* Schulden machen; *on the ~ of* wegen; **2.** *v/t.* (ein)kerben; *a. ~ up* Zeche, Punktzahl u. *fig.* anschreiben, verzeichnen; *Sport:* Punkte machen; gewinnen (*a. fig.*); ♪ in Partitur setzen, instrumentieren; *Am.* F scharfe Kritik üben an; *v/i.* gerechnet werden; *Sport:* Punkte machen, gewinnen; *Fußball:* ein Tor schießen; *Karten:* zählen; *sl.* Schwein haben; *~ off s.o.* F *j-m* e-e Abfuhr erteilen; **'~·board** *Sport:* Anzeigetafel *f*; **'scor·er** Anschreiber(in); *Fußball:* Torschütze *m*.

sco·ri·a, pl. **sco·ri·ae** ⊕ ['skɔːriə, '‿riiː] Schlacke f.

scorn [skɔːn] **1.** Verachtung f; Spott m; laugh s.o. to ‿ j. verspotten; **2.** verachten; verschmähen, von sich weisen; '**scorn·er** Verächter(in); Spötter(in); **scorn·ful** □ ['‿ful] verächtlich.

Scor·pi·o ast. ['skɔːpiəu] Skorpion m.

scor·pi·on zo. ['skɔːpjən] Skorpion m.

Scot[1] [skɔt] Schotte m.

scot[2] [‿]: pay ‿ and lot sich an den Kosten beteiligen.

Scotch[1] [skɔtʃ] **1.** schottisch; **2.** Schottisch n; the ‿ pl. die Schotten m/pl.

scotch[2] [‿] (nur) verwunden.

Scotch·man ['skɔtʃmən] Schotte m.

scot-free ['skɔt'friː] straflos.

Scots [skɔts] = Scotch[1]; '**Scots·man** = Scotchman.

Scot·tish ['skɔtiʃ] schottisch (bsd. in gewählter Sprache u. in Schottland).

scoun·drel ['skaundrəl] Schurke m; '**scoun·drel·ly** adj. schurkisch.

scour[1] ['skauə] scheuern; reinigen; sich ein Bett graben.

scour[2] [‿] v/i. eilen; jagen; ‿ about (suchend) umherstreifen; v/t. durchstreifen, absuchen.

scourge [skəːdʒ] **1.** Geißel f (a. fig.); **2.** geißeln.

scout[1] [skaut] **1.** Späher m, Kundschafter m; ⚓ Aufklärungsfahrzeug n; ✈ Aufklärer m; univ. Aufwärter m; mot. Mitglied n der Straßenwacht; (Boy) ♀ Pfadfinder m; ‿ party ⚜ Spähtrupp m; **2.** (aus-) kundschaften, spähen.

scout[2] [‿] verächtlich zurückweisen.

scout·mas·ter ['skautmɑːstə] Pfadfinderführer m.

scow ⚓ [skau] Schute f, Flachboot n.

scowl [skaul] **1.** finsteres Gesicht n; **2.** finster blicken.

scrab·ble ['skræbl] (be)kritze'n; scharren; krabbeln.

scrag [skræg] **1.** fig. Gerippe n (dürrer Mensch etc.); a. ‿-end (of mutton Hammel)Hals m; **2.** sl. (er)würgen; '**scrag·gi·ness** Magerkeit f; '**scrag·gy** □ dürr.

scram sl. [skræm] verdufte!

scram·ble ['skræmbl] **1.** klettern; sich reißen od. balgen (for um); ‿d eggs pl. Rührei n; **2.** Kletterei f; Balgerei f, Kampf m.

scrap [skræp] **1.** Stückchen n, Brocken m; (Zeitungs)Ausschnitt m, Bild n zum Einkleben; Altmaterial n; Schrott m; ‿s pl. Reste m/pl.; ‿ of paper Fetzen m Papier (a. fig.); **2.** zum alten Eisen werfen; ausrangieren; verschrotten; '**‿-book** Sammelalbum n.

scrape [skreip] **1.** Kratzen n, Scharren n; Kratzfuß m; Not f, Klemme f; **2.** v/t. schrap(p)en; (ab)schaben; (ab)kratzen; ‿ together, ‿ up zs.-scharren, -kratzen; ‿ acquaintance with sich mit j-m anfreunden; v/i. kratzen; scharren; Kratzfüße machen; '**scrap·er** Kratzer m; Schab-, Kratzeisen n, Kratze f; '**scrap·ing** Scharren n; ‿s pl. Abschabsel n/pl.; Zs.-gekratzte n; fig. Spargroschen m/pl.

scrap…: '**‿-heap** Abfall-, Schrotthaufen m; '**‿-i·ron** Alteisen n, Schrott m; '**scrap·py** □ zs.-gestoppelt; bruchstückartig; '**scrap·yard** Schrottplatz m.

scratch [skrætʃ] **1.** Ritz m; Riß m, Schramme f; Sport: Startlinie f; Gekritzel n der Feder; come up to ‿ s-n Mann stellen, durchhalten; up to ‿ auf der Höhe; start from ‿ fig. von vorne anfangen; **2.** zs.-gewürfelt; Rennsport: ohne Vorgabe; **3.** v/t. (zer)kratzen; (zer)schrammen; parl. u. Sport: streichen; ‿ out auskratzen; ausradieren; ausstreichen; ‿ the surface fig. an der Oberfläche bleiben; v/i. kratzen; Sport: streichen (Meldung zurückziehen); '**scratch·y** kratzig; kritz(e)lig; Sport: unausgeglichen.

scrawl [skrɔːl] **1.** kritzeln; **2.** Gekritzel n.

scraw·ny Am. F ['skrɔːni] dürr.

scream [skriːm] **1.** Schrei m; Gekreisch n; he is a ‿ F er ist zum Schreien (komisch); **2.** schreien, kreischen; '**scream·ing** □ kreischend; F zum Totlachen, zum Schreien (komisch).

scree [skriː] Geröll(halde f) n.

screech [skriːtʃ] = scream; '**‿-owl** orn. Käuzchen n.

screed [skriːd] Tirade f; langatmiges Schreiben n.

screen [skriːn] **1.** Wandschirm m, spanische Wand f; Ofenschirm m; Schutzschirm m; △ Lettner m; fig. Schleier m; (Film)Leinwand f; der

Film; Sandsieb *n*; (Fliegen)Gitter *n*; **2.** schirmen; (be)schützen; ✗ verschleiern, tarnen; auf der Leinwand zeigen; verfilmen; (durch-)sieben; sortieren; *fig.* durchleuchten; **~ play** Drehbuch *n*; Fernsehfilm *m*; **~ test** *Film*: Probeaufnahmen *f/pl.*

screev·er ['skriːvə] Pflastermaler *m*.

screw [skruː] **1.** Schraube *f* (*a. fig. u.* ⏁); ✖ Propeller *m*, Luftschraube *f*; Tütchen *n Tabak etc.*; *he has a ~ loose* F bei ihm ist e-e Schraube locker; **2.** (fest)schrauben; *fig.* drücken, bedrängen, pressen; ver-, umdrehen; V ficken, vögeln; *~ round* ganz herumdrehen; *~ up* festschrauben; hochschrauben; *~ up one's courage* Mut fassen; '**~-ball** *Am. sl.* Spinner *m*, komischer Kauz *m*; '**~-driv·er** Schraubenzieher *m*; '**~-jack** Wagenheber *m*; '**~-pro'pel·ler** Schiffsschraube *f*.

scrib·ble ['skribl] **1.** Gekritzel *n*; **2.** kritzeln; *~ over* bekritzeln; '**scrib·bler** Schmierer *m*; Skribent *m*; '**scrib·bling-block** Schmierblock *m*.

scribe [skraib] Schreiber *m*; Kopist *m*; *Bibel*: Schriftgelehrte *m*.

scrim [skrim] leichter Leinenstoff *m*.

scrim·mage ['skrimidʒ] Handgemenge *n*; Getümmel *n*; *Rugby*: Gedränge *n*.

scrimp [skrimp], '**scrimp·y** = *skimp etc.*

scrip † [skrip] Interimsschein(e *pl.*) *m*; Besatzungsgeld *n*.

script [skript] Schrift(art) *f*; Schreibschrift *f*; Manuskript *n*; *Film*: Drehbuch *n*; *~s pl.* (schriftliche) Prüfungsarbeiten *f/pl.*; *~-writer* Rundfunkautor *m*.

Scrip·tur·al ['skriptʃərəl] biblisch; **Scrip·ture** ['~tʃə] *mst the Holy ~s pl.* die Heilige Schrift.

scrof·u·la ✖ ['skrɔfjulə] Skrofeln *f/pl.*; '**scrof·u·lous** □ skrofulös.

scroll [skrəul] Schriftrolle *f*, Liste *f*; △ Schnecke *f*; Schnörkel *m*.

scro·tum ['skrəutəm] Hodensack *m*.

scrounge F [skraundʒ] organisieren, sich aneignen.

scrub[1] [skrʌb] Gestrüpp *n*, Busch (-werk *n*) *m*; Knirps *m*, Zwerg *m*.

scrub[2] [~] **1.** schrubben, scheuern; **2.** *Am. Sport*: zweite (Spieler-)Garnitur *f*.

scrub·bing-brush ['skrʌbiŋbrʌʃ] Scheuerbürste *f*; Schrubber *m*.

scrub·by ['skrʌbi] struppig; schäbig, armselig.

scruff [skrʌf]: *~ of the neck* Genick *n*.

scrum [skrʌm], '**scrum·mage** = *scrimmage.*

scrump·tious *sl.* ['skrʌmpʃəs] fabelhaft, prima.

scrunch [skrʌntʃ] *v/t.* zermalmen; *v/i.* knirschen.

scru·ple ['skruːpl] **1.** Skrupel *n* (= *20 Gran = 1,296 Gramm*); Skrupel *m*; Zweifel *m*, Bedenken *n*; *make no ~ to do* keine Bedenken haben, zu tun; **2.** Bedenken haben; **scru·pu·lous** □ ['~pjuləs] (allzu) bedenklich (*about in dat.*); gewissenhaft, peinlich; ängstlich.

scru·ti·neer [skruːti'niə] Wahlprüfer *m*; '**scru·ti·nize** (genau) prüfen; '**scru·ti·ny** Forschen *n*; forschender Blick *m*; genaue (*bsd.* Wahl)Prüfung *f*.

scu·ba ['skuːbə]: *~ diving* Sporttauchen *n*.

scud [skʌd] **1.** (Dahin)Jagen *n*; (dahintreibende) Wolkenfetzen *m/pl.*; Bö *f*; **2.** eilen, jagen; ⏁ lenzen.

scuff [skʌf] schlurfen, schlorren.

scuf·fle ['skʌfl] **1.** Balgerei *f*, Rauferei *f*; **2.** sich balgen, raufen.

scull ⏁ [skʌl] **1.** kurzes Ruder *n*; **2.** rudern, skullen.

scul·ler·y ['skʌləri] Spülküche *f*; *~maid* Scheuermagd *f*; **scul·lion** † ['skʌljən] Küchenjunge *m*.

sculp·tor ['skʌlptə] Bildhauer *m*.

sculp·ture ['skʌlptʃə] **1.** Plastik *f*, Bildhauerei *f*, Skulptur *f*; **2.** (heraus)meißeln, formen.

scum [skʌm] (*fig.* Ab)Schaum *m*.

scup·per ⏁ ['skʌpə] Speigatt *n*.

scurf [skəːf] (Haut-, *bsd.* Kopf-)Schuppen *f/pl.*; '**scurf·y** □ schuppig.

scur·ril·i·ty [skʌ'riliti] Gemeinheit *f*, Pöbelhaftigkeit *f*, Unflätigkeit *f*; '**scur·ril·ous** gemein, pöbelhaft; unflätig.

scur·ry ['skʌri] **1.** *v/i.* hasten, rennen; *v/t.* jagen; **2.** Hasten *n*.

scur·vy[1] ✖ ['skəː'viː] Skorbut *m*.

scur·vy[2] ['~] (hunds)gemein.

scut [skʌt] kurzer Schwanz *m*.

scutch·eon ['skʌtʃən] = *escutcheon.*

scut·tle[1] ['skʌtl] Kohlenbehälter *m*.

scut·tle² [~] **1.** ⚓ Springluke *f*; **2.** *Schiff* anbohren, (selbst) versenken.
scut·tle³ [~] **1.** Drückebergerei *f*; **2.** eilen; *fig.* sich drücken.
scythe ⚮ [saið] **1.** Sense *f*; **2.** (ab-) mähen.
sea [si:] See *f*; Meer *n* (*a. fig.*); hohe Welle *f*; *at* ~ auf See; *fig.* ratlos; *by the* ~ am Meer; *go to* ~ zur See gehen; *s. put* 2; '~·**board** Küste(n-gebiet *n*) *f*; ~ **cap·tain** Schiffs-kapitän *m*; ~ **coast** Küste *f*; '~·**dog** alter Seebär *m*; *elisabethanischer* Seeheld *m*; = *seal¹*; '~·**far·ing** see-fahrend; ~ **food** *Am.* eßbare Meerestiere *n/pl.*; '~·**front** Strand(prome-nade *f*) *m*; '~·**go·ing** Hochsee..., Ozean...; '~·**gull** (See)Möwe *f*.
seal¹ *zo.* [si:l] Seehund *m*, Robbe *f*.
seal² [~] **1.** Siegel *n*, Petschaft *n*; Stempel *m*; Bestätigung *f*, Versi-cherung *f*; *great* ~, *broad* ~ großes Staatssiegel *n*; **2.** versiegeln; *fig.* besiegeln; ~ *off fig.* abschließen; ~ *up* (fest) verschließen; ⊕ abdich-ten.
seal·er ['si:lə] Robbenfänger *m*.
sea-lev·el ['si:levl] Meeresspiegel *m*.
seal·ing ['si:liŋ] Robbenfang *m*.
seal·ing-wax ['si:liŋwæks] Siegel-lack *m*.
seal·skin ['si:lskin] Seehundsfell *n*.
seam [si:m] **1.** Saum *m*, Naht *f*; ⊕ Fuge *f*; *geol.* Flöz *n*; Narbe *f*; *burst at the* ~s aus den Nähten platzen (*a. fig.*); **2.** schrammen; furchen.
sea·man ['si:mən] Seemann *m*, Matrose *m*; '**sea·man·ship** See-mannskunst *f*.
sea-mew ['si:mju:] Sturmmöwe *f*.
seam·less □ ['si:mlis] nahtlos.
seam·stress ['semstris] Näherin *f*.
seam·y ['si:mi] narbig; ~ *side fig.* Schattenseite *f*.
sea...: '~·**piece** *paint.* Seestück *n*; '~·**plane** Wasserflugzeug *n*; '~·**port** Seehafen *m*; Hafenstadt *f*; '~·**pow·er** Seemacht *f*.
sear [siə] **1.** dürr, welk; **2.** austrock-nen; versengen; ⚶ brennen; *fig.* verhärten.
search [sə:tʃ] **1.** Suchen *n*, Forschen *n* (*for* nach); Unter-, Durch-suchung *f*; *in* ~ *of* auf der Suche nach; **2.** *v/t.* durch-, untersuchen; ⚶ sondieren; *Gewissen etc.* prüfen; erforschen; durchdringen (*Kälte*,

Geschoß etc.); ~ *out* ausfindig machen; *v/i.* suchen, forschen (*for* nach); ~ *into* ergründen; '**search·er** (Unter)Sucher *m*; Erforscher *m*; '**search·ing** □ forschend, prüfend (*Blick*); eingehend (*Prüfung etc.*); '**search-light** (Such)Scheinwerfer *m*; **search par·ty** Suchtrupp *m*; '**search-war·rant** ⚖ Haussu-chungsbefehl *m*.
sea...: '~·**rov·er** Seeräuber(schiff *n*) *m*; ~·**scape** ['si:skeip] *s. sea-piece*; '~·**ser·pent** Seeschlange *f*; '~·**shore** Seeküste *f*; '~·**sick** see-krank; '~·**sick·ness** Seekrankheit *f*; '~·**side** Strand *m*, Küste *f*; ~ *place*, ~ *resort* Seebad *n*; *go to the* ~ an die See gehen.
sea·son ['si:zn] **1.** Jahreszeit *f*; (rechte) Zeit *f*; Hauptzeit *f*, Saison *f*; F = ~·*ticket*; *height of the* ~ Hochsaison *f*; *in* (*good od. due*) ~ zur rechten Zeit; *cherries are in* ~ jetzt ist die Kirschenzeit; *out of* ~ außer der Zeit; zur Unzeit, unge-legen; *for a* ~ eine Zeitlang; *with the compliments of the* ~ mit den besten Wünschen zum Fest; **2.** *v/t.* reifen (lassen); würzen; abhärten (*to gegen*); *v/i.* ablagern (*Bauholz etc.*); '**sea·son·a·ble** □ zeitgemäß, passend; **sea·son·al** □ ['si:zənl] von der Jahreszeit *od.* (*bsd.* ♈) Saison abhängig; Saison...; saison-bedingt; '**sea·son·ing** Würze *f*; '**sea·son·tick·et** ⛻ Zeitkarte *f*; *thea.* Abonnement *n*.
seat [si:t] **1.** Sitz *m* (*a. fig.*); Sessel *m*, Stuhl *m*, Bank *f*; (Sitz)Platz *m*; Wohnsitz *m*; Landsitz *m*; Gesäß *n*; Schauplatz *m*; **2.** (hin)setzen; *Wür-denträger* einsetzen; fassen, Sitz-plätze haben für; mit e-m neuen Sitz versehen; ~ *o.s.* sich setzen; *be* ~*ed* sitzen; sich setzen; s-n Sitz haben (*in* in *dat.*); liegen (*Ort*); '~·**belt** ⛐ Sicherheitsgurt *m*; '**seat·ed** sitzend; ...sitzig; '**seat·er** *bsd. mot.*, ⛐ ...sitzer *m*.
sea-ur·chin ['si:'ə:tʃin] Seeigel *m*; **sea·ward** ['~wəd] *adj.* seewärts ge-richtet; *adv. a.* **sea·wards** ['~wədz] seewärts.
sea...: '~·**weed** ♧ (See)Tang *m*; '~·**wor·thy** seetüchtig.
se·ba·ceous *physiol.* [si'beiʃəs] Fett-..., Talg...
se·cant ⚕ ['si:kənt] **1.** schneidend;

2. Sekante *f.*

séc·a·teur ✄ [sekə'tɔ:] *mst (a pair of)* ⁓s *pl.* (eine) Baumschere *f.*

se·cede [si'si:d] sich trennen, sich lossagen, abfallen; **se'ced·er** Abtrünnige *m.*

se·ces·sion [si'seʃən] Lossagung *f;* Spaltung *f;* Abfall *m;* **se'ces·sion·ist** [⁓ʃnist] Abtrünnige *m;* Sezessionist *m.*

se·clude [si'klu:d] abschließen, absondern; **se'clud·ed** einsam; zurückgezogen; abgelegen; **se'clu·sion** [⁓ʒən] Abgeschlossen-, Abgeschiedenheit *f.*

sec·ond[1] ['sekənd] **1.** □ zweite(r, -s); nächste(r, -s); geringer (*to* als); *he is* ⁓ *to none* er steht keinem nach; *on* ⁓ *thoughts* bei genauerer Überlegung; **2.** Zweite *m, f, n;* Sekundant *m;* Beistand *m;* Sekunde *f;* ⁓s *pl.* ✝ zweite Sorte *f;* ⁓ *of exchange* ✝ Sekundawechsel *m;* **3.** sekundieren, beistehen (*dat.*); unterstützen.

se·cond[2] ⚔ [si'kɔnd] *Offizier* abkommandieren.

sec·ond·ar·i·ness ['sekəndərinis] *das* Sekundäre, Zweitrangigkeit *f;* **'sec·ond·ar·y** □ sekundär; in zweiter Linie kommend, untergeordnet; Neben...; Hilfs...; Sekundär...; **sec·ond·ar·y school** höhere Schule *f;* weiterführende Schule *f;* **'sec·ond·'best** zweitbest; *come off* ⁓ F den kürzeren ziehen; **'sec·ond·'class** zweitklassig, -rangig; 🚆 zweiter Klasse; **'sec·ond·er** Unterstützer *m (bsd. parl.);* **sec·ond-hand 1.** ['sekənd'hænd] aus zweiter Hand; *schon* gebraucht; antiquarisch; ⁓ *bookseller* Antiquar *m;* ⁓ *bookshop* Antiquariat *n;* **2.** ['sekəndhænd] Sekundenzeiger *m;* **'sec·ond·ly** zweitens; **'sec·ond·'rate** zweiten Ranges; zweitklassig; ✝ ⁓ *quality* zweite Wahl *f.*

se·cre·cy ['si:krisi] Heimlichkeit *f;* Verschwiegenheit *f;* **se·cret** ['si:krit] **1.** □ geheim; Geheim...; verschwiegen; verborgen; ⁓ *agent* Geheimagent *m;* **2.** Geheimnis *n; in* ⁓ insgeheim; *be in the* ⁓, *be taken into the* ⁓ eingeweiht sein.

sec·re·tar·i·at(e) [sekrə'tɛəriət] Sekretariat *n.*

sec·re·tar·y ['sekrətri] Schriftführer *m;* Sekretär(in); ♀ *of State* Staatssekretär *m,* Minister *m; Am.* Außen-

minister *m;* **'sec·re·tar·y·ship** Sekretariat *n,* Schriftführeramt *n.*

se·crete [si'kri:t] verbergen; *physiol.* absondern, ausscheiden; **se'cre·tion** *physiol.* Absonderung *f,* Sekretion *f;* Sekret *n;* **se'cre·tive** *fig.* verschlossen; geheimtuerisch.

sect [sekt] Sekte *f;* **sec·tar·i·an** [⁓'tɛəriən] **1.** sektiererisch; **2.** Sektierer(in).

sec·tion ['sekʃən] 🔬 Sektion *f,* Zerlegung *f; mikroskopischer* Schnitt *m;* ⚕ Schnitt *m;* △ Durchschnitt *m;* Teil *m;* Abschnitt *m,* Paragraph *m; typ.* Absatz *m; s.* ⁓-*mark;* Sektion *f,* Abteilung *f;* Gruppe *f; shopping (residential)* ⁓ Einkaufs- (Wohn-) viertel *n;* **sec·tion·al** ['⁓ʃnl] Durchschnitts...; Teil...; Abschnitts...; Abteilungs...; ⊕ zs.-setzbar; partikularistisch, Lokal...; **'sec·tion·al·ism** Gruppenegoismus *m;* **'sec·tion-mark** Paragraph(enzeichen *n*) *m.*

sec·tor ['sektə] (Kreis)Sektor *m;* ⚔ Abschnitt *m.*

sec·u·lar □ ['sekjulə] säkular; hundertjährig; weltlich; **sec·u·lar·i·ty** [⁓'læriti] Weltlichkeit *f;* **sec·u·lar·ize** ['⁓ləraiz] säkularisieren; *geistliche Güter* einziehen; verweltlichen.

se·cure [si'kjuə] **1.** □ sicher (*of gen.; against, from* vor *dat.*); **2.** sichern; schützen (*from, against* vor *dat.*); *j., et.* sicherstellen; festmachen; *sich et.* sichern *od.* verschaffen; verwahren.

se·cu·ri·ty [si'kjuəriti] Sicherheit *f;* Sorglosigkeit *f;* Gewißheit *f;* Schutz *m;* Bürgschaft *f,* Kaution *f;* ⁓ *check* Sicherheitskontrolle *f;* ♀ *Council* Sicherheitsrat *m;* ♀ *Force* Friedenstruppe *f; securities pl.* Wertpapiere *n/pl.; public securities* Staatspapiere *n/pl.*

se·dan [si'dæn] Limousine *f; a.* ⁓-*chair* Sänfte *f.*

se·date □ [si'deit] gesetzt; ruhig; **se'date·ness** Gesetztheit *f,* Ruhe *f.*

se·da·tion ♂ [si'deiʃən] Beruhigung *f* der Nerven durch Sedativa.

sed·a·tive *mst* ♂ ['sedətiv] **1.** beruhigend; **2.** Beruhigungsmittel *n.*

sed·en·tar·i·ness ['sedntərinis] sitzende Lebensweise *f;* Seßhaftigkeit *f;* **'sed·en·tar·y** □ sitzend; seßhaft.

sedge ♥ [sedʒ] Riedgras *n*, Segge *f*.
sed·i·ment ['sedimənt] (Boden-) Satz *m*, Niederschlag *m*; *geol.* Ablagerung *f*, Sediment *n*; **sed·i·men·ta·ry** [∼'mentəri] *geol.* sedimentär; Ablagerungs...
se·di·tion [si'diʃən] Aufruhr *m*.
se·di·tious ☐ [si'diʃəs] aufrührerisch.
se·duce [si'dju:s] verführen; **se·duc·er** Verführer(in); **se·duc·tion** [∼'dʌkʃən] Verführung *f*; **se'duc·tive** ☐ verführerisch.
sed·u·lous ☐ ['sedjuləs] emsig.
see[1] [si:] (*irr.*) *v/i.* sehen; *fig.* einsehen; *I* ∼ ich verstehe; ∼ *about s.th.* sich um et. kümmern; ∼ *through s.o. od. s.th. j. od. et.* durchschauen; ∼ *to* sorgen für, achten auf (*acc.*); ∼ *for yourself!* Überzeugen Sie sich selbst!; *v/t.* sehen; ansehen, beobachten; einsehen, begreifen; sorgen (*daß et. geschieht*); *Patienten* besuchen; *Arzt* aufsuchen; ∼ *s.th. done* dafür sorgen, daß et. geschieht; **go to** ∼ *s.o. j.* besuchen; ∼ *s.o. home j.* nach Hause bringen *od.* begleiten; ∼ *off Besuch etc.* wegbringen; ∼ *out Besuch* hinausbegleiten; *et.* zu Ende erleben; ∼ *over s.th.* et. besichtigen; ∼ *s.th. through* et. durchhalten *od.* -fechten; ∼ *s.o. through* j-m durchhelfen; *live to* ∼ erleben.
see[2] [∼] (Erz)Bischofssitz *m*; *Holy* ♀ *der* Heilige Stuhl.
seed [si:d] **1.** Same(n) *m*, Saat(gut *n*) *f*; (Obst)Kern *m*; Keim *m* (*a. fig.*); *go od.* run to ∼ in Samen schießen; *fig.* herunterkommen; **2.** *v/t.* (be)säen; *Obst* entkernen; *Sport*: *Spieler* setzen; *v/i.* in Samen schießen; '∼·bed = seed-plot; 'seed·i·ness Schäbigkeit *f*; F Katzenjammer *m*; 'seed·less kernlos (*Obst*); 'seed·ling ✗ Sämling *m*; 'seed-plot ✗ Samenbeet *n*; *fig.* Brutstätte *f*; seeds·man ['∼zmən] Samenhändler *m*; 'seed·y schäbig; F unwohl, elend.
see·ing ['si:iŋ] **1.** Sehen *n*; worth ∼ sehenswert; **2.** *cj.* ∼ *that* da ja; angesichts der Tatsache, daß.
seek [si:k] (*irr.*) *a.* ∼ *after*, ∼ *for* suchen (nach); begehren (nach); streben *od.* trachten nach; 'seek·er Suchende *m, f*; Sucher(in).
seem [si:m] scheinen, erscheinen; 'seem·ing **1.** ☐ anscheinend;

scheinbar; **2.** Anschein *m*; 'seem·li·ness Anstand *m*, Schicklichkeit *f*; 'seem·ly geziemend, schicklich.
seen [si:n] *p.p. von* see[1].
seep [si:p] durchsickern, tropfen, lecken; 'seep·age Durchsickern *n*, Tropfen *n*, Lecken *n*.
seer ['si:ə] Seher(in), Prophet(in).
see·saw ['si:sɔ:] **1.** Wippen *n*; Wippe *f*, Wippschaukel *f*; **2.** wippen; *fig.* schwanken.
seethe [si:ð] sieden, kochen.
seg·ment ['segmənt] Abschnitt *m*; *bsd.* ♈ Segment *n*.
seg·re·gate ['segrigeit] absondern, trennen; **seg·re'ga·tion** Absonderung *f*; Rassentrennung *f*.
seine [sein] *Fischerei*: Schlagnetz *n*.
sei·sin ⚖ ['si:zin] Besitz *m*.
seis·mic ['saizmik] seismisch.
seis·mo·graph ['saizməgrɑːf] Erdbebenmesser *m*, Seismograph *m*; **seis·mol·o·gy** [∼'mɔlədʒi] Seismologie *f*, Erdbebenkunde *f*.
seize [si:z] *v/t.* ergreifen, fassen, packen; sich *et.* aneignen, sich *e-r Sache* bemächtigen; mit Beschlag belegen; *mit dem Verstand* erfassen; ♣ (bei)zeisen; *v/i.* ⊕ sich festfressen; ∼ *upon* sich *e-r Sache od. j-s* bemächtigen; 'seiz·ing Ergreifen *n etc.*; *mst* ∼s *pl.* ♣ Bändsel *n*; **sei·zure** ['∼ʒə] Ergreifung *f*; ⚖ Beschlagnahme *f*; ✗ plötzlicher Anfall *m*.
sel·dom ['seldəm] *adv.* selten.
se·lect [si'lekt] **1.** auswählen, -lesen, -suchen; **2.** auserwählt; erlesen; exklusiv (*Verein etc.*); **se'lec·tion** Auswahl *f*, -lese *f*; *zo.*, ♥ Zuchtwahl *f*; *a. musical* ∼ Potpourri *n*; **se'lec·tive** ☐ auswählend; Auswahl...; *Radio*: trennscharf; **se·lec·tiv·i·ty** *Radio*: Trennschärfe *f*; **se·lect·man** *Am.* Stadtrat *m in den Neuenglandstaaten*; **se'lec·tor** Auswählende *m, f*; *Radio*: Sucher *m*.
self [self] **1.** *pron.* selbst; ✝ *od.* F = *myself etc.*; **2.** *adj.* ♥ einfarbig; **3.** *pl.* **selves** [selvz] Selbst *n*, Ich *n*; Persönlichkeit *f*; *my poor* ∼ meine Wenigkeit; '∼-a'base·ment Selbsterniedrigung *f*; '∼-'act·ing selbsttätig; '∼-ad'he·sive selbstklebend; '∼-as'ser·tion Geltendmachen *n s-r* Meinung, s-s Willens *etc*; '∼-as'ser·tive: ∼ *person* j., der sich

durchzusetzen *od.* zu behaupten versteht; '**~as'sur·ance** Selbstbewußtsein *n*; '**~'ca·ter·ing** Selbstverpflegungs...; '**~'cen·tred**, *Am.* '**~'centered** egozentrisch, ichbezogen; '**~ -'col·o(u)red** einfarbig; uni (*Stoff*); '**~com'mand** Selbstbeherrschung *f*; '**~con'ceit** Eigendünkel *m*; '**~ -con'ceit·ed** dünkelhaft; '**~con-'fessed** eingestanden; '**~'con·fi·dence** Selbstvertrauen *n*; '**~'con·scious** befangen, gehemmt; '**~'con·scious·ness** Befangenheit *f*; '**~con-'tained** (in sich) abgeschlossen; verschlossen (*Charakter*); **~ country** Selbstversorgerland *n*; **~ house** Einfamilienhaus *n*; '**~con'trol** Selbstbeherrschung *f*; '**~de'fence** Selbstverteidigung *f*; *in ~* in (der) Notwehr; '**~ -de'ni·al** Selbstverleugnung *f*; '**~ -de·ter·mi'na·tion** Selbstbestimmung *f*; '**~'ed·u·cat·ed: ~ person** Autodidakt *m*; '**~em'ployed** selbständig (*Handwerker etc.*); '**~'ev·i·dent** selbstverständlich; '**~ex'plan·a·to·ry** ohne Erläuterung verständlich; '**~'gov·ern·ment** Selbstverwaltung *f*, Autonomie *f*; '**~im'port·ance** Eigendünkel *m*; '**~im'port·ant** eingebildet, aufgeblasen; '**~in-'dul·gent** genießerisch, bequem; '**~ -'in·ter·est** Eigennutz *m*; '**self·ish** □ selbstsüchtig; '**self·ish·ness** Selbstsucht *f*.

self...: '**~'made** selbstgemacht; **~ man** j., der durch eigene Kraft et. geworden ist, Selfmademan *m*; '**~ -pos'ses·sion** Selbstbeherrschung *f*; '**~pre·ser'va·tion** Selbsterhaltung *f*; '**~re'gard** Eigennutz *m*; '**~re'li·ance** Selbstsicherheit *f*; '**~re'li·ant** selbstsicher; '**~re-'spect** Selbstachtung *f*; '**~re-'spect·ing:** *every ~ nation* jede Nation, die etwas auf sich hält; '**~ -'right·eous** selbstgerecht; '**~ -'sac·ri·fice** Selbstaufopferung *f*; '**~same** *lit.* ebenderselbe; '**~ -'seek·ing** eigennützig; '**~'serv·ice res·tau·rant** Selbstbedienungsrestaurant *n*; '**~'start·er** *mot.* Anlasser *m*; '**~'suf'fi·cien·cy** Selbstversorgung *f*; Selbstgenügsamkeit *f*; '**~sup'pli·er** Selbstversorger(in); '**~sup'port·ing** selbständig; (wirtschaftlich) unabhängig; '**~'will** Eigenwille *m*; '**~ -'willed** eigenwillig.

sell [sel] **1.** (*irr.*) *v/t.* verkaufen (*a. fig.*); *Am.* F anpreisen, beibringen; **~ (out)** F j. reinlegen; **~ off** ✝ ausverkaufen; **~ up** j. auspfänden; *v/i.* handeln; sich verkaufen, gehen (*Ware*); **~ off, ~ out** ✝ ausverkaufen; **2.** F Schwindel *m*; Reinfall *m*; '**sell·er** Verkäufer *m*; *good etc.* **~** gut *etc.* gehende Ware *f*; '**sell-out** F ausverkaufte Veranstaltung *f*; *fig.* Riesenerfolg *m*; Verrat *m*.

selt·zer ['seltsə] *a.* **~ water** Selterswasser *n*.

sel·vage, sel·vedge ⊕ ['selvidʒ] Salband *n*, Webekante *f*.

selves [selvz] *pl. von* self 3.

se·man·tics [si'mæntiks] *sg.* Wortbedeutungslehre *f*, Semantik *f*.

sem·a·phore ['seməfɔ:] **1.** Zeichentelegraph *m*; ✗ (*bsd.* Flaggen-) Winken *n*; 🚂 Signalmast *m*; **2.** (*bsd.* durch Winkzeichen) signalisieren.

sem·blance ['sembləns] Anschein *m*; Gestalt *f*.

se·men ['si:mən] Samenflüssigkeit *f*.

se·mes·ter *univ.* [si'mestə] Semester *n*.

sem·i... ['semi] halb...; Halb...; '**~breve** ♩ ganze Note *f*; '**~cir·cle** Halbkreis *m*; '**~'cir·cu·lar** halbkreisförmig; '**~'co·lon** Strichpunkt *m*, Semikolon *n*; '**~con'duc·tor** ⚡ Halbleiter *m*; '**~de'tached house** Doppelhaus(hälfte *f*) *n*; '**~'fi·nal** *Sport*: Vorschlußrunde *f*; Halbfinale *n*; '**~man·u'fac·tured** halbfertig.

sem·i·nal ['si:minl] Samen...; Keim...; *fig.* keimtragend.

sem·i·nar·y ['seminəri] (Priester-) Seminar *n*; *fig.* Schule *f*.

sem·i·of·fi·cial ['semiə'fiʃəl] halbamtlich.

sem·i·pre·cious ['semi'preʃəs]: **~ stone** Halbedelstein *m*.

sem·i·qua·ver ♩ ['semikweivə] Sechzehntel(note *f*) *n*.

Sem·ite ['si:mait] Semit(in); **Se·mit·ic** [si'mitik] semitisch.

sem·i·tone ♩ ['semitəun] Halbton *m*.

sem·i·vow·el ['semivauəl] Halbvokal *m*.

sem·o·li·na [semə'li:nə] Grieß *m*.

semp'stress ['sempstris] Näherin *f*.

sen [sen] Sen *m* (*japanische Münze*).

sen·ate ['senit] Senat *m*.

sen·a·tor ['senətə] Senator *m*; **sen·a·to·ri·al** □ [~'tɔ:riəl] senatorisch.

send [send] (*irr.*) senden, schicken; (*mit adj. od. p.pr.*) machen; *Ball etc.* werfen; *Kugel wohin* schießen; *s. pack* 2; ~ *for* kommen lassen, holen (lassen); ~ *forth* aussenden; von sich geben; *fig.* veröffentlichen; ~ *in* einsenden; einreichen; ~ *in one's name* sich melden lassen; ~ *off* wegschicken; absenden; aussenden; ~ *up* hinaufsenden; *fig.* in die Höhe treiben; ~ *word* mitteilen, Nachricht geben; **'send·er** (Ab)Sender(in); *tel.* Sender *m*; **'send-'off** Abschied(sfeier *f*) *m*.

sen·e·schal ['seniʃəl] Seneschall *m*, Majordomus *m*.

se·nile ['si:nail] greisenhaft, senil; **se·nil·i·ty** [si'niliti] Greisenalter *n*.

sen·ior ['si:njə] **1.** älter (*to* als); dienstälter; Ober...; ~ *citizens pl.* Senioren *m/pl.*, ältere Mitbürger *m/pl.*; ~ *partner* ✝ Chef *m*; **2.** Ältere *m*; Dienstältere *m*; Senior *m*; *he is my* ~ *by a year, he is a year my* ~ er ist ein Jahr älter als ich; **sen·ior·i·ty** [si:ni'ɔriti] höheres (Dienst)Alter *n*.

sen·sa·tion [sen'seiʃən] (Sinnes-) Empfindung *f*, Gefühl *n*; Eindruck *m*; Aufsehen *n*; Sensation *f*; **sen'sa·tion·al** □ [~ʃənl] Empfindungs...; aufregend, sensationell; **sen'sa·tion·al·ism** [~ʃnəlizəm] Effekthascherei *f*, Sensationslust *f*.

sense [sens] **1.** *allg.* Sinn *m* (*of* für); Empfindung *f*, Gefühl *n*; Verstand *m*; Bedeutung *f*; Ansicht *f*; *in* (*out of*) *one's* ~*s* bei (von) Sinnen; *bring s.o. to his* ~*s* zur Vernunft bringen; *make* ~ Sinn haben (*Sache*); *talk* ~ vernünftig reden; **2.** spüren. **sense·less** □ ['senslis] sinnlos, unsinnig; bewußtlos; gefühllos; **'sense·less·ness** Sinnlosigkeit *f*; Bewußt-, Gefühllosigkeit *f*.

sen·si·bil·i·ty [sensi'biliti] Sensibilität *f*, Empfindungsvermögen *n*; Empfindlichkeit *f* (*to, a. of* für); *sensibilities pl.* Empfindsamkeit *f*, Zartgefühl *n*.

sen·si·ble □ ['sensəbl] verständig, vernünftig, klug; empfänglich (*of* für); fühlbar; *be* ~ *of* sich *e-r Sache* bewußt sein; *et.* empfinden; **'sen·si·ble·ness** Fühlbarkeit *f*; Vernünftigkeit *f*.

sen·si·tive □ ['sensitiv] empfindlich (*to* für); empfindungsfähig; Empfindungs...; feinfühlend; leicht verletzt; *phot.* lichtempfindlich; **'sen·si·tive·ness, sen·si'tiv·i·ty** Empfindlichkeit *f* (*to* für).

sen·si·tize *phot.* ['sensitaiz] lichtempfindlich machen.

sen·so·ri·al [sen'sɔːriəl], **sen·so·ry** ['~səri] Empfindungs...; Sinnes...; *sensory nerve* Gefühlsnerv *m*.

sen·su·al □ ['sensjuəl] sinnlich; **'sen·su·al·ism** Sinnlichkeit *f*; **'sen·su·al·ist** sinnlicher Mensch *m*; **sen·su·al·i·ty** [~'æliti] Sinnlichkeit *f*.

sen·su·ous □ ['sensjuəs] sinnlich (*die Sinne betreffend*); sinnenfreudig.

sent [sent] *pret. u. p.p. von* send.

sen·tence ['sentəns] **1.** ⚖ Richterspruch *m*, Urteil *n*; *gr.* Satz *m*; *serve one's* ~ s-e Strafe absitzen; *s. life*; **2.** das Urteil fällen über (*acc.*); verurteilen (*to* zu).

sen·ten·tious □ [sen'tenʃəs] sententiös; salbungsvoll; salbaderisch.

sen·tient ['senʃənt] empfindend.

sen·ti·ment ['sentimənt] (seelische) Empfindung *f*, Gefühl *n*; Meinung *f*, Ansicht *f*; *s.* ~*ality*; **sen·ti·men·tal** □ [~'mentl] empfindsam, gefühlvoll; sentimental, rührselig; ~ *value* Liebhaberwert *m*; **sen·ti·men·tal·ist** [~'mentəlist] Gefühlsmensch *m*; **sen·ti·men·tal·i·ty** [~men'tæliti] Sentimentalität *f*; Empfindsamkeit *f*; Rührseligkeit *f*.

sen·ti·nel ['sentinl], **sen·try** ['sentri] ✗ Schildwache *f*, Posten *m*. **sen·try...:** '~**box** Schilderhaus *n*; '~**go** Postengang *m*.

se·pal ♀ ['sepəl] Kelchblatt *n*.

sep·a·ra·bil·i·ty [sepərə'biliti] Trennbarkeit *f*; **'sep·a·ra·ble** □ trennbar; **sep·a·rate 1.** □ ['seprit] (ab)getrennt, gesondert, besonder, separat, für sich; ~ *property* ⚖ Gütertrennung *f*; **2.** ['~əreit] (sich) trennen; (sich) absondern; (sich) scheiden; **sep·a'ra·tion** Trennung *f*, Scheidung *f*; **sep·a·ra·tist** ['~ərətist] *eccl.* Sektierer *m*; *pol.* Separatist *m*; **sep·a·ra·tor** ⊕ ['~əreitə] Scheider *m*; (Milch-) Zentrifuge *f*.

se·pi·a *paint.* ['si:pjə] Sepia *f*.

sep·sis ⚕ ['sepsis] Sepsis *f*, Blutvergiftung *f*.

Sep·tem·ber [sep'tembə] September *m*.

sep·ten·ni·al □ [sep'tenjəl] siebenjährig.

sep·tic ✵ ['septik] septisch.

sep·tu·a·ge·nar·i·an [septjued3i-'neəriən] Siebzigjährige *m, f*.

se·pul·chral [si'pʌlkrəl] Grab...; Toten...; *fig.* düster; **sep·ul·chre** ['sepəlkə] **1.** Grab(stätte *f*) *n*; **2.** begraben; **sep·ul·ture** ['⸚tʃə] Begräbnis *n*.

se·quel ['si:kwəl] Folge *f*; Nachspiel *n*; (Roman)Fortsetzung *f*; *in the* ⸚ in der Folge.

se·quence ['si:kwəns] Aufeinander-, Reihenfolge *f*; *Film*: Szene *f*; ⸚ *of tenses gr.* Zeitenfolge *f*; **'se·quent** aufeinanderfolgend.

se·ques·ter [si'kwestə] *s. sequestrate*; ⸚ *o.s.* sich zurückziehen (*from* von); ⸚*ed* zurückgezogen; einsam.

se·ques·trate ⚖ [si'kwestreit] *Eigentum* einziehen; beschlagnahmen; **se·ques·tra·tion** [si:kwes'treiʃən] Absonderung *f*; ⚖ Beschlagnahme *f*; **'se·ques·tra·tor** ⚖ Zwangsverwalter *m*.

se·quin ['si:kwin] Paillette *f*.

se·quoi·a ♧ [si'kwɔiə] Mammutbaum *m*.

se·ragl·io [se'rɑ:liəu] Serail *n*.

ser·aph ['serəf], *pl. a.* **ser·a·phim** ['⸚fim] Seraph *m*; **se·raph·ic** [se-'ræfik] (⸚*ally*) seraphisch; engelgleich; verzückt.

Serb, Ser·bi·an ['sə:b(jən)] **1.** serbisch; **2.** Serbe *m*, Serbin *f*; Serbisch *n*.

sere *poet.* [siə] dürr, welk.

ser·e·nade [seri'neid] **1.** ♪ Serenade *f*, Ständchen *n*; **2.** ein Ständchen bringen (*dat.*).

se·rene □ [si'ri:n] klar, heiter; ruhig; **se·ren·i·ty** [si'reniti] Heiterkeit *f*; Ruhe *f*.

serf [sə:f] Leibeigene *m, f*, Hörige *m, f*; *fig.* Sklave *m*; **'serf·age, 'serf·dom** Leibeigenschaft *f*.

serge [sə:dʒ] Serge *f* (*Stoff*).

ser·geant ⚔ ['sɑ:dʒənt] Feldwebel *m*, Wachtmeister *f*; Polizeisergeant *m*; **'⸚'ma·jor** ⚔ Hauptfeldwebel *m*.

se·ri·al □ ['siəriəl] **1.** fortlaufend, reihenweise, Serien...; Fortsetzungs...; ⸚*ly* reihen-, lieferungsweise; **2.** Fortsetzungsroman *m*.

se·ries ['siəri:z] *sg. u. pl.* Reihe *f* (*a.* ⚡); Serie *f*; Folge *f*; *biol.* Gruppe *f*;

in ⸚ ⚡ in Reihe geschaltet.

se·ri·ous □ ['siəriəs] *allg.* ernst (*aufrichtig*; *eifrig*; *schwerwiegend*; *beträchtlich*; *bedenklich*; *gefährlich*); ernsthaft, -lich; *be* ⸚ *es im Ernst* meinen; **'se·ri·ous·ness** Ernst *m*; Ernsthaftigkeit *f*.

ser·jeant *parl.* ['sɑ:dʒənt]: ⸚*-at-arms* Ordnungsbeamte *m*.

ser·mon ['sə:mən] Predigt *f*; *iro.* Strafpredigt *f*; **'ser·mon·ize** *v/i.* predigen; *v/t.* abkanzeln.

se·rol·o·gy ✵ [siə'rɔlədʒi] Serologie *f*, (Blut)Serumkunde *f*.

se·rous ['siərəs] serös.

ser·pent ['sə:pənt] Schlange *f*; **ser·pen·tine** ['⸚tain] **1.** Schlangen...; schlangengleich (*bsd. fig.*); schlangenförmig; gewunden; **2.** *min.* Serpentin *m*.

ser·rate ['serit], **ser·rat·ed** [se-'reitid] gezackt; **ser·ra·tion** Auszackung *f*.

ser·ried ['serid] dichtgedrängt.

se·rum ['siərəm] Serum *n* (*physiol.* Blutwasser; ✵ Impfstoff).

serv·ant ['sə:vənt] Diener(in); *a. domestic* ⸚ Dienstbote *m*, Bedienstete *m, f*; **'⸚-girl** Dienstmädchen *n*.

serve 1. [sə:v] *v/t.* dienen (*dat.*); bedienen (*with* mit); *j-m* aufwarten; *Amt* verwalten; *Speisen* reichen; *a.* ⸚ *up Speisen* auftragen; *schlecht etc.* behandeln; helfen, nützen, dienlich sein (*dat.*); *Zweck* erfüllen; *Tennis:* aufschlagen; (*it*) ⸚*s him right* (das) geschieht ihm recht; *s. sentence* 1; ⸚ *out et.* austeilen; F *es j-m* besorgen; ⸚ *a writ on s.o.*, ⸚ *s.o. with a writ* ⚖ *j-m* e-n Gerichtsbefehl zustellen; *v/i.* dienen (*a.* ⚔); aufwarten, servieren; nützen, passen, zweckmäßig sein; dienen (*as, for* als, zu); ⸚ *at table* servieren; **2.** *Tennis:* Aufschlag *m*; **'serv·er** *Tennis:* Aufschläger *m*; *eccl.* Meßdiener *m*.

serv·ice ['sə:vis] **1.** Dienst *m*; Aufwartung *f*; Bedienung *f*; Gefälligkeit *f*; ✝ Dienst *m am* Kunden; *a. divine* ⸚ Gottesdienst *m*; Betrieb *m*; Verkehr *m*; Nutzen *m*; Gang *m von Speisen*; Service *n*, Tafelgerät *n*; ⚓ Bekleidung *f e-s Taues*; ⚖ Zustellung *f*; *Tennis:* Aufschlag *m*; *be at s.o.'s* ⸚ *j-m* zu Diensten stehen; **2.** betreuen; *j-m* Hilfe leisten; ⊕ warten, pflegen; **'serv·ice·a·ble** ☐ dienlich, nützlich; benutzbar, betriebsfähig; strapazierfähig; **'serv·ice·a·ble·ness** Dienlichkeit *f*.

serv·ice...: ~ **ar·e·a** Raststätte *f* mit Tankstelle; **'~-ball** *Tennis:* Aufschlag(ball) *m*; ~ **charge** Bedienung(sgeld *n*) *f*; Bearbeitungsgebühr *f*; ~ **flat** Etagenwohnung *f* mit Bedienung; **'~-line** *Tennis:* Aufschlaglinie *f*; ~ **pipe** ⊕ Zweig-, Anschlußrohr *n*; ~ **sta·tion** Tankstelle *f*; Werkstatt *f*.

ser·vile ☐ ['sə:vail] sklavisch (*a. fig.*); unterwürfig; kriecherisch; **ser·vil·i·ty** [~'viliti] Unterwürfigkeit *f*, Kriecherei *f*.

serv·ing ['sə:vin] Portion *f*.

ser·vi·tude ['sə:vitju:d] Knechtschaft *f*; Sklaverei *f*; ⚖ Servitut *n*; *s. penal.*

ser·vo-brake *mot.* ['sə:vəubreik] Servobremse *f*.

ses·a·me ♀ *u. fig.* ['sesəmi] Sesam *m*.

ses·sion ['seʃən] (*a.* Gerichts)Sitzung *f*; be in ~ tagen; **ses·sion·al** ['seʃənl] Sitzungs...

set [set] **1.** (*irr.*) *v/t.* setzen; stellen; legen; zurechtmachen *od.* -stellen; (ein)richten, ordnen; bringen; pflanzen; *Aufgabe, Wecker* stellen; *Hund* hetzen (*at, on* auf *acc.*); *Messer* abziehen; *Säge* schränken; *Edelstein* fassen; *Zeit* festsetzen; gerinnen *od.* erstarren lassen; *Haar* legen; ✂ *Knochenbruch* einrichten; ~ *s.o. laughing* j. zum Lachen bringen; ~ *an example* ein Beispiel geben; ~ *the fashion* in der Mode bestimmend sein; ~ *sail* Segel setzen; ~ *one's teeth* die Zähne zs.-beißen; ~ *against* gegenüberstellen (*dat.*); *s. apart*; ~ *aside* beiseite setzen; auf die Seite legen, reservieren; *fig.* verwerfen; ~ *at defiance j-m* Trotz bieten; ~ *at ease* beruhigen; ~ *at liberty* in Freiheit setzen; ~ *at rest* beruhigen; *Frage* entscheiden; ~ *store by* Wert legen auf (*acc.*); ~ *down* niedersetzen; absetzen (*aus e-m Wagen etc.*); aufschreiben; zuschreiben (*to s.o.* j-m); ~ *forth* dartun, -legen; ~ *off* hervorheben, -treten lassen; auf-, anrechnen (*against* gegen); ausgleichen; ~ *on* setzen auf (*acc.*); anstiften; ~ *out* auslegen, zeigen; aus-

einandersetzen, darlegen; pflanzen; ~ *up* auf-, er-, einrichten; *Meinung etc.* aufstellen; *j-m* aufhelfen; *j.* etablieren; *Geschäft etc.* anfangen; ~ *up in type typ.* setzen; **2.** (*irr.*) *v/i.* untergehen (*Sonne etc.*); gerinnen, fest werden; fließen, laufen (*Flut etc.*); *hunt.* (vor)stehen; sitzen (*Kleid etc.*); ~ *about s.th.* sich an et. machen; ~ *about s.o.* F über j. herfallen; ~ *forth* aufbrechen; ~ *forward* sich auf den Weg machen; ~ *in* beginnen, einsetzen; ~ *off* sich in Bewegung setzen; sich aufmachen, aufbrechen; fahren (*for* nach); ~ (*up*)*on* anfangen; angreifen; ~ *out* abreisen, aufbrechen; *fig.* ausgehen (*from* von); ~ *to* sich daran machen, anfangen; ~ *up* sich niederlassen (*as* als); ~ *up for* sich ausgeben für; sich aufspielen als; **3.** fest; starr, unbeweglich; festgesetzt, bestimmt; regelmäßig; vorgeschrieben; formell; ~ (*up*)*on* versessen auf (*acc.*), entschlossen zu; ~ *with* besetzt mit; ~ *fair Barometer:* beständig; *hard* ~ in großer Not; ~ *piece* Gruppenbild *n*; ~ *speech* wohlüberlegte Rede *f*; **4.** Reihe *f*, Folge *f*, Serie *f*, Sammlung *f*, Satz *m* zs.-*gehöriger Dinge*; Garnitur *f*; Besteck *n*; Service *n*; (Radio)Gerät *n*; ✝ Kollektion *f*; Gesellschaft *f*; Sippschaft *f*, Rotte *f*; ✔ Setzling *m*; *Tennis:* Satz *m*; Neigung *f*; Richtung *f*; Schnitt *m e-s Kleides etc.*; *poet.* Untergang *m der Sonne*; *thea.* Bühnenausstattung *f*; *make a dead ~ at fig.* über *j.* herfallen; es auf *e-n Mann* abgesehen haben (*Frau*).

set·back ['setbæk] *fig.* Rückschlag *m*; △ Mauervorsprung *m*; **'set·down** Dämpfer *m*; **'set-'off** Kontrast *m*; Schmuck *m*; ✝ *u.* ⚖ Gegenrechnung *f*, -forderung *f*; *fig.* Ausgleich *m*; **'set-square** ◬ Zeichendreieck *n*.

set·tee [se'ti:] *kleines Sofa n*.

set·ter ['setə] Setzer(in); *hunt.* Setter *m* (*Vorstehhund*).

set the·o·ry ◬ Mengenlehre *f*.

set·ting ['setin] Setzen *n etc.* (*s. set 1 u. 2*); Erstarren *n*; Gerinnen *n*; *ast.* Untergang *m*; Richtung *f des Windes etc.*; Fassung *f e-s Edelsteins*; Umgebung *f*, Lage *f*; *thea.*

Ausstattung *f*; *fig.* Umrahmung *f*; ♪ Komposition *f*; '~-lo·tion (Haar-) Fixativ *n*.

set·tle ['setl] **1.** Sitzbank *f*; **2.** *v/t.* (fest)setzen; *Kind etc.* versorgen, ausstatten; *j.* etablieren; regeln; *Geschäft* abschließen, abmachen, erledigen; *Frage* entscheiden; *Rechnung* begleichen; ordnen; beruhigen; *Streit* beilegen; *Rente* aussetzen (on *s.o.* j-m); ansiedeln; *Land* besiedeln; *v/i.* oft ~ down, *a.* ~ *o.s.* sich niederlassen; sich ansiedeln; *a.* ~ *in* sich (wohnlich) einrichten; sich setzen (*a. Haus, Boden*); ♣ wegsacken; nachlassen, sich legen (*Wut etc.*); beständig werden (*Wetter*); sich entschließen (on für, zu); sich begnügen (with mit); *it is settling for a frost es* wird Frost geben; ~ down to sich widmen (*dat.*).

set·tled ['setld] fest, bestimmt; entschieden; beständig (*Wind etc.*); (*auf Rechnung*) bezahlt.

set·tle·ment ['setlmənt] Regelung *f*; Erledigung *f*; Klärung *f*; Schlichtung *f*; Übereinkunft *f*; Niederlassung *f*; (Be)Siedlung *f*; ₰ (Eigentums)Übertragung *f*; ✝ Ausgleich(ung *f*) *m*; Mission *f*; soziales Hilfswerk *n*.

set·tler ['setlə] Siedler *m*; entscheidender Schlag *m*.

set·tling ['setliŋ] Festsetzung *f etc.* (*s.* settle 2); ✝ Abrechnung *f*.

set...: '~-'to Kampf *m*; Schlägerei *f*; '~-up F Aufbau *m*, Einrichtung *f*.

sev·en ['sevn] **1.** sieben; **2.** Sieben *f*; 'sev·en·fold siebenfach; **sev·en·teen** ['~'ti:n] siebzehn; **sev·enth** ['sevnθ] **1.** ~ siebente(r, -s); **2.** Siebentel *n*; ♪ Septime *f*; **se·ven·ti·eth** ['~tiiθ] siebzigste(r, -s); 'sev·en·ty **1.** siebzig; **2.** Siebzig *f*.

sev·er ['sevə] (sich) trennen; (auf-) lösen; zerreißen.

sev·er·al □ ['sevrəl] mehrere, verschiedene; einige; einzeln; besonder; getrennt; *joint and* ~ ₰ solidarisch; 'sev·er·al·ly besonders, einzeln.

sev·er·ance ['sevərəns] Trennung *f*.

se·vere □ [si'viə] streng; rauh (*Winter*); hart (*Winter*); scharf (*Tadel*); ernst (*Mühe*); heftig (*Schmerz etc.*); herb (*Stil, Schönheit etc.*); schlimm, schwer (*Unfall, Verlust,*

Wunde); **se·ver·i·ty** [si'veriti] Strenge *f*, Härte *f*; Schwere *f*; Ernst *m*.

sew [səu] (*irr.*) nähen; *Buch* heften; ~ up zu-, vernähen.

sew·age ['sju:idʒ] Abwasser *n*; ~ *farm* Rieselfelder *n/pl.*

sew·er[1] ['səuə] Näherin *f*.

sew·er[2] ['sjuə] Abwasserkanal *m*; 'sew·er·age Kanalisation *f*.

sew·ing ['səuiŋ] **1.** Nähen *n*; Näherei *f*; **2.** Näh...

sewn [səun] *p.p. von* sew.

sex [seks] *natürliches* Geschlecht *n*; Sex(ualität *f*) *m*; Geschlechtsverkehr *m*; *attr.* Geschlechts...; ~ *appeal* erotische Anziehungskraft *f*, Sex-Appeal *m*; ~ *education* sexuelle Aufklärung *f*, Sexualerziehung *f*; ~ *object* Lustobjekt *n*.

sex·a·ge·nar·i·an [seksədʒi'neəriən] Sechzigjährige *m*, *f*; **sex·en·ni·al** □ [sek'senjəl] sechsjährig; sechsjährlich; **sex·tant** ['sekstənt] Sextant *m*.

sex·ton ['sekstən] Küster *m*, *zugleich* Totengräber *m*.

sex·tu·ple ['sekstjupl] sechsfach.

sex·u·al □ ['seksjuəl] sexuell; Sexual...; geschlechtlich; Geschlechts...; ~ *desire* (geschlechtliche) Begierde *f*; ~ *intercourse* Geschlechtsverkehr *m*; ~ *urge* Geschlechtstrieb *m*; **sex·u·al·i·ty** [~'æliti] Sexualität *f*.

sex·y F ['seksi] sexy; sexuell anregend; erotisch (*Witz, Buch etc.*).

shab·bi·ness ['ʃæbinis] Schäbigkeit *f*; 'shab·by □ schäbig; gemein.

shack *bsd. Am.* [ʃæk] Hütte *f*, Bude *f*.

shack·le ['ʃækl] **1.** Fessel *f* (*fig. mst* ~*s pl.*); ♣, ⊕ Schäkel *m* (*Kettenglied*); **2.** fesseln.

shad *ichth.* [ʃæd] Alse *f*.

shade [ʃeid] **1.** Schatten *m*, Dunkel *n* (*a. fig.*); Lampen- *etc.* Schirm *m*; Schattierung *f*; *Am.* Rouleau *n*; *fig.* Spur *f*, Kleinigkeit *f*; **2.** beschatten; verdunkeln (*a. fig.*); *Licht* abschirmen; schützen (*from gegen Licht etc.*); *paint.* schattieren; ~ *away*, ~ *off* allmählich übergehen (lassen) (*into in acc.*); **shades** *pl.* F Sonnenbrille *f*; 'shad·ing *paint.* Schattierung *f*; *fig.* Nuance *f*.

shad·ow ['ʃædəu] **1.** Schatten *m* (*a. fig.*); Phantom *n*; Spur *f*, Kleinigkeit *f*; **2.** beschatten; *mst* ~ *forth*, ~ *out* andeuten; versinnbildlichen; *j.* beschatten, überwachen;

share

~ **cab·i·net** *pol.* Schattenkabinett *n*; **'shad·ow·y** schattig; dunkel; schattenhaft; wesenlos.

shad·y ['ʃeidi] schattenspendend; schattig; dunkel; F zweifelhaft; *on the ~ side of forty* F über die Vierzig hinaus.

shaft [ʃɑːft] Schaft *m*; Stiel *m*; Pfeil *m* (*a. fig.*); *poet.* Strahl *m*; ⊕ Welle *f*, Spindel *f*; Deichsel *f*; ✗ Schacht *m*.

shag [ʃæg] Krüllschnitt *m* (*Tabak*).

shag·gy ['ʃægi] zottig.

sha·green [ʃæ'griːn] Chagrin(leder|

Shah [ʃɑː] Schah *m*. [*n*) *m*.∫

shake [ʃeik] **1.** (*irr.*) *v/t.* schütteln, rütteln; erschüttern; ~ *down* herunterschütteln; *Stroh etc.* hinschütten; zs.-rütteln; ~ *hands* sich die Hände geben *od.* schütteln; ~ *up Bett* aufschütteln; *fig.* aufrütteln; *v/i.* zittern, beben, wanken, wackeln (*with* vor *dat.*); ♪ trillern; ~ *down* sich einleben; **2.** Schütteln *n*; Erschütterung *f*; Beben *n*; ♪ Triller *m*; F Augenblick *m*; ~ *of the hand* Händedruck *m*; *no great* ~s F nichts Besonderes; **'~'down** Notlager *n*; *Am. sl.* Erpressung *f*; ~ *cruise* ⚓ Probefahrt *f*; **'~-hands** Händedruck *m*; **'shak·en 1.** *p.p. von shake* 1; **2.** *adj.* erschüttert; **'shak·er** Schüttler(in); Mix-, Mischbecher *m*.

shake-up F ['ʃeik'ʌp] Aufrüttelung *f*; Umgruppierung *f*.

shak·i·ness ['ʃeikinis] Wacklichkeit *f*; Gebrechlichkeit *f*; **'shak·y** □ *mst* wacklig (*a. fig.*); *engS.* (sch)wankend; zitternd, zitterig.

shale *geol.* [ʃeil] Schiefer *m*.

shall [ʃæl] (*irr.*) *v/aux.* soll; werde.

shal·lot ♣ [ʃə'lɒt] Schalotte *f*.

shal·low ['ʃælou] **1.** seicht; flach; *fig.* oberflächlich; **2.** Untiefe *f*; **3.** (sich) verflachen; **'shal·low·ness** Seichtigkeit *f* (*a. fig.*).

shalt † [ʃælt] *du sollst*.

sham [ʃæm] **1.** falsch, unecht; Schein...; **2.** Trug *m*, leerer Schein *m*; Lüge *f*, Täuschung *f*; Schwindler(in); **3.** *v/t.* (er)heucheln, vortäuschen; *v/i.* sich verstellen; simulieren; ~ *ill* sich krank stellen.

sham·ble ['ʃæmbl] watscheln.

sham·bles *fig.* ['ʃæmblz] *sg.* Schlacht-, Trümmerfeld *n*.

sham·bling □ ['ʃæmbliŋ] wackelig.

shame [ʃeim] **1.** Scham *f*; Schande *f*; ~*!*, *for* ~*!*, ~ *on you!* pfui!, schäme dich!; *cry* ~ *upon s.o.* pfui über j. rufen; *put to* ~ beschämen; **2.** beschämen, schamrot machen; schänden; *j-m* Schande machen.

shame·faced □ ['ʃeimfeist] schamhaft, schüchtern; **'shame·faced·ness** Schamhaftigkeit *f*.

shame·ful □ ['ʃeimful] schändlich, schmachvoll, beschämend; **'shame·ful·ness** Schändlichkeit *f*.

shame·less □ ['ʃeimlis] schamlos; **'shame·less·ness** Schamlosigkeit *f*.

sham·my ['ʃæmi] Wildleder *n*.

sham·poo [ʃæm'puː] **1.** Shampoo *n*, Haarwaschmittel *n*; Haarwäsche *f*; ~ *and set Haare*: Waschen *n* und Legen *n*; *have a* ~ *and set* sich die Haare waschen und legen lassen; **2.** *Haare* schamponieren, waschen.

sham·rock ['ʃæmrɔk] ♣ weißer Feldklee *m*; Kleeblatt *n* (*irisches Nationalzeichen*).

shan·dy ['ʃændi] *Getränk aus Bier und Limonade*.

shang·hai ⚓ *sl.* [ʃæŋ'hai] schanghaien (*gewaltsam heuern*).

shank [ʃæŋk] (Unter)Schenkel *m*; ⚓ Stiel *m*; ⚓ (Anker)Schaft *m*; *go on ♘'s mare od. pony* auf Schusters Rappen reiten; **shanked** ...schenkelig.

shan't [ʃɑːnt] = *shall not*.

shan·tung [ʃæn'tʌŋ] Schantungseide *f*.

shan·ty ['ʃænti] Hütte *f*, Bude *f*; = *chanty*.

shape [ʃeip] **1.** Gestalt *f*, Form *f*; Art *f*; *in bad* ~ in schlechtem Zustand; **2.** *v/t.* bilden, formen, gestalten; anpassen (*to dat.*); ~ *one's course* nür Kurs nehmen auf (*acc.*); *v/i.* sich entwickeln, sich anlassen; **shaped** ...förmig; **'shape·less** formlos; unförmig; **'shape·li·ness** schöne Form *f*; **'shape·ly** wohlgestaltet, hübsch, schöne.

share [ʃeə] **1.** Teil *m*, Anteil *m*; Beitrag *m*, Kontingent *n*; ✠ Anteilschein *m*, Aktie *f*; ✗ Kux *m*; *original* ~, *ordinary* ~, *primary* ~ ✠ Stammaktie *f*; *preference* ~, *preferred* ~, *priority* ~ ✠ Vorzugsaktie *f*; *have a* ~ *in* teilhaben an (*dat.*); *go* ~s teilen (*with s.o.* mit j-m; *in s.th.* et.); ~ *and* ~ *alike* zu gleichen Teilen; **2.** *v/t.* teilen (*among*

sharecropper

unter *acc.*; *with* mit); teilhaben an
(*dat.*); *v/i.* teilhaben (*in* an *dat.*);
'**~·crop·per** *Am. kleiner* Farm-
pächter *m*; '**~·hold·er** ♔ Aktionär
(-in); '**shar·er** Teiler(in); Teil-
haber(in).

shark [ʃɑːk] *ichth.* Hai(fisch) *m*;
fig. Gauner *m*; *Am. sl.* Kanone *f*
(*Experte*).

sharp [ʃɑːp] **1.** □ *allg.* scharf (*a.
fig.*); spitz; schneidend, stechend
(*Schmerz*); herb (*Wein*); schrill
(*Schrei*); hitzig (*Temperament*);
schnell, flott; pfiffig, schlau, gewitzt, *b.s.* gerissen; ♪ um e-n
halben Ton erhöht; *F* ~ Fis *n*;
2. *adv.* ♪ (einen halben Ton) zu
hoch; *F* pünktlich; *look* ~! (mach)
schnell!; **3.** ♪ Kreuz *n*; durch ein
Kreuz erhöhte Note *f*; *F* Gauner *m*;
'**sharp·en** (ver)schärfen; *Bleistift*
spitzen; *Appetit* anregen; ♪ erhöhen; '**sharp·en·er** *Messer*-
Schärfer *m*; *Bleistift*-Spitzer *m*;
'**sharp·er** Gauner *m*; '**sharp-'eyed**
scharfsichtig; '**sharp·ness** Schärfe *f*
(*a. fig.*); Strenge *f*, Härte *f*; *fig.* Heftigkeit *f* e-s *Schmerzes*; Scharfsinn *m*;
Pfiffigkeit *f*.

sharp...: '**~-'set** hungrig; erpicht
(*on* auf *acc.*); '**~-shoot·er** Scharf-
schütze *m*; '**~-'sight·ed** scharfsichtig; '**~-'wit·ted** scharfsinnig.

shat·ter ['ʃætə] zerschmettern, -bre-
chen, -schlagen, -trümmern (*a.
fig.*); *Nerven etc.* zerrütten; '**~proof**
splitterfrei, -sicher.

shave [ʃeiv] **1.** (*irr.*) *v/t.* rasieren;
bsd. Holz (ab)schälen; haarscharf
vorbeigehen *od.* -fahren *od.* -kom-
men an (*dat.*); *v/i.* sich rasieren; ~
through durchschlüpfen; **2.** Rasieren
n, Rasur *f*; *have a* ~ sich rasieren
(lassen); *by a* ~ um ein Haar;
a close ~, *a narrow* ~ ein Entkommen *n* mit knapper Not;
'**shav·en** *p.p. von shave* 1; *a* ~ *head*
ein geschorener Kopf *m*; '**shav·er**
Barbier *m*; *young* ~ *F* Grünschnabel *m*.

Sha·vi·an ['ʃeivjən] Shawsch, charakteristisch für G. B. Shaw.

shav·ing ['ʃeiviŋ] **1.** Rasieren *n*;
~*s pl.* (*bsd.* Hobel)Späne *m/pl.*,
Schnitzel *n pl.*; **2.** Rasier..., Barbier...; ~*brush* Rasierpinsel *m*; ~
cream Rasiercreme *f*; ~ *soap*, ~ *stick*
Rasierseife *f*.

shawl [ʃɔːl] Schal *m*, Kopftuch *n*.
shawm ♪ [ʃɔːm] Schalmei *f*.
shay † *od.* F [ʃei] Chaise *f*, Kutsche *f*.
she [ʃiː, ʃi] **1.** sie; **2.** Weib *n*, Sie *f*;
she-... Weibchen *n von Tieren.*

sheaf [ʃiːf], *pl.* **sheaves** [ʃiːvz]
Garbe *f*; Bündel *n*.

shear [ʃiə] **1.** (*irr.*) scheren, abschneiden; *fig.* rupfen; **2.** (*a pair of*)
~*s pl.* (eine) *große* Schere *f*; '**shear·
er** (Schaf)Scherer *m*; Schnitter *m*;
'**shear·ing** Scheren *n*, Schur *f*; ~*s
pl.* Scherwolle *f*.

sheath [ʃiːθ], *pl.* **sheaths** [ʃiːðz]
Scheide *f* (*a.* ♀ *u. anat.*); *zo.* Flü-
geldecke *f*; **sheathe** [ʃiːð] (in die
Scheide) stecken; einhüllen; ⊕ be-
kleiden, beschlagen; '**sheath·ing**
⊕ Bekleidung *f*, Beschlag *m*.

sheave ⊕ [ʃiːv] Scheibe *f*, Rolle *f*.
sheaves [ʃiːvz] *pl. von sheaf.*
she·bang *Am. sl.* [ʃə'bæŋ] Bruchbude *f*; *the whole* ~ der ganze
Laden.

shed¹ [ʃed] (*irr.*) ausgießen; *Blut,
Tränen etc.* vergießen; *Licht, Frie-
den etc.* verbreiten (*upon* über *acc.*);
Blätter, Zähne etc. abwerfen.

shed² [~] Schuppen *m*; Stall *m*;
Flugzeughalle *f*.

sheen [ʃiːn] Glanz *m* (*bsd. von
Stoffen*); '**sheen·y** glänzend.

sheep [ʃiːp] Schaf *n*; *coll.* Schafe *pl.*;
Schafleder *n*; '**~-cot** = *sheep-fold*;
'**~-dog** Schäferhund *m*; '**~-fold**
Schafhürde *f*; '**sheep·ish** □ blöd(e),
einfältig; '**sheep·ish·ness** Blödig-
keit *f*.

sheep...: '**~-man** *Am.* Schafzüchter
m; '**~-run** = *sheep-walk*; '**~-skin**
Schaffell *n*; Schafleder *n*; *Am.*
Diplom *n*; '**~-walk** Schafweide *f*.

sheer¹ [ʃiə] *adj. u. adv.* rein, lauter;
gänzlich, völlig, glatt; steil; senkrecht; direkt.

sheer² [~] **1.** ⚓ gieren, scheren
(*vom Kurs abweichen*); ~ *off fig.* sich
davonmachen; **2.** ⚓ Ausscheren *n*.

sheet [ʃiːt] **1.** Bett-, Leintuch *n*,
Laken *n*; (*Glas-, Metall- etc.*)Platte
f; Blatt *n*, Bogen *m* Papier; weite
Fläche *f* (*von Wasser etc.*); ⚓
Schot(e) *f*; *the rain came down in* ~*s*
es regnete in Strömen; ~ *iron*
Eisenblech *n*; **2.** einhüllen; '**~-an-
chor** ⚓ Notanker *m* (*a. fig.*).
'**sheet·ing** Leinwand *f* für Bett-
tücher; '**sheet-light·ning** Flächen-

blitz *m*, Wetterleuchten *n*; **sheet mu·sic** Notenblätter *n/pl.*

sheik(h) [ʃeik] Scheich *m*.

shelf [ʃelf], *pl.* **shelves** [ʃelvz] Brett *n*, Regal *n*, Fach *n*, Sims *m*; Riff *n*, Sandbank *f*; *on the* ~ *fig.* ausrangiert, abgetan; *get on the* ~ *fig.* sitzenbleiben (*Mädchen*); ~ **life** Lagerfähigkeit *f*.

shell [ʃel] **1.** Schale *f*, Hülse *f*; Muschel *f*; Schneckenhaus *n*; ⊕ Gehäuse *n*; Gerippe *n e-s Hauses*; ✕ Bombe *f*, Granate *f*; Renn-(ruder)boot *n*; **2.** schälen, enthülsen; ✕ bombardieren; ~ *out sl.* Geld herausrücken.

shel·lac [ʃəˈlæk] Schellack *m*.

shell-cra·ter [ˈʃelkreitə] Granattrichter *m*; **shelled** [ʃeld] ...schalig.

shell...: '~**-fire** Granatfeuer *n*; '~**-fish** Schalentier *n*; '~**-proof** bombensicher; '~**-shock** Kriegsneurose *f*.

shel·ter [ˈʃeltə] **1.** Schuppen *m*; Schutz-, Obdach *n*; *fig.* Schutz *m*, Schirm *m*; **2.** *v/t.* (be)schützen; (be)schirmen; Zuflucht gewähren (*dat.*); *v/i.* Schutz suchen; '**shelter·less** schutzlos.

shelve[1] [ʃelv] mit Brettern *od.* Regalen versehen; auf ein Brett stellen; *fig.* zu den Akten legen; *fig.* außer Dienst stellen; *fig.* beiseite lassen, weglassen; F links liegen lassen.

shelve[2] [~] sich allmählich neigen.

shelves [ʃelvz] *pl. von* shelf.

shelv·ing [ˈʃelviŋ] **1.** Regal(e *pl.*) *n*; **2.** schräg.

she·nan·i·gan *Am.* F [ʃiˈnænigən] Gaunerei *f*; Humbug *m*.

shep·herd [ˈʃepəd] **1.** Schäfer *m*, Hirt *m*; **2.** (be)hüten; leiten, bugsieren; '**shep·herd·ess** Schäferin *f*.

sher·bet [ˈʃəːbət] Sorbett *m*, *n* (*Fruchtgetränk*); Brauselimonade *f*.

sher·iff [ˈʃerif] Sheriff *m*.

sher·ry [ˈʃeri] Sherry *m*.

shew ⚲ [ʃou] = show.

shib·bo·leth [ˈʃibəleθ] Erkennungszeichen *n*; Schlagwort *n*; überholte Anschauung *f*.

shield [ʃiːld] **1.** (Schutz)Schild *m*; Wappenschild *m*, *n*; **2.** (be)schirmen, schützen (*from* vor *dat.*, gegen); '**shield·less** schild-, schutzlos.

shift [ʃift] **1.** Veränderung *f*,

-schiebung *f*, Wechsel *m*; Notbehelf *m*; List *f*, Kniff *m*; Ausflucht *f*; (Arbeits)Schicht *f*; *make* ~ es möglich machen (*to inf.* zu *inf.*); sich behelfen (*with* mit; *without* ohne); sich durchschlagen; **2.** *v/t.* (ver-, weg)schieben; ⚓ wenden, umlegen; umladen; *Platz, Szene etc.* verlegen, verändern, verlagern; *Betrieb etc.* umstellen (*to* auf *acc.*); *mot. Gang* schalten; *v/i.* den Ort verändern; sich verlagern; umspringen (*Wind*); ⚓ überschießen (*Ballast*); sich behelfen; ~ *for o.s.* für sich sorgen; sich selbst helfen; '**shift·ing** □ veränderlich; ~ *sands pl.* Flugsand *m*; '**shift·less** □ hilflos; *fig.* ungewandt; faul; '**shift·y** □ schlau, verschlagen, gerissen; unzuverlässig.

shil·ling [ˈʃiliŋ] *engl.* Schilling *m*; *cut off with a* ~ enterben.

shil·ly-shal·ly [ˈʃiliʃæli] unentschlossen (sein).

shim·mer [ˈʃimə] flimmern, schimmern.

shin [ʃin] **1.** *a.* ~-*bone* Schienbein *n*; **2.** ~ *up* hinaufklettern.

shin·dy F [ˈʃindi] Radau *m*, Krach *m*.

shine [ʃain] **1.** Schein *m*; Glanz *m*; *give one's shoes a* ~ s-e Schuhe polieren; *rain or* ~ bei jedem Wetter; **2.** (*irr.*) scheinen; leuchten; *fig.* glänzen, strahlen; blank putzen.

shin·gle[1] [ˈʃiŋgl] **1.** Schindel *f*; Herrenschnitt *m* (*Damenfrisur*); *Am.* F (Aushänge)Schild *n*; **2.** mit Schindeln decken; *Haar* kurz schneiden.

shin·gle[2] *coll.* [~] Strandkiesel *m/pl.*; Strand *m*.

shin·gles ⚕ [ˈʃiŋglz] *pl.* Gürtelrose *f*.

shin·gly [ˈʃiŋgli] kies(el)ig, Kies...

shin·y □ [ˈʃaini] blank, glänzend.

ship [ʃip] **1.** Schiff *n*; *Am.* F Flugzeug *n*; ~'*s company* Schiffsbesatzung *f*; **2.** *v/t.* an Bord nehmen *od.* bringen; verschiffen, versenden; (ver)schicken; transportieren; *Matrosen* heuern; ~ *the oars* die Riemen einlegen; ~ *a sea* e-e Sturzsee bekommen; *v/i.* sich anheuern lassen; sich einschiffen; '~**-board:** *on* ~ ⚓ an Bord; '~**-brok·er** Schiffsmakler *m*; -händler *m*; '~**-build·er** Schiffbauer *m*, Schiff-

baumeister *m*; '**~-build·ing** Schiff-
bau *m*; '**~-ca·nal** Schiffahrtskanal
m; '**~-chan·dler** Schiffslieferant*m*;
'**~-chan·dler·y** Schiffsproviant *m*;
'**~-load** Schiffsladung *f*; '**shipment** Verschiffung *f*, Verladung *f*;
Versand *m*; Schiffsladung *f*; '**ship-
own·er** Reeder *m*; '**ship·per** Ver-
schiffer *m*, Verlader *m*.
ship·ping ['∫ipiŋ] **1.** Verschiffung *f*;
Schiffe *n*/*pl.*, Flotte *f* *e*-*s* *Landes*;
2. Schiffs...; Verschiffungs..., Ver-
lade...; '**~-a·gent** Reedereiver-
treter *m*, Schiffsagent *m*; ~ **fore·cast**
Seewetterbericht *m*; '**~-of·fice**
Heuerbüro *n*.
ship...: '**~shape** sauber, ordentlich; '**~way** Helling *f*; '**~wreck**
1. Schiffbruch *m*; **2.** scheitern
(lassen); *be* ~*ed* Schiffbruch erleiden, scheitern; '**~wrecked**
schiffbrüchig; '**~wright** Schiffbauer *m*; Schiffszimmermann *m*;
'**~yard** Schiffswerft *f*.
shire ['∫aiə, *in Zssgn* ...∫iə] Grafschaft *f*; ~ **horse** schweres Zugpferd *n*.
shirk [∫ə:k] sich drücken (um *e*-*e*
Aufgabe); '**shirk·er** Drückeberger
m.
shirt [∫ə:t] Herrenhemd *n*; *a*.
~-*waist* *Am.* Hemdbluse *f*; *keep*
one's ~ *on* *sl.* sich nicht aufregen;
'**shirt·ing** ✝ Hemdenstoff; '**shirt-
-sleeve** **1.** Hemdsärmel *m*; **2.**
hemdsärmelig, informell; ~ *diplomacy* *bsd.* *Am.* offene Diplomatie *f*;
'**shirt·y** *sl.* aus dem Häuschen,
wütend.
shit [∫it] **1.** ∨ Scheiße *f*; P Shit *n*,
Hasch(isch) *n*; **2.** ∨ scheißen.
shiv·er[1] ['∫ivə] **1.** Splitter *m*; *break
to* ~*s* = **2.** *v*/*t*. *u*. *v*/*i*. zersplittern.
shiv·er[2] [~] **1.** Schauer *m*; *the* ~*s* *pl.*
das Fieber; *it gives me the* ~*s* es
läuft mir kalt über den Rücken;
2. schau(d)ern; (er)zittern; frösteln; ~*ing* *fit* Fieberschauer *m*,
Schüttelfrost *m*; '**shiv·er·y** fröstelnd.
shoal[1] [∫əul] **1.** Schwarm *m*, Schar *f*
(*Fische*; *a.* *fig.*); **2.** sich scharen.
shoal[2] [~] **1.** Untiefe *f*; **2.** flacher *od.*
seichter werden; **3.** = '**shoal·y**
seicht, flach.
shock[1] ⚡ [∫ɔk] Garbenhaufen *m*,
Mandel *f*.
shock[2] [~] **1.** Stoß *m*; Anstoß *m*,

Ärgernis *n*; Erschütterung *f*,
Schlag *m*; ⚕ (Nerven)Schock *m*;
2. *fig.* verletzen, empören, schok-
kieren, Anstoß erregen bei; *Nervensystem* erschüttern.
shock[3] [~] (*of hair* Haar)Schopf *m*.
shock...: '**~-ab·sorb·er** *mot.* Stoß-
dämpfer *m*; '**~-bri·gade** Stoß-
brigade *f*.
shock·er *sl.* ['∫ɔkə] Schauerroman *m*.
shock·ing □ ['∫ɔkiŋ] anstößig; verletzend, empörend; haarsträubend.
shock...: '**~-proof** stoßsicher; ~ **ther-
a·py**, ~ **treat·ment** ⚕ Schockthera-
pie *f*; ~ **wave** Druckwelle *f*; *fig.*
Schock *m*, Erschütterung *f*.
shod [∫ɔd] *pret. u. p.p. von* shoe 2.
shod·dy ['∫ɔdi] **1.** Reißwolle *f*; *fig.*
Schund *m*, Kitsch *m*; **2.** unecht,
falsch; minderwertig; kitschig.
shoe [∫u:] **1.** Schuh *m*; Hufeisen *n*;
Beschlag *m*; Hemmschuh *m*;
2. (*irr.*) beschuhen; beschlagen;
'**~black** Schuhputzer *m*; '**~black-
ing** Schuhwichse *f*; '**~horn**
Schuhanzieher *m*; '**~-lace** Schnürsenkel *m*; '**~mak·er** Schuhmacher
m; '**~string** Schnürsenkel *m*; *on
a* ~ F mit ein paar Groschen; '**~tree**
Schuhspanner *m*.
shone [∫ɔn] *pret. u. p.p. von* shine 2.
shoo [∫u:] *Vögel* scheuchen.
shook [∫uk] *pret. von* shake 1.
shoot [∫u:t] **1.** *fig.* Schuß *m* (*schnelle
Bewegung*); 🌱 Schößling *m*; Jagd*f*;
Rutsche *f*; Stromschnelle *f*; **2.** (*irr.*)
v/t. schießen; abschießen, ab-
feuern; werfen, stoßen; *Film* aufnehmen, drehen; durchschießen;
fig. unter *e*-*r Brücke etc.* hindurch-,
über *et.* hinwegschießen; ⚓ treiben;
Riegel vorschieben; *Müll, Karren*
ausschütten; *Faß* schroten; ⚕
(ein)spritzen; *v/i.* schießen (*at*
nach); stechen (*Schmerz, Glied*);
fliegen, daherschießen; stürzen;
fallen; *a.* ~ *forth* sprossen, ausschlagen; ⚓ überschießen (*Ballast*); ~ *ahead* vorwärtsschießen;
~ *ahead of* überholen, hinter sich
lassen; ~ *up* emporschnellen;
'**shoot·er** Schütze *m*.
shoot·ing ['∫u:tiŋ] **1.** Schießen *n*;
Schießerei *f*; Jagd *f*; Jagdrecht *n*;
Film: Dreharbeiten *f*/*pl.*; **2.** stechend (*Schmerz*); '**~-box** Jagd-
häuschen *n*; '**~-brake** Jagdwagen
m; Kombiwagen *m*; '**~-gal·ler·y**

Schießstand *m*, -bude *f*; '~-**range** Schießplatz *m*; ~ **star** Sternschnuppe *f*; '~-**war** heißer Krieg *m*.

shoot-out F ['ʃuːtaut] Schießerei *f*.

shop [ʃɔp] **1.** Laden *m*, Geschäft *n*; Werkstatt *f*, Betrieb *m*; *set up* ~ ein Geschäft eröffnen; *talk* ~ fachsimpeln; **2.** *mst go* ~*ping* einkaufen gehen; '~-**as·sist·ant** Verkäufer(in); ~ **floor** Produktionsstätte *f*; *fig.* Arbeiter *m/pl.* (*Ggs. management*); '~-**keep·er** Ladeninhaber(in); Krämer *m*; '~-**lift·er** Ladendieb *m*; '~-**man** Ladengehilfe *m*; '**shop·per** Käufer (-in); '**shop·ping** Einkaufen *n*; Einkaufs...; ~ *centre*, *Am.* ~ *center* Einkaufszentrum *n*.

shop...: '~-**soiled** angestaubt (*Ware*); '~-'**stew·ard** Betriebsobmann *m der Gewerkschaft*; '~-**walk·er** Aufsichtsherr *m*, -dame *f in großen Geschäften*; '~-'**win-dow** Schaufenster *n*.

shore¹ [ʃɔ:] Küste *f*, Gestade *n*, Ufer *n*; Strand *m*; *on* ~ an Land.

shore² [~] **1.** Stütze *f*, Strebe *f*; **2.** ~ *up* (ab)stützen.

shore...: '~-**line** Küstenlinie *f*; '~-**ward** ['~wəd] küstenwärts (gelegen).

shorn [ʃɔ:n] *p.p. von shear* 1; ~ *of e-r Sache* beraubt.

short [ʃɔ:t] **1.** kurz; klein (*Figur*); knapp; mürbe (*Gebäck*); brüchig (*Metall*); kurz angebunden, wortkarg; ✝ kurzfristig; *s. circuit*; ~ *wave Radio:* Kurzwelle *f*; *in* ~ kurz(um); ~ *of* knapp *an* (*dat.*), ohne; abgesehen von; *nothing* ~ *of* nichts als; geradezu; ~ *of London* kurz vor London; ~ *of lying* ehe ich lüge; *come od. fall* ~ *of* nicht erreichen, es fehlen lassen an (*dat.*); unter *dat.* bleiben; *cut* ~ plötzlich unterbrechen; *fall od. run* ~ ausgehen (*Vorräte*); *stop* ~ *of* innehalten vor (*dat.*); **2.** *gr.* kurzer Vokal *m*, kurze Silbe *f*; Kurzfilm *m*; ⚡ Kurzschluß *m*; *s. shorts*; ~*circuit*; '**short·age** Fehlbetrag *m*; Gewichtsverlust *m*, Abgang *m*; Mangel *m*, Knappheit *f*.

short...: '~-**cake** Mürbekuchen *m*; ~-'**change** F *j-m* zu wenig (Wechselgeld) herausgeben; '~-'**cir·cuit** ⚡ kurzschließen; ~-'**com·ing** Unzulänglichkeit *f*; Fehler *m*; Mangel *m*; ~ **cut** Abkürzungsweg *m*; '~-'**dat·ed** ✝

auf kurze Sicht; '**short·en** *v/t.* ab-, verkürzen; *v/i.* kürzer werden; '**short·en·ing** Backfett *n*.

short...: '~-'**fall** Fehlbetrag *m*; '~-**hand** Kurzschrift *f*, Stenographie *f*; ~ *typist* Stenotypistin *f*; '~-'**hand·ed** knapp an Arbeitskräften; ~ **list** Auswahlliste *f*; *be on the* ~ in der engeren Wahl sein; '~-**list** in die engere Wahl ziehen; '~-'**lived** kurzlebig, von kurzer Dauer; '**short·ly** *adv.* kurz; in Kürze, bald; '**short·ness** Kürze *f*; Mangel *m*; **short or·der** *Am.* Schnellgericht *n im Restaurant*; '**short-range** Kurzstrecken..., Nah...; *fig.* kurzfristig.

shorts [ʃɔ:ts] *pl.* Shorts *pl.*, kurze Hose *f*.

short...: '~-'**sight·ed** kurzsichtig; '~-'**tem·pered** aufbrausend, reizbar; '~-**term** kurzfristig; ~ **time** Kurzarbeit *f*; *be on* ~ Kurzarbeit haben; '~-**wave** *Radio:* Kurzwellen...; '~-'**wind·ed** kurzatmig.

shot¹ [ʃɔt] **1.** *pret. u. p.p. von shoot* 2; **2.** *adj.* schillernd (*Seide*).

shot² [~] Schuß *m*; Geschoß *n*, Kugel *f*; *a. small* ~ Schrot *n*; *pl. mst* ~ Schrotkorn *n*; Schütze *m*; *Sport:* Stoß *m*, Schlag *m*, Wurf *m*; *phot., Film:* Aufnahme *f*; 💉 Einspritzung *f*, Spritze *f*; *sl.* Schuß *m Rum etc.*; *have a* ~ *at* et. versuchen; *not by a long* ~ F noch lange nicht; *within* (*out of*) ~ in (außer) Schußweite; *like a* ~ F wie aus der Pistole geschossen; *big* ~ F großes Tier *n*; *Bonze m*; *make a bad* ~ fehlschießen; (*fig. falsch raten*); '~-**gun** Schrotflinte *f*; ~ *marriage Am.* F Mußheirat *f*; '~-'**proof** kugelfest; '~-**put** Kugelstoßen *n*.

shot·ten her·ring ['ʃɔtn'heriŋ] Hohlhering *m*.

should [ʃud] *pret. von shall.*

shoul·der ['ʃəuldə] **1.** Schulter *f* (*a. von Tieren*; *fig. Vorsprung*); Achsel *f*; *give s.o. the cold* ~ j. über die Achsel ansehen; *put one's* ~ *to the wheel* sich tüchtig ins Zeug legen; *rub* ~*s with* in Berührung kommen mit; ~ *to* ~ Schulter an Schulter; **2.** auf die Schulter (*fig. auf sich*) nehmen; 🪖 schultern; drängen; ~ *one's way* sich e-n Weg bahnen; '~-**bag** Umhäng(e)tasche *f*; '~-**blade** *anat.* Schulterblatt *n*; '~-**strap** Träger *m am Kleid*; 🪖 Schulter-, Achselstück *n*.

shout [ʃaut] **1.** lauter Schrei *m od.* Ruf *m*; Geschrei *n*; **2.** laut schreien *od.* rufen; jauchzen.

shove [ʃʌv] **1.** Schub *m*, Stoß *m*; **2.** schieben, stoßen.

shov·el [ˈʃʌvl] **1.** Schaufel *f*; **2.** schaufeln; '**~-board** Beilketafel *f*; Beilkespiel *n*.

show [ʃou] **1.** (*irr.*) *v/t.* zeigen; ausstellen; *Gnade etc.* erweisen; *Gründe* angeben; beweisen; **~** *forth* darlegen; **~** *in* hereinführen; **~** *off* zur Geltung bringen; **~** *out* hinausgeleiten; **~** *round* herumführen; **~** *up* hinaufführen; bloßstellen, entlarven; *v/i. a.* **~** *up* sich zeigen, erscheinen; zu sehen sein; **~** *off* angeben, prahlen, sich aufspielen; **2.** Schau(stellung) *f*; Ausstellung *f*; Auf-, Vorführung *f*; Anschein *m*, Anblick *m*; *sl.* Sache *f*, Geschichte *f*; **~** *of hands* Handzeichen *n bei Abstimmungen*; *dumb* **~** Pantomime *f*, Gebärdenspiel *n*; *on* **~** zu besichtigen; *run the* **~** *sl.* den Laden schmeißen; **~** **busi·ness** Unterhaltungsindustrie *f*; Schaugeschäft *n*; '**~-card** Geschäftsanzeige *f*; '**~-case** Schaukasten *m*, Vitrine *f*; '**~-down** Aufdecken *n* der Karten (*a. fig.*); *fig.* Kraftprobe *f*.

show·er [ˈʃaua] **1.** (Regen-, Hagel-) Schauer *m*; Dusche *f*; *fig.* Fülle *f*, Menge *f*; **2.** herabschütten (*a. fig.*); übergießen, -schütten (*with* mit); sich ergießen; **~-bath** [ˈ~bɑ:θ] Brausebad *n*, Dusche *f*; '**show·er·y** regnerisch; Regen...

show·i·ness [ˈʃouinis] Gepränge *n*; Auffälligkeit *f*; '**show·man** Zirkus-, Varietéunternehmer *m*; j., der sich *od. et.* in Szene zu setzen versteht; '**show·man·ship** Kunst *f*, sich *od. et.* in Szene zu setzen; **shown** [ʃoun] *p.p. von show* 1; '**show·piece** Schau-, Paradestück *n*; '**show-place** Sehenswürdigkeit *f*; '**show-room** Ausstellungsraum *m*; '**show-win·dow** Schaufenster *n*; '**show·y** □ prächtig; prunkhaft; auffällig.

shrank [ʃræŋk] *pret. von shrink*.

shrap·nel ✕ [ˈʃræpnl] Schrapnell *n*.

shred [ʃred] **1.** Stückchen *n*; Schnitz(el *n*) *m*; Fetzen *m* (*a. fig.*); **2.** (*irr.*) (zer)schnitzeln; zerfetzen; ausfasern; **~ded** *wheat* fertige Frühstücksnahrung *f* aus Weizen.

shrew [ʃru:] zänkisches Weib *n*; *a.* **~-mouse** *zo.* Spitzmaus *f*.

shrewd □ [ʃru:d] scharfsinnig, klug, schlau; '**shrewd·ness** Scharfsinn *m*, Schlauheit *f*.

shrew·ish □ [ˈʃru:iʃ] zänkisch.

shriek [ʃri:k] **1.** (Angst)Schrei *m*; Gekreisch *n*; *fig.* Pfeifen *n*; **2.** kreischen, schreien.

shrift [ʃrift]: *give s.o. short* **~** mit j-m kurzen Prozeß machen, j. kurz abfertigen.

shrike *orn.* [ʃraik] Würger *m*.

shrill [ʃril] **1.** □ schrill, gellend; **2.** schrillen, gellen; schreien.

shrimp *zo.* [ʃrimp] Garnele *f*, Krabbe *f*; *fig.* Knirps *m*.

shrine [ʃrain] (Reliquien)Schrein *m*; Altar *m*.

shrink [ʃriŋk] (*irr.*) *v/i.* (ein-, zs.-) schrumpfen; einlaufen (*Stoff*); sich zurückziehen; *a.* **~** *back* zurückschrecken (*from, at vor dat.*); *v/t.* einschrumpfen lassen; ⊕ Stoff krump(f)en, einlaufen lassen; '**shrink·age** Einlaufen *n*, Zs.-schrumpfen *n*; Schrumpfung *f*; *fig.* Verminderung *f*.

shriv·el [ˈʃrivl] *a.* **~** *up* einschrumpfen (lassen); *fig.* vergehen (lassen).

shroud[1] [ʃraud] **1.** Leichentuch *n*, Totenhemd *n*; *fig.* Gewand *n*, Umhüllung *f*; **2.** in ein Leichentuch einhüllen; *fig.* hüllen.

shroud[2] ⊕ [~] Want(tau *n*) *f*; *mst* **~s** *pl.* Wanten *f*/*pl.*

Shrove·tide [ˈʃrouvtaid] Fastnachtszeit *f*; **Shrove Tues·day** Fastnachtsdienstag *m*.

shrub [ʃrʌb] Staude *f*, Strauch *m*; Busch *m*; '**shrub·ber·y** Strauchpflanzung *f*; Gebüsch *n*; '**shrub·by** strauch(art)ig.

shrug [ʃrʌg] **1.** (die Achseln) zucken; **~** *s.th. off et.* abtun; **2.** Achselzucken *n*.

shrunk [ʃrʌŋk] *p.p. von shrink*; '**shrunk·en** *adj.* (ein)geschrumpft; eingefallen (*Wangen*).

shuck *Am.* [ʃʌk] **1.** Hülse *f*, Schote *f*; **~s!** F Quatsch!; **2.** enthülsen, -schoten.

shud·der [ˈʃʌdə] **1.** schaudern; (er-) beben; *2.* Schauder *m*; Erbeben *n*.

shuf·fle [ˈʃʌfl] **1.** *v/t.* schieben; *Karten* mischen; **~** *away* wegpraktizieren; **~** *off* von sich schieben; abstreifen; *v/i.* schieben, stoßen; *Karten*: mischen; schlurren, schlurfen; sich herauszureden suchen, Ausflüchte machen; ~ *through one's work* s-e Arbeit flüchtig tun, pfuschen; **2.** Schieben *n*; Mischen *n der Karten*; Schlurfen *n*; *pol.* Umbesetzung *f*; Schiebung *f*; '**shuffler** Mischer *m*; Ausflüchtemacher *m*, Schwindler *m*; '**shuf·fling** □ schleppend (*Gang*); ausweichend; unredlich.

shun [ʃʌn] (ver)meiden.

shunt [ʃʌnt] **1.** ⛭ Rangieren *n*; ⛭ Weiche *f*; ⚡ Nebenschluß *m*; **2.** ⛭ rangieren, verschieben *od.* (*v/i.*) verschoben werden; ⚡ nebenschließen; *fig.* ver-, aufschieben; '**shunt·er** ⛭ Rangierer *m*; '**shunt·ing sta·tion** ⛭ Verschiebe-, Rangierbahnhof *m*.

shut [ʃʌt] (*irr.*) *v/t.* (ver)schließen, zumachen; ~ *one's eyes* to die Augen verschließen vor; ~ *down Betrieb* schließen, stillegen; ~ *in* einschließen; *Finger etc.* einklemmen in (*acc.*); ~ *out* ausschließen; ~ *up* ein-, verschließen; einsperren; ~ *up shop* das Geschäft schließen; *v/i.* sich schließen, zugehen; ~ *up!* F halt den Mund!; '~·**down** Betriebsschließung *f*, Stillegung *f*; '~·**out** *Sport*: Zu-Null-Niederlage *f*; '**shut·ter** Fensterladen *m*; *phot.* Verschluß *m*; ~ *speed phot.* Belichtungszeit *f*; *put up the* ~s den Laden dicht machen, schließen; *rolling* ~ Rolladen *m*.

shut·tle ['ʃʌtl] **1.** Weberschiff *n*; Schiffchen *n der Nähmaschine*; ⛭ *etc.* Pendelverkehr *m*; ~ *diplomacy pol.* Pendeldiplomatie *f*; ~ *service* Pendelverkehr *m*; ~ *train* Pendelzug *m*; **2.** *Verkehr*: pendeln; '~·**cock** Federball(spiel *n*) *m*.

shy[1] [ʃai] **1.** □ scheu; schüchtern; *be od.* fight ~ *of* sich scheuen *od.* hüten vor (*dat.*); **2.** (zurück)scheuen (*at* vor *dat.*).

shy[2] F [~] **1.** werfen; **2.** Wurf *m*; Hieb *m*; *have a* ~ *at* e-n Versuch machen mit.

shy·ness ['ʃainis] Schüchternheit *f*; Scheu *f*.

shy·ster *bsd. Am. sl.* ['ʃaistə] gerissener Kerl *m*; Winkeladvokat *m*.

Si·a·mese [saiə'mi:z] **1.** siamesisch; **2.** Siamese *m*, Siamesin *f*; Siamesisch *n*.

Si·be·ri·an [sai'biəriən] **1.** sibirisch; **2.** Sibirier(in).

sib·i·lant ['sibilənt] **1.** □ zischend; **2.** *gr.* Zischlaut *m*.

sib·yl ['sibil] Sibylle *f*, Seherin *f*; Wahrsagerin *f*; **sib'yl·line** [~lain] sibyllinisch.

Si·cil·ian [si'siljən] **1.** sizilianisch; **2.** Sizilianer(in).

sick [sik] krank (*of an dat.*; *with* vor *dat.*); (zum Erbrechen) übel, unwohl; überdrüssig (*of gen.*); *be* ~ *for* sich sehnen nach; *be* ~ *of* genug haben von; *go* ~, *report* ~ sich krank melden; '~·**bay** Lazarett *n*, Krankenrevier *n*; '~·**bed** Krankenbett *n*; '**sick·en** *v/i.* krank werden; kränkeln; ~ *at* sich ekeln vor (*dat.*); ~ *of* (*ger.*) es müde *od.* überdrüssig werden zu (*inf.*); *v/t.* krank machen; anekeln.

sick·le ['sikl] Sichel *f*.

sick-leave ['sikli:v] Krankheitsurlaub *m*; '**sick·li·ness** Kränklichkeit *f*; Ungesundheit *f des Klimas etc.*; '**sick·ly** kränklich; schwächlich; bleich, blaß; ungesund (*Klima etc.*); widerlich (*Geruch etc.*); matt (*Lächeln etc.*).

sick·ness ['siknis] Krankheit *f*; Übelkeit *f*; ~ **ben·e·fit** Krankengeld *n*.

sick pay ['sik'pei] Krankengeld *n*.

side [said] **1.** *allg.* Seite *f*; Ufer *n*, Rand *m*; Flanke *f* e-s *Berges*; Partei *f*; ~ *by* ~ Seite an Seite, nebeneinander; *fig.* daneben; *by one's* ~ zur Seite; ~ *by* ~ *with* neben; *at od. by s.o.'s* ~ an j-s Seite; *put on* ~ F angeben; **2.** Seiten...; Neben...; **3.** Partei ergreifen (*with* für); '~·**arms** *pl.* ⚔ Seitengewehre *n/pl.*; '~·**board** Anrichte(tisch *m*) *f*; Sideboard *n*; ~·**burns** *Am.* ['~bə:nz] *pl.* Koteletten *n/pl.* (*Backenbart*); '~·**car** *mot.* Beiwagen *m*; '**sid·ed** ...seitig.

side...: ~ **ef·fect** Nebenwirkung *f*; '~·**face** Seitenansicht *f*, Profil *n*; ~ **is·sue** Nebenfrage *f*, Randproblem *n*; '~·**kick** F Kumpel *m*; Gehilfe *m*; '~·**light** Seiten-, *fig.* Streiflicht *n*; '~·**line** ⛭ Nebenbahn *f*; Nebenbeschäftigung *f*; '~·**long** **1.** *adv.* seitwärts; **2.** *adj.* seitlich; Seiten...; *fig.* versteckt (*Lächeln etc.*).

si·de·re·al *ast.* [sai'diəriəl] siderisch; Stern(en)...

side...: '~·**road** Seiten-, Nebenstraße

side-saddle

f; '**~·sad·dle** Damensattel *m*; '**~·slip** ✂ seitlich abrutschen; *mot.* schleudern; **sides·man** ['~zmən] Kirchendiener *m*.

side...: '**~·split·ting** zwerchfellerschütternd; '**~·step** 1. Schritt *m* zur Seite; 2. beiseite treten; *e-r Sache* ausweichen; '**~·street** = side-road; '**~·stroke** Seitenschwimmen *n*; '**~·track** 1. 🚂 Nebengleis *n*; 2. auf ein Nebengleis schieben; *bsd. Am. fig.* zur Seite schieben; '**~·walk** *bsd. Am.* Bürgersteig *m*, Gehweg *m*; **side·ward** ['~wəd] 1. *adj.* seitlich; 2. *adv.* = side·wards ['~wədz], '**side·ways**, '**side·wise** seitwärts.

sid·ing 🚂 ['saidiŋ] Ausweichstelle *f*; Nebengleis *n*.

si·dle ['saidl] seitwärts *od.* mit der Seite voran gehen.

siege [si:dʒ] Belagerung *f*; *lay* ~ *to* belagern. [kette *f*.]

si·er·ra ['siərə] Sierra *f*, Gebirgs]

sieve [siv] 1. Sieb *n*; 2. (durch-)sieben.

sift [sift] sieben; *fig.* sichten; prüfen.

sift·er ['siftə] Sieber(in); Sichter (-in); Sieb *n*.

sigh [sai] 1. Seufzer *m*; 2. seufzen; sich sehnen (*for, after* nach).

sight [sait] 1. Sehvermögen *n*, -kraft *f*; *fig.* Auge *n*; Ansicht *f*, Anblick *m*; Schauspiel *n*; Visier *n am Gewehr*; Sicht *f*; F Masse *f*, Menge *f* (*sehr viel*); ~s *pl.* Sehenswürdigkeiten *f/pl.*; *second* ~ zweites Gesicht *n*, Hellsehen *n*; *at od. on* ~ beim Anblick; ♪ vom Blatt; ✝ nach Sicht; *catch* ~ *of* erblicken, zu Gesicht bekommen; *lose* ~ *of* aus den Augen verlieren; *within* ~ in Sicht; *out of* ~ aus den Augen; *außer Sicht*; *take* ~ visieren; *not by a long* ~ bei weitem nicht; *know by* ~ vom Sehen kennen; 2. *v/t.* sichten; anvisieren; *v/i.* visieren; '**sight·ed** ...sichtig; '**sight·ing-line** Visierlinie *f*; '**sight·less** blind; '**sight·li·ness** Ansehnlich-, Stattlichkeit *f*; '**sight·ly** ansehnlich, stattlich.

sight...: '**~·read** (*irr. read*) ♪ vom Blatt spielen *od.* singen; '**~·see·ing** Besuchen *n* von Sehenswürdigkeiten; '**~·see·er** Tourist(in); '**~·sing·ing** ♪ (Vom)Blattsingen *n*.

sign [sain] 1. (Kenn-, Vor)Zeichen *n*; Wink *m*; (Aushänge)Schild *n*;

in ~ *of* zum Zeichen (*gen.*); 2. *v/i.* winken, Zeichen geben; ~ *on* (*off*) *Radio:* (*mit e-r Melodie*) den Beginn (das Ende) e-r Sendung ankündigen; *v/t.* (unter)zeichnen, unterschreiben; ~ *on* (*v/i.* sich) vertraglich verpflichten.

sig·nal ['signl] 1. Signal *n*; Zeichen *n*; ~s *pl.* ✕ Fernmeldetruppe *f*; *busy* ~ *teleph.* Besetztzeichen *n*; 2. ☐ bemerkenswert, außerordentlich; 3. signalisieren; *j-m* Zeichen geben; melden; anzeigen; '**~·box** 🚂 Stellwerk *n*; **sig·nal·ize** ['~nəlaiz] bemerkenswert machen, auszeichnen; = *signal* 3; '**sig·nal·man** 🚂 Bahnwärter *m*; Funker *m*.

sig·na·to·ry ['signətəri] 1. Unterzeichner *m*, Signatar *m*; 2. unterzeichnend; *powers* ~ *to an agreement* Signatarmächte *f/pl.* e-s Abkommens.

sig·na·ture ['signitʃə] Signatur (*a. typ.*, ♪, ✝); Unterschrift *f*; ~ *tune Radio:* Kennmelodie *f*.

sign·board ['sainbɔ:d] (Aushänge-)Schild *n*; '**sign·er** Unterzeichner (-in). [Siegelring *m*.]

sig·net ['signit] Siegel *n*; '**~·ring**]

sig·nif·i·cance, **sig·nif·i·can·cy** [sig'nifikəns(i)] Bedeutung *f*; Wichtigkeit *f*; **sig'nif·i·cant** ☐ bedeutsam; bezeichnend (*of* für); **sig·ni·fi'ca·tion** Bedeutung *f*; **sig'nif·i·ca·tive** [~kətiv] bezeichnend (*of* für); bedeutsam.

sig·ni·fy ['signifai] bezeichnen, andeuten; kundgeben; bedeuten; *it does not* ~ es hat nichts auf sich.

si·gnor ['si:njɔ:] Signor *m*, Herr *m*; **si'gnor·a** [~rə] Signora *f*, Frau *f*; **si·gno·ri·na** [~'ri:nə] Signorina *f*, Fräulein *n*.

sign...: '**~·paint·er** Schildermaler *m*; '**~·post** Wegweiser *m*.

si·lage ['sailidʒ] Silofutter *n*.

si·lence ['sailəns] 1. (Still)Schweigen *n*; Stille *f*, Ruhe *f*; ~! Ruhe!; *put od. reduce to* ~ = 2. zum Schweigen bringen; '**si·lenc·er** ⊕ Schalldämpfer *m*; *mot.* Auspufftopf *m*.

si·lent ☐ ['sailənt] still; schweigend; schweigsam; stumm (*Buchstabe*); ~ *film* Stummfilm *m*; ~ *partner bsd. Am.* ✝ stiller Teilhaber *m*.

Si·le·sian [sai'li:zjən] 1. schlesisch; 2. Schlesier(in).

sil·hou·ette [silu:'et] **1.** Silhouette *f*; Schattenriß *m*; **2.** *be* ~*d against* sich abheben gegen.

sil·i·ca 🜍 ['silikə] Kieselerde *f*; Silikat *n*; **sil·i·cat·ed** ['~keitid] kieselsauer; **si'li·ceous** [~ʃəs] kieselartig; **sil·i·con** ['~kən] Silizium *n*; **sil·i·cone** ['~kəun] Silikon *n*; **sil·i·co·sis** ✚ [~'kəusis] Staublunge *f*.

silk [silk] **1.** Seide *f*; 👗 Seidentalar *m*; Kronanwalt *m*; *take* ~ Kronanwalt werden; **2.** Seiden...; **silk·en** □ seiden; *s. silky;* **'silk·i·ness** Seidenartigkeit *f*; **'silk-** **-'stock·ing** *Am.* vornehm; **'~-worm** Seidenraupe *f*; **'silk·y** □ seid(enart)ig; seidenweich.

sill [sil] Schwelle *f*; Fensterbrett *n*.

sil·li·ness ['silinis] Albernheit *f*.

sil·ly □ ['sili] albern, töricht, dumm; ~ *season* Sauregurkenzeit *f*.

si·lo ['sailəu] Futtersilo *m*.

silt [silt] **1.** Schlamm *m*; **2.** *mst* ~ *up* verschlammen.

sil·ver ['silvə] **1.** Silber *n* (*a. Silbergeld, -gerät u. fig.*); **2.** silbern; Silber...; **3.** versilbern; silberig *od.* silberweiß werden (lassen); **'~--'plate** ⊕ versilbern; **'~·ware** *Am.* Tafelsilber *n*; **'sil·ver·y** silberig; silberglänzend; *zo. u.* 🐟 Silber...; silberhell (*Stimme*).

sim·i·lar □ ['similə] ähnlich, gleich; **sim·i·lar·i·ty** [~'læriti] Ähnlichkeit *f*.

sim·i·le ['simili] Gleichnis *n*.

si·mil·i·tude [si'militju:d] Gestalt *f*; Ebenbild *n*; Gleichnis *n*.

sim·mer ['simə] sieden, brodeln (lassen); *fig.* gären (*Gefühl, Aufstand*); ~ *down* ruhig(er) werden.

Si·mon ['saimən] Simon *m*; *the real* ~ *Pure* F der wahre Jakob; *simple* ~ F Einfaltspinsel *m*; **si·mo·ny** ['~ni] Simonie *f*, Ämterkauf *m*.

si·moom *meteor.* [si'mu:m] Samum *m*.

sim·per ['simpə] **1.** einfältiges Lächeln *n*; **2.** einfältig lächeln.

sim·ple □ ['simpl] einfach; schlicht; einfältig; arglos; **'~--'heart·ed**, **'~-** **-'mind·ed** arglos, naiv; **sim·ple·ton** ['~tən] Einfaltspinsel *m*.

sim·plic·i·ty [sim'plisiti] Einfachheit *f*; Klarheit *f*, Schlichtheit *f*; Einfalt *f*; **sim·pli·fi·ca·tion** [~fi-

'keiʃən] Vereinfachung *f*; **sim·pli·fy** ['~fai] vereinfachen.

sim·ply ['simpli] *adv.* einfach *etc.* (*s. simple*); bloß, nur; schlechthin.

sim·u·late ['simjuleit] vortäuschen; (er)heucheln; *j-s* Aussehen annehmen, sich tarnen als; **sim·u'la·tion** Vortäuschung *f*; Heuchelei *f*; **'sim·u·la·tor** Simulator *m*, Übungsgerät *n*.

si·mul·ta·ne·i·ty [siməltə'niəti] Gleichzeitigkeit *f*.

si·mul·ta·ne·ous □ [siməl'teinjəs] gleichzeitig; **si·mul'ta·ne·ous·ness** Gleichzeitigkeit *f*.

sin [sin] **1.** Sünde *f*; **2.** sündigen.

since [sins] **1.** *prp.* seit; **2.** *adv.* seitdem; *long* ~ schon lange; *how long* ~? seit wann?; *a short time* ~ vor kurzem; **3.** *cj.* seit(dem); da (ja), weil.

sin·cere □ [sin'siə] aufrichtig; *Yours* ~*ly* Ihr ergebener; **sin·cer·i·ty** [~'seriti] Aufrichtigkeit *f*.

sine 🜔 [sain] Sinus *m*.

si·ne·cure ['sainikjuə] Sinekure *f*, Pfründe *f*.

sin·ew ['sinju:] Sehne *f*; *fig. mst* ~*s pl.* Nerv(kraft *f*) *m/pl.*; Seele *f*; **'sin·ew·y** sehnig; nervig, stark.

sin·ful □ ['sinful] sündig, sündhaft, böse; **'sin·ful·ness** Sündhaftigkeit *f*.

sing [siŋ] (*irr.*) singen (*fig. = dichten*); *j-, et.* besingen; summen (*Kessel*); klingen (*Ohr*); ~ *out* F laut rufen, schreien; ~ *small*, ~ *another song od. tune* kleinlaut werden, klein beigeben.

singe [sindʒ] (ver)sengen.

sing·er ['siŋə] Sänger(in).

sing·ing ['siŋiŋ] Gesang *m*, Singen *n*; ~ *bird* Singvogel *m*.

sin·gle ['siŋgl] **1.** □ einzig; einzeln; Einzel...; einfach; ledig, unverheiratet; ~ *bill* 🜍 Solawechsel *m*; ~ *combat* Zweikampf *m*; *bookkeeping by* ~ *entry* einfache Buchführung *f*; ~ *file* Gänsemarsch *m*; **2.** *Tennis:* Einzel(spiel) *n*; einfache Fahrkarte *f*; **3.** ~ *out* auswählen, -suchen; **'~--'breast·ed** einreihig (*Jacke etc.*); **'~--'en·gin·ed** 🜍 einmotorig (*Flugzeug*); **'~--'hand·ed** eigenhändig, allein; **'~--'heart·ed** □, **'~--'mind·ed** □ aufrichtig, grundehrlich; zielstrebig; **'~--'line** eingleisig; **'single-'seat·er** Einsitzer *m*; **'sin·gle-**

stick Stockrapier *n*; **sin·glet** ['siŋglit] Unterhemd *n*; **sin·gle·ton** ['ᴗtən] *Karten*: Singleton *m* (*einzige Karte e-r Farbe*); **'sin·gle·-'track** eingleisig; **'sin·gly** einzeln, allein.

sing·song ['siŋsɔŋ] Singsang *m*.

sin·gu·lar ['siŋgjulə] **1.** □ einzigartig, ungewöhnlich; eigenartig; sonderbar; *gr.* singularisch; **2.** *gr. a.* ᴗ *number* Singular *m*, Einzahl *f*; **sin·gu·lar·i·ty** [ᴗˈlæriti] Einzigartigkeit *f*; Sonderbarkeit *f*.

Sin·ha·lese [siŋhəˈliːz] **1.** singhalesisch; **2.** Singhalese *m*, Singhalesin *f*.

sin·is·ter □ ['sinistə] unheilvoll; unheimlich, finster.

sink [siŋk] **1.** (*irr.*) *v/i.* sinken; nieder-, unter-, versinken; sich senken; eindringen (*into* in *acc.*); erliegen (*beneath, under* unter *dat.*); *v/t.* (ver)senken; ⚒ abteufen; *Brunnen* bohren; *Schuld* abtragen; *Geld* festlegen; *et.* weglassen; *Namen, Anspruch* aufgeben; *Streit* beilegen; **2.** Senkgrube *f*; Ausguß *m in Küchen*; *fig.* Pfuhl *m*; **'sink·er** ⚒ Schachtarbeiter *m*; Senkblei *n*; **'sink·ing** Sinken *n etc.*; ⚓ Schwäche(gefühl *n*) *f*; ᴗ *fund* (Schulden-)Tilgungsfonds *m*.

sin·less ['sinlis] sündenlos, -frei.

sin·ner ['sinə] Sünder(in).

Sinn Fein ['ʃinˈfein] Sinn Fein *m* (*irische Partei*).

Sin·o... ['sinəu] chinesisch; China...; Chinesen...

sin·u·os·i·ty [sinjuˈɔsiti] Windung *f*, Krümmung *f*; **'sin·u·ous** □ gewunden, krumm (*a. fig.*).

si·nus *anat.* ['sainəs] Nebenhöhle *f*; **si·nus·i·tis** [ᴗˈsaitis] (Neben)Höhlenentzündung *f*.

Sioux [suː], *pl.* ᴗ [suːz] Sioux(indianer) *m*.

sip [sip] **1.** Schlückchen *n*; **2.** schlürfen; nippen; langsam trinken.

si·phon ['saifən] **1.** (Saug)Heber *m*, Siphon(flasche *f*) *m*; **2.** saugen.

sir [sə:] Herr *m* (*als Anrede*); ♀ Sir *m* (*Titel e-s baronet od. knight*).

sire ['saiə] *mst poet.* Vater *m*; Vorfahr *m*, Ahnherr *m*; *zo.* Vater(tier *n*) *m*; † Herr *m*, Gebieter *m*.

si·ren ['saiərən] Sirene *f*.

sir·loin ['sə:lɔin] Lendenstück *n*.

sir·rah *contp.* † ['sirə] Bursche *m*.

sir·up ['sirəp] Sirup *m*.

sis F [sis] *Kurzform für sister.*

sis·al ['saisəl] Sisal *m*.

sis·kin *orn.* ['siskin] Zeisig *m*.

sis·sy *Am.* ['sisi] Weichling *m*.

sis·ter ['sistə] Schwester *f*; (Ordens)Schwester *f*; Oberschwester *f im Krankenhaus*; ᴗ *of charity od.* mercy Barmherzige Schwester *f*; **sis·ter·hood** ['ᴗhud] Schwesternschaft *f*; **'sis·ter-in-law** Schwägerin *f*; **'sis·ter·ly** schwesterlich.

sit [sit] (*irr.*) *v/i.* sitzen; Sitzung halten, tagen; ᴗ *down* sich setzen; ᴗ-*down strike* Sitzstreik *m*; ᴗ (*up*)*on* untersuchen; F *j-m* aufs Dach steigen; ᴗ *up* aufrecht sitzen; aufbleiben; sich aufrichten; *make s.o.* ᴗ *up* j. aufrütteln; j. aufhorchen lassen; *v/t.* sitzen auf (*dat.*); ᴗ *a horse well* gut zu Pferde sitzen; ᴗ *s.th. out* e-r Sache bis zu Ende beiwohnen; ᴗ *s.o. out* länger bleiben *od.* aushalten als j.

sit·com F ['sitkɔm] Situationskomödie *f*.

site [sait] **1.** Lage *f*; (Bau)Platz *m*; **2.** legen.

sit·ter ['sitə] Sitzende *m, f*; Bruthenne *f*; *sl.* sichere Sache *f*; **'ᴗ-'in** Babysitter *m*.

sit·ting ['sitiŋ] Sitzung *f*; *at one* ᴗ in einem Zug; ᴗ *duck fig.* leichte Beute *f* (*Person*); **'ᴗ-room** Wohnzimmer *n*.

sit·u·ate ['sitjueit] *in e-e Lage* versetzen; **'sit·u·at·ed** gelegen; *be* ᴗ liegen, gelegen sein; *thus* ᴗ in dieser Lage; **sit·u·a·tion** Lage *f*; Stellung *f*, Stelle *f*.

six [siks] **1.** sechs; **2.** Sechs *f*; *be at* ᴗes *and sevens in* Verwirrung sein; **'ᴗ-fold** sechsfach; **'ᴗ-pence** Sixpence(stück *n*) *m*; **six·teen** ['ᴗˈtiːn] sechzehn; **six·teenth** ['ᴗ-ˈtiːnθ] **1.** sechzehnte(r, -s); **2.** Sechzehntel *n*; **sixth** [ᴗθ] **1.** sechste(r, -s); **2.** Sechstel *n*; **'sixth·ly** sechstens; **six·ti·eth** ['ᴗtiəθ] sechzigste(r, -s); **'six·ty 1.** sechzig; **2.** Sechzig *f*.

siz·a·ble □ ['saizəbl] ziemlich groß.

size[1] [saiz] **1.** Größe *f*, Umfang *m*; Format *n*; *Schuh- etc.* Nummer *f*; **2.** nach der Größe ordnen; ᴗ *up* F *j.* abschätzen; **sized** von ... Größe.

size[2] [ᴗ] **1.** Leim *m*; **2.** leimen.

size·a·ble □ ['saizəbl] = *sizable.*

siz·zle ['sizl] zischen; knistern; brutzeln; *sizzling hot* glühend heiß.

skate [skeit] **1.** Schlittschuh *m*; ~board Skateboard *n*, Rollerbrett *n* (*Sportgerät*); roller-~ Rollschuh *m*; **2.** Schlittschuh *od.* Rollschuh laufen; '**skat·er** Schlittschuh-, Rollschuhläufer(in); '**skat·ing-rink** Eisbahn *f*; Rollschuhbahn *f*.

ske·dad·dle F [ski'dædl] türmen, ausreißen, abhauen.

skein [skein] Strähne *f Garn etc.*

skel·e·ton ['skelitn] **1.** Skelett *n*; Gerippe *n*; Gestell *n e-s Schirms etc.*; *Sport*: Skeleton *m* (*Schlitten*); ✗ Stammtruppe *f*; ~ in the cupboard (*Am. closet*) *fig.* dunkler Punkt *m*, streng gehütetes (Familien)Geheimnis *n*; **2.** Skelett...; im Entwurf, skizziert; ✗ Stamm...; ~ crew Notbelegschaft *f*, Restmannschaft *f*; ~ key Nachschlüssel *m*, Dietrich *m*.

skep·tic ['skeptik] = sceptic.

sketch [sketʃ] **1.** Skizze *f*; Entwurf *m*; Auf-, Umriß *m*; **2.** skizzieren, entwerfen; '**sketch·y** □ skizzenhaft.

skew [skju:] schief; schräg.

skew·er ['skuə] **1.** Speiler *m*, Fleischspieß *m*; **2.** aufspeilern.

ski [ski:] **1.** *pl. a.* ~ Schi *m*, Ski *m*; **2.** Schi *od.* Ski laufen.

skid [skid] **1.** Hemmschuh *m*, Bremsklotz *m*; ✗ (Gleit)Kufe *f*; Rutschen *n*; *mot.* Schleudern *n*; **2.** *v/t.* hemmen; *v/i.* ausrutschen, gleiten; *mot.* schleudern; ✗ abrutschen; ~ **mark** *mot.* Bremsspur *f*; ~ **row** F Pennergegend *f*; be on ~ Penner sein.

ski·er ['ski:ə] Schiläufer(in), Skiläufer(in).

skiff ⚓ [skif] Nachen *m*; Skiff *n* (*Rennboot*).

ski·ing ['ski:iŋ] Schilauf(en *n*) *m*, Skilauf(en *n*) *m*; '**ski-jump** Skisprung *m*, Schisprung *m*; Sprungschanze *f*; '**ski-jump·ing** Skispringen *n*, Schispringen *n*.

skil·ful □ ['skilful] geschickt, gewandt; kundig; '**skil·ful·ness**, **skill** [skil] Geschicklichkeit *f*, Fertigkeit *f*.

skilled [skild] geschickt; gelernt; ~ worker Facharbeiter *m*.

skil·let ['skilit] Tiegel *m*, Kasserolle *f*.

skill·ful ['skilful] *etc. Am. für skilful.*

skim [skim] **1.** *a.* ~ off abschöpfen;

Milch abrahmen; dahingleiten über (*acc.*); überfliegen (*flüchtig lesen*); ~ through durchblättern; **2.** ~ milk Magermilch *f*; '**skim·mer** Schaumlöffel *m*.

skimp [skimp] *j.* knapp halten; sparen (mit *et.*); '**skimp·y** □ knapp, dürftig.

skin [skin] **1.** Haut *f* (*a.* ⚓); Fell *n*; Pelz *m*; *Ballon*-Hülle *f*; Schale *f*, Hülse *f*; *Wein- etc.* Schlauch *m*; by *od.* with the ~ of one's teeth mit knapper Not; have a thick (thin) ~ ein dickes Fell haben (empfindlich sein); **2.** *v/t.* (ent)häuten; abbalgen; schälen; F betrügen (of um); ~ off F *Strumpf etc.* abstreifen; keep one's eyes ~ned F die Augen offenhalten; *v/i. a.* ~ over zuheilen; '~-'**deep** (nur) oberflächlich; '~-**div·ing** Sporttauchen *n*; '~-**flick** *sl.* Sexfilm *m*; '~-**flint** Knicker *m*; '~-**graft·ing** ✚ Hauttransplantation *f*; '**skin·ner** Kürschner *m*; '**skin·ny** häutig; mager; F knickerig; '**skin·ny-dip** *Am.* F nackt baden.

skint P [skint] pleite, blank.

skin·tight ['skintait] hauteng.

skip [skip] **1.** Sprung *m*; ✗ Förderkorb *m*; **2.** *v/i.* hüpfen, springen; seilhüpfen; *v/t. a.* ~ over überspringen; '~-**jack** Stehaufmännchen *n*; *zo.* Springkäfer *m*.

skip·per[1] ['skipə] Hüpfer(in).

skip·per[2] [~] ⚓ Schiffer *m*, Kapitän *m*; F *Sport*: Mannschaftsführer *m*.

skip·ping-rope ['skipiŋrəup] Springseil *n*.

skir·mish ✗ ['skə:miʃ] **1.** Scharmützel *n*; **2.** plänkeln; '**skir·mish·er** Plänkler *m*.

skirt [skə:t] **1.** (Damen)Rock *m*; (Rock-, Hemd)Schoß *m*; *oft* ~s *pl.* Rand *m*, Saum *m*; **2.** *v/t.* umsäumen; *v/t. u. v/i. a.* ~ along (sich) entlangziehen (an *dat.*); entlangfahren; '**skirt·ing-board** Fuß-, Scheuerleiste *f*.

ski-run ['skirʌn] Skipiste *f*.

skit[1] [skit] Stichelei *f*, Hieb *m* (at gegen); Satire *f* (on, upon auf *acc.*).

skit[2] F [~] Haufen *m*, Masse *f*.

skit·tish □ ['skitiʃ] ungebärdig (*bsd. Pferd*); ausgelassen; mutwillig.

skit·tle ['skitl] Kegel *m*; play (at) ~s Kegel schieben; '~-**al·ley** Kegelbahn *f*.

skive F [skaiv] blaumachen; schwänzen; **'skiv·er** F Drückeberger *m*.

skiv·vy F *contp.* ['skivi] Besen *m* (*Dienstmädchen*).

skul·dug·er·y *Am.* F [skʌl'dʌgəri] Gemeinheit *f*, Schuftigkeit *f*.

skulk [skʌlk] schleichen; sich verstecken; lauern; sich um *et.* drükken; **'skulk·er** Drückeberger *m*.

skull [skʌl] Schädel *m*; ~ and cross--bones Totenkopf *m*; have a thick ~ dumm sein.

skunk [skʌŋk] *zo.* Stinktier *n*; Skunk *m* (*Pelz*); F Schuft *m*.

sky [skai] *oft* skies *pl.* Himmel *m*; Himmelsstrich *m*; *praise to the skies fig.* in den Himmel heben; **'~·blue** himmelblau; **'~·div·ing** *Sport:* Fallschirmspringen *n*; **'~·jack** im Flugzeug entführen; **'~·lark** 1. *orn.* Feldlerche *f*; 2. Ulk treiben; **'~·light** Oberlicht *n*; Dachfenster *n*; **'~·line** Horizont(linie *f*) *m*; Silhouette *f*; **'~·rock·et** F steil ansteigen, emporschnellen; **'~·scrap·er** Wolkenkratzer *m*, Hochhaus *n*; **sky'ward(s)** ['~wəd(z)] himmelwärts; **'sky-writ·ing** ✈ Himmelsschrift *f*.

slab [slæb] Platte *f*, Tafel *f*; Scheibe *f*; Streifen *m*; Fliese *f*; ⊕ Holzschwarte *f*.

slack [slæk] 1. schlaff; lose, locker; (nach)lässig; ✝ flau; ~ water ⚓ Stillwasser *n*; 2. ⚓ Lose *n* (*loses Tauende*); ✝ Flaute *f*; Kohlengrus *m*; *s.* ~s; 3. = ~en; = slake; F trödeln; **'slack·en** schlaff machen *od.* werden; verringern; *Tau etc.* nachlassen (*a.* v/i.); (sich) lockern; (sich) entspannen; (sich) verlangsamen; **'slack·er** F Drückeberger *m*; Faulenzer *m*; **'slack·ness** Schlaffheit *f etc.*; **slacks** *pl.* Damenhose *f*.

slag [slæg] Schlacke *f*; **'slag·gy** schlackig; **'slag-heap** Schlackenhalde *f*.

slain [slein] *p.p. von* slay.

slake [sleik] *Durst, Kalk* löschen; *Sehnsucht etc.* stillen.

sla·lom ['sleiləm] *Sport:* Slalom *m*, Torlauf *m*.

slam [slæm] 1. Zuschlagen *n*; Knall *m*; *Bridge, Whist:* Schlemm *m*; 2. *Tür etc.* zuschlagen, -knallen; *et. auf den Tisch etc.* knallen.

slan·der ['slɑ:ndə] 1. Verleumdung *f*; 2. verleumden; **'slan·der·er** Verleumder(in); **'slan·der·ous** □ verleumderisch.

slang [slæŋ] 1. Slang *m*, *n*; Berufssprache *f*; lässige Umgangssprache *f*; 2. *j.* wüst beschimpfen; ~ing match wüste gegenseitige Beschimpfungen *f/pl.*; **'slang·y** □ Slang...; vulgär.

slant [slɑ:nt] 1. schräge Fläche *f*; Abhang *m*; Neigung *f*; *Am.* F Einstellung *f*; Sicht *f*; 2. v/t. schräg legen; v/i. schräg liegen, sich neigen; **'slant·ing** □ *adj.*, **'slant·wise** *adv.* schief, schräg.

slap [slæp] 1. Klaps *m*, Schlag *m*; ~ in the face Ohrfeige *f* (*a. fig.*); 2. klapsen; schlagen; klatschen; 3. direkt, geradewegs, stracks; **'~-bang** Knall u. Fall; **'~·dash** hastig, übereilt, ungestüm; *adv. a.* Hals über Kopf; **'~·jack** *Am. Art* Pfannkuchen *m*; **'~·stick** *thea.* (Narren)Pritsche *f*; *a.* ~ comedy Posse *f*, Burleske *f*; **'~-up** F piekfein, erstklassig.

slash [slæʃ] 1. Hieb *m*; Schnitt *m*; Schlitz *m in e-m Kleid*; 2. v/t. (auf-) schlitzen; einschlagen auf (*acc.*); peitschen; Schlitze machen in (*acc.*); *fig.* geißeln, *Buch etc.* verreißen (*Kritiker*); F *Gehalt* drastisch kürzen; v/i. schlagen, hauen (*at* nach); **'slash·ing** □ scharf, vernichtend (*Kritik*).

slat [slæt] Lamelle *f e-r Jalousie*.

slate [sleit] 1. Schiefer *m*; Schiefertafel *f*; *bsd. Am.* Kandidatenliste *f*; *start with a clean* ~ e-n neuen Anfang machen; 2. mit Schiefer decken; heftig kritisieren; *Am.* F *für e-n Posten* vorschlagen; **'~-'pen·cil** Schieferstift *m*, Griffel *m*; **'slat·er** Schieferdecker *m*; **'slat·ing** heftige Kritik *f*.

slat·tern ['slætə:n] Schlampe *f*; **'slat·tern·ly** schlampig.

slat·y □ ['sleiti] schieferig.

slaugh·ter ['slɔ:tə] 1. Schlachten *n von Vieh*; *fig.* Hinschlachten *n*, Morden *n*; Gemetzel *n*, Blutbad *n*; 2. Schlacht...; 3. schlachten; niedermetzeln; **'slaugh·ter·er** Schlächter *m*; Mörder *m*; **'slaughter-house** Schlachthaus *n*; **'slaughter·ous** □ *rhet.* mörderisch.

Slav [slɑ:v] 1. Slawe *m*, Slawin *f*; 2. slawisch.

slave [sleiv] 1. Sklave *m*, Sklavin *f* (*a. fig.*); ~ driver *a. fig.* Sklaventreiber *m*; 2. sich placken, schuften.

slav·er[1] ['sleivə] Sklavenschiff *n*;
Sklavenhändler *m*.

slav·er[2] ['slævə] **1.** Geifer *m*, Sabber *m*; **2.** (be)geifern, (be)sabbern
(*a. fig.*).

slav·er·y ['sleivəri] Sklaverei *f*;
Plackerei *f*, Schinderei *f*.

slav·ey *sl.* ['slævi] dienstbarer Geist
m.

Slav·ic ['slɑːvik] **1.** slawisch; **2.** Slawisch *n*.

slav·ish □ ['sleiviʃ] sklavisch; **'slavish·ness** sklavisches Wesen *n*.

slaw [slɔː] Krautsalat *m*.

slay *rhet.* [slei] (*irr.*) erschlagen;
töten; **'slay·er** Mörder *m*.

slea·zy ['sliːzi] verschlissen, dünn
(*Gewebe*); *fig.* schäbig, heruntergekommen (*Hotel etc.*).

sled [sled] = *sledge*[1].

sledge[1] [sledʒ] **1.** Schlitten *m*;
2. Schlitten fahren; mit Schlitten
befördern.

sledge[2] [~] *a.* ~-*hammer* Schmiedehammer *m*.

sleek [sliːk] **1.** □ glatt, geschmeidig
(*Haut etc.*; *a. fig.*); **2.** glätten;
'sleek·ness Glattheit *f*; Glätte *f*.

sleep [sliːp] **1.** (*irr.*) *v/i.* schlafen;
stehen (*Kreisel*); ~ (*up*)*on od. over*
et. beschlafen; *v/t. j.* für die Nacht
unterbringen; ~ *away Zeit* verschlafen; ~ *off s-n Rausch etc.* ausschlafen; **2.** Schlaf *m*; *go to* ~ einschlafen; *put to* ~ einschläfern (*Tier
schmerzlos töten, a. Person vor Operation narkotisieren*); **'sleep·er** Schläfer(in); 🚪 Schwelle *f*; Schlafwagen
m; *be a light* ~ e-n leichten Schlaf
haben; **'sleep·i·ness** Schläfrigkeit *f*.

sleep·ing ['sliːpiŋ] schlafend;
Schlaf...; **'~-bag** Schlafsack *m*;
♀ **Beau·ty** Dornröschen *n*; **'~-car**,
'~-'car·riage 🚪 Schlafwagen *m*;
'~-draught Schlaftrunk *m*; ~
part·ner ✝ stiller Teilhaber *m*; ~ **pill**
Schlaftablette *f*; **'~-'sick·ness** Schlafkrankheit *f*.

sleep·less □ ['sliːplis] schlaflos;
ruhelos; **'sleep·less·ness** Schlaflosigkeit *f*.

sleep·walk·er ['sliːpwɔːkə] Nachtwandler(in).

sleep·y □ ['sliːpi] schläfrig; verschlafen (*a. Ort*); **'~-head** F *fig.*
Schlafmütze *f*.

sleet [sliːt] **1.** Schloßen *f/pl.*,
Graupelregen *m*; **2.** graupeln;

'sleet·y graupelig; Graupel...

sleeve [sliːv] **1.** Ärmel *m*; ⊕ Muffe
f; *attr.* Muffen...; *have something*
up one's ~ etwas in Bereitschaft
halten; etwas im Schilde führen;
laugh in one's ~ sich ins Fäustchen
lachen; **2.** Ärmel einsetzen in (*acc.*);
sleeved ...ärmelig; **'sleeve·less**
ärmellos, ohne Ärmel; **'sleeve
-link** Manschettenknopf *m*.

sleigh [slei] **1.** (*bsd.* Pferde)Schlitten
m; **2.** im Schlitten fahren *od.* befördern.

sleight [slait]: ~ *of hand* Taschenspielerei *f*; Kunststück *n*.

slen·der □ ['slendə] schlank, dünn;
schmächtig; gering, schwach; dürftig; **'slen·der·ness** Schlankheit *f*
etc.

slept [slept] *pret. u. p.p. von sleep* **1**.

sleuth [sluːθ], **'~-hound** Blut-,
Spürhund *m* (*mst fig. Detektiv*).

slew[1] [sluː] *pret. von slay.*

slew[2] [~] *a.* ~ *round* (sich) drehen.

slice [slais] **1.** Schnitte *f*, Scheibe *f*,
Stück *n*; Teil *m*; *Küche*: Wender
m; Fischheber *m*; **2.** in Scheiben
zerschneiden; *a.* ~ *off* (in Scheiben)
abschneiden.

slick F [slik] **1.** *adj.* glatt, glitschig;
fig. raffiniert; **2.** *adv.* direkt, genau;
3. *a.* ~ *paper Am. sl.* vornehme
Zeitschrift *f*; **'slick·er** *Am.* F
Regenmantel *m*; gerissener Kerl *m*.

slid [slid] *pret. u. p.p. von slide* **1**.

slide [slaid] **1.** (*irr.*) *v/i.* gleiten;
rutschen; schlittern; ausgleiten;
hineinschlittern (*into* in *acc.*); *let
things* ~ die Dinge laufen lassen;
v/t. gleiten lassen; **2.** Gleiten *n*;
Rutsche *f*; ⊕ Schieber *m*; Diapositiv *n*; *a. land* ~ Erdrutsch *m*;
'slid·er Gleitende *m*; Schieber *m*;
'slide-rule Rechenschieber *m*.

slid·ing ['slaidiŋ] **1.** Gleiten *n*;
2. gleitend; Schiebe...; ~ *roof*
Schiebedach *n*; ~ *rule* Rechenschieber *m*; ~ *scale* gleitende
(Lohn- *od.* Preis)Skala *f*; ~ *seat*
Rollsitz *m* im Ruderboot.

slight [slait] **1.** □ schmächtig;
schwach; leicht; gering(fügig), unbedeutend; **2.** Nichtachtung *f*, Geringschätzung *f*; **3.** geringschätzig
behandeln; unbeachtet lassen;
'slight·ing □ geringschätzig;
'slight·ly etwas, ein wenig; **'slightness** Dünnheit *f*; Schwäche *f*;

Geringfügigkeit *f.*

slim [slim] **1.** ☐ schlank; dünn; schmächtig; dürftig; *sl.* schlau, gerissen; **2.** e-e Schlankheitskur machen. [*m.*\

slime [slaim] Schlamm *m;* Schleim\

slim·i·ness ['slaiminis] schlammige *od.* schleimige Beschaffenheit *f.*

slim·ness ['slimnis] Schlankheit *f.*

slim·y ☐ ['slaimi] schlammig; schleimig (*a. fig.*).

sling [sliŋ] **1.** Schleuder *f;* Tragriemen *m;* ✝ Schlinge *f,* Binde *f;* Wurf *m;* **2.** (*irr.*) schleudern; auf-, umhängen; *a.* ~ *up* hochziehen.

slink [sliŋk] (*irr.*) schleichen; sich *wohin* stehlen.

slip [slip] **1.** *v/i.* schlüpfen, gleiten, rutschen; ausgleiten; ausrutschen; *oft* ~ *away* entschlüpfen; sich versehen; *v/t.* schlüpfen *od.* gleiten lassen; loslassen; entschlüpfen, -gleiten (*dat.*); ~ *in Bemerkung* dazwischenwerfen; ~ *into* hineinstecken *od.* -schieben in (*acc.*); ~ *on* (*off*) *Kleid etc.* über-, (ab-) streifen; **2.** (Aus)Gleiten *n,* (Aus-) Rutschen *n;* Fehltritt *m* (*a. fig.*); Versehen *n;* (Flüchtigkeits)Fehler *m;* Verstoß *m;* Streifen *m; a.* ~ *of paper* Zettel *m;* ⚘ Steckreis *n; fig.* Sproß *m;* Unterkleid *n;* ~*s pl. od.* ~*way* ⚓ Helling *f;* (Kissen)Überzug *m;* ~*s pl.* Badehose *f; a* ~ *of a girl* ein schmächtiges junges Mädchen *n;* ~ *of the pen* Schreibfehler *m; it was a* ~ *of the tongue* ich habe mich (er hat sich) versprochen; *give s.o. the* ~ j-m entwischen; '~-**knot** Laufknoten *m;* Schleife *f;* '~-**on** loser Mantel *m;* '**slip·per** Pantoffel *m,* Hausschuh *m;* '**slip·per·y** ☐ schlüpfrig; *fig.* aalglatt; '**slip-road** (Autobahn)Einfahrt *f,* (-)Ausfahrt *f;* **slip·shod** ['~ʃɔd] schlampig, nachlässig; **slip·slop** ['~slɔp] labberiges Zeug *n* (*fig. Gewäsch*); '**slip-stream** ✈ Luftschraubenstrahl *m,* Nachstrom *m;* '**slip-up** F Fehler *m.*

slit [slit] **1.** Schlitz *m,* Spalte *f;* **2.** (*irr.*) (auf-, zer)splittern.

slith·er ['sliðə] schlittern, rutschen; gleiten.

sliv·er ['slivə] Splitter *m,* dünne Scheibe *f.*

slob·ber ['slɔbə] **1.** Sabber *m;* Gesabber *n;* **2.** (be)sabbern; '**slob-**

ber·y sabberig; matschig.

sloe ♀ [sləu] Schlehe *f;* Schwarzdorn *m.*

slog F [slɔg] **1.** hauen; schuften; **2.** Hieb *m.*

slo·gan ['sləugən] *fig.* Schlagwort *n,* Losung *f;* (Werbe)Slogan *m.*

sloop ⚓ [slu:p] Schaluppe *f.*

slop[1] [slɔp] **1.** Pfütze *f;* ~*s pl.* Spülicht *n;* Krankenspeise *f;* **2.** *a.* ~ *over v/t.* verschütten; *v/i.* überlaufen (*a. fig.*).

slop[2] [~]: ~*s pl.* billige Konfektionskleidung *f;* ⚓ Kleidung *f* u. Bettzeug *n.*

slop-ba·sin ['slɔpbeisn] Gefäß *n* für Teereste.

slope [sləup] **1.** (Ab)Hang *m;* Neigung *f;* **2.** *v/t.* schräg *od.* schief machen *od.* legen; neigen; ⊕ abschrägen; ~ *arms!* ⚔ Gewehr über!; *v/i.* schräg verlaufen; abfallen, sich neigen; ~ *off, a. do a* ~ *sl.* abhauen, türmen; '**slop·ing** ☐ schräg.

slop-pail ['slɔppeil] Spül-, Ausgußeimer *m;* '**slop·py** ☐ naß, schmutzig; wässerig; schlampig; labberig (*Nahrung*); rührselig.

slop-shop ['slɔpʃɔp] Laden *m* mit billiger Konfektionsware.

slosh [slɔʃ] *v i.* im Matsch herumpatschen; *v/t. sl. j.* verhauen; **sloshed** *sl.* voll, besoffen.

slot [slɔt] *hunt.* Fährte *f;* Schlitz *m am Automaten etc.;* ⊕ Nut *f.*

sloth [sləuθ] Faulheit *f; zo.* Faultier *n;* **sloth·ful** ☐ ['~ful] faul, träg.

slot-ma·chine ['slɔtməʃi:n] (Waren- *od.* Spiel)Automat *m.*

slouch [slautʃ] **1.** faul herumhängen; herumlatschen; **2.** schlaffe Haltung *f;* latschiger Gang *m;* ~ *hat* Schlapphut *m.*

slough[1] [slau] Sumpf(loch *n*) *m.*

slough[2] [slʌf] **1.** *zo.* abgeworfene Haut *f;* ⚕ Schorf *m;* **2.** *v/i.* sich ablösen (*Schorf etc.*); sich häuten (*Schlange etc.*); *v/t.* Haut *etc.* abwerfen.

slough·y ['slaui] sumpfig.

Slo·vak ['sləuvæk] **1.** Slowake *m,* Slowakin *f;* **2.** = **Slo'va·ki·an** slowakisch.

slov·en ['slʌvn] unordentlicher Mensch *m;* Schlampe *f;* '**slov·en·li·ness** Schlampigkeit *f;* '**slov·en-**

smash

ly liederlich, schlampig.
slow [sləu] **1.** □ langsam (*of* in *dat.*);
nachgehend (*Uhr*); schwerfällig;
lässig; schleichend (*Fieber*); langweilig; *Sport*: schwer (*die Bewegung hemmend*); *be* ~ *to do* s.th.
nicht schnell *et.* tun; *my watch is
ten minutes* ~ meine Uhr geht
10 Minuten nach; **2.** *adv.* langsam;
3. *oft* ~ *down*, ~ *up*, ~ *off v/t.* verlangsamen; *v/i.* langsam(er) werden *od.*
gehen *od.* fahren; '~-**coach** Lang-
weiler *m*; altmodischer Mensch *m*;
~ **lane** *mot.* Kriechspur *f*; '~-**match**
Lunte *f*; '~-'**mo·tion film** Zeitlu-
penaufnahme *f*; '**slow·ness** Langsamkeit *f*; **slow train** Bummelzug *m*;
'**slow·worm** *zo.* Blindschleiche *f*.
sludge [slʌdʒ] Schlamm *m*; Matsch
m.
slue [slu:] = *slew*[2].
slug[1] [slʌg] Stück *n* Rohmetall;
typ. Zeilensatz *m*.
slug[2] *zo.* [~] Wegschnecke *f*.
slug[3] [~] *Am. für slog* 1.
slug·gard ['slʌgəd] Faulenzer(in);
'**slug·gish** □ träge, faul.
sluice [slu:s] **1.** Schleuse *f*; **2.** ausströmen (lassen); ausspülen; wa-
schen; '~-'**gate** Schleusentor *n*;
'~-'**way** Schleusenkanal *m*.
slum [slʌm] schmutzige Gasse *f*;
~*s pl.* Elendsviertel *n*, Slums *pl.*
slum·ber ['slʌmbə] **1.** *a.* ~*s pl.*
Schlummer *m*; **2.** schlummern.
slum·brous, **slum·ber·ous** □
['slʌmbrəs, '~bərəs] einschläfernd;
schläfrig.
slump [slʌmp] *Börse*: **1.** fallen,
stürzen; **2.** (Kurs-, Preis)Sturz *m*;
Wirtschaftskrise *f*.
slung [slʌŋ] *pret. u. p.p. von sling* 2.
slunk [slʌŋk] *pret. u. p.p. von slink.*
slur [slə:] **1.** Fleck *m*; *fig.* Tadel *m*,
Vorwurf *m*; ♩ Bindezeichen *n*;
2. *v/t. oft* ~ *over* hinweggehen über,
übergehen; ♩ *Töne* binden; *Silben
etc.* verschleifen.
slurp F [slə:p] schlürfen.
slush [slʌʃ] Schlamm *m*; Matsch
m; Gefühlsduselei *f*; F Kitsch *m*;
'**slush·y** matschig; F kitschig.
slut [slʌt] Schlampe *f*; Nutte *f*;
'**slut·tish** schlampig.
sly □ [slai] schlau, verschmitzt;
hinterlistig, tückisch; *on the* ~
heimlich; '~-**boots** F Schlauberger
m; '**sly·ness** Schläue *f*; Ver-

schmitztheit *f*; Hinterlist *f*.
smack[1] [smæk] **1.** (Bei)Geschmack
m; Prise *f Salz etc.*; *fig.* Spur *f*;
2. schmecken (*of* nach); e-n Beigeschmack haben (*of* von).
smack[2] [~] **1.** Schmatz(kuß) *m*;
Schlag *m*, Klatsch *m*, Klaps *m*;
2. klatschen, knallen (mit); schmat-
zen (mit *den Lippen*); *j-m* e-n Klaps
geben; **3.** *int.* klatsch!
smack[3] ♫ [~] Schmack(e) *f*.
smack·er *Am. sl.* ['smækə] Dollar *m*.
small [smɔ:l] **1.** *allg.* klein; gering,
unbedeutend; *fig.* kleinlich; niedrig; wenig; ~ *eater* schlechter
Esser *m*; *feel* ~, *look* ~ sich gedemütigt fühlen; *the* ~ *hours pl.* die
frühen Morgenstunden *f/pl.*; *in a* ~
way bescheiden; **2.** dünner Teil *m*; ~*s
pl.* F Leib- und Tischwäsche *f*; ~
of the back anat. Kreuz *n*; '~-**arms**
pl. Handfeuerwaffen *f/pl.*; ~ **beer**
Dünnbier *n*; *think no* ~ *of o.s.* F
sich hübsch was einbilden; *be* ~
unbedeutend sein; ~ **change** Kleingeld *n*; *fig.* triviale Bemerkungen
f/pl.; Geplätscher *n*; '~-'**hold·er**
Kleinbauer *m*; '~-'**hold·ing** bäuer-
licher Kleinbetrieb *m*; '**small·ish**
ziemlich klein; '**small·ness** Kleinheit *f*.
small...: '~-**pox** *pl.* ♣ Pocken *f pl.*; ~
print Kleingedruckte *n*; ~ **talk** Plauderei *f*; '~-**time** *Am.* F unbedeutend,
drittklassig.
smalt ⊕ [smɔ:lt] Schmalte *f*.
smarm·y F ['smɑ:mi] schmierig
(*schmeichelnd*).
smart [smɑ:t] **1.** □ scharf; heftig
(*Schmerz*, *Kampf*); munter, flink;
geschickt; gerissen; sauber;
schmuck, elegant, fein, adrett,
schick; forsch, patent; ~ *aleck Am.*
Neunmalkluge *m*; **2.** Schmerz *m*;
3. schmerzen; leiden; *you shall* ~
for it das sollst du büßen; '**smart·en**
mst ~ *up* herausputzen; '**smart-
-mon·ey** Schmerzensgeld *n*;
'**smart·ness** Klugheit *f*; Schärfe *f*,
Heftigkeit *f*; Gewandtheit *f*; Gerissenheit *f*; Schick *m*, Eleganz
f.
smash [smæʃ] **1.** *v/t. oft* ~ *up* zertrümmern, zerschmettern, zer-
schlagen; ~ *in* einschlagen; *fig.* vernichten; schmettern; *v/i.* zerschmettern, *fig.* zs.-brechen; (dahin)stürzen; *oft* ~ *up* Bankrott

machen; **2.** Zerschmettern *n*;
Krach *m*; Zs.-bruch *m* (*a.* ✝);
Tennis: Schmetterball *m*; '**~-and-
-'grab raid** Schaufenstereinbruch
m; '**smash·er** *sl.*
m, vernichtende Kritik *f*; **smash hit**
F Bombenerfolg *m*; '**smash·ing** F
super, toll; '**smash-up** Zs.-stoß *m*;
Zs.-bruch *m*.

smat·ter·ing ['smætəriŋ] oberflächliche Kenntnis *f*.

smear [smiə] **1.** beschmieren, bestreichen; einschmieren; *Schrift*
verschmieren; *Fett etc.* schmieren
(*on a.* *acc.*); *fig.* besudeln, beschmutzen; **~(**ing) *campaign* Ver-
leumdungskampagne *f*; **2.** Schmiere
f; Fleck *m*; ~ **test** ⚛ Abstrich *m*.

smell [smel] **1.** Geruch *m*; **2.** (*irr.*)
riechen (an *dat.*, *a.* ~ **at**; *of* nach
et.); '**smell·ing-salt** Riechsalz *n*;
'**smell·y** übelriechend.

smelt¹ [smelt] *pret. u. p.p. von*
smell 2.

smelt² *ichth.* [~] Stint *m*.

smelt³ [~] schmelzen; '**smelt·er**
Schmelzer *m*; '**smelt·ing-'furnace** Schmelzofen *m*.

smile [smail] **1.** Lächeln *n*; **2.** lächeln (*at* über *acc.*); ~ **on**, ~ **at** *j-m*
zulächeln.

smirch *rhet.* [smɔ:tʃ] beschmieren;
fig. besudeln.   [sen *n.*\

smirk [smɔ:k] **1.** grinsen; **2.** Grin-\

smite [smait] (*irr.*) *poet. od. co.*
schlagen; vernichten; heimsuchen;
schwer treffen; quälen (*Gewissen*);
~ *upon bsd. fig.* an *das* Ohr *etc.*
schlagen.

smith [smiθ] Schmied *m*.

smith·er·eens F ['smiðə'ri:nz] *pl.*
kleine Stücke *n/pl.*, Splitter *m/pl.*,
Fetzen *m/pl.*; *smash to* ~ in Stücke
hauen.

smith·y ['smiði] Schmiede *f*.

smit·ten ['smitn] **1.** *p.p. von* smite;
2. ergriffen; betroffen; *fig.* hingerissen (*with* von).

smock [smɔk] **1.** fälteln; **2.** *a.*
~*frock* Arbeitskittel *m*, Bluse *f*;
'**smock·ing** Smokarbeit *f*.

smog [smɔg] Smog *m*, Gemisch *n*
von Nebel und Rauch.

smoke [smouk] **1.** Rauch *m*; Qualm
m; ⚔ (Tarn)Nebel *m*; F Rauchen *n*
e-r Zigarre etc.; F Zigarre *f*, Zigarette *f*, Tabak *m*; *have a* ~ (eine)
rauchen; **2.** *v/i.* rauchen; dampfen;

v/t. Tabak rauchen; (aus)räuchern;
⚔ einnebeln; '**~-bomb** Nebel-,
Rauchbombe *f*; **smoked**, '**smoke-
-dried** geräuchert; '**smoke·less** □
rauchlos; '**smok·er** Raucher *m*;
Räucherer *m*; 🚃 Raucherwagen *m*,
-abteil *n*; '**smoke-screen** ⚔ Rauch-,
Nebelvorhang *m*; '**smoke-stack** 🚃
u. ⚓ Schornstein *m*.

smok·ing ['smoukiŋ] **1.** Rauchen
n; *no* ~! Rauchen verboten!; **2.**
Rauch(er)...; Räucher...; '**~-com-
part·ment** 🚃 Raucher(abteil *n*) *m*;
'**~-room** Rauchzimmer *n*.

smok·y □ ['smouki] rauchig; ver-
räuchert.

smol·der *Am.* ['smouldə] = smoul-
der.

smooth [smu:ð] **1.** □ glatt; *fig.*
fließend; sanft, mild; schmeichle-
risch; **2.** *oft* ~ **out**, ~ **down** glätten;
ebnen (*a. fig.*); plätten; *a.* ~ **down**
mildern; *a.* ~ **over**, ~ **away** Schwierigkeit *etc.* wegräumen; ~ **down** sich
glätten; '**smooth·ing 1.** Glätten *n*;
2. Glätt..., Plätt...; ~ *iron* Bügeleisen *n*; ~ *plane* Schlichthobel *m*;
'**smooth·ness** Glätte *f* (*a. fig.*);
'**smooth-tongued** schmeichlerisch.

smote [smout] *pret. von* smite.

smoth·er ['smʌðə] **1.** Qualm *m*;
2. *a.* ~ *up* ersticken (*a. fig.*).

smoul·der ['smouldə] glimmen,
schwelen.

smudge [smʌdʒ] **1.** *v/t.* beschmutzen; (be)schmieren; *v/i.* schmieren;
schmutzen; **2.** Schmutzfleck *m*;
'**smudg·y** □ schmutzig, schmierig.

smug [smʌg] selbstzufrieden, selbstgefällig.

smug·gle ['smʌgl] schmuggeln;
'**smug·gler** Schmuggler(in);
'**smug·gling** Schmuggel(ei *f*) *m*.

smut [smʌt] **1.** Schmutz *m*; Ruß
(-fleck) *m*; Zoten *f/pl.*; ⚘ Getreide-
Brand *m*; **2.** beschmutzen; ⚘ brandig machen.

smutch [smʌtʃ] **1.** schwarz machen;
beflecken; **2.** schwarzer Fleck *m*.

smut·ty □ ['smʌti] schmutzig;
rußig; zotig, obszön; ⚘ brandig.

snack [snæk] Imbiß *m*; '**~-bar**,
'**~-coun·ter** Snackbar *f*, Imbiß-
stube *f*.

snaf·fle¹ ['snæfl] Trense *f*.

snaf·fle² *sl.* [~] klauen (*stehlen*).

snaf·fle-bit ['snæflbit] Trensen-
gebiß *n*.

snooze

sna·fu *Am. sl.* ✗ [snæ'fu:] **1.** total
drunter und drüber; **2.** tolles
Durcheinander *n*.

snag [snæg] Aststumpf *m*; Zahn-
stumpf *m*, Raffzahn *m*; *fig.* Haken *m*
(*Schwierigkeit*); *Am.* Baumstamm *m*
in Flüssen; **snag·ged** ['~gid], **'snag-
gy** ästig; knorrig.

snail *zo.* [sneil] Schnecke *f*.

snake *zo.* [sneik] Schlange *f* (*a. fig.*);
'~-charm·er Schlangenbeschwö-
rer *m*; **'~-weed** ♀ Natterwurz *f*.

snak·y □ ['sneiki] schlangengleich,
-artig; Schlangen...; *fig.* hinterhältig.

snap [snæp] **1.** Schnappen *n*, Biß *m*;
Knack(s) *m*, Krach *m*, Knall *m*; *fig.*
Schwung *m*, Schmiß *m*; Schnapp-
schloß *n*; *phot.* Schnappschuß *m*;
Plätzchen *n*, Keks *m*, *n*; *cold* ~
Kältewelle *f*; **2.** *v/i.* schnappen
(*at nach*); zuschnappen (*Schloß*);
knacken; (zer)springen, reißen;
(*at s.o.* j. an)schnauzen; ~ *into it*
Am. sl. mach schnell, Tempo!;
~ *out of it Am. sl.* hör auf damit;
komm, komm!; *v/t.* (er)schnappen;
(zu)schnappen lassen; *phot.* knipsen; zerknicken, -brechen; ~ *one's
fingers at s.o.* mit Verachtung auf j.
herabblicken; ~ *out Wort* hervor-
stoßen; ~ *up et.* wegschnappen; *j.*
anschnauzen; *j-m* ins Wort fallen;
3. knacks!; schwapp!; **'~-drag·on**
♀ Löwenmaul *n*; Rosinenfischen *n*
aus brennendem Branntwein (*Spiel*);
'~-fas·ten·er Druckknopf *m am
Kleid*; **'snap·pish** □ bissig, beißend; schnippisch; **'snap·pish-
ness** bissiges *od.* schnippisches
Wesen *n*; **'snap·py** = *snappish*; F
flott, forsch; *make it* ~! F mach mal
fix!; **'snap·shot 1.** Schnappschuß
m, Photo *n*, Momentaufnahme *f*;
2. Momentaufnahmen machen
(von).

snare [snɛə] **1.** Schlinge *f*; **2.** (mit e-r
Schlinge) fangen; *fig.* umgarnen.

snarl [snɑ:l] **1.** knurren; murren; verfitzen; **2.** Knurren *n*; Gewirr *n*; **'~-up**
Durcheinander *n*; *bsd.* Verkehrs-
chaos *n*.

snatch [snætʃ] **1.** schneller Griff *m*;
Ruck *m*; Stückchen *n*; Augenblick
m; *by* ~*es* in Absätzen, ruckweise;
2. schnappen; ergreifen; an sich
reißen; nehmen, bekommen; ~ *at*
greifen nach; ~ *from s.o.* j-m ent-

reißen.

sneak [sni:k] **1.** *v/i.* (sich *wohin*)
schleichen; F petzen; *v/t.* F stibitzen; **2.** Schleicher *m*; F Petzer *m*;
'sneak·ers *pl.* F leichte Segeltuch-
schuhe *m/pl.*; **'sneak·ing** □ schleichend; heimlich, still (*Gefühl*);
'sneak-thief Gelegenheitsdieb *m*;
'sneak·y F hinterlistig; raffiniert.

sneer [sniə] **1.** Hohnlächeln *n*; Spott
m; **2.** hohnlächeln; spotten, spötteln (*at über acc.*); **'sneer·er**
Spötter(in); **'sneer·ing** □ höhnisch.

sneeze [sni:z] **1.** niesen; *not to be* ~*d
at* F nicht zu verachten; **2.** Niesen *n*.

snick·er ['snikə] kichern; wiehern.

sniff [snif] **1.** *v/i.* schnüffeln,
schnuppern (*at an dat.*); die Nase
rümpfen (*at über acc.*); *v/t.* riechen;
2. Schnüffeln *n*; Naserümpfen *n*;
Nasevoll *f*; **snif·fles** ['sniflz] *pl.*
Schnupfen *m*; *have the* ~ Schnupfen
haben; **'sniff·y** F hochnäsig, verächtlich; übelriechend.

snif·ter F ['sniftə] Schnäpschen *n*;
Am. Kognakschwenker *m*.

snig·ger ['snigə] kichern (*at über
acc.*).

snip [snip] **1.** Schnitt *m*; Schnippel
m, Schnipsel *n*; **2.** schnippe(l)n,
schnipseln; *Fahrkarte* knipsen.

snipe [snaip] **1.** *orn.* Bekassine *f*,
(Sumpf)Schnepfe *f*; *coll.* Schnep-
fen *pl.*; **2.** ✗ aus dem Hinterhalt
(ab)schießen; **'snip·er** ✗ Scharf-
b. s. Heckenschütze *m*.

snip·pets ['snipits] *pl.* Schnipsel
n/pl.; *fig.* Bruchstücke *n/pl.*

snitch *sl.* [snitʃ] ~ *on s.o.* j. ver-
petzen (*verraten*).

sniv·el ['snivl] aus der Nase triefen;
schluchzen; plärren; **'sniv·el·(l)ing**
triefnasig; wehleidig; jämmerlich.

snob [snɔb] Großtuer *m*; Snob *m*;
'snob·ber·y Vornehmtuerei *f*;
Snobismus *m*; **'snob·bish** □ vornehm tuend; snobistisch.

snog F [snɔg] knutschen.

snook·er ['snu:kə] **1.** *Art* Billard-
spiel *n*; **2.** *be* ~*ed* F in die Enge
getrieben sein.

snoop *Am. sl.* [snu:p] **1.** *fig.* (umher-)
schnüffeln (*upon in dat.*); **2.** Schnüf-
felei *f*; Schnüffler *m*.

snoot·y F ['snu:ti] hochnäsig.

snooze F [snu:z] **1.** Schläfchen *n*;
2. dösen; ein Nickerchen machen.

snore [snɔː] **1.** Schnarchen *n*; **2.** schnarchen.

snor·kel ⚓ ['snɔːkəl] Schnorchel *m*.

snort [snɔːt] **1.** Schnauben *n*, Schnaufen *n*; **2.** schnauben, schnaufen.

snot P [snɔt] Rotz *m*; **'snot·ty** P rotzig; *fig.* gemein.

snout [snaut] Schnauze *f*; Rüssel *m*.

snow [snəu] **1.** Schnee *m*; **2.** (be-) schneien; *be* ~*ed under with fig.* erdrückt werden von; ~*ed in od.* up eingeschneit; **'~·ball 1.** Schneeball *m*; **2.** (sich) mit Schneebällen bewerfen; **'~-bound** eingeschneit; **'~-capped**, **'~-clad**, **'~-cov·ered** schneebedeckt; **'~-drift** Schneewehe *f*; **'~-drop** ♀ Schneeglöckchen *n*; **'~-fall** Schneefall *m*; **'~-flake** Schneeflocke *f*; **'~-gog·gles** *pl.* (*a pair of* eine) Schneebrille *f*; **'~-line** Schneegrenze *f*; ~·mo·bile ['~məbiːl] Motorschlitten *m*, Schneemobil *n*; **'~-plough**, *Am.* **'~-plow** Schneepflug *m*; **'~-shoe** Schneeschuh *m*; **'~-storm** Schneesturm *m*; **'~-'white** schneeweiß; **'snow·y** ☐ schneeig; schneebedeckt; schneeweiß.

snub [snʌb] **1.** schelten, anfahren; **2.** Verweis *m*; **snub nose** Stupsnase *f*; **'snub-nosed** stupsnasig.

snuff [snʌf] **1.** Schnuppe *f e-r Kerze*; Schnupftabak *m*; *up to* ~ F gerissen; *give s.o.* ~ F j-m Saures geben; **2.** *a.* *take* ~ schnupfen; *Kerze* putzen; **'~-box** Schnupftabaksdose *f*; **'snuff·ers** *pl.* Lichtputzschere *f*; **snuf·fle** ['~fl] schnüffeln; schnauben; näseln; **'snuff·y** mit Schnupftabak beschmutzt; schnupftabakartig; F *fig.* verschnupft.

snug ☐ [snʌg] geborgen; behaglich, gemütlich; eng anliegend (*Kleid*); **'snug·ger·y** gemütliches Zimmer *n*, warmes Nest *n*; **snug·gle** ['~gl] *a.* ~ *up* (sich) schmiegen *od.* kuscheln (*to an, in in acc.*).

so [səu] so; deshalb; also, so ... denn; *I hope* ~ ich hoffe (es); *are you tired?* ~ *I am* bist du müde? ja; *you are tired*, ~ *am I* du bist müde, ich auch; *a mile or* ~ etwa eine Meile; ~ *as to* ... so daß ...; um zu ...; ~ *far* bisher; ~ *far as I know* soviel ich weiß.

soak [səuk] **1.** *v/t.* einweichen; durchnässen; (durch)tränken; vollsaugen; *sl. j.* schröpfen; ~ *up od. in* auf-, einsaugen; *v/i.* weichen; durchsickern (*into*, *in* in *acc.*); F saufen; **2.** Einweichen *n*; Durchweichung *f*; = **'soak·er** F Regenguß *m*; Sauferei *f*.

so-and-so ['səuənsəu] so und so; *Mr.* ♀ *Herr m* Soundso.

soap [səup] **1.** Seife *f*; *soft* ~ Schmierseife *f*; **2.** (ein)seifen; **'~-box** Seifenkiste *f*; *fig.* (Redner-) Plattform *f*; ~ *orator* Volksredner *m*; ~ *race* Seifenkistenrennen *n*; **'~-dish** Seifenschale *f*; **'~-bub·ble** Seifenblase; **'~-op·er·a** *Am.* rührseliges Hör- *od.* Fernsehspiel *n in Fortsetzungen*; **'~-suds** *pl.*, *a. sg.* Seifenlauge *f*; **'soap·y** ☐ seifig; *fig.* ölig, unterwürfig.

soar [sɔː] sich erheben; sich aufschwingen (*a. fig.*); schweben; ✈ segelfliegen, gleiten.

sob [sɔb] **1.** Schluchzen *n*; **2.** schluchzen.

so·ber ['səubə] **1.** ☐ nüchtern (*a. fig.* mäßig; *sachlich denkend*; *unauffällig*); **2.** *oft* ~ *down* ernüchtern; nüchtern werden; **'so·ber·ness**, **so·bri·e·ty** [~'braiəti] Nüchternheit *f*.

so·bri·quet ['səubrikei] Spitzname *m*.

sob...: ~ *sis·ter* F Briefkastentante *f*; ~ *sto·ry* F rührselige Geschichte *f*; **'~-stuff** F Gefühlsduselei *f*.

so-called ['səu'kɔːld] sogenannt.

soc·cer F ['sɔkə] Fußball *m* (*Spiel*; *im Ggs. zu Rugby*).

so·cia·bil·i·ty [səuʃə'biliti] Geselligkeit *f*; **'so·cia·ble** ☐ **1.** gesellig; Gesellschafts...; gemütlich; **2.** Kremser *m*; Plaudersofa *n*; geselliges Beisammensein *n*.

so·cial ['səuʃəl] **1.** ☐ gesellschaftlich; gesellig; sozial; Sozial...; ~ *activities pl.* gesellschaftliche Veranstaltungen *f/pl.*; ~ *insurance* Sozialversicherung *f*; ~ *services pl.* Sozialeinrichtungen *f/pl.*; **2.** geselliges Beisammensein *n*; **'so·cial·ism** Sozialismus *m*; **'so·cial·ist 1.** Sozialist(in); **2.** *a.* **so·cial·'is·tic** sozialistisch; **so·cial·ite** F ['~lait] Angehörige *f*, *f* der oberen Zehntausend; **'so·cial·ize** sozialisieren; verstaatlichen; **so·cial se·cu·ri·ty** Sozialhilfe *f*; *be on* ~ Sozialhilfe bekommen.

solidarity

so·ci·e·ty [sə'saiəti] Gesellschaft *f*; Verein *m*, Klub *m*; secret ~ Geheimbund *m*.

so·ci·o·log·i·cal □ [sousjə'lɔdʒikəl] soziologisch; so·ci·ol·o·gist [~si-'ɔlədʒist] Soziologe *m*; so·ci·ol·o·gy Sozialwissenschaft *f*, Soziologie *f*.

sock¹ [sɔk] Socke *f*; Einlegesohle *f*.

sock² *sl.* [~] **1.** Keile *f*, Senge *f* (*Prügel*); give s.o. ~s = **2.** *j.* versohlen.

sock·er F ['sɔkə] = soccer.

sock·et ['sɔkit] (Augen-, Zahn-) Höhle *f*; (Gelenk)Pfanne *f*; ⊕ Muffe *f*; ≠ Fassung *f*; Steckdose *f*.

so·cle ['sɔkl] Sockel *m*; Untersatz *m*.

sod [sɔd] **1.** Grasnarbe *f*; Rasen (-stück *n*) *m*; **2.** mit Rasen belegen.

so·da ⚗ ['səudə] Soda *f*; '~-fountain Siphon *m*; Erfrischungshalle *f*, Eisdiele *f*; '~-wa·ter Soda-, Mineralwasser *n*.

sod·den ['sɔdn] durchweicht; teigig (*Brot*); durch Trinken verblödet.

so·di·um ⚗ ['səudjəm] Natrium *n*.

so·ev·er [səu'evə] ... auch immer.

so·fa ['səufə] Sofa *n*. [Leibung *f*.]
sof·fit △ ['sɔfit] Untersicht *f*;]
soft [sɔft] **1.** □ *allg.* weich; *engS.* mild; sanft; sacht, leise, leicht; zart, zärtlich; weichlich; F einfältig; ~ drink F alkoholfreies Getränk *n*; ~ furnishings Teppiche, Gardinen, Möbelbezüge etc.; *a* ~ thing *sl.* e-e ruhige Sache (*einträgliches Geschäft*); *s.* soap 1; **2.** *adv.* weich; **3.** F Trottel *m*; '~-'boiled weich (*Ei*).

soft·en ['sɔfn] weich machen (*a. fig.*); (sich) erweichen; mildern; Ton, Farbe dämpfen; ⊕ enthärten; 'soft·en·er Weichmacher *m*; Wasserenthärtungsanlage *f*; soft-head·ed ['sɔft'hedid] blöd(e), schwachsinnig; 'soft-'heart·ed weichherzig, gutmütig; 'soft·ness Weichheit *f*; Sanftmut *f*; Milde *f*; 'soft--'ped·al ♩ mit dem Pianopedal spielen; *fig.* abschwächen; 'soft--'saw·der **1.** *j-m* schmeicheln; **2.** Schmeichelei *f*; 'soft-'soap *j-m* schmeicheln, um den Bart gehen; 'soft-'spok·en: be ~ eine sanfte Stimme haben; 'soft·ware *Computer*: Software *f*, Programmausstattung *f*; 'soft·y F Trottel *m*; Softie *m*.

sog·gy ['sɔgi] durchnäßt, -weicht; feucht.

so·ho ['səu'həu] holla!

soil¹ [sɔil] Boden *m*, Erde *f*.

soil² [~] **1.** Fleck *m*; Schmutz *m*; **2.** (be)schmutzen; (be)flecken; 'soil-pipe Fallrohr *n* am *Klosett*.

so·journ ['sɔdʒə:n] **1.** Aufenthalt *m*; **2.** sich aufhalten; 'so·journ·er Fremde *m*, Gast *m*.

sol ♩ [sɔl] Sol *n* (*Solmisationssilbe*).

sol·ace ['sɔləs] **1.** Trost *m*; **2.** trösten.

so·lar ['səulə] Sonnen...; ~ plex·us *anat.* ['pleksəs] Solarplexus *m*; *weitS.* Magengrube *f*.

sold [səuld] *pret. u. p.p. von* sell **1.**
sol·der ⊕ ['sɔldə] **1.** Lötmetall *n*; **2.** löten; 'sol·der·ing-i·ron Lötkolben *m*.

sol·dier ['səuldʒə] **1.** Soldat *m*; **2.** Soldat sein; go ~ing Soldat werden; 'sol·dier·like, 'sol·dier·ly soldatisch; Soldaten...; 'sol·dier·ship soldatische Tüchtigkeit *f*; 'sol·dier·y Militär *n*; *contp.* Soldateska *f*.

sole¹ □ [səul] alleinig, einzig; ~ agent Alleinvertreter *m*.

sole² [~] **1.** Sohle *f*; **2.** besohlen.

sole³ *ichth.* [~] Seezunge *f*.

sol·e·cism ['sɔlisizəm] Sprachschnitzer *m*; Verstoß *m*, Fauxpas *m*.

sol·emn □ ['sɔləm] feierlich; ernst; so·lem·ni·ty [sə'lemniti] Feierlichkeit *f*; Steifheit *f*; sol·em·ni·za·tion ['sɔləmnai'zeiʃən] Feier *f*; 'sol·em·nize feiern; feierlich vollziehen.

so·lic·it [sə'lisit] (dringend) bitten (*s.o. j.*; *s.th.* um et.; *s.o. for s.th.* od. *s.th. of s.o. j.* um et.); ansprechen, belästigen; so·lic·i·ta·tion Ansuchen *n*; dringende Bitte *f*; so·lic·i·tor ⚖ Anwalt *m*, Rechtsbeistand *m*; *Am.* Agent *m*, Werber *m*; ♀ *General* Kronanwalt *m*; so-'lic·it·ous □ besorgt, in Sorge (*about, for* um); ~ *of* begierig nach; ~ *to inf.* bestrebt zu *inf.*; so'lic·i·tude [~tju:d] Sorge *f*, Besorgnis *f*; Bemühung *f*.

sol·id ['sɔlid] **1.** □ fest; dauerhaft; haltbar; derb; kräftig; massiv, gediegen; ♪ körperlich, Raum...; *fig.* gediegen, zuverlässig; *bsd.* ✝ solid; triftig (*Grund*); solidarisch; einmütig, einstimmig; *a* ~ *hour* eine geschlagene *od.* volle Stunde; ~ geometry ♪ Stereometrie *f*; ~ leather Kernleder *n*; **2.** (fester) Körper *m*; sol·i·dar·i·ty [~'dæriti]

Solidarität *f*; **so·'lid·i·fy** [ˌdifai] (sich) verdichten; fest machen *od.* werden; **so·'lid·i·ty** Festigkeit *f*, Solidität *f*; Gediegenheit *f*; Zuverlässigkeit *f*; Triftigkeit *f*; **'sol·id--'state** ⚡ Festkörper..., Halbleiter...

so·lil·o·quize [sə'liləkwaiz] Selbstgespräche führen; **so·'lil·o·quy** Selbstgespräch *n*, Monolog *m*.

sol·i·taire [sɔli'tɛə] Solitär *m*, einzeln gefaßter Edelstein *m*; Patience *f* (*Spiel*); **sol·i·tar·y** □ ['ˌtəri] einsam; einzeln; einsiedlerisch; ~ *confinement* Einzelhaft *f*; **sol·i·tude** ['ˌtjuːd] Einsamkeit *f*; Verlassenheit *f*; Öde *f*.

so·lo ['səuləu] ♪ *u. Kartenspiel*: Solo *n*; ✈ Alleinflug *m*; **'so·lo·ist** Solist (-in).

sol·stice ['sɔlstis] Sonnenwende *f*.

sol·u·bil·i·ty [sɔlju'biliti] Löslichkeit *f*; Auflösbarkeit *f*; **sol·u·ble** ['ˌbl] löslich; (auf)lösbar.

so·lu·tion [sə'luːʃən] (Auf)Lösung *f* (*a. ♞ u. ♘*); ⊕ Gummilösung *f*.

solv·a·ble ['sɔlvəbl] auflösbar; **solve** *Aufgabe, Zweifel etc.* lösen; **sol·ven·cy** ✝ ['ˌvənsi] Zahlungsfähigkeit *f*; **'sol·vent 1.** (auf)lösend; ✝ zahlungsfähig; **2.** Lösungsmittel *n*.

som·bre, *Am.* **som·ber** □ ['sɔmbə] düster, trübe, dunkel (*a. fig.*).

some [sʌm, səm] **1.** *pron. u. adj.* irgendein; ein gewisser; etwas; einige, manche *pl.*; ~ *bread* (etwas) Brot; ~ *few* einige wenige, ein paar; ~ *20 miles* etwa 20 Meilen; *in* ~ *degree*, *to* ~ *extent* in gewissem Grade, einigermaßen; *this is* ~ *speech!* das ist mal 'ne Rede!; **2.** *adv.* etwas; *Am.* F prima; **'~·bod·y** jemand; **'~·day** eines Tages; **'~·one** jemand; **'~·how** irgendwie; ~ *or other* so oder so.

som·er·sault ['sʌməsɔːlt] Salto *m*; Rolle *f*, Purzelbaum *m*; *turn a* ~ e-n Purzelbaum schlagen.

some...: **~·thing** ['sʌmθiŋ] (irgend) etwas; *that is* ~ das ist doch etwas; ~ *like* so etwas wie, so ungefähr; **'~·time 1.** einmal, dereinst; **2.** ehemalig; **'~·times** zuweilen, manchmal; **'~·what** etwas, ziemlich; **'~·where** irgendwo(hin); **'~·while** gelegentlich, eine Weile.

som·nam·bu·lism [sɔm'næmbjulizəm] Nachtwandeln *n*; **som·nam·bu·list** Nachtwandler(in).

som·nif·er·ous □ [sɔm'nifərəs] einschläfernd.

som·no·lence ['sɔmnələns] Schläfrigkeit *f*; **'som·no·lent** schläfrig; einschläfernd.

son [sʌn] Sohn *m*.

so·na·ta ♪ [sə'nɑːtə] Sonate *f*.

song [sɔŋ] Gesang *m*; Lied *n*; Gedicht *n*; *for a mere od.* an old ~ für e-n Pappenstiel; *nothing to make a* ~ *about* F nichts Besonderes; **'~·bird** Singvogel *m*; **'~·book** Liederbuch *n*; **'~·hit** Schlager *m*; **song·ster** ['ˌstə] Singvogel *m*; Sänger *m*; **song·stress** ['ˌstris] Sängerin *f*.

son·ic ['sɔnik] Schall...; ~ **bang** Knall *m* beim Durchbrechen der Schallmauer; ~ **bar·ri·er** Schallgrenze *f*, -mauer *f*.

son-in-law, *pl.* **sons-in-law** ['sʌn(z)inlɔː] Schwiegersohn *m*.

son·net ['sɔnit] Sonett *n*.

son·ny F ['sʌni] Kleiner *m* (*Anrede*).

so·nor·i·ty [sə'nɔriti] Klang-, Tonfülle *f*; **so·no·rous** □ [sə'nɔːrəs] klangvoll, vollklingend, sonor.

soon [suːn] bald; früh; gern; *as od.* so ~ *as* sobald wie; **'soon·er** eher; früher; lieber; *no* ~ ... *than* kaum ... als; *no* ~ *said than done* gesagt, getan.

soot [sut] **1.** Ruß *m*; **2.** be-, verrußen.

sooth [suːθ]: *in* ~ in Wahrheit, fürwahr; **soothe** [suːð] beruhigen, besänftigen; mildern; **sooth·say·er** ['suːθseiə] Wahrsager(in).

soot·y □ ['suti] rußig.

sop [sɔp] **1.** eingeweichter Brocken *m*; *fig.* Besänftigungsmittel *n*, Bestechung *f*; **2.** eintunken; durchweichen; ~ *up Wasser* aufnehmen, -wischen.

soph·ism ['sɔfizəm] Sophismus *m*; Trugschluß *m*.

soph·ist ['sɔfist] Sophist *m*; **so·phis·tic, so·phis·ti·cal** □ [sə-'fistik(əl)] sophistisch; **so·phis·ti·cate** [ˌkeit] verdrehen; verfälschen; **so·phis·ti·cat·ed** kultiviert, raffiniert; intellektuell; hochgestochen, blasiert; hochentwickelt, kompliziert; **so·phis·ti·ca·tion** Spitzfindigkeit *f*; Verfälschung *f*; Intellektualismus *m*; Kompliziertheit *f*; **soph·ist·ry** ['sɔfistri] Sophisterei *f*, Spitzfindigkeit *f*.

soph·o·more *Am.* ['sɔfəmɔː] Student(in) im zweiten Studienjahr.
so·po·rif·ic [sɔpə'rifik] **1.** (~*ally*) einschläfernd; **2.** Schlafmittel *n*.
sop·ping ['sɔpiŋ] *a.* ~ *wet* patschnaß; **'sop·py** durchweicht; F rührselig; fad.
so·pran·o ♪ [sə'prɑːnəu] Sopran *m*.
sor·cer·er ['sɔːsərə] Zauberer *m*; **'sor·cer·ess** Zauberin *f*; Hexe *f*; **'sor·cer·y** Zauberei *f*.
sor·did □ ['sɔːdid] schmutzig, schäbig (*bsd. fig.*); **'sor·did·ness** Schmutzigkeit *f*.
sore [sɔː] **1.** □ schlimm, entzündet; wund; weh; empfindlich; schmerzend; *fig.* schlimm, arg; ~ *throat* Halsweh *n*, -entzündung *f*; **2.** wunde Stelle *f*, Schaden *m* (*a. fig.*); **'sore·head** *Am.* F mürrischer *od.* enttäuschter Mensch *m*; **'sore·ly** *adv.* heftig; äußerst, sehr; **'sore·ness** Empfindlichkeit *f*.
so·ror·i·ty [sə'rɔriti] Schwesternschaft *f*; *Am. univ.* Studentinnenverbindung *f*.
sor·rel¹ ['sɔrəl] **1.** rötlichbraun (*bsd. Pferd*); **2.** Fuchs *m* (*Pferd*).
sor·rel² ♣ [~] Sauerampfer *m*.
sor·row ['sɔrəu] **1.** Sorge *f*; Kummer *m*, Leid *n*; Trauer *f*; **2.** trauern; sich grämen; **sor·row·ful** □ ['sɔrəful] traurig, betrübt; elend.
sor·ry □ ['sɔri] betrübt, bekümmert; traurig, erbärmlich; (*I am*) (*so*) ~! es tut mir (sehr) leid, (ich) bedaure!; Verzeihung!; *I am* ~ *for him* er tut mir leid; ich bemitleide ihn; *we are* ~ *to say* wir müssen leider sagen; wir bedauern, sagen zu müssen.
sort [sɔːt] **1.** Sorte *f*, Gattung *f*, Art *f*; Weise *f*; *what* ~ *of* was für; *of a* ~, *of* ~*s* so was wie; ~ *of* F gewissermaßen; *out of* ~*s* F unpäßlich, verdrießlich; *a good* ~ ein guter Kerl; (*a*) ~ *of peace* so etwas wie ein Frieden; **2.** sortieren; ✝ assortieren; aussuchen; ~ *out* (aus-) sondern.
sor·tie ✕ ['sɔːtiː] Ausfall *m*; ✈ Einsatz *m*.
sot [sɔt] Trunkenbold *m*.
sot·tish □ ['sɔtiʃ] versoffen.
sou [suː] Sou *m* (*französische Münze*); *fig.* Heller *m*.
sou·bri·quet ['suːbrikei] = *sobriquet*.
souf·flé ['suːflei] Soufflé *n*, Auflauf *m*.

sough [sau] **1.** Sausen *n*, Rauschen *n*; **2.** rauschen (*bsd. Wind*).
sought [sɔːt] *pret. u. p.p. von seek*; **'~-'aft·er** gesucht, begehrt.
soul [səul] Seele *f* (*a. fig.*); **'~-de·stroy·ing** geisttötend; **'soul·less** □ seelenlos.
sound¹ □ [saund] *allg.* gesund (*a. fig.*); ganz (*unbeschädigt*); vernünftig; tüchtig, gründlich; fest (*Schlaf*); derb (*Schlag etc.*); ✝ sicher; ⚖ gültig.
sound² [~] **1.** Ton *m*, Schall *m*, Laut *m*, Klang *m*; **2.** *v/i.* tönen, klingen; ertönen, erklingen; erschallen; *v/t.* erschallen lassen, ertönen lassen; (aus)sprechen; ~ *the charge* ✕ zum Angriff blasen.
sound³ [~] Sund *m*, Meerenge *f*; Fischblase *f*.
sound⁴ [~] **1.** ✚ Sonde *f*; **2.** ✚ sondieren (*a. fig.*); ⚓ loten; ✚ abhorchen; ~ *s.o. out* j. ausholen, -horchen.
sound...: ~ *bar·ri·er* Schallmauer *f*; **'~-box** Schalldose *f*; ~ *broad·cast·ing* Tonrundfunk *m*; ~ *ef·fects pl.* Klang-, Toneffekte *m/pl.*; **'~-film** Tonfilm *m*.
sound·ing ⚓ ['saundiŋ] Lotung *f*; ~*s pl.* lotbare Wassertiefe *f*.
sound·ing-board ['saundiŋbɔːd] Resonanz-, Schallboden *m*.
sound·less □ ['saundlis] lautlos.
sound·ness ['saundnis] Gesundheit *f* (*a. fig.*).
sound...: **'~-proof**, **'~-tight** schalldicht; **'~-track** *Film:* Tonspur *f*; **'~-wave** Schallwelle *f*.
soup¹ [suːp] Suppe *f*.
soup² *Am. sl.* [~] **1.** Pferdestärke *f*; **2.** ~ *up* Motor frisieren (*Leistung erhöhen*).
sour ['sauə] **1.** □ sauer; *fig.* bitter; *fig.* sauer(töpfisch), mürrisch; **2.** *v/t.* säuern; *fig.* ver-, erbittern; *v/i.* sauer (*fig.* bitter) werden.
source [sɔːs] Quelle *f*; Ursprung *m*; ~ *language gr.* Ausgangssprache *f*.
sour·ish □ ['sauəriʃ] säuerlich; **'sour·ness** Säure *f*; *fig.* Bitterkeit *f*; **'sour·puss** Miesepeter *m*.
souse [saus] **1.** eintauchen; (mit Wasser) begießen; *Fisch etc.* einlegen, -pökeln; **2.** Plumps *m*; **soused** *sl.* besoffen.
sou·tane *eccl.* [suː'tɑːn] Soutane *f*.

south [sauθ] **1.** Süden *m*; *to the ~ of* südlich von; **2.** Süd...; südlich, südwärts; '**~·bound** in Richtung Süden fahrend.

south-east ['sauθ'i:st] **1.** Südosten *m*; **2.** *a.* **south-'east·ern** südöstlich.

south·er·ly ['sʌðəli], **south·ern** ['~ən] südlich; Süd...; '**south·ern·er** Südländer(in); *Am.* Südstaatler(in).

south·ern·most ['sʌðənməust] südlichst.

south·ing ['sauðiŋ] ⚓ (zurückgelegter) südlicher Kurs *m*; *ast.* Kulmination(szeit) *f*.

south...: '**~·land** Süden *m*; '**~·paw** *Am. Baseball:* Linkshänder *m*; ♀ **Pole** Südpol *m*.

south·ward(s) ['sauθwəd(z)] *adv.* südwärts, nach Süden.

south...: '**~·'west 1.** Südwesten *m*; **2.** *a.* **~·'west·er·ly**, **~·'west·ern** südwestlich; **~·'west·er** Südwestwind *m*; = **sou'west·er** ⚓ [sau-'westə] Südwester *m* (*wasserdichter Ölhut*).

sou·ve·nir ['su:vəniə] Andenken *n* (*of* an *acc.*).

sov·er·eign ['sɔvrin] **1.** □ höchst; unübertrefflich; hochwirksam (*Arznei*); unumschränkt, souverän; **2.** Landesherr(in), Herrscher(in), Souverän *m*; Sovereign *m* (*20-Schilling-Stück*); **sov·er·eign·ty** ['~rənti] Oberherrschaft *f*, Landeshoheit *f*, Souveränität *f*.

so·vi·et ['səuviət] Sowjet *m*.

sow¹ [sau] *zo.* Sau *f*, (Mutter-)Schwein *n*; ⊕ Sau *f*, Massel *f*.

sow² [səu] (*irr.*) (aus)säen, ausstreuen; *Land* besäen, bestreuen; '**sow·er** Sämann *m*; Sämaschine *f*; *fig.* Verbreiter(in); **sown** [səun] *p.p. von* sow².

so·ya ♀ ['sɔiə] Soja *f*; **~ bean** Sojabohne *f*.

soz·zled *sl.* ['sɔzld] besoffen.

spa [spa:] Heilbad *n*; Kurort *m*.

space [speis] **1.** Weltraum *m*; Platz *m*; Zwischenraum *m*; Zeitraum *m*; *typ.* Spatium *n*; **2.** *a.* **~ out** in Abständen anordnen, verteilen; *typ.* sperren; gesperrt drucken; '**~·craft** Raumschiff *n*; '**~·lab** Weltraumlabor *n*; **~ race** Weltraum-Wettrennen *n*; '**~·ship** Raumschiff *n*; **~ shot** Start *m e-s Satelliten etc.*;

~ shut·tle Raumfähre *f*; '**~·suit** Raumanzug *m*; '**~·'time** Zeit-Raum *m*, vierte Dimension *f*.

spa·cious □ ['speiʃəs] geräumig; weit, umfassend; '**spa·cious·ness** Weite *f*, Weiträumigkeit *f*.

spade [speid] **1.** Spaten *m*; *call a ~ a ~* das Kind beim rechten Namen nennen; *mst ~s pl. Karten:* Pik *n*, Schippe *f*; **2.** graben; '**~·work** mühevolle Vorarbeit *f*.

spa·ghet·ti [spə'geti] Spaghetti *pl.*

spake † *od. poet.* [speik] *pret. von* speak.

span¹ [spæn] **1.** (*a.* Zeit)Spanne *f*; ⚔ Spannung *f*, Spannweite *f*; *Am.* Gespann *n*; **2.** (um-, über)spannen; überwölben; (aus)messen.

span² [~] *pret. von* spin 1.

span·gle ['spæŋgl] **1.** Flitter *m*; **2.** (mit Flitter) besetzen; *fig.* übersäen.

Span·iard ['spænjəd] Spanier(in).

span·iel ['spænjəl] Spaniel *m*.

Span·ish ['spæniʃ] **1.** spanisch; **2.** Spanisch *n*; *the ~ pl.* die Spanier *pl.*

spank F [spæŋk] **1.** *v/t.* verhauen, -sohlen; *v/t.* **~ along** dahineilen; **2.** Klaps *m*, Schlag *m*; '**spank·er** ⚓ Gieksegel *n*; '**spank·ing 1.** □ tüchtig; schnell, scharf; F toll; **2.** F Haue *f*, Tracht *f* Prügel.

span·ner ⊕ ['spænə] Schraubenschlüssel *m*; *throw a ~ into the works fig.* querschießen.

spar¹ [spa:] ⚓ Spiere *f*; ✕ Holm *m*.

spar² [~] *Boxen:* sparren; Scheinhiebe machen (*at* nach); *fig.* sich streiten; kämpfen (*Hähne*); **~·ring partner** *Boxen:* Sparringspartner *m*.

spar³ *min.* [~] Spat *m*.

spare [spɛə] **1.** □ spärlich, kärglich, sparsam; mager; überzählig; überschüssig; Ersatz...; Reserve...; **~ hours** *pl.* Mußestunden *f/pl.*; **~ room** Gastzimmer *n*; **~ time** Freizeit *f*; **2.** ⊕ Ersatzteil *n*, *m*; **3.** *v/t.* (ver-)schonen; erübrigen; entbehren; (übrig) haben für; (er)sparen; sparen mit; *enough and to ~* mehr als genug; *v/i.* sparen, sparsam sein; Schonung üben; '**spare·ness** Dürftigkeit *f*; Magerkeit *f*; **spare part** Ersatzteil *n*, *m*; '**spare·rib** *Fleischerei:* Rippe(n)speer *m*, *n*.

spar·ing □ ['spɛəriŋ] sparsam (*in, of* mit); knapp, dürftig; '**spar·ing·ness** Sparsamkeit *f*.

spark¹ [spɑːk] **1.** Funke(n) *m* (*a. fig.*); **2.** *v/i.* Funken sprühen; *v/t.* ~ *s.th. off* et. auslösen.
spark² [~] flotter Kerl *m*; Galan *m*.
spark·ing-plug *mot.* ['spɑːkiŋplʌg] Zündkerze *f.*
spar·kle ['spɑːkl] **1.** Funke(n) *m*; Funkeln *n*; *fig.* sprühendes Wesen *n*; **2.** funkeln; blitzen; sprühen (*Witz*); perlen, moussieren (*Wein*), schäumen; *sparkling wine* Schaumwein *m*; **spar·klet** ['~klit] Fünkchen *n* (*a. fig.*).
spark-plug *mot.* ['spɑːkplʌg] Zündkerze *f.*
spar·row *orn.* ['spærəu] Sperling *m*, Spatz *m*; '~-hawk *orn.* Sperber *m.*
sparse □ [spɑːs] spärlich, dünn.
Spar·tan ['spɑːtən] **1.** spartanisch; **2.** Spartaner(in).
spasm ✸ ['spæzəm] Krampf *m* (*a. fig.*); **spas·mod·ic, spas·mod·i·cal** □ [~'mɔdik(əl)] krampfhaft, -artig, spasmodisch; *fig.* sprunghaft, unregelmäßig; **spas·tic** ['~tik] **1.** (~*ally*) spastisch; **2.** Spastiker(in).
spat¹ [spæt] Schaltierlaich *m.*
spat² [~] (Schuh)Gamasche *f.*
spat³ [~] *pret. u. p.p. von* spit² 2.
spatch-cock ['spætʃkɔk] *Bemerkung etc.* einstreuen, -fügen.
spate [speit] Hochwasser *n*; *fig.* Flut *f*; *be in* ~ Hochwasser führen.
spa·tial □ ['speiʃəl] räumlich, Raum...
spat·ter ['spætə] **1.** (be)spritzen; klatschen, prasseln; **2.** Schauer *m* (*a. fig.*).
spat·u·la ['spætjulə] Spatel *m.*
spav·in *vet.* ['spævin] Spat *m.*
spawn [spɔːn] **1.** Laich *m*; *fig. mst contp.* Brut *f*; 2. laichen; *contp.* aushecken; '**spawn·er** Rog(e)ner *m* (*weiblicher Fisch*); '**spawn·ing 1.** Laichen *n*; 2. Laich...; Brut...
spay [spei] *weibliches Tier* sterilisieren.
speak [spiːk] (*irr.*) *v/i.* sprechen; reden; ♪ erklingen; ~*ing! teleph.* am Apparat!; *Brown* ~*ing!* hier Brown!; ~ *out* laut sprechen; offen reden; ~ *to j. od.* mit *j-m* sprechen; ~ *up* kein Blatt vor den Mund nehmen; ~ *up!* (sprich) lauter!; ~ *up against* auftreten gegen; *that* ~*s well for him* das spricht sehr für ihn; *v/t.* sprechen; *Gedanken etc.* ausspre-

chen, äußern; verkünden; '~-eas·y *Am. sl.* Flüsterkneipe *f* (*ohne Konzession*); '**speak·er** Sprecher(in); Redner(in); *parl.* Sprecher *m*, Vorsitzende *m.*
speak·ing ['spiːkiŋ] sprechend; sprechend ähnlich (*Bild*); *be on* ~ *terms with* oberflächlich bekannt sein mit; '~-**trum·pet** Sprachrohr *n.*
spear [spiə] **1.** Speer *m*, Spieß *m*; Lanze *f*; **2.** (auf)spießen; '~**head 1.** Speerspitze *f*; *fig.* (Angriffs-)Spitze *f*, Vortrupp *m*; **2.** *Angriff* beginnen.
spec ✝ *sl.* [spek] Spekulation *f.*
spe·cial ['speʃəl] **1.** □ besonder; Sonder...; speziell; extra; Spezial...; ~ *envoy* Sonderbotschafter *m*; 2. *a.* ~ *constable* Hilfspolizist *m*; *a.* ~ *edition* Sonderausgabe *f*; *a.* ~ *train* Sonderzug *m*; *Am.* Sonderangebot *n* (*in e-m Geschäft*); *Am.* (Tages)Spezialität *f* (*in e-m Restaurant*); '**spe·cial·ist** Spezialist *m*; Fachmann *m*; ✸ Facharzt *m*; **spe·ci·al·i·ty** [speʃi'æliti] Besonderheit *f*; Spezialfach *n*; ✝ Spezialität *f*; **spe·cial·i·za·tion** [speʃəlai-'zeiʃən] Spezialisierung *f*; '**spe·cial·ize** *v/t.* besonders *od.* einzeln anführen; besonders ausbilden; *v/i.* sich spezialisieren (*in* in *dat.*, auf *acc.*), sich besonders verlegen auf (*acc.*); **spe·cial·ty** ['~ti] *s.* speciality; ⚖ besiegelter Vertrag *m.*
spe·cie ['spiːʃiː] Metallgeld *n*, Hartgeld *n*; '**spe·cies** *pl. u. sg.* Art *f*, Spezies *f.*
spe·cif·ic [spi'sifik] **1.** (~*ally*) spezifisch, eigen(tümlich); besonder; bestimmt; ~ *gravity phys.* spezifisches Gewicht *n*; ~ *name* Artname *m*; **2.** ✸ spezifisches Mittel *n.*
spec·i·fi·ca·tion [spesifi'keiʃən] Spezifizierung *f*; ⚖ Patentschrift *f*; ~*s pl.* nähere Angaben *f/pl.*; (technische) Beschreibung *f*; **spec·i·fy** ['~fai] spezifizieren, einzeln angeben *od.* nennen.
spec·i·men ['spesimin] Probe *f*, Muster *n*, Exemplar *n.*
spe·cious □ ['spiːʃəs] äußerlich blendend, bestechend; trügerisch; Schein...; '**spe·cious·ness** trügerischer Schein *m.*
speck [spek] **1.** Fleck *m*; Stückchen *n*; **2.** flecken, sprenkeln; **speck·le** ['~kl] **1.** Fleckchen *n*; **2.** *s.* speck 2.

specs F [speks] *pl.* Brille *f.*

spec·ta·cle ['spektəkl] Schauspiel *n*; Anblick *m*; (*a pair of*) ⁓s *pl.* (eine) Brille *f*; ⁓ *frame* Brillenfassung *f*; '**spec·ta·cled** bebrillt.

spec·tac·u·lar □ [spek'tækjulə] **1.** eindrucksvoll; auffallend, spektakulär; **2.** *Am.* F Galarevue *f.*

spec·ta·tor [spek'teitə] Zuschauer *m*; ⁓ *sport* Zuschauersport *m.*

spec·tral □ ['spektrəl] gespenstisch; *opt.* Spektral...; **spec·tre,** *Am.* **spec·ter** ['⁓tə] Gespenst *n*; **spec·tro·scope** *opt.* ['⁓trəskəup] Spektroskop *n*; **spec·trum** *opt.* ['⁓trəm] Spektrum *n.*

spec·u·late ['spekjuleit] grübeln, nachsinnen (*on, upon* über *acc.*); ✝ spekulieren; **spec·u·la·tion** theoretische Betrachtung *f*; Grübelei *f*; ✝ Spekulation *f*; **spec·u·la·tive** □ ['⁓lətiv] spekulativ, grüblerisch; theoretisch; ✝ spekulierend; **spec·u·la·tor** ['⁓leitə] Denker *m*; ✝ Spekulant *m.*

spec·u·lum ♣, *opt.* ['spekjuləm] (Metall)Spiegel *m*; Spekulum *n.*

sped [sped] *pret. u. p.p. von* speed 2.

speech [spi:tʃ] Sprache *f*; Rede, Ansprache *f*; *make a* ⁓ e-e Rede halten; '⁓-day *Schule*: (Jahres-) Schlußfeier *f*; ⁓ **de·fect** Sprachfehler *m*; **speech·i·fy** *contp.* ['⁓ifai] viel Worte machen; '**speech·less** □ sprachlos.

speed [spi:d] **1.** Geschwindigkeit *f*; Schnelligkeit *f*; Eile *f*; ⊕ Drehzahl *f*; *phot.* Lichtempfindlichkeit *f*; **2.** (*irr.*) *v/i.* schnell fahren, rasen; ⁓ *up* (*pret. u. p.p.* ⁓ed) die Geschwindigkeit erhöhen; *v/t. j-m* Glück verleihen; befördern; ⁓ *up* (*pret. u. p.p.* ⁓ed) beschleunigen; '⁓-boat Rennboot *n*; '⁓-cop motorisierter Verkehrspolizist *m*; '⁓-in·di·ca·tor = *speedometer*; '⁓-lim·it Geschwindigkeitsbegrenzung *f*; **speed-om·e·ter** *mot.* [spi'dɔmitə] Geschwindigkeitsmesser *m*, Tachometer *n*; **speed trap** Radarfalle *f*; '**speed·way** Motorradrennbahn *f*; *bsd. Am.* Schnellstraße *f*; '**speed·well** ♀ Ehrenpreis *n, m*; '**speed·y** □ schnell, rasch.

spell[1] [spel] **1.** (Arbeits)Zeit *f*, ⊕ Schicht *f*; Weilchen *n*, Bißchen *n*; Periode *f*; **2.** abwechseln mit *j-m* (*at* bei).

spell[2] [⁓] **1.** Zauber(spruch) *m*; **2.** (*irr.*) buchstabieren; richtig schreiben; bedeuten; ⁓ *out* entziffern; '⁓-bind·er *Am.* fesselnder Redner *m*; '⁓-bound *fig.* (fest)gebannt, verzaubert; '**spell·er:** *he is a bad* ⁓ er kann nicht richtig schreiben.

spell·ing ['speliŋ] Rechtschreibung *f*; '⁓-book Fibel *f.*

spelt[1] [spelt] *pret. u. p.p. von spell*[2] 2.

spelt[2] ♀ [⁓] Spelt *m*, Dinkel(weizen)⟩ **spel·ter** ['speltə] Zink *n.* [*m.*⟩

spen·cer ['spensə] Spenzer *m* (*Jäckchen*).

spend [spend] (*irr.*) *v/t.* verwenden (*on, upon* für, auf *acc.*); *Geld etc.* ausgeben (*on* für); verbrauchen, *b.s.* verschwenden; *Zeit* verbringen; (*bsd.* ⁓ *o.s.* sich) erschöpfen; ⁓ *the night* übernachten; *v/i.* Geld ausgeben; '**spend·er** Verschwender (-in).

spend-thrift ['spend⁰rift] **1.** Verschwender(in); **2.** verschwenderisch.

spent [spent] **1.** *pret. u. p.p. von* spend; **2.** *adj.* erschöpft, entkräftet, matt.

sperm [spə:m] *menschlicher u. tierischer* Same(n) *m*; **sper·ma·ce·ti** [⁓mə'seti] Walrat *m, n*; **sper·ma·to·zo·on** *biol.* [⁓ətəu'zəuɔn] Spermatozoon *n*, Spermium *n.*

spew [spju:] (sich) erbrechen.

sphere [sfiə] Kugel *f*; Erd-, Himmelskugel *f*; *fig.* Sphäre *f*, (Wirkungs)Kreis *m*; Bereich *m*; Gebiet *n*; **spher·i·cal** □ ['sferikəl] sphärisch; kugelförmig.

sphinc·ter *anat.* ['sfiŋktə] Schließmuskel *m.*

sphinx [sfiŋks] Sphinx *f* (*a. fig.*).

spice [spais] **1.** Gewürz(e *pl.*) *n*; *fig.* Würze *f*; Beigeschmack *m*; Anflug *m*; **2.** würzen; ⁓ *rack* Gewürzregal *n*; '**spic·er·y** Gewürze *n/pl.*

spic·i·ness ['spaisinis] Würzigkeit *f*; *fig.* Pikantheit *f.*

spick and span ['spikən'spæn] frisch u. sauber; schmuck; funkelnagelneu.

spic·y □ ['spaisi] gewürzreich, würzig; *fig.* pikant.

spi·der *zo.* ['spaidə] Spinne *f*; '**spi·der·y** spinnengleich.

spiel *Am. sl.* [spi:l] Gequassel *n.*

spiff·y *sl.* ['spifi] schick; toll.

spig·ot ['spigət] (Faß)Zapfen *m*;

Hahn *m*.
spike [spaik] **1.** Stift *m*; Spitze *f*;
Dorn *m*; Stachel *m*; *Sport*: Lauf-
dorn *m*; *mot.* Spike *m*; ♃ Ähre *f*;
2. festnageln; ✂ *Geschütz* vernageln; mit *eisernen* Stacheln versehen; **spike·nard** ['‿nɑːd] Laven-
del-, Nardenöl *n*; '**spik·y** ☐ spitzig.
spill[1] [spil] **1.** (*irr.*) *v/t.* verschütten;
Blut vergießen; F *Reiter etc.* ab-
werfen; *weitS.* schleudern; *v/i.* ver-
schüttet werden; überlaufen; **2.** F
Sturz *m vom Pferd etc.*
spill[2] [‿] Fidibus *m*.
spill·o·ver ['spiləuvə] Bevölkerungsüberschuß *m*.
spill·way ['spilwei] Abflußkanal *m*.
spilt [spilt] *pret. u. p.p. von spill*[1] **1**;
cry over ‿ milk über etwas jammern,
was doch nicht zu ändern ist.
spin [spin] **1.** (*irr.*) *v/t.* spinnen (*a.
fig.*); wirbeln, (herum)drehen;
Münze hochwerfen; sich *et.* ausdenken; erzählen; ‿ *s.th. out* et. in
die Länge ziehen; *v/i.* spinnen; *a.* ‿
round sich drehen, herumwirbeln;
✿ trudeln; ‿ *along* dahinsausen;
send s.o. (*s.th.*) ‿*ning* j. (et.) schleudern; **2.** Wirbeln *n*, Drehung *f*;
Spritztour *f*; ✿ Trudeln *n*.
spin·ach ♃ ['spinidʒ] Spinat *m*.
spi·nal ['spainl] Rückgrat...; ‿ *column* Wirbelsäule *f*; ‿ *cord*, ‿ *marrow* Rückenmark *n*; ‿ *curvature*
Rückgratverkrümmung *f*.
spin·dle ['spindl] Spindel *f*; '**spin·
dly** spindeldürr.
spin·dri·er ['spindraiə] Wäsche-
schleuder *f*.
spin-drift ['spindrift] Gischt *m*.
spin-dry ['spin'drai] *Wäsche* schleudern.
spine [spain] Rückgrat *n*; Dorn *m*;
(Gebirgs)Grat *m*; (Buch)Rücken *m*;
'**spine·less** rückgratlos (*a. fig.*).
spin·et ♪ [spi'net] Spinett *n*.
spin·na·ker ⚓ ['spinəkə] Spinnaker
m, Dreiecksegel *n*.
spin·ner ['spinə] Spinner(in);
Spinnmaschine *f*; **spin·ner·et** *zo.*
['spinəret] Spinndrüse *f*.
spin·ney ['spini] Dickicht *n*.
spin·ning...: ‿·jen·ny ⊕ ['spiniŋ-
'dʒeni] Feinspinnmaschine *f*; '‿·
-mill Spinnerei *f*; '‿·**wheel** Spinn-
rad *n*.
spin-off ['spinɔf] Nebenprodukt *n*.
spin·ster ['spinstə] unverheiratete

Frau *f*; *engS.* alte Jungfer *f*; *nach
dem Namen*: ledig.
spin·y ['spaini] dornig.
spi·ra·cle ['spaiərəkl] Luftloch *n*.
spi·rae·a ♃ [spai'riə] Spierstaude *f*.
spi·ral ['spaiərəl] **1.** ☐ spiralig;
Spiral...; schnecken-, schrauben-
förmig; **2.** Spirale *f*; *fig.* Wirbel *m*,
Welle *f*; **3.** sich spiralförmig bewegen; sich schrauben; wirbeln.
spire ['spaiə] Turmspitze *f*; *Berg-,
Baum- etc.* Spitze *f*; Spitzturm *m*.
spir·it ['spirit] **1.** *allg.* Geist *m*;
Sinn *m*; Temperament *n*, Leben *n*;
Mut *m*; Gesinnung *f*; ♏ Spiritus
m; Sprit *m*, Benzin *n*; ‿*s pl.* Stimmung *f*, Laune *f*; geistige Getränke
n/pl., Spirituosen *pl.*; ‿ *of wine*
Weingeist *m*; *in* (*high*) ‿*s* in gehobener Stimmung, gut aufgelegt;
in low ‿*s* in gedrückter Stimmung,
schlecht aufgelegt; **2.** ‿ *away*, ‿ *off*
verschwinden lassen, wegzaubern;
‿ *up* aufmuntern.
spir·it·ed ☐ ['spiritid] geistvoll; lebhaft, lebendig, temperamentvoll;
mutig; ...gesinnt; ...gestimmt;
'**spir·it·ed·ness** Lebhaftigkeit *f*;
Mut *m*.
spir·it·ism ['spiritizəm] Spiritismus
m; '**spir·it·ist** Spiritist(in).
spir·it·less ☐ ['spiritlis] geistlos;
temperament-, lustlos; mutlos.
spir·it-lev·el ['spiritlevl] Wasserwaage *f*.
spir·it·u·al ☐ ['spiritjuəl] geistig;
geistlich; geistvoll; '**spir·it·u·al·
ism** Spiritualismus *m*; Spiritismus
m; **spir·it·u·al·i·ty** [‿'æliti] Gei-
stigkeit *f*; geistige Natur *f*; **spir·it·
u·al·ize** ['‿əlaiz] ver-, durch-
geistigen.
spir·it·u·el(le) [spiritju'el] geist-
reich, -sprühend. [lisch.|
spir·it·u·ous ['spiritjuəs] alkoho-|
spirt [spəːt] **1.** (hervor)spritzen,
(hervor)schießen (lassen); **2.** (Was-
ser- *etc.*)Strahl *m*.
spit[1] [spit] **1.** Bratspieß *m*; Landzunge *f*; **2.** aufspießen.
spit[2] [‿] **1.** Speichel *m*, Spucke *f*;
be the very ‿ of s.o. F j-m wie aus
dem Gesicht geschnitten sein;
2. (*irr.*) *v/i.* spucken; fauchen
(*Katze*); sprühen (*fein regnen*); ‿ *at*
anspucken; ‿ *upon* bespucken; *v/t.*
(*mst ‿ out aus*)spucken; ‿ *it out!* F
heraus mit der Sprache!

spit 528

spit³ [↲] Spatenstich *m*.

spite [spait] **1.** Bosheit *f*; Groll *m*; **in** ~ **of** trotz (*gen.*); **2.** ärgern; kränken.

spite·ful □ ['spaitful] boshaft, gehässig; **'spite·ful·ness** Bosheit *f*.

spit·fire ['spitfaiə] Hitzkopf *m*; Kratzbürste *f*.

spit·tle ['spitl] Speichel *m*, Spucke *f*.

spit·toon [spi'tu:n] Spucknapf *m*.

spiv *sl.* [spiv] Schieber *m*.

splash [splæʃ] **1.** Spritzfleck *m*; P(l)atschen *n*; **make a** ~ F Aufsehen erregen; **2.** (be)spritzen; p(l)atschen; planschen; *Farbe etc.* (hin-)klecksen, (auf)klatschen; ~ **one's money about** *sl.* mit Geld um sich werfen; **'~-board** Spritzbrett *n*; **'~-down** Wasserung(sstelle) *f e-s Raumfahrzeugs*; **'splash·y** □ platschend; matschig; klecksig.

splay [splei] **1.** Ausschrägung *f*; **2.** auswärts gebogen; **3.** ausschrägen; ausgeprägt sein; **'~-foot** Spreizfuß *m*.

spleen [spli:n] *anat.* Milz *f*; üble Laune *f*, Ärger *m*; **spleen·ful** ['~ful], **'spleen·y** ärgerlich, launisch.

splen·did □ ['splendid] glänzend, prächtig, herrlich, großartig, wunderbar; **splen·dif·er·ous** F ['~difərəs] = *splendid*; **'splen·do(u)r** Glanz *m*, Pracht *f*, Herrlichkeit *f*.

sple·net·ic [spli'netik] **1.** *a.* **sple-'net·i·cal** □ ärgerlich; launisch; **2.** Hypochonder *m*.

splice [splais] **1.** Verspleißung *f*; ⚓ Spleiß *m*; **2.** (ver)spleißen; ⚓ splissen; ⊕ einfalzen; *sl.* verheiraten.

splint 🎇 [splint] **1.** Schiene *f*; **2.** schienen; **'~-bone** *anat.* Wadenbein *n*.

splin·ter ['splintə] **1.** Splitter *m*; **2.** (zer)splittern; **'splin·ter-proof** splittersicher.

split [split] **1.** Spalt *m*, Riß *m*; *fig.* Spaltung *f*; ~**s** *pl.* Grätsche *f*; Spagat *m*; **2.** gespalten; **3.** (*irr.*) *v/t.* (zer)spalten; zerreißen; platzen lassen; (sich) *et.* teilen; ~ **hairs** Haarspalterei treiben; ~ **one's sides with laughter** sich vor Lachen biegen, sich totlachen; ~ **up** aufspalten; platzen; *fig.* sich entzweien; ~ **on** *sl.* *j.* hochgehen lassen (*verraten*); **'~-'lev·el** ⌂ mit versetzten Ebenen;

'split·ting sehr heftig; F rasend (schnell).

splotch [splotʃ] Fleck *m*, Klecks *m*.

splurge [splə:dʒ] Angabe *f*, Getue *n*.

splut·ter ['splʌtə] *s.* sputter; 🚗 kotzen (*Motor*).

spoil [spɔil] **1.** *oft* ~**s** *pl.* Beute *f*, Raub *m*; *fig.* Ausbeute *f*; Schutt *m*; **2.** (*irr.*) *v/t.* (be)rauben; plündern; verderben; verwöhnen; *Kind* verziehen; *v/i.* verderben; ~**ing for a fight** streitlustig; **'spoil·er** Räuber *m*; Verderber *m*; **spoils·man** *Am. pol.* ['~zmən] Postenjäger *m*; **'spoil-sport** Spielverderber(in); **spoils sys·tem** *Am. pol.* Futterkrippensystem *n*.

spoilt [spɔilt] *pret. u. p.p. von spoil* 2.

spoke¹ [spəuk] *pret. von speak.*

spoke² [↲] Speiche *f*; (Leiter-) Sprosse *f*; ⚓ Spake *f*.

spo·ken ['spəukən] *p.p. von speak.*

spokes·man ['spəuksmən] Wortführer *m*, Sprecher *m*.

spo·li·a·tion [spəuli'eiʃən] Beraubung *f*, Plünderung *f*.

spon·dee ['spɔndi:] Spondeus *m*.

sponge [spʌndʒ] **1.** Schwamm *m*; **throw up the** ~ *Boxen u. fig.* sich geschlagen geben; **2.** *v/t.* mit e-m Schwamm (ab)wischen *od.* reiben; ~ **up** aufsaugen; *v/i.* schmarotzen (on bei); **'~-bag** Waschbeutel *m*; **'~-'cake** Biskuitkuchen *m*; **'spong·er** Schmarotzer(in).

spon·gi·ness ['spʌndʒinis] Schwammigkeit *f*; **'spon·gy** schwammig; porös.

spon·sor ['spɔnsə] **1.** Taufzeuge *m*, Pate *m*; Bürge *m*; Förderer *m*, Gönner *m*; Auftraggeber *m* für Werbesendung; **2.** Pate stehen bei; aus der Taufe heben; finanzieren; fördern; **'spon·sor·ship** Paten-, Gönnerschaft *f*.

spon·ta·ne·i·ty [spɔntə'ni:iti] Freiwilligkeit *f*; Unmittelbarkeit *f*; Spontaneität *f*; Selbstentstehung *f*, Selbstentwick(e)lung *f*; **spon·ta-ne·ous** □ ['~teinjəs] freiwillig, von selbst (entstanden); Selbst...; spontan; unwillkürlich; unmittelbar; unüberlegt; ♀ wild wachsend; ~ **combustion** Selbstverbrennung *f*; ~ **generation** Urzeugung *f*.

spoof *sl.* [spu:f] **1.** *j.* verkohlen; **2.** Mumpitz *m*; Schwindel *m*.

spook [spu:k] Spuk *m*; **'spook·y**

geisterhaft, Spuk...

spool [spu:l] **1.** Spule *f*; **2.** spulen.

spoon [spu:n] **1.** Löffel *m*; *sl.* verliebter Narr *m*; *be* ~s *on sl.* verschossen sein in *j.*; **2.** löffeln; *sl.* schmusen; '~**-drift** Gischt *m*, *f*; '**spoon·er·ism** Schüttelreim *m*; '**spoon-fed** *fig.* hochgepäppelt; verhätschelt, verwöhnt; **spoon·ful** ['~ful] Löffel(voll) *m*; '**spoon-meat** (Kinder-, Kranken)Brei *m*; '**spoon·y** □ F verschossen (*on* in *acc.*).

spoor *hunt.* [spuə] Spur *f*, Fährte *f*.

spo·rad·ic [spə'rædik] (~*ally*) sporadisch, verstreut.

spore ♀ [spɔ:] Spore *f*, Keimkorn *n*.

spor·ran ['spɔrən] Felltasche *f der Schottentracht*.

sport [spɔ:t] **1.** Sport *m*; Spiel *n*; *fig.* Spielball *m*; Unterhaltung *f*; Scherz *m*; ~s *pl. allg.* Sport *m*; Sportfest *n*; *a. good* ~ feiner Kerl *m*; *make* ~ *of* sich lustig machen über (*acc.*); **2.** *v/i.* sich belustigen; spielen, scherzen; *v/t.* F protzen mit; ~ *one's oak* die Tür verschlossen halten; '**sport·ing** □ Sport...; Jagd...; sportlich; ~ *chance* knappe Chance *f*; '**spor·tive** □ lustig; scherzhaft; '**sports-car** *mot.* Sportwagen *m*; '**sports-coat**, '**sports-jack·et** Sportsakko *m*; '**sports·man** Sportler *m*; Weidmann *m*; '**sports·man·like** sportlich; anständig, fair; weidmännisch; '**sports·man·ship** Sportlichkeit *f*; *fig.* faires Benehmen *n*; '**sports-wear** Sportkleidung *f*; '**sports·wom·an** Sportlerin *f*.

spot [spɔt] **1.** *allg.* Fleck *m*; Tupfen *m*; Makel *m*; Stelle *f*; Platz *m*; Leberfleck *m*, Pickel *m*; Tropfen *m*; ~s *pl.* † Lokowaren *f/pl.*; *a* ~ *of* F etwas, ein bißchen; *on the* ~ auf der Stelle; sofort, sogleich; *be on the* ~ zur Stelle sein; **2.** † sofort lieferod. zahlbar; Loko...; **3.** *v/t.* (be-) flecken, sprenkeln; ausfindig machen; (genau) erkennen; *v/i.* fleckig werden; F regnen; ~ *check* Stichprobe *f beim Zoll, der Steuer etc.*; '**spot·less** □ fleckenlos; '**spot·less·ness** Unbeflecktheit *f*; '**spot·light** *thea.* Scheinwerfer(licht *n*) *m*; *mot.* Suchscheinwerfer *m*; *in the* ~ *fig.* im Brennpunkt des Interesses; '**spot·ted** gefleckt, getupft; ~ *fever* ⚕ Fleck-

fieber *n*; '**spot·ter** Beobachter *m* (*bsd. zur Luftraumsicherung*); *Am.* Kontrolleur *m bsd. e-r Verkehrsgesellschaft*; '**spot·ti·ness** Fleckigkeit *f*; '**spot·ty** fleckig, sprenklig.

spouse [spauz] Gatte *m*; Gattin *f*.

spout [spaut] **1.** Tülle *f*, Schnauze *f*; Strahlrohr *n*; ⚠ Wasserspeier *m*; (Wasser)Strahl *m*; **2.** (aus)spritzen; F salbadern.

sprain [sprein] **1.** Verstauchung *f*; **2.** verstauchen.

sprang [spræŋ] *pret. von* spring 2.

sprat *ichth.* [spræt] Sprotte *f*.

sprawl [sprɔ:l] *v/i.* ausgestreckt daliegen, sich rekeln (*a. fig.*); ♀ wuchern; *fig.* sich ausdehnen; *v/t.* ~ *out* ausstrecken.

spray[1] [sprei] Zweig(verzierung *f*) *m*.

spray[2] [~] **1.** zerstäubte Flüssigkeit *f*; Sprühregen *m*; Gischt *m*; Spray *m*; = ~*er*; **2.** *Flüssigkeit* zerstäuben; *et.* besprühen; spritzen; '**spray·er** Zerstäuber *m* (*Gerät*).

spread [spred] **1.** (*irr.*) *v/t. a.* ~ *out* ausbreiten; (aus)dehnen; *Gerücht, Krankheit etc.* verbreiten; (be-) decken, belegen, überziehen; *Butter etc.* aufstreichen; *Brot etc.* bestreichen; *v/i.* sich aus-, verbreiten; ~ *the table* den Tisch decken; sich aus-, verbreiten; **2.** ~ *eagle* fliegender Adler *m als Abzeichen*; **3.** Aus-, Verbreitung *f*; Spannweite *f*; Weite *f*; Fläche *f*; *Am.* Decke *f*; Brotaufstrich *m*; F Festschmaus *m*; '~**-ea·gle** F bombastisch; hurrapatriotisch; '**spread·er** Aus-, Verbreiter(in); '**spread·ing** ausgebreitet, weit.

spree F [spri:] Spaß *m*, Jux *m*; Zechgelage *n*; Orgie *f*; (*Kauf- etc.*)Welle *f*; *go on a* ~ e-e Sauftour machen.

sprig [sprig] **1.** Sproß *m*, Reis *n* (*a. fig.*); Zweigverzierung *f*; ⊕ Zwecke *f*, Stift *m*; **2.** mit Stiften befestigen; ~*ged* geblümt (*Stoff*).

spright·li·ness ['spraitlinis] Lebendigkeit *f*; '**spright·ly** lebhaft, munter.

spring [spriŋ] **1.** Sprung *m*; Satz *m*; (Sprung)Feder *f*; Feder-, Sprungkraft *f*, Elastizität *f*; Triebfeder *f*; Springquell *m*, Quelle *f*; *fig.* Ursprung *m*; Frühling *m*; **2.** (*irr.*) *v/t.* springen lassen; (zer)sprengen; plötzlich herauskommen mit *et.*; *Wild* aufjagen; ~ *a leak* ⚓ leck werden; ~ s.th. on s.o. j. mit et. überraschen; v/i. springen; entspringen, entstehen (from aus, von); ♀ sprießen; ~ up aufspringen; aufkommen (Ideen etc.); aus dem Boden schießen; ~ into existence plötzlich entstehen; '~-'bal·ance Federwaage f; '~-board Sprungbrett n; '~--'clean·ing Frühjahrsputz m.

springe hunt. [sprind3] Schlinge f.

spring gun ['spriŋʌn] Selbstschuß m; '**spring·i·ness** Elastizität f; **spring mat·tress** Sprungfedermatratze f; **spring tide** Springflut f; '**spring·tide, 'spring·time** Frühling(szeit f) m; '**spring·y** □ federnd, elastisch.

sprin·kle ['spriŋkl] v/t. (be)streuen; (be)sprengen; v/i. sprühen (Regen); '**sprin·kler** Berieselungsanlage f; Rasensprenger m; eccl. Weihwedel m; '**sprin·kling** Sprühregen m; a ~ of fig. ein wenig, ein paar.

sprint [sprint] Sport: 1. sprinten; spurten; 2. Sprint m; Kurzstreckenlauf m; Endspurt m; '**sprint·er** Sprinter m, Kurzstreckenläufer m.

sprit ⚓ [sprit] Spriet n.

sprite [sprait] Geist m, Kobold m.

sprit·sail ⚓ ['spritsl] Sprietsegel n.

sprock·et-wheel ⊕ ['sprɔkitwiːl] Kettenrad n.

sprout [spraut] 1. sprießen, wachsen (lassen); 2. ♀ Sproß m; a. Brussels ~s pl. Rosenkohl m.

spruce[1] □ [spruːs] 1. schmuck, sauber; 2. (sich) fein machen.

spruce[2] ♀ [~] a. ~ fir Fichte f, Rottanne f.

sprung [sprʌŋ] pret. (✎) u. p.p. von spring 2.

spry [sprai] munter, flink.

spud [spʌd] Jätmesser n; F Kartoffel f.

spume lit. [spjuːm] Schaum m; '**spu·mous, 'spum·y** □ schaumig.

spun [spʌn] pret. u. p.p. von spin 1.

spunk [spʌŋk] Zunder m; F Feuer n, Mumm m; '**spunk·y** mutig.

spur [spəː] 1. Sporn m (a. zo., ♀); fig. Ansporn m; Vorsprung m, Ausläufer m e-s Berges; on the ~ of the moment der Eingebung des Augenblicks folgend; spornstreichs; put od. set ~s to dem Pferd die Sporen geben; fig. j. (an)spornen; win one's ~s sich die Sporen verdienen; ~ gear ⊕ Stirnrad n; 2. a. ~ on (an)spornen

(a. fig.); poet. sprengen, eilen.

spurge ♀ [spəːdʒ] Wolfsmilch f.

spu·ri·ous □ ['spjuəriəs] unecht, gefälscht; '**spu·ri·ous·ness** Unechtheit f.

spurn [spəːn] verschmähen, verächtlich zurückweisen.

spurred [spəːd] gespornt.

spurt [spəːt] 1. alle s-e Kräfte zs.-nehmen; Sport: spurten; s. spirt; 2. plötzliche Anstrengung f, Ruck m; Sport: Spurt m; s. spirt.

sput·nik ['sputnik] Sputnik m, Satellit m.

sput·ter ['spʌtə] 1. Gesprudel n; 2. v/i. sprudeln; spritzen; (at s.o. j. an)blubbern; v/t. a. ~ out hervorsprudeln.

spy [spai] 1. Späher(in); Spion(in); 2. (er)spähen; erblicken; spionieren; ~ (up)on s.o. j-m nachspionieren; '~·glass kleines Fernrohr n; '~-hole Guckloch n.

squab [skwɔb] Jungvogel m, bsd. ungefiederte Taube f.

squab·ble ['skwɔbl] 1. Zank m, Zwist m, Kabbelei f; 2. (sich) zanken; '**squab·bler** Zänker(in).

squad [skwɔd] Rotte f, Trupp m; **squad·ron** ['~rən] ⚔ Schwadron f; ✈ Staffel f; ⚓ Geschwader n.

squal·id □ ['skwɔlid] schmutzig, armselig.

squall[1] [skwɔːl] 1. Schrei m; ~s pl. Geschrei n; 2. schreien.

squall[2] ⚓ [~] Bö f; '**squall·y** ⚓ böig, stürmisch.

squa·lor ['skwɔlə] Schmutz m.

squa·mous ['skweiməs] schuppig.

squan·der ['skwɔndə] verschwenden; '~·'ma·ni·a Verschwendungssucht f.

square [skwɛə] 1. □ viereckig; quadratisch; senkrecht; im rechten Winkel (to, with zu); passend, stimmend; in Ordnung; direkt, unzweideutig, glatt; quitt, gleich (with mit); F ehrlich, redlich, offen; Am. F altmodisch, spießig; ~ measure Flächenmaß n; ~ mile Quadratmeile f; (take a) ~ root ✗ Quadratwurzel f (ziehen); ~ sail ⚓ Rahsegel n; 2. Quadrat n (a. e-r Zahl); Viereck n; Feld n (Schachbrett etc.); △ Säulenplatte f; ⚔ Karree n; öffentlicher Platz m; Winkelmaß n; Am. F altmodischer Spießer m; 3. v/t. viereckig machen; ✗ qua-

stage

drieren; einrichten (*with* nach), anpassen (*dat.*); ✝ begleichen, ausgleichen; bestechen; *v/i.* (*with*)
passen (zu); übereinstimmen (mit);
im Einklang stehen (mit); '~
-'built vierschrötig; ~ **dance**
Quadrille *f*; '~-'rigged ⚓ mit
Rahen getakelt; '~-toes F *sg*. Pedant *m*.

squash¹ [skwɔʃ] **1.** Gedränge *n*;
Fruchtsaft *m*; Platsch(en *n*) *m*;
Squash *n* (*ein Rakettspiel*); *mst*
~-*hat* Schlapphut *m*; **2.** (zer-,
zs.-)quetschen; drücken, pressen;
fig. erdrücken; F mundtot machen.

squash² ♀ [~] Kürbis *m*.

squat [skwɔt] **1.** kauernd; untersetzt; **2.** hocken, kauern; '**squatter** Hausbesetzer *m*; Siedler *m* ohne
Rechtstitel; *Australien*: Schafzüchter
m.

squaw [skwɔ:] (Indianer)Frau *f*,
Squaw *f*.

squawk [skwɔ:k] **1.** kreischen,
schreien; **2.** Gekreisch *n*, Geschrei *n*.

squeak [skwi:k] **1.** quieken, quiet-
schen; *sl.* pfeifen, petzen; **2.** Ge-
quieke *n etc.*; *a narrow* ~ F ein
knappes Entrinnen *n*; '**squeak·y** □
quiekend *etc.*

squeal [skwi:l] quäken; gell schreien;
s. squeak.

squeam·ish □ ['skwi:miʃ] empfindlich; mäkelig; Übelkeit empfindend; heikel; penibel; '**squeam-
ish·ness** Überempfindlichkeit *f*.

squee·gee ['skwi:'dʒi:] Scheiben-
reiniger *m* mit Gummilippe; *phot.*
Rollenquetscher *m*.

squeez·a·ble ['skwi:zəbl] gefügig.

squeeze [skwi:z] **1.** (sich) drücken,
(sich) pressen, (sich) quetschen;
auspressen; *fig.* (be)drängen, quälen; **2.** Druck *m* (*a. fig.*); kräftiger
Händedruck *m*; Gedränge *n*;
'**squeez·er** Presse *f*.

squelch [skweltʃ] platschen; zermalmen.

squib [skwib] Schwärmer *m*, Frosch
m; Spottgedicht *n*.

squid *zo.* [skwid] Tintenfisch *m*.

squif·fy *sl.* ['skwifi] beschwipst.

squig·gle F ['skwigl] Schnörkel *m*.

squill ♀ [skwil] Meerzwiebel *f*.

squint [skwint] **1.** schielen; **2.** Schielen *n*; F flüchtiger *od.* schiefer
Blick *m*; '~-**eyed** schielend; *fig.*

scheel, böse.

squire ['skwaiə] **1.** Gutsbesitzer *m*;
(Land)Junker *m*; *Am.* F (Friedens-)
Richter *m*; *hist.* Schildknappe *m*;
co. Kavalier *m*; Frauenheld *m*;
2. *e-e Dame* begleiten.

squir(e)·arch·y ['skwaiərɑ:ki] Jun-
kertum *n*; Junkerherrschaft *f*.

squirm F [skwə:m] sich winden.

squir·rel *zo.* ['skwirəl] Eichhörnchen *n*.

squirt [skwə:t] **1.** Spritze *f*; Strahl
m; F Wichtigtuer *m*; **2.** spritzen.

squish F [skwiʃ] Marmelade *f*.

stab [stæb] **1.** Stich *m*; ~ *in the back*
fig. verleumderischer Angriff *m*;
2. *v/t.* (er)stechen; *v/i.* stechen
(*at* nach).

sta·bil·i·ty [stə'biliti] Stabilität *f*;
Standfestig-, Beständig-, Stetigkeit *f*; ⚖ dynamisches Gleichgewicht *n*.

sta·bi·li·za·tion [steibilai'zeiʃən]
Stabilisierung *f*.

sta·bi·lize ['steibilaiz] stabilisieren
(*a.* ⚖); '**sta·bi·liz·er** ⚖, ⚓ Stabilisator *m*.

sta·ble¹ □ ['steibl] stabil; (stand-)
fest; dauerhaft; beständig; stetig.

sta·ble² [~] **1.** Stall *m*; **2.** einstallen.

sta·bling ['steibliŋ] Stallung *f*.

stac·ca·to ♪ [stə'kɑ:təu] stakkato.

stack [stæk] **1.** ✗ (Heu-, Stroh-,
Getreide)Schober *m*; Stapel *m*,
Stoß *m*; Schornsteinreihe *f*; ✗ Ge-
wehrpyramide *f*; Regal *n*; ~*s pl.*
bsd. Am. Hauptmagazin *n e-r*
Bibliothek; F Haufen *m*, Menge *f*;
blow one's ~ F *fig.* in die Luft gehen;
2. aufstapeln; aufstellen.

sta·di·um ['steidjəm] *Sport*: Stadion *n*, Sportplatz *m*, Kampfbahn *f*.

staff [stɑ:f] **1.** Stab *m*, Stock *m*;
Stütze *f*; ✗ Stab *m*; Personal *n*; Belegschaft *f*; Beamten-, Lehrkörper
m; ♪ *pl.* **staves** [steivz] Notensystem
n; **2.** (mit Personal, Beamten *od.*
Lehrern) besetzen; ~ **man·a·ger**
Personalchef *m*; ~ **room** Lehrerzim-
mer *n*.

stag [stæg] *zo.* **1.** Hirsch *m*; F Herr *m*
ohne Dame; ✝ Konzertzeichner *m*
an der Börse.

stage [steidʒ] **1.** Bühne *f*, Theater *n*;
fig. Schauplatz *m*; Stufe *f*, Stadium
n; Teilstrecke *f*, Etappe *f*; Gerüst
n, Gestell *n*; *go on the* ~ zur Bühne
gehen; **2.** *v/t.* inszenieren; *v/i.* für

die Bühne geeignet sein; '~·box Proszeniumsloge *f*; '~·coach Postkutsche *f*; '~·craft dramatisches Talent *n*; Theatererfahrung *f*; ~ di·rec·tion Bühnenanweisung *f*; ~ fright Lampenfieber *n*; '~·hand Bühnenarbeiter *m*; ~ man·ag·er Regisseur *m*; 'stag·er: *old* ~ alter Hase *m*; 'stage-struck theaterbesessen; stage ver·sion Bühnenfassung *f*; 'stag·ey = *stagy*.

stag·ger ['stægə] 1. *v/i.* (sch)wanken, taumeln; *fig.* stutzen; *v/t.* wankend machen; ⊕ *u. weitS.* staffeln; 2. Schwanken *n*, Wanken *n*; ⊕ *u. weitS.* Staffelung *f*; ~s *pl. vet.* Koller *m*; 'stag·ger·ing *fig.* umwerfend.

stag·nan·cy ['stægnənsi] Stockung *f*; 'stag·nant □ stehend (*Wasser*); stagnierend; stockend; träg; ✝ still; stag·nate [~'neit] stagnieren; stocken; stag'na·tion Stockung *f*.

stag-par·ty F ['stægpɑ:ti] Herrengesellschaft *f*.

stag·y □ ['steidʒi] theatralisch.

staid □ [steid] gesetzt, ruhig; 'staid·ness Gesetztheit *f*.

stain [stein] 1. Fleck(en) *m* (*a. fig.*); (Holz)Beize *f*; 2. fleckig machen; *fig.* beflecken, beschmutzen; ⊕ beizen, färben; ~ed glass buntes Glas *n*; 'stain·less □ ungefleckt; *fig.* fleckenlos; ⊕ rostfrei, nichtrostend (*Stahl*).

stair [stɛə] Stufe *f*; ~s *pl.* Treppe *f*, Stiege *f*; '~-car·pet Treppenläufer *m*; '~-case Treppe(nhaus *n*) *f*; '~-rod Läuferstange *f*; '~-way = *staircase*.

stake [steik] 1. Pfahl *m*; Marterpfahl *m*; (Spiel)Einsatz *m* (*a. fig.*); ~s *pl.* Pferderennen: Preis *m*, Einlage *f*; Rennen *n*; *pull up* ~s *Am.* F abhauen; *be at* ~ auf dem Spiele stehen; *place one's* ~ *on* setzen auf (*acc.*); 2. (um)pfählen; aufs Spiel setzen; *Geld etc.* setzen; ~ *out*, ~ *off* abstecken.

stal·ac·tite ['stæləktait] Stalaktit *m*, hängender Tropfstein *m*; stal·ag·mite ['stæləgmait] Stalagmit *m*, stehender Tropfstein *m*.

stale¹ □ [steil] alt (*Ggs. frisch*); schal, abgestanden (*Wasser, Neuigkeit*); altbacken (*Brot*); verbraucht (*Luft, Kraft*); fad (*Geruch*); alt (*Witz*); überanstrengt.

stale² [~] 1. stellen, harnen (*Pferd etc.*); 2. Harn *m*.

stale·mate ['steil'meit] 1. *Schach*: Patt *n*; *fig.* Stillstand *m*; 2. patt setzen; *fig.* zum Stillstand bringen.

stalk¹ [stɔ:k] Stengel *m*, Stiel *m*; Halm *m*.

stalk² [~] 1. *v/i.* einherschreiten; (einher)stolzieren; *hunt.* pirschen; *v/t.* beschleichen; 2. *hunt.* Pirsch *f*; 'stalk·er Pirschjäger *m*; 'stalking-horse *fig.* Deckmantel *m*.

stall [stɔ:l] 1. (Pferde)Box *f*; (Verkaufs)Stand *m*, Marktbude *f*; *thea.* Sperrsitz *m*; *eccl.* Chorstuhl *m*; 2. *v/t.* einstallen; ⚡ überziehen; *Motor* abwürgen; *v/i. mot.* aussetzen; ⚡ durchsacken; *fig.* Ausflüchte machen; '~-feed·ing Stallfütterung *f*.

stal·lion ['stæljən] Hengst *m*.

stal·wart ['stɔ:lwət] 1. □ stramm; handfest; 2. *pol.* Unentwegte *m*.

sta·men ⚘ ['steimen] Staubfaden *m*, -gefäß *n*; stam·i·na ['stæminə] Ausdauer *f*, Widerstandsfähigkeit *f*, Vitalität *f*; stam·i·nate ⚘ ['~nit] mit Staubfäden.

stam·mer ['stæmə] 1. stottern, stammeln; 2. Stottern *n*; 'stammer·er Stotter(in).

stamp [stæmp] 1. (Auf)Stampfen *n*; ⊕ Stampfe(r *m*) *f*; Stempel *m* (*a. fig.*); (Brief)Marke *f*; Gepräge *n* (*a. fig.*); Art *f*, Schlag *m*; 2. *v/t.* stampfen; prägen; stanzen; (ab-)stempeln (*a. fig.*); *Brief* frankieren; ~ *on the memory* dem Gedächtnis einprägen; ~ *out* zertreten; *fig.* niederschlagen; *v/i.* (auf)stampfen; '~-al·bum Briefmarkenalbum *n*; '~-col·lec·tor Briefmarkensammler *m*; '~-deal·er Briefmarkenhändler *m*; '~-du·ty Stempelgebühr *f*.

stam·pede [stæm'pi:d] 1. Panik *f*, wilde Flucht *f*; 2. durchgehen; in Panik versetzen.

stamp·er ['stæmpə] Stampfer *m*; Stempel *m*; stamp·ing ground F Revier *n*; *fig.* Tummelplatz *m*, Treff (-punkt) *m*; 'stamp(·ing)-mill *metall.* Pochwerk *n*.

stance [stæns] *Golf etc.*: Stellung *f*, Haltung *f*.

stanch [stɑ:ntʃ] 1. hemmen; stillen; 2. *adj.* = *staunch 1*; stan·chion ['stɑ:nʃən] Stütze *f*, Pfosten *m*.

stand [stænd] 1. (*irr.*) *v/i. allg.*

stehen; sich befinden; bestehen, beharren; *mst* ~ *still* stillstehen, stehenbleiben; bestehen (bleiben); ~ *against* bestehen gegen, *j-m* widerstehen; ~ *aside* abseits stehen; beiseite treten; ~ *back,* ~ *clear* zurücktreten; ~ *by* dabeistehen, dabei sein; *fig.* (fest) stehen zu; helfen; bereitstehen; ~ *for* sich bewerben um *ein Amt,* kandidieren für *e-n Sitz im Parlament;* bedeuten; eintreten für; vertreten; F sich *et.* gefallen lassen; ~ *in* einspringen (*for* für); ⚓ landwärts anliegen; ~ *in with* sich gut stellen mit; sich mit *j-m* beteiligen (*in an dat.*); ~ *off* abstehen; sich entfernt halten; zurücktreten (von); ⚓ seewärts anliegen; ~ *off!* weg da!; ~ *on* (*fig.* be-) stehen auf (*dat.*); ~ *out* hervorstehen; *fig.* deutlich hervortreten, sich abheben (*against* gegen); sich fernhalten; standhalten (*against* gegen); bestehen (*for* auf *dat.*); ⚓ nach See zu liegen; ~ *over für später* stehen *od.* liegen bleiben; *j.* beaufsichtigen; ~ *pat Am.* F stur bleiben; ~ *to* bleiben bei, beharren bei; *s. reason;* ~ *to!* ⚔ an die Gewehre!; ~ *up* aufstehen; sich erheben (*a. fig.*); ~ *up for* eintreten für; ~ *up to* sich zur Wehr setzen gegen; standhalten (*dat.*); ~ *upon* (*fig.* be-) stehen auf (*dat.*); *v/t.* (hin)stellen; aushalten, (v)ertragen; über sich ergehen lassen; *s. ground;* ~ *s.o. a dinner* F j-m ein Mittagessen spendieren; *s. treat;* **2.** Stand *m;* Standplatz *m;* Bude *f;* Standpunkt *m;* Stellung *f;* Stillstand *m;* Ständer *m,* Gestell *n;* Tribüne *f für Zuschauer; bsd. Am.* Zeugenstand *m; make a od. one's* ~ *against* standhalten (*dat.*).

stand·ard ['stændəd] **1.** Standarte *f,* Fahne *f;* Standard *m,* Norm *f;* Regel *f,* Maßstab *m;* Niveau *n,* Grad *m;* Stufe *f,* Klasse *f der Grundschule;* Münzfuß *m;* Währung *f;* Ständer *m,* Mast *m;* senkrechtes Rohr *n;* ♀ Hochstamm *m;* ~ *lamp* Stehlampe *f;* ~ *of living* Lebenshaltung *f,* -standard *m;* **2.** maßgebend; Muster..., Normal...; Einheits...; '~**-bear·er** *bsd. fig.* Bannerträger *m,* Vorkämpfer *m;* '~**-ga(u)ge** 🚂 normalspurig; **stand·ard·i·za-tion** [~ai'zeiʃən] Norm(ier)ung *f;*

'**stand·ard·ize** norm(ier)en, festsetzen, vorschreiben; vereinheitlichen.

stand-by ['stændbai] Beistand *m.*

stand·ee [stæn'di:] Stehende *m; Am.* Stehplatzinhaber *m.*

stand·er-by ['stændə'bai] Dabeistehende *m,* Zuschauer(in).

stand-in ['stænd'in] *Film:* Double *n.*

stand·ing ['stændiŋ] **1.** □ stehend; fest; (be)ständig; ~ *jump* Sprung *m* aus dem Stand; ~ *committee pol.* ständiger Ausschuß *m;* ~ *orders pl. parl.* Geschäftsordnung *f;* **2.** Stehen *n,* Stellung *f,* Rang *m;* Ruf *m* (*Ansehen*); Dauer *f; of long* ~ alt; '~**-room** Stehplatz *m.*

stand...: '~**-off** *Am.* Unentschieden *n;* Gegengewicht *n;* '~**-'off·ish** zurückhaltend; ~'**pat·ter** *Am.* F *pol.* sture Konservative *m;* '~**-pipe** Standrohr *n;* '~**-point** Standpunkt *m;* '~**-still** Stillstand *m; be at a* ~ stillstehen; *come to a* ~ zum Stehen kommen; '~**-up:** ~ *collar* Stehkragen *m;* ~ *fight* regelrechter Kampf *m;* ~ *supper* kaltes Büfett (*im Stehen eingenommen*).

stank [stæŋk] *pret. von* stink 2.

stan·nic 🜛 ['stænik] Zinn...

stan·za ['stænzə] Stanze *f;* Strophe *f.*

sta·ple[1] ['steipl] **1.** Haupterzeugnis *n; fig.* Hauptgegenstand *m;* Stapel *m* (*Faserwuchs der Wolle etc.*); **2.** Haupt...

sta·ple[2] [~] Haspe *f,* Krampe *f;* Heftklammer *f.*

sta·pler ['steiplə] (Büro)Heftmaschine *f.*

star [sta:] **1.** *allg.* Stern *m* (*fig.* Schicksal*); thea.* Star *m;* ♀s *and Stripes pl. Am.* Sternenbanner *n;* **2.** besternen; *thea.* die Hauptrolle spielen; ~ (*it*) glänzen; *thea.* gastieren; ~*ring mit ...* in der Hauptrolle.

star·board ⚓ ['sta:bəd] **1.** Steuerbord *n;* **2.** *Ruder* steuerbord legen.

starch [sta:tʃ] **1.** (Wäsche)Stärke *f; fig.* Steifheit *f;* ~ *flour* Stärkemehl *n;* **2.** stärken; ~*ed fig.* steif; '**starch·i-ness** Steifheit *f;* '**starch·y** □ steif; stärkehaltig.

star·dom ['sta:dəm] (Star)Ruhm *m.*

stare [steə] **1.** Starren *n;* Staunen *n;* starrer Blick *m;* **2.** große Augen machen; (*at an*)starren, (an)staunen.

star·fish *zo.* ['sta:fiʃ] Seestern *m.*

star·ing □ ['stɛəriŋ] starr (*Blick*); auffallend; grell.

stark [stɑːk] starr; völlig; ~ *naked* splitternackt.

star·light ['stɑːlait] Sternenlicht *n*.

star·ling¹ *orn*. ['stɑːliŋ] Star *m*.

star·ling² [~] Eisbrecher *m* e-r *Brücke*.

star·lit ['stɑːlit] sternenklar.

star·ry ['stɑːri] gestirnt; Stern(en)...; ~-'**eyed** *fig*. romantisch, wirklichkeitsfremd, verträumt.

star-span·gled ['stɑːspæŋgld] sternenbesät; *Star-Spangled Banner Am*. Sternenbanner *n*.

start [stɑːt] **1.** Auffahren *n*, Stutzen *n*; Ruck *m*; *Sport:* Start *m*; Aufbruch *m*; Anfang *m*; *fig*. Vorsprung *m*; *get the ~ of s.o.* j-m zuvorkommen; *give a ~* zs.-, auffahren; *s. fit²;* **2.** *v/i.* aufspringen, auffahren; stutzen (*at* vor *dat.*, bei); *Sport:* starten; abgehen, abfahren; aufbrechen, abreisen, sich aufmachen (*for* nach); *fig. von e-m Gedanken* ausgehen; anfangen (*on* mit *e-r Arbeit; doing* zu tun); *to ~ with* zunächst; *v/t.* in Gang bringen; *Maschine* anlassen; *Sport:* starten (lassen); *Wild* aufjagen; *fig*. anfangen; veranlassen (*doing* zu tun); *Geschäft* gründen, errichten; *Frage* aufwerfen.

start·er ['stɑːtə] *Sport:* Starter *m*; Läufer *m*, Rennteilnehmer *m*; *mot*. Anlasser *m*.

start·ing ['stɑːtiŋ] Ausgangs..., Anfangs...; '~-**point** Ausgangspunkt *m*; ~ **sal·a·ry** Anfangsgehalt *n*.

star·tle ['stɑːtl] (er-, auf)schrecken; '**star·tling** □ bestürzend, überraschend, aufsehenerregend.

star·va·tion [stɑː'veiʃən] (Ver-)Hungern *n*, Hungertod *m*; *attr*. Hunger...; **starve** verhungern (lassen); *fig*. verkümmern (lassen); **starve·ling** ['~liŋ] **1.** Hungerleider *m*; *fig*. Kümmerling *m*; **2.** verhungert; *fig*. verkümmert.

state [steit] **1.** Zustand *m*; Stand *m*; Pomp *m*, Staat *m*; *pol. mst* ⚇ Staat *m*; ~ *of life* Lebensstellung *f*; ~ *of the art* ⊕ neueste Stand *m* der Technik; *in ~* feierlich; *get into a ~* F sich aufregen; **2.** angeben; darlegen, -stellen; feststellen; melden; *s-e Regel etc.* aufstellen; ~ **a·part·ment** Prunkzimmer *n*; ~ **coach** Staatskarosse *f*; '~-**craft** *pol*. Staatskunst *f*; ⚇ **De·part·ment** *Am*.

pol. Außenministerium *n*; ~ **fu·ner·al** Staatsbegräbnis *n*; '**state·less** staatenlos; '**state·li·ness** Stattlichkeit *f*; Würde *f*; Pracht *f*; '**state·ly** stattlich; prächtig; erhaben; '**state·ment** Angabe *f*; Aussage *f*; Erklärung *f*; Darlegung *f*, Darstellung *f*; Feststellung *f*; Aufstellung *f*, ✝ (*of account* Konto)Auszug *m*; ⊕, ✝ Tarif *m*; **state mourn·ing** Staatstrauer *f*; '**state·room** Prunk-, Staatszimmer *n*; ⚓ Einzelkabine *f*; '**state·side** *Am*. F USA...; *go ~* heimkehren.

states·man ['steitsmən] Staatsmann *m*; '**states·man·like** staatsmännisch; '**states·man·ship** Staatskunst *f*; '**state-'sub·si·dized** staatlich subventioniert.

stat·ic ['stætik] statisch, Ruhe...; '**stat·ics** *pl. od. sg.* Statik *f*; *nur pl. Radio:* atmosphärische Störungen *f/pl.*

sta·tion ['steiʃən] **1.** Stand(ort) *m*; Stelle *f*; Stellung *f*; ✗, ⚓, 🚂 Station *f*; Bahnhof *m*; (Rundfunk-, Fernseh)Sender *m*; Rang *m*, Stand *m*; ⚒ Beruf *m*, Geschäft *n*; **2.** aufstellen, postieren, stationieren; **sta·tion·ar·y** □ ['~ʃnəri] stillstehend; feststehend, stationär; ~ *engine* Standmotor *m*; '**sta·tion·er** Schreibwarenhändler *m*; ⚇*s'* Hall Buchhändlerbörse *f in London*; '**sta·tion·er·y** Schreib- und Papierwaren *f/pl.*; **sta·tion-mas·ter** ['~ʃənmɑːstə] 🚂 Stationsvorsteher *m*; **sta·tion wag·on** *Am. mot.* Kombiwagen *m*.

stat·ism *pol.* ['steitizəm] staatlicher Dirigismus *m*, Planwirtschaft *f*; '**stat·ist** Anhänger *m* der Planwirtschaft.

sta·tis·ti·cal □ [stə'tistikəl] statistisch; **stat·is·ti·cian** [stætis'tiʃən] Statistiker *m*; **sta'tis·tics** *pl.* (*als Wissenschaft sg.*) Statistik *f*; *vital ~* Bevölkerungsstatistik *f*; weiblicher Körpermaße *f/pl.*

stat·u·ar·y ['stætjuəri] **1.** Bildhauer..., Statuen...; **2.** Bildhauerei *f*; Bildhauer *m*; **stat·ue** ['~tju:] Standbild *n*, Plastik *f*, Statue *f*; **stat·u·esque** □ [~tju'esk] statuenhaft; **stat·u·ette** [~tju'et] Statuette *f*.

stat·ure ['stætʃə] Statur *f*, Wuchs *m*, Gestalt *f*.

sta·tus ['steitəs] Zustand *m*; Stellung *f*, Rang *m*, Stand *m*; Status *m*; ~ symbol, symbol of ~ Statussymbol *n*.

stat·ute ['stætju:t] Statut *n*, Satzung *f*; (Landes)Gesetz *n*; '~-book Gesetzessammlung *f*; ~ law Gesetzesrecht *n*; ~ mile Meile *f* (*1,609 km*). **stat·u·to·ry** □ ['stætjutəri] gesetzlich.

staunch [stɔːntʃ] 1. □ fest; zuverlässig, standhaft; treu; 2. hemmen, stillen.

stave [steiv] 1. Faßdaube *f*; Strophe *f*; 2. *(irr.) mst* ~ *in (dat.)* den Boden einschlagen; ~ off abwehren; aufschieben.

staves ♪ [steivz] *pl. von staff 1.*

stay [stei] 1. ♎ Stag *n*; Stütztau *n*; *fig.* Stütze *f*; Aufschaub *m*, Frist *f*; Aufenthalt *m*; ~s *pl.* † Korsett *n*; 2. bleiben; wohnen; (sich) aufhalten; Ausdauer haben; hemmen, *(dat.)* Einhalt gebieten; aufschieben; *Hunger* vorläufig stillen; stützen; ~ *in zu* Hause bleiben; nachsitzen; ~ *for* warten auf *(acc.)*; ~ *(for) supper* zum Abendessen bleiben; ~ *put* F an Ort und Stelle bleiben; ~ *up* aufbleiben; ~ *the course* (bis zum Ende) durchhalten; ~*ing power* Ausdauer *f*; '~-at-home Stubenhocker *m*; '~-'down strike Sitzstreik *m der Bergleute*; 'stay·er *Sport*: Steher *m*; *be a good* ~ Stehvermögen haben.

stead [sted] Stelle *f*, Statt *f*; *in his* ~ an seiner Stelle, statt seiner; *stand s.o. in good* ~ j-m zustatten kommen.

stead·fast □ ['stedfəst] fest, unerschütterlich; standhaft; unverwandt *(Blick)*; '**stead·fast·ness** Festigkeit *f*, Standhaftigkeit *f*.

stead·i·ness ['stedinis] Festigkeit *f*.

stead·y ['stedi] 1. □ (be)ständig; stetig; sicher; fest; ruhig; gleichmäßig; ✝ fest; unerschütterlich; zuverlässig; *go* ~ *with s.o.* mit j-m fest gehen; 2. stetig *od.* sicher machen *od.* werden; (sich) festigen; stützen; (sich) beruhigen; halten; 3. *Am.* F feste Freundin *f*.

steak [steik] (Beef)Steak *n*; Fischfilet *n*.

steal [stiːl] 1. *(irr.) v/t.* stehlen *(a. fig.)*; ~ *a march on s.o.* j-m zuvorkommen; *v/i.* sich stehlen *od.* schleichen; ~ *into* sich einschleichen in *(acc.)*; 2. *Am.* Korruptionsgeschäft *n*.

stealth [stelθ] Heimlichkeit *f*; *by* ~ heimlich; '**stealth·i·ness** Heimlichkeit *f*; '**stealth·y** □ verstohlen, heimlich.

steam [stiːm] 1. Dampf *m*; Dunst *m*; *let off* ~ ⊕ Dampf ablassen; *fig.* sich Luft machen; 2. Dampf...; 3. *v/i.* dampfen; ~ *up* beschlagen *(Glas)*; *v/t.* ausdünsten; mit Dampf behandeln, dämpfen; '~-boat Dampfschiff *n*; '~-boil·er Dampfkessel *m*; **steamed** beschlagen *(Fenster)*; '**steam-en·gine** Dampfmaschine *f*; '**steam·er** ♎ Dampfer *m*; ⊕ Dämpfer *m*; '**steam·i·ness** Dunstigkeit *f*.

steam...: '~-roller 1. Dampfwalze *f*; 2. *fig.* niederwalzen; '~-ship = steamboat; ~ *tug* ♎ Schleppdampfer *m*; '**steam·y** □ dampfig; dampfend; dunstig.

ste·a·rin ⚗ ['stiərin] Stearin *n*.

steed *rhet.* [stiːd] (Streit)Roß *n*.

steel [stiːl] 1. Stahl *m*; Wetzstahl *m*; 2. stählern; Stahl...; 3. (ver)stählen; '~-clad stahlgepanzert; ~ en·grav·ing Stahlstich *m*; '~-plat·ed gepanzert; '~-works *sg.* Stahlwerk *n*; '**steel·y** *mst fig.* stählern; '**steel·yard** Laufgewichtswaage *f*.

steep[1] [stiːp] 1. steil, jäh; F toll, stark *(unerhört)*; 2. *poet.* jäher Abhang *m*.

steep[2] [~] einweichen; einlegen; eintauchen; tränken; *fig.* versenken *(in* in *acc.*).   [*od.* werden.]

steep·en ['stiːpən] steiler machen]

stee·ple ['stiːpl] Kirchturm *m*; '~-chase Hindernisrennen *n*; '~-jack Turm-, Schornsteinarbeiter *m*.

steep·ness ['stiːpnis] Steilheit *f*.

steer[1] [stiə] junger Ochse *m*.

steer[2] [~] steuern; ~ *clear of fig.* vermeiden; '**steer·a·ble** lenkbar.

steer·age ♎ ['stiəridʒ] Steuerung *f*; Zwischendeck *n*; '~-way ♎ Steuerfähigkeit *f*, -fahrt *f*.

steer·ing... ['stiərin]: ~ col·umn *mot.* Lenksäule *f*; '~-gear ♎ Ruderanlage *f*; '~-wheel Steuerrad *n*.

steers·man ♎ ['stiəzmən] Rudergänger *m*.

stein [stain] Maßkrug *m*.

stel·lar ['stelə] Stern(en)...

stem[1] [stem] 1. (Baum-, Wort-) Stamm *m*; Stiel *m*; Stengel *m*;

2. abstielen; *Am.* (ab)stammen (*from* von).

stem² [~] **1.** ⚓ Vordersteven *m*; **2.** *v/t.* sich stemmen *od.* ankämpfen gegen; *v/i. Schilauf*: stemmfahren; ~(ming) turn Stemmbogen *m*.

stench [stentʃ] Gestank *m*.

sten·cil ['stensl] **1.** Schablone *f*; Matrize *f*; **2.** schablonieren; hektographieren.

ste·nog·ra·pher [ste'nɔgrəfə] Stenograph(in); **sten·o·graph·ic** [~nə-'græfik] (~ally) stenographisch; **ste·nog·ra·phy** [~'nɔgrəfi] Stenographie *f*, Kurzschrift *f*.

step¹ [step] **1.** Schritt *m*, Tritt *m*; *fig.* (kurze) Strecke *f*; Fußstapfe *f*; (Treppen)Stufe *f*; Trittbrett *n*; (*a pair of*) ~s *pl.* (eine) Trittleiter *f*; *in* ~ with in gleichem Schritt mit; *take* ~s Schritte unternehmen; **2.** *v/i.* schreiten; treten, gehen; ~ down von *e-m Posten* zurücktreten; ~ in *fig.* einschreiten; ~ on it! *sl.* mach fix!; ~ out ausschreiten, sich beeilen; *v/t.* ~ out, ~ off abschreiten; ~ up in die Höhe bringen, ankurbeln.

step² [~] *in Zssgn* Stief...; '~·fa·ther Stiefvater *m*; '~·moth·er Stiefmutter *f*.

steppe [step] Steppe *f*.

step·ping-stone ['stepinstɔun] Trittstein *m*; *fig.* Sprungbrett *n*.

ster·e·o ['stiəriɔu] **1.** *typ.* Klischee *n*; **2.** ♪ Stereo...

ster·e·o... [~'stiəriə]: ~·phon·ic [~-'fɔnik] stereophonisch, Stereo...; '~·scope Stereoskop *n*; '~·type **1.** Stereotype *f*; **2.** stereotypieren; ~d stereotyp.

ster·ile ['sterail] steril; unfruchtbar; keimfrei; **ste·ril·i·ty** [~'riliti] Unfruchtbarkeit *f*; **ster·il·i·za·tion** [sterilai'zeiʃən] Sterilisierung *f*; **'ster·i·lize** sterilisieren; unfruchtbar machen; entkeimen.

ster·ling ['stə:liŋ] vollwertig, echt; gediegen; ✝ Sterling...; *pound* ~ Pfund *n* Sterling; ~ **a·re·a** Sterlingblock *m*.

stern¹ □ [stə:n] ernst; finster; streng, hart.

stern² ⚓ [~] Heck *n*, Spiegel *m*.

stern·ness ['stə:nnis] Ernst *m*; Strenge *f*.

stern-post ⚓ ['stə:npɔust] Hintersteven *m*.

ster·num *anat.* ['stə:nəm] Brustbein *n*.

steth·o·scope ⚕ ['steθəskɔup] Stethoskop *n* (*Hörrohr*).

ste·ve·dore ⚓ ['sti:vidɔ:] Schauermann *m*, Stauer *m*.

stew [stju:] **1.** schmoren, dämpfen; **2.** Schmorgericht *n*; F Aufregung *f*.

stew·ard ['stjuəd] Verwalter *m*; Haushofmeister *m*; ⚓ Steward *m*; (Fest)Ordner *m*; **stew·ard·ess** ⚓, ✈ Stewardeß *f*.

stew...: '~·pan, '~·pot Schmorpfanne *f*, -topf *m*.

stick¹ [stik] **1.** Stock *m*; Stecken *m*; Stab *m*; (*Besen- etc.*)Stiel *m*; Stange *f Siegellack etc.*; F Klotz *m* (*unbeholfener Mensch*); ~s *pl.* Kleinholz *n*; *the* ~s *pl. Am.* F hinterste Provinz *f*; **2.** ✗ mit Stöcken stützen.

stick² [~] (*irr.*) *v/i.* stecken (bleiben); haften; kleben (*to an dat.*); *fig.* sich stoßen (*at an dat.*); ~ *at nothing* vor nichts zurückschrecken; ~ out, ~ up hervorragen, -stehen; F standhalten; F bestehen (*for auf dat.*); ~ *to* bleiben bei, festhalten an (*dat.*); ~ up *for s.o.* j-m die Stange halten; *v/t.* (ab)stechen; (an)stecken, (an)heften; (an)kleben; F aushalten, ertragen; ~ *it on sl.* unverschämte Preise verlangen; ~ out herausstrecken; ~ *it out* F durchhalten, nicht nachgeben; ~ up sl. Bank etc. überfallen; **'stick·er** Klebezettel *m*; **'stick·i·ness** Klebrigkeit *f*; **'stick·ing-plas·ter** Heftpflaster *n*; **'stick-in-the-mud 1.** rückschrittlich; **2.** Rückschrittler *m*; Spießer *m*.

stick·le ['stikl] Partei nehmen; **'stick·le·back** *ichth.* Stichling *m*; **'stick·ler** Eiferer *m*, Verfechter *m* (*for gen.*).

stick-up ['stikʌp] *a.* ~ *collar* F Stehkragen *m*; *sl.* Raubüberfall *m*.

stick·y □ ['stiki] kleb(e)rig; schmierig, schmutzig; zäh; *come to a* ~ *end sl.* ein schlimmes Ende nehmen; *be* ~ *about doing* F et. ungern tun.

stiff □ [stif] steif; starr; hartnäckig; hart, mühsam; stark (*Getränk*); *be bored* ~ F zu Tode gelangweilt sein; *keep a* ~ *upper lip* die Ohren steifhalten; **'stiff·en** (sich) steifen; (sich) versteifen (*bsd.* ✝); erstarren (lassen); *fig.* stärken; **'stiff·en·er** steife Einlage *f*; **'stiff-'necked** halsstarrig.

sti·fle¹ *vet.* ['staifl] Kniegelenk *n*.

sti·fle[2] [ˑ] ersticken (a. *fig.*).

stig·ma ['stigmə] (Brand-, Schand-) Mal *n*; Stigma *n*; ⚥ Symptom *n*; ⚘ Narbe *f*; **stig·ma·tize** ['ˑtaiz] brandmarken.

stile [stail] Zauntritt *m*, -übergang *m*; ⊕ Seitenpfosten *m e-r Tür etc.*

sti·let·to [stiˈletəu] Stilett *n*; ˑ *heel* Pfennigabsatz *m*.

still[1] [stil] **1.** *adj.* still; ˑ *wine* Stillwein *m*; **2.** Photographie *f* (*im Gegensatz zum Film*); **3.** *adv.* noch immer; *bei comp.* noch; **4.** *cj.* doch, dennoch, trotzdem; **5.** stillen; beruhigen.

still[2] [ˑ] Destillierapparat *m*.

still...: 'ˑ**birth** Totgeburt *f*; 'ˑ**born** totgeboren; 'ˑ**hunt** pirschen; 'ˑ**hunt·ing** Pirschjagd *f*; ˑ *life* Stillleben *n*; '**still·ness** Stille *f*, Ruhe *f*.

still-room ['stilrum] Vorratskammer *f*.

still·y *poet.* ['stili] still, ruhig.

stilt [stilt] Stelze *f*; '**stilt·ed** gespreizt, hochtrabend, geschraubt.

stim·u·lant ['stimjulənt] **1.** ⚕ stimulierend; **2.** ⚕ Reizmittel *n*; Genußmittel *n*; Anreiz *m*; **stim·u·late** ['ˑleit] (an)reizen; anregen; **stim·u·la·tion** Reizung *f*, Antrieb *m*; **stim·u·la·tive** ['ˑlətiv] (an)reizend; **stim·u·lus** ['ˑləs] Antrieb *m* (*to zu*); Reizmittel *n*.

sting [stiŋ] **1.** Stachel *m von Insekten*; Stich *m*, Biß *m*; *fig.* Schärfe *f*; Antrieb *m*; **2.** (*irr.*) stechen; *fig.* schmerzen; peinigen; (an)treiben; *be stung sl.* geneppt werden (*for* um); '**sting·er** F schmerzhafter Schlag *m*.

stin·gi·ness ['stindʒinis] Geiz *m*; Kargheit *f*.

sting(·ing)-net·tle ⚘ ['stiŋ(iŋ)netl] Brennessel *f*.

stin·gy □ ['stindʒi] geizig; knapp, karg.

stink [stiŋk] **1.** Gestank *m*; **2.** (*irr.*) *v/i.* stinken (*of nach*; *sl. a. fig.*); *v/t.* verstänkern; '**stink·er** F Ekel *n*, ekelhafter Kerl *m*, gemeiner Typ *m*; geharnischter Brief *m*; vertrackte Problem *n*.

stint [stint] **1.** Einschränkung *f*; zugewiesene Arbeit *f*; **2.** kargen *od.* knausern mit; einschränken; *j.* knapp halten.

sti·pend ['staipend] Gehalt *n* (*bsd. e-s Pfarrers*); **sti·pen·di·ar·y** [ˑ-**

djəri] **1.** besoldet; **2.** Polizeirichter *m.*

stip·ple *paint.* ['stipl] punktieren.

stip·u·late ['stipjuleit] *a.* ˑ *for* zur Bedingung machen, ausbedingen, festsetzen; **stip·u·la·tion** Abmachung *f*; Festsetzung *f*; Klausel *f*, Bedingung *f*.

stir[1] [stəː] **1.** Regung *f*; Bewegung *f*; Rühren *n*; Aufregung *f*; Aufsehen *n*; **2.** *v/t.* (um)rühren, bewegen; (an)schüren; aufregen; ˑ *up* aufrühren; reizen, aufhetzen; *v/i.* sich rühren *od.* regen.

stir[2] *sl.* [ˑ] Kittchen *n* (*Gefängnis*).

stir·ring ['stəːriŋ] auf-, erregend; bewegt.

stir·rup ['stirəp] Steigbügel *m.*

stitch [stitʃ] **1.** Stich *m*; Masche *f*; Seitenstechen *n*; *not have a dry ˑ on one* keinen trockenen Faden am Leibe haben; *a ˑ in time saves nine* gleich getan ist viel gespart; **2.** nähen; heften; *Buchbinderei*: heften, broschieren.

stoat *zo.* [stəut] Hermelin *n.*

stock [stɔk] **1.** (Baum)Strunk *m*; Pfropfunterlage *f*; Griff *m*, Schaft *m e-s Gerätes*, Kolben *m e-s Gewehrs*; Stamm *m*, Geschlecht *n*, Her-, Abkunft *f*; Roh-, Grundstoff *m*; Suppenstock *m*, (Fleisch-, Gemüse)Brühe *f*; Vorrat *m*, (Waren)Lager *n*; (Wissens)Schatz *m*; *a. live ˑ* Vieh(bestand *m*) *n*; *hist.* Halsbinde *f*; ⚘ Levkoje *f*; ✝ (Stamm-, Anleihe)Kapital *n*; ˑ*s pl.* Effekten *pl.*, Aktien *f/pl.*; Staatspapiere *n/pl.*; ˑ*s pl.* ⚓ Stapel *m*; ˑ*s pl. hist.* Stock *m* (*für Gefangene*); *in* (*out of*) ˑ (nicht) vorrätig; *take* ˑ ✝ Inventur machen; *take ˑ of fig.* sich klarwerden über (*acc.*), *et.* abschätzen; **2.** auf Lager, vorrätig; Lager...; *bsd. thea.* stehend, ständig; gängig; Standard...; stereotyp; ˑ *play* Repertoirestück *n*; **3.** versehen, versorgen; *Waren* führen; vorrätig haben.

stock·ade [stɔˈkeid] **1.** Einpfählung *f*, Staket *n*; **2.** einpfählen.

stock...: 'ˑ**breed·er** Viehzüchter *m*; 'ˑ**brok·er** Börsenmakler *m*; 'ˑ**car** Viehwagen *m*; ˑ **com·pa·ny** *thea.* ständiges Ensemble *n*; ˑ **ex·change** Börse *f*; 'ˑ**farm·er** Viehzüchter *m*; 'ˑ**hold·er** Aktionär *m.*

stock·i·net [stɔkiˈnet] Trikot *n.*

stock·ing ['stɔkiŋ] Strumpf *m.*
stock·ist † ['stɔkist] Lagerhalter *m.*
stock...: '~-in-'trade Werk-, Rüstzeug *n;* '~job·ber Börsenmakler *m;* ~ **mar·ket** Börse *f;* '~-pil·ing (staatliche) Vorratshaltung *f;* '~-'still unbeweglich, mäuschenstill; '~·tak·ing Inventur *f.*
stock·y ['stɔki] untersetzt, stämmig.
stock·yard ['stɔkjɑːd] Viehhof *m.*
stodge *sl.* [stɔdʒ] (sich) vollstopfen; '**stodg·y** □ schwer, unverdaulich; *fig.* schwerfällig; langweilig.
sto·gy, sto·gie *Am.* ['stəugi] billige Zigarre *f.*
sto·ic ['stəuik] **1.** stoisch; **2.** Stoiker *m;* '**sto·i·cal** □ *fig.* stoisch; **sto·i·cism** ['~sizəm] Stoizismus *m;* Gleichmut *m,* Gelassenheit *f.*
stoke [stəuk] *Feuer* (an)schüren; heizen, feuern; '~-hold, '~-hole ⚓ Heizraum *m;* '**stok·er** Heizer *m.*
stole[1] [stəul] Stola *f.*
stole[2] [_] *pret.,* '**sto·len** *p.p. von* steal 1.
stol·id □ ['stɔlid] unerschütterlich, gleichmütig; stur; **sto'lid·i·ty** Unerschütterlichkeit *f,* Gleichmut *m;* Sturheit *f.*
stom·ach ['stʌmək] **1.** Magen *m;* Leib *m,* Bauch *m; fig.* Neigung *f,* Lust *f* (for zu); **2.** verdauen, -tragen; *fig.* ertragen; '~-ache Magen-, Bauchschmerzen *m/pl.;* **sto·mach·ic** [stəu'mækik] **1.** (~ally) Magen...; magenstärkend; **2.** magenstärkendes Mittel *n.*
stomp *Am.* [stɔmp] (auf)stampfen.
stone [stəun] **1.** Stein *m;* (Obst-) Kern *m; a. precious ~* Edelstein *m; Gewichtseinheit von 6,35 kg;* **2.** steinern; Stein...; **3.** steinigen; *Obst* entsteinen; ♀ **Age** *die* Steinzeit; '~-'blind stockblind; '~-'cold eiskalt; '~-crop ♀ Mauerpfeffer *m.*
stoned *sl.* [stəund] (stink)besoffen; *durch Drogen:* weg.
stone...: '~-'dead mausetot; '~-'deaf stocktaub; '~-fruit ♀ Steinfrucht *f;* '~-ma·son Steinmetz *m;* '~-pit Steinbruch *m;* '~-wall·ing *Sport:* Mauern *n; pol.* Obstruktionspolitik *f;* '~-ware Steingut *n;* '~-work Steinmetzarbeit *f.*
ston·i·ness ['stəuninis] Härte *f.*
ston·y ['stəuni] steinig; *fig.* steinern; *a.* ~-broke *sl.* völlig pleite.
stood [stud] *pret. u. p.p. von* stand.

stooge *sl.* [stuːdʒ] **1.** *thea.* Stichwortgeber *m; fig.* Handlanger *m;* Prügelknabe *m;* **2.** den Dummen machen.
stool [stuːl] Schemel *m,* Hocker *m;* ⚶ Stuhlgang *m;* ♀ Wurzelstock *m;* ♀ Wurzelschößling *m;* '~-pi·geon *bsd. Am.* Spitzel *m,* Lockvogel *m.*
stoop [stuːp] **1.** *v/i.* sich bücken; sich erniedrigen *od.* herablassen; krumm gehen; *v/t. Kopf* neigen; **2.** gebeugte Haltung *f; Am.* Vorplatz *m,* Veranda *f.*
stop [stɔp] **1.** *v/t.* anhalten; hindern (from an *dat.*); aufhören (mit); *a.* ~ up (ver)stopfen; *Zahn* füllen, plombieren; *Weg* versperren; *Scheck* sperren; *Zahlung* einstellen; *Lohn* einbehalten; ♪ *Saite, Ton* greifen; *v/i.* stehenbleiben, aufhören; halten; F bleiben; ~ *dead,* ~ *short* plötzlich *od.* unvermittelt anhalten; ~ *at home* F zu Hause bleiben; ~ *over* haltmachen, die Reise unterbrechen; ~ *up late* F lange aufbleiben; **2.** Halt *m,* Einhalt *m;* Pause *f;* Hemmung *f;* ⊕ Anschlag *m;* Aufhören *n,* Ende *n;* Haltestelle *f; mst full* ~ *gr.* Punkt *m;* ♪ Klappe *f;* ♪ Griff *m; gr.* Verschlußlaut *m;* '~-cock ⊕ Absperrhahn *m;* '~-gap Notbehelf *m,* Lückenbüßer *m;* '~-light *Am.* Verkehrsampel *f;* '~-o·ver Aufenthalt *m,* Fahrtunterbrechung *f;* ✈ Zwischenlandung *f;* '**stop·page** Verstopfung *f;* (Arbeits-, Betriebs-, Zahlungs-) Einstellung *f;* Sperrung *f;* (Lohn-) Abzug *m;* Aufenthalt *m;* ⊕ Hemmung *f;* Betriebsstörung *f;* (Verkehrs)Stockung *f;* '**stop·per 1.** Stöpsel *m;* ⊕ Hemmer *m;* ~ *circuit* ⚡ Sperrkreis *m;* **2.** (zu)stöpseln; '**stop·ping** Zahnfüllung *f,* Plombe *f;* '**stop·press** (Spalte *f* für) neueste Nachrichten *f/pl.;* '**stop·watch** Stoppuhr *f.*
stor·age ['stɔːridʒ] Lagerung *f,* Aufbewahrung *f;* ⚡ Speicherung *f;* Lagergeld *n;* ~ *battery* Akkumulator *m.*
store [stɔː] **1.** Vorrat *m; a.* ~s *pl. fig.* Fülle *f;* Lagerhaus *n; Am.* Laden *m;* ~s *pl.* Kauf-, Warenhaus *n;* ~s *pl.* ⚔, ⚓ Militär-, Schiffsbedarf *m; in* ~ vorrätig, auf Lager; *be in* ~ *for* auf *j.* warten; *have in* ~ *for* bereit halten für; *set od. put great* ~

by Gewicht legen auf (*acc.*); **2.** *a.*
~ up (auf)speichern; unterbringen;
verstauen; (ein)lagern; versehen,
versorgen (*with* mit); '~·**house**
Lagerhaus *n*; *mst fig.* Schatzkammer *f*; '~·**keep·er** Lagerverwalter *m*; *Am.* Ladenbesitzer *m*;
'~-**room** Vorratskammer *f*.
sto·rey(ed) ['stɔːri(d)] *s.* story[2],
storied[2].
sto·ried[1] ['stɔːrid] in Geschichten
od. Sagen gefeiert.   [...stöckig.\
sto·ried[2] [~] mit ... Stockwerken;/
stork [stɔːk] Storch *m*.
storm [stɔːm] **1.** Sturm *m* (*a.* ✕);
Gewitter *n*; Unwetter *n*; *take by* ~
im Sturm nehmen; **2.** stürmen (*a.*
✕); toben, wüten (*at* gegen, *über*
acc.); '**storm·y** ☐ stürmisch; ~ petrel
zo. Sturmschwalbe; *fig.* Unruhestifter *m*.
sto·ry[1] ['stɔːri] Geschichte *f*; Erzählung *f*; Märchen *n*; Darstellung
f; Handlung *f* *e-r Dichtung*; F
Lüge *f*; *short* ~ Erzählung *f*.
sto·ry[2] [~] Stock(werk *n*) *m*, Geschoß *n*.
sto·ry-tell·er ['stɔːriteləl] (Märchen)Erzähler(in); F Lügner(in).
stout [staut] **1.** ☐ stark, kräftig,
stämmig; derb; dick; tapfer;
2. Starkbier *n*; '~·**heart·ed** beherzt; '**stout·ness** Stärke *f*; Mut *m*,
Mannhaftigkeit *f*; *Sport:* Ausdauer *f*.
stove [stəuv] **1.** Ofen *m*; Herd *m*; ♪
Treibhaus *n*; **2.** trocknen; (durch
Hitze) desinfizieren; **3.** *pret. u. p.p.*
von stave 2; '~·**pipe** Ofenrohr *n*;
Am. F Zylinder(hut) *m*.
stow [stəu] (ver)stauen, packen;
'**stow·age** Stauen *n*, Packen *n*;
♣ Stauraum *m*; '**stow·a·way** ♣
blinder Passagier *m*.
stra·bis·mus ✱ [strə'bizməs] Schielen *n*.
strad·dle ['strædl] (die Beine) spreizen; rittlings sitzen auf (*dat.*); mit
gespreizten Beinen stehen über
(*dat.*); ✕ eingabeln; *Am. fig.* es
mit beiden Parteien halten; schwan-
keň.
strafe [strɑːf] (be)strafen; ✕ bombardieren; ✈ mit Bordwaffen beschießen.
strag·gle ['strægl] verstreut *od.*
einzeln liegen; umherstreifen;
bummeln; *fig.* abschweifen; ♀

wuchern; '**strag·gler** Umher-
streifer *m*; ✕ Nachzügler *m*;
'**strag·gling** ☐ weitläufig, lose.
straight [streit] **1.** *adj.* gerade; *fig.*
aufrichtig, ehrlich; glatt (*Haar*);
Am. pur, unverdünnt; *Am. pol.*
hundertprozentig; *put* ~ in Ordnung bringen; **2.** *Rennsport:* (Ziel-)
Gerade *f*; **3.** *adv.* gerade(wegs);
geradeaus; direkt; sofort, stracks;
~ *away* sofort; ~ *out* rundheraus;
'**straight·en** gerademachen *od.*
-werden; ~ *out* in Ordnung bringen; entwirren; **straight'for-**
ward ☐ gerade; ehrlich, redlich;
'**straight·way** sofort, unverzüglich.
strain[1] [strein] **1.** ⊕ (verformende)
Spannung *f*, Dehnung *f*; Anspannung *f*, (Über)Anstrengung *f*;
starke Inanspruchnahme *f* (*on*
gen.); Druck *m* (*on* auf *acc.*); ✱
Zerrung *f*; Ton *m*; *mst* ~*s pl.* ♪
Weise *f*; Art und Weise *f*; Hang *m*
(*of* zu); *put a great* ~ *on* starke Anforderungen stellen an (*acc.*); **2.** *v/t.*
(an)spannen; anstrengen (*a. fig.*);
überspannen, -anstrengen; ⊕ beanspruchen; ✱ zerren; durchseihen, -drücken, -pressen; *v/i.* sich
spannen; sich anstrengen; sich abmühen (*after* um); zerren (*at* an
dat.).
strain[2] [~] Abstammung *f*, Geschlecht *n*; Art *f*.
strain·er ['streinə] Durchschlag *m*;
Seihtuch *n*; Filter *m*; Sieb *n*.
strait [streit] **1.** (*in Eigennamen* ♀*s*
pl.) Meerenge *f*, Straße *f*; ~*s pl.*
Klemme *f*, Not *f*; **2.** ~ *jacket*
Zwangsjacke *f*; '**strait·en** beschränken; ~*ed* dürftig; in Not (*for*
um); **strait-laced** ['~leist] engherzig, prüde; '**strait·ness** Enge *f*;
Beschränktheit *f*; Not *f*.
strand[1] [strænd] **1.** Strand *m*; **2.** *v/t.*
auf den Strand setzen; *fig.* stranden
lassen; ~*ed* gestrandet (*a. fig.*); *mot.*
steckengeblieben; *v/i.* stranden.
strand[2] [~] Ducht *f* *e-s Taus*;
(Haar)Strähne *f*; *fig.* Ader *f*.
strange ☐ [streindʒ] fremd (*a. fig.*);
seltsam, befremdend, sonderbar,
merkwürdig; '**strange·ness** Fremd-
heit *f*; Seltsamkeit *f*; '**stran·ger**
Fremde *m*, Unbekannte *m*; Neuling *m* (*to* in *dat.*).
stran·gle ['stræŋgl] erwürgen; *fig.*

unterdrücken; '~·hold Würge-
griff m.

stran·gu·late ✵ ['stræŋgjuleit] ab-
schnüren; strangulieren, erwürgen;
stran·gu·la·tion Erwürgung f; ✵
Abschnürung f.

strap [stræp] 1. Riemen m; Gurt m;
Band n; 2. an-, festschnallen; mit
Riemen peitschen; '~·hang·er F
stehender Fahrgast m; '**strap·less**
trägerlos (Kleid); '**strap·ping** 1.
drall (Mädchen); stramm, stämmig;
2. ✻ Heftpflasterverband m.

stra·ta ['strɑːtə] pl. von stratum.

strat·a·gem ['strætidʒəm] (Kriegs-)
List f.

stra·te·gic [strə'tiːdʒik] (~ally) stra-
tegisch; **strat·e·gist** ['strætidʒist]
Stratege m; '**strat·e·gy** Kriegs-
kunst f, Strategie f.

strat·i·fy ['strætifai] schichten.

stra·to·cruis·er ⚔ ['strætəukruːzə]
Stratosphärenflugzeug n.

strat·o·sphere phys. ['strætəusfiə]
Stratosphäre f.

stra·tum geol. ['strɑːtəm], pl. **strata** ['~tə] Schicht f (a. fig.),Lage f.

straw [strɔː] 1. Stroh n; Strohhalm
m (a. fig.); I don't care a ~ ich
mache mir gar nichts daraus; a man
of ~ fig. ein Strohmann m; 2.
Stroh...; ~ vote Am. pol. Probe-
abstimmung f; '~·ber·ry Erdbeere
f; '**straw·y** strohig.

stray [strei] 1. irregehen; sich verirren; abirren (from von; a. fig.);
umherschweifen; 2. a. ~ed verirrt;
vereinzelt; 3. verirrtes Tier n; ~s
pl. ✻ atmosphärische Störungen
f/pl.

streak [striːk] 1. Strich m, Streifen
m; fig. Ader f, Spur f; kurze
Periode f; ~ of lightning Blitzstrahl
m; 2. streifen; jagen; '**streak·y** ☐
streifig; durchwachsen (Speck etc.).

stream [striːm] 1. Wasserlauf m;
Bach m; Strom m; Strömung f;
Schule: (Leistungs)Zug m; go with
the ~ fig. mit dem Strom schwimmen; 2. v/i. strömen; überströmen
(Augen); triefen (Schirm etc.); flattern (Flagge, Haar); v/t. strömen
lassen; ausströmen; '**stream·er**
Wimpel m; (fliegendes) Band n;
Papierschlange f; Lichtstrahl m beim
Nordlicht; Zeitung: Schlagzeile f;
'**stream·ing** Schule: Einteilung f
in Leistungsgruppen; **stream·let**

['~lit] Bächlein n.

stream·line ['striːmlain] 1. Strom-
linie f; 2. stromlinienförmig machen; fig. modernisieren.

street [striːt] Straße f; not in the
same ~ with F nicht zu vergleichen
mit; '~·car bsd. Am. Straßenbahnwagen m; '~·walk·er Straßen-
dirne f.

strength [streŋθ] Stärke f, Kraft f
(a. fig.); ✗, ⚓ (Ist)Stärke f; on the ~
of auf (acc.) hin, auf Grund od. kraft
(gen.); '**strength·en** v/t. stärken,
kräftigen; bestärken; v/i. erstarken.

stren·u·ous ☐ ['strenjuəs] rührig,
emsig; eifrig; anstrengend; '**stren-
u·ous·ness** Eifer m, Emsigkeit f.

stress [stres] 1. Druck m; Nachdruck m; Betonung f; Schwergewicht n; Ton m; ⊕ Spannung f,
Beanspruchung f; psych. Stress m;
lay ~ (up)on Nachdruck legen auf
(acc.), betonen; 2. betonen; ⊕
spannen, beanspruchen.

stretch [stretʃ] 1. v/t. strecken;
(aus)dehnen; mst ~ out die Hand
etc. ausstrecken; (an)spannen; fig.
überspannen; ~ one's legs sich die
Beine vertreten; v/i. sich (er)strek-
ken; sich dehnen (lassen) (into [bis]
zu); fig. aufschneiden; a. ~ one's
powers sich bis zum äußersten anstrengen; 2. Strecken n; Dehnung f;
Spannung f; Anspannung f; Übertreibung f; Überschreitung f; Strecke
f, Fläche f; at a ~ in e-m Zug,
hintereinander, ohne Unterbrechung; on the ~ (an)gespannt;
'**stretch·er** Tragbahre f; Streckvor-
richtung f; Stemmbrett n im Boot;
'**stretch·er-bear·er** Krankenträger
m.

strew [struː] (irr.) (be)streuen;
strewn [struːn] p.p. von strew.

stri·ate ['straiit], **stri·at·ed** ['~'eitid]
gerieft.

strick·en ['strikən] ge-, betroffen,
befallen, heimgesucht (with von);
~ in age bejahrt.

strict [strikt] streng; genau; ~ly
speaking streng genommen; '**strictness** Genauigkeit f; Strenge f;
stric·ture ['~tʃə] oft ~s pl. kritische Bemerkung f, scharfe Kritik
f; ✻ Verengung f.

strid·den ['stridn] p.p. von stride 1.

stride [straid] 1. (irr.) v/t. über-,
durchschreiten; v/i. a. ~ out aus-

schreiten; **2.** (weiter) Schritt *m*; *get into one's* ~ richtig in Schwung kommen.

stri·dent □ ['straidənt] knarrend, kreischend; grell (*Stimme*).

strife *lit.* [straif] Streit *m*, Hader *m*.

strike [straik] **1.** Ausstand *m*, Streik *m*; (Öl-, Erz)Fund *m*; *fig.* Treffer *m*; ⚔ (Luft)Angriff *m auf ein Einzelziel*; *Am. Baseball*: Verlustpunkt *m bei Schlagfehler etc.*; *be on* ~ streiken; *go on* ~ in den Ausstand treten; **2.** (*irr.*) *v*/*t.* treffen, stoßen; schlagen; prägen; gegen *od.* auf *et.* (*acc.*) schlagen *od.* stoßen; stoßen auf (*acc.*), (auf)finden; *Wort, Flagge, Segel* streichen; *Zelt* abbrechen; *Schlag* führen, tun; *Ton* anschlagen; auffallen (*dat.*); ergreifen; *Handel* abschließen; *Streichholz, Licht* anzünden; *Wurzel* schlagen; *j. blind, sprachlos etc.* machen; *s. attitude*; ~ *a balance* die Bilanz *od.* den Saldo ziehen; ~ *oil* Erdöl finden; F Glück haben); ~ *off* ausstreichen; ~ *out Plan etc.* entwerfen; ausstreichen; ~ *through* durchstreichen; ~ *up* anstimmen; *Freundschaft* schließen; *v*/*i.* schlagen (*at* nach); ⚓ auf Grund stoßen, auflaufen; ⚓, ⚔ die Flagge streichen; die Arbeit einstellen, streiken; schlagen (*Uhr*); einschlagen (*Blitz*); angehen (*Streichholz*); *Wurzel* schlagen; *in e-r Richtung* gehen; ~ *home* (richtig, *fig.* empfindlich) treffen; ~ *in* nach innen schlagen; sich einmischen; ~ *into* verfallen in (*acc.*); ~ *up* einsetzen (*Orchester etc.*); ~ *upon the ear* das Ohr treffen; ~ **bal·lot** Urabstimmung *f*; '~**bound** durch Streik lahmgelegt; '~**break·er** Streikbrecher *m*; '~**pay** Streikgeld *n*; '**strik·er** Schläger(in); Streikende *m*, *f*; ⊕ Schlagbolzen *m*; *Sport*: Stürmer *m*.

strik·ing □ ['straikiŋ] Schlag...; auffallend; eindrucksvoll; treffend; ausständig, streikend.

string [striŋ] **1.** Schnur *f*; Bindfaden *m*; Band *n*; Gängelband *n*; *Am.* F Bedingung *f*; Haken *m*; (Bogen)Sehne *f*; ♀ Faser *f*, (Blatt-) Rippe *f*; ♪ Saite *f*; Reihe *f*, Kette *f*; Schar *f*; ~*s pl.* ♪ Saiteninstrumente *n*/*pl.*, Streicher *m*/*pl.*; *harp on the same* ~ auf ein u. derselben Sache herumreiten; *have two* ~*s to one's*

bow zwei Eisen im Feuer haben; *pull the* ~*s* der Drahtzieher sein; *there are* ~*s attached to it* F die Sache hat e-n Haken; **2.** (*irr.*) *Bogen* spannen; *Perlen etc.* aufreihen; *Geige etc.* besaiten (*a. fig.*), bespannen; *grüne Bohnen* abziehen; *Am. sl. j.* verkohlen; ~ *up* F aufknüpfen, -hängen; *be strung up* angespannt *od.* erregt sein; ~ **bag** Einkaufsnetz *n*; ~ **band** ♪ Streichorchester *n*; ~ **bean** ♀ grüne Bohne *f*; ~ **cor·re·spon·dent** *Am.* freier Mitarbeiter *m e-r Zeitung*; **stringed** ♪ Saiten...; ...-saitig.

strin·gen·cy ['strindʒənsi] Strenge *f*, Schärfe *f*; bindende *od.* zwingende Kraft *f*; ✝ Knappheit *f*; '**strin·gent** □ streng, scharf; bindend, zwingend; starr, fest; ✝ knapp (*Geld*).

string·er ['striŋə] = *string correspondent.*

string·y ['striŋi] faserig; zäh.

strip [strip] **1.** *v*/*t.* entkleiden (*a. fig.*; *of gen.*), *j.* ausziehen; *Rinde etc.* abziehen; *fig.* entblößen, berauben (*of gen.*); ⊕ auseinandernehmen; ⚓ abtakeln; *a.* ~ *off Kleid etc.* ausziehen, abstreifen; *v*/*i.* F sich ausziehen; **2.** *schmaler* Streifen *m*; ~ **car·toon** = comics.

stripe [straip] *andersfarbiger* Streifen *m*; ⚔ Tresse *f*; **striped** gestreift.

strip-light·ing ['striplaitiŋ] Neonbeleuchtung *f*.

strip·ling ['stripliŋ] Bürschchen *n*.

strip-tease ['stripti:z] Striptease *n* (*Entkleidungsnummer*).

strive [straiv] (*irr.*) streben (*after, for* nach), sich bemühen (um); ringen (*against* gegen, *for* um); **striv·en** ['strivn] *p.p. von* strive.

strode [stroud] *pret. von* stride 1.

stroke [strouk] **1.** Schlag *m*; Streich *m*, Hieb *m*; Stoß *m*; ⚕ Schlaganfall *m*; ⊕ (Kolben)Hub *m*; (Pinsel-, Feder)Strich *m* (*a. fig.*); Schlag *m der Uhr*; *Rudern*: Schlagmann *m*; ~ *of genius* genialer Einfall *m*; ~ *of luck* glücklicher Zufall *m*; **2.** streiche(l)n; *Boot* als Schlagmann rudern.

stroll [stroul] **1.** schlendern, bummeln; spazierengehen; umherziehen; **2.** Bummel *m*; Spaziergang *m*; '**stroll·er** Bummler(in), Spa-

ziergänger(in); *Am.* (Falt)Sport-
wagen *m*.

strong ☐ [strɔŋ] *allg.* stark; kräftig,
kraftvoll; *fig.* tüchtig; energisch,
eifrig; fest (*Überzeugung*); stark
(*an Zahl*; *Getränk*, *Geruch*, *Geschmack*); schwer (*Zigarre*, *Speise
etc.*); *gr.* stark (*ablautend*); *s.
language*; feel ~(*ly*) about sich aufregen über (*acc.*); s-e besondere
Meinung haben über; *be going* ~
F s-n Mann stehen; (noch) rüstig
sein; '~-box Stahlkassette *f*; '~-
hold Festung *f*; *fig.* Bollwerk *n*,
Hochburg *f*; '~-'mind·ed willens-
stark; '~-room Stahlkammer *f*;
'~-'willed eigenwillig; dickköpfig.

strop [strɔp] **1.** Streichriemen *m*;
⚓ Stropp *n*; **2.** *Messer* abziehen.

stro·phe ['strəufi] Strophe *f*.

strop·py F ['strɔpi] patzig, unwirsch.

strove [strəuv] *pret. von* strive.

struck [strʌk] *pret. u. p.p. von*
strike 2.

struc·tur·al ☐ ['strʌktʃərəl] baulich; Bau...; organisch; strukturell;
'struc·ture Bau(werk *n*) *m*; Struktur *f*, Gefüge *n*; Gebilde *n*.

strug·gle ['strʌgl] **1.** kämpfen,
ringen (*for* um); sich (ab)mühen;
sich quälen; sich sträuben; zappeln; **2.** Kampf *m*; Ringen *n* (*for*
um) Anstrengung *f*; 'strug·gler
Kämpfer(in).

strum [strʌm] **1.** klimpern; **2.** Geklimper *n*.

strum·pet † ['strʌmpit] Hure *f*,
Dirne *f*.

strung [strʌŋ] *pret. u. p.p. von*
string 2.

strut [strʌt] **1.** *v/i.* stolzieren; *v/t.*
⊕ verstreben, abstützen; **2.** Stolzieren *n*; ⊕ Strebe(balken *m*) *f*;
Stütze *f*.

strych·nine ⚕ ['strikni:n] Strychnin *n*.

stub [stʌb] **1.** (Baum)Stumpf *m*;
Stummel *m*; *Am.* Kontrollab-
schnitt *m*; **2.** *mst* ~ *up* ausroden;
Land roden; sich *den Fuß* stoßen;
~ *out Zigarette* ausdrücken.

stub·ble ['stʌbl] Stoppel(n *pl.*) *f*.

stub·bly ['stʌbli] stopp(e)lig.

stub·born ☐ ['stʌbən] eigensinnig;
widerspenstig; halsstarrig, stur;
hartnäckig (*a. Widerstand*); unerbittlich (*Tatsachen*); 'stub·born·
ness Halsstarrigkeit *f etc.*

stub·by ['stʌbi] stummelhaft.

stuc·co ['stʌkəu] **1.** Stuck *m*; **2.** mit
Stuck verzieren, stuckieren.

stuck [stʌk] *pret. u. p.p. von* stick²;
~ *on Am.* F verschossen in *j.*; '~-'up
F hochnäsig.

stud¹ [stʌd] **1.** (Wand)Pfosten *m*;
Beschlagnagel *m*, Buckel *m*, Knauf
m; *herausnehmbarer* Kragenknopf
m; **2.** beschlagen; besetzen.

stud² [~] Gestüt *n*; '~-book Ge-
stütbuch *n*.

stud·ding △ ['stʌdiŋ] Fachwerk *n*.

stu·dent ['stju:dənt] Student(in);
Studierende *m*, *f*; Forscher(in); Gelehrte *m*, *f*; Büchermensch *m*; ~ hostel Studentenwohnheim *n*; 'stu·
dent·ship Stipendium *n*.

stud·ied ☐ ['stʌdid] einstudiert (*Pose*); gesucht (*Stil*); gewollt (*Kränkung*).

stu·di·o ['stju:diəu] Atelier *n*; Studio
n; *Radio*: Aufnahme-, Senderaum *m*;
~ couch Schlafcouch *f*.

stu·di·ous ☐ ['stju:djəs] fleißig; bedacht (*of* auf *acc.*); bemüht (*to inf.*
zu *inf.*); geflissentlich; 'stu·di·ous·
ness Fleiß *m*, Eifer *m*, Beflissen-
heit *f*.

stud·y ['stʌdi] **1.** Studium *n*; Stu-
dier-, Arbeitszimmer *n*; *paint. etc.*
Studie *f*; *be in a brown* ~ versunken *od.* geistesabwesend sein;
2. *v/i.* studieren (*for acc.*); *v/t.* studieren (*a. fig.*); sich *et.* genau ansehen; sich bemühen um; einstudieren.

stuff [stʌf] **1.** Stoff *m*; Zeug *n* (*a.
contp.*); † Wollstoff *m*; *fig.* Unsinn
m; **2.** *v/t.* stopfen (*into* in *acc.*);
voll-, ausstopfen; ~ *up* verstopfen;
~ed shirt *Am. sl.* Fatzke *m*; *v/i.* sich
vollstopfen; 'stuff·ing Füllung *f*;
⊕ Polsterung *f*; Füllsel *n*; 'stuff·y
☐ dumpf(ig), muffig, stickig (*Luft
etc.*); F verschnupft, verärgert; F
etepetete.

stul·ti·fi·ca·tion [stʌltifi'keiʃən]
Veralberung *f*, Blamage *f*; **stul·
ti·fy** ['~fai] lächerlich machen,
blamieren; *et.* hinfällig machen.

stum·ble ['stʌmbl] **1.** Stolpern *n*;
Versehen *n*; Fehltritt *m*; **2.** stolpern; straucheln (*a. fig.*); ~ *upon*
stoßen auf (*acc.*); 'stum·bling·
-block *fig.* Stein *m* des Anstoßes.

stump [stʌmp] **1.** Stumpf *m*, Stummel *m*; *Zeichnen*: Wischer *m*;

Kricket: Torstab *m*; F Wahlpropaganda *f*; ⁓*s pl*. F Stelzen *f/pl.* (*Beine*); *stir one's* ⁓*s* F sich beeilen; **2.** *v/t. Kricket*: *Schläger* abwerfen; F verblüffen; *Am*. F herausfordern; ⁓ *up sl*. berappen (*zahlen*); ⁓ *the country* als Wahlredner im Land herumziehen; ⁓*ed for* verlegen um; *v/i.* (daher)stapfen, stelzen; '⁓-'or-a-tor Wahl-, Volksredner *m*; 'stump-y □ gedrungen (*Körperbau*); plump.

stun [stʌn] betäuben (*a. fig.*); ⁓ned *fig.* verdutzt, sprachlos.

stung [stʌŋ] *pret. u. p.p. von* sting 2.

stunk [stʌŋk] *pret. u. p.p. von* stink 2.

stun-ner F ['stʌnə] Bombenkerl *m*; Mordsding *n*; 'stun-ning □ F toll, famos.

stunt¹ F [stʌnt] **1.** Kraft-, Kunststück *n*; (Reklame)Trick *m*; Sensation *f*; Schlager *m*; ✈ Kunstflug *m*; **2.** kunstfliegen.

stunt² [⁓] im Wachstum hindern; 'stunt-ed verkümmert.

stupe ✍ [stju:p] **1.** heißer Umschlag *m*; **2.** heiße Umschläge legen auf (*acc.*).

stu-pe-fac-tion [stju:piˈfækʃən] Betäubung *f*; Verblüffung *f*; **stu-pe-fy** ['⁓fai] *fig.* betäuben; verblüffen; verdummen.

stu-pen-dous □ [stju:ˈpendəs] erstaunlich.

stu-pid □ ['stju:pid] dumm, einfältig, stumpfsinnig; blöd (*langweilig*); **stu'pid-i-ty** Dummheit *f etc.*

stu-por ['stju:pə] Erstarrung *f*, Betäubung *f*.

stur-di-ness ['stə:dinis] Derbheit *f*; Handfestigkeit *f*; 'stur-dy derb, kräftig, stark; stämmig; stramm; handfest.

stur-geon *ichth.* ['stə:dʒən] Stör *m*.

stut-ter ['stʌtə] **1.** stottern; **2.** Stottern *n*; 'stut-ter-er Stotterer *m*.

sty¹ [stai] Schweinestall *m*, Koben *m*.

sty² [⁓] Gerstenkorn *n am Auge*.

style [stail] **1.** Griffel *m* (*a.* ⚘); Stichel *m*; Sonde *f*; Stil *m*; *Schneiderei*: Machart *f*; Betitelung *f*; Zeitrechnung *f*; *in* ⁓ vornehm; *under the* ⁓ *of* ... ♱ unter der Firma ...; **2.** (be)nennen, betiteln.

styl-ish □ ['stailiʃ] stilvoll; stilgerecht, elegant; 'styl-ish-ness

Eleganz *f*.

styl-ist ['stailist] Stilist(in).

sty-lo F ['stailəu], **sty-lo-graph** ['⁓grɑ:f] Tintenkuli *m*.

sty-lus ['stailəs] *Plattenspieler*: Nadel *f*.

styp-tic ['stiptik] blutstillend(es Mittel *n*).

sua-sion ['sweiʒən] Überredung *f*.

suave □ [swɑ:v] verbindlich (*Wesen etc.*); mild (*Wein etc.*); 'suav-i-ty Verbindlichkeit *f*; Milde *f*.

sub F [sʌb] *abbr. für* subordinate 2; subscription; substitute 2; submarine 2.

sub... [⁓] *mst* Unter...; *unter...*; Neben...; Hilfs...; ein wenig ...; fast ...

sub-ac-id ['sʌbˈæsid] säuerlich; *fig.* bissig.

sub-al-tern ['sʌbltən] Untergebene *m*; ✕ Subalternoffizier *m*.

sub-a-tom-ic ['sʌbəˈtɔmik] subatomisch, innerhalb des Atoms.

sub-com-mit-tee ['sʌbkəmiti] Unterausschuß *m*.   [unterbewußt.|

sub-con-scious □ ['sʌbˈkɔnʃəs]|

sub-con-tract [sʌbˈkɔntrækt] Nebenvertrag *m*.

sub-cu-ta-ne-ous □ ['sʌbkju:teinjəs] subkutan, unter der *od.* die Haut.

sub-deb *Am*. F [sʌbˈdeb] Backfisch *m*, junges Mädchen *n*.

sub-di-vide [sʌbdiˈvaid] (sich) unterteilen; **sub-di-vi-sion** ['⁓viʒən] Unterteilung *f*; Unterabteilung *f*.

sub-due [səbˈdju:] unterwerfen; bezwingen; bändigen; unterdrücken, verdrängen; *Licht etc.* dämpfen.

sub-head(-ing) ['sʌbhed(iŋ)] Untertitel *m*.

sub-ja-cent [sʌbˈdʒeisənt] darunter *od.* tiefer liegend.

sub-ject ['sʌbdʒikt] **1.** unterworfen (*to dat.*); untergeben, abhängig; *pred.* untertan; unterliegend (*to dat.*); *be* ⁓ *to* neigen zu; ⁓ *to a fee od.* duty gebührenpflichtig; **2.** *adv.* ⁓ *to* vorbehaltlich (*gen.*); ⁓ *to change without notice* Änderungen vorbehalten; ⁓ *to this* mit diesem Vorbehalt; **3.** Untertan *m*, Staatsangehörige *m*; *phls.*, *gr.* Subjekt *n*; *a.* ⁓ *matter* Thema *n*, Gegenstand *m*; ♪ Satz *m*, Thema *n*; *paint*. Sujet *n*; Vorgang *m* (*Akte*); Anlaß *m*; (Lehr-, Studien)Fach *n*; **4.** [səbˈdʒekt] unterwerfen; ⁓ *to e-r Prü-*

fung etc. unterziehen; *e-r Gefahr etc.* aussetzen; ~ **cat·a·logue** Schlagwortkatalog *m*; **sub'jec·tion** Unterwerfung *f*; **sub'jec·tive** ☐ subjektiv.

sub·join ['sʌb'dʒɔin] noch beifügen.

sub·ju·gate ['sʌbdʒugeit] unterjochen; **sub·ju'ga·tion** Unterjochung *f*.

sub·junc·tive *gr.* [səb'dʒʌŋktiv] *a.* ~ *mood* Konjunktiv *m*.

sub·lease ['sʌb'li:s], **sub·let** ['ʌ·'let] (*irr. let*) untervermieten, -verpachten.

sub·li·mate ⚗ 1. ['sʌblimit] Sublimat *n*; 2. ['ʌmeit] sublimieren; **sub·li'ma·tion** Sublimierung *f*; **sub·lime** [sə'blaim] 1. ☐ erhaben, sublim; großartig; 2. *the* ~ das Erhabene; 3. ⚗ sublimieren; *fig.* läutern.

sub·lim·i·nal *psych.* [səb'liminəl] unterschwellig.

sub·lim·i·ty [sə'blimiti] Erhabenheit *f*.

sub-ma·chine gun ['sʌbmə'ʃi:ngʌn] Maschinenpistole *f*.

sub·ma·rine [sʌbmə'ri:n] 1. unterseeisch; Untersee...; 2. ⚓ Unterseeboot *n*.

sub·merge [səb'mə:dʒ] untertauchen (*a. v/i.*); überschwemmen; **sub·mers·i·bil·i·ty** [ʌsə'biliti] Tauchfähigkeit *f*; **sub'mer·sion** Untertauchen *n*; Überschwemmung *f*.

sub·mis·sion [səb'miʃən] Unterwerfung *f* (*to* unter *acc.*); Unterbreitung *f*, Vorlage *f*; **sub'mis·sive** ☐ unterwürfig.

sub·mit [səb'mit] *v/t.* unterwerfen; anheimstellen; vorlegen, unterbreiten, einreichen; *bsd. parl.* ergebenst bemerken; *v/i. a.* ~ *o.s.* sich unterwerfen *od.* unterordnen (*to dat.*); sich *e-r Operation* unterziehen; *fig.* sich fügen *od.* ergeben (*to in acc.*).

sub·nor·mal [səb'nɔ:məl] von unterdurchschnittlicher Intelligenz; schwachsinnig.

sub·or·di·nate 1. ☐ [sə'bɔ:dnit] untergeordnet; untergeben; ~ *clause gr.* Nebensatz *m*; 2. [ʌ] Untergebene *m*; 3. [sə'bɔ:dineit] unterordnen; **sub·or·di'na·tion** Unterordnung *f* (*to* unter *acc.*).

sub·orn ⚖ [sʌ'bɔ:n] verleiten, anstiften (*to* zu); **sub·or'na·tion** Anstiftung *f*, Verleitung *f*.

sub·p(o)e·na ⚖ [səb'pi:nə] 1. Vorladung *f*; 2. vorladen.

sub·scribe [səb'skraib] *Geld* stiften (*to* für); *Summe* zeichnen; *s-n Namen* setzen (*to* unter *acc.*), unterschreiben mit; ~ *to Zeitung etc.* abonnieren; *e-r Meinung* zustimmen, *et.* unterschreiben; **sub'scrib·er** (Unter)Zeichner(in) (*to, for gen.*); Abonnent(in); *teleph.* Teilnehmer(in).

sub·scrip·tion [səb'skripʃən] Unterzeichnung *f etc.*; gezeichnete Summe *f*; Abonnement *n*.

sub·sec·tion ['sʌbsekʃən] Unterabteilung *f*.

sub·se·quence ['sʌbsikwəns] späteres Eintreten *n*; **'sub·se·quent** ☐ folgend; später (*to* als); ~*ly* hinterher; in der Folge, anschließend.

sub·serve [səb'sə:v] dienen (*dat.*); befördern; **sub'ser·vi·ence** [ʌvjəns] Dienlichkeit *f*; Unterwürfigkeit *f*; **sub'ser·vi·ent** ☐ dienlich; dienstbar; unterwürfig.

sub·side [səb'said] sinken, sich senken; sich setzen (*Haus etc.*); sich legen (*nachlassen*); ~ *into* verfallen in (*acc.*); **sub·sid·ence** ['sʌbsidəns] Senkung *f*; Abflauen *n*; **sub·sid·i·ar·y** [səb'sidjəri] 1. ☐ Hilfs...; Neben...; als Hilfe dienend (*to* für); *be* ~ *to* ergänzen, unterstützen; 2. Filiale *f*; *a.* ~ *company* Tochtergesellschaft *f*; **sub·si·dize** ['sʌbsidaiz] mit Geld unterstützen; subventionieren; **'sub·si·dy** Beihilfe *f*, Zuschuß *m*; Subvention *f*.

sub·sist [səb'sist] *v/i.* bestehen; leben (*on* von *e-r Nahrung*; *by* von *e-m Beruf*); *v/t. e-n* ~, unterhalten, **sub'sist·ence** Dasein *n*; (Lebens-) Unterhalt *m*; ~ *wage* Minimallohn *m*.

sub·soil ['sʌbsɔil] Untergrund *m*.

sub·son·ic [sʌb'sɔnik] Unterschall...

sub·stance ['sʌbstəns] Substanz *f*; Wesen *n*; *fig.* Hauptsache *f*; Inhalt *m*; Kern *m*; Wirklichkeit *f*; Stoff *m*; Vermögen *n*.

sub·stan·dard [səb'stændəd] nicht hochsprachlich; unzulänglich (*Qualität*).

sub·stan·tial ☐ [səb'stænʃəl] wesentlich; wirklich; nahrhaft, kräftig; stark; solid; vermögend; namhaft (*Summe*); **sub·stan·ti·al·i·ty**

[ˌʃiˈæliti] Wesenheit *f*; Wirklichkeit *f*; Gediegenheit *f*; Wesentlichkeit *f*.

sub·stan·ti·ate [səbˈstænʃieit] beweisen, begründen, dartun.

sub·stan·ti·val □ *gr.* [sʌbstənˈtaivəl] substantivisch; **sub·stan·tive** [ˈˌtiv] **1.** □ selbständig; *gr.* substantivisch; wirklich; fest; **2.** *gr.* Substantiv *n*, Hauptwort *n*.

sub·sti·tute [ˈsʌbstitjuːt] **1.** an die Stelle setzen *od.* treten (*for* von); *b.s.* unterschieben (*for* statt); **2.** Stellvertreter *m*; Ersatzmann *m*; Ersatz *m*; **sub·sti·tu·tion** Einsetzung *f*, *mst b.s.* Unterschiebung *f*; Stellvertretung *f*; Ersatz *m*.

sub·stra·tum [ˈsʌbˈstrɑːtəm] Substrat *n*; Grundlage *f*; ⊕, *geol.* Unterlage *f*; Substanz *f*.

sub·struc·ture [ˈsʌbstrʌktʃə] Unterbau *m*.

sub·ten·ant [ˈsʌbˈtenənt] Untermieter *m*, Unterpächter *m*.

sub·ter·fuge [ˈsʌbtəfjuːdʒ] Ausflucht *f*.

sub·ter·ra·ne·an □ [sʌbtəˈreinjən] unterirdisch.

sub·til·ize [ˈsʌtilaiz] *v/t.* verfeinern; überspitzen; *v/i.* klügeln.

sub·ti·tle [ˈsʌbtaitl] Untertitel *m*.

sub·tle □ [ˈsʌtl] fein(sinnig); subtil scharfsinnig; spitzfindig; ingeniös; **'sub·tle·ty** Feinheit *f*; Spitzfindigkeit *f*.

sub·to·pia [sʌbˈtəupiə] zersiedelte *od.* urbanisierte Landschaft *f*.

sub·tract [səbˈtrækt] abziehen, subtrahieren; **sub'trac·tion** Abziehen *n*, Subtraktion *f*.

sub·urb [ˈsʌbəːb] Vorstadt *f*, -ort *m*; **sub·ur·ban** [səˈbəːbən] vorstädtisch; Vorstadt..., -ort...; *contp.* spießbürgerlich; **Sub'ur·bia** [ˌbjə] *die* Vorstädte *f/pl.*; *das* Leben in den Vorstädten.

sub·trop·i·cal [ˈsʌbˈtrɔpikəl] subtropisch.

sub·ven·tion [səbˈvenʃən] **1.** Subvention *f*, Zuschuß *m*, Beihilfe *f*; Unterstützung *f*; **2.** subventionieren.

sub·ver·sion [sʌbˈvəːʃən] Umsturz *m*; **sub'ver·sive** umstürzend, zerstörend (*of acc.*); subversiv.

sub·vert [sʌbˈvəːt] umstürzen; *Regierung* stürzen; untergraben.

sub·way [ˈsʌbwei] (*bsd.* Fußgänger-)

Unterführung *f*; *Am.* Untergrundbahn *f*.

sub–ze·ro [ˈsʌbˈziərəu] unter null Grad, unter dem Gefrierpunkt.

suc·ceed [səkˈsiːd] Erfolg haben (*Person od. Sache*); glücken, gelingen (*Sache*); (nach)folgen (*dat.*); ~ *to* auf *dem Thron* folgen; *Amt* übernehmen; *Gut etc.* erben; *he* ~*s in ger.* es gelingt ihm, zu *inf.*

suc·cess [səkˈses] Erfolg *m*; glückliches Ergebnis *n*; Glanzleistung *f*; *he was a great* ~ er hatte großen Erfolg; **suc'cess·ful** □ [ˌful] erfolgreich; glücklich; *be* ~ Erfolg *od.* Glück haben; **suc·ces·sion** [ˌseʃən] (Nach-, Erb-, Reihen)Folge *f*; Nachkommenschaft *f*; ~ *to the* throne Thronfolge *f*; *in* ~ nacheinander; ~ *duty* Erbschaftssteuer *f*; **suc'ces·sive** □ aufeinanderfolgend; **suc'ces·sor** Nachfolger(in); ~ *to the* throne Thronfolger *m*.

suc·cinct □ [səkˈsiŋkt] bündig, kurz.

suc·co·ry ♀ [ˈsʌkəri] Zichorie *f*.

suc·co(u)r [ˈsʌkə] **1.** Hilfe *f*, Beistand *m*; ✗ Entsatz *m*; **2.** helfen (*dat.*); beistehen (*dat.*); ✗ entsetzen.

suc·cu·lence [ˈsʌkjuləns] Saftigkeit *f*; **'suc·cu·lent** □ saftig, wohlschmeckend (*Frucht*); fleischig (*Blatt, Stiel*).

suc·cumb [səˈkʌm] unter-, erliegen.

such [sʌtʃ] **1.** *adj.* solch; derartig; so groß; ~ *a man* ein solcher Mann; *s. another*; *no* ~ *thing* nichts dergleichen; ~ *as* die, welche; ~ *and* ~ der und der, die und die; ~ *is life* so ist nun mal das Leben; **2.** *pron.* (ein) solch(er, -es), (eine) solche, *pl.* solche; der, die, das; **'such-like** dergleichen.

suck [sʌk] **1.** (ein)saugen; saugen an (*dat.*); aussaugen; lutschen; ~ *up to Schul-sl.* sich anbiedern *od.* einschmeicheln bei; ~ *s.o.'s brains* j. ausholen; **2.** Saugen *n*; *give* ~ säugen; **'suck·er** Saugorgan *n*; ⊕ Pumpenschuh *m*; ♀ Wurzelsproß *m*; *Am.* Einfaltspinsel *m*; **'suck·ing** saugend; Saug...; ~ *pig* Spanferkel *n*; **suck·le** [ˈˌl] säugen, nähren, stillen; **'suck·ling** Säugling *m*.

suc·tion [ˈsʌkʃən] **1.** Saugen *n*; Ansaugen *n*; Sog *m*; **2.** Saug...; ~ *cleaner*, ~ *sweeper* Staubsauger *m*.

sud·den □ [ˈsʌdn] plötzlich; *on a* ~,

(*all*) *of a* ⌣ (ganz) plötzlich; **'sud-den·ness** Plötzlichkeit *f*.

su·dor·if·ic [sju:də'rifik] schweiß-treibend(es Mittel *n*).

suds [sʌdz] *pl.* Seifenlauge *f*; Seifenschaum *m*; **'suds·y** *Am.* schaumig, seifig.

sue [sju:] *v/t.* verklagen; ⌣ *out* auf dem Rechtsweg erwirken; *v/i.* nachsuchen (*for* um); klagen (*for* auf *acc.*).

suède [sweid] feines Wildleder *n*.

su·et ['sjuit] Nierenfett *n*; Talg *m*; **'su·et·y** talgig.

suf·fer ['sʌfə] *v/i.* leiden (*from* an *dat.*); *v/t.* erdulden, erleiden; dulden, (zu)lassen; **'suf·fer·ance** Duldung *f*; *on* ⌣ nur geduldet(erweise); **'suf·fer·er** Leidende *m*, *f*; Dulder (-in); **'suf·fer·ing** Leiden *n*.

suf·fice [sə'fais] genügen, (aus-) reichen; ⌣ *it to say* es sei nur gesagt.

suf·fi·cien·cy [sə'fiʃənsi] Hinlänglichkeit *f*; auskömmliches Vermögen *n*; *a* ⌣ *of money* genug Geld; **suf'fi·cient** ☐ genügend, ausreichend, genug; *be* ⌣ genügen.

suf·fix *gr.* ['sʌfiks] **1.** anhängen; **2.** Nachsilbe *f*, Suffix *n*.

suf·fo·cate ['sʌfəkeit] ersticken; **suf·fo'ca·tion** Erstickung *f*; **suf·fo·ca·tive** ☐ ['⌣kətiv] erstickend.

suf·fra·gan *eccl.* ['sʌfrəgən] Weihbischof *m*; **'suf·frage** (Wahl-) Stimme *f*; Abstimmung *f*; Wahl-, Stimmrecht *n*; **suf·fra·gette** [⌣ə-'dʒet] Frauenrechtlerin *f*, Suffragette *f*.

suf·fuse [sə'fju:z] übergießen; überziehen; **suf'fu·sion** [⌣ʒən] Übergießung *f*; Überzug *m*.

sug·ar ['ʃugə] **1.** Zucker *m*; **2.** zuckern; **'⌣-ba·sin** Zuckerdose *f*; **'⌣-beet** Zuckerrübe *f*; **'⌣-bowl** *Am.* Zuckerdose *f*; **'⌣-cane** Zuckerrohr *n*; **'⌣-coat** überzuckern, versüßen; **⌣ dad·dy** *älterer, reicher* Liebhaber *m*; **'⌣-free** ohne Zucker; **'⌣-loaf** Zuckerhut *m*; **'⌣-lump** Zuckerwürfel *m*; **'⌣-plum** Bonbon *m*, *n*; **'⌣-tongs** *pl.* (*a pair of* eine) Zuckerzange *f*; **'sug·ar·y** zuckerig; zuckersüß.

sug·gest [sə'dʒest] vorschlagen, anregen; nahelegen; vorbringen; *Gedanken* eingeben; andeuten; denken lassen an (*acc.*); **sug'ges·tion** Anregung *f*; Wink *m*, Rat *m*, Vor-schlag *m*; Suggestion *f*; Eingebung *f*; Andeutung *f*.

sug·ges·tive ☐ [sə'dʒestiv] anregend (*of* zu); andeutend (*of acc.*); gehaltvoll; vielsagend; zweideutig (*Witz etc.*); **sug'ges·tive·ness** Gedankenreichtum *m*; Zweideutigkeit *f*.

su·i·cid·al ☐ [sjui'saidl] selbstmörderisch; **su·i·cide** ['⌣said] **1.** Selbstmord *m*; Selbstmörder(in). **2.** *Am.* Selbstmord begehen.

suit [sjuit] **1.** (Herren)Anzug *m*; (Damen)Kostüm *n*; Anliegen *n*, Bitte *f*; (Heirats)Antrag *m*; *Karten:* Farbe *f*; *t⁵₂* Prozeß *m*; *follow* ⌣ Farbe bekennen; dasselbe tun; **2.** *v/t.* j-m passen, zusagen, recht sein, entsprechen, zuträglich sein, bekommen; *j.* kleiden, *j-m* stehen, passen zu (*Kleidungsstück etc.*); ⌣ *oneself* tun, was e-m beliebt; ⌣ *s.th. to et.* anpassen (*dat.*); *be* ⌣*ed* geeignet sein (*for* für), passen (*to* zu); *v/i.* passen; **suit·a'bil·i·ty** Eignung *f*; **'suit·a·ble** ☐ passend, geeignet (*to, for* für); entsprechend; **'suit·a·ble·ness** = *suitability*; **'suit·case** Handkoffer *m*; **suite** [swiit] Gefolge *n*; (Reihen)Folge *f*; ♪ Suite *f*; *a.* ⌣ *of rooms* Zimmerflucht *f*; Garnitur *f*, (Zimmer-) Einrichtung *f*; **suit·ing** ♱ ['sjuitiŋ] Anzugstoff *m*; **'suit·or** Freier *m*; *t⁵₂* Kläger(in), Prozessierende *m*, *f*.

sulk [sʌlk] **1.** *a.* be in the ⌣s schmollen, bocken; **2.** sulks *pl.*, **'sulk·i·ness** üble Laune *f*, Bockigkeit *f*; **'sulk·y 1.** ☐ verdrießlich; mürrisch, launisch; schmollend, bockig; **2.** *Sport:* Traberwagen *m*, Sulky *n*.

sul·len ☐ ['sʌlən] verdrossen, finster, mürrisch; widerspenstig; trotzig; **'sul·len·ness** Verdrießlichkeit *f*.

sul·ly *mst fig.* ['sʌli] beflecken.

sul·pha ['sʌlfə] *pl.* = *sulphona-mides*.

sul·phate ♑ ['sʌlfeit] schwefelsaures Salz *n*, Sulfat *n*; **sul·phide** ♑ ['⌣faid] Schwefelverbindung *f*, Sulfid *n*.

sul·pho·na·mides ✗ [sʌl'fɔnə-maidʒ] *pl.* Sulfonamide *pl.*

sul·phur ♑ ['sʌlfə] **1.** Schwefel *m*; **2.** schwefeln; **sul·phu·re·ous** [sʌl-'fjuəriəs] schwef(e)lig; **sul·phu-**

ret·ted hy·dro·gen [' fjuretid-'haidridʒən] Schwefelwasserstoff *m*;
sul·phu·ric ['fjuərik] Schwefel...; ~ *acid* Schwefelsäure *f*; **'sul·phu·rize** ⊕ schwefeln, vulkanisieren; **sul·phur·ous** [' fərəs] Schwefel..., schwefelhaltig.

sul·tan ['sʌltən] Sultan *m*; **sul·tan·a** [sʌl'taːnə] Sultanin *f*; [sɔl-'taːnə] Sultanine *f*.

sul·tri·ness ['sʌltrinis] Schwüle *f*; **'sul·try** □ schwül; *fig.* heftig, hitzig.

sum [sʌm] **1.** Summe *f*; Betrag *m*; *fig.* Inbegriff *m*, Inhalt *m*; Rechenaufgabe *f*; *do* ~*s* rechnen; *in* ~ mit e-m Wort; **2.** *mst* ~ *up* zs.-rechnen, -zählen; *fig.* zs.-fassen, resümieren.

su·mac(h) ♣ ['suːmæk] Sumach *m*, Färberbaum *m*.

sum·ma·rize ['sʌməraiz] (kurz) zs.-fassen; **'sum·mar·y 1.** □ summarisch, kurz (zs.-gefaßt); ⚡ Schnell...; **2.** (kurze) Inhaltsangabe *f*, Auszug *m*.

sum·mer[1] ['sʌmə] **1.** Sommer *m*; ~ *resort* Sommerfrische *f*; **2.** den Sommer verbringen; **'~-house** (Garten)Laube *f*.

sum·mer[2] △ [ ] Trägerbalken *m*; Oberschwelle *f*.

sum·mer·like ['sʌmməlaik], **'summer·ly** sommerlich.

summer...: '~-school Ferienkurs *m*; **'~-time** Sommer(szeit *f*) *m*; **'~-'time** Sommerzeit *f* (*um 1 Std. vorgerückt*); **'sum·mer·y** sommerlich.

sum·mit ['sʌmit] Gipfel *m* (*a. fig.*); ~ **con·fe·rence** *pol.* Gipfelkonferenz *f*.

sum·mon ['sʌmən] auffordern; (be)rufen, einberufen; ⚡ vorladen; *fig. mst* ~ *up* aufbieten; **'sum·mon·er** Bote *m*; **sum·mons** [' z] Aufforderung *f* (*a.* ✕ *zur Übergabe*); (gerichtliche) Vorladung *f*.

sump *mot.* [sʌmp] Ölwanne *f*.

sump·ter ['sʌmptə] *a.* **'~-horse**, **'~-mule** † Saumtier *n*.

sump·tu·ar·y ['sʌmptjuəri] Aufwand(s)..., Luxus...

sump·tu·ous □ ['sʌmptjuəs] kostbar, prächtig, luxuriös; **'sump·tu·ous·ness** Pracht *f*.

sun [sʌn] **1.** Sonne *f*; **2.** (sich) sonnen; **'~-baked** von der Sonne getrocknet; **'~-bath** Sonnenbad *n*;

'~-bathe sonnenbaden; **'~-beam** Sonnenstrahl *m* (*a. fig.*); **'~-blind** Markise *f*; **'~-burn** Sonnenbräune *f*; Sonnenbrand *m*; **'~-burnt** sonn(en)verbrannt.

sun·dae ['sʌndi] Früchte-Eisbecher *m*.

Sun·day ['sʌndi] Sonntag *m*; ~ **school** Sonntagsschule *f*.

sun·der *poet.* ['sʌndə] (sich) trennen.

sun·di·al ['sʌndaiəl] Sonnenuhr *f*.

sun·down ['sʌndaun] Sonnenuntergang *m*; **'sun·down·er** F Dämmerschoppen *m*.

sun·dry ['sʌndri] **1.** verschiedene; **2. sun·dries** *pl. bsd.* ✝ [' driz] Verschiedenes *n*; Extraausgaben *f/pl.*

sun·flow·er ♣ ['sʌnflauə] Sonnenblume *f*.

sung [sʌŋ] *pret. u. p.p. von* sing.

sun...: '~-glass·es *pl.* (*a pair of* eine) Sonnenbrille *f*; **'~-god** Sonnengott *m*; **'~-hel·met** Tropenhelm *m*.

sunk [sʌŋk] *pret. u. p.p. von* sink **1.**

sunk·en ['sʌŋkən] **1.** ⚓ *p.p. von* sink **1**; **2.** *adj.* versunken; *fig.* eingefallen (*Wangen etc.*); tiefliegend (*Augen*); ⊕ versenkt.

sun-lamp ['sʌnlæmp] ⚡ künstliche Höhensonne *f*; *Film*: Jupiterlampe *f*.

sun·less ['sʌnlis] sonnen-, lichtlos, dunkel; **'sun·light** Sonnenlicht *n*; **'sun·lit** sonnenbeschienen.

sun·ni·ness ['sʌninis] Sonnigkeit *f* (*a. fig.*); **'sun·ny** □ sonnig (*a. fig.*).

sun...: '~·rise Sonnenaufgang *m*; **'~·room** Glasveranda *f*; **'~·set** Sonnenuntergang *m*; **'~·shade** Sonnenschirm *m*; **'~·shine** Sonnenschein *m*; ~ *roof mot.* Schiebedach *n*; **'~·shin·y** sonnig; heiter; **'~·spot** *ast.* Sonnenfleck *m*; **'~·stroke** ⚡ Sonnenstich *m*; **'~·up** Sonnenaufgang *m*.

sup[1] [sʌp] *v/i.* zu Abend essen (*off od. on s.th. et.*).

sup[2] [ ] **1.** schlückchenweise trinken, nippen; löffeln; **2.** Schlückchen *n*; *neither bite nor* ~ nichts zu essen u. zu trinken.

su·per[1] ['suːpə] **1.** *thea. sl.* Statist (-in); **2.** F erstklassig, super, prima; Riesen...

su·per[2] [ ] Über...; über...; Ober..., ober...; Groß...

su·per...: ˈˌ‿aˈbound im Überfluß vorhanden sein; Überfluß haben (in, with an dat.); ˌ‿aˈbun·dant ☐ überreichlich; überschwenglich; ˌ‿ˈadd noch hinzufügen; ˌ‿an·nu·ate [ˌ‿ˈrænjueit] pensionieren; ‿d überaltert; ausgedient; veraltet (Sache); ˌ‿an·nuˈa·tion Pensionierung f; Ruhegehalt n; ‿ fund Pensionsfonds m.

su·perb ☐ [sjuːˈpɜːb] prächtig; herrlich.

su·per...: ˈˌ‿car·go ⚓ Ladungsaufseher m; ˈˌ‿charg·er mot. Gebläse n, Kompressor m; **su·per·cil·i·ous** ☐ [ˌ‿ˈsiliəs] hochmütig; **su·perˈcil·i·ous·ness** Hochmut m; **su·per-ˈdread·nought** Großkampfschiff n; **su·per·er·o·ga·tion** [ˌ‿rerəˈgeiʃən] Mehrleistung f; **su·per·e·rog·a·to·ry** ☐ [ˌ‿reˈrɔgətəri] über das Pflichtmaß hinausgehend; **su·per·fi·cial** ☐ [ˌ‿ˈfiʃəl] oberflächlich; **su·per·fi·ci·al·i·ty** [ˌ‿fiʃiˈæliti] Oberflächlichkeit f; **su·per·fi·ci·es** [ˌ‿ˈfiʃiːz] Oberfläche f; ˈsu·perˈfine extrafein; **su·per·flu·i·ty** [ˌ‿ˈfluːiti] Überfluß m (of an dat.); **su·perˈflu·ous** ☐ [ˌ‿fluəs] überflüssig; **su·perˈheat** ⊕ überhitzen; **su·per·het** [ˈˌ‿het] Radio: Überlagerungsempfänger m, Super(het) m.

su·per...: ˌ‿ˈhu·man ☐ übermenschlich; ˌ‿im·pose [ˈˌ‿rimˈpəuz] darauf-, darüberlegen; ˌ‿in·duce [ˈˌ‿rinˈdjuːs] noch hinzufügen (on, upon zu); ˌ‿in·tend [ˌ‿rinˈtend] die Oberaufsicht haben über (acc.); überwachen; ˌ‿in·ˈtend·ence Oberaufsicht f; ˌ‿inˈtend·ent 1. Leiter m, Direktor m; (Ober)Aufseher m, Inspektor m; 2. aufsichtführend.

su·pe·ri·or [suːˈpiəriə] 1. ☐ ober; höher(stehend); vorgesetzt; besser; hochwertiger; überlegen (to dat.); vorzüglich; ‿ officer höherer Beamter m od. Offizier m; 2. Höherstehende m, bsd. Vorgesetzte m; eccl. Obere m, Superior m; mst lady ‿ Oberin f; **su·pe·ri·or·i·ty** [ˌ‿ˈɔriti] Überlegenheit f.

su·per·la·tive [suːˈpɜːlətiv] 1. ☐ höchst; überragend; gr. superlativisch; 2. ‿ ‿ degree gr. Superlativ m; **su·per·man** [ˈsuːpəmæn] Übermensch m; ˈsu·per·mar·ket Supermarkt m; **su·per·nal** [suː-ˈpɔːnl] überirdisch, himmlisch; **su·per·nat·u·ral** ☐ [suːpɔˈnætʃrəl] übernatürlich; **su·per·nu·mer·ar·y** [ˌ‿ˈnjuːmərəri] 1. überzählig; 2. Überzählige m, f; thea. Statist(in); ˈsu·perˈpose obenauf legen; überlagern; ˈsu·per·poˈsi·tion Auflagerung f; geol. Schichtung f; ˈsu·perˈpow·er pol. Supermacht f; ˈsu·perˈscribe überschreiben; adressieren; **su·per·scrip·tion** [ˌ‿ˈskripʃən] Über-, Aufschrift f; **su·per·sede** [ˌ‿ˈsiːd] ersetzen; verdrängen; absetzen; fig. überholen; **su·per·ses·sion** Ersetzung f, Ablösung f; **su·per·son·ic** phys. [ˌ‿ˈsɔnik] Überschall...; **su·per·sti·tion** [ˌ‿ˈstiʃən] Aberglaube m; **su·per·sti·tious** ☐ [ˌ‿ˈstiʃəs] abergläubisch; **su·per·struc·ture** [ˈˌ‿strʌktʃə] Oberbau m; **su·per·vene** [ˌ‿ˈviːn] noch hinzukommen (on, upon zu); unerwartet eintreten; **su·per·ven·tion** [ˌ‿ˈvenʃən] Hinzukommen n; **su·per·vise** [ˈˌ‿vaiz] beaufsichtigen, überwachen; **su·per·vi·sion** [ˌ‿ˈviʒən] (Ober)Aufsicht f; Beaufsichtigung f, Überwachung f; **su·per·vi·sor** [ˈˌ‿vaizə] Aufseher m, Inspektor m; univ. Tutor m.

su·pine 1. gr. [ˈsjuːpain] Supinum n; 2. ☐ [ˌ‿ˈpain] auf dem Rücken liegend; zurückgelehnt; lässig, gleichgültig; **suˈpine·ness** Lässigkeit f, Gleichgültigkeit f.

sup·per [ˈsʌpə] Abendessen n; the (Lord's) ♀ das Heilige Abendmahl.

sup·plant [səˈplɑːnt] verdrängen; fig. ausstechen; ersetzen.

sup·ple [ˈsʌpl] 1. ☐ biegsam, geschmeidig; 2. geschmeidig machen.

sup·ple·ment 1. [ˈsʌplimənt] Supplement n, Ergänzung f; Nachtrag m; (Zeitungs- etc.)Beilage f; 2. [ˈ‿ment] ergänzen; **sup·ple·men·tal** ☐, **sup·ple·men·ta·ry** Ergänzungs...; nachträglich; Nachtrags...; ‿ benefit Sozialhilfe f; ‿ order Nachbestellung f.

sup·ple·ness [ˈsʌplnis] Biegsamkeit f; Schmiegsamkeit f (a. fig.).

sup·pli·ant [ˈsʌpliənt] 1. ☐ demütig bittend, flehend; 2. Bittsteller(in).

sup·pli·cate [ˈsʌplikeit] demütig bitten, anflehen; **sup·pli·ca·tion** demütige Bitte f; **sup·pli·ca·to·ry** [ˈ‿kətəri] flehend; Bitt...

sup·pli·er [sə'plaiə] Versorger(in); ✝ Lieferant(in).

sup·ply [sə'plai] **1.** liefern; *e-m Mangel* abhelfen; *e-e Stelle* ausfüllen, vertreten; ausstatten, versehen, versorgen (*with* mit); ergänzen; **2.** Lieferung *f*; Versorgung *f*; Zufuhr *f*; Menge *f*; Vorrat *m*; Bedarf *m*; ✝ Angebot *n* (*Ggs.* demand); (Stell-) Vertretung *f*; *mst* supplies *pl.* ✝ Versorgungsgüter *n/pl.*; *parl.* Etat *m*, Budget *n*; ✗ Nachschub *m*; *in short* ～ knapp, schwer zu haben; *on* ～ in Vertretung; *Committee of* ♀ *parl.* Haushaltsausschuß *m*; **sup-'ply-'side:** ～ economics *sg. od. pl. bsd. Am.* angebotsorientierte Wirtschaftspolitik *f*.

sup·port [sə'pɔːt] **1.** Stütze *f* (*a. fig.*); Hilfe *f*; Fußstütze *f*, Einlage *f*; ⊕ Träger *m*, Halter *m*; Unterstützung *f*; Lebensunterhalt *m*; **2.** (unter)stützen (*a. fig.*); *sich, e-e Familie etc.* unterhalten, ernähren; *Debatte etc.* aufrechterhalten; *e-e Sache* verteidigen; *Meinung, Würde* behaupten; (v)ertragen; ～ing actor Nebendarsteller *m*; ～ing evidence ⚖ erhärtendes Beweismaterial *n*; ～ing part Nebenrolle *f*; ～ing programme *Film:* Beiprogramm *n*; **sup'port·a·ble** ☐ erträglich; aufrechtzuerhalten(d), haltbar; **sup'port·er** Unterstützer(in); Anhänger(in); Helfer(in).

sup·pose [sə'pəuz] annehmen; voraussetzen; vermuten; *he is* ～*d to* man erwartet *od.* verlangt von ihm, daß er tut; er soll tun; ～ *od. supposing (that)* ... angenommen (daß) ...; ～ *we go* gehen wir; wie wär's, wenn wir gingen; *he is rich, I* ～ er wird wohl reich sein.

sup·posed ☐ [sə'pəuzd] vermeintlich; **sup'pos·ed·ly** [～idli] vermutlich.

sup·pos·ing [sə'pəuziŋ] angenommen, falls.

sup·po·si·tion [sʌpə'ziʃən] Voraussetzung *f*; Annahme *f*; Vermutung *f*; **sup·pos·i·ti·tious** ☐ [səpɔzi-'tiʃəs] untergeschoben; **sup'pos·i·to·ry** ⚕ [～təri] Zäpfchen *n*, Suppositorium *n*.

sup·press [sə'pres] unterdrücken; **sup·pres·sion** [sə'preʃən] Unterdrückung *f*; **sup'pres·sive** ☐ [～siv] unterdrückend; **sup'pres·sor** ⚡ Entstörungselement *n*; *Radio:*

Entstörer *m*.

sup·pu·rate ['sʌpjuəreit] eitern; **sup·pu'ra·tion** Eiterung *f*.

su·pra·na·tion·al ['sjuːprə'næʃənl] überstaatlich.

su·prem·a·cy [su'preməsi] Obergewalt *f*, -hoheit *f*; Überlegenheit *f*; Vorrang *m*; **su'preme** ☐ [suː-'priːm] höchst; oberst; Ober...; größt; kritisch (*Zeitpunkt*).

sur·charge [səː'tʃɑːdʒ] **1.** überladen; *e-n* Strafzuschlag erheben von *j-m*; **2.** ['～] Überladung *f*; (Straf)Zuschlag *m*; Strafporto *n*; Überdruck *m* auf *Briefmarken*.

surd ⚹ [səːd] irrational(e Zahl *f*).

sure ☐ [ʃuə] *allg.* sicher, gewiß, bestimmt; *to be* ～*!*, F ～ *enough!*, *Am.* ～*!* sicher(lich)!, natürlich!; *I'm* ～ *I don't know* ich weiß wirklich nicht; *he is* ～ *to return* er wird sicher(lich) zurückkommen; *make* ～ sich vergewissern; *sich versichern* (*of gen.*); '～-**foot·ed** sicher auf den Füßen; **'sure·ly** sicherlich; **'sure·ness** Sicherheit *f*; **'sure·ty** Bürge *m*.

surf [səːf] Brandung *f*.

sur·face ['səːfis] **1.** Oberfläche *f*; Fläche(ninhalt *m*) *f*; ✈ Tragfläche *f*; *control* ～ ✈ Steuerfläche *f*; *below the* ～ unter Tage; **2.** auftauchen (*U-Boot*); ～ *mail* auf dem Land- und Seeweg beförderte Post *f*; '～-**man** ⚒ Streckenarbeiter *m*; '～-**to--air** ['～tə'ɛə]: ～ *missile* ✗ Boden-Luft-Rakete *f*.

surf...: '～-**board** Wellenreiterbrett *n*; '～-**boat** Brandungsboot *n*.

sur·feit ['səːfit] **1.** Übersättigung *f*, Ekel *m*; **2.** (sich) überladen, -sättigen (*on, fig. with* mit).

surf·rid·ing ['səːfraidiŋ] *Sport:* Wellenreiten *n*.

surge [səːdʒ] **1.** Woge *f*; Brandung *f*; **2.** wogen, branden.

sur·geon ['səːdʒən] Chirurg *m*, Operateur *m*; ✗ Stabs-, ⚓ Schiffsarzt *m*; **sur·ger·y** ['səːdʒəri] Chirurgie *f*; chirurgische Behandlung *f*; Sprechzimmer *n*; ～ *hours pl.* Sprechstunden *f/pl.*

sur·gi·cal ☐ ['səːdʒikəl] chirurgisch; Operations...

sur·li·ness ['səːlinis] mürrisches Wesen *n*, Unfreundlichkeit *f*; Bärbeißigkeit *f*; **'sur·ly** ☐ unfreundlich; bärbeißig; zäh (*Boden*).

sur·mise 1. ['sə:maiz] Vermutung *f*; Argwohn *m*; **2.** [sə:'maiz] vermuten; argwöhnen.

sur·mount [sə:'maunt] übersteigen; überragen; *fig.* überwinden; ⁓*ed by od. with* überragt *od.* überdeckt von; **sur'mount·a·ble** übersteigbar, überwindlich.

sur·name ['sə:neim] **1.** Zu-, Nach-, Familienname *m*; **2.** *j-m* den Zunamen ... geben; ⁓*d* mit Zunamen.

sur·pass *fig.* [sə:'pa:s] übersteigen, -treffen; ⁓*ed by* überragt von; **sur'pass·ing** □ unübertrefflich, außerordentlich.

sur·plice *eccl.* ['sə:pləs] Chorhemd *n*.

sur·plus ['sə:pləs] **1.** Überschuß *m*, Mehr *n*; **2.** überschüssig; Über...; Mehr...; ⁓ *population* Bevölkerungsüberschuß *m*; **'sur·plus·age** = *surplus* 1; etwas Überflüssiges *n*.

sur·prise [sə'praiz] **1.** Überraschung *f*; ✕ Überrump(e)lung *f*; *take by* ⁓ überrumpeln; **2.** Überraschungs...; überraschend; **3.** überraschen; ✕ überrumpeln; **sur'pris·ing** □ überraschend.

sur·re·al·ism [sə'riəlizəm] *Kunst*: Surrealismus *m*; **sur're·al·ist** Surrealist *m*.

sur·ren·der [sə'rendə] **1.** Übergabe *f*, Ergebung *f*; Kapitulation *f*; Aufgeben *n*; **2.** *v/t.* übergeben, ausliefern; *Besitz* aufgeben; *v/i. a.* ⁓ *o.s.* sich ergeben.

sur·rep·ti·tious □ [sʌrəp'tiʃəs] erschlichen; heimlich; unecht.

sur·ro·gate ['sʌrogit] Stellvertreter *m bsd. e-s Bischofs.*

sur·round [sə'raund] umgeben; ✕ umzingeln; **sur'round·ing** umliegend; **sur'round·ings** *pl.* Umgebung *f*; Umwelt *f*.

sur·tax ['sə:tæks] (Einkommen-) Steuerzuschlag *m*.

sur·veil·lance [sə:'veiləns] Überwachung *f*.

sur·vey 1. [sə:'vei] überblicken; besichtigen; mustern; begutachten; *surv.* vermessen; **2.** ['⁓] Überblick *m* (*a. fig.*); Besichtigung *f*; Gutachten *n*; Umfrage *f*; *surv.* Vermessung *f*, Aufnahme *f*; **sur'vey·or** Aufseher *m*; Inspektor *m*; Land-, Feldmesser *m*, Geometer *m*; Gutachter *m*; *Board of* ⁓s Baupolizei *f*.

sur·viv·al [sə'vaivəl] Über-, Fortleben *n*; Überbleibsel *n*; **sur'vive**

v/t. überleben; *v/i.* noch (*od.* fort-) leben; am Leben bleiben; bestehen bleiben; **sur'vi·vor** Überlebende *m, f.*

sus·cep·ti·bil·i·ty [səseptə'biliti] Empfänglichkeit *f* (*to* für); *oft* *susceptibilities pl.* Empfindlichkeit *f*, empfindliche Stelle *f*; **sus'cep·ti·ble** □, **sus'cep·tive** empfänglich (*to* für); empfindlich (gegen); *be* ⁓ *of* zulassen (*Sache*).

sus·pect 1. [səs'pekt] (be)argwöhnen; im Verdacht haben, verdächtigen; zweifeln an (*dat.*); vermuten, befürchten; **2.** ['sʌspekt] Verdächtige *m, f*; **3.** = **sus'pect·ed** verdächtig.

sus·pend [səs'pend] (auf)hängen; aufschieben; unentschieden lassen; *Tätigkeit, Zahlung* einstellen; *Urteil* aussetzen; *Beamten, Gesetz* suspendieren; *Sportler* sperren; ⁓*ed* schwebend; ⁓*ed animation* Scheintod *m*; **sus'pend·er** Strumpf-, Sockenhalter *m*; ⁓*s pl. Am.* Hosenträger *m*.

sus·pense [səs'pens] Ungewißheit *f*; Unentschiedenheit *f*; Spannung *f*; ⁓ *account* † vorläufiges Konto *n*; **sus·pen·sion** [⁓'penʃən] Aufhängung *f*; Aufschub *m*; Einstellung *f e-r Tätigkeit etc.*; Suspendierung *f*; Amtsenthebung *f*; einstweilige Aufhebung *f e-s Gesetzes*; *Sport*: Sperre *f*; **sus·pen·sion bridge** Hängebrücke *f*; **sus'pen·sive** □ aufschiebend; **sus·pen·so·ry** [⁓'pensəri] Hänge...; aufschiebend; ⁓ *bandage* ✕ Suspensorium *n*.

sus·pi·cion [səs'piʃən] Verdacht *m*; Argwohn *m*; Ahnung *f*; *fig.* Spur *f*; **sus'pi·cious** □ argwöhnisch, mißtrauisch; verdächtig; **sus'pi·cious·ness** mißtrauisches Wesen *n od.* Gefühl *n*; Verdächtigkeit *f*.

sus·tain [səs'tein] stützen; *fig.* aufrecht erhalten; aushalten; *Verlust, Schaden* erleiden; ♪ aushalten; ♫ anerkennen; *thea. e-r Rolle* gerecht werden (*Schauspieler*); **sus'tain·a·ble** haltbar (*Anklage*); **sus'tained** anhaltend; ununterbrochen.

sus·te·nance ['sʌstinəns] (Lebens-) Unterhalt *m*; Nahrung *f*; Nährwert *m*.

sut·ler ✕ ['sʌtlə] Marketender *m*.

sweeping

su·ture ['suːtʃə] **1.** ⚲, *anat.*, ⚕ Naht *f*; **2.** nähen.

su·ze·rain ['suːzərein] Oberlehnsherr *m*.

svelte [svelt] schlank (*Frau*).

swab [swɔb] **1.** Aufwischmop *m*; ⚓ Schwabber *m*; ⚕ Tupfer *m*; Abstrich *m*; **2.** *a.* ~ *down* aufwischen; ⚓ schwabbern.

Swa·bi·an ['sweibjən] **1.** Schwabe *m*, Schwäbin *f*; Schwäbisch *n*; **2.** schwäbisch.

swad·dle ['swɔdl] *Baby* wickeln; 'swad·dling-clothes *pl. mst fig.* Windeln *f/pl.*

swag·ger ['swægə] **1.** (umher)stolzieren; großtun, aufschneiden; **2.** F elegant; **3.** Großtuerei *f*; '~-cane ✗ Ausgehstöckchen *n*.

swain *poet. od.* † [swein] (Bauern-) Bursche *m*; Schäfer *m*; *co.* Liebhaber *m*. [rung *f*.\
swale *Am.* [sweil] Mulde *f*, Niede-\
swal·low[1] *orn.* ['swɔləu] Schwalbe *f*.

swal·low[2] [~] **1.** Schlund *m*; Schluck *m*; **2.** *v/t.* (*fig. mst* ~ *up*) (hinunter-, ver)schlucken; *fig. Ansicht etc.* begierig aufnehmen; *Behauptung* zurücknehmen; *v/i.* schlucken.

swam [swæm] *pret. von* swim 1.

swamp [swɔmp] **1.** Sumpf *m*, Morast *m*; **2.** überschwemmen (*a. fig.*); ⚓ zum Sinken bringen; *fig.* überhäufen; 'swamp·y sumpfig.

swan [swɔn] Schwan *m*.

swank *sl.* [swæŋk] **1.** Angabe *f*, Protzerei *f*; **2.** angeben, protzen; 'swank·y protzig, angeberisch, snobistisch.

swan-neck ['swɔnnek] Schwanenhals *m*; 'swan·ner·y Schwanenteich *m*; 'swan-song Schwanengesang *m*.

swap F [swɔp] (ver-, aus)tauschen.

sward [swɔːd] Rasen *m*.

sware † [swɛə] *pret. von* swear.

swarm[1] [swɔːm] **1.** Schwarm *m*; Haufe(n) *m*, Gewimmel *n*; **2.** schwärmen; wimmeln (*with* von).

swarm[2] [~] ~ *up* hochklettern an (*dat.*).

swarth·i·ness ['swɔːθinis] dunkle Gesichtsfarbe *f*; 'swarth·y ☐ schwärzlich; dunkelfarbig, -häutig.

swash [swɔʃ] **1.** *v/i.* plan(t)schen; prahlen; *v/t.* (be)spritzen; **2.** Pla(n)tschen *n*, Klatschen *n des*

Wassers; ~·buck·ler ['~bʌklə] großmäuliger Draufgänger *m*.

swas·ti·ka ['swɔstikə] Hakenkreuz *n*.

swat [swɔt] **1.** *Fliege etc.* klatschen; **2.** Schlag *m*.

swath ⚲ [swɔːθ] Schwade(n *m*) *f*.

swathe [sweiδ] **1.** Wickelband *n*; Binde *f*; *s. swath;* **2.** (ein)wickeln, einhüllen.

sway [swei] **1.** Schaukeln *n*; Wiegen *n*; Einfluß *m*; Macht *f*, Herrschaft *f*; **2.** *v/t.* schaukeln; wiegen; beeinflussen; beherrschen; *v/i.* schaukeln; sich wiegen; schwanken.

swear [swɛə] **1.** (*irr.*) *v/i.* schwören (*by* bei, F auf *j. od. et.*); beschwören (*to s.th.* et.); fluchen (*at* auf *acc.*); *v/t.* (be)schwören; ~ *s.o. in j.* vereidigen; **2.** *a.* ~-word F Fluch *m*.

sweat [swet] **1.** Schweiß *m*; *old* ~ *sl.* alter Hase *m*; *by the* ~ *of one's brow* im Schweiße s-s Angesichts; **2.** (*irr.*) *v/i.* schwitzen; *v/t.* (aus-) schwitzen; in Schweiß bringen; *Arbeiter* ausbeuten; ⊕ *Kabel* schweißen; 'sweat·ed für Hungerlöhne hergestellt; 'sweat·er Sweater *m*, Pullover *m*; Trainingsjacke *f*; Leuteschinder *m*; 'sweat-shirt Sweatshirt *n*; Trainingshemd *n*; 'sweat-shop Ausbeutungsbetrieb *m*; sweat suit Trainingsanzug *m*; 'sweat·y schweißig; verschwitzt.

Swede [swiːd] Schwede *m*, Schwedin *f*; Swed·ish ['swiːdiʃ] **1.** schwedisch; **2.** Schwedisch *n*.

sweep [swiːp] **1.** (*irr.*) *v/t.* fegen, kehren; *fig.* (*mst mit adv.*) reißen, jagen, treiben; streifen; bestreichen (*a.* ✗); schleppen, hinter sich herziehen; *v/i.* fegen, kehren; *fig.* (*mst mit adv.*) (dahin)fegen, eilen, stürmen, schießen, sausen; (majestätisch) (dahin)rauschen; sich erstrecken, streichen; *be swept off one's feet fig.* hingerissen sein; **2.** Fegen *n*, Kehren *n*; *fig.* Dahinfegen *n*, Stürmen *n*; Schwung *m*; ♪ Tusch *m*; glänzender Sieg *m*; Schwenkung *f*; Krümmung *f*; Bogen *m*; Fläche *f*; Spielraum *m*, Bereich *m*; Schornsteinfeger *m*; Auffahrt *f vor e-m Hause*; langes Ruder *n*; (Pumpen)Schwengel *m*; *make a clean* ~ (*of*) reinen Tisch machen (mit); hinauswerfen; 'sweep·er (Straßen)Feger *m*; Kehrmaschine *f*; 'sweep·ing ☐

ausgedehnt; umfassend; weitgehend (*Behauptung etc.*); schwungvoll; durchgreifend; '**sweep·ings**
pl. Kehricht *m*; **sweep·stakes** ['⌣-
steiks] *pl.* (*bsd.* Pferde)Toto *n*.

sweet [swi:t] **1.** □ süß; lieblich,
hold; freundlich, lieb(enswürdig);
leicht, bequem; frisch; duftend;
have a ⌣ *tooth* ein Leckermaul sein;
2. Liebling *m*; Süßigkeit *f*, Bonbon
n; Nachtisch *m*; ⌣s *pl.* Freuden *f/pl.*;
'⌣-**bread** (*bsd.* Kalbs)Bries *n*; '⌣-
'**bri·ar** ♀ Weinrose *f*; '**sweet·en**
(ver)süßen; *fig.* angenehm machen;
mildern; '**sweet·en·er** Süßstoff *m*;
'**sweet·heart** Liebling *m*, Liebchen
n, Liebste *m*, *f*; Freund(in); '**sweet·-
ish** süßlich; '**sweet·meat** Bonbon *m*,
n; kandierte Frucht *f*; '**sweet·ness**
Süßigkeit *f*; Lieblichkeit *f*; Annehmlichkeit *f*; Freundlichkeit *f*; Frische *f*;
sweet pea ♀ Gartenwicke *f*; '**sweet-
shop** Süßwarengeschäft *n*; '**sweet-
-'wil·liam** ♀ Studentennelke *f*.

swell [swel] **1.** (*irr.*) *v/i.* (an-, auf-)
schwellen (*into* zu) (*a. fig.*); sich
blähen (*Segel*); sich (aus)bauchen;
v/t. (an)schwellen lassen; aufblähen; vergrößern, erhöhen; **2.** F
flott, elegant; feudal; *sl.* prima;
3. *bsd.* ♪ Anschwellen *n*; Schwellung
f, Ausbauchung; ⚓ Dünung *f*; Anhöhe *f*; F feudaler Herr *m*, feudale
Dame *f*; '**swell·ing 1.** Anschwellen
n; Geschwulst *f*; **2.** □ schwellend;
schwülstig (*Stil etc.*).

swel·ter ['sweltə] sehr heiß sein; vor
Hitze umkommen; schwitzen.

swept [swept] *pret. u. p.p. von*
sweep 1.

swerve [swə:v] *v/i.* sich seitwärts
wenden; abweichen; plötzlich ab-
od. ausbiegen (*Wagen*); *v/t.* ablenken; *Sport:* Ball schneiden.

swift 1. □ schnell, eilig, geschwind,
flink; **2.** *orn.* Turmschwalbe *f*;
'**swift·ness** Schnelligkeit *f*.

swig F [swig] **1.** (tüchtiger) Schluck
m; **2.** schlucken; saufen.

swill [swil] **1.** Spülicht *n* (*a. fig.*);
Schweinetrank *m*; *contp.* Gesöff *n*;
2. spülen; saufen.

swim [swim] **1.** (*irr.*) *v/i.* schwimmen; schweben; *my head* ⌣*s* mir
schwindelt; *v/t.* durchschwimmen;
schwimmen lassen; schwemmen;
2. Schwimmen *n*; *be in the* ⌣ auf
dem laufenden *od.* eingeweiht sein;

'**swim·mer** Schwimmer(in).

swim·ming ['swimiŋ] **1.** Schwimmen *n*; **2.** Schwimm...; '⌣-**bath**
(*bsd.* Hallen)Schwimmbad *n*; '⌣-
-**cos·tume** Badeanzug *m*; '**swim-
ming·ly** *adv.* leicht; glatt; '**swimming-pool** Frei-, Schwimmbad *n*;
'**swim-suit** Badeanzug *m*.

swin·dle ['swindl] **1.** *v/t.* beschwindeln (*out of* um *et.*); *v/i.* schwindeln;
2. Schwindel *m*; '**swin·dler**
Schwindler(in).

swine *nur rhet.*, *zo. od. fig. contp.*
[swain], *pl.* ⌣ Schwein *n*; '**swine-
herd** Schweinehirt *m*.

swing [swiŋ] **1.** (*irr.*) *v/i.* schwingen,
schwanken; F baumeln, gehängt
werden; (sich) schaukeln; schwenken; sich drehen, ⚓ schwaien; ⌣
into motion in Gang kommen; *v/t.*
schwingen, (herum)schwenken;
schaukeln; **2.** Schwingen *n*;
Schwung *m*; Schaukel *f*; freier
Lauf *m*; Spielraum *m* (*a. fig.*); ♪
Swing *m*; *Boxen:* Schwinger *m*; *in
full* ⌣ in vollem Gange; *go with a* ⌣
Schwung haben; *wie am* Schnürchen gehen; **3.** Schwing...; ⌣
bridge Drehbrücke *f*; ⌣ **door**
Drehtür *f*.

swinge·ing □ F ['swindʒiŋ] riesig,
mächtig.

swing·ing □ ['swiŋiŋ] schwingend;
Schwing...; schwungvoll.

swin·gle ⊕ ['swiŋgl] **1.** *Flachs*
schwingen; **2.** Flachsschwinge *f*;
'⌣-**tree** Ortscheit *n*.

swin·ish □ ['swainiʃ] schweinisch.

swipe [swaip] **1.** aus vollem Arm
schlagen; *sl.* klauen; **2.** kräftiger
Schlag *m*; ⌣s *pl.* Dünnbier *n*.

swirl [swə:l] **1.** (herum)wirbeln,
strudeln; **2.** Wirbel *m*, Strudel *m*.

swish [swiʃ] **1.** sausen (lassen);
zischen (*Sense*); rascheln; peitschen;
2. Sausen *n etc.*; **3.** F forsch.

Swiss [swis] **1.** schweizerisch,
Schweizer; **2.** Schweizer(in); *the* ⌣
pl. die Schweizer *m/pl.*

switch [switʃ] **1.** Gerte *f*; 🚃 Weiche
f; ∮ Schalter *m*; falscher Zopf *m*;
2. peitschen; 🚃 rangieren; ∮ (um-)
schalten; *fig.* wechseln, überleiten;
⌣ *on* (*off*) ∮ ein- (aus)schalten; '⌣-
back Berg- und Talbahn *f*; '⌣-
board ∮ Schaltbrett *n*, -tafel *f*;
Telefonvermittlung *f*; ⌣ **box** ∮
Schaltkasten *m*.

synoptical

swiv·el ⊕ ['swivl] Drehring *m*; Spannschloß *n*; *attr*. Dreh...

swol·len ['swəulən] *p.p. von* swell *1*.

swoon [swu:n] *1*. Ohnmacht *f*; *2*. in Ohnmacht fallen.

swoop [swu:p] *1*. ~ *down on od. upon* (herab)stoßen (auf *acc.*) (*Raubvogel*); **2**. Stoß *m*.

swop F [swɔp] (ver-, aus)tauschen.

sword F [sɔːd] Schwert *n*, Degen *m*; Säbel *m*; '~-**cane** Stockdegen *m*; '~-**play** Fechten *n*; *fig.* Wortgefecht *n*.

swords·man ['sɔːdzmən] Fechter *m*; '**swords·man·ship** Fechtkunst *f*.

swore [swɔː] *pret. von* swear *1*.

sworn [swɔːn] *1*. *p.p. von* swear *1*; **2**. ⚷ gerichtlich vereidigt; ~ *expert* ⚷ gerichtlich vereidigter Sachverständiger *m*.

swot *Schul-sl.* [swɔt] *1*. Paukerei *f*; Streber *m*; **2**. pauken, büffeln.

swum [swʌm] *p.p. von* swim *1*.

swung [swʌŋ] *pret. u. p.p. von* swing *1*.

syb·a·rite ['sibərait] Weichling *m*, Genüßling *m*.

syc·a·more ⚘ ['sikəmɔː] Bergahorn *m*; *Am*. Platane *f*.

syc·o·phant ['sikəfənt] Kriecher *m*, Speichellecker *m*, Schmarotzer *m*; **syc·o·phan·tic** [~'fæntik] (~*ally*) kriecherisch.

syl·lab·ic [si'læbik] (~*ally*) silbenmäßig; Silben...; **syl·la·ble** ['siləbl] Silbe *f*.

syl·la·bus ['siləbəs] Auszug *m*, Abriß *m*; (*bsd.* Vorlesungs)Verzeichnis *n*; (*bsd.* Lehr-, Unterrichts)Plan *m*.

syl·lo·gism *phls.* ['silədʒizəm] Syllogismus *m*, Vernunftschluß *m*.

sylph [silf] Sylphe *f*, Luftgeist *m*.

syl·van ['silvən] waldig, Wald...

sym·bi·o·sis *biol.* [simbi'əusis] Symbiose *f* (*Zusammenleben artverschiedener Lebewesen*).

sym·bol ['simbəl] Symbol *n*, Sinnbild *n*; **sym·bol·ic**, **sym·bol·i·cal** □ [~'bɔlik(l)] symbolisch, sinnbildlich; **sym·bol·ism** ['~bəlizəm] Symbolik *f*; '**sym·bol·ize** sinnbildlich darstellen, symbolisieren, versinnbildlichen.

sym·met·ri·cal □ [si'metrikəl] symmetrisch, ebenmäßig; **sym·me·try** ['simitri] Symmetrie *f*, Ebenmaß *n*.

sym·pa·thet·ic [simpə'θetik] (~*ally*)

ein-, mitfühlend; geistesverwandt; sympathisch; sympathetisch (*Nerv, Tinte*); ~ *strike* Sympathiestreik *m*; '**sym·pa·thize** sympathisieren, mitfühlen, empfinden; wohlwollend gegenüberstehen (*with dat.*); übereinstimmen; '**sym·pa·thiz·er** Anhänger(in); **sym·pa·thy** ['~θi] Sympathie *f*, Mitgefühl *n*; (An)Teilnahme *f*; *letter of* ~ Beileidsbrief *m*.

sym·phon·ic ♪ [sim'fɔnik] symphonisch; **sym·pho·ny** ♪ ['~fəni] Symphonie *f*.

sym·po·sium [sim'pəuzjəm] Symposion *n*, Sammlung *f* von Beiträgen.

symp·tom ['simptəm] Symptom *n*, (An)Zeichen *n*; **symp·to·mat·ic** [~'mætik] (~*ally*) symptomatisch; bezeichnend (*of* für).

syn·a·gogue ['sinəgɔg] Synagoge *f*.

sync(h) F [sink] Synchronisation *f*; *out of* ~ nicht synchron, nicht im Einklang.

syn·chro·flash *phot.* ['sinkrəuflæʃ] Synchronblitzlicht *n*.

syn·chro·mesh *gear mot.* ['sinkrəumeʃ'giə] Synchrongetriebe *n*.

syn·chro·nism ['sinkrənizəm] Gleichzeitigkeit *f*; '**syn·chro·nize** *v/i*. gleichzeitig sein, zeitlich zs.-fallen; *v/t*. als gleichzeitig zs.-stellen; *Uhren, Tonfilm* synchronisieren; '**syn·chro·nous** gleichzeitig; gleichlaufend.

syn·chro·tron *phys.* ['sinkrəutrɔn] Synchrotron *n*, Beschleuniger *m*.

syn·co·pate ['sinkəpeit] verkürzen, synkopieren; **syn·co·pe** ['~pi] Synkope *f*.

syn·dic ['sindik] Syndikus *m*; **syn·di·cate** *1*. ['~kit] Syndikat *n*; **2**. ['~keit] zu e-m Syndikat verbinden; '**syn·di·cat·ed** syndikalisiert, in mehreren Zeitungen erscheinend.

syn·od *eccl.* ['sinəd] Synode *f*; **syn·od·al** ['~dəl], **syn·od·ic**, **syn·od·i·cal** □ *eccl.* [si'nɔdik(l)] synodal.

syn·o·nym ['sinənim] Synonym *n*, sinnverwandtes Wort *n*; **syn·on·y·mous** □ [si'nɔniməs] sinnverwandt.

syn·op·sis [si'nɔpsis], *pl.* **syn'op·ses** [~si:z] *zs.-fassende* Übersicht *f*; Synopse *f*.

syn·op·tic, **syn·op·ti·cal** □ [si'nɔptik(əl)] synoptisch, übersichtlich.

syn·tac·tic, syn·tac·ti·cal ⬚ gr. [sin'tæktik(əl)] syntaktisch; **syn·tax** gr. ['sintæks] Syntax f, Satzlehre f.
syn·the·sis ['sin'θisis], pl. **syn·the·ses** ['ˌsiːz] Synthese f, Verbindung f; **syn·the·size** ⊕ ['ˌsaiz] künstlich herstellen.
syn·thet·ic, syn·thet·i·cal ⬚ [sin'θetik(əl)] synthetisch; künstlich, Kunst...
syn·to·nize ['sintənaiz] Radio: abstimmen; **syn·to·ny** Abstimmung f.
syph·i·lis ⚕ ['sifilis] Syphilis f.

syph·i·lit·ic ⚕ [sifi'litik] syphilitisch.
sy·phon ['saifən] = siphon.
Syr·i·an ['siriən] 1. syrisch; 2. Syr(i)er(in).
sy·rin·ga ⚘ [si'riŋgə] Flieder m.
syr·inge ['sirindʒ] 1. Spritze f; 2. (be-, ein-, aus)spritzen.
syr·up ['sirəp] Sirup m.
sys·tem ['sistim] System n; Organismus m, Körper m; Plan m, Ordnung f; **sys·tem·at·ic** [ˌ'mætik] (ˌally) systematisch, planmäßig; folgerichtig.

T

T [tiː]: to a ˷ F haargenau.
tab [tæb] Streifen m; Schildchen n, Anhänger m; Schlaufe f, Aufhänger m; (Kartei)Reiter m; F Rechnung f, Konto n; keep a ˷ on, keep ˷s on Buch führen über; fig. im Auge behalten.
tab·ard ['tæbəd] Heroldsrock m.
tab·by ['tæbi], a. 'ˌ-cat getigerte Katze f.
tab·er·nac·le ['tæbɔːnækl] Tabernakel n; Stiftshütte f.
ta·ble ['teibl] 1. Tisch m, Tafel f; Tisch-, Tafelrunde f; Tabelle f, Verzeichnis n; Bibel: Gesetzestafel f; s. ˷-land; at ˷ bei Tisch; lay s.th. on the ˷ parl. et. zurückstellen; turn the ˷s den Spieß umdrehen (on gegen); 2. auf den Tisch legen; tabellarisch anordnen; parl. zurückstellen, ruhen lassen.
tab·leau ['tæblɔu], pl. **tab·leaux** ['tæblɔuz] lebendes Bild n.
ta·ble...: 'ˌ-cloth Tischtuch n; 'ˌ-land Tafelland n, Hochebene f; 'ˌ-lin·en Tischwäsche f.
ta·bles ⅍ ['teiblz] pl. das Einmaleins.
ta·ble-spoon ['teiblspuːn] Eßlöffel m; 'ˌ-ful Eßlöffel(voll) m.
tab·let ['tæblit] Täfelchen n; (Gedenk)Tafel f; (Notiz-, Schreib-, Zeichen)Block m; Stück n Seife; pharm. Tablette f.
ta·ble...: 'ˌ-talk Tischgespräch(e pl.) n; 'ˌ-ten·nis Tischtennis n; 'ˌ-top Tischplatte f; 'ˌ-ware Ge-

schirr n und Besteck n; ˷ wine Tisch-, Tafelwein m.
tab·loid ['tæblɔid] Revolverblatt n.
ta·boo [tə'buː] 1. tabu, unantastbar, verboten; 2. Tabu n; Verbot n; 3. verbieten; für tabu erklären.
ta·bor ♪ ['teibə] Tamburin n.
tab·u·lar ⬚ ['tæbjulə] tafelförmig, tabellarisch; **tab·u·late** ['ˌleit] tabellarisch ordnen; **tab·u·la·tion** tabellarische Anordnung f.
tac·it ⬚ ['tæsit] stillschweigend; **tac·i·turn** ⬚ ['ˌtəːn] schweigsam; **tac·i·tur·ni·ty** Schweigsamkeit f.
tack [tæk] 1. Stift m, Zwecke f; Näherei: Heftstich m; ♣ Halse f; Gang m beim Lavieren; fig. Kurs m, Weg m; ♣ Essen n; on the wrong ˷ auf dem Holzweg; 2. v/t. (an)heften; fig. (an)hängen (to, on an acc.); v/i. ♣ wenden, über Stag gehen; fig. lavieren.
tack·le ['tækl] 1. Gerät n; ♣ Takel-, Tauwerk n; ♣ Talje f; ⊕ Flaschenzug m; 2. (an)packen; in Angriff nehmen; fertig werden mit; j. angehen (for um).
tack·y ['tæki] klebrig; Am. F schäbig.
tact [tækt] Takt m, Feingefühl n; **tact·ful** ['ˌful] taktvoll.
tac·ti·cal ⬚ ✗ ['tæktikəl] taktisch; **tac·ti·cian** [ˌ'tiʃən] Taktiker m; **tac·tics** ['ˌiks] pl., a. sg. Taktik f.
tac·tile ['tæktail] taktil, Tast...
tact·less ⬚ ['tæktlis] taktlos.
tad·pole zo. ['tædpəul] Kaulquappe f.

take

taf·fe·ta [ˈtæfitə] Taft *m*.

taf·fy *Am*. [ˈtæfi] = **toffee**; F Schmus *m*, Schmeichelei *f*.

tag [tæg] **1.** (Schnürsenkel)Stift *m*; Schildchen *n*, Etikett *n*; Redensart *f*, Zitat *n*; Zusatz *m*; loses Ende *n*; Fangen *n* (*Kinderspiel*); **2.** etikettieren, auszeichnen; anhängen (*to*, *on to* an *acc*.); ⏷ *after* hinter (*dat*.) herlaufen; ⏷ *along* F hinterherlaufen, unaufgefordert mitgehen; ⏷ *together* aneinanderreihen.

tail [teil] **1.** Schwanz *m*; Schweif *m*; hinteres Ende *n*, Schluß *m*; ⏷s *pl*. Rückseite *f e-r Münze*; F Frack *m*; *from the* ⏷ *of one's eye* aus den Augenwinkeln; *turn* ⏷ davonlaufen; ⏷s *up* in Hochstimmung; **2.** ⏷ *after* s.o. j-m nachlaufen; ⏷ s.o. *Am*. j. beschatten; ⏷ *off*, ⏷ *away* abflauen, sich verlieren; zögernd enden; sich auseinanderziehen; 'ˌ⏷-**back** *mot*. Rückstau *m*; 'ˌ⏷-**board** *mot*. Ladeklappe *f*; 'ˌ⏷-'**coat** Frack *m*; **tailed** geschwänzt; '**tail**-'**end** hinteres Ende *n*, Schluß *m*; '**tail**·**gate** *mot*. **1.** Heckklappe *f*; **2.** dicht auffahren; '**tail**·**less** schwanzlos; '**tail**·**light** Rück-, Schlußlicht *n*.

tai·lor [ˈteilə] **1.** Schneider *m*; **2.** schneidern; ⏷ed *suit* Maßanzug *m*; 'ˌ⏷-**made** vom Schneider gearbeitet, Schneider...; ⏷ *costume* Schneiderkostüm *n*.

tail...: 'ˌ⏷-**piece** *typ*. Schlußvignette *f*; 'ˌ⏷-**spin** ⚔ (Ab)Trudeln *n*; ⏷ **wind** Rückenwind *m*.

taint [teint] **1.** Flecken *m*, Makel *m*; Ansteckung *f*; Verderbnis *f*; **2.** *v/t*. beflecken; verderben, vergiften; 🐟 anstecken; *v/i*. verderben.

take [teik] **1.** (*irr*.) *v/t*. nehmen; an-, ab-, auf-, ein-, fest-, hin-, wegnehmen; (weg)bringen; *Speise* (zu sich) nehmen; *Mahlzeit* einnehmen; *Maßnahme, Gelegenheit* ergreifen; *Aufgabe etc*. übernehmen; *Eid, Gelübde, Examen* ablegen; *phot*. aufnehmen; *et. gut etc*. aufnehmen; *Beleidigung* hinnehmen; fassen, ergreifen; *Fisch etc*. fangen; sich *e-e Krankheit* holen; gewinnen; erfordern; brauchen; *gewisse Zeit* dauern; F verstehen; auffassen, auslegen; halten, ansehen (*for* für); *the devil* ⏷ *it!* hol's der Teufel!; *I* ⏷ *it that* ich nehme an, daß; ⏷ *breath* verschnaufen; ⏷ *comfort* sich trö-

sten; ⏷ *compassion on* Mitleid empfinden mit; sich erbarmen (*gen*.); *s. consideration*; ⏷ *counsel* beraten; *s. decision*; ⏷ *a drive* e-e Fahrt machen; *s. effect*; *s. exercise*; ⏷ *fire* Feuer fangen; ⏷ *in hand* unternehmen; *s. heart*; ⏷ *a hedge* über e-e Hecke setzen; ⏷ *hold of* ergreifen; ⏷ *it* F es kriegen; *s. liberty*; *s. note*; *s. notice*; ⏷ *pity on* Mitleid haben mit; ⏷ *place* stattfinden; spielen (*Handlung*); ⏷ *s.o.'s place* an j-s Stelle treten; ⏷ *a rest* (eine) Rast machen; *s. rise*; ⏷ *a seat* Platz nehmen; ⏷ *a walk* e-n Spaziergang machen; ⏷ *my word for it* verlaß dich drauf; ⏷ *about* herumführen; ⏷ *along* mitnehmen; ⏷ *down Gerüst etc*. abnehmen; herunternehmen; einreißen; *j*. demütigen; *j-m* e-n Dämpfer geben; niederschreiben, notieren; ⏷ *for* halten für, ansehen als; ⏷ *from j-m* wegnehmen; abziehen von; ⏷ *in* einnehmen; *Segel* bergen; einnähen, enger machen; *Zeitung* halten; aufnehmen (*als Gast etc*.); *Arbeit* übernehmen; einschließen; verstehen; erfassen, geistig aufnehmen; überblicken; F *j*. 'reinlegen; ⏷ *off* ab-, wegnehmen; *Kleid* ausziehen, *Hut* absetzen; *Steuer* aufheben; fortführen, wegholen; F nachäffen; *be* ⏷*n off* 🎭 nicht mehr verkehren; ⏷ *on* an-, übernehmen; *Arbeiter etc*. einstellen; *Fahrgäste* zusteigen lassen; ⏷ *out* heraus-, entnehmen; *Fleck* entfernen; *Kind* spazieren-, ausführen; *Patent etc*. sich geben lassen; *Entscheid etc*. erwirken; *Versicherung* abschließen; ⏷ *it out of* s.o. *fig*. j. mitnehmen; j. strapazieren; es j-m austreiben; ⏷ *over* übernehmen; ⏷ *to* mitnehmen nach; ⏷ *to pieces* auseinandernehmen, zerlegen (*a. fig*.); ⏷ *up* aufnehmen, -heben; *Waffen etc*. ergreifen; sich *e-r Sache* annehmen; *Tätigkeit* aufnehmen; sich befassen mit, sich verlegen auf; *j*. protegieren; aufreißen, -brechen; *Wechsel* akzeptieren; *Aktien* zeichnen; festnehmen, aufgreifen, verhaften; *Raum, Zeit* wegnehmen, in Anspruch nehmen; *Wohnsitz* aufschlagen; *j*. unterbrechen, korrigieren; *et*. unterbreiten (*with dat*.); *be* ⏷*n up with fig*. angetan sein von; ⏷ *upon o.s.* auf sich nehmen; **2.** (*irr.*) *v/i.* wirken, ein-, anschlagen; Eindruck machen; gefallen, ziehen (*Theaterstück, Ware etc.*); Feuer fangen; sich *gut etc.* photographieren lassen; ~ *after* j-m nachschlagen; ~ *from* abziehen von; Abbruch tun (*dat.*); ~ *off* abspringen; 💥 aufsteigen; starten; ~ *on* F Anklang finden; ~ *over* die Amtsgewalt übernehmen; ~ *to* sich begeben nach; liebgewinnen; *fig.* sich verlegen auf (*acc.*); Zuflucht nehmen zu; sich zuwenden (*dat.*); sich ergeben (*dat.*); ~ *to ger.* dazu übergehen zu inf.; ~ *up* F sich bessern (*Wetter*); ~ *up with* sich anfreunden mit; *that won't* ~ *with me* das verfängt bei mir nicht; **3.** Fang *m*; *Geld*-Einnahme *f*; *Film*: Szene(naufnahme) *f*.

take...: '~**·a·way** *1.* zum Mitnehmen (*Essen*); *2.* Essen *n* zum Mitnehmen; Restaurant *n* mit Straßenverkauf; '~**·home pay** Nettogehalt *n*, -lohn *m*; '~**·in** F Reinfall *m*; '**tak·en** *p.p. von take*; *be* ~ besetzt sein; *be* ~ *with* entzückt sein von; *be* ~ *ill* krank werden; '**take-off** Nachahmung *f*, Karikatur *f*; Absprung *m*; 💥 Start *m*; '**tak·er** Nehmer(in).

tak·ing ['teikiŋ] *1.* ☐ F anziehend, fesselnd, einnehmend; *2.* Nehmen *n etc.*; F Aufregung *f*; ~*s pl.* ✝ Einnahmen *f/pl.*

talc *min.* [tælk] Talk *m*; **tal·cum** ['~kəm] = *talc.*

tale [teil] Erzählung *f*, Geschichte *f*; Märchen *n*, Sage *f*; *it tells its own* ~ es spricht für sich selbst; '~**·bear·er** Zuträger(in).

tal·ent ['tælənt] Talent *n*, Begabung *f*, Anlage *f*; '**tal·ent·ed** talentvoll, talentiert, begabt; **tal·ent scout** Talentsucher *m*.

ta·les ⚖ ['teili:z] *pl.* Hilfs-, Ersatzgeschworenen *pl.*

tal·is·man ['tælizmən] Talisman *m*.

talk [tɔ:k] *1.* Gespräch *n*; Unterredung *f*; Plauderei *f*; Vortrag *m*; Geschwätz *n*; *give a* ~ e-n Vortrag halten; *have a* ~ sich unterhalten; *2.* sprechen, reden (von *et.*); plaudern; ~ *to s.o.* F j-m die Meinung sagen; ~ *back* frech antworten; ~ *down* herablassend reden (*to* mit); **talk·a·tive** ☐ ['~ətiv] gesprächig, geschwätzig, redselig; **talk·ee-talk·ee**

F ['tɔ:ki'tɔ:ki] Geschwätz *n*, Kauderwelsch *n*; '**talk·er** Schwätzer(in); Sprechende *m, f*; *he is a good* ~ er kann (*gut*) reden; **talk·ie** F ['~i] Tonfilm *m*; '**talk·ing** Geplauder *n*; **talk·ing-to** F ['~tu:] Standpauke *f* (*Schelte*).

tall [tɔ:l] groß, lang, hoch (*Mensch, Baum etc.*); F übertrieben, unglaublich; *that's a* ~ *order* F das ist ein bißchen viel verlangt; '**tall·boy** Aufsatzkommode *f*; '**tall·ness** Größe *f*, Länge *f*, Höhe *f*.

tal·low ['tæləu] *ausgelassener* Talg *m*; '**tal·low·y** talgig.

tal·ly ['tæli] *1.* Kerbholz *n*; Gegenstück *n* (*of* zu); Kennzeichen *n*; Kupon *m*; *2.* übereinstimmen.

tal·ly-ho ['tæli'həu] *1.* hallo!; *2. hunt.* Weidruf *m*; *3.* hallo rufen.

tal·on *orn.* ['tælən] Kralle *f*, Klaue *f*.

ta·lus¹ ['teiləs] Böschung *f*; *geol.* Schuttkegel *m*.

ta·lus² *anat.* [~] Sprungbein *n*.

tam·a·ble ['teiməbl] zähmbar.

tam·a·rind ♀ ['tæmərind] Tamarinde(nfrucht) *f*.

tam·a·risk ♀ ['tæmərisk] Tamariske *f*.

tam·bour ['tæmbuə] *1.* Stickrahmen *m*; △ Säulentrommel *f*; *2.* (auf dem Rahmen) sticken; **tam·bou·rine** ♪ [~bə'ri:n] Tamburin *n*.

tame [teim] *1.* ☐ zahm; folgsam; harmlos; lahm, fad(e); *2.* (be)zähmen, bändigen; '**tame·ness** Zahmheit *f*; '**tam·er** Zähmer(in), Bändiger(in).

Tam·ma·ny *Am.* ['tæməni] New Yorker Demokraten-Vereinigung *f*.

tam-o'-shan·ter [tæmə'ʃæntə] Baskenmütze *f*.

tamp [tæmp] ✕ *Bohrloch* verdämmen; ⊕ *Lehm etc.* feststampfen.

tam·per ['tæmpə]: ~ *with* sich (unbefugt) zu schaffen machen mit; intrigieren mit *j-m*; *j.* zu bestechen suchen; *Urkunde* fälschen.

tam·pon ✗ ['tæmpən] Tampon *m*.

tan [tæn] *1.* Lohe *f*; Lohfarbe *f*; (Sonnen)Bräune *f*; *2.* lohfarben; *3.* gerben; bräunen; F *j-m das Fell gerben* (*prügeln*).

tan·dem ['tændəm] Tandem *n*; ~ *connexion* ✗ Serienschaltung *f*; *in* ~ *with* in Zusammenarbeit mit.

tang¹ [tæŋ] Angel *f*, Heftzapfen *m* *e-s Messers etc.*; *fig.* besonderer Bei-, Nachgeschmack *m*.

tang[2] [˘] **1.** *scharfer* Klang *m*; Schrillen *n*; **2.** *scharf* klingen (lassen); schrillen (lassen).

tan·gent Ⱥ [ˈtændʒənt] Tangente *f*; **go** (*a. fly*) *off at a* ~ vom Thema abkommen; **tan·gen·tial** □ Ⱥ [˘ˈdʒenʃəl] Tangential...

tan·ger·ine ⚘ [tændʒəˈriːn] Mandarine *f*.

tan·gi·bil·i·ty [tændʒiˈbiliti] Fühlbarkeit *f*; **tan·gi·ble** □ [ˈ˘dʒəbl] fühlbar, greifbar (*a. fig.*); klar.

tan·gle [ˈtæŋgl] **1.** Gewirr *n*; Verwicklung *f*; **2.** (sich) verwirren, verwickeln.

tan·go [ˈtæŋgəu] Tango *m* (*Tanz*).

tank [tæŋk] **1.** Zisterne *f*, Wasserbehälter *m*; ⊕, ⚔ Tank *m*; **2.** tanken; **ˈtank·age** Fassungsvermögen *n* e-s Tanks.

tank·ard [ˈtæŋkəd] Kanne *f*, bsd. (Bier)Krug *m*.

tank-car 🚃 [ˈtæŋkkɑː] Kesselwagen *m*; **ˈtank·er** Tanker *m*, Tankschiff *n*; **ˈtank-top** Pullunder *m*.

tan·ner[1] [ˈtænə] Gerber *m*.

tan·ner[2] *sl.* [˘] Sixpence(stück *n*) *pl.*

tan·ner·y [ˈtænəri] Gerberei *f*.

tan·nic ac·id ⚗ [ˈtænikˈæsid] Gerbsäure *f*.

tan·nin ⚗ [ˈtænin] Tannin *n*.

tan·noy [ˈtænɔi] Lautsprecheranlage *f*.

tan·ta·lize [ˈtæntəlaiz] quälen, peinigen.

tan·ta·mount [ˈtæntəmaunt] von gleichem Wert (*to* wie); gleichbedeutend (*to* mit).

tan·trum F [ˈtæntrəm] Rappel *m*, Koller *m*.

tap[1] [tæp] **1.** leichtes Klopfen *n*; **2.** pochen, klopfen; tippen (auf, an, gegen *acc.*).

tap[2] [˘] **1.** (Wasser-, Gas-, Zapf-) Hahn *m*; Zapfen *m*; Wasserleitung *f*; F Sorte *f*, Marke *f* e-s *Getränkes*; ⊕ Gewindebohrer *m*; F *s.* ~-*room*; *on* ~ frisch vom Faß (*Bier*); *fig.* verfügbar; **2.** an-, abzapfen; ~ *the wire(s)* ⚡ Strom stehlen; *teleph.* mithören.

tap-dance [ˈtæpdɑːns] Stepptanz *m*.

tape [teip] schmales Band *n*; *Sport:* Zielband *n*; Tonband *n*; *tel.* Papierstreifen *m*; *red* ~ Bürokratismus *m*; **ˈ~-meas·ure** Bandmaß *n*; **tape re·cord·er** Tonbandgerät *n*; **tape re·cord·ing** Tonbandaufnahme *f*.

ta·per [teipə] **1.** dünne Wachskerze

f; **2.** *adj.* spitz (zulaufend); schlank (*Finger*); **3.** *v/i.* spitz zulaufen; ~*ing* = ~ **2**; *v/t.* zuspitzen.

tap·es·tried [ˈtæpistrid] gobelingeschmückt; **ˈtap·es·try** Gobelin *m*, Wandteppich *m*.

tape·worm [ˈteipwəːm] Bandwurm *m*.

tap·i·o·ca [tæpiˈəukə] Tapioka *f*.

ta·pir *zo.* [ˈteipə] Tapir *m*.

tap·pet ⊕ [ˈtæpit] Stößel *m*; Daumen *m*, Nocken *m*.

tap-room [ˈtæprum] Schankstube*f*.

tap-root ⚘ [ˈtæpruːt] Pfahlwurzel *f*.

taps *Am.* ⚔ [tæps] *pl.* Zapfenstreich *m*.

tap·ster [ˈtæpstə] Schankkellner *m*.

tap-wa·ter [ˈtæpwɔːtə] Leitungswasser *n*.

tar [tɑː] **1.** Teer *m*; *Jack* ♀ F Teerjacke *f*, Matrose *m*; **2.** teeren.

ta·ran·tu·la *zo.* [təˈræntjulə] Tarantel *f*.

tar-board [ˈtɑːbɔːd] Teerpappe *f*.

tar·di·ness [ˈtɑːdinis] Langsamkeit *f*; **ˈtar·dy** □ langsam; spät.

tare[1] ⚘ [tɛə] *mst* ~*s pl.* Wicke *f*.

tare[2] ✝ [˘] **1.** Tara *f*; **2.** tarieren.

tar·get [ˈtɑːgit] (Schieß)Scheibe *f*; *fig.* Ziel(scheibe *f*) *n*; Ziel(leistung *f*) *n*; Soll *n*; ~ *date* ✝ Stichtag *m*, Termin *m*; ~ *language* Zielsprache *f*; ~ *practice* Scheibenschießen *n*.

tar·iff [ˈtærif] (*bsd.* Zoll)Tarif *m*.

tar·mac [ˈtɑːmæk] Asphalt *m* *als Straßenbelag*.

tarn [tɑːn] Bergsee *m*.

tar·nish [ˈtɑːniʃ] **1.** *v/t.* ⊕ trüb *od.* blind machen; *fig.* trüben; *v/i.* trüb werden, anlaufen; **2.** Trübung *f*; Belag *m*.

tar·pau·lin [tɑːˈpɔːlin] ⚓ Persenning *f*; Plane *f*, Wagendecke *f*.

tar·ra·gon [ˈtærəgən] Estragon *m*.

tar·ry[1] *lit.* [ˈtæri] säumen, zögern; weilen.

tar·ry[2] [ˈtɑːri] teerig.

tart [tɑːt] **1.** □ sauer, herb; *fig.* scharf, schroff; **2.** (Obst)Torte *f*; *sl.* Nutte *f*, Dirne *f*.

tar·tan [ˈtɑːtən] Tartan *m*; Schottentuch *n*; Schottenmuster *n*; ~ *plaid* Schottenplaid *n*.

Tar·tar[1] [ˈtɑːtə] Tatar *m*; *fig.* Hitzkopf *m*; *catch a* ~ an den Unrechten kommen.

tar·tar[2] [˘] ⚗ Weinstein *m*; Zahnstein *m*.

task [tɑːsk] **1.** Aufgabe *f*; *aufgege-bene* Arbeit *f*; Tagewerk *n*, Ge-schäft *n*; *take to* ~ *(for)* zur Rede stellen (wegen); **2.** beschäftigen; in Anspruch nehmen; **task force** ✕ Kampfgruppe *f für Sonderopera-tion*; **'task·mas·ter** (strenger) Ar-beitgeber *m*; ⊕ Anweiser *m*.

tas·sel ['tæsəl] **1.** Troddel *f*, Quaste *f*; **2.** mit Troddeln schmücken.

taste [teist] **1.** Geschmack *m*; (Kost)Probe *f* (*of gen.*, von); Nei-gung *f*, Lust *f* (*for* zu); *to* ~ nach Belieben; **2.** *v/t.* kosten, schmecken; versuchen; genießen; erleben; *v/i.* kosten (*of* von, *a. acc.*); schmecken (*of* nach); **taste·ful** □ [~'ful] ge-schmackvoll.

taste·less □ ['teistlis] geschmack-los; **'taste·less·ness** Geschmack-losigkeit *f*.

tas·ter ['teistə] (Tee-, Wein- *etc.*) Schmecker *m*, Koster *m*, Prüfer *m*.

tast·y □ F ['teisti] schmackhaft.

tat¹ [tæt] *s. tit¹*.

tat² [~] Frivolitäten (*Spitzen*) an-fertigen.

ta·ta ['tæ'tɑː] F *Kindersprache u. co.* adda (*adieu*).

tat·ter ['tætə] **1.** zerfetzen; **2.** ~s *pl.* Fetzen *m/pl.*; **tat·ter·de·mal·ion** [~də'meiljən] zerlumpter Kerl *m*.

tat·tle ['tætl] **1.** schwatzen, plaudern; *b.s.* tratschen; **2.** Geschwätz *n*; *b.s.* Tratsch *m*; **'tat·tler** Plauderer(in), Schwätzer(in).

tat·too¹ [tə'tuː] **1.** ✕ Zapfenstreich *m*; *beat the devil's* ~ *fig.* mit den Fingern trommeln; **2.** *fig.* trom-meln. [wierung *f*.]

tat·too² [~] **1.** tätowieren; **2.** Täto-

tat·ty F ['tæti] schäbig.

taught [tɔːt] *pret. u. p.p. von teach.*

taunt [tɔːnt] **1.** Stichelei *f*, Spott *m*; **2.** verhöhnen, spotten; ~ *s.o. with s.th.* j-m et. vorwerfen; **'taunt·ing** □ spöttisch, höhnisch.

Tau·rus *ast.* ['tɔːrəs] Stier *m*.

taut [tɔːt] ⚓ steif, straff; schmuck; **'taut·en** (sich) straffen.

tau·tol·o·gy [tɔː'tɔlədʒi] Tauto-logie *f*.

tav·ern ['tævən] Schenke *f*, Ta-verne *f*.

taw¹ ⊕ [tɔː] weißgerben.

taw² [~] Murmel(spiel *n*) *m*, *f*.

taw·dri·ness ['tɔːdrinis] Flitter-haftigkeit *f*, Kitsch *m*; **'taw·dry** ⸱

flitterhaft, billig (aufgeputzt); kitschig.

taw·ny ['tɔːni] lohfarben.

tax [tæks] **1.** Steuer *f*, Abgabe *f* (*on* auf *acc.*); *fig.* Inanspruchnahme *f* (*on, upon gen.*); ~ *allowance* Steuer-freibetrag *m*; ~ *bracket* Steuerklasse *f*; ~ *evasion* Steuerhinterziehung *f*; **2.** besteuern; *fig.* stark in Anspruch nehmen; ⚖ *Kosten* schätzen; auf e-e harte Probe stellen; *j.* zur Rede stel-len; mit *j-m* ins Gericht gehen; ~ *s.o. with s.th.* j. e-r Sache beschuldigen; **'tax·a·ble** □ besteuerbar; **tax'a-tion** Besteuerung *f*; Steuer(n *pl.*) *f*; *bsd.* ⚖ Schätzung *f*; **'tax·col·lec·tor** Steuereinnehmer *m*; **'tax·de'duct-i·ble** von der Steuer absetzbar; **tax dodg·er** Steuersünder *m*; **'tax-free** steuerfrei; **tax ha·ven** Steuerpara-dies *n*.

tax·i F ['tæksi] **1.** = '~**cab** Taxi *n*, (Auto)Droschke *f*; **2.** mit e-m Taxi fahren; ✈ rollen; **'~danc·er** Ein-tänzer *m*; Taxigirl *n*.

tax·i·der·mist ['tæksidəːmist] Tier-präparator *m*.

tax·i...: '~**driv·er** Taxichauffeur *m*; '~**me·ter** Taxameter *m* (*Fahrpreis-anzeiger*); ~ **rank**, ~ **stand** Taxistand *m*.

tax...: '~**pay·er** Steuerzahler *m*; ~ **re·lief** Steuererleichterung(en *pl.*) *f*; ~ **return** Steuererklärung *f*.

tea [tiː] Tee *m*; *high* ~, *meat* ~ frühes Abendbrot *n* mit Tee; '~**bag** Teebeutel *m*; '~**break** Teepause *f*; '~**cad·dy** Teedose *f*.

teach [tiːtʃ] (*irr.*) lehren, unter-richten, *j-m et.* beibringen; **'teach-a·ble** gelehrig; lehrbar; **'teach-er** Lehrer(in); **'teach·er-'train-ing col·lege** Lehrerbildungsan-stalt *f*; **'teach-'in** (politische) Dis-kussion *f* (*mst als Großveranstal-tung*); **'teach·ing** Unterrichten *n*; ~s *pl.* die Lehren *pl.*

tea...: '~**co·sy** Teewärmer *m*; '~**cup** Teetasse *f*; *storm in a* ~ *fig.* Sturm *m* im Wasserglas; '~**-gown** Nachmittagskleid *n*.

teak ⸶ [tiːk] Teakbaum *m*, -holz *n*.

tea-ket·tle ['tiːketl] Wasserkessel *m*.

team [tiːm] Team *n*, Arbeitsgruppe *f*; Gespann *n*; *bsd. Sport:* Mann-schaft *f*; ~ **ef·fort** *by a* ~ mit gemein-samen Kräften; ~ **spir·it** Gemein-schafts-, Korpsgeist *m*; **team·ster**

['ˌstə] Gespannführer *m*; *Am*. Lkw-Fahrer *m*; **'team—work** Zusammenarbeit *f*, Teamwork *n* (*a. Sport*); *thea.* Zusammenspiel *n*.

tea·pot ['tiːpɔt] Teekanne *f*.

tear[1] [teə] **1.** (*irr.*) *v/t.* zerren, reißen; zerreißen; *Loch* reißen; *v/i.* (zer)reißen; F *mit adv. od. prep.* rasen, stürmen; **2.** Riß *m*; *s.* wear.

tear[2] [tiə] Träne *f*; **'ˌ~·drop** Träne *f*.

tear·ful □ ['tiəful] tränenreich.

tear–gas ['tiəgæs] Tränengas *n*.

tear·ing *fig.* ['teəriŋ] rasend.

tear–jerk·er F ['tiədʒəːkə] Schnulze *f*.

tear·less ⸬ ['tiəlis] tränenlos.

tea·room ['tiːrum] Tearoom *m*, Teestube *f*, Café *n*.

tease [tiːz] **1.** *Wolle etc.* kämmen, zupfen; *Tuch* rauhen; *fig.* necken, hänseln; **2.** Necker *m*; Quälgeist *m*; **tea·sel** ⚘ ['tiːzl] Karde(ndistel) *f*; ⊕ Karde *f*, Krempel *f*; **'teas·er** F *fig.* harte Nuß *f*.

tea...: **'ˌ~–spoon** Teelöffel *m*; **'ˌ~–spoon·ful** Teelöffel(voll) *m*; **'ˌ~–-strain·er** Teesieb *n*.

teat [tiːt] Zitze *f*, Brustwarze *f*; (Gummi)Sauger *m*.

tea...: **'ˌ~–things** *pl.* Teegeschirr *n*; ~ **tow·el** Geschirrtuch *n*; **'ˌ~–urn** Teemaschine *f*.

tech·nic ['teknik] *a.* ˌ~s *pl. od. sg.* = *technique*; **'tech·ni·cal** □ technisch; gewerblich, Gewerbe... (*Schule etc.*); fachlich, Fach... (*Ausdruck etc.*); **tech·ni·cal·i·ty** [ˌ~'kæliti] technische Eigentümlichkeit *f*; Fachausdruck *m*; **tech-'ni·cian** [ˌ~ʃən] Techniker(in).

tech·ni·col·or ['teknikˌʌlə] Technikolor...; **2.** Technikolor(verfahren) *n*.

tech·nique [tek'niːk] Technik *f*; Methode *f*; Art *f* der Ausführung; mechanische Fertigkeit *f*.

tech·no·cra·cy [tek'nɔkrəsi] Technokratie *f*.

tech·nol·o·gy [tek'nɔlədʒi] Technologie *f*; Gewerbekunde *f*; *school of* ~ Technische Hochschule *f*.

tech·y ['tetʃi] = *testy*.

ted·der *Am*. ['tedə] Heuwendemaschine *f*.

ted·dy boy F ['tedibɔi] Halbstarke *m*.

te·di·ous ⸬ ['tiːdjəs] langweilig, ermüdend; weitschweifig; **'te·di·ous·ness** Langweiligkeit *f*; Weitschweifigkeit *f*.

te·di·um ['tiːdjəm] Lang(e)weile *f*; Langweiligkeit *f*.

tee [tiː] **1.** *Sport*: Mal *n*, Ziel *n*; *Golfspiel*: Abschlagmal *n*; **2.** ~ *off* das Spiel eröffnen.

teem [tiːm] wimmeln; strotzen (*beide: with* von).

teen·ag·er ['tiːneidʒə] Jugendliche *m*, *f* von 13 bis 19 Jahren, Teenager *m*.

teens [tiːnz] *pl.* Lebensjahre *n/pl.* von 13 bis 19; *in one's* ~ noch nicht 20 Jahre alt.

tee·ny F ['tiːni] *Kindersprache*: winzig; **~·bop·per** F *oft contp.* ['ˌbɔpə] Teenybopper *m* (*nur an Pop und Mode interessierter jüngerer Teenager*).

tee·ter F ['tiːtə] wanken.

teeth [tiːθ] *pl. von* tooth.

teethe [tiːð] zahnen; *teething troubles pl.* Beschwerden *f/pl.* beim Zahnen.

tee·to·tal [tiːˈtəutl] abstinent, Abstinenzler...; **tee'to·tal·(l)er** Abstinenzler(in), Antialkoholiker(in).

tee·to·tum ['tiːtəu'tʌm] Drehwürfel *m*.

tel·au·to·gram [te'lɔːtəgræm] Bildtelegramm *n*; **tel'aut·o·graph** [ˌ~·grɑːf] Bildbriefsender *m*.

tel·e·cast ['telikɑːst] **1.** Fernsehsendung *f*; **2.** im Fernsehen übertragen.

tel·e·com·mu·ni·ca·tions ['telikəmjuːniˈkeiʃənz] *pl.* Fernmeldewesen *n*.

tel·e·course *Am*. F ['telikɔːs] Fernsehlehrgang *m*.

tel·e·gram ['teligræm] Telegramm *n*.

tel·e·graph ['teligrɑːf] **1.** Telegraph *m*; **2.** Telegraphen...; Telegramm...; **3.** telegraphieren; **tel·e·graph·ic** [ˌ~'græfik] (ˌ~ally) telegraphisch; telegrammäßig (*Stil*); **te·leg·ra·phist** [ti'legrəfist] Telegraphist(in)); **te'leg·ra·phy** Telegraphie *f*.

te·lep·a·thy [ti'lepəθi] Telepathie *f*, Gedankenübertragung *f*.

tel·e·phone ['telifəun] **1.** Telephon *n*, Fernsprecher *m*; *by* ~ telephonisch; *be on the* ~ Telephonanschluß haben; am Telefon sein; **2.** telephonieren; *j.* anrufen; **'ˌ~–an·swer·ing ma·chine** Anrufbeantworter *m*; ~ **booth** Telephonzelle *f*; ~

charg·es pl. Telephongebühren f/pl.; **tel·e·phon·ic** [˷'fɔnik] (˷ally) telephonisch; Fernsprech...; **te·leph·o·nist** [ti'lefənist] Telephonist(in); **te·'leph·o·ny** Fernsprechwesen n.

tel·e·pho·to phot. ['teli'fəutəu] a. ˷ lens Teleobjektiv n.

tel·e·print·er ['teliprintə] Fernschreiber m.

tel·e·scope ['teliskəup] **1.** opt. Teleskop n, Fernrohr n; **2.** (sich) ineinanderschieben; **tel·e·scop·ic** [˷'kɔpik] teleskopisch; ˷ aerial, Am. ˷ antenna Teleskopantenne f; ˷ sight Zielfernrohr n.

tel·e·typ·er ['teli'taipə] Fernschreiber m.

tel·e·vise ['telivaiz] im Fernsehen übertragen; **tel·e·vi·sion** ['˷viʒən] Fernsehen n; attr. Fernseh...; watch ˷ fernsehen; ˷ set Fernsehapparat m; **tel·e·vi·sor** ['˷vaizə] Fernsehapparat m.

tell [tel] (irr.) v/t. (bsd. Stimmen) zählen; sagen, berichten, erzählen, unterscheiden; erkennen; ˷ s.o. to do s.th. j-m sagen, er solle et. tun; j. et. tun heißen; I have been told mir ist gesagt worden; ˷ off abzählen; auswählen (for s.th. zu et.; to do um zu tun); F heruntermachen, abkanzeln; ˷ the world sl. hinausposaunen; v/i. erzählen (of, about von); (aus)plaudern (on, of über acc.); Wirkung tun, sich auswirken; sitzen (Hieb etc.); sich geltend machen; **'tell·er** Zähler m; Erzähler m; Kassierer m; **'tell·ing** ☐ wirkungsvoll; wirksam; **'tell·ing-'off**: give s.o. a ˷ F j. ausschimpfen; **tell·tale** ['˷teil] **1.** verräterisch; kennzeichnend; fig. sprechend (Ähnlichkeit); **2.** Zuträger(in), Klatschbase f; ⊕ Anzeiger m; ˷ clock Kontrolluhr f.

tel·ly F ['teli] Fernsehen n; Fernseher m.

tel·pher ['telfə] Hängebahn(wagen m) f.

te·mer·i·ty [ti'meriti] Unbesonnenheit f, Verwegenheit f.

temp F [temp] Aushilfskraft f; bsd. Aushilfssekretärin f.

tem·per ['tempə] **1.** mäßigen, mildern; ♪ temperieren; Farbe, Kalk anmachen; Stahl anlassen, vergüten; **2.** ⊕ gehörige Mischung f; metall. Härte(grad m) f; (Gemüts-) Ruhe f, Gleichmut m; Temperament n, Wesen(sart f) n, Natur f; Stimmung f, Laune f; Gereiztheit f, Wut f; hot ˷ Jähzorn m; lose one's ˷ wütend werden; **tem·per·a·ment** ['˷rəmənt] Temperament n, (Gemüts)Art f; **tem·per·a·men·tal** ☐ [˷'mentl] anlagebedingt; launisch; **'tem·per·ance 1.** Mäßigkeit f; Enthaltsamkeit f; **2.** alkoholfrei (Gasthaus); Enthaltsamkeits...; **tem·per·ate** ☐ ['˷rit] gemäßigt; zurückhaltend; maßvoll; mäßig im Essen etc.; ˷ zone gemäßigte Zone f; **tem·per·a·ture** ['tempritʃə] Temperatur f; have od. run a ˷ Fieber haben; **tempered** ['tempəd] ...geartet; ...mütig; ...gelaunt; hot-˷ jähzornig.

tem·pest ['tempist] Sturm m; Gewitter n; **tem·pes·tu·ous** ☐ [˷'pestjuəs] stürmisch; ungestüm.

Tem·plar ['templə] hist. Tempelherr m; ♔ univ. Student m der Rechte am Londoner Temple.

tem·ple[1] ['templ] Tempel m, Kirche f; ♔ Rechtsinstitut u. Rechtskollegien in London.

tem·ple[2] anat. [˷] Schläfe f.

tem·po ['tempəu] Geschwindigkeit f, Tempo n.

tem·po·ral ☐ ['tempərəl] zeitlich, weltlich; **tem·po·ral·i·ties** [˷'rælitiz] pl. weltliche Güter n/pl.; Temporalien n/pl.; **tem·po·ra·ri·ness** ['˷rərinis] zeitweilige Dauer f; **'tem·po·rar·y** ☐ zeitweilig; vorläufig; vorübergehend; ˷ bridge Notbrücke f; ˷ work Gelegenheitsarbeit f; **'tem·po·rize** Zeit zu gewinnen suchen; auf Zeit spielen.

tempt [tempt] j. versuchen; verleiten; verlocken; be ˷ed versucht sein; **temp'ta·tion** Versuchung f; Reiz m; **'tempt·er** Versucher m; **'tempt·ing** ☐ verführerisch; **'tempt·ress** Versucherin f.

ten [ten] **1.** zehn; **2.** Zehn f.

ten·a·ble ['tenəbl] haltbar (Theorie etc.); verliehen (Amt).

te·na·cious ☐ [ti'neiʃəs] zäh; festhaltend (of an dat.); treu (Gedächtnis); fig. beharrlich (of in dat.); **te·nac·i·ty** [ti'næsiti] Zähigkeit f; Festhalten n (of an dat.); Treue f des Gedächtnisses.

ten·an·cy ['tenənsi] Pachtbesitz m.

ten·ant ['tenənt] **1.** Pächter m;

Mieter *m*; *fig.* Bewohner *m*, Insasse *m*; ∾ right Mietrecht *n*; **2.** bewohnen; **'ten·ant·ry** Pächter *m/pl.*; Mieter *m/pl.*

tench *ichth.* [tenʃ] Schleie *f.*

tend[1] [tend] **1.** gerichtet sein (*towards* nach, auf *acc.*), hinstreben (zu); abzielen (*to* auf *acc.*); neigen, den Hang haben (*to* zu); ∾ *from* wegstreben von; ∾ *upwards* sich nach oben bewegen (*Preise*).

tend[2] [∾] *Kranke* pflegen; *Vieh* hüten; *Maschine etc.* bedienen; **'tend·ance** Pflege *f*; Bedienung *f.*

tend·en·cy ['tendənsi] Richtung *f*; Neigung *f*; Tendenz *f*; Zweck *m*; **ten·den·tious** [∾'denʃəs] tendenziös, zweckbestimmt, einseitig.

ten·der[1] □ ['tendə] zart; weich; empfindlich; heikel (*Thema*); zärtlich; schwächlich.

ten·der[2] □ **1.** (*bsd.* Zahlungs-) Angebot *n*; ✝ (Lieferungs)Angebot *n*, Offerte *f*, Ausschreibung *f*; Kostenanschlag *m*; *legal* ∾ gesetzliches Zahlungsmittel *n*; **2.** v/t. anbieten; *Entlassung* einreichen; v/i. ein Angebot machen.   [der *m*.]

ten·der[3] [∾] Wärter *m*; 🚂, ⚓ Ten-]

ten·der·foot *Am.* F ['tendəfut] Anfänger *m*, Neuling *m*; **'ten·der·ize** *Fleisch* zart machen; **ten·der·loin** ['∾lɔin] *bsd. Am.* Filet *n*; *Am.* berüchtigtes Viertel *n*; **'ten·der·ness** Zartheit *f*; Zärtlichkeit *f.*

ten·don *anat.* ['tendən] Flechse *f*, Sehne *f.*

ten·dril ♀ ['tendril] Ranke *f.*

ten·e·ment ['tenimənt] Wohnhaus *n*; (*bsd.* Miet)Wohnung *f*; ⚖ *jeder* beständige Besitz *m*; ∾ *house* Mietshaus *n.*

ten·et ['tiːnet] Grund-, Lehrsatz *m.*

ten·fold ['tenfəuld] zehnfach.

ten·nis ['tenis] Tennis(spiel) *n*; **'∾-court** Tennisplatz *m.*

ten·on ⊕ ['tenən] Zapfen *m*; **'∾-saw** ⊕ Fuchsschwanz *m.*

ten·or ['tenə] Fortgang *m*, Verlauf *m*; Inhalt *m*; ♪ Tenor *m.*

tense[1] *gr.* [tens] Zeit(form) *f*, Tempus *n.*

tense[2] □ [∾] gespannt (*a. fig.*); straff; **'tense·ness** Gespanntheit *f*; **ten·sile** ['tensail] dehnbar; Dehnungs...; ∾ *strength* Zugfestigkeit *f*; **ten·sion** ['∾ʃən] Spannung *f*; *high* ∾ ⚡ Hochspannung *f*; ∾ *test* Zer-

reißprobe *f.*

tent[1] [tent] Zelt *n*; *pitch one's* ∾s s-e Zelte aufschlagen (*a. fig.*).

tent[2] [∾] Tintowein *m.*

ten·ta·cle *zo.* ['tentəkl] Fühler *m*; Fangarm *m e-s Polypen.*

ten·ta·tive ['tentətiv] **1.** □ versuchend; Versuchs...; ∾*ly* versuchsweise; **2.** Versuch *m.*

ten·ter ['tentə] Spannrahmen *m*; **'∾·hook** Spannhaken *m*; *be on* ∾s *fig.* auf die Folter gespannt sein.

tenth [tenθ] **1.** zehnte(r, -s); **2.** Zehntel *n*; **'tenth·ly** zehntens.

tent-peg ['tentpeg] Zeltpflock *m*, Hering *m.*

ten·u·ous □ ['tenjuəs] dünn; zart; fein; dürftig.

ten·ure ['tenjuə] Besitz(art *f*, -dauer *f*, -anspruch *m*) *m*; ∾ *of office* Amtszeit *f.*

te·pee ['tiːpiː] Indianerzelt *n.*

tep·id □ ['tepid] lau(warm); **te·pid·i·ty**, **'tep·id·ness** Lauheit *f.*

ter·cen·te·nar·y [təːsen'tiːnəri], **ter·cen·ten·ni·al** [∾'tenjəl] **1.** dreihundertjährig; **2.** Dreihundertjahrfeier *f.*

ter·gi·ver·sa·tion [təːdʒivəː'seiʃən] völlige Kehrtwendung *f*; Ausflucht *f*; Zweideutigkeit.

term [təːm] **1.** (bestimmte) Zeit *f*, Frist *f*, Termin *m*; Zahltag *m*; Amtszeit *f*; ⚖ Sitzungsperiode *f*; Semester *n*, Quartal *n*, Trimester *n an Universitäten, Schulen*; ♙, *phls.* Glied *n*; (Fach)Ausdruck *m*, Wort *n*, Bezeichnung *f*; Begriff *m*; ∾s *pl.* Bedingungen *f/pl.*; Honorar *n*; Preise *m/pl.*; Verhältnis *n*, Beziehungen *f/pl.*; *in* ∾s *of praise* in lobenden Worten; *be on good (bad)* ∾s *with* gut (schlecht) *od.* auf gutem (schlechtem) Fuße stehen mit; *come to* ∾s, *make* ∾s sich einigen; **2.** (be)nennen; bezeichnen (als).

ter·ma·gant ['təːməgənt] **1.** □ zanksüchtig; **2.** Zankteufel *m* (*Weib*).

ter·mi·na·ble □ ['təːminəbl] begrenzt; befristet; **ter·mi·nal** ['∾nl] **1.** □ End..., letzt; (Ab)Schluß...; ♀ gipfelständig; Termin...; ∾*ly* terminweise; **2.** Endstück *n*, -teil *m*; ⚡ Pol *m*; ⚡ Klemme *f*; 🚂 *etc.* Endstation *f*; *Computer:* Terminal *n*; **ter·mi·nate** ['∾neit] v/t. begrenzen; beendigen; v/i. endigen; **ter·mi·na·tion** Beendigung *f*; Ende *n*; *gr.* Endung *f.*

ter·mi·nol·o·gy [təːmiˈnɔlədʒi] Terminologie *f*, Fachsprache *f*.

ter·mi·nus [ˈtəːminəs], *pl.* **ter·mi·ni** [ˈ‿nai] Endpunkt *m*; 🚂 Endstation *f*.

ter·mite *zo.* [ˈtəːmait] Termite *f*.

tern *orn.* [təːn] Seeschwalbe *f*.

ter·na·ry [ˈtəːnəri] aus je drei bestehend, dreifältig.

ter·race [ˈterəs] Terrasse *f*; Häuserreihe *f in Städten*; **'ter·raced** terrassenförmig; flach (*Dach*); ~ **house** Reihenhaus *n*.

ter·rain [ˈterein] Gelände *n*, Terrain *n*.

ter·ra·cot·ta [ˈterəˈkɔtə] Terrakotta *f*.

ter·res·tri·al □ [tiˈrestriəl] irdisch; Erd...; *bsd. zo.*, 🌿 Land...

ter·ri·ble □ [ˈterəbl] schrecklich; **'ter·ri·ble·ness** Schrecklichkeit *f*.

ter·ri·er *zo.* [ˈteriə] Terrier *m*.

ter·rif·ic [təˈrifik] (~*ally*) fürchterlich, furchtbar, schrecklich; F ungeheuer, großartig, toll; **ter·ri·fy** [ˈterifai] *v/t.* erschrecken.

ter·ri·to·ri·al [teriˈtɔːriəl] **1.** □ territorial; Land...; Bezirks...; ~ *waters pl.* Hoheitsgewässer *n/pl.*; ♀ *Army*, ♀ *Force* Territorialarmee *f*; **2.** ✕ Angehöriger *m* der Territorialarmee; **ter·ri·to·ry** [ˈ‿təri] Gebiet *n*; Territorium *n*.

ter·ror [ˈterə] Schrecken *m*, Entsetzen *n*, Furcht *f*; **'ter·ror·ism** Schreckensherrschaft *f*; **'ter·ror·ize** terrorisieren.

ter·ry(-cloth) [ˈteri(klɔθ)] Frottee *n*, *m*.

terse □ [təːs] knapp; kurz u. bündig; prägnant; **'terse·ness** Knappheit *f*.

ter·tian 🩺 [ˈtəːʃən] dreitägig(es Fieber *n*); **'ter·ti·ar·y** tertiär.

tes·sel·ate [ˈtesileit] mosaikartig zs.-setzen; ~*d pavement* Mosaikfußboden *m*.

test [test] **1.** Probe *f*; Untersuchung *f*; (Eignungs)Prüfung *f*; Test *m*; *fig.* Prüfstein *m*; 🧪 Reagens *n*; *put to the* ~ auf die Probe stellen; **2.** probieren, prüfen, testen.

tes·ta·ceous *zo.* [tesˈteiʃəs] hartschalig; Schal...

tes·ta·ment *Bibel*, ⚖ [ˈtestəmənt] Testament *n*; **tes·ta·men·ta·ry** [‿ˈmentəri] testamentarisch.

tes·ta·tor [tesˈteitə] Erblasser *m*.

tes·ta·trix [tesˈteitriks] Erblasserin *f*.

test...: ~ **ban** (Atombomben)Versuchsverbot *n*; ~ *treaty* Teststoppabkommen *n*; ~ **card** *Fernsehen:* Testbild *n*; ~ **case** Muster-, Schulbeispiel *n*; Präzedenzfall *m*; ~ **drive** *mot.* Probefahrt *f*.

tes·ter[1] [ˈtestə] Betthimmel *m*.

test·er[2] [‿] Prüfer *m* (*a. Gerät*).

tes·ti·cle *anat.* [ˈtestikl] Hode *f*.

tes·ti·fi·er [ˈtestifaiə] Zeuge *m*, Zeugin *f* (*to für*); **tes·ti·fy** [ˈ‿fai] *v/t.* bezeugen (*a. fig.*); *v/i.* zeugen (*to für*); (als Zeuge) aussagen (*on über acc.*).

tes·ti·mo·ni·al [testiˈməunjəl] (Führungs)Zeugnis *n*; Zeichen *n* der Anerkennung; **tes·ti·mo·ny** [ˈ‿məni] Zeugnis *n* (*Zeugenaussage*; *Beweis*) (*to für*).

tes·ti·ness [ˈtestinis] Gereiztheit *f*.

test...: **'~-match** *Kricket:* internationaler Vergleichskampf *m*; **'~-pa·per** 🧪 Reagenzpapier *n*; **'~-pi·lot** ✈ Testpilot *m*; **'~-print** *phot.* Probeabzug *m*; ~ **run** Probelauf *m e-r Maschine etc.*; **'~-tube** 🧪 Reagenzglas *n*; ~ *baby* 🧪 Retortenbaby *n*.

tes·ty □ [ˈtesti], **tetch·y** □ [ˈtetʃi] reizbar, gereizt, heftig, kribbelig.

teth·er [ˈteðə] **1.** Haltestrick *m*; *fig.* Spielraum *m*; *at the end of one's* ~ *fig.* am Ende s-r Kraft; **2.** anbinden.

tet·ra·gon ◿ [ˈtetrəgən] Viereck *n*; **te·trag·o·nal** [‿ˈtrægənl] viereckig.

tet·ter 🩺 [ˈtetə] Flechte *f*.

Teu·ton [ˈtjuːtən] Germane *m*, Teutone *m*; **Teu·ton·ic** [‿ˈtɔnik] germanisch, teutonisch.

text [tekst] Text *m*; Bibelstelle *f*; Bibelspruch *m*; **'~-book** Leitfaden *m*, Lehrbuch *n*.

tex·tile [ˈtekstail] **1.** Textil..., Web...; **2.** ~*s pl.* Webwaren *f/pl.*, Textilien *pl.*

tex·tu·al □ [ˈtekstjuəl] Text...; textlich; textgemäß.

tex·ture [ˈtekstʃə] Gewebe *n*; Gefüge *n*; Struktur *f*.

tha·lid·o·mide [θəˈlidəmaid] Contergan *n*; ~ *baby*, ~ *child* Contergankind *n*.

than [ðæn, ðən] *nach comp.*: als.

thane *hist.* [θein] Than *m*, Lehensmann *m*.

thank [θæŋk] **1.** danken (*dat.*); ~ *you, bei Ablehnung* no, ~ *you* danke;

I will thank you for ich wäre Ihnen
dankbar für; ~ *you for nothing iro.*
ich danke dafür; **2.** ~*s pl.* Dank *m*;
~*s!* vielen Dank!; danke (schön)!;
give ~*s* das Tischgebet sprechen;
~*s to* dank (*dat.*); **thank·ful**
['~ful] dankbar; **'thank·less** ˈ⸗
undankbar; **thanks·giv·ing** ['~s-
giviŋ] Danksagung *f*; Dankfest *n*;
ℨ (*Day*) *bsd. Am.* (Ernte)Dankfest *n*
(*letzter Donnerstag im November*);
'thank·wor·thy dankenswert.

that [ðæt, ðət] **1.** *pron.* (*pl. those*)
jene(r, -s); der *od.* die *od.* das(jenige);
der, die, das, welche(r, -s); so ~'s ~!
damit basta!; ... *and* ~ und zwar;
at ~ zudem, noch dazu; **2.** *cj.* daß;
damit; weil.

thatch [θætʃ] **1.** Dachstroh *n*;
Strohdach *n*; **2.** mit Stroh decken.

thaw [θɔ:] **1.** Tauwetter *n*; (Auf-)
Tauen *n*; **2.** (auf)tauen.

the [ði:; *vor Vokal* ði, *vor Konson.*
ðə] **1.** *Artikel:* der, die, das;
2. *adv.* ~ ... ~ je ... desto, um so.

the·a·tre, *Am.* **the·a·ter** ['θiətə]
Theater *n*; *fig.* Schauplatz *m*; ✗
Kriegsschauplatz *m*; ~ *nuclear war
bsd. Am.* taktischer Atomkrieg *m*; ~
nuclear weapons pl. bsd. Am. taktische
Atomwaffen *f/pl.*; **'~-go·er** Theater-
besucher(in); **the·at·ric, the·at·ri-
cal** □ [θi'ætrik(əl)] Theater...; büh-
nenmäßig; theatralisch; **the'at·ri-
cals** *pl.* Theater-, *bsd.* Liebhaberauf-
führungen *f/pl.*

The·ban ['θi:bən] **1.** thebanisch;
2. Thebaner(in).

thee † *od. lit.* [ði:] dich; dir.

theft [θeft] Diebstahl *m*.

their [ðeə] ihr(e); **theirs** [~z] der,
die, das ihrige *od.* ihre.

the·ism ['θi:izəm] Theismus *m*.

them [ðem, ðəm] sie (*acc. pl.*);
ihnen.

theme [θi:m] Thema *n* (*a.* ♩); ✎
Aufgabe *f*, Aufsatz *m*; *gr.* Stamm
m; ~ **mu·sic** *Film etc.*: Titelmelodie
f; ~ **song** Hauptmelodie *f e-s Musicals
etc.*

them·selves [ðəm'selvz] sie (*acc.
pl.*) selbst; sich selbst.

then [ðen] **1.** *adv.* dann, alsdann;
damals; da; *by* ~ bis dahin; inzwischen; *every now and* ~ alle
Augenblicke; *there and* ~ sogleich;
now ~ nun denn; **2.** *cj.* denn, also,
folglich; **3.** *adj.* damalig.

thence *lit.* [ðens] daher; von da.
thence·forth ['ðens'fɔ:θ], **thence-
for·ward** ['~'fɔ:wəd] seitdem, von
da an.

the·oc·ra·cy [θi'ɔkrəsi] Theokratie
f; **the·o·crat·ic** [θiə'krætik] (~*ally*)
theokratisch.

the·o·lo·gi·an [θiə'ləudʒjən] Theo-
loge *m*; **the·o·log·i·cal** □ [~-
'lɔdʒikəl] theologisch; **the·ol·o·gy**
[θi'ɔlədʒi] Theologie *f*.

the·o·rem ['θiərəm] Lehrsatz *m*;
the·o·ret·ic, the·o·ret·i·cal □
[~'retik(əl)] theoretisch; **'the·o·rist**
Theoretiker *m*; **'the·o·rize** theore-
tisieren; **'the·o·ry** Theorie *f*.

the·os·o·phy [θi'ɔsəfi] Theosophie
f.

ther·a·peu·tic [θerə'pju:tik] **1.** the-
rapeutisch; **2.** ~*s mst sg.* Thera-
peutik *f* (*praktische Heilkunde*);
'ther·a·py Therapie *f* (*Heilver-
fahren*); **'ther·a·pist** Therapeut
(-in); *mental* ~ Psychotherapeut
(-in).

there [ðeə] **1.** *adv.* da, dort; darin;
dorthin; ~ *is*, ~ *are* [ðə'riz, ðə'ra:]
es gibt, es ist, es sind; ~'*s* [ðeəz] *a
good fellow!* so bist du lieb!; sei
doch lieb!; ~ *you are!* da hast du
es!; **2.** *int.* na!
there...: '~·a·bout(s) da herum;
so ungefähr ...; ~'af·ter danach;
'~'by dadurch, damit; dabei;
~'for dafür; '~'fore darum, deswegen; deshalb, daher; ~'from
davon; ~'in darin; ~'of davon;
dessen, deren; ~'on darauf, dazu;
~'to dazu; '~·up'on darauf(hin);
~'with damit; ~·with'al überdies;
damit.

ther·mal □ ['θə:məl] **1.** Thermal...
(*Bad etc.*); *phys.* Wärme...; ~ *value*
Heizwert *m*; **2.** Thermik *f*, Aufwind *m*; **'ther·mic** (~*ally*) ther-
misch; Hitze...; **therm·i·on·ic**
[~'ɔnik] *Radio:* ~ *valve* Elektronen-,
Glühkathodenröhre *f*.

ther·mo·e·lec·tric cou·ple *phys.*
['θə:məui'lektrik'kʌpl] Thermo-
element *n*; **ther·mom·e·ter** [θə-
'mɔmitə] Thermometer *n*; **ther-
mo·met·ric, ther·mo·met·ri·cal**
□ [θə:məu'metrik(əl)] thermome-
trisch; **ther·mo·pile** *phys.* ['~məu-
pail] Thermosäule *f*; **Ther·mos**
['~mɔs] *a.* ~ *flask*, ~ *bottle* Thermosflasche *f*; **ther·mo·stat** ['~mə-

stæt] Thermostat *m* (*automatischer Wärmeregler*).

the·sau·rus [θiˈsɔːrəs] Thesaurus *m*; Wörterbuch *n*; Sammlung *f*.

these [ðiːz] (*pl. von this*) diese; ~ *three years* seit drei Jahren.

the·sis [ˈθiːsis], *pl.* **the·ses** [ˈ~siːz] Leitsatz *m*, These *f*; Dissertation *f*.

they [ðei] sie (*pl.*); ~ *who* die (-jenigen), welche.

thick [θik] **1.** ⎕ *allg.* dick; dicht (*Nebel, Haar etc.*); trüb (*Flüssigkeit*); legiert (*Suppe*); heiser, belegt (*Stimme*); dumm; *oft as ~ as thieves* F *pred.* dick befreundet; ~ *with* dicht besetzt mit; *that's a bit ~!* *sl.* das ist ein bißchen stark!; **2.** dickster Teil *m*; *fig.* Brennpunkt *m*; *in the ~ of* mitten in (*dat.*); **'thick·en** *v/t.* dick(er) machen, verdicken; verstärken; *Küche:* legieren; *v/i.* dick(er) od. dicht(er) werden; sich verdichten; sich trüben; sich verstärken; **thick·et** [ˈθikit] Dickicht *n*; **'thick·'head·ed** dumm; **'thick·ness** Dicke *f*; Dichtigkeit *f*; Heiserkeit *f*, Belegschaft *f*; ⊕, ⚹ Lage *f*, Schicht *f*; **'thick·'set** dicht (gepflanzt); untersetzt; **'thick·'skinned** *fig.* dickfellig.

thief [θiːf], *pl.* **thieves** [θiːvz] Dieb (-in); **thieve** [θiːv] stehlen; **'thiev·er·y** Dieberei *f*.

thiev·ish ⎕ [ˈθiːviʃ] diebisch; verstohlen; **'thiev·ish·ness** diebisches Wesen *n*, Spitzbüberei *f*.

thigh [θai] (Ober)Schenkel *m*.

thim·ble [ˈθimbl] Fingerhut *m*; **thim·ble·ful** [ˈ~ful] Fingerhut (-voll) *m*.

thin [θin] **1.** ⎕ *allg.* dünn; leicht; mager; spärlich, dürftig; schwach; fadenscheinig (*bsd. fig.*); *he had a ~ time* F es ging ihm dreckig *od.* miserabel; **2.** *v/t.* verdünnen; *Wald, Schlachtreihe etc.* lichten; *Bevölkerung* dezimieren; *v/i.* dünn werden; abnehmen; sich lichten.

thine † *od. poet.* [ðain] dein; der, die, das deinige *od.* deine.

thing [θiŋ] Ding *n*; Sache *f*; Wesen *n*, Geschöpf *n*; ~s *pl.* Sachen *f/pl.* (*Kleider, Gepäck, Geräte etc.*); die Dinge *n/pl.* (*Umstände*); *such a ~* so etwas; *the ~* F das Richtige; richtig; die Hauptsache *f*; *the ~ is* die Frage ist; *know a ~ or two* F

Bescheid wissen, Erfahrung haben; *of all ~s* vor allen Dingen; ~*s are going better* es geht jetzt besser; *I don't feel quite the ~* F ich bin nicht so ganz auf Deck.

thing·um(·a)·bob F [ˈθiŋəm(i)bɔb], **thing·um·my** F [ˈ~əmi] Dingsda *m*, *f*, *n*.

think [θiŋk] (*irr.*) *v/i.* denken (*of an acc.*); nachdenken (*about, over* über *acc.*); sich besinnen (*of* auf *acc.*); meinen, glauben; gedenken (*to inf.* zu *inf.*); *v/t.* denken; sich *et.* denken; halten für; ~ *much etc. of* viel *etc.* halten von; ~ *out* (sich) *et.* ausdenken; ~ *s.th. over* (sich) et. überlegen, über et. nachdenken; **'think·a·ble** denkbar; **'think·er** Denker(in); **'think·ing** denkend; Denk...

thin·ness [ˈθinnis] Dünne *f*.

third [θəːd] **1.** dritte(r, -s); ~ *degree* Folterverhör *n*; **2.** Drittel *n*; ♩ Terz *f*; **'third·ly** drittens; **'third·'par·ty in·sur·ance** Haftpflichtversicherung *f*; **'third·'rate** drittklassig.

thirst [θəːst] **1.** Durst *m* (*a. fig.*); **2.** dürsten (*for, after* nach); **'thirst·y** ⎕ durstig (*a. fig.*); dürr (*Boden etc.*); F Durst machend (*Arbeit*).

thir·teen [ˈθəːˈtiːn] dreizehn; **'thir·'teenth** [~θ] dreizehnte(r, -s); **thir·ti·eth** [ˈθəːtiiθ] dreißigste(r, -s); **'thir·ty** dreißig; *the thirties pl.* die Dreißigerjahre *pl. des Lebens*; die dreißiger Jahre *pl. e-s Jahrhunderts*.

this [ðis] (*pl.* **these**) diese(r, -s); ⚹ laufend; *in ~ country* hierzulande; ~ *morning* heute morgen; ~ *day week* heute in acht Tagen.

this·tle ⚘ [ˈθisl] Distel *f*; **'~-down** Distelwolle *f*.

thith·er(·ward) † *od. poet.* [ˈðiðə (-wəd)] dorthin.

tho' [ðəu] = *though*.

thole ⚓ [θəul] Dolle *f*, Ruderpflock *m*; **'~-pin** *fig.* Angelpunkt *m*.

thong [θɔŋ] (Leder-, Peitschen-) Riemen *m*.

tho·rax *anat.* [ˈθɔːræks] Brust(korb *m*, -kasten *m*) *f*, Thorax *m*.

thorn ⚘ [θɔːn] Dorn *m*; **'thorn·y** dornig, stach(e)lig; beschwerlich, dornenvoll.

thor·ough ⎕ [ˈθʌrə] vollkommen; vollständig; vollendet; gründlich;

eingehend; ⁓ly *a.* durchaus; '⁓-
-'**bass** ♪ Generalbaß *m;* '⁓·**bred**
1. Vollblut...; gründlich; **2.** Voll-
blüter *m;* '⁓·**fare** Durchgang *m,*
-fahrt *f;* Hauptverkehrsstraße *f;*
'⁓·**go·ing** gründlich; tatkräftig;
'**thor·ough·ness** Vollständigkeit *f;*
Gründlichkeit *f;* '**thor·ough-
paced** vollendet; ausgemacht.

those [ðəuz] (*pl. von that 1*) jene,
die; diejenigen; *are* ⁓ *your parents?*
sind das Ihre Eltern?

thou †, *Bibel, poet.* [ðau] du.

though [ðəu] obgleich, obwohl,
wenn auch; zwar; (*mst am Satz-
ende*) aber, doch; freilich; *as* ⁓ als
ob.

thought [θɔ:t] **1.** *pret. u. p.p. von*
think; **2.** Gedanke *m;* (Nach-)
Denken *n; give* ⁓ *to* sich Gedanken
machen über (*acc.*); *on second* ⁓*s*
nach nochmaliger Überlegung;
take ⁓ *for* Sorge tragen für.

thought·ful □ ['θɔ:tful] gedankenvoll, nachdenklich; besorgt (*of* um);
rücksichtsvoll(*of* gegen); '**thought-
ful·ness** Nachdenklichkeit*f;* Rück-
sichtnahme *f;* Besorgtheit *f.*

thought·less □ ['θɔ:tlis] gedankenlos; unbesonnen; rücksichtslos (*of*
gegen); '**thought·less·ness** Ge-
dankenlosigkeit *f;* Rücksichtslosigkeit *f.*

thought-read·ing ['θɔ:tri:diŋ] Ge-
dankenlesen *n.*

thou·sand ['θauzənd] **1.** tausend;
2. Tausend *n;* **thou·sandth** ['⁓-
zəntθ] **1.** tausendste(r, -s); **2.** Tausendstel *n.*

Thra·cian ['θreiʃjən] **1.** Thrakier
(-in); **2.** thrakisch.

thral(l)·dom ['θrɔ:ldəm] Knechtschaft *f.*

thrall [θrɔ:l] Sklave *m.*

thrash [θræʃ] *v/t.* (ver)dreschen,
(ver)prügeln; F schlagen, besiegen;
v/i. dreschen; (hin u. her) schlagen;
⚓ sich vorwärtsquälen; = *thresh;*
'**thrash·er** = *thresher;* '**thrashing** Dresche *f,* Tracht *f* Prügel; =
threshing.

thread [θred] **1.** Faden *m* (*a. fig.*);
Zwirn *m,* Garn *n;* (Schrauben-)
Gewinde *n;* **2.** einfädeln; aufreihen; sich durchwinden durch;
durchziehen; '⁓·**bare** fadenscheinig
(*a. fig.*); '**thread·y** fadenartig;
fadendünn.

threat [θret] Drohung *f;* '**threat·en**
v/t. j. bedrohen, *j-m* drohen; *et.*
androhen; *v/i.* drohen; '**threat·en-
ing** bedrohlich.

three [θri:] **1.** drei; **2.** Drei *f;*
'⁓-'**col·our** Dreifarben...; '⁓·**fold**
dreifach; ⁓·**pence** ['θrepəns] Drei-
pence(stück *n*) *m/pl.;* '⁓-**pen·ny**
Dreipence...; *fig.* gering; ⁓-**phase**
cur·rent ⚡ ['θri:feiz'kʌrənt] Drehstrom *m;* '⁓-**piece** dreiteilig; ⁓ *suit*
dreiteiliger Anzug *m;* ⁓ *suite* Sitz-
garnitur *f;* '⁓-'**score** sechzig.

thresh [θreʃ] *Korn* (aus)dreschen;
= *thrash;* ⁓ *out fig.* Angelegenheit
gründlich erörtern.

thresh·er ['θreʃə] Drescher *m;*
Dreschmaschine *f.*

thresh·ing ['θreʃiŋ] Dreschen *n;*
'⁓-**floor** (Dresch)Tenne *f;* '⁓-**machine** Dreschmaschine *f.*

thresh·old ['θreʃhəuld] Schwelle *f.*

threw [θru:] *pret. von throw 1.*

thrice ⚘ [θrais] dreimal.

thrift, thrift·i·ness [θrift, '⁓inis]
Sparsamkeit *f,* Wirtschaftlichkeit *f;*
Sparsinn *m;* '**thrift·less** □ verschwenderisch; '**thrift·y** □ sparsam; *poet.* gedeihend.

thrill [θril] **1.** *v/t.* durchdringen,
-schauern; *fig.* packen, aufwühlen;
aufregen; *v/i.* (er)beben (*with* vor);
2. Schauer *m;* Beben *n;* aufregendes
Erlebnis *n;* Sensation *f;* '**thrill·er**
F Reißer *m,* Thriller *m,* Schauerroman *m,* -drama *n;* '**thrill·ing**
aufwühlend, packend; aufregend;
spannend; sensationell.

thrive [θraiv] (*irr.*) gedeihen, geraten; *fig.* blühen; Glück haben;
thriv·en ['θrivn] *p.p. von thrive;*
thriv·ing □ ['θraiviŋ] gedeihend,
blühend, erfolgreich.

thro' [θru:] *abbr. für through.*

throat [θrəut] *allg.* Kehle *f;* Gurgel
f; Hals *m;* Schlund *m; clear one's* ⁓
sich räuspern; '**throat·y** □ kehlig;
heiser.

throb [θrɔb] **1.** pochen, schlagen,
klopfen (*Herz etc.*); pulsieren;
2. Pochen *n,* Schlagen *n;* Pulsschlag *m.*

throe [θrəu] Schmerz *m;* ⁓*s pl.*
Geburtswehen *f/pl.* (*mst fig.*).

throm·bo·sis ⚕ [θrɔm'bəusis]
Thrombose *f.*

throne [θrəun] **1.** Thron *m;* **2.** *v/t.*
auf den Thron setzen; *v/i.* thronen.

throng 566

throng [θrɔŋ] **1.** Gedränge *n*; Menge *f*, Schar *f*; **2.** sich drängen (in *dat.*, *a. acc.*); anfüllen mit.

thros·tle *orn.* ['θrɔsl] Drossel *f*.

throt·tle ['θrɔtl] **1.** erdrosseln; ⊕ (ab)drosseln; **2.** = '**∼-valve** ⊕ Drosselklappe *f*.

through [θru:] **1.** durch; **2.** Durchgangs…; durchgehend (*Zug etc.*); ∼ **flight** Direktflug *m*; ∼'**out 1.** *prp.* überall in (*dat.*); während; ∼ *the year* das ganze Jahr hindurch; **2.** durch u. durch, ganz u. gar, durchweg; '∼·**way** = *thruway*.

throve [θrəuv] *pret. von thrive*.

throw [θrəu] **1.** (*irr.*) *v/t. allg.* werfen, schleudern; *Wasser* gießen; *Reiter* abwerfen; ⊕ *Seide* zwirnen; *Brücke* schlagen; *Töpferei*: formen, drehen; *Am.* F *Wettspiel, Boxkampf etc.* absichtlich verlieren; ∼ *at* werfen nach; ∼ *away* wegwerfen; vergeuden; verwerfen; ∼ *in* hineinwerfen; *Wort etc.* einwerfen; mit in den Kauf geben; ∼ *off* abwerfen; *Kleid etc., Scham* ablegen; ∼ *out* (hin)auswerfen; *bsd. parl.* verwerfen; *e-n Wink* geben; ⊕ ausschalten; ∼ *over* aufgeben, fallen lassen; ∼ *up* in die Höhe werfen; erbrechen; *Amt, Karten etc.* hinwerfen; *s. sponge*; *v/i.* werfen; würfeln; ∼ *off* (die Jagd) beginnen; **2.** Wurf *m*; ⊕ (Kolben)Hub *m*; '∼-**back** *biol.* Atavismus *m*; **thrown** [θrəun] *p.p. von throw*; '**throw-'off** Aufbruch *m* (zur Jagd); *weitS.* Beginn *m*.

thru *Am.* [θru:] = *through*.

thrum[1] [θrʌm] *Weberei*: Trumm *m*, Saum *m*; Franse *f*; loser Faden *m*, Fussel *f*.

thrum[2] [∼] klimpern (auf *dat.*).

thrush[1] *orn.* [θrʌʃ] Drossel *f*.

thrush[2] [∼] ✿ Mundschwamm *m*; *vet.* Strahlfäule *f*.

thrust [θrʌst] **1.** Stoß *m*; ✗ *u. fig.* Vorstoß *m*; ⊕ Druck *m*, Schub *m*; **2.** (*irr.*) *v/t.* stoßen; ∼ *o.s. into* sich drängen in (*acc.*); ∼ *out* (her-, hin-) ausstoßen; *Zunge* herausstrecken; ∼ *upon s.o.* j-m aufdrängen; *v/i.* stoßen (*at* nach).

thru·way *Am.* ['θru:wei] Schnellstraße *f*.

thud [θʌd] **1.** dumpf aufschlagen, bumsen; **2.** dumpfer (Auf)Schlag *m*, Bums *m*, Plumps *m*.

thug [θʌg] (Gewalt)Verbrecher *m*, Gangster *m*; Rowdy *m*.

thumb [θʌm] **1.** Daumen *m*; *Tom* ♀ *Däumling m im Märchen*; **2.** *Buch etc.* abgreifen; ∼ *one's nose at s.o.* j-m e-e lange Nase machen; ∼ *a lift* per Anhalter fahren; '∼-**nail** Daumennagel *m*; ∼ *sketch* kleine, flüchtige Skizze *f*; '∼-**print** Daumenabdruck *m*; '∼-**screw** Daumenschraube *f*; ⊕ Flügelschraube *f*; '∼-**stall** Däumling *m* (*Schutzhülle*); '∼-**tack** *Am.* Reißnagel *m*.

thump [θʌmp] **1.** Bums *m*; Puff *m*; **2.** *v/t.* bumsen *od.* pochen auf (*acc.*) *od.* gegen; knuffen, puffen; *v/i.* (auf)bumsen; '**thump·er** *sl.* Mordsding *n*; '**thump·ing** *sl.* kolossal.

thun·der ['θʌndə] **1.** Donner *m* (*fig. oft* ∼*s pl.*); **2.** donnern; '∼-**bolt** Blitz *m* (*u. Donner m*); '∼-**clap** Donnerschlag *m*; '∼-**cloud** Gewitterwolke *f*; '**thun·der·er** *myth.* Donnerer *m* (*Jupiter*).

thun·der…: '∼-**head** schwere Gewitterwolke(n *pl.*) *f* (*a. fig.*); '**thun·der·ing** *sl.* kolossal; '**thun·der·ous** □ *fig.* donnernd; gewitterschwül; gewaltig; '**thun·der·storm** Gewitter *n*; '**thun·der·struck** wie vom Donner gerührt; '**thun·der·y** gewitterschwül.

Thu·rin·gi·an [θjuə'rindʒiən] **1.** thüringisch; **2.** Thüringer(in).

Thurs·day ['θə:zdi] Donnerstag *m*.

thus [ðʌs] so, auf diese Weise; also, somit.

thwack [θwæk] = *whack*.

thwart [θwɔ:t] **1.** durchkreuzen; hintertreiben; *j-m* entgegenarbeiten; **2.** Ducht *f*, Ruderbank *f*.

thy *Bibel, poet.* [ðai] dein(e).

thyme ✿ [taim] Thymian *m*.

thy·roid *anat.* ['θairɔid] **1.** Schilddrüsen…; ∼ *extract* Schilddrüsenextrakt *m*; ∼ *gland* = **2.** Schilddrüse *f*.

thy·self *Bibel, poet.* [ðai'self] du selbst; dir, dich (selbst).

ti·a·ra [ti'ɑ:rə] Tiara *f* (*Papstkrone*); Stirnreif *m*, Diadem *n*.

tib·i·a *anat.* ['tibiə] Schienbein *n*.

tic ✿ [tik] nervöser (Gesichts)Krampf *m*.

tich F [titʃ] Knirps *m*.

tick[1] *zo.* [tik] Zecke *f*.

tick[2] [∼] (Inlett)Überzug *m*.

tick[3] F [∼]: *on* ∼ auf Pump.

tick⁴ [_] **1.** Ticken *n*; F Augenblick *m*; Vermerkhäkchen *n*; *to the* _ mit dem Glockenschlag; **2.** *v/i.* ticken; _ *over mot.* leerlaufen; *v/t.* anmerken, anhaken; _ *off* abhaken; *sl. j.* heruntermachen, zs.-stauchen.

tick·er ['tikə] Börsentelegraph *m*; F Uhr *f*; '_**-tape** *coll.* Luftschlangen *f/pl.*

tick·et ['tikit] **1.** Fahrkarte *f*, -schein *m*; Flugkarte *f*; Eintrittskarte *f*; (Straf)Zettel *m*, (Preis- *etc.*) Schildchen *n*; *pol.* (Wahl-, Kandidaten)Liste *f*; *the* _ F das Richtige; _ *of leave* ꬞ Freilassung *f* auf Bewährung; **2.** mit e-m Zettel *etc.* versehen, kennzeichnen; _ **a·gen·cy** *thea. etc.* Vorverkaufsstelle *f*; *Reisebüro:* Fahrkartenverkaufsstelle *f*; '_**-col·lec·tor** Bahnsteigschaffner *m*; '_**-in·spec·tor** Fahrkartenkontrolleur *m*; '_**-ma·chine** Fahrkartenautomat *m*; '_**-of·fice**, '_**-win·dow** *bsd. Am.* Fahrkartenschalter *m*; '_**-punch** Lochzange *f*.

tick·ing ['tikiŋ] (Inlett)Drell *m*.

tick·le ['tikl] kitzeln (*a. fig.*); '**tick·ler** schwierige Situation *f*; *a.* _ *coil* Rückkopplungsspule *f*; '**tick·lish** kitzlig; heikel.

tid·al [‿ ['taidl] Gezeiten...; Flut...; _ *wave* Flutwelle *f* (*a. fig.*).

tid·bit ['tidbit] = *titbit*.

tid·dly-winks ['tidliwiŋks] Floh-(hüpf)spiel *n*.

tide [taid] **1.** Gezeit(en *pl.*) *f* (*a. fig.*); (*low* _) Ebbe und (*high* _) Flut *f*; *fig.* Strom *m*, Flut *f*; *in Zssgn: rechte* Zeit *f*; *turn of the* _ Flut-, *fig.* Glückswechsel *m*; **2.** mit dem Strom treiben; _ *over fig.* hinwegkommen od. -helfen über (*acc.*).

tide·mark ['taidmɑːk] Flutmarke *f*; *fig. co.* schwarzer Rand *m* an der Badewanne od. am Hals.

ti·di·ness ['taidinis] Sauberkeit *f*.

ti·dings ['taidiŋz] *pl. od. sg.* Neuigkeiten *f/pl.*, Nachrichten *f/pl.*

ti·dy ['taidi] **1.** ordentlich, sauber, reinlich; F ganz schön, beträchtlich (*Summe*); **2.** Behälter *m*; Abfallkorb *m*; **3.** *a.* _ *up* zurechtmachen; ordnen; *Zimmer etc.* aufräumen, in Ordnung bringen.

tie [tai] **1.** Band *n* (*a. fig.*); Schleife *f*; Halstuch *n*, Krawatte *f*, Schlips *m*; Bindung *f* (*bsd.* ♩); ⚓ Anker *m*; *fig.* Fessel *f*, Verpflichtung *f*; *Sport:*

Unentschieden *n*; *parl.* Stimmengleichheit *f*; *Sport:* Entscheidungsspiel *n*; ⚓ *Am.* Schwelle *f*; **2.** *v/t. allg.* binden (*a.* ♩); verbinden; ⚓ verankern; _ *down fig.* binden (*to an e-e Pflicht etc.*); _ *up* zu-, an-, ver-, zs.-binden; *v/i. Sport:* unentschieden spielen (*with* gegen).

tier [tiə] Reihe *f*; *thea.* Sitzreihe *f*; Rang *m*.   [Terz *f.*\
tierce [tiəs] *fenc.*, *Kartenspiel:*\
tie-up ['taiʌp] (Ver)Bindung *f*; ✝ Fusion *f*; Stockung *f*; Stillstand *m*; *bsd. Am.* Streik *m*.

tiff F [tif] **1.** *kleine* Meinungsverschiedenheit *f*; **2.** schmollen.

tif·fin ['tifin] Mittagessen *n*.

ti·ger ['taigə] Tiger *m*; *Am.* F Beifallsgebrüll *n*; *three cheers and a* _! hoch, hoch, hoch und nochmals hoch!; '**ti·ger·ish** ☐ *fig.* tigerhaft; Tiger...

tight ☐ [tait] dicht (*bsd. in Zssgn*); fest *gebaut od. gefügt*; eng; knapp (sitzend) (*Jacke etc.*); straff (*Seil etc.*), prall (*Backen etc.*); knapp (*bsd.* ✝ *Geld*); F beschwipst; *be in a* _ *place od. corner* F in der Klemme sein; *hold* _ festhalten; *it is a* _ *fit* es paßt knapp; '**tight·en** *a.* _ *up* (sich) zs.-ziehen; *Schraube, Zügel etc.* anziehen; *Gürtel* enger schnallen; *Feder* spannen; (sich) straffen; '_**-fist·ed** knick(e)rig; '_**-laced** fest geschnürt; engherzig, prüde; '_**-lipped** verschwiegen; verkniffen; '**tight·ness** Festigkeit *f*, Dichtigkeit *f etc.*; '**tight-rope** gespanntes Seil *n*; **tights** [_s] *pl.* Trikot *n der Akrobaten etc.*; Strumpfhose *f*; '**tight·wad** *sl.* Knauser *m*, Knicker *m*.

ti·gress ['taigris] Tigerin *f*.

tile [tail] **1.** (Dach)Ziegel *m*; Kachel *f*; Fliese *f*; *sl.* Deckel *m* (*Hut*); *he has a* _ *loose sl.* bei ihm ist e-e Schraube locker; **2.** mit Ziegeln *etc.* decken; kacheln; '_**-lay·er**, '**til·er** Dachdecker *m*.

till¹ [til] Laden(tisch)kasse *f*.

till² [_] **1.** *prp.* bis (zu); **2.** *cj.* bis.

till³ ⚘ [_] bestellen, beackern, bebauen; '**till·age** (Land)Bestellung *f*, Beackerung *f*; Ackerbau *m*; Ackerland *n*.

till·er¹ ['tilə] Bauer *m*, Pflüger *m*.

till·er² ⚓ [_] Ruderpinne *f*.

tilt¹ [tilt] Plane *f*.

tilt² [⌣] **1.** Neigung *f*, schiefe Lage *f*; Stoß *m*; Lanzenbrechen *n* (*a. fig.*); *on the* ⌣ *auf der Kippe*; (*at*) *full* ⌣ mit voller Geschwindigkeit; *have a* ⌣ *at s.o.* mit j-m e-e Lanze brechen; **2.** *v/t.* kippen; *v/i.* kippen; Lanzen brechen (*a. fig.*); stechen (*at* nach); ⌣ *against* anrennen gegen; '**tilt·ing** Kipp...; Turnier...

tilth [tilθ] Bebauungstiefe *f*; Ackerland *n*.

tim·bal ♪ ['timbəl] (Kessel)Pauke *f*.

tim·ber ['timbə] **1.** (Bau-, Nutz-) Holz *n*; Baum(bestand) *m*; ⚓ Inholz *n*; **2.** zimmern; ⌣ed holzgezimmert; Fachwerk...; bewaldet; '**⌣-line** Baumgrenze *f*; '**⌣-work** Gebälk *n*, Holzwerk *n*; '**⌣-yard** Zimmerplatz *m*.

time [taim] **1.** Zeit *f*; Mal *n*; Takt *m*; Zeitmaß *n*, Tempo *n*; ⌣! *parl.* Schluß!; ⌣ *and again* immer wieder; *at* ⌣*s* zu Zeiten; *at a* ⌣, *at the same* ⌣ zugleich; *at one* ⌣ einstmals; *before one's* ⌣ verfrüht; *behind one's* ⌣ verspätet; *behind the* ⌣*s* hinter der Zeit zurück; *by that* ⌣ zu der Zeit; *bis dahin*; unterdessen; *do* ⌣ F *im Gefängnis sitzen*; *for the* ⌣ *being* für den Augenblick, einstweilen; zunächst; *have a good* ⌣ es gut haben; sich amüsieren; *in* (*good*) ⌣ zur rechten Zeit; *in no* ⌣ im Nu; *in a month's* ⌣ nach e-m Monat; *s. mean*² 1; *on* ⌣ rechtzeitig; *out of* ⌣ zur Unzeit; aus dem Takt *od.* Schritt; *beat the* ⌣ Takt schlagen; *s. keep*; **2.** *v/t.* die Zeit bestimmen für; zeitlich abpassen *od.* einrichten; den richtigen Zeitpunkt wählen für; ♪ den Takt angeben für; *a. take the* ⌣ *of die Zeit(dauer) e-s Rennens etc.* messen; regeln (*to* nach); *Uhr* stellen; *the train is* ⌣*d to leave at* 7 der Zug soll um 7 abfahren; *v/i.* Takt halten (*to* mit); zs.-stimmen (*with* mit); '**⌣-and-'mo·tion stud·y** Zeitstudie *f*; '**⌣-bar·gain** Termingeschäft *n*; '**⌣-clock** Stempel-, Stechuhr *f*; '**⌣-con·sum·ing** zeitraubend; ⌣ **cred·it** Zeitguthaben *n bei gleitender Arbeitszeit*; ⌣ **deb·it** Fehlzeit *f bei gleitender Arbeitszeit*; '**⌣-ex·po·sure** *phot.* Zeitaufnahme *f*; '**⌣-hon-o(u)red** altehrwürdig; '**⌣-keep·er** Zeitmesser *m*, *bsd.* Uhr *f*; (Arbeits-) Zeitnehmer *m*; '**⌣-lag** zeitliche Verzögerung *f*; '**⌣-'lim·it** Befristung *f*; '**time·ly** (recht)zeitig; aktuell, zeitgemäß; '**time·piece** Uhr *f*; '**tim·er** *Sport*: Zeitnehmer *m*; *phot.* Zeitauslöser *m*.

time...: ⌣**-serv·er** ['taimsə:və] Achselträger *m*, Opportunist *m*; '**⌣-sheet** Anwesenheitsliste *f*; Stempel-, Kontrollkarte *f*; '**⌣-sig·nal** *bsd. Radio*: Zeitzeichen *n*; '**⌣-ta·ble** Terminkalender *m*; 🚂 Fahrplan *m*; *Schule*: Stundenplan *m*.

tim·id ☐ ['timid] furchtsam, ängstlich; schüchtern; **ti'mid·i·ty** Furchtsamkeit *f*; Schüchternheit *f*.

tim·ing ['taimiŋ] Wahl *f* des Zeitpunkts.

tim·or·ous ☐ ['timərəs] = timid.

tin [tin] **1.** Zinn *n*; Weißblech *n*; (Blech-, Konserven)Büchse *f*, (-)Dose *f*; *sl.* Piepen *pl.* (*Geld*); **2.** zinnern; Zinn...; Blech...; blechern (*a. fig. contp.*); ⌣ *solder* Lötzinn *n*; **3.** verzinnen; in Büchsen einmachen, eindosen; ⌣ned meat Dosenfleisch *n*.

tinc·ture ['tiŋktʃə] **1.** Farbe *f*; *fig.* Anstrich *m*; *pharm.* Tinktur *f*; **2.** färben; e-n Anstrich geben (*dat.*).

tin·der ['tində] Zunder *m*.

tine [tain] Zinke *f*; Zacke *f*; (Geweih)Sprosse *f*.

tin·foil ['tin'fɔil] Stanniol *n*.

ting F [tiŋ] = tinkle.

tinge [tindʒ] **1.** Farbe *f*, Färbung *f*; *fig.* Anflug *m*, Spur *f*; **2.** färben; *fig.* e-n Anstrich geben (*dat.*); *be* ⌣*d with* etwas von ... an sich haben.

tin·gle ['tiŋgl] klingen; prickeln, kribbeln; flirren; surren.

tin...: ⌣ **god** F Götze *m*, Idol *n*; ⌣ **hat** *sl.* Stahlhelm *m*.

tink·er ['tiŋkə] **1.** Kesselflicker *m*; **2.** *v/t.* zs.-flicken; *v/i.* (*herum*)pfuschen (*at* an *dat.*); (*up* zurecht-) basteln. [**2.** Geklingel *n*.]

tin·kle ['tiŋkl] **1.** klingeln (*mit*);]

tin·man ['tinmən] Klempner *m*; '**tin·ny** blechern (*Klang*); '**tin-o·pen·er** Dosenöffner *m*; '**tin-plate** Weißblech *n*.

tin·sel ['tinsl] **1.** Flitter *m*; Rauschgold *n*; Lametta *f*; *fig.* Flitter(werk *n*) *m*; **2.** Flitter...; flitterhaft; **3.** mit Flitterwerk verzieren.

tint [tint] **1.** *hellgetönte* Farbe *f*; (Farb)Ton *m*, Schattierung *f*;

2. färben; (ab)tönen; ~ed paper Tonpapier n.

tin·tin·nab·u·la·tion ['tintinæbju-'leiʃən] Geklingel n.

tin·ware ['tinwɛə] Blechwaren f/pl.

ti·ny ☐ ['taini] winzig, klein.

tip [tip] **1.** Spitze f; Mundstück n e-r Zigarette; Trinkgeld n; Tip m, Wink m, Fingerzeig m; leichter Schlag m od. Stoß m; Schuttablade-platz m; give s.th. a ~ et. kippen; **2.** v/t. mit e-r Spitze versehen; beschlagen; (um)kippen; j-m ein Trinkgeld geben; a. ~ off j-m e-n Wink geben; v/i. (um)kippen; '~--cart Kippkarren m; '~-off Wink m.

tip·pet ['tipit] Pelerine f.

tip·ple ['tipl] **1.** zechen, picheln; **2.** Getränk n; '**tip·pler** Zechbruder m.

tip·si·ness ['tipsinis] Trunkenheit f.

tip·staff ['tipstɑːf] Gerichtsdiener m.

tip·ster ['tipstə] (Wett)Berater m.

tip·sy ['tipsi] angeheitert; wack(e)lig.

tip·toe ['tiptəu] **1.** auf Zehenspitzen gehen; **2.** on ~ auf Zehenspitzen.

tip·top F ['tip'tɔp] **1.** höchster Punkt m; **2.** höchst, vorzüglich; fein.

tip-up seat thea. ['tipʌp'siːt] Klappsitz m.

ti·rade [tai'reid] Tirade f, Wortschwall m.

tire[1] ['taiə] (Rad-, Auto)Reifen m.

tire[2] [~] ermüden, müde machen od. werden (of ger. zu inf.).

tired ☐ ['taiəd] müde (fig. of gen.); verbraucht; '**tired·ness** Müdigkeit f.

tire·less ☐ ['taiəlis] unermüdlich.

tire·some ☐ ['taiəsəm] ermüdend; langweilig, unangenehm, lästig.

ti·ro ['taiərəu] Anfänger m.

'tis [tiz] = it is.

tis·sue ['tiʃuː] Gewebe n; ✝ (durchwirkter) Schleierstoff m; '~-'pa·per Seidenpapier n.

tit[1] [tit]: ~ for tat wie du mir, so ich dir; Wurst wider Wurst.

tit[2] Am. [~] = teat.

tit[3] orn. [~] Meise f.

Ti·tan ['taitən] Titan(e) m; '**Ti·tan·ess** Titanin f; **ti·ta·nic** [~'tænik] (~ally) titanisch, titanenhaft.

ti·ta·ni·um ⚕ [tai'teinjəm] Titan n.

tit·bit ['titbit] Leckerbissen m.

titch [titʃ] = tich.

tithe [taið] Zehnt(e) m; mst fig. Zehntel n.

tit·il·late ['titileit] kitzeln; **tit·il la·tion** Kitzel(n n) m.

tit·i·vate F ['titiveit] (sich) schön-od. zurechtmachen.

ti·tle ['taitl] **1.** (Buch-, Ehren)Titel m; Überschrift f; (bsd. Rechts-) Anspruch m (to auf acc.); **2.** betiteln; (be)nennen; ~d bsd. ad(e)lig; '~-deed ⚖ Besitztitel m; '~-holder bsd. Sport: Titelinhaber(in); '~-page Titelseite f; '~-role Titelrolle f.

tit·mouse orn. ['titmaus], pl. **tit·mice** ['~mais] Meise f.

ti·trate ⚗ ['titreit] titrieren; **ti'tra·tion** Titrieren n.

tits V [tits] pl. Titten f/pl.

tit·ter ['titə] **1.** kichern; **2.** Kichern n.

tit·tle ['titl] Pünktchen n; fig. Tütelchen n; to a ~ bis aufs Tüpfelchen; '~-tat·tle **1.** Schnickschnack m (leeres Geschwätz); **2.** schnickschnacken.

tit·u·lar ☐ ['titjulə] Titular...; dem Namen nach.

to [tuː; im Satz mst tu, vor Konsonant tə] **1.** zur Bezeichnung des Infinitivs: zu; **2.** prp. zu (a. adv.); Richtung, Ziel: zu, gegen, nach, an, in, auf; Vergleich: gegen; Gemäßheit: nach; Grenze: bis zu (od. an acc., in acc., nach, auf acc.); zeitlich: bis zu, bis an (acc.); Absicht: um zu; Zweck, Ende, Wirkung: zu, für; zur Bildung des (betonten) Dativs: ~ me, ~ you etc. mir, Ihnen etc.; he gave it ~ his friend er gab es seinem Freund; it happened ~ me es geschah mir; Beziehung, Zugehörigkeit: alive ~ s.th. empfänglich für et.; cousin ~ Vetter des Königs etc. od. der Frau N. od. von N.; heir ~ Erbe des etc.; secretary ~ Sekretär des etc.; Verkürzung e-s Nebensatzes: I weep ~ think of it ich weine, wenn ich daran denke; here's ~ you! auf Ihr Wohl!, Prosit!; ~ and fro hin und her, auf und ab.

toad zo. [təud] Kröte f; '~-stool (größerer Blätter)Pilz m; Giftpilz m.

toad·y ['təudi] **1.** Speichellecker m; **2.** vor j-m kriechen od. scharwenzeln; '**toad·y·ism** Speicheleckerei f.

to-and-fro ['tuːən'frəu] Kommen n und Gehen n.

toast [təust] **1.** Toast m, geröstetes Brot n; Trinkspruch m; **2.** toasten, rösten; fig. wärmen; trinken auf (*acc.*); **'toast·er** Toaster *m*, Brot-röster *m*.

to·bac·co [tə'bækəu] Tabak *m*; **to-'bac·co·nist** [⸓kənist] Tabakhänd-ler *m*. ⋅

to·bog·gan [tə'bɔgən] **1.** Toboggan *m*; Rodelschlitten *m*; **2.** rodeln.

toc·sin ['tɔksin] Sturmglocke *f*.

tod *sl.* [tɔd]: *on one's* ⸯ ganz allein.

to·day [tə'dei] heute.

tod·dle ['tɔdl] watscheln; zotteln; tappen; unsicher gehen; **'tod·dler** Taps *m*, unsicher gehendes Baby *n*.

tod·dy ['tɔdi] *Art* Grog *m*.

to-do F [tə'du:] Lärm *m*, Aufheben *n*.

toe [təu] **1.** Zehe *f*; Spitze *f*; *from top to* ⸯ von Kopf bis Fuß; *on one's* ⸯs *fig.* auf Draht; **2.** mit den Zehen berühren; *Schuh* bekappen; ⸯ *the line Sport*: zum Start antreten; *pol.* sich der Parteidisziplin unterwer-fen.

toed [təud] ...zehig.

toff P [tɔf] feiner Pinkel *m* (*Stutzer*).

tof·fee ['tɔfi] Sahnebonbon *m*, *n*, Tof-fee *n*; **'ⸯ-nosed** F hochnäsig; auf-geblasen.

tof·fy ['tɔfi] = *toffee*.

tog F [tɔg] **1.** anziehen; **2.** *s. togs*.

to·ga [təugə] Toga *f*.

to·geth·er [tə'geðə] *örtlich*: zusam-men; *zeitlich*: zugleich; nachein-ander, ohne Unterbrechung.

tog·gle ⚓ *u.* ⊕ ['tɔgl] **1.** Knebel *m*; ⸯ *switch* ⚡ Kippschalter *m*; **2.** (fest-) knebeln.

togs F [tɔgz] *pl.* Kluft *f* (*Kleidung*).

toil [tɔil] **1.** schwere Arbeit *f*, Mühe *f*, Plackerei *f*; **2.** sich plagen, schwer arbeiten, sich abmühen; sich mühsam bewegen.

toil·er *fig.* ['tɔilə] Arbeitspferd *n*.

toi·let ['tɔilit] Toilette *f* (*Ankleiden*; *Anzug*; *Kleid*; *Badezimmer*, *Klo-sett*); *make one's* ⸯ Toilette machen; ⸯ *bag* Kulturbeutel *m*; **'ⸯ-pa·per** Toilettenpapier *n*; ⸯ *seat* Toiletten-sitz *m*, Brille *f*; **'ⸯ-set** Toilettengarni-tur *f*; **'ⸯ-ta·ble** Frisiertoilette *f*.

toils [tɔilz] *pl.* Schlingen *f/pl.*, Netz *n*.

toil·some ☐ ['tɔilsəm] mühsam.

toil-worn ['tɔilwɔːn] abgearbeitet.

to-ing and fro-ing F ['tu:iŋən'frəuiŋ] Hin und Her *n*.

to·ken ['təukən] Zeichen *n*; Andenken *n*, Geschenk *n*; ⸯ *money* Ersatz-, Not-geld *n*; ⸯ *payment* ✝ Pro-forma-Zah-lung *f*; ⸯ *strike* Warnstreik *m*; *in* ⸯ *of*

zum Zeichen (*gen.*).

told [təuld] *pret. u. p.p. von tell*; *all* ⸯ alles in allem.

tol·er·a·ble ☐ ['tɔlərəbl] erträglich; leidlich; **'tol·er·ance** Duldung *f*; Duldsamkeit *f*, Toleranz *f*; **'tol·er·ant** ☐ duldsam (*of* gegen); **tol·er·ate** ['⸓reit] dulden; ertragen; **tol-er'a·tion** Duldung *f*.

toll[1] [təul] Zoll *m* (*a. fig.*); Wege-, Brücken-, Marktgeld *n*; *fig.* Tribut *m*; ⸯ *call teleph.* Ferngespräch *n*; ⸯ *of the road* die Verkehrsopfer *n/pl.*

toll[2] [ⸯ] läuten (*bsd. Totenglocke*).

toll...: **'ⸯ-bar**, **'ⸯ-gate** Schlagbaum *m*; ⸯ *road* gebührenpflichtige Auto-straße *f*, Mautstraße *f*.

tom·a·hawk ['tɔməhɔ:k] **1.** Kriegs-beil *n*, Streitaxt *f der Indianer*; **2.** mit der Streitaxt töten *od.* schla-gen.

to·ma·to ♗ [tə'ma:təu, *Am.* tə'mei-təu], *pl.* **to'ma·toes** Tomate *f*.

tomb [tu:m] Grab(mal) *n*.

tom·boy ['tɔmbɔi] Range *f*, Wild-fang *m* (*Mädchen*).

tomb·stone ['tu:mstəun] Grab-stein *m*.

tom·cat ['tɔm'kæt] Kater *m*.

tome [təum] Band *m*, Buch *n*.

tom·fool ['tɔm'fu:l] **1.** Hansnarr *m*; **2.** den Hansnarren spielen; **tom-'fool·er·y** Narretei *f*, Albernheit *f*.

tom·my *sl.* ['tɔmi] Tommy *m* (*bri-tischer Soldat*); Fressalien *pl.*; ⸯ *gun* Maschinenpistole *f*; ⸯ *rot* richtiger Quatsch *m*.

to·mor·row [tə'mɔrəu] morgen.

tom·tom ['tɔmtɔm] Tamtam *n*.

ton [tʌn] Tonne *f* (*Gewichtseinheit*); ⸯs *pl.* F Massen *f/pl.*

to·nal·i·ty [təu'næliti] Tonart *f*; *paint.* Tönung *f*.

tone [təun] **1.** Ton *m beim Sprechen* (*a.* ♫, ♩, *paint.*, *fig.*); Klang *m*, Laut *m*; *out of* ⸯ verstimmt; **2.** *v/t.* e-n Ton *od.* e-e Färbung geben (*dat.*); stimmen; *paint.* abtönen; *phot.* tonen; ⸯ *down* abschwächen; mildern; *v/i.* stimmen (*with* zu) (*bsd. Farbe*); ⸯ *down* sich mildern.

tongs [tɔŋz] *pl.* (*a pair of* eine) Zange *f*.

tongue [tʌŋ] *allg.* Zunge *f*; *fig.* Sprache *f*; Landzunge *f*; Zunge *f der Waage etc.*; (Schuh)Lasche *f*;

hold one's ~ den Mund halten; *speak with one's* ~ *in one's cheek* es nicht ernst meinen, unaufrichtig sein; '**tongue·less** ohne Zunge; *fig.* stumm; '**tongue-tied** zungenlahm; *fig.* sprachlos; schweigsam; '**tongue-twist·er** Zungenbrecher *m.*

ton·ic ['tɔnik] **1.** (~*ally*) ♪ tonisch; ♪ tonisch, die Spannkraft erhöhend; stärkend; ~ *chord* ♪ Grundakkord *m*; **2.** ♪ Grundton *m*, Tonika *f*; ♪ Stärkungsmittel *n*, Tonikum *n*.

to·night [tə'nait] heute abend *od.* nacht.

ton·ing so·lu·tion *phot.* ['təuniŋ sə'lu:ʃən] Tonbad *n.*

ton·nage ♪ ['tʌnidʒ] Tonnengehalt *m*, Tonnage *f*; Lastigkeit *f*; Tonnengeld *n.*

ton·sil *anat.* ['tɔnsl] Mandel *f*; **ton·sil·li·tis** [‿si'laitis] Mandelentzündung *f.*

ton·sure ['tɔnʃə] **1.** Tonsur *f*; **2.** tonsurieren, scheren.

ton·y *Am. sl.* ['təuni] schick.

too [tu:] zu, allzu; auch, noch dazu.

took [tuk] *pret. von* take.

tool [tu:l] **1.** Werkzeug *n* (*a. fig.*), Instrument *n*, Gerät *n*; **2.** mit e-m Werkzeug (be)arbeiten; '~**-bag**, '~**-kit** Werkzeugtasche *f*; ~ **shed** Geräteschuppen *m.*

toot [tu:t] **1.** blasen, tuten; **2.** Tuten *n.*

tooth [tu:θ], *pl.* **teeth** [ti:θ] Zahn *m*; ~ *and nail* mit aller Kraft; *cast s.th. in s.o.'s teeth* j-m et. vorwerfen; '~**·ache** Zahnweh *n*; '~**-brush** Zahnbürste *f*; **toothed** mit (...) Zähnen; Zahn...; '**tooth·ing** ⊕ (Ver)Zahnung *f*; '**tooth·less** ☐ zahnlos; '**tooth-paste** Zahnpasta *f*; '**tooth·pick** Zahnstocher *m.*

tooth·some ☐ ['tu:θsəm] schmackhaft.

too·tle ['tu:tl] tuten; dudeln; schwatzen.

top¹ [tɔp] **1.** oberstes Ende *n*; Oberteil *n*; Gipfel *m*, Spitze *f*; Wipfel *m*, Krone *f*; (Haus)Giebel *m*; Kopf *m* *e-r Seite*; *fig.* Gipfel *m* (*höchster Grad*); Oberfläche *f* *des Wassers*; (Bett)Himmel *m*; *mot. Am.* Verdeck *n*; ♪ Mars *m*; Scheitel *m*; Haupt *n*, Erste *m*; Stulpe *f* *e-s Stiefels*; *at the* ~ obenan; *at the* ~ *of* oben an *od.* auf (*dat.*); *at the* ~ *of one's speed* in

höchster Eile; *at the* ~ *of one's voice* aus voller Kehle, so laut man kann; *on* ~ obenauf; dazu noch; *on* ~ *of* oben auf (*dat.*); **2.** ober(er, -e, -es); oberst; Haupt...; *the* ~ *right corner* die rechte obere Ecke; **3.** oben bedecken, krönen; *fig.* übertragen, -treffen; vorangehen in (*dat.*); als erste(r) stehen auf *e-r Liste*; ✂ stutzen, kappen; ~ *up* auffüllen.

top² [‿] Kreisel *m*; *sleep like a* ~ wie ein Murmeltier schlafen.

to·paz *min.* ['təupæz] Topas *m.*

top...: '~**-boots** *pl.* Stulpenstiefel *m/pl.*; Langschäfter *m/pl.*; ~ **dog** *sl.* *der* Überlegene, *der* Herr; ~ **earn·er** Spitzenverdiener *m.*

to·pee ['təupi] Tropenhelm *m.*

top·er ['təupə] Zecher *m.*

top...: '~**-flight** F prima, erstklassig; ~**gal·lant** ♪ [‿'gælənt, ♪ tə'gælənt] **1.** Bram...; **2.** *a.* ~ *sail* Bramsegel *n*; ~ *hat* Zylinderhut *m*; '~**-heav·y** kopflastig; '~**-hole** *sl.* ganz groß (*erstklassig*).

top·ic ['tɔpik] Gegenstand *m*, Thema *n*; '**top·i·cal** ☐ örtlich, lokal (*a.* ♪); aktuell.

top·knot ['tɔpnɔt] Haarknoten *m*; *orn.* Haube *f.*

top·less ['tɔplis] oben ohne.

top...: '~**-mast** ♪ Marsstenge *f*; '~**-most** höchst, oberst; '~**-notch** F prima, erstklassig.

to·pog·ra·pher [tə'pɔgrəfə] Topograph *m*; **top·o·graph·ic**, **top·o·graph·i·cal** ☐ [tɔpə'græfik(əl)] topographisch; **to·pog·ra·phy** [tə'pɔgrəfi] Topographie *f*, Ortsbeschreibung *f.*

top·per F ['tɔpə] Zylinder *m*; '**top·ping** F prima, toll, fabelhaft.

top·ple ['tɔpl] *mst* ~ *over*, ~ *down* (um)kippen, umfallen.

top·sail ♪ ['tɔpsl] Marssegel *n.*

top...: ~ **se·cret** streng geheim; ~ **speed** Höchstgeschwindigkeit *f.*

top·sy-tur·vy ☐ ['tɔpsi'tə:vi] auf den Kopf gestellt; das Unterste zuoberst; drunter und drüber.

toque [təuk] Toque *f* (*Damenhut*).

tor [tɔ:] Felsturm *m.*

torch [tɔ:tʃ] Fackel *f*; *a. electric* ~ Taschenlampe *f*; '~**-light** Fackelschein *m*; ~ *procession* Fackelzug *m.*

tore [tɔ:] *pret. von* tear¹ 1.

tor·ment 1. ['tɔ:mənt] Qual *f*, Folter *f*, Pein *f*, Marter *f*; **2.** [tɔ:-

'ment] peinigen, foltern, martern, quälen; **tor'men·tor** Quälgeist *m*, Folterer *m*, Peiniger *m*.

torn [tɔːn] *p.p. von tear¹* 1.

tor·na·do [tɔː'neidəu], *pl.* **tor'na·does** [ﹾz] Wirbelsturm *m*, Tornado *m*.

tor·pe·do [tɔː'piːdəu], *pl.* **tor'pe·does** [ﹾz] 1. ⚓, ⚔ Torpedo *m*; *a.* toy ﹾ Knallerbse *f*; *a.* ﹾ-fish *ichth.* Zitterrochen *m*; 2. ⚓ torpedieren (*a. fig.*); ﹾ-boat ⚓ Torpedoboot *n*; ﹾ-tube Torpedorohr *n*.

tor·pid ☐ ['tɔːpid] starr, erstarrt; *fig.* stumpf, apathisch; träg, schlaff; **tor'pid·i·ty**, **'tor·pid·ness**, **tor·por** ['tɔːpə] Erstarrung *f*, Betäubung *f*.

torque ⊕ [tɔːk] Drehmoment *n*.

tor·rent ['tɔrənt] Sturz-, Gießbach *m*; (reißender) Strom *m* (*a. fig.*); **tor·ren·tial** ☐ [tɔ'renʃəl] gießbachartig; Gießbach...; strömend; *fig.* ungestüm.

tor·rid ['tɔrid] dörrend; brennend heiß; ﹾ zone heiße Zone *f*.

tor·sion ['tɔːʃən] Drehung *f*; **tor·sion·al** ['ﹾ_ʃənl] Drehungs...

tor·so ['tɔːsəu] Torso *m*; Rumpf *m*; Bruchstück *n*.

tort ⚖ [tɔːt] Unrecht *n*.

tor·toise *zo.* ['tɔːtəs] Schildkröte *f*; ﹾ-shell ['tɔːtəʃel] Schildpatt *n*.

tor·tu·os·i·ty [tɔːtju'ɔsiti] Gewundenheit *f*; Windung *f*; **'tor·tu·ous** ☐ gewunden (*a. fig.*); *fig.* krumm.

tor·ture ['tɔːtʃə] 1. Folter *f*, Marter *f*, Tortur *f*, Qual *f*; 2. foltern, martern; **'tor·tur·er** Folterer *m*; Peiniger *m*.

To·ry ['tɔːri] 1. Tory *m* (*engl. Konservativer*); 2. konservativ; Tory...; **'To·ry·ism** Torytum *n*.

tosh *sl.* [tɔʃ] Quatsch *m*.

toss [tɔs] 1. Werfen *n*, Wurf *m*; Zurückwerfen *n des Kopfes*; Hochwerfen *n e-r Münze etc.*; win the ﹾ beim Losen gewinnen; 2. *v/t. a.* ﹾ about hin und her werfen; schütteln; (*in Verbindung mit adv.*) werfen; *a.* ﹾ up hochwerfen; ﹾ off *Getränk* hinunterstürzen; *Arbeit* hinhauen; ﹾ the oars ⚓ die Riemen pieken; *v/i.* sich hin und her werfen; geschüttelt werden; *a.* ﹾ up losen (*for* um); 'ﹾ-up Losen *n mit e-r Münze*; *fig. et.* Zweifelhaftes *n*; *it's a* ﹾ es ist fraglich.

tot¹ F [tɔt] Knirps *m* (*kleines Kind*); Schlückchen *n*.

tot² F [ﹾ] 1. (Gesamt)Summe *f*; 2. ﹾ up zs.-zählen; sich belaufen (*to auf acc.*).

to·tal ['təutl] 1. ☐ ganz, gänzlich; total; gesamt, Gesamt...; 2. Gesamtbetrag *m*, -summe *f*; grand ﹾ Endsumme *f*; 3. insgesamt betragen, sich belaufen auf (*acc.*); summieren; **to·tal·i·tar·i·an** [ﹾtæli'tɛəriən] totalitär; **to·tal·i'tar·i·an·ism** Totalitarismus *m*; **to'tal·i·ty** Gesamtheit *f*; Vollständigkeit *f*; **to·tal·i·za·tor** ['ﹾtəlaizeitə] Totalisator *m*; **to·tal·ize** ['ﹾtəlaiz] zs.-zählen.

tote F [təut] (mit sich) schleppen, tragen.

to·tem ['təutəm] Totem *n*; 'ﹾ-pole Totempfahl *m*.

tot·ter ['tɔtə] wanken, wackeln; **'tot·ter·ing** ☐, **'tot·ter·y** wack(e)lig.

touch [tʌtʃ] 1. *v/t.* be-, anrühren; (an)stoßen, stoßen an (*acc.*); betreffen; *fig.* rühren; erreichen; spielen, *Saiten* rühren; *Ton* anschlagen; färben; ﹾ one's hat to s.o. j. grüßen; ﹾ bottom auf Grund kommen; *fig.* den Tiefstpunkt erreichen; ﹾ the spot F gerade das Rechte sein; den Finger auf die Wunde legen; ﹾ s.o. for sl. j. anbetteln um; a bit ﹾed *fig.* ein bißchen verrückt; ﹾ off skizzieren; *Geschütz* abfeuern; *fig.* auslösen; ﹾ up auffrischen; *phot.* retuschieren; *v/i.* sich berühren; ﹾ at ⚓ anlegen bei *od.* in (*dat.*), berühren; ﹾ (up)on *fig.* berühren; (kurz) erwähnen, betreffen; 2. Berührung *f*; Gefühl(s-sinn *m*) *n*; Anfall *m von Krankheit*; Anflug *m*, Anstrich *m*, Zug *m*; Fertigkeit *f*, Hand *f*; ♪ Anschlag *m*; (Pinsel)Strich *m*; get in(to) ﹾ with sich in Verbindung setzen mit; to the ﹾ beim Anfassen; 'ﹾ-and-'go 1. gewagte Sache *f*; *it is* ﹾ es steht auf des Messers Schneide; 2. unsicher; riskant, gewagt; 'ﹾ-down ⚔ Aufsetzen *n*, Landung *f*; 'touch·i·ness Empfindlichkeit *f*; 'touch·ing 1. ☐ rührend; 2. *prp.* betreffend, in betreff; 'touch·line *Fußball:* Seiten-, Marklinie *f*; 'touch·stone Probierstein *m*; *fig.* Prüfstein *m*; 'touch-type blindschreiben; 'touch·y ☐ empfindlich; heikel; = testy.

tough [tʌf] **1.** zäh (*a. fig.*); unnachgiebig; schwer, hart, schwierig (*Arbeit etc.*); grob, brutal, übel; *a* ~ *customer* F ein übler Bursche *m*; **2.** schwerer Junge *m*; '**tough·en** zäh machen *od.* werden; '**tough·ie** F ['tʌfi] = *tough* 2; '**tough·ness** Zähigkeit *f*.

tour [tuə] **1.** (Rund)Reise *f*, Tour (-nee) *f*; *conducted* ~ Führung *f*; ~ *operator* Reiseveranstalter *m*; **2.** (be)reisen; **tour·ing** ['tuəriŋ] Reise..., Touren...; ~ *car mot.* Touren-, Reisewagen *m*; '**tour·ism** Tourismus *m*; '**tour·ist** Tourist(in), (Vergnügungs)Reisende *m*; ~ *agency*, ~ *office*, ~ *bureau* Reisebüro *n*; ~ *industry* Fremdenindustrie *f*; ~ *season* Reisezeit *f*; ~ *ticket* Rundreisekarte *f*.

tour·ma·line *min.* ['tuəməlin] Turmalin *m*.

tour·na·ment ['tuənəmənt], **tour·ney** ['ˌni] Turnier *n*. [presse *f*.\
tour·ni·quet ⚕ ['tuənikei] Ader-/
tou·sle ['tauzl] (zer)zausen.

tout [taut] **1.** Schlepper *m*, (Kunden)Werber *m*; **2.** Kunden werben, schleppen.

tow¹ ⚓ [təu] **1.** Schleppen *n*; Schleppzug *m*; *take in* ~ ins Schlepptau nehmen; **2.** (ab)schleppen; treideln; ziehen.

tow² [ˌ] Werg *n zum Spinnen*.

tow·age ⚓ ['təuidʒ] Schleppen *n*, Bugsieren *n*; Schleppgebühr *f*.

to·ward(s) [tə'wɔ:d(z), tɔ:d(z)] gegen; nach ... zu, auf ... (*acc.*) zu; (als Beitrag) zu.

tow·bar *mot.* ['tɔubɑ:] Anhängerkupplung *f*.

tow·el ['tauəl] **1.** Handtuch *n*; **2.** abreiben; *sl. j-m* e-e Abreibung geben (*prügeln*); ~ **dis·pens·er** Handtuchautomat *m*; 'ˌ**horse** Handtuchständer *m*; 'ˌ**rack** Handtuchhalter *m*.

tow·er ['tauə] **1.** Turm *m*; *fig.* Hort *m*, Bollwerk *n*; **2.** sich (empor)türmen, sich erheben; ~ *above mst fig.* überragen; ~ **block** Hochhaus *n*; '**tow·ered** hochgetürmt; '**tow·er·ing** □ turmhoch; *fig.* hoch; rasend (*Wut*).

tow(·ing)... ['təu(iŋ)]... 'ˌ**line** Schlepptau *n*; 'ˌ**path** Treidelpfad *m*.

town [taun] **1.** Stadt *f*; *man about* ~ Lebemann *m*; **2.** Stadt...; städtisch; ~ **cen·tre**, *Am.* ~ **cen·ter** Behördenviertel *n*; ~ **clerk** Stadtsyndikus

m; ~ **coun·cil** Stadtrat *m* (*Versammlung*); ~ **coun·cil·lor** Stadtrat *m* (*Person*); ~ **cri·er** Ausrufer *m*; ~ **hall** Rathaus *n*; 'ˌ'**plan·ning** Städtebau *m*, -planung *f*; ~**scape** ['ˌskeip] Stadtbild *n*.

towns·folk ['taunzfəuk] Stadtleute *pl.*, Städter *m/pl.*

town·ship ['taunʃip] Stadtgemeinde *f*; Stadtgebiet *n*.

towns·man ['taunzmən] Bürger *m*; *univ.* Philister *m*; *fellow* ~ Mitbürger *m*; '**towns·people** = *townsfolk*.

tow...: 'ˌ**path** Treidelpfad *m*; 'ˌ**rope** Schlepptau *n*; ~ **truck** *mot.* Abschleppwagen *m*.

tox·ic, tox·i·cal □ ['tɔksik(əl)] giftig, toxisch, Gift...; **tox·in** ['tɔksin] Toxin *n*, Giftstoff *m*.

toy [tɔi] **1.** Spielzeug *n*; Tand *m*; ~*s pl.* Spielwaren *f/pl.*; **2.** Spiel(zeug)...; Miniatur...; Zwerg...; **3.** spielen (*mst fig.*); 'ˌ**book** Bilderbuch *n*; 'ˌ**box** Spielzeugschachtel *f*; 'ˌ**shop** Spielwarenhandlung *f*.

trace¹ [treis] **1.** Spur *f* (*a. fig.*); Grundriß *m*; **2.** nachspüren (*dat.*); *fig.* verfolgen; auf-, herausfinden, ausfindig machen; *et.* feststellen, nachweisen; (auf)zeichnen; (durch-)pausen; *surv.* abstecken; ~ *back et.* zurückverfolgen (*to* bis zu); ~ *out* aufspüren.

trace² [ˌ] Strang *m*, Zugtau *n*; *kick over the* ~*s fig.* über die Stränge schlagen.

trace·a·ble □ ['treisəbl] zurückzuverfolgen(d); nachweisbar; **trace el·e·ment** Spurenelement *n*; '**trac·er** *a.* ~ *ammunition* Leuchtspurmunition *f*; *a.* ~ *element* Isotopenindikator *m*; '**trac·er·y** ⛪ Maßwerk *n an gotischen Fenstern*.

tra·che·a *anat.* [trə'ki:ə] Luftröhre *f*.

trac·ing ['treisiŋ] Aufzeichnung *f*; Durchpausen *f*; Pauszeichnung *f*; 'ˌ**pa·per** Pauspapier *n*.

track [træk] **1.** Spur *f*; *bsd. Sport*: Bahn *f*; Rennstrecke *f*; Pfad *m*; Geleise *n* (*a.* 🚂); *hunt.* Fährte *f*; ⊕ Raupenkette *f*; ~ *events pl.* Lauf (-disziplinen *f/pl.*) *m*; **2.** *v/t.* nachspüren (*dat.*); verfolgen; ~ *down*, ~ *out* aufspüren; *v/i.* Spur halten; 'ˌ**and-**-'**field** *sports* Leichtathletik *f*; **tracked ve·hi·cle** Raupenfahrzeug *n*; '**track·er** *bsd. hunt.* Spurhalter *m*; Verfolger(in); '**track·ing** **sta-**

tion *Raumfahrt*: Bodenstation *f*; **'track·less** spur-, pfadlos; ⊕ schienenlos; **track suit** Trainingsanzug *m*.

tract¹ [trækt] Fläche *f*, Strecke *f*, Gegend *f*; *anat.* Trakt *m*.

tract² [⌣] Traktat *m*, *n*, Abhandlung *f*.

trac·ta·bil·i·ty [træktə'biliti], **'trac·ta·ble·ness** Lenksamkeit *f*; **'trac·ta·ble** □ lenk-, fügsam.

trac·tion ['trækʃən] Ziehen *n*, Zug *m*; ~ *engine* Zugmaschine *f*; **'trac·tive** Zug...; **'trac·tor** ⊕ Trecker *m*, Zugmaschine *f*, Schlepper *m*, Traktor *m*.

trade [treid] **1.** Handel *m*; Geschäft *n*; Gewerbe *n*; Handwerk *n*; *Am.* Schiebung *f*, Kompensationsgeschäft *n*; *Board of* ♀ Handelsministerium *n*; *the* ♀*s pl.* ⚓ die Passatwinde *m/pl.*; *do a good* ~ gute Geschäfte machen; **2.** *v/i.* Handel treiben; handeln (*with* mit *j-m*; *in* mit *e-r Ware*); ~ *on* ⊦ reisen auf (*acc.*), ausnutzen; *v/t.* tauschen (*for* gegen); ~ *s.th. in* et. in Zahlung geben; ~ **cy·cle** Konjunkturzyklus *m*; **'~·fair** ♱ Messe *f*; ~ **mark** Warenzeichen *n*, Schutzmarke *f*; ~ **name** Firmenname *m*; Warenbezeichnung *f*; ~ **price** Händlerpreis *m*; **'trad·er** Händler *m*; Handelsschiff *n*; **trade re·la·tions** *pl.* Handelsbeziehungen *f/pl.*; **trade school** Gewerbeschule *f*; **trade se·cret** Geschäfts- *od.* Betriebsgeheimnis *n*; **trade show** Filmvorführung *f* für Verleiher u. Kritiker; **trades·man** ['⌣zmən] Händler *m*, Geschäftsmann *m*; **'trades·peo·ple** Geschäftsleute *pl.*; **trade un·ion** Gewerkschaft *f*; **trade·'un·ion·ism** Gewerkschaftswesen *n*; **trade·'un·ion·ist 1.** Gewerkschaftler *m*; **2.** gewerkschaftlich; **trade war** Handelskrieg *m*; **trade wind** ⚓ Passatwind *m*.

trad·ing ['treidiŋ] Handels...

tra·di·tion [trə'diʃən] Tradition *f*, Überlieferung *f*; alter Brauch *m*; **tra'di·tion·al** □ [⌣ʃənl], **tra·'di·tion·ar·y** [⌣ʃnəri] □ traditionell, überliefert; herkömmlich.

traf·fic ['træfik] **1.** Verkehr *m*; Handel *m*; **2.** handeln (*in* mit); **traf·fi·ca·tor** ['⌣keitə] *mot.* Winker *m*; **traf·fic cone** *mot.* Leitkegel *m*; **traf·fic jam** Verkehrsstauung *f*;

'traf·fick·er Händler *m*, *b.s.* Schacherer *m*; **traf·fic light** Verkehrsampel *f*; **traf·fic news** *pl.* Verkehrsmeldungen *f/pl.*; **traf·fic war·den** Politesse *f*.

tra·ge·di·an [trə'dʒi:djən] Tragiker *m*; *thea.* Tragöde *m*, Tragödin *f*; **trag·e·dy** ['trædʒidi] Tragödie *f* (*a. fig.*); Trauerspiel *n*.

trag·ic, trag·i·cal □ ['trædʒik(əl)] tragisch (*a. fig.*).

trag·i·com·e·dy ['trædʒi'kɔmidi] Tragikomödie *f*; **trag·i'com·ic** (⌣*ally*) tragikomisch.

trail [treil] **1.** *fig.* Schwanz *m*, Schweif *m*; Schleppe *f*; Spur *f*, *hunt.* Fährte *f*; Pfad *m*; ~ *of smoke* Rauchfahne *f*; **2.** *v/t.* hinter sich (her)ziehen; auf der Spur verfolgen; *v/i.* (sich) schleppen; (sich) hin)ziehen; ♀ kriechen; wehen, flattern; ~ **blaz·er** *Am.* Pistensucher *m*; Bahnbrecher *m*; **'trail·er** (Wohnwagen)Anhänger *m*; ♀ Kriechpflanze *f*; *Film:* Voranzeige *f*, Vorschau *f*.

train [trein] **1.** (Eisenbahn)Zug *m*; *allg.* Zug *m*; Gefolge *n*; Reihe *f*, Folge *f*, Kette *f*; Schleppe *f am Kleid*; **2.** *v/t.* erziehen; schulen; abrichten; ausbilden; einexerzieren; *Sport:* trainieren; *Geschütz* richten; *v/i.* (sich) üben; trainieren; *a.* ~ *it* ⊦ mit der Eisenbahn fahren; **'~·ac·ci·dent, '~·dis·as·ter** Eisenbahnunglück *n*; **train'ee** in der Ausbildung Begriffene *m*; **'train·er** Ausbilder *m*; Zureiter *m*; Trainer *m*; **'train-'fer·ry** Eisenbahnfähre *f*.

train·ing ['treiniŋ] Ausbildung *f*; Übung *f*; *Sport:* Training *n*; *physical* ~ körperliche Ertüchtigung *f*; **'~·col·lege** Lehrerbildungsanstalt *f*; **'~·ship** Schulschiff *n*.

train-oil ['treinɔil] Fischtran *m*.

trait [treit] (Charakter)Zug *m*.

trai·tor ['treitə] Verräter *m* (*to an dat.*); **'trai·tor·ous** □ verräterisch.

trai·tress ['treitris] Verräterin *f*.

tra·jec·to·ry *phys.* ['trædʒiktəri] Flugbahn *f*.

tram [træm] ⚒ Förderwagen *m*, Hund *m*; ~ *car*, ~ *way*; '**~·car** Straßenbahnwagen *m*; '**~·line** Straßenbahnlinie *f*.

tram·mel ['træml] **1.** Art Fischnetz *n*; ~*s pl. fig.* Fesseln *f/pl.*; **2.** fesseln,

translate

hemmen.

tramp [træmp] **1.** Getrampel *n*; (schwerer) Tritt *m*; Wanderung *f*; Tramp *m*; Landstreicher *m*; *a.* ~ *steamer* Trampschiff *n*; *on the* ~ auf der Wanderschaft; **2.** *v/i.* trampeln, treten; (zu Fuß) wandern; *v/t.* durchwandern; **tram·ple** ['~l] (zer)trampeln.

tram·way ['træmwei] Straßenbahn *f*.

trance [trɑːns] Trance *f*, (hypnotischer) Traumzustand *m*; Verzückung *f*.

tran·ny *sl.* ['træni] Kofferradio *n*.

tran·quil ☐ ['træŋkwil] ruhig; gelassen; **tran'quil·(l)i·ty** Ruhe *f*; Gelassenheit *f*; **tran·quil·i·za·tion** [~lai'zeiʃən] Beruhigung *f*; **'tran·quil·(l)ize** beruhigen; **'tran·quil·(l)i·zer** Beruhigungsmittel *n*, Sedativum *n*.

trans·act [træn'zækt] abwickeln; abmachen; ~ *business* Geschäfte machen; **trans'ac·tion** Verrichtung *f*; Geschäft *n*, Transaktion *f*; ~s *pl.* (Sitzungs-, Tätigkeits)Bericht(e *pl.*) *m*.

trans·al·pine ['trænz'ælpain] transalpin(isch).

trans·at·lan·tic ['trænzət'læntik] transatlantisch, Transatlantik...

tran·scend [træn'send] überschreiten, -steigen; -treffen; hinausgehen über (*acc.*); **tran'scend·ence, tran'scend·en·cy** Überlegenheit *f*; *phls.* Transzendenz *f*; **tran'scend·ent** ☐ überragend, vorzüglich; *a.* = **tran·scen·den·tal** ☐ [~'dentl] *A* transzendent; *phls.* transzendental; P phantastisch.

trans·con·ti·nen·tal ['trænzkɔnti-'nentl] transkontinental.

tran·scribe [træns'kraib] abschreiben; *Kurzschrift* umschreiben; *♪* umsetzen; *Radio:* aufnehmen.

tran·script ['trænskript] Abschrift *f*; **tran'scrip·tion** Abschreiben *n*; Umschrift *f*; *♪* Umsetzung *f*; *Radio:* Aufnahme *f*.

tran·sept△ ['trænsept] Querschiff *n*.

trans·fer 1. [træns'fəː] *v/t.* übertragen (*bsd.* ⚖, to auf *acc.*); versetzen, verlegen (*to* nach; *in, into* in *acc.*); *Druck, Stich etc.* umdrucken; *v/i.* übertreten; **2.** ['~] Übertragung *f* (*bsd.* ⚖); *✝* Transfer *m*, Überweisung *f*, Versetzung *f*, Verlegung *f*; Abzug *m*, Umdruck *m*; Abziehbild *n*; Umsteiger *m* (*Fahrschein*); **trans'fer·a·ble** übertragbar *etc.*; **trans·fer·ee** ⚖ [~fə'riː] Zessionar *m*, Übernehmer *m*; **trans·fer·ence** ['~fərəns] Übertragung *f*; **'trans·fer fee** Ablösesumme *f für e-n Sportler*; **'trans·fer·or** ⚖ Zedent *m*; **trans·fer·pic·ture** ['~fəːpiktʃə] Abziehbild *n*.

trans·fig·u·ra·tion [trænsfigjuə-'reiʃən] Umgestaltung *f*; Verklärung *f*; **trans·fig·ure** [~'figə] umgestalten; verklären.

trans·fix [træns'fiks] durchstecken; ~ed *fig.* versteinert, starr (*with* vor *dat.*).

trans·form [træns'fɔːm] umformen; um-, verwandeln; umgestalten; **trans·for·ma·tion** [~fə'meiʃən] Umformung *f*; Um-, Verwandlung *f*; Haarersatz *m*; **trans·form·er** *⚡* [~'fɔːmə] Umformer *m*, Transformator *m*.

trans·fuse [træns'fjuːz] *⚕* Blut *etc.* übertragen (*into* in, auf *acc.*); *fig.* einflößen (*dat.*); *fig.* durchtränken (*with* mit); **trans'fu·sion** [~ʒən] (*bsd.* ⚕ Blut)Übertragung *f*, Transfusion *f*.

trans·gress [træns'gres] *v/t.* überschreiten; übertreten, verletzen; *v/i.* sich vergehen; **trans'gres·sion** Überschreitung *f etc.*; Vergehen *n*; **trans'gres·sor** [~sə] Übertreter *m*.

tran·sience, tran·sien·cy ['trænziəns(i)] Vergänglichkeit *f*.

tran·sient ['trænziənt] **1.** *zeitlich* vorübergehend; vergänglich, flüchtig; **2.** *Am.* Durchreisende *m*.

tran·sis·tor [trən'zistə] Transistor *m*; ~ (*radio*) Transistor-, Kofferradio *n*.

trans·it ['trænsit] Durchgang *m*; Durchgangsverkehr *m*; *in* ~ unterwegs, auf dem Transport; ~ **camp** Durchgangslager *n*.

tran·si·tion [træn'siʒən] Übergang *m*; **tran·si·tion·al** ☐ [~ʒənl] Übergangs...; e-n Übergang bildend.

tran·si·tive ☐ *gr.* ['trænsitiv] transitiv.

tran·si·to·ri·ness ['trænsitərinis] Vergänglichkeit *f*, Flüchtigkeit *f*; **'tran·si·to·ry** ☐ vergänglich, flüchtig.

trans·lat·a·ble [træns'leitəbl] übersetzbar; **trans·late** *Buch etc.* über-

translation

setzen, -tragen; *fig.* umsetzen, -arbeiten (*into* in *acc.*, zu); *Geistliche* versetzen; entrücken; **trans·'la·tion** Übersetzung *f etc.*; **trans'la·tor** Übersetzer(in).

trans·lu·cence, trans·lu·cen·cy [trænz'luːsns(i)] Durchscheinen *n*; **trans'lu·cent** durchscheinend; *fig.* hell.

trans·ma·rine [trænzmə'riːn] überseeisch.

trans·mi·grant ['trænzmigrənt] Durchwanderer *m*; **trans·mi·grate** ['trænzmai'greit] (aus)wandern; *fig.* wandern (*Seele*); **trans·mi·gra·tion** (Aus)Wanderung *f*; ~ *of souls* Seelenwanderung *f*.

trans·mis·si·ble [trænz'misəbl] übertragbar; **trans'mis·sion** Übermittlung *f*, *biol.* Vererbung *f*; *phys.* Fortpflanzung *f*; ⊕ Transmission *f*; *mot.* Getriebe *n*; *Radio:* Übertragung *f*, Sendung *f*.

trans·mit [trænz'mit] übermitteln, -senden; übertragen; *tel.*, *Radio:* senden; *biol.* vererben; *phys.* fortpflanzen; **trans'mit·ter** Übermittler(in); *tel. etc.* Sender *m*; **trans'mit·ting** *Radio:* Sende...; ~ *station* Sendestelle *f*.

trans·mog·ri·fy F [trænz'mɔgrifai] umkrempeln.

trans·mut·a·ble □ [trænz'mjuːtəbl] umwandelbar; **trans·mu·ta·tion** Um-, Verwandlung *f*; **trans'mute** um-, verwandeln.

trans·o·ce·an·ic ['trænzəuʃi'ænik] überseeisch; Ozean...

tran·som △ ['trænsəm] Querholz *n*; Oberlicht *n*.

trans·par·en·cy [træns'pɛərənsi] Durchsichtigkeit *f*; Transparent *n*; Dia(positiv) *n*; **trans'par·ent** □ durchsichtig (*a. fig.*).

tran·spi·ra·tion [trænspi'reiʃən] Ausdünstung *f*; **tran·spire** [~'paiə] ausdünsten, -schwitzen; *fig.* durchsickern, verlauten; V passieren.

trans·plant [træns'plɑːnt] um-, verpflanzen; **trans·plan·ta·tion** Verpflanzung *f*.

trans·port 1. [træns'pɔːt] fortschaffen, befördern, transportieren; *fig.* hinreißen, entzücken; **2.** ['~] Fortschaffen *n*; Beförderung *f*; Transport *m*; Verkehr *m*; Beförderungsmittel *n*; Transportschiff *n*;

Entzücken *n*; *Minister of* ♀ Verkehrsminister *m*; *in* ~*s* (*vor Freude od. Wut*) außer sich; **trans'port·a·ble** transportabel; **trans·por·'ta·tion** Beförderung *f*, Fortschaffung *f*, Versendung *f*, Transport *m*.

trans·pose [træns'pəuz] versetzen, umstellen; ♪ transponieren; **trans·po·si·tion** [~pə'ziʃən] Umstellung *f*; ♪ Transposition *f*.

trans·ship ⚓, 🚂 [træns'ʃip] umladen.

tran·sub·stan·ti·ate [trænsəb'stænʃieit] stofflich umwandeln; *eccl. Brot u. Wein* verwandeln; **'tran·sub·stan·ti·a·tion** Stoffverwandlung *f*; *eccl.* Transsubstantiation *f*.

trans·ver·sal [trænz'vəːsəl] **1.** □ quer hindurchgehend; **2.** ⅄ Transversale *f*; **'trans·verse** □ quer laufend; Quer...; ~ *section* Querschnitt *m*; ~ *strength* ⊕ Querbiegefestigkeit *f*.

trap¹ [træp] **1.** Falle *f* (*a. fig.*); Klappe *f*; Wurfmaschine (*bsd. beim Tontaubenschießen*); ⊕ Wasserverschluß *m*; Geruchverschluß *m*; Gig *n* (*leichte Kutsche*); = ~*door*; **2.** (*in e-r Falle*) fangen, in die Falle locken; *fig.* ertappen; mit Fallen besetzen; ⊕ mit Wasserverschluß versehen.

trap² *min.* [~] Trapp *m*.

trap·door ['træp'dɔː] Falltür *f*; *thea.* Versenkung *f*.

trapes F [treips] latschen.

tra·peze [trə'piːz] *Zirkus:* Trapez *n*; **tra·pe·zi·um** ⅄ [~zjəm] Trapez *n*; **trap·e·zoid** ⅄ ['træpizɔid] Trapezoid *n*.

trap·per ['træpə] Trapper *m*, Pelzjäger *m*.

trap·pings ['træpinz] *pl.* Paradegeschirr *n e-s Pferdes*; Schabracke *f*; *fig.* Schmuck *m*, Putz *m*.

trap·pist *eccl.* ['træpist] Trappist *m*.

trap·py ['træpi] heimtückisch.

traps F [træps] *pl.* Siebensachen *pl.*

trash [træʃ] Abfall *m*; *fig.* Plunder *m*; Unsinn *m*, Blech *n*; Kitsch *m*; ~ **can** *Am.* Mülltonne *f*; **'trash·y** □ wertlos, kitschig.

trau·ma ['trɔːmə] Trauma *n*; **trau·mat·ic** [~'mætik] traumatisch; ~ *experience psych.* traumatisches Erlebnis *n*; ~ *medicine* Unfallmedizin *f*.

trav·ail † ['træveil] (Geburts-)

Wehen pl.

trav·el ['trævl] **1.** v/i. bsd. weit reisen (a. ✝); weitS. sich bewegen; wandern; v/t. bereisen, durchwandern; **2.** das Reisen; ⊕ Lauf m, Bewegung f; ∿s pl. Reisen f/pl.; ∿ **a·gen·cy,** ∿ **a·gent's** Reisebüro n; ∿ **al·low·ance** Reise-, Fahrtkostenzuschuß m.

trav·e·la·tor ['trævəleitə] rollender Gehsteig m (Beförderungsband für Fußgänger); **'trav·el(l)ed** weitgereist; **'trav·el·(l)er** Reisende m (a. ✝); ⊕ Laufkran m, Läufer m; ∿'s cheque Reisescheck m; **'trav·el-(l)ing** Reise...; ⊕ Lauf...; ∿ allowance = travel allowance; ∿ rug Reisedecke f; ∿ salesman Handlungsreisende m.

trav·e·log(ue) ['trævələg] Reisebericht m (Lichtbildervortrag).

trav·erse ['trævə:s] **1.** Durchquerung f; mount. Quergang m; 𝔯 Bestreitung f; ✖ Querwall m; ⊕ Querstück n; **2.** v/t. (über-) queren; durchqueren, -ziehen; fig. durchkreuzen; 𝔯 bestreiten; Geschütz (seitwärts) schwenken; v/i. mount. queren.

trav·es·ty ['trævisti] **1.** Travestie f; Karikatur f; Zerrbild n; **2.** travestieren (scherzhaft umgestalten); verulken.

trawl [trɔ:l] **1.** (Grund)Schleppnetz n; **2.** mit dem Schleppnetz fischen; **'trawl·er** Trawler m.

tray [trei] (Servier)Brett n, Tablett n; Ablegekasten m, Ablage f; pen-∿ Federschale f.

treach·er·ous □ ['tretʃərəs] verräterisch, treulos; (heim)tückisch; trügerisch (Wetter, Gedächtnis etc.); **'treach·er·ous·ness, 'treach·er·y** Verrat m, Verräterei f, Treulosigkeit f; Tücke f.

trea·cle ['tri:kl] Sirup m; Melasse f; **'treac·ly** sirupartig; fig. zuckersüß.

tread [tred] **1.** (irr.) v/i. treten (on, upon auf acc.); einhertreten, schreiten; v/t. treten (a. vom Hahn); rhet. betreten; **2.** Tritt m, Schritt m; Hahnentritt m; Trittstufe f; Lauffläche f e-s Rades etc.; **trea·dle** ['∿dl] **1.** Pedal n, Tritt m; **2.** treten; **'tread·mill** Tretmühle f.

trea·son ['tri:zn] Verrat m; **'trea-son·a·ble** □ verräterisch (bsd. Sache).

treas·ure ['treʒə] **1.** Schatz m,

Reichtum m; ∿s of the soil Bodenschätze m/pl.; ∿-house Schatzkammer f; ∿ hunt Schatzsuche f; ∿ trove Schatzfund m; **2.** oft ∿ up Schätze sammeln, aufhäufen; fig. schätzen; **'treas·ur·er** Schatzmeister m, Kassenwart m.

treas·ur·y ['treʒəri] Schatzkammer f; (bsd. Staats)Schatz m; ♀ (Board), Am. ♀ Department Finanzministerium n; ♀ **Bench** parl. Ministerbank f; ∿ **bill** Schatzwechsel m; ∿ **note** Kassenschein m (Papiergeld).

treat [tri:t] **1.** v/t. behandeln; betrachten; ∿ s.o. to s.th. j-m et. spendieren; ∿ o.s. to s.th. sich et. genehmigen; v/i. ∿ of handeln von, et. behandeln; ∿ with unterhandeln mit (for über acc.); **2.** (Extra-) Vergnügen n, Hochgenuß m; school ∿ Schulausflug m; it is my ∿ F es geht auf meine Rechnung; stand ∿ F (die Zeche) bezahlen; **trea·tise** ['∿tiz] Abhandlung f; **'treat·ment** Behandlung f; **'trea·ty** Vertrag m; be in ∿ with in Unterhandlung stehen mit; ∿ port Vertragshafen m.

tre·ble ['trebl] **1.** □ dreifach; ♪ Diskant...; **2.** Dreifache n; ♪ Diskant m, Sopran m; **3.** (sich) verdreifachen; ∿ **con·trol** Radio: Höhenregler m.

tree [tri:] **1.** Baum m; s. family; at the top of the ∿ fig. auf der höchsten Stufe; up a ∿ F in der Klemme; **2.** auf e-n Baum treiben; fig. in die Enge treiben; **'tree·less** baumlos; **'tree·top** Baumkrone f, -wipfel m. **tre·foil** ['trefoil] ♧ Klee m; ⚑ Kleeblatt n.

trek [trek] Südafrika: **1.** trecken, (im Ochsenwagen) reisen od. ziehen; **2.** Treck m.

trel·lis ['trelis] **1.** ⚘ Spalier n; **2.** vergittern; ⚘ am Spalier ziehen. **trem·ble** ['trembl] **1.** zittern (at bei; with vor dat.); **2.** Zittern n. **tre·men·dous** □ [tri'mendəs] schrecklich, furchtbar; F kolossal, riesig, fürchterlich, ungeheuer. **trem·or** ['tremə] Zittern n, Beben n. **trem·u·lous** □ ['tremjuləs] zitternd, bebend; **'trem·u·lous·ness** Zittern n, Beben n.

trench [trentʃ] **1.** Graben m; fig. Furche f; ✖ Schützengraben m;

~ *warfare* Grabenkrieg *m*; **2.** *v/t.*
mit Gräben durchziehen; *fig.*
durchfurchen; ✗ umgraben; *v/i.*
✗ Gräben ausheben; ~ (*up*)*on* eingreifen in (*acc.*); *fig.* hart grenzen
an (*acc.*); **'trench·ant** □ schneidend, scharf; bündig, markig
(*Sprache*); **trench coat** Wettermantel *m*, Trenchcoat *m*.

trench·er ['trentʃə] Schneidebrett *n*;
fig. Tafel *f*; ~ **cap** Studentenmütze *f*.

trend [trend] **1.** Richtung *f*; *fig.*
Lauf *m*; *fig.* Strömung *f*; Tendenz
f; **2.** sich erstrecken, laufen; '~
-set·ter *Mode*: Schrittmacher *m*;
'trend·y modisch, im Trend; *be* ~ als
schick gelten; ,in' sein; *the trendies pl.*
die Schickeria.

tre·pan [tri'pæn] **1.** ✍ *hist.* Schädelbohrer *m*; **2.** ✍ trepanieren; ⊕ anfräsen.

trep·i·da·tion [trepi'deiʃən] Zittern
n, Beben *n*; Bestürzung *f*.

tres·pass ['trespəs] **1.** Vergehen *n*,
Übertretung *f*; unbefugtes Betreten *n od.* Verletzen *n fremden
Eigentums*; Eingriff *m*; **2.** unbefugt
eindringen (*on*, *upon* in *fremdes
Eigentum etc.*); *Zeit etc.* über Gebühr in Anspruch nehmen; **'tres-pass·er** Rechtsverletzer *m*; unbefugter Eindringling *m*; ~*s will be
prosecuted* unbefugtes Betreten bei
Strafe verboten.

tress [tres] Haarlocke *f*, -flechte *f*.

tres·tle ['tresl] Gestell *n*, Bock *m*;
~ *bridge* Bockbrücke *f*.

trey [trei] Drei *f im Karten- u.
Würfelspiel.*

tri·ad ['traiəd] Dreizahl *f*, Triade *f*.

tri·al ['traiəl] Versuch *m* (*of* mit);
Probe *f*, Prüfung (*f*); *fig.* Prüfung *f*,
Plage *f*; ⚖ Verhandlung *f*, Prozeß
m, (Gerichts)Verfahren *n*; ~ *match*
Sichtungsspiel *n*; *on* ~ auf Probe;
vor Gericht; *prisoner on* ~ Untersuchungsgefangene *m*, *f*; ~ *of
strength* Kraftprobe *f*; *bring to* ~
vor Gericht bringen; *give s.o. od.
s.th. a* ~ es mit j-m *od.* e-r Sache
versuchen; *send for* ~ vor Gericht
stellen; *stand* ~ sich (vor Gericht)
verantworten (*for* wegen); ~ **marriage** Ehe *f* auf Probe; ~ **of·fer**
Einführungsangebot *n*; ~ **pe·ri·od**
Probezeit *f*; ~ **run** Probefahrt *f*.

tri·an·gle ['traiæŋgl] Dreieck *n*; ♪

Triangel *m*; **tri·an·gu·lar** □
[~'æŋgjulə] dreieckig; **tri'an·gulate** *surv.* [~leit] triangulieren.

trib·al □ ['traibəl] den Stamm betreffend; Stammes...; **tribe** Stamm
m; Geschlecht *n*; *bsd. contp.* Zunft
f, Sippe *f*; ♥, *zo.* Klasse *f*; **tribes-man** ['~zmən] Stammesangehörige
m, -genosse *m*.

trib·u·la·tion [tribju'leiʃən] Drangsal *f*, Leiden *n*.

tri·bu·nal [tri'bju:nl] Richterstuhl
m; Gericht(shof *m*) *n*; Tribunal *n*
(*a. fig.*); **'trib·une** Tribun *m*;
Tribüne *f*.

trib·u·tar·y ['tribjutəri] **1.** □ zinspflichtig; *fig.* helfend; *weitS.* untergeordnet; Neben...; **2.** Tributpflichtige *m*; Nebenfluß *m*; **trib-ute** ['~bju:t] Tribut *m*, Zins *m*;
fig. Tribut *m*, Zoll *m*; Anerkennung *f*; Hochachtung *f*; Huldigung *f*.

trice¹ [trais]: *in a* ~ im Nu.

trice² [~]: ~ *up* aufwinden.

tri·chi·na *zo.* [tri'kainə] Trichine *f*.

trick [trik] **1.** Kniff *m*, Pfiff *m*, List *f*,
Trick *m*; Kunstgriff *m*, -stück *n*;
Streich *m*, Possen *m*; Eigenheit *f*;
Karten: Stich *m*; ~ *film* Trickfilm
m; **2.** betrügen (*out of* um); hereinlegen; verleiten (*into* zu); ~ *out*,
~ *up* herausputzen; **'trick·er**,
trick·ster ['~stə] Gauner *m*, Betrüger *m*, Schwindler *m*; **'trick·er·y**
Betrügerei *f*; **'trick·ish** □ betrügerisch; verschmitzt.

trick·le ['trikl] **1.** tröpfeln, rieseln;
F *fig.* spritzen (*schnell gehen*);
2. Tröpfeln *n*; Tropfen *m*.

trick·si·ness ['triksinis] Mutwilligkeit *f*; **'trick·sy** □ mutwillig; =
'trick·y □ verschlagen; F heikel;
verzwickt, knifflig, verwickelt,
schwierig.

tri·col·o(u)r ['trikələ] Trikolore *f*.

tri·cy·cle ['traisikl] Dreirad *n*.

tri·dent ['traidənt] Dreizack *m*.

tri·en·ni·al □ [trai'enjəl] dreijährig;
dreijährlich.

tri·er ['traiə] Untersucher *m*, Prüfer *m*.

tri·fle ['traifl] **1.** Kleinigkeit *f*; Lappalie *f*; *Küche*: Biskuitauflauf *m*;
a ~ ein bißchen, ein wenig, etwas;
2. *v/i.* spielen, spaßen, scherzen;
v/t. ~ *away* vertrödeln, verschwenden; **'tri·fler** oberflächlicher

Mensch *m*.

tri·fling ['traifliŋ] □ geringfügig; unbedeutend.

trig[1] [trig] **1.** hemmen; ˷ *up* stützen; **2.** Hemmschuh *m*.

trig[2] [˷] schmuck; fest.

trig·ger ['trigə] **1.** Abzug *m am Gewehr*; *phot.* Auslöser *m*; **2.** ˷ *off fig.* auslösen; **'˷-hap·py** schießwütig; kriegslüstern; *be* ˷ (*a. fig.*) gleich losschießen.

trig·o·no·met·ric, trig·o·no·met·ri·cal □ Ⱥ [trigənə'metrik(əl)] trigonometrisch; **trig·o·nom·e·try** Ⱥ [˷'nɔmitri] Trigonometrie *f*.

tri·lat·er·al □ Ⱥ ['trai'lætərəl] dreiseitig.

tril·by F ['trilbi] großer Schlapphut *m*.

tri·lin·gual □ ['trai'liŋgwəl] dreisprachig.

trill [tril] **1.** Triller *m*; gerolltes R *n*; **2.** trillern; *bsd.* das R rollen.

tril·lion ['triljən] Trillion *f*; *Am.* Billion *f*.

tril·o·gy ['trilədʒi] Trilogie *f*.

trim [trim] **1.** □ ordentlich; schmuck; gepflegt (*Bart etc.*); **2.** (richtiger) Zustand *m*; Ordnung *f*; ⚓ richtige Lage *f od.* Stellung *f*; (richtige) Verfassung *f*; Putz *m*, Staat *m*; *in* (*out of*) ˷ in guter (schlechter) Verfassung; **3.** *v/i.* in Ordnung bringen, zurechtmachen; (*up* heraus)putzen, schmücken; *Kleid etc.* besetzen; *Bart etc.* stutzen; *Hecke etc.* beschneiden; *Lampe* putzen; 🖝, ⚓ trimmen (*gleichmäßig verteilen*); *v/i. fig.* schwanken, lavieren; **'trim·mer** Putzer(in); ⚓ Trimmer *m*; *pol.* Achselträger *m*; **'trim·ming** Putzen *n*; *mst* ˷*s pl.* Besatz *m*, Garnierung *f*; **'trim·ness** gute Ordnung *f*; gutes Aussehen *n*, Gepflegtheit *f*.

tri·mo·tor ['traimɔutə] dreimotoriges Flugzeug *n*; **'tri·mo·tored** dreimotorig.

Trin·i·ty ['triniti] Dreieinigkeit *f*.

trin·ket ['triŋkit] wertloses Schmuckstück *n*; ˷*s pl.* Kinkerlitzchen *pl.*

tri·o ♪ ['tri:ɔu] Trio *n*.

trip [trip] **1.** Reise *f*, Fahrt *f*; Ausflug *m*, Spritztour *f*; Stolpern *n*, Fallen *n*; Fehltritt *m* (*a. fig.*); ˷ *of the tongue* Versprechen *n*; **2.** *v/i.* trip-

peln, tänzeln; stolpern (*over* über *acc.*); e-n Fehltritt tun (*a. fig.*); *fig.* e-n Fehler *od.* Fauxpas machen; *catch s.o.* ˷*ping j.* bei e-m Fehler ertappen; *v/t. a.* ˷ *up j-m* ein Bein stellen (*a. fig.*).

tri·par·tite ['trai'pɑ:tait] dreiteilig.

tripe [traip] Kaldaunen *f/pl.*, Kutteln *f/pl.*; *sl.* Quatsch *m*, Mist *m*.

tri·phase ['trai'feiz] dreiphasig; ˷ *current* ⚡ Drehstrom *m*.

tri·plane 🛪 ['traiplein] Dreidecker *m*.

tri·ple □ ['tripl] dreifach; ˷ **jump** *Sport:* Dreisprung *m*.

tri·plet ['triplit] Dreiergruppe *f*; *poet.* Dreireim *m*; ♪ Triole *f*; ˷*s pl.* Drillinge *m/pl.*

tri·plex ['tripleks] dreifach; ˷ *glass* Verbundglas *n*.

trip·li·cate 1. ['triplikit] dreifach; **2.** ['˷keit] verdreifachen.

tri·pod ['traipɔd] Dreifuß *m*; *phot.* Stativ *n*.

tri·pos ['traipɔs] letztes Examen *n* für e-n *honours degree in Cambridge*.

trip·per F ['tripə] Ausflügler(in); **'trip·ping 1.** □ flink, flott; **2.** Trippeln *n*; Beinstellen *n*.

trip·tych ['triptik] Triptychon *n*, dreiteiliges Altarbild *n*.

tri·sect [trai'sekt] in drei (gleiche) Teile teilen.

tris·yl·lab·ic ['traisi'læbik] (˷*ally*) dreisilbig; **'tri'syl·la·ble** dreisilbiges Wort *n*.

trite □ [trait] abgedroschen, platt.

trit·u·rate ['tritjureit] zerreiben.

tri·umph ['traiəmf] **1.** Triumph *m*, Sieg *m* (*over* über *acc.*) (*a. fig.*); **2.** triumphieren, den Sieg davontragen (*over* über *acc.*) (*a. fig.*); **tri·um·phal** [˷'æmfəl] Sieges..., Triumph...; ˷ *arch* Triumphbogen *m*; ˷ *procession* Triumphzug *m*; **tri'um·phant** □ triumphierend, frohlockend.

tri·um·vi·rate [trai'ʌmvirit] Triumvirat *n*.

tri·une ['traiju:n] dreieinig.

triv·et ['trivit] Dreifuß *m zum Kochen*; *as right as a* ˷ in schönster Ordnung; pudelwohl.

triv·i·al □ ['triviəl] bedeutungslos; unbedeutend; trivial; gewöhnlich, alltäglich; **triv·i·al·i·ty** [˷'æliti]

Belanglosigkeit *f*; Plattheit *f*, Trivialität *f*. [(*Versfuß*).
tro·chee ['trəuki:] Trochäus *m*
trod [trɔd], *pret.*, **'trod·den** *p.p. von* tread 1.
trog·lo·dyte ['trɔglədait] Höhlenbewohner *m*.
Tro·jan ['trəudʒən] **1.** trojanisch; **2.** Trojaner(in); *work like a* ~ wie ein Pferd arbeiten.
troll¹ [trəul] mit der Schleppangel fischen; (vor sich hin) trällern.
troll² [~] Troll *m*, Kobold *m*.
trol·l(e)y ['trɔli] Handwagen *m*, Karren *m*; Draisine *f*; *a.* tea-~ Tee-, Servierwagen *m*; Kontaktrolle *f* e-s Oberleitungsfahrzeugs; *Am.* Straßenbahnwagen *m*; **'~-bus** O(berleitungs)bus *m*.
trol·lop *contp.* ['trɔləp] **1.** Schlampe *f*; Hure *f*; **2.** latschen.
trom·bone ♪ [trɔm'bəun] Posaune*f*.
troop [tru:p] **1.** Truppe *f*; Schar *f*, Gruppe *f*, Trupp *m*; ✕ (Reiter)Zug *m*; ~s *pl.* Truppen *f/pl.*; **2.** sich scharen, sich sammeln; in Scharen ziehen; ~ *away*, ~ *off* abziehen; ~*ing the colour(s)* ✕ Fahnenparade *f*; **'~-carri·er** ⚓, ✈ Truppentransporter *m*; **'troop·er** Kavallerist *m*; Kavalleriepferd *n*; *swear like a* ~ wie ein Landsknecht fluchen.
trope [trəup] bildlicher Ausdruck *m*, Tropus *m*.
tro·phy ['trəufi] Trophäe *f*, Siegeszeichen *n*.
trop·ic ['trɔpik] Wendekreis *m*; ~s *pl.* Tropen *pl.*; **'trop·ic**, **'trop·i·cal** □ tropisch; Wendekreis...
trot [trɔt] **1.** Trott *m*, Trab *m*; *keep s.o. on the* ~ *fig.* j. in Trab halten; **2.** traben (lassen); trotten; ~ *out* F vorführen; ~ *s.o. round* j. herumführen; j. mitnehmen.
troth † [trəuθ]: *in* ~ meiner Treu, wahrlich; *plight one's* ~ sein Wort verpfänden.
trot·ter ['trɔtə] Traber *m*; ~*s pl.* Hammel-, Schweinsfüße *m/pl. als Speise*.
trou·ble ['trʌbl] **1.** Unruhe *f*; Störung *f* (*a.* ⊕); Kummer *m*, Sorge *f*, Not *f*; Mühe *f*, Beschwerde *f*; Plage *f*; *weitS.* Unannehmlichkeiten *f/pl.*; ~*s pl. pol.* Unruhen *f/pl.*; *be in* ~ in Nöten sein; *ask od. look for* ~ sich (selbst) Schwierig-

keiten machen; das Schicksal herausfordern; *take (the)* ~ sich (die) Mühe machen; **2.** *v/t.* stören, beunruhigen, belästigen; quälen, plagen; Mühe machen (*dat.*); ~ *s.o. for* j. bemühen um; *v/i.* F sich bemühen; **'~-mak·er** Unruhestifter *m*; **'~-man**, **'~-shoot·er** *Am.* F Störungssucher *m*; **trou·ble·some** ['~səm] beschwerlich, lästig; **'trou·ble-spot** *pol.* Krisenherd *m*; **'troub·lous** unruhig.
trough [trɔf] (Futter)Trog *m*; Backtrog *m*, Mulde *f*; ~ *of the sea* Wellental *n*.
trounce F [trauns] *j.* verhauen.
troupe [tru:p] (Schauspieler-, Zirkus)Truppe *f*.
trou·sered ['trauzəd] behost; **trou·sers** ['~z] *pl.* (*a pair of* eine) (lange) Hose *f*, Hosen *f/pl.*; **trou·ser suit** Hosenanzug *m*.
trous·seau ['tru:səu] Aussteuer *f*.
trout *ichth.* [traut] Forelle *f*.
tro·ver ⚖ ['trəuvə] rechtswidrige Aneignung *f*.
trow † *od. co.* [trau] glauben, meinen.
trow·el ['trauəl] Maurerkelle *f*.
troy (**weight**) ['trɔi(weit)] Feingewicht *n für Edelmetalle u. -steine*.
tru·an·cy ['tru:ənsi] (Schul)Schwänzerei *f*; **'tru·ant 1.** müßig, bummelnd; **2.** Schulschwänzer *m*; *fig.* Bummler *m*; *play* ~ die Schule schwänzen; bummeln.
truce [tru:s] Waffenstillstand *m*; *political* ~ Burgfriede *m*.
truck¹ [trʌk] (offener) Güterwagen *m*; Last(kraft)wagen *m*, Lkw *m*; Transportkarren *m*.
truck² [~] **1.** (ver)tauschen, handeln, (ver)schachern; **2.** Tausch(-handel) *m*; Verkehr *m*; *mst* ~ *system* Naturallohnsystem *n*; ~ *farm Am.* Gemüsegärtnerei *f*; *garden* ~ *Am.* Gemüse *n*.
truck·er *Am.* ['trʌkə] Fernfahrer *m*; Spediteur *m*; Gemüsegärtner *m*.
truck·le¹ ['trʌkl] zu Kreuze kriechen (*to* vor *dat.*).
truck·le² [~] *mst* ~-*bed* Unterschiebbett *n*.
truck...: **'~·man** Lkw-Fahrer *m*, Lastwagenfahrer *m*; ~ **stop** *bsd. Am.* Raststätte *f* (*bsd. für Fernfahrer*); ~ **trail·er** Lkw-Anhänger *m*; Lastzug *m*.
truc·u·lence, **truc·u·len·cy** ['trʌk-

juləns(i)] Wildheit *f*; '**truc·u·lent**
□ wild, roh; grob; grausam.
trudge [trʌdʒ] wandern; sich
(dahin)schleppen, mühsam gehen.
true [truː] (*adv. truly*) wahr; echt,
wirklich; treu; wahrheitsgetreu;
genau; richtig, (regel)recht; *be* ～ *of*
zutreffen auf (*acc.*), gelten für;
it is ～ gewiß, freilich, zwar, allerdings; *come* ～ sich bewahrheiten;
～ *to life* (*nature*) lebenstreu (naturgetreu); *prove* ～ (sich) bewahrheiten; '～-'**blue** *fig.* 1. waschecht;
treu; 2. treuer Anhänger *m*; '～-
-**bred** reinrassig; '～-**love** Lieb
(-chen) *n*; '**true·ness** Wahrheit *f*;
Treue *f*; Echtheit *f etc.*
truf·fle ♣ ['trʌfl] Trüffel *f*.
tru·ism ['truːizəm] Binsenwahrheit *f*.
tru·ly ['truːli] wirklich; wahrhaft;
aufrichtig; genau; treu; *Yours* ～
Ihr ergebener, Ihre ergebene.
trump [trʌmp] 1. *Karten:* Trumpf
m; F feiner Kerl *m*; 2. (über-)
trumpfen, *Karte* stechen; ～ *up* erdichten, zs.-schwindeln; '**trump-
er·y** 1. Plunder *m*, Trödel *m*;
Kitsch *m*; 2. lumpig; kitschig.
trum·pet ['trʌmpit] 1. ♪ Trompete
f; Schalltrichter *m*; *blow one's
own* ～ *fig.* sein eigenes Lob singen
s. ear-～, *speaking-*～; 2. trompeten;
～ *forth fig.* ausposaunen; '**trum-
pet·er** Trompeter *m*.
trun·cate ['trʌŋkeit] stutzen; verstümmeln; **trun'ca·tion** Verstüm-
melung *f*.
trun·cheon ['trʌntʃən] (Polizei-,
Gummi)Knüppel *m*; Kommando-
stab *m*.
trun·dle ['trʌndl] 1. Rolle *f*; 2. rollen, (sich) wälzen; *Reifen* schlagen.
trunk [trʌŋk] (Baum)Stamm *m*;
Rumpf *m*; Rüssel *m des Elefanten*;
großer Koffer *m*; *s.* ～-*line*; '～-**call**
teleph. Ferngespräch *n*; '～-**exchange** *teleph.* Fernamt *n*; '～-**line**
▦ Hauptlinie *f*; *teleph.* Fern-
leitung *f*; '～-**road** Fernstraße *f*;
trunks *pl.* Turnhose *f*; Badehose *f*;
Herrenunterhose *f*.
trun·nion ⊕ ['trʌnjən] Zapfen *m*.
truss [trʌs] 1. Bündel *n*, Bund *n*;
⚕ Bruchband *n*; ⌂ Hängewerk *n*,
Binder *m*, Gerüst *n*; 2. (zs.-)binden,
zs.-schnüren; ⌂ stützen; '～-
-**bridge** Fachwerkbrücke *f*.

trust [trʌst] 1. Vertrauen *n* (*in* auf
acc.); Glaube *m*; Kredit *m*; De-
positum *n*, Pfand *n*; Verwahrung *f*,
Obhut *f*; ⚖ Treuhand *f*; ⚖ Treu-
gut *n*; ♱ Ring *m*, Trust *m*; ～ *company* Treuhandgesellschaft *f*; *in* ～
treuhänderisch, zu treuen Händen;
on ～ auf Treu und Glauben; ♱ auf
Kredit; *position of* ～ Vertrauens-
stellung *f*; 2. *v/t.* (ver)trauen (*dat.*);
anvertrauen, übergeben (*s.o. with
s.th., s.th. to s.o.*); zuversichtlich hoffen; ～ *s.o. to do s.th.*
j-m zutrauen, daß er et. tut; *v/i.*
vertrauen (*in*, *to* auf *acc.*).
trus·tee [trʌs'tiː] Sach-, Verwalter
m; ⚖ Pfleger *m*, Treuhänder *m*,
Kurator *m*; ～ *security*, ～ *stock*
mündelsicheres Papier *n*; **trus'tee-
ship** Sachwalterschaft *f*; Treu-
händerschaft *f*; Kuratorium *n*.
trust·ful □ ['trʌstful], '**trust·ing** □
vertrauensvoll, zutraulich.
trust·wor·thi·ness ['trʌstwəːðinis]
Vertrauenswürdigkeit *f*; Zuverlässigkeit *f*; '**trust·wor·thy** vertrauenswürdig; zuverlässig; '**trust-
y** zuverlässig, treu.
truth [truːθ], *pl.* **truths** [truːðz]
Wahrheit *f*; Wirklichkeit *f*; Wahrhaftigkeit *f*; Genauigkeit *f*; ～ *to life*
Lebenstreue *f*.
truth·ful □ ['truːθful] wahrhaft(ig);
'**truth·ful·ness** Wahrhaftigkeit *f*,
Wahrheitsliebe *f*.
try [trai] 1. *v/t.* versuchen; probieren; prüfen (*a. fig.*); ⚖ verhandeln
über *et.* (*acc.*) *od.* gegen *j.* (*for
wegen*); *j.* vor Gericht stellen; ab-
urteilen; *die Augen etc.* angreifen;
～ *on Kleid* anprobieren; ～ *it on
with s.o.* F es bei j-m probieren;
～ *one's hand at* sich versuchen an
(*dat.*); ～ *out* erproben, ausprobie-
ren; *v/i.* versuchen (*at acc.*); sich
bemühen *od.* bewerben (*for* um);
2. F Versuch *m*; *have a* ～ e-n Versuch machen; '**try·ing** □ anstrengend; kritisch; '**try-'on** Anprobe *f*;
F Schwindelmanöver *n*; '**try-'out**
Erprobung *f*; *Sport:* Ausschei-
dungsspiel *n*; **try·sail** ⚓ ['traisl]
Gaffelsegel *n*.
tryst *schott.* [traist] 1. Stelldichein *n*;
2. (sich) verabreden.
Tsar [zɑː] Zar *m*.
T-shirt ['tiːʃəːt] kurzärmeliges
Sporthemd *n*.

T-square ['tiːskwɛə] Reißschiene f.
tub [tʌb] **1.** Faß n, Zuber m; Kübel m; Badewanne f; F (Wannen)Bad n; F co. Kahn m; *Sport*: Ruderkasten m; **2.** *Pflanzen* in Kübel setzen; *Butter* in ein Faß tun; F baden; im Ruderkasten trainieren; '**tub·by** tonnenartig.
tube [tjuːb] Rohr n; (*Am. bsd.* Radio)Röhre f; Tube f; *mot.* (Luft-) Schlauch m; Tunnel m; F Untergrundbahn f (*bsd. in London*).
tu·ber ♀ ['tjuːbə] Knolle f; **tu·ber·cle** ['ˌbəːkl] *anat., zo.* Knötchen n; ♣ Tuberkel f; **tu·ber·cu·lo·sis** ♣ [ˌbəːkjuˈləusis] Tuberkulose f; **tu'ber·cu·lous** ♣ tuberkulös; **tu·ber·ous** ♀ ['ˌbərəs] knollig.
tub·ing ['tjuːbiŋ] Röhrenmaterial, -werk n.
tub-thump·er ['tʌbθʌmpə] Volksredner m, Kanzelpauker m.
tu·bu·lar □ ['tjuːbjulə] röhrenförmig; Röhren...; Rohr...
tuck [tʌk] **1.** Falte f; Abnäher m; *sl.* Leckereien f/pl.; **2.** ab-, aufnähen; ~ in reinhauen, kräftig essen; (*mit adv. od. prp.*) packen, stecken; ~ up aufschürzen, -krempeln; *Beine* unterschlagen; *in e-e Decke etc.* einwickeln.
tuck·er *hist.* ['tʌkə] Brusttuch n.
tuck...: '~-in *sl.* großes Essen n; '~-shop *sl.* Süßwarengeschäft n.
Tues·day ['tjuːzdi] Dienstag m.
tu·fa *min.* ['tjuːfə], **tuff** [tʌf] Tuff (-stein) m.
tuft [tʌft] Büschel n, Busch m; (Haar)Schopf m; '~-hunt·er gesellschaftlicher Streber m, Schmarotzer m; '**tuft·y** □ büschelig.
tug [tʌg] **1.** Zug m, Ruck m; ⚓ Schlepper m; *fig.* Anstrengung f; ~ of war *Sport u. fig.* Tauziehen n; **2.** ziehen, zerren (*at* an *dat.*); ⚓ schleppen; sich mühen (*for* um).
tu·i·tion [tjuːˈiʃən] Unterricht m; Schulgeld n.
tu·lip ♀ ['tjuːlip] Tulpe f.
tulle [tjuːl] Tüll m.
tum·ble ['tʌmbl] **1.** v/i. fallen, purzeln; taumeln; sich wälzen; ~ to F kapieren, spitzkriegen; v/t. werfen; (um)stürzen; durchwühlen, zerknüllen; **2.** Sturz m, Fall m; Wirrwarr m; '~-down baufällig; '~-'dri·er Wäschetrockner m; '**tum·bler** Trinkglas n, Becher m; ⊕

Zuhaltung f *am Schloß*; *orn.* Tümmler m.
tum·brel ['tʌmbrəl], **tum·bril** ['ˌbril] Schutt-, Dungkarren m.
tu·mid ['tjuːmid] geschwollen; *fig.* schwülstig; **tu'mid·i·ty** Schwellung f; Geschwollenheit f.
tum·my F ['tʌmi] *Kindersprache*: Bäuchlein n, Magen m.
tu·mo(u)r ♣ ['tjuːmə] Geschwulst f, Tumor m.
tu·mult ['tjuːmʌlt] Tumult m; Lärm m; Aufruhr m (*a. fig.*); **tu'mul·tu·ous** □ [ˌtjuəs] lärmend; stürmisch, ungestüm.
tu·mu·lus ['tjuːmjuləs] Grabhügel m, Tumulus m.
tun [tʌn] Tonne f, Faß n; Maischbottich m.
tu·na *ichth.* ['tuːnə] Thunfisch m.
tun·dra ['tʌndrə] Tundra f.
tune [tjuːn] **1.** Melodie f, Lied n, Weise f, Tonstück n; ♪ Stimmung f (*a. fig.*); *in* ~ (gut) gestimmt; *fig.* übereinstimmend (*with* mit); *out of* ~ verstimmt (*a. fig.*); *to the* ~ *of* £ 100 in Höhe von 100 Pfd.; *change one's* ~ *fig.* andere Saiten aufziehen; **2.** stimmen (*a. fig.*); ~ *in Radio*: einstellen (*to* auf *acc.*); ~ *out Radio*: ausschalten; ~ *up* (die Instrumente) stimmen; *fig. Befinden etc.* heben; *mot.* tunen, die Leistung erhöhen; ♪ anstimmen; **tune·ful** □ ['ˌful] melodisch; klangvoll; '**tune·less** □ unmelodisch; '**tun·er** ♪ Stimmer m; *Radio*: Abstimmvorrichtung f.
tung·sten ♠ ['tʌŋstən] Wolfram m.
tu·nic ['tjuːnik] Tunika f; ✕ Uniformrock m; *anat.*, ♀ Häutchen n.
tun·ing...: '~-coil *Radio*: Abstimmspule f; '~-fork ♪ Stimmgabel f.
tun·nel ['tʌnl] **1.** Tunnel m; ⚒ Stollen m; **2.** e-n Tunnel bohren (durch).
tun·ny *ichth.* ['tʌni] Thunfisch m.
tun·y F ['tjuːni] melodisch.
tur·ban ['təːbən] Turban m.
tur·bid ['təːbid] trüb; dick; verworren; '**tur·bid·ness** Trübheit f *etc.*
tur·bine ⊕ ['təːbin] Turbine f; '~-pow·ered mit Turbinenantrieb; **tur·bo-jet** ['təːbəuˈdʒet] Strahlturbine f; **tur·bo-prop** ['~prɔp] Propellerturbine f.
tur·bot *ichth.* ['təːbət] Steinbutt m.
tur·bu·lence ['təːbjuləns] Unruhe f;

Ungestüm *n*; **'tur·bu·lent** ☐ unruhig; ungestüm; stürmisch, turbulent.

turd V [təːd] Haufen *m* Scheiße; Dreckskerl *m*.

tu·reen [tə'riːn] Terrine *f*.

turf [təːf] **1.** Rasen *m*; Torf *m*; Rennbahn *f*; Rennsport *m*; **2.** mit Rasen belegen; ~ out *sl. j.* 'rausschmeißen; **turf·ite** ['⌣ait] Rennsportliebhaber *m*; **'turf·y** rasenbedeckt; torfartig; rennsportlich.

tur·gid ☐ ['təːdʒid] geschwollen, schwülstig (*mst fig.*); **tur'gid·i·ty** Geschwollenheit *f*.

Turk [təːk] Türke *m*, Türkin *f*; *fig.* Wüterich *m*.

tur·key ['təːki] **1.** ♀ *carpet* türkischer Teppich *m*; **2.** *orn.* Truthahn *m*, -henne *f*, Pute(r *m*) *f*; *Am. sl. thea.*, *Film:* Pleite *f*, Versager *m* (*schlechtes Stück*).

Turk·ish ['təːkiʃ] türkisch; ~ *bath* türkisches Bad *n*, Schwitzbad *n*; ~ *delight* Geleefrüchte *f/pl.*; ~ *towel* Frottier(hand)tuch *n*.

tur·moil ['təːmɔil] Aufruhr *m*, Unruhe *f*; Getümmel *n*.

turn [təːn] **1.** *v/t.* drehen; (um-)wenden, umkehren; lenken; richten; verwandeln (*into* in *acc.*); abbringen (*from* von); abhalten, abwehren; übertragen (*into English* ins Englische); formen, bilden; (*a. fig. Verse etc.*) drechseln; schwindlig machen; verrückt machen; *he has* ~*ed 50, he is* ~*ed (of) 50* er ist über 50 Jahre alt; ~ *s.o.'s brain* j-m den Kopf verdrehen; ~ *colour* die Farbe wechseln; ~ *a corner* um eine Ecke biegen; *he can* ~ *his hand to anything* er ist zu allem zu gebrauchen; ~ *tail* F ausreißen; ~ *s.o. against* j. aufhetzen gegen; ~ *aside* abwenden; ~ *away* abwenden; abweisen; wegjagen; ~ *down* umkehren; *Buchseite etc.* umkniffen; *Gas etc.* herunterschrauben, kleinstellen; *Bettdecke etc.* zurückschlagen; *Vorschlag etc.* ablehnen; *j-m* e-n Korb geben; ~ *in* einwärts drehen; F ab-, zurückgeben; ~ *off* ableiten (*a. fig.*); hinauswerfen; wegjagen; ~ *off (on)* ab- (an)drehen, ab- (ein)schalten; ~ *out* auswärts drehen; hinauskehren; *Taschen etc.* umkehren; wegjagen, hinauswerfen, vertreiben; *Fabrikat etc.* her-

ausbringen, produzieren, herstellen; *Gas etc.* ausdrehen; ~ *over* umwenden; *fig.* übertragen; ✝ umsetzen; überlegen; ~ *over a new leaf* ein neues Leben beginnen; ~ *up* nach oben wenden *od.* richten; *Kragen etc.* hochklappen; umwenden; *Spielkarte* aufdecken; *Hose etc.* auf-, umschlagen; *Gas etc.* aufdrehen; ⚔ umpflügen; F *j-m* den Magen umdrehen, zum Erbrechen bringen; *v/i.* sich drehen, sich wenden; sich umdrehen; sich verwandeln (*into* in *acc.*); umschlagen (*Wetter etc.*; *a. fig.*); *Christ, Soldat, grau etc.* werden; *a.* ~ *sour* sauer werden (*Milch*); ~ *about* sich umdrehen; ⚔ kehrt machen; ~ *away* sich abwenden; ~ *back* zurückgehen, -kehren; ~ *in* sich einbiegen; hineingehen, einkehren; F zu Bett gehen; ~ *off* abbiegen; ~ *on* sich drehen um, abhängen von; ~ *out* sich nach außen wenden *od.* kehren; die Arbeit einstellen; ausfallen, ablaufen; (schließlich) werden; sich erweisen als, sich herausstellen als; F *aus dem Bett* aufstehen; aus dem Hause gehen; ⚔ ausrücken; ~ *over* sich umwenden; ~ *round* sich herumdrehen; ~ *to* sich (*dat.*) zuwenden, sich wenden an (*acc.*); sich verwandeln in (*acc.*); werden *od.* gereichen zu; ~ *to* (*adv.*) sich an die Arbeit machen; ~ *up* sich zeigen, auftauchen; ~ *upon* sich drehen um (*a. fig.*); sich wenden *od.* richten gegen; **2.** (Um)Drehung *f*; Krümmung *f*; Serpentine *f*; Wendung *f*, Richtung *f* (*a. fig.*); Neigung *f*, Hang *m* (*for* zu); Wechsel *m*, Veränderung *f*; Gestalt *f*; Beschaffenheit *f*, Art *f*; Spaziergang *m*; Reihe(nfolge) *f*; (Programm)Nummer *f*; F Schreck *m*, Schock *m*; *at every* ~ auf Schritt und Tritt; *by od. in* ~*s* der Reihe nach, abwechselnd; *do s.o. a good (bad)* ~ *j-m* e-n guten (schlechten) Dienst erweisen; *in* ~ abwechselnd, der Reihe nach; *in my* ~ meinerseits; *it is my* ~ ich bin an der Reihe; *take a* ~ sich ändern; *take a* ~ *at s.th.* et. versuchen; *take a few* ~*s* ein paar Schritte tun; *take one's* ~ et. tun, wenn die Reihe an e-n kommt; *take* ~*s* miteinander abwechseln; *to a* ~ aufs Haar; *a friendly* ~ ein Freundschaftsdienst *m*; *does it serve your* ~? entspricht das Ihren Zwecken?; '~·a·bout Kehrt(wendung *f*) *n*; '~-buck·le ⊕ Spannschraube *f*; '~-coat Abtrünnige *m*; 'turn-down col·lar Umlegekragen *m*; 'turn·er Drechsler *m*; Dreher *m*; 'turn·er·y Drechslerarbeit *f*.

turn·ing ['tə:niŋ] Drechseln *n*; Wendung *f*; Biegung *f*; Straßenecke *f*; (Weg)Abzweigung *f*; Querstraße *f*; *take a* ~ um die Ecke biegen; '~-lathe ⊕ Drehbank *f*; '~-point *fig*. Wendepunkt *m*.

tur·nip ♀ ['tə:nip] (*bsd*. weiße) Rübe *f*.

turn-key ['tə:nki:] Schließer *m*, Gefangenenwärter *m*; 'turn-off Abzweigung *f*; Ausfahrt *f e-r Autobahn*; 'turn-'out Ausstaffierung *f*; Kutsche *f*; Arbeitseinstellung *f*; Versammlung *f*; ✝ Gesamtproduktion *f*; 🐞, ⚓ Ausweichstelle *f*; 'turn·o·ver ✝ Umsatz *m*; Umgruppierung *f*, Verschiebung *f*; (Apfel- *etc*.)Tasche *f* (*Gebäck*); 'turn·pike Schlagbaum *m*; *Am*. (gebührenpflichtige) Schnellstraße *f*; 'turn-screw Schraubenzieher *m*; 'turn·spit Bratenwender *m*; 'turn·stile Drehkreuz *n*; 'turn-ta·ble 🎵 Drehscheibe *f*; Plattenteller *m am Plattenspieler*; 'turn-'up 1. aufklappbar; 2. Umschlag *m an der Hose*; F Krach *m*; F Keilerei *f*.

tur·pen·tine 🜍 ['tə:pəntain] Terpentin *n*.

tur·pi·tude *lit*. ['tə:pitju:d] Schändlichkeit *f*.

turps F [tə:ps] = *turpentine*.

tur·quoise *min*. ['tə:kwɑ:z] Türkis *m*.

tur·ret ['tʌrit] Türmchen *n*; ⚔, ⚓ (*mst* drehbarer) Panzerturm *m*; ⚔ Kanzel *f*; ⊕ Revolverkopf *m*; ~ *lathe* ⊕ Revolverdrehbank *f*; 'tur·ret·ed mit Türmchen *etc*. besetzt.

tur·tle¹ *zo*. ['tə:tl] Schildkröte *f*; *turn* ~ kentern.

tur·tle² *orn*. [~] *mst* ~-dove Turteltaube *f*.

tur·tle·neck ['tə:tlnek] Rollkragen (-pullover) *m*.

Tus·can ['tʌskən] 1. toskanisch; 2. Toskaner(in); Toskanisch *n*.

tush [tʌʃ] *int*. pah!

tusk [tʌsk] Fangzahn *m*; Stoßzahn *m des Elefanten etc*.; Hauer *m des*

Wildschweins.

tus·sle ['tʌsl] 1. Rauferei *f*, Balgerei *f*; 2. raufen, sich balgen.

tus·sock ['tʌsək] Büschel *n*.

tut [tʌt] ach was!, Unsinn!

tu·te·lage ['tju:tilidʒ] Vormundschaft *f*; Bevormundung *f*.

tu·te·lar·y ['tju:tiləri] schützend; Schutz...

tu·tor ['tju:tə] 1. (Privat-, Haus-) Lehrer *m*; *univ*. Tutor *m*; *Am. univ*. Assistent *m mit Lehrauftrag*; 🏛 Vormund *m*; 2. unterrichten; schulen, erziehen; *fig*. beherrschen; tu·to·ri·al [~'to:riəl] 1. Lehrer...; Tutor...; 2. *univ*. Unterrichtsstunde *f* e-s Tutors; tu·tor·ship ['~tə∫ip] (*bsd*. Haus)Lehrerstelle *f* (*of* bei).

tux·e·do *Am*. [tʌk'si:dəu] Smoking *m*.

TV ['ti:'vi:] 1. Fernsehen *n*; Fernsehapparat *m*; 2. Fernseh...

twad·dle ['twɔdl] 1. Geschwätz *n*; 2. schwatzen, quatschen.

twain ✝ [twein] zwei.

twang [twæŋ] 1. Schwirren *n*; *mst* nasal ~ näselnde Aussprache *f*; 2. schwirren (lassen), klimpern; näseln.

'twas [twɔz, twəs] = *it was*.

tweak [twi:k] zwicken.

tweed [twi:d] Tweed *m* (*Wollgewebe*).

'tween [twi:n] = *between*.

tween·y ['twi:ni] Aushilfsmädchen *n*.

tweet [twi:t] zwitschern; 'tweet·er *Radio*: Hochtonlautsprecher *m*.

tweez·ers ['twi:zəs] *pl.* (*a pair of* eine) Haarzange *f*; Pinzette *f*.

twelfth [twelfθ] 1. zwölfte(r, -s); 2. Zwölftel *n*; '2-night Dreikönigsabend *m*.

twelve [twelv] zwölf; ~·fold ['~fəuld] zwölffach; '~-month ein Jahr *n*.

twen·ti·eth ['twentiiθ] 1. zwanzigste(r, -s); 2. Zwanzigstel *n*.

twen·ty ['twenti] zwanzig; ~·fold ['~fəuld] zwanzigfach.

'twere [twə:] = *it were*.

twerp *sl*. [twə:p] Kerl *m*, Knülch *m*.

twice [twais] zweimal; ~ *the sum* die doppelte Summe; ~ *as much* zweimal *od*. noch einmal soviel.

twid·dle ['twidl] 1. (*v/i*. sich) drehen; mit ... spielen; 2. Schnörkel *m*.

twig¹ [twig] Zweig *m*, Rute *f*.

twig² F [~] kapieren, spitzkriegen.

twi·light ['twailait] **1.** Zwielicht *n*; Dämmerung *f* (*a. fig.*); ⁓ *of the gods* Götterdämmerung *f*; **2.** Dämmer(ungs)...; dämmerig; ⁓ *sleep* 𝕁 Dämmerschlaf *m*.

twill [twil] **1.** Köper *m* (*Gewebe*); **2.** köpern.

'twill [⏜] = *it will*.

twin [twin] **1.** Zwillings...; doppelt; ⁓-**engined** 𝓩 zweimotorig; **2.** Zwilling *m*; ⁓ **beds** *pl.* zwei Einzelbetten *n pl.*

twine [twain] **1.** Bindfaden *m*; Schnur *f*; Zwirn *m*; Windung *f*; **2.** *v/t.* zwirnen; zs.-drehen; *fig.* verflechten; schlingen, winden; umwinden, -schlingen, -ranken (*with* mit); *v/i. a.* ⁓ *o.s.* sich winden *od.* schlingen; sich schlängeln.

twinge [twind3] Zwicken *n*; Stechen *n*, Stich *m*; bohrender Schmerz *m*.

twin·kle ['twiŋkl] **1.** funkeln, blitzen; huschen; zwinkern; *in the twinkling of an eye* im Nu; **2.** Funkeln *n etc.*; *in a* ⁓ im Nu.

twirl [twɔ:l] **1.** Wirbel *m*; Schnörkel *m*; **2.** wirbeln; drehen; **'twirl·ing--stick** Quirl. *m*.

twirp [twɔ:p] = *twerp*.

twist [twist] **1.** Drehung *f*; Drall *m*; Windung *f*; Verdrehung *f*; Verdrehtheit *f*; Neigung *f*, Veranlagung *f*; (Gesichts)Verzerrung *f*; Garn *n*; Rollentabak *m*; Kringel *m*, Zopf *m* (*Backwaren*); Tüte *f*; Twist *m* (*Tanz*); **2.** *v/t.* drehen, winden; zs.-drehen; zwirnen; verdrehen; verkrümmen; *Gesicht* verziehen, verzerren; *Ball* anschneiden; *v/i.* sich drehen *od.* winden (*a. fig.*); sich verziehen; '**twist·er** Seiler *m*; Zwirner *m*; *Sport:* (an)geschnittener Ball *m*; *Billard:* Effetstoß *m*; F etwas zum Kopfzerbrechen; *Am.* Tornado *m*.

twit *fig.* [twit] *j.* aufziehen (*with* mit).

twitch [twitʃ] **1.** reißen; zupfen; zwicken; zucken (mit); **2.** Zupfen *n*; Ruck *m*; Zuckung *f*; *vet.* Nasenbremse *f*; = *twinge*.

twit·ter ['twitə] **1.** zwitschern; piepsen; **2.** Gezwitscher *n*; *be in a* ⁓ zittern, beben.

'twixt [twikst] = *betwixt*.

two [tu:] **1.** zwei; *in* ⁓ entzwei; *put* ⁓ *and* ⁓ *together* sich et. zs.-reimen; seine eignen Schlüsse ziehen;

2. Zwei *f*; *in* ⁓*s* zu zweien; '⁓-**bit** *Am.* F 25-Cent...; *fig.* unbedeutend, Klein...; '⁓-**edged** zweischneidig; '⁓-**'faced** falsch, heuchlerisch; ⁓-**fold** ['⁓fəuld] zweifach; '⁓-**hand·ed** zweihändig; für zwei Personen; '⁓-**'job man** Doppelverdiener *m*; ⁓-**pence** ['tʌpəns] zwei Pence; ⁓-**pen·ny** ['tʌpni] zwei Pence wert; Zweipenny...; '⁓-**phase** 𝓕 zweiphasig; '⁓-**'piece** zweiteilig; '⁓-**ply** zweischäftig (*Tau*); doppelt (*Tuch etc.*); '⁓-**'seat·er** *mot.* Zweisitzer *m*; '⁓-**·some** F Pärchen *n*, Gespann *n*; *play a* ⁓ zu zweit spielen; '⁓-**'step** Twostep *m* (*Tanz*); '⁓--**'sto·rey** zweistöckig; '⁓-**stroke** *mot.* Zweitakt...; '⁓-**'thirds** Zweidrittel...; '⁓-**time** F Ehepartner, Komplizen *etc.* betrügen, hintergehen; '⁓-**way** ⊕ Zweiweg...; ⁓ *adapter* 𝓕 Doppelstecker *m*; ⁓ *traffic* Gegenverkehr *m*.

'twould [twud] = *it would*.

ty·coon *Am.* F [tai'ku:n] Industriekapitän *m*, Magnat *m*.

tyke [taik] Köter *m*; Lümmel *m*.

tym·pa·num ['timpənəm] *anat.* Trommelfell *n*; △ Giebelfeld *n*, Tympanon *n*.

type [taip] **1.** Typ(us) *m*; Urbild *n*; Vorbild *n*; Muster *n*; Art *f*; ⊕ Ausführung *f*; Sinnbild *n*; *typ.* Letter *f*, Type *f*, Buchstabe *m*; *in* ⁓ gesetzt; ⁓ *area* Satzspiegel *m*; *true to* ⁓ artecht; *set in* ⁓ setzen; **2.** = ⁓*write*; '⁓-**face** *typ.* Schrift(bild *n*) *f*; '⁓-**found·er** Schriftgießer *m*; '⁓--**script** (Schreib)Maschinenschrift *f*; '⁓-**set·ter** Schriftsetzer *m*; '⁓-**write** (*irr. write*) mit der Schreibmaschine schreiben; '⁓-**writer** Schreibmaschine *f*; ⁓ *face* Schreibmaschinenschrift *f*; ⁓ *ribbon* Farbband *n*; '⁓-**writ·ten** maschinengeschrieben.

ty·phoid 𝓕 ['taifɔid] **1.** typhös; ⁓ *fever* = **2.** (Unterleibs)Typhus *m*.

ty·phoon *meteor.* [tai'fu:n] Taifun *m*.

ty·phus 𝓕 ['taifəs] Flecktyphus *m*.

typ·i·cal ☐ ['tipikəl] typisch; (vor-)bildlich; richtig, echt; kennzeichnend, chrakteristisch; bezeichnend (*of* für); **typ·i·fy** ['⁓fai] typisch sein für; versinnbildlichen.

typ·ing ['taipiŋ] Maschine(n)schreiben *n*; *pool* Schreibzentrale *f*; '**typ·ist** *a.* shorthand ⁓ Stenotypistin *f*.

ty·pog·ra·pher [tai'pɔgrəfə] Buchdrucker *m*; **ty·po·graph·ic, ty·po·graph·i·cal** ⸗ [ˌpə'græfik(əl)] typographisch; Druck...; **ty·pog·ra·phy** [ˑ'pɔgrəfi] Buchdruckerkunst *f*, Typographie *f*.

ty·ran·nic, ty·ran·ni·cal ⬜ [ti-'rænik(əl)] tyrannisch; **ty'ran·ni·cide** [ˌsaid] Tyrannenmörder *m*; Tyrannenmord *m*; **tyr·an·nize** ['tirənaiz] als Tyrann herrschen;

⸗ *over* tyrannisieren; **'tyr·an·nous** tyrannisch; **'tyr·an·ny** Tyrannei *f*, Gewaltherrschaft *f*.

ty·rant ['taiərənt] Tyrann(in).

tyre ['taiə] *s. tire¹*.

ty·ro ['taiərəu] *s. tiro*.

Tyr·o·lese [tirə'li:z] **1.** Tiroler(in); **2.** tirolisch, Tiroler(...).

Tzar [zɑ:] Zar *m*.

U

u·biq·ui·tous ⬜ [ju:'bikwitəs] allgegenwärtig, überall zu finden(d); **u'biq·ui·ty** Allgegenwart *f*.

U-boat ⚓ ['ju:bəut] *deutsches* U-Boot *n*.

ud·der ['ʌdə] Euter *n*.

ugh [ʌx, uh, ə:h] hu! (*Schreck*); puh! (*Ekel*).

ug·li·fy ['ʌglifai] entstellen.

ug·li·ness ['ʌglinis] Häßlichkeit *f*.

ug·ly ⸗ ['ʌgli] häßlich, garstig; gefährlich, schlimm (*z.B. Wunde*).

U·krain·i·an [ju:'kreinjən] **1.** ukrainisch; **2.** Ukrainer(in).

u·ku·le·le ♩ [ju:kə'leili] Ukulele *n*, Hawáiigitarre *f*.

ul·cer ⚕ ['ʌlsə] Geschwür *n*; Ulkus *m*; (Eiter)Beule *f*; **ul·cer·ate** ['ˌreit] eitern (lassen); **ul·cer'a·tion** Geschwürbildung *f*; **'ul·cer·ous** geschwürig.

ul·lage ⬦ ['ʌlidʒ] Flüssigkeitsverlust *m*, Leckage *f*.

ul·na *anat.* ['ʌlnə], *pl.* **ul·nae** ['ˌni:] Elle *f*.

ul·ster ['ʌlstə] Ulster *m* (*Mantel*).

ul·te·ri·or [ʌl'tiəriə] jenseitig; *fig.* weiter; anderweitig; tiefer liegend, versteckt; ⸗ *motive* Hintergedanke *m*.

ul·ti·mate ⬜ ['ʌltimit] letzt; endlich; End...; **'ul·ti·mate·ly** zu guter Letzt.

ul·ti·ma·tum [ʌlti'meitəm], *pl. a.* **ul·ti'ma·ta** [ˌtə] Ultimatum *n*.

ul·ti·mo ⬦ ['ʌltiməu] im letzten Monat, vorigen Monats.

ul·tra ['ʌltrə] übermäßig; Ultra..., ultra...; **'ˌfash·ion·a·ble** hyper-

modern; **'ˌhigh fre·quen·cy** *Radio*: Ultrakurzwelle *f*, Ultrahochfrequenz *f*; ⸗ **ma'rine 1.** überseeisch; **2.** ⚛ *paint.* Ultramarin *n*; **'ˌmod·ern** hypermodern; ⸗ **mon·tane** *eccl., pol.* [ˌ'mɔntein] **1.** ultramontan; **2.** Ultramontane *m*; **'ˌred** ultrarot; **'ˌ'short wave** Ultrakurzwelle *f*; **'ˌson·ic** Überschall...; **'ˌvi·o·let** ultraviolett.

ul·u·late ['ju:ljuleit] heulen.

um·bel ⚘ ['ʌmbəl] Dolde *f*.

um·ber *min., paint.* ['ʌmbə] Umber *m*, Umbra *f* (*brauner Farbstoff*).

um·bil·i·cal ⬜ [ʌm'bilikəl, ⚕ ˌlai-kəl] Nabel...; ⸗ *cord* Nabelschnur *f*.

um·brage ['ʌmbridʒ] Anstoß *m* (*Ärger*); *poet.* Schatten *m*; **um·bra·geous** ⬜ [ˌ'breidʒəs] schattig; *fig.* empfindlich.

um·brel·la [ʌm'brelə] Regenschirm *m*; *fig.* Schirm *m*, Schutz *m*; ✕ Abschirmung *f*; Jagdschutz *m*; ⸗ **or·gan·i·za·tion** Dachorganisation *f*; ⸗ **stand** Schirmständer *m*.

um·pire ['ʌmpaiə] **1.** Schiedsrichter *m*; **2.** Schiedsrichter sein.

ump·teen ['ʌmpti:n], **'ump·ty** *sl.* zig, viele, zahlreiche.

un... [ʌn] un...; Un...; ent...; nicht...

'un F [ʌn, ən] = one.

un·a·bashed ['ʌnə'bæʃt] unverfroren; unerschrocken.

un·a·bat·ed ['ʌnə'beitid] unvermindert.

un·a·ble ['ʌn'eibl] unfähig, außerstande (*to inf.* zu *inf.*).

un·a·bridged ['ʌnə'bridʒd] ungekürzt.

un·ac·cept·a·ble [ˈʌnəkˈseptəbl] unannehmbar.

un·ac·com·mo·dat·ing [ˈʌnəˈkɔmədeitiŋ] nicht entgegenkommend.

un·ac·count·a·ble □ [ˈʌnəˈkauntəbl] unerklärlich; seltsam; nicht zur Rechenschaft verpflichtet.

un·ac·cus·tomed [ˈʌnəˈkʌstəmd] ungewohnt; ungewöhnlich; ~ to nicht gewöhnt an (acc.).

un·ac·knowl·edged [ˈʌnəkˈnɔlidʒd] nicht anerkannt od. zugestanden.

un·ac·quaint·ed [ˈʌnəˈkweintid]: ~ with nicht vertraut mit, unkundig e-r Sache. [schmückt.)

un·a·dorned [ˈʌnəˈdɔːnd] unge-)

un·a·dul·ter·at·ed □ [ˈʌnəˈdʌltəreitid] unverfälscht.

un·ad·vis·a·ble □ [ˈʌnədˈvaizəbl] unratsam; **'un·ad·vised** □ [~zd, adv. ~zidli] unbedacht; unberaten.

un·af·fect·ed □ [ˈʌnəˈfektid] unberührt; fig. ungerührt; ungekünstelt.

un·a·fraid [ˈʌnəˈfreid] furchtlos.

un·aid·ed [ˈʌnˈeidid] ohne Unterstützung; (ganz) allein; unbewaffnet, bloß (Auge).

un·al·ien·a·ble [ˈʌnˈeiljənəbl] unveräußerlich.

un·al·loyed [ˈʌnəˈlɔid] unlegiert; fig. unvermischt.

un·al·ter·a·ble □ [ʌnˈɔːltərəbl] unveränderlich; **un·al·tered** unverändert.

un·am·big·u·ous □ [ˈʌnæmˈbigjuəs] unzweideutig.

un·am·bi·tious □ [ˈʌnæmˈbiʃəs] ohne Ehrgeiz; anspruchslos.

un·a·me·na·ble [ˈʌnəˈmiːnəbl] unzugänglich.

un·A·mer·i·can [ˈʌnəˈmerikən] unamerikanisch.

un·a·mi·a·ble □ [ˈʌnˈeimjəbl] unliebenswürdig.

u·na·nim·i·ty [juːnəˈnimiti] Einmütigkeit f; **u·nan·i·mous** □ [juːˈnæniməs] einmütig, -stimmig.

un·an·nounced [ˈʌnəˈnaunst] unangemeldet.

un·an·swer·a·ble □ [ʌnˈɑːnsərəbl] unwiderleglich; **'un·an·swered** unbeantwortet; offen (Frage); unerwidert.

un·ap·palled [ˈʌnəˈpɔːld] unerschrocken.

un·ap·peal·a·ble ⚖ [ˈʌnəˈpiːləbl]

unanfechtbar.

un·ap·peas·a·ble □ [ˈʌnəˈpiːzəbl] unversöhnlich.

un·ap·proach·a·ble □ [ˈʌnəˈprəutʃəbl] unzugänglich.

un·ap·pro·pri·at·ed [ˈʌnəˈprəuprieitid] nicht verwendet; herrenlos.

un·apt □ [ˈʌnˈæpt] untauglich, ungeeignet; ~ to inf. nicht dazu neigend, zu inf.; be ~ to learn nicht leicht lernen.

un·armed [ˈʌnˈɑːmd] unbewaffnet.

un·a·shamed □ [ˈʌnəˈʃeimd]; adv. ~midli] schamlos.

un·asked [ˈʌnˈɑːskt] unverlangt; ungebeten.

un·as·sail·a·ble □ [ʌnəˈseiləbl] unangreifbar.

un·as·sist·ed □ [ˈʌnəˈsistid] ohne Hilfe od. Unterstützung.

un·as·sum·ing [ˈʌnəˈsjuːmiŋ] anspruchslos, bescheiden.

un·at·tached [ˈʌnəˈtætʃt] nicht gebunden, nicht organisiert; ungebunden, ledig, frei.

un·at·tain·a·ble □ [ˈʌnəˈteinəbl] unerreichbar.

un·at·tend·ed [ˈʌnəˈtendid] unbegleitet; unbeaufsichtigt.

un·at·trac·tive [ʌnəˈtræktiv] wenig anziehend, reizlos, uninteressant.

un·au·thor·ized [ˈʌnˈɔːθəraizd] unberechtigt, unbefugt.

un·a·vail·a·ble [ˈʌnəˈveiləbl] nicht verfügbar; unbrauchbar; **'un·a·vail·ing** vergeblich, nutzlos.

un·a·void·a·ble □ [ʌnəˈvɔidəbl] unvermeidlich.

un·a·ware [ˈʌnəˈwɛə] ohne Kenntnis; be ~ of et. nicht merken; be ~ that nicht wissen, daß; **'un·a'wares** unversehens; versehentlich; unvermutet; ohne es zu wissen od. zu merken.

un·backed [ˈʌnˈbækt] ohne Unterstützung; ungedeckt (Scheck); ~ horse Pferd n, auf das nicht gesetzt wurde.

un·bag [ˈʌnˈbæg] aus dem Sack holen od. lassen.

un·bal·ance [ˈʌnˈbæləns] Unausgeglichenheit f; **'un'bal·anced** nicht im Gleichgewicht befindlich; unausgeglichen; geistesgestört.

un·bap·tized [ˈʌnbæpˈtaizd] ungetauft.

un·bar [ˈʌnˈbɑː] aufriegeln, -schließen.

un·bear·a·ble ☐ [ʌn'bɛərəbl] unerträglich.

un·beat·en ['ʌn'biːtn] ungeschlagen; unbetreten (*Weg*).

un·be·com·ing ☐ ['ʌnbi'kʌmiŋ] unkleidsam; unziemlich, unschicklich (*to od. for s.o.* für j.).

un·be·friend·ed ['ʌnbi'frendid] freundlos; hilflos.

un·be·known ['ʌnbi'nəun] unbekannt; ~ *to s.o.* ohne j-s Wissen.

un·be·lief ['ʌnbi'liːf] Unglaube *m*, Ungläubigkeit *f*; **un·be'liev·a·ble** ☐ unglaublich; **un·be'liev·er** Ungläubige *m, f*; **un·be'liev·ing** ☐ ungläubig.

un·be·loved ['ʌnbi'lʌvd] ungeliebt.

un·bend ['ʌn'bend] (*irr. bend*) *v/t.* entspannen (*a. fig.*); ⊕ gerade richten; *v/i.* sich entspannen; freundlich werden, auftauen; '**un'bend·ing** ☐ unbiegsam; *fig.* unbeugsam.

un·be·seem·ing ☐ ['ʌnbi'siːmiŋ] unpassend.

un·bi·as(s)ed ☐ ['ʌn'baiəst] vorurteilsfrei, unbefangen, unbeeinflußt.

un·bid(·den) ['ʌn'bid(n)] ungeheißen, unaufgefordert; ungebeten.

un·bind ['ʌn'baind] (*irr. bind*) losbinden, befreien; lösen.

un·bleached ['ʌn'bliːtʃt] ungebleicht.

un·blem·ished [ʌn'blemiʃt] unbefleckt.

un·blush·ing ☐ [ʌn'blʌʃiŋ] nicht errötend; schamlos.

un·bolt ['ʌn'bəult] aufriegeln; '**un·'bolt·ed** unverriegelt; ungebeutelt (*Mehl*). [boren.\

un·born ['ʌn'bɔːn] (noch) unge-/

un·bos·om [ʌn'buzəm] *Gefühl etc.* offenbaren; ~ *o.s.* sich offenbaren, sein Herz ausschütten (*to s.o.* j-m).

un·bound ['ʌn'baund] ungebunden.

un·bound·ed ☐ [ʌn'baundid] unbegrenzt; schrankenlos.

un·bowed *fig.* ['ʌn'baud] ungebeugt, ungebrochen.

un·brace ['ʌn'breis] losmachen; schlaff machen; entspannen.

un·break·a·ble ['ʌn'breikəbl] unzerbrechlich.

un·bri·dled [ʌn'braidld] ungezäumt; *fig.* ungezügelt.

un·bro·ken ['ʌn'brəukən] ungebrochen; unversehrt; ununterbrochen;

unzugeritten (*Pferd*).

un·buck·le ['ʌn'bʌkl] auf-, losschnallen.

un·bur·den ['ʌn'bəːdn] *mst fig.* entlasten; *sein Herz* ausschütten.

un·bur·ied ['ʌn'berid] unbegraben.

un·burned ['ʌn'bəːnd], **un·burnt** ['‿'bəːnt] unverbrannt; ungebrannt.

un·busi·ness·like [ʌn'biznislaik] nicht geschäftsmäßig.

un·but·ton ['ʌn'bʌtn] aufknöpfen.

un·called ['ʌn'kɔːld] unaufgefordert; ✝ nicht aufgerufen; **un·'called-for** ungerufen; unverlangt (*Sache*); unpassend (*Bemerkung etc.*).

un·can·did ☐ ['ʌn'kændid] unaufrichtig.

un·can·ny ☐ [ʌn'kæni] unheimlich.

un·cared-for ['ʌn'kɛədfɔː] unbeachtet, vernachlässigt.

un·case ['ʌn'keis] auspacken.

un·ceas·ing ☐ [ʌn'siːsiŋ] unaufhörlich.

un·cer·e·mo·ni·ous ☐ ['ʌnseri'məunjəs] ungezwungen; formlos.

un·cer·tain ☐ [ʌn'səːtn] *allg.* unsicher; ungewiß; unbestimmt; unzuverlässig (*a. Wetter*); be ~ *of e-r Sache* nicht sicher sein; **un·'certain·ty** Unsicherheit *f etc.*

un·chain ['ʌn'tʃein] entfesseln.

un·chal·lenge·a·ble ['ʌn'tʃælindʒəbl] unanfechtbar; '**un·'challenged** unangefochten.

un·change·a·ble ☐ [ʌn'tʃeindʒəbl], **un·'chang·ing** ☐ unveränderlich, unwandelbar; **un·'changed** unverändert.

un·char·i·ta·ble ☐ [ʌn'tʃæritəbl] lieblos; unbarmherzig; unfreundlich.

un·charm ['ʌn'tʃɑːm] entzaubern.

un·chart·ed ['ʌn'tʃɑːtid] unerforscht; auf keiner Landkarte verzeichnet, nicht vermessen.

un·chaste ☐ ['ʌn'tʃeist] unkeusch; **un·chas·ti·ty** ['ʌn'tʃæstiti] Unkeuschheit *f*.

un·checked ['ʌn'tʃekt] ungehindert.

un·chris·tian ☐ ['ʌn'kristjən] unchristlich.

un·civ·il ☐ ['ʌn'sivl] unhöflich; '**un·'civ·i·lized** [‿vilaizd] unzivilisiert.

un·claimed ['ʌn'kleimd] nicht beansprucht; unzustellbar (*Brief*).

un·clasp ['ʌn'klɑːsp] auf-, loshaken, -schnallen; aufmachen.

un·clas·si·fied [ˈʌnˈklæsifaid] nicht (ein)geordnet; ✗ nicht geheim; ~ **road** Landstraße f.

un·cle [ˈʌŋkl] Onkel m; sl. Pfandleiher m.

un·clean [ˈʌnˈkliːn] unrein (a. fig.).

un·clench [ˈʌnˈklentʃ] (sich) öffnen.

un·cloak [ˈʌnˈkləuk] (j-m) den Mantel abnehmen; fig. enthüllen.

un·close [ˈʌnˈkləuz] (sich) öffnen.

un·clothe [ˈʌnˈkləuð] entkleiden.

un·cloud·ed [ˈʌnˈklaudid] unbewölkt; wolkenlos (a. fig.).

un·coil [ˈʌnˈkɔil] (sich) aufrollen.

un·col·lect·ed [ˈʌnkəˈlektid] nicht gesammelt (a. fig.).

un·col·o(u)red [ˈʌnˈkʌləd] ungefärbt; fig. ungeschminkt.

un·come-at-a·ble F [ˈʌnkʌmˈætəbl] unerreichbar, unzugänglich; schwer erreichbar.

un·come·ly [ˈʌnˈkʌmli] reizlos; unpassend.

un·com·fort·a·ble □ [ʌnˈkʌmfətəbl] unbehaglich, ungemütlich; unangenehm.

un·com·mit·ted [ʌnkəˈmitid] unabhängig, nicht gebunden; pol. blockfrei.

un·com·mon □ [ʌnˈkɔmən] (a. F adv.) ungewöhnlich.

un·com·mu·ni·ca·tive [ˈʌnkəˈmjuːnikətiv] wenig mitteilsam, verschlossen; schweigsam.

un·com·plain·ing [ˈʌnkəmˈpleiniŋ] klaglos; ohne Murren; geduldig.

un·com·pro·mis·ing □ [ʌnˈkɔmprəmaiziŋ] kompromißlos; unnachgiebig; fig. entschieden.

un·con·cern [ˈʌnkənˈsəːn] Unbekümmertheit f; Gleichgültigkeit f; 'un·con'cerned [adv. ~idli] unbekümmert (about um); uninteressiert (with an dat.); unbeteiligt (in an dat.).

un·con·di·tion·al □ [ˈʌnkənˈdiʃənl] unbedingt; bedingungslos.

un·con·fined [ˈʌnkənˈfaind] unbegrenzt; ungehindert.

un·con·firmed [ˈʌnkənˈfəːmd] unbestätigt; eccl. unkonfirmiert.

un·con·gen·ial [ˈʌnkənˈdʒiːnjəl] ungleichartig, unsympathisch.

un·con·nect·ed □ [ˈʌnkəˈnektid] unverbunden.

un·con·quer·a·ble □ [ʌnˈkɔŋkərəbl]

---

unüberwindlich; 'un'con·quered unbesiegt, nicht erobert.

un·con·sci·en·tious [ˈʌnkɔnʃiˈenʃəs] nicht gewissenhaft, nachlässig.

un·con·scion·a·ble □ [ʌnˈkɔnʃnəbl] gewissenlos; F unverschämt, übermäßig.

un·con·scious □ [ʌnˈkɔnʃəs] 1. unbewußt; bewußtlos; be ~ of nichts ahnen von; 2. the ~ psych. das Unbewußte; **un'con·sciousness** Bewußtlosigkeit f.

un·con·se·crat·ed [ˈʌnˈkɔnsikreitid] ungeweiht.

un·con·sid·ered [ˈʌnkənˈsidəd] unberücksichtigt; unbedacht.

un·con·sti·tu·tion·al □ [ˈʌnkɔnstiˈtjuːʃənl] verfassungswidrig.

un·con·strained □ [ˈʌnkənˈstreind] ungezwungen.

un·con·test·ed □ [ˈʌnkənˈtestid] unbestritten.

un·con·tra·dict·ed [ˈʌnkɔntrəˈdiktid] unwidersprochen.

un·con·trol·la·ble □ [ʌnkənˈtrəuləbl] unkontrollierbar; unbändig; nicht zu meistern(d); 'un·con·'trolled unbeaufsichtigt; fig. unbeherrscht.

un·con·ven·tion·al □ [ˈʌnkənˈvenʃənl] unkonventionell; ungezwungen.

un·con·vert·ed [ˈʌnkənˈvəːtid] unbekehrt; ✝ nicht konvertiert.

un·con·vinced [ˈʌnkənˈvinst] nicht überzeugt; 'un·con'vinc·ing nicht überzeugend.

un·cooked [ˈʌnˈkukt] ungekocht, roh.

un·cord [ˈʌnˈkɔːd] auf-, losbinden.

un·cork [ˈʌnˈkɔːk] entkorken.

un·cor·rupt·ed [ˈʌnkəˈrʌptid] unverdorben; unbestochen.

un·count·a·ble [ˈʌnˈkauntəbl] unzählbar; 'un'count·ed ungezählt.

un·cou·ple [ˈʌnˈkʌpl] los-, auskoppeln.

un·couth □ [ʌnˈkuːθ] grob, ungeschlacht, linkisch; seltsam.

un·cov·er [ʌnˈkʌvə] aufdecken, freilegen; Körperteil entblößen.

un·crit·i·cal □ [ˈʌnˈkritikəl] unkritisch.

un·crowned [ˈʌnˈkraund] ungekrönt.

unc·tion [ˈʌŋkʃən] Salbung f (a. fig.); Salbe f; extreme ~ eccl. Letzte

Ölung *f*; **unc·tu·ous** □ [ˈʌŋktjuəs] fettig, ölig; *fig.* salbungsvoll.

un·cul·ti·vat·ed [ˈʌnˈkʌltiveitid] unbebaut, unkultiviert; *fig.* ungebildet.

un·cured [ˈʌnˈkjuəd] ungeheilt; ungesalzen, ungepökelt.

un·curl [ˈʌnˈkəːl] (sich) entkräuseln.

un·cut [ˈʌnˈkʌt] ungeschnitten; unbeschnitten; unaufgeschnitten (*Buch*).

un·dam·aged [ˈʌnˈdæmidʒd] unbeschädigt.

un·damped [ˈʌnˈdæmpt] ungedämpft; ungeschwächt.

un·dat·ed [ˈʌnˈdeitid] undatiert.

un·daunt·ed □ [ʌnˈdɔːntid] unerschrocken, kühn, furchtlos.

un·de·ceive [ˈʌndiˈsiːv] *j.* aufklären, *j-m* die Augen öffnen (*of* über *acc.*).

un·de·cid·ed □ [ˈʌndiˈsaidid] unentschieden; unentschlossen.

un·de·ci·pher·a·ble [ˈʌndiˈsaifərəbl] unentzifferbar.

un·de·fend·ed [ˈʌndiˈfendid] unverteidigt.

un·de·filed [ˈʌndiˈfaild] unbefleckt.

un·de·fined □ [ˈʌndiˈfaind] *adv.* ˷nidli] unbegrenzt; unbestimmt.

un·de·mon·stra·tive □ [ˈʌndiˈmɔnstrətiv] zurückhaltend.

un·de·ni·a·ble □ [ʌndiˈnaiəbl] unleugbar, unbestreitbar.

un·de·nom·i·na·tion·al □ [ˈʌndinɔmiˈneiʃənl] konfessionslos; paritätisch; Simultan...

un·der [ˈʌndə] **1.** *adv.* unten; darunter; **2.** *prp.* unter; *from* ˷ ... unter ... hervor; ˷ *sentence of* ⚡ ... zu ... verurteilt; **3.** *in Zssgn*: unter...; Unter...; mangelhaft ...; '˷**act** *thea.* zu zurückhaltend spielen; '˷**age** minderjährig, unmündig; '˷**bid** (*irr.* bid) unterbieten; '˷**bred** unfein, ungebildet; '˷**brush** Unterholz *n*, Gesträuch *n*; '˷**carriage** (Flugzeug)Fahrwerk *n*; *mot.* Fahrgestell *n*; '˷**charge** *j-m* zu wenig berechnen; '˷**clothes** *pl.*, '˷**clothing** Unterbekleidung *f*, -wäsche *f*; '˷**cov·er** Geheim...; '˷**cur·rent** Unterströmung *f*; '˷**cut** Preise unterbieten; '˷**dog** Unterlegene *m*; Unterdrückte *m*; '˷**done** nicht gar; '˷**dress** (sich) zu einfach kleiden; '˷**em·ploy·ment** Unterbeschäftigung *f*; '˷**es·ti·mate** unterschätzen; '˷**ex·pose** *phot.* unterbelichten; '˷

'˷**fed** unterernährt; '˷**feed·ing** Unterernährung *f*; '˷**foot** unter den Füßen, unter die Füße; '˷**gar·ments** *pl.* Leibwäsche *f*; '˷**go** (*irr.* go) erdulden; sich unterziehen (*dat.*); '˷**grad·u·ate** *univ.* Student(in); '˷**ground 1.** unterirdisch; Untergrund...; ˷ *movement* Untergrundbewegung *f*; *go* ˷ in den Untergrund gehen; **2.** *a.* ˷ *railway* Untergrundbahn *f*; '˷**growth** Unterholz *n*; '˷**hand** unter der Hand; heimlich; heimtückisch; ˷ *service* *Tennis:* Aufschlag *m* aus der Hüfte; '˷**hung** unter dem Oberkiefer hervorstehend; mit vorstehendem Unterkiefer; ˷**lay 1.** [ʌndəˈlei] (*irr.* lay) unterlegen; **2.** [ˈ˷] wasserdichte Unterlage *f*; '˷**let** (*irr.* let) unterverpachten, -vermieten; unter dem Werte verpachten *od.* vermieten; ˷**lie** (*irr.* lie) unter *et.* (*dat.*) liegen; *fig.* zugrunde liegen (*dat.*); unterstehen (*dat.*); ˷**line 1.** [ʌndəˈlain] unterstreichen; **2.** [ˈ˷] Unterstreichung *f*; '˷**lin·en** Leibwäsche *f*.

un·der·ling [ˈʌndəliŋ] Untergeordnete *m*, Kuli *m*; **un·der'ly·ing** zugrundeliegend; **un·der·manned** [ˈ˷ˈmænd] unterbelegt; **under'men·tioned** unten erwähnt; **under'mine** unterminieren; *fig.* untergraben; schwächen, aushöhlen; '˷**most 1.** *adj.* unterst; **2.** *adv.* zuunterst; **un·der·neath** [˷ˈniːθ] **1.** *prp.* unter(halb); **2.** *adv.* unten, unterwärts; darunter; '**un·der'nour·ished** unterernährt.

un·der...: '˷**pants** *pl.* Unterhose *f*; '˷**pass** Unterführung *f*; '˷**pay** (*irr.* pay) unterbezahlen; ˷**pin** ⊕ untermauern (*fig.* stützen); ˷**pinning** ⊕ Untermauerung *f*; Unterbau *m*; ˷**play** (seine Karten) nicht voll ausspielen; *thea.* (die Rolle) (zu) verhalten spielen; *fig.* sich zurückhalten (in *od.* mit); '˷**plot** Nebenhandlung *f*; '˷**print** *phot.* unterkopieren; '˷**priv·i·leged** benachteiligt, schlechtgestellt; '˷**rate** unterschätzen; ˷**score** unterstreichen; '˷**sec·re·tar·y** Unterstaatssekretär *m*; '˷**sell** ✝ (*irr.* sell) *j.* unterbieten; *Ware* verschleudern; '˷**shoot** (*irr.* shoot): ˷ *the runway* ✈ vor der Landebahn aufkommen; '˷**shot** unterschlächtig (*Mühlrad*); '˷**side** Unterseite *f*; ˷**signed** Unterzeichnete *m, f*; '˷

'**sized** unter Normalgröße, zu klein; '~'**slung** *mot.* Hänge...; ~ *frame* Unterzugrahmen *m*; '~'**staffed** unterbesetzt; ~'**stand** (*irr.* stand) *allg.* verstehen; sich verstehen auf (*acc.*); (als sicher) annehmen; auffassen; *fig.* hören; sinngemäß ergänzen; *make o.s. understood* sich verständlich machen; *it is understood* es heißt, es verlautet; *that is understood* das ist selbstverständlich; *an understood thing* e-e ausod. abgemachte Sache; ~'**stand·a·ble** verständlich; ~'**stand·ing** 1. Verstand *m*; Einvernehmen *n*; Verständigung *f*; Vereinbarung *f*, Abkommen *n*, Abmachung *f*; *on the ~ that* unter der Voraussetzung, daß; 2. verständig; '~'**state** zu gering angeben; unterbewerten; *Tatsache* verkleinern; '~'**state·ment** zu niedrige Angabe *f*; Unterbewertung *f*; Understatement *n*, Untertreibung *f*. **un·der...:** '~'**strap·per** = *underling*; '~'**stud·y** *thea.* **1.** Rollenvertreter(in); **2.** einspringen für; ~'**take** (*irr.* take) unternehmen; übernehmen; sich verpflichten (*to inf.* zu *inf.*); ~ *that* sich dafür verbürgen, daß; '~'**tak·er** Bestattungsinstitut *n*, Leichenbestatter *m*; ~'**tak·ing** Unternehmung *f*; Verpflichtung *f*, Zusicherung *f*; ['~'teikiŋ] Leichenbestattung *f*; '~'**ten·ant** Untermieter *m*, -pächter *m*; ~'**-the-'coun·ter** unter der Hand, heimlich; '~'**tone** leiser Ton *m*; Unterton *m*; *in an ~* halblaut; '~'**val·ue** unterschätzen; '~'**wear** Unterkleidung *f*, -wäsche *f*; '~'**weight** Untergewicht *n*; '~'**wood** Unterholz *n*, Gestrüpp *n* (*a. fig.*); '~'**world** Unterwelt *f*; '~'**write** † (*irr.* write) *Versicherung* abschließen; '~'**wri·ter** Versicherer *m*.

un·de·served □ ['ʌndi'zə:vd] unverdient; '**un·de'serv·ing** unwürdig.

un·de·signed □ ['ʌndi'zaind] unbeabsichtigt, absichtslos.

un·de·sir·a·ble ['ʌndi'zaiərəbl] **1.** □ unerwünscht; **2.** unerwünschte Person *f*.

un·de·terred ['ʌndi'tə:d] nicht abgeschreckt.

un·de·vel·oped ['ʌndi'veləpt] unentwickelt; unerschlossen (*Gelände*).

un·de·vi·at·ing □ [ʌn'di:vieitiŋ]

unentwegt.

un·dies F ['ʌndiz] *pl.* Damenunterwäsche *f*.

un·di·gest·ed ['ʌndi'dʒestid] unverdaut.

un·dig·ni·fied □ [ʌn'dignifaid] würdelos.

un·di·min·ished ['ʌndi'miniʃt] unvermindert.

un·di·rect·ed ['ʌndi'rektid] führungslos; ungelenkt.

un·dis·cerned □ ['ʌndi'sə:nd] unbemerkt; '**un·dis'cern·ing** einsichtslos.

un·dis·charged ['ʌndis'tʃɑ:dʒd] (noch) nicht entlastet; unerledigt.

un·dis·ci·plined [ʌn'disiplind] zuchtlos, undiszipliniert; ungeschult.

un·dis·cov·ered ['ʌndis'kʌvəd] unentdeckt.

un·dis·crim·i·nat·ing □ ['ʌndis-'krimineitiŋ] unterschiedlos.

un·dis·guised □ ['ʌndis'gaizd] unverkleidet; unverhohlen.

un·dis·posed ['ʌndis'pəuzd] nicht geneigt (*to* zu); nicht vergeben, † unverkauft.

un·dis·put·ed □ ['ʌndis'pju:tid] unbestritten.

un·dis·tin·guished ['ʌndis'tiŋ-gwiʃt] unbedeutend, gewöhnlich.

un·dis·tort·ed ['ʌndis'tɔ:tid] unverzerrt.

un·dis·turbed □ ['ʌndis'tə:bd] ungestört.

un·di·vid·ed □ ['ʌndi'vaidid] ungeteilt.

un·do ['ʌn'du:] (*irr.* do) aufmachen (*öffnen*); aufknöpfen; (auf)lösen; *j-m das Kleid* aufmachen; auftrennen; ungeschehen machen, aufheben; ⚓ vernichten; '**un'do·ing** Aufmachen *n* etc.; Verderben *n*.

un·do·mes·ti·cat·ed ['ʌndə'mesti-keitid] am Haushalt nicht interessiert (*Frau*).

un·done ['ʌn'dʌn] ungetan, ungeschehen *etc.*; erledigt, vernichtet; *he is ~* es ist aus mit ihm; *come ~* auf-, losgehen.

un·doubt·ed □ [ʌn'dautid] unzweifelhaft, zweifellos.

un·dreamt [ʌn'dremt]: ~-*of* ungeahnt.

un·dress ['ʌn'dres] **1.** (sich) entkleiden *od.* ausziehen; **2.** Hauskleid *n*; ⚔ Interimsuniform *f*; '**un-**

'dressed unbekleidet; nicht ordentlich angezogen; unzugerichtet, nicht zurechtgemacht; unverbunden (*Wunde*); ungegerbt.

un·due ['ʌn'dju:] ungebührlich, unangemessen; übermäßig; unzulässig; † noch nicht fällig.

un·du·late ['ʌndjuleit] wogen; wallen; wellenförmig verlaufen, wellig sein; **'un·du·lat·ing** □ wogend; well(enförm)ig; **un·du'la·tion** wellenförmige Bewegung *f*; **un·du·la·to·ry** ['‿lətəri] wellenförmig; Wellen...

un·du·ly ['ʌn'dju:li] *adv. von undue.*

un·du·ti·ful □ ['ʌn'dju:tiful] ungehorsam, pflichtvergessen.

un·dy·ing □ [ʌn'daiiŋ] unsterblich, unvergänglich.

un·earned ['ʌn'ə:nd] nicht aus Arbeit herrührend; *fig.* unverdient; ~ *income* Kapitaleinkommen *n*.

un·earth ['ʌn'ə:θ] ausgraben; *fig.* auftreiben, -stöbern; **un'earth·ly** übernatürlich, -irdisch; unheimlich; F unheimlich früh.

un·eas·i·ness [ʌn'i:zinis] Unruhe *f*; Unbehagen *n*; **un'eas·y** □ unbehaglich; unruhig, ängstlich (*about wegen*); unsicher.

un·eat·a·ble ['ʌn'i:təbl] ungenießbar.

un·e·co·nom·ic, un·e·co·nom·i·cal □ ['ʌni:kə'nɔmik(əl)] unwirtschaftlich.

un·ed·i·fy·ing □ ['ʌn'edifaiiŋ] wenig erbaulich *od.* erhebend.

un·ed·u·cat·ed ['ʌn'edjukeitid] unerzogen; ungebildet.

un·em·bar·rassed ['ʌnim'bærəst] ungehindert; nicht verlegen.

un·e·mo·tion·al □ ['ʌni'məuʃənl] leidenschaftslos; passiv; nüchtern.

un·em·ployed ['ʌnim'plɔid] **1.** unbeschäftigt; arbeits-, erwerbslos; unbenutzt; **2.** *the* ~ *pl.* die Arbeitslosen *pl.*; **'un·em'ploy·ment** Arbeitslosigkeit *f*; ~ *benefit*, ~ *pay* Arbeitslosenunterstützung *f*.

un·en·cum·bered ['ʌnin'kʌmbəd] unbelastet.

un·end·ing □ [ʌn'endiŋ] endlos.

un·en·dowed ['ʌnin'daud] nicht ausgestattet (*with* mit).

un·en·dur·a·ble ['ʌnin'djuərəbl] unerträglich.

un·en·gaged ['ʌnin'geidʒd] frei;

nicht gebunden; unbeschäftigt.

un·Eng·lish ['ʌn'iŋgliʃ] unenglisch.

un·en·light·ened ['ʌnin'laitnd] *fig.* unerleuchtet, nicht aufgeklärt.

un·en·ter·pris·ing ['ʌn'entəpraiziŋ] ohne Unternehmungsgeist.

un·en·vi·a·ble □ ['ʌn'enviəbl] nicht beneidenswert.

un·e·qual □ ['ʌn'i:kwəl] ungleich; nicht gewachsen (*to dat.*); **'un·e·qual(l)ed** unvergleichlich, unerreicht.

un·e·quiv·o·cal □ ['ʌni'kwivəkəl] unzweideutig, eindeutig.

un·err·ing □ ['ʌn'ə:riŋ] unfehlbar.

un·es·sen·tial □ ['ʌni'senʃəl] unwesentlich, -wichtig (*to* für).

un·e·ven □ ['ʌn'i:vən] uneben; ungleich(mäßig); unausgeglichen (*Charakter etc.*); ungerade (*Zahl*).

un·e·vent·ful □ ['ʌni'ventful] ereignislos; *be* ~ ohne Zwischenfälle verlaufen.

un·ex·am·pled [ʌnig'zɑ:mpld] beispiellos.

un·ex·cep·tion·a·ble □ [ʌnik'sepʃnəbl] untadelig; einwandfrei.

un·ex·cep·tion·al ['ʌnik'sepʃənl] (nicht un)gewöhnlich, durchschnittlich.

un·ex·pect·ed □ ['ʌniks'pektid] unerwartet.

un·ex·pired ['ʌniks'paiəd] noch nicht abgelaufen.

un·ex·plained ['ʌniks'pleind] unerklärt. [unbelichtet.]

un·ex·posed *phot.* ['ʌniks'pəuzd])

un·ex·plored ['ʌniks'plɔ:d] unerforscht.

un·ex·pressed ['ʌniks'prest] unausgesprochen.

un·fad·ing □ [ʌn'feidiŋ] nicht welkend; unvergänglich; echt (*Farbe*).

un·fail·ing □ [ʌn'feiliŋ] unfehlbar; nie versagend; unerschöpflich; *fig.* treu.

un·fair □ ['ʌn'fɛə] unehrlich; unanständig, unfair (*Spiel etc.*); unbillig, ungerecht; **'un'fair·ness** Unehrlichkeit *f*; Ungerechtigkeit *f etc.*

un·faith·ful □ ['ʌn'feiθful] un(ge)-treu, treulos; nicht wortgetreu; **'un'faith·ful·ness** Untreue *f*.

un·fal·ter·ing □ [ʌn'fɔ:ltəriŋ] nicht schwankend; unentwegt.

un·fa·mil·iar □ ['ʌnfə'miljə] unbekannt; ungewohnt.

un·fash·ion·a·ble □ [ˈʌnˈfæʃnəbl] unmodern, altmodisch.

un·fas·ten [ˈʌnˈfɑːsn] aufmachen.

un·fath·om·a·ble □ [ʌnˈfæðəmbl] unergründlich.

un·fa·vo(u)r·a·ble□ [ˈʌnˈfeivərəbl] ungünstig.

un·feel·ing □ [ʌnˈfiːliŋ] gefühllos.

un·feigned □ [ʌnˈfeind, *adv.* ~nidli] ungeheuchelt, unverstellt.

un·felt [ˈʌnˈfelt] ungefühlt.

un·fer·ment·ed [ˈʌnfəːˈmentid] unvergoren.

un·fet·ter [ˈʌnˈfetə] entfesseln; **'un·'fet·tered** *fig.* ungefesselt, frei.

un·fil·i·al □ [ˈʌnˈfiljəl] respektlos, pflichtvergessen (*Kind*).

un·fin·ished [ˈʌnˈfiniʃt] unvollendet; unfertig.

un·fit 1. □ [ˈʌnˈfit] ungeeignet, untauglich, unpassend (*for* s.th. für et.; *to inf.* zu *inf.*); **2.** [ʌnˈfit] untauglich machen; **'un·'fit·ness** Untauglichkeit *f*; **un·'fit·ted** ungeeignet; nicht (gut) ausgerüstet.

un·fix [ˈʌnˈfiks] losmachen, lösen; **'un·'fixed** unbefestigt.

un·flag·ging □ [ʌnˈflægiŋ] nicht erschlaffend (*Aufmerksamkeit etc.*).

un·flat·ter·ing□ [ˈʌnˈflætəriŋ] nicht schmeichelhaft, ungeschminkt.

un·fledged [ˈʌnˈfledʒd] ungefiedert; (noch) nicht flügge; *fig.* unreif.

un·flick·er·ing [ˈʌnˈflikəriŋ] nicht flackernd; *fig.* beständig.

un·flinch·ing □ [ʌnˈflintʃiŋ] fest entschlossen, unnachgiebig.

un·fly·a·ble [ˈʌnˈflaiəbl]: ~ weather ✈ kein Flugwetter.

un·fold [ˈʌnˈfould] (sich) entfalten *od.* öffnen; [ʌnˈfould] enthüllen.

un·forced □ [ˈʌnˈfɔːst, *adv.* ~sidli] ungezwungen.

un·fore·see·a·ble [ʌnfɔːˈsiːəbl] unvorhersehbar.

un·fore·seen [ˈʌnfɔːˈsiːn] unvorhergesehen.

un·for·get·ta·ble □ [ˈʌnfəˈgetəbl] unvergeßlich.

un·for·giv·ing [ˈʌnfəˈgiviŋ] unversöhnlich.

un·for·got, un·for·got·ten [ˈʌnfəˈgɔt(n)] unvergessen.

un·for·ti·fied [ˈʌnˈfɔːtifaid] unbefestigt.

un·for·tu·nate [ʌnˈfɔːtʃnit] **1.** □ unglücklich; unselig; Unglücks...; **2.** Unglückliche *m*, *f*; **un·'for·tu-**

nate·ly unglücklicherweise, leider.

un·found·ed □ [ˈʌnˈfaundid] unbegründet; grundlos.

un·fre·quent [ʌnˈfriːkwənt] nicht häufig, selten.

un·fre·quent·ed [ˈʌnfriˈkwentid] nicht *od.* wenig besucht; einsam.

un·friend·ed [ˈʌnˈfrendid] freundlos; **'un·'friend·ly** unfreundlich; ungünstig.

un·frock [ˈʌnˈfrɔk] *j-m* das Priesteramt entziehen.

un·fruit·ful □ [ˈʌnˈfruːtful] unfruchtbar.

un·ful·filled [ˈʌnfulˈfild] unerfüllt.

un·furl [ˈʌnˈfɔːl] *Fahne, Segel etc.* entfalten, aufrollen.

un·fur·nished [ˈʌnˈfəːniʃt] unmöbliert (*Wohnung*); ~ *with* nicht versehen mit.

un·gain·li·ness [ʌnˈgeinlinis] Unbeholfenheit *f*; **un·'gain·ly** unbeholfen, plump.

un·gal·lant □[ˈʌnˈgælənt] ungalant (*to* gegen).

un·gat·ed [ˈʌnˈgeitid] unbeschrankt (*Bahnübergang*).

un·gear ⊕ [ˈʌnˈgiə] auskuppeln.

un·gen·er·ous □ [ˈʌnˈdʒenərəs] unedelmütig; nicht freigebig.

un·gen·ial □ [ˈʌnˈdʒiːnjəl] unfreundlich.

un·gen·tle □ [ˈʌnˈdʒentl] unsanft, unzart.

un·gen·tle·man·ly [ʌnˈdʒentlmənli] ungebildet, unfein, ohne Lebensart, e-s Gentleman unwürdig.

un·get-at·able [ˈʌnget'ætəbl] unzugänglich.

un·glazed [ˈʌnˈgleizd] unglasiert; nicht verglast.

un·gloved [ˈʌnˈglʌvd] unbehandschuht.

un·god·li·ness [ʌnˈgɔdlinis] Gottlosigkeit *f*; **un·'god·ly** □ gottlos; F abscheulich, schrecklich, unmenschlich.

un·gov·ern·a·ble □ [ʌnˈgʌvənəbl] unlenksam; zügellos, unbändig; **'un·'gov·erned** unbeherrscht.

un·grace·ful □ [ˈʌnˈgreisful] ungraziös, ohne Anmut; unbeholfen.

un·gra·cious □ [ˈʌnˈgreiʃəs] ungnädig; unfreundlich.

'un·'gram·mat·i·cal □ gegen die Regeln der Grammatik verstoßend.

un·grate·ful □ [ʌnˈgreitful] undankbar.

un·ground·ed [ʌn'graundid] unbegründet; ⚡ ungeerdet.

un·grudg·ing □ ['ʌn'grʌdʒiŋ] ohne Murren, willig; neidlos.

un·gual anat. ['ʌŋgwəl] Nagel...

un·guard·ed □ ['ʌn'gɑːdid] unbewacht; unvorsichtig, unbedacht; ⊕ ungeschützt.

un·guent ['ʌŋgwənt] Salbe f.

un·guid·ed □ ['ʌn'gaidid] ungeleitet; führerlos.

un·gu·late ['ʌŋgjuleit] a. ~ animal Huftier n.

un·hal·lowed [ʌn'hæləud] unheilig, böse; ungeweiht.

un·ham·pered ['ʌn'hæmpəd] ungehindert.

un·hand·some □ [ʌn'hænsəm] unschön (a. fig.).

un·hand·y □ [ʌn'hændi] ungeschickt; unhandlich (Sache); unbeholfen (Person).

un·hap·pi·ness [ʌn'hæpinis] Unglück(seligkeit f) n; **un'hap·py** □ unglücklich; un(glück)selig; unpassend.

un·harmed ['ʌn'hɑːmd] unversehrt.

un·har·mo·ni·ous □ ['ʌnhɑː'məunjəs] unharmonisch.

un·har·ness ['ʌn'hɑːnis] abschirren.

un·health·y □ [ʌn'helθi] ungesund.

un·heard ['ʌn'hɔːd] ungehört; **un·heard-of** [ʌn'hɔːdɔv] unerhört.

un·heat·ed ['ʌn'hiːtid] ungeheizt.

un·heed·ed ['ʌn'hiːdid] unbeachtet; unbewacht; **'un'heed·ing** sorglos, unachtsam.

un·hes·i·tat·ing □ [ʌn'heziteitiŋ] ohne Zögern; unbedenklich; anstandslos; ~ly ohne zu zögern.

un·hin·dered ['ʌn'hindəd] ungehindert.

un·hinge [ʌn'hindʒ] aus den Angeln heben; fig. zerrütten.

un·his·tor·ic, un·his·tor·i·cal □ ['ʌnhis'tɔrik(əl)] unhistorisch; ungeschichtlich. [spannen.⟩

un·hitch ['ʌn'hitʃ] losmachen; aus-⟩

un·ho·ly [ʌn'həuli] unheilig; gottlos; F scheußlich, schrecklich.

un·hon·o(u)red ['ʌn'ɔnəd] ungeehrt; uneingelöst (Pfand, Scheck).

un·hook ['ʌn'huk] auf-, aushaken.

un·hoped-for [ʌn'həuptfɔː] unverhofft.

un·horse ['ʌn'hɔːs] aus dem Sattel heben; Reiter abwerfen.

un·house ['ʌn'hauz] (aus dem Hause) vertreiben; obdachlos machen.

un·hung [ʌn'hʌŋ] un(auf)gehängt.

un·hurt ['ʌn'hɔːt] unverletzt.

u·ni·corn ['juːnikɔːn] Einhorn n.

un·i·den·ti·fied ['ʌnai'dentifaid] nicht identifizierbar od. identifiziert; ~ flying object Ufo n.

u·ni·fi·ca·tion [juːnifi'keiʃən] Vereinigung f; Vereinheitlichung f.

u·ni·form ['juːnifɔːm] **1.** □ gleichförmig, -mäßig; einheitlich; ~ price Einheitspreis m; **2.** Dienstkleidung f; Uniform f; **3.** uniformieren; **u·ni'form·i·ty** Gleichförmigkeit f, -mäßigkeit f.

u·ni·fy ['juːnifai] verein(ig)en; vereinheitlichen.

u·ni·lat·er·al ['juːni'lætərəl] einseitig.

un·im·ag·i·na·ble □ [ʌni'mædʒinəbl] undenkbar; **'un·im'ag·i·na·tive** □ [ˌ~nətiv] ohne Phantasie, phantasielos, einfallslos.

un·im·paired ['ʌnim'pɛəd] unvermindert, ungeschwächt.

un·im·peach·a·ble □ [ʌnim'piːtʃəbl] einwandfrei, unanfechtbar.

un·im·ped·ed □ ['ʌnim'piːdid] ungehindert.

un·im·por·tant □ ['ʌnim'pɔːtənt] unwichtig.

un·im·proved ['ʌnim'pruːvd] nicht kultiviert, unbebaut (Land); unverbessert.

un·in·flu·enced ['ʌn'influənst] unbeeinflußt. [unterrichtet.⟩

un·in·formed ['ʌnin'fɔːmd] nicht⟩

un·in·hab·it·a·ble ['ʌnin'hæbitəbl] unbewohnbar; **'un·in'hab·it·ed** unbewohnt.

un·in·jured ['ʌn'indʒəd] unbeschädigt, unverletzt.

un·in·struct·ed ['ʌnin'strʌktid] nicht unterrichtet; nicht instruiert.

un·in·sured ['ʌnin'ʃuəd] unversichert.

un·in·tel·li·gi·bil·i·ty ['ʌnintelidʒə'biliti] Unverständlichkeit f; **'un·in'tel·li·gi·ble** □ unverständlich.

un·in·tend·ed □ ['ʌnin'tendid] unbeabsichtigt.

un·in·ten·tion·al ['ʌnin'tenʃənl] unabsichtlich.

un·in·ter·est·ing □ ['ʌn'intristiŋ] uninteressant.

un·in·ter·rupt·ed □ ['ʌnintə'rʌptid] ununterbrochen; ~ working hours

pl. durchgehende Arbeitszeit *f.*
un·in·vit·ed [ˈʌninˈvaitid] un(ein)-geladen; 'un·in'vit·ing ☐ wenig einladend.
un·ion [ˈjuːnjən] Vereinigung *f;* (*engS.* *eheliche*) Verbindung *f; pol. etc.* Union *f,* Bund *m; univ.* (De-battier)Klub *m;* Einigung *f;* Einig-keit *f;* Verein *m,* Verband *m;* Armenhaus *n;* ⚓ Gösch *f;* ⊕ Rohrverbindung *f;* Gewerkschaft *f;* ~ **dues** *pl.* Gewerkschaftsbeitrag *m;* 'un·ion·ism *pol. etc.* Unionismus *m;* Gewerkschaftswesen *n;* 'un·ion·ist *pol. etc.* Anhänger *m* der Union; Gewerkschaftler *m;* 'un·ion·ize ge-werkschaftlich organisieren.
un·ion...: ⚥ **Jack** Union Jack *m* (*britische Nationalflagge*); ~ **of·fi·cial** Gewerkschaftsfunktionär *m;* ~ **suit** *Am.* Hemdhose *f.*
u·nique [juːˈniːk] **1.** ☐ einzigartig; einmalig; **2.** Unikum *n.*
u·ni·son ♩ *u. fig.* [ˈjuːnizn] Einklang *m; in* ~ *unisono* (*einstimmig*); **u·nis·o·nous** ♩ [juːˈnisənəs] gleich-tönend.
u·nit [ˈjuːnit] Einheit *f* (*a.* ✕); ⅍ Einer *m;* ⊕ Anlage *f;* ~ **furniture** Anbaumöbel *pl.;* **U·ni·tar·i·an** [ˌ-ˈtɛəriən] **1.** Unitarier *m;* **2.** uni-tarisch; **u·ni·tar·y** [ˈˌ-təri] Ein-heits...; ⅍ Einer...; **u·nite** [juː-ˈnait] (sich) vereinigen, verbinden.
u·nit·ed [juːˈnaitid] vereinigt, ver-eint; ⚥ **King·dom** *das* Vereinigte Königreich (*Großbritannien u. Nordirland*); ⚥ **Na·tions** *pl. die* Vereinten Nationen *pl.;* ⚥ **States** *pl. die* Vereinigten Staaten *pl.*
u·ni·ty [ˈjuːniti] Einheit *f;* Einig-keit *f.*
u·ni·ver·sal ☐ [juːniˈvɔːsəl] allge-mein; allumfassend; Universal...; Welt...; ~ **heir** Universalerbe *m;* ~ **joint** ⊕ Universalgelenk *n;* ~ **language** Weltsprache *f;* ⚥ **Postal Union** Weltpostverein *m;* ~ **suffrage** allgemeines Wahlrecht *n;* **u·ni·ver·sal·i·ty** [ˌ-ˈsæliti] Allgemeinheit *f;* umfassende Bildung *f,* Vielseitig-keit *f;* **u·ni·verse** [ˈjuːnivɔːs] Weltall *n,* Universum *n;* **u·ni·ver·si·ty** Universität *f; Open* ⚥ Fern-universität *f* (*in England*).
un·just ☐ [ˈʌnˈdʒʌst] ungerecht; **un'jus·ti·fi·a·ble** ☐ [ˌ-tifaiəbl] nicht zu rechtfertigen(d), unverant-

wortlich.
un·kempt [ˈʌnˈkempt] ungekämmt; *fig.* ungepflegt, verwahrlost.
un·kind ☐ [ʌnˈkaind] unfreundlich; rücksichtslos.
un·knit *bsd. fig.* [ˈʌnˈnit] (*irr. knit*) (auf)lösen.   [knüpfen.]
un·knot [ˈʌnˈnɔt] entknoten; los-]
un·know·ing ☐ [ˈʌnˈnəuiŋ] un-wissend; unbewußt; 'un'known **1.** unbekannt; unbewußt; **2.** *adv.* ~ *to me* ohne mein Wissen; **3.** Unbe-kannte *m, f;* ⅍ Unbekannte *f.*
un·lace [ˈʌnˈleis] aufschnüren.
un·lade [ˈʌnˈleid] (*irr. lade*) aus-, entladen; ⚓ löschen.
un·la·dy·like [ˈʌnˈleidilaik] nicht damenhaft, unfein. [deckt (*Tisch*).]
un·laid [ˈʌnˈleid] ungelegt; unge-]
un·la·ment·ed [ˈʌnləˈmentid] un-beklagt.
un·latch [ˈʌnˈlætʃ] aufklinken.
un·law·ful ☐ [ˈʌnˈlɔːful] ungesetz-lich; rechtswidrig; *weitS.* unrecht-mäßig.
un·learn [ˈʌnˈlɔːn] (*irr. learn*) ver-lernen; 'un'learn·ed ☐ [ˌ-nid] un-gelehrt, unwissend.
un·leash [ˈʌnˈliːʃ] losbinden, *Hund* loskoppeln; *fig.* entfesseln.
un·leav·ened [ˈʌnˈlevnd] unge-säuert.
un·less [ənˈles] wenn nicht, außer wenn; es sei denn, daß.
un·let·tered [ˈʌnˈletəd] ungebildet, unwissend.
un·li·censed [ˈʌnˈlaisənst] unbe-rechtigt, unkonzessioniert.
un·licked *mst fig.* [ˈʌnˈlikt] unbe-leckt, unreif; ~ *cub* grüner Junge *m.*
un·like ☐ [ˈʌnˈlaik] ungleich, un-ähnlich (*s.o.* j-m), anders als; im Gegensatz zu; **un'like·li·hood** [ˌhud] Unwahrscheinlichkeit *f;* **un'like·ly** unwahrscheinlich.
un·lim·it·ed [ʌnˈlimitid] unbe-grenzt; unbeschränkt; *fig.* grenzen-los.   [unliniiert.]
un·lined [ˈʌnˈlaind] ungefüttert;]
un·liq·ui·dat·ed [ˈʌnˈlikwideitid] unbeglichen, unbezahlt.
un·load [ˈʌnˈləud] ent-, ab-, aus-laden; *Ladung* löschen; *Börse:* ab-stoßen.
un·lock [ˈʌnˈlɔk] aufschließen (*a. fig.*); *Schußwaffe* entsichern; 'un-'locked unverschlossen.
un·looked-for [ʌnˈluktfɔː] uner-

wartet.

un·loose, un·loos·en [ˈʌnˈluːs(n)] lösen, losmachen.

un·lov·a·ble [ˈʌnˈlʌvəbl] nicht liebenswert; **'un'love·ly** reizlos, unschön; **'un'lov·ing** ⸫ lieblos.

un·lucky ⸪ [ʌnˈlʌki] unglücklich.

un·made [ˈʌnˈmeid] ungemacht.

un·make [ˈʌnˈmeik] (*irr. make*) vernichten; rückgängig machen; umbilden; *Herrscher* absetzen.

un·man [ˈʌnˈmæn] entmannen; entmutigen; verrohen (lassen).

un·man·age·a·ble □ [ʌnˈmænidʒəbl] unlenksam, widerspenstig; unhandlich; schwierig (*Lage*).

un·man·ly [ˈʌnˈmænli] unmännlich.

un·manned [ˈʌnˈmænd] unbemannt.

un·man·ner·ly [ʌnˈmænəli] unmanierlich.

un·marked [ˈʌnˈmɑːkt] unbezeichnet; unbemerkt.

un·mar·ried [ˈʌnˈmærid] unverheiratet, ledig.

un·mask [ˈʌnˈmɑːsk] (sich) demaskieren; *fig.* entlarven.

un·matched [ˈʌnˈmætʃt] unerreicht; unvergleichlich.

un·mean·ing □ [ʌnˈmiːniŋ] nichtssagend; **un'meant** [ˈʌnˈment] unbeabsichtigt.

un·meas·ured [ʌnˈmeʒəd] ungemessen; unermeßlich.

un·meet [ˈʌnˈmiːt] ungeeignet, unpassend.

un·men·tion·a·ble [ʌnˈmenʃnəbl] **1.** nicht zu erwähnen(d), unnennbar; **2.** ⸝s *pl.* F (Unter)Hosen *f/pl.*

un·mer·ci·ful □ [ʌnˈməːsiful] unbarmherzig.

un·mer·it·ed [ˈʌnˈmeritid] unverdient.

un·me·thod·i·cal [ˈʌnmiˈθɔdikəl] unmethodisch.

un·mil·i·tar·y [ˈʌnˈmilitəri] unmilitärisch.

un·mind·ful □ [ʌnˈmaindful] unbedacht(sam); sorglos; ohne Rücksicht (*of* auf *acc.*).

un·mis·tak·a·ble □ [ˈʌnmisˈteikəbl] unverkennbar; unmißverständlich, eindeutig.

un·mit·i·gat·ed [ʌnˈmitigeitid] ungemildert; richtig; *fig.* Erz...

un·mixed [ˈʌnˈmikst] unvermischt.

un·mod·i·fied [ˈʌnˈmɔdifaid] nicht abgeändert.

un·mo·lest·ed [ˈʌnməuˈlestid] unbelästigt.

un·moor [ˈʌnˈmuə] *Schiff* losmachen.

un·mor·al [ˈʌnˈmɔrəl] amoralisch.

un·mort·gaged [ˈʌnˈmɔːgidʒd] unverpfändet.

un·mount·ed [ˈʌnˈmauntid] unberitten; nicht gefaßt (*Stein*); unaufgezogen (*Bild*); unmontiert (*Geschütz*).

un·mourned [ˈʌnˈmɔːnd] unbetrauert.

un·moved ⸪ [ˈʌnˈmuːvd] *mst fig.* unbewegt, ungerührt; **un'mov·ing** regungslos.

un·mu·si·cal ⸪ [ˈʌnˈmjuːzikəl] unmusikalisch; unmelodisch.

un·muz·zle [ˈʌnˈmʌzl] *e-m Hund* den Maulkorb abnehmen; ⸝d ohne Maulkorb.

un·named [ˈʌnˈneimd] ungenannt.

un·nat·u·ral □ [ʌnˈnætʃrəl] unnatürlich.

un·nav·i·ga·ble [ˈʌnˈnævigəbl] nicht schiffbar.

un·nec·es·sar·y □ [ʌnˈnesisəri] unnötig.

un·neigh·bo(u)r·ly [ˈʌnˈneibəli] nicht gutnachbarlich.

un·nerve [ˈʌnˈnəːv] entnerven.

un·not·ed [ˈʌnˈnəutid] unbemerkt; unbekannt, unberühmt.

un·no·ticed [ˈʌnˈnəutist] unbemerkt.

un·num·bered [ˈʌnˈnʌmbəd] unnumeriert; *poet.* ungezählt.

un·ob·jec·tion·a·ble □ [ˈʌnəbˈdʒekʃnəbl] einwandfrei.

un·ob·serv·ant □ [ˈʌnəbˈzəːvənt] unachtsam (*of* auf *acc.*); **'un·ob·'served** ⸝ unbemerkt.

un·ob·tain·a·ble [ˈʌnəbˈteinəbl] unerreichbar; nicht zu bekommen(d).

un·ob·tru·sive ⸪ [ˈʌnəbˈtruːsiv] unaufdringlich, bescheiden.

un·oc·cu·pied [ˈʌnˈɔkjupaid] unbesetzt; unbewohnt; unbeschäftigt.

un·of·fend·ing [ˈʌnəˈfendiŋ] nicht anstößig, harmlos.

un·of·fi·cial □ [ˈʌnəˈfiʃəl] nichtamtlich, inoffiziell.

un·o·pened [ˈʌnˈəupənd] ungeöffnet.

un·op·posed [ˈʌnəˈpəuzd] ungehindert; ohne Widerstand (zu finden).

un·or·gan·ized [ˈʌnˈɔːgənaizd] unorganisch; unorganisiert.

un·os·ten·ta·tious ⌐ ['ʌnɔsten-'teiʃəs] anspruchslos; ohne Prunk; unauffällig.

un·owned ['ʌn'əund] herrenlos.

un·pack ['ʌn'pæk] auspacken.

un·paid ['ʌn'peid] unbezahlt; unbelohnt; ⌐ unfrankiert.

un·pal·at·a·ble [ʌn'pælətəbl] nicht schmackhaft, schlecht (schmekkend); *fig.* widerwärtig.

un·par·al·leled ['ʌn'pærəleld] beispiellos, ohnegleichen.

un·par·don·a·ble ⌐ [ʌn'pɑ:dnəbl] unverzeihlich.

un·par·lia·men·ta·ry ⌐ ['ʌnpɑ:lə-'mentəri] unparlamentarisch.

un·pat·ent·ed ['ʌn'peitəntid] unpatentiert.

un·pa·tri·ot·ic ['ʌnpætri'ɔtik] (⌐ally) unpatriotisch.

un·paved ['ʌn'peivd] ungepflastert.

un·per·ceived ⌐ ['ʌnpə'si:vd] unbemerkt.

un·per·formed ['ʌnpə'fɔ:md] unausgeführt.

un·per·plexed ['ʌnpə'plekst] nicht verwirrt.

un·per·turbed ['ʌnpə:'tə:bd] nicht beunruhigt *od.* verwirrt, ruhig, gelassen, unerschüttert.

un·phil·o·soph·i·cal ⌐ ['ʌnfilə'sɔfikəl] unphilosophisch.

un·pick ['ʌn'pik] *Naht* (auf)trennen.

un·picked ['ʌn'pikt] unsortiert.

un·pin ['ʌn'pin] losstecken.

un·pit·ied ['ʌn'pitid] unbemitleidet.

un·placed ['ʌn'pleist] ohne Platz; *Rennsport*: unplaziert; nichtangestellt.

un·pleas·ant ⌐ [ʌn'pleznt] unangenehm; unerfreulich; **un'pleas·ant·ness** Unannehmlichkeit *f.*

un·plumbed ['ʌn'plʌmd] unergründlich.

un·po·et·ic, **un·po·et·i·cal** ⌐ ['ʌnpəu'etik(əl)] unpoetisch, prosaisch.

un·po·lished ['ʌn'pɔliʃt] unpoliert; *fig.* ungebildet.

un·polled ['ʌn'pəuld] nicht in die Wählerliste eingetragen.

un·pol·lut·ed ['ʌnpə'lu:tid] unbefleckt.

un·pop·u·lar ⌐ ['ʌn'pɔpjulə] unpopulär, unbeliebt; **un·pop·u·lar·i·ty** ['⌐læriti] Unbeliebtheit *f.*

un·pos·sessed ['ʌnpə'zest]: ⌐ *of s.th.* nicht im Besitz e-r Sache.

un·prac·ti·cal ⌐ ['ʌn'præktikəl] un-

praktisch; **un'prac·ticed**, **un'prac·tised** [⌐tist] ungeübt.

un·prec·e·dent·ed ☐ [ʌn'presidəntid] beispiellos, unerhört; noch nie dagewesen.

un·prej·u·diced ⌐ [ʌn'predʒudist] unbefangen, unvoreingenommen.

un·pre·med·i·tat·ed ☐ ['ʌnpri-'mediteitid] nicht vorbedacht, unbeabsichtigt; aus dem Stegreif.

un·pre·pared ⌐ ['ʌnpri'pɛəd, *adv.* ⌐ridli] unvorbereitet.

un·pre·pos·sess·ing ['ʌnpri:pə'zesiŋ] nicht einnehmend, reizlos.

un·pre·sent·a·ble ['ʌnpri'zentəbl] nicht vorzeigbar; nicht salonfähig.

un·pre·tend·ing ☐ ['ʌnpri'təndiŋ], **'un·pre'ten·tious** ⌐ anspruchslos, bescheiden.

un·prin·ci·pled [ʌn'prinsəpld] ohne Grundsätze; gewissenlos.

un·print·a·ble ['ʌn'printəbl] nicht wiederzugeben(d), nicht salonfähig (*Wort*).

un·priv·il·eged *Am.* [ʌn'privilidʒd] sozial benachteiligt, arm.

un·pro·duc·tive ⌐ ['ʌnprə'dʌktiv] unfruchtbar, unergiebig (*of* an *dat.*); ✝ unproduktiv.

un·pro·fes·sion·al ⌐ ['ʌnprə'feʃənl] nicht berufsmäßig, berufswidrig.

un·prof·it·a·ble ⌐ [ʌn'prɔfitəbl] nicht einträglich; nutzlos, unnütz; **un'prof·it·a·ble·ness** Nutzlosigkeit *f.*

un·prom·is·ing ☐ ['ʌn'prɔmisiŋ] nicht vielversprechend, aussichtslos.

un·prompt·ed [ʌn'prɔmptid] unbeeinflußt, spontan.

un·pro·nounce·a·ble ☐ ['ʌnprə-'naunsəbl] schwer auszusprechen(d).

un·pro·pi·tious ⌐ ['ʌnprə'piʃəs] ungünstig, ungeeignet.

un·pro·tect·ed ☐ ['ʌnprə'tektid] ungeschützt.

un·proved ['ʌn'pru:vd] unerwiesen.

un·pro·vid·ed ['ʌnprə'vaidid] nicht versehen (*with* mit); ⌐ *for* unversorgt, mittellos.

un·pro·voked ⌐ ['ʌnprə'vəukt] unprovoziert; ohne Grund.

un·pub·lished ['ʌn'pʌbliʃt] unveröffentlicht.

un·punc·tu·al ☐ ['ʌn'pʌŋktjuəl] unpünktlich; **un·punc·tu·al·i·ty** ['⌐æliti] Unpünktlichkeit *f.*

un·pun·ished [ˈʌnˈpʌnɪʃt] ungestraft; go ⁓ straflos ausgehen.
un·qual·i·fied □ [ˈʌnˈkwɔlifaid] ungeeignet, unqualifiziert; unberechtigt; unbeschränkt; F ausgesprochen (*Lügner etc.*).
un·quench·a·ble □ [ʌnˈkwentʃəbl]
unlöschbar; *fig.* unstillbar.
un·ques·tion·a·ble □ [ʌnˈkwestʃə-
nəbl] unfraglich, fraglos; **un·ques-
tioned** ungefragt; unbestritten;
un·ques·tion·ing □ ohne zu
fragen; bedingungslos.
un·qui·et [ʌnˈkwaiət] unruhig, ruhelos.
un·quote [ˈʌnˈkwəut] *Zitat* be-
endend; **un·quot·ed** *Börse*: nicht
notiert.
un·rav·el [ʌnˈrævəl] (sich) entwirren; enträtseln.
un·read [ˈʌnˈred] ungelesen; un-
belesen (*Person*); **un·read·a·ble**
[ˈʌnˈriːdəbl] unleserlich; unlesbar.
un·read·i·ness [ˈʌnˈredinis] man-
gelnde Bereitschaft *f*; **'un·read·y**
□ nicht bereit *od.* fertig; unlustig,
zögernd.
un·re·al □ [ˈʌnˈriəl] unwirklich;
un·re·al·is·tic [ˈʌnriəˈlistik] wirklichkeitsfremd, unrealistisch; **un-
re·al·i·ty** [⌣ˈælit i] Unwirklichkeit
f; **'un·re·al·iz·a·ble** [⌣əlaizəbl]
nicht zu verwirklichen(d), nicht
realisierbar; ✝ unverkäuflich.
un·rea·son [ˈʌnˈriːzn] Unvernunft *f*;
un·rea·son·a·ble □ unvernünftig;
grundlos; unmäßig.
un·re·claimed [ˈʌnriˈkleimd] un-
gebessert; nicht kultiviert, unbebaut (*Land*).
un·rec·og·niz·a·ble □ [ˈʌnˈrekəg-
naizəbl] nicht wiederzuerken-
nen(d); **'un·rec·og·nized** nicht
(an)erkannt.
un·rec·om·pensed [ˈʌnˈrekəmpenst]
unbelohnt.
un·rec·on·ciled [ˈʌnˈrekənsaild] un-
versöhnt.
un·re·cord·ed [ˈʌnriˈkɔːdid] (geschichtlich) nicht aufgezeichnet.
un·re·dee·med □ [ˈʌnriˈdiːmd] un-
erlöst; uneingelöst (*Pfand, Versprechen*); *fig.* ungemildert (*by
durch*).
un·re·dressed [ˈʌnriˈdrest] nicht
abgestellt (*Mißstand*); ungesühnt.
un·reel [ˈʌnˈriːl] (sich) abhaspeln.
un·re·fined [ˈʌnriˈfaind] ungeläu-

tert; *fig.* ungebildet.
un·re·flect·ing □ [ˈʌnriˈflektiŋ] gedankenlos.
un·re·formed [ˈʌnriˈfɔːmd] unverbessert; nicht reformiert.
un·re·gard·ed [ˈʌnriˈgɑːdid] unbeachtet; unberücksichtigt; **'un-
re·gard·ful** [⌣ful] unachtsam (*of
auf acc.*).
un·reg·is·tered [ˈʌnˈredʒistəd] un-
aufgezeichnet; nicht approbiert
(*Arzt etc.*); nicht eingeschrieben
(*Brief*).
un·re·gret·ted [ˈʌnriˈgretid] unbe-
klagt, unbetrauert.
un·re·lat·ed [ˈʌnriˈleitid] ohne Beziehung (*to zu*).
un·re·lent·ing □ [ˈʌnriˈlentiŋ] erbarmungslos; unerbittlich.
un·re·li·a·ble [ˈʌnriˈlaiəbl] unzuverlässig.
un·re·lieved □ [ˈʌnriˈliːvd] unge-
lindert; nicht unterbrochen, ununterbrochen.
un·re·mit·ting □ [ˈʌnriˈmitiŋ] un-
ablässig, unaufhörlich; unermüdlich.
un·re·mu·ner·a·tive □ [ˈʌnriˈmjuː-
nərətiv] nicht lohnend.
un·re·pealed [ˈʌnriˈpiːld] unwider-
rufen.
un·re·pent·ed [ˈʌnriˈpentid] un-
bereut.
un·re·pin·ing □ [ˈʌnriˈpainiŋ] klaglos; unverdrossen.
un·re·quit·ed □ [ˈʌnriˈkwaitid] unerwidert; unbelohnt.
un·re·served □ [ˈʌnriˈzəːvd, *adv.*
⌣vidli] rückhaltlos; unbeschränkt;
ohne Vorbehalt.
un·re·sist·ing □ [ˈʌnriˈzistiŋ] wider-
standslos.
un·re·spon·sive [ˈʌnrisˈpɔnsiv] unempfänglich (*to für*).
un·rest [ˈʌnˈrest] Unruhe *f*; **'un-
'rest·ing** □ rastlos.
un·re·strained □ [ˈʌnrisˈtreind]
ungehemmt; unbeherrscht; unbeschränkt; ungezwungen.
un·re·strict·ed □ [ˈʌnrisˈtriktid]
uneingeschränkt.
un·re·vealed [ˈʌnriˈviːld] nicht of-
fenbart.
un·re·ward·ed [ˈʌnriˈwɔːdid] unbelohnt.
un·rhymed [ˈʌnˈraimd] ungereimt,
reimlos.
un·rid·dle [ˈʌnridl] enträtseln.

un·rig ⚓ [ˈʌnˈrig] abtakeln.
un·right·eous ☐ [ʌnˈraitʃəs] ungerecht; unredlich.
un·rip [ˈʌnˈrip] auftrennen; aufschlitzen.
un·ripe [ˈʌnˈraip] unreif.
un·ri·val(1)ed [ʌnˈraivəld] unvergleichlich, unerreicht, einzigartig.
un·roll [ˈʌnˈrəul] auf-, entrollen.
un·roof [ˈʌnˈruːf] *Haus* abdecken.
un·rope *mount.* [ˈʌnˈrəup] (sich) ausseilen.
un·ruf·fled [ˈʌnˈrʌfld] glatt; unerschüttert; ruhig.
un·ruled [ˈʌnˈruːld] unbeherrscht; unliniiert (*Papier*).
un·rul·y [ʌnˈruːli] ungebärdig, unbändig.
un·sad·dle [ˈʌnˈsædl] absatteln.
un·safe ☐ [ˈʌnˈseif] unsicher.
un·said [ˈʌnˈsed] ungesagt.
un·sal·a·ried [ˈʌnˈsælərid] unbezahlt, ehrenamtlich.
un·sal(e)·a·ble [ˈʌnˈseiləbl] unverkäuflich.
un·salt·ed [ˈʌnˈsɔːltid] ungesalzen.
un·sanc·tioned [ˈʌnˈsæŋkʃənd] unbestätigt; unerlaubt.
un·san·i·tar·y [ˈʌnˈsænitəri] unhygienisch.
un·sat·is·fac·to·ry ☐ [ˈʌnsætisˈfæktəri] unbefriedigend; unzulänglich; **ˈun·ˈsat·is·fied** [ˌfaid] unbefriedigt; **ˈun·ˈsat·is·fy·ing** ☐ [ˌfaiiŋ] = *unsatisfactory*.
un·sa·vo(u)r·y ☐ [ˈʌnˈseivəri] unappetitlich (*a. fig.*), widerwärtig.
un·say [ˈʌnˈsei] (*irr. say*) zurücknehmen, widerrufen.
un·scathed [ˈʌnˈskeiðd] unbeschädigt, unversehrt.
un·schooled [ˈʌnˈskuːld] ungeschult; unverbildet.
un·sci·en·tif·ic [ˈʌnsaiənˈtifik] (ˌally) unwissenschaftlich.
un·screw [ˈʌnˈskruː] (sich) ab-, los-, aufschrauben.
un·script·ur·al ☐ [ˈʌnˈskriptʃərəl] schriftwidrig, nicht biblisch.
un·scru·pu·lous ☐ [ʌnˈskruːpjuləs] bedenkenlos; gewissenlos; skrupellos.
un·seal [ˈʌnˈsiːl] entsiegeln.
un·search·a·ble ☐ [ʌnˈsəːtʃəbl] unerforschlich; unergründlich.
un·sea·son·a·ble ☐ [ʌnˈsiːznəbl] unzeitig, *fig.* ungelegen; **ˈun·ˈsea·soned** nicht abgelagert (*Holz*); *fig.*

nicht abgehärtet; ungewürzt.
un·seat [ˈʌnˈsiːt] aus dem Amt entfernen; aus dem Sattel heben, abwerfen; *be* ～*ed* s-n Sitz *im Parlament* verlieren; (vom Pferd) stürzen.
un·sea·wor·thy ⚓ [ˈʌnˈsiːwəːði] seeuntüchtig.
un·see·ing *fig.* [ˈʌnˈsiːiŋ] blind.
un·seem·li·ness [ʌnˈsiːmlinis] Unziemlichkeit *f*; **un·ˈseem·ly** unziemlich, unpassend.
un·seen [ˈʌnˈsiːn] **1.** ungesehen; unsichtbar; **2.** *Schule*: Übersetzung *f* e-s unbekannten Textes; *the* ～ die unsichtbare Welt.
un·self·ish ☐ [ˈʌnˈselfiʃ] selbstlos, uneigennützig; **ˈun·ˈself·ish·ness** Selbstlosigkeit *f*.
un·sen·ti·men·tal [ˈʌnsentiˈmentl] unsentimental.
un·serv·ice·a·ble ☐ [ˈʌnˈsəːvisəbl] undienlich; unbrauchbar.
un·set·tle [ˈʌnˈsetl] in Unordnung bringen; verwirren; erschüttern; **ˈun·ˈset·tled** nicht festgesetzt, unbestimmt; unbeständig, schwankend (*a. Wetter*, ✝ *Markt*); ✝ unbezahlt; unerledigt (*Frage*); ohne festen Wohnsitz; unbesiedelt (*Land*).
un·sex [ˈʌnˈseks] entweiben.
un·shack·le [ˈʌnˈʃækl] entfesseln.
un·shak(e)·a·ble [ʌnˈʃeikəbl] unerschütterlich.
un·shak·en [ˈʌnˈʃeikən] unerschüttert; unerschütterlich.
un·shape·ly [ˈʌnˈʃeipli] ungestalt.
un·shav·en [ˈʌnˈʃeivn] unrasiert.
un·sheathe [ˈʌnˈʃiːð] aus der Scheide ziehen.
un·shell [ˈʌnˈʃel] (ab)schälen.
un·ship [ˈʌnˈʃip] ausschiffen, ausladen; F *fig. j.* ausbooten.
un·shod [ˈʌnˈʃɔd] unbeschuht; unbeschlagen (*Pferd*).
un·shorn [ˈʌnˈʃɔːn] ungeschoren.
un·shrink·a·ble [ˈʌnˈʃriŋkəbl] nicht einlaufend (*Stoff*); **ˈun·ˈshrink·ing** ☐ unverzagt.
un·sight [ˈʌnˈsait] die Sicht nehmen; **un·ˈsight·ly** häßlich.
un·signed [ˈʌnˈsaind] nicht unterzeichnet.
un·sized[1] [ˈʌnˈsaizd] ungrundiert; ungeleimt (*Papier*).
un·sized[2] [ˌ] nicht nach Größen geordnet; unsortiert.
un·skil(1)·ful ☐ [ˈʌnˈskilful] un-

unskilled

geschickt; **'un'skilled** ungelernt (*Arbeit, Arbeiter*).

un·skimmed ['ʌn'skimd] nicht entrahmt.

un·sleep·ing ['ʌn'sliːpiŋ] schlaflos.

un·so·cia·ble [ʌn'səuʃəbl] ungesellig; **un'so·cial** ungesellig; unsozial.

un·sold ['ʌn'səuld] unverkauft.

un·sol·der ['ʌn'sɔldə] los-, ablöten.

un·sol·dier·ly *adj.* ['ʌn'səuldʒəli] unsoldatisch, unkriegerisch.

un·so·lic·it·ed ['ʌnsə'lisitid] unverlangt (*Sache*); unaufgefordert (*Person*).

un·solv·a·ble ['ʌn'sɔlvəbl] unlösbar; **'un'solved** ungelöst.

un·so·phis·ti·cat·ed ['ʌnsə'fistikeitid] unverfälscht; ungekünstelt; unverdorben, unverbildet.

un·sought ['ʌn'sɔːt] ungesucht.

un·sound □ ['ʌn'saund] ungesund; verdorben; wurmstichig; morsch; nicht stichhaltig (*Beweis*); verkehrt; *of* ~ *mind* geistig nicht gesund; ~ *doctrine* Irrlehre *f*.

un·spar·ing □ ['ʌn'spɛəriŋ] nicht kargend, freigebig (*of, in* mit); schonungslos, unbarmherzig (*of* gegen).

un·speak·a·ble □ [ʌn'spiːkəbl] unsagbar; unsäglich.

un·spec·i·fied ['ʌn'spesifaid] nicht spezifiziert.

un·spent ['ʌn'spent] unverbraucht; unerschöpft.

un·spoiled ['ʌn'spɔild], **'un'spoilt** [~t] unverdorben; unbeschädigt; nicht verzogen (*Kind*).

un·spo·ken ['ʌn'spəukən] ungesagt; ~*of* unerwähnt.

un·sport·ing ['ʌn'spɔːtiŋ], **un·sports·man·like** ['ʌn'spɔːtsmənlaik] unsportlich, unfair, unkameradschaftlich; unweidmännisch.

un·spot·ted ['ʌn'spɔtid] ungefleckt; *fig.* unbefleckt.

un·sta·ble □ ['ʌn'steibl] nicht (stand)fest; unbeständig; unstet(ig); labil.

un·stained *fig.* ['ʌn'steind] unbefleckt.

un·stamped ['ʌn'stæmpt] ungestempelt; ⊗ unfrankiert.

un·states·man·like ['ʌn'steitsmənlaik] unstaatsmännisch.

un·stead·y □ ['ʌn'stedi] unstet(ig), unsicher; schwankend; unbeständig; unsolid; unregelmäßig.

un·stint·ed [ʌn'stintid] unverkürzt, unbeschränkt.

un·stitch ['ʌn'stitʃ] auftrennen.

un·stop ['ʌn'stɔp] durchgängig machen.

un·strained ['ʌn'streind] ungefiltert; *fig.* ungezwungen.

un·strap ['ʌn'stræp] los-, abschnallen.

un·stressed ['ʌn'strest] unbetont.

un·string ['ʌn'striŋ] (*irr.* string) Bogen, Saite entspannen; *Perlen etc.* abfädeln; **un·strung** ['ʌn'strʌŋ] saitenlos; entspannt; *fig.* abgespannt, nervös, überdreht.

un·stuck ['ʌn'stʌk]: *come* ~ aufgehen, sich lösen; *sl.* ins Wasser fallen, danebengehen.

un·stud·ied ['ʌn'stʌdid] ungesucht, ungekünstelt, natürlich.

un·sub·dued ['ʌnsəb'djuːd] unbesiegt, nicht unterjocht.

un·sub·mis·sive □ ['ʌnsəb'misiv] nicht unterwürfig, widerspenstig.

un·sub·stan·tial □ ['ʌnsəb'stænʃəl] wesenlos; gegenstandslos; unsolid; gehaltlos; dürftig.

un·suc·cess·ful □ ['ʌnsək'sesful] erfolglos, ohne Erfolg; **'un·suc·'cess·ful·ness** Erfolglosigkeit *f*.

un·suit·a·ble □ ['ʌn'sjuːtəbl] unpassend; unangemessen; **'un'suit·ed** ungeeignet (*for, to* für, zu).

un·sul·lied ['ʌn'sʌlid] unbefleckt.

un·sup·port·ed ['ʌnsə'pɔːtid] ungestützt; nicht bestätigt; ohne Unterstützung.

un·sure ['ʌn'ʃuə] unsicher.

un·sur·passed ['ʌnsə'pɑːst] unübertroffen.

un·sus·pect·ed ['ʌnsəs'pektid] unverdächtig; unvermutet; **'un·sus·'pect·ing** nichts ahnend, *pred.* ohne Ahnung (*of* von); arglos.

un·sus·pi·cious □ ['ʌnsəs'piʃəs] nicht argwöhnisch, arglos.

un·swear ['ʌn'swɛə] (*irr.* swear) abschwören.

un·swerv·ing □ ['ʌn'swɜːviŋ] unentwegt.

un·sworn ['ʌn'swɔːn] ungeschworen; unvereidigt (*Zeuge*).

un·tack ['ʌn'tæk] losmachen.

un·taint·ed ['ʌn'teintid] unbefleckt; *fig.* fleckenlos; unverdorben.

un·tam(e)·a·ble ['ʌn'teiməbl] unbezähmbar; **'un'tamed** ungezähmt.

un·tan·gle ['ʌn'tæŋgl] entwirren.
un·tanned ['ʌn'tænd] ungegerbt.
un·tar·nished ['ʌn'tɑːnɪʃt] unbefleckt; ungetrübt.
un·tast·ed ['ʌn'teistid] ungekostet.
un·taught ['ʌn'tɔːt] ungelehrt.
un·taxed ['ʌn'tækst] unbesteuert.
un·teach·a·ble ['ʌn'tiːtʃəbl] unbelehrbar (*Person*); unlehrbar (*Sache*).
un·tem·per·a·men·tal ['ʌntempərə'mentl] temperamentlos.
un·tem·pered ['ʌn'tempəd] ⊕ ungehärtet; ungemildert.
un·ten·a·ble ['ʌn'tenəbl] unhaltbar.
un·ten·ant·ed ['ʌn'tenəntid] unvermietet, unbewohnt.
un·thank·ful □ ['ʌn'θæŋkful] undankbar.
un·think·a·ble [ʌn'θiŋkəbl] undenkbar; **un·think·ing** □ gedankenlos.
un·thought ['ʌn'θɔːt] unbedacht; ~-of unvermutet.
un·thread ['ʌn'θred] ausfädeln; *fig.* sich hindurchfinden durch.
un·thrift·y □ ['ʌn'θrifti] verschwenderisch; nicht gedeihend.
un·ti·dy □ [ʌn'taidi] unordentlich.
un·tie ['ʌn'tai] aufbinden, -knoten, -knüpfen; *Knoten etc.* lösen; *j.* losbinden.
un·til [ən'til] **1.** *prp.* bis; **2.** *cj.* bis (daß); *not* ~ erst wenn *od.* als.
un·tilled ['ʌn'tild] unbebaut (*Acker*).
un·time·ly [ʌn'taimli] unzeitig; vorzeitig; früh(zeitig); ungelegen.
un·tir·ing □ [ʌn'taiəriŋ] unermüdlich.
un·to ['ʌntu] = *to.*
un·told ['ʌn'tould] unerzählt; ungezählt; unermeßlich, unsäglich.
un·touched ['ʌn'tʌtʃt] unberührt; *fig.* ungerührt; *phot.* unretuschiert.
un·to·ward [ʌn'touəd] unglücklich; ungünstig; widerspenstig.
un·trained ['ʌn'treind] undressiert; unerzogen; untrainiert.
un·tram·mel(l)ed [ʌn'træməld] ungebunden, ungehindert.
un·trans·fer·a·ble ['ʌntræns'fəːrəbl] nicht übertragbar.
un·trans·lat·a·ble ['ʌntræns'leitəbl] unübersetzbar.
un·trav·el(l)ed ['ʌn'trævld] unbereist; ungereist (*Person*).
un·tried ['ʌn'traid] unversucht; unerprobt; ⚖ ununtersucht (*Fall*); nicht vernommen; nicht abgeurteilt (*Angeklagter*).

un·trimmed ['ʌn'trimd] nicht in Ordnung (gebracht); unbeschnitten (*Haar etc.*); ungeschmückt.
un·trod, un·trod·den ['ʌn'trɔd(n)] unbetreten.
un·trou·bled ['ʌn'trʌbld] ungestört, unbelästigt.
un·true □ ['ʌn'truː] unwahr; untreu.
un·trust·wor·thy □ ['ʌn'trʌstwəːði] nicht vertrauenswürdig.
un·truth ['ʌn'truːθ] Unwahrheit *f.*
un·tu·tored ['ʌn'tjuːtəd] unerzogen, ungebildet.
un·twine ['ʌn'twain], **un·twist** ['ʌn'twist] *v/t.* aufdrehen; aufflechten; entwirren; *v/i.* aufgehen.
un·used ['ʌn'juːzd] ungebraucht; ['ʌn'juːst] nicht gewöhnt (*to* an *acc.*; zu *inf.*); **un·u·su·al** □ [ʌn'juːʒuəl] ungewöhnlich; ungewohnt.
un·ut·ter·a·ble □ [ʌn'ʌtərəbl] unaussprechlich.
un·val·ued ['ʌn'væljuːd] nicht (ab-) geschätzt.
un·var·ied [ʌn'vɛərid] unverändert.
un·var·nished ['ʌn'vɑːnɪʃt] ungefirnißt; *fig.* ungeschminkt.
un·var·y·ing □ [ʌn'vɛəriiŋ] unveränderlich.
un·veil [ʌn'veil] entschleiern, enthüllen.
un·versed ['ʌn'vəːst] unbewandert, unerfahren (*in* in *dat.*).
un·voiced ['ʌn'vɔist] nicht ausgesprochen; stimmlos (*Konsonant*)⸜
un·vouched ['ʌn'vautʃt] *a.* ~-*for* unverbürgt, unbezeugt.
un·want·ed ['ʌn'wɔntid] unerwünscht.
un·war·i·ness [ʌn'wɛərinis] Unbedachtsamkeit *f.*
un·war·like ['ʌn'wɔːlaik] unkriegerisch.
un·war·rant·a·ble □ [ʌn'wɔrəntəbl] unverantwortlich; **'un'war·rant·ed** unberechtigt; unverbürgt.
un·war·y □ ['ʌn'wɛəri] unbedachtsam.
un·washed ['ʌn'wɔʃt] ungewaschen.
un·wa·tered ['ʌn'wɔːtəd] unbewässert; unverwässert (*Milch, Kapital*).
un·wa·ver·ing [ʌn'weivəriŋ] unerschütterlich.
un·wea·ried [ʌn'wiərid], **un·wea·ry·ing** □ [ʌn'wiəriiŋ] unermüdlich.
un·wel·come [ʌn'welkəm] unwillkommen.

un·well [ˈʌnˈwel] unwohl.

un·whole·some [ˈʌnˈhəulsəm] ungesund; schädlich.

un·wiecl·y ☐ [ʌnˈwiːldi] unhandlich; ungefüge; ⸙ sperrig.

un·will·ing ☐ [ˈʌnˈwiliŋ] un-, widerwillig, abgeneigt; *be ⌣ to do* nicht tun wollen; *be ⌣ for s.th. to be done* nicht wollen, daß et. getan wird.

un·wind [ˈʌnˈwaind] (*irr. wind*) auf-, loswickeln; (sich) auf-, abwickeln.

un·wis·dom [ˈʌnˈwizdəm] Unklugheit *f*; **un·wise** ☐ [ˈʌnˈwaiz] unklug.

un·wished [ʌnˈwiʃt] ungewünscht; *⌣-for* unerwünscht.

un·wit·ting ☐ [ʌnˈwitiŋ] unwissentlich; unwillentlich, unbeabsichtigt.

un·wom·an·ly [ʌnˈwumənli] unweiblich.

un·wont·ed ☐ [ʌnˈwəuntid] ungewohnt; nicht gewöhnt (*to an acc.*).

un·work·a·ble [ˈʌnˈwəːkəbl] nicht zu bearbeiten(d); undurchführbar; ⊕ betriebsunfähig.

un·world·ly [ˈʌnˈwəːldli] unweltlich.

un·wor·thy ☐ [ʌnˈwəːði] unwürdig.

un·wound·ed [ˈʌnˈwuːndid] unverwundet.

un·wrap [ˈʌnˈræp] auswickeln, -packen; aufwickeln.

un·wrin·kle [ˈʌnˈriŋkl] entrunzeln.

un·writ·ten [ˈʌnˈritn] ungeschrieben (*Gesetz*); unbeschrieben (*Seite*).

un·wrought [ˈʌnˈrɔːt] unbearbeitet; roh; Roh...

un·yield·ing ☐ [ʌnˈjiːldiŋ] unnachgiebig.

un·yoke [ˈʌnˈjəuk] ausspannen.

un·zip [ʌnˈzip] den Reißverschluß aufmachen an.

up [ʌp] **1.** *adv.* (her-, hin)auf; aufwärts, empor; oben, in der Höhe; auf(gestanden); aufgegangen (*Sonne etc.*); abgelaufen (*Zeit*); in Aufregung, in Wallung; nach London *od.* Oxford *od.* Cambridge; *Am. Baseball*: am Schlag; *come ⌣ to s.o.* auf j. zukommen; *⌣ and about* wieder auf den Beinen; *be hard ⌣* in Geldschwierigkeiten *od.* schlecht bei Kasse sein; *⌣ against a task* einer Aufgabe gegenüber; *⌣ to* bis an (*acc.*), bis auf (*acc.*); *s.* date² 1; *be ⌣ to s.th.* e-r Sache gewachsen sein; *fig.* an et. herankommen; et. im

Schilde führen; *it is ⌣ to me to do* es ist meine Sache zu tun; *s.* mark 1; *the time is ⌣* die Zeit ist um; *what are you ⌣ to there?* was macht ihr da?; *what's ⌣ sl.* was ist los?; *⌣ with* auf gleicher Höhe mit; *it's all ⌣ with him* es ist aus mit ihm; **2.** *int.* auf!; herauf!; heran!; hoch!; **3.** *prp.* hinauf, auf; *⌣ the hill* den Berg hinauf, bergan; **4.** *adj. ⌣ train* Zug *m* nach der Stadt; **5.** *the ⌣s and downs* das Auf und Ab, die Höhen und Tiefen *des Lebens*; **6.** F (sich) erheben, hochfahren; hochtreiben.

up-and-com·ing *Am.* F [ˈʌpənˈkʌmiŋ] unternehmungslustig; vielversprechend.

up·beat [ˈʌpbiːt] ♪ Auftakt *m*; Anakrusis *f*.

up·braid [ʌpˈbreid] vorwerfen (*s.o. with od. for s.th. j-m et.*).

up·bring·ing [ˈʌpbriŋiŋ] Aufziehen *n*, Aufzucht *f*; Erziehung *f*.

up·build [ˈʌpˈbild] (*irr. build*) aufbauen.

up·cast [ˈʌpkaːst] Hochwurf *m*; *a. ⌣ shaft* ⚒ Luftschacht *m*.

up·com·ing *Am.* [ˈʌpkʌmiŋ] bevorstehend, kommend.

up·coun·try [ˈʌpˈkʌntri] landeinwärts (gelegen).

up·cur·rent ⚡ [ˈʌpkʌrənt] Aufwind *m*.

up·date 1. [ʌpˈdeit] auf den neuesten Stand bringen; **2.** [ˈʌpdeit] neuester Bericht *m*.

up·end [ʌpˈend] hochkant stellen.

up·grade 1. [ˈʌpgreid] Steigung *f*; *on the ⌣ fig.* im Aufsteigen; **2.** [ʌpˈgreid] höher einstufen, aufwerten.

up·heav·al [ʌpˈhiːvəl] *geol.* Hebung *f*; *fig.* Umwälzung *f*, Umsturz *m*.

up·hill [ˈʌpˈhil] bergan; mühsam.

up·hold [ʌpˈhəuld] (*irr. hold*) aufrecht(er)halten; stützen; **up·hold·er** *fig.* Stütze *f*, Verteidiger *m*.

up·hol·ster [ʌpˈhəulstə] *Möbel* (auf)polstern; *Zimmer* dekorieren; **up·hol·ster·er** Tapezierer *m*, Dekorateur *m*, Polsterer *m*; **up·hol·ster·y** Polstermöbel *n/pl.*; Polsterung *f*, Tapezierarbeit *f*; Zimmerdekoration *f*.

up·keep [ˈʌpkiːp] Instandhaltung(skosten *pl.*) *f*; Unterhalt *m von Personen*.

up·land [ˈʌplənd] **1.** *oft ⌣s pl.*

Hoch-, Oberland *n*; **2.** Hoch-, Oberland(s)...

up·lift 1. [ʌpˈlift] *fig.* emporheben; **2.** [ˈ‿] Erhebung *f*; *fig.* Aufschwung *m*; moralische Unterstützung *f*.

up·most [ˈʌpməust] = **uppermost.**

up·on [əˈpɔn] = *on*.

up·per [ˈʌpə] **1.** ober; Ober...; *the* ‿ *ten* (*thousand*) die oberen Zehntausend *pl.*; **2.** *mst* ‿*s pl.* Oberleder *n*; F *be* (*down*) *on one's* ‿*s* F total pleite *od.* abgebrannt sein; 'ˌ‿**class** ... der Oberschicht; vornehm; ‿ **class** (**-es** *pl.*) Oberschicht *f*; ‿ **crust** Erdkruste *f*; *the* ‿ F die oberen Zehntausend *pl.*; 'ˌ‿**cut** *Boxen*: Aufwärts-, Kinnhaken *m*; 'ˌ‿**most** oberst, höchst.

up·pish □ F [ˈʌpiʃ] hochnäsig, eingebildet.

up·pi·ty F [ˈʌpiti] eingebildet; dreist.

up·raise [ʌpˈreiz] erheben.

up·rear [ʌpˈriə] aufrichten.

up·right 1. □ [ˈʌpˈrait] aufrecht (stehend); senkrecht; *fig.* [ˈ‿] aufrecht, aufrichtig, gerade; **2.** [ˈ‿] Pfosten *m*; Ständer *m*; = ‿ **pia·no** ♪ Klavier *n*.

up·ris·ing [ʌpˈraiziŋ] Aufstehen *n*; Erhebung *f*, Aufstand *m*.

up·roar *fig.* [ˈʌprɔ:] Aufruhr *m*, Tumult *m*; Lärm *m*; Toben *n*; **up-ˈroar·i·ous** □ lärmend, tobend; tosend (*Beifall etc.*).

up·root [ʌpˈru:t] entwurzeln; (her-) ausreißen.

up·set [ʌpˈset] **1.** (*irr. set*) umwerfen (*a. fig.*); (um)stürzen; außer Fassung *od.* in Unordnung bringen; stören; verwirren; beunruhigen; ⊕ stauchen; *be* ‿ außer sich sein; **2.** Aufregung *f*, Ärger *m*; *Sport*: Überraschung *f*; *stomach* ‿ Magenverstimmung *f*; ‿ **price** Anschlagspreis *m bei Auktionen*.

up·shot [ˈʌpʃɔt] Ausgang *m*, Ende *n*, Ergebnis *n*; *in the* ‿ am Ende.

up·side *adv.* [ˈʌpsaid]: ‿ *down* das Oberste zuunterst; *fig.* drunter und drüber; verkehrt; *turn* ‿ *down* auf den Kopf stellen.

up·stage F *fig.* [ˈʌpˈsteidʒ] von oben herab; hochnäsig, eingebildet.

up·stairs [ˈʌpˈstɛəz] oben *im Hause*; nach oben.

up·stand·ing [ʌpˈstændiŋ] aufrecht; stramm.

up·start [ˈʌpstɑ:t] **1.** Emporkömm-

ling *m*; **2.** emporkommen.

up·state *Am.* [ˈʌpˈsteit] Hinterland *n e-s Staates, bsd. nördlich New York.*

up·stream [ˈʌpˈstri:m] fluß-, stromaufwärts (gelegen, gerichtet).

up·stroke [ˈʌpstrəuk] Aufstrich *m beim Schreiben.*

up·surge [ˈʌpsə:dʒ] Aufwallung *f*.

up·swing [ˈʌpswiŋ] Aufschwung *m*.

up·take [ˈʌpteik] Auffassung(svermögen *n*) *f*; *be slow* (*quick*) *in od. on the* ‿ F e-e lange (kurze) Leitung haben.

up·throw [ˈʌpθrəu] Umwälzung *f*.

up·tight F [ʌpˈtait] verärgert; nervös; steif, förmlich; puritanisch; verklemmt.

up-to-date [ˈʌptəˈdeit] modern, neuzeitlich.

up-to-the-min·ute [ˈʌptəðəˈminit] modernst, allerneu(e)st.

up-town [ˈʌpˈtaun] im *od.* in den oberen Stadtteil; *Am.* im Wohn- *od.* Villenviertel.

up·turn [ʌpˈtə:n] emporrichten; nach oben kehren.

up·ward [ˈʌpwəd] **1.** *adj.* nach oben gerichtet; **2.** *adv.* = **up·wards** [ˈ‿z] aufwärts; darüber (hinaus); ‿ *of* mehr als.

u·ra·ni·um ⚛ [juəˈreinjəm] Uran *n*.

ur·ban [ˈə:bən] städtisch; Stadt...; ‿ *guerilla* Stadtguerilla *m*; **ur·bane** □ [ə:ˈbein] höflich; gebildet, urban, weltmännisch; **ur·ban·i·ty** [ə:ˈbæniti] Höflichkeit *f*; Bildung *f*; **ur·ban·i·za·tion** [ə:bənaiˈzeiʃən] Verstädterung *f*; **ˈur·ban·ize** verstädtern.

ur·chin [ˈə:tʃin] Bengel *m*.

u·re·thra *anat.* [juəˈri:θrə] Harnröhre *f*.

urge [ə:dʒ] **1.** *oft* ‿ *on j.* drängen, (an)treiben; *fig.* nötigen (*to zu*), dringen in *j.* (*to inf. zu inf.*); dringen auf *e-e Sache*; nachdrücklich betonen; geltend machen; ‿ *s.th. on s.o.* j-m et. eindringlich vorstellen; j-m et. einschärfen; **2.** *innerer* Drang *m*; **ur·gen·cy** [ˈə:dʒənsi] Dringlichkeit *f*; Drängen *n*; **ˈurgent** □ dringend; dringlich; eilig; *be* ‿ *with s.o. to inf.* in j. dringen zu *inf.*

u·ric ⚛ [ˈjuərik] Harn...   [*inf.*]

u·ri·nal [ˈjuərinl] Harnglas *n*; Bedürfnisanstalt *f*; **ˈu·ri·nar·y** Harn- ...; **u·ri·nate** [ˈ‿neit] urinieren; **ˈu·rine** Urin *m*, Harn *m*.

urn [ə:n] Urne *f*; Kaffee- *od.* Teemaschine *f*.

us [ʌs, əs] uns; *all of* ~ wir alle.

us·a·ble [' juːzəbl] brauch-, verwendbar.

us·age ['juːzidʒ] Brauch *m*, Gepflogenheit *f*, Usus *m*; Sprachgebrauch *m*; Behandlung *f*, Verwendung *f*, Gebrauch *m*.

us·ance ✝ ['juːzəns] Wechselfrist *f*, Uso *m*; *bill at* ~ Usowechsel *m*.

use 1. [juːs] Gebrauch *m*; Benutzung *f*; Verwendung *f*; Gewohnheit *f*, Übung *f*; Brauch *m*; Nutzen *m*; *be of* ~ von Nutzen *od.* nützlich sein; *it is* (*of*) *no* ~ *ger. od. to inf.* es ist unnütz *od.* es hat keinen Zweck zu *inf.*; *have no* ~ *for* keine Verwendung haben für; *Am.* F nicht mögen; *put to* ~ nutzbar anwenden; **2.** [juːz] gebrauchen; benutzen; ver-, anwenden; behandeln; ~ *up* ver-, aufbrauchen; *I* ~ *d* ['juːs(t)] *to do* ich pflegte zu tun, früher tat ich; *used* ['juːst] *to* gewöhnt an (*acc.*); **use·ful** □ ['juːsful] brauchbar; nützlich; von Nutzen; ⊕ Nutz...; **'use·ful·ness** Nützlichkeit *f etc.*; **'use·less** □ nutz-, zwecklos, unnütz; unbrauchbar; **'use·less·ness** Nutzlosigkeit *f*; **us·er** ['juːzə] Benutzer(in).

ush·er ['ʌʃə] **1.** Türhüter *m*, Pförtner *m*; Gerichtsdiener *m*; Platzanweiser *m*; *contp.* Hilfslehrer *m*; **2.** *mst* ~ *in* (hin)einführen, anmelden; *fig.* einleiten; **ush·er·ette** [~'ret] Platzanweiserin *f*.

u·su·al □ ['juːʒuəl] gewöhnlich; üblich; gebräuchlich; **'u·su·al·ly** gewöhnlich, normalerweise.

u·su·fruct ⚖ ['juːsjuːfrʌkt] Nutznießung *f*; **u·su'fruc·tu·a·ry** [~tjuəri] Nutznießer(in).

u·su·rer ['juːʒərə] Wucherer *m*; **u·su·ri·ous** □ [juːˈzjuəriəs] wucherisch; Wucher...

u·surp [juːˈzəːp] sich *et.* widerrechtlich aneignen, an sich reißen; **u·sur'pa·tion** widerrechtliche Aneignung *f*, Usurpation *f*; **u'surp·er** unrechtmäßiger Machthaber *m od.* Besitzer *m*, Usurpator *m*; **u'surp·ing** □ eigenmächtig.

u·su·ry ['juːʒuri] Wucher *m*; Wucherzinsen *m/pl*.

u·ten·sil [juːˈtensl] Gerät *n*; Geschirr *n*; ~*s pl.* Utensilien *pl.*

u·ter·ine ['juːtərain] Gebärmutter...; ~ *brother* Halbbruder *m*; **u·ter·us** *anat.* ['~rəs] Gebärmutter *f*.

u·til·i·tar·i·an [juːtili'tɛəriən] **1.** Utilitarist *m*, Vertreter *m* des Nützlichkeitsprinzips; **2.** utilitaristisch; **u'til·i·ty 1.** Nützlichkeit *f*, Nutzen *m*; *public* ~ öffentlicher Versorgungsbetrieb *m*; **2.** Gebrauchs..., Einheits... (*Kleidung, Wagen etc.*).

u·ti·li·za·tion [juːtilai'zeiʃən] Nutzbarmachung *f*, Nutzanwendung *f*; **'u·ti·lize** sich *et.* nutzbar *od.* zunutze machen.

ut·most ['ʌtməust] äußerst.

U·to·pi·an [juːˈtəupjən] **1.** utopisch; **2.** Utopist(in), Schwärmer (-in).

ut·ter ['ʌtə] **1.** □ *fig.* äußerst, völlig, gänzlich; ausgesprochen, entschieden; **2.** äußern; *Seufzer etc.* ausstoßen, von sich geben; *Falschgeld etc.* in Umlauf setzen; **'ut·ter·ance** Äußerung *f*, Ausdruck *m*; Aussprache *f*; *give* ~ *to* Ausdruck geben (*dat.*); **'ut·ter·er** Äußernde *m*; Verbreiter(in); **'ut·ter·most** äußerst.

U-turn ['juːtəːn] Wende *f auf der Straße*; F *fig.* (totale) Kehrtwendung *f*, (völliger) Umschwung *m*.

u·vu·la *anat.* ['juːvjulə] Zäpfchen *n*; **'u·vu·lar** Zäpfchen...

ux·o·ri·ous [ʌkˈsɔːriəs] treuergeben (*Ehemann*).

V

vac F [væk] = *vacation*.

va·can·cy ['veikənsi] Leere *f* (*a. fig.*); leerer *od.* freier Platz *m*, Lücke *f*; Vakanz *f*, offene Stelle *f*; *gaze into* ~ ins Leere starren; **'va·can·cies** *pl. Zeitung:* Stellenangebote *n/pl.*;

ˈva·cant ☐ leer (a. fig.); frei (Zeit, Zimmer); offen (Stelle); unbesetzt, vakant (Amt); ⌣ possession sofort beziehbar.

va·cate [vəˈkeit, Am. ˈveikeit] Haus räumen; Stelle aufgeben, aus e-m Amt scheiden; vaˈca·tion 1. (Schul)Ferien pl.; Räumung f; Niederlegung f e-s Amtes; 2. Am. Urlaub machen; va·ˈca·tion·ist Am. Ferienreisende m, f.

vac·ci·nate [ˈvæksineit] impfen; vac·ci·na·tion Impfung f; ˈvac·ci·na·tor Impfarzt m; vac·cine [ˈ⌣siːn] Impfstoff m.

vac·il·late [ˈvæsileit] schwanken; vac·il·ˈla·tion Schwanken n.

va·cu·i·ty [væˈkjuːiti] Leere f (mst fig.); vac·u·ous [ˈvækjuəs] fig. leer, geistlos; vac·u·um [ˈ⌣əm] 1. phys. Vakuum n (bsd. luft)leerer Raum m; ⌣ brake Unterdruckbremse f; ⌣ cleaner Staubsauger m; ⌣ flask, ⌣ bottle Thermosflasche f; ⌣-packed vakuumverpackt; ⌣ tube Vakuumröhre f; 2. (mit dem Staubsauger) saugen.

va·de·me·cum [ˈveidiˈmiːkəm] Vademekum n, Handbuch n.

vag·a·bond [ˈvægəbɔnd] 1. vagabundierend (a. ✍); umherstreifend; Vagabunden...; 2. Landstreicher m, Vagabund m; Strolch m; ˈvag·a·bond·age Landstreicherei f.

va·gar·y [ˈveigəri] wunderlicher Einfall m, Laune f, Schrulle f.

va·gi·na anat. [vəˈdʒainə] Scheide f.

va·gran·cy [ˈveigrənsi] Landstreicherei f; ˈva·grant 1. wandernd; fig. unstet; 2. = vagabond 2.

vague ⌐ [veig] vag, unbestimmt; verschwommen, unklar; ˈvague·ness Unbestimmtheit f.

vail † od. poet. [veil] Fahne senken; Hut abnehmen.

vain ⌐ [vein] eitel, eingebildet (of auf acc.); fig. eitel, leer; nichtig; vergeblich; in ⌣ vergebens, umsonst; ⌣·glo·ri·ous ⌐ [⌣ˈɡlɔːriəs] prahlerisch; ⌣ˈglo·ry Prahlerei f.

val·ance [ˈvæləns] Volant m.

vale [veil] poet. od. in Namen: Tal n.

val·e·dic·tion [væliˈdikʃən] Abschied(sworte n pl.) m; val·e·ˈdic·to·ry [⌣təri] 1. Abschieds...; 2. Abschiedsrede f.

va·lence ⌢ [ˈveiləns] Wertigkeit f.

val·en·tine [ˈvæləntain] Valentinsschatz m, -gruß m (am Valentinstag, 14. Februar, erwählt, gesandt).

va·le·ri·an ⚕ [vəˈliəriən] Baldrian m.

val·et [ˈvælit] 1. (Kammer)Diener m; 2. Diener sein bei j-m; j. bedienen.

val·e·tu·di·nar·i·an [ˈvælitjuːdiˈnɛəriən] 1. kränklich; hypochondrisch; 2. kränklicher Mensch m; Hypochonder m.

val·iant ⌐ [ˈvæljənt] tapfer.

val·id ⌐ [ˈvælid] triftig, richtig, stichhaltig; (rechts)gültig; be ⌣ gelten; val·i·date [ˈ⌣deit] für gültig erklären; va·lid·i·ty [vəˈliditi] Gültigkeit f; Triftig-, Richtigkeit f.   [Tornister m.)

va·lise [vəˈliːz] Reisetasche f; ✗)

val·ley [ˈvæli] Tal n.

val·or·i·za·tion [væləraiˈzeiʃən] Aufwertung f; ˈval·or·ize aufwerten.

val·or·ous ⌐ [ˈvælərəs] tapfer.

val·o(u)r [ˈvælə] Tapferkeit f.

val·u·a·ble [ˈvæljuəbl] 1. ⌐ wertvoll; 2. ⌣s pl. Wertsachen f pl.

val·u·a·tion [væljuˈeiʃən] Abschätzung f; Taxwert m; ˈval·u·a·tor Taxator m, Schätzer m.

val·ue [ˈvæljuː] 1. Wert m (a. fig.); Währung f, Valuta f; give (get) good ⌣ (for one's money) ✝ reell bedienen (bedient werden); ⌣-added tax Mehrwertsteuer f; 2. (ab-)schätzen; werten; fig. schätzen, achten; ˈval·ued (hoch)geschätzt: -wertig; val·ue judg(e)·ment Werturteil n; ˈval·ue·less wertlos; val·u·er [ˈvæljuə] (Ab)Schätzer m, Taxator m.

valve [vælv] Klappe f (a. anat., ⚕); Ventil n; Radio: Röhre f.

va·moose Am. sl. [væˈmuːs] abhauen; fluchtartig verlassen.

vamp¹ [væmp] 1. Vorschuh m; 2. vorschuhen; zurechtflicken; ♪ improvisieren.

vamp² F [⌣] 1. Vamp m (verführerische Frau); 2. aussaugen, neppen.

vam·pire [ˈvæmpaiə] Vampir m.

van¹ [væn] Möbelwagen m; Lieferwagen m; ⛢ Packwagen m, (geschlossener) Güterwagen m.

van² ✗ od. fig. [⌣] Vorhut f.

Van·dal [ˈvændəl] hist. Vandale m; ⌣ fig. Vandale m, Barbar m; ˈvan·dal·ism Vandalismus m; ˈvan·dal-

ize mutwillig zerstören.

van·dyke [væn'daik] Zackenmuster *n*; *attr.* ⚹ Van-Dyck-...

vane [vein] Wetterfahne *f*; (Windmühlen-, Propeller)Flügel *m*; *surv.* Visier *n*.

van·guard ✕ ['vængɑːd] Vorhut *f*.

va·nil·la ♀ [və'nilə] Vanille *f*.

van·ish ['væniʃ] (ver)schwinden; ↙*ing cream* Tagescreme *f*.

van·i·ty ['væniti] Eitelkeit *f*, Einbildung *f*; Nichtigkeit *f*; Frisiertoilette *f*; ↙ *bag* Kosmetiktäschchen *m*.

van·quish ['væŋkwiʃ] besiegen; bezwingen.

van·tage ['vɑːntidʒ] *Tennis*: Vorteil *m*; '↙**-ground** günstige Stellung *f*.

vap·id ˍ ['væpid] schal.

va·po(u)r·ize ['veipəraiz] verdampfen, verdunsten (lassen); '**va·po(u)r·iz·er** ⊕ Verdampfer *m*; ⚸ Zerstäuber *m*.

va·por·ous ˍ ['veipərəs] dunstig; dampfig; *fig.* nebelhaft; duftig (*Gewebe*).

va·po(u)r ['veipə] Dunst *m* (*a. fig.*); Dampf *m*; ↙ **bath** Dampfbad *n*; ↙ **trail** Kondensstreifen *m e-s Flugzeugs*; '**va·po(u)r·y** = *vaporous*.

var·i·a·bil·i·ty [veəriə'biliti] Veränderlichkeit *f*; '**var·i·a·ble** ˍ veränderlich; '**var·i·ance** Veränderung *f*; Uneinigkeit *f*; *be at ↙ un*einig sein; (sich) widersprechen; *set at ↙ entzweien*; '**var·i·ant 1.** abweichend; **2.** Variante *f*; verschiedene Lesart *f*; **var·i'a·tion** Abänderung *f*; Schwankung *f*; Abwechs(e)lung *f*; Abweichung *f*; ♪ Variation *f*.

var·i·cose ⚕ ['værikəus] krampfaderig; ↙ *vein* Krampfader *f*.

var·ied ˍ ['veərid] verschieden, verändert, mannigfaltig; **var·i·e·gate** ['↙rigeit] bunt gestalten; '**var·i·e·gat·ed** bunt; **var·i·e'ga·tion** Buntheit *f*; **va·ri·e·ty** [və'raiəti] Mannigfaltigkeit *f*, Vielheit *f*, -zahl *f*; Abwechslung *f*; *biol.* Varietät *f*, Spiel-, Abart *f*; *bsd.* ⚜ Auswahl *f*; Menge *f*; ↙ *show* Varietévorstellung *f*; ↙ *theatre* Varietétheater *n*.

va·ri·o·la ⚕ [və'raiələ] Pocken *f/pl.*

var·i·ous ˍ ['veəriəs] verschiedene, mehrere; mannigfaltig; verschiedenartig; wechselvoll.

var·let † ['vɑːlit] Schurke *m*.

var·mint V, *co.* ['vɑːmint] *kleiner* Racker *m*.

var·nish ['vɑːniʃ] **1.** Firnis *m*, Lack *m*; *fig.* (äußerer) Anstrich *m*; **2.** firnissen, lackieren; *fig.* bemänteln, beschönigen.

var·si·ty F ['vɑːsiti] Uni *f*.

var·y ['veəri] *v/t.* (ver)ändern; wechseln mit *et.*; *bsd.* ♪ variieren; *v/i.* sich (ver)ändern, wechseln; abweichen, verschieden sein (*from* von).

vas·cu·lar ♀, *anat.* ['væskjulə] Gefäß...

vase [vɑːz] Vase *f*.

vas·sal ['væsəl] Vasall *m*; *attr.* Vasallen...; '**vas·sal·age** Vasallentum *n* (*to gegenüber dat.*).

vast ˍ [vɑːst] ungeheuer, gewaltig, riesig, umfassend, weit; '**vast·ness** ungeheure Größe *f*; Weite *f*.

vat [væt] **1.** *großes* Faß *n*; Bottich *m*; Kufe *f*; (Färber)Küpe *f*; **2.** in ein Faß tun; im Faß behandeln.

vat·ted ['vætid] faßreif (*Wein etc.*).

vaude·ville ['vəudəvil] *Am.* Varieté *n*.

vault[1] [vɔːlt] **1.** Gewölbe *n*; Wölbung *f*; Stahlkammer *f*; Gruft *f*; **2.** (über)wölben.

vault[2] [↙] **1.** *v/i.* springen; *v/t.* springen über (*acc.*); **2.** Sprung *m*.

vault·ing ⚖ ['vɔːltiŋ] Gewölbe *n*.

vault·ing-horse ['vɔːltiŋhɔːs] *Turnen*: Pferd *n*.

vaunt *lit.* [vɔːnt] **1.** (sich) rühmen; **2.** Prahlerei *f*; '**vaunt·ing** ˍ prahlerisch.

veal [viːl] Kalbfleisch *n*; *roast* ↙ Kalbsbraten *m*.

veer [viə] **1.** (sich) drehen; ↙ *round* sich herumdrehen; *fig.* (her)umschwenken; **2.** Schwenkung *f*.

veg F [vedʒ] *mst gekochtes* Gemüse *n*.

veg·e·ta·ble ['vedʒitəbl] **1.** Pflanzen..., pflanzlich; **2.** Pflanze *f*; *mst* ↙s *pl.* Gemüse *n*; **veg·e·tar·i·an** [↙'teəriən] **1.** Vegetarier(in); **2.** vegetarisch; **veg·e·tate** ['↙teit] vegetieren; **veg·e'ta·tion** Vegetation *f*; **veg·e·ta·tive** ˍ ['↙tətiv] vegetativ, Wachstums...; wachstumsfördernd.

ve·he·mence ['viːiməns] Heftigkeit *f*; Gewalt *f*; Ungestüm *n*; Vehemenz *f*; '**ve·he·ment** ˍ heftig; ungestüm; vehement.

ve·hi·cle ['viːikl] Fahrzeug *n*, Be-

förderungsmittel *n*; *pharm.* Löse-
mittel *n*; *fig.* Vermittler *m*, Träger
m; Ausdrucksmittel *n*; **ve·hic·u·lar**
□ [vi'hikjulə] Fahrzeug...
veil [veil] **1.** Schleier *m* (*a. phot.*);
Hülle *f*; **2.** (sich) verschleiern; *fig.*
verhüllen; '**veil·ing** Verschleierung
f (*bsd. phot.*); ✝ Schleierstoff *m*.
vein [vein] Ader *f* (*a. fig.*), Vene *f*;
Anlage *f*; Neigung *f*; Stimmung *f*
(*for* zu); **veined** geädert; '**vein·ing**
Äderung *f*.
vel·le·i·ty [ve'li:iti] bloßes Wollen *n*,
schwacher Wille *m*.
vel·lum ['veləm] Pergament *n*; *a.*
~ *paper* Velinpapier *n*.
ve·loc·i·pede [vi'lɔsipi:d] *Am.* (Kinder)Dreirad *n*; *hist.* Veloziped *n*.
ve·loc·i·ty [vi'lɔsiti] Geschwindigkeit *f*.
ve·lour(s) [və'luə] Velours *m* (*Samt*).
vel·vet ['velvit] **1.** Samt *m*; *hunt.*
Bast *m am neuen Geweih*; **2.** Samt...;
samten; **vel·vet·een** [‿'ti:n] Baum-
wollsamt *m*; Manchester *m*; '**vel-
vet·y** samtig.
ve·nal ['vi:nl] käuflich, feil; **ve·nal-
i·ty** [vi:'næliti] Käuflichkeit *f*.
vend [vend] verkaufen; '**vend·er**,
'**vend·or** Verkäufer *m*, Händler *m*;
'**vend·i·ble** verkäuflich, gangbar;
'**vend·ing ma·chine** (Waren-,
Verkaufs)Automat *m*.
ve·neer [vi'niə] **1.** Furnier *n*; *fig.*
(äußerer) Anstrich *m*; **2.** furnieren;
fig. bemänteln.
ven·er·a·ble □ ['venərəbl] ehrwürdig; **ven·er·ate** ['‿reit] (ver)ehren;
ven·er·a·tion Verehrung *f*; '**ven-
er·a·tor** Verehrer *m*.
ve·ne·re·al [vi'niəriəl] geschlechtlich; Geschlechts...; ♂ *a.* venerisch;
~ *disease* Geschlechtskrankheit *f*.
Ve·ne·tian [vi'ni:ʃən] **1.** venetia-
nisch; ~ *blind* (Stab)Jalousie *f*;
2. Venetianer(in).
venge·ance ['vendʒəns] Rache *f*;
with a ~ F nicht zu knapp, und wie,
ganz gehörig; **venge·ful** □ ['‿ful]
rachgierig, -süchtig.
ve·ni·al □ ['vi:njəl] verzeihlich; ent-
schuldbar; läßlich (*Sünde*).
ven·i·son ['venzn] Wildbret *n*.
ven·om ['venəm] (*bsd.* Schlangen-)
Gift *n*; *fig.* Gift *n*, Gehässigkeit *f*;
'**ven·om·ous** □ giftig.
ve·nous ['vi:nəs] Venen...; venös.
vent [vent] **1.** Öffnung *f*; Luft-,

Spundloch *n*; Ausweg *m*; Schlitz *m*;
give ~ *to s-m Zorn etc.* Luft machen;
find ~ sich Luft machen (*Gefühl*);
2. *fig.* Luft machen (*dat.*); *Zorn* auslassen (*on an dat.*); '**~-hole** Abzugs-
öffnung *f*.
ven·ti·late ['ventileit] ventilieren,
(be-, ent-, durch)lüften; *fig.* erörtern; **ven·ti'la·tion** Ventilation *f*,
Lüftung *f*; ♨ Wetterführung *f*;
fig. Erörterung *f*; '**ven·ti·la·tor**
Ventilator *m*.
ven·tral ['ventrəl] Bauch...
ven·tri·cle *anat.* ['ventrikl] Kammer *f*.
ven·tril·o·quist [ven'trilɔkwist]
Bauchredner *m*; **ven'tril·o·quize**
bauchreden.
ven·ture ['ventʃə] **1.** Wagnis *n*;
Risiko *n*; gewagtes Unternehmen *n*;
Abenteuer *n*; Spekulation(sobjekt
n) *f*; *at a* ~ auf gut Glück; **2.** *v/t.*
wagen, aufs Spiel setzen, riskieren;
v/i. sich *wohin* wagen; ~ (*up*)*on* sich
wagen an (*acc.*); *I* ~ *to say* ich wage
zu behaupten; **ven·ture·some** □
['‿səm], '**ven·tur·ous** □ verwegen,
kühn.
ven·ue ['venju:] zuständiger Ge-
richtsort *m*; *fig.* Schauplatz *m*;
F Treffpunkt *m*.
ve·ra·cious □ [və'reiʃəs] wahrhaft;
ve·rac·i·ty [ve'ræsiti] Wahrhaftigkeit *f*.
ve·ran·da(h) [və'rændə] Veranda *f*.
verb *gr.* [və:b] Zeitwort *n*, Verb(um)
n; '**ver·bal** □ wörtlich; mündlich;
Wort...; verbal; '**ver·bal·ize** in Worten ausdrücken; *gr.* in ein Verb umwandeln; **ver·ba·tim** [‿'beitim]
wörtlich, wortgetreu; **ver·bi·age** ['‿-
biidʒ] Wortschwall *m*; **ver·bose** □
[‿'bəus] wortreich; **ver·bos·i·ty** [‿-
'bɔsiti] Wortschwall *m*.
ver·dan·cy ['və:dənsi] Grün *n*; *fig.*
Grünheit *f*, Unreife *f*; '**ver·dant** □
grün; *fig.* unerfahren, unreif.
ver·dict ['və:dikt] ♨ (Urteils-)
Spruch *m der Geschworenen*; *fig.*
Urteil *n* (*on* über *acc.*); *bring in od.*
return a ~ *of guilty* auf schuldig erkennen.
ver·di·gris ['və:digris] Grünspan *m*.
ver·dure ['və:dʒə] Grün *n*.
verge[1] ['və:dʒ] (Amts- *etc.*)Stab *m*.
verge[2] □ **1.** *mst fig.* Rand *m*, Grenze *f*; *on the* ~ *of* am Rande (*gen.*);
dicht vor (*dat.*); nahe daran, zu *inf.*;

2. sich (hin)neigen; ~ (up)on streifen, grenzen an (acc.).

ver·ger ['vɔːdʒə] Kirchendiener m; Amtsstabträger m.

ver·i·fi·a·ble ['verifaiəbl] nachweisbar; **ver·i·fi·ca·tion** [ˌfiˈkeiʃən] Nachprüfung f; Bestätigung f; **ver·i·fy** ['ˌfai] (nach)prüfen, verifizieren; beweisen, belegen; bestätigen; **'ver·i·ly** † wahrlich; **ver·i·si·mil·i·tude** [ˌsiˈmilitjuːd] Wahrscheinlichkeit f; **ver·i·ta·ble** ['ˌtəbl] wahr(haftig), wirklich; **'ver·i·ty** Wahrheit f.

ver·mi·cel·li [vɔːmiˈseli] Fadennudeln f/pl.; **ver·mi·cide** pharm. ['ˌsaid] Wurmmittel n; **ver'mic·u·lar** [ˌkjulə] wurmartig, -förmig; **ver·mi·form** ['ˌfɔːm] wurmförmig; Wurm...; **ver·mi·fuge** pharm. ['ˌfjuːdʒ] Wurmmittel n.

ver·mil·ion [vɔˈmiljən] **1.** Zinnoberrot n; **2.** zinnoberrot.

ver·min ['vɔːmin] Ungeziefer n; hunt. Raubzeug n; fig. Gesindel n; **'ˌkill·er** Kammerjäger m; **'ver·min·ous** voller Ungeziefer; verlaust.

ver·m(o)uth ['vɔːməθ] Wermut m.

ver·nac·u·lar □ [vɔˈnækjulə] **1.** einheimisch; Landes...; landes-, muttersprachlich; **2.** Landes-, Muttersprache f; Jargon m.

ver·nal ['vɔːnl] Frühlings...

ver·ni·er ['vɔːnjə] ♣ Gradteiler m; ⊕ Fein(ein)steller m.

ver·ru·ca [veˈruːkə] mst auf der Fußsohle befindliche Warze f.

ver·sa·tile □ ['vɔːsətail] wandelbar; wandlungsfähig; beweglich (Geist); vielseitig, gewandt; **ver·sa·til·i·ty** [ˌˈtiliti] Wandelbarkeit f; Beweglichkeit f; Vielseitigkeit f.

verse [vɔːs] Vers m; Strophe f; coll. Verse m/pl.; weitS. Dichtung f; Poesie f; **versed** bewandert, erfahren (in in dat.).

ver·si·fi·ca·tion [vɔːsifiˈkeiʃən] Verskunst f; Versbau m; **ver·si·fy** ['ˌfai] v/t. in Verse bringen; v/i. Verse machen.

ver·sion ['vɔːʃən] Übersetzung f; Fassung f, Darstellung f; Lesart f.

ver·so ['vɔːsəu] Verso n, Rückseite f e-s Blattes.

ver·sus bsd. ⟨⟩ ['vɔːsəs] gegen.

vert F eccl. [vɔːt] übertreten, konvertieren.

ver·te·bra anat. ['vɔːtibrə], pl. **ver·te·brae** ['ˌbriː] Wirbel m; **ver·te·bral** ['ˌbrəl] Wirbel...; **ver·te·brate** ['ˌbrit] **1.** Wirbel...; ~ animal = **2.** Wirbeltier n.

ver·tex ['vɔːteks], pl. mst **ver·ti·ces** ['ˌtisiːz] Scheitel(punkt) m; **'ver·ti·cal** □ vertikal, senkrecht; Scheitel...; ~ take-off aircraft ✈ Senkrechtstarter m.

ver·tig·i·nous □ [vɔˈtidʒinəs] schwindlig; schwindelnd (Höhe); Schwindel...; **ver·ti·go** ['ˌtigəu] Schwindel(anfall) m.

verve [vɔːv] künstlerische Begeisterung f, Schwung m, Verve f.

ver·y ['veri] **1.** adv. sehr; the ~ best das allerbeste; **2.** adj. wahrhaftig; wirklich; gerade, eben; schon, bloß; the ~ same ebenderselbe; in the ~ act auf frischer Tat; gerade dabei; to the ~ bone bis auf den Knochen; the ~ thing gerade das; the ~ thought schon der Gedanke, der bloße Gedanke; the ~ stones sogar die Steine; the veriest baby (selbst) das kleinste Kind; the veriest rascal der ärgste od. größte Schuft; ~ high fre·quen·cy Radio: Ultrakurzwelle f.

ves·i·ca ['vesikə] Blase f; **ves·i·cle** ['ˌkl] Bläschen n.

ves·per ['vespə] poet. Abend m; ~s pl. eccl. Vesper f, Abendandacht f.

ves·sel ['vesl] Gefäß n (a. anat., ♀, fig.); ♣ Fahrzeug n, Schiff n.

vest [vest] **1.** Unterhemd n; ✝ Weste f; **2.** v/t. mst fig. j. bekleiden (with mit); j. einsetzen (in in acc.); et. übertragen (in s.o. j-m); v/i. verliehen werden (in s.o. j-m); ~ed rights pl. wohlerworbene Rechte n/pl.

ves·tal ['vestl] **1.** vestalisch; jungfräulich; **2.** Vestalin f.

ves·ti·bule ['vestibjuːl] Vorhof m (a. fig.); Vorhalle f; Hausflur m; 🚃 bsd. Am. Korridor m zwischen zwei D-Zug-Wagen; ~ train D-Zug m.

ves·tige ['vestidʒ] Spur f; **ves·tig·i·al** [ˌdʒiəl] rudimentär; verkümmert.

vest·ment ['vestmənt] (bsd. Amts-) Gewand n, Kleid n.

vest-pock·et ['vestˈpɔkit] Westentaschen..., Klein...

ves·try ['vestri] *eccl.* Sakristei *f*; Gemeindevertretung *f*; Gemeindesaal *m*; '∿·**man** Gemeindevertreter *m*.

ves·ture *poet.* ['vestʃə] **1.** Kleid(er *pl.*) *n*; **2.** kleiden.

vet F [vet] **1.** Tierarzt *m*; *Am.* ✗ Veteran *m*; **2.** verarzten; *fig.* gründlich prüfen.

vetch ⚘ [vetʃ] Wicke *f*.

vet·er·an ['vetərən] **1.** ausgedient; erfahren; **2.** Veteran *m*; ehemaliger Soldat *m*; ∿ **car** *mot.* Oldtimer *m*, Autoveteran *m*.

vet·er·i·nar·i·an *Am.* [vetəri'nɛəriən] Tierarzt *m*.

vet·er·i·nar·y ['vetərinəri] **1.** tierärztlich; **2.** *a.* ∿ **surgeon** Tierarzt *m*.

ve·to ['viːtəu] **1.** *pl.* **ve·toes** ['∿z] Veto *n*; Einspruch *m*; *put a od.* one's ∿ (*up*)*on* = **2.** sein Veto einlegen gegen.

vex [veks] ärgern; quälen; *bsd.* 🎓 schikanieren; **vex'a·tion** Verdruß *m*, Ärger *m*; Ärgernis *n*; Schikane *f*; **vex'a·tious** ☐ ärgerlich, verdrießlich; schikanös; **vexed** ☐ ärgerlich (*at s.th., with s.o.* über *acc.*); ∿ *question* Streitfrage *f*; '**vex·ing** ☐ ärgerlich.

vi·a ['vaiə] über, via.

vi·a·ble ['vaiəbl] lebensfähig.

vi·a·duct ['vaiədʌkt] Viadukt *m*, Überführung *f*.

vi·al ['vaiəl] Phiole *f*, Fläschchen *n*; Ampulle *f*.

vi·and ['vaiənd] *mst* ∿*s pl.* Lebensmittel *n/pl.*

vi·at·i·cum *eccl.* [vai'ætikəm] Wegzehrung *f*.

vibes [vaibz] *pl.* F Vibraphon *n*; *sl.* Atmosphäre *f*, Wirkung *f*, Ausstrahlung *f*.

vi·brant ['vaibrənt] vibrierend; zitternd (*with* vor *dat.*).

vi·bra·phone ♩ ['vaibrəfəun] Vibraphon *n*.

vi·brate [vai'breit] vibrieren; schwingen; zittern; **vi'bra·tion** Schwingung *f*, Zittern *n*, Vibrieren *n*, Erschütterung *f*; **vi'bra·tor** Vibrator *m*; **vi·bra·to·ry** ['∿brətəri] schwingend; Schwingungs...

vic·ar *eccl.* ['vikə] Vikar *m*, (Unter-) Pfarrer *m*; ∿ *general* Generalvikar *m*; '**vic·ar·age** Pfarrhaus *n*; **vi·car·i·ous** ☐ [vai'kɛəriəs] stellvertretend.

vice¹ [vais] Laster *n*; Fehler *m*;

Unart *f*.

vice² ⊕ [∿] Schraubstock *m*.

vice³ ['vaisi] *prp.* an Stelle von.

vice⁴ [vais] **1.** Vize..., Unter...; **2.** F Stellvertreter *m*; '∿·'**ad·mi·ral** Vizeadmiral *m*; '∿·'**chair·man** stellvertretender Vorsitzender *m*; Vizepräsident *m*; '∿·'**chan·cel·lor** Vizekanzler *m*; *univ.* Rektor *m*; '∿·'**con·sul** Vizekonsul *m*; ∿·**ge·rent** ['∿'dʒerənt] Statthalter *m*, Stellvertreter *m*; '∿·'**pres·i·dent** Vizepräsident *m*; '∿·'**re·gal** vizeköniglich; ∿·**reine** ['∿'rein] Gemahlin *f* des Vizekönigs; ∿·**roy** ['∿rɔi] Vizekönig *m*.

vi·ce ver·sa ['vaisi'vəːsə] umgekehrt.

vic·i·nage ['visinidʒ] Nachbarschaft *f*; Nähe *f* (*to* bei); *in the* ∿ *of 40* um 40 herum.

vi·cious ☐ ['viʃəs] lasterhaft; verwerflich; bösartig (*Tier*); boshaft (*Kritik*); fehlerhaft; ∿ *cir·cle* Circulus *m* vitiosus, Teufelskreis *m*; ∿ *spi·ral* *fig.* Schraube *f* ohne Ende.

vi·cis·si·tude [vi'sisitjuːd] Wandel *m*, Wechsel *m*; ∿*s pl.* Wechselfälle *m/pl.*

vic·tim ['viktim] Opfer *n*; '**vic·tim·ize** (hin)opfern; *fig. j.* hereinlegen; drangsalieren, verfolgen.

vic·tor ['viktə] Sieger *m*; **Vic·to·ri·an** *hist.* [vik'tɔːriən] Viktorianisch; **vic'to·ri·ous** ☐ siegreich; Sieges...; **vic·to·ry** ['∿təri] Sieg *m*.

vict·ual ['vitl] **1.** (sich) mit Lebensmitteln versehen; **2.** *mst* ∿*s pl.* Lebensmittel *n/pl.*, Proviant *m*; **vict·ual·(l)er** ['vitlə] Lebensmittellieferant *m*; *licensed* ∿ Schankwirt *m*.

vi·de ['vaidiː] siehe!

vi·de·li·cet [vi'diːliset] (*abbr. viz.*; *lies: namely, that is*) nämlich.

vid·e·o ['vidiəu] Fernseh...; Video...; ∿ **disc** Bildplatte *f*; ∿ **re·cord·er** Videorecorder *m*; ∿ **tape** Videoband *n*; *video-tape library* Videothek *f*.

vie [vai] wetteifern.

Vi·en·nese [vie'niːz] **1.** Wiener(in); **2.** Wiener, wienerisch.

view [vjuː] **1.** Sehen *n*, Sicht *f*, Auge(n *pl.*) *n*, Blick *m*; Besichtigung *f*; Aussicht *f* (*of auf acc.*); Anblick *m*; Ansicht *f* (*a. paint., phot.*); Absicht *f*; *fig.* Ansicht *f* (*Meinung*); Anschauung *f*; *at first* ∿ auf den ersten Blick; *in* ⌣ sichtbar, zu sehen; *in* ⌣ *of* im Hinblick auf (*acc.*); *fig.* angesichts (*gen.*); *in my* ⌣ in meinen Augen; *on* ⌣ zu besichtigen *od.* sehen; *on the long* ⌣ auf weite Sicht, auf die Dauer; *out of* ⌣ unsichtbar, nicht zu sehen; *with a* ⌣ *to ger.*, *with the* ⌣ *of ger.* mit *od.* in der Absicht zu *inf.*; zu dem Zweck (*gen.*); im Hinblick auf (*acc.*); *come into* ⌣ sichtbar werden, in Sicht kommen; *have* (*keep*) *in* ⌣ im Auge haben (behalten); **2.** an-, besehen, besichtigen; *geistig* (an)sehen, betrachten; '**view·er** Betrachter(in), (Fernseh-) Zuschauer(in); '**view-find·er** *phot.* Sucher *m*; '**view·less** ohne eigene Meinung; *poet.* unsichtbar; '⌣**point** Gesichts-, Standpunkt *m*; '**view·y** ☐ F schrullig.

vig·il *bsd. eccl.* ['vidʒil] Nachtwache *f*; '**vig·i·lance** Wachsamkeit *f*; ⌣ **committee** *Am. hist.* Wachkomitee *n*; '**vig·i·lant** ☐ wachsam; **vig·i-lan·te** *Am.* [⌣'lænti] Angehörige *m* e-s Wachkomitees.

vi·gnette *typ., phot.* [vi'njet] **1.** Vignette *f*; **2.** vignettieren.

vig·or·ous ☐ ['vigərəs] kräftig, kraftvoll; energisch; lebhaft; *fig.* nachdrücklich; '**vig·o(u)r** Kraft *f*; Vitalität *f*; Energie *f*; Lebenskraft *f*; *fig.* Nachdruck *m*.

vi·king ['vaikiŋ] **1.** Wiking(er) *m*; **2.** wikingisch, Wikinger...

vile ☐ [vail] gemein, niedrig, nichtswürdig.

vil·i·fi·ca·tion [vilifi'keiʃən] Verunglimpfung *f*; **vil·i·fy** [⌣'fai] verunglimpfen, schlechtmachen.

vil·la ['vilə] Villa *f*, Landhaus *n*.

vil·lage ['vilidʒ] Dorf *n*; ⌣ **green** Dorfanger *m*, -wiese *f*; '**vil·lag·er** Dorfbewohner(in).

vil·lain ['vilən] Schurke *m*, Schuft *m*, Bösewicht *m* (*a. co.*); '**vil·lain-ous** ☐ schurkisch, schändlich; F miserabel, scheußlich; '**vil·lain·y** Schurkerei *f*.

vil·lein *hist.* ['vilin] Leibeigene *m, f*.

vim F [vim] Schwung *m*, Schneid *m*.

vin·di·cate ['vindikeit] rechtfertigen (*from* gegen); verteidigen; beanspruchen (*to, for* für); **vin·di·ca·tion** Rechtfertigung *f*; **vin·di·ca·to·ry** ☐ ['⌣təri] rechtfertigend; Rechtfertigungs...

vin·dic·tive ☐ [vin'diktiv] rach-

süchtig; nachtragend.

vine ♣ [vain] Wein(stock) *m*, Rebe *f*; Kletterpflanze *f*; '⌣**-dress·er** Winzer *m*; **vin·e·gar** ['vinigə] **1.** (Wein-) Essig *m*; **2.** mit Essig behandeln; '**vin·e·gar·y** *mst fig.* (essig)sauer; **vine-grow·er** ['vaingrəuə] Weinbauer *m*; '**vine-grow·ing** Weinbau *m*; '**vine-louse** Reblaus *f*; **vine-yard** ['vinjəd] Weinberg *m*.

vi·nous ['vainəs] weinig; Wein...

vin·tage ['vintidʒ] **1.** Weinlese *f*; (Wein)Jahrgang *m*; **2.** klassisch; erlesen; altmodisch; ⌣ **car** *mot.* Veteran *m*; '**vin·tag·er** Winzer *m*; **vint·ner** ['vintnə] Weinhändler *m*.

vi·ol ♪ ['vaiəl] Viole *f*.

vi·o·la[1] ♪ [vi'əulə] Bratsche *f*, Viola *f*.

vi·o·la[2] ♣ ['vaiələ] Viole *f*.

vi·o·la·ble ☐ ['vaiələbl] verletzbar.

vi·o·late ['vaiəleit] verletzen; *Eid etc.* brechen; *Frau* vergewaltigen (*a. fig.*); *Tempel* schänden; **vi·o'la-tion** Verletzung *f*; (Eid- *etc.*) Bruch *m*; Vergewaltigung *f*; Schändung *f*; '**vi·o·la·tor** Verletzer *m etc.*

vi·o·lence ['vaiələns] Gewalttätigkeit *f*; Gewalttat *f*; Gewaltsamkeit *f*; Heftigkeit *f*, Gewalt *f*; *do od. offer* ⌣ *to* Gewalt antun (*dat.*); '**vi·o·lent** ☐ gewaltsam; gewalttätig; heftig, ungestüm.

vi·o·let ['vaiəlit] **1.** ♣ Veilchen *n*; **2.** veilchenblau, violett, lila.

vi·o·lin ♪ [vaiə'lin] Violine *f*, Geige *f*; '**vi·o·lin·ist** Violinist(in), Geiger (-in).

vi·o·lon·cel·list ♪ [vaiələn'tʃelist] Cellist(in); **vi·o·lon'cel·lo** [⌣'ləu] Cello *n*.

VIP *sl.* ['vi:ai'pi:] hohes Tier *n*.

vi·per *zo.* ['vaipə] Viper *f*, Natter *f* (*a. fig.*); **vi·per·ine** ['⌣rain], '**vi-per·ous** ☐ *mst fig.* viperartig; giftig.

vi·ra·go [vi'rɑːgəu] Zankteufel *m*, Drachen *m*.

vir·gin ['vəːdʒin] **1.** Jungfrau *f*; **2.** ☐ jungfräulich (*fig. unberührt*); *fig. u.* ⊕ Jungfern...; '**vir·gin·al** ['vəː-dʒin] **1.** ☐ jungfräulich; Jungfern-...; **2.** ♪ Virginal *n* (*Spinett*); **Vir-gin·ia** [və'dʒinjə] *a.* ⌣ **tobacco** Virginiatabak *m*; ⌣ **creeper** wilder Wein *m*; **Vir'gin·i·an** Virginia...; virginisch; **vir·gin·i·ty** [vəː'dʒiniti] Jungfräulichkeit *f*.

Vir·go *ast.* ['vəːgəu] Jungfrau *f.*

vir·ile ['virail] männlich; Mannes...;
mannhaft; viril; **vi·ril·i·ty** [vi'riliti]
Mannesalter *n*; Mannheit *f*; Männlichkeit *f*; Mannhaftigkeit *f*.

vir·tu [vəː'tuː]: *article of* ⸋ Kunstgegenstand *m*; **vir·tu·al** ⸋ ['ⸯtjuəl]
dem Wesen nach, eigentlich; '**vir-
tu·al·ly** praktisch; **vir·tue** ['ⸯtjuː]
Tugend *f*; Wirksamkeit *f*; Kraft *f*;
Vorzug *m*, Wert *m*; *in od. by* ⸋ *of*
kraft, vermöge *(gen.)*; auf Grund
von; *make a* ⸋ *of necessity* aus der
Not e-e Tugend machen; **vir·tu-
os·i·ty** [vəːtju'ɔsiti] Virtuosität *f*;
vir·tu·o·so [ⸯ'əuzəu] *bsd. ♩* Vir-
tuose *m*; Kunstliebhaber *m*; **vir-
tu·ous** ⸋ tugendhaft.

vir·u·lence ['viruləns] Giftigkeit *f*,
Virulenz *f*; *fig.* Bösartigkeit *f*; '**vir-
u·lent** ⸋ giftig; virulent; *fig.* bösartig.

vi·rus ⚶ ['vaiərəs] Virus *n*; *fig.*
Gift *n*.

vi·sa ['viːzə] **1.** Visum *n*, Sichtvermerk *m*; **2.** *pret. u. p.p.* '**vi·saed** mit
e-m Sichtvermerk *od.* Visum ver-
sehen.

vis·age *lit.* ['vizidʒ] (An)Gesicht *n*.

vis·cer·a *anat.* ['visərə] Eingeweide *pl.*

vis·cid ⸋ ['visid] = *viscous.*

vis·cose ⚘ ['viskəus] Viskose *f*; ⸋
silk Zellstoffseide *f*; **vis·cos·i·ty**
[ⸯ'kɔsiti] (Grad *m* der) Zähflüssig-
keit *f*, Viskosität *f*.

vis·count ['vaikaunt] Vicomte *m*
(englischer Adelstitel); '**vis·count-
ess** Vicomtesse *f*.

vis·cous ⸋ ['viskəs] zäh-, dick-
flüssig; klebrig.

vise [vais] *Am. für vice²*.

vi·sé ['viːzei] = *visa.*

vis·i·bil·i·ty [vizi'biliti] Sichtbar-
keit *f*; Sichtweite *f*; '**vis·i·ble** ⸋
sichtbar; *fig.* (er)sichtlich; *pred.* zu
sehen *(Sache)*; zu sprechen *(Person)*.

vi·sion ['viʒən] Sehvermögen *n*,
-kraft *f*; *fig.* Einsicht *f*, Seherblick
m; Vision *f*, Erscheinung *f*; Traum
(-bild *n*) *m (a. fig.)*; **vi·sion·ar·y**
['ⸯnəri] **1.** phantastisch; **2.** Geister-
seher(in); Phantast(in), Träumer
(-in).

vis·it ['vizit] **1.** *v/t.* besuchen; besichtigen; *fig.* heimsuchen *(with
mit)*; *et.* ahnden *(upon an j-m)*; *v/i.*

---

vivid

Besuche machen; ⸋ *with Am.* sich
unterhalten *od.* plaudern mit;
2. Besuch *m (to* bei; *gen.)*; '**vis·it-
ant** Besuch(er) *m*; *orn.* Strichvogel
m; **vis·it'a·tion** Besuch *m*; Besichtigung *f*; *fig.* Heimsuchung *f*; **vis-
it·a·to·ri·al** [ⸯtə'tɔːriəl] Besichti-
gungs...; Aufsichts...; '**vis·it·ing**
Besuchs...; ⸋ *card* Visitenkarte *f*;
⸋ *professor* Gastprofessor *m*; ⸋ *team
Sport:* Gastmannschaft *f*, *die* Gäste
m/pl.; '**vis·i·tor** Besuch(er) *m (to
gen.)*; Gast *m*; Inspektor *m*; ⸋s' *book*
Fremden-, Gästebuch *n*.

vi·sor ['vaizə] Helmvisier *n*; Müt-
zenschirm *m*; *mot.* Blendschirm *m*.

vis·ta ['vistə] Durchblick *m*; Rück-
od. Ausblick *m (a. fig.*; *of* auf *acc.)*;
Allee *f*; Galerie *f*; Reihe *f*.

vis·u·al ⸋ ['vizjuəl] Seh...; Gesichts...; '**vis·u·al·ize** (sich) vor
Augen stellen, sich ein Bild machen
von.

vi·tal ⸋ ['vaitl] Lebens...; lebens-
wichtig, wesentlich *(to* für); lebens-
gefährlich *(Wunde)*; ⸋s *pl.*, ⸋ *parts pl.*
lebenswichtige Organe *n/pl.*, edle
Teile *m/pl.*; *s. statistics*; **vi·tal·i·ty**
[ⸯ'tæliti] Lebenskraft *f*, -fähigkeit *f*;
Vitalität *f*; **vi·tal·ize** ['ⸯtəlaiz] beleben.

vi·ta·min(e) ['vitəmin] Vitamin *n*;
vi·ta·mi·nized ['ⸯnaizd] *(künstlich)*
mit Vitaminen angereichert.

vi·ti·ate ['viʃieit] verderben; beeinträchtigen; hinfällig *od.* 🜊 ungültig
machen.

vit·i·cul·ture ['vitikʌltʃə] Weinbau
m.

vit·re·ous ⸋ ['vitriəs] Glas...; gläsern.

vit·ri·fac·tion [vitri'fækʃən] Verglasung *f*; **vit·ri·fy** ['ⸯfai] verglasen.

vit·ri·ol ⚘ ['vitriɔl] Vitriol *n*; **vit·ri-
ol·ic** [vitri'ɔlik] Vitriol...; *fig.* ätzend,
bissig.

vi·tu·per·ate [vi'tjuːpəreit] schelten; schmähen, beschimpfen; **vi-
tu·per'a·tion** Schmähung *f*, Beschimpfung *f*; **vi'tu·per·a·tive** ⸋
[ⸯrətiv] schmähend; Schmäh...

vi·va *(vo·ce)* ['vaivə('vəusi)] **1.**
mündlich; **2.** mündliche Prüfung
f.

vi·va·cious ⸋ [vi'veiʃəs] lebhaft,
munter; **vi·vac·i·ty** [vi'væsiti] Lebhaftigkeit *f.*

viv·id ⸋ ['vivid] lebhaft, lebendig;

'**viv·id·ness** Lebhaftigkeit *f*.
viv·i·fy ['vivifai] (sich) beleben;
vi'vip·a·rous □ [‿pərəs] lebendgebärend; **viv·i·sec·tion** [‿'sekʃən]
Vivisektion *f*.
vix·en ['viksn] Füchsin *f*; zänkisches
Weib *n*.
viz. ['neimli] = *videlicet*.
vi·zier [vi'ziə] Wesir *m*.
vi·zor ['vaizə] = *visor*.
vo·cab·u·lar·y [vəu'kæbjuləri] Wörterverzeichnis *n*; Wortschatz *m*,
Vokabular *n*.
vo·cal □ ['vəukəl] stimmlich;
Stimm...; gesprochen; laut; ♪ Vokal..., Gesang...; sprechend; klingend; *gr*. stimmhaft; ‿ c(h)ord
Stimmband *n*; ‿ part Singstimme *f*;
'**vo·cal·ist** Sänger(in); '**vo·cal·ize**
(*gr*. stimmhaft) aussprechen; singen; '**vo·cal·ly** *adv*. mittels der
Stimme; laut.
vo·ca·tion [vəu'keiʃən] *innere* Berufung *f*; Beruf *m*; **vo'ca·tion·al** □
[‿ʃənl] beruflich; Berufs...; ‿
guidance Berufsberatung *f*.
voc·a·tive *gr*. ['vɔkətiv] Vokativ *m*.
vo·cif·er·ate [vəu'sifəreit] schreien;
laut rufen; brüllen; **vo·cif·er'a·tion** *a*. ‿s *pl*. Geschrei *n*; **vo'cif·er·ous** □ schreiend, laut.
vogue [vəug] Beliebtheit *f*; Mode *f*.
voice [vɔis] **1.** Stimme *f*; *active*
(*passive*) ‿ *gr*. Aktiv *n* (Passiv *n*); *in*
(*good*) ‿ (gut) bei Stimme; *give* ‿ *to*
Ausdruck geben (*dat*.); **2.** äußern,
ausdrücken; *gr*. stimmhaft aussprechen; '‿box ⊦ Kehlkopf *m*;
voiced *gr*. stimmhaft; *in Zssgn*
...stimmig; '**voice·less** □ *bsd*. *gr*.
stimmlos; stumm.
void [vɔid] **1.** leer; ⁑ nichtig, ungültig; ‿ of frei von; arm an (*dat*.);
ohne; **2.** Leere *f*; Lücke *f*; **3.** entleeren; ungültig machen, aufheben;
'**void·ness** Leere *f*.
voile [vɔil] Voile *m*, Schleierstoff *m*.
vol·a·tile ['vɔlətail] ⚗ flüchtig (*a*.
fig.); flatterhaft; **vol·a·til·i·ty** [‿'tiliti] Flüchtigkeit *f*; **vol·a·til·ize**
[vɔ'lætilaiz] (sich) verflüchtigen.
vol·can·ic [vɔl'kænik] (‿ally) vulkanisch; **vol·ca·no** [vɔl'keinəu], *pl*.
vol'ca·noes [‿z] Vulkan *m*.
vole *zo*. [vəul] Wühlmaus *f*.
vo·li·tion [vəu'liʃən] Wollen *n*;
Wille(nskraft *f*) *m*; *on one's own* ‿
aus eigenem Entschluß.

vol·ley ['vɔli] **1.** Salve *f*; (Geschoß-
etc.) Hagel *m*; *fig*. Schwall *m*, Strom
m; *Tennis*: Volley-, Flugball *m*;
2. *v/t*. *mst* ‿ out e-n Schwall von
Worten etc. von sich geben; *Ball*
volley nehmen; *v/i*. Salven abgeben;
sich entladen; *fig*. hageln; dröhnen;
'**vol·ley-ball** *Sport*: Volleyball *m*,
Flugball *m*.
vol·plane ✈ ['vɔlplein] **1.** Gleitflug
m; **2.** im Gleitflug niedergehen.
volt ⚡ [vəult] Volt *n*; '**volt·age** ⚡
Spannung *f*; **vol·ta·ic** ⚡ [vɔl'teiik]
voltaisch.
volte-face *fig*. ['vɔlt'fɑːs] völlige
Kehrtwendung *f*.
volt·me·ter ⚡ ['vəultmiːtə] Voltmeter *n*, Spannungsmesser *m*.
vol·u·bil·i·ty [vɔlju'biliti] Zungenfertigkeit *f*, Redegewandtheit *f*;
vol·u·ble □ ['‿bl] zungenfertig,
(rede)gewandt.
vol·ume ['vɔljum] Band *m* e-s Buches; *phys. etc*. Volumen *n*; *fig*.
Masse *f*, große Menge *f*; (*bsd*.
Stimm)Umfang *m*; ‿ of sound Radio: Lautstärke *f*; ‿ control, ‿ regulator Lautstärkeregler *m*; **vo·lu·mi·nous** □ [və'ljuːminəs] vielbändig; umfangreich; voluminös.
vol·un·tar·y □ ['vɔləntəri] **1.** freiwillig; *physiol*. willkürlich; ‿ death
Freitod *m*; **2.** freiwillige Arbeit *f*;
♪ Orgelsolo *n*; **vol·un·teer** [‿'tiə]
1. Freiwillige *m*; *attr*. Freiwilligen-
...; **2.** *v/i*. freiwillig dienen; sich
freiwillig melden; sich erbieten;
v/t. anbieten; sich e-e Bemerkung
erlauben.
vo·lup·tu·ar·y [və'lʌptjuəri] Genußmensch *m*; Wollüstling *m*.
vo·lup·tu·ous [və'lʌptjuəs] wollüstig; üppig; sinnlich; **vo'lup·tu·ous·ness** Wollust *f*; Sinnlichkeit *f*.
vo·lute ⌂ [və'ljuːt] Volute *f*,
Schnecke *f*; **vo'lut·ed** voluten-,
schneckenförmig.
vom·it ['vɔmit] **1.** (sich) erbrechen;
fig. (aus)speien, ausstoßen; **2.** Erbrochene *n*; Ausgespiene *n*; Auswurf *m*.
voo·doo ['vuːduː] **1.** Wodu *m*, Zauberkult *m*; Hexerei *f*; **2.** behexen.
vo·ra·cious □ [və'reiʃəs] gefräßig;
gierig; **vo'ra·cious·ness**, **vo·rac·i·ty** [və'ræsiti] Gefräßigkeit *f*; Gier *f*
(*of* nach).
vor·tex ['vɔːteks], *pl. mst* **vor·ti·ces**

['_tisiːz] Wirbel *m*, Strudel *m* (*mst fig.*).

vo·ta·ry ['vəutəri] Geweihte *m*; Anhänger(in); Verehrer(in).

vote [vəut] **1.** (Wahl)Stimme *f*; Abstimmung *f*; Stimmrecht *n*; *Abstimmungs*-Beschluß *m*, Votum *n*; _ *of no confidence* Mißtrauensvotum *n*; *cast a* _ (s)eine Stimme abgeben; *put to the* _ zur Abstimmung bringen, abstimmen lassen über; *take a* _ *on s.th.* über et. abstimmen; **2.** *v/t.* stimmen für; F erklären für; *v/i.* (ab)stimmen; wählen; _ *for* stimmen für; F für *et.* sein; *et.* vorschlagen; **'vot·er** Stimmberechtigte *m*, *f*; Wähler(in).

vot·ing...: _-**booth** ['vəutiŋbuːð] Wahlzelle *f*; '_-**box** Wahlurne *f*; '_-**pa·per** Stimmzettel *m*.

vo·tive ['vəutiv] Votiv...; Weih...

vouch [vautʃ] verbürgen; _ *for* bürgen für; '**vouch·er** Beleg *m*, Unterlage *f*; Gutschein *m*; Zeuge *m*, Gewährsmann *m*; **vouch'safe** *v/t.* gewähren; sich herablassen zu; *v/i.* geruhen.

vow [vau] **1.** Gelübde *n*; (Treu-)Schwur *m*; **2.** *v/t.* geloben.

vow·el ['vauəl] Vokal *m*.

voy·age ['vɔiidʒ] **1.** *längere* (See-, Luft)Reise *f*; **2.** *zur See, in der Luft* reisen, fahren; **voy·ag·er** ['vɔiədʒə] (See)Reisende *m*.

vul·can·ite ['vʌlkənait] Vulkanit *m* (*Hartgummi*); **vul·can·i'za·tion** ⊕ Vulkanisierung *f*; '**vul·can·ize** ⊕ vulkanisieren; _d *fibre* Vulkanfiber *f*.

vul·gar ['vʌlgə] **1.** □ gewöhnlich, gemein, vulgär, pöbelhaft; _ *tongue* Volkssprache *f*; **2.** *the* _ *der* Pöbel; '**vul·gar·ism** vulgärer Ausdruck *m*; **vul·gar·i·ty** [_'gæriti] Gemeinheit *f*; **vul·gar·ize** ['_gəreiz] gemein machen, erniedrigen; populär machen, verbreiten.

vul·ner·a·bil·i·ty [vʌlnərə'biliti] Verwundbarkeit *f etc.*; '**vul·ner·a·ble** □ verwundbar; *fig.* angreifbar; ungeschützt; '**vul·ner·ar·y** **1.** Wund..., Heil...; **2.** Wundmittel *n*.

vul·pine ['vʌlpain] Fuchs...; fuchsartig; *fig.* schlau, listig.

vul·ture *orn.* ['vʌltʃə] Geier *m*; **vul·tur·ine** ['_tʃurain] geierartig.

vy·ing ['vaiiŋ] wetteifernd.

W

wab·ble ['wɔbl] = *wobble*.

wack·y *Am. sl.* ['wæki] verrückt.

wad [wɔd] **1.** (Watte)Bausch *m*; Polster *n*; Pfropf(en) *m*); Banknotenbündel *n*; **2.** wattieren; polstern; zu-, verstopfen; '**wad·ding** Wattierung *f*; Watte *f*.

wad·dle ['wɔdl] watscheln, wackeln.

wade [weid] *v/i.* waten; *fig.* sich hindurcharbeiten; *v/t.* durchwaten; '**wad·er** Watvogel *m*; _s *pl.* Wasserstiefel *m/pl.*

wa·fer ['weifə] Waffel *f*; *a. consecrated* _ *eccl.* Oblate *f*, Hostie *f*.

waf·fle ['wɔfl] **1.** Waffel *f*; **2.** F quasseln.

waft [wɑːft] **1.** wehen, tragen; (ent-)senden; **2.** Hauch *m*.

wag[1] [wæg] **1.** *v/t.* wackeln mit, schütteln; wedeln mit *dem Schwanz*;

v/i. wackeln; **2.** Schütteln *n*; Wedeln *n*.

wag[2] [_] Spaßvogel *m*, Schalk *m*; *play* _ *sl.* die Schule schwänzen.

wage [weidʒ] **1.** *Krieg* führen, unternehmen; **2.** *mst* _s *pl.* Lohn *m*; _ **de·mands** *pl.* Lohnforderungen *f/pl.*; _ **dis·pute** Lohnkampf *m*; _**earn·er** ['_əːnə] Lohnempfänger *m*; _ **in·crease** Lohnerhöhung *f*; _ **pack·et** Lohntüte *f*; _ **re·straint** Lohnbeschränkung *f*; '_**sheet**, '**wag·es·sheet** Lohnliste *f*; **wage slip** Lohnstreifen *m*.

wa·ger *lit.* ['weidʒə] **1.** Wette *f*; **2.** wetten; *Geld* verwetten (*on* für).

wag·ger·y ['wægəri] Schelmerei *f*; Spaß *m*; '**wag·gish** □ schelmisch, schalkhaft.

wag·gle F ['wægl] = *wag*[1] *1*; '**wag-**

gly F wacklig; sich windend.
wag·(g)on ['wægən] (Roll-, Güter-) Wagen *m*; Waggon *m*; Pferdefuhrwerk *n*; *be od.* go on the (*water*) ~ F nicht trinken; **'wag·(g)on·er** Fuhrmann *m*.
wag·tail *orn.* ['wægteil] Bachstelze *f*.
waif [weif] herrenloses Gut *n*; weggeworfenes Diebesgut *n*; Strandgut *n*; Heimatlose *m*, *f*; **~s** *and strays pl.* verwahrloste Kinder *n/pl.*; Reste *m/pl.*
wail [weil] **1.** (Weh)Klagen *n*; **2.** *v/t.* bejammern; *v/i.* (weh)klagen.
wain *poet.* [wein] Wagen *m*; Charles's ♀, the ♀ *ast.* der Große Wagen.
wain·scot ['weinskət] **1.** Holzverkleidung *f*, (-)Täfelung *f*; **2.** täfeln.
waist [weist] Taille *f*; schmalste Stelle *f*; ♱ Mitteldeck *n*; **'~·band** Taillen-, Gurtband *n*; **~·coat** ['weiskout] Weste *f*; **~·deep** ['weist'di:p] bis über die Hüften (reichend; **'waist·ed** tailliert; **'waist·line** Taille *f*.
wait [weit] **1.** *v/i.* warten; *a.* ~ *at* (*Am.* on) *table* bedienen, servieren; ~ for warten auf (*acc.*); ~ (up)on s.o. j. bedienen; j. besuchen; *keep* ~ing warten lassen; ~ *and see* abwarten; ~ *in line* Schlange stehen; *v/t.* abwarten; mit *dem Essen* warten (*for* auf *j.*); **2.** Warten *n*, Aufenthalt *m*; ~s *pl.* Weihnachtssänger *m/pl.*; *have a long* ~ lange warten müssen; *lie in* ~ *for s.o.* j-m auflauern; **'wait·er** Kellner *m*; Tablett *n*.
wait·ing ['weitiŋ] Warten *n*; Dienst *m*; *in* ~ diensttuend; *no* ~ Parken verboten; **'~·maid** Kammermädchen *n*; **'~·room** Wartezimmer *n*, -saal *m*.
wait·ress ['weitris] Kellnerin *f*.
waive [weiv] verzichten auf (*acc.*), aufgeben, ⚖ sich *e-s Rechtes* begeben; **'waiv·er** ⚖ Verzicht *m*.
wake[1] [weik] ♱ Kielwasser *n* (*a. fig.*); ✈ Luftsog *m*; *fig.* Spur *f*.
wake[2] [~] **1.** (*irr.*) *v/i. a.* ~ *up* aufwachen; *v/t. a.* ~ *up* (auf)wecken; erwecken; *fig.* wachrufen; **2.** Totenwache *f*; Kirmes *f*; **wake·ful** □ ['~ful] wachend; wachsam; schlaflos; **'wak·en** *v/i.* (auf)wachen; *v/t.* (auf)wecken; *fig.* anregen.
wale [weil] *bsd. Am.* für *weal*[2].
walk [wɔ:k] **1.** *v/i.* (zu Fuß) gehen;

spazierengehen; wandern; Schritt gehen; ~ *about* umhergehen, -wandern; ~ *into sl.* herfallen über (*acc.*); ~ *out* F die Arbeit niederlegen, streiken; ~ *out on sl.* im Stich lassen; *v/t.* führen; *Pferd* Schritt gehen lassen; begleiten; spazieren führen; (durch)wandern; umhergehen auf *od.* in (*dat.*); ~ *the hospitals* s-e klinischen Semester machen (*Mediziner*); **2.** (Spazier)Gang *m*; Spazierweg *m*; Schritt *m* (*Gangart*); *go for a* ~ e-n Spaziergang machen, spazierengehen; ~ *of life* Lebensstellung *f*, Beruf *m*; **'~·a·bout:** *go on a* ~ ein Bad in der Menge nehmen (*wichtige Person*); **'walk·er** Fuß-, Spaziergänger(in); *Sport:* Geher *m*; *be a good* ~ gut zu Fuß sein; **'walk·er·on** *thea.* Statist(in).
walk·ie-talk·ie ⚔ ['wɔ:ki'tɔ:ki] tragbares Sprechfunkgerät *n*.
walk·ing ['wɔ:kiŋ] **1.** Spazierengehen *n*, Wandern *n*; *attr.* Spazier-...; Wander...; ~ *pa·pers pl. Am.* F Entlassung(spapiere *n/pl.*) *f*; Laufpaß *m*; **'~·stick** Spazierstock *m*; **'~·tour** (Fuß)Wanderung *f*.
walk...: **'~·out** *Am.* Ausstand *m*; **'~·over** Kinderspiel *n*, leichter Sieg *m*; **'~·up** ohne Fahrstuhl (*Haus*).
wall [wɔ:l] **1.** Wand *f*; Mauer *f*; *give s.o. the* ~ j-m den Vorrang lassen; *go to the* ~ *fig.* an die Wand gedrückt werden; ~·to·~ *carpeting* Teppichboden *m*; **2.** mit Mauern umgeben; (ein-, um)mauern (*mst mit adv.*); *fig.* ein-, abschließen; ~ *up* zumauern.
wal·la·by *zo.* ['wɔləbi] kleines Känguruh *n*.
wal·let ['wɔlit] Brieftasche *f*; Werkzeugtasche *f*; † Ränzel *n*.
wall...: **'~·eye** *vet.* Glasauge *n*; **'~·flow·er** ♀ Goldlack *m*; *fig.* Mauerblümchen *n*; **'~·fruit** Spalierobst *n*; **'~·map** Wandkarte *f*.
Wal·loon [wɔ'lu:n] **1.** Wallone *m*, Wallonin *f*; Wallonisch *n*; **2.** wallonisch.
wal·lop F ['wɔləp] **1.** *v/i.* brodeln; poltern; *v/t. j.* verdreschen; **2.** kräftiger Schlag *m*, Hieb *m*; *sl.* Bier *n*; **'wal·lop·ing** F riesig.
wal·low ['wɔləu] **1.** sich wälzen; *fig.* schwelgen (*in in dat.*); **2.** Sichwälzen *n*; *hunt.* Suhle *f*.
wall...: **'~·pa·per** Tapete *f*; **'~-**

-sock·et *⚡* Steckdose *f.*
wal·nut *♀* ['wɔ:lnʌt] Walnuß(baum *m*) *f.*
wal·rus *zo.* ['wɔ:lrəs] Walroß *n.*
waltz [wɔ:ls] **1.** Walzer *m*; **2.** Walzer tanzen, walzen.
wam·pum ['wɒmpəm] Wampum *n (Muschelornament u. Geld der Indianer)*; *sl.* Moneten *pl.*
wan □ [wɒn] blaß, bleich, fahl.
wand [wɒnd] Zauberstab *m*; Amtsstab *m.*
wan·der ['wɒndə] wandern; *a.* ~ *about* umherschweifen, -wandern; *fig.* abschweifen *(from* von); irregehen, umherirren; phantasieren; **'wan·der·er** Wanderer(in); **'wan·der·ing 1.** □ wandernd; *fig.* unstet; **2.** ~s *pl.* Wanderung(en *pl.*) *f,* Wanderschaft *f*; *(Fieber)*Phantasie *f.*
wane [wein] **1.** abnehmen *(Mond)*; *fig.* schwinden; **2.** Abnahme *f*; *on the* ~ im Abnehmen *od.* Schwinden.
wan·gle *sl.* ['wæŋgl] schieben, deichseln, drehen, organisieren; **'wan·gler** Schieber *m.*
wan·ness ['wɒnnis] Blässe *f.*
want [wɒnt] **1.** Mangel *m (of* an *dat.)*; Bedürfnis *n*; Not *f*; *for* ~ *of* aus Mangel an *(dat.)*, mangels *(gen.)*; **2.** *v/i.* be ~*ing* fehlen; be ~*ing in* es fehlen lassen an *(dat.)*; be ~*ing to der Lage etc.* nicht gewachsen sein; *he does not* ~ *for* es mangelt ihm nicht an *(dat.)*; *it* ~*s of* es mangelt *od.* fehlt an *(dat.)*; *v/t.* bedürfen *(gen.)*, nötig haben, brauchen; ermangeln *(gen.)*, nicht haben; verlangen; wünschen, (haben) wollen; *it* ~*s s.th.* es fehlt an et.; *he* ~*s energy* es fehlt ihm an Energie; *you* ~ *to be careful* du mußt vorsichtig sein; ~ *s.o. to do* wollen *od.* wünschen, daß j. tut; ~*ed* gesucht; **'~-ad** Kleinanzeige *f*; Stellenangebot *n,* -gesuch *n.*
wan·ton ['wɒntən] **1.** □ wollüstig, geil; üppig; mutwillig; übermütig; **2.** Wollüstling *m*; Dirne *f*; **3.** *♀* geil wachsen; herumtollen; **'wan·ton·ness** Geilheit *f*; Mutwille *m.*
war [wɔ:] **1.** Krieg *m*; *attr.* Kriegs...; *at* ~ im Krieg(szustand); *make* ~ Krieg führen *(upon* gegen); ~ *criminal* Kriegsverbrecher *m*; **2.** *lit.* Krieg führen; *fig.* streiten; einander widerstreiten.
war·ble ['wɔ:bl] **1.** trillern; singen

(bsd. Vogel); **2.** Getriller *n*; **'war·bler** Sänger *m*; Singvogel *m.*
war...: **'~-blind·ed** kriegsblind; **'~-cry** Schlachtruf *m*; *fig.* Parole *f.*
ward [wɔ:d] **1.** Gewahrsam *m*; Vormundschaft *f*; Mündel *n*; *weitS.* Schützling *m*; *fenc.* Parade *f*; Gefängniszelle *f*; Abteilung *f,* Station *f in e-m Krankenhaus etc.*, Krankenzimmer *n*; (Stadt)Bezirk *m*; ⊕ Einschnitt *m im Schlüsselbart*; Bart *m*; *casual* ~ Obdachlosenasyl *n*; *in* ~ unter Vormundschaft; **2.** ~ *off* abwehren, abwenden; **'ward·en** Aufseher *m*; (Luftschutz)Wart *m*; Herbergsvater *m*; *univ.* Rektor *m*; **'ward·er** (Gefangenen)Wärter *m,* Aufseher *m*; **'ward·robe** Garderobe *f*; Kleiderschrank *m*; ~ *dealer* Kleidertrödler *m*; ~ *trunk* Schrankkoffer *m*; **'ward·room** *⚓* Offiziersmesse *f*; **'ward·ship** Vormundschaft *f.*
ware [wɛə] Ware *f*; Geschirr *n.*
ware·house 1. ['wɛəhaus] (Waren-)Lager *n*; Lagerhaus *n,* Speicher *m*; **2.** ['~hauz] auf Lager bringen, einlagern; **~·man** ['~hausmən] Lagerverwalter *m*; Großhändler *m*; (Möbel)Spediteur *m*; Speicherarbeiter *m.*
war...: **'~-fare** Krieg(führung *f*) *m*; **'~-grave** Soldatengrab *n*; **'~-head** Gefechtskopf *m.*
war·i·ness ['wɛərinis] Vorsicht *f*; Behutsam-, Achtsamkeit *f.*
war·like ['wɔ:laik] kriegerisch; Kriegs...
war-loan ['wɔ:ləun] Kriegsanleihe *f.*
warm [wɔ:m] **1.** □ warm *(a. fig.)*; *a.* heiß; *fig.* hitzig; *fig.* glühend; *make things* ~ *for s.o.* j-m die Hölle heiß machen; **2.** *F* Erwärmung *f*; **3.** *v/t.* (er)wärmen *(a. fig.)*; *sl.* vermöbeln *(prügeln)*; ~ *up* aufwärmen; *v/i. a.* ~ *up* warm werden, sich erwärmen *(to für)*; **'~-'heart·ed** herzlich, warmherzig; **'warm·ing** *sl.* Senge *f (Prügel).*
war-mon·ger ['wɔ:mʌŋgə] Kriegstreiber *m,* -hetzer *m*; **'war-mon·ger·ing, 'war-mon·ger·y** Kriegshetze *f.*
warmth [wɔ:mθ] Wärme *f.*
warm-up ['wɔ:mʌp] Sichwarmlaufen *n.*
warn [wɔ:n] warnen *(of, against* vor *dat.)*; verwarnen; ermahnen *(to inf.*

warning

zu *inf.*); verständigen (*of* von), aufmerksam machen (*of* auf *acc.*); **'warn·ing** Warnung *f*, Mahnung *f*; Verwarnung *f*; Kündigung *f*; *give* ∼ kündigen; *take* ∼ *from* sich ein warnendes Beispiel nehmen an (*dat.*).

War Of·fice ['wɔːrɔfis] Heeresministerium *n*.

warp [wɔːp] **1.** *Weberei:* Kette *f*; ⚓ Bugsiertau *n*; Verwerfung *f* des *Holzes*; *fig.* Verkehrtheit *f*; **2.** *v/i.* sich werfen (*Holz*); ⚓ werpen, warpen; *Weberei:* anscheren; *v/t. Holz etc.* werfen, verziehen; ✈ *Tragflächen* verwinden; *Weberei:* anscheren; ⚓ verholen; verzerren, entstellen; *j.* beeinflussen; *j.* abbringen (*from* von).

war-paint ['wɔːpeint] Kriegsbemalung *f* (*a. fig.*); *in full* ∼ in Gala.

war-path ['wɔːpɑːθ] Kriegspfad *m*.

warp·ing ✈ ['wɔːpiŋ] Verwindung *f*.

war...: '∼**-plane** Kampfflugzeug *n*; '∼**-prof·it·eer** Kriegsgewinnler *m*.

war·rant ['wɔrənt] **1.** Vollmacht *f*; Rechtfertigung *f*, Berechtigung *f*; ⚖ (Vollziehungs)Befehl *m*; Berechtigungsschein *m*; Lagerschein *m*; *a.* ∼ *of apprehension* Steckbrief *m*; ∼ *of arrest* Haftbefehl *m*; **2.** bevollmächtigen; *j.* berechtigen; *et.* rechtfertigen; verbürgen, *bsd.* ♰ garantieren; **'war·rant·a·ble** ☐ zu rechtfertigen(d), vertretbar; *hunt.* jagdbar (*Hirsch*); **'war·rant·a·bly** *adv.* billigerweise; **'war·rant·ed** garantiert; **war·ran'tee** ⚖ Sicherheitsempfänger *m*; **'war·rant-offi·cer** ⚓ Deckoffizier *m*; ✕ Portepeeunteroffizier *m*; **war·ran·tor** ⚖ ['∼tɔː] Sicherheitsgeber *m*; **'war·ran·ty** Garantie *f*; Bürgschaft(s-schein *m*) *f*; Berechtigung *f*.

war·ren ['wɔrən] Kaninchengehege *n*.

war·ri·or ['wɔriə] Krieger *m*.

war·ship ['wɔːʃip] Kriegsschiff *n*.

wart [wɔːt] Warze *f*; *bsd.* ♃ Auswuchs *m*; **'wart·y** warzig.

war·time ['wɔːtaim] **1.** Kriegszeit(en *pl.*) *f*; **2.** Kriegs...

war·y ☐ ['weəri] vorsichtig, behutsam; wachsam.

was [wɔz, wəz] *pret.* von *be*; *im Passiv:* wurde; *he* ∼ *to have come* er hätte kommen sollen.

wash [wɔʃ] **1.** *v/t.* waschen; (um-)spülen; ∼*ed out* verwaschen, aus-

geblaßt; F erledigt, fertig; ∼ *up* abwaschen, spülen; *v/i.* sich waschen (lassen); waschecht sein (*a. fig.*); spülen, schlagen (*Wellen*); **2.** Waschen *n*; Wäsche *f*; Wellenschlag *m*; ⚓ Kielwasser *n*; ✈ Luftstrudel *m hinter Tragflächen*; Seichtwasser *n*; Schwemmland *n*; Spülwasser *n*; *contp.* Gewäsch *n*; *mouth-*∼ Mundwasser *n*; *s. white*∼; **'wash·a·ble** waschbar; **'wash-and-'wear** bügelfrei, pflegeleicht; **'wash-ba·sin** Waschbecken *n*; **'wash-cloth** Waschlappen *m*; **'wash-draw·ing** Art Aquarell *n*.

wash·er ['wɔʃə] Wäscherin *f*; Waschmaschine *f*; ⊕ Unterlagscheibe *f*, Dichtungsring *m*; '∼-wom·an Waschfrau *f*, Wäscherin *f*.

wash·ing ['wɔʃiŋ] **1.** Waschen *n*; Waschung *f*; Wäsche *f*; ∼*s pl.* Spülicht *n*; **2.** Wasch...; '∼-ma·chine Waschmaschine *f*; ∼ pow·der Waschpulver *n*; '∼-silk Waschseide *f*; ∼'up Geschirrspülen *n*, Abwaschen *n*; ∼ machine Geschirrspülmaschine *f*.

wash...: '∼-'out *sl.* Versager *m*, Niete *f*; Fiasko *n*; '∼-rag *bsd.* Am. Waschlappen *m*; '∼-stand Waschtisch *m*; '∼-tub Waschbottich *m*; **'wash·y** wässerig (*a. fig.*).

was·n't [wɔznt] = *was not*.

wasp [wɔsp] Wespe *f*; **'wasp·ish** gereizt; reizbar, giftig.

was·sail † ['wɔseil] Trinkgelage *n*; Würzbier *n*.

wast·age ['weistidʒ] Abgang *m*, Verlust *m*; Vergeudung *f*.

waste [weist] **1.** wüst, öde; unbebaut, brach; unfruchtbar; unnütz; ⊕ unbrauchbar; überflüssig; Abfall...; *lay* ∼ verwüsten; ∼ *paper* Altpapier *n*; **2.** Verschwendung *f*, Vergeudung *f*; Abfall *m*; Einöde *f*, Wüste *f*, *go od. run to* ∼ verfallen; **3.** *v/t.* verwüsten, verheeren; verschwenden, vergeuden; verzehren; *v/i.* verschwendet werden; ∼ *away* dahinsiechen, verfallen (*Kranker*); ∼ **dis·pos·al** Müllbeseitigung *f*; *waste-disposal unit* Müllschlucker *m*; **waste·ful** ☐ ['∼ful] verschwenderisch; kostspielig; **waste heat** Abwärme *f*; **'waste·land** Ödland *n*; **'waste-pa·per bas·ket** Papierkorb *m*; **'waste-pipe** Abflußrohr *n*; Fall-

rohr *n am Klosett*; **waste pro·duct**
Abfallprodukt *n*; *biol.* Ausscheidungsstoff *m*; **'wast·er** Verschwender(in); = *wastrel.*
wast·rel ['weistrəl] Ausschuß(ware
f) *m*; Taugenichts *m*.
watch [wɔtʃ] **1.** Wache *f* (*a.* ⚓);
Taschenuhr *f*; *be on the* ⌁ *for* achtgeben auf *et.*; **2.** *v i.* wachen (*with*
bei, *over über acc.*); ⌁ *for* warten
auf (*acc.*), auflauern (*dat.*); ⌁ *out* F
aufpassen; *v t.* bewachen; (be-)
hüten; beobachten, sehen; achtgeben *od.* aufpassen auf (*acc.*); ⌁
one's time s-e Gelegenheit abpassen; **'⌁·boat** ⚓ Wachtboot *n*;
'⌁·brace·let Uhrarmband *n*; **'⌁-
-case** Uhrgehäuse *n*; **'⌁·dog** Wachhund *m*; **'watch·er** Wächter *m*;
Wärter *m*; **watch·ful** ⌁ ['⌁ful]
wachsam, achtsam.
watch...: **'⌁-mak·er** Uhrmacher *m*;
'⌁·man (Nacht)Wächter *m*; **'⌁-
-tow·er** Wachtturm *m*; **'⌁·word**
Losung *f*, Schlagwort *n*, Parole *f*.
wa·ter ['wɔ:tə] **1.** Wasser *n*; Gewässer *n*; ⌁ *supply* Wasserversorgung *f*; Wasserleitung *f*; *high* ⌁
Hochwasser *n*, Flut *f*; *low* ⌁ Niedrigwasser *n*, Ebbe *f*; *by* ⌁ auf dem
Wasserweg; *drink od. take the* ⌁*s*
Brunnen trinken; *of the first* ⌁ vom
reinsten Wasser (*a. fig.*); *be in hot* ⌁
F in der Patsche sitzen; *be in low* ⌁
F auf dem trocknen sitzen; *hold* ⌁
fig. stichhaltig sein; *make* ⌁ Wasser
lassen; lecken (*Schiff*); **2.** *v/t. Land*
bewässern; *Straße* (be)sprengen;
Pflanze (be)gießen; mit Wasser
versorgen; tränken; *oft* ⌁ *down* verwässern (*a. fig.*); ⊕ moirieren; *v i.*
wässern (*Mund*); tränen (*Augen*);
Wasser einnehmen; ⚓ wässern;
make s.o.'s mouth ⌁ j-m den Mund
wässerig machen; **'⌁-blis·ter** ⚕
Wasserblase *f*; **'⌁-borne** zu Wasser
befördert; **'⌁-bot·tle** Feldflasche *f*;
⌁ **butt** Regentonne *f*; ⌁ **can·non**
Wasserwerfer *m*; **'⌁-cart** Sprengwagen *m*; **'⌁-clos·et** (Wasser)Klosett *n*;
'⌁-col·o(u)r Aquarell *n*; Aquarellmalerei *f*; ⌁*s pl.* Wasserfarben *f pl.*;
'⌁-cool·ing Wasserkühlung *f*; **'⌁-
course** Wasserlauf *m*; Kanal *m*;
Bach-, Flußbett *n*; **'⌁-cress** ⚘ Brunnenkresse *f*; **'⌁-fall** Wasserfall *m*; **'⌁-
fowl** *pl.* Wasservögel *m pl.*; **'⌁-front**
Ufer *n*; *bsd. Am. städtisches* Hafen-

gebiet *n*; **'⌁-ga(u)ge** ⊕ Wasserstandsanzeiger *m*; Pegel *m*; **'⌁-glass** ⚗
Wasserglas *n*; **'⌁-hose** Wasserschlauch *m*; **'wa·ter·i·ness** Wässerigkeit *f*.
wa·ter·ing ['wɔ:təriŋ] Wässern *n*
etc.; **'⌁-can**, **'⌁-pot** Gießkanne *f*;
'⌁-place Wasserloch *n*; Tränke *f*,
Schwemme *f*; Bad(eort *m*) *n*; Seebad *n*.
water...: **'⌁-jack·et** ⊕ Wasser(kühl)mantel *m*; **'⌁-lev·el** Wasserspiegel
m; Wasserstand(slinie *f*) *m*; ⊕
Wasserwaage *f*; **'⌁-lil·y** ⚘ Wasserrose *f*; **'⌁-logged** voll Wasser (gelaufen); **'⌁-main** Haupt(wasser)rohr *n*; **'⌁-man** Fährmann *m*; Flußschiffer *m*; Bootsführer *m*; Wasserträger *m*; **'⌁-mark** Wassermarke *f*;
Wasserzeichen *n im Papier*; **'⌁-
-mel·on** ⚘ Wassermelone *f*; **'⌁-
-pipe** Wasser(leitungs)rohr *n*; **'⌁-
-plane** Wasserflugzeug *n*; ⌁ **pol·lu-
tion** Wasserverschmutzung *f*; **'⌁-po-
lo** Wasserball(spiel *n*) *m*; **'⌁-pow·er**
Wasserkraft *f*; ⌁ *station* Wasserkraftwerk *n*; **'⌁-proof 1.** wasserdicht; **2.**
Regenmantel *m*; **3.** imprägnieren; **'⌁-
-re'pel·lent** wasserabstoßend; **'⌁-
shed** Wasserscheide *f*; *weitS.* Stromgebiet *n*; **'⌁-side 1.** Fluß-, Seeufer *n*;
2. am Wasser (gelegen); **'⌁-spout**
Wasserhose *f*; Abtraufe *f*; **'⌁-ta·ble**
Grundwasserspiegel *m*; **'⌁-tight** wasserdicht; *fig.* eindeutig, unangreifbar; **'⌁-wave 1.** Wasserwelle *f* (*Frisur*); **2.** Wasserwellen legen; **'⌁-way**
Wasserstraße *f*; Schiffahrtsweg *m*;
'⌁-wings *pl.* Schwimmflügel *m pl.*;
'⌁-works *pl., a. sg.* Wasserwerk *n*;
'wa·ter·y wässerig (*a. fig.*).
watt ⚡ [wɔt] Watt *n*.
wat·tle ['wɔtl] **1.** Flechtwerk *n*;
Hürde *f*; *orn.* Kehllappen *m*; **2.** aus
Flechtwerk herstellen.
waul [wɔ:l] mauzen, miauen.
wave [weiv] **1.** Welle *f* (*a. phys. u.*
von Haar); Woge *f* (*a. fig.*);
Schwenken *n*; Winken *n*; **2.** *v/t.*
wellig machen; *Haar* wellen;
schwingen; schwenken; (*j-m* zu-)
winken; ⌁ *s.o. aside* j. beiseite
winken; *v/i.* wogen; wehen, flattern; (⌁ *to s.o.* j-m zu)winken; **'⌁-
-length** ⚡ Wellenlänge *f*; *be on the*
same ⌁ *fig.* auf der gleichen Wellenlänge liegen.
wa·ver ['weivə] (sch)wanken (*a.*

fig.); flackern.
wave...: '**~-range** *Radio*: Wellen-
bereich *m*; '**~-trap** *Radio*: Sperrkreis *m.*
wav·y ['weivi] wellig; wogend.
wax[1] [wæks] **1.** Wachs *n*; Siegellack
m; Ohrenschmalz *n*; Schusterpech
n; ~ *candle* Wachskerze *f*; ~ *doll*
Wachspuppe *f*; **2.** wachsen; bohnern; pichen (*Schuhmacher*).
wax[2] [~] (*irr.*) wachsen, zunehmen
(*Mond*); † (*vor adj.*) werden.
wax·en *fig.* ['wæksn] wächsern,
Wachs...; '**wax·work** Wachsfiguren
f|*pl.*; ~s *pl.*, ~ *show* Wachsfiguren-
kabinett *n*; '**wax·y** ☐ wachsartig;
weich.
way [wei] **1.** *mst* Weg *m*; Straße *f*;
Art u. Weise *f*, Methode *f*; *eigene*
Art *f*; Stück *n* (*Weg*), Strecke *f*,
Entfernung *f*; Richtung *f*; F Gegend *f*; ⚓ Fahrt *f*; *fig.* Hinsicht *f*,
Beziehung *f*; Zustand *m*, Verhält-
nisse *n*|*pl.*; ⚓ Helling *f*; ~ *in* Ein-
gang *m*; ~ *out* Ausgang *m*; *fig.* Ausweg *m*; ~s *and means* Mittel und
Wege *pl. zur Geldbeschaffung*; *right*
of ~ ⚓ Wegerecht *n*; *bsd. mot.* Vor-
fahrt(srecht *n*) *f*; ~ *of life* Lebensweise *f*, -form *f*; *this* ~ hierher, hier
entlang; *the wrong* ~ falsch (herum);
in some ~, *in a* ~ in gewisser Hinsicht;
in no ~ keineswegs; *go a great* ~ *towards ger.*, *go a long* (*some*) ~ *to*
inf. viel (etwas) dazu beitragen zu
inf.; *by the* ~ im Vorbeigehen;
übrigens, nebenbei (bemerkt); *by* ~
of durch, (auf dem Weg) über (*acc.*);
by ~ *of excuse* als Entschuldigung;
on the ~, *on one's* ~ unterwegs; *out*
of the ~ abwegig; ungewöhnlich;
under ~ im Gange, ⚓ in Fahrt; *give*
~ sich zurückziehen, zurückgehen;
mot. Vorfahrt lassen (*to dat.*); nachgeben; *fig.* stattgeben (*to dat.*); ab-
gelöst werden (*to* von), übergehen
(*to* in); sich hingeben (*to dat.*); *have*
one's ~ s-n Willen haben; *if I had*
my ~ wenn es nach mir ginge; *have*
a ~ *with* umzugehen wissen mit;
lead the ~ vorangehen; *s. make*; *pay*
one's ~ glatt auskommen; sich selbst
weiterhelfen; *see one's* ~ *to ger. od.*
inf. e-e Möglichkeit für sich sehen,
zu *inf.*; **2.** *adv.* (weit) weg; weit;
'**~-bill** Beförderungsschein *n*;
Frachtbrief *m*; '**~-far·er** Wanderer
m; ~'**lay** (*irr. lay*) auflauern (*dat.*);

'**~-leave** Wegerecht *n*; '**~-side**
1. Weg-, Straßenrand *m*; *by the* ~
am Wege, an der Straße; **2.** am
Wege, an der Straße (befindlich);
~ **sta·tion** *Am.* Zwischenstation *f*;
~ **train** *Am.* Bummelzug *m.*
way·ward ['weiwəd] starrköp-
fig, eigensinnig; '**way·ward·ness**
Starr-, Eigensinn *m.*
we [wiː, wi] wir.
weak ☐ [wiːk] *allg.* schwach;
schwächlich; dünn (*Getränk*);
'**weak·en** *v*/*t.* schwächen; *v*/*i.*
schwach werden; '**weak·ling**
Schwächling *m*; '**weak·ly** schwächlich; '**weak-'mind·ed** schwachsinnig; charakterschwach; '**weak·
ness** Schwäche *f.*
weal[1] [wiːl] Wohl *n.*
weal[2] [~] Strieme *f.*
wealth [welθ] Wohlstand *m*; Reichtum *m*; *fig.* Fülle *f*; '**wealth·y** ☐
reich; wohlhabend.
wean [wiːn] *Kind* entwöhnen; *fig.*
~ *s.o. from od. of s.th.* j-m et. abgewöhnen.
weap·on ['wepən] Waffe *f*; '**weap·
on·less** waffen-, wehrlos.
wear [wɛə] **1.** (*irr.*) *v*/*t.* *am Körper*
tragen; *ein Lächeln* zur Schau tra-
gen; *ein Gesicht* zeigen; *a.* ~ *away*, ~
down, ~ *off*, ~ *out* abnutzen; verbrauchen; *Kleid etc.* abtragen; Geduld
etc. erschöpfen; ermüden; zermür-
ben; ausnagen; *v*/*i.* sich *gut etc.*
tragen *od.* halten; sich abnutzen *od.*
abtragen; ~ *away* abnehmen; vergehen; ~ *off* sich abnutzen *od.* abtragen; *fig.* sich verlieren; ~ *on* vergehen (*Zeit*); ~ *out* sich abnutzen
od. abtragen; sich erschöpfen;
2. Tragen *n*; Gebrauch *m*; Abnutzung *f*, Verschleiß *m*; *gentlemen's* ~ Herrenbekleidung *f*; *for*
hard ~ zum Strapazieren, strapazierfähig; *s. worse* 1; *there is plenty*
of ~ *in it yet* es läßt sich noch gut
tragen; '**wear·a·ble** tragbar; zu tra-
gen(d); **wear and tear** Verschleiß
m; '**wear·er** Träger(in) (*e-s Klei-
dungsstücks*).
wea·ri·ness ['wiərinis] Müdigkeit *f*;
Ermüdung *f*; *fig.* Überdruß *m.*
wea·ri·some ☐ ['wiərisəm] ermüdend; langweilig.
wea·ry ['wiəri] **1.** ☐ müde (*with*
von); *fig.* überdrüssig (*of s.th.* e-r
Sache); ermüdend; beschwerlich,

anstrengend; **2.** v/t. ermüden; langweilen; Geduld etc. erschöpfen; v/i. müde werden.

wea·sel zo. ['wi:zl] Wiesel n.

weath·er ['weðə] **1.** Wetter n, Witterung f; s. permit; **2.** ⚓ Luv...; **3.** v/t. dem Wetter aussetzen; lüften; ⚓ luvwärts umschiffen; a. ⌐ out ⚓ Sturm abwettern, fig. überstehen; ⌐ed verwittert; v/i. verwittern; ⌐-**beat·en** ['⌐bi:tn] vom Wetter mitgenommen; wetterhart; '⌐- -**board** Wasserschenkel m; Schalbrett n; '⌐-**board·ing** Verschalung f; '⌐-**bound** durch schlechtes Wetter behindert; '⌐-**bu·reau** Wetteramt n; '⌐-**chart** Wetterkarte f; '⌐- **cock** Wetterhahn m, -fahne f; '⌐- -**fore·cast** Wetterbericht m, -vorhersage f; '⌐-**proof**, '⌐-**tight** wetterfest; '⌐-**sta·tion** Wetterwarte f; '⌐-**strip** Dichtungsstreifen m am Fenster etc.; '⌐-**vane** Wetterfahne f; '⌐-**worn** verwittert.

weave [wi:v] **1.** (irr.) weben; wirken; flechten; fig. ersinnen, erfinden; sich schlängeln od. winden; **2.** Gewebe n, Webart f; '**weav·er** Weber m; '**weav·ing** Weben n, Weberei f; attr. Web... [schrump(e)lig.\ **wea·zen** ['wi:zn] verhutzelt,/ **web** [web] Gewebe n; Gespinst n; orn. Schwimmhaut f; Gurt m; Papierbahn f, -rolle f; **webbed** mit Schwimmhäuten; '**web·bing** Gurtband n; '**web·foot·ed** mit Schwimmfüßen.

wed [wed] heiraten; fig. verbinden (to mit).

we'd F [wi:d] = we had; we should; we would.

wed·ded ['wedid] ehelich; Ehe...; ⌐ to fig. verhaftet (dat.); '**wed·ding 1.** Hochzeit f; **2.** Hochzeits...; Braut...; Trau...; ⌐ anniversary Hochzeitstag m (Jahrestag); ⌐ ring Ehe-, Trauring m.

wedge [wedʒ] **1.** Keil m; the thin end of the ⌐ fig. der erste kleine Anfang; ⌐ heel Keilabsatz m am Schuh; **2.** (ver)keilen; a. ⌐ in (hin)einzwängen, einkeilen; '⌐-**shaped** keilförmig.

wed·lock ['wedlɔk] Ehe f; out of ⌐ unehelich.

Wednes·day ['wenzdi] Mittwoch m.

wee [wi:] klein, winzig; a ⌐ bit ein klein wenig.

weed [wi:d] **1.** Unkraut n; F Kraut n (Tabak); Kümmerling m; **2.** jäten; säubern (of von); ⌐ out ausmerzen; '**weed·er** Jäter(in); Jätwerkzeug n; '**weed-kill·er** Unkrautvertilgungsmittel n.

weeds [wi:dz] pl. mst widow's ⌐ Witwenkleidung f.

weed·y ['wi:di] voll Unkraut, verkrautet; fig. lang aufgeschossen.

week [wi:k] Woche f; this day ⌐ heute in acht Tagen; heute vor acht Tagen; '⌐-**day** Wochentag m; '⌐-'**end 1.** Wochenende n; ⌐ ticket Sonntagsfahrkarte f; **2.** das Wochenende verbringen; '⌐-'**end·er** Wochenendausflügler m; '**week·ly 1.** wöchentlich; **2.** a. ⌐ paper Wochenblatt n, -(zeit)schrift f.

weep [wi:p] (irr.) weinen (for vor Freude etc.; um j.); tropfen; nässen; '**weep·er** Weinende m; Leidtragende m; Trauerflor m, -schleier m, -schleife f; '**weep·ing 1.** weinend; Trauer...; ⌐ willow ♀ Trauerweide f; **2.** Weinen n.

wee·vil ['wi:vil] Rüsselkäfer m; Kornwurm m.

weft [weft] Weberei: Einschlag m, Schuß m; poet. Gewebe n.

weigh [wei] **1.** v/t. (ab)wiegen; a. ⌐ up fig. abwägen (with, against gegen); erwägen; ⌐ anchor ⚓ den Anker lichten; ⌐ down et. überwiegen; ⌐ed down niedergebeugt; v/i. wiegen (a. fig.); fig. Gewicht haben, ausschlaggebend sein (with bei); ⌐ in (out) vor (nach) dem Rennen gewogen werden (Jockei); ⌐ in with Argumente vorbringen; ⌐ (up)on lasten auf (dat.); **2.** get under ⌐ (= way) ⚓ unter Segel gehen; '**weigha·ble** wägbar; '**weigh·bridge** Brükkenwaage f; '**weigh·er** Wäger m; Waagemeister m; '**weigh·ing-** -**ma·chine** (bsd. Brücken-, Tafel-) Waage f.

weight [weit] **1.** Gewicht n (a. fig.); Last f (a. fig.); fig. Bedeutung f; Wucht f; carry great ⌐ fig. großes Gewicht haben, viel gelten; give short ⌐ zu knapp wiegen; putting the ⌐ Kugelstoßen n; **2.** beschweren; fig. belasten; '**weight·i·ness** Gewichtigkeit f; '**weight·y** ☐ (ge-) wichtig, bedeutend; schwerwiegend; wuchtig.

weir [wiə] Wehr n; Fischreuse f.

weird [wiəd] Schicksals...; unheimlich; F sonderbar, seltsam.

wel·come ['welkəm] **1.** ☐ willkommen; *you are ~ to inf.* es steht Ihnen frei zu *inf.*; *you are ~ to it* es steht Ihnen zur Verfügung; *(you are) ~!* gern geschehen!, bitte sehr!; **2.** Willkomm(en *n*) *m*; **3.** willkommen heißen, bewillkommnen; *fig.* begrüßen.

weld ⊕ [weld] **1.** (zs.-)schweißen (*into* zu); **2.** *a. ~ing seam* Schweißnaht *f*; **'weld·ing** ⊕ Schweißen *n*; *attr.* Schweiß...; *~ goggles pl.* Schweißbrille *f*.

wel·fare ['welfɛə] Wohlfahrt *f*; *~ cen·tre* Fürsorgeamt *n*; *~ state* Wohlfahrtsstaat *m*; *~ work* Fürsorge *f*, Wohlfahrtspflege *f*; *~ work·er* Fürsorger(in).

well¹ [wel] **1.** Brunnen *m*; *fig.* Quelle *f*; ⊕ (Senk)Schacht *m*; ⊕ Bohrloch *n*; Treppen-, Aufzugs-, Licht-, Luftschacht *m*; **2.** quellen.

well² [~] **1.** *adv.* wohl; gut; ordentlich, tüchtig, gründlich; *s. as; ~ off* in guten Verhältnissen, wohlhabend; *~ past fifty* weit über fünfzig; **2.** *pred. adj.* wohl, gesund; *I am not ~* mir ist nicht wohl; *that's ~* das ist gut; **3.** *int.* nun!, F na!

we'll F [wi:l] = *we will; we shall*.

well...: **'~-ad'vised** wohlbedacht; wohlberaten; **'~-'bal·anced** ausgeglichen; ausgewogen; **'~-'be·ing** Wohl(sein) *n*; **'~-'born** von guter Herkunft; **'~-'bred** wohlerzogen; **'~-de'fined** deutlich, klar umrissen; **'~-dis'posed** wohlgesinnt (*to, towards dat. od.* gegen); **'~-'fa·vo(u)red** gut aussehend; **'~-in-'formed** gut unterrichtet.

Wel·ling·tons ['weliŋtənz] *pl.* Langschäfter *m/pl.* (*Stiefel*).

well...: **'~-in'ten·tioned** wohlmeinend; wohlgemeint (*Rat*); **'~-'judged** wohlberechnet; **'~-'knit** festgefügt; *~ known*, **'~-'known** bekannt; *~ made* gutgebaut (*Figur*); **'~-'man·nered** mit guten Manieren; **'~-'marked** deutlich (erkennbar); **'~-'nigh** beinahe; **'~-'off** wohlhabend; gut d(a)ran; **'~-'or·dered** wohlgeordnet; **'~-'read** ['~'red] belesen; *weitS.* gebildet; **'~-'sea·soned** gut gewürzt; **'~-'spok·en:** *be ~* sich gewählt ausdrücken; **'~-'thumbed**

abgegriffen (*Buch*); *~ timed* rechtzeitig; zeitlich wohlberechnet; **'~-to--'do** wohlhabend; **'~-'trained** gut ausgebildet; *~ turned fig.* gedrechselt; **'~-'wish·er** Gönner *m*, Freund *m*; **'~-'worn** abgetragen; *fig.* abgedroschen.

wel·ly F ['weli] Gummistiefel *m*.

Welsh¹ [welʃ] **1.** walisisch; **2.** Walisisch *n*; *the ~ pl.* die Waliser *m/pl.*

welsh² [~] *Rennsport:* *j-m* mit dem Wettgeld durchbrennen; **'welsh·er** Wettbetrüger *m*; *weitS.* Schwindler *m*.

Welsh...: **'~-man** Waliser *m*; *~ rab·bit* überbackene Käseschnitte *f*; **'~-wom·an** Waliserin *f*.

welt [welt] **1.** ⊕ Rahmen *m*, Rand *m e-s Schuhes*; Einfassung *f am Kleid etc.*; Strieme *f*; **2.** *Schuh* auf Rahmen arbeiten; F durchbleuen; *~ed* randgenäht (*Schuh*).

wel·ter ['weltə] **1.** rollen, sich wälzen; *~ in fig.* schwimmen in *s-m Blut etc.*; **2.** Wirrwarr *m*, Durcheinander *n*; **'~-weight** *Boxen:* Weltergewicht *n*.

wen [wen] ♣ Balggeschwulst *f*; *bsd.* Grützbeutel *m am Kopf*; *fig.* Pfannkuchen *m* (*unverhältnismäßig angewachsene Stadt*).

wench [wentʃ] Mädchen *n*; Dirne *f*.

wend [wend]: *~ one's way* s-n Weg nehmen (*to nach, zu*).

went [went] *pret. von* **go 1.**

wept [wept] *pret. u. p.p. von* **weep.**

were [wə:, wə] *pret. von* **be.**

we're F [wiə] = *we are.*

weren't F [wə:nt] = *were not.*

west [west] **1.** Westen *m*; **2.** West...; westlich; westwärts; *go ~ sl.* hops gehen (*sterben*); **'~-bound** in Richtung Westen fahrend.

west·er·ly ['westəli] westlich.

west·ern ['westən] **1.** westlich; West...; abendländisch; **2.** Wildwestgeschichte *f*, -film *m*, Western *m*; = **'west·ern·er** Westländer(in); *Am.* Weststaatler(in); Abendländer (-in); **'west·ern·most** westlichst.

West In·dian ['west'indjən] **1.** westindisch; **2.** Westindier(in).

west·ing ⚓ ['westiŋ] (zurückgelegter) westlicher Kurs *m*; Westrichtung *f*.

West·pha·li·an [west'feiljən] **1.** westfälisch; **2.** Westfale *m*, Westfälin *f*.

west·ward(s) ['westwəd(z)] west-

wärts (gelegen).
wet [wet] **1.** naß, feucht; *Am.* den Alkoholhandel gestattend; *s. blanket 1*; ~ *dressing* feuchter Umschlag *m*; ~ *steam* gesättigter Dampf *m*; ~ *through* durchnäßt; **2.** Nässe *f*; Feuchtigkeit *f*; **3.** (*irr.*) nässen, naß machen; anfeuchten, benetzen; F *Geschäft etc.* begießen; ~ *through* durchnässen.
wet·back *Am. sl.* ['wetbæk] illegaler Einwanderer *m aus Mexiko.*
weth·er ['weðə] Hammel *m.*
wet-nurse ['wetnə:s] Amme *f.*
we've F [wi:v] = *we have.*
whack F [wæk] **1.** verhauen; **2.** Schlag *m*, Hieb *m*; voller Anteil *m*; *have od. take a* ~ *at* 'rangehen an (*acc.*); 'whack·er F Mordsding *n*; 'whack·ing F **1.** Haue *f* (*Prügel*); **2.** kolossal.
whale [weil] Wal *m*; *a* ~ *of* F e-e Riesenmenge; *a* ~ *at* F e-e Kanone in (*dat.*); '~·bone Fischbein *n*; '~·-fish·er, '~·man, *mst* 'whal·er Walfischfänger *m*; 'whale-oil Tran *m.*
whal·ing ['weilin] Walfischfang *m.*
whang F [wæŋ] **1.** Krach *m*, Bums *m*; **2.** krachen, bumsen; hauen.
wharf [wɔ:f] **1.** *pl. a.* **wharves** [wɔ:vz] Kai *m*, Anlegeplatz *m*; **2.** ausladen, löschen; 'wharf·age Kaianlage *f*; Kaigeld *n*; **wharf·in·ger** ['~indʒə] Kaimeister *m.*
what [wɔt] **1.** was; das, was; *know* ~'*s* ~ wissen, was los ist; Bescheid wissen; ~ *money I had* was ich an Geld hatte; ... *and* ~ *not* ... und was nicht sonst noch; **2.** was?; wie?; wieviel?; welch(er, -e, -es)?; was für ein(e)?; ~ *about* ...? wie wär's mit ...?, wie steht's mit ...?; ~ *for?* wozu?; ~ *of it?* was ist denn dabei?; ~ *if* ...? wie wäre es, wenn ...?; und wenn nun ...?; ~ *though* ...? was tut's, wenn ...?; *what-d'you--call-him*, ~'*s-his-name* Dingsda *m*, Dingsbums *m*; ~ *next?* was sonst noch?; *iro.* was denn noch alles?; ~ *a blessing!* was für ein Segen!; ~ *impudence!* was für eine Unverschämtheit!; **3.** ~ *with* ... ~ *with* ... teils durch ... teils durch ...;
what·e'er *poet.* [wɔt'ɛə], **what-'ev·er** = *whatsoever*; 'what·not Etagere *f*; **what·so·e'er** *poet.* [wɔtsəu'ɛə], **what·so'ever 1.** was

auch (immer); **2.** welche(r, -s) auch (immer); überhaupt.
wheat ♣ [wi:t] Weizen *m*; 'wheat-en Weizen...
whee·dle ['wi:dl] beschwatzen (*into* zu); ~ *s.th. out of s.o.* j-m et. abschwatzen.
wheel [wi:l] **1.** Rad *n*; Steuer *n*; *bsd. Am.* F Fahrrad *n*; Töpferscheibe *f*; Drehung *f*, Kreis *m*; ✗ Schwenkung *f*; **2.** *v/t.* rollen, fahren, schieben; *v/i.* rollen, sich drehen; sich umwenden; ✗ schwenken; F radeln; '~·bar·row Schubkarren *m*; ~ **base** *mot.* Radstand *m*; ~ **chair** Rollstuhl *m*; 'wheeled mit Rädern; 'wheel·er-'deal·er F Schlitzohr *n*; 'wheel·wright Stellmacher *m.*
wheeze [wi:z] **1.** schnaufen, keuchen; krächzen; **2.** Schnaufen *n etc.*; *thea. sl.* Witz *m*, Gag *m*; 'wheez·y schnaufend, keuchend.
whelk *zo.* [welk] Wellhornschnecke *f.*
whelp *rhet.* [welp] **1.** Welpe *m*; *allg.* Junge *n*; Balg *m, n* (*ungezogenes Kind*); **2.** (Junge) werfen.
when [wen] **1.** wann?; **2.** wenn; als; während *od.* da doch; und da.
whence [wens] woher, von wo.
when·e'er *poet.* [wen'ɛə], **when-(so·)ev·er** [wen(səu)'evə] wann (auch) immer; immer *od.* jedesmal wenn; sooft (als).
where [wɛə] wo; wohin; ~·**a·bout**, *mst* ~·**a·bouts 1.** ['wɛərə'baut(s)] wo etwa; **2.** ['~] Aufenthalt *m*; Verbleib *m*; ~'**as** wohingegen, während (doch); ✗ in Anbetracht dessen, daß; ~'**at** wobei, worüber, worauf; ~'**by** wodurch; '~·**fore** weshalb; ~'**in** worin; ~'**of** wovon; ~'**on** worauf; ~·**so'ev·er** wo(hin) (auch) immer; ~·**up'on** worauf(hin); **wher-'ev·er** wo(hin) (auch) immer, überall wo; **where'whith** womit; **where·with·al 1.** [wɛəwi'ðɔ:l] womit; **2.** F ['~] Erforderliche *n*; Mittel *n/pl.*
wher·ry ['weri] Fährboot *n*; Jolle *f.*
whet [wet] **1.** wetzen, schärfen; anstacheln; **2.** Wetzen *n*, Schärfen *n*; appetitanregendes Mittel *n.*
wheth·er ['weðə] ob; ~ *or no* so oder so.
whet·stone ['wetstəun] Wetz-, Schleifstein *m.*
whew [hwu:] hui!; hu!
whey [wei] Molke *f.*

which [witʃ] **1.** welche(r, -s)?;
2. welche(r, -s); der, die, das; *auf
den vorhergehenden Satz bezüglich*:
was; **~'ev·er** welche(r, -s) (auch)
immer.

whiff [wif] **1.** Hauch *m*; Zug *m beim
Rauchen*; Zigarillo *n*; **2.** wehen;
rauchen, paffen.

Whig [wig] **1.** Whig *m* (*engl. Libe-
raler*); **2.** Whig...; whiggistisch.

while [wail] **1.** Weile *f*; Zeit *f*; *for
a ~ e-e* Zeitlang; *worth ~* der Mühe
wert; **2.** *mst ~ away Zeit* verbringen;
sich *die Zeit* vertreiben; **3.** *a.* **whilst**
[wailst] während.

whim [wim] = *whimsy.*

whim·per ['wimpə] **1.** wimmern;
winseln; **2.** Wimmern *n*; Winseln *n*.

whim·si·cal ⌐ ['wimzikəl] wunderlich; schrullig; **whim·si·cal·i·ty**
[‿'kæliti], **whim·si·cal·ness** ['‿kəl-
nis] Wunderlichkeit *f*.

whim·s(e)y ['wimzi] Grille *f*,
Laune *f*, Schrulle *f*, Einfall *m*.

whin ♀ [win] Stechginster *m*.

whine [wain] **1.** winseln; wimmern;
heulen; plärren; **2.** Gewinsel *n etc.*

whin·ny ['wini] wiehern.

whip [wip] **1.** *v/t.* peitschen; geißeln
(*a. fig.*); *j.* verprügeln; F *j.* schlagen;
j. übertreffen; *Sahne etc.* schlagen;
werfen, schleudern; übernähen,
umsäumen; umwickeln; ♣ beta-
keln; *mit adv. od. prp.* werfen; reißen; *~ away* wegreißen; *~ from*
wegreißen von; *~ in parl.* zs.-trom-
meln; *~ off* schnell weg- *od.* herunterreißen; entführen; *~ on Kleidungsstück* überwerfen; *~ up* antreiben; aufraffen; *v/i.* springen, rennen, flitzen; **2.** Peitsche *f*; Geißel
f; *parl.* Einpeitscher *m*; Aufforde-
rungsschreiben *n*; überwendliche
Naht *f*; '**~cord** Peitschenschnur *f*;
'**~'hand** rechte Hand *f des Reiters*;
have the ~ of s.o. Gewalt über *j.*
haben.

whipped [wipt]: *~ cream* Schlagsahne
f, -rahm *m*.

whip·per... ['wipə]: '**~'in** *hunt.*
Pikör *m*; *parl.* Einpeitscher *m*; '**~-
-snap·per** Dreikäsehoch *m*.

whip·pet *zo.* ['wipit] Whippet *m*
(*kleiner engl. Rennhund*).

whip·ping ['wipiŋ] Peitschen *n*;
Prügel *pl.*; '**~-boy** Prügelknabe *m*;
'**~-post** *hist.* Stäupsäule *f*; '**~-top**

Kreisel *m*.

whip·poor·will *orn.* ['wippuəwil]
Ziegenmelker *m*.

whip-round F ['wipraund]: *have a ~
Geld* zs.-legen.

whip-saw ⊕ ['wipsɔ:] *zweihändige*
Schrotsäge *f*.

whir [wə:] = *whirr.*

whirl [wə:l] **1.** wirbeln; (sich) drehen; **2.** Wirbel *m*, Strudel *m*;
whirl·i·gig ['‿ligig] Kreisel *m*;
Karussell *n*; *fig.* Wirbel *m*; '**whirlpool** Strudel *m*; '**whirl·wind** Wir-
belwind *m*; Windhose *f*.

whirr [wə:] **1.** schwirren (lassen);
2. Schwirren *n*.

whisk [wisk] **1.** Wisch *m*; Staub-,
Fliegenwedel *m*; *Küche:* Schneebesen *m*; Schwung *m*; Husch *m*;
2. *v/t.* (ab-, weg)wischen, (-)fegen,
(-)kehren; schwingen, wirbeln (mit);
Küche: Schnee schlagen; *~ away*
schnell wegtun; *v/i.* huschen, flitzen, wischen; '**whis·ker** *zo.* Bart-,
Schnurrhaar *n*; *mst (a pair of) ~s pl.*
(ein) Backenbart *m*; '**whis·kered**
mit Backenbart.

whis·k(e)y ['wiski] Whisky *m*.

whis·per ['wispə] **1.** flüstern, wispern; raunen; **2.** Geflüster *n*;
'**whis·per·er** Flüsterer *m*; Zuträger
(-in); **whis·per·ing cam·paign**
Verleumdungs-, Flüsterkampagne *f*.

whist[1] [wist] pst!, st!

whist[2] [‿] Whist *n* (*Kartenspiel*).

whis·tle ['wisl] **1.** pfeifen; **2.** Pfeife *f*;
Pfiff *m*; F Kehle *f*; *~ stop Am.*
Kleinstadt *f*; *pol.* kurzes Auftreten
n e-s Kandidaten im Wahlkampf.

whit[1] [wit]: *not a ~* nicht ein bißchen, keinen Deut.

Whit[2] [‿] Pfingst...; *~ week* Pfingst-
woche *f*.

white [wait] **1.** *allg.* weiß; rein; F
anständig; Weiß...; *~ coffee* Kaffee *m*
mit Milch; *~ meat* helles Fleisch *n von
Geflügel, Kalb etc.*; **2.** Weiß(e) *n*; *typ.*
Lücke *f*; Weiße *m* (*Rasse*); *~ ant zo.*
Termite *f*; '**~-bait** *ichth. Art* Weißfisch *m*, Breitling *m*; *~ book pol.*
Weißbuch *n*; '**~-caps** *pl.* schaum-
gekrönte Wellen *f/pl.*; '**~-col·lar** geistig, Kopf..., Büro...; *~ crime* Wirt-
schaftskriminalität *f*; *~ workers pl.*
Angestellten *pl.*; '**~-'faced** blaß; '**~-
-'haired** weißhaarig; *~ heat* Weiß-
glut *f*; '**~'hot** weißglühend; *~ lie*
Höflichkeitslüge *f*; '**~-liv·ered**

wide-open

feig(e); ~ **man** Weiße *m*; **'whit·en**
v/t. weiß machen; ⊕ weißen; bleichen; *v/i.* weiß *od.* blaß werden;
'whit·en·er Tüncher *m*; **'white·ness**
Weiße *f*; Blässe *f*; **'whit·en·ing**
Schlämmkreide *f*.

white...: ~ pa·per *pol.* Weißbuch *n*;
~ **sheet** Büßerhemd *n*; **'~·smith**
Klempner *m*; **'~·wash 1.** Tünche *f*;
2. weißen, tünchen; *fig.* weiß *od.*
rein waschen; **'~·wash·er** Tüncher
m.

whith·er *lit.* ['wiðə] wohin; **whith-**
er·so'ev·er *lit.* wohin auch immer.

whit·ing ['waitiŋ] Schlämmkreide
f; *ichth.* Weißfisch *m*.

whit·ish ['waitiʃ] weißlich.

whit·low ✞ ['witləu] Nagelgeschwür
n, Umlauf *m*.

Whit·sun ['witsn] pfingstlich;
Pfingst...; **~·day** ['wit'sʌndi]
Pfingst(sonn)tag *m*; **~·tide** ['witsn-
taid] Pfingsten *pl*.

whit·tle ['witl] schnitze(l)n, schnip-
peln; ~ *away* verkleinern; schwächen; ~ *down* beschneiden.

whit·y ['waiti] *bei Farben*: hell...

whiz(z) [wiz] **1.** zischen, sausen;
2. Zischen *n*, Sausen *n*.

who [huː] **1.** welch(r, -s); der, die,
das; **2.** wer?; *Who's Who?* Wer
ist's? (*biographisches Nachschlagewerk*).

whoa [wəu] brr!

who·dun·(n)it *sl.* [huː'dʌnit] Kriminalroman *m*, -film *m*.

who·ev·er [huː'evə] wer auch immer.

whole [həul] **1.** ☐ ganz; heil, unversehrt; † gesund; *made out of* ~ *cloth*
Am. F frei erfunden; **2.** Ganze *n*;
the ~ *of London* ganz London; *the* ~
of them sie alle; (*up*)*on the* ~ alles
in allem, im ganzen; im allgemeinen; schließlich; **'~-'bound** in
Ganzleder (gebunden); **'~-'heart-**
ed [ ] aufrichtig, ehrlich; rückhaltlos; **'~-'hog·ger** *sl.* kompromißloser
Anhänger *m*; Hundert(fünfzig)pro-
zentige *m*; **'~-'length** *a.* ~ *portrait*
Ganzbild *n*; **'~-meal bread** Voll-
korn-, Schrotbrot *n*; **'~·sale 1.** *mst*
~ *trade* Großhandel *m*; **2.** im großen; Großhandels...; Engros...; *fig.*
Massen...; ~ *dealer* **'~-'sal·er**
Großhändler *m*; **whole·some**
['~səm] gesund, bekömmlich; heilsam; **'whole·time** vollbeschäftigt;

hauptberuflich (tätig); Ganztags...;
'whole·wheat Weizenschrot...

who'll F [huːl] = *who will*; *who shall.*

whol·ly ['həulli] *adv.* ganz, gänzlich.

whom [huːm, hum] *acc. von who.*

whoop [huːp] **1.** Schrei *m*, Geschrei
n; **2.** laut schreien; ~ *it up Am. sl.*
Rabatz machen, laut feiern; **whoop-**
ee *Am.* F ['wupiː] Freudenfest *n*;
make ~ auf die Pauke hauen;
whoop·ing-cough ✞ ['huːpiŋkɔf]
Keuchhusten *m*.

whop *sl.* [wɔp] vertrimmen; **'whop-**
per *sl.* Mordskerl *m*, -ding *n*; *bsd.*
faustdicke Lüge *f*; **'whop·ping** *sl.*
kolossal, mächtig.

whore [hɔː] Hure *f*.

whorl [wɔːl] ⊕ Wirtel *m*; ♀ Quirl *m*;
zo., anat. Windung *f*.

whor·tle·ber·ry ♀ ['wəːtlberi] Heidelbeere *f*; *red* ~ Preiselbeere *f*.

who's F [huːz] = *who is.*

whose [huːz] *gen. von who*; **who·so**
(**-ev·er**) ['huːsəu; huːsəu'evə] wer
auch immer.

why [wai] **1.** warum, weshalb; ~ *so?*
wieso?; *that is why* deshalb; **2.** ei!,
ja!; (je) nun.

wick [wik] Docht *m*.

wick·ed ☐ ['wikid] *moralisch* böse,
schlimm, gottlos, sündhaft,
schlecht; schalkhaft; **'wick·ed·ness**
Bosheit *f* etc.

wick·er ['wikə] aus Weide geflochten; Weiden...; Korb...; ~ *basket*
Weidenkorb *m*; ~ *chair* Korbstuhl
m; ~ *furniture* Korbmöbel *pl.*; **'~-**
work 1. Flechtwerk *n*; **2.** =
wicker.

wick·et ['wikit] Pförtchen *n*; *Krik-*
ket: Dreistab *m*, Tor *n*; **'~-keep·er**
Torhüter *m*.

wide [waid] *a.* [ ] *u. adv.* weit; ausgedehnt; weitgehend; umfassend;
weitherzig, großzügig; *bei Maß-*
angaben: breit; weitab, weit entfernt
vom Ziel; ~ *awake* völlig *od.* hellwach; *3 feet* ~ *3* Fuß breit; ~ *differ-*
ence großer Unterschied *m*; **'~-an-**
gle *phot.* Weitwinkel...; **~-a·wake**
1. ['waidə'weik] hellwach; aufmerksam; F hell(e) (*schlau*); **2.** ['~]
Kalabreser *m* (*Schlapphut*); **~-**
-'eyed mit großen Augen; verwundert; **'wid·en** (sich) erweitern;
'wide·ness Weite *f*; **'wide-'o·pen**
weit geöffnet; *Am. sl.* großzügig,
lax *in der Gesetzesdurchführung*;

'**wide·spread** weitverbreitet, ausgedehnt.

wid·ow ['widəu] Witwe *f*; *attr*. Witwen...; '**wid·owed** verwitwet; *fig*. verwaist; '**wid·ow·er** Witwer *m*; **wid·ow·hood** [' ⌣hud] Witwenstand *m*.

width [widⁱ] Breite *f*, Weite *f*.

wield *lit*. [wiːld] *Schwert etc.* handhaben, führen; *fig*. ausüben.

wife [waif], *pl*. **wives** [waivz] (Ehe-) Frau *f*; Gattin *f*; Weib *n*; '**wife·ly** frauenhaft, fraulich.

wig [wig] Perücke *f*; **wigged** mit Perücke; '**wig·ging** F Schelte *f*, Anschnauzer *m*.

wig·gle ['wigl] wackeln (mit *et.*).

wight † *od. co.* [wait] Wicht *m*, Kerl *m*.

wig·wag F ['wigwæg] (durch Flaggen *etc.*) signalisieren.

wig·wam ['wigwæm] Wigwam *m*, Indianerhütte *f*, -zelt *n*.

wild [waild] 1. □ *allg*. wild; *engS*. toll; unbändig; abenteuerlich; planlos; *run ~* wild (auf)wachsen; ⚥ ins Kraut schießen; *talk ~* (wild) darauflos reden; *~ for od. about s.th.* (ganz) wild nach et.; 2. *mst the ~s pl.* die Wildnis; '**wild·cat** 1. *zo*. Wildkatze *f*; *Am*. Schwindelunternehmen *n*; *bsd. Am*. wilde Ölbohrung *f*; 2. *fig*. wild; Schwindel...; **wil·der·ness** ['wildənis] Wildnis *f*, Wüste *f*; Einöde *f*; **wild·fire** ['waildfaiə]: *like ~* wie ein Lauffeuer; '**wild-goose chase** *fig*. vergebliche Mühe *f*; '**wild·ing** ⚥ Wildling *m*; '**wild·ness** Wildheit *f*.

wile [wail] 1. List *f*; *mst ~s pl.* Tücke *f*; 2. (ver)locken; *~ away = while* 2. [sätzlich.]

wil·ful □ ['wilful] eigensinnig; vor-)
wil·i·ness ['wailinis] List *f*, Arglist *f*.

will [wil] 1. Wille *m*; Wunsch *m*; letzter Wille *m*, Testament *n*; *at ~* nach Belieben; *of one's own free ~* aus freien Stücken; 2. (irr.) *v/aux.*: *he ~ come* er wird kommen; er pflegt zu kommen, er kommt gewöhnlich; *I ~ do it* ich will es tun; 3. *v/t. u. v/i.* wollen; durch Willenskraft zwingen; **willed** mit e-m ... Willen, ...willig.

will·ing □ ['wiliŋ] willig, bereit (-willig); *pred*. willens, gewillt (*to inf.* zu *inf.*); *I am ~ to believe* ich glaube gern; '**will·ing·ly** bereit-

willig, gern; '**will·ing·ness** (Bereit)Willigkeit *f*, Bereitschaft *f*, Geneigtheit *f*.

will-o'-the-wisp ['wiləðəwisp] Irrlicht *n*.

wil·low ['wiləu] ⚥ Weide *f*; ⊕ Reißwolf *m*; *attr*. Weiden...; '**~-herb** ⚥ Weiderich *m*; '**wil·low·y** weidenbestanden; *fig*. weidengleich; gertenschlank.

will·pow·er ['wilpauə] Willenskraft *f*.

wil·ly-nil·ly ['wili'nili] wohl oder übel.

wilt¹ † [wilt] *du* willst.

wilt² [⌣] *v/i*. (ver)welken; schlaff werden; *v/t*. welk machen; schlaff machen.

Wil·ton car·pet ['wiltən'kaːpit] Velourteppich *m*.

wil·y □ ['waili] schlau, verschmitzt.

wim·ple ['wimpl] (Nonnen)Schleier *m*.

win [win] 1. (irr.) *v/t*. gewinnen; erringen; erlangen, erreichen; ⚔ *sl*. organisieren; *j*. dazu bringen (*to inf.* zu *inf.*); *~ s.o. over j.* für sich gewinnen; *v/i*. gewinnen; siegen; *~ through to* sich durchringen zu; 2. *Sport*: Sieg *m*.

wince [wins] 1. (zs.-)zucken, zs.-fahren; 2. Zs.-fahren *n*.

winch [wintʃ] Haspel *m, f*, Winde *f*; Kurbel *f*.

wind¹ [wind, *poet. a.* waind] 1. Wind *m*; *fig*. Atem *m*, Luft *f*; ⚕ Blähung *f*; ♪ Blasinstrumente *n/pl*.; *be in the ~* heimlich im Gange sein; *have a long ~* e-e gute Lunge haben; *throw to the ~s fig*. in den Wind schlagen; *raise the ~ sl*. Geld auftreiben; *get od. have the ~ up sl*. Schiß kriegen; 2. *hunt*. wittern; außer Atem bringen; verschnaufen lassen; *be ~ed* außer Atem sein.

wind² [waind] (irr.) *v/t*. winden; wickeln; *Horn* blasen (*pret. u. p.p. a. ~ed*); *~ up* aufwickeln, -winden; *Uhr* aufziehen; *fig*. spannen; *Geschäft* abwickeln; † liquidieren; abschließen; *v/i. a. ~ o.s., ~ one's way* sich winden; sich schlängeln.

wind... [wind]: '**~-bag** *contp*. Windbeutel *m*, Schwätzer *m*; '**~-bound** ⚓ vom Wind zurückgehalten; '**~-break** Windschutz *m*; '**~-cheat·er** Windjacke *f*; '**~-fall** Fallobst *n*; (unverhoffter) Glücksfall *m*; '**~-ga(u)ge** Windstärkemesser *m*;

'wind·i·ness Windigkeit *f*; Aufgeblasenheit *f*.

wind·ing ['waindiŋ] **1.** Winden *n*; Windung *f*; ⊕ Wicklung *f*; **2.** □ sich windend; ⸺ staircase, ⸺ stairs *pl.* Wendeltreppe *f*; '⸺-sheet Leichentuch *n*; '⸺-'up Aufziehen *n*; *fig.* Abschluß *m*; Ende *n*; ✝ Liquidation *f*.

wind-in·stru·ment ♪ ['windinstrumənt] Blasinstrument *n*.

wind-jam·mer ⚓ F ['winddʒæmə] Segler *m* (Segelschiff); *Am.* Windmacher *m* (Schwätzer).

wind·lass ⊕ ['windləs] Winde *f*.

wind·mill ['winmil] Windmühle *f*.

win·dow ['windəu] Fenster *n*; Schaufenster *n*; '⸺-dress·ing Schaufensterdekoration *f*; *fig.* Aufmachung *f*, Mache *f*; 'win·dowed mit Fenstern.

win·dow...: ⸺ en·ve·lope Fensterbriefumschlag *m*; '⸺-frame Fensterrahmen *m*; '⸺-ledge Fenstersims *n*; '⸺-pane Fensterscheibe *f*; '⸺-shade *Am.* Rouleau *n*; '⸺-shop·ping Schaufensterbummel *m*; '⸺-shut·ter Fensterladen *m*; '⸺-sill Fensterbrett *n*.

wind... [wind]: '⸺-pipe Luftröhre *f*; '⸺-screen, *Am.* '⸺-shield *mot.* Windschutzscheibe *f*; ⸺ wiper Scheibenwischer *m*; '⸺-tun·nel ✈ Windkanal *m*.

wind·ward ['windwəd] **1.** windwärts; Wind..., Luv...; **2.** Luv(-seite) *f*.

wind·y ⸺ ['windi] windig (*a. fig. inhaltslos*); ✈ blähend; geschwätzig.

wine [wain] Wein *m*; '⸺-grow·er Weinbauer *m*; '⸺-mer·chant Weinhändler *m*; '⸺-press Kelter *f*; win·e·ry *Am.* ['wainəri] Weinkellerei *f*; 'wine-vault Weinkeller *m*.

wing [wiŋ] **1.** Flügel *m* (*a.* ✖ *u.* △); Schwinge *f*; F *co.* Arm *m*; *mot.* Kotflügel *m*; ✈ Tragfläche *f*; ✖, ✖ Geschwader *n*; *Fußball:* Außenstürmer *m*; ⸺s *pl. thea.* Kulissen *f/pl.*; take ⸺ weg-, auffliegen; be on the ⸺ im Flug sein; *fig.* auf dem Sprung sein; **2.** *v/t.* mit Flügeln versehen; *fig.* beflügeln; *Strecke* (durch)fliegen; flügellahm schießen; *v/i.* fliegen; '⸺-case, '⸺-sheath *zo.* Flügeldecke *f*; '⸺-chair Ohrensessel *m*; winged geflügelt; Flügel...; ...flügelig; 'wing-span Flü-

gelspannweite *f*.

wink [wiŋk] **1.** Blinzeln *n*, Zwinkern *n*; not get a ⸺ of sleep kein Auge zutun; tip s.o. the ⸺ sl. j-m e-n Wink geben; *s. forty*; **2.** blinzeln, zwinkern (mit *et.*); *fig.* blinken; ⸺ at ein Auge zudrücken bei *et.*; *j-m* zublinzeln; 'wink·ing light *mot.* Blinker *m*.

win·ner ['winə] ' Gewinner(in); *Sport:* Sieger(in).

win·ning ['winiŋ] **1.** □ einnehmend, gewinnend; **2.** ⸺s *pl.* Gewinn *m im Spiel*; '⸺-post *Sport:* Ziel(pfosten *m*) *n*.

win·now ['winəu] *Getreide* schwingen, worfeln; *fig.* sondern; sichten.

win·some ['winsəm] gefällig, einnehmend.

win·ter ['wintə] **1.** Winter *m*; ⸺ sports *pl.* Wintersport *m*; **2.** überwintern; win·ter·ize ['⸺təraiz] *Am.* winterfest machen.

win·try ['wintri] winterlich; *fig.* frostig.

wipe [waip] **1.** (ab-, auf)wischen; reinigen; (ab)trocknen; ⸺ off abwischen; *Rechnung* bezahlen; ⸺ out auswischen; *fig.* vernichten; *Schande* tilgen; **2.** Abwischen *n*; F Wischer *m* (*Hieb*); 'wip·er Wischer *m*; Wischtuch *n*.

wire ['waiə] **1.** Draht *m*; Leitung *f*; F Telegramm *n*; *attr.* Draht...; pull the ⸺s der Drahtzieher sein; s-e Beziehungen spielen lassen; *s. live 2*; **2.** *v/t.* (ver)drahten; ⚡ (be-)schalten; (*a. v/i.*) *tel.* drahten, telegraphieren; '⸺-drawn spitzfindig; '⸺-ga(u)ge ⊕ Drahtlehre *f*; '⸺-haired drahthaarig; 'wire·less **1.** □ drahtlos; Funk...; **2.** *a.* ⸺ set Radio(apparat *m*) *n*; on the ⸺ im Rundfunk *od.* Radio; ⸺ station (Rund)Funkstation *f*; **3.** funken; 'wire'net·ting Maschendraht *m*, Drahtgeflecht *n*; 'wire-pull·er Marionettenspieler(in); *fig.* Drahtzieher *m*; 'wire-tap·ping *teleph.* Anzapfen *n der Leitung*; Abhören *n*; 'wire-wove Velin...

wir·ing ['waiəriŋ] Drahtnetz *n*; ⚡ Verdrahtung *f*; Beschaltung *f*; ✖ Verspannung *f*; ⸺ diagram ⚡ Schaltschema *n*; 'wir·y □ drahtig, sehnig.

wis·dom ['wizdəm] Weisheit *f*; Klugheit *f*; ⸺ tooth Weisheitszahn *m*.

wise¹ □ [waiz] weise, verständig; klug; gelehrt; erfahren; ~ guy Am. sl. Schlauberger m; put s.o. ~ j. aufklären (to, on über acc.).

wise² † [~] Weise f, Art f.

wise·a·cre ['waizeikə] Klugtuer(in);

'wise-crack F **1.** witzige Bemerkung f; **2.** witzeln.

wish [wiʃ] **1.** wünschen; wollen; ~ s.o. joy (of) j-m Glück wünschen (zu); ~ for (sich) et. wünschen, sich sehnen nach; ~ well (ill) wohl-(übel)wollen (to dat.); **2.** Wunsch m; good ~es pl. (Glück)Wünsche m/pl.; **wish·ful** □ ['~ful] voll Verlangen (to inf. zu inf.); sehnsüchtig; ~ thinking Wunschdenken n; **'wish(·ing)-bone** Gabelbein n des Geflügels.

wish-wash F ['wiʃwɔʃ] labb(e)riges Zeug n; **'wish·y-wash·y** F labb(e)rig, saft- u. kraftlos, seicht.

wisp [wisp] Wisch m; Strähne f; **'wisp·y** dünn, schmächtig; Haare: sehr fein.

wist·ful □ ['wistful] gedankenvoll, versonnen; sehnsüchtig.

wit [wit] **1.** Witz m; a. ~s pl. Verstand m; witziger Kopf m; be at one's ~'s end mit seiner Weisheit zu Ende sein; have one's ~s about one seine fünf Sinne beisammen haben; keep one's ~s about one e-n klaren Kopf behalten; live by one's ~s sich durchs Leben schlagen; out of one's ~s von Sinnen; **2.** to ~ nämlich, das heißt.

witch [witʃ] Hexe f, Zauberin f; **'~·craft**, **'witch·er·y** Hexerei f; **'witch-doc·tor** Medizinmann m; **witch hunt** Am. politische Diffamierung f, Hexenjagd f.

with [wið] mit; nebst; bei; von; durch; vor (dat.); nach Verben der Gemütsbewegung: vor; it is just so ~ me es geht mir geradeso; ~ it sl. auf Draht, schwer auf der Höhe.

with·al † [wi'ðɔ:l] **1.** adv. dabei, obendrein; **2.** prp. mit.

with·draw [wið'drɔ:] (irr. draw) v/t. ab-, ent-, zurückziehen; heraus-, zurücknehmen; Geld abheben; v/i. sich zurückziehen (from von); abtreten; **with'draw·al** Ein-, Zurückziehung f; bsd. ⚔ Rückzug m; (Geld)Abhebung f; ⚔ Entzug m; ~ symptoms pl. 💉 Entzugserscheinungen f/pl.

withe [wiθ] Weidenrute f.

with·er ['wiðə] a. ~ up, ~ away v/i. (ver)welken; verdorren; ver-, austrocknen; fig. vergehen; v/t. welk machen.

with·ers ['wiðəz] pl. Widerrist m.

with·hold [wið'həuld] (irr. hold) zurückhalten (s.o. from j. von et.); et. vorenthalten (from s.o j-m);

with'in 1. lit. adv. im Innern, drin (-nen); zu Hause; from ~ von innen (her); **2.** prp. innerhalb, binnen, in; ~ doors im Hause; ~ a mile of bis auf eine Meile von; ~ call, ~ sight, ~ hearing in Ruf-, Seh-, Hörweite;

with'out 1. lit. adv. (dr)außen; äu'ßerlich; from ~ von außen (her); **2.** prp. ohne; lit. außerhalb; **with·'stand** (irr. stand) widerstehen, trotzen; aushalten.

with·y ['wiði] = withe.

wit·less □ ['witlis] witzlos; geistlos; gedankenlos.

wit·ness ['witnis] **1.** Zeuge m; Zeugin f; bear ~ Zeugnis ablegen (to für; of von); in ~ of zum Zeugnis (gen.); marriage ~ Trauzeuge m; **2.** v/t. bezeugen; Zeuge sein von et.; erleben; v/i. zeugen (for, to für; against gegen); **'~-box**, Am. **~·stand** Zeugenstand m.

wit·ti·cism ['witisizəm] Witz m; witzige Bemerkung f; **'wit·ti·ness** Witzigkeit f; **'wit·ting·ly** wissentlich, geflissentlich; **'wit·ty** □ witzig; geistreich.

wives [waivz] pl. von wife.

wiz Am. sl. [wiz] Genie n; **wiz·ard** ['~əd] **1.** Zauberer m, Hexenmeister m; fig. Genie n; financial ~ Finanzgenie n; **2.** Schul-sl. prima; **'wiz·ard·ry** (a. fig.) Zauberei f, Hexerei f.

wiz·en(·ed) ['wizn(d)] verhutzelt, schrump(e)lig.

wo(a) [wəu] brr!

woad ♀, ⊕ [wəud] (Färber)Waid m.

wob·ble ['wɔbl] schwanken; wakkeln; ⊕ flattern.

wo(e) rhet. od. co. [wəu] Weh n, Leid n; ~ is me! wehe mir!; **'~-be·gone** jammervoll; **wo(e)·ful** □ rhet. od. co. ['~ful] jammervoll, traurig, elend; **'wo(e)·ful·ness** Elend n, Jammer m.

wog sl. contp. [wɔg] Farbige m, f (bsd. Asiat. od. Araber).

woke [wəuk] pret. u. p.p. von wake² **1.**

wold [wəuld] (hügeliges) Heideland *n.*

wolf [wulf], *pl.* **wolves** [wulvz]
1. *zo.* Wolf *m*; *sl.* Schürzenjäger *m*;
cry ~ blinden Alarm schlagen; ~ *whistle* bewundernder Pfiff *m e-s Mannes*;
give s.o. a ~ *whistle e-r attraktiven
Frau* nachpfeifen; 2. F *gierig* verschlingen; **'wolf·ish** □ wölfisch;
Wolfs...; F *fig.* gefräßig.

wolf·ram *min.* ['wulfrəm] Wolfram
n.

wolves [wulvz] *pl. von* wolf.

wom·an ['wumən], *pl.* **wom·en**
['wimin] 1. Frau *f*; Weib *n*; ~'s
rights pl. Frauenrechte *n/pl.*;
2. weiblich; ~ *doctor* Ärztin *f*; ~
student Studentin *f*; ~ *suffrage*
Frauenstimmrecht *n*; **'wom·an-
-hat·er** Weiberfeind *m*; **wom·an-
hood** ['~hud] (die) Frauen *f/pl.*;
Weiblichkeit *f*; *reach* ~ zur Frau
heranreifen; **'wom·an·ish** □ weibisch; **'wom·an·kind** Frauen(welt
f) *f/pl.*; **'wom·an·like** frauenhaft;
'wom·an·ly weiblich.

womb [wu:m] *anat.* Gebärmutter *f*;
Mutterleib *m*; *fig.* Schoß *m*.

wom·en ['wimin] *pl. von* woman;
~'s *rights pl.* Frauenrechte *n/pl.*;
~'s *team Sport:* Damenmannschaft
f; **wom·en·folk(s)** ['~fəuk(s)],
'wom·en·kind *die* Frauen *f/pl. (bsd.
e-r Familie);* Weibervolk *n*; **Women's Lib** [lib] Frauenbewegung *f*;
wom·en's lib·ber F ['libə] Emanze *f*.

won [wʌn] *pret. u. p.p. von* win 1.

won·der ['wʌndə] 1. Wunder(werk)
n; Verwunderung *f*; *for a* ~ erstaunlicherweise; 2. sich wundern
(at über acc.); gern wissen mögen,
neugierig sein, sich fragen *(whether,
if* ob); **won·der·ful** [⸏ ['~ful]
wunderbar, -voll, erstaunlich; wunderschön; herrlich; **'won·der·ing**
1. □ staunend, verwundert; 2. Verwunderung *f*; **'won·der·land**
Märchenland *n*; Wunderland *n*;
'won·der·ment Verwunderung *f*;
'won·der·struck von Staunen ergriffen; **'won·der·work·er** Wundertäter(in).

won·drous □ *lit.* ['wʌndrəs] wunderbar, erstaunlich.

won·ky *sl.* ['wɔŋki] wack(e)lig *(a.
fig.).*

won't [wəunt] = *will not.*

wont [wəunt] 1. *pred.* gewohnt; *be*
~ *to do* zu tun pflegen; 2. Gewohn

heit *f*; **'wont·ed** gewohnt.

woo [wu:] freien; werben um, umwerben *(a. fig.)*; locken, drängen
(to zu).

wood [wud] Wald *m*, Gehölz *n*;
Holz *n*; Faß *n*; ♪ Holzblasinstrumente *n/pl.*; ~s *pl. Schisport:* Hölzer
n/pl., Bretter *n/pl.*; *touch* ~*!* unberufen!; *out of the* ~ *fig.* über den
Berg; *from the* ~ vom Faß; **~·bine**,
a. **~·bind** ♀ ['~bain(d)] Geißblatt *n*;
'~·carv·ing Holzschnitzerei *f*;
'~·chuck *zo.* Waldmurmeltier *m*;
'~·cock *orn.* Waldschnepfe *f*; **'~·
craft** Weidmannskunst *f*; Kenntnis *f* des Waldes; (Geschicklichkeit
f in der) Holzbearbeitung *f*; **'~·cut**
Holzschnitt *m*; **'~·cut·ter** Holzfäller *m*, -hauer *m*; *Kunst:* Holzschneider *m*; **'wood·ed** bewaldet;
'wood·en hölzern *(a. fig.);* Holz...;
'wood·en·grav·er *Kunst:* Holzschneider *m*; **'wood·en·grav·ing**
Holzschnitt *m (Technik u. Bild);*
'wood·i·ness Waldreichtum *m*;
Holzigkeit *f*.

wood...: **'~·land** 1. Waldung *f*,
Waldland *n*; 2. Wald...; **'~·lark**
orn. Heidelerche *f*; **'~·louse** *zo.*
Rollassel *f*; **'~·man** Förster *m*;
Holzfäller *m*; Waldbewohner *m*;
'~·peck·er *orn.* Specht *m*; **'~·pile**
Holzstapel *m*; **'~·pulp** Holzschliff
m; **'~·ruff** ♀ Waldmeister *m*;
'~·shav·ings *pl.* Hobelspäne *m/pl.*;
'~·shed Holzschuppen *m*; **'woodsman** *Am. für* woodman; **'wood
-wind**, *a.* ~ *instruments pl.* ♪ Holzblasinstrumente *n/pl.*; **'~·work**
Holzwerk *n (bsd.* △); **'~·work·ing machine** Holzbearbeitungsmaschine *f*;
'wood·y waldig; Wald...; holzig;
Holz...; **'wood·yard** Holzplatz *m*.

woo·er ['wu:ə] Freier *m*.

woof [wu:f] *s.* weft.

woof·er ♪ ['wu:fə] Tieftonlautsprecher *m*.

wool [wul] Wolle *f (co. Kopfhaar);*
dyed in the ~ in der Wolle gefärbt;
fig. waschecht; *pull the* ~ *over s.o.'s
eyes* j. hinters Licht führen; *lose
one's* ~ F ärgerlich werden; **'~·gather·ing** 1. Geistesabwesenheit *f*,
Zerstreutheit *f*; *go* ~ spintisieren;
2. geistesabwesend; **'wool·len** 1.
wollen; Woll(en)...; 2. ~s *pl.* Wollsachen *f/pl.*, -kleidung *f*; **'wool-**

(1)**y 1.** wollig; Woll...; belegt (*Stim-me*); *paint. u. fig.* verschwommen; **2.** woollies *pl.* F Wollsachen *f/pl.*, -kleidung *f.*

wool...: '**~·sack** Wollsack *m* (*Sitz des Lordkanzlers im Oberhaus*); '**~-sta·pler** Wollgroßhändler *m*; '**~-work** Wollstickerei *f.*

Wop *Am. sl.* [wɔp] *eingewanderter Italiener.*

word [wə:d] **1.** *mst* Wort *n*; *engS.* Nachricht *f*; Zusage *f*, Versprechen *n*; ⚔ Losung(swort *n*) *f*; Spruch *m*; ~s *pl.* Wörter *n/pl.*; Worte *n/pl.*; *fig.* Wortwechsel *m*; Text *m e-s Liedes*; *by ~ of mouth* mündlich; *eat one's ~s* das Gesagte zurück-nehmen; *have a ~ with* mit *j-m* sprechen; *have ~s* sich zanken (*with* mit); *leave ~* Bescheid hinterlassen; *send* (*bring*) *~* Nachricht geben (bringen); *be as good as one's ~* Wort halten; *take s.o. at his ~ j.* beim Wort nehmen; **2.** (in Worten) ausdrücken, (ab)fassen; *~ed as follows* mit folgendem Wortlaut; '**~-book** Wörterbuch *n*, Glossar *n*; Libretto *n*; '**word·i·ness** Wortfülle *f*, -schwall *m*; '**word·ing** Ausdruck *m*; Wortlaut *m*, Fassung *f*; '**word-less** wortlos, stumm; **word or·der** *gr.* Wortstellung *f*; '**word-'per·fect** *thea.* rollensicher; **word pro·ces·sor** *Computer:* Textverarbeitungsanlage *f*; '**word-split·ting** Wortklauberei *f.*

word·y □ ['wə:di] wortreich; Wort...

wore [wɔ:] *pret. von wear 1.*

work [wə:k] **1.** Arbeit *f*; Werk *n*; ~s *sg.* Fabrik *f*, Werk *n*; ~s *pl.* ⊕ (Uhr-, Feder)Werk *n*; ⚔ Befesti-gungen *f/pl.*, Festungswerk *n*; *pub-lic ~s pl.* öffentliche Bauten *pl.*; ~ *of art* Kunstwerk *n*; *at ~* bei der Arbeit; *in Tätigkeit*, im Gange, im Betrieb; *be in ~* Arbeit haben; *be out of ~* arbeitslos sein; *make sad ~ of* arg wirtschaften mit; *make short ~ of* kurzen Prozeß machen mit; *put out of ~* arbeitslos machen; *set to ~*, *set od. go about one's ~* an die Arbeit gehen; ~s *council* Be-triebsrat *m*; **2.** (*irr.*) *v/i.* arbeiten (*a. fig. in heftiger Bewegung sein*); funk-tionieren; wirken; gären; sich *hin-durch- etc.* arbeiten; ~ *at* arbeiten an (*dat.*); ~ *out* sich auswirken; heraus-kommen (*Summe*); *v/t.* (be)arbeiten;

tüchtig arbeiten lassen, zur Arbeit anhalten; abnutzen; *Bergwerk etc.* ausbeuten; *Fabrik etc.* betreiben; *Gut etc.* bewirtschaften; in Betrieb *od.* Bewegung setzen, in Gang bringen; *Maschine etc.* bedienen; gären lassen; (hervor)bringen, (be-) wirken; anrichten; *Wagen etc.* führen, lenken; *Summe* ausrechnen, *Aufgabe* lösen; ~ *one's way* sich e-n Weg bahnen, sich durcharbeiten; *he is ~ing his way through college* er arbeitet, um sein Studium zu finan-zieren; ~ *one's will* s-n Willen durchsetzen (*upon* bei); ~ *it sl.* es deichseln, es hinkriegen; ~ *off* weg-, aufarbeiten; *Energie* abarbeiten; *Gefühl* abreagieren; † abstoßen; ~ *out* ausarbeiten; abnutzen; heraus-bekommen; lösen; ausrechnen; ~ *up Geschäft etc.* hochbringen; *Ge-fühl, Nerven* aufpeitschen, -wühlen; verarbeiten (*into* zu); *Thema* aus-, bearbeiten; sich einarbeiten in (*acc.*).

work·a·ble □ ['wə:kəbl] bearbei-tungs-, betriebsfähig; aus-, durch-führbar; brauchbar, nützlich; '**work·a·day** Alltags...; *fig.* pro-saisch; **work·a·hol·ic** F [wə:kə'hɔlik] Arbeitssüchtige *m*; '**work·day** Werktag *m*; '**work·er** Arbeiter(in); Urheber(in); ~s *pl.* Belegschaft *f*; **work force** Arbeiterschaft *f*; '**work-house** Armenhaus *n*; *Am.* Besse-rungsanstalt *f*, Arbeitshaus *n.*

work·ing ['wə:kiŋ] **1.** Bergwerk *n*; Steinbruch *m*; *mst pl.* Funktions-, Arbeits-, Wirkungsweise *f*; arbei-tend; Arbeits...; brauchbar; ~ *knowl-edge* ausreichende Kenntnisse *f/pl.*; *in ~ order* in betriebsfähigem Zu-stand; ~ *cap·i·tal* Betriebskapital *n*; '**~-class** Arbeiter...; ~ *day* Werk-, Arbeitstag *m*; ~ *draw·ing* △ Werk-plan *m*; ~ *hours pl.* Arbeitszeit *f*; ~ *man* Arbeiter *m*; '**~-out** Ausarbeiten *n*, -rechnen *n*; Ausführung *f*; ~ *plan* △ Werkplan *m.*

work·man ['wə:kmən] Arbeiter *m*; Handwerker *m*; '**~-like** kunst-gerecht, geschickt; fachmännisch; '**work·man·ship** Kunstfertigkeit *f*, Geschicklichkeit *f*; Ausführung *f*; Werk *n.*

work...: '**~-out** *Am.* F *mst Sport:* (Konditions)Training *n*; Erpro-bung *f*; ~ *per·mit* Arbeitserlaubnis

wrack

f; '~·**room** Arbeitsraum *m;* '~·**sheet**
Schule: Arbeitsunterlage *f;* ✝ Rohbilanz *f;* '~·**shop** Werkstatt *f;* '~·**shy**
1. arbeitsscheu; 2. Arbeitsscheue *m;*
'~·**wom·an** Arbeiterin *f.*

world [wɔ:ld] *allg.* Welt *f; a* ~ *of* e-e
Unmenge (von); *in the* ~ auf der
Welt; *what in the* ~? was in aller
Welt?; *bring* (come) *into the* ~ zur
Welt bringen (kommen); *for all the*
~ *like od. as if* genau so wie *od.* als
ob; *a* ~ *too wide* viel zu weit; *think
the* ~ *of* alles halten von; *man of the*
~ Weltmann *m;* ~ **cham·pi·on** *Sport:*
Weltmeister(in); ~ **cham·pi·on·ship**
Sport: Weltmeisterschaft *f;* ♀ **Cup**
Fußballweltmeisterschaften *f/pl.;*
♀ **Fair** Weltausstellung *f;* **world·**
li·ness ['~linis] Weltlichkeit *f;* Weltsinn *m;* '**world·ling** Weltkind *n.*

world·ly ['wɔ:ldli] weltlich; Welt...;
irdisch; ~ *innocence* Weltfremdheit
f; ~ *wisdom* Weltklugheit *f;* '~·
'**wise** weltklug.

world...: '~·**pow·er** *pol.* Weltmacht
f; '~·'**wear·y** lebensmüde; '~·
·**wide** über die ganze Welt verbreitet; weltweit; weltumspannend;
Welt...

worm [wɔ:m] 1. Wurm *m (a. fig.);*
⊕ (Kühl)Schlange *f;* ⊕ Schnekke(ngewinde *n) f;* 2. ~ *a secret out of
s.o.* j-m ein Geheimnis entlocken; ~
o.s. sich schlängeln; *fig.* sich einschleichen *(into in acc.);* '~·**drive**
⊕ Schneckenantrieb *m;* '~·**eat·en**
wurmstichig *(a. fig.);* '~·**gear** ⊕
Schneckengetriebe *n;* = '~·**wheel**
⊕ Schneckenrad *n;* '~·**wood** Wermut *m; fig.* Wermutstropfen *m,*
Bitterkeit *f;* '**worm·y** wurmig.

worn [wɔ:n] *p.p. von* wear 1; '~·'**out**
abgenutzt; abgetragen; verbraucht
(a. fig.); müde, matt, erschöpft; abgezehrt; verhärmt.

wor·ri·ment F ['wʌrimənt] Quälerei
f; **wor·rit** V ['wʌrit] quälen; ärgern;
'**wor·ry** 1. (sich) beunruhigen;
(sich) ärgern; sich sorgen, sich Sorgen machen; sich aufregen; bedrücken, bekümmern; zerren, (ab-)
würgen; plagen, quälen; 2. Unruhe
f; Sorge *f;* Ärger *m;* Qual *f,* Plage *f;*
Quälgeist *m.*

worse [wɔ:s] 1. schlechter; ärger;
schlimmer *(a. ♣);* (all) the ~ desto
schlimmer; ~ *luck!* leider!; um so
schlimmer!; *he is none the* ~ *for it*

er ist darum nicht übler dran; *the*
~ *for wear* abgetragen; 2. Schlimmere *n; from bad to* ~ vom Regen
in die Traufe; '**wor·sen** (sich)
verschlechtern *od.* -schlimmern;
schädigen.

wor·ship ['wɔ:ʃip] 1. Verehrung *f,*
Anbetung *f;* Gottesdienst *m;* Kult
m; Your ♀ Euer Würden; *place of* ~
Kultstätte *f;* 2. *v/t.* verehren; anbeten; *v/i.* den Gottesdienst besuchen; **wor·ship·ful** ☐ ['~ful] *in
Titeln:* verehrlich; '**wor·ship·(p)er**
Verehrer(in), Anbeter(in); Gottesdienstbesucher(in), Kirchgänger
(-in).

worst [wɔ:st] 1. schlechtest; ärgst;
schlimmst; 2. *das* Schlimmste; *at*
(the) ~ schlimmstenfalls; *do your* ~!
mach, was du willst!; *get the* ~ *of it*
den kürzeren ziehen; *if the* ~ *comes
to the* ~ wenn es ganz schlimm
kommt; 3. überwältigen, besiegen.

wor·sted ['wustid] Woll-, Kammgarn *n;* Kammgarnstoff *m.*

wort[1] ♀ [wɔ:t] ...kraut *n,* ...wurz *f.*
wort[2] [~] (Bier)Würze *f.*

worth [wɔ:θ] 1. wert; *he is* ~ *a
million* er hat e-e Million; ~ *reading*
lesenswert; 2. Wert *m;* Würde *f;*
wor·thi·ness ['wɔ:ðinis] Würdigkeit *f;* **worth·less** ☐ ['wɔ:θlis]
wertlos; unwürdig; '**worth·'while**
der Mühe wert, lohnend; **wor·thy**
☐ ['wɔ:ði] 1. würdig; *oft co.* ehrbar;
~ *of s.th.* e-r Sache würdig *od.* wert;
2. Mann *m* von Verdienst.

would [wud, wəd] *pret. von* will;
wollte; würde, möchte, pflegte.

would-be ['wudbi:] an-, vorgeblich,
sogenannt; möglich, potentiell;
Schein..., Pseudo...; ~ *aggressor*
möglicher Angreifer *m;* ~ *buyer*
Kauflustige *m;* ~ *painter* Farbenkleckser *m;* ~ *poet* Dichterling *m;* ~
politician Kannegießer *m.*

wouldn't ['wudnt] = *would not.*

wound[1] [wu:nd] 1. Wunde *f,* Verwundung *f,* Verletzung *f; fig.* Kränkung *f;* 2. verwunden, verletzen *(a.
fig.).*   [wind[2].\

wound[2] [waund] *pret. u. p.p. von*|
wove *pret.,* **wo·ven** ['wəuv(ə)n] *p.p.*
von weave 1.

wow *Am.* [wau] 1. Mensch!; toll!;
2. *thea. sl.* Bombenerfolg *m; weitS.*
Bombensache *f.*

wrack[1] ♀ [ræk] Seetang *m.*

wrack[2] [⌐] = *rack*[3].

wraith [reiθ] Geist *m* e-s Sterbenden *od. Verstorbenen*.

wran·gle ['ræŋgl] **1.** streiten, (sich) zanken; **2.** Streit *m*, Zank *m*.

wrap [ræp] **1.** *v/t.* wickeln; *oft* ⌐ *up* einwickeln; *fig.* einhüllen; *be* ⌐*ped up in* gehüllt sein in; *fig.* ganz aufgehen in (*dat.*); *v/i.* ⌐ *up* sich einhüllen; **2.** Hülle *f*; *engS.* Decke *f*; Schal *m*; Mantel *m*; '**wrap·per** Hülle *f*, Umschlag *m*; Morgenrock *m*; Deckblatt *n der Zigarre*; *a. postal* ⌐ Streifband *n*; '**wrap·ping** Umhüllung *f*; Verpackung *f*; ⌐ *paper* Einwickel-, Packpapier *n*.

wrath *lit.* [rɔθ] Zorn *m*, Grimm *m*; **wrath·ful** □ ['⌐ful] zornig, grimmig. [lassen (*upon an j-m*).\

wreak [ri:k] *Rache* üben, *Zorn* aus-⌐

wreath [ri:θ], *pl.* **wreaths** [ri:ðz] (Blumen)Gewinde *n*; Kranz *m*, Girlande *f*; Ring *m*, Kreis *m*; Schneewehe *f*; **wreathe** [ri:ð] *v/t.* winden; umwinden; *v/i.* sich ringeln.

wreck [rek] **1.** ⚓ Wrack *n* (*a. fig.*); Trümmer *pl.* (*oft fig.*); Schiffbruch *m*; *fig.* Untergang *m*; **2.** zum Scheitern bringen; *Zug* zum Entgleisen bringen; zertrümmern; vernichten; zugrunde richten; *be* ⌐*ed* ⚓ scheitern; Schiffbruch erleiden; '**wreck·age** Trümmer *pl.*; Wrackteile *m/pl.*; **wrecked** schiffbrüchig; gestrandet; zerstört, ruiniert; '**wreck·er** ⚓ Bergungsschiff *n*; -arbeiter *m*; Strandräuber *m*; *fig.* Saboteur *m*; *Am.* Abbrucharbeiter *m*; *mot.* Abschleppwagen *m*; '**wreck·ing** Strandraub *m*; ⌐ *company* Abbruchfirma *f*; ⌐ *service mot.* Abschlepp-, Hilfsdienst *m*.

wren *orn.* [ren] Zaunkönig *m*.

wrench [rentʃ] **1.** winden, drehen; reißen; entwinden (*from s.o.* j-m); verdrehen (*a. fig.*); verrenken; ⌐ *open* aufreißen; ⌐ *out* herausreißen⌐; **2.** *drehender* Ruck *m*; Verdrehung *f* (*a. fig.*); Verrenkung *f*; *fig.* (Trennungs)Schmerz *m*; ⊕ Schraubenschlüssel *m*.

wrest [rest] *drehend* reißen; verdrehen; entreißen, abringen (*from s.o.* j-m).

wres·tle ['resl] **1.** *v/i.* ringen; *fig.* kämpfen; *v/t.* ringen mit; **2.** = *wrestling*; '**wres·tler** Ringer(in);

'**wres·tling** Ringkampf *m*, Ringen *n*.

wretch [retʃ] Elende *m*; Schuft *m*; *co.* Schelm *m*, Kerl *m*; *poor* ⌐ armer Teufel *m*.

wretch·ed ◌ ['retʃid] elend, unglücklich; erbärmlich; '**wretch·ed·ness** Elend *n*; Erbärmlichkeit *f*.

wrick [rik] **1.** verdrehen, verrenken; **2.** Verdrehung *f*, -renkung *f*.

wrig·gle ['rigl] (sich) hin und her drehen *od.* bewegen; sich winden *od.* schlängeln *od.* ringeln; ⌐ *out of* sich herauswinden aus.

wright [rait] ...macher *m*, ...bauer *m*.

wring [riŋ] **1.** (*irr.*) Hände ringen; *Wäsche* (aus)wringen; pressen; *Hals* umdrehen; ⌐ *s.th. from s.o.* j-m et. abringen *od.* entreißen; ⌐ *s.o.'s heart* j-m zu Herzen gehen; ⌐*ing wet* klatschnaß; **2.** Wringen *n*; Druck *m*; '**wring·er**, '**wring·ing- -ma·chine** Wringmaschine *f*.

wrin·kle[1] ['riŋkl] **1.** Runzel *f*; Falte *f*; **2.** (sich) runzeln; (sich) falten; ⌐*d* runz(e)lig. [Trick *m*.\

wrin·kle[2] F [⌐] Wink *m*; Kniff *m*;\

wrist [rist] Handgelenk *n*; ⌐ *watch* Armbanduhr *f*; '**wrist·band** Bündchen *n*, (Hemd)Manschette *f*; = **wrist·let** ['⌐lit] Armband *n*; *Sport*: Handgelenkschützer *m*.

writ [rit] (behördlicher) Erlaß *m*; (gerichtlicher) Befehl *m*; *Holy* ⌐ Heilige Schrift *f*; ⌐ *of attachment* ⚖ Haftbefehl *m*; ⌐ *of execution* ⚖ Vollstreckungsbefehl *m*.

write [rait] (*irr.*) *v/t.* schreiben; *Bogen etc.* voll-, beschreiben; ⌐ *down* auf-, niederschreiben; ⌐ *in full* ausschreiben; ⌐ *off Brief etc.* (schnell) herunterschreiben; † abschreiben; ⌐ *out* aus-, abschreiben; ⌐ *up* ausführlich niederschreiben; ausarbeiten; hervorheben; *fig.* lobend erwähnen, herausstreichen; *ergänzend* nachtragen; *v/i.* schreiben; schriftstellern; ⌐ *for* schriftlich bestellen, kommen lassen; ⌐ *home about fig.* Staat machen mit; '⌐**-off** † Abschreibung *f*; *a complete* ⌐ F ein Totalschaden *m*.

writ·er ['raitə] Schreiber(in); Verfasser(in); Autor(in); Schriftsteller (-in); ⌐ *to the signet in Schottland*: Notar *m*; ⌐*'s cramp*, ⌐*'s palsy* Schreibkrampf *m*.

write-up ['raitʌp] Bericht *m*, Besprechung *f* in der Presse.

writhe [raið] sich (*vor Schmerz*) krümmen; *fig.* leiden.

writ·ing ['raitiŋ] Schreiben *n*; Aufsatz *m*; Schrift *f*, Werk *n*; (Hand-) Schrift *f*; Schriftstück *n*; Urkunde *f*; Schreibart *f*, Stil *m*; *attr.* Schreib-...; *in ~* schriftlich; '~-block Schreibblock *m*; '~-case Schreibmappe *f*; '~-desk Schreibtisch *m*; '~-pad Schreibblock *m*; '~-pa·per Schreibpapier *n*.

writ·ten ['ritn] **1.** *p.p. von* write; **2.** *adj.* schriftlich.

wrong [rɔŋ] **1.** ☐ unrecht; verkehrt; unrichtig, falsch; *be ~* unrecht haben, im Irrtum sein; sich irren; in Unordnung sein; falsch gehen (*Uhr*); *go ~* den Weg verfehlen; daneben-, schiefgehen; *fig.* auf Abwege geraten; *there is something ~* irgend etwas ist nicht in Ordnung; *what's ~ with ...?* F was fehlt denn ...

(*dat.*)?; was ist los mit ...?; *on the ~ side of sixty* über die 60 hinaus; **2.** Unrecht *n*; Beleidigung *f*; *be in the ~* im Unrecht sein, unrecht haben; *put s.o. in the ~* j. ins Unrecht setzen; **3.** unrecht tun (*dat.*); ungerecht behandeln; '~'do·er Übel-, Missetäter(in); '~'do·ing Übel-, Missetat *f*; **wrong·ful** ☐ ['~ful] ungerecht; unrechtmäßig; 'wrong'head·ed verdreht, verschroben; querköpfig; 'wrongness Ungerechtigkeit *f*; Verkehrtheit *f*.

wrote [rəut] *pret. von* write.

wroth *poet. od. co.* [rəuθ] erzürnt.

wrought *lit.* [rɔːt] *pret. u. p.p. von* work 2; '~-'i·ron **1.** Schmiedeeisen *n*; **2.** schmiedeeisern; '~-up erregt.

wrung [rʌŋ] *pret. u. p.p. von* wring 1.

wry ☐ [rai] schief, krumm, verzerrt.

X

X & *u. fig.* [eks] X *n* (*unbekannte Größe*).

x-(cer·tif·i·cate) film † ['eks(sə-'tifikit)'film] für Jugendliche ab 18 Jahren freigegebener Film *m*.

xen·o·pho·bi·a [zenə'fəubiə] Xenophobie *f*, Fremdenhaß *m*.

Xmas ['krisməs] = Christmas.

X-ray ['eks'rei] **1.** ~s *pl.* Röntgenstrahlen *m/pl.*; **2.** Röntgen...; **3.** durchleuchten; röntgen.

X-shaped ['eksʃeipt] x-förmig.

xy·log·ra·phy [zai'lɔgrəfi] Xylographie *f*, Holzschneidekunst *f*.

xy·lo·nite ['zailənait] Zelluloid *n*.

xy·lo·phone ♪ ['zailəfəun] Xylophon *n*.

Y

yacht ⚓ [jɔt] **1.** (Motor)Jacht *f*; Segelboot *n*; **2.** auf e-r Jacht fahren; segeln; '~-club Segel-, Jachtklub *m*; 'yacht·er, yachts·man ['~smən] Jachtsegler *m*; (Sport)Segler *m*; 'yacht·ing Segelsport *m*; *attr.* Segel...

yah [jɑː] *int.* äh!; puh!; pfui!

ya·hoo [jə'huː] Rohling *m*; Tölpel *m*.

yam & [jæm] Jamswurzel *f*.

yank¹ [jæŋk] **1.** *v/t.* (weg-, heraus-) reißen; *v/i.* flink hantieren; rührig sein; **2.** Ruck *m*.

Yank² *sl.* [~] = Yankee.

Yan·kee F ['jæŋki] Yankee *m* (Nordamerikaner); ~ Doodle amerikanisches Volkslied.

yap [jæp] **1.** kläffen; F quasseln;

2. Gekläff *n*; F Gequassel *n*.
yard¹ [jɑːd] Yard *n*, *engl.* Elle *f* (= 0,914 *m*); ⚓ Rah(e) *f*.
yard² [⌐] Hof *m*; (Bau-, Stapel-) Platz *m*; *Am.* Garten *m* (*um das Haus*); the ⚲ Scotland Yard *m*; *marshalling* ⌐, *railway* ⌐ Rangierbahnhof *m*.
yard…: '⌐**-arm** ⚓ Rahnock *f*; '⌐**-man** ⚘ Rangierer *m*; '⌐**-measure**, '⌐**-stick** Yardstock *m*, -maß *n*.
yarn [jɑːn] **1.** Garn *n*; ⚓ Kabelgarn *n*; F Seemannsgarn *n*; abenteuerliche Geschichte *f*; *spin a* ⌐ ein Seemannsgarn spinnen, e-e Geschichte erzählen; **2.** F (Geschichten) erzählen.
yar·row ⚘ ['jærəu] Schafgarbe *f*.
yaw ⚓, ✕ [jɔː] gieren (*vom Kurs abweichen*).
yawl ⚓ [jɔːl] Jolle *f*.
yawn [jɔːn] **1.** gähnen; **2.** Gähnen *n*.
ye † *od. poet. od. co.* [jiː, ji] ihr.
yea † *od. prov.* [jei] **1.** ja; **2.** Ja *n*.
year [jəː] Jahr *n*; ⌐ *of grace* Jahr *n* des Heils; *he bears his* ⌐*s well* er ist für sein Alter (noch) recht rüstig; '**year·ling** Jährling *m* (*einjähriges Tier*); '**year-long** einjährig, ein Jahr dauernd; '**year·ly** jährlich.
yearn [jəːn] sich sehnen, verlangen (*for, after* nach; *to inf.* danach, zu *inf.*); '**yearn·ing 1.** Sehnen *n*, Sehnsucht *f*; **2.** ☐ sehnsüchtig.
yeast [jiːst] Hefe *f*; Schaum *m*, Gischt *m*; '**yeast·y** ☐ hefig; schaumig; *fig.* gärend; schaumschlägerisch.
yegg(·man) *Am. sl.* ['jeg(mən)] Stromer *m*; Einbrecher *m*, Geldschrankknacker *m*.
yell [jel] **1.** (gellend) schreien; aufschreien; **2.** (gellender) Schrei *m*; anfeuernder Ruf *m*.
yel·low ['jeləu] **1.** gelb; F hasenfüßig (*feig*); *sl.* chauvinistisch; Sensations…; Hetz…; ⌐ *pages pl.* Gelbe Seiten *f/pl.*, Branchenfernsprechbuch *n*; **2.** Gelb *n*; **3.** (sich) gelb färben; ⌐*ed* vergilbt; '⌐**-back** Schmöker *m* (*billiger Roman*); ⌐ **fe·ver** ✿ Gelbfieber *n*; '⌐**-ham·mer** *orn.* Goldammer *f*; '**yel·low·ish** gelblich; **yel·low press** Sensations-, Boulevardpresse *f*.
yelp [jelp] **1.** Gekläff *n*; **2.** kläffen.
yen *Am. sl.* [jen] brennendes Verlangen *n*.

yeo·man ['jəumən] Yeoman *m*, freier Bauer *m*, Freisasse *m*; ⌐ *of the guard* Leibgardist *m*; '**yeo·man·ry** Freisassen *m/pl.*, freie Bauernschaft *f*; ✕ berittene Miliz *f*.
yep *Am.* F [jep] ja.
yes [jes] **1.** ja; doch; **2.** Ja *n*; ⌐**-man** *sl.* ['⌐mæn] Jasager *m*.
yes·ter·day ['jestədi] **1.** gestern; **2.** der gestrige Tag, das Gestern; **yes·ter'year** voriges Jahr *n*.
yet [jet] **1.** *adv.* noch; jetzt noch; bis jetzt; schon; selbst, sogar, *as* ⌐ bis jetzt; bisher; *not* ⌐ noch nicht; **2.** *cj.* doch, jedoch, dennoch, gleichwohl, trotzdem.
yew ⚘ [juː] Eibe *f*, Taxus *m*.
Yid·dish ['jidiʃ] Jiddisch *n*.
yield [jiːld] **1.** *v/t. als Ertrag* hervorbringen, liefern; *Resultat* ergeben; *Gewinn* (ein)bringen, abwerfen; gewähren; übergeben, -lassen; zugestehen; ⌐ *up the ghost* den Geist aufgeben; *v/i. bsd.* ✓ tragen; sich fügen; weichen, nachgeben (*Person u. Sache*); **2.** Ertrag *m*; Ausbeute *f*; '**yield·ing** ☐ nachgebend (*Erdreich etc.*); *fig.* nachgiebig.
yip *Am.* F [jip] jaulen.
yob F [jɔb], **yob·bo** F ['jɔbəu] Halbstarke *m*.
yo·del, yo·dle ['jəudl] **1.** Jodler *m*; **2.** jodeln.
yog·hourt, yog·(h)urt ['jɔgət] Joghurt *m*.
yo·gi ['jəugi] Jogi *m*.
yo-ho [jəu'həu] hau ruck!
yoicks *hunt.* [jɔiks] hussa!
yoke [jəuk] **1.** Joch *n* (*a. fig.*); Paar *n* (Ochsen); Schultertrage *f*; **2.** anjochen, anspannen; zs.-jochen, -spannen; *fig.* paaren (*to* mit); '⌐**-fel·low** (*bsd.* Lebens)Gefährte *m*, (-)Gefährtin *f*.
yo·kel F ['jəukəl] Tölpel *m*.
yolk [jəuk] (Ei)Dotter *m*, Eigelb *n*; Wollfett *n*.
yon † *od. poet.* [jɔn], **yon·der** *lit.* ['jɔndə] **1.** jene(r, -s); jenseitig; **2.** da *od.* dort drüben.
yore [jɔː]: *of* ⌐ ehemals, ehedem.
you [juː, ju] ihr; du, Sie; man.
you'd F [juːd] = *you had*; *you would*;
you'll F [juːl] = *you will*; *you shall*.
young [jʌŋ] **1.** ☐ jung (*fig. frisch; neu; unerfahren*); *von Kindern a.* klein; Jung…; **2.** Junge(n) *pl.*; *with*

~ trächtig; '**young·ish** ziemlich jung; **young·ster** ['~stə] Kind *n*, *bsd.* Junge *m*.

your [jɔː, jə] euer(e); dein(e), Ihre; **you're** F [juə] = *you are*; **yours** [jɔːz] der (die, das) eurige, deinige, Ihrige; euer; dein, Ihr; **your'self**, *pl.* **your·selves** [~'selvz] (ihr, du, Sie) selbst; euch, dich, Sie (selbst), sich (selbst).

youth [juːθ], *pl.* **youths** [juːðz] Jugend *f*; Jüngling *m*; junge Leute *pl.*; ~ **hostel** Jugendherberge *f*; go ~*-hostelling* e-e Jugendherbergswanderung machen; in Jugendherbergen übernachten.

youth·ful □ ['juːθful]ˈ jugendlich, jung; Jugend...; '**youth·ful·ness** Jugendlichkeit *f*; Jugend *f*.

you've F [juːv, juv] = *you have*.

yuc·ca ♀ ['jʌkə] Yucca *f*, Palmlilie *f*.

Yu·go-Slav ['juːgəu'slaːv] **1.** Jugoslawe *m*, Jugoslawin *f*; **2.** jugoslawisch.

yule *lit.* [juːl] Weihnacht *f*; ~ *log* Weihnachts-, Julblock *m im Kamin*; '~·**tide** *lit.* Weihnachtszeit *f*.

yup·pie ['jʌpi] *in Großstädten: junger, karrierebewußter und ausgabefreudiger Mensch (häufig auch bestimmten Modetrends folgend)*.

Z

za·ny ['zeini] Dummkopf *m*, Hanswurst *m*.

zeal [ziːl] Eifer *m*; **zeal·ot** ['zelət] Eiferer *m*; *bsd. eccl.* Zelot *m*; '**zeal·ot·ry** blinder Eifer *m*; Zelotismus *m*; '**zeal·ous** □ eifrig; eifrig bedacht (*for* auf *acc.*; *to inf.* darauf zu *inf.*); innig, heiß.

ze·bra *zo.* ['ziːbrə] Zebra *n*; ~ **crossing** Zebrastreifen *m*, Fußgängerüberweg *m*.

ze·bu *zo.* ['ziːbuː] Zebu *n*, Buckelochse *m*. [punkt *m*.]

ze·nith ['zeniθ] Zenit *m*; *fig.* Höhe-]

zeph·yr ['zefə] Zephir *m*, Westwind *m*; sanfte Brise *f*; † Zephirwolle *f*; Zephirgarn *n*; Sporttrikot *n*.

ze·ro ['ziərəu] **1.** Null *f* (*a. fig.*); Nullpunkt *m* (*a. fig.*); Anfangspunkt *m*; **2.** ~ *in on* ✕ sich einschießen auf; *fig. Thema* herausgreifen; ~ **growth** Nullwachstum *n*; ~ **hour** ✕ festgelegter Zeitpunkt *m* für eine geplante Operation, Stunde *f* Null; ~ **op·tion** *bsd. Am.* Nullösung *f*.

zest [zest] **1.** Würze *f* (*a. fig.*); Lust *f*, Freude *f* (*for* an *dat.*); Genuß *m*, Behagen *n*; ~ *for life* Lebenshunger *m*; **2.** würzen.

zig·zag ['zigzæg] **1.** Zickzack *m*; **2.** im Zickzack (laufend), zickzackförmig; Zickzack...; **3.** im Zickzack gehen.

zinc [ziŋk] **1.** *min.* Zink *n*; **2.** verzinken.

Zi·on ['zaiən] Zion *m*; '**Zi·on·ism** Zionismus *m*; '**Zi·on·ist 1.** Zionist (-in); **2.** zionistisch.

zip [zip] **1.** Schwirren *n*; F Schmiß *m*, Schwung *m*; **2.** den Reißverschluß auf- *od.* zumachen von; **zip code** *Am.* Postleitzahl *f*; '~·**fas·ten·er** = *zipper 1*; '**zip·per 1.** Reißverschluß *m*; **2.** mit Reißverschluß versehen; '**zip·py** F schmissig.

zith·er ♪ ['ziθə] Zither *f*.

zo·di·ac *ast.* ['zəudiæk] Tierkreis *m*; **zo·di·a·cal** [zəu'daiəkəl] Tierkreis...

zon·al □ ['zəunl] zonenförmig; Zonen...; **zone** Zone *f*; Erdgürtel *m*; *fig.* Gürtel *m*; *fig.* Gebiet *n*.

Zoo F [zuː] Zoo *m*.

zo·o·log·i·cal □ [zəuə'lɔdʒikəl] zoologisch; ~ *garden(s pl.)* Zoologischer Garten *m*; **zo·ol·o·gist** [~'ɔlədʒist] Zoologe *m*; **zo'ol·o·gy** Zoologie *f*.

zoom ≤̌ *sl.* [zuːm] **1.** das Flugzeug hochdrücken; steil (empor)steigen; **2.** plötzliches steiles Steigen *n*; ~ *lens phot.* Gummilinse *f*, Vario-Objektiv *n*, Zoom-Objektiv *n*.

Zu·lu ['zuːluː] Zulu *m*, Zulufrau *f*; Zulu(sprache *f*) *n*.

zy·mot·ic [zai'mɔtik] ⚕ zymotisch; Gärung erregend; Gärungs...; ⚕ Infektions...

Proper Names with Phonetic Transcriptions and Explanations

A

Ab·er·deen [æbə'di:n] *Stadt in Schottland.*

Ab·(o)u·kir [æbu:'kiə] Abukir *n (Hafenstadt in Ägypten)* [*m.*]

A·bra·ham ['eibrəhæm] Abraham *f*

Ab·ys·sin·i·a [æbi'sinjə] Abessinien *n (früherer Name von Äthiopien).*

Ad·am ['ædəm] Adam *m.*

Ad·di·son ['ædisn] *englischer Autor.*

Ad·e·laide ['ædəleid] *weiblicher Vorname; Stadt in Australien.*

A·den ['eidn] *Hauptstadt des Südjemen.*

Ad·i·ron·dack [ædi'rɔndæk] *Gebirgszug in U.S.A.*

Ad·olf ['ædɔlf], **A·dol·phus** [ə'dɔlfəs] Adolf *m.*

A·dri·at·ic (Sea) [eidri'ætik('si:)] *das Adriatische Meer.*

Af·ghan·i·stan [æf'gænistæn] Afghanistan *n.*

Af·ri·ca ['æfrikə] Afrika *n.*

Ag·a·tha ['ægəθə] Agathe *f.*

Aix-la-Cha·pelle ['eikslɑ:ʃæ'pæl] Aachen *n.*

Al·a·bam·a [ælə'bæmə] *Staat der U.S.A.*

A·las·ka [ə'læskə] *Staat der U.S.A.*

Al·ba·ni·a [æl'beinjə] Albanien *n.*

Al·ba·ny ['ɔ:lbəni] *Hauptstadt des Staates New York (U.S.A.).*

Al·bert ['ælbət] Albert *m.*

Al·ber·ta [æl'bə:tə] *Provinz in Kanada.*

Al·der·ney ['ɔ:ldəni] *e-e der Kanalinseln.*

Al·ex·an·der [ælig'zɑ:ndə] Alexander *m.*

Al·ex·an·dra [ælig'zɑ:ndrə] Alexandra *f.*

Al·fred ['ælfrid] Alfred *m.*

Al·ger·non ['ældʒənən] *männlicher Vorname.*

Al·ice ['ælis] Alice *f.*

Al·le·ghe·ny ['æligeni] *Fluß u. Gebirge in U.S.A.*

Al·len ['ælin] *männlicher Vorname.*

Al·sace ['ælsæs], **Al·sa·ti·a** [æl'seiʃjə] das Elsaß.

A·me·lia [ə'mi:ljə] Amalie *f.*

A·mer·i·ca [ə'merikə] Amerika *n.*

A·my ['eimi] *weiblicher Vorname.*

An·des ['ændi:z] *pl. die* Anden.

An·dor·ra [æn'dɔrə] Andorra *n.*

An·drew ['ændru:] Andreas *m.*

An·gle·sey ['æŋglsi] *Grafschaft in Wales.*

An·nap·o·lis [ə'næpəlis] *Hauptstadt von Maryland (U.S.A.).*

Ann(e) [æn] Anna *f.*

An·tho·ny ['æntəni; 'ænθəni] Anton *m.*

An·til·les [æn'tili:z] *pl. die* Antillen.

An·to·ni·a [æn'təunjə] Antonia *f.*

An·to·ny ['æntəni] Anton *m.*

Ap·en·nines ['æpinainz] *pl. die* Apenninen.

Ap·pa·la·chians [æpə'leitʃjənz] *pl. die* Appalachen.

A·ra·bi·a [ə'reibjə] Arabien *n.*

Ar·chi·bald ['ɑ:tʃibəld] Archibald *m.*

Ar·den ['ɑ:dn] *englischer Familienname.*

Ar·gen·ti·na [ɑ:dʒən'ti:nə], **the Argen·tine** [ðiˈɑ:dʒəntain] Argentinien *n.*

Ar·is·tot·le ['æristɔtl] Aristoteles *m.*

Ar·i·zo·na [æri'zəunə] *Staat der U.S.A.*

Ar·kan·sas ['ɑ:kənsɔ:] *Fluß in U.S.A.; Staat der U.S.A.*

Ar·ling·ton ['ɑ:liŋtən] *Nationalfriedhof bei Washington (U.S.A.).*

Ar·thur ['ɑ:θə] Art(h)ur *m.*

As·cot ['æskət] *Stadt in England mit berühmter Rennbahn.*

A·sia ['eiʃə] Asien *n*; ∼ Minor Kleinasien *n.*

Ath·ens ['æθinz] Athen *n.*

At·lan·tic [ət'læntik] *der* Atlantik.

Auck·land ['ɔ:klənd] *Hafenstadt in Neuseeland.*

Aus·ten ['ɔstin] *englische Autorin.*

Aus·tin ['ɔstin] *Hauptstadt von Texas (U.S.A.).*

Aus·tra·lia [ɔs'treiljə] Australien *n.*

Aus·tri·a ['ɔstriə] Österreich *n.*

A·von ['eivən] *Fluß in England.*

Ax·min·ster ['æksminstə] *Stadt in England.*

A·zores [ə'zɔ:z] *pl. die* Azoren.

B

Ba·con ['beikən] *englischer Staatsmann u. Philosoph.*

Ba·den-Pow·ell ['beidn'pəuəl] *Begründer der Pfadfinderbewegung.*

Ba·ha·mas [bə'hɑ:məz] *pl. die* Bahamainseln.

Bald·win [bɔ:ldwin] *männlicher Vorname; amerikanischer Autor.*

Bâle [bɑ:l] Basel *n.*

Bal·kans ['bɔ:lkənz] *pl. der* Balkan.

Bal·mor·al [bæl'mɔrəl] *Königsschloß in Schottland.*

Bal·ti·more ['bɔ:ltimɔ:] *Hafenstadt in U.S.A.*

Bar·thol·o·mew [bɑ:'θɔləmju:] Bartholomäus *m.*

Bath [bɑ:θ] *Badeort in England.*

Ba·ton Rouge ['bætən'ru:ʒ] *Hauptstadt von Louisiana (U.S.A.).*

Ba·var·ia [bə'veəriə] Bayern *n.*

Bea·cons·field ['bi:kənzfi:ld] *Adelstitel Disraelis.*

Beck·y ['beki] *Kurzform von* Rebecca.

Bed·ford ['bedfəd] *Stadt in England; a.* **Bed·ford·shire** ['⁓ʃiə] *Grafschaft in England.*

Bee·cham ['bi:tʃəm] *englischer Dirigent.*

Bel·fast [bel'fɑ:st] *Hauptstadt von Nordirland.*

Bel·gium ['beldʒəm] Belgien *n.*

Bel·grade [bel'greid] Belgrad *n.*

Bel·gra·vi·a [bel'greivjə] *Stadtteil von London.*

Ben [ben] *Kurzform von* Benjamin.

Ben·e·dict ['benidikt; 'benit] Benedikt *m.*

Ben·gal [beŋ'gɔ:l] Bengalen *n.*

Ben·ja·min ['bendʒəmin] Benjamin *m.*

Ben Ne·vis [ben'nevis] *höchster Berg in Großbritannien.*

Berk·shire ['bɑ:kʃiə] *Grafschaft in England;* ⁓ *Hills pl. Gebirgszug in Massachusetts (U.S.A.).*

Ber·lin [bə:'lin] Berlin *n.*

Ber·mu·das [bə:'mju:dəz] *pl. die* Bermudainseln.

Ber·nard ['bə:nəd] Bern(h)ard *m.*

Bern(e) [bə:n] Bern *n.*

Bern·stein ['bə:nstain] *amerikanischer Komponist u. Dirigent.*

Ber·tha ['bə:θə] Bertha *f.*

Ber·trand ['bə:trənd] Bertram *m.*

Bess, Bes·sy ['bes(i)], **Bet·s(e)y** ['betsi], **Bet·ty** ['beti] Lieschen *n.*

Bill, Bil·ly ['bil(i)] *Kurzform von* William.

Bir·ken·head ['bə:kənhed] *Industrie- u. Hafenstadt in England.*

Bir·ming·ham ['bə:miŋəm] *Industriestadt in England.*

Bis·cay ['biskei]: *Bay of*⁓ *der* Golf von Biskaya.

Blooms·bur·y ['blu:mzbəri] *Künstlerviertel in London.*

Bob [bɔb] *Kurzform von* Robert.

Bo·he·mi·a [bəu'hi:mjə] Böhmen *n.*

Boi·se ['bɔisi] *Hauptstadt von Idaho (U.S.A.).*

Bol·eyn ['bulin]: Anne ⁓ *Mutter Elizabeths I.*

Bo·liv·i·a [bə'liviə] Bolivien *n.*

Bom·bay [bɔm'bei] *Hafenstadt in Indien.*

Bonn [bɔn] *Hauptstadt der Bundesrepublik Deutschland.*

Bos·ton ['bɔstən] *Hauptstadt von Massachusetts (U.S.A.).*

Bourne·mouth ['bɔ:nməθ] *Badeort in England.*

Brad·ford ['brædfəd] *Industriestadt in England.*

Bra·zil [brə'zil] Brasilien *n.*

Breck·nock(·shire) ['breknɔk(ʃiə)] *Grafschaft in Wales.*

Bridg·et ['bridʒit] Brigitte *f.*

Brigh·ton ['braitn] *Badeort in England.* [*land.*⧵

Bris·tol ['bristl] *Hafenstadt in England.*⧵

Bri·tan·ni·a [bri'tænjə] Großbritannien *n.* [*nist.*⧵

Brit·ten ['britn] *englischer Komponist.*⧵

Broad·way ['brɔ:dwei] *Straße in New York (U.S.A.).*

Bron·të ['brɔnti] *Name dreier englischer Autorinnen.*

Brook·lyn ['bruklin] *Stadtteil von New York (U.S.A.).*

Bruges [bru:ʒ] Brügge *n.*

Bruns·wick [ˈbrʌnzwik] Braun-
schweig *n.*

Brus·sels [ˈbrʌslz] Brüssel *n.*

Bu·cha·rest [bjuːkəˈrest] Bukarest *n.*

Buck [bʌk] *amerikanische Autorin.*

Buck·ing·ham [ˈbʌkiŋəm] *Grafschaft in England;* ⁓ *Palace Königsschloß in London;* **Buck·ing·ham-
shire** [ˈ⁓ʃiə] *s.* Buckingham.

Bu·da·pest [ˈbjuːdəˈpest] Budapest
n.

Bud·dha [ˈbudə] Buddha *m.*

Bul·gar·i·a [bʌlˈgɛəriə] Bulgarien *n.*

Bur·ma [ˈbɜːmə] Birma *n.*

Burns [bɜːnz] *schottischer Dichter.*

By·ron [ˈbaiərən] *englischer Dichter.*

C

Caer·nar·von(·shire) [kəˈnɑːvən
(-ʃiə)] *Grafschaft in Wales.*

Cae·sar [ˈsiːzə] (*Julius*) Cäsar *m.*

Cai·ro [ˈkaiərəu] Kairo *n.*

Cal·cut·ta [kælˈkʌtə] Kalkutta *n.*

Cal·i·for·nia [kæliˈfɔːnjə] Kalifornien *n* (*Staat der U.S.A.*).

Cam·bridge [ˈkeimbridʒ] *englische
Universitätsstadt; Stadt in U.S.A.,
Sitz der Harvard-Universität;* **Cam-
bridge·shire** [ˈ⁓ʃiə] *Grafschaft in
England.*

Can·a·da [ˈkænədə] Kanada *n.*

Ca·nar·y Is·lands [kəˈnɛəriˈailəndz]
pl. die Kanarischen Inseln.

Can·ber·ra [ˈkænbərə] *Hauptstadt
von Australien.*

Can·ter·bur·y [ˈkæntəbəri] *Stadt in
England.*

Cape·town [ˈkeiptaun] Kapstadt *n.*

Ca·pote [kəˈpəuti] *amerikanischer
Autor.*

Car·diff [ˈkɑːdif] *Hauptstadt von
Wales.*

Car·di·gan(·shire) [ˈkɑːdigən(ʃiə)]
Grafschaft in Wales.

Ca·rin·thi·a [kəˈrinθiə] Kärnten *n.*

Car·lyle [kɑːˈlail] *englischer Autor.*

Car·mar·then(·shire) [kəˈmɑːðən
(-ʃiə)] *Grafschaft in Wales.*

Car·ne·gie [kɑːˈnegi] *amerikanischer Industrieller.*

Car·o·li·na [kærəˈlainə]: *North* ⁓
Nordkarolina *n* (*Staat der U.S.A.*);
South ⁓ Südkarolina *n* (*Staat der
U.S.A.*).

Car·o·line [ˈkærəlain] Karoline *f.*

Car·rie [ˈkæri] *Kurzform von Caro-
line.*

Cath·er·ine [ˈkæθərin] Katharina *f.*

Ce·cil [ˈsesl; ˈsisl] *männlicher Vorname.*

Ce·cil·ia [siˈsiljə], **Cec·i·ly** [ˈsisili;
ˈsesili] Cäcilie *f.*

Cey·lon [siˈlɔn] Ceylon *n.*

Cham·ber·lain [ˈtʃeimbəlin] *Name
mehrerer britischer Staatsmänner.*

Char·ing Cross [ˈtʃæriŋˈkrɔs] *Stadtteil von London.*

Char·le·magne [ˈʃɑːləˈmein] Karl
der Große.

Charles [tʃɑːlz] Karl *m.*

Charles·ton [ˈtʃɑːlstən] *Hauptstadt
von West Virginia (U.S.A.).*

Char·lotte [ˈʃɑːlət] Charlotte *f.*

Chau·cer [ˈtʃɔːsə] *englischer Dichter.*

Chel·sea [ˈtʃelsi] *Stadtteil von London.* [*England.*]

Chesh·ire [ˈtʃeʃə] *Grafschaft in*

Ches·ter·field [ˈtʃestəfiːld] *Industriestadt in England.*

Chev·i·ot Hills [ˈtʃeviətˈhilz] *pl.
Grenzgebirge zwischen England u.
Schottland.*

Chi·ca·go [ʃiˈkɑːgəu; *Am. a.* ʃiˈkɔː-
gəu] *Industriestadt in U.S.A.*

Chil·e, Chil·i [ˈtʃili] Chile *n.*

Chi·na [ˈtʃainə] China *n.*

Chris·ti·na [krisˈtiːnə] Christine *f.*

Chris·to·pher [ˈkristəfə] Christoph
m.

Chrys·ler [ˈkraizlə] *amerikanischer
Industrieller.*

Church·ill [ˈtʃɜːtʃil] *britischer Staatsmann.*

Cin·cin·nat·i [sinsiˈnæti] *Stadt in
U.S.A.*

Cis·sie [ˈsisi] *Kurzform von Cecilia.*

Clar·a [ˈklɛərə], **Clare** [klɛə] Kla-
ra *f.*

Clar·en·don [ˈklærəndən] *Name
mehrerer britischer Staatsmänner.*

Cle·o·pat·ra [kliəˈpætrə] Kleopa-
tra *f.*

Cleve·land [ˈkliːvlənd] *Industrie- u.
Hafenstadt in U.S.A.*

Clive [klaiv] *Begründer der britischen
Macht in Indien.*

Clyde [klaid] *Fluß in Schottland.*

Cole·ridge [ˈkəulridʒ] *englischer
Dichter.*

Co·logne [kəˈləun] Köln *n.*

Col·o·ra·do [kɔləˈrɑːdəu] *Name
zweier Flüsse u. Staat der U.S.A.*

Co·lum·bi·a [kəˈlʌmbiə] *Fluß in
U.S.A.; Bundesdistrikt der U.S.A.;
Hauptstadt von Südkarolina
(U.S.A.).*

Con·cord [ˈkɔŋkɔːd] *Hauptstadt von New Hampshire* (*U.S.A.*).

Con·naught [ˈkɔnɔːt] *Provinz in Irland.*

Con·nect·i·cut [kəˈnetikət] *Fluß in U.S.A.; Staat der U.S.A.*

Con·stance [ˈkɔnstəns] Konstanze *f;* Konstanz *n; Lake of* ~ Bodensee *m.*

Coo·per [ˈkuːpə] *amerikanischer Autor.*

Co·pen·ha·gen [kəupnˈheigən] Kopenhagen *n.*

Cor·dil·le·ras [kɔːdiˈljeərəz] *pl. die* Kordilleren.

Cor·ne·lia [kɔːˈniːljə] Kornelia *f.*

Corn·wall [ˈkɔːnwəl] *Grafschaft in England.*

Cov·ent Gar·den [ˈkɔvəntˈgɑːdn] *die Londoner Oper.*

Cov·en·try [ˈkɔvəntri] *Industriestadt in England.*

Cri·me·a [kraiˈmiə] *die Krim.*

Crom·well [ˈkrɔmwəl] *englischer Staatsmann.*

Croy·don [ˈkrɔidn] *früherer Flughafen von London.*

Cu·ba [ˈkjuːbə] Kuba *n.*

Cum·ber·land [ˈkʌmbələnd] *Grafschaft in England.*

Cy·prus [ˈsaiprəs] Zypern *n.*

Czech·o·slo·va·ki·a [ˈtʃekəuslɔuˈvækiə] *die Tschechoslowakei.*

D

Da·ko·ta [dəˈkəutə]: *North* ~ Norddakota *n* (*Staat der U.S.A.*); *South* ~ Süddakota *n* (*Staat der U.S.A.*).

Dan·iel [ˈdænjəl] Daniel *m.*

Dan·ube [ˈdænjuːb] *die Donau.*

Dar·da·nelles [dɑːdəˈnelz] *pl. die* Dardanellen.

Dar·jee·ling [dɑːˈdʒiːliŋ] *Stadt in Indien.*

Dart·moor [ˈdɑːtmuə] *Bergmassiv in England.*

Dar·win [ˈdɑːwin] *englischer Naturforscher.*

Da·vid [ˈdeivid] David *m.*

Dee [diː] *Fluß in England.*

De·foe [diˈfəu] *englischer Autor.*

Del·a·ware [ˈdeləwɛə] *Fluß in U.S.A.; Staat der U.S.A.*

Den·bigh(·shire) [ˈdenbi(ʃiə)] *Grafschaft in Wales.*

Den·mark [ˈdenmɑːk] Dänemark *n.*

Den·ver [ˈdenvə] *Hauptstadt von Colorado* (*U.S.A.*).

Der·by(·shire) [ˈdɑːbi(ʃə)] *Grafschaft in England.*

Des Moines [diˈmɔin] *Hauptstadt von Iowa* (*U.S.A.*).

De·troit [dəˈtrɔit] *Industriestadt in U.S.A.*

Dev·on(·shire) [ˈdevn(ʃiə)] *Grafschaft in England.*

Dew·ey [ˈdjuːi] *amerikanischer Philosoph.*

Dick [dik] *Kurzform von Richard.*

Dick·ens [ˈdikinz] *englischer Autor.*

Dis·rae·li [disˈreili] *britischer Staatsmann.*

Dol·ly [ˈdɔli] *Kurzform von Dorothy.*

Don·ald [ˈdɔnld] *männlicher Vorname.*

Don Quix·ote [dɔnˈkwiksət] Don Quijote *m.*

Dor·o·the·a [dɔrəˈθiə], **Dor·o·thy** [ˈdɔrəθi] Dorothea *f.*

Dor·set(·shire) [ˈdɔːsit(ʃiə)] *Grafschaft in England.*

Dos Pas·sos [dəsˈpæsəs] *amerikanischer Autor.*

Doug·las [ˈdʌgləs] *schottisches Adelsgeschlecht.*

Do·ver [ˈdəuvə] *Hafenstadt in England; Hauptstadt von Delaware* (*U.S.A.*).

Down·ing Street [ˈdauniŋˈstriːt] *Straße in London mit der Amtswohnung des Prime Ministers.*

Drei·ser [ˈdraisə] *amerikanischer Autor.*

Dry·den [ˈdraidn] *englischer Dichter.*

Dub·lin [ˈdʌblin] *Hauptstadt der Republik Irland.*

Dun·kirk [dʌnˈkəːk] Dünkirchen *n.*

Dur·ham [ˈdʌrəm] *Grafschaft in England.*

E

Ed·die [ˈedi] *Kurzform von Edward.*

E·den [ˈiːdn] Eden *n, das Paradies.*

Ed·in·burgh [ˈedinbərə] Edinburg *n.*

Ed·i·son [ˈedisn] *amerikanischer Erfinder.*

Ed·ward [ˈedwəd] Eduard *m.*

E·gypt [ˈiːdʒipt] Ägypten *n.*

Ei·leen [ˈailiːn] *weiblicher Vorname.*

Ei·re [ˈɛərə] *Name der Republik Irland.*

Ei·sen·how·er [ˈaizənhauə] *34. Präsident der U.S.A.*

El·ea·nor [ˈelinə] Eleonore *f.*

E·li·as [i'laiəs] Elias *m.*
El·i·nor ['elinə] Eleonore *f.*
El·i·ot ['eljət] *englische Autorin; englischer Dichter.*
E·liz·a·beth [i'lizəbəθ] Elisabeth *f.*
Em·er·son ['eməsn] *amerikanischer Philosoph:*
Em·i·ly ['emili] Emilie *f.*
Eng·land ['iŋglənd] England *n.*
E·noch ['i:nɔk] *männlicher Vorname.*
Ep·som ['epsəm] *Stadt in England mit Pferderennplatz.*
E·rie ['iəri]: *Lake* ～ Eriesee *m (e-r der fünf Großen Seen Nordamerikas).*
Er·nest ['ə:nist] Ernst *m.*
Es·sex ['esiks] *Grafschaft in England.*
Eth·el ['eθəl] *weiblicher Vorname.*
E·thi·o·pi·a [i:θi'əupjə] Äthiopien *n.*
E·ton ['i:tn] *berühmte Public School.*
Eu·gene, [ju:'ʒein; 'ju:dʒi:n] Eugen *m.*
Eu·ge·ni·a [ju:'dʒi:njə] Eugenie *f.*
Eu·rope ['juərəp] Europa *n.*
Eus·tace ['ju:stəs] *männlicher Vorname.*
Ev·ans ['evənz] *englischer Familienname.*
Eve [i:v] Eva *f.*

F

Falk·land Is·lands ['fɔ:lklənd'ailəndz] *pl. die Falklandinseln.*
Faulk·ner ['fɔ:knə] *amerikanischer Autor.*
Fawkes [fɔ:ks] *Haupt der Pulververschwörung (1605).*
Fe·li·ci·a [fi'lisiə] *weiblicher Vorname.*
Fe·lix ['filiks] Felix *m.*
Fin·land ['finlənd] Finnland *n.*
Flint·shire ['flintʃiə] *Grafschaft in Wales.*
Flor·ence ['flɔrəns] Florenz *n; weiblicher Vorname.*
Flor·i·da ['flɔridə] *Staat der U.S.A.*
Flush·ing ['flʌʃiŋ] Vlissingen *n.*
Folke·stone ['fəukstən] *Seebad in England.*
Ford [fɔ:d] *amerikanischer Industrieller.*
France [frɑ:ns] Frankreich *n.*
Fran·ces ['frɑ:nsis] Franziska *f.*
Fran·cis [～] Franz *m.*
Frank·fort ['fræŋkfət] *Hauptstadt von Kentucky (U.S.A.).*
Frank·lin ['fræŋklin] *amerikanischer Staatsmann und Physiker.*

Fred(·dy) ['fred(i)] *Kurzform von Alfred, Frederic(k).*
Fred·er·ic(k) ['fredrik] Friedrich *m.*
Fry [frai] *englischer Dramatiker.*
Ful·ton ['fultən] *amerikanischer Erfinder.*

G

Gains·bor·ough ['geinzbərə] *englischer Maler.*
Gals·wor·thy ['gɔ:lzwə:ði] *englischer Autor.*
Gal·ves·ton ['gælvistən] *Hafenstadt in U.S.A.*
Gan·ges ['gændʒi:z] *der Ganges.*
Ge·ne·va [dʒi'ni:və] Genf *n; Lake of* ～ Genfer See *m.*
Geof·frey ['dʒefri] Gottfried *m.*
George [dʒɔ:dʒ] Georg *m.*
Geor·gia ['dʒɔ:dʒə] *Staat der U.S.A.*
Ger·ald ['dʒerəld] Gerhard *m.*
Ger·al·dine ['dʒerəldi:n; '～dain] *weiblicher Vorname.*
Ger·ma·ny ['dʒə:məni] Deutschland *n.*
Gersh·win ['gə:ʃwin] *amerikanischer Komponist.*
Ger·trude ['gə:tru:d] Gertrud *f.*
Get·tys·burg ['getizbə:g] *Stadt in U.S.A.*
Gha·na ['gɑ:nə] *Staat in Afrika.*
Ghent [gent] Gent *n.*
Gi·bral·tar [dʒi'brɔ:ltə] Gibraltar *n.*
Giles [dʒailz] Julius *m.*
Gill [dʒil] Julie *f.*
Glad·stone ['glædstən] *britischer Staatsmann.*
Gla·mor·gan(·shire) [glə'mɔ:gən (-ʃiə)] *Grafschaft in Wales.*
Glas·gow ['glɑ:sgəu] *Hafenstadt in Schottland.*
Glouces·ter ['glɔstə] *Stadt in England; a.* **Glouces·ter·shire** ['～ʃiə] *Grafschaft in England.*
Gold·smith ['gəuldsmiθ] *englischer Autor.*
Gor·don ['gɔ:dn] *englischer Familienname.*
Gra·ham ['greiəm] *englischer Familienname; männlicher Vorname.*
Great Brit·ain ['greit'britn] *Großbritannien n.*
Great Di·vide ['greit di'vaid] *die Rocky Mountains (U.S.A.).*
Greece [gri:s] Griechenland *n.*
Greene [gri:n] *englischer Autor.*
Green·land ['gri:nlənd] Grönland *n.*

Green·wich ['grinidʒ] *Vorort von London;* ~ *Village Künstlerviertel von New York (U.S.A.).*

Greg·o·ry ['gregəri] Gregor m.

Gri·sons ['gri:zɔ̃:ŋ] Graubünden n.

Gros·ve·nor ['grəuvnə] *Straße u. Platz in London.*

Guern·sey ['gə:nzi] *e-e der Kanalinseln.*

Guin·ness ['ginis; gi'nes] *englischer Familienname.*

Guy [gai] Guido m.

Gwen·do·len, Gwen·do·lyn ['gwendəlin] *weiblicher Vorname.*

H

Hague [heig]: *the* ~ Den Haag.

Hai·ti ['heiti] Haiti n.

Hal·i·fax ['hælifæks] *Name zweier Städte in England u. Kanada.*

Ham·il·ton ['hæmiltən] *englischer Familienname.*

Hamp·shire ['hæmpʃiə] *Grafschaft in England.*

Hamp·stead ['hæmpstid] *Stadtteil von London.*

Han·o·ver ['hænəuvə] Hannover n.

Har·ri·et ['hæriət] Henriette f.

Har·ris·burg ['hærisbə:g] *Hauptstadt von Pennsylvanien (U.S.A.).*

Har·row ['hærəu] *berühmte Public School.*

Har·ry ['hæri] *Kurzform von Henry.*

Har·vard U·ni·ver·si·ty ['hɑ:vədju:ni'və:siti] *amerikanische Universität.* [England.]

Har·wich ['hæridʒ] *Hafenstadt in*

Has·tings ['heistiŋz] *Stadt in England; britischer Staatsmann.*

Ha·wai·i [hə'waii:] *pl. Staat der U.S.A.*

Heb·ri·des ['hebridi:z] *pl. die Hebriden.*

Hel·en ['helin] Helene f.

Hel·i·go·land ['heligəulænd] Helgoland n.

Hel·sin·ki ['helsiŋki] Helsinki n.

Hem·ing·way ['hemiŋwei] *amerikanischer Autor.*

Hen·ley ['henli] *Stadt in England mit berühmter Regattastrecke.*

Hen·ry ['henri] Heinrich m.

Her·e·ford(·shire) ['herifəd(ʃiə)] *Grafschaft in England.*

Hert·ford(·shire) ['hɑ:fəd(ʃiə)] *Grafschaft in England.*

Hi·ma·la·ya [himə'leiə] *der Himalaya.*

Hin·du·stan [hindu'stɑ:n] Hindustan n.

Ho·garth ['həugɑ:θ] *englischer Maler.*

Hol·born ['həubən] *Stadtteil von London.*

Hol·land ['hɔlənd] Holland n.

Hol·ly·wood ['hɔliwud] *Filmstadt in Kalifornien (U.S.A.).*

Home [hju:m]: *Sir Alec Douglas-*~ *britischer Politiker.*

Ho·mer ['həumə] Homer m.

Hon·o·lu·lu [hɔnə'lu:lu:] *Hauptstadt von Hawaii (U.S.A.).* [U.S.A.]

Hoo·ver ['hu:və] 31. *Präsident der*

Hous·ton ['hju:stən] *Stadt in U.S.A.*

Hud·son ['hʌdsn] *Fluß in U.S.A., an seiner Mündung New York; englischer Familienname.*

Hugh [hju:] Hugo m.

Hull [hʌl] *Hafenstadt in England.*

Hume [hju:m] *englischer Philosoph.*

Hun·ga·ry ['hʌŋgəri] Ungarn n.

Hun·ting·don(·shire) ['hʌntiŋdən (-ʃiə)] *Grafschaft in England.*

Hu·ron ['hjuərən]: *Lake* ~ Huronsee m *(e-r der fünf Großen Seen Nordamerikas).*

Hux·ley ['hʌksli] *englischer Biologe; englischer Autor.* [London.]

Hyde Park ['haid'pɑ:k] *Park in*

I

Ice·land ['aislənd] Island n.

I·da·ho ['aidəhəu] *Staat der U.S.A.*

I·dle·wild ['aidlwaild] *ehemaliger Name von Kennedy Airport.*

Il·li·nois [ili'nɔi] *Fluß in U.S.A.; Staat der U.S.A.*

In·di·a ['indjə] Indien n.

In·di·an·a [indi'ænə] *Staat der U.S.A.*

In·di·an O·cean ['indjən'əuʃən] *der Indische Ozean.*

In·dies ['indiz] *pl.: the (East, West)* ~ (Ost-, West)Indien n.

In·dus ['indəs] *der Indus.*

I·o·wa ['aiəuə] *Staat der U.S.A.*

I·rak, I·raq [i'rɑ:k] der Irak.

I·ran [i'rɑ:n] der Iran.

Ire·land ['aiələnd] Irland n.

I·rene [ai'ri:ni; 'airi:n] Irene f.

Ir·ving ['ə:viŋ] *amerikanischer Autor.*

I·saac ['aizək] Isaak m.

Is·a·bel ['izəbel] Isabella f.

Is·ra·el ['izreiəl] Israel n.

It·a·ly ['itəli] Italien n.

J

Jack [dʒæk] Hans *m.*
James [dʒeimz] Jakob *m.*
Jane [dʒein] Johanna *f.*
Ja·net ['dʒænit] Johanna *f.*
Ja·pan [dʒə'pæn] Japan *n.*
Jean [dʒiːn] Johanna *f.*
Jef·fer·son ['dʒefəsn] 3. *Präsident der U.S.A., Verfasser der Unabhängigkeitserklärung von 1776;* ∼ *City Hauptstadt von Missouri (U.S.A.).*
Jen·ny ['dʒeni] Hanne *f.*
Jer·e·my ['dʒerimi] *männlicher Vorname.*
Jer·sey ['dʒəːzi] *e-e der Kanalinseln;* ∼ *City Stadt in U.S.A.*
Je·ru·sa·lem [dʒə'ruːsələm] Jerusalem *n.*
Je·sus (Christ) ['dʒiːzəs('kraist)] Jesus (Christus) *m.*
Jill [dʒil] Julia *f.*
Jim(·my) ['dʒim(i)] *Kurzform von James.*
Joan [dʒəun] Johanna *f.*
Jo(e) [dʒəu] *Kurzform von Joseph.*
John [dʒɔn] Johann(es) *m.*
John·ny ['dʒɔni] Hans *m.*
John·son ['dʒɔnsn] *englischer Autor;* 36. *Präsident der U.S.A.*
Jo·nah ['dʒəunə] *männlicher Vorname.*
Jon·a·than ['dʒɔnəθən] *männlicher Vorname.*
Jon·son ['dʒɔnsn] *englischer Dramatiker.*
Jor·dan ['dʒɔːdn] Jordanien *n.*
Jo·seph ['dʒəuzif] Joseph *m.*
Josh·u·a ['dʒɔʃwə] *männlicher Vorname.*
Joyce [dʒɔis] *englischer Autor.*
Jul·ia ['dʒuːljə], **Ju·li·et** ['∼jət] Julia *f.*
Jul·ius ['dʒuːljəs] Julius *m.*
Ju·neau ['dʒuːnəu] *Hauptstadt von Alaska (U.S.A.).*

K

Kan·sas ['kænzəs] *Fluß in U.S.A.; Staat der U.S.A.*
Ka·ra·chi [kə'rɑːtʃi] *Stadt in Pakistan.*
Kash·mir [kæʃ'miə] Kaschmir *n.*
Kate [keit] *Kurzform von Catherine, Katharine, Katherine, Kathleen.*
Kath·a·rine, Kath·er·ine ['kæθərin] Katharina *f.*

Kath·leen ['kæθliːn] Katharina *f.*
Keats [kiːts] *englischer Dichter.*
Ken·ne·dy ['kenidi] 35. *Präsident der U.S.A.;* Cape ∼ *Landspitze in Florida (U.S.A.), Raketenversuchsgelände;* ∼ *Airport Flughafen von New York (U.S.A.).*
Ken·sing·ton ['kenziŋtən] *Stadtteil von London.*
Kent [kent] *Grafschaft in England.*
Ken·tuck·y [ken'tʌki] *Fluß in U.S.A.; Staat der U.S.A.*
Ken·ya ['kenjə] *Staat in Afrika.*
Kip·ling ['kipliŋ] *englischer Dichter.*
Kit·ty ['kiti] *Kurzform von Catherine.*
Klon·dike ['klɔndaik] *Fluß u. Landschaft in Kanada u. Alaska.*
Ko·re·a [kə'riə] Korea *n.*
Krem·lin ['kremlin] *der* Kreml.
Ku·weit [ku'weit] Kuwait *n.*

L

Lab·ra·dor ['læbrədɔː] *Halbinsel Nordamerikas.*
Lan·ca·shire ['læŋkəʃiə] *Grafschaft in England.*
Lan·cas·ter ['læŋkəstə] *Name zweier Städte in England u. U.S.A.; s.* Lancashire.
Law·rence ['lɔrəns] Lorenz *m; Name zweier englischer Autoren.*
Leb·a·non ['lebənən] *der* Libanon.
Leeds [liːdz] *Industriestadt in England.*
Leg·horn ['leg'hɔːn] Livorno *n.*
Leices·ter ['lestə] *Stadt in England;* a. **Leices·ter·shire** ['∼ʃiə] *Grafschaft in England.*
Le·man ['lemən]: Lake ∼ *Genfer See m.*
Leon·ard ['lenəd] Leonhard *m.*
Les·lie ['lezli] *männlicher Vorname.*
Lew·is ['luːis] Ludwig *m; englischer Dichter; amerikanischer Autor.*
Lin·coln ['liŋkən] 16. *Präsident der U.S.A.; Hauptstadt von Nebraska (U.S.A.); Stadt in England;* a. **Lin·coln·shire** ['∼ʃiə] *Grafschaft in England.*
Li·o·nel ['laiənl] *männlicher Vorname.*
Lis·bon ['lizbən] Lissabon *n.*
Lit·tle Rock ['litl'rɔk] *Hauptstadt von Arkansas (U.S.A.).*
Liv·er·pool ['livəpuːl] *Industrie- u. Hafenstadt in England.*

Liz·zie ['lizi] *Kurzform von Eliza-beth.*

Lloyd [lɔid] *männlicher Vorname; englischer Familienname.*

Locke [lɔk] *englischer Philosoph.*

Lon·don ['lʌndən] London *n.*

Lor·raine [lɔ'rein] Lothringen *n.*

Los An·ge·les [lɔs'ændʒili:z; *Am. a.* ˏ'æŋgələs] *Hafenstadt in Kalifornien (U.S.A.).*

Lou·i·sa [lu:'i:zə] Luise *f.*

Lou·i·si·an·a [lu:i:zi'ænə] *Staat der U.S.A.*

Lu·cerne [lu:'sə:n] *Lake of* ⁓ Vierwaldstätter See *m.* [*name.*⟩

Lu·cius ['lu:sjəs] *männlicher Vor-*⟩

Lu·cy ['lu:si] Lucie *f.*

Luke [lu:k] Lukas *m.*

Lux·em·b(o)urg ['lʌksəmbə:g] Luxemburg *n.*

Lyd·i·a ['lidiə] Lydia *f.*

M

Mab [mæb] *Feenkönigin.*

Ma·bel ['meibəl] *weiblicher Vorname.*

Ma·cau·lay [mə'kɔ:li] *englischer Hi-*⟩ *storiker.* [*Kanada.*⟩

Mac·ken·zie [mə'kenzi] *Fluß in*⟩

Mac·leod [mə'klaud] *britischer Politiker.*

Ma·dei·ra [mə'diərə] Madeira *n.*

Madge [mædʒ] Margot *f,* Marg(r)it *f.*

Mad·i·son ['mædisn] *4. Präsident der U.S.A.; Hauptstadt von Wisconsin (U.S.A.).*

Ma·dras [mə'drɑ:s] *Hafenstadt in Indien.*

Ma·drid [mə'drid] Madrid *n.*

Mag·da·len ['mægdəlin] Magdalene *f.* [g(r)it *f.*⟩

Mag·gie ['mægi] Margot *f,* Mar-⟩

Ma·hom·et [mə'hɔmit] Mohammed⟩

Maine [mein] *Staat der U.S.A.* [*m.*⟩

Mal·ta ['mɔ:ltə] Malta *n.*

Man·ches·ter ['mæntʃistə] *Industriestadt in England.*

Man·hat·tan [mæn'hætən] *Stadtteil von New York (U.S.A.).*

Man·i·to·ba [mæni'təubə] *Provinz in Kanada.*

Mar·ga·ret ['mɑ:gərit] Margarete *f.*

Mark [mɑ:k] Markus *m.*

Marl·bor·ough ['mɔ:lbərə] *englischer General.*

Mar·lowe ['mɑ:ləu] *englischer Dramatiker.*

Mar·tha ['mɑ:θə] Martha *f.*

Mar·y ['meəri] Maria *f.*

Mar·y·land ['meərilænd; *Am.* 'merilənd] *Staat der U.S.A.*

Mas·sa·chu·setts [mæsə'tʃu:sits] *Staat der U.S.A.*

Ma·t(h)il·da [mə'tildə] Mathilde *f.*

Ma(t)·thew ['mæθju:; 'meiθju:] Matthäus *m.*

Maud [mɔ:d] *Kurzform von Magdalene,* Mat(h)ilda.

Maugham [mɔ:m] *englischer Autor.*

Mau·rice ['mɔris] Moritz *m.*

May [mei] *Kurzform von Mary.*

Mel·bourne ['melbən] *Hafenstadt in Australien.* [*Autor.*⟩

Mel·ville ['melvil] *amerikanischer*⟩

Mer·i·on·eth(·shire) [meri'ɔniθ (-ʃiə)] *Grafschaft in Wales.*

Mex·i·co ['meksikəu] Mexiko *n.*

Mi·am·i [mai'æmi] *Badeort in Florida (U.S.A.).*

Mi·chael ['maikl] Michael *m.*

Mich·i·gan ['miʃigən] *Staat der U.S.A.; Lake* ⁓ Michigansee *m* (e-r *der fünf Großen Seen Nordamerikas).*

Mid·dle·sex ['midlseks] *Grafschaft in England.*

Mid·west ['midwest] *der* Mittlere Westen·(U.S.A.).

Mil·dred ['mildrid] *weiblicher Vorname.*

Mil·ton ['miltən] *englischer Dichter.*

Mil·wau·kee [mil'wɔ:ki:] *Stadt in U.S.A.*

Min·ne·ap·o·lis [mini'æpəlis] *Stadt in U.S.A.* [*U.S.A.*⟩

Min·ne·so·ta [mini'səutə] *Staat der*⟩

Mis·sis·sip·pi [misi'sipi] *Fluß in U.S.A.; Staat der U.S.A.*

Mis·sou·ri [mi'zuəri] *Fluß in U.S.A.; Staat der U.S.A.*

Mo·ham·med [məu'hæmed] Mohammed *m.*

Moll [mɔl] *Kurzform von Mary.*

Mon·a·co ['mɔnəkəu] Monaco *n.*

Mon·mouth(·shire) ['mɔnməθ(ʃiə)] *Grafschaft in England.*

Mon·roe [mən'rəu] *5. Präsident der U.S.A.*

Mon·tan·a [mɔn'tænə] *Staat der U.S.A.*

Mont·gom·er·y [mənt'gʌməri] *britischer Feldmarschall; a.* **Mont·gom·er·y·shire** [⁓ʃiə] *Grafschaft in Wales.*

Mont·re·al [mɔntri'ɔ:l] *Stadt in Kanada.*

Moore [muə] *englischer Bildhauer.*

Mos·cow ['mɔskəu] Moskau n.
Mo·selle [məu'zel] die Mosel.
Mu·nich ['mju:nik] München n.
Mur·ray ['mʌri] Fluß in Australien.

N

Nan·cy ['nænsi] Ännchen n.
Na·ples ['neiplz] Neapel n.
Na·tal [nə'tæl] Natal n.
Ne·bras·ka [ni'bræskə] Staat der U.S.A.
Nell, Nel·ly ['nel(i)] Kurzform von Eleanor, Helen.
Nel·son ['nelsn] britischer Admiral.
Ne·pal [ni'pɔ:l] Nepal n.
Neth·er·lands ['neðələndz] pl. die Niederlande. [U.S.A.]
Ne·vad·a [ne'va:də] Staat der]
New Bruns·wick [nju:'brʌnzwik] Provinz in Kanada.
New·cas·tle ['nju:ka:sl] Hafenstadt in England.
New Del·hi [nju:'deli] Hauptstadt von Indien.
New Eng·land [nju:'iŋglənd] Neuengland n.
New·found·land [nju:fənd'lænd] Neufundland n.
New Hamp·shire [nju:'hæmpʃiə] Staat der U.S.A.
New Jer·sey [nju:'dʒə:zi] Staat der U.S.A.
New Mex·i·co [nju:'meksikəu] Neumexiko n (Staat der U.S.A.).
New Or·le·ans [nju:'ɔ:liənz] Hafenstadt in U.S.A.
New·ton ['nju:tn] englischer Physiker.
New York ['nju:'jɔ:k] Stadt in U.S.A.; Staat der U.S.A.
New Zea·land [nju:'zi:lənd] Neuseeland n.
Ni·ag·a·ra [nai'ægərə] der Niagara (Fluß zwischen Erie- u. Ontariosee).
Nich·o·las ['nikələs] Nikolaus m.
Ni·ge·ri·a [nai'dʒiəriə] Staat in Afrika.
Nile [nail] der Nil.
Nix·on ['niksn] 37. Präsident der U.S.A.
Nor·folk ['nɔ:fək] Grafschaft in England; Hafenstadt in U.S.A.
North·amp·ton [nɔ:'θæmptən] Stadt in England; a. **North·amp·ton·shire** [ˌ-ʃiə] Grafschaft in England.
North Sea ['nɔ:θ'si:] die Nordsee.

North·um·ber·land [nɔ:'θʌmbələnd] Grafschaft in England.
Nor·way ['nɔ:wei] Norwegen n.
Not·ting·ham ['nɔtiŋəm] Stadt in England; a. **Not·ting·ham·shire** ['ˌ-ʃiə] Grafschaft in England.
No·va Sco·tia ['nəuvə'skəuʃə] Provinz in Kanada.
Nu·rem·berg ['njuərəmbə:g] Nürnberg n.

O

O·ce·an·i·a [əuʃi'einjə] Ozeanien n.
O·hi·o [əu'haiəu] Fluß in U.S.A.; Staat der U.S.A.
O·kla·ho·ma [əuklə'həumə] Staat der U.S.A.; ~ City Hauptstadt von Oklahoma (U.S.A.).
O·ma·ha ['əuməha:] Stadt in U.S.A.
O'Neill [əu'ni:l] amerikanischer Dramatiker.
On·tar·i·o [ɔn'tɛəriəu] Provinz in Kanada; Lake ~ Ontariosee m (e-r der fünf Großen Seen Nordamerikas).
Or·ange ['ɔrindʒ] der Oranje.
Or·e·gon ['ɔrigən] Staat der U.S.A.
Ork·ney Is·lands ['ɔ:kni'ailəndz] pl. die Orkneyinseln.
Or·well ['ɔ:wəl] englischer Autor.
Os·borne ['ɔzbən] englischer Dramatiker.
Os·lo ['ɔzləu] Oslo n.
Ost·end [ɔs'tend] Ostende n.
Ot·ta·wa ['ɔtəwə] Hauptstadt von Kanada.
Ox·ford ['ɔksfəd] englische Universitätsstadt; a. **Ox·ford·shire** ['ˌ-ʃiə] Grafschaft in England.
O·zark Moun·tains ['əuza:k'mauntinz] pl. Bergmassiv in U.S.A.

P

Pa·cif·ic [pə'sifik] der Pazifik.
Pak·i·stan [pa:kis'ta:n] Pakistan n.
Pall Mall ['pæl'mæl] Straße in London.
Palm Beach ['pa:m'bi:tʃ] Badeort in Florida (U.S.A.).
Palm·er·ston ['pa:məstən] britischer Staatsmann.
Pan·a·ma [pænə'ma:] Panama n.
Par·is ['pæris] Paris n.
Pa·tri·cia [pə'triʃə] weiblicher Vorname. [name.]
Pat·rick ['pætrik] männlicher Vor-]
Paul [pɔ:l] Paul m.
Pau·line [pɔ:'li:n; 'pɔ:li:n] Pauline f.

644

Pearl Har·bor [ˈpəːlˈhɑːbə] *Hafenstadt auf den Hawaiinseln (U.S.A.).*
Peel [piːl] *britischer Staatsmann.*
Pe·kin [ˈpiːkin], **Pe·king** [ˈpiːkiŋ] Peking *n.*
Peg(·gy) [ˈpeg(i)] Margot *f.*
Pem·broke(·shire) [ˈpembruk(ʃiə)] *Grafschaft in Wales.*
Penn·syl·va·nia [pensilˈveinjə] Pennsylvanien *n (Staat der U.S.A.).*
Per·cy [ˈpəːsi] *männlicher Vorname.*
Per·sia [ˈpəːʃə] Persien *n.*
Pe·ru [pəˈruː] Peru *n.*
Pe·ter [ˈpiːtə] Peter *m.*
Phil·a·del·phi·a [filəˈdelfjə] *Stadt in U.S.A.*
Phil·ip [ˈfilip] Philipp *m.*
Phil·ip·pines [ˈfilipiːnz] *pl. die Philippinen.*
Phoe·nix [ˈfiːniks] *Hauptstadt von Arizona (U.S.A.).*
Pic·ca·dil·ly [pikəˈdili] *Straße in London.*
Pin·ter [ˈpintə] *englischer Dramatiker.*
Pitts·burgh [ˈpitsbəːg] *Stadt in U.S.A.*
Pla·to [ˈpleitəu] Plato(n) *m.*
Plym·outh [ˈpliməθ] *Hafenstadt in England; Stadt in U.S.A.*
Poe [pəu] *amerikanischer Autor.*
Po·land [ˈpəulənd] Polen *n.*
Pope [pəup] *englischer Dichter.*
Port·land [ˈpɔːtlənd] *Name zweier Städte in U.S.A.*
Ports·mouth [ˈpɔːtsməθ] *Hafenstadt in England.*
Por·tu·gal [ˈpɔːtjugəl] Portugal *n.*
Po·to·mac [pəˈtəumək] *Fluß in U.S.A.*
Prague [prɑːg] Prag *n.*
Prus·sia [ˈprʌʃə] Preußen *n.*
Pul·itz·er [ˈpulitsə] *amerikanischer Journalist.*
Pun·jab [pʌnˈdʒɑːb] Pandschab *n.*
Pur·cell [ˈpəːsl] *englischer Komponist.*

Q

Que·bec [kwiˈbek] *Stadt u. Provinz in Kanada.*
Queens [kwiːnz] *Stadtteil von New York (U.S.A.).*

R

Ra·chel [ˈreitʃəl] Rachel *f.*
Rad·nor(·shire) [ˈrædnə(ʃiə)] *Grafschaft in Wales.*
Ra·leigh [ˈrɔːli; ˈrɑːli; ˈræli] *englischer Seefahrer;* [ˈrɔːli] *Hauptstadt von Nordkarolina (U.S.A.).*
Ralph [reif; rælf] Ralph *m.*
Rat·is·bon [ˈrætizbɔn] Regensburg *n.*
Ra·wal·pin·di [ˈrɔːlpindi] *Hauptstadt von Pakistan.*
Read·ing [ˈrediŋ] *Industriestadt in England; Stadt in U.S.A.*
Rea·gan [ˈreigən] *40. Präsident der U.S.A.*
Reg·i·nald [ˈredʒinld] Reinhold *m.*
Rey·kja·vik [ˈreikjəviːk] Reykjavik *n.*
Reyn·olds [ˈrenldz] *englischer Maler.*
Rhine [rain] *der Rhein.*
Rhode Is·land [rəudˈailənd] *Staat der U.S.A.*
Rhodes [rəudz] Rhodos *n.*
Rho·de·sia [rəuˈdiːzjə] Rhodesien *n.*
Rich·ard [ˈritʃəd] Richard *m*; ~ the Lionhearted Richard Löwenherz.
Rich·mond [ˈritʃmənd] *Hauptstadt von Virginia (U.S.A.); Stadtteil von London.*
Rob·ert [ˈrɔbət] Robert *m.*
Rob·in [ˈrɔbin] *Kurzform von Robert.*
Rock·e·fel·ler [ˈrɔkifelə] *amerikanischer Industrieller.*
Rock·y Moun·tains [ˈrɔkiˈmauntinz] *pl. Gebirge in U.S.A.*
Rog·er [ˈrɔdʒə; ˈrəudʒə] Rüdiger *m.*
Rome [rəum] Rom *n.*
Roo·se·velt [ˈrəuzəvelt] *Name zweier Präsidenten der U.S.A.*
Rug·by [ˈrʌgbi] *berühmte Public School.* [*n.*]
Ru·ma·ni·a [ruːˈmeinjə] Rumänien
Rus·sell [ˈrʌsl] *englischer Philosoph.*
Rus·sia [ˈrʌʃə] Rußland *n.*
Rut·land(·shire) [ˈrʌtlənd(ʃiə)] *Grafschaft in England.*

S

Sac·ra·men·to [sækrəˈmentəu] *Hauptstadt von Kalifornien (U.S.A.).*
Salis·bur·y [ˈsɔːlzbəri] *Stadt in England.*
Sal·ly [ˈsæli] *Kurzform von Sarah.*
Salt Lake Cit·y [ˈsɔːltˈleikˈsiti] *Hauptstadt von Utah (U.S.A.).*
Sam [sæm] *Kurzform von Samuel.*
Sam·u·el [ˈsæmjuəl] Samuel *m.*
San Fran·cis·co [sænfrənˈsiskəu] *Hafenstadt in U.S.A.*
Sar·a(h) [ˈsɛərə] Sarah *f.*

Sas·katch·e·wan [səs'kætʃiwər] *Provinz in Kanada.*

Sax·o·ny ['sæksni] Sachsen *n.*

Scan·di·na·vi·a [skændi'neivjə] Skandinavien *n.*

Sche·nec·ta·dy [ski'nektədi] *Stadt in U.S.A.*

Scot·land ['skɔtlənd] Schottland *n;* ~ *Yard Polizeipräsidium in London.*

Scott [skɔt] *englischer Autor; englischer Polarforscher.*

Se·at·tle [si'ætl] *Hafenstadt in U.S.A.*

Sev·ern ['sevən] *Fluß in England.*

Shake·speare ['ʃeikspiə] *englischer Dichter.*

Shaw [ʃɔ:] *englischer Dramatiker.*

Shef·field ['ʃefi:ld] *Industriestadt in England.*

Shel·ley ['ʃeli] *englischer Dichter.*

Shet·land Is·lands ['ʃetlənd'ailəndz] *pl. die* Shetlandinseln.

Shrop·shire ['ʃrɔpʃiə] *Grafschaft in England.*

Sib·yl ['sibil] Sibylle *f.*

Sic·i·ly ['sisili] Sizilien *n.*

Sid·ney ['sidni] *männlicher Vorname; englischer Familienname.*

Si·le·sia [sai'li:zjə] Schlesien *n.*

Sin·clair ['siŋkl(ɛ)ə] *männlicher Vorname; amerikanischer Autor.*

Sin·ga·pore [siŋgə'pɔ:] Singapur *n.*

Sing-Sing ['siŋsiŋ] *Staatsgefängnis von New York (U.S.A.).*

Snow·don ['snəudn] *Berg in Wales.*

So·fia ['səufjə] Sofia *n.*

Sol·o·mon ['sɔləmən] Salomo(n) *m.*

Som·er·set(·shire) ['sʌməsit(ʃiə)] *Grafschaft in England.*

So·phi·a [səu'faiə] Sophie *f.*

South·amp·ton [sauθ'æmptən] *Hafenstadt in England.*

South·wark ['sʌðək; 'sauθwək] *Stadtteil von London.*

Spain [spein] Spanien *n.*

Staf·ford(·shire) ['stæfəd(ʃiə)] *Grafschaft in England.*

Steele [sti:l] *englischer Autor.*

Stein·beck ['stainbek] *amerikanischer Autor.*

Ste·phen ['sti:vn] Stephan *m.*

Ste·ven·son ['sti:vnsn] *englischer Autor.*

St. Law·rence [snt'lɔ:rəns] *der* St.-Lorenz-Strom.

St. Lou·is [snt'lu:is] *Stadt in U.S.A.*

Stock·holm ['stɔkhəum] Stockholm *n.*

Strat·ford on A·von ['strætfədɔn-'eivən] *Geburtsort Shakespeares.*

Stu·art [stjuət] *schottisch-englisches Herrschergeschlecht.*

Styr·i·a ['stiriə] die Steiermark.

Su·dan [su:'dɑ:n] *der* Sudan.

Sue [sju:] *Kurzform von Susan.*

Su·ez ['su:iz] Sues *n.* [*land.*]

Suf·folk ['sʌfək] *Grafschaft in England.*

Su·pe·ri·or [sju:'piəriə]: *Lake* ~ Oberer See *m (e-r der fünf Großen Seen Nordamerikas).*

Sur·rey ['sʌri] *Grafschaft in England.*

Su·san ['su:zn] Susanne *f.*

Sus·que·han·na [sʌskwə'hænə] *Fluß in U.S.A.*

Sus·sex ['sʌsiks] *Grafschaft in England.* [*Wales.*]

Swan·sea ['swɔnzi] *Hafenstadt in Wales.*

Swe·den ['swi:dn] Schweden *n.*

Swift [swift] *englischer Autor.*

Swit·zer·land ['switsələnd] die Schweiz.

Syd·ney ['sidni] *Hafen- u. Industriestadt in Australien.*

Syr·i·a ['siriə] Syrien *n.*

T

Tal·la·has·see [tælə'hæsi] *Hauptstadt von Florida (U.S.A.).*

Ted(·dy) ['ted(i)] *Kurzform von Edward, Theodore.*

Ten·nes·see [tenə'si:] *Fluß in U.S.A.; Staat der U.S.A.*

Ten·ny·son ['tenisn] *englischer Dichter.*

Tex·as ['teksəs] *Staat der U.S.A.*

Thack·er·ay ['θækəri] *englischer Autor.*

Thames [temz] *die* Themse.

The·o·dore ['θiədɔ:] Theodor *m.*

The·re·sa [ti'ri:zə] Therese *f.*

Thom·as ['tɔməs] Thomas *m.*

Tho·reau ['θɔ:rəu] *amerikanischer Philosoph.* [*gen n.*]

Thu·rin·gi·a [θjuə'rindʒiə] Thürin-

Tim·o·thy ['timəθi] Timotheus *m.*

Ti·ra·na [ti'rɑ:nə] *Hauptstadt von Albanien.*

To·bi·as [tə'baiəs] Tobias *m.*

To·by ['təubi] *Kurzform von Tobias.*

Tom(·my) ['tɔm(i)] *Kurzform von Thomas.*

To·pe·ka [təu'pi:kə] *Hauptstadt von Kansas (U.S.A.).*

To·ron·to [tə'rɔntəu] *Stadt in Kanada.*

Toyn·bee ['tɔinbi] *englischer Historiker*.

Tra·fal·gar [trə'fælgə] *Vorgebirge bei Gibraltar*.

Trent [trent] *Fluß in England*.

Treves [tri:vz] *Trier n*.

Trol·lope ['trɔləp] *englischer Autor*.

Tru·man ['tru:mən] *33. Präsident der U.S.A.* [schergeschlecht.\

Tu·dor ['tju:də] *englisches Herr-\

Tur·key ['tə:ki] *die Türkei*.

Tur·ner ['tə:nə] *englischer Maler*.

Tus·ca·ny ['tʌskəni] *die Toskana*.

Twain [twein] *amerikanischer Autor*.

Ty·rol ['tirəl]: *the ~ Tirol n*.

U

Ul·ster ['ʌlstə] *Provinz in Irland*.

U·nit·ed States of A·mer·i·ca [ju:'naitid'steitsəvə'merikə] *die Vereinigten Staaten von Amerika*.

U·tah ['ju:tɑ:] *Staat der U.S.A.*

V

Val·en·tine ['vælənt(a)in] *Valentin m; Valentine f*.

Van·cou·ver [væn'ku:və] *Hafenstadt in Kanada*.

Vat·i·can ['vætikən] *der Vatikan*.

Vaughan Wil·liams ['vɔ:n'wiljəmz] *englischer Komponist*.

Ven·ice ['venis] *Venedig n*.

Ver·mont [və'mɔnt] *Staat der U.S.A.*

Vic·to·ri·a [vik'tɔ:riə] *Viktoria f*.

Vi·en·na [vi'enə] *Wien n*.

Vi·et·nam ['vjet'næm] *Vietnam n*.

Vir·gin·ia [və'dʒinjə] *Virginien n (Staat der U.S.A.); West ~ Staat der U.S.A.*

Vis·tu·la ['vistjulə] *die Weichsel*.

Vosges [vəuʒ] *pl. die Vogesen*.

W

Wales [weilz] *Wales n*.

Wal·lace ['wɔlis] *englischer Autor; amerikanischer Autor*.

Wall Street ['wɔ:l'stri:t] *Finanzzentrum in New York (U.S.A.)*.

War·saw ['wɔ:sɔ:] *Warschau n*.

War·wick(·shire) ['wɔrik(ʃiə)] *Grafschaft in England*.

Wash·ing·ton ['wɔʃiŋtən] *1. Präsident der U.S.A.; Staat der U.S.A.; Bundeshauptstadt der U.S.A.*

Wa·ter·loo [wɔ:tə'lu:] *Ort in Belgien*.

Watt [wɔt] *englischer Erfinder*.

Wedg·wood ['wedʒwud] *englischer Keramiker*.

Wel·ling·ton ['weliŋtən] *englischer Feldherr u. Staatsmann; Hauptstadt von Neuseeland*.

West·min·ster ['westminstə] *Stadtteil von London*.

West·mor·land ['westmələnd] *Grafschaft in England*.

White·hall ['wait'hɔ:l] *Straße in London*.

White House ['wait'haus] *das Weiße Haus (Amtssitz des Präsidenten der U.S.A.)*.

Whit·man ['witmən] *amerikanischer Dichter*.

Wight [wait]: *Isle of ~ Insel vor der Südküste Englands*.

Wilde [waild] *englischer Dichter*.

Wil·der ['waildə] *amerikanischer Autor*. [helm m.\

Will [wil], **Wil·liam** ['wiljəm] *Wil-\

Wil·son ['wilsn] *britischer Politiker; 28. Präsident der U.S.A.*

Wilt·shire ['wiltʃiə] *Grafschaft in England*.

Wim·ble·don ['wimbldən] *Vorort von London (Tennisturniere)*.

Win·ni·peg ['winipeg] *Stadt in Kanada*.

Wis·con·sin [wis'kɔnsin] *Fluß in U.S.A.; Staat der U.S.A.*

Wolfe [wulf] *amerikanischer Autor*.

Woolf [wulf] *englische Autorin*.

Worces·ter ['wustə] *englische Industriestadt; a. Worces·ter·shire ['~ʃiə] Grafschaft in England*.

Words·worth ['wə:dzwə:θ] *englischer Dichter*.

Wyc·liffe ['wiklif] *englischer Reformator*.

Wy·o·ming [wai'əumiŋ] *Staat der U.S.A.*

Y

Yale U·ni·ver·si·ty ['jeilju:ni'və:siti] *amerikanische Universität*.

Yeats [jeits] *irischer Dichter*.

Yel·low·stone ['jeləustəun] *Fluß in U.S.A.; Nationalpark*.

York [jɔ:k] *Stadt in England; a. York·shire ['~ʃiə] Grafschaft in England*.

Yo·sem·i·te [jəu'semiti] *Naturschutzgebiet in U.S.A.*

Yu·go·sla·vi·a ['ju:gəu'slɑ:vjə] *Jugoslawien n*.

Z

Zach·a·ri·ah [zækə'raiə], **Zach·a·ry** ['~ri] *Zacharias m*.

British and American Abbreviations

A

a. *acre* Acre *m (4046,8 m²).*

A.A. *anti-aircraft* Flugabwehr *f;* *Brit. Automobile Association* Kraftfahrerverband *m.*

A.A.A. *Brit. Amateur Athletic Association* Leichtathletikverband *m;* *Am. American Automobile Association* Amerikanischer Kraftfahrerverband *m.*

A.B. *able-bodied seaman* Vollmatrose; *s. B.A. (Bachelor of Arts).*

abbr. *abbreviated* abgekürzt; *abbreviation* Abk., Abkürzung *f.*

A.B.C. *American Broadcasting Company* Amerikanische Rundfunkgesellschaft *f.*

A.B.M. *anti-ballistic missile* Anti-Rakete *f (zur Abwehr von Raketen).*

A.C. *alternating current* Wechselstrom *m.*

A/C *account (current)* Kontokorrent *n,* Rechnung *f.*

acc(t). *account* Kto., Konto *n,* Rechnung *f.*

A.D. *Anno Domini (Lat. = in the year of our Lord)* im Jahr des Herrn, n. Chr., nach Christus.

A.D.A. *Brit. Atom Development Administration* Atomforschungsverwaltung *f.* [Admiralität *f.*\]

Adm. *Admiral* Admiral *m; Admiralty*⌉

advt. *advertisement* Anzeige *f,* Ankündigung *f.*

AEC *Atomic Energy Commission* Atomenergiekommission *f.*

A.E.F. *American Expeditionary Forces* Amerikanische Streitkräfte *f/pl.* in Übersee.

AFL-CIO *American Federation of Labor & Congress of Industrial Organizations (größter amerikanischer Gewerkschaftsverband).*

A.F.N. *American Forces Network (Rundfunkanstalt der amerikanischen Streitkräfte).*

Ala. *Alabama.*

Alas. *Alaska.*

Am. *America* Amerika *n; American* amerikanisch.

A.M. *amplitude modulation* Mittelwelle *f; s.* M.A. *(Master of Arts).*

a.m. *ante meridiem (Lat. = before noon)* morgens, vormittags.

A.P. *Associated Press (amerikanisches Nachrichtenbüro).*

A/P *account purchase* Einkaufsabrechnung *f.*

A.P.O. *Am. Army Post Office* Heerespostamt *n.*

A.R.C. *American Red Cross* Amerikanisches Rotes Kreuz *n.*

Ariz. *Arizona.*

Ark. *Arkansas.*

A.R.P. *air-raid precautions* Luftschutz *m.*

arr. *arrival* Ank., Ankunft *f.*

A/S *account sales* Verkaufsabrechnung *f.*

ASA *American Standards Association* Amerikanische Normungs-Organisation *f.*

av. *average* Durchschnitt *m;* Havarie *f.*

avdp. *avoirdupois* Handelsgewicht *n.*

A.W.O.L. *Am. absent without leave* abwesend ohne Urlaub.

B

b. *born* geb., geboren.

B.A. *Bachelor of Arts* Bakkalaureus *m* der Philosophie; *British Academy* Britische Akademie *f.*

BA *British Airways (britische Fluggesellschaft).*

B.A.O.R. *British Army of the Rhine* Britische Rheinarmee *f.*

Bart. *Baronet* Baronet *m.*

B.B.C. *British Broadcasting Corporation* Britische Rundfunkgesellschaft *f.*

bbl. *barrel* Faß *n.*

B.C. *before Christ* v. Chr., vor Christus.

B.D. *Bachelor of Divinity* Bakkalaureus *m* der Theologie.

B.E. *Bachelor of Education* Bakkalaureus *m* der Erziehungswissenschaft; *Bachelor of Engineering* Bakkalaureus *m* der Ingenieurwissenschaft(en).

B/E *Bill of Exchange* Wechsel *m*.

Beds. *Bedfordshire.*

Benelux ['benilʌks] *Belgium, Netherlands, Luxemburg* Benelux, Belgien, Niederlande, Luxemburg (*Zollunion*).

Berks. *Berkshire.*

b/f *brought forward* Übertrag *m*.

B.F.A. *British Football Association* Britischer Fußballverband *m*.

B.F.N. *British Forces Network* (*Sender der britischen Streitkräfte in Deutschland*).

B.I.F. *British Industries Fair* Britische Industriemesse *f*.

B.L. *Bachelor of Law* Bakkalaureus *m* des Rechts.

B/L *bill of lading* (See)Frachtbrief *m*.

bl. *barrel* Faß *n*.

B.Lit. *Bachelor of Literature* Bakkalaureus *m* der Literatur.

bls. *bales* Ballen *m/pl.*; *barrels* Fässer *n/pl.*

B.M. *Bachelor of Medicine* Bakkalaureus *m* der Medizin.

B.M.A. *British Medical Association* Britischer Ärzteverband *m*.

B/O *Branch Office* Zweigstelle *f*, Filiale *f*.   [kauft.]

bot. *bottle* Flasche *f*; *bought* ge-]

B.O.T. *Brit. Board of Trade* Handelsministerium *n*.

B.R. *British Railways* Britische Eisenbahn *f*.

B/R *bills receivable* ausstehende Wechselforderungen *f/pl.*

B.R.C.S. *British Red Cross Society* Britisches Rotes Kreuz *n*.

Br(it). *Britain* Großbritannien *n*; *British* britisch.

Bros. *brothers* Gebr., Gebrüder *pl.* (*in Firmenbezeichnungen*).

B.S. *Bachelor of Science* Bakkalaureus *m* der Naturwissenschaften; *British Standard* Britische Norm *f*.

B/S *bill of sale* Kaufvertrag *m*, Übereignungsurkunde *f*.

B.Sc. *Bachelor of Science* Bakkalaureus *m* der Naturwissenschaften.

B.Sc.Econ. *Bachelor of Economic Science* Bakkalaureus *m* der Wirtschaftswissenschaft(en).

bsh., bu. *bushel* Scheffel *m* (*Brit.* 36,36 l, *Am.* 35,24 l).

Bucks. *Buckinghamshire.*

B.U.P. *British United Press* (*Nachrichtenbüro*).

bus(h). *bushel(s)* Scheffel *m* (*od. pl.*) (*Brit.* 36,36 l, *Am.* 35,24 l).

C

C. *Celsius* C Celsius, *centigrade* hundertgradig (*Thermometereinteilung*).

c. *cent(s)* Cent *m* (*od. pl.*) (*amerikanische Münze*); *circa* ca., circa, ungefähr; *cubic* Kubik…

C.A. *chartered account* Frachtrechnung *f*; *Brit. Chartered Accountant* vereidigter Buchprüfer *m*; Wirtschaftsprüfer *m*.

C/A *current account* laufendes Konto *n*.

c.a.d. *cash against documents* Zahlung *f* gegen Aushändigung der Dokumente.

Cal(if). *California.*

Cambs. *Cambridgeshire.*

Can. *Canada* Kanada *n*; *Canadian* kanadisch.

Capt. *Captain* Kapitän *m*, Hauptmann *m*, Rittmeister *m*.

C.B. *cash book* Kassenbuch *n*; *Brit. Companion of the Bath* Ritter *m* des Bathordens.

C/B *cash book* Kassenbuch *n*.

C.B.C. *Canadian Broadcasting Corporation* Kanadische Rundfunkgesellschaft *f*.

C.C. *continuous current* Gleichstrom *m*; *Brit. County Council* Grafschaftsrat *m*.

C.E. *Church of England* Anglikanische Kirche *f*; *Civil Engineer* Bauingenieur *m*.

cert. *certificate* Bescheinigung *f*.

CET *Central European Time* MEZ, mitteleuropäische Zeit *f*.

cf. *confer* vgl., vergleiche.

ch. *chain* (*Länge einer*) Meßkette *f* (*20,12 m*); *chapter* Kap., Kapitel *n*.

Ches. *Cheshire.*

CIA *Am. Central Intelligence Agency* (*US-Geheimdienst*).

C.I.D. *Brit. Criminal Investigation Department* (*Kriminalpolizei*).

c.i.f. *cost, insurance, freight* Kosten, Versicherung und Fracht einbegriffen.

CINC, C. in C. *Commander-in--Chief* Oberkommandierende(r) *m* (*dem Land-, Luft- und Seestreitkräfte unterstehen*).

cl. *class* Klasse *f.*

C.O. *Commanding Officer* Kommandeur *m.*

Co. *Company* Kompanie *f,* Gesellschaft *f; county* Grafschaft *f,* Kreis *m.*

c/o *care of* p.A., per Adresse, bei.

C.O.D. *cash* (*Am. a. collect*) *on delivery* Zahlung *f* bei Empfang, gegen Nachnahme.

Col. *Colonel* Oberst *m; Colorado.*

Colo. *Colorado.*

Conn. *Connecticut.*

Cons. *Conservative* konservativ.

Corn. *Cornwall.*

Corp. *Corporal* Korporal *m,* Unteroffizier *m.*

C.P. *Canadian Press* (*Nachrichtenbüro*).

cp. *compare* vgl., vergleiche.

C.P.A. *Am. Certified Public Accountant* beeidigter Bücherrevisor *m;* Wirtschaftsprüfer *m.*

ct(s). *cent(s)* Cent *m* (*od. pl.*) (*amerikanische Münze*).

cu(b). *cubic* Kubik...

Cum(b). *Cumberland.*

c.w.o. *cash with order* Barzahlung *f* bei Bestellung.

cwt. *hundredweight* (*etwa 1*) Zentner *m* (*Brit. 50,8 kg, Am. 45,36 kg*).

D

d. (*Lat. denarius*) *penny, pence* (*britische Münze*); *died* gest., gestorben.

D.A. *deposit account* Depositenkonto *n.*

D.A.R. *Daughters of the American Revolution* Töchter *f/pl.* der amerikanischen Revolution (*patriotischer Frauenverband*).

D.B. *Day Book* Tage-, Kassenbuch *n.*

D.C. *direct current* Gleichstrom *m; District of Columbia* Distrikt Columbia (*mit der amerikanischen Hauptstadt Washington*).

D.C.L. *Doctor of Civil Law* Dr. jur., Doktor *m* des Zivilrechts.

D.D. *Doctor of Divinity* Dr. theol., Doktor *m* der Theologie.

d-d *damned* verdammt!

DDD *Am. direct distance dialing* Selbstwählferndienst *m.*

DDT *dichloro-diphenyl-trichloroethane* DDT, Dichlordiphenyltrichloräthan *n* (*Insekten- und Seuchenbekämpfungsmittel*).

Del. *Delaware.*

dep. *departure* Abf., Abfahrt *f.*

dept. *department* Abt., Abteilung *f.*

Derby. *Derbyshire.*

Devon. *Devonshire.*

dft. *draft* Tratte *f.*

disc(t). *discount* Diskont *m,* Abzug *m.*

div. *dividend* Dividende *f.*

do. *ditto* do., dito, dgl., desgleichen.

doc. *document* Dokument *n,* Urkunde *f.*

dol. *dollar* Dollar *m.*

Dors. *Dorsetshire.*

doz. *dozen(s)* Dtzd., Dutzend *n* (*od. pl.*).

d/p *documents against payment* Dokumente *n/pl.* gegen Zahlung.

dpt. *department* Abt., Abteilung *f.*

Dr. *debtor* Schuldner *m; Doctor* Dr., Doktor *m.*

dr. *dra(ch)m* Dram *n,* Drachme *f* (*1,77 g*); *drawer* Trassant *m.*

d.s., d/s *days after sight* Tage *m/pl.* nach Sicht (*bei Wechseln*).

Dur(h). *Durham.*

D.V. *Deo volente* (*Lat. = God willing*) so Gott will.

dwt. *pennyweight* Pennygewicht *n* (*1,5 g*).

dz. *dozen(s)* Dtzd., Dutzend *n* (*od. pl.*).

E

E. *east* O, Ost(en) *m; eastern* östlich; *English* englisch.

E. & O.E. *errors and omissions excepted* Irrtümer und Auslassungen vorbehalten.

E.C. *East Central* (London) Mitte-Ost (*Postbezirk*).

ECE *Economic Commission for Europe* Wirtschaftskommission *f* für Europa (*des ECOSOC*).

ECOSOC *Economic and Social Council* Wirtschafts- und Sozialrat *m* (*der U.N.*).

ECSC *European Coal and Steel Community* EGKS, Europäische Gemeinschaft *f* für Kohle und Stahl.

Ed., ed. *edited* h(rs)g., herausgegeben; *edition* Aufl., Auflage *f*; *editor* H(rs)g., Herausgeber *m.*

EE., E./E. *errors excepted* Irrtümer vorbehalten.

EFTA *European Free Trade Association* EFTA, Europäische Freihandelsgemeinschaft *f od.* -zone *f.*

Eftpos *electronic funds transfer at point of sale* Zahlungsart *f* „ec-Kasse".

e.g. *exempli gratia* (*Lat.* = *for instance*) z.B., zum Beispiel.

ELDO *European Launcher Development Organization* Europäische Trägerraketen-Entwicklungsorganisation *f.*

EMA *European Monetary Agreement* EWA, Europäisches Währungsabkommen *n.*

Enc. *enclosure(s)* Anlage(n *pl.*) *f.*

Eng(l). *England* England *n*; *English* englisch.

E.R.P. *European Recovery Program(me)* Europäisches Wiederaufbauprogramm *n*, Marshall-Plan *m.*

Esq. *Esquire* Wohlgeboren (*in Briefadressen*).

ESRO *European Space-Research Organization* Europäische Weltraumforschungsorganisation *f.*

Ess. *Essex.*

etc., &c. *et cetera, and the rest, and so on* etc., usw., und so weiter.

EUCOM *Am. European Command* Hauptquartier *n* für den Befehlsbereich Europa.

EURATOM *European Atomic Energy Community* Euratom, Europäische Atomgemeinschaft *f.*

exam. *examination* Prüfung *f.*

excl. *exclusive, excluding* ausschl., ausschließlich, ohne.

ex div. *ex dividend* ohne *od.* ausschließlich Dividende.

ex int. *ex interest* ohne *od.* ausschließlich Zinsen.

F

f. *fathom* Faden *m*, Klafter *f*, *m*, *n* (*1,83 m*); *feminine* weiblich; *following* folgend; *foot* (*feet*) Fuß *m* (*od. pl.*) (*30,48 cm*).

F. *Fahrenheit* F, Fahrenheit (*Thermometereinteilung*); *univ. Fellow* Mitglied *n.*

F.A. *Brit. Football Association* Fußballverband *m.*

Fahr. *Fahrenheit* F, Fahrenheit (*Thermometereinteilung*).

F.A.O. *Food and Agriculture Organization* Organisation *f* für Ernährung und Landwirtschaft (*der U.N.*).

f.a.s. *free alongside ship* frei längsseits Schiff.

FBI *Am. Federal Bureau of Investigation* (*Bundeskriminalamt*).

F.B.I. *Federation of British Industries* Britischer Industrieverband *m.*

F.C.C. *Am. Federal Communications Commission* Bundeskommission *f* für das Nachrichtenwesen.

fig. *figure(s)* Abb., Abbildung(en *pl.*) *f.*

Fla. *Florida.*

F.M. *frequency modulation* UKW, Ultrakurzwelle *f.*

fm. *fathom* Faden *m*, Klafter *f*, *m*, *n* (*1,83 m*).

F.O. *Brit. Foreign Office* Auswärtiges Amt *n.*

fo. *folio* Folio *n*; Blatt *n*, Seite *f.*

f.o.b. *free on board* frei Schiff.

FOBS *Fractional Orbital Bombardment System* Orbitalraketensystem *n.*

fol. *folio* Folio *n*; Blatt *n*, Seite *f.*

f.o.q. *free on quay* frei Kai.

f.o.r. *free on rail* frei Bahn.

f.o.t. *free on truck* frei Waggon.

f.o.w. *free on waggon* frei Waggon.

F.P. *fire-plug* Hydrant *m*; *freezing-point* Gefrierpunkt *m.*

Fr. *France* Frankreich *n*; *French* französisch.

fr. *franc(s)* Frank(en *pl.*) *m.*

ft. *foot* (*feet*) Fuß *m* (*od. pl.*) (*30,48 cm*).

FTC *Am. Federal Trade Commission* Bundeshandelskommission *f.*

fur. *furlong* Achtelmeile *f* (*201,17 m*).

G

g. *gauge* Normalmaß *n*; 🚆 Spurweite *f*; *grain* Gran *n* (*0,0648 g*); *gram(me)* g, Gramm *n*; *guinea* Guinee *f* (*21 Shilling*).

G.A. *General Agent* Generalvertreter *m*; *General Assembly* Generalversammlung *f.*

Ga. *Georgia.*

gal. *gallon* Gallone *f* (*Brit. 4,546 l*, *Am. 3,785 l*).

GATT *General Agreement on Tariffs and Trade* Allgemeines Zoll- und Handelsabkommen *n.*

G.B. *Great Britain* Großbritannien *n.*

G.B.S. *George Bernard Shaw.*
G.C.B. *(Knight) Grand Cross of the Bath* (Ritter *m* des) Großkreuz(es) *n* des Bathordens.
GDR *German Democratic Republic* DDR, Deutsche Demokratische Republik *f.*
Gen. *General* General *m.*
gen. *generally* allgemein.
GFR *German Federal Republic* BRD, Bundesrepublik *f* Deutschland.
G.I. *government issue* von der Regierung ausgegeben, Staatseigentum *n*; *fig. der amerikanische Soldat.*
gi., gl. *gill* Viertelpinte *f (Brit. 0,142 l, Am. 0,118 l).*
G.L.C. *Greater London Council* Stadtrat *m* von Groß-London.
Glos. *Gloucestershire.*
G.M.T. *Greenwich mean time* WEZ, westeuropäische Zeit *f.*
gns. *guineas* Guineen *f/pl. (s. g.).*
G.O.P. *Am.' Grand Old Party* Republikanische Partei *f.*
Gov. *Government* Regierung *f; Governor* Gouverneur *m.*
G.P. *general practitioner* praktischer Arzt *m.*
G.P.O. *General Post Office* Hauptpostamt *n.*
gr. *grain* Gran *n (0,0648 g); gross* brutto; Gros *n (12 Dutzend).*
gr.wt. *gross weight* Bruttogewicht *n.*
gs. *guineas* Guineen *f/pl. (s. g.).*
Gt.Br. *Great Britain* Großbritannien *n.*
guar. *guaranteed* garantiert.

H

h. *hour(s)* Std., Stunde(n *pl.*) *f,* Uhr *(bei Zeitangaben).*
Hants. *Hampshire.*
H.B.M. *His (Her) Britannic Majesty* Seine (Ihre) Britannische Majestät *f.*
H.C. *Brit. House of Commons* Unterhaus *n.*
H.C.J. *Brit. High Court of Justice* Hoher Gerichtshof *m.*
H.E. *high explosive* hochexplosiv; *His Excellency* Seine Exzellenz *f.*
Heref. *Herefordshire.*
Herts. *Hertfordshire.*
hf. *half* halb.
hhd. *hogshead* Oxhoft *n (etwa 240 l).*
H.I. *Hawaiian Islands* Hawaii-Inseln *f/pl.*

H.L. *Brit. House of Lords* Oberhaus *n.*
H.M. *His (Her) Majesty* Seine (Ihre) Majestät *f.*
H.M.S. *His (Her) Majesty's Service* Dienst *m,* ℔ Dienstsache *f; His (Her) Majesty's Ship (Steamer)* Seiner (Ihrer) Majestät Schiff *n* (Dampfer *m).*
H.M.S.O. *Brit. His (Her) Majesty's Stationery Office (Staatsdruckerei).*
H.O. *Brit. Home Office* Innenministerium *n.*
Hon. *Honorary* ehrenamtlich; *Honourable* Ehrenwert *(Anrede und Titel).*
H.P., h.p. *horse-power* PS, Pferdestärke *f; high pressure* Hochdruck *m; hire purchase* Abzahlungskauf *m.*
H.Q., Hq. *Headquarters* Stab(squartier *n) m,* Hauptquartier *n.*
H.R. *Am. House of Representatives* Repräsentantenhaus *n.*
H.R.H. *His (Her) Royal Highness* Seine (Ihre) Königliche Hoheit *f.*
hrs. *hours* Stunden *f/pl.*
H.T., h.t. *high tension* Hochspannung *f.*
Hunts. *Huntingdonshire.*

I

I. *Idaho (Staat der U.S.A.); Island, Isle* Insel *f.*
Ia. *Iowa.*
IAAF *International Amateur Athletic Federation* Internationaler Leichtathletikverband *m.*
I.A.T.A. *International Air Transport Association* Internationaler Luftverkehrsverband *m.*
I.B. *Invoice Book* Fakturenbuch *n.*
ib(id). *ibidem (Lat. = in the same place)* ebd., ebenda.
IBRD *International Bank for Reconstruction and Development* Internationale Bank *f* für Wiederaufbau und Entwicklung, Weltbank *f.*
I.C.A.O. *International Civil Aviation Organization* Internationale Zivilluftfahrt-Organisation *f.*
I.C.B.M. *intercontinental ballistic missile* interkontinentaler ballistischer Flugkörper *m.*
I.C.F.T.U. *International Confederation of Free Trade Unions* Internationaler Bund *m* Freier Gewerkschaften.
ICPC *International Criminal Police*

Commission Interpol, Internationale Kriminalpolizei-Kommission *f.*

ICRC *International Committee of the Red Cross* Internationales Komitee *n* des Roten Kreuzes.

I.D. *Am. Intelligence Department* ✗ Nachrichtendienst *m.*

id. *idem* (*Lat.* = the same author od. word) id., idem, derselbe, dasselbe.

Id(a). *Idaho.*

i.e. *id est* (*Lat.* = that is to say) d. h., das heißt.

IFT *International Federation of Translators* Internationaler Bund *m* der Übersetzer.

I.H.P., i.h.p. *indicated horse-power* i. PS, indizierte Pferdestärke *f.*

Ill. *Illinois.*

I.L.O. *International Labo(u)r Organization* Internationale Arbeitsorganisation *f.*

I.M.F. *international Monetary Fund* IWF, Internationaler Währungsfonds *m.*

in. *inch(es)* Zoll *m* (*od. pl.*) (2,54 cm).

Inc. *inclosure* Anlage *f*; *Incorporated* (amtlich) eingetragen.

incl. *inclusive, including* einschl., einschließlich.

incog. *incognito* incognito.

Ind. *Indiana.*

inst. *instant* d. M., dieses Monats.

I.O.C. *International Olympic Committee* IOK, Internationales Olympisches Komitee *n.*

I. of M. *Isle of Man* (*englische Insel*).

I. of W. *Isle of Wight* (*englische Insel*).

I.O.U. *I owe you* Schuldschein *m.*

I.P.A. *International Phonetic Association* Weltlautschriftverein *m* (*Internationale Phonetische Gesellschaft*).

I.Q. *intelligence quotient* Intelligenzquotient *m.*

Ir. *Ireland* Irland *n*; *Irish* irisch.

I.R.C. *International Red Cross* IRK, Internationales Rotes Kreuz *n.*

I.R.O. *International Refugee Organization* Internationale Flüchtlingsorganisation *f.*

ISO *International Organization for Standardization* Internationale Organisation *f* für Normung.

I.T.O. *International Trade Organization* Internationale Handelsorganisation *f.*

I.U.S. *International Union of Students* Internationaler Studentenverband *m.*

I.U.S.Y. *International Union of Socialist Youth* Internationale Vereinigung *f* sozialistischer Jugend.

I.V.S.(P.) *International Voluntary Service (for Peace)* Internationaler freiwilliger Hilfsdienst *m* (für den Frieden).

I.W.W. *Industrial Workers of the World* Weltverband *m* der Industriearbeiter.

I.Y.H.F. *International Youth Hostel Federation* Internationaler Jugendherbergsverband *m.*

J

J. *Judge* Richter *m*; *Justice* Justiz *f*; Richter *m.*

J.C. *Jesus Christ* Jesus Christus *m.*

J.I.B. *Brit. Joint Intelligence Bureau* ✗ Nachrichtendienst *m.*

J.P. *Justice of the Peace* Friedensrichter *m.*

Jr. *junior* (*Lat.* = the younger) jr., jun., der Jüngere.

jun(r). *junior* (*Lat.* = the younger) jr., jun., der Jüngere.

K

Kan(s). *Kansas.*

K.C. *Brit. Knight Commander* Großoffizier *m* (*eines Ordens*); *King's Counsel* Kronanwalt *m.*

K.C.B. *Brit. Knight Commander of the Bath* Großoffizier *m* des Bathordens.

kg. *kilogram(me)* kg, Kilogramm *n.*

K.K.K. *Ku Klux Klan* (*geheime Terrororganisation in U.S.A.*).

km. *kilometre* km, Kilometer *m, n.*

k.o., KO *knock(ed) out* k.o.; *Boxen*: durch Niederschlag kampfunfähig; *fig.* erledigt.

k.v. *kilovolt* kV, Kilovolt *n.*

k.w. *kilowatt* kW, Kilowatt *n.*

Ky. *Kentucky.*

L

l. *left* links; *line* Zeile *f*, Linie *f*; *link* (20,12 cm); *litre* l, Liter *n, m.*

£ *pound sterling* Pfund *n* Sterling.

La. *Louisiana.*

Lancs. *Lancashire.*

lat. *latitude* geographische Breite *f.*

lb. (*Lat. libra*) *pound* Pfund *n* (*Gewicht*).

L.C. *letter of credit* Kreditbrief *m*.

l.c. *loco citato* (*Lat.* = *at the place cited*) a.a.O., am angeführten Ort.

L.C.J. *Brit. Lord Chief Justice* Lordoberrichter *m*.

Leics. *Leicestershire*.

Lincs. *Lincolnshire*.

ll. *lines* Zeilen *f/pl.*, Linien *f/pl.*

LL.D. *legum doctor* (*Lat.* = *Doctor of Laws*) Dr. jur., Doktor *m* der Rechte.

loc.cit. *loco citato* (*Lat.* = *at the place cited*) a.a.O., am angeführten Ort.

lon(g). *longitude* geographische Länge *f*.

LP *long-playing* (*record*) Langspiel(-platte *f*). [partei *f*.⟩

L.P. *Brit. Labour Party* Arbeiter-⟨

l.p. *low pressure* Tiefdruck *m*.

L.S.O. *London Symphony Orchestra* Londoner Sinfonieorchester *n*.

L.S.S. *Am. Life Saving Service* Lebensrettungsdienst *m*.

Lt. *Lieutenant* Leutnant *m*.

L.T., l.t. *low tension* Niederspannung *f*.

Lt.-Col. *Lieutenant-Colonel* Oberstleutnant *m*. [tung.⟩

Ltd. *Limited* mit beschränkter Haf-⟨

Lt.-Gen. *Lieutenant-General* Generalleutnant *m*.

M

m *minim* (*Apothekermaß*, *Brit.* 0,0592 *ml*, *Am.* 0,0616 *ml*).

m. *masculine* männlich; *metre* Meter *n*, *m*; *mile* Meile *f* (*1609,34 m*); *minute* Min., min, Minute *f*.

M.A. *Master of Arts* Magister *m* der Philosophie; *Military Academy* Militärakademie *f*.

Maj. *Major* Major *m*.

Maj.-Gen. *Major-General* Generalmajor *m*.

Man. *Manitoba*.

Mass. *Massachusetts*.

M.C. *Master of Ceremonies* Zeremonienmeister *m*; *Am. Conférencier m*; *Am. Member of Congress* Kongreßmitglied *n*.

MCP *male chauvinist pig* Chauvi *m*.

M.D. *medicinae doctor* (*Lat.* = *Doctor of Medicine*) Dr. med., Doktor *m* der Medizin.

Md. *Maryland*.

Me. *Maine*. [gramm *n*.⟩

mg. *milligram(me)* mg, Milli-⟨

mi. *mile* Meile *f* (*1609,34 m*).

Mich. *Michigan*.

Middx. *Middlesex*.

Min. *minute* Min., min, Minute *f*.

Minn. *Minnesota*.

Miss. *Mississippi*. [*n*, *m*.⟩

mm. *millimetre* mm, Millimeter⟨

Mo. *Missouri*.

M.O. *money order* Geldanweisung *f*.

Mon. *Monmouthshire*.

Mont. *Montana*.

MP, M.P. *Member of Parliament* Parlamentsabgeordnete(r) *m*; *Military Police* Militärpolizei *f*.

m.p.h. *miles per hour* Stundenmeilen *f/pl.*

Mr *Mister* Herr *m*.

Mrs *Mistress* Frau *f*.

Ms (*briefliche*) *Anredeform falls unbekannt, ob* Mrs *oder* Miss.

MS. *manuscript* Ms., Manuskript *n*.

M.S. *motorship* Motorschiff *n*.

MSA *Am. Mutual Security Agency* Verwaltung *f* für gemeinsame Sicherheit.

MSS. *manuscripts* Mss., Manuskripte *n/pl.*

mt. *megaton* Mt, Megatonne *f*.

Mt. *Mount* Berg *m*.

Mx. *Middlesex*.

N

N. *north* N, Nord(en) *m*; *northern* nördlich.

n. *noon* Mittag *m*.

N.A.A.F.I. *Navy, Army and Air Force Institutes* (*Marketenderei- und Truppenbetreuungsinstitution der britischen Streitkräfte*).

NASA *Am. National Aeronautics and Space Administration* Nationale Luft- und Raumfahrtbehörde *f*.

NATO *North Atlantic Treaty Organization* Nordatlantikpakt-Organisation *f*.

N.B.C. *Am. National Broadcasting Corporation* Nationale Rundfunkgesellschaft *f*.

N.C. *North Carolina*.

N.C.B. *Brit. National Coal Board* Nationale Kohlenbehörde *f*.

n.d. *no date* ohne Datum.

N.D(ak). *North Dakota*.

N.E. *northeast* NO, Nordost(en) *m*; *northeastern* nordöstlich.

Neb(r). *Nebraska.*
Nev. *Nevada.*
N.F. N/F *no funds* keine Dek-⎫
N.H. *New Hampshire.* [kung.⎰
N.H.S. *Brit. National Health Service* Nationaler Gesundheitsdienst *m* (*Krankenversicherung*).
N.J. *New Jersey.*
N.M(ex). *New Mexico.*
No. *north* N, Nord(en) *m*; *number* Zahl *f*; *numero* Nr., Nummer *f.*
Norf. *Norfolk.*
Northants. *Northamptonshire.*
Northumb. *Northumberland.*
Notts. *Nottinghamshire.*
n.p. or d. *no place or date* ohne Ort oder Datum.
N.S.P.C.A. *Brit. National Society for the Prevention of Cruelty to Animals* (*Tierschutzverein*).
N.T. *New Testament* Neues Testament *n.*
Nt.wt. *net weight* Nettogewicht *n.*
N.U.M. *Brit. National Union of Mineworkers* Nationale Bergarbeitergewerkschaft *f.*
N.W. *northwest* NW, Nordwest(en) *m*; *northwestern* nordwestlich.
N.Y. *New York* (*Staat der U.S.A.*).
N.Y.C. *New York City* Stadt *f* New York.
N.Z. *New Zealand* Neuseeland *n.*

O

O. *Ohio*; *order* Auftrag *m.*
o/a *on account* für Rechnung von.
O.A.S. *Organization of American States* Organisation *f* amerikanischer Staaten.
ob. *obiit* (*Lat.* = *died*) gest., gestorben.
OECD *Organization for Economic Co-operation and Development* Organisation *f* für wirtschaftliche Zusammenarbeit und Entwicklung.
O.H. *on hand* vorrätig.
O.H.M.S. *On His* (*Her*) *Majesty's Service* im Dienst Seiner (Ihrer) Majestät; ⚭ Dienstsache *f.*
O.K. (*möglicherweise aus:*) *all correct* in Ordnung.
Okla. *Oklahoma.*
O.N.A. *Overseas News Agency* Überseenachrichtenagentur *f* (*ein amerikanischer Pressedienst*).
O.N.S. *Overseas News Service* Überseenachrichtendienst *m* (*ein britischer Pressedienst*).

Ore(g). *Oregon.*
O.T. *Old Testament* Altes Testament *n.*
Oxon. *Oxfordshire.*
oz. *ounce(s)* Unze(n *pl.*) *f* (*28,35 g*).

P

p (*new*) *penny*, (*new*) *pence.*
Pa. *Pennsylvania.*
p.a. *per annum* (*Lat.* = *yearly*) jährlich.
Panam. *Pan American Airways* Panamerikanische Luftfahrtgesellschaft *f.*
par. *paragraph* Paragraph *m*, Abschnitt *m.*
P.A.Y.E. *Brit.* *pay as you earn* Lohnsteuerabzug *m.*
P.C. *police constable* Polizist *m*, Schutzmann *m*; *postcard* Postkarte *f.*
p.c. *per cent.* Prozent *n od. pl.*
p/c *price current* Preisliste *f.*
P.D. *Police Department* Polizeibehörde *f.*
p.d. *per diem* (*Lat.* = *by the day*) pro Tag.
P.E.N., PEN Club *Poets, Playwrights, Editors, Essayists, and Novelists* PEN-Club *m* (*internationale Vereinigung von Dichtern, Dramatikern, Redakteuren, Essayisten und Romanschriftstellern*).
Penn(a). *Pennsylvania.*
per pro(c). *per procurationem* (*Lat.* = *by proxy*) pp., ppa., per Prokura.
P.f.c. *Am. private first class* Obergefreite *m.*
Ph.D. *Philosophiae Doctor* (*Lat.* = *Doctor of Philosophy*) Doktor *m* der Philosophie.
pk. *peck* (*9,087 l*).
P./L. *profit and loss* Gewinn *m* und Verlust *m.*
plc *Brit. public limited company* Aktiengesellschaft *f.*
p.m. *post meridiem* (*Lat.* = *after noon*) nachmittags, abends.
P.O. *postal order* Postanweisung *f*; *Post Office* Postamt *n.*
P.O.B. *Post-Office Box* Post(schließ)-fach *n.*
p.o.d. *pay on delivery* Nachnahme *f.*
P.O.O. *post-office order* Postanweisung *f.*
P.O.S.B. *Post-Office Savings Bank* Postsparkasse *f.*

P.O.W. *Prisoner of War* Kriegsge-fangene *m*.

p.p. *per procurationem* (*Lat.* = *by proxy*) pp., ppa., per Prokura.

Pref. *Preface* Vorwort *n*.

Pres. *President* Präsident *m*.

Prof. *Professor* Professor *m*.

prox. *proximo* (*Lat.* = *next month*) n. M., nächsten Monats.

P.S. *Passenger Steamer* Passagier-dampfer *m*; *postscript* PS, Post-skript(um) *n*, Nachschrift *f*.

pt. *pint* Pinte *f* (*Brit.* 0,57 *l*, *Am.* 0,47 *l*).

P.T.A. *Parent-Teacher Association* Eltern-Lehrer-Vereinigung *f*.

Pte. *Private* Soldat *m* (*Dienstgrad*).

P.T.O., p.t.o. *please turn over* b.w., bitte wenden.

Pvt. *Private* Soldat *m* (*Dienstgrad*).

P.W. *Prisoner of War* Kriegsge-fangene *m*.

PX *Post Exchange* (*Marketenderei und Verkaufsläden der amerikanischen Streitkräfte*).

Q

q. *query* Anfrage *f*.

Q.C. *Brit. Queen's Counsel* Kron-anwalt *m*.

qr. *quarter* (*etwa 1*) Viertelzentner *m*.

qt. *quart* Quart *n* (*etwa 1 l*).

qu. *query* Anfrage *f*.

quot. *quotation* Kurs-, Preisnotie-rung *f*.

qy. *query* Anfrage *f*.

R

R. *Réaumur* R, Réaumur (*Thermo-metereinteilung*); *River* Strom *m*, Fluß *m*; *Road* Str., Straße *f*.

r. *right* rechts.

R.A. *Brit. Royal Academy* König-liche Akademie *f*.

R.A.C. *Brit. Royal Automobile Club* Königlicher Automobilklub *m*.

RADWAR *Am. radiological warfare* Atomkriegführung *f*.

R.A.F. *Royal Air Force* Königlich-(-Britisch)e Luftwaffe *f*.

R.C. *Red Cross* Rotes Kreuz *n*.

Rd. *Road* Str., Straße *f*.

rd. *rod* Rute *f* (5,029 *m*).

recd. *received* erhalten.

ref(c). (*in*) *reference* (*to*) (mit) Bezug *m* (auf); Empfehlung *f*.

regd. *registered* eingetragen; ℞ ein-geschrieben.

reg.tn. *register ton* RT, Register-tonne *f*.

resp. *respective(ly)* bzw., bezie-hungsweise.

ret. *retired* i.R., im Ruhestand, a.D., außer Dienst.

Rev. *Reverend* Ehrwürden.

R.I. *Rhode Island*.

R.L.O. *Brit. Returned Letter Office* Amt *n* für unzustellbare Briefe.

R.N. *Royal Navy* Königlich(-Bri-tisch)e Marine *f*.

R.P. *reply paid* Rückantwort be-zahlt.

r.p.m. *revolutions per minute* U/min., Umdrehungen *pl.* pro Minute.

R.R. *Am. railroad* Eisenbahn *f*.

R.S. *Brit. Royal Society* Königliche Gesellschaft *f*.

R.S.V.P. *répondez s'il vous plaît* (*Fr.* = *please reply*) u.A.w.g., um Antwort wird gebeten.

Rt.Hon. *Right Honourable* Sehr Ehrenwert.

Rutl. *Rutlandshire*.

Ry. *Brit. railway* Eisenbahn *f*.

S

S. *south* S, Süd(en) *m*; *southern* südlich.

s. *second* Sek., sek, Sekunde *f*; *shilling* Shilling *m*.

$ *dollar* Dollar *m*.

S.A. *Salvation Army* Heilsarmee *f*; *South Africa* Südafrika *n*; *South America* Südamerika *n*.

SACEUR *Supreme Allied Commander Europe* Oberbefehlshaber *m* der Alliierten Streitkräfte in Euro-pa.

SACLANT *Supreme Allied Commander Atlantic* Oberbefehlshaber *m* der Alliierten Streitkräfte im Atlantik.

Salop. *Shropshire*.

Sask. *Saskatchewan*.

S.B. *Sales Book* Verkaufsbuch *n*.

S.C. *Security Council* Sicherheitsrat *m* (*der U.N.*); *South Carolina*.

S.D(ak). *South Dakota*.

S.E. *southeast* SO, Südost(en) *m*; *southeastern* südöstlich; *Stock Exchange* Börse *f*.

SEATO *South East Asia Treaty Organization* Südostasienpakt-Or-ganisation *f*.

Sec. *Secretary* Sekretär *m*, Minister *m*.

sec. *second* Sek., sek, Sekunde *f*.

sen(r). *senior* (*Lat.* = *the elder*) sen., der Ältere.

S(er)gt. *Sergeant* Feldwebel *m*, Wachtmeister *m*.

sh. *sheet* Blatt *n*; *shilling* Schilling *m*.

SHAPE *Supreme Headquarters Allied Powers Europe* Oberkommando *n* der Alliierten Streitkräfte in Europa.

S.M. *Sergeant-Major* Oberfeldwebel *m*, Oberwachtmeister *m*.

S.N. *shipping note* Frachtannahme-, Ladeschein *m*, Schiffszettel *m*.

Soc. *society* Gesellschaft *f*, Verein *m*.

Som(s). *Somersetshire*.

SOS *SOS* (*internationales Seenotzeichen*).

sov. *sovereign* Sovereign *m* (*britische 20-Schilling-Goldmünze*).

sp.gr. *specific gravity* spezifisches Gewicht *n*.

S.P.Q.R. *small profits, quick returns* kleine Gewinne, große Umsätze.

Sq. *Square* Pl., Platz *m*.

sq. *square* ... Quadrat...

Sr. *senior* (*Lat.* = *the elder*) sen., der Ältere.

S.S. *steamship* Dampfer *m*.

st. *stone* (*6,35 kg*).

St. *Saint* ... St. ..., Sankt ...; *Station* Bhf., Bahnhof *m*; *Street* Str., Straße *f*.

Staffs. *Staffordshire*.

S.T.D. *Brit. subscriber trunk dialling* Selbstwählferndienst *m*.

St. Ex. *Stock Exchange* Börse *f*.

stg. *sterling* Sterling *m* (*britische Währungseinheit*).

sub. *substitute* Ersatz *m*.

Suff. *Suffolk*.

suppl. *supplement* Nachtrag *m*.

Suss. *Sussex*.

S.W. *southwest* SW, Südwest(en) *m*; *southwestern* südwestlich.

Sy. *Surrey*.

T

t. *ton* t, Tonne (*Brit. 1016 kg, Am. 907,18 kg*).

T.B. *tuberculosis* Tb, Tbc, Tuberkulose *f*.

T.C. *Trusteeship Council of the United Nations* Treuhandschaftsrat *m* der Vereinten Nationen.

T.D. *Am. Treasury Department* Finanzministerium *n*.

Tenn. *Tennessee*.

Tex. *Texas*.

tgm. *telegram* Telegramm *n*.

T.G.W.U. *Brit. Transport and General Workers' Union* Transportarbeiterverband *m*.

T.M.O. *telegraph money order* telegraphische Geldanweisung *f*.

TNT *trinitrotoluene* TNT, Trinitrotoluol *n*.

T.O. *Telegraph* (*Telephone*) *Office* Telegraphenamt *n* (Fernsprechamt *n*); *turn-over* Umsatz *m*.

t.o. *turn-over* Umsatz *m*.

T.P.O. *Travelling Post Office* Bahnpost *f*.

T.U. *Trade(s) Union(s)* Gewerkschaft(en *pl*.) *f*.

T.U.C. *Brit. Trade(s) Union Congress* Gewerkschaftsverband *m*.

T.V. *television* Fernsehen *n*; Fernseh...

T.V.A. *Tennessee Valley Authority* Tennesseetal-Behörde *f*.

T.W.A. *Am. Trans World Airlines* (*Luftfahrtgesellschaft*).

U

U.H.F. *ultra-high frequency* UHF, Dezimeterwelle(nbereich *m*) *f*.

U.K. *United Kingdom* Vereinigtes Königreich *n* (*England, Schottland, Wales und Nordirland*).

ult. *ultimo* (*Lat.* = *last day of the month*) ult., ultimo, am Letzten des Monats.

UMW *Am. United Mine Workers* Vereinigte Bergarbeiter *m/pl.* (*Gewerkschaftsverband*).

UN, U.N. *United Nations* Vereinte Nationen *f/pl.*

UNESCO *United Nations Educational, Scientific, and Cultural Organization* Organisation *f* der Vereinten Nationen für Erziehung, Wissenschaft und Kultur.

UNICEF *United Nations International Children's Emergency Fund* Kinderhilfswerk *n* der Vereinten Nationen.

U.N.S.C. *United Nations Security Council* Sicherheitsrat *m* der Vereinten Nationen.

U.P.I. *Am. United Press International* (*Nachrichtenagentur*).

U.S.(A.) *United States* (*of America*)

US(A), Vereinigte Staaten *m/pl.* (von Amerika).

USAF(E) *United States Air Force (Europe)* Luftwaffe *f* der Vereinigten Staaten (in Europa).

U.S.S.R. *Union of Socialist Soviet Republics* UdSSR, Union *f* der Sozialistischen Sowjetrepubliken.

Ut. *Utah.*

V

v. *verse* V., Vers *m*; *versus (Lat. = against)* contra, gegen; *vide (Lat. = see)* s., siehe.

V *volt* V, Volt *n.*

Va. *Virginia.*

V.A.T. *value-added tax* Mehrwertsteuer *f.*

V.D. *venereal disease* Geschlechtskrankheit *f.*

V.H.F. *very high frequency* UKW, Ultrakurzwelle(nbereich *m*) *f.*

V.I.P. *very important person* hohes Tier *n*, bedeutende Persönlichkeit *f.*

Vis. *viscount(ess)* Vicomte *m* (Vicomtesse *f*).

viz. *videlicet (Lat. = namely)* nämlich.

vol. *volume* Bd., Band *m.*

vols. *volumes* Bde., Bände *m/pl.*

vs. *versus (Lat. = against)* contra, gegen.

V.S. *veterinary surgeon* Tierarzt *m.*

V.S.O.P. *very superior old pale (Qualitätsbezeichnung für Kognak).*

Vt. *Vermont.*

V.T.O.(L.) *vertical take-off (and landing) (aircraft)* Senkrechtstart (-er) *m.*

v.v. *vice versa (Lat. = conversely)* umgekehrt.

W

W *watt* W, Watt *n.*

W. *west* W, West(en) *m*; *western* westlich.

War. *Warwickshire.*

Wash. *Washington.*

W.C. *West Central* (London) Mitte-West *(Postbezirk)*; *water-closet* WC, Wasserklosett *n*, Toilette *f.*

WCC *World Council of Churches*

Ökumenischer Rat *m* der Kirchen, Weltkirchenrat *m.*

WFPA *World Federation for the Protection of Animals* Welttierschutzverband *m.*

W.F.T.U. *World Federation of Trade Unions* WGB, Weltgewerkschaftsbund *m.*

WHO *World Health Organization* WGO, Weltgesundheitsorganisation *f.*

W.I. *West Indies* Westindien *n.*

Wilts. *Wiltshire.*

Wis. *Wisconsin.* [*f.*}
W/L., w.l. *wave length* Wellenlänge}

W.O.M.A.N. *World Organization of Mothers of All Nations* Weltbund *m* der Mütter aller Nationen.

Worcs. *Worcestershire.*

W.P. *weather permitting* bei günstigem Wetter.

w.p.a. *with particular average* mit Teilschaden.

W.S.R. *World Students' Relief* Internationales Studentenhilfswerk *n.*

W/T *wireless telegraphy (telephony)* drahtlose Telegraphie *f* (Telephonie *f*).

wt. *weight* Gewicht *n.*

W.Va. *West Virginia.*

Wyo. *Wyoming.*

X

x-d. *ex dividend* ausschließlich *od.* ohne Dividende.

x-i. *ex interest* ausschließlich *od.* ohne Zinsen.

Xmas *Christmas* Weihnachten *n.*

Xroads *cross roads* Straßenkreuzung *f.*

Xt. *Christ* Christus *m.*

Y

yd. *yard(s)* Elle(n *pl.*) *f (91,44 cm).*

YMCA *Young Men's Christian Association* CVJM, Christlicher Verein *m* junger Männer.

Yorks. *Yorkshire.*

yr(s). *year(s)* Jahr(e *pl.*) *n.*

YWCA *Young Women's Christian Association* Christlicher Verein *m* junger Mädchen.

American Orthography

Gegenüber dem britischen Englisch (BE) weist die Rechtschreibung im amerikanischen Englisch (AE) hauptsächlich folgende Eigenheiten auf:

1. Häufige Weglassung des **Bindestrichs**, z. B. newsstand, breakdown, soapbox, coed, cooperate.

2. Wegfall des **u** in der Endung **-our**, z. B. color, humor, honorable, favor.

3. **-er** statt BE **-re** in Endsilben, z. B. center, fiber, theater, aber nicht bei massacre.

4. Verdopplung des Endkonsonanten **l** erfolgt nur, wenn der Hauptakzent auf der Endsilbe liegt, daher z. B. AE councilor, jewelry, quarreled, traveled, woolen; andererseits findet sich im AE enroll(s), fulfill(s), skillful, installment = BE enrol(s), fulfil(s), skilful, instalment.

5. AE **s** statt BE **c**, besonders in der Endsilbe **-ence**, z. B. defense, offense, license, aber auch AE practice und practise als Verb.

6. Verbreitet sind Vereinfachungen oder Wegfall fremdsprachlicher Endungen, z. B. dialog(ue), prolog(ue) catalog(ue), program(me).

7. Verbreitet ist ferner die Vereinfachung von **ae** und **oe** zu **e**, z. B. an(a)emia, an(a)esthesia, subp(o)ena.

8. Die Endung **-ction** wird statt **-xion** bevorzugt, z. B. connection, inflection.

9. Verbreitet findet sich Konsonantenvereinfachung, z. B. wagon, kidnaped, worshiped, benefited.

10. AE bevorzugt **-o-** statt **-ou-**, z. B. mo(u)ld, smo(u)lder, plow statt BE plough.

11. Stummes **e** entfällt in Wörtern wie abridg(e)ment, judg(e)ment, acknowledg(e)ment.

12. AE gebraucht die Vorsilbe **in-** statt **en-** häufiger als BE, z. B. inclose, infold, incase.

13. AE bevorzugt die folgende Schreibweise in Einzelfällen: *check* = BE cheque, *hello* = BE hallo, *cozy* = BE cosy, *mustache* = BE moustache, *skeptical* = BE sceptical, *peddler* = BE pedlar, *gray* = BE grey.

14. Neben although, all right, through finden sich die informell-familiären Formen *altho, alright, thru*.

Numerals

Cardinal Numbers

0 nought, zero, cipher; *teleph.* 0
[əu] *null*
1 one *eins*
2 two *zwei*
3 three *drei*
4 four *vier*
5 five *fünf*
6 six *sechs*
7 seven *sieben*
8 eight *acht*
9 nine *neun*
10 ten *zehn*
11 eleven *elf*
12 twelve *zwölf*
13 thirteen *dreizehn*
14 fourteen *vierzehn*
15 fifteen *fünfzehn*
16 sixteen *sechzehn*
17 seventeen *siebzehn*
18 eighteen *achtzehn*
19 nineteen *neunzehn*
20 twenty *zwanzig*
21 twenty-one *einundzwanzig*
22 twenty-two *zweiundzwanzig*
30 thirty *dreißig*
31 thirty-one *einunddreißig*
40 forty *vierzig*
41 forty-one *einundvierzig*
50 fifty *fünfzig*
51 fifty-one *einundfünfzig*

60 sixty *sechzig*
61 sixty-one *einundsechzig*
70 seventy *siebzig*
71 seventy-one *einundsiebzig*
80 eighty *achtzig*
81 eighty-one *einundachtzig*
90 ninety *neunzig*
91 ninety-one *einundneunzig*
100 a *od.* one hundred *hundert*
101 hundred and one *hundert(und)-
eins*
200 two hundred *zweihundert*
300 three hundred *dreihundert*
572 five hundred and seventy-two
fünfhundert(und)zweiundsiebzig
1000 a *od.* one thousand *(ein)tausend*
1066 ten sixty-six *tausendsechsund-
sechzig*
1971 nineteen (hundred and) seventy-one *neunzehnhundertein-
undsiebzig*
2000 two thousand *zweitausend*
5044 *teleph.* five 0 double four *fünfzig vierundvierzig*
1 000 000 a *od.* one million *eine Million*
2 000 000 two million *zwei Millionen*
1 000 000 000 a *od.* one milliard, *Am.*
billion *eine Milliarde*

Ordinal Numbers

1. first *erste*
2. second *zweite*
3. third *dritte*
4. fourth *vierte*
5. fifth *fünfte*
6. sixth *sechste*
7. seventh *siebente*
8. eighth *achte*
9. ninth *neunte*
10. tenth *zehnte*
11. eleventh *elfte*
12. twelfth *zwölfte*

13. thirteenth *dreizehnte*
14. fourteenth *vierzehnte*
15. fifteenth *fünfzehnte*
16. sixteenth *sechzehnte*
17. seventeenth *siebzehnte*
18. eighteenth *achtzehnte*
19. nineteenth *neunzehnte*
20. twentieth *zwanzigste*
21. twenty-first *einundzwanzigste*
22. twenty-second *zweiundzwanzig-
ste*
23. twenty-third *dreiundzwanzigste*

30.	thirtieth *dreißigste*
31.	thirty-first *einunddreißigste*
40.	fortieth *vierzigste*
41.	forty-first *einundvierzigste*
50.	fiftieth *fünfzigste*
51.	fifty-first *einundfünfzigste*
60.	sixtieth *sechzigste*
61.	sixty-first *einundsechzigste*
70.	seventieth *siebzigste*
71.	seventy-first *einundsiebzigste*
80.	eightieth *achtzigste*
81.	eighty-first *einundachtzigste*
90.	ninetieth *neunzigste*
100.	(one) hundredth *hundertste*

101.	hundred and first *hundertund-erste*
200.	two hundredth *zweihundertste*
300.	three hundredth *dreihundertste*
572.	five hundred and seventy-second *fünfhundertundzwei-undsiebzigste*
1000.	(one) thousandth *tausendste*
1950.	nineteen hundred and fiftieth *neunzehnhundertfünfzigste*
2000.	two thousandth *zweitausendste*
1 000 000.	millionth *millionste*
2 000 000.	two millionth *zwei-millionste*

Fractions and other Numerical Values

$^1/_2$ one *od.* a half *ein halb*

$1^1/_2$ one and a half *anderthalb*

$2^1/_2$ two and a half *zweieinhalb*

$^1/_3$ one *od.* a third *ein Drittel*

$^2/_3$ two thirds *zwei Drittel*

$^1/_4$ one *od.* a quarter, one fourth *ein Viertel*   [*drei Viertel*⎫

$^3/_4$ three quarters, three fourths ⎬

$^1/_5$ one *od.* a fifth *ein Fünftel*

$3^4/_5$ three and four fifths *drei vier Fünftel*

$^5/_8$ five eighths *fünf Achtel*

$^{12}/_{20}$ twelve twentieths *zwölf Zwan-zigstel*

$^{75}/_{100}$ seventy-five hundredths *fünf-undsiebzig Hundertstel*

.45 point four five *null Komma vier fünf*   [*fünf*⎫

2.5 two point five *zwei Komma* ⎬

once *einmal*

twice *zweimal*

three (four) times *drei- (vier)mal*

twice as much (many) *zweimal od. doppelt so viel(e)*

firstly (secondly, thirdly), in the first (second, third) place *erstens (zweitens, drittens)*

$7 + 8 = 15$ seven and eight are fifteen *sieben und od. plus acht ist fünfzehn*

$9 - 4 = 5$ nine less four are five *neun minus od. weniger vier ist fünf*

$2 \times 3 = 6$ twice three are *od.* make six *zweimal drei ist sechs*

$20 : 5 = 4$ twenty divided by five make four *zwanzig dividiert od. geteilt durch fünf ist vier*

Weights and Measures

1. Längenmaße
Linear Measures

1 inch (in.)
= 2,54 cm

1 foot (ft.)
= 12 inches = 30,48 cm

1 yard (yd.)
= 3 feet = 91,44 cm

2. Wege- und Vermessungsmaße
Distance and Surveyors' Measures

1 link (li., l.)
= 7.92 inches = 20,12 cm

1 rod (rd.), pole *od.* **perch (p.)**
= 25 links = 5,03 m

1 chain (ch.)
= 4 rods = 20,12 m

1 furlong (fur.)
= 10 chains = 201,17 m

1 (statute) mile (mi.)
= 8 furlongs = 1609,34 m

3. Nautische Maße
Nautical Measures

1 fathom (fm.)
= 6 feet = 1,83 m

1 cable('s) length
= 100 fathoms = 183 m
US 120 fathoms = 219 m

1 nautical mile (n. m.)
= 10 cables' length = 1852 m

4. Flächenmaße
Square Measures

1 square inch (sq. in.)
= 6,45 cm²

1 square foot (sq. ft.)
= 144 square inches
= 929,03 cm²

1 square yard (sq. yd.)
= 9 square feet = 0,836 m²

1 square rod (sq. rd.)
= 30.25 square yards = 25,29 m²

1 rood (ro.)
= 40 square rods = 10,12 a

1 acre (a.)
= 4 roods = 40,47 a

1 square mile (sq. mi.)
= 640 acres = 2,59 km²

5. Raummaße
Cubic Measures

1 cubic inch (cu. in.)
= 16,387 cm³

1 cubic foot (cu. ft.)
= 1728 cubic inches
= 0,028 m³

1 cubic yard (cu. yd.)
= 27 cubic feet = 0,765 m³

1 register ton (reg. tn.)
= 100 cubic feet = 2,832 m³

6. Britische Hohlmaße
British Measures of Capacity

Trocken- und Flüssigkeitsmaße
Dry and Liquid Measures

1 British *od.* **Imperial gill (gi., gl.)**
= 0,142 l

1 British *od.* **Imperial pint (pt.)**
= 4 gills = 0,568 l

1 British *od.* **Imperial quart (qt.)**
= 2 Imp. pints = 1,136 l

1 British *od.* **Imp. gallon (Imp. gal.)**
= 4 Imp. quarts = 4,546 l

Trockenmaße
Dry Measures

1 British *od.* **Imperial peck (pk.)**
= 2 Imp. gallons = 9,092 l

1 Brit. *od.* **Imp. bushel (bu., bsh.)**
= 4 Imp. pecks = 36,36 l

1 Brit. *od.* **Imperial quarter (qr.)**
8 Imp. bushels = 290,94 l

Flüssigkeitsmaß
Liquid Measure

1 Brit. *od.* **Imp. barrel (bbl., bl.)**
= 36 Imp. gallons = 1,636 hl

7. Hohlmaße der USA
U.S. Measures of Capacity

Trockenmaße
Dry Measures

1 U.S. dry pint
= 0,550 l

1 U.S. dry quart
= 2 dry pints = 1,1 l

1 U.S. peck
= 8 dry quarts = 8,81 l

1 U.S. bushel (Getreidemaß)
= 4 pecks = 35,24 l

Flüssigkeitsmaße
Liquid Measures

1 U.S. liquid gill
= 0,118 l

1 U.S. liquid pint
= 4 gills = 0,473 l

1 U.S. liquid quart
= 2 liquid pints = 0,946 l

1 U.S. gallon
= 4 liquid quarts = 3,785 l

1 U.S. barrel
= 31½ gallons = 119 l

1 U.S. barrel petroleum
= 42 gallons = 158,97 l

8. Apothekermaße
Apothecaries' Fluid Measures

1 minim (min., m.)
= 0,0006 dl

1 fluid drachm, *US* **dram (dr. fl.)**
= 60 minims = 0,0355 dl

1 fluid ounce (oz. fl.)
= 8 fluid dra(ch)ms = 0,284 dl

1 pint (pt.)
= 20 fluid ounces = 0,568 l
US 16 fluid ounces = 0,473 l

9. Handelsgewichte
Avoirdupois Weight

1 grain (gr.)
= 0,0648 g

1 drachm, *US* **dram (dr. av.)**
= 27.34 grains = 1,77 g

1 ounce (oz. av.)
= 16 dra(ch)ms = 28,35 g

1 pound (lb. av.)
= 16 ounces = 0,453 kg

1 stone (st.)
= 14 pounds = 6,35 kg

1 quarter (qr.)
= 28 pounds = 12,7 kg
US 25 pounds = 11,34 kg

1 hundredweight (cwt.)
= 112 pounds = 50,8 kg
(*a.* long hundredweight:
cwt. l.)

US 100 pounds = 45,36 kg
(*a.* short hundredweight:
cwt. sh.)

1 ton (tn., t.)
= 2240 pounds (= 20 cwt. l.) =
1016 kg (*a.* long ton: tn. l.)

US 2000 pounds (= 20 cwt. sh.) =
907,18 kg (*a.* short ton: tn. sh.)

10. Fein- und Apothekergewichte
Troy and Apothecaries' Weight

1 grain (gr.)
= 0,0648 g

1 scruple (s. ap.)
= 20 grains = 1,296 g

1 pennyweight (dwt.)
= 24 grains = 1,555 g

1 dra(ch)m (dr. t. *od.* **dr. ap.)**
= 3 scruples = 3,888 g

1 ounce (oz. ap.)
= 8 dra(ch)ms = 31,104 g

1 pound (lb. t. *od.* **lb. ap.)**
= 12 ounces = 0,373 kg

Irregular Verbs

Die an erster Stelle stehende Form bezeichnet das Präsens (present tense), nach dem ersten Gedankenstrich steht das Präteritum (past tense), nach dem zweiten das Partizip Perfekt (past participle).

abide - abode - abode
arise - arose - arisen
awake - awoke - awoke, awaked
be (am, is, are) - was (were) - been
bear - bore - borne *getragen*, born *geboren*
beat - beat - beaten, beat
become - became - become
beget - begot - begotten
begin - began - begun
belay - belayed, belaid - belayed, belaid
bend - bent - bent
bereave - bereaved, bereft - bereaved, bereft
beseech - besought - besought
bet - bet, betted - bet, betted
bid - bade, bid - bidden, bid
bind - bound - bound
bite - bit - bitten
bleed - bled - bled
blow - blew - blown
break - broke - broken
breed - bred - bred
bring - brought - brought
build - built - built
burn - burnt, burned - burnt, burned
burst - burst - burst
buy - bought - bought
can - could
cast - cast - cast
catch - caught - caught
chide - chid - chid, chidden
choose - chose - chosen
cleave - clove, cleft - cloven, cleft
cling - clung - clung
clothe - clothed, *lit.* clad - clothed, *lit.* clad
come - came - come
cost - cost - cost
creep - crept - crept
crow - crowed, crew - crowed
cut - cut - cut
dare - dared, durst - dared
deal - dealt - dealt
dig - dug - dug
do - did - done

draw - drew - drawn
dream - dreamt, dreamed - dreamt, dreamed
drink - drank - drunk
drive - drove - driven
dwell - dwelt - dwelt
eat - ate - eaten
fall - fell - fallen
feed - fed - fed
feel - felt - felt
fight - fought - fought
find - found - found
flee - fled - fled
fling - flung - flung
fly - flew - flown
forbear - forbore - forborne
forbid - forbad(e) - forbidden
forget - forgot - forgotten
forgive - forgave - forgiven
forsake - forsook - forsaken
freeze - froze - frozen
geld - gelded, gelt - gelded, gelt
get - got - got, *Am. a.* gotten
gild - gilded, gilt - gilded, gilt
gird - girded, girt - girded, girt
give - gave - given
go - went - gone
grave - graved - graved, graven
grind - ground - ground
grow - grew - grown
hang - hung - hung
have (has) - had - had
hear - heard - heard
heave - heaved, ⚓ hove - heaved, ⚓ hove
hew - hewed - hewed, hewn
hide - hid - hidden, hid
hit - hit - hit
hold - held - held
hurt - hurt - hurt
keep - kept - kept
kneel - knelt, kneeled - knelt, kneeled
knit - knitted, knit - knitted, knit
know - knew - known
lade - laded - laded, laden
lay - laid - laid

lead - led- led
lean - leaned, leant - leaned, leant
leap - leaped, leapt - leaped, leapt
learn - learned, learnt - learned, learnt
leave - left - left
lend - lent - lent
let - let - let
lie - lay - lain
light - lighted, lit - lighted, lit
lose - lost - lost
make - made - made
may - might
mean - meant - meant
meet - met - met
mow - mowed - mowed, mown
must - must
kein Präsens - **ought**
pay - paid - paid
pen - penned, pent - penned, pent
put - put - put
read - read - read
rend - rent - rent
rid - rid - rid
ride - rode - ridden
ring - rang - rung
rise - rose - risen
rive - rived - riven
run - ran - run
saw - sawed - sawn, sawed
say - said - said
see - saw - seen
seek - sought - sought
sell - sold - sold
send - sent - sent
set - set - set
sew - sewed - sewed, sewn
shake - shook - shaken
shall - should
shave - shaved - shaved, (*mst adj.*) shaven
shear - sheared - shorn
shed - shed - shed
shine - shone - shone
shoe - shod - shod
shoot - shot - shot
show - showed - shown
shred - shredded - shredded, shred
shrink - shrank - shrunk
shut - shut - shut
sing - sang - sung
sink - sank - sunk
sit - sat - sat
slay - slew - slain
sleep - slept - slept
slide - slid - slid
sling - slung - slung
slink - slunk - slunk

slit - slit - slit
smell - smelt, smelled - smelt, smelled
smite - smote - smitten
sow - sowed - sown, sowed
speak - spoke - spoken
speed - sped, ⊕ speeded - sped, ⊕ speeded
spell - spelt, spelled - spelt, spelled
spend - spent - spent
spill - spilt, spilled - spilt, spilled
spin - spun, span - spun
spit - spat - spat
split - split - split
spoil - spoiled, spoilt - spoiled, spoilt
spread - spread - spread
spring - sprang - sprung
stand - stood - stood
stave - staved, stove - staved, stove
steal - stole - stolen
stick - stuck - stuck
sting - stung - stung
stink - stunk, stank - stunk
strew - strewed - (have) strewed, (be) strewn
stride - strode - stridden
strike - struck - struck
string - strung - strung
strive - strove - striven
swear - swore - sworn
sweat - sweat, sweated - sweat, sweated
sweep - swept - swept
swell - swelled - swollen
swim - swam - swum
swing - swung - swung
take - took - taken
teach - taught - taught
tear - tore - torn
tell - told - told
think - thought - thought
thrive - throve - thriven
throw - threw - thrown
thrust - thrust - thrust
tread - trod - trodden
wake - woke, waked - waked, woke(n)
wear - wore - worn
weave - wove - woven
weep - wept - wept
wet - wetted, wet - wetted, wet
will - would
win - won - won
wind - wound - wound
work - worked, *bsd.* ⊕ wrought - worked, *bsd.* ⊕ wrought
wring - wrung - wrung
write - wrote - written

Punctuation and Capitalisation

1. Der Punkt

a) Der Punkt steht am Ende eines vollständigen Satzes, wenn dieser nicht in die Form der Frage oder des Ausrufes gekleidet ist.

Three removes are as bad as a fire.

Er beschließt aber auch unvollständige Sätze, also Wortgruppen und Einzelwörter, die anstelle eines Satzes stehen.

All rights reserved.
Have you locked the shed? Certainly.

b) Der Punkt wird meist nach Abkürzungen gesetzt.

gr.; Mon.; pop. 1028.

Im Gegensatz zum Amerikanischen fehlt im britischen Gebrauch der Punkt vielfach hinter *Mr*, *Mrs* und *Dr*.

Mr W. Smith, son of the Rev. J. Smith,
...

Die Zeichen für Pfund Sterling, Pence und Dollar haben keinen Punkt.

She paid £4.12 for her food.
That's 30 p!
He paid $ 14.15 for his coat.

c) Nach Büchertiteln, Überschriften etc. steht weder ein Punkt noch irgendein anderes Satzzeichen mit Ausnahme unbedingt notwendiger Frage- und Ausrufezeichen.

d) Bei Dezimalstellen bleibt der Punkt auf der Zeile. Ausnahme: Bei Geldbeträgen werden im britischen Englisch Dezimalstellen durch einen zentrierten, von der Zeile abgehobenen Punkt abgetrennt.

10.41 m
£5·30

e) Römische Zahlen zur Bezeichnung von Seiten oder Kapiteln können mit oder ohne Punkt verwendet werden; stehen sie jedoch hinter Eigennamen, wird der Punkt nicht gesetzt.

James I

f) Auslassungen oder Unterbrechungen werden in einem Satz gewöhnlich durch drei gesperrt gedruckte Punkte angezeigt.

Ausnahmen:
Die einzelnen Buchstaben von Abkürzungen zusammengesetzter Namen internationaler Organisationen etc. werden in der Hauptsache ohne Punkt und Abstand voneinander geschrieben.

ILO; UN; UNESCO; USSR; IPA; WHO

Die Symbole der chemischen Elemente erhalten keinen Punkt.
Die Schreibweisen *1st*, *2(n)d*, *3(r)d* etc. gelten nicht als Abkürzungen und bleiben deshalb ohne Punkt.

2. Das Komma

a) Wörter, Wortgruppen und Sätze werden in einer Aufzählung durch Kommas voneinander getrennt. Bei einer Aufzählung von mehr als zwei Gliedern steht das Komma auch, wenn das letzte Glied durch eine Konjunktion (*and* oder *or*) angeschlossen ist.

He entered a small, tidy, well-lighted room.
Horses and cows, goats and sheep, dogs and cats were shown on this agricultural fair.
All the expenses fell on William, John, and Walter.

Bisweilen findet man auch, daß das Komma vor *and* oder *or* ausgelassen wird.

b) Treffen zwei Adjektive zusammen, von denen das zweite mit dem zu bestimmenden Substantiv in engerer Verbindung steht als das erste, so wird kein Komma gesetzt.

His vivid brown eyes.

c) Geraten *etc., or the like, and so on* bei einer Aufzählung in die Endstellung, ohne damit gleichzeitig den Satz zu beenden, folgt ihnen ein Komma, es sei denn, es ergibt sich aus dem Gesamtsatz eine besondere Zeichensetzung.

Any bookshop selling, lending, copying, etc., this book will be prosecuted.

d) Treffen zwei gleiche Wörter oder Wendungen in einem Satzgefüge zusammen, so trennt sie ein Komma. Das gleiche gilt auch für Zahlengruppen.

He who asks, asks not in vain.
In the year 1962, 650 people frequented this place.

e) Wörter oder Wendungen, die einen Gegensatz ausdrücken, werden durch Kommas abgetrennt. Werden solche Einzelwörter jedoch durch eine adversative Konjunktion (*but, yet, though*) eingeleitet, fällt das Komma fort.

Bread, not words, is what we are hoping for.
It was small yet well made.

f) das Komma deutet die Auslassung eines Wortes (oder einer Gruppe von Wörtern) an, das zwei Satzteilen gemeinsam ist, aber nicht wiederholt wird.

Harold failed in French; Hazel, in mathematics.

g) Beziehen sich Adverbien auf einen ganzen Satz und nicht nur auf ein einzelnes Wort, so werden sie durch Komma abgetrennt.

Unfortunately, she could not come to see it.
The affair was something that could, after all, be overlooked.

h) Hinter längere Adverbialbestimmungen, die nicht an gewohnter Stelle stehen, tritt oft ein Komma.

What he was thinking about his neighbour's behaviour, no one will ever know.

i) Werden Wörter wie *however, moreover, therefore, nevertheless, then, indeed, too, now, of course, no doubt, consequently, accordingly* in einen Satz eingefügt, ohne dessen Sinn zu verändern, so daß sie auch weggelassen werden könnten, trennt man sie durch Kommas ab.

He was, as a matter of fact, on his way to the station.
Still, I am not sure whether he was right.

Allerdings lassen einige Schreiber diese Kommas auch aus.
Bei sehr kurzen Sätzen, in denen die Wörter ohnehin nahe dem Verb stehen, ist die Abtrennung nicht nötig.

Consequently he decided to return.

Wenn einige der in dieser Regel aufgeführten Wörter, z. B. *however, indeed, too,* nicht weggelassen werden können, ohne den Sinn zu verändern, steht kein Komma.

However great the difficulties, he never gave in.
The water was too cold.

j) Nach Ausdrücken wie *namely, viz., that is, i.e., as, e.g., etc.,* die nicht eine Aufzählung einführen, sondern eine Erläuterung, steht ein Komma.

There were only three persons present at the meeting: namely, Mr. Kingstone, Mrs. Turner, and Mr. Williams.

k) Anreden, Eigennamen, akademische oder Ehrentitel, auch mehrere hintereinander, werden durch Komma abgetrennt.

I think, my love, we should go now.
Percy J. Grant, M.Sc., D.Sc., President.

Anreden in persönlichen Briefen und die formelhaften Briefschlüsse werden zumeist durch Komma getrennt.

Dear Bob, ... Sincerely yours,

l) Nachgestellte Vornamen in Bibliographien etc. trennt das Komma ab.

Carvell, Edward C. John.

m) das Komma trennt den Monat vom Jahr und untergliedert größere Zahlen von rechts in Dreiergruppen. Im britischen Englisch trennt es auch die einzelnen Glieder einer vollen Adresse.

It was dated 21st July, 1963.
The total number of the inhabitants of the city is 1,236,178.
Mr John Smith,
32, Pelaw Terrace,
London, N. 1.

n) Appositionell, parenthetisch oder auch unabhängig gebrauchte Wörter, Wendungen und Satzglieder werden durch Komma abgetrennt.

The notes were taken by Mr. Gunn, Clerk to the Council.
Her mother, a native of Germany, had preferred Switzerland to her country.
Fiddlesticks, I don't want that.

Besteht jedoch eine enge Gedankenverbindung zwischen dem Substantiv und seiner Apposition, so wird kein Komma gesetzt.

William the Conqueror; the architect Christopher Wren.

o) Hauptsätze, die durch eine nebenordnende Konjunktion verbunden sind, werden durch Komma getrennt. Das Komma entfällt bei sehr kurzen Sätzen und besonders dann, wenn beide Sätze das gleiche Subjekt haben.

He came early, as he had been asked.
She worked hard but she failed.

p) Als allgemeine Regel gilt, daß ein Komma nach einem Satz gesetzt wird, der nicht an gewohnter Stelle steht.

What had happened during those days, he could not remember.

q) Durch ein Komma getrennt werden Adverbialsätze immer, wenn sie dem Hauptsatz vorangehen, und für gewöhnlich, wenn sie an einer anderen Stelle im Satz stehen.

If it is possible, you may be sure that the work will be done.
Try and meet me at six o'clock, when you can make it.

Das Komma kann entfallen, wenn der Adverbialsatz kurz ist und Haupt- und Nebensatz das gleiche Subjekt haben.

But if you want to win a prize you must before all things strive to win it.

Das Komma entfällt auch, wenn es sich um einen kurzen nachgestellten Adverbialsatz handelt oder überhaupt um einen, der keinen Bruch im Verlauf des Satzes verursacht.

I will leave when he turns up.
He is a great deal cleverer than you are.

Ist die Anfügung jedoch unwesentlich, d. h. schließt sie noch eine zusätzliche Begründung oder Einräumung mit *because, since, as, though* an, muß das Komma stehen.

She has bought a new hat, though I doubt if she can afford it.

r) Während ein Subjekt für gewöhnlich nicht von seinem Verb getrennt wird, ist ein Komma zwischen Subjektsatz und Hauptsatz zulässig.

That the man was an ignoramus of the worst sort in this particular field of learning, is something which admits of no dispute.

s) Nicht notwendige Attributsätze, Relativsätze oder Partizipialsätze werden durch Komma abgetrennt.

I had a look at the stadium outside the town, which was only opened last summer.
Walter, feeling ill, went home soon afterwards.

Ein notwendiger Relativsatz dagegen darf nicht durch Komma abgetrennt werden.

The woman who won the swimming championship was given a medal.

t) Objekt- oder notwendige Attributsätze werden in einer Aufzählung durch Komma voneinander, aber nicht vom Hauptsatz getrennt.

He told me that he had lived in England these four months, that he had come to Germany to pass his examination, and that he wanted to return as soon as possible.
It is a house which had been built in 1925, which was damaged during the war, and which was rebuilt ten years ago.

u) Ein Komma trennt absolute Partizipial- und Infinitivkonstruktionen ab.

The visitors having left, normal life returned to the house.
Granted everything which was said in her favour, she cannot be saved.
They were all, to tell you what has happened, taken in by his words.

v) Bei der direkten Rede sowie bei kurzen Zitaten, Fragen und Maximen werden einleitende, eingeschobene oder nachgestellte *he said, she replied* etc. durch Komma abgetrennt.

"Bacchus' blessings are a treasure," says Dryden.
She asked him hurriedly, "What measure do you propose?"

3. Der Strichpunkt

a) Der Strichpunkt steht zwischen gedanklich zusammenhängenden Hauptsätzen.

Speech is silver; silence is golden.

b) Der Strichpunkt trennt die nebengeordneten Sätze in einer Satzverbindung:

ba) besonders vor den als Konjunktionen verwendeten Adverbien wie *accordingly, also, consequently, for, furthermore, hence, however, indeed, moreover, nevertheless, otherwise, so, still, then, therefore, thus, yet.*
You'll have to ask for it; otherwise you won't get it.

bb) wenn ein Gegensatz zwischen den einzelnen Sätzen besteht.

Heaven and earth will pass away; but my words will never pass away. (Matthew 24:35)

bc) wenn die einzelnen Sätze in sich noch durch Kommas unterteilt sind.

The dilapidated houses, apparently deserted years ago, looked grey and dreary; and neither cats nor dogs were straying about, looking for some food.

bd) wenn keine Konjunktion vorhanden ist.

Keep it under your hat; don't tell him anything about it.

c) Der Strichpunkt trennt die Einzelsätze in einer Reihe von Sätzen oder Ausdrücken, besonders wenn ihnen ein Doppelpunkt vorangeht.

It was in 1929: he had been fired; he had run short of money; and he did not know what to do.

d) Der Strichpunkt wird bei Namen- und Adressenlisten gesetzt und trennt Zahlengruppen etc., wenn die Trennung durch das Komma nicht klar genug erscheint.

John Smith, 41, Oxford Rd., Grantchester; William Fairways, 39, North Street, Dunstable.

4. Der Doppelpunkt

a) Der Doppelpunkt steht vor direkten Zitaten oder Fragen.

And then he cited this line from Pope:
The Proper study of mankind is man.

Stehen die Worte, die das Zitat kennzeichnen, an einer anderen Stelle als
am Anfang, so wird ein Komma gesetzt.

b) Ein Doppelpunkt geht detaillier-
ten Aufzählungen voran, besonders
wenn Wörter oder Wendungen wie
viz., *namely*, *i.e.*, *that is*, *e.g.*, *for
example*, *for instance* eingesetzt werden könnten oder tatsächlich dastehen.

*Some of the most famous of Thomas
Hardy's novels are the following: Under the Greenwood Tree, The Mayor of
Casterbridge, Tess of the D'Urber-
villes, Jude the Obscure.*

c) Der Doppelpunkt trennt zwei Aussagen, die nicht durch eine Konjunktion verbunden sind, von denen aber
die zweite die erste erweitern oder
erklären hilft.

*It is a most interesting book: a vivid
description of rural life in Elizabethan
England.*

d) Der Doppelpunkt steht im Amerikanischen nach der Anrede in Ge-
schäftsbriefen oder auch sonst nach
Anreden.

Sirs:
Ladies and Gentlemen:

e) Er steht auch zwischen Verhältnis-
zahlen sowie zwischen Kapitel- und
Versangaben aus der Bibel.

$10:20 = 1:2$
St. Luke 6:12—18

Statt eines Punktes findet sich der
Doppelpunkt bei Zeitangaben zwischen Stunden und Minuten.

10:35 a.m.

5. Das Ausrufezeichen

a) Das Ausrufezeichen steht nach
Ausrufen, ganz gleich, ob diese aus
Einzelwörtern, Wendungen oder
vollständigen Sätzen bestehen.

Oh! I see what you mean.
I can never understand why he did this!

b) In einer Serie von Ausrufen steht
hinter jedem einzelnen Ausruf ein
Ausrufezeichen.

Oh, lift me as a wave, a leaf, a cloud!
I fall upon the thorns of life! I bleed!
(Shelley)

c) Ein Ausrufezeichen wird auch gesetzt nach Wendungen oder Sätzen,
die einem Wunsch, einem Befehl
oder der Ironie und anderen starken
Äußerungen Ausdruck verleihen.

*"Stop this nonsense!" he shouted at the
crowd.*
So this is what you want me to believe!

6. Großschreibung

Großschreibung wird angewandt bei:

a) dem ersten Wort eines vollständigen oder unvollständigen Satzes,
dem ersten Wort eines Zitates oder
einer Verszeile.

Let's get hold of him.
*As if you could kill time without injur-
ing eternity.*

b) Eigennamen und Wörtern, die als
solche gebraucht werden, sowie bei
deren Ableitungen im ursprüng-
lichen Sinne.

Elizabeth, Elizabethan
Roman Empire. **Aber:** *roman types.*

c) Namen von Völkern, Rassen,
Stämmen und Sprachen und bei von
ihnen abgeleiteten Adjektiven.

Italian; Germanic; Apache tribe.

d) Ehrentiteln, akademischen und
kirchlichen Titeln und Berufs- und
Geschäftstiteln, die mit Eigennamen
zusammen gebraucht werden.

*Queen Anne; Dean Swift; Treasurer
M.J.P. Hough of the Mermaid Company.*

e) offiziellen und Regierungstiteln sowie Adelstiteln.

President; Chancellor; Speaker of the House; Prince Philip.

f) den amtlichen Bezeichnungen nationaler oder internationaler Regierungsgremien oder bei Dokumenten.

The Twentieth Congress; the United Nations; Charter of the United Nations.

g) Substantiven und oft auch Adjektiven, die auf eine Gottheit Bezug nehmen; bei Pronomen und pronominalen Adjektiven, wenn sie nicht dicht vor oder hinter dem Beziehungswort stehen.

God; the Almighty; Allah; Providence; Holy Ghost.
Now, God be thanked who has matched us with His hour . . .

h) Namen von heiligen Schriften, ihren Teilen und Ausgaben sowie bei adjektivischen Ableitungen, die sich ausdrücklich auf diese Schriften beziehen.

Koran; Old Testament.

i) Namen von Glaubensbekenntnissen, kirchlichen Bezeichnungen und Mönchsorden sowie dem Wort *Church*, wenn es auf ein bestimmtes Kirchengebäude gemünzt ist.

Buddhist; Apostles' Creed; order of Our Lady of Mount Carmel; Church of St. David's.

j) Feiertagen, Monaten und Wochentagen.

Ascension Day; February; Wednesday.

k) Namen von Kongressen, Versammlungen und Ausstellungen.

The Potsdam Conference; Congress of Horticultural Organizations; Brussels' World Fair.

l) Namen von Gerichtshöfen, Verträgen, Gesetzen, Erlassen, wichtigen Ereignissen, historischen Epochen und literarischen Perioden etc.

London Court of Appeals; Magna Charta; Napoleonic Wars; Middle Ages; Victorian Age of Literature.

m) Namen von geologischen Zeitaltern, Perioden, Epochen, Formationen etc. sowie bei Namen prähistorischer Zeitalter.

Mesozoic; Cambrian; Upper Triassic; Age of Coal; Bronze Age.

n) geographischen Gattungsnamen, die ein integrierter Bestandteil eines bestimmten Eigennamens sind: *bay, borough, colony, continent, country, district, hemisphere, island, lake, mountain, ocean, pass, peninsula, river, sea;* und in der gleichen Weise: *avenue, boulevard, bridge, park, road, square, street.*

The Cromwell Current; the Southern Hemisphere; the Red Sea; St. Denis Drive.
Aber: *The Pacific coast of the USA; Bavarian mountains.*

Dennoch finden sich solche Begriffe auch in Kleinschreibung, allerdings selten, wenn sie einem Eigennamen vorausgehen. – Werden sie von zwei oder mehreren Eigennamen begleitet, schwankt der Schreibgebrauch zwischen Groß- und Kleinschreibung.

o) politischen Gattungsnamen, die ein integrierter Bestandteil eines bestimmten Eigennamens sind und ein politisches Einteilungsprinzip andeuten: *colony, department, dominion, empire, kingdom, republic, state, territory* etc.

The Holy Roman Empire; the Third Republic.

p) Namen bestimmter geographischer Gliederungen:

The Orient; the Middle East.

q) Himmelsrichtungen, die, geographisch gesehen, einen Teil eines Landes oder der Welt bezeichnen, sowie bei deren adjektivischen und substantivischen Ableitungen.

The Southeast; a Southerner.

r) personifizierten abstrakten Ideen oder toten Gegenständen und bei personifizierten Jahreszeiten.

To Mercy, Pity, Peace and Love
All pray in their distress.

(Blake)

s) allen Wörtern in den Titeln von Büchern, (Monats)Zeitschriften, Essays, Gedichten mit Ausnahme der weniger betonten Präpositionen, Konjunktionen und Artikel; ferner bei akademischen Graden und ihren Abkürzungen.

Shakespeare's Two Gentlemen of Verona;
Journal of the American Language Association;
Doctor of Philosophy (Ph.D.).

t) dem Artikel *the,* wenn er zu einem Eigennamen oder Titel gehört oder wenn er Teil eines gesetzlich geschützten Namens ist. Die Großschreibung wird nicht angewandt, wenn im laufenden Text auf Tageszeitungen und Zeitschriften Bezug genommen wird.

The Very Reverend C.T. Curtis;
... was to be found in the Saturday Evening Post.

Film Certificates – GB

U   Universal. Suitable for all ages.
Für alle Altersstufen geeignet.

PG   Parental Guidance. Some scenes may be unsuitable for young children.
Einige Szenen ungeeignet für Kinder. Erklärung und Orientierung durch Eltern sinnvoll.

15   No person under 15 years admitted when a "15" film is in the programme.
Nicht freigegeben für Jugendliche unter 15 Jahren.

18   No person under 18 years admitted when an "18" film is in the programme.
Nicht freigegeben für Jugendliche unter 18 Jahren.

Film Certificates – USA

G   All ages admitted. General audiences.
Für alle Altersstufen geeignet.

PG   Parental guidance suggested. Some material may not be suitable for children.
Einige Szenen ungeeignet für Kinder. Erklärung und Orientierung durch Eltern sinnvoll.

R   Restricted. Under 17 requires accompanying parent or adult guardian.
Für Jugendliche unter 17 Jahren nur in Begleitung eines Erziehungsberechtigten.

X   No one under 17 admitted.
Nicht freigegeben für Jugendliche unter 17 Jahren.

Second Part

German-English

by

PROF. EDMUND KLATT
GISELA KLATT
HEINZ MESSINGER

Contents

Copyright 1884, 1911, 1929, 1951, © 1959, 1973, 1984

by Langenscheidt KG, Berlin and Munich

Printed in Germany

Preface

Since it first appeared a hundred years ago, the German-English Taschenwörterbuch has been one of Langenscheidt's best-known publications. There have been six completely revised editions of it.

The present enlarged and updated edition offers its users the very latest vocabulary of the eighties. Thousands of neologisms from all fields have been added to this widely-used and popular dictionary.

A few examples may serve to indicate the scope of these new entries, taken from both everyday and specialized fields of vocabulary: *Bioladen, Biomasse, Digitalaufnahme, Genmanipulation, Kabelfernsehen, Lauschangriff, Lichtgriffel, Marschflugkörper, ökologisches Gleichgewicht, Rucksacktourismus, saurer Regen, Waldsterben.*

Besides the addition of individual words, the basic vocabulary of entire subject-areas, such as data processing, has been taken into consideration. Colloquialisms popular with the younger generation have also been included (e.g. *ich bin total auf Reggae abgefahren* I'm really into Reggae).

It need hardly be said that this new edition has preserved the long-established principles on which the German-English Pocket Dictionary's reputation as a valuable source of information is based. Thus importance continues to be placed on idiomatic phrases (cf. for example the article *sagen*), the inclusion of American English, the precise labelling of stylistic register, phonetic transcription of the German headwords and clear, concise explanations.

The dictionary is supplemented by eight appendices. The lists of proper names and abbreviations have been brought up to date, and a new and undoubtedly welcome addition are the temperature conversion charts. The foreign user will find the German declension and conjugation tables and the comprehensive list of irregular verbs of invaluable help.

The neologisms were compiled by the English editorial department of Langenscheidt and Christian Nekvedavicius.

We have endeavoured in this new enlarged edition of the German-English Pocket Dictionary to do justice to the rapid developments in today's vocabulary and we hope that as a result it will be of benefit to an even wider range of users.

LANGENSCHEIDT

Vorwort

Seit seinem ersten Erscheinen vor 100 Jahren gehört das deutsch-englische Taschenwörterbuch zu den bekanntesten Werken des Langenscheidt-Verlags. Sechsmal wurde es vollständig neu bearbeitet, neu gesetzt und wesentlich erweitert.

Die vorliegende erweiterte Neuausgabe bietet dem Benutzer den modernen Wortschatz der achtziger Jahre. Tausende von Neuwörtern aus allen Lebensbereichen mußten daher neu aufgenommen werden; das bedingte wiederum eine Erweiterung des Umfangs dieses in Millionen von Exemplaren verbreiteten Standardwörterbuchs.

Einige Stichwort-Beispiele mögen die Spannweite der im Bereich der Allgemeinsprache und Fachsprachen durchgeführten Neuwortarbeit für dieses Wörterbuch verdeutlichen: *Bioladen, Biomasse, Digitalaufnahme, Genmanipulation, Kabelfernsehen, Lauschangriff, Lichtgriffel, Marschflugkörper, ökologisches Gleichgewicht, Rucksacktourismus, saurer Regen, Waldsterben.*

Neben diesen Einzelwort-Neologismen wurden auch ganze Fachgebiete neu erarbeitet, so die Terminologie der Datenverarbeitung mit ihrem Kernwortschatz. Auch die familiäre Umgangssprache der jungen Generation wurde bei den Neuaufnahmen berücksichtigt (z. B. *ich bin total auf Reggae abgefahren* I'm really into Reggae).

Selbstverständlich wurden in der vorliegenden Neuausgabe die bewährten Grundsätze beibehalten, denen das deutsch-englische Taschenwörterbuch seinen Ruf und seinen Nachschlagewert verdankt: Die Idiomatik (vgl. z. B. das Stichwort *sagen*), die starke Einbeziehung des Amerikanischen Englisch, die genaue Kennzeichnung der Sprachgebrauchsebenen, die Ausspracheangabe für die deutschen Stichwörter und die ausgefeilten Erläuterungen hatten schon immer einen beträchtlichen Anteil an dem hohen Informationswert dieses Wörterbuchs.

Das Wörterbuch enthält acht Anhänge. Die Anhänge „Eigennamen" und „Abkürzungen" wurden auf den neuesten Stand gebracht. Neu aufgenommen und sicherlich willkommen sind die praktischen Temperatur-Umrechnungstabellen. Dem Ausländer werden die Tabellen zur deutschen Deklination und Konjugation und die umfangreiche Liste der unregelmäßigen Verben sicherlich von Nutzen sein.

Der moderne Wortschatz wurde von der Redaktion Anglistik des Verlags und Christian Nekvedavicius erarbeitet. Wir hoffen, mit der vorliegenden erweiterten Neuausgabe der raschen Entwicklung des Wortschatzes Rechnung zu tragen. Möge das deutsch-englische Taschenwörterbuch in dieser erweiterten Fassung noch zusätzliche Freunde gewinnen!

LANGENSCHEIDT

Directions for the Use of the Dictionary

Hinweise für die Benutzung des Wörterbuches

1. Arrangement. Alphabetical order has been maintained throughout the dictionary. Note that the umlaut-forms ä, ö, ü are treated like a, o, u. (Thus "Müll" will be found directly after "Mull" but not under "muell"). ß is treated like ss. The following forms are also listed alphabetically:

a) the irregular forms of comparatives and superlatives;

b) the various forms of pronouns;

c) the principal parts (infinitive, past tense and past participle) of strong and irregular weak verbs.

Proper names and abbreviations are listed separately at the end of the dictionary.

2. Tilde or swung dash as mark of repetition (~ ♀ ~ ♀). Words belonging to the same group, derivatives or homographs and words with partly identical spelling are frequently combined with the aid of a tilde to save room. The bold-faced tilde stands for the entry word or the part of it preceding the vertical bar (|). In the examples printed in *lightface* type or in the explanations printed in *italics* the simple tilde (~) stands for the bold-faced word immediately preceding, which itself may have been formed with aid of a bold-faced tilde.

When the initial letter changes from a capital to a small letter, or vice-versa, the tilde is replaced by the sign ♀ or ♀.

1. Anordnung: Die alphabetische Reihenfolge ist überall beachtet worden. Dabei wurden die Umlautbuchstaben ä, ö, ü wie a, o, u behandelt. („Müll" z. B. suche man hinter „Mull", nicht unter „muell"). ß wird wie ss eingeordnet. An ihrem alphabetischen Platz sind gegeben:

a) die unregelmäßigen Formen des Komparativs und Superlativs;

b) die verschiedenen Formen der Fürwörter;

c) die Stammformen (Grundform, Vergangenheit, Mittelwort der Vergangenheit) der starken und der unregelmäßigen schwachen Verben.

Eigennamen und Abkürzungen sind am Schluß des Bandes in besonderen Verzeichnissen zusammengestellt.

2. Das Wiederholungszeichen oder die **Tilde** (~ ♀ ~ ♀). Zusammengehörige und verwandte Wörter, sowie Wörter, die ganz oder teilweise im Schriftbild übereinstimmen, sind häufig zum Zwecke der Raumersparnis unter Verwendung der Tilde zu Gruppen vereinigt. Die fette Tilde (~) vertritt dabei entweder das ganze Stichwort oder den vor dem Strich (|) stehenden Teil des Stichwortes. Bei den in *Auszeichnungsschrift* gesetzten Redewendungen oder in *Kursivschrift* gesetzten Erläuterungen vertritt die einfache Tilde (~) stets das unmittelbar voraufgegangene Stichwort, das seinerseits wiederum mit Hilfe der fetten Tilde gebildet sein kann.

Wenn sich die Anfangsbuchstaben ändern (groß zu klein oder umgekehrt), steht statt der Tilde das Zeichen: ♀ *od.* ♀.

Examples: **Drama**, ⸚**tiker**, ⸰⸚**tisch; duld|en**, ⸰⸚**er**, ⸚**sam; essen** (eat), ⸰⸚ (eating; food); **Selbst|-kostenpreis** etc., ⸚**verlag:** im ⸚ published by the author; **fassen:** e-n Plan ⸚.

The tilde (⸚) may also stand for the part of the entry word that is not repeated in the phonetic transcription; other parts of the word are replaced by a short dash (-): **Origin|al** [origi'nɑːl], ⸚**altreue** [⸚-'nɑːl-]; **neutral** [nɔʏ'trɑːl], ⸚**i'sieren** [⸚trɑli-].

3. Phonetic transcription (see the remarks at the head of the Key to Pronunciation, page 685) has usually been omitted:

a) in the case of compounds whose constituent elements are independent words which appear in their normal alphabetical position with pronunciation. Examples: Handbuch, Absicht, see Hand and Buch, ab and Sicht;

b) for suffixes (see list on page 688).

4. The **shortened hyphen** [-] is placed in entry words:

a) before a vowel to mark the glottal stop (e.g. be'-antworten);

b) between two consonants to indicate that they must be pronounced separately (e.g. Häus-chen, gesinnungs-treu).

5. Inflexion. The number in parentheses following simple words subject to inflexion refers to the corresponding paradigm in the declension and conjugation tables at the end of the book.

In order to save space the number has frequently been omitted:

a) when nouns have the following endings: -ei, -heit, -ion, -keit, -schaft, -ung; these are inflected according to (16); all feminine nouns ending in -in (e.g. Freundin) are inflected according to (16[1]);

Beispiele: **Drama**, ⸚**tiker**, ⸰⸚**tisch; duld|en**, ⸰⸚**er**, ⸚**sam; essen** (eat), ⸰⸚ (eating; food); **Selbst|kosten-preis** usw., ⸚**verlag:** im ⸚ published by the author; **fassen:** e-n Plan ⸚.

In der Aussprachebezeichnung wird der ausgelassene Teil des phonetischen Umschrift des Stichwortes durch die Tilde (⸚) wiedergegeben; weitere Wortteile werden durch einen kurzen Strich (-) ersetzt: **Origin|al** [origi'nɑːl], ⸚**altreue** [⸚'nɑːl-]; **neutral** [nɔʏ'trɑːl], ⸚**i-'sieren** [⸚trɑli-].

3. Die **Aussprachebezeichnung** fällt meistens weg bei

a) Wortzusammensetzungen wie Handbuch, Absicht, deren einzelne Bestandteile (Hand und Buch, ab und Sicht) als Grundwörter an alphabetischer Stelle mit Aussprache gegeben sind;

b) häufig wiederkehrenden Nachsilben (s. die Liste Seite 688).

4. Der **verkürzte Bindestrich** [-] steht in Stichwörtern:

a) vor einem Vokal zur Bezeichnung des Knacklautes (z. B. be'-antworten);

b) zwischen zwei Konsonanten, um anzuzeigen, daß sie getrennt auszusprechen sind (z. B. Häus-chen, gesinnungs-treu).

5. Deklination und Konjugation. Bei jedem einfachen abwandelbaren Wort steht in runden Klammern eine Ziffer als Hinweis auf das entsprechende Beispiel der Deklinations- und Konjugationstabellen am Schluß des Bandes.

Aus Gründen der Raumersparnis ist die Ziffer häufig weggelassen worden:

a) bei Substantiven mit den Endungen -ei, -heit, -ion, -keit, -schaft, -ung, die nach (16) abgewandelt werden; alle femininen Substantive auf -in (z. B. Freundin) sind abwandelbar nach (16[1]);

b) when adjectives act as nouns, e.g. Uneingeweihte *m, f*; these are inflected according to (18);

c) when verbs act as nouns (verbal nouns), e.g. Geschehen; all verbal nouns are neuter and are inflected according to (6);

d) when verbs end in -ieren, e.g. radieren; these are inflected according to (25).

The abbreviation (sn) means that the intransitive verb in question forms its perfect with the auxiliary "sein". All other verbs form their perfect with the auxiliary "haben".

Proper names are inflected according to (17) if no other numbers are given.

The abbreviations *sg.* or *pl.* following a noun indicate that these nouns take singular or plural verbs respectively.

6. Semantic differences (printed in *italics*) are made clear:

a) by synonyms in parentheses, e.g.: **rein** pure; (*sauber*) clean;

b) by preceding German explanations, e.g.: **Blick** *flüchtiger*: glance; **dämpfen** *Stoß, Schall*: deaden; **Abfall** *der Blätter*: fall; *beim Schlachten*: offal;

c) by additions that supply grammatical information and/or illustrate the use of a word but are left untranslated, e.g.: **abkommen** ... *von et.* ~ give up, drop; ~ *von e-r Ansicht* change; *von e-m Thema* digress from;

d) by preceding symbols and abbreviated definitions (see list, pp. 683–684);

e) by giving the opposite of the word in question, e.g.: **Land** (*Ggs. Wasser*) land; (*Ggs. Stadt*) country.

A semicolon separates one given meaning from another essentially different meaning.

b) bei den substantivierten Adjektiven (z. B. Uneingeweihte *m, f*); sie werden nach (18) abgewandelt;

c) bei den substantivierten Verben (z. B. Geschehen); sie sind Neutra und abwandelbar nach (6);

d) bei den Verben auf -ieren (z. B. radieren); sie werden nach (25) abgewandelt.

Der Vermerk (sn) bedeutet, daß das betreffende intransitive Verb das Perfekt usw. mit „sein" bildet. Die übrigen Verben werden mit „haben" konjugiert.

Die Eigennamen werden, falls keine andere Ziffer angegeben ist, nach (17) dekliniert.

Die Bezeichnungen *sg.* bzw. *pl.* nach einem Substantiv bedeuten singularische bzw. pluralische Konstruktion der abhängigen Verben.

6. Bedeutungsunterschiede (in *Kursivschrift*) sind gekennzeichnet:

a) durch sinnverwandte Wörter in runden Klammern, z. B.: **rein** pure; (*sauber*) clean;

b) durch vorgesetzte deutsche Erklärungen, z. B.: **Blick** *flüchtiger*: glance; **dämpfen** *Stoß, Schall*: deaden; **Abfall** *der Blätter*: fall; *beim Schlachten*: offal;

c) durch Einschübe, die einen grammatischen oder bedeutungsmäßigen Zusammenhang verdeutlichen sollen, jedoch unübersetzt bleiben, z. B.: **abkommen** ... *von et.* ~ give up, drop; ~ *von e-r Ansicht* change; *von e-m Thema* digress from;

d) durch vorgesetzte bildliche Zeichen und abgekürzte Begriffsbestimmungen (s. Verzeichnis S. 683 u. 684);

e) durch Angabe des Gegensatzes, z. B.: **Land** (*Ggs. Wasser*) land; (*Ggs. Stadt*) country.

Das Semikolon trennt eine gegebene Bedeutung von einer neuen, wesentlich verschiedenen.

Symbols and Abbreviations
Erklärung der Zeichen und Abkürzungen

1. Symbols — Bildliche Zeichen

~ } v. Directions for Use, p. 680,
○ } section 2.
~ } s. *Hinweise S. 680, Absatz 2.*

F   familiar, colloquial language, *familiär, Umgangssprache.*

P   low colloquialism, *populär, Sprache des (einfachen) Volkes.*

V   indecent, *unanständig.*

†   archaic, *altertümlich.*

✎   rare, little used, *selten.*

⚕   scientific term, *wissenschaftlich.*

✿   botany, *Pflanzenkunde.*

⊕   handicraft; engineering, *Handwerk, Technik.*

⚒   mining, *Bergbau.*

⚔   military term, *militärisch.*

⚓   nautical (sailors' or watermen's) term, *Schiffahrt.*

†   commercial term, *Handelswesen.*

🚂   railroad, railway, *Eisenbahn.*

✈   aviation, *Luftfahrt.*

✉   postal affairs, *Postwesen.*

♪   musical term, *Musik.*

⌂   architecture, *Baukunst.*

⚡   electrical engineering, *Elektrotechnik.*

⚖   jurisprudence, *Rechtswissenschaft.*

⚹   mathematics, *Mathematik.*

⚘   farming, *Landwirtschaft.*

⚗   chemistry, *Chemie.*

♏   medicine, *Heilkunde, Medizin.*

2. Abbreviations — Abkürzungen

a., a.   *also*, auch.

abbr.   *abbreviation*, Abkürzung.

acc.   *accusative (case)*, Akkusativ, 4. Fall.

adj.   *adjective*, Adjektiv, Eigenschaftswort.   [wort.]

adv.   *adverb*, Adverb, Umstands-]

allg.   allgemein, *commonly.*

Am.   *Americanism*, im amerikanischen Englisch gebräuchlicher Ausdruck.

anat.   *anatomy*, Anatomie.

art.   *article*, Artikel, Geschlechtswort.

ast.   *astronomy*, Astronomie.

attr.   *attributively*, als Attribut od. Beifügung.

biol.   *biology*, Biologie.

Brt.   *in British usage only*, nur im britischen Englisch gebräuchlich.

b.s.   *bad sense*, in schlechtem Sinne.

bsd.   besonders, *particularly.*

cj.   *conjunction*, Konjunktion, Bindewort.

co.   *còmic(al)*, komisch, scherzhaft.

comp.   *comparative*, Komparativ.

contp.   *contemptuously*, verächtlich.

dat.   *dative (case)*, Dativ, 3. Fall.

dem.   *demonstrative*, hinweisend.

ea., ea.   einander, *one another, each other.*

eccl.   *ecclesiastical*, kirchlich, geistlich.

e-e   eine, *a (an).*

ehm.   ehemals, *formerly.*

e-m }
e-m } einem, *to a (an).*

e-n }
e-n } einen, *a (an).*

engS.   in engerem Sinne, *more strictly taken.*

e-r }
e-r } einer, *of a (an), to a (an).*

e-s }
e-s } eines, *of a (an).*

et. }
et. } etwas, *something.*

etc., etc.   et cetera, *and others, and so forth*, und so weiter.

f	*feminine,* weiblich.
fenc.	*fencing,* Fechtkunst.
fig.	*figuratively,* figürlich, bild-}
fr.	französisch, *French.* [lich.]
gen.	*genitive (case),* Genitiv, 2. Fall.
geogr.	*geography,* Erdkunde.
geol.	*geology,* Geologie.
ger.	*gerund,* Gerundium.
Ggs.	Gegensatz, *antonym.*
gr.	*grammar,* Grammatik.
h.	haben, *have.*
hist.	*history,* Geschichte.
hunt.	*hunting,* Jagdwesen. [tiv.}
imp.	*imperative (mood),* Impera-}
ind.	*indicative (mood),* Indikativ.
inf.	*infinitive (mood),* Infinitiv.
int.	*interjection,* Empfindungswort, Ausruf.
interr.	*interrogative,* fragend.
inv.	*invariable,* unveränderlich.
iro.	*ironically,* ironisch.
j., j-s,	jemand(es *of;* -em *dat. to;*
j-m, j-n	-en *acc.) somebody.*
l.	lassen, *let.*
lit.	*literary,* nur in der Schriftsprache vorkommend.
m	*masculine,* männlich.
m-e	meine, *my.*
metall.	*metallurgy,* Hüttenwesen.
min.	*mineralogy,* Mineralogie.
m-n	meinen, *my.*
mot.	*motoring,* Kraftfahrwesen.
mount.	*mountaineering,* Bergsteigerei.
m-r	meiner, *of my, to my.*
mst	meistens, *mostly, usually.*
n	*neuter,* sächlich.
nom.	*nominative (case),* Nominativ, 1. Fall.
o.	ohne, *without.*
od.	oder, *or.*
opt.	*optics,* Optik.
o.s.	*oneself,* sich.
P.	Person, *person.*
p., p.	*person,* Person.
paint.	*painting,* Malerei.
parl.	*parliamentary term,* parlamentarischer Ausdruck.
perf.	*perfect,* Perfekt(um), vollendete Gegenwart.
pharm.	*pharmacy,* Apothekerkunst.
phls.	*philosophy,* Philosophie.
phot.	*photography,* Photographie.
phys.	*physics,* Physik.
physiol.	*physiology,* Physiologie.
pl.	*plural,* Mehrzahl.
poet.	*poetry,* Dichtkunst.

pol.	*politics,* Politik.
p.p.	*past participle,* Partizip der Vergangenheit.
p.pr.	*present participle,* Partizip der Gegenwart.
pred.	*predicative,* prädikativ.
pret.	*preterit(e),* Präteritum, Vergangenheit. [wort.}
pron.	*pronoun,* Pronomen, Für-}
prp.	*preposition,* Verhältniswort.
prs.	*present (tense),* Präsens, Gegenwart.
refl.	*reflexive,* reflexiv, rückbezüglich.
rel.	*relative,* bezüglich.
rhet.	*rhetoric,* Rhetorik.
S., S.	Sache, *thing.*
s., s.	siehe, man sehe, *see, refer to.*
s-e	seine, *his, one's.*
sg.	*singular,* Einzahl.
sl.	*slang,* Slang.
s-m	seinem, *to his, to one's.*
sn	sein (Verb), *be.*
s-n	seinen, *his, one's.*
s-r	seiner } *of his,*
s-s	seines } *of one's.*
su.	*substantive,* Hauptwort.
subj.	*subjunctive (mood),* Konjunktiv.
sup.	*superlative,* Superlativ.
surv.	*surveying,* Landvermessung.
tel.	*telegraphy,* Telegraphie.
teleph.	*telephony,* Fernsprechwesen.
th., th.	*thing,* Ding, Sache.
thea.	*theatre,* Theater.
typ.	*typography,* Buchdruck.
u., u.	und, *and.*
univ.	*university,* Hochschulwesen, Studentensprache.
usw.	und so weiter, *etc. and so forth.*
v.	vón, vom, *of, by, from.*
vb.	*verb,* Verb(um), Zeitwort.
v/aux.	*auxiliary verb,* Hilfszeitwort.
vet.	*veterinary art,* Tierheilkunde.
vgl., vgl.	vergleiche, *compare.*
v/i.	*verb intransitive,* intransitives Zeitwort.
v/refl.	*verb reflexive,* reflexives Zeitwort. [Zeitwort.}
v/t.	*verb transitive,* transitives}
weitS.	im weiteren Sinne, *more widely taken.*
z.B.	zum Beispiel, *for instance.*
zo.	*zoology,* Zoologie.
Zssg(n)	Zusammensetzung(en), *compound word(s).*

Key to Pronunciation

The phonetic alphabet used in this German-English dictionary is that of the Association Phonétique Internationale (A. P. I. or I. P. A. = International Phonetic Association).

The length of vowels is indicated by [ː] following the vowel symbol, the stress by ['] preceding the stressed syllable.

The glottal stop [ʔ] is the forced stop between one word or syllable and a following one beginning with a stressed vowel, as in "beobachten" [bə'ʔoːbaxtən].

Symbol	Examples	Nearest English Equivalents	Remarks
		A. Vowels	
a	Mann [man]		short a as in French "carte" or in British English "cast" said quickly
ɑː	Wagen ['vɑːgən]	father	long a
e	Edikt [e'dikt]	bed	
eː	Weg [veːk]		unlike any English sound, though it has a resemblance to the sound in "day"
ə	bitte ['bitə]	ago	a short sound, that of unaccented e
ɛ	Männer ['mɛnər] Geld [gɛlt]	fair	There is no -er sound at the end. It is one pure short vowel-sound.
ɛː	wählen ['vɛːlən]		same sound, but long
i	Wind [vint]	it	
iː	hier [hiːr]	meet	
ɔ	Ort [ɔrt]	long	
ɔː	Komfort [kɔm'fɔːr]	draw	
o	Advokat [atvo'kɑːt]	molest [mo'lest]	
oː	Boot [boːt]		[oː] resembles the English sound in go [gou] but without the [u]

Symbol	Examples	Nearest English Equivalents	Remarks
ø:	schön [ʃøːn]		as in French "feu". The sound may be acquired by saying [e] through closely rounded lips.
ø	Ödem [øˈdeːm]		same sound, but short
œ	öffnen [ˈœfnən]		as in French "neuf". The sound has a resemblance to the English vowel in "her". Lips, however, must be well rounded as for ɔ.
u	Mutter [ˈmutər]	book	
u:	Uhr [uːr]	boot	
y	Glück [glyk]		almost like the French u as in sur. It may be acquired by saying i through fairly closely rounded lips.
y:	führen [ˈfyːrən]		same sound, but long

B. Diphthongs

aɪ	Mai [maɪ]	like	
aʊ	Maus [maʊs]	mouse	
ɔʏ	Beute [ˈbɔʏtə] Läufer [ˈlɔʏfər]	boy	

C. Consonants

b	besser [ˈbɛsər]	better	
d	du [duː]	dance	
f	finden [ˈfindən] Vater [ˈfɑːtər] Philosoph [filoˈzoːf]	find	
g	Gold [gɔlt] Geld [gɛlt]	gold	
ʒ	Genie [ʒeˈniː] Journalist [ʒurnaˈlist]	measure	
h	Haus [haʊs]	house	
ç	Licht [liçt] Mönch [mœnç] lustig [ˈlustiç]		An approximation to this sound may be acquired by assuming the mouth-configuration for [i] and emitting a strong current of breath.

Symbol	Examples	Nearest English Equivalents	Remarks
x	Loch [lɔx]	Scotch: loch	Whereas [ç] is pronounced at the front of the mouth, x is pronounced in the throat.
j	ja [jɑ:]	year	
k	keck [kɛk] Tag [tɑ:k] Chronist [kroˈnɪst] Café [kaˈfe:]	kick	
l	lassen [ˈlasən]	lump	pronounced like English initial "clear l"
m	Maus [maʊs]	mouse	
n	nein [naɪn]	not	
ŋ	singen [ˈziŋən] trinken [ˈtriŋkən]	sing, drink	
p	Paß [pas] Weib [vaɪp] obgleich [ɔpˈglaɪç]	pass	
r	rot [ro:t]	rot	There are two pronunciations: the frontal or lingual r and the uvular r (the latter unknown in England).
s	Glas [glɑ:s] Masse [ˈmasə] Mast [mast] naß [nas]	miss	unvoiced when final, doubled, or next to a voiceless consonant
z	Sohn [zo:n] Rose [ˈro:zə]	zero	voiced when initial in a word or a syllable
ʃ	Schiff [ʃif] Charlotte [ʃarˈlɔtə] Spiel [ʃpi:l] Stein [ʃtaɪn]	shop	
t	Tee [te:] Thron [tro:n] Stadt [ʃtat] Bad [bɑ:t] Findling [ˈfɪntlɪŋ] Wind [vint]	tea	
v	Vase [ˈvɑ:zə] Winter [ˈvɪntər]	vast	

ã, ɛ̃, õ are nasalized vowels. Examples: Ensemble [ãˈsã:bl], Terrain [tɛˈrɛ̃], Bonbon [bõˈbõ].

List of Suffixes
often given without Phonetic Transcription

Suffix	Phonetic Tran-scription	Examples	Remarks
-bar	-bɑːr	'schein**bar**	
-chen	-çən	'Städt**chen**	
-d	-t	'fessel**nd**	
-de	-də	'Zier**de**	
-ei	-aɪ	Reede'**rei**	
-en	-ən	zer'stör**en**	
-end	-ənt	'ätz**end**	
-er	-ər	Trans'port**er** be'reich**ern**	
-haft	-haft	'zwergen**haft**	
-heit	-haɪt	Be'sonder**heit**	
-ie	-iː	Orange'**rie**	
-ieren	-iːrən	organi'**sieren** salu'**tieren** mystifi'**zieren**	
-ig	-iç	'lust**ig**	but lust**ige** [-igə], lust**iger** [-igər], lust**iges** [-igəs], etc.
-ik	-ik	Belle'trist**ik**	
-in	-in	'Säuger**in**	
-isch	-iʃ	'belg**isch**	
-ist	-ist	Pessi'm**ist**	
-keit	-kaɪt	'Männlich**keit**	
-lich	-liç	'sach**lich**	
-losigkeit	-loːziçkaɪt	'Rücksichts**losigkeit**	
-nis	-nis	'Wirr**nis**	
-sal	-zɑːl	'Trüb**sal**	
-sam	-zɑːm	'furcht**sam**	
-schaft	-ʃaft	'Wähler**schaft**	
-ste	-stə	'dreißig**ste**	
-tät	-tɛːt	Morali'**tät**	
-tum	-tuːm	'Wachs**tum**	
-ung	-uŋ	Ge'sinn**ung**	
-ungs-	-uŋs-	Ge'**sinnungs**wechsel	

A

A, a [ɑ:] *n* A, a (*a. ♪*); *fig. das A u. O*
the most important thing; *von A
bis Z* from A to Z; *wer A sagt, muß
auch B sagen* in for a penny, in for a
pound; ♪ *A-Dur* A major; *a-Moll*
A minor.

à [a] *prp.* ✝ (at) ... each.

Aal [ɑ:l] *m* (3) eel; '₂en *v/refl.* laze
(about); '₂glatt slippery (as an eel).

Aar *poet.* [ɑ:r] *m* (3) eagle.

Aas [ɑ:s] *n* (4, *pl. a.* Äser ['ɛ:zər] 1²)
carrion; (*Köder*) bait; P *Schimpfwort*: beast; ₂en F ['a:zən] (27):
mit et. ~ squander; '₋geier *m*
carrion kite; *fig.* vulture.

ab [ap] *adv. u. prp.* off; down; from;
thea. exit, *pl.* exeunt; *zeitlich*: (*von
...*) *ab* from ... on(wards), *amtlich*:
as from, on and after *May 1st, etc.*
~ *und zu* now and then; *weit* ~ far
off; ✝ ~ *Berlin, Fabrik, Lager usw.*
ex Berlin, factory, store, *etc.*; 🚂 ~
dep. (= departs, departure); ~
Brüssel from Brussels; ~ *dort* (to be)
delivered at yours; ~ *Unkosten* less
charges; *Hut* ~*!* hat(s) off!; *von
jetzt* ~ from now on.

abänder|lich ['apˀɛndərliç] alter-
able; '₋n alter; change; modify;
parl. amend; *jur.* commute; '₂ung *f*
alteration; modification; amendment; '₂ungsantrag *parl. m*
amendment.

'**ab-arbeiten** *Schuld*: work out; *sich*
~ overwork o.s., slave; *abgearbeitet*
worn-out.

'**Ab-art** *f* variety; '₂en (sn) degenerate; (*variieren*) vary; '₂ig abnormal; *sexuell*: perverted; '₋ung *f*
degeneration; variation.

'**Abbau** *m* ⊕ dismantling; ⚒ working; *der Preise, des Personals*:
reduction, *Am.* cutback; *einzelner
Angestellten*: retrenchment, dismissal; ⚙ decomposition; '₂en *v/t.*
Gebäude usw.: pull down, *a.* ⊕
dismantle; ⚒ work, mine; *Preise,
Personal*: reduce, cut down; *einzelne Angestellte*: retrench, dismiss;
⚙ reduce.

'**abbeißen** bite off.

'**abbeizen** strip.

'**Abbeizmittel** *n* paint stripper.

'**abbekommen** get off; *s-n Teil
(od. et.)* ~ get (*od.* come in for)
one's share; *et.* ~ (*verletzt werden*)
get hurt, *S.*: be damaged.

'**abberuf|en** recall; '₂ung *f* re-
call.

'**abbestell|en** countermand, cancel
(orders for); *Zeitung*: discontinue;
'₂ung *f* countermand, cancellation.

'**abbetteln:** *j-m et.* ~ wheedle a th.
out of a p.

'**abbiegen** *v/t.* bend off; *fig. e-e
Sache*: avert, ward off; *v/i.* (sn)
turn off; *Straße*: branch off.

'**Abbild** *n e-r S.*: copy; *e-r P.*: likeness; (*Ebenbild*) image; '₂en represent; model; copy *a th.*; portray
a p.; '₋ung *f* representation; picture;
illustration; *Computer*: mapping.

'**abbinden** unbind, untie; ⚓ tie up
od. off; *Zement*: set.

'**Abbitte** *f* apology; ~ *tun* = '₂n
v/t. u. v/i. apologize (*j-m et.* to a p.
for a th.).

'**abblasen** *v/t. Dampf*: blow off;
Angriff: break off; *fig.* call off,
cancel.

'**abblättern** *v/refl. u. v/i.* (sn) shed
the leaves; *fig.* flake *od.* peel off.

'**abblend|en** *v/t.* screen (off), dim;
phot. stop down; *Film, Radio*: fade
down; *v/i. mot.* dip the (head)lights;
'₂licht *mot. n* dipped (*Am.* dimmed)
headlights *pl.*; '₂schalter *mot. m* dip
switch; '₂vorrichtung *f im Kino
usw.*: dimmer.

'**abblitzen** F (sn) meet with a rebuff
(*bei j-m* from a p.); ~ *lassen* rebuff,
send *a p.* packing.

'**abbrausen** *v/t.* (*a. sich* ~) shower;
v/i. F (sn) buzz off.

'**abbrechen** *v/t. u. v/i.* (sn) break
off (*a. fig.*); *Haus usw.*: pull down,
demolish; *Lager*: break (up); *Zelt*:
strike; *kurz* ~ *v/t.* cut short, *v/i.*
stop short; *alle Brücken hinter sich* ~
burn one's boats.

'**abbremsen** slow down; *mot.* brake.

'**abbrennen** *v/t. Haus*: burn down;

Feuerwerk: let off; *v/i.* (sn) burn down; *s. abgebrannt.*

'**abbringen** get off, deflect, divert; *fig.* j-n ~ von put a p. off doing (*a th.*), *von e-r Meinung usw.* talk a p. out of; (*abraten*) dissuade from; *s. ausreden; von e-m Thema*: lead away from; *vom (rechten) Wege* ~ (*a. fig.*) lead astray; *sich nicht* ~ *lassen von etwas abide by* (*od.* stick to) a th.; *davon lasse ich mich nicht* ~ nothing can change my mind about that.

'**abbröckeln** (sn) crumble away *od.* off; *Kurse, Preise*: crumble.

'**Abbruch** *m* breaking off (*a. fig. von Beziehungen*); *e-s Hauses*: pulling down, demolition; (*Schaden*) damage, injury; *auf* ~ *verkaufen* sell for the material; ~ *tun* (*dat.*) damage, impair, prejudice; ~ *erleiden* be impaired; '**~unternehmer** *m* demolition contractor, wrecker.

'**abbrühen** *Gemüse*: (par)boil; *Geflügel, Schwein*: scald; *s. abgebrüht.*

'**abbuchen** † charge off; (*abschreiben*) write off.

'**abbüß|en** expiate, atone for; *Strafe*: serve; '**2ung** *f* expiation, atonement.

Abc [ɑ:be'tse:] *n* ABC, alphabet; **~Buch** *n* primer, spelling book.

'**abchecken** F (25) tick (*Am.* check) off.

Abc-Schütze *m* (school) beginner.

ABC-Waffen *f/pl.* NBC-weapons.

abdach|en ['apdaxən] (25) slant, slope; *sich* ~ slope off; '**2ung** *f* slope, declivity.

'**abdämmen** (25) dam up.

'**abdampf|en** (h. *u.* sn) evaporate; F *Zug*: steam off, *Person*: *sl.* beat it; '**2ung** *f* evaporation.

'**abdank|en** resign; *Herrscher*: abdicate; '**2ung** *f* resignation; abdication; retirement.

'**abdecken** uncover; *Dach*: untile; *Haus*: unroof; *Tisch*: clear; ⊕ mask, cover; *phot.* screen off; *Vieh*: flay; *Sport*: *s.* decken.

'**Abdecker** *m* (7) knacker, flayer; **~ei** [~'raɪ] *f* knackery, *Am.* boneyard. [dust cover.⟩

'**Abdeckhaube** *f e-s Plattenspielers*: ⟩

'**abdicht|en** (26) seal (up); *Maschinenteil*: pack; ⚓ ca(u)lk; '**2gummi** *mot. m, n* body rubber; '**2ung** *f*

sealing; packing.

'**abdienen** *Schuld*: work out; *s-e Zeit* ~ serve one's time.

'**abdrehen** *v/t.* twist off; *Gas usw.*: turn off; ⚡ switch off; *v/i.* ✈, ⚓ turn away, sheer off.

'**abdrosseln** ⊕ throttle (down *fig.*).

'**Abdruck** *m* impression (*a. typ.*), imprint; (*Nachdruck*) reprint; (*Exemplar*) copy; *typ.* (*Probe2*) proof; (*Abguß*) cast; *e-s Petschafts usw.*: stamp; mark; '**2en** print; *wieder* ~ reprint.

'**abdrücken** squeeze off; (*abformen*) mo(u)ld; *Gewehr*: pull the trigger of *a gun*, fire; (*umarmen*) hug; *j-m das Herz* ~ break a p.'s heart; *sich* ~ leave an imprint.

'**abdunkeln** dim; *Farben*: darken.

'**abdüsen** F (27, sn) clear off, take off.

'**ab-ebben** *a. fig.* ebb (away).

Abend ['ɑ:bənt] *m* (3^1) evening; night; *des* ~s, 2s in the evening, at night; *s. essen; man soll den Tag nicht vor dem* ~ *loben* don't halloo till you are out of the wood; *es ist noch nicht aller Tage* ~ things may take a turn yet.

'**Abend...** *mst* evening ...; '**~andacht** *f* evening prayer(s *pl.*); '**~anzug** *m* evening dress; '**~blatt** *n* evening paper; '**~brot** *n*, '**~essen** *n* evening meal; dinner; supper; '**~dämmerung** *f* dusk; '**2füllend** *Film usw.*: full-length; '**~gesellschaft** *f* (evening) party; '**~gymnasium** *n* night-school; '**~kasse** *f* box-office; '**~kleid** *n* evening dress *od.* gown; '**~kurs(us)** *m* evening class(es *pl.*); '**~land** *n* occident; '**~länder(in** *f*) *m* Occidental, Westerner; **2ländisch** ['~lɛndiʃ] western, occidental; '**2lich** evening, of (*od.* in) the evening; '**~mahl** *eccl. n the* Holy Communion, *the* Lord's Supper; '**~mahlskelch** *m* Eucharist cup, chalice; '**~rot** *n*, '**~röte** *f* sunset glow; '**~schule** *f* night-school; '**~sonne** *f* setting sun; '**~stern** *m* evening star; '**~toilette** *f* evening dress; '**~zeit** *f* night-time; '**~zeitung** *f s.* Abendblatt.

Abenteuer ['ɑ:bəntɔʏər] *n* (7) adventure; '**2lich** adventurous; *fig.* odd, wild, fantastic; '**~lichkeit** *f* adventurousness; *fig.* strangeness, oddity; '**~lust** *f* spirit of adventure; '**~spielplatz** *m* adventure playground.

'**Abenteurer** *m* adventurer; '**~in** *f*

adventuress; '**~leben** n: ein ~ führen lead an adventurous life.

aber ['a:bər] **1.** adv. again; tausend und ~ tausend thousands and (od. upon) thousands; **2.** cj. but; nun ~ but now; nein ~! I say!; ~, ~! come, come!; oder ~ otherwise, (or) else; ~ d(enn)och (but) yet, however; **3.** ♀ n but; er hat immer (ein Wenn und) ein ~ he is always full of "ifs" and "buts".

'**Aber|glaube** m superstition; ♀-**gläubisch** ['~gləʏbiʃ] superstitious.

aberkenn|en ['ap'ɛrkɛnən]: j-m et. ~ deny a p. a th.; ⚖ deprive a p. of a th.; '♀**ung** f denial; ⚖ deprivation.

aber|malig ['a:bərma:liç] repeated; **~mals** ['~s] again, once more.

abernten ['ap'ɛrntən] reap.

Aberwitz ['a:bərvits] m madness, folly; '♀**ig** crazy, foolish.

abessen ['ap'ɛsən] v/t. eat clean.

abfackeln ['apfakəln] Erdgas: burn off.

abfahren ['apfa:rən] v/i. (sn) leave, depart, set out od. off, start (nach for); Ski: descend, run downhill; F j-n ~ lassen send a p. packing; sl. ich bin total auf Reggae abgefahren F I'm really into Reggae; v/t. Last: carry off; (abnützen) wear (out); Strecke: drive through, cover; patrol; ihm wurde ein Bein abgefahren he lost a leg in a motor-accident.

'**Abfahrt** f start, departure; ⚓ sailing; Ski: downhill (race od. run); bei ~ des Zuges at traintime; '~**slauf** m Ski: downhill race; '~**släufer** m Ski: downhiller; '~**(s)zeit** f time of departure.

'**Abfall** m falling-off; (Böschung) slope; der Blätter: fall; (Trennung) defection, secession (von from), desertion (of); eccl. apostasy; (Abnahme) decrease, a. ♀ drop; fig. contrast (gegen to, with); (Unbrauchbares) (oft pl.) waste; (Müll) refuse, bsd. Am. garbage; (Schnitzel) clippings pl.; beim Schlachten: offal; '~**eimer** m dustbin, Am. ashcan; '♀**en** (sn) fall off (schräg sein) slope, decline; pol. defect, desert; eccl. apostatize; ♀ drop; (mager werden) lose flesh; (übrigbleiben) be left; im Vergleich: compare badly (gegen with); (sich ergeben) result; et. fällt dabei für ihn

ab there will be something in it for him; '♀**end** Gelände: sloping; '~**haufen** m rubbish heap.

'**abfällig** fig. disapproving; Bemerkung: disparaging; Kritik: adverse; ~ über j-n sprechen speak disparagingly of a p.; ~ urteilen über (acc.) criticize unfavo(u)rably, run down.

'**Abfall|produkt** n waste product; by-product; '~**verwertung** f recycling.

'**abfang|en** catch, snatch; j-n, Brief, ✗ usw.: intercept; ⊕ Stöße: absorb; △, ✗ prop; hunt. stab; ✈ flatten out; mot. get under control; '♀**jäger** ✗ m interceptor.

'**abfärben** v/i. stain; lose colo(u)r; ~ auf (acc.) stain; fig. rub off on, influence.

'**abfass|en** Werk: compose, write, pen; Vertrag usw.: draft, bsd. ⚖ draw up; j-n: catch; '♀**ung** f composition; drawing up.

'**ab|faulen** (sn) rot off; '~**federn** ⊕ cushion, spring(-load); suspend; '~**feilen** file off.

'**abfertig|en** dispatch (a. 🚂, ✈); j-n: attend to, ✚ a. serve, a. weitS. serve, deal with; (abweisen) snub; j-n kurz ~ send a p. about his business; '♀**ung** f dispatch(ing); Zoll: clearance; (Abweisung) snub; (Bedienung) service; '♀**ungsschalter** m check-in counter (od. desk); '♀**ungsstelle** f dispatching office.

'**abfeuern** fire (off), discharge.

'**abfinden** satisfy, pay off, Gläubiger: a. compound with; Partner: buy out; (entschädigen) compensate, indemnify; sich mit s-m Los usw. ~ resign o.s. to one's fate, etc.; sich mit e-r unangenehmen P. od. S. ~ put up with.

Abfindung ['apfɪnduŋ] f settlement, satisfaction; composition (der Gläubiger with the creditors); '~**(s-summe**) f indemnity.

abflach|en ['~flaxən] flatten (a. sich); '♀**ung** f flattening; slope.

abflauen ['~flauən] (25; sn) Wind usw.: abate; fig. a. slacken (off); Interesse: flag; ✚ Kurse: fall off.

'**abfliegen** v/i. (sn) fly off; ✈ start, take off; v/t. ✈ patrol, cover.

'**abfließen** (sn) flow off.

'**Abflug** ✈ m start, take-off; departure; '~**hafen** m departure airport; '~**halle** f departure lounge.

'**Abfluß** m flowing off, discharge; drain (a. fig.); (~stelle) outlet; '~**graben** m drain(ing-ditch); '~**rohr** n waste-pipe; ⊕ drain-pipe.

'**abfordern:** j-m et. ~ demand a th. from a p.

'**abformen** mo(u)ld, model.

'**abfragen:** j-m et. ~ question a p. about a th.; e-m Schüler die Grammatik ~ hear a boy's grammar.

'**abfressen** eat off; Wild usw.: browse on, crop, eat bare.

'**abfrieren** (sn) be bitten off by cold.

Abfuhr ['apfuːr] f (16) removal; F (Abweisung) rebuff; fenc. disablement; Sport u. fig. beating.

'**abführen** v/t. j-n: lead off; ins Gefängnis: march off; vom (rechten) Wege ~ lead astray (a. fig.); Geld: branch (od. draw) off; v/i. ⚕ loosen the bowels; '~d ⚕ purgative.

'**Abführmittel** ⚕ n laxative.

'**Abfüll-anlage** f bottling plant.

'**abfüllen** fill; Bier, Wein: draw (od. rack) off; in Flaschen: bottle.

'**abfüttern** feed; ⊕ line.

'**Abgabe** f delivery; der Wahlstimme: casting, polling; (bsd. Zoll) duty; (Steuer) tax, lokale: rate; soziale ~ social contribution; Sport: pass; ✝ sale; phys. emission; ⚡ output; '2nfrei duty-free; tax-free; 2npflichtig ['~pfliçtiç] taxable; dutiable.

'**Abgang** m departure; thea. exit; aus e-r Stellung: retirement; von der Schule: leaving (school), mit Erfolg: graduation; von Waren: sale; (Verlust) loss, wastage; (Fehlen) deficiency, shortage; ⚕ discharge; (Abfall) refuse, offal.

abgängig ['apgɛŋiç] missing.

'**Abgangs|prüfung** f leaving examination; '~**zeugnis** n (school-) leaving certificate.

'**Abgase** n/pl. exhaust fumes.

'**Abgas|-entgiftungsanlage** f anti-pollution device; '~**katalysator** mot. m (8) catalytic converter; '~**test** m fume emission test; '~**turbolader** mot. m (7) turbocharger.

'**abgeben** deliver, hand over (an acc., bei to); Schriftstück: submit (to), a. Schulhefte: hand in; Ware: sell; Erklärung: make; Gepäck: deposit; Meinung usw.: give, pass; e-n Politiker usw.: make; Schuß: fire; Fußball: pass (a. v/i.); s. Stimme; von et.: give some of; (dienen als) act as; sich ~ mit et. occupy o.s. with, deal with; sich ~ mit j-m associate with, have dealings with; können Sie mir e-e Zigarette ~? can you spare me a cigarette?; du willst mir nie was ~ you never want to give me anything.

abge|brannt F ['apgɔbrant] (ohne Geld) (stony-)broke; ~**brüht** ['~gɔbryːt] fig. hardened; ~**droschen** ['~gɔdrɔʃən] trite, hackneyed; '~**fahren** ['~gɔfaːrən] Reifen: worn down, F bald; ~**feimt** ['~gɔfaimt] cunning, crafty; ~**griffen** ['~gɔgrifən] Buch: well-thumbed; Münze: worn; fig. hackneyed; ~**hackt** ['~gɔhakt] fig. abrupt, disjointed; '~**härtet** s. abhärten.

'**abgehen** (sn) go off; a. 🚂 usw.: leave, depart, start; Post: go; (Amt aufgeben) retire, resign; v. e-r Schule: leave (school), mit Erfolg: graduate (von from); (sich ablösen) come off; Seitenweg: branch off; (fehlen) be missing; thea. make one's exit; ⚡ be discharged; ✝ Ware: sell; reißend ~ F sell like hot cakes; ~ von e-m Vorhaben drop; ~ von e-r Meinung change; ~ von e-m Thema digress (od. swerve) from; vom (rechten) Wege ~ go astray, deviate (beide a. fig.); davon kann ich nicht ~ I must insist (up)on that; hiervon geht ... ab ... must be deducted; er geht mir sehr ab I miss him badly; ihm geht nichts ab he does not go short of anything; fig. gut ~ pass off well; schlecht ~ turn out badly; ~ lassen forward, dispatch; sich et. ~ lassen deny o.s. a th.

abgekämpft ['~gɔkempft] worn-out, spent.

'**abgelegen** remote; out of the way.

'**abgelten** Forderung: meet, satisfy.

abgemessen ['~gɔmesɔn] measured.

abgeneigt ['~gɔnaikt] disinclined od. unwilling (dat. for od. to a th.; zu inf. to), averse (to); j-m ~ ill-disposed towards a p.; '2**heit** f s. Abneigung.

abgenutzt ['~gɔnutst] worn-out.

Abgeordnete ['~gɔ°ɔrdnɔtɔ] m, f (18) delegate, deputy; parl. Member of Parliament (abbr. M.P.), Am. representative.

'**abgepackt** Lebensmittel: packaged, prepacked.

abgerissen [ˈ~gərisən] (zerrissen) torn; (zerlumpt) ragged; (schäbig) shabby; Person: seedy, out-at--elbows; Sprache, Stil: abrupt, disjointed.

'Abgesandte m, f messenger; pol. envoy; geheimer: emissary.

'abgeschieden secluded, retired; (tot) defunct, deceased; **'2heit** f retirement, seclusion.

'abgeschlafft F whacked.

'abgeschlossen (zurückgezogen) secluded; Wohnung: self-contained; Ausbildung usw.: complete; **'2heit** f seclusion.

abgeschmackt [ˈ~gəʃmakt] insipid, absurd; **'2heit** f insipidity, absurdity.

abgesehen [ˈ~gəzeːən]: ~ von apart (Am. a. aside) from, except for.

'abgespannt fig. exhausted, run down; **'2heit** f exhaustion.

abgestanden [ˈ~gəʃtandən] stale.

abgestorben [ˈ~gəʃtɔrbən] (erstarrt) numb; gänzlich ~ dead.

abgestumpft [ˈ~gəʃtumpft] blunt (-ed); ⚔ truncated; fig. dull(ed), indifferent (gegen to).

'abgewinnen j-m et. ~ win a th. from (od. off) a p.; e-r S. Geschmack ~ acquire a taste for a th.

abgewirtschaftet [ˈ~gəvirtʃaftət] run down, finished, ruined.

'abgewöhnen: j-m et. ~ cure a p. of a th.; make a p. stop ger.; sich et. ~ leave off, give up.

abgezehrt [ˈ~gətseːrt] emaciated.

'abgießen pour off; in Gips: cast.

'Abglanz m reflection; fig. schwacher ~ pale reflection, feeble copy.

'abgleichen equalize; Konten: square; ⚙ trim.

'abgleiten, **'abglitschen** (sn) slip off, glide off; Vorwürfe usw. gleiten von ihm ab he is deaf to.

'Abgott m idol.

Abgött|erei [~gœtəˈraɪ] f idolatry; mit j-m ~ treiben idolize a p.; **'2isch** idolatrous; ~ lieben idolize, adore.

'abgraben dig off; fig. j-m das Wasser ~ cut the ground from under a p.'s feet.

'abgrämen: sich ~ grieve, eat one's heart out.

'abgrasen graze (off); fig. scour.

'abgrenz|en mark off; demarcate; (de)limit; Begriff: define; **'2ung** f delimitation, demarcation; definition.

'Abgrund m abyss, chasm, precipice; **'2tief** abysmal (a. fig.).

'abgucken F: j-m et. ~ copy a th. from a p.

'Abguß m in Gips usw.: cast, mo(u)ld.

'abhaben: etwas ~ von have a share of; den Hut usw.: have ... off.

'abhacken chop (od. cut) off; Worte: chop; s. abgehackt.

abhaken [ˈaphaːkən] (25) unhook; in e-r Liste: tick (od. check) off.

'abhalftern unhalter; fig. sack.

'abhalt|en v/t. hold (od. keep) off, fig. detain, (hindern) keep, restrain, prevent; (abwehren) ward off; Sitzung, Fest usw.: hold; Lehrstunde: give; Kind: hold out; v/i. ♣ vom Lande ~ bear off; ~ auf (acc.) head for; **'2ung** f e-r Versammlung usw.: holding; e-s Festes: celebration; (Hindernis) hindrance; e-e ~ haben be otherwise engaged.

'abhand|eln: j-m etwas vom Preise ~ beat a p. down in price (od. by a sum); j-m et. ~ purchase a th. of a p.; (erörtern) treat of, discuss; (erledigen) deal with; **'2lung** f treatise, article, (Vortrag in e-m gelehrten Verein) paper; wissenschaftliche: a. dissertation.

abhanden [~ˈhandən]: ~ kommen get lost.

'Abhang m slope; jäher: precipice.

'abhängen v/t. take off od. down; 🎪, 🚇 uncouple; Anhänger: unhook; Verfolger usw.: shake off; v/i. ~ von depend on.

abhängig [ˈ~hɛnic] dependent (von on); (vorbehaltlich) subject (to); **'2keit** f dependence.

'abhärmen (sich) pine away; sich ~ über (acc.) grieve at, for, over; abgehärmt careworn, haggard.

'abhärt|en harden (gegen against); gegen Strapazen: inure (to); **'2ung** f hardening; inurement.

'abhaspeln reel off (a. fig.).

'abhauen v/t. cut off; v/i. (sn) sl. make off, bsd. Am. beat it.

'abhäuten skin, flay.

'abheb|en v/t. lift (off); Geld: (with)draw; Karten: cut (a. v/i.); sich vom Hintergrund usw. ~ contrast (von with), stand out (against); v/i. 🛫 take off, become airborne; **'2ung** f von Geld: withdrawal.

'abheften file away.
'abheilen (sn) heal.
'abhelfen *e-r S.*: help, remedy; *e-r Beschwerde, e-m Mißstand, e-r Notlage*: redress; *e-m Mangel* ~ supply a want.
'abhetzen drive hard, harass; *Pferd*: override; *sich* ~ tire o.s. out, rush, hurry.
'Abhilfe *f* (*vgl. abhelfen*) help; remedy; redress; ~ *schaffen* take remedial measures.
'abhold *j-m*: ill-disposed towards; *e-r S.*: averse to.
'abhol|en fetch; *P., Brief, Paket*: call (*od.* come) for, pick up, collect; ~ *lassen* send for; *j-n von der Bahn* ~ go to meet a p. at the station; **'Ꝗung** *f* fetching; pick-up; collection.
'abholzen (27) *Wald*: cut down.
'abhorchen ✆ auscultate; ✗ *usw. s. abhören.*
'Abhör-anlage *f* bugging system.
'abhören (*abfragen*) hear (*e-m Schüler die Aufgabe* a pupil's lesson); *Gespräch*: listen in on, *mit Mikrophon*: bug; *Telephonleitung*: tap.
'abhör|sicher *Telephonleitung*: safe from interception; **'Ꝗskandal** *m* bugging scandal.
'ab-irren (sn) go astray (*a. fig.*).
'ab-isolieren *Draht*: strip.
Abitur [abi'tuːr] *n* (3) school-leaving (*Am.* final) examination at German secondary schools.
Abiturient(in *f*) [~turi'ent(in)] *m* (12) candidate for the matriculation, *Am.* high-school graduate.
abjagen ['apjɑːgən] *Pferd*: override, overdrive; *P.*: rush about; *j-m et.* ~ snatch a th. away from a p.
abkanzeln ['~kantsəln] (29) lecture, F tell *a p.* off.
abkarten ['~kartən] (26) plot; *abgekartete Sache* prearranged affair, F put-up job.
'abkaufen *j-m*: buy from.
Abkehr ['~keːr] *f* turning away, departure (*von* from); **'Ꝗen 1.** (*abwenden*) turn away (*a. sich*); **2.** sweep off.
'abklappern F *v/t.* scour, F do.
'abklär|en clear, clarify; ✆ filter; *abgeklärt Urteil*: detached, *Charakter*: mellow; **'Ꝗung** *f* clarification; *fig.* detachment of mind.

Abklatsch ['~klatʃ] *m* *typ.* impression; *fig.* (*schwacher*) ~ (poor) copy.
'abklemmen pinch off.
'abklingen (sn) fade away; *Krankheit*: ease off; *Wirkung*: wear off.
'Abklingzeit *f* fade-out time.
'abklopfen *v/t.* beat (*od.* knock) off; ✿ percuss; (*abstauben*) dust down; *v/i.* ♪ stop the music.
'abknabbern nibble off.
'abknallen P bump off.
abknappen, abknapsen ['~knap(s)ən] pinch, stint; *sich et.* ~ stint o.s. of a th.
'abknicken crack (*od.* snap) off; (*beugen*) bend.
'abknöpfen (25) unbutton; F *j-m et.* ~ do a p. out of a th.
abknutschen F (have a) snog with.
'abkochen *v/t.* boil; ✆ decoct; *Milch*: scald; *v/i.* cook out.
'abkommandieren ✗ detach, detail; *Offizier*: second.
'Abkomme *m* (13) descendant.
'abkommen 1. (sn) come (*od.* get) away; *beim Schießen*: mark; *vom Wege* ~ lose one's way; *fig. von et.* ~ give up, drop; ~ *von e-r Ansicht* change; ~ *von e-m Thema* digress from; *von e-m Verfahren* ~ depart from; ⚓ *s.* abheben; *Sport*: gut ~ get a good start; *er kann nicht* ~ *s.* abkömmlich; **2.** Ꝗ *n* (*Vertrag*) agreement, *pol. a.* treaty, convention.
abkömmlich ['~kœmliç]: *er ist nicht* ~ he cannot be spared, he cannot get away.
Abkömmling ['~kœmliŋ] *m* (3) descendant, offspring (*a. pl.*).
'abkoppeln uncouple; *fig. sich* ~ *von et.* dissociate o.s. from a th.
'abkratzen scratch (*od.* scrape) off; P (*sterben*) *sl.* peg out.
'abkriegen *s.* abbekommen.
'abkühl|en cool; *sich* ~ cool down; **'Ꝗung** *f* cooling; *fig.* damper.
Abkunft ['~kunft] *f* (14, *o. pl.*) descent; extraction; (*Geburt*) birth.
'abkürz|en *v/t.* shorten; *Inhalt, Unterredung*: abridge; *Wort*: abbreviate; *Besuch, Geschichte*: cut short; ⚭ reduce; *v/i.* take a short-cut; **'Ꝗung** *f* abridgment; abbreviation; *des Weges*: short-cut (*a. fig.*); ⚭ reduction; **'Ꝗungsverzeichnis** *n* list of abbreviations; **'Ꝗungszeichen** *n* (sign of) abbreviation; *s.* Kürzel.

'**abküssen** *j-n*: smother with kisses.
'**abladen** unload; *Schutt usw.*: dump.
'**Abladeplatz** *m* unloading point; *für Schutt*: dump(ing-ground).
'**Ablage** *f* place of deposit; *von Akten*: filing.
'**ablager|n** *v/t.* deposit; ~ *lassen* store, season well; *v/i.* (sn) settle; *Wein usw.*: mature; *abgelagert Tabak, Holz*: well-seasoned; '**Qung** *f* maturing; *geol.*, ⚒ deposition, sedimentation, (*Abgelagertes*) deposit, sediment.
Ablaß *eccl.* ['~las] *m* (4²) indulgence; '**~brief** *eccl. m* letter of indulgence; '**~ventil** ⊕ *n* drain valve.
'**ablassen** *v/t.* let off; *Teich usw.*: drain; *Zug usw.*: start; *vom Preis* ~ take *od.* knock off the price; (*überlassen*) let *a p.* have *a th.*; *käuflich*: sell; *v/i.* leave off (*von et.* doing a th.), desist (from).
Ablativ *gr.* ['ablati:f] *m* (3¹) ablative.
'**Ablauf** *m e-r Frist*: lapse; *e-s Vertrages, e-r Frist*: expiration; *für Wasser usw.*: drain; ✝ *e-s Wechsels*: maturity; *Sport*: start; *nach ~ von* at the end of; '**Qen** *v/i.* (sn) *Wasser*: run off; *Frist, Vertrag, usw.*: lapse, expire, terminate; ✝ *Wechsel*: become due; *Sport*: start (*a.* ~ *lassen*); *Uhr*: run down; ~ *lassen Flüssigkeit*: drain off; *fig. j-n*: snub; *Schiff*: launch; *gut usw.* ~ come to a good, *etc.* end, pass (*od.* go) off well, *etc.*; *v/t. Schuhe*: wear out; *sich die Beine* ~ run o.s. off one's legs; *s. Horn, Rang*; *die Stadt* ~ scour the town.
'**Ablaut** *gr. m* vowel-gradation, ablaut; '**Qen** *gr.* change the radical vowel.
'**Ableben** *n* death, decease.
'**ablecken** lick off.
'**ablegen** lay down, off *od.* aside, *Kleidungsstück (ausziehen)*: put (*od.* take) off; *altes Kleidungsstück, Vorurteil*: discard; *Gewohnheit*: give up, drop; *Akten, Brief*: file; *Bekenntnis, Gelübde*: make; *Eid*: take; *Prüfung*: pass; *Raumfähre*: separate; *s. Rechenschaft, Probe, Zeugnis*; *bitte legen Sie ab!* take off your coat, please.
Ableger ✐ ['~le:gər] *m* (7) layer, scion (*a. fig. Person*); ✝ branch.
'**ablehn|en** *v/t. u. v/i.* decline, re-

fuse; *als unannehmbar, unbrauchbar usw.*: reject; *Gesuch, Angebot usw.*: turn down; (*nicht anerkennen*) disown; (*ungünstig beurteilen*) object to; *parl. Antrag*: defeat; ⚖ *Zeugen usw.*: challenge; *Theaterstück*: condemn; *dankend* ~ decline with thanks; '**~end** negative; '**Qung** *f* declining, refusal, *Am.* declination; rejection; *parl.* defeat; ⚖ challenge; *thea.* condemnation.
'**ableisten** *Dienstzeit*: pass, ✗ serve.
'**ableiten** *Fluß usw.*: divert; *Wasser*: drain, draw off; ⚡ shunt (off); *gr.*, ⅄, *fig.* derive.
'**Ableitung** *f* (*vgl. ableiten*) diversion; ⚡ shunt; *gr.*, ⅄ derivation; (*Abgeleitetes*) derivative; (*Folgerung*) deduction; '**~ssilbe** *gr. f* derivative affix.
'**ablenk|en** turn away, off *od.* aside, *bsd. Aufmerksamkeit*: take off, divert, distract (*a. j-n*); *Auge, Gedanken, bsd. Verdacht*: avert; *phys., opt.* deflect; *Stoß*: parry; '**Qung** *f* turning away *od.* off; averting; diversion, distraction; deflection; '**Qungsmanöver** ✗ *n* diversion; *fig. a.* red herring.
'**ables|en** *Obst, Raupen usw.*: gather, pick off; *Rede usw.*: read off; *Skala*: read; '**Qung** ⊕ *f* reading.
'**ableugn|en** deny, disavow; '**Qung** *f* denial, disavowal.
'**Ablichtung** *f* photostat.
'**abliefern** deliver.
'**Ablieferung** *f* delivery; *bei* ~ on delivery; '**~ssoll** *n* delivery quota.
'**abliegen** (sn) lie at a distance; *s. abgelegen*.
'**ablohn|en** pay off; '**Qung** *f* paying off; (*Entlassung*) dismissal.
'**ablösbar** *Rente usw.*: redeemable.
'**ablöschen** extinguish; *Schreibtafel*: clean; *Geschriebenes*: wipe off, *mit Löschpapier*: blot; *Kalk*: slake; *Stahl*: temper.
'**ablös|en** loosen, detach; ✗ relieve; *Amtsvorgänger*: supersede; *Schuld*: discharge; *Anleihe*: redeem; *sich* ~ come off; *sich od. ea.* ~ alternate, relieve one another; '**Qesumme** *f Sport*: transfer fee; '**Qung** *f* loosening; detaching; ✗ relief; supersession; discharge; redemption.
'**Abluft** *f* waste air.
'**ablutschen** lick (off).
'**abmach|en** undo, loosen; *s. ablösen*;

fig. settle, arrange; (*ausbedingen*) stipulate; *abgemacht!* agreed!, all right!, *bsd. Am.* O.K.!; '♀**ung** *f* arrangement.

abmager|n ['∾mɑːgərn] (29) (*sn*) grow lean *od.* thin; *abgemagert* emaciated; '♀**ung** *f* emaciation; '♀**ungskur** *f* diet; *e-e ∾ machen* go on a diet; (*auf ∾ sein*) be on a diet.

'**abmalen** paint, portray; *fig. a.* depict; *nach Vorlage*: copy.

'**Abmarsch** *m* departure; '♀**ieren** (*sn*) march off, depart.

'**abmeld|en** give notice of *a p.'s* departure; *sein Telephon ∾* have one's telephone disconnected; '♀**ung** *f* notice of leaving; (*Bescheinigung*) leaving-certificate.

'**abmess|en** measure (off); *Worte*: weigh; '♀**ung** *f* measurement.

'**abmildern** moderate.

'**abmontieren** *Fabrikanlage*: strip, dismantle; *Geschütz, Maschine*: dismount; *Reifen usw.*: remove, detach.

'**abmühen**: *sich ∾* exert o.s., struggle.

'**abmustern** ♣ *Mannschaft*: pay off.

'**abnagen** gnaw (off).

'**abnäh|en**, '♀**er** *m im Kleid*: tuck.

Abnahme ['∾nɑːmə] *f* (15) taking off; (*Verminderung*) decrease, drop; ♣ amputation; ✝ (*Übernahme*) taking, (*Verkauf*) sale; *des Mondes*: wane; *der Reifen usw.*: removal; *e-s Eides*: administering; *der Tage*: shortening; ⊕ acceptance (test); *des Körpergewichts*: loss of weight; ✝ *bei ∾ von ...* on orders of ...

'**abnehm|bar** detachable; '∾**en** *v/t.* take off *od.* down; (*ablösen*) detach; *teleph. Hörer*: unhook; *Glied*: amputate; *Bart*: shave off; ✝ *Strom*: collect; (*wegnehmen*) take *a th.* from *a p.*; *Ware*: take (*dat.* from); ⊕ *Material*: accept, (*prüfen*) inspect; *Obst*: gather; *Rechnung*: audit; *j-m e-n Eid ∾* administer an oath to *a p.*; *Maschen ∾* narrow; *j-m e-e Mühe ∾* relieve a p. of a trouble; *e-e Parade ∾* take (*od.* hold) a review; *j-m ein Versprechen ∾* make a p. promise (a th.); ✝ *j-m zuviel ∾* overcharge a p.; *v/i.* decrease, diminish; (*verfallen*) decline; *Kräfte usw.*: begin to fail, dwindle; *an Körpergewicht*: lose weight, *absichtlich*: reduce; *Mond*: wane;

Tage: shorten; '♀**er(in** *f*) *m* buyer; (*Kunde*) customer, client.

'**Abneigung** *f* aversion, disinclination, dislike (*gegen* to); *natürliche*: antipathy (*against*, to).

abnorm [ap'nɔrm] abnormal, exceptional, unusual.

Abnormität [∾i'tɛːt] *f* (16) abnormity.

'**abnötigen** (*erpressen*) extort (*dat.* from); *j-m Bewunderung ∾* compel a p.'s admiration.

'**abnutz|en**, '**abnütz|en** (*a. sich ∾*) wear out; ♀**ung** *f* wear (and tear); (*Zermürbung*) attrition.

Abonnement [abɔn(ə)'mɑ̃] *n* (11) subscription (*auf acc.* to); ∾**karte** *f* 🚃 *usw.*: season-ticket, *Am.* commutation ticket; ∾**vorstellung** *f* subscription performance.

Abonnent(in *f*) *m* [∾'nɛnt(in)] subscriber (*gen.* to).

abon'nieren subscribe (*auf acc.* to); *abonniert sein auf e-e Zeitung* take (in).

'**ab-ord|nen** depute, delegate, *Am. a.* deputize; '♀**nung** *f* delegation.

'**Ab-ort**[1] *m* (3) (water-)closet, W.C., lavatory, privy, toilet.

Abort[2] 🕀 [a'bɔrt] *m* (3), ∾**us** [∾us] *m* (*inv.*) abortion.

'**abpachten** rent, lease (*j-m from*)

'**abpassen** measure; fit; *j-n, Gelegenheit*: wait (*od.* watch) for; *zeitlich*: *gut* (*od. schlecht*) *∾* time well (*od.* ill).

'**abperlen** (*sn*) drip off (*von et.* a th.).

'**abpfeifen**: (*das Spiel*) *∾* stop the game.

'**Abpfiff** *m Sport*: final whistle.

'**abpflücken** pluck off, gather.

'**abplacken**, '**abplagen**: *sich ∾* toil, drudge; struggle (*mit* with).

abplatten ['∾platən] (26) flatten off.

Abprall ['∾pral] *m* (3, *o. pl.*) bounce; '♀**en** (*sn*) bounce off (*a. fig.*).

'**abputzen** clean; (*polieren*) polish.

'**abquälen** (*sich*) *arbeitend*: toil, drudge; *seelisch*: worry o.s.

'**abquetschen** squeeze off.

abrackern F ['∾rakərn] (29) (*sich*) drudge, slave.

'**abrahmen** *Milch*: skim.

'**abrasieren** shave off; *fig. Gebäude etc.*: raze to the ground.

'**abraten**: *j-m* ([*von*] *et.*) *∾* dissuade a p. (from a th.), advise *od.* warn a p. against a th.

'**Abraum** ⚒ *m* (3, *o. pl.*) mining debris.

'**abräumen** clear away, remove; *den Tisch* ~ clear the table.

'**Abraumsalze** *n/pl.* potassium salts.

'**abreagieren** abreact; (*a. sich*) work off (one's feelings *od.* bad temper); *sich* ~ *a.* let off steam.

'**abrechnen** *v/i.* settle (up) (*od.* square) accounts; *v/t.* (*abziehen*) deduct, discount; *Spesen usw.*: account for; ... *abgerechnet* apart from ..., discounting ...

'**Abrechnung** *f* settlement (of accounts); (*Abzug*) deduction, discount; *auf* ~ on account; ~ *halten* balance (*od.* settle) accounts; '~s-**tag** *m* settling-day; '~**sverkehr** ✝ *m* clearing (system).

'**Abrede** *f* agreement, stipulation; *in* ~ *stellen* deny; '2n *v/i.*: *j-m* (*von et.*) dissuade a p. (from a th.).

'**Abreib|buchstabe** *m* rub-on letter; '2en rub off; *Körper*: rub down; '~**ung** *f* rubbing off; 🪨 rub-down; *nasse*: sponge-down; F (*Prügel, Niederlage*) beating.

'**Abreise** *f* departure; '2n (sn) depart, start, leave, set out (*nach* for).

'**Abreiß|birne** ⊕ *f* wrecking ball; '2en *v/t.* tear off; *Kleider*: wear out; *Gebäude*: pull down; *s. abgerissen*; *v/i.* (sn) break off (*a. fig.*), snap; *Knopf usw.*: come off; *die Arbeit reißt nicht ab* there is no end of work; '~**kalender** *m* tear-off (*Am.* pad) calendar; '~(**notiz**)**block** *m* tear-off pad.

'**abreiten** *v/i.* (sn) ride away; *v/t.* (*zuviel reiten*) override; *Strecke*: ride; ⚔ *Front*: ride down.

'**abrennen**: *sich* ~ run o.s. off one's legs; *s. a. ablaufen*.

'**abricht|en** *Tier*: train; *Pferd*: break in; ⊕ dress; '2er *m* trainer; '2ung *f* training; breaking-in.

'**abriegeln** (29) *Tür*: bolt, bar; *Straße*: block (off), *durch Polizei*: cordon off; ⚔ seal off.

'**abringen** wrest (*j-m* from a p.).

'**Abriß** *m* (*kurze Darstellung*) summary, epitome, abstract; (*Übersicht*) digest; (*Buch*) compendium; *von Gebäude*: demolition.

'**abrollen** *v/t. u. v/i.* (sn) unroll; uncoil; *v. e-r Rolle*: unwind, unreel; (*wegrollen*) roll off; ✝ (*v/t.*) cart away; *fig.* (*v/i.*) unfold, pass.

'**abrücken** *v/t. u. v/i.* (sn) move off (*a.* ⚔); remove; *fig. von j-m* ~ dissociate o.s. from.

'**Abruf** *m*: ✝ *auf* ~ on call; *Geld auf* ~ call money; '2**bar** ready on call; *Computer*: retrievable; '2**en** call off (*a.* ✝) *od.* away; ⚙ *Zug*: call out; *Computer*: retrieve.

'**abrunden** round (off); *abgerundet Leistung*: well-rounded, finished; *Zahl*: round.

'**abrupfen** pluck off.

'**abrüst|en** *v/t. Gerüst*: take down; *v/i.* ⚔ disarm; '2**ung** ⚔ *f* disarmament, arms reduction; '2**ungskonferenz** *f* disarmament conference; '2**ungsverhandlungen** *f/pl.* disarmament (*od.* arms reduction) talks.

'**abrutschen** (sn) slip off *od.* down; ✈ sideslip.

'**absäbeln** hack off.

absacken ['~zakən] (25, sn) ⚓ sag; ✈ pancake.

'**Absage** *f* cancellation; (*Ablehnung*) refusal; *fig.* repudiation (*an acc.* of); '2n cancel, call off; *unerwartet*: cry off (*v/i.*); (*ablehnen*) decline, refuse; (*entsagen*) renounce.

'**absägen** saw off; F *fig.* ax(e).

'**absahnen** F (25) rake in.

'**absatteln** *v/t.* unsaddle.

'**Absatz** *m* stop, pause; ✝ sale(s *pl.*), market(ing), outlet; *typ.* period, break; (*kurzer Abschnitt*) paragraph; (*Stiefel*2) heel; (*Treppen*2) landing; *in Absätzen* intermittently, at intervals; *guten* (*od.* reißenden*) ~ finden* meet with a ready sale, F sell like hot cakes; '2**fähig** ✝ marketable; '~**gebiet** ✝ *n* marketing area; '~**krise** *f* sales crisis; '~**markt** *m* outlet, market; '~**möglichkeit** *f* marketing potentiality; *engS.* outlet; '~**steigerung** *f* sales increase; '~**stockung** *f* stagnation of trade.

'**absaugen** suck off; *Gas*: exhaust; *Teppich usw.*: vacuum.

'**abschab|en** scrape off; *abgeschabt* (*schäbig*) shabby, threadbare; 2**sel** ['~ʃɑːpsəl] *n/pl.* (7) scrapings *pl.*

'**abschaff|en** (25) abolish, do away with; *Gesetz*: abrogate; (*loswerden*) get rid of; *Auto usw.*: give up; '2**ung** *f* abolition; abrogation.

'**abschälen** *s.* schälen.

'**abschalt|en** *v/t.* switch *od.* turn off; ⚡ *Kontakt*: disconnect; *v/i.* F *fig.* relax; '⚥**ung** *f* switching off, disconnection.

'**abschätz|en** estimate, value; (*taxieren*) appraise; *bsd. für die Steuer*: assess; '⚥**ig** disparaging; '⚥**ung** *f* valuation, estimation; appraisal; assessment.

'**Abschaum** *m* scum; *fig. a.* dregs *pl.*

'**abscheiden** *v/t.* separate (*a. Metall*); 🐝 secrete; 🔩 disengage, (*fällen*) precipitate; *v/i.* (sn) depart (*von dieser Welt this life*); *sich* ~ 🔩 be precipitated.

'**abscheren** *s.* scheren.

'**Abscheu** *m* abhorrence, abomination, detestation (*vor dat.* of), disgust (at, for; *gegen* against), horror (of); ~ **haben vor** (*dat.*) abhor, detest, loathe.

'**abscheuern** scour (*od.* scrub) off; (*abnutzen*) wear away *od.* off (*a. sich*); *Haut*: abrade, chafe.

abscheulich [⚥'ʃɔʏlɪç] abominable, detestable; ⚥**keit** *f* abomination.

'**abschicken** send off, dispatch; 🕯 post, *Am.* mail.

'**Abschieb|ehaft** 🔩 *f* remand pending deportation; *j-n in* ~ *nehmen* put a p. on remand pending deportation; '⚥**en** *v/t.* shove off; *Ausländer*: deport; ⚒ evacuate; (*loswerden*) get rid of; *v/i.* (sn) F *fig.* push off; '⚥**ung** 🔩 *f* deportation.

Abschied ['apʃiːt] *m* (3) (*Abreise*) departure; (*~nehmen*) leave-taking, farewell; (*Entlassung*) dismissal; ⚒ discharge, *freiwillig*: resignation; ~ *nehmen* take leave (*von* of), bid farewell (to); ⚒ *s-n* ~ *erhalten* be put on half-pay; *s-n* ~ *nehmen* resign, retire, ⚒ *a.* quit the service; *j-m den* ~ *geben* dismiss (*od.* discharge) a p.; '⚥**nehmen** *n* leave-taking.

'**Abschieds|besuch** *m* farewell visit; '⚥**brief** *m* farewell letter; '⚥**essen** *n* farewell dinner; '⚥**feier** *f* farewell party; '⚥**gesuch** *n* resignation; '⚥**kuß** *m* parting kiss; '⚥**rede** *f* valedictory (address); '⚥**schmerz** *m* wrench; '⚥**szene** *f* farewell scene.

'**abschießen** *Glied*: shoot off; *Schußwaffe*: shoot, fire (off), discharge; *Pfeil*: let fly; *Rakete*: launch; *Wild*: shoot, *j-n*: *a.* pick off; *Flugzeug*: (shoot *od.* bring) down; *fig. s.* Vogel; F *Beamten usw.*:

oust.

abschilfern ['⚥ʃɪlfərn] (29) peel (*od.* scale) off.

'**ab|schinden** *s.* abrackern; '⚥**schirmdienst** ⚒ *m* counter-intelligence; '⚥**schirmen** screen; ⚥**schirren** ['⚥ʃɪrən] (25) unharness; '⚥**schlachten** slaughter, butcher.

'**Abschlag** *m Börse*: discount; (*Preisnachlaß*) reduction; *der Preise*: fall in prices; *auf* ~ on account; *Fußball*: goal kick; '⚥**en** *v/t.* beat (*od.* strike) off; *Baum, Kopf*: cut off; *Bitte*: refuse; *Angriff*: repulse; ⊕ take down; *Lager, Zelt*: strike; *Fußball*: (*a. v/i.*) kick off; *Läufer*: leave far behind.

abschlägig ['⚥ʃlɛːgɪç] negative; ~**e** *Antwort* refusal, denial; ~ **bescheiden** reject, turn down.

'**Abschlagszahlung** *f* part-payment, instal(l)ment.

'**abschleifen** grind off; *fig.* polish, refine; *fig. sich* ~ acquire polish.

'**Abschlepp|dienst** *m* recovery (*Am.* wrecker) service; '⚥**en** drag off; ⚓, *mot.* take in tow, tow off; *sich* ~ struggle under a load; '⚥**öse** *f* towing eye; '⚥**seil** *n* towrope; '⚥**wagen** *m* break-down lorry, *Am.* wrecker (truck).

'**abschließen** *v/t.* lock (up); (*abdichten*) seal (off); *Angelegenheit*: close, settle; (*vollenden*) complete; *Brief, Rede usw.*: conclude, close; *Rechnung*, 🕯 *Bücher*: balance; *Konto*: close; *Vertrag*: conclude, sign; *Versicherung, Verkauf*: effect; (*absondern*) isolate; 🕯 *e-n Handel* ~ strike a bargain, close a deal; *e-n Vergleich mit e-m Gläubiger* ~ compound with a creditor; *sich* ~ seclude o.s.; *v/i.* conclude; *mit dem Leben abgeschlossen haben* have done with life; *ich habe mit allem abgeschlossen* I've done with all that; '⚥**d** concluding; final(ly *adv.*).

'**Abschluß** *m* closing (*a.* 🕯 ~ *der Bücher*), settlement; (*Ende*; *a.* 🕯 ~ *e-s Geschäfts*) conclusion; (*Geschäft*) deal; (*Verkauf*) sale; '⚥**prüfung** *f* leaving (*Am.* final) examination.

'**ab|schmelzen** *v/t.* melt off (*a. v/i.* [sn]); '⚥**schmieren** scribble off; ⊕ grease, lubricate; *v/i.* (sn) ⚒ *sl.* crash; '⚥**schmiernippel** *mot. m* grease nipple; '⚥**schmierpresse** *mot. f* grease gun; '**⁓schminken:** *sich* ⁓ remove one's make-up; F *fig. sich et.* ⁓ get a th. out of one's head; '**⁓schmirgeln** *s. schmirgeln;* '**⁓schnallen** unbuckle.

'**abschneiden** *v/t.* cut off (*a. fig. Rückzug, Zufuhr usw.*); (*scheren*) clip; *j-m die Ehre* ⁓ damage a p.'s reputation; *j-m die Möglichkeit* ⁓ deprive a p. of the chance; *s.* Wort; *v/i. gut, schlecht usw.* ⁓ come off (*od.* do) well, badly, *etc.;* 2 *n* (*Leistung*) performance.

'**Abschnitt** *m* cut; ⩍ segment; ✗ sector; ✝ coupon; *im Scheckbuch:* counterfoil, *Am.* stub; *in e-r Schrift:* section, paragraph; *e-r Reise:* leg; (*Zeit*) period.

'**ab|schnüren** *s.* abbinden; '**⁓schnurren** rattle off; '**⁓schöpfen** skim off (*a.* ✝ *Gewinne*); *Kaufkraft:* absorb; *fig.* den Rahm ⁓ take the cream off; '**⁓schrägen** ['⁓ʃrɛ:gən] (25) slope; bevel; '**⁓schrauben** screw off.

'**abschreck|en** scare away; *Metall, Eier:* chill; *j-n* ⁓ von deter a p. from; '**⁓end** deterrent; (*a.* ⁓ *häßlich*) repulsive; *⁓es Beispiel* warning; '**2ung** *f* deterrence; '**2ungsmittel** *n* deterrent; '**2ungs-potential** *n* deterrent potential.

'**abschreib|en** *v/t.* copy; *Schuld usw., a. fig. j-n:* write off; *Literaturwerk: b. s.* plagiarize; *in der Schule: b. s.* crib; *v/i.* (*absagen*) send a refusal; '**2er** *m* copyist; *b. s.* plagiarist; '**2ung** ✝ *f* writing-off; write-off; (*Wertminderung*) depreciation; '**2ungskünstler** F *m* tax fiddler.

'**abschreiten** pace off; ✗ *die Front* ⁓ receive the military hono(u)rs.

'**Abschrift** *f* copy; *beglaubigte* ⁓ certified copy; '**2lich** *adj.* copied; *adv.* by (*od.* as a) copy.

'**abschrubben** *s.* schrubben.

'**abschuften:** *sich* ⁓ drudge.

'**abschuppen** (*a. sich*) scale (off).

'**abschürf|en:** *sich die Haut* ⁓ graze (*od.* chafe) one's skin; '**2ung** *f* abrasion, graze (*an dat.* on).

'**Abschuß** *m e-r Schußwaffe:* discharge; *e-r Rakete, e-s Torpedos:* launching; *hunt.* shooting; *e-s Flugzeuges:* downing; *e-s Panzers:* disabling; '**⁓rampe** *f* launcher, launching pad.

abschüssig ['⁓ʃysiç] sloping; (*steil*) steep, precipitous.

'**ab|schütteln** shake off (*a. Verfolger*); *fig. a.* get rid of; '**⁓schwächen** weaken, diminish (*beide a. sich*); *phot.* reduce; *Sturz:* cushion; *fig.* (*mildern*) mitigate; (*beschönigen*) extenuate; *Ausdruck:* qualify.

'**abschweif|en** (sn) stray; *fig. a.* digress (*von* from); '**2ung** *f* digression.

'**ab|schwenken** *v/i.* (sn) *bsd.* ✗ wheel off *od.* aside; *fig.* veer off; *v/t.* rinse, wash off; '**⁓schwören** abjure; (*leugnen*) deny by oath; '**⁓segeln** (sn) set sail (*nach* for), sail away; '**⁓segnen** F give one's blessing to.

absehbar ['⁓ze:baːr]: *in* ⁓*er Zeit* in the foreseeable future; *nicht* ⁓ not to be foreseen.

'**absehen** *v/t. Gelegenheit:* watch (for); *in der Schule:* crib; *j-m et.* ⁓ copy a th. from a p.; *Künftiges:* foresee, tell; *es ist kein Ende abzusehen* there is no end in sight; *es abgesehen haben auf* (*acc.*) aim at, have one's eye on; *abgesehen sein auf* (*acc.*) be aimed at; *das war auf mich abgesehen* that was meant for me; *v/i.* ⁓ *von* refrain from; *s. abgesehen.*

'**abseifen** (25) soap down.

'**abseihen** *s.* seihen.

abseilen ['⁓zaɪlən] (25) (*a. sich*) mount. rope down.

'**absein** F (*erschöpft sein*) be all in.

abseits ['⁓zaɪts] **1.** *adv.* aside, apart; *Fußball:* offside; ⁓ *vom Wege* off the road; *fig.* ⁓ *stehen* stand aloof; **2.** *prp.* (*gen. od. von*) aside from, off; '**2tor** *n Fußball:* goal scored from an off-side position.

'**absend|en** send (off), (*bsd.* ✝) dispatch; (*befördern*) forward; *Brief usw.:* post, *Am.* mail; '**2er(in** *f*) *m* sender; '**2ung** *f* sending (off), dispatch(ing).

'**absengen** singe off.

'**Absenker** ⚹ *m* (7) layer.

'**absetz|bar** ✝ sal(e)able; *Betrag:* deductible; *Beamter:* removable; '**⁓en** *v/t.* set down, put down, deposit (*a.* ⌂, *a. sich*); *Hut:* put off; *Beamte:* remove; *König:* depose; *Flugzeug:* set down; *Fahrgast:* set down, drop; *Fallschirm-*

truppen: drop; *Betrag*: deduct; *Bucheintrag, Termin*: cancel; *Ware*: dispose of, sell; *typ.* set up (in type); *Wörter*: separate; *von der Tagesordnung, vom Spielplan* ~ take off ...; *sich* ~ ✗ retreat; *v/i.* break off, stop, pause; F *es wird et.* ~ there will be trouble; **'⒉ung** *f* deposition; *von Beamten*: removal.

'absichern *s. sichern.*

'Absicht *f* intention; *a.* 🜨 intent; (*a. böse* ~) design; (*Ziel*) aim, object; *in der* ~ *zu* with intent to, with a view to; ~*en haben auf* (*acc.*) have designs upon; *sich mit der* ~ *tragen, zu inf.* have thoughts of ger.; **'⒉lich** intentional; *adv. a.* on purpose; **'~s-erklärung** *f* declaration of intent.

'absitzen *v/i. Reiter*: dismount; *v/t.* sit out; *Strafzeit*: do, serve.

absolut [apzo'lu:t] absolute; ~ *nicht* by no means; **⒉ion** [~lu'tsjo:n] *f* absolution; **⒉ismus** [~'tismus] *m* absolutism.

Absolv|ent(in *f*) [apzɔl'vent(in)] *m* (12) school-leaver, *Am.* graduate; **~'ieren** (*lossprechen*) absolve; *Studien*: complete; *Schule*: get through; *höhere Schule, Hochschule*: graduate from; *Prüfung*: pass.

ab'sonderlich peculiar, odd.

'absonder|n separate; *e-n Kranken*: isolate; 🜊 secrete; *sich* ~ seclude o.s.; **'⒉ung** *f* separation; isolation; seclusion; 🜊 secretion.

absorbieren [~zɔr'bi:rən] absorb.

'abspalten (*a. sich*) split off, separate (*a.* 🜮).

'abspann|en *Pferd*: unhitch; ⊕ stay; *s. abgespannt*; **'⒉ung** *f* (*Erschöpfung*) exhaustion.

'absparen: *sich et.* ~ pinch o.s. for a th.

'abspecken (25) lose weight.

'abspeisen *v/i.* finish dinner; *v/t.* feed; *fig.* fob *a p.* off (*mit leeren Worten* with fair words).

abspenstig ['~ʃpenstiç]: ~ *machen* entice away, alienate (*dat.* from); ~ *werden* desert.

'absperr|en shut off; *Tür, Haus*: lock; *Straße*: block (off); *durch Polizei*: cordon off; (*abdrehen*) turn off; *Dampf, Strom usw.*: cut off; *sich* ~ shut o.s. off; **'⒉gitter** *n der Polizei*: crowd barrier; **'⒉hahn** *m* stop-cock; **'⒉ung** *f* shutting off;

blocking; cordoning off; turning off; cutting off; isolation.

'abspiegeln *s. widerspiegeln.*

'abspielen ♪ play; *Tonaufnahme*: play back; (*abnützen*) wear out; *sich* ~ *fig.* take place, happen, pass.

'absplittern *v/t. u. v/i.* (sn) splinter off.

'Absprache *f* arrangement.

'absprechen: *j-m et.* ~ deny a p. a th., deprive a p. of a th.; (*regeln*) settle, agree; **'~d** unfavo(u)rable, disparaging, adverse.

'abspringen (sn) leap (*od.* jump) off; *mit Fallschirm*: a) jump, parachute, b) *im Notfall*: bail (*od.* bale) out; *Splitter, Glasur usw.*: crack (*od.* chip) off; (*abprallen*) bounce off; ~ (*von e-m Thema*) digress, drop (*a subject*) abruptly; *von e-r Partei usw.*: quit, desert.

'Absprung *m* jump; *Sport*: take-off; **'~balken** *m* take-off board.

'abspulen wind off, unspool.

'abspülen wash off *od.* up; rinse.

'abstamm|en (sn): ~ *von* descend from; *gr.* be derived from; **'⒉ung** *f* descent; birth; *gr.* derivation; *deutscher* ~ of German extraction; **'⒉ungslehre** *f* theory of evolution.

'Abstand *m räumlich, zeitlich, fig.*: distance; (*Zwischenraum*) interval; *fig.* (*Unterschied*) difference; ~ *nehmen von* stand away from, *fig.* refrain *od.* desist from; ~ *halten od. wahren a. fig.* keep one's distance; *mit* ~ *besser* far and away better; *mit* ~ *gewinnen* by a wide margin.

abstatten ['~ʃtatən] make, give; *Besuch*: pay; *Dank*: return, render.

'abstauben *v/t.* (25) dust.

'abstech|en *v/t.* cut (off); (*töten*) stick, stab; *v/i.* contrast (strongly) (*gegen od. von* with); **'⒉er** *m* (7) (*Ausflug*) excursion (*a. fig.*), (side-) trip.

'absteck|en *Haar*: unpin; *Kleid*: fit, pin; *Grundriß*: trace out; *Gelände*: mark out, *mit Pfählen*: stake out.

'abstehen stand at a distance; *Ohren usw.*: stick out; (sn) (*verzichten*) desist (von from); (sn) (*schal werden*) get stale; *s. abgestanden*; **'~d** projecting.

'absteifen ⊕ stiffen, strut, prop.

'Absteige F *f* dosshouse, *Am.* flophouse; **'⒉n** (sn) descend; *vom Wagen,*

Pferd: alight; *in e-m Wirtshaus*: put up at; *Sport*: go down, be relegated; '**⊸quartier** *n* (temporary) lodgings; '**⊸r** *m* (7) *Fußball*: relegated team.

abstell|en put down; ⊕ turn off, stop; *Radio usw.*: switch off; *Telephon*: disconnect; *(parken)* park; ⚞ sidetrack; *Mißstand*: abolish, put an end to; ⚒ detach; *darauf abgestellt sein, zu inf.* be calculated to; '**⁀gleis** ⚞ *n* siding; '**⁀tisch** *m* dumb waiter.

'**abstempeln** stamp *(a. fig. als* as).

'**absteppen** stitch, quilt.

'**absterben** (sn) die off; *Glied*: go numb; *Motor*: conk out.

Abstieg ['⊸ʃtiːk] *m* (3) descent; *Sport*: relegation; '**⁀sbedroht** threatened by relegation.

'**abstimm|en** *v/i.* vote *(über acc.* on); **⊸ lassen über** *(acc.)* put to the vote; *v/t. fig.* harmonize *(auf acc.* with), coordinate (with); *zeitlich*: time; ♪, *Radio*: tune (in); ✝ *Bücher*: balance; *Konto*: check off; '**⁀ung** *f* voting; vote; ballot; tuning; coordination; timing; '**⁀ungsregler** *m Radio*: tuning control.

abstinen|t [⊸sti'nɛnt] *allg.* abstemious; *im Alkoholgenuß*: teetotal; **⁀z** [⊸ts] *f inv.* (total) abstinence, teetotalism; **⁀zler** [⊸tslɔr] *m* (7), **⁀zlerin** *f* (16¹) total abstainer, teetotal(l)er.

'**abstoppen** stop; *Sport*: time, clock.

'**Abstoß** *m Sport*: goal-kick; '**⁀en** *v/t.* push off; *phys. u. fig.* repel; ⚔ *Gewebe*: reject; *Aktien, Ware*: dispose of; *e-e Schuld*: discharge; *(abnutzen)* wear (away); *sich* ⊸ get worn; *v/i. Schiff*: push off; *Sport*: make a goal--kick; '**⁀end** *fig.* repulsive, forbidding; '**⊸ung** *f* repulsion.

'**abstottern** F pay off bit by bit.

abstrahieren [⊸stra'hiːrən] abstract.   [*Wärme*: emit.]

'**abstrahlen** *Rost etc.*: sandblast;

abstrakt [⊸'strakt] abstract; **⁀ion** [⊸'tsjoːn] *f* abstraction; **⁀um** *gr.* [⊸'straktum] *n* abstract noun.

'**abstreichen** *Rechnungsposten usw.*: strike off; *(abhaken)* tick off; *Rasiermesser*: strop; *Schuhe*: wipe; *Schaum usw.*: skim off; *Gebiet*: scour.

'**abstreifen** slip off; *Geweih, Haut*: cast, shed; *fig.* cast off; *Schuhe*: wipe; *(absuchen)* patrol.

'**abstreiten** contest, dispute; *Schuld, Tatsache*: deny.

'**Abstrich** *m beim Schreiben*: down stroke; *(Abzug)* cut; ⚔ *von Mandeln*: swab, *von Gebärmutter*: smear; *e-n ⊸ machen* take a swab *od.* smear; *fig. ⊸e machen müssen* have to lower one's sights.

abstuf|en ['⊸ʃtuːfən] (25) *(a. sich)* grad(u)ate; *Farben*: shade off; '**⁀ung** *f* grad(u)ation; shade.

abstumpfen . ['⊸ʃtumpfən] (25) blunt; ⚕ truncate; *fig. die Sinne*: dull; *Gefühle*: deaden *(a. v/i.)*; *sich* ⊸ get blunted.

'**Absturz** *m* fall, plunge; ⚞ crash; *(Abhang)* precipice.

'**abstürzen** (sn) fall *od.* plunge (down); ⚞ crash; *(abschüssig sein)* descend steeply.

'**abstützen** ⚠ prop, support.

'**absuchen** search all over, scour, comb; *mit Scheinwerfer, Radar*: sweep, scan.

Absud ['apzuːt] *m* (3) decoction.

absurd [⊸'zurt] absurd; **⁀e** [⊸'zurdə] *n*, **⁀ität** [⊸zurdi'tɛːt] *f* (16) absurdity.

Abszeß [aps'tsɛs] *m* abscess.

Abt [apt] *m* (3³) abbot.

'**abtakeln** (29) unrig, dismantle.

'**abtasten** feel; ♪, *TV* scan; *fig.* probe; *Boxer*: feel out.

'**abtau|en** defrost; '**⁀vorrichtung** *f* defroster.

Abtei [ap'taɪ] *f* (16) abbey.

Ab'teil ⚞ *n* compartment.

'**abteil|en** divide; *durch e-e Wand*: partition off; '**⁀ung** *f* division.

Ab'teilung *f e-r Behörde, e-s Kaufhauses*: department; *e-s Krankenhauses*: ward; ⚒ detachment, detail, *(Bataillon)* battalion; *von Arbeitern*: gang; *(Verschlag)* partition; *(Fach)* compartment; *(Abschnitt)* section; **⊸sleiter** *m* head of department, departmental manager.

'**abtelegraphieren** wire refusal.

'**abtippen** F type out, *Manuskript etc.*: type up.

Äbtissin [ɛp'tisin] *f* (16) abbess.

'**abtön|en** *paint.* tint, tone (down), shade; '**⁀ung** *f* tint, shading.

'**abtöten** kill *(a. fig. Gefühle)*; *Zahnnerv*: deaden.

Abtrag ['⊸traːk] *m* (3³): ⊸ *tun (dat.)* prejudice, impair, detract from.

'**abtragen** carry off; *Gebäude*: pull down; *Kleid*: wear out; *Schuld*: pay off; *(die Speisen)* ⊸ clear the table.

abträglich [ˈʌtrɛːklɪç] detrimental, prejudicial (*dat.* to); *Kritik*: unfavo(u)rable.

'Abtransport *m* transportation.

'abtreib|en *v/t.* drive off; *Pferd*: jade; (*ein Kind, die Leibesfrucht*) ⌐ procure abortion; *v/i.* (sn) drift off; '2**ung** *f* (ӻt criminal) abortion; e-e ⌐ *machen lassen* have an abortion; '2**ungsklinik** *f* abortion clinic; '2**ungsparagraph** *m* abortion law(s *pl.*).

'abtrenn|en sever; separate; detach; *Genähtes*: rip (off); '2**ung** *f* severance; separation; detachment.

'abtret|en *v/t. Schuh*: wear down; *Stufe usw.*: wear out; (*aufgeben*) cede (*a. Gebiet*), *Anspruch, Eigentum*: yield, assign, transfer (*alle*: *an acc.* to); *sich die Füße* ⌐ wipe (*od.* scrape) one's shoes; *v/i.* (sn) retire (*vom Amt* from office), resign; *thea.* go off (the stage); '2**er** *m* (7) ӻt assignor; (*Fußmatte*) doormat; '2**ung** ӻt *f* cession, transfer.

'Abtritt *m* (3) withdrawal; *thea.* exit; *s. Abort[1]*.

'abtrocknen dry (*sich die Hände* one's hands).

'abtröpfeln, 'abtropfen (sn) drip (*od.* trickle) down *od.* off.

'Abtropfgestell *n* dish (*od.* washing-up) rack.

'abtrudeln ⫯ go into a spin.

abtrünnig [ˈʌtrʏnɪç] unfaithful, disloyal; rebellious; *eccl.* apostate; ⌐ *werden s. abfallen*; 2**e** [ˈʌgə] *m, f* deserter, renegade; *eccl.* apostate; 2**keit** [ˈʌçkaɪt] *f* defection; *eccl.* apostasy.

'abtun (*ablegen*) take off, remove; (*töten*) dispatch; (*erledigen*) dispose of, settle; (*von sich weisen*) dismiss (*als untunlich usw.* as); *Gewohnheit*: cast off.

'abtupfen mop up; dab (*a. ⫸*).

'ab-urteilen try, bring to trial; pass sentence on; *s. verurteilen, aberkennen*.

'abverdienen *Schuld*: work off.

'abverlangen *s. abfordern*.

'abwägen weigh (*a. fig.*).

'abwälzen roll off; *fig.* shift (*von sich* from o.s.); *die Schuld von sich* ⌐ clear o.s. of the charge; *die Schuld auf j-n* ⌐ lay the blame on a p.; *die Verantwortung auf e-n anderen* ⌐ shift the responsibility to someone else, F pass the buck to someone else.

'abwandel|bar *gr. Hauptwort*: declinable; *Zeitwort*: capable of conjugation; '⌐**n** modify, vary; *gr.* decline; conjugate.

'abwander|n *v/i.* (sn) migrate; drift away; '2**ung** *f* migration; drift; *des Kapitals usw.*: exodus; *von Wissenschaftlern*: brain-drain.

'Abwandlung *f* modification; *gr. Hauptwort*: declension; *Zeitwort*: conjugation.

'Abwärme *f* waste heat.

'abwarten wait (for); *s-e Zeit, e-e Gelegenheit*: bide; ⌐! wait and see!; *das bleibt abzuwarten* that remains to be seen; ⌐**de** *Haltung* wait-and-see attitude.

abwärts [ˈʌvɛrts] down, downward(s); F *mit ihm geht's* ⌐ a) he is going downhill, b) *Greis*: he is on the decline; *damit geht es* ⌐ it is going to the bad; '2**trend** *m* downward trend.

'Abwasch *m* (3) washing-up.

'abwaschen wash (off); *Geschirr*: wash up; *fig. Schande*: wipe out.

'Abwaschwasser *n* dish-water.

'Abwasser *n* (7[1]) waste water; sewage; '⌐**kanal** *m* sewer; '2**n** ⫯ take off from water.

'abwechseln *v/t. u. v/i.* alternate (*mit ea. od. sich* with each other); (*verschiedenartig sein*) vary (*a.* ⌐ *mit den Darbietungen usw.*); *mit j-m* ⌐ take turns with a p.; '⌐**d** alternate; *adv.* by turns, alternately.

'Abwechs(e)lung *f* change; alternation; variation; (*Mannigfaltigkeit*) variety; (*Zerstreuung*) diversion; ⌐ *bringen in* (*acc.*) relieve, liven up; *zur* ⌐ for a change; '2**s-arm** monotonous; '2**sreich** varied; *Leben usw.*: diversified; (*ereignisreich*) eventful; '2**sweise** *adv.* by turns, alternately.

'Abweg *m*: *auf* ⌐**e** *geraten* (*führen*) go (lead) astray; 2**ig** [ˈʌgɪç] (*irrig*) erroneous; (*unangebracht*) inept, out of place; (*belanglos*) not to the point, irrelevant.

'Abwehr *f* defen|ce, *Am.* -se (*a. Sport*); *e-s Stoßes, e-s Gefahr usw.*: warding off; *e-s Angriffs, e-r Frage*: parrying; (*Verhütung*) prevention; (*Widerstand*) resistance; ⫻ (⌐**dienst**) counter-espionage service; '2**en** ward off; parry; prevent; *Unglück usw.*: avert; *Angriff*: repulse; *v/i.*

fig. (ablehnen) refuse; '⸝**maßnahme** *f* defence reaction; '⸝**mechanismus** *m* defence mechanism; '⸝**re-aktion** *f* defensive reaction (*gegen* to); '⸝**spieler** *m* defender; '⸝**stoff** *m biol.* antibody.

'**abweich|en** *v/i.* (sn) deviate, diverge (*von* from); *fig.* deviate, depart (from), *von der Wahrheit a.*: swerve from; (*verschieden sein*); *in der Meinung*) differ (*von ea.* from one another); vary (*von* from); *Magnetnadel*: decline; '⸝**ung** *f* deviation, defle|xion, *Am.* -ction; (*Verschiedenheit*) difference; ℞ divergence; declination; departure (*von e-r Meinung, Regel* from).

'**abweis|en** reject, refuse; ℞ dismiss; *Angriff*: repulse; *schroff*: rebuff; (*fortschicken*) turn *a p.* away; '⸝**end** unfriendly, cool; '⸝**ung** *f* refusal, rejection; ℞ dismissal; repulse; rebuff.

'**abwend|en** turn off; *Unglück*: avert; *sich* ⸝ turn away (*von* from), *fig. s.* abkehren; '⸝**ig** *s.* abspenstig; '⸝**ung** *f* turning off; averting.

'**abwerben** ✝ entice away.

'**abwerfen** cast (*od.* throw) off; *Bomben usw.*: drop; *Reiter*: throw; *Blätter, Geweih, Haut usw.*: shed; *Gewinn*: yield; *Spielkarte*: discard.

'**abwert|en** devaluate; '⸝**ung** *f* devaluation.

abwesen|d ['⸝veːzənt] absent; *fig.* absent-minded; *die* ⸝**en** those absent; '⸝**heit** *f* absence; *fig.* absent-mindedness; *durch* ⸝ *glänzen* be conspicuous by one's absence.

'**abwick|eln** unroll, wind off; ✝ *Geschäft*: transact; *Schuld*: liquidate; *Firma*: wind up; (*durchführen*) effect; '⸝**lung** *f* transaction; winding-up, *Am.* wind-up.

'**ab|wiegen** weigh out; '⸝**winken** give a sign of refusal; '⸝**wirtschaften** *v/i.* get ruined (by mismanagement); '⸝**wischen** wipe off; ⸝**wracken** ['⸝vrakən] (25) break up.

Abwurf ['⸝vurf] *m* dropping.

'**abwürgen** strangle; *mot.* stall.

'**abzahl|en** pay off; *in Raten*: pay by instal(l)ments; '⸝**ung** *f* payment (in full); *in Raten*: payment by (*Am.* on) instal(l)ments; (*Rate*) instal(l)ment; *auf* ⸝ on the instal(l)ment system (*Am.* plan).

'**abzählen** *Geld*: count, tell; *Per-*

sonen usw.: tell off; *das kann man sich an den Fingern* ⸝ that's not hard to guess.

'**Abzahlungs|geschäft** *n* hire-purchase (firm); '⸝**kauf** *m* hire-purchase.

'**abzapfen** *Bier usw.*: tap; *Blut*: draw; *j-m Blut* ⸝ bleed a p.

abzäunen ['⸝tsɔynən] fence off *od.* in.

'**Abzehrung** *f* emaciation; ⚕ consumption.

'**Abzeichen** *n* distinguishing mark; *am Anzug usw.*: badge; ✠ marking.

'**abzeichnen** copy; draw; (*abhaken*) tick off; *sich* ⸝ appear in outlines; *Gefahr*: loom; *deutlich*: stand out (*gegen den Himmel usw.* against).

'**Abziehbild** *n* transfer(-picture); ⊕ decalcomania.

'**abziehen** *v/t.* draw (*od.* pull) off; *Hut*: take off; *Aufmerksamkeit*: divert; *Summe*: deduct, ℞ subtract; *Bett*: strip; *Bier*: draw; *typ. Bogen*: pull (off); (*vervielfältigen*) mimeograph; *phot.* print; *Bilder*: transfer; *Tier* ⸝, *e-m Tier das Fell* ⸝ skin; *Rasiermesser*: strop; (*abhobeln*) plane off; *Schlüssel*: take out; *Wein*: rack (off); *Truppen*: withdraw; *s-e Hand von j-m* ⸝ withdraw one's support from a p.; *v/i.* (sn) move off, withdraw; *Rauch usw.*: escape; (*schießen*) pull the trigger.

'**abzielen:** ⸝ *auf* (*acc.*) aim at.

'**abzirkeln** (29) measure with compasses; *fig.* be very precise in.

'**Abzug** *m* withdrawal, departure; *für Wasser usw.*: outlet; *v. Rauch usw.*: escape; *des Gewehrs*: trigger; *e-r Summe*: deduction; (*Rabatt*) rebate, reduction; *phot.* print; *typ.* (galley-)proof; (*Vervielfältigung*) (mimeographed) copy; *nach* ⸝ *der Kosten* charges deducted; *in* ⸝ *bringen* deduct.

abzüglich ['⸝tsyːkliç] *prp.* (*gen. od. acc.*) less, deducting.

'**Abzugs|bügel** *m am Gewehr usw.*: trigger-guard; '⸝**fähig** *Betrag*: deductible; '⸝**haube** *f über dem Herd*: cooker hood; '⸝**rohr** *n* drain- (*od.* waste-)pipe; escape-pipe.

Abzweig|dose ⚡ ['aptsvaɪk-] *f* distribution (*od.* junction) box; ⸝**en** ['⸝tsvaɪgən] (25) (*a. sich*) branch off (*a. fig.*); '⸝**ung** *f* junction, turn-off; ⚡ branch, shunt.

abzwicken

'abzwicken nip (*od.* pinch) off.

ach! [ax] ah!, alas!; ~ (so)! oh (, I see)!; ~ wo! not a bit of it!; ~ was! nonsense!; mit ♀ u. Krach barely, by the skin of one's teeth.

Achat [a'xɑːt] m (3) agate.

'Achs-antrieb mot. m final drive.

Achse ['aksə] f (15) axis; ⊕ axle; per ~ ⊤ by road, 🚃 by rail; F auf der ~ on the move.

Achsel ['aksəl] f (15) shoulder; mit den ~n zucken shrug one's shoulders; über die ~ ansehen look down upon; auf die leichte ~ nehmen fig. make light of; '~höhle f armpit; '~zucken n shrug (of one's shoulders).

acht¹ [axt] eight; heute in ~ Tagen today week; vor ~ Tagen a week ago; alle ~ Tage every other week.

Acht² f (16) **1.** (Obacht) außer ♀ lassen disregard; in ♀ nehmen take care of; sich in ♀ nehmen take care, beware (vor dat. of); **2.** (Bann) ban, outlawry; in die ~ erklären outlaw.

'achtbar respectable, reputable; '♀keit f respectability.

'achte eighth.

'Acht-eck n (3) octagon; '♀ig octagonal.

'Achtel n (7) eighth (part); '~note ♪ f quaver; '~takt ♪ m quaver time.

'achten (26) v/t. respect; (schätzen) esteem; v/i. ~ auf (acc.) s. achtgeben.

ächten ['ɛçtən] (26) outlaw, proscribe; gesellschaftlich: ostracise.

achtens ['axtəns] eighthly.

'achter¹ ⚓ aft.

'Achter² m (7) a. Rudern: eight; '~bahn f switchback, Am. roller coaster; '~deck ⚓ n quarterdeck; '♀lei of eight kinds; '~steven ⚓ m stern-post.

achtfach ['~fax] eightfold.

'achtgeben pay attention (auf acc. to), attend (to); (sich et. merken) mark, mind (auf acc. a th.); (sorgen für) take care (auf acc. of; daß that); ~ auf (acc.) (beobachten) watch; gib acht! look (Am. watch) out!

'achtjährig eight years old, attr. eight-year-old.

'achtlos careless, unmindful; '♀igkeit f carelessness.

'achtmal eight times.

'Achtmi'nutentakt teleph. m eight-minute limit.

'achtsam careful, mindful (auf acc. of); '♀keit f carefulness.

'Acht||'stundentag m eight-hour day; ♀stündig ['~ʃtyndiç] eight-hour; ♀tägig ['~tɛːgiç] lasting a week, a week's trip, etc.

Achtung ['axtuŋ] f esteem, regard, respect (vor dat. for); (Aufmerksamkeit) attention; ~! look out!, Am. watch out!; ✂ attention!; ~! Lebensgefahr! Caution! Danger of death!; ~, Stufe! mind the step!; j-m ~ bezeigen pay respect to a p.; (j-m) ~ einflößen command (a p.'s) respect; sich ~ verschaffen make o.s. respected; alle ~ (vor)! hats off (to)! '~s-erfolg m succès d'estime (fr.); ♀svoll respectful.

Ächtung ['ɛçtuŋ] f proscription.

'achtzehn eighteen; '~te eighteenth.

achtzig ['axtsiç] eighty; in den ~er Jahren in the eighties; j-n auf ~ bringen get a p. hopping mad; ♀er ['~gər] m, ~jährig ['~çjɛːriç] octogenarian; '~ste eightieth.

'Achtzylinder mot. m eight-cylinder car.

ächzen ['ɛçtsən] (27) groan; ♀ n groan(s pl.).

Acker ['akər] m (7¹) field, land; (Boden) soil; (Maß) acre; '~bau m (3, o. pl.) agriculture, farming; '~bauer m husbandman, farmer; '♀bautreibend agricultural; '~gaul m farm-horse; '~gerät n agricultural implements pl.; '~land n arable land; bestelltes: tilled (od. cultivated) land; '♀n (29) v/t. u. v/i. plough, Am. plow, till; fig. toil, drudge; '~salat ♀ m lamb's lettuce.

Acryl||farbe [a'kryːl-] f acrylic paint; ~glas n acrylic glass.

ad absurdum [at ap'zurdum]: ~ führen reduce to absurdity.

ad acta [at 'akta]: ~ legen file away; fig. shelve, Am. table a matter.

Adam ['aːdam] m: den alten ~ ausziehen cast off the old Adam; nach ~ Riese according to Spoker.

'Adams||apfel m anat. Adam's apple; im '~kostüm (n) in one's buff, sky-clad.

addier|en [a'diːrən] add, sum up; ♀maschine f adding machine.

Addition [adi'tsjoːn] f (16) addition.

ade [a'deː] s. adieu.

Adel ['aːdəl] m (7, o. pl.) nobility; von ~ sein be of noble birth.

ad(e)lig ['a:d(ə)liç] noble, titled; **2e(r)** ['⁓ligər] *m* nobleman, aristocrat; **'2e** *f* noblewoman; *die* ⁓*n pl.* the nobility.

'adeln (29) ennoble (*a. fig.*); *Brt.* knight.

'Adels|krone *f* coronet; **'⁓stand** *m* nobility; *Brt.* peerage; *in den* ⁓ *erheben* knight.

Ader ['a:dər] *f* (15) vein (*a.* ✂, ⚕, *im Holz, Marmor usw. u. fig.*); (*Schlag2*) artery; *zur* ⁓ *lassen* bleed; **'⁓laß** *m* (4²) blood-letting (*a. fig.*).

ädern ['ɛ:dərn] (29) vein.

adieu [a'djø:] **1.** *int.* farewell, good-by(e); **2.** ⚲ *n* farewell, adieu.

Adjektiv ['atjɛkti:f] *n* (3¹) adjective; **2isch** [⁓'ti:viʃ] adjectival.

Adjutant [atju'tant] *m* (12) adjutant; *e-s Generals*: aide(-de-camp).

Adler ['a:dlər] *m* (7) eagle; **'⁓auge** *n* eagle eye; ⁓*n haben* be eagle-eyed; **'⁓horst** *m* aerie; **'⁓nase** *f* aquiline nose.

Admiral [atmi'ra:l] *m* (3¹) admiral; **⁓ität** [⁓rali'tɛ:t] *f* admiralty; **⁓stab** [⁓'ra:lʃta:p] *m* naval staff.

adopt|ieren [adɔp'ti:rən] adopt; **2ion** [⁓'tsjo:n] *f* adoption.

Adoptiv... [⁓'ti:f] adoptive.

Adressat [adrɛ'sa:t] *m* (12) addressee; *e-r Warensendung*: consignee; *e-s Wechsels*: drawee; **⁓engruppe** *f* target group.

A'dreßbuch *n* directory.

Adresse [a'drɛsə] *f* (15) address, direction; *falsche* ⁓ misdirection; *s. per*; *fig. an die falsche* ⁓ *geraten* come to the wrong shop, *weitS.* catch a Tartar.

A'dressenkartei *f* mailing list.

A'dreß-etikett *n* address label.

adres'sieren address, direct; ⚕ consign; *falsch* ⁓ misdirect.

Adres'siermaschine *f* addressograph.

adrett [a'drɛt] smart.

adsorbieren [atzɔr'bi:rən] 🜍 adsorb.

Advent [at'vɛnt] *m* (3) Advent; **⁓skranz** *m* Advent wreath; **⁓(s)zeit** *f* Advent season.

Adverb [at'vɛrp] *n* (8²) adverb; **2ial** [⁓vɛr'bja:l] adverbial.

Advokat [atvo'ka:t] *m* (12) advocate; *s. Anwalt.*

Aerobic [ɛ'rɔbik] *n* (11¹) *Sport*: aerobics *pl.*

aerodynamisch   [aerody'na:miʃ] aerodynamic.

Aerogramm ⓥ [aero'gram] *n* (3¹) air letter.

Affäre [a'fɛ:rə] *f* (15) (*a. Liebes2*) affair; *sich aus der* ⁓ *ziehen* wriggle out, *gut*: master the situation.

Affe ['afə] *m* (13) ape, *bsd. kleiner*: monkey; ✂ *sl.* (*Tornister*) pack; F silly ass; F *e-n* ⁓*n haben* be drunk.

Affekt [a'fɛkt] *m* (3) emotion, passion; **⁓handlung** ⚖ *f* act committed in the heat of passion; **2iert** [⁓'ti:rt] affected; **⁓iertheit** *f* affectation.

äffen ['ɛfən] *v/t.* (25) ape; (*necken*) mock; (*täuschen*) fool.

'affen|-artig simian; F *mit* ⁓*er Geschwindigkeit* like a greased lightning; **'2liebe** *f* doting love; **'2schande** F *f* crying shame; **'2theater** *n fig.* utter farce; *weitS.* crazy business; **'2zahn** F *m*: *der hat e-n* ⁓ *drauf!* he's going some lick!

affig ['afiç] F silly.

Äffin ['ɛfin] *f* (16) she-ape, she-monkey.

Afrikan|er [afri'ka:nər] *m* (7), **⁓erin** *f*, **2isch** African.

After *anat.* ['aftər] *m* (7) anus; **'⁓kritik** *f* pseudo-criticism; **'⁓mieter(in** *f) m* subtenant; **'⁓rede** *f*, **'2reden** slander.

ägäisch [ɛ:'gɛ:iʃ]: **2es** *Meer* Aegean Sea.

Agent [a'gɛnt] *m* (12), **⁓in** *f* (16¹) ⚔ *u. pol.* agent; **⁓enring** *m* spy ring; **⁓ur** [⁓'tu:r] *f* (16) agency.

Aggregat [agre'ga:t] *n phys.* aggregate; ⊕ set (of machines); unit; **⁓zustand** *m* (physical) state.

Aggression [agrɛ'sjo:n] *f pol. u. psych.* aggression.

aggressiv [⁓'si:f] aggressive; **2i'tät** [⁓sivi'tɛ:t] *f* (16) aggressiveness.

Ägide [ɛ:'gi:də] *f*: *unter der* ⁓ (*gen.*) under the auspices of.

agieren [a'gi:rən] act, function.

agil [a'gi:l] agile.

Agio ['a:ʒio:] *n* (11) agio, premium; **⁓tage** [⁓'ta:ʒə] *f* stock-jobbing.

Agitation [agita'tsjo:n] *f* agitation.

Agitator [⁓'ta:tɔr] *m* (8¹) agitator.

agitatorisch [⁓ta'to:riʃ] fomenting, demagogical.

agi'tieren agitate.

Agraffe [a'grafə] *f* (15) brooch, clasp.

A'grar|minister *m* Minister (*Am.* Secretary) of Agriculture; **~staat** *m* agrarian state.

Ägypt|er [ɛ'gyptər] *m* (7), **~erin** *f* (16¹), **2isch** Egyptian.

ah! [ɑː] ah!; **äh!** [ɛ(ː)] *Ekel*: ugh!; *stotternd*: er!; **aha!** [a'hɑː] aha!, I see!

A'ha-Erlebnis *n* sudden insight; *Psychologie*: aha-experience.

Ahle ['ɑːle] *f* (15) awl, pricker.

Ahn [ɑːn] *m* (5 *u.* 12) ancestor, forefather (*a.* '**~herr** *m*); '**~e** *f* (15) ancestress (*a.* '**~frau** *f*).

ahnd|en ['ɑːndən] (26) (*rächen*) avenge; (*strafen*) punish; **2ung** *f* revenge; punishment.

ähneln ['ɛːnəln] (26) (*dat.*) be (*od.* look) like, resemble.

ahnen ['ɑːnən] (25) have a presentiment (*Am.* F hunch) of (*od.* that ...); (*erfassen*; *erraten*) divine; (*vorhersehen*) foresee, anticipate; (*spüren*) sense; (*argwöhnen*) suspect; *et.* ~ *lassen* foreshadow, *weitS.* give an idea of; *nichts* ~*d s. ahnungslos*.

'Ahnen|forschung *f* ancestry research; '**~tafel** *f* genealogical table.

ähnlich ['ɛːnliç] (*dat.*) like, resembling; *bsd. v. Dingen u.* Å similar (to); *j-m* ~ *sehen* look like a p.; *iro.* *das sieht ihm* ~ that's just like him; **2keit** *f* likeness, resemblance; similarity.

Ahnung ['ɑːnuŋ] *f* presentiment, *Am.* F hunch; *bsd. v. Unheil*: foreboding, misgiving; (*Argwohn*) suspicion; F *keine* ~! no idea!; F *keine* ~ *haben von* have not the slightest notion (*od.* idea) of; '**2slos** unsuspecting; '**2svoll** full of misgivings.

Ahorn ['ɑːhɔrn] *m* (3) maple.

Ähre ['ɛːrə] *f* (15) ear; *Blume*: spike; *Gras*: head; ~*n lesen* glean.

Ais ♪ ['ɑːʔis] *n* A sharp.

Akademie [akade'miː] *f* (15) academy.

Akademiker [~'deːmikər] *m* (7) (*Studierter*) university-bred man, *Am.* (university) graduate; *im freien Beruf*: professional man; (*Mitglied e-r Akademie*) academician.

aka'demisch academic; ~ *gebildet* university-trained *od.* -bred.

Akazie [a'kɑːtsjə] *f* (15) acacia.

akklimatisier|en [aklimati'ziːrən]

acclimatize, *Am.* acclimate; *sich* ~ become acclimatized; **2ung** *f* acclimatization, *Am.* acclimation.

Akkord [a'kɔrt] *m* (3) ♪ chord; ♥ (*Vereinbarung*) contract; ♥ (*Vergleich*) composition; *auf* ~, *im* ~ by the piece (*od.* job); **~arbeit** *f* piece-work; **~arbeiter(in** *f*) *m* piece-worker.

Ak'kordeon [~deɔn] *n* (11) accordion.

akkor'dieren *v/t.* arrange; *v/i.* agree, compromise (*mit* with; *über acc.* upon); ♥ arrange, compound (*mit* with; *wegen* for).

Ak'kordlohn *m* piece wages *pl.*

akkredit|ieren [akredi'tiːrən] accredit (*bei* to); ♥ open a credit for; **2iv** [~'tiːf] *n* (3¹) ♥ letter of credit; *j-m ein* ~ *eröffnen* open a credit in favo(u)r of a p.

Akku F ['aku] *m* (11), **~mulator** [~mu'lɑːtɔr] *m* (18¹) accumulator, storage battery.

akkurat [~'rɑːt] accurate.

Akkusativ *gr.* ['akuzatiːf] *m* (3¹) accusative (case); '**~objekt** *n* direct object.

Akne ['aknə] ♪ *f* (15) acne.

Akontozahlung [a'kɔntotsɑːluŋ] *f* payment on account.

Akquisiteur ♥ [akvizi'tøːr] *m* canvasser, agent.

Akrib|ie [akri'biː] *f* (15, *o. pl.*) scientific precision, meticulosity; **2isch** [a'kriːbiʃ] meticulous.

Akrobat [akro'baːt] *m* (12), **~in** *f* acrobat; **~ik** *f* acrobatics *pl.*; **2isch** acrobatic.

Akt [akt] *m* (3) act(ion); *thea.* act; ∫²z̄, ♥ *s.* Aktenstück; *paint.* nude; ~ *der Verzweiflung* desperate deed.

Akte ['aktə] *f* (15) *s.* Aktenstück.

'Akten *pl.* records, papers, deeds, documents; *abgelegte*: files; *Notiz*: *zu den* ~ *to be filed*; *zu den* ~ *legen s. ad acta*; '**~deckel** *m* folder; '**~klammer** *f* paper-clip; '**2kundig** on record; '**~mappe** *f*, '**~tasche** *f* document-case, portfolio, brief-case; '**2mäßig** documentary; ~ *festlegen* put on record; '**~mensch** *m* red-tapist; '**~notiz** *f* memo (-randum); *sich von et. e-e* ~ *machen* write a memo about a th.; '**~ordner** *m* file; '**~stück** *n einzelnes*: document; (*Aktenband*) file; '**~zeichen** *n* reference (*od.* file) number.

Akteur [ak'tø:r] *m* (3¹) *thea. u. fig.* actor.

Aktie ['aktsjə] *f* (15) share, *Am.* stock; ∼*n besitzen* hold shares (*Am.* stock); *s-e* ∼*n sind gestiegen* (*a. fig.*) his stock has gone up; '∼**nbesitz** *m* (share, *Am.* stock) holdings *pl.*; '∼**ngesellschaft** *f* joint-stock company, *Am.* (stock-)corporation; '∼**n-inhaber(in** *f*) *m* shareholder, *bsd. Am.* stockholder; '∼**nkapital** *n* share capital, *Am.* capital stock; '∼**n-unternehmen** *n* joint-stock undertaking.

Aktion [ak'tsjo:n] *f* (16) action; (*Werbungs⌾ usw.*) drive, campaign; *polizeiliche* ∼ police raid; *in* ∼ *treten* take action; ∼**är** [∼'nɛ:r] *m* (3¹), ∼**ärin** *f* (16¹) *s.* Aktieninhaber; ∼**sradius** [∼'tsjo:nsra:djus] *m* radius of action, range (*a. fig.*).

aktiv [ak'ti:f] active; *Bilanz*: favo(u)rable; ✗ regular; ∼*es Wahlrecht* franchise; ∼*er Wortschatz* using vocabulary.

Aktiv *gr.* ['akti:f] *n* (3¹) active voice; ∼**a** ✝ [∼'ti:va] *n/pl.* assets, *Am. a.* resources; ∼**handel** [∼'ti:f-] *m* active trade; ⌾**ieren** [∼ti'vi:rən] activate; ∼**ist** [∼ti'vist] *m* (12) activist; ∼**kohle** [∼'ti:f-] *f* activated carbon; '∼**posten** *m* asset; ∼**-urlaub** [∼'ti:f-] *m* sporting holiday.

'**Aktstudie** *f* study from the nude.

aktuell [aktu'ɛl] current, up-to--date, topical, present-day; *Problem usw.*: acute.

Akupunktur [akupuŋk'tu:r] 🏥 *f* (16²) acupuncture.

Akust|ik [a'kustik] *f* (16, *o. pl.*) acoustics; ⌾**isch** acoustic.

akut [a'ku:t] 🏥 *u. fig.* acute.

Akzent [ak'tsɛnt] *m* (3) accent; (*Betonung*) *a.* stress.

akzentuieren [∼tu'i:rən] accent; *bsd. fig.* accentuate, stress.

Ak'zentverschiebung *f* shift of emphasis.

Akzept [∼'tsɛpt] ✝ *n* (3) acceptance; ∼**ant** [∼'tant] *m* (12) acceptor; ⌾**ieren** [∼'ti:rən] accept; ∼**ierung** [∼'ti:ruŋ] *f* acceptance.

Akzise [∼'tsi:zə] *f* (15) excise.

Alabaster [ala'bastər] *m* (7), ⌾*n* alabaster.

Alarm [a'larm] *m* (3¹) alarm; *s.* Flieger⌾; ∼ *blasen, schlagen* ✗ sound (*fig.* give) the alarm; ∼**anlage** *f* alarm system; ⌾**bereit** in constant readiness; *on the alert;* ∼**bereit-schaft** *f: in* ∼ on the alert; ∼**glocke** *f* alarm-bell; ⌾**ieren** [∼'mi:rən] alarm (*a. fig.*); ✗, *die Polizei:* alert; ∼**zone** *f* alert zone; ∼**zustand** *m* alert; *in den* ∼ *versetzen* put on the alert.

Alaun 🜍 [a'laun] *m* (3¹) alum; ∼**-erde** *f* alumina.

albern ['albərn] silly, foolish; '⌾**heit** *f* foolishness, silliness.

Album ['album] *n* (9 *u.* 11) album.

Alchim|ie [alçi'mi:] *f* (15) alchemy; ∼**ist** [∼'mist] *m* (12) alchemist.

Alge ['algə] *f* (15) seaweed, alga.

Algebra ['algebra] *f* (15, *o. pl.*) algebra.

algebra-isch [∼'bra:-] algebraic(al).

Alibi 🜊 ['a:libi] *n* (2) alibi.

Aliment [ali'mɛnt] *n, mst* ∼*e n/pl.* (3) alimony.

alkalisch 🜍 [al'ka:liʃ] alcaline.

Alkohol ['alkohol] *m* (3¹) alcohol; '⌾**frei** non-alcoholic, F *bsd. Am.* soft; ∼*es Gasthaus* temperance hotel; '∼**gehalt** *m* alcoholic strength; ∼**iker** [∼'ho:likər] *m* alcoholic; ⌾**isch** [∼'ho:liʃ] alcoholic; ∼*es Getränk* alcoholic (*Am.* hard) liquor; ⌾**i'sieren** alcoholize; '∼**mißbrauch** *m* excessive drinking; '∼**schmuggler** *m* liquor-smuggler, *Am.* bootlegger; '⌾**süchtig** alcoholic; '∼**test** *m* breathalyzer; *j-n e-m* ∼ *unterziehen* give a p. a breathalyzer; '∼**verbot** *n* prohibition; '∼**vergiftung** *f* alcoholic poisoning.

Alkoven [al'ko:vən] *m* (16) alcove.

all [al] **1.** *indef. pron.* all; (*jeder*) every; (*jeder beliebige*) any; *sie* ∼*e* all of them; ∼*e beide* both of them; ∼ *und jeder* all and sundry; ∼*es aussteigen!* all change, please!; *auf* ∼*e Fälle* in any case, at all events; ∼*e Tage* every day; ∼*es in* ∼*em* on the whole; *vor* ∼*em* above (*od.* first of) all; ∼*e zwei Minuten* every two minutes; F *hast du sie noch* ∼*e?* have you gone mad?; **2.** *su. das* **All** the universe.

'**all'-abendlich** every evening.

'**allbe'kannt** notorious.

'**alle** all gone, at an end; *Geld:* all spent; ∼ *machen* finish.

Allee [a'le:] *f* (15) avenue, *schmale:* (tree-lined) walk.

Allegorie [alego'ri:] *f* allegory.

allegorisch [∼'go:riʃ] allegoric(al).

allein [a'lain] **1.** *pred. adj.* alone,

(*ohne Hilfe a.*) single-handed, by o.s.; **2.** *adv.* alone, only; (*ausschließlich*) exclusively; **3.** *cj.* only, yet, but, however; ⌂**besitz** *m* exclusive possession; ⌂**-erbe** *m*, ⌂**-erbin** *f* sole (*od.* universal) heir(ess *f*); ⌂**gang** *m Sport*: solo attempt; *fig.* e-n ⁓ **machen** go it alone; ⌂**herrschaft** *f* absolute monarchy, autocracy; ⌂**herrscher(in** *f*) *m* absolute monarch, autocrat; ⁓**ig** (*einzig*) only; (*ausschließlich*) sole, exclusive; ⌂**-inhaber(in** *f*) *m* sole owner; ⌂**sein** *n* loneliness; being alone; ⁓**'seligmachend** *the* true (*Glaube* faith, *Kirche* church); *P.*: alone (in the world); (*unverheiratet*) single; *Gebäude usw.*: isolated, detached; ⌂**unterhalter** *m* (7) solo entertainer; ⌂**verkauf** *m* exclusive sale, monopoly; ⌂**vertreter** † *m* sole agent *od.* distributor; ⌂**vertretung** *f* sole agency; ⌂**vertrieb** *m* sole distribution.

'**alle**'**mal** always, every time; ⁓! F any time!, *ein für* ⁓ once (and) for all.

'**allen**'**falls** (*zur Not*) if need be; (*vielleicht*) possibly, perhaps; (*höchstens*) at best.   [where.]

allenthalben ['alant'halbən] every-∫

'**aller...** ... of all; *bsd. im Titel*: most ...; '⁓**best** best of all, very best; *aufs* ⁓**e** in the best possible manner; ⁓'**dings** (*dennoch*) nevertheless; (*in der Tat*) indeed; (*auf jeden Fall*) at any rate; (*freilich*) it is true; (*ich muß zugeben*) to be sure; ⁓! certainly!, *Am.* F sure!; '⁓**-erst** (*a. zu* ⁓) first of all; '⁓'**hand** of all kinds *od.* sorts, various; F *das ist ja* ⁓! I say!; ⌂'**heiligen(fest)** *n* All Saints' Day; ⌂'**heiligste** *n* Holy of Holies; ⁓'**höchst** highest of all; '⁓**höchstens** *adv.* at the very most; ⁓'**lei** *s. allerhand*; miscellaneous; ⌂'**lei** *n* medley; ⁓'**letzt** last of all (*a. zu* ⁓), very last; ⁓'**liebst** dearest of all; most lovely, sweet; *am* ⁓**en** *möchte ich* I should like best of all; ⁓'**meist** most; *am* ⁓**en** most(ly); (*besonders*) chiefly; ⁓'**nächst** very next; ⁓'**neu(e)st** the very latest *od.* newest; ⁓**e** *Ausgabe!* (*Zeitung*) latest edition.

Allerg|ie [aler'giː] ♂ *f* (15) allergy; ⌂**isch** [a'lɛrgiʃ] allergic (*für, gegen* to).

Aller|'**seelen** *n* All Souls' Day; ⌂**seits** ['⁓zaıts] on all sides; universally; to all (of you); ⁓'**weltskerl** *m* devil of a fellow; ⌂**wenigst** [⁓'veːniçst] least of all; '⁓'**werteste** F *m* posterior, rear.

'**alle**'**samt** all of them, all together.

'**Alles**|**kleber** *m* all-purpose glue; '⁓**schneider** *m* food slicer.

'**allezeit** always, at all times.

'**All**|'**gegenwart** *f* omnipresence, ubiquity; '⌂'**gegenwärtig** omnipresent, ubiquitous; '⌂**ge**'**mein** general; common; universal; ⁓**e** *Redensarten pl.* generalities; *im* ⁓**en** in general, generally; *s. Wehrpflicht*; '⁓**ge**'**meinbildung** *f* general education; '⌂**ge**'**meingültig** generally accepted; ⁓**ge**'**meinheit** *f* generality, universality; (*Öffentlichkeit*) general public; ⁓**ge**'**meinmedizin** *f* general medicine; *Arzt für* ⁓ general practitioner; '⌂**ge**'**waltig** all-powerful; ⁓'**heilmittel** *n* panacea, cure-all (*a. fig.*).

Allianz [ali'ants] *f* (16) alliance.

alli'**-ier**|**en** *v/refl.* ally o.s. (*mit* to, with); ⌂**te** *m* ally.

'**all**|'**jährlich** annual, yearly; *adv. a.* every year; '⌂**macht** *f* omnipotence; ⁓'**mächtig** omnipotent, almighty; ⁓**mählich** [⁓'mɛːliç] gradual; *adv. a.* by degrees; '⁓'**nächtlich** every night.

Allopath [alo'paːt] *m* allopathist; ⁓**ie** [⁓pa'tiː] *f* allopathy; ⌂**isch** [⁓'paːtiʃ] allopathic.

'**Allrad**|**-antrieb** *mot. m* four-wheel drive; '⁓**lenkung** *f* all-wheel steering.

Allroundman [ɔːl'raʊndmən] *m* all-rounder.

all|**seitig** ['⁓zaıtiç] universal; *Am.* all-round; '⌂**strom...** *Radio*: AC-DC... (alternating current-direct current); '⌂**tag**(**sleben** *n*) *m* everyday life; ⁓'**täglich** daily; *fig.* everyday, common, trivial; ⌂'**täglichkeit** *f* commonness, triviality; '⌂**tags...** common(place), everyday; '⁓**umfassend** all-embracing; ⌂'**wetter...** all--weather; ⁓'**wissend** omniscient; ⌂'**wissenheit** *f* omniscience; ⁓'**wöchentlich** weekly; '⁓**zu** (much) too; ⁓**zu**'**viel** too much, overmuch; ⁓ *ist ungesund* enough is as good as a feast; '⌂**zweck...** all-purpose..., all-duty...

Alm [alm] *f* (16) Alpine pasture, alp.

Almanach ['almanax] *m* (3¹) almanac.

Almosen ['ˌmoːzən] *n* (6) alms, charity; '**ˌbüchse** *f* poor-box; '**ˌempfänger(in** *f*) *m* pauper.

Alp [alp] *m* (3), '**ˌdrücken** *n* (*haben have a*) nightmare.

Alpen ['alpən] *pl.* Alps; '**ˌglühen** *n* alp-glow; '**ˌrose** *f* Alpine rose; '**ˌveilchen** *n* cyclamen; '**ˌver·ein** *m* Alpine Club; '**ˌvorland** *n* foothills *pl.* of the Alps.

Alphabet [alfaˈbeːt] *n* (3) alphabet; **ˌisch** alphabetical.

alphanumerisch [alfanuˈmeːriʃ] alphanumeric.

alpin [alˈpiːn] Alpine.

Alpi'nis|t(in *f*) *m* Alpinist; **ˌmus** *m* (16, *o. pl.*) mountaineering.

Alraun ♀ [alˈraun] *m* (3), **ˌe** *f* (15) mandrake.

als [als] *nach comp.*: than; (*ganz so wie*) as, like; (*in der Eigenschaft* ˌ) as; (*statt*) for; *nach Negation*: but, except; *zeitlich*: when, as; *s. ob*; ˌ *Geschenk* for a present; *er starb* ˌ *Bettler* he died a beggar; *schon* ˌ *Kind* when only a child; *er bot zu wenig*, ˌ *daß ich es hätte annehmen können* he offered too little for me to accept it; ˌ'**bald** immediately, forthwith; ˌ'**dann** then.

also ['alzoː] *adv.* thus, so; *cj.* therefore, consequently; *na* ˌ*!* there you are!; *es ist* ˌ *wahr?* it is true then?

alt[1] [alt] old; (*Ggs. modern*) ancient, antique; (*Ggs. frisch*) stale; (*schon gebraucht, z. B. Kleider*) second-hand; ˌe *Sprachen* ancient languages, classics; *wie* ˌ *bist du?* how old are you?, what is your age?; *es bleibt alles beim* ˌ*en* everything stands as it was.

Alt[2] ♪ *m* (3) alto.

Altan [alˈtaːn] *m* (3¹) balcony.

Altar [alˈtaːr] *m* (3¹ *u.* 3³) altar; ˌ**blatt** *n*, ˌ**gemälde** *n* altar-piece.

'**alt**|**backen** stale; '**ˌbau** *m* old building; '**ˌbausanierung** *f* redevelopment of old buildings; '**ˌbekannt** well-known; '**ˌbewährt** well-tried; '**ˌdeutsch** Old German; ˌ'**ehrwürdig** time-hono(u)red; '**ˌeisen** *n* scrap iron.

'**Alte** *m* (18) old man; ˌ *f* old woman; F *der* ˌ (*Vater*) the old man, (*Chef*) the boss; F *m-e* ˌ my old lady; *die* ˌ*n pl.* the old; *hist.* the

ancients; *das* ˌ *n* old things *pl.*; *etwas* ˌ*s* an old thing; '**ˌnheim** *n* old people's home, rest-home; '**ˌnpflegeheim** *n* geriatric care cent|re, *Am.* -er; '**ˌnteil** *n: fig. sich aufs* ˌ *zurückziehen* retire.

Alter ['altər] *n* (7) age; (*Greisen*♀) old age; (*Dienst*♀) seniority; *im* ˌ *von 20 Jahren* at an age of 20 years; *von* ♀*s her* of old, from ancient times; *er ist in meinem* ˌ he is my age; *von mittlerem* ˌ middle-aged.

älter ['ɛltər] older; *der* ˌ*e Bruder* the elder brother; *e-e* ˌ*e Dame* an elderly lady; *er ist (3 Jahre)* ˌ *als ich* he is my senior (by 3 years); *er sieht (20 Jahre)* ˌ *aus, als er ist* he looks (20 years) more than his age.

'**altern** (29) (h. *u.* sn) grow old, (*a.* ⊕) age.

alternativ [altɛrnaˈtiːf] alternative; ♀**e** [ˌˈtiːvə] *f* (15) alternative.

'**Alters**|**erscheinung** *f* symptom of old age; '**ˌgenosse** *m*, '**ˌgenossin** *f* contemporary; '**ˌgrenze** *f* age-limit; *für Beamte*: retirement age; *flexible* ˌ flexible retirement age; '**ˌgründe** *m/pl.*: *aus* ˌ*n* for reasons of age; '**ˌgruppe** *f* age-group (*od.* -bracket); '**ˌheim** *n* old people's home; '**ˌklasse** *f* age group; '**ˌrente** *f* old-age pension; '♀**schwach** decrepit; '**ˌschwäche** *f* senile decay, decrepitude; '**ˌsitz** *m: s-n* ˌ *in Berchtesgaden nehmen* spend one's retirement in Berchtesgaden; '**ˌstufe** *f* stage of life; *s. Altersklasse*; '**ˌversorgung** *f* old-age pension (scheme).

'**Altertum** *n* (1²) antiquity; '**ˌsforscher** *m* arch(a)eologist; '**ˌskunde** *f* arch(a)eology.

altertümlich ['ˌtyːmliç] ancient, antique; (*veraltet*) archaic, antiquated.

ältest ['ɛltəst] oldest; *in der Reihenfolge*: eldest; '♀**e** *m* elder, senior; *mein* ˌ*r* my eldest son.

'**alt**|'**hergebracht** [ˌgəbraxt] traditional; time-hono(u)red; '**ˌhochdeutsch** Old High German.

Altist(in *f*) *m* (12) alto (-singer).

'**alt**|**jüngferlich** old-maidish; '**ˌklug** precocious.

ältlich ['ɛltliç] elderly, oldish.

'**Alt**|**material** *n* junk, scrap; '**ˌmeister** *m* past master; *Sport*:

ex-champion; '~**metall** *n* scrap metal; '♀**modisch** old-fashioned; '~**öl** *n* waste oil; '~**papier** *n* waste paper; '~**philologe** *m* classical philologist; '~**reifen** *m* old tyre (*Am.* tire); '♀**sprachlich** classical; '~**stadt** *f* old town, city; '~**stimme** *f* alto (voice); ♀**väterisch** ['~fɛ:təriʃ] *s.* altmodisch; '~**warenhändler**(**in** *f*) *m* second-hand dealer; ~'**weibersommer** *m* Indian summer; (*Sommerfäden*) gossamer.

Alufolie ['a:lufo:liə] *f* aluminium (*Am.* aluminum) foil, tin foil.

Aluminium [alu'mi:njum] *n* (9, *o. pl.*) aluminium, *Am.* aluminum.

am [am] = *an dem*, *s. an*.

amalgamieren ⚗ [amalga'mi:rən] amalgamate (*a. fig.*).

Amateur [ama'tø:r] *m* (3¹) amateur; ~**photograph** *m* amateur photographer.

Amazone [~'tso:nə] *f* (15) Amazon.

ambitioniert [ambitsjo'ni:rt] ambitious.

Amboß ['ambɔs] *m* (4) anvil.

Ambra ['ambra] *f* (16, *o. pl.*) amber; *graue* ~ ambergris.

ambulan|**t** [ambu'lant] out-patient (*a. su.* = ~ *behandelter Patient*); ~**es** *Gewerbe* itinerant trade; ♀**z** [~ts] *f* (16) (*Klinik*) out-patient department; (*Wagen*) ambulance.

Ameise ['a:maizə] *f* (15) ant; '~**nbär** *m* ant-eater; '~-**ei** *n* ant's egg; '~**n-haufen** *m* ant-hill; '~**nnest** *n* ants' nest; '~**nplage** *f* plague of ants; '~**n-säure** ⚗ *f* formic acid.

Amen ['a:mən] *int. u. n* (16) amen.

Amerikan|**er** [ameri'ka:nər] *m* (7), ~**erin** *f*, ♀**isch** American; ♀**i'sieren** Americanize; ~**ismus** [~ka'nismus] *m* (16²) Americanism.

Amethyst [ame'tʏst] *m* (3) amethyst.

Amme ['amə] *f* (15) nurse, wet-nurse; '~**nmärchen** *contp. n* old wives' tale.

Ammer *zo.* ['amər] *f* (15) bunting.

Ammoniak ⚗ [amon'jak] *n* (3¹, *o. pl.*) ammonia.

Amnesie [amne'zi:] ⚕ *f* (15) amnesia.

Amnestie [amnɛs'ti:] *f* (15) amnesty, general pardon; ♀**ren** (grant a) pardon.

Amok ['a:mɔk] *inv.*: ~ *laufen* (*fahren*) run (drive) amuck; '~**fahrt** *f* mad ride; '~**läufer** *m* mad gunman.

Amor ['a:mər] *m* Cupid.

amorph [a'mɔrf] amorphous.

Amortisation [amɔrtiza'tsjo:n] *f* amortization; *e-r Anleihe*: redemption.

amorti'sier|**bar** redeemable; ~**en** amortize; *e-e Anleihe*: redeem.

Ampel ['ampəl] *f* (15) hanging lamp; (*Verkehrs♀*) traffic light.

Ampere|**meter** ⚡ [ãpɛ:r'me:tər] *n* ammeter; ~**stunde** [ã'pɛ:r-] *f* ampere-hour.

Ampfer ⚘ ['ampfər] *m* (7) dock.

Amphibie [am'fi:bjə] *f* (15), ~**n**... amphibian.

Amphitheater [am'fi:tea:tər] *n* amphithea|tre, *Am.* -ter.

Ampulle [am'pulə] *f* (12) ampoule.

Ampu|**tation** [amputa'tsjo:n] *f* (16) amputation; ♀**tieren** amputate; ~'**tierte** *m* amputee.

Amsel ['amzəl] *f* (15) blackbird.

Amt [amt] *n* (1²) office; (*Posten*) post; (*Behörde*) office, board, agency; (*Pflicht*) official duty, function; (*Aufgabe*) task; (*Gerichts♀*) court; (*Fernsprech♀*) exchange; *s. antreten, auswärtig, bekleiden, entheben, niederlegen*; *von* ~**s** *wegen* officially, ex officio; ♀**ieren** [~'ti:rən] hold office; *eccl. od. fig.* officiate; ~ *als* act as; ~**d** acting, *official* in charge; '♀**lich** official; '~**mann** *m* (1²) bailiff.

'**Amts**... official, of (an) office; '~-**antritt** *m* entering upon office; '~-**arzt** *m* public-health officer; '~**befugnis** *f* authority; '~**bereich** *m*, '~**bezirk** *m* jurisdiction; '~**blatt** *n* official gazette; '~**bruder** *m* colleague; '♀**dauer** *f* term of office; '~**diener** *m* usher; '~-**eid** *m* oath of office; '~**enthebung** *f* removal from office, dismissal; '~**führung** *f* administration (of an office); '~**geheimnis** *n* official secret; '~**gericht** *n* Inferior Court; '~**geschäfte** *n/pl.* official duties; '~**gewalt** *f* official authority; '~**handlung** *f* official act; '~**kollege** *pol. m* opposite number; '~**miene** *f* solemn air; '♀**müde** weary of one's office; '~**niederlage** *f* resignation; '~**richter** *m* *etwa*: district judge; '~**schimmel** *m* red tape; '~**stunden** *f/pl.* official hours; '~**tracht** *f* official attire; ♰, *eccl.* robe; *univ.* gown; '~**träger** *m* office-holder; '~-**überschreitung** *f* abuse of authority; '~-**unterschla**-

gung f ŽƗ malversation; '**~verletzung** f misconduct in office; '**~verwalter** m administrator of an office, substitute, deputy; '**~vorgänger** m predecessor in office; '**~vormund** m public guardian; '**~vorsteher** m head official; '**~weg** m: den ~ beschreiten go through the official channels; den ~ (nicht) einhalten (not to) act through the proper channels; '**~zeichen** n teleph. dial(ling) tone; '**~zeit** f term of office.

Amulett [amu'let] n (3) charm.

amüs|ant [amy'zant] amusing; **~ieren** [~'zi:rən] amuse, entertain; sich ~ (sich die Zeit vertreiben) amuse o.s.; (sich gut unterhalten) enjoy o.s., have a good time.

an [an] (wo? dat.; wohin? acc.) **1.** prp. at; on, upon; by; against; to; (bis ~) as far as, up to; (etwa) near(ly); am Fenster at (od. by) the window; ~ der Themse on the Thames; am 1. März on March 1st; am Morgen in the morning; ~ Anfang at the beginning; ~ e-m Orte in a place; ~ der Grenze on the frontier; ~ der Hand führen by the hand; am Ufer on the shore; ~ der Wand on (od. against) the wall; am Leben alive; s. Reihe; es ist ~ dir, zu sagen, ob ... it is up to you now to say whether ...; **2.** adv. on, onward; up; von heute ~ from today (onwards); von nun (od. jetzt) ~ from now on; ⊕ ~-aus on-off.

Anachronismus [anakro'nismus] m (16²) anachronism.

analog [ana'lo:k] analogous.

Analogie [~lo'gi:] f (15) analogy.

Ana'logrechner m Computer: analogue computer.

Analphabet|(in f) [an⁹alfa'be:t] m (12) illiterate; **~entum** n illiteracy.

Analyse [ana'ly:zə] f (15) analysis.

analy'sieren analy|se, bsd. Am. -ze.

Analyt|iker [ana'ly:tikər] m (6) analyst; **Žisch** analytic(al).

Ananas ['ananas] f (inv. od. 14²) pineapple.

Anarchie [anar'çi:] f (15) anarchy.

Anar'chis|mus m (16²) anarchism; **~t** m (12), **~tin** f (16¹) anarchist; **Žtisch** anarchic(al).

Anästhesist [anɛstе'zist] m (12), **~in** f (16¹) an(a)esthetist.

Anatom [~'to:m] m (12) anatomist.

Anatomie [~to'mi:] f (15) anatomy.

anatomisch [~'to:miʃ] anatomical.

'**anbahn|en** pave the way for, initiate; sich ~ be at hand; Beziehungen, Verhandlungen usw.: open (up); '**Žer** m initiator.

anbändeln ['~bendəln] (29): ~ mit make up to, pick up with; (Streit suchen) s. anbinden (v/i.).

'**Anbau** ✗ m cultivation; Δ annex, extension, bsd. Am. addition, (Flügel) wing; '**Žen** ✗ cultivate, grow; Δ add, annex (an [acc.] to); ⊕ attach; sich ~ settle; '**~fläche** f arable land; area under cultivation.

'**Anbeginn** m earliest beginning, outset; von ~ from the outset.

'**anbehalten** Kleid usw.: keep on.

an'bei im Brief: enclosed.

'**anbeißen** v/t. bite; v/i. bite; fig. take the bait.

'**anbelangen** concern; was mich anbelangt as to (od. for) me.

'**anbellen** bark at.

anberaum|en ['~bəraumən] (25) appoint, fix; '**Žung** f appointment.

'**anbet|en** worship, fig. a. adore; '**Žer(in** f) m worship(p)er, adorer, fig. a. admirer.

'**Anbetracht**: in ~ (gen.) considering, in consideration (od. view) of.

'**anbetreffen** s. anbelangen.

'**anbetteln** solicit alms of.

Anbetung ['~be:tuŋ] f worship, adoration; '**Žswürdig** adorable.

'**anbiedern** (29): sich ~ mit od. bei cotton (od. F chum) up to.

'**anbiet|en** v/t. offer; sich ~ P.: offer one's services, Gelegenheit: present itself; '**Žer** ✝ m (7) supplier.

'**anbinden** v/t. bind, tie up; ~ an (acc.) tie to; v/i. mit j-m ~ pick a quarrel with, tangle with; kurz angebunden sein fig. be curt od. short (gegen with).

'**anblasen** blow at od. upon; Hochofen: blow in; F (rüffeln) blow up.

'**Anblick** m (Blick, Aussehen) look; (Bild) sight, view, aspect; beim ersten ~ at first sight; '**Žen** look at; flüchtig: glance at; (besehen) view; (mustern) eye.

'**an|blinzeln** blink od. (schlau) wink at; '**~bohren** bore, pierce; '**~braten** roast gently; '**~brechen** v/t. Vorrat: break into; Flasche: open, crack; v/i. (sn) begin; Tag: dawn; Nacht: come on; '**~brennen** v/t. burn; Zigarre usw.: light; v/i. (sn) kindle, catch fire; *Speise*: burn (*a*. ~ *lassen*).

'**anbringen** (*herbeibringen*) bring in *od.* on; (*befestigen*) fix, attach, mount, fit (*an dat.* to); *Stempel, Unterschrift*: affix (to); *Gründe*: put forward; *e-n Schlag*: bring home; *ein Wort*: put in; *Sohn usw.*: get a place for; ⚓ *Ware*: dispose of, (*los-schlagen*) knock off; *e-e Klage* ~ bring an action; *e-e Beschwerde* ~ lodge a complaint; *das ist bei ihm nicht angebracht* that won't do with him; *s. angebracht*.

'**Anbruch** *m* break, beginning; (*bei*) ~ *des Tages* (at) daybreak; (*bei*) ~ *der Nacht* (at) nightfall.

'**anbrüllen** roar at, bawl at.

Andacht ['~daxt] *f* (16) devotion; (*Handlung*) prayers *pl.*, service; *s. verrichten*.

andächtig ['~dεçtiç] devout; (*bei e-r Andacht anwesend*) devotional; *fig.* rapt, absorbed, religious.

'**andauern** last; continue; *hart-näckig*: persist; '~**d** lasting; continuous; persistent.

'**Andenken** *n* (6) (*Gedächtnis*) memory, (*a. Gegenstand*) remembrance; (*nur Gegenstand*) keepsake; *mit-genommenes*: souvenir (*an acc.* of); *zum* ~ *an* (*acc.*) in memory of.

ander ['andər] (18) other; (*ver-schieden*) different; (*zweit*) second; (*folgend*) next; (*gegenüberliegend*) opposite; *der* ~*e Strumpf usw.* the pair to (*od.* the fellow of) this sock, *etc.*; *am* ~*en Tag* (on) the next day; *e-n Tag um den* ~*n* every other day; *et.* ~*es* another thing, something else; *das ist etwas* ~*es* that is different; *alles* ~*e* everything else; *alles* ~*e als* anything but; *kein* ~*er* no one else (*als* but), *rühmend*: no lesser person (than); *nichts* ~*es* nothing else; ~*er Ansicht sein* differ; *ein* ~*es Hemd anziehen* change one's shirt; *s. unter* 1; ~**erseits** ['~zaɪts] *s. anderseits*.

ändern ['ɛndərn] (29) (*a. sich*) alter, (*wechseln*) change; *teilweise*: modify; (*verschieden gestalten*) vary; *ich kann es nicht* ~ I can't help it; *es läßt sich nicht* ~ it cannot be helped.

'**andern|falls** otherwise; '~**teils** on the other hand.

anders ['~s] otherwise; (*verschieden*)

differently (*als* from); *bei pron.*: else; *wer* ~? who else?; *er ist* ~ *als sein Vater* he is unlike (*od.* different from) his father; *ich kann nicht* ~, *ich muß weinen* I cannot help crying; ~ *werden* change; *s. besinnen* 1; '~**denkend** dissenting.

anderseits ['~zaɪts] on the other hand.

'**anders|ge-artet** different; '~**gläu-big** of a different faith, heterodox; '~**herum** the other way round; F (*homosexuell*) bent; '~**wo** elsewhere; '~**woher** from elsewhere; '~**wohin** to some other place, elsewhere.

anderthalb ['~thalp] one and a half.

'**Änderung** *f s. ändern*: alteration; change; modification; variation.

ander|wärts ['~vεrts] elsewhere; '~**weitig** *adj.* other, further; *adv.* in another way *od.* manner.

'**andeuten** indicate; (*anspielen*) hint; (*zu verstehen geben*) give to understand, intimate, imply; (*zu bedenken geben*) suggest; *paint. u. fig.* outline.

'**Andeutung** *f* indication; hint (*a. fig. Spur*); intimation; suggestion; '~**sweise** by way of intimation; in outlines.

'**andichten**: *j-m et.* ~ impute (*od.* attribute) a th. falsely to a p.

'**Andrang** *m* rush, press; (*Zulauf*) concourse; ⚕ congestion.

'**andrehen** *Gas usw.*: turn on; ⚡ *Licht*: switch on; *Motor*: start up; *Schraube usw.*: tighten; F *j-m et.* ~ palm a th. off on a p.

'**androh|en**: *j-m et.* ~ menace (*od.* threaten) a p. with; '~**ung** *f* threat; ⚖ *unter* ~ *von od. gen.* under penalty of.

aneign|en ['~ʔaɪgnən] (*sich*) appropriate, make one's own; *Gebiet*: annex; *Gewohnheit*: contract; *Kenntnisse*: acquire; *Meinung anderer*: adopt; *widerrechtlich*: usurp; '~**ung** *f* appropriation; acquisition; adoption; usurpation.

an-ei'nander together; ~**geraten** (*in Streit kommen*) clash (*mit* with); (*handgemein werden*) come to blows.

Anekdote [anεk'do:tə] *f* (15) anecdote; ~**nhaft** anecdotic(al).

'**an-ekeln** disgust, sicken; *es ekelt mich an* I am disgusted with it, I loathe it.

'**an-empfehlen** recommend.

'**An·erbieten** *n* (6) offer.

'**an·erkannter**'**maßen** admittedly.

'**an·erkenn|en** acknowledge; recognize (*beide*: *als* as); *Anspruch*, *Schuld*: admit; (*lobend* ~) appreciate; (*billigen*) approve; *Kind*: (*nicht* ~ dis)own; accept; *Wechsel*: hono(u)r; *nicht* ~ repudiate; '**~ens·wert** commendable; '**Qung** *f* acknowledgment; recognition (*a. pol.*); (*lobende* ~) appreciation; (*Zeichen der Hochachtung*) tribute (*gen.* to); *e-s Wechsels*: acceptance; (*Zulassung*) admission; *in* ~ *gen.* in recognition of.

'**an·erziehen**: *j-m et.* ~ breed a th. into a p.; *anerzogen* acquired.

anfachen ['~faxən] (25) fan (*a. fig.*).

'**anfahr|en** *v/i.* (sn) (*losfahren*) start; *v/t.* (*rammen*) run into, hit, ✥ run foul of; (*herbeibringen*) carry up, convey to the spot; *fig. j-n*: bellow at; '**Qt** *f* journey; (*Ankunft*) arrival; (*~weg*) approach, *vor e-m Hause*: drive(way *Am.*).

'**Anfall** *m* attack (*a. ✗*); ✗ fit; (*Ertrag*) yield; *v. Gewinn, Zinsen*: accrual; (*Menge*) amount, number; '**Qen** *v/t.* (*angreifen*) attack; *v/i.* (sn) result, occur; *Gewinn, Zinsen*: accrue.

anfällig ['~fɛliç] *allg.* susceptible (*für* to); ✗ prone to disease.

'**Anfang** *m* beginning, start; *förmlich*: commencement; *am, im, zu* ~ *s. anfangs*; *von* ~ *an* from the beginning (*od.* start, outset); ~ *Mai* early in May; *den* ~ *machen* begin, lead off; *in den Anfängen stecken* be in its infancy; '**Qen** begin; start (*mit e-r Arbeit usw.* on; *zu inf. ger.*); commence; (*tun*) do; *was soll ich* ~? what am I to do?; *was wirst du morgen* ~? what are you going to do with yourself tomorrow?; *das hast du schlau angefangen* that was a clever trick.

Anfäng|er(in *f*) ['~fɛŋər] *m* beginner; (*Neuling*) tiro; '**Qlich** *adj.* initial; (*ursprünglich*) original; *adv.* in the beginning.

anfangs ['~faŋs] in the beginning; '**Q...** initial, early; '**Qbuchstabe** *m* initial letter; *großer* (*kleiner*) ~ capital (small) letter; '**Qgehalt** *n* starting (*od.* initial) salary; '**Qgründe** *m/pl.* elements, rudiments; '**Qkapital** *n* opening capital; (*Aktien*Q)

original stock; '**Qstadium** *n* initial stage; '**Q-unterricht** *m* elementary instruction.

'**anfassen** *v/t.* take hold of, seize, grasp; (*berühren*) touch, handle (*a. fig.*); *fig.* approach, tackle; *scharf* ~ handle *a p.* roughly; *sich* (*ea.*) ~ take hands; *v/i.* (*helfen, a. mit* ~) lend a hand.

'**anfaulen** (sn) (begin to) rot; *angefault* partially decayed.

anfecht|bar ['~fɛçtba:r] contestable; '**~en** contest, ⚖ *a.* avoid; *Urteil*: appeal from; *Meinung*: oppose; (*beunruhigen*) trouble; '**Qung** *f* contestation; appeal (*gen.* from); *eccl.* (*Versuchung*) temptation.

anfeind|en ['~faɪndən] be hostile to; '**Qung** *f* persecution (*gen.* of), hostility (*gen.* to).

'**anfertig|en** make, manufacture; '**Qung** *f* making, manufacture.

'**an|feuchten** moisten, wet, damp; '**~feuern** fire (*a. fig.*); *fig.* ginger up; *Sport*: cheer (on); '**~flehen** implore; '**~flicken** patch on (*an acc.* to); '**~fliegen** *v/t. Ziel*: ✈ approach, head for, (*landen*) land at; *angeflogen kommen* come flying.

'**Anflug** *m* approach (flight); *fig.* touch, tinge; ~ *von Bart* down; '**~schneise** *f* approach corridor.

'**anforder|n** demand, claim; call for; ✗ requisition; '**Qung** *f* demand, claim; ✗ requisition; *allen* ~*en genügen* meet all requirements, *Am.* fill the bill; *den* ~*en nicht genügen* not to be up to standard; *hohe* ~*en stellen* be very exacting.

'**Anfrage** *f* inquiry; *parl.* interpellation; '**Qn** *v/i.* ask (*bei j-m a p.*); inquire (*nach* for; *bei j-m nach et.* of a p. about a th.).

'**an|fressen** gnaw; *Metall*: corrode; '**~freunden** ['~frɔyndən]: *sich* ~ become friends; *sich* ~ *mit* make friends with; '**~frieren** (sn) freeze on (*an acc.* to); '**~fügen** join, attach, add, annex (*an acc.* to); '**~fühlen** feel, touch; *sich* ~ feel.

'**Anfuhr** ['~fu:r] *f* (16) conveyance, carriage; (*Zufuhr*) supply.

'**anführ|en** lead; ✗ *Truppe*: command; (*erwähnen*) mention, state; *einzeln*: specify; *Gründe*: put forward; *Worte, Beispiele*: quote, cite; (*täuschen*) dupe, fool; *zur Entschul-*

digung ~ plead (in excuse); '**♀er(in** *f*) *m* leader; (*Rädelsführer*) ringleader.

'**Anführung** *f s.* anführen: lead(ership); allegation; quotation; '**~szeichen** *n* quotation mark, inverted comma.

'**anfüllen** fill (up).

'**Angabe** *f* declaration, statement; (*Anweisung*) instruction; (*Auskunft*) information, *pl. a.* data *pl.*; (~ *v.* *Einzelheiten*) specification; F (*Prahlerei*) showing off; *bewußt falsche* ~ misrepresentation; *besondere* ~*n* particular items; *genauere* (*od. nähere*) ~*n* particulars.

'**angaffen** gape at.

angängig ['~gɛnɪç] possible.

'**angeben** *v/t.* Namen, Grund, Tatsachen: give; *bestimmt:* state; *im einzelnen:* specify; (*erklären*), *engS.* *Zollware:* declare; (*vorbringen, behaupten*) allege (*daß* that); (*anzeigen*) denounce, inform against; (*vorgeben*) pretend; ✝ Preis: quote; *s. Tempo, Ton; zu gering* ~ understate; *zu hoch* ~ overstate; *v/i.* *Kartenspiel:* deal first; *Tennis:* serve; F (*prahlen*) show off, brag (*mit* with).

'**Angeber|(in** *f*) *m* informer; F (*Prahler*) show-off; '**~ei** [~'raɪ] *f* denunciation; F (*Prahlerei*) *s.* Angabe; '**♀isch** F boastful; showy.

'**Angebinde** *n* gift, present.

angeblich ['~geːplɪç] *adj.* pretended, alleged, ostensible; *adv.* pretendedly *usw.*; ~ *ist er* ... he is said (*od.* reputed) to be ...

'**angeboren** innate, inborn; ♂ congenital.

'**Angebot** *n* offer; *Auktion:* bid; ✝ (*Ggs. Nachfrage*) supply; (*Lieferungs-, Preis-, Zahlungs♀*) tender, *Am.* bid.

angebracht ['~gəbraxt] advisable; *gut* ~ appropriate, opportune; *schlecht* ~ inopportune, out of place.

'**angedeihen:** *j-m et.* ~ *lassen* bestow upon a p., grant to a p.

angegossen ['~gəgɔsən]: *wie* ~ *sitzen* fit like a glove.

angeheiratet ['~gəhaɪraːtət]: *~er Vetter* cousin by marriage.

angeheitert ['~gəhaɪtərt] slightly tipsy, mellow, *Am.* F happy.

'**angehen** *v/i.* (sn) begin; ♂ begin to take root; (*leidlich sein*) be tolerable; (*zulässig sein*) be admissible; (*schlecht werden*) spoil; *angegangen Fleisch:* tainted; *das geht* (*nicht*) *an* that will (not) do; *v/t.* *ein Unternehmen, e-n Gegner:* tackle; *fig. j-n* ~ (*betreffen*) concern; *das geht dich nichts an* that is no business of yours; *j-n um et.* ~ apply to (*od.* solicit) a p. for; '**~d** (*werdend*) budding, would-be, future.

'**angehör|en** (*dat.*) belong to; *als Mitglied:* a. be member of; '**~ig** (*dat.*) belonging to; '♀**ige** *m*, *f* (*Mitglied*) member; (*Unterhaltsberechtigter*) dependant; *s-e* '♀**igen** *pl.* his relations, his people, F his folks; *die nächsten* ~ the next of kin.

Angeklagte ['~gəklaːktə] *m*, *f* defendant.

angeknackst ['~gəknakst] *fig.* ich bin *etwas* ~ I'm in a bad way.

Angel ['aŋəl] *f* (*Tür♀*) hinge; *s.* Angelgerät, -rute.

angelegen: *sich et.* ~ *sein lassen* make a th. one's business; *es sich* ~ *sein lassen, zu inf.* make a point of ger.; '♀**heit** *f* business, concern, affair, matter; '**~tlich** urgent.

'**Angel|gerät** *n* fishing-gear *od.* -tackle; '**~haken** *m* fish(ing)-hook; '♀**n** (29) (*a. fig.*) angle, fish (*nach* for); '**~punkt** *m* pivot; *fig.* crucial point; '**~rute** *f* fishing-rod; '**~sachse** *m*, '♀**sächsisch** Anglo-Saxon; '**~schein** *m* fishing permit; '**~schnur** *f* fishing-line.

'**angemessen** suitable, appropriate (*dat.* to); (*annehmbar*) reasonable, fair; (*ausreichend*) adequate; '♀**heit** *f* suitableness; reasonableness; adequacy.

'**angenehm** pleasant, agreeable; (*behaglich*) comfortable; (*willkommen*) welcome (*alle: dat.* to).

'**angenommen** *s.* annehmen.

Anger ['aŋər] *m* (7) meadow; (*Dorf♀*) common, (village) green.

ange|regt ['~gəreːkt] animated; '**~schlagen** Boxen: groggy; *Geschirr:* chipped; ♀**schuldigte** ['~ʃuldɪçtə] ⚖ *m*, *f* accused; '**~sehen** respected; esteemed; (*ausgezeichnet*) distinguished; '**~säuselt** F *s.* angeheitert.

'**Angesicht** *n* face; *von* ~ by sight; *von* ~ *zu* ~ face to face; '♀**s** (*gen.*) in the presence of, (*a. fig.*) in view of; *fig.* considering.

ange|stammt ['⁓gəʃtamt] hereditary; innate; ⁀**stellte** ['⁓ʃtɛltə] m, f (salaried) employee; die ⁓n the staff; '⁀**stelltenversicherung** f employees' insurance; '⁓**strengt** strained, intense; ⁓ arbeiten (nachdenken) work (think) hard; ⁓**tan** ['⁓ta:n]: ⁓ (gekleidet) mit attired in; danach ⁓, zu apt to; ⁓ von pleased with; ⁓**trunken** ['⁓truŋkən] tipsy; ⁓**wandt** ['⁓vant] Kunst, Wissenschaft: applied; ⁓**wiesen** ['⁓vi:zən]: ⁓ sein auf be dependent (up)on; '⁓**wöhnen** accustom (j-m et. a p. to a th.); sich das Rauchen usw. ⁓ get into the habit of smoking etc., take to smoking etc.; '⁀**wohnheit** f habit, custom; ⁓**wurzelt** ['⁓vurtsəlt]: wie ⁓ dastehen stand rooted to the ground.

'angleich|en (a. sich) assimilate, adjust (dat. to); '⁀**ung** f assimilation; adjustment.

Angler ['aŋlər] m (7) angler.

'anglieder|n (annektieren) annex; (aufnehmen) affiliate; '⁀**ung** f annexion; affiliation.

Anglist [aŋ'glist] m (12) professor (od. student) of English, Anglicist.

An'glistik f (16) English language and literature, Am. English philology.

Anglizismus [aŋgli'zismus] m (16²) Anglicism, Am. Briticism.

Anglo... ['aŋglo-] Anglo-...

anglotzen ['anglɔtsən] goggle at.

Angorawolle [aŋ'go:ra-] angora wool, mohair.

angreif|bar ['an-] assailable; fig. vulnerable; ⁓**en** (anfassen) handle; Kapital, Vorräte: draw on, break into; Aufgabe: set about, approach, tackle; feindlich: assail, attack, charge; ⚔ j-n, den Körper: weaken, affect; ⚙ corrode; Augen, Nerven: try, strain; sich rauh ⁓ feel rough; angegriffen aussehen look poorly; '⁓**end** aggressive, offensive; körperlich: trying; '⁀**er(in** f) m aggressor (a. pol.).

'angrenzen border, abut (an acc. on, upon); '⁓**d** adjacent, adjoining (an acc. to).

'Angriff m attack (a. Sport u. fig.); charge, assault (auf acc. on); in ⁓ nehmen start on, tackle; zum ⁓ übergehen take the offensive; '⁓**skrieg** m offensive war; '⁀**slustig** aggressive; '⁓**s-punkt** m point of attack; ⊕ working point; '⁓**swaffe** f offensive weapon.

'angrinsen grin at.

Angst [aŋst] f (14¹) anxiety, fear; (Schreck) fright; (große ⁓) dread, terror; ⁓ haben s. (sich) ängstigen; mir ist ⁀ I am afraid (vor dat. of); ⁀ und bange terribly frightened; j-m ⁀ machen, j-n in ⁓ versetzen alarm od. scare a p.; '⁓**gegner** m formidable opponent; '⁓**hase** m coward, sl. chicken.

ängstigen ['ɛŋstigən] (25) alarm; sich ⁓ be afraid od. in fear (vor dat. of); be alarmed (um about).

'Angstkäufe m/pl. panic buying.

ängstlich ['ɛŋstliç] anxious, nervous; (besorgt) uneasy; (schüchtern) timid; (sorgfältig) scrupulous; '⁀**keit** f anxiety, nervousness; timidity; scrupulousness.

'Angst|macher m (7) scaremonger; '⁓**neurose** f anxiety neurosis; '⁓**röhre** F f stove-pipe hat; '⁓**schweiß** m cold sweat; '⁀**voll** anxious, fearful; '⁓**zustände** m/pl. state of anxiety, Am. sl. jitters.

angucken ['an-] look at.

'angurten (26): sich ⁓ fasten one's seat belt.

'anhaben Kleid: have on; sie konnten ihm nichts ⁓ they could find (od. do) nothing against him, they could do him no harm.

'anhaften stick, adhere (dat. to).

'anhaken hook on; in e-r Liste: tick off.

'Anhalt m (Stütze) hold, support; s. ⁓spunkt; '⁀**en** v/t. stop; (hindern) check; polizeilich: arrest, seize; den Atem ⁓ hold (od. bate) one's breath; j-n ⁓ zu et. keep a p. to a th.; v/i. (andauern) continue, last; (stillstehen) stop, halt; ⁓ um ein Mädchen propose to; '⁀**end** continuous, sustained, lasting; (beharrlich) persistant; ⁓er Fleiß assiduity; '⁓**er** m (7) hitch-hiker; per ⁓ fahren hitch-hike; '⁓**s-punkt** m clue, Am. a. lead.

'Anhang m appendage; (Buch usw.) appendix, supplement; (Nachtrag) annex; (Angehörige) dependants pl., family; (Gefolgschaft) adherents pl., following; '⁀**en** (dat.) adhere (od. cling) to.

'anhäng|en v/t. hang on; (hinzufügen) append, affix, add (an acc. to); sich ⁓ hang on, cling (an acc.

to); *fig. j-m et.* ~ implicate a p.; *v/i. s. anhangen;* 2**er** ['~hεŋər] *m* (7) adherent, follower (*a.* 2**in** *f*); (*Schmuck*) pendant; *am Koffer usw.*: label, taǧ; (*~wagen*) trailer; '2**er-kupplung** *f* trailer coupling, tow--bar; '2**erschaft** *f* following; '~**ig:** ɟⁱₜ ~ *sein* be pending; *e-n Prozeß gegen j-n* ~ *machen* bring an action against; '~**lich** attached (*an acc.* to); affectionate; devoted; '2**lichkeit** *f* attachment (*an acc.* to); '2**sel** *n* (7) appendage; (*Etikett*) tag.

'**anhauchen** breathe on; *die Finger:* blow; F (*rüffeln*) blow *a p.* up.

'**anhauen** F: *j-n um et.* ~ scrounge a th. off *a p.*

'**anhäuf|en** heap up; (*a. sich*) accumulate; '2**ung** *f* accumulation; *phys.* aggregation.

'**anheben** *v/t.* lift (up); *fig.* (*a. v/i.*) begin.

'**anheften** fasten, affix (*an acc.* to); (*annähen*) tack, baste, stitch (*an acc.* to); *mit Reißzwecken:* tack on.

'**anheilen** (sn) heal on *od.* up.

anheimeln ['~haiməln] (29) remind *a p.* of home; '~**d** homelike, hom(e)y, friendly, cosy.

an'heim|fallen (sn): *j-m* ~ fall to, devolve on; ~**geben,** ~**stellen:** *j-m et.* ~ leave to a p.('s discretion); *dem Urteil j-s:* submit to.

anheischig ['~haiʃiç]: *sich* ~ *machen* offer, volunteer.

Anhieb ['~hi:p] *m:* F *auf* ~ at the first go; *sagen können:* off the cuff.

'**anhimmeln** (29) *v/t.* idolize.

'**Anhöhe** *f* rise, hill, elevation.

'**anhör|en** listen to, hear; *sich schlecht* ~ sound badly; *man hört ihm den Ausländer an* one can tell by his accent that he is a foreigner; '2**ung** *f* hearing.

Anilin [ani'li:n] *n* (3, *o. pl.*) anilin(e); ~**farbe** *f* anilin(e) dye.

animalisch [ani'mɑːliʃ] animal.

Animateur [anima'tør] *m* (3¹) *im Ferienclub:* host; ~**in** *f* (16¹) hostess.

animier|en [ani'miːrən] incite, encourage, stimulate; 2**mädchen** *n* hostess.

Animosität [animozi'tεːt] *f* animosity.

Anis ⚕ [a'niːs] *m* (4) anise.

'**ankämpfen:** ~ *gegen* struggle *od.* battle against, combat.

'**Ankauf** *m* buying, purchase; '2**en**

buy, purchase; *sich* ~ settle.

Anker ['aŋkər] *m* (7) ⚓ *u.* ⊕ anchor; ⚡ armature; *vor* ~ *gehen* cast *od.* drop anchor; *den* ~ *lichten* weigh anchor; *vor* ~ *liegen* ride at anchor; '~**boje** *f* anchor buoy; '~**grund** *m* anchorage; '~**kette** *f* chain cable; '2**n** (29) anchor; '~**platz** *m* berth; '~**tau** *n* cable; '~**uhr** *f* lever watch; '~**wicklung** ⚡ *f* armature winding; '~**winde** *f* capstan.

'**anketten** chain (*an acc.* to).

'**Anklage** *f* accusation, charge; ɟⁱₜ *a.* indictment (*wegen* for); *wegen Amtsvergehens:* impeachment; *s. erheben; unter* ~ *stehen* be on trial (*wegen* for); '~**bank** *f*: *auf der* ~ in the dock; '2**n** accuse (*wegen* of), charge (with); impeach (of, for); indict (for).

'**Ankläger(in** *f*) *m* accuser; *s. Kläger;* öffentlicher ~ public prosecutor, *Am. a.* district attorney.

'**Anklage|schrift** *f* (bill of) indictment; '~**vertreter** *m* counsel for the prosecution.

'**anklammern** ⊕ clamp (*an acc.* to); *mit Büroklammer:* clip on; *sich* ~ cling (*an acc.* to).

'**Anklang** *m:* ~ *an* (*acc.*) reminiscence (*od.* suggestion) of; ~ *finden* meet approval *od.* a favo(u)rable response, catch on; ~ *finden bei* appeal to; *keinen* ~ *finden* fall flat, *sl.* (be a) flop.

'**ankleben** *v/t.* stick on; *mit Leim:* glue on; *mit Kleister:* paste (on); *mit Gummi:* gum on (*alle: an acc.* to); *v/i.* (sn) stick (*an dat.* to).

'**Ankleide|kabine** *f* changing cubicle; '2**n** (*a. sich*) dress; '~**raum** *m* dressing-room.

'**an|klingeln** *teleph. j-n:* ring up, give *a p.* a ring; '~**klingen:** ~ *an* (*acc.*) be suggestive of; ~ *lassen* call up; '~**klopfen** knock (*an acc.* at); '~**knipsen** ⚡ switch on.

'**anknüpf|en** *v/t.* tie (*an acc.* to); *fig.* begin, enter into; *Beziehungen:* establish; *wieder* ~ resume; *v/i.* (*an acc.*) link up (with), continue; *Sprecher:* refer to; '2**ungs-punkt** *m* point of contact, starting-point.

'**ankommen** *v/i.* (sn) arrive; ~ *bei e-r Firma* get a job at; *fig.* ~ (*bei j-m*) (*verstanden werden*) go down (with), (*Erfolg haben*) make a hit (with); ~ *auf* (*acc.*) depend (up)on;

bei j-m gut (schlecht) ⌇ be well (ill) received by; *es darauf* ⌇ *lassen* run the risk, take a (*od.* one's) chance; *darauf kommt es an* that is the point; *es kommt (ganz) darauf an* it (all) depends; *es kommt nicht darauf an* it is (a matter) of no consequence; *es kommt mir viel darauf an* it is very important to me; *es kommt darauf an, ob* the question is whether; *es kommt mir darauf an, zu inf. od. daß* I am concerned to *inf. od.* that; *es kommt mir nicht auf ... an* I don't mind ...; *v/t.* befall; *es kommt mich hart an* it is hard on me; *es kam mich (mir) die Lust an, zu ...* I felt like *ger.*

Ankömmling ['⌇kœmlin] *m* (3¹) newcomer, arrival.

'**ankoppeln** couple (*an acc.* to); *Raumfähre:* link up (*an acc.* with, to), dock.

'**Ankopplungsmanöver** *n e-r Raumfähre:* link-up manœuvre (*Am.* maneuver).

ankreiden ['⌇kraɪdən] (26) chalk up (*j-m* against a p.).

'**ankreuzen** tick *od.* check off.

'**ankündig|en** announce; *fig.* herald; '**⨀ung** *f* announcement.

Ankunft ['⌇kunft] *f* (14¹) arrival; '**⌇s-flughafen** *m* arrival airport.

'**ankurbeln** *mot.* crank up; *fig.* stimulate, *sl.* pep up; *Produktion usw.:* step up.

'**anlächeln,** '**anlachen** smile at.

'**Anlage** *f* (*Anlegen*) *e-s Gartens usw.:* laying-out; (*Bau*) construction; (*Einbau, Einrichtung*) installation; (*Anordnung*) plan, arrangement, layout; (*Fabrik⨀*) plant, works *pl. u. sg.;* (*Betriebs⨀*) equipment, facility; (*Maschinen⨀ usw.*) plant, unit; (*Hi-Fi-⌇*) stereo system; (*Garten⨀*) pleasure-ground, park; (*Fähigkeit*) talent, ability; (*Natur⨀*) tendency, bent, *a.* ⚕ (pre)disposition; (*Kapital⨀*) investment; (*zu e-m Schreiben*) enclosure; *öffentliche ⌇n pl.* public gardens *pl.; im Brief: in der ⌇* enclosed; '**⨀bedingt** inherent; '**⌇berater** *m* advisor on investments; '**⌇beratung** *f* investment advice; '**⌇kapital** *n* invested capital; '**⌇papiere** *n/pl.* investment securities; '**⌇vermögen** *n* capital assets *pl.*

'**anlangen** *v/i.* (sn) arrive; *v/t.* concern, regard; *was ... anlangt* as to

(*od.* for) ...

Anlaß ['⌇las] *m* (4²) occasion; (*Grund*) reason (*zu* for); (*Ursache*) cause (of); *aus ⌇ gen. s. anläßlich; bei diesem ⌇* on this occasion; *ohne allen ⌇* for no reason at all; *dem ⌇ entsprechend* to fit the occasion; *⌇ geben zu et.* give rise to; *j-m ⌇ geben zu* give a p. reason for; *et. zum ⌇ nehmen, zu inf.* take occasion to *inf.; allen ⌇ haben zu* have every reason for.

'**anlass|en** *Kleid usw.:* keep on; ⊕ start; *Wasser usw.:* turn on; *Stahl:* temper; *j-n hart ⌇* rebuke sharply; *sich gut ⌇* promise well; '**⨀er** ⊕ *m* (7) starter.

anläßlich ['⌇lɛsliç] (*gen.*) on the occasion of.

'**anlasten:** *j-m et. ⌇* blame a th. on a p.

'**Anlauf** *m* start, run; ⚡ *beim Start:* take-off run; *Sport:* run-up; *fig.* e-n ⌇ *nehmen* take a run; '**⨀en** *v/i.* (sn) *Sport:* run up; (*beginnen*) start; *Film:* open; (*in Schwung kommen*) get underway; (*anwachsen*) run up, accumulate; (*sich trüben*) *Metall:* tarnish, *Glas:* (get) dim; ⌇ *lassen* start; *angelaufen kommen* come running (up); *rot ⌇* turn red; *v/t. s.* anrennen; ⚓ *Hafen:* call at; '**⌇phase** *f* initial phase; '**⌇schwierigkeiten** *f/pl.* initial problems.

'**Anlaut** *m* initial sound; '**⨀en:** ⌇ *mit* begin with.

'**anläuten** *s.* anklingeln.

'**anleg|en** *v/t.* (*an acc.*) put against, to; *Feuerung:* put on; *Garten, Straße usw.:* lay out; (*planen*) design, plan; (*bauen*) construct, set up; (*einrichten*) instal(l); *Geld:* invest; *Konto:* open; *Gewehr:* level (*auf acc.* at); *Hund:* tie up; *Kleid, Schmuck usw.:* put on; *typ.* feed; *Maßstab, Verband:* apply (*an acc.* to); *Vorrat:* lay in; *sich ⌇ lean* (*an acc.* against); *Feuer ⌇ an (acc.) od. in* (*dat.*) set fire to; *Hand ⌇* (*helfen*) lend hands; *es ⌇ auf (acc.)* aim at, make *it* one's object; *darauf angelegt sein zu inf.* be calculated to; *v/i. Schütze:* (take) aim (*auf acc.* at); ⚓ land; '**⨀er** ⚶ *m* (7) investor; '**⨀estelle** ⚓ *f* landing-place; (*Hafendamm*) pier; '**⨀ung** *f* laying out; setting up; foundation; ⚶ investment; application.

'**anlehnen** (*a. sich*) lean (*an acc.*

against); *Tür*: leave ajar; *fig. sich* ⌣ *an* (*acc.*) take pattern from.

Anleihe [ˈ⌣laɪə] *f* (15) loan; *s. aufnehmen*; *eine* ⌣ *bei j-m machen* borrow money of a p., *fig.* borrow from a p.

ˈanleimen glue on (*an acc.* to).

ˈanleit|en guide (*zu* to); (*lehren*) instruct (in); **ˈ2ung** *f* guidance; instruction; *s. a. Leitfaden*.

ˈanlern|en teach, train, break in; **ˈ2ling** *m* trainee.

ˈanliefern deliver.

ˈanlieg|en 1. *s. angrenzen*; *Kleid*: fit well, cling; **2.** ⌣ *n* (6) request; *fig.* concern; **ˈ⌣end** adjacent; *Kleid*: tight-fitting; *im Brief*: enclosed; **ˈ2er** *m* abutter; *mot.* local resident; **ˈ2erstaat** *m* neighbo(u)ring state.

ˈanlocken allure, entice, attract.

ˈanlöten solder (*an acc.* to).

ˈanlügen: *j-n* ⌣ tell a p. a lie.

ˈanmachen fasten, fix, attach (*an acc.* to); *Feuer*: make, light; *Licht*: switch on; (*mischen*) mix; *Kalk, Farbe*: temper; *Salat*: dress; F *j-n* ⌣ *sexuell*: give a p. the come-on.

ˈanmalen paint.

ˈAnmarsch *m*, **ˈ2ieren** (sn) approach.

anmaß|en [ˈ⌣maːsən] (27): *sich et.* ⌣ usurp, presume; *sich* ⌣ *zu tun* pretend to, have the impudence to; **ˈ⌣end** arrogant; **ˈ2ung** *f* arrogance, presumption.

ˈanmeld|en announce, *a. polizeilich*: notify, report (*bei* to); *sich* ⌣: *beim Arzt usw.* make an appointment with, *zur Teilnahme* book for, *Schüler usw.*: enrol(l) for, *Sport*: enter for; *sich* ⌣ *lassen als Besucher* have o.s. announced; *s. Patent*; **ˈ⌣epflichtig** notifiable; **ˈ2eschein** *m* entry-form; **ˈ2ung** *f* announcement, notification, report; booking; enrol(l)ment; entry.

ˈanmerk|en (*anstreichen*) mark; (*aufschreiben*) note down; *j-m et.* ⌣ observe (*od.* notice) a th. in a p.; *sich et. nicht* ⌣ *lassen* not to betray a th.; *laß dir nichts* ⌣*!* F don't let on!; **ˈ2ung** *f* comment, remark; *schriftlich*: note; *erklärend*: annotation; *Text mit* ⌣*en versehen* annotate.

ˈanmessen: *j-m et.* ⌣ measure a p. for; *s. angemessen*.

ˈAnmut *f* (16, *o. pl.*) grace, charm,

sweetness; **ˈ2ig** graceful, charming, lovely; *Gegend*: pleasant.

ˈannageln nail on (*an acc.* to).

ˈannähen sew on (*an acc.* to).

annähernd [ˈ⌣nɛːərnt] approximate, *adv. a.* (*nicht* ⌣ not) nearly.

ˈAnnäherung *f* approach; *pol.* rapprochement (*fr.*); *fig.* approximation; **ˈ⌣sversuche** *m/pl.* approaches *pl.*; *amourös*: advances.

Annahme [ˈ⌣naːmə] *f* (15) acceptance; *e-s Kindes, a. e-s Antrags, e-s Plans*: adoption; *e-s Gesetzes*: passing, *bsd. Am.* passage; (⌣*stelle*) receiving office; (*Vermutung*) assumption, supposition; *ich habe Grund zu der* ⌣ I have reasons to believe; *in der* ⌣, *daß* on the supposition that; **ˈ⌣schluß** *m Anzeigenwerbung*: deadline; **ˈ⌣verweigerung** *f* non-acceptance.

Annalen [aˈnaːlən] *f/pl.* annals.

ˈannehm|bar acceptable; *Preis usw.*: reasonable; (*leidlich*) passable; **ˈ⌣en** accept, take; (*vermuten*) assume, suppose, think, *Am.* guess; *Glauben, Meinung*: embrace; *Gestalt*: assume; *Farbe*: take (on); *Bedienten*: engage; *Schüler usw.*: admit; *Wechsel*: accept; *Gewohnheit*: contract; *Antrag, Kind, Haltung, Meinung*: adopt; *Gesetz*: pass; *sich j-s od. e-r S.* ⌣ take care of; *angenommen, es wäre so* supposing (*od.* suppose) it were so; **ˈ2lichkeit** *f* amenity, agreeableness; ⌣*en pl. des Lebens* comforts *pl.* of life.

anne|ktieren [anɛkˈtiːrən] annex; **2xion** [⌣ˈksjoːn] *f* annexation.

Anno [ˈano] *in the year*; ⌣ *dazumal* in the olden times.

Annon|ce [aˈnõːsə] *f* (15) advertisement, F ad; **2ˈcieren** advertise.

annullier|en [anuˈliːrən] annul; ✝ *Auftrag*: cancel; **2ung** *f* annulment. [⌣*n... anode ...*]

Anode ⚡ [aˈnoːdə] *f* (15) anode;

ˈan-öden (26) F bore stiff.

anomal [ˈanomaːl] anomalous.

anonym [anoˈnyːm] anonymous; **2iˈtät** [⌣nymiˈtɛːt] *f* anonymity.

Anorak [ˈ⌣rak] *m* (11) anorak, parka.

ˈan-ordn|en arrange; *fig.* order, direct; **ˈ2ung** *f* arrangement; *fig.* direction, order; *auf* ⌣ *von* by order of; ⌣*en treffen* make dispositions.

ˈan-organisch inorganic.

ˈanpacken *s. anfassen*.

'anpass|en fit, adapt (*a. geistig*), *e-r Norm, e-m Zweck*: adjust (*alle*: *dat.* to); *s.* anprobieren; *sich* ~ (*dat.*) adapt o.s. to; adjust to; **'ℒung** *f* adaptation; adjustment.

'anpassungsfähig adaptable (*an acc.* to); **'ℒkeit** *f* adaptability.

'anpeilen take the bearings of, locate.

'Anpfiff *m Sport*: whistle; F *e-n* ~ *kriegen* get a ticking-off.

'anpflanz|en plant, cultivate; **'ℒung** *f* planting; *konkret*: plantation.

'anpöbeln molest, mob.

Anprall ['~pral] *m* (3¹) impact, (*a.* ✕) shock; **'ℒen** (sn) bound, strike (*an acc.* against).

anprangern ['~praŋərn] (29) pillory, denounce, brand.

'anpreis|en (*empfehlen*) (re)commend; (*loben*) praise; *durch Reklame*: boost, *Am. a.* push; **'ℒung** *f* praising; boosting.

'Anprob|e *f* try-on, fitting; **'ℒieren** try (*od.* fit) on.

'anpumpen F: *j-n* ~ *um* touch a p. for.

'anraten advise; (*empfehlen*) recommend; ℒ *n*: *auf sein* ~ at his suggestion *od.* advice.

'anrechn|en charge; (*gutschreiben*) credit; (*abziehen*) deduct; *j-m zuviel* ~ overcharge a p.; *fig. j-m et. hoch* ~ think highly of a p. for a th.; *j-m et. in* **'ℒung** (*f*) *bringen* put a th. to a p.'s account.

'Anrecht *n* right, title, claim (*auf acc.* to).

'Anrede *f* address; *im Brief*: salutation; **'ℒn** address, speak to.

'anreg|en (*berühren*) touch; *geistig, a. physiol.*: stimulate; (*vorschlagen*) suggest; *j-n zu e-m Werk usw.* ~ give a p. the idea of; *s.* angeregt; **'~end** stimulating; **'ℒung** *f* stimulation; (*Vorschlag*) suggestion; **'ℒungsmittel** *n* stimulant.

anreicher|n ['~raiçərn] (29) enrich; (*sättigen*) concentrate; **'ℒung** *f* enrichment; concentration; **'ℒungsanlage** *f für Uran*: enrichment plant.

'anreihen join; *sich* ~ (*dat.*) join, rank with; (*sich anstellen*) queue (*Am.* line) up.

'Anreiz *m* incentive, stimulus, inducement; **'ℒen** incite, stimulate; (*verlocken*) induce.

anrempeln ['~rɛmpəln] (29) jostle (*od.* bump) against.

'anrennen *v/t. u. v/i.* (sn): ~ *gegen* run against; ✕ assault; *angerannt kommen* come running (up).

'anrichte|n *Speisen*: prepare, dish, dress, serve; *Unheil usw.*: cause, do; *es ist angerichtet* dinner *etc.* is served; **'ℒ(tisch m)** *f*(15) sideboard.

anrüchig ['~ryçiç] disreputable.

'anrücken (sn) approach.

'Anruf *m* call (*a. teleph.*); **'~be-antworter** *teleph. m* (7) telephone answering machine; **'ℒen** call, shout to; *teleph.* call (up), ring (up), (tele-)phone; *Schiff, Taxi*: hail; ✕ *v. Posten*: challenge; *Gott usw.*: invoke; *j-s Hilfe,* ⚖ *höhere Instanz*: appeal to; **'~ung** *f* invocation; ⚖ *usw.* appeal (*gen.* to).

'anrühren touch; *Brei usw.*: mix.

'Ansag|e *f*(15) announcement; **'ℒen** announce (*a. Radio*); *sein Spiel*: call; *Trumpf* ~ declare trumps; *s. Kampf*; **'~er(in** *f*) *m* (7) announcer (*a. Radio*); *s. a. Conférencier*.

'ansamm|eln (*a. sich*) collect; gather, assemble (*a. Personen*); (*anhäufen*) accumulate, amass; *Truppen*: concentrate; **'ℒlung** *f* gathering; accumulation; assembly; concentration.

ansässig ['~zɛsiç] resident (*in dat.* at *od.* in); *sich* ~ *machen* settle down; **'ℒe** ['~gə] *m, f* resident.

'Ansatz *m an e-m Blasinstrument*: embouchure; ⊕ *s.* ~stück; (*Anfang, Anlauf*) start; *in e-r Rechnung*: rate, charge; ⚕ statement; (*Voranschlag*) estimate; (*Anlage*) disposition; *biol.* rudiment; *geol.* deposit; **'~punkt** *m* starting point; **'~stück** ⊕ *n* extension.

'ansaugen suck in.

'anschaff|en procure, provide; (*kaufen*) buy, purchase (*a. sich et.* ~); **'ℒung** *f* procuring, buying *usw.*; purchase; acquisition; **'ℒungskosten** *pl.* prime (*od.* purchase) cost; **'ℒungspreis** *m* cost price; **'ℒungswert** *m* cost value.

'anschalten *Licht, Radio*: switch on; ⚡ *mit Draht*: connect.

'anschau|en look at, view; **'~lich** graphic(ally *adv.*), clear, vivid.

'Anschauung *f* view, opinion; (*Einstellung*) approach, point of view; (*Vorstellung*) conception, idea; '**~smaterial** *n* illustrative material; (*Ton- u. Bildapparate*) audio-visual aids *pl.*; '**~s-unterricht** *m* visual instruction, object-teaching; *fig.* object-lesson; '**~sweise** *f* point of view.

'**Anschein** *m* appearance; *allem ~ nach* to all appearances; *den ~ erwecken* give the impression; *sich den ~ geben* pretend, make believe; *den ~ haben* seem; '**2end** apparent, seeming.

'**anschicken:** *sich ~ (zu)* prepare (for); set about doing *a th.*; *gerade:* be going to.

'**anschießen** wound, shoot, *bsd. Vogel:* wing; *Gewehr:* test, try.

anschirren ['~∫irən] (25) harness.

'**Anschiß** *sl. m:* *j-m e-n ~ verpassen* give a p. a bollocking.

'**Anschlag** *m* stroke; (*Schätzung*) estimate; (*Berechnung*) calculation; (*Komplott*) plot; (*Attentat*) attempt; *♪, a. Schwimmen:* touch; ✗ *des Gewehrs:* aiming (*od.* firing) position; ⊕ stop, detent; *s. ~zettel; in ~ bringen* take into account; *Gewehr im ~ halten* level (*auf acc.* at); *e-n ~ verüben auf (acc.)* make an attempt on; '**~brett** *n* notice-board, *Am.* bulletin board, billboard; '**2en** *v/t.* strike (*an acc.* at, against); (*befestigen*) fasten, affix (*an on*); *Plakat:* post up, put up; (*schätzen*) estimate (*hoch* highly), rate; *♪* touch, strike; *Gewehr:* level (*auf acc.* at); *Faß Bier usw.:* tap; *zu hoch ~* overestimate; *zu niedrig ~* underrate; *e-n andern Ton ~ change* one's tune; *s. angeschlagen; v/i. Glocke:* ring; (*bellen*) give tongue; *Schwimmer:* touch; (*wirken*) take (effect); *Essen:* agree (*bei j-m* with); (*zielen*) take aim (*auf acc.* at); (*sn*) *mit dem Kopf an die Wand ~* strike one's head against; '**~säule** *f* advertisement (*Am.* advertising) pillar; '**~zettel** *m* bill, placard, poster.

'**anschließen** *v/t.* fix with a lock; (*anketten*) chain; (*anfügen*) add, join, attach, annex; ⊕ join (*an acc.* to), link up (with); *♪* connect (to), *mit Stecker:* plug in; *sich ~: j-m, j-s Bitte, e-r Gesellschaft usw.:* join, *e-r Meinung:* subscribe to, *e-m Beispiel:* follow; *sich ~ an (acc.) Sache:* follow; *v/i. Kleid:* fit close; '**~d** subsequent(ly *adv.*; *an acc.* to).

'**Anschluß** *m* joining; ☎, *♪, teleph.* connection; (*Gas- usw.* ⚲) supply; *~ an e-n Zug haben* meet a train, have a connection with a train; *im ~ an* (*acc.*) following; *teleph. ~ bekommen* get through; *fig. ~ finden* (*suchen*) meet (seek) company; *den ~ verpassen* (*a. fig.*) miss one's connection, *fig. sl.* miss the bus; '**~arbeiten** *f/pl.* (*weitere Arbeiten*) follow-up work *sg.*; (*Anschließungsarbeiten*) connection work *sg.*; '**~dose** *♪ f* junction box; '**~flug** *m* connecting flight; '**~gebühr** *f* connection fee; '**~klemme** *♪ f* terminal; '**~rohr** *n* service-pipe; '**~schnur** *♪ f* flex(ible cord); '**~station** ☎ *f* junction; '**~treffer** *m* goal that leaves one more to level the score; '**~zug** ☎ *m* connecting train.

'**an|schmiegen** (25): *sich ~ an (acc.)* nestle against; *Kleid:* cling to; '**~schmiegsam** *Kleidung:* soft (and comfortable); *fig.* affectionate; '**~schmieren** (be)smear, daub; grease; F (*betrügen*) cheat; '**~schnallen** (25) buckle on; ✗, *mot. sich ~* fasten one's seat belts.

'**anschnauzen** F (27) blow up, snap at, *Am.* bawl out.

'**an|schneiden** cut (from); *Thema:* broach; '**2schnitt** *m* first cut *od.* slice; '**~schrauben** screw on (*an acc.* to); '**~schreiben 1.** write down; *✝ j-n:* write to; *Stand e-s Spiels:* score (*a. v/i.*; *h.*); *Schuld:* charge; *j-m et. ~* put to a p.'s account; *et. ~ lassen* buy on credit; *bei j-m gut (schlecht) angeschrieben sein* be in a p.'s good (bad) books; **2.** ⚲ *n* cover note; '**~schreien** shout at; '**2schrift** *f* address.

anschuldig|en ['~∫uldigən] (25) accuse, incriminate; '**2ung** *f* accusation, incrimination.

'**anschwärzen** *fig.* blacken, calumniate, F sneak against.

'**anschweißen** ⊕ weld on.

'**anschwell|en** *v/i.* (sn) swell; (*zunehmen*) increase, rise; '**2ung** *f* swelling. [*Land:* deposit.]

'**anschwemmen** wash ashore;]

'**ansegeln** *Hafen:* make for; *angesegelt kommen* come up (sailing).

'**ansehen 1.** look at; *s. scharf, scheel; sich et. ~* take (*od.* have) a look at; (*besichtigen*) view; (*beobachten*) watch; *fig. ~ für od. als* regard as, consider, *fälschlich:* take for; *et.*

mit ~ witness, (*ertragen*) bear; *j-m et.* ~ read a th. in a p.'s face; *man sieht ihm sein Alter nicht an* he does not look his age; **2.** ♀ *n* (6) (*Anschein*) appearance, aspect; (*Geltung*) authority, prestige, standing; (*Achtung*) esteem, reputation; *sich ein* ~ *geben* put on airs; *j-n von* ~ *kennen* know a p. by sight; *ohne* ~ *der Person* without respect of persons.

ansehnlich ['~ze:nliç] considerable; *Person*: fine-looking.

anseilen *mount.* ['~zaɪlən] rope.

'ansengen singe.

'ansetz|en *v/t.* (*an acc.*) put on (to), apply (to); *Glas, Flöte usw.*: put to one's lips; (*anstücken*) add (to); *Frist*: appoint, fix; (*abschätzen*) rate, assess; *Preis*: fix, quote; (*berechnen*) charge; (*entwickeln*) produce; *Blätter usw.*: put forth; *Fleisch* (*am Körper*), *Speise* (*zum Kochen*), *a. thea. Stück*: put on; *Essig, Likör usw.*: prepare; *Rost*: gather; *die Feder* ~ set pen to the paper; *v/i.* (*versuchen*) try; (*Fett* ~) grow fat; *zu et.* ~ prepare for *od.* to do; *zum Sprung* ~ get ready for the jump; '♀ung *f e-s Preises*: quotation; *e-s Termins*: appointment.

'Ansicht *f* sight, view; *fig.* view, opinion; *meiner* ~ *nach* in my opinion; ✝ *zur* ~ on approval; *der* ~ *sein, daß* be of opinion that; *zu der* ~ *kommen, daß* decide that; *ich bin anderer* ~ I beg to differ; '♀ig: *j-s* ~ *werden* catch sight of; '~s(post)-karte *f* picture postcard; '~ssache *f* matter of opinion.

'ansied|eln (29) (*a. sich*) settle, colonize; *fig.* place; '♀ler *m* settler; '♀lung *f* settlement.

'Ansinnen *n* (6) request, demand.

'anspann|en stretch; *Muskeln*: flex; *Pferd*: harness; *fig.* tense (*a. sich*); (*anstrengen*) strain; '♀ung *fig. f* strain; *unter* ~ *aller Kräfte* by exerting all one's energies.

'anspeien spit (up)on *od.* at.

'anspiel|en *v/i.* play first, lead; *Sport*: lead off; *Fußball*: kick off; ~ *auf* (*acc.*) allude to, hint at; *v/t. Karte*: lead; *Fußball*: *j-n* ~ pass to; '♀ung *f* allusion, hint.

'anspinnen: *fig. sich* ~ develop.

'anspitzen point, sharpen.

'Ansporn *m* spur, encouragement;

(*Anreiz*) incentive; '♀en spur; *fig. a.* goad (on), encourage.

'Ansprache *f* address, speech (*an acc.* to); *e-e* ~ *halten* deliver an address.

'ansprechen speak to, address; *fig.* ~ *als* regard as; (*gefallen*) appeal to; (*reagieren, a.* ⊕) respond (*auf acc.* to); '~d appealing.

'anspringen *v/t.* leap against; *v/i.* (sn) *Motor*: start; *angesprungen kommen* come skipping along.

'anspritzen besprinkle, spray.

'Anspruch *m* (*auf acc.*) claim, pretension (to); ⚖ title, (*a. Patent*♀) claim (to); *hohe Ansprüche* high demands; *s. aufgeben*; ~ *haben auf* (*acc.*) be entitled to; ~ *machen* (*od. erheben*) *auf* (*acc.*), *in* ~ *nehmen* lay claim to, pretend to; *claim to be*; *j-s Hilfe usw. in* ~ *nehmen* call on, *Vorräte usw.*: draw (up)on; *Zeit, Aufmerksamkeit, Kredit in* ~ *nehmen* take up; *ganz in* ~ *nehmen* engross; *ganz u. gar für sich in* ~ *nehmen* monopolize; (*starke*) *Ansprüche stellen an* (*acc.*) tax severely; '♀slos unpretentious; (*schlicht*) unassuming, modest; *Essen*: frugal; (*geistig*) ~ *S.*: undemanding; '~slosigkeit *f* unpretentiousness; '♀svoll pretentious; (*streng*) exacting; (*wählerisch*) fastidious; *v. Sachen*: ambitious; *geistig*: demanding.

'anspucken spit (up)on *od.* at.

'anspülen *s.* anschwemmen.

'anstacheln goad on, prod, incite.

Anstalt ['~ʃtalt] *f* (16) establishment; institution; *s. Irren(heil)*♀, *Heil*♀, *Lehr*♀; ~ *machen zu* prepare to *inf.*; ~*en treffen zu* make arrangements for.

'Anstand *m* (3³, *o. pl.*) *hunt.* stand; (*Schicklichkeit*) decency, propriety, decorum; (*Einwendung*) objection (*an dat.* to); ~ *nehmen zu* hesitate to.

anständig ['~ʃtendiç] *allg.* decent; (*schicklich*) proper; (*achtbar*) respectable; (*beträchtlich*) fair, handsome; *adv.* F (*sehr*) thoroughly; '♀keit *f* decency; propriety.

'Anstands|besuch *m* formal call; '~dame *f* chaperon; '~formen *f/pl.* proprieties *pl.*; '~gefühl *n* tact; '♀halber for decency's sake; '♀slos *adv.* unhesitatingly; (*ungehindert*) freely.

'anstarren stare at.

anstatt [~'ſtat] (*gen.*) instead of.

'**anstauen** dam up; *sich* ~ accumulate.

'**anstaunen** gape at.

'**anstechen** prick; *Faß*: broach, tap.

'**ansteck|en** *v/t.* stick on; *mit e-r Nadel*: pin on; *Ring*: slip on; ♂ infect; (*anzünden*) set on fire; *Feuer*: kindle; *Kerze, Zigarre usw.*: light; *v/i.* be catching; '**~end** ♂ infectious; contagious; '**♀nadel** *f* badge; (*Schmucknadel*) pin; '**♀ung** *f* infection; *durch Berührung*: contagion; '**♀ungsgefahr** *f* danger of infection; '**♀ungsstoff** *m* infectious matter.

'**anstehen** *in e-r Reihe*: queue (up), *Am.* stand in line (*nach* for); *j-m*: suit, become; (*zögern*) hesitate; (*zu erwarten sein*) be due; ~ *lassen* put off, delay.

'**ansteigen** (*sn*) *Boden usw.*: rise, ascend; *fig.* rise, increase; ♀ *n* rising, rise; increase.

'**anstell|en** place (*an acc.* against); *P.*: engage, employ; *Mechanismus*: start; *Licht, Radio usw.*: switch on; *Unfug*: do; *Versuch usw.*: make; *Vergleich*: draw; (*fertigbringen*) manage; *sich* ~ queue on *od.* up, *Am.* line up (*nach* for); *sich* ~ *als ob* act as if; *sich geschickt* (*ungeschickt*) ~ set to work (*od.* act) cleverly (clumsily); *angestellt bei* in the employ of; '**~ig** handy, clever; '**♀igkeit** *f* (25) skill; '**♀ung** *f* place; employment, job.

'**ansteuern** steer (*od.* head) for.

Anstieg ['anſti:k] *m* (3) ascent; *fig.* rise, increase.

'**anstieren** (25) stare at.

'**anstift|en** *j-n, et.*: instigate; *et.*: cause, do, stir up; '**♀er(in** *f*) *m* instigator; '**♀ung** *f* instigation.

'**anstimmen** strike up.

'**Anstoß** *m* (*Antrieb*) impulse; (*Ärgernis*) offence, *Am.* offense; *Fußball*: kick-off; *Stein des* ~*es* stumbling-block; ~ *erregen* give offence (*bei* to), scandalize (*a p.*); ~ *nehmen an* (*dat.*) take offence at, be scandalized at; take exception to; *den* ~ *geben zu* start, initiate; '**♀en** *v/t.* push, knock, bump (against); *heimlich*: nudge; *v/i. s. angrenzen; mit der Zunge* ~ lisp; ~ *bei j-m* offend, shock; *mit den Gläsern* ~ clink glasses; *auf j-s Gesundheit* ~ drink a p.'s health; '**♀end** *s. angrenzend.*

anstößig ['~ſtø:siç] offensive, shocking.

'**anstrahlen** beam on (*fig.* at); ⚡ floodlight.

'**anstreben** aspire to, strive for.

'**anstreich|en** paint, coat; *Textstelle*: mark; *Fehler*: underline; *fig. j-m et.* ~ make a p. pay for; '**♀er** *m* (7) house-painter.

anstreng|en ['~ſtrɛŋən] (25) exert; (~*d sein für*) *Geist, Körper*: tax, try; *j-n*: fatigue; *sich* ~ exert (*Am.* drive) o.s., (*sich bemühen*) endeavo(u)r (*zu tun* to do); *alle Kräfte* ~ strain every nerve; *s. Prozeß, angestrengt*; '**~end** strenuous; trying (*für* to); '**♀ung** *f* exertion, effort; strain.

'**Anstrich** *m* paint; (*Überzug*) coat (-ing); *fig.* varnish; (*leiser* ~) tinge; (*Anschein*) air, appearance.

'**An|sturm** *m* assault, charge; ~ *auf e-e Bank* run on; '**♀stürmen** (*sn*) storm, rush (*gegen* against).

'**ansuchen 1.** (*bei j-m*) *um et.* ~ apply (to a p.) for; **2.** ♀ *n* (6) request, application; *auf* ~ by request; *auf j-s* ~ at a p.'s request.

Antarkt|is [ant'ʔarktis] *f the* Antarctic (regions *pl.*); **♀isch** antarctic.

'**antasten** touch; *fig. a.* attack.

'**Anteil** *m* share (*a.* ♱), portion; (*Quote*) quota; *fig.* interest; ~ *share an* (*dat.*) share *od.* participate in; ~ *nehmen an* (*dat.*) take an interest in, *mitleidig*: sympathize with; (*sich interessieren für*) take an interest in; '**♀mäßig** proportional; '**~nahme** *f* sympathy; interest; '**~schein** *m* share certificate.

'**antelephonieren** ring up.

Antenne [an'tɛnə] *f* (15) *Radio*: aerial, *bsd. Am.* antenna.

Anthrazit *min.* [~tra'tsi:t] *m* (3[1]) anthracite; **♀farben** charcoal.

Anti..., anti... [anti-] anti...

Anti-alko'holiker(in *f*) *m* teetotaller.

Anti-'Baby-Pille *f the* pill.

Anti-Be'schlagtuch *n* anti-mist cloth.

Antibiotikum ♂ [antibi'o:tikum] *n* (9[2]) antibiotic.

Anti-Blockier-System *mot. n* anti--brake-locking system.

Antifaschi|smus [antifa'ſismus] *m* (16, *o. pl.*) antifascism; **~st** *m* (12), **♀stisch** *adj.* antifascist.

Anti'haftbeschichtung *f e-r Pfanne*:

non-stick surface; *mit* ~ non-stick.
antik [an'ti:k] antique; 2e *f* (15)
Kunstwerk: antique; *Zeitalter*: *die* ~
the (classical) antiquity.
'**Antikörper** *m* anti-body.
Antilope [anti'lo:pə] *f* (15) antelope.
Antipathie [~pa'ti:] *f* antipathy
(*gegen* against, to), aversion (to, for).
'**antippen** touch lightly, tap.
Antiqua *typ*. [~'ti:kva] *f inv*. Roman
(type).
Antiquar [anti'kva:r] *m* (3[1]) second-
-hand bookseller; *s. Antiquitäten-
händler*; ~**iat** [~kvar'ja:t] *n* (3[1])
second-hand bookshop; 2isch [~-
'kva:riʃ] second-hand.
Antiquitäten|händler[~kvi'te:tən-]
m antique dealer; ~**laden** *m* antique
shop.
Antisemit [~ze'mi:t] *m* (12) anti-
-Semite; 2isch anti-Semitic; ~**ismus** [~mi'tismus] *m* anti-Semitism.
anti'statisch antistatic.
Antlitz ['antlits] *n* (3[2]) face.
Antrag ['antra:k] *m* (3[3]) (*Angebot*)
offer, (*a. Heirats*2) proposal; (*Gesuch*) application, request, *parl*.
motion, *ᵗᵗ* petition; *e-n* ~ *stellen auf*
(*acc.*) *s*. beantragen; 2en ['~gən] offer; '~**sformular** *n* application
form; ~**steller(in** *f*) ['~ʃtɛlər] *m*
applicant, *ᵗᵗ a*. petitioner; *parl*.
mover.
'**antrauen**: *j-m* ~ wed to a p.
'**antreffen** meet (*et*. with), find.
'**antreiben** *v/i*. (sn) drift (*od*. float)
ashore; *v/t*. drive (*od*. push) on;
Pferd: urge on; *Maschine*: drive;
Schiff usw.: propel; *fig*. impel.
'**antreten** *v/t. Amt, Dienst, Erbschaft*: enter (up)on; *Reise*: set out
on; *die Arbeit* (*den Dienst*) ~ report
for work (duty); *s. Beweis*; *v/i*. (sn)
take one's place; ✕ fall in, line up.
'**Antrieb** *m* motive, impulse; (*Anreiz*) incentive; ⊕ drive, propulsion; *aus eigenem* ~ of one's own
accord; ⊕ *mit* ...~ ...-powered;
'~**s-achse** ⚙ *f* propeller shaft; '~**s-
schwäche** *f* ab(o)ulia; '~**swelle** *f*
driving shaft.
'**Antritt** *m fig*. commencement; *e-s
Amtes usw*.: entrance upon; *e-r Reise*: setting out on; '~**sbesuch** *m* courtesy call; '~**srede** *f* inaugural speech;
parl. maiden speech.
'**antun**: *j-m et*. ~ do a th. to a p.;
sich et. ~ lay hands upon o.s.; *es*

j-m ~ bewitch (*od*. charm) a p.;
s. angetan.
'**Antwort** *f* (16) answer, reply (*auf
acc*. to); 2en *v/t. u. v/i*. (26) answer,
reply (*j-m* a p.; *auf acc*. to); '~**karte**
f reply postcard; '2lich (*gen*.) ✝ in
reply to; '~**schein** *m* reply coupon;
'~**schreiben** *n* reply.
'**anvertrauen** confide (*a. Geheimnis*), entrust (*beide: dat*. to); *j-m et*. ~
a. trust a p. with a th.; *fig. sich
j-m* ~ confide in a p.
'**anverwandt** related; '2e *m, f* relation.
'**anwachsen** (sn) grow on (*an acc*.
to); (*Wurzel schlagen*) take root;
fig. increase; 2 *n fig*. increase.
Anwalt ['~valt] *m* (3[3]) lawyer, *bsd.
Am*. attorney(-at-law); *beratender*:
solicitor; *plädierender*: barrister,
Am. counselor-at-law; *vor Gericht*:
counsel (*des Angeklagten* for the
defence); *fig*. advocate; '~**schaft** *f*
the Bar; '~**skammer** *f* Board of
Attorneys; '~**skosten** *pl*. legal expenses.
'**anwandeln** come over, seize; *ihn
wandelte die Lust an, zu inf*. the
fancy took him to; '2lung *f* fit;
(*Antrieb*) impulse.
'**anwärmen** warm up; preheat.
'**Anwärter(in** *f*) *m* (3[3]) (*auf acc*.) candidate (for), aspirant (to); *ᵗᵗ* ex-
pectant, claimant (of).
Anwartschaft ['~vartʃaft] *f* (*auf
acc*.) candidacy, qualification (for);
ᵗᵗ expectancy (of), claim (to).
'**anweis|en** (*zuteilen*) assign; (*be-
lehren*) instruct; (*beauftragen*) direct; *s. angewiesen*; '2ung *f* assignment; instruction; direction; ✝
cheque, *Am*. check, draft; *s. Post*2.
anwend|bar ['~ventba:r] practi-
cable; applicable (*auf acc*. to);
'2**barkeit** *f* applicability; ~**en** ['~-
dən] employ, use; apply (*auf acc*.to);
Vorsicht: take; *s. angewandt*; '2er *m*
(7) *a. Computer*: user; '2ung *f* application; *zur* ~ *bringen s. anwenden*;
'2**ungsbeispiel** *n* example of use,
illustrative example; '2**ungs-pro-
gramm** *n Computer*: application
program.
'**anwerb|en** ✕ enlist, recruit, *Am*.
levy, enrol(l); *Arbeiter*: recruit, engage; '2**estopp** *m* recruitment stop;
'2ung *f* ✕ enlistment, recruitment;
engagement.

'**Anwesen** n property; ✓ farm, (*Gut*) estate.

'**anwesen|d** present (*bei* at); *die* ℒen the persons (*od.* those) present; ℒe *ausgenommen* present company excepted; *verehrte* ℒe! Ladies and Gentlemen!; '**ℒheit** f presence; *in* ~ *gen.* in the ~ of; '**ℒheitsliste** f attendance list.

anwidern ['~viːdərn] (29) s. *anekeln.*

'**Anwohner** m neighbo(u)r; s. *Anlieger.*

'**Anwurf** m (*Verleumdung*) aspersion.

'**Anzahl** f number; quantity.

'**anzahl|en** pay on account, pay a first instal(l)ment; *et.* ~ (*als Angeld*) pay a deposit; '**ℒung** f *bei Ratenzahlung:* down payment, payment on account, (first) instal(l)ment; *als Sicherheit:* deposit.

'**anzapfen** tap (*a. ✗ teleph.*), broach.

'**Anzeichen** n sign, indication, *a.* ✗ symptom (*für* of).

Anzeig|e ['antsaɪgə] f (15) notice; (*Zeitungsℒ usw.*) advertisement, F ad; (*Ankündigung*) announcement, ✦ advice; ⚖ information; ⊕ signal, (*Ablesung*) reading; *kleine* ~*n* pl. classified ads; *s. erstatten; e-e* ~ *aufgeben* place an advertisement in a newspaper; '**ℒen** announce, notify, ✦ advise; *in der Zeitung usw.:* advertise; (*deuten auf*) indicate; *j-n:* denounce, inform against, *et.:* report (*bei* to); *es erscheint angezeigt, zu inf.* it seems expedient *od.* indicated to *inf.*; '**~en-annahme** f advertising office; '**~en-auftrag** m insertion order; '**~enbüro** n advertising agency *od.* office; '**~enteil** m *in der Zeitung:* advertisements pl., ads pages pl.; '**ℒepflichtig** notifiable; '**~er** m advertiser (*a.* '**~enblatt** n); ⚖ informer; ⊕ indicator; '**~etafel** f *Sport:* scoreboard.

anzetteln ['~tsetəln] (29) *fig.* plot.

'**anziehen** v/t. draw, pull; *Zügel:* draw in; *Schraube:* tighten; *Kleid:* put on; *j-n:* dress; *fig.* attract; v/i. draw; *Preise:* rise; *im Brettspiel:* make the first move; '**~d** attractive.

'**Anziehung** f attraction; '**~skraft** f attractive power, pull; *der Erde usw.:* gravitation(al pull); *fig.* attraction, appeal.

'**Anzug** m (*Kleidung*) dress; (*Herren*ℒ) suit; ✗ dress, uniform; *beim Brettspiel:* first move; *im* ~ *sein* be

approaching.

anzüglich ['~tsyːkliç] suggestive; (*stichelnd*) personal; '**ℒkeit** f suggestiveness; personal remark.

'**Anzugstoff** m suiting.

'**anzünd|en** light, kindle; *Streichholz:* strike; *Haus:* set on fire; '**ℒer** m (7) lighter.

'**anzweifeln** doubt, (call in) question.

apart [a'part] exquisite.

Apath|ie [apa'tiː] f apathy; **ℒisch** [a'paːtiʃ] apathetic.

Apfel ['apfəl] m (7¹) apple; *s. sauer;* '**~baum** m apple-tree; '**~kompott** n stewed apple; '**~mus** n apple-sauce; '**~saft** m apple-juice; '**~schimmel** m dapple-grey horse; **~sine** [~'ziːnə] f (15) orange; '**~tasche** f apple turnover; '**~wein** m cider.

Apostel [a'pɔstəl] m (7) apostle; **~geschichte** f *the* Acts pl. of the Apostles.

apostolisch [apɔ'stoːliʃ] apostolical; *das* ℒe *Glaubensbekenntnis* The Apostles' Creed, The Belief.

Apostroph [apɔ'stroːf] m (3¹) apostrophe.

Apotheke [apo'teːkə] f (15) chemist's shop, *Am.* pharmacy.

Apo'theker m (7) (dispensing) chemist, *Am.* druggist, pharmacist; **~gewicht** n apothecaries' weight.

Apparat [apa'raːt] m (3) *allg.* apparatus; instrument; (*Gerät*) appliance; (*Vorrichtung*) device; *phot.* camera; *Radio:* set; *teleph.* telephone; *fig.* apparatus, organization; *teleph. am* ~! speaking!; *am* ~ *bleiben* hold the line (*Am.* wire); **~ur** [~'tuːr] f apparatus; outfit; (*Zubehör*) fixtures pl.

Appartement [apartə'mãː] n (11) flat, *bsd. Am.* apartment; **~haus** n block of flats, *Am.* apartment house.

Appell [a'pɛl] m (3¹) ✗ roll-call; inspection; parade; *fig.* appeal (*an acc.* to).

appel'lieren appeal (*an acc.* to).

Appetit [ape'tiːt] m (3) appetite (*auf acc.* for); ~ *machen* give (an) appetite; **ℒlich** appetizing (*a. fig.*); **~zügler** m (7) appetite suppressant.

applaudieren [aplau'diːrən] cheer, applaud (*j-m* a p.).

Applaus [a'plaus] m (4) applause.

apport [a'pɔrt] go fetch!; **~ieren** [~'tiːrən] fetch, retrieve.

appret|ieren [apre'tiːrən] dress, finish; *Papier*: glaze; 2ur [~'tuːr] *f* (16) dressing, finish.
approbiert [apro'biːrt] *Arzt*: qualified, *Am.* licensed.
Aprikose [apri'koːzə] *f* (15) apricot.
April [a'pril] *m* (3¹) April; *j-n in den ~ schicken* make an April-fool of a p.; **~scherz** *m* April-fool joke; **~wetter** *n* April weather.
Aquaplaning [akva'plaːniŋ] *n* (11¹, *o. pl.*) aquaplaning.
Aquarell [akva'rɛl] *n* (3¹) water--colo(u)r; **~farbe** *f* water-colo(u)r; **~maler**(in *f*) *m* aquarellist, water--colo(u)rist.
Äquator [ɛ'kvaːtɔr] *m* (8, *o. pl.*) equator.
Äquivalent [ɛːkviva'lɛnt] *n*, 2 *adj.* equivalent.
Ar [aːr] *n* (3¹, *nach Zahlen inv.*) are.
Ära ['ɛːra] *f* (16²) era.
Arab|er ['arabər] *m* Arab; *Pferd*: [a'raːbər] Arab; **~erin** *f* Arabian (woman); **~eske** [ara'bɛskə] *f* (15) arabesque; **2isch** [a'raːbiʃ] Arabian; Arabic.
Arbeit ['arbaɪt] *f* (16) work; (*mühevolle ~*) labo(u)r, toil; (*Beschäftigung*) employment, job; (*Tätigkeit, Geschäft*) business; (*aufgegebene ~, Schul*2) task; (*schriftliche ~*) paper; (*Fabrikat*) make; (*Ausführungsart*) workmanship; *phys.* work; *ƒ* energy; ⊕ performance; *e-e gute* (*schlechte*) *~ a* good (bad) piece of work; *bei der ~* at work; *sich an die ~ machen*, *an die ~ gehen* set to work; (*keine*) *~ haben* be in (out of) work; *s. antreten, niederlegen; et. in ~ geben* (*nehmen*) put (take) a. th. in hand; *in ~ sein* (*S.*) be in hand; *bei j-m in ~ stehen* be in the employ of a p.; *gute ~ leisten* make a good job of it; **2en** *v/i.* (26) work (*a. v/t.*); (*schwer ~*) labo(u)r, toil; *~ an* (*dat.*) be working at; ✝ *mit e-r Firma ~* do business with; *Kapital ~ lassen* employ, invest.
'Arbeiter *m* worker (*a. zo.*); (*Hand*2) workman; *ungelernt:* labo(u)rer, hand; *die ~ s. ~schaft*; '**~in** *f* (female) worker; working woman, workwoman; '**~klasse** *f* working class(es *pl.*); '**~mangel** *m* shortage of workers; '**~partei** *f* Labo(u)r Party; '**~schaft** *f*, '**~stand** *m* working class(es *pl.*), *a. pol.* labo(u)r.

'**Arbeit|geber**(in *f*) *m* employer; **~-geber-anteil** *m* employer's contribution; '**~nehmer**(in *f*) *m* employee.
'**arbeitsam** industrious, diligent; '2**keit** *f* industry, diligence.
'**Arbeits...** *mst* working ...; '**~amt** *n* Labo(u)r Exchange; '**~anzug** *m* working clothes *pl.*; overall; '**~ausschuß** *m* working committee; '**~bedingungen** *f/pl.* working (⊕ operating) conditions; '**~beschaffung** *f* provision of work; '**~beschaffungsprogramm** *n* job creation scheme; '**~bescheinigung** *f* certificate of employment; '**~bogen** *m* Schule: work folder; '**~buch** *n* employment record; '**~dienst** *m* labo(u)r service; ✗ fatigue; '**~dienstpflicht** *f* industrial conscription; '**~direktor** *m* workers' representative; '**~einkommen** *n* earned income; '**~einstellung** *f* stoppage of work; *e-s Betriebs:* closure; (*Streik*) strike; '**~erlaubnis** *f* work permit; '**~essen** *n* working lunch; '2**fähig** fit (*od.* able) to work; '**~fähigkeit** *f*: *j-s ~ feststellen* declare a p. fit to work; '**~feld** *n* field (*od.* sphere) of work *od.* activity; '**~fläche** *f* work-surface; '2**freudig** willing to work; '**~frieden** *m* industrial peace; '**~gang** *m* working operation, process; '**~gemeinschaft** *f* study group; ✝ working pool; *Schule:* seminar group; '**~gericht** *n* industrial court; '**~kleidung** *f* work clothes *pl.*; '**~klima** *n* work climate; '**~konflikt** *m* labo(u)r dispute; '**~kosten** *pl.* work cost; *~anteil* work cost per unit; '**~kraft** *f* capacity for work; (*Arbeiter*) workman, hand; *pl. a.* labo(u)r *sg.*, manpower; '**~lager** *n* labo(u)r camp; '**~leistung** *f* working capacity, efficiency; *a.* ⊕ performance, output; '**~lohn** *m* wages *pl.*, pay; '2**los** out of work, unemployed, jobless; *~ machen* put out of work; '**~lose** *m, f* unemployed person; '**~losenquote** *f* unemployment rate; '**~losenunterstützung** *f* unemployment benefit; *~ beziehen* be on the dole; '**~losenversicherung** *f* unemployment insurance; '**~losigkeit** *f* unemployment; '**~markt** *m* labo(u)r market; '**~methode** *f* working method; '**~minister** *m* Minister of Labour, *Am.* Secretary for Labor; '**~moral** *f* (working) morale; '**~nachweis(stelle** *f*) *m* employment registry office;

'**~niederlegung** f strike; '**~platz** m place of employment; (*Stelle*) job; *Sicherheit des* ~*es* job security; '**~platzbeschreibung** f job description; '**~platzgarantie** f job guarantee; '**~platzteilung** f job sharing; '**~raum** m workroom; '**~recht** n industrial law; '**²scheu** work-shy; '**~scheu** f aversion to work; '**~soll** n target; '**²sparend** labo(u)r-saving; '**~streit(igkeit** f) f labo(u)r dispute; '**~stunde** f *als Maßeinheit:* man--hour; *pl.* working hours; '**~suche** f job hunting; *auf* ~ *sein* be job hunting; '**~süchtige** m, f workaholic; '**~tag** m working day; '**~takt** *mot.* m power stroke; '**~teilung** f division of labo(u)r; '**~tier** F n demon for work; '**²-unfähig** unfit for work; *dauernd:* disabled; '**~unfall** m industrial accident; '**~vertrag** m employment contract; '**~weise** f working method; ⊕ (mode of) operation; '**~vermittlung** f employment exchange; '**~vorbereitung** f operations scheduling; '**~willige** m (18) non-striker; '**~zeit** f working time; working hours *pl.*; *gleitende* ~ flexible working hours *pl.*; '**~zeitregelung** f regulation of working hours; '**~zeitverkürzung** f reduction in working hours; '**~zeug** n tools *pl.*, kit; '**~zimmer** n study.

Archäolog|e [arçɛo'loːgə] m (13) arch(a)eologist; ~**ie** [~lo'giː] f arch(a)eology; **²isch** [~'loːgiʃ] arch(a)eological.

Arche ['arçə] f (15) ark.

Archipel [arçi'peːl] m (3¹) archipelago.

Architekt [arçi'tɛkt] m (12) architect; **²onisch** [~'toːniʃ] architectural; ~**ur** [~'tuːr] f architecture.

Archiv [ar'çiːf] n (3¹) archives *pl.*; record-office; ~**ar** [~çi'vaːr] m (3¹) archivist, registrar; ~**exemplar** n record copy.

Areal [are'aːl] n (3¹) area.

Arena [a'reːna] f (16²) arena.

arg [ark] **1.** (18²) *allg.* bad; (*moralisch schlecht*) wicked; *Sünder:* hopeless; *Versehen:* gross; *sein ärgster Feind* his worst enemy; ~ *enttäuscht* badly disappointed; *das ist zu* ~ that is too much; *²es denken von* think ill of; *im* ~*en liegen* be in a sorry state; **2.** ² n (11, *o. pl.*) malice, harm.

Ärger ['ɛrgər] m (7, *o. pl.*) (*Ver-druß*) vexation, annoyance, chagrin; (*Zorn*) anger; *j-m* ~ *machen* give a p. trouble; '**²lich** *Sache:* annoying, vexatious; *Person:* angry, vexed, irritated (*auf, über acc. et.* at, *j-n* with); '**²n** (29) make angry, annoy, vex, anger, irritate; *sich* ~ (*über acc.*) feel angry (at, about *a th.*; *with a p.*) *od.* vexed (by); '**~nis** n (4¹) scandal, offen|ce, *Am.* -se; (*Mißstand*) (*öffentliches* public) nuisance; ~ *erregen* cause offence; ~ *an dat. nehmen* be scandalized at.

'**Arg|list** f craft(iness), malice; ** zⁱ⁄₂** fraud; '**²listig** crafty, insidious, deceitful; **zⁱ⁄₂** fraudulent; '**²los** guileless, innocent; (*nichtsahnend*) unsuspecting; (*ohne Argwohn*) unsuspicious; '**~losigkeit** f guilelessness.

Argumen|t [argu'mɛnt] n (3) argument; ~**tieren** argue, reason.

Arg|wohn ['~voːn] m (3, *o. pl.*) suspicion (*gegen* of); **²wöhnen** ['~vøː-nən] (25) suspect; **²wöhnisch** suspicious.

Arie ♪ ['aːrjə] f (15) aria. [Aryan.]

Arier ['aːrjər] m (7), '~**in** f, '**arisch** ∫

Aristokrat [aristo'kraːt] m (12), ~**in** f aristocrat; ~**ie** [~kra'tiː] f aristocracy; **²isch** [~'kraːtiʃ] aristocratic(ally *adv.*).

Arithme|tik [arit'meːtik] f (16) arithmetic; **²tisch** arithmetical.

Arkt|is ['arktis] f *the* Arctic (regions *pl.*); **²isch** arctic.

arm¹ [arm] (18²) poor (*an dat.* in); *ein ²er a poor* man; *die ²en pl. the* poor; *ich ²er!* poor me!

Arm² m (3) arm; *Fluß, Leuchter:* branch; *auf den* ~ *nehmen Kind:* take in one's arms, F *fig. j-n:* pull a p.'s leg; *in die* ~*e schließen* clasp in one's arms; *j-m unter die* ~*e greifen* help a p. (out).

Armatur ⚡ [arma'tuːr] f (16) armature; ~**en** *pl.* fittings; ~**enbrett** n instrument panel, dashboard.

'**Arm|band** n bracelet; *als Halt od. Schutz:* wristlet; '**~band-uhr** f wrist watch; '**~binde** f (arm-)sling; *als Abzeichen:* armlet; '**~bruch** m fracture of the arm; '**~brust** f cross-bow.

Armee [ar'meː] f (15) army; ~**korps** n army corps.

Ärmel ['ɛrməl] m (7) sleeve; *fig. aus dem* ~ *schütteln* do offhand; '**~auf**-

schlag *m* cuff; '**~kanal** *m the* (English) Channel; '**Ϙlos** sleeveless.
'**Armen|haus** *n* poorhouse; *neuerdings*: public assistance institution; '**~kasse** *f* relief-fund; *eccl.* poor--box; '**~pflege** *f* poor-relief; '**~pfleger(in** *f*) *m* relieving officer; '**~recht** *n* poor-law; ᵗᵗᶻ *auf ~ klagen* sue in forma pauperis.
Arme'sündergesicht *n* hangdog look.
armieren [ar'mi:rən] ⚔ arm; ⊕ armo(u)r; *Beton*: reinforce.
...armig ...-armed; ...-branched.
'**Arm|lehne** *f* arm; '**~leuchter** *m* chandelier; F *fig.* idiot.
ärmlich ['ɛrmliç] *s. armselig.*
'**Armreif** *m* (3), '**~en** bangle.
'**armselig** poor; (*schäbig*) shabby; *fig. a.* miserable; (*dürftig*) paltry; '**Ϙkeit** *f* poorness.
'**Arm|sessel** *m*, '**~stuhl** *m* arm-chair, easy chair.
Armut ['armu:t] *f* (16, *o. pl.*) poverty; '**~szeugnis** *n*: *sich ein ~ ausstellen* give a poor account of o.s.
Aroma [a'ro:ma] *n* (11²) aroma, flavo(u)r; **Ϙtisch** [aro'ma:tiʃ] aromatic.
Arrak ['arak] *m* (3¹) arrack.
arrangieren [arã'ʒi:rən] arrange.
Arrest [a'rest] *m* (3²) (*Haft*) arrest; confinement, (*a. Schul*Ϙ) detention; ᵗᵗᶻ (*Beschlagnahme*) attachment; *mit ~ bestrafen* put under arrest; **~ant** [~'tant] *m* (12) prisoner.
arretieren [are'ti:rən] arrest; ⊕ (*sperren*) arrest, lock.
arrogant [aro'gant] arrogant.
Arsch V [arʃ] *m* (3² *u.* ³) arse, bum; *leck mich am ~!* fuck you!; '**~loch** *n* arsehole.
Arsenal [arze'na:l] *n* (3¹) arsenal.
Art [a:rt] *f* (16) (*Gattung*) kind, sort, ⏁ species, *zo. a.* race, breed; (*Typ*) type; (*äußere Form*) style; (*Weise*) manner, way, fashion; (*Natur*) nature; (*Benehmen*) manners *pl.*; *~ und Weise* way, mode; *Fortpflanzung der ~* propagation of the species; *auf die(se) ~* in this way; *das ist keine ~* this is bad form; *aus der ~ schlagen* degenerate.
'**art-eigen** characteristic.
'**arten** (26, sn): *~ nach* take after; *s. geartet.*
'**arten|-arm** with few animal (*od.* plant) species; '**~reich** with a richly

varied animal (*od.* plant) population.
Arterie [ar'te:rjə] *f* (15) artery; **~nverkalkung** *f* hardening of the arteries, arteriosclerosis.
'**artfremd** alien.
artig ['a:rtiç] (*hübsch, nett*) nice, pretty; *Kind*: good, well-behaved; (*höflich*) civil, polite; *sei ~!* be (*od.* there's) a good child!; '**Ϙkeit** *f* prettiness; good behavio(u)r; polite- ness, (*a. pl.*) civility.
Artikel [ar'ti:kəl] *m* (7) *allg., a.* ✝ article.
artikulieren [~tiku'li:rən] articulate.
Artiller|ie [artilə'ri:] *f* (15) artillery; **~ist** [~'rist] *m* (12) artilleryman, gunner.
Artischocke [arti'ʃɔkə] *f* (15) artichoke.
Artist [ar'tist] *m* (12), **~in** *f* acrobat, variety artist, circus performer.
Arznei [arts'nai] *f* (16) medicine; **~kunde** *f*, **~kunst** *f* pharmaceutics *sg.*; **~mittel** *n* medicine, medicament; drug; **~mittel-abhängigkeit** *f* drug dependence; **~mittellehre** *f* pharmacology; **~mittelmißbrauch** *m* drug abuse; **~schrank** *m* medicine cabinet.
Arzt [a:rtst] *m* (3² *u.* ³) medical practitioner, doctor, F medical man; *Berufsbezeichnung*: physician; *s. praktisch.*
'**Ärztemuster** *n* sample.
'**Arzthelferin** *f* doctor's receptionist.
Ärztin ['ɛ:rtstin] *f* (16¹) woman (*od.* lady) doctor *od.* physician.
'**ärztlich** medical.
As¹ [as] *n* (4¹) *Spiel*: ace (*a. fig. P.*).
As² ♪ *n inv.* A flat; *As-Dur* (*as-Moll*) A flat major (minor).
Asbest [as'best] *m* (3²) asbestos.
'**aschblond** ashy-fair.
Asche ['aʃə] *f* (15) ashes *pl.*
'**Aschen...** *mst* ash...; '**~bahn** *f* cinder track; '**~becher** *m* ash-tray; '**~brödel** *n* (7) Cinderella (*a. fig.*); '**~platz** *m Sport*: cinder pitch.
Ascher'mittwoch *m* Ash Wednesday.
'**asch|fahl** ashen; '**~farben**, '**~farbig** ash-colo(u)red; '**~grau** ash- -grey (*Am.* -gray).
äsen ['ɛ:zən] (27) *v/i. u. v/t. hunt.* graze, browse, feed (*et.* on).
Asiat [az'ja:t] *m* (12), **~in** *f*, Ϙisch Asiatic.

Askese [as'ke:zə] *f* (15, *o. pl.*) asceticism.

As'ket *m* (12), **~in** *f* (16¹), ⚥**isch** ascetic.

asozial ['azotsja:l] antisocial.

Aspekt [as'pɛkt] *m* (3¹ *u.* ²) aspect.

Asphalt [as'falt] *m* (3) asphalt; ⚥**ieren** [~'ti:rən] asphalt; **'~presse** *f* yellow press.

aß [a:s] *pret. von* essen 1.

Asservat [asɛr'va:t] ɪ̃ɪ̃ *n* (3) court exhibit.

Assessor [a'sɛsɔr] *m* (8¹) assessor; ɪ̃ɪ̃ assistant judge.

Assisten|t [asis'tɛnt] *m* (12), **~tin** *f* assistant; **~z-arzt** [~ts-] *m* assistant doctor (*od.* surgeon); *Am. im Krankenhaus:* intern.

assis'tieren assist.

Ast [ast] *m* (3² *u.* ³) bough; *schwacher:* branch; *im Holz:* knot; *s. lachen.*

Aster ['astər] *f* (15) aster.

Asteroid [astero'i:t] *m* (12) asteroid.

Ästhet|ik [ɛ'ste:tik] *f* (16) (a)esthetics *sg.;* **~iker**(**in** *f*) *m* (a)esthete; ⚥**isch** (a)esthetic(al).

Asthma ['astma] *n* (11, *o. pl.*) asthma.

Asthma|tiker [~'ma:tikər] *m* (7), **~tikerin** *f*, ⚥**tisch** asthmatic.

'Astloch *n* knot-hole.

Astro|log(e) [astro'lo:k, ~gə] *m* (12 [13]) astrologer; **~logie** [~lo'gi:] *f* (15, *o. pl.*) astrology; **~naut** [~'naut] *m* (12) astronaut; **~nautik** [~'nautik] *f* astronautics *sg.;* **~nom** [~'no:m] *m* (12) astronomer; **~nomie** [~no'mi:] *f* (15, *o. pl.*) astronomy; ⚥**nomisch** [~'no:m-] astronomical; **~physik** [~fy'zi:k] *f* astrophysics *sg.*

Asyl [a'zy:l] *n* (3¹) asylum; *fig.* sanctuary; (*politisches*) ~ *suchen* seek (political) asylum; **~bewerber**(**in** *f*) *m* person seeking (political) asylum; **~recht** *n* right of asylum.

Atelier [atɛ'lje:] *n* (11) studio.

Atem ['a:təm] *m* (6, *o. pl.*) breath; ~ *holen* pause for breath; *außer* ~ (*kommen* get) out of breath *od.* winded; *wieder zu* ~ *kommen* recover one's breath; *j-n in* ~ *halten* keep a p. busy (*od. in Spannung:* in suspense); *s. anhalten;* **'~beschwerden** *f/pl.* difficulty *sg.* in breathing; **'~gerät** *n* breathing apparatus; 🩺 respirator; **'~geräusch** *n* respiratory sounds *pl.;* **'~holen** *n* respiration; **'⚥los** breathless (*a. fig.*); **'~not** *f* shortness of

breath; **'~pause** *f* breathing-time, breathing-space, breather; **'⚥raubend** breath-taking; **'~technik** *f* breathing technique; **'~übungen** *f/pl.* breathing exercises *pl.;* **'~wege** *m/pl.* respiratory tract *sg.;* **'~zug** *m* breath.

Atheismus [ate'⁹ismus] *m* (16, *o. pl.*) atheism.

Atheist [~'⁹ist] *m* (12), **~in** *f* (16¹) atheist; ⚥**isch** atheistic(al).

Athen [a'te:n] *n* (17) Athens; *Eulen nach* ~ *tragen* carry coals to Newcastle.

Äther ['ɛ:tər] *m* (7, *o. pl.*) ether (*a.* ⚗); *Radio: über den* ~ on the air; *mit* ~ *betäuben* etherize.

ätherisch [ɛ'te:r-] ethereal; *phys., Radio:* etheric; **~es** *Öl* essential oil.

'Äther|krieg *m* radio war; **'~wellen** *phys. f/pl.* ether waves *pl.*

Athlet [at'le:t] *m* (12), **~in** *f* (16¹) athlete; **~ik** *f* (16) athletics *pl.;* ⚥**isch** athletic.

Atlant [at'lant] *m* (12) *s. Atlas* 1.; ⚥**isch** Atlantic; *der* ⚥e *Ozean* the Atlantic (Ocean).

Atlas ['atlas] *m* (4¹, *sg. a. inv.*) 1. *geogr.* atlas; 2. *Seiden*⚥: satin; *Baumwoll*⚥: sateen. [breathe.⟩

atmen ['a:tmən] (26) *v/i. u. v/t.*⟩

Atmosphär|e [atmɔ'sfɛ:rə] *f* (15) atmosphere; ⚥**isch** atmospheric; **~e** *Störungen* *f/pl. Radio:* atmospherics, statics *pl.*

'Atmung *f* breathing, respiration; **'~s-organ** *n*, **'~swerkzeug** *n* respiratory organ.

Atom [a'to:m] *n* (3¹) atom; **~antrieb** *m* atomic propulsion; ⚥**ar** [ato'ma:r] atomic, nuclear; **~bombe** *f* atomic (*od.* atom-, *abbr.* A-)bomb, fission bomb; ⚥**bombensicher** atom-bomb-proof; **~bombenversuch** *m* A-bomb test; **~bunker** *m* fall-out shelter; **~-energie** *f* atomic energy; **~forscher** *m* nuclear scientist; **~forschung** *f* nuclear research; **~gemeinschaft** *f* Atomic Community; **~geschoß** *n* atomic shell; **~geschütz** *n* atomic gun; **~gewicht** *n* atomic weight; **~kern** *m* atomic nucleus; **~kraft** *f* atomic power; **~kraftwerk** *n* atomic power plant; **~krieg** *m* nuclear war(fare); **~meiler** *m* atomic pile; **~müll** *m* radioactive waste; **~mülldeponie** *f* radioactive waste dump; ~**pilz** *m* mushroom cloud; ~**re-aktor** *m* atomic reactor; ~**spaltung** *f* atomic fission, atom-splitting; ~**sprengkopf** *m* nuclear warhead; ~**staub** *m* atomic dust; ~**teilchen** *n* atomic particle; ~**U-Boot** *n* nuclear submarine; ~**versuch** *m* atomic test; ~**waffe** *f* atomic weapon; ₂**waffenfrei** nuclear-free; ~**waffenlager** *n* atomic weapon depot; ~**waffensperrvertrag** *m* non--proliferation treaty; ~**wissenschaft** *f* atomics *sg.*, nuclear science; ~**zeitalter** *n* atomic age; ~**zerfall** *m* atomic decay; ~**zertrümmerung** *f* atom--smashing.

Attaché [ata'ʃeː] *m* (11) attaché.

Attack|e [a'takə] *f* (15), ₂**ieren** [~'kiːrən] (25) attack.

Attentat [aten'taːt] *n* (3) attempt upon a p.'s life, (attempted) assassination; *fig.* outrage.

Atten'täter *m* assassin.

Atte|st [a'tɛst] *n* (3²) (medical) certificate; ₂'**stieren** attest, certify.

Attrak|tion [atrak'tsjoːn] *f* attraction; ₂**tiv** [~'tiːf] attractive.

Attrappe [a'trapə] *f* (15) dummy.

Attribut [atri'buːt] *n* (3) attribute; *gr.* attributive; ₂**iv** *gr.* [~bu'tiːf] attributive.

atz|en ['atsən] (27) feed; ₂'**ung** *f* feeding; (*Nahrung*) food.

ätz|en ['ɛtsən] (27) corrode; ⚕ cauterize; *auf Kupfer usw.*: etch; '~**end** corrosive; (*a. fig.*) caustic; '₂**kalk** *m* caustic lime, quicklime; '₂**kunst** *f* art of etching; '₂**mittel** *n*, '₂**stoff** *m* corrosive; *bsd.* ⚕ caustic; '₂**ung** *f* corrosion; ⚕ cauterization; (*Zeichnung*) etching.

au! [au] oh!, ouch!

auch [aux] also; too; likewise; (*selbst, sogar*) even; *du glaubst es — ich ~!* you believe it — so do I!; *er hat keine Freude — wir ~ nicht* he has no pleasure — nor (*od.* neither) have we; *wenn ~ even if, even though, although; mag er ~ noch so reich sein* let him be ever so rich; ~ *nur ein Mensch* nothing but a human being.

Audienz [au'djɛnts] *f* (16) audience.

audiovisuell [audiovizu'ɛl] audio--visual.

Auditorium [audi'toːrjʊm] *n* (9) (*Raum*) lecture-hall; (*Zuhörerschaft*) audience.

Aue ['auə] *f* (15) fertile plain; (*Wiese*) meadow, *poet.* mead.

Auer|hahn ['auər-] *m* capercaillie; '~**ochs** *m* aurochs.

auf [auf] **1.** *prp.* **a)** *mit dat.*: on, upon; in; at; of; by; ~ *dem Tisch* on *od.* upon; ~ *dem Markt* in; ~ *der Universität*, ~ *einem Ball* at; ~ *s-r Seite* at (*od.* on) his side; ~ *dem nächsten Wege* by the nearest way; **b)** *mit acc.*: on; in; at; to; towards (*a.* ~ ... *zu*); up; ~ *deutsch* in German; ~ *e-e Entfernung von* at a range of; ~ *die Post usw. gehen* go to; ~ *eine Mark gehen 100 Pfennige* ... go to a mark; *es geht* ~ *neun* it is getting on to nine; ~ ... *hin* on the strength of; ~ *Jahre hinaus* for years to come; ~ *morgen* for tomorrow; **2.** *adv.* up, upwards; ~ *und ab gehen* walk up and down *od.* to and fro; **3.** *cj.* ~ *daß* (in order) that; ~ *daß nicht* that not, lest; **4.** *int.* ~*!* up!, arise!; (*los!*) let's go!

'**auf-arbeiten** *Rückstand:* work (*od.* clear) off; (*auffrischen*) work (*od.* furbish) up; *Kleid:* F do up.

'**auf-atmen** draw a deep breath; *fig.* breathe again *od.* freely; recover.

aufbahren ['~baːrən] (25) *Sarg:* put on the bier; *Leiche:* lay out (in state).

'**Aufbau** *m* building(-up); *a. e-s Dramas usw.*: construction; *e-r Organisation usw.*: structure, *bsd. Am.* setup; *mot.* body; △, ⚓ superstructure; '₂**en** erect, *a. fig. e-e Theorie, Existenz usw.*: build up; *Drama usw.*: construct; *sich* ~ *auf dat.* be based (up)on; *sich* ~ *vor P.*: plant o.s. before; '₂**end** constructive.

'**aufbäumen:** *sich* ~ rear; *fig.* rebel.

'**Aufbauphase** *f* development stage.

'**aufbauschen** puff up; *fig.* exaggerate, magnify, F play up.

'**aufbegehren** flare up; rebel, revolt (*gegen* against).

'**aufbehalten** *Hut:* keep on.

'**aufbekommen** *Tür usw.*: get open; *Knoten:* get undone; *Arbeit:* be given *a task.*

'**aufbereit|en** prepare, process; *Erz, Häute:* dress; *Kohle:* upgrade; '₂**ung** *f* preparation, processing; dressing; upgrading; '₂**ungs-anlage** *f* (re)processing plant.

'**aufbessern** *Gehalt*: raise.
'**aufbewahr|en** keep; *im Lager*: store (up); (*haltbar machen*) preserve; '❑**ungs-ort** *m* depository.
'**aufbiet|en** summon; *Kräfte, Mut, etc.*: *a.* muster; ✗ raise, levy, (*a. fig.*) mobilize; *Brautpaar*: publish (*od.* put up) the banns of; *alles* ~ move heaven and earth; '❑**ung** *f* summoning; exertion; *unter* ~ *aller Kräfte* by supreme effort.
'**aufbinden** tie up; (*lösen*) untie; *fig. j-m et. od.* e-n *Bären* ~ hoax a p.; *sich etwas* ~ *lassen* be taken in.
'**aufbläh|en** puff up, swell; *a. Währung usw.*: inflate; *sich* ~ *fig.* be puffed up (*vor dat.* with); ❑**ung** *f* inflation.
'**aufblasen** blow up, inflate.
'**aufbleiben** (sn) (*wachen*) sit (*od.* stay) up; *Tür usw.*: remain open.
'**aufblenden** *mot.* turn (the head-lights) on; *Film*: fade in.
'**aufblicken** raise one's eyes; look up (*fig. zu* j-m to a p.).
'**aufblitzen** (sn *u.* h.) flash (up).
'**aufblühen** (sn) (begin to) bloom; *fig.* blossom (out); *wirtschaftlich usw.*: flourish, prosper, thrive.
'**aufbocken** *mot.* jack up.
'**aufbrauchen** use up, consume.
'**aufbrausen** (h. *u.* sn) *Gelächter, Sturm*: roar; ⚗ effervesce; *fig.* fly into a passion; '**~d** effervescent; *fig.* irritable, irascible.
'**aufbrechen** *v/t.* break (*od.* force) open; *v/i.* (sn) burst open; (*weggehen*) start, set out (*beide*: *nach* for).
'**aufbringen** bring up; *Mode*: introduce; *Geld, Truppen usw.*: raise; *Schiff*: capture; *Mut*: summon up; *j-n*: provoke, infuriate, anger.
'**Aufbruch** *m* departure, start, outset (*nach, zu* for); *fig.* awakening.
'**aufbrummen** F: *j-m* et. ~ land a p. with a th.
'**aufbügeln** iron; *Hose*: press; *Kenntnisse*: brush up.
'**aufbürden**: (26) *j-m* et. ~ burden a p. with a th.
'**aufbürsten** brush up.
'**aufdecken** *v/t.* uncover; *fig. a.* expose; (*aufklären*) clear up; *v/i.* lay the table.
'**aufdonnern** F: *sich* ~ get dolled up.
'**aufdrängen** S. *od.* P.: force, obtrude (*j-m* [up]on a p.).

'**aufdrehen** *v/t. Schraube*: loosen; *Hahn, Gas usw.*: turn on; *v/i.* F *mot.* step on the gas; (*loslegen*) open up.
'**aufdringen** *s. aufdrängen.*
'**aufdringlich** obtrusive (*a. S.*); '❑**keit** *f* obtrusiveness.
'**Aufdruck** *m* (im)print; *auf Postmarken*: surcharge; '❑**en** imprint.
'**aufdrücken** (*öffnen*) press open; *Stempel usw.*: impress (*dat. od. auf acc.* on).
auf-einander [~ʔaɪ'nandər] one after (*od.* upon) another; ~ *böse sein* be cross with one another; ❑**folge** *f* succession; **~folgen** (sn) succeed (one another); **~folgend** successive, consecutive; *an 3* ~*en Tagen* on 3 days running; **~prallen** (sn) collide; *fig. Meinungen, a. P.*: clash.
Aufenthalt ['~ɛnthalt] *m* (3) *vorübergehend*: stay, sojourn; whereabouts (*a.* '**~s-ort** *m*); (*Wohnsitz*) residence, abode, domicile; (*Verzögerung*) delay, hindrance; 🚆 *usw.*: stop; '**~sgenehmigung** *f* residence permit; '**~sraum** *m* lounge; day-room.
'**auf-erlegen**: *j-m als Pflicht* ~ enjoin on a p. (*et.* a th.; *zu inf.* to *inf.*); *Aufgabe, Bedingung, Pflicht, Steuer, s-n Willen usw.*: impose (*j-m* on a p.); *Strafe*: inflict (*j-m* on a p.); *s. Zwang.*
'**auf-ersteh|en** (sn) rise (from the dead); '❑**ung** *f* resurrection.
'**auf-erwecken** raise (from the dead).
'**auf-essen** eat up.
'**auffädeln** (29) thread, string.
'**auffahren** *v/i.* (sn) *Schiff*: run aground, (*auf acc.*) run (up)on; *Wagen*: run *od.* drive (*auf acc.* against); (*vorfahren*) drive up; *P.*: *zornig*: fly out, *erschreckt*: start (up); *v/t. Wagen*: park; *Kanonen*: mount; *Speisen usw.* (*a.* ~ *lassen*) dish up; '**~d** passionate, irritable.
'**Auffahrt** *f* (16) ✗ ascent; *in e-m Wagen*: driving up; (*Platz vor e-m Haus*) drive; '**~srampe** *f* ramp.
'**Auffahr-unfall** *m* rear-end collision.
'**auffallen** *v/i.* (sn) fall (*auf acc.* upon); *fig.* be conspicuous; *j-m* ~ strike; *es fällt allgemein auf* it is generally noticed; *mit dem Kopf* ~ fall on one's head; '**~d**, '**auffällig** striking; (*sichtbar*) conspicuous;

(*sensationell*; *a. Kleid*) flashy; *b.s.* shocking; ~ *gekleidet* showily dressed.

'**auffang|en** catch (up); *Brief, Funkspruch usw.*: intercept; *Hieb*: parry; *fig. Entwicklung*: absorb; '♀**lager** *n* reception camp.

'**auffärben** redye.

'**auffassen** *v/t. fig.* conceive; (*begreifen*) understand, comprehend; *Bühnenrolle usw.*: interpret, (*deuten*) *a.* read; *falsch* ~ misconceive; *v/i. leicht* ~ be quick of understanding.

'**Auffassung** *f* conception; (*Deutung*) interpretation; (*Fassungskraft*) apprehension; (*Meinung*) opinion, view; *falsche* ~ misconception; *nach meiner* ~ as I see it, from my point of view; *die* ~ *vertreten, daß* hold that; '~**svermögen** *n* perceptive faculty.

auffind|bar ['~fintbɑːr] discoverable, traceable; ~**en** ['~dən] find out, trace, discover, locate; '♀**ung** *f* discovery, finding.

'**auffischen** fish (up).

'**aufflackern** (sn) flare up (*a. fig.*).

'**aufflammen** (sn) flame up.

'**auffliegen** (sn) fly up(wards); *Vogel*: take wing; *Tür*: fly open; *Mine usw.*: explode, (*a. fig.*) burst; *Verein usw.*: be dissolved.

'**aufforder|n** ask, request; (*einladen*) invite; (*drängen*) urge; *anordnend*: order; *bsd.* ⚖ summon; *j-n* ~, *zu inf.* call (up)on a p. to *inf.*; '♀**ung** *f* request; invitation; order; *bsd.* ⚖ summons *sg.*

aufforsten ['~fɔrstən] afforest.

'**auffressen** eat up; devour.

'**auffrischen** (25) refresh (*a. sich*; *a. Gedächtnis*); *Bild*: touch up; *Kenntnisse*: brush up; (*wieder*) ~ *Andenken, Kummer*: revive.

'**aufführ|en** *Bau*: erect, build; *Schauspiel*: perform, act, *a. Film*: present, show; (*aufzählen*) enumerate; *in e-r Liste*: state, show, list; *Zeugen*: produce; put forward; *einzeln* ~ specify, *Am.* itemize; *sich* ~ behave; '♀**ung** *f* erection; *thea.* performance; *Film*: showing; (*Darbietung*) show; enumeration; entry; specification; (*Benehmen*) conduct; *von Zeugen*: production; '♀**ungsrecht** *n* performing rights *pl.*

'**auffüllen** fill (*od.* top) up, refill; *Vorräte usw.*: replenish.

'**Aufgabe** *f* (*Arbeit*) task, assignment, job; (*Pflicht*) duty, function; (*Sendung*) mission; (*Denk♀*) problem; (*Schul♀*) lesson, task; *e-s Briefes*: posting, *Am.* mailing; *von Gepäck*: booking, *Am.* checking; *von Telegrammen*: dispatch; ✝ (*Mitteilung*) advice; *e-s Amtes*: resignation; (*Preisgabe*) abandonment; (*Geschäfts♀*) giving up business; *Tennis*: service; *es sich zur* ~ *machen, zu inf.* make it one's business to *inf.*

aufgabeln *fig.* ['~gɑːbəln] pick up.

'**Aufgabe|nheft** *n* book for homework notes; '~**nkreis** *m* scope of duties, functions *pl.*; '~**schein** *m* certificate of delivery; receipt; '~**zeit** *f* time of dispatch.

'**Aufgang** *m* ascent; *ast.* rising, rise; (*Treppe*) staircase.

'**aufgeben** *Sache, Geschäft, Geist, Gewohnheit, Kranke, im Sport usw.*: give up; *Amt*: resign; *Anspruch*: give up, waive; *Anstellung*: quit; *Brief*: post, *Am.* mail; *Gepäck*: book, register, *Am.* check; *Anzeige*: insert, run; *Telegramm*: dispatch; ✝ *Bestellung*: give, place; (*mitteilen*) advise; *Preise*: quote; *Aufgabe*: set, assign; *Rätsel*: ask, set; *Tennis*: serve; *j-m e-e Aufgabe* ~ set a p. a task; (*es, den Kampf, das Spiel usw.*) ~ give in (*od.* up).

aufgeblasen ['~gəblɑːzən] puffed up; *fig.* arrogant; bumptious.

'**Aufgebot** *n* public notice; ✗ levy, (*Streitmacht*) body (of men); (*Ehe♀*) banns *pl.*; (*stattliche Reihe*) array; *das* ~ *bestellen* ask the banns.

aufgebracht ['~gəbraxt] angry (*über et.* at, about; *über j-n* with).

'**aufgedonnert** F dressed up to the nines, dolled up.

aufgedunsen ['~gədunzən] bloated.

'**aufgehen** (sn) (*sich öffnen*) open; *Knoten usw.*: come undone, get loose; *Naht*: come open; Ⱥ leave no remainder; *Eis, Geschwür*: break (up); *Teig, Gestirn, Vorhang*: rise; *Pflanze*: come up; *fig.* prove right; ~ *in et.* be merged in; ~ *in e-r Arbeit, e-m Gedanken* be absorbed (*od.* wrapt up) in; *in Flammen* ~ go up in flames; *in Rauch* ~ end in smoke; *die Augen gehen mir auf, mir geht ein Licht auf* I begin to see daylight; *5 geht nicht* *in 9 auf five* will not divide into nine.

aufgeklärt ['ˌ‿gəklɛːrt] enlightened; '**⸰heit** *f* enlightenment.

aufgeknöpft ['ˌ‿gəknœpft] F affable, chatty, expansive.

aufgekratzt ['ˌ‿gəkratst] F in high spirits, chipper.

aufgelegt ['ˌ‿gəleːkt] disposed (*zu* for *a th.*; *to do*), inclined (to); *~ sein* (*zu*) be in the mood (to), feel like (*doing*); *gut* (*schlecht*) *~* in a good (bad) mood; F *~er Schwindel* blatant swindle.

aufgeräumt *fig.* ['ˌ‿gərɔ˸ʏmt] in high spirits, cheerful.

aufgeregt ['ˌ‿gəreːkt] excited; *als Charaktereigenschaft*: excitable.

aufgeschlossen *fig.* ['ˌ‿gəʃlɔsən] open-minded; open (*dat.* to); (*mitteilsam*) communicative; '**⸰heit** *f* open-mindedness.

aufgeschmissen F ['ˌ‿gəʃmisən]: *~ sein* be stuck.

aufgestaut ['ˌ‿gəʃtaʊt] *Zorn usw.*: pent-up.

aufgeweckt *fig.* ['ˌ‿gəvɛkt] bright.

aufgeworfen ['ˌ‿gəvɔrfən] *Lippe*: pouting; *Nase*: turned-up.

'**aufgießen** pour (*auf acc.* upon); *Tee*: infuse, make.

'**aufgliedern** subdivide, break down.

'**aufgraben** dig up.

'**aufgreifen** *et.*: snatch up; *j-n*: pick up, seize; *fig.* take up.

'**Aufguß** *m* infusion; '**⸰beutel** *m* tea (*Kräuter*: herb) bag.

'**aufhaben** *Hut usw.*: have on; *Tür*: have open; *Aufgabe*: have to do.

'**aufhacken** hoe up; pick.

'**aufhaken** unhook.

'**aufhalten** *Tür usw.*: keep open; (*anhalten*) stop; *j-n*: hold up (*a. Auto, Verkehr*), detain; (*hemmen*) check, stay; (*verzögern*) delay, retard; *sich ~* (*Reise unterbrechen*) stop; (*wohnen, verweilen*) stay, dwell (*fig. bei et.* on); *sich ~ über* (*acc.*) find fault with; *ich kann mich damit nicht ~* I cannot waste any time on it.

'**aufhäng|en** hang (up); ⊕ suspend (*an dat.* from); *fig. j-m et. ~* palm off a th. on a p.; '**⸰er** ['ˌ‿hɛŋər] *m* (7) (*Rock⸰*) tab; *fig.* a peg to hang a th. on; '**⸰ung** *f* suspension.

'**aufhäufen** pile up, heap up, (*a. sich ~*) accumulate.

'**Aufhäufung** *f* accumulation.

'**aufheb|en** (*emporheben*) lift (up), raise, *vom Boden*: pick up; *Belagerung, Blockade, Maßnahme usw.*: raise; (*bewahren*) keep, preserve; *Vertrag usw.*: cancel, annul, abolish, *zeitweilig*: suspend; *Erlaß, Verbot*: cancel, remove; *Gesetz*: repeal, abrogate; *Urteil*: quash; *Verlobung*: break off; *Ehe*: annul; *Versammlung*: break up; *Wirkung*: cancel, neutralize; *sich gegenseitig ~* cancel each other out; *die Tafel ~* rise from the table; *viel ⸰s machen* (*von*) make a fuss (about); *gut aufgehoben sein* be well taken care of; '**⸰ung** *f e-r Belagerung usw.*: raising; (*Abschaffung*) abolition; *e-s Gesetzes*: repeal; *e-s Vertrages, der Ehe usw.*: annulment; *e-r Versammlung*: breaking up; *der Schwerkraft*: neutralization.

'**aufheitern** (29) cheer (up); *sich ~ Wetter*: clear up, *Gesicht*: brighten.

'**Aufheiterung** *f Wetter*: brighter period, sunny interval.

'**aufhelfen**: *j-m ~* help a p. up.

'**aufhellen** (25) (*a. sich*) brighten, clear (up), lighten; *fig.* clarify.

'**aufhetz|en** *j-n*: incite, instigate, stir up; *~ gegen* set *a p.* against; '**⸰er(in** *f*) *m* instigator; '**⸰ung** *f* instigation, incitement; *pol.* agitation, fomenting.

'**aufheulen** yowl.

'**aufholen** *v/t.* make up (for); *v/i.* pull up; ⚓ haul (*od.* hoist) up.

'**aufhorchen** listen attentively; *fig.* sit up and take notice.

'**aufhören 1.** (*zu Ende gehen*) cease; (*ablassen*; *a. ~ mit*) cease, stop; leave off, have done (with); *~ zu inf.* cease to *inf. od. ger.*, stop, leave off, *Am.* quit *ger.*; F *da hört doch alles auf!* that's the limit!; *hör auf damit!* stop it!; **2.** ⸰ *n* (6) cessation, stop.

'**aufjauchzen** shout with joy.

'**Aufkauf** *m* buying up; '**⸰en** buy up; *um zu spekulieren*: corner.

'**Aufkäufer** *m* speculative buyer, forestaller.

'**aufklappen** *Buch, Messer*: open; *Sitz*: tip up.

'**aufklär|en** clear up (*a. sich ~*); *j-n*: enlighten (*über acc.* on), (*unterrichten*) inform (about); ✕ (*a. v/i.*) reconnoit|re, *Am.* -er, scout; *j-n* (*se-*

xuell) ~ tell a p. about the facts of life (*od.* the birds and the bees); *alles hat sich aufgeklärt* everything has been explained; '2er *m* (7) enlightener (*a.* '2erin *f*); ✕ scout; '2ung *f* clearing--up; (*Erklärung*) explanation; (*Bildung*) enlightenment; *hist. the* Enlightenment; ✕ reconnaissance; *sexuelle* ~ sex enlightenment.

'Aufklärungs|-aktion *f* educational campaign; '~flug *m* reconnaissance flight; '~flugzeug *n* scout plane, air scout; '~satellit *m* reconnaissance satellite; '~zeit-alter *n* Age of Enlightenment.

'aufkleb|bar adhesive; '~en paste, stick (*auf acc.* to, on); '2er *m* sticker.

'aufklinken (25) unlatch.

'aufknacken crack (open).

'aufknöpfen unbutton; *s. aufgeknöpft.*

'aufknüpfen (*lösen*) untie; *j-n:* hang.

'aufkochen *v/t. u. v/i.* (sn, h.) boil (up); *v/t.* ~ (*lassen*) bring to the boil.

'aufkommen 1. (sn) (*aufstehen*) get up, rise; *Wind:* spring up; *Wetter:* come up; (*genesen*) recover (*von* from); *Mode, Brauch:* come into fashion *od.* use; *Gedanke:* arise; *für et.* ~ answer for; *für die Kosten* ~ pay, defray; *für den Schaden:* compensate for, make good; *für Schulden, Verluste:* make o.s. liable for; *gegen j-n* ~ prevail against; *Zweifel* ~ *lassen* give rise to; *j-n nicht* ~ *lassen* give a p. no chance; *keinen* ~ *lassen* admit no rival; 2. 2 *n* (6) (*Entstehen*) rise; (*Erscheinen*) advent; (*Genesung*) recovery; (*Steuer-* 2) (tax) yield.

'aufkrempeln *Hose, Hutrand:* turn up; *Ärmel:* tuck up.

'aufkreuzen F *fig. v/i.* (sn) turn up.

'aufkriegen F *s. aufbekommen.*

'aufkündig|en *s. kündigen; Kapital:* recall; *Freundschaft:* renounce, *s. a. absagen; Gehorsam:* refuse; '2ung *f* warning, notice.

'auflachen burst out laughing.

'aufladen load; ⚡ charge; *Motor:* boost, supercharge; *j-m et.* ~ burden (*od.* charge) a p. with a th.; *sich et.* ~ saddle o.s. with a th.

'Auflader *m* loader, packer; *e-s Motors:* supercharger, *Am.* booster.

'Auflage *f* (*Steuer*) tax, duty; (*amtlicher Befehl*) injunction; (*Bedin-*

gung) condition; *e-s Buches:* edition; *e-r Zeitung* (*a.* '~nziffer *f*) circulation, run; (*Schicht*) layer; (*Stütze*) rest, support.

'auflass|en leave open; ⚡ convey; '2ung *f* conveyance.

'auflauern: *j-m* ~ lie in wait for a p.

'Auflauf *m* gathering of people, crowd; ⚡ unlawful assembly; (*Tumult*) riot; *Speise:* soufflé (*fr.*).

'auflaufen *v/i.* (sn) rise, swell; *Summen:* accumulate, run up; *Zinsen usw.:* accumulate, accrue; ⚓ run aground; *v/t. sich die Füße* ~ get footsore.

'Auflaufform *f* ovenproof dish.

'aufleben 1. *v/i.* (sn): (*wieder*) ~ (*lassen*) revive; 2. 2 *n* (6) revival.

'auflegen put, lay (*auf acc.* on); *Buch:* print, publish; *wieder* ~ reprint; *Schiff, Waren:* lay up; *Zeitung:* lay out; *Last:* impose (*j-m* on a p.); *Strafe:* inflict (*j-m* on a p.); *Feuerung:* put on; *teleph.* (*v/i.*) ring off; *sich* ~ lean (*auf acc.* on); *Schminke* ~ lay on rouge; *teleph.* (*den Hörer*) ~ hang up (the receiver).

'auflehn|en (*a. sich*) lean (*auf acc.* on); *fig. sich* ~ (*gegen*) rebel, revolt (against); '2ung *f* rebellion.

'auflesen gather, pick up (*a.* F *fig.*); *Ähren:* glean.

'aufleuchten flash (*od.* light) up.

'aufliegen lie *od.* lean (*auf dat.* on); *zur Besichtigung usw.:* be laid out (*zu* for); ⚕ *sich* ~ get bedsore.

'auflockern loosen; ✕, *a.* ✈ disperse.

'auflodern (sn) blaze up.

'auflösbar solvable; ⚗ soluble.

'auflösen *Knoten:* undo, untie; *Versammlung:* break up; *Heer usw.:* disband; *Salz usw., Ehe, Geschäft, Parlament, Verein usw.:* dissolve (*a. sich*); (*sich*) *in s-e Bestandteile* ~ disintegrate; *e-e Verbindung:* sever; *Firma, Geschäft:* wind up, liquidate; *Rätsel,* ♪ *Gleichung, Klammer:* solve; ♫ *Bruch:* reduce; *gr.,* ⚗ analyse; *aufgelöst fig.* (*außer Fassung*) upset.

'Auflösung *f vgl. auflösen:* (dis-) solution; disbandment; liquidation; disintegration; '~szeichen ♪ *n* natural.

'aufmach|en open; *Kleid, Paket usw.:* a. undo; *Schirm:* put up;

(*zurechtmachen*) get up; *Geschäft*: open; *sich* ~ *Wind*: rise; *Wanderer usw.*: set out (*nach* for); (*die Tür*) ~, *wenn es läutet*: answer the door; ⊕ *Dampf* ~ get up steam; '2ung *f* (*Äußeres*) make-up (*a. e-s Buches, e-r Zeitung*), get-up; *fig.* display, splash; *in großer* ~ *herausbringen* highlight.

'**Aufmarsch** *m* marching-up; ✗ concentration; *zur Gefechtslinie*: deployment; (*Parade*) parade, marchpast; '2**ieren** (sn) draw up; form into line; *zur Gefechtslinie*: deploy (*a.* ~ *lassen*).

'**aufmerken** attend, pay attention (*auf acc.* to); *s.* aufhorchen.

'**aufmerksam** attentive (*auf acc.* to); *fig.* (*zuvorkommend*) kind (*gegen* to); *j-n* ~ *machen auf* (*acc.*) call a p.'s attention to; '2**keit** *f* attention (*a. fig.*); *fig.* (*Höflichkeit*) kindness; (*kleines Geschenk*) small token; *s-e* ~ *richten auf* (*acc.*) focus one's attention on; ~ *schenken* (*dat.*) pay attention to.

'**aufmöbeln** F pep up.

'**aufmunter|n** (29) rouse; *fig.* (*ermutigen*) encourage; (*aufheitern*) cheer up; '~**nd** encouraging; ~**e** Worte pep talk; '2**ung** *f* encouragement.

aufmüpfig ['~mypfiç] rebellious.

'**aufnäh|en** sew (*auf acc.* on); (*verkürzen*) tuck; '2**er** *m im Kleid*: tuck.

Aufnahme ['~nɑ:mə] *f* (15) *der Arbeit, v. Kapital*: taking up; (*Empfang, geistige* ~) reception; (*Zulassung*) admission; (*Einbeziehung*) inclusion; ~ *v. Beziehungen*: establishing; *v. Nahrung*: intake; *v. Schulden*: contraction; *surv.* survey; *geogr.* mapping out; *phot. Vorgang*: taking, *Film*: shooting; *Bild*: photo(graph), *bsd. Film*: shot; (*Ton*2) recording; *e-e* ~ *machen* take a photograph *od.* picture, shoot a film; '2**fähig** capacious; *geistig*: receptive (*für* of); '~**fähigkeit** *f* capacity; *geistige*: receptivity; '~**gebühr** *f* admission (*Am.* initiation) fee; '~**gerät** *n phot., Film*: pick-up unit; (*Ton*2) recorder; '~**land** *n* host country; '~**leiter** *m Film*: production manager; '~**prüfung** *f* entrance examination; '~**studio** *n Film*: (film) studio; (*Tonstudio*) (recording) studio.

'**aufnehmen** take up; *vom Boden*:

pick up; *j-n*: take in; *Diktat, Stenogramm*: take (down); *geistig*: take in; *Gast*: receive; *phot.* take (*j-n a p.'s picture*); *Film*: shoot; *auf Tonband usw.*: record; *Geld*: borrow; *Anleihe*: raise; *Verzeichnis, Protokoll*: draw up; *Verbindung*: establish; *in e-e Liste usw.*: enter; 🜂 absorb (*a. fig.*); *surv.* survey; *geogr.* map out; *gut* (*übel*) ~ take well (ill); *in e-n Verein* ~ admit to (*od.* enrol[l] in) a club; *in sich* ~ absorb; *es* ~ *mit* cope with, be a match for; *wieder* ~ *e-e Rede*: resume.

'**aufnötigen**: *j-m et.* ~ force upon a p.

'**auf-opfer|n**, '2**ung** *f* sacrifice.

'**aufpass|en** *v/i.* attend (*auf acc.* to); (*beobachten*) watch; (*aufmerken*) be attentive; *paß auf!, aufgepaßt!* attention!, (*Vorsicht!*) look out!; *paß* (*mal*) *auf!* look (*Am.* see) here!; *auf j-n* ~ take care of a p.; '2**er(in**f) *m* (12) watcher; (*Spion*) spy.

'**aufpeitschen** whip up; *j-n, Nerven*: rouse, stimulate.

'**aufpflanzen** set up; *Seitengewehr*: fix; *sich* ~ plant o.s.

'**aufplatzen** (sn) burst (open).

'**aufpolieren** polish up (*a. fig.*).

'**aufprägen** imprint, stamp (*dat.* on).

aufprallen ['~pralən] (sn) bound, bounce (*auf acc.* against); ~ *auf a.* strike.

'**Aufpreis** *m* extra charge, surcharge.

'**aufprobieren** try on.

'**aufpumpen** pump (*od.* blow) up.

'**aufputschen** (27*) stimulate; (*aufhetzen*) rouse; *sich* ~ pep o.s. up.

'**Aufputsch|mittel** *n* stimulant; '~**tablette** *f* pep pill.

'**Aufputz** *m* attire, get-up; '2**en** dress (*od.* smarten) up.

'**aufraffen** snatch up; *sich* ~ pull o.s. together (*zu* for), brace o.s. up (for); *vom Krankenbett*: recover.

'**aufragen** tower up, loom (up).

'**aufräumen** *v/t.* put in order; *Zimmer*: tidy (up), *Am.* straighten up; (*wegräumen*) clear away; *v/i.* ~ *mit et.* do away with; ~ *unter* (*dat.*) play havoc among.

'**aufrechnen** reckon up; (*gegen*) set off (against).

'**aufrecht** upright (*a. fig.*), erect; '~**erhalten** maintain, uphold; '2**erhaltung** *f* maintenance.

'**aufreg|en** excite; (*ärgern*) irritate; *s. aufgeregt*; '**ꜱung** *f* excitement, agitation.

'**aufreiben** rub sore, gall; (*verschleißen*) wear out; (*vernichten*) wipe out; (*sich*) ～ *fig.* wear (o.s.) out, worry (o.s.) to death; '**～d** exhausting, wearing.

'**aufreihen** thread, string.

'**aufreißen** *v/t.* rip (*od.* tear) open; *Tür*: fling open; *Straße*: take up; *Augen usw.*: open (wide); *sl. Mädchen*: pick up; *v/i.* (sn) split open, burst.

'**aufreiz|en** incite, provoke, stir up; '**～end** provocative; *Rede*: inflammatory; '**ꜱung** *f* incitement, instigation.

'**aufrichten** set up, erect; (*aufhelfen*) help up; (*trösten*) comfort; *sich* ～ arise, straighten o.s.; *im Bett*: sit up.

'**aufrichtig** sincere; upright; '**ꜱkeit** *f* sincerity, uprightness.

'**aufriegeln** unbolt.

'**Aufriß** *m* lay-out; (*äußere Ansicht*) elevation; (*Skizze*) sketch; ⚓ vertical section.

'**aufritzen** slit (*od.* rip) open; *die Haut*: scratch open.

'**aufrollen** roll up; (*entfalten*) unroll.

'**aufrücken** (sn) move up, advance; *im Rang usw.*: be promoted.; ✕ *in Reih und Glied*: close the ranks.

'**Aufruf** *m* call, summons; *an die Bevölkerung*: proclamation; '**ꜱen** call up; *j-n zu et.*: call upon; *einzeln beim Namen*: call over; *Banknoten usw.*: call in; *zum Streik* ～ call a strike.

Aufruhr ['～ruːr] *m* (3) rebellion, revolt; (*Meuterei*) mutiny; (*Tumult*) riot; *fig.* uproar.

'**aufrühren** stir up; *alte Geschichte*: rake up; *Erinnerungen*: revive.

'**Aufrührer** *m* (7), '**～in** *f* rebel, insurgent, mutineer; '**ꜱisch** rebellious; *Rede*: inflammatory.

aufrunden ['～rundən] round off.

'**aufrüst|en** ✕ (re)arm; '**ꜱung** *f* (re)armament.

'**aufrütteln** shake up; *aus dem Schlaf usw.*: rouse (up).

'**aufsagen** say, repeat; *Gedicht*: recite; *s. aufkündigen*.

'**aufsammeln** pick up, collect.

aufsässig ['～zɛsiç] restive; (*widerspenstig*) refractory, rebellious.

'**Aufsatz** *m* essay; (*Schulꜱ*) essay, *Grundschule*: composition; (*Zeitungsꜱ*) article; *e-s Schrankes usw.*: top; (*Tafelꜱ*) epergne, cent|re-(*Am.* -er)-piece.

'**aufsaug|en** suck up; ⚗ *u. fig.* absorb; '**ꜱung** *f* absorption.

'**aufschauen** look up (*zu* to; *a. fig.*).

'**aufscheuchen** scare.

'**aufscheuern** scour; *Haut*: chafe.

'**aufschichten** pile up, stack (up).

'**aufschieben** push open; *fig.* put off; defer, postpone; *zögernd*: delay; *auf kurze Zeit*: adjourn.

'**aufschießen** (sn) shoot up; (*schnell wachsen*) grow tall; *hoch aufgeschossen* lanky, gangling.

'**Aufschlag** *m* striking (*auf acc.* [up]on *a th.*); *e-s Geschosses*: impact; (*Rockꜱ*) lapel; (*Ärmelꜱ*) cuff; (*Hosenꜱ*) turn-up; (*Preisꜱ*) increase, (*Zuschlag*) additional charge; (*Steuerꜱ*) additional duty; *Tennis*: (*a.* '**～ball** *m*) service, (*～art*) serve.

'**aufschlagen** *v/t.* (*öffnen*) break open; *Ei*: crack; *Karte, Hosen, Ärmel usw.*: turn up; (*errichten*) put up; *Zelt*: pitch; *Buch, Augen*: open; *Wohnsitz*: take up; *sein Hauptquartier* ～ *in* (*dat.*) make one's headquarters at; *sich den Kopf usw.* ～ bruise one's head *etc.*; *v/i.* (sn) strike (violently) (*auf acc.* [up]on); ↑ rise in price; *Tennis*: serve.

'**Aufschläger** *m Tennis*: server.

'**aufschließen** unlock, open (*a. fig.*); ⚗ disintegrate; *fig. sich j-m* ～ open one's heart to.

'**aufschlitzen** slit, rip up.

'**Aufschluß** *m fig.* information; ⚗ disintegration; '**ꜱreich** informative, revealing.

'**aufschlüsseln** subdivide, break down; *Kosten*: allocate.

'**aufschnallen** unbuckle; (*anschnallen*) buckle (*od.* strap) on (*auf acc.* to).

'**aufschnappen** *v/t.* snap up; *fig.* pick up; *v/i.* spring open.

'**aufschneid|en** *v/t.* cut open; *Braten*: cut up, carve; *v/i. fig.* brag, boast, show off; '**ꜱer** *m* (7) braggart, boaster; **ꜱerei** [～'raɪ] *f* (16) brag(ging), boast(ing).

'**Aufschnitt** *m*: *kalter* ～ (slices *pl.* of) cold meat, *Am.* cold cuts *pl.*

'**aufschnüren** untie; *Schuh*: unlace; *Knoten*: undo.

'**aufschrauben** screw (*auf acc.* on); (*losschrauben*) unscrew, loosen.

'**aufschrecken** *v/t.* frighten up; *v/i.* (sn) start up.

'**Aufschrei** *m* cry, yell, scream; *fig.* outcry.

'**aufschreiben** write down, make a note of; *amtlich:* book; *j-n polizeilich* ~ take a p.'s name.

'**aufschreien** cry out, scream.

'**Aufschrift** *f* inscription; (*Überschrift*) heading; *e-s Briefes:* address, direction; *e-r Flasche usw.:* label.

'**Aufschub** *m* deferment; (*Verzögerung*) delay; *beabsichtigter:* adjournment; *gewährter:* respite; ♂♭ *der Vollstreckung:* reprieve.

'**aufschürfen** *Haut:* graze, skin.

'**aufschütteln** shake up.

'**aufschütten** pour (*od.* put) on; *Sand usw.:* heap up; *Damm:* raise.

'**aufschwatzen** *j-m et.* ~ talk a p. into buying a th.; *Ware:* palm off a th. on a p.

'**aufschwellen** (sn) swell (up).

'**aufschwemmen** bloat.

'**aufschwingen:** *sich* ~ soar (up), rise; *fig. sich* ~ *zu* brace o.s. up for.

'**Aufschwung** *m Turnen:* upward circle; *fig.* rise, *Am.* upswing, *bsd.* ♣ boom; (*Besserung*) improvement; *e-n* ~ *nehmen* receive a fresh impetus, revive.

'**aufsehen** 1. look up (*zu* to; *a. fig.*); 2. ♀ *n* (6) sensation, stir; ~ *erregen* cause a sensation, make a stir; '~**erregend** startling, sensational.

'**Aufseher** *m* (7), '~**in** *f* (16¹) overseer, inspector; (*Wächter*) guard, attendant.

'**aufsein** (sn) be up; *Tür usw.:* be open.

'**aufsetzen** (*aufrichten*) set up; *Hut, Kessel, Flicken usw., Miene:* put on; (*schriftlich abfassen*) draw up, compose; *Telegramm, Urkunde:* draft; make out; *s. Horn; sich* ~ sit up; *s-n Kopf* ~ be obstinate; *Schneiderei: aufgesetzte Taschen pl.* patch pockets; *v/i.* ✈ touch down.

'**Aufsicht** *f* inspection, supervision, control; *im Kaufhaus:* shop- (*Am.* floor-)walker; (*Polizei*♀) surveillance; (*Fürsorge*) care; '~**sbe·amte** *m* supervisor, inspector; '~**sbehörde** *f* board of control, supervising authority; '~**srat** *m* ♣ supervisory

board; '~**sratsvorsitzende** *m*, *f* chairman (*f* chairwoman) of the board.

'**aufsitzen** sit, rest (*auf dat.* on); *nachts:* sit up; *Reiter:* (sn) mount; *fig.* ℱ (sn) be taken in (*j-m* by); *j-n lassen* let a p. down.

'**aufspalt|en** *v/t. u. v/refl.* (sn) split up, cleave; ℳ disintegrate; '♀**ung** *f biol. e-r Zelle:* fission; ℳ disintegration.

'**aufspannen** stretch; *Schirm:* put up; *Saite:* put on; *Segel:* spread.

'**aufsparen** save; *fig.* reserve.

'**aufspeicher|n** (29) store up; '♀**ung** *f* storage.

'**aufsperren** open wide; (*aufschließen*) unlock; *fig. s.* Mund.

'**aufspielen** *v/t. u. v/i.* strike up; *sich* ~ put on airs; *sich* ~ *als* pose as, set up for.

'**aufspießen** spit; (*durchbohren*) pierce; *mit den Hörnern:* gore.

'**aufsprengen** burst (*od.* force) open; *mit Pulver:* blow up.

'**aufspringen** (sn) leap up, jump up; (*landen*) land; *Ball:* bounce; *Knospe, Tür usw.:* burst open; (*rissig werden*) crack; *Haut:* chap; (*auf e-n Zug*) ~ jump on (to a train).

'**aufspritzen** splash up.

'**aufsprudeln** bubble up.

'**aufspulen** (25) wind (up), reel.

'**aufspüren** *a. fig.* hunt up, track down; ferret out.

'**aufstacheln** goad (*a. fig.*); *fig.* incite, *bsd. b.s.* instigate.

'**aufstampfen** stamp (one's foot *od.* feet).

'**Aufstand** *m* insurrection, rebellion, uprising, revolt.

aufständisch ['~ʃtendiʃ] rebellious; *ein* ♀*er* an insurgent, a rebel.

'**aufstapeln** (29) pile up, stack (up); ♣ store up.

'**aufstechen** puncture, prick open; *Geschwür:* lance.

'**aufstecken** fix; *mit Nadeln:* pin up; *Haar, Gardine usw.:* put up; ℱ (*aufgeben*) give up (*a. v/i.*); *j-m ein Licht* ~ open a p.'s eyes (*über acc.* to).

'**aufstehen** (sn) stand up; rise, *bsd. aus dem Bett:* get up; *vom Sitz:* rise to one's feet; (*offenstehen, mst* h.) stand open; *von e-r Krankheit:* recover; *Volk:* rise, revolt.

'**aufsteigen** (sn) rise, ascend; *Flug-*

zeug: take the air, take off; *Reiter*: mount; *beruflich*: be promoted; *Gefühl*: well up; *ein Gedanke (Verdacht) stieg in mir auf* a thought struck me (I had a suspicion).

'**Aufsteiger** *m in der Gesellschaft*: social climber; *Sport*: league climber.

'**aufstell|en** set up; ✕ *usw.* line up, *Wachposten*: post, station, *Einheit*: organize; *Behauptung*: make; *Beispiel*: set; *Bildsäule usw.*: erect; *Falle*: set; *als Kandidaten*: nominate; *Leiter*: raise; *Maschine*: set up, mount; *Liste*: make out; *Rechnung*: draw (*od.* make) up; *Kosten*: specify; *Grundsatz*: lay down; *Problem, Regel*: state; *Lehre, Theorie*: propound, advance; *Rekord*: set, establish; *Waren*: expose; *Mannschaft*: compose; *sich ~ take one's stand*, place o.s.; *sich ~ lassen für e-n Sitz im Parlament* stand (*Am.* run) for; '**2ung** *f* setting up (*a.* ⊕); (*Anordnung*) formation (*a.* ✕); *Sport*: team composition; *e-r Behauptung*: assertion; *pol.* nomination; mounting; ✝ statement (of account); (*Liste*) list, schedule.

Aufstieg ['~ʃtiːk] *m* (3) ascent, *Am. mst* ascension; *fig.* rise; (*Beförderung*) promotion; '**~s-chancen** *f/pl.* promotion prospects; '**~srunde** *f* league-qualifying round; '**~sspiel** *n* league-qualifying game.

'**aufstöbern** *Wild*: start, rouse; *fig.* ferret out, hunt up.

'**aufstocken** ✝ step up; *Vorräte*: stock up on.

'**aufstören** rouse up, disturb.

'**aufstoßen** *v/t. Tür usw.*: push open; ~ *auf (acc.)* knock against; *v/i.* (h. u. sn) *Speise*: rise up, repeat; *P.*: belch; ⚓ run aground; ~ *auf (acc.)* strike on; *fig. j-m*: meet with *a th.*, come across *a th.*

'**aufstreben** rise, tower up; *fig.* aspire.

'**aufstreichen** *auf Brot*: spread.

'**aufstreuen** strew (*auf acc.* on).

'**Aufstrich** *m beim Schreiben*: upstroke; *auf Brot*: spread.

'**aufstülpen** turn up; *sich den Hut ~* clap on one's hat.

'**aufstützen** (*stützen*) prop up; *sich ~ auf (dat. u. acc.)* lean (up)on *the table etc.*

'**aufsuchen** search for; *in e-m Buche*: look up; *j-n ~* (go to) see a

p., look a p. up; *Ort*: visit; *vom Boden*: pick up.

'**auftakeln** rig; *fig. sich ~ rig* o.s. up; *aufgetakelt s. aufgedonnert.*

'**Auftakt** *m* ♪ upbeat, pickup; *fig.* prelude (*zu* to).

'**auftanken** fill up.

'**auftauchen** (sn) emerge, appear, turn up; *U-Boot*: surface; *Frage usw.*: crop up; *Gerücht*: get afloat.

'**auftauen** *v/t., v/i.* (sn) *a.fig.* thaw.

'**aufteilen** divide up, partition; *Land*: parcel out, allot; (*verteilen*) distribute.

auftischen ['~tiʃən] (27) dish up (*a. fig.*), serve up.

Auftrag ['~traːk] *m* (3¹) commission; (*Befehl, Pflicht*) charge; (*Weisung*) instruction; (*Sendung*) mission; ⚙ mandate; ✝ (*Bestellung*) order; *v. Farbe*: application; *im ~ von* by order of; *abbr. i. A. vor Unterschriften*: on instruction, *im Behördenbrief*: by order; *e-n ~ erteilen* give an order; *im ~ handeln* von act on (*od.* in) behalf of; '**2en** *Speisen*: serve (up); *Farbe*: lay on; *Kleid usw.*: wear out; *j-m et. ~* charge a p. with; *fig. dick ~* lay it on thick; **~geber** ['~traːk-] *m* employer; (*Besteller*) orderer; (*Kunde*) customer; ⚙ mandator; *Börse*: principal; '**~sbestand** *m* orders in hand; '**~sbestätigung** *f* confirmation of order; '**~sbuch** ✝ *n* order-book; '**~s-eingang** *m* incoming orders *pl.*; '**~s-erteilung** *f* placing of order; *bei Ausschreibung*: award; contract; '**~sformular** *n* order form, *Am.* blank; '**2sgemäß** as ordered; '**~srückgang** *m* drop in orders.

'**auftreffen** strike, hit.

'**auftreiben** drive up; (*aufblähen*) swell up, distend; (*beschaffen*) hunt up, get hold of; *Geld*: raise.

'**auftrennen** rip (up); *Naht*: undo.

'**auftreten** **1.** *v/t. Tür usw.*: kick open; *v/i.* (sn) *leise up*: tread; *thea., als Zeuge usw.*: appear (*als* as); *als Redner od. Sänger*: take the floor; (*sich benehmen*) act, behave; *fig.* (*eintreten*) occur; *Schwierigkeit usw.*: arise; *plötzlich*: crop up; ~ *als* (*sich brüsten als*) pose as; ~ *gegen* rise against, oppose; *energisch ~* F put one's foot down; *thea. zum ersten Mal ~* make one's debut;

2. ♀ *n* (6) (*Erscheinen*) appearance; (*Vorkommen*) occurrence; *bsd. e-r Krankheit*: incidence; (*Benehmen*) behavio(u)r, demeano(u)r, bearing.

'**Auftrieb** *m phys. u. fig.* buoyancy; ⚓ lift; (*Anstoß*) impetus; *neuen ~ verleihen* give a fresh impetus (*dat.* to).

'**Auftritt** *m thea.* scene; *e-s Schauspielers*: appearance; *fig. einen ~ mit j-m haben* have a row with a p.; *j-m einen ~ machen* make a p. a scene.

'**auftrumpfen** *fig.* put one's foot down.

'**auftun** open (*a. sich ~*); F *sich ~ Verein usw.*: get started.

'**auftürmen** pile (*od.* heap) up; *sich ~ tower up*; *Schwierigkeiten usw.*: mount (up), accumulate.

'**aufwachen** (sn) awake, wake up.

'**aufwachsen** (sn) grow up.

'**aufwallen** (sn) boil up; *See*: rage; *Blut, Leidenschaft*: boil.

Aufwand ['~vant] *m* (3) expense, (*a. fig.*) expenditure (*an dat.* of); (*Prunk*) pomp; *von Worten, Luxus*: display.

'**aufwärmen** warm up; *fig.* bring up again, rake up, rehash.

'**Aufwartefrau** *f* charwoman.

'**aufwarten** *j-m*: wait (up)on, attend on; *bei Tische*: wait; *~ mit* offer, *fig. a.* come up with.

aufwärts ['~vɛrts] upward(s); (*bergan*) uphill; *Fahrstuhl*: going up!; '♀-**entwicklung** *f* upward trend; '♀-**haken** *m Boxen*: uppercut.

'**Aufwartung** *f* attendance, service; (*Besuch*) visit; *j-m s-e ~ machen* pay one's respects to a p.

'**aufwaschen** wash (up).

'**aufwecken** wake up, (*a. fig.*) rouse.

'**aufweichen** *v/t. u. v/i.* (sn) soften; *mit Flüssigkeit*: soak.

'**aufweisen** show, have.

'**aufwend|en** spend, expend; (*anwenden*) use, apply; *Mühe ~ take* pains; *viel Geld ~* go to great expense; '**~ig** costly; large-scale; '♀**ungen** *f/pl.* expenditure(s).

'**aufwerfen** *Schanze usw.*: throw up; *Graben*: dig; *Tür usw.*: throw open; *Blasen*: raise; *Frage*: raise, pose; *Kopf*: toss; *sich ~ als* set up for.

aufwert|en ['~veːrtən] revalorize; '♀**ung** *f* revalorization.

'**aufwickeln** (*a. sich ~*) wind (up);

Haar: curl up, roll up; (*loswickeln*) unwind; *Paket*: unwrap; ⚓ *Tau*: coil.

aufwiegel|n ['~viːɡəln] (29) stir up, incite, instigate; '♀**ung** *f* instigation, sedition.

'**aufwiegen** *fig.* outweigh, make up for.

Aufwiegler ['~viːɡlər] *m* (7), '**~in** *f* (16[1]) *s*. Aufrührer; '♀**isch** *s*. aufrührerisch.

'**Aufwind** ⚓ *m* upwind.

'**aufwinden** wind up; *mit e-r Winde usw.*: hoist; *Anker*: weigh.

'**aufwirbeln** whirl up (*a. v/i.*); *Staub*: raise; *fig. viel Staub ~ create* quite a stir.

'**aufwischen** mop up.

'**aufwühlen** *Erde*: turn up; *von Schweinen*: root up; *Meer*: toss up; *Seele*: stir, agitate; '**~d** *fig.* heart-stirring.

'**aufzähl|en** enumerate, *Am. a.* call off; *einzeln*: specify, *Am.* itemize; *Geld*: count down; '♀**ung** *f* enumeration; specification.

'**aufzäumen** bridle; *s*. Pferd.

'**aufzehren** consume (*a. fig.*), eat up.

'**aufzeichn|en** draw (*auf acc.* upon); (*notieren*) note down; *amtlich*: register, record; *geschichtlich*: chronicle, record; ⊕ *v. Geräten*: record; '♀**ung** *f* drawing; note; record; ⊕ recording.

'**aufzeigen** show, point out.

'**aufziehen** *v/t.* draw (*od.* pull) up; *Flagge usw.*: hoist; *Anker*: weigh; (*öffnen*) (pull) open; *Kind*: bring up, *a. Tier*: rear, breed; *Bild usw.*: mount; *Perlen usw.*: thread; *Pflanze*: cultivate; *Saite*: put on; *Uhr*: wind up; F *j-n*: chaff, tease, F kid; *fig. andere Saiten ~* change one's tune; *v/i.* (sn) ⚔ draw up; *Gewitter*: approach.

'**Aufzucht** *f* breeding.

'**Aufzug** *m* procession, parade; *thea.* act; ⊕ hoist; (*Fahrstuhl*) lift, *Am.* elevator; (*Gewand*) attire, F get-up; (*Pomp*) show, pomp; *Turnen*: pull-up.

'**auf**|**zwängen** force open; '**~zwingen**: *j-m et.*: force upon a p.

Aug·apfel ['auk-] *m* (7[1]) eyeball; *fig.* apple of the eye.

Auge ['auɡə] *n* (10) eye; (*Sehkraft*) sight; ⚘ bud; *auf Karten, Würfeln*: pip, spot; *ganz ~ sein* be all eyes;

fig. ~ *um* ~ an eye for an eye; *in m-n* ~*n* in my view; *nur fürs* ~ just for show; *et. im* ~ *behalten* keep one's eye on, keep in mind; *j-m schöne* ~*n machen* give a p. the glad eye; *aus den* ~*n verlieren* lose sight of; *aus den* ~*n, aus dem Sinn* out of sight, out of mind; *bei et. ein* ~ *zudrücken* wink at, turn a blind eye to; *j-m ins* ~ *fallen od. in die* ~*n stechen* catch (*od.* strike) a p.'s eye; *ins* ~ *fallend* striking, evident, obvious; *große* ~*n machen* gape, stare; *Ziel usw. ins* ~ *fassen* envisage; *j-m ins* ~ *sehen* look a p. full in the face; *e-r Gefahr (Tatsache) ins* ~ *sehen* look a danger (fact) in the face, envisage a danger (fact); *unter vier* ~*n* face to face, privately; *vor* ~*n führen* demonstrate; *vor* ~*n haben* have in view; *sich vor* ~*n halten* bear in mind; *kein* ~ *zutun* not to get a wink of sleep; *s. blau.*

äugeln [ɔʏgəln] (29) ogle.

'Augen|-arzt *m* eye specialist; **'~bank** *f* eye-transplant bank; **'~blick** *m* moment, instant; *alle*~*e* every now and then; *im* ~ at the moment, at present, (*im Nu*) in the twinkling of an eye; *im ersten* ~ for a moment; *in diesem* ~ at this moment *od.* instant; **'2blicklich** instantaneous, immediate; (*vorübergehend*) momentary; (*gegenwärtig*) present; *adv.* instantaneously, immediately, instantly; at (*od.* for the) present; **'~braue** *f* eyebrow; **'~brauenstift** *m* eyebrow pencil; **'~-entzündung** *f* inflammation of the eye; **'2fällig** conspicuous; *s. augenscheinlich;* **'~flimmern** *n* flickering before the eyes; **'~glas** *n* eye-glass; **'~höhle** *f* eye-socket, *$* orbit; **'~klappe** *f* eye patch; **'~klinik** *f* ophthalmic hospital, *Am.* eye-clinic; **'~leiden** *n* eye-complaint; **'~licht** *n* eyesight; **'~lid** *n* eyelid; **'~maß** *n* sense of proportion; *ein gutes* ~ a sure eye; *nach dem* ~ by eye; **'~merk** *n* attention; (*Ziel*) aim; *sein* ~ *richten auf* (*acc.*) direct one's attention to; **'~nerv** *m* optic nerve; **'~schein** *m* inspection; (*Anschein*) appearance, evidence; *in* ~ *nehmen* inspect; **'2scheinlich** evident, obvious, apparent; **'~scheinlichkeit** *f* obviousness; **'~schirm** *m* eye-shade; **'~stern** *m* pupil; **'~täu-**

schung *f* optical illusion; **'~tropfen** *m*/*pl.* eyedrops; **'~wasser** *n* eye-lotion; **'~weide** *f* feast for the eyes, sight for sore eyes; **'~wimper** *f* eyelash; **'~winkel** *m* corner of the eye; **'~wischerei** *f* *fig.* eyewash; **'~zahn** *m* eye-tooth; **'~zeuge** *m* eye-witness; ~*nbericht* eye-witness report; **'~zwinkern** *n* winking.

...äugig [-ɔʏgiç] ...-eyed.

August [aʊ'gust] *m* (3) *Monat:* August; *im* ~ in August.

Auktion [aʊk'tsjoːn] *f* (16) auction, public sale; **~ator** [~jo'naːtɔr] *m* (8¹) auctioneer; **~slokal** [aʊk-'tsjoːnslokaːl] *n* sale-room.

Aula ['aʊla] *f* (16² *u.* 11¹) great hall, assembly-hall, *Am.* auditorium.

aus [aʊs] **1.** *prp.* out of; from; of; by; for; on, upon; in; ~ *Achtung* out of respect; ~ *London kommen* come from London; ~ *diesem Grunde* for this reason; ~ *Ihrem Brief ersehe ich* I see by your letter; *von mir* ~ I don't mind, for all I care; **2.** *adv.* out; over; (*erledigt*) done with, finished; ⊕ (*abgeschaltet*) off; *die Kirche ist* ~ church is over; *auf et.* ~ *sein* be set (*od.* bent, keen) on a th.; *es ist* ~ *mit ihm* it is all over (*od.* up) with him; *das Spiel ist* ~! the game is up!; *er weiß weder ein noch* ~ he is at his wits' end.

Aus *n Sport: im* ~ out (of play).

'aus-arbeit|en work out, elaborate; (*entwerfen*) prepare, draw up; **'2ung** *f* preparation, working out, elaboration.

'aus-arten (sn) degenerate (*in acc.* into); *Spiel usw.:* get out of hand.

'aus-atmen *v/t.* exhale.

'ausbaden *fig.* pay (*od.* suffer) for; *die Sache* ~ face the music.

'ausbaggern dredge.

'ausbalancieren balance (out).

'Ausbau *m* development, extension; (*Festigung*) consolidation; *Haus:* (inside) finish; ⊕ (*Abbau*) removal; **'2en** (*erweitern*) develop, extend; (*fertigstellen*) finish; (*festigen*) consolidate; ⊕ remove; **'~phase** *f* consolidation (*od.* extension) stage.

'ausbauch|en (*a. sich*), **'2ung** *f* bulge.

'ausbedingen stipulate; *sich et.* ~ reserve to o.s., (*bestehen auf*) insist on.

'ausbesser|n mend, repair, fix; *Bild:*

touch up; '**2ung** f mending, repair.

'**ausbeulen** v/t. (25) beat out; *Kleidung*: make baggy; v/i. *Kleidung*: go baggy.

'**Ausbeut|e** f gain, profit; (*Ertrag*) yield; output (a. ⊕, ✗); '**2en** (26) exploit (*allg. a. fig. b.s.*); '**~ung** f exploitation (a. b.s.).

'**ausbiegen** v/t. bend out(wards); v/i. turn aside; j-m, e-m *Wagen usw.* ~ make way for.

'**ausbieten** offer (*zum Verkauf* for sale).

'**ausbild|en** develop; *Geist usw.*: cultivate; (*schulen*) train; (*lehren*) instruct, educate; ✗ (*exerzieren*) drill; ⊕ design; *sich* ~ *zu* train (*od.* study) for; *sich im Gesang* ~ train to be a singer; '**2er** (7) m instructor; '**2ung** f development; cultivation; instruction, education; training, ✗ a. drill; '**2ungsförderung** f grant(s pl.); '**2ungsgang** m training; '**2ungslehrgang** m training course.

'**ausbitten**: *sich* ~ request; *das bitte ich mir aus* I must insist on this.

'**ausblasen** blow out.

'**ausbleiben 1.** (sn) stay away, fail to appear *od.* come; (*fehlen*) be wanting; (*nicht*) *lange* ~ be (not) long in coming; *es konnte nicht* ~, *daß* it was inevitable that; **2.** ♀ *n* non-appearance, absence; non-arrival.

'**ausbleichen** (25) *s.* bleichen.

'**ausblenden** *Film, Radio*: fade out.

'**Ausblick** m outlook, prospect, view (*auf acc.* of); (*a. fig.*) vista (*auf acc.* of); *fig.* outlook (*in die Zukunft* on).

'**ausbluten** v/i. *Wunde*: cease bleeding; *P.*: bleed to death; *Wunde* ~ *lassen* allow to bleed; v/t. bleed to death.

'**ausbohren** bore.   [oust.}

'**ausbooten** (26) disembark; *fig.*}

'**ausborgen**: *sich et.* ~ borrow (*von* from); *j-m et.* ~ lend to a p.

'**ausbrechen** v/t. break out; (*erbrechen*) vomit; v/i. (sn) break out (a. *fig. Feuer, Krieg usw.*); *fig.* burst out (*in Gelächter* laughing; *in Tränen* crying); *in Beifall* (*Schweiß*) ~ break into applause (a sweat).

'**ausbreit|en** spread (out); *Macht, Geschäft usw.*: expand; *Lehre*: propagate; *sich* ~ spread; (*ausführlich werden*) enlarge (*über acc.* upon); *s. a.* verbreiten; '**2ung** f

spread(ing); expansion; propagation.

'**ausbrennen** v/t. burn out; ✗ cauterize; v/i. (sn) cease burning; *Haus usw.*: burn out, be gutted; *ausgebrannt* (*Vulkan*) extinct; *Haus*: gutted; *P.*: exhausted.

'**ausbringen** bring out; j-s *Gesundheit* ~ propose a p.'s health.

'**Ausbruch** m outbreak; *e-s Vulkans*: eruption; *e-s Gefangenen*: escape; (*Gefühls*♀) outburst; ✗ break-out; *fig. zum* ~ *kommen* break out.

'**ausbrüten** hatch (a. *fig.*).

'**Ausbuchtung** f bulge.

'**ausbuddeln** dig out.

'**ausbügeln** iron out (a. F *fig.*).

'**Ausbund** m paragon *of beauty etc.*; *ein* ~ *von Bosheit* a regular demon.

'**ausbürgern** (29) deprive of citizenship; (*ausweisen*) expatriate.

'**ausbürsten** brush out.

'**Ausdauer** f perseverance; *im Ertragen*: endurance; *bsd.* *Sport*: stamina, staying power; (*Zähigkeit*) tenacity; '**2n** hold out, last; *fig.* persevere; '**2nd** persevering; tenacious; ♀ perennial.

'**ausdehnbar** extensible; expansible; '**2keit** f *Länge*: extensibility; *Raum*: expansibility.

'**ausdehnen** (a. *sich*) extend (*auf acc.* to); enlarge; expand; (*strecken*) stretch.

'**Ausdehnung** f expansion; *phys.* extension; ♪ dimension; ✗ dilatation; (*Umfang*) extent; '**~svermögen** n expansive force.

'**ausdenken** (*zu Ende denken*) think out; (*erdenken, a. sich* ~) think out (*Am.* up), contrive, devise, invent, (*vorstellen*) imagine; *nicht auszudenken* inconceivable, (*verheerend*) disastrous.

'**ausdeuten** interpret, explain.

'**ausdienen** serve one's time; *s. ausgedient.*

'**ausdorren** (25) v/i. (sn) dry up.

'**ausdörren** v/t. dry up, parch; (*versengen*) scorch; *ausgedörrt* a. arid.

'**ausdrehen** *Lampe, Gas*: turn off; *elektr. Licht*: a. switch off.

'**Ausdruck**[1] m (3³) expression; *bsd. fachlicher*: term; *das ist gar kein* ~! that's putting it mildly; (3, *o.pl.*) *auf dem Gesicht, in Worten*: expression; *e-m Gefühl usw.* ~ *geben* give utterance (*od.* voice) to; *zum* ~ *bringen* express, voice; *zum* ⌁ *kommen* be expressed.

'Ausdruck² *m* (3) (*Ausgedrucktes*) *typ.* printing; *Computer:* printout; **'≗en** *Computer:* print out.

'ausdrück|en press (out); squeeze out; *Zigarette:* stub (out); *fig.* express (*sich o.s.*); *sich kurz* ⌁ be brief; **'⌁lich** express, explicit.

'ausdrucks|fähig expressionable; **'≗kraft** *f* expressiveness; **'⌁los** inexpressive, blank; **'⌁voll** expressive; **'≗weise** *f* style, diction; *weitS.* language.

'ausdünst|en *v/i.* (sn) *u. v/t.* (26) evaporate; *Körper:* transpire, perspire; *v/t.* (*ausatmen*) exhale; (*ausschwitzen*) sweat out; **'≗ung** *f* evaporation; exhalation; (*Schweiß*) perspiration.

aus·ei'nander apart; separate(d); ⌁**brechen** *v/t.* break in two; *v/i.* (sn) break up; ⌁**bringen** separate; ⌁**fallen** fall apart; ⌁**gehen** (sn) come apart; *Versammlung:* break up; *Menge:* disperse; *Freunde usw.:* part (company); *Meinungen:* differ, be divided; ⌁**d** divergent; ⌁**halten** keep apart; *fig.* distinguish between; ⌁**jagen** scatter; ⌁**leben** *v/refl.* drift apart; ⌁**nehmen** take to pieces; ⊕ strip, dismantle; ⌁**reißen** tear apart; ⌁**setzen** separate; *fig.* explain; *sich mit j-m* ⌁ *über Ansichten:* argue with, *gründlich:* have it out with; (*sich einigen*) come to terms with; *über Ansprüche:* arrange with, ✝ compound with; *sich mit e-m Problem* ⌁ get down to a problem; ≗**setzung** *f* (*Erörterung*) discussion; (*Streit*) argument, dispute; (*kriegerische*) ⌁ (armed) conflict; (*Übereinkommen*) arrangement, ✝ composition; ⌁**treiben** *v/t.* disperse, scatter; *mit e-m Keil:* cleave asunder; *v/i.* drift apart.

'aus·erkoren chosen, selected, elect.

'aus·erlesen 1. *s.* ausersehen; **2.** *adj.* choice; picked; select(ed).

'aus·ersehen (30) choose, select.

'aus·erwählen select, choose; *s-e Auserwählte* the girl of his choice; (*Braut*) his bride elect; *das Auserwählte Volk* the chosen people.

'aus·essen eat up; *Schüssel:* clear; *fig.* pay for.

'ausfahren *v/t. Weg:* wear out, rut; *j-n* ⌁ take out for a drive; ⚞ *Fahrgestell:* lower, extend; ⚓ *Sehrohr:*

lift; *mot.* run (*the engine*) up to top speed; *Kurve:* round; *ausgefahren Weg:* rutted, rutty; *v/i.* (sn) drive out; 🚋 pull out; ⚓ put to sea; ⚒ ascend.

'Ausfahrt *f* drive, excursion; (*Tor*) doorway, gateway; *e-r Autobahn:* turn-off, exit; (*Hafen≗*) mouth; (*Abfahrt*) departure (*a.* ⚓).

'Ausfall *m* falling out; (*Ergebnis*) result; ⚛ precipitate; (*radioaktiver Niederschlag*) fall-out; (*Verlust*) loss; (*Fehlbetrag*) deficit; ⊕ (*Versagen*) failure, breakdown; *fenc.* pass, lunge; *fig.* attack; ⚔ sally, sortie; ⚔ (*Verlust*) casualty; **'≗en** *v/i.* (sn) fall out; (*nicht stattfinden*) not (*od.* fail) to take place, be cancelled (*od.* called off); (*ausgelassen werden*) be omitted; ⊕ (*versagen*) fail, break down; *Sport:* drop out; *fenc.* lunge; ⚔ sally out; *Ergebnis:* turn out, prove; *die Haare fallen ihm aus* he is losing his hair; *die Schule fällt aus* there is no school; *e-e Stunde, Sitzung usw.* ⌁ *lassen* drop; **'≗end, 'ausfällig** aggressive; ⌁ *werden* become abusive; **'⌁s·erscheinung** ✴ *f* outfall symptom; **'⌁straße** *f* radial route.

'ausfasern (sn) ravel out, fray (out).

'ausfechten fight out; *et. mit j-m* ⌁ have it out with a p.

'ausfegen sweep (out).

'ausfeilen file out; *fig.* file.

'ausfertig|en *Schriftstück:* draw up; *Paß:* issue; ⚖ *Urkunde:* execute; *Rechnung:* make out; **'≗ung** *f* drawing up; issue; execution; (*Abschrift*) copy; *in doppelter* ⌁ in duplicate.

'ausfindig: ⌁ *machen* find out; (*entdecken*) discover; (*örtlich feststellen*) locate; (*aufspüren*) ferret out.

'ausflicken patch up.

'ausfliegen (sn) fly out; *fig.* leave home; go on a trip.

'ausfließen (sn) flow out; *fig.* emanate.

ausflippen *sl.* ['⌁flipən] (sn) freak out.

'Ausflucht *f* evasion, subterfuge; (*Vorwand*) excuse, pretext; *Ausflüchte machen* prevaricate, shuffle, dodge.

'Ausflug *m* excursion (*a. fig.*), outing, trip.

Ausflügler ['⌁fly:glər] *m* excursionist, F tripper, *bsd. Am.* tourist.

'**Ausfluß** *m* flowing out, effluence;
♂ discharge; (*Mündung*) outfall;
issue, outlet; ♈, *fig.* emanation;
fig. (*Ergebnis*) result.

'**ausforschen** investigate, inquire
into; *j-n:* sound.

'**ausfragen** *j-n:* interrogate, question; *prüfend:* bsd. *Am.* quiz; *neugierig:* sound, pump.

ausfransen ['⁓franzən] fray (out).

'**ausfressen** *s.* ausessen; ♈ corrode;
F et. ⁓ make mischief.

Ausfuhr ['⁓fuːr] *f* (16) export
(-ation); (*Waren*) exports *pl.*; '⁓-
artikel *m* export(ed article).

'**ausführbar** practicable, feasible,
workable; ✝ exportable; '⁓**keit** *f*
practicability; ✝ exportability.

'**Ausfuhrbewilligung** *f* export per-
mit *od.* licen|ce, *Am.* -se.

'**ausführen** execute, carry out, perform, *Auftrag:* Am. a. fill; *Ware:*
export; (*darlegen*) explain, point
out, state; *j-n:* take out.

'**Ausfuhr|handel** *m* export trade;
'⁓**land** *n* exporting country.

'**ausführlich** full(-length), detailed;
(*umfassend*) comprehensive; *adv.* in
detail; *sehr* ⁓ at full (*od.* great)
length; *ziemlich* ⁓ at some length;
⁓ *schreiben* write fully; '⁓**keit** *f*
(*Genauigkeit*) minuteness of detail;
in Einzelheiten: particularity; (*Weitschweifigkeit*) copiousness.

'**Ausfuhr|papiere** *n/pl.* export
documents; '⁓**prämie** ✝ *f* (export)
bounty; '⁓**sperre** *f* embargo on exports.

'**Ausführung** *f* ✝ exportation; *fig.*
execution, performance (*a. e-s Vertrags*); *e-s Gesetzes:* implementa-
tion; (*Fertigstellung*) completion;
⊕ (*Konstruktion*) design; *hand-
werklich:* workmanship; (*Type*)
type, model; (*Darlegung*) explanation, statement.

'**Ausfuhr|verbot** *n* prohibition of
exportation; '⁓**waren** *f/pl.* exports
pl.; '⁓**zoll** *m* export duty.

'**ausfüllen** fill out; *Formular usw.:*
fill in *od.* up; *fig.* fill; *j-n:* absorb.

'**ausfüttern** line (*a.* ⊕).

'**Ausgabe** *f von Briefen usw.:* delivery; (*Verteilung*) distribution; *Computer:* output; *e-s Buches:* edition,
(*Exemplar*) copy; (*Geld⁂*) expense,
expenditure; *von Aktien, Papiergeld
usw.:* issue; (⁓*stelle*) issuing office;

'⁓**daten** *n/pl.* (computer) output
data.

'**Ausgang** *m* (*Ausgehen*) going out,
exit; (*Tür usw.*) way out, exit; (*Auslaß*) outlet; (*Ende*) end; (*Ergebnis*)
result, upshot; ⁓ *haben Hauspersonal:*
have one's day (*od.* evening) off;
'⁓**sbasis** *f fig.* starting point, working
basis; '⁓**smaterial** *n* source material; '⁓**s-punkt** *m* starting-point;
'⁓**ssperre** *f* curfew; '⁓**ssprache** *f*
source language.

'**ausgeben** *v/t.* give out; (*verteilen*)
distribute; *Befehl, Aktien, Papiergeld, Fahrkarten:* issue; *Briefe,
Waren:* deliver; *Spielkarten:* deal;
Geld: spend; *fig.* extend o.s. (*bei
in*); *s. a. verausgaben; sich* ⁓ *für*
pass o.s. off for, pose as; *v/i.* gut
usw. ⁓ (*Tee usw.*) yield well *etc.*

'**ausgebeult** *Hose:* baggy.

ausgebombt ['⁓gəbɔmpt] bombed
out.

ausgebufft ['⁓gəbuft] *sl.* fly, sharp.

'**Ausgeburt** *f* (monstrous) product;
P.: monster; *der Phantasie:* phantom.

ausgedient ['⁓gədiːnt] *P.:* pen-
sioned-off; past use, worn-out; ⁓
(*haben*) *P. u. S.:* (be) superannuated;
⁓er *Soldat* ex-serviceman, veteran.

'**ausgefallen** *fig.* eccentric, odd.

'**ausgefeilt** *fig.* elaborate.

'**ausgeflippt** *sl.* freaked (*od.* flipped)
out. [(out).]

ausgefranst ['⁓gəfranst] frayed

ausgeglichen ['⁓gəgliçən] *fig.* well-
-balanced, well-poised.

'**Ausgeh-anzug** *m* outdoor-dress; ✕
dress uniform.

'**ausgehen** (sn) go out; (*spazierengehen*) take a walk; (*enden*) end (*auf
acc.* in); *Farbe:* fade; *Haar:* fall
out; *Geld, Vorrat:* run short, give
out; *Feuer, Licht:* go out; *gut usw.*
⁓ turn out well *etc.*; *frei* ⁓ get off
scot-free; *leer* ⁓ come away empty-
-handed; *von et.* ⁓ start (*od.* proceed) from; *von j-m* ⁓ *Vorschlag
usw.:* come from; *auf et.* (*acc.*) ⁓
(*suchen*) seek, look for, (*anstreben*)
be out to *inf.*, aim at *ger.*; *ihm ging
das Geld aus* he ran short of money.

Ausgehverbot ['⁓geː-] *n* curfew.

ausgeklügelt ['⁓gəklyːgəlt] ingenious, clever.

'**ausgekocht** *fig.* hard-boiled; (*erfahren*) seasoned.

ausgelassen [ˈ∼gəlasən] frolicsome; wild; '**Qheit** f (16) frolicsomeness.
ausgeleiert [ˈ∼gəlaɪərt] a. fig. worn-out.
ausgemacht [ˈ∼gəmaxt] settled; (sicher) confirmed, established; Gauner usw.: downright, thorough; ∼e Sache foregone conclusion.
ausgenommen [ˈ∼gənɔmən] except; du nicht ∼ not excepting you.
ausgerechnet [ˈ∼gərɛçnət] fig. exact(ly), just; ∼ er of all people.
ausgeschlossen [ˈ∼gəʃlɔsən] impossible, out of the question.
'**ausgeschnitten** Kleid: low-cut.
Ausgesiedelte [ˈ∼gəziːdəltə] m, f evacuee.
ausgesprochen [ˈ∼gəʃprɔxən] decided, pronounced.
'**ausgestalten** s. gestalten.
'**ausgesucht** exquisite (a. Höflichkeit), choice; P.: (hand-)picked; Worte: well-chosen.
ausgetreten [ˈ∼gətreːtən]: fig. ∼er Weg beaten (od. trodden) path; Schuh: trodden-down.
'**ausgewachsen**: fig. ein ∼er Unsinn utter nonsense.
Ausgewiesene [ˈ∼gəviːzənə] m, f expellee.
ausgezeichnet [ˈ∼gətsaɪçnət] excellent, first-class; F capital.
ausgiebig [ˈ∼giːbiç] s. reichlich, ergiebig; ∼en Gebrauch machen von make full use of.
'**ausgießen** pour out.
Ausgleich [ˈ∼glaɪç] m (3) equalization (a. Sport); Tennis: deuce; (Vergleich) arrangement, compromise; (Ersatz) compensation, offset; s. ∼ung; '∼**behälter** mot. m expansion tank; '**Qen** equalize; Verlust: compensate; ✝ balance; Streit: settle; '∼**er** m Sport: handicapper; '∼**s-tor** n equalizer; '∼**ung** f equalization; compensation; balance.
'**ausgleiten** (30, sn) slip, lose one's footing; fig. slip.
'**ausgrab|en** dig out od. up (a. fig.); excavate; Leiche: exhume; '**Qung** f excavation; exhumation.
'**ausgreifen** Pferd: step out.
Ausguck [ˈ∼guk] m (3) look-out.
'**Ausguß** m (∼becken) sink; (Tülle) spout; '∼**-eimer** m slop-pail.
'**aushacken** hew (od. hack) out; die Augen: pick out.
'**aushaken** unhook.

'**aushalten** v/t. endure, bear; Angriff, Hitze, Probe, Vergleich usw.: stand; Ton: hold, sustain; v/i. hold out; fig. a. persevere; nicht zum Q beyond endurance.
aushändig|en [ˈ∼hendigən] (25) deliver up, hand over (dat. to); '**Qung** f delivery, surrender.
'**Aushang** m (3³) notice, bulletin.
'**aushänge|n** v/t. hang out (a. v/i.); Tür: unhinge; Plakat: post (up); '**Qschild** n sign-board, shop sign; fig. front; (Paradestück) show-piece.
'**ausharren** hold out, persevere.
'**aushauen** hew out, carve; Wald: thin.
'**ausheb|en** lift out; Tür: unhinge; Truppen:levy, den einzelnen:enrol(l), enlist, draft; Erde, Grube: excavate; Verbrechernest usw.: raid, mop up; '**Qung** ✕ f draft(ing), conscription.
'**aushecken** fig. hatch, F cook up.
'**ausheilen** v/t. u. v/i. (sn) heal (up).
'**aushelfen** help out (j-m a p.); supply a p. (mit with).
'**Aushilf|e** f help (a. P.), assistance; (Notbehelf) stopgap; '∼**skraft** f temporary worker, help; **Qsweise** [ˈ∼hilfsvaɪzə] as a stopgap; weitS. temporarily.
aushöhl|en [ˈ∼høːlən] (25) hollow out, excavate; fig. sap, erode; '**Qung** f excavation.
'**ausholen** v/i. swing, strike out; Erzählung: weit ∼ go far back; v/t. j-n: sound, pump.
'**aushorchen** j-n: sound, draw.
'**Aushub** m Erdarbeiten: digging, excavations pl.
'**aushungern** starve (out); ausgehungert famished, starved.
'**aushusten** cough up, expectorate.
'**auskämpfen** fight out.
'**auskehren** (25) sweep out.
'**auskennen**: sich ∼ in e-m Ort know (one's way about) a place; in e-r S.: be quite at home in a th., know all about a th.
'**ausklammern** fig. leave out of consideration, shelve.
'**Ausklang** m end.
'**ausklauben** pick out.
'**auskleiden** (a. sich) undress; ⊕ line, coat.
'**ausklingen** fade away; fig. ∼ in (acc.) end in.
'**ausklopfen** beat (out); Kleid usw.: dust; Pfeife: knock out.

ausklügeln ['‿kly:gəln] puzzle out; s. *ausgeklügelt*.

auskneifen F v/i. decamp, bolt.

'ausknipsen F ⚡ switch off.

'ausknobeln F dice (*od.* toss) for; *fig.* puzzle (*od.* figure) out.

'auskochen boil (out); *Saft usw.*: decoct; *s.* ausgekocht.

'auskommen 1. v/i. (sn) come out; *Feuer*: break out; *geldlich*: make both ends meet; *mit (ohne) et.* ‿ do *od.* manage with(out); *mit j-m* ‿ get on (*od.* along) with; **2.** ⚤ n (6) competency; *sein* ‿ *haben* make a living, have a competency; *sein gutes* ‿ *haben* be well off; *es ist kein* ‿ *mit ihm* there is no getting on with him.

auskömmlich ['‿kœmliç] sufficient.

'auskosten *fig.* enjoy thoroughly, *a. ironisch*: taste fully.

'auskramen rummage out; *fig.* bring up; *Wissen*: *co.* trot out.

'auskratzen v/t. scratch out; ✂ curette; v/i. (sn) F bolt.

'auskundschaften explore; ✕ reconnoit|re, *Am.* -er, scout.

Auskunft ['‿kunft] f (14[1]) information; (‿*schalter*) inquiry-office, *Am.* information desk; ‿ei [‿'tai] f (16) inquiry-agency, *Am.* information bureau; '‿s-pflicht f obligation to give information.

'auskuppeln ⊕ disconnect, uncouple; *mot.* declutch.

'auslachen laugh at, deride.

'ausladen v/t. unload, discharge; *Truppen, Passagiere*: disembark; *Gast*: put off; v/i. (sn) ⚓ project.

'Auslage f (*Geld*⚤) outlay; ‿n *pl.* expenses *pl.*; (*Waren*⚤) display; *Boxen, fenc.* guard; *die* ‿n *ansehen* go window-shopping.

'Ausland n foreign country *od.* countries *pl.*; *ins* ‿, *im* ‿ abroad.

Ausländ|er ['‿lɛndər] m, '‿erin f foreigner; *im Lande seßhafter, nicht naturalisierter*: alien; '⚤erfeindlich hostile to foreigners; '‿erfeindlichkeit f hostility to foreigners; '‿erhaß m xenophobia; '⚤isch foreign; ⚤, zo. exotic.

'Auslands... *mst* foreign; '‿-aufenthalt m stay abroad; '‿flug m international flight; '‿gespräch n *teleph.* international call; '‿reise f trip abroad; '‿verschuldung f foreign debts *pl.*

'auslass|en let out; *Wort usw.*: leave out, omit, skip; *Fett*: melt (down); *Kleid*: let out; *s-e Wut usw.*‿ *an (dat.)* vent ... on; *sich* ‿ express o.s. (*über acc.* about), *weitläufig*: enlarge (upon); '⚤ung f omission; (*Äußerung*) utterance.

'Auslauf m *für Tiere*: run; *Tennis*: margin; '⚤en (sn) run out; *Gefäß*: leak; ⚓ put to sea; (*enden*) (come to an) end; *sich* ‿ have a good run; *fig.* ‿ *lassen* taper off.

'Ausläufer m errand-boy; ⚘ runner; *pl. e-s Gebirges*: foothills *pl.*; *e-r Stadt*: outskirts *pl.*

'Auslaufmodell n phase-out model.

'Auslaut m terminal sound; *im* ‿ when final; '⚤en terminate, end (*auf acc.* in).

'ausleben (*sich*) live one's life fully.

'auslecken lick out, lick clean.

'ausleer|en empty, clear; ✂ evacuate; '⚤ung f emptying.

'auslegen lay out; (*zur Schau stellen*) display; (*deuten*) interpret, construe, read, explain; *Geld*: advance; (*entwerfen*) design; ⊕ line, cover; (*verzieren*) inlay; *falsch* ‿ misinterpret.

'Ausleger m (7), '‿in f expositor, expounder; ⊕ arm; *e-s Krans*: jib; ⚓ cantilever; '‿(boot n) m outrigger.

'Auslegeware f floor coverings *pl.*

'Auslegung f laying out; (*Deutung*) interpretation, construction.

'ausleihen lend (out), *bsd. Am.* loan; *sich et.* ‿ borrow.

'auslernen complete one's training; *man lernt nie aus* we live and learn.

'Auslese f (15) choice, selection; *fig.* pick, cream, élite; '⚤n a) (*sortieren*) pick out, select; b) *Buch*: finish.

'ausliefern deliver (up); *Gefangenen*: give up; *ausländischen Verbrecher*: extradite; *j-m ausgeliefert sein* be at the mercy of a p.

'Auslieferung f delivery; *von Verbrechern*: extradition; '‿shaft f custody pending extradition; '‿slager n supply depot; '‿sstelle f distribution cent|re, *Am.* -er; '‿svertrag m extradition treaty.

'ausliegen *Ware*: be displayed; *Zeitung*: be kept; (*zur Einsichtnahme*) ‿ be open to inspection.

'auslöffeln spoon out; *s.* Suppe.

'auslöschen *Licht*: put out; *Feuer*

u. fig.: extinguish; *Schrift*: efface; *(auswischen)* wipe out *(a. fig.)*.

'**auslos|en** draw lots for; *Staatspapiere*: draw; '**ꞁung** *f* draw.

'**auslös|en** loosen; *Gefangene*: redeem, ransom; *Pfand, Wechsel*: redeem; ⊕ release, *(betätigen)* a. actuate; *fig.* start, trigger; *Wirkung*: produce; *Beifall usw.*: arouse; '**ꞁer** *m* (7) release; *phot.* trigger; '**ꞁung** *f* redeeming, redemption; *(Trennungsgeld)* severance pay; *s.* **Auslöser.**

'**auslüften** air, ventilate.

'**ausmachen** *Feuer, Licht*: put out; ⚡ switch off; *Hülsenfrüchte*: husk, shell; *(betragen)* come to, amount to; *(bilden)* make up, constitute; *Streitsache*: settle; *(erkennen)* make out; *(vereinbaren)* agree upon, arrange; *es macht nichts aus* it does not matter; *würde es Ihnen etwas ꞁ, wenn ...?* would it make any difference to you if ...?; *wenn es Ihnen nichts ausmacht* if you don't mind; *s.* **ausgemacht.**

'**ausmalen** paint; *(illustrieren, bunt ꞁ)* illuminate; *sich et. ꞁ* picture a th. (to o.s.), visualize a th.

'**Ausmarsch** *m* departure; '**ꞁieren** (sn) march out.

'**Ausmaß** *n* dimension(s *pl.*), measurement(s *pl.*); *fig.* extent; *erschreckende ꞁe* alarming proportions; *in großem ꞁ* on a large scale, *fig.* to a great extent.

ausmergeln ['ꞁmɛrgəln] emaciate.

ausmerzen ['ꞁmɛrtsən] reject; *Fehler*: expunge; *(ausrotten)* eradicate.

'**ausmess|en** measure; *Grundstück*: survey; *Gefäß*: ga(u)ge; '**ꞁung** *f* measuring; survey; ga(u)ge.

'**ausmisten** ⚑ clear (of dung); F *fig.* clear up (the mess).

'**ausmustern** ⚔ discharge; *weitS.* discard, reject; *Maschine*: scrap.

Ausnahme ['ꞁnɑːmə] *f* (15) exception; *mit ꞁ von od. gen.* with the exception of; '**ꞁ... mst** exceptional; '**ꞁzustand** *m* (state of) emergency; ⚔ (state of) martial law.

'**ausnahms|los** without exception; '**ꞁweise** exceptionally, by way of exception; *(für diesmal)* for once.

'**ausnehmen** take out; *(ausschließen)* except, exempt; *(ausweiden)* disembowel, *Fisch*: gut, *Geflügel*: draw; *fig.* fleece; *sich gut ꞁ* look well;

'**ꞁd** *adv.* exceedingly.

'**Ausnüchterungszelle** *f* drying-out cell.

ausnutz|en ['ꞁnutsən] utilize; profit by; *Gelegenheit, b.s. j-n*: take advantage of, *a.* ⚒, ⚒ exploit; '**ꞁung** *f* utilization; exploitation.

'**auspacken** unpack; F *fig.* talk; *zornig*: speak one's mind.

'**auspeitschen** whip, scourge, flog.

'**auspfänd|en** *j-n*: distrain (up)on a p.('s goods); '**ꞁung** *f* distraint.

'**aus|pfeifen** boo; *thea.* hiss (off the stage); '**ꞁplaudern** blab (*od.* let) out; '**ꞁplündern** *s.* plündern; '**ꞁpolstern** stuff, pad; *(wattieren)* wad; '**ꞁposaunen** (25) trumpet (forth); noise abroad; **ꞁpowern** ['ꞁpoːvərn] impoverish; '**ꞁprägen** coin, stamp; *ausgeprägt fig.* marked; '**ꞁpressen** squeeze out; '**ꞁprobieren** try, test.

Auspuff ['ꞁpuf] *m* (3) *mot.* exhaust; '**ꞁgas** *n* exhaust gas; '**ꞁrohr** *n* exhaust pipe; '**ꞁtopf** *m* silencer, *Am.* muffler.

'**aus|pumpen** pump out; *Luft*: exhaust; '**ꞁpunkten** (26) *Boxen*: beat by points; '**ꞁputzen** *(reinigen)* clean; *(schmücken)* adorn; '**ꞁputzer** *m Fußball*: sweeper; '**ꞁquartieren** dislodge; ⚔ billet out; '**ꞁquetschen** squeeze out; F *fig.* grill; '**ꞁradieren** erase; '**ꞁrangieren** discard; *Schiff usw.*: scrap; '**ꞁrauben** rob; '**ꞁräuchern** fumigate; *Bienen usw., a.* ⚒: smoke out; '**ꞁraufen** tear out; *s. Haar*; '**ꞁräumen** *Zimmer usw.*: clear; *Möbel usw.*: remove.

'**ausrechn|en** calculate; *Am.* figure out; *s.* ausgerechnet; '**ꞁung** *f* calculation.

'**Ausrede** *f* excuse, pretext; evasion; '**ꞁn** *v/i.* finish speaking; *j-n ꞁ lassen* hear a p. out; *v/t. j-m et. ꞁ* dissuade a p. from a th., talk a p. out of a th.

'**ausreichen** suffice; *das reicht aus* that will do; '**ꞁd** sufficient; '**ꞁd** *n (Schulzensur)* satisfactory.

'**Ausreise** *f* departure, exit; ⚓ voyage out; '**ꞁerlaubnis** *f* exit permit.

'**ausreiß|en** *v/t.* pull (*od.* tear) out; *v/i.* (sn) *(fliehen)* run away, decamp, *a. Pferd*: bolt; '**ꞁer** *m* (7), '**ꞁerin** *f* runaway.

'**aus|reiten** (sn) ride out, go for a ride; **ꞁrenken** ['ꞁrɛŋkən] (25) dislocate; '**ꞁrichten** straighten; *(fluch-*

ten) align; ✂ dress; *Karte:* orient; *fig.* orientate, *pol. a.* streamline; *Botschaft:* deliver; *(bewirken)* do, effect; *(vollbringen)* accomplish; *(erlangen)* obtain; *Veranstaltung:* organize; *Benehmen usw.:* ~ *nach* adjust to; *Grüße von j-m* ~ present a p.'s compliments; **'~ringen** *Wäsche:* wring out; **'♀ritt** *m* ride; **'~roden** root out, stub up; **'~rollen 1.** *v/t. Teig:* roll out; *v/i.* ⚑ (sn) taxi to a standstill; **2.** ♀ ♂ *n* landing run.

'ausrott|en (26) *Pflanze, a. fig.:* root out; *fig.* eradicate, extirpate; *Volk:* exterminate; **'♀ung** *f* eradication, extermination.

'ausrücken *v/i.* (sn) march out; F *(weglaufen)* run away, bolt; *v/t.* ⊕ disengage.

'Ausruf *m* cry, outcry, *mit Worten:* exclamation; **'♀en** *v/i.* cry out, exclaim; *v/t.* proclaim.

'Ausrufung *f* proclamation; **'~s-wort** *gr. n* interjection; **'~szeichen** *n* exclamation-mark *(Am.* -point).

'ausruhen *v/i. (a. sich)* (take a) rest.

'ausrupfen pluck out.

'ausrüst|en equip; **'♀ung** *f* fitting out; *(Sport♀ usw.)* outfit, *(a.* ✂ *u.* ⊕) equipment; *des Soldaten:* kit; *(Zubehör)* accessories *pl.*

'ausrutschen *s. ausgleiten.*

'Aussaat *f* sowing; *konkret:* seed.

'aussäen sow; *fig.* spread, disseminate.

'Aussage *f* (15) statement *(a.* ⚖ *u. literarisch)*; *(Erklärung)* declaration; ⚖ *(Zeugnis)* testimony; *gr.* predicate; *e-e* ~ *machen s. aussagen;* **'~kraft** *f (Beweiskraft)* validity, strength; *(Ausdruckskraft)* expressiveness; **'♀n** state, declare; ⚖ testify, give evidence; *gr.* predicate; **'~satz** *m* affirmative proposition.

'Aussatz ♂ *m* (3², *o. pl.)* leprosy.

aussätzig ♂ ['~zetsiç] leprous; **♀e** ['~gə] *m, f* leper.

'aussaugen suck (out); *fig.* drain, exhaust; *j-n.:* bleed *a p.* white.

'Ausschabung ♂ *f* scrape.

ausschachten ['~ʃaxtən] (26) excavate; ⚒, *Brunnen:* sink.

'ausschalt|en *j-n od. et.:* eliminate; ⚡ break, cut out, *Licht, Gerät:* switch *(od.* turn) off; *Kupplung:* throw out; **'♀er** ⚡ *m* (7) cut-out, circuit-breaker; **'♀ung** *f* elimination.

'Ausschank *m* (3¹) retail; *(Schankstätte)* public house, F pub.

'Ausschau *f:* ~ *halten* be on the look-out *(nach* for); **'♀en** *nach j-m:* look out for; *s. aussehen.*

'ausscheid|en *v/t.* eliminate *(a.* ♈, ♌); *(wegtun)* discard; *physiol.* secrete; ♂ excrete; *v/i.* (sn) *aus e-m Amt usw.:* retire, *a. aus e-m Klub usw.:* withdraw (from); *Sport:* drop out, be eliminated; *fig. das scheidet aus* that's out (of the question); **'♀ung** *f (a. Sport)* elimination; *physiol.* secretion; ♂ excretion; **'♀ungskampf** *m Sport:* eliminating contest, tie; **'♀ungsspiel** *n Sport:* tie.

'aus|schelten scold, chide; **'~schenken** pour out; *als Schankwirt:* retail; **'~scheren** veer out; *fig.* step out of line; **'~schicken** send out.

'ausschiff|en *(a. sich)* disembark, debark; **'♀ung** *f* disembarkation.

'aus|schimpfen scold, upbraid; **'~schlachten** cut up; F ♂ salvage, *Auto usw.:* cannibalize; *(ausnutzen)* exploit; **'~schlafen** *v/i.* sleep one's fill; *v/t. Rausch usw.:* sleep off.

'Ausschlag *m* ♂ eruption, rash; *e-s Zeigers:* deflection; *des Pendels:* swing; *der Waage:* turn of the scale(s); *den* ~ *geben* turn the scale, settle it; **'♀en** *v/t.* beat out; knock out; *mit Tuch usw.:* line; *(ablehnen)* refuse, decline; *Erbschaft:* waive; *v/i.* (h., sn) ⚘ sprout, bud; *Bäume:* break into leaf; *(feucht werden)* grow moist; *Pferd:* kick; *Zeiger:* deflect; *Pendel:* swing; *Waage:* turn; *fig. (gut, schlecht)* turn out; **'♀gebend** decisive; *~e Stimme* casting vote.

'ausschließ|en shut *(od.* lock) out; *fig.* exclude; *v. e-r Schule, aus e-m Verein usw.:* expel; *Sport:* disqualify, *zeitweilig:* suspend; *sich* ~ exclude o.s. (von from); *s. ausgeschlossen;* **'~lich** exclusive; **'♀ung** *f,* **'Ausschluß** *m* exclusion; expulsion; disqualification, suspension; *unter* ~ *der Öffentlichkeit* in camera.

'aus|schlüpfen (sn) *aus dem Ei:* hatch; **'~schmelzen** melt out; *Erz:* fuse; **'~schmieren** *Fugen:* point.

'ausschmück|en adorn, decorate; *Erzählung:* embroider; **'♀ung** *f* adornment; *fig.* embellishment.

'**ausschnauben:** *sich die Nase* ~ blow one's nose.
'**ausschneiden** cut out; *tief ausgeschnitten Kleid*: low-necked.
'**Ausschnitt** *m* cut; (*Zeitungs*♀) cutting, *Am.* clipping; *am Kleid*: neck-line; (*Kreis*♀) sector; *fig.* section.
'**ausschöpfen** scoop; ladle out; *Boot*: bale out; *fig. Thema*: exhaust.
'**ausschreib|en** write out; *Brief usw.*: finish; *Heft*: fill; *Wort usw.*: write in full; *Zahl, Abkürzung*: expand; *Kurzschrift*: extend; *Rechnung*: make out; (*abschreiben*) copy; (*ankündigen*) announce; (*zs.-berufen*) convoke; *Steuern*: impose; *Stelle usw.*: advertise; *Wahlen* ~ issue the writs for elections; *e-n Wettbewerb*: invite entries for (*a competition*), ✝ invite tenders (for); *sich* ~ write o.s. out; '♀**ung** *f* convocation; announcement; advertisement; ✝ call for tenders; *Sport*: invitation to a competition.
'**ausschreit|en** (sn) step out; '♀**ung** *f* excess, outrage; ~**en** *pl.* riots *pl.*
'**Ausschuß** *m* refuse, waste; *s.* ~**ware**; ⚕ (~**wunde**) exit wound; (*Vertretung*) committee, board; '~**sitzung** *f* committee meeting; '~**ware** *f* rejects *pl.*
'**aus|schütten** pour (*od.* dump) out; (*verschütten*) spill; *Dividende*: distribute; (*j-m*) *sein Herz* ~ pour out one's heart (to a p.); *sich vor Lachen* ~ split one's sides with laughing; '~**schwärmen** (sn) swarm (out); ✕ ~ (*lassen*) extend, deploy; '~**schwatzen** blab out; '~**schweben** ⚡ *v/i.* (sn) flatten out.
'**ausschweif|end** *Phantasie*: extravagant; (*liederlich*) dissolute, licentious; '♀**ung** *f* extravagance; debauch, excess.
'**ausschweigen:** *sich* ~ be silent (*über acc.* on). [exudation.)
'**ausschwitz|en** exude; '♀**ung** *f*∫
'**aussehen 1.** *v/i.* look; *nach j-m* ~ look out for a p.; ~, *als ob* ... look as if ...; *bleich (gesund)* ~ look pale (well); *er sieht sehr gut aus* he is very good-looking; *sie sieht nicht übel aus* she is not bad-looking; *wie sieht er aus?* what does he look like?; *wie siehst du nur aus!* what a sight you are!; *es sieht nach Regen aus* it looks like rain; F *damit es nach et. aussieht* just for

looks; *es sieht schlimm mit ihm aus* he is in a bad way; **2.** ♀ *n* (6) appearance, look(s *pl.*); *j-n dem* ~ *nach kennen* know a p. by sight; *nach dem* ~ *urteilen* judge by appearances.
'**außen** ['aʊsən] out; (*außerhalb*) without, (on the) outside; (*im Freien*) out of doors; *von* ~ *her* from (the) outside; *nach* ~ (*hin*) outwards; '♀-**ansicht** *f* outside view; '♀-**anstrich** *m* façade; '♀-**aufnahme** *f* *Film*: outdoor shot; '♀**bezirk** *m* outlying district; ~**e** *pl. e-r Stadt* outskirts *pl.*; '♀**bordmotor** ⚓ *m* outboard motor.
'**aussenden** send out.
'**Außen|dienst** ✝ *m* external duty; '~**dienstmitarbeiter(in** *f*) *m* representative; '~**durchmesser** *m* outside diameter; '~**hafen** *m* outport; '~**handel** *m* foreign trade; ~**sbilanz** balance of trade; '~**minister** *m* Foreign Minister; *Brt.* Foreign Secretary; *Am.* Secretary of State; '~**ministerium** *n* Foreign Ministry; *Brt.* Foreign Office; *Am.* Department of State; '~**politik** *f* foreign policy; '♀-**politisch** (*od.* referring to, *adv.* with regard to) foreign policy; '~**rand** *m* outer margin; '~**seite** *f* outside, surface; '~**seiter** *m* (7) outsider; '~**spiegel** *m* outside mirror; ~**stände** ['~ʃtɛndə] *m/pl.* outstanding debts; '~**stelle** *f* branch office; '~**stürmer** *m* wing; '~**tasche** *f* outer pocket; '~**verteidiger** *m* outside defender; '~**welt** *f* outer (*od.* outside) world; '~**winkel** *m* external angle; '~**wirtschaft** *f* foreign trade.
außer ['aʊsər] **1.** *prp.* out of; (*neben, hinzukommend zu*) besides, apart from; in addition to; (*ausgenommen*) except; ~ *Zweifel* beyond all doubt; *alle* ~ *e-m* all but one; ~ *sich sein od. geraten* be *od.* get beside o.s. (*vor* with); **2.** *cj.* ~ *daß* except that, save that; ~ *wenn* unless; *s. Betrieb usw.*; '~**beruflich** private; '~**dem** besides.
äußere ['ɔysərə] **1.** *adj.* exterior, outer, external, outward; **2.** ♀ *n* outward appearance, exterior; *Minister des* ~*n s.* Außenminister.
'**außer|-ehelich** *Kind*: illegitimate; *Verkehr*: extramarital; '~**gerichtlich** extrajudicial; '~**gewöhnlich** exceptional, uncommon; *et.* ♀*es* something out of the ordinary; '~**halb** *prp.* out-

side; out of; (*jenseits*) beyond; *adv.*
(on the) outside; '**~-irdisch** extra-
terrestrial; '**~-irdische** *m*, *f* extra-
terrestrial being.

äußerlich ['ɔysərliç] external, outward; (*oberflächlich*) superficial;
(*schon*) rein ~ betrachtet on the face
of it; '**~keit** *f* superficiality; (*Formalität*) formality; '**~keiten** *pl.* ex-
ternals; formalities.

'**äußern** (29) utter, express, voice;
sich ~ *P.*: express o.s.; *S.*: manifest
(*od.* show) itself.

'**außer|-ordentlich** extraordinary;
~er Professor senior lecturer, *Am.*
associate professor; '**~parlamen-
tarisch** *adj.* extra-parliamentary
(*opposition*); '**~planmäßig** extra-
ordinary; *Beamte*: supernumerary;
Budget: extra-budgetary.

äußerst ['ɔysərst] outermost; *fig.*
utmost, extreme; *adv.* extremely,
exceedingly; *sein* ~es tun do one's
utmost; *auf das* ~e *gefaßt* prepared
for the worst; *bis zum* ~en *gehen*
go to extremes, *Am.* go the limit;
zum ~en *entschlossen* desperate;
zum ~en *treiben* drive to extremes.

außerstande ['~'ʃtandə] unable.

Äußerung ['ɔysərun] *f* (16) utterance, declaration, remark; *fig.*
manifestation.

aussetz|en ['auszetsən] *v/t.* set (*od.*
put) out; *Boot*: lower; (*an Land
setzen*) put ashore; *Belohnung*: offer; *Rente*: settle (*j-m* on a p.);
(*vermachen*) bequeath; (*aufschieben*)
defer; *Tätigkeit usw.*: interrupt,
stop; *Zahlung*, *Urteil*: suspend;
Verfahren: stay; *Kind*: expose;
dem Wetter, e-r Gefahr usw.: expose
to; *et.* ~ *an* (*dat.*) find fault with,
object to; *was ist daran auszusetzen?* what's wrong with it?; *v/i.*
intermit, (*versagen*) fail; *Motor*:
stall, misfire; ~ *mit et.* interrupt;
(*sich Ruhe gönnen*) take a rest; ~
müssen im Spiel: lose a turn; '**~en** *n*
(6) intermission, interruption; failure; misfiring; '**~ung** *f* offer; settlement; bequest; stay; suspension;
exposure; disembarkation; (*Tadel*)
objection, criticism.

'**Aussicht** *f* view (*auf acc.* of); *fig.*
prospect, outlook; *nicht die geringste* ~ not the slightest chance;
das Zimmer hat ~ *nach Süden* ...
looks towards the south; *in* ~ *haben*

have in prospect; *in* ~ *nehmen* consider, plan; *et. in* ~ *stellen* hold out
a prospect of, promise; '**~slos**
hopeless; '**~s-punkt** *m* vantage
point; '**~sreich**, '**~svoll** promising;
'**~s-turm** *m* look-out tower, *Am.*
observatory.

'**aussieben** sift out; *fig.* screen.

'**aussied|eln** evacuate; '**~ler(in** *f*)
m evacuee; '**~lung** *f* compulsory
transfer, evacuation.

'**aussinnen** *s.* ausdenken.

aussöhn|en ['~zøːnən] (25) recon-
cile (*sich* o.s.) (*mit* to, with); '**~ung**
f reconciliation.

'**aussondern** (*auswählen*) single out;
(*trennen*) separate; *s.* ausscheiden.

'**ausspähen** *v/t.* spy out; *v/i.* look
out (*nach* for); ✕ scout.

'**ausspann|en** *v/t.* stretch; extend;
Zugtier: unharness; ⊕ *Werkstück*:
unclamp; *v/i. fig.* relax, (take a)
rest; '**~ung** *f fig.* relaxation.

'**ausspeien** spit out; *fig.* vomit.

'**aussperr|en** *j-n*: shut out, *a. Ar-
beiter*: lock out; *typ.* space out;
'**~ung** *f* lock-out.

'**ausspielen** *v/t. Karte*: lead; *Preis*:
play for; *gegeneinander* ~ play off
against each other; *v/i.* finish playing; *wer spielt aus?* whose lead is
it?; *ausgespielt haben fig.* be done
for.

'**ausspionieren** spy out.

'**Aussprache** *f* pronunciation; accent; (*Erörterung*) discussion; talk;
'**~bezeichnung** *f* phonetic transcription.

'**aussprechen** pronounce (*a.* 👄),
deutlich: articulate; (*ausdrücken*)
express; *gr. nicht ausgesprochen
werden* be silent *od.* mute; *sich* ~
speak (out) one's mind (*über acc.*
about), (*sein Herz ausschütten*) unburden o.s.; (*sich erklären*) declare
o.s. (*für* for, *gegen* against); *sich
mit j-m über et.* ~ talk a th. over
with a p.; *v/i.* finish (speaking);
s. ausgesprochen.

'**aus|sprengen** *Gerücht*: spread; '**~-
spritzen** squirt out; 🦻 *Ohr*: syringe; '**~spruch** *m* utterance, saying, remark; '**~spülen** rinse; '**~-
spüren** track down, trace.

'**ausstaffier|en** (25) fit out; (*schmük-
ken*) dress up, rig out; '**~ung** *f* outfit, equipment; trimming.

'**Ausstand** *m* (*Arbeitseinstellung*)

strike, *Am. a.* walkout; *Ausstände pl.*
outstanding debts; *in den ~ treten*
go on strike, *Am. a.* walk out.
'**ausständig** outstanding; *Arbeiter*:
striking, on strike; '♀e *m* striker.
'**ausstanzen** ⊕ punch out.
ausstatten ['~ʃtatən] (26) fit out,
equip; provide, supply (*mit* with);
Buch usw.: get up; (*möblieren*)
furnish; *mit Befugnissen*: vest;
Tochter: portion (off); *fig.* (*begaben*)
endow.
'**Ausstattung** *f* (16) outfit, equipment; supply; get-up; *s. Aussteuer*; furniture, appointments *pl.*;
⊕ fittings *pl.*; *thea.* setting, décor
(*fr.*); '~**sstück** *n thea.* spectacular
show; (*Gegenstand*) fitment.
'**ausstechen** *Torf usw., fig. Rivalen*:
cut out; *Auge*: put out; *Apfel*: core;
fig. outdo.
'**ausstehen** *v/i.* be overdue; have not
yet come; (*noch ~*) *Geld*: be owing;
~de Schulden f/pl. outstanding
debts; *v/t.* (*ertragen*) endure, bear,
stand (*a th. or p.*).
'**aussteigen** (sn) get out (*aus* of; *a.*
F *fig.*); alight (from); ⏚, ✈ disembark; F ⛵ bale (*bsd. Am.* bail) out.
'**Aussteiger** F *m* (7) drop-out.
'**ausstell|en** *zur Schau*: exhibit, dis-
play; *Wache*: post; *Quittung usw.*:
give, issue; *Wechsel*: draw (*auf j-n*
on, upon); *Rechnung, Scheck, Urkunde*: make out; '♀er *m* (7), '♀erin *f*
(16¹) exhibitor; issuer; drawer; '♀-
fenster *mot. n* quarterlight.
'**Ausstellung** *f* exhibition, show, *Am.
a.* exposition; drawing; issue; '~**s-
datum** *n* date of issue; '~**sgelände** *n*
exhibition grounds *pl.*; '~**sraum** *m*
show-room; '~**sstück** *n* exhibit.
'**ausstempeln** clock out.
'**aussterben** (sn) die out; *ausgestorben*
extinct; *Straße usw.*: deserted.
'**Aussteuer** *f* (*Geld*) dowry; (*Wäsche
usw.*) trousseau; '♀n portion (off);
Radio: modulate; *s. ausstatten.*
'**Ausstieg** *m* (3) exit.
'**ausstopfe|n** stuff; '♀r *m* taxider-
mist.
'**Ausstoß** *m* ✝ output; ⊕ ejection.
'**ausstoß|en** thrust out, eject; (*aus-
schließen*) expel (*aus* from); (*ausscheiden*) eliminate; *gr.* elide; *Verwünschung, Schrei*: utter; *Seufzer*:
heave; *phys.* emit, give off; '♀ung *f*
expulsion; elimination; utterance.

'**ausstrahl|en** *v/i.* (sn) *u. v/t.* radiate
(*a. fig.*); *Radio*: broadcast; '♀ung *f*
radiation; *fig. e-r P.*: aura, personal
magnetism; '♀**ungskraft** *f* charisma.
'**ausstrecken** stretch (out).
'**ausstreichen** strike (*od.* cross) out;
(*glätten*) smooth down.
'**ausstreuen** scatter; *Gerücht*: spread.
'**ausström|en** *v/t.* pour forth; *Gas
usw.*: emit; *phys.* emanate (*a. fig.*);
v/i. (sn) stream forth; *phys.* emanate; *Gas, Dampf*: escape; '♀ung *f*
emanation; escape.
'**ausstudieren** finish one's studies.
'**aussuchen** choose, select.
'**Austausch** *m* exchange; interchange; *v. Gütern*: a. barter; *im ~
gegen* in exchange for; '♀**bar** ex-
changeable; interchangeable; '♀**en**
exchange (*gegen* for); (*unter-ea.*)
interchange; *Güter*: a. barter; '~**
motor** *m* replacement engine; '~**
schüler(in** *f*) *m*, '~**student(in** *f*) *m*
exchange student.
'**austeil|en** distribute, hand out; *Be-
fehle*: issue, give; *Hiebe*: deal out;
(*spenden*) dispense; '♀ung *f* distribution.
Auster ['austər] *f* (15) oyster; '~**n-
bank** *f* oyster-bed; '~**nfischerei** *f*
oyster-dredging; '~**ngabel** *f* oyster
fork; '~**nschale** *f* oyster-shell; '~**n-
zucht** *f* oyster-culture.
'**austilg|en** (25) exterminate; '♀ung
f extermination.
'**austoben** *v/i.* cease raging; *v/t. s-e
Wut*: give vent to; *v/refl. Jugend*:
sow one's wild oats; *weit S.* let off
steam; *Sturm*: spend itself.
Austrag ['~tra:k] *m* (3³) (*Entscheidung*) decision; ♀**en** ['~gən] carry
out; *Briefe usw.*: deliver; *Klatsch
usw.*: retail; *Streit*: settle; *Wettkampf*: hold; *Buchungsposten*: cancel.
'**Austräger(in** *f*) *m* carrier, *Am.*
roundsman; *b.s. fig.* telltale.
'**Austragung** *f Sport*: holding; '~**s-
ort** *m* venue.
Austral|ier [au'stra:ljər] *m*, ♀**isch**
Australian.
austreib|en ['austraibən] drive out;
(*vertreiben*) expel; *Teufel*: exorcize;
fig. j-m et. ~ cure a p. of a th.;
'♀**ung** *f* expulsion; exorcism.
'**aus|treten** *v/t.* tread out; *Schuh,
Treppe*: wear out; *s. ausgetreten*;
v/i. (sn) come forth; (*überfließen*)

overflow; (*sich abmelden*) retire (*aus* from); *aus e-r Partei, Schule usw.*: leave; (*ein Bedürfnis verrichten*) F spend a penny; '⁔**tricksen** (27) F outwit; '⁔**trinken** drink up; (*leeren*) empty; '⁔**tritt** *m* retirement, withdrawal, leaving; '⁔**tritts-erklärung** *f* resignation; '⁔**trocknen** *v/t.* dry up (*a. v/i.*, sn); *Holz*: season; *Kehle, Land*: parch; '⁔**trommeln** publish by beat of drum; *fig.* noise abroad; '⁔**trompeten** *s. ausposaunen*; '⁔**tüfteln** puzzle out.

'**aus-üb|en** *Aufsicht, Macht, Recht usw.*: exercise; *Beruf*: practise; *Druck, Einfluß usw.*: exert; *Gewerbe*: carry on; *Verbrechen*: commit; '⁔**end** practising; *Gewalt*: executive; '⁔**ung** *f* exercise; practise.

'**Ausverkauf** *m* selling off, clearance (*od.* bargain) sale; *fig.* sellout; '⁔**en** sell out; *um den Rest zu räumen*: sell off, clear out (stock); '⁔**t** ✝, *thea.* sold out.

'**auswachsen** *v/i.* (sn) grow up; *v/t. Kleid*: outgrow; *sich* ⁔ grow up; *sich* ⁔ *zu* grow (*od.* develop) into; F *zum* ⁔ awful.

'**Auswahl** *f* choice, selection; ✝ assortment, collection, range; *Hunderte von Büchern zur* ⁔ hundreds of books to choose from.

'**auswählen** choose, select.

'**Auswahl|mannschaft** *f Sport*: select team; '⁔**sendung** ✝ *f* samples *pl.* (sent for selection).

'**Auswander|er** *m* (7), '⁔**in** *f* (16¹) emigrant; '⁔**n** emigrate; '⁔**ung** *f* emigration.

auswärt|ig ['⁔vertiç] (*aus der Provinz*) out-of-town; (*nicht ansässig*) non-resident; (*ausländisch, fremd*) foreign; *das* ⁔e *Amt s.* Außenministerium; ⁔e *Angelegenheiten pl.* foreign affairs; ⁔**s** ['⁔verts] outward(s); (*außer dem Hause*) not at home, away; (*außer der Stadt*) out of town; (*im Ausland*) abroad; ⁔ *essen usw.*: dine *etc.* out; '⁔**sspiel** *n Sport*: away match.

'**auswaschen** wash out; *geol.* erode.

'**auswechsel|bar** interchangeable, exchangeable; '⁔**n** exchange, interchange; *Rad, Batterie usw.*: change; (*ersetzen*) replace; '⁔**spieler** *m Sport*: substitute; '⁔**ung** *f* exchange, interchange; replacement.

'**Ausweg** *m* way out (*a. fig.*); exit;

outlet; *fig.* expedient; *letzter* ⁔ last resort; '⁔**los** hopeless.

ausweichen (sn; *dat.*) make way (for); *e-m Schlag, Wagen usw., a. fig.* avoid, dodge; *fig.* elude, evade, avoid; ⁔ *auf* switch over to; '⁔**d** evasive.

'**Ausweich|gleis** 🚋 *n* siding; '⁔**möglichkeit** *f fig.* alternative.

'**ausweiden** disembowel, eviscerate.

'**ausweinen** *v/i.* cease weeping; *v/t. sich* ⁔ have a good cry; *sich die Augen* ⁔ cry one's eyes out.

Ausweis ['⁔vais] *m* (4) (*Beleg*) voucher; (*Bank*⁔, *Rechnungs*⁔) statement; (*Personal*⁔) identity card; '⁔**en** turn out, expel; *aus Besitz*: evict; (*verbannen*) banish; *lästige Ausländer*: deport; (*zeigen*) show, prove; *j-n als USA-Bürger usw.* ⁔ identify a p. as; *sich* ⁔ prove one's identity; *sich* ⁔ *über* (*acc.*) give an account of; '⁔**karte** *f* identity card; (*Zulassungskarte*) (admission) ticket; '⁔**kontrolle** *f* identity check; '⁔**ung** *f* expulsion; eviction; deportation; '⁔**ungsbefehl** *m* deportation order.

'**ausweiten** (*a. sich* ⁔) widen, stretch; expand (*a. fig.*); *fig.* spread.

'**auswendig** outward, outside; *fig.* by heart, *mechanisch*: by rote.

'**auswerfen** throw out; *Anker*: cast; 🩺 expectorate; ⊕, *Lava usw.*: eject; *Summe*: allow, grant.

'**auswert|en** *Daten*: evaluate; (*ausnützen*) make full use of, *a.* ✝ exploit; *Karte, Luftbild*: interpret; '⁔**ung** *f* evaluation; utilization; exploitation; interpretation.

'**aus|wickeln** unwrap; '⁔**wiegen** weigh out; '⁔**winden** wring out; '⁔**wirken** *v/t. fig.* effect, obtain; *sich* ⁔ take effect, operate; *sich* ⁔ *auf* (*acc.*) affect; '⁔**wirkung** *f* effect; '⁔**wischen** wipe out; *sich die Augen* ⁔ wipe one's eyes; F *j-m eins* ⁔ F put one over on a p.; '⁔**wringen** *Wäsche*: wring out; '⁔**wuchs** *m* (4²) outgrowth (*a. der Phantasie*); (*a. fig.*) excrescence; (*Höcker*) protuberance; (*Mißstand*) abuse; '⁔**wurf** *m* 🩺 expectoration; sputum; *v. Lava usw.*: eruption; *fig.* dregs *pl.*, scum.

'**auszacken** jag; ⊕ indent, tooth.

'**auszahlen** pay (out); *j-n*: pay off; *bar* ⁔ pay in cash; *sich* ⁔ *fig.* pay.

'auszählen *parl. u. Boxen*: count out.

'Auszahlung *f* payment.

'auszanken scold.

'auszehr|en *v/t.* consume; *v/i.* (sn) waste away; '♀ung *f* consumption.

'auszeichn|en mark; *mit Orden*: decorate; *fig.* distinguish (*sich o.s.*); '♀ung *f* marking; distinction; hono(u)r; (*Orden*) decoration; *mit ∼ bestehen* take first-class hono(u)rs.

'auszieh|bar extensible, telescopic; '∼en *v/t. Kleid*: take off; (*herausziehen*) draw out, (a. ℞, ⚕ *u. aus Büchern*) extract; *Rechnung*: make out; *Zeichnung*: trace; *Farbe*: fade (*a. v/i.*); *j-n, a. sich*: undress; *v/i.* (sn) set out; (*aus e-r Wohnung*) (re-)move (from); *Farbe*: fade; '♀leiter *f* extension ladder; '♀platte *f e-s Tisches*: leaf; '♀tisch *m* pull-out table; '♀tusche *f* drawing ink.

'auszischen *thea.* hiss (at).

'Auszubildende *m, f* trainee.

'Auszug *m* departure; *biblisch u. fig.*: exodus; *aus e-m Buch, a.* ⚕: extract; (*Abriß*) epitome; (*Hauptinhalt*) summary; *einzelne Stellen*: excerpt; *aus e-r Rechnung*: abstract; (*Konto♀*) statement (of account); *aus e-r Wohnung*: removal; '♀sweise by (way of) extract, in extracts.   [unravel.]

'auszupfen pluck out; pick; *Fäden*:

autark [au'tark] self-supporting, (economically) self-sufficient.

Autarkie [autar'ki:] *f* (15) autarky, self-sufficiency.

authentisch [au'tentiʃ] authentic (-ally *adv.*).

Auto ['auto] *n* (11) (motor-)car, *Am. a.* auto(mobile); *∼ fahren* drive (a car); *sich im ∼ mitnehmen lassen* hitch-hike; '∼-abstellplatz *m*: *überdachter ∼* carport; '∼-apotheke *f* first-aid kit; '∼-atlas road atlas; '∼-ausstellung *f* motor-show; '∼bahn *f* motorway, *Am.* superhighway; '∼bahn-abschnitt *m* section; '∼bahn-auffahrt *f* entrance; '∼bahn-ausfahrt *f* exit; '∼bahnbe'nützungsgebühr *f* toll; '∼bahndreieck *n* motorway junction; '∼bahnkreuz *n* intersection; ∼biogra'phie *f* autobiography; ∼bus ['∼bus] *m* (4¹) (motor) bus, autobus, motor coach; ∼didakt [∼di'dakt] *m* self-educated person; '∼dieb *m* car thief; '∼fähre *f* car ferry;

'∼fahrer *m* (7) motorist, (car-)driver; '∼falle *f* police-trap; '∼friedhof *m* car dump; ♀gen ⊕ [∼'ge:n] autogenous; ∼'gramm *n* autograph; ∼'grammjäger *m* autograph hunter; '∼hof *m* motor-court, *Am.* auto court; '∼karte *f* road map; '∼kino *n* drive-in cinema; ∼krat [∼'kra:t] *m* (12) autocrat; ∼kratie [∼kra'ti:] *f* (15) autocracy; ∼mat [∼'ma:t] *m* (12) automaton; ⊕ automatic machine, robot; ⚡ slot-machine; *s. Musik♀*; ∼'matenrestaurant *n* self-service restaurant, *Am.* automat; ∼matik [∼'ma:tik] *f* (16) automatism; ⊕ automatic; *mot.* automatic transmission; ∼'matikgurt *m* inertia reel seat belt; ∼mation ⊕ [∼ma'tsjo:n] *f* (16) automation; ♀matisch [∼'ma:tiʃ] automatic(ally); ♀matisieren [∼mati'zi:rən] automatize; ∼matisierung [∼mati'zi:ruŋ] *f* automation; ∼mo'bil [∼mo'bi:l] *n* (3¹) *s. Auto*; ∼mo'bil-industrie *f* car (*Am.* auto) industry; ♀nom [∼'no:m] autonomous; ∼nomie [∼no'mi:] *f* (15) autonomy; '∼nummer *f* registration number.

Autor ['autɔr] *m* (8¹), ∼in [∼'to:rin] *f* (16¹) author, writer.

'Autoreisezug *m* motorail train.

autor|isieren [∼tori'zi:rən] authorize; ∼itär [∼i'tε:r] authoritarian; ♀ität [∼i'tε:t] *f* authority; ∼itativ [∼ita'ti:f] authoritative.

'Auto|schalter ⚡ *m* drive-in counter; '∼schlosser *m* car-mechanic; '∼skooter *m* (7) dodgem; '∼straße *f* motor-road, *Am.* highway; ∼suggesti'on *f* auto-suggestion; '∼telephon *n* car telephone; '∼unfall *m* car accident; '∼verleih *m*, '∼vermietung *f* car-hiring service, rent-a-car (service); '∼veteran *m* veteran-car; '∼wäsche *f* car wash.

avantgardistisch [avãgar'distiʃ] avant-garde.

Avers [a'vεrs] *m* obverse.

Avis [a'vi:] *m* (4) advice.

avisieren [avi'zi:rən] advise.

Axt [akst] *f* (14¹) axe, *Am.* ax.

Azalee ⚘ [atsa'le:ə] *f* (15) azalea.

Azetatseide [atse'ta:t-] *f* acetate (*od.* cellulose) silk.

Azeton [atse'to:n] *n* (9, *o. pl.*) acetone.

Azetylen ⚕ [atsety'le:n] *n* (3¹) acetylene.

Azur [a'tsu:r] *m*, ♀(e)n azure.

B

B, b [be:] B, b; ♪ B flat; *B-Dur* B flat major; *b-Moll* B flat minor.

Baby ['be:bi] *n* (11) baby; '**~ausstattung** *f* layette; '**~bad** *n* baby bath oil; '**~hös-chen** *n* (*pl.*) baby pants; '**~nahrung** *f* baby food; '**~öl** *n* baby oil; '**~schuhe** *m/pl.* bootees; '**~sitter** *m* (7) baby-sitter; '**~speck** *m* F puppy fat; '**~sprache** *f* baby-talk; '**~tragetasche** *f* carrycot.

Bacchant [ba'xant] *m* (12), **~in** *f* bacchant(e *f*); **isch** bacchanal.

Bach [bax] *m* (3³) brook.

'**Bachstelze** *zo. f* (water) wagtail.

back ⚓ [bak] 1. aback; 2. *f* forecastle; (*Schüssel*) bowl; (*gemeinsamer Tisch*) mess; '**blech** *n* baking-tin; '**bord** ⚓ *n* port.

Backe ['bakə] *f* (15) cheek; ⊕ **~n** *pl.* *e-s Schraubstocks*: jaws; (*Schneid*) die; *am Schi*: toe-piece.

backen ['bakən] (30) *v/t. u. v/i.* bake; *in der Pfanne*: fry; *Obst*: dry; *Schnee usw.*: cake, stick.

Backen|bart *m* sideburns *pl.*; '**~knochen** *m* cheek-bone; '**~tasche** *f* cheek-pouch; '**~zahn** *m* molar (tooth), grinder.

Bäcker ['bɛkər] *m* (7) baker; **~ei** [~'raɪ] *f* (16) bakery; '**~laden** *m* bakery, baker's (shop); '**~meister** *m* master baker.

'**Back|fett** *n* shortening; '**~fisch** *m* fried fish; *fig.* † teenage girl; '**~huhn** *n* fried chicken; '**~obst** *n* dried fruit; '**~ofen** *m* (baking) oven; '**~pfeife** *f* box on the ear; '**~pflaume** *f* prune; '**~pulver** *n* baking-powder; '**~stein** *m* brick; '**~trog** *m* kneading-trough; '**~waren** *f/pl.* bread and cakes; '**~werk** *n* pastries *pl.*

Bad [ba:t] *n* (1²) bath; *im Freien*: bathe; *s. a. Badeanstalt, Badeort, Badezimmer.*

Bade|anstalt ['ba:dəʔanʃtalt] *f* public baths *pl.*; '**~anzug** *m* bathing-costume (*od.* -suit); '**~gast** *m* visitor (at a watering-place); '**~hose** *f* (*eine* **~** a pair of) bathing-trunks *pl.* (*od.* -shorts *pl.*); '**~kappe** *f* bathing-cap; '**~kur** *f* bathing-cure; '**~mantel** *m* bathing-gown, *bsd. Am.* bathrobe; '**~matte** *f* bath-mat; '**~meister** *m* bath attendant; *Schwimmbad*: swimming instructor; **n** (26) *v/t.* Kind, Kranke: bath; *v/i. im Freien*: bathe;

in der Wanne: take (*od.* have) a bath; '**~nde** *m, f* bather; '**~ofen** *m* bath-heater; (*Gas*) geyser, *Am.* hot-water heater; '**~ort** *m* watering-place; *mit Heilquellen*: spa; '**~salz** *n* bath-salts *pl.*; '**~schuhe** *m/pl.* bathing shoes; '**~strand** *m* bathing-beach; '**~tuch** *n* bath-towel; '**~wanne** *f* bath, (bath-)tub; '**~zeug** *n* swimming things *pl.*; '**~zimmer** *n* bathroom; '**~zimmerschrank** *m* bathroom cabinet.

Bagage [ba'ga:ʒə] *f* (15) ✕ baggage; *fig. contp.* rabble, lot.

Bagatell|e [baga'tɛlə] *f* (15) trifle, bagatelle; i'**sieren** play down.

Bagger ['bagər] *m* (7), '**~maschine** *f* dredge(r), excavator; '**~eimer** *m* bucket; '**~löffel** *m* shovel; '**n** (29) *v/i. u. v/t.* dredge.

Bahn [ba:n] *f* (16) course; (*Pfad*) path, road; *Sport*: course, track; *ast.* orbit; *fig.* (*Laufbahn*) career; *Tuch usw.*: breadth, width; (*Flug*) trajectory; (*Eisen*) railway, *bsd. Am.* railroad, (*Strecke*) line; *mot.* (*Fahr*) lane (*a. Sport: des Läufers usw.*); *mit der* **~** by train; *j-n zur* **~** bringen see a p. off; *zur* **~** *gehen* go to the station; '**~arbeiter** *m* railwayman, *Am.* railroader; '**~beamte** *m* railway official; **brechend** pioneer(ing), epoch-making; '**~brecher** *m* pioneer; '**~damm** *m* railway embankment; **en** (25) *e-n Weg*: open (up), beat; *fig.* pave *the way* (*dat.* for); *sich einen Weg* **~** force one's way; '**~fahrt** *f* train-journey; '**~fracht** ✝ *f* rail carriage (*Am.* freight); '**~gleis** *n* track; '**~hof** *m* (railway) station; '**~hofsmission** *f* travel(l)er's aid; '**~hofsvorsteher** *m* station-master, *Am.* station agent; '**~körper** *m* permanent way; **lagernd** to be collected from the station; '**~linie** *f* railway line; '**~polizei** *f* railway police; '**~steig** *m* platform; '**~steigkarte** *f* platform ticket; '**~strecke** *f* line, *bsd. Am.* track; '**~übergang** *m* level (*Am.* grade) crossing; '**~verbindung** *f* train connection; '**~wärter** *m* linesman (*Schrankenwärter*) gatekeeper.

Bahre ['ba:rə] *f* (15) barrow; (*Kranken*) stretcher; (*Toten*) bier.

Baiser [beˈzeː] n (11) meringue.

Baisse ✝ [ˈbɛːs(ə)] f (15) slump (in prices); *auf* ~ *spekulieren* (sell) bear, *Am.* sell short; '~**spekulation** f bear speculation; '~**stimmung** f downward tendency.

Bajonett ✕ [bajoˈnɛt] n (3) bayonet; ~**verschluß** ⊕ m bayonet catch.

Bake ⚓ [ˈbɑːkə] f (15) beacon.

Bakterie [bakˈteːrjə] f (15) bacterium (*pl.* -ia), germ; ~**nbombe** f bacteria bomb; ~**nkrieg** m germ warfare.

Bakteriologe [~terjoˈloːgə] m (13) bacteriologist.

Balance [baˈlɑ̃ːsə, baˈlaŋsə] f (15) balance, equilibrium; ~**-akt** m *fig.* balancing act.

balancier|en [~ˈsiːrən] v/t. u. v/i. balance; Ꝯ**stange** f balancing-pole.

bald [balt] soon; (*in Kürze*) shortly; (*beinahe*) almost, nearly; *so* ~ *als möglich s. baldigst*; ~ ..., ~ ... now..., now...   [opy.]

Baldachin [ˈbaldaxiːn] m (3¹) can-⌉

baldig [ˈbaldiç] early, speedy; '~**st** as soon as possible.

Baldrian [ˈbaldriːn] m (3¹) valerian.

Balg [balk] m (3³) skin; F (*Kind*) [*pl. Bälger*] brat, urchin; [*pl. Bälge*] (*OrgelꝮ*) bellows *pl.*; *phot.* (*mst* ~**en** [ˈ~gən] m) bellows *pl.*; Ꝯ**en** [ˈ~gən] (25): *sich* ~ scuffle, scramble, tussle (*um* for); *Kinder*: romp; ~**erei** [~gə-ˈraɪ] f scuffle, scramble (*um* for); romp.

Balken [ˈbalkən] m (6) beam.

Balkon [balˈkõ, ~ˈkoːn] m (11; 3¹) balcony; *thea.* dress-circle, *Am.* balcony; ~**tür** f French window.

Ball m (3³) **1.** ball; **2.** ball, dance; *auf dem* ~ at the ball.

Ballade [baˈlɑːdə] f (15) ballad.

Ballast [ˈbalast] m (3²) ballast; ~**stoffe** m/pl. roughage *sg.*

ballen¹ [ˈbalən] (25) (*a. sich*) (form into a) ball; *Faust*: clench; Ꝯ² m (6) bale; *anat.* ball; ꝲ (*entzündeter Fuß-*Ꝯ) bunion; '~**weise** by the bale.

Ballermann [ˈbalər-] m *sl.* shooter.

ballern [ˈbalərn] (29) bang; *j-m e-e* ~ F clout a p. one.

Ballett [baˈlɛt] n (3) ballet; ~**tänzer** (**-in** *f*) m ballet-dancer.

'**ball|förmig** ball-shaped; 'Ꝯ**junge** m ball-boy; 'Ꝯ**kleid** n ball-dress.

Ballon [baˈlõ, ~ˈloːn] m (11; 3¹) balloon; (*große Flasche*) carboy;

~**sperre** f balloon barrage.

'**Ball|saal** m ball-room; '~**spiel** n ball-game.

'**Ballung** f concentration; (*Überfüllung*) overcrowding, congestion; '~**sgebiet** n overcrowded region.

Balsam [ˈbalzaːm] m (3¹) balsam, (*a. fig.*) balm; Ꝯ**ieren** [~zaˈmiːrən] embalm; Ꝯ**isch** [~ˈzɑːmiʃ] balmy.

baltisch [ˈbaltiʃ] Baltic.

balzen [ˈbaltsən] (27) mate, pair; (*den Balzruf ausstoßen*) call.

Bambus [ˈbambus] m (*inv. od.* 4¹), '~**rohr** n bamboo (cane).

banal [baˈnɑːl] commonplace, banal; Ꝯ**ität** [~naliˈtɛːt] f banality.

Banane [baˈnɑːnə] f (15) banana; ~**nstecker** ꝲ m banana plug.

Banause [baˈnaʊzə] m (13) Philistine, low-brow.

Band [bant] **1.** m (3³) volume; *dicker*: tome; (*Einband*) binding; **2.** n (1²) band; (*FarbꝮ, SchmuckꝮ*) ribbon; (*IsolierꝮ, MeßꝮ, TonꝮ, ZielꝮ*) tape; ⊕ (*FörderꝮ*) (conveyor) belt; (*MontageꝮ*) assembly line; *anat.* ligament; *am laufenden* ~ on the assembly line, *fig.* continuously; **3.** n (*pl.* '~**e**) *fig.* tie, bond; **4.** Ꝯ *pret. v.* **binden.**

Bandag|e [banˈdɑːʒə] f (15) bandage; Ꝯ**ieren** [~daˈʒiːrən] bandage.

'**Band|-aufnahme** f tape recording; '~**breite** f ꝲ band-width; *fig.* spread.

Bande [ˈbandə] f (15) *Billard*: cushion; *fig.* gang (*a. contp.*); '~**n-krieg** m guerilla war(fare).

Band-eisen [ˈbant-] n band iron.

Banderole [~dəˈroːlə] f (15) *Steuerwesen*: revenue stamp; (*Klebeband*) adhesive tape.

Bänder|riß [ˈbɛndəris] m torn ligament; ~**zerrung** [ˈ~tsɛruŋ] f pulled ligament.

bändig|en [ˈbɛndigən] (25) tame; *fig. a.* subdue, restrain, master; 'Ꝯ**ung** f taming.

Bandit [banˈdiːt] m (12) bandit.

'**Band|maß** n tape-measure; '~**säge** f band-saw; '~**scheibe** *anat.* f (intervertebral) disc; '~**scheibenschaden** ꝲ m damaged disc; '~**wurm** m tapeworm; '~**zählwerk** n tape counter.

bang, ~**e** [baŋə] anxious (*um* about); *mir ist* ~ I am afraid (*vor dat.* of); *j-m* ~ *machen* make a p. afraid, frighten a p.; *keine Bange!*

don't worry!; **2emacher** ['~-maxər] *m* alarmist; '**~en** (25) be afraid (*vor dat.* of); *sich ~ um* be anxious (*od.* worried) about; '**2igkeit** *f* (16, *o. pl.*) anxiety, fear.

Bank [baŋk] *f* **1.** (14¹) bench; *Schule*: form; *auf die lange ~ schieben* put off; F *durch die ~* without exception, down the line; **2.** (16) ✝ bank; '**~aktie** *f* bank share (*Am.* stock); '**~anweisung** *f* cheque, *Am.* check; '**~ausweis** *m* bank return (*Am.* statement); '**~beamte** *m* bank clerk; '**~direktor** *m* bank manager; '**~diskont** *m* bank discount; (*~satz*) bank-rate.

Bänkelsänger ['beŋkəlzeŋər] *m* ballad-singer.

bank(e)rott [baŋk(ə)'rɔt] **1.** bankrupt; *~ werden* go (*od.* become) bankrupt; **2.** 2 *m* (3) bankruptcy (*a. fig.*), failure, F crash; *~ machen* go (*od.* become) bankrupt; **2-erklärung** *f* declaration of bankrupty; *fig.* sell-out; **2eur** [~rɔ'tøːr] *m* (3¹) bankrupt.

Bankett [baŋ'kɛt] *n* (3) banquet.

'**bankfähig** bankable, negotiable.

'**Bank|gebühren** *f/pl.* banking charges; '**~geheimnis** *n* banker's discretion; '**~geschäft** *n* banking transaction; (*Bankwesen*) banking (business), banking trade; '**~guthaben** *n* bank balance; '**~halter** *m* banker; '**~haus** *n* bank(ing-house).

Bankier [~'je:] *m* (11) banker.

'**Bank|kaufmann** *m* bank clerk; '**~konto** *n* banking-account, *Am.* bank account; '**~leitzahl** *f* bank code number; '**~note** *f* bank-note, *Am.* bill; '**~räuber** *m* bank robber; '**~überfall** *m* bank raid (*od.* holdup); '**~wechsel** *m* bank-bill, draft; '**~wesen** *n* banking.

Bann [ban] *m* (3) ban; *fig.* spell; *eccl.* excommunication; *in den ~ tun* put under the ban, *eccl.* excommunicate; '**2en** (25) banish (*a. fig. Sorgen usw.*); *Gefahr*: avert; (*fesseln*) spellbind; (*festhalten*) *auf Bild, Papier usw.*: capture, record; *gebannt* spellbound.

Banner ['banər] *n* (7) standard, banner (*a. fig.*); '**~träger** *m* standard-bearer.

'**Bann|fluch** *m* anathema; '**~meile** *f* boundary.

bar¹ [baːr] *e-r S. ~* destitute (*od.* devoid) of; *~es Geld* ready money,

cash; *~er Unsinn* sheer nonsense; *~ bezahlen* pay cash (down); *gegen ~* for cash; *s. Münze.*

Bar² [~] *f* (11¹) (*Ausschank*) bar.

Bär [beːr] *m* (12) bear; *der Große ~* the Great(er) Bear; *der Kleine ~* the Little (*od.* Lesser) Bear; *fig.* j-m *e-n ~en aufbinden* hoax a p.

Baracke [ba'rakə] *f* (15) (wooden) hut, barrack.

Barbar [bar'baːr] *m* (12), **~in** *f* (16¹) barbarian; **~ei** [~ba'raɪ] *f* (16) barbarism; (*Grausamkeit*) barbarity; **2isch** [~'baːriʃ] barbarian; *contp.* barbarous; *fig.* barbaric.

'**Bar|bestand** *m* cash in hand; '**~betrag** *m* amount in cash.

Barbier [bar'biːr] *m* (3¹) barber; **2en** (25) shave; F *fig.* j-n *über den Löffel ~* do a p. in the eye.

'**Bar|dame** *f* barmaid; '**~einnahme** *f* cash receipts *pl.*

'**Bären|dienst** *m*: j-m *e-n ~ leisten* do a p. a disservice; '**~führer** *m* bear-leader (*a. fig.*); '**~hunger** F *m* ravenous hunger; *e-n ~ haben* be ravenous, be starving.

Barett [ba'rɛt] *n* (3) cap, beret.

bar|fuß ['baːrfuːs] bare-foot(ed); **~füßig** ['~fyːsiç] bare-footed.

barg [bark] *pret. v.* bergen.

'**Bar|geld** *n* cash, ready money; '**2geldlos** cashless; **2häuptig** ['~-hɔyptiç] bare-headed.

Bärin ['beːrin] *f* (16¹) she-bear.

Bariton ['baːritɔn] *m* (3¹) baritone.

Barkasse ⚓ [bar'kasə] *f* (15) launch.

'**Barkauf** *m* cash purchase.

Barke ⚓ ['barkə] *f* (15) barque.

'**Barkredit** *m* cash loan.

barmherzig [barm'hɛrtsiç] merciful, charitable; *der ~e Samariter* the good Samaritan; *~e Schwester* sister of charity; **2keit** *f* mercy, charity.

'**Barmittel** *n/pl.* cash (funds *pl.*).

'**Barmixer** *m* cocktail waiter, barman.

barock [ba'rɔk] **1.** baroque; *fig.* grotesque, odd; **2.** 2 *n* Baroque.

Barometer [baro'me:tər] *n* (7) barometer (*a. fig.*); '**~säule** *f* barometric column; '**~stand** *m* barometer reading.

Baron [ba'roːn] *m* (3¹) baron; **~in** *f* (16¹) baroness.

Barre ['barə] *f* (15) bar; '**~n** *m* (6)

metall. billet; (*Gold*♀, *Silber*♀) bullion, ingot; *Turnen*: parallel bars *pl.*; '~ngold *n* gold bullion.

Barriere [bar'jɛːrə] *f* (15) barrier.

Barrikade [bari'kɑːdə] *f* (15) barricade.

Barsch[1] [barʃ] *m* (3²) perch.

barsch[2] [~] gruff, brusque.

Bar|schaft ['bɑːrʃaft] *f* (16) ready money, cash; '~scheck ✝ *m* uncrossed cheque (*Am.* check).

'**Barschheit** *f* gruffness.

barst [barst] *pret. v.* bersten.

Bart [bɑːrt] *m* (3³) beard; (*Schlüssel*♀) bit; *fig.* j-m um den ~ gehen cajole a p.; *sich* e-n ~ wachsen (*od.* stehen) *lassen* grow a beard.

bärtig ['bɛːrtiç] bearded.

'**bartlos** beardless.

'**Bar|verkauf** *m* cash sale; '~verlust *m* clear loss; '~zahlung *f* cash payment; *gegen* ~ cash down.

Basar [ba'zɑːr] *m* (3¹) (*a. Wohltätigkeits*♀) bazaar.

Base ['bɑːzə] *f* (15) **1.** (female) cousin; **2.** 🜨 base.

basieren [ba'ziːrən] *v/t.* base, found (*auf dat.* upon); *v/i.* ~ *auf* (*dat.*) be based upon.

Basilikum ⚕ [ba'ziːlikum] *n* (11, 9) basil.

Bas|is ['bɑːzis] *f* (16²) base, *mst fig.* basis; '♀isch basic.

'**Basislager** *mount. n* base camp.

Baskenmütze ['baskən-] *f* beret.

Baß [bas] *m* (4²) bass; '~geige *f* bass viol; *große*: contrabass; '~gitarre *f* bass guitar.

Bassin [ba'sɛ̃] *n* (11) basin; reservoir; (*Schwimm*♀) swimming-pool.

Bassist [~'sist] *m* (12) bass(-singer).

'**Baß|schlüssel** ♪ *m* bass clef; '~stimme *f* bass voice.

Bast [bast] *m* (3²) bast.

basta [~'basta]: *und damit* ~! so that's that!, so there!

Bastard ['bastart] *m* (3) bastard; *zo.*, ⚕ hybrid. [wark.]

Bastei [ba'staɪ] *f* (16) bastion, bul-⌡

bast|eln ['bastəln] (29) tinker (*an dat.* at); (*bauen*) rig up; '♀ler *m* (7) amateur constructor, hobbyist, home-mechanic.

'**Bastseide** *f* raw silk.

bat [bɑːt] *pret. v. bitten.*

Bataillon [batal'joːn] *n*(3¹) battalion.

Batik ['bɑːtik] *f* (16) batik.

Batist [ba'tist] *m* (3³) batiste,

48*

cambric.

Batterie [batə'riː] *f*(15) battery; ♀betrieben battery-operated; ~lader *mot. m* (7) battery charger.

Bau [baʊ] *m* (3; *pl. a.* '~ten) (*Bauen*) building, construction (*a.* ⊕); (*Gebäude*) building, edifice; structure (*a. Gefüge*); (*o. pl.*) ✔ cultivation; (*Körper*♀) build, frame; (*pl.* '~e) (*Tier*♀) burrow, (*a. fig.*) den, earth; *im* ~ (*begriffen*) being built, under construction; '~amt *n* Surveyor's Office; '~arbeiten *f|pl.* construction work *sg.*; *an Straßen*: roadworks; '~arbeiter *m* construction worker; '~art *f* structure; build; ⊕ construction, design, (*Typ*) type, model; △ (style of) architecture; '~beginn *m* start of building.

Bauch [baʊx] *m* (3³) belly (*a. fig.*); *anat.* abdomen; '~fell *n* peritoneum; '~fell-entzündung *f* peritonitis; '♀ig bulgy; ...-bellied; '~klatscher ['~klatʃər] *m* (7) belly-flop; '~landung *f* belly-landing; '~muskel *m* abdominal muscle; '~nabel *m* navel, F belly button; '♀reden ventriloquize; '~redner *m* ventriloquist; '~redne'rei *f* ventriloquism; '~schmerzen *m|pl.*, '~weh *n* stomach-ache; '~speicheldrüse *f* pancreas; '~tanz *m* belly dance.

'**Bau|denkmal** *n* historical monument; '~element *n Fertigbau*: construction element.

bauen ['baʊən] (25) *v/t.* build; construct; ✔ cultivate, grow; *Hoffnung usw.*: base (*auf acc.* on); *v/i.* ~ *auf* (*acc.*) rely (*od.* build) on.

Bauer ['baʊər] **1.** *n* (7) cage; **2.** *m* (7) builder; **3.** *m* (10 *od.* 13) ✔ farmer, peasant; *fig.* boor; *Schach*: pawn; *Karten*: knave.

Bäuerin ['bɔʏərin] *f* (16¹) countrywoman; *engS.* farmer's wife.

'**bäu(e)risch** *contp.* boorish.

'**Bau-erlaubnis** *f* building permit.

'**bäuerlich** rural, rustic.

'**Bauern|bursche** *m* country lad; '~fänger *m* (7) sharper, confidence man; '~fängerei *f* confidence trick (*Am.* game); '~frau *f s. Bäuerin*; '~gut *n* farm; '~haus *n* farm-house; '~hof *m* farm; '~regel *f* weather maxim; '~schaft *f*, '~stand *m* peasantry.

'**Bau|-erwartungsland** *n* development area; '~fach *n* architecture;

building trade; '⌐**fällig** out of repair, dilapidated, tumble-down; '⌐**fällig-keit** f dilapidation, state of decay; '⌐**firma** f, '⌐**geschäft** n builders and contractors pl.; '⌐**gelände** n building land; '⌐**genehmigung** f planning and building permission; '⌐**gerüst** n scaffolding; '⌐**gewerbe** n building trade; '⌐**grube** f excavation; '⌐**handwerker** m craftsman in the building trade; '⌐**herr** m building owner; '⌐**holz** n timber, Am. lumber; '⌐**ingenieur** m constructional engineer; '⌐**jahr** n year of construction; Auto: model; '⌐**kasten** m box of bricks; (Stabil⌐) construction set; '⌐**kastensystem** n unit construction system; '⌐**kunst** f architecture; '⌐**land** n building land; '⌐**lich** architectural; in gutem ⌐em Zustand in good repair.

Baum [baʊm] m (3³) tree; (Hebe⌐, Weber⌐ usw.) beam; ⚓ boom; '⌐**bestand** m stand (of timber-trees).

'**Baumeister** m architect; master-builder.

baumeln ['baʊməln] (29) dangle, swing (an dat. from); mit den Beinen ⌐ swing one's legs.

bäumen ['bɔʏmən] v/refl. (25) rear, prance; P. vor Schmerzen: writhe (with).

'**Baum|grenze** f timber-line; '⌐**lang** (as) tall as a lamp-post; '⌐**schere** f (eine a pair of) pruning--shears pl.; '⌐**schule** f tree-nursery; '⌐**stamm** m trunk; '⌐**stark** (as) strong as an ox; '⌐**sterben** n (6) death of trees; '⌐**wolle** f cotton; '⌐**wollen** (made of) cotton; '⌐**wollsamt** m velveteen.

'**Bau|plan** m architect's plan; ⊕ blueprint; '⌐**platz** m (building) site (od. plot).

Bausch [baʊʃ] m (3² u. 3³) pad, bolster; Watte: wad; in ⌐ und Bogen in the lump; '⌐**en** (27) swell out (a. sich), puff; bag; '⌐**ig** puffy, swelled; baggy.

'**Bau|schlosser** m building fitter, locksmith; '⌐**schule** f school of architecture; '⌐**sparkasse** f building society, Am. building and loan association; '⌐**sparvertrag** m building society savings agreement; '⌐**stein** m building-stone, a. für Kinder: brick; '⌐**stelle** f (building) site; '⌐**stil** m (architectural) style;

'⌐**stoff** m building material; '⌐**stopp** m building freeze; e-n ⌐ verhängen impose a halt on building; '⌐**techniker** m constructional engineer; '⌐**teil** n structural member, component part; '⌐**ten** m/pl. buildings pl., structures pl.; thea. setting sg., Film: a. architecture; öffentliche ⌐ public works; '⌐-**unternehmer** m building contractor; '⌐**vorhaben** n building project; '⌐**weise** f method of construction; '⌐**werk** n edifice, building; '⌐**wesen** n s. Baufach; '⌐**zeichnung** f construction drawing.

Bayer ['baɪər] m (13), '⌐**in** f (16¹), '**bay(e)risch** Bavarian.

Bazill|enträger [ba'tsiləntrɛːgər] m carrier; ⌐**us** [⌐'tsilus] m (16²) bacillus (pl. -cilli), germ.

beabsichtigen [bə'ʔapziçtigən] (25) intend, mean, propose (zu tun to do, doing).

be'-acht|en (26) note, pay attention to; j-n: notice; (berücksichtigen) consider; Vorschrift usw.: observe; nicht ⌐ ignore; ⌐**enswert** noteworthy, remarkable; ⌐**lich** noticeable, considerable; ⌐**ung** f notice, attention; consideration; observance.

Beamt|e [bə'ʔamtə] m (18), ⌐**in** f (16¹) official; höherer: functionary, officer; (Staats⌐) civil (Am. public) servant; ⌐**enschaft** f civil servants pl.

be'-ängstig|en make anxious, alarm; ⌐**ung** f anxiety, uneasiness.

beanspruch|en [⌐'ʔanʃpruxən] (25) claim; Mühe, Platz, Zeit: require, take; ⊕ stress; ⌐**ung** f claim (gen. to); demand (on); ⊕ stress, strain.

beanstand|en [⌐'ʔanʃtandən] (26) object to; Wahl: contest; ✝ complain of; ⌐**ung** f objection (gen. to); complaint.

beantragen [⌐'ʔantraːgən] (25) apply for (bei j-m to); (vorschlagen) propose; parl., ⚖ move.

be'-antwort|en answer; ⌐**ung** f answer(ing); in ⌐ (gen.) in reply to.

be'-arbeit|en work; maschinell: a. machine, tool; ✎ cultivate; thea. usw. adapt (nach from), bsd. ♪ arrange; Thema: treat; Buch: revise; Antrag usw.: act upon, deal with, handle; j-n ⌐ work on, a. mit Schlägen: belabo(u)r; ⌐**ung** f working; cultivation; adaptation, bsd. ♪ arrangement; treatment; revision; handling; **₂ungsgebühr** f handling charge.

be'-argwöhnen be suspicious of.

Be'-atmung f: künstliche ∼ artificial respiration.

beaufsichtig|en [∼¹ⁿaʊfziçtigən] (25) supervise, superintend; control; Kind: look after; **₂ung** f supervision; control.

beauftrag|en [∼¹ⁿaʊftraːgən] commission, charge; (berufen) appoint; **₂te** [∼traːktə] m, f (18) commissioner; authorized representative, agent, deputy.

be'bau|en build on; ✓ cultivate; **₂ungs-plan** m development scheme.

beben ['beːbən] 1. (25) shake, tremble; (schaudern) shiver; Erde: quake (alle: vor dat. with); 2. ₂ n (6) (Erd₂) earthquake.

be|bildern [bə'bildərn] (29) illustrate; ∼**brillt** [∼'brilt] spectacled.

Becher ['bɛçər] m (7) cup; ohne Fuß: tumbler, mug.

Becken ['bɛkən] n (6) basin, Am. a. bowl; ♪ cymbal(s pl.); anat. pelvis; '∼**knochen** m/pl. pelvic bones.

Bedacht [∼'daxt] 1. m (3, o. pl.) consideration, care; mit ∼ deliberately; ∼ nehmen auf (acc.) take a th. into consideration; 2. ₂: ∼ auf (acc.) intent on; darauf ∼ sein, zu inf. be careful to inf.

bedächtig [∼'dɛçtiç], **bedachtsam** [∼'daxtzaːm] (überlegt) deliberate; (vorsichtig) careful; (langsam) slow; **₂keit** f deliberateness.

Be'dachung f roofing.

be'danken sich ∼ (bei j-m; für et.) thank (a p.; for a th.); ablehnend: dafür bedanke ich mich! thank you for nothing!

Bedarf [bə'darf] m (3) need, want (an dat. of); ♥ demand (for); requirements pl.; (Verbrauch) consumption; bei ∼ if required; nach ∼ as required; ∼ haben an (dat.) be in need (od. want) of; s-n ∼ decken cover one's requirements; ∼**s-artikel** m (essential) commodity, pl. a. supplies pl., requisites pl.; ∼**sfall** m: im ∼ if required; ∼**shalte-stelle** f request stop.

bedauerlich [∼'daʊərliç] regrettable, deplorable; ∼**erweise** unfortunately.

be'dauern (29) 1. j-n: be sorry for,

pity; et.: regret, deplore; ich bedaure sehr, daß ... I am very sorry for ger. od. that ...; 2. ₂ n (6) regret (über acc. for); (Mitleid) pity (mit for); ∼**swert** pitiable.

be'deck|en cover; ∼t Himmel: overcast; **₂ung** f covering; bsd. ⚔ escort; bsd. ⚓ convoy.

be'denken 1. consider; (beachten) (bear in) mind; im Testament: remember; j-n mit et. ∼ endow a p. with a th.; sich ∼ deliberate; sich anders ∼ change one's mind; 2. ₂ n (6) (Erwägung) consideration; (Einwand) objection; (Zaudern) hesitation; (Zweifel) doubt, scruple; ∼ haben hesitate; kein ∼ tragen zu tun make no scruple to do; ∼**los** adj. unscrupulous; adv. without hesitation.

be'denklich doubtful; stärker: critical, serious; (heikel) delicate; Lage usw.: a. precarious; P.: doubtful; thoughtful; **₂keit** f doubtfulness; critical state; precariousness.

Be'denkzeit f time for reflection.

be'deuten mean, signify; stand for; (in sich schließen) imply, involve; (vorbedeuten) (fore)bode; j-m (od. j-n) ∼ zu inf. give a p. a sign to inf., intimate a p. to inf.; es hat nichts zu ∼ it is of no consequence; ∼**d** important; Person: a. eminent; (beträchtlich) considerable.

be'deutsam significant; **₂keit** f significance.

Be'deutung f meaning, signification; (Wichtigkeit) importance; **₂s-los** insignificant; (ohne Sinn) meaningless; **₂svoll** significant.

be'dien|en v/t. serve, wait on; ♥ attend to; Maschine usw.: work, attend, operate; sich ∼ bei Tisch: help o.s.; sich e-r S. ∼ make use of; v/i. bei Tisch: wait (at table); Karten: follow suit, nicht ∼ revoke; **₂stete** m, f (18) employé(e f) m (fr.), employee; **₂te** m (18) (man-) servant.

Be'dienung f service, ♥ a. attendance; ⊕ working, operation; (Dienerschaft) servants pl.; (Kellner[in]) waiter (f waitress); (Bedienungsgeld) service charge; ∼**s-anleitung** f directions pl. for use, operating instructions pl.; ∼**sknopf** m control knob; ∼**skomfort** m easy operation.

beding|en [bə'diŋən] stipulate; (in

sich schließen) imply; (*erfordern*) require; (*bewirken*) cause; ‿t conditional (*durch* on); ‿ *sein durch* be conditioned by.

Be'dingung f condition; *pl.* ‿en ✝, ⚖ terms *pl.*; *unter der* ‿, *daß* on condition that; *es zur* ‿ *machen, daß* make it a condition that; *unter keiner* ‿ on no account; ⚹slos unconditional.

be'dräng|en press hard; *fig. a.* afflict, beset; *bedrängte Lage* distress; ⚹nis [‿'drɛŋnis] f (14²) distress, trouble, plight.

be'droh|en threaten, menace; ‿lich threatening; ⚹ung f threat, menace (*gen.* to).

be'drucken print (on).

be'drück|en oppress; *seelisch*: depress; ⚹er(*in* f) m oppressor; ⚹ung f oppression; depression.

be'dürfen (*gen.*) need, want, require.

Be'dürfnis n (4¹) need, want; necessity, requirement; (*s*)*ein* ‿ *verrichten* relieve nature; ‿anstalt f (public) lavatory; ⚹los frugal.

be'dürftig needy, indigent; *e-r Sache*: in need of; ⚹keit f indigence, neediness.

Beefsteak ['biːfsteˑ(ː)k] n (11) (beef-)steak; *deutsches* ‿ s. Frikadelle.

be'-ehren hono(u)r; ✝ *mit Aufträgen usw.*: favo(u)r; *ich beehre mich zu ...* I have the hono(u)r to ...

beeid|(ig)en [bə'ʔaɪd(ig)ən] (26 [25]) *et.*: affirm by oath, swear to; *j-n*: swear in; ‿igt, ‿et sworn; ⚹igung f confirmation by oath.

be'-eilen: *sich* ‿ hurry, make haste; *beeil dich!* hurry up!

beeindrucken [‿'ʔaɪndrukən] v/t. impress.

beeinfluss|en [‿'ʔaɪnflusən] (28) influence; *nachteilig*: affect; ⚹ung f influence (*gen.* on).

beeinträchtig|en [‿'ʔaɪntrɛçtigən] (25) impair, affect (adversely); *Ruf, Schönheit usw.*: detract from; *Recht, Wert*: prejudice; (*behindern*) hamper; ⚹ung f impairment (*gen.* of); prejudice (to); detraction (from).

be'-end(ig)|en (bring to an) end, finish, conclude, terminate; ⚹ung f termination, close.

beengen [‿'ʔɛŋən] (25) cramp, narrow; *fig. a.* confine.

be'-erben *j-n*: be a p.'s heir.

beerdigen [‿'ʔeˑrdigən] (25) bury.

Be'-erdigung f burial, interment; ‿s-**institut** n undertaker's, funeral directors *pl.*; ‿s**kosten** *pl.* funeral expenses.

Beere ['beːrə] f (15) berry.

Beet [beːt] n (3) bed.

befähig|en [bə'fɛːigən] (25) enable (*to do*); qualify (*für, zu* for); ‿t able; ⚹ung f qualification; (*Fähigkeit*) ability; ⚹ungsnachweis m certificate of qualification.

befahr|bar [‿'faːrbaːr] *Weg*: practicable, negotiable; *Wasser*: navigable; ‿en travel on, pass over; *Fluß, Meer*: navigate, ply; *eine stark* ‿e *Straße* a much frequented road.

be'fallen (30) befall, attack; *Krankheit*: strike; ‿ *werden von Krankheit, Furcht* be seized with; *von Insekten usw.*: be infested by.

be'fangen embarrassed; (*schüchtern*) shy, self-conscious; (*voreingenommen*) prejudiced, bias(s)ed (*a.* ⚖); *in e-m Irrtum* ‿ *sein* be mistaken; ⚹heit f embarrassment; shyness, self-consciousness; prejudice.

be'fassen touch, handle; *sich* ‿ *mit* occupy o.s. with; *a. S.*: deal with.

befehden [‿'feːdən] (26) make war upon, (*a. fig.*) fight against.

Befehl [bə'feːl] m (3) order (*a.* ⚖); (*a. Ober*⚹) command; *auf* ‿ (*gen.*) by order (of); ⚹en (30) order, command; *wie Sie* ‿ as you wish; ⚹igen [‿'feːligən] (25) command.

Be'fehls|form *gr.* f imperative (mood); ⚹gemäß as ordered; ‿**haber** m (7) commander(-in-chief); ⚹haberisch imperious, dictatorial.

befestig|en [‿'fɛstigən] fasten, fix, attach (*an dat.* to); ⚓, *fig.* fortify; *fig.* strengthen; *sich* ‿ ✝ *Preise*: stiffen, harden; ⚹ung f fastening; ⚓ fortification; strengthening.

befeuchten [‿'fɔʏçtən] (26) moisten, damp; *stärker*: wet.

be'find|en 1. find, deem; *sich* ‿ be; *gesundheitlich*: be, feel; **2.** ⚹ n (6) (state of) health; (*Meinung*) opinion; ‿lich [‿'fint-] being; ‿ *in* (*dat.*) (contained) in.

be'flaggen flag.

beflecken [‿'flekən] (25) spot, stain; (*besudeln*) pollute; *nur fig.* sully, tarnish, defile.

befleißigen [‿'flaɪsigən] (25): *sich e-r S.* ‿ apply o.s. to; take pains to *inf.*, be studious to *inf.*

beflissen [ˌ'flisən] (*gen.*) studious (of); **2heit** *f* studiousness, assiduity.
beflügeln [ˌ'fly:gəln] (29) wing (*a. fig.*); *fig.* lend wings to.
befohlen [ˌ'fo:lən] *p. p. v.* befehlen.
be'folg|en follow, obey, observe; comply with; **2ung** *f* observance (of), compliance (with).
be'förder|n convey; carry; transport, *bsd. Am.* ship; (*spedieren*) *Güter*: forward; *im Amt od. Rang*: promote (*zum Major usw.* [to be] major *etc.*), *a.* prefer (*zu* to); (*fördern*) further, promote; **2ung** *f* conveyance; transport(ation); forwarding; shipment; preferment, promotion; furtherance; **2ungsmittel** *n* (means of) transport(ation *Am.*).
befrachten [ˌ'fraxtən] (26) load; ⚓ freight, charter.
be'fragen question, interrogate; interview; *um Rat*: consult.
be'frei|en (25) free; deliver; liberate (*alle*: von from); (*von e-r Verpflichtung* ˌ release (*od.* exempt) from; **2er(in** *f*) [ˌ'fraiər(in)] *m* liberator; **2ung** *f* liberation, deliverance; release, exemption; **2ungsfront** *f* liberation front; **2ungskrieg** *m* war of liberation; **2ungsversuch** *m* escape attempt.
befremd|en [ˌ'frɛmdən] (26) **1.** surprise, astonish, shock; **2.** 2 *n* (6) surprise; **˜lich** [ˌ'frɛmtliç] strange.
befreunde|n [bəˈfrɔyndən] (26): *sich* ˜ become friends; *sich* ˜ *mit* make friends with; *fig.* reconcile o.s. to; **˜t** friendly; ˜ *sein* be on friendly terms, be friends.
befried|en [ˌ'fri:dən] (26) pacify; **2ung** *f* pacification.
be'friedig|en [ˌdigən] (25) satisfy; *Erwartungen, Nachfrage*: meet; *schwer zu* ˜ hard to please; **˜end** satisfactory; **2ung** *f* satisfaction.
befrist|en [ˌ'fristən] limit (in time), set a time-limit on, *Am. a.* deadline; **2ung** *f* (setting a) time-limit.
be'frucht|en (26) fecundate, fertilize, fructify (*alle a. fig.*); (*schwängern*) impregnate; *e-e Blüte*: pollinate; **2ung** *f* fecundation; fertilization; impregnation; ⚕ *künstliche* ˜ artificial insemination.
Befug|nis [ˌ'fu:knis] (14²) *f* authority, power, *bsd.* ⚖ competence; **˜se** *pl.* powers *pl.*; **2t** authorized, em-

powered, *bsd.* ⚖ competent.
be'fühlen feel, touch, handle.
Be'fund *m* (3) state (*gen.* of *a th.*); *bsd.* ⚖ *u.* ⚕ finding(s *pl.*).
be'fürcht|en fear, apprehend; **2ung** *f* fear, apprehension.
befürwort|en [ˌ'fy:rvɔrtən] (26) plead for, advocate; (*anraten*) recommend; *Antrag*: support; **2er(in** *f*) *m* advocate, supporter; **2ung** *f* recommendation; support.
begab|en [ˌ'ga:bən] (25): ˜ *mit* endow with; **˜t** [ˌpt] gifted, talented; **2ung** [ˌbuŋ] *f* aptitude; talent(s *pl.*), endowment(s *pl.*).
begann [ˌ'gan] *pret. v.* beginnen[1].
begatt|en [ˌ'gatən] (26) couple *od.* copulate with; **2ung** *f* copulation.
begaunern [ˌ'gaunərn] (29) cheat, swindle, *Am. sl.* gyp.
be'geben (30) *Wechsel*: negotiate; *sich* ˜ *nach* go to, betake o.s. to; *zu j-m*: join a p.; *sich* ˜ (*sich ereignen*) happen, occur; *sich e-r S.* ˜ give up, renounce, ⚖ waive; *sich zur Ruhe* ˜ go to rest; *sich auf die Flucht* ˜ take to flight; *sich auf die Reise* ˜ set out (on one's journey); *sich in Gefahr* ˜ expose o.s. to danger; **2heit** *f* event, occurrence.
begegn|en [ˌ'ge:gnən] (26, sn) (*dat.*) (*treffen*) meet (*a p.*; *zufällig*: with); *dem Feind, Schwierigkeiten*: encounter; (*widerfahren*) happen (to); (*vorbeugen*) prevent; obviate; *e-m Wunsch, der Nachfrage usw.*: meet; *j-m freundlich* (*grob*) ˜ treat a p. kindly (rudely); **2ung** *f* meeting; *feindlich*: encounter.
begeh|bar [ˌ'ge:ba:r] *Weg*: passable; **˜en** (30) walk (on); *besichtigend*: inspect; *Fehler, Verbrechen*: commit; *Fest*: celebrate.
Begehr [bəˈge:r] *m, n* (3) desire; **2en** (25) desire, crave for; (*fordern*) demand; ✝ (*sehr*) *begehrt* in (great) demand; **2enswert** desirable; **2lich** covetous, greedy; **˜lichkeit** *f* covetousness, greed(iness).
Be'gehung *f vgl.* begehen: inspection; celebration; commission.
begeister|n [ˌ'gaistərn] (29) inspire, fill with enthusiasm, enthuse, thrill; *sich* ˜ *für* be(come) enthusiastic about; **˜t** enthusiastic(ally *adv.*); **2ung** *f* enthusiasm.
Begier *f*, **˜de** [bəˈgi:r(də)] *f* (16, 15)

desire, appetite, craving (*nach* for);
2**ig** [~'giːriç] eager (*nach* for; to *do*),
desirous (of; to *do*); (*habgierig*) covetous (of); ~ *zu erfahren* anxious to
know.

be'gießen water, sprinkle; *Braten*:
baste; F (*feiern*) wet, celebrate.

Beginn [bə'gin] *m* (3) beginning;
(*Ursprung*) origin; 2**en** *v/t. u. v/i.*
(30) begin, *förmlich*: commence;
(*tun*) do; (*den Anfang machen*) lead
off; ~**en** *n* (6) beginning; (*Unternehmen*) enterprise, undertaking.

beglaubig|en [~'glaubigən] (25)
attest, certify, authenticate; *j-n*:
accredit (*bei* to); ~**t** [~biçt] certified; 2**ung** *f* certification, authen-
tication; 2**ungsschreiben** *n* cre-
dentials *pl.*

be'gleich|en balance; *Rechnung*:
pay, settle; 2**ung** *f* settlement.

Begleit|adresse [bə'glaɪtʔadresə] *f*
declaration form, *Am.* pass-bill;
~**brief** *m* covering letter; 2**en** (26)
accompany (*a. ♩*); (*höflich od. zum
Schutz, a. ✗* escort; *j-n* heim-,
hinaus-, *zur Bahn usw.* ~ see a p.
home, out, off *etc.*; ~**er(in** *f*) *m*
companion, attendant; ♩ accom-
panist; ~**erscheinung** *f* accom-
paniment, concomitant; ~**-instru-
ment** *n* accompanying instrument;
~**musik** *f* incidental music; ~**schein**
✝ *m* way-bill; (*Zollfreischein*) pass-
-bill, permit; ~**schiff** *n* escort vessel;
~**schreiben** *n* covering letter; ~**umstand** *m* attendant circumstance,
concomitant; ~**ung** *f* company; (*Gefolge*) attendants *pl.*; retinue; ♩ ac-
companiment; *bsd.* ✗ escort.

be'glück|en make happy; bless; ~**
wünschen** (27) congratulate (*zu* on);
2**wünschung** *f* congratulation.

begnadet [~'gnaːdət] inspired, highly gifted; ~ *mit* blessed with.

begnadig|en [~'gnaːdigən] (25) par-
don; *pol.* amnesty; 2**ung** *f* pardon;
amnesty; 2**ungsgesuch** *n* plea for a
reprieve (*od.* pardon).

begnügen [~'gnyːgən]: (25) *sich* ~
content o.s. (*mit* with), be satisfied
(with).

begonnen [~'gɔnən] *p.p. v.* beginnen.

be'graben bury (*a. fig.*), inter.

Begräbnis [~'grɛːpnis] *n* (4[1]) burial;
(*Leichenbegängnis*) funeral, *feier-
liches*: obsequies *pl.*

begradigen [~'graːdigən] (*a.* ✗ *die*

Front) straighten; align.

be'greifen (*verstehen*) comprehend,
understand, grasp; *in sich* ~ comprise, include; *s.* begriffen.

be'greiflich understandable, conceivable; *j-m et.* ~ *machen* make a
p. understand a th.; ~**er'weise**
logically, naturally.

be'grenz|en bound, form the
boundary of; *fig.* limit (*auf acc.* to);
2**theit** *f* limitation; *fig.* narrowness;
2**ung** *f* bounds *pl.*; limitation; ⊕
stop; 2**ungsstreifen** *mot. m* white
line.

Be'griff *m* (3) idea, notion; (*Vorstellung*) conception; (*Ausdruck*)
term; *sich e-n* ~ *machen von* get (*od.*
form) an idea of; *das geht über
meine* ~**e** that's beyond me; *du
machst dir keinen* ~! you have no
idea!; *im* ~ *sein zu inf.* be about
(*od.* going) to *inf.*, be on the point
of *ger.*; F *schwer von* ~ *s.* begriffs-
stutzig; 2**en:** ~ *sein in* (*dat.*) be
doing (*a th.*); *im Fortgehen* ~ leaving; *s.* Bau, Entstehen; ~**sbestim-
mung** *f* definition (of terms); 2**s-
stutzig** F slow in the uptake, dense;
~**svermögen** *n* comprehension;
~**sverwirrung** *f* confusion of ideas.

be'gründ|en found; establish, set
up; *Behauptung usw.*: give reasons
for, prove, substantiate; *Handlung*:
motivate, explain; ♩♩ *Rechte usw.*:
create, vest; 2**er(in** *f*) *m* founder;
2**ung** *f* establishment; *fig.* argu-
ment(ation), reason(s *pl.*), proof(s
pl.); substantiation; *mit der* ~, *daß*
on the grounds that.

be'grüß|en greet, salute; *freudig*:
welcome (*a. fig.*); 2**ung** *f* greeting,
salutation; welcome.

begünstig|en [~'gynstigən] (25)
favo(u)r; (*fördern*) promote; (*helfen*) aid (*a.* ♩♩); 2**ung** *f* favo(u)r;
promotion; aid, patronage; ♩♩ acting as an accessory after the fact.

be'gut-achten (26) give an opinion
on; (*prüfen*) examine; ~ *lassen* obtain expert opinion on, submit to
an expert.

begütert [~'gyːtərt] well-to-do.

begütigen [~'gyːtigən] (25) soothe,
appease, placate.

behaart [bə'haːrt] hairy.

behäbig [~'hɛːbiç] sedate; (*Gestalt*)
portly.

behaftet [~'haftət] *mit e-r Krank-*

heit: affected with; *mit Haaren usw.*: covered with; *mit Fehlern usw.*: full of; *mit Schulden*: burdened with.

behag|en [~'ha:gən] **1.** (25) (*dat.*) please, suit; **2.** ♀ *n* (6) ease, comfort; (*Vergnügen*) pleasure; *mit ~* with relish; **~lich** [~'ha:kliç] comfortable; (*traulich*) cosy, snug; *sich ~ fühlen* feel at one's ease; **♀lichkeit** *f* ease, comfortableness; cosiness.

be'halten retain, keep (*für sich* to o.s.); (*im Gedächtnis ~*) remember, retain; *recht ~* be right, be confirmed.

Behält|er [bə'heltər] *m* (7), **~nis** *n* (4¹) container; receptacle; (*Kiste*) case, box; (*Kasten*) bin; *für Öl usw.*: tank.

be'hand|eln treat; (*verfahren mit*) *a.* handle, deal with (*alle a. Thema usw.*); ♪ *Patienten*: treat, attend, *Wunde*: *a.* dress; **♀lung** *f* treatment; handling; *in* (*ärztlicher*) *~* under medical treatment.

Be'hang *m* (3³) (*Wand♀*) hangings *pl.*; (*Anhängsel*) appendage.

be'hängen hang; (*drapieren*) drape.

beharr|en [~'harən] persevere (*bei* in); continue; *hartnäckig*: persist (*bei, auf dat.* in); *~ auf e-m Grundsatz usw.*: stick to, *s-r Meinung*: *a.* stand to; **~lich** [~'harliç] persevering, persistent; **♀lichkeit** *f* perseverance, persistence.

be'hauen hew; ⊕ dress, trim.

behaupt|en [~'hauptən] (26) assert, maintain, hold, claim, contend, say (*daß* that); *Recht usw.*: assert; *Stellung, Ruf, Meinung*: maintain; *das Feld ~* hold the field; *sich ~* hold one's ground (*od.* own); *Preise*: remain firm; **♀ung** *f* assertion; statement, contention (*daß* that); maintaining.

Behausung [~'hauzuŋ] *f* lodging, quarters *pl.*, accommodation.

be'heb|en remedy, repair; **♀ung** *f* reparation.

beheimatet [~'haima:tət] native (*in dat.* of); domiciled (in).

Behelf [bə'helf] *m* (3) expedient, (make)shift; *s. Notbehelf*; **♀en:** *sich ~ make* do, manage; *sich ~ ohne* do without; **~sheim** *n* temporary home; **~s...**, **♀smäßig** makeshift, improvised, temporary.

behellig|en [~'heligən] (25) trouble,

bother; importune, molest; **♀ung** *f* trouble, bother; molestation.

behend, **~e** [~'hent, ~de] nimble, agile; (*gewandt*) adroit, dexterous; **♀igkeit** [~diç-] *f* agility, nimbleness; dexterity.

beherbergen [~'herbergən] (25) lodge, accommodate, shelter, put up.

be'herrsch|en rule, govern (*a. fig.*); *die Lage, Leidenschaft,* † *Markt usw.*: control; (*überragen,* v. *e-m Berg usw.*) command, dominate; *Sprache, Thema*: master, have (a good) command of; *sich ~ control* o.s.; **♀er** (*in f*) *m* ruler; master, *f* mistress (*alle*: *gen.* over, of); **♀ung** *f* rule, domination; command (*a. e-r Sprache*); control; *fig.* mastery; (*Selbst♀*) self-control.

beherzigen [~'hertsigən] (25) take to heart, (bear in) mind, remember; **~swert** worth remembering.

be'herzt courageous, stout-hearted; **♀heit** *f* courage; intrepidity.

be'hexen bewitch.

behilflich [~'hilfliç]: *j-m ~ sein* help (*od.* assist) a p. (*bei* in); be of service to a p.

be'hinder|n hinder, hamper; *a. Sicht, Verkehr*: obstruct; **~t** handicapped; *körperlich* (*geistig*) *~* physically (mentally) handicapped; **♀te** *m, f* handicapped person; **♀tenwerkstatt** *f* sheltered workshop; **♀ung** *f* hindrance; impediment; obstruction; handicap.

Behörd|e [bə'hø:rdə] *f* (15) authority (*mst pl.*); *engS.* agency, board; **♀lich** [~'hø:rtliç] official.

Behuf [~'hu:f] *m* (3): *zu diesem ~* for this purpose; **♀s** (*gen.*) for the purpose of, with a view to.

be'hüt|en guard, protect, keep (*vor dat.* from); watch over, look after; *behüte!* by no means!; *Gott behüte!* God forbid!

behutsam [~'hu:tza:m] cautious, careful, wary; (*sacht*) gentle; gingerly; **♀keit** *f* caution, care.

bei [bai] by; near; at; with; about; among(st); in; on; of; to; (*wohnhaft bei*) *Anschrift*: care of (*abbr.* c/o); *~ j-m sitzen usw.* sit *etc.* by a p.; *~ der Hand usw. nehmen* take by the hand *etc.*; *j-n ~m Namen nennen* call a p. by his name; *~ Gott!* by God!; *~ der Kirche* near the church; *~* (*trotz*) *aller Gelehrsamkeit* for all his learning; ~*m Buchhändler* at the bookseller's; ~ *Brauns* at the Browns; ~ *Hofe* at court; ~*m Essen* at dinner; ~*m Spiel* at play; ~ *Tagesanbruch* at dawn; ~ *uns* with us; ~ *offenen Fenstern* with the windows open; *ich habe kein Geld* ~ *mir* I have no money about me; ~ *den Griechen* among (*od.* with) the Greeks; ~ *guter Gesundheit* in good health; *ich lese* ~ *Horaz* in Horace; *man fand e-n Brief* ~ *ihm* a letter was found on him; *gleich* ~ *m-r Ankunft* on my arrival; *die Schlacht* ~ *Waterloo* the battle of Waterloo; ~ *sich behalten* keep to o.s.; *Besuch* ~ *visit* to; ~ *e-m Glase Wein* over a glass of wine; ~ *alledem* for all that; *Stunden nehmen* ~ take lessons from *od.* of; ~ *günstigem Wetter* weather permitting.

'**beibehalt|en** keep, retain; '**2ung** *f* keeping, retention, maintenance.

'**Beiblatt** *n* supplement (*gen.* to).

'**beibringen** furnish, supply, provide; *Zeugen, Beweis*: produce; *j-m eine Niederlage, Wunde* ~ inflict on a p.; *j-m et.* ~ *lehrend*: impart a th. to a p., teach a p. a th.; *erklärend*: explain a th. to a p.; *nachdrücklich*: bring a th. home to a p.; *schonend*: break a th. (gently) to a p.; *j-m* ~, *daß* make a p. understand that.

Beicht|e ['baɪçtə] *f* (15) confession; *j-m die* ~ *abnehmen* confess a p.; '**2en** (26) *v/t. u. v/i.* confess; '**~geheimnis** *n* confessional secret; '**~kind** *n* penitent; '**~stuhl** *m* confessional; '**~vater** *m* father confessor.

beide ['baɪdə] (18) the two; *betont*: both; (*jeder von zweien*) either (*sg.*); *wir* ~ both of us, we two; *alle* ~ both of them; *in* ~*n Fällen* in either case.

beider|lei ['~dərlaɪ] (of) both kinds, (of) either sort; '**~seitig** *adj.* on both sides; (*gegenseitig*) mutual; *adv.* (= '**~seits**) on both sides; mutually.

'**beidrehen** ♲ heave to.

bei-ei'nander together.

'**Beifahrer** *m* front passenger; *im Lkw, a. beim Rennen*: co-driver; '**~sitz** *m* front-passenger seat.

'**Beifall** *m* (3, *o. pl.*) approval; *durch Händeklatschen*: applause; *durch Zuruf*: acclaim, cheers *pl.*; ~ *ernten*

od. finden meet with approval, *beim Publikum*: earn applause; ~ *klatschen od. spenden* applaud (*j-m* a p.); *stürmischen* ~ *hervorrufen thea.* bring down the house.

'**beifällig** approving.

'**Beifalls|ruf** *m* acclaim; *pl.* cheers; '**~sturm** *m* thundering applause.

'**Beifilm** *m* supporting film.

'**beifüg|en** add; *e-m Brief*: enclose; '**2ung** *f* addition; *gr.* attributive.

'**Beigabe** *f* addition; extra.

'**beigeben** add, join (*dat.* to); *klein* ~ knuckle under, eat humble pie.

Beigeordnete ['~gə'ʔɔrdnətə] *m, f* assistant, deputy.

'**Beigeschmack** *m* (*a. fig.*) smack.

'**beigesellen** join (*dat.* to); *sich j-m* ~ join a p.

'**Beihilfe** *f* aid, assistance; (*Geld2*) allowance, grant; subsidy; ♄ aiding and abetting.

'**beikommen** (sn) (*dat.*) get at.

Beil [baɪl] *n* (3) hatchet; (*Hack2*) chopper; (*Fleischer2*) cleaver; (*Henker2*) ax(e).

'**Beilage** *f e-s Briefes*: enclosure (*gen.* to); *e-r Zeitung*: supplement (*gen.* to); (*Reklame2*) inset; *zu e-r Speise*: garnishing, vegetables *pl.*

beiläufig ['~lɔyfiç] incidental; *Bemerkung*: casual; (*übrigens*) by the way.

'**beileg|en** adjoin, add (*dat.* to); *e-m Brief*: enclose (with); (*zuschreiben*) attribute (to); *Titel*: confer (on); *Namen*: give; *Streit*: settle; *Bedeutung, Wert*: attach importance (to); *sich e-n Titel usw.* ~ assume; '**2ung** *f* addition; attribution; conferment; settlement.

beileibe [~'laɪbə]: ~ *nicht!* certainly not!, by no means!; ~ *kein Narr* certainly no fool.

Beileid ['baɪlaɪt] *n* (3, *o. pl.*) condolence; *weitS.* sympathy; *j-m* (*sein*) ~ *bezeigen* offer a p. one's condolences; '**~sbrief** *m* letter of condolence.

'**beiliegen** be enclosed (*e-m Brief* with); '**~d** enclosed; ~ *sende ich* ... enclosed please find ...

'**beimengen** *s.* beimischen.

'**beimessen**: *j-m et.* ~ attribute (*od.* ascribe) a th. to a p.; *e-r S. Glauben* ~ give credence (*od.* credit) to a th.; *e-r S. Bedeutung usw.* ~ attach importance *etc.* to a th.

'**beimisch|en:** *e-r S.* et. ~ admix (*od.* add) a th. to, mix with a th.; '**Qung** *f* admixture; *fig.* tinge.

Bein [baɪn] *n* (3) leg; (*Knochen*) bone; *den ganzen Tag auf den ~en* on the trot; *j-m auf die ~e helfen* help a p. up, *fig.* give a p. a leg up; *j-m ein ~ stellen* trip a p. (up); *fig.* et. *auf die ~e stellen* set a th. on foot; F *j-m ~e machen* make a p. find his legs; *sich auf die ~e machen* be (*od.* toddle) off; *die ~e in die Hand nehmen* take to one's heels.

bei'nah(e) almost; nearly; et. ~ *tun* come near doing a th.; Q**-unfall** *m*, Q**zusammenstoß** *m* near-miss.

'**Beiname** *m* surname; (*Spitzname*) nickname.

'**Bein|-arbeit** *f Sport:* leg-work; *Boxen:* foot-work; '**~bruch** *m* fracture of the leg; *fig. das ist kein ~!* that's no tragedy!; '**~freiheit** *f* leg-room.

beinhalten [bə'?ɪnhaltən] contain; (*ausdrücken*) express, say.

'**bei·ordnen** adjoin; (*an die Seite stellen*) coordinate (*a. gr.*); *j-n:* assign (*dat.* to).

'**Beipackzettel** *m* instructions *pl.*

beipflicht|en ['~pflɪçtən] (26) *j-m:* agree with; *e-r Ansicht usw.:* assent to; *e-r Maßregel:* approve of; '**Qung** *f* agreement; approbation.

'**Beiprogramm** *n Film:* supporting program(me).

'**Beirat** *m Person:* adviser; *Körperschaft:* advisory board.

beirren [bə'?ɪrən] confuse; (*erschüttern*) disconcert, fluster; (*ablenken*) divert; *er läßt sich nicht ~* F he sticks to his guns.

beisammen [baɪ'zamən] together; Q**sein** *n* (6, *o. pl.*) being together; *geselliges ~* (social) gathering.

'**Beischlaf** *m* sexual intercourse, coition; '**Qen** (*dat.*) sleep with.

'**beischließen** enclose.

'**Beisein** *n:* im ~ *von* (*od. gen.*) in the presence of.

bei'seite aside (*a. thea.*), apart; ~ *bringen od. schaffen* remove; ~ *lassen* disregard; ~ *legen* put aside; *Geld:* put by; ~ *schieben fig.* brush aside; ~ *treten* step (*od.* stand) aside.

'**beisetz|en** *Leiche:* inter, bury; (*hinzusetzen*) add; '**Qung** *f s. Bestattung.*

'**Beisitzer** *m* (7) assessor.

'**Beispiel** *n* (*Muster, Vorbild*) ex-

ample, model; (*Beleg*) example, instance; *zum ~* for example, for instance; *ein ~ geben, mit gutem ~ vorangehen* set an example; *sich ein ~ an j-m nehmen* take example by a p.; '**Qhaft** exemplary; '**Qlos** unprecedented, unparalleled, matchless; '**~losigkeit** *f* singularity; matchlessness; '**Qsweise** for (*od.* by way of) example.

'**beispringen** (sn) *s. beistehen.*

beißen ['baɪsən] (30) *v/t. u. v/i.* bite (*auf, in* et. [*acc.*] on, into a th.; *nach* at); *Pfeffer usw.:* sting (*auf der Zunge* a p.'s tongue); '**~d** biting, pungent (*beide a. fig.*).

'**Beißerchen** F ['baɪsərçən] *n/pl.* (6) toothy-pegs.

'**Beiß|korb** *m* muzzle; '**~ring** *m für Babys:* teething ring; '**~zange** *f* (*eine a pair of*) nippers *od.* pincers *pl.*

Beistand ['baɪʃtant] *m* (3^1) assistance, aid; *Person:* assistant, standby; *s. RechtsQ*; *j-m ~ leisten* lend assistance to a p.; **⚔** attend a p.; '**~s-pakt** *m* mutual assistance treaty, *Am.* mutual aid pact.

'**beistehen:** *j-m ~* stand by (*od.* assist, aid) a p., come to a p.'s aid.

'**Beistelltisch** *m* side (*od.* occasional) table. [tribute (zu to).)

'**Beisteuer** *f* contribution; '**Qn** con-)

'**beistimm|en** *j-m:* agree with; *e-r Meinung usw.:* assent (to), agree (to); '**Qung** *f* agreement; assent.

'**Beistrich** *gr. m* comma.

Beitrag ['~traːk] *m* contribution; (*~santeil*) share; (*MitgliedsQ*) (membership) fee (*od.* subscription), *Am.* dues *pl.*; *e-n ~ leisten* make a contribution; **Qen** ['~gən] *v/t. u. v/i.* contribute (*zu* to); **Qspflichtig** ['~spflɪçtɪç] liable to subscription.

'**beitreib|en** collect, enforce payment of; *Abgaben:* exact; '**Qung** *f* collection; exaction.

'**bei|treten** (sn) *e-r Meinung usw.:* assent to; *e-m Vertrag:* accede to; *e-r Partei usw.:* join; '**Qtritt** *m* accession (zu to); joining.

'**Beiwagen** *mot. m* side-car; (*Anhänger*) trailer; *s. a. Motorrad.*

'**Beiwerk** *n* accessories *pl.*

'**beiwohnen** (*dat.*) assist (*od.* be present) at, attend; *geschlechtlich:* cohabit with.

'**Beiwort** *n* epithet; *gr.* adjective.

Beize ['baɪtsə] *f* (15) *Vorgang:* cor-

rosion; *Mittel*: corrosive; mordant;
(*Holz*♀) stain; *Gerberei*: bate;
metall. pickle; (*Tabak*♀) sauce;
(*Falken*♀) hawking.

beizeiten [baɪˈtsaɪtən] (*früh*) early;
(*rechtzeitig*) in (good) time.

beizen [ˈbaɪtsən] (27) (*ätzen*) corrode; *Holz*: stain; *Häute*: bate;
metall. pickle; ✠ cauterize.

bejah|en [bəˈjaːən] (25) answer in
the affirmative (*a. v/i.*), affirm; *fig.*
say yes to; **~end** affirmative; ♀**ung**
f affirmation, affirmative answer.

bejahrt [~ˈjaːrt] aged, advanced in
be**ˈjammern** *s. beklagen.* [years.]

be**ˈkämpf|en** fight (against), combat; *Meinung usw.*: *a.* attack, oppose, resist; ♀**ung** *f* fight(ing), combat (*gen.* against).

bekannt [~ˈkant] known; (*berühmt*)
well-known, noted (*wegen* for);
~ *mit e-r P. od. S.* acquainted with;
j-n mit j-m ~ *machen* introduce a p.
to a p.; *j-n mit e-r S.* ~ *machen* acquaint a p. with; *als* ~ *voraussetzen*
take for granted; *er ist* ~ *als ...* he
is known to be; ♀**e** *m, f* acquaintance, *mst* friend; ♀**gabe** *f s.* Bekanntmachung; **~geben** *s.* bekanntmachen; **~lich** as everybody knows;
~machen make known, notify;
publish, announce; *in der Zeitung*:
a. advertise; ♀**machung** *f* publication; proclamation; announcement;
notification; advertisement; *durch*
Anschlag: public notice, bulletin;
♀**schaft** *f* acquaintance; ♀**schaftsanzeige** *f* lonely hearts advertisement.

be**ˈkehr|en** convert; *sich* ~ become
a convert (*zu* to); *fig. a.* come round
to; (*sich bessern*) turn over a new
leaf; ♀**er(in** *f*) *m* converter; ♀**te** *m,f*
(18) convert, proselyte; ♀**ung** *f*
conversion.

be**ˈkenn|en** confess, avow; (*zugestehen*) admit; *sich* ~ *zu* confess,
fig. declare o.s. for; *eccl.* profess;
sich schuldig ~ plead guilty; *Farbe*
~ *Karten*: follow suit, *fig.* show
one's hand; ♀**er** *m* confessor.

Be'kenntnis *n* (4¹) confession;
(*Glaubens*♀) creed; **~schule** *f* denominational school.

be**ˈklagen** lament, deplore; (*bemitleiden*) pity; *sich* ~ complain (*über*
acc. of); **~swert** deplorable.

Beklagte [~ˈklɑːktə] *m, f* (18) im

Zivilprozeß: defendant.

be**ˈklatschen** applaud, clap.

be**ˈkleben** paste; *mit Zettel*: label.

be**ˈkleckern, beˈklecksen** stain,
blotch; *mit Tinte*: blot; *allg.* soil,
bespatter.

be**ˈkleid|en** clothe, dress; *mit Marmor usw.*: line, face; *Amt usw.*:
hold, fill; *fig.* ~ *mit* invest with;
♀**ung** *f* clothing; clothes *pl.*; lining,
facing; holding, administration; *mit*
e-m Amt usw.: investiture; ♀**ungsindustrie** *f* clothing industry.

be**ˈklemm|en** *fig.* oppress; ♀**ung** *f*
oppression, anguish, anxiety.

be**klommen** [~ˈklɔmən] oppressed,
uneasy, anxious; ♀**heit** *f* uneasiness;
s. a. Beklemmung.

be**ˈklopfen** tap; ✠ percuss.

bekloppt [~ˈklɔpt] F, **beknackt** [~-
ˈknakt] F mad, crazy, *Person*: *a.*
round the bend *pred.*

be**ˈkommen** *v/t. allg.* get; receive;
be given; have; (*erlangen*) obtain;
Krankheit: get; *Ansteckung*: catch,
contract; *Kind, Junge*: have; *e-n*
Zug usw.: catch; *das ist nicht zu* ~
that is not to be had; *sie bekommt*
ein Kind she is going to have a baby;
Zähne ~ cut one's teeth; *wieviel* ~
Sie (von mir)? how much do I owe
you?; *v/i.* (sn) *j-m*: agree with;
nicht (od. schlecht) ~ disagree with;
j-m gut ~ do a p. good; *wohl be-*
komm's! your health!, cheers!; *fig.*
es wird ihm schlecht ~ he will pay
for it.

bekömmlich [~ˈkœmliç] wholesome; *Klima, Luft*: salubrious.

beköstig|en [~ˈkœstiɡən] (25) board;
sich selbst ~ find o.s.; ♀**ung** *f*
board(ing); *Wohnung und* ~ board
and lodging; *ohne* ~ without meals.

be**ˈkräftig|en** confirm; ♀**ung** *f* confirmation.

be**ˈkränzen** wreathe, festoon.

be**ˈkreuz(ig)en**: *sich* ~ cross o.s.

be**ˈkriegen** make war (up)on.

be**ˈkritteln** carp (*od.* cavil) at.

be**ˈkritzeln** scribble over.

be**ˈkümmern** afflict, grieve, trouble; *sich* ~ *um* concern o.s. with,
take care of; ♀**is** *f* (14²) grief, trouble, affliction.

bekunden [~ˈkundən] (26) state, ⚖
a. testify; (*offenbaren*) manifest,
show.

be**ˈlächeln** smile at.

be'laden load; *fig.* burden.

Belag [bə'lɑ:k] *m* (3³) covering; ⊕ coat(ing) (*Brems℥ usw.*) lining; (*Brot℥*) spread; (*Zungen℥*) fur; (*Zahn℥*) film; (*Spiegel℥*) foil.

Belager|er [~'lɑ:gərər] *m* (7) besieger; ℥n besiege, beleaguer (*beide a. fig.*), lay siege to; **~ung** *f* siege; **~ungszustand** *m* state of siege *od.* of martial law.

Belang [~'laŋ] *m* (3) importance, relevancy; **~e** *pl.* interests *pl.*; *von* (*ohne*) ~ (*für*) of (of no) consequence (to); ℥en concern; ⚖ sue, prosecute; *was mich belangt* as for me; ℥los irrelevant (*für* to); (*unwichtig*) unimportant; (*gering*) negligible; **~losigkeit** *f* irrelevance; insignificance; ℥reich important, relevant (*für* to); **~ung** *f* prosecution.

belasten [~'lastən] load, charge (*beide a.* ⊕, *⚡*); *fig.* burden; ✝ charge (*j-n mit e-r Summe* a sum to a p.), debit; ⚖ incriminate; *Grundstück, Haus:* encumber; *erblich belastet* tainted with a hereditary disease; *politisch belastet* politically incriminated.

belästig|en [~'lɛstigən] (25) molest; (*stören*) trouble, annoy, bother; *unabsichtlich:* inconvenience, incommode; *mit Bitten od. Fragen:* importune, pester; ℥ung *f* molestation; trouble; inconvenience.

Be'lastung *f* load (*a. ⚡, ⊕*); ⊕ stress, *fig.* burden, strain; (*Sorge*) worry; ✝ debit; *e-s Grundstücks:* encumbrance; *erbliche ~* hereditary taint; *politische ~* political incrimination; **~s-probe** *f* load-test; *fig.* (severe) test; **~szeuge** *m* witness for the prosecution.

belaubt [~'laupt] in leaf, covered in leaves.

be'laufen: *sich ~ auf* (*acc.*) amount to, run up to, total.

be'lauschen overhear, listen to.

be'leb|en enliven, animate; *a. Getränk usw.:* stimulate; **~t** [~pt] animated, lively; *Straße usw.:* crowded, busy; ℥t-heit *f* animation; liveliness (*a. e-r Straße*); ℥ung *f* animation, stimulation; *s. Wieder℥*.

be'lecken lick.

Beleg [bə'le:k] *m* (3) proof; (*~schein, Unterlage*) voucher; (*Quittung*) receipt; (*Beispiel*) example; ℥en [~gən] overlay, cover; *Platz:* engage, occupy, (*vorherbestellen*) reserve, book; *Sport:* be placed (*first, etc.*); *Stute usw.:* cover; (*beweisen*) prove, verify, substantiate; *Vorlesung:* enter one's name for; ~ *mit e-m Teppich, Stroh usw.:* lay with; *durch Beispiele* ~ exemplify; *mit Strafe* ~ inflict punishment on; *einen Ort mit Truppen* ~ quarter (*od.* billet) troops in a place; **~-exemplar** *n* voucher copy; **~schaft** *f* personnel, staff; workers *pl.*; **~stelle** *f* reference, quotation; ℥t *Platz:* engaged, reserved; *Stimme:* husky; *Zunge:* furred; *teleph.* engaged, *Am.* busy; **~es Brot** sandwich.

be'lehr|en inform; instruct; *sich ~ lassen* take advice; *eines Bessern ~ set right*; **~end** instructive; ℥ung *f* instruction; (*Rat*) advice.

be'leibt [bə'laipt] corpulent, stout; ℥heit *f* corpulence.

beleidig|en [~'laidigən] (25) offend (*a. fig.*); *gröblich:* insult; *ich wollte Sie nicht ~* no offence (*Am.* offense) (*meant*); **~end** insulting; ℥ung *f* offen|ce, *Am.* -se; insult; affront; ⚖ defamation.

be'leihen (grant a) loan on.

be'lesen well-read; ℥heit *f* extensive (*od.* wide) reading.

be'leucht|en light (up); *festlich:* illuminate; *fig.* elucidate, illustrate; *näher ~* examine more closely; ℥er *m thea. usw.:* lighter.

Be'leuchtung *f* lighting; illumination; *fig.* elucidation, illustration; *konkret:* lights *pl.*; **~skörper** *m* lighting fixture, lamp.

Belg|ier ['bɛlgjər] *m*, '**~ierin** *f*, '℥isch Belgian.

belicht|en [bə'liçtən] *phot.* expose; ℥ung *f* exposure; ℥ungsdauer *f*, ℥ungszeit *f* time of exposure; ℥ungsmesser *m* exposure meter; ℥ungs-tabelle *f* exposure table.

be'lieb|en 1. *v/t.* deign, choose; *v/i.* please; *wie es Ihnen beliebt* as you please; 2. ℥ *n* (6) will, pleasure; *nach* (*Ihrem*) ~ at pleasure, at will, as you like; *es steht in Ihrem* ~ it rests with you; **~ig:** *ein ~er usw.* any; *jedes ~e Land* any given country; *adv.* at pleasure; ~ *viele* as many as you *etc.* like; **~t** [~pt] liked, favo(u)rite; (*allgemein* ~) popular (*bei* with); *Ware*: sought-after; *Mode*: ~ *sein* be in vogue; *sich bei j-m* ~ *machen* ingratiate o.s. with a p.; ℒt-**heit** *f* popularity.

be'**liefer|n**, ℒ**ung** *f* supply.

bellen ['bɛlən] (25) bark (*a. fig.*).

Belletrist [bɛlɛ'trist] *m* (12) literary man, belletrist; ~**ik** *f* (16) belles--lettres *pl.*; fiction; ℒ**isch** belletristic; ~**e** *Zeitschrift* *f* literary magazine.

be'**lob|en** praise, commend; ℒ**(ig)ung** *f* praise, commendation.

be'**lohn|en**, ℒ**ung** *f* reward.

be'**lügen**: *j-n* ~ tell a p. a lie.

belustig|en [~'lustigən] (25) amuse, divert, entertain; *sich* ~ amuse o.s., make merry; ℒ**ung** *f* amusement, diversion, entertainment.

bemächtigen [~'mɛçtigən] (25): *sich e-r P. od. S.* ~ seize.

be'**mäkeln** cavil (*od.* carp) at.

be'**malen** paint (over).

bemängeln [~'mɛŋəln] (29) find fault with, criticize.

bemann|en [~'manən] (25) man; ~**t**: ~*er Raumflug* manned space flight; ℒ**ung** *f* manning; (*Mannschaft*) crew.

bemäntel|n [~'mɛntəln] (29) (*verdecken*) cloak; (*beschönigen*) palliate; ℒ**ung** *f* cloaking, palliation.

bemerk|bar [~'mɛrkbaːr] perceptible, noticeable; *sich* ~ *machen P.*: attract attention, *S.*: make itself felt; ~**en** observe, notice, feel, perceive; (*äußern*) remark, observe; ~**enswert** remarkable; ℒ**ung** *f* remark, observation; *schriftliche*: note.

be'**messen** measure; (*verhältnismäßig zuteilen*) proportion (*nach* to); *zeitlich*: time; ⊕ dimension; *Leistung*: rate; *meine Zeit ist knapp* ~ I am short of time.

bemitleiden [~'mitlaɪdən] (25) pity, commiserate; ~**swert** pitiable.

bemittelt [~'mitəlt] well-off, well--to-do; *pred.* well off.

be'**mogeln** F cheat, trick.

bemüh|en [~'myːən] trouble (*j-n um et.* a p. for a th.); *sich* ~ take pains, endeavo(u)r, exert o.s.; *sich für j-n* ~ exert o.s. on behalf of; *sich um et.* ~ exert o.s. for, strive for; *sich um e-n Verletzten usw.* ~ attend to; *sich um j-s Gunst od. um j-n* ~ woo a p.; *sich um e-e Stellung* ~ apply for, seek; *sich zu j-m* ~

betake o.s. to a p.; *bemüht sein zu inf.* be anxious to *inf.*, be endeavo(u)red to *inf.*; ~ *Sie sich nicht!* don't trouble *od.* bother!; ℒ**ung** *f* trouble, endeavo(u)r, pains *pl.*; (*Anstrengung*) effort (*um et.* for, toward).

bemüßigt [~'myːsiçt]: *sich* ~ *fühlen zu inf.* feel bound to.

be'**muttern** [~'mutərn] (29) mother.

be'**nachbart** neighbo(u)ring.

benachrichtig|en [~'naːxriçtigən] (25) inform (*von* of; *daß* that), send *a p.* word (that); *formell*: notify (of; that); † advise (of); ℒ**ung** *f* information; notification; † advice.

benachteilig|en [~'naːxtaɪligən] (25) place *a p.* at a disadvantage, handicap; discriminate against; (*schädigen*) injure; ℒ**ung** *f* disadvantage (*gen.* to); discrimination (against); injury (to).

be'**nagen** gnaw (at).

benebel|n [~'neːbəln] (29) (be)fog (*a. fig.*); ~**t** *fig. co.* fuddled.

Benediktiner [benedik'tiːnər] *m* Benedictine (*a. Likör*).

Benefiz [bene'fiːts] *n* (3³) benefit; ~**spiel** *n Sport*: charity game, benefit (match); ~**vorstellung** *f* benefit (-night).

be'**nehmen**: **1.** take away (*j-m den Atem usw.* a p.'s breath *etc.*); *j-m die Hoffnung usw.* ~ deprive a p. of; *sich* ~ behave (o.s.); **2.** ℒ *n* (6) behavio(u)r, conduct; manners *pl.*; *im* ~ *mit* in agreement with; *sich ins* ~ *setzen mit* contact *a p.*, confer (*od.* consult) with (*über acc.* about).

be'**neiden** envy (*j-n um et.* a p. a th.); ~**swert** enviable.

be'**nenn|en** *j-n, et.*: name; *et.*: *a.* designate, term; *e-n Termin*: fix; *benannt* ⅋ concrete; ℒ**ung** *f* naming, name; denomination; (*Fachsprache*) nomenclature.

be'**netzen** wet, moisten.

Bengel ['bɛŋəl] *m* (7) lout; (*Schelm*) rascal; *kleiner*: urchin; *dummer* ~ silly fool, booby.

benommen [bə'nɔmən] benumbed; (*schwindlig*) dizzy; ℒ**heit** *f* numbness; dizziness.

be'**nötigen** want, need, require.

benutz|en [~'nutsən] use, make use of, utilize; (*sich zunutze machen*) *a.* profit by; *die Gelegenheit* ~ seize the opportunity; ℒ**er** *m* user; ~**er-**

freundlich user-friendly; Ωung *f* use; utilization.
Benzin [bɛn'tsiːn] *n* (3¹) benzine; *mot.* petrol, *Am.* gas(oline); ~**gutschein** *m* petrol coupon; ~**kanister** *m* (7) petrol (*Am.* gas) container; ~**leitung** *f* fuel pipe; ~**motor** *m* petrol (*Am.* gasoline) engine; ~**pumpe** *f* fuel pump; *an Tankstelle:* petrol pump; ~**tank** *m* fuel tank; ~**uhr** *f* fuel gauge; ~**verbrauch** *m* petrol (*Am.* gasoline) consumption.
Benzol [bɛn'tsoːl] *n* benzene, benzol(e).
beobacht|en [bə'ʔoːbaxtən] (26) observe (*a. fig. Stillschweigen, Vorschrift usw.*); *genau:* watch; Ωer(**in** *f*) *m* observer; ✈ navigator; ⚒ *a.* spotter; Ωung *f* observation; *fig.* observance (*gen.* of), compliance (with); Ωungsgabe *f* (power of) observation; Ωungsposten *m* ⚔ observation post; Ωungsstation *f* *ast.* observatory; ⚒ observation ward.
beordern [ʌ'ʔɔrdərn] (29) order.
be'packen load, pack.
be'pflanzen plant.
bequem [bə'kveːm] convenient; (*behaglich*) comfortable; (*leicht*) easy; *Schuh usw.:* easy; *P.:* easy-going, *b.s.* indolent; *es sich* ~ *machen* relax, make o.s. at home; ~**en** (25): *sich* ~ *zu et.* comply with, submit to; *b.s.* condescend to; Ωlichkeit *f* convenience; comfort, ease; *b.s.* indolence. [fork out.〕
berappen F [ʌ'rapən] (25) pay up,〕
be'rat|en *j-n:* advise, counsel; *et.:* deliberate on; (*sich*) ~, **be'ratschlagen** (25) deliberate (*über acc.* on, about); (*mit j-m*) consult, confer (with); *gut* (*schlecht*) ~ well- (ill-)-advised; ~**end** advisory, consultative; Ωer *m* adviser; consultant; Ωung *f* advice, counsel (*j-s* to a p.); consultation (*a.* ⚒, ✝); deliberation; (*Konferenz*) conference; Ωungsfirma *f* consultancy firm; Ωungsstelle *f* advisory board; information cent|re, *Am.* -er; *soziale:* welfare cent|re, *Am.* -er.
be'raub|en rob, *fig. a.* deprive (*gen.* of); Ωung *f* robbing, deprivation.
be'rauschen intoxicate; *sich* ~ *get* drunk; *fig.* be (*od.* get) intoxicated (*an dat.* with); ~**d** intoxicating (*a. fig.*).

be'rechn|en calculate, compute; (*schätzen*) estimate (*auf acc.* at); ✝ charge; *darauf berechnet sein, zu inf.* be calculated to *inf.*; ~**end** calculating; Ωung *f* calculation.
berechtig|en [ʌ'rɛçtigən] (25) *v/t.* *j-n:* entitle (*zu* to *a th.*; to *inf.*); (*ermächtigen*) authorize (to *inf.*); (*befähigen*) qualify (to); *v/i. zu et.* ~ justify; *zu Hoffnungen* ~ bid fair, promise well; ~**t** entitled, *etc.*, *s.* berechtigen; *attr. Anspruch, Hoffnung usw.:* legitimate; Ωung *f* right, title (*zu* to); authorization; justification; Ωungsschein *m* permit; ✝ *für Dividende, Zinsen:* warrant.
be'red|en (*überreden*) persuade; (*über et. reden*) talk *a th.* over; *sich* ~ *mit* confer with; Ωsamkeit [ʌ'reːt-] *f* eloquence; ~**t** eloquent.
Be'reich *m, n* (3) reach, area; *fig. a.* compass, scope, (*a.* ⚒) range; (*Gebiet*) field, sphere, domain; Ωern (29) enrich; ~**erung** *f* enrichment.
bereif|en¹ [ʌ'raɪfən] cover with hoarfrost; ~**en**² *Faß:* hoop; *Rad:* tyre, *Am.* tire; Ωung *f* *mot.* tyres, *mst* tires *pl.*
be'reinig|en settle, straighten out; Ωung *f* settlement.
be'reisen travel, tour; ✝ *a.* work.
bereit [bə'raɪt] ready, prepared; *sich* ~ *erklären od. finden zu* agree to; *sich* ~ *machen zu* get ready (*od.* prepare o.s.) for; ~**en** (26) prepare, make ready; *Freude, Verdruß usw.:* give; *Niederlage:* inflict (*dat.* upon); ~**halten** keep ready; *fig. für j-n* have in store for; ~**s** already; (*bei Fragen und Verneinungen*) yet; Ωschaft *f* (16) readiness; (*Polizeimannschaft*) squad; Ωschafts-arzt *m* duty doctor; Ωschaftsdienst *m* stand-by service; Ωschafts-polizei *f* riot police; ~**stehen** be ready; ~**stellen** make available, provide; Ωung *f* preparation; ~**willig** ready, willing; Ωwilligkeit *f* readiness, willingness.
be'reuen repent; (*bedauern*) regret.
Berg [bɛrk] *m* (3) mountain, (*Hügel*) hill; *fig.* ~*e von ...* heaps of ...; ~*e versetzen* move mountains; *hinterm* ~ *halten mit* hold back, keep *a th.* dark; *die Haare standen mir zu* ~*e* my hair stood on end; *über alle* ~*e sein* be off and away; *wir sind noch nicht über den* ~ we are not yet out of the wood; Ω'-**ab**

downhill (*a. fig.*); '**~-akademie** *f* mining college; '**~-amt** *n* mining office; **♀'-an**, **♀'-auf** uphill (*a. fig.*); '**~-arbeiter** *m s.* **~mann**; '**~bahn** **🚇** *f* mountain-railway; '**~bau** *m* mining; '**~besteigung** *f* climb; '**~-bewohner(in** *f*) *m* highlander.

bergen ['bɛrɡən] (30) save; **⚓** salv(ag)e; *mot.* recover; (*enthalten*) contain; *fig.* harbo(u)r; (*verbergen*) conceal; *s.* geborgen.

Berg|führer ['bɛrk-] *m* mountain guide; **♀ig** ['~ɡiç] mountainous, (*hügelig*) hilly; '**~-ingenieur** *m* mining engineer; '**~kette** *f* mountain range; '**~knappe** *m* miner; '**~-krankheit** *f* mountain sickness; '**~kristall** *m* rock crystal; '**~land** *n* mountainous (*od.* hilly) country; '**~mann** *m* (*pl.* Bergleute) miner; *im Kohlenbergwerk*: pitman, collier; '**~predigt** *f* Sermon on the Mount; '**~recht** *n* mining laws *pl.*; '**~rennen** *n Sport*: mountain race; '**~rücken** *m* ridge; '**~rutsch** *m* landslip, *Am. od. pol.* landslide; '**~salz** *n* rock salt; '**~schuh** *m* climbing boot; '**~spitze** *f* mountain peak; '**~steigen** *n* mountaineering; '**~steiger(in** *f*) *m* mountaineer; '**~stock** *m* alpenstock; '**~sturz** *m s.* Bergrutsch; '**Berg-und-Tal-Bahn** *f* switchback (railway), *Am.* roller-coaster; **~ung** ['~ɡuŋ] *f* saving, **⚓** salvage; *mot.* recovery; *von Menschen*: rescue; '**~ungs-arbeiten** *f*/*pl.* **⚓** salvage operations; *für Menschen*: rescue work; '**~ungsfahrzeug** *n mot.* recovery vehicle, *Am.* wrecker truck; **⚓** salvage vessel; **🚑** crash tender; '**~ungsmannschaft** *f* salvage crew; *für Menschen*: rescue party; '**~werk** *n* mine; (*Kohlengrube*) pit; '**~werksgesellschaft** *f* mining company; '**~wesen** *n* mining.

Bericht [bə'riçt] *m* (3) report, account; *statistische* **~e** *pl.* official returns; **~** *erstatten s.* berichten; **♀en** report (*über acc.* on; *j-m* to a p.); *in der Presse*: *Am. a.* cover (*über et. a th.*); (*erzählen*) relate; *j-m et.* **~** (*melden*) inform a p. of a th.; **~-erstatter** *m* (7) reporter; *auswärtiger*: correspondent; *Radio*: commentator; *Referent*: reporter, *Am.* refeee; **~erstattung** *f* reporting, *Am. a.* coverage; (*Bericht*) report.

be'richtig|en [~igən] (25) *et.*: rec-

tify; *et.*, *j-n*: correct, set right; *Rechnung usw.*: settle; **⊕** adjust; *Schuld*: settle; **♀ung** *f* rectification; correction; settlement; adjustment.

Be'richtsjahr *n* year under review.

be'riechen smell at.

be'riesel|n *Land*: irrigate; (*besprengen*) sprinkle; **♀ung** *f* irrigation; sprinkling.

beritten [~'rɪtən] mounted.

Berliner [bɛr'li:nər] **1.** *m* (7), **~in** *f* Berlinian, Berliner; **2.** *adj.* Berlin.

Bernstein ['bɛrnʃtaɪn] *m* amber.

bersten ['bɛrstən] (30, sn) burst (*fig. vor dat.* with).

berüchtigt [bə'rʏçtɪçt] notorious (*wegen* for), ill-famed.

be'rücken captivate; **~d** captivating; *Schönheit*: fascinating.

be'rücksichtig|en [~ziçtigən] (25) *et.*: take into consideration (*od.* account), a. *j-n*: consider; (*an-, abrechnen*) allow for; **♀ung** *f* consideration (*gen.* of), regard (to); *unter* **~** (*gen.*) in consideration of.

Beruf [bə'ru:f] *m* (3) calling; (*Tätigkeit*) occupation, job; (*Geschäft*) business; (*Gewerbe*) trade; (*Amt*) office; (*höherer* **~**) profession; (*innerer* **~**) vocation, mission; *von* **~** by occupation; by profession; by trade; *freier* **~** liberal profession; **♀en¹** *v/t.* call; *Versammlung*: convene; *Parlament usw.*: convoke; *j-n zu e-m Amt*: appoint (to); *sich* **~** *auf* (*acc.*) appeal to, *entschuldigend*: plead, (*sich beziehen auf*) refer to; **♀en²** *adj.* competent (*zu* for *a th.*; *to inf.*); *sich* **~** *fühlen zu inf.* feel called upon to *inf.*; **♀lich** *s.* Berufs...

Be'rufs... vocational, occupational, professional; **~ausbildung** *f* vocational training; **~be-amtentum** *n* officialdom; **~berater(in** *f*) *m* careers adviser; **~beratung** *f* vocational guidance; **~kleidung** *f* work (-ing) clothes *pl.*; **~krankheit** *f* occupational disease; **~offizier** *m* regular officer; **~risiko** *n* occupational hazard; **~schule** *f* vocational school; **~spieler** *m Sport*: professional; **~sport** *m* professional sport(s *pl.*); **♀tätig** working; (*gainfully*) employed; practising a profession; **~verbot** *n* professional ban; **~verbrecher** *m* professional criminal.

Be'rufung f (16) s. berufen: call; convocation; appointment (zu to); appeal (auf acc., ⅌ an acc. to, gegen from); reference (auf acc. to); s. einlegen; ⟋sgericht n, ⟋s‑instanz f court of appeal; ⟋sklage f appeal; ⟋skläger(in f) m appellant; ⟋srecht n right of appeal.

be'ruhen: ⟋ auf (dat.) rest (od. be based od. depend) on; et. auf sich ⟋ lassen let a th. rest (od. pass).

beruhig|en [⟋'ru:igən] (25) quiet, calm, soothe; Ängstliche: ease, set at rest; Erregte: appease; P. od. S.: sich ⟋ calm down; ℒung f quieting, calming; appeasement; (Trost) consolation; ℒungsmittel n, ℒungspille 🕂 f sedative; fig. placebo.

berühmt [⟋'ry:mt] famous (wegen for), celebrated; renowned; ℒheit f renown; Person: celebrity, star.

be'rühr|en touch; fig. (erwähnen) touch (up)on, allude to; (wirken auf) affect; j‑s Interessen usw.: concern; Hafen, Haltestelle: touch at; sich (od. ea.) ⟋ touch, meet; j‑n (un)angenehm ⟋ (dis)please a p.; es berührt seltsam, daß it is strange that; ℒung f touching; touch, contact; mit j‑m in ⟋ bleiben keep in touch with; in ⟋ kommen mit come in(to) contact (od. touch) with; ℒungsfläche f surface of contact; ℒungslinie ⅄ f tangent; ℒungspunkt m point of contact.

be'sä|en sow; ⟋t fig. studded, dotted; mit Sternen ⟋ star-spangled.

be'sag|en say; (bedeuten) mean, signify, imply; das will wenig ⟋ it little matters; ⟋t [⟋kt] (afore-)said.

besaiten [⟋'zaɪtən] string; zart besaitet fig. very sensitive.

Besan ⚓ [bə'za:n] m (3¹) miz(z)en.

besänftig|en [bə'zɛnftigən] (25) soothe; assuage; appease; sich ⟋ calm down; ℒung f soothing; appeasement.

Be'satz m border; (Garnierung) trimming; (Borte) braid.

Be'satzung f garrison; ⚓, ✈ crew; (Besetzung) occupation; ⟋smacht f occupying power; ⟋sstreitkräfte f/pl. occupation forces; ⟋szone f occupation zone.

be'saufen: F sich ⟋ get drunk.

Be'säufnis n (4¹) F booze-up.

be'schädig|en S.: damage, injure;

P.: injure, hurt; ℒung f damage, injury (gen. to); ⚓ average.

be'schaff|en 1. v/t. procure, make available; **2.** adj. constituted; gut (schlecht) ⟋ well‑ (ill‑)conditioned; die Sache ist so ⟋ the matter stands thus; ℒenheit f condition; (Eigenschaft) quality; (Natur) nature; ℒung f procurement.

beschäftig|en [⟋'ʃɛftigən] (25) occupy, engage; Angestellte: employ; geistig: preoccupy; sich ⟋ mit busy (od. occupy) o.s. with, be engaged in, be busy ger.; ⟋t [⟋tiçt]: ⟋ bei in the employ of, working for; ⟋ mit engaged in, occupied with; ℒung [⟋guŋ] f occupation; employment, job; (Geschäft) business; ⟋ungslos unemployed, out of work; ℒungstherapeut 🕂 m occupational therapist; ℒungs‑therapie 🕂 f occupational therapy.

be'schäl|en Stute: cover; ℒer m (7) stallion, stud(-horse).

be'schäm|en make ashamed, (put to) shame; (verlegen machen) embarrass; ⟋d humiliating; ⟋t a‑shamed (über acc. of); ℒung f confusion; Zustand: shame.

beschatten [⟋'ʃatən] (26) shade; (heimlich verfolgen) shadow.

be'schau|en look at; view; prüfend: examine; Fleisch usw.: inspect; fig. contemplate; ⟋lich contemplative; (friedlich) tranquil; (behaglich) leisurely; ℒlichkeit f contemplativeness; tranquillity.

Bescheid [bə'ʃaɪt] m (3) answer; ⅌ usw. decision; (Mitteilung, Auskunft) information (über acc. about); j‑m ⟋ geben send a p. word, let a p. know (about); j‑m gehörig ⟋ sagen (abkanzeln) give a p. a piece of one's mind; j‑m trinkend ⟋ tun pledge a p.; ⟋ wissen (be in the) know; ⟋ wissen mit od. in (dat.) od. über (acc.) know all about, be aware of; ich weiß hier ⟋ I know this place.

be'scheiden 1. v/t. (zuteilen) allot; j‑n wohin: direct, order; (benachrichtigen) inform; j‑n abschlägig ⟋ give a p. a refusal; sich ⟋ be content; sich mit et. ⟋ resign o.s. to; es war mir nicht beschieden it was not granted to me; **2.** adj. modest; ℒheit f modesty.

be'scheinen shine (up)on.

bescheinig|en [ˌˈʃaɪnɪgən] (25) certify (*j-m* to a p.), (*a. fig.*) attest; den Empfang (*gen.*) ~ acknowledge receipt (of *a letter, etc.*); (give a) receipt (for *money paid*); es wird hiermit bescheinigt, daß ... this is to certify that ...; 2ung *f* certificate; receipt.

be'scheißen P cheat.

be'schenken *j-n:* make a p. a present; *j-n mit et.*: present a p. with a th.

be'scher|en *j-m et.* ~ give a p. a th., bestow a th. (up)on a p.; 2ung *f* distribution of presents; *fig.* eine schöne ~! a nice mess!; da haben wir die ~! there we are! die ganze ~ the whole bag of tricks.

bescheuert [ˌˈʃɔʏərt] F s. bekloppt.

be'schick|en *Parlament usw.*: send deputies to; *Ausstellung, Messe*: exhibit at; ⊕ charge; 2ung *f* (*gen.*) sending of delegates (to); representation (at); ⊕ charging (of).

be'schieß|en fire on; *mit Kanonen*: bombard (*a. phys.*), shell; 2ung *f* fire; bombardment, shelling.

be'schimpf|en insult, call a p. names; 2ung *f* insult (*gen.* to).

be'schirm|en (25) protect, shield, shelter (*vor dat.* from).

be'schlafen *et.*: sleep on.

Be'schlag *m* metal (*od.* iron) fittings *pl.*; mounting; (*Huf*2) shoeing, *konkret*: shoes *pl.*; ⚕ efflorescence; 𝕥𝕥 s. ~nahme; in ~ nehmen, mit ~ belegen seize, *fig. a.* monopolize; ~ legen auf distrain (up)on; ⚓ embargo.

be'schlagen 1. *v/t.* mount; *Pferd*: shoe; *Stock*: tip; *mit Ziernägeln*: stud; *v/i.* (sn) *Eßware*: grow mo(u)ldy; *Fenster*: get covered with damp; **2.** *adj. Glas*: clouded, steamed, in e-r S. gut ~ sein be well versed (*od.* up) in; 2heit *f* experience, (profound) knowledge (*in dat.* of).

Be'schlagnahm|e [ˌknɑːmə] *f* (15, *o. pl.*) seizure, confiscation; sequestration; ✕ requisition; ⚓ embargo; 2en seize, confiscate; sequestrate; ✕ requisition.

be'schleichen sneak up to; *Wild, Feind*: stalk; *fig.* steal (*od.* creep) (up)on.

beschleunig|en [bəˈʃlɔʏnɪgən] (25) accelerate; hasten, speed up; 2er

mot. phot. m accelerator (*a. Kernphysik*); 2ung *f* acceleration (*a. phys.*); speeding up; 2ungsspur *mot. f* acceleration lane; 2ungsvermögen *n* acceleration.

be'schließen (*beenden*) close, conclude; (*sich entscheiden*) determine, decide (*beide a.* 𝕥𝕥), resolve.

Be'schluß *m* (4²) (*Entscheidung*) decision, resolution (*a. parl.*), Am. resolve; 𝕥𝕥 (court) order, decree; 2fähig: e-e ~e Anzahl od. Versammlung a quorum; das Haus ist (nicht) ~ there is a (no) quorum; ~fähigkeit *f* quorum, competence; ~fassung *f* (passing of a) resolution.

be'schmieren (be)smear; *s.* bestreichen.

be'schmutzen soil (*a. fig.*), dirty.

be'schneid|en clip; cut; *Baum*: lop; *Fingernägel*: pare; ⚕ circumcise; *fig.* cut (down), curtail; 2ung *f* clipping; circumcision; cut.

be'schneit snowy.

be'schnüffeln, be'schnuppern sniff at.

beschönig|en [ˌˈʃøːnɪgən] (25) palliate, extenuate, gloss over; 2ung *f* palliation, extenuation.

beschränk|en [ˌˈʃrɛŋkən] (25) confine, limit, restrict, Am. a. curb; sich ~ auf (*acc.*) restrict o.s. to; ~t [ˌkt] limited, restricted; *geistig*: narrow(-minded), (*dumm*) obtuse; 2t-heit *f* narrowness; dul(l)ness; 2ung *f* limitation, restriction.

be'schreib|en *Blatt*: write (up)on; (*schildern*) describe (*a. Kreis usw.*); ~end descriptive; 2ung *f* description; ⊕ specification; jeder ~ spotten beggar all description.

be'schreiten walk on; *fig.* e-n Weg ~ follow a course; neue Wege ~ apply new methods; *s. Rechtsweg.*

beschrift|en [ˌˈʃrɪftən] (26) inscribe, letter; *Kiste usw.*: mark; 2ung *f* lettering; (*Inschrift*) inscription; *erläuternde*: caption, legend.

beschuldig|en [ˌˈʃʊldɪgən] (25) accuse (*gen.* of), charge (with); 2te [ˌdɪçtə] *m, f* (18) accused; 2ung [ˌgʊŋ] *f* accusation, charge.

beschummeln F [ˌˈʃʊməln] (29) cheat, trick (*um* out of).

Be'schuß *m* (4²) fire; bombardment (*a. phys.*), shelling.

be'schütz|en (*vor dat.*) protect

(from), defend (against); ℒ**er** *m*
(7) protector; ℒ**erin** *f* (16¹) protectress.
be'**schwatzen** talk *a p.* over; coax
(*zu to inf.*; into *ger.*); ~ *zu* talk *a p.*
into *ger.*
Beschwerde [bə'ʃveːrdə] *f* (15)
trouble; (*Klage*) complaint; (~-
grund) grievance; ⚖ appeal (*gegen*
from); (*Krankheit*) complaint,
trouble; ~**buch** *n* complaints book;
~**führer(in** *f*) *m* complainant.
beschwer|en [~'ʃveːrən] (25) bur-
den, charge (*a. fig.*); *lose Papiere
usw.*: weight; *Magen*: lie heavy on;
sich ~ complain (*über acc.* about,
of; *bei* to); ~**lich** troublesome; *j-m*
~ *fallen* give a p. trouble.
beschwichtigen [~'ʃviçtigən] (25)
appease; *Gewissen*: silence.
Be'schwichtigungspolitik *f* ap-
peasement policy.
be'**schwindeln** cheat, swindle (*um
et.* out of).
beschwingt [~'ʃviŋt] winged; *fig.*
elated, buoyant; *Melodie*: racy.
beschwipst F [~'ʃvipst] tipsy.
be'**schwör|en** *et.*: confirm by oath,
swear (to); *Geister*: conjure, (*bannen*) conjure away; *Gefahr*: banish;
j-n: (*anflehen*) implore; ℒ**ung** *f* confirmation by oath, swearing; con-
juration; banishment; imploring.
beseel|en [~'zeːlən] (25) animate;
~**t** animated; *fig.* soulful.
be'**sehen** look at; *prüfend*: inspect.
beseitig|en [bə'zaɪtigən] (25) re-
move; (*abschaffen*) *a.* abolish, do
away with (*a. j-n*); ℒ**ung** *f* removal.
beseligen [~'zeːligən] (25) make
happy, fill with bliss.
Besen ['beːzən] *m* (6) broom;
(*Reisig*ℒ) besom; *kleiner* ~ (hand-)
-brush; *fig. mit eisernem* ~ with a
rod of iron; *neue* ~ *kehren gut* a
new broom sweeps clean; F *ich
fresse e-n* ~, *wenn* ... I'll eat my
hat if ...; '~**schrank** *m* broom-cup-
board; '~**stiel** *m* broom-stick.
besessen [~'zɛsən] obsessed, pos-
sessed (*von* by, with); *wie* ~ like
mad; ℒ**e** *m*, *f* man (woman) pos-
sessed, maniac; ℒ**heit** *f* obsession;
(*Raserei*) frenzy.
be'**setz|en** *Kleid usw.*: trim; *mit
Edelsteinen usw.*: set; ⚔ occupy;
⚓ man; *Amt, Stelle*: fill; (*Sitz-*)
Platz: engage; *thea. Rolle, Stück*:

cast; ~**t** *Platz, Gebiet*: occupied;
Bus usw.: full up; *dicht* ~ crowded,
packed; *teleph.* engaged, *Am.* busy;
meine Zeit ist ~ occupied; ℒ**tzei-
chen** *n* engaged (*Am.* busy) signal;
ℒ**ung** *f* occupation; filling; *thea.*
cast; (*Personal*) staff; *Sport*: team
composition.
besichtig|en [~'ziçtigən] (25) view,
inspect, survey; *zu* ~ *sein* be on
view; ℒ**ung** *f* inspection (*a.* ⚔); *von
Sehenswürdigkeiten*: sightseeing,
visit (*gen.* to).
be'**siedel|n** settle, colonize; ℒ**ung** *f*
settlement, colonization.
be'**siegeln** seal (*a. fig.*).
be'**sieg|en** defeat; ℒ**er(in** *f*) *m* (7)
conqueror; ℒ**te** *m*, *f* loser; ℒ**ung** *f*
defeat; conquest.
be'**singen** sing (of).
be'**sinn|en** 1. *sich* ~ (*überlegen*) re-
flect, consider; (*sich erinnern*) recollect, remember (*auf et.* a thing);
sich anders (*od. e-s andern*) ~ change
one's mind; *sich e-s Besseren* ~
think better of it; 2. ℒ *n* (6) reflection; ~**lich** contemplative, reflec-
tive.
Be'sinnung *f* consciousness; (*Überlegung*) reflection, consideration;
die ~ *verlieren* lose consciousness,
fig. lose one's head; *wieder zur* ~
kommen recover consciousness, *fig.*
come to one's senses; *j-n zur* ~
bringen bring a p. to his senses; ~**s-
aufsatz** *m* contemplative essay;
ℒ**slos** unconscious; *fig.* senseless,
blind; ~**slosigkeit** *f* unconsciousness; *fig.* senselessness.
Be'sitz *m* (3²) possession; *s.* ~**tum**;
~ *ergreifen von, in* ~ *nehmen* take
possession of, occupy, *Person*: take
hold of; *im* ~ *e-r S. sein* be in possession of a th.; *im* ~ *e-r P. sein*
be in the possession of a p.; *in den*
~ *e-r S. setzen* put in possession of;
ℒ-**anzeigend** *gr.* possessive; ℒ**en**
possess, have; ℒ**end** propertied;
~**er(in** *f*) *m* possessor; (*Eigentümer*
[-*in*]) owner, propriet|or, *f* -ress;
e-s Wertpapiers, Passes usw.: holder;
den ~ *wechseln* change hands; ~**-er-
greifung** *f*, ~**nahme** *f* taking possession (*von* of), occupation; ℒ**erlos**
abandoned; ℒ**los** unpropertied; ~**-
stand** *m* ownership; † assets *pl.*;
~**störung** *f* trespass; ~**titel** *m* pos-
sessory title; ~**tum** *n* (1²), ~**ung** *f*

49*

possession; property, estate; **~-urkunde** f title-deed.

besoffen P [bə'zɔfən] (roaring) drunk.

besohlen [~'zo:lən] (25) sole.

besold|en [~'zɔldən] (26) pay (a salary); **~et** salaried; **2ung** f (16) pay; salary.

be'sonder particular, special; *(einmalig)* singular; *(eigenartig)* peculiar; *(gesondert)* separate; et. **2es** something special; *nichts* **2es** nothing out of the way; *im* **~en** in particular; **2heit** f particularity; peculiarity; special quality *(od.* feature); **~s** especially, particularly; separately, apart.

besonnen [~'zɔnən] prudent; *(bedacht)* considerate; *(vernünftig)* sensible, level-headed; **2heit** f prudence; considerateness; *(Geistesgegenwart)* presence of mind.

be'sorgen *(fürchten)* apprehend, fear; *(Sorge tragen für)* take care of; *(erledigen)* attend to; *(beschaffen)* get *(j-m et.* a p. a th., a th. for a p.), procure, provide (a th. for a p.); *Haushalt usw.:* manage; F *es j-m* ~ settle a p.'s hash.

Besorgnis [bə'zɔrknis] f (14²) apprehension, fear, anxiety; **2-erregend** alarming.

be'sorgt [~kt] *(fürchtend)* alarmed *(um* for); *(ängstlich bemüht)* anxious, solicitous *(um* about, for); **2heit** f *s. Besorgnis;* solicitude.

Be'sorgung [~guŋ] f *(Erledigung)* handling, management; *(Beschaffung)* procurement; *(Einkauf)* purchase; *(Auftrag)* errand; **~en** *machen* go shopping; **~sgebühr** f service charge.

be'spann|en put (the) horses to; *mit Saiten:* string; *mit Stoff:* cover; **2ung** f stringing; covering.

be'speien spit on *od.* at.

be'spiegeln: *sich* ~ look at o.s. (F admire o.s.) in the glass.

be'spielt *Musik-, Videokassette:* prerecorded.

be'spitzeln (29) spy on *a. p.*

be'spötteln (29) ridicule.

be'sprech|en discuss, talk *a th.* over; *Buch usw.:* review; *(vereinbaren)* arrange, agree upon; *Schallplatte usw.:* make a recording on; *sich* ~ *mit* confer with; **2er(in** f) *m e-s Buches usw.:* reviewer; **2ung** f discussion;

review; conference; **2ungs-exemplar** *n e-s Buches:* review copy.

be'sprengen sprinkle, spray.

be'spritzen (be)spatter, splash.

be'spucken spit at *od.* (up)on.

besser ['bɛsər] better; *(überlegen)* superior; *es* ~ *haben als ein anderer* be better off than; *es geht (wirtschaftlich)* ~ things are looking up; *es geht ihm heute* ~ he is better today; *ich täte* ~ *(daran) zu gehen* I had better go; *es* ~ *wissen* know better; ~ *gesagt* or rather; *um so* ~ all the better; *du könntest nichts* **2es** *tun* you could not do better; *s. belehren, besinnen, Hälfte;* '**~n** (29) improve; *moralisch:* reform; *sich* ~ (grow) better, improve; *moralisch:* reform, mend one's ways.

'**Besserung** f improvement *(a.* ⚕ *u.* ✝); *(Wendung)* change for the better; *moralisch:* reform; *gute* ~! hope you will be better soon; '**~s-anstalt** f *für Jugendliche:* reformatory, *Am. mst* reform school.

'**Besserverdienende** *m/pl.* (18) better earners, higher income bracket *sg.*

'**Besserwisser** *m* know-all.

best [bɛst] best; *der erste* **~e** the first comer; *am* **~en** best; *aufs* **~e,** **~ens** in the best way; *auf dem* **~en** *Wege sein zu inf.* be in a fair way to *inf.; zum* **~en** *geben Lied:* oblige with, *Geschichte:* tell, relate, entertain with; *j-n zum* **~en** *haben* make fun of a p.; *nach* **~en** *Kräften* to the best of one's power; *nach meinem* **~en** *Wissen* to the best of my knowledge; *sich von der* **~en** *Seite zeigen* show o.s. *(od.* be) at one's best; *zu Ihrem* **2en** in your interest; *zum* **2en** *der Armen* for the benefit of the poor; *in den* **~en** *Jahren* in the prime of life; *fig. das* **2e** *herausholen* make the best of it; *sein* **2es** *geben* do one's best; *ich täte am* **~en** *zu gehen* I had best go; *empfehlen Sie mich* **~ens!** remember me most kindly!; *ich danke* **~ens** thank you very much!, *ablehnend:* I would rather be excused!, *contp.* thank you for nothing!

bestall|en [bə'ʃtalən] (25) appoint (zu to); **2ung** f appointment; **2ungs-urkunde** f certificate of appointment.

Be'stand *m* (3³) *(Bestehen)* existence;

(*Fortdauer*) continuance, duration; (*Haltbarkeit*) stability, durability; (*Vorrat*) stock; (*Kapital♀*) assets *pl.*; (*Aktien♀ usw.*) holdings *pl.*; (*Kassen♀*) cash (*od.* balance) in hand; (*Waren♀*) stock on hand; (*Fahrzeug♀*) rolling stock, fleet; ✂ (*Mannschafts♀*) strength; (*Rest♀*) rest, remainder; *von* ~ *sein,* ~ *haben* be durable (*od.* lasting), endure, last.

be'ständig constant, steady; (*unveränderlich*) invariable; (*dauerhaft*) lasting, permanent, stable; (*andauernd*) continual; (*beharrlich*) persistent; *Wetter*: settled; *Barometerstand*: set fair; ~e *Valuta* stable currency; ♀keit *f* constancy, steadiness; stability, permanence; continuance.

Be'stand|s-aufnahme ✝ *f* stock-taking (*a. fig.*), *Am.* inventory; ~teil *m* component (part), constituent (part); element; *e-r Mischung*: ingredient; (*Einzelteil*) part; *s. auflösen*

be'stärken *j-n, e-e Vermutung usw.*: confirm; (*ermutigen*) encourage; (*verstärken*) strengthen.

bestätig|en [~'ʃtɛːtigən] (25) confirm; *amtlich*: attest; (*erhärten*) corroborate; *Vertrag, Gesetz*: ratify; ⚖ *Urteil*: uphold; *Empfang*: acknowledge; *sich* (*nicht*) ~ (not) to be confirmed, prove true (false); ♀ung *f* confirmation; attestation; corroboration; ratification; acknowledg(e)ment.

bestatt|en [~'ʃtatən] (26) bury, inter; ♀ung *f* funeral; (*Beerdigung*) burial, interment; (*Feuer♀*) cremation; ♀ungs-institut *n* (firm of) undertakers *pl., Am.* funeral home.

be'stäub|en dust, spray; ♣ pollinate; ♀ung *f* dusting, spraying; ♣ pollination.

be'stechen bribe, corrupt; *fig.* be fascinating, impress; ~d brilliant, fascinating, impressive; *Wesen*: engaging.

be'stechlich corruptible; ♀keit *f* corruptibility.

Be'stechung *f* bribery, corruption; ~s-affäre *f* bribery scandal; ~sgeld *n* bribe.

Besteck [bə'ʃtɛk] *n* (3) ⚔ set of instruments; (*Eß♀*) knife, fork and spoon, (set of) cutlery; ⚓ reckoning.

be'stecken stick (*mit* with).
be'stehen 1. *v/t.* overcome, conquer; (*durchmachen*) undergo, endure, go through; *Kampf*: win; *Probe*: stand; *Prüfung*: pass; *e-e Prüfung nicht* ~ fail in an examination; *v/i.* be, exist; subsist; (*fort~*) last, continue; ~ *auf* (*acc.*) insist (up)on; ~ *aus* consist of, be composed of; ~ *in* (*dat.*) consist in; *nicht* ~ *Prüfling*: fail; 2. ♀ *n* existence; *e-r Prüfung*: passing; (*j-s*) ~ *auf* (*acc.*) insistence (by a p.) on; ~d existing; (*gegenwärtig*) present.

be'stehlen rob, steal from.
be'steig|en ascend (*a. Thron*), climb (on); *Pferd, Fahrrad*: mount; *Schiff*: (go on) board a ship; *Wagen usw.*: enter, *bsd. Am.* board; ♀ung *f* ascent.

Be'stell|buch ✝ *n* order-book; ♀en *Ware, Speise usw.*: order; *Zeitung*: subscribe to; *Platz, Zimmer*: book; (*kommen lassen*) ask *a p.* to come; send for; (*ernennen*) appoint (*zum Statthalter usw.* [to be] governor *etc.*); *Brief, Botschaft*: deliver; *Feld*: till, cultivate; *Grüße*: give; *sein Haus* ~ put one's house in order; *es ist schlecht mit ihm* (*od. um ihn*) *bestellt* he is in a bad way; ~er *m* orderer; *e-r Zeitung*: subscriber; ~karte *f*, ~schein *m*, ~zettel *m* order form (*od.* slip); ~ung *f* order, commission; subscription (*gen.* to); appointment; ✒ cultivation; *e-s Briefes*: delivery; *auf* ~ *gemacht* made to order, *Am.* custom-made.

'bestenfalls at best.
be'steuer|n tax; ♀ung *f* taxation.
bestial|isch [bɛst'jɑːliʃ] beastly; bestial; ♀ität [~jali'tɛːt] *f* bestiality.
Bestie ['bɛstjə] *f* (15) beast, brute.
bestimm|en [bə'ʃtimən] (*entscheiden*) determine; decide; *Preis*: fix; *Ort, Zeit usw.*: appoint; *vom Gesetz*: lay down; *v. höherer Gewalt*: ordain; *Begriff*: define; *Daten, Werte*: determine; *j-n zu, für et.* ~ destine (*od.* intend) for; *j-n* ~ *et. zu tun* determine (*od.* induce) a p. to do a th.; ~ *über* (*acc.*) dispose of; ~t *Zeit*: appointed; *Summe usw.*: fixed; (*entschlossen*) decided, determined; (*sicher*) certain, positive; *Antwort, Begriff, gr.*: definite; ~ *sein für od. zu* be intended for; *sich* ~ *ausdrücken* express o.s. distinctly;

(*ganz*) ~ decidedly; certainly!, *Am.* sure!; *et.* ~ *wissen* know a th. for certain; ~ *nach* ⚓, ✈ bound for; 2t-heit *f* exactitude; determination; certainty; *mit* ~ positively; 2ung *f* determination; destination (*a. Ort*); (*Geschick*) destiny; (*Beruf*) vocation; (*Begriffs*2) definition; (*Vorschrift*) direction, instruction; 🖈 provision; *amtliche* ~en *pl.* regulations; 2ungsland † *n* country of destination; 2ungs-ort *m* (point of) destination.

'Best|leistung *f* record (performance); '2möglich best possible.

be'straf|en punish; 2ung *f* punishment; (*Strafe*) *a.* penalty.

be'strahl|en irradiate; 🖋 ray-treat, *mit Radium*: radio; 2ung *f* irradiation; 🖋 ray-treatment.

be'streb|en 1. *sich* ~ (*od. bestrebt sein*) *zu inf.* endeavo(u)r (*od.* strive) to *inf.*, *begierig*: be anxious to *inf.*; 2. 2 *n* (6) (*Neigung*) tendency; = 2ung *f* effort, endeavo(u)r, attempt.

be'streichen spread; ✕ *mit Feuer*: rake, sweep; *mit Butter* ~ butter.

be'streiken *Betrieb*: strike; *bestreikt* strikebound, struck.

be'streit|bar contestable, disputable; ~en (*anfechten*) contest, dispute; (*leugnen*) deny; *Ausgaben*: bear, defray; *Bedürfnisse*: supply; *Unterhaltung*: do (*the talking*); 2ung *f der Kosten*: defrayal.

be'streuen strew; *mit Salz usw.* ~ sprinkle with salt, *etc.*; *mit Kies* ~ gravel; *mit Zucker* ~ sugar.

be'stricken *fig.* ensnare; (*berücken*) charm, bewitch.

Bestseller ['bɛstzɛlər] *m* (7) bestseller; '~-autor *m* bestselling author.

be'stück|en ✕, ⚓ arm (with guns); 2ung *f* armament, guns *pl.*

be'stürm|en storm, assail; *fig. mit Bitten, Fragen usw.*: assail (with); 2ung *f* storming, assault.

bestürz|t [~'ʃtyrtst] dismayed (*über acc.* at); perplexed; 2ung *f* consternation, dismay.

Besuch [~'zu:x] *m* (3) visit (*gen.*; *bei*, *in dat.* to); *kurzer*: call (*bei* on); (*Besucher*) visitor(s *pl.*), company; *gewohnheitsmäßiger* ~ *e-s Gasthauses usw.*: frequentation; *der Schule usw.*: attendance (*gen.* at); (*Besichtigung*) visit (*gen.* to); *auf* (*od. zu*) ~ on a visit; *e-n* ~ *machen* pay a visit *od.*

call; 2en visit; *P.*: go (*od.* come) to see, call on; *Ort, Gasthaus usw. gewohnheitsgemäß* ~: frequent; *Schule, Versammlung usw.*: attend; *Kino, Theater*: go to; *gut besucht* well attended; ~er(in *f*) *m* visitor (*gen.* to); caller; (*Gast*) guest; (*Zuschauer*) spectator; ~szeit *f* visiting hours *pl.*; ~szimmer *n* visitors' room.

be'sudeln soil; *fig. a.* sully; (*bekritzeln*) scribble over.

betagt [~'ta:kt] *s.* bejahrt.

be'takel|n ⚓ rig; 2ung *f* rigging.

be'tasten finger, feel, touch.

betätig|en [~'tɛ:tigən] (25) ⊕ manipulate; *Bremse usw.*: actuate, operate; *sich* ~ busy o.s.; *als*: act as; *bei et.*: take an active part in, participate in; 2ung *f* operation, actuation; (*Tätigkeit*) activity.

betäub|en [~'tɔʏbən] (25) *durch Lärm, e-n Schlag usw. od. fig.*: stun, daze; *durch Schlafmittel usw. od. fig.*: drug; 🖋 an(a)esthetize, narcotize; *Schmerz*: deaden, dull; *fig. sich* ~ divert o.s.; ~end stunning (*a. fig.*); *Lärm*: deafening; 🖋 narcotic; 2ung *f* stunning; stupefaction; 🖋 narcotization, an(a)esthesia, (*Zustand*) narcosis; 2ungsmittel *n* narcotic.

Betbruder ['be:t-] *m* devotee, bigot.

Bete 🌱 ['be:tə] *f* (15) beet(-root).

beteilig|en [bə'taɪligən] (25): *j-n* ~ give a p. a share *od.* interest (*an od. bei dat.* in); *sich* ~ *an od.* bei participate (*od.* take part) in; *beteiligt sein bei* have a share (*od.* interest) in, be interested in, (*verwickelt sein*) be involved in; 2te [~çtə] *m, f* party (*od.* person) concerned, participant; 🖈 party (*an dat.* to); 2ung [~guŋ] *f* participation; † *a.* (*Teilhaberschaft*) partnership; (*Anteil*) share, interest; (*Teilnehmerzahl*) attendance.

beten ['be:tən] (26) *v/i.* pray (*um* for), say one's prayers; *bei Tische*: say grace; *v/t.* say (*a prayer*).

beteuer|n [bə'tɔʏərn] (29) protest, affirm; '2ung *f* protestation; affirmation (*a.* 🖈).

betiteln [~'ti:təln] (29) *P., Buch usw.*: entitle; (*nennen*) style, call.

Beton ⊕ [be'tõ, ~'to:n] *m* (11) concrete.

beton|en [bə'to:nən] (25) stress (*a.*

fig.), accent; *fig. nachdrücklich* ~ emphasize; *fig. betont* studied, emphatic(ally); ⚥**ung** *f* accentuation; (*Silbenton*) accent, stress; emphasis (*alle a. fig.*).
betonieren [beto'niːrən] concrete.
Be'ton|klotz *m* concrete block; *contp.* (*Haus*) concrete pile; ~**mischmaschine** *f* cement mixer; ~**wüste** *f* *contp.* concrete jungle.
betören [bə'tøːrən] (25) befool; (*verliebt machen*) bewitch, infatuate, charm.
Betracht [~'traxt] *m* (3, *o. pl.*): *in* ~ *ziehen* take into consideration, consider; (*einkalkulieren*) allow (*od.* make allowance) for; *außer* ~ *lassen* disregard; (*nicht*) *in* ~ *kommen* (not) to come into question, (not) to be concerned; ⚥**en** view (*a. fig.*); (*genau*) inspect; *sinnend*: contemplate; *fig.* ~ *als* consider; ~**er(in** *f*) *m* viewer, observer; ~**ung** *f* view; contemplation; consideration; ~**ungsweise** *f* way of looking at things.
beträchtlich [~'trɛçtliç] considerable.
Betrag [~'traːk] *m* (3³) amount; (*Gesamt*⚥) (sum) total; *im* ~*e von* to the amount of; ⚥**en** [~gən] **1.** amount to; (*insgesamt* ~) total; *sich* ~ behave (o.s.); **2.** ⚥ *n* (6) behavio(u)r, conduct.
be'trauen entrust (*mit* with).
be'trauern mourn (for), deplore.
Betreff [bə'trɛf] *m am Briefanfang*: subject, re; *in* ⚥, ⚥s (*gen.*) with regard to, in respect of, concerning; ⚥**en** (*befallen*) befall; (*fig. berühren*) affect, touch; (*angehen*) concern; (*sich beziehen auf*) refer (*od.* relate) to; (*behandeln*) deal with; *was mich betrifft* as for me, as far as I am concerned; *was das betrifft* as to that; *betrifft* (*am Briefanfang*) subject, re; ⚥**end** concerning *a th.*; *die* ~*e Person* the person concerned *od.* in question; *das* ~*e* (*erwähnte*) *Buch* the book referred to.
be'treiben 1. *Geschäft*: carry on, run; *Studien, Gewerbe usw.*: pursue; *Eisenbahn usw.*: work, *Am.* operate; (*beschleunigen*) urge *a th.* on, push forward; **2.** ⚥ *n*: *auf* ~ *von* (*od. gen.*) at the instigation of.
be'treten 1. set foot on *od.* in, step on (to); *Raum*: enter; *Schwelle*:

cross; ⚥ *des Rasens usw. verboten!* keep off the grass *etc.*!; **2.** *adj. fig.* embarrassed.
betreu|en [~'trɔyən] (25) care for; attend (on), look after; ⚥**ung** *f* care (*gen.* of, for).
Betrieb [bə'triːp] *m* (3) (*Betreiben*) management, working, running, *bsd. Am.* operation; (*Unternehmen*) enterprise, concern; (*Anlage*) plant; (*Werkstatt*) workshop; (*Fabrikanlage*) works, factory, *Am.* plant; (*Eisenbahn*⚥, *Schiffs*⚥ *usw.*) service; (*Geschäftigkeit*) activity; (*lebhaftes Treiben*) bustle; *öffentlicher* ~ public utility; *außer* ~ out of operation, (*defekt*) out of order; *in* ~ working, operating, in operation; *in* ~ *setzen* start; *den* ~ *einstellen* shut down; *den* ~ *wiederaufnehmen* reopen.
be'triebsam active, industrious; ⚥**keit** *f* activity, bustle; industry.
Be'triebs|-anleitung *f* operating instructions *pl.*; ~**-ausflug** *m* works outing; ⚥**fähig** serviceable; ⚥**fertig** ready for service; ~**führer** *m s.* *Betriebsleiter*; ~**geheimnis** *n* trade secret; ~**-ingenieur** *m* production engineer; ~**kapital** *n* working capital; ~**klima** *n* working conditions *pl.*; ~**kosten** *pl.* running expense(s *pl.*), *Am.* operating cost; ~**leiter** *m* (works) manager; ~**material** *n* working stock; ~**obmann** *m* shop steward; ~**rat** *m* (*P.*: member of the) works council; ⚥**sicher** safe (to operate); (*zuverlässig*) reliable (in service); ~**sicherheit** *f* safety (in operation); reliability; ~**stoff** *m mot.* fuel; ~**störung** *f* trouble; breakdown, stoppage; ~**-unfall** *m* industrial accident; ~**wirtschaft(slehre)** *f* management.
betrinken: *sich* ~ get drunk.
betroffen [~'trɔfən] *fig.* shocked, startled; *von Krankheit usw.* ~ *stricken* (*od.* afflicted) with; *s. betreffend*; ⚥**heit** *f* perplexity, shock.
betrüb|en [~'tryːbən] grieve, afflict; ~**lich** [~'tryːp-] sad; ⚥**nis** *f* (14²) affliction, grief; ~**t** sad, grieved (*über acc.* at, about).
Be'trug *m* (3) cheat; ŗŧ, *a.fig.* fraud, deceit; *bsd. fig.* deception.
be'trüg|en cheat, deceive, defraud; *j-n um et.* ~ cheat a p. out of; ⚥**er** (**-in** *f*) *m* cheat, deceiver, swindler;

Ջe'rei f cheating, fraud(ulence); ⸃erisch deceitful, fraudulent.
be'trunken drunken, pred. drunk; Ջe m (18) drunken man; Ջheit f drunkenness, intoxication.
Bet|saal ['beːtsaːl] m chapel, oratory; '⸃stuhl m praying-desk.
Bett [bɛt] n (5) bed (a. geol., ⊕); am ⸃ at the bedside; das ⸃ hüten keep one's bed; zu ⸃ bringen put to bed; zu ⸃ gehen go to bed, F turn in; krank zu ⸃ liegen be laid up; '⸃couch ['⸃kautʃ] f (16, pl. inv. ⸃es) bed--couch, divan bed; '⸃decke f bedspread, coverlet, counterpane; wollene ⸃ blanket; gesteppte ⸃ quilt.
Bettel ['bɛtəl] m (7, o. pl.) (Plunder) trash; der ganze ⸃ the whole lot; 'Ջ'-arm desperately poor; '⸃brief m begging letter; '⸃brot n bread of charity; ⸃ei [⸃'laɪ] f (16) begging; mendicancy; '⸃kram m s. Bettel; '⸃mönch m mendicant friar; 'Ջn (29) beg (um for); ⸃ gehen go begging; '⸃stab m: an den ⸃ bringen reduce to beggary, ruin.
'betten (26) bed (a. ⊕); fig. embed; sich ⸃ make one's bed; wie man sich bettet, so liegt man as you make your bed so you must lie on it.
'Bett|flasche f hot-water bottle; '⸃lade f bedstead.
bettlägerig ['⸃lɛːgəriç] bedridden, confined to bed, Am. a. bedfast; 'Ջkeit f confinement to bed.
'Bettlaken n sheet.
'Bettler m (7) beggar; '⸃in f beggar (-woman).
Bett|nässer ['⸃nɛsər] m (7) bed--wetter; '⸃stelle f bedstead; '⸃tuch n sheet; '⸃überzug m pillow--case; '⸃ung ⊕ f bed(ding), bed--plate; '⸃vorleger m (7) bedside rug; '⸃wäsche f bed-linen; '⸃zeug n bedding.
betucht [⸃'tuːxt] F well-heeled.
betupfen [bə'tupfən] dab.
beug|en ['bɔʏgən] (25) bend, bow (a. sich ⸃; vor dat. to); Stolz: humble; durch Kummer: bow down, afflict; gr. inflect; das Recht ⸃ pervert justice; vom Alter gebeugt bowed down by age; 'Ջung f bending; gr. inflexion, inflection.
Beule ['bɔʏlə] f (15) bump, swelling; (Geschwür) boil; in Blech usw.: dent; '⸃npest f bubonic plague.
be-unruhig|en [bə'⁹unruːigən] (25)

disturb, trouble; fig. a. worry, disquiet, alarm; sich ⸃ über (acc.) worry about; Ջung f trouble; anxiety, alarm; worry.
be-urkund|en [⸃'⁹uːrkundən] (26) authenticate, certify, legalize; Ջung f authentication, legalization.
be-urlaub|en [⸃'⁹uːrlaubən] (25) grant leave (of absence); vom Amt: suspend; sich ⸃ take (one's) leave; ⸃t [⸃pt] (absent) on leave; Ջung [⸃buŋ] f (granting of a) leave; suspension.
be-urteil|en [⸃'⁹urtaɪlən] judge (nach by); Ջer(in f) m (7) judge; critic; Ջung f judg(e)ment, opinion (gen. of, on).
Beute ['bɔʏtə] f (15) booty, spoil; (a. Diebs⸃) loot; e-s Tieres: prey (a. fig.: gen. to); hunt. bag; auf ⸃ ausgehen go plundering.
Beutel ['bɔʏtəl] m (7) bag; (zo.; Tabaks⸃) pouch; (Geld⸃) purse; biol. sac; beim Billard: pocket; 'Ջig baggy; 'Ջn (29) shake; Mehl: bolt; '⸃schneider m s. Betrüger; '⸃tier n marsupial.
'Beutezug m raid.
bevölker|n [bə'fœlkərn] (29) people, populate; Ջung f population.
Be'völkerungs|dichte f density of population; ⸃-explosion f population explosion; ⸃politik f population policy; ⸃stand m (level of) population; ⸃-überschuß m surplus population.
bevollmächtig|en [⸃'fɔlmɛçtigən] (25) authorize, empower; Ջte [⸃tiçtə] m (18) authorized agent; proxy, deputy; Ջung [⸃guŋ] f authorization; s. Vollmacht.
be'vor before.
be'vormund|en (26) keep in tutelage, hold in leading-strings; Ջung f tutelage.
be'vorraten (25) stock up.
be'vorrecht(ig)en (26) privilege.
Be'vorschussung f advance.
be'vorstehen be near od. forthcoming, lie ahead; Gefahr: be imminent; j-m: be in store for; ⸃d forthcoming, approaching; Gefahr: imminent; (nächst) next (week, etc.).
bevorzug|en [⸃'foːrtsuːgən] (25) prefer; favo(u)r; 🕮 privilege; Ջung f preference.
be'wach|en guard, watch; Sport: mark; Ջung f guard; custody.

be'wachsen: ~ *mit* grown (over) with.

be'waffn|en arm; **~et** armed; *Auge*: aided; *mit ~er Hand* by force of arms; **²ung** *f* armament (*a. e-s Schiffes*); (*Waffen*) arms *pl.*

be'wahren (*erhalten*) keep, preserve; (*behüten*) preserve (*vor dat.* from); (*Gott*) *bewahre!* Heaven forbid!

be'währen prove; *sich ~* stand the test; prove good *od.* a success; *Grundsatz*: hold good.

Be'wahrer(in *f*) *m* (7) keeper.

bewahrheiten [~'va:rhaɪtən] (26) verify; *sich ~* come (*od.* prove) true.

bewährt [~'vɛ:rt] (well) tried, tested, proved; (*zuverlässig*) reliable.

Be'wahrung *f* keeping, preservation (*vor dat.* from).

Be'währung *f* proof, trial, (crucial) test; ⚖ = **~sfrist** *f* probation(ary period); **~shelfer(in** *f*) *m* probation officer; **~s-probe** *f* test; **~szeit** *f s. Bewährungsfrist.*

bewaldet [~'valdət] wooded, woody.

bewältigen [~'vɛltigən] (25) cope with, master, handle.

bewandert [~'vandərt] versed; skilled; experienced (*in dat.* in).

Bewandtnis [~'vantnis] *f* (14²): *damit hat es folgende ~* the case is this; *das hat seine eigene ~* that is a matter apart, thereby hangs a tale.

bewässer|n [~'vɛsərn] *Garten*: water; *Land*: irrigate; **²ung** *f* watering; irrigation; **²ungs-anlage** *f* irrigation plant.

beweg|en [~'ve:gən] (30) (*a. sich*) move, stir (*beide a. seelisch*); *sich im Kreise* (*fig. in feinen Kreisen*) ~ move in a circle (in good society); (*sich*) *von der Stelle ~* budge; *sich ~ lassen* be moved (*von, durch* with *pity etc.*); *j-n zu et. ~* induce, get; *s. bewogen*; **~end** moving (*a. fig.*); *~de Kraft* motive power; **²grund** [~'ve:k-] *m* motive; **~lich** movable; *P., Geist*: versatile; (*behend*) agile, nimble; *Zunge*: voluble; *~e Habe* movables *pl.*; **²lichkeit** *f* mobility; movableness; versatility; agility; volubility; **~t** *See*: agitated; *fig.* (*gerührt*) moved, touched; *Leben*: eventful; *Zeit*: stirring, turbulent.

Be'wegung [~guŋ] *f* movement (*a. pol. usw.*); *unruhige*: stir; *phys.* motion; (*Gemüts²*) emotion, *stärker*: agitation; *körperliche ~* (*Sport usw.*) physical exercises *pl.*; *in ~ setzen* set in motion; *sich in ~ setzen* start, get going; *sich ~ machen* take exercise; *s. Hebel*; **~sfreiheit** *f* freedom of movement; *fig.* liberty of action; **~skrieg** *m* mobile warfare; **²slos** motionless; **~s-therapie** ⚕ *f* kinesiotherapy; **²s-unfähig** unable to move.

be'wehren arm (*a. zo.*, ⚘, ⊕); *Beton*: reinforce.

be'weihräuchern cense; *fig.* adulate.

be'weinen deplore, mourn.

Beweis [bə'vaɪs] *m* (4) proof (*für* of); evidence (of); *s. ~grund*; *zum ~ e-r S.* in proof of a th.; *den ~ für et. antreten* undertake to prove a th.; *den ~ für et. erbringen* furnish proof of, prove; **~-aufnahme** *f* taking of evidence; **²bar** provable, demonstrable; **²en** [~zən] prove; demonstrate; *Interesse usw.*: show; **~führung** *f* reasoning, argumentation; **~grund** *m* argument; **~kraft** *f* argumentative (*bsd.* ⚖ probative) force; **~material** *n* evidence; **~-stück** *n* (piece of) evidence; *vor Gericht*: exhibit.

be'wenden 1. *es ~ lassen bei* leave it at; **2.** **²** *n*: *dabei hat es sein ~* there the matter rests.

be'werb|en: *sich ~ um* apply for (*bei* to); (*kandidieren*) stand for, *Am. a.* run for; *um Stimmen*: canvass; ✝ *um Aufträge*: solicit; *sich* (*mit andern*) *~* (*um e-n Preis*) compete (with *others* for *a prize*); *sich um e-e Dame ~* court, woo; **²er** *m um ein Amt*: applicant; candidate; *um e-n Preis*: competitor (*alle a.* **²erin** *f*; *um* for); (*Freier*) suitor, wooer; **²ung** *f* application; candidature; competition; courtship (*um* of); **²ungsformular** *n* application sheet; **²ungsschreiben** *n* letter of application; **²ungsverfahren** *n* application procedure.

be'werfen pelt; ⚠ plaster.

bewerkstellig|en [~'vɛrkʃtɛligən] (25) manage, bring about, contrive; **²ung** *f* effecting, accomplishment.

bewert|en [~'ve:rtən] value (*auf acc.* at; *nach* by); (*einschätzen*) rate; **²ung** *f* valuation; rating.

bewillig|en [~'viligən] (25) grant, allow; **²ung** *f* grant, allowance.

bewirken 778

be'wirken effect; (*verursachen*) cause (*daß j. tut a p.* to do; *daß et. geschieht a th.* to be done); (*hervorrufen*) produce, give rise to.

bewirt|en [~'virtən] (25) entertain; 2ung f entertainment.

be'wirtschaft|en *Betrieb*: manage, run; *Mangelware*: ration, a. *Devisen*: control; 2ung f management, running; rationing, control.

bewog [~'vo:k] *pret. v. fig.* bewegen; ~en [~'vo:gən] *p.p. v. fig.* bewegen; *sich ~ fühlen zu* feel bound to *inf.*

bewohn|bar [~'vo:nba:r] habitable; 2barkeit f habitableness; ~en inhabit, live in; occupy; 2er(in f) m (7 [16¹]) inhabitant; *e-s Hauses*: occupant, *bei mehreren*: a. inmate.

bewölk|en [~'vœlkən] (25) cloud; *sich ~* cloud over; ~t cloudy; 2ung f clouding.

Bewunder|er [~'vundərər] m (7), ~in f admirer; 2n admire; 2nswert [~sve:rt], 2nswürdig admirable; ~ung f admiration.

bewußt [~'vust] conscious; (*bekannt*) known; (*absichtlich*) deliberate, *adv. a.* knowingly; *sich e-r S. ~ sein* be conscious (*od.* aware) of; *die ~e Sache* the matter in question; ~los unconscious; ~ werden lose consciousness; 2losigkeit f unconsciousness; 2sein n consciousness; *in dem ~* conscious (*gen.* of; *daß* that); *bei ~ sein* be conscious; *j-m et. zum ~ bringen* bring a th. home to a p.; *j-m zum ~ kommen* come home to a p.; *wieder zum ~ bringen* (*kommen*) bring a p. (come) round to; ~seins-erweiternd *Droge*: mind-expanding.

be'zahl|en pay; *Gekauftes*: pay for; *sich bezahlt machen* (*S.*): pay (for itself); 2ung f pay(ment).

be'zähmen tame; *fig.* restrain.

be'zauber|n bewitch, enchant; *fig. a.* charm, fascinate; ~t *von* enchanted with; 2ung f enchantment.

be'zeichn|en mark; *fig.* (*bedeuten*) denote, signify; (*benennen, a. für ein Amt*) designate (*als* as); call, name; (*zeigen*) point out; (*kennzeichnen*) characterize; ~end typical, characteristic (*für* of); ~enderweise typically enough; 2ung f marking, *konkret*: mark; denotation; designation; name, term; sign.

be'zeig|en show, express, manifest;

2ung f expression, manifestation.

be'zeug|en (*a.* ⚖) bear witness to, testify to *od.* that; (*bescheinigen*) certify; 2ung f attestation.

bezichtigen [bə'tsiçtigən] (25) *s.* beschuldigen.

be'zieh|bar *Wohnung*: ready for occupation; *Ware*: obtainable; ~en *Schirm usw.*: (neu ~ re)cover; *mit Saiten*: string; *Wohnung*: move into, occupy; *Universität usw.*: enter, go up to; *Ware*: obtain, procure, get; *Zeitung*: take in; *Lohn usw.*: draw, receive; *Bett*: sheet; ⚔ *Stellung*: take up; ⚔ *ein Lager ~* encamp; *~ auf* (*acc.*) apply (*od.* relate) to; *sich ~ Himmel*: become overcast; *sich ~ auf* (*acc.*) refer (*od.* relate) to; *sich auf j-n ~* use a p.'s name as (a) reference; 2er(in f) m (7) *e-s Wechsels*: drawer; *e-r Zeitung*: subscriber (*gen.* to); (*Käufer*) buyer, taker.

Be'ziehung f relation, reference (*zu* to); *persönliche ~en pl.* connexions, relations (*zu j-m* with); *gute ~en haben* be well connected; *in dieser usw. ~* in this etc. respect; *in politischer, wirtschaftlicher usw. ~* politically, economically *etc.*; *in ~ stehen zu* (*S.*) be related to; *in guten ~en stehen* be on good etc. terms (*zu j-m* with); 2slos irrelative, unconnected; 2svoll suggestive; 2sweise respectively.

beziffern [~'tsifərn] (29) figure; *~ auf* (*acc.*) figure at; *sich ~ auf* figure (*od.* work) out at, amount to.

Bezirk [bə'tsirk] m (3) district; *Am.* (*Polizei2, Wahl2*) precinct; *fig. s.* Bereich.

Bezogene ✝ [~'tso:gənə] m (18) drawee.

Be'zug [bə'tsu:k] m (3³) cover(ing), case; (*Kissen2*) slip; *v. Ware*: purchase, supply; *e-r Zeitung, a. von Aktien*: subscription (*gen.* to); *fig.* relation, reference; *bei ~ von 25 Stück* on orders for; *in 2 auf* (*acc.*) as for, as to; with regard to, in relation to; *~ haben* (*od.* nehmen) refer to.

Bezüg|e [~'tsy:gə] m/pl. emoluments, drawings, income *sg.*; (*Gehalt*) pay, salary; (*Lieferungen*) supplies; 2lich [~'tsy:kliç] adj. (*auf acc.*), *prp.* (*gen.*) relative to; *gr. ~es Fürwort* relative pronoun.

Be'zugnahme [∼nɑːmə] *f* (15) reference; *unter* ∼ *auf (acc.)* with reference to, referring to.
Bezugs... [∼'tsuːks-]: ∼**bedingungen** *f/pl.* terms of delivery; ∼**person** *f* person to whom one relates most closely; ∼**preis** *m* subscription (*od.* issue) price; ∼**punkt** *m* reference point; ∼**quelle** *f* source of supply; ∼**schein** *m* purchase permit.
bezwecken [∼'tsvɛkən] (25) aim at; *et.* ∼ *mit* intend by.
be'zweifeln doubt, question.
be'zwing|en master, overcome; conquer; subdue; *sich* ∼ restrain o.s.; 2**er(in** *f*) *m* (7 [16¹]) subduer.
Bibel ['biːbəl] *f* (15) Bible; '∼spruch *m* verse from the Bible, text; '∼stelle *f* scriptural passage, text.
Biber ['biːbər] *m* (7) beaver; '∼pelz *m* beaver fur (fur).
Biblio|graph [biːbliˈoˈgrɑːf] *m* (12) bibliographer; ∼**graphie** ['∼graˈfiː] *f* (15) bibliography; ∼**thek** [∼'teːk] *f* (15) library; ∼**thekar** [∼teˈkɑːr] *m* (3¹) librarian.
biblisch ['biːbliʃ] biblical, scriptural; ∼e *Geschichte* scripture.
bieder ['biːdər] honest, upright; *a. ironisch*: worthy; '2**keit** *f* honesty, uprightness; '2**mann** *m* (1²) honest (*od.* upright) man; worthy.
bieg|en ['biːgən] (30) *v/t.* (*a. sich*) bend; *gr.* inflect; *sich vor Lachen* ∼ be doubled up with laughter; *v/i.* (sn): *um e-e Ecke* ∼ turn (round) a corner; *auf* 2 *oder Brechen* by hook or by crook; ∼**sam** ['∼kzaːm] flexible, supple; *fig. a.* pliant; '2**samkeit** *f* flexibility, suppleness; pliancy; 2**ung** [∼gun] *f* bend(ing); *gr.* inflexion; (*Weg*2, *Fluß*2) bend, turn.   [doll.⟩
Biene ['biːnə] *f* (15) bee; F (*Mädel*)⟩
'**Bienen|fleiß** *m* assiduity; '∼**haus** *n* apiary, bee-house; '∼**königin** *f* queen bee; '∼**korb** *m* bee-hive; '∼**schwarm** *m* swarm of bees; '∼**stich** *m* bee's sting; '∼**stock** *m* bee-hive; '∼**wachs** *n* beeswax; '∼**zucht** *f* bee-keeping; '∼**züchter** *m* bee-keeper.
Bier [biːr] *n* (3) beer; *helles* ∼ pale ale; *dunkles* ∼ dark ale; ∼ *vom Faß* beer on draught; (*Lager*2) lager; F *das ist dein* ∼ that's your problem; '∼**baß** F *m* beery voice; '∼**bauch** *m*

beer-belly; '∼**brauer** *m* brewer; '∼**brauerei** *f* brewery; '∼**deckel** *m* beer mat; '∼**dose** *f* beer can; '∼**eifer** *m* excessive zeal; '∼**fahrer** *m* beer lorry (*Am.* truck) driver; '∼**faß** *n* beer-barrel; '∼**garten** *m* beer garden; '∼**hefe** *f* brewer's yeast, barm; '∼**krug** *m* beer-mug, *Am.* stein; '∼**kutscher** *m* drayman; '∼**reise** F *f* pub-crawl; '∼**ruhe** F *f* imperturbable calm; '2**selig** F beery, tiddly; '∼**stube** *f*, '∼**wirtschaft** *f* public house, F pub, *Am.* beer-saloon.
Biese ['biːzə] *Schneiderei*: (pin) tuck; ✂ piping.
Biest [biːst] *n* (1¹) beast (*a.* F *fig.*).
bieten ['biːtən] (30) offer; *e-n guten Morgen*, ✝, *bei Auktion*: bid; *sich* ∼ (*Gelegenheit*) present (*od.* offer) itself; *das läßt er sich nicht* ∼ he won't stand that; *s. Stirn.*
Bigamie [biːgaˈmiː] *f* (15) bigamy.
bigott [biˈgɔt] bigoted; 2e'**rie** *f* (15) bigotry.
Bilanz [biˈlants] *f* (16) balance; (*Aufstellung*) balance-sheet; *Am. a.* statement; *die* ∼ *ziehen* strike the balance; 2**ieren** [∼'tsiːrən] balance, show in the balance-sheet.
Bild [bilt] *n* (1) *allg.* picture; (*Ab*2, *Eben*2) image (*a. opt., TV*); *in e-m Buch*: illustration; (*Bildnis*) portrait; *rhet.* metaphor; (*Vorstellung*) idea; *im* ∼e *sein* be in the picture; *im* ∼ *sein über (acc.)* be aware of, know about; *j-n ins* ∼ *setzen* inform a p., put a p. in the picture; *sich ein* ∼ *machen von et.* picture a th. to o.s.; '∼**archiv** *n* photo library; '∼**band** *m* illustrated book; '∼**bericht** *m Presse*: picture-story.
bilden ['bildən] (26) *allg.* (*a. sich*) form; (*gestalten*) *a.* shape, fashion; *Geist*: cultivate; *Ausschuß, Gruppe*: constitute; *sich geistig* ∼ educate o.s.; '∼**d** (*belehrend*) instructive; ∼e *Künste f/pl.* fine (*od.* plastic) arts.
'**Bilder|-anbetung** *f* image-worship; '∼**bogen** *m* picture-sheet; '∼**buch** *n* picture-book; '∼**galerie** *f* picture-gallery; '∼**rätsel** *n* rebus; '2**reich** rich in pictures; *Sprache*: flowery; '∼**schrift** *f* picture-writing; '∼**sprache** *f* imagery; '∼**stürmer** *m* iconoclast.
Bild|fläche ['bilt-] *f* image area *od.* plane; *Film*: screen; *auf der* ∼ *erscheinen* appear on the scene, turn

up; *von der* ~ *verschwinden* vanish; '~**funk** *m* (3¹) radio picture transmission; *TV* television; '²**haft** plastic; '~**hauer(in** *f*) *m* sculptor; ~**haue'rei** *f* sculpture; '²'**hübsch** very pretty; '~**karte** *f Karten:* court-card, *Am.* face card; '²**lich** pictorial, graphic; *Ausdruck usw.:* figurative; ~**ner** ['~dnər] *m* (7), '~**nerin** *f* sculptor; *fig.* mo(u)lder; ~**nis** ['bilt-] *n* (4¹) portrait, likeness; effigy; '~**platte** *f* videodisc; '~**plattenspieler** *m* videodisc player; '~**qualität** *f* image (*phot.* picture) quality; '~**röhre** *f* picture tube; '²**sam** (*a. fig.*) plastic; '~**säule** *f* statue; '~**schirm** *m* (television) screen; '~**schirmgerät** *n Computer:* (video) display (terminal); '~**schirmtext** *m* videotex; '~**schnitzer** *m* (wood-)carver; '²'**schön** most beautiful; '~**sendung** *f*, '~**übertragung** *f* picture transmission; '~**streifen** *m* film strip; (*Zeichnung*) strip cartoon; '~**telegraphie** *f* phototelegraphy; '~**telephon** *n* videophone.

Bildung ['bilduŋ] *f* (16) *allg.* formation; *des Körpers:* form, shape; (*Gründung*) foundation, organization; *e-s Ausschusses usw.:* constitution; (*Aus²*) education; (*Kultur*) culture; (*Kenntnisse*) knowledge, information; (*Gelehrsamkeit*) learning; (*feine Sitte*) refinement, good breeding; '²**sfähig** cultivable; '~**sgang** *m* course of education; '~**sgrad** *m* educational standard; '~**slücke** *f* gap in *a p.'s* education; '~**snotstand** *m* educational crisis; '~**s-politik** *f* educational policy; '~**s-urlaub** *m* educational holiday.

'**Bildwerk** *n* sculpture; imagery; (*Buch*) book of plates.

Billard ['biljart] *n* (3¹ *u.* 11) billiards *sg.*; (~*tisch*) billiard-table; '~**kugel** *f* billiard-ball; '~**stock** *m* cue.

Billett [bil'jet] *n* (3) ticket; ~**-ausgabe** *f*, ~**schalter** *m* ticket-office; *s. Karten...*

Billiarde [bil'jardə] *f* (15) *a* thousand billions, *Am.* quadrillion.

billig ['biliç] (*gerecht*) equitable, fair, just; (*vernünftig, mäßig*) reasonable; (*wohlfeil*) cheap (*a. fig. contp.*); '²**-angebot** *n* cut-price offer; '~**en** (25) approve (of); (*genehmigen*) sanction; '²**keit** *f* equitableness, fairness, justice, *bsd.* ⚖️ equity;

cheapness; ²**ung** ['~guŋ] *f* approval; sanction.

Billion [bil'jo:n] *f* (16) billion, *Am.* trillion.

bimbam! ['bim'bam] ding-dong!

bimmeln F ['biməln] (29) tinkle.

Bimsstein ['bims∫tain] *m* pumice (-stone).

Binde ['bində] *f* (15) band; ⚕️ bandage, *für den Arm:* sling; (*Hals²*) (neck)tie; (*Kopf²*) fillet; (*Stirn²*) bandeau; *j-m e-e* ~ *vor die Augen tun* blindfold a p.; *fig. j-m die* ~ *von den Augen nehmen* open a p.'s eyes; '~**gewebe** *anat.* n connective tissue; '~**glied** *n* connecting link; '~**haut** *f* conjunctiva; '~**haut-entzündung** *f* conjunctivitis; '~**mittel** *n* binding agent; △ *u. fig.* cement; '²**n** (30) (*a. fig.*) bind, tie (*an acc.* to); *Buch:* bind; *Knoten, Schlips, Schnürband:* tie; *Besen, Strauß:* make; *Faß:* hoop; ♪ slur; *sich* ~ bind o.s.; '²**nd** binding (*für* upon); '~**r** *m* (*Schlips*) (neck-)tie; '~**strich** *m* hyphen; *mit* ~ *schreiben* hyphen(-ate); '~**wort** *n* conjunction.

Bind|faden ['bint-] *m* string; *stärker:* packthread, twine; ~**ung** ['~duŋ] *f a.* Ski: binding; △, *fig.:* bond; ♪ slur, ligature; *fig., a.* ♪ tie; (*Verpflichtung*) commitment; *fig.* ~**en** *pl.* bonds, ties.

binnen ['binən] (*dat. od. gen.*) within; ~ *kurzem* before long.

'**Binnen|gewässer** *n* inland water; '~**hafen** *m* inner harbo(u)r; '~**handel** *m* inland (*od.* home) trade; '~**land** *n* inland, interior; '~**länder** (-**in** *f*) *m* inlander; '²**ländisch** inland, internal; '~**markt** *m* home market; '~**meer** *n* inland sea; '~**schiffahrt** *f* inland navigation; '~**schiffer** *m* bargee, *Am.* bargeman; '~**verkehr** *m* inland traffic.

Binse ['binzə] *f* (15) rush; F *in die* ~*n gehen* go to pot; '~**nwahrheit** *f*, '~**nweisheit** *f* truism.

Biochem|ie [bioçe'mi:] *f* biochemistry; ~**iker** [~'çe:mikər] *m* biochemist; ²**isch** biochemical.

Bio|-Chip ['bi:o-] *m Computer:* bio-chip; '~**gas** *n* biogas; '~**gas-anlage** *f* biogas (heating) system.

Biograph [bio'gra:f] *m* (12), ~**in** *f* biographer; ~**ie** [~gra'fi:] *f* biography; ²**isch** [~'gra:fi∫] biographical.

'**Bioladen** *m* health food shop.

Biolog|e [bio'lo:gə] *m* (13) biologist;
~ie [~lo'gi:] *f* biology; **2isch** [~'lo:giʃ]
biological.
'Bio|masse *f* biomass; **'~physik** *f*
biophysics *sg.*; **'~rhythmus** *m* bio-
rhythm; **~'top** [-'to:p] *n* (3) biotope.
Birke ['birkə] *f* (15) birch(-tree).
'Birk|hahn *m* black-cock; **'~henne**
f, **'~huhn** *n* grey-hen.
'Birnbaum *m* (3¹) pear-tree.
Birne ['birnə] *f* (15) ♀ pear; *(Glüh2)*
bulb; *sl. (Kopf)* pate, *Am.* bean.
birnenförmig ['~fœrmiç] pear-
-shaped.
bis [bis] **1.** *prp. räumlich*: to; up to;
(~ *nach*) as far as; *zeitlich*: till;
until; down to; (~ *spätestens*) by;
zwei ~ *drei* two or three; ~ *an*, ~
auf (acc.) to, up to; ~ *auf weiteres*
until further notice; ~ *auf (acc.) s.*
abgesehen von; *alle* ~ *auf drei* all
but three; ~ *dahin* so far; ~ *hierher*
thus far; ~ *heute* up to this day,
Am. F todate; ~ *jetzt* till now, up
to the present; ~ *jetzt noch nicht*
not as yet; ~ *vier zählen* count up
to four; **2.** *cj.* till, until.
Bisam ['bi:zam] *m* (3¹) musk; *(Pelz)*
musquash; **'~ratte** *f* musk-rat.
Bischof ['biʃɔf] *m* (3¹ *u.* 3³) bishop.
bischöflich ['~ʃø:fliç] episcopal.
'Bischofs|-amt *n* episcopate; **'~sitz**
m (episcopal) see; cathedral town;
'~stab *m* crosier.
bisher [bis'he:r] hitherto, till *(od.*
up to) now, so far, as yet; **~ig**
hitherto existing; previous; *(jetzig)*
present.
Biskuit [bis'kvi:t] *n* biscuit; **~-**
kuchen *m* sponge-cake.
Biß¹ [bis] *m* (4) bite *(a. ~wunde)*.
biß² *pret. v.* beißen.
bißchen ['~çən]: *ein* ~ a little (bit).
Bissen ['bisən] *m* (6) bit, morsel.
'bissig biting; *Hund., a. P.*: snappish; *Bemerkung usw.*: cutting; *Vorsicht, ~er Hund!* Beware of the dog!;
'2keit *f* snappishness.
Bistum ['bistu:m] *n* (1²) bishopric.
bisweilen [bis'vailən] sometimes.
Bit [bit] *n* (11) *Computer*: bit.
Bitte ['bitə] *f* (15) request; *(dringende* ~) entreaty; *auf j-s* ~ at a p.'s
request; *ich habe e-e* ~ *an Sie*
I have a favo(u)r to ask of you.
'bitten (30) *v/t.* ask, request; *dringend*: entreat; *(einladen)* invite; *j-n
um Verzeihung* ~ beg a p.'s pardon;

sich (lange) ~ *lassen* want a lot of
asking; *v/i.* ~ *für j-n* intercede for;
~ *um et.* ask for; *bitte* please; *nach
danke!*: (you're) welcome, don't
mention it; *(wie) bitte?* (I beg your)
pardon!; *Spiel: bitte!* play!; *dürfte
ich Sie um ... ~?* may I trouble you
for ...?; *Wünschen Sie noch eine
Tasse Tee? Bitte (sehr)!* Yes, thank
you!
bitter ['bitər] bitter; *fig. a.* severe,
sharp; *Schokolade*: plain; ~er *Ernst*
bitter earnest; **'~böse** furious;
(schlimm) very wicked; **'~'ernst** dead
serious; **'2keit** *f* bitterness *(a. fig.)*;
'~lich bitterish; *adv.* bitterly; **'2salz**
⚕ *n* Epsom salts *pl.*; **'2wasser** *n*
bitter mineral water.
'Bitt|gang *m* procession; **'~gesuch**
n, **'~schrift** *f* petition; **'~steller**
(**-in** *f*) *m* petitioner.
Biwak ['bi:vak] *n* (3¹), **2ieren**
[~'ki:rən] bivouac.
bizarr [bi'tsar] bizarre.
Bizeps ['bi:tsɛps] *m* (3²) biceps.
bläh|en ['blɛ:ən] (25) *v/t.* inflate,
(a. sich) swell *(a. fig.: vor dat.* with);
v/i. **⚕** cause flatulence; **'~end** **⚕**
flatulent; **'2ung** **⚕** *f* flatulence,
wind.
Blam|age [bla'ma:ʒə] *f* (15) shame,
disgrace; **2ieren** [~'mi:rən] *(bloßstellen)* compromise *(sich o.s.)*;
(lächerlich machen) ridicule; *sich* ~
make a fool of o.s.
blank [blaŋk] bright, shining; (~
geputzt) polished; *Schuh*: shiny;
(bloß) naked, bare *(a. ⊕)*; *(abgetragen)* shiny; F *(ohne Geld)* broke;
~er *Unsinn* sheer nonsense; ~ *ziehen* draw (one's sword).
Blankett [blaŋ'kɛt] *n* blank form,
Am. a. blank; *s. Blankovollmacht.*
blanko ✝ ['blaŋko] *(adv.* in) blank;
'2... blank; **'2vollmacht** *f* full dis-
cretionary power, carte blanche *(fr.)*.
Bläs-chen ['blɛ:s?çən] *n* (6) small
bubble; **⚕** pustule.
Blase ['bla:zə] *f* (15) *(Luft2)* bubble;
(Harn2 usw.) bladder; *(Haut2)*
blister, **⚕** vesicle; *im Glas usw.*:
flaw; F *contp.* gang; **'~balg** *m* bellows *pl.*; **'2n** (30) blow; *Horn usw.*:
sound *(zum Angriff usw.* the charge
etc.); **'~n-entzündung** *f* cystitis;
'~nkrebs *m* bladder cancer; **'~n-
leiden** *n* bladder trouble; **'2nzie-
hend** **⚕** vesicant.

Bläser ['blɛ:zər] *m* (7) blower; ♩ *die* ~ *pl. im Orchester* the wind.

blasiert [bla'zi:rt] blasé (*fr.*).

blasig ['blɑ:ziç] bubbly; blistery.

'**Blas|-instrument** ♩ *n* wind-instrument; *die* ~*e pl. im Orchester* the wind; '~**kapelle** *f* brass-band; '~**rohr** *n* blowpipe; *zum Schießen*: a. pea-shooter.

Blasphemie [blasfe'mi:] (15) *f* blasphemy.

blaß [blas] pale; ~*rot usw.* pale red *etc.*; ~ *werden* (turn) pale, *Farbe*: fade; *blasser Neid* green envy; *keine blasse Ahnung* not the faintest idea.

Blässe ['blɛsə] *f* (15) paleness, pallor.

Blatt [blat] *n* (1², *als Maß im pl. inv.*) *Pflanze, Buch*: leaf; *Papier*: sheet; *Schulter, Ruder, Schwert*: blade; (*Zeitung*) (news)paper; *Karten*: *ein gutes* ~ a good hand; ♩ *vom* ~ *spielen* play at sight; *kein* ~ *vor den Mund nehmen* not to mince matters; *fig. das* ~ *hat sich gewendet* the tables are turned.

Blatter ['blatər] *f* (15) pustule; pock; '~*n pl.* smallpox.

blätt(e)rig ['blɛt(ə)riç] leafy, *in Zssgn* ...-leaved; *min.* laminate(d).

blättern ['blɛtərn] (29) turn over the leaves (*in dat. of*).

'**Blatter|narbe** *f* pock-mark; '2**narbig** pock-marked.

'**Blätterteig** *m* puff-paste.

'**Blatt|gold** *n* gold-leaf; '~**grün** *n* chlorophyll; '~**laus** *f* plant-louse; '~**pflanze** *f* foliage plant; '~**stiel** *m* leaf-stalk; '~**werk** *n* foliage.

blau [blau] **1.** blue; F (*betrunken*) *sl.* tight, plastered; ~*es Auge fig.* black eye; *mit e-m* ~*en Auge davonkommen* get off cheaply; F ~ *machen* take a day off; *s. Blut, Dunst, Wunder*; **2.** 2 *n* blue; *ins* ~*e hinein* at random; '~**äugig** ['~ˀɔygiç] blue-eyed; *fig.* gullible, naive; '2**beere** *f* bilberry, *Am.* blueberry; '~**blütig** blue-blooded.

Bläue ['blɔyə] *f* (15, *o. pl.*) blue(-ness).

bläuen ['blɔyən] (25) (dye) blue.

'**Blau|fuchs** *m* arctic (♱ blue) fox; '2**grau** bluish grey; '~**kraut** *n* red cabbage.

'**bläulich** bluish.

'**Blau|meise** *f* bluetit; '~**pause** *f* blueprint; '~**säure** *f* prussic acid; '~**stift** *m* blue pencil; '~**strumpf** *fig. m* blue-stocking.

Blech [blɛç] *n* (3) sheet metal; *s. Feinblech usw.*; F (*Unsinn*) rot, bosh, *Am.* blah; '~**büchse** *f* tin (box), *Am.* (tin) can.

'**blechen** F (25) pay (up).

'**blechern** (of) tin; *Klang*: tinny.

'**Blech|geschirr** *n* tin-plate vessels *pl.*; '~**instrument** ♩ *n* brass instrument; *die* ~*e pl. im Orchester* the brass; '~**musik** *f* (music of a) brass band; '~**schere** *f* plate-shears *pl.*; '~**schmied** *m* tinsmith; '~**verkleidung** *f* sheeting; '~**ware(n** *pl.*) *f* tinware.

blecken ['blɛkən] (25): *die Zähne* ~ show one's teeth.

Blei [blai] *n* (3) lead; ⚓ plummet; (~*stift*) (lead) pencil; (*Geschoß*) shot.

bleiben ['blaibən] (30, sn) remain, stay; (*übrig*~) be left, remain; *in der Schlacht*: fall; (*andauern*) continue; *treu usw.* ~ remain; *bei et.* ~ keep to, stick to, abide by; *dabei muß es* ~ there the matter must rest; *es bleibt dabei!* agreed!; '~**d** lasting, permanent; '~**lassen** leave (*od.* let) *a th.* alone.

bleich [blaiç] pale; ~ *werden* turn pale; '2**e** *f* (15) paleness; *der Wäsche*: bleaching; (*Bleichplatz*) bleaching-ground; '~**en** (25) *v/t. u. v/i.* (sn) bleach, blanch; *Farbe*: fade; '2**sucht** *f* greensickness, ⚕ chlorosis; ~**süchtig** ['zyçtiç] greensick, ⚕ chlorotic.

bleiern ['blaiərn] leaden (*a. fig.*).

'**blei|farben** lead-colo(u)red; '~**frei** *Benzin*: unleaded; *Am.* lead-free; '2**gehalt** *m* lead content; '~**haltig** containing lead, plumbiferous; *Benzin*: leaded; '2**kugel** *f* (lead-)bullet; '2**lot** *n* plumb(-line); ⚓ lead, plummet; '2**rohr** *n* lead pipe; '2**satz** *typ. m* hot-metal setting; '2**soldat** *m* tin soldier; '2**stift** *m* (lead) pencil; '2**stiftspitzer** *m* pencil-sharpener; '2**vergiftung** *f* lead poisoning; '2**weiß** *n* white lead.

Blend|e ['blɛndə] *f* (15) blind; △ blind window *od.* door; ⚒ blend; *phot.* diaphragm, stop; '2**en** (26) blind; *auf kurze Zeit od. fig.*: dazzle; '~**er** *m fig.* bluffer, F dazzler; '2**frei** ⊕ dazzle-free; '~**laterne** ['blɛnt-] *f* dark lantern; '~**ling** *zo. m* bastard, mongrel; '~**rahmen** *m* blind frame; '~**schutzscheibe** *f* anti-dazzle screen, *Am.* (sun) visor; '~**schutz-zaun** *m Autobahn:* anti-dazzle barrier; ~**ung** ['~duŋ] *f* blinding; dazzling; '~**werk** ['blɛnt-] *n* delusion; (*Betrug*) deception.

Blesse ['blɛsə] *f* (15) blaze, white spot;(*Pferd*) horse with a blaze.

Blick [blik] *m* (3) look; *flüchtiger:* glance; (*Aussicht*) view (*auf acc.* of); *auf den ersten* ~ at first sight; *mit einem* ~ at a glance; *einen (keinen)* ~ *für et.* haben have an (no) eye for; *e-n* ~ *werfen auf* cast a glance (*od.* take a look) at; '²**en** (25) look, glance (*auf acc., nach* at); *sich* ~ *lassen* show o.s., appear; '~**fang** *m* eye-catcher; '~**feld** *n* field of vision; *fig.* range (of vision); '~**punkt** *m* visual focus; *fig.* focus; *im* ~ in the cent|re (*Am.* -ter) of interest; '~**winkel** *m* visual angle; *fig.* point of view.

blieb [bli:p] *pret. v.* **bleiben**.

blies [bli:s] *pret. v.* **blasen**.

blind [blint] blind (*a. fig.:* für, gegen to); (*trübe*) tarnished, dull; *Patrone:* blank; *Gehorsam, Glaube, Liebe, Wut:* blind; ⚠ blind, sham; *auf e-m Auge* ~ blind of (*Am.* in) one eye; ~*er Alarm* false alarm; ~*er Passagier* deadhead, ⚓ stowaway.

'**Blinddarm** *m* blind gut, 🔲 caecum; (*Wurmfortsatz*) appendix; '~**ent-zündung** *f* appendicitis; '~**opera-tion** *f* appendectomy.

'**Blinde** *m* blind man, *f* blind woman.

'**Blindekuh** *f* blind-man's-buff.

'**Blinden**|-**anstalt** *f* blind asylum, home for the blind; '~**hund** *m* blind man's dog, guide-dog, *Am.* seeing--eye dog; '~**schrift** *f* braille; '~**stock** *m* blind man's cane.

blind|**fliegen** 🛫 ['blint-] fly blind, fly on instruments; '²**flug** *m* instrument (*od.* blind) flying; ²**gän-ger** 🔲 ['~gɛŋər] *m* (7) blind (shell), *sl.* dud; F *fig.* washout; '²**heit** *f* blindness; *mit* ~ *geschlagen* struck blind; ~**lings** ['~liŋs] blindly; ²~**schleiche** ['~ʃlaɪçə] *f* (15) slow--worm; '~**schreiben** *Schreibma-schine:* touch-type.

blink|**en** ['bliŋkən] (25) blink; gleam, *bsd. Sterne:* twinkle; 🔲, ⚓ (*signalisieren*) flash; '²**feuer** *n* intermittent light; '²**licht** *n* 🔲 inter-

mittent light; *mot.,* 🛫 indicator; '²**zeichen** *n* flash signal.

blinzeln ['blintsəln] (29) blink; *mit einem Auge, a. lustig:* wink.

Blitz [blits] *m* (3²) lightning; *fig.* flash; *s.* ~**strahl;** *phot.* flash(-light); *wie der* ~ like a shot; *vom* ~ *getrof-fen* struck by lightning; *ein* ~ *aus heiterem Himmel* a bolt from the blue; ~**ableiter** ['~⁹aplaɪtər] *m* (7) lightning-rod; '~**besuch** *m* flying visit; '²**blank** shining; *pred.* spick and span; '²**en** (27) *v/i.* flash; *es blitzt* there is lightning; '~**gerät** *phot. n* flash gun; '~**gespräch** *teleph. n* special priority call; '~**krieg** *m* blitz; '~**licht** *phot. n* flash-light; '~**schlag** *m* lightning-stroke; '²**schnell** as quick as lightning; *adv. a.* with lightning speed; '~**strahl** *m* thunder-bolt; '~**würfel** *phot. m* flash cube.

Block [blɔk] *m* (3³) block (*a. von Häusern usw.*); (*Holz²*) log; (*Fahr-karten²*) book; (*Schreib²*) pad, book; *pol.* bloc; ~**ade** [~'ka:də] *f* (15) block-ade; ~**debrecher** *m* blockade-run-ner; '~**flöte** *f* recorder; '²**frei** *pol.* non-aligned; '~**haus** *n* log-house; 🞨 blockhouse; ²**ieren** [~'ki:rən] block (up); ⊕ jam; '~**säge** *f* pit-saw; '~**satz** *typ. m* justified lines *pl.*; '~**schrift** *f* block letters.

blöd|**e** ['blø:də] (*schwachsinnig*) im-becile; (*dumm*) stupid, dull; (*albern*) silly; (*schüchtern*) shy; (*unangenehm*) awkward, stupid; ²**heit** ['blø:t-] *f* imbecility; stupidity, dul(l)ness; sil-liness; '²**mann** F *m* dimwit, jerk; ²**sinn** ['blø:tzin] *m* imbecility, idi-ocy; (*Unsinn*) nonsense, *sl.* rot; '~**sinnig** silly, idiotic; *adv.* F awfully; ²**sinnige** ['~zinigə] *m, f* idiot.

blöken ['blø:kən] (25) bleat; *Kalb:* low.

blond [blɔnt] blond(e *f*), fair; '~**ge-lockt** blond and curly-haired; ²**ine** [~'di:nə] *f* (15) blonde.

bloß [blo:s] **1.** bare, naked; (*nichts als*) mere, simple; *Schwert, Auge:* naked; *mit* ~*em Kopf* bare-headed; **2.** *adv.* merely, only, simply.

Blöße ['blø:sə] *f* (15) bareness, nakedness; 🞨, *fenc.,* *fig.* weak point *od.* spot, opening; (*Lichtung*) glade; *sich e-e* ~ *geben* expose o.s.; *sich j-m gegenüber e-e (empfindliche)* ~ *geben* leave o.s. (wide) open to a p.

'**bloß**|**legen** lay bare; '~**stellen** ex-

pose, show up; *sich* ~ compromise
o.s.; '2stellung *f* exposure.
blühen ['bly:ən] (25) bloom, blossom; *fig.* flourish; F *j-m* ~ be in
store for a p.; '~d *Aussehen*: rosy;
Unternehmen: flourishing.
Blume ['blu:mə] *f* (15) flower; *des
Weins*: bouquet; *des Biers*: froth;
hunt. tail; *durch die* ~ *sagen* say a
th. under the rose; *laßt* ~*n sprechen!* say it with flowers!
'**Blumen**|**-ausstellung** *f* flower-
-show; '~**beet** *n* flower-bed; '~**blatt**
n petal; '~**draht** *m* florist's wire;
'~**dünger** *m* plant fertilizer; '~**erde**
f garden-mo(u)ld; '~**händler(in** *f*) *m*
florist; '~**kelch** *m* calyx; '~**kohl** *m*
cauliflower; '~**korso** *m* carnival of
flowers; '~**krone** ⚥ *f* corolla; '2**reich**
flowery (*a. fig.*); '~**strauß** *m* bunch
of flowers, bouquet; '~**topf** *m* flow-
er-pot; '~**zucht** *f* floriculture; '~**-
züchter(in** *f*) *m* florist; '~**zwiebel** *f*
flower-bulb.
'**blumig** flowery (*a. fig.*).
Bluse ['blu:zə] *f* (15) blouse.
Blut [blu:t] *n* (3, *o. pl.*) blood;
blaues (junges) ~ blue (young)
blood; *bis aufs* ~ to the quick;
böses ~ *machen* breed bad blood;
~ *lecken (schwitzen)* taste (sweat)
blood; *ruhig* ~! keep cool!; '~**alkohol** *m* blood alcohol; '~**andrang**
m rush of blood (to the head), ⚕
congestion; '2**-arm** an(a)emic; *blut-*
'**arm** extremely poor, penniless; '~**
armut** *f* an(a)emia; '~**bad** *n* carnage,
massacre; '~**bank** ⚕ *f* blood bank;
'~**bild** ⚕ *n* blood picture (*od.* count);
'~**blase** *f* blood blister; '~**buche** *f*
copper-beech; '~**druck** *m* blood-
-pressure; '~**durst** *m* bloodthirsti-
ness; 2**dürstig** ['~dyrstiç] blood-
thirsty.
Blüte ['bly:tə] *f* (15) blossom,
bloom; flower (*a. fig. Elite*); *der
Jahre*: prime; (*Wohlstand*) prosperity; *s.* ~*zeit*; *e-e neue* ~ *erleben*
go through a time of revival.
'**Blut-egel** *m* leech.
'**bluten** (26) *a. fig.* bleed (*aus* from).
'**Blüten**|**knospe** *f* bud; '~**lese** *f*
anthology; '~**staub** *m* pollen; '~**
stengel** *m* peduncle.
'**Blut**|**-entnahme** *f* (taking of a)
blood sample; '~**erguß** *m* effusion
of blood.
'**Blütezeit** *f* (16) flowering time; *fig.*

a. heyday.
'**Blut**|**farbstoff** *m* h(a)emoglobin;
'~**fleck** *m* blood-stain; '~**gefäß** *n*
blood-vessel; '~**gerinnsel** *n* clot of
blood; '~**geschwür** *n* boil; '~**gier** *f
s. Blutdurst*; '~**gruppe** *f* blood-
-group; '~**hund** *m* bloodhound;
'2**ig** bloody; *Schlacht*: sanguinary;
fig. cruel; ~*er Anfänger* greenhorn;
~*er Ernst* deadly earnest; '2'**jung**
very young; '~**konserve** *f* unit of
stored blood; '~**körperchen** ['~kœr-
pərçən] *n* (6) blood-corpuscle; '~**
kreislauf** *m* blood circulation; '2**
leer**, 2**los** bloodless; '~**pfropfen** *m*
blood clot; '~**plasma** *n* blood plasma; '~**probe** *f* blood test; (*entnomme-
nes Blut*) blood sample; '~**rache** *f*
blood revenge, vendetta; 2**reinigend** purifying the blood, depura-
tive; '2'**rot** blood-red; 2**rünstig** ['~
rynstiç] bloody; '~**sauger** *m* blood-
-sucker, vampire; '~**schande** *f* in-
cest; 2**schänderisch** ['~ʃɛndəriʃ] in-
cestuous; '~**schuld** *f* blood-guilti-
ness; '~**senkung** *f* blood sedimenta-
tion; '~**spender(in** *f*) *m* blood donor;
'2**stillend** blood-sta(u)nching, styp-
tic; '~**s-tropfen** *m* drop of blood;
'~**sturz** *m* h(a)emorrhage; '2**sver-
wandt** related by blood (*mit* to);
'~**sverwandte** *m*, *f* blood relation;
'~**sverwandtschaft** *f* consanguini-
ty; '~**tat** *f* bloody deed; '2**triefend**
dripping with blood; '2**-über-
strömt** covered with blood; '~**
übertragung** *f* blood transfusion;
'~**ung** *f* bleeding, h(a)emorrhage;
'2**-unterlaufen** bloodshot; '~**vergießen** *n* bloodshed; '~**vergiftung** *f*
blood-poisoning; '~**verlust** *m* loss of
blood; '2**verschmiert** smeared with
blood; '~**wäsche** *f* dialysis; '2**wurst** *f*
black pudding; '~**zoll** *m* toll of lives;
'~**zucker** *m* blood sugar.
Bö [bø:] *f* (16) gust, squall.
Bob [bɔp] *m* (11) *Sport*: bob(sleigh).
Bock [bɔk] *m* (3⁹) buck; (*Widder*)
ram; (*Ziegen*2) he-goat; *Gerät*:
trestle, (*Turnen*: buck-)horse; (*Kut-
schersitz*) box; *e-n* ~ *schießen* commit a blunder, *Am.* F pull a boner;
den ~ *zum Gärtner machen* set the
fox to keep the geese; 2**beinig**
['~baıniç] *fig.* stubborn (as a mule).
bock|en ['bɔkən] (25) buck (*a. mot.*);
Mensch: sulk; '~**ig** obstinate.
'**Bock**|**leder** *n*, '2**ledern** buckskin;

'**⁓leiter** f step-ladder; '**⁓shorn** n: ins ⁓ jagen scare; '⁰springen play (at) leap-frog; '**⁓sprung** m caper, gambol; Bocksprünge machen caper, gambol.

Boden ['bo:dən] m (6¹) (Erde) ground; ✓ u. fig. soil; e-s Gefäßes, des Meeres: bottom; e-s Zimmers: floor; e-s Hauses: garret, loft; (festen) ⁓ fassen get a (firm) footing; ⁓ gewinnen (verlieren) gain (lose) ground; zu ⁓ schlagen (gehen) knock (go) down; '**⁓abwehr** ✕ f ground defen|ce, Am. -se; '**⁓belag** m floor covering; '**⁓erhebung** f rise, elevation; '**⁓ertrag** m crop yield; '**⁓fläche** f acreage; △ u. ⊕ floor-space; '**⁓haftung** mot. f road traction; '**⁓kammer** f garret; '**⁓kre'dit-anstalt** f land mortgage bank; '**⁓-'Luft-Rakete** f ground (od. surface)-to-air missile; '⁰los bottomless; fig. enormous; '**⁓personal** ⚰ n ground personnel, Am. ground crew; '**⁓radar** n ground-based radar; '**⁓reform** f land reform; '**⁓satz** m grounds, dregs pl., sediment; ⁓schätze ['⁓ʃɛtsə] m/pl. treasures of the soil, (mineral) resources; '⁰ständig native; racy of the soil; mil. home; '**⁓station** f Raumfahrt: tracking station; '**⁓streitkräfte** f/pl. ground forces; '**⁓turnen** n mat-work. [bottomry}

Bodmerei ⚓ [bo:dmə'raɪ] f (16)}
bog [bo:k] pret. v. biegen.

Bogen ['bo:gən] m (6) bow; e-s Flusses usw.: bend, curve; ⅄ arc; △ arch, vault; v. Papier: sheet; e-n großen ⁓ um j-n machen give a p. a wide berth; fig. den ⁓ überspannen go too far; '**⁓fenster** n bow window; '⁰förmig arched; '**⁓führung** ♪ f bowing; '**⁓gang** △ m arcade; '**⁓lampe** ⚡ f arc-lamp; '**⁓schießen** n archery; '**⁓schütze** m archer; '**⁓sehne** f bow-string; '**⁓zirkel** m bow compasses pl.

Bohle ['bo:lə] f (15) plank, thick board; '⁰n (25) plank.

Böhm|e ['bø:mə] m (13), '**⁓in** f, '⁰isch Bohemian; das sind mir ⁓e Dörfer that's all Greek to me.

Bohne ['bo:nə] f (15) bean; grüne ⁓n pl. French (Am. string) beans; weiße ⁓n pl. haricot beans; (Sau⁰) broad bean; fig. blaue ⁓ bullet.

'**Bohnen|kaffee** m pure coffee; '⁓-

kraut ♣ n savory; '**⁓stange** f bean-pole (a. F fig.).

Bohner ['bo:nər] m (7) (floor-)polisher; '⁰n (29) wax, polish; '⁓-wachs n floor-wax.

bohr|en ['bo:rən] (25) bore, drill; Brunnen: sink; nach Öl ⁓ prospect (od. drill) for oil; fig. (forschen) bore; (quälen) harass; '⁰er m (7) borer, drill; '⁰-insel f oil rig; '⁰loch n drill-hole; '⁰maschine f boring (od. drilling) machine; '⁰turm m derrick; '⁰ung f drilling; boring; (Loch) (drill)hole; (Durchmesser) diameter (of bore); mot. bore; (Kaliber) cali|bre, Am. -ber.

böig ['bø:iç] squally.

Boje ['bo:jə] f (15) buoy.

Böller ['bœlər] m (7) small mortar.

Bollwerk ['bɔlvɛrk] n (3) bulwark.

Bolschewis|mus [bɔlʃə'vismus] m (16) Bolshevism; ⁓t(in f) [⁓'vist] m (12 [16¹]) Bolshevist; ⁰tisch Bolshevist(ic).

Bolzen ['bɔltsən] m (6) bolt (a. ⊕).

Bombard|ement [bɔmbardə'mã] n (11) bombardment; ⁰ieren [⁓'di:rən] bombard (a. fig.); bomb.

Bombast [bɔm'bast] m (3²) bombast; ⁰isch bombastic(ally adv.).

Bombe ['bɔmbə] f (15) bomb (a. mit ⁓n belegen); fig. bombshell; Fußball: cracker; '**⁓n-alarm** m bomb alert; '**⁓n-angriff** m bomb-raid; '**⁓n-anschlag** m bomb attempt; '**⁓ndrohung** f bomb threat; '**⁓n-erfolg** m huge success, sl. smash hit; '⁰nfest, '⁰nsicher bomb-proof; fig. F dead sure; '**⁓nflugzeug** n, '**⁓r** m bomber; '**⁓ngeschäft** F n roaring trade; '**⁓n-leger** m (7) bomber; '**⁓nräumkom-mando** n bomb disposal squad; '**⁓n-sache** F f sl. knockout; '**⁓nschaden** m bomb-damage; '**⁓ntrichter** m bomb-crater.

Bon [bõ] m (11) coupon; voucher; (Gutschein) credit note.

Bonbon [bõ'bõ] m, n (11) bonbon, sweet(meat), Am. (hard) candy.

Bonbonniere [bõbɔ'njɛːrə] f (15) sweetmeat-box.

bongen ['bɔŋən] (25) F Registrierkasse: ring up; gebongt! sure!

Bonus ✝ ['bo:nus] m (14² od. inv.) bonus.

Bonze F ['bɔntsə] m (13) bigwig, big bug, big shot, bsd. pol. (party-)boss.

Boot [boːt] n (3) boat; '**~shaus** n boat-
-house; '**~smann** m boatswain; ✗,
⚓ petty officer.
Bor ♫ [boːr] n (3¹, o. pl.) boron; **~ax**
['boːraks] m (11¹ od. 3², o. pl.) borax.
Bord [bɔrt] m (3) ⚓, 🐎 board; (Rand)
edge, border, rim; an ~ e-s Schiffes on
board a ship; an ~ nehmen take
aboard; über ~ werfen throw over-
board (a. fig.); '**~computer** mot. m
dashboard computer; '**~elektronik**
🐎 f avionics sg.
Bordell [bɔr'dɛl] n (3¹) brothel.
'**Bord|flugzeug** n ship-plane, ship-
-borne aircraft; '**~funker** 🐎 m air
wireless (Am. radio) operator; '**~
karte** 🐎 f boarding card; '**~mecha-
niker** m, '**~monteur** 🐎 m air mechanic; '**~radar** n air-borne radar;
'**~schwelle** f, '**~stein** m kerb(stone),
Am. curb(stone); '**~wand** f ship's
side; '**~werkzeug** mot. n tool kit.
Bordüre [bɔr'dyːrə] f (15) border,
braiding.
Borg [bɔrk] m (3) borrowing; auf ~
on credit, F on tick; **⚩en** ['bɔrgən]
borrow; j-m et.: lend, bsd. Am. loan.
Borke ['bɔrkə] f (15) bark, rind;
(Kruste) crust.
Born [bɔrn] m (3) spring, well.
borniert [bɔr'niːrt] narrow-minded.
Bor|salbe ['bɔrzalbə] f borax oint-
ment; '**~säure** f boric acid.
Börse ['bøːrzə] f (15) purse; ✝ Exchange, 🏛 (')Change; (Effekten⚩)
Stock Exchange; an (od. auf) der ~
on the Exchange; '**~nbericht** m
Exchange (od. market) report; in
der Zeitung: City article od. news;
'**~nblatt** n Stock Exchange journal; '**⚩nfähig** negotiable (od. marketable) on the Stock Exchange;
'**~ngeschäft** n (Stock) Exchange
transaction; '**~nkrise** f crisis of the
(Stock) Exchange; '**~nkurs** m Exchange rate; '**~nmakler** m stock-
-broker; '**~nnotierung** f (market-)
quotation; '**~npapiere** n/pl. stocks
pl.; '**~nschluß** m close of the Exchange; '**~nspekulant** m stock-
-jobber; '**~nzeitung** f financial
paper; '**~nzettel** m stock-list, mar-
ket-report.
Borste ['bɔrstə] f (15) bristle.
'**borstig** bristly; fig. surly.
Borte ['bɔrtə] f (15) border; (Be-
satz⚩) braid.
Borwasser ['boːrvasər] n boric acid

solution.
bös [bøːs] s. böse; '**~artig** ill-na-
tured, malicious, Am. F ugly; Tier:
vicious; 🖤 malignant; '⚩**-artigkeit**
f malignity; viciousness; 🖤 malig-
nancy.
Böschung ['bœʃuŋ] f slope; (Fluß⚩
usw.) embankment; bsd. ✗ scarp.
böse ['bøːzə] allg. bad; (verrucht)
evil; (boshaft) malicious, wicked;
(zornig) angry, cross (über et. at,
about; auf j-n, mit j-m, F j-m with),
Am. mad (at a p.); er meint es nicht
~ he means no harm; der ⚩ (18) the
Evil One; '⚩n (18) evil; '⚩**wicht** m
villain (a. fig. co.).
bos|haft ['boːs-haft] malicious;
(mutwillig) mischievous; (tückisch)
spiteful; '⚩**heit** f malice; malignity;
aus ~ out of spite.
bossieren [bɔ'siːrən] emboss.
'**böswillig** malevolent; ~e Absicht ⚖
malice prepense; adv. ⚖ wilfully;
'⚩**keit** f malevolence.
bot [boːt] pret. v. bieten.
Botanik [bo'taːnik] f (16) botany;
~er m (7) botanist.
bo'tanisch botanic(al).
botanisier|en [~ni'ziːrən] botanize;
⚩**trommel** f vasculum.
Bot|e ['boːtə] m (13), '**~in** f (16¹)
messenger.
'**Botengang** m errand.
'**botmäßig** subject; (gehorsam) obedient; '⚩**keit** f dominion, rule,
sway.
'**Botschaft** f message; Amt: em-
bassy; gute ~ good tidings pl. od.
sg.; '**~er** m (7) ambassador; '**~erin** f
ambassadress; '**~erkonferenz** f
ambassadors' conference.
Böttcher ['bœtçər] m (7) cooper;
~ei [~'raɪ] f cooper's workshop;
Handwerk: cooper's trade.
Bottich ['bɔtiç] m (3) tub, vat.
Bouillon [bul'jõ] f (11¹) broth,
clear soup, beef-tea; **~würfel** m
beef-tea cube.
Boutique [bu'tiːk] f (16) boutique.
Bowle ['boːlə] f (15) bowl; (Getränk)
spiced wine, cup.
Box [bɔks] f (16) 1. (a. **~e** [15]) für
Pferde: box; mot. pit; 2. (**~kamera**)
box-camera; 3. (Lautsprecher⚩)
speaker.
box|en ['bɔksən] (27) box; '⚩**er** (7)
m boxer; '⚩**handschuh** m boxing-
-glove; '⚩**kampf** m boxing-match;

'Ꝛring *m* ring; 'Ꝛsport *m* boxing.
Boykott [bɔy'kɔt] *m* (3), Ꝛieren
[~'tiːrən] boycott.   [mutter.⟩
brabbeln F ['brabəln] (29) babble,⟩
brach[1] [braːx] *pret. v.* brechen.
brach[2] fallow (*a. fig.*); 'Ꝛ-**acker** *m*,
'Ꝛfeld *n* fallow land.
Brachialgewalt [brax'jaːlɡəvalt] *f*
(*mit ~ by*) brute force (*od.* strength).
'**brach**|**legen** lay fallow; '~**liegen**
v/i. lie fallow; *fig.* lie idle, be neg-
lected; 'Ꝛschnepfe *f*, 'Ꝛvogel *m*
curlew.
brachte ['braxtə] *pret. v.* bringen.
Brahman|**e** [bra'maːnə] *m* (13),
Ꝛisch Brahman, *mst* Brahmin.
Bramsegel ⚓ ['braːm-] *n* top-
gallant sail.
Branche ⅂ ['brɑ̃ːʃə] *f* (15) branch,
line, trade; industry; '~**nkenntnis** *f*
knowledge of the trade; 'Ꝛn-**üblich**
customary in the industry concerned; '~**nverzeichnis** *n* classified
directory.
Brand [brant] *m* (3[2] *u.* [3]) burning;
(*Feuersbrunst*) fire, conflagration;
🞛 gangrene, (*kalter ~*) mortifica-
tion; ♀ blight, mildew; 🞛 smut;
in ~ geraten catch fire; *in ~ stecken*
set on fire; '~-**anschlag** *m* arson
attack; '~**blase** *f* blister; '~**bombe** *f*
incendiary bomb; '~**brief** *m* *fig.*
threatening (*od.* urgent) letter; Ꝛen
['~dən] (26) surge (*a. fig.*); '~**er** *m* (7)
fireship; '~**flasche** *f* Molotov cocktail; '~**fleck(en)** *m* burn; '~**geruch** *m*
burnt smell; Ꝛig ['~diç] ♀ blighted,
blasted; 🞛 gangrenous; *~ riechen*
have a burnt smell; ~**mal** ['brant-] *n*
brand; *fig.* stigma; ~**male'rei** *f*
poker-work; 'Ꝛmarken (25) brand;
fig. a. stigmatize, denounce; '~**mar-
kung** *f fig.* stigmatization; '~**mauer**
f fire-proof wall; '~**rede** *f* incendiary
speech; '~**schaden** *m* damage caused
by fire; 'Ꝛschatzen (27) lay under
contribution; (*plündern*) sack, pillage; '~**sohle** *f* insole; '~**stätte** *f*,
'~**stelle** *f* scene of fire; '~**stifter(in** *f*)
m incendiary; '~**stiftung** *f* arson.
Brandung ['~duŋ] *f* breakers *pl.*,
surf, surge; '~**swelle** *f* breaker.
'**Brand**|**wache** *f* fire-watch; '~-
wunde *f* burn; '~**zeichen** *n* brand.
brannte ['brantə] *pret. v.* brennen.
Branntwein ['brantvain] *m* brandy,
spirits *pl.*; '~**brennerei** *f* distillery.
Brasil [bra'ziːl] *f* (*inv.*) Brazil cigar.

Brasilianer [brazil'jaːnər] *m* (7),
~**in** *f*, **Brasilier** [~'ziːljər] *m* (7),
~**in** *f*, brasili'anisch, bra'silisch
Brazilian.
brassen ⚓ ['brasən] (28) brace.
'**Brat**-**apfel** *m* baked apple.
braten[1] ['braːtən] *v/t. u. v/i.* (30)
roast; *im Ofen:* bake; *auf dem
Roste:* grill, broil; *in der Pfanne:*
fry; F (*nur v/i.*) (*in der Sonne ~*) roast
(in the sun).
'**Braten**[2] *m* (6) roast, joint; *fig.* den
~ riechen smell a rat; '~**fett** *n* dripping; '~**platte** *f* meat-dish; '~-
soße *f* gravy; '~**topf** *m* roaster.
'**brat**|**fertig** oven-ready; 'Ꝛfisch *m*
fried fish; 'Ꝛhuhn *n* roaster, broiler;
'Ꝛkartoffeln *f/pl.* fried potatoes; 'Ꝛ-
ofen *m* oven; 'Ꝛpfanne *f* frying-pan;
'Ꝛröhre *f s.* Bratofen.
Bratsche ♪ ['braːtʃə] *f* (15) viola;
'~**r** *m* (7) violist.
'**Brat**|**spieß** *m* spit; '~**wurst** *f* sau-
sage (for frying); fried sausage.
Bräu [brɔy] *n* (3) (*Gebräu*) brew;
(*~haus*) brewery.
Brauch [braux] *m* (3[3]) (*Sitte*)
custom; (*Gewohnheit*) use, practice,
bsd. ⅂ *od. sprachlich:* usage; 'Ꝛbar
useful; *P.: a.* able; *S.: a.* serviceable, handy; '~**barkeit** *f* usefulness; 'Ꝛen (25) (*nötig haben*) want,
need; (*erfordern*) require; *Zeit:*
take; *s.* gebrauchen, verbrauchen;
er braucht nicht zu gehen he need
not go; *ich brauche drei Tage dazu*
it will take me three days; '~**tum** *n*
(1[2]) customs *pl.*; folklore.
Braue ['brauə] *f* (15) eyebrow.
brau|**en** ['brauən] (25) brew; 'Ꝛer *m*
(7) brewer; Ꝛerei [~ə'rai] *f*, 'Ꝛhaus
n brewery.
braun [braun] brown; *Pferd:* bay;
(*sonngebräunt*) (sun-)tanned; *~e
Butter* fried butter; 'Ꝛe *m* (18) bay
(horse).
Bräune ['brɔynə] *f* (15) brownness;
🞛 quinsy, angina; *häutige ~* croup;
'Ꝛn *v/t.* (25) brown; *v. der Sonne:*
a. tan, bronze; *v/i. od. sich ~* (grow
od. become) brown; tan.
'**braun**|**gelb** brownish yellow; 'Ꝛ-
kohle *f* brown coal, lignite.
bräunlich ['brɔynliç] brownish.
'**braunrot** brownish red.
Braus [braus] *m* (4, *o. pl.*) *s.* Saus.
Brause ['brauzə] *f* (15) (*Gießkannen*Ꝛ) rose; *s. ~bad; s. ~limonade;*

'~bad n shower-bath; '~kopf m hothead, hotspur; '~limonade f fizzy drink, Am. soda pop; '2n (27) roar, bluster; (eilen, stürmen) rush, sweep; Orgel: peal; ⚙ effervesce; (sich ab~) take a shower(-bath); '~pulver n sherbet powder; '~tablette f effervescent tablet.

Braut [braut] f (14¹) fiancée, bride--to-be; lit. a. betrothed; am Hochzeitstag: bride; '~ausstattung f trousseau; '~bett n bridal bed; '~führer m best man.

Bräutigam ['brɔytigam] m (3¹) fiancé; am Hochzeitstag: bridegroom, Am. a. groom.

'**Braut|jungfer** f bridesmaid; '~kleid n wedding-dress; '~leute pl. s. Brautpaar.

bräutlich ['brɔytliç] bridal.

'**Braut|paar** n engaged couple; am Hochzeitstag: bride and bridegroom; '~schau f: auf ~ gehen look out for a wife; '~schleier m bridal veil; '~zug m bridal procession.

brav [bra:f] honest, upright; (tapfer) brave, gallant; (artig) good; ~ gemacht! well done!; '2heit f honesty; good behavio(u)r.

bravo! ['brɑːvo] bravo!, well done!

Bravour [bra'vuːr] f bravado; mit ~ brilliantly; ~stück n feat of daring, stunt; ♪ bravura.

Brech|bohnen ['brɛç-] f/pl. broken French beans; '~durchfall m diarrh(o)ea with vomiting, cholerine; '~eisen n jemmy, Am. jimmy; '2en v/t. (30) break (a. fig. Eid, Eis, Gesetz, Rekord, Stille usw.); Blume: pluck, pick; Lichtstrahl: refract; Papier: fold; Steine: quarry; (er~) vomit; die Ehe ~ commit adultery; sich ~ break; opt. be refracted; sich den Arm ~ break one's arm; v/i. (sn) break; (h.) mit j-m ~ break with; (er~) vomit, be sick; '~er ⚓ m (7) breaker; '~mittel n emetic, vomitive; F fig. pest; '~nuß f vomit-nut; '~reiz m nausea, retching; '~stange f crowbar; '~ung f breaking; opt. refraction; '~ungswinkel m angle of refraction.

Brei [brai] m (3) (bsd. Kinder2) pap; (bsd. Hafer2) porridge; (~masse) pulp, squash; (Mus) mash; (Teig) paste; s. Katze; '2ig pulpy; pasty.

breit [brait] broad (a. Akzent, Lachen usw.), (a. ⊕) wide; (weit-

schweifig) diffuse; ~es Publikum wide public; s. Masse; '~beinig straddle-legged, straddling.

Breite ['~tə] f (15) vgl. breit: breadth; width; diffuseness; ast., geogr. latitude; '2n spread; '~ngrad m degree of latitude; '~nkreis m parallel (of latitude).

'**breit|machen**: sich ~ spread o.s.; fig. obtrude o.s.; '~schlagen F: j-n ~ talk a p. round, zu et.: talk a p. into; '~schult(e)rig broad--shouldered; '2seite f broadside; '~spurig 🚂 broad-ga(u)ge; fig. F bumptious; '~treten fig. expatiate on; '2wandfilm m wide-screen picture.

Bremse¹ zo. ['brɛmzə] f (15) gad--fly, horse-fly.

'**Bremse²** f (15) (Wagen2 usw.) brake; '2n (27) v/t. brake; fig. a. check; v/i. (put on the) brake; fig. go slow; '~r m (7) brake(s)man.

Brems|fußhebel ['brɛms-] m brake pedal; '~klotz m brake-block; '~leuchte f, '~licht mot. n stop light; '~pedal n brake pedal; '~scheibe f brake disc (Am. disk); '~schuh m brake-shoe; '~spur f skid mark; '~vorrichtung f brake-mechanism; '~weg m braking distance.

brenn|bar ['brɛn-] combustible; '2dauer f burning-time; '2-element n Kernreaktor: fuel element; '~en v/t. (30) burn; Branntwein: distil(l Am.); das Haar: curl; Kaffee, Mehl: roast; 🌾 cauterize; Ziegel usw.: bake; F sich ~ (täuschen) be mistaken; v/i. burn (a. fig. Augen, Wunde usw.); Nessel: sting; Pfeffer usw.: bite, be hot; vor Ungeduld ~ burn with impatience; F darauf ~, zu inf. be dying (od. itching) to inf.; es brennt! fire!; ~d burning (a. fig. Durst, Frage, Leidenschaft usw.); '2er m (7) distiller; (Gas2) burner; (Schweiß2) torch; (Atom2) pile; 2erei [~'rai] f distillery; '2glas n burning-glass; '2holz n firewood; '2material n fuel; '2nessel f stinging nettle; '2-öl n lamp-oil; (Heiz2) fuel oil; '2punkt m focus; in den ~ rücken bring into focus (a. fig.); '2schere f (eine a pair of) curling tongs pl.; '2spiegel m burning-mirror; '2spiritus m methylated spirit; '2stab m Kernenergie: fuel rod; '2stoff m combustible; bsd. mot., ✈ fuel; '2weite opt. f focal distance.

brenzlig ['brɛntsliç] *Geruch, Geschmack*: burnt; F *fig.* ticklish.
Bresche ['brɛʃə] *f* (15) breach; **e-e ~ schlagen** *od. schießen* make a breach; *fig. in die ~ springen* stand in the breach.
Brett [brɛt] *n* (1) board; *dickes*: plank; (*Regal*) shelf; **~er** *pl.* (*Bühne*) boards *pl.*; (*Skier*) woods *pl.*; *Boxen: auf die ~er schicken* (knock) down; *fig. ein ~ vor dem Kopf haben* be very dense; '**~erbude** *f* wooden shed *od.* hut, shack; '**~erzaun** *m* hoarding, *Am.* board fence; '**~spiel** *n* board game.
Brevier [bre'viːr] *n* (3[1]) breviary.
Brezel ['breːtsəl] *f* (15) pretzel.
Brief [briːf] *m* (3) letter; (*Sendschreiben*) epistle; '**~aufschrift** *f* address; '**~beschwerer** *m* (7) paper-weight; '**~bogen** *m* sheet of note-paper; '**~bombe** *f* letter bomb; '**~fach** *n* pigeon-hole; '**~freund(in** *f*) *m* pen friend; '**~geheimnis** *n* privacy (*od.* secrecy) of letters; '**~kasten** *m* letter-box, pillar-box, *Am.* mailbox; *Zeitungsrubrik*: Question and Answer Column; *den ~ leeren* clear the letter-box, *Am.* collect the mail; '**~kastentante** F *f* sob sister; '**~kopf** *m* letter-head; '**~lich** *adj. u. adv.* by letter; **~er** *Verkehr* correspondence; '**~marke** *f* (postage) stamp; '**~markensammler** *m* stamp-collector, philatelist; '**~markensammlung** *f* stamp collection; '**~öffner** *m* (7) letter-opener, paper knife; '**~ordner** *m* letter-file; '**~papier** *n* note- (*od.* letter-)paper; '**~porto** *n* postage; '**~post** *f* mail, post, *Am. a.* first--class matter; '**~tasche** *f* wallet; *mit Notizbuch*: pocket-book; '**~taube** *f* carrier pigeon, homing pigeon; '**~telegramm** *n* letter telegram, *Am.* lettergram; '**~träger** *m* postman, *Am. a.* mailman; '**~umschlag** *m* envelope; '**~waage** *f* letter-balance; '**~wahl** *f* postal vote, *bsd. Am.* absentee ballot; '**~wähler** *m* postal voter, *bsd. Am.* absentee voter; '**~wechsel** *m* correspondence.
brief [briːf] *pret. v.* braten[1].
Brigade [bri'gaːdə] *f* (15) brigade.
Brigg ⚓ [brik] *f* (11[1]) brig.
Brikett [bri'kɛt] *n* (3 *od.* 11) briquet(te).
Brillant [bril'jant] *m* (12), ⚥ *adj.* brilliant; **~ring** *m* diamond ring.

Brille ['brilə] *f* (15) (*eine* a pair of) spectacles *pl.*, glasses *pl.*, F specs *pl.*; (*Schutz⚥*) goggles *pl.*; (*Klosett⚥*) seat; '**~nfutteral** *n* spectacle-case; '**~nschlange** *f* cobra; '**~nträger(in** *f*) *m*: *~ sein* wear glasses.
bringen ['brinən] (30) (*her~*) bring; (*fort~*) take; (*geleiten*) conduct; *s. begleiten; thea. usw.* present, show; *Zeitung*: print, contain; (*ein~, verursachen*) bring, cause; *Opfer*: make; *Zinsen*: yield; *an sich ~* acquire, appropriate; *j-n wieder auf die Beine* (*od. zu sich*) *~* bring a p. round; *auf einen Nenner ~* reduce to a common denominator; *es bis zum Major usw. ~* rise to the rank of major *etc.*; *j-n dahin ~, daß* induce (*od.* prevail upon) a p. to *inf.*; *es dahin ~, daß* manage (*od.* contrive) to *inf.*; *fig. es mit sich ~* involve; *es weit ~, es zu etwas ~* get on (*od.* succeed) in the world; *es zu nichts ~* fail (in life); *j-n um et. ~* deprive (*od.* rob) a p. of a th.; *j-n zum Lachen usw. ~* make a p. laugh *etc.*
brisan|t [bri'zant] high-explosive; **⚥z** *f* explosive effect; *in Zssgn* high-explosive.
Brise ⚓ ['briːzə] *f* (15) breeze.
Brit|e ['britə] *m* (13), '**~in** *f* Briton, *Am.* Britisher; *die Briten pl.* the British; '**⚥isch** British.
bröck|(e)lig ['brœk(ə)liç] crumbly, *feiner*: friable; '**~eln** *v/t. u. v/i.* (29, sn) crumble.
Brocken ['brɔkən] *m* (6) piece; *Brot*: crumb; (*Bissen*) morsel; (*Teilchen*) bit, scrap; (*Klumpen*) lump; *fig. ~ pl. e-r Sprache*: scraps *pl.*, e-r *Unterhaltung*: snatches *pl.*; *harter ~* hard nut.
brodeln ['broːdəln] (29) bubble, simmer, seethe (*a. fig.*).
Brokat [bro'kaːt] *m* (3) brocade.
Brom ⚗ [broːm] *n* (3[1]) bromine.
Brombeer|e ['brɔmbeːrə] *f* blackberry; '**~strauch** *m* bramble.
'**Brom|säure** *f* bromic acid; '**~silber** *n* bromide of silver.
Bronch|ialkatarrh [brɔn'çiaːlkatar] *m* bronchial catarrh; **~ien** ['~çiən] *m/pl.* bronchi *pl.*; **~itis** [~'çiːtis] *f* bronchitis.
Bronze ['brõːsə] *f* (15) bronze; '**~plastik** *f* bronze sculpture.
bronzieren [~'siːrən] bronze.
Brosame ['broːzamə] *f* (15) crumb.

Brosche ['brɔʃə] f (15) brooch.
broschier|en [~'ʃiːrən] stitch; ~t in paper cover, stitched.
Broschüre [~'ʃyːrə] f (15) booklet, pamphlet, brochure.
Brot [broːt] n (3) bread; *ganzes:* loaf; *fig.* bread, livelihood; *belegtes* ~ sandwich; '~**aufstrich** m spread; '~**beutel** m haversack.
Brötchen ['brøːtçən] n (6) roll; '~**geber** F m employer, boss.
'**Brot|-erwerb** m bread-winning, (making a) living; '~**korb** m bread-basket; *j-m den* ~ *höher hängen* put a p. on short allowance; '~**krume** f bread-crumb; '**⊙los** unemployed; *Tätigkeit:* unprofitable; '~**neid** m trade jealousy, professional envy; '~**rinde** f crust (of bread); '~**röster** m (7) toaster; '~**schneidemaschine** f bread-cutter; '~**schnitte** f slice of bread; '~**studium** n utilitarian study.
brr! *(halt)* whoa!, wo!; *(pfui)* ugh!
Bruch¹ [bruːx] m, n (3²) bog, fen.
Bruch² [brux] m (3³) breach *(a. fig.)*; *(Brechen)* breaking; *(Knochen⊙)* fracture; *(Unterleibs⊙)* rupture, ⛵ hernia; *im Papier:* fold; *im Stoff:* crease; ⚓ fraction; *des Eides, des Friedens usw.:* violation; *(~schaden)* breakage; *(Schrott)* scrap; F *(Schund)* trash, rubbish; ⚓ *gewöhnlicher* ~ vulgar fraction, *echter* ~ proper fraction; *in die Brüche gehen* come to grief, *bsd. Ehe:* go on the rocks; ✂ ~ *machen* crash; '~**band** n truss; '~**bude** F f tumbledown shanty, ramshackle house.
brüchig ['bryçiç] brittle, fragile.
'**Bruch|landung** ✂ f crash landing; '~**rechnung** f fractions *pl.*; '~**schaden** m breakage; '~**stein** m quarry-stone; '~**stelle** f point of fracture; '~**strich** ⚓ m fraction stroke; '~**stück** n fragment; *pl. fig. a.* scraps, snatches *pl.*; '⊙**stückhaft** fragmentary; '⊙**stückweise** in fragments; '~**teil** m fraction; *im* ~ *e-r Sekunde* in a split second; '~**zahl** f fractional number.
Brücke ['brykə] f (15) bridge *(a.* ⚓, ✂; *a. beim Ringen u. Zahnprothese)*; *(kleiner Teppich)* rug; *Sport:* back-bend; *e-e* ~ *schlagen über (acc.)* throw a bridge across; *fig. s. abbrechen;* '~**nkopf** m bridge-head; '~**npfeiler** m bridge pier; '~**n-**

waage f weigh-bridge.
Bruder ['bruːdər] m (7¹) brother; *(Mönch)* friar; *lustiger* ~ jolly fellow; '~**krieg** m fratricidal war.
brüderlich ['bryːdərliç] brotherly, fraternal; '⊙**keit** f brotherliness.
'**Bruder|liebe** f brotherly love; '~**mord** m, '~**mörder(in** f) m fratricide.
'**Brüderschaft** f (16) brotherhood, fellowship; ~ *trinken* pledge close friendship.
'**Brudervolk** n sister nation.
Brüh|e ['bryːə] f (15) broth; *(Soße)* sauce; *(Fleischsaft)* gravy; *als Suppengrundlage:* stock; *contp.* slop; '⊙**en** (25) scald; '⊙**heiß** scalding (hot); '~**kartoffeln** f/pl. potatoes *pl.* boiled in broth; '⊙**warm** *fig.* red hot *(news)*; *j-m et.* ~ *wiedererzählen* take a story straight away to a p.; '~**würfel** m beef-cube.
brüllen ['brylən] (25) roar; *Rind:* bellow; *(muhen)* low; *Mensch:* roar, *(a. heulen)*; howl, bawl; *vor Lachen usw.* ~ roar with laughter *etc.*; F *er (es) ist zum* ⊙ he (it) is a scream.
'**Brumm|bär** m grumbler, growler, *Am.* F grouch; '~**baß** m ♪ double-bass; *fig.* rumbling bass; ⊙**en** ['brumən] v/i. u. v/t. (25) *Tier:* growl; *Fliege usw.:* buzz; *Mensch:* grumble, *Am.* grouch; F *(im Gefängnis sein)* do time; *in den Bart* ~ mutter to o.s.; *mir brummt der Kopf* my head is buzzing; '~**er** m (7) *(Fliege)* blowfly, bluebottle; *(Käfer)* dung-beetle; '⊙**ig** grumbling, *Am.* F grouchy; '~**kreisel** m humming-top;' ~**schädel** F m headache.
brünett [bry'nɛt] dark(-complexioned); *Frau:* brunette *(a. ⊙e* [~'nɛtə] *f)*.
Brunft [brunft] f (14¹) *hunt.* rut; '⊙**en** (26) rut; '⊙**ig** rutting; '~**schrei** m bell; '~**zeit** f rutting-season.
brünieren [bry'niːrən] (25) brown.
Brunnen ['brunən] m (6) well *(a. fig.)*; *(Quelle)* spring; *(Spring⊙)* fountain; ♨ *(mineral)* waters *pl.*; ~ *trinken* take the waters; '~**kresse** f water-cress; '~**kur** f mineral-water cure; '~**vergiftung** f *fig.* vitiating the political atmosphere.
Brunst [brunst] f (14¹) *zo.* rut, *des weiblichen Tieres:* heat; *v. Menschen:* lust; *fig. s.* **Inbrunst.**
brünstig ['brynstiç] *(vgl.* **Brunst***) zo.*

rutting, on (*od.* in) heat; lustful; *fig. s.* inbrünstig.

Brust [brust] *f* (14¹) breast; (~*kasten*) chest; (*Busen*) bosom; *am Braten*: brisket; *sich in die* ~ *werfen* give o.s. airs, bridle (up); ~ *an* ~ neck and neck; '~**bein** *n* breastbone; '~**beschwerden** *f/pl.* chest-trouble; '~**bild** *n* half-length portrait *od.* photo; '~**bonbon** *m* pectoral lozenge; '~**drüse** *f* mamma(ry gland).

brüsten ['brystən] (26): *sich* ~ give o.s. airs; boast, brag (*mit* with); *sich* ~ *als* ... pose as. [*f* pleurisy.)

'**Brustfell** *n* pleura; '~-**entzündung** ...brüstig ...breasted, ...chested.

'**Brust|kasten** *m*, '~**korb** *m* chest; '~**kind** *n* breast-fed child; '2**krank** suffering from chest-trouble; '~**krebs** *m* breast cancer; '~**schwimmen** *n* breast-stroke; '~**stimme** *f* chest-voice; '~**stück** *n am Braten*: brisket; '~**tasche** *f* breast pocket; '~**tee** *m* pectoral herb-tea; '~**ton** *m* chest-note; *fig.* ~ *der Überzeugung* true ring of conviction; '~**-umfang** *m s.* Brustweite.

Brüstung ['brystuŋ] *f* balustrade; parapet; (*Fenster*2) sill.

'**Brust|warze** *f* nipple; '~**wehr** *f* breastwork; '~**weite** *f* chest-measurement; *der Frau*: bust(-measurement).

Brut [bru:t] *f* (16) brood (*a. fig.*); (*Fisch*2) fry, spawn; *fig. b.s.* scum, lot.

brutal [bru'tɑ:l] brutal; 2**ität** [~tali'tɛ:t] *f* brutality.

'**Brut|-apparat** *m*, '~-**ofen** *m* incubator; '~-**ei** *n* egg for hatching.

brüten ['bry:tən] (26) brood, sit, incubate; *fig.* brood .*(über dat.* over, on); *s.* Rache.

'**Brüter** *m* (7) (*Brutreaktor*) schneller ~ fast breeder (reactor).

'**Brut|henne** *f* sitting hen; '~**kasten** *m* incubator; '~**re-aktor** *m* breeder reactor; '~**stätte** *f* breeding-place; *fig.* hotbed.

brutto ['bruto] gross, in gross; 2-**einkommen** *n* gross income; '2**gewicht** *n* gross weight; '2**registertonne** *f* gross register ton; '2**sozialprodukt** *n* gross national product; '2**verdienst** *m* gross earnings *pl.*

Bube ['bu:bə] *m* (13) boy, lad; (*Schurke*) rascal; *Karten*: knave, *bsd. Am. a.* jack; '~**nstreich** *m*,

'~**nstück** *n* knavish trick.

Bubikopf ['bu:bikɔpf] *m* bobbed hair.

bübisch ['by:biʃ] knavish.

Buch [bu:x] *n* (1²) book; ~ *Papier* quire; *s.* Dreh2; '~**besprechung** *f* book review; '~**binder** *m* (book-)binder; ~**binde'rei** *f* bookbinder's (work)shop, *Am.* (book)bindery; *Gewerbe*: bookbinding; '~**druck** *m* letterpress printing; '~**drucker** *m* (letterpress) printer; ~**drucke'rei** *f* printing-office, *Am. a.* print(ing) shop; *Gewerbe*: printing (of books).

Buch|e ['bu:xə] *f* (15) beech(-tree); ~**ecker** ['~²ɛkər] *f* (15) beech-nut.

buchen ['bu:xən] (25) † enter, post; *e-n Platz usw.*: book; *fig. als Erfolg usw.*: count as.

Bücher|-abschluß † ['by:çər-] *m* balancing of the books; '~**brett** *n* bookshelf; ~**ei** [~'raɪ] *f* (16) library; '~**freund** *m* book-lover, bibliophile; '~**gutschein** *m* book token; '~**kunde** *f* bibliography; '~**mappe** *f* satchel; '~**narr** *m* bibliomaniac; '~**regal** *n* bookshelf; '~**revisor** *m* auditor, accountant; '~**schrank** *m* bookcase; '~**stand** *m* bookstall, *Am.* bookstand; '~**stütze** *f* book-end; '~**weisheit** *f* book-learning; '~**wurm** *m* bookworm.

'**Buch|fink** *m* chaffinch; '~**forderungen** † *f/pl.* book claims; '~**führer** *m*, '~**halter** *m* book-keeper; '~**führung** *f*, '~**haltung** *f* book-keeping; *doppelte* ~ book-keeping by double entry; '~**gemeinschaft** *f* book club; ~**halterei** [~'raɪ] *f* (16) book-keeping department; '~**halterin** *f* (lady) book-keeper; '~**handel** *m* booktrade; '~**händler** *m* bookseller; '~**handlung** *f* bookseller's shop, bookshop, *Am. a.* bookstore; '~**hülle** *f* book wrapper; '~**macher** *m* bookmaker; '~**messe** *f* book fair; '2**mäßig** according to the books; '~**prüfer** *m* auditor, accountant.

Buchsbaum ['buksbaum] *m* box (-tree).

Buchse ⊕ ['buksə] *f* bush(ing); (*Muffe*) sleeve; (*Fett*2) cup; ⚡ socket.

Büchse ['byksə] *f* (15) box, case; *aus Blech*: tin (box), *Am.* can; *für Salben*: pot, jar; (*Gewehr*) rifle; '~**nfleisch** *n* tinned (*Am.* canned) meat; '~**nmacher** *m* gunsmith;

'**~n-öffner** m (7) tin-opener, Am. can opener.

Buchstabe ['buːxʃtaːbə] m (13¹) letter; (Schriftzug) character; typ. type; großer (kleiner) ~ capital (small) letter; '**~nrätsel** n logogriph; '**~nrechnung** f algebra; '**~nschloß** n puzzle lock.

buchstabieren [~ʃtaˈbiːrən] spell; (mühsam lesen) spell out.

buchstäblich ['~ʃtɛːpliç] literal.

Bucht [buxt] f (16) inlet, bay; kleine: creek.

'**Buch|-umschlag** m (book) wrapper od. jacket; '**~ung** f booking, entry.

'**Buchweizen** m buckwheat.

Buckel ['bukəl] m 1. (7) hump (-back), F (Rücken) back; e-n ~ machen stoop, Katze: put up its back; 2. Verzierung: boss, stud.

'**buck(e)lig** humpbacked; **2e** ['~(ə)ligə] m, f (18) hunchback.

bücken ['bykən] (25) (mst sich) bend, stoop; sich vor j-m ~ bow to, kriecherisch: cringe to.

Bück(l)ing¹ ['byk(l)iŋ] m (3¹) bloater, red herring, kipper.

'**Bückling²** m (3¹) bow, obeisance.

buddeln F ['budəln] (29) dig.

Bude ['buːdə] f (15) stall, booth, F (Hütte) shanty, shack; (Studenten2) pad, digs pl.; (Laden) shop.

Budget [byˈdʒeː] n (11) budget; im ~ vorsehen budget for.

Büfett [byˈfeː, byˈfɛt] n (3) buffet, sideboard; (Schenktisch) bar, Am. counter; kaltes ~ cold buffet; '**~ier** [byfɛtˈjeː] m barkeeper, barman, Am. bartender.

Büffel ['byfəl] m (7) buffalo; '**2n** F v/i. (29) grind, sl. mug, Am. F bone; (a. v/t.) cram, sl. swot.

Büffler F ['byflər] m (7) sl. swot.

Bug [buːk] m (3³) bow (a. ⚓), bend; (Knie2) hock; (Vorder2) shoulder.

Bügel ['byːgəl] m (7) bow; s. Kleider2, Steig2; '**~-eisen** n flat-iron; '**~falte** f crease; '**2frei** non-iron; '**2n** (29) Wäsche: iron; Kleid: press.

Bugsier|dampfer [bukˈsiːr-] m (steam-)tug; **2en** v/t. tow; fig. steer, manœuvre, Am. maneuver.

Bugspriet ⚓ ['buːkʃpriːt] n (3) bowsprit.

Buhle ['buːlə] m (13), f (15) lover; jetzt mst b.s. paramour; '**2n** (25) um et.: court, woo; mit j-m: sleep (od. wanton) with; um j-s Gunst ~ curry favo(u)r with a p.

Buhmann ['buː-] m fig. bogeyman.

Buhne ['buːnə] f (15) groyne.

Bühne ['byːnə] f (15) scaffold; (Redner2) od. ⊕ platform; thea. stage; fig. scene, arena; zur ~ gehen go on the stage; '**~n-anweisung** f stage direction; '**~n-arbeiter** m stage-hand; '**~n-ausstattung** f, '**~nbild** n scene(ry); '**~nbe-arbeitung** f dramatization; '**~nbildner(in** f) m stage designer; '**~ndichter** m playwright, dramatist; '**2nfähig** stage-worthy; '**~nfassung** f stage version; '**~nkünstler(in** f) m stage actor (f actress); '**~nlaufbahn** f theatrical career; '**~nleiter** m stage manager; '**~nmaler** m scene-painter; '**~nrecht** n dramatic right; '**~nschriftsteller** m s. Bühnendichter; '**~nstück** n stageplay.

buk [buːk] pret. v. backen.

Bukett [buˈkɛt] n (3) bouquet.

Bulette [buˈlɛtə] f (15) meatball, rissole, hamburger.

Bulgar|e [bulˈgɑːrə] m (13), **~in** f (16¹) Bulgarian; **2isch** Bulgarian.

'**Bull|-auge** n bull's eye, porthole; '**~dogge** f bulldog.

Bulle¹ ['bulə] m (13) bull; sl. die ~n (Polizei) the fuzz pl.; '**~²** eccl. f (15) bull; '**~nbeißer** m (7) bulldog.

bullern ['bulərn] (29) rumble; Feuer im Ofen: roar.

bum(m)! [bum] boom!, bang!

Bumerang ['buːməraŋ] m (3¹) boomerang.

Bummel F ['buml] m (7) (Spaziergang) stroll; (Bierreise usw.) spree, binge; e-n ~ machen go for a stroll; auf den ~ gehen go on the spree; '**~ei** [~ˈlaɪ] f (16) dawdling, loafing; (Nachlässigkeit) slackness; '**2ig** dawdling; careless; '**2n** (29) (müßig gehen) loaf; (trödeln) dawdle; (gemächlich gehen) stroll, saunter; (Berufsarbeit aussetzen) (be) idle; (sich amüsieren) be on the spree; '**~streik** m go-slow; '**~zug** m slow train.

'**Bummler** m (7) loafer.

bums! [bums] bang!; **2** m bang; '**~en** bang, bump; V ball, have it off; '**2lokal** F n sl. dive.

Bund [bunt] 1. n (3, nach Zahlen im pl. inv.) bundle; Schlüssel: bunch; Heu, Stroh (als Maß): truss; 2. m (3³) (Band) band, tie; Schnei-

derei: waistband; *fig.* union (*a. Ehe*); (*Bündnis*) alliance; *pol. a.* league, federation, confederacy; (*Bundesregierung*) Federal Government; *bsd. eccl.* covenant; *im* ~*e mit* in league with.

Bündel ['byndəl] *n* (7) bundle; '2n (29) bundle (up); '2weise by bundles.

'**Bundes...** *in Zssgn* federal; '~bahn *f* Federal Railway(s *pl.*); '~gebiet *n* Federal Territory; ~**genosse** *m* confederate, ally; '~kanzler *m* Federal Chancellor; '~liga *f* National League; '~präsident *m* President of the Federal Republic; '~rat *m* Federal Council; *parl.* Upper House; '~regierung *f* Federal Government; '~republik *f* **Deutschland** Federal Republic of Germany; '~staat *m einzelner*: federal state; *Gesamtheit der einzelnen*: (con)federation; '~straße *f* Federal Highway; '~tag *m* Lower House (of the Federal Parliament); ~**trainer** *m* national coach; *der neue* ~ Germany's new coach; '~wehr ✕ *f* Federal Armed Forces *pl.*; '2weit nationwide.

bündig ['byndiç] (*gültig*) binding; (*überzeugend*) conclusive; *Stil, Rede*: concise, terse; *kurz und* ~ succinctly; '2keit *f* conclusiveness; conciseness.

Bündnis ['byntnis] *n* (4¹) alliance; '2frei nonaligned; '~freiheit *f* nonalignment.

Bungalow ['buŋgalo] *m* (11) bungalow, *Am.* ranch house.

Bunker ['buŋkər] *m* (7) ⚓ (*Kohlenvorratsraum*) bunker; (*Schutzraum*) shelter, refuge, ✕ bunker, pillbox; ⚓ *für U-Boote*: pen.

bunt [bunt] colo(u)rful (*a. fig.*); (*farbig*) (many)colo(u)red; (~*gefleckt*) variegated; (*scheckig*) motley; (*lebhaft gefärbt*) gay; (*grell*) gaudy; *Glas*: stained; *gewürfelt*: chequered; (*gemischt*) motley, mixed (*crowd etc.*); (*abwechslungsreich*) varied; ~*er Abend*, ~*e Unterhaltung* variety show; ~*e Reihe machen* pair off ladies and gentlemen; *er treibt es zu* ~ he goes too far; *es ging* ~ *zu* there were fine goings-on; '2druck *m* colo(u)r-printing; (*Bild*) chromolithograph; '~fleckig spotted, (*a. fig.*) motley; '2metall *n* nonferrous metal; '2stift *m* colo(u)red pencil, crayon.

Bürde ['byrdə] *f* (15) burden (*a. fig.*: *für j-n* to), load.

Burg [burk] *f* (16) castle; (*Festung, a. fig.*) citadel, stronghold.

Bürge ['byrgə] *m* (13) bail, surety; guarantor (*a. fig.*); *e-n* ~*n stellen* give (*od.* offer) bail, *Am. a.* post bond; '2n (25) *für j-n*: go bail for, stand surety for, *Am.* bond *a p.*; *für et.*: guarantee (*od.* vouch for) a th.

Bürger ['~gər] *m* (7), '~**in** *f* citizen; (*Stadtbewohner*) townsman, *f* townswoman, *pl.* townsfolk; (*Einwohner*) inhabitant; (~*licher*) commoner; '~**initiative** *f* civic action group; '~**krieg** *m* civil war; '~**kunde** *f* civics *sg.*; '2**lich** civil; middle-class; (*nichtadlig*) common, untitled; *Küche usw.*: plain; ~*e Ehrenrechte n/pl.* civic rights *pl.*; ~*es Gesetzbuch* code of civil law; '~**liche** *m*, *f* (18) commoner; '~**meister** *m* mayor; *in Deutschland*: burgomaster; '~**meister-amt** *n* mayor's office; '~**pflicht** *f* civic duty; '~**recht** *n* civic rights *pl.*; freedom of a city; '~**rechtler(in** *f*) *m* civil rights activist; '~**rechtsbewegung** *f* civil rights movement; '~**schaft** *f* (16) citizens *pl.*; '~**sinn** *m* public spirit; '~**stand** *m* middle classes *pl.*; '~**steig** *m* pavement, *Am.* sidewalk; '~**tum** *n* (1², *o. pl.*) citizenship; *konkret*: middle classes *pl.*; *contp.* bourgeoisie; '~**wehr** *f* militia.

'**Burg|friede(n)** *m* public peace; *pol.* truce; '~**graf** *m* burgrave.

Bürgschaft ['byrk∫aft] *f* (16) (*Sicherheit*) security, surety, guarantee; *im Strafrecht*: bail; ~ *leisten od.* übernehmen give (*od.* provide) security, stand surety; *im Strafrecht*: go bail (*Bürge*), give bail (*Angeklagter*).

Burgunder [bur'gundər] *m* (7) Burgundian; *Wein*: burgundy.

'**Burgverlies** *n* (4) keep, dungeon.

burlesk [bur'lɛsk], 2e *f* burlesque.

Büro [by'roː] *n* (11) office; ~**angestellte** *m*, *f* clerk, office worker; ~**automatisierung** *f* office automation; ~**be-amte** *m* clerk; ~**bedarf(s-artikel** *m/pl.*) *m* office supplies *pl.*; ~**chef** *m* head clerk; ~**gehilfe** *m*, ~**gehilfin** *f* office junior, clerical assistant; ~**klammer** *f* (paper)clip; ~**krat** [~ro'kraːt] *m* (12) red-tapist, bureaucrat; ~**kratie** [~kra'tiː] *f* (15) red-tapism, bureaucracy; **⚲kratisch** [~'krɑːtiʃ] bureaucratic; **~kratismus** [~kra'tismus] m bureaucratism; **~maschine** [by-'roː-] f office machine; **~möbel** n/pl. office furniture; **~personal** n office personnel; **~stunden** f/pl. office--hours, Am. a. duty hours; **~technik** f office technology; **~vorsteher** m s. Bürochef.

Bursch(e) ['burʃə] m (13) boy, lad, fellow; (Kerl) a. freundschaftlich: chap, Am. guy; ✗ orderly, batman; univ. senior man, weitS. student.

burschikos [~ʃi'koːs] pert.

Bürste ['byrstə] f (15), **⚲n** (26) brush; '**~n-abzug** typ. m brush--proof; '**~nbinder** m brush--maker; '**~nhaarschnitt** m crew cut.

Bürzel ['byrtsəl] m (7) rump; am Brathuhn usw.: parson's noꞁe.

Bus [bus] F m (4¹) bus; '**~halte-stelle** f bus-stop.

Busch [buʃ] m (3² u. ³) bush (a. Urwald); (kleines Gehölz) copꞁe, thicket; s. Büschel; bei j-m auf den ~ klopfen sound a p.; sich (seitwärts) in die Büsche schlagen slip away.

Büschel ['byʃəl] n (7) bunch; Haare usw.: tuft, wisp.

'**Busch|hemd** n jacket-shirt; '**~holz** n underwood; '**⚲ig** bushy; Haar: shaggy; '**~klepper** m bush-ranger; '**~werk** n bushes pl., Am. brush; '**~windrös-chen** n wood-anemone.

Busen ['buːzən] m (6) bosom, breast; (Meer⚲) bay, gulf; '**~freund** (-in f) m bosom-friend.

Bussard ['busart] m (3) buzzard.

Buße ['buːsə] f (15) penance; (Sühne) atonement; (Geldstrafe) fine; ~ tun s. büßen.

büßen ['byːsən] (27) do penance (for), atone (for); Verbrechen: expiate; mit Geld: be fined for; fig. pay (od. suffer) for.

'**Büßer** m (7), '**~in** f (16¹) penitent; '**~bank** f penitent bench.

'**bußfertig** penitent, repentant; '**⚲-keit** f penitence, repentance.

'**Bußgeld** n fine; '**~bescheid** m notice of fine due; '**~katalog** m list of fines.

Bussole [bu'soːlə] f (15) compass.

'**Buß|predigt** f penitential sermon; '**~tag** m day of repentance.

Büste ['bystə] f (15) bust; '**~nhalter** m brassière, F bra; '**~nhebe** f uplift brassière.

Butan 🜔 [bu'taːn] n (11, o. pl.) butane.

Butt [but] m (3) (Fisch) butt.

Butte ['butə] f, **Bütte** ['bytə] f (15) tub, vat.

Büttel ['bytəl] m (7) beadle, bailiff.

Büttenpapier ['bytənpapiːr] n handgeschöpft: hand-made paper; (Werks⚲) mo(u)ld paper.

Butter ['butər] f (15) butter; F alles in ~! everything's okay!; '**~blume** f buttercup; '**~brot** n (slice of) bread and butter; fig. für ein ~ for a song; '**~brotpapier** n greaseproof paper; '**~dose** f butter-dish; '**~faß** n churn; '**~milch** f butter-milk; '**⚲n** v/t. u. v/i. (29) churn; (bestreichen) (spread with) butter.

Button ['batən] m (11) badge.

Butzen ['butsən] m (6) im Geschwür, Obst usw.: core; '**~scheibe** f bull's--eye pane.

Byzantin|er [bytsan'tiːnər] m (7), **~e-rin** f, **⚲isch** Byzantine; **~ismus** [~ti-'nismus] m (16, o. pl.) fig. Byzantinism.

C

C [tseː], **c** n inv. C, c; ♪ C.

Café [ka'feː] n (11) coffee-house, café.

Camping|-ausrüstung ['kɛmpiŋ-] f camping gear; '**~bus** m camper; '**~platz** m camping site, campsite; für Wohnwagen: caravan site.

Canaille [ka'naljə] f (15) (Pöbel) rabble, mob; (Schurke) rascal.

Cape [keːp] n (11) cape.

C-Dur ♪ n C major.

Cellist [tʃɛ'list] m (12) cellist.

Cello ['tʃɛlo] n (11) cello.

Cellophan [tsɛlo'faːn] n cellophane.

Celsius ['tsɛlzjus] m (inv., o. pl.)

(degree) centigrade, Celsius (abbr. °C).

Cembalo ['tʃɛmbalo] n (11) harpsichord.

Ces ♪ [tsɛs] n C flat.

Chagrinleder [ʃa'grɛ̃-] n shagreen.

Chaiselongue [ʃɛːz(ə)'lõ(g)] f (11¹) lounge-chair.

Chamäleon [ka'mɛːleɔn] n (11) chameleon.

Champagner [ʃam'panjər] m (7) champagne.

Champignon ['ʃampinjõ] m (11) (field) mushroom.

Chance ['ʃãsə] f (15) chance; j-m eine ~ geben give a p. a chance (F a break); die ~n sind gleich the odds are even; '~ngleichheit f equal opportunities pl.

changieren [ʃã'ʒiːrən] Seide: be shot; ~d shot.

Chaos ['kaːɔs] n inv. chaos.

chaotisch [ka'oːtiʃ] chaotic.

Charakter [ka'raktər] m (3¹, pl. Charaktere [~'teːrə]) character; ~-bild n portrait; ~-eigenschaft f characteristic; 2bildend adj., ~bildung f character-building; ~fehler m defect in a p.'s character, weakness; 2fest m of firm character; 2i-'sieren characterize; ~i'sierung f, ~istik [~'ristik] f (16) characterization; ⊕, ⅍ characteristic; 2istisch [~'ristiʃ] characteristic (für of); ~kopf m fine head; 2lich (adv. in) character; 2los unprincipled; (schwach) weak, spineless; ~losigkeit f want of principles; ~schwäche f weakness of character; ~stärke f strength of character; 2voll full of personality; ~zug m characteristic, feature, trait.

Charge ['ʃarʒə] f (15) mil. post, rank; P.: (bsd. non-commissioned) officer; thea. (small) character part; metall. charge.

Charlatan ['ʃarlatan] m s. Scharlatan.

charm|ant [ʃar'mant] charming; 2e [ʃarm] m (11, o.pl.) charm, grace.

Charter ['ʃartər] f inv. charter; '~flug m charter(ed) flight; '~flugzeug n, '~maschine f charter plane; '2n (29) charter.

Chassis [ʃa'siː] n (11) chassis.

Chauff|eur [ʃɔ'føːr] m (3¹) chauffeur, driver; 2ieren [~'fiːrən] drive.

Chaussee [ʃo'seː] f (15) high road,

Am. highway.

Chauvi F ['ʃoːvi] m (11) male chauvinist (pig); ~nismus [ʃovi'nismus] m (16) chauvinism, Brt. a. jingoism; ~'nist(in f) m chauvinist, Brt. a. jingo; 2'nistisch chauvinistic.

Chef [ʃɛf] m (11) chief; head; ✠ principal, employer; F governor, bsd. Am. boss; '~arzt m medical superintendent; '~dirigent m principal conductor; '~etage f executive floor; '~ideologe m chief ideologist; '~pilot m chief pilot; '~redakteur m chief editor; '~sekretärin f director's secretary.

Chemie [çe'miː] f (15) chemistry; ~faser f synthetic fib|re, Am. -er; ~müll m chemical waste.

Chemikalien [çemi'kaːljən] f/pl. (15) chemicals.

Chemiker ['çeːmikər] m (7) (analytical) chemist.

chemisch ['çeːmiʃ] chemical; ~ reinigen dry-clean. [chicory]

Chicorée ['ʃikore] f, m (11, o. pl.)

Chiffre ['ʃifrə] f (15) cipher, code; '~anzeige f box-number advertisement; '~nummer f box-number; '~schrift f cryptography.

chiffrieren [ʃi'friːrən] (en)cipher, (en)code.

China|kohl ['çina-] m Chinese cabbage; '~rinde f Peruvian bark.

Chines|e [çi'neːzə] m (13), ~in f (16¹), 2isch Chinese.

Chinin [çi'niːn] n (11, o. pl.) quinine.

Chintz [tʃints] m (3) chintz.

Chip ['tʃip] m (11) (Kartoffel🅡) crisp, Am. potato chip; (Spiel🅡), Computer: chip.

Chirurg [çi'rurk] m (12) surgeon; ~ie [~'giː] f (15) surgery; (Station) surgical ward; 2isch [~'rurgiʃ] surgical.

Chlor [kloːr] n (3²) chlorine; '2en chlorinate; ~'kalium n potassium chloride; '~kalk m, ~'kalzium n chloride of lime, calcium chloride.

Chloroform [kloro'fɔrm] n (11), 2ie-ren [~'miːrən] chloroform.

Chlorophyll [kloro'fyl] n (11, o. pl.) chlorophyll.

'Chlorsäuresalz n chlorate.

Choke ['tʃoːk] mot. m (11) choke.

Cholera ['koːləra] f inv. cholera.

cholerisch [ko'leːriʃ] choleric.

Cholesterin 🅡 [kolɛste'riːn] n (11, o. pl.) cholesterol; ~spiegel m cholesterol level.

Chor [koːr] *m* (3⁸) chorus; (*Sänger*♀) choir; ♪ *m* (*od. n*) chancel, choir; *im ~ a. fig.* in chorus.
Choral [ko'rɑːl] *m* (3¹ *u.* ³) hymn, choral(e).
'**Chor-altar** *m* high altar.
Choreograph [koreo'grɑːf] *m* (12), **~in** *f* (16¹) choreographer; **~ie** [~gra'fiː] *f* (15) choreography.
Chor|gang ['koːr-] *m* aisle; '**~gesang** *m* choral singing (*od.* song); chorus; **~gestühl** ['~gəʃtyːl] *n* (3) choir-stalls *pl.*; '**~hemd** *n* surplice; '**~herr** *m* canon.
Chorist [ko'rist] *m* (12), **~in** *f* (16¹) chorister; *thea.* chorus-singer.
Chor|knabe ['koːr-] *m* choir-boy; '**~sänger** *m* chorus-singer; '**~stuhl** *m* stall.
Christ [krist] 1. *m* (3¹) Christ; 2. *m* (12), '**~in** *f* (16¹) Christian.
Christ... *s.* Weihnachts...
'**Christen|heit** *f* (16) Christendom; '**~tum** *n* (1²) Christianity; '**~verfolgung** *f* persecution of Christians.
'**Christkind** *n* Infant Jesus, Christ-child.
'**christlich** Christian.
Chrom [kroːm] *n* (3¹) (*Metall*) chromium; (*Farbe*) chrome.
chromatisch [kro'mɑːtiʃ] chromatic.
chromgelb ['kroːm-] chrome yellow.
Chromosom [kromo'zoːm] *n* (5²) chromosome.
'**Chromsäure** *f* chromic acid.
Chronik ['kroːnik] *f* (16) chronicle.
'**chronisch** chronic.
Chronist [kro'nist] *m* (12) chronicler.
Chronolog|ie [~nolo'giː] *f* (15) chronology; **♀isch** [~'loːgiʃ] chronological.
Chronometer [~no'meːtər] *n* (7) chronometer.
circa ['tsirka] about, circa.

Cis ♪ [tsis] *n* C sharp.
Claque *thea.* ['klakə] *f* (15) claque.
Clique ['klikə] *f* (15) clique, coterie; '**~nwesen** *n* cliquism.
Clou [kluː] *m* (11) highlight. (*Höhepunkt*) climax; (*Pointe*) point.
Cod|e [koːt] *m* (11) code; **♀ieren** [ko'diːrən] (en)code; **~ierung** *f* coding.
Coeur [køːr] *n* Karten: heart(s *pl.*).
Collaborateur *pol.* [kɔlabora'tøːr] *m* (3¹) collaborationist.
Computer [kɔm'pjuːtər] *m* (7) computer; **♀gesteuert** computer-controlled; **♀isieren** [~pjuːtəri'ziːrən] computerize; **~kasse** *f* computerised cash register; **~spiel** *n* computer game.
Conférencier [kõferã'sjeː] *m* compère, *Am.* master of ceremonies (*abbr.* M.C.); *als ~ leiten* compère (*Am.* emcee) *a* show.
Container [kɔn'teːnər] *m* (7) container; **♀isieren** containerize; **~schiff** *n* container ship.
Contergan [kɔntɛr'gaːn] *n* (11, *o. pl.*) thalidomide; **~kind** *n* thalidomide child.
Couch [kautʃ] *f* (16) couch; '**~garnitur** *f* lounge (*od.* three-piece) suite; '**~tisch** *m* coffee table.
Coupé [ku'peː] *n* (11) 🚃 compartment; (*Wagen*) coupé (*a. mot.*).
Couplet [~'pleː] *n* (11) comic (*od.* music-hall) song; *politisches usw.*: topical song.
Coupon [ku'põ] *m* (11) coupon.
Cour [kuːr] *f bei Hofe*: levee; *j-m die ~ machen* court; **~age** [ku'rɑːʒə] *f inv.* courage.
Cousin [ku'zɛ̃] *m* (11), **~e** [~'ziːnə] *f* (15) cousin.
Creme ['kreːm(ə)] *f* (11¹) cream (*a. fig.*); '**♀farben** cream-colo(u)red; '**~torte** *f* cream tart.
Cutaway ['katəveː] *m*, F **Cut** *m* (11) morning coat, cutaway.

D

D [deː], **d** *n* D, d; ♪ D.
da [dɑː] 1. *adv. räumlich:* (*dort*) there; (*hier*) here; *zeitlich:* then; *in der Erzählung:* now; *du ~* you there; *der Mann ~* that man there; *~ drüben* over there; *~ sein* be there (*vgl. dasein*); (*zur Hand*) be at hand; (*angekommen*) have (*od.* be)

arrived; ~ *bin ich* here I am; *dein Vater war* ~ was here; *ist j.* ~*gewesen?* has anybody called?; *wieder* ~ here (*od.* back) again, back once more; ~ *und* ~ at such and such a place; *von* ~ *an od. ab räumlich:* from there; *zeitlich:* from that time on; *was läßt sich* ~ *machen?* what can be done in such a case?; *wer* ~*?* who is (✕ goes) there?; *nichts* ~*!* nothing of the kind!, on no account!; ~ *haben wir's!* there we are!; **2.** *cj. Zeit:* when; while; *Grund:* as; (*da ja*) since; ~ *nun,* ~ *doch* now since, since indeed.

dabei [da'baɪ] near by, close by; (*anwesend*) there, present; (*überdies*) besides, moreover, as well; (*noch dazu; trotzdem*) yet, for all that; (*währenddessen*) all the time, in doing so; (*bei diesem Anlaß*) on the occasion, then; ~ *sein bei der Arbeit:* be at it; ~ *sein zu inf.* be about to *inf.,* be on the point of *ger.;* *darf ich mit* ~ *sein?* may I join the party?; *ich bin* ~*!* agreed!, count me in!, F I'm on; *was ist denn* ~*?* what harm is there in it?; ~ *bleiben* persist; *s. a. bleiben;* ~**sein** present (*od.* there), take part; ~**stehen** stand by.

'**dableiben** (sn) stay.

da capo [da'ka:po] da capo, encore; ~ *rufen* encore; *s. Dakapo.*

Dach [dax] *n* (1^2) roof; *mot. a.* top; *fig.* shelter, house; *unter* ~ *und Fach* under cover, *fig.* all settled; *fig.* F *eins aufs* ~ *kriegen* cop it; '~**balken** *m* roof-tree; rafter; '~**boden** *m* loft; '~**decker** *m* roofer; (*Ziegeldecker*) tiler; (*Schieferdecker*) slater; '~**fenster** *n* dormer-window; '~**first** *m* ridge (of a roof); '~**garten** *m* roof-garden; '~**gepäckträger** *mot. m* roof rack; '~**geschoß** *n* attic stor(e)y; loft; '~**gesellschaft** ✝ *f* holding company; '~**himmel** *mot. m* roof lining; '~**kammer** *f* attic, garret; '~**organisation** *f* umbrella organization; '~**pappe** *f* roofing (felt); '~**pfanne** *f* pantile; '~**reiter** *m* (ridge-)turret; '~**rinne** *f* gutter, eaves *pl.*

Dachs [daks] *m* (4) badger.

'**Dach|schiefer** *m* roofing slate; '~**schindel** *f* roof shingle.

Dachshund *m* dachshund.

'**Dach|sparren** *m* rafter; '~**stube** *f* attic, garret; '~**stuhl** *m* roof-truss.

dachte ['daxtə] *pret. v.* denken.

'**Dach|traufe** *f* eaves *pl.*; '~**werk** *n* roofing; '~**wohnung** *f* attic flat; '~**ziegel** *m* (roofing) tile.

Dackel ['dakəl] *m* (7) dachshund.

'**dadurch** *örtlich:* through that *od.* it; *Mittel:* through (*od.* by) it; thereby; by this means, thus; ~ *daß ...* by *ger.*

dafür [da'fy:r] for that; for it *od.* them; (*als Ersatz*) in return (for it), in exchange; (*statt dessen*) instead of it; *ich kann nichts* ~ it is not my fault; ~ *sein* be in favo(u)r of it; (~ *stimmen*) vote for it; ♀**halten:** *nach meinem* ♀ in my opinion, as I see it.

da|gegen 1. *adv.* against that; against it; *Vergleich:* in comparison with it; *Tausch, Ersatz:* in return *od.* exchange (for it); (*anderseits*) on the other hand; *ich habe nichts* ~ I have no objection (to it), I don't mind; ~ *sein* be against it; (~ *stimmen*) vote against it; **2.** *cj. Gegensatz:* on the contrary, on the other hand.

daheim [~'haɪm] at home; (*in der Heimat*) in one's own country; ♀ *n* home.

daher ['da:he:r, da'he:r] from there; *Ursache:* hence; therefore; *bei Verben der Bewegung:* along.

daherum ['da:hɛrum] thereabouts.

dahin ['da:hin, da'hin] there; to that place; (*vergangen*) gone, past, over; (*verloren*) gone, lost; *bei Verben bisweilen = weg...:* away; *bei Verben der Bewegung:* along; *j-n* ~ *bringen, daß* make a p. *do a th.;* *es* ~ *bringen, daß j. od. et. ...* cause a p. *od.* a th. to *inf.;* succeed in *ger.;* ~**fliegen** [da'hin-] (sn) fly along; *Zeit:* fly; ~**gehen** (sn) walk along; *Zeit:* pass; (*sterben*) pass away; ~**gehend** ['da:hin-] to the effect (*that*); ~**gestellt** [da'hin-]: ~ *sein lassen* leave undecided; ~**reden** speak thoughtlessly; ~**siechen** *v/i.* (sn) waste away; ~**stehen** remain to be seen.

da|hinten back there.

da|hinter behind it (*a. fig.*); ~**kommen** (sn) find out (about it); ~**machen** *od.* ~**setzen:** *sich* ~ set to work, get down to it; ~**stecken** be at the bottom of it.

Dakapo *n* repeat; encore; *s. da capo.*

damal|ig ['da:ma:liç] of that time;

der ~*e Besitzer* the then owner; '~**s** then, at that time.

Damas|t [da'mast] *m* (3²), ♀**ten** damask; ♀'**zieren** *Stoff:* damask; *Stahl:* damascene.

Dambrett ['dɑːm-] *n* draught--bord, *Am.* checkerboard.

Dämchen ['dɛːmçən] *n* (6) damsel.

Dame ['dɑːmə] *f* (15) lady; *beim Tanz usw.:* partner; (*Karte*) queen; *s.* ~*spiel*; *im Damespiel:* king; *meine* ~*!* madam!; *meine* ~*n* (*und Herren*)*!* ladies (and gentlemen)!

'**Damen|besuch** *m* lady-visitor(s *pl.*); '~**binde** *f* sanitary towel (*Am.* napkin); '~'**doppel(spiel)** *n Tennis:* the women's doubles *pl.*; '~'**-einzel** (**-spiel**) *n Tennis:* the women's singles *pl.*; '~**friseur** *m* ladies' hairdresser; ♀**haft** ladylike; '~**kleidung** *f* ladies' wear; '~**konfektion** *f* ladies' ready-made (*Am.* ready--to-wear) clothing; '~**mannschaft** *f Sport:* women's team; '~**schneider** *m* ladies' tailor; '~**toilette** *f* ladies' toilet (*Am.* restroom); '~-**unterwäsche** *f* ladies' underwear; *feine:* lingerie; '~**wahl** *f* ladies' choice; '~**welt** *f the* ladies *pl., the* fair sex.

'**Damespiel** *n* draughts *sg., Am.* checkers *sg.*

Damhirsch ['damhirʃ] *m* (3²) (fallow-)buck.

da'mit 1. *adv.* with it; with that, by it *od.* this, thereby; **2.** *cj.* (in order) that *od.* to; ~ *nicht* lest, (in order) that ... not; for fear that.

dämlich F ['dɛːmliç] stupid, silly.

Damm [dam] *m* (3²) dam; (*Deich*) dike; (*Bahn*♀, *Fluß*♀) embankment; (*Hafen*♀) mole; (*Straßen*♀) bank; (*Fahr*♀) roadway; *anat.* perineum; *fig.* barrier; *fig.* F *j-n wieder auf den* ~ *bringen* set a p. on his feet again; *auf dem* ~ *sein* be all right, feel up to it; '~**bruch** *m* bursting of a dam; (*Lücke*) break in a dam.

dämmen ['dɛmən] (25) dam (up); *fig.* stem, check.

dämmer|ig ['dɛməriç] dusky; ♀**licht** *n* twilight; *morgens:* grey dawn of day; *weitS.* dim light; '~**n** (29) grow dusky; *morgens:* dawn (*a. fig.*); *fig.* es *dämmert bei ihm* it is beginning to dawn on him; ♀**schein** *m s.* ♀*licht*; '♀**schoppen** *m* F sundowner; '♀**stunde** *f* hour of twilight; *in der* ~ in the dusk of the

evening; '♀**ung** *f* (*Morgen*♀) dawn (**-ing**); (*Abend*♀, *Dämmerlicht*) twilight, dusk.

Dämon ['dɛːmɔn] *m* (8¹) demon; ♀**isch** [dɛ'moːniʃ] demoniac(al).

Dampf [dampf] *m* (3³) steam; *weitS.* vapo(u)r; (*Rauch*) smoke; '~**bad** *n* steam-bath; '~**boot** *n* steamboat; '~**bügeleisen** *n* steam iron; '~**druck** *m* steam-pressure; '♀**en** (25) steam; F (*rauchen*) smoke.

dämpfen ['dɛmpfən] (25) (*abschwächen*) damp; *Farbe, Ton, Licht:* soften (down), subdue; *Feuer:* quench; *Stoß, Schall:* deaden; ✗ stabilize; (*mit Dampf behandeln; im Dampfbad kochen*) steam; *mit gedämpfter Stimme* in an undertone.

'**Dampfer** *m* (7) steamer.

'**Dämpfer** *m* (7) damper (*a. am Klavier*); ♪ *bsd. für Geige:* mute; *Radio:* baffle; *Kernphysik:* moderator; *s. Schall*♀, *Stoß*♀; *fig. j-m* *e-n* ~ *aufsetzen* damp a p.'s enthusiasm.

'**Dampfheizung** *f* steam-heating.

'**dampfig** steamy.

'**dämpfig** (*schwül*) sultry; *vet.* broken-winded.

'**Dampf|kessel** *m* (steam-)boiler; '~**kochtopf** *m* pressure cooker; '~**kraft** *f* steam power; '~**maschine** *f* steam-engine; '~**nudel** *f* yeast dumpling; '~**schiff** *n* steamer, steamship, steamboat; *vor dem Schiffsnamen:* S. S.; '~**schiffahrt** *f* steam navigation.

Dämpfung ['dɛmpfuŋ] *f s. dämpfen:* damping *usw.*; (*a. fig.*) suppression; ✗ stabilization; '~**s-flosse** ✗ *f* stabilizer.

'**Dampfwalze** *f* steam-roller.

Damwild ['damvilt] *n* fallow-deer.

da'nach after that *od.* it; (*nachher*) afterwards; (*demgemäß*) accordingly, according to that; *er trägt Verlangen* ~ he has a desire for it; *er sieht ganz* ~ *aus* he looks very much like it; *es ist aber auch* ~ don't ask what it is like.

Dän|e ['dɛːnə] *m* (13), '~**in** *f* Dane.

daneben [da'neːbən] beside (*od.* near) it, next to it *od.* that; (*außerdem*) besides; (*gleichzeitig*) at the same time; ~**gehen** (sn) miss (the mark); *fig.* go amiss; ~**liegen** *fig.* (*sich irren*) be off beam; ~**treffen** miss (the mark).

dang [daŋ] *pret. v.* dingen.
daniederliegen [ˌ∼'niːdərliːgən]:
(*krank*) ∼ be laid up (*an dat.* with);
Handel usw.: languish, stagnate.
dänisch ['dɛːniʃ] Danish.
Dank [daŋk] *m* (3) thanks *pl.*; (∼*barkeit*) gratitude; (*Lohn*) reward; *j-m
∼ sagen* thank a p., return thanks
to a p.; *j-m ∼ wissen für* be obliged
to a p. for; *Gott sei ∼!* thank God!;
vielen (*od.* schönen) ∼*!* many thanks!,
Am. F thanks a lot!; *zum ∼* by way
of thanks, in reward (*für* for); *iro.
das ist der* (*ganze*) ∼ *dafür!* that's
all the thanks one gets!; ♀ *seiner
Güte* owing (*od.* [*a. iro.*] thanks) to
his kindness; '∼-adresse *f* vote of
thanks.
'**dankbar** thankful, grateful (*j-m* to
a p.; *für* for); (*lohnend*) profitable;
(*befriedigend*) *Aufgabe*: rewarding;
ich wäre Ihnen ∼ für I will thank
you for; '♀keit *f* gratitude.
'**danken** *v/i.* thank (*j-m* a p.), return
thanks; ∼ *für* (*ablehnen*) decline
with thanks; *danke!* thank you!, F
thanks!; *bei Ablehnung*: no thank
you!; *danke schön!* many thanks!;
v/t. j-m et. ∼ (*lohnen*) reward a p.
for a th.; (*ver∼*) owe a th. to a p.;
∼*d erhalten* received with thanks;
'∼swert meritorious.
'**Dank|e-schön** *n* (11, *o. pl.*) thank-
-you; '∼eswort *n* (3) words *pl.* of
thanks.
'**Dank|gebet** *n* thanksgiving
(prayer); '∼gottesdienst *m* thanksgiving service; '∼-opfer *n* thank-
-offering; ∼sagung ['∼zaːguŋ] *f*
thanks; *eccl.* thanksgiving; '∼-
schreiben *n* letter of thanks.
dann [dan] then; ∼ *und wann* now
and then; '∼en: *von ∼* (from) thence;
(*weg*) off, away.
daran [da'ran] *at* (*od.* by, in, on, to)
that *od.* it; *sich ∼ machen s.* ∼gehen;
nahe ∼ sein zu inf. be on the point
of *ger.*; *was liegt ∼?* what does it
matter?; *es ist nichts ∼* there is
nothing in it; *er ist gut* (*übel*) ∼
he is well (badly) off; *er tut gut ∼*
(*zu inf.*) he does well (to *inf.*); *wie
ist er mit Kleidern ∼?* how is he
off for clothes?; *ich bin* (*od.* komme)
∼ it is my turn; *Spiel: wer ist ∼?*
whose turn is it?; ∼gehen (sn) go
(*od.* set) about it; ∼ *zu inf.* proceed
to *inf.*; ∼setzen stake, risk.

darauf [ˌ∼'rauf] *räumlich*: on it *od.*
them, upon that; *zeitlich*: then,
after that; *den Tag ∼* the next day;
gleich ∼ directly afterwards; *gerade
∼ zu* straight towards it; ∼folgend
following; 'darauf'hin thereupon.
daraus [ˌ∼'raus] from this *od.* that
od. them; ∼ *folgt* hence it follows;
es kann nichts ∼ werden nothing
can come of it; ∼ *wird nichts!* F
nothing doing!
darben ['darbən] (25) suffer want;
stärker: starve.
darbiet|en ['daːr-] offer, present;
'♀ung *f thea. usw.* performance;
weitS. entertainment, event.
'**darbringen** present, offer, give.
darein [da'rain] into that *od.* it;
∼finden, ∼fügen, ∼schicken: *sich
∼* resign o.s. to it, put up with it;
∼geben give into the bargain; ∼-
mischen: *sich ∼* meddle (with it),
interfere (with it); *vermittelnd*:
intervene; ∼reden *v/i.* interrupt;
fig. interfere; ∼willigen consent
(to it).
darin [ˌ∼'rin] in that, in it *od.* them;
(*in dieser Hinsicht*) in this respect;
∼, *daß* ... in that ...
darleg|en ['daːr-] lay open, expose;
(*auseinandersetzen*) explain, point
out; (*ausführen*) state; (*offen ∼, anführen*) set forth, show; '♀ung *f*
exposition; explanation; statement,
showing.
Darleh(e)n ['daːrleːən] *n* (6) loan;
'∼skasse *f* loan-office, loan bank.
Darm [darm] *m* (3³) gut; (*Wurst-
haut*) skin; *Därme pl.* intestines,
bowels; '∼geschwür *n* intestinal
ulcer; '∼-infektion *f* intestinal infection; '∼krebs *m* cancer of the
intestine; '∼saite *f* catgut string; '∼-
verschlingung *f* twisting of the
guts; '∼verschluß ♂ *m* ileus.
Darre ['darə] *f* (15) (*Vorgang*) kiln-
-drying; (*Darrofen*) (drying-)kiln;
(*Vogelkrankheit*) roup, pip.
darreichen ['daːr-] offer, present;
♂ *u. eccl.* administer.
darren ['darən] (25) kiln-dry.
darstell|bar ['daːrʃtɛlbaːr] repre-
sentable; '∼en *allg.* represent; (*abbilden*; *graphisch ∼*) figure; *thea.
Rolle*: (im)personate, do; ♂ disengage; *sich ∼* present itself; ∼de
Kunst interpretative art; '♀er(in *f*)
thea. m performer; '♀ung *f* repre-

sentation; (im)personation, acting; ♫ disengagement; *graphische* ~ diagram, graph.

dartun ['dɑ:r-] show; demonstrate.

darüber [da'ry:bər] over that, over it *od.* them; *(querüber)* across it; *(was dies anbetrifft)* about that *od.* it, on that point; *zeitlich:* meanwhile; *zwei Pfund* ~ two pounds more; *zwei Jahre und* ~ two years and upward; *past it, fig. a.* in addition (to this); *wir sind* ~ *hinweg* we got over it; *es geht nichts* ~ there is nothing like it.

darum [~'rum] **1.** *adv.* around that *od.* it *od.* them; about that; *er weiß* ~ he is aware of it; *es ist mir sehr* ~ *zu tun, daß* I set great store by *ger.*; *es ist mir nur* ~ *zu tun* my only object is; **2.** *cj.* ['da:rum] *(deshalb)* therefore, that's why.

darunter [da'rontər] under that *od.* it *od.* them; *unter e-r Anzahl:* among them; *(einschließlich)* including; *(weniger)* less; *zwei Jahre und* ~ two years and under; *was verstehst du* ~? what do you understand by it?

das [das] *s.* der.

dasein ['da:-] **1.** (sn) be there; *(anwesend sein)* be present; *(vorhanden sein)* exist; *noch nie dagewesen* unprecedented; *vgl.* da; **2.** ♀ *n* (6) existence, being; life; *(Gegenwart, Anwesenheit)* presence; *ins* ~ *treten* come into being; '♀sberechtigung *f* raison d'être *(fr.)*; '♀skampf *m* struggle for existence.

da'selbst [da-] there, in that very place.

daß [das] that; ~ *nicht* lest; *bis* ~ till.

dastehen ['da:-] stand (there).

Daten ['dɑ:tən] *n/pl.* (9²) data, facts; particulars; '~ausgabe *f* data output; '~bank *f* data bank; '~eingabe *f* data input; '~schreiber *m* data printer; '~schutz *m* data protection; '~träger *m* data medium; '~typist (-in *f*) *m* terminal operator; '~übertragung *f* data transmission; '♀verarbeitend, '~verarbeitung *f* data processing; '~verbund *m* aggregate.

datieren [da'ti:rən] date.

Dativ ['dɑ:ti:f] *m* (3¹) dative (case).

dato ['dɑ:to]: *bis* ~ to date, hitherto; *(nach)* ~ after date.

Dattel ['datəl] *f* (15) date.

Datum ['dɑ:tum] *n* (9²) date; *welches* ~ *haben wir heute?* which day of the month is it?; '~stempel *m* date stamp; *(Gerät)* dater.

Daube ['daobə] *f* (15) stave.

Dauer ['daoər] *f* (15) duration; *(Fortdauer)* continuance; *(Ständigkeit)* permanence; *auf die* ~ in the long run; *für die* ~ *von* for a period *(od.* term) of ...; *von kurzer* ~ of short duration; *von* ~ *sein* last; '~auftrag ✝ *m* standing order; '~betrieb ⊕ *m* continuous operation; '~brenner *m (Ofen)* slow-combustion stove; *(Erfolg)* long-running hit; F *(Kuß)* long kiss; '~feuer ⚔ *n* sustained fire; '~flug *m* endurance flight; non-stop flight; '♀haft durable, lasting; ~ *sein Stoff:* wear well; '~haftigkeit *f* durability; '~karte *f* season-ticket, *Am.* commutation ticket; '~lauf *m* endurance run; *leichter:* jog-trot; '~leistung *f* continuous output; '~lutscher *m* lollipop; '♀n (29) **1.** continue, last; *e-e gewisse Zeit* ~ take; ~d lasting, permanent, *(ständig)* constant; **2.** *er (es) dauert mich* I feel sorry for him (it); I pity him (it); '~stellung *f* permanent position, permanency; '~welle *f im Haar:* permanent wave, F perm; '~zustand *m* permanent condition.

Daumen ['daomən] *m* (6) thumb; F *j-m den* ~ *drücken* keep one's fingers crossed for a p.; *die* ~ *drehen* twiddle one's thumbs; '~breite *f* thumb's breadth; '~register *n* thumb index; '~schraube *f* thumbscrew *(a. fig.)*.

Daune ['daonə] *f* (15) down; '~ndecke *f* eider-down.

davon [da'fɔn] of that *od.* it *od.* them; by that *od.* it; *(fort, weg)* off; *was habe ich* ~? what does it get me?; ~*kommen* get away *od.* off; *s.* Schreck; ~*laufen* (sn) run away; ~*machen: sich* ~ make off; ~*schleichen: sich* ~ steal away *od.* off; ~*tragen* carry off; *fig.* incur, get; *s.* Sieg.

da'vor before that *od.* it *od.* them; of it.

dazu [da'tsu:] to that *od.* it *od.* them; *(zu dem Zweck)* for that purpose; *(außerdem)* in addition to that; *noch* ~ at that; moreover, into the bargain; ~ *gehört Zeit* that requires time; ~ *kommt* add to this; *wie kommst du* ~? how could you?; *ich kam nie* ~ I never got (a)round to

do it; ~**gehören** belong to it *od.*
them; ~**gehörig** belonging to it;
~**kommen** (sn) come along; *unvermutet*: supervene; *s. a. dazu.*

dazumal ['daːtsumaːl] at that time.

da'zutun add (to it).

dazwischen [da'tsviʃən] between
(them); ~**fahren** (sn), ~**funken** F
interfere; ~**kommen** (sn) intervene;
♀**kunft** *f* (16) intervention; ~**liegend**
intermediate; ~**treten** (sn) intervene.

Dealer *sl.* ['diːlər] *m* (7) (drug) pusher.

Debatte [de'batə] *f* (15) debate; *zur* ~
stehen be under discussion, be at
issue.

debat'tieren debate.

Debet ✝ ['deːbɛt] *n* (11) debit.

Debüt [de'byː] *n* (11) first appearance, début (*fr.*); ~**ant(in** *f*) *m*
[~by'tant(in)] débutant(e *f*) (*fr.*);
♀**ieren** [~'tiːrən] make one's début.

dechiffrieren [deʃif'riːrən] decipher, decode.

Deck ⚓ [dɛk] *n* (3) deck; '~-**adresse**
f cover (address); '~**bett** *n* feather-
-bed; '~**blatt** *n* e-r *Zigarre*: wrapper; *zu Büchern usw.*: errata slip.

Decke ['dɛkə] *f* (15) cover; (*Bett*♀)
coverlet, *wollene*: blanket; *e-s Zim-
mers*: ceiling; *mot.* (*Reifen*♀) casing;
unter e-r ~ *stecken* conspire together; *sich nach der* ~ *strecken*
cut one's coat according to one's
cloth, make both ends meet.

Deckel ['dɛkəl] *m* (7) lid, (*a. Buch*♀)
cover; F (*Hut*) lid.

decken ['dɛkən] (25) cover (*a.* ✗,
✝, *Stute usw.*; *a. Boxen*); *Dach*:
(*mit Ziegeln* ~) tile, (*mit Schiefer* ~)
slate; *Sport*: mark; *fig. j-n*: shield;
Bedarf: meet, supply; *den Tisch* ~
lay the cloth *od.* table; *für sechs
Personen* ~ lay covers for six persons; *e-n Wechsel* ~ meet a bill;
hinlänglich gedeckt sein have sufficient security; *a.* ⚤ *sich* ~ coincide; *fenc. usw.* guard (*a. fig.*);
gegen against).

'**Decken|beleuchtung** *f* ceiling
lighting; '~**gemälde** *n* ceiling fresco.

'**Deck|farbe** *f* body-colo(u)r; '~-
mantel *m fig.* cloak; '~**name** *m*
cover name, pseudonym; '~**ung** *f*
covering; ✝ (*Sicherheit*) cover, security, (*Mittel*) funds *pl.*; *des Be-
darfs*: supply; (*Zahlung*) payment;

fenc. usw. guard; (*Schutz*) cover; '~-
weiß *n* (4, 16, *o. pl.*) opaque white.

defekt [de'fɛkt] **1.** defective; **2.** ♀ *m*
(3) defect.

defensiv [defɛn'ziːf] defensive; ♀**e**
[~'ziːvə] *f* (15) defensive; *in der* ~
on the defensive.

defilieren [defi'liːrən] (h. *u.* sn)
march past, pass in review, parade.

defi'nier|bar definable; ~**en** [~'niː-
rən] define.

Definition [~ni'tsjoːn] *f* (16) definition.

definitiv [~'tiːf] (*bestimmt*) definite;
(*endgültig*) definitive, final.

Defizit ['deːfitsit] *n* (3) deficit, deficiency; *ein* ~ *decken* make good a
deficiency.

Deflation [defla'tsjoːn] *f* deflation.

Degen ['deːgən] *m* (6) sword; *Sport*:
épée (*fr.*).

degenerieren [degene'riːrən] degenerate.

degradier|en [degra'diːrən] de-
grade, *Am.* demote; ♀**ung** *f* degradation, *Am.* demotion.

dehn|bar ['deːnbaːr] extensible;
elastic (*a. fig.*); *fig.* (*vage*) vague;
'♀**barkeit** *f* extensibility; elasticity;
vagueness; '~**en** (25) extend;
elastisch: stretch (*a. sich*); *phys.* expand (*a. sich*); *die Worte*: drawl;
Vokal: lengthen; '♀**ung** *f* extension;
stretch(ing); expansion; lengthen-
ing.

dehydrieren [dehy'driːrən] de-
hydrate.

Deich [daɪç] *m* (3) dike, dam.

Deichsel ['daɪksəl] *f* (15) pole, shaft;
(*Gabel*♀) thill; '♀**n** F (29) manage,
F wangle, engineer.

dein [daɪn] (20) your; *eccl., poet.*
thy; *pred. od. der* (*die, das*) *dein(ig)e*
yours; *eccl., poet.* thine; *die* ♀**en**
your family *od.* people; '~**er** (20)
a) of you; *refl.* of yourself; **b)** yours;
~**erseits** ['~ərzaɪts] for (*od.* on) your
part; ~**esgleichen** ['~əs'glaɪçən]
your like(s *pl.*), F the like(s *pl.*) of
you; ~**ethalben** ['~əthalbən], '~**et-
wegen**, (um) '~**etwillen** for your
sake; on your account; ~**ige** ['~igə]
(18b) *s.* dein.

Dekade [de'kaːdə] *f* (15) decade;
(*zehn Tage*) ten-day period.

dekaden|t [deka'dɛnt] decadent;
biol. degenerate; ♀**z** *f* (16) deca-
dence.

Dekan [de'kɑːn] *m* (3¹) dean.

dekatieren [deka'tiːrən] decatize.

Deklam|ation [deklama'tsjoːn] *f* declamation; **~ator** [~'mɑːtɔr] *m* (8¹) declaimer; **2atorisch** [~ma'toːriʃ] declamatory; **2ieren** [~'miːrən] *v/t.* recite; *mst v/i.* declaim.

deklarieren [~'riːrən] declare.

Dekli|nation [deklina'tsjoːn] *f* (16) declension; *phys.* declination; **2-'nierbar** declinable; **2'nieren** decline.

Dekolle|té [dekɔlte:] *n* (low) neckline; **2'tiert** low-necked, décolleté (*fr.*).

Dekorateur [dekora'tøːr] *m* (3¹) (*Maler*) decorator; (*Tapezierer*) upholsterer; (*Schaufenster2*) window--dresser; *thea.* scene-painter.

Dekoration [~'tsjoːn] *f* (16) decoration; (*Schaufenster2*) window-dressing; *thea.* scenery; **~smaler** *m* decorator; *thea.* scene-painter; **~stoff** *m* furnishing fabric.

dekorativ [dekora'tiːf] decorative.

deko'rieren decorate (*a. j-n mit Orden*); (*behängen*) drape; *Schaufenster*: dress.

Dekret [de'kreːt] *n* (3), **2ieren** [~kre'tiːrən] decree.

Deleg|ation [delega'tsjoːn] *f* delegation; **2ieren** [~'giːrən] delegate; **~ierte** [~'giːrtə] *m, f* delegate.

delikat [deli'kɑːt] delicate (*a. fig.*), dainty; (*köstlich*) delicious.

Delikatesse [~ka'tɛsə] *f* (15) delicacy (*a. fig.*); (*Leckerbissen*) *a.* dainty, titbit (*a. fig.*); *~n pl. bsd. Am.* delicatessen *pl.*; **~nhandlung** *f* delicatessen (store) *sg.*

Delikt [de'likt] *n* (3) delict.

Delirium [de'liːrjum] *n* (9) delirium.

Delle ['dɛlə] *f* (15) dent.

Delphin [dɛl'fiːn] *m* (3¹) dolphin.

Delta ['dɛlta] *n* (11[1]) delta.

dem [deːm]: *wie ~ auch sei* however that may be; *wenn ~ so ist* if that be true.

Demagog [dema'goːk], **~e** [~gə] *m* (12) demagog(ue); **~ie** [~go'giː] *f* (15) demagogy; **2isch** [~'goːgiʃ] demagogic.

Demarkationslinie [demarka-'tsjoːnsliːnjə] *f* line of demarcation.

demaskieren [demas'kiːrən] unmask.

Dement|i [de'mɛnti] *n* (11) (official) denial; **2ieren** [~'tiːrən] deny.

'dem|gegen'·über in contrast to this; **'~gemäß** accordingly; **'~nach** therefore, hence; accordingly; **'~-'nächst** shortly, soon, before long.

Demo ['deːmo] *f* (11¹) F demo.

demobilisier|en [demobili'ziːrən] *v/t. u. v/i.* demobilize; **2ung** *f* demobilization.

'Demokassette F *f* demo (tape).

Demokrat [demo'krɑːt] *m* (12), **~in** *f* (16¹) democrat; **~ie** [~kra'tiː] *f* (15) democracy; **2isch** [~'krɑːtiʃ] democratic; **2isieren** [~krati'ziːrən] democratize.

demolier|en [demo'liːrən] demolish; **2ung** *f* demolition.

Demonstr|ant [demɔn'strant] *m* (12) demonstrator; **~ation** [~stra'tsjoːn] *f* (16) demonstration; **~ationsmaterial** *n* teaching aids *pl.*; **~ationsrecht** *n* right to demonstrate; **~ationsverbot** *n* ban on demonstrating; **~ationszug** *m* protest march; **2ieren** [~'striːrən] *v/t. u. v/i.* demonstrate.

Demont|age [~'tɑːʒə] *f* (15) disassembly; dismantling; **2ieren** [~'tiːrən] disassemble; *a. Fabrik usw.:* dismantle.

demoralisieren [demorali'ziːrən] demoralize.

Demoskopie [~sko'piː] *f* (15) opinion poll(ing).

Demut ['deːmuːt] *f* (16) humility.

demütig ['~myːtiç] humble; **~en** ['~gən] (25) humble (*sich o.s.*), humiliate; **2ung** *f* humiliation.

'demzufolge accordingly.

denaturieren ⌐ [denatu'riːrən] (25) denature.

'Denk|-anstoß *m* a th. to start one thinking; *j-m e-n ~ geben* set a p. thinking about a th.; **'~-art** *f* way of thinking, mentality; **'2bar** thinkable; (*vorstellbar*) imaginable; (*faßbar*) conceivable; **'2en** *v/t.* (30) think; (*vermuten*) suppose, *Am.* F guess (*alle a. v/i.*); (*beabsichtigen*) intend; *~ an* (*acc.*) think of; (*sich erinnern*) remember *a p., a th.*; *~ über* (*acc.*) think about; *sich et. ~* think, (*vorstellen*) imagine, fancy; *j-m zu ~ geben* set a p. thinking; *~ Sie nur!* just fancy!; *ich denke nicht daran!* I wouldn't think of it!; **'~er** *m* (7) thinker; **'2fähig** intelligent; **'2faul** too lazy to think, mentally inert;

'**∼fehler** *m* false reasoning; '**∼freiheit** *f* freedom of thought; '**∼lehre** *f* logic; '**∼mal** *n* (1³ *u.* 3) monument; (*Ehrenmal*) memorial; '**∼malschutz** *m*: unter ∼ listed; '**∼modell** *n* (theoretical) model, blueprint; '**∼münze** *f* commemorative medal; '**∼prozeß** *m* process of reasoning; '**∼schrift** *f* memoir; memorial; memorandum; '**∼sport** *m* mental exercise; ∼aufgabe problem, brain-twister, *Am.* quiz; '**∼spruch** *m* motto, sentence; '**∼stein** *m* memorial stone; '**∼vermögen** *n* intellectual power; '**∼weise** *f s.* Denkart; '**?würdig** memorable; '**∼würdigkeit** *f* memorableness; *pl.* memorabilia; '**∼zettel** *m fig.* reminder; lesson.

denn [dɛn] for; *nach comp.*: than; (*tonlos* = *also, schließlich*) then.

'**dennoch** nevertheless, yet, still.

Dentist [dɛn'tist] *m* (12), **∼in** *f* (16¹) dentist.

Denun|ziant [denun'tsjant] *m* (12), **∼ziantin** *f* (16¹) informer; **∼ziation** [∼tsja'tsjoːn] *f* (16) denunciation; **?zieren** inform against, denounce.

Deo|dorant [deodo'rant] *n* (3¹, 11) deodorant; '**∼Roller** *m* roll-on (deodorant); '**∼spray** *m*, *n* deodorant spray; '**∼stift** *m* deodorant stick.

Depesch|e [de'pɛʃə] *f* (15) dispatch; *telegraphisch*: telegram, wire; *drahtlos*: wireless, radio; (*Kabel⬡*) cable (-gram); **?ieren** [∼'ʃiːrən] telegraph, wire, cable.

Deponie [depo'niː] *f* (15) (*Müll⬡*) dump, tip; **?ren** [∼'niːrən] deposit.

deportieren [∼pɔr'tiːrən] deport.

Depositen [∼'ziːtən] *pl.* (9) deposits *pl.*; **∼bank** *f* deposit bank; **∼kasse** *f* branch-office *of a bank*; **∼konto** *n* deposit account.

Depot [de'poː] *n* (11) ✝ deposit; ✗ (*a. Straßenbahn⬡*) depot; **∼-effekt** *pharm. m* controlled sustained release.

Depress|ion [deprɛ'sjoːn] *f* (16) depression (*a.* ✝); **?iv** [∼'siːf] depressed; *Stimmung etc.*: depressing, gloomy.

deprimieren [depri'miːrən] depress.

Depu|tation [deputa'tsjoːn] *f* (16) deputation; **?tieren** depute; **∼'tierte** *m*, *f* (18) deputy.

der [deːr], **die** [diː], **das** [das] **1.** *art.* (22) the; **2.** *dem. pron.* (22¹) that, this, he, she, it; *die pl.* these, those, they; *der und der usw.*: *adj.* such-and-such (a); *su.* so-and-so; **3.** *rel. pron.* (23) who, which, that.

'**der-art** in such a manner; to such a degree; '**∼ig** such, of such a kind; *nichts* ?es nothing of the kind.

derb [dɛrp] firm, solid; (*kräftig*) robust; (*stämmig*) sturdy; (*scharf*) severe; (*grob*) coarse (*a. zotig*), rough; (*unverblümt*) blunt; '**?heit** *f* robustness; sturdiness; roughness.

der'∼einst some day, in (the) future; **∼ig** future.

derent|halben ['deːrənthalbən], '**∼wegen**, '**∼willen** on her (their, whose) account.   [*daß so that.*]

'**dergestalt** in such a manner; ∼ }

der'gleichen such; *su.* the like; *und* ∼ and the like; *nichts* ∼ nothing of the kind.

der-, die-, dasjenige ['∼jeniɡə] (22¹) he *who*, she *who*, that *which*; *pl.* those *who*, *S.*: those *which*.

dermaßen ['∼maːsən] *s. derart.*

der-, die-, dasselbe [∼'zɛlbə] (22¹) the same; he, she, it.

'**derzeit** at present; '**∼ig** present.

Des ♪ [dɛs] *n* D flat.

desensibilisieren [dezɛnzibili'ziːrən] ⬡, *phot.* desensitize.

Desert|eur [dezɛr'tøːr] *m* (3¹) deserter; **?ieren** [∼'tiːrən] (sn) desert.

desgleichen [dɛs'ɡlaɪçən] *adv.* likewise.

deshalb ['dɛshalp] therefore, for that reason, that is why.

Desinfektion [dɛsʔinfɛk'tsjoːn] *f* disinfection; **∼smittel** *n* disinfectant.

des-infizieren [∼fi'tsiːrən] disinfect.

'**Des|-information** *f* disinformation; '**∼-interesse** *n* lack of interest.

desodorisieren [dɛsʔodori'ziːrən] deodorize.

Despot [dɛs'poːt] *m* (12), **∼in** *f* despot; **?isch** despotic; **∼ie** [∼po'tiː] *f* (16), **∼ismus** [∼'tismus] *m* (16, *o. pl.*) despotism.

dessenungeachtet ['desən'ʔunɡeʔaxtət] notwithstanding (that), nevertheless.

Dessert [dɛ'seːr] *n* (11) dessert.

Dessin [dɛ'sɛ̃] *n* (11) design, pattern.

Destill|ation [dɛstila'tsjoːn] *f* (16) distillation; **?ieren** [∼'liːrən] *v/i. u. v/t.* distil(l); **∼ierung** *f* distillation.

desto ['dɛsto] the; ∼ *besser* all (*od.* so much) the better; *s. je.*

destruktiv [destruk'ti:f] destructive.
deswegen ['dɛsveːgən] *s. deshalb.*
Detail [de'taj] *n* (11) detail; ✝ retail; **~geschäft** *n* retail business; (*Laden*) retail shop; **~handel** *m* retail trade; **~händler** *m* retail dealer; ⚲**lieren** [~'jiːrən] specify; **~list** [~'jist] *m* (12) retailer.
Detektiv [detɛk'tiːf] *m* (3¹) detective.
Detektor [de'tɛktɔr] *m* (8¹) *Radio:* detector.
Deto|nation [detona'tsjoːn] *f* (16) detonation; ⚲**nieren** detonate.
deuchte ['dɔʏçtə] *pret. v. dünken.*
Deut [dɔʏt] *m:* keinen ~ wert not worth a farthing.
deut|eln ['~əln] (29) *v/i.* subtilize; ~ *an* (*dat.*) quibble at; '**~en** *v/i.* (26): ~ *auf* (*acc.*) point to, *fig. a.* signify; *v/t.* interpret, construe, explain; *Traum, Zeichen:* read; *falsch* ~ misinterpret; '**~lich** clear, distinct; *fig.* ~ *werden* (*mit j-m*) be outspoken (with a p.); '⚲**lichkeit** *f* clearness, distinctness.
deutsch [dɔʏtʃ], ⚲ *n* German; '⚲**e** *m, f* (18) German; '⚲**tum** *n* (1²) German character, Germanity; *konkret:* Germans *pl.*
'**Deutung** *f* (16) interpretation; construction.
Devise [de'viːzə] *f* (15) device, motto; ✝ (*a. pl.*) foreign exchange *od.* currency; **~nausgleichsfonds** *m* exchange equalization funds; **~n-handel** *m* foreign exchange dealing; **~nkontrollstelle** *f* foreign exchange control office; **~nmarkt** *m* currency market; **~nschmuggel** *m* currency smuggling; **~nsperre** *f* exchange embargo.
devot [de'voːt] submissive.
Dezember [de'tsɛmbər] *m* (7) December.
dezent [de'tsɛnt] discreet; (*unaufdringlich*) unobtrusive; *Farbe, Licht usw.:* subdued, mellow.
dezentralisieren [detsɛntrali'ziːrən] decentralize.
Dezernat [detsɛr'naːt] *n* (3) department.
dezimal [detsi'maːl] decimal; ⚲**bruch** *m* decimal fraction; ⚲**stelle** *f* decimal place; ⚲**system** *n* decimal system.
dezi'mieren decimate.
Dia ['diːa] *n* (11) *s. Diapositiv.*
Diabe|tiker [dia'beːtikər] *m* (7),

⚲**tisch** diabetic.
diabolisch [dia'boːliʃ] diabolic(al).
'**Diabetrachter** *m* slide viewer.
Diadem [dia'deːm] *n* (3¹) diadem.
Diagnose [~'gnoːzə] *f* (15) diagnosis.
diagnostizieren [~gnɔsti'tsiːrən] diagnose.
diagonal [~go'naːl], ⚲**e** *f* (15) diagonal; ⚲**reifen** *mot. m* crossply tyre (*Am.* tire).
Diagramm [dia'gram] *n* (3) diagram.
Diakon [dia'koːn] *m* (3¹ *u.* 8), **Diakonus** [di'aːkonus] *m* (14³ *u.* 16²) deacon.
Diako'niss|e [diako'nisə] *f* (15), **~in** (16¹) Protestant (nursing) sister.
Dialekt [dia'lɛkt] *m* (3) dialect; **~ik** *f* (16, *no pl.*) dialectic(s *pl.*); ⚲**isch** dialectal.
Dialog [~'loːk] *m* (3¹) dialog(ue).
Dialyse [dia'lyːzə] 🜚 *f* (15) dialysis.
Diamant [~'mant] *m* (12), ⚲**en** diamond.
diametral [~me'traːl] diametrical.
Dia|positiv [diapozi'tiːf] *n* (3¹) slide, transparency; **~projektor** ['~projɛktɔr] *m* (8¹) slide projector.
Diarrhöe [dia'røː] *f* (15) diarrh(o)ea.
Diät [di'ɛːt] *f* (16) (special) diet, regimen; ⚲ *leben* diet *one's* o.s.; **~assistent**(**in** *f*) *m* dietician; **~en** *f/pl.* daily allowance *sg.*; **~kost** *f* dietary food.
dich [diç] you; *refl.* yourself.
dicht [diçt] (*undurchlässig*) tight; (*zusammengedrängt*) compact; *phys., Nebel, Verkehr, Wald, Bevölkerung:* dense; *Haar, Laub, Gedränge:* thick; *Stoff:* thick, close; ~ *an* (*dat.*) *od.* bei close by; ~ *hinter* (*dat.*) close behind; '⚲**e** *f* (15) *a. phys.* density; *s. Dichtheit.*
'**dichten 1.** (26) make tight; ⊕ seal; *Fuge:* flush; **2.** *v/t.* compose (*a. v/i.*); *v/i.* write poetry.
'**Dichter** *m* (7) poet; '**~in** *f* poetess; '**~lesung** *f* reading; *e-e* ~ *halten* give a reading; '**~ling** *m* (3) would-be poet, poetaster; '⚲**isch** poetic(al).
'**Dicht|heit** *f,* '**~igkeit** *f* (16) tightness; compactness; density; thickness; closeness.
'**Dichtkunst** *f* poetry.
'**dichtmachen** F *v/i.* shut up shop; *v/t.* shut (up).
'**Dichtung** *f* (16) **1.** ⊕ sealing; *konkret:* seal; packing; *aus Werg:*

gasket; **2.** poetry; (*Einzel♀*) poem; work of fiction; (*Er♀*) fiction; '**∼s-masse** ⊕ *f* sealing compound; '**∼s-ring** ⊕ *m*, '**∼sscheibe** ⊕ *f* washer.

dick [dik] thick; (*massig*) big; (*umfangreich*) voluminous; (*beleibt*) stout, corpulent; F *das ∼e Ende kommt noch* the worst is yet to come; F *sie sind ∼e Freunde* as thick as thieves; *∼e Milch* curdled milk; F *∼e Luft!* trouble's brewing!; *durch ∼ und dünn* through thick and thin; F (*sich*) *∼ tun* talk big; *mit et.* brag of; *∼ auftragen* lay it on thick.

dick|bäuchig ['∼bɔʏçiç] big-bellied; '**♀darm** *m* great gut, ⬚ colon; '**♀e** *f* (15, *o. pl.*) thickness; stoutness; '**♀erchen** F *n* (6) fatso; **∼fellig** ['∼fɛliç] thick-skinned; '**∼flüssig** viscous; **♀häuter** ['∼hɔʏtər] *m* (7) pachyderm; **♀icht** ['∼içt] *n* (3¹) thicket; '**♀kopf** *m* pig-headed fellow; **∼köpfig** ['∼kœpfiç] pig-headed; **∼leibig** ['∼laɪbiç] corpulent; *fig.* bulky; '**♀leibigkeit** *f* corpulency; bulkiness; '**♀milch** *f* sour milk; '**♀wanst** *m* paunch.

Didaktik [di'daktik] *f* (16) didactics *sg.*

die [di:] *s.* der.

Dieb [di:p] *m* (3) thief; **∼erei** [∼bə'raɪ] *f* (16) thieving, thievery.

Diebes|bande ['di:bəs-] *f* gang of thieves; '**∼höhle** *f* nest of thieves; '**♀sicher** theft-proof.

Dieb|in ['di:bin] *f* (16¹) (female) thief; **♀isch** ['di:biʃ] thievish; F *Freude usw.*: devilish; **∼stahl** ['di:pʃtɑ:l] *m* (3³) theft, ⱥ larceny; '**∼stahlsicherung** *f* theft prevention device; '**∼stahlversicherung** *f* insurance against theft.

Diele ['di:lə] *f* (15) (*Brett*) board; (*Fußboden*) floor; (*Vorraum*) hall; '**♀n** board; floor.

dienen ['di:nən] *v/i.* (25) serve (*j-m a p.*; *als* as; *zu* for; *dazu, zu inf. to inf.*); *zu nichts ∼* be of no use; ✝ *womit kann ich ∼?* what can I do for you?, *Am.* may I help you?

'**Diener** *m* (7) (man-)servant; (*Verbeugung*) bow; *stummer ∼* (*Nebentischchen*) dumb-waiter; '**∼in** *f* (16¹) maid-servant, maid; *fig.* handmaid; '**∼schaft** *f* domestics *pl.*

'**dienlich** useful, helpful, serviceable (*dat.* to).

Dienst [di:nst] *m* (3²) service (*a.* ✗ *u. Einrichtung*); (*Stelle*) post, employment; *im* (*außer*) *∼ on* (off) duty; *∼ am Kunden* prompt service to the customer; *j-m e-n ∼ erweisen* do a p. a good turn; *gute ∼e leisten* render good services; *j-m zu ∼en stehen* be at a p.'s service; *s.* stellen.

Dienstag ['di:nsta:k] *m* (3) Tuesday.

'**Dienst|-alter** *n* seniority; '**♀-ältest** *adj.*, '**∼-älteste** *m* senior; '**∼-antritt** *m* entering upon service; '**∼-anzug** ✗ *m* service uniform *od.* dress; '**♀bar** subservient (*dat.* to); *∼er Geist fig.* factotum; *s-n Zwekken ∼ machen* make *a p. od. th.* serve one's purpose; '**∼barkeit** *f* servitude, bondage; '**♀beflissen** *s.* *∼eifrig*; '**♀bereit** ready for service; (*gefällig*) obliging; '**∼bote** *m* domestic (servant); '**∼-eid** *m* oath of office; '**∼-eifer** *m* zeal; obligingness; '**♀-eifrig** zealous, assiduous; obliging; '**♀fähig** *s.* *∼tauglich*; '**♀fertig** *s.* *∼eifrig*; '**♀frei**: *∼ sein* be off duty; '**∼geheimnis** *n* official secret; '**∼gespräch** *n* official call; '**∼grad** *m* ✗ rank; *der Unteroffiziere u. Mannschaften*: *Am.* grade; ⚓ rating; '**♀habend** (on) duty; '**∼herr** *m* master, employer; '**∼jahre** *n/pl.* years of service; '**∼leistung** *f* service; '**∼leistungsbetrieb** *m* service company; '**♀lich** official; on business; '**∼mädchen** *n* maid-servant, help; '**∼mann** *m* porter, commissionaire; '**∼-ordnung** *f* official regulations *pl.*; '**∼pflicht** *f* official duty;✗ compulsory (military) service; '**∼plan** *m* roster; '**∼reise** *f* official journey; '**∼stelle** *f* office, agency; '**∼stunden** *f/pl.* duty (*od.* office) hours; '**♀tauglich** fit for (✗ active) service; **♀tuend** ['∼tu:ənt] acting; (*im Dienst*) on duty; '**♀-unfähig**, '**♀-untauglich** unfit for service; '**∼vergehen** *n* official misdemeano(u)r; '**∼verhältnis** *n* (contract of) employment; '**♀verpflichtet** conscripted for essential service; '**∼vertrag** *m* contract of employment; '**∼vorschrift** *f* regulations *pl.*; '**∼wagen** *m* official car; '**∼weg** *m* official channels *pl.*; '**♀willig** *s.* *∼bereit*; '**∼wohnung** *f* official residence; '**∼zeit** *f* (period of) service.

'**diesbezüglich** relevant (to this); referring to this.

Dieselmotor ['diːzəlmoːtɔr] *m* Diesel engine.

dies|er ['diːzər], '**~e**, '**~es** *od.* **dies** [diːs] (21) *adj.* this; *su.* this one; '**~e** *pl.* these; **~jährig** ['~jɛːriç] this year's, of this year; '**~mal** this time; **~seitig** ['~zaⁱtiç] on this (*od.* my, our) side; **~seits** ['~zaⁱts] on this side (*gen.* of).

diesig ['diːziç] hazy, misty.

Dietrich ['diːtriç] *m* (3) skeleton key; *des Einbrechers*: picklock.

diffamieren [difaˈmiːrən] defame.

Differential... [difərənˈtsjɑːl] differential.

Diffe'renz *f* (16) difference.

differenzieren [~ˈtsiːrən] differentiate.

diffe'rieren differ.

Digital|-anzeige [digiˈtɑːl-] *f* digital display; **~aufnahme** *f* digital recording; **~rechner** *m* digital computer; **~technik** *f* Computer: digital computing system; **~uhr** *f* digital clock (*od.* watch).

Diktat [dikˈtɑːt] *n* (3) dictation; (*Befehl*) dictate; *nach ~ schreiben* write from dictation; **~or** [~tɔr] *m* (8¹) dictator; **Qorisch** [~taˈtoːriʃ] dictatorial; **~ur** [~ˈtuːr] *f* (16) dictatorship.

dik'tier|en dictate; **Qgerät** *n* dictating machine.

Dilemma [diˈlema] *n* (11) dilemma.

Dilettant [dileˈtant] *m* (12), **~in** *f* amateur, dilettante; **Qisch** amateurish, dilettante.

Dill ♣ [dil] *m* (3) dill.

Dimension [dimenˈzjoːn] *f* (16) dimension.

Ding [diŋ] *n* (3) thing; *vor allen ~en* first of all; *das geht nicht mit rechten ~en zu* there's something wrong about it; '**Qen** *v/t.* (30) hire; '**Qfest**: *j-n ~ machen* arrest a p.; '**Qlich** 🕵 real.

dinieren [diˈniːrən] dine.

Diode ⚡ [diˈoːdə] *f* (15) diode.

Diözese [diøˈtseːzə] *f* (15) diocese.

Diphtherie [diftəˈriː] *f* (15, *o. pl.*) diphtheria.

Diphthong [difˈtɔŋ] *m* (3¹ *u.* 12) diphthong; **Qisch** diphthongal.

Diplom [diˈploːm] *n* (3¹) diploma; **~arbeit** *f* dissertation.

Diplomat [~ploˈmɑːt] *m* (12) diplomat; **~enkoffer** *m* executive case; **~ie** [~maˈtiː] *f* (16) diplomacy; **Qisch**

[~ˈmɑːtiʃ] diplomatic.

Di'plom-ingenieur *m* graduated engineer.

dir [diːr] (*to*) you; *refl.* (*to*) yourself.

direkt [diˈrɛkt] direct; **~er** *Wagen* 🚃 through carriage; **Q-antrieb** ⊕ *m* direct drive; **Qflug** *m* through flight, non-stop flight.

Direktion [dirɛkˈtsjoːn] *f* (16) direction; (*Verwaltung*) management; *s. Direktorium*; **~s-etage** *f* executive floor.

Direktive [dirɛkˈtiːvə] *f* (16) directive, (general) instruction.

Di'rektmandat *pol. n* direct mandate.

Direktor [diˈrɛktɔr] *m* (8¹) manager, director; (*Schul2*) headmaster, *Am.* principal; **~at** [~ˈrɑːt] *n* (3) directorship; **~ium** [~ˈtoːrium] *n* (9) board of directors.

Direktrice [~ˈtriːsə] *f* (15) manageress, directress.

Di'rekt-übertragung *f* live broadcast.

Dirig|ent ♪ [diriˈgɛnt] *m* (12) conductor, leader; **Qieren** [~ˈgiːrən] direct, manage; ♪ conduct; **~ismus** [~ˈgismus] ♥ *m* (14, *o. pl.*) planned economy. [whore)

Dirne ['dirnə] *f* (15) prostitute, ∫

Dis ♪ [dis] *n* D sharp.

Dishar|monie [disharmoˈniː] *f* (15) discord; **Qmonisch** [~ˈmoːniʃ] discordant.

Diskant ♪ [disˈkant] *m* (3) treble, soprano.

Diskette [disˈkɛtə] *f* (15) *Computer*: diskette, disk.

Diskjockey ['diskdʒɔke] *m* (11) disc jockey.

Diskont ♥ [~ˈkɔnt] *m* (3), **~o** *m* (11), **Qieren** [~ˈtiːrən] discount; **~satz** *m* discount rate; bank-rate.

Diskothek [diskoˈteːk] *f* (15) discotheque.

diskret [disˈkreːt] discreet; **Qion** [~kreˈtsjoːn] *f* (16) discretion.

Diskriminierung [~krimiˈniːruŋ] *f* discrimination.

Diskussion [~kuˈsjoːn] *f* (16) discussion; **~sleiter** *m* chairman; **~sveranstaltung** *f* discussion meeting, *Am.* forum.

Diskuswerfen ['diskusvɛrfən] *n* (6) discus-throwing.

diskutieren [diskuˈtiːrən] discuss, debate.

Dispens [dis'pɛns] m (4) dispensation; **2ieren** [~'ziːrən] dispense (*von* from), exempt (from).

disponieren [~po'niːrən] dispose (*über acc.* of); plan ahead.

Disposition [~zi'tsjoːn] f (16) disposition; (*Anordnung*) a. arrangement; s-e ~en treffen make one's arrangements; **~skredit** m overdraft facilities pl.

disputieren [dispu'tiːrən] debate.

disqualifizieren [~kvalifi'tsiːrən] disqualify.

Dissertation [disɛrta'tsjoːn] f (16) dissertation; (*Doktor2*) a. thesis.

Distanz [di'stants] f (16) distance (a. *fig.*); **2ieren** [~'tsiːrən]: sich ~ keep one's distance; *weitS.* dissociate o.s. (*von* from).

Distel ['distəl] f (15) thistle; '**~fink** m goldfinch.

Distrikt [di'strikt] m (3) district.

Disziplin [distsi'pliːn] f (16) discipline; (*Sparte*) branch; *Sport:* event; **2arisch** [~pli'naːriʃ] disciplinary; **~arstrafe** [~'naːr-] f disciplinary punishment; **~arverfahren** n disciplinary action; **2iert** [~'niːrt] disciplined; **2los** undisciplined, unruly.

dito ['diːto] ditto.

divers [di'vɛrs] sundry.

Dividend ∦ [divi'dɛnt] m (12) dividend; **~e** [~də] f (15) dividend.

divi'dieren divide.

Division [~'zjoːn] f (16) division.

Divisor [di'viːzɔr] m (8[1]) divisor.

Diwan ['diːvaːn] m (3[1]) divan.

doch [dɔx] (*dennoch*) yet; however; nevertheless; (*je~*) but; auffordernd: do (z. B. setz dich ~! do sit down); nach verneinter Frage: siehst du's nicht? ~! yes, I do!; willst du nicht kommen? ~! O, yes, I will!; du kommst ~? surely you will come?; ja ~ yes, indeed; nicht ~! don't!, (gewiß nicht) certainly not!

Docht [dɔxt] m (3) wick.

Dock [dɔk] n (3[1] u. 11) dock; '**~arbeiter** m docker, Am. dock laborer.

'**docken** ⚓ (25) dock.

Dogge ['dɔgə] f (15): deutsche ~ Great Dane; englische ~ mastiff.

Dogma ['dɔgma] n (9[1]) dogma.

Dogma|tiker [~'maːtikər] m (7) dogmatist; **2tisch** dogmatic.

Dohle zo. ['doːlə] f (15) (jack)daw.

Doktor ['dɔktɔr] m (8[1]) doctor (abbr.

Dr.); den ~ machen take one's (doctor's) degree; **~and** [~o'rant] m (12) doctoral (od. PhD, DSc etc.) candidate; '**~arbeit** f doctoral thesis; '**~frage** f fig. vexed question; '**~grad** m doctorate; '**~prüfung** f viva; '**~vater** m supervisor; '**~würde** f doctorate.

Doktrin [dɔk'triːn] f (16) doctrine.

Dokument [doku'mɛnt] n (3) document, ⚘ a. deed, instrument; **~ar-film** [~'taːr-] m documentary (film); **2arisch** [~'taːriʃ] documentary; **2en-echt** waterproof; **2ieren** [~'tiːrən] document; fig. reveal.

Dolch [dɔlç] m (3) dagger; '**~messer** n case-knife, Am. bowie-knife; '**~stich** m, '**~stoß** m stab with a dagger.

Dolde ['dɔldə] f (15) umbel.

Dollar ['dɔlar] m (11, pl. nach Zahlen inv.) dollar.

Dolle ⚓ ['dɔlə] f (15) rowlock.

dolmetsch|en ['dɔlmɛtʃən] v/i. u. v/t. (27) interpret; '**2(er)** m (4 u. [7]), '**2erin** f (16[1]) interpreter; fig. mouthpiece.

Dom [doːm] m (3) cathedral.

Domäne [do'mɛːnə] f (15) domain.

dominieren [domi'niːrən] v/i. dominate.

Domino ['doːmino] (11): **a)** m (*Kleidung*) domino; **b)** n (*Spiel*) (game of) dominoes sg.

Domizil [domi'tsiːl] n (3[1]) domicile.

'**Dompfaff** m bullfinch.

Donner ['dɔnər] m (7) thunder; wie vom ~ gerührt thunder-struck; '**2n** (26) thunder (a. fig.); '**~schlag** m clap (od. peal) of thunder; fig. thunderclap; '**~s-tag** m Thursday; '**~stimme** f thundering voice; '**~wetter** n thunderstorm; (zum) ~! hang it (all)!, staunend: wow!

doof F [doːf] silly; '**2mann** F m thick-head.

dop|en ['dɔpən, 'doːpən] (25) Sport: dope; '**2ing** n (11) doping.

Doppel ['dɔpəl] n (6) double, duplicate; s. ~spiel 1; '**~adler** m double eagle; '**~agent** m double agent; '**~belichtung** phot. f double exposure; '**~bett** n double bed; '**~decker** m (7) biplane; F (Bus) double-decker; '**~ehe** f bigamy; '**~fehler** m Tennis: double fault; '**~fenster** n double window; **~gänger** [~'gɛŋər] m (7) double; '**~haushälfte** f semi-detached (house); '**~kinn** n double chin; '~laut *m* diphthong; '~moral *f* double standards *pl.*; '~mord *m* double murder; '~punkt *m* colon; ♀reihig ['~raıç] *Jackett*: double--breasted; ♀seitig ['~zaıtıç] *Stoff*: double-faced, reversible; '~sinn *m* double meaning, ambiguity; '♀sinnig ambiguous, equivocal; '~sohle *f* clump sole; '~spiel *n* 1. *Tennis*: double; 2. *fig.* double game; '~stecker ⚡ *m* two-way adapter; '♀t double; ~ *adv.* doubly; ~ *so groß* twice as big; '~tür *f* double-door; (*Flügeltür*) folding doors *pl.*; '~verdiener *m/pl.* dual-income family *sg.*; '~verglasung *f* double glazing; '~währung *f* double standard; '~zentner *m* quintal; '~zimmer *n* double (-bedded) room; ♀züngig ['~tsyŋıç], '~züngigkeit *f* double-dealing.

Dorf [dɔrf] *n* (1²) village; '~bewohner(in *f*) *m* villager; '~trottel *m* village idiot.

Dorn [dɔrn] *m* (5) thorn; (*Stachel*) prickle; ♀ *a.* spine; ⊕ mandrel; *e-r Schnalle*: tongue; *j-m ein ~ im Auge sein* be a thorn in a p.'s side; '~enhecke *f* thorn-hedge; '~enkrone *f* crown of thorns; '♀envoll, '♀ig thorny (*a. fig.*); '~rös-chen [~'røːsçən] *n* Sleeping Beauty; '~strauch *m* brier, bramble.

dörr|en ['dœrən] (25) dry; '♀fleisch *n* dried meat; '♀gemüse *n* dried vegetables *pl.*; '♀-obst *n* dried fruit.

Dorsch [dɔrʃ] *m* (3²) cod.

dort [dɔrt] there; (*drüben*) over there; '~her from there; '~hin there, that way; '~ig of that place, there.

Dose ['doːzə] *f* (15) box; (*Konserven*♀) tin, *Am.* can; '~n-öffner *m* (7) tin-opener, *Am.* can opener.

dösen F['døːzən] (27) doze.

dosieren [do'ziːrən] dose.

Dosis ['doːzıs] *f* (16²) dose; *zu starke ~* overdose.

dotier|en [do'tiːrən] endow; ♀ung *f* endowment.

Dotter ['dɔtər] *m* (7) yolk; '~blume *f* marsh-marigold.

Double ['duːbl] *n* (11) *Film*: double.

Doz|ent [do'tsɛnt] *m* (12) university teacher, lecturer, reader, *Am.* assistant professor, instructor; ♀ieren [~'tsiːrən] lecture.

Drache ['draxə] *m* (13) dragon; '~n *m* (6) (*Papier*♀) kite; *Sport*: hang--glider; *fig.* (*böses Weib*) termagant, shrew; *e-n ~ steigen lassen* fly a kite; '~fliegen *n Sport*: hang-gliding; '~nflieger(in *f*) *m Sport*: hang--glider.

Dragée [dra'ʒeː] *n* (11) coated tablet.

Draht [draːt] *m* (3³) wire; F *auf ~ sein* be in good form, (*wachsam*) be on the ball; *pol. heißer ~* hot line; '~-anschrift *f* cable address; '~-antwort *f* reply by telegram; '~bürste *f* wire brush; '♀en (27) wire; '~-esel *m* F bike; '~gaze *f* wire gauze; '~geflecht *n* wire netting; '~gitter *n* wire grating; '~haarterrier *m* wire-haired terrier; '♀ig wiry; '♀los wireless, radio-...; '~nachricht *f* wire; '~puppe *f* puppet; '~saite *f* wire string; '~schere *f* (*eine a pair of*) wire-shears *pl.*; '~seil *n* wire rope; '~seilbahn *f* funicular (railway); '~stift *m* wire--tack; '~zange *f* (*eine a pair of*) wire--pliers *pl.*; '~zieher ['~tsiːər] *m* (7) wire-drawer; *fig.* wire-puller.

drakonisch [dra'koːnıʃ] Draconian.

Drall[1] ⊕ [dral] *m* (3) twist; *im Gewehr*: a. rifling; *Ball*: spin.

drall[2] buxom, strapping.

Drama ['draːma] *n* (9¹) drama; ~tik [dra'maːtik] *f* (16, *o. pl.*) dramatic art; *weit S. u. fig.* drama; ~tiker *m* (7) dramatist; ♀tisch [~'maːtiʃ] dramatic; ♀tisieren [~mati'ziːrən] dramatize (*a. fig.*).

Dramaturg [drama'turk] *m* (12 *u.* 5²) dramatic adviser; ~ie [~'giː] *f* dramaturgy.

dran F [dran] *s. daran*.

Dränage [drɛ'naːʒə] *f* (15) drainage.

Drang[1] [draŋ] *m* (3) *fig. der Geschäfte*: pressure, rush; (*Antrieb*) impulse, impetus; (*Trieb*) urge; (*Bedrängnis*) distress; (*Eile*) hurry.

drang[2] *pret. v. dringen*.

dräng|eln F ['drɛŋəln] (29) push, jostle; '~en (25) press, push, shove; *sich ~* crowd, throng; *fig.* urge (*auf acc.* a th.); *auf Eile*: urge, hurry; *es drängt mich, zu inf.* I feel moved to *inf.*; *die Zeit drängt* time presses; *s. gedrängt*.

Drangsal ['draŋzaːl] *f* (14) affliction, distress; ~e *pl.* hardships *pl.*; ♀ieren [~za'liːrən] persecute.

dränieren [drɛ'niːrən] drain.

'**dran|kommen** F (sn) (*erreichen*) be able to reach; (*an e-e S. a th.*); (*an die*

Reihe kommen) have one's turn; *in der Schule*: be called on; '**~nehmen** see; *in der Schule*: ask.

drapieren [dra'pi:rən] drape.

drastisch ['drasti∫] drastic(ally *adv.*).

drauf F [drauf] *s. darauf*; *~ und dran sein, zu inf.* be on the point of *ger.*; ♀**gänger** ['~gɛŋər] *m* (7) daredevil; (*Erfolgsmensch*) go-ahead fellow, *Am.* go-getter; '♀**gängertum** *n* pluck; go-aheadedness; '**~gehen** (sn) go, be lost; (*kaputtgehen*) go to pot; (*sterben*) be killed; **~'los** straight ahead; (*wild*) recklessly, blindly.

draußen ['drausən] outside; out of doors; (*in der Fremde*) abroad.

drechseln ['drɛksəln] (29) turn; *gedrechselt fig.* well-turned.

'**Drechsler** *m* (7) turner; '**~-arbeit** *f* turnery; **~ei** [~'rai] *f* (16) turnery; turner's shop.

Dreck F [drɛk] *m* (3) dirt; (*Schlamm*) mud; (*Unflat*) filth; *fig. contp.* rubbish; '♀**ig** dirty; muddy; filthy; '**~s-kerl** F *m* bastard; '**~spatz** F *m* mucky pup.

Dreh|-arbeit ['dre:-] *f Film*: (*a. pl.*) shooting; '**~bank** *f* (turning-)lathe; '♀**bar** revolving; '**~bleistift** *m* propelling pencil; '**~brücke** *f* swing-bridge; '**~buch** *n Film*: scenario, *bsd. Am. a.* script; '**~bühne** *thea. f* revolving stage; '♀**en** (25) (*a. sich* ~) turn (*a.* ⊕); *Film*: shoot; *Szene*: take; *Zigarette*: roll; *sich* ~ *um e-n Mittelpunkt, e-e Achse* revolve (*um round a centre, on an axis*); *fig. Thema*: be about; *es dreht sich darum, daß* the point is whether; *die Frage dreht sich um* the question turns (*od.* hinges) on; *mir dreht sich der Kopf* my head swims; '**~er** ⊕ *m* (7) turner; '**~griff** *m* turning handle; '**~knopf** ⊕ *m* (control) knob; '**~kran** *m* swing crane; '**~kreuz** *n* turnstile; '**~-orgel** *f* barrel-organ; '**~punkt** *m* cent|re (*Am.* -er) of rotation, fulcrum; (*a. fig.*) pivot; '**~schalter** ⚡ *m* turn (*od.* rotary) switch; '**~scheibe** *f* 🚂 turntable; (*Töpfer*♀) potter's wheel; '**~strom** ⚡ *m* three-phase current; '**~stuhl** *m* revolving chair; '**~tür** *f* revolving door; '**~ung** *f* turn(ing); *um e-e Achse*: rotation; *um e-n Körper*: revolution; '**~zahl** ⊕ *f* number of revolutions; ~ *per Minute*

revolutions *pl.* per minute (*abbr.* r.p.m.); '**~zahlregler** ⊕ *m* speed governor; '**~zapfen** *m* pivot.

drei [drai] **1.** three; ~ *Viertel zehn* a quarter to (*Am.* of); *sie waren zu* ~*en* there were three of them; *er sieht aus, als ob er nicht bis* ~ *zählen kann* he looks as if butter would not melt in his mouth; **2.** ♀ *f* (16) (number) three; (*Schulzensur*) fair; '♀**-akter** *thea. m* three-act play; **~ar-mig** ['~ʔarmiç] three-armed; **~bei-nig** ['~bainiç] three-legged; '♀**blatt** *n* (*Klee*) trefoil; **~blätterig** ['~blɛtəriç] three-leaved; **~dimensional** ['~dimɛnzjo'na:l] three-dimensional; '♀**-eck** *n* (3) triangle; '**~-eckig** three--cornered; ⚔ triangular; ♀'**-einig-keit** *f* Trinity.

dreierlei ['draiər'lai] of three kinds.

drei|fach ['~fax], **~fältig** ['~fɛltiç] threefold, treble; ♀**faltigkeit** [~'fal-tiçkait] *f* Trinity; ♀'**farben...** three-colo(u)r; '**~farbig** tricol-o(u)red; '♀**fuß** *m* tripod; '♀**ge-spann** *fig. n* trio; '**~'hundert** three hundred; ♀**käsehoch** F [~'kɛ:zə-ho:x] *m* (3) hop-o'-my-thumb, whipper-snapper; '♀**klang** ♪ *m* triad; ♀'**königsfest** *n* Epiphany; '**~mal** three times; **~malig** ['~ma:-liç] thrice repeated; '♀'**meilenzone** ♻, ⚓ *f* three-mile limit; **~monatig** ['~mo:natiç] three-months, lasting three months; '**~monatlich** three--monthly; *adv.* every three months; **~motorig** ['~moto:riç] three-en-gine(d).

drein [drain] *s. darein*; '**~schlagen** lay about one.

'**Drei|rad** *n* tricycle; '**~satz** ⚔ *m* rule of three; ♀**seitig** ['~zaitiç] three-sided, 🔲 trilateral; ♀**silbig** ['~zilbiç] trisyllabic; ♀**sprachig** ['~∫pra:xiç] in three languages, 🔲 trilingual; '**~sprung** *m* triple jump.

dreißig ['draisiç] thirty; ♀**er** ['~gər] *m* (7) man of thirty; **~jährig** ['~jɛ:riç] thirty-year-old; *of* thirty years; *der* ♀*e Krieg* the Thirty Years' War; '**~ste** thirtieth.

dreist [draist] bold; (*frech*) impu-dent.

dreistellig ['~∫tɛliç] of three places; ~*e Zahl a.* three-figure number.

'**Dreistigkeit** *f* boldness; (*Frechheit*) impudence.

drei|stimmig ['~∫timiç] for (*od.* in)

three voices; '⚲**stufenrakete** *f* three-stage rocket; **⚲tägig** ['⚲tɛːgiç] three days', three-day; **⚲teilig** ['⚲taɪliç] (consisting) of three parts, ◫ tripartite; *Anzug*: three-piece; ⚲'**vierteltakt** ♪ *m* three-four time; '⚲**zack** *m* (3) trident; '⚲**zehn(te)** thirteen(th).

Dresch|e F ['drɛʃə] *f* (15, *o. pl.*) thrashing; '⚲**en** (30) thresh; (*prügeln*) thrash; '⚲**er** *m* (7) thresher; '⚲**flegel** *m* flail; '⚲**maschine** *f* threshing-machine.

Dress|eur [drɛ'søːr] *m* (3¹) trainer; (*Bändiger*) tamer; ⚲**ieren** [drɛ'siːrən] train; *Pferd*: break in; ⚲**man** ['drɛsmən] *m* male model; ⚲**ur** [⚲'suːr] *f* (16) training; breaking in.

Drill [dril] ✖ *m* (3, *o. pl.*) drill; '⚲**bohrer** *m* drill; '⚲**en** ✖, ✔ (25) drill; ⚲**ich** ['⚲liç] *m* drill; denim, canvas; '⚲**ich-anzug** ✖ *m* fatigues *pl.*; '⚲**ing** ['⚲iŋ] *m* (3¹) (*Kind*) triplet; ✖ *hunt.* three-barrel(l)ed gun; '⚲**lings...** ⊕ triple...

drin F [drin] *s. darin.*

dringen ['driŋən] (30): **a)** (sn) *durch et.*: force one's way through, get through; penetrate through; pierce; *aus et.*: break forth from; *in et.* (*acc.*): penetrate into; *in die Öffentlichkeit* ⚲ leak out; *zum Herzen*: go to; **b)** (h.) ⚲ *auf* (*acc.*) urge, insist on; ⚲ *in j-n* urge (*od.* press) a p.; '⚲**d** urgent(ly *adv.*); *Gefahr*: imminent; *Verdacht*: strong; ⚲ *verdächtig* highly suspect; ⚲ *notwendig* imperative; ⚲ *brauchen* want badly; ⚲ *bitten* entreat.

'**dringlich** urgent; '⚲**keit** *f* urgency; (*Vor*⚲) priority; '⚲**keits-antrag** *parl. m* motion of urgency; '⚲**keitsstufe** *f* priority; ⚲ *1* top priority.

drinnen ['drinən] inside, within.

dritte ['dritə], '⚲**l** *n* (7) third; '⚲**ns** thirdly.

'**dritt|letzt** last but two; '⚲**rangig** third-rate.

droben ['droːbən] above (there); up there; (*im Himmel*) on high.

Droge ['droːgə] *f* (15) drug; '⚲**n-abhängig** addicted to drugs; '⚲**n-abhängige** *m, f* drug addict; '⚲**n-handel** *m* drug traffic(king); '⚲**n-händler(in** *f*) *m sl.* pusher; '⚲**n-mißbrauch** *m* drug abuse; '⚲**n-szene** *f* drug scene; ⚲**rie** [drogə'riː] *f* (15) chemist's (shop), *Am.* drug-store.

Drogist [⚲'gist] *m* (12) chemist, *Am.* druggist.

'**Drohbrief** *m* threatening letter.

drohen ['droːən] (25) threaten (*a. fig.*), menace (*j-m* a p.); '⚲**d** threatening, menacing; (*bevorstehend*) imminent.

Drohne ['droːnə] *f* (15) (*a. fig.*) drone.

dröhnen ['drøːnən] (25) boom, roar; *Raum*: resound (*von* with).

Drohung ['droːuŋ] *f* threat, menace.

drollig ['droliç] droll, funny.

Dromedar [dromeˈdaːr] *n* (3¹) dromedary.

Drops [drops] (*m/pl. inv.*) (*saure* acid) drops.

drosch [droʃ] *pret. v.* dreschen.

Droschke ['droʃkə] *f* (15) cab; (*Auto*) *a.* taxi(-cab).

Drossel *zo.* ['drosəl] *f* (15) thrush.

'**Drossel|klappe** ⊕ *f*, '⚲**ventil** ⊕ *n* throttle (-valve); '⚲**n** ⊕ (29) throttle (*a. fig.*); *Heizung*: turn down; '⚲**spule** ⚡ *f* choke coil.

drüben ['dryːbən] over there; on the other side.

Druck [druk] *m* **a)** (3³) pressure; *der Hand*: squeeze; (*Last*) weight, burden; ⚲ *ausüben auf* (*acc.*) exert pressure on; *j-n unter* ⚲ *setzen* put pressure on a p.; **b)** *typ.* (3) impression, print; (⚲*en*) printing; *großer* (*kleiner*) ⚲ large (small) print *od.* type; *im* ⚲ *sein* be printing; *in* ⚲ *geben* (*gehen*) send (go) to the press; '⚲**bogen** *m* printed sheet; '⚲**buchstabe** *m* block letter; *in* ⚲*n schreiben* print.

Drückeberger F ['drykəbɛrgər] *m* (7) shirker; ⚲**ei** F [⚲'raɪ] *f* (16) shirking; *im Betrieb*: absenteeism.

'**druck-empfindlich** sensitive to pressure, 🌶 *a.* tender.

drucken ['drukən] (25) print.

drücken ['drykən] (25) press; *Hand*: *a.* squeeze; *fig.* (*nieder*⚲) oppress; pinch (*Schuh*); *Markt, Preise*: bring (*od.* force) down; *Rekord*: lower, better; *j-n an sich* ⚲ give a p. a hug; *auf den Knopf* ⚲ press the button; F *sich* ⚲ sneak away; *sich in e-e Ecke usw.* ⚲ dodge into; *sich von e-r Pflicht* ⚲ shirk, dodge *a* duty; *sich um e-e Antwort, Verpflichtung usw.* ⚲ evade, dodge; '⚲**d** heavy, oppressive.

'**Drucker** *m* (7) *a. Computer*: printer.
'**Drücker** *m* (7) push-button; *am Gewehr*: trigger; (*Tür♀*) door--handle.
Drucke'rei *f* (16) printing-office, *bsd. Am.* printing shop.
'**Druck-erlaubnis** *f* printing licence (*Am.* license); imprimatur.
'**Drucker|presse** *f* printing-press; '**~schwärze** *f* printer's ink.
'**Druck|fahne** *f* (galley-)proof; '**~farbe** *f* printing-ink; '**~fehler** *m* misprint, erratum; '**~fehlerteufel** *m* demon of misprints; '**~fehlerverzeichnis** *n* errata *pl.*; '**♀fertig** ready for the press; '**♀frisch** fresh from the press; '**~kammer** *f* pressure chamber; '**~knopf** *m am Kleid*: press-stud, snap-fastener; **⚡** push--button; '**~legung** *f* printing; '**~luft** *f* compressed air; *attr.* compressed--air *cylinder*; pneumatic, air *brake, etc.*; '**~maschine** *f typ.* printing machine; '**~messer** *m* pressure--ga(u)ge; '**~mittel** *n fig.* lever; '**~probe** *f typ.* proof; '**~pumpe** *f* force-pump; '**♀reif** ready for the press; '**~sache(n** *pl.*) **⚡** *f* printed matter, *Am. a.* second-class matter; '**~schalter** **⚡** *m* push- (*od.* press-)button switch; '**~schrift** *f* print, type; (*Abhandlung*) publication; '**~taste** *f* push-button; '**~welle** *f* *e-r Explosion*: shock wave.
drum [drum] *s. darum*; *das ♀ und Dran* the paraphernalia *pl.*
drunten ['druntən] below (there).
'**drunter und 'drüber** upside down, topsy-turvy, F higgledy-piggledy.
Drüse ['dry:zə] *f* (15) gland; **~n...** glandular.
Dschungel ['dʒuŋəl] *m, n* (7) jungle.
du [du:] you; *eccl., poet.* thou; *auf ~ und ~ stehen* be on intimate terms.
Dübel ⊕ ['dy:bəl] *m* (7) dowel, peg.
Dublee(gold) [du'ble:-] *n* (11) rolled gold.
Dublette [du'blɛtə] *f* (15) duplicate; *hunt.* right-and-left (shot).
ducken ['dukən] (25) *den Kopf*: duck; *j-n*: *fig.* take *a p.* down a peg or two; *sich ~* crouch, *ausweichend*: duck, *fig.* knuckle under.
Duckmäuser ['~mɔyzər] *m* (7) sneak; (*Scheinheiliger*) hypocrite; '**♀ig** sneaking; hypocritical.
dudeln ['du:dəln] (29) tootle.

'**Dudelsack** *m* bagpipe.
Duell [du'⁹ɛl] *n* (3¹) duel (*auf Degen usw.* with); **~ant** [~'lant] *m* (12) duellist; **♀ieren** [~'li:rən]: *sich ~* (fight a) duel.
Duett [du'⁹ɛt] *n* (3) duet.
Duft [duft] *m* (3³) scent; fragrance; perfume; '**♀en** (26) be fragrant, smell (*süß* sweet); '**♀end** fragrant; '**♀ig** (*leicht, zart*) flimsy, filmy, dainty; '**~stoff** *m* odorous substance.
duld|en ['duldən] (26) (*ertragen*) bear, endure; (*leiden*) suffer (*a. v/i.*); (*zulassen*) tolerate; '**♀er(in** *f*) *m* sufferer; **~sam** ['dultza:m] tolerant (*gegen* of); '**♀samkeit** *f* tolerance, toleration; **♀ung** ['~duŋ] *f* toleration.
dumm [dum] stupid, dull, *Am.* F dumb; (*einfältig*) silly, foolish; (*unangenehm*; *ungeschickt*) awkward; (*schwindlig*) dizzy (*von, vor dat.* with); **~er** *Junge* young shaver; **~er** *Streich* foolish prank; **~es** *Zeug* nonsense; *der ♀e sein* be the loser; *die ♀en werden nicht alle* fools never die out; '**~dreist** impertinent; '**♀heit** *f* stupidity; (*a. dumme Handlung usw.*) folly; (*Fehler*) blunder; (*Unbesonnenheit*) indiscretion; **~en** *machen* (play the) clown; *fig.* get into trouble; '**♀kopf** *m* fool, stupid, *Am. a.* sap(head).
dümmlich ['dymliç] silly, dumb.
dumpf [dumpf] *Schall*: hollow; *Geräusch, Gefühl, Schmerz*: dull; *Donner*: rumbling; (*düster*) gloomy; (*feucht*) damp; *Luft*: heavy, *im Zimmer*: close; '**~ig** (*feucht*) damp; (*modrig*) mo(u)ldy, musty; (*muffig*) fusty; (*stickig*) stuffy, close.
Düne ['dy:nə] *f* (15) sandhill, dune.
Dung [duŋ] *m* (3), **Dünger** ['dyŋər] *m* (7) dung, manure; (*Misch♀*) compost; *bsd. künstlicher*: fertilizer.
Dünge|mittel ['dyŋə-] *n* fertilizer; '**♀n** (25) dung, manure, fertilize.
'**Dunggrube** *f* manure pit.
dunkel ['duŋkəl] **1.** *allg.* dark; (*trüb*) dim; (*finster*) gloomy; (*unklar*) obscure; *Erinnerung*: vague; **2.** ♀ *n* (7) *the* dark; *fig. j-n im ♀n lassen* leave a p. in the dark (*über acc.* about).
Dünkel ['dyŋkəl] *m* (7) conceit.
'**dunkelblau** dark-blue.
'**dünkelhaft** conceited, arrogant.

'**Dunkel|heit** *f* darkness; *fig.* obscurity; *bei anbrechender* ~ at nightfall; '**~kammer** *phot. f* darkroom.
'**dunkeln** (29) grow dark, darken.
'**Dunkelziffer** *f* number of undetected cases.
dünken ['dyŋkən] (30) seem; *es dünkt mich (a. mir)* it seems to me; *sich ... ~* imagine (*od.* fancy) o.s. ...
dünn [dyn] *allg.* thin; (*schmächtig*) slim; *Flüssigkeit:* a. weak; (*spärlich*) sparse; *Luft, phys.* rare; '**2darm** *m* small gut; '**2e** *f* (15, *o. pl.*) *s.* Dünnheit; '**~flüssig** thin, fluid; '**2heit** *f* thinness; *der Luft, phys.* rarity.
Dunst [dunst] *m* (3² *u.* ³) vapo(u)r; (*Ausdünstung*) exhalation; *in der Luft:* haze; *über e-r Stadt:* F smog; *des Alkohols usw.:* fume; *sl. blauer* ~ hot air; *j-m blauen* ~ *vormachen* humbug a p.
dünsten ['dynstən] (26) *Speise:* steam.
'**dunstig** vaporous; (*feucht*) damp; (*nebelig*) hazy.
'**Dunstkreis** *m* atmosphere.
Dünung ⚓ ['dy:nuŋ] *f* swell.
düpieren [dy'pi:rən] dupe.
Duplikat [dupli'ka:t] *n* (3) duplicate.
Duplizität [duplitsi'tɛ:t] *f* (16) duplicity.
Dur ♪ [du:r] *n inv.* major.
durch [durç] **1.** *prp.* through; (*quer* ~) across; *Mittel, Ursache:* through, by; *Zeitdauer:* through(out); **2.** *adv.:* *das ganze Jahr* ~ throughout the year; *die ganze Nacht* ~ all night long; *es ist drei (Uhr)* ~ it is past three; ~ *und* ~ through and through, *fig. a.* to the backbone; *ein Schurke* ~ *und* ~ a thorough scoundrel.
'**durch-ackern** *fig.* plough (*Am.* plow) through.
'**durch-arbeiten** work through; *sich* ~ make one's way through.
'**durch'-aus** throughout, thoroughly; (*ganz und gar*) out and out; (*geradezu*) downright; (*unbedingt*) absolutely, quite; by all means; ~ *nicht* not at all, by no means.
'**durchbeißen** bite through; *sich* ~ struggle through.
'**durchbilden** educate (*od.* train) thoroughly.
'**durchblättern** leaf (*od.* glance, skim) through.
'**Durchblick** *m* vista; '**2en** *v/i.* look

through; *fig.* appear, show; ~ *lassen* give to understand.
durch'bluten supply with blood.
durch'bohren *v/t.* pierce; (*durchlöchern*) perforate; *j-n mit (den) Blicken* ~ look daggers at a p.; *v/i.* '**durchbohren** bore through.
'**durchbraten** roast thoroughly; *durchgebraten* well done; *nicht durchgebraten* underdone, rare.
'**durchbrechen** *v/i.* (sn) break through; *v/t.* durch'brechen break through; pierce; penetrate.
'**durchbrennen** (sn) burn through; ⚡ *Sicherung:* fuse, blow; *Radioröhre:* burn out; F *fig.* run away, bolt (*mit et.* with); *Frau:* elope.
'**durchbringen** bring through; *Gesetz:* pass; *Geld:* dissipate; *sich* ~ make both ends meet; *sich ehrlich* ~ get an honest living; *sich kümmerlich* ~ make a poor living; *e-n Kranken:* pull a p. through.
'**Durchbruch** *m* breach; *e-s Dammes, a.* ✠ rupture; *der Zähne:* cutting; ✗ break-through (*a. fig. Erfolg*); *e-r Mauer:* break.
durchdacht [~'daxt]: *gut* ~ *Rede usw.:* well-reasoned; *Plan:* well-devised.
durch'denken think over (*od.* out).
'**durchdrängen** force through; *sich* ~ force one's way through.
'**durchdrehen** *v/t. Fleisch:* pass through the mincer; ✗ swing; *v/i.* F P.: crack up; *mot. Räder:* spin.
'**durchdringen** **1.** *v/i.* (sn) get through; penetrate; *Flüssigkeit:* percolate, permeate; *Meinung:* prevail; **2.** durch'dringen *v/t.* penetrate; pierce; *durch'drungen von e-m Gefühl usw.* imbued with; **~d** ['~driŋənt] penetrating; piercing.
Durch'dringung *f* penetration.
'**durchdrücken** press through; F *fig. s.* durchsetzen.
durch'eilen hasten (*od.* hurry) through.
durch-ei'nander **1.** in confusion; in a jumble; pell-mell; (*wahllos*) promiscuously; *ganz* ~ *sein* P.: be all mixed up, be all upset; **2.** ♀ *n* muddle, jumble; confusion; medley *of voices;* **~bringen** muddle up; *j-n:* upset, bewilder; *Begriffe:* mix up; **~geraten** get mixed up; **~werfen** jumble up; *fig.* mix up.
'**durchfahr|en 1.** *v/i.* (sn) pass (*od.*

drive *od.* sail) through; **2.** *durch-*
'*fahren* v/t. = ~ 1.; *fig.* rush
through; '*2t* f passage; (*Tor*) gate
(-way); ~ *verboten!* no thoroughfare!

'**Durchfall** m ✻ diarrh(o)ea; (*Miß-*
erfolg) failure, *Am.* F flunk, *thea.*
usw. sl. flop; '*2en* (sn) fall through;
im Examen usw.: fail, be rejected,
Am. F flunk; *thea.* (turn out a)
flop; ~ *lassen* reject, *Am.* F flunk;
thea. damn.

'**durchfechten** fight *a th.* through,
see *a th.* through.

'**durchfeilen** file through.

'**durchfinden:** *sich* ~ find one's way
through.

durch'flechten interweave.

durch'fliegen fly through; *fig. Buch*
usw.: run through.

durch'fließen, durch'fluten flow
(*od.* run) through (*a. fig.*).

durch'forsch|en search through,
investigate; *Land*: explore; *2ung* f
investigation; exploration.

'**durchfragen:** *sich* ~ ask one's way
through.

'**durchfressen** eat through; *geol.*,
ätzend: corrode.

'**durchfrieren** (sn) freeze (*od.* chill)
through.

durchführ|bar ['~fyːrbɑːr] practi-
cable, feasible; '*~en* lead (*od.* convey) through; *Draht usw.*: pass
through; *fig.* carry through *od.* out;
Gesetz usw.: implement, (*a.* 🕸)
enforce; '*2ung* f carrying-out; realization; enforcement; '*2ungsbe-*
stimmungen f/pl. implementing
regulations.

'**Durchgabe** f transmission; (*Be-*
kanntgabe) special announcement,
(radio) flash.

'**Durchgang** m passage; *v. Waren*
od. ast.: transit; *Sport*: heat; ~ *ver-*
boten! no thoroughfare!, no tres-
passing!

durchgängig ['~gɛŋiç] general(ly
adv.).

'**Durchgangs|handel** m transit
trade; '*~lager* n transit camp; '*~-*
straße f through road; '*~verkehr*
m through traffic; ✝ transit trade;
'*~zoll* m transit duty; '*~zug* m corridor train.

'**durchgeben** pass on; *Nachricht*:
transmit; *Radio*: announce.

'**durchgehen** v/i. (sn) go (*od.* walk)

through, pass (through); (*fliehen*)
abscond, *a. Pferd*: bolt, *Liebende*:
elope; *Antrag, Gesetz*: pass, be
carried; (*geduldet werden*) pass; *et.*
~ *lassen* overlook; *j-m nichts* ~
lassen pass a p. nothing; *mit j-m* ~
Gefühl usw.: run away with a p.;
v/t. (*erörtern*; *prüfen*) go through
a th.; (*durchlesen*) go over *a th.*; '*~d*
through; *zeitlich*: continuous; 🚂
~er Wagen (*Zug*) through carriage
(train); *adv.* generally; (*durchweg*)
throughout; ~ *geöffnet* open
throughout.

durch'geistigt spiritual, highly intellectual.

'**durchgreifen** pass one's hand
through; *fig.* take drastic measures;
'*~d* drastic; radical, sweeping.

'**durchhalte|n** v/i. hold out (to the
end), see it through; '*2vermögen*
n staying power, stamina.

'**durchhecheln** *fig.* gossip about *a p.*

'**durchhelfen** (*dat.*) help through;
sich ~ manage, make shift.

'**durchkämmen** comb (thoroughly);
fig. comb (out).

'**durchkämpfen** fight out; *sich* ~
fight one's way through.

'**durchkochen** boil thoroughly;
'*durchgekocht* well done.

'**durchkommen** (sn) come (*od.* get)
through; *durch Krankheit usw.*:
pull through; *im Examen*: pass,
knapp: scrape through; (*auskom-*
men) get along; *fig.* succeed.

durch'kreuzen cross; *fig. a.* thwart.

Durch|laß ['durçlas] m (1²) passage;
outlet; '*2lassen* let through, allow
to pass; *Licht*: transmit; *im Exa-*
men: pass; '*2lässig* permeable (*für*
to).

Durchlaucht ['~lauxt] f (16) Serene
Highness; *2ig* [~'lauxtiç] serene.

'**durchlaufen** v/i. (sn) run through;
s. durchsickern; v/t. *Schuhe*: wear
through; *durch'laufen* v/t. run
through (*a. fig. Gefühl*); *Schule*:
pass through; *Strecke*: cover.

'**Durchlauf·erhitzer** ⚡ m (7) con-
tinuous-flow water heater.

durch'leben live (*od.* pass) through.

'**durchlesen** read through *od.* over;
sorgfältig: peruse; *flüchtig*: skim.

durch'leucht|en (flood with) light,
illuminate; ✻ X-ray, screen; *Ei*:
test, *Am.* candle; *fig.* investigate,
screen; *2ung* f illumination; X-ray

examination; screening; **੨ungs-schirm** ⚡ *m* fluorescent screen.

'durchliegen: *sich* ~ get bedsore.

durch|lochen [~'lɔxən] (25) *Fahrkarte usw.*: punch; **~löchern** [~'lœçərn] (29) perforate; (*durchbohren*) pierce; *mit Kugeln*: riddle.

'durchlüften, *a.* durch'lüften air.

'durchmachen go (*od.* pass) through; suffer.

'Durchmarsch *m* march(ing) through; F ⚡ diarrh(o)ea; **੨ieren** (sn) march through.

durch'messen traverse.

'Durchmesser *m* (7) diameter.

'durchmustern, *a.* durch'mustern pass in review, examine carefully, scrutinize.

'durchnässen, *a.* durch'nässen wet through, drench, soak.

'durchnehmen *Thema*: go through *od.* over, deal with, treat.

'durchpausen trace, calk.

'durchpeitschen whip soundly; *fig.* hurry through; *parl.* rush *a bill* through.

'durchprügeln beat soundly, thrash.

durchqueren [durç'kve:rən] (25) pass through, cross, traverse.

'durchrechnen count (*od.* calculate, go) over; check.

'durchreiben *s.* durchscheuern.

Durchreiche ['~raiçə] *f* (15) (service) hatch; **੨n** hand (*od.* pass) through.

'Durchreise *f* passage, transit; **੨n** *v/i.* (sn) travel (*od.* pass) through; **durch'reisen** *v/t.* travel over; **~nde** *m, f* travel(l)er, *Am. a.* transient; ⚯ through passenger.

'durchreißen *v/i.* (sn) get torn; *Faden*: break; *a.* durch'reißen *v/t.* rend, tear.

'durchreiten *Pferd*: gall by riding; *sich* ~ chafe o.s. by riding; *durch-'reiten* ride through.

durch'rieseln *v/t.* run through; *fig. a.* thrill *a p.*; *v/i.* '**durchrieseln** trickle through.

'durchringen: *sich* ~ struggle through (*zu* to); *sich zu e-m Entschluß* ~ make up one's mind (after long inner struggles).

'durchsacken ⚡ *v/i.* (sn) pancake.

'Durchsage *f s.* Durchgabe; **੨n** pass on; *Radio*: announce.

'durchsägen saw through.

durch'schaubar clear; *schwer* ~ in-

scrutable; '**durchschauen** *v/i.* look through; *fig.* durch'schauen *v/t.* see through.

'durchscheinen shine through; '**~d** translucent, transparent.

'durchscheuern rub through, gall, chafe; *Stoff*: wear through; *sich* ~ get chafed.

'durchschießen *v/i.* shoot through (*a. fig.*); (*durcheilen*) dash through; *durch'schießen* *v/t.* shoot through; *typ.* lead; *mit Papier*: interleave.

'durchschimmern shine through.

'Durchschlag *m* (*Sieb*) strainer; *v. Maschinenschrift*: (carbon) copy, F carbon; *e-s Geschosses*: penetration; ⚡ disruptive discharge; ⊕ punch; **੨en** ['~gən] *v/i.* (*durchdringen*) get through; (*wirken*) have (*od.* take) effect; *Papier*: blot; *Farbe*: show through; ⚡ break down, spark; *fig.* be dominant; (*sich zeigen*) show; *v/t.* beat through; *Erbsen usw.*: strain; *sich* ~ fight one's way through; *fig. s. sich durchbringen*; *durch'schlagen* beat through; (*durchbohren*) pierce; *Geschoß*: penetrate; '**੨end** (*wirkungsvoll*) effective, telling; **~er Erfolg** striking (*od.* complete) success; '**~papier** *n* copying paper, flimsy; (*Kohlepapier*) carbon paper; '**~skraft** *f* penetrating power; *fig.* force, impact.

'durchschlängeln: *sich* ~ wind through; *fig. P.*: wriggle through.

'durchschleichen: *sich* ~ sneak through.

'durchschleusen pass through (the lock); *fig.* pass (through).

'durchschlüpfen (sn) slip through.

'durchschmelzen melt, fuse.

'durchschneiden cut through; *fig.* intersect; *durch'schneiden* (*kreuzen*) cross, traverse.

'Durchschnitt *m* cutting through; ⊕ section, profile; ⚠ *u. fig.* average; *über* (*unter*) *dem* ~ above (below) average; *im* ~ *s.* ੨lich *adv.*; '**੨lich** average; *adv.* on an average; ~ *betragen* (*leisten usw.*) average; '**~s...** average ...

'Durchschreibe|block *m* carbon copy pad; '**~buch** *n* transfer copying (*od.* duplicating) book; '**~verfahren** *n* copying process.

durch'schreiten walk through; pass (through); cross.

'Durchschrift *f* (carbon) copy.

'**Durchschuß** *m typ.* lead; *Weberei:* weft; (*a.* '**~blatt** *n*) interleaf; ~ des Armes shot through the arm.
durch'schwimmen swim (through *od.* across).
'**durchschwitzen** soak with sweat.
durch'segeln sail (through).
'**durchsehen** *v/i.* look (*od.* see) through; *v/t.* look *a th.* over; (*prüfen*) examine; *bsd. typ. Korrekturbogen:* read.
'**durchseihen** strain, filter.
'**durchsetzen:** *fig. et.* ~ carry through; (*erzwingen*) enforce; (*es*) ~, *daß et. geschieht* cause a th. to be done; *s-n Kopf* ~ have one's way; *sich* ~ assert o.s.; win through, prevail, succeed; *durch'setzen* intersperse (*mit* with).
'**Durchsicht** *f s.* durchsehen: looking over; examination; inspection; *bsd. typ.* reading; revision; '**2ig** transparent (*a. fig.*); *fig.* perspicuous, lucid; '**~igkeit** *f* transparency (*a. fig.*); *fig.* perspicuity, lucidity.
'**durchsickern** (sn) ooze (*od.* seep) through *od.* out (*a. fig.*); *fig. Nachricht:* leak out.
'**durchsieben** sift, screen (*beide a. fig.*); *mit Kugeln durch'sieben* riddle with.
'**durchsprechen** talk over, discuss.
'**durchstech|en** pierce through; *durch'stechen* perforate; *mit e-r Nadel:* prick; *Damm:* cut; **2erei** [~'raɪ] *f* (16) underhand dealing(s *pl.*).
'**durchstecken** pass through.
'**durchstehen** *fig.* see *a th.* through.
'**Durchstich** *m* cut(ting).
durch'stöbern rummage through; *Gebiet:* scour.
'**durchstoßen** push (*od.* thrust) through; *durch'stoßen* pierce.
'**durchstreichen**, *a. durch'streichen* cross (*od.* strike, score) out, cancel.
durch'streifen roam through; *suchend:* scour.
'**durchströmen** *v/i.* (sn) *u. durch-'strömen v/t.* run through (*a. fig.*).
durch'such|en search; *Gebiet: a.* scour, comb; **2ung** *f* search.
durch'tränken impregnate, soak.
durchtrieben [durç'tri:bən] cunning, sly, tricky; (*schalkhaft*) mischievous; **2heit** *f* cunning, trickiness, slyness.
durch'wachen pass (*od.* spend) the

night waking.
'**durchwachsen** (sn) grow through; *adj. durch'wachsen Fleisch, Speck:* streaky; *fig.* mixed.
'**Durchwahl** *teleph. f* direct dial(l)ing.
'**durchwählen** *teleph.* dial through.
durch'wandern *v/t.* wander through (*a. v/i.* [sn] '**durchwandern**); traverse.
durch'wärmen, *a.* '**durchwärmen** warm through.
durch'waten *v/t. u.* '**durchwaten** *v/i.* (sn) wade (through), ford.
durch'weben interweave.
durchweg ['durç'vɛk] throughout; without exception.
durch'weichen (25) soak through (*a. v/i.* [sn] '**durchweichen**), drench.
'**durchwinden:** *sich* ~ worm (*od.* thread) one's way through.
durch'wühlen *Erde:* rake (*od.* root) up; (*durchsuchen*) search, rummage; (*a. plündern*) ransack.
'**durchwursteln** F: *sich* ~ muddle through.
'**durchzählen** count over.
'**durchzeichnen** trace.
'**durchziehen** *v/t.* pull through; *Faden:* pass through; *sich* ~ run through (*a. fig.*); *durch'ziehen* pass through; *mit Fäden usw.:* interlace; *v/i.* '**durchziehen** (sn) pass (*od.* march) through.
durch'zucken flash through.
'**Durchzug** *m* passage; (*Luft*) draught, *Am.* draft; circulation; △ girder; ~ *machen* let in fresh air.
durch'zwängen (25) force through; *sich* ~ squeeze o.s. through.
dürfen ['dyrfən] (30) be permitted *od.* allowed; (*wagen*) dare; *ich darf* I may; *darf ich?* may I?; *ich darf nicht* I must not; *wenn ich bitten darf* (if you) please; *es dürfte ein leichtes sein* it should be easy; *er dürfte recht haben* he is probably right.
durfte ['durftə] *pret. v.* dürfen.
dürftig ['dyrftɪç] (*bedürftig*) needy; (*ungenügend*) poor, inadequate; (*spärlich*) scanty, meag|re (*Am.* -er); (*erbärmlich, gering*) paltry, measly; *in ~en Verhältnissen* in needy circumstances; '**2keit** *f* neediness; *fig.* poorness, scantiness, paltriness.
dürr [dyr] dry; *Baum usw.:* dead; *Boden:* arid, barren; (*mager*) lean,

spindly; *mit* ~en Worten in plain terms, bluntly.

'**Dürre** *f* (15) dryness; aridity; barrenness; leanness; (*Regenmangel*) drought.

Durst [durst] *m* (3²) thirst (*nach* for); ~ *haben* be thirsty; ~ *bekommen* get thirsty.

dürsten ['dyrstən] *v/i.* (26) be thirsty; *fig.* thirst (*nach* for, after).

'**durstig** thirsty (*nach* for); F dry.

'**Durststrecke** *f fig.* hard times *pl.*

Dusch|e ['duːʃə] *f* (15) douche (*a.* ✶), shower; (*Brausebad*) shower-bath; '**₂en** (27) douche, have (*Am.* take) a shower; **~gel** ['~geːl] *n* shower foam; '**~kabine** *f* shower cubicle; '**~raum** *m* shower room; '**~vorhang** *m* shower curtain.

Düse ['dyːzə] *f* (15) *allg.* nozzle; (*Spritz₂, Strahl₂*) jet.

Dusel ['duːzəl] *m* (7) dizziness; F luck, fluke; ~ *haben* be lucky.

'**dus(e)lig** dizzy.

'**Düsen|-antrieb** *m* jet propulsion; *mit* ~ jet-powered, jet-propelled; '**~flugzeug** *n* jetplane; '**~jäger** *m* jetfighter; '**~triebwerk** *n* jet engine.

Dussel F ['dusəl] *m* (7) idiot.

düster ['dyːstər] dark, gloomy (*a. fig.*); (*traurig*) sad; '**₂heit** *f,* '**₂keit** *f* gloom(iness).

Dutzend ['dutsənt] *n* (3¹) dozen; '**~mensch** *m* commonplace man; '**₂weise** by the dozen, in dozens.

Duz|bruder ['duːts-] *m* intimate friend; '**₂en** (27) *j-n* ~ be on familiar terms with a p.

Dynam|ik [dy'naːmik] *f* (16) dynamics *sg.*; *fig.* dynamic force; **₂isch** dynamic(al); *Rente*: index-linked.

Dynamit [dyna'miːt] *n* (3) dynamite (*a. v/t. mit* ~ *sprengen*).

Dynamo *m* (11), **~maschine** [dy-'naːmoma'ʃiːnə] *f* dynamo (machine), generator.

Dynastie [dynas'tiː] *f* (16) dynasty.

D-Zug ['deːtsuːk] *m* corridor-train, *Am. a.* vestibule-train.

E

E [eː], **e** *n inv.* E, e; ♪ E.

Ebbe ['ɛbə] *f* (15) ebb(-tide); low tide, low water; *es ist* ~ the tide is out *od.* down; *es tritt* ~ *ein* the tide is going out; *fig. bei mir ist* ~ I am broke; '**₂n** (25) ebb.

eben ['eːbən] **1.** *adj.* even; (*flach*) plain, level; ♉ plane; *zu* ~*er Erde* on the ground (*Am.* first) floor; **2.** *adv.* evenly; (*genau*) exactly; (*gerade*) just; (*schließlich*) after all; ~ *tun wollen* be just going to do; ~ *erst* just now; '**₂bild** *n* image, (exact) likeness; '**₂bürtig** ['~byrtiç] of equal birth; *fig. j-m* ~ *sein* be a match for a p., be a p.'s equal; **~der**'**selbe** the very same; **~'deswegen** for that very reason.

'**Ebene** *f* (15) plain; ♉ plane; *fig.* level; *s. schief.*

'**eben|falls** likewise; '**₂heit** *f* evenness; '**₂holz** *n* ebony; '**₂maß** *n* symmetry; '**~mäßig** symmetrical; '**~so** just so; just as ...; (*auch*) likewise; '**~sogut** *adv.* just as well; '**~soviel** just as much; '**~sowenig** just as little *od. pl.* few.

Eber ['eːbər] *m* (7) boar; '**~esche** ♣ *f* mountain-ash.

ebnen ['eːbnən] (26) even, level; (*glätten*) smooth; *fig. j-m den Weg* ~ smooth the way for a p.

Echo ['ɛço] *n* (11) echo; '**~lot** *n* ♏ echo sounder; ♏ sonic altimeter.

echt [ɛçt] genuine; (*wahr*) true; (*rein*) pure; (*wirklich*) real; (*rechtmäßig*) legitimate; *Farbe*: (*haltbar*) fast; *Gold, Silber*: sterling; *Haar*: natural; (*glaubwürdig*) authentic; ♉ ~*er Bruch* proper fraction; '**₂heit** *f* genuineness; purity; reality; legitimacy; fastness; authenticity.

Eck|ball ['ɛk-] *m Sport*: corner-kick; '**~e** *f* (15) corner; (*Kante*) edge; (*kurzer Weg*) short distance; *in die* ~ *drängen* (*a. fig.*) corner; F *um die* ~ *bringen* do in; *um die* ~ *gehen* turn (round) the corner, F *fig.*

go west; *an allen* ~*n und Enden*
everywhere; *von allen* ~*n und Enden*
from all parts; '~**ensteher** *m* (7)
loafer.
Ecker ♀ ['ɛkər] *f* (15) acorn.
'**eck|ig** angular (*a. fig.*); ...~ ...-cornered; '♀**pfeiler** *m* corner-pillar;
'♀**platz** *m* corner-seat; '♀**stein** *m*
corner-stone; '♀**zahn** *m* canine
tooth, eye-tooth; '♀**zins** *m* prime
rate.
edel ['eːdəl] noble; *Metall*: precious;
edles Pferd thorough-bred (horse);
physiol. edle Teile m/pl. vital parts
pl.; '~**denkend,** '~**gesinnt** noble-minded; '♀**frau** *f* noblewoman; '♀-**gas** *n* inert gas; '♀**hirsch** *m* stag;
'♀**holz** *n* rare wood; '♀**leute** *pl.* noblemen, nobles; '♀**mann** *m* nobleman; '♀**metall** *n* precious metal;
'♀**mut** *m* noble-mindedness,
generosity; ~**mütig** ['~myːtiç]
noble-minded, generous; '♀-**obst** *n*
choice fruit; '♀**stahl** *m* high-grade
steel; '♀**stein** *m* precious stone; *geschliffener*: gem; '♀**tanne** *f* silver fir;
'♀**weiß** ♀ *n* (3²) edelweiss.
Edikt [e'dikt] *n* (3) edict.
Edition [edi'tsjoːn] *f* critical edition.
EDV-Anlage ['eː'deːfaU-] *f* electronic data processing equipment.
Efeu ['eːfɔy] *m* (11) ivy; *mit* ~ *bewachsen* ivy-clad.
Eff-eff F ['ɛf'ʔɛf] *n inv.*: *et. aus dem*
~ *können* have a th. at one's fingers'
ends *od.* finger-tips.
Effekt [ɛ'fɛkt] *m* (3) effect; *nach* ~
haschen strain after effect; ~**en** *pl.*
effects; ✝ securities; ~**enbörse** *f*
Stock Exchange; ~**enhandel** *m*
stock(-exchange) business; ~**enhändler** *m* stock-jobber; ~**enmakler** *m* stock-broker; ~**hasche'rei** *f*
(16) claptrap, sensationalism.
effektiv [ɛfɛk'tiːf] effective, actual.
ef'fektvoll effective, striking.
egal [e'gaːl] (*gleich*) equal; (*einerlei*)
all the same (*mir* to me); *ganz* ~ *wo*
no matter where.
Egel *zo.* ['eːgəl] *m* (7) leech.
Egge ['ɛgə] *f* (15), '♀**n** (25) harrow.
Egoismus [ego'ʔismus] *m* (16)
egoism.
Ego'-ist *m* (12), ~**in** *f* (16¹) egotist;
♀**isch** egotistic(al), selfish.
egozentrisch [~'tsɛntriʃ] self-centred, *Am.* -centered. [ere.]
eh' [eː], **ehe¹** ['eːə] *cj.* before, *lit.* }

'**Ehe²** (15) marriage; *s. Ehestand*:
wedlock; *Kind aus erster usw.* ~
child by the first *etc.* marriage; *die*
~ *brechen* commit adultery; '~**-anbahnung** *f* match-making; '~**berater** *m* marriage guidance counsellor; '~**bett** *n* nuptial bed; '♀-**brechen** (*nur im inf.*) commit
adultery; '~**brecher** *m* (7) adulterer; '~**brecherin** *f* (16¹) adulteress; '♀**brecherisch** adulterous;
'~**bruch** *m* adultery.
ehedem ['~deːm] formerly.
'**Ehe|frau** *f* wife; '~**gatte** *m*, '~**gattin** *f*
spouse; '~**glück** *n* wedded bliss; '~-**hälfte** *f* better half; '~**leben** *n* married life; '~**leute** *pl.* married couple(s
pl.); '♀**lich** conjugal; matrimonial;
Kind: legitimate; '♀**lichen** (25) marry; '♀**los** unmarried, single; '~**losigkeit** *f* celibacy.
ehemal|ig ['~maːliç] (*früher*) former,
bsd. Am. one-time; (*verstorben*; *pensioniert*) late; *ex-*... (*z. B. ex-president*); '~**s** formerly.
'**Ehe|mann** *m* husband; '♀**mündig**
marriageable; '~**paar** *n* married couple; '~**partner** *m* (*Mann*) husband;
(*Frau*) wife.
'**eher** sooner, earlier; (*lieber*) rather;
(*leichter*) more easily; *je* ~, *je lieber*
the sooner the better.
'**Ehe|recht** *n* marriage law; '~**ring**
m wedding ring.
ehern ['eːərn] brazen, of brass; *fig.*
iron (*law, etc.*); *mit* ~*er Stirn* brazen-faced.
'**Ehe|scheidung** *f* divorce; '~**scheidungsklage** *f* divorce-suit; '~-**schließung** *f* (contraction of) marriage; '~**stand** *m* married state,
matrimony, *gewählt*: wedlock.
ehestens ['eːəstəns] at the earliest;
(*möglichst bald*) as soon as possible.
'**Ehe|stifter(in** *f*) *m* match-maker;
'~**vermittlung** *f s. Eheanbahnung*.
'~**versprechen** *n* promise of marriage; '~**vertrag** *m* marriage settlement.
Ehrabschneider(in *f*) ['eːr'ʔapʃnaɪdər] *m* slanderer.
'**ehrbar** hono(u)rable, respectable;
Benehmen: decent, modest; '♀**keit** *f*
honesty, respectability; decency.
Ehre ['eːrə] *f* (15) hono(u)r; *zu* ~*n*
(*gen.*) in hono(u)r of; *mit wem*
habe ich die ~ (*zu sprechen*)? whom
have I the hono(u)r to address?;

j-m (e-e) ~ *antun* (*erweisen*) do (*od.* pay) hono(u)r to a p.; *j-m* ~ *machen* do a p. credit; *j-n bei s-r* ~ *packen* put a p. on his hono(u)r; *s. einlegen*; '♀**n** (25) hono(u)r.

'**Ehren**|-**amt** *n* honorary post; '♀-**amtlich** honorary; '~**bezeigung** *f* mark of respect; ⚔ salute; '~**bür-ger** *m* honorary citizen, freeman; '~**bürgerrecht** *n* freedom (of a city); '~**doktor** *m* honorary doctor; '~-**erklärung** *f* (full) apology; '~**gast** *m* guest of hono(u)r; '~**gericht** *n* court of hono(u)r; '♀**haft** hono(u)r-able; honest; ♀**halber** ['~halbər] for hono(u)r's sake; *Doktor* ~ *Doctor honoris causa*; '~**handel** *m* affair of hono(u)r; '~**kränkung** *f* insult to *a p.'s* hono(u)r; '~**mal** *n* memorial; '~**mann** *m* man of hono(u)r, hono(u)rable man; '~**mitglied** *n* honorary member; '~**pflicht** *f* honorary obligation; *es ist für mich e-e* ~ I am in hono(u)r bound; '~**platz** *m* place (*engS.* seat) of hono(u)r; '~**preis** *m* prize; ♀ speedwell; '~**recht** *n: Verlust* (*od. Aberkennung*) *der bürgerlichen* ~*e* loss of civil rights, civic degradation; '~**rettung** *f* vindication (of *a p.'s* hono[u]r); '♀**rührig** defamatory; '~**runde** *f Sport*: lap of hono(u)r; '~**sache** *f s. Ehrenhandel; es ist für mich* ~ it is a point of hono(u)r with me; '~**schuld** *f* debt of hono(u)r; '~**tag** *m* great day; '~**titel** *m* honorary title; '~**tor** *n Sport*: consolation goal; '♀**voll** hono(u)rable; '~**vorsitzende** *m* (18) honorary chairman; '♀**wert** hono(u)rable; (*achtbar*) respectable; '~**wort** *n* word of hono(u)r; *auf* ~ *entlassen usw.* on parole; '~**zeichen** *n* decoration.

ehr|**erbietig** ['~ʔɛrbiːtiç] respectful, deferential; '♀-**erbietung** *f*, '♀-**furcht** *f* respect, deference, reverence; *stärker*: awe (*vor dat.* of); '~**furchtgebietend** awe-inspiring, awesome; ~**fürchtig** ['~fyrçtiç], '~**furchtsvoll** respectful, reverential; '♀**gefühl** *n* sense of hono(u)r; (*Selbstachtung*) self-respect; '♀**geiz** *m* ambition; '~**geizig** ambitious.

'**ehrlich** honest; (*aufrichtig*) sincere; (*echt*) genuine; *Handel, Spiel*: fair; *Meinung*: frank; *Handlungsweise*: plain-dealing; ~ *währt am längsten* honesty is the best policy; F ~! really!, indeed!; '♀**keit** *f* honesty; fairness; frankness; plain dealing.

'**ehrlos** dishono(u)rable, infamous; '♀**igkeit** *f* dishonesty, infamy.

'**ehrsam** hono(u)rable, respectable; '♀**keit** *f* respectability.

'**Ehr**|**sucht** *f* immoderate ambition; '♀**süchtig** (over-)ambitious; '♀**ung** *f* hono(u)r (conferred on *a p.*); '♀-**vergessen** infamous, disgraceful; '~**verlust** ♫ *m s. Ehrenrecht*; '~-**würden**: *Ew.* ~ Reverend Sir; '♀-**würdig** venerable, reverend; '~-**würdigkeit** *f* venerableness.

ei[1] [aɪ] ah!, indeed!

Ei[2] *n* (1) egg; ⚕ ovum; ∨ ~*er pl.* (*Hoden*) balls; (*wie*) *auf* ~*ern gehen* walk gingerly; *wie ein* ~ *dem andern gleichen* be as like as two peas; F *wie aus dem* ~ *gepellt* spick-and-span; *wie ein rohes* ~ *behandeln* handle with kid--gloves.

Eibe ♀ ['aɪbə] *f* (15) yew(-tree).

Eibisch ♀ ['aɪbiʃ] *m* (4) marsh--mallow.

Eichamt ['aɪçʔamt] *n* Office of Weights and Measures, *Am.* Bureau of Standards.

Eiche ['aɪçə] *f* (15) oak.

Eichel ['aɪçəl] *f* (15) acorn; *anat.* glans; *Karte*: club; ~**häher** *zo.* ['~hɛːər] *m* (7) jay.

eichen[1] ['aɪçən] (25) *v/t. Gewichte*: ga(u)ge; *Rohre*: calibrate.

'**eichen**[2] *adj.* of oak, oaken.

'**Eichen...**[3] *in Zssgn* oak ....

'**Eich**|**hörnchen** *n*, '~**kätzchen** *n* squirrel; '~**maß** *n* standard; ga(u)ge; '~**meister** *m* ga(u)ger.

Eid [aɪt] *m* (3) oath; *an* ~*es Statt* in lieu of oath; *unter* ~ on oath.

Eidechse ['aɪdɛksə] *f* (15) lizard.

Eider|**daunen** ['aɪdər-] *f/pl.* eiderdown; '~**ente** *f* eider (duck).

eidesstattlich ['aɪdəs-] in lieu of (an) oath; ~*e Erklärung* affidavit.

Eid|**genosse** ['aɪt-] *m* confederate; '~**genossenschaft** *f* (Swiss) Confederation; ♀**genössisch** ['~gənœsiʃ] Federal; Swiss; '♀**lich** sworn; *adv.* on oath.

Eidotter ['aɪdɔtər] *m* (7) yolk.

Eidschwur ['aɪt-] *m* oath.

'**Eier**|**becher** *m* egg-cup; '~**kuchen** *m* omelet, pancake; '~**likör** *m* advocaat; '~**schale** *f* egg-shell; '~**stock** *m* ovary; '~**uhr** *f* egg-timer.

Eifer ['aɪfər] *m* (7, *o. pl.*) zeal; eagerness; *stärker*: ardo(u)r; (*Zorn*) passion; *blinder* ~ rashness; *blinder* ~ *schadet nur* haste is waste; '~**er** *m* (7) zealot, fanatic; '⚥**n** (29) (*heftig streben*) be eager (*nach* for); (*schmähen*) declaim, inveigh (*gegen* against); *s.* **wetteifern**; '~**sucht** *f* jealousy (*auf acc.* of); '⚥**süchtig** jealous (*auf acc.* of).

eifrig ['aɪfrɪç] zealous, eager, keen; *stärker*: ardent.

'**Eigelb** *n* (3) yellow of an egg, yolk.

eigen ['aɪgən] own, proper; (*besonder*; *genau*; *wählerisch*) particular; *j-m* ~ peculiar (to); (*seltsam*) strange, odd; *in Zssgn* ...-owned; *z. B.* *staats*~ state-owned; *ein* ~*es Zimmer* a room of one's own; *sich e-e Ansicht usw. zu* ~ *machen* adopt; '⚥-**art** *f* peculiarity; (*Originalität*) originality; '~-**artig** peculiar; original; '⚥**bedarf** *m* one's own requirements *pl.*; ⚥**brötler** ['~brøːtlər] *m* (7) eccentric; '⚥**dünkel** *m* self-conceit; '⚥**fabrikat** *n* self-produced article; '⚥**gewicht** *n* dead weight; '~**händig** with one's own hand; ~**e** *Unterschrift* one's own signature, autograph; ~ *übergeben* deliver personally; '⚥**heim** *n* home of one's own; owner-occupied house.

'**Eigen|heit** *f* peculiarity; (*Seltsamkeit*) oddity; *der Sprache*: idiom; '~**kapital** *n* privately owned capital; capital resources *pl.*; '~**liebe** *f* self-love; '~**lob** *n* self-praise; '⚥-**mächtig** arbitrary; '~**mächtigkeit** *f* arbitrariness; '~**name** *m* proper name; '~**nutz** *m* (3², *o. pl.*) self-interest; '⚥**nützig** self-interested, selfish; '⚥**s** expressly, specially, on purpose.

'**Eigenschaft** *f* quality; (*Merkmal*) attribute, *e-r S.*: property; *in s-r* ~ *als* in his capacity as; '~**swort** *n* adjective.

'**Eigen|sinn** *m* wil(l)fulness; (*Hartnäckigkeit*) obstinacy; '⚥**sinnig** wil(l)ful; obstinate.

'**eigentlich** (*genau*) proper; (*tatsächlich*) actual; (*wirklich*) true, real; (*dem Wesen nach*) virtual; *adv.* properly; (*eigentlich*) actually, really; (*genau gesagt*) properly speaking; *das* ~*e London* London proper; *was wollen Sie* ~? what do you want anyhow?

'**Eigentor** *n* *Sport*: own goal.

Eigentum ['~tuːm] *n* (1²) property.

Eigentüm|er ['~tyːmər] *m* (7) owner,

proprietor; '~**erin** *f* owner, proprietress; '⚥**lich** proper; (*eigenartig*) peculiar (*dat.* to); (*seltsam*) queer, odd; '~**lichkeit** *f* peculiarity.

'**Eigentums|recht** *n* proprietary right, title (*an dat.* to); '~**wohnung** *f* freehold flat, *Am.* condominium apartment.

'**Eigen|wechsel** ✝ *m* promissory note; '~**wille** *m* wil(l)fulness; '⚥**willig** self-willed, wil(l)ful.

eign|en ['aɪgnən] (29): *sich* ~ (*für j-n*) suit (a p.); (*für et.*) be suitable (for), *P.*: be qualified (for); *j-m* ~ be peculiar to; *s.* **geeignet**; '⚥**er** *m* (7) owner; '⚥**ung** *f* aptitude, qualification; suitability, fitness; '⚥**ungsprüfung** *f* aptitude test.

Eiland ['aɪlant] *n* (3) island.

'**Eil|-auftrag** ✝ *m* rush order; '~**bote** *m* express (*od.* special) messenger; *durch* ~*n* by special delivery; '~**brief** *m* express letter, *Am.* special delivery letter.

Eile ['aɪlə] *f* (15) haste, speed; *große*: hurry; ~ *haben P.*: be in a hurry; *S.*: be urgent.

'**eilen** (25, *sn u. h.*) hasten, (*a. sich*) make haste; hurry; *S.*: be urgent; *Aufschrift*: eilt! urgent!; *eile mit Weile* more haste, less speed; ~**ds** ['~ts] quickly, speedily, in haste.

'**eil|fertig** hasty; rash; '⚥**fertigkeit** *f* hastiness; rashness; '⚥**fracht** *f*, '⚥**gut** *n* express (*od.* dispatch) goods *pl.*, *Am.* fast freight.

'**eilig** hasty, speedy; (*dringend*) pressing, urgent; ~*st* in great haste; *es* ~ *haben* be in a hurry.

'**Eil|marsch** *m* forced march; '~**paket** *n* express parcel; '~**schrift** *f* high-speed shorthand; '~**tempo** *n* (11, *o. pl.*): *im* ~ at top speed; '~**zug** *m* semi-fast train; '~**zustellung** *f* express (*Am.* special) delivery.

Eimer ['aɪmər] *m* (7) bucket (*a.* ⊕), pail; '⚥**weise** in buckets.

ein [aɪn] (20) 1. one; 2. *art.* a, an; 3. *pron.* one; *s. allemal*.

'**Ein-akter** *thea.* *m* (7) one-act play.

einander [aɪ'nandər] one another, each other.

'**ein-arbeit|en** work (*od.* break) in; *sich* ~ work o.s. in; *sich* ~ *in* (*acc.*) make o.s. acquainted with; '⚥**ungszeit** *f* training period.

'**ein-armig** one-armed.

einäscher|n ['~ʔɛʃərn] (29) burn to

ashes; *Leiche*: cremate, incinerate; '♀ung *f* cremation, incineration.
' **ein-atmen** breathe in, inhale.
einäugig ['ᵕˀᵓʏgiç] one-eyed.
'**Einbahnstraße** *f* one-way street.
' **einbalsamier|en** embalm; '♀ung*f* embalming.
'**Einband** *m* (3³) binding; 'ᵕdecke *f* cover.
einbändig ['ᵕbɛndiç] in one volume.
' **einbauen** build in(to in *acc.*); install, fit, fix.
'**Einbau|küche** *f* fitted kitchen; 'ᵕmöbel *n*/*pl.* built-in furniture; 'ᵕschrank *m* fitted cupboard; 'ᵕspüle *f* fitted sink.
einbegriffen ['ᵕbəgrifən] included, inclusive (of).
' **einbehalten** detain, keep back.
' **einberuf|en** convene; *parl.* convoke; ✗ call up, *Am.* draft, induct; '♀ung *f* convocation; ✗ call(ing)-up, *Am.* draft, induction; '♀ungs-bescheid ✗ *m* call-up order, *Am.* induction order.
'**Einbett|...** *Zimmer*: single-bed; ⚓ *Kabine*: single-berth; '♀en embed (*a.* ⊕); 'ᵕzimmer *n* single.
einbeulen ['aɪnbɔʏlən] (25) dent.
' **einbeziehen** comprise, include, embrace, cover.
' **einbiegen** *v/t.* bend inwards; *v/i.* (sn) turn (in *acc.* into).
'**einbilden:** *sich et.* ᵕ fancy, imagine; *sich et.* ᵕ *auf* (*acc.*) pride (*od.* pique) o.s. on; *sich viel* ᵕ conceited; *darauf kann er sich et.* ᵕ that is a feather in his cap.
'**Einbildung** *f* imagination, fancy; (*Dünkel*) conceit; 'ᵕskraft *f* (power of) imagination.
' **einbinden** *Buch*: bind; *neu* ᵕ rebind.
' **einblasen** blow in; *fig.* prompt (*j-m et.* a th. to a p.).
'**einblend|en** *Film*, *Radio*: fade in; '♀ung *f Fernsehen*: insert.
' **einbleuen** (25): *j-m et.* ᵕ pound (*od.* hammer) into a p.'s head.
'**Einblick** *m* insight (in *acc.* into); ᵕ *gewähren in* afford an insight into; ᵕ *nehmen in* inspect.
'**einbrech|en** *v/t.* break open *od.* down; *v/i.* (sn) break in, collapse; *Dieb*: break in(to in *ein Haus*), burglarize (*in ein Haus* a house); (*einsetzen*) set in, come suddenly; ✗

penetrate, breach; *in ein Land*: invade; ᵕ *bei j-m*, *in ein Haus*: burgle; '♀er *m* (7) housebreaker; *bei Nacht*: burglar.
Einbrenne ['ᵕbrɛnə] *f* (15) (*Mehlschwitze*) roux.
' **einbrennen** burn in(to in *acc.*).
' **einbringen** bring in; *Gewinn*: yield; *et.* wieder ᵕ retrieve; *verlorene Zeit usw.*: make up for; *eingebrachtes Gut* dowry.
' **einbrocken** (25) crumble (in *acc.* into); *fig. j-m* (*a.* sich) *et.* ᵕ get into trouble; *das hast du dir selbst eingebrockt* that's your own doing.
'**Einbruch** *m* breaking-in; *in ein Land*: invasion (in *acc.* of); (*Haus♀*) housebreaking, burglary (*a.* 'ᵕs-diebstahl *m*); ✗ penetration, breach; *fig.* inroad; ᵕ *der Nacht* nightfall.
Einbuchtung ['ᵕbuxtuŋ] *f* (*Bucht*) inlet; (*Auszackung*) indentation.
einbürger|n ['ᵕbyrgərn] (29) naturalize; *sich* ᵕ become naturalized; '♀ung *f* naturalization.
'**Einbuße** *f* loss, damage.
'**einbüßen** lose, forfeit. [in.]
einchecken [ᵕtʃɛkən] ✈ (25) check ⌡
eincremen [ᵕkre:mən] (25) cream.
'**eindämm|en** (25) dam up (*a. fig.*); *Fluß usw.*: embank; '♀ung *f* damming(-up); embankment; '♀ungs-politik *f* policy of containment.
' **eindampfen** evaporate.
' **eindecken** cover; *mit Artilleriefeuer*: straddle; *sich* ᵕ provide o.s. (*mit* with); stock up (on).
'**Eindecker** ✈ *m* (7) monoplane.
' **eindeutig** unequivocal, definite, clear-cut; clear(ly *adv.*).
' **eindicken** thicken; *durch Eindampfen*: condense, inspissate.
' **eindosen** (27) tin, *Am.* can.
' **eindrängen:** *sich* ᵕ intrude (in *acc.* into).
'**eindring|en** (sn) enter (in *et.* a th.); *unbefugt*: intrude (into); (*a. fig.*) penetrate (into); 'ᵕlich urgent; forceful; ♀ling ['ᵕliŋ] *m* (3¹) intruder; (*Angreifer*) invader.
'**Eindruck** *m* (3¹) impression (*a.fig.*); *den* ᵕ *haben*, *daß* be under the impression that; *s. schinden.*
' **eindrücken** press in; (*einprägen*) impress; (*zermalmen*) crush; *Glasscheibe*: break; *Sporen*: dig in.
'**eindrucksvoll** impressive, striking.

'Ein-ehe f monogamy.

eineiig biol. ['~ʔaiiç] uniovular; ~e Zwillinge identical twins.

'ein-engen (25) narrow (a. fig.).

einer ['aɪnər] **1.** s. ein; **2.** ♀ m (7) ♣ digit, unit; ⚓ single (sculler).

'einer'lei 1. of the same kind; (unwesentlich) immaterial; es ist (mir) ~ it is all the same (to me); it is all one to me; ~ wer usw. whoever etc., no matter who etc.; **2.** ♀ n (6, o.pl.) sameness; (Eintönigkeit) monotony, humdrum.

einerseits ['aɪnərzaɪts], **eines-teils** ['aɪnəstaɪls] on the one hand.

einfach ['~fax] simple; (einzeln) single; (schlicht) plain; Mahlzeit: frugal; Fahrkarte: single, Am. one-way; ✝ ~e Buchführung book-keeping by single entry; adv. simply, just (wonderful, etc.); '♀heit f simplicity.

'einfädeln (29) thread; fig. contrive; mot. sich (in den Verkehr) ~ filter in, Am. merge.

'einfahr|en v/t. carry in; Pferd: break in; Auto: run in; ✈ Fahrgestell: retract; v/i. (sn) drive in; enter (in den Bahnhof usw. the station, etc.); ✗ descend; '♀t f entrance; (Torweg) gateway; (Hafen♀) mouth; ✗ descent.

'Einfall m (3³) ✗ invasion (in ein Land of a country), raid (into); fig. idea; glücklicher ~ brain-wave; '♀en (sn) fall in, collapse; Hohlraum: cave in; feindlich: invade (in ein Land a country); in die Rede: break in; ♪ join in; j-m ~ occur to a p., come to a p.'s mind; sich ~ lassen take into one's head; sich nicht ~ lassen not to dream of; F (das) fällt mir nicht ein! catch me!; '♀sreich imaginative; '~swinkel m angle of incidence.

Einfalt ['~falt] f (16) (Einfachheit) simplicity; (Unschuld) innocence; (Dummheit) silliness.

einfältig ['~fɛltiç] (dumm) dull; (arglos) simple; (albern) silly.

'Einfalts-pinsel m simpleton.

'Einfamilienhaus n one-family house.

'einfangen catch; (a. fig.) capture.

'einfarbig one-colo(u)red, unicolo(u)red.

'einfass|en border, edge; mit e-m Zaun usw.: enclose; Schneiderei:

trim; Edelstein: set, mount (mit in); (einrahmen, a. fig.) frame; '♀ung f bordering, edging; enclosure; trimming; setting, mounting; framing.

einfetten ['aɪnfɛtən] (26) grease.

'einfinden: sich ~ appear, arrive, F turn up.

'einflechten interlace; Haar: braid; fig. put in, insert.

'einfliegen ✈ v/i. enter (by air); v/t. Flugzeug: test, fly in.

'einfließen (sn) flow in(to in acc.); fig. ~ lassen drop, mention in passing.

'einflößen (27) j-m et.: pour into a p.'s mouth; feed; fig. j-m Mut usw. ~ inspire a p. with courage; j-m Angst usw. ~ fill a p. with fear etc.

'Einflugschneise f approach corridor.

'Einfluß m influx; fig. influence (auf acc. on, bei with); ~ haben auf influence; '~bereich m sphere of influence; '♀reich influential.

'einflüstern j-m: whisper to; fig. a. insinuate (od. suggest) to.

'einfordern call in.

einförmig ['~fœrmiç] monotonous; '♀keit f monotony.

einfriedig|en ['~friːdigən] (25) enclose; '♀ung f enclosure.

'einfrieren v/i. (sn) freeze in; v/t. Lebensmittel: deep-freeze; ✝ Guthaben, Löhne etc.: freeze.

'einfüg|en put in; insert (in acc. in[to]); (sich) ~ fit in; Person: sich ~ adapt o.s. (in acc. to); '♀ung f insertion; adaptation.

'einfühl|en: sich ~ project o.s. (in j-n into a p.'s mind); in et.: get into the spirit of; '♀ungsvermögen n sympathetic understanding, ⬚ empathy.

Einfuhr ['~fuːr] f (16) import (-ation); konkret: imports pl.; '~genehmigung f import licence (Am. license); '~handel m import trade; '~verbot n import ban; '~waren f/pl. imports; '~zoll m import duty.

'einführ|en allg., a. j-n, Brauch: introduce; ⊕ usw. a. insert; ✝ import; (einweihen) initiate (in acc. into); in Amt: install (in); ✝ (gut) eingeführt sein Firma: be (well) established; '♀ung f insertion; importation; introduction; initiation; installation, establishment; '♀ungs-

angebot ✝ *n* trial offer; **'⭢ungs-preis** ✝ *m* introductory price.
'einfüllen fill in(to *in acc.*).
'Eingabe *f* application (*an acc.* to; *um* for); (*Bittschrift*) petition (to; for); *Computer*: input; **'⭢daten** *n/pl. Computer*: input data; **'⭢gerät** *n Computer*: terminal.
'Eingang *m Ort*: entrance; (*Eintreten*) entry; (*Anfang*) beginning; *v. Waren*: arrival; *nach* ⭢ on receipt; *Eingänge m/pl. v. Waren*: goods, *v. Post*: mail *sg.* received, *v. Geld*: receipts; **'⭢s** at the beginning; **'⭢sbuch** *n* book of entries; **'⭢s-empfindlichkeit** *f Radio*: input sensitivity; **'⭢s-formel** *f* preamble; **'⭢szoll** *m* import duty.
'eingeben *Arznei*: give; *Gedanken usw.*: prompt, suggest (*dat.* to); *Computer*: enter.
eingebildet ['⭢gəbɪldət] imaginary; (*dünkelhaft*) conceited (*auf acc.* about).
'eingeboren native; *Sohn Gottes*: only begotten; **'⭢e** *m, f* native.
Eingebung ['⭢geːbʊŋ] *f* inspiration.
eingedenk ['⭢gədeŋk] mindful (*gen.* of); ⭢ *sein* (*gen.*) remember, bear in mind.
'eingefallen *Augen*: sunken; *Wangen*: hollow; (*abgezehrt*) emaciated.
eingefleischt ['⭢gəflaɪʃt] inveterate, ingrained, confirmed.
'eingehen *v/i.* (sn) *Brief, Ware*: come in, arrive; ☿, *Tier*: die; (*aufhören*) cease, F fizzle out; *Betrieb*: close down; *Zeitung*: perish; *Stoff*: shrink; *j-m* ⭢ go down with a p.; ⭢ *auf* (*acc.*) agree to; *auf Einzelheiten*: enter into; ⭢ *lassen* (*aufgeben*) give up, drop, discontinue; *v/t.* (h., sn) *Beziehungen, Vertrag usw.*: enter into; *Ehe*: contract; *e-n Vergleich* ⭢ *mit* settle with; *Verpflichtungen* ⭢ incur liabilities; *e-e Wette* ⭢ make a bet, lay a wager; *eingegangene Gelder n/pl.* receipts *pl.*; **'⭢d** detailed; (*gründlich*) thorough; *Prüfung*: close.
Eingemachte ['⭢gəmaxtə] *n* (18) *in Zucker*: preserves *pl.*; *in Essig*: pickles *pl.*
eingemeind|en ['⭢gəmaɪndən] (26) incorporate (*dat.* into); **'⭢ung** *f* incorporation.
eingenommen ['⭢gənɔmən] prepossessed (*für in* favo[u]r of), par-

tial (to); prejudiced (*gegen* against); *von sich* ⭢ self-conceited; **'⭢heit** *f* prepossession; prejudice, bias; self--conceit. [cross, peeved.]
eingeschnappt F ['⭢gəʃnapt] *fig.*
'eingesessen, **'⭢e** *m, f* resident.
eingestandenermaßen ['⭢gəʃtandənər'maːsen] admittedly.
'Eingeständnis *n* confession, avowal, admission.
'eingestehen confess, avow.
eingetragen ['⭢gətraːgən] *amtlich*: registered.
Eingeweide ['⭢gəvaɪdə] *n/pl.* (7) *allg. anat.* viscera; (*Gedärme*) bowels; *bsd. v. Vieh*: entrails; *anat.* intestines.
Eingeweihte ['aɪngəvaɪtə] *m, f* initiate.
'eingewöhnen (*a. sich*) acclimatize, *Am.* acclimate (*in dat. u. acc.* to); accustom (to); *sich* ⭢ get accustomed (to).
eingewurzelt ['⭢gəvurtsəlt] deep--rooted, engrained.
'eingießen pour in(to *in acc.*); (*einschenken*) pour out.
eingleisig ['⭢glaɪzɪç] single-track.
'eingliedern incorporate, integrate (*in acc.* in[to]); *Gebiet*: annex (to).
'eingraben dig in; (*beerdigen*) bury; *in Stein usw., fig. ins Gedächtnis*: engrave (*in acc.* upon); ⚔ *sich* ⭢ entrench o.s.
'eingravieren engrave.
'eingreifen 1. ⊕ engage (*in acc.* in *od.* with); *Getriebe usw.*: gear in(to), mesh; *fig.* take action; ⚔ come into action; *vermittelnd*: intervene; *störend*: interfere (*in acc.* with); *fig.* interfere (with); *in die Debatte* ⭢ join in the debate; **2.** ⚲ *n* (6) engagement; meshing; action; intervention; interference.
'Eingriff *m s. eingreifen*: gearing; ⚔ operation; *fig. s. Eingreifen*.
'einhaken hook in(to *in acc.*); *fig. sich bei j-m* ⭢ link arms with a p.; *fig.* cut in; *bei et.*: take a th. up.
'Einhalt *m*: ⭢ *gebieten od. tun* (*dat.*) put a stop to; **'⭢en** *v/t.* (*hemmen*) stop, check; (*genau beachten*) observe, comply with, keep; *Kurs usw.*: follow; *Versprechen*: keep; *Verpflichtung*: meet; *die Zeit* ⭢ be punctual; *v/i.* stop, leave off; **'⭢ung** *f* (*gen.*) observance (of), compliance (with).

'**einhandeln** obtain; trade in.
einhändig|en['∼hendigən](25)hand over, deliver; '**Sung** f delivery.
'**einhängen** v/t. hang in; (aufhängen) hang (up); Tür: put on its hinges; sich bei j-m ∼ link arms with a p.; v/i. teleph. hang up.
'**einhauen** v/t. hew in; (aufbrechen) cut open; v/i. ∼ auf (acc.) fall upon; F beim Essen: F tuck in.
'**einheften** sew (od. stitch) in; Akten: file.
'**einhegen** s. einfriedigen.
'**einheimisch** native (in dat. to), (a. ♥) indigenous (to); domestic (a. ✝); home-made; Krankheit: endemic; '**Se** m, f native; resident.
einheimsen ['∼haimzən] (27) Ernte: reap; fig. a. pocket.
'**Einheirat** f: ∼ in (acc.) marriage into; '**Sen** v/i.: ∼ in (acc.) marry into.
'**Einheit** f unity; (Gleichheit) oneness; A⌃, phys., ⊕, ✕ unit; '**Slich** uniform; '**∼lichkeit** f uniformity; '**∼s-partei** f united party; '**∼s-preis** m standard (od. flat) price; '**∼sschule** f comprehensive school; '**∼sstaat** m centralized state; '**∼swert** m ✝ rateable value.
'**einheizen** light a fire; heat; F fig. j-m ∼ make it hot for a p.
einhellig ['ainheliç] unanimous; '**Skeit** f unanimity.
einher [∼'heːr] along.
'**einholen** v/t. (erreichen) catch up with, overtake; Versäumtes: make up for; Genehmigung: apply for; Gutachten usw.: obtain; Befehl: take; Rat: seek, take; (einkaufen) buy; Segel: strike; Flagge: haul down; v/i. go shopping.
'**Einhorn** n unicorn.
Einhufer ['∼huːfər] m (7) solid--hoofed animal, soliped.
'**einhüllen** wrap (up); envelop.
einig ['ainiç] united; (sich) ∼ sein be at one, be agreed, agree; (sich) nicht ∼ sein (über acc.) differ (about); (sich) ∼ werden come to an agreement od. to terms.
einige ['ainigə] some, a few; several; '**∼n** (25) (vereinigen) unite; sich ∼ come to terms; agree (mit with a p.; auf acc., über acc. [up]on); **∼rmaßen** ['∼r'maːsən] to some extent; (ziemlich) rather, fairly; '**∼s** something, several things.

'**Einigkeit** f (16) unity; (Übereinstimmung) agreement; (Eintracht) concord; (Einmütigkeit) unanimity.
'**Einigung** ['∼guŋ] f union; (Übereinstimmung) agreement; (Vergleich) settlement; pol. unification.
'**ein-impf|en** inoculate (a. fig. j-m into a p.); '**Sung** f inoculation.
'**einjagen**: j-m Furcht ∼ frighten a p.
'**einjährig** (one-)year-old; Dauer: of one year, one year's; bsd. ♥ annual.   [allow for.)
'**einkalkulieren** take into account;(
'**einkassier|en** cash; Schulden: collect; '**Sung** f cashing; collection.
'**Einkauf** m purchase; Einkäufe machen go shopping; '**Sen** buy, purchase; v/i. ∼ (gehen) go shopping.
'**Einkäufer** ✝ m buyer.
'**Einkaufs|liste** f shopping list; '**∼-möglichkeit** f shopping facility; **∼-netz** n string bag; '**∼passage** f shopping arcade, Am. shopping mall; '**∼preis** m cost-price, first (od. prime) cost; '**∼straße** f shopping street, Am. mall; '**∼tasche** f shopping bag; '**∼-wagen** m trolley, Am. shopping cart; '**∼zentrum** n shopping cent|re (Am. -er).
Einkehr ['∼keːr] f (16) putting up (in dat., bei at); fig. contemplation; fig. ∼ bei sich halten commune with o.s.; '**Sen** (25) in e-m Gasthaus: stop at an inn (for drink, food); (übernachten) put up (in dat., bei at).
einkeilen ['∼kailən] fig. wedge in.
einkellern ['∼kelərn] (29) lay in.
'**einkerb|en** (25), '**Sung** f notch.
einkerker|n ['∼kerkərn] (29) imprison, incarcerate; '**Sung** f imprisonment, incarceration.
'**einklagen** Schuld: sue for.
'**einklammern** Wort usw.: bracket, put in parentheses.
'**Einklang** m unison; harmony; accord; in ∼ bringen bring into line, harmonize, square (mit with); im ∼ stehen be compatible od. in keeping, coincide, square (mit with).
'**einkleben** paste in(to in acc.).
'**einkleid|en** clothe; (a. fig.) invest; '**Sung** f clothing; investiture.
'**einklemmen** squeeze in; jam (od. wedge) in.
'**einklinken** latch; ⊕ engage.
'**einknicken** v/t. u. v/i. (sn) bend in, break; a. Knie: buckle.

'**einkochen** v/t. u. v/i. (sn) (eindicken) boil down; (einmachen)
preserve.
'**einkommen 1.** (sn): bei j-m: petition, apply to (um for); s. Abschied;
2. ♀ n (6) income; pol. revenue;
'♀**sgefälle** n income differential; '**~s-
schwach** low-income attr.; '**~sstark**
high-income attr.; '**~(s)steuer** f income-tax; '**~(s)stufe** f income class
(Am. bracket).
'**einkreis|en** encircle; '♀**ung** f en-
circlement.
Einkünfte ['~kynftə] pl. (14¹) proceeds, receipts; (Einkommen) income; pol. revenue sg.
'**einkuppeln** ⊕ clutch, couple, mot.
(let in or engage the) clutch.
'**einlad|en** et.: load in; j-n: invite;
'**~end** inviting; '♀**ung** f invitation.
'**Einlage** f im Brief: enclosure; ⊕
insert; (Schicht) layer; (Zahn♀)
temporary filling; Schneiderei: padding; Küche: garnish; (Schuh♀)
(arch-)support; ♥ investment;
(Bank♀) deposit; Spiel: stake; thea.
insert(ed piece), extra; (a. fig.)
interlude.
'**einlagern** lay in; ♥ warehouse,
store, put into stock.
Einlaß ['~las] m (4) admission, admittance; ⊕ inlet.
'**einlassen** let in, admit; (einfügen)
put in; sich in (od. auf) et. (acc.) ~
engage in, enter into; embark on;
leichtsinnig: meddle with; sich mit
j-m ~ have dealings with, feindselig:
tangle with.
'**Einlauf** ☀ m enema.
'**einlaufen** (sn) come in, arrive;
Schiff: enter; Stoff: shrink; nicht
~d shrink-proof; Bad ~ lassen run
the bath.
'**einläuten** ring in.
'**einleben**: sich ~ accustom o.s. (in
dat. u. acc. to).
'**Einlege-arbeit** f inlaid work.
'**einlegen** lay (od. put) in; ⊕ mit et.:
inlay; Geld: deposit; in Salz: salt;
pickle; Früchte: preserve; Berufung
~ lodge an appeal (bei with); Ehre ~
mit gain hono(u)r (od. credit) by; ein
Wort ~ für intercede for.
'**Einlegesohle** f insole, Brt. a. sock.
'**einleit|en** introduce; start, launch;
Verhandlungen usw.: open; ⚖ institute; '**~end** introductory; '♀**ung** f

introduction; ⚖ institution.
'**einlenken** turn in; fig. come round.
'**einlernen:** sich et. ~ learn thoroughly; j-m et. ~ teach a p. a th.
'**einleuchten** be evident od. obvious;
das will mir nicht ~ I cannot see
that; '**~d** evident, obvious, clear.
'**einliefer|n** deliver (up); e-n Ge-
fangenen: commit (to prison); in
ein Krankenhaus ~ take to a hospital, Am. hospitalize; '♀**ung** f delivery; '♀**ungsschein** m receipt of
delivery.
'**einliegend** im Brief: enclosed.
'**einlochen** F lock up.
'**einlös|en** redeem; Schuld, Rech-
nung: discharge; ♥ Wechsel: hon-
o(u)r, take up; Scheck: cash; '♀**ung**
f redemption; discharge, payment;
cashing, passing.
'**einlullen** ['~lulən] (25) lull to sleep;
fig. lull.
'**einmach|en** Früchte: preserve,
bottle; Fleisch: pot; '♀**glas** n pre-
serving jar.
'**einmal** once; (künftig) one day,
some time; auf ~ (plötzlich) all at
once, (gleichzeitig) at the same time;
es war ~ once (upon a time) there
was; nicht ~ not even, not so much
as; stellen Sie sich ~ vor just fancy;
~ ist keinmal one and none is all
one.
Einmal'-eins n (Tabelle) multiplica-
tion-table; großes (kleines) ~ compound (simple) multiplication.
'**Einmalhandtuch** n disposable
towel.
'**einmalig** single, one; Zahlung usw.:
non-recurring; fig. singular; ~e
Gelegenheit unique opportunity.
'**Einmal|rasierer** m (7) disposable
razor; '**~spritze** f disposable syringe.
'**Einmarsch** m marching-in, entry;
'♀**ieren** (sn) march in, enter.
'**einmauern** immure, wall in.
'**einmeißeln** chisel in, engrave.
'**einmengen** mix in; sich ~ meddle,
interfere (in acc. with), F bsd. Am.
butt in.
'**einmieten** take lodgings (j-n for a
p.; bei j-m with a p.); Kartoffeln
usw.: pit.
'**einmischen** s. einmengen.
'**Einmischung** f interference.
einmotorig ✈ ['~mo'to:riç] single-
-engine(d). [usw.).}
'**einmotten** mothball (a. Schiff}

'**einmünd|en:** ~ *in* (*acc.*) *Straße*: run into, join; *Fluß*: flow into; '**2ung** *f Straße*: junction; *Fluß*: mouth.

einmütig ['~myːtiç] unanimous; '**2keit** *f* unanimity.

Einnahme ['~naːmə] *f* (15) ✕ taking, conquest, capture; (*Geld*2) receipt, *mst* ~*n pl.* takings, receipts.

'**einnebeln** (29) smoke-screen.

'**einnehmen** take in; *Geld usw.*: receive; *Steuern*: collect; ✕ take; *Raum*: take up, occupy; *Arznei, Mahlzeit, s-n Platz*: take; *Haltung*: assume; *Stelle*: hold; *fig.* captivate, charm; *j-n* ~ *für* (*gegen*) prejudice in favo(u)r of (against); '~**d** winning, engaging, charming.

'**einnicken** (sn) doze off.

'**einnisten:** *sich* ~ nestle (down); *fig.* settle (down).

'**Ein-öde** *f* desert, solitude.

'**ein-ölen** oil.

'**ein·ordnen** arrange in (proper) order; *Brief usw.*: file; *in Klassen*: classify; *ins Ganze*: integrate (*in acc.* into); *mot. sich* (*rechts*) ~ get into (the right) lane.

'**einpacken** *v/t.* pack up; (*einwickeln*) wrap up; *v/i.* F *fig.* pack up.

'**einpassen** fit in(to *in acc.*).

'**einpauken** F cram.

'**Einpeitscher** *m* (7) slave-driver.

'**einpendeln:** *sich* ~ *fig.* even out, come right.

'**einpferchen** pen in; *fig.* cram (*od.* pack) together.

'**einpflanzen** plant; *fig.* implant (*j-m in a p.*'s mind).

einphasig ⚡ ['~faːziç] single-phase, monophase.

'**einplanen** include, allow for.

'**einpökeln** pickle, salt, corn.

einpolig ⚡ ['~poːliç] unipolar.

'**einpräg|en** imprint; *j-m et.*: impress on a p.'s mind; *sich* ~ sink into the mind *od.* memory; *sich et.* ~ commit a th. to one's memory; ~**sam** ['~prɛːkzaːm] impressive.

'**einprogrammieren** *Computer*: feed in.

'**einquartier|en** quarter, billet (*in e-n Ort, bei j-m* on; *in e-e Wohnung* in); '**2ung** *f* billeting; soldiers *pl.* billeted *od.* quartered, billetees.

'**einrahmen** (25) frame.

'**einrammen** ram in(to *in acc.*).

'**einrasten** (sn) engage (*in acc.* in).

'**einräum|en** (*wegpacken*) clear away; *Möbel*: place (*od.* put) in; *Zimmer*: put the furniture in *a room*; (*abtreten*) give up, cede (*j-m* to); (*zugestehen*) grant, concede; ✝ *Frist, Kredit usw.*: grant, allow; '~**end** *gr.* concessive; '**2ung** *f* grant (-ing), concession.

'**einrechnen** include; (*einkalkulieren*) allow for; (*nicht*) *eingerechnet* ... (not) including ...

'**Einrede** *f* objection; ⚖ demurrer, plea; '**2n** *v/t. j-m et.*: make a p. believe *a th.*, talk a p. into; *sich et.* ~ imagine a th.; *v/i. auf j-n* ~ talk (insistently) to a p., *drängend*: urge a p.

'**einreiben** rub in(to *in acc.*); ~ *mit* rub with; *mit Fett* ~ grease.

'**einreichen** hand in; *Gesuch, Rechnung usw.*: submit, file, present; *s-e Entlassung*: hand in, tender (*one's resignation*); *Klage*: file, lodge.

'**einreihen** range (*in acc.* in; *unter acc.* among).

einreihig ['~raiiç] *Jacke*: single--breasted.

'**Einreise** *f* entry (*in acc.* into); '~**erlaubnis** *f* entry permit; '~**verbot** *n*: *j-m* ~ *erteilen* refuse a p. entry; '~**visum** *n* entry visa.

'**einreißen** *v/t.* tear; *Haus*: pull down, demolish; *v/i.* (sn) tear; *fig.* spread, gain ground.

einrenken ['~rɛŋkən] (25) set; *fig.* set right; *sich* ~ come right.

'**einrennen** crash through; *j-m das Haus* ~ pester a p.; *offene Türen* ~ force an open door.

'**einricht|en** *Glied*: set; *Wohnung*: fit up, furnish; ⊕ install; *Geschäft, Schule usw.*: establish; set up; (*ausstatten*) equip; (*errichten*) establish; (*ermöglichen*) arrange (*a. ♪*), manage; *es* (*so*) ~, *daß* arrange (*od.* see to) it that; *sich* ~ establish o.s., settle down; *sparsam*: economize; *sich* ~ *auf* (*acc.*) prepare for; *sich* ~ *mit* manage with; *sich* ~ *nach* adapt o.s. to; *es läßt sich* ~ it can be arranged; '**2ung** *f* (*Ausstattung*) equipment; *e-s Hauses etc.*: furnishings *pl.*, appointments *pl.*; (*Laden*2) fittings *pl.*; ⊕ (*Anlage od. Einbau*) installation; (*bequeme* ~) facility; (*Anordnung*) arrangement; (*Gründung od. Anstalt*) establishment; (*öffentliche* ~ public) institution; '**2ungsgegenstand** *m* piece of furniture; *mst pl. Einrichtungsgegenstände* fixtures, fittings.

'**einrosten** (sn) get rusty (*a. fig.*).

'**einrücken** *v/i.* (sn) enter, march in; ✕ *zur Truppe*: be called up; *v/t. in die Zeitung*: insert; *typ. Zeile*: indent; ⊕ *Kupplung usw.*: engage; *Gang*: shift.

'**einrühren** stir, mix in.

eins [aıns] **1.** one; *es ist mir alles* ~ it is all one (*od.* the same) to me; ~ *ums andere* one after the other, *abwechselnd*: by (*od.* in) turns; ~ *trinken* have a glass; ~ *sein fig.* be at one; *nicht* ~ *sein* differ; **2.** ♀ *f* (16³) one; *auf Würfeln*: ace; (*Schulnote*) alpha, grade one.

einsacken ['aınzakən] (25) bag, sack; *fig.* pocket.

'**einsalzen** salt.

'**einsam** lonely, solitary; '**2keit** *f* loneliness, solitude.

'**einsammeln** gather; *Geld usw.*: collect.

'**Einsatz** *m* ⊕ inset; *am Hemd*: shirt-front; *am Kleid*: insertion; *im Koffer*: tray; (*Gefäß usw.*) insert; (*Spiel2*) stake, *gemeinsamer*: pool; ♪ striking in, intonation; (*Verwendung*) use, employment; *v. Truppen*: engagement, action; ✕ (*Auftrag*) mission, operation; *v. Arbeitskräften*: employment; (*Anstrengung*) effort; *im* ~ in action (*a.* ⊕); ✕, ✈ ~ *fliegen* fly a sortie *od.* mission; *mit vollem* ~ all out; *unter* ~ *s-s Lebens* at the risk of one's life; '**2bereit** ready for action (⊕ for operation); *fig.* devoted; '**2fähig** serviceable; (*verfügbar*) available; ✕ fit for action; '**~gruppe** ✕ *f* task force.

'**einsäumen** hem in.

'**einschalt|en** insert; ∮, *Radio*: switch (*od.* turn) on; *Kupplung*: throw in; *mot.* start; *fig.* (*einschieben*) insert; *j-n*: call in; *sich* ~ intervene; '**2quote** *f* program(me) rating; '**2ung** *f* insertion; intervention.

'**einschärfen** enjoin (*dat.* upon).

'**einscharren** bury.

'**einschätz|en** estimate, assess (*auf acc.* at); *fig. j-n*: appraise, F size up; '**2ung** *f* estimation, assessment; appraisal.

'**einschenken** pour out *od.* in(to *in*

acc.); *j-m Wein usw.* ~ help a p. to; *s. rein*.

'**einschicken** send in.

'**einschieb|en** push (*od.* slip) in; insert (*a. fig. Worte usw.*); '**2ung** *f* insertion.

'**einschießen** shoot (*od.* batter) down; *ein Gewehr*: test, try; *Fußball*: score, net; *Geld*: contribute; *sich* ~ *auf ein Ziel* find the range of, bracket.

'**einschiff|en** (*a. sich*) embark (*nach* for); '**2ung** *f* embarkation.

'**einschlafen** (sn) fall asleep; *Glied*: go to sleep; *fig.* (*sterben*) pass away; *Briefwechsel usw.*: drop, fizzle out; ~ *lassen* drop.

'**einschläf(e)rig** *Bett*: single.

einschläfern ['aınʃlɛːfərn] (29) lull to sleep; *fig.* lull (into security); narcotize; *Tier*: put to sleep; '**~d** soporific, narcotic.

'**Einschlag** *m* (*Hülle*) wrapper, cover, envelope; *Weberei*: woof, weft; *am Kleid*: tuck; *e-s Geschosses*: impact; *fig.* infusion, streak, touch.

'**einschlagen** *v/t. Nagel*: drive in(to *in acc.*); (*zerbrechen*) break (in); *Fenster, Schädel*: smash (in); (*einhüllen*) envelop, wrap up; *Weg*: take; *Laufbahn*: enter upon; (*zs.-falten*) tuck in; *v/i.* shake hands; *Blitz*: strike (*in ein Haus* a house); *Geschoß*: hit; (*Erfolg haben*) be a success *od.* hit; *nicht* ~ fail; ~ *auf* (*acc.*) strike out at.

'**Einschlag(e)papier** *n* wrapping paper.

einschlägig ['~ʃlɛːgiç] pertinent, relevant.

'**einschleichen** (sn) *mst sich* ~ creep (*od.* sneak) in(to *in acc.*); *fig. sich* ~ *Fehler usw.*: creep in; *in j-s Vertrauen usw.* worm o.s. into.

'**einschleppen** drag in; *Krankheit*: import.

'**einschleusen** channel (*od.* let) in; *Spione*: infiltrate.

'**einschließ|en** lock in *od.* up; (*umgeben*; *in e-n Brief* ~) enclose; ✕ surround, encircle; *fig.* include; '**~lich** (*gen.*) including, inclusive (of); *Seite 1 bis 10* ~ pages 1 to 10 inclusive.

'**einschlummern** (sn) doze off.

'**Einschluß** *m*: *mit* ~ (*gen.*) including, inclusive of.

'**einschmeicheln:** *sich* ~ ingratiate o.s. (*bei* with); '~d ingratiating.
'**einschmelzen** melt down.
'**einschmieren** smear; *mit Fett*: grease; *mit Krem*: cream.
'**einschmuggeln** smuggle in.
'**einschnappen** (sn) catch, click; *fig. s.* eingeschnappt.
'**einschneiden** cut in; *Namen usw.*: carve (*in acc.* in); (*einkerben*) notch; (*auszacken*) indent; '~d *fig.* incisive.
'**einschneien** snow up *od.* in.
'**Einschnitt** *m* cut, incision; (*Kerbe*) notch; *fig.* cut, turning-point.
'**einschnüren** *Taille*: lace; *Hals*: strangle; *s.* schnüren, einengen.
'**einschränk|en** (25) restrict, confine (*auf acc.* to); *Ausgaben, Produktion, Umfang*: reduce; *Behauptung usw.*: qualify; *sich* ~ economize; '~end restrictive; '2ung *f* restriction; reduction; qualification; *mit* (*ohne*) ~ (*Vorbehalt*) with (without) reservation.
'**einschrauben** screw in(to *in acc.*).
'**Einschreibe|brief** *m* registered (*od.* recorded delivery) letter; '~gebühr *f* registration-fee.
'**einschreiben** 1. (*eintragen*) enter; (*buchen*) book; *als Mitglied u.* ✗: enrol(l); ✆ register; *e-n Brief* ~ *lassen* have a letter registered; *sich* ~ enter one's name; 2. 2 *n* registered (*od.* recorded delivery) letter; *per* ~ by recorded delivery (*od.* registered mail).
'**einschreiten** 1. (sn) *fig.* step in, interfere, intervene; ~ *gegen* proceed against; 2. 2 *n* (6) intervention.
'**einschrumpfen** (sn) shrink.
'**einschüchter|n** (29) intimidate, cow; *durch Gewalttätigkeit*: bully; *durch Drohungen*: browbeat; '2ung *f* intimidation; '2ungsversuch *m* attempt at intimidation.
'**einschulen** put to school.
'**Einschuß** *m* bullet-hole; (*Wunde*) entry wound; ✝ capital invested (*od.* paid in); *Weberei*: woof, weft.
'**einschütten** pour in(to *in acc.*).
'**einschweißen** *Waren*: shrink-wrap.
'**einsegn|en** consecrate; *Kinder*: confirm; '2ung *f* consecration; confirmation.
'**einsehen** 1. look into *od.* over; (*prüfen*) inspect; (*verstehen*) see, understand; (*erkennen*) realize; (*richtig einschätzen*) appreciate;

2. 2 *n*: *ein* ~ *haben* show consideration.
'**einseifen** soap; *beim Rasieren*: lather; *fig.* F (*betrügen*) take in.
einseitig ['aɪnzaɪtɪç] one-sided (*a. fig.*); ☐, *pol.*, ⚡ unilateral; ~e Lungenentzündung single pneumonia; '2keit *f* one-sidedness.
'**einsend|en** send in; (*einreichen*) hand in, submit; *Fußball*: net; '2er(in *f*) *m* sender; *an e-e Zeitung*: contributor; '~eschluß *m* closing date (for entries); '2ung *f* sending in; (*Zuschrift*) letter.
'**einsetz|en** *v/t.* set (*od.* put) in; *Geld*: stake; (*einfügen; inserieren*) insert; (*stiften, gründen*) institute; *in ein Amt*: install (*in acc.* in), appoint (to); (*anwenden*) use, apply, (*a.* ✗) employ, bring into action; *Leben*: risk, stake; *sich* ~ extend o.s.; *sich* ~ *für* stand up for; (*bitten, plädieren*) plead for, advocate; *v/i.* ♪ strike (*fig.* chime) in; *Fieber, Wetter usw.*: set in; '2ung *f* insertion; appointment, installation; *s.* Einsatz.
'**Einsicht** *f* (16) inspection; *fig.* insight; judg(e)ment; understanding; '2ig *s.* einsichtsvoll; ~nahme ['~naːmə] *f* (15): *zur* ~ for inspection; *nach* ~ on sight; '2svoll judicious; (*verständig*) sensible.
'**einsickern** (sn) infiltrate (*a.* ✗ *usw.*), ooze (*od.* soak, seep) in(to *in acc.*).
'**Einsiedler** *m* (7), '~in *f* (16¹) hermit; '2isch recluse, solitary.
einsilbig ['~zɪlbɪç] monosyllabic; (*wortkarg*) taciturn; ~es Wort monosyllable; '2keit *f fig.* taciturnity.
'**einsinken** (sn) sink in(to *in acc.*).
Einsitz|er ['~zɪtsər] *m* (7) single-seater; '2ig single-seated.
'**einspannen** stretch (*in e-n Rahmen* in a frame); ⊕ clamp, chuck; *Pferd, a. fig.*: harness (*für, in acc.* to); *j-n*: make *a p.* work; *an den Wagen*: put to.
Einspänner ['~ʃpɛnər] *m* (7) one-horse carriage; F *fig.* recluse.
'**einspar|en** economize; *Material, Zeit*: save; '2ung *f* economization; saving(s *pl.*); economies *pl.*
'**einsperren** lock up.
'**einspielen** *Waage*: (*a. sich*) balance (out); *Geld*: realize, net; *sich* ~ *Sport*: play o.s. in, warm up; *fig.*

S.: get into its stride; *sich aufein-ander* ~ become co-ordinated; *sie sind gut aufeinander eingespielt* they are a fine team.

'**Einsprache** *f* s. *Einspruch.*

'**einsprechen** *v/t.*: *j-m Mut* ~ en-courage a p.; *j-m Trost* ~ comfort a p.; *v/i. s. einreden.*

'**einsprengen** *Wäsche*: sprinkle; *geol.* intersperse (*a. fig.*).

'**einspringen** (*sn*) ⊕ catch, snap; *Stoff*: shrink; (*sich einbiegen*) bend in; *fig.* (*aushelfen*) step in(to the breach), help out; *für j-n* ~ substi-tute (*Am. a.* pinchhit) for a p.; ~ *auf* (*acc.*) fly at; ~*der Winkel* re--entrant angle.

'**einspritz|en** inject; '**2motor** *m* fuel injection engine; '**2ung** *f* in-jection.

'**Einspruch** *m* objection (*a.* ⚖); protest, veto; (*Berufung*) appeal; ~ *erheben* enter a protest (*gegen* against), take exception (to), veto (*gegen et.* a thing); '~**srecht** *n* veto.

einspurig ['~ʃpuːriç] ⛟ single-track; *Straße*: single-lane.

einst [aɪnst] (*vormals*) once; (*künftig*) one (*od.* some) day.

einstampfen ['aɪnʃtampfən] *Schrif-ten*: pulp.

'**Einstand** *m* (*Antritt*) entrance; *Tennis*: deuce.

'**einstechen** prick, puncture; *Nadel*: stick in.

'**einstecken** put in; *in die Tasche, a. Beleidigung*: pocket; *ins Gefäng-nis*: put in; *Schwert*: sheathe.

'**einstehen** (*sn*): ~ *für* answer for.

'**Einsteig|dieb** *m* cat burglar; '~**dieb-stahl** *m* burglary; '**2en** (*sn*) get in; ⛟ *alles* ~! all aboard!

'**einstell|bar** ⊕ adjustable; '~**en** put in; ✕ enrol(l), enlist; *Arbeiter, Hausgehilfin*: engage, *Am.* hire; (*aufgeben*) give up, drop, discon-tinue; *Zahlung, Feindseligkeiten usw.*: suspend, stop; *Mechanismus, a. fig.*: adjust (*auf acc.* to); *Radio*: tune in (to); *Arbeit*: stop; *Fabrik-betrieb*: shut down; *opt., a. fig. Gedanken usw.*: focus (*auf acc.* on); *Auto*: garage; *Rekord*: tie; ✕ *das Feuer* ~ cease fire; *sich* ~ appear, turn up, show up; *Wetter usw.*: set in; *fig. sich* ~ *auf* (*acc.*) adjust (*od.* adapt) o.s. to, *vorbereitend*: prepare for; *sozial usw.* eingestellt

socially *etc.* minded; *eingestellt auf* (*acc.*) prepared for *a th.*, to *inf.*; *eingestellt gegen* opposed to; '~**ig** ♃ of one place *od.* figure; '**2ung** *f* recruiting, enlistment; engagement; suspension; adjustment; strike; focus; *geistig*: mental attitude, men-tality, outlook.

'**einstempeln** clock in.

einstig ['aɪnstiç] (*künftig*) future; (*ehemalig*) former, one-time; (*ver-storben*) late.

'**einstimm|en** chime (*od.* join) in; *fig. a.* agree (*in acc.* to); '~**ig** ♪ of (*od.* for) one voice; (*einmütig*) un-animous; '**2igkeit** *f* unanimity.

einstmals ['aɪnstmɑːls] s. *einst.*

einstöckig ['~ʃtœkiç] one-storied.

'**einstöpseln** ⚡ plug in.

'**einstoßen** push (*od.* thrust) in; *Fensterscheibe usw.*: smash in.

'**einstreichen** *Geld*: pocket.

'**einstreuen** strew in(to *in acc.*); *fig.* intersperse.

'**einströmen** (*sn*) stream (*od.* pour) in.

'**einstudieren** study; *thea. Stück*: rehearse; *Rolle*: get up.

'**einstuf|en** (25) classify; grade, rate; '**2ung** *f* classification; rating; '**2ungs-prüfung** *f* placement test.

'**einstürmen** (*sn*) rush in; *fig. auf j-n* ~ rush at a p., assail a p.

'**Einsturz** *m* falling-in, collapse.

'**einstürzen** *v/i.* (*sn*) fall in, break (*od.* tumble) down, collapse; *fig. auf j-n*: overwhelm.

einstweil|en ['aɪnstvaɪlən] in the meantime; (*für jetzt*) for the present; '~**ig** temporary; ⚖ ~*e Verfügung* re-straining order.

eintägig ['aɪntɛːgiç] one-day.

Eintagsfliege ['~tɑːks-] *f* ephemera (*a. fig.*).

'**eintasten** *Computer*: key in.

'**eintauchen** *v/t. u. v/i.* (*sn*) dip in.

'**eintauschen** exchange, barter (*beide*: *gegen* for).

'**einteil|en** divide (*in acc.* into); (*ver-teilen*) distribute; (*planen*) plan; *in Klassen*: classify; *zeitlich*: time; *zur Arbeit*: assign (to); detail; '~**ig** ['~taɪliç] one-piece; '**2ung** *f* divi-sion; distribution; classification.

eintönig ['~tøːniç] monotonous; '**2keit** *f* monotony.

'**Eintopf(gericht** *n*) *m* hot-pot.

'**Eintracht** *f* harmony, concord.

einträchtig [ˈ‿trɛçtiç] harmonious; peaceful.

Eintrag [ˈ‿trɑːk] *m* (3³) *s*. *Eintragung*; (*Abbruch*) prejudice; (*Schaden*) damage; ‿ *tun* (*dat*.) prejudice, injure; **‿en** [ˈ‿trɑːɡən] *schriftlich*: enter; *amtlich*: register; *als Mitglied*: enrol(l); *Gewinn*: bring in, yield; *sich* ‿ (*P*.) enter one's name; register (*bei* with); *fig. j-m Böses*: bring on.

einträglich [ˈ‿trɛːkliç] profitable.

Eintragung [ˈ‿trɑːɡuŋ] *f* entry; (*Posten*) item; *amtlich*: registration.   [make you pay for it.⎫

'eintränken: *ich werde es dir* ‿ I'll⎰

'eintreffen (sn) arrive; (*geschehen*) happen; *Voraussagung*: come true; **'♀** *n* arrival.

'eintreiben drive in *od*. home; *Schulden, Steuern*: collect.

'eintreten *v/i*. (sn) enter (*in ein Haus* a house); step in; *in das Heer, ein Geschäft usw.*: join; *in ein Amt*: enter on; *in Verhandlungen*: enter into; (*sich ereignen*) occur (*a. Tod*), happen, take place; *Fall, Umstände*: arise; *Wetter usw.*: set in; *für j-n*: answer (*od*. stand up *od*. intercede) for; *v/t. Tür*: kick in; *sich et*. ‿ *run a* th. into one's foot.

eintrichtern [ˈ‿triçtərn] (29) *fig. j-m et*.: drum into a p.'s head.

'Eintritt *m* entry, entrance; (*Einlaß*) admittance; (*Anfang*) beginning; *des Winters usw.*: setting in; ‿ *frei!* admission free!; ‿ *verboten!* no admittance!; **'‿sgeld** *n* entrance-fee; **'‿skarte** *f* admission ticket.

'eintrocknen (sn) dry in *od*. up.

eintunken [ˈ‿tuŋkən] (25) dip in; *Brot usw.*: sop, dunk.

'ein-üben *et*.: (*a. sich*) practise; *j-n*: train, coach, drill.

einverleib|en [ˈ‿fɛrlaɪbən] (25) incorporate (*dat. od. in acc.* in, with); (*aneignen*) annex (to); **'♀ung** *f* incorporation; annexation.

Einver|nehmen [ˈ‿fɛrneːmən] *n* (6), **'‿ständnis** *n* agreement, understanding; *in gutem* ‿ on friendly terms; *sich mit j-m ins* ‿ *setzen* come to an understanding with a p.; **♀standen** [ˈ‿fɛrʃtandən]: ‿! agreed!; (*nicht*) ‿ *sein* (dis)agree.

Einwand [ˈ‿vant] *m* (3³) objection (*gegen* to); ‿ *erheben* raise an objection.

'Einwander|er *m* (7) immigrant; **'♀n** (sn) immigrate; **'‿ung** *f* immigration.

'einwandfrei *adj*. unobjectionable; (*unanfechtbar*) incontestable; (*tadellos*) blameless; ✝ faultless; ‿*e Führung* irreproachable conduct; *nicht* ‿ objectionable; *adv*. absolutely.

einwärts [ˈ‿vɛrts] inward(s).

'einwechseln change; (*tauschen*) exchange.

'Einwegflasche *f* non-returnable bottle.

'einweichen (25) steep, soak.

'einweih|en *eccl*. consecrate; *Denkmal usw.*: inaugurate; *in* (*acc*.) ‿ initiate into, *in ein Geheimnis* ‿ *a.* let into; *eingeweiht* (*Mitwisser*) *sein* be in the secret, F be in the know; **'♀ung** *f* consecration; inauguration; initiation; **'♀ungsfeier** *f* (official) opening.

'einweis|en install (*in ein Amt* in); assign (*in e-e Wohnung* in[to]); (*lenken*) direct; ⚔ *am Boden*: marshal, *in der Luft*: vector; (*unterweisen*) instruct, brief; **'♀ung** *f* installation; assignment; instruction, briefing.

'einwend|en object (*gegen* to); ‿, *daß* ... argue that ...; **'♀ung** *f* objection.

'einwerfen throw in (*a. fig*.); *Fenster*: smash, break; *Bemerkung usw.*: interject; (*einwenden*) object.

'einwickel|n wrap (up), envelop (*in acc.* in); F *fig. j-n*: *sl.* bamboozle; **'♀papier** *n* wrapping paper.

einwillig|en [ˈ‿amviliɡən] consent, agree (*in acc.* to); **'♀ung** *f* consent.

'einwirk|en: *fig.* ‿ *auf* (*acc*) act (up)on; (*angreifen*) affect; (*beeinflussen*) influence, work (up)on *a p.*; **'♀ung** *f* action; effect; influence.

einwöchig [ˈaɪnvœçiç] one-week.

Einwohner [ˈ‿voːnər] *m* (7), **'‿in** *f* inhabitant, resident; **'‿melde-amt** *n* registration office; **'‿schaft** *f* inhabitants *pl*.

'Einwurf *m Sport*: throw-in; *fig*. objection; *für Briefe usw.*: opening, slit; *für Münzen*: slot.

'einwurzeln (sn) take root; *s. eingewurzelt*.

'Einzahl *f* singular (number); **'♀en** pay in; **'‿ung** *f* payment; *Bank*: deposit; **'‿ungsschein** *m* paying-in slip, *Am*. deposit slip.

einzäun|en ['ˌtsɔʏnən] (25) fence in; **ˈ2ung** *f* enclosure; fence.
ˈeinzeichn|en draw in; *sich* ∼ enter one's name; **ˈ2ung** *f* entry.
Einzel ['aɪntsəl] *n s.* **ˌspiel**; **ˈ∼aufhängung** *mot. f* independent suspension; **ˌaufstellung** *f* itemized list; **ˈ∼fall** *m* individual case; **ˈ∼firma ♰** *f* one-man firm; **ˌgänger** *m* outsider, F lone wolf; **ˈ∼haft** *f* solitary confinement; **ˈ∼handel** *m* retail trade; **ˈ∼händler** *m* retailer; **ˈ∼haus** *n* detached house; **ˈ∼heit** *f* particular point, detail, item; **ˌen** *pl.* particulars, details; *bis in alle* **ˌen** down to the smallest detail; **ˈ∼kampf** *m* single combat *od.* fight; **ˈ2n** single; (*besonder*) particular; (*für sich allein*) individual, isolated; (*abgetrennt*) separate; *Schuh usw.*: odd; *im* **ˌen** in detail; ∼ *angeben od. aufführen* specify, *bsd. Am.* itemize; *ins* **ˌe** *gehen* go into detail(s); *der* **2e** the individual; *jeder* **ˌe** each man; each (one); **ˈ2nstehend** *s. allein- stehend*; **ˈ∼persönlichkeit** *f* individual; **ˈ∼spiel** *n Tennis*: single; **ˈ∼teil** *m* component (part); **ˈ∼verkauf** *m* sale by retail; **ˈ∼wesen** *n* individual; **ˈ∼zelle** *f* solitary cell; **ˈ∼zimmer** *n* single room.
einzieh|bar ✘ ['aɪntsiːbaːr] *Fahrgestell:* retractable; **ˈ∼en** *v/t.* draw in; *bsd.* ⊕ retract; *Flagge:* strike; *Segel:* take in; ✘ call up, *Am.* draft, induct; ⚖ seize, confiscate; *Steuer usw.*: collect; *Geldscheine, Münzen:* withdraw; *Erkundigungen* ∼ make inquiries (*über acc.* on, about), gather information (on, about); *v/i.* (*sn*) enter, march in; *in e-e Wohnung:* move in; *Flüssigkeit:* soak in; **ˈ2ung** *f* ✘ calling-up, *Am.* drafting, induction; ⚖ confiscation; collection; withdrawal.
einzig ['aɪntsɪç] *adj.* only; (*einzeln*) single; (*alleinig*) sole; *s. einzigartig*; *der* **ˌe** the only one; *das* **ˌe** the only thing; *adv.* ∼ *und allein* solely; **ˈ∼artig** unique, singular.
ˈEinzimmerwohnung *f* one-room flat (*Am.* apartment).
ˈEinzug *m* entry, entrance; *in ein Haus usw.*: moving-in(to *in acc.*), occupation (of); *v. Truppen:* marching-in; *s. Einziehung*.
ˈeinzwängen squeeze (in).
Eis [aɪs] *n* (4) ice; (*Speise2*) ice-cream; ∼ *am Stiel* ice-lolly; *fig. das* ∼ *brechen* break the ice; *auf* ∼ *legen* put into cold storage (*a. fig.*).
Eis ♪ ['eːʔɪs] *n* E sharp.
ˈEis|bahn *f* skating-rink; **ˈ∼bär** *m* polar bear; **ˈ∼becher** *m* sundae; **ˈ∼bein** *n* pig's knuckles *pl.*; **ˈ∼berg** *m* iceberg; **ˈ∼beutel** *m* ice-bag; **ˈ∼blume** *f am Fenster:* frost-flower; **ˈ∼bombe** *f* ice-cream bombe; **ˈ∼brecher** *m* (7) ice-breaker; **ˈ∼creme** *f* ice-cream; **ˈ∼decke** *f* sheet of ice; **ˈ∼diele** *f* ice-cream parlo(u)r.
Eisen ['aɪzən] *n* (6) iron; (*Huf2*) horseshoe; *altes* ∼ scrap-iron; *zum alten* ∼ *werfen* (*a. fig.*) throw on the scrap-heap; *zwei* ∼ *im Feuer haben* have two strings to one's bow; (*man muß*) *das* ∼ *schmieden, solange es heiß ist* strike the iron while it is hot.
Eisenbahn ['ˌbaːn] *f* railway, *Am.* railroad; *mit der* ∼ by rail, by train; *s. Bahn...*; **ˈ∼abteil** *n* railway compartment; **ˈ∼er** *m* (7) railwayman; **ˈ∼erstreik** *m* rail strike; **ˈ∼knotenpunkt** *m* (railway) junction; **ˈ∼netz** *n* railway (*Am.* railroad) network; **ˈ∼schwelle** *f* sleeper, *Am.* tie; **ˈ∼station** *f* railway (*Am.* railroad) station, *Am. a.* depot; **ˈ∼strecke** *f* (railway) line, *Am.* road; **ˈ∼überführung** *f* railway overpass; **ˈ∼unglück** *n* railway accident, train disaster; **ˈ∼unterführung** *f* railway underpass; **ˈ∼wagen** *m* railway carriage *od.* coach, *Am.* railroad car.
ˈEisen|bergwerk *n* iron mine, iron pit; **ˈ∼beschlag** *m* iron-mounting; **ˈ∼beton** *m* reinforced concrete; **ˈ∼blech** *n* sheet-iron; **ˈ∼erz** *n* iron-ore; **ˈ∼gießerei** *f* iron-foundry; **ˈ∼guß** *m* iron casting; (*Gußeisen*) cast iron; **ˈ2haltig** ferruginous; **ˈ∼hammer** *m* iron-works *sg.*; **ˈ2hart** (as) hard as iron; **ˈ∼hütte** *f* iron- -works *sg.*; **ˈ∼oxyd** *n* ferric oxide; **ˈ∼stange** *f* iron rod; **ˈ∼träger** *m* iron girder; **ˈ∼vitriol** *m*, *n* green vitriol; **ˈ∼waren** *f/pl.* ironware, *bsd. Am.* hardware; **ˈ∼warenhändler** *m* ironmonger, *Am.* hardware dealer; **ˈ∼warenhandlung** *f* ironmonger's (shop), *Am.* hardware store; **ˈ∼werk** *n* iron-work; *Fabrik:* iron-works *pl. od. sg.*
eisern ['aɪzərn] (*of*) iron (*a. fig.*); *fig. Gesundheit:* cast-iron; **ˌe** *Ra-*

tion iron ration; ~er *Bestand* permanent stock; ~er *Fleiß* untiring industry; ~er *Wille* iron will; *s. Besen, Lunge, Vorhang.*

'**eis|frei** free from ice; '~**gang** *m* ice-drift; '~**gekühlt** iced; '~**grau** hoary; '2**heiligen** *m/pl.* Ice Saints; '2**hockey** *n Sport:* ice-hockey.

eisig ['aızıç] icy, glacial (*a. fig.*).

'**eis|kalt** icy-cold; *fig.* cool; '2**kunstlauf** *m* figure skating; '2**lauf(en** *n) m* skating; '2**läufer(in** *f) m* skater; '2**maschine** *f* ice-machine; '2**meer** *n* polar sea; *Nördliches* ~ Arctic, *Südliches* ~ Antarctic Ocean; '2**pickel** *m* ice-ax(e).

'**Ei-sprung** *biol. m* ovulation.

'**Eis|revue** *f* ice-show; '~**schießen** *n* curling; '~**schnellauf** *m* speed skating; '~**scholle** *f* ice-floe; '~**schrank** *m* refrigerator, icebox; '~**segeln** *n* ice-yachting; '~**stockschießen** *n* curling; '~**verkäufer** *m* ice-cream man; '~**verkäuferin** *f* ice-cream lady; '~**würfel** *m* ice-cube; '~**zapfen** *m* icicle; '~**zeit** *f* ice-age, glacial epoch.

eitel ['aıtəl] vain (*auf acc.* of); *fig.* (*leer*) vain, empty; (*fruchtlos*) vain, futile; (*bloß*) mere; *eitles Gerede* idle talk; ~ *Gold* pure gold; *eitle Hoffnung* idle (*od.* vain) hope; '2**keit** *f* vanity.

Eiter ['aıtər] *m* (7) matter, pus; '~**beule** *f* abscess; '~**pfropf** *m* core; '~**pustel** *f* pustule.

eit(e)rig ['aıt(ə)rıç] purulent.

'**eiter|n** (29) fester, discharge matter, ⬚ suppurate; '2**ung** *f* suppuration.

'**Eiweiß** *n* (3²) white of egg, ⬚ albumen; '2**-arm** low in protein, low-protein *attr.*; 2**haltig** ['~haltıç] albuminous; '2**reich** high in protein, high-protein *attr.*; '~**stoff** *m* albumen.

Ekel ['e:kəl] **1.** *m* (7) disgust (*vor dat.* at), nausea; *er ist mir ein* ~ he is my aversion; **2.** *n* F *Person:* nasty fellow, pest; '2**haft**, '**ek(e)lig** nauseous, disgusting; nasty; '2**n** (29) disgust, sicken; *sich* ~ *vor* (*dat.*) loathe, be disgusted with *od.* at; be nauseated at.

eklatant [ekla'tant] spectacular; (*auffällig*) striking.

Eksta|se [ɛk'staːzə] *f* (15) ecstasy;

2**tisch** ecstatic(ally *adv.*).

Ekzem ⬚ [ɛk'tseːm] *n* (3¹) eczema.

Elan [e'lã] *m* (11) élan (*fr.*), verve, vim, dash, spirit.

elast|isch [e'lastıʃ] elastic; 2**izität** [~tsi'tɛːt] *f* elasticity.

Elch *zo.* [ɛlç] *m* (3) elk.

Elefant [ele'fant] *m* (12) elephant; F ~ *im Porzellanladen* bull in a china shop; *s. Mücke;* ~**enrüssel** *m* elephant's trunk; ~**enzahn** *m* elephant's tusk.

elegan|t [ele'gant] elegant (*a. fig.*), fashionable; *Kleidung:* a. stylish, smart; 2**z** *f* (16) elegance.

Elegie [ele'giː] *f* (15) elegy.

elegisch [e'leːgıʃ] elegiac.

elektrifizier|en [elɛktrifi'tsiːrən] electrify; 2**ung** *f* electrification.

E'lektriker *m* (7) electrician.

e'lektrisch electric(al).

elektrisier|en [~zi'rən] electrify (*a. fig.*); 2**maschine** *f* electrical machine.

Elektrizität [~tsi'tɛːt] *f* (16) electricity; ~**sgesellschaft** *f* electric supply company; ~**swerk** *n* (electric) power station; ~**szähler** *m* electricity meter.

Elektro|chemie [elɛktroçe'miː] *f* electrochemistry; 2**chemisch** [~'çeːmıʃ] electrochemical.

Elektrode [elɛk'troːdə] *f* (15) electrode.

Elektro|dy'namik *f* electrodynamics *sg.*; ~**geschäft** [e'lɛktro-] *n* electrical shop; ~**herd** *m* electric range; ~**ingenieur** *m* electrical engineer; ~**installateur** *m* electrician; ~**lyse** [~'lyːzə] *f* electrolysis; ~**motor** *m* (electric) motor.

Elektron ⚡ [e'lɛktrɔn] *n* (8¹) electron; ~**enblitz** [~'troːnən-] *phot. m* electronic flash; ~**engehirn** *n* electronic brain; ~**enmikroskop** *n* electron microscope; ~**enröhre** *f* electron valve (*Am.* tube); ~**entechnik** *f*, ~**ik** [elɛk'troːnik] *f* (16, *o. pl.*) electronics *sg.*; 2**isch** electronic; ~**e** *Datenverarbeitung* electronic data processing.

E'lektro|rasenmäher *m* electric lawn-mower; ~**rasierer** *m* electric razor; ~**technik** *f* electrical engineering; ~**techniker** *m* electrical engineer; 2**technisch** electrotechnical.

Element [ele'mɛnt] *n* (3) *allg.* element; ⚡ *a.* cell.

elementar [ˌtɑːr] elementary; ∼e *Gewalt* elemental force; ♀**klasse** *f* junior form; ♀**schule** *f* elementary (*a.* primary, *Am.* grade) school; ♀**unterricht** *m* elementary instruction.

Elen [ˈeːlɛn] *m, n* (6), '∼**tier** *n* elk.

Elend [ˈeːlɛnt] **1.** *n* (3, *o.pl.*) misery; (*Not*) need, distress; F *das graue* ∼ the blues *sg.*; *s.* stürzen; **2.** ♀ miserable, wretched (*beide a. contp.*); ∼ *aussehen* look very poorly; *sich* ∼ *fühlen* feel miserable *od.* wretched; '∼**sviertel** *n* slums *pl.*

elf [ɛlf] **1.** eleven; **2.** ♀ *f* (16) *Fußball*: eleven, team.

Elf *m* (12), ∼**e** [ˈɛlfə] *f* (15) elf, fairy. '**Elfenbein** *n*, '♀**ern** ivory.

Elf'**meter** *m Fußball*: penalty kick; ∼**marke** *f* penalty spot; ∼**schießen** *n* sudden-death play-off; ∼**tor** *n* penalty goal.

'**elfte** eleventh; '♀**l** *n* (6) eleventh (part); '∼**ns** in the eleventh place.

Elite [eˈliːtə] *f* (15) *the* élite (*fr.*); ∼**denken** *n* elitism.

Elixier [eliˈksiːr] *n* (3¹) elixir.

'**Ellbogen** *m* elbow; '∼**freiheit** *f* elbow-room.

Elle [ˈɛlə] *f* (15) yard; *anat.* ulna; '♀**n**'**lang** *fig.* incredibly long (*Person*: tall); interminable.

Ellip|**se** [ɛˈlɪpsə] *f* (15) ⅋ ellipse; *gr.* ellipsis; ♀**tisch** elliptic(al).

Elsäss|**er** [ˈɛlzɛsər] *m* (7), '∼**erin** *f* (16¹), '♀**isch** Alsatian.

Elster [ˈɛlstər] *f* (15) magpie.

elter|**lich** [ˈɛltərlɪç] parental; '♀**n** *pl. inv.* parents; '♀**n**-**abend** *m* parent-teacher meeting; '♀**nbeirat** *m* Parents' Council; '∼**nlos** parentless, without parents; '♀**nsprechstunde** *f* consultation hour (for parents); '♀**nsprechtag** *m* open day (for parents).

Email [eˈmɑːj] *n* (11), ∼**le** [*a.* eˈmaljə] *f* (15), ♀**lieren** [ema(l)ˈjiːrən] enamel.

Émanze [eˈmantsə] F *f* (15) women's libber.

Emanzi|**pation** *f* [emantsipaˈtsjoːn] *f* emancipation; ∼**pationsbewegung** *f* emancipatory movement; ♀**patorisch** [ˌtoˈriʃ] emancipatory; ♀**i**'**pieren** emancipate.

Embargo [ɛmˈbargo] *n* (11) (*Ausfuhrverbot*) embargo.

Embolie ⚕ [ɛmboˈliː] *f* (15) embolism.

Embryo *biol.* [ˈɛmbryo] *m* (8¹) embryo; ♀**nal** [ˌˈnɑːl] embryonic.

Emigr|**ant** [emiˈgrant] *m* (12) emigrant; ♀**ieren** [ˌgriːrən] emigrate.

Emotion [emoˈtsjoːn] *f* emotion; ♀**al** [ˌtsjoˈnɑːl], ♀**ell** [ˌnɛl] emotional; ♀**sgeladen** emotionally charged.

empfahl [ɛmˈpfɑːl] *pret. v. empfehlen*.

Empfang [ɛmˈpfaŋ] *m* (3³) reception (*a. Radio*); *e-s Briefes usw.*: receipt; *nach (od. bei)* ∼ (*gen.*) on receipt of; *in* ∼ *nehmen* receive; ♀**en** *v/t.* (30) receive; *freundlich*: *a.* welcome; *v/i.* (*schwanger werden*) conceive.

Empfänger [ˌˈpfɛŋər] *m* (7) *P. u. Gerät*: receiver; *v. Waren*: consignee; *e-s Briefes*: addressee.

em'**pfänglich** impressionable; susceptible (*für* to); receptive (to, of); ♀**keit** *f* susceptibility.

Em'**pfängnis** *f* (14²) conception; ♀**verhütend** ∼**es** *Mittel* contraceptive; ∼**verhütung** *f* contraception.

Em'**pfangs**|**bereich** *m Radio*: reception area; ∼**bescheinigung** *f* receipt; ∼**chef** *m* reception (*Am.* room) clerk; ∼**dame** *f*, ∼**herr** *m* receptionist; ∼**gerät** *n* receiving set; ∼**schein** *m* receipt; ∼**station** *f Radio*: receiving station; ∼**tag** *m* at-home; ∼**zimmer** *n* reception-room.

empfehlen [ɛmˈpfeːlən] (30) (*als geeignet* ∼) recommend; (*anvertrauen*) (re)commend; ∼ *Sie mich* (*dat.*) please remember me to; *sich j-m* ∼ present one's respects (*od.* compliments) to; *sich* ∼ (*gehen*) take leave; *S.*: commend itself; *es empfiehlt sich* it is (re)commendable; ∼**swert** (re)commendable.

Em'**pfehlung** *f* recommendation; (*Gruß*) compliments *pl.*; ∼**sschreiben** *n* letter of recommendation.

empfinden [ˌˈpfɪndən] (30) feel (*als lästig usw.* to be troublesome *etc.*); (*gewahren*) perceive, sense.

empfindlich [ˌˈpfɪntlɪç] sensitive (*a. phot.*, ♪, ⊕; *für*, *gegen* to); *pred. a.* susceptible (*gegen* to); (*zart*) delicate; (*reizbar*) irritable; (*leicht gekränkt*) touchy; (*fühlbar*) sensible; *Kälte, Strafe, Verlust*: severe; *Kränkung*: grievous; *Schmerz*: acute; *fig. s-e* ∼**ste** *Stelle* his sore spot; ♀**keit** *f* sensitiveness; irritability; sensibility; touchiness; delicacy.

empfindsam [~'pfintzɑːm] sensitive; sentimental; ♀**keit** f sensitiveness; sentimentality.

Empfindung [~'pfinduŋ] f sensation; (*Wahrnehmung*) perception; *weitS.* feeling; ♀**slos** insensitive (*für, gegen* to); insensible; *bsd. fig.* unfeeling; ~**slosigkeit** f insensitiveness (*für, gegen* to); insensibility; ~**svermögen** n sensitive (*od.* perceptive) faculty.

empfohlen [ɛm'pfoːlən] *p.p. v.* empfehlen.

empor [ɛm'poːr] up, upwards; ~**arbeiten:** *sich* ~ work one's way up; ~**blicken** look up (*zu* to).

Empore △ [ɛm'poːrə] f (15) gallery.

empören [ɛm'pøːrən] (*aufbringen*) (rouse to) anger, incense; scandalize, shock; *sich* ~ revolt, rebel (*beide a. fig.; über acc.* at); (*zornig werden*) grow furious; **empört** indignant, shocked, scandalized (*über acc.* at); ~**d** outrageous; shocking.

Em'pörer m (7), ~**in** f insurgent, rebel; ♀**isch** rebellious, mutinous.

em'por|kommen (sn) rise (in the world); ♀**kömmling** m upstart; ~**ragen** (h.) tower (*über acc.* above), rise; ~**schießen** (sn) shoot up; *sich* ~**schwingen** rise, soar up; ~**steigen** (sn) rise, ascend; ~**streben** (h.) strive upward(s); *fig.* aspire (*zu* to); ~**treiben** force up(wards).

Empörung [ɛm'pøːruŋ] f rebellion, revolt; (*Unwille*) indignation.

emsig ['ɛmziç] (*tätig*) busy, active; (*fleißig*) industrious, assiduous; ♀**keit** f industry, activity; assiduity.

Emulsion [emul'zjoːn] f (16) emulsion.

End-abnehmer ['ɛntʔapneːmər] m, ~**in** f ultimate buyer, consumer.

Ende ['ɛndə] n (10) *allg.* end; *zeitlich a.* close; (*Ergebnis*) *a.* upshot; *am Geweih:* antler; *am* ~ at (*od.* in) the end, (*doch*) after all, (*schließlich*) eventually, at length, (*vielleicht*) perhaps, maybe; *s.* dick; *zu* ~ gehen (come to an) end, (*ablaufen*) expire, (*knapp werden*) run short; *zu* ~ *sein* be at an end; *s.* Weisheit; *e-r S. ein* ~ *machen* put an end to; *ein böses* ~ *nehmen* come to a bad end.

'enden (26) *v/t. s.* beend(ig)en; *v/i.* (h.) end, terminate; (*aufhören*) cease, finish; *nicht* ~ *wollend* unending.

Endergebnis ['ɛntʔɛrgeːpnis] n final

result, upshot.

Endes-unterzeichnete ['ɛndəs-] m, f (18) *the* undersigned.

'Endfassung f final version.

endgültig ['ɛnt-] final, definitive, conclusive.

'Endhaltestelle f terminus.

endigen ['ɛndigən] (25) *s.* enden; *gr.* ~ *auf* (*acc.*) terminate in.

Endivie ♀ [ɛn'diːvjə] f (15) endive.

End|kampf ['ɛntkampf] m *Sport:* final (contest); '~**lagerung** f final storage; '~**lauf** m final (heat).

'endlich *adj.* final, ultimate; *phls.* finite; *adv.* finally, at last, at length; ~ *doch* after all; '♀**keit** f finiteness.

'end|los endless (*a.* ⊕); '♀**losigkeit** f endlessness; '♀**montage** f final assembly; '♀**phase** f final stage; '♀**produkt** n end (*od.* final) product; '♀**punkt** m final point; '♀**reim** m end-rhyme; '♀**resultat** n final result, upshot; '♀**runde** f *Sport:* final; '♀**rundenteilnehmer(in** f) m *Sport:* finalist; '♀**silbe** f final syllable; '♀**spiel** n final (match); '♀**spurt** ['~ʃpurt] m *Sport:* final spurt, finish; '♀**station** 🚇 f terminus, *Am.* terminal; '♀**summe** f (sum) total.

Endung ['ɛnduŋ] f ending.

End|verbraucher ✝ ['ɛnt-] m ultimate consumer; '~**ziel** n, '~**zweck** m ultimate object.

Energie [enɛr'giː] f (15) energy; ~**bedarf** m energy requirement; ~**krise** f energy crisis; ♀**los** lacking (in) energy; ~**quelle** f source of energy; ~**sparen** n energy saving; ♀**sparend** energy-saving; ~**sparmaßnahme** f energy-saving measure; ~**träger** m energy source; ~**verbrauch** m energy consumption; ~**verschwendung** f waste of energy; ~**wirtschaft** f power industry; ~**zufuhr** f energy supply.

e'nergisch energetic(ally *adv.*); ~ *werden* put one's foot down.

eng [ɛŋ] narrow; *Kleidung:* tight; (~ *anliegend*) clinging; (*dicht; nah*) close; (*innig*) intimate; ~ *befreundet sein* be great friends; ~ *sitzen* (*od.* stehen) sit (*od.* stand) closely together; *im* ~*eren Sinne* strictly speaking; *s.* Wahl.

Engag|ement [ãgaʒ'mã] n (11) engagement; *fig.* commitment; ♀**ieren** [~'ʒiːrən] engage, *Am. a.* hire; ♀**iert** *fig.* committed.

Enge ['ɛŋə] f (15) narrowness; *der Kleidung*: tightness; (*Engpaß*) bottle-neck (*a. fig.*); *fig.* straits *pl.*; *in die ~ treiben* corner.

Engel ['ɛŋəl] m (7) angel; '2**haft** angelic; '~**macher(in** f) m back-street abortionist; '~**sgeduld** f angelic patience.

Engerling ['ɛŋərliŋ] m (3¹) grub of the cockchafer.

'**engherzig** narrow-minded, hidebound.

Engländer ['ɛŋlɛndər] m (7) Englishman, *Am. a.* Britisher; *pl.* (*als Volk*) *the* English; ⊕ m (*Schraubenschlüssel*) monkey-wrench; '~**in** f (16¹) Englishwoman.

englisch ['ɛŋliʃ] English; *weitS.* British; *~e Kirche* Church of England, English (*od.* Anglican) Church; *~e Krankheit* rickets *pl. od. sg.*; *~es Pflaster* court-plaster; 2 n: *ins ~e* into English; *aus dem ~en* from (the) English.

engmaschig ['ɛŋmaʃiç] close-meshed.

'**Engpaß** m defile, narrow pass, *Am. a.* notch; *bsd. fig.* bottle-neck.

en gros [ã'gro:], **En'gros...** wholesale.

engstirnig ['ɛŋʃtirniç] narrow-minded.

Enkel ['ɛŋkəl] m (7) grandchild; (*~sohn*) grandson; *weitS.* (*Nachkomme*) descendant; '~**in** f (16¹) granddaughter.

enorm [e'nɔrm] enormous; F (*famos*) terrific.

Ensemble *thea.* [ã'sã:bl(ə)] n (11) ensemble; (*Besetzung*) cast.

ent'-art|en [ɛnt-] (26) degenerate; *~et* degenerate; decadent; 2**ung** f degeneration. [of, part with.}

ent'-äußern: *sich e-r S. ~* dispose{

entbehr|en [ɛnt'be:rən] (25) (*nicht haben, vermissen*) lack, miss, want; (*auskommen ohne*) dispense with, do without; *ich kann ihn nicht ~* I cannot spare him; *~lich* dispensable; 2**ung** f want, privation.

ent'bieten: *j-m s-n Gruß ~* present one's compliments to a p.; *j-n zu sich ~* send for, summon.

ent'binden dispense, release (*von* from); *Frau*: deliver (of).

Ent'bindung f dispensation, release (*von* from); *e-r Frau*: delivery; *~s-anstalt* f, *~s-heim* n maternity

hospital (*od.* clinic); *~ssaal* m delivery room; *~sstation* f delivery ward.

ent'blättern strip of leaves; *sich ~* shed its leaves; F *fig.* strip.

entblöden [ɛnt'blø:dən] (26): *sich nicht ~ zu inf.* not to be ashamed to *inf.*

entblöß|en [~'blø:sən] (27) denude, strip (*gen.* of); *das Haupt*: uncover; ✕ expose; *~t* bare; *fig.* destitute (*gen.* of); 2**ung** f denudation; *fig.* destitution.

ent'brennen (sn) *fig.* be inflamed (*in Liebe zu j-m* with love for a p.); *Zorn*: blaze up; *Kampf usw.*: break out, flare up.

ent'decken discover; (*herausfinden*) detect; (*aufdecken*) reveal; *sich j-m ~* confide in a p.

Ent'decker m (7), *~in* f discoverer.

Ent'deckung f discovery; *~sreise* f voyage of discovery, expedition.

Ente ['ɛntə] f (15) duck; *fig.* (*Zeitungs2*) canard, hoax.

entehr|en [ɛnt'⁹e:rən] dishono(u)r; *~end* dishono(u)ring, disgraceful; 2**ung** f disgrace; degradation.

enteign|en [~'⁹aignən] (25) *j-n, et.*: expropriate; *j-n*: dispossess; 2**ung** f expropriation; dispossession.

ent'-eilen (sn) hasten away.

enteis|en [~'⁹aizən] *mot.*, ✈ *usw.* de-ice; 2**ungs-anlage** f de-icer.

'**Enten|braten** m roast duck; '~**jagd** f duck-shooting.

'**Enterbeil** ⚓ n boarding-ax(e).

ent'-erb|en disinherit; 2**ung** f disinheritance.

'**Enterhaken** ⚓ m grapnel.

Enterich ['ɛntəriç] m (3) drake.

entern ['ɛntərn] (29) board, grapple.

entfachen [ɛnt'faxən] (25) kindle.

ent'fahren (sn): *j-m ~* drop from a p.'s *hand etc.*

ent'fallen *v/i.* (sn): *j-m ~* escape a p.; *fig.* slip a p.'s memory; *s. wegfallen*; (*nicht in Frage kommen*) be inapplicable; *auf j-n ~* fall to a p.'s share.

ent'falt|en (*a. sich*) unfold; *fig.* (*a. sich*) develop (*zu* into); (*zeigen*) display; ✕ *Truppen*: deploy; 2**ung** f display; development.

ent'färbe|n decolorize; (*bleichen*) bleach; *sich ~ s. verfärben*; 2**r** m (7) decolorant.

entfern|en [~'fɛrnən] (25) *allg.* remove; *bsd. Fleck*: take out; *sich ~*

withdraw; ~t distant, remote (a. fig. Ähnlichkeit usw.); weit davon~ zu inf. far from ger.; nicht im ~esten not in the least; 2ung f removal; (Abstand, Ferne) distance; (Reichweite) range; in e-r gewissen~ at a distance; 2ungsmesser m range-finder.

ent'fessel|n unchain; fig. unleash; 2ungskünstler m escape artist.

entfetten [~'fɛtən] (26) degrease; Wolle: scour.

Entfettungskur [ɛnt'fɛtuŋskuːr] f slimming-cure.

ent'flammen inflame.

ent'flecht|en ✝ decartelize; 2ung f decartelization.

ent'fliegen (sn) fly away (dat. from).

ent'fliehen (sn) flee, escape (aus od. dat. from); Zeit: fly.

entfremd|en [~'frɛmdən] (26) estrange, alienate (j-m from a p.); 2ung f estrangement, alienation.

entfrosten [~'frɔstən] (26) defrost.

ent'führ|en carry off; ein Mädchen: elope with; mit Gewalt: abduct, bsd. Kind: kidnap; Flugzeug: hijack, F skyjack; 2er m (7), 2erin f abductor, kidnap(p)er; (Flugzeug2) hijacker, F skyjacker; 2ung f abduction, kidnap(p)ing; elopement; hijacking.

entgasen [ɛnt'gaːzən] (27) degas.

entgegen [ɛnt'geːgən] 1. adv., prp. (dat.) Gegensatz: in opposition to, contrary to; Richtung: towards; 2. adj. s. entgegengesetzt; ~arbeiten counteract, work against, oppose (e-r S. a th., j-m a p.); ~bringen j-m et.: carry towards a p.; j-m ein Gefühl ~ meet a p. with a feeling; ~-eilen (sn) hasten to meet; ~gehen (sn) go to meet (a p.); e-r Gefahr, e-r Zukunft: face, be in for (a th.); dem Ende ~ be drawing to a close; ~gesetzt opposite; fig. contrary, opposed (dat. to); ~halten (einwenden) object; zum Vergleich: contrast (e-r S. et. anderes a th. with another th.); ~handeln act against; e-m Gesetz usw.: contravene (a th.); ~kommen (sn) come to meet (a p.); fig. j-m ~ meet a p.('s wishes) halfway; 2kommen n obligingness; ~kommend adj. obliging, accommodating; ~laufen (sn) run to meet (a p.); ~nehmen accept, receive; ~sehen look forward to, expect (a th.); e-r baldigen Antwort ~d awaiting an early reply; ~setzen

oppose (dat. to); Widerstand: put up; ~stehen (h.) be opposed (dat. to); (ausschließen) bar; ~stellen oppose (dat. to); fig. sich e-r S. ~ set o.s. against; ~strecken hold out (dat. to); ~treten (sn) meet (a p.), face (a. e-r Gefahr); feindlich: oppose a p.; ~wirken s. entgegenarbeiten.

entgegn|en [~'geːgnən] (25) reply; return; schlagfertig: retort; 2ung f reply; retort.

ent'gehen (sn) escape (j-m a p.; e-r S. [from] a th.); fig. j-m ~ escape a p.('s notice); sich die Gelegenheit ~ lassen miss one's opportunity.

entgeistert [~'gaistərt] aghast.

Entgelt [ɛnt'gɛlt] n (3) (Lohn) recompense, remuneration; (vertragliche Gegenleistung) consideration; (Ersatz) compensation; gegen ~ for a (valuable) consideration; 2en (büßen) atone (od. suffer) for.

ent'giften decontaminate (a. fig.).

entgleis|en [~'glaizən] (27 sn) run off the rails, be derailed; fig. (make a) slip; ~ lassen derail; 2ung f derailment; fig. slip, faux pas (fr.).

ent'gleiten (sn) slip (dat. from).

entgräten [~'grɛːtən] (26) bone.

ent'haaren (25) depilate.

Ent'haarungsmittel n depilatory.

ent'halt|en contain, hold, include; sich ~ (gen.) abstain (od. refrain) from; er konnte sich des Lachens nicht ~ he could not help laughing; 2ung f abstention; ~sam abstinent; (keinen Alkohol trinkend) teetotal; 2samkeit f abstinence; teetotalism.

ent'härten ⊕ soften; metall. anneal.

enthaupt|en [ɛnt'hauptən] (26) behead, decapitate; 2ung f beheading, decapitation.

ent'heb|en (gen.) relieve of; e-r Pflicht usw.: exempt from; des Amtes: remove from, vorläufig: suspend from; 2ung f relief; exemption; removal.

ent'heilig|en profane, desecrate; 2ung f profanation, desecration.

ent'hemmen: j-n ~ free a p. from his (od. her) inhibitions.

ent'hüll|en uncover; Gesicht, Denkmal, a. fig.; unveil; fig. reveal, disclose; (zeigen) show; (aufdecken) expose; 2ung f unveiling; fig. revelation, disclosure; exposure.

enthülsen [~'hylzən] (27) husk.

Enthusias|mus [ɛntuzi'asmus] *m* (16²) enthusiasm; **~t** *m* (12), **~tin** *f* enthusiast; *für Film, Sport:* F fan; **2tisch** enthusiastic(ally *adv.*).

ent'jungfer|n (25) deflower; **2ung** *f* defloration.

ent'kalken (25) decalcify; *Boiler etc.:* descale.

ent'keimen *v/t.* sterilize; *v/i.* & germinate, sprout (*dat.* from); *fig.* spring (from).

entkernen [~'kɛrnən] (25) stone; *Äpfel:* core.

ent'kleiden unclothe; (*a. fig.*) strip (*gen.* of); (*a. sich*) undress; *bsd. fig.* divest (*gen.* of).

ent'kommen 1. (sn) escape (*j-m* a p.; *aus* from), get away (*od.* off); **2.** ♀ *n* escape, getaway.

entkorken [~'kɔrkən] (25) uncork.

entkräft|en [~'krɛftən] (26) enfeeble, debilitate; ♯♯ (*ungültig machen*) invalidate; (*widerlegen*) refute; **~et** exhausted; **2ung** *f* enfeeblement, debilitation; ♯♯ invalidation; refutation.

ent'lad|en unload; (*bsd.* ✈, ⚡; *a. sich*) discharge; *sich ~ Wolke usw.:* burst; *Gewehr:* go off; **2erampe** *f* unloading platform; **2ung** *f* unloading; discharge; *fig.* explosion; *zur ~ bringen* explode.

ent'lang along; *hier ~!* this way.

entlarv|en [ɛnt'larfən] (25) unmask, *fig. a.* expose; **2ung** *f* unmasking; *fig.* exposure.

ent'lass|en dismiss; *bsd.* ✕, ✈, ♯♯ discharge; *Gefangene:* release; **2ung** *f* dismissal; discharge; **2ungsgesuch** *n* resignation; **2ungspapiere** *n/pl.* discharge papers; **2ungszeugnis** *n Schule:* school-leaving certificate.

ent'lasten unburden; (*befreien*) relieve (*von* of); ♯♯ clear, exonerate; ✝ *Vorstand usw.:* discharge; *j-n für et. ~* credit a p. with.

Ent'lastung *f* relief; exoneration; ✝ discharge; credit (*of* a p.'s account); **~sstraße** *f* by-pass (road); **~szeuge** *m* witness for the defen|ce, *Am.* -se; **~szug** *m* relief train.

ent'laub|en (25) defoliate; **2ung** *f* defoliation.

ent'laufen (sn) run away (*dat.* from).

entlausen [~'lauzən] delouse.

entledig|en [ɛnt'le:digən] (25) release (*gen.* from); *sich j-s, e-r S. ~* rid o.s. (*od.* get rid) of; *e-r Pflicht, e-s Auftrags:* acquit o.s. of; **2ung** *f* release; *fig.* discharge.

ent'leeren empty.

ent'legen remote, distant, out-of--the-way; **2heit** *f* remoteness.

ent'lehnen borrow (*dat.* of, from).

entleiben [~'laɪbən] (25): *sich ~* commit suicide.

ent'leihen *s. entlehnen.*

ent'lob|en *sich ~* break off one's engagement; **2ung** *f* disengagement.

ent'locken draw, elicit (*dat.* from).

ent'lohn|en pay (off); **2ung** *f* pay (-ing off); *s. Entgelt.*

ent'lüften evacuate the air from; (*lüften*) air, ventilate.

entmachten [~'maxtən] (26) deprive a p. of *his* power.

entmagneti'sieren demagnetize.

entmann|en [~'manən] (25) castrate; *fig.* emasculate; **2ung** *f* castration; emasculation.

entmenscht [~'mɛnʃt] inhuman, brutish.

entmilitarisier|en [~militari'zi:rən] demilitarize; **2ung** *f* demilitarization.

entmündigen [~'myndigən] (25) ♯♯ incapacitate, put under tutelage *od.* restraint.

entmutig|en [~'mu:tigən] (25) discourage; **2ung** *f* discouragement.

Entnahme [~'na:mə] *f* (15) taking; *v. Geld:* drawing, withdraw; ✝ *bei ~ von* by taking *od.* ordering.

ent'nehmen take (*dat.* from); *Geld:* (with)draw (*aus* from); *e-m Buch usw.:* draw, borrow (*dat.* from); *fig.* (*schließen, erfahren*) gather, learn (*dat. od. aus* from); (*folgern*) infer (from).

entnerven [ɛnt'nɛrfən] (25) enervate, unnerve.

ent'-ölen free from oil.

entpuppen [~'pupən] (25): *sich ~* burst the cocoon; *fig.* reveal o.s.; *sich ~ als* turn out to be.

ent'rahmen skim.

enträtseln [~'rɛ:tsəln] (29) puzzle out, solve; (*entziffern*) decipher.

ent'recht|en: *j-n ~* deprive a p. of his (own) rights; **2ung** *f* deprivation of rights.

Entree [ã'tre:] *n* (11) entrance money.

ent'reißen *j-m et.*: tear *od.* snatch (away) from a p.; *a. fig.* wrench from; *dem Tode usw.*: save from.

ent'richt|en pay; ℒung *f* payment.

ent'ringen: *j-m et.* ~ wrest a th. from a p.; *sich j-s Lippen usw.* ~ escape from.

ent'rinnen (sn) escape (*dat.* from).

ent'rollen *v/i.* (sn) roll (down) (*dat.* from); *v/t.* (*a.* sich) unroll; *Fahne, Segel usw.*: unfurl; *ein Bild von et.* ~ unfold a picture of a th.

ent'rücken remove (*dat.* from).

entrümpeln [~'rympəln] (29) clear of lumber.

ent'rüst|en fill with indignation, anger; (*schockieren*) scandalize, shock; *sich* ~ become angry *od.* indignant, be scandalized (*über acc.* at); ℒung *f* anger, indignation (*über acc.* at *a th.*; with *a p.*).

ent'saft|en (26) extract the juice (from); ℒer *m* (7) liquidizer.

ent'sag|en (*dat.*) renounce, resign; *dem Thron* ~ abdicate; ℒung *f* renunciation, resignation; abdication.

Ent'satz *m* relief.

ent'schädig|en *j-n*: indemnify, compensate; *für et.* ~ make up (*od.* compensate) for a th.; ℒung *f* indemnity, compensation.

ent'schärfen *Bombe usw.*: deactivate.

Entscheid [~'ʃaɪt] *m* ⚖ decree; *s. a.* Entscheidung; ℒen [~'ʃaɪdən] decide; *sich* ~ *Sache*: be decided, *P.*: decide (*für, gegen, über acc.* for, against, on); ℒend decisive.

Ent'scheidung *f* decision; *der Geschworenen*: verdict; *e-s Schiedsgerichts*: award; (*gerichtliche Verfügung*) ruling; *eine* ~ *treffen* come to (*od.* take) a decision; ~s... decisive; ~sspiel *n* Sport: deciding game, tie; (*Endspiel*) final.

entschieden [ɛnt'ʃiːdən] decided; (*entschlossen*) determined, firm; *adv.* decidedly; firmly; ℒheit *f* determination.

ent'schlafen (sn) fall asleep; *fig.* die, pass away; *der (die)* ℒe the deceased.

entschleiern [~'ʃlaɪərn] (29) unveil.

ent'schließ|en: *sich* ~ decide, determine (*zu et.* on; *zu tun* to do), make up one's mind (to do); ℒung *f s.* Entschluß.

entschlossen [~'ʃlɔsən] resolute, determined; ℒheit *f* determination.

ent'schlüpfen (sn) *s.* entfallen, entgehen.

Ent'schluß *m* resolve, resolution; (*Entscheidung*) decision, determination; *zu e-m* ~ *kommen* come to a decision; *zu dem* ~ *kommen, zu inf.* make up one's mind to *inf.*

ent'schlüsseln decipher, decode.

Ent'schlußkraft *f* determination, strength of purpose, initiative.

ent'schuldbar [~'ʃult-] excusable.

entschuldig|en [~'ʃuldigən] (25) excuse; *sich* ~ *a.* apologize (*bei j-m* to a p.; *für et.* for a th.); *sich* ~ *lassen* beg to be excused; *es läßt sich nicht* ~ it admits (*od.* allows) of no excuse; ℒung *f* excuse; apology; *Schule*: excuse note; *ich bitte (Sie) um* ~ (I am) sorry!; *als* (*od.* zur) ~ *für* in excuse of; ℒungsgrund *m* excuse.

Ent'schuldung *f* liquidation of *a p.'s* indebtedness.

ent'schwinden (sn) disappear, vanish (*dat.* from); *j-s Gedächtnis* ~ slip a p.'s memory.

entseelt [~'zeːlt] dead, lifeless.

ent'senden send off; *als Vertreter* ~ delegate, depute.

ent'setz|en 1. *des Amtes*: remove (*gen.* from); *Festung*: relieve; (*erschrecken*) terrify, horrify; shock; *sich* ~ be terrified *od.* shocked (*über acc.* at); 2. ℒ *n* (6) (*Furcht*) terror, horror, dismay; ~lich terrible, horrible (F *beide a. fig.*); shocking; ℒlichkeit *f* frightfulness; (*Greuel*) atrocity; ℒung *f* removal (from office); ✗ relief.

entseuch|en [~'zɔyçən] decontaminate; ℒung *f* decontamination.

ent'sichern ✗ *Gewehr*: unlock; *v/i.* release the safety catch.

ent'sinken (sn; *dat.*) drop (from); *Mut*: fail (*j-m* a p.).

ent'sinnen: *sich* ~ (*gen.*) remember, recall, recollect.

entsittlich|en [~'zɪtlɪçən] demoralize; deprave; ℒung *f* demoralization; depravation.

Ent'sorgung *f* disposal of nuclear waste.

ent'spann|en relax (*a. Muskeln, Nerven usw.*), ⊕ relieve, release; *Bogen*: unbend; *sich* ~ *P.*, *Gesicht*: relax; *Lage*: ease; ℒung *f* relaxation, slackening; unbending; easing; *pol.* détente (*fr.*).

ent'spinnen: *sich* ~ arise, develop.

ent'sprech|en (*dat.*) answer, correspond to; meet (*e-m Verlangen* a demand); *Anforderungen*: come (*od.* be) up to; **~end** *adj.* corresponding; (*angemessen*) appropriate; (*gleichwertig*) equivalent; *adv.* accordingly; (*gemäß dat.*) according to; **2ung** *f* equivalent.

ent'sprießen (sn) sprout, spring up (*dat.* from); *s. abstammen*.

ent'springen (sn) escape (*dat., aus* from); *Fluß*: rise, spring; (*Ursprung haben*) *s. entstehen*.

ent'stammen (*dat.*) (*abstammen von*) be descended from; (*herrühren von*) come from *od.* of, originate from.

ent'steh|en (sn) arise, develop, originate (*aus* from, in); grow (out of), result (from); come into being; spring up; *im 2 begriffen* in the making, in process of development; **2ung** *f* origin, rise, formation; **2ungsgeschichte** *f* genesis.

ent'stell|en disfigure; deface, deform; *Tatsachen usw.*: distort; **2ung** *f* disfigurement; defacement; distortion.

ent'stör|en *Radio*: free from interference, clear, dejam; **2er** *m* (7) *Radio*: suppressor; **2ung** *f* interference suppression; **2ungsstelle** *teleph. f* fault-clearing service.

ent'täusch|en disappoint; disillusion; **2ung** *f* disappointment; disillusionment.

ent'thron|en dethrone; **2ung** *f* dethronement.

entvölker|n [~'fœlkərn] (29) depopulate, unpeople; **2ung** *f* depopulation.

ent'wachsen (sn; *dat.*) outgrow.

ent'waffn|en disarm; **2ung** *f* disarming.

entwalden [~'valdən] (26) clear of forests, dis(af)forest, deforest.

ent'warn|en sound the all-clear (signal); **2ung** *f* all-clear signal.

ent'wässer|n drain; **2ung** *f* drainage; **2ungs-anlage** *f* drainage plant.

entweder [ɛnt've:dər]: ~ ... *oder* either ... or; ~ — *oder!* take it or leave it!

ent'weichen (sn) escape (*aus* from).

ent'weih|en desecrate, profane; **2ung** *f* desecration, profanation.

ent'wend|en (26) purloin, steal, pilfer; misappropriate; **2ung** *f* purloining, misappropriation.

ent'werf|en *Schriftstück, Vertrag*: draft, draw up; (*skizzieren*) sketch, trace (out), outline (*a. fig.*); *Muster, Konstruktion usw.*: design; *Plan*: make, devise; *Gesetz*: frame; **2er** ⊕ *m* designer.

ent'wert|en depreciate; *Briefmarke*: cancel; *fig.* render valueless; **2er** *m* (ticket) cancel(l)ing machine; **2ung** *f* depreciation; cancellation.

ent'wick|eln (*a. sich*) develop (*a. phot.*) (zu into); *Gedanken usw.*: (*darlegen*) explain, set forth; *Tatkraft usw.*: display; ⚔ deploy; **2ler** *phot. m* (7) developer.

Ent'wicklung *f* development; evolution; ⚔ deployment; display; **2s-fähig** capable of development; **~geschichte** *f* history of (the) development; *biol.* biogenetics; **~helfer** *m* adviser (in developing countries); **~shilfe** *f* economic aid to developing countries; **~sland** *n* developing country; **~slehre** *f* theory of evolution; **~sstufe** *f* stage of development; **~szeit** *f* period of development.

ent'winden: *j-m et.* ~ wrest a th. from a p.

entwirren [~'virən] (25) disentangle, unravel.

ent'wischen (sn) slip away (*dat.* from), escape (*j-m* a p.; *aus* from); *j-m* ~ give a p. the slip.

entwöhnen [~'vø:nən] (25) disaccustom (*gen.* to); *Kind, Trinker usw.*: wean (from).

ent'würdig|en degrade, disgrace; **2ung** *f* degradation.

Ent'wurf *m* (*Skizze*) (rough) sketch; (*Gestaltung*) design, *schriftlich*: draft; (*Plan*) plan, project, outline, sketch; **~sstadium** *n* planning (*od.* blueprint) stage.

ent'wurzeln uproot (*a. fig.*).

ent'zerr|en *Radio*: equalize; *phot.* rectify; **2ung** *f* equalization; rectification.

ent'zieh|en: *j-m et.* ~ deprive a p. of a th.; withdraw a th. from a p.; (*vorenthalten*) withhold a th. from a p.; *sich e-r Pflicht usw.* ~ shirk, evade; *das entzieht sich meiner Kenntnis* that is beyond my knowledge; *s. Wort*; **2ung** *f* deprivation, withdrawal; **2ungskur** 💊 *f* withdrawal treatment.

entziffer|n [~'tsifərn] (29) decipher,

make out; (*entschlüsseln*) decode; ♀ung *f* deciphering; decoding.
ent'zück|en **1.** charm, enchant, delight; *entzückt über* (*acc.*) *od. von* delighted with; **2.** ♀ *n s.* *Entzückung*; ‿end delightful, charming; ♀ung *f* rapture, transport; (*entzücktes Gebaren*) raptures *pl.*, transports *pl.*; *in* ‿*en geraten* go into raptures.
Ent'zug *m* (3, *o. pl.*) *von Arznei, Droge:* withdrawal; *von Genehmigung:* revocation; ‿s-**erscheinung** *f* withdrawal symptom.
entzünd|bar [ent'tsyntbɑːr] (in-)flammable; ♀barkeit *f* (in)flammability; ‿en [‿'tsyndən] inflame (*a.* ⚕), kindle; *sich* ‿ catch fire; ⚕ become inflamed; ♀ung *f* kindling; ⚕ inflammation.
ent'zwei asunder, in two, in (*od.* to) pieces; (*zerbrochen*) broken; ‿brechen break in two; ‿en (25) disunite, set at variance; *sich* ‿ quarrel, fall out (*mit* with); ‿gehen break, go to pieces; ♀ung *f* disunion, quarrel, split.
Enzian ⚘ ['entsjɑːn] *m* (5) gentian.
Enzyklopäd|ie [entsyklopɛ'diː] *f* (15) encyclop(a)edia; ♀isch [‿'pɛːdiʃ] encyclop(a)edic(ally *adv.*).
Enzym *biol.* [ɛn'tsyːm] *n* (3) enzyme.
Epide|mie [epide'miː] *f* (15) epidemic (disease); ♀misch [‿'deːmiʃ] epidemic(ally *adv.*).
Epigone [epi'goːnə] *m* (13) epigone.
Epigramm [‿'gram] *n* (3[1]) epigram.
Epik ['eːpik] *f* (16) epic poetry; '‿er *m* epic poet.
Epilep|sie [epilɛp'siː] *f* (15) epilepsy; ‿tiker [‿'lɛptikər] *m* (7), ♀tisch epileptic.
Epilog [‿'loːk] *m* (3) epilog(ue).
episch ['eːpiʃ] epic.
Episode [epi'zoːdə] *f* (15) episode.
Epistel [e'pistəl] *f* (15) epistle.
Epoche [e'pɔxə] *f* (15) epoch; ♀-machend epoch-making.
Epos ['eːpɔs] *n* (16[2]) epic (poem).
er [eːr] (19) he; ‿ *selbst* he himself.
erachten [ɛr'⁹axtən] **1.** consider, judge, deem, think; **2.** ♀ *n* (6) opinion, judg(e)ment; *m-s* ‿*s* to my mind, in my opinion. •
er'-arbeiten gain by working; *Wissen usw.:* acquire.
Erb|adel ['ɛrp⁹ɑːdəl] *m* hereditary nobility; '‿anspruch *m* claim to

an inheritance.
erbarmen [ɛr'barmən] **1.** (25) *j-n:* move (to pity); *sich j-s* ‿ pity (*od.* commiserate) a p.; show mercy to a p.; **2.** ♀ *n* (6) pity, compassion, commiseration; mercy; ‿swert, ‿swürdig pitiable.
erbärmlich [‿'bɛrmliç] pitiful, pitiable; *contp. a.* miserable; *Verhalten:* mean; (*kläglich*) piteous; ♀keit *f* pitifulness, pitiableness; meanness.
erbarmungslos [‿'barmuŋsloːs] pitiless, merciless, relentless.
er'bau|en build (up), construct, raise; *fig.* edify; *sich* ‿ be edified (*an dat.* by); *nicht erbaut sein von* not to be pleased with; ♀er *m* (7) builder; constructor; (*Gründer*) founder; ‿lich edifying; ♀ung *fig. f* edification, *Am. a.* uplift.
erbberechtigt ['ɛrp-] entitled to the inheritance.
Erbe ['ɛrbə] **1.** *m* (13) heir (*gen.* to *a p. od. th.*); **2.** *n* (10, *o. pl.*) inheritance, (*a. fig.*) heritage.
er'beben (sn) tremble, shake, quake.
erben ['ɛrbən] (25) inherit.
er'betteln get (*od.* obtain) by begging, wheedle (*von j-m* out of).
erbeuten [ɛr'bɔytən] (26) capture.
erb|fähig ['ɛrp-] capable of inheriting; '♀faktor *m* gene; '♀fehler *m* hereditary defect; '♀feind *m* traditional enemy; '♀folge *f* (*gesetzliche* intestate) succession; '♀folgekrieg *m* war of succession.
er'bieten: *sich* ‿ offer to do.
'Erbin *f* (16[1]) heiress.
er'bitten beg (*od.* ask) for, request.
erbitter|n [ɛr'bitərn] (29) embitter, exasperate; ‿t embittered (*über acc.* at); (*heftig*) fierce; *Gegner usw.:* bitter; ♀ung *f* exasperation.
Erbkrankheit ['ɛrp-] *f* hereditary disease.
erblassen [ɛr'blasən] (28, sn) grow (*od.* turn) pale, blanch.
Erb-lasser ['ɛrplasər] *m* (7) testator; '‿in *f* (16[1]) testatrix.
er'bleichen (30, sn) *s.* erblassen.
erblich[1] ['ɛrpliç] hereditary; '♀keit *biol. f* heredity.
erblich[2] [ɛr'bliç] *pret.*, ‿en *p.p. v.* erbleichen.
er'blicken catch sight of, see.
erblind|en [ɛr'blindən] (26, sn) grow blind; ♀ung *f* loss of sight.

er'blühen s. aufblühen.

Erbmasse ['ɛrp-] f ⚮ estate; biol. idioplasm.

erbosen [ɛr'boːzən] (27) infuriate; sich ~ grow angry (über acc. with a p., at, about a th.).

erbötig [~'bøːtiç] willing, ready.

Erb|pacht ['ɛrp-] f hereditary tenure; '~pächter m hereditary tenant; '~prinz m hereditary prince.

erbrechen [ɛr'brɛçən] 1. break (od. force) open; ⚕ (a. sich) vomit, puke; 2. ♀ ♂ n (6) vomiting.

Erb-recht ['ɛrp-] n law (des Erben: right) of succession.

'Erbschaft f inheritance; fig. heritage; '~ssteuer f estate duty, Am. succession tax.   [hunter.]

'Erbschleicher(in f) m legacy⌟

Erbse ['ɛrpsə] f (15) pea; '~nbrei m pease-pudding; '~nsuppe f pea-soup.

'Erb|stück n heirloom; '~sünde f original sin; '~teil n, m (portion of) inheritance.

Erd|-achse ['eːrt-] f axis of the earth; '~-antenne f ground aerial (Am. antenna); '~-arbeiten f/pl. earth works pl.; '~-arbeiter m digger, excavator, Am. laborer; '~-atmosphäre f earth's atmosphere; '~bahn f orbit of the earth; '~ball m globe; '~beben n earthquake; '~beere f strawberry; '~bestattung f interment, burial; '~boden m ground, soil; dem ~ gleichmachen level with the ground, raze.

Erde ['eːrdə] f (15) earth; (Boden) ground; (Bodenart) soil, a. dirt; (Humus) mo(u)ld; (Welt) world; ⍗n ⚡ (26) earth, Am. ground.

er'denk|en think out, devise; (erdichten) invent; '~lich imaginable.

Erd|gas ['eːrt-] n natural gas; '~gasleitung f gas pipeline; '~geschoß n ground-floor, Am. first floor; '~gürtel m zone; '~halbkugel f hemisphere; '~harz n asphalt.

er'dicht|en invent (a. b.s.); ~et fictitious.

erdig ['eːrdiç] earthy.

Erd|kabel ['eːrt-] n underground cable; '~kampf ✕ m ground fighting; '~karte f map of the earth; '~kreis m, '~kugel f (terrestrial) globe; '~krume f topsoil; '~kunde f geography; '~leitung ⚡ f earth-connexion, earth-wire, Am. ground connection

od. wire; '~nähe ast. f perigee; '~nuß f peanut; '~nußbutter f peanut butter; '~-öl n mineral oil, petroleum.

erdolchen [ɛr'dɔlçən] (25) stab (with a dagger).

Erd|-ölraffinerie ['eːrt-] f oil refinery; '~pech n mineral pitch, bitumen; '~pol m pole (of the earth); '~reich n ground, soil, earth.

erdreisten [ɛr'draɪstən] (26): sich ~ dare, presume.

er'dröhnen s. dröhnen.

er'drosseln strangle, throttle.

er'drücken crush (to death); fig. crush; ⚖ ~des Beweismaterial damning evidence; ~de Mehrheit overwhelming majority.

Erd|rutsch ['eːrtrutʃ] m landslip, (a. fig.) landslide; '~satellit m earth satellite; '~schicht f layer of earth, stratum; '~schluß ⚡ m earth (connexion), Am. ground (leakage); '~scholle f clod; '~stoß m earth-tremor; '~strich m region, zone; '~teil m part of the world; geogr. continent.

er'dulden suffer, endure.

Erd-umlaufbahn ['eːrt-] f earth orbit.

Erdung ⚡ ['eːrduŋ] f earth(ing), Am. ground(ing).

Erdwärme ['eːrt-] f geothermal energy; '~kraftwerk n geothermal power station.

er'-eifern: sich ~ get excited, fly into a passion.

ereignen [ɛr'ʔaɪgnən]: sich ~ happen, come to pass od. about, occur.

Ereignis [ɛr'ʔaɪknis] n (4¹) event; (Vorfall) occurrence, incident; 2~reich eventful.

er'-eilen overtake.

Eremit [ere'miːt] m (12) hermit.

er'-erben inherit (von from).

er'fahr|en 1. learn, come to know, be told; (hören) hear, understand; (erleben) experience; 2. adj. experienced, expert; (geübt) skilled; 2ung f experience; (Praxis) practice; (Übung) skill; (Fachkenntnis) know-how; in ~ bringen learn, (herausfinden) find out, discover; durch ~ klug werden learn it the hard way; s-e ~en machen gain experience; aus ~ by (od. from) experience; ~ungsgemäß adv. according to (my, our) experience; ~ungsmäßig empiric(ally adv.).

er'fass|en seize, catch, grasp (*alle a. geistig*); lay hold of; (*in sich schließen*) cover; *statistisch*: register, record; **Sung** *f* registration, recording.

er'finden invent; *b.s. a.* fabricate, cook up; *erfunden Nachricht usw.*: *a.* fictitious.

Er'finder *m* (7) inventor; **~in** *f* (16¹) inventress; **Sisch** inventive.

Er'findung *f* invention; **~sgabe** *f* inventiveness; **Ssreich** inventive; resourceful.

er'flehen implore.

Erfolg [ɛr'fɔlk] *m* (3) success; (*Wirkung*) result; **~** haben succeed, be successful; *keinen* **~** *haben* fail, be unsuccessful; **Sen** [~gən] (sn) ensue, follow, result (*aus* from); (*sich ereignen*) happen, take place; *Antwort*: be given; *Zahlung*: be made; **Slos** unsuccessful, ineffective; *adv.* (*umsonst*) in vain; **~losigkeit** *f* unsuccessfulness; failure; **Sreich** successful; **~s-autor(in** *f)* *m* bestselling author; **~sbeteiligung** *f* profit-sharing; **~s-erlebnis** *n* success experience; **~srechnung †** *f* profit and loss account; **Sversprechend** promising.

er'forderlich requisite, required, necessary; **~enfalls** if need be, if necessary *od.* required.

er'forder|n require, demand; **Snis** *n* (4¹) requirement, exigency.

er'forsch|en inquire into, investigate; *Land*: explore (*a. fig.*); **Ser** *m* (7) investigator; explorer; **Sung** *f* investigation; exploration.

er'fragen ask for, ascertain; *zu* **~** *bei* inquire at, apply to.

erfrechen [ɛr'frɛçən] (25): *sich* **~** *zu inf.* have the impudence to *inf.*

er'freu|en please, delight; *sich* **~** *an* (*dat.*) rejoice (*od.* delight) in *od.* at, enjoy *a th.*; *sich e-r S.* **~** enjoy a th.; **~lich** pleasing, gratifying; glad, welcome (*news, etc.*); **~licher-'weise** fortunately; **~t** glad (*über acc.* of; *zu* to *inf.*); pleased (*with*; to *inf.*); rejoiced (at; to *inf.*); delighted (with, at; to *inf.*).

er'frier|en (sn) freeze to death, die from (*od.* perish with) cold; *sich die Ohren* **~** have one's ears frozen; *erfroren Körperteil usw.*: frost-bitten; **Sung** *f* *e-s Körperteils*: frost-bite.

er'frisch|en (27) refresh; **Sung** *f* refreshment; **Sungsraum** *m* refreshment-room; **Sungs-tuch** *n* refresher tissue.

er'füll|en fill; *Bedingung, Pflicht, Versprechen, Wunsch, Zweck usw.*: fulfil(l); *Aufgabe*: accomplish, perform; *Vertrag*: fulfil(l), perform; *Bitte*: comply with; *Erwartungen*: meet; *sich* **~** be fulfilled; (*wahr werden*) come true; **Sung** *f* fulfil(l)ment; accomplishment; performance; **Sungs-ort** *m* place of performance.

ergänzen [~'gɛntsən] (27) complete; complement (*sich gegenseitig* one another); *hinzufügend*: supplement; *Summe*: make up; **†** *Lager*: replenish; **~d** complementary; supplementary (*beide acc.* to).

Er'gänzung *f* completion; (*das Ergänzte*) supplement; replenishment; *gr.* complement; **~s...** supplementary; complementary; **~s-abgabe †** *f* supplementary tax.

ergattern [~'gatərn] (29) (manage to) get hold of, grab, secure.

er'geben 1. result in; (*liefern*) yield; give; (*erweisen*) prove; ⚔ *sich* **~** surrender (*dat.* to); *Schwierigkeit usw.*: arise; *sich e-r S.* **~** devote o.s. to, *e-m Laster*: take to; *sich* **~** *aus* result (*od.* follow) from; *sich* **~** (*in ein Schicksal*) resign o.s. (to); 2. *adj.* devoted (*dat.* to); *e-m Laster*: addicted to; (*untertänig*) humble; (*gefaßt*) resigned (to); **~st** *adv.* respectfully; *Brief*: Yours faithfully; **Sheit** *f* devotion; resignation.

Ergebnis [~'ge:pnis] *n* (4¹) result, outcome; *Sport*: (*Punktzahl*) score; **Slos** resultless, negative; without result.

Ergebung [~'ge:buŋ] *f* resignation, submission; ⚔ surrender.

er'gehen 1. (sn) *Gesetz usw.*: come out, be published; **~** *lassen* issue, publish; *ein Urteil* **~** *lassen* pass a sentence; *über sich* **~** *lassen* submit to; *sich* **~** (*spazierengehen*) stroll about; *fig. sich* **~** *in* (*dat.*) indulge in; *es wird ihm schlecht* **~** he will come off badly, it will go hard with him; *es ist mir gut* (*schlecht*) *ergangen* I fared well (ill); 2. **S** *n* (state of) health.

ergiebig [~'gi:biç] productive, rich (*an dat.* in); *s. einträglich*; **Skeit** *f* productiveness, richness.

er'**gießen** pour *od.* gush forth (*a. sich*); *sich ~ in* (*acc.*) discharge into.

er'**glühen** (sn) glow; *Gesicht*: a. blush, flush (*vor dat.* with).

ergötz|en [~'gœtsən] (27) delight; *sich ~ an* (*dat.*) (take) delight in; 2en *n* (6) delight; *zu j-s ~* to a p.'s amusement; ~lich diverting, delightful; amusing; 2ung *f s.* Ergötzen.

er'**grauen** *v/i.* (sn) (become) grey, *Am.* gray.

er'**greifen** seize, grasp, grip; lay hold of; *Beruf*: choose; *die Waffen, Feder*: take up; *Gemüt*: move, touch, stir; *Maßregeln, Besitz*: take; *die Flucht ~* take to flight; *s. Partei usw.*

er**griffen** [~'grifən] moved, touched, deeply stirred *od.* affected (*von* with); *vom Fieber usw. ~ werden* be struck with fever *etc.*; 2heit *f* emotion.

er**grimmen** [ɛr'grimən] (25, sn) grow angry, flare up.

er'**gründen** fathom (*a. fig.*); *fig.* penetrate, get to the bottom of.

Er'**guß** *m* outpour (*a. fig.*); *physiol. u. fig.* effusion.

er'**haben** elevated; *fig.* exalted, sublime; ~e *Arbeit* embossed work, (*Relief*) relief; ~ *sein über* (*acc.*) be above; 2heit *f* elevation; relief; *fig.* sublimity; loftiness.

er'**halt|en 1.** *v/t.* get; *förmlich*: obtain; *Nachricht usw.*: receive; (*bewahren*) conserve; (*dauernd machen*) preserve, keep (*am Leben* alive); (*unterhalten*) support, maintain; *sich ~ von* subsist on; **2.** *adj. gut ~ Haus usw.*: in good repair *od.* condition; ~ *bleiben* be preserved; 2er *m* (7), 2erin *f* preserver; supporter; 2ung *f* conservation; preservation; maintenance, upkeep.

erhältlich [~'hɛltliç] obtainable.

er'**hängen** hang.

er'**härt|en** (*bestätigen*) confirm, corroborate; 2ung *f* corroboration.

er'**haschen** catch, seize.

er'**heben** lift, raise (*beide a. Augen, Stimme*); *Anspruch, Einwand, Frage, Geschrei usw.*: raise; (*erhöhen*) elevate; (*preisen*) exalt; *Steuern usw.*: levy, raise, (*einziehen*) collect; *e-e Forderung ~* enter (*od.* put in) a claim; *Geld ~* raise money; *Klage* (*Anklage*) ~ bring an action (accu-

sation); *ins Quadrat ~* square; *s. Adelsstand*; *sich ~* rise, start; *Wind*: spring up; *Frage usw.*: arise; (*sich empören*) rise; ~d *fig.* elevating.

erheblich [ɛr'he:pliç] considerable; 2keit *f* consequence, importance.

Er'**hebung** *f* elevation; exaltation; *v. Steuern*: levy, collecting; (*Empörung*) revolt; (*Boden2*) rise; (*Untersuchung*) inquiry, inquest.

erheiter|n [~'haitərn] (29) cheer; amuse, exhilarate; 2ung *f* amusement.

erhell|en [~'hɛlən] (25) *v/t.* light up, illuminate; *fig.* clear up, elucidate; *v/i. fig.* appear, become evident; 2ung *f* illumination.

er'**hitzen** (27) (*a. sich*) heat (*a. fig.*); *sich ~* grow hot, *fig.* become heated.

er'**hoffen** hope for.

erhöh|en [~'hø:ən] (25) raise, lift, elevate; *fig.* (*steigern*) allg. increase, raise (*auf acc.* to; *um* by); enhance; *im Rang od. rühmend*: exalt; *sich ~* (be) increase(d); 2ung *f* (*Anhöhe*) elevation; exaltation; (*Steigerung*) increase, rise; *der Preise*: a. advance.

er'**hol|en**: *sich ~* recover (*von* from); *nach der Arbeit*: (take a) rest, relax; *Preise*: recover, rally; ~sam restful; 2ung *f* recovery (*a.* ✝); (*Entspannung*) recreation, relaxation; (*Ferien*) holiday, *bsd. Am.* vacation; 2ungsgebiet *n* recreational area; 2ungsheim *n* rest home; 2ungsurlaub *m* recreation leave; *nach Krankheit*: convalescence leave; 2ungswert *m* recreational value.

er'**hören** hear; *Bitte*: grant.

er'**-inner|lich** present to one's mind; *soviel mir ~ ist* as far as I can remember; ~n [~'ʔinərn] (29) *v/i. ~ an* (*acc.*) be reminiscent of, recall; *v/t. j-n an* (*acc.*) ~ remind a p. of, call to a p.'s mind; *j-n daran ~, daß od. wie usw. ...* remind a p. that *od.* how *etc.*; *sich ~* (*gen. od. an acc.*) remember, recollect (*a th. od. a p.*).

Er'**-innerung** *f* remembrance; (*Gedächtnis*) recollection; (*Mahnung*) reminder; ~en *pl.* reminiscences; memoirs; *zur ~ an* (*acc.*) in memory of; ~sstück *n* keepsake (*an acc.* from); ~svermögen *n* memory, power of recollection.

er'**jagen** hunt down; *fig.* catch.

er'**kalten** (26, sn) cool down, get cold; *fig.* cool (off).

erkält|en [⟨ˈkɛltən] (26): *sich (sehr)* ⟨ catch (a bad) cold; 2ung *f* cold.

er'**kämpfen** obtain by fighting.

er'**kaufen** purchase, buy; *(bestechen)* bribe, corrupt.

er'**kenn|bar** recognizable; *(wahrnehmbar)* perceptible; 2barkeit *f* perceptibility; ⟨en recognize *(an dat.* by); *(wahrnehmen)* perceive, discern; *(geistig erfassen)* know *(an dat.* by); *(sich vergegenwärtigen)* realize, see; ✝ credit (*j-n für* a p. with a *sum*); ⚖ judge, find *a p. guilty etc.*; ⟨ *lassen, zu* ⟨ geben indicate, suggest; give to understand; *sich zu* ⟨ geben disclose one's identity; ⚖ ⟨ *auf (acc.)* pass a sentence of.

er'**kenntlich** *(dankbar)* grateful; 2keit *f* gratitude.

Er'**kenntnis** *vgl.* erkennen: 1. *f* (14²) perception; realization; 2. ⚖ *n* (4¹) judg(e)ment, sentence, finding; ⟨theorie *f* theory of cognition; ⟨vermögen *n* intellectual power.

Er'**kennung** *f* recognition; ⟨sdienst *m Polizei*: police records department; ⟨smarke ⚔ *f* identity disk, *Am.* identification tag; ⟨smelodie *f Radio*: signature (tune); ⟨swort *n* password; ⟨szeichen *n* identification sign; distinctive mark, *(Abzeichen)* badge; ⚔ *u. fig.* symptom.

Erker [ˈɛrkər] *m* (7) bay; '⟨fenster *n* bay-window.

er'**klär|bar** explicable; ⟨en explain; *(Rechenschaft ablegen über, Gründe angeben für)* account for; *(aussprechen)* declare, state; *sich* ⟨ *für, gegen* declare for, against; 2er *m* (7) commentator, expounder; ⟨lich explicable, accountable; ⟨t professed, declared; 2ung *f* explanation; declaration.

erklecklich [ɛrˈklɛklɪç] considerable.

er'**klettern**, er'**klimmen** climb.

er'**klingen** (sn) sound; *(widerhallen)* resound; ⟨ *lassen* sound, *Lied*: strike up.

erkor [⟨ˈkoːr] *pret.*, ⟨en *p.p. v.* erkiesen: chosen, *adj. a.* (s)elect.

er'**krank|en** (sn) fall *(od.* be taken) ill *(an dat.* of, with); *Organ*: be affected; 2ung *f* illness, sickness; *e-s Organs*: affection.

er'**kühnen** [⟨ˈkyːnən] (25): *sich* ⟨ venture, presume, make bold.

erkunden [⟨ˈkundən] (26) explore; ⚔ reconnoiter, *Am.* reconnoiter.

erkundig|en [⟨ˈkundɪɡən]: *sich* ⟨ inquire *(über acc., nach P.*: after, for; *S.*: about); 2ung *f* inquiry.

Er'**kundung** ⚔ *f* reconnaissance.

er'**künsteln** (29) affect.

er'**lahmen** (sn) *fig.* weary, tire; *Interesse usw.*: wane, flag.

er'**langen** (25) *(fassen)* reach; *fig. a.* achieve; *(sich verschaffen)* obtain, get, secure.

Erlaß [ɛrˈlas] *m* (4²) exemption *(gen.* from); *e-r Schuld, Strafe usw.*: remission (of); *(Verordnung)* decree; *e-s Gesetzes*: enactment.

er'**lassen** *Schuld usw.*: remit; *Verpflichtung*: release, dispense (*j-m* et. a p. from a th.); *Verordnung usw.*: issue, publish; *Gesetz*: enact.

erlauben [ɛrˈlaubən] (25) allow, permit; *sich* et. ⟨ *(gönnen)* indulge in a th.; *sich* ⟨ *zu inf.* ✝ beg to *inf.*, *s. a.* sich erkühnen; *das kann ich mir nicht* ⟨ I cannot afford that; *was* ⟨ *Sie sich!* how dare you!

Erlaubnis [⟨ˈlaupnɪs] *f* (14²) permission; *(Ermächtigung)* authority; *a.* = ⟨schein *m* permit.

erlaucht [⟨ˈlauxt] illustrious, noble.

er'**läuter|n** explain, illustrate; *(kommentieren)* comment (up)on; 2ung *f* explanation, illustration.

Erle ♣ [ˈɛrlə] *f* (15) alder.

er'**leb|en** (live to) see; *(erfahren)* experience; *Schlimmes*: go through; *(mit ansehen)* see, witness; *schöne Tage usw.*: have, spend; 2ensversicherung *f* pure endowment insurance; 2nis [⟨ˈleːpnɪs] *n* (4¹) occurrence, event; *(Abenteuer)* adventure; *(Erfahrung)* experience; ⟨nisreich eventful.

erledig|en [⟨ˈleːdɪɡən] (25) finish *(a.* F *fig.)*; *Auftrag*: execute; *Streitfall*: settle, adjust; *Geschäft*: deal with, handle; *sich* ⟨ be settled; ⟨t finished *(a.* F *fig.)*; 2ung *f* handling; execution; settlement.

er'**legen** *hunt.* kill, shoot.

erleichter|n [⟨ˈlaiçtərn] (29) make easy; *e-e Bürde*: lighten; *Not, Schmerz*: relieve, alleviate; *Aufgabe*: facilitate; *j-n, das Herz*: relieve; 2ung *f* ease; lightening; relief; facilitation; ⟨en *pl. (Vorteile)* facilities.

er'leiden suffer, endure; *Schaden, Verlust*: sustain.

er'lernen learn.

er'lesen *adj.* select, choice.

er'leucht|en light (up), illuminate; *fig.* enlighten; **2ung** *f* illumination; enlightenment.

er'liegen (sn) succumb (*dat.* to).

Erlkönig [ˈɛrlkøːniç] *m* erlking; *mot.* mystery model.

erlogen [ˌ~'loːgən] false, untrue.

Erlös [ˌ~'løːs] *m* (4) proceeds *pl.*

erlosch [ˌ~'lɔʃ] *pret.*, **~en** *p.p. v.* erlöschen; *adj.* extinct.

er'löschen [ˌ~'lœʃən] (30, sn) go out, be extinguished; *fig.* become extinct; *Vertrag, Patent*: expire.

er'lös|en save, redeem; (*frei machen*) deliver; **2er** *m* (7) redeemer, deliverer; *eccl.* Redeemer, Savio(u)r; **2ung** *f* redemption; deliverance.

ermächtig|en [ˌ~'mɛçtigən] (25) empower, authorize; **2ung** *f* authorization; (*Befugnis*) authority, power.

er'mahn|en admonish, exhort; **2ung** *f* exhortation, admonition.

er'mangel|n *e-r S.*: be wanting in; **~ zu tun** fail to do; **2ung** *f*: **in ~** (*gen.*) in default of, failing.

ermannen [ɛr'manən] (25): *sich ~* take courage *od.* heart.

er'mäßig|en abate, reduce; **2ung** *f* abatement, reduction.

ermatt|en [ˌ~'matən] (26) *v/t.* tire, fatigue; (*erschöpfen*) exhaust; *v/i.* (sn) grow weary *od.* tired; (*nachlassen*) slacken (*in dat.* in); *Interesse usw.*: flag; **2ung** *f* weariness, fatigue, exhaustion, lassitude.

er'messen 1. judge; **2.** **2** *n* (6) judg(e)ment, opinion; *nach freiem ~* at one's (free) discretion; **2sfrage** *f* matter of discretion; **2sspielraum** *m* latitude, leeway.

ermitt|eln [ˌ~'mitəln] (29) ascertain, determine; find out; *ħ* investigate; **2(e)lung** *f* ascertainment; *ħ* investigation; **~en anstellen** make inquiries; **2lungsverfahren** *ħ* *n* judicial inquiry.

ermöglichen [ˌ~'møːk-] (25) render (*od.* make) possible; *es j-m ~ zu tun* enable (*od.* make it possible for) a p. to do.

er'mord|en, **2ung** *f* murder.

ermüd|en [ˌ~'myːdən] (26) *v/t.* tire, fatigue; *v/i.* (sn) get tired *od.* fatigued; **2ung** *f* fatigue, tiredness.

ermunter|n [ˌ~'muntərn] (29) rouse; (*anfeuern*) incite, encourage, animate; (*erheitern*) cheer (up); *sich ~* rouse o.s.; **2ung** *f* encouragement, animation.

ermutig|en [ˌ~'muːtigən] (25) encourage; **2ung** *f* encouragement.

er'nähr|en nourish, feed; (*erhalten*) support; **2er** *m* (7) bread-winner, supporter; **2ung** *f* nourishment; support; *♣* nutrition; **2ungswissenschaft** *f* nutritional science.

er'nenn|en nominate, appoint (*zum Botschafter usw.* ambassador *etc.*); **2ung** *f* nomination, appointment.

erneu|e(r)n [ˌ~'nɔyə(r)n] (25 [29]) renew; (*wieder aufleben lassen*) revive; **2erung** *f* renewal; revival; **~t** *adj.* renewed; *adv.* once more, anew.

erniedrig|en [ˌ~'niːdrigən] (25) lower; *im Rang*: degrade; *fig.* humiliate, humble; **2ung** *f* lowering; degradation; humiliation.

Ernst¹ [ɛrnst] *m* (3¹, *o.pl.*) seriousness, earnest; (*Würdigkeit, Wichtigkeit*) gravity; (*Strenge*) severity; *es im ~* (*od.* **2**) *meinen* be in earnest, be serious; **~ machen mit et.** go ahead with a th.; *es ist mein voller ~* I mean it; **'~fall** *m* emergency; *im ~* in case of emergency; *⚔* in case of war.

ernst², **'~haft**, **'~lich** serious, earnest; (*würdig*) grave; (*streng*) stern; *es ernst meinen s. Ernst¹*; *et. ernst nehmen* take a th. seriously; **'2haftigkeit** *f s. Ernst¹*.

Ernte [ˈɛrntə] *f* (15) harvest; (*Ertrag*) crop; **~dankfest** *n* harvest festival, *Am.* Thanksgiving Day; **'~fest** *n* harvest home; **'2n** *v/t. u. v/i.* (26) harvest, gather (in), (*a. fig.*) reap.

ernüchter|n [ɛr'nyçtərn] (28) sober; *fig. a.* disillusion; **2ung** *f* sobering; *fig.* disillusionment.

Er'ober|er *m* (7) conqueror; **2n** [ˌ~'ʔoːbərn] (29) conquer; **~ung** *f* conquest; **~ungskrieg** *m* war of conquest.

er'-öffn|en *allg.* open (*a. Konto, Kredit, Sitzung usw.*); *feierlich*: inaugurate; *⚔ Feuer*: open; *j-m et.*: disclose, reveal, *förmlich*: notify (to); *ein Geschäft ~* (*als*) set up a business (as); *sich ~ Möglichkeit*: present itself; **2ung** *f* opening; inauguration; disclosure; notification.

erogen [ero'ge:n] erogenous.

erörter|n [~'⁷œrtərn] (29) discuss; 2**ung** f discussion.

Erosion [ero'zjo:n] geol. f erosion.

Erot|ik [e'ro:tik] f eroticism; 2**isch** erotic.

Erpel ['ɛrpəl] m (7) drake.

erpicht [ɛr'piçt]: ~ auf (acc.) bent (od. intent, keen) on; darauf ~ sein zu inf. be anxious to inf.

er'press|en Geld usw.: extort; j-n: blackmail; 2**er(in** f) m extortioner; blackmailer; 2**erbrief** m blackmail letter; ~**erisch** extortionate; 2**ung** f extortion; blackmail(ing); 2**ungsversuch** m attempted extortion.

er'proben try, (put to the) test.

erquick|en [~'kvikən] (25) refresh; ~**lich** refreshing; 2**ung** f refreshment.

er'raten guess, divine; find out; ~! you guessed!

er'rechnen calculate, compute, figure out.

erreg|bar [~'re:kba:r] excitable, irritable; 2**barkeit** f excitability, irritability; ~**en** [~gən] excite (a. ∮); (erzürnen) irritate, infuriate; (verursachen) cause, call forth; sich ~ get excited; ~**end** exciting; 2**er** m (7), 2**erin** f (16¹) ∮ germ, virus; 2**erkreis** m Radio: exciting circuit; 2**ung** f excitation; Zustand: excitement.

erreich|bar [ɛr'raiçba:r] get-at-able, within reach od. call; fig. attainable; (verfügbar) available; ~**en** reach; Ziel, Zweck usw.: achieve, attain; (erlangen) obtain; Zug usw.: catch; ein gewisses Maß: come up to; j-n telephonisch ~ get a p. on the phone; von der Bahn leicht zu ~ within easy reach of the station; 2**ung** f reach(ing).

er'rett|en save, rescue; (befreien) deliver; 2**er(in** f) m rescuer, deliverer; 2**ung** f rescue, deliverance; eccl. Salvation.

er'richt|en erect, raise (a. ∮ das Lot); (gründen) establish; Geschäft: set up; 2**ung** f erection; establishment.

er'ringen obtain; Erfolg, Ruhm usw.: achieve, gain; Preis: win; s. Sieg.

er'röten 1. (sn) blush; 2. 2 n (6) blush(ing).

Errungenschaft [ɛr'ruŋənʃaft] f (16) achievement; (Erwerbung) acquisition.

Er'satz m (3², o. pl.) (Vergütung) compensation; (Schadloshaltung) indemnification; (Schadens2) damages pl.; (Austausch) replacement, konkret: a. substitute (für for); ✗ replacement(s pl.); (Rekruten) recruits pl., draft(s pl.); ~... ersatz (z.B. ~kaffee); s. Ersetzung, ~mann, ~mittel, ~teil; ~ leisten make restitution od. amends (für for); ~-anspruch m claim for compensation; ~befriedigung f compensation; ~dienst m s. Wehrersatzdienst; ~mann m substitute, Am. a. alternate; Sport: reserve, ∮ spare; ✗ replacement, filler; ~mine f für Bleistift: refill; ~mittel n substitute; minderwertig: ersatz; ~pflicht f liability (to pay damages); ~rad mot. n spare wheel; ~reifen mot. m spare tyre; ~stück n, ~teil ⊕ n, m replacement part; mitgeliefert: spare (part); ~liste parts list; ~wahl f by-election.

er'saufen P (sn) be drowned.

ersäufen P [~'zoyfən] (25) drown.

er'schaff|en create; 2**er(in** f) m creator; 2**ung** f creation.

er'schallen (sn) (re)sound; ring.

er'schein|en (sn) appear (a. Geist; j-m to a p.); Buch usw.: a. come out, be published; ratsam ~ appear advisable; 2**en** n appearance; 2**ung** f appearance; (Geister2) apparition; (Traumbild) vision; (Natur2) phenomenon; (Krankheits2) symptom; e-e glänzende ~ sein cut a fine figure; in ~ treten make one's appearance, fig. appear, come to the fore; 2**ungsbild** n Person: outward appearance; 2**ungsjahr** n year of publication; 2**ungstermin** m date of publication.

er'schießen shoot (dead).

erschlaff|en [~'ʃlafən] v/i. (25, sn) Muskel: go limp; P.: tire, wilt; fig. flag, slacken; v/t. relax; exhaust; 2**ung** f relaxation; enervation.

er'schlagen kill, slay.

er'schleichen obtain surreptitiously; Gunst: creep into.

er'schließen open (a. sich); Gegend: open up; Baugelände: develop.

er'schöpf|en exhaust; ∮ Batterie:

run down; **～end** *fig.* exhaustive;
2ung *f* exhaustion.
erschrak [～'ʃrɑːk] *pret. v.* erschrecken 2.
er'schrecken 1. *v/t.* (25) frighten,
terrify, scare; **2.** *v/i.* (30, sn) (*a.*
sich ～) be frightened *od.* startled
(*über acc.* at); **3.** **2** *n* fright, terror;
～d alarming, startling.
erschrocken [ɛr'ʃrɔkən] **1.** *p.p. v.*
erschrecken 2.; **2.** *adj.* frightened,
terrified, scared; startled.
er'schütter|n (29) shake; *fig.* shock,
(*rühren*) move; **2ung** *f* shaking;
shock; (*Rührung*) emotion; **✗** concussion; **⊕** percussion.
erschweren [～'ʃveːrən] (25) render
more difficult; *Schuld*: aggravate.
er'schwindeln obtain by trickery;
von j-m ～ swindle out of a p.
er'schwing|en afford; **～lich** attain-
able, within *a p.'s* means; *Preis*:
reasonable.
er'sehen learn, gather (*aus* from).
er'sehnen long for.
er'setz|bar, **～lich** *P.*: replaceable;
Schaden, Verlust: reparable; **～en**
(*wiedergutmachen*) repair; (*entschädigen für*) make up for, compensate
(for), make good; *j-m et.*: indemnify a p. for a th.; (*an die Stelle
setzen od. treten*) replace, substitute,
supersede; *j-m Unkosten ～* reimburse a p. for his expenditure; *er
ersetzt ihn nicht* he is not equal to
him; *den Schaden ersetzt bekommen*
recover damages; **2ung** *f* compensation; replacement.
er'sichtlich evident, obvious.
er'sinnen contrive, devise.
er'spähen (e)spy, F spot.
er'spar|en *Geld*: save; *j-m Geld,
Zeit, Ärger usw. ～* save a p. money,
time, trouble, *etc.*; *j-m e-e Demütigung usw. ～* spare a p. a humiliation,
etc.; **2nis** *f* (14²) saving (*an dat.* of);
～se *pl.* savings.
ersprießlich [～'ʃpriːslɪç] useful,
profitable, beneficial.
erst [eːrst] **1.** (18) *der* (*die*) **～e** (*od.* **2e**)
first; *fig.* first, foremost, leading; **～e**
Qualität prime quality; **～e** *Hilfe*
first aid; *in ～er Linie, an ～er Stelle* in
the first place, primarily; *aus ～er
Hand* first-hand (*mit su. nur attr.*);
der, die **2e** *e-r Klasse* the head (*od.*
top) boy *od.* girl; *fig. die* **～e** *Geige
spielen* play first fiddle; *fürs* **～e** for

the time being; *bei Auktionen*: *zum
～en, zum zweiten, zum dritten!*
going, going, gone!; **2.** *adv.* first;
(*anfangs*) at first; (*bloß*) only, but;
(*nicht früher als*) not before, not
till *od.* until; *～ als* only when; *jetzt
～ but now; ～ recht* more than ever;
'2-angriff ✗ *m* first strike.
erstarken [ɛr'ʃtarkən] (25, sn) grow
strong(er), gain strength.
er'starr|en (sn) grow stiff, stiffen;
Glieder: grow numb; *vor Schreck*:
freeze (with), be paralysed; *metall.*
solidify; *Fett*: congeal; *Zement*: set;
Blut: coagulate, *fig.* run cold; *erstarrt* stiff, numb; **2ung** *f* torpidity;
numbness; solidification; congeal-
ment; setting.
erstatt|en [～'ʃtatən] (26) restore,
return; *Geld*: (re)pay; *s. a.* ersetzen; **t̪t̪** *Anzeige ～* file an information; *s. Bericht*; **2ung** *f* restitution,
compensation; *e-s Berichts*: delivery.
'Erst-aufführung *thea.* *f* first (*od.*
opening) night; **'～-auflage** *f* first
printing.
er'staunen 1. *v/i.* (sn) be astonished
(*über acc.* at); *v/t.* astonish; **2.** **2** *n*
(6) astonishment; *in ～ setzen* aston-
ish.
er'staunlich astonishing, amazing.
'Erst-ausgabe *f* first edition.
'erst'beste: *der, die, das ～* the first
comer.
er'stechen stab.
er'stehen 1. *v/i.* (sn) arise, rise; **2.**
v/t. buy, purchase. [ascent.]
er'steig|en ascend, climb; **2ung** *f*∫
erstens ['eːrstəns] first, firstly.
er'sterben (sn) die (away) (*a. fig.*).
'erstere: *der, die, das ～* the former.
erstgeboren ['～gəboːrən] first-born.
'Erstgeburtsrecht *n* birthright.
er'stick|en *v/t. u. v/i.* (sn) choke
(*an dat.* on; *vor Wut usw.* with),
suffocate; stifle; *gewaltsam*: smother; *im Keime ～* nip in the bud;
2ung *f* suffocation.
erstklassig ['eːrstklasɪç] first-class.
'erstlich firstly, in the first place.
'Erstling *m* (3¹) first-born (child);
Tier: firstling; **'～s...** first; **'～swerk** *n*
first publication.
erstmal|ig ['～mɑːlɪç] *adj.* first; *adv.*
= **～s** ['～mɑːls] (for) the first time.
er'streben [ɛr-] strive after; **～swert**
desirable.

er'**strecken**: sich ~ extend (bis zu to); fig. a. sich ~ auf (acc.) refer to; sich ~ über (acc.) cover.

'**Erstschlag** ✗ m first-strike; **~s-potential** n first-strike potential; **~swaffe** f first-strike weapon.

er'**stürmen** take (by storm).

'**Erstwähler**(**in** f) m first-time voter.

er'**suchen 1.** ask, request; **2.** ♀ n (6) (auf j-s ~ at a p.'s) request.

er'**tappen** catch, surprise; s. frisch.

er'**teilen** give; s. Auftrag, Wort.

er'**tönen** (sn) (re)sound.

Ertrag [ɛr'traːk] m (3³) produce, yield; (Einnahmen) proceeds, returns pl.; ✗ output.

er'**trag|en** bear, endure; (leiden) suffer; (vertragen) support, stand; **♀fähigkeit** [~k-] f productiveness.

er**träglich** [~'trɛːkliç] bearable, endurable; (leidlich) tolerable, passable.

Er'tragslage f profit situation.

er'**tränken** drown.

er'**träumen** dream of.

er'**trinken** (sn) drown, be (od. get) drowned.

er**tüchtig|en** [~'tyçtigən] (25) make fit, train; **♀ung** f: körperliche ~ physical training.

er**übrigen** [~¹⁹yːbrigən] (25) save; Zeit: spare; sich ~ be superfluous.

er'**wachen** (sn) awake.

er'**wachsen 1.** v/i. (sn) arise; spring; Vorteil usw.: accrue (aus from); **2.** adj. grown-up, adult (a. ♀e m, f); **♀enbildung** f adult education.

er'**wäg|en** consider; **♀ung** f consideration; in der ~, daß considering that; in ~ ziehen take into consideration.

er'**wählen** choose, elect.

er'**wähn|en** mention; **~enswert** worth mentioning; **♀ung** f mention.

er'**wärmen** (a. sich) warm, heat; fig. sich ~ für warm to.

er'**wart|en** expect; await; ein Kind ~ be expecting; et. zu ~ haben be in for; **♀ung** f expectation; **~ungsvoll** expectant.

er'**weck|en** awaken (a. fig.); vom Tode: resuscitate, a. fig. Erinnerung, Hoffnung usw.: raise; fig. cause; Eindruck: give; Interesse, Verdacht: arouse; s. Anschein; **♀ung** f awakening; resuscitation; revival.

er'**wehren**: sich ~ (gen.) ward off; sich der Tränen ~ restrain one's

tears; ich konnte mich des Lachens nicht ~ I could not help laughing.

er'**weichen** (25) soften; fig. j-n: a. mollify; (rühren) move; **~d**(es Mittel) emollient.

er'**weis|en** prove; Achtung: show; e-n Dienst, Gehorsam: render; Ehre: do, pay; Gunst: grant, bestow (j-m on a p.); sich ~ als prove (od. turn out) to be; **~lich** [~'vaɪsliç] provable.

er**weiter|n** [~'vaɪtərn] (29) (a. sich) extend (a. fig.), expand, widen; **~bar** a. Computer: expandable; **♀ung** f expansion, (a. gr.) extension; **✗** dila(ta)tion.

Erwerb [ɛr'vɛrp] m (3) (Erwerben) acquisition; (Unterhalt)living;(Verdienst) earnings pl.; **♀en** [~bən] acquire; gain; durch Arbeit: earn; sich Verdienste ~ um deserve well of.

er'**werbs|fähig** capable of gainful employment; **♀fähigkeit** f earning capacity; **~los** usw. s. arbeitslos usw.; **♀quelle** f source of income; **♀sinn** m, **♀trieb** m acquisitiveness; **~tätig** working (for a living), gainfully employed; **♀tätige(r** m) f person gainfully employed; **♀tätigkeit** f occupational activities pl., gainful employment; **~unfähig** incapable of earning one's living; **♀-unfähigkeit** f incapacity of earning one's living; **♀zweig** m branch of industry (od. trade); line (of business), trade.

Er'**werbung** [~buŋ] f acquisition.

er**wider|n** [~'viːdərn] (29) return; Gefälligkeit, Glückwunsch, Zuneigung usw.: a. reciprocate; (antworten) reply (auf acc. to), bsd. ⚖ rejoin; Beleidigung usw., scharf ~: retort; **♀ung** f return; answer, reply; reciprocation; bsd. ⚖ rejoinder.

er**wiesen** [~'viːzən] p.p. v. erweisen; **~er'maßen** as has been proved.

er'**wirken** obtain, procure, effect; e-n Entscheid usw.: take out.

er'**wischen** catch, get.

er**wünscht** [~'vynʃt] desired; (wünschenswert) desirable; (willkommen) welcome.

er'**würgen** strangle, throttle.

Erz [eːrts] n (3²) ✗ ore; (Metall) brass, bronze; '**~-ader** f vein of ore.

er'**zähl|en** tell; (berichten) relate; bsd. formgerecht: narrate; man erzählt sich people (od. they) say;

Ջer(in f) m narrator; (*Schriftsteller*) story-teller, writer; **Ջung** f narration; (*Bericht*) report; (*Geschichte*) tale, story, narrative.

'**Erz|bischof** m archbishop; '**Ջbischöflich** archiepiscopal; '**ᴗbistum** n archbishopric; '**ᴗ-engel** m archangel.

er'zeug|en (*zeugen*) beget; (*hervorbringen, -rufen*) produce; (*fabrizieren*) make, manufacture; *Gefühl:* engender; *phys.,* 🜨 generate; **Ջer** m (7) begetter; producer, manufacturer; generator; **Ջnis** [ᴗ'tsɔyk-] n product; (*BodenՋ*) *mst pl.* ᴗse produce; *des Geistes, der Kunst:* production; *eigenes* ᴗ my *etc.* own make; *deutsches* ᴗ made in Germany; **Ջung** [ᴗɡuŋ] f production; manufacture; *phys.,* 🜨 generation.

'**Erz|feind** m arch-enemy; '**ᴗgang** m vein of ore; '**ᴗgauner** m arrant swindler; '**Ջhaltig** ore-bearing; '**ᴗherzog** m archduke; '**ᴗherzogin** f archduchess; '**ᴗherzogtum** n archduchy; '**ᴗhütte** f smelting works *pl. od. sg.* [rear; *geistig:* educate.)

er'ziehen (*aufziehen*) bring up,) **Er'zieher** m (7) educator; (*Lehrer*) teacher; **ᴗin** f governess; **Ջisch** educational, pedagogic(al).

Er'ziehung f (*Aufziehen*) upbringing; (*geistige* ᴗ) education; (*Lebensart*) breeding; *von guter* ᴗ well--bred; '**ᴗs-anstalt** f reformatory; **ᴗsberater** m educational adviser; **ᴗsberatung** f child guidance; **ᴗsberechtigte** m, f parent or guardian; **ᴗswissenschaft** f pedagogics *sg.*

er'zielen obtain, reach; *Preis:* realize, fetch; *Erfolg:* achieve; *Treffer:* score.

er'zittern *s.* zittern.

'**erz|konservativ** ultraconservative.

'**Erz|lager** n ore deposit *od.* bed; '**ᴗlügner** m arch liar; '**ᴗprobe** f assay; '**ᴗvater** m patriarch.

er'zürn|en *v/t.* make angry, infuriate; *sich* ᴗ = *v/i.* grow angry; **ᴗt** angry.

er'zwingen force, *bsd. gesetzlich:* enforce; *Gehorsam usw.:* compel; *von j-m:* extort from.

es [ɛs] (19) it; *als Ergänzung des Prädikats:* so; *ich bin's* it is I *od.* F me; *sie sind* ᴗ it is they; *wer ist der Junge?* — ᴗ *ist mein Freund* who is the boy? — he is my friend;

er sagt ᴗ he says so; *ich hoffe* ᴗ I hope so; *er sagte, ich sollte gehen, und ich tat* ᴗ he told me to go, and I did so; *er ist reich, ich bin* ᴗ *auch* he is rich, so am I; ᴗ *gibt* there is, there are; ᴗ *wurde getanzt* there was dancing; *ich will* ᴗ *versuchen* I will try; *ich weiß* ᴗ I know; *ich ziehe* ᴗ *vor zu gehen* I prefer to go; ᴗ *lebe der König!* long live the King!

Es ♩ n E flat.

Esche ['ɛʃə] f (15) ash(-tree); '**Ջn** ash(en); '**ᴗnholz** n ash-wood.

Esel ['eːzəl] m (7) ass, *mst* donkey; F *fig.* (silly) ass; **ᴗei** [ᴗ'laɪ] f stupidity; '**Ջhaft** asinine, stupid; '**ᴗin** f (16¹) she-ass.

'**Esels|brücke** f *Schule:* crib, *Am.* F pony; '**ᴗohr** n *im Buch:* dog's ear.

Eskal|ation [ɛskala'tsjoːn] f escalation; **Ջieren** [ᴗ'liːrən] escalate.

Eskorte [ɛs'kɔrtə] f (15), **eskor'tieren** escort, convoy.

Espe 🜂 ['ɛspə] f (15) asp(en); *wie* ᴗ*nlaub zittern* tremble like an aspen-leaf.

eßbar ['ɛsbɑːr] eatable, edible.

'**Eßbesteck** n *s.* Besteck.

Esse ['ɛsə] f (15) chimney, flue; (*SchmiedeՋ*) forge.

essen ['ɛsən] **1.** (30) eat; *zu Mittag* ᴗ (have) lunch; *zu Abend* ᴗ have supper (*od.* dinner); *auswärts* (*im Restaurant*) ᴗ eat (*od.* dine) out; **2.** Ջ n (6) eating; (*Speise*) food; (*Mahlzeit*) meal; (*MittagՋ*) lunch; (*AbendՋ*) supper, dinner; (*FestՋ*) dinner, banquet; ᴗ *auf Rädern* meals on wheels; '**Ջgutschein** m luncheon voucher; '**Ջszeit** f meal-time; lunch-hour; *abends:* dinner-time.

Essenz [ɛ'sɛnts] f (16) essence.

'**Esser(in** f) m eater; *schwache(r)* ᴗ poor eater; *starke(r)* ᴗ great eater.

'**Eß|geschirr** n dinner-service; ✗ mess-tin, *Am.* mess kit; '**ᴗgewohnheiten** f/pl. eating habits.

Essig ['ɛsiç] m (3¹) vinegar; '**ᴗgurke** f pickled cucumber, gherkin; '**Ջsauer** 🜨 acetic, *in Zssgn:* acetate of; *s.* Tonerde; '**ᴗsäure** f acetic acid.

'**Eß|kastanie** f edible chestnut; '**ᴗlöffel** m table-spoon; '**ᴗlust** f appetite; '**ᴗnische** f dinette; '**ᴗtisch** m dining-table; '**ᴗwaren** f/pl. eatables, victuals, food *sg.*; '**ᴗzimmer** n dining-room.

Estrade [ɛ'strɑːdə] f (15) estrade.

Estragon ['ɛstragɔn] *m* (3¹ *o. pl.*) tarragon.

Estrich ['ɛstriç] *m* (3¹) cement (*od.* plaster *od.* asphalt) floor(ing).

etabl|ieren [eta'bli:rən] establish; *sich* ⌄ set up in business; ⌾**issement** [⌄blis(ə)'mã] *n* (11) establishment.

Etage [e'tɑ:ʒə] *f* (15) floor, stor(e)y; ⌄**nbett** *n* bunk bed; ⌄**nwohnung** *f* flat, *Am.* apartment.

Etappe [e'tapə] *f* (15) ✕ base, communications zone; *fig.* (*Teilstrecke*) stage, leg; ⌾**nweise** by stages.

Etat [e'tɑ:] *m* (11) (*Haushaltplan*) budget, *parl. a. the* Estimates *pl.*; *parl.* (*bewilligter* ⌄) supplies *pl.*; ⌾**mäßig** *Beamter usw.*: permanent; ⌄**sjahr** *n* fiscal year.

Ethik ['e:tik] *f* (16) ethics *pl. od. sg.* '**ethisch** ethical.

Ethnographie [ɛtnogra'fi:] *f* (15) ethnography. [ogy.]
Ethnologie [⌄lo'gi:] *f* (15) ethnol-⌡

Etikett [eti'kɛt] *n* (11) label, ticket; *gummiertes: Am. a.* sticker; ⌄**e** *f* (15) etiquette; ⌾**ieren** [⌄'ti:rən] label.

etliche ['ɛtliçə] *pl.* some, several.

Etüde ♪ [e'ty:də] *f* (15) study.

Etui [e'tvi:] *n* (11) case.

etwa ['ɛtva] perhaps, by chance; (*ungefähr*) about, say, *Am. a.* around; ⌄**ig** ['⌄vaʔiç] possible, eventual, any.

etwas ['ɛtvas] *pron.* something; *verneinend, fragend od. bedingend*: anything; *adj.* some; any; *adv.* somewhat; ⌾ *n: ein gewisses* ⌄ a certain something.

Etymolog|ie [etymolo'gi:] *f* (15) etymology; ⌾**isch** [⌄'lo:giʃ] etymological.

euch [ɔyç] (19) you; to you; *refl.* yourselves.

euer ['ɔyər] (19) of you; (20) '⌄, '⌄**e** your; *pred.* yours.

Eule ['ɔylə] *f* (15) owl; ⌄*n nach Athen tragen* carry coals to Newcastle; '⌄**nspiegel** *m* Owlglass; '⌄**nspiegelstreich** *m* roguish trick.

euresgleichen ['ɔyrəs'glaiçən] your likes *pl.*, people *pl.* of your kind.

euret|halben ['ɔyrəthalbən], '⌄**wegen,** (*um*) ⌄**willen** ['⌄vilən] for your sake.

'**eurig** (*od. der, die, das* ⌄**e**) yours.

Euro|dollar ['ɔyro-] *m* eurodollar; '⌄**kommunismus** *m* Eurocom-

munism; '⌄**markt** *m* euromarket.

Europä|er [ɔyro'pɛ:ər] *m* (7), ⌄**erin** *f*, ⌾**isch** European; ⌾**isieren** [⌄pɛi'zi:-rən] Europeanize.

Europa|meister [ɔy'ro:pa-] *m* European champion; ⌄**meisterschaft** *f* European championship; ⌄**parlament** *n* European parliament; ⌄**pokal** *m* European cup; ⌄**rat** *pol. m* Council of Europe.

Euroscheck ['ɔyro-] *m* Eurocheque; ⌄**heft** *n* Eurocheque-book; ⌄**karte** *f* Eurocheque-card.

Euter ['ɔytər] *n* (7) udder.

evakuier|en [evaku'ʔi:rən] evacuate; ⌾**te** *m*, *f* evacuee.

evangel|isch [evaŋ'ge:liʃ] evangelic(al); Protestant; ⌾**ist** [⌄ge'list] *m* (12) evangelist; ⌾**ium** [⌄'ge:ljum] *n* (9) gospel.

Eventu|alität [eventuali'tɛ:t] *f* (16) eventuality, contingency; ⌾**ell** [⌄'ɛl] possible, contingent, potential; *adv.* possibly; perhaps; if necessary.

Ewer ⚓ ['e:vər] *m* (7) lighter.

ewig ['e:viç] eternal; (*unaufhörlich*) everlasting, perpetual; *auf* ⌄ for ever; '⌾**keit** *f* eternity; F *seit einer* ⌄ for ages; ⌄**lich** ['e:vikliç] eternally.

ex [ɛks]: ⌄ (*trinken*)! bottoms up!; '⌾... ex-...

exakt [ɛ'ksakt] exact; ⌾**heit** *f* exactitude, exactness.

Exam|en [ɛ'ksɑ:mən] *n* (11; *pl. Examina*) examination, F exam; ⌄**ens-angst** *f* exam(ination) nerves *pl.*; ⌄**inator** [ɛksami'nɑ:tɔr] *m* (8) examiner; ⌾**inieren** [⌄mi'ni:rən] examine; *fig.* question, quiz.

Exekutive [ɛksəku'ti:və] *f* (15) executive power.

Exempel [ɛ'ksɛmpəl] *n* (7) example; Å problem; *s. statuieren*.

Exemplar [ɛksɛm'plɑ:r] *n* (3) specimen; *e-s Buches:* copy; ⌾**isch** exemplary; *j-n* ⌄ *bestrafen* make an example of a p.

exerzier|en [ɛksɛr'tsi:rən] *v/t. u. v/i.* drill; ⌾**platz** *m* drillground.

Exil [ɛ'ksi:l] *n* (3¹) exile (*a. fig.*); banishment; *im* ⌄ in exile.

Existenz [ɛksi'stɛnts] *f* (16) existence; (*wirtschaftliche Grundlage*) livelihood; ⌄**berechtigung** *f* right to exist; ⌄**grundlage** *f* basis of subsistence; ⌄**kampf** *m* struggle for existence; ⌄**minimum** *n* subsistence level; living wage.

exi'stieren exist; *(bestehen können)* subsist.

exklusiv [ɛksklu'zi:f] exclusive.

exkommunizieren [‿kɔmuni'tsi:-rən] excommunicate.

exotisch [ɛ'kso:tiʃ] exotic.

Exped|ient [ɛkspe'djɛnt] *m* (12) forwarding agent *(od. clerk)*; ℒieren [‿'di:rən] dispatch, forward.

Expedition [‿di'tsjo:n] *f (Versand)* dispatch, forwarding; *(Kriegszug, Forschungsreise)* expedition; *(Versandstelle)* forwarding department.

Experiment [ɛksperi'mɛnt] *n* (3) experiment; ℒell [‿'tɛl] experimental; ℒieren [‿'ti:rən] experiment.

Experte [ɛks'pɛrtə] *m* (13) expert.

explo|dieren [ɛksplo'di:rən] (sn) explode, burst; ℒsion [‿'zjo:n] *f* explosion; ‿siv [‿'zi:f], ℒ'siv... explosive; ℒ'sivstoff *m* explosive.

exponieren [ɛkspo'ni:rən] (25) expose.

Export [ɛks'pɔrt] *m* (3) export (-ation); *(Waren)* exports *pl.*; *in Zssgn mst* export; ‿**artikel** *m* export article, *pl. mst* exports *pl.*; ‿**eur** [‿'tø:r] *m* (3¹) exporter; ℒ**ieren** [‿'ti:rən] export.

expreß [ɛks'prɛs], ℒ... express.

Ex'preß 🚃 *m* (4, *pl.* ‿züge) express (train); ‿**bote** *m*, ‿**gut** *n s.* Eilbote *usw.*

extra ['ɛkstra] extra; 'ℒ... extra, special; 'ℒ**blatt** *n* supplement; *e-r Zeitung:* special edition, *Am.* extra.

extrahieren [ɛkstra'hi:rən] extract.

Extrakt [ɛks'trakt] *m* (3) extract.

'**Extrawurst** F *f* something (extra-) special.

Extrem [ɛks'tre:m] **1.** *n* (3) extreme; **2.** ℒ *adj.* extreme; ‿**ist** [‿tre-'mist] *m* (12) extremist; ‿**itäten** [‿tremi'tɛ:tən] *f/pl.* extremities.

Exzellenz [ɛkstsɛ'lɛnts] *f* (16) Excellency.

exzentrisch [‿'tsɛntriʃ] eccentric.

Exzeß [ɛks'tsɛs] *m* (3) excess.

F

F [ɛf], **f** *n inv.* F, f; ♪ F.

Fabel ['fɑ:bəl] *f* (15) fable; *e-s Dramas usw.:* a. plot; *fig.* tale; '‿**dichter** *m* fabulist; 'ℒ**haft** fabulous; *fig. a.* capital, marvellous, stunning; 'ℒ**n** (29) *v/i.* tell stories *(von about)*; '‿**wesen** *n* fabulous creature.

Fabrik [fa'bri:k] *f* (16) factory, mill, works *(pl., oft sg.)*; ‿**anlage** *f* (manufacturing) plant; ‿**ant** [‿bri-'kant] *m* (12) manufacturer, maker; ‿**arbeit** *f* work in a factory; *s. Fabrikware*; ‿**arbeiter(in** *f) m* factory worker *od.* hand; ‿**at** [‿bri-'ka:t] *n* (3) make, manufacture, brand; ‿**ationsfehler** [‿ka'tsjo:ns-] *m* flaw; ‿**ati'onsnummer** *f* serial number; ‿**besitzer(in** *f) m* factory-owner; ‿**marke** *f* trade mark; ℒ**neu** brand-new; ‿**stadt** *f* manufacturing town; ‿**ware** *f* manufactured *(od.* factory-made) goods *pl. od.* article.

fabrizieren [fabri'tsi:rən] manufacture, make; *fig.* fabricate.

Facett|e ⊕ [fa'sɛtə] *f* (15) facet; ℒ**iert** [‿'ti:rt] faceted.

Fach [fax] *n* (2) compartment; *im Schrank usw.:* partition; *im Schreibtisch:* pigeon-hole; *im Bücherbrett usw.:* shelf; *(Schubfach)* drawer; 🚪 panel; *fig.* department, province, branch, field (of activity), line; *(Geschäft)* business; *(Unterrichtsℒ)* subject; *Musiker usw. von ~* by profession; *s. schlagen*; '‿**arbeiter(in** *f) m* skilled worker; '‿**arzt** *m* (medical) specialist; '‿**(-aus)bildung** *f* specialist training; '‿**ausdruck** *m* technical term; '‿**bereich** *univ. m* department.

fächeln ['fɛçəln] (29) fan.

Fächer ['fɛçər] *m* (7) fan; 'ℒ**förmig** fan-shaped.

'**Fach|gebiet** *n* (special) field *od.* subject; '‿**gelehrte** *m* specialist; 'ℒ**gemäß**, 'ℒ**gerecht** workmanlike, expert; '‿**geschäft** *n* (specialized) dealer; '‿**kenntnisse** *f/pl.* specialized knowledge; '‿**kreis** *m*: *in* ‿*en* among experts; '⍦**kundig** competent, expert; '⍦**lehrer** *m* specialist teacher; '⍦**lich** technical, specialist; '⍦**literatur** *f* technical literature; '⍦**mann** *m* expert, specialist; ⍦**männisch** ['⍦mɛniʃ] expert; *Arbeit:* workmanlike; '⍦**schule** *f* technical school; ⍦**simpeln** ['⍦zimpəln] (29) talk shop; '⍦**sprache** *f* technical terminology; '⍦**studium** *n* specialized study; '⍦**welt** *f* experts *pl.*; '⍦**werk** ⚒ *n* framework, half-timbering; '⍦**wissenschaft** *f* special branch of science; '⍦**zeitschrift** *f* technical (*od.* trade) journal.

Fackel ['fakəl] *f* (15) torch; '⍦**n** F (29) *fig.* hesitate; *ohne lange zu* ⍦ without further ado; '⍦**schein** *m* torch-light; '⍦**träger** *m* torch-bearer; '⍦**zug** *m* torch-light procession.

fad(e) ['fɑːd(ə)] (*schal*) stale; (*geschmacklos*) insipid; (*langweilig*) boring, dull.

Faden ['fɑːdən] *m* (6[1]) thread (*a. fig.*); ⚡ filament; *opt.* hairline; ⚓ *Maß:* fathom; *an e-m* ⍦ *hängen* hang by a thread; '⍦**kreuz** *n* cross wires *pl.*, spider lines *pl.*, retic(u)le; '⍦**netz** *opt. n* graticule; '⍦**nudeln** *f/pl.* vermicelli *pl.*; ⍦**scheinig** ['⍦ʃaɪniç] threadbare (*a. fig.*).

Fading ['feːdiŋ] *n* (11) *Radio:* fading.

Fagott ♪ [fa'gɔt] *n* (3) bassoon; ⍦**ist** [⍦'tist] *m* bassoonist.

fähig ['feːiç] (*zu*) able (to), capable (of), fit (for); *speziell:* qualified; '⍦**keit** *f* ability, capacity; *bsd. geistige:* faculty.

fahl [fɑːl] (*bleich*) pale; *Gesichtsfarbe, Himmel:* livid; (*düster*) lurid.

fahnd|en ['fɑːndən] *v/i.* (26) search, look (*nach* for); '⍦**ung** *f Polizei:* criminal investigation (department); (*Suche*) search.

Fahne ['fɑːnə] *f* (15) flag, standard, banner; ✂, ⚓, *fig.* colo(u)rs *pl.*; *typ.* (galley) proof.

'**Fahnen**|-**eid** *m* oath of allegiance; '⍦**flucht** *f* desertion; '⍦**flüchtig:** ⍦ *werden* desert; '⍦**flüchtige** *m* (18) deserter; '⍦**stange** *f* flag-staff, *Am. a.* flagpole; '⍦**träger** *m* standard-bearer; [⚓ midshipman.]

Fähnrich ['feːnriç] *m* (3) ✂ cadet;⎰
'**Fahr**|**bahn** *f* roadway, *Am. a.* driveway; '⍦**bar** *Maschine usw.:* portable; movable; *Weg usw.:* practicable; ⚓ navigable; '⍦**bereit** ready to start, in running order; '⍦**bereitschaft** *f* car pool; '⍦**damm** *m*, '⍦**weg** *m s. Fahrbahn.*

Fähre ['feːrə] *f* (15) ferry(-boat).

fahren ['fɑːrən] (30) **1.** *v/i.* (sn) *allg.* go; *selbst lenkend:* drive; *auf e-m Fahrrad od. mit e-m öffentlichen Beförderungsmittel:* ride; ⚓ sail, cruise; *Wagen, Schiff, Zug:* go, run; (*in Fahrt sein*) be moving; *gen Himmel* ⍦ ascend to heaven; *zur Hölle* ⍦ descend to hell; *mit der Eisenbahn* ⍦ go by rail *od.* by train; *über e-n Fluß* ⍦ cross a river; *aus dem Hafen* ⍦ clear the port; *s. Haut; auf Grund* ⍦ run aground; *aus dem Bette* ⍦ start up from one's bed; *in die Kleider* ⍦ slip on one's clothes; *mit der Hand* ⍦ *über* (*acc.*) pass one's hand over; ⍦ *lassen fig.* let go, abandon; *gut* (*schlecht*) ⍦ *bei et.* fare well (ill) at *od.* with; *fahr(e) wohl!* farewell!; **2.** *v/t.* drive; ⚓ navigate; (*befördern*) convey; *Boot:* sail, row; '⍦**d** *adj.* vagrant; ⍦*er Ritter* knight errant; ⍦*e Habe* movables *pl.*

'**Fahrer** *m* (7) driver; '⍦**flucht** *f* hit-and-run offen|ce, *Am.* -se; driving away from an accident.

'**Fahr-erlaubnis** *f s. Führerschein.*

'**Fahrgast** *m* passenger.

'**Fahrgeld** *n* fare; '⍦**zuschuß** *m* travel allowance.

'**Fahr**|**gelegenheit** *f* conveyance; '⍦**gemeinschaft** *f* car pool; '⍦**geschwindigkeit** *f* speed; '⍦**gestell** *n* ✈ under-carriage, landing gear; *mot.* chassis; '⍦**ig** fidgety, nervous; '⍦**karte** *f* ticket; '⍦**karten-ausgabe** *f*, '⍦**kartenschalter** *m* booking-office, *Am.* ticket office; '⍦**lässig** reckless, negligent; ⍦*e Tötung* manslaughter (*in the second degree Am.*); '⍦**lässigkeit** *f* (*grobe gross*) negligence; '⍦**lehrer** *mot. m* driving instructor.

'**Fährmann** *m* (1²) ferryman.

'**Fahr**|**plan** *m* time-table (*a. fig.*), *Am.* schedule; '⍦**planmäßig** regular, *Am.* scheduled; *adv.* on time, according to schedule; '⍦**preis** *m* fare; '⍦**preis-anzeiger** *m* taximeter; '⍦**prüfung** *mot. f* driving test; '⍦**rad** *n* bicycle, F bike; '⍦**rinne** ⚓ *f* fairway; '⍦**schein** *m* ticket; '⍦**schein-automat** *m* ticket machine; '⍦**scheinentwerter** *m* ticket cancel(l)ing machine; '~**schule** *mot. f* driving school; '~**schüler** *m* learner; '~**stuhl** *m* lift, *Am.* elevator; '~**stuhlführer** *m* lift-attendant, *Am.* elevator operator; '~**stunde** *f* driving lesson.

Fahrt [faːrt] *f* (16) *im Wagen*: ride, drive; (*Reise*) journey; (*See*⌓) voyage, passage; (*Ausflug*) trip; ⚓ (*Kurs*) course; ~ *ins Blaue* mystery trip; *in voller* ~ (at) full speed; ~ *aufnehmen* gather speed; *in* ~ *kommen* get under way; *fig.* get into one's stride.

Fährte ['fɛːrtə] *f* (15) track, trace; *hunt.* scent (*alle a. fig.*); *auf falscher* ~ *sein* be on the wrong track.

'**Fahrten|buch** *mot. n* (driver's) log-book; '~**schreiber** *mot. m* tachograph.

'**Fahrt|kosten** *pl.* travel(l)ing expenses; '~**richtungs-anzeiger** *m* direction indicator.

'**fahrtüchtig** fit to drive; *Fahrzeug*: roadworthy; '⌓**keit** *f* driving capability; *e-s Fahrzeugs*: roadworthiness.

'**Fahrt|-unterbrechung** *f* break of journey, *Am.* stopover; '~**wind** *m* head wind.

'**Fahr|-unterricht** *m* driving instruction; '~**verbot** *n* driving ban; '~**wasser** *n* navigable water; *s. Fahrrinne*; *fig.* track; '~**weg** *m* carriage-road; '~**werk** ✈ *n s. Fahrgestell*; '~**zeug** *n* vehicle; ⚓ vessel, craft; '~**zeughalter** *m* car-owner; '~**zeugpark** *m* fleet.

Fäkalien [fɛˈkɑːljən] *pl.* (8²) f(a)eces, f(a)ecal matter.

Faksimile [fakˈziːmile] *n* (11) facsimile.

faktisch ['faktiʃ] (f)actual.

Faktor ['faktɔr] *m* (8¹) factor.

Faktotum [~ˈtoːtum] *n* (9²) factotum; *altes* ~ old retainer.

Faktum ['faktum] *n* (9²) fact.

Faktur|(a) [~ˈtuːr(a)] *f* (16²) invoice; ⌓**ieren** [~tuˈriːrən] invoice.

Fakultät *univ.* [fakulˈtɛːt] *f* (16) faculty, *Am.* department.

fakultativ [~taˈtiːf] optional.

falb [falp] dun; ⌓**e** ['~bə] *m* dun (horse).

Falke ['falkə] *m* (13) falcon; '~**n-beize** *f*, '~**njagd** *f* falconry, hawking.

Fall [fal] *m* (3²) fall, drop; (*Vorfall*) case, event; *gr.*, ♪♫, ⚔ case; *den* ~

setzen, *a. gesetzt den* ~ suppose; *auf alle Fälle* at all events, by all means; *auf jeden* ~ in any case, at any rate; *auf keinen* ~ on no account; *im* ~*e* (*wenn*) ... in case ...; *im* ~*e e-s Krieges usw.* in the event of a war *etc.*; *von* ~ *zu* ~ in each case, singly; *den* ~ *setzen* put the case; *zu* ~ *bringen* bring down *od.* low, *fig.* ruin, *parl. Gesetz usw.*: defeat; *zu* ~ *kommen* have a fall, *fig.* come to grief; '~**beil** *n* guillotine; '~**brücke** *f* drawbridge.

Falle ['falə] *f* (15) trap; *fig. a.* pitfall; (*Schlinge*) snare; *j-m e-e* ~ *stellen* set a trap for; *in die* ~ *gehen* walk into the trap.

fallen ['falən] **1.** (30, sn) fall, drop (*a. Preise usw.*); ✗ fall, be killed in action; *Festung usw.*: fall; *Schuß*: be fired *od.* heard; *Bemerkung*: fall; ~ *lassen* drop, let fall; *fig.* dismiss, drop; *es fällt mir schwer* it is difficult for me; *j-m in die Rede* ~ interrupt a p.; ~ *unter ein Gesetz*, *e-e Kategorie usw.* come under; *s. Auge*, *Last usw.*; **2.** ⌓ *n* (6) fall, drop.

fällen ['fɛlən] (25) fell, cut; *Gegner*: fell; *Urteil*: pronounce, pass; *Bajonett*: lower; ⚗ *das Lot*: draw, drop; ⚗ precipitate.

'**Fallensteller** *m* (7) trapper.

'**Fall|geschwindigkeit** *f* rate of fall; '~**gesetz** *phys. n* law of falling bodies; '~**grube** *f* pitfall.

fallieren † [faˈliːrən] fail.

fällig ['fɛliç] due; *Geld*: *a.* payable; *Wechsel*: *a.* mature; *längst* ~ overdue; ~ (*zahlbar*) *sein* (*od. werden*) fall (*od.* become) due, *Wechsel*: *a.* mature; '⌓**keits-termin** *m* maturity, due date.

'**Fall|-obst** *n* windfall; ~**reep** ⚓ ['~reːp] *n* (3) gangway; jack ladder; '~**rohr** ⊕ *n* down-pipe.

falls [fals] in case, if.

'**Fall|schirm** *m* parachute; '~**schirm-absprung** *m* parachute jump; '~**schirmjäger** *m* paratrooper; '~**schirmspringen** *n* parachuting; *Sport*: skydiving; '~**schirmspringer** *m* (7) parachutist; *Sport*: skydiver; '~**schirmtruppen** *f/pl.* paratroops; '~**strick** *m* snare; *fig. a.* trap, pitfall; '~**sucht** *f* falling sickness; ⌓**süchtig** ['~zyçtiç] epileptic; '~**tür** *f* trap-door; '~**wind** *m* katabatic wind.

falsch [falʃ] *allg.* false (*a. Eid, Freund, Haar, Name, Scham, Stolz, Zähne*); (*verkehrt*) wrong; (*unecht*) counterfeit, *Am.* F phon(e)y, fake; (*nachgemacht, vorgetäuscht*) mock, sham; *Münze*: base; *Wechsel*: forged; *Mensch*: deceitful; e-e *S.* ~ anpacken do a th. the wrong way; ~ *auffassen* misconceive; ~ *aussprechen* mispronounce; ~ *darstellen* misrepresent; ~ *gehen Uhr*: go (*od.* be) wrong; ~ *singen* sing out of tune; *j-n* ~ *unterrichten* misinform a p.; *ohne* ♀ guileless; *s. Kehle, Spiel.*

fälschen ['fɛlʃən] (27) falsify; *Geld*: counterfeit; *Bücher, Rechnung*: fake; *Nahrungsmittel*: adulterate; *Urkunde, Unterschrift*: forge.

'**Fälscher** *m* (7), '~**in** *f* falsifier; faker; adulterator; forger.

'**Falschgeld** *n* counterfeit (*od.* bogus) money.

'**Falschheit** *f* falseness, falsity.

'**fälschlich** (*adv. a.* ~*erweise*) false(ly *adv.*); wrong(ly).

'**Falsch|meldung** *f* false report; '~**münzer** *m* (7) counterfeiter; ~**münze'rei** *f* counterfeiting; '~**spieler** *m* card-sharper.

'**Fälschung** *f vgl. fälschen*: falsification; fake; adulteration; forgery.

'**Falt|boot** *n* collapsible boat, folding canoe; '~**dach** *mot. n* folding top.

Falte ['faltə] *f* (15) fold; *am Kleid*: pleat; (*Bügel*♀) crease; (*Runzel*) wrinkle; *der Stirn*: furrow.

fältel|n ['fɛltəln] (29) pleat; '♀**ung** *f* pleat(ing).

falten ['faltən] (26) fold; *Hände*: fold, clasp, join; '♀**rock** *m* pleated skirt; '♀**wurf** *m* drapery.

'**Falter** *m* (7) butterfly, moth.

'**faltig** folded; pleated; *Stirn*: wrinkled.

'**Faltkarte** *f* folding (*od.* pull-out) map.

Falz [falts] *m* (3²) fold; *Tischlerei*: rabbet; *Buchbinderei*: guard; '~**bein** *n* folder; paper-knife; '♀**en** (27) fold; *Tischlerei*: rabbet.

Fama ['faːma] *f* fame; (*Gerücht*) rumo(u)r.

familiär [famil'jɛːr] familiar.

Familie [fa'miːljə] *f* (15) family.

Fa'milien|-ähnlichkeit *f* family likeness; ~**angelegenheit** *f* family

affair; ~'**anschluß** *m*: ~ *haben* live as one of the family; ~**betrieb** *m* family business; ~**feier** *f* family celebration (*od.* party); ~**gericht** ⚖ *n* Family Court; ~**glück** *n* domestic happiness; ~**leben** *n* family life; ~**nachrichten** *f/pl. in Zeitungen*: births, marriages, and deaths; ~**name** *m* family (*Am. a.* last) name, surname; ~**planung** *f* family planning; ~**stand** *m* family status; (*Ehestand*) marital status; ~**vater** *m* father of (a) family, family man; ~**zuwachs** *m* addition to the family.

famos [fa'moːs] excellent, capital, F grand, great.

Fan F [fɛn] *m* (11) fan.

Fanal [fa'naːl] *n* (3¹) *bsd. fig.* beacon.

Fanatiker [fa'naːtikər] *m* (7), ~**in** *f* (16¹) fanatic; *für Sport usw.*: F fan.

fa'natisch fanatic(al).

Fanatismus [fana'tismus] *m* (16, *o. pl.*) fanaticism.

fand [fant] *pret. v. finden.*

Fanfare [fan'faːrə] *f* (15) fanfare, flourish of trumpets.

Fang [faŋ] *m* (3³) catch; capture (*beide a. konkret*); (*Zahn*) fang; (*Kralle*) claw, talon; (*Beute*) booty; '~**ball** *m* catch-ball; '~**eisen** *n* iron trap; '♀**en** (30) catch; *engS.* capture; *sich* ~ be caught; *fig.* rally; settle down; '~**frage** *f* trick question; '~**zahn** *m* fang; *des Ebers*: tusk.

Fant [fant] *m* (3) coxcomb, fop.

Farb|band ['farpbant] *n* typewriter ribbon; '~**beilage** *f* colo(u)r supplement; '~**bild** *n* colo(u)r photo; '~**druck** *m* colo(u)r print.

Farbe ['~bə] *f* (15) colo(u)r; (*Farbstoff*) dye; (*Färbung, Farbton*) hue; (*Anstrich*) paint; (*Haut*♀) complexion; *Kartenspiel*: suit.

farb-echt ['farp-] colo(u)r-fast.

Färbemittel ['fɛrbə-] *n* dye(-stuff).

färben ['fɛrbən] (25) colo(u)r (*a. sich u. fig.*); *Haar, Stoff*: dye; *Papier, Glas, mit Blut*: stain; (*tönen*) tint, tinge.

'**farben|blind** colo(u)r-blind; '♀**druck** *m* colo(u)r-printing; *Bild*: colo(u)r-print; '~**freudig**, '~**froh** colo(u)rful, gaily colo(u)red; '♀**lehre** *f* theory of colo(u)rs, 🕮 chromatics *pl. u. sg.*; '~**prächtig**, '~**reich** colo(u)rful; '♀**spiel** *n* play of colo(u)rs, 🕮 iridescence; '♀**zusammenstellung** *f* colo(u)r scheme.

Färber ['fɛrbər] *m* (7) dyer.
Färberei [~'raɪ] *f* (16) dye-house.
Farb|fernsehen ['farp-] *n* colo(u)r television; '**~film** *m* colo(u)r film; '**~filter** *phot. m* colo(u)r filter.
farbig ['farbiç] colo(u)red; *fig.* colo(u)rful.
Farb|kopierer ['farp-] *m* colo(u)r copier; '**2los** colo(u)rless; '**~photographie** *f Bild:* colo(u)r photo; *Verfahren:* colo(u)r photography; '**~stift** *m* colo(u)red pencil; '**~stoff** *m* pigment (*a. physiol.*), colo(u)ring matter; ⊕ dye(-stuff); '**~ton** *m* tone; *vorherrschender:* hue; *bsd. heller:* tint; (*Schattierung*) shade.
Färbung ['fɛrbun] *f* colo(u)ring; hue; *bsd. leichte:* tinge.
Far|ce ['farsə] *f* (15) farce; *Küche:* forcemeat, stuffing; 2**'cieren** stuff.
Farm [farm] *f* (16) farm; *Am. bsd. zur Viehzucht:* ranch; '**~er** *m* (7) farmer; *Am. a.* rancher.
Farn [farn] *m* (3), '**~kraut** *n* fern.
Fasan [fa'za:n] *m* (3 *u.* 8) pheasant; **~erie** [~ə'ri:] *f* (15) pheasantry.
Fasching ['faʃɪŋ] *m* (3¹) carnival.
Faschis|mus [fa'ʃɪsmus] *m* Fascism; **~t** *m* (12), **~tin** *f* (16¹) Fascist; 2**tisch** Fascist(ic).
Fasel|ei [fa:zə'laɪ] *f* drivel, twaddle; '2**n** (29) drivel, babble.
Faser ['fa:zər] *f* (15) fib|re, *Am.* -er; *im Holz:* grain; ⚥ string; '2**ig** fibrous; *Fleisch etc.:* stringy; '2**n** *v/t. u. v/i.* (29) (*a. sich*) ravel (out), fray, fuzz.
Faß [fas] *n* (2¹) cask, barrel; (*Bütte*) vat, tub; (*frisch*) *vom ~ beer* on draught, *wine* from the wood; F *das schlägt dem ~ den Boden aus!* that is the last straw!
Fassade [fa'sa:də] *f* (15) façade, front (*a. fig.*); **~nkletterer** *m* cat burglar.
'**Faßbier** *n* draught beer.
Fäßchen ['fɛsçən] *n* (6) small cask *od.* barrel, keg.
fassen ['fasən] (28) seize, get (*od.* take) hold of; *s. einfassen;* (*fangen*) catch (*a. fig.*); (*begreifen*) grasp; (*enthalten*) hold, contain; *Entschluß:* take; *s. Auge usw.;* *e-n Plan ~* form a plan; *Tritt ~* fall into step; *in Worte ~* word; *sich ~* compose o.s.; *sich schnell wieder ~* rally quickly; *sich kurz ~* be brief, cut it short; *zum Hund: faß ihn!* sick him!;

s. gefaßt.
'**faßlich** conceivable, intelligible.
Fasson [fa'sõ] *f* (11¹) shape, form, style.
'**Fassung** *f s. Einfassung; der Brille:* frame; ⚡ holder, socket; *fig.* composure; *schriftliche:* draft(ing); (*Lesart*) version; (*Wortlaut*) wording; *aus der ~ bringen* disconcert, upset; *die ~ verlieren* lose hold of o.s.
'**Fassungs|gabe** *f,* '**~kraft** *f* power of comprehension, (mental) capacity, grasp; '2**los** shaken, speechless; '**~vermögen** *n* capacity; *fig. s. Fassungsgabe.*
fast [fast] *vor su. u. adj.* mst almost; *vor Zahlen, Maß- u. Zeitangaben* mst nearly; *~ nichts* next to nothing; *~ nie* hardly ever; *ich habe es ~ erwartet* F I kind of expected it.
fasten ['fastən] **1.** (26) fast; **2.** ⚥ *n* (6) fasting; *pl.* fast(ing); *s. ~zeit;* '2**zeit** *f* Lent.
'**Fast|nacht** *f* Shrove Tuesday; (*Fasching*) Shrovetide, carnival; '**~tag** *m* fast(ing)-day.
faszinieren [fastsi'ni:rən] fascinate.
fatal [fa'ta:l] disastrous; (*peinlich*) awkward, annoying.
Fatalismus [fata'lismus] *m* (16, *o. pl.*) fatalism.
Fatum ['fa:tum] *n* (9²) fate.
fauchen ['fauxən] (25) hiss (*a. fig. P.*).
faul [faul] (*modrig, verdorben*) rotten, putrid, bad; *Zahn:* carious, decayed; (*stinkend*) foul; (*träge*) idle, lazy; (*verdächtig*) fishy; *~er Kunde* bad customer; *~er Witz bad* (*od.* stale) joke; *~er Zauber* humbug.
Fäule ['fɔylə] *f* (15) *s. Fäulnis.*
faulen ['faulən] (25) rot, decay.
faulenz|en ['~lɛntsən] (27) loaf, laze; '2**er(in** *f*) *m* idler, sluggard, do-nothing, F lazy-bones (*sg.*); 2**erei** [~'raɪ] *f* loafing, laziness.
'**Faul|heit** *f* laziness; '2**ig** rotten, putrid.
Fäulnis ['fɔylnɪs] *f* (14², *o. pl.*) rot, rottenness, decay; *in ~ übergehen* rot, putrefy.
'**Faul|pelz** *m s. Faulenzer;* '**~tier** *n* sloth (*a. fig.*).
Faust [faust] *f* (14¹) fist; *auf eigene ~* on one's own (account); *s. ballen;* *e-e ~ machen* double up one's hand; *mit der ~ auf den Tisch schlagen* *fig.* put one's foot down; *wie die*

~ *aufs Auge* like a square peg in a round hole.

Fäustchen ['fɔʏstçən] *n* (6): *sich ins ~ lachen* laugh up one's sleeve.

'**faust|dick** (as) big as a fist; *Lüge: sl.* whopping; *es ~ hinter den Ohren haben* be a deep one; '♀**feuerwaffe** *f* handgun; '♀**handschuh** *m* mitten; '♀**kampf** *m* boxing; *einzelner*: boxing-match; '♀**kämpfer** *m* boxer, pugilist; '♀**pfand** *n* dead pledge, pawn; '♀**recht** *n* club-law; '♀**regel** *f* rule of thumb; '♀**schlag** *m* punch.

Favorit [favo'riːt] *m* (12), **~in** *f* (16¹) favo(u)rite.

Faxe ['faksə] *f* (15) foolery, antic; **~n** *machen* clown; '**~nmacher** *m* clown, buffoon.

Fazit ['faːtsit] *n*(3¹ *u.* 11) result, sum (total); *das ~ ziehen* sum (it) up.

Februar ['feːbruaːr] *m* (3¹), *a.* **Feber** ['feːbər] *m* (7) February.

Fecht|boden ['fɛçt-] *m* fencing--room; '♀**en** *v/i.* (30) fight (*a. v/t.*); *fenc.* fence; (*betteln*) cadge; '**~er** *m* (7) fighter; fencer; swordsman; (*Bettler*) cadger; '**~kunst** *f* (art of) fencing; '**~meister** *m* fencing--master; '**~schule** *f* fencing-school.

Feder ['feːdər] *f* (15) feather; (*Schmuck♀*) plume; (*Schreib♀*) pen; ⊕ spring; '**~ball** *m* 1. shuttlecock; 2. = '**~ballspiel** *n* badminton; '**~bett** *n* feather-bed; '**~brett** *n Sport*: springboard; '**~busch** *m*, '**~büschel** *n* tuft of feathers, plume; '**~fuchser** ['~fuksər] *m* (7) quill--driver, scribbler; '♀**führend** *fig.* responsible, in charge; '**~gewicht** (**-ler** *m*) *n Boxen*: featherweight; '**~halter** *m* penholder; '**~kasten** *m* pencil box; '**~kernmatratze** *f* spring-interior mattress; '**~kiel** *m* quill; '**~kraft** *f* resilience; '**~krieg** *m* literary feud; '♀**leicht** (as) light as a feather; '**~lesen** *n*: *nicht viel ~s machen mit* make short work of; **~mäppchen** ['~mɛpçən] *n* (6) pencil case; '**~messer** *n* penknife; '♀**n** (29) *v/i.* lose feathers; ⊕ be elastic *od.* resilient; (*schnellen*) jerk, bounce; *v/t.* ⊕ spring; *Holz*: tongue; *gut gefedert* well sprung; '♀**nd** elastic, resilient; ⊕ springy (*a. fig.*); '**~strich** *m* stroke of the pen; '**~ung** *f* springing; springs *pl.*; *mot.* spring-suspension; '**~vieh** *n* poultry; '**~waage** *f* spring-balance; '**~wild** *n* winged

game; '**~wolke** *f* cirrus; '**~zeichnung** *f* pen-and-ink drawing.

Fee [feː] *f* (15) fairy; *gute ~* fairy godmother; '♀**nhaft** fairylike; '**~n-reigen** *m* fairy-ring.

'**Fegefeuer** *n* purgatory.

fegen ['feːgən] (25) *v/t.* sweep; *v/i.* (*sausen*) rush, flit.

Fehde ['feːdə] *f* (15) feud; '**~hand-schuh** *m* gauntlet; *den ~ aufnehmen* take up the gauntlet.

Fehl [feːl] *m*: *ohne ~ P.*: without fault, *S.*: without blemish, flawless; ♀ *am Platze* out of place; '**~anzeige** *f a.* ✕ nil return; '**~ball** *m Tennis*: fault; '♀**bar** fallible; '**~besetzung** *f* wrong choice (*od.* man); *thea.* miscast(ing); '**~bestand** *m* deficiency; '**~betrag** *m* deficit, shortage; '**~bitte** *f*: *eine ~ tun* meet with a refusal; '**~diagnose** ⚕ *f* false diagnosis; '**~einschätzung** *f* miscalculation.

fehlen ['feːlən] 1. (25) (*nicht anwesend sein*) be absent (*in der Schule, bei e-r Feier usw.* from); (*irren*) err; (*fehlschlagen*; *im Stich lassen*) fail; (*sündigen*) do wrong; (*nicht vorhanden sein*) be missing (*od.* lacking, wanting); (*vorbeischießen*) miss (*a. v/t.*); *~ gegen* offend against; *es fehlt* (*an dat.*) *et.* a th. is wanting *od.* lacking; *es fehlt mir an* (*dat.*) I want *od.* lack *a th.*, I am lacking in; *es ~ lassen an* (*dat.*) fail in; *er fehlt mir sehr* I miss him badly; *was fehlt Ihnen?* what ails you?, what is the matter with you?, what is wrong with you?; *es fehlte nicht viel, und ich hätte ... a* little more and I would have ...; *das fehlte gerade noch!* it only wanted that!; *wo fehlt's* (*denn*)? what's wrong?; *weit gefehlt!* far from the mark!; 2. ♀ *n* absence.

'**Fehl-entscheidung** *f* incorrect (*od.* wrong) decision; mistake.

Fehler ['feːlər] *m* (7) (*Mangel*) defect, flaw (*a.* ⊕); (*Charakter♀*; *Verstoß*; *Schuld*; *~ beim Tennis*) fault; (*Mißgriff, Versehen*) mistake; (*Irrtum*) error; *grober*: blunder; '♀**frei**, '♀**los** faultless, *a.* ⊕ flawless; '♀**haft** faulty, defective; (*unrichtig*) incorrect; '**~quelle** *f* source of error; '**~quote** *f* error rate.

'**Fehl|farbe** *f* off shade; '**~geburt** *f* miscarriage; '♀**gehen** (sn) miss one's way, (*a. fig.*) go wrong;

Schuß: miss (its mark); (*mißlingen*) fail; '♀**greifen** miss one's hold; *fig.* make a mistake; '**~griff** *m fig.* mistake, blunder; '**~kalkulation** *f* miscalculation; '**~leistung** *f* slip, blunder; '♀**schießen** miss (one's aim *od.* the mark); '**~schlag** *m* miss; *fig.* failure; (*Enttäuschung*) disappointment; '♀**schlagen** miss; *fig.* (sn) fail; '**~schluß** *m* wrong conclusion, fallacy; **~schuß** *m* miss; '**~start** *m* false start; '♀**treten** make a false step; '**~tritt** *m* false step; *fig.* blunder, faux pas (*fr.*); *moralisch*: slip, lapse; '**~urteil** *n* error of judg(e)ment; ♀♀ incorrect sentence; '**~verhalten** *n* abnormal behavio(u)r; '**~zeit** *f bei gleitender Arbeitszeit*: time debit; '♀**zünden** *v/i.*, '**~zündung** *mot. f* misfire.

Feier ['faɪər] *f* (15) (*Arbeitsruhe*) rest; (*Feiertag*) holiday; *e-s Festes*: celebration; *konkret*: ceremony; (*Festlichkeit*) festival; *zur ~ des Tages* to mark the occasion; '**~abend** *m* closing time; *weitS.* leisure-time; *~ machen* leave off work, F knock off; '♀**lich** solemn; '**~lichkeit** *f* solemnity; (*Feier*) ceremony; (*Aufwand*) pomp; '♀**n** (29) *v/t.* celebrate; *v/i.* rest (from work), make holiday; (*faulenzen*) take it easy; *s. streiken*; '**~stunde** *f* festive hour; '**~tag** *m* holiday; *gesetzlicher ~* public (*od.* bank) holiday.

feig(e[1]**)** [faɪk, 'faɪɡə] cowardly.
'**Feige**[2] *f* (15) fig; '**~nbaum** *m* fig-tree; '**~nblatt** *n* fig-leaf.

Feig|heit ['faɪkhaɪt] *f* cowardice; '**~ling** *m* (3[1]) coward.

feil [faɪl] for sale, to be sold; *fig.* venal; '**~bieten** offer for sale; *contp.* prostitute.

Feile ['faɪlə] *f* (15) file; '♀**n** (25) file (*a. fig.*).

'**feilhalten** have on sale.
'**Feilheit** *f* venality.

feilschen ['faɪlʃən] (27) (*um*) bargain (for), haggle (about).

fein [faɪn] *allg.* fine; (*verfeinert; gebildet*) refined; *Benehmen*: polite; *Gebäck*: fancy; (*geschmackvoll*) elegant; (*zart*) delicate; (*subtil*) subtle; F (*famos*) excellent, splendid; *~er Ton* good form; '♀**-abstimmung** *f* fine tuning; '♀**bäckerei** *f* fancy bakery; '♀**blech** *n* (thin) sheet.

Feind [faɪnt] **1.** *m* (3), **~in** ['~dɪn] *f* (16[1]) enemy; *rhet.* foe; **2.** ♀ hostile (*dat.* to).

feindlich ['~tlɪç] hostile (*gegen* to); '♀**keit** *f* hostility.
'**Feindschaft** *f* enmity; hostility; (*Streit*) feud, quarrel; (*Zwietracht*) discord.
'**feindselig** hostile; '♀**keit** *f* hostility.
'**fein|fühlend**, '**~fühlig** sensitive; (*zartfühlend*) delicate; tactful; '♀**gefühl** *n* sensitiveness; delicacy; tact; '♀**gehalt** *m* standard.
'**Feinheit** *f s. fein*: fineness; refinement; politeness; delicacy; subtlety; elegance; *die ~en pl.* niceties.
fein|hörig ['~høːrɪç] quick of hearing; '♀**kost** *f s. Delikatessen*; '**~maschig** ['~maʃɪç] fine-meshed; '♀**mechanik** *f* precision engineering; '♀**mechaniker** *m* precision-instrument maker; '**~mechanisch** precision ...; '♀**schmecker** *m* (7) gourmet; '♀**schnitt** *m* (*Tabak*) fine cut; '**~sinnig** subtle; sensitive; '♀**wäsche** *f* (dainty) lingerie; (*Waschen*) fine laundering.

feist [faɪst] fat, stout.

Feld [fɛlt] *n* (1) field (*a. fig.* ✕, ⚔, *Sport*); (*Grund, Boden*) ground; △, ⊕, panel, compartment; *Schach*: square; *aus dem ~e schlagen fig.* defeat, outstrip; *ins ~ führen* advance (*arguments*); *fig. freies ~* a clear field; '**~arbeit** *f* agricultural work; ✠ *usw.* field work; '**~bahn** *f* field-railway; '**~bau** *m* agriculture, tillage; '**~bett** *n* camp-bed; '**~bluse** ✕ *f* service blouse; '**~dienst** *m* field duty; '**~flasche** *f* canteen, water-bottle; '**~frucht** *f* fruit of the earth; '**~geistliche** *m* army chaplain; '**~gendarmerie** *f* (15) military police; '**~herr** *m allg.* general; *als Titel*: commander-in-chief; '**~herrnkunst** *f* strategy, generalship; '**~hüter** *m* field-guard; '**~küche** *f* field-kitchen; '**~lager** *n* bivouac, camp; '**~lazarett** *n* casualty clearing station, *Am.* evacuation hospital; '**~marschall** *m* Field Marshal; '♀**marschmäßig** in (heavy) marching order; '**~maus** *f* field-mouse; '**~messer** *m* (7) surveyor; '**~mütze** *f* forage-cap; '**~salat** *m* lamb's lettuce; '**~schlacht** *f* battle; '**~spat** ['~ʃpaːt] *m* fel(d)spar; '**~stecher** *m* field-glasses *pl.*; '**~studie** *f Soziologie etc.*: field study; '**~stuhl** *m* camp-stool; '**~we-**

bel ['ˌveːbəl] *m* (7) sergeant; '**ˌweg** *m* field-path; '**ˌzeichen** *n* ensign, standard; '**ˌzug** *m* campaign (*a. fig.*), expedition.

Felge ['fɛlɡə] *f* (15) felloe, felly, *bsd. mot.* rim; *Turnen*: circle.

Fell [fɛl] *n* (3) (*Haut des lebenden Tieres mit Haaren*) coat; (*abgezogenes* ˌ) *v. größeren Tieren*: hide, *v. kleineren Tieren*: skin; (*rohes* ˌ *v. Pelztieren*) pelt; (*Pelz*) fur; *v. Menschen*: hide, skin; *s. abziehen*; *fig.* er hat ein sehr dickes ˌ he is very thick-skinned; *fig.* F j-m das ˌ gerben give a p. a good hiding; j-m das ˌ über die Ohren ziehen fleece a p.; *fig. s-e* ˌe davonschwimmen sehen see a cake turn into dough.

Fels [fɛls] *m* (12¹), **ˌen** ['ˌzən] *m* (6) rock; '**ˌblock** *m* rock, boulder.

'**felsen|fest** rock-like; *Glaube usw.*: unshakeable; ˌ überzeugt firmly convinced; '**ˌklippe** *f* cliff; '**ˌriff** *n* reef.

felsig ['fɛlzɪç] rocky.

Fem|e ['feːmə] *f* (15) vehme; '**ˌgericht** *n* vehmic court.

Femininum *gr.* [femi'niːnum] *n* (9²) feminine noun.

Feminis|mus [femi'nɪsmus] *m* (16) feminism; **ˌt** *m* (12), **ˌtin** *f* (16¹) feminist.

Fenchel ['fɛnçəl] *m* (7) fennel.

Fenn [fɛn] *n* (3¹) fen, bog.

Fenster ['fɛnstər] *n* (7) window; '**ˌbrett** *n* window-sill; '**ˌbrüstung** *f* window-ledge; '**ˌflügel** *m* casement (*od.* wing) of the window; '**ˌgitter** *n* window-grate; '**ˌglas** *n* window-glass; '**ˌkreuz** *n* cross-bar(s *pl.*); '**ˌladen** *m* window shutter; '**ˌleder** *n* chamois (leather); '**ˌpfosten** *m* mullion; '**ˌplatz** *m* seat by the window; '**ˌrahmen** *m* window-frame; *des Schiebefensters*: sash; '**ˌrose** △ *f* rose window; '**ˌscheibe** *f* window-pane; '**ˌsims** *n* window-sill.

Ferien ['feːrjən] *pl. inv.* holidays *pl.*; ⁂, *univ. od. Am.* vacation; *parl.* recess; ˌ machen, in die ˌ gehen take one's holidays, *Am.* (take a) vacation; '**ˌdorf** *n* holiday camp; '**ˌhaus** *n* holiday home; '**ˌreisende** *m, f* holiday-maker; '**ˌwohnung** *f* holiday flat; '**ˌzeit** *f* holiday season.

Ferkel ['fɛrkəl] *n* (7) young pig; *fig.* pig; '**ˌn** (29) farrow, pig.

Fermate ♩ [fɛr'maːtə] *f* (15) pause.

fern [fɛrn] far (*a. adv.*); distant, remote (*beide a. fig.*); (*weit fort*) far off; *von* ˌ from afar; *das sei* ˌ *von mir* far be it from me.

'**Fern|-amt** *teleph. n* trunk (*Am.* long-distance *od.* toll) exchange; '**ˌ-aufnahme** *f*, '**ˌbild** *n* telephoto(graph); '**ˌbleiben** (sn) keep away (*dat.* from), absent o.s. (from); '**ˌbleiben** *n* (6) absence; *vom Arbeitsplatz*: absenteeism; '**ˌe** *f* (15) distance, remoteness; *aus der* ˌ from a distance, from afar; *in der* ˌ in the (*od.* at a) distance.

ferner ['fɛrnər] farther; *fig.* further (-more), moreover; *Sport*: ˌ liefen ... also ran ...; '**ˌhin** for the future; henceforth; *auch* ˌ *et.* tun continue to do.

'**Fern|fahrer** *m* long-distance lorry (*Am.* truck) driver; '**ˌflug** ✈ *m* long-distance flight; '**ˌgelenkt** ['ˌɡəlɛŋkt] remote-controlled; *Geschoß*: guided; '**ˌgespräch** *teleph. n* trunk call, *Am.* long-distance (*od.* toll) call; '**ˌgesteuert** *s.* ferngelenkt; '**ˌglas** *n* binocular(s *pl.*); *s. a.* Fernrohr; '**ˌhalten** (*a. sich*) keep away (*von* from); '**ˌheizung** *f* district heating; '**ˌkamera** *f* telecamera; '**ˌkopie** *teleph. f* facsimile; '**ˌkopierer** *teleph. m* facsimile machine; '**ˌkurs(us)** *m* correspondence course; '**ˌlaster** *m*, '**ˌlastwagen** *m* long-distance lorry, *Am.* long haul truck; '**ˌleitung** *f* *teleph.* trunk-line, *Am.* long-distance line; (*Röhren*⚲) pipeline; '**ˌlenkung** *f* remote control; '**ˌlicht** *mot. n* full beam; '**ˌliegen** (*dat.*) be far from; '**ˌmeldetechnik** *f*, '**ˌmeldewesen** *n* telecommunications *pl.*; '**ˌmündlich** telephonic; *adv.* by telephone; '**ˌrohr** *n* telescope; '**ˌruf** *m* telephone call; *s.* Ferngespräch; '**ˌschnellzug** *m* long-distance express train; '**ˌschreiben** *n* teleprint, *Am.* teletype (message); '**ˌschreiber** *m* teleprinter; '**ˌsehen** *n* (6) television (*abbr.* TV); *im* ˌ on television; '**ˌsehen** *v/i.* watch television; '**ˌseher** *m P.*: viewer; *s.* Fernsehgerät; '**ˌsehfilm** *m* telefilm; '**ˌsehgebühren** *f/pl.* television licence fee *sg.*; '**ˌsehgerät** *n* television set, F telly; '**ˌsehkamera** *f* television camera; '**ˌsehschirm** *m* television screen; '**ˌsehsender** *m* television transmitter;

(*Fernsehanstalt*) television station; '**~sehsendung** *f* television program(me), telecast; '**~sehserie** *f* television series; '**~sehspiel** *n* teleplay; '**~sehturm** *m* television tower; '**~sicht** *f* (distant) view; 2**sichtig** ['~ziçtiç] long-sighted.

'**Fernsprech|-amt** *n* telephone exchange; '**~anschluß** *m* telephone connection; '**~apparat** *m* telephone set; '**~auskunft** *f* directory enquiries *pl.*; '**~automat** *m* coin-box telephone, *Am.* pay station; '**~buch** *n* telephone directory; '**~er** *m* (7) telephone; *s. a.* Telephon; '**~stelle** *f* (public) call-office; '**~teilnehmer** *m* telephone subscriber; '**~wesen** *n* telephony; '**~zelle** *f* telephone box (*Am.* booth).

'**fern|stehen** (*dat.*) be a stranger to, not to be close to; '2**steuerung** *f* remote (*od.* distant) control; 2**studium** *n*, '2**-unterricht** *m* correspondence course(s *pl.*); '2**verkehr** *m* long-distance traffic; '2**verkehrsstraße** *f* trunk road, *Am.* highway; '2**waffe** *f* long-range weapon; '2**wahl** *teleph.* *f* trunk (*Am.* direct distance) dial(l)ing; '2**zug** *m* long--distance train.

Ferse ['fɛrzə] *f* (15) heel; *fig. auf den ~n* (*dat.*) on the heels of; '**~ngeld** *n* geben take to one's heels.

fertig ['fɛrtiç] ready; (*beendet*) finished; (*~gekauft*) *Kleid:* ready-made, F reach-me-down; *fig.* (*vollendet*) accomplished, perfect; F (*erschöpft*) all in, (*ruiniert*) done for, (*verblüfft*) flabbergasted; ~ werden mit, ~ machen finish; mit j-m od. et. ~ werden deal (*od.* cope) with, manage, handle; *s.* fertigmachen; mit et. ~ sein have done; mit j-m ~ sein have done (F *bsd. Am.* be through) with a p.; ohne et. ~ werden manage (*od.* do) without a th.; es ~, zu *inf.* manage to *inf.*; '2**bauweise** *f* prefab(ricated) construction; '**~bekommen,** '**~bringen** manage (et. a th.); '**~en** ['~gən] (25) *s.* anfertigen; '2**fabrikat** *n s.* Fertigware; '2**gericht** *n* instant meal; '2**haus** *n* prefab(ricated house); '2**keit** *f* skill; (*Können*) proficiency; (*Sprech*2) fluency; '**~machen** ready (zu for); F *fig.* fix, do for, (*erschöpfen*, *a. seelisch*) finish, (*abkanzeln*) tick *a p.* off; '**~stellen** complete; '2**stellung** *f*

completion; 2**ung** ['~guŋ] *f* (16) manufacture, production; '2**ungsstraße** ⊕ *f* production line; '2**ware** *f* finished article *od.* product.

Fes ♩ [fɛs] *n* F flat.

fesch [fɛʃ] smart, chic, stylish; (*schneidig*) dashing.

Fessel ['fɛsəl] *f* (15) (*a. fig.*) fetter, chain; *pl.* (*Hand*2*n*) handcuffs, manacles; *anat.* ankle; *vet.* fetlock, pastern; '**~ballon** *m* captive balloon; '**~gelenk** *vet. n* pastern-joint.

fesseln ['fɛsəln] (29) fetter, chain; (*binden*) tie, bind; *fig.* (*bezaubern*) captivate, fascinate; *Aufmerksamkeit*, *Auge usw.*: catch, arrest, rivet; *ans Bett, Zimmer ~* confine to one's bed, room; '**~d** *fig.* captivating, fascinating; (*spannend*) gripping.

fest[1] [fɛst] *allg.* firm (*a. ♣*); (*nicht flüssig; festgefügt*) solid; (*unbeweglich*) fixed (*a. Preis*); (*nicht losgehend*) fast; (*festhaltend*) tight; (*unerschütterlich*) firm, steady; ⊕ (*orts~*) stationary; ⚔ *Ort usw.*: fortified; *Schlaf:* sound; *Berufsstellung, Wohnsitz:* permanent; ~ *schlafen* sleep fast, be fast asleep; *in e-r Wissenschaft ~ sein* be well versed in; *die Tür ist ~ zu* the door is fast; F *~(e)! go it!; ~ mit j-m gehen* go steady with a p.

Fest[2] [~] *n* (3²) festival; fête, festivity; (*kirchliches ~; ~mahl*) feast; '**~akt** *m* ceremony; 2**besoldet** salaried; '2**binden** fasten, tie (*an dat.* to); '**~e** *f* (15) stronghold; '**~essen** *n* feast, banquet; *sich* '2**fahren** get stuck; *sich* '2**fressen** ⊕ seize; '**~gelage** *n* feast, banquet; '**~halle** *f* *s.* Festsaal; '2**halten** *v/t.* hold fast; (*packen*) seize; *polizeilich:* detain; *in Bild, Wort, Ton:* record, *Stimmung usw.*: capture; *j-n ~ (auf j-n einreden)* buttonhole a p.; *v/i. ~ an* (*dat.*) keep (*od.* cling, adhere) to; (*a. sich ~ an*) hold fast to.

festig|en ['~igən] (25) (*sichern*) secure; (*stärken*) strengthen; *Macht usw.*: establish (firmly), consolidate; *Währung:* stabilize; *sich ~* grow stronger; 2**keit** ['~içkait] *f* firmness; solidity; steadiness (*s. fest*); 2**ung** ['~iguŋ] *f s.* festigen: strengthening; establishment; consolidation; stabilization.

'**fest|kleben** *v/i.* adhere, stick (*an dat.* to); *v/t.* fasten (*od.* stick) with glue *od.* gum; '❬kleid *n* festive dress; '❬körper... ⚇ solid-state; '❬land *n* mainland; continent; '❬legen fix; *Geld:* tie up, freeze; *Regel usw.:* lay down; *j-n auf et.* ❬ pin a p. down to a th.; *sich auf et.* ❬ commit o.s. to a th.

'festlich festive, solemn; '❬keit *f* festivity, solemnity; *s. Fest²*.

'fest|machen fix, fasten; *Handel:* close; '❬mahl *n* feast, banquet; ❬-nahme ['❬na:mə] *f* (15) arrest; '❬nehmen seize, arrest; '❬-ordner *m* steward; '❬-ordnung *f* table of events; '❬platte *f Computer:* hard disk; '❬preis ✞ *m* fixed price; '❬rede *f* speech of the day; '❬saal (banqueting-)hall; ballroom; '❬setzen fix; *sich* ❬ settle (down); '❬spiele *n/pl.* Festival *sg.*; '❬stecken pin; '❬stehen be steady; *fig.* be certain; '❬stehend stationary, fixed; *Regel, Tatsache:* established; '❬stellen establish; (*ermitteln*) ascertain, find out; *Ort, Lage:* locate; *Personalien:* identify; (*konstatieren*) state; (*erklären*) declare; '❬stellung *f* establishment; statement; ascertainment; location; identification; '❬tag *m* festive day, holiday; (*Glückstag*) red-letter day.

'Festung *f* (16) fortress; '❬s-anlagen *f/pl.* fortifications.

'fest|verzinslich ✞ fixed interest bearing; '❬wochen *f/pl.*: *Berliner usw.* ❬ Festival; '❬wurzeln become firmly rooted; '❬zug *m* (festive) procession.

fett [fɛt] 1. fat; *fig.* rich; *Boden: a.* fertile; *typ.* extra bold; 2. ❬ *n* (3) fat; (*Schmalz*) lard; (*Schmier❬*) grease.

'Fett|-auge *n* speck of fat; '❬bauch *m* paunch; '❬druck *typ. m* extra bold print, heavy-faced type; '❬en grease; '❬fleck *m* spot of grease; '❬gehalt *m* fat content; '❬ig fat(ty); (*schmierig*) greasy; '❬kohle *f* fat coal; ❬leibig ['❬laɪbɪç] corpulent; '❬näpfchen *n*: *fig.* ins ❬ treten drop a brick, put one's foot in it; '❬sack *m sl.* fat slob; '❬spritze *mot. f* grease-gun; '❬sucht *f* obesity.

Fetzen [ˈfɛtsən] *m* (6) shred; (*Lumpen*) rag, *Am. a.* frazzle; *ein* ❬ *Papier* a scrap of paper; *in* ❬ in rags.

feucht [fɔʏçt] moist; *bsd. Luft:* humid; (*unangenehm* ❬) damp; '❬en (26) moisten; damp.

'Feuchtigkeit *f* moisture; humidity;

dampness; '❬screme *f* moisturizing cream; '❬sgehalt *m* moisture content; '❬smesser *m* hygrometer.

feudal [fɔʏˈdaːl] feudal; F (*großartig*) sumptuous, *sl.* ritzy.

Feuer [ˈfɔʏər] *n* (7) fire (*a. fig.*); *fig.* ardo(u)r; (*feuriges Temperament*) mettle; ❬ *bekommen* ⚇ be fired at; *j-m* ❬ *geben* (*für die Zigarre*) give a p. a light; ❬ *machen* make (*Am.* build) a fire; '❬-alarm *m* fire--alarm; '❬bestatten cremate; '❬bestattung *f* cremation; '❬bohne ♣ *f* scarlet runner; '❬-eifer *m* ardent zeal, ardo(u)r; '❬-einstellung ⚇ *f* cessation of fire; '❬fest fire--proof, fire-resistant; *Baustoff usw.:* refractory; '❬garbe ⚇ *f* sheaf (*od.* cone) of fire; '❬gefährlich inflammable; '❬gefecht *n* gun-fight; '❬hahn *m* fire-plug; '❬kraft ⚇ *f* fire power; '❬leiter *f* fire-ladder; (*Nottreppe*) fire-escape; '❬löscher *m* fire-extinguisher; '❬melder *m* fire-alarm; '❬n (29) fire (*a. fig. entlassen*); F (*werfen*) hurl; '❬probe *f fig.* crucial (*od.* acid) test; *die* ❬ *bestehen* stand the test; '❬rad *n* Catherine-wheel; '❬rot flaming red; '❬sbrunst *f* (great) fire, conflagration; '❬schaden *m* damage (caused) by fire; '❬schiff *n* lightship; '❬sgefahr *f* danger (*od.* risk) of fire; '❬sglut *f* burning heat; '❬snot *f* danger from fire; '❬speiend vomiting fire; volcanic; ❬er *Berg* volcano; '❬spritze *f* fire-engine; '❬stelle *f* fireplace, hearth; '❬stein *m min. u. im Feuerzeug:* flint; '❬stoß ⚇ *m* burst of fire; '❬strahl *m* flash of fire; '❬taufe *f* baptism of fire; '❬teufel *m* (*Brandstifter*) fire bug; '❬treppe *f* fire escape.

'Feuerung *f* firing; (*Heizung*) heating; (*Ofen*) furnace; (*Brennmaterial*) fuel.

'Feuer|versicherung(sgesellschaft) *f* fire insurance (company); '❬verzinken ⊕ hot-galvanize; '❬vorhang *thea. m* fire-curtain; '❬wache *f* fire-station; '❬waffe *f* fire-arm; '❬wehr *f* fire-brigade, *Am.* fire department; '❬wehrmann *m* fireman; '❬werk *n* fireworks *pl.* (*a. fig.*); '❬werker *m* (7) pyrotechnician; ⚇ artificer, ordnance technician; '❬werke'rei *f* pyrotechnics *sg.*; '❬werkskörper *m* firecracker; '~**zange** f (*eine* a pair of) fire-tongs *pl.*; '~**zeichen** n fire--signal; '~**zeug** n (cigarette-, pocket-)lighter.

Feuilleton ['fœj(ə)tõ] n (11) feuilleton (*fr.*), features section.

feurig ['fɔʏriç] fiery; *fig. a.* ardent.

Fex [fɛks] m faddist; *in Zssgn* ... fan.

Fiaker [fi'akər] m (7) cab.

Fiasko [fi'asko] n (11) fiasco, failure.

Fibel ['fiːbəl] f (15) spelling-book, primer.

Fiber ['fiːbər] f (15) fib|re, *Am.* -er.

Fichte ['fiçtə] f (15) spruce; '~**n-holz** n pine-wood; '~**nnadel** f pine--needle.

ficken V ['fikən] (25) fuck.

fidel [fi'deːl] merry, jolly.

Fidibus ['fiːdibus] m (*inv. od.* 4¹) spill.

Fieber ['fiːbər] n (7) fever (*a. fig.*); ~ haben *s. fiebern; das* ~ messen take the temperature; '~**anfall** m attack of fever; '2~**artig** febrile; '~**frost** m chill; '2**haft** feverish (*a. fig.*), febrile; '2**hitze** f fever heat; '2**krank** feverish; '~**kurve** f temperature--curve; *s. Fiebertabelle;* '~**mittel** n febrifuge; '2**n** (29) be feverish, have (*od.* run) a temperature; *fig.* ~ *nach* yearn for; (*vor Erwartung*) ~ be in a fever (of expectation); '~**rinde** f Peruvian bark; '~**schauer** m shivering fit; '~**tabelle** f temperature--chart; '~**thermometer** n clinical thermometer; '~**traum** m feverish dream.

fiebrig ['fiːbriç] *s.* fieberhaft.

Fiedel ['fiːdəl] f (15) fiddle; '~**bogen** m fiddle-stick *od.* -bow; '2**n** *v/t u. v/i.* (29) fiddle.

fiel [fiːl] *pret. v. fallen* 1.

fies F [fiːs] F awful, filthy.

Figur [fi'guːr] f (16) figure (*a. Eislauf, Tanz, a.* ♟, ♁, ⊕); *Schach:* chessman; *e-e gute* (*schlechte*) ~ *machen* cut a fine (poor) figure; '2**bewußt** figure--conscious.

figürlich [~'gyːrliç] figurative.

Fiktion [fik'tsjoːn] f (16) fiction.

fiktiv [fik'tiːf] fictitious.

Filet [fi'leː] n (11) *Handarbeit:* network; *Kochkunst:* fillet; '~**braten** m roast fillet.

Filial|e [fil'jɑːlə] f (15) branch (office *od.* establishment); ~**geschäft** n multiple shop, chain store; *s. Filiale;* ~**leiter** m branch manager.

Filigran(-**arbeit** f) [fili'grɑːn-] n (3¹) filigree.

Film [film] m (3¹) *allg.* film; (~*stück*) *Am. a.* (motion) picture, F movie; *beim* (*od. im*) ~ on the films; *phot.* e-n ~ *einlegen* load the camera; '~**atelier** n (film)studio; '~**aufnahme** f (film) shot; *Vorgang:* shooting (of a film); '~**band** n reel; '~**bauten** *pl.* sets; ~**diva** ['~diːva] f film star; '2**en** (25) film, screen, shoot; '~**gesellschaft** f film company; '~**industrie** f film industry; '~**kamera** f film camera; '~**kunst** f cinematic art; '~**regisseur** m film director; '~**reklame** f screen advertising; ~**reportage** ['~reportɑːʒə] f screen record; '~**riß** m fig. (mental) blackout; '~**schauspieler**(**in** f) m film (*od.* screen) actor m (actress f); '~**spule** f (film) reel; '~**star** m film (*Am.* F movie) star; '~**streifen** m film-strip, reel; '~**theater** n cinema; '~**verleih** m film distribution; (*Firma*) film distributors *pl.*; '~**vorführer** m projectionist; '~**vorschau** f (film) trailer; '~**vorstellung** f film (*Am.* movie) show(ing); '~**welt** f film world.

Filter ['filtər] m, n (7), '2**n** (29) filter; '~**kaffee** m filtered coffee; '~**tüte** f filter bag; '~**zigarette** f filter-tipped cigarette.

filtrieren [~'triːrən] filter, strain.

Filz [filts] m (3²) felt; *fig.* niggard; '~**hut** m felt hat; '2**ig** feltlike; (*geizig*) niggardly, stingy; '~**laus** f crab-louse; '~**schreiber** m, '~**stift** m felt(-tipped) pen.

Fimmel F ['fiməl] m craze.

Finale [fi'nɑːle] n (11, *pl. inv.* -le) ♪ finale; *Sport:* final(s *pl.*).

Finanz|amt [fi'nants?amt] n (inland) revenue office; ~**en** f/pl. (16) finances; 2**iell** [~'tsjɛl] financial; 2**ieren** [~'tsiːrən] finance; ~**jahr** n fiscal year; ~**lage** f financial state *od.* standing; ~**mann** m financier; ~**minister** m Minister of Finance; *Brt.* Chancellor of the Exchequer, *Am.* Secretary of the Treasury; ~**ministerium** n Ministry of Finance; *Brt.* Exchequer, *Am.* Treasury Department; ~**wesen** n finances *pl.*, financial system.

Findelkind ['findəlkint] n foundling.

finden ['findən] (30) find; (*antreffen*) meet with; *sich* ~ *S.:* be found, *P.:* find o.s.; *sich* ~ *in* (*acc.*) accommodate o.s. to; *wie ~ Sie ...?* how do you like ...? *~ Sie nicht?* don't you think so?; *das wird sich ~* we shall see.

'**Finder** *m*, '*~in* *f* finder; '*~lohn* *m* finder's reward.

'**findig** resourceful; '2**keit** *f* resourcefulness.

Findling ['fintliŋ] *m* (3¹) foundling; *geol.* erratic block, boulder.

fing [fiŋ] *pret. v.* fangen.

Finger ['fiŋər] *m* (7) finger; *sich die ~ verbrennen (a. fig.)* burn one's fingers; *die ~ davon lassen* keep one's hands off; *s. rühren;* '*~ab-druck* *m* finger-print; '*~fertig-keit* *f* dexterity; '*~glied* *n* finger--joint; '*~handschuh* *m* (fingered) glove; '*~hut* *m* thimble; ♀ foxglove; '*~ling* *m* (3¹) finger-stall; '2**n** (29) finger; F *fig. e-e S. ~ wangle a th.;* '*~nagel* *m* finger-nail; '*~satz* ♩ *m* fingering; '*~spitze* *f* finger-tip; '*~spitzengefühl* *n fig.* flair, subtle intuition; '*~übung* ♩ *f* fingering--exercise; *~zeig* ['~tsaɪk] *m* hint, cue, tip.

fingieren [fiŋ'giːrən] feign.

Fink [fiŋk] *m* (12) finch.

Finne¹ ['finə] *f* (15) pimple; *pl. der Schweine:* measles *pl.;* (*Flosse*) fin.

'**Finne**² *m* (13), '**Finnin** *f* (16¹) Fin (-lander).

'**finnisch** Finnish.

finster ['finstər] dark; *fig. a.* gloomy; (*grimmig*) grim; *~er Blick* scowl; *j-n ~ ansehen* scowl (*od.* look black) at a p., frown at a p.; '2**nis** *f* (14²) darkness, obscurity.

Finte ['fintə] *f* (15) feint (*a. fig.*).

Firlefanz ['fɪrləfants] *m* (3²) (*Albernheit*) (tom)foolery, nonsense; (*Flitterkram*) frippery, gew-gaws *pl.; ~ treiben* play the fool.

Firma ['fɪrma] *f* (16²) firm, (commercial) house; company; *Brief-anschrift: ~ Langenscheidt* Messrs. Langenscheidt.

Firmament [fɪrma'mɛnt] *n* (3) firmament.

firm|en ['fɪrmən] (25) confirm; '2**ung** *f* confirmation.

'**Firmen|-inhaber** *m* principal; '*~schild* *n* sign(board), facia; '*~spre-cher* *m* company spokesman; '*~sprecherin* *f* company spokeswoman; '*~wagen* *m* company car; '*~wert* *m* goodwill.

Firn [fɪrn] *m* (3), '*~feld* *n* névé.

Firnis ['fɪrnis] *m* (4¹), '2**sen** (28) varnish.

First [fɪrst] *m* (3²) ridge.

Fis ♩ [fis] *n* F sharp.

Fisch [fiʃ] *m* (3²) fish; *~e pl. ast.* Fishes, Pisces; F *kleine ~e* child's play; '*~-auge* *phot. n* fish-eye lens; '*~bein* *n* whalebone; '*~blase* *f* fish--bladder; '*~dampfer* *m* trawler.

'**fischen** *v/t. u. v/i.* (27) fish; *s. trüb.*

'**Fischer** *m* (7) fisherman; '*~boot* *n* fishing-boat; '*~dorf* *n* fishing-village; *~ei* [~'raɪ] *f* (*Gewerbe*) fishery; (*Fischen*) fishing.

'**Fisch|fang** *m* fishing; '*~gerät* *n* fishing-tackle; '*~gericht* *n* fish dish; '*~geruch* *m* fishy smell; '*~gräte* *f* fish-bone; '*~grätenmuster* *n* herring-bone pattern; '*~händler* *m* fishmonger, *Am.* fishdealer; '*~kon-serve* *f* tinned (*Am.* canned) fish; '*~kunde* *f* ichthyology; '*~laich* *m* spawn; '*~leim* *m* fish-glue; '*~mehl* *n* fish-meal; '*~milch* *f* milt; '*~otter* *m* otter; '2**reich** abounding in fish; '*~reiher* *m* heron; '*~rogen* *m* roe; '*~schuppe* *f* scale; *~stäbchen* ['~-ʃtɛːpçən] *n* (6) fish finger; '*~teich* *m* fish-pond; '*~tran* *m* train-oil; '*~ver-giftung* *f* fish-poisoning; '*~zucht* *f* fish-hatching, ♲ pisciculture; '*~zug* *m* draught (of fishes), haul.

fiskalisch [fis'kaːliʃ] fiscal.

Fiskus ['fiskus] *m inv.* Exchequer, *bsd. Am.* Treasury.

Fistel ['fistəl] *f* (15) ✚ fistula; ♩ (*od.* '*~stimme* *f*) falsetto.

Fitnesscenter ['fitnɛstsɛntər] *n* (7) *Sport:* health cent|re, *Am.* -er.

Fittich ['fitiç] *m* (3) wing.

fix [fiks] quick; (*Gehalt, Preise usw.:* fixed; *~e Idee* fixed idea; *~ u. fertig* quite ready; all finished (*a.* F *fig. erledigt, erschöpft*); *ein ~er Bursche* a smart fellow; F *mach (mal) ~!* make it snappy!; '*~en* (27) *an der Börse:* bear; *sl.* (*Drogen spritzen*) fix, shoot; '2**er** *m* (7) bear; *sl.* junkie; 2**ierbad** *phot.* [~'ksiːrbaːt] *n* fixer; *~ieren* [~'ksiːrən] fix; *j-n:* stare at; 2**ier-mittel** [~'ksiːrmitəl] *n* fixative; 2**ie-rung** [~'ksiːruŋ] *f* fixation; '2**stern** *m* fixed star; '2**um** *n* (9²) fixed sum *od.* salary.

FKK-|Anhänger(in *f*) *m* [ɛfkaː'kaː-] nudist, naturist; *~Strand* *m* nudist beach.

flach [flax] flat; (*eben*) plain; *Wasser, Teller u. fig.*: shallow; *Schuhe*: heelless; *die* ⁓e *Hand* the flat of the hand; '⁀bahn ✗ *f* flat trajectory; '⁀dach *n* flat roof.

Fläche ['flɛçə] *f* (15) (*Ebene*) plain, level; (*Ober⁀*) surface; (*weite* ⁓) expanse, tract; (*Wasser⁀ usw.*) sheet; (⁓*raum*) area; ⅍ plane; '⁀nblitz *m* sheet lightning; '⁀n-inhalt *m*, '⁀n-raum *m* area, superficies; '⁀nmaß *n* square (*od.* surface) measure.

'**Flachheit** *f* flatness; *Wasser u. fig.*: shallowness.

'**Flachmann** F *m* (*Taschenflasche*) hip-flask.

'**Flachrennen** *n* flat race.

Flachs [flaks] *m* (4) flax; '⁀en F wisecrack; '⁀haarig flaxen-haired; '⁀kopf *m* flaxen-haired person.

'**Flachzange** *f* flat-nose(d) pliers *pl.*

flackern ['flakərn] (29) flare, flicker.

Fladen ['flɑːdən] *m* (6) flat cake.

Flagge ['flagə] *f* (15) flag, colo(u)rs *pl.*; *unter falscher* ⁓ under false colo(u)rs; '⁀n... *mst* flag; '⁀n (25) *v/i.* hoist (the) flag; *v/t.* dress; '⁀nstock *m* flagstaff.

'**Flagg|leine** *f* flag-line; '⁀offizier *m* flag-officer; '⁀schiff *n* flagship.

Flakon [fla'kõ] *n*, *m* (11) small bottle, flask.

Flam|e ['flɑːmə] *m* (12), ⁀länder ['⁀lɛndər] *m* (7), '⁀in *f* (16¹) Fleming.

flämisch ['flɛmiʃ] Flemish.

Flamm|e ['flamə] *f* (15) flame (*a.* F *Geliebte*); (*lodernde* ⁓) blaze; *s. aufgehen*; '⁀en *v/i.* (25) flame; blaze; *v/t. Stoff*: water; '⁀end flaming; *fig. Rede*: *a.* stirring; '⁀enmeer *n* sea of flames; '⁀(en)-ofen ⊕ *m* reverberatory (puddling) furnace; '⁀enwerfer ✗ *m* flame-thrower.

Flammeri ['flaməri] *m* (11) blancmange, flummery.

'**Flammpunkt** *m* flash point.

Flanell [fla'nɛl] *m* (3¹) flannel; ⁀anzug *m*, ⁀hose *f* flannels *pl.*

flanieren [fla'niːrən] (sn) saunter.

Flanke ['flaŋkə] *f* (15) flank (*a.* △, ✗, *mount.*); '⁀n-angriff *m* flank attack; '⁀ndeckung *f* flank protection.

flan'kieren flank; ✗, *pol.* ⁓*de Maßnahmen* supporting measures.

Flansch ⊕ [flanʃ] *m* (3) flange.

Flaps F [flaps] *m* (4) boor, lout.

Fläschchen ['flɛʃçən] *n* (6) small bottle, flask; *pharm.* phial.

Flasche ['flaʃə] *f* (15) bottle; *kleine*: flask; F *Sport usw.*: dud; '⁀nbier *n* bottled beer; '⁀ngärung *f* fermentation in the bottle; '⁀nhals *m* neck of a bottle; '⁀nkind *n* bottle-fed baby; '⁀n-öffner *m* bottle-opener; '⁀npost *f* message in a bottle; '⁀nregal *n* bottle rack; '⁀nzug *m* block and tackle, pulley(-block).

Flatter|geist ['flatər-] *m* **1.** fickle person; **2.** = '⁀sinn *m* fickleness; '⁀haft fickle, inconstant; '⁀haftigkeit *f* fickleness, inconstancy; '⁀n (29, h. *u.* sn) flutter (*a.* ⊕); *mot. Räder*: shimmy, wobble.

flau [flau] (*schwach*) feeble, faint; *Getränk*: stale, flat; *phot.* weak; ✝ flat, dull; ⁓e *Zeit* slack time; ⁓er *werden Wind*: calm down.

Flaum [flaum] *m* (3) fluff; = '⁀feder *f* down; '⁀ig downy, fluffy.

Flausch [flauʃ] *m* (3) (*Woll-, Haarbüschel*) tuft; (*dicker Wollstoff*) fleece fabric; ⁀ig fluffy.

Flause ['flauzə] *f* (15) fib, shift; (*Unsinn*) nonsense; '⁀nmacher (-*in* *f*) *m* shuffler.

Flaute ['flautə] *f* (15) ⚓ dead calm, lull; ✝ slackness.

Flechse ['flɛksə] *f* (15) sinew, tendon.

Flecht|e ['flɛçtə] *f* (15) braid; (*Haar⁀*) *a.* tress, plait; ♀ lichen; ⚕ herpes; '⁀en (30) twist; *Korb*: weave; *Kranz*: bind; *Haare*: braid, plait; *sich* ⁓ twine, wind (*um* round); '⁀werk *n* plaiting; (*Weiden⁀*) wicker-work.

Fleck [flɛk] *m* (3) (*Stelle*) spot; (*Flicken*) patch; (*Stück Land*) patch; (*Schmutz⁀*) stain, blot, spot; (*Makel*) spot, blemish, blur; (*Kaldaunen*) tripe; (*Schuhabsatz⁀*) heel (-piece); *schöner* ⁓ *Erde* beauty spot; *auf dem* ⁓ on the spot; *wir kommen nicht vom* ⁓ we are not getting on.

'**Flecken**[1] *m* (6) *s.* Fleck; (*Ortschaft*) market-town, borough.

'**flecken**[2] (25) spot, stain; '⁀los spotless; *fig. a.* stainless.

'**Fleck|-entferner** *m* (7) spot (*od.* stain) remover; '⁀fieber *n* spotted fever; '⁀ig spotted; (*befleckt*) stained; '⁀typhus *m* typhus; '⁀wasser *n s.* Fleckentferner.

Fledermaus ['fleːdər-] *f* bat.

Flegel ['fleːgəl] *m* (7) flail; *fig.* lout, boor; **'⁓-alter** *n*, **'⁓jahre** *n/pl.* awkward age *sg.*; **⁓ei** [⁓'laɪ] *f* rudeness, churlish conduct; **'⁓haft** churlish, rude; *sich* **'⁓n** sprawl, loll.

flehen ['fleːn] **1.** (25) implore, entreat (*um et.* [*for*] a th., *zu j-m* a p.); **2.** ♀ *n* (6) supplication, entreaty; **'⁓tlich** suppliant, imploring(ly *adv.*), beseeching(ly).

Fleisch [flaɪʃ] *n* (3²) flesh; (*Schlacht-*♀) meat; (*Frucht*♀) pulp; *fig. sich ins eigne* ⁓ *schneiden* cut one's own throat; **'⁓bank** *f* butcher's stall, *Am.* meat-counter; **'⁓beschauer** ['⁓bəʃauər] *m* meat inspector; **'⁓brühe** *f* (meat-)broth; *v. Rindfleisch*: beef tea; **'⁓er** *m* (7) butcher; **⁓erei** [⁓'raɪ] *f*, **'⁓erladen** *m* butcher's (*Am.* butcher) shop.

'Fleischeslust *f* carnal desire.

'Fleisch|-extrakt *m* meat extract; **'⁓farbe** *f* flesh-colo(u)r; **'♀farben** flesh-colo(u)red; **'♀fressend** carnivorous; **'♀ig** fleshy; ♀ pulpous, pulpy; **'⁓kloß** *m* meat-ball; **'⁓konserven** *f/pl.* potted (*od.* tinned, *Am.* canned) meat; **'⁓kost** *f* meat diet; **'♀lich** carnal, fleshly; **'♀los** fleshless; *Kost*: meatless; **'⁓pastete** *f* meat-pie; **'⁓schnitte** *f* slice of meat; steak; **'⁓speise** *f* (course of) meat; **'⁓vergiftung** *f* ptomaine poisoning; **⁓werdung** ['⁓veːrduŋ] *f* incarnation; **'⁓wolf** *m* meat mincer (*Am.* grinder); **'⁓wunde** *f* flesh-wound.

Fleiß [flaɪs] *m* (3²) diligence, industry; (*Beharrlichkeit*) application, assiduity; *mit* ⁓ intentionally, on purpose; *viel* ⁓ *verwenden auf* (*acc.*) take great pains with; **'♀ig** assiduous; diligent, industrious, hard-working; (*sorgfältig*) painstaking; *ein* ⁓*er Besucher* a frequent visitor.

flektieren *gr.* [flɛk'tiːrən] inflect.

flennen ['flɛnən] (25) cry.

fletschen ['flɛtʃən] (27): *die Zähne* ⁓ show one's teeth, snarl.

Flexion *gr.* [flɛks'joːn] *f* inflexion; **⁓s...** inflectional.

Flick|-arbeit ['flik-] *f* patchwork; **'⁓en** *m* patch; **'♀en** (25) mend, patch (up), repair; *fig. j-m et. am Zeug* ⁓ pick holes in a p.; **'⁓er(in** *f*) *m* patcher, mender; **⁓erei** [⁓ə'raɪ] *f* patchwork; **'⁓schuster** *m* cobbler;

'⁓werk *n* patchwork; **'⁓wort** *n* expletive; **'⁓zeug** *n* sewing (⊕ repair) kit.   [lilac; (*Holunder*) elder.)

Flieder ['fliːdər] *m* (7) (*spanischer*)∫ **Fliege** ['fliːgə] *f* (15) fly; (*Bärtchen*) imperial; F (*Krawatte*) bow-tie; *ein* ⁓*n beschmutzt* fly-blown; *zwei* ⁓*n mit e-r Klappe schlagen* kill two birds with one stone.

'fliegen 1. *v/i.* (sn) *u. v/t.* (30) fly; *Fahne usw.*: *a.* stream; (*eilen*) fly, rush; F (*entlassen werden*) get the sack, *Am.* get fired; *Sport*: ⁓*der Start* flying start; **2.** ♀ *n* (6) flying; ✈ *a.* aviation.

'Fliegen|fänger ['⁓fɛŋər] *m* fly-paper; **'⁓fenster** *n* fly-screen; **'⁓gewicht(ler** *m*) *n Boxen*: fly-weight; **'⁓klappe** *f* **'⁓klatsche** *f* fly-flap, *Am.* fly swatter; **'⁓pilz** *m* toadstool; **'⁓schrank** *m* meat-safe.

'Flieger *m* (7) flyer, airman, aviator; *berufsmäßiger*: pilot; *s. Flugzeug*; *Rad-, Rennsport*: sprinter; **'⁓-abwehr** *f* anti-aircraft defen∫ce, *Am.* -se; ⁓... anti-aircraft...; **'⁓alarm** *m* air-raid warning, air alert; **'⁓bombe** *f* aircraft bomb; **'⁓dreß** *m* flying suit; **'⁓horst** *m* air station, *Am.* air base; **'⁓in** *f* (16¹) airwoman, aviatrix; **'♀isch** aeronautic(al), flying; **'⁓offizier** *m* air-force officer; **'⁓schule** *f* flying school.

fliehen ['fliːən] *v/i.* (30, sn) flee (*statt* flee[ing] *mst* fly[ing]) (*vor dat.* from); *v/t.* avoid, shun; **⁓d** *Stirn, Kinn*: receding.

'Fliehkraft *f* centrifugal power.

Fliese ['fliːzə] *f* (15) flag(stone), tile.

Fließ|band ['fliːsbant] *n* assembly line; (*Förderband*) conveyor belt; **'⁓bandfertigung** *f* assembly-line production; **'♀en** (30, sn) flow, run; **'♀end** flowing; *Sprache*: fluent; **'⁓heck** *mot. n a. Wagen mit* ⁓ fastback; **'⁓papier** *n* blotting-paper.

Flimmer ['flimər] *m* (7), **'♀n** (29) glimmer, glitter; *bsd. Film*: flicker; *es flimmert mir vor den Augen* my head swims.

flink [fliŋk] quick, nimble, brisk; **'♀heit** *f* quickness, nimbleness.

Flinte ['flintə] *f* (15) (shot)gun; *fig. die* ⁓ *ins Korn werfen* throw up the sponge.

'Flinten|kolben *m* butt-end (of a gun); **'⁓lauf** *m* gun-barrel; **'⁓schuß** *m* gunshot.

Flipper ['flipər] m (7) (*Spielautomat*) pinball machine.

Flirt [flœrt] m (11) flirtation; '~en (26) flirt.

Flitter ['flitər] m (7) tinsel, spangle; '~gold n tinsel, leaf-brass; '~kram m cheap finery, tinsel; '~wochen f/pl. honeymoon sg.

Flitzbogen ['flits-] m boy's bow.

flitzen ['flitsən] (27, sn) flit, whisk.

flocht [flɔxt] pret. v. flechten.

Flock|e ['flɔkə] f (15) (*Schnee♀*) flake; (*Woll♀*) flock; '~enblume f centaury; '♀ig flaky; flocky, fluffy.

flog [flo:k] pret. v. fliegen.

Floh[1] [flo:] m (3²) flea; j-m e-n ~ ins Ohr setzen put ideas into a p.'s head; '~stich m flea-bite.

floh[2] pret. v. fliehen.

Floppy-Disc ['flɔpidisk] f (11¹) Computer: floppy-disk.

Flor [flo:r] m (3¹) **1.** bloom; fig. bloom, prime; (*Blumenmenge*) display of flowers; fig. v. Damen: bevy; **2.** auf Samt usw.: nap, pile; (*dünnes Gewebe*) gauze, crépe; (*Trauer♀*) crape. [~seide f floss-silk.}

Florett fenc. [flo'rɛt] n (3) foil;}

florieren [flo'ri:rən] flourish, prosper.

Floskel ['flɔskəl] f (15) flourish; contp. empty phrase

Floß[1] [flo:s] n (3³) raft, float; '~brücke f floating bridge.

floß[2] [flɔs] pret. v. fließen.

Flosse ['flɔsə] f (15) fin.

flößen ['flø:sɛn] (27) float, raft.

'Flößer m (7) raftsman.

Flöte ['flø:tə] f (15) flute; Kartenspiel: flush; '♀n (26) v/i. u. v/t. play (on) the flute; fig. F ~ gehen go to the dogs od. to pot; '~nbläser m, '~nspieler m flute-player, flutist.

flott [flɔt] floating, afloat; (*lustig*) gay; Bursche: dashing; Tänzer usw.: good; Tanz: lively; Kleidung: stylish, smart; (*schnell*) quick, snappy; ~ leben lead a jolly (od. gay) life, F go the pace.

Flotte ['flɔtə] f (15) fleet; (*Marine*) navy; '~n-abkommen n naval agreement; '~nschau f naval review; '~nstation f naval station; '~nstützpunkt m naval base.

'flottgehend Geschäft usw.: brisk, lively, flourishing.

Flottille [flɔ'tiljə] f (15) flotilla; ~n-admiral m commodore.

'flottmachen ♻ float, set afloat.

Flöz [flø:ts] n (3²) seam, layer, stratum.

Fluch [flu:x] m (3³) curse, malediction; (*Redensart*) (profane) oath, F swear-word; '♀beladen under a curse; '♀en (25) curse (j-m a p.), swear (auf acc. at); '~er m curser.

Flucht [fluxt] f (16) flight (vor dat. from); e-s Gefangenen: escape; wilde: rout, stampede; (*Reihe*) range, row; s. Zimmer♀; in die ~ schlagen (od. jagen od. treiben) put to flight; s. begeben, ergreifen; '♀-artig hasty, headlong.

fluchten ['fluxtən] (26) ⊕ align.

flüchten ['flyçtən] (26, sn) flee; (a. sich) ~ take refuge; Gefangener: escape.

'Fluchthelfer m escape agent.

'flüchtig fugitive (a. fig.); (*vergänglich*) fleeting, transitory; Lächeln: fleeting; Mensch: flighty; (*unsorgfältig*) careless; (*eilig*) hasty; 🜂 volatile; ~er Bekannter nodding acquaintance; ~er Blick (cursory) glance; ~ durchlesen skim (through); ~ werden abscond; '♀keit f transitoriness; flightiness; carelessness; volatility; '♀keitsfehler m slip, oversight.

Flüchtling ['flyçtliŋ] m (3¹) fugitive; pol. refugee; '~slager n refugee camp.

'Flucht|linie △ f alignment; '~versuch m attempt to escape; '~wagen m get-away car; '~weg m escape route.

fluchwürdig ['flu:x-] execrable.

Flug [flu:k] m (3³) flight; (*Schar*) flock, swarm; auf dem (od. im) ~e on the wing, fig. in haste; '~abwehr... anti-aircraft ...; '~bahn f trajectory; ✗ flight path; '~ball m Tennis: volley; '~betrieb m flying (operations pl.); '~blatt n leaflet, pamphlet; '~boot n flying boat; '~deck n flight deck; '~dienst m air-service.

Flügel ['fly:gəl] m (7) wing (a. ✗, △, pol. u. Sport); (*Fenster♀*) casement; (*Tür♀*) leaf, half; (*Windmühlen♀*) sail; (*Propeller♀*) blade; ♩ grand (piano); '~fenster n casement-window; '♀lahm broken-winged; fig. lame; '♀los wingless; '~mann ✗ m flank man, marker; '~mutter ⊕ f wing nut; '~schlag

m beat of the wings; '˷**schraube** ⊕ *f* thumb screw; '˷**stürmer** *m Fußball*: winger; '˷**tür** *f* folding-door.
Fluggast ['fluːk-] *m* air-passenger.
flügge ['flygə] fledged.
Flug|geschwindigkeit ['fluːk-] *f* flying speed; '˷**gesellschaft** *f* airline; '˷**hafen** *m* airport; '˷**höhe** *f* altitude; '˷**kapitän** *m* aircraft captain; '˷**karte** *f s.* Flugticket; '˷**lehrer** *m* flying instructor; '˷**linie** *f* air-route, airway; (*Gesellschaft*) airline; e-e ˷ *benutzen* ride an airline; '˷**lotse** *m* air-traffic controller; '˷**maschine** *f* flying-machine; '˷**platz** *m* aerodrome, airfield, *Am. a.* airdrome; '˷**post** *f* air-mail; '˷**preis** *m* (air) fare.
flugs [fluːks] quickly, swiftly.
'**Flug|sand** *m* quicksand; '˷**schalter** *m* flight desk; '˷**schreiber** *m* flight recorder; '˷**schrift** *f* pamphlet; '˷**sicherung** *f* air traffic control; '˷**sport** *m* aviation; '˷**strecke** *f* flying distance; air-route; '˷**stützpunkt** *m* airbase; '˷**ticket** *n* plane ticket; '˷**verkehr** *m* air traffic; *planmäßiger*: air service; '˷**weg** *m* flight path; '˷**wetter** *n* flying weather; '˷**zeug** *n* aeroplane, *F* plane, *bsd. Am.* airplane, (*a.* ˷e *pl.*) aircraft.
'**Flugzeug|bau** *m* aircraft construction; '˷**-entführer** *m* hijacker, *F* skyjacker; '˷**-entführung** *f* hijacking, *F* skyjacking; '˷**führer** *m* pilot; '˷**halle** *f* hangar; '˷**katastrophe** *f* air disaster; '˷**motor** *m* aircraft engine; '˷**rumpf** *m* fuselage; '˷**träger** *m* aircraft carrier.
Fluidum ['fluːidum] *n* (9²) *fig.* aura.
fluktuieren [fluktuˈiːrən] fluctuate.
Flunder ['flundər] *f* (15) flounder.
Flunker|ei [fluŋkəˈraɪ] *f* fib(bing); '˷**n** (29) fib, tell fibs.
Fluor ['fluːɔr] ⚗ *n* (3¹, *o.pl.*) fluorine; ⚗**eszieren** [˷ɛsˈtsiːrən] fluoresce.
Flur [fluːr] **1.** *f* (16) field, plain, *poet.* lea; **2.** *m* (3) (*Haus*⚥) (entrance-)hall; (*Gang*) passage, corridor; '˷**bereinigung** *f* consolidation (of farmland); '˷**garderobe** *f* hall-stand; '˷**schaden** *m* damage to crops.
Fluß [flus] *m* (4²*) river, stream; (*das Fließen*) flow(ing); *metall.* melting, fusion; *der Rede*: fluency, flow; ⊕ (˷*mittel*) flux; *in* ˷ *bringen* (*kommen*) *fig.* get going, get under way; ⚥-

'**abwärts** downstream; ⚥'-**aufwärts** upstream; '˷**bett** *n* river-bed, channel; '˷**diagramm** *n Computer*: flowchart.
flüssig ['flysiç] liquid (*a. Kapital*), fluid; *Geld*: ready; *Stil*: flowing, fluent; ˷ *machen Geld*: disengage; *Wertpapier*: realize; ⚥**keit** *f* liquid; *Zustand*: liquidity (*a. fig.*); ⚥**keits-bremse** *f* hydraulic brake; ⚥**keits-getriebe** *n* fluid drive; ⚥**kristall** *m Computer*: liquid crystal; ⚥**kristall-anzeige** *f* liquid crystal display.
'**Fluß|lauf** *m* course of a river; '˷**mündung** *f* river-mouth; '˷**pferd** *n* hippopotamus; '˷**schiffahrt** *f* river-navigation; '˷**stahl** *m* ingot steel.
flüster|n ['flystərn] (29) *v/i. u. v/t.* whisper; '⚥**propaganda** *f* whispering campaign; '⚥**ton** *m* whisper.
Flut [fluːt] *f* (16) flood; (*Ggs. Ebbe*) high tide, flood-tide; (*Überschwemmung*) inundation; *fig.* flood, spate, deluge; '⚥**en** (26, h. u. sn) flow; '˷**licht** *n* floodlight; '˷**lichtspiel** *n Sport*: floodlit match; '˷**marke** *f* tidemark; '˷**wechsel** *m* turn of the tide; '˷**welle** *f* tidal wave; '˷**zeit** *f* flood-tide.
focht [fɔxt] *pret. v.* fechten.
Fock|mast ⚓ ['fɔkmast] *m* foremast; '˷**segel** *n* foresail.
Födera|lismus [fødəraˈlismus] *m* (16², *o. pl.*) federalism; ˷**tion** [˷ˈtsjoːn] *f* (16) federation.
Fohlen ['foːlən] **1.** *n* (6) foal; *s.* Füllen²; **2.** ⚥ (25) foal.
Föhn [føːn] *m* (3) föhn (wind), foehn.
Föhre ['føːrə] *f* (15) pine.
Folge ['fɔlgə] *f* (15) (*Wirkung, logische* ˷) consequence; (*Ergebnis*) result; (*Fortsetzung*) continuation; (*Aufeinander*⚥) sequence, succession; (*Reihe, Serie*) series; (˷*zeit*) future; (*Zs.-gehöriges*) set; *in der* ˷ in the sequel, subsequently; *die* ˷ *war* the result was; *zur* ˷ *haben* result in, entail, bring about; *e-r Bitte, e-r Vorschrift*: comply with; *e-r Einladung*: accept; *die* ˷*n tragen* take the consequences; '˷**erscheinung** *f* consequence.
'**folgen** (25, sn; *dat.*) *allg.* (*a. geistig*) follow; *Nachfolger*: succeed (*j-m* a p.; *auf acc.* to a *th.*); (*sich ergeben*) follow, ensue (*aus* from); (*h.*) (*ge-*

horchen) obey; *s.* befolgen; *j-m auf Schritt und Tritt*~ dog a p.'s footsteps, *polizeilich usw.*: shadow a p.; '~**d** following; (*später*) subsequent; (*nächst*) next; ~**es** the following; ~**dermaßen** ['~dərmɑːsən] as follows; '~**schwer** of great consequence, momentous.

'**folgerichtig** logical, consistent; '**2~keit** *f* logic(al consistency).

folger|n ['fɔlgərn] (29) infer, conclude, gather (*aus* from); '**2ung** *f* inference, deduction, conclusion.

'**Folge|satz** *m gr.* consecutive clause; **A** corollary; '**2widrig** inconsistent; '~**widrigkeit** *f* inconsistency.

folglich ['fɔlk-] consequently.

'**folgsam** obedient, docile; '**2keit** *f* obedience.

Foliant [fol'jant] *m* (12) folio (-volume); *weit S.* (heavy) tome.

Folie ['foːljə] *f* (15) foil; *fig. als* ~ *dienen* serve as a foil (*dat.* to); '~**kartoffeln** *f/pl.* baked potatoes.

Folter ['fɔltər] *f* (15) torture; rack; *fig. auf die* ~ *spannen* torture, keep *a p.* in suspense; '~**bank** *f* rack; '~**instrument** *n* instrument of torture; '~**kammer** *f* torture-chamber; '~**knecht** *m* torturer; '**2n** (29) torture, torment; '~**qual** *f* torture; *fig. a.* torment.

Fön [føːn] *m* (3) hair-dryer.

Fond [fõ] *m* (11) (*Grundlage*) bottom, ground; (*Hintergrund*) background; *mot. usw.* back (of the car).

Fonds [fõ] *m* (11) **☩** funds *pl.*; *fig.* fund; '~**börse** *f* stock-exchange.

fönen ['føːnən] (25) blow-dry.

Fontäne [fɔn'tɛːnə] *f* (15) fountain.

fopp|en ['fɔpən] (25) (*necken*) tease; (*täuschen*) fool, hoax; **2erei** [~ə'raɪ] *f* teasing; hoaxing.

forcieren [fɔr'siːrən] force.

'**Förder|-anlage** *f* conveyor equipment; '~**band** *n* conveyor belt; '~**er** *m*, '~**in** *f* sponsor, *bsd. der Künste*: patron; '~**kohle ☓** *f* pit-coal; '~**korb** *m* cage; '**2lich** conducive (*dat.* to); (*nützlich*) useful (for), beneficial (to).

fordern ['fɔrdərn] (29) ask, demand, call for; require (*von j-m of* a p.); *vor Gericht*: summon; *als Eigentum, Recht*: claim; *Preis*: charge; (*heraus*~) challenge; *zuviel* ~ overcharge.

fördern ['fœrdərn] (29) further, advance, promote, *a. Verdauung*: aid;

☓ mine, *bsd. Kohle*: haul.

'**Forderung** *f* demand; claim; requirement; charge; challenge.

'**Förderung** *f* furtherance, promotion, advancement; **☓** hauling, haulage; mining.

Forelle [fo'rɛlə] *f* (15) trout.

Forke ['fɔrkə] *f* (15) (pitch)fork.

Form [fɔrm] *f* (16) form; (*Gestalt*) figure, shape; *bsd.* **⊕** design; (*Muster*) model; (*Gieß*2) mo(u)ld; *Sport*: condition; *in* ~ *sein* (*kommen, bleiben*) be in ~ (get into, keep in) form; *die* ~ *wahren* observe the proprieties.

formal [fɔr'mɑːl] formal; technical; **2ien** [~'mɑːljən] *pl.*, **2itäten** [~mali'tɛːtən] *f/pl.* (16) formalities.

Format [~'mɑːt] *n* (3) size; *fig.* calib|re, *Am.* -er; *von großem* ~ large-sized.

Formation [~a'tsjoːn] *f* (16) formation; **☓** (*Verband*) *a.* unit.

'**Formblatt** *n s.* Formular.

Formel ['fɔrməl] *f* (15) form, formula; '~**buch** *n* formulary.

formell [fɔr'mɛl] formal.

'**formen** (25) form, shape, model, fashion, (*a.* **⊕**) mo(u)ld.

'**Formen|lehre** *gr. f* accidence; '~**mensch** *m* formalist.

'**Form|fehler** *m* informality; **☒** formal defect; '~**gebung** **⊕** *f*, '~**gestaltung** *f* design(ing).

for'mieren form; **☓** *sich* ~ fall in.

förmlich ['fœrmliç] formal; ceremonial; *P.*: ceremonious; *ein* ~*er Aufruhr* a regular uproar; '**2keit** *f* formality, ceremony.

'**form|los** formless, shapeless; *fig.* informal; '~**schön** beautifully shaped; '~**sache** *f* formality; '**2tief** *n* *Sport*: loss of form; *ein* ~ *haben* be badly off-form.

Formular [fɔrmu'lɑːr] *n* (3[1]) (printed) form, blank (form).

formu'lier|en formulate; **2ung** *f* formulation.

'**formvollendet** perfect, finished.

forsch [fɔrʃ] smart, dashing; (*schwungvoll*) brisk, peppy.

forschen ['fɔrʃən] (27) (*nach*) search (for); inquire (after).

'**Forscher** *m* (7), '~**in** *f* investigator; (*Wissenschaftler*) (research) scientist; researcher; *s.* Forschungsreisende.

'**Forschung** *f* inquiry, investigation;

gelehrte: research; '**~s-arbeit** *f* research work; '**~s-auftrag** *m* research assignment; '**~sreise** *f* exploring expedition; '**~sreisende** *m* (18) explorer; '**~ssatellit** *m* research satellite.

Forst [fɔrst] *m* (3²) forest; '**~-amt** *n* forestry superintendent's office; '**~-aufseher** *m* (forest-)keeper, gamekeeper; '**~be-amte** *m* forest-officer.

Förster ['fœrstər] *m* (7) forester, forest ranger; **~ei** [~'raɪ] *f* forester's house.

'**Forst|frevel** *m* infringement of the forest-laws; '**~haus** *n* forester's house; '**~mann** *m* forester; '**~meister** *m* forestry superintendent; '**~revier** *n* forest district; '**~wesen** *n*, '**~wirtschaft** *f* forestry.

Fort¹ ✕ [fo:r] *n* (11) fort.

fort² [fɔrt] (*weg*) away; gone; (*weiter*) on; (*vorwärts*) forward; *in* e-m ~ uninterruptedly; ~ *und* ~ continually; *und so* ~ and so forth *od.* on; *sie sind schon* ~ they have already left; *ich muß* ~ I must be off.

'**fort...** (*vgl. a. die Zssgn mit weg...*): **~'-an** henceforth; '**~bestehen** *v/i.* continue, survive; '**~bewegen** move (*a. sich* ~); drive; '**2bewegung** *f* locomotion; *sich* '**~bilden** continue one's studies; '**2bildungs-anstalt** (*od.* **-schule**) *f* continuation school *od.* classes *pl.*; '**~bleiben** stay away; '**2dauer** *f* continuance; '**~dauern** continue, last; '**~dauernd** lasting, permanent; continuous; '**2-entwick(e)lung** *f* (further) development; '**~fahren** depart; *fig.* continue, go on; '**2fall** *m* s. *Wegfall*; '**~fallen** s. *wegfallen*; '**~führen** continue, go on with; *Geschäft, Krieg*: carry on; '**2führung** *f* continuation; carrying on; '**2gang** *m* departure; *s. Fortschritt, Fortdauer*; '**~gehen** (sn) go (away), leave; (*weitergehen*) go on; (*fortschreiten*) proceed; (*fortdauern*) continue; '**~geschritten** *Schüler usw.*: advanced; '**~gesetzt** continual; '**~helfen** (*j-m*) help *a. p.* on; '**~kommen** (sn) s. *wegkommen*; (*weiterkommen*) get on *od.* along; F *mach, daß du fortkommst!* be off!, *sl.* beat it!; '**2-kommen** *n* getting on, progress; (*Lebensunterhalt*) living; '**~lassen** s. *weglassen*; '**~laufen** (sn) run away ([*vor*] *j-m* from a p.); (*weitergehen*)

run on, be continued; '**~laufend** continuous, running; '**~leben** live on; '**~pflanzen** (*a. sich*) propagate; '**2pflanzung** *f* propagation; *biol. a.* reproduction; '**2pflanzungs-trieb** *m* reproductive instinct; '**~reißen**: *j-n mit sich* ~ *fig.* carry a p. (away) with o.s.; '**2satz** *m* (*Vorsprung*) projection; *anat.,* ♀ process; '**~schaffen** remove; '**~schreiten** (sn) advance, proceed; '**~schreitend** progressive; '**2schritt** *m* progress; ~*e machen* make progress *od.* headway; *große* ~*e machen* make great strides; '**~schrittlich** progressive; '**~setzen** continue (*a. sich*), pursue; '**2setzung** *f* continuation, pursuit; ~ *folgt* to be continued; *sich* '**~stehlen** steal (*od.* sneak) away; '**~stoßen** push away; '**~während** continual, continuous; (*ewig*) perpetual; '**~ziehen** *v/t.* draw away; *v/i.* (sn) *aus der Wohnung*: remove; ✕ march off; *Vögel*: migrate.

Forum ['fo:rum] *n* (9²) forum.

fossil [fɔ'si:l], ♀ *n* (8²) fossil.

Fötus ['fø:tus] *m* (4¹) f(o)etus.

'**Foto...** *s. Photo...*

Foul [faʊl] *n* (11) *Sport:* foul; '**2en** (25) foul.

Foyer [foa'je:] *n* (11) *thea.* foyer, *Am. od. parl.* lobby; *im Hotel:* foyer, lounge.

Fracht [fraxt] *f* (16) (~*ladung*) load, goods *pl.*, freight; ♣ cargo; (~*beförderung*) carriage, *Am.* freight (-age); *s.* ~*geld*; '**~brief** *m* way-bill; ♣ *u. Am.* bill of lading; '**~dampfer** *m* cargo-steamer; '**2en** (26) freight, load; '**~er** *m* freighter; '**2frei** carriage paid; '**~geld** *n* carriage, freight (-age); '**~gut** *n* goods *pl., Am.* ordinary freight; *als* ~ by goods train, *Am.* by freight train; '**~raum** *m* cargo compartment; (*Ladefähigkeit*) freight capacity; '**~satz** *m* freight rate; '**~schiff** *n* cargo-ship, freighter; '**~stück** *n* package; '**~verkehr** *m* goods traffic.

Frack [frak] *m* (11 *u.* 3³) dress- (*od.* tail-)coat; *im* ~ in full evening dress; '**~anzug** *m* dress-suit; '**~hemd** *n* dress-shirt.

Frage ['fra:gə] *f* (15) question (*a. fig. Problem*); *gr., rhet.* interrogation; (*Erkundigung*) inquiry; *e-e* ~ *tun od. stellen* ask a question; *außer* ~ *stehen* be beyond question; *in* ~

kommen come into question; *das kommt nicht in* ~ that's out (of the question); *in* ~ *stellen* make dubious *od.* uncertain; *in* ~ *ziehen* (call in) question; *ohne* ~ beyond question; '~**bogen** *m* questionnaire; '~**form** *gr. f* interrogative form; '~**fürwort** *n* interrogative pronoun; 'Qn *v/t u. v/i.* (25) ask; (*ausfragen*) question; interrogate; (*j-n*) et. ~ ask (a p.) a question; ~ *nach* ask for; *s.* erkundigen; (*sich kümmern um*) care about; *j-n nach s-m Namen, dem Wege usw.* ~ ask a p. his name, the way *etc.*; *ich frage mich, warum usw.* I wonder why *etc.*; *es fragt sich, ob it* is a question whether; *gefragt* † in demand.

'**Frager** *m* (7), '~**in** *f* questioner.

'**Frage|satz** *m* interrogative sentence; '~**steller** *m* (7) questioner; '~**stunde** *parl. f* question-time; '~**wort** *n* interrogative; '~**zeichen** *n* question-mark, mark of interrogation, *Am. mst* interrogation point.

frag|lich ['fraːkliç] (*zweifelhaft*) questionable; (*in Rede stehend*) in question (*hinter su.*); '~**los** unquestionably, beyond (all) question.

Fragment [frag'ment] *n* (3) fragment; Qarisch [~'taːriʃ] fragmentary.

fragwürdig ['fraːk-] questionable.

Fraktion *parl.* [frak'tsjoːn] *f* (16) parliamentary party; '~**s-vorsitzende** *m* leader (*od.* chairman) of the (parliamentary) group, *Am.* floor leader.

Fraktur [frak'tuːr] *f* fracture; *typ.* (*a.* ~**schrift** *f*) German type.

frank[1] [fraŋk] frank, free; ~ *und frei* frankly, plainly.

Frank[2] *m* (12), '~**en** *m* (6) *Münze:* franc.   [Franconian.]

'**Franke** *m* (13), **Fränkin** *f* (16[1])

fran'kier|en stamp, prepay; Q~**maschine** *f* franking machine.

franko ['fraŋko] post-paid, prepaid, post-free; *Paket:* carriage paid.

Franse ['franzə] *f* (15) fringe.

Franz|band ['frants-] *m* calf-binding; ~**branntwein** ['~brant-] *m* surgical spirit.

Franziskaner [frantsis'kaːnər] *m* (7) Franciscan friar.

Franzose [fran'tsoːzə] *m* (13) Frenchman; *die* ~*n pl.* the French.

Franzö|sin [~'tsøːzin] *f* French-

woman; Qsisch French.

frappant [fra'pant] striking.

fräsen ['frɛːzən] (27) *v/t.* mill.

Fräsmaschine ['frɛːs-] *f* milling machine.

Fraß [fraːs] **1.** *m* (3[2]) (*Essen*) *sl.* grub; (*Viehfutter*) feed; caries; **2.** Q *pret. v.* fressen 1.

Fratze ['fratsə] *f* (15) grimace; F (*Gesicht*) mug; (*Zerrbild*) caricature; *e-e* ~ *schneiden* make a grimace; Qnhaft grotesque.

Frau [frau] *f* (16) woman; (*Herrin*) mistress; (*Edelfrau; Dame*) lady; (*EheQ*) wife; *vor Namen:* Mrs. (*Aussprache:* 'misiz); *gnädige* ~ madam; *m-e* ~ my wife, *förmlich:* *Mrs Brown etc.*; *zur* ~ *begehren, geben, nehmen* ask, give, take in marriage.

'**Frauen|-arzt** *m* gyn(a)ecologist; '~**bewegung** *f* Women's Lib; 'Qhaft womanly; '~**klinik** *f* hospital for women; '~**kloster** *n* nunnery; '~**krankheit** *f* women's disease; '~**leiden** *n* women's complaint; '~**rechte** *n/pl.* women's rights *pl.*; '~**rechtlerin** *f* suffragette; '~**sport** *m* women's sports *pl.*; '~**stimmrecht** *n* women's suffrage; '~**welt** *f* womankind, women *pl.*; '~**zimmer** *n mst contp.* woman, *sl.* skirt.

Fräulein ['frɔylain] *n* (6) young lady; unmarried lady; *Titel:* Miss; (*Kellnerin*) waitress; *Ihr* ~ *Tochter* your daughter; *teleph. das* ~ *vom Amt* the operator.

'**fraulich** womanly.

frech [frɛç] impudent, insolent; F saucy, cheeky, *Am. sl.* fresh; 'Qheit *f* impudence, insolence; F sauciness.

Fregatte [fre'gatə] *f* (15) frigate; ~**kapitän** *m* commander.

frei [frai] free (*von* from, of); (*offen*) frank; (*unabhängig*) independent; (*von Lasten*) exempt (*von* from); *Stelle:* vacant; *Feld, Himmel:* open; (*unentgeltlich*) free (of charge); (*porto~*) (pre)paid; ~*er Beruf* liberal (*od.* independent) profession; *Journalist, Künstler:* free-lance; *Straße usw.:* clear; † ~ (*ins*) *Haus* free of charge; † ~ *an Bord* free on board (*abbr.* f.o.b.); ~ *heraus* (*offen*) frankly, plainly; *im* Qen, *unter* ~*em Himmel* in the open air; *ich bin so* ~ I take the liberty (*zu inf.* of *ger.*); ~ *umherlaufen* be at large; *im* Qen *la-*

gern camp out; ⁓*er Mensch* free agent; ⁓*e Künste f/pl.* liberal arts; ⁓*er Nachmittag* afternoon off, half--holiday; ⁓*er Tag* day off, holiday; ⁓ *sprechen Redner*: speak offhand *od.* extempore; *Straße* ⁓*!* road clear!; *s. ausgehen, Fuß, Hand, Stück usw.*

'**Frei|bad** *n* open-air swimming pool; '⁓**beruflich** free-lance; '⁓**betrag** *m* allowance; ⁓**beuter** ['⁓bɔʏtǝr] *m* (7) freebooter, filibuster; '⁓**billett** *n s.* Freikarte; '⁓**bleibend** *Preis*: without engagement; '⁓**brief** *m* charter, (letters *pl.*) patent; *fig.* warrant; '⁓**denker** *m* free-thinker; '⁓**denke'rei** *f*, '⁓**denkerisch** free--thinking.

freien ['fraɪǝn] (25) *v/i.*: ⁓ *um* court, woo; *v/t.* marry.

'**Freier** *m* (7) suitor; *rhet.* wooer; *auf* '⁓**sfüßen** *gehen* go courting.

'**Frei|exemplar** *n* free copy, presentation copy; '⁓**fahrschein** 🚋 *m* free (travel) ticket; '⁓**frau** *f* baroness; '⁓**gabe** *f* release; *bewirtschafteter Ware*: decontrol; '⁓**geben** release; *s. freilassen*; *gesperrtes Konto*: deblock; *Schule*: give a holiday; *Straße usw.*: open; *Ware*: decontrol; '⁓**gebig** liberal, generous; '⁓**gebigkeit** *f* liberality, generosity; '⁓**gehege** *n* open-air enclosure; '⁓**geist** *m* free-thinker; '⁓**gepäck** *n* allowed (*od.* free) luggage; '⁓**grenze** ✝ *f* duty exemption limit; '⁓**haben** *Schule*: have a holiday; *Dienst*: have a day off; '⁓**hafen** *m* free port; '⁓**halten** *j-n*: pay for; *e-n Platz*: keep free; ✝ *Angebot*: keep open; '⁓**handel** *m* free trade; '⁓**händig** without support; *Zeichnen*: freehand; ꝛꞇ privately; ✝ direct.

'**Freiheit** *f* (16) liberty, freedom (*von* from); *v. Lasten*: exemption (from); *bürgerliche* ⁓ civil liberty; *dichterische* ⁓ poetic licen|ce, *Am.* -se; *sich die* ⁓ *nehmen zu tun* take the liberty of doing; *in* ⁓ *setzen, j-m die* ⁓ *schenken* set at liberty; '⁓**lich** liberal; '⁓**sberaubung** *f* deprivation of liberty; '⁓**s-entzug** ꝛꞇ *m* detention; '⁓**skampf** *m* struggle for freedom; '⁓**skrieg** *m* war of independence; '⁓**sstrafe** *f* prison sentence; imprisonment.

freihe'raus frankly.

'**Frei|herr** *m* baron; '⁓**in** *f* baroness; '⁓**karte** *f* free (*thea. a.* complimen-

tary) ticket; '⁓**körperkultur** *f* nudism, naturism; '⁓**korps** *n* volunteer corps; '⁓**lassen** release, liberate, set free; *Sklaven*: emancipate; '⁓**lassung** *f* release, liberation; emancipation; '⁓**lauf** *m* free-wheel; '⁓**legen** lay open; '⁓**lich** certainly, to be sure; *einräumend*: of course, though; '⁓**lichtbühne** *f* open-air stage; '⁓**machen** get free; *Weg usw.*: clear; ✉ prepay, stamp; *sich* ⁓ disengage o.s.; *vom Dienst usw.*: take time off; '⁓**marke** *f* (postage) stamp; '⁓**maurer** *m* freemason; '⁓**maure'rei** *f* freemasonry; '⁓**maurerloge** *f* freemason's lodge; '⁓**mut** *m* frankness; '⁓**mütig** ['⁓myːtɪç] frank, candid, open; '⁓**schaffend**: ⁓*er Künstler* free-lance artist; '⁓**schar** *f s.* Freikorps; ⁓**schärler** ['⁓ʃɛːrlǝr] *m* gue(r)-rilla, irregular; '⁓**schwimmen**: *sich* ⁓ pass one's 15 minute swimming test; '⁓**setzen** release; *Arbeitnehmer*: make redundant; '⁓**sinn** *m* liberalism; '⁓**sinnig** liberal; '⁓**sprechen** absolve (*von* from), ꝛꞇ acquit (of); *Lehrling*: release from his articles; '⁓**sprechung** *f* absolutism, acquittal; release *of an apprentice*; '⁓**spruch** ꝛꞇ *m* acquittal; '⁓**staat** *m* free state; republic; '⁓**statt** *f*, '⁓**stätte** *f* asylum, refuge; '⁓**stehen**: *es steht dir frei zu tun* you are free (*od.* at liberty) to; '⁓**stehend** *Haus*: detached; '⁓**stelle** *f* scholarship; '⁓**stellen** ✗ exempt (from military service); *Angestellte*: lay off; *j-m et.* ⁓ leave to a p.('s discretion); '⁓**stil** *m Sport*: free style; '⁓**stilringen** *n* free-style wrestling; catch-as-catch-can; '⁓**stoß** *m Fußball*: free kick; '⁓**stunde** *f* leisure hour; '⁓**tag** *m* Friday; '⁓**tod** *m* voluntary death, suicide; '⁓**tragend** cantilever, self-supporting; '⁓**treppe** *f* outside staircase, perron, *Am.* stoop; '⁓**übungen** *f/pl.* free exercises; '⁓**umschlag** *m* stamped envelope; '⁓**wild** *n* fair game; '⁓**willig** free, voluntary, spontaneous; *adv. a.* of one's own free will; *sich* ⁓ *erbieten od. melden* volunteer; '⁓**willige** ['⁓viligǝ] *m* (18) volunteer; '⁓**willigkeit** *f* voluntariness, spontaneity; '⁓**wurf** *m Basketball etc.*: free throw; '⁓**zeit** *f* free (*od.* spare, leisure, off) time; '⁓**zeitkleidung** *f* leisure wear; ⁓**zügig** ['⁓tsyːgɪç] free to move; *fig.* unhampered; (*großzügig*) permissive; '**~zügigkeit** *f* freedom of movement; permissiveness.

fremd [frɛmt] strange; (*ausländisch*) foreign; (*nicht dazugehörig*) extraneous; *fig.* (*zuwider*) alien; *~es Gut* other people's property; *ich bin hier* *~* I am a stranger here.

'**fremd-artig** strange, odd; '**2keit** *f* strangeness, oddness.

Fremde[1] ['frɛmdə] *f* (15) foreign country; *in der* (*od. die*) *~* abroad; '**~**[2] *m, f* (18) stranger; (*Ausländer*) foreigner, *nicht naturalisiert*: alien; (*Gast*) guest, visitor; '**~nbuch** *n* visitors' book; '**~nführer** *m* guide; '**~nheim** *n* boarding house, private hotel; '**~n-industrie** *f* tourist industry; '**~nlegion** ⚔ *f* Foreign Legion; '**~nverkehr** *m* tourist traffic; '**~nzimmer** *n* spare (bed)room, guest room.

'**fremdgehen** F (sn) two-time.

'**Fremd|herrschaft** *f* foreign rule; '**~körper** *m* ⚕ foreign body; *fig.* alien element; **2ländisch** ['~lɛndiʃ] foreign; '**~ling** ['~liŋ] *m* (3[1]) *s. Fremde*[2]; '**~sprache** *f*, '**2sprachlich** foreign language; '**~sprachenkorrespondent** *m* foreign correspondence clerk; '**~sprachensekretärin** *f* linguist-secretary; '**~wort** *n* foreign word. [frequent.)

frequentieren [frekvɛn'ti:rən]}
Fre'quenz [~ts] *f* (16) *phys.* frequency; (*Besucherzahl*) attendance.

fressen ['frɛsən] **1.** eat, feed; (*a. v/i.* [30]); *Raubtier*: devour, F *Mensch*: devour, (*a. v/i.*) gorge; 🐍 corrode; *nur v/i.* (h.) ⊕ *Lager usw.*: seize; *fig.* swallow, consume; *e-m Tier* (*Gras usw.*) *zu ~ geben* feed an animal (on grass *etc.*); **2.** 🐍 *n* (6) feed, food; *ein gefundenes ~ für ihn* just what he wanted.

'**Fresser** *m* (7) voracious eater, glutton; **~ei** [~'raɪ] *f* gluttony.

'**Freß|gier** *f* gluttony, greediness; '**2gierig** gluttonous, greedy; '**~napf** *m* feeding dish.

Frettchen ['frɛtçən] *n* (6) ferret.

Freude ['frɔʏdə] *f* (15) joy, gladness; (*Wonne*) delight; (*Vergnügen*) pleasure; *~ haben* (*od. finden*) *an* (*dat.*) take pleasure in; *mit ~n* gladly, with pleasure.

'**Freuden...** *in Zssgn mst* ... of joy; '**~botschaft** *f* glad tidings *pl.*; '**~feier** *f*, '**~fest** *n* feast, rejoicing; '**~-**

feuer *n* bonfire; '**~geschrei** *n* shouts *pl.* of joy; '**~haus** *n* brothel, disorderly house; '**~mädchen** *n* prostitute; '**~rausch** *m*, '**~taumel** *m* transports *pl.* of joy; '**~tag** *m* day of rejoicing, red-letter day.

'**freudestrahlend** radiant with joy.

'**freudig** joyful; *~es Ereignis* happy event; '**2keit** *f* joyfulness.

freudlos ['frɔʏtlo:s] joyless, cheerless.

'**freuen** (25): *es freut mich, zu inf.* I am glad (*od.* pleased) to ...; *es freut mich, daß du gekommen bist* I am glad (*od.* happy) you have come; *sich ~* (*über acc., zu inf.*) be glad (of, at; to *inf.*), be pleased (with; to *inf.*), be happy (about; to *inf.*); *sich ~ an* (*dat.*) delight in, enjoy; *sich ~ auf* (*acc.*) look forward to; *ich freue mich darüber* I am glad of it.

Freund [frɔʏnt] *m* (3) (*engS.* boy) friend; **~in** ['~din] *f* (16[1]) (*engS.* girl) friend; *~ der Musik usw.* lover; **2lich** ['frɔʏnt-] friendly, kind, genial (*a. Klima*); *Zimmer*: cheerful; '**~lichkeit** *f* kindness; *j-m e-e ~ erweisen do a p. a* kindness; '**2los** friendless; '**~schaft** *f* friendship; *~ schließen mit* make friends with; '**2schaftlich** friendly; '**~schaftsspiel** *n* *Sport*: friendly match.

Frevel ['fre:fəl] *m* (7) outrage (*an dat., gegen on*); (*Mutwille*) wantonness; '**2haft** wicked, outrageous, wanton, impious; '**2n** (29) commit a crime; *~ an dat., gegen* outrage; '**~tat** *f* outrage.

freventlich ['~fəntliç] *s.* frevelhaft.

Frevler ['~flər] *m* (7), '**~in** *f* (16[1]) offender, transgressor.

Friede(n) ['fri:də(n)] *m* (13[1][6]) peace; *im ~* at peace; *~ schließen* make peace; *laß mich in ~!* leave me alone!

'**Friedens|bewegung** *f* peace movement; '**~bruch** *m* breach of (the) peace; '**~forschung** *f* peace research; '**~gespräche** *n/pl.* peace talks; '**~pfeife** *f* peace-pipe; '**~produktion** *f* peace-time production; '**~schluß** *m* conclusion of peace; '**~stärke** ⚔ *f* peace establishment; '**~stifter(in** *f*) *m* peace-maker; '**~truppe** *f* peace-keeping force; '**~verhandlungen** *f/pl.* peace-negotiations; '**~vertrag** *m* peace-treaty.

fried|fertig ['fri:t-] peaceable, pacific; '**Qfertigkeit** f peaceableness; '**Qhof** m churchyard, cemetery; '**~lich**, '**~sam** peaceable; *(ungestört)* peaceful; '**~liebend** peace-loving; '**~los** peaceless.

frieren ['fri:rən] v/t. u. v/i. (30, h. u. sn) freeze; *mich friert* I am *(od. feel)* cold; *mich friert an den Füßen* my feet are cold.

Fries [fri:s] m (4) △ frieze *(a. Tuch).*

Fries|e ['fri:zə] m (13), '**~in** (16¹) f, '**Qisch**, **~länder** ['fri:slendər] m (7), '**~länderin** f (16¹) Frisian.

Frikadelle [frika'dɛlə] f (15) (meat) rissole.

Frikass|ee [frika'se:] n (11), Qieren [~'si:rən] fricassee.

frisch [friʃ] *allg.* fresh; *Brot:* new; *Ei:* new-laid; *Wäsche:* clean; *(kühl)* cool; *(neu)* new; *(kürzlich geschehen)* recent; *(kräftig)* vigorous; *(blühend)* florid; *(munter)* brisk, lively; *von ~em* afresh; *j-n auf ~er Tat ergreifen od. ertappen* take a p. in the very act, take a p. red-handed; *~ gestrichen!* wet paint!; '**Qe** f (15) freshness; **vigo(u)r**; '**~en** (27) *Eisen:* refine; '**Qfleisch** n butcher's meat; '**Qhaltebeutel** m keep-fresh bag.

Friseur [fri'zø:r] m (3¹) hairdresser, *Am. (für Herren)* a. barber; '**~laden** m hairdresser's shop, *Am. (für Herren)* barbershop.

Friseuse [~'zø:zə] f (15) ladies' hairdresser.

fri'sieren: *j-n~* dress a p.'s hair; *F fig. Bericht usw.:* cook, doctor; *Motor etc.:* F hype *(od. soup)* up.

Fri'sier|mantel m peignoir *(fr.);* **~salon** m hairdressing saloon; **~tisch** m, **~toilette** f dressing-table, *Am.* dresser.

Frist [frist] f (16) (space of) time; *(festgesetzter Zeitpunkt)* appointed *od.* fixed) time, (set) term; time-limit; *(Aufschub)* respite, delay; '**Qen** (26): *sein Leben ~* barely manage to exist; make a bare living; '**Q-gerecht** timely; '**Qlos** without notice.

Frisur [fri'zu:r] f (16) hair-style, coiffure *(fr.), Am.* hairdo.

Fri|teuse [fri'tø:zə] f (15) deep-frying *(od. chip)* pan; **Qtieren** deep-fry.

frivol [fri'vo:l] frivolous, flippant; **Qität** [~i'tɛ:t] f frivolity, flippancy.

froh [fro:] glad, cheerful, happy; *(freudig)* joyful; *s-s Lebens nicht ~ werden* have no end of trouble.

fröhlich ['frø:liç] merry, gay, cheerful; '**Qkeit** f gaiety, cheerfulness.

froh'locken exult *(über acc.* at); *(triumphieren)* triumph (over).

'**Frohsinn** m cheerfulness.

fromm [frɔm] (18²) pious, religious; *Pferd:* quiet; **~er** *Betrug* pious fraud; **~er** *Wunsch* idle wish.

Frömmelei [frœmə'lai] f (16) affected piety, bigotry.

frömmeln (29) be bigoted.

'**Frömm|igkeit** f piety; '**~ler(in** f) m bigot, sanctimonious person.

Fron [fro:n] f (16), '**~arbeit** f, '**~dienst** m compulsory labo(u)r *od.* service; *fig.* drudgery.

frönen ['frø:nən] (25) *(dat.)* indulge in.   [Corpus Christi.)

Fron'leichnamsfest n (feast of)∫

Front [frɔnt] f (16) front *(bsd. ~ u. △), △ a.* face; *an der ~ at the front; ~ machen gegen* turn against; *Sport: in ~ gehen* take the lead; **Qal** [frɔn-'ta:l] frontal; head-on; **~alzusammenstoß** *mot. m* head-on collision; '**~antrieb** *mot. m* front-wheel drive; '**~kämpfer** m combatant; *ehemaliger:* ex-serviceman, *Am.* veteran; '**~lader** m (7) *Video, Hi-Fi:* frontloader; '**~soldat** m front-line soldier; '**~wechsel** m change of front, face-about.

fror [fro:r] *pret. v.* frieren.

Frosch [frɔʃ] m (3² u. 3³) frog; *Feuerwerk:* squib; '**~perspektive** f worm's-eye view.

Frost [frɔst] m (3² u. 3³) frost; *(Kältegefühl)* chill, coldness; '**Qbeständig** frost-resistant; '**~beule** f chilblain.   [shiver (with cold).)

frösteln ['frœstəln] (29) feel chilly,∫

'**frostig** frosty, chilly *(beide a. fig.);* '**Qkeit** f frostiness.

'**Frost|salbe** f chilblain ointment; '**~schaden** m damage done by frost; *am Körper:* frostbite; '**~schutzmittel** n anti-freezing agent; anti-freeze; '**~schutzscheibe** *mot. f* anti-frost screen; '**~wetter** n frosty weather.

Frottee [frɔ'te:] n (11) terry (cloth).

frottier|en [frɔ'ti:rən] rub; Q(**hand**)-**tuch** n Turkish *(od. terry)* towel.

Frucht [fruxt] f (14¹) fruit *(a. fig.); (Getreide)* corn; *fig.* effect, result.

'**frucht|bar** fruitful *(a. biol.),* fertile

(beide a. fig.; an dat. in); *(produktiv)* prolific; ~ **machen** fertilize; '2**barkeit** *f* fruitfulness, fertility; '~**bringend** fruit-bearing; *fig.* productive; '~**en** (26) be of use, have effect; '2**knoten** ♀ *m* seed-vessel; '~**los** fruitless; '2**losigkeit** *f* fruitlessness; '2**presse** *f* fruit press; '2**saft** *m* fruit-juice.

frugal [fru'ga:l] frugal.

früh [fry:] *(zeitig)* early; *(morgens)* in the morning; *von* ~ *bis spät* from morning till night; ~**er** earlier, sooner; *(ehemals)* former; ~**er als** *a.* prior to; ~**er oder später** sooner or later; ~**er habe ich geraucht** *(jetzt nicht mehr)* I used to smoke; ~**est** earliest, soonest; ~**estens** at the earliest; ~**e Morgenstunden** *(1—4 Uhr)* small hours; '2**-aufsteher(in** *f*) *m* early riser.

Früh|e ['fry:ə] *f* (15) early hour *od.* morning; *in aller* ~ very early; '~**erkennung** ♂ *f* early diagnosis; '~**geburt** *f* premature birth; '~**gemüse** *n* early vegetable(s *pl.*); '~**gottesdienst** *m* morning service; '~**jahr** *n*, '~**ling** *m* (3¹) spring; '~**konzert** *n* morning concert; '~**messe** *f* morning prayer, mat(t)ins *pl.*; 2'**morgens** early in the morning; '~'**obst** *n* early fruit; '2**reif** early(-ripe); *fig.* precocious; '~**reife** *f* earliness; *fig.* precocity; '~**rentner(in** *f*) *m* person who has retired early; '~**schicht** *f* early (morning) shift; '~**schoppen** *m* morning pint; '~**sport** *m* early morning exercises *pl.*; '~**stadium** *n* early stage; '~**stück** *n* breakfast; '2**stücken** (25) (have) breakfast; '~**warnsystem** *n* early warning system; '2**zeitig** early; *fig.* premature; '~**zeitigkeit** *f* earliness; *fig.* prematurity; '~**zug** 🚂 *m* early train; '~**zündung** *f* pre-ignition, advanced ignition.

frustrieren [frus'tri:rən] frustrate.

Fuchs [fuks] *m* (4²) fox (*a. fig.*); *Pferd:* sorrel (horse); *univ.* freshman; '~**bau** *m* fox-earth; '2**en** (27) F madden; *sich* ~ be furious (*über acc.* at, about); ~**ie** ♀ ['fuksjə] *f* (15) fuchsia; '2**ig** foxy; F *(ärgerlich)* furious.

Füchsin ['fyksin] *f* she-fox, vixen.

'**Fuchs|jagd** *f* fox-hunt(ing); '~**pelz** *m* (fur of a) fox; '2**rot** fox-col-o(u)red; '~**schwanz** *m* foxtail;

(Säge) pad-saw; ♀ amarant(h); '2**teufels'wild** mad with rage.

Fuchtel ['fuxtəl] *f* (15) rod; *unter j-s* ~ under a p.'s thumb; '2**n** (29) *mit* wave (about), brandish.

Fuder ['fu:dər] *n* (7) cart-load.

fuchtig ['fuxtiç] furious.

Fug [fu:k] *m* (3): *mit* ~ *und Recht* with full right.

Fuge ['fu:gə] *f* (15) joint, seam; *(Falz)* rabbet; ♪ fugue; *aus den* ~*n bringen* put out of joint, disjoint; '2**n** (25) join; rabbet.

fügen ['fy:gən] (25) *s. an*~, *hinzu*~, *zusammen*~; *(verfügen)* ordain, dispose; *sich* ~ *(dat.)* *od.* *in* *(acc.)* *(nachgeben)* comply with, resign o.s. to; submit to; *(sich anpassen)* accommodate o.s. to; *es fügt sich* it (so) happens.   [justly.)

füglich ['fy:k-] *adv.* conveniently,}

'**fügsam** pliant, supple; *(lenksam)* tractable; *(folgsam)* obedient; '2**keit** *f* pliancy; obedience.

Fügung ['~guŋ] *f (Zs.-treffen)* coincidence; *(in acc.)* resignation (to), submission (to); ~ *Gottes* dispensation (of Providence).

'**fühlbar** sensible, palpable, tangible; *geistig:* perceptible, noticeable; ~**er Mangel** felt want; '2**keit** *f* sensibility; perceptibility.

fühl|en ['fy:lən] (25) feel; *sich glücklich usw.* ~ feel happy *etc.*; '2**er** *m* (7), '2**horn** *n* feeler; '2**ung** *f* touch, contact; ~ *haben (verlieren)* *mit* be in (lose) touch with; ~ *nehmen* *mit j-m* get in(to) touch with a p., contact a p.

fuhr [fu:r] *pret. v. fahren.*

Fuhre ['fu:rə] *f* (15) cart-load.

führen ['fy:rən] (25) lead; *e-m Ziele zu:* conduct, guide; ⚔ *(befehligen)* command; *(weg*~) take; *thea. j-n an seinen Platz:* usher; *(tragen)* carry; *Bücher, Liste:* keep; *Geschäft, Gespräch, Prozeß:* carry on; *Namen:* bear; *Feder, Waffe: (handhaben)* wield; *Ware:* keep, carry; *Wagen:* drive; *e-e Sprache:* use; *e-n Schlag:* strike; *e-n Titel:* bear, hold; *(beaufsichtigen, verwalten)* manage; *sich gut usw.* ~ conduct o.s.; *Besuch hinein*~ show in; *durch das Haus* ~ show over the house; *zum Munde* ~ raise to one's lips; *die Aufsicht* ~ *über* *(acc.)* superintend; *den Beweis* ~ prove; *ein Geschäft* ~ carry on (*od.*

run) a business *od.* shop; (*j-m*) den Haushalt (*od. die Wirtschaft*) ~ keep house (for a p.); *Klage* (*od. Beschwerde*) ~ complain (*über acc.* of); *Krieg* (*mit j-m*) ~ wage war (with a p.), make war ([up]on a p.); *ein Leben* ~ live a life; *s. Licht, Schild, Vorsitz, Wort usw.*; *v/i.* lead (*zu* to; *a. fig.*); *Sport:* (hold the) lead; *Sport: mit Punkten* ~ be ahead (*z. B. 6 : 2*).

'**führend** leading, (top-)ranking, prominent, top; ~ *sein* (hold the) lead, be at the top.

'**Führer** *m* (7), '~in *f* leader; (*Leiter*) conductor; (*Wegweiser*) guide (*a. als Buch u.* ⊕); (*Verwalter*) manager(ess *f*); *e-s Wagens:* driver; ✗ pilot; *Sport:* captain; ✗ (*Zug* ♀, *Gruppen* ♀) leader, (*Kompanie* ♀) commander; '♀los guideless; *Wagen:* driverless; ✗ pilotless; '~raum ✗ *m* cockpit; '~schaft *f* leadership; '~schein *m mot.* driving licence, *Am.* driver's license; ✗ pilot's licence, *Am.* pilot's certificate; '~sitz *m* driver's seat; ✗ (pilot's) cockpit.

'**Fuhr|geld** *n*, '~lohn *m* carriage, cartage; '~mann *m* (*pl. Fuhrleute*) carrier; (*Kutscher*) driver; '~park *m* park; (*Wagen*) fleet.

'**Führung** *f e-m Ziele zu:* guidance; *Sport u. fig.:* lead; (*Leitung*) conduct, direction, management; leadership, ✗ command; *in e-m Museum usw.:* showing round; *e-s Titels:* use; (*Benehmen*) conduct; ~ *der Bücher* book-keeping; ✗ *innere* ~ moral leadership; ⊕ guide; *die* ~ *übernehmen* take the lead (*a. Sport*); *in* ~ *liegen* be in the lead; '~szeugnis *n* certificate of conduct; *für Personal:* character.

'**Fuhr|-unternehmen** *n* (firm of) carriers *pl. od.* haul(i)ers *pl.*; '~-unternehmer** *m* carrier, haul(i)er, *Am. a.* teamster; '~werk *n* vehicle, cart, wag(g)on.

'**Füllbleistift** *m* propelling pencil.

'**Fülle** ['fylə] *f* (15) ful(l)ness (*a. fig.*); (*reicher Vorrat*) plenty, abundance; (*Körper* ♀) stoutness; '♀n[1] (25) fill (*a. sich*); *Braten usw.:* stuff; *Zahn:* stop, fill; *auf Flaschen* ~ bottle.

'**Füllen**[2] ['fylən] *n* (6) foal; (*Hengst* ♀) colt; (*Stuten* ♀) filly.

'**Füll|er** F *m* (7) = '~feder(halter

m) *f* fountain-pen; '~horn *n* horn of plenty; ~sel ['~zəl] *n* (7) stuffing; '~ung *f* filling (*a. Zahn* ♀); (*Tür* ♀) panel; (*Ladung*) charge; *s. Füllsel*; '~wort *n* expletive.

fummeln F ['fuməln] (29) fumble; (*knutschen*) pet.

Fund [funt] *m* (3) finding, discovery; (*Gefundenes*) find; *einen* ~ *tun od. machen* have a find.

Fundament [funda'mɛnt] *n* (3) foundation(s *pl.*); ♀al [~mɛn'taːl] fundamental; ♀ieren [~'tiːrən] lay the foundation(s) of.

'**Fund|büro** *n* lost property office; '~grube *f fig.* mine, storehouse.

fundieren [fun'diːrən] found; *Schuld:* fund, consolidate.

'**Fund|-ort** *m* place where a th. was found; '~sachen *f/pl.* lost property *sg.*

fünf [fynf] **1.** five; ~ *gerade sein lassen* stretch a point; **2.** ♀ *f* (16) (number) five; *auf Würfeln u. Spielkarten: a.* cinque; '~blätt(e)rig five-leaved; '♀-eck *n* pentagon; '~-eckig pentagonal; '~erlei of five kinds; '~fach, ~fältig ['~fɛltiç] fivefold; '~hundert five hundred; ~jährig ['~jɛːriç] five-year-old; '~jährlich every five years; '♀kampf *m Sport:* pentathlon; '♀linge *m/pl.* quintuplets *pl.*; '~mal five times; '~malig done (*od.* occurring) five times; '~-seitig five-sided; '~stellig *Zahl:* of five digits; ~stöckig ['~ʃtœkiç] five-storied; ~tägig ['~tɛːgiç] of five days; '~te fifth; *fig. das* ~ *Rad am Wagen sein* be the fifth wheel on the coach; '♀tel *n* (7) fifth (part); '~tens fifthly.

'**fünfzehn** fifteen; '~te fifteenth.

fünfzig ['~tsiç] fifty; ♀er ['~tsigər] *m* (7), '♀erin *f* quinquagenarian; '~ste fiftieth.

'**Fünfzylinder** *mot. m* five-cylinder car.

fungieren [fuŋ'giːrən] (25): ~ *als* act as.

Funk [fuŋk] *m* (3[1], *o. pl.*) radio, *Brt. a.* wireless; '~-anlage *f* wireless (*od.* radio) equipment; '~-apparat *m s. Funkgerät*; '~-ausstellung *f* radio show; '~bastler *m* radio amateur *od.* fan; '~bild *n* photoradiogram.

Fünkchen ['fyŋkçən] *n* (6) small spark; *fig.* grain.

'**Funkdienst** *m* radio service.

Funke

Funke ['fuŋkə] *m* (13), '**∼n** *m* (6) spark (*a. fig.*).

'**Funk-einrichtung** *f* radio equipment.

'**funkeln** (29) sparkle (*a. fig.*), glitter.

'**funkel(nagel)'neu** brand-new.

'**funken** (25) radio.

'**Funker** *m* (7) radio operator.

'**Funk|feuer** ✠ *n* radio beacon; '**∼gerät** *n* radio (*od.* wireless) set; '**∼haus** *n* broadcasting cent|re, *Am.* -er; '**∼ortung** *f* radio location; '**∼peilung** *f* radio bearing; '**∼sprechgerät** *n* radiophone; *tragbares*: walkie-talkie; '**∼spruch** *m* radio message, radiogram; '**∼station** *f* radio (*od.* wireless) station; '**∼stille** *f* radio silence; '**∼streife(nwagen** *m*) *f* radio patrol (car); '**∼technik** *f* radio engineering; '**∼telegramm** *n* radio telegram, radiogram.

Funktion [fuŋk'tsjoːn] *f* (16) function; **∼är** [∼tsjo'nɛːr] *m* (3¹) functionary; ♀**ieren** [∼'niːrən] function, operate, work; ♀**sfähig** functioning; **∼sstörung** ✠ *f* malfunction.

'**Funk|turm** *m* radio tower; '**∼verbindung** *f* radio connection; '**∼verkehr** *m* wireless (*od.* radio) traffic; '**∼wagen** *m* radio car *od.* truck; '**∼wesen** *n* radio (telegraphy).

für [fyːr] *allg.* for; (*als Ersatz*) *a.* in exchange for; (*zugunsten von*) *a.* in favo(u)r of; *Jahr ∼ Jahr* year by year; *Stück ∼ Stück* piece by piece; *Tag ∼ Tag* day after day; *ich habe* (*esse usw.*) *es ∼ mein Leben gern* I am exceedingly fond of it; *ich ∼ meine Person I for one*; *∼ sich* (*leise*) in an undertone, *thea.* aside; *∼ sich leben* live by o.s.; *an und ∼ sich* in itself; *das* ♀ *und Wider* the pros and cons *pl.*; *was ∼* (*ein*) ...? what (kind of) ...?; *s. was*; *sich ∼ sich halten* stand aloof.

'**Fürbitte** *f* intercession; *∼ einlegen für* intercede (*od.* plead) for.

Furche ['furçə] *f* (15) furrow; (*Runzel*) wrinkle; (*Wagenspur*) rut; '♀**n** (25) furrow; wrinkle.

Furcht [furçt] *f* (16, *o. pl.*) fear, dread, fright; *aus ∼ vor* (*dat.*) for (*od.* from) fear of; *in ∼ setzen* frighten; '♀**bar** terrible, *stärker*: dreadful, frightful, formidable, horrible (*alle a.* F *ungemein*); F (*sehr groß usw.*) *a.* awful, tremendous.

fürchten ['fyrçtən] (26) fear, dread; *sich ∼* be afraid (*vor dat.* of).

'**fürchterlich** *s.* furchtbar.

'**furcht|-erregend** fearsome; '**∼los** fearless; ♀**losigkeit** *f* fearlessness; '**∼sam** fearful, timid, timorous; '♀**samkeit** *f* timidity.

Furie ['fuːrjə] *f* (15) fury.

Furier ✠ [fu'riːr] *m* (3¹) ration N.C.O. (= noncommissioned officer).

für'liebnehmen: *∼ mit* be content with, put up with.

Furnier [fur'niːr] *n* (3¹), ♀**en** veneer.

Furore [fu'roːre] *f* (15, *o. pl.*) *od. n* (10, *o. pl.*): *∼ machen* create a sensation.

'**Für|sorge** *f* care; *öffentliche ∼* public assistance, welfare work; *s. sozial*; '**∼sorge-amt** *n* welfare cent|re, *Am.* -er; '**∼sorge-erziehung** *f* trustee (*als Strafe*: correctional) education; '**∼sorger(in** *f*) *m* welfare officer *od.* worker; '♀**sorglich** solicitous; '**∼sprache** *f* intercession; '**∼sprecher** *m* advocate.

Fürst [fyrst] *m* (12) prince; (*Herrscher*) sovereign; '**∼engeschlecht** *n* dynasty; '**∼enstand** *m* princely rank; '**∼entum** *n* (1²) principality; '**∼enwürde** *f s.* Fürstenstand; '**∼in** *f* (16¹) princess; '♀**lich** princely; '**∼lichkeit** *f* princeliness; *∼en f/pl.* princely personages.

Furt [furt] *f* (16) ford.

Furunkel [fu'ruŋkəl] *m* (7) boil, furuncle; **Furunkulose** [furuŋku-'loːzə] ✠ *f* (15) furunculosis.

für|'wahr in truth; '♀**witz** *m s.* Vorwitz; '♀**wort** *n* (1²) pronoun.

Furz V [furts] *m* (3² *u.* ³), ♀**en** (27) fart.

Fusel F ['fuːzəl] *m* (7) *sl.* rotgut.

Fusion ✠ [fu'zjoːn] *f* (16) fusion, amalgamation, merger; ♀**ieren** [∼'niːrən] merge.

Fuß [fuːs] *m* (3² *u.* 3³) foot; *e-r Säule*: base; *e-s Stuhls, Tisches usw.*: leg; *s. Münz*♀; *festen ∼ fassen* gain a foothold; *auf gutem* (*schlechtem*) *∼ stehen mit* be on good (bad) terms with; *auf großem ∼e leben* live in grand style; *auf freien ∼ setzen* set at liberty; *auf eignen Füßen stehen* stand on one's own legs; *auf schwachen Füßen stehen* rest on a weak foundation; *mit beiden Füßen auf der Erde* *stehen* keep both feet on the ground; *stehenden* ~es on the spot, forthwith; *zu* ~ *on foot; zu* ~ *gehen* walk; *gut zu* ~ *sein* be a good walker.

'**Fuß|-abdruck** *m* (3³) footprint; '~**abstreicher** *m,* '~-**abtreter** *m* shoe scraper; '~**angel** *f* man-trap; '~**bad** *n* foot-bath; '~**ball** *m* football; '~**ballmannschaft** *f* football team; '~**ballplatz** *m* football field; '~**ballspiel** *n* (*Sportart*) (association) football, F soccer; (*Kampf*) soccer match; '~**ballspieler** *m* football-player, footballer; '~**ballstadion** *n* football stadium; '~**bank** *f* footstool; '~**bekleidung** *f* footwear; '~**boden** *m* floor(ing); '~**bodenbelag** *m* floor covering; '~**bodenheizung** *f* underfloor heating; '~**bremse** *f* foot brake.

Fussel F ['fusəl] *f* (15) fluff, fuzz.

fußen ['fu:sən] (27) *auf* (*dat.*) *Sache:* be based (*od.* rest) on.

'**Fuß|fall** *m* prostration; *e-n* ~ *tun* prostrate o.s.; '2**fällig** prostrate, on one's knees; ~**gänger** ['~gɛŋər] *m* (7) pedestrian; '~**gänger-überweg** *m* pedestrian crossing, *Am.* crosswalk; '~**gängerzone** *f* pedestrian zone (*Am.* precinct); '~**gelenk** *n* ankle-joint; '~**gestell** *n* pedestal; '~**knöchel** *m* ankle(-bone); '~**marsch** *m* walk; '~**matte** *f* doormat; *mot.* floormat; '~**note** *f* footnote; '~**pfad** *m* footpath; '~**pflege** *f* pedicure; '~**pilz**

🦶 *m* athlete's foot; '~**punkt** *m ast.* nadir; 🦶 foot; '~**schemel** *m* footstool; '~**sohle** *f* sole of the foot; '~**spur** *f einzelne:* footprint; *Reihe v.* ~*en*: track; '~**stapfe** *f* footstep; '~**steig** *m* footpath; '~**tour** *f* walking tour; '~**tritt** *m* kick; '~**volk** *n* foot; *fig.* rank and file; '~**wanderung** *f* hike; '~**weg** *m* footpath; '~**wurzel** *f* tarsus.

futsch F [futʃ] lost, gone; (*kaputt*) broken; ~ *gehen* go phut.

Futter ['futər] *n* (7) **1.** (*Nahrung*) food, F grub, *Am.* F chow; *für das Vieh:* feed, (*Trocken*2) fodder; **2.** (*Rock*2) lining (*a.* ⊕); 🔺 casing.

Futteral [~'rɑ:l] *n* (3) case; (*Schachtel*) box; (*Scheide*) sheath.

'**Futter|beutel** *m* nosebag; '~**kasten** *m* feedbox; '~**krippe** *f* crib, manger; '~**krippensystem** *pol. n Am.* spoils system; '~**mittel** *n* feed(ing) stuff; '~**napf** *m* feeding dish; '~**neid** *m* envy, (professional) jealousy.

fütter|n ['fytərn] (29) **1.** feed; **2.** (*innen bekleiden*) line; 🔺 case; *mit Pelz:* fur; (*auspolstern*) stuff; '2**ung** *f* feeding; lining; casing.

'**Futter|stoff** *m* lining (material); '~**trog** *m* feeding-trough.

Futurologie [futurolo'gi:] *f* (15, *o. pl.*) futurology.

Futur(um) *gr.* [fu'tu:r(um)] *n* (9²) future (tense).

G

G [ge:], **g** *n inv.* G, g; ♪ G.

gab [gɑ:p] *pret. v.* geben.

Gabardine [gabar'di:n] *m* (6) gabardine.

Gabe ['gɑ:bə] *f* (15) gift, present; *milde:* alms; (*Schenkung*) donation; 🦶 (*Dosis*) dose; (*Talent*) gift, talent; (*Fähigkeit*) skill.

Gabel ['gɑ:bəl] *f* (15) fork; (*Deichsel*2) (e-e a pair of) shafts *pl.;* ✕ bracket; 2**förmig** ['~fœrmiç], '2**ig** forked, bifurcated; '~**frühstück** *n* early lunch; '2**n** (*a. sich*) (29) fork, bifurcate; '~**stapler** *m* fork-lift truck; '~**ung** *f* bifurcation.

gackern ['gakərn] (29) cackle.

Gaffel ⚓ ['gafəl] *f* (15) gaff; '~**segel** *n* gaff-sail, trysail.

gaffen ['gafən] (25) gape; (*stieren*) stare.

Gage ['gɑ:ʒə] *f* (15) pay, salary.

gähnen ['gɛ:nən] **1.** (25) yawn; **2.** 2 *n* (6) yawn(ing).

Gala ['gala] *f inv.* gala; *in* (*großer*) ~ in full dress.

Galan [ga'lɑ:n] *m* gallant, squire.

galant [ga'lant] gallant; (*höflich*) courteous; ~*es Abenteuer* love adventure.   [courtesy.}

Galanterie [~ə'ri:] *f* (15) gallantry;}

'Gala|uniform f full(-dress) uni-
form; **'~vorstellung** thea. f gala
performance.

Galaxis [ga'laksis] f (16², pl. -ien wie
15) galaxy.

Galeere [ga'leːrə] f (15) galley; **~n-
sklave** m galley-slave.

Galerie [galə'riː] f (15) gallery.

Galgen ['galgən] m (6) gallows sg.,
gibbet; **'~frist** f respite, short grace;
'~humor m gallows humo(u)r; **'~
strick** m, **'~vogel** m gallows-bird.

Gall-apfel ['gal-] m gall-nut.

Galle ['galə] f (15) bile; v. niederen
Tieren: gall; **'~nblase** f gallbladder;
'~nkolik f bilious colic; **'~nleiden** n
bilious complaint; **'~nstein** m gall-
-stone.

Gallert ['galərt] n (3), **~e** [ga'lɛrtə] f
(15) gelatine, jelly; **'2-artig** gelati-
nous, jelly-like.

Gallier ['galjər] m (7) Gaul.

'gallig gall-like; fig. bilious.

'gallisch Gallic, Gaulish.

Galopp [ga'lɔp] m (3) gallop; im
kurzen ~ at an easy canter; im ge-
streckten ~ at full gallop od. speed;
2ieren [~'piːrən] gallop.

Galosche [ga'lɔʃə] f (15) galosh
(mst pl.), pl. Am. a. rubbers.

galt [galt] pret. v. gelten.

galvan|isch [gal'vaːniʃ] galvanic;
~ versilbern electroplate; **~
golden** electrogild; **~isieren** [~vani-
'ziːrən] galvanize; **2ismus** [~'nis-
mus] m (16, o. pl.) galvanism.

Galvano [~'vaːno] n (11) (galvani-
sierter Druckstock) electro(type);
~'plastik f galvanoplastics sg.; typ.
electrotypy.

Gamasche [ga'maʃə] f (15) gaiter,
legging; kurze: spat.

gamm|eln F ['gaməln] (29*) loaf
around; **'2ler** m (7) drop-out.

Gang¹ ['gaŋ] m (3³) walk; s. Gangart;
fig. (Bewegung, Tätigkeit) motion;
e-r Maschine: movement, running,
(Wirkungsweise) action; (Boten2)
errand; (Weg) way; (Baum2) alley;
(Bahn, Lauf; Verlauf; bei Tafel)
course; ⚓ beim Lavieren: tack;
(Röhre) duct; (Verbindungsweg) passage; im Hause: corridor; gallery;
zwischen Sitzreihen: gangway, bsd.
Am. aisle; 🚌 corridor, Am. aisle;
Fechten usw.: bout; round; anat.
duct; ⊕ e-r Schraube: worm,
thread; mot. speed; erster, zweiter,

dritter ~ low (od. bottom), second,
third gear; ✗ vein; in ~ bringen od.
setzen set going od. in motion; in ~
kommen get under way; in ~ halten keep going; im ~ sein be in
motion, fig. be (going) on, be in
progress, be afoot; in vollem ~ in full
swing.

gang²: ~ und gäbe ['gɛːbə] usual,
customary, traditional.

'Gang-art f Mensch: gait, walk;
Pferd: pace (a. weitS. Tempo).

'gangbar Weg: practicable (a. fig.);
Münze: current; ✝ marketable,
salable.

Gängel|band ['gɛŋəlbant] n lead-
ing-strings pl.; am ~ führen keep in
leading-strings; sich am ~ führen
lassen be in leading-strings; **'2n**
(29) fig. lead by the nose.

'Gang|(schalt)hebel mot. m gear
(-change) lever; **'~schaltung** f
gear-change, Am. gear-shift.

Gangster ['gɛŋstər] m (7) gangster;
'~bande f band of criminals; **'~
braut** f gang moll.

Gans [gans] f goose (pl. geese).

Gäns-chen ['gɛnsçən] n (6) gosling.

Gänse|blümchen ['gɛnzə-] n daisy;
~braten m roast goose; **'~feder** f
goose-quill; **~füßchen** ['~fyːsçən]
n/pl. quotation-marks, inverted
commas; **'~haut** f goose-skin; fig.
a. goose-flesh, Am. a. goose pimples
pl.; ich bekam e-e ~ my flesh began
to creep; **'~klein** n (goose-)giblets
pl.; **'~leberpastete** f pâté de foie
gras (fr.); **'~marsch** m single (od.
Indian) file; **~rich** ['~riç] m (3) gan-
der; **'~schmalz** n goose-dripping.

ganz [gants] **1.** adj. all; (ungeteilt)
entire, whole; (vollständig) complete, total, full; ~ Deutschland all
Germany, the whole of Germany;
~e Zahl Å integer; den ~en Tag all
day (long); das ~e Jahr hindurch
throughout the year; von ~em Herzen with all my etc. heart; er ist ein
~er Mann he is a real man; ~e fünf
Stunden full five hours; die ~e Zeit
all the time; **2.** adv. quite; (s. 1.)
entirely, wholly; completely; (sehr)
very; (ziemlich) pretty; nicht ~ 10
less than 10, just under 10; ~ Auge
(Ohr) all eyes (ears); ~ und gar
wholly, totally; ~ und gar nicht not
at all, by no means; ~ durch
throughout; ~ gut quite good, F not

bad; *im ~en* on the whole, generally; **✝** *in the lump; ich bin ~ naß* I am wet all over; '**Ωe** *n* (18) whole; (*Gesamtheit*) totality; *aufs ~ gehen* go all out, *bsd. Am.* go the whole hog. '**Ganz**|-**aufnahme** *f*, '**~bild** *n* full--length (portrait); '**~fabrikat** *n* finished product; '**~heitsmethode** *f Schule*: 'look and say' method; '**~leder** *n*: *in ~ gebunden* whole-bound. **gänzlich** ['gɛntsliç] complete, total, entire; *a.* wholly, absolutely. '**ganz**|**seitig** full-page; '**Ωtagsbeschäftigung** *f* full-time job *od.* occupation; '**Ωtagsschule** *f* all-day school.

gar [gɑːr] **1.** *adj. Speise*: done; *Leder*: dressed; *Metall*: refined; *nicht ~ Fleisch*: underdone, rare; **2.** *adv.* quite, entirely, very; (*sogar*) even; *~ nicht* not at all; *~ keiner* not a single one; *warum nicht ~!* and why not, indeed?

Garage [ga'rɑːʒə] *f* (15) garage.
Garant [ga'rant] *m* (12) guarantor.
Garantie [~'tiː] *f* (15) guarantee, warranty; **Ωren** guarantee, warrant; **~schein** *m* guarantee.
Garaus ['gɑːr'ʔaʊs] *m inv.*: *j-m den ~ machen* dispatch (*od.* finish) a p.
Garbe ['garbə] *f* (15) sheaf (*a.* ✖).
Garde ['gardə] *f* (15) guard; *der britische Königin: the* Guards *pl.*
Garderobe [gardə'roːbə] *f* (15) wardrobe; (*Kleiderablage*) cloak--room, *Am.* checkroom; *e-s Schauspielers*: dressing-room; **~nfrau** *f* (*a. thea.* **Garderobiere** [~ro'bjɛːrə] *f*) cloak-room attendant; **~nmarke** *f* cloak-room ticket, *Am.* check; **~nschrank** *m* wardrobe; **~nständer** *m* hat (*od.* hall) stand.
Gardine [gar'diːnə] *f* (15) curtain; **~npredigt** *f* curtain-lecture; **~nstange** *f* curtain rail.
gären ['gɛːrən] (30) ferment (*a. ~ lassen*).
Garküche ['gɑːr-] *f* cook-shop.
'**Gär**|**mittel** *n*, '**~stoff** *m* ferment.
Garn [garn] *n* (3) yarn; (*Faden*) thread; (*BaumwollΩ*) cotton; (*Netz*) net; *ins ~ gehen* fall into the snare; *ins ~ locken* decoy, trap.
Garnele [gar'neːlə] *f* (15) shrimp.
garnier|**en** [gar'niːrən] trim; *bsd. Speise*: garnish; **Ωung** *f* trimming; *e-r Speise*: trimmings *pl.*, garnish.
Garnison [garni'zoːn] *f* (16), **Ωieren** [~zo'niːrən] garrison; **~stadt** [~'zoːn-] *f* garrison-town.
Garnitur [~'tuːr] *f* (16) (*Besatz*) trimming; (*Zubehör*) fittings *pl.*; (*Zs.gehöriges*) set; *fig. die erste ~ the* élite.
garstig ['garstiç] nasty, ugly.
Garten ['gartən] *m* (6[1]) garden; '**~arbeit** *f* gardening; '**~architekt** *m* landscape gardener; '**~bau** *m* horticulture; '**~bau...** horticultural; '**~erde** *f* (garden-)mo(u)ld; '**~fest** *n* garden (*Am. a.* lawn) party; '**~geräte** *n/pl.* gardening-tools; '**~haus** *n* summer-house; '**~laube** *f* arbo(u)r; '**~lokal** *n* open-air café (*od.* restaurant); (*Biergarten*) beer--garden; '**~schau** *f* horticultural show; '**~schere** *f* (eine a pair of) pruning-shears *pl.*; '**~stadt** *f* garden city; '**~zaun** *m* garden fence.
Gärtner ['gɛrtnər] *m* (7), '**~in** *f* (16[1]) gardener; **~ei** [~'raɪ] *f* gardening, horticulture; (*Betrieb*) nursery, market garden.
Gärung ['gɛːruŋ] *f* fermentation; *sich in ~ befinden* (*a. fig.*) be in a state of ferment; '**~s-prozeß** *m* process of fermentation.
Gas [gɑːs] *n* (4) gas; *mot. u. fig. ~ geben* step on the gas; *mot. ~ wegnehmen* throttle down; '**~angriff** ✖ *m* gas attack; '**~anzünder** *m* gas lighter; '**Ω-artig** gaseous; '**~behälter** *m* gasometer, gas-container; '**~beleuchtung** *f* gas-light(ing); '**~brenner** *m* gas-burner; '**~explosion** *f* gas explosion; '**~feuerzeug** *n* gas lighter; '**~flasche** *f* gas cylinder; **Ωförmig** ['~fœrmiç] gaseous; '**~fußhebel** *m s. Gaspedal*; '**~hahn** *m* gas-cock; '**~hebel** *mot. m* throttle (hand) lever; *s. Gaspedal*; '**~heizung** *f* gas-heating; '**~herd** *m* gas-stove *od.* -range; '**~kammer** *f* gas-chamber; '**~kocher** *m* gas cooker; '**~leitung** *f* gas main; '**~licht** *n* gaslight; '**~Luftgemisch** *n* gas-air mixture; '**~mann** *m* gas--man; '**~maske** ✖ *f* gas-mask; '**~messer** *m* gas-meter; '**~ofen** *m* gasoven; **~ometer** [gazo'meːtər] *m* (7) gasometer; (*Gasbehälter*) gas--holder; '**~pedal** *mot. n* accelerator (pedal).
Gäßchen [gɛsçən] *n* (6) narrow alley *od.* lane.
Gasse ['gasə] *f* (15) lane (*a. fig.*).
'**Gassen**|**bube** *m*, '**~junge** *m* street

arab, gutter-snipe, urchin; '⹀hauer
m popular song.
Gast [gast] *m* (3² *u.* 3³) guest (*a. thea.
usw.*); (*Besucher*) visitor; (*Wirts-
haus⹀*) customer; (*regelmäßiger* ⹀)
frequenter; *s.* ungebeten; zu ⹀e bitten
invite; Gäste haben have company;
'⹀·arbeiter *m* foreign worker; '⹀bett
n spare bed; '⹀dirigent *m* guest
conductor; '⹀dozent *m* visiting lecturer.
Gäste|buch ['gɛstə-] *n* visitors' book;
'⹀haus *n*, '⹀heim *n* guest-house.
'**gast|frei** hospitable; '⹀freiheit *f* hos-
pitality; '⹀freundlich *s.* gastfrei; '⹀-
freundschaft *f* hospitality; '⹀geber
m host; *pl. Sport:* home team *sg.*;
'⹀geberin *f* hostess; '⹀haus *n*, '⹀hof
m restaurant; *mit Unterkunft:* inn,
hotel; '⹀hörer *univ. m* guest (*od.*
extramural) student; ⹀ieren *thea.*
[⹀'tiːrən] give a guest performance;
'⹀land *n* host country; '⹀lich hospitable; ⹀ aufnehmen receive as guest,
entertain; '⹀lichkeit *f* hospitality;
'⹀mahl *n* feast, banquet; '⹀mann-
schaft *f Sport:* visiting team; '⹀-
recht *n* right of hospitality.
Gastritis [gas'triːtis] *𝒮 f* (16, *pl. inv.*
⹀i'tiden) gastritis.
'**Gast|redner** *m* guest speaker; '⹀-
rolle *thea. f* guest part; e-e ⹀ geben *s.*
gastieren; *fig.* show up briefly.
Gastronomie [gastrono'miː] *f* (15)
gastronomy; (*Gewerbe*) catering
trade.
'**Gast|spiel** *n* guest performance; '⹀-
spielreise *f* tour; '⹀stätte *f* restaurant; '⹀stube *f* (bar) parlo(u)r; '⹀-
vorlesung *f* guest lecture; '⹀vor-
stellung *s.* Gastspiel; '⹀wirt *m* landlord, host, innkeeper; '⹀wirtin *f*
landlady, hostess; '⹀wirtschaft *f*
inn; '⹀zimmer *n* lounge; *weitS.*
spare (bed)room.
'**Gas|·uhr** *f* gas-meter; '⹀vergiftung
f gas poisoning; '⹀vorkommen *n*
gas field; '⹀werk *n* gasworks *pl.*
Gatte ['gatə] *m* (13) husband; spouse.
Gatter ['gatər] *n* (7) railing, grating;
'⹀säge *f* frame-saw; '⹀tor *n* lattice
gate; '⹀werk *n* lattice-work.
'**Gattin** *f* wife; spouse.
Gattung ['gatuŋ] *f* kind, sort; *biol.*
race, species, genus; *Kunst:* genre
(*fr.*); '⹀sname *m* generic name;
gr. appellative.
Gau [gaʊ] *m* (3) district, region.

Gaudi ['gaʊdi] F *f* (11), **Gaudium**
['gaʊdjum] *n* (9, *o. pl.*) (bit of) fun.
Gaukel|bild ['gaʊkəl-] *n* illusion,
phantasm; ⹀ei [⹀'laɪ] *f*, '⹀spiel *n*,
'⹀werk *n* jugglery; (*Täuschung*)
trick(ery), delusion; '⹀n (29) juggle;
(*hin und her flattern*) flutter.
Gaukler ['gaʊklər] *m* (7), '⹀in *f*
juggler; (*Spaßmacher*) buffoon.
Gaul [gaʊl] *m* (3³) (farm-)horse,
nag; *contp. alter* ⹀ (old) jade.
Gaumen ['gaʊmən] *m* (6) palate;
'⹀laut *m* palatal; '⹀platte *f* Zahnheilkunde: (dental) plate.
Gauner ['gaʊnər] *m* (7), '⹀in *f* (16¹)
swindler, crook; *co.* rascal; ⹀ei
[⹀'raɪ] *f* swindling, sharp practice,
trickery; '⹀n (29) cheat, swindle;
'⹀sprache *f* thieves' cant.
Gaze ['gaːzə] *f* (15) gauze; *feine* ⹀
✝ gossamer; '⹀-artig gauzy.
Gazelle [ga'tsɛlə] *f* (15) gazelle.
Geächtete [gə'⁹ɛçtətə] *m* (18) outlaw.
Geächze [⹀'⁹ɛçtsə] *n* (3) groans *pl.*
ge'**artet:** anders ⹀ sein be of different nature.
Geäst [gə'⁹ɛst] (3, *o. pl.*) *n* branches
pl.
Gebäck [gə'bɛk] *n* (3) baker's
goods *pl.*; *feines:* pastry, fancy
cakes *pl.*
ge'**backen** *p.p. v.* backen.
Gebälk [⹀'bɛlk] *n* (3) timber-work.
geballt [⹀'balt] *s.* ballen; ⹀e Ladung
concentrated charge.
gebar [gə'baːr] *pret. v.* gebären.
Gebärde [⹀'bɛːrdə] *f* (15) gesture;
⹀n (26): sich ⹀ behave, act; ⹀nspiel
n gesticulation; *bsd. thea.* dumb
show; ⹀nsprache *f* language of
gestures.
gebaren [⹀'baːrən] **1.** (26): sich ⹀
behave, act; **2.** ⹀ *n* (6) deportment,
behavio(u)r.
gebären [⹀'bɛːrən] (30) bear, bring
forth (*a. fig.*), give birth to; *ich bin
am ... geboren* I was born on ...
Ge'bärmutter *f* womb, ⍾ uterus;
⹀hals *m* cervix; ⹀halskrebs *m* cancer
of the cervix; ⹀krebs *m* cancer of the
uterus.
Gebäude [gə'bɔʏdə] *n* (7) building,
edifice (*a. fig.*); ⹀komplex *m* complex (of buildings).
gebefreudig ['geːbə-] open-handed.
Gebein (e *pl.*) [gə'baɪn] *n* (3) bones *pl.*
Gebell [gə'bɛl] *n* (3) barking.
geben ['geːbən] **1.** (30) *j-m et.:* give

a p. a th.; (*schenken*) present *a p.* with *a th.*; *Ertrag*: yield; *Karten*: deal; (*veranstalten*) give, hold; *thea.* give, perform; ge~ werden be on; *Antwort* ~ (give an) answer; *s. Anlaß, Beispiel, Mühe, Pflege usw.*; *von sich* ~ give out, emit, *Laut*: utter, *Speise*: bring up; *sein Wort* ~ pledge one's word; *et.* (*nichts*) ~ *auf* (*acc.*) set great (no) store by; *sich* ~ (*nachgeben*) yield, (*nachlassen*) abate, settle (down); *sich gefangen* ~ surrender; *s.* denken, erkennen *usw.*; *Tennis*: serve (*v/i.*); *es gibt* there is, there are; *was gibt es?* what is the matter?; F *was es nicht alles gibt!* F it takes all kinds!; F *ich habe es ihm tüchtig ge*~ I gave it him hot; **2.** ♀ *n* (6) giving; *Kartenspiel*: *am* ~ *sein* (have the) deal.

'Geber *m* (7), **'~in** *f* giver, donor, donator.

Gebet [gə'be:t] *n* (3) prayer; **~buch** *n* prayer-book.

ge'beten *p.p. v.* bitten.

Gebiet [gə'bi:t] *n* (3) territory; (*Bezirk*) district, region; (*Fläche*) area; *fig.* (*Fach*♀) field, domain; province; (*Bereich*) sphere.

ge'bieten (30) *v/t.* order, *a. Achtung usw.*: command; *v/i.* (*herrschen*) rule (*über acc.* over), govern.

Ge'bieter *m* (7) master, lord, ruler; **~in** *f* (16¹) mistress; ♀**isch** imperious, commanding.

Ge'biets|-anspruch *m* territorial claim; **~hoheit** *f* territorial sovereignty; **~reform** *f* regional reorganization.

Gebilde [gə'bildə] *n* (7) *oft nur*: thing; (*Schöpfung*) creation; (*Form*) form; (*Bau, Gefüge*) structure; (*Bildung, a. geol.*) formation; ♀t educated, well-bred, cultivated; well-informed, well-read; *die* ♀en *pl.* the educated classes.

Gebimmel [gə'biməl] *n* (7) (continual) ringing *od.* tinkling.

Gebirg|e [gə'birgə] *n* (7) (range of) mountains *pl.*; ♀ig mountainous.

Gebirgs|bewohner [gə'birks-] *m* mountain-dweller; **~gegend** *f* mountainous region; **~kamm** *m*, **~rücken** *m* mountain-ridge; **~kette** *f* chain of mountains; **~zug** *m* mountain-range.

Gebiß [gə'bis] *n* (4) (set of) teeth *pl.*; *künstliches*: denture, (set of) false teeth *pl.*; *am Zaum*: bit; **~abdruck** *m* denture impression.

ge'bissen *p.p. v.* beißen.

Gebläse [~'blɛ:zə] *n* (7) blower, blast; *mot.* supercharger.

ge'blasen *p.p. v.* blasen.

geblieben [~'bli:bən] *p.p. v.* bleiben.

geblümt [~'bly:mt] flowered, flowery; ♀ floriated, sprigged.

Geblüt [~'bly:t] *n* (3) blood; (*Geschlecht*) lineage, race; *Prinz von* ~ prince of the blood.

gebogen [~'bo:gən] **1.** *p.p. v.* biegen; **2.** *adj.* bent, curved.

geboren [~'bo:rən] **1.** *p.p. v.* gebären; **2.** *adj.* born; *ein* ~er *Deutscher* German by birth; ~e *Schmidt* née Smith; ~ *sein für e-n Beruf* be cut out for; ~er *Künstler* born artist.

geborgen [~'borgən] **1.** *p.p. v.* bergen; **2.** *adj.* safe, sheltered; ♀**heit** *f* safety, security.

geborsten [~'borstən] *p.p. v.* bersten.

Gebot [~'bo:t] *n* (3) order; *stärker*: command; (*Angebot*) bid(ding), offer; *die Zehn* ~e *pl.* the Ten Commandments; *j-m zu* ~e *stehen* be at a p.'s disposal; *Not kennt kein* ~ necessity knows no law; *das* ~ *der Vernunft* the dictates *pl.* of reason; *dem* ~ *der Stunde gehorchen* fit in with the needs of the present; ♀**en 1.** *p.p. v.* bieten; **2.** *adj.* necessary, required; (*gehörig*) due.

gebracht [~'braxt] *p.p. v.* bringen.

gebrannt [~'brant] *p.p. v.* brennen.

ge'braten *p.p. v.* braten¹.

Gebräu [gə'brɔy] *n* (3) brew (*a. fig.*).

Gebrauch [~'braux] *m* (3³) use; usage (*a. Herkommen*); (*Sitte*) custom; ~ *machen von* (make) use (of); *in* ~ *kommen* come into use; ♀**en** use, employ; *er ist zu allem* (*zu nichts*) *zu* ~ he can turn his hand to anything (he is good for nothing); *gebrauchte Kleidung usw.*: second--hand.

gebräuchlich [~'brɔyçliç] common (-ly used), in use; current; (*üblich*) usual, customary.

Ge'brauchs|-anweisung *f* directions *pl.* for use; **~artikel** *m*, **~gegenstand** *m* article for daily use, utility article; **~fahrzeug** *n* utility vehicle; ♀**fertig** ready for use; **~graphik** *f* commercial art; **~graphiker** *m* commercial (*od.* industrial) artist; **~güter** *n/pl.* commodities; **~muster** *n* registered design; **~musterschutz** *m* legal protection for registered designs.

Ge'braucht|wagen *mot. m* used *od.* second-hand car; **~waren** *f/pl.* second-hand articles.

Ge'brechen *n* (6) defect, infirmity.

ge'brechlich fragile; *P.*: frail, feeble; **⩜keit** *f* fragility; frailty, infirmity.

gebrochen [gə'brɔxən] **1.** *p.p. v.* brechen; **2.** *adj.* broken (*a. fig. Herz, Mensch, Sprache, Stimme*).

Gebrüder [gə'bry:dər] *m/pl.* (7): **~ Schmidt** Smith Brothers (*abbr.* Bros.).

Gebrüll [~'bryl] *n* (3) roaring; *des Rindes*: lowing.

Gebühr [~'by:r] *f* (16) duty, rate; fee, charge; **~en** *pl.* fee(s *pl.*), dues *pl.*; (*das j-m Zukommende*) due; *nach ~* duly, deservedly; *über ~* unduly, immoderately.

ge'bühren (25) (*dat.*) be due to, belong to; *sich ~* be fit *od.* proper; **~d** (*schuldig*) due; (*geziemend*) becoming; (*entsprechend*) proper; **⩜einheit** *teleph. f* unit; **⩜erhöhung** *f* increase in charges; **⩜erlaß** *m* remission of fees; **~frei** free of charges; **⩜ordnung** *f* schedule of fees, tariff; **~pflichtig** chargeable; **~e** *Autostraße* toll road.

ge'bührlich *s.* gebührend.

gebunden [gə'bundən] **1.** *p.p. v.* binden; **2.** *adj.* bound; *Rede*: metrical; (*gelenkt, a.* ✝) controlled; *Kapital*: tied.

Geburt [~'bu:rt] *f* (16) birth; **~enbeschränkung** *f*, **~enkontrolle** *f*, **~enregelung** *f* birth-control; **~enrückgang** *m* drop in the birth-rate; **⩜enschwach: ~er** *Jahrgang* cohort with a low birth-rate; **⩜enstark: ~er** *Jahrgang* cohort with a high birth-rate; **~enziffer** *f* birth-rate.

gebürtig [~'byrtiç]: **~** *aus* a native of, born in, (*German- usw.*) born.

Ge'burts|-anzeige *f* announcement of (a) birth; **~fehler** *m* congenital defect; **~helfer** *m* obstetrician; **~helferin** *f* midwife; **~hilfe** *f* midwifery, ◫ obstetrics; **~jahr** *n* year of birth; **~land** *n* native country; **~ort** *m* birthplace; **~schein** *m*, **~urkunde** *f* birth-certificate; **~stadt** *f* native town; **~tag** *m* birthday; **~wehen** *f/pl.* labo(u)r(-pains *pl.*) *sg.*;

throes *pl.*

Gebüsch [gə'byʃ] *n* (3²) bushes *pl.*, underbrush, thicket.

Geck [gɛk] *m* (12) fop, dandy.

'geckenhaft foppish, dandyish.

gedacht [gə'daxt] **1.** *p.p. v.* denken; **2.** *adj.* imaginary, fictitious.

Gedächtnis [gə'dɛçtnis] *n* (4¹) memory; (*Erinnerung*) remembrance, recollection; *im ~ behalten* keep in mind; *ins ~ rufen* call to mind, recall; *zum ~* (*gen.*) in memory of; **~feier** *f* commemoration; **~hilfe** *f*, **~stütze** *f* memory-aid; **~lücke** *f* gap in one's memory; **~rede** *f* commemorative address; **~schwäche** *f* weakness of memory; **~schwund** *m*, **~störung** *f* temporary amnesia, disturbed memory; **~verlust** *m* amnesia, loss of memory.

Gedanke [~'daŋkə] *m* (13¹) thought; idea; *in ~n sein* be absorbed in thought; *j-n auf den ~n bringen, daß ...* make a p. think that, give a p. the idea that; *ich kam auf den ~n* the thought occurred to me, it came to my mind; *sich ~n machen über* (*acc.*) worry about; *sich mit dem ~n tragen zu tun* consider doing.

ge'danken|-arm lacking in ideas; **⩜austausch** *m* exchange of ideas; **⩜blitz** *m* brainwave; **⩜freiheit** *f* freedom of thought; **⩜gang** *m* train of thought, reasoning; **⩜leser(in** *f*) *m* thought-reader; **~los** thoughtless; **⩜losigkeit** *f* thoughtlessness; **~reich** rich in ideas; **⩜reichtum** *m* wealth of ideas; **⩜splitter** *m/pl.* aphorisms; **⩜strich** *m* dash; **⩜übertragung** *f* telepathy; **~voll** thoughtful; **⩜welt** *f* world of ideas, *weit S.* ideal (*od.* intellectual) world.

ge'danklich intellectual, mental.

Gedärm [gə'dɛrm] *n* (3¹ *u.* 3²), **~e** *n* (7) *mst pl.* entrails, bowels *pl.*

Gedeck [~'dɛk] *n* (3) (*Tischzeug*) cover; (*Speisenfolge*) menu; *ein ~ auflegen* lay a place.

gedeihen [~'daɪən] **1.** (30, sn) thrive, prosper, *fig. a.* flourish; (*gelingen*) succeed; (*vorwärtskommen*) progress, get on (well); **2. ⩜** *n* (6) thriving, prosperity; success.

gedeihlich [~'daɪlɪç] thriving, prosperous; successful; profitable.

ge'denk|en (30; *gen.*) think of; be mindful of; (*sich erinnern*) remember, recollect; (*feiern*) commemorate; *(ehren)* hono(u)r; *(erwähnen)* mention; ~ *zu tun* think of doing, intend to do; **2en** *n* (6) memory; **2feier** *f* commemoration; **2rede** *f* commemorative address; **2stätte** *f* memorial place; **2stein** *m* commemorative stone; **2tafel** *f* commemorative tablet; **2tag** *m* commemoration (day).

Gedicht [gə'diçt] *n* (3) poem; F *fig.* dream, beauty; **~sammlung** *f* collection of poems; *in Auswahl:* anthology.

gediegen [~'diːgən] solid; *(rein)* pure; *(echt)* genuine, true; **2heit** *f* solidity; purity.

gedieh [~'diː] *pret.*, **~en** *p.p. v. gedeihen 1.*

Gedränge [~'drɛŋə] *n* (7) press, crowd, throng; *(Not)* trouble.

ge'drängt crowded, packed, crammed; *Sprache:* concise; **~e** *Übersicht* condensed review; ~ *voll* cramfull; **2heit** *f* conciseness.

ge'droschen *p.p. v. dreschen.*

gedrückt [~'drykt] *fig.* depressed.

gedrungen [~'druŋən] **1.** *p.p. v. dringen;* **2.** *adj.* compact; *P.:* squat, stocky; *Sprache:* concise; *sich* ~ *fühlen* feel compelled.

Geduld [~'dult] *f (inv. o. pl.)* patience; *die* ~ *verlieren* lose patience; *sich in* ~ *fassen s.* gedulden; *j-s* ~ *auf die Probe stellen* try one's patience; *s. reißen, üben;* **2en** [~'duldən] (26): *sich* ~ have patience, wait (patiently); **2ig** [~'duldiç] patient; **~spiel** [~'dult-] *n* puzzle; **~s·probe** *f* trial of (a p.'s) patience; ordeal.

gedungen [~'duŋən] *p.p. v. dingen.*

gedunsen [~'dunzən] bloated.

gedurft [~'durft] *p.p. v. dürfen.*

geeignet [~'ʔaɪgnət] fit *(für, zu, als* for *a th., inf);* suited, suitable (to, for), proper (for); qualified (for).

Geest [geːst] *f* (16), **'~land** *n* sandy heath-land.

Gefahr [gə'faːr] *f* (16) danger, peril; *(Wagnis)* risk, jeopardy; *auf meine* ~ at my peril *od.* risk; *s. begeben, schweben;* ~ *laufen zu verlieren* run the risk of losing; **2bringend** dangerous.

gefährden [gə'fɛːrdən] endanger; *(aufs Spiel setzen)* risk, jeopardize.

ge'fahren *p.p. v. fahren.*

Ge'fahren│zone *f* danger area; **~zulage** *f* danger-money;

gefährlich [~'fɛːrliç] dangerous *(für* to), perilous, risky; *ein* ~*es Spiel treiben* skate on thin ice.

ge'fahr│los without risk, safe; **2losigkeit** *f* safety.

Gefährt [~'fɛːrt] *n* (3) vehicle.

Ge'fährte *m* (13), **Ge'fährtin** *f* companion, fellow, mate.

ge'fahrvoll perilous, dangerous.

Gefälle [~'fɛlə] *n* (7) fall, descent; gradient, *bsd. Am.* grade; *fig. (Unterschiede)* differentials *pl.*

Gefallen [~'falən] **1.** *m* (6) *(Gefälligkeit)* favo(u)r, kindness; *dir zu* ~ to please you; **2.** *n* (6): ~ *finden an (dat.)* take pleasure in, take a fancy to; **3.** **2** *v/i.* (30) please *(j-m* a p.); *er (es) gefällt mir* I like him (it); *wie gefällt es Ihnen in B.?* how do you like B.?; *sich* ~ *lassen (sich in et. fügen)* put up with; *das lasse ich mir nicht* ~ I won't stand *(Am.* for) that; *sich in e-r Rolle usw.* ~ fancy o.s. in, be pleased with; **4.** **2** *p.p. v. fallen;* **5.** **2** *adj.* fallen *(a. Engel, Mädchen, Soldat);* **~e** *m* (18) fallen person; **✕** *die* ~*n pl.* the killed, the fallen.

gefällig [gə'fɛliç] pleasing, agreeable; *(verbindlich)* obliging; *(zuvorkommend)* kind; **~st** *(if you)* please; *Zigaretten* ~*?* cigarettes, please?; **2keit** *f* complaisance, kindness; *Handlung:* favo(u)r; **2keitswechsel ✝** *m* accommodation bill.

Ge'fallsucht *f* desire to please; *weibliche:* coquetry.

ge'fallsüchtig [~zyçtiç] coquettish.

ge'fangen 1. *p.p. v. fangen;* **2.** *adj.* captive, imprisoned; *s. geben;* **2e** *m* prisoner, captive.

Ge'fangen│en-austausch *m* exchange of prisoners; **~enlager** *n* prison(ers') camp; **~enwagen** *m der Polizei:* prison van, *Am.* patrol wagon; **2halten** keep *a p.* (a) prisoner; **~haltung** *f* detention, confinement; **~nahme** ['~naːmə] *f* (15) capture, seizure; **2nehmen** take prisoner; *fig.* captivate; **~schaft** *f mil.* captivity; **↯** imprisonment, custody; **2setzen** imprison, jail.

Gefängnis [gə'fɛŋnis] *n* (4¹) prison, jail, *Brt. a.* gaol; *s.* ~*strafe;* **~direktor** *m* governor, *Am.* warden; **~strafe** *f* (term of) imprisonment; **~wärter** *m* jailer, *Am. a.* (prison) guard.

Gefasel [ˌ'faːzəl] *n* (7) twaddle.
Gefäß [ˌ'fɛːs] *n* (3²) vessel (*a. anat.*).
gefaßt [ˌ'fast] *adj.* calm, composed;
~ *auf* (*acc.*) prepared for; *sich* ~
machen auf (*acc.*) prepare (o.s.) for.
Gefecht [ˌ'fɛçt] *n* (3) engagement;
combat, fight; (~*s-tätigkeit*) action;
außer ~ *setzen* put out of action;
♀**sbereit** combat-ready; ♀**sklar**:
♣ ~ *machen* clear *a ship* for action;
~**skopf** *m* warhead; ~**s-schießen** *n*
field firing; ~**s-stand** *m* command
post; *im Flugzeug*: turret; ~**s-
übung** *f* combat practice.
gefeit [gə'faɪt] immune (*gegen* from,
against), proof (against).
Gefieder [gə'fiːdər] *n* (7) plumage,
feathers *pl.*; ♀**t** feathered.
Gefilde *poet.* [ˌ'fildə] *n* (7) fields
pl., regions *pl.*
Geflecht [ˌ'flɛçt] *n* (3) plaited work,
plait; (*Weiden*♀) wickerwork.
gefleckt [ˌ'flɛkt] spotted.
geflissentlich [ˌ'flisəntliç] intentional, deliberate, studious.
geflochten [ˌ'flɔxtən] *p.p. v. flechten.*
geflogen [ˌ'floːgən] *p.p. v. fliegen.*
geflohen [ˌ'floːən] *p.p. v. fliehen.*
geflossen [ˌ'flɔsən] *p.p. v. fließen.*
Ge'flügel *n* (7) poultry, fowl(s *pl.*);
~**farm** *f* poultry farm; ~**händler** *m*
poulterer; ~**schere** *f* poultry dis-
sectors *pl.*; ♀**t** winged; ~**e Worte**
n/pl. winged words; ~**zucht** *f*
poultry-farming.
Geflunker [gə'fluŋkər] *n* (7) fib-
bing; lies *pl.*, humbug.
Geflüster [ˌ'flystər] *n* (7) whisper
(-ing), whispers *pl.*
gefochten [ˌ'fɔxtən] *p.p. v. fechten.*
Gefolg|**e** [ˌ'fɔlgə] *n* (7) *e-s Fürsten*:
suite; (*Geleit*) retinue; *von Be-
diensteten*: attendance; *im* ~ *von fig.*
in the wake of; ~**schaft** [ˌ'fɔlk-] *f*
followers *pl.*, following; *im Betrieb*:
staff, employees *pl.*
gefräßig [ˌ'frɛːsiç] greedy, voracious; ♀**keit** *f* gluttony, voracity.
Gefreite [ˌ'fraɪtə] *m* (18) lance-
-corporal, *Am.* private first class.
ge'fressen *p.p. v. fressen* 1.
Gefrier|**-anlage** [gə'friːr-] *f* freezing
plant; ~**beutel** *m* freezer bag; ♀**en**
(sn) congeal, freeze (*a.* ~ *lassen*);
~**fach** *n* freezing compartment; ~
fleisch *n* frozen meat; ♀**getrocknet**
freeze-dried; ~**punkt** *m* freezing-
-point; *auf dem* ~ *stehen* be at zero;

~**schrank** *m* (upright) freezer; ~
truhe *f* freezer, deep-freeze.
gefroren [ˌ'froːrən] *p.p. v. frieren;*
♀**e** *n* (18) ice(-cream).
Gefüge [gə'fyːgə] *n* (7) structure (*a.
fig.*); (*Gewebe*) texture; (*Schicht*)
layer; *fig.* make-up, fabric.
ge'fügig pliable, flexible; *P.*: pliant,
docile, obedient.
Gefühl [ˌ'fyːl] *n* (3) feeling; (*Tast-
sinn*) touch; (*Empfänglichkeit*) sense
(*für* of); *als Wahrnehmung*: sensation; ♀**los** *Hand usw.*: numb; *P.*:
unfeeling, insensible (*gegen* to); ~
losigkeit *f* unfeelingness; ♀**sbe-
tont** emotional; ~**sduselei** [ˌ-duːzə-
'laɪ] *f* (16) sentimentalism; ♀**sduse-
lig** sentimental; ~**smensch** *m*
emotional character; ♀**voll** (full of)
feeling; (*zärtlich*) tender; (*rührselig*)
sentimental.
gefunden [gə'fundən] *p.p. v. finden.*
gegangen [gə'gaŋən] *p.p. v. gehen.*
gegeben [gə'geːbən] **1.** *p.p. v. geben;*
2. *adj.* given (*a.* ♂); *zu* ~**er** *Zeit* at
the proper time; *die* ~**e** *Methode* the
best (*od.* obvious) method; ~**enfalls**
[ˌ-ən'fals] if need be, should the occasion arise; ♀**heit** *f* (given) fact,
reality.
gegen ['geːgən] *örtlich, zeitlich*: towards; *gegensätzlich*: against, ⚖
versus; (*ungefähr*) about, nearly,
Am. around; *Zeitpunkt*: by; *Mittel*
~ *e-e Krankheit usw.*: for; *vergleichend*: compared with, as against;
(*als Entgelt für*) (in exchange) for;
freundlich, grausam usw. ~ kind,
cruel *etc.* to; ~ *die Vernunft usw.*
contrary to reason *etc.*; *hundert* ~
eins a hundred to one; ~ *Quittung*
on receipt.
'Gegen|**-angriff** *m* counter-attack;
'~**anklage** *f*, '~**beschuldigung** *f*
counter-charge; '~**antrag** *m* coun-
ter-motion; '~**antwort** *f* rejoinder;
'~**argument** *n* counter-argument;
'~**befehl** *m* counter-order; '~**besuch**
m return visit; '~**bewegung** *f* coun-
ter-movement; '~**beweis** *m* proof to
the contrary; ⚖ counter-evidence;
'~**bild** *n* counterpart.
Gegend ['geːgənt] *f* (16) region (*a.
anat.*), country; (*Bezirk*) district,
area; (*Himmels*♀) quarter; (*Um*♀) environs *pl.*
Gegen|**darstellung** ['geːgən-] *f*
counter-statement; '~**dienst** *m* re-

turn (*od.* reciprocal) service; *j-m e-n*
~ **erweisen** return a p.'s favo(u)r;
'~**druck** *m* counter-pressure; *fig.*
reaction; ♀-**einander** ['~aɪ'nandər]
against one another *od.* each other;
'~**erklärung** *f* counter-statement;
'~**fahrbahn** *f* oncoming carriage-
way (*Am.* highway); '~**forderung** *f*
counter-claim; '~**frage** *f* counter-
-question; '~**füßler** *m* (7) antipode;
'~**gerade** *f Sport:* back straight; '~-
geschenk *n* return gift; '~**gewicht** *n*
counterbalance, counterpoise; *das* ~
halten (*dat.*) counterbalance; '~**gift** *n*
antidote; '~**kandidat** *m* rival candidate; '~**klage** *f* counter-charge; '~-
leistung *f* equivalent; ♂♂, ✝ consideration; *als* ~ in return; '~**licht** *n*
back light; '~**licht-aufnahme** *f* con-
tre-jour photograph; '~**lichtblende**
f lens hood; '~**liebe** *f* return of love;
keine ~ *finden* not to be reciprocated;
'~**maßnahme** *f* counter-measure;
'~**mittel** *n* remedy (*gegen* for), antidote (against, for); '~**partei** *f* opposite party; '~**probe** *f* check-test;
'~**re-aktion** *f* counter-reaction; '~-
rechnung *f* counter-claim; *zum*
Ausgleich: set-off, *Am.* offset; '~**rede**
f reply, objection; '~**revolution** *f*
counter-revolution; '~**satz** *m* contrast, opposite; (*Widerspruch*) opposition; antithesis; *im* ~ *zu* in contrast
to *od.* with, in opposition to; unlike
(*a th. od. p.*); '♀**sätzlich** contrary,
opposite; '~**schlag** ✖ *m* reprisal; '~-
seite *f* opposite side; '♀**seitig** mutual, reciprocal; '~**seitigkeit** *f* reci-
procity, mutuality; *auf* ~ *beruhen* be
mutual; *das beruht ganz auf* ~ *a.* same
here; '~**spieler** *m* opposite number;
fig. opponent; '~**spionage** *f* counter-
-espionage; '~**sprech-anlage** *f* intercom; '~**stand** *m* object; (*Thema*)
subject, topic; ~ *des Mitleids usw.*
object of pity, *etc.*; ♀**ständlich** ['~-
ʃtɛntlɪç] objective; (*anschaulich*)
graphic(ally *adv.*); ♀**standslos** ['~-
ʃtantslɔːs] abstract; *Kunst: a.* non-
-representational; (*sinnlos*) meaningless, irrelevant; (*zwecklos*) to no
purpose; '~**standswort** *gr. n* noun;
'~**stimme** *f* vote against; (*Meinung*)
objection, opposing voice; '~**stoß** *m*
(*a.* ✖) counter-thrust; '~**strömung** *f*
counter-current; '~**stück** *n* counterpart; '~**teil** *n* contrary, reverse; *e-s*
Begriffes: opposite; *im* ~ on the con-

trary; '♀**teilig** contrary, opposite; ♀-
'**über** (*dat.*) opposite (to) *a th. od. p.*;
P.: face to face (with); (*im Vergleich*
zu) compared with, as against; (*im*
Gegenteil zu) contrary to; *j-m* ~
freundlich usw. kind *etc.* to a p.; *sich*
e-r Aufgabe usw. ~ *sehen* be con-
fronted (*od.* faced) with, be up
against; ~'-**über** *n* (7) vis-à-vis; *fig.*
a. opposite number; ♀'-**überliegend**
(*dat.*) opposite; ♀'-**überstehen** (*dat.*)
stand opposite, face; *feindlich:* be
opposed to; ♀'-**überstellen** (*dat.*)
opose (to); *a.* ♂♂ confront (with); *fig.*
contrast (with); ~'-**überstellung** *f*
opposition; confrontation; comparison; ♀'-**übertreten** (*dat.*) *bsd.*
fig. face; '~**verkehr** *m* two-way traffic; oncoming traffic; '~**vorschlag** *m*
counter-proposal; ~**wart** ['~vart] *f*
(14, *o. pl.*) presence; (*jetzige*
Zeit) present time; *gr.* present
(tense); ♀**wärtig** ['~vɛrtɪç] (*anwe-*
send) present; (*jetzig*) present, actual; current (*a.* ✝); *adv.* at present;
'~**wartskunde** *f* current affairs, *Am.*
social studies *pl.*; '~**wartsliteratur** *f*
contemporary literature; '♀**warts-**
nah topical; '~**wehr** *f* opposition;
'~**wert** *m* equivalent; '~**wind** *m* head
wind; '~**winkel** *m* corresponding
angle; '~**wirkung** *f* counter-effect,
reaction; '♀**zeichnen** countersign;
'~**zeichnung** *f* countersignature; '~-
zeuge *m* counterwitness; '~**zug** *m*
countermove; 🚂 opposite train.

gegessen [gə'gɛsən] *p.p. v.* essen.
geglichen [gə'glɪçən] *p.p. v.* gleichen.
gegliedert [gə'gliːdərt] articulate;
fig. organized.
geglitten [gə'glɪtən] *p.p. v.* gleiten.
ge'glommen *p.p. v.* glimmen.
Gegner ['geːgnər] *m* (7) adversary,
opponent; rival; ♀**isch** antagonis-
tic, adverse; ♂♂ opposing; (*nach su.*)
of the enemy; '~**schaft** *f* opponents
pl.; (*Widerstand*) antagonism, opposition.
gegolten [gə'gɔltən] *p.p. v.* gelten.
gegoren [gə'goːrən] *p.p. v.* gären.
gegossen [gə'gɔsən] *p.p. v.* gießen.
ge'graben *p.p. v.* graben.
gegriffen [gə'grɪfən] *p.p. v.* greifen.
Gehackte [gə'haktə] *n s.* Hackfleisch.
Gehalt [gə'halt] **1.** *m* (3) content;
(*Fassungsvermögen*) capacity; (*Fein*♀
v. Münzen) standard; *fig.* content,
substance; (*innerer Wert*) merit; **2.** *n*

(1^2) salary, pay; 2**en 1.** *p.p. v. halten;*
2. *adj.:* ~ *sein zu tun* be bound (*od.*
obliged) to do; 2**los** empty, hollow;
~losigkeit *f* emptiness; 2**reich**, 2-
voll *Nahrung:* substantial (*a. fig.*
Buch usw.); *Wein:* full-bodied.

Ge'halts|-abzug *m* salary deduction;
~-empfänger *m* salaried employee;
~-erhöhung *f*, **~zulage** *f* increase in
salary, *Am.* raise; **~forderung** *f* pay
claim; **~gruppe** *f*, **~stufe** *f* salary
bracket.

Gehänge [gə'hɛŋə] *n* (7) (*Abhang*)
slope, declivity; (*Blumen*2) festoon;
(*Schmuck*) pendants *pl.*

gehangen [gə'haŋən] *p.p. v. hängen.*

geharnischt [~'harnıʃt] (clad) in
armo(u)r; **~e** *Antwort* sharp reply.

gehässig [~'hɛsıç] malicious, spiteful; 2**keit** *f* malice, spitefulness.

ge'hauen *p.p. v. hauen.*

Gehäuse [gə'hɔʏzə] *n* (7) case, box;
⊕ casing, housing; *v. Obst:* core;
e-r Schnecke: shell.

Gehege [gə'he:gə] *n* (7) enclosure;
fence; *hunt. u. fig.* preserve; *fig. j-m*
ins ~ kommen encroach upon a p.'s
preserves, get in a p.'s way.

geheim [~'haım] secret; *et.* **~halten**
keep a th. secret; 2**agent** *m* secret
agent; 2**bund** *m* secret society; 2-
dienst *m* secret service; 2**fach** *n*
secret drawer; 2**haltung** *f* secrecy;
2**konto** *n* secret account.

Ge'heimnis *n* (4^1) secret; (*Rätsel-
haftes*) mystery; **~krämer** *m* secret-
-monger; **~kräme'rei** *f* secret-
-mongering; **~träger** *m* bearer of
secrets; 2**umwittert**, 2**umwoben**
shrouded in secrecy; 2**voll** mysterious; **~** *tun* be secretive (*mit et.* about).

Ge'heim|nummer *f* secret number;
teleph. ex-directory (*Am.* unlisted)
number; **~polizei** *f* secret police;
~polizist *m* detective, plain-clothes
man; **~rat** *m* Privy Councillor; **~-
sache** *f* secret (*od.* security) matter;
~schrift *f* secret code; **~treffen** *n*
secret meeting; **~tuerei** [~tu:ə'raı] *f*
(16) secretiveness; 2**tuerisch** secretive, mysterious; **~tür** *f* secret door;
~waffe *f* secret weapon.

Geheiß [gə'haıs] *n* (3^3) command,
order; *auf j-s ~* at a p.'s bidding.

ge'heißen *p.p. v. heißen.*

gehen ['ge:ən] (30, sn) go; *zu Fuß:*
walk; (*weg~*) leave; *Maschine:*
work; *Uhr:* go; *Ware:* sell; *Wind:*

blow; *Teig:* rise; (*reichen*) *bis an*
(*acc.*) reach; *wie geht es Ihnen?* how
are you?; *es geht mir gut* (*schlecht*)
I am well (not well); *es geht mir*
gerade so F same here; *es geht* (*ist*
möglich) it can be done, (*funktio-
niert*) it works, (*ganz gut*) fairly
well; *das geht nicht* that will not
do; ~ *lassen* let go; *an die Arbeit*
usw. ~ set about; *s-e Worte usw.* ~
dahin, daß ... aim at *ger.*; *du mußt*
jetzt ~ you will have to leave; F *ach,*
geh doch! go on!; *mit e-m Mädchen*
~ go with a girl; *das Fenster geht*
auf die Straße (*hinaus*) the window
opens (*od.* gives, looks) into the
street; *in sich* ~ commune with o.s.,
reuig: repent; *er geht ins zwanzigste*
Jahr he is entering upon his twentieth year; *vor sich* ~ happen; *wenn*
es nach mir ginge if I had my way;
es geht nichts über (*acc.*) ... there is
nothing like ...; *s. Horizont; um was*
geht es? what is it (all) about?; *es*
geht um dein Leben your life is at
stake; 2 *n* walking (*a. sport*); '**~las-
sen:** *sich* ~ take it easy, *b.s.* take
leave of one's manners.

geheuer [~'hɔʏər]: *nicht* ~ (*riskant*)
risky; (*unheimlich*) uncanny, eerie;
(*verdächtig*) *sl.* fishy; *hier ist es*
nicht ~ this place is haunted; *ihm*
war nicht recht ~ *zu Mute* he did not
feel quite at his ease.

Geheul [~'hɔʏl] *n* (3) howling.

Gehilf|e [~'hılfə] *m* (13), **~in** *f*
(16^1) assistant; *fig.* helpmate.

Gehirn [gə'hırn] *n* (3) brain(s *pl. fig.*);
~blutung *f* cerebral h(a)emorrhage;
~-erschütterung *f* concussion (of
the brain); **~hälfte** *f* cerebral hemisphere; **~schlag** *m* cerebral apoplexy; **~schwund** *m* atrophy of the
brain; **~tumor** *m* cerebral tumo(u)r;
~wäsche *f* brain-washing; *j-n e-r* ~
unterziehen brainwash a p.

gehoben [~'ho:bən] **1.** *p.p. v. heben;*
2. *adj. Sprache usw.:* elevated;
Stellung: high, senior; *in* **~er** *Stimmung* in high spirits.

Gehöft [~'hø:ft] *n* (3) farm(stead).

geholfen [gə'hɔlfən] *p.p. v. helfen.*

Gehölz [~'hœlts] *n* (3^2) wood, copse.

Gehör [~'hø:r] *n* (3) hearing; ear;
musikalisches ~ musical ear; *nach*
dem ~ by (the) ear; ~ *haben für* have
an ear for; *j-m* ~ *schenken* lend an
ear (*od.* listen) to a p.; *sich* ~ *ver-*

schaffen make o.s. heard; ♪ *zu ~ bringen* perform.

ge'**horchen** (25) obey (*j-m* a p.).

ge'**hören** (25, *dat. od.* zu) belong to; *es gehört sich* it is proper *od.* right *od.* fit; *die Sachen ~ in den Schrank* these things go into the cupboard; *dazu gehört Geld* that requires (*od.* takes) money; *das gehört nicht hierher* that's not to the point.

Ge'**hörgang** *m* auditory passage.

ge'**hörig** (*dat. od.* zu) belonging to; (*wie sich's gehört*) fit, proper, right; due; (*tüchtig*) good; *adv.* duly, in due form; (*tüchtig*) thoroughly; *s.* Meinung.

ge'**hörlos** deaf; ♀**enschule** *f* school for the deaf.

Gehörn [~'hœrn] *n* (3) horns *pl.*; *hunt.* antlers *pl.*; ♀**t** horned.

gehorsam [~'ho:rza:m] **1.** *adj.* obedient; **2.** ♀ *m* (3) obedience.

'**Geh**|**steig** *m* pavement, *Am.* sidewalk; '~**versuch** *m* attempt at walking; '~**weg** *m s. Gehsteig;* '~**werk** ⊕ *n* works *pl.*, clockwork.

Geier ['gaɪər] *m* (7) vulture.

Geifer ['gaɪfər] *m* (7) slaver, drivel; *fig.* venom; '♀**n** (29) drivel, slaver; *fig.* foam; *fig.* ~ *gegen* vituperate against.

Geige ['gaɪgə] *f* (15) violin, F fiddle; *s. erst, zweit;* '♀**n** (25) play (on) the violin, F fiddle; '~**nbogen** *m* (violin-)bow; '~**nharz** *n* colophony, rosin; '~**nkasten** *m* violin-case; '~**nmacher** *m* violin-maker; '~**r** *m* (7), '~**rin** *f* (16¹) violinist.

'**Geigerzähler** *phys. m* Geiger counter.

geil [gaɪl] lascivious, wanton, lewd; *sl.* horny, randy; (*üppig*) luxuriant, rank; '♀**heit** *f* lewdness, wantonness; rankness, luxuriance.

Geisel ['gaɪzəl] *f* (15) hostage; '~**drama** *n* hostage drama; ~**nahme** ['~na:mə] *f* (15) taking of hostages; '~**nehmer** *m* (7) kidnapper.

Geiß [gaɪs] *f* (16) goat; '~**blatt** ♀ *n* honeysuckle, woodbine; '~**bock** *m* he-goat, billy-goat.

Geißel ['gaɪsəl] *f* (15) whip, lash; *fig.* scourge; '♀**n** (27) whip, lash; *fig.* lash, castigate; '~**ung** *f* whipping, lashing; *fig.* castigation.

Geist [gaɪst] *m* (1¹) spirit; (*Verstand*) mind, intellect; (*Genius*) genius; (*Witz*) wit; *ein großer ~ P.:* a great

mind; (*Gespenst*) ghost; (*Kobold*) sprite; *der Heilige ~* the Holy Ghost; *den ~ aufgeben* give up the ghost, *fig. a.* conk out (*sl.*); *im ~e bei j-m sein usw.* in (the) spirit *od.* in mind.

'**Geister**|**bahn** *f* ghost train; '~**beschwörer** *m* (7) (*Geisteranrufer*) necromancer; (*Austreiber*) exorcist; '~**bilder** *n/pl. Fernsehen:* ghosting *sg.*; '~**erscheinung** *f* apparition; '♀**haft** ghostly; '~**hand** *f: wie von ~* as if by magic; '~**stunde** *f* witching hour; '~**welt** *f* world of spirits.

'**geistes**|-**abwesend** absent-minded; '♀-**abwesenheit** *f* absent-mindedness; '♀-**arbeit** *f* brain-work; '♀-**arbeiter** *m* brain-worker; '♀**blitz** *m* flash of genius, brainwave; '♀**gabe** *f* talent; '♀**gegenwart** *f* presence of mind; '~**gegenwärtig** alert, quick-witted; '♀**geschichte** *f* intellectual history; '~**gestört** mentally deranged; '♀**größe** *f* greatness of mind; '♀**haltung** *f* mental attitude, mentality; '♀**kraft** *f* power of mind; '~**krank** insane, mentally ill; '♀-**kranke** *m*, *f* lunatic; '♀**krankheit** *f* insanity, mental disorder; '♀**produkt** *n* brain-child; '~**schwach** imbecile; '♀**schwäche** *f* feeble-mindedness, imbecility; '♀**störung** *f* mental disorder; '♀**verfassung** *f* frame of mind; '~**verwandt** congenial (*mit* to); '♀**verwandtschaft** *f* congeniality; '♀**verwirrung** *f* mental disturbance; '♀**wissenschaften** *f/pl. the* humanities, *the* Arts; '♀**zustand** *m* state of mind.

'**geistig** intellectual, mental; (*unkörperlich*) spiritual; ~**es** *Auge* mind's eye; ~**es** *Eigentum* intellectual property; ~**e** *Getränke* *n/pl.* spirits.

'**geistlich** spiritual; *Orden:* religious; (♀**e** *betreffend*) ecclesiastical, clerical; *Musik usw.:* sacred; ~**es** *Amt* ministry; '♀**e** *m* (18) clergyman, cleric; *e-r Sekte:* minister; ⚔, ⚓, 🕂 chaplain; '♀**keit** *f* clergy.

'**geist**|**los** mindless; (*langweilig*) dull; (*dumm*) stupid; '♀**losigkeit** *f* mindlessness; dul(l)ness; *Redensart:* platitude; '~**reich**, '~**voll** witty; '~**tötend** soul-destroying.

Geiz [gaɪts] *m* (3²) avarice; (*Knauserei*) stinginess; '♀**en** (27) be avaricious *od.* stingy; *nach et. ~* covet; *mit et. ~* be sparing with, stint *a th.*;

'**~hals** *m*, '**~kragen** *m* miser; '**~ig**
avaricious; (*knickerig*) niggardly,
stingy, mean.
Gejammer [gə'jamər] *n* (7) (endless) lamentation, wailing.
Gejohle [~'joːlə] *n* (7) hooting.
gekannt [~'kant] *p.p. v. kennen.*
Gekeife [~'kaɪfə] *n* (3) scolding.
Gekicher [~'kiçər] *n* (7) tittering.
Gekläff [~'klɛf] *n* (3) yelping.
Geklapper [~'klapər] *n* (7) rattling.
Geklatsche [~'klatʃə] *n* (7) clapping;
fig. gossiping.
Geklimper [~'klimpər] *n* (7) *auf
dem Klavier*: strum(ming).
Geklirr(e) [~'klir(ə)] *n* (3) clashing,
clanking.
ge'klommen *p.p. v. klimmen.*
geklungen [~'kluŋən] *p.p. v. klingen.*
Geknatter [~'knatər] *n s.* Geknister.
gekniffen [~'knifən] *p.p. v. kneifen.*
Geknister [~'knistər] *n* (7) crackling.
ge'kommen *p.p. v. kommen.*
gekonnt [gə'kɔnt] **1.** *p.p. v. können;*
2. *adj.* competent, expert(ly *adv.*).
geköpert [gə'køpərt] twilled.
Gekreisch [~'kraɪʃ] *n* (4) screaming,
screams *pl.*; shrieking, shrieks *pl.*
Gekritzel [~'kritsəl] *n* (7) scrawl
(-ing), scribbling, scribble.
gekrochen [~'krɔxən] *p.p. v. kriechen.*
Gekröse [~'krøːzə] *n* (7) tripe; *anat.*
mesentery.
gekünstelt [~'kynstəlt] artificial.
Gel [geːl] *n* (3) gel.
Gelächter [~'lɛçtər] *n* (7) laughter.
ge'laden *p.p. v. laden*[1].
Gelage [gə'laːgə] *n* (7) feast, banquet; (*Zecherei*) drinking-bout.
Gelände [~'lɛndə] *n* (7) tract of land,
area; country; (*Boden*) ground; *bsd.*
⚔ terrain; **~fahrt** *f* cross-country
drive; **~fahrzeug** *n* cross-country
vehicle; **Ǫgängig** [~gɛnɪç] cross-
-country *car*; **~kunde** *f* topography;
~lauf *m Sport*: cross-country race.
Geländer [~'lɛndər] *n* (7) railing,
balustrade; (*Treppen*Ǫ) banisters *pl.*;
(*~stange*) handrail.
ge'lang *pret. v. gelingen* 1.
ge'langen (25, sn): **~** *an* (*acc.*), *nach*,
zu arrive at, get (*od.* come) to, reach;
zu e-m Ziele (*a. gewinnen*): attain
(to), gain, (*bekommen*) obtain; *s.
Macht; auf die Nachwelt*: come (*od.*
be handed) down to; *in j-s Hände* **~**
get into a p.'s hands.

Gelaß [gə'las] *n* (4) room, space.
ge'lassen 1. *p.p. v. lassen;* **2.** *adj.*
calm, composed; **Ǫheit** *f* calmness.
Gelatin|e [ʒela'tiːnə] *f* (15) gelatine;
Ǫieren [~ti'niːrən] gelatinize.
Gelaufe [gə'laufə] *n* (7) running
(to and fro).
ge'laufen *p.p. v. laufen.*
ge'läufig fluent, easy; *Zunge*: vol-
uble; (*allgemein bekannt*) current;
das ist ihm **~** that is familiar to him;
Ǫkeit *f* fluency, ease.
gelaunt [gə'launt] disposed; *gut* **~**
good-humo(u)red, in good hu-
mo(u)r; *schlecht* **~** ill-humo(u)red,
out of humo(u)r, bad-tempered.
Geläut(e) [gə'lɔʏt(ə)] *n* (3 [7]) ringing; (*die Glocken*) chime.
gelb [gɛlp] yellow; *Verkehrsampel*:
amber; **Ǫe** ['gɛlbə] *n im Ei*: yolk;
'**Ǫfilter** *phot. m* yellow filter; '**~-
grün** yellowish-green; '**~lich** yel-
lowish; '**Ǫschnabel** *m fig.* greenhorn, whipper-snapper; '**Ǫsucht** *f*
jaundice; **~süchtig** ['~zyçtiç] jaun-
diced.
Geld [gɛlt] *n* (1) money; *s. bar, klein,
knapp; bei* **~***e sein* be in cash; *ins*
~ *laufen* run into money; *zu* **~**
machen turn into cash; *nicht für* **~**
und gute Worte neither for love nor
money.
'**Geld**|**-angelegenheit** *f* money-
matter; '**~-abwertung** *f* devalua-
tion; '**~-anlage** *f* investment; '**~-
anleihe** *f* loan (of money); '**~-an-
weisung** *f* remittance; '**~-aufwer-
tung** *f* revaluation of money; '**~-
ausgabe** *f* expense; '**~-automat** ✝
m cash dispenser; '**~betrag** *m*
amount *od.* sum (of money); '**~beu-
tel** *m* purse; '**~brief** *m* money-letter;
'**~buße** *f* fine; '**~-entwertung** *f*
depreciation of money; *s. Geldabwer-
tung*; '**~-erwerb** *m* money-making;
'**~forderung** *f* monetary claim; ✝
outstanding debt; '**~geber** *m* (7) financial backer, financier, investor;
'**~geschäfte** *n/pl.* money transac-
tions; '**~geschenk** *n* gratuity, donation; '**~gier** *f* greed for money, avarice; '**Ǫgierig** greedy for money, avaricious; '**~heirat** *f* money-match;
'**~klemme** F *f* squeeze; '**~knapp-
heit** *f* shortness (✝ scarcity) of money; '**~krise** *f* monetary crisis; '**Ǫlich**
pecuniary; '**~makler** *m* money-
-broker; '**~mangel** *m* lack of money;

'**~mann** *m* financier; '**~markt** *m* money market; '**~mittel** *n/pl.* funds, means, resources; '**~not** *f* financial straits *pl.*; '**~quelle** *f* pecuniary resource; '**~sache** *f* money matter; '**~schein** *m* bank-note, *Am.* bill; '**~schrank** *m* safe, strong-box; '**~schrankknacker** *m* (7) safe-cracker; '**~sendung** *f* (cash) remittance; '**~sorte** *f* denomination; *pl.* coins and notes; '**~spende** *f* donation, contribution; '**~strafe** *f* fine; *mit e-r ~ belegen* fine, mulct; '**~stück** *n* coin; '**~tasche** *f* money-bag, purse; *für Scheine*: note-case, pocketbook, *Am.* billfold; '**~-überhang** *m* surplus money; '**~verlegenheit** *f* pecuniary embarrassment; *in ~ sein* be pressed for money, F be hard up; '**~verlust** *m* pecuniary loss; '**~verschwendung** *f* waste of money; '**~wert** *m* value (of money), value of currency.

Gelee [ʒe'le:] *n* (11) jelly.

ge'legen 1. *p.p. v. liegen;* **2.** *adj.* situated, *Am. a.* located; (*passend*) convenient, suitable; *Zeit:* opportune; *es kommt mir gerade ~* it just suits me, it comes in handy; *s. liegen.*

Gelegenheit [gə'le:gənhaɪt] *f* occasion; *gute:* opportunity; (*Zufall*) chance; (*Wasch♀ usw.*) facility; *bei ~ s. gelegentlich adv.; bei dieser ~ on this occasion; bei jeder ~ at every turn; j-m ~ bieten* give a p. an opportunity; *die ~ (beim Schopf) ergreifen* seize the opportunity; *~ nehmen zu inf.* take occasion to; **~s-arbeit** *f* casual (*od.* odd) job; **~s-arbeiter** *m* casual labo(u)rer, odd-job worker; **~sdieb** *m* casual thief; **~skauf** *m* chance purchase, bargain.

gelegentlich [~'le:gəntliç] *adj.* occasional; (*zufällig*) casual; chance; *adv.* some time, at one's convenience; *prp.* (*gen.*) on the occasion of.

gelehrig [gə'le:riç] docile; clever; ♀-**keit** *f* docility; cleverness.

Ge'lehrsamkeit *f* erudition, learning.

ge'lehrt learned; F **~es Haus** pundit; ♀**e** *m, f* learned (wo)man, scholar.

Geleise [gə'laɪzə] *n* (7, *mst pl.*) rut, track; 🚉 rails *pl.*, *Am.* track; *fig. im alten ~ in the same old rut; auf ein totes ~ geraten* reach a deadlock.

Geleit [~'laɪt] *n* (3) *a.* ✕ escort; ⚓ convoy; (*Gefolge*) attendance; *j-m das ~ geben* accompany (*schützend*:

escort) a p., *zum Abschied*: see a p. off; *freies ~* safe-conduct; **~brief** *m* (letter of) safe-conduct; ✝ letter of consignment; ♀**en** accompany, conduct; *bsd.* ✕ escort; ⚓ convoy; **~schiff** *n* convoy (vessel); **~wort** *n* foreword; **~zug** ⚓ *m* convoy.

Gelenk [~'lɛŋk] *n* (3) joint; *anat. a.* (*~fügung*) articulation; ⊕ joint; (*Scharnier*) hinge; (*Bindeglied*) link; **~bus** *m* articulated bus; **~entzündung** ⚕ *f* arthritis; **~ig** lissom(e), agile, (*a.* ⊕) flexible; **~igkeit** *f* agility; flexibility; **~rheumatismus** ⚕ *m* articular rheumatism.

gelernt [~'lɛrnt] *Arbeit(er)*: skilled.

ge'lesen *p.p. v. lesen.*

Gelichter [~'liçtər] *n* (7) lot, riff-raff, rabble.

Geliebte [gə'li:ptə] (18) *m* lover; ~ *f* love(r), sweetheart; (*Mätresse*) mistress.

geliehen [gə'li:ən] *p.p. v. leihen.*

gelieren [ʒe'li:rən] gelatinize.

ge'lind(e) soft, gentle, mild (*alle a. fig.*); *Strafe*: mild, lenient; *gelinde gesagt* to put it mildly.

gelingen [gə'liŋən] **1.** (30, sn) succeed; *es gelingt mir, zu tun* I succeed in doing; *es gelingt mir nicht, zu tun* I fail in doing *od.* to do; **2.** ♀ *n* (6) success.

Gelispel [~'lispəl] *n* (7) lisping; (*Geflüster*) whispering.

gelitten [~'litən] *p.p. v. leiden 1.*

gellen ['gɛlən] (25) shrill; (*gellend schreien*) *a.* yell, scream; *Ohr*: tingle; '**~d** shrill, piercing.

ge'loben (25) promise; *feierlich*: vow, pledge; *das Gelobte Land* the Land of Promise.

Gelöbnis [gə'lø:pnis] *n* (4¹) (solemn) promise, pledge; vow.

gelogen [gə'lo:gən] *p.p. v. lügen.*

gelt¹ [gɛlt] giving no milk; (*unfruchtbar*) *Tier*: barren.

gelt² F *int.* F isn't it?

gelt|en ['gɛltən] (30) *v/t.* be worth; *v/i.* be of value; (*gültig sein*) be valid *od.* good; (*zählen*) count; *Gesetz*: be in force; *Grund usw.*: hold (good *od.* true); *Münze*: be current; *fig. etwas ~* carry weight, have influence; *j-m ~ be meant for a p.; ~ für a)* (*od. ~ als*) pass for, be reputed (*od.* thought, supposed) to be, rank as, b) (*sich anwenden lassen*) apply to; be right for, be true of; *~ lassen* let pass; allow; ~ *lassen als* pass off as; *s-n Einfluß* ~*d machen* bring one's influence to bear; ~*d machen* a) assert, b) *als Entschuldigung*: plead, c) *(daß)* maintain (that); *das gilt nicht* that is not allowed, that is not fair *od.* does not count; *es gilt!* done!; *es galt unser Leben* our life was at stake; *es gilt zu inf.* the question is to *inf.*, it is necessary to *inf.*; *s.* Wette; '2ung *f (Gültigkeit)* validity; *e-r Münze*: currency; *e-r P.*: authority, credit, *(Achtung)* prestige, respect; *zur ~ bringen* bring to bear; *Gesetz usw.*: enforce; *zur ~ kommen* (begin to) tell, take effect, *(herausragen)* stand out; '2ungsbedürfnis *n*, '2ungsdrang *m* craving for recognition.

Gelübde [gə'lypdə] *n* (7) vow.

gelungen [~'luŋən] **1.** *p.p. v.* gelingen; **2.** *adj.* successful; *(vortrefflich)* capital; *du bist ~!* you are funny!

Gelüst [~'lyst] *n* (3¹) desire, craving, appetite *(alle: nach* for); 2en: *mich gelüstet nach* I crave (for).

gemach¹ [~'ma:x] *int.*: ~! *(sachte!)* gently!

Ge'mach² *n* (1², *poet.* 3) room, apartment, chamber.

gemächlich [~'mɛ:çliç] *adj. u. adv.* leisurely; 2keit *f* leisureliness, ease.

Gemahl [gə'ma:l] *m* (3) husband, consort; *Ihr Herr ~* Mr. X.; ~in *f* wife, consort; *Ihre Frau ~* Mrs. X.

gemahnen [~'ma:nən]: ~ *an (acc.)* remind of.

Gemälde [~'mɛ:ldə] *n* (7) painting, picture; ~**ausstellung** *f* exhibition of pictures; ~**galerie** *f* picture-gallery, *Am. a.* museum.

gemäß [~'mɛ:s] **1.** *adj.* conformable; **2.** *prp. (dat.)* according to, in accordance with, *bsd.* ⚖ pursuant to; ~igt moderate; *geogr.* temperate.

Gemäuer [gə'mɔyər] *n* (7): *altes ~* decayed building(s *pl.*); ruins *pl.*

gemein [~'main] common; *(allgemein)* a. general; *b.s.* low, mean, dirty; *(pöbelhaft)* vulgar; ~*er Kerl* beast of a fellow; ~*er Soldat, Gemeine m* private (soldier), *Am.* (basic) private; *et.* ~ *haben mit* have a th. in common with; *sich ~ machen mit* keep company with.

Gemeinde [~'maində] *f* (15) community; *(Kirchen2)* parish, *(Kirchgänger)* congregation; *(Stadt2)* mu-

nicipality; ~**bezirk** *m* district; ~**haus** *n* municipal hall; *eccl.* parish hall; ~**rat** *m* municipal council *(od. P.*: councillor); ~**schwester** *f* district nurse; ~**steuer** *f* (local) rate, *Am.* local tax; ~**vorstand** *m* local board; ~**wahl** *f* communal election; ~**zentrum** *n* community cent|re, *Am.* -er.

ge'mein|faßlich *s.* gemeinverständlich; ~**gefährlich** dangerous to the public; ~*er Mensch* public danger, *Am.* public enemy; 2**geist** *m* public spirit; ~**gültig** generally accepted; 2**gut** *n* common property; 2**heit** *f (Niedrigkeit)* vulgarity, meanness; *(niedrige Tat)* mean trick; ~**hin** commonly; 2**kosten** *pl.* overhead (costs); 2**nutz** *m* (3², *o. pl.*) common good; ~**nützig** [~nytsiç] of public utility; *Verein*: non-profit; ~e Betriebe public utilities *pl.*; 2**nützigkeit** *f* public utility; 2**platz** *m* commonplace; 2**er Markt** *m* Common Market; ~ *mit* in common with; ~e *Sache machen mit* make common cause with; 2**samkeit** *f*, 2**schaft** *f* (16) community; *(Verkehr)* intercourse; ~**schaftlich** common, joint; *v. zweien*: mutual; *adv. a.* in common.

Ge'meinschafts|-anschluß *m* party line; ~**antenne** *f* communal aerial; ~**arbeit** *f* teamwork; ~**erziehung** *f* coeducation; ~**geist** *m* esprit de corps *(fr.)*, community spirit; 2**konto** *n* joint account; ~**praxis** *f* joint practice; ~**produktion** *f* co-production; ~**raum** *m* common room; ~**sendung** *f* simultaneous broadcast.

Ge'mein|schuldner *m* bankrupt; ~**sinn** *m* public spirit; 2**verständlich** intelligible to all, popular; ~**wesen** *n* community; polity; ~**wohl** *n* public weal.

Gemeng|e [gə'mɛŋə] *n* (7) mixture; *(Hand2)* scuffle; ~**sel** [~zəl] *n* (7) medley, hotchpotch.

ge'messen 1. *p.p. v.* messen; **2.** *adj.* measured; *(förmlich)* formal; *(feierlich)* grave; 2**heit** *f* measuredness; formality; gravity.

Gemetzel [gə'mɛtsəl] *n* (7) slaughter, carnage, massacre.

gemieden [~'mi:dən] *p.p. v.* meiden.

Gemisch [~'miʃ] *n* (3²) mixture.

gemischt [~'miʃt] mixed (*a.* Tennis; *a. fig.* Gefühl *usw.*); 2**warenhand-**

lung *f* grocery, *Am.* general (merchandise) store.
Gemme ['gɛmə] *f* (15) gem.
gemocht [gə'mɔxt] *p.p. v. mögen.*
gemolken [gə'mɔlkən] *p.p. v. melken.*
Gemse ['gɛmzə] *f* (15) chamois.
Gemurmel [gə'murməl] *n* (7) murmur(ing), mutter(ing).
Gemüse [ˍ'myːzə] *n* (7) vegetable; greens *pl.*; ˍ**bau** *m* vegetable gardening, *Am.* ˍ**beet** *n* vegetable bed; ˍ**garten** *m* kitchen-garden; ˍ**händler(in** *f)* *m* greengrocer; ˍ**konserven** *f/pl.* preserved (*od.* tinned, *Am.* canned) vegetables; ˍ**schale** *f im Kühlschrank:* salad drawer.
gemüßigt [ˍ'myːsiçt]: *sich ˍ sehen, zu inf.* feel (*od.* find o.s.) obliged to *inf.*
gemußt [ˍ'must] *p.p. v. müssen.*
gemustert [ˍ'mustərt] *Stoff:* figured, patterned.
Gemüt [ˍ'myːt] *n* (1) mind; (*Gefühl*) feeling; (*Seele*) soul; (*Herz*) heart; (ˍ*s-art*) disposition, temper; *j–m et. zu ˍe führen* bring a th. home to a p.; F *sich e–e Flasche Wein usw. zu ˍe führen* discuss.
ge'mütlich (*gutmütig*) good-natured; (*freundlich*) genial; (*behaglich*) comfortable, snug, cosy, restful; ˍ*es Beisammensein* social gathering; ˍ *werden* unbend; *es sich ˍ machen* make o.s. at home, relax; ℒ**keit** *f* good nature; geniality; cosiness, snugness.
Ge'müts|-art *f*, ˍ**beschaffenheit** *f* (mental) disposition, temper, character; ˍ**bewegung** *f* emotion; ℒ**krank** mentally diseased, emotionally disturbed; (*schwermütig*) melancholy; ˍ**krankheit** *f* mental disorder, melancholia; ˍ**mensch** *m* emotional (*od.* warm-hearted) person; ˍ**ruhe** *f* calmness; composure; ˍ**verfassung** *f*, ˍ**zustand** *m* state of mind, humo(u)r.
ge'mütvoll *P.*: warm(-hearted); *S.*: full of feeling.
gen[1] [gɛn] *prp.* towards.
Gen[2] [geːn] *biol. n* (3[1]) gene.
genannt [gə'nant] *p.p. v. nennen.*
genas [gə'naːs] *pret. v. genesen.*
genau [gə'nau] exact, accurate, precise; (*streng*) strict; (*sorgfältig*) care-

ful, scrupulous; *Bericht usw.*: detailed; ˍ*so gut* just as good (*od.* well); *es ˍ nehmen* (*mit*) be particular (about); ℒ*eres* full particulars *pl.*; ˍ**genommen** strictly speaking; ℒ**igkeit** *f* accuracy, exactness; precision; strictness.
Gendarm [ʒã'darm] *m* (12) country policeman; ˍ**erie** [ˍmə'riː] *f* (15) rural constabulary.
Genealogie [genealo'giː] *f* (16) genealogy.
genehm [gə'neːm] agreeable, convenient (*dat.* to); ˍ**igen** [ˍmigən] (*bewilligen*) grant; consent to; (*gutheißen*) approve (of), authorize; *behördlich*: a. license; ℒ**igung** *f* grant; approval; licen|ce, *Am.* -se, permit; (*Erlaubnis*) permission, authorization; (*Einwilligung*) consent.
geneigt [ˍ'naikt] inclined (*fig. zu* to); (*j–m*) well disposed (to[wards] a p.); *ein ˍes Ohr* a willing ear; *der ˍe Leser* the gentle reader.
General [genə'raːl] *m* (3[1] *u.* 3[2]) general; ˍ**-agent** *m* agent-general; ˍ**-amnestie** *f* general amnesty; ˍ**-anzeiger** *m* (*Zeitung*) General Gazette; ˍ**baß** ♪ *m* thorough-bass; ˍ**bevollmächtigte** *m* chief representative *od.* agent; ˍ**direktor** *m* general manager; ˍ'**feldmarschall** ✕ *m* Field Marshal; ˍ**-intendant** *thea. m* director; ˍ**ität** ✕ [ˍrali'tɛːt] *f* (16) (body of) generals *pl.*; ˍ**konsul** [ˍ'rɔːl-] *m* consul-general; ˍ**konsulat** *n* consulate-general; ˍ**leutnant** *m* lieutenant-general; ˍ**major** *m* major-general; ˍ**oberst** *m* colonel-general; ˍ**probe** *f* dress rehearsal; ˍ**sekretär** *m* secretary general; ˍ'**staatsanwalt** *m* Chief State Counsel; ˍ**stab** *m* General Staff; ˍ**stabskarte** *f* ordnance (survey) map, *Am.* strategic map; ˍ**streik** *m* general strike; ˍ**überholung** *f* complete overhaul; ˍ**versammlung** *f* general meeting; ˍ**vertreter** *m* agent-general; ˍ**vollmacht** ⚖ *f* general power of attorney.
Generation [genəra'tsjoːn] *f* (16) generation; ˍ**skonflikt** *m* generation gap.
Generator [ˍ'raːtɔr] *m* (8[1]) generator; (*Gas*ℒ) *a.* producer.
generell [ˍ'rɛl] general(ly *adv.*).
gene|sen [gə'neːzən] **1.** (30, sn) recover (*von* from); **2.** *p.p. v.* 1.; ℒ**sende**

m, f convalescent; ♀**sung** *f* recovery; convalescence; ♀**sungsheim** *n* convalescent home.

Genet|ik [ge'ne:tik] *f* (16, *o. pl.*) genetics *sg.*; ♀**isch** genetic.

Genfer ['gɛnfər]: ~ **Abkommen** *n*, ~ **Konventi'on** *f* Geneva Convention.

genial [gen'jɑːl] ingenious, brilliant; ♀**ität** [~jali'tɛːt] *f* (16) genius, brilliancy.

Genick [gə'nik] *n* (3) (back of the) neck, nape (of the neck); (*sich*) *das* ~ *brechen* break one's neck; *fig. das brach ihm das* ~ that finished him off, that was the last straw; ~**schuß** *m* shot in the neck; ~**starre** ⚕ *f* cerebrospinal meningitis.

Genie [ʒe'niː] *n* (11) genius (*a. P.*).

ge'nieren (25) trouble, disturb; *sich* ~ feel embarrassed; *zu tun*: be too timid to do; *sich nicht* ~ *zu inf.* not to be ashamed to *inf.*; ~ *Sie sich nicht* don't be shy.

ge'nieß|bar [gə'niː-s] *Speise*: eatable; *Getränk*: drinkable; *fig.* agreeable; ~**en** (30) enjoy; *Speise*: eat; *Getränk*: drink; *et.* ~ take some food *od.* some refreshments; *j-s Vertrauen* ~ be in a p.'s confidence.

Genitalien [geni'tɑːljən] *pl.* genitals.

Genitiv *gr.* ['ge:niti:f] *m* (3¹) genitive (case); possessive (case).

Genius ['ge:nius] *m* (16²) genius; *guter* ~ guardian angel.

'Gen|manipulation *f* genetic engineering; **'~mutation** *f* gene mutation.

genommen [gə'nɔmən] *p.p. v. nehmen.*

genormt [gə'nɔrmt] standardized.

genoß [gə'nɔs] *pret. v. genießen.*

Genoss|e [gə'nɔsə] *m* (13), ~**in** *f* companion, mate, (*a. pol.*) comrade; ♀**en** *p.p. v. genießen;* ~**enschaft** ✝ *f* co-operative (society).

Genre|bild ['ʒɑ̃r(ə)-] *n* genre-picture; '~**maler** *m* genre-painter.

genug [gə'nuːk] enough, sufficient (-ly); ~ (*davon*)! enough (of that)!; no more of this!; *ich habe* ~ *davon* I am sick of it.

Genüg|e [~'nyːgə] *f* (15): *j-m* ~ *tun* satisfy a p.; *e-r S.* come up to a th.; *zur* ~ enough, sufficiently; ♀**en** (25) be enough; *das genügt* that will do; *j-m* ~ satisfy a p.; (*nicht*) ~ (not to) give satisfaction; *sich* ~ *lassen* be

satisfied with; ♀**end** sufficient; ♀**sam** [~'nyːk-] easily satisfied; (*mäßig*) frugal; ~**samkeit** *f* contentedness; frugality.

Genugtu-ung [gə'nuːktuːuŋ] *f* satisfaction; (*Wiedergutmachung*) reparation.

Genus *gr.* ['genus] *n* (16, *pl.* '**Genera**) gender.

Genuß [gə'nus] *m* (4²) (*Freude; Besitz*) enjoyment; (*Nutznießung*) use; *v. Speisen usw.*: taking; *fig. ein wahrer* ~ a real treat; ~**mittel** *n* semi-luxury; *anregendes*: stimulant; ♀**reich** delightful, enjoyable; ~**sucht** *f* thirst for pleasure; ♀**süchtig** pleasure-seeking.

Geo|däsie [geodɛ'siː] *f* (16) geodesy; ~**graph** [~'grɑːf] *m* (12) geographer; ~**graphie** [~grɑ'fiː] *f* geography; ♀**graphisch** [~'grɑːfiʃ] geographical; ~**log(e)** [~'loːk, ~gə] *m* (12 [13]) geologist; ~**logie** [~lo'giː] *f* geology; ♀**logisch** [~'loːgiʃ] geological; ~**meter** [~'meːtər] *m* (7) surveyor; ~**metrie** [~me'triː] *f* geometry; ♀**metrisch** [~'meːtriʃ] geometric(al); ~**phy'sik** *f* geophysics *sg.*; ~**poli'tik** *f* geopolitics *sg.*; ♀**po'litisch** geopolitical.

ge-ordnet [gə'¹⁷ɔrdnət] orderly.

Gepäck [gə'pɛk] *n* (3) luggage; ✗ *od. Am.* baggage; ~**annahme(stelle)** *f* luggage (registration) office, *Am.* baggage checking counter; ~**auf-bewahrung(stelle)** *f* cloak-room, left-luggage office, *Am.* checkroom; ~**ausgabe(stelle)** *f* luggage delivery office, *Am.* baggage room; *am Flughafen*: baggage reclaim; ~**netz** *n* luggage (*Am.* baggage) rack; ~**raum** *m* luggage (*Am.* baggage) hold, belly-hold; ~**schein** *m* luggage-ticket, *Am.* baggage check; ~**stück** *n* piece of luggage (*Am.* baggage); ~**träger** *m* (railway) porter; *mot.* roof-rack; *am Fahrrad*: carrier; ~**wagen** *m* luggage-van, *Am.* baggage car.

gepanzert [gə'pantsərt] armo(u)red, iron-clad.

gepfeffert [~'pfɛfərt] *fig. Rechnung*: steep; *Witz*: fruity.

gepfiffen [~'pfifən] *p.p. v. pfeifen.*

gepflegt [~'pfleːkt] *P.*: well-groomed; *S.*: well cared-for; *Stil usw.*: cultivated, refined.

gepflogen [~'pfloːgən] *p.p. v. pflegen;* ♀**heit** *f* habit; custom.

Geplänkel [ˌ'plɛŋkəl] *n* (7) skirmish.
Geplapper [ˌ'plapər] *n* (7) babbling, chattering, prattle.
Geplätscher [ˌ'plɛtʃər] *n* (7) splashing.
Geplauder [ˌ'plaudər] *n* (7) chatting, small talk.
Gepolter [ˌ'pɔltər] *n* (7) rumble, rumbling.
Gepräge [ˌ'prɛːgə] *n* (7) impression; (*a. fig.*) stamp; *e-r Münze*: coinage.
Gepränge [ˌ'prɛŋə] *n* (7) pomp.
Geprassel [ˌ'prasəl] *n* (7) crackling.
gepriesen [ˌ'priːzən] *p.p. v.* preisen.
gequollen [ˌ'kvɔlən] *p.p. v.* quellen.
gerade [gə'raːdə] **1.** *adj.* straight (*a. fig.*); (*eben*) even; (*unmittelbar*) direct; (*aufrichtig*) upright, plain, straightforward; *Gang*, *Haltung*: upright, erect; *Zahl*: even; **2.** *adv. s.* ~ **1.**; just; *ich bin* ~ *gekommen* I have just come; *er schrieb* ~ *he was* (just) writing; *ich war* ~ (*zufällig*) *dort* I happened to be there; ~ *das Gegenteil* the very opposite; *nun* ~ now more than ever; ~ *an dem Tage* on that very day; **3.** ♀ *f* (18) ♙ straight line; *Lauf-*, *Rennsport:* die ~ the straight; **4.** ♀ *f*, *a.* ♀r *m Boxen:* straight; ~'-**aus** straight on *od.* ahead; ~**he'raus** freely, frankly, point-blank; ~**(n-)wegs** [ˌveːks] directly, straight(away); ~**stehen** stand erect; *fig.* für etwas ~ answer for a th.; ~'**zu** (*geradeaus*) straight on, directly; (*nichts andres als*) downright *nonsense, etc.*
Geradheit [ˌ'raːthaɪt] *f* straightness; *fig.* straightforwardness.
geradlinig [ˌ'raːtliːnɪç] rectilinear.
gerammelt [ˌ'raməlt]: ~ *voll* chock--ful, crammed.
Gerangel [ˌ'raŋəl] *n* (3¹) wrangling.
gerannt [ˌ'rant] *p.p. v.* rennen.
Gerassel [gə'rasəl] *n* (7) rattling, rattle; *Kette: a.* clanking.
Gerät [ˌ'rɛːt] *n* (3) tool, implement, utensil; *technisches:* gear, device; (*Apparat*) appliance, apparatus; *teleph.*, *Radio usw.*: set; ✗ (*Ausrüstung*) equipment; *s.* Angel♀, Fisch♀, Haushalts♀, Turn♀; *elektrisches* ~ electric appliance.
geraten [gə'raːtən] **1.** *v/i.* (30, sn) *örtlich:* come, fall, get (*in acc.* in[to]; *auf acc.* [up]on *etc.*); (*ausfallen*) turn out *well etc.*; *nach j-m* ~ take

after a p.; *über et.* (*acc.*) ~ come across a th.; *s.* Abweg, aneinander, außer, Brand, Konkurs, Stocken, Vergessenheit usw.; **2.** *adj.* successful; (*ratsam*) advisable; **3.** *p.p. v.* raten.
Ge'räte|stecker ⚡ *m* connector plug; ~**turnen** *n* apparatus gymnastics *pl.*
Gerate'wohl *n:* aufs ~ at random, on the off-chance.
geraum [gə'raum]: ~e *Zeit* long time.
geräumig [gə'rɔymɪç] spacious, roomy; ♀keit *f* spaciousness.
Geräusch [ˌ'rɔyʃ] *n* (3²) noise; ~**dämpfung** *f* sound damping; ~**kulisse** *f* background noise; ♀los noiseless, silent; ~**losigkeit** *f* noiselessness; ~**pegel** *m* noise level; ♀voll noisy, loud.
gerb|en ['gɛrbən] (25) tan (*a. fig.* = *prügeln*); *weiß* ~ taw; '♀er *m* (7) tanner; ♀**erei** [ˌ'raɪ] *f* tannery; ♀-**säure** ['gɛrp-] *f* tannic acid.
gerecht [gə'rɛçt] just; (*rechtschaffen*) righteous; (*billig*) fair; *j-m* ~ *werden* do justice to a p. (*a. fig.*); *e-r Anforderung, e-m Wunsch usw.* ~ *werden* meet; *allen Seiten* ~ *werden* deal with all aspects; ~**fertigt** justified, justifiable; ♀**igkeit** *f* justice; righteousness; fairness; *j-m* ~ *widerfahren lassen* do a p. justice; ♀**igkeitssinn** *m* sense of justice.
Gerede [gə'reːdə] *n* (7) talk; (*Geschwätz*) gossip; (*Gerücht*) rumo(u)r; *ins* ~ *kommen* get talked about.
ge'regelt regulated, ordered; orderly.
ge'reichen (25): *zu et.* ~ (turn out to) be a th.; redound to a th.
gereizt [ˌ'raɪtst] irritated, nettled, piqued; ♀**heit** *f* irritation.
ge'reuen: *es gereut mich* I repent (of) it, I am sorry for it; *sich keine Mühe* ~ *lassen* spare no trouble.
Gericht [ˌ'rɪçt] *n* (3) **1.** (*Speise*) dish, course; **2.** ⚖ law-court, court (of justice), *mst rhet. u. fig.* tribunal; (*Rechtsspruch*) judg(e)ment; *s.* jüngst; *fig. mit j-m ins* ~ *gehen* take a p. to task; *vor* ~ *bringen* bring to trial; *vor* ~ *fordern* summon; *zu* ~ *sitzen über* (*acc.*) sit in judg(e)ment over *od.* on; ♀**lich** judicial, legal; ~ *vereidigt* sworn.

Ge'richts|barkeit f jurisdiction; ~**beschluß** m court order; durch ~ by order of the court; ~**diener** m (court) usher; ~**gebäude** n law-court, court--house; ~**hof** m law-court, court of justice; mst rhet. u. fig. tribunal; ~**kosten** pl. (law-)costs; ~**medizin** f forensic medicine; ~**mediziner** m medical expert (Am. examiner); ~**saal** m court-room; ~**schreiber** m clerk of the court; ~**stand** m (legal) venue; ♱ legal domicile; ~**urteil** n judg(e)ment (of the court); ~**verfahren** n legal proceedings pl.; (law-)suit; ~**verhandlung** f (judicial) hearing; (Straf♀) trial; ~**vollzieher** m bailiff, Am. marshal; ~**weg** m: auf dem ~ by legal proceedings.

gerieben [gə'riːbən] **1.** p.p. v. reiben; **2.** adj. fig. smart, crafty, wily.

Geriesel [gə'riːzəl] n (7) purling; Regen: drizzling.

gering [gə'riŋ] little, small; (unbedeutend) trifling, slight, negligible; (niedrig) mean, low; (ärmlich) poor; (minderwertig) inferior; mein ~es Verdienst my humble merit; mit ~en Ausnahmen with but few exceptions; ~ denken von think little of; ~**achten** think little of; disregard, slight; ~**er** inferior, less, minor; kein ♀er als no less a person than; ~**fügig** [~fy:giç] insignificant, trifling, negligible, slight; ♀**fügigkeit** f littleness, insignificance; ~**haltig** [~haltiç] of low standard, low--grade; ~**schätzen** s. geringachten; ~**schätzig** [~ʃetsiç] depreciatory, disparaging, slighting; ♀**schätzung** f disdain, contempt; ~**st** least; slightest; minimum; nicht im ~en not in the least; ~**wertig** [~ve:rtiç] low-value, low-quality, inferior.

ge'rinn|en (30, sn) curdle, coagulate; bsd. Blut: clot; ♀**sel** [~zəl] n (7) clot; ♀**ung** f coagulation.

Geripp|e [gə'ripə] n (7) skeleton (a. fig.); (dürrer Mensch) a. scrag; ⊕ framework; ♀t ribbed; Säule usw.: fluted; Stoff: corded.

gerissen [gə'risən] **1.** p.p. v. reißen 1.; **2.** adj. fig. s. gerieben 2.

geritten [gə'ritən] p.p. v. reiten.

German|e [ger'ma:nə] m (13) Teuton; ♀**isch** Germanic, Teutonic; ~**ist** [~ma'nist] m (12) German scholar, Germanist; ~**istik** [~'nistik] f (16, o. pl.) Germanistics

pl., Am. Germanics pl.

gern(e) ['gɛrn(ə)] willingly, gladly, with pleasure; als Antwort: sehr ~! I should be delighted!, I should love to!; ~ haben, mögen od. tun be fond of, like; F du kannst mich ~ haben! go to blazes!; ich möchte ~ wissen I should like to know; ~ gesehen sein be welcome; ~ geschehen! don't mention it!, (you are) welcome!

'**Gernegroß** m (14) show-off.

gerochen [~'rɔxən] p.p. v. riechen.

Geröll [gə'rœl] n (3) rubble.

geronnen [~'rɔnən] p.p. v. gerinnen.

Gerste ['gɛrstə] f (15) barley.

'**Gersten|graupen** f/pl. peeled barley; '~**korn** n barleycorn; ⚕ sty.

Gerte ['gɛrtə] f (15) switch, twig; '♀**nschlank** (slim and) willowy.

Geruch [gə'rux] m (3³) smell, (a. fig.) odo(u)r; angenehmer: scent; fig. odo(u)r, reputation; ♀**los** odo(u)rless; ~**snerv** m olfactory nerve; ~(s)**sinn** m (sense of) smell.

Gerücht [gə'ryçt] n (3) rumo(u)r, report; es geht das ~ it is rumo(u)red; ~**emacher** m rumo(u)r--monger.

ge'ruchtilgend [~tilgənt], ~**es** [~dəs] **Mittel** n deodorant.

ge'rufen p.p. v. rufen; das kommt wie ~ that comes in handy.

ge'ruhen deign, condescend.

Gerümpel [gə'rympəl] n (7) lumber, junk.

Gerundium gr. [ge'rundjum] n (9) gerund.

gerungen [gə'ruŋən] p.p. v. ringen.

Gerüst [gə'ryst] n (3¹) (Bau♀) scaffold(ing); (Schau♀) stage; (Tragewerk) frame; (Gestell) trestle; ∆ (Hängewerk) truss; fig. frame(work).

Ges ♪ [gɛs] n G flat.

gesalzen [gə'zaltsən] salted; fig. spicy; Preise usw.: exorbitant, F steep.

gesamt [gə'zamt] whole, entire, total, all; ♀**ansicht** f general view; ♀**auflage** f total circulation; e-s Buchs: total number of copies published; ♀**ausgabe** f e-s Werkes: complete edition; ♀**betrag** m (sum) total; ♀**bild** fig. n overall picture; ~**deutsch** all-German; ♀**eindruck** m overall impression; ♀**einnahme** f total receipts pl.; ♀**ertrag** m total proceeds pl.; ♀**heit** f total(ity); the whole;

ⵉ**konzept** *n* overall plan; ⵉ**länge** *f* overall length; ⵉ**note** *f Schule:* aggregate mark; ⵉ**preis** *m* total (*od.* inclusive) price; ⵉ**schule** *f* comprehensive school; ⵉ**sieger(in** *f*) *m* overall winner; ⵉ**summe** *f* (sum) total; ⵉ-**umsatz** *m* total turnover; ⵉ**zahl** *f* total number.

gesandt [gə'zant] *p.p. v.* senden; ⵉe *m* (18) envoy; ⵉ**schaft** *f* legation.

Gesang [gə'zaŋ] *m* (3³) singing; (*Lied*) song; (*Lob*ⵉ) hymn; (*Teil e-r Dichtung*) canto; ⵉ**buch** *n* book of songs; *eccl.* hymn-book; ⵉ**lehrer(in** *f*) *m* singing teacher; ⵉ**s-einlage** *thea. f* song insert; ⵉ**ver-ein** *m* choral society, *Am.* glee club.

Gesäß [gə'zɛːs] *n* (3²) seat, bottom; ⵉ**tasche** *f* hip pocket.

ge'schaffen *p.p. v.* schaffen.

Geschäft [gə'ʃɛft] *n* (3) business; (*Unternehmung*) *a.* transaction, deal; (*Angelegenheit*) affair; (*Beschäftigung*) occupation, trade, job; (*Firma*) business, firm; (*Laden*ⵉ) shop, *Am.* store; ein ⵉ tätigen do a business; ein ⵉ (*Notdurft*) verrichten relieve nature; ⵉe machen mit j-m do business with; ein gutes ⵉ machen make a bargain; ⵉ**emacher** *m* profiteer; ⵉ**ig** busy, active; ⵉ**igkeit** *f* activity; ⵉ**lich** commercial, business; *adv.* on business; ⵉe Beziehungen business relations.

Ge'schäfts|-abschluß *m* (business) transaction *od.* deal; ⵉ**-anteil** *m* share *od.* interest (in a company); ⵉ**aufsicht** *f* legal control; ⵉ**bedingungen** *f/pl.* terms of business; ⵉ**bereich** *m* sphere of activity, scope; *e-s Ministers:* portfolio; ᵗᵗᵥ jurisdiction; ⵉ**bericht** *m* business report; ⵉ**brief** *m* business letter; ⵉ**fähigkeit** *f* legal (*od.* disposing) capacity; ⵉ**frau** *f* businesswoman; ⵉ**freund** *m* business friend; ⵉ**führend** managing, executive; ⵉ**führer** *m* manager; *e-s Vereins usw.:* secretary; ⵉ**führung** *f* management; ⵉ**gang** *m* course of business; routine; ⵉ**gebaren** *n* business methods *pl.*; ⵉ**geheimnis** *n* business secret; ⵉ**geist** *m* business acumen; ⵉ**haus** *n* (*Gebäude*) shop (*od.* office) building; (*Firma*) commercial firm; ⵉ**inhaber** *m* owner of a business; ⵉ**jahr** *n* business (*parl.* financial, *Am.* fiscal) year; ⵉ**kosten** *pl.*: auf ⵉ on expense account; ⵉ**kundig** experienced *od.* versed in

business; ⵉ**lage** *f* business situation; ⵉ**leute** *pl.* businessmen; ⵉ**lokal** *n* business premises *pl.*; (*Laden*) shop, *Am.* store; (*Büro*) office; ⵉ**mann** *m* (1, *pl.* Geschäftsleute) businessman; ⵉ**mäßig** businesslike; ⵉ**ordnung** *f* rules *pl.* (of procedure); *parl.* standing orders *pl.*; zur ⵉ sprechen rise to order; ⵉ**papiere** *n/pl.* business papers; ⵉ**partner(in** *f*) *m* (business) partner; ⵉ**räume** *m/pl.* business premises; ⵉ**reise** *f* business trip; auf einer ⵉ sein be away on business; ⵉ**reisende** *m* commercial traveller; *Am.* traveling salesman; ⵉ**schädigend** damaging (*od.* detrimental) to business; ⵉ**schluß** *m* closing time; ⵉ**sitz** *m* place of business; ⵉ**stelle** *f* office, agency; ⵉ**straße** *f* shopping street; ⵉ**teilhaber(in** *f*) *m* partner; ⵉ**träger** *m* agent, representative; *pol.* chargé d'affaires (*fr.*); ⵉ**tüchtig** smart, efficient (in business); ⵉ**-unkosten** *pl.* business expenses; ⵉ**-unternehmen** *n* business enterprise; ⵉ**verbindung** *f* business connection; ⵉ**viertel** *n* business (*od.* shopping) centre, *Am. a.* downtown; ⵉ**welt** *f* business (world); ⵉ**wert** *m e-r* Firma: goodwill; ᵗᵗᵥ *s.* Streitwert; ⵉ**zeit** *f* business (*od.* office) hours *pl.*; ⵉ**zimmer** *n* office; ⵉ**zweig** *m* branch *od.* line (of business).

geschah [gə'ʃaː] *pret. v.* geschehen 1.

geschehen [gə'ʃeːən] **1.** (30, sn) happen, occur, take place; (*getan werden*) be done; ⵉ lassen allow, suffer; es geschehe so be it; es ist um mich ⵉ I am done for; es geschieht ihm recht it serves him right; Dein Wille geschehe Thy will be done; **2.** *p.p. v.* 1.; **3.** ⵉ *n* happenings *pl.*, events *pl.*

Ge'schehnis *n* occurrence, event.

gescheit [gə'ʃaɪt] clever, intelligent, smart, brainy, bright; nicht recht ⵉ a bit cracked *od.* touched.

Geschenk [gə'ʃɛŋk] *n* (3) present, gift; j-m et. zum ⵉ machen make a p. a present of a th.; ⵉ**packung** *f* gift-box.

Geschichte [gə'ʃɪçtə] *f* (15) story; (*Erzählung*) *a.* narrative; tale; *bsd. als Wissenschaft:* history; e-e schöne ⵉ! a nice affair!; die ganze ⵉ the whole business; ⵉ**nbuch** *n* story-book; ⵉ**n-erzähler(in** *f*) *m* story-teller.

ge'schichtlich historical; (~ *bedeutsam*) historic.
Ge'schichts|fälschung *f* falsification of history; **~forscher** *m* historian; **~forschung** *f* historical research; **~schreiber** *m* historian.
Geschick [gə'ʃik] *n* (3) **1.** fate, destiny; **2.** = **~lichkeit** *f* skill; (*Gewandtheit*) dexterity, adroitness; (*Befähigung*) aptitude; **~lichkeitsprüfung** *f* test of skill; **≈t** skil(l)ful (*zu* at; *in dat.* in), clever (at), able; dexterous, adroit.
geschieden [gə'ʃi:dən] *p.p. v. scheiden.*
ge'schienen *p.p. v. scheinen.*
Geschirr [~'ʃir] *n* (3) (*Gefäß*) vessel; (*Tafel≈*) table-ware; (*Silber≈*) plate; (*Porzellan*) china; *oft nur*: things *pl.*; *irdenes ~* earthenware, crockery; (*Pferde≈*) harness; *das ~ abwaschen* wash up (*od.* do) the dishes; **~spüler** *m*, **~spülmaschine** *f* dish-washer, washing-up machine; **~spülmittel** *n* washing-up liquid; **~tuch** *n* tea towel.
ge'schissen V *p.p. v. scheißen.*
ge'schlafen *p.p. v. schlafen.*
ge'schlagen *p.p. v. schlagen.*
Geschlecht [gə'ʃlɛçt] *n* (1) sex; (*Art*) kind, species; (*Abstammung*) race; (*Familie*) family; (*Menschenalter*) generation; *gr.* gender; *s. schön usw.*; *beiderlei ~s* of both sexes; **≈lich** sexual.
Ge'schlechts|-akt *m* sexual act; **~bestimmung** *f* sex determination; **~hormon** *n* sex hormone; **≈krank** suffering from venereal disease; **~krankheit** *f* venereal disease; **~leben** *n* sex life; **≈los** sexless; *biol.* asexual; **~merkmal** *n* sex characteristic; **~-organ** *n* sexual organ; **~reife** *f* sexual maturity; **≈spezifisch** sex-specific; **~teil** *n mst. pl.* genitals *pl.*; **~trieb** *m* sexual instinct (*od.* urge); **~-umwandlung** *f* sex change; **~verkehr** *m* sexual intercourse; **~wort** *gr. n* article.
ge'schlichen *p.p. v. schleichen.*
ge'schliffen **1.** *p.p. v. schleifen* 1.; **2.** *adj. Glas*: cut; *fig.* polished.
ge'schlissen *p.p. v. schleißen.*
ge'schlossen **1.** *p.p. v. schließen*; **2.** *adj.* closed; ⚔, *hunt.*, *gr.* close; (*gemeinsam*) united, *adv.* in a body; ⊕ self-contained; *~e Gesellschaft* private party; *~e Veranstaltung* private meeting.
geschlungen [gə'ʃluŋən] *p.p. v. schlingen.*
Geschmack [~'ʃmak] *m* (3^3) taste (*a. fig. an dat.* for); (*Aroma*) flavo(u)r; *fig.* (*guter*) ~ (good) taste; *~ finden an* (*dat.*) take a fancy to; **≈los** tasteless; (*fad*) insipid; *fig.* tasteless; (*pred.*) in bad taste; **~losigkeit** *f* tastelessness; *fig.* bad taste; **~srichtung** *f* trend in taste; **~(s)sache** *f* matter of taste; **~ssinn** *m* (sense of) taste; **~sverirrung** *f* lapse of taste; **≈voll** tasteful, elegant, *pred.* in good taste.
Geschmeide [gə'ʃmaɪdə] *n* (7) trinkets, jewels *pl.*; jewel(le)ry.
ge'schmeidig supple, pliant; flexible; **≈keit** *f* suppleness, flexibility.
Geschmeiß [~'ʃmaɪs] *n* (3^2) vermin; *fig. a.* rabble, scum.
Ge'schmiere *n* (7) smearing; (*Gekritzel*) scrawl, scribbling.
ge'schmissen *p.p. v. schmeißen.*
ge'schmolzen *p.p. v. schmelzen.*
Geschnatter [~'ʃnatər] *n* (7) cackling; *fig. a.* chatter(ing).
ge'schnitten *p.p. v. schneiden.*
geschnoben [gə'ʃno:bən] *p.p. v. schnauben.*
geschoben [~'ʃo:bən] *p.p. v. schieben.*
gescholten [~'ʃɔltən] *p.p. v. schelten.*
Geschöpf [~'ʃœpf] *n* (3) creature.
geschoren [~'ʃo:rən] *p.p. v. scheren.*
Geschoß [gə'ʃɔs] *n* (4) projectile; (*Wurf≈*) missile; (*Gewehr≈*, *Pistolen≈*) bullet; (*Granate*) shell; (*Stockwerk*) stor(e)y, floor; **~bahn** *f* trajectory.
ge'schossen *p.p. v. schießen.*
geschraubt [~'ʃraupt] *Stil*: stilted.
Ge'schrei *n* (3) cries *pl.*; shouting; *fig.* noise, fuss; *viel ~ und wenig Wolle* much ado about nothing.
Geschreibsel [gə'ʃraɪpsəl] *n* (7, *o. pl.*) scribble (*a. fig.*).
geschrieben [~'ʃri:bən] *p.p. v. schreiben* 1.
ge'schrie(e)n *p.p. v. schreien.*
ge'schritten *p.p. v. schreiten.*
geschunden [gə'ʃundən] *p.p. v. schinden.*
Geschütz [gə'ʃyts] *n* (3^2) gun; **~feuer** *n* gun-fire, shelling; **~turm** *m* turret.
Geschwader [~'ʃva:dər] *n* (7) ⚓ squadron; ✈ group, *Am.* wing.

Geschwafel F [ʌˈʃvɑːfəl] *n* waffle.
Geschwätz [ʌˈʃvɛts] *n* (3²) idle talk, twaddle, prattle; (*Klatsch*) gossip.
ge'schwätzig talkative, *Am. a.* gabby; **♀keit** *f* talkativeness.
geschweige [gəˈʃvaɪgə]: (ʌ *denn*) not to mention, let alone, much less.
geschwiegen [gəˈʃviːgən] *p.p. v. schweigen* 1.
geschwind [gəˈʃvint] fast, quick, swift.
Ge'schwindigkeit [ʌdiç-] *f* speed, *bsd. phys.* velocity; (*Maß der Fortbewegung*) rate; *mit e-r* ʌ *von* ... *at a* speed (*od.* rate) of ...; **ʌsbegrenzung** *f* speed limit; **ʌsmesser** *mot. m* speedometer, tachometer; **ʌsrekord** *m* speed record; **ʌs-überschreitung** *f* speeding.
Geschwister [gəˈʃvistər] *pl.* (7) brother(s) and sister(s), siblings; **♀lich** brotherly; sisterly; **ʌpaar** *n* brother and sister.
ge'schwollen 1. *p.p. v. schwellen;* **2.** *adj.* swollen; *fig. Sprache:* pompous.
geschwommen [ʌˈʃvɔmən] *p.p. v. schwimmen.*
ge'schworen *p.p. v. schwören;* **♀e** *m* (18) juror; **♀en** *pl.* jury (*a.* **♀engericht** *n*); **♀enliste** *f* panel.
Geschwulst [ʌˈʃvulst] *f* (14¹) swelling; (*Gewächs*) tumo(u)r.
geschwunden [ʌˈʃvundən] *p.p. v. schwinden.*
geschwungen [ʌˈʃvuŋən] *p.p. v. schwingen.*
Geschwür [ʌˈʃvyːr] *n* (3) abscess, boil; (*Magenʌ usw.*) ulcer; *fig.* sore.
ge'sehen *p.p. v. sehen.*
Gesell(e) [ʌˈzel(ə)] *m* (12[13]) companion, fellow; (*Handwerksʌ*) journeyman.
ge'sellen (25) (*a. sich*) (*zu*) associate (with), join (with, to).
Ge'sellen|jahre *n/pl.,* **ʌzeit** *f* journeyman's years *pl.* of service.
ge'sellig gregarious (*a. fig.*); (*umgänglich*) sociable; **ʌes** *Leben usw.* social life *etc.*; *er ist ein* **ʌer** *Mensch* F he is a good mixer; **♀keit** *f* sociability; (*Verkehr*) sociality.
Ge'sellschaft *f* (16) society; (*Zs.sein mit anderen; Besucher, Gäste*) company; *geladene:* party; *allg.* social gathering; **✝** company; *fig. iro.* lot, bunch; *Dame der* ʌ society lady; ʌ *mit beschränkter Haftung* limited

(*liability*) company; *s. geschlossen;* *e-e* ʌ *geben* give (*Am. a.* throw) a party; *j-m* ʌ *leisten* bear (*od.* keep) a p. company; *in guter* (*schlechter*) ʌ *in good* (bad) company; *in j-s* ʌ *in a* p.'s company; **ʌer** *m* (7) companion; **✝** partner; **♀lich** social; **ʌe** *Manieren pl.* company manners.
Ge'sellschafts|-anzug *m* evening dress, dress-suit, ✖ dress uniform; **ʌdame** *f* lady companion; **♀fähig** presentable (*in society*); **ʌkleid** *n* evening gown; **ʌkritik** *f* social criticism; **ʌkritisch** socio-critical; **ʌ-ordnung** *f* social order; **ʌrecht** ⚥ *n* company law; **ʌreise** *f* party tour; **ʌschicht** *f* (social) class; **ʌspiel** *n* parlo(u)r game; **ʌtanz** *m* ballroom dance; **ʌvermögen** **✝** *n* company assets *pl.;* **ʌzimmer** *n* reception room.
Gesenk ⊕ [gəˈzɛnk] *n* (3¹) die; (*Flachhammer*) swage.
gesessen [gəˈzɛsən] *p.p. v. sitzen.*
Gesetz [gəˈzɛts] *n* (3²) *allg.* law; *geschriebenes:* statute; *parl.* Act; **ʌblatt** *n* law gazette; **ʌbuch** *n* (legal) code; statute-book; **ʌ-entwurf** *m* bill; **ʌeskraft** *f* legal force; ʌ *erhalten* pass into law; **ʌeslücke** *f* loophole in the law; **♀gebend** legislative; **ʌgeber** *m* legislator; **ʌgebung** *f* legislation; **♀lich** legal, statutory; (*rechtmäßig*) lawful, legitimate; ʌ *geschützt* patent(ed), registered, proprietary; **ʌlichkeit** *f* lawfulness; legality.
ge'setz|los lawless; anarchic(al); **♀losigkeit** *f* lawlessness; anarchy; **ʌmäßig** *Macht:* legal; *Rechtsmittel:* lawful; *Anspruch:* legitimate; (*satzungsgemäß*) statutory; *fig.* regular; **♀mäßigkeit** *f* legality; lawfulness; legitimacy; *fig.* regularity, law.
ge'setzt (*maßvoll*) sedate, staid; (*zuverlässig*) steady; (*besonnen*) composed, staid; *Sport:* seeded; *von* **ʌem** *Alter* of mature age; ʌ (*den Fall*), *es sei wahr* suppose (*od.* supposing) *it were* (*od.* it to be) true; **♀heit** *f* sedateness; steadiness.
Ge'setz|vorschlag *m* bill; **♀widrig** unlawful, illegal; **ʌwidrigkeit** *f* illegality.
Gesicht [gəˈziçt] *n* (1) (*Sehvermögen*) (eye)sight; (*Angesicht*) face; (*Miene*) countenance; (*Aussehen*) look; (3) (*Erscheinung*) apparition, vision; *zweites* ʌ second sight; *ein*

saures ~ machen look surly; *~er ziehen od. schneiden* make (*od.* pull) faces; *fig. das ~ wahren* save one's face; *j-m wie aus dem ~ geschnitten be* the spit and image of a p.; *j-m et.* (*Unangenehmes*) *ins ~ schleudern* fling a th. into a p.'s face; *zu ~ bekommen* catch sight of.

Ge'sichts|-ausdruck *m* facial expression; **~creme** *f* face-cream; **~farbe** *f* complexion; **~feld** *opt. n* field of vision; **~kreis** *m* horizon; **~massage** *f* facial massage, F facial; **~muskel** *m* facial muscle; **~pakkung** *f* face-pack, F facial; **~punkt** *m* point of view, viewpoint, perspective, angle; **~wasser** *n* face-lotion; **~winkel** *m anat.* facial angle; *opt.* visual angle; **~zug** *m mst pl.* feature(s), lineament(s).

Gesims [gə'zims] *n* (4) ledge; (*Zierleiste*) mo(u)lding; (*Kranz⁀*) cornice.

Gesinde [~'zində] *n* (7) servants *pl.*, domestics *pl.*

Ge'sindel *n* (7) rabble, riff-raff.

gesinnt [gə'zint] *well etc.* disposed; *in Zssgn …*-minded.

Ge'sinnung *f* mind, sentiment(s *pl.*); (*Überzeugung*) conviction; (*Ansichten*) opinions *pl.*; **~sgenosse** *m*, **~sgenossin** *f* like-minded person; **⁀slos** unprincipled; **⁀s-treu** loyal; **⁀stüchtig** sta(u)nch; **~swechsel** *m* change of mind; *bsd. pol.* volteface.

gesitt|et [~'zitət] civilized; (*wohlerzogen*) well-bred, well-mannered; (*höflich*) polite; **⁀ung** *f* civilization.

Gesöff [~'zœf] F *n* (3) (vile) brew.

gesoffen [~'zɔfən] *p.p. v. saufen.*

gesogen [~'zo:gən] *p.p. v. saugen.*

gesonnen [~'zɔnən] **1.** *p.p. v. sinnen;* **2.** *adj.* minded; *~ sein* have a mind (*zu inf.* to).

gesotten [~'zɔtən] *p.p. v. sieden.*

Gespann [~'ʃpan] *n* (3) team, *Am. a.* span; *v. Ochsen:* yoke; *fig.* (*Paar*) pair, couple, duo.

ge'spannt stretched, (*a. fig.*) tense; *Seil:* taut; *fig.* intent; *Aufmerksamkeit:* a. close; *Beziehungen:* strained; *Lage, Nerven:* tense; *~ sein auf* (*acc.*) be anxious (*od.* on edge) for; *~ sein, ob usw.* be anxious to know if *etc.*; *auf ~em Fuße mit* on bad terms with; **⁀heit** *f* tenseness, tension.

Gespenst [gə'ʃpɛnst] *n* (1¹) ghost, spect|re, *Am.* -er (*a. fig.*); **⁀erhaft** ghostly; **~erstunde** *f* ghostly hour; **⁀isch** ghostly; nightmarish (*a. fig.*).

Gespiel|(e) [gə'ʃpi:l(ə)] *m* (13), **~in** *f* (16¹) playmate.

gespien [gə'ʃpi:n] *p.p. v. speien.*

Gespinst [~'ʃpinst] *n* (3²) (*Gewebe*) web; (*Gesponnenes*) spun yarn.

gesponnen [~'ʃpɔnən] *p.p. v. spinnen.*

Gespött [~'ʃpœt] *n* (3) mockery, derision; *sich zum ~ machen* make a fool of o.s.; *zum ~ der Leute werden* become the laughing-stock of people.

Gespräch [~'ʃprɛ:ç] *n* (3) talk (*a. pol.*); conversation, *teleph. a.* call; (*Zwie⁀*) dialog(ue); **⁀ig** talkative, communicative; **~igkeit** *f* talkativeness; **~s-einheit** *teleph. f* unit; **~s-leiter** *m* chairman (of the discussion); **~s-partner** *m* interlocutor; **~srunde** *pol. f* round of talks; **~s-stoff** *m* topic(s *pl.*) of conversation; **⁀sweise** in conversation; (*vom Hörensagen*) by hearsay.

gespreizt [gə'ʃpraitst] *s. spreizen; fig.* affected, stilted; **⁀heit** *f* affectation. [*sprechen.⁀*]

gesprochen [gə'ʃprɔxən] *p.p. v.*

ge'sprossen *p.p. v. sprießen.*

ge'sprungen *p.p. v. springen.*

Gespür [~'ʃpy:r] *n* (3¹, *o. pl.*) nose (*für* for).

Gestade [gə'ʃta:də] *n* (7) shore.

Gestalt [~'ʃtalt] *f* (16) form, figure, shape; (*Wuchs*) stature; (*Weise*) manner, way; *in ~ von* in the form of; (*feste*) *~ annehmen* take shape; **⁀en** (26) form, shape; ⊕ design; (*einrichten, organisieren*) arrange, organize; *schöpferisch:* create, produce; *zu et.:* make, turn into; *sich ~* develop (*zu* into), turn out; **~er** *m* shaper; organizer; creator; ⊕ designer.

Ge'staltung *f* shaping; arrangement, organization; creation; ⊕ design(ing); (*Form*) shape; (*Merkmale*) features *pl.*; (*Zustand*) state.

Gestammel [~'ʃtaməl] *n* (7) stammering.

gestanden [~'ʃtandən] *p.p. v. stehen.*

geständ|ig [~'ʃtɛndiç] confessing; *~ sein* confess; **⁀nis** [~'ʃtɛnt-] *n* (4¹) (*a. ⚖*) confession; admission.

Gestank [gə'ʃtaŋk] *m* (3, *o. pl.*) stench, F stink.

gestatten [gə'ʃtatən] (26) allow, permit.

Geste ['gɛstə] f (15) gesture.
ge'stehen confess.   [cost.⟩
Ge'stehungskosten ✝ pl. prime⟩
Ge'stein n (3) rock, stone.
Gestell [gə'ʃtɛl] n (3) stand, rack;
(*Rahmen, Gerippe*) frame; (*Bock♈*)
trestle, horse.
Ge'stellung ✖ f reporting for service; **∼sbefehl** m calling-up (*Am.*
induction) order.
gestern ['gɛstərn] yesterday; ∼
abend last night.
ge'stiefelt booted, in boots.
gestiegen [∼'ʃti:gən] p.p. v. steigen.
gestielt [∼'ʃti:lt] helved; ♉ stalked.
gestikulieren [gɛstiku'li:rən] gesticulate.
Gestirn [gə'ʃtirn] n (3) star; (*Sternbild*) constellation; ♉t starred, starry.
gestoben [∼'ʃto:bən] p.p. v. stieben.
Gestöber [∼'ʃtø:bər] n (7) drift(ing),
flurry (of snow).
gestochen [∼'ʃtɔxən] p.p. v. stechen.
gestohlen [∼'ʃto:lən] p.p. v. stehlen.
gestorben [∼'ʃtɔrbən] p.p. v. sterben.
ge'stoßen p.p. v. stoßen.
Gestotter [∼'ʃtɔtər] n (7) stuttering.
Gesträuch [∼'ʃtrɔyç] n (3) bushes pl.,
shrubs pl.
gestreckt [∼'ʃtrɛkt] 1. p.p. v. strekken; 2. adj. ✖ Ladung: elongated
(*charge*); s. Galopp.
gestreift [∼'ʃtraift] striped, streaky.
gestreng [gə'ʃtrɛŋ] severe.
ge'strichen p.p. v. streichen.
gestritten [∼'ʃtritən] p.p. v. streiten.
gestrig ['gɛstriç] of yesterday; die ∼e
Zeitung yesterday's paper.
Gestrüpp [gə'ʃtryp] n (3) scrub, undergrowth, *Am.* brush; fig. jungle.
gestunken [∼'ʃtuŋkən] p.p. v. stinken.
Gestüt [gə'ʃty:t] n (3) stud.
Gesuch [∼'zu:x] n (3) application,
request; (*Bittschrift*) petition; ♉t
wanted (a. 🔒); (*begehrt*) (much)
sought-after, in (great) demand;
(*absichtlich*) studied; (*geziert*) affected; (*weit hergeholt*) far-fetched.
Gesudel [∼'zu:dəl] n (7) (*Schrift*)
scribble, scrawl; *paint.* daubing.
gesund [gə'zunt] healthy (a. fig.),
sound (a. Ansicht, Firma usw.), in
good health; (*geistig* ∼) sane; (*heilsam; a. fig.*) wholesome; ∼ und munter fit as a fiddle; ∼ wie ein Fisch im
Wasser sound as a roach; s. Menschenverstand; ♉beter(in f) m

faith-healer; ♉bete'rei f faith-healing; ♉brunnen m mineral spring;
∼en [∼'zundən] (26, sn) recover,
regain one's health.
Gesundheit [gə'zunt-] f (16) health;
fig. a. soundness; (*geistige* ∼) sanity;
(*Heilsamkeit*) wholesomeness; ∼!
beim Niesen: bless you!; s. ausbringen; ♉lich sanitary, hygienic; ∼er
Zustand state of health; ∼ geht es ihm
gut he is in good health; **∼s-amt** n
public health office; **∼s-apostel** m
health fanatic; **∼s-pflege** f (personal)
hygiene; ♉sschädlich unhealthy,
bad for one's health; **∼swesen** n
öffentliches: Public Health; **∼szeugnis** n certificate of health; **∼szustand** m state of health.
Gesundung [gə'zunduŋ] f recovery
(a. fig. ✝ usw.).
gesungen [gə'zuŋən] p.p. v. singen.
gesunken [gə'zuŋkən] p.p. v. sinken.
Getäfel [gə'tɛ:fəl] n (7) wainscot.
getan [gə'ta:n] p.p. v. tun 1.
Getier [∼'ti:r] n (3, o. pl.) animals pl.
Getöse [gə'tø:zə] n (7) noise, din.
ge'tragen 1. p.p. v. tragen; 2. adj.
fig. measured, slow; (*feierlich*)
solemn.
Getrampel [gə'trampəl] n (7)
stamping, trampling.
Getränk [gə'trɛŋk] n (3) drink,
beverage; ♈ potion; s. geistig; **∼e-automat** m drinks machine; **∼e-karte** f list of beverages, oft wine list;
∼esteuer f alcohol tax.
Getrappel [∼'trapəl] n (7) pattering;
(*Pferde♈*) clatter (of hooves).
Getratsche [∼'tra:tʃə] f (7) gossip.
ge'trauen: sich ∼ dare, venture.
Getreide [gə'traidə] n (7) corn, grain;
∼arten f/pl. cereals; **∼bau** m graingrowing; **∼feld** n grain-field; **∼-händler** m grain-merchant; **∼land** n
grain-growing country; **∼pflanze** f
cereal plant; **∼silo** m, **∼speicher** m
granary.
ge'treten p.p. v. treten.
ge'treu, ∼lich faithful, true, loyal.
Getriebe [gə'tri:bə] n (7) ⊕ gearing,
gear unit; (*∼räder*) gears pl.; (*Räderwerk*) wheelwork; fig. wheels pl.;
(*reges Leben*) bustle.
getrieben [∼'tri:bən] p.p. v. treiben.
getroffen [∼'trɔfən] p.p. v. treffen.
getrogen [∼'tro:gən] p.p. v. trügen.
getrost [gə'tro:st] confident.
ge'trunken p.p. v. trinken.

Getto [ˈgɛto] *n* (11) ghetto.
Getue [gəˈtuːə] *n* (7) fuss.
Getümmel [ˈtyməl] *n* (7) turmoil.
Gevatter [ˈfatər] *m* (7 *u.* 13) god-father; ~ *Tod* Goodman Death; ~in *f* (16¹) godmother.
geviert [gəˈfiːrt] 1. squared; 2. ♀ *n* (3) square.
Gewächs [gəˈvɛks] *n* (4) (*Pflanze*) plant, vegetable; (*Kraut*) herb; (*Erzeugnis*) growth (*a.* ✿); (*Weinsorte*) vintage; ~haus *n* greenhouse.
ge'wachsen 1. *p.p. v. wachsen*; 2. *adj.* j-m ~ *sein* be a p.'s equal, be a match for a p.; e-r *Sache* ~ *sein* be equal to a th.; *sich der Lage* ~ *zeigen* rise to the occasion.
gewagt [gəˈvɑːkt] daring (*a. fig.*), risky; *Witz*: risqué (*fr.*), *Am.* off--color.
gewählt [ˈvɛːlt] choice; *Sprache*: selected; *Gesellschaft*: select.
ge'wahr *werden* ~ ~en perceive, notice, become aware of (*od. daß* that); (*entdecken*) discover.
Gewähr [ˈvɛːr] *f* (16) warrant(y), guarantee, security; *ohne* ~ without guarantee, ✝ *a.* without engagement; ~ *bieten für* guarantee; ♀en (25) grant; (*geben*) give, yield, afford; ~ *lassen* let *a p.* have his way; ♀leisten guarantee; ~leistung *f* guaranty.
Ge'wahrsam *m, n* (3) custody.
Ge'währsmann *m* authority; *für Nachrichten*: informant.
Gewalt [ˈvalt] *f* (16) power; *amtliche*: *a.* authority; (*Aufsicht*) control; (*Gewalttätigkeit*) force, violence; *höhere* ~ force majeure (*fr.*), act of God; *s. roh*; j-m ~ *antun* do violence to a p.; ~ *anwenden* resort to force; *sich in der* ~ *haben* have o.s. under control; *in j-s* ~ *sein* be in a p.'s power *od.* grip; *mit* ~ by force; *mit aller* ~ with might and main; *er verlor die* ~ *über den Wagen* his car got out of hand; ~-akt *m* act of violence; ~bremsung *f*: e-e ~ *machen* slam on the brakes; ~enteilung *f* separation of powers; ~herrschaft *f* tyranny; ~herrscher *m* despot; ♀ig powerful, mighty; (*heftig*) vehement; (*ungeheuer*) enormous, F tremendous; ~kur *f* drastic measures *pl.*; ♀los *pol.* non-violent; ~marsch *m* forced march; ~maßnahme *f* violent (*fig.* drastic) measure; ~

mensch *m* brute; ♀sam violent, forcible; ~samkeit *f* violence; ~streich *m* bold stroke; ~tat *f* act of violence; ♀tätig violent; brutal; ~tätigkeit *f* violence; ~verbrechen *n* violent crime; ~verbrecher *m* violent criminal; ~verzichtsabkommen *pol. n* non-aggression treaty.
Gewand [gəˈvant] *n* (1², *poet.* 1³) garment, dress; *wallendes*: robe.
ge'wandt 1. *p.p. v. wenden*; 2. *adj. bsd. körperlich*: dexterous, adroit; *bsd. geistig*: clever; ♀heit *f* adroitness, dexterity; cleverness.
ge'wann *pret. v. gewinnen*.
gewärtig [ˈvɛrtiç] (*gen.*) expectant (of); e-r *Sache* ~ *sein*, *et. od. e-e Sache* ~gen expect, reckon with; *zu* ~ *haben* be in for, face.
Gewäsch [gəˈvɛʃ] *n* (3²) twaddle.
ge'waschen *p.p. v. waschen*.
Gewässer [ˈvɛsər] *n* (7) waters *pl.*; ~verschmutzung *f* pollution of rivers and seas.
Gewebe [gəˈveːbə] *n* (7) (*Stoff*) woven) fabric, textile, web (*a. fig.*); (*feines* ~) tissue (*a. anat. u. fig.*); (*Webart*) texture (*a. fig.*); ~probe ✿ *f* tissue sample; ♀schonend kind to fabrics.
Ge'wehr *n* (3) gun; ⚔ rifle; ~feuer *n* rifle fire; ~kolben *m* (rifle) butt; ~lauf *m* (rifle) barrel; ~riemen *m* rifle sling.
Geweih [ˈvai] *n* (3) horns, antlers *pl.*
Gewerbe [gəˈvɛrbə] *n* (7) trade, business; (*Beruf*) occupation; (*Industrie*) industry; ~ausstellung *f* industrial exhibition; ~betrieb *m* industrial enterprise; ~freiheit *f* freedom of trade; ~ordnung *f* industrial code; ~schein *m* trade licen|ce, *Am.* -se; ~schule *f* vocational school; ~steuer *f* trade tax; ♀tätig industrial; ~tätigkeit *f* industry; ♀treibend engaged in trade; industrial; ~treibende *m* person carrying on a trade or business; ~zweig *m* (branch of) trade or industry.
gewerblich [ˈvɛrp-] industrial.
ge'werbsmäßig professional.
Ge'werkschaft *f* trade union, *Am.* labor union; ~ler *m* (7) trade-unionist; ♀lich *attr.* trade- (*Am.* labor-) union; *adv. sich* ~ *organisieren* unionize; ~ *nicht organisiert* unorganized, not unionized; ~sbeitrag *m*

union dues *pl.*; ～**sbund** *m* federation of trade (*Am.* labor) unions; *Brt. etwa* Trades Union Congress, *Am. etwa* American Federation of Labor and Congress of Industrial Organizations; ～**sfunktionär** *m* trade union (*Am.* labor union) official; ～**s- mitglied** *n* union member; ～**swesen** *n* trade-unionism.

gewesen [gə've:zən] **1.** *p.p. v.* sein; **2.** *adj.* former, ex-...

gewichen [gə'viçən] *p.p. v.* weichen.

Gewicht [gə'viçt] *n* (3) weight (*a. fig.*); ～ haben (*bei*) carry weight (with); ～ legen auf (*acc.*) attach importance to; nicht ins ～ fallen be of no consequence; ～**heben** *n* Sport: weight-lifting; 2**ig** weighty (*a. fig.*); ～**s-abnahme** *f*, ～**sverlust** *m* loss in weight; ✝ shortage; ～**sklasse** *f* weight(-class); ～**szunahme** *f* increase in weight.

Gewieher [～'vi:ər] *n* (7) neighing.

gewiesen [～'vi:zən] *p.p. v.* weisen.

gewillt [～'vilt] willing.

Gewimmel [～'viməl] *n* (7) swarming; (*Menge*) swarm, crowd, throng.

Gewimmer [～'vimər] *n* (7) whimpering.

Gewinde [～'vində] *n* (7) winding; (*Blumen*2) garland, wreath; (*Schrauben*2) thread; ～**bohrer** *m* (screw-) -tap.

Gewinn [～'vin] *m* (3) winning; (*Gewonnenes*) gain, profit; (*Lotterie*- 2) prize; (*Spiel*2) winnings *pl.*; (*Vorteil*) advantage; ～- und Verlust- konto *od.* -rechnung profit-and- -loss account (*Am.* statement); ～ ziehen aus profit by; ～**anteil** *m* dividend; ～**beteiligung** *f* profit- -sharing; 2**bringend** profitable, paying; ～**chancen** *f/pl.* chances of winning; beim Wetten: odds; 2**en** (30) *v/t.* win; gain; Vorteil, Vor- sprung: gain (*a. Zeit*), get; ✗ usw.: win, produce; an Bedeutung usw. ～ gain in ...; j-n für sich ～ win a p. over; *v/i.* gain; er hat sehr gewonnen he has greatly improved; durch et. ～ gain by a th.; 2**end** winning, engaging; ～**er** *m* (7), ～**erin** *f* winner; ～**(n)ummer** *f* winning number; ～**spanne** *f* profit margin; ～**sucht** *f* greed; 2**süchtig** greedy, profit-seeking; ～**ung** *f* winning; production; ～**zahl** *f* winning number.

Gewinsel [gə'vinzəl] *n* (7) whining.

Gewirr [～'vir] *n* (3) confusion, entanglement; (*Labyrinth*) maze.

gewiß [～'vis] certain, sure; ～! certainly!, to be sure!, *Am.* sure!; aber ～! by all means!; ein gewisser Herr N. a certain Mr. N.

Gewissen [gə'visən] *n* (6) conscience; ein reines (*schlechtes*) ～ a good (bad) conscience; s. Wissen, reden; 2**haft** conscientious (in dat. about); ～**haftigkeit** *f* conscientiousness; 2**los** unscrupulous; ～**losigkeit** *f* unscrupulousness.

Ge'wissens|bisse *m/pl.* remorse *sg.*, pangs *pl.* of conscience; ～**frage** *f* matter of conscience; ～**freiheit** *f* freedom of conscience; ～**konflikt** *m*, ～**not** *f* moral dilemma; ～**zwang** *m* moral constraint; ～**zweifel** *m* scruple. [speak, as it were.\] **gewissermaßen** [～'ma:sən] so to/

Ge'wißheit *f* certainty; sich ～ ver- schaffen über (*acc.*) make certain on.

ge'wißlich certainly, surely.

Gewitter [gə'vitər] *n* (7) (thunder-) storm; 2**n** (29) thunder; ～**regen** *m* thunder-shower; ～**wolke** *f* thun- der-cloud.

gewitzt [gə'vitst] taught by experience; (*pfiffig*) shrewd, smart.

gewoben [～'vo:bən] *p.p. v.* weben.

gewogen [～'vo:gən] **1.** *p.p. v.* wie- gen[1], wägen; **2.** *adj.* (*dat.*) well (*od.* kindly) disposed (to[wards]), fa- vo(u)rable (to); 2**heit** *f* goodwill; kindness.

gewöhnen [gə'vø:nən] (25) accus- tom, habituate (an acc. to); an Stra- pazen: inure (to); j-n ～ an (acc.) get a p. used to; sich ～ get accustomed *od.* used (an acc. to).

Gewohnheit [gə'vo:nhaɪt] *f* wont; (*Herkommen*) custom; persönliche: habit; zur ～ werden grow into a habit; 2**smäßig** habitual; ～**s- mensch** *m* creature of habit; ～**s- recht** *n* common law; weitS. estab- lished right; ～**s-trinker** *m* habitual drunkard; ～**sverbrecher** *m* habitual criminal.

gewöhnlich [～'vø:nliç] (*allgemein*) common; (*alltäglich*) ordinary; (*üb- lich*) usual, customary; (*gewohnt*) habitual, wonted; *b.s.* (*gemein*) com- mon, vulgar.

gewohnt [gə'vo:nt] habitual, wont- ed; et. ～ sein be accustomed *od.* used to, be in the habit of ger.

Ge'wöhnung f accosting, habituation (a. 🖋); inurement (alle an acc. to); s. Gewohnheit.

Gewölb|e [gə'vœlbə] n (15) vault; (Bogen) arch; 2t [~pt] vaulted; arched.

Gewölk [~'vœlk] n (3) clouds pl.

gewollt [~'vɔlt] 1. p.p. v. wollen; 2. adj. deliberate, conscious.

gewonnen [~'vɔnən] p.p. v. gewinnen.

geworben [~'vɔrbən] p.p.v. werben.

geworden [~'vɔrdən] p.p.v. werden.

geworfen [~'vɔrfən] p.p. v. werfen.

gewrungen [~'vruŋən] p.p. v. wringen.

Gewühl [~'vy:l] n (3) bustle; (Menge) milling crowd.

gewunden [~'vundən] 1. p.p. v. winden; 2. adj. twisted; bsd. fig. tortuous.

Gewürm [~'vyrm] n (3) worms pl.; (Ungeziefer) vermin.

Gewürz [~'vyrts] n (3²) spice; Kochkunst: condiment, seasoning; **~bord** n, **~ständer** m spice rack; **~gurke** f pickled gherkin; **~händler** m spice dealer; 2ig spicy, aromatic; **~mischung** f mixed herbs pl.; **~nelke** f clove.

gewußt [gə'vust] p.p. v. wissen.

ge'zahnt toothed; ⚕ dentate.

Gezänk [~'tsɛŋk] n (3) squabble.

Ge'zeit f, mst **~en** pl. inv. tide; **~en...** tidal.

Gezeter [gə'tse:tər] n (7) shrill clamo(u)r; hue and cry.

geziehen [gə'tsi:ən] p.p.v. zeihen.

ge'ziemen (25, dat.) (a. sich ~ [für]) become; **~d** becoming, seemly, fit(ting); (schuldig) proper, due.

geziert [~'tsi:rt] affected; (geckenhaft) foppish; (förmlich) prim; 2heit f affectation; primness.

Gezisch [~'tsiʃ] n (3²) hissing; **~el** n (7) whispering.

gezogen [~'tso:gən] p.p. v. ziehen.

Gezücht [~'tsyçt] n (7) brood, breed.

Gezwitscher [~'tsvitʃər] n (7) chirping, twitter.

gezwungen [~'tsvuŋən] 1. p.p. v. zwingen; 2. adj. fig. forced, constrained; (geziert) affected; ~ lachen force a laugh; **~er'maßen** under compulsion.

Gicht [giçt] f (16) gout; 2**brüchig**, 2**isch** gouty; **~knoten** m gout node.

Giebel ['gi:bəl] m (7) gable(-end).

Gier [gi:r] f (16) greed(iness) (nach of); 2**ig** greedy (nach of).

Gießbach ['gi:sbax] m torrent.

gieß|en ['gi:sən] (30) pour; (verschütten) spill; ⊕ cast, found; Pflanze, Garten: water; es gießt it is pouring (with rain); '2er m (7) founder; 2erei [~'raɪ] f (Gießhaus) foundry; Tätigkeit: casting; '2-kanne f watering-can.

Gift [gift] n (3) poison; (bsd. Schlangen2, a. fig.) venom; (Bosheit) malice; F darauf kannst du ~ nehmen! F you bet your life on it!; '**~gas** n poison-gas; '2**haltig** adj. toxic.

'**giftig** (a. fig.) poisonous; (boshaft) malicious, spiteful.

'**Gift|mischer(in** f) m poisoner; '**~mord** m (murder by) poisoning; '**~müll** m toxic waste; '**~pfeil** m poisoned arrow; '**~pflanze** f poisonous plant; '**~pilz** m poisonous mushroom, toadstool; '**~schlange** f venomous (od. poisonous) snake; '**~stoff** m toxic substance; '**~zahn** m venom-tooth.

Gigant [gi'gant] m (12) giant; **~in** f giantess; 2**isch** gigantic.

Gilde ['gildə] f (15) guild, corporation.

Gimpel ['gimpəl] m (7) zo. bullfinch; fig. simpleton, dupe, fool.

ging [giŋ] pret. v. gehen.

Ginster ⚕ ['ginstər] m (7) broom.

Gipfel ['gipfəl] m (7) summit, top; (Spitze) peak; fig. a. acme; '**~konferenz** pol. f summit conference; '2**n** culminate (a. fig.); '**~treffen** n summit meeting.

Gips [gips] m (4) gypsum; ⊕ plaster (of Paris); '**~abdruck** m, '**~abguß** m plaster-cast; '**~bein** F n leg in plaster; '2**en** (27) plaster; '**~er** m (7) plasterer; '**~figur** f plaster figure; '**~verband** m plaster dressing od. cast.

Giraffe [gi'rafə] f (15) giraffe.

Gir|ant ✝ [ʒi'rant] m (12) endorser; **~at** [~'ra:t] m (12) endorsee; 2**ieren** [~'ri:rən] circulate; Wechsel: endorse.

Girlande [gir'landə] f (15) garland.

Giro ✝ ['ʒi:ro] n (11) endorsement; '**~bank** f clearing bank; '**~konto** n giro (transfer) account; '**~verkehr** m giro transfer business; '**~zentrale** f (central) clearing-house.

girren ['girən] (25) coo.
Gis ♪ [gis] *n inv.* G sharp.
Gischt [giʃt] *m* (3²) foam, spray.
Gitarre [gi'tarə] *f* (15) guitar.
Gitter ['gitər] *n* (7) grating; lattice; (*Zaun*) fence; (*Geländer*) railing; *Radio, a. Landkarte:* grid; *fig.* hinter ~n behind bars; '~fenster *n* lattice-window; '**2förmig** latticed; '~netz *n Landkarte:* grid; '~tor *n* trellised gate; '~zaun *m* lattice-work fence.
Glacéhandschuhe [gla'se:hantʃu:ə] *m/pl.* kid gloves (*a. fig.*).
Glanz [glants] *m* (3²) brightness, lust|re, *Am.* -er; brilliancy; (*Herrlichkeit*) splendo(u)r; '~bürste *f* polishing brush.
glänzen ['glɛntsən] (27) glitter, shine (*a. fig. vor dat.* with); *s. Abwesenheit;* '~d bright, brilliant; (*a. glatt*) glossy; (*poliert*) polished; *fig.* splendid, brilliant.
'**Glanz|leder** *n* patent leather; '~leinen *n* glazed linen; '~leistung *f* brilliant performance *od.* feat; '~lichter *n/pl.* high lights; '**2los** lustreless; '~papier *n* glazed paper; '~periode *f* brightest period, glorious days *pl.*; '~politur *f* gloss polish; '~punkt *m* highlight; (*Höhepunkt*) acme; '~stück *n* gem; *weitS.* brilliant feat; '**2voll** splendid, magnificent; '~zeit *f* heyday.
Glas [glɑ:s] *n* (2¹; *als Maß im pl. inv.*) glass; '~auge *n* glass eye; '~bläser *m* glass-blower.
Glaser ['glɑ:zər] *m* (7) glazier; ~ei [~'rai] *f* glazier's workshop.
gläsern ['glɛːzərn] of glass; *fig.* glassy.
Glas|faser ['glɑ:s-] *f* fibreglass, *Am.* fiberglass; '~glocke *f* bell-glass, (*glass*) shade; '~hütte *f* glass-works.
glasieren [gla'zi:rən] glaze; *Kochkunst:* ice, frost.
glasig ['glɑ:ziç] glassy (*a. fig.*), vitreous.
Glas|kasten ['glɑ:s-] *m* glass case; '~malerei *f* glass painting; (*Kunstwerk*) stained glass window; '~perle *f* glass bead; '~platte *f* glass top; '~scheibe *f* pane of glass; '~scherben *f/pl.* (pieces *pl.* of) broken glass *sg.*; '~schneider *m* glass cutter; '~schrank *m* glass cupboard; '~splitter *m* splinter of glass.
Glasur [gla'zu:r] *f* (16) glaze; (*Schmelz*) enamel; *auf Backwerk:*

icing, frosting.
Glas|veranda ['glɑ:s-] *f* glass veranda(h); '**2weise** in glasses, by glassfuls; '~wolle *f* glass wool.
glatt [glat] **1.** *adj.* (18²) *allg.* smooth (*a. fig. gewandt*); (*eben*) even; (*poliert*) polished, glossy; (*gefällig*) smooth; *Absage, Lüge usw.*: flat, blunt, downright; (*schlüpfrig*) slippery; **2.** *adv.* smoothly; (*ganz*) entirely, clean (*through, etc.*); (*ohne weiteres*) without ado; ~ anliegen fit close; ~ rasiert clean-shaven; *et.* ~ ableugnen deny a th. flatly; ~ heraussagen tell frankly *od.* bluntly.
Glätte ['glɛtə] *f* (15) smoothness; (*Politur*) polish; (*Schlüpfrigkeit*) slipperiness.
'**Glatt-eis** *n* black ice; *fig. j-n aufs* ~ führen trip a p. up.
glätten ['glɛtən] (26) smooth; (*polieren*) polish.
'**glatt|streichen** smooth down; '~züngig** ['~tsyniç] smooth-tongued.
Glatz|e ['glatsə] *f* (15) bald head; '**2köpfig** ['~kœpfiç] bald(-headed).
Glaube ['glaubə] (13¹) *m,* '~n¹ (6) *m* (*a. eccl.*) faith, belief (*an acc.* in); ~n schenken (*dat.*) give credence to, believe; *auf Treu und* ~n on trust; *in gutem* ~n in good faith; '**2n²** (26) *v/t.* believe; (*meinen, annehmen*) *a.* think, suppose, *Am. a.* guess; *es ist nicht zu* ~ it is past belief; *v/i.* believe (*j-m* a p.; *an acc.* in); (*Vertrauen haben zu*) put faith in; F *dran* ~ müssen have to die (*od. Sache:* go).
'**Glaubens|bekenntnis** *n* creed (*a. fig.*), confession of faith; '~freiheit** *f* religious liberty; '~genosse** *m* fellow-believer; '~lehre** *f,* '~satz** *m* dogma; '~zeuge** *m* martyr.
glaubhaft ['glauphaft] credible; (*verbürgt*) authentic; *ть* ~ machen substantiate; '**2igkeit** *f* credibility; authenticity.
gläubig ['glɔybiç] believing, faithful; **2e** ['~bigə] *m, f* (18) believer; '**2er** ♦ *m* (7), '**2erin** *f* (16¹) creditor.
glaub|lich ['glaup-] credible, believable; '~würdig** credible, reliable; *P.: a.* trustworthy; '**2würdigkeit** *f* credibility.
gleich [glaiç] **1.** *adj.* equal (*an dat.* in); (*ebenso beschaffen*) like; (*derselbe*) the same; (*eben, auf* ~*er Höhe*) even, level; (*~bleibend*) constant; (*einheitlich*) uniform; *in* ~*er Weise*

likewise; *zu* ~*er Zeit* at the same time; *es ist (mir) ganz* ~ it is all the same (to me); *s. Münze*; **2.** *adv.* alike, equally; *(so~)* at once, immediately; *es ist* ~ *acht Uhr* it is close on eight o'clock; *s.* ⏀e; '~**alt-rig** (of) the same age; '~**artig** of the same kind; homogeneous; *(ähnlich)* like, similar; '⏀**artigkeit** *f* homogeneousness; '~**bedeutend** synonymous *(mit* with); equivalent (to), tantamount (to); '⏀**behandlung** *f* equal treatment; '~**berechtigt** having equal rights; '⏀**berechtigung** *f* equality, equal rights *pl.*; '~**bleibend** constant, steady, stable; '⏀e[1] *m* peer; '⏀e[2] *n the* same thing; *(j-m)* ~*s mit* ~*m vergelten* give (a p.) tit for tat.

'**gleichen** (30, *dat.*) equal; *(ähnlich sein)* resemble, be *(od.* look) like.

gleicher | **ge'stalt**, ~'**maßen**, ~'**weise** in like manner, likewise.

'**gleich** | **falls** also, likewise; *danke*, ~! thanks, the same to you!; ~**förmig** ['~fœrmiç] uniform; *(regelmäßig)* regular; *(eintönig)* monotonous; '⏀-**förmigkeit** *f* uniformity; '~**gesinnt** like-minded; '~**gestellt** on a par *(dat.* with); ~**gestimmt** ['~gə-ʃtimt] ♪ (tuned) in unison; *fig.* congenial; '⏀**gewicht** *n* (*a. fig.*) balance, equilibrium, equipoise; *politisches* ~ balance of power; *seelisches* ~ mental balance; *aus dem* ~ *bringen* unbalance, *fig. a.* upset; *ins* ~ *bringen*, *im* ~ *erhalten* balance; *das* ~ *verlieren* lose one's balance; '~**gültig** indifferent *(gegen* to); unconcerned; ~, *ob usw.* no matter if *etc.*; *es ist mir* ~ I don't care; '⏀**gültigkeit** *f* indifference; '⏀**heit** *f* equality; *völlige*: identity; *(Ähnlichkeit)* likeness; *(Einheitlichkeit)* uniformity; '⏀**klang** *m* unison, harmony; '~**kommen** *(dat.)* equal, come up to, match; '~**laufend** parallel; *(zeitlich)* synchronous; '⏀-**laut** *m* consonance; '~**lautend** consonant; *Inhalt:* of the same tenor, identical; ~*e Abschrift* duplicate, true copy; '~**machen** make equal *(dat.* to); '⏀**mache'rei** egalitarianism, levelling; '⏀**maß** *n* symmetry, proportion; '~**mäßig** equal, symmetrical; *(ausgeglichen)* even; *s. gleichförmig*; *(stetig)* steady; '⏀**mut** *m*, ⏀-**mütigkeit** ['~my:tiçkaıt] *f* equanimity, calmness; '~**mütig** calm, imper-

turbable; ~**namig** ['~na:miç] of the same name; ⏀ homonymous; ⅍ correspondent; '⏀**nis** *n* (4[1]) *(Bild)* image; *rhet.* simile; *biblisch:* parable; ~**rangig** ['~raŋiç] of the same rank; equal; '⏀**richter** ⚡ *m* rectifier; '~**sam** as it were; '~**schalten** coordinate, bring into line; ~**schenk(e)lig** ['~ʃeŋk(ə)liç] isosceles; '⏀**schritt** ⚔ *m* marching in step, *Am.* cadence; '~**seitig** equilateral; '~**setzen** *(dat.)* equate with; '~**stellen** *(dat.)* equate (with), equalize (to, with); *P.:* put on a par (with), *staatsbürgerlich:* assimilate in status (to); '⏀**stellung** *f* equalization; '⏀**strom** ⚡ *m* direct current; '~**tun**: *es j-m* ~ equal *(od.* match) a p.; '⏀**ung** *f* equation; '~**viel**: ~, *ob usw.* no matter if *etc.*; '~**wertig** equivalent *(mit* to), of the same value; '~**wohl** yet, nevertheless, however, all the same; '~**zeitig** simultaneous; *(zeitgenössisch)* contemporary; *adv.* at the same time; '⏀**zeitigkeit** *f* simultaneousness; '~**ziehen** *Sport: (einholen)* catch up *(mit* with); *(ausgleichen)* equalize.

Gleis [glaıs] *n* (4) *s. Geleise*; '~-**anschluß** *m* siding; '~**körper** *m* railway embankment.

Gleisner ['glaısnər] *m* (7) hypocrite; '⏀**isch** hypocritical.

Gleit | **bahn** ['glaıt-] *f* slide; shoot, chute; ⊕ guide(way); '~**boot** *n* gliding boat, glider; '⏀**en** (30, sn) glide, slide; '~**fläche** *f* gliding plane *od.* surface; '~**flug** *m* gliding flight, glide, volplane; '~**flugzeug** *n* glider; '~**klausel** † *f* escalator clause; '~-**mittel** *n* lubricant; '~**rolle** *f* trolley; '~**zeit** *f* flexible working hours *pl.*; '~**zeitkarte** *f* timecard.

Gletscher ['glɛtʃər] *m* (7) glacier; '⏀-**artig** glacial; '~**spalte** *f* crevasse.

glich [gliç] *pret. v. gleichen.*

Glied [gli:t] *n* (1) limb; *(a. Mit⏀)* member; *(Ketten⏀, Binde⏀)* link; ⅍, *Logik:* term; ⚔ rank.

'**glieder** | **lahm** lame in the limbs; ⚕ paralytic; '~**n** (29) joint, articulate; *(anordnen)* arrange; *(einrichten)* organize; *in Teile:* (sub)divide *(in acc.* into); *(gruppieren)* group; '⏀-**puppe** *f* jointed doll; *(Marionette)* puppet; *für Maler:* lay figure; *für Kleider:* mannequin; '⏀**reißen** *n*, '⏀**schmerz** *m* pain(s *pl.*) in the

limbs, rheumatism; '**⍵ung** f (*An-ordnung*) arrangement; (*Aufbau*) structure; (*Einteilung*) division; formation.
Glied|maßen ['gliːtmɑːsən] pl. limbs, extremities; '**⍵staat** m member state.
glimmen ['glimən] (30) *Feuer*: smo(u)lder (*a. fig.*); (*glühen*) glow; (*schimmern*) glimmer, gleam; ⍵de *Asche* embers pl.
'**Glimmer** min. m (7) mica.
'**Glimmstengel** F m fag.
glimpflich ['glimpfliç] lenient, mild; ⍵ *behandeln* deal gently with; ⍵ *davonkommen* get off lightly.
glitsch|en F ['glitʃən] (27, sn) slide; '**⍵ig** slippery.
glitt [glit] pret. v. *gleiten*.
glitzern ['glitsərn] (29) glitter.
global [gloˈbɑːl] global.
Globus ['gloːbus] m (16² u. 4¹) globe.
Glöckchen ['glœkçən] n, '**Glöcklein** n (6) small bell.
Glocke ['glɔkə] f (15) bell; (*Glas⍵*) shade; (*Uhr*) clock; *fig. et. an die große* ⍵ *hängen* noise a th. abroad, make a fuss about a th.
'**Glocken|blume** f bell-flower; ⍵förmig ['⍵fœrmiç] bell-shaped; '**⍵geläut** n bell-ringing; *abgestimmtes*: chime; '**⍵gießer** m bell-founder; '**⍵rock** m wide flared skirt; '**⍵schlag** m stroke (of the clock); '**⍵spiel** n chime(s pl.); '**⍵stuhl** m belfry; '**⍵turm** m bell-tower, belfry.
Glöckner ['glœknər] m (7) bell-ringer, sexton.
glomm [glɔm] pret. v. *glimmen*.
Glorie ['gloːrjə] f (15) glory; '**⍵n-schein** m *fig.* halo, aureola.
glorreich ['gloːraiç] glorious.
Gloss|ar [glɔˈsɑːr] n (3) glossary; '**⍵e** f (15) gloss, comment; ⍵**ieren** [⍵ˈsiːrən] gloss, comment (up)on.
'**Glotz-auge** n goggle-eye, *Am. a.* pop-eye.
Glotze F ['glɔtsə] f (15) (*Fernsehgerät*) goggle-box, *Am.* tube; '⍵**n** (27) goggle, stare.
Glück [glyk] n (3) fortune; (*Glücksfall*) good luck; (*Gefühl von* ⍵) happiness; (*Wohlstand*) prosperity; *auf gut* ⍵ at haphazard; *zu meinem* ⍵ luckily for me; ⍵ *haben* be lucky, succeed; *das* ⍵ *haben zu inf.* have the good fortune to *inf.*; ⍵ *wünschen* congratulate (*j-m zu et.* a p. [up]on

a th.); *zum Geburtstag:* wish many happy returns (of the day); *da können Sie von* ⍵ *sagen* you may call yourself lucky; *viel* ⍵! good luck!; *zum* ⍵ fortunately.
'**glückbringend** lucky.
Glucke ['glukə] f (15) clucking hen; '⍵**n** (25) cluck.
'**glücken** (25, sn) succeed; *mir glückt et.* I succeed in a th.
'**gluckern** (29) *wie Wasser*: gurgle.
'**glücklich** happy; (*von Glück begünstigt*) lucky, fortunate; (*günstig*) a. favo(u)rable, auspicious; '**⍵er'weise** fortunately, luckily; *s. preisen.*
'**Glücksbringer(in** f) m mascot; (*Gegenstand*) lucky charm.
'**glück'selig** blissful, very happy; ⍵**keit** f blissfulness.
glucksen ['gluksən] (27) gurgle.
'**Glücks|fall** m lucky chance, stroke of luck; *unverhoffter*: windfall; '**⍵göttin** f Fortune; '**⍵kind** n lucky person; '**⍵klee** m four-leaf clover; '**⍵pfennig** m lucky penny; '**⍵pilz** F m lucky dog; '**⍵ritter** m soldier of fortune; '**⍵sache** f (matter of) luck; '**⍵spiel** n game of chance; *fig.* gamble; '**⍵stern** m lucky star; '**⍵strähne** f streak of good luck; '**⍵tag** m lucky (*od.* happy) day.
'**glück|strahlend** radiant with happiness; '⍵**s-treffer** m *Sport*: fluke, lucky shot; *fig.* stroke of (good) luck, (*Geldgewinn*) windfall; '**⍵verheißend** auspicious; '⍵**wunsch** m congratulation, good wishes pl.; *zum Geburtstag: s. Glück; pl. zu Neujahr usw.*: (season's) greetings pl.; '⍵**wunsch** congratulatory; '⍵**wunschkarte** f greetings card; '⍵**wunschtelegramm** n greetings telegram.
Glüh|birne ⚡ ['glyː-] f (incandescent) bulb; '⍵**en** v/t. u. v/i. (25) glow; v/t. ⊕ anneal; '⍵**end** glowing (*a. fig.*); *Eisen: a.* red-hot; *Kohle*: live; *fig.* ardent, fervid; '**⍵faden** m filament; '⍵'**heiß** red-hot; '**⍵lampe** f, '**⍵licht** n incandescent lamp; '**⍵strumpf** m incandescent mantle; '**⍵wein** m mulled claret; '**⍵wurm** m glow-worm.
Glut [gluːt] f (16) heat; *konkret*: glowing fire; live coal; *fig.* glow, ardo(u)r.   [in(e).}
Glyzerin [glytsəˈriːn] n (3) glycer-}
Gnade ['gnɑːdə] f (15) grace;

(*Gunst*) favo(u)r; (*Barmherzigkeit*) mercy; (*Milde*) clemency; ohne ~ without mercy; *von Gottes* ~n by the grace of God; *Euer* ~n Your Grace; *auf* ~ *oder Ungnade* at discretion; *s. walten.*

'**Gnaden**|-**akt** *m* act of grace; '~**bild** *n* miraculous image; '~**brot** *n* bread of charity; '~**frist** *f* reprieve, respite, grace; '~**gesuch** *n* petition for mercy; '~**schuß** *m*, '~**stoß** *m* coup de grâce (*fr.*); '~**weg** *m*: *auf dem* ~ by way of grace.

gnädig ['gnɛdiç] gracious; (*freundlich*) kind; (*barmherzig*) merciful; ~**e Frau** madam.

Gnom [gnoːm] *m* (12) gnome, goblin; '**2enhaft** gnomish, gnomelike.

Gobelin [gobə'lɛ̃] *m* (11) Gobelin (tapestry).

Gockel F ['gɔkəl] *m* (7) cock.

Gold [gɔlt] *n* (3) gold; '~**ader** *f* vein of gold; '~**barren** *m* gold ingot, bullion; '~**barsch** *m* ruff; ♥ redfish; '~**bergwerk** *n* gold-mine.

golden ['~dən] (of) gold; *fig.* golden; (*vergoldet*) gilt; ~**e Hochzeit** golden wedding; ♣ ~**er Schnitt** medial section.

'**gold**|**farben** gold-colo(u)red, golden; '**2fasan** *m* golden pheasant; '2~**fisch** *m* goldfish; '~**gelb** golden; '2~**gewicht** *n* troy (weight); '**2gräber** *m* (7) gold-digger; '**2grube** *f*, **2mine** *f* gold-mine (*a. fig.*); ~**ig** ['~diç] sweet, lovely, *Am. a.* cute; '**2kind** *n* darling; '**2klumpen** *m* lump of gold, nugget; '**2lack** *m* gold-varnish; ♀ wallflower; '**2medaille** *f* gold medal; '**2münze** *f* gold coin; '**2regen** ♀ *m* laburnum; '**2reserve** *f* gold reserve; '**2schmied** *m* goldsmith; '**2schnitt** *m* gilt edge(s *pl.*); *mit* ~ *Buch:* gilt--edged; '**2stück** *n* gold coin; '**2waage** *f* gold-balance; *fig. jedes Wort auf die* ~ *legen* weigh every word; '**2währung** *f* gold standard; '**2waren** *f*/*pl.* gold articles.

Golf¹ *geogr.* [gɔlf] *m* (3) gulf.

Golf² *n*, '~**spiel** *n* golf; '~**platz** *m* golf--course, (golf-)links *pl.*; '~**schläger** *m* golf-club; '~**spieler**(**in** *f*) *m* golfer.

'**Golfstrom** *geogr. m* Gulf Stream.

Gondel ['gɔndəl] *f* (15) gondola; *am Ballon, Luftschiff: mst* car; '~**bahn** *f* cable-car; '**2n** F bowl (*od.* tool) along.

gönnen ['gœnən] (25): *j-m et.* ~ allow (*od.* grant *od.* not to grudge)

a p. a th.; *j-m et. nicht* ~ grudge a p. a th.; *wir* ~ *es ihm von Herzen* we wish him every joy with it; *sich et.* ~ treat o.s. to (*od.* allow o.s.) a th.; *sich et. nicht* ~ grudge (*od.* not to allow) o.s. a th.

'**Gönner** *m* (7) patron, *Am. a.* sponsor; '**2haft** patronizing; '~**in** *f* patroness; '~**miene** *f* patronizing air; '~**schaft** *f* patronage.

gor [goːr] *pret. v. gären.*

Gör F [gøːr] *n* (5), '**Göre** *contp. f* (15) brat.

Gorilla [go'rila] *m* (11) gorilla.

goß [gɔs] *pret. v. gießen.*

Gosse ['gɔsə] *f* (15) gutter.

Got|**e** ['goːtə] *m* (13) Goth; '**2isch** Gothic.

Gott [gɔt] *m* (1¹ *u.* ²) God; (*Gottheit*) god, deity; ~ *sei Dank!* thank God!; *leider* ~*es* unfortunately; *s. bewahren, behüten;* '2~**ähnlich** godlike; '**2begnadet** god-gifted, inspired.

Götter|**bild** ['gœtərbilt] *n* image of a god, idol; '~**dämmerung** *f* twilight of the gods.

'**Götter**|**speise** *f fig.* ambrosia; '~**trank** *m fig.* nectar.

'**Gottes**|**acker** *m* churchyard; '~**dienst** *m* divine service; '~**furcht** *f* fear of God; **2fürchtig** ['~fyrçtiç] godfearing; '~**haus** *n* house of God; '~**lästerer** *m* blasphemer; '**2läster-lich** blasphemous; F unholy; '~**lästerung** *f* blasphemy; '~**leugner** *m* atheist; '~**lohn** *m* God's blessing; '~**urteil** *n* ordeal.

'**gott**|**gefällig** pleasing to God; '~**gleich** godlike; '**2heit** *f* deity, divinity, god(dess *f*); (*Gottnatur*) godhead.

Göttin ['gœtin] *f* goddess.

göttlich divine, godlike; F *fig.* divine; *Spaß:* capital.

gott|'**lob!** thank God!; '~**los** godless; impious; F *fig.* godless, unholy; '2~**losigkeit** *f* ungodliness; **2seibei-uns** [~zaɪ'baɪʔuns] *m inv.* Old Nick, *the* Devil; '~**s-erbärmlich** pitiful; '~**vergessen** *s. gottlos;* '~**verlassen** god-forsaken; '**2vertrauen** *n* trust in God; '~**voll** F divine; *Spaß:* capital, very funny.

Götze ['gœtsə] *m* (13) idol.

'**Götzen**|**bild** *n* idol; '~**diener**(**in** *f*) *m* idolater; '~**dienst** *m* idolatry; '~**tempel** *m* temple of an idol.

Gouvern|**ante** [guvɛr'nantə] *f* (15)

governess; ~eur [~'nøːr] m (3¹) governor.

Grab [graːp] n (1²) grave, rhet. (u. ~mal) tomb; das Heilige ~ the Holy Sepulchre; j-n zu ~e geleiten attend a p.'s funeral; verschwiegen wie das ~ (as) secret as the grave.

Graben ['graːbən] **1.** m (6¹) ditch; bsd. ✕ trench; **2.** ♀ (30) dig; Tier: burrow; '~krieg m trench war(fare).

Gräber ['grɛːbər] m (7) digger.

'**Grabes|ruhe** f, ~'stille f deathly silence; '~stimme f sepulchral voice.

Grab|geläute ['graːp-] f (death-)knell (a. fig.); '~gesang m funeral song; '~gewölbe f n vault, tomb; '~kammer f burial chamber; '~legung f interment, burial; '~mal n tomb, sepulch|re, Am. -er; '~rede f funeral speech; '~schrift f epitaph; '~stätte f, '~stelle f burial-place, tomb; '~stein m tombstone, gravestone.

Grad [graːt] m (3, als Maß im pl. inv.) allg., a. univ. u. fig. degree; (Rang) grade; in (od. bis zu) e-m gewissen ~ to a certain degree, up to a point; '~bogen ♀ m protractor; '~einteilung f graduation.

gradieren [~'diːrən] graduate.

grad|linig ['graːt-] s. geradlinig; '♀messer m graduator; fig. indicator, barometer; '♀netz n Landkarte: grid. [nichtenglischer: count.)

Graf [graːf] m (12) englischer: earl;)

Gräf|in ['grɛfin] f countess; '♀lich of an earl od. a count(ess).

'**Grafschaft** f county.

Gral [graːl] m (3, o. pl.): der Heilige ~ the Holy Grail.

Gram [graːm] **1.** m (3) grief, sorrow; **2.** j-m ♀ sein bear a p. ill-will od. a grudge.

grämen ['grɛːmən] (25) (a. sich) grieve; sich zu Tode ~ die with grief.

'**grämlich** morose, peevish.

Gramm [gram] n (3, im pl. nach Zahlen inv.) gramme, Am. gram.

Grammatik [gra'matik] f (16) grammar; ♀alisch [~'kaːliʃ], gram-'matisch grammatical; '~er m grammarian.

Grammophon [gramo'foːn] n (3¹) gramophone, Am. phonograph; ~platte f (gramophone) disk od. record.

'**gramvoll** sorrowful, grief-stricken.

Gran [graːn] n (3¹, im pl. nach Zahlen inv.) grain.

Granat min. [gra'naːt] m garnet; ~apfel m pomegranate; ~e f (15) (Geschütz♀) shell; (Gewehr♀, Hand♀) grenade; ~splitter m shell-splinter; ~trichter m shell-crater; ~werfer m mortar.

Grande ['grandə] m (13) grandee.

grandios [gran'djoːs] adj. grand(iose), overwhelming.

Granit [gra'niːt] m (3) granite.

Granne ♀['granə] f (15) awn, beard.

Graph|ik ['graːfik] f (16, o. pl.) graphic arts pl.; (Darstellung) s. graphisch; '~iker m (7) commercial artist; '♀isch graphic(ally adv.); ~e Darstellung graph(ic representation), diagram, chart.

Graphit [gra'fiːt] m (3) black lead, graphite, plumbago.

Grapholog|e [grafo'loːgə] m (13), ~in f (16¹) graphologist; ~ie [~loˈgiː] f graphology.

Gras [graːs] n (2¹) grass; fig. F das ~ wachsen hören hear the grass grow; fig. F ins ~ beißen bite the dust; '♀-bewachsen grass-grown.

grasen ['graːzən] (27) graze.

'**gras|fressend** graminivorous; '~grün grass-green; '♀halm m blade of grass; '♀hüpfer m (7) grasshopper; ~ig ['~ziç] grassy; '♀land n grassland; '♀mücke zo. f warbler; '♀narbe f turf, sod; '♀platz m grassplot, lawn, green.

grassieren [gra'siːrən] rage, be rampant, spread.

gräßlich ['grɛsliç] horrible, ghastly; (scheußlich) hideous, atrocious; '♀-keit f horribleness; atrocity.

Grat [graːt] m (3) edge; Berg: ridge.

Gräte ['grɛːtə] f (15) (fish-)bone.

Gratifikation [gratifika'tsjoːn] f (16) gratuity, bonus, extra pay.

gratis ['graːtis] gratis, free (of charge); '♀-exemplar n presentation copy; '♀probe ✝ f free sample.

Grätsche ['grɛːtʃə] f (15) Turnen: straddling vault; '♀n (27) straddle.

Gratul|ant [gratu'lant] m (12) congratulator; ~ation [~la'tsjoːn] f congratulation; ♀ieren [~'liːrən] congratulate (j-m zu et. a p. on a th.); j-m zum Geburtstag ~ wish a p. many happy returns (of the day); (ich) gratuliere! (my) congratulations!   [walk.)

'**Gratwanderung** fig. f tightrope)

grau [grau] grey, *Am.* gray; *Vorzeit*: remote; *fig.* grey, bleak; *der* ~*e Alltag* the drab monotony of everyday life; *s. Haar*; '~**blau** greyish blue; '⚲**brot** *n* rye bread; '~**en**¹ (25) *Tag*: dawn.

'**grauen**² **1.** *mir graut vor (dat.)* I have a horror of, I shudder at; **2.** ♀ *n* (6) horror (*vor dat.* of); '~**haft**, '~**voll** horrible, dreadful.

'**grauhaarig** grey- (*Am.* gray-) haired.

graulen ['graulən] (25): *sich* ~ (*vor*) be afraid (of); *s. grauen*².

gräulich ['grɔʏliç] greyish, *Am.* grayish.

graumeliert ['~meˈliːrt] tinged with grey (*Am.* gray), grey-flecked.

Graupe ['graupə] *f* (15) (peeled) barley; '⚲**lig** sleety; '~**ln** 1. *f/pl.* sleet *sg.*; **2.** ♀ (29) sleet; '~**lwetter** *n* sleety weather.

'**Graupensuppe** *f* barley broth.

Graus [graus] *m* (4) horror.

'**grausam** cruel; '⚲**keit** *f* cruelty.

'**Grau|schimmel** *m* grey (*Am.* gray) horse; '~**schleier** *fig. m* greyness, *Am.* grayness.

graus|en ['grauzən] **1.** (27) *s. grauen*² 1.; **2.** ♀ *n* (6) horror (*vor dat.* of); '~**ig** horrible.

'**Grau|tier** *n* ass, donkey; '~**zone** *f* grey (*Am.* gray) area.

Graveur [graˈvøːr] *m* (3¹) engraver.

Gravier|anstalt [graˈviːr-] *f* engraving establishment; ⚲**en** engrave; ♀**end** serious; ~**ung** *f* engraving.

Gravitations|gesetz [gravitaˈtsjoːns-] *n* law of gravitation; ~**kraft** *f* gravitational force.

gravitätisch [~viˈtɛːtiʃ] grave, solemn; *Gang*: stately.

Grazie ['graːtsjə] *f* (15) grace; *die drei* ~*n* the three Graces.

graziös [graˈtsjøːs] graceful.

Greif [graif] *m* (3 *u.* 12) griffin.

'**Greif|arm** ⊕ *m* claw arm; '~**bagger** *m* grab dredger; '⚲**bar** seizable; ✝ available, on hand; (*offenbar*) tangible, palpable, obvious; *fig. nicht* ~ impalpable; *in* ~*er Nähe* near at hand; '⚲**en** (30) *v/t.* seize; ♪ *Saite*: hold down, *Note*: strike; *fig. man kann es mit Händen* ~ it meets the eye; *v/i. an den Hut* ~ touch; *fig. ans Herz* ~ touch deeply; ~ *in* (*acc.*) put one's hand(s) in(to); ~ *nach* reach for, grasp at, *hastig*: snatch at; *fig. um sich* ~ gain ground, spread; *zu e-m Mittel*

~ resort to; *zur Feder* ~ take up pen; *zu den Waffen* ~ take up arms; *s.* Arm; '~**er** *m* (7) ⊕ claw; *Kran*: grab; *P.*: (*Spürer*) bloodhound; '~**vogel** *m* bird of prey; '~**zange** *f* tongs *pl.*

greinen ['grainən] (25) whine.

Greis [grais] *m* (4) old man.

Greisen|-alter ['~zən-] *n* old age, senility; '⚲**haft** senile; '~**haftigkeit** *f* senility.

'**Greisin** *f* (16¹) old woman.

grell [grɛl] *Farbe, Licht*: glaring (*a. fig.*); *Farbe*: *a.* loud, flashy; *Ton*: shrill.

Gremium ['greːmjum] *n* (9) body, group.

Grenadier [grenaˈdiːr] *m* (3¹) infantryman, rifleman; *Traditionsbezeichnung*: grenadier; ~... infantry ...

'**Grenz|-abfertigung** *f* border clearance; '~**bereich** *m* border area; *fig.* borderline; '~**bewohner** *m* borderer, frontiersman.

Grenze ['grɛntsə] *f* (15) limit; (*Scheidelinie*) boundary; (*Ländergrenze*) frontier, border(s *pl.*); (*äußerstes Ende*) extreme point; *fig. e-e* ~ *ziehen* draw the line; *in* ~*en* within (certain) limits.

'**grenzen** (27) border (*an acc.* on; *a. fig.*); '~**los** boundless; *adv.* ~ *dumm* infernally stupid; '⚲**losigkeit** *f* boundlessness.

'**Grenz|fall** *m* borderline case; ~**gänger** ['~gɛŋər] *m* (7) (illegal) border crosser; (*Arbeiter*) frontier commuter; '~**konflikt** *m* border dispute; '~**kontrolle** *f* border control; '~**land** *n* borderland; '~**linie** *f* boundary-line; demarcation line; *fig.* borderline; '~**pfahl** *m* boundary-post; '~**posten** *m* border guard; '~**schutz** *m* frontier defen|ce, *Am.* -se; *Truppe*: border police; '~**sperre** *f* closing of the frontier, frontier ban; '~**stadt** *f* frontier town; '~**stein** *m* boundary-stone; '~**übergang** *m* border crossing(-point); '~**verkehr** *m* border traffic; '~**wert** *m* limiting value; '~**zwischenfall** *m* border incident.

Greuel ['grɔʏəl] *m* (7) horror, abomination; *s. Greueltat*; *er (es) ist mir ein* ~ I loathe him (it); '~**märchen** *n* atrocity tale; '~**propaganda** *f* atrocity propaganda; '~**tat** *f* atrocity.

'**greulich** horrid, dreadful.

Grieben ['gri:bən] *f/pl.* (15) greaves *pl.*

Griebs [gri:ps] *m* (4) core.

Griech|e ['gri:çə] *m* (13), '**~in** *f* (16[1]) Greek; '**♀isch** Greek; △ *paint.* Grecian; **~-römischer Ringkampf** Gr(a)eco-Roman wrestling.

Gries|gram ['gri:sgrɑ:m] *m* (3) grumbler, crab, *Am.* F grouch; **♀grämig** ['~gre:miç] morose, grumpy, *Am.* F grouchy.

Grieß [gri:s] *m* (3[2]) gravel (*a.* ♂[x]), grit; (*Weizen*♀) semolina; '**~brei** *m* semolina pudding; '**~kloß** *m* semolina dumpling.

Griff [grif] **1.** *m* (3) grip, grasp, hold; ♪ touch; ⊕ grip; knob; (*Hebel*) lever; *Schirm, Messer usw.*: handle; *Schwert*: hilt; *v. Stoff*: feel, handle; *Ringen*: hold; ✗ **~e** üben *od.* F *kloppen* do rifle drill; *fig. ein guter ~ a hit; fig. et. im ~ haben* have the knack of a th.; **2.** ♀ *pret. v.* greifen; '**♀bereit** handy; '**~brett** *n e-r Geige usw.*: finger-board; '**~el** *m* (7) slate pencil; ♀ pistil; '**♀ig** affording a firm hold; *Tuch*: of good feel; *Werkzeug*: wieldy; *mot.* non-skid.

Grill [gril] *m* (11) *elektrischer etc.*: grill; (*offener Rost*) grill, barbecue.

Grille ['grilə] *f* (15) *zo.* cricket; *fig.* whim, fancy.

grill|en ['grilən] (25) *elektrisch etc.*: grill; *auf dem Rost*: grill, barbecue; '**♀party** *f* barbecue; '**♀restaurant** *n* grillroom.

Grimasse [gri'masə] *f* (15) grimace; **~n schneiden** pull faces, grimace.

Grimm [grim] *m* (3) rage, wrath; '**~en** ♂[x] *n* (6) gripes *pl.*, colic; '**♀ig** grim, fierce (*beide a. fig.*); furious.

Grind [grint] *m* (3) scab, scurf; ♀ig ['~diç] scabbed, scabby, scurfy.

grinsen ['grinzən] (27), ♀ *n* (6) grin (*über acc.* at); *höhnisch*: sneer (at).

Grippe ['gripə] *f* (15) influenza, F flu; grippe.

Grips [grips] F *m* (3) brains *pl.*

grob [grɔp] (18[2]) coarse; (*unhöflich*) rude; (*rauh*; *roh*; *ungeschliffen*; *ungefähr*) rough; *Fehler, Irrtum, Fahrlässigkeit usw.*: gross (*od.* bad) mistake; **~es Geschütz** heavy guns *pl.*; **~ gegen j-n sein** be hard on a p.; *aus dem Gröbsten heraus sein* have broken the back of it.

'**Grob|blech** *n* (heavy) plate; '**~**

einstellung ⊕ *f* coarse adjustment; '**~heit** *f* coarseness; grossness; roughness; rudeness; **~en** *pl.* rude things.

Grobian ['gro:bjɑ:n] *m* (3) rude fellow, boor, ruffian.

grobkörnig ['grɔp-] coarse-grained.

gröblich ['grø:pliç] ~ *beleidigen* insult grossly.

grob|maschig ['grɔpmaʃiç] wide-meshed; '**♀schmied** *m* blacksmith; '**♀schnitt** *m* (*Tabak*) coarse cut.

grölen F ['grø:lən] (25) bawl.

Groll [grɔl] *m* (3) grudge, ill-will, ranco(u)r; '**♀en** (25) *Donner*: rumble; *j-m ~* have a grudge (*od.* spite) against a p.

Gros[1] [grɔs] *n* (4[1], *pl. nach Zahlen inv.*) (*12 Dutzend*) gross.

Gros[2] [gro:] *n inv.* main body.

Groschen ['grɔʃən] *m etwa*: penny; F *der ~ ist gefallen!* the penny has dropped!; '**~automat** *m* (penny-in-the-)slot machine; '**~roman** *m* penny dreadful, *Am.* dime novel.

groß [gro:s] (18[2]) great, large; (*umfangreich*; *bedeutend*) big; *von Wuchs*: tall; (*ungeheuer*) huge; *fig.* great, (*~artig*) grand; *Hitze*: intense; *Kälte*: severe; *Verlust*: heavy; *die* ♀*en pl.* the grown-ups; *das* **~e** *Publikum* the general public; *im* **~en** ✝ wholesale, *allg.* on a large scale; *im* **~en** *und ganzen* on the whole, by and large; **~er** *Buchstabe* capital (letter); **~e** *Ferien* long vacation; *das* ♀*e Los* the jackpot; *der* ♀*e Ozean* the Pacific (Ocean); *Rechtschreibung*: **~** *schreiben* capitalize; *ich bin kein* **~er** *Tänzer* I am not much of a dancer; *~. klein, Terz, Tier*; '**♀-abnehmer** *m* bulk purchaser; '**♀-aktionär** ✝ *m* principal shareholder; '**~-angelegt** large-scale; '**♀-angriff** *m* large-scale attack; '**~-artig** grand, great; splendid, marvellous; enormous; '**♀-aufnahme** *f Film*: close-up; '**♀-auftrag** *m* bulk (*od.* substantial) order; '**♀-betrieb** *m* large-scale enterprise; '**♀-brand** *m s. Großfeuer*; '**♀-buchstabe** *m* capital (letter); '**♀druck-ausgabe** *f* (*Buch*) large-print edition.

Größe ['grø:sə] *f* (15) (*Umfang*) size, largeness; *des Wuchses*: tallness, height; ✝ *e-s Kleides usw.*: size; (*Menge*; *bsd.* ♂[x]) quantity; *fig.*

greatness; *a. ast.* magnitude; (*Person*) celebrity, notability; *thea., Sport*: star.

'**Groß|-einkauf** ✝ *m* bulk purchase; '**~-einsatz** *m* large-scale operation; '**~-eltern** *pl.* grand-parents; '**~-enkel** *m* great-grandson; '**~-enkelin** *f* great-granddaughter.

'**Größen-ordnung** *f* order.

'**großenteils** to a large (*od.* great) extent, largely.

'**Größen|verhältnisse** *n/pl.* proportions, dimensions; '**~wahn** *m* megalomania; '**≈wahnsinnig** megalomaniac.

'**Groß|fahndung** *f* dragnet operation; '**~familie** *f* extended (*od.* kinship) family; '**~feuer** *n* large fire, conflagration; '**~format** *n* large size; '**~fürst** *m* grand duke; '**~fürstentum** *n* grand duchy; '**~grundbesitz** *m* large landed property; '**~handel** *m* wholesale trade; '**~handels-preis** *m* wholesale price; '**~händler** *m* wholesale dealer; '**~handlung** *f* wholesale firm; '**≈herzig** magnanimous; '**~herzigkeit** *f* magnanimity; '**~herzog** *m* grand duke; '**~herzogin** *f* grand duchess; '**≈herzoglich** grand-ducal; '**~herzogtum** *n* grand duchy; '**~hirn** *n* cerebrum; '**~-industrie** *f* big industry; '**~industrielle** *m* (7) big industrialist.

Grossist [grɔ'sist] *m* (12) wholesaler.

'**groß|jährig** of age; **~ werden** come of age; '**≈jährigkeit** *f* full age, majority; '**≈kampfschiff** *n* capital ship; '**≈kapitalist** *m* big capitalist; '**≈kaufmann** *m* wholesale merchant; '**≈kraftwerk** ⚡ *n* super power station; '**≈kreuz** *n* Grand Cross; '**≈küche** *f* canteen kitchen; '**≈macht** *f* great power; '**~mächtig** mighty; '**≈mannssucht** *f* megalomania; '**≈maul** *n* bigmouth; '**~mäulig** [-mɔylic] big-mouthed; '**~mut** *f* magnanimity, generosity; '**~mütig** [-mytic] generous, magnanimous; '**≈mutter** *f* grandmother; '**≈neffe** *m* grand-nephew; '**≈nichte** *f* grand-niece; '**≈-onkel** *m* great-uncle, grand-uncle; '**≈raumbüro** *n* open-plan office; '**≈rechner** *m* *Computer:* mainframe; **≈'reinemachen** *n* (6) wholesale house-cleaning; '**≈schreibung** *f* capitalization; '**≈sprecher** *m* boaster; **≈sprecherei** *f* big talk; '**~sprecherisch** boastful; '**~spurig** arrogant; '**≈stadt** *f* large city, metropolis; '**≈städter(in** *f*) *m* inhabitant of a large city, metropolitan; '**~städtisch** (characteristic) of a large city, metropolitan; '**≈tante** *f* great-aunt, grand-aunt; '**≈tat** *f* great deed *od.* exploit, feat.

größtenteils ['grøːstəntaɪls] for the most part, mostly.

'**Groß|tuer** *m* (7) boaster, show-off; '**≈tuerisch** boastful; '**≈tun** talk big; *sich mit et. ~* brag of; '**~unternehmen** *n* large-scale enterprise; '**~unternehmer** *m* big industrialist, entrepreneur (*fr.*); '**~vater** *m* grandfather; '**~vaterstuhl** *m* arm-chair; '**~verdiener** *m* (7) big earner; '**~vertrieb** *m* distribution in bulk; '**~wildjagd** *f* big game hunt(ing); '**≈ziehen** bring up; **≈zügig** ['~tsyːgiç] liberal, generous (*beide a. freigebig*), broad-minded (*Plan usw.*: large-scale; '**~zügigkeit** *f* broad-mindedness; liberality; generosity.

grotesk [gro'tesk] grotesque.

Grotte ['grɔtə] *f* (15) grotto.

grub [gruːp] *pret. v.* graben 2.

Grübchen ['gryːpçən] *n* (6) dimple.

Grube ['gruːbə] *f* (15) pit; ⚒ *a.* mine.

Grübelei [gryːbə'laɪ] *f* (16) brooding, pondering, rumination.

grübeln ['gryːbəln] (29) brood, ponder, pore (*über dat.* over).

'**Gruben|-arbeiter** *m* miner; '**~brand** *m* pit fire; '**~gas** *n* fire-damp; '**~holz** ⚒ *n* pit-props *pl.*; '**~lampe** *f* miner's lamp; '**~-unglück** *n* mine disaster.

Grübler ['gryːblər] *m* (7), '**~in** *f* (16¹) ponderer.

Gruft [gruft] *f* (14¹) tomb, vault.

Grum(me)t ['grum(ə)t] *n* (3) aftermath, *Am.* rowen.

grün [gryːn] 1. green (*a. fig. unreif, unerfahren*); *Hering:* green, fresh; *~er Junge* greenhorn; *~es Licht Verkehr u. fig.*: green light; *j-m ~es Licht geben* give s.o. the green light (*od.* the go-ahead); *e-e Entscheidung etc. vom ~en Tisch an* armchair decision *etc.*; *j-n ~ und blau schlagen* beat a p. black and blue; *fig. auf e-n ~en Zweig kommen* get somewhere, make it; 2. ⚥ *n* (3¹) green; *der Natur:* verdure; *dasselbe in ~* practically the same thing.

Grund [grunt] *m* (3³) ground; (*Erdboden*) soil; *~ und Boden* s.

Grundbesitz; (*Meeresboden usw.*) bottom; (*Tal*) valley; (*Fundament*) foundation; (*Kaffeesatz*) grounds *pl.*; (*Ursache*) cause; (*Beweg♀*) motive; (*Vernunft♀*) reason; (*Beweis♀*) argument; *auf ~ von* on grounds of, on the strength of, based on, (*wegen*) because of, due to; *aus gesundheitlichen Gründen* for reasons of health; *aus diesem ~e* for this reason; *im ~e* (*genommen*) at (the) bottom, fundamentally; strictly speaking; *jeden* (*keinen*) *~ haben zu inf.* have every (no) reason to *inf.*; *e-r Sache auf den ~ gehen od.* kommen get to the bottom of a th.; *von ~ aus* thoroughly, fundamentally, radically; '*~ausbildung* ✗ *f* basic training; '*~bau m* foundation; '*~bedeutung f* original meaning; '*~bedingung f* basic condition; '*~bedürfnis n* basic requirement (*od.* need); '*~begriff m* basic idea; *~e pl.* fundamentals *pl.*; '*~besitz m* landed property, real estate; '*~besitzer m* landed proprietor; '*~bestandteil m* basic component; '*~buch n* land (title and charges) register; '*~buch-amt n* land registry; '♀-ehrlich thoroughly honest; '*~-eigentum n s. Grundbesitz*; '*~-eis n* ground-ice.

gründen ['gryndən] (26) found, establish; *fig.* base, ground (*auf acc.* on); ✝ promote, float; *sich ~ auf* (*acc.*) be based (*od.* founded) on.

'**Gründer** *m* (7), '*~in f* (16¹) founder; ✝ *a.* promoter.

'**grund**|'**falsch** absolutely wrong; '♀**farbe** *f* ground-colo(u)r; *phys.* primary colo(u)r; '♀**fehler** *m* basic fault; fundamental mistake; '♀**fläche** *f* base; ⊕ floor-space; '♀**gebühr** *f* basic rate *od.* fee; '♀**gedanke** *m* fundamental (*od.* root) idea; '♀**gehalt** *n* basic salary; '♀**gesetz** *pol. n* basic (constitutional) law; '♀**herr** *m* landlord.

grund|**ieren** *paint.* [~'di:rən] ground, prime; ♀**ierfarbe** *f* primer; ♀**ierung** *f* priming; *Kosmetik:* foundation.

'**Grund**|**kapital** *n* (original) stock; '*~kenntnisse f/pl.* basic knowledge *sg.*; '*~lage f* basis, foundation; '*~lagenforschung f* pure research; '♀**legend** fundamental, basic(ally *adv.*); '*~legung f* laying the foundation.

gründlich ['gryntliç] thorough; (*zuverlässig*) solid; *Wissen:* profound; (*durchgreifend*) radical; '♀**keit** *f* thoroughness.

'**Grund**|**linie** *f* base-line; '*~lohn m* basic wage(s *pl.*); '♀**los** bottomless; *fig.* groundless; (*unbegründet*) unfounded; *adv.* for no reason (at all); '*~losigkeit f* groundlessness; '*~mauer f* foundation(-wall); '*~nahrungsmittel n* staple food.

Grün|'**donners-tag** *m* (3) Maundy Thursday.

'**Grund**|**pfeiler** *m* bottom pillar; *weitS.* main support; '*~platte* ⊕ *f* base-plate; '*~prinzip n* basic principle; '*~rechte pol. n/pl.* basic rights; '*~regel f* fundamental rule; '*~riß m* ⚠ ground-plan; (*Lehrbuch*) compendium; *fig.* outline(s *pl.*); '*~satz m* principle; *unbestreitbarer:* axiom; (*Lebensregel*) maxim; '♀**sätzlich** fundamental; *adv.* on principle; '*~schuld f* mortgage; '*~schule f* primary (*od.* elementary) school; '*~schullehrer(in f) m* primary (*Am.* elementary) school teacher; '*~stein* ⚠ *m* foundation-stone; *fig.* den *~ legen zu* lay the foundations of; '*~steinlegung f* laying (of) the foundation-stone; '*~steuer f* land tax; '*~stock m* basis; '*~stoff m* element; (*Rohstoff*) raw material; *fig.* basic material; '*~stoff-industrie f* basic industry; '*~strich m* down-stroke; '*~stück n* piece of land; (landed *od.* real) estate; (*Parzelle*) plot, *Am.* lot; (*Haus u. Zubehör*) the premises *pl.*; '*~stücksmakler m* real estate agent, *Am.* realtor; '*~stücks-preis m* land price; '*~text m* original text; '*~ton ♩ m* keynote; '*~übel n* basic evil; '*~umsatz m* ✝ basic turnover; *physiol.* basal metabolic rate.

Gründung ['grynduŋ] *f* foundation, establishment, creation; '*~smitglied n* founding member.

'**grund**|**ver**|'**kehrt** utterly wrong; '*~ver*'**schieden** entirely different; '♀**wahrheit** *f* fundamental truth; '♀**wasser** *n* (under)ground water; '♀**wasserspiegel** *m* ground water level; '♀**wehrdienst** *m* basic military service; '♀**wortschatz** *m* basic vocabulary; '♀**zahl** *f* cardinal number; '♀**zins** *m* ground-rent; '♀**zug** *m* characteristic (feature); '♀**züge** *m/pl.* fundamentals *pl.*

Grüne ['gryːnə] *m*, *f* (13) *mst. pl. the Greens pl.*

grünen ['gryːnən] (25) be (*od.* grow) green; *fig.* flourish.

'**Grün|fläche** *f* green space; '**~futter** *n* green food *od.* fodder; '**~gürtel** *m* green belt; '**~kohl** *m* (curly) kale.

'**grünlich** greenish.

'**Grün|schnabel** *fig. m* greenhorn, whippersnapper; '**~span** *m* verdigris; '**~specht** *m* green woodpecker.

grunzen ['gruntsən] (27) grunt.

'**Grünzeug** *n* greens *pl.*; greenstuff.

Gruppe ['grupə] *f* (15) group (*a.* ✞); ✗ section, *Am.* squad; ✈ wing, *Am.* group; '**~n-arbeit** *f* teamwork; *Schule*: working in teams (*od.* groups); '**~nbild** *phot. n* group photograph; '**~ndynamik** *f* group dynamics *sg.*; '**~nreise** *f* organized (group) tour; '**~nsex** *m* group sex; '**~ntherapie** *f* group therapy; '**~nweise** in groups; ✗ in sections, *etc.*

grup'pier|en group; **2ung** *f* grouping.

Grus [gruːs] *m* (4, *o. pl.*) (coal-)slack.

'**Grusel|film** ['gruːzəl-] *m* horror film; '**~geschichte** *f* horror story; '**2ig** creepy; '**2n 1.** (29) *mir* (*od. mich*) *hat's gegruselt* it made my flesh creep; **2.** *~ n* (6) *the creeps pl.*

Gruß [gruːs] (3² *u.* ³) (*Grüßen*) salutation; *vertraulicher*: greeting; *bsd.* ✗, ⚓ salute; *mst pl.* *Grüße im Brief*: regards, *förmlich*: respects, compliments *pl.*

grüßen ['gryːsən] (27) greet, *bsd.* ✗ salute; (*anrufen*) hail; (*j-n*) *~ lassen* send one's compliments *od.* regards (to a p.); *~ Sie ihn von mir* remember me to him.

Grütz|beutel 𝕤ˢ ['gryts-] *m* wen; '**~e** *f* (15) (*bsd. Hafer*2) grits *pl.*, groats *pl.*; F (*Verstand*) gumption.

gucken ['gukən] (25) look, peep.

'**Guckloch** *n* peep-hole.

Guerillakrieg [ge'riljakriːk] *m* guerrilla war(fare).

Gulasch ['gulaʃ] *n* (3) goulash; '**~suppe** *f* goulash soup.

Gulden ['guldən] *m* (6) florin.

gültig ['gyltiç] valid; (*in Kraft*) effective, in force; (*gesetzlich*) legal; *Münze*: current, good; *Fahrkarte*: available; *für ~ erklären* validate; '**2keit** *f* validity; currency; availability; *Vertrag*: *mst* term.

Gummi ['gumi] *m*, *n* (11) (*Kleb*2) gum; (*Kautschuk*) (India) rubber; '**~arabikum** [~a'rɑːbikum] *n* gum Arabic; '**2-artig** gummy; '**~ball** *m* rubber ball; '**~band** *n* elastic; '**~bärchen** ['~bɛːrçən] *n* (6) jelly bear; '**~baum** *m* gum (*od.* rubber) tree; (*Zimmerpflanze*) rubber plant; '**~boot** *n* rubber dinghy; '**~druck** *typ. m* offset.

gum'mieren gum; ⊕ rubberize.

'**Gummi|handschuh** *m* rubber glove; '**~knüppel** *m* (rubber) truncheon; *Am.* club, F billy; '**~mantel** *m* mackintosh, plastic mac; '**~paragraph** *m* elastic clause; '**~reifen** *m* (rubber) tyre, *Am.* tire; '**~ring** *m* rubber band; '**~schlauch** *m für Wasser*: rubber hose; *mot. usw.*: rubber tube; '**~schnur** *f* elastic; '**~schuhe** *m/pl.* galoshes, rubber shoes, *Am.* rubbers; '**~schwamm** *m* rubber sponge; '**~sohle** *f* rubber sole; '**~stempel** *m* rubber stamp; '**~strumpf** *m* elastic stocking; '**~zelle** *f* padded cell; '**~zug** *m* elastic.

Gunst [gunst] *f* (16) favo(u)r (*a.* '**~bezeigung** *f*); *s. erweisen*; *in ~ stehen bei j-m* be in a p.'s favo(u)r (*od.* good graces); *zu m-n ~en* (*a.* ✞) to my favo(u)r (*od.* credit); *s. zugunsten.*

günstig ['gynstiç] favo(u)rable (*für* to); *~e Gelegenheit* opportunity; *im ~sten Fall* at best; ✝ *zu ~en Bedingungen* on easy terms; *~es Angebot* bargain.

Günstling ['~liŋ] *m* (3¹) favo(u)rite; *contp.* minion; '**~swirtschaft** *f* favo(u)ritism.

Gurgel ['gurgəl] *f* (15) throat; (*Schlund*) gullet; '**2n** *v/i.* (29) *u.* *v/t.* gargle; '**~wasser** *n* gargle.

Gurke ['gurkə] *f* (15) cucumber; *s. sauer*; '**~nhobel** *m* cucumber slicer; '**~nsalat** *m* cucumber salad.

gurren ['gurən] coo.

Gurt [gurt] *m* (3) belt (*a.* ✗ *Patronen*2); ⚓ (*u. Sattel*2) girth; (*Trage*2) strap; ⊕ web(bing); *mot.* seat-belt; '**~band** *n* webbing.

Gürtel ['gyrtəl] *m* (7) belt, girdle (*beide a. fig.*); *geogr.* zone; '**~linie** *f* waistline; *a. fig. unter der* (*od. die*) *~* below the belt; '**~reifen** *m* radial (-ply) tyre, *Am.* tire; '**~rose** 𝕤ˢ *f* shingles *pl.*; '**~schnalle** *f* belt-buckle; '**~tier** *n* armadillo.

'**gurten** *mot.* put one's seat-belt on.
'**gürten** (26) gird.

Guß [gus] *m* (4²) (*Gießen*) founding, casting, (*Gegossenes*) cast(ing); *typ.* fount, *Am.* font; (*Regen*) downpour, shower (of rain); *aus einem* ~ of a piece; *s.* Zucker♀; '~**beton** *m* cast concrete; '~**eisen** *n* cast iron; '♀-**eisern** cast-iron; '~**form** *f* casting mo(u)ld; '~**stahl** *m* cast steel; '~**waren** *f/pl.* castings *pl.*

gut¹ [guːt] good; *adv.* well; ~*es* Wetter fine weather; ~*er Dinge od.* ~*en Mutes sein* be of good cheer; *ein* ~*gehendes Geschäft* a flourishing business; *es ist* ~*!, schon* ~*!* never mind!: all right!; F *mach's* ~*!* (*als Gruß*) cheerio!; *es* ~ *haben* be well off; *für* ~ *finden* think proper; *j-m* ~ *sein* love (*od.* like) a p.; *laß es* ~ *sein!* never mind!; *Sie haben* ~ *lachen* it is very well for you to laugh; *im* ~*en* in a friendly manner; ~*e Miene zum bösen Spiel machen* grin and bear it; *so* ~ *wie fertig usw.* as good as finished, *etc.*; *s. gehen, kurz, lassen, tun; s. a. zugute.*

Gut² *n* (1²) (*Besitz*) goods *pl.*, possession, property; (*Land*) (landed) estate; Güter ✝ *n/pl.* goods *pl.*, merchandise, 🚲 goods.

'**Gut**|-**achten** *n* (6) (*engS.* expert) opinion; *schriftlich*: report; '~-**achter** *m* (7) expert; '♀-**artig** good-natured; 🌶 benign; '~-**artigkeit** *f* good nature; 🌶 benignity; '♀-**aussehend** good-looking, attractive; ♀-**be'tucht** well-heeled; '♀**bürgerlich**: ~*e Küche* good home cooking; '~**dünken** *n* (6) opinion, discretion; *nach* ~ at pleasure, at (one's own) discretion.

'**Gute** *n* (18) *the* good; ~*s tun* do good; *des* ~*n zuviel tun* overdo it; *alles* ~*!* all the best!

Güte ['gyːtə] *f* (15) goodness, kindness; ✝ class, quality; (*Reinheit*) purity; *in* ~ amicably; *haben Sie die* ~, *zu* be so kind as; *durch die* ~ *des Herrn S.* by favo(u)r (*od.* by the kind offices) of Mr. S.; F *meine* ~*!* good gracious!; '~**klasse** *f* grade, quality.

Gute'nacht|**geschichte** *f* bedtime story; ~**kuß** *m* goodnight kiss.

'**Güter**|-**abfertigung** *f*, '~-**annahme** *f* goods office; '~**bahnhof** *m* goods station, *Am.* freight depot *od.*

yard; '~**gemeinschaft** *f* community of property; '~**kraftverkehr** *m* road haulage; '~**schuppen** *m* goods (*Am.* freight) shed; '~**trennung** *f* separation of property; '~**verkehr** *m* goods (*Am.* freight) traffic; '~-**wagen** *m* wag(g)on, *Am.* freight car; *offener*: (goods) truck; *geschlossener*: (goods) van, *Am.* boxcar; '~**zug** *m* goods (*Am.* freight) train.

'**Gütesiegel** *n* seal of quality.

gut|**gebaut** ['~gəbaut] well-built; *P.*: with a good figure; '~**gehend** flourishing, prospering; ~**gelaunt** ['~gəlaunt] in a good mood; ~**gemeint** ['~gəmaint] well-meant; ~**gesinnt** ['~gəzint] well-disposed (*dat.* to); '~**gläubig** acting (*od.* done) in good faith, bona fide; *s. leichtgläubig*; '♀~**haben** *n* credit (balance); (*Konto*) account; '♀**habenzins** *m* interest; '~**heißen** approve (of), F okay; '~**herzig** kind(-hearted).

gütig ['gyːtiç] good, kind.

'**gütlich** amicable, friendly; ~*er Vergleich* amicable settlement; *sich* ~ *tun an* (*dat.*) do o.s. well on.

'**gut**|**machen**: *wieder*~ make good, make up for, compensate, repair; ~**mütig** ['~myːtiç] good-natured; '♀**mütigkeit** *f* good nature; '~**sagen** *für* be good for.

'**Gutsbesitzer(in** *f*) *m* landowner, landed proprietor (*f* proprietress).

'**Gut**|**schein** *m* credit note *od.* slip; *j-m* '♀**schreiben** credit a p. with *an amount*; place to a p.'s credit; '~**schrift** ✝ *f* credit; '~**schrifts**-**anzeige** *f* credit note.

'**Guts**|**haus** *n* farm-house; '~**herr(in** *f*) *m* lord (*f* lady) of the manor; '~**hof** *m* farmyard; '~**verwalter** *m* (landowner's) steward.

Guttapercha [guta'pɛrça] *f* (11²) gutta-percha.

'**Gut**|**tat** *f* good action, kindness; '♀**tun** (*j-m*) do *a p.* good.

'**gutwillig** voluntary, willing; '♀**keit** *f* willingness.

Gymnasialbildung [gymna'zjɑːl-] *f* secondary (*engS.* classical) education.

Gymnasiast [~'zjast] *m* (12), ~**in** *f* (16¹) grammar-school boy (*f* girl).

Gymnasium [~'nɑːzjum] *n* (9) (*humanistisches* classical) secondary school.

Gymnast|**ik** [~'nastik] *f* (16)

gymnastics *pl. u. sg.*, physical exercises *pl.*; **~ik-anzug** *m* leotard; **²isch** gymnastic.

Gynäkolo|ge [gynɛ:ko'lo:gə] *m* (13) gyn(a)ecologist; **~gie** [~lo'gi:] *f* gyn(a)ecology.

H

H [hɑ:], **h** *n inv.* H, h; ♪ B.
ha! [hɑ:] ha!, ah!
Haar [hɑ:r] *n* (3) hair; *am Tuch:* nap, pile; *die ~e verlieren* lose one's hair; *sich die ~e machen* do (*od.* dress, *Am.* fix) one's hair; *sich die ~e (aus)raufen* tear one's hair; *sich die ~e schneiden lassen* have one's hair cut; *sich das ~ waschen* shampoo one's hair; *fig. aufs ~* to a hair; *um ein ~* within a hair's breadth; *fig.* F *er fand ein ~ in der Suppe* he found a fly in the ointment; *um kein ~ besser* not a bit better; *~e lassen müssen* be fleeced; *sich in den ~en liegen* be at loggerheads; *laß dir darüber keine grauen ~e wachsen* don't give yourself any grey hair; *j-m kein ~ krümmen* not to touch a hair of a p.'s head; *fig. an den ~en herbeiziehen* drag in (by the head and shoulders); *fig. an den ~en herbeigezogen* far-fetched; *kein gutes ~ an j-m lassen* pull a p. to pieces; *~e auf den Zähnen haben* be a Tartar.
'Haar... *mst* hair-...; **'~-ansatz** *m* hair-line; **'~-ausfall** *m* loss of hair; **'~boden** *anat. m* hair bed; **'~bürste** *f* hairbrush; **'~büschel** *n* tuft of hair; **'²en** (25) lose (*od.* shed) one's hair; **'~-entferner** *m* (7) depilatory; **'~ersatz** *m* hair-piece, wig; **'~esbreite** *fig. f: um ~* within a hair's breadth; **'~färbemittel** *n* hair-dye; **'²fein** (as) fine as a hair; *fig.* subtle; **'~festiger** *m* (7) setting lotion; **'~gefäß** *n* capillary vessel; **'²ge'nau** to a T, precise (-ly *adv.*); **'²ig** hairy; *in Zssgn* ...-haired; F (*schwierig*) tough; **'²klein** *adv.* to the last detail; **'~klemme** *f* hair clip, *Am.* bobby pin; **'~künstler** *m* hair stylist; **'²los** hairless; **'~nadel** *f* hairpin; **'~nadelkurve** *mot. f* hairpin bend; **'~netz** *n* hair-net; **'~pflege** *f* hair care; **'²scharf** razor-sharp; *fig.* by a hair's breadth; **'~schnitt** *m*

haircut; **'~schwund** *m* loss of hair; **'~sieb** *n* hair sieve; **~spalterei** ['~-[paltə'raɪ] *f* (16) hair-splitting; ~ *treiben* split hairs; **'²sträubend** hair-raising; shocking; **'~strich** *m* hair-stroke; **'~teil** *n* hair-piece; **'~tracht** *f* coiffure (*fr.*), hair-style, F hairdo; **'~transplantation** *f*, **'~verpflanzung** *f* hair transplant; **'~trockner** *m* (7) hair-dryer; **'~wäsche** *f*, **'~waschmittel** *n* shampoo; **'~wasser** *n* hair lotion; **'~wickel** *m* (7) curler; **'~wuchs** *m* growth of hair; (*Kopf voller Haar*) head of hair; **'~wuchsmittel** *n* hair-restorer; **'~zange** *f* tweezers *pl.*
Habe ['hɑ:bə] *f* (15) property, (personal) belongings *pl.*, goods *pl.*; *bewegliche ~* movables *pl.*; *unbewegliche ~* immovables *pl.*, real estate; *Hab und Gut* goods and chattels *pl.*
haben ['hɑ:bən] **1.** (30) have; *s. gern, gut, recht, unrecht; ~ wollen* want; *sich ~* make a fuss; *etwas (nichts) auf sich ~* be of (no) consequence; *unter sich ~ fig.* be in control of; (*befehligen*) command; *Ware: zu ~* obtainable; *ich hab's!* I have got it; *was hast du?* what is the matter with you?; *da ~ wir's!* there we are!; **2.** ♀ ✝ *n* (6) credit; *s.* Soll.
'Habenichts *m* (4 *od. inv.*) beggar, have-not.
'Haben|saldo *m* credit balance; **'~seite** *f* credit side; **'~zinsen** *m/pl.* credit interest.
Habicht ['hɑ:bɪçt] *m* (3) hawk.
Habili|tation *univ.* [habilita'tsjo:n] *f* (16) habilitation; *sich* **²'tieren** habilitate.
Habgier ['hɑ:p-] *f* greed, avarice; **'²ig** greedy, avaricious.
'habhaft: *~ werden* (*gen.*) get hold of.
Hab|seligkeit ['hɑ:p-] *f* property; *~en pl.* things, belongings *pl.*; **'~-**

sucht f, '♀**süchtig** s. Habgier, habgierig.

Hachse ['haksə] f (15) knuckle.

'**Hack|beil** n chopper, cleaver; '∼**block** m chopping-block; '∼**braten** m mince loaf; '∼**brett** n chopping--board; ♪ dulcimer.

Hacke ['hakə] f **1.** (15) hoe, mattock; **2.** = '∼n¹ m (6) heel.

hacken² ['hakən] (25) hack, chop; (klein∼) mince; (picken) pick.

'**Hack|fleisch** n minced (Am. ground) meat; '∼**frucht** ✔ f root vegetable; '∼**ordnung** zo. f pecking order (a. fig.).

Häcksel ['hɛksəl] m, n (7) chaff; '∼**maschine** f chaff-cutter.

Hader ['haːdər] m (7) discord, strife, quarrel; '♀**n** (29) quarrel.

Hafen ['haːfən] m (7¹) port; bsd. als Schutz: harbo(u)r; '∼**anlagen** ⚓ f/pl. docks pl.; '∼**arbeiter** m docker, Am. longshoreman; '∼**damm** m jetty, pier; '∼**meister** m harbo(u)r-master; '∼**sperre** f blockade (of a harbo[u]r), embargo; (Vorrichtung) barrage; '∼**stadt** f seaport; '∼**viertel** n dock area, waterfront.

Hafer ['haːfər] m (7) oats pl.; in Zssgn mst oat-...; '∼**brei** m (oatmeal) porridge; '∼**flocken** f/pl. rolled oats; '∼**grütze** f grits, (oat) groats pl.; '∼**schleim** m gruel.

Haff [haf] n (3) haff, bay.

Haft [haft] f (16) custody, detention; (Verhaftung) arrest; '♀**bar** responsible, answerable, liable (für for); '∼**befehl** m warrant of arrest; '♀**en** (26) stick, adhere (an dat. to); ∼ für answer for, be liable for.

Häftling ['hɛftliŋ] m (3¹) prisoner.

'**Haftpflicht** f liability; mit beschränkter ∼ limited; '♀**ig** s. haftbar; '∼**versicherung** f liability insurance; mot. third-party insurance.

'**Haft|reifen** mot. m traction tyre, Am. tire; '∼**richter** m committing magistrate; '∼**schale** opt. f contact lens.

'**Haftung** f liability.

'**Haft|-urlaub** m parole from prison; '∼**vermögen** ⊕ n adhesive power.

Hag [haːk] m (3) enclosure; (Hain) grove; (Wald) wood.

Hage|butte ['haːgəbutə] f hip; '∼**dorn** m hawthorn.

Hagel ['haːgəl] m (7) hail; (Schrot)

small shot; fig. shower; '♀**dicht** as thick as hail; '∼**korn** n hailstone; '♀**n** (29) hail; '∼**schauer** m shower of hail; '∼**schlag** m damage by hail; '∼**wetter** n hailstorm.

hager ['haːgər] lean, gaunt; '♀**keit** f leanness, gauntness.

'**Hagestolz** m (3²) (old) bachelor.

Häher ['hɛːər] m (7) jay.

Hahn [haːn] m (3²) cock, rooster; ⊕ (stop)cock, tap, Am. faucet; am Gewehr: cock; es kräht kein ∼ danach nobody cares a fig for that; s. Korb.

Hähnchen ['hɛːnçən] n (6) cockerel.

'**Hahnen|fuß** ♣ m crowfoot; '∼**kamm** m (a. ♣) cockscomb; '∼**kampf** m cock-fight; '∼**schrei** m cock-crow; '∼**tritt** m im Ei: (cock-)tread.

Hahnrei ['haːnraɪ] m (3) cuckold.

Hai [haɪ] m (3), '∼**fisch** m shark.

Hain poet. [haɪn] m (3) grove.

Häkchen ['hɛːkçən] n (6) small hook.

'**Häkel|-arbeit** f crochet-work; '♀**n** v/i. u. v/t. (29) crochet; '∼**nadel** f crochet-hook.

Haken ['haːkən] **1.** m (6) hook (a. beim Boxen); (Spange) clasp; fig. (Hindernis) snag, hitch; fig. da(s) ist der ∼ F there's the rub; die Sache hat e-n ∼ there is a catch to it; **2.** ♀ (2) hook; '∼**kreuz** n swastika; '∼**wurm** m hookworm.

halb [halp] **1.** adj. half; eine ∼e Stunde half an hour, Am. a half-hour; ∼ 3 Uhr half past two; es schlägt ∼ the half-hour strikes; ♪ ∼er Ton semitone; j-m auf ∼em Wege entgegenkommen meet a p. halfway; **2.** adv. by halves, half; ∼ entschlossen half determined; ∼ soviel half as much; die Sache ist ∼ so schlimm things are not as bad as all that.

'**halb|-amtlich** semi-official; '♀**bildung** f superficial education, smattering; '♀**blut** n half-blood; v. Volksrassen a.: half-breed, half-caste; (Pferd) half-bred; '♀**bruder** m half-brother; '♀**dunkel** n semi--darkness; dusk, twilight; '♀**-edelstein** m semi-precious stone; ... ∼**er** ['halbər] (wegen) on account of, owing to; (um ... willen) for the sake of; ♀**fabrikat** ['halp-] n semi--manufactured product; '∼**fertig** half-finished; ✝ semi-manufactured; '∼**fett** typ. semi-bold; '♀-

finale *n Sport*: semi-final; '♀-**franzband** *m* half-calf (binding); '~**gar** underdone, *Am.* rare; '~**gebildet** semi-cultured; '♀**geschwister** *pl.* half-brothers and -sisters; '♀**gott** *m* demigod; '♀**heit** *f* (16) half-measure.

halbieren [~'biːrən] halve; ♣ bisect.
'**Halb**|-**insel** *f* peninsula; '~**jahr** *n* half-year, six months *pl.*; '♀**jährig** of six months; '♀**jährlich** half--yearly; '~**kreis** *m* semicircle; '~**kugel** *f* hemisphere; '♀**laut** in an undertone; '~**leder** *n*: in ~ *gebunden* half-bound (*od.* -calf); '~**lederband** *m* half-binding; '~**leinen** *n* half-linen; '**~leiter** ⚡ *m* semiconductor; ~... solid-state; '♀**mast** *od. auf* ♀ (at) half-mast; '~**messer** *m* radius; '♀-**monatlich**, '~**monats...** fortnightly; '~**mond** *m* half-moon, crescent; '♀**nackt** half-naked; ♀'-**offen** *Tür*: ajar; '♀**part**: ~ *machen* go halves, F go fifty-fifty; '~**pension** *f* demi-pension, half board; '~**profil** *n* semi--profile; '~**schlaf** *m* doze; '~**schuh** *m* (*Damen*♀ flat) shoe; '~**schwergewicht(ler** *m*) *n* light-heavyweight; '~**schwester** *f* half-sister; '~**seide** *f* half silk; '~**starke** *m* (18) hooligan; '♀**starr** ⚙ semi-rigid; '~**stiefel** *m* ankle boot; '♀**stündlich** half-hourly; '~**tagsbeschäftigte** *m, f* part-timer; '~**tagsbeschäftigung** *f* part-time job *od.* employment; '~**ton** ♪, *phot. m* half-tone; '♀**tot** half-dead; '~**vokal** *m* semivowel; ♀**wegs** ['~veːks] half--way; (*ziemlich*) tolerably; '~**welt** *f* demi-monde; '~**wertszeit** *phys. f* half-life; '~**wissen** *n s. Halbbildung*; ♀**wüchsig** ['~vyːksiç] adolescent, teenage; '~**wüchsige** *m, f* adolescent, teenager; '~**zeit** *f Sport*: half-time; '~**zeug** ⊕ *n* semi-product; *Papier*: half-stuff.

Halde ['haldə] *f* (15) slope, declivity; ⚒ dump.

half [half] *pret. v. helfen.*

Hälfte ['hɛlftə] *f* (15) half; F *m-e bessere* ~ my better half; *die* ~ *der Leute* half the men; *um die* ~ *mehr* (*weniger*) half as much again (less by half); *zur* ~ half.

Halfter ['halftər] *m od. n* (7) halter.

Halle ['halə] *f* (15) hall; (*Vor*♀) porch; *e-s Hotels*: lounge; *Tennis*: covered court; (*Markt*♀) market--hall; ✈ hangar.

hallen ['halən] (25) (re)sound, echo.
'**Hallen**|**handball** *m* indoor handball (game); '~(**schwimm**)**bad** *n* indoor swimming-pool.

hallo! [ha'loː] hallo!, hullo!, hello!; ♀ *n* (11) *fig.* hullabaloo.

Halluzin|**ation** [halutsina'tsjoːn] *f* hallucination; ~**a'torisch** hallucinatory; ~**o'gen** hallucinogenic.

Halm [halm] *m* (3) blade; (*Getreide*♀) stalk; (*Stroh*♀) straw.

Halogen 🜚 [halo'geːn] *n* (3[1]) halogen; ~**scheinwerfer** *m* halogen headlight.

Hals [hals] *m* (4[2]) neck; (*Kehle*) throat; ~ *über Kopf* head over heels, (*hastig*) headlong, helter-skelter; *auf dem* ~*e haben* have on one's back, be saddled with; *sich vom* ~*e schaffen* get rid of; *j-m um den* ~ *fallen* fall on a p.'s neck; *sich j-m an den* ~ *werfen* throw o.s. at the head of a p.; *aus vollem* ~*e lachen* have a good laugh; *aus vollem* ~*e schreien* shout at the top of one's voice; *bis über den* ~ over head and ears, up to the eyes; F *es hängt mir zum* ~*e heraus* I am fed up (to the teeth) with it, I am sick of it; *sich den* ~ *verrenken aus Neugier* crane one's neck (*nach for*); '~-**abschneider** *m* cut-throat; '~-**ausschnitt** *m* (*tiefer* low) neck; '~**band** *n* necklace; *bsd. für Tiere*: collar; '~**binde** *f* (neck)tie; '~**bräune** *f* quinsy; '♀**brecherisch** breakneck; '~-**entzündung** *f* inflammation of the throat; '~**kette** *f* necklace; '~**kragen** *m* collar; neckband; '~'**Nasen**-**Ohren-Arzt** *m* ear, nose and throat specialist; '~**schlag-ader** *f* carotid artery; '~**schmerzen** *m/pl. s. Halsweh*; '♀**starrig** obstinate, stubborn; '~**starrigkeit** *f* obstinacy; '~**tuch** *n* scarf, neckerchief; '~**weh** *n* sore throat; '~**wirbel** *m* cervical vertebra; '~**wirbelsäule** *f* cervical vertebrae *pl.*

Halt [halt] **1.** *m* (3) hold; (*Innehalten*) halt, stop; (*Stütze*) support (*a. fig.*); *s. haltmachen*; **2.** ♀! *int.* stop!, ⚒ *usw.* halt!; **3.** ♀ *adv.* you know; *das ist* ~ *so* that's how it is, it can't be helped.

'**haltbar** (*dauerhaft*) durable, lasting; *fig.* tenable; *es ist* ~ it wears well; '♀**keit** *f* durability; '♀**keitsdatum** *n auf Lebensmitteln*: pull date.

'**Haltebucht** *f für Busse etc.*: bay.

halten ['haltən] (30) *v/t.* (*fest~, auf~, zurück~, an~, ent~*) hold; (*beibe~, fest~, an~, zurück~, feil~, ver~*) keep; *den Körper gerade usw. ~; Sitzung, Versammlung*: hold; *Feiertag, Schule, Personal, Tier, Versprechen*: keep; (*stützen*) support; (*enthalten*) contain; *Predigt, Rede*: deliver; *Vorlesung*: give; *Zeitung*: take in; *sich ~ (stand~)* hold (out); (*in e-r bestimmten Richtung bleiben, in e-m* [*guten*] *Zustand bleiben*) keep; *sich bereit~* be ready; *~ für* hold, think, take to be, *irrtümlich*: take for; *es ~ mit* side with; *Frieden ~* keep peace; *s. kurz, Mund, Narr, Ordnung, Schach, Schritt; große Stücke od. viel (wenig) ~ auf (acc.) od. von* make much (little) of, think highly (little) of; *sich ~ an (acc.)* keep to; *sich gut ~ S.*: keep well, *P.*: stand one's ground; *das kannst du ~, wie du willst* you can please yourself; *was ~ Sie von ...?* what do you think of ...?; *v/i.* stop; (*ganz bleiben*) last; (*aushalten, dauern*) hold out, endure; (*festsitzen*) hold; *Eis*: bear; *es hält schwer* it is difficult; *dafür ~, daß* hold that; *zu j-m ~* adhere (*od.* stick) to; *auf et. ~* insist on, set store by.

'**Halte|platz** *m*, '**~punkt** *m*, '**~stelle** *f* stop; (*Droschken♀*) taxi-rank; '**~verbot** *n* no stopping area.

'**halt|los** without support; *Charakter*: unsteady; '**♀losigkeit** *f* unsteadiness; '**~machen** (make a) halt, stop.

'**Haltung** *f* (*Körper♀*) bearing, carriage; (*Benehmen*) deportment; (*Stellung*) posture, (*a. Geistes♀*) attitude; *der Börse*: tone; *~ bewahren* remain composed, control o.s.; *s-e ~ wiedergewinnen* recover one's composure.

'**Haltzeichen** *n im Straßenverkehr*: stop-signal.

Halunke [ha'luŋkə] *m* (13) rascal.

hämisch ['hɛmiʃ] malicious.

Hammel ['haməl] *m* (7[1]) wether; '**~braten** *m* roast mutton; '**~fleisch** *n* mutton; '**~keule** *f* leg of mutton; '**~sprung** *parl. m* division.

Hammer ['hamər] *m* (7[1]) hammer (*a. Sport*); *~ des Auktionators usw.*: gavel; *a. = ~werk; unter den ~ kommen* come under the hammer.

'**hämmer|bar** malleable; '**~n** ['hɛmərn] *v/t. u. v/i.* (29) hammer; *Motor*: knock; (*stampfen*) pound.

'**Hammer|schlag** *m* stroke with a hammer; (*Abgang vom Eisen*) hammer-scales *pl.*; '**~schmied** *m* blacksmith; '**~werk** *n* forge shop, hammer mill; '**~werfen** *n Sport*: throwing the hammer.

Hämorrhoiden [hɛmɔro'i:dən] *f/pl.* (15) h(a)emorrhoids *pl.*, piles *pl.*

Hampelmann ['hampəlman] *m* (1[2]) jumping jack; *fig.* puppet; *contp.* clown.

Hamster ['hamstər] *m* (7) hamster; **~ei** [~'raɪ] *f* hoarding; '**~er** *m* (7) hoarder; '**♀n** *v/i. u. v/t.* (29) hoard.

Hand [hant] *f* (14[1]) hand; *s. flach, hohl; j-m die ~ drücken* shake hands with a p.; *j-m freie ~ lassen* give a p. a free hand; *sich die Hände reichen* join hands; *~ an j-n legen* lay hands on a p.; *~ an et. legen* put one's hand to a th.; *~ ans Werk legen* set to work; *s. letzt; an ~ von* by means of, guided by; *auf eigene ~* of one's own accord; *an die ~ geben* supply with; *aus der ~ geben* part with; *aus erster ~* at first hand; *bei der ~, zur ~* at hand, handy; *die Hände in den Schoß legen* rest upon one's oars; *in die ~ nehmen* take in hand; *j-m et. in die Hände spielen* help a p. to a th.; *mit der ~ gemacht usw.* by hand; *von langer ~* for a long time past; *von der ~ in den Mund leben* live from hand to mouth; *von der ~ weisen* decline, reject; *unter den Händen haben* have in hand; *unter der ~* in secret, privately; *auf Brief*: *zu Händen* (*gen.*) care of (*abbr.* c/o), *Am.* attention; *fig. ~ und Fuß haben* hold water; *ohne ~ und Fuß* without rhyme or reason; *s-e ~ im Spiele haben* have a finger in the pie; *s-e ~ ins Feuer legen für etwas od. j-n* put one's hand into the fire for a th. *od.* a p.; *eine ~ wäscht die andere* one good turn deserves another; *s. öffentlich*; '**~arbeit** *f* manual labo(u)r; (*Ggs. Maschinenarbeit*) handwork; *weibliche*: needlework; *das ist ~* it is handmade; '**~arbeiter** *m* manual labo(u)rer, (handi)craftsman; '**~aufheben** *n bei Abstimmungen*: show of hands; '**~ausgabe** *f* concise edition; '**~**

ball *m* handball; '**∼beil** *n* hatchet; '**∼bibliothek** *f* reference library; '**⊙breit** of a hand's breadth; '**∼breit(e)** *f* hand's breadth; '**∼bremse** *f* hand-brake; '**∼buch** *n* manual, handbook; '**∼creme** *f* hand cream.

Hände|druck ['hɛndə-] *m* shaking of hands, handshake; '**∼klatschen** *n* (6) clapping of hands.

Handel ['handəl] *m* (7¹) (*geschäftlicher Verkehr*) trade; *in großem Maßstab*: commerce; *weitS.* traffic; (*Geschäft*) transaction, business; (*abgeschlossener* ∼) bargain; (*schlimme usw. Sache*) affair; ⚹ lawsuit; ∼ *treiben* trade; *im* ∼ on the market; *nicht mehr im* ∼ off the market; *ein ehrlicher* ∼ a square deal.

Händel ['hɛndəl] *m/pl.* quarrel *sg.*; ∼ *suchen* pick a quarrel.

handeln ['handəln] (29) act; (*Handel treiben*) trade (*mit* with *a p.*; *in* goods); deal (*nur in* goods); (*feilschen*) bargain (*um* for); *in e-r Rede usw.*: ∼ *von od. über* (*acc.*) treat of, deal with; *es handelt sich um* it is a question (*od.* matter) of, ... is concerned; *es handelt sich darum, wer usw.* the question is who *etc.*; *worum handelt es sich?* what is the (point in) question?, what is it all about?

'**Handels|-abkommen** *n* trade agreement; '**∼adreßbuch** *n* commercial directory; '**∼artikel** *m* commodity; '**∼bank** *f* commercial bank; '**∼beziehungen** *f/pl.* trade relations; '**∼bilanz** *f* balance of trade; '**∼blatt** *n* trade journal; ∼**bücher** ['∼by:çər] *n/pl.* commercial books, account books; '⊙**einig** *werden* come to terms; '**∼flotte** *f* merchant (*od.* mercantile) fleet; '**∼gärtner** *m* market-gardener, *Am.* truck farmer; '**∼genossenschaft** *f* traders' co-operative (society); '**∼gericht** *n* commercial court; '**∼gesellschaft** *f* trading company; *offene* ∼ general partnership; '**∼gesetzbuch** *n* Commercial Code; '**∼hafen** *m* commercial port; '**∼haus** *n* commercial house; '**∼hochschule** *f* commercial academy; '**∼kammer** *f* Chamber of Commerce, *Am. a.* Board of Trade; '**∼mann** *m* tradesman; '**∼marine** *f* mercantile marine; '**∼marke** *f* trade-mark;

'**∼metropole** *f* cent|re (*Am.* center) of commerce; '**∼minister** *m* *allg.* Minister of Commerce; *Brt.* President of the Board of Trade, *Am.* Secretary of Commerce; '**∼ministerium** *n* *allg.* Ministry of Commerce; *Brt.* Board of Trade, *Am.* Department of Commerce; '**∼müll** *m* commercial refuse, trade waste; '**∼nation** *f* trading nation; '**∼platz** *m* emporium, trading cen|tre, *Am.* -er; '**∼politik** *f* trade policy; '**∼produkt** *n* commercial product; '**∼recht** *n* commercial law; '**∼register** *n* commercial register; *im* ∼ *eintragen* register, *Am.* incorporate; '**∼richter** *m* commercial judge; '**∼schiff** *n* trading vessel; '**∼schiffahrt** *f* merchant shipping; '**∼schule** *f* commercial school, *Am.* business college; '**∼spanne** *f* trade margin; '**∼sperre** *f* embargo; '**∼stadt** *f* commercial town; '⊙**üblich** customary in the trade.

händelsüchtig ['hɛndəl-] quarrelsome.

'**Handels|verkehr** *m* traffic, trade; '**∼vertrag** *m* commercial treaty; '**∼vertreter** *m* commercial representative; '**∼ware** *f* commodity; '**∼wechsel** *m* commercial bill; '**∼weg** *m* trade route; '**∼wert** *m* trading value; '**∼zeichen** *n* trade-mark; '**∼zweig** *m* branch of trade.

'**handeltreibend** trading.

'**Hand|feger** *m* hand-brush; '**∼fertigkeit** *f* manual skill; handicraft; '**∼fesseln** *f/pl.* handcuffs, manacles; '⊙**fest** sturdy, robust; *fig.* sound; '**∼feuerwaffe** *f* hand gun; *pl.* small arms *pl.*; '**∼fläche** *f* flat of the hand, palm; '⊙**ge-arbeitet** handmade; '**∼geld** *n* handsel; 🕈 earnest money; ⚔ bounty; '**∼gelenk** *n* wrist; *fig. aus dem* ∼ offhand, just like that; '⊙**gemein** *werden* come to blows (*od.* grips); '**∼gemenge** *n* fray, mêlée (*fr.*); (*Balgerei*) scuffle; '**∼gepäck** *n* hand luggage (*Am.* baggage); '⊙**gerecht** handy; '⊙**geschrieben** hand-written, written by hand; '⊙**gesteuert** manually operated; '⊙**gestrickt** hand-knitted; F *fig.* home-made; '**∼granate** ⚔ *f* hand-grenade; '⊙**greiflich** palpable; (*offensichtlich*) obvious; ∼ *werden* turn violent, F get rough; '**∼griff** *m* grasp; grip, manipulation; *konkret*: grip, handle; '**~habe** f (15) handle (a. fig.); '**⁀haben** (25) handle, manipulate; Maschine: operate; Rechtspflege: administer; fig. handle; '**~habung** f handling, manipulation; operation. ...**händig** [hɛndiç] ...-handed.

'**Hand|karren** m hand-cart; '**~koffer** m (small) suitcase, attaché case, Am. valise; '**~korb** m hand-basket; '**~kuß** m kiss on the hand; F mit ~ gladly; '**~langer** m (7) handy man, odd--jobber, Am. hand; △ hodman; contp. underling.

Händler ['hɛndlər] m (7), '**~in** f (16¹) dealer, trader.

'**Handleser(in** f) m palmist.
'**Handlesekunst** f palmistry.
handlich ['hantliç] handy.
Handlung ['handluŋ] f act(ion), deed; e-s Dramas usw.: action, a. plot; (Laden) shop, Am. store; strafbare ~ punishable act; '**~sbevollmächtigte** m authorized agent; '**~sfreiheit** f liberty of action, a free hand; '**~sgehilfe** m (commercial) clerk; (Verkäufer) shop-assistant; '**~sreisende** m commercial traveller, bsd. Am. traveling salesman; '**~sweise** f way of acting, conduct; (Verfahren) procedure; (Methoden) methods pl.

'**Hand|pflege** f manicure; '**~reichung** f help, assistance; '**~rücken** m back of the hand; '**~säge** f hand--saw; '**~schelle** f handcuff; '**~schlag** m handshake; '**~schreiben** n autograph letter; '**~schrift** f handwriting; (geschriebenes Werk) manuscript; '**~schriftendeutung** f graphology; '**⁀schriftlich** adj. hand--written, in writing, manuscript; adv. in writing; in manuscript; '**~schuh** m glove; '**~schuhfach** mot. n glove compartment; '**~spiegel** m hand-glass; '**~stand** m handstand; '**~staubsauger** m portable vacuum cleaner; '**~streich** m coup de main (fr.), surprise raid; '**~tasche** f handbag, Am. purse; '**~teller** m palm (of the hand); '**~tuch** n towel; '**~tuchautomat** m towel dispenser; '**~tuchhalter** m towel-rail od. -rack; '**~umdrehen** n: im ~ in a jiffy, in no time; '**~voll** f handful; '**~waffe** f hand weapon; '**~wagen** m hand--cart; '**~waschbecken** n wash-hand basin; '**~werk** n trade, (handi)craft; j-m das ~ legen put a stop to a p.'s

practices; sein ~ verstehen know one's business; s. pfuschen; '**~werker** m (7) craftsman, artisan; weit S. workman; '**~werksbursche** m (travel[l]ing) journeyman; '**~werkskammer** f chamber of handicrafts; '**⁀werksmäßig** workmanlike; bsd. fig. mechanical; '**~werksmeister** m master craftsman; '**~werkszeug** n (set of) tools pl.; '**~wörterbuch** n concise dictionary; '**~wurzel** f wrist; '**~zeichen** n hand signal; statt Unterschrift: initials pl.; '**~zeichnung** f hand drawing; '**~zettel** m handbill.

Hanf [hanf] m (3) hemp; in Zssgn mst hemp-...; '**⁀en** hempen.
Hänfling ['hɛnfliŋ] m (3¹) linnet.
Hang [haŋ] m (3²) slope; (Abdachung) declivity; fig. inclination, propensity (zu to, for); tendency (to).
Hänge|backe ['hɛŋə-] f flabby cheek; '**~bahn** f suspension railway (Am. railroad); '**~bauch** m paunch; '**~boden** m loft; '**~brücke** f suspension bridge; '**~busen** m drooping breasts pl.; '**~lampe** f hanging-lamp; '**~matte** f hammock.

hangeln ['haŋəln] (29) climb (od. travel) hand over hand.
hängen ['hɛŋən] v/t. (30) hang; suspend; s. Herz; v/i. hang; be suspended; (haften) adhere, stick, cling (an dat. to); fig. ~ an (dat.) cling to, be attached to; den Kopf ~ lassen hang one's head, be down in the mouth; '**~bleiben** (sn) be caught (an dat. by), catch (on).

'**Hängeschrank** m wall cabinet.
Hansdampf [hans'dampf] m: ~ in allen Gassen Jack-of-all-trades.
hänseln ['hɛnzəln] (29) tease, chaff.
'**Hansestadt** f Hanse town.
Hans|'narr m tomfool; ~'**wurst** m (3²) clown (a. contp.).
Hantel ['hantəl] f (15) dumb-bell.
han'tier|en v/i.: ~ mit work with, operate, handle, wield; (geschäftig sein) be busy.
hapern ['haːpərn] (29): es hapert mit there is a problem with; bei ihm hapert's im Englischen he is weak in English; es hapert uns an Geld we are short of money.
Hap|pen ['hapən] m (6) mouthful, morsel, bite; fetter ~ juicy morsel, fig. fine catch; '**⁀ig** F Preis etc.: steep, hefty.
Harfe ['harfə] f (15) harp.

Harfenist(in)

Harfe'nist(in f) m harp-player, harpist.

Harke ['harkə] f (15) rake; j-m zeigen, was e-e ~ ist show a p. what's what; '**2n** v/t. u. v/i. (25) rake.

Harm [harm] m (3) grief, sorrow; (Kränkung) injury, wrong.

härmen ['hermən]: sich ~ grieve (um about, over).

'**harmlos** harmless (a. fig.).

'**Harmlosigkeit** f harmlessness.

Harmon|ie [harmo'ni:] f (15) harmony; **2ieren** [~'ni:rən] harmonize; fig. a. agree; **~ika** [~'mo:nika] f (16² u. 11) accordion; **2isch** harmonious; **2isieren** [~moni'zi:rən] v/i. u. v/t. harmonize; **~ium** ♪ [~'mo:njum] n (11¹, 9) harmonium.

Harn [harn] m (3) urine; '**~blase** f (urinary) bladder.

'**harnen** (25) pass water, urinate.

'**Harn|fluß** m incontinence of urine; '**~glas** n urinal; '**~grieß** m gravel.

Harnisch ['harniʃ] m (3²) armo(u)r; fig. j-n in ~ bringen infuriate a p.; in ~ geraten fly into a rage.

'**Harn|leiter** anat. m ureter; '**~röhre** f urethra; '**~säure** f uric acid; '**~stoff** m urea; '**~untersuchung** f uranalysis, Am. urinalysis; '**~wege** m/pl. urinary tract sg.

Harpun|e [har'pu:nə] f (15), **2ieren** [~'ni:rən] harpoon.

harren ['harən] (25, gen. od. auf acc.) wait (for); fig. hope (for).

harsch [harʃ] harsh, rough; '**2schnee** m crusted snow.

hart [hart] hard; fig. a. severe; ~ werden harden; adv. ~ arbeiten work hard; es ging ~ auf ~ it was either do or die; s. Nuß.

Härte ['hɛrtə] f (15) hardness; fig. a. severity; unbillige ~ undue hardship; '**~fall** m case of hardship.

'**härten** (a. sich) harden.

'**Hart|faserplatte** f fibreboard, Am. fiberboard; '**~geld** n coined money, coins pl., specie; '**2gesotten** fig. hard-boiled; '**~gummi** m, n hard rubber; ✝ vulcanite, ebonite; '**2herzig** hard-hearted; '**~holz** n hard wood; **2leibig** [~'laibiç] constipated, costive; '**~leibigkeit** ♪ f constipation, costiveness; '**2löten** braze, hard-solder; **2mäulig** [~'mɔyliç] hard-mouthed; **2näckig** [~'nɛkiç] obstinate, pertinacious, bsd. Krank-

heit: refractory; '**~näckigkeit** f obstinacy, pertinacity; '**~pappe** f hardboard; '**~platz** m Tennis: hard court; '**~spiritus** m solid alcohol; '**~wurst** f hard sausage.

Harz [ha:rts] n (3²) resin; (Geigen2) rosin; **2en** v/t. (27) resin; Geigenbogen: rosin; '**2ig** resinous.

Hasardspiel [ha'zartʃpi:l] n (3) game of chance; fig. gamble.

Häs-chen ['hɛ:sçən] n (6) young hare, leveret.

haschen¹ ['haʃən] (27) v/t. snatch, catch; v/i. ~ nach snatch at; fig. a. aim at; nach Komplimenten: fish for.

haschen² F ['haʃen] (27) smoke hash.

Häscher ['heʃər] m (7) catchpole.

Haschisch ['haʃiʃ] n (inv., o. pl.) hashish, F hash.

Hase ['ha:zə] m (13) hare; fig. alter ~ old hand; F da liegt der ~ im Pfeffer there's the rub; sehen, wie der ~ läuft see which way the cat jumps.

Hasel|huhn ['ha:zəlhu:n] n hazel--hen; '**~maus** f dormouse; '**~nuß** f hazel-nut; '**~strauch** m hazel(-tree).

'**Hasen|braten** m roast hare; '**~fuß** m hare's foot; fig. coward; '**~jagd** f hare-hunt(ing); '**~klein** n, '**~pfeffer** m jugged hare; '**~panier** n: das ~ ergreifen take to one's heels; '**~scharte** f harelip.

Häsin ['hɛ:zin] f female hare, doe.

Haspe ['haspə] f (15) hasp, hinge.

Haspel ['haspəl] f (15) reel; (Winde) windlass; '**2n** (29) reel.

Haß [has] m (4) hatred.

'**hass|en** (28) hate; '**~enswert** hateful, odious; '**2er(in** f) m hater.

häßlich ['hesliç] ugly; fig. a. mean, nasty; '**2keit** f ugliness; meanness.

'**Haßliebe** f love-hate relationship.

Hast [hast] f (16) haste, hurry; '**2en** (26, sn) hasten, hurry; '**2ig** hasty, hurried; '**~igkeit** f hastiness.

hätscheln ['hɛ:tʃəln] (29) caress, fondle, cuddle, pet; (verzärteln) pamper, coddle.

hatte ['hatə] pret. v. haben 1.

Haube ['haubə] f (15) bonnet, cap; (Schwestern2) cornet; zo. tuft, crest; ⊕ u. mot. bonnet, mot. Am. hood; unter die ~ bringen find a husband for; unter die ~ kommen get married.

Hauch [haux] m (3) breath; (leiser Luftzug) breeze, whiff; (leiser Duft) waft; *fig.* (*Spur*) touch, tinge; *gr.* aspiration; '♀**dünn** wafer-thin; '♀**en** (25) *v/i.* breathe; *v/t.* exhale; *gr.* aspirate; '**～laut** *m* aspirate.

'**Haudegen** *m* (6) *fig.* (old) blade.

Haue ['hauə] *f* (15) **1.** ✔ hoe, mattock; **2.** F (*Prügel*) hiding, spanking.

'**hauen** (30) *v/t.* (*hacken*) hew, chop, *Holz*: a. cut; *Loch, Stufen, Weg*: cut; (*schlagen*) strike; F (*prügeln*) thrash, hide; *sich ～* fight; *v/i. ～ nach* strike at; *um sich ～* lay about one.

'**Hauer** *m* (7) hewer (*a.* ✗); *zo.* tusk.

häufeln ✔ ['hɔyfəln] (29) hill (up).

Haufen ['haufən] *m* (13¹ [6]) heap (F *a. fig.*: *Menge, Zahl*), pile; (*Schwarm*) crowd; F *ein ～ ... a lot of ...*; *e-n ～* (*Geld*) *verdienen* make a pile (of money); *der große ～* the multitude; *über den ～ werfen* overthrow, *bsd. fig.* upset.

häufen ['hɔyfən] (25) heap (up), (*a. sich*) accumulate.

'**haufen**|**weise** in heaps; (*scharenweise*) in crowds; '♀**wolke** *f* cumulus (cloud).

'**häufig** frequent(ly *adv.*); '♀**keit** *f* frequency.

'**Häufung** *f* accumulation.

'**Hauklotz** *m* (3¹ u. ³) chopping block.

Haupt [haupt] *n* (1²) head; (*Ober♀*) head, chief; '**～...** principal, chief, main; '**～aktionär** ✦ *m* principal shareholder (*Am.* stockholder); '**～akzent** *m* main stress; '**～altar** *m* high altar; '♀**amtlich** full-time; *adv.* on a full-time basis; '**～anliegen** *n* main (*od.* chief) concern; '**～anschluß** *m* teleph. main station; ✦ *usw.* mains connection; '**～anteil** *m* main share; '**～bahnhof** *m* main (*od.* central) station; '**～beruf** *m*, '**～beschäftigung** *f* main occupation; '♀**beruflich** full-time; '**～bestandteil** *m* chief ingredient (*od.* component); '**～buch** *n* ledger; '**～darsteller(in** *f*) *thea. m* leading man (*f* lady), lead; '**～eingang** *m* main entrance; '**～fach** *n Studium*: main subject, *Am.* major; *... als ～ studieren* take ... as one's main subject, *Am.* major in ...; '**～feldwebel** *m* sergeant major, *Am.* first sergeant; '**～film** *m des Programms*: feature (film); '**～gang** *m* main corridor; *beim Essen*: main course; '**～gebäude** *n* main building; '**～geschäft** *n* main business; '**～geschäftszeit** *f* rush hours *pl.*; '**～ge-**

～winn *m* first prize; '**～haar** *n* hair of the head; '**～hahn** *m* mains tap; '**～leitung** *f* ✦, *Wasser*: main(s *pl.*); '**～lieferant** *m* main supplier.

Häuptling ['hɔyptliŋ] *m* (3¹) chief, chieftain.

'**Haupt**|**mahlzeit** *f* main meal; '**～mann** *m* (1, *pl.* Hauptleute) captain; '**～masse** *f* bulk; '**～merkmal** *n* chief characteristic; '**～nahrung** *f* staple food; '**～nenner** & *m* common denominator; '**～person** *f* most important person; *thea. usw.* main character; '**～post-amt** *n* General (*Am.* Main) Post Office; '**～probe** *f* dress rehearsal; '**～punkt** *m* main (*od.* cardinal) point; '**～quartier** *n* headquarters *pl.*; '**～rolle** *f* leading part (*bsd. Film*: rôle), *ein Film mit N. N. in der ～* a film featuring N.N.; '**～sache** *f* main point *od.* thing; *in der ～* mainly; '♀**sächlich** chief, main, principal; '**～saison** *f* peak season; '**～satz** *gr. m* main *od.* principal clause; '**～schalter** ✦ *m* main (*od.* master) switch; '**～schlag-ader** *f* aorta; '**～schlüssel** *m* master-key; '**～schuldige** *m* chief culprit; '**～sendezeit** *f* prime time; '**～spaß** *m* great fun; '**～stadt** *f* capital; '♀**städtisch** metropolitan; '**～straße** *f* main street; major road; '**～täter** ♫ *m* principal offender; '**～ton** *m* principal (*od.* main) stress; '**～treffer** *m* jackpot; '**～verhandlung** ♫ *f* main hearing, trial; '**～verkehrsstraße** *f* arterial road, thoroughfare, *Am.* highway; '**～verkehrsstunden** *f*|*pl.*, '**～verkehrszeit** *f* peak (*od.* rush) hour(s *pl.*); '**～versammlung** *f* general meeting; '**～verwaltung** *f* central office; '**～waschgang** *m* main wash; '**～werk** *n* main work; '**～wort** *gr. n* noun, substantive; '**～zeuge** *m*, '**～zeugin** *f* main (*od.* chief) witness.

Haus [haus] *n* (2¹) house; (*Heim*) home; ✦ house, firm; *～ und Hof* house and home; *nach ～e* home; *zu ～e* at home; *er ist (nicht) zu ～* F he is (not) in; *fig. in e-r S. zu ～e sein* be at home (*od.* well versed) in a th.; *fig. ein fideles ～* a jolly fellow; *ein großes ～ führen* live in great style; *aus gutem ～ sein* come of a good house (*od.* family); *so tun, als ob man zu ～ wäre* make o.s. at home; '**～angestellte** *m, f* domestic (servant), household help; '**～an-**

schluß *m allg.* house connection; *für Wasser*: service pipe; '**~apotheke** *f* (household) medicine-cabinet *od.* -chest; '**~arbeit** *f* housework; *Schule*: homework; '**~arrest** *m* house arrest; '**~arzt** *m* family doctor; '**~aufgabe** *f* homework; '**⚬backen** home-made; *fig.* plain, homely; (*langweilig*) humdrum; '**~bar** *f* cocktail cabinet; '**~bedarf** *m* household requirements *pl.*; *für den ~* for the home; '**~besetzer** *m* squatter; '**~besitzer(in** *f*) *m* house-owner; '**~bewohner(in** *f*) *m* occupant (of the house); '**~boot** *n* house-boat.

Häus-chen ['hɔysçən] *n* (6) small house; *fig. aus dem ~ sein* be beside o.s. (*vor* with); *aus dem ~ geraten* go mad (*vor* with).

'**Haus|detektiv** *m* store detective; '**~diener** *m im Hotel*: boots.

hausen[1] ['haʊzən] (27) live, house, dwell; *arg ~ in* (*dat.*), *mit, unter* (*dat.*) play havoc among, *mit Vorräten*: be heavy on *supplies*.

'**Hausen**[2] *zo.* [~] *m* (6) sturgeon; '**~blase** *f* isinglass.

Häuser|block ['hɔyzərblɔk] *m* block (of houses); '**~makler** *m* house agent, *Am.* realtor; '**~reihe** *f* row of (terraced) houses.

'**Haus|flur** *m* (entrance-)hall, *Am. a.* hallway; '**~frau** *f* housewife; (*Herrin*) lady of the house; '**~friedensbruch** *m* trespass (in a p.'s house); '**~garten** *m* back garden; '**~gebrauch** *m* domestic use; '**~gehilfin** *f* s. *Hausangestellte*; '**~genosse** *m* (fellow-)tenant; '**~hahn** *m* domestic cock, rooster; '**~halt** *m* household; *parl.* budget; *fig.* economy; *s. führen*; '**⚬halten** keep house; *~ mit* husband, economize; **~hälter** ['~hɛltər] *m* (7), '**~hälterin** *f* (16[1]) housekeeper; '**⚬hälterisch** economical; '**~halts-artikel** *m* domestic (*od.* household) article; '**~halts-ausschuß** *parl. m* Budget Committee; *Brt.* Estimates Committee, *Am.* Appropriations Committee; '**~haltsdebatte** *parl. f* budget debate; '**~haltsdefizit** *parl. n* budgetary deficit; '**~haltsgeräte** *n/pl.* household appliances; '**~haltsjahr** *n* fiscal (*od.* financial) year; '**~halts-packung** *f* economy pack; '**~halts-plan** *parl. m* budget; '**~halts-politik** *f* budgetary policy; '**~**

halts('**vor**)-**anschlag** *parl. m the* Estimates *pl.*; '**~haltung** *f* housekeeping; *s. Haushalt*; '**~haltungskosten** *pl.* household expenses; '**~haltungsvorstand** *m* head of the household; '**~herr** *m* master of the house, head of the family; *als Gastgeber*: host; *als Vermieter*: landlord; '**⚬hoch** as high as a house; *fig.* vast; *~ überlegen* (*dat.*) head and shoulders above *a p.*, vastly superior (to); '**~huhn** *n* domestic fowl; '**~hund** *m* house-dog.

hausier|en [~'ziːrən] hawk, peddle (*mit et.* a th.); *~ gehen* be a hawker, *a. fig.* peddle (*mit a th.*); **⚬er** *m* (7) hawker, pedlar.

'**Haus|katze** *f* domestic cat; '**~kleid** *n* house dress; '**~lehrer** *m*, '**~lehrerin** *f* private tutor.

'**häuslich** domestic; home, *a.* household; (*sparsam*) economical; (*zu Hause bleibend*) home-loving, domesticated; *~e Arbeit s. Hausarbeit*; '**⚬keit** *f* domesticity; family life; (*Heim*) home.

'**Haus|mädchen** *n* housemaid; '**~mann** *m* house-husband; '**~mannskost** *f* simple (*od.* plain) fare; '**~mantel** *m* house coat; '**~meister** *m s. Hausverwalter*; '**~miete** *f* house-rent; '**~mittel** *n* household medicine; '**~müll** *m* domestic waste; '**~mutter** *f* mother of the family, housewife; (*Heimleiterin*) warden; '**~ordnung** *f* rules *pl.* of the house; '**~pflege** *f* home-nursing; '**~rat** *m* household effects *pl.*; '**~recht** *n* domestic authority; '**~sammlung** *f* house-to-house collection; '**~schlachtung** *f* home slaughtering; '**~schlüssel** *m* latch-key; '**~schuh** *m* slipper; '**~schwamm** *m* dry rot; '**~schwein** *n* domestic pig.

Hausse ✝ ['hoːsə] *f* (15) rise (in prices), boom; *auf ~ spekulieren* speculate for a rise; '**~markt** *m* boom market.

Haussier ✝ [hos'jeː] *m* bull.

'**Haus|stand** *m* household; *e-n ~ gründen* set up house; '**~suchung** *f* house search, *Am.* house check; '**~suchungsbefehl** *m* search-warrant; '**~tarif** *m* internal pay scale; '**~tarifvertrag** *m* internal pay agreement; '**~telephon** *n im Geschäftshaus usw.*: intercom(munication system); '**~tier** *n* domestic animal; '**~tochter** *f* lady help; '**~tor** *n* gate; '**~tür** *f* front-

-door; '~**vater** m father of the family; (*Heimleiter*) warden; '~**verwalter** m, '~**wart** m (3) care-taker, janitor, *Am.* superintendent; '~**wirt** m landlord; '~**wirtin** f landlady; '~**wirtschaft** f housekeeping; *weitS.* domestic economy; (*a.* '~**wirtschaftslehre** f) domestic science; '♀**wirtschaftlich** domestic; household.

Haut [haʊt] f (14¹) skin; (*abgezogene Tier*♀) hide; ♀, *anat.*, *zo.* membrane, cuticle; *auf Flüssigkeit*: film; *bis auf die* ~ to the skin; *fig.* *ehrliche* ~ honest fellow; *s-e* (*eigene*) ~ *retten* F save one's bacon; *aus der* ~ *fahren* jump out of one's skin; *ich möchte nicht in s-r* ~ *stecken* I wouldn't like to be in his shoes; *mit* ~ *und Haar* completely; '~**abschürfung** f skin-abrasion, excoriation; '~**arzt** m dermatologist; '~**ausschlag** m rash.

Häutchen ['hɔytçən] n (6) membrane, pellicle, film.

'**Hautcreme** f skin cream.

'**häuten** (26) skin; *sich* ~ cast one's skin; *Schlange usw.*: slough.

'**haut**|**-eng** *Kleid*: skin-tight; '♀**farbe** f complexion.

Hautgout [oː'guː] m (11, *o. pl.*) high smell; ~ *haben* be high.

'**Haut**|**krankheit** f skin disease; '~**krebs** ♂ m cancer of the skin; '~**pflege** f care of the skin; '~**schere** f (e-e ~ a pair of) cuticle scissors *pl.*; ~**transplantation** ['~transplanta-'tsjoːn] f (16) skin grafting.

'**Häutung** f casting of the skin.

'**Hautwunde** f skin-wound.

Havanna(**zigarre**) [ha'vanatsigarə] f Havana (cigar).

Havarie [hava'riː] f (15) (*große* general, *besondere od. partielle* particular) average.

'**H-Bombe** f H-bomb (= hydrogen bomb).

he! [heː] hey!, I say!

Hebamme ['heːpʔamə] f midwife.

Hebe|**baum** ['heːbə-] m lever; '~**bock** m (lifting-)jack; '~**bühne** *mot.* f lifting ramp; '~**kran** m hoist(ing crane).

Hebel ['heːbəl] m (7) lever (*a. Ringen*); *fig. alle* ~ *in Bewegung setzen* move heaven and earth; *fig. am längeren* ~ *sitzen* have the better leverage; '~**arm** m lever-arm; '~**kraft** f

leverage; '~**schalter** ⚡ m lever switch; '~**wirkung** f lever action, leverage.

heben ['heːbən] (30) lift, (*a. fig.*) raise; *mit Mühe*: heave; (*hochwinden*) hoist; (*steigern*) increase; (*fördern*) further; *s. Sattel, Taufe*; *sich* ~ rise; *s. gehoben*.

'**Heber** *phys.* m (7) siphon; (*Stech*♀) pipette.

'**Hebeschiff** n salvage ship.

Hebräer [he'brɛːər] m (7), ~**in** f (16¹), **he'bräisch** Hebrew.

'**Hebung** f *vgl.* heben; raising, lifting; increase; furtherance; *des Bodens*: elevation.

Hechel ['hɛçəl] f (15) hatchel. hackle, flax-comb; '♀**n** (25) hackle.

Hecht [hɛçt] m (3) pike; F *fig.* (*Qualm*) fug; '♀**en** *Sport*: dive; *Schwimmen*: do a pike-dive.

Heck [hɛk] n (3) ⚓ stern; *mot.* rear; ✈ tail; '~**antrieb** *mot.* m rear (-wheel) drive.

Hecke ['hɛkə] f (15) **1.** ✦ hedge; **2.** *zo.* brood, breed, hatch.

'**hecken** *v*/*t. u. v*/*i.* (25) hatch, breed.

'**Hecken**|**rose** f dog-rose; '~**schere** f hedge-shears *pl.*; '~**schütze** ✗ m sniper.

'**Heck**|**klappe** *mot.* f tailgate, hatchback; '~**licht** n ⚓ stern-light; ✈, *mot.* tail-light; '~**motor** m rear engine; '~**scheibe** *mot.* f rear window (*od.* windscreen, *Am.* windshield); '~**scheibenheizung** f rear window heating (*od.* defroster); '~**scheibenwischer** m rear windscreen wiper; '~**spoiler** m rear spoiler.

heda! ['heːdɑː] hey!

Heer [heːr] n (3) Army; (*große Schar*) host; '~**es...** *mst* Army ...; '~**esdienst** m military service; '~**(es-)zug** m (military) expedition, campaign; '~**führer** m general, commander-in-chief; '~**lager** n army camp; *fig.* camp; '~**schar** f host; '~**straße** f highway.

Hefe ['heːfə] f (15) yeast; (*Bodensatz u. fig.*) dregs *pl.*; '~**kuchen** m yeast cake.

Heft [hɛft] n (3) haft, handle; *e-s Schwertes*: hilt; (*Schreib*♀) exercise book, copy-book; *e-r Zeitschrift*: number, issue; (*Broschüre*) booklet, paper book; *das* ~ *in der Hand haben* (*behalten*) have (keep) the reins in one's hand.

'heft|en (26) fasten, fix (an acc. to; Augen: on); Näherei: baste, tack; Buch: stitch, sew; sich ~ an (acc.) attach (od. cling) to; geheftet Buch: in sheets; '♀er m für Akten: folder; s. Heftmaschine.

'Heftfaden m tacking thread.

'heftig vehement, violent, impetuous; (reizbar) irritable; Kälte: sharp; Regen: heavy; '♀keit f vehemence, violence.

'Heft|klammer f paper-clip; der Heftmaschine: staple; '~maschine f stapling machine; '~nadel f stitching needle; '~pflaster n sticking plaster, adhesive plaster od. tape; '~stich m tack; '~zwecke f drawing-pin, Am. thumbtack.

Hegemonie [hegəmo'ni:] (15) f hegemony, supremacy.

hege|n ['he:gən] (25) cherish; hunt. preserve; Pflanzen usw.: tend; Zweifel usw.: have, entertain; ~ und pflegen lavish care on; '♀r hunt. m (7) gamekeeper.

Hehl [he:l] n (3): kein ~ machen aus make no secret of; '♀en r̷t̷ (25) v/i. receive stolen goods.

'Hehler r̷t̷ m (7), '~in f receiver (of stolen goods), sl. fence; ~ei r̷t̷ [~'raɪ] f receiving (of stolen goods).

hehr [he:r] noble; lofty, sublime.

Heide[1] ['haɪdə] m (13), 'Heidin f heathen, pagan; biblisch: Gentile.

Heide[2] [~] f (15) heath; '~kraut n heather; '~land n moor(land).

'Heidelbeere f bilberry Am. blueberry, huckleberry.

'Heidelerche f woodlark.

'Heiden|-angst F f mortal fright, F blue funk; '~geld n piles pl. of money; '~lärm m tremendous noise; '♀mäßig enormous, tremendous; '~spaß m great fun; '~tum n (1²) paganism.

Heiderös-chen ['~rø:sçən] n (6) wild briar, dog-rose.

heidnisch ['haɪdnɪʃ] heathen, pagan; biblisch: Gentile.

heikel ['haɪkəl] delicate; (wählerisch) particular, fussy; fastidious, (over-)nice (mit about); S.: (schwierig) delicate, ticklish.

heil [haɪl] 1. (ganz) whole, intact; (unversehrt) sound, unhurt; (geheilt) healed, restored; 2. ♀ n (3) welfare; eccl. salvation; ♀! hail!; Jahr des ~s year of grace; sein ~ in der Flucht

suchen seek safety in flight; sein ~ versuchen try one's luck.

Heiland ['haɪlant] m (3) Savio(u)r.

'Heil|-anstalt f sanatorium, Am. sanitarium; für Alkoholiker usw.: home, (mental) hospital; '~bad n medicinal bath; (Kurort) spa; '♀bar curable; '~barkeit f curableness; '♀bringend salutary, salubrious; '~butt m (3) halibut; '♀en (25) v/t. j-n: cure (von of; a. fig.); Krankheit: cure; Wunde: (a. v/i.; sn) heal; '~gymnastik f physiotherapy.

heilig ['haɪlɪç] holy, sacred; (fromm) saintly; (feierlich) solemn; ♀er Abend Christmas Eve; ♀e Jungfrau Blessed Virgin; ♀e Nacht Holy Night; ♀er Vater Holy Father; fig. ~e Pflicht sacred duty; s. Geist, Grab, Gral, Schrift, Stuhl; ♀e ['~lige] m, f saint; ~en ['~ligən] (25) hallow, (a. fig. = gutheißen) sanctify; '♀enschein m halo, glory, gloriole; '♀keit f holiness, sanctity; '~sprechen canonize; '♀tum n (1²) Ort: sanctuary; Reliquie: relic.

Heiligung ['~guŋ] f sanctification.

'Heil|kraft f healing power; '♀kräftig curative; '~kraut n officinal herb; '~kunde f medical science; praktische: therapeutics mst sg.; '♀los unholy (F a. fig. = fürchterlich); F adv. hopelessly, frightfully; '~mittel n remedy (gegen for; a. fig.), medicament; '~pädagogik f therapeutic pedagogy; '~praktiker m healer; '~quelle f (medicinal) mineral spring.

'heilsam wholesome, salutary; '♀keit f wholesomeness, salutariness.

'Heils-armee f Salvation Army.

'Heil|serum n antiserum; '~stätte f sanatorium, Am. sanitarium; '~ung f vgl. heilen; curing, cure; healing; '~ungs-chancen f/pl. chances of being cured; '~ungs-prozeß m healing process; '~ungsquote f cure rate; '~verfahren n medical treatment, therapy.

heim [haɪm] 1. adv. home; 2. ♀ n (3) home (a. Anstalt); (Jugend♀, Studenten♀) hostel; '♀-arbeit f home-work, outwork; '♀-arbeiter (-in f) m homeworker.

Heimat ['~a:t] f (16) home, native place od. country; '~kunde f local history and geography; '~land n native country; '♀lich native; Ge-

fühl: homelike; '⸠los homeless; '⸠-ort *m* native place; '⸠stadt *f* home town; '⸠vertriebene *m, f* (18) expellee.

'**heimbegleiten:** *j-n* ⸠ see home.

'**Heimbuchung** *f Computer*: home banking.

Heimchen ['⸠çən] *n* (6) cricket.

'**Heimcomputer** *m* home computer.

heimelig ['haɪməlɪç] cosy.

'**Heim|fahrt** *f* journey home; '⸠fall ɫ⸠ *m* reversion; '⸠gang *m* going home; *fig.* death; '⸠gehen go home; '⸠isch *s.* einheimisch; (*vertraut*) homelike; *sich* ⸠ *fühlen* feel at home (*a. fig. in dat.* in); ⸠ *werden* settle down, *S.*: become established; ⸠kehr ['⸠ke:r] *f* (16), ⸠kunft ['⸠kunft] *f* (14¹) return (home); '⸠kehren, '⸠kommen (sn) return home; '⸠kehrer *m* home--comer, returnee; '⸠kind *n* child in care, institutional child; '⸠leuchten: *j-m* ⸠ send a p. packing.

'**heimlich** (*verborgen*) secret; (*verstohlen*) stealthy; *s.* heimelig; '⸠keit *f* secrecy; (*Geheimnis*) secret; ⸠tuerei [⸠'raɪ] *f* secretive behavio(u)r; '⸠tun be secretive (*mit et.* about).

'**Heim|niederlage** *f Sport*: home defeat; '⸠reise *f* homeward journey; journey home; '⸠sieg *m* home win; '⸠spiel *n* home match; '⸠stätte *f* home; (*Siedlung*) home-croft, *Am.* homestead; '⸠suchen *Geist usw.*: haunt; (*plagen*) afflict, plague; *biblisch*: visit; '⸠suchung *f bibl.* visitation; *fig. a.* affliction; '⸠trainer *m* (*Gerät*) home exerciser; '⸠tücke *f* malice, treachery; '⸠tückisch malicious; (*a. fig.*) treacherous, insidious; ⸠wärts ['⸠vɛrts] homeward; '⸠weg *m* way home; '⸠weh *n* homesickness; ⸠ *haben* be homesick; '⸠werker *m* hobbyist; *Heimwerker...* do-it-yourself; '⸠zahlen F: *j-m et.* ⸠ pay a p. back for a th.

Hein [haɪn] *m: Freund* ⸠ Goodman Death.

Heinzelmännchen ['haɪntsəlmençən] *n* brownie; *pl. a.* little people.

Heirat ['haɪra:t] *f* (16) marriage; '⸠en *v/t. u. v/i.* (26) marry.

'**Heirats|-antrag** *m* offer (*od.* proposal) of marriage; *e-n* ⸠ *machen* propose (*dat.* to); '⸠fähig marriageable; '⸠kandidat *m* suitor; eligible bachelor; '⸠lustig eager to

get married; '⸠markt *m* marriage market; '⸠schwindler *m* marriage impostor; '⸠urkunde *f* marriage certificate; '⸠vermittler(in *f*) *m* marriage broker; '⸠versprechen *n* promise of marriage.

heischen ['haɪʃən] (27) demand.

heiser ['haɪzər] hoarse; '⸠keit *f* hoarseness.

heiß [haɪs] hot; *fig. a.* ardent; (*heftig*) fierce; ⸠e Zone torrid zone; *mir ist* ⸠ I am hot; *s. Hölle*; '⸠blütig hot-blooded.

heißen¹ ['haɪsən] (30) *v/t.* call, name; (*befehlen*) bid, command, order, tell; *j-n willkommen* ⸠ bid a p. welcome; *v/i.* be called; (*bedeuten*) mean, signify; *das heißt* that is (to say); *es heißt, daß* ... it is said (*od.* reported) that ...; *wie* ⸠ *Sie?* what is your name?; *wie heißt das auf englisch?* what's that in English?; *was soll das* ⸠? what is the meaning of this?

heißen² ['haɪsən] (27) ⚓ hoist (*the flag, etc.*).

'**Heiß|hunger** *m* ravenous hunger; '⸠hungrig ravenous; '⸠geliebt (dearly) beloved; (*sich*) '⸠laufen ⊕ run hot, overheat; '⸠luftherd *m* convection oven; '⸠sporn *m* hotspur; '⸠-umstritten highly controversial; '⸠wasser... *s. Warmwasser...*

heiter ['haɪtər] cheerful, merry, serene; *Wetter usw.*: clear, bright; '⸠keit *f* cheerfulness, mirth; serenity.

Heiz|-anlage ['haɪts-] *f* heating plant; '⸠bar to be heated; with heating facilities; *Heckscheibe:* defrosting; '⸠batterie *f* filament (*Am.* A-) battery; '⸠decke *f* electric blanket; '⸠en *v/t. u. v/i.* (27) heat; '⸠er *m* (7) fireman, stoker; (*Gerät*) heater; '⸠kessel *m* boiler; '⸠kissen *n* electric (heating) pad; '⸠körper *m der Zentralheizung:* radiator; ⚡ heater; '⸠kosten *pl.* heating costs; '⸠kostenabrechnung *f* heating bill; '⸠lüfter *m* fan heater; '⸠material *n* fuel; '⸠-öl *n* fuel oil; '⸠platte *f* hot plate; '⸠rohr *n* heating pipe; '⸠sonne *f* bowl-fire; '⸠ung *f* heating.

hektisch ['hɛktiʃ] hectic(ally *adv.*).

Hekto... [hɛkto-] *in Zssgn* hecto...

Held [hɛlt] *m* (12) hero (*a. thea., etc.*).

Helden... ['⸠dən]: *in Zssgn mst* heroic ...; '⸠gedicht *n* heroic epic;

'♀**haft** heroic(ally *adv.*); '⁓**mut** *m* heroism, valo(u)r; ♀**mütig** ['⁓my:- tiç] heroic; '⁓**tat** *f* heroic deed, exploit; '⁓**tenor** *m* heroic tenor; '⁓**tod** *m* heroic death; *den* ⁓ *erleiden* die a hero; '⁓**tum** *n* (1) heroism.

'**Heldin** *f* heroine.

helfen ['hɛlfən] (30, *dat.*) help; (*unterstützen*) aid; (*beistehen*) assist; (*nützen*) avail, profit; *sich zu* ⁓ *wissen* be full of resource; *sich nicht zu* ⁓ *wissen* be at one's wits' end; *ich kann mir nicht* ⁓ I can't help it; *es hilft* (*zu*) *nichts* it is of no use, it is no good.

'**Helfer** *m* (7), '⁓**in** *f* helper, assist- ant; ⁓ *in Steuersachen* tax-consult- ant; '⁓**s-helfer** *m* accomplice.

hell [hɛl] bright (*a. gescheit*), clear (*a. Klang*); *Haar*: fair; *Bier*: light; *Neid, Unsinn usw.*: sheer; *am* ⁓*en Tage* in broad daylight; *es wird* ⁓ it is getting light; '⁓**blau** light-blue; '⁓**blond** very fair.

'**Helle** *f* (15) brightness, clearness.

Hellebarde [hɛlə'bardə] *f* (15) halberd.

Hellen|e [hɛ'le:nə] *m* (13) Hellene; ♀**isch** Hellenic.

Heller ['hɛlər] *m* (7) farthing, penny; *auf* ⁓ *und Pfennig bezahlen* pay to the last penny; *keinen* ⁓ *wert* not worth a penny.

'**hell|glänzend** brightly shining; '⁓**hörig** quick of hearing; *fig.* per- ceptive.

Helligkeit ['hɛliçkaɪt] *f* brightness.

Helling ['hɛliŋ] *f* (16) ⚓ slip(way).

'**Hell|seher(in** *f*) *m*, '♀**seherisch** clairvoyant; ⁓**seherei** [⁓'raɪ] *f* clairvoyance; ♀**sichtig** ['⁓zɪçtiç] *fig.* clear-sighted; '♀'**wach** wide awake (*a. fig.*).

Helm [hɛlm] *m* (3) ✕ helmet; ⚓ helm, rudder; △ dome.

Hemd [hɛmt] *n* (5) (*Männer♀*) shirt; (*Frauen♀*) *a.* chemise; *j-n bis aufs* ⁓ *ausziehen* strip a p. to the shirt; '⁓**bluse** *f* shirt(-blouse); '⁓**blusen- kleid** *n* shirt dress; '⁓**hose** ['hɛmt-] *f* (*eine a pair of*) combinations *pl., Am. a.* union suit; (*Damen♀*) (pair of) cami-knickers *pl.*; '⁓**knopf** *m* shirt button; '⁓**(s)-ärmel** *m* shirtsleeve; *in* ⁓*n* in one's shirtsleeves.

Hemisphäre [he:mi'sfɛ:rə] *f* (15) hemisphere.

hemmen ['hɛmən] (25) stop, check;

(*behindern*) hinder, hamper; im- pede; (*bremsen*) brake; *seelisch*: in- hibit.

'**Hemm|nis** *n* (4¹) hindrance; '⁓- **schuh** *m* drag (*a. fig. gen.* on); '⁓**ung** *f* stop(ping), check(ing); obstruction; *Uhr*: escapement; *see- lisch*: inhibition; '♀**ungslos** unre- strained, without restraint.

Hengst [hɛŋst] *m* (3²) stallion.

Henkel ['hɛŋkəl] *m* (7) handle; '⁓**korb** *m* basket with handles.

henken ['hɛŋkən] (25) hang.

'**Henker** *m* (7) hangman, execu- tioner; *zum* ⁓! the deuce!; *zum* ⁓ *mit* ...! hang ...!; '⁓**sknecht** *m fig.* henchman; '⁓**smahl(zeit** *f*) *n* last meal.

Henne ['hɛnə] *f* (15) hen.

her [he:r] here; *zeitlich*: *es ist schon ein Jahr* ⁓, *daß* ... it is now a year ago since ...; *wie lange ist es* ⁓? how long is it ago?; *von weit* ⁓ from afar; *s. hin*; ⁓ *sein von* be (*od.* come) from; *hinter* (*dat.*) ⁓ *sein* be after; ⁓ *damit!* out with it!; *s. Alter, hin, weit.*

herab [hɛ'rap] down, downward; *s. oben*; ⁓**drücken** press down; *Preis*: force down, depress; ⁓**las- sen** let down; *sich* ⁓ *fig.* conde- scend; ⁓**lassend** condescending; ♀**lassung** *f* condescension; ⁓**sehen** *auf* (*acc.*) look down upon; ⁓**setzen** lower; *im Rang*: degrade, reduce (in rank); (*verächtlich machen*) dis- parage; *Preis*: reduce, mark (*od.* cut) down; ♀**setzung** *f* lowering; degradation; disparagement; reduc- tion; cut; ⁓**sinken** sink, descend; ⁓**steigen** (sn) climb down, de- scend; *vom Pferde*: dismount; ⁓- **würdigen** degrade; ♀**würdigung** *f* abasement, degradation.

Herald|ik [he'raldik] *f* (16) herald- ry; ♀**isch** heraldic.

heran [hɛ'ran] on, near, up; *er ging an sie* ⁓ he went up to them; *nur* ⁓! come on!; ⁓**bilden** train, educate; ⁓**bringen** bring up; ⁓**gehen** (sn) approach (*an et. a th.*), go up (to); ⁓ *an e-e Arbeit usw.*: set about, tackle; ⁓**kommen** (sn) come on (*od.* near); ⁓ *an* (*acc.*) come up to (*a. fig.*), (*bekommen*) get at; *die Dinge an sich* ⁓ *lassen* wait and see; *sich* ⁓**machen** *an* (*acc.*) *et.*: set about, *j-n*: make up to; ⁓**nahen**

(sn) *a. zeitlich:* approach, draw near; *sich* ~**pirschen** creep up (*an acc.* to); ~**reichen** *an* (*acc.*) reach (up to); *fig.* measure up to; ~**schaffen** bring up, move to the spot; supply; ~**schleichen:** *sich* ~ *an* (*acc.*) sneak up to; ~**treten** approach (*an j-n* a p.; *a. fig.*); ~**wachsen** (sn) grow up; ♀**wachsende** *m*, *f* (18) adolescent; ~**ziehen** draw near; *fig. Stelle, Werk:* quote, cite; *j-n:* call *a* p. in; *j-n zu e-r Arbeit usw.* ~ call (up)on a p. to *do work*, etc.

herauf [hɛ'rauf] up, upwards; (*hier*~) up here; ~**beschwören** conjure up; *fig. a.* bring on; ~**kommen** (sn) come up; *Unwetter:* approach; ~**setzen** increase, raise; ~**steigen** (sn) climb up, ascend; ~**ziehen** *v/t.* pull up; *v/i.* (sn) *Unwetter usw.:* approach.

heraus [hɛ'raus] out; ~*!* come out!, turn out!; ~ *damit!* out with it!; *s. frei; die Handhabung von et.* ~ *haben* have got the knack (*Am.* hang) of *a* th.; *Lösung, Sinn* ~ *haben* have found out; ~**bekommen** get out; *Geld:* get back; *fig.* find out; ~**bringen** bring out; (*herausbekommen*) get out; *fig.* find out; *Fabrikat usw.:* launch; *Buch:* s. *herausgeben;* ~**finden** find out; ♀**forderer** *m* challenger; ~**fordern** defy, provoke; *zum Zweikampf:* challenge; ♀**forderung** *f* challenge (*a. fig.*); provocation; ~**fühlen** feel, sense; ♀**gabe** *f* delivery; *e-s Buches usw.:* publication; ~**geben** surrender; (*zurückgeben*) give back; *Buch:* publish, *als Bearbeiter:* edit; *Geld:* give ... in change; *Geld* ~ *auf* (*acc.*) give change for; *Vorschrift usw.:* issue; ♀**geber** *m* publisher; (*Redakteur*) editor; ♀**geberin** *f* editress; ~**greifen** pick out; ~**gehen** (sn) *Nagel usw.:* go out; *Fleck:* come out; *fig. aus sich* ~ liven up; ~**kommen** (sn) come out; (*ruchbar werden*) become known, leak out; *Buch:* be published, appear; (*sich ergeben*) result (*bei* from), come (of); work out; *es kommt auf eins (od. dasselbe) heraus* it comes to the same thing; *es kommt nichts dabei heraus* it is of no use; *es ist nichts Gutes dabei herausgekommen* nothing good has come

(out) of it; ~**kriegen** *s. herausbekommen;* ~**machen** take out, remove; *fig. sich* ~ turn out well; ~**nehmen** take out; *sich* ~ *zu* presume; *sich Freiheiten* ~ take liberties (*gegen* with); ~**platzen** (sn): *mit et.* ~ *fig.* blurt a th. out; ~**putzen** dress up; ~**ragen** *a. fig.* stand out (*aus dat.* from); ~**reden:** *frei* ~ speak out; *sich* ~ make excuses, wriggle out; ~**reißen** pull (*od.* tear) out; *fig.* extricate, save; ~**rücken** *v/t. u. v/i.* (sn): ~ *mit* hand over; *mit Geld:* F shell out; *mit der Wahrheit usw.:* come out with; *mit der Sprache* ~ speak out (freely); ~**rufen** call out; ~**rutschen** (sn) slip out (*a. fig.*); ~**schlagen** *fig.* get, *sl.* wangle; *etwas* ~ *bei* get out of; ~**springen** (sn) jump out; *fig.* result, be gained; ~**stellen** put out; *Spieler:* turn out; *fig.* give prominence to; feature; *sich* ~ appear, turn out, prove (*als* to be), be found (out); ~**strecken** put (*od.* stick) out; ~**streichen** praise, crack up; ~**treten** (sn) step out; ⚚ protrude; *Flüssigkeit usw.:* exude; *sich* ~**wagen** venture out; *sich* ~**winden** (*aus dat.*) *fig.* extricate o.s. (from), wriggle out (of); ~**wirtschaften** obtain; *et.* ~ make a profit; ~**ziehen** *v/t.* draw (*od.* pull) out; extract.

herb [hɛrp] harsh (*a. fig.*); (*sauer*) acid, sour; *Wein usw.:* dry; *Enttäuschung, Worte:* bitter, harsh; *Schönheit, Stil:* austere.

Herbarium [hɛr'ba:rjum] *n* (9) herbarium.

herbei [hɛr'bai] hither, *mst* here; ~*!* (*komm*[*t*] *her!*) come on *od.* here!; ~ *zu mir* up to me; *s. heran...;* ~**eilen** (sn) approach in haste; ~**führen** *fig.* bring about *od.* on, cause; ~**lassen:** *sich* ~ condescend; ~**rufen** call; ~**schaffen** bring on; procure; ~**sehnen** long for.

herbemühen ['hɛ:rbəmy:ən] trouble to come (here); *sich* ~ take the trouble of coming.

Herberge ['hɛrbergə] *f* (15) shelter, lodging; (*Gasthaus*) inn; (*Jugend*♀) hostel; ²**n** (25) *v/i.* put up, lodge (*bei* at); *v/t. s.* beherbergen.

Herbergsvater ['~ksfa:tər] *m* warden (of a hostel).

herbestellen 926

'**her|bestellen** send for, summon; '**⁓beten** rattle off.
Herbheit ['hɛrphaɪt] harshness (a. fig.); fig. bitterness, severity; austerity; Wein: dryness.
'**herbringen** bring here, bring (up).
Herbst [hɛrpst] m (3²) autumn, Am. fall; '**⁓anfang** m beginning of autumn; '**⁓lich** autumnal; '**⁓tag** m autumn day; **⁓zeitlose** ♀ ['⁓tsaɪt-loːzə] f (15) meadow saffron.
Herd [heːrt] m (3) hearth (a. = Heim); offener: fireplace; (Kochmaschine) cooking-stove, großer: range; fig. (Sitz) seat.
Herde ['heːrdə] f (15) Großvieh: herd (contp. a. fig.); getriebene: drove; Kleinvieh: flock; fig. crowd; '**⁓ntier** n gregarious animal; '**⁓ntrieb** m herd instinct.
herein [hɛˈraɪn] in; ⁓! come in!; **⁓bemühen** trouble to come in; **⁓bitten** ask (od. invite) in; **⁓brechen** fig. (sn) Nacht: close in (über acc. upon); Unglück usw.: ⁓ über overtake, befall; **⁓bringen** bring in; Verlust wieder ⁓ make good; **⁓fall** m s. Reinfall; **⁓fallen** (sn) taken in (auf acc. by); ⁓ auf Am. F fall for; **⁓führen** show (od. usher) in; **⁓kommen** (sn) come in (a. ✛); **⁓lassen** let in, admit; **⁓legen** F take a p. in, fool (od. dupe) a p.; **⁓platzen** F (sn) burst in; **⁓schauen** look in (F bei j-m on a p.); **⁓schneien** fig. (sn) blow in.
her|fallen ['heːr-] (sn): über j-n fall (od. set) (up)on; '**⁓gang** m course of events, circumstances pl.; tell me what happened; '**⁓geben** deliver, give (away); fig. (gewähren) yield; sich (s-n Namen) ⁓ zu lend o.s. (one's name) to; '**⁓gebracht** handed down to us, traditional; (üblich) customary; '**⁓gehören** belong to the matter; '**⁓gelaufen** adj. vagabond; '**⁓halten** v/t. hold out; v/i. suffer (für for); ⁓ müssen F stand the racket; '**⁓holen** fetch; weit hergeholt far-fetched.
Hering ['heːrɪŋ] m (3¹) herring; (Zeltpflock) tent peg; zusammengedrängt wie die ⁓e packed like sardines; s. grün; '**⁓ssalat** m pickled-herring salad.
her|kommen ['heːr-] (sn): komm her! come here!; ⁓ von come (od. originate) from; S.: a. be due to;

Wort: be derived from; '**⁓kommen** n (6) (Sitte) convention, custom; (Abstammung) origin, extraction; **⁓kömmlich** ['⁓kœmlɪç] conventional (a. ✗ Waffe); s. hergebracht; '**⁓kunft** f (14¹) P.: origin, extraction; S.: origin, provenance; '**⁓laufen** (sn): hinter j-m ⁓ run after; '**⁓leiern** F reel off; '**⁓leiten** (von) derive (from); sich ⁓ von (be) derive(d) from; '**⁓leitung** f derivation; sich '**⁓machen** über (acc.) set about, tackle; j-n: set on, attack.
Hermelin [hɛrməˈliːn] n (3¹) ermine.
hermetisch [hɛrˈmeːtiʃ] hermetic (-ally adv.).
hernach [hɛrˈnɑːx] after(wards).
hernehmen ['heːr-] (von) take (from), get (from); fig. j-n ⁓ take a p. to task.
hernieder [hɛrˈniːdər] down; s. herab, herunter.
Heroin [heroˈiːn] n (3¹, o. pl.) heroin.
hero|isch [heˈroːiʃ] heroic(ally adv.); **⁓ismus** [heroˈismus] m (16) heroism.
Herold ['heːrɔlt] m (3) herald.
Heros ['heːrɔs] m (16²) hero.
herplappern ['heːr-] rattle off.
Herr [her] m (12²) master; (bsd. adliger ⁓) lord; (Herrscher) ruler; (feiner Mann, a. allg.) gentleman; (Gott) Lord; Anrede: Sir, vor Eigennamen: Mr.; mein ⁓ Sir; meine ⁓en gentlemen; aus aller ⁓en Länder(n) from all over the world; fig. ⁓ werden (gen.) master, get under control; ⁓ der Lage master of the situation.
'**Herren|-anzug** m (gentle)man's suit; '**⁓artikel** m/pl. gentlemen's outfitting, Am. haberdashery sg.; '**⁓bekleidung** f (gentle)men's wear; '**⁓doppel** n Tennis: men's doubles pl.; '**⁓-einzel** n Tennis: men's singles pl.; '**⁓friseur** m (gentle)men's hairdresser, barber; '**⁓haus** n mansion, manor(-house); '**⁓konfektion** f (gentle)men's ready--to-wear clothes; '**⁓los** ownerless; Tier: stray; ⁓e Güter n/pl. derelicts; '**⁓mode** f men's fashion; '**⁓reiter** m gentleman rider; '**⁓schneider** m (gentlemen's) tailor; '**⁓schnitt** m bei Damen: Eton crop, shingle; '**⁓toilette** f men's toilet (Am. restroom); '**⁓zimmer** n study.

'**Herrgott** *m* (1¹ *u.* ²) *the* Lord (God), God.

herrichten ['hɛ:rrɪçtən] arrange, prepare, get *a th.* ready; *Zimmer*: tidy; (*instand setzen*) do up, repair; *sich* ~ smarten o.s. up.

Herrin ['hɛrɪn]*f*(16¹) mistress, lady.

'**herrisch** imperious.

herrje! [hɛr'je:] goodness!, dear me!

'**herrlich** marvellous, glorious, magnificent, splendid; '♀**keit** *f* magnificence, splendo(u)r, glory.

'**Herrschaft** *f* rule, dominion (*über acc.* of); *a. fig.* mastery, power, control; (*Regierung*) government, *e-s Fürsten*: reign; *der Dienstboten*: master and mistress; *meine* ~*en!* ladies and gentlemen!; *die* ~ *verlieren über* lose control of; '♀**lich** belonging (*od.* referring) to a master *od.* lord; (*grundherrlich*) manorial; (*vornehm*) high-class, elegant.

herrschen ['hɛrʃən] (27) rule (*über acc.* over); (*regieren*) govern (*über e-n Staat usw.* a State *etc.*); *als Fürst*: reign (*über* over); (*vor*~) prevail, reign; (*bestehen*) be, exist.

'**Herrscher** *m* (7) ruler, sovereign; '~**haus** *n* dynasty.

'**Herrsch|sucht** *f* thirst for power; F bossiness; '♀**süchtig** greedy of power; *weit S.* domineering, F bossy.

her|rufen ['hɛ:r-] call (here); '~**rühren** *s.* herkommen; '~**sagen** recite, say; '~**schreiben**: *sich* ~ *von* come from; '~**sehen** look here *od.* this way; '~**stammen** *s.* abstammen; *s.* herkommen; '~**stellen** place (*od.* put) here; (*erzeugen*) manufacture, produce, make; *fig.* produce, bring about; *Frieden, Ordnung, Verbindungen*: establish; (*wieder*~) restore, repair; *Kranke*: restore to health; '♀**steller** *m* (7) manufacturer, maker, producer; '♀**stellerfirma** *f* manufacturing firm, manufacturers *pl.*; '♀**stellung** *f* manufacture, production; establishment; (*Abteilung*) production department; '♀**stellungskosten** † *pl.* production costs; '♀**stellungsleiter**(**in** *f*) *m* production manager; '♀**stellungsverfahren** *n* manufacturing method (*od.* process).

Hertz *phys.* [hɛrts] *n inv.* cycles *pl.* per second.

herüber [hɛ'ry:bər] over, across; ~**kommen** (sn) come over (here), come across.

herum [hɛ'rum] *ziellos*: about, *Am. a.* around; (*rings*~) (a)round; (*ungefähr*) about; *hier* ~ hereabout(s); (*vorbei*) over, finished; ~**bekommen** *s.* herumkriegen; ~**bringen** *Zeit*: pass, kill; *j-n*: *s.* herumkriegen; ~**doktern** *an j-m* physic (*od.* doctor) *a p.*; ~**drehen** turn round; *sich* ~**drücken** *s.* herumlungern; ~**fuchteln** *v/i.* saw the air; mit *et.*: fidget with; ~**führen**: *j-n* ~ (*zur Orientierung*) show a p. round; *j-n* ~ *in* (*dat.*) show a p. over *a house etc.*; *s.* Nase; ~**kommen** (sn) come round; *weit* ~ see much of the world, get about (*Am.* around); *fig.* ~ *um e-e Notwendigkeit usw.* avoid, dodge; ~**kommandieren** order *a p.* about; *j-n* ~**kriegen** win a p. over, talk a p. round; ~**lungern** loaf (*od.* loiter, hang) about; ~**reden**: um *et.* ~ talk (*od.* argue) round a th.; ~**reichen** hand round; ~**reisen** (sn) travel about; ~**reiten** *auf* (*dat.*) *fig.* harp (up)on; ~**scharwenzeln** um *j-n* dance attendance on; *sich* ~**schlagen** mit grapple with; ~**spionieren** snoop about; *sich* ~**sprechen** get about; *es hat sich herumgesprochen, daß* it is rumo(u)red that; ~**stehen** stand about; ~ um stand (a)round *a th. od. p.*; ~**treiben**: *sich* ~ gad (F knock) about; *s.* herumlungern; ~**ziehen***v/t.* draw (*od.* pull) (a)round; *v/i.* (sn) wander about; um *et.*: march round.

herunter [hɛ'runtər] *s. herab*; *den Hut* ~! off with your hat!; ~**bringen** bring down; *fig. a.* lower, reduce; ~**hauen**: *j-m e-e* ~ F fetch a p. one; ~**kommen** (sn) come down (in the world *fig. v. P.*); (*verfallen*) decay; heruntergekommen *fig.* in reduced circumstances, out-at-elbows, *gesundheitlich*: in poor health; ~**machen** F run (*Am.* F call) down; ~**reißen** pull down; *fig.* (*scharf kritisieren*) pull to pieces; ~**schrauben** *fig.* lower; ~**sein** *fig. gesundheitlich*: be run down; ~**spielen** ♪ F rattle off; *fig.* play down; ~**wirtschaften** run down.

hervor [hɛr'fo:r] forth, out; ~**bringen** produce; *Worte*: utter; ♀**brin-**

gung f production; **~gehen** (sn) *als Sieger*: come off, emerge (*aus* from); *als Folge*: result *od.* follow (*aus* from); (*ersichtlich sein*) be evident, follow (*aus* from); **~heben** render prominent; *Kunst*: set off; (*herausstreichen*) show off; (*betonen*) emphasize; **~holen** produce; **~ragen** project; stand out, be prominent; *fig. a.* excel; **~ragend** prominent; *nur fig.* excellent, outstanding, eminent; **⒉ruf** *thea.* m call; **~rufen** call forth; *thea.* call for; *fig.* cause; **~stechen** stick out; *fig.* stand forth; **~stechend** prominent; conspicuous; **~stehen** stand out; *Augen usw.*: protrude; **~treten** (sn) step forth; *s. a.* hervorragen, -stechen; *sich* **~tun** distinguish o.s.; **~ziehen** draw forth, produce.

her|wagen ['heːr-]: *sich* **~** venture to come here; **⒉weg** m way here.

Herz [hɛrts] *n* (12²) heart; (*Mut*) *a.* courage, spirit; (*Seele*) *a.* soul; (*Gemüt, Geist*) mind; *Kartenspiel*: hearts *pl.*; *Anrede*: darling, love; *sich ein* **~** *fassen* take heart; *s. ausschütten, schließen*; *auf* **~** *und Nieren prüfen* put to the acid-test; *etwas auf dem* **~**en haben have something on one's mind; *j-m et. ans* **~** *legen* enjoin a th. on a p.; *das* **~** *auf der Zunge haben* wear one's heart on one's sleeve; F *mir ist das* **~** *in die Hosen gefallen* my heart is in my boots; *s-m* **~**en *Luft machen* give vent to one's feelings; *mit ganzem* **~**en *dabeisein usw.* with one's whole heart; *ich kann es nicht über das* **~** *bringen* I cannot find it in my heart; *von ganzem* **~**en *danken usw.* with all my *etc.* heart; *sich et. zu* **~**en *nehmen* take a th. to heart; *sein* **~** *an et. hängen* set one's heart on a th.; *ein* **~** *und eine Seele sein* be as thick as thieves, be hand in glove; **~...** ⚕ cardiac (*z. B. cardiac asthma*).

'Herz|-anfall m heart-attack; **'~asthma** n cardiac asthma; **'~beschwerden** f/pl. heart trouble; **'~chen** n *Anrede*: darling.

'Herzeleid n deep sorrow.

'herzen (27) press to one's heart; (*umarmen*) hug, embrace; (*liebkosen*) caress, cuddle.

'Herzens|-angelegenheit f love-affair; **'~angst** f anguish of mind;

'~brecher m lady-killer; **'⒉froh** very glad; **'⒉gut** very kind; **'~güte** f kindness of heart; *nach* **'~lust** f to one's heart's content, to the top of one's bent; **'~wunsch** m heart's desire.

'herz|-erfrischend heart-warming; **'~-ergreifend** heart-moving; **'⒉-erweiterung** f dilatation of the heart; **'⒉fehler** m cardiac defect; **~förmig** ['~fœrmiç] heart-shaped; **'⒉gegend** f cardiac region; **'⒉-grube** f pit of the stomach; **'~haft** courageous; (*kräftig*) hearty; **⒉haftigkeit** f courage; heartiness.

herziehen ['heːrtsiːən]: **~** *über j-n* run a p. down.

herzig ['hɛrtsiç] sweet, lovely, *Am.* cute.

'Herz|-infarkt m coronary (thrombosis), ⚕ cardiac infarction; **'~kammer** f ventricle; **'~katheter** ⚕ m (*Gerät*) cardiac catheter; (*Untersuchung*) heart (*od.* cardiac) catheter; **'~kirsche** f heart cherry; **'~klopfen** n beating (*od.* palpitation) of the heart; **'⒉krank** having heart trouble; **'~leiden** n heart complaint.

'herzlich heartfelt, warm, sincere; **~** *gern* with the greatest of pleasure; **~** *wenig* precious little; *im Brief*: *mit* **~**en *Grüßen* *pl.* yours sincerely, *intimer*: (yours with) love; **~**e *Grüße an* (*acc.*) kind regards to; **'⒉keit** f heartiness, cordiality, warmth. [heartlessness.)

herz|los heartless; **'⒉losigkeit** f)

Herzog ['hɛrtsoːk] m (3[³]) duke; **~in** ['~tsoːgin] f (16¹) duchess; **⒉lich** ['~kliç] ducal; **'~tum** n (1²) dukedom, duchy.

'Herz|schlag m heartbeat; ⚕ heart attack (*od.* failure); **'~schrittmacher** m pace-maker; **'~schwäche** f cardiac weakness; **'~spezialist** m heart specialist; **'⒉stärkend** cordial; **'~stillstand** m heart stoppage, ⚕ cardiac arrest; **'~tod** m cardiac death.

herzu [hɛr'tsuː] = heran, herbei.

'Herzverpflanzung f heart transplant.

'herzzerreißend heart-rending.

Hesse ['hɛsə] m (13), **'Hessin** f, **'hessisch** Hessian.

heterogen [hetero'geːn] heterogeneous.

Hetze ['hɛtsə] f (15) s. Hetzjagd;

(*Eile*) hurry, rush; (*Aufreizung*) instigation, agitation (*gegen* against); '**2n** (27) *v/t. hunt.* course, hunt, chase (*a. fig.*); *fig.* (*umherjagen*) hurry, rush (*a. v/i.*); (*aufreizen*) incite; *e-n Hund auf j-n* ~ set a dog at a p.; *v/i.* cause discord; *gegen j-n* ~ agitate against a p.

'**Hetzer** *m* (7), '**~in** *f fig.* instigator, agitator; '**2isch** inflammatory.

'**Hetz|jagd** *f* coursing, baiting; *fig.* rush, *Am. sl.* rat race; '**~rede** *f* inflammatory speech.

Heu [hɔʏ] *n* (3) hay; F *Geld wie* ~ pots of money; '**~boden** *m* hay-loft.

Heuchel|ei [hɔʏçə'laɪ] *f* (16) hypocrisy; dissimulation; '**~n** (29) *v/t.* simulate, feign; *v/i.* play the hypocrite; dissemble, sham.

'**Heuchler** *m* (7), '**~in** *f* (16¹) hypocrite; '**2isch** hypocritical.

heuen ['hɔʏən] (25) make hay.

heuer¹ ['hɔʏər] (in) this year.

'**Heuer²** *m* haymaker.

'**Heuer³** ⚓ *f* (15) wages *pl.*; '**2n** (29) hire.

'**Heu|-ernte** *f* hay-harvest; '**~gabel** *f* hay-fork, pitch-fork.

heul|en ['hɔʏlən] (25) howl; (*weinen*) cry; (*jammern*) wail; *Sirene*: hoot; **2suse** F ['~zu:zə] *f* cry-baby.

heurig ['hɔʏriç] of this year.

'**Heu|schnupfen** *m* hay fever; '**~schober** *m* haystack, hayrick; '**~schrecke** *f* (15) locust, grasshopper.

heute ['hɔʏtə] today, this day; ~ *abend* this evening, tonight; ~ *früh*, ~ *morgen* this morning; ~ *über* (*vor*) *acht Tage*(*n*) this day week; ~ *übers Jahr* a year from today; ~ *vor acht Tagen* a week ago (today); *von* ~ *auf morgen fig.* overnight.

'**heutig** of this day, this day's, today's; (*gegenwärtig*) present(-day), modern.

'**heutzutage** nowadays.

Hexe ['hɛksə] *f* (15) witch, sorceress; *fig.* (*altes Weib*) *a.* hag; (*böses Weib*) hell-cat; '**2n** (27) practise witchcraft; *fig.* work miracles.

'**Hexen|jagd** *f fig.* witch-hunt; '**~kessel** *m* inferno; '**~meister** *m* wizard, sorcerer; '**~sabbath** *m* Witches' Sabbath; *fig.* inferno; '**~schuß** ⚕ *m* lumbago.

Hexerei [~'raɪ] *f* (16) witchcraft, (*a. fig.*) magic.

Hieb [hi:p] **1.** *m* (3) stroke, blow; *mit e-m Schwert usw.*: cut; (*Anzüglichkeit*) hit (*gegen, auf acc.* at); **~e** *pl.* (*Prügel*) a thrashing *sg.*; **2.** 2 *pret. v. hauen*; '**2- und** '**stichfest** *fig.* watertight, cast-iron.

hielt [hi:lt] *pret. v. halten.*

hienieden [hi:'ni:dən] here below.

hier [hi:r] here; (*am Ort*) in this place; ~ *und da* here and there; ~ *sein* be here *od.* present; *Appell*: ~! present!; ~ *entlang!* this way!; ~, *bitte!* here you are!

hieran ['hi:ran] at (*od.* by, in, on, to) this.

Hierarchie [hi:erar'çi:] *f* (15) hierarchy.

hier|auf ['hi:r-] hereupon, after this *od.* that, next; '**~aus** from (*od.* out of) this; '**~bei** at (*od.* in *od.* with) this; (*inliegend*) enclosed; '**~durch** by this, hereby; '**~für** for this, for it; '**~gegen** against this *od.* it; '**~her** here, hither; this way; *bis* ~ hitherto, so far, till now; '**~herum** hereabout(s); '**~in** herein, in this; '**~mit** herewith, with this; '**~nach** after this; (*dementsprechend*) according to this; '**~-orts** in this place *od.* country; '**~über** over here; (*über dieses Thema*) about this; '**~um** (a)round this; '**~unter** under this; among these; *bei verstehen usw.*: by this; '**~von** of (*od.* from) this; '**~zu** (in addition) to this *od.* it; '**~zulande** in this country.

hiesig ['hi:ziç] of this place *od.* country; local.

hieß [hi:s] *pret. v. heißen.*

Hilfe ['hilfə] *f* (15) help (*a. P.*); (*Beistand*) aid, assistance; (*Rettung*) succour; (*Armen*2) relief (*für* to); *Erste* ~ first aid; *j-m zu* ~ *kommen* (*eilen*) come (run) to a p.'s assistance (*od.* aid); *j-m* ~ *leisten* help (*od.* assist) a p.; *et. zu* ~ *nehmen* make use of, resort to; *mit* ~ (*gen. od.*) *von* with the help of *a p.*, with (*od.* by) the aid of *a th.*; *ohne* ~ (*selbständig*) unaided, single-handed; '**2flehend** imploring (help), suppliant; '**~leistung** *f* aid, assistance, help; '**~ruf** *m* cry for help; '**2suchend** seeking (for) help.

'**hilf|los** helpless; '**2losigkeit** *f* helplessness; '**~reich** helpful.

'**Hilfs|-aktion** *f* relief action; '**~-arbeiter(in** *f*) *m* unskilled (*od.* auxiliary) worker; '**2bedürftig** needy, indigent; '~bedürftigkeit f indigence; '2bereit willing to help, co--operative; '~geistliche m curate; '~gelder n/pl. subsidies; '~kraft f help(er), auxiliary; '~kreuzer ⚓ m auxiliary cruiser; '~lehrer m supply teacher; untrained teacher; '~linie ⵏ f subsidiary line; '~maschine f, '~motor m auxiliary engine; '~mittel n aid; (Heilmittel) remedy; s. Hilfsquelle; '~organisation f relief organization; '~quelle f resource; '~schule f school for backward children, Am. ungraded classes; '~truppen f/pl. auxiliaries; '~werk n relief (work); '~zeitwort n auxiliary verb.

Himbeere ['himbe:rə] f raspberry. 'Himbeer|saft m raspberry-juice; '~strauch m raspberry-bush.

Himmel ['himəl] m (7) sky, heavens pl.; s. ~sstrich; fig. heaven; (Trag2 usw.) canopy; in den ~ heben fig. praise to the skies; am ~ in the sky; fig. im ~ in heaven; ~ auf Erden heaven on earth; unter freiem ~ in the open air; aus heiterem ~ out of a clear sky; um ~s willen! goodness!; '2-angst: F ihm ist ~ he is scared to death; '~bett n tester--bed, four-poster; '2blau sky-blue; '~fahrt f Ascension; Mariä ~ Assumption; '~fahrtsnase F f tip--tilted nose; '~fahrts-tag m Ascension Day; '~reich n kingdom of heaven; '~schlüssel ♀ m primrose; '2schreiend outrageous, terrible; ~e Schande crying shame.

'Himmels... in Zssgn mst heavenly, celestial; '~gegend f quarter (of the heavens); die vier ~en the four cardinal points of the compass; '~körper m celestial body; '~kugel f celestial globe; '~richtung f cardinal point; weitS. direction; '~strich m climate, zone; '~zelt n (canopy of) heaven.

himmel|wärts ['~verts] skyward(s); fig. heavenward(s); '~weit fig. vast; ~ verschieden sein differ widely; es ist ein ~er Unterschied zwischen ... there is all the difference in the world between ...

'himmlisch celestial, heavenly.

hin [hin] there; (weg) gone, lost; (kaputt) gone, broken; an ... ~ along; ~ und her to and fro, Am. back and forth; ~ und zurück there and back; ~ und wieder now and

then; er ist ~ (ruiniert usw.) he is done for, (tot) he is dead; ~ und her überlegen turn a th. over in one's mind.

hinab [hi'nap] down; ~gehen, ~steigen (sn) go down, descend.

hinan [hi'nan] up; s. hinauf(...).

'hin-arbeiten auf (acc.) aim at.

hinauf [hi'nauf] up; den Berg ~ up the hill, uphill; sich ~arbeiten work one's way up; ~gehen (sn) go up (a. Preise); die Treppe ~ go upstairs; ~setzen Preis: raise; ~steigen (sn) ascend, mount.

hinaus [~'naus] out; ~ mit euch! out with you!; auf (viele) Jahre ~ for many years to come; ~begleiten Besuch: see out; ~gehen (sn) go (od. walk) out; ~ über e-e S.: go beyond, exceed; ~ auf (acc.) Fenster usw.: look out on, face; Absicht: aim at; ~kommen (sn) come out; fig. auf dasselbe ~ come (down) to the same thing; ~laufen (sn) run out; ~ auf (acc.) amount to; Absicht: aim at; auf eins (od. dasselbe) ~ come to the same thing; ~schieben put off, postpone; ~sein: fig. über et. hinaussein be past (od. beyond) a th.; ~werfen throw out, expel; (zur Tür) ~ turn od. F kick out (of doors); (entlassen) sl. throw out, Am. fire; ~wollen wish to go out; hoch ~ aim high; worauf will er hinaus? what is he driving at?

'Hin|blick m: im ~ auf (acc.) with regard to, in view of; '2bringen take, carry (beide: zu to); Zeit: spend, pass.

hinder|lich ['hindər-] hindering; troublesome; '~n (29) prevent (an dat. from doing), hinder; Verkehr: block, obstruct; '2nis n (4¹) hindrance; (Hemmnis) impediment; äußerliches: obstacle; belastendes: encumbrance; Rennsport: hurdle, obstacle (beide a. fig.); '2nisrennen n steeple-chase.

'hindeuten auf (acc.) point to.

hin'durch through(out); across; s. ganz; in Zssgn = durch...

hinein [hi'nain] in; ~arbeiten: sich in e-e S. ~ get into a matter; ~denken: sich ~ in et. go deeply into; ~gehen (sn; in acc.) go in(to a th.), enter (a th.); in den Topf gehen ... hinein the pot holds ...; in *den Saal gehen* ... *hinein* the hall seats *500 persons*; **~leben:** *in den Tag ~* take it easy; **~legen** put in(to *in acc.*); F *fig. s. hereinlegen; sich* **~mischen** *s. einmischen;* **~stecken, ~stellen, ~tun** put in(to *in acc.*); **~ziehen** *a. fig.* drag in(to *in acc.*).

'**Hin|fahrt** *f* journey there; *auf der ~* on the way there; '**⸰fallen** (sn) fall (down); '**⸰fällig** (*gebrechlich*) frail, weak, decrepit; *Grund:* futile; (*ungültig*) invalid; *~ machen* invalidate; '**~fälligkeit** *f* frailty, weakness; **⸰'fort** henceforth, in (the) future; '**~führen** *a. fig.* lead (*nach, zu* to).

hing [hiŋ] *pret. v. hängen.*

'**Hin|gabe** *f* devotion (*an acc.* to); (*Opfer*) sacrifice; '**~gang** *m* death; '**⸰geben** give away; (*überlassen*) give up, surrender; (*opfern*) sacrifice; *sich ~* (*dat.*) devote o.s. (*od.* give o.s. up) to); *e-m Laster:* indulge in; '**~gebung** *f* devotion; '**⸰gebungsvoll** devoted; **⸰'gegen** on the other hand; '**⸰gehen** (sn) go there; (*vergehen*) pass; *~ lassen* let pass; *über et. ~* pass over a th.; '**⸰geraten** (sn) *zu usw.* get to; '**~gerichtete** *m, f* executed man (*od.* woman); '**⸰halten** hold out; (*vertrösten*) put off; (*verzögern*) delay; '**⸰haltend** *Taktik usw.:* delaying; '**⸰hauen** F *Arbeit:* knock off; *sich ~* flop down, *zum Schlafen:* turn in; *das haut hin!* it works!, that does the trick!; '**⸰hören** listen.

hinken ['hiŋkən] (25, h. *u.* sn) limp, go lame; '**~d** lame, limping.

'**hin|knien** kneel down; '**~länglich** sufficient; '**⸰länglichkeit** *f* sufficiency; '**~legen** lay down; *sich ~* lie down; (*dulden*) suffer, put up with; (*sich*) '**~neigen** *nach, zu* incline to(wards).

hinnen ['hinən]: *von ~* from hence.

'**hin|raffen** snatch away; '**~reichen** *v/t.* reach (out); *v/i.* (*genügen*) suffice, do; '**~reißen** carry away (*a. fig.*); *fig.* (*begeistern*) enrapture, thrill; *sich ~ lassen* let o.s. be carried away; **~d** breath-taking; '**~richten** execute, put to death; '**⸰richtung** *f* execution; '**⸰richtungskommando** *n* execution squad; '**~scheiden**[1] (sn) die, pass away; '**⸰scheiden**[2] *n* (6) decease; '**~schlagen**

(sn) fall down heavily; '**~schleppen:** *sich ~* drag on; '**~schreiben** write down; *an j-n:* write to *him, etc.*; '**~schwinden** (sn) vanish *od.* dwindle (away); '**~sehen** *nach, zu* look to(wards) *od.* at; '**~setzen** put down; *j-n:* seat; *sich ~* sit down, take a seat; '**⸰sicht** *f:* *in ~ auf* (*acc.*) *s.* hinsichtlich; *in anderer ~* in other respects; *in dieser (einer, jeder) ~* in this (one, every) respect; *in gewisser ~* in a way; '**~sichtlich** (*gen.*) with regard to, as to, concerning; '**~siechen** waste away; '**~stellen** place; (*niederstellen*) put down; *~ als* represent as; '**~strecken** stretch out; *j-n: a.* fell; *sich ~* stretch o.s. out.

hintan|setzen [hint'?an-], **~stellen** *fig.* put last.

hinten ['hintən] behind; (*im Hintergrunde*) in the background; (*am Ende*) in the rear; *von ~* from behind; *~ und vorn fig.* everywhere; '**~herum** *fig.* on the quiet; **~'-über** backwards.

hinter ['hintər] behind, *Am.* F *a.* back of; *~ sich lassen allg.* leave behind; *sich ~ et. machen* get down to (*od.* tackle) *a th.*; '**⸰-achse** *f* rear-axle; '**⸰-achsen-antrieb** *mot. m* rear-axle drive; '**⸰-ansicht** *f* back view; '**⸰backe** *f* buttock; '**⸰bänkler** *parl. m* back-bencher; '**⸰bein** *n* hind leg; '**⸰bliebene(n)** [~'bli:bə-nə(n)] *pl.* surviving dependants; *in Traueranzeigen: the* bereaved; **~'bringen:** *j-m et. ~* inform a p. of a th.; '**⸰deck** *n* after-deck; '**~drein** [~'drain] *s.* hinterher; '**~e** *adj.* back, rear; '**~ei'nander** one after another; *successively;* **≠** in series; *fünfmal ~* five times running; '**~ei'nanderschalten** **≠** connect in series; '**⸰-eingang** *m* rear (*od.* back) entrance; '**~fragen** examine, question in depth; '**⸰fuß** *m* hind foot; '**⸰gebäude** *n s.* Hinterhaus; '**⸰gedanke** *m* ulterior motive, arrière pensée (*fr.*); '**~gehen** deceive; **⸰'gehung** *f* deception; '**⸰grund** *m* background; *fig. sich im ~ halten* keep in the background; *in den ~ drängen* thrust into the background; '**~gründig** cryptic; '**⸰halt** *m* ambush; '**~hältig** ['~hɛltiç] *s.* hinterlistig; '**⸰hand** *f Pferd:* hind quarters *pl.*; *Kartenspiel:* youngest hand; '**⸰haupt** *n* back of the head, ⫐ occiput; '**⸰haus** *n* back-building, back part (of the house); ~'**her** behind; after; *nur zeitlich*: afterwards; '2**hof** *m* backyard; '2**kopf** *m s. Hinterhaupt*; '2**lader** *m* (7) breech-loader; '2**land** *n* hinterland, interior; ~'**lassen** 1. *v/t*. leave (behind); 2. *adj.* posthumous; 2'**lassenschaft** *f* estate; '2**lauf** *m* hind leg; ~'**legen** deposit; 2'**legung** *f* deposition; '2**leib** *zo*. *m* hind quarters *pl*.; '2**list** *f* insidiousness; underhand trick; '~**listig** insidious, deceitful, crafty; '2**mann** *m* ✕ rear-rank man; ✝ subsequent endorser; *fig.* backer; (*Drahtzieher*) wire-puller; '2**mannschaft** *f Sport*: defen|ce, *Am.* -se; '2**n** F *m* backside, bottom, behind; '2**rad** *n* rear wheel; '2**rad-antrieb** *mot. m* rear-wheel drive; ~**rücks** ['~ryks] from behind; *fig.* behind a *p*.'s back; '2**seite** *f* back; '~**ste** rearmost, backmost; '2**teil** *n* back part; ♣ stern; *zo*. hind quarters *pl*.; *s. Hintern*; '2**treffen** *n*: *ins* ~ *geraten* lag (*od. fall*) behind; *weit S.* get the worst of it; ~'**treiben** prevent, thwart; 2~'**treibung** *f* prevention, frustration; '2**treppe** *f* backstairs *pl*.; '2**tür** *f* (*a. fig.*) backdoor; 2**wäldler** ['~vɛldlər] *m* (7) yokel, *Am. a.* hick; '2**wand** *f* back (wall); ~**wärts** ['~vɛrts] backward(s); ~'**ziehen** evade; 2'**ziehung** *f* (tax) evasion; '2**zimmer** *n* back room.

hinüber [hi'ny:bər] over, across.
'**Hin- und** '**Rückfahrt** *f* journey there and back; *Fahrkarte für* ~ return (*Am.* roundtrip) ticket.

hinunter [hi'nuntər] down; *den Berg* ~ down the hill, downhill; ~**gehen** (sn) go down (*a. Preise*); *die Treppe* ~ go downstairs; ~**schlucken** swallow down; *fig.* swallow.

Hinweg ['~ve:k] *m* way (there).
hinweg [~'vɛk] *adv.* away, off; ~**gehen** *über* (*acc.*) pass over (*a. fig.*); *s. hinwegsetzen*; ~**helfen**: *j-m* ~ *über* (*acc.*) help a p. get (*od.* tide) over; ~**kommen** *über* (*acc.*) get over (*a. fig.*); ~**sehen**: *fig. über et.* ~ overlook a th.; *sich* ~**setzen** *über* (*acc.*) make light of (*od.* disregard) a th.; override a rule, objection, *etc.*; *lachend* (*gleichgültig*): laugh (shrug) a th. off; ~**täuschen**: *j-n über et.* ~ deceive a p. about a th.
Hin|weis ['~vaɪs] *m* (4) hint, direc-

tion, F pointer; ~ *auf* (*acc.*) reference to; '2**weisen** *v/t*. direct (*nach, zu* to); *v/i.* ~ *auf* (*acc.*) point to; (*verweisen*) refer to; *darauf* ~, *daß* point out that; '2**weisend**: ~*es Fürwort* demonstrative pronoun; '2**werfen** throw down; *flüchtig, a. Wort*: drop, *Brief, Zeichnung usw.*: dash off; *fig. Arbeit usw.*: chuck; *j-m et.* ~ throw a th. to a p.; 2'**wiederum** again; (*andererseits*) on the other hand; '2**wirken** *auf* (*acc.*) work towards; '2**ziehen** *v/t*. draw, attract; *räumlich*: extend (*bis* to); *zeitlich*: drag out, protract; *sich* ~ *räumlich*: extend, *Zeit usw.*: drag on; '2**zielen** *auf* (*acc.*) aim at.

hin'zu near; there; (*außerdem*) in addition; ~**fügen** add; 2**fügung** *f* addition; ~**kommen** (sn) *unvermutet*: supervene; (*noch* ~) be added; *es kommt hinzu, daß* add to this that; ~**setzen** add; ~**treten** (sn) approach; *s. hinzukommen*; ~**tun**, ~**zählen** add; ~**ziehen** *Arzt usw.*: call in, consult.

Hiobs|botschaft *f*, ~**post** ['hi:ɔps-] *f* bad news.

Hirn [hɪrn] *n* (3) brain; (~*substanz*) *fig. Verstand*) brains *pl.*; '~**gespinst** *n* figment of the mind, (mere) fancy; '~**haut-entzündung** *f* meningitis; '2**los** brainless; '~**masse** *f* brain matter; '2**rissig** whacky, weird, crazy; '~**schale** *f* brain-pan, cranium; '~**schlag** *m* apoplexy (of the brain); '2**tod** *m* cerebral death; '~**tumor** *m* brain tumo(u)r; '2**verbrannt** mad, crazy.

Hirsch [hɪrʃ] *m* (3²) stag, hart; *als Gattung*: deer; '~**braten** *m* roast venison; ~**fänger** ['~fɛŋər] *m* hunting-knife; '~**geweih** *n* antlers *pl.*; '~**horn** *n* hartshorn; '~**hornsalz** *n* salt of hartshorn; '~**jagd** *f* stag-hunt(ing); '~**käfer** *m* stag-beetle; '~**kalb** *n* calf of deer; '~**kuh** *f* hind; '~**leder** *n* buckskin; '~**talg** *m* suet (of deer).

Hirse ['hɪrzə] *f* (15) millet; '~**brei** *m* millet gruel.

Hirt [hɪrt] *m* (12) herdsman; (*Schaf*2) shepherd.
'**Hirten|brief** *eccl. m* pastoral letter; '~**junge** *m*, '~**knabe** *m* shepherd-boy; '~**stab** *m* shepherd's staff; *eccl.* crosier; '~**volk** *n* pastoral tribe.
'**Hirtin** *f* (16) shepherdess.

His ♪ [his] *n* B sharp.
hissen ['hisən] (28) hoist.
Historie [hi'stoːrjə] *f* (15) history;
~**nmaler** *m* historical painter.
Hi'storiker *m* (7) historian.
hi'storisch historical; (*geschichtlich bedeutsam*) historic.
'**Hitzbläs-chen** *n* heat spot (*od.* vesicle); *pl.* heat rash.
Hitze ['hitsə] *f* (15) heat; '♀**beständig** heat-resistant; '~**grad** *m* degree of heat; '~**welle** *f* heat-wave.
'**hitzig** hot (*a. fig.*); *fig.* heated, fierce *discussion, etc.*; ~ werden fly into a passion.
'**Hitz|kopf** *m* hothead; ♀**köpfig** ['~kœpfiç] hot-headed; '~**pickel** *m s. Hitzbläschen*; '~**schlag** *m* heat-stroke.
'**H-Milch** *f* long-life milk.
hob [hoːp] *pret. v.* heben.
Hobby ['hɔbi] *n* (11) hobby.
Hobel ['hoːbəl] *m* (7) plane; '~**bank** *f* carpenter's bench; '~**messer** *n* planing knife; '♀**n** (29) plane; ~**späne** ['~ʃpɛːnə] *m/pl.* shavings.
hoch [hoːx] **1.** high; (*hochgewachsen*) tall; *fig. a.* noble, sublime; *hohes Alter* great age; *hohe See* open sea; *hohe Strafe* severe punishment, heavy penalty; *hoher Offizier* high (-ranking) officer; *drei Mann* ~ three of them; *das ist mir zu* ~ that's beyond me; *hohe Ehre* great hono(u)r; *in hoher Fahrt* at full speed; *Hände* ~! hands up!; e-e *hohe Meinung von j-m haben* think highly of a p.; ~ *zu stehen kommen* cost dear; ~ *lebe die Königin!* long live the queen!; ♃ 4 ÷ 3 (4³)· four in the third (power); **2.** ♀ *n* (11) (~*ruf*) cheer; (*Trinkspruch*) toast; *barometrisches*: high; *ein* ~ *auf j-n ausbringen* cheer a p., *bei Tisch*: toast a p.
'**hoch|-achtbar** most respectable; '~-**achten** esteem highly; '♀-**achtung** *f* esteem, respect; '~-**achtungsvoll** (most) respectful; *adv. Briefschluß*: Yours very truly; '~**adel** *m* nobility; '♀-**altar** *m* high altar; '♀-**amt** *n* high mass; '♀-**antenne** *f* overhead (*od.* outdoor) aerial; '♀**bahn** *f* overhead railway, *Am.* elevated (railroad); '♀**bau** *m* surface engineering; (*Gebäude*) multi-stor(e)y building; '~**be'gabt** highly gifted; '~**berühmt** very

famous; '~**be'tagt** very aged, well advanced in years; '♀**betrieb** *m* intense activity, big rush; '~**bezahlt** highly paid; '~**bringen** *fig.* raise; '~**brisant** *fig. Thema etc.*: explosive; '♀**burg** *fig. f* stronghold; '♀**deutsch** *n* High German; '♀**druck** *m* high pressure; *mit* ~ at high pressure; *mit* ~ *arbeiten* hustle; '~**drükken** push up; '♀**druckgebiet** *n* high (-pressure area); '♀-**ebene** *f* plateau, tableland; '~-**empfindlich** highly sensitive; '~-**entwickelt** highly developed; '~-**erfreut** delighted; '~**fahrend** high-handed; '~**fein** very refined; '♀**finanz** *f* high finance; '~**fliegend** high-flying, lofty; '♀**flut** *f* high tide; '♀**form** *f*: *in* ~ in top form; '♀**format** *n* (3) upright format; '♀**frequenz** ≠ *f* high frequency; '♀**frisur** *f* upswept hair-style; '♀**garage** *f* multi-stor(e)y car park; '~**gebildet** highly educated; '♀**gebirge** *n* high mountain region, high mountains *pl.*; '~**gehen** *a. Vorhang, Preise usw.*: go up, rise; *See:* run high; *Bombe, a.* F *Person*: explode; '~**gemut** ['~gəmuːt] high-spirited; '♀**genuß** *m* great enjoyment, F real treat; *mit* ~ with relish; '♀**geschwindigkeits...** high-speed; '~**gesinnt** ['~gəzint] high-minded; '~**gespannt** *fig. Plan usw.*: ambitious; *Erwartung*: great; '~**gestellt** high-ranking; '~**gestochen** jumped-up, sophisticated; '♀**glanz** *m* high lustre; high polish; ~**gradig** ['~graːdiç] extreme; severe; ~**hackig** ['~hakiç] *Schuhe*: high-heeled; '~**halten** hold up; *fig.* hono(u)r, treasure; '♀**haus** *n* high-rise flats *pl.*, (*Wolkenkratzer*) skyscraper; '~**heben** lift (up), raise; '~**herzig** generous; '♀**herzigkeit** *f* generosity; '~**kant** on edge *od.* end; ~ *stellen* upend; '~**karätig** high-carat; *fig.* top-calibre; '~**kommen** (sn) come up; *vom Boden usw.*: get up; *fig.* get on; '♀**konjunktur** *f* boom; '♀**land** *n* highlands *pl.*; *s. Hochebene*; '~**laufen** run up; '~**leben**: ~ *lassen give a p.* three cheers; '♀**leistung** *f* high performance; '♀**leistungs...** high-power(ed); high-speed ...; heavy-duty ...
höchlich ['høːçliç] highly.
'**Hoch|mut** *m* haughtiness, arrogance; ♀**mütig** ['~myːtiç] haughty, supercilious; ♀**näsig** F ['~nɛːziç] stuck-up; '~-**ofen** *m* blast-furnace;

'2**prozentig** *Alkohol*: high-proof; '2**qualifiziert** highly qualified; '2-**ragen** tower up, rise; '2**rappeln:** *sich* ~ struggle to one's feet; '2**rech-nen** project, make a computer pre-diction of; '~**rechnung** *f* projection; '2**rot** flaming red; '~**ruf** *m* cheer; '~**saison** *f* peak season; '2**schätzen** esteem highly; '2**schnellen** leap up (*a. fig.*); '2**schrauben** *Preise*: force up; *Forderungen*: step up; '~**schule** *f* university; (*Akademie*) academy, college; *s. technisch*; '~**schullehrer** *m* university (*od.* college) teacher; '~**schulreife** *f* university entrance qualifications *pl.*; '2**schwanger** far advanced in pregnancy; '~**see** *f* high seas *pl.*; '~**seefischerei** *f* deep-sea fishing; '~**seeflotte** *f* high-seas fleet; '~**seejacht** *f* ocean-going (*od.* sea-going) yacht; '~**sitz** *hunt.* *m* raised hide; '~**sommer** *m* midsummer; '~**spannung** *≠* *f* high tension *od.* voltage; '2**spielen** F *fig.* play up; '~**sprache** *f* standard language; *die deutsche* ~ standard German; '2**sprachlich** standard; *nicht* ~ substandard; '~**sprung** *m* high jump.

höchst [hø:çst] *allg.* highest; *fig. a.* greatest, supreme; (*äußerst*) ex-treme; *s.* Zeit; *adv.* highly; most, extremely; '2-**alter** *n* maximum age.

Hoch|stapelei [~ʃtɑ:pə'laɪ] *f* (16) (high-class) swindling, imposture; '~**stapler** *m* (7) impostor, confidence trickster.

'**Höchstbelastung** *f* maximum load.
'**hochstehend** *fig.* high(-ranking); *geistig* ~ of high intellect.
höchstens ['hø:çstəns] at (the) most, at best, at the outside (*bei Zahlen-angaben alle nachgestellt*).

'**Höchst|fall** *m*: *im* ~ *s.* höchstens; '~**geschwindigkeit** *f* top (*od.* maxi-mum) speed; '~**grenze** *f* maximum limit, ceiling; '~**leistung** *f* *Sport*: record; *e-r Fabrik*: maximum out-put, *e-r Maschine usw.*: *a.* maximum efficiency; '~**maß** *n* maximum; '2-'**möglich** highest possible; '2**per-sönlich** personal(ly); *adv. a.* in per-son; '~**preis** *m* maximum price, ceil-ing price; '~**stand** *m* peak (level); '2**wahrscheinlich** most probably; '~**wert** *m* peak (*od.* maximum) value; '~**zahl** *f* maximum (number).
'**Hoch|touren** *f/pl.*: *auf* ~ ⊕ at full speed *od.* pressure, *fig.* in full swing, at full blast; '2**tourig** high-speed; '2**trabend** high-sounding, pomp-ous; '~ **und** '**Tiefbau** *m* civil engi-neering; '2**verdient** highly deserv-ing; '2**ver-ehrt** (highly) esteemed; ~*es Publikum!* ladies and gentlemen!; '~**verrat** *m* high treason; '~**verräter** *m* person guilty of high treason, traitor; '2**verräterisch** treasonable; '~**wald** *m* timber(-forest); '~**wasser** *n* high water; (*Überschwemmung*) flood; '~**wasserkatastrophe** *f* flood-disaster; '~**wassermarke** *f* flood mark, high-water mark; '2**wertig** of high value, high-class, high-grade; '~**wild** *n* large game.

Hochzeit ['hɔxtsaɪt] *f* wedding; (*Trauung*) marriage; '2**lich** nuptial, bridal; '~**sgeschenk** *n* wedding pres-ent; '~**snacht** *f* wedding night; '~**s-reise** *f* honeymoon (trip); '~**s-tag** *m* wedding day; (*Jahrestag*) wedding anniversary.

Hocke ['hɔkə] *f* (15) *✿* shock; *Turnen*: crouch, (*Sprung*) squat-vault; '2**n** (25) squat; F (*sitzen*) sit; *sich* ~ squat (*od.* sit) down; '~**r** *m* (7) (*Schemel*) stool.

Höcker ['hœkər] *m* (7) *zo. u.* *☞* hump; *anat.* tubercle; *allg.* bump, knob; '2**ig** bumpy; *Rücken*: hump-backed, hunchbacked.

Hockey|schläger ['hɔki-] *m* hockey-stick; '~**spieler** *m* hockey-player.

Hode ['ho:də] *f* (15) testicle; '~**n-sack** *m* scrotum.

Hof [ho:f] *m* (3³) court(yard), yard; (*Bauern*2) farm; *e-s Fürsten*: court; *um Sonne, Mond, a.* *☞*: halo, corona; *j-m den* ~ *machen s.* hofie-ren; '~**dame** *f* lady at court; *im Dienst der Königin usw.*: lady-in-waiting.

Hoffart ['hɔfart] *f* (16) haughtiness, arrogance, pride.
hoffärtig ['~fertiç] haughty, proud.
hoffen ['hɔfən] *v/t. u. v/i.* (25) hope (*auf acc.* for); '~**tlich** let us hope, I hope (that) ..., *bsd. Am.* hopefully.
Hoffnung ['hɔfnuŋ] *f* hope (*auf acc.* for, of); *guter* ~ *sein* be full of hope, *Frau*: be expecting a baby; *j-m* ~(*en*) *machen* raise a p.'s hopes (*auf* of); *sich* ~*en machen* be hope-ful; (*neue*) ~ *schöpfen* gather fresh hope; *s-e* ~ *setzen auf* (*acc.*) pin one's hopes on; *e-e* ~ *zerstören*

dash a hope; '≗sfreudig hopeful; '≗slos hopeless (a. fig.); '⸗sstrahl m ray of hope; '≗svoll hopeful; (vielversprechend) promising.

hofieren [ho'fi:rən] court, pay one's addresses to; contp. flatter, fawn (up)on.

höfisch ['hø:fiʃ] courtly.

höflich ['hø:fliç] polite, courteous, civil (gegen to); '≗keit f courtesy, politeness, civility; '≗keitsbesuch m courtesy call.

Höfling ['hø:fliŋ] m (3¹) courtier.

'**Hof|narr** m court jester; '⸗staat m royal (od. princely) household; (Gefolge) retinue; (Kleid) court-dress.

Höhe ['hø:ə] f (15) height; ⅄, ast., geogr. altitude; (Niveau) level; (Anhöhe) hill; (Gipfel) summit; ♪ pitch; e-r Summe: amount; e-r Strafe: degree; ✝ ~ der Preise level of prices; Summe in ~ von ... to the amount of; auf gleicher ~ mit on a level with; fig. auf der ~ up to the mark, der Zeit: up to date; ⚓ auf der ~ von off; in die ~ up, upward, aloft; in die ~ steigen rise; Preise in die ~ treiben force up, Am. boost; aus der ~ from above; F das ist die ~! that's the limit!

Hoheit ['ho:haɪt] f (16) pol. sovereignty; Titel: Seine (Ihre) ~ His (Her) Highness; fig. grandeur; '⸗s(-ab)zeichen n national emblem; '⸗sgebiet n territory; '⸗sgewässer n/pl. territorial waters; '≗svoll majestic(ally adv.).

'**Höhen|flosse** 🛩 f stabilizer; '⸗flug m high-altitude flight; '⸗krankheit f altitude sickness; '⸗kur-ort m high-altitude health--resort; '⸗leitwerk 🛩 n elevator unit; '⸗linie f Karte: contour line; '⸗luft f mountain air; '⸗messer m altimeter; '⸗regler m Radio etc.: treble control; '⸗sonne f Alpine sun; Gerät: sun-ray lamp; '⸗unterschied m difference in altitude; '≗verstellbar with adjustable height; '⸗zug m hill-range.

'**Höhepunkt** m highest point; ast., fig. culmination; fig. climax, peak; height, zenith.

höher ['hø:ər] higher (a. fig.); ~er Beruf (learned) profession; ~e Mathematik higher mathematics; ~e Schule secondary school; s. Ge-

walt; '≗e n fig. higher things pl.

hohl [ho:l] hollow (a. Klang u. fig.); (vertieft) concave; die ~e Hand the hollow of the hand; ⸗äugig ['⸗ʔɔʏgiç] hollow-eyed.

Höhle ['hø:lə] f (15) cave; (Tier≗) den; bsd. ⚕ cavity; '≗n hollow; '⸗nforschung f spel(a)eology; '⸗nmensch m cave-man.

'**hohlgeschliffen** hollow-ground.

'**Hohlheit** f hollowness.

'**Hohl|kehle** f channel, groove; '⸗maß n dry measure; '⸗raum m hollow (space), cavity; '⸗saum m hemstitched hem; '⸗schliff m hollow grinding; '⸗spiegel m concave mirror.

Höhlung ['hø:luŋ] f hollow, cavity.

'**Hohl|weg** m (narrow) pass, defile; '⸗ziegel m hollow brick.

Hohn [ho:n] m (3) scorn, derision; (⸗lächeln; höhnische Bemerkung) sneer; ein ~ auf (acc.) ... sein be a mockery of; j-m zum ~ in defiance of a p.

höhnen ['hø:nən] v/i. u. v/t. (25) sneer, scoff, jeer (j-n at a p.).

'**Hohngelächter** n scornful (od. mocking) laughter.

'**höhnisch** sneering, scornful.

'**hohn|lächeln**, '⸗lachen sneer; '⸗sprechen (dat.) (trotzen) defy; (verspotten) mock; fig. make a mockery of.

Höker ['hø:kər] m (7) hawker, huckster; '≗n (29) hawk, huckster.

Hokuspokus [ho:kus'po:kus] m inv. hocus-pocus; ~! a. hey presto!

hold [hɔlt] kindly disposed (dat. to); (lieblich) lovely, sweet; das Glück war ihm ~ fortune smiled upon him, he was lucky.

'**holdselig** lovely, sweet.

holen ['ho:lən] (25) fetch, get; go for; (ab~) come for, pick up; die Polizei usw.: call; ~ lassen send for; sich ~ (sich zuziehen) catch; s. Atem, Rat.

holla! ['hɔla] hey!

Holländer ['hɔlɛndər] m (7) Dutchman; '⸗in f (16¹) Dutchwoman.

'**holländisch** Dutch.

Hölle ['hœlə] f (15) hell; die ~ ist los the fat is in the fire; j-m die ~ heiß machen make it hot for a p.

'**Höllen|-angst** f mortal fright; '⸗lärm m infernal noise; '⸗maschine f infernal machine, time bomb;

'**~qual** f torment of hell; '**~stein** 🜍 m lunar caustic.

'**höllisch** (a. F fig.) hellish, infernal.

Holm [hɔlm] m (3¹) beam; (Barren♀) bar; 💥 spar.

holper|ig ['hɔlpəriç] rough, bumpy; fig. stumbling; '**~n** (sn) Wagen: jolt, bump; s. stolpern.

Holunder [ho'lundər] m (7) elder.

Holz [hɔlts] n (1¹ u. ²) wood; (Nutz♀) timber, Am. lumber; fig. aus demselben (e-m anderen) ~ geschnitzt of the same (of a different) stamp; '**~apfel** m crab-apple; '**~arbeit(en** pl.) f woodwork; '♀artig ligneous, woody; '**~axt** f (felling-)ax(e); '**~bau** m wooden structure, timber-work; '**~be-arbeitung** f woodworking; '**~bild-hauer** m wood-carver; '**~blas-instrument** n woodwind instrument; die ~e pl. im Orchester: the wood(-wind).

'**holzen** (27) fell (od. cut) wood; F Fußball: play rough.

hölzern ['hœltsərn] wooden; fig. (linkisch) a. awkward, clumsy, stiff.

'**Holz|-essig** m wood-vinegar; '**~fäller** m (7) wood-cutter, Am. lumberman; '**~faserplatte** f wood-fib|re (Am. -fiber) board; '♀**frei** Papier: wood-free; '**~hacker** m, '**~hauer** m (7) wood-cutter; '**~hammer** m mallet; F fig. sledge-hammer; '**~handel** m timber-trade; '**~händler** m timber merchant; '**~haus** n wooden (Am. frame) house; '♀**ig** woody; '**~kohle** f charcoal; '**~nagel** m wooden peg; '**~platz** m timber (Am. lumber) yard; '**~schliff** m mechanical pulp; '**~schnitt** m woodcut; '**~schnitzer** m wood-carver; '**~schuh** m clog; '**~span** m wood-chip; '**~stapel** m, '**~stoß** m wood-pile; '**~stoff** m lignin; '**~taube** f wood-pigeon; '**~verklei-dung** f timber lining; '**~weg** m wood-path; fig. auf dem ~ sein be on the wrong track; '**~werk** n wood-work; '**~wolle** f wood-wool, Am. excelsior; '**~wurm** m woodworm.

homogen [homo'ge:n] homogene-ous.

Homöopath [homøo'pɑːt] m (12) hom(o)eopathist; **~ie** [~pa'tiː] f (16) hom(o)eopathy; ♀**isch** [~'pɑːtiʃ] hom(o)eopathic(ally adv.).

Homosex|ualität [homozɛksuali-

'**te:t**] f homosexuality; ♀**u'ell**, **~u'elle** m homosexual.

Honig ['ho:niç] m (3¹) honey; '**~biene** f honey-bee; '**~kuchen** m gingerbread; '♀**süß** honey-sweet; '**~wabe** f honeycomb.

Honorar [hono'rɑːr] n (3¹) fee.

Honoratioren [~ra'tsjoːrən] m/pl. notabilities.

hono'rieren pay a fee (j-n: to; et.: for); Wechsel: hono(u)r; fig. show o.s. appreciative of.

Hopfen ['hɔpfən] m (6) hop; Braue-rei: hops pl.; '**~bau** m hop-culture.

hopp! [hɔp] hop!; quick!

hoppla! ['hɔpla] whoops!

hops [hɔps]: ~ gehen ⚔ sl. go west.

hops|a! ['hɔpsa] whoops!; '**~en** (27, sn) hop; ♀**er** m (7) hop; (Tanz) hop-waltz.

hörbar ['hø:rbɑːr] audible.

horch|en ['hɔrçən] (25) listen (auf acc. to); b.s. eavesdrop; ♀**er** m (7) listener; b.s. eavesdropper; '♀**gerät** n listening apparatus, sound detec-tor; ♀**posten** ⚔ m listening post.

Horde ['hɔrdə] f (15) horde, gang.

hör|en ['hø:rən] v/t. u. v/i. (25) hear (von j-m from); (zu~, hin~) listen; (zufällig mit an~) overhear; Radio: listen (in); Vorlesung, Messe: hear, attend; (erfahren) hear, learn; ~ auf (acc.) listen to; schwer ~ be hard of hearing; sich ~ lassen als Künstler: perform; von sich ~ lassen give news of o.s.; das läßt sich ~ there's something in that; hören Sie mal! I say!, Am. say!, listen!; auf den Namen ... ~ answer to the name of ...; s. vergehen; ♀**ensagen** n: vom ~ by hearsay; ♀**er** m (7) hearer; bsd. Radio: listener; (Ap-parat) receiver; e-s Professors: student; ♀**erbrief** m letter from a listener; ♀**erschaft** f audience; ♀**frequenz** f audio frequency; ♀**funk** m radio, sound broadcasting; ♀**gerät** n (für Schwerhörige) hearing aid; '**~ig**: j-m ~ sein be enslaved to a p.; ♀**igkeit** f bondage.

Horizont [hori'tsɔnt] m (3) horizon; (~linie) skyline; seinen ~ erweitern broaden one's mind; das geht über m-n ~ that is beyond me; ♀**al** [~'tɑːl] horizontal.

Hormon [hɔr'moːn] n (3) hormone.

'**Hörmuschel** teleph. f earpiece.

Horn [hɔrn] n (1²) horn (a. ♪);

(*Signal⚥*) bugle; (*Bergspitze*) peak; (*Fühl⚥*) feeler; *fig. sich die Hörner abstoßen* sow one's wild oats; *j-m Hörner aufsetzen* cuckold a p.; '**⚥-artig** like horn, horny; '**⚥brille** *f* (*eine* a pair of) horn-rimmed glasses.

Hörnchen ['hœrnçən] *n* (6) small horn, cornicle; (*Gebäck*) crescent. '**Hornhaut** *f* horny skin; *des Auges*: cornea.

Hornisse [hɔr'nisə] *f* (15) hornet.

Hor'nist *m* (12) bugler.

Horn|späne ['⚥pɛːnə] *m/pl.* horn parings; '**⚥vieh** *n* horned cattle.

Horoskop [horo'skoːp] *n* (3[1]) horoscope; *j-m das* ⚥ *stellen* cast a p.'s horoscope.

horrend [hɔ'rɛnt] enormous.

'**Hör-rohr** *n* ear-trumpet.

Horror ['hɔrɔr] *m* (11, *o. pl.*) horror (*vor dat.* of); '**⚥film** horror film.

'**Hör|saal** *m* lecture-hall; '**⚥spiel** *n* radio play.

Horst [hɔrst] *m* (3[2]) eyrie; *s. Flieger⚥*; '⚥**en** (26) build an eyrie.

Hort [hɔrt] *m* (3) hoard, (*sicherer Ort*) sanctuary; (*Schutz*) bulwark, stronghold, refuge; *s. Kinder⚥*; '⚥**en** (26) hoard; '**⚥ung** *f* hoarding.

'**Hör|verlust** *m* hearing loss; '**⚥weite** *f*: *in* (*außer*) ⚥ within (out of) hearing *od.* earshot.

Hös-chen ['høːsçən] *n* (6) shorts *pl.*, F pants *pl.*; *s. Unterhose, Schlüpfer*.

Hose ['hoːzə] *f* (15) *mst* ⚥*n pl.* (eine a pair of) trousers, F *od. Am.* pants *pl.*; (*Damen⚥*) slacks *pl.*; (*Knie⚥*) breeches *pl.*; (*kurze* ⚥) shorts *pl.*; *fig.* F *die* ⚥*n anhaben* wear the trousers *od.* pants; *s. Herz, Jacke, kurz*.

'**Hosen|-anzug** *m* trouser suit, pant(s) suit; '**⚥bein** *n* trouser-leg; '**⚥boden** *m* (trouser-)seat; '**⚥rock** *m* (a pair of) culottes *pl.*, pant skirt; '**⚥rolle** *f* breeches part; '**⚥schlitz** *m* fly; '**⚥tasche** *f* trouser pocket; '**⚥träger** *m* (*a. pl.*) (*ein a* pair of) braces *pl.*, *Am.* suspenders *pl.*

Hospit|al [hɔspi'taːl] *n* (1[2] *u.* 3[1]) hospital; **⚥ant** [⚥'tant] *m* (12), **⚥antin** *f* guest student.

Hospiz [hɔs'piːts] *n* (3[2]) hospice.

Hostie ['hɔstjə] *f* (15) host, eucharistic wafer.

Hotel [ho'tɛl] *n* (11) hotel; **⚥ier** [⚥'jeː] *m* (11), **⚥besitzer(in** *f*) *m* hotel proprietor; **⚥boy** *m* (11), **⚥page** *m* (13) page(-boy), *Am.* bellboy; **⚥direktor** *m* hotel manager; **⚥führer** *m* hotel guide; **⚥gewerbe** *n* hotel industry; **⚥halle** *f* foyer, lobby.

hott! [hɔt], **hü!** [hyː] gee up!

Hub [huːp] *m* (3[3]) lift; ⊕ (*Kolben⚥*) stroke.

hüben ['hyːbən] on this side.

'**Hub|pumpe** *f* lifting pump; '**⚥raum** *m* piston displacement; '**⚥raumsteuer** *f* tax on engine volume.

hübsch [hypʃ] pretty; (*a. = beträchtlich*) handsome; (*nett*) nice; (*anziehend*) attractive, good-looking.

'**Hubschrauber** 🛩 *m* helicopter; '**⚥landeplatz** *m* heliport, helipad.

huckepack ['hukəpak] pick-a-back.

hudeln ['huːdəln] (29) scamp one's work.

Huf [huːf] *m* (3) hoof; '**⚥beschlag** *m* shoeing; *a. =* '**⚥eisen** *n* horseshoe; '**⚥lattich** ♀ *m* coltsfoot; '**⚥nagel** *m* hobnail; '**⚥schlag** *m* horse's kick; (*Geräusch*) hoof-beat; '**⚥schmied** *m* farrier; '**⚥tier** *n* hoofed mammal, ungulate.

Hüft|bein ['hyft-] *n* hip-bone; '**⚥e** *f* (15) hip; '**⚥gelenk** *n* hip-joint; '**⚥gürtel** *m* suspender (*Am.* garter) belt; '**⚥halter** *m* roll-on girdle; '⚥**lahm** hip-shot; '**⚥umfang** *m* hip-measurement; '**⚥weh** *n* sciatica.

Hügel ['hyːgəl] *m* (7) hill, hillock; '⚥**ig** hilly; '**⚥land** *n* hilly country.

Huhn [huːn] *n* (1[2]) hen, *a. Küche*: chicken; *junges* ⚥, **Hühnchen** ['hyːnçən] *n* (6) pullet, chicken; *ein* ⚥ *zu rupfen haben mit* have a bone to pick with.

Hühner|-auge ['hyːnər-] *n* corn; '**⚥brühe** *f* chicken-broth; '**⚥ei** *n* hen's egg; '**⚥habicht** *m* goshawk; '**⚥hof** *m* chicken-run, *Am.* -yard; '**⚥hund** *m* pointer; '**⚥leiter** *f* roost-ladder; '**⚥schrot** *n* partridge-shot; '**⚥stall** *m* hen-house; '**⚥vögel** *m/pl.* gallinaceous birds *pl.*; '**⚥zucht** *f* chicken-farming.

hui! [hui] whoosh!; (*erstaunt*) ooh!; *in e-m* ⚥ in a trice *od.* flash.

Huld [hult] *f* (16) grace, favo(u)r.

huldig|en ['⚥digən] (25) pay homage; *fig.* pay tribute to; *e-m Laster usw.*: indulge in.

huld|reich, ⚥voll ['hult-] gracious.

Hülle ['hylə] *f* (15) cover(ing), wrap, envelope; (*Schleier*) veil; *in* ⚥ *und*

Fülle in abundance, plenty of; *die sterbliche* ~ the mortal frame; ♀**n** (25) cover, wrap (up); (*kleiden*) clothe; *fig.* shroud; *in Nebel usw.*: envelop.

Hülse ['hylzə] *f* (15) hull, husk; (*Schote*) pod; (*Gehäuse, a.* ✕) shell; ⊕ sleeve; (*Steck*♀) socket; '**~nfrucht** *f* legume; '**~nfrüchte** *f/pl. a.* pulse.

human [hu'ma:n] humane; ♀**ismus** [huma'nismus] *m* (16, *o. pl.*) humanism; **~istisch** [~'nistiʃ] humanistic, classical; **~itär** [~ni'tɛ:r] humanitarian; ♀**ität** [~ni'tɛ:t] *f* (16) humanity.   [humbug.)

Humbug ['humbuk] *m* (6, *o. pl.*))

Hummel ['huməl] *f* (17) bumble--bee.

Hummer ['humər] *m* (7) lobster.

Humor [hu'mo:r] *m* (3¹) (sense of) humo(u)r; **~eske** [~mo'reskə] *f* (15) humorous sketch; **~ist** [~'rist] *m* (12) humorist; *thea.* comedian; ♀**istisch** [~'ristiʃ], ♀**voll** humorous.

humpeln ['humpəln] (29, h. *u.* sn) hobble, limp.

Humpen ['humpən] *m* (6) tankard.

Humus(erde *f*) ['hu:mus(ʔe:rdə)] *m* (16, *o. pl.*) vegetable mo(u)ld.

Hund [hunt] *m* (3) dog (*a.* ✕; *a.fig. v. Menschen*); (*Jagd*♀) hound; *Schimpfwort*: cur; *da liegt der* ~ *begraben* there's the rub; *fig. auf den* ~ *kommen* reach rock-bottom; *vor die* ~*e gehen* go to the dogs; F *wie* ~ *und Katze leben* lead a cat-and--dog life.

Hunde|-abteil 🚋 ['hundə-] *n* dog--box; **~ausstellung** *f* dog-show; '♀'**-elend** F: *sich* ~ *fühlen* feel lousy; '**~hütte** *f* dog-kennel; '**~kälte** F *f* biting cold; '**~kuchen** *m* dog-biscuit; '**~leben** F *n* dog's life; '**~leine** *f* (dog-)lead, leash; '**~loch** F *n* dog-hole; '**~marke** *f* dog-tag; '♀'**~müde** dog-tired; '**~peitsche** *f* dog-whip; '**~rasse** *f* dog-breed.

hundert ['hundərt] (a) hundred; *4 vom* ♀ four per cent (4%); *zu* ♀**en** by hundreds; ♀**er** *m* (7) hundred; **~erlei** ['~ər'lai] of a hundred different sorts; '**~fach**, **~fältig** ['~fɛltiç] hundredfold; **~gradig** ['~gra:diç] centigrade; ♀'**jahrfeier** *f* centenary, *Am.* centennial; '**~jährig** centenary; '**~mal** a hundred times; ♀'**markschein** *m* hundred-mark (bank-)note; '**~prozentig** a hundred per cent; *fig. a.* absolute(ly *adv.*); '♀**satz** *m* percentage; '**~st** hundredth; '♀**stel** *n* (7) one hundredth (part); '**~weise** by hundreds.

'**Hunde|wetter** *n* filthy weather; '**~zucht** *f* dog-breeding; (*~zwinger*) kennel (of dogs).

Hündin ['hyndin] *f* she-dog, bitch.

'**hündisch** *fig.* servile.

Hunds|fott ['huntsfɔt] *m* (1²) scoundrel; '♀**gemein** dirty, mean; '♀**-mise'rabel** F lousy; **~tage** ['~ta:-gə] *m/pl.* dog-days.

Hüne ['hy:nə] *m* (13) giant; '**~ngestalt** *f* (person of) Herculean stature; '**~ngrab** *n* megalithic grave; ♀**nhaft** gigantic.

Hunger ['huŋər] *m* (7) hunger (*fig. nach* for); ~ *bekommen* get hungry; ~ *haben* be hungry; ~*s sterben* starve (to death); '**~kur** *f* fasting cure; '**~leider** *m* (7) starveling; '**~lohn** *m* starvation wage(s *pl.*), *a.* pittance.

'**hungern** (29) hunger (*fig. nach* for), be hungry; (*schlecht leben*) starve; *freiwillig*: starve o.s., fast; *j-n* ~ *lassen* starve a p.

Hunger|ödem 🜍 ['~ʔø'de:m] *n* (3¹) hunger (o)edema; '**~snot** *f* famine; '**~streik** *m* hunger-strike; '**~tod** *m* (death from) starvation; '**~tuch** *n*: *am* ~ *nagen* be starving.

'**hungrig** hungry (*fig. nach* for).

Hupe ['hu:pə] *f* (15) horn, hooter; ♀**n** (25) hoot, honk.

hüpfen ['hypfən] (25, sn) hop, skip.

Hürde ['hyrdə] *f* (15) hurdle; (*Pferch*) fold, pen; '**~nlauf** *m*, '**~n-rennen** *n* hurdle-race, hurdles *pl.*; '**~nläufer** *m* hurdler.

Hure ['hu:rə] *f* (15) whore, prostitute; ♀**n** (25) whore; **~rei** [~'rai] *f* (15) whoring; prostitution.

hurra! [hu'ra:] hurrah!; ♀**patriot** *m* patrioteer, jingo(ist); ♀**patriotismus** *m* patrioteering, jingoism.

hurtig ['hurtiç] quick, swift; (*flink und gewandt*) agile, nimble; ♀**keit** *f* swiftness, quickness; agility.

Husar [hu'za:r] *m* (12) hussar.

husch! [huʃ] (*plötzlich*) in a flash; *scheuchend*: shoo!; '**~en** (27, sn) scurry, whisk, flit.

hüsteln ['hy:stəln] **1.** (29) cough slightly; **2.** ♀ *n* (6) slight cough.

husten ['hu:stən] **1.** (26) cough; F *fig.* ~ *auf* (*acc.*) not to care a rap; *ich werde dir was* ~! go to hell! **2.** ⚲ *m* (6) cough; '⚲-**anfall** *m* coughing fit; '⚲**bonbon** *m* cough drop; '⚲**reiz** *m* urge to cough; '⚲-**saft** *m* cough-mixture.

Hut[1] [hu:t] *m* (3³) hat; *den* ~ *abnehmen* take off one's hat (*fig. vor j-m* to a p.); ~ *ab!* hat(s) off (*vor* to)!; *fig. unter einen* ~ *bringen* reconcile; F *ihm ging der* ~ *hoch* he blew his top.

Hut[2] *f* (16) (*Obhut, Aufsicht*) care, charge; (*Schutz*) protection; *auf der* ~ *sein s.* (*sich*) *hüten.*

hüten ['hy:tən] (26) (*bewachen*) guard, watch (over); *Vieh:* tend; *s. Bett; sich* ~ be on one's guard (*vor dat.* against), look (*Am.* watch) out (for); *sich* ~ *zu tun* be careful not to do; *hüte dich vor ... beware of ...*

'**Hüter** *m* (7), '~**in** *f* keeper, guardian; (*Vieh*⚲) herdsman.

'**Hut**|**futter** *n* hat-lining; '~**geschäft**, *n*, '~**laden** *m* hat shop; '~**krempe** *f* brim (of a hat); '~**macher** *m* hatter; '~**schachtel** *f* hat--box; '~**schnur** *f* hat-string; F *das geht über die* ~ that's (really) too much!

Hütte ['hytə] *f* (15) hut, cabin; (*Bude*) shanty, *Am.* F shack; ⊕ *s. Hüttenwerk.*

'**Hütten**|-**erz** *n* dressed ore; '~**käse** *m* cottage cheese; '~**kunde** *f* metallurgy; '~**werk** *n* metallurgical plant, smelting-works; '~**wesen** *n* metallurgy.

Hyäne [hy'ɛ:nə] *f* (15) hyena.

Hyazinthe [hya'tsintə] *f* (15) hyacinth.

hybrid [hy'bri:t], ⚲**e** [~də] *f, m* hybrid.

Hydrant [hy'drant] *m* (12) hydrant, fire-plug.

Hydrauli|**k** [hy'draʊlik] *f* (16) hydraulics *pl.*; ⚲**sch** hydraulic(ally *adv.*).

hydrieren [hy'dri:rən] hydrogenate.

Hygien|**e** [hy'gje:nə] *f* (15) hygiene, *a.* hygienics *pl.*; ⚲**isch** hygienic(ally *adv.*), sanitary.

Hymne ['hymnə] *f* (15) hymn.

hypermodern ['hypər-] hyper- *od.* ultra-modern.

Hyperbel [hy'pɛrbəl] *f* (15) 𝒜 hyperbola; *rhet.* hyperbole.

Hypno|**se** [hyp'no:zə] *f* (15) hypnosis; ⚲**tisch** hypnotic; ~**tiseur** [~noti'zø:r] *m* (3¹) hypnotist; ⚲**tisieren** hypnotize.

Hypochon|**der** [hypo'xɔndər] *m* (7) hypochondriac; ~'**drie** *f* hypochondria; ⚲**drisch** hypochondriacal.

Hypotenuse 𝒜 [~te'nu:zə] *f* (15) hypotenuse.

Hypothek [~'te:k] *f* (16) mortgage; *e-e* ~ *aufnehmen* raise a mortgage; *mit* ~*en belastet* mortgaged; ⚲**arisch** [~te'ka:riʃ] hypothecary; *adv.* by (*od.* on) mortgage; ~**enbank** [~'te:kən-] *f* mortgage bank; ~**enbrief** *m* mortgage(-deed); ~**engläubiger** *m* mortgagee; ~**enpfandbrief** *m* mortgage debenture (*od.* bond); ~**enschuldner** *m* mortgagor.

Hypothe|**se** [hypo'te:zə] *f* (15) hypothesis; ⚲**tisch** hypothetic(al).

Hysterie [hyste'ri:] *f* (15) hysteria.

hysterisch [~'ste:riʃ] hysterical.

I

I [i:], **i** *n inv.* I, i.

i! why!; *i nun!* well!; *i freilich!* of course!; *i wo!* certainly not!, not at all!

iah! [i:a:], ⚲ *n* (*Eselsschrei*) hee-haw.

Iamb|**e** ['jambə] *f* (15), ~**us** ['~us] *m* (16²) iambus; '⚲**isch** iambic.

ich [iç] **1.** (19) I; ~ *bin's!* it is I!,

F *it's me!*; **2.** ⚲ *n inv.* self; ego; '~**bezogen** egocentric; *in der* '⚲-**form** *f* in the first person (singular); '⚲**sucht** *f* selfishness.

Ideal [ide'a:l] **1.** *n* (3¹) ideal; F *fig. a.* dream; **2.** ⚲ *adj.* ideal; ~**fall** *m* ideal state of affairs; *im*~ ideally; ⚲**i'sieren** [~ali-] idealize; ~**ismus** [~'lismus] *m*

(16, *o. pl.*) idealism; **~ist** [~'list] *m* (12), **~istin** *f* (16¹), **2istisch** idealist; **~vorstellung** *f* ideal.

Idee [i'de:] *f* (15) idea, notion; *gute* ~ good idea!; *ich kam auf die* ~ *zu inf.* I got the idea to *inf.*, it occurred to me to *inf.*

ideell [ide'ɛl] ideal, imaginary.

I'deen|losigkeit *f* lack of ideas *od.* imagination; **2reich** full of ideas *od.* imagination.

identi|fizieren [idɛntifi'tsi:rən] identify; **2fi'zierung** *f* identification; **~sch** [i'dɛntiʃ] identical; **2tät** [~'tɛ:t] *f* (16) identity; **2'tätsnachweis** *m* proof of identity.

Ideo|logie [ideolo'gi:] *f* (16) ideology; **2logisch** [~'lo:giʃ] ideological.

Idiom [idi'o:m] *n* (3¹) idiom; (*Sprache*) language; **2atisch** [~o-'ma:tiʃ] idiomatic.

Idiot [idi'o:t] *m* (12) idiot; **~en-arbeit** *f* donkey work; **~enhang**, **~enhügel** *co. m* nursery slope; **2ensicher** foolproof; **~ie** [~o'ti:] *f* (15) idiocy; **2isch** [~'o:tiʃ] idiotic(al).

Idol [i'do:l] *n* (3¹) idol.

Idyll [i'dyl] *n* (3¹), **~e** *f* (15) idyl(l); **2isch** idyllic(ally *adv.*).

Igel ['i:gəl] *m* (7) hedgehog; ✕ = **'~stellung** *f* allround defen|ce, *Am.* -se; hedgehog position.

Ignor|ant [igno'rant] *m* (12) ignorant person, ignoramus; **~anz** [~'rants] *f* (16) ignorance; **2ieren** [~'ri:rən] ignore, take no notice of.

ihm [i:m] (to) him; *S.*: (to) it.

ihn [i:n] him; *S.*: it.

'ihnen (to) them; **2** (to) you.

ihr [i:r] 1. (*dat. von sie sg.*) (to) her; (*nom. pl. von du, im Brief* **2**) you; 2. (20) *besitzanzeigend*: her; *S.* its; *pl.* their; **2** your; 3. der (die, das) ~e *od.* ~ige ['~igə] hers; *pl.* theirs; der (die, das) **2**e, **2**ige yours.

ihrerseits ['~ərzaɪts] on her (*pl.* their, **2** your) part.

ihresgleichen [~əs'glaɪçən] the like(s) of her *od.* them; their like; her (*od.* their) equals.

ihret|halben ['i:rəthalbən], '**~wegen**, (um) '**~willen** for her (*pl.* their, **2** your) sake; on her (their, **2** your) account.

ihrig ['i:riç] *s.* ihr 3.

illegal ['ilega:l] illegal.

illegitim [ilegi'ti:m] illegitimate.

illuminieren [ilumi'ni:rən] illuminate.

Illu|sion [ilu'zjo:n] *f* illusion; **2so-risch** [~'zo:riʃ] illusory.

Illu|stration [ilustra'tsjo:n] *f* illustration; **~strator** [ilu'stra:tɔr] *m* illustrator; **2strieren** [~'stri:rən] illustrate; **~'strierte** *f* (illustrated) magazine.

Iltis ['iltis] *m* (4¹) fitchew, polecat.

im [im] = *in dem* in the.

imaginär [imagi'nɛ:r] imaginary.

Imbiß ['imbis] *m* (4) snack; '**~stube** *f* snack-bar.

Imit|ation [imita'tsjo:n] *f* imitation; **2ieren** [~'ti:rən] imitate.

Imker ['imkər] *m* (7) bee-master; **~ei** [~'raɪ] *f* (7) bee-farming.

Immatrikul|ation [imatrikula-'tsjo:n] *f* registration, enrol(l)ment; **2ieren** [~'li:rən] (*a. sich* ~ *lassen*) register, enrol(l).

immer ['imər] always; *auf* ~, *für* ~ for ever, for good; ~ *mehr* more and more; ~ *noch* still; ~ *noch nicht* not yet, not even now; ~ *weiter* on and on; ~ *reden usw.*: keep *talking, etc.*; ~ *wieder* again (*od.* time) and again; **~dar** ['~da:r] always, for ever; '**~fort** always, continually; '**2grün** *n* evergreen; '**~hin** still, yet; '**~während** everlasting, perpetual; '**~zu** always.

Immobilien [imo'bi:ljən] *pl. inv.* immovables *pl.*, real estate *sg.*; **~fonds** *m* real estate investment trust; **~makler** *m s. Grundstücksmakler*; **~markt** *m* property market.

immun [i'mu:n] immune (*gegen* from); **~i'sieren** immunize; **2ität** [~'tɛ:t] *f* (16) immunity (from).

Imperativ ['imperati:f] *m* (3¹) imperative (mood); **2isch** [~'ti:viʃ] imperative.

Imperfekt(um) ['imperfɛkt(um)] *n* (3 [9²]) imperfect tense.

Imperialis|mus [imperja'lismus] *m* (16, *o. pl.*) imperialism; **2tisch** imperialist(ic).

impertinen|t [imperti'nɛnt] impertinent, insolent; **2z** [~'nɛnts] *f* (16) impertinence.

Impf|-arzt ['impf-] *m* vaccinator; '**2en** (25) ♀ vaccinate, (*a.* ♠) inoculate; '**~ling** *m* (3¹) person due to be vaccinated; '**~paß** *m* vaccination document; '**~pistole** *f* vaccination gun; '**~schein** *m* vaccination certificate; '~stoff *m* vaccine; '~ung *f* 🗲 vaccination; *a.* 🖉 inoculation.

Imponderabilien [impɔndera'biːljən] *n*/*pl. inv.* imponderables.

imponieren [impo'niːrən]: *j-m* ~ impress a p. strongly; ~**d** imposing.

Import [im'pɔrt] *m* (3) import (-ation); *konkret:* = ~**e** *pl.* imports; ~**beschränkungen** *f*/*pl.* import restrictions; ~**eur** [~'tøːr] *m* (3¹) importer; **♀ieren** [~'tiːrən] import; ~**ware** *f einzelne:* imported article; *als Sammelbegriff:* imported goods *pl.*

imposant [impo'zant] imposing.

impoten|t ['impotɛnt] impotent; **♀z** [~ts] *f* (16) impotence.

imprägnier|en [imprɛ:g'niːrən] impregnate; *(wasserdicht machen)* (water)proof; **♀ung** *f* impregnation.

Impresario [impre'zaːrio] *m* (11) impresario, manager.

improvisieren [improvi'ziːrən] improvise.

Impuls [im'puls] *m* (4) impulse; **♀iv** [~'ziːf] impulsive; ~ *handeln* act on impulse, act on the spur of the moment.

imstande [im'ʃtandə]: ~ *sein* be able.

in [in] *(acc.)* in, into; *(dat.)* in, at; *(innerhalb)* within.

In'-angriffnahme *f* (15) taking in hand, tackling.

In'-anspruchnahme *f* (15) *e-s Rechts usw.:* laying claim *(gen.* to), assertion (of); *(Benutzung)* utilization; *(Zuhilfenahme)* resort (to); *v. Geldmitteln, Kraft, Material usw.:* strain *(gen.* on); *(Anforderungen)* demands *pl. (gen.* on).

'Inbegriff *m* essence; *(Verkörperung)* embodiment; *(Muster)* paragon; **'♀en** included, inclusive of.

Inbe'sitznahme *f* taking possession, occupation.

Inbe'triebnahme *f* putting into operation, starting, opening.

'Inbrunst *f* (14¹) ardo(u)r, fervo(u)r.

'inbrünstig ardent, fervent.

in'dem whilst, while; *(dadurch, daß)* mst by *mit Gerundium;* ~ *er mich ansah, sagte er* looking at me he said.

Inder ['indər] *m* (7), '~**in** *f* (16¹) Indian.

in'des(sen) 1. *adv.* meanwhile; 2. *cj.* while; *(jedoch)* however, yet.

Index ['indɛks] *m* (3², *sg. a. inv., pl. a.* 'Indizes) *(Verzeichnis, a.* ~*ziffer)* index.

Indianer [in'djaːnər] *m* (7) Red Indian.

indifferent ['indifɛrɛnt] indifferent.

indigniert [indi'gniːrt] indignant.

Indigo ['indigo] *m, n* (11) indigo.

Indikation 🗲 [indika'tsjoːn] *f* indication.

Indikativ ['indikatiːf] *m* (3¹) indicative (mood); **♀isch** [~'tiːviʃ] indicative.

indirekt ['indirɛkt] indirect; *gr.* ~**e** *Rede* reported speech.

indisch ['indiʃ] Indian.

indiskret ['indiskreːt] indiscreet; **♀ion** [~e'tsjoːn] *f* (16) indiscretion.

indiskutabel ['indiskutaːbəl] *pred.* out of the question.

indisponiert ['indisponiːrt] indisposed, unwell.

Individualist [individua'list] *m* individualist; **♀isch** individualist(ic).

Individu|alität [~li'tɛːt] *f* (16) individuality; **♀'ell** individual; ~**um** [~'viːduum] *n* (9) individual.

Indizienbeweis [in'diːtsjənbəvaɪs] *m* circumstantial evidence.

Indoss|ament ✝ [indɔsa'mɛnt] *n* (3) endorsement; ~**ant** [~'sant] *m* (12) indorser; ~**at** [~'saːt] *m* (12) endorsee; ~**ieren** [~'siːrən] endorse.

Induktion [induk'tsjoːn] *f* induction; ~**sstrom** 🗲 *m* induced current.

industrialisier|en [industriali'ziːrən] industrialize; **♀ung** *f* industrialization.

Industrie [~'striː] *f* (15) industry; ~**anlage** *f* industrial plant; ~**arbeiter** *m* industrial worker; ~**ausstellung** *f* industrial exhibition; ~**denkmal** *n* industrial monument; ~**erzeugnis** *n* industrial product; ~**gebiet** *n* industrial area.

industriell [~stri'ɛl] industrial; **♀e** *m* (13) industrialist.

Indu'strie|magnat [~magnaːt] *m* (12) business magnate, tycoon; ~**müll** *m* industrial refuse *(od.* waste); ~**nation** *f* industrial nation; ~**roboter** *m* industrial robot; ~**staat** *m* industrial nation; ~**zeit-alter** *n* industrial age; ~**zweig** *m* (branch of) industry.

in-ei'nander into one another; ~**greifen** ⊕ interlock, intermesh; ~**schieben** *(a. sich)* telescope.

infam [in'faːm] shameful; **♀ie** [~fa-'miː] *f* (15) infamy.

Infanter|ie [ʌə'riː] *f* (15) infantry; **ist** [ʌ'rist] *m* (12) infantryman.
infantil [infan'tiːl] infantile.
Infarkt [in'farkt] 𝕰 *m* (3) infarct.
Infektion [infɛk'tsjoːn] *f* infection; **sgefahr** *f* danger of infection; **s-herd** *m* focus of infection; **skrankheit** *f* infectious disease; **s-träger** (**-in** *f*) *m* infection agent (*od.* carrier).
Infinitiv ['infinitiːf] *m* (3¹) infinitive (mood); **isch** [ʌ'tiːviʃ] infinitive.
infizieren [infi'tsiːrən] infect.
Inflation [infla'tsjoːn] *f* (16) inflation; **är** [ʌtsjo'nɛːr] inflationary; **istisch** [ʌtsjo'nistiʃ] inflationary; **sausgleich** *m* indexation, *Am.* indexing; **s-politik** *f* inflationary policy (*od.* policies *pl.*); **srate** *f* rate of inflation.
Influenza [ʌflu'ɛntsa] *f inv.* influenza, F flu.
infolge [in'fɔlgə] (*gen.*) in consequence of, as a result of, owing to, due to; **ʌ'dessen** consequently, as a result.
Informatik [infɔr'maːtik] *f* (16, *o. pl.*) information (*od.* computer) science; **er(in** *f*) *m* information scientist (*od.* specialist).
Inform|ation [informa'tsjoːn] *f* (16) information; **ativ** [ʌ'tiːf] informative; **atorisch** [ʌ'toːriʃ] informatory; **ieren** [ʌ'miːrən] inform; *falsch* ʌ misinform.
infra|rot ['infraroːt] infrared; **rot-bestrahlung** 𝕰 [infra'roːtʌ] *f* infrared heat treatment; **rot-Fernbedienung** [infra'roːtʌ] *f* infrared remote control (unit); **schall...** infrasonic; **struktur** *f* infrastructure.
Infusorien [infu'zoːrjən] *n/pl.* infusoria.
In'gangsetzung *f* starting.
Ingenieur [inʒe'njøːr] *m* (3¹) engineer; **schule** *f* engineering college.
'Ingrimm *m* (3) anger, wrath; **'ig** wrathful, furious.
Ingwer ['iɲvər] *m* (7) ginger.
Inhaber ['inhaːbər] *m* (7), **'in** *f* (16¹) holder; (*Eigentümer*) owner, proprietor; (*Wohnungs*ℒ) occupant; (*Laden*ℒ) keeper; *e-s Amtes, e-r Aktie, e-s sportlichen Titels od. Preises usw.*: holder; *e-s Wechsels, Schecks*: bearer; '**aktie** *f* bearer share; '**scheck** *m* bearer cheque (*Am.* check).

Inhalation [inhala'tsjoːn] *f* (16) inhalation; **s-apparat** *m* inhaler.
inha'lier|en inhale; **gerät** *n* inhalator.
'Inhalt *m* (3) contents *pl.* (*a. fig.*); (*Gehalt*) content; (*Raum*ℒ) capacity; (*Körper*ℒ) volume; *e-r Rede, Urkunde usw.*: tenor, content; *des* ʌs, *daß* ... to the effect that; '**s-angabe** *f* summary; **slos** empty; '**sreich** copious; significant; pregnant; '**s-schwer** momentous; '**s-verzeichnis** *n* table of contents, index.
Initiale [ini'tsjaːlə] *f* (15) initial.
Initiative [initsja'tiːvə] *f* (15) initiative; *die* ʌ *ergreifen* take the initiative; *aus eigener* ʌ of one's own accord, on one's own initiative.
Injektion [injɛk'tsjoːn] *f* injection, F shot.
injizieren [inji'tsiːrən] inject.
Inkasso [in'kaso] *n* (11) encashment, collection.
Inkognito [ʌ'kɔgnito] *n* (11), ℒ *adv.* incognito.
inkonsequen|t ['inkɔnzəkvɛnt] inconsistent; **z** [ʌts] *f* inconsistency.
'inkorrekt incorrect.
In'krafttreten *n* (6) coming into force; *Tag des* ʌs effective day.
inkriminieren [inkrimi'niːrən] incriminate.
Inkubationszeit 𝕰 [inkuba'tsjoːnstsaɪt] *f* incubation period.
'Inland *n* (1) inland; (*Ggs. Ausland*) home (*od.* native) country; '**ʌ...** home, domestic, internal.
Inländer ['inlɛndər] *m* (7), '**in** *f* inlander; (*Ggs. Ausländer*) native.
'Inlandflug *m* domestic flight.
'inländisch native, indigenous; domestic; *Handel*: inland; † *Erzeugnis*: home-made.
'Inlaut *m* (3) medial sound.
Inlett ['inlɛt] *n* (3¹) bedtick; '**stoff** *m* ticking.
'inliegend enclosed.
in'mitten (*gen.*) in the midst of, amidst, *Am. mst* amid.
inne ['inə] within; '**haben** *Rekord, Stelle*: hold; *Amt, Wohnung*: occupy; '**halten** *v/i.* stop, pause; *v/t.* keep to, observe.
innen ['inən] (*innerhalb*) (on the) inside, within; (*im Hause*) within doors; *nach* ʌ inwards; *von* ʌ from within, from the inside.

'**Innen**|-**ansicht** f interior view; '**~-antenne** f indoor aerial od. antenna; '**~-architekt** m interior decorator; '**~-architektur** f interior decoration; '**~-aufnahme** phot. f indoor photograph od. shot; '**~-ausstattung** f interior equipment; '**~dekoration** f interior decoration; '**~leben** n inner life; '**~leuchte** mot. f courtesy light; '**~minister** m Minister of the Interior; Brt. Home Secretary; Am. Secretary of the Interior; '**~ministerium** n Ministry of the Interior; Brt. Home Office; Am. Department of the Interior; '**~politik** f home politics pl.; bestimmte: domestic policy; '**2politisch** home affairs ...; domestic (political) ...; adv. with regard to home affairs; '**~raum** m interior; '**~seite** f inner side, inside; '**~spiegel** mot. m driver's (od. rear-view) mirror; '**~stadt** f town (od. city) cent|re, Am. -er, Am. a. downtown.

inner ['inər] interior; (innerlich) inward, inner; a. 🦶, pol. internal; ⊕ a. inside; **~e** Angelegenheit internal affair; **~e** Stimme inner voice; '**~betrieblich** internal, Am. a. in--plant; '**2e** n interior; fig. (Geist) mind; Minister(ium) des **~n** s. Innenminister(ium) **2eien** ['~raɪən] f/pl. offal(s); '**~halb** prp. (gen.) within; adv. (on the) inside; '**~lich** s. inner; P.: introspective, contemplative; '**~parteilich** intra-party; internal.

'**innerst** inmost; '**2e** n the innermost (part); fig. the very heart.

'**innewerden** (gen.) perceive, become aware of.

'**innewohnen** v/i. be inherent (dat. in); '**~d** inherent (dat. in).

innig ['iniç] (herzlich) hearty; (tief empfunden) heartfelt, profound; (inbrünstig) ardent, fervent; (zärtlich) tender; Beziehung: intimate; '**2keit** f heartiness; fervo(u)r; intimacy.

Innung ['inuŋ] f (16) guild, corporation.

inoffiziell ['in?ɔfitsjɛl] unofficial.

ins [ins] = in das into the.

Insasse ['inzasə] m (13) inmate, occupant; e-s Wagens usw.: a. passenger.

insbesondere [insbə'zɔndərə] in particular; especially.

'**Inschrift** f inscription; e-r Münze usw.: legend.

Insekt [in'zɛkt] n (5) insect; **~enkunde** f entomology; **~enpulver** n insect-powder.

Insektizid [inzɛkti'tsiːt] n (3) insecticide, pesticide.

Insel ['inzəl] f (15) island; '**~bewohner(in** f) m islander; '**~gruppe** f archipelago; '**~staat** m insular state.

Inser|**at** [inzə'raːt] n (3) advertisement, F ad; ein **~** aufgeben put an ad in; **2ieren** [~'riːrən] advertise.

ins|**ge'heim** secretly; **~ge'mein** generally; **~ge'samt** altogether.

Insignien [in'ziɡnjən] pl. insignia.

insofern [in'zoːfɛrn] adv. so far; cj. **~** als as (a. so) far as, in so far as, in that.

insolven|**t** ['inzɔlvɛnt] insolvent; '**2z** [~ts] f (16) insolvency.

Inspekteur [inspɛk'tøːr] m (3[1]) inspector; ✗ Chief of the Army (od. Air Force od. Navy) Staff.

Inspektion [inspɛk'tsjoːn] f (16) inspection; (Amt) inspectorate; **~sreise** f tour of inspection.

Inspektor [in'spɛktɔr] m (8[1]) inspector; (Aufseher) overseer.

Inspir|**ation** [inspira'tsjoːn] f inspiration; **2ieren** [~'riːrən] inspire.

Inspiz|**ient** thea. [~'tsjɛnt] m (12) stage-manager; **2ieren** [~'tsiːrən] inspect, superintend.

Install|**ateur** [instala'tøːr] m (3[1]) installer, plumber; für Gas: gas fitter; **~ation** [~'tsjoːn] f (15) installation, plumbing; **2ieren** [~-'liːrən] install.

instand [in'ʃtant]: **~** halten maintain, keep up; **~** setzen et.: repair, restore; (wieder **~** setzen) a. recondition, Am. fix; **2haltung** f maintenance, upkeep.

'**inständig** urgent, instant.

In'standsetzung f repair(ing), restoration; reconditioning.

Instanz [in'stants] f (16) instance; ⚖ court of first etc. instance; letzte **~** last resort; **~enweg** m stages pl. of appeal; s. Dienstweg.

Instinkt [in'stiŋkt] m (3) instinct; **2mäßig**, **2iv** [~'tiːf] instinctive.

Institut [~sti'tuːt] n (3) institute.

Institution [~stitu'tsjoːn] f institution.

instru|**ieren** [~stru'iːrən] instruct; **2ktion** [~struk'tsjoːn] f (15) instruction; **~ktiv** [~'tiːf] instructive.

Instrument [ˌstruˈmɛnt] n (3) instrument; **~almusik** [ˌ~ˈtaːl-] f instrumental music; **~enbrett** n instrument panel, dashboard; **~enflug** instrument flying; **2ieren** ♪ [ˌ~ˈtiːrən] instrument, score.

Insulaner [inzuˈlaːnər] m (7) islander.

inszenier|en [instseˈniːrən] (put on the) stage; *fig.* stage; **2ung** f staging.

intakt [inˈtakt] intact.

Integralrechnung ⅍ [inteˈgraːlreçnuŋ] f integral calculus.

Inte|gration [integraˈtsjoːn] f integration; **2grieren** [ˌ~ˈgriːrən] integrate; **~der Bestandteil** integral part.

intellektuell [intɛlɛktuˈɛl], **2e** m, f (18) intellectual, F highbrow.

intelligen|t [ˌ~liˈgɛnt] intelligent; **2z** [ˌ~ts] f (16) intelligence; **2zbestie** F f egghead; **2zquotient** m intelligence quotient, I. Q.; **2ztest** m intelligence test.

Intendant [intɛnˈdant] m (12) superintendent; *thea.* director.

Inten|sität [intɛnziˈtɛːt] f (16, *o. pl.*) intensity; **2siv** [ˌ~ˈziːf] intensive; **~'sivkurs** m crash course; **~'sivstation** ⅍ f intensive care unit.

Intercity 🚄 [intərˈsiti] m (11) inter-city train.

interessant [intərɛˈsant] interesting.

Interesse [intəˈrɛsə] n (10) interest (*an dat.*, *für* in); **2los** uninterested, indifferent; **~ngebiet** n field of interest; **~ngemeinschaft** f community of interests; (*Kartell*) pool, combine; **~ngruppe** *pol.* f pressure group, lobby.

Interess|ent [ˌ~ˈsɛnt] m (12) interested party; *für e-n Kauf:* prospect; **~envertretung** [ˌ~ˈrɛsən-] f representation of interests; **2ieren** [ˌ~ˈsiːrən] interest (*für* in); *sich ~ für* take an interest in; *interessiert sein an* (*dat.*) be interested in.

'Interims|regierung f provisional *od.* interim government; **'~schein** ✝ m scrip.

interkontinental [intərkontinɛnˈtaːl] intercontinental; **2rakete** f intercontinental ballistic missile.

intern [inˈtɛrn] internal.

Internat [ˌ~ˈnaːt] n (3) boarding-school.

inter|national [internatsjoˈnaːl] international; **~'nieren** intern; **2-**

'nierte m internee; **2'nierung** f internment; **2'nierungslager** n internment camp; **2'nist** ⅍ m (12) internal specialist; **~pellieren** [ˌ~pɛˈliːrən] interpellate; **~plane'tarisch** interplanetary; **2pretation** [ˌ~pretaˈtsjoːn] f interpretation; **~pretieren** [ˌ~preˈtiːrən] interpret; **2punktion** [ˌ~puŋkˈtsjoːn] f (16) punctuation; **2punk'tionszeichen** n punctuation mark; **2vall** [ˌ~ˈval] n (3) interval; **~venieren** [ˌ~veˈniːrən] intervene; **2vention** [ˌ~venˈtsjoːn] f intervention; **2view** [ˌ~ˈvjuː] n (11¹), **~viewen** (25) interview.

Interzonen|handel [intərˈtsoːnənhandəl] m interzonal trade; **~paß** m (inter)zonal pass *od.* permit; **~verkehr** m interzonal traffic.

intim [inˈtiːm] intimate (*mit* with); **2ität** [ˌ~timiˈtɛːt] f (16) intimacy; **2sphäre** f privacy.

intoleran|t ['intolərant] intolerant; **'2z** [ˌ~ts] f (16) intolerance.

intransitiv ['intranzitiːf] intransitive.

intravenös ⅍ [intraveˈnøːs] intravenous.

intrigant [ˌ~triˈgant] **1.** intriguing; **2.** **2** m (13), **2in** f (16¹) intriguer.

Intrig|e [inˈtriːgə] f (15) intrigue; **2ieren** [ˌ~ˈgiːrən] intrigue, plot.

introvertiert [introvɛrˈtiːrt] introverted.

intus F ['intus]: *et. ~ haben* have got a th. into one's head; (*Essen etc.*) have downed a th.; *e-n ~ haben* have had one too many.

Invalide [invaˈliːdə] m (13) invalid; *engS.* disabled worker *od.* soldier *od.* sailor; **~nrente** f disability pension; **~nversicherung** f disablement insurance.

Invalidität [invalidiˈtɛːt] f disablement, disability.

Invasion [ˌ~vaˈzjoːn] f invasion.

Inventar [ˌ~vɛnˈtaːr] n (3¹) inventory, stock; *lebendes und totes ~* live and dead stock; **2isieren** [ˌ~tariˈziːrən] inventory.

Inventur [ˌ~ˈtuːr] f (16) stock-taking; *~ machen* take stock; **~ausverkauf** m stock-taking sale.

investier|en ✝ [ˌ~vesˈtiːrən] invest; **2ung** f investment.

Investition [investiˈtsjoːn] f investment; **~s-anreiz** m investment incentive.

Investment [in'vɛstmənt] n (11) investment; **～fonds** m investment fund.

inwärts ['invɛrts] inwards.

inwendig inward.

inwie'fern, inwie'weit (in) how far.

'Inzucht f (16) inbreeding.

in'zwischen in the meantime, meanwhile; (seither) since.

Ion phys. ['i'ɔn] n (8) ion.

ird|en ['irdən] earthen; **'～isch** earthly; (weltlich) worldly; (sterblich) mortal.

Ire ['iːrə] m (13) s. Irländer.

irgend ['irgənt] in Zssgn some; allg. u. bei Frage u. so rasch wie ～ möglich as soon as ever possible; wenn ich ～ kann if I possibly can; **'～-ein, '～-eine, '～-eins** some; any; **'～-einer, '～ 'jemand, '～wer** somebody, someone; anybody, anyone; **'～-einmal** some time; **'～ 'etwas** something; anything; **'～'wann** some time (or other); **'～'wie** somehow; anyhow; **'～'wo** somewhere; anywhere; **'～-wo'her** from somewhere; from anywhere; **'～wo'hin** somewhere; anywhere.

irisch ['iːriʃ] Irish.

Irländer ['irlɛndər] m (7) Irishman; **'～in** f (16¹) Irishwoman.

Iron|ie [iro'niː] f (15) irony; **♀isch** [i'roːniʃ] ironic(al).

irrational ['iratsjonɑːl] irrational.

irre ['irə] **1.** astray; fig. wrong; (verwirrt) confused; (verrückt) lunatic, mad, **♂** insane; sl. (ausgefallen) way-out; ～ werden get confused; ～ werden an (dat.) not to know what to make of, begin to doubt; **2.** ♀ m, f (18) insane person, lunatic; F wie ein ～r like mad; **3.** ♀ f (15): in der (od. die) ～ astray; **'～führen** lead astray; fig. a. mislead; **'～gehen** (sn) go astray; **'～machen** puzzle, bewilder, perplex, confound.

irren ['irən] (25) err, go astray; (umherschweifen) wander; geistig: err, make a mistake (a. sich); sich ～ be mistaken (in dat. in a p., about a th.); be wrong.

'Irren|-arzt m mental specialist, alienist; **'～haus** n, **'～(heil)-anstalt** f lunatic asylum, mental home.

'irrereden rave.

'Irr|fahrt f wandering; **'～gang** m, **'～garten** m labyrinth, maze; **'♀-gläubig** heretical.

'irrig erroneous; (falsch) false, wrong.

irritieren [iri'tiːrən] (ärgern) irritate; (be-irren) puzzle, intrigue.

'Irr|lehre f false doctrine, heterodoxy; (Ketzerei) heresy; **'～licht** n will-o'-the-wisp, jack-o'-lantern; **'～pfad** m wrong path; **'～sinn** m insanity; **'♀sinnig** insane, mad; **'～tum** m (1²) error, mistake; im ～ sein be mistaken; in e-m ～ befangen sein labo(u)r under a mistake; Irrtümer vorbehalten errors excepted; **♀tümlich** ['～tyːm-] erroneous; **'～ung** f error, mistake; **'～weg** m wrong way; **'～wisch** m s. Irrlicht; F P.: flibbertigibbet.

Ischias ♂ ['isçias, 'iʃ-] f F a. n, m inv. sciatica.

Islam [is'lɑːm] m (11) Islam(ism).

Isländ|er ['iːslɛndər] m Icelander; **♀isch** Icelandic.

Isolation [izolaˈtsjoːn] f isolation; von Häftlingen: confinement; ⚡ insulation.

Isolator ⚡ [izoˈlɑːtɔr] m (8¹) insulator.

Isolier... ⚡ [～'liːr] insulating; **～band** n insulating tape; **♀en** isolate; ⚡ insulate; **～haft** f solitary confinement; **～kanne** f thermos jug; **～station** ♂ f isolation ward; **～ung** f isolation; ⚡ insulation.

isometrisch [izo'meːtriʃ] isometric; **～e Übungen** isometrics pl.

Isotop ⚛ [izo'toːp] n (3) isotope.

Israel|i [isra'eːli] m (11) Israeli; **～it** [～e'liːt] m (12) Israelite.

Ist|bestand ['ist-] m actual inventory od. stock; **'～stärke** f effective strength; **'～wert** m actual value.

Italien|er [ital'jeːnər] m (7) Italian; **～erin** f Italian (woman); **♀isch** Italian.

'I-Tüpfelchen n fig.: bis aufs ～ to a T.

J

J [jɔt], **j** *n inv.* J, j.

ja [jɑː] yes; ~ *freilich* yes, indeed; to be sure; ~ *sogar*, ~ *selbst* even; *wenn* ~ if so; ~ *sagen* say yes, consent; *er ist* ~ *mein Freund* why, he is my friend; *da ist er* ~*!* well, there he is!; *ich sagte es Ihnen* ~ I told you so; *tun Sie es* ~ *nicht!* don't you do it!; *vergessen Sie es* ~ *nicht!* be sure not to forget it!

Jacht [jaxt] *f* (16) yacht.

Jäckchen ['jɛkçən] *n* (6) (short) jacket, coatee.

Jacke ['jakə] *f* (15) jacket; *fig.* F *das ist* ~ *wie Hose* that's six of one and half a dozen of the other; '~**nkleid** *n* lady's suit.

Jackett [ʒa'kɛt] *n* (11) jacket.

Jagd [jɑːkt] *f* (16) hunt(ing); *mit der Flinte:* shooting; *(Verfolgung)* chase, *s. Jagdbezirk; fig.* hunt *(nach* for); *weit S.* pursuit (of); *die* ~ *aufnehmen* give chase; *auf* ~ *gehen* go hunting *od.* shooting; ~ *machen auf (acc.)* hunt after *od.* for; '~**aufseher** *m* gamekeeper; '♀**bar** fit for hunting, fair; '~**berechtigung** *f* shooting; '~**bezirk** *m* shoot, hunting-ground; '~**bomber** ✕ *m* fighter-bomber; '~**büchse** *f* sporting rifle; '~**flieger** *m* fighter pilot; '~**flinte** *f* sporting gun; *leichte:* fowling-piece; '~**flugzeug** *n* fighter; '~**geschwader** *n* fighter wing *(Am.* group); '~**gesellschaft** *f* hunting *(od.* shooting) party; '~**haus** *n* shooting *(od.* hunting) lodge; '~**horn** *n* bugle, hunting-horn; '~**hund** *m* hound; '~**hütte** *f* shooting *(od.* hunting) box; '~**messer** *n* hunting knife; '~**pächter** *m* game-tenant; '~**recht** *n* game-laws *pl.;* hunting right(s *pl.*); '~**rennen** *n* steeple-chase; '~**revier** *n s. Jagdbezirk;* '~**schein** *m* shooting-licenc|e, *Am.* -se; '~**schloß** *n* hunting seat.

jagen ['jaːgən] *v/i.* (25) hunt; *(rennen usw.)* rush, dash; *fig.* ~ *nach* hunt after; *v/t.* hunt; *(hetzen)* chase, *fig. a.* rush; *(weg~)* drive away, turn out *(aus dem Hause* of doors); *Messer in den Leib usw.:* drive, thrust; *Kugel:* send; *s. Flucht, Luft.*

Jäger ['jɛːgər] *m* (7) hunter, sportsman; *(Wildhüter)* gamekeeper; ✕ rifleman; ❦ fighter; ~**ei** [~'raɪ] *f*

(16) hunting; ~**in** ['~rin] *f* huntress; '~**latein** *n* sportsman's slang; *(Aufschneiderei)* huntsman's yarn.

Jaguar ['jaːguɑːr] *m* (3¹) jaguar.

jäh [jɛː] abrupt; *(steil)* a. precipitous, steep; *(plötzlich)* a. sudden; ~**lings** ['~lɪŋs] precipitously; *(plötzlich)* suddenly.

Jahr [jaːr] *n* (3) year; *ein halbes* ~ half a year, six months; *einmal im* ~ once a year; *im* ~ *1900* in 1900; *mit (od. im Alter von)* 18 ~*en* at the age of eighteen; *letztes* ~ last year; *bei* ~*en* advanced in years; *das ganze* ~ *hindurch od. über* all the year round; *s. hinaus;* ♀'**-aus:** ~, *jahrein* year in, year out; '~**buch** *n* yearbook, annual.

'**jahrelang** for years.

jähren ['jɛːrən] *(sich)* (25) be a year ago.

'**Jahres...** *in Zssgn mst* annual, yearly; '~**-abschluß** ✝ *m* annual statement of accounts; '~**bericht** *m* annual report; '~**-einkommen** *n* annual income; '~**-ergebnis** ✝ *n* annual balance; '~**feier** *f* anniversary; '~**gehalt** *n* annual salary; '~**tag** *m* anniversary; '~**wechsel** *m*, '~**wende** *f* turn of the year; '~**zahl** *f* date, year; '~**zeit** *f* season.

'**Jahr|gang** *m e-r Zeitschrift:* annual set; *v. Menschen u. Tieren:* age-class; *v. Wein:* vintage; ~'**hundert** *n* century; ♀'**hunderte-alt** centuries old.

jährig ['jɛːrɪç] a year old; ...~ ...-year-old.

'**jährlich** annual, yearly.

'**Jahr|markt** *m* fair; ~'**tausend** *n* millennium; ~'**tausendfeier** *f* millenary; ~'**zehnt** *n* (3¹) decade.

Jähzorn ['jɛːtsɔrn] *m (Ausbruch)* sudden anger; *(Eigenschaft)* irascibility; ♀**ig** hot-tempered, irascible.

Jakob ['jaːkɔp]: F *der wahre* ~ the real McCoy.

Jalousie [ʒalu'ziː] *f* (15) Venetian blind, *Am. a.* window shade.

'**Jamb|e** ['~us, ♀**isch** *s.* Iambe *usw.*

Jammer ['jamər] *m* (7) lamentation; *(Elend)* misery; *es ist ein* ~ it is a great pity; '~**bild** *n* picture of misery; '~**geschrei** *n* lamentation; '~**gestalt** *f* miserable figure; '~**lappen** *contp. m* F sissy.

jämmerlich ['jɛmərliç] miserable, wretched.

jammern ['jamərn] (29) lament (*um* for; *über acc.* over); (*ächzen, wimmern*) wail, whine; *er jammert mich* I pity him.

'**Jammer...**: *es ist* '2'**schade** it is a great pity; '⌣**tal** *n* vale of tears; '2**voll** *s. jämmerlich.*

Jänner, Januar ['jɛnər, 'januːr] *m* (3¹) January.

Japan|er [ja'paːnər] *m* (7), ⌣**erin** *f* (16¹), 2**isch** Japanese.

jappen ['japən], **japsen** ['japsən] (27) gasp, pant.

Jargon [ʒar'gõ] *m* (11) jargon, slang.

Jasager ['jaːzaːgər] *m* (7) yes-man.

Jasmin [jas'miːn] *m* (3¹) jasmine.

Jaspis ['jaspis] *m* (4¹) jasper.

'**Ja-stimme** *parl. f* aye, *Am.* yea.

jäten ['jɛːtən] *v/t. u. v/i.* (26) weed.

Jauche ['jauxə] *f* (15) liquid manure.

jauchzen ['jauxtsən] **1.** (27) shout with joy, jubilate, exult; **2.** 2 *n* (6) jubilation, exultation.

jaulen ['jaulən] (25) howl.

ja'wohl yes(, indeed).

'**Jawort** *n* (1) consent; *e-m Freier das* ⌣ *geben* accept a suitor.

Jazz [jats, dʒɛz] *m* (3²) jazz; '⌣-**kapelle** *f* jazz band.

je [jeː] ever, at any time; (*beziehungsweise*) respectively; ⌣ *nachdem* a) *adv.* as the case may be, it depends, b) *cj.* according as; ⌣ *zwei* two at a time, (*zu zweien*) in pairs, by twos; *er gab den drei Knaben* ⌣ *zwei Äpfel* he gave the three boys two apples each; *für* ⌣ *zehn Wörter* for every ten words; ⌣ *eher,* ⌣ *lieber* the sooner the better; ⌣ *mehr,* ⌣ (*od. desto*) *besser* the more the better.

je'doch however, yet, nevertheless.

jedweder ['jeːtveːdər], **jeglicher** ['jeːkliçər] *s. jeder.*

jeher ['jeːheːr]: *von* ⌣ at all times.

jemals ['jeːmɑːls] ever, at any time.

jemand ['jeːmant] (24) somebody, someone; *bei Frage u. Verneinung*: anybody, anyone; *s. sonst.*

jene ['jeːnə], '⌣**r**, '⌣**s** (21) that; (*Ggs. dieser*) the former.

jenseitig ['jɛnzaitiç] opposite.

'**jenseit(s) 1.** *adv.* on the other side; **2.** *prp.* (*gen.*) on the other side of, beyond; **3.** 2 *n the* other world, *the* beyond.   [2**isch** Jesuitic(al).

Jesuit [jezu'iːt] *m* (12) Jesuit;

jetzig ['jetsiç] present, existing; (*gegenwärtig*) actual, current.

jetzt [jetst] now, at present; *für* ⌣ for the present; *von* ⌣ *an* from now on; '2**zeit** *f*: *die* ⌣ the present (time), the present day.

jeweil|ig ['jeːvailiç] respective; *der* ⌣*e Präsident usw.* the president *etc.* of the day; '⌣**s** at a time; respectively, in each case.

Jiu-Jitsu ['dʒiːu'dʒitsu] *n* j(i)u-jitsu.

Joch [jɔx] *n* (3; *im pl. als Maß inv.*) yoke; (*Berg2*) pass; ⚠ bay; '⌣**bein** *n* cheek-bone.

Jockei ['dʒɔki] *m* (11) jockey.

Jod [joːt] *n* (3) iodine.

jod|eln ['joːdəln] (29) yodel; '2**ler** *m* (7) yodel(l)er; (*Jodelruf*) yodel.

Jodoform [jodo'fɔrm] *n* (11) iodoform.

Jodtinktur ['joːt-] *f* tincture of iodine.

Joga ['joːga] *m* (11[¹], *o. pl.*) yoga.

Joghurt ['jɔgurt] *m, n* (3¹, *o. pl.*) yog(ho)urt.

Johanni [jo'hani:], ⌣**s** [⌣is] *n inv.* St. John's Day, Midsummer (Day) (*auch* ⌣**s-tag** *m,* ⌣**sfest** *n*); ⌣**sbeere** *f* (red) currant; ⌣**sbrot** *n* carob.

johlen ['joːlən] (25) bawl, howl.

Jolle ['jɔlə] *f* (15) jolly(-boat).

Jon|gleur [ʒõ'gløːr] *m* (3¹) juggler; 2**glieren** juggle (*a. fig.*).

Joppe ['jɔpə] *f* (15) jacket.

Journal [ʒur'naːl] *n* (3¹) journal; ⌣**ismus** [⌣na'lismus] *m* (16, *o. pl.*) journalism; ⌣**ist** [⌣na'list] *m* (12), ⌣**istin** *f* (16¹) journalist.

jovial [jovi'aːl] jovial.

Jubel ['juːbəl] *m* (7) jubilation, rejoicing; '⌣**feier** *f,* '⌣**fest** *n* jubilee; '2**n** (29) shout with joy, rejoice, exult (*alle*: *über acc.* at).

Jubil|ar [ju:bi'laːr] *m* (3¹), ⌣**arin** *f* person celebrating his (her) jubilee; ⌣**äum** [⌣'lɛːum] *n* (9) jubilee; ⌣**äumsband** *m* anniversary edition.

juchhe(i)! [jux'heː, ~'haɪ] hurray!, whoopee!

Juchten ['juxtən] *n, m* (6) Russia leather.

jucken ['jukən] (25) itch; *fig.* es *juckt mich zu inf.* I'm itching to *inf.*

Jude ['juːdə] *m* (13) Jew; *der ewige* ~ the Wandering Jew; '~ntum *n* (1²) Judaism; *coll.* Jewry; '~nverfolgung *f* Jew-baiting.

Jüd|in ['jyːdin] *f* Jewess; '♀isch Jewish.

Judo ['juːdo] *n* (11[¹], *o. pl.*) judo.

Jugend ['juːgənt] *f* (16) youth; '~-alter *n* (days *pl.* of) youth; '~-amt *n* Youth Welfare Office; '~buch *n* book for young people; '~-erinnerung *f* reminiscence from one's youth; '~freund(in *f*) *m* friend of one's youth; '~fürsorge ~ youth welfare; '~gericht *n* juvenile court; '~herberge *f* youth hostel; '~jahre *n/pl.* early years, youth; '~kraft *f* youthful strength; ~kriminalität ['~kriminali'tɛːt] *f* juvenile delinquency; '♀lich youthful; juvenile; '~liche *m, f* (18) juvenile, young person; '~liebe *f* first love, *co.* calf-love; '~schutz *m* protection of the young; '~stil *m Kunst:* Art Nouveau (*fr.*); '~streich *m* youthful prank; '~sünde *f* sin of one's youth; '~werk *n e-s Autors:* early work; ~e *pl. a.* juvenilia; '~zeit *f* youth.

Jugoslaw|e [ju:go'slɑːvə] *m* (13), ~in *f* (16¹), ♀isch Yugoslav.

Juli ['juːli] *m* (11) July.

jung [juŋ] (18²) young; (*jugendlich*) youthful; *fig.* young, new, fresh; ~ *bleiben* stay young; '♀brunnen *m* fountain of youth.

'Junge 1. *m* (13) boy, lad; *Kartenspiel:* knave; **2.** *n* (18) young; *ein* ~s a young one; *Hunde♀:* puppy; *Katzen♀:* kitten; *Raubtier♀:* cub; '♀n (25) bring forth young; *Katze:* have kittens; '♀nhaft boyish; '~n-streich *m* boyish prank.

jünger ['jyŋər] **1.** younger; junior; *er ist drei Jahre* ~ *als ich* he is three years younger than I, he is my junior by three years; **2.** ♀ *m* (7) disciple (*a. bibl.*), follower.

Jungfer ['juŋfər] *f* (15) virgin, maid(en); (*ledige Frau*) spinster; *alte* ~ old maid.

jüngferlich ['jyŋfərliç] maidenly.

'Jungfern|fahrt *f* maiden voyage; '~rede *f* maiden speech; '~schaft *f* (16) virginity, maidenhood.

'Jung|frau *f* maid; *eng S.* virgin; *ast.* Virgin, Virgo; ♀fräulich ['~frɔʏliç] maiden(ly), virginal; *fig. Boden, Schnee usw.:* virgin; '~geselle *m* bachelor; '~gesellenstand *m* bachelorhood; '~gesellin *f* bachelor girl.

Jüngling ['jyŋliŋ] *m* (3¹) youth, young man; '~s-alter *n* youth.

jüngst [jyŋst] **1.** *adj. sup.* youngest; *Ereignis, Zeit:* recent, latest; ♀er *Tag,* ♀es *Gericht* doomsday, Last Judg(e)ment; **2.** *adv.* recently, lately, of late.

'Jungwähler *pol. m* young voter.

Juni ['juːni] *m* (11) June.

junior ['juːnjɔr] junior.

Junker ['juŋkər] *m* (7) young nobleman; (*Land♀*) squire.

Jupiterlampe ['juːpitər-] *f Film:* Jupiter lamp, *Am. a.* klieg light.

Jura¹ ['juːra] (*pl. v. Jus*): ~ *studieren* study law.

Jura² *geol.* ['juːra] *m* (11, *o. pl.*) Jurassic (period).

Jurist [ju'rist] *m* (12) lawyer, jurist; (*Student*) law-student; ♀isch legal, juridical, of (the) law; ~e *Person* legal entity, body corporate.

Jury [ʒyˈriː, ˈjuːri] *f* (11¹, *pl. a. Juries*) jury.

Jus [juːs] *n* law; *s. Jura.*

just [just] just; (*eben erst*) just now; ~ieren ⊕ [~'tiːrən] adjust; ♀ierung [~'tiːruŋ] *f* adjustment.

Justiz [ju'stiːts] *f* (16) justice; ~beamte *m* officer of justice; ~gewalt *f* judicial power; ~-irrtum *m* judicial error; ~minister *m* Minister of Justice, *Brt.* Lord Chancellor, *Am.* Attorney General; ~ministerium *n* Ministry of Justice, *Brt.* Lord Chancellor's Office(s *pl.*), *Am.* Department of Justice; ~mord *m* judicial murder; ~rat *m Brt.* King's (*od.* Queen's) Counsel (*abbr.* K.C., Q.C.); ~wesen *n* judicial system, judiciary.

Jute ['juːtə] *f* (15) jute.

Juwel [ju've:l] *n* (5²) jewel; gem (*a. fig.*); ~en *n/pl.* jewels, jewel(le)ry *sg.*; ~ier [juve'liːr] *m* (3¹) jewel(l)er; ~ier-geschäft [~ve'liːr-] *n* jewel(l)er's shop.

Jux F [juks] *m* (3²) joke, prank, F lark.

K

K [kɑ:], **k** *n inv.* K, k.
Kabale [ka'bɑ:lə] *f* (15) cabal, intrigue.
Kabarett [kaba'rɛt] *n* (3¹) cabaret; (~*vorführung*) cabaret (show), *Am.* floor show; *satirisches*: (satirical) review; ~**ist** [~rɛ'tist] *m* (12) review artiste.
Kabel ['kɑ:bəl] *n* (7) cable; '~**anschluß** *m* cable connection; '~**fernsehen** *n* cable television.
Kabeljau ['kɑ:bəljaʊ] *m* (3¹ *u.* 11) cod(fish).
'**kabel|n** (29) cable; '2**netz** *n* cable network.
Kabine [ka'bi:nə] *f* (15) cabin; (*Abteil*) compartment; (*Fahrstuhl*) cage; ✈ (*Führerraum*) cockpit.
Kabinett [kabi'nɛt] *n* (7) cabinet (*a. pol.*); *als Raum a.* closet; ~**ssitzung** *f* cabinet meeting; ~**s-umbildung** *f* cabinet reshuffle.
Kabriolett [kabrio'lɛt] *n* (3) cabriolet, *bsd. Am.* convertible.
Kachel ['kaxəl] *f* (15) (Dutch) tile; '2**n** tile; '~**ofen** *m* tiled stove.
Kadaver [ka'dɑ:vər] *m* (7) carcass; ~**gehorsam** *m* blind obedience.
Kader ['kɑ:dər] ✕ *m* (7) cadre (*a. fig.*).
Kadett [ka'dɛt] *m* (12) cadet; ~**en-schiff** *n* cadet ship.
Kadi ['kɑ:di] F *m* (11) judge, *the court.*
Käfer ['kɛ:fər] *m* (7) beetle, *Am.* bug.
Kaff [kaf] F *n* (11) god-forsaken place.
Kaffee ['kafe] *m* (11) coffee; ~ *verkehrt* milk with a dash; '~**bohne** *f* coffee-bean; '~**gebäck** *n* cakes to serve with coffee; '~**haus** *n* coffee--house; '~**kanne** *f* coffee-pot; '~**klatsch** F *m* hen-party; '~**löffel** *m* tea-spoon, coffee-spoon; '~**maschine** *f* coffee-percolator; '~**mühle** *f* coffee-mill *od.* -grinder; '~**rösterei** *f* coffee-roasting establishment; '~**satz** *m* coffee-grounds *pl.*; '~**tasse** *f* coffee-cup; '~**wärmer** *m* (coffee-pot) cosy.
Käfig ['kɛ:fiç] *m* (3) cage.
kahl [kɑ:l] bald; *fig. a.* bare, naked; *Baum*: bare; *Landschaft*: barren; '2**heit** *f* baldness; *fig. a.* bareness; '2**kopf** *m* bald head; bald-headed person; ~**köpfig** ['~

kœpfiç] bald-headed; '2**schlag** *m* complete deforestation; (*Lichtung*) clearing.
Kahn [kɑ:n] *m* (3³) boat; *kleiner*: skiff; (*Last2*) barge; F (*Gefängnis*) clink, jug.
Kai [kaɪ] *m* (11), '~**anlage** *f* quay, wharf; '~**gebühr** *f* wharfage; '~**meister** *m* wharfinger.
Kaiser ['kaɪzər] *m* (7) emperor; '~**adler** *m* imperial eagle; '~**in** *f* (16¹) empress; '~**krone** *f* imperial crown; '2**lich** imperial; *die* '~**lichen** *pl.* the Imperialists; '~**reich** *n*, ~**tum** ['~tu:m] *n* (1²) empire; '~**schnitt** ♂ *m* Caesarean (section).
Kajak ['kɑ:jak] ⚓ *m, n* (11) kayak.
Kajüte [ka'jy:tə] *f* (15) cabin.
Kakadu ['kakadu:] *m* (3¹ *u.* 11) cockatoo.
Kakao [ka'kɑ:o] *m* (11) cocoa; F *j-n durch den* ~ *ziehen* (*necken*) pull a p.'s leg, (*schlechtmachen*) run a p. down.
Kakerlak ['kɑ:kərlak] *m* albino; *Insekt*: cockroach.
Kaktee [kak'te:ə] *f* (15), **Kaktus** ['~tus] *m* (14, *pl. Kak'teen* [15]) cactus.
Kalamität [kalami'tɛ:t] *f* (16) calamity.
Kalauer ['kɑ:laʊər] *m* (7) stale joke *od.* pun, Joe Miller.
Kalb [kalp] *n* (1²) calf; 2**en** ['~bən] (25) calve.
kalbern, kälbern ['kalbərn, 'kɛlbərn] *v/i.* (29) *fig.* frolic.
Kalb|fell ['kalp-] *n* calfskin; '~**fleisch** *n* veal; '~**leder** *n* calf(-leather); *in* ~ *gebunden* calf-bound.
'**Kalbs|braten** *m* roast veal; ~**bries(chen)** ['~bri:s(çən)] *n*, ~**bröschen** ['~brø:sçən] *n*, '~**milch** *f* calf's sweetbread; '~**keule** *f* leg of veal; '~**kotelett** *n* veal chop; '~**nierenbraten** *m* loin of veal; '~**schnitzel** *n* veal cutlet.
Kaldaunen [kal'daʊnən] *f/pl.* (15) tripe(s *pl.*) *sg.*
Kalender [ka'lɛndər] *m* (7) calendar, almanac; ~**jahr** *n* calendar year; ~**methode** *f bei Empfängnisverhütung*: rhythm method.
Kali ['kɑ:li] *n* (11) potash, potassium carbonate.

Kalib|er [ka'liːbər] *n* (7) cali|bre, *Am.* -ber (*a. fig.*), bore; (*Maß*) ga(u)ge; **⁀rieren** ⊕ [⌐li'briːrən] calibrate, ga(u)ge.

Kalium ['kaːlium] *n* (11) potassium.

Kalk [kalk] *m* (3) lime; (*Tünche*) whitewash; (⌐*putz*) lime plaster; *physiol.* calcium; (*un*)*gelöschter* ⌐ (*un*)slaked lime; '⌐**brenner** *m* lime--burner; '⌐**en** (25) (*tünchen*) white-wash; ✓ lime; '⌐**erde** *f* calcareous earth; '⌐**ig** limy; '⌐**mangel** ✂ *m* calcium deficiency; '⌐**ofen** *m* lime-kiln; '⌐**stein** *m* limestone.

Kalkulation [kalkula'tsjoːn] *f* calculation.

kalkulieren [kalku'liːrən] calculate.

Kalorie *phys.* [kalo'riː] *f* (15) calorie; **⁀nreich** [⌐'riːən-] rich in calories; ⌐**nwert** *m* calorific value.

kalt [kalt] (18²) cold (*a. fig.*); *bsd. geogr., a. fig.* frigid; ⌐**er** *Krieg* cold war; ⌐**e** *Küche*, ⌐**e** *Platte* cold meats *od.* dishes *pl.*; *mir ist* ⌐ I am (*od.* feel) cold; *j-m die* ⌐**e** *Schulter zeigen* give a p. the cold shoulder; *das läßt mich* ⌐ that leaves me cold.

kaltblütig ['⌐blyːtiç] cold-blooded (*a. fig.*); *adv.* in cold blood; '**⁀keit** *f* cold blood, sangfroid (*fr.*).

Kälte ['kɛltə] *f* (15) cold, chill (*a. fig.*); *fig.* coldness; '**⁀beständig** cold--resistant; '⌐-**einbruch** *m* sudden cold spell; '⌐-**erzeuger** *m*, '⌐-**maschine** *f* refrigerator; '⌐**grad** *m* degree of frost; '⌐**technik** *f* refrigeration engineering; '⌐**welle** *f* cold wave, *bsd. Am.* cold snap.

'**kalt|herzig** cold-hearted; '**⁀leim** *m* cold glue; '**⁀luft** *f* cold air; '⌐**machen** F: *j-n* ⌐ (*ermorden*) bump a p. off; '**⁀schale** *f* cold beer (*od.* fruit *od.* wine) soup; ⌐**schnäuzig** ['⌐ʃnɔytsiç] cool; '⌐**schweißen** cold-weld; '**⁀start** *mot. m* cold start; '⌐**stellen** keep cool, put on ice; *fig.* relegate to the background, shelve.

Kalt'wasserkur *f* coldwater cure.

kalzinieren ⌐ [kaltsi'niːrən] calcine.

kam [kaːm] *pret. v.* kommen.

Kamel [ka'meːl] *n* (3) camel; ⌐**garn** *n* mohair; ⌐**haar** *n* camel hair (*a.* ✿).

Kamera *phot.* ['kaːmərə] *f* (11¹) camera.

Kamerad [kamə'raːt] *m* (12) comrade, companion, fellow, mate; F chum, pal, *Am.* bud(dy); ⌐**schaft** *f*

(16) comradeship, companionship; **⁀schaftlich** comradely; (*gesellig*) companionable; ⌐**schaftlichkeit** *f* comradeliness; ⌐**schafts-ehe** *f* companionate marriage; ⌐**schafts-geist** *m* esprit de corps (*fr.*).

'**Kameramann** *m* cameraman.

Kamille ♧ [ka'milə] *f* (15) camomile; ⌐**ntee** *n* camomile tea.

Kamin [ka'miːn] *m* (3¹) (*Schornstein u. mount.*) chimney; (*offene Feuerstätte im Zimmer*) fire-place, fireside; *fig. et. in den* ⌐ *schreiben* write a th. off; ⌐**feger** *m* chimney--sweep.

Kamm [kam] *m* (3³) comb; *zo.* crest; (*Gebirgs⁀*) ridge; *fig.* alle(s) *über* '*einen* ⌐ *scheren* treat all alike.

kämmen ['kɛmən] (25) comb.

Kammer ['kamər] *f* (15) chamber (*a. anat., zo.,* ⊕), small room, cabinet, closet; *pol. usw.* board, chamber; ✕ unit stores *pl.*; '⌐**diener** *m* valet; '⌐**gericht** *n* supreme court of justice; '⌐**jäger** *m* vermin exterminator; '⌐**konzert** *n* chamber concert; '⌐**musik** *f* chamber music; '⌐**ton(höhe** *f*) ♪ *m* concert pitch; '⌐**zofe** *f* lady's maid.

'**Kamm|garn** *n* worsted (yarn); '⌐**rad** *n* cog-wheel.

Kampagne [kam'panjə] *f* (15) campaign.

Kampf [kampf] *m* (3³) fight, combat, battle; *Sport:* contest; *schwerer:* struggle; *der Meinungen usw.:* conflict; ⌐ *ums Dasein* struggle for existence; *j-m (den)* ⌐ *ansagen* challenge; *s. stellen*; '⌐-**ansage** *f* challenge (*an acc.* to); '⌐**bahn** *f* *Sport:* stadium; arena; '**⁀bereit** ready for battle (*Sport:* to fight); '⌐-**einsatz** ✕ *m* operational mission.

kämpfen ['kɛmpfən] (25) fight; *a. fig.* struggle, battle (*mit* with).

Kampfer ['kampfər] *m* (7) camphor.

Kämpfer ['kɛmpfər] *m* (7), '⌐**in** *f* 1. fighter; ✕ combatant; 2. △ *m* impost; abutment; '**⁀isch** fighting; pugnacious.

'**kampf|fähig** fit to fight; ✕ fit for action; '**⁀flugzeug** *n* tactical aircraft; '**⁀geist** *m* fighting spirit; '**⁀gruppe** *f* brigade (*Am.* combat) group; '**⁀hahn** *m* fighting-cock; *fig.* quarrelsome fellow; '**⁀handlung** *f* fighting; action; '**⁀hubschrauber** *m* gunship; '⁓lust *f* pugnacity; '⁓lustig pugnacious; '⁓maßnahme *f bei Tarifkonflikt*: industrial action; '⁓platz *m* battlefield; *Sport u. fig.*: arena; '⁓preis *m* prize; '⁓richter *m* umpire; '⁓schwimmer *m* frogman; '⁓sport *m* combatant sport; '⁓stoff *m* chemical warfare agent; '⁓truppe *f* combat troops *pl.*; '⁓-unfähig disabled, out of action; '⁓verband *m* fighting (*Am.* combat) unit; '⁓wagen *m* combat car, armo(u)red vehicle; tank.

kampieren [kam'pi:rən] camp.

Kanad|ier[1] [ka'nɑ:djər] *m* (7), **⁓ierin** *f* (16[1]), **⁓isch** Canadian.

Kanadier[2] *m* (7) (*Boot*) Canadian (canoe).

Kanal [ka'nɑ:l] *m* (3[1] *u.* [3]) *künstlicher*: canal; *natürlicher*: channel (*a.* ⊕ *od. fig.*); ⊕ (*Röhre*) duct; (*Abzugs⁓*) sewer, drain; *geogr. the* British Channel; **⁓isation** [⁓naliza'tsjo:n] *f* (15) *e-s Flusses*: canalization; (*Entwässerung*) drainage; *e-r Stadt*: sewerage; (*⁓sanlage*) sewers *pl.*, drains *pl.*; **⁓isieren** [⁓'zi:rən] *Fluß*: canalize; *Stadt*: sewer; **⁓wähler** *TV m* channel selector.

Kanapee ['kanape:] *n* (11) sofa, settee.

Kanarienvogel [ka'nɑ:rjən-] *m* canary.

Kandare [kan'dɑ:rə] *f* (15) curb (-bit); *fig. j-n an die ⁓ nehmen* put a tight rein on.

Kandelaber [kandə'lɑ:bər] *m* (7) candelabrum.

Kandidat [kandi'dɑ:t] *m* (12) candidate; **⁓enliste** *f* list of candidates; (⁓ *e-r Partei*) *Am.* ticket; **⁓ur** [⁓da'tu:r] *f* candidature, *Am.* candidacy.

kandi'dieren be a candidate, *parl.* contest a seat; *für e-e Wahl ⁓* stand (*Am.* run) for election.

kandieren [kan'di:rən] candy.

Kandis ['kandis] *m inv.*, '**⁓zucker** *m* (sugar-)candy.

Kaneel [ka'ne:l] *m* (3[1]) cinnamon.

Känguruh ['kɛŋguru:] *n* (3[1] *u.* 11) kangaroo.

Kaninchen [ka'ni:nçən] *n* (6) rabbit; **⁓bau** *m* rabbit-burrow; **⁓stall** *m* rabbit-hutch.

Kanister [ka'nistər] *m* (7) container, can.

Kanne ['kanə] *f* (15) can, pot; (*Krug*) jug; (*Bier⁓*) tankard.

kannelieren [⁓'li:rən] channel, flute.

Kannibal|e [kani'bɑ:lə] *m* (13), **⁓isch** cannibal; *adv. a.* F *fig.* beastly.

kannte ['kantə] *pret. v. kennen.*

Kanon ['kɑ:nɔn] *m* (11) canon.

Kanonade [kano'nɑ:də] *f* (15) bombardment, cannonade.

Kanone [ka'no:nə] *f* (15) cannon, gun; F (*Könner*) wizard, genius; *bsd. Sport*: ace; F *unter aller ⁓* beneath contempt, *sl.* lousy; **⁓nboot** *n* gunboat; **⁓nfutter** F *n* cannon-fodder; **⁓nrohr** *n* gun-barrel; **⁓nschuß** *m* cannon-shot.

Kanonier [⁓no'ni:r] *m* (3[1]) gunner.

Kanon|ikus [ka'no:nikus] *m* (14[2]) canon; **⁓isch** canonical.

Kante ['kantə] *f* (15) edge; (*Rand*) *a.* brim; *des Tuches*: list, selvage; (*Spitze*) lace; '**⁓l** *m* (7) square ruler; '**⁓n**[1] *m* (6) *des Brotes*: crust; '**⁓n**[2] (26) cant, tilt; *Holz usw.*: square; chamfer.

'**Kantholz** ⊕ *n* square(d) timber.

'**kantig** angular, edged, square.

Kantine [kan'ti:nə] *f* (15) canteen.

Kanton [⁓'to:n] *m* (3[1]) canton; **⁓ist** [⁓to'nist] *m* (12): F *fig. ein unsicherer ⁓* an unreliable fellow.

Kantor ['kantɔr] *m* (8[1]) precentor.

Kanu [ka'nu:] *n* (11) canoe; **⁓te** ['ka'nu:tə] *m* (13) canoeist.

Kanüle ⚕ [⁓'ny:lə] *f* (15) drain tube.

Kanzel ['kantsəl] *f* (15) pulpit; ✈ cockpit; ⚔ turret.

Kanzlei [kants'laɪ] *f* (16) (government-)office, chancellery; (*Büro*) office; chancery.

'**Kanzler** *m* (7) chancellor.

Kap [kap] *n* (3[1] *u.* 11) cape.

Kapaun [ka'paʊn] *m* (3[1]) capon.

Kapazität [kapatsi'tɛ:t] *f* (16) capacity; ⚡ capacitance; *fig.* authority.

Kapell|e [ka'pɛlə] *f* (15) chapel; (*Musik⁓*) band; **⁓meister** *m* conductor; band-master, band leader.

Kaper[1] ⚘ ['kɑ:pər] *f* (15) caper;

'**Kaper**[2] ⚓ *m* (7) privateer, corsair; '**⁓brief** *m* (letters *pl.* of) marque; **⁓ei** [⁓'raɪ] *f* privateering; '**⁓n** (29) capture, seize; '**⁓schiff** *n* privateer.

kapieren F [ka'pi:rən] get (it); *kapiert?* (have you) got it?

Kapillar|gefäß *anat.* [kapi'lɑ:r-] *n* capillary vessel; **⁓röhrchen** [⁓-rø:rçən] *n* (6) capillary tube.

Kapital [kapi'tɑ:l] **1.** *n* (3[1] *u.* 8[2]) capital; *fig. a.* asset; *⁓ und Zinsen* principal and interest; *⁓ schlagen* *aus* capitalize on; *s. tot*; **2.** ♀ capital; **~-abwanderung** *f* exodus of capital; **~-anlage** *f* investment; **~-anleger(in** *f*) *m* investor; **~bildung** *f* accumulation of capital; **~-einkommen** *n* investment income; **~-er-'tragssteuer** *f* capital yield tax; **~-flucht** *f* flight of capital; **~geber(in** *f*) *m* financier; **~gesellschaft** *f* joint--stock company; ♀**isieren** [~tali'zi:rən] capitalize; **~ismus** [~'lismus] *m inv.* capitalism; **~ist** [~'list] *m* (12) capitalist; ♀**istisch** capitalistic(ally *adv.*); ♀**kräftig** [~'tɛ:l-] financially sound; **~markt** *m* capital market; **~steuer** *f* tax on capital; **~verbrechen** *n* capital crime; **~zins** *m* interest on capital.

Kapitän [~'tɛ:n] *m* (3¹) captain (*a. Sport*); **~** *zur See* (naval) captain; **~leutnant** *m* (naval) lieutenant.

Kapitel [ka'pitəl] *n* (7) chapter (*a. eccl.*); *das ist ein* **~** *für sich* that's another story.

Kapitu|lation [~tula'tsjo:n] *f* (16) capitulation, surrender; (*Dienstverlängerung*) re-enlistment; ♀**'lieren** capitulate, surrender (*vor dat.* to); re-enlist. [lain.\]

Kaplan [ka'pla:n] *m* (3¹ *u.* ³) chap-⟩

Kappe ['kapə] *f* (15) cap, (*Kapuze*) hood (*beide a.* ⊕); (*oberer Teil*) top--piece; *fig. et. auf s-e* **~** *nehmen* take the responsibility for; '♀**n** (25) *Tau*: cut; *Baum*: lop, top; *Hahn*: caponize.

Käppi ['kɛpi] *n* (11) cap, ✗ *a.* kepi.

Kapri|ole [kapri'o:lə] *f* (15) caper; **~n** *machen* cut capers, *fig.* play tricks; ♀**'zieren**: *sich* **~** *auf* (*acc.*) set one's heart on; ♀**ziös** [~'tsjø:s] capricious.

Kapsel ['kapsəl] *f* (15) case, box; *anat., pharm.*, ♀ capsule; *e-r Flasche*: cap; *s. Raumkapsel*.

kaputt [ka'put] broken; *out of order*, (*verdorben*) spoilt; *fig.* done for; ruined; (*erschöpft*) worn out, all in; (*tot*) dead; **~gehen** (sn) get smashed *od.* ruined, go phut; **~machen** smash, wreck; *fig.* ruin, bust; *P.*: (*sich*) **~** *fag* (o.s.) out, kill o.s.

Kapuze [ka'pu:tsə] *f* (15) hood; *der Mönche usw.*: cowl.

Kapuziner [kapu'tsi:nər] *m* (7) Capuchin.

Karabiner [kara'bi:nər] *m* (7) car-

(a)bine; **~haken** *m* spring-hook.

Karaffe [ka'rafə] *f* (15) carafe, decanter.

Karambol|age [karambo'la:ʒə] *f* (15) collision; *Billard*: cannon, *Am.* carom; ♀**ieren** [~'li:rən] *Billard*: cannon, *Am.* carom; *fig.* collide.

Karat [ka'ra:t] *n* (3, *als Maß im pl. inv.*) carat.

Karate [ka'ra:tə] *n* (*inv., o. pl.*) karate; **~schlag** *m* karate-chop.

...karätig [ka'rɛ:tiç] ... carat.

Karawane [kara'va:nə] *f* (15) caravan.

Karbid [kar'bi:t] *n* (3¹) carbide.

Karbonade [~bo'na:də] *f* (15) carbonado.

Karbunkel [kar'buŋkəl] *m* (7) carbuncle.

Kardan|gelenk ⊕ [kar'da:n-] *n* cardan (*od.* universal) joint; **~welle** ⊕ *f* cardan shaft.

Kardätsche [~'dɛ:tʃə] *f* (15) (*Woll*♀) card; (*Striegel*) curry-comb; ♀**n** (27) card; curry.

Karde ♀, ⊕ ['kardə] *f* (15) teasel.

Kardinal [kardi'na:l] *m* (3¹ *u.* ³) cardinal; **~fehler** *m* cardinal fault; **~frage** *f* cardinal question.

Kardiogramm ♂ [kardio'gram] *n* (3¹) cardiogram.

Karenzzeit [ka'rɛntstsait] *f* waiting period.

Kar'freitag [ka:r-] *m* (3) Good Friday.

karg [kark] (18[²]) (*knickerig*) niggardly, stingy; (*dürftig*) scanty, poor; *Boden*: sterile, poor; **~en** ['~gən] (25) be stingy (*mit* with), be sparing (of); ♀**heit** ['kark-] *f* stinginess, parsimony.

kärglich ['kɛrkliç] scanty, paltry, poor.

kariert [ka'ri:rt] check(ed), chequered, *Am.* checkered.

Karies ['ka:ries] *f* (16, *o. pl.*) caries.

Karikatur [karika'tu:r] *f* (16) caricature (*a. fig.*), cartoon; **~ist** [~tu'rist] *m* (12) caricaturist, cartoonist.

kari'kieren caricature.

kariös ♂ [kari'ø:s] decayed, carious.

karitativ [karita'ti:f] charitable.

karmesin [karme'zi:n] crimson.

Karmin [~'mi:n] *n* (3¹) carmine.

Karneval ['karnəval] *m* (3¹) carnival.

Karnickel F [kar'nikəl] *n* (7) rabbit; *fig.* F silly ass.

Karo ['kɑːro] *n* (11) square; *Karte*: diamonds *pl*.; '**~muster** *n* check(ed) pattern.

Karosserie *mot*. [karɔsəˈriː] *f* (15) body.

Karotin ⚕ [karoˈtiːn] *n* carotine.

Karotte ⚕ [kaˈrɔtə] *f* (15) carrot.

Karpfen ['karpfən] *m* (6) carp.

Karre ['karə] *f* (15) *s. Karren.*

Karree [kaˈreː] *n* (11) square.

karren ['karən] **1.** (25) wheel, cart; **2.** ⚕ *m* (6) cart; (*Hand*⚕) (wheel-)barrow; F (*Auto*) car; '⚕**gaul** *m* cart-horse.

Karriere [karˈjɛːrə] *f* (15) gallop; (*Laufbahn*) career; *in voller ~ at* full gallop, at a rattling pace; **~macher** *m* careerist.

Kar'samstag [kɑːr-] *m* Holy Saturday.

Karte ['kartə] *f* (15) card; (*Land*⚕) map; (*See*⚕) chart; (*Ausweis*⚕, *Fahr*⚕, *Zulassungs*⚕) ticket; *s. Speisekarte; alles auf eine ~ setzen* put all one's eggs in one basket; *s. legen.*

Kartei [~'taɪ] *f* (16) card-index; **~karte** *f* filing (*od.* index) card; **~kasten** *m* card-index box; **~schrank** *m* card-index (*od.* filing) cabinet.

Kartell [~'tɛl] *n* (3¹) cartel; ✝ *a.* combine, *Am. a.* trust.

'**Karten|brief** *m* letter-card; '**~haus** *n* house of cards; '**~kunststück** *n* card-trick; '**~legerin** *f* fortune-teller; '**~spiel** *n* card-playing; (*Karten*) pack (*Am. a.* deck) of cards; '**~vorverkauf(s-stelle** *f*) *m* advance booking (office); '**~zeichen** *n* conventional sign.

Kartoffel [karˈtɔfəl] *f* (15) potato; **~bau** *m* cultivation of potatoes; **~brei** *m* mashed potatoes *pl*.; **~chips** *m/pl*. potato crisps (*Am.* chips); **~käfer** *m* potato-beetle, *Am.* -bug; **~puffer** *m* potato-pancake; **~salat** *m* potato salad; **~schalen** *f/pl*. potato peelings; **~schäler** *m* (7) potato peeler; **~stampfer** *m* (7) potato masher.

Kartograph [kartoˈgrɑːf] *m* (12) cartographer, map-maker; **~ie** [~graˈfiː] *f* (16) cartography.

Karton [karˈtɔ̃] *m* (11) (**~papier**) cardboard; (*Zeichnung*) cartoon; (*Schachtel*) carton, (cardboard) box; *Buchbinderei*: boards *pl*.; ⚕**ieren** [~toˈniːrən] bind in boards.

Kartothek [~toˈteːk] *f* (15) *s. Kartei.*

Kartusche [karˈtuʃə] *f* (16) cartridge.

Karussell [karuˈsɛl] *n* (3¹) round-about, *bsd. Am.* merry-go-round.

Karwoche ['kɑːrvɔxə] *f* Passion (*od.* Holy) Week.

Karzer *univ.* ['kartsər] *m* (7) lock-up; (*Strafe*) detention.

Karzinom [kartsiˈnoːm] ⚕ *n* (3¹) carcinoma.

Käse ['kɛːzə] *m* (7) cheese; '**~blatt** F *n* rag; '**~gebäck** *n* cheese biscuits *pl*.; '**~glocke** *f* cheese-cover; '**~händler** *m* cheesemonger.

Kasematte [kazəˈmatə] *f* (15) casemate.

'**Käseplatte** *f* cheeseboard.

Käserei [~ˈraɪ] *f* (16) cheese-dairy.

Kasern|e [kaˈzɛrnə] *f* (15) barracks *pl*.; **~enhof** *m* barrack-yard *od.* -square; ⚕**ieren** [~ˈniːrən] barrack; ⚕**iert** [~ˈniːrt] quartered in barracks.

'**Käsestange** *f* (*Gebäck*) cheese-straw.

'**käsig** cheesy; *Gesicht usw.*: pasty.

Kasino [kaˈziːno] *n* (11) club, casino; (*Offiziers*⚕) (officers') mess.

Kaskoversicherung ['kasko-] *mot. f* comprehensive insurance.

Kasperle ['kaspɛrlə] *n* (7) Punch; *fig.* clown; '**~theater** *n* Punch and Judy (show).

Kassa ✝ ['kasa] *f* (16²): *per ~ in* cash; '**~buch** *n* cash-book.

Kasse ['kasə] *f* (15) cash-box; (*Laden*⚕) till, cash-register; (*Zahlstelle*) pay-office; (*~nschalter*) cash-desk; (*Theater*⚕ *usw*.) ticket-office, booking-office, *thea. a.* box-office; *s. Kranken*⚕; (*Bargeld*) cash; ✝ *~ gegen Dokumente* cash against documents; *bei (nicht bei) ~ in* (out of) cash; *gut bei ~ sein* F be flush.

'**Kassen|-abschluß** *m* balancing of the cash (accounts); cash-balance; '**~anweisung** *f* cash order; '**~arzt** *m* panel doctor; '**~bericht** *m* cash '**~bon** *m* receipt, sales slip; '**~buch** *n* cash-book; '**~erfolg** *m* *thea. etc.* box-office success; '**~führer** *m* cashier; '**~patient** *m* panel patient; '**~preis** *m* cash price; '**~prüfung** *f* cash audit; '**~schalter** *m* cash-desk; *e-r Bank*: teller's counter; '**~schein** *m* (*Quittung*) cash voucher; (*Banknote*) treasury note; '**~sturz** *m*: *~ machen* check the cash accounts, F *weit S.* tot up one's cash; '**~wart** *m* treasurer; '**~zettel** *m* sales slip.

Kasserolle [kasəˈrɔlə] f (15) casserole.
Kassette [kaˈsɛtə] f (15) casket; *für Bücher*: slip-case; *phot.* cartridge; (*Video♀, Audio♀*) cassette; ⚠ coffer; **⁓ndeck** n cassette deck; **⁓nrecorder** m (7) cassette recorder.
kassier|en [kaˈsiːrən] v/i. cash, collect; (*aufheben*) annul; *Urteil*: quash; (*entlassen*) cashier; **♀er** m (7), **♀erin** f cashier; (*Bank♀*) a. teller. [castanet.♀
Kastagnette [kastanˈjɛtə] f (15)♀
Kastanie [kasˈtaːnjə] f (15) chestnut; *fig. die* ⁓*n für j-n aus dem Feuer holen* act as a p.'s cat's-paw; **⁓nbaum** m chestnut-tree; **♀nbraun** chestnut.
Kästchen [ˈkɛstçən] n (6) little box (*od.* case), casket; *in Zeitungen usw.*: box.
Kaste [ˈkastə] f (15) caste.
kastei|en [kaˈstaɪən] (25): *sich* ⁓ chasten o.s., mortify the flesh; **♀ung** f mortification of the flesh.
Kasten [ˈkastən] m (6) chest, box, case; *s. Schrank*; *für Bier usw.*, a. F (*Fahrzeug*) crate; F (*Haus*) box; **'⁓geist** m caste-spirit; **'⁓wesen** n caste-system.
Kastr|at [kaˈstraːt] m (12) eunuch; **♀ieren** [⁓ˈstriːrən] castrate.
Kasus [ˈkaːzus] m *inv.* case.
Katalog [⁓ˈloːk] m (3¹), **♀isieren** [⁓logiˈziːrən] catalog(ue).
Katalys|ator [katalyˈzaːtɔr] m (8¹) 🜚 catalyst; *mot.* catalytic converter; **♀ieren** [⁓ˈziːrən] catalyse.
Katapult [⁓ˈpult] m, n (3) catapult (a. ✈); **⁓start** ✈ m catapult take-off.
Katarrh [kaˈtar] m (3¹) (common) cold, catarrh; **♀alisch** [⁓ˈraːliʃ] catarrhal.
Kataster [kaˈtastər] m u. n (7) land-register.
katastro|phal [katastroˈfaːl] catastrophic(ally *adv.*), disastrous; **♀phe** [⁓ˈstroːfə] f (15) catastrophe, disaster; **♀phengebiet** n disaster area; **♀phenhilfe** f disaster relief.
Katechismus [kateˈçismus] m (16²) catechism.
Kateg|orie [⁓goˈriː] f (16) category; **♀orisch** [⁓ˈgoːriʃ] categorical.
Kater [ˈkaːtər] m (7) tom cat; F *vom Trinken*: hangover.
Katheder [kaˈteːdər] n, m (7) reading desk; **⁓blüte** f howler.

Kathedrale [kateˈdraːlə] f (15) cathedral.
Katheter 🜛 [kaˈteːtər] m (7) catheter.
Kathode ⚡ [kaˈtoːdə] f cathode; **⁓nröhre** f cathode ray tube.
Katholik [katoˈliːk] m (12), **⁓in** f (16¹), **katholisch** [⁓ˈtoːliʃ] (Roman) Catholic.
Katholizismus [katoliˈtsismus] m (16, *o. pl.*) Catholicism.
Kattun [kaˈtuːn] m (3¹) calico; *bedruckt*: print; (*Möbel♀*) chintz; **⁓kleid** n print-dress.
'katzbuckeln (29) crouch, cringe (*vor dat.* to), bow and scrape.
Kätzchen [ˈkɛtsçən] n (6) kitten; ♀ catkin.
Katze [ˈkatsə] f (15) cat; F *das ist für die Katz* that's all for nothing; *die* ⁓ *im Sack kaufen* buy a pig in a poke; *die* ⁓ *aus dem Sack lassen* let the cat out of the bag; *wie die* ⁓ *um den heißen Brei gehen* beat about the bush.
'Katzen|-auge n a. ⊕ cat's eye; **'⁓buckel** m cat's (arched) back; **'♀freundlich** oversweet; **'♀haft** catlike, feline; **'⁓jammer** F m hangover; *moralischer*: a. the dumps, the blues *sg.*; **'⁓klo** n cat tray; **'⁓musik** f charivari, *Am.* shivaree; **'⁓sprung** m *fig.*: *ein* ⁓ a stone's throw; **'⁓streu** f cat litter; **'⁓wäsche** F f cat's lick.
Kauderwelsch [ˈkaʊdərvɛlʃ] n (3²) gibberish, double Dutch; lingo; **♀en** (27) talk gibberish.
kauen [ˈkaʊən] v/t. u. v/i. (25) chew.
kauern [ˈkaʊərn] (29) (a. *sich* ⁓) cower, squat.
Kauf [kaʊf] m (3³) buying, purchase, *Am.* a. buy; (*Handel*) bargain; *in* ⁓ *nehmen* take into the bargain, *fig.* put up with; *leichten* ⁓*es davonkommen* get off cheaply; **'⁓auftrag** m buying order; **'⁓brief** m purchase-deed; **'♀en** (25) buy (*bei j-m* from a p.), purchase; F (*bestechen*) bribe, buy; F *sich j-n* ⁓ give a p. hell.
Käufer [ˈkɔʏfər] m (7), **'⁓in** f (16¹) buyer, purchaser.
'Kauf|haus n commercial house; (*Warenhaus*) (department) store; **'⁓kraft** f purchasing power; **'♀kräftig** able to buy; **'⁓laden** m shop, store.
käuflich [ˈkɔʏfliç] purchasable; *fig.*

                             kein

b.s. venal, corrupt; *adv.* by purchase; '9keit *f fig.* venality.

'Kauf|mann *m* (*pl. Kaufleute*) merchant; businessman, trader, dealer; *im Laden*: shopkeeper, *Am. a.* storekeeper; (*Angestellter*) commercial clerk; 9männisch ['~mɛniʃ] commercial, mercantile; '~vertrag *m* contract of purchase; '~zwang *m* obligation to buy.

'Kaugummi *m* chewing-gum.

Kaulquappe ['kaʊlkvapə] *f* (15) tadpole.

kaum [kaʊm] scarcely, hardly; (*nur gerade*) barely; *zeitlich*: ~ ... *als* no sooner ... than, hardly ... when.

kausal [kaʊ'zaːl] causal; 9zusammenhang *m* causal connection.

'Kautabak *m* chewing-tobacco.

Kaution [kaʊ'tsjoːn] *f* (16) security; *im Strafrecht*: bail.

Kautschuk ['kaʊtʃuk] *m* (3¹) caoutchouc, India rubber.

'Kauwerkzeuge *n/pl.* masticatory organs.

Kauz [kaʊts] *m* (3¹ *u.* ³) screech-owl; *fig.* (*a. komischer* ~) (odd) character, queer fish; *alter* ~ old codger.

Kavalier [kava'liːr] *m* (3¹) cavalier, gentleman; ~sdelikt *n* peccadillo.

Kavallerie [ˌ·lə'riː] *f* (15) cavalry, horse; ~pferd *n* troop-horse.

Kavalle'rist *m* (12) cavalryman, trooper.

Kaviar ['kaːviar] *m* (3¹) caviar(e).

keck [kɛk] bold, pert, F saucy; '9heit *f* boldness; F sauciness.

Kegel ['keːgəl] *m* (7) cone; *Spiel*: skittle, pin; *s. Kind*; ~ *schieben s. kegeln*; '~bahn *f* skittle- (*Am.* bowling) alley; 9förmig ['~fœrmiç] conical, cone-shaped; '~klub *m* skittles club; '~kugel *f* skittle-ball; '9n (29) play (at) skittles *od.* ninepins; '~rad ⊕ *n* bevel gear; '~schnitt *m* conic section; '~spiel *n*, '~sport *m* skittles, ninepin bowling; '~stumpf *m* truncated cone.

Kegler ['keːglər] *m* skittle-player.

Kehle ['keːlə] *f* (15) throat; ⊕ groove; *das Messer sitzt ihm an der* ~ he feels the knife at his throat; *etwas in die falsche* ~ *bekommen* swallow a morsel the wrong way, *fig.* take a th. amiss; *das Wort blieb mir in der* ~ *stecken* the word stuck in my throat; *s. zuschnüren.*

'Kehl|kopf *m* larynx; '~kopf-entzündung ⚕ *f* laryngitis; '~kopfkrebs ⚕ *m* cancer of the larynx, F throat cancer; '~kopfspiegel *m* laryngoscope; '~laut *m* guttural; '~leiste *f* ogee, mo(u)lding.

'Kehr|-aus *m inv.* last dance; *fig.* clean-out; '~besen *m* broom.

Kehre ['keːrə] *f* (15) turn; *Sport*: back-vault; *des Weges*: turn, sharp (*od.* hairpin) bend; '9n (25) sweep; brush; (*um*~) turn; ⚔ *kehrt!* (right) about, turn! (*Am.* face!); *das Oberste zuunterst* ~ turn (everything) upside down; *sich nicht* ~ *an* (*acc.*) ignore, disregard; *fig. j-m den Rücken* ~ turn one's back on a p.; *in sich gekehrt* withdrawn, introverted.

Kehricht ['keːriçt] *m, n* (3¹) sweepings *pl.*, rubbish; '~eimer *m* dustbin, *Am.* trash-can; '~schaufel *f* dust-pan.

'Kehr|reim *m* burden, refrain; '~seite *f* reverse, back; *fig. a.* seamy side; '~wert ⅍ *m* reciprocal.

'kehrt|machen turn round *od.* back; ⚔ face about; '9wendung *f* about-face (*a. fig.*).

keif|en ['kaɪfən] (25) scold (*mit j-m* a p.); '9erin *f* scold.

Keil [kaɪl] *m* (3) wedge; *typ.* quoin; *Näherei*: gore, gusset; '~absatz *m* wedge heel; '~e F *f* thrashing; '9en (25) fasten with wedges; F thrash; '~er *hunt. m* (7) wild boar; ~e'rei F *f* scrap.

keil|förmig ['~fœrmiç] wedge-shaped, cuneiform; '9hacke *f* pick-ax(e); '9hosen *f/pl.* tapered trousers; '9riemen ⊕ *m* V-belt; '9schrift *f* cuneiform characters *pl.*

Keim [kaɪm] *m* (3) *biol., a. fig.* germ; ⚘ *a.* seed, bud; *s. ersticken*; '~blatt *n* ⚘ cotyledon; *biol.* germ-layer; '~drüse *f* genital gland, gonad; '9en (25, h. *u.* sn) germinate; ⚘ *a.* sprout.

'keim|fähig germinable; '~frei sterile; ~ *machen* sterilize; '9ling *m* (3) seed-plant; sprout; '~tötend germicidal; '9träger ⚕ *m* (germ-)carrier; '9zelle *f* germ-cell.

kein [kaɪn] (20) *als adj.* no, not any; *als su.* ~er *m*, ~e *f* no one, none, not (any)one, nobody, not anybody; ~(e)s *n* nothing, not anything; ~er (*von beiden*) neither; ~ *Ding* nothing.

keinerlei ['ˌɔrlaɪ] of no sort; no ... whatever; *auf ~ Weise* in no way.
'keines'|falls on no account; **~wegs** ['~'veːks] by no means, not at all.
'keinmal not once, never.
Keks [keːks] *m, n* (4) biscuit, *Am.* cookie, *(knuspriger ~)* cracker.
Kelch [kɛlç] *m* (3) cup; ♀ calyx; *eccl.* chalice.
Kelle ['kɛlə] *f* (15) ladle; *(Maurer♀)* trowel; *(Signal♀)* signal(l)ing disk.
Keller ['kɛlər] *m* (7) cellar; **~ei** [~'raɪ] *f* (16) (wine-)cellars *pl.*; **'~geschoß** *n* basement; **'~lokal** *n* wine- *od.* beer-cellar; **'~meister** *m* cellarer, cellar man.
Kellner ['kɛlnər] *m* (7) waiter; **'~in** *f* waitress.
Kelte ['kɛltə] *m* (12) Celt.
Kelter ['kɛltər] *f* (15) wine-press; **'♀n** (29) press (out).
'keltisch Celtic.
'kennbar recognizable.
kennen ['kɛnən] (30) know; **'~lernen** become acquainted with, get *(od.* come) to know, meet.
'Kenner *m* (7), **'~in** *f* (16¹) connoisseur; *(Fachmann)* expert.
'Kennkarte *f* identity card.
'Kennmelodie *f Radio:* signature tune.
'kenntlich recognizable; **~ machen** mark.
'Kenntnis *f* (14²) knowledge; *~ nehmen von* take note of; *j-n in ~ setzen von* inform a p. of; **~nahme** ['~naːmə] *f inv.:* zur *~* for your information; **'~se** *pl. (Wissen)* knowledge *sg.*; *oberflächliche ~* a smattering.
'Kennwort *n* code word; ✂ *a.* password.
'Kennzeich|en *n* (distinguishing) mark, sign; characteristic; *fig. a.* criterion; *mot.* registration *(Am.* license) number; *besondere ~ pl.* distinguishing marks; **'♀nen** (26) mark; *fig. a.* characterize, typify.
'Kennziffer *f* code number; ✝ reference number.
kentern ⚓ ['kɛntərn] *v/i.* (29, sn) capsize; *a. ~ lassen* overturn.
Keramik [keˈraːmik] *f* (16) ceramics *sg.*; *(Ware)* ceramic article.
Kerbe ['kɛrbə] *f* (15) notch, score.
Kerbel ♀ ['kɛrbəl] *m* (7) chervil.
'kerben (25) notch, score.
Kerb|holz ['kɛrp-] *n*: *et. auf dem ~*

haben have done something bad; **'~tier** *n* insect.
Kerker ['kɛrkər] *m* (7) gaol, jail; **'~meister** *m* gaoler, jailer.
Kerl [kɛrl] *m* (3; P *a.* 11) fellow, F bloke, chap, *Am.* guy; *contp.* type; *feiner ~* splendid fellow, *Am.* great guy; *ein lieber od. netter ~* a dear.
Kern [kɛrn] *m* (3) kernel; *v. Apfel usw.:* pip; *v. Steinobst:* stone, *Am.* pit; *fig.* core *(a. ⊕),* nucleus *(a. phys.);* *(Wesen)* essence; *~ der Sache* crux of the matter; *pol. harter ~* hard core; **'~chemie** *f* nuclear chemistry; **'~energie** *f* nuclear energy; **'~fach** *n Schule, univ.* basic subject; **'~forscher** *m* nuclear scientist; **'~forschung** *f* nuclear research; **'~forschungszentrum** *n* nuclear research cent|re, *Am.*-er; **'~frage** *f* crucial question; **'~frucht** *f* stone-fruit; **'~fusion** *f* nuclear fusion; **'~gehäuse** *n* core; **'♀gesund** thoroughly healthy, F as sound as a bell; **'~holz** *n* heartwood.
'kernig full of pips; *fig. (markig)* pithy, robust.
'Kern|kraftwerk *n* nuclear power station *(od.* plant); **'~leder** *n* bend leather; **'~los** seedless; **'~physik** *f* nuclear physics *sg.*; **'~plasma** *phys. n* (9) nucleoplasm; **'~punkt** *m* central point *(od.* issue); **'~re-aktor** *m* nuclear reactor; **'~seife** *f* curd *(od.* hard) soap; **'~spaltung** *f* nuclear fission; **'~spruch** *m* pithy saying; **'~stück** *n* essential part; **'~truppen** *f/pl.* picked *(od.* elite) troops; **'~waffe** *f* nuclear weapon; **'~zeit** *f (Arbeitszeit)* core time.
Kerosin 🜊 [keroˈziːn] *n* (3¹, *o. pl.*) kerosene.
Kerze ['kɛrtsə] *f* (15) candle *(a. phys.);* *s.* Zündkerze; **'♀ngeˈrade** bolt upright; *auf et. zu:* straight; **'~halter** *m* candlestick, candleholder; **'~licht** *n (bei ~* by) candlelight; **'~nstärke** *f* candle-power.
Kessel ['kɛsəl] *m* (7) kettle; *großer:* cauldron, ⊕ vat; *(Dampf♀)* boiler; *geol. (Vertiefung)* hollow; *(Becken)* basin; ✂ pocket; **'~haus** *n* boilerhouse; **'~pauke** *f* kettledrum; **'~raum** *m* boiler room; **'~stein** *m* scale, fur; **'~treiben** *hunt. n* battue; *fig.* hunt *(gegen* for); *pol.* witch-hunt.

Kette ['kɛtə] *f* (15) chain (*a. Schmuck*♀; *a.* ⚓, ⚓ *u. fig.*); (*Gebirgs*♀) *a.* range; (*Folge*) series, train; (*Weber*♀) warp; ⚓, ⚓ flight; ⚓ *e-s Panzers*: track; '♀n (26) chain (*an acc.* to).

'**Ketten|-antrieb** *m* chain-drive; '♀brief *m* chain letter; '♀fahrzeug *n* tracked vehicle; '♀geschäft *n*, '♀laden *m* multiple shop, chain store; '♀glied *n* chain link; '♀hund *m* watch--dog; '♀raucher *m* chain-smoker; '♀re-aktion *phys. f* chain reaction; '♀rechnung *f*, '♀regel Å *f* chain rule.

Ketzer ['kɛtsər] *m* (7), '♀in *f* heretic; ♀ei [♀'raɪ] *f* heresy; '♀isch heretical.

keuch|en ['kɔʏçən] (25) pant, gasp; '♀husten *m* (w)hooping-cough.

Keule ['kɔʏlə] *f* (15) club; *Fleisch*: leg; '♀nschlag *m* blow with a club; *fig.* crushing blow.

keusch [kɔʏʃ] chaste; (*rein*) pure; (*sittsam*) modest; '♀heit *f* chastity.

'**Kicher-erbse** *f* chick-pea.

kichern ['kiçərn] (29) titter, giggle.

kicken ['kikən] (25) kick.

Kiebitz ['kiːbɪts] *m* (3²) peewit, lapwing; (*Zugucker*) F kibitzer.

Kiefer¹ ♀ ['kiːfər] *f* (15) pine.

'**Kiefer**² *anat. m* (7) jaw; '♀höhle *anat. f* maxillary sinus; '♀-orthopäde *m*, '♀-orthopädin *f* orthodontist.

Kiel [kiːl] *m* (3) ⚓ keel; (*Feder*♀) quill; '♀holen ⚓ careen; ♀'-oben keeled over, bottom up; '♀raum *m* bilge; '♀wasser *n* wake (*a. fig.*).

Kieme ['kiːmə] *f* (15) gill.

Kien [kiːn] *m* (3) resinous pine--wood; '♀-apfel *m* pine-cone; '♀fackel *f* pine-torch; '♀holz *n s.* Kien; '♀-öl *n* pine-oil; '♀ruß *m* pine--soot; '♀span *m* chip of pine-wood.

Kiepe ['kiːpə] *f* (15) back-basket.

Kies [kiːs] *m* (4) gravel, grit; *mit* ♀ *bestreuen* gravel.

Kiesel ['kiːzəl] *m* (7) flint, pebble; '♀-artig siliceous; '♀-erde *f* siliceous earth; '♀säure ⚗ *f* (9, *o.pl.*) silicic acid.

kiesig ['kiːzɪç] gravelly.

'**Kiesweg** *m* gravel walk.

'**kiffen** *sl.* ['kifən] (25) (*Haschisch rauchen*) smoke pot (*od.* hash).

Killer *sl.* ['kilər] *m* (7) hitman; '♀satellit ⚓ *m* killer satellite.

Kilo ['kiːlo] *n* (11['])), ♀'gramm *n* kilo|gramme, *Am.* -gram; ♀hertz [♀'hɛrts] *n* kilo-cycle per second;

♀'meter *n* kilomet|re, *Am.* -er; ♀'metergeld *n* mileage (allowance); ♀'meterstand *m* mileage; ♀'meterstein *m* milestone; ♀'metertarif *m* Nahverkehr: distance fare; ♀'meterweit for miles (and miles); ♀'meterzähler *m* mileage indicator, odometer; ♀'watt *n* kilowatt; ♀'wattstunde *f* kilowatt hour (*abbr.* kWh).

Kimme ['kimə] *f* (15) notch (⚓ in the backsight).

Kind [kint] *n* (1) child, F kid; (*kleines* ♀) baby; *mit* ♀ *und Kegel* (with) bag and baggage; *das* ♀ *beim rechten Namen nennen* call a spade a spade; *wes Geistes* ♀ *ist er?* what sort of a fellow is he?; *s.* bekommen, erwarten; '♀bett *n* childbed; '♀bettfieber *n* puerperal fever; '♀chen *n* (6) little child, baby.

'**Kinder|-arzt** ['♀dər-] *m*, '♀ärztin *f* p(a)ediatrician, p(a)ediatrist; '♀buch *n* children's book.

Kinderei [♀də'raɪ] *f* (16) childishness; (*dummer Streich*) childish trick; (*Kleinigkeit*) trifle, *Am. a.* chicken feed.

Kinder|-ermäßigung ['♀dər-] *f* reduction for children; '♀frau *f* nurse; '♀fräulein *n* (children's) governess; '♀freund(in *f*) *m*: *ein* ♀ *sein* be fond of children; '♀funk *m* children's program(me); '♀fürsorge *f* child welfare; '♀garten *m* kindergarten; *für 2–5jährige*: nursery-school; *für 5–7jährige*: infant-school; '♀gärtnerin *f* kindergarten teacher; '♀geld *n s.* Kinderzulage; '♀gesicht *n* baby--face; '♀gottesdienst *m* children's service; '♀hort *m* day-nursery; '♀kleid *n* child's dress; '♀kleidung *f* children's wear; '♀krankheit *f* children's disease; *fig.* teething troubles *pl.*; '♀lähmung *f*: (*spinale* ♀) infantile paralysis, polio(myelitis); *zerebrale* ♀ polioencephalitis; ♀'leicht dead easy; ♀'lieb fond of children; '♀lied *n* nursery-rhyme; ♀'los childless; '♀mädchen *n* nurse(maid); '♀märchen *n* nursery-tale; '♀mord *m* child-murder; '♀pflege *f* child care; '♀psychologe *m*, '♀psychologin *f* child psychologist; ♀'reich large (*family*); '♀schreck *m* bugbear; ♀'sicher *Schloß etc.*: child-proof; '♀spiel *n fig.* child's play; '♀sterblichkeit *f* infant mortality; '♀stube *fig. f* (*good, bad*) upbringing *od.* manners *pl.*; '*tagesstätte* f day nursery, *Am.* day-care center; '*wagen* m perambulator, F pram, *Am.* baby carriage; '*zeit* f childhood; '*zimmer* n nursery, *Am. a.* play-room; '*zulage* f allowance for children.

Kindes|-alter ['kindəs-] n infancy; '*bein:* von *en* an from infancy, from a child; '*-entführung* f kidnap(p)ing; '*kind* n grandchild; '*liebe* f filial love; '*mißhandlung* f child abuse; '*mord* m child-murder; '*mutter* f mother (of illegitimate child); '*tötung* ɟ̃ f infanticide.

Kindheit ['kint-] f (16) childhood; von ∼ an from a child.

kindisch ['kindiʃ] childish; ∼es Wesen childishness.

Kindlein ['kintlain] n s. Kindchen.

'**kindlich** childlike, childish; *im Verhältnis zu den Eltern:* filial.

'**Kindskopf** F m (big) child, silly.

'**Kindtaufe** f christening.

Kinet|ik [ki'ne:tik] f (16, o. pl.) kinetics *sg.*; ♀isch kinetic; ∼e Energie kinetic energy.

Kinkerlitzchen F ['kiŋkərlitsçən] pl. inv. gewgaws, knick-knacks pl.; *fig.* trivialities pl.

Kinn [kin] n (3) chin; '*backen* m, '*lade* f jaw(-bone); '*bart* m imperial; '*haken* m Boxen: hook to the chin; uppercut.

Kino ['ki:no] n (11) cinema, *the* pictures *od.* F flicks pl., *Am.* motion picture theater, F movies pl.; '*besucher(in* f) m cinema-goer; '*reklame* f s. Filmreklame; '*vorstellung* f cinema-show.

Kintopp ['ki:ntɔp] F m (3¹) s. Kino.

Kiosk [ki'ɔsk] m (3²) kiosk.

Kipfel ['kipfəl] n (7) crescent.

Kippe ['kipə] f (15) (Zigarettenstummel) F fag-end, stub, bsd. Am. butt; *Turnen:* upstart, Am. kip; auf der ∼ on the tilt; fig. es steht auf der ∼ it is touch and go; '♀n (25) v/t. tilt, tip; v/i. (h. u. sn) tip, topple (over).

'**Kipp|fenster** n bottom-hung window; '*frequenz* ɟ f sawtooth (*TV* sweep) frequency; '*karren* m tipcart; '*lore* f tipping truck, tipper; '*schalter* ɟ m toggle switch; '*wagen* m s. Kipplore.

Kirche ['kirçə] f (15) church.

'**Kirchen|-älteste** m church-

warden, elder; '*bann* m excommunication; in den ∼ tun excommunicate; '*buch* n parochial register; '*chor* m church choir; '*diener* m sexton, sacristan; '*fürst* m prince of the church; '*gemeinde* f parish; '*geschichte* f ecclesiastical history; '*jahr* n ecclesiastical year; '*konzert* n church concert; '*licht* F n: kein (großes) ∼ not very bright; '*lied* n hymn; '*musik* f sacred music; '*rat* m parish council; *P.:* parish councillor; '*recht* n ecclesiastical law; '*schiff* n nave; '*spaltung* f schism; '*steuer* f church rate; '*stuhl* m pew; '*tag* m Church congress; '*vater* m Father of the Church; '*vorsteher* m churchwarden, elder.

'**Kirch|gang** m church-going; '*hof* m churchyard; '♀lich ecclesiastical, church...; '*spiel* n, '*sprengel* m parish; '*turm* m church-tower, steeple; '*turmpolitik* f parish-pump politics pl.; '*turmspitze* f spire; '*weih* ['∼vai] f parish fair.

Kirmes ['kirməs] f (16³) kermis.

kirre ['kirə] tame; ∼ machen tame.

'**kirren** (25) tame; (ködern) bait.

Kirsch m [kirʃ] (3²) kirsch; '∼e f (15) cherry; mit ihm ist nicht gut ∼n essen it's best not to tangle with him; '*kern* m cherry-stone; '*kuchen* m cherry cake; '*likör* m cherry brandy; '♀rot cherry-red, cherry-colo(u)red, cerise; '*wasser* n kirsch.

Kissen ['kisən] n (6) cushion; (Kopf-♀) pillow; '*bezug* m pillow-case.

Kiste ['kistə] f (15) chest, box; (Latten♀) crate; mot. u. ✈ sl. bus.

Kitsch [kitʃ] m (3²) trash, kitsch; '♀ig trashy.

Kitt [kit] m (3) cement; (Glaser♀) putty. [clink.] }

Kittchen ['kitçən] F n (6): im ∼ in }

Kittel ['kitəl] m (7) smock, frock; (Arbeits♀) overall; weißer: (white) coat; '*kleid* n house frock; '*schürze* f pinafore-type overall.

kitten ['kitən] (26) cement; Glaserei: putty; fig. patch up.

Kitz(chen) ['kits(çən)] n (3² [6]) kid; (small) fawn.

Kitzel ['kitsəl] m (7) tickling, tickle; fig. desire, longing; '♀n (29) tickle.

'**kitzlig** ticklish (a. fig.).

Kladde ['kladə] *f* (15) waste-book, *Am.* blotter.

klaffen ['klafən] (25, h. *u.* sn) gape.

kläff|en ['klɛfən] (25) yap, yelp; 'Ωer *m* (7) yelping dog.

Klafter ['klaftər] *f* (15) fathom; *Holz:* cord; 'holz *n* cord-wood.

klagbar ['kla:kba:r] actionable; werden (gegen *j-n*) sue (a p.).

Klage ['kla:gə] *f* (15) (*Beschwerde*) complaint, grievance; (*Wehklage*) lament(ation); 𝕤𝕥𝕤 suit, action (*auf acc.* for); *s.* erheben, führen *usw.*; 'grund *m* cause of action; 'laut *m* plaintive sound; 'lied *n* lamentation, elegy; 'Ωn *v/t.* (25): *j-m* et. complain to a p. of (*od.* about) a th.; *v/i.* lament (*um* for; *über acc.* over); 𝕤𝕥𝕤 sue (*auf acc.* for), bring an action (*gegen* against); *über acc.* (*leiden an*) complain of.

Kläger ['klɛ:gər] *m* (7), 'in *f* (16¹) plaintiff, complainant; (*Scheidungs-*Ω) petitioner; 'Ωisch of the plaintiff.

'**Klageschrift** *f* statement of claim.

kläglich ['klɛ:kliç] pitiful, piteous (*a. Stimme usw.*), miserable, wretched.

klamm[1] [klam] (*feuchtkalt*) clammy; (*erstarrt*) numb; F sein (*geldlos*) be hard up.

Klamm[2] *f* (16) gorge.

Klammer ['klamər] *f* (15) ⊕ clamp, cramp; (*Büro*Ω, *Haar*Ω *usw.*) clip; 𝕤 (*Zahn*Ω) brace; (*Wäsche*Ω) peg; *gr., typ.* bracket (*a.* 𝔸⟩), parenthesis; *in* n setzen put in parentheses; bracket; 'Ωn (29) clamp; clasp; *sich* *an* (*acc.*) cling to (*a. fig.*).

Klamotte [kla'mɔtə] F *f* (15): *alte* F oldie; *pl.* (*Kleider, Sachen*) things, rags *pl.*

Klang [klaŋ] **1.** *m* (3³) sound; *Glocke:* ringing; *Geld, Stimme usw.:* ring; (farbe) timbre; **2.** Ω *pret. v.* *klingen;* 'fülle 𝔍 *f* sonority; 'lich tonal; 'Ωlos toneless; 'regler *m Radio etc.:* tone control; 'Ωreich sonorous; 'Ωvoll sonorous; *fig.* illustrious.

'**Klappbett** *n* folding bed.

Klappe ['klapə] *f* (15) *allg.* flap (*a.* ⊕); (*Deckel*) lid; 𝔍 key, stop; ⊕, *anat.* valve; (*Tisch*Ω, *Visier*Ω) leaf; F mouth, trap; *halt die* ! shut up!; F *in die* *gehen* go to bed, F turn in; 'Ωn (25) *v/t.*: *in die Höhe* tip up; *v/i.* clap, flap (*mit* et. a th.);

F (*gutgehen*) work (out well); *zum* Ω kommen (*bringen*) come (bring) to a head; *das klappt!* that works!; *s. klappern;* 'ntext *m Buch:* blurb.

'**Klapper** *f* (15) rattle; 'Ωdürr (as) lean as a rake.

'**klapp(e)rig** F *fig.* shaky, rickety.

'**Klapper|kasten** *m*, 'kiste *f*, 'mühle F *f* rattletrap.

klappern ['klapərn] (29) clatter, rattle (*mit* et. a th.); *mit den Zähnen* chatter one's teeth.

'**Klapper|schlange** *f* rattlesnake; 'storch *m* stork.

'**Klapp|horn** 𝔍 *n* key-bugle; 'hornvers *m* nonsense rhyme; 'hut *m* opera-hat; 'messer *n* jack knife; 'rad *n* folding bicycle; 'sitz *m* tip-up seat; 'stuhl *m* folding chair; 'tisch *m* folding table; drop-leaf table; 'tür *f* snap-action door.

Klaps [klaps] *m* (4[²]) slap, smack; F *fig.* e-n haben be mad; 'Ωen (27) slap, smack; 'mühle F *f* F loony bin.

klar [kla:r] *allg.* clear (*a. fig.*); *fig. a.* lucid; (*offenbar*) obvious, plain; ⚓, ✕ clear, ready (*zu* for); en *Kopf* behalten keep a clear head; *sich über* et. sein realize a th., be aware of a th.; *s. klarmachen usw.*; F (*na*) ! of course, *Am.* sure!; *das geht* (*schon*) ! that will be all right.

'**Klär-anlage** *f* purification plant.

'**klarblickend** clear-sighted.

klären ['klɛ:rən] (25) (*a. sich*) clarify; clear (up) (*beide a. fig.*).

'**Klarheit** *f* clearness, clarity.

Klarinette [klari'nɛtə] *f* (15) clarinet.

'**klar|kommen** (sn) manage, get by; 'legen, 'machen make *a th.* clear (*dat.* to); 'Ωschriftbeleg *m Computer:* hard copy.

'**Klarsicht|folie** *f* transparent film; 'hülle *f* transparent cover (*od.* folder); 'packung *f* transparent pack.

'**klar|stellen** clear up; (*sagen*) state clearly; 'Ωtext *m* clear text; *fig. im* in (the) clear.

'**Klärung** *f* clarification.

'**klarwerden** become clear (*dat.* to); *sich* *über* (*acc.*) realize (*a th.*); get (*a th.*) clear in one's mind.

Klasse ['klasə] *f* (15) *allg.* class; *e-r Schule:* class, form, *Am. bsd. e-r Volksschule:* a. grade; F (*ganz große*) marvellous, terrific; 'n-arbeit *f*

(written) class test; '~nbeste *m*, *f*
best pupil; '~nbewußtsein *n* class-
-consciousness; '~ngesellschaft *f*
class society; '~nhaß *m* class hatred;
'~nkamerad *m* classmate; '~n-
kampf *pol. m* class war(fare) *od.*
struggle; '~nlehrer *m* class-teacher,
form-master; 'Qnlos classless; '~n-
lotterie *f* class (*od.* Dutch) lottery;
'~nsprecher *m* class representative;
'~n-unterschied *m* class distinction; '~nzimmer *n* classroom.

klassifizier|en [klasifi'tsiːrən] clas-
sify; Qung *f* classification.

Klass|iker ['~ikər] *m* (7) classic,
classical author; 'Qisch classic(al);
fig. classic (*mistake, etc.*).

klatsch! [klatʃ] **1.** smack!; (*in*)
Wasser: splash!; **2.** Q *m* (3²) (*Schlag*)
clap; (*Gerede*) gossip; 'Qbase *f*
gossip; 'Qe *f* (15) fly-flap; F *s.*
Klatschbase; '~en *v/t. u. v/i.* (27)
clap (*in die Hände* one's hands);
slap; (*in*) *Wasser*: splash; *fig.* gossip; *s. Beifall*; 'Qer *m* (7) clapper;
(*Beifall*Q) applauder; Qerei [~ə'raɪ]
f (16) gossip(ing); '~haft gossipy;
'Qmaul F *n* gossip, scandalmonger;
'Qmohn ♀ *m* (corn-)poppy; '~naß
sopping wet; 'Qspalte *f* gossip column; '~süchtig gossip-mongering;
'Qtante *f* gossip.

klauben F ['klaʊbən] (25) pick.

Klaue ['klaʊə] *f* (15) claw (*a.* ⊕);
(*Pfote*) paw (*a. contp. s. Hand*); *fig.*
b.s. clutch; F (*schlechte Schrift*)
scrawl; 'Qn P (*stehlen*) F pinch,
swipe; '~nfett *n* neat's-foot oil;
'~nseuche *f* foot-rot.

Klause ['klaʊzə] *f* (15) cell, her-
mitage.

Klausel ['~zəl] *f* (15) clause; (*Vorbehalt*) proviso; stipulation.

Klausner ['klaʊsnər] *m* hermit.

Klausur [klaʊ'zuːr] *f* (16) seclusion;
a. = '~arbeit *f* work written under
supervision; ~sitzung *f* closed session; ~tagung *f* closed meeting.

Klaviatur [klavja'tuːr] *f* (16) keyboard.

Klavier [kla'viːr] *n* (3¹) piano(forte);
auf dem (*am*) ~ on (at) the piano;
'~auszug ♪ *m* piano-score; ~kon-
zert *n* piano recital; ~lehrer(in *f*)
m piano-teacher; ~schule *f* (*Buch*)
piano tutor; ~sonate *f* piano
sonata; ~spieler(in *f*) *m* pianist;
~stimmer *m* (7) tuner; ~stunde *f*

piano lesson.

'Klebe|band *n* adhesive tape; '~-
folie *f* self-adhesive plastic sheet-
ing; '~mittel *n* adhesive.

klebe|n ['kleːbən] (25) *v/t.* stick,
paste; F *j-m eine* ~ paste a p. one;
v/i. (*a. ~bleiben*) stick, adhere (*an
dat.* to); 'Qpflaster *n* adhesive (*od.*
sticking) plaster; 'Qr *m* (7) **1.** *s.*
Klebstoff; **2.** ♀ gluten; 'Qzettel *m*
stick-on label, *Am.* sticker.

'klebrig adhesive, sticky; Ⓤ viscous; 'Qkeit *f* stickiness.

Kleb|stoff ['kleːp-] *m* adhesive;
'~streifen *m* adhesive tape.

Klecks [klɛks] *m* (4) blot, blotch;
(*Masse*) blob; 'Qen (27) blot, make
splodges; *Malerei contp.* daub.

Klee [kleː] *m* (3¹) clover, trefoil; '~-
blatt *n* clover-leaf; *fig.* trio.

Kleid [klaɪt] *n* (1) dress, garment;
langes: robe, *elegantes*: gown; *pl.*
clothes; Qen ['~dən] (26) dress; (*a.
fig.*) clothe, dress; *j-n gut usw.* ~
suit, become, look *well etc.* on;
sich ~ dress.

Kleider|-ablage ['~dər-] *f* cloak-
room, *Am.* checkroom; *im Haus*:
hall-stand; '~bügel *m* coat- *od.*
dress-hanger; '~bürste *f* clothes-
brush; '~haken *m* clothes-peg,
coat-hook; '~schrank *m* wardrobe; '~schürze *f* house frock;
'~ständer *m* (hat and) coat stand;
'~stoff *m* dress material.

kleidsam ['klaɪt-] becoming.

'Kleidung *f* clothing, dress, clothes
pl.; '~sstück *n* article of clothing,
garment.

Kleie ['klaɪə] *f* (15) bran.

klein [klaɪn] small, *nur attr.*: little;
fig. (*unbedeutend*) petty; ~(er *comp.*)
(*minder*) minor; ~es *Geld* (small)
change; *ein* ~ *wenig* a little (bit);
groß und ~ great and small, (*jung
u. alt*) old and young; *von* ~ *auf*
from a child; *s. beigeben*; *im* ~en
verkaufen (sell by) retail; *Wort* ~
schreiben write in small letters; *bis
ins* ~ste (down) to the last detail; 'Qe *m* little boy; *f* little girl;
n (*Kind*) little one; *die* ~n *pl.* the
little ones.

'Klein|-anzeige *f* classified ad(ver-
tisement); '~arbeit *f* spade-work;
'~auto *n* small car; '~bahn *f* narrow-
-ga(u)ge railway; '~bauer *m* small-
holder; '~betrieb *m* small(-scale)

enterprise; ✓ smallholding; '**~bild-kamera** f miniature camera; '**~buchstabe** m small letter; '**~bürger** m, '≗**bürgerlich** petty bourgois; '**~bus** m minibus; '**~computer** m minicomputer; '≗**denkend** small--minded; '**~format** m small size; '**~garten** m allotment (garden); '**~gärtner** m allotment gardener; '**~gebäck** n fancy biscuits pl.; '**~gedruckte** n: das ~ the small print; '**~geld** n (small) change; '≗**gläubig** of little faith, faint-hearted; '**~handel** † m retail trade; '**~händler** m retailer; '**~heit** f littleness, smallness; '**~hirn** n cerebellum; '**~holz** n matchwood.

'**Kleinigkeit** f trifle; '**~skrämer** m pedant, fuss-pot; '**~skrämerei** f pedantry.

'**Klein|kaliberbüchse** f small-bore (od. sub-calibre) rifle; '≗**kariert** small-check(ed); fig. small-minded; '**~kind** n infant; '**~kram** m trifles pl.; '**~krieg** m guer(r)illa warfare; '**~kunstbühne** f cabaret; '≗**laut** subdued.

'**kleinlich** pedantic; (engstirnig) narrow-minded.

'**Klein|mut** m pusillanimity, faint--heartedness; ≗**mütig** ['~myːtiç] pusillanimous, faint-hearted.

Kleinod ['~noːt] n (3; pl. a. -ien [~'noːdiən]) jewel, gem; fig. a. treasure.

'**Klein|staat** m minor state; '**~staaterei** f particularism; '**~stadt** f small town; '**~städter(in** f) m, '≗**städtisch** provincial; '**~st...** very small, miniature ...; '**~vieh** n small cattle; '**~wagen** m small car.

Kleister ['klaɪstər] m (7), '≗**n** (29) paste.

Klemm|e ['klɛmə] f (15) ⊕ clamp, (a. Haar≗ usw.) clip; ⚡ terminal; F fig. in der ~ sein be in a jam od. fix; '≗**en** (25) jam (a. ⊕), squeeze, pinch; F (stehlen) pinch; sich den Finger ~ get one's finger jammed; fig. sich ~ hinter get down to (work, etc.); '**~er** m (7) pince-nez (fr.); '**~schraube** ⊕ f setscrew; ⚡ binding screw.

Klempner ['klɛmpnər] m (7) tinman, tinsmith; (Installateur) plumber; **~ei** [~'raɪ] f (16) tinman's trade od. workshop; plumbing.

Klepper ['klɛpər] m (7) nag, hack.

klerikal [kleri'kɑːl] clerical.

Kleriker ['kleː-] m (7) cleric.

Klerus ['kleːrus] m clergy.

Klette ['klɛtə] f (15) bur(r) (a. fig.), burdock.

Kletter|er ['klɛtərər] m (7) climber; '≗**n** (29, sn) climb (auf e-n Baum usw. [up] a tree, etc.); '**~pflanze** f climber, creeper; '**~rose** f rambler; '**~stange** f climbing-pole.

Klient [kli'ent] m (12), **~in** f client.

Klima ['kliːma] n (11²) climate; fig. a. atmosphere; '**~anlage** f air--conditioning (system); ≗**tisch** [~'mɑːtiʃ] climatic(ally adv.); **~ti'sierung** f (15) air conditioning; **~tologe** [~to'loːgə] m (13) climatologist; **~tologie** [~tolo'giː] f (15, o. pl.) climatology; '**~wechsel** m change of climate.

Klimbim [klim'bim] F m (3¹, o. pl.) junk; (Getue) fuss.

klimm|en ['klimən] (30, sn) climb (s. klettern); '≗**zug** m pull-up.

klimpern ['klimpərn] v/i. (29) jingle, tinkle (beide a. ~ mit); (a. v/t.) auf dem Klavier usw.: strum.

Klinge ['kliŋə] f (15) blade; mit j-m die ~n kreuzen (a. fig.) cross swords with a p.

Klingel ['kliŋəl] f (15) (small) bell; (Tür≗) (door)bell; '**~knopf** m bell--push; '≗**n** (29) tinkle (Glocke: ring; P.: ring the bell; es klingelt the bell rings; '**~zug** m bellpull.

klingen ['kliŋən] (30) sound (a. fig.); Metall: tinkle; Glas: clink; Glocke: ring; ~de Münze hard cash.

Klin|ik ['kliːnik] f (16) hospital (department); (Privat≗) nursing home, clinic; '≗**isch** clinical.

Klinke ['kliŋkə] f (15) (Türgriff) (door-)handle; weitS. latch; ✓ jack.

'**Klinker** m (7) (Dutch) clinker.

klipp [klip]: ~ und klar perfectly clear; adv. say plainly, straight out.

Klipp|e ['klipə] f (15) reef; weitS. cliff; fig. hurdle; '≗**ig** craggy.

'**klipp'klapp** click-clack, flip-flap.

klirren ['kliːrən] (25) Glas: clink; Porzellan usw.: clatter; Kette usw.: clank, clash (alle a. ~ mit); Fensterscheibe: rattle.

Klischee [kli'ʃeː] n (11) (stereotype) block od. plate, (a. fig.) cliché; **~vorstellung** f stereotyped idea.

Klistier [kli'stiːr] n (3¹) enema; **~spritze** f rectal syringe.

klitschig ['klitʃiç] *Brot*: doughy.
klitzeklein ['klitsə-] F tiny little, teeny-weeny.
Klo [klo:] F *n* (11) F loo, *Am.* john.
Kloake [klo'ɑ:kə] *f* (15) sewer; (*Grube*) cesspool (*a. fig.*).
Klob|en ['klo:bən] (6) *m* ⊕ block; (*Holz*) log; '⸗**ig** (*massig*) bulky, massy; (*plump*) clumsy.
klomm [klɔm] *pret. v.* klimmen.
klönen ['klønən] F chin-wag.
klopf|en ['klɔpfən] *v/t. u. v/i.* (25) knock (*a. mot.*), rap; (*sanft* ⸗) tap; *Steine*: break; *Teppich*: beat (*v/i. a. Herz*); es klopft there's a knock at the door; *s.* Busch; '⸗**er** *m* (7) beater; (*Tür*⸗) knocker; *tel.* sounder; '⸗**fest** *mot.* knockproof.
Klöppel ['klœpəl] *m* (7) *der Glocke*: clapper; (*Spitzen*⸗) bobbin; ✐ swingle; '⸗**arbeit** *f*, **⸗ei** [⸗'laɪ] *f* bobbin lace work; '⸗**kissen** *n* (lace-)pillow; '⸗**n** *v/i.* (29) make lace; '⸗**spitzen** *f/pl.* bobbin- (*od.* pillow-)lace *sg.*
Klops [klɔps] *m* (4) meat ball.
Klosett [klo'zet] *n* (3) toilet, closet, W.C., lavatory; **⸗becken** *n* closet-bowl; **⸗papier** *n* toilet-paper.
Kloß [klo:s] *m* (3² *u.* ³) *Küche*: dumpling.
Kloster ['klo:stər] *n* (7¹) (*Mönchs*⸗) monastery; (*Nonnen*⸗) convent, nunnery; '⸗**bruder** *m* friar; '⸗**frau** *f* nun; '⸗**leben** *n* monastic life.
klösterlich ['kløstərliç] monastic; convent(ual).
Klotz [klɔts] *m* (3² *u.* ³) block, (*a. fig.*) log; *fig. contp.* oaf; '⸗**ig** (*sehr groß*) mighty; *s.* klobig.
Klub [klup] *m* (11) club; '⸗**jacke** *f* blazer; '⸗**kamerad** *m* fellow club-member; '⸗**sessel** *m* club chair.
Kluft [kluft] *f* (14¹) gap, cleft; (*grundlose Tiefe*) gulf, abyss, chasm (*alle a. fig.*); F (*Kleidung*) togs *pl.*
klug [klu:k] (*gescheit*) clever, shrewd; (*verständig*) wise, intelligent, judicious, sensible; (*vorsichtig*) prudent; (*schlau*) cunning; ich kann nicht ⸗ daraus werden I can't make head or tail of it; ich werde aus ihm nicht ⸗ I cannot make him out; er hat ⸗ reden it is easy for him to say so; der Klügere gibt nach the wiser head gives in; '⸗**heit** *f* cleverness; intelligence; judiciousness; prudence.

klüglich ['kly:kliç] wisely.
'**Klug|redner** *m*, '⸗**schnacker** *m* (7) wiscacre, *Am.* wise guy, smart aleck.
Klump|en ['klumpən] *m* (6) lump, clot; (*Erde*) clod; (*Haufen*) heap; '⸗**fuß** *m* club-foot; '⸗**ig** lumpy.
Klüngel ['klyŋəl] *m* (7) clique.
Klüver ⚓ ['kly:vər] *m* (7) jib; '⸗**baum** ⚓ *m* jib-boom.
knabbern ['knabərn] *v/i. u. v/t.* (29) gnaw, nibble (*an dat.* at).
Knabe ['knɑ:bə] *m* (13) *allg.* boy; (*Bursche*) lad; F *alter* ⸗ old chap; '⸗**n-alter** *n* boyhood; '⸗**nchor** *m* boys' choir; '⸗**nhaft** boyish.
Knack(s) [knak(s)] *m* (4) crack.
Knäckebrot ['knɛkə-] *n* crispbread.
'**knack|en** 1. *v/t.* (25) crack (*a. fig.*); F *Auto*: break into; *v/i.* crack; snap; *Schloß usw.*: click; 2. ⸗ *n* (6) crack; click; '⸗**laut** *gr. m* glottal stop; '⸗**mandel** *f* shell-almond; '⸗**wurst** *f* saveloy.
Knall [knal] *m* (3) bang; (*Schuß*) *a.* report; *bsd. Peitsche*: crack; (*Explosion*) detonation; ⸗ *und Fall* abruptly; F *e-n* ⸗ *haben* be mad (*od.* nuts); '⸗**bonbon** *m* (party) cracker; '⸗**effekt** *m* sensation, bang; '⸗**en** (25) bang, crack, pop (*alle a.* ⸗ mit); (*explodieren*) explode, detonate; ⸗ *gegen* crash against; '⸗**erbse** *f* (toy-)torpedo; '⸗**frosch** *m* jumping cracker; '⸗**gas** *n* oxyhydrogen gas; '⸗**hart** F tough; *Schuß*: powerful; (*unmißverständlich*) brutal; '⸗**ig** F flashy; '⸗**kopf** F *m* idiot; '⸗**körper** *m* banger; '⸗**rot** glaring red.
knapp [knap] (*eng*) *Kleidung*: close, tight; (*spärlich*) scanty, *mst pred.* scarce; *Stil*: concise; *Gewicht*: short; *Mehrheit*: bare; *mit* ⸗*er Not* barely, with great difficulty; *mit* ⸗*er Not entrinnen od. davonkommen* have (*od.* make) a narrow escape; ⸗ *an Geld sein* be short of money, be hard up; ⸗ *werden* *Vorrat*: run short; ⸗ *10 Minuten* just (*od.* barely) ten minutes; '⸗**e** *m* (13) *hist.* page, squire; ⚒ miner; '⸗**halten** keep *a p.* short; '⸗**heit** *f s.* knapp; tightness; scarcity; conciseness; *an Vorräten*: shortage; '⸗**schaft** *f* (16) miners' society.
Knarre ['knarə] *f* (15) rattle; F (*Schußwaffe*) gun, F pea-shooter; '⸗**n** (25) creak, rattle; *Stimme*: grate.
Knast [knast] *m* (3) (*Holz*) knag;

Brot: crust; F *alter* ~ old fogey; *sl.* (3, *o. pl.*) (*Gefängnis*) clink; *sl.* ~ *schieben* do time.

Knaster ['knastər] *m* (7) canaster; F *contp.* bad tobacco.

knattern ['knatərn] (29) crackle; *Gewehrfeuer*: rattle; *mot.* roar.

Knäuel ['knɔʏəl] *m, n* (7) ball; *fig.* tangle; (*Menschen*♀) cluster, crowd.

Knauf [knauf] *m* (3³) knob; ⚠ capital; (*Degen*♀) pommel.

Knauser ['knauzər] *m* (7) miser; **~ei** [~'rai] *f* niggardliness, stinginess; '♀**ig** niggardly, stingy; '♀**n** (29) be stingy (*mit* with).

knautsch|en F ['knautʃən] (27) crumple; '♀**zone** *f* crushable bin.

Knebel ['kne:bəl] *m* (7) ⊕ lever; (*Mund*♀) gag; '~**bart** *m* turned-up moustache; '♀**n** (29) gag; *fig.* muzzle; (*lähmen*) fetter.

Knecht [knɛçt] *m* (3) servant; ✓ farm-hand; (*Unfreier*) slave; '♀**en** (26) enslave; '♀**isch** servile, slavish; '~**schaft** *f* servitude, slavery; '~**ung** *f* enslavement.

kneif|en ['knaifən] (30) pinch, nip; F *fig.* back (*Am.* chicken) out; ~ *vor* dodge; '♀**er** *m* (7) pince-nez (*fr.*); '♀**zange** *f* (*eine* a pair of) nippers *pl.*, pincers *pl.*

Kneipe ['knaipə] *f* (15) public house, F pub, *Am.* saloon; (*Studenten*♀) beer-party, (*Ort*) students' club; '♀**n** (*zechen*) tipple, booze; '~**nwirt** *m* publican, *Am.* saloon keeper.

Kneippkur ['knaip-] *f* Kneipp('s) cure.

knet|en ['kne:tən] (26) knead; '♀**-masse** *f* plasticine.

Knick [knik] *m* (3) (*Biegung*) bend; (*Riß*) crack; *in Draht usw.*: kink; *in Papier usw.*: fold, crease; '♀**en** *v/i. u. v/t.* (25) bend; crack; crease; *fig.* crush; *geknickt fig.* crestfallen.

Knicker ['knikər] *m* (7), **~ei** [~'rai] *f*, '♀**ig** *s. Knauser usw.*

'**Knickfuß** *m* pes valgus.

Knicks [kniks] *m* (4) curts(e)y; *e-n* ~ *machen*, '♀**en** (27) (drop a) curtsy.

Knie [kni:] *n* (3) knee (*a.* ⊕); (*Biegung*) bend; *et. übers* ~ *brechen* rush a th.; ~**beuge** ['~bɔʏɡə] *f* (15) *Turnen*: knee-bend; '~**fall** *m* genuflection, prostration; '♀**fällig** on one's bended knees; '~**gelenk** *n* knee-joint (*a.* ⊕); '~**hose** *f* (*eine* a

pair of) knee-breeches; '~**kehle** *f* hollow of the knee; '♀**n** (25) kneel (*vor dat.* to); '~**scheibe** *f* knee--cap, knee-pan; '~**schützer** *m* knee--pad; '~**strumpf** *m* knee-length stocking.

Kniff [knif] **1.** *m* (3) *im Stoff usw.*: crease, fold; *fig.* trick, knack; **2.** ♀ *pret. v.* kneifen; '♀**(e)lig** tricky; '♀**en** (25) fold (down), crease.

knipsen ['knipsən] (27) *v/i.* snap (*mit den Fingern* one's fingers); *v/t.* 🎫 punch; F *phot.* (*a. v/i.*) snap (-shot), take a shot (*v/t.* of).

Knirps [knirps] *m* (4) F hop-o'-my--thumb.

knirschen ['knirʃən] (27) grate, creak; *Kies usw.*: crunch; *mit den Zähnen* ~ gnash one's teeth.

knistern ['knistərn] (29) crackle; *bsd. Seide*: rustle.

knitter|frei ['knitər-] creaseproof, non-creasing, crease-resistant; '~**n** *v/i. u. v/t.* (29) crumple, crease.

knobeln F ['kno:bəln] (29) throw dice (*um* for); (*tüfteln*) puzzle (*an dat.* over).

Knoblauch ['kno:b-] *m* (3) garlic; '~**zehe** *f* clove of garlic.

Knöchel ['knœçəl] *m* (7) knuckle; (*Fuß*♀) ankle; '~**bruch** *m* ankle fracture.

Knochen ['knɔxən] *m* (6) bone; '~**-bruch** *m* fracture (of a bone); '~**fraß** *m* caries; '~**gerüst** *n* skeleton; '~**mark** *n* (bone) marrow; '~**mehl** *n* bone meal; '~**splitter** *m* bone--splinter.

knöchern ['knœçərn] bone ...; bony, 🏛 osseous.

knochig ['knɔxiç] bony.

Knödel ['knø:dəl] *m* (7) dumpling.

Knolle ['knɔlə] *f* (15) tuber; (*Zwiebel*) bulb; '~**n** *m* (6) lump.

'**knollig** knobby, cloddy; 🌿 tuberous; 🌿 bulbous.

Knopf [knɔpf] *m* (3³) button; (*Degen*♀, *Sattel*♀, *Turm*♀) pommel; (*Griff an der Tür usw.*) knob; (*Nadel*♀) head; *s. Hemd*♀, *Manschetten*♀.

Knöpf|chen ['knœpfçən] *n* (6) small button; '♀**en** (25) button.

'**Knopf|druck** *m*: *auf* ~ at the press of a button; '~**loch** *n* buttonhole.

Knorpel ['knɔrpəl] *m* (7) cartilage, gristle; '♀**ig** cartilaginous, gristly.

Knorr|en ['knɔrən] *m* (6) knot, knag; '♀**ig** knobby, gnarled.

Knosp|e ['knɔspə] *f* (15) bud; '♀**en** (25) bud.
Knoten ['knoːtən] **1.** *m* (6) knot (*a. fig.* = *Schwierigkeit*; ♏ = *Seemeile*); (*Haarfrisur*) knot, chignon; *e-s Dramas*: plot; **2.** ♀ (26) knot; '**~punkt** *m* ⬚ junction.
knotig ['knoːtiç] knotty (*a. fig.*).
Knuff [knuf] *m* (3³) cuff, thump; '♀**en** (25) cuff, poke. [*Am.* guy.⟨
Knülch [knylç] F *m* (3¹) *sl.* bird,⟨
knüllen ['knylən] (25) crumple.
Knüller F ['knylər] *m* F (big) hit.
knüpfen ['knypfən] (25) tie, knot.
Knüppel ['knypəl] *m* (7) cudgel; club, stick; (*Brötchen*) (small) roll; *s.* Polizei♀, Steuer♀; '**~damm** *m* log-road, *Am.* corduroy road; '♀**n** cudgel, beat; '**~schaltung** *mot. f: mit* **~** with floor-mounted gear change.
knurren ['knurən] (25) snarl, growl; *fig.* grumble (*alle:* über *acc.* at); *Magen, Eingeweide*: rumble.
'**knurrig** F grumpy.
knusp(e)rig ['knusp(ə)riç] crisp.
Knute ['knuːtə] *f* (15) knout.
knutsch|en F ['knuːtʃən] (27) hug, cuddle, F neck, pet; '♀**fleck** *m* love bite.
Knüttel ['knytəl] *m* (7) cudgel; '**~vers** *m* doggerel rhyme *od.* verse.
Koalition [koˑʔaliˈtsjoːn] *pol. f* coalition.
Kobalt *min.* ['koːbalt] *m* (3) cobalt.
Koben ['koːbən] *m* (6) pigsty.
Kobold ['koːbɔlt] *m* (3) (hob)goblin, imp (*a. fig.*).
Koch [kɔx] *m* (3³) (man-)cook; '**~birne** *f* cooking pear; '**~buch** *n* cookery-book, *Am.* cookbook; '♀**echt** fast to boiling; '♀**en** (25) *v/i.* be cooking; *Flüssigkeit*: boil (*a.fig. vor Wut usw.*); *v/t.* cook; boil; '**~er** *m* (7) cooker.
Köcher ['kœçər] *m* (7) quiver.
'**Koch|fett** *n* shortening; '**~gelegenheit** *f* cooking facilities *pl.* '**~geschirr** ✗ *n* mess tin, *Am.* mess kit; '**~herd** *m* (cooking-)range, *Am.* cook stove.
Köchin ['kœçin] *f* (16¹) cook.
'**Koch|kiste** *f* haybox; '**~kunst** *f* art of cooking, culinary art; '**~löffel** *m* (wooden) spoon; '**~nische** *f* kitchenette; '**~platte** *f* hot-plate; '**~salz** *n* common salt; '**~topf** *m* cooking-pot.
Köder ['køːdər] *m* (7) (*a. fig.*) bait,

lure; '♀**n** (29) (*a. fig.*) bait, lure.
Kodex ['koːdeks] *m* (3², *sg. a. inv.*, *pl. a.* Kodizes) code.
Koffein [kɔfeˈʔiːn] *n* (3¹) caffeine; ♀**frei** decaffeinated.
Koffer ['kɔfər] *m* (7) (*Hand*♀) suitcase, case *Am. a.* grip; *großer*: trunk; '**~anhänger** *m* address tag; '**~gerät** *n*, '**~radio** *n* portable radio (set); '**~raum** *mot. m* boot, *Am.* trunk.
Kognac ['kɔnjak] *m* (3¹ *u.* 11) cognac, (French) brandy.
Kohl [koːl] *m* (3) cabbage; F *fig.* twaddle, rubbish.
Kohle ['koːlə] *f* (15) coal; *s.* Holz♀, Stein♀; *zum Zeichnen*, ⚡ *usw.:* carbon; *glühende* **~n** red-hot (*od.* live) coals; *fig.* wie *auf* **~n** sitzen be on tenterhooks; '**~faden(lampe** *f*) *m* carbon filament (lamp); '**~hydrat** ⚗ *n* carbohydrate; '**~kraftwerk** *n* coal power plant (*od.* station); '♀**n** *v/i.* (25) (*ver*~, *an*~) char, carbonize; ♏ coal.
'**Kohlen|becken** *n* brazier; ✗ *s.* Kohlenrevier; '**~bergwerk** *n* coal-mine, colliery; '**~bunker** *m* (coal)bunker; '**~dioxyd** ⚗ *n* carbon dioxide; '**~eimer** *m* coal-scuttle; '**~flöz** ✗ *n* coal seam; '**~gas** *n* coal-gas; '**~händler** *m* coal merchant; '**~oxyd** *n* carbon monoxide; '**~revier** *n* coal-field *od.* -district; '♀**sauer** carbonate of ...; '**~säure** *f* carbonic acid; *weit S.* carbon dioxide; '**~schiff** *n* collier; '**~staub** *m* coal-dust; '**~stoff** *m* carbon; '**~stoffaser** *f* carbon fibre; '**~wasserstoff** *m* hydrocarbon.
'**Kohlepapier** *n* carbon paper.
Köhler ['køːlər] *m* (7) charcoal--burner.
'**Kohle|stift** *m* charcoal pencil; ⚡ carbon-rod; '**~vorkommen** *n* coal field; '**~zeichnung** *f* charcoal-drawing.
'**Kohl|kopf** *m* cabbage; '♀**raben-'schwarz** coal-black; **~rabi** [~ˈraːbi] *m* (11) kohlrabi; '**~rübe** *f* Swedish turnip, swede, *Am. a.* rutabaga; **~weißling** ['~vaisliŋ] *m* cabbage-butterfly.
Ko-itus ['koˑʔiːtus] *m* (*inv.*) coition.
Koje ♏ ['koːjə] *f* (15) berth, bunk.
Kokain [kokaˈʔiːn] *n* (3¹) cocaine.
Kokarde [koˈkardə] *f* (15) cockade.
kokett [koˈkɛt] coquettish; ♀**erie** [~ə'riː] *f* coquetry, coquettishness; **~ieren** [~'tiːrən] coquet, flirt.

Kokon [ko'kõ] *m* (11) cocoon.

Kokos|baum ['ko:kɔs-] *m* coconut tree; '~fett *n* coconut oil; '~matte *f* coir mat(ting); '~nuß *f* coconut; '~palme *f* coconut palm.

Koks [ko:ks] *m* (4) coke (*a. sl. Kokain*); 'Ǝen *sl.* (27) sniff coke.

Kolben ['kɔlbən] *m* (6) (*Gewehrǝ*) butt(-end); (*Keule*) mace, club; (*Maschinenǝ*) piston; ♀ spike; ⚗ flask; '~hub *m* piston stroke; '~motor *m* piston engine; '~ring *m* piston ring; '~stange *f* piston rod.

Kolchose [kɔl'ço:zə] *f* (15) kolkhoz, collective farm.

Kolik ['ko:lik] *f* (16) colic.

Kollaborateur [kɔlabora'tø:r] *m* (3¹) collaborator.

Kollaps ['kɔlaps] *m* (3²) collapse.

Kolleg [kɔ'le:k] *n* (8²) course of lectures; lecture; ~e [~gə] *m* (13), ~in [~] (16¹) colleague; ǝial [~'gja:l] collegial; *weitS.* helpful; ~ium [~'le:gjum] *n* (9) board, staff; *s. Lehrkörper.*

Kollek|te [kɔ'lɛktə] *f* (15) collection; (*Gebet*) collect; ~tion ♦ [~'tsjo:n] *f* (16) collection, range; Ǝtiv [~'ti:f] 1. *adj.*, 2. ♀ *n* (3¹) collective; ~'tiv-vertrag *m* collective agreement.

Koller ['kɔlər] *m* (7) *vet.* staggers *pl.*; *fig.* rage, tantrum; 'Ǝn *v/i.* (29, sn; *a. v/t.*) roll; (h.) *Puter:* gobble.

kolli|dieren [kɔli'di:rən] (sn) collide; Ǝsion [~'zjo:n] *f* (16) collision.

Kollo ['kɔlo] *n* (11, *pl. a. Kolli* ['~li]) parcel, package.

Kölnischwasser [kœlniʃ'vasər] *n* eau-de-Cologne.

Kolon ['ko:lɔn] *n* (11 *u.* 9²) colon.

Kolonial... [kolo'nja:l-] colonial ...; ~waren *f/pl.* colonial produce; groceries *pl.*; ~warenhändler *m* grocer; ~warenhandlung *f* grocer's shop, grocery.

Kolon|ie [kolo'ni:] *f* (15) colony; Ǝisieren [~ni'zi:rən] colonize; ~ist [~'nist] *m* (12) colonist, settler.

Kolonnade [kolɔ'na:də] *f* (15) colonnade.

Kolonne [ko'lɔnə] *f* (15) column (*a. typ.*); (*Arbeiterǝ*) gang; ~nspringer *mot.* F *m* queue-jumper.

Kolophonium [kolo'fo:njum] *n* (9) colophony, rosin.

Koloratur [kolora'tu:r] *f* (16) coloratura; ~sängerin *f* coloratura singer.

kolor|ieren [~'ri:rən] colo(u)r; Ǝit [~'ri:t] *n* (3) colo(u)r(ing).

Koloß [ko'lɔs] *m* (4) colossus.

kolossal [~'sa:l] colossal, huge; *fig. a.* enormous, F terrific.

Kolport|age [kɔlpɔr'ta:ʒə] *f* (15, *o. pl.*) hawking (of books); *fig.* (*Schund*) trash; (*Verbreiten*) spreading; Ǝieren [~'ti:rən] hawk; *fig.* spread.

Kolum|ne [ko'lumnə] *f* (15) column; ~nentitel *typ. m* running head; ~'nist [~'nist] *m* (12) columnist.

Kombination [kɔmbina'tsjo:n] *f allg.* combination (*a. Sport*); (*Schutzanzug*) overall, ⚙ flying suit; *fig.* (*Folgerung*) deduction; ~sgabe *f* power of deduction; ~sschloß *n* combination (*od.* puzzle) lock.

kombinieren [~'ni:rən] combine; (*folgern*) deduce.

Kombiwagen ['kɔmbi-] *m* estate car, *bsd. Am.* station wagon.

Kombüse ⚓ [kɔm'by:zə] *f* (15) galley.

Komet [ko'me:t] *m* (12) comet; Ǝenhaft comet-like; ~enschweif *m* comet's tail.

Komfort [kɔm'fo:r, kõ-] *m* (7, *o.pl.*) comfort(s *pl.*); luxury; Ǝabel [~fɔr'ta:bəl] comfortable; ~wohnung *f* luxury flat.

Komik ['ko:mik] *f* (16) comicality, funniness; fun; '~er *m* (7) comedian, comic (actor).

'**komisch** comic(al); *fig. a.* funny, queer, odd.

Komitee [komi'te:] *n* (11) committee.

Komma ['kɔma] *n* (11²) comma; *im Dezimalbruch:* decimal point.

Kommand|ant [kɔman'dant] *m* (12), ~eur [~'dø:r] *m* (3¹) commander, *Am.* commanding officer; ~antur [~'tu:r] *f* garrison (*od. Am.* post) headquarters *pl.*; Ǝieren [~'di:rən] *v/t. u. v/i.* command; *v/t.* ✗ (*abstellen*) detach; (*einteilen*) detail; *vorübergehend:* attach; ~itgesellschaft [~'di:t-] *f* limited partnership; ~itist [~di'tist] *m* (12) limited partner.

Kommando [~'mando] ✗ *n* (11) command; (*Abteilung*) detachment; (~*truppe*) commando (unit); ~brücke ⚓ *f* (navigating) bridge; ~kapsel *f Raumfahrt:* command module; ~stab *m* baton; ~turm *m* ⚓

conning tower; ✈ ⚔ control-tower.
kommen ['kɔmən] (30, sn) come;
(*gelangen*) get; (*an~*) arrive; (*sich
zutragen*) come (to pass); ~ *lassen*
P.: send for, S.: order; ~ *sehen*
foresee; *gegangen* ~ come on foot;
gelaufen ~ come running; s. *Atem,
Fall, Kosten, Reihe, Schluß, Verlegenheit*; *es komme, wie es wolle* come
what may; *auf et. (acc.)* ~ hit on,
find out; *wie kommst du darauf?*
what put this idea into your head?;
auf soundsoviel ~ (*sich belaufen*)
amount to; *auf einen Knaben* ~ *zwei
Äpfel* there are two apples to one
boy; *hinter et. (acc.)* ~ find out;
um et. ~ lose a th.; ~ *von e-r Ursache*
be due to; *zu et.* ~ (*bekommen*) come
by a th.; *wieder zu sich* ~ come
round *od.* to; *drohend*: *wie* ~ *Sie
dazu?* how dare you?; *ich komme
nie dazu* I can never find time (to
do it); *wie kommt es, daß die Tür
offen ist?* how come(s it that) the
door is open?; *das kommt davon* F
that's what comes of it; s. *kurz*;
'~**d** coming; ~**es** *Jahr* a. next year.
Kommen|tar [kɔmɛn'taːr] m (3¹)
commentary; ~ *überflüssig!*, *kein
~!* no comment!; ~'**tator** [~tɔr] m
commentator; ♀**tieren** comment
on.
Kommers [kɔ'mɛrs] m (4) drinking-
-bout; ~**buch** n students' songbook.
kommerz|ialisieren [kɔmɛrtsjali-
'ziːrən] commercialize; ~**iell** [~-
'tsjɛl] commercial.
Kommilitone [kɔmili'toːnə] m (13)
fellow student.
Kommis [kɔ'miː] m inv. (*Schreiber*)
clerk; (*Verkäufer*) salesman, shop-
man, Am. salesclerk.
Kommiß [kɔ'mis] F m (4, o. pl.)
military service *od.* life, army.
Kommissar [kɔmi'saːr] m (3¹) com-
missioner; s. *Kriminal*♀; (*Sowjet*♀)
commissar; ♀**isch** deputy; temporary.
Kommission [~'sjoːn] f commission (a. ✝), committee; ~**är** ✝
[~'nɛːr] m (3¹) commission agent;
~**sgeschäft** n commission business.
Kommode [kɔ'moːdə] f (15) chest
of drawers, Am. bureau.
Kommunal... [kɔmu'naːl-] local,
communal, municipal; ~**be-amte** m
municipal officer; ~**politik** f local
politics *pl.*; ~**wahlen** f/pl. local elec-

tions.
Kommune [kɔ'muːnə] f (15) commune; *weitS.* the Communists *pl.*
Kommunikat|ionsmittel [kɔmuni-
ka'tsjoːns-] n means of communication; *pl. a.* mass media *pl.*; ~**ions-
technik** f communications technology; ♀**iv** [~'tiːf] communicative.
Kommunion [~'njoːn] f (16) (Holy)
Communion.
Kommuniqué [kɔmyni'keː] n (11)
communiqué.
Kommunismus [kɔmu'nismus] m
(16, o. pl.) communism.
Kommu'nist m (12), ~**in** f (16¹)
communist; ♀**isch** communist(ic).
Komödiant [kɔmø'djant] m (12)
comedian; *contp. a. fig.* play-actor;
~**in** f (16¹) comedienne.
Komödie [~'møːdjə] f (15) comedy;
~ *spielen* fig. play-act.
Kompagnon ['kɔmpanjõ] m (11)
partner.
kompakt [kɔm'pakt] compact.
Kompanie [kɔmpa'niː] f (15) company; ~**chef** m company commander; ~**geschäft** n joint business.
Komparativ gr. ['kɔmparatiːf] m
(3¹) comparative (degree).
Kompars|e [kɔm'parzə] m (13), ~**in**
f (16¹) extra, F super.
Kompaß ['kɔmpas] m (4) compass;
~**häus-chen** ⚓ ['~hɔʏsçən] n bin-
nacle; '~**nadel** f compass-needle;
'~**rose** f compass-card.
Kompen|sation [kɔmpɛnza'tsjoːn]
f (16) compensation; ~**sati'ons-
geschäft** ✝ n barter transaction;
~'**sator** ⚡ n potentiometer; ♀**sieren** compensate for.
kompeten|t [kɔmpe'tɛnt] compe-
tent; ♀**z** [~ts] f (16) competence;
♀**zstreitigkeit** f dispute about
competence.
Komplementärfarbe[kɔmplemɛn-
'tɛːr-] f complementary colo(u)r.
komplett [kɔm'plɛt] complete.
Komplex [~'plɛks] m (3²) allg. complex (a. psych).
Komplikation [kɔmplika'tsjoːn] f
complication.
Kompliment [~pli'mɛnt] n (3)
compliment.
Komplize [kɔm'pliːtsə] m (13) accomplice.
komplizieren [~pli'tsiːrən] compli-
cate; 🩺 *komplizierter Bruch* compound fracture.

Komplott [ˌ'plɔt] n (3) plot; ℒ**ieren** [ˌ'tiːrən] plot.

Kompo|nente [ˌpo'nɛntə] f (15) component; ℒ**nieren** [ˌpo'niːrən] compose; ˌ**nist** [ˌ'nist] m (12) composer; ˌ**sition** [ˌzi'tsjoːn] f (16) composition.

Kompositum gr. [kɔm'poːzitum] n (9) compound (word).

Kompost ✗ [kɔm'pɔst] m (3) compost; ˌ**haufen** m compost-heap.

Kompott [kɔm'pɔt] n (3) compote, stewed fruit, Am. sauce.

Kompress|e [ˌ'prɛsə] f (15) compress; ˌ**or** [ˌɔr] m (8[1]) ⊕ compressor; mot. supercharger.

kompri'mieren [ˌpri-] compress.

Komprom|iß [ˌpro'mis] m (4) compromise; ℒ**ißlos** uncompromising (-ly adv.); ˌ**ißlösung** f compromise solution; ℒ**it'tieren** compromise.

Kondens|at [kɔndɛn'zaːt] n (3) condensate; ˌ**ator** [ˌ'zaːtɔr] m (8[1]) condenser, capacitor; ℒ**ieren** [ˌ'ziːrən] condense; kondensierte Milch = ˌ**milch** [kɔn'dɛns-] f evaporated milk; ˌ**streifen** m vapo(u)r trail; ˌ**wasser** n condensed water.

Kondition [kɔndi'tsjoːn] f a. Sport: condition; ˌ**al** [ˌtsjo'naːl] gr. m conditional (mood); ˌ**alsatz** gr. m conditional clause; ˌ**s-training** n Sport: fitness training.

Konditor [kɔn'diːtɔr] m (8[1]) confectioner, pastry-cook; ˌ**ei** [ˌto'raɪ] f (16) confectioner's shop, pastry-shop; ˌ**waren** [ˌ'diːtɔr-] f/pl. confectionery products.

Konferenz [ˌfe'rɛnts] f (16) conference; ˌ**dolmetscher** m conference interpreter; ˌ**tisch** m conference table.

konferieren [ˌ'riːrən] confer (über acc. on).

Konfession [ˌfɛ'sjoːn] f confession; creed, denomination; ℒ**ell** [ˌjo'nɛl] denominational; ℒ**slos** [ˌ'sjoːns-]

undenominational; ˌ**sschule** f denominational school.

Konfetti [kɔn'fɛti] n (11[1]) confetti.

Konfirm|and [kɔnfir'mant] m (12), ˌ**andin** [ˌ'mandin] f (16[1]) confirmand, confirmee; ˌ**ation** [ˌma'tsjoːn] f confirmation; ℒ**ieren** [ˌ'miːrən] confirm.

konfiszieren [ˌfis'tsiːrən] confiscate.

Konfitüre [ˌfi'tyːrə] f (15) jam.

Konflikt [kɔn'flikt] m (3) conflict.

Konföderation [kɔnfødəra'tsjoːn] f (16) confederation.

konform [ˌ'fɔrm] concurring (dat. od. mit with); ~ gehen mit agree with.

Konfront|ation [ˌfrɔnta'tsjoːn] f confrontation; ℒ**ieren** [ˌ'tiːrən] confront (mit with).

konfus [ˌ'fuːs] (18[1]) confused; muddle-headed, F muddled.

Kongreß [ˌ'grɛs] m (4) congress, Am. a. convention; ˌ**halle** f Congress Hall; ˌ**mitglied** n Am. congressman.

kongru|ent [ˌgru'ɛnt] congruent; ℒ**'enz** [ˌts] f (16) congruity; ˌ**ieren** [ˌgru'iːrən] coincide.

König ['køːniç] m (3) king (a. Karten, Schach); ˌ**in** ['ˌgin] f queen (a. zo.); ℒ**lich** ['ˌkliç] royal; (hoheitsvoll) kingly; Insignien u. fig.: regal; '**ˌreich** n kingdom; rhet. realm; '**ˌshaus** n (royal) dynasty; '**ˌs-würde** f royal dignity.

konisch ['koːniʃ] conical.

Konju|gation gr. [kɔnjuga'tsjoːn] f (16) conjugation; ℒ'**gieren** conjugate.

Konjunkt|ion [kɔnjuŋk'tsjoːn] f (16) conjunction; ˌ**iv** ['ˌjuŋktiːf] m (3[1]) subjunctive (mood).

Konjunktur [ˌ'tuːr] ✝ f (16) business cycle; (Hoch ℒ) boom; (Tendenz, Lage) economic trend (od. situation); ˌ**aufschwung** m economic upswing; ˌ**barometer** n business barometer; ℒ**dämpfend** countercyclical; ℒ**ell** [ˌtu'rɛl] cyclical; economic; ˌ**politik** f policy for controlling the trade cycle; ˌ**rück-gang** m recession.

konkav [ˌ'kaːf] concave.

Konkordat [ˌkɔr'daːt] n (3[1]) concordat.

konkret [ˌ'kreːt] concrete.

Konkubin|at [ˌkubi'naːt] n (3)

concubinage; **~e** [⌣ku'biːnə] f concubine.

Konkurrent [⌣ku'rɛnt] m (12), **~in** f (16¹) competitor, (✝ a. business) rival.

Konkur'renz [⌣ts] f competition; (*sportliche Veranstaltung*) event; ✝ competitor(s pl.), (business) rival(s pl.); j-m ~ **machen** enter into competition with a p.; **2fähig** able to compete, competitive; **~geschäft** n rival firm; **~kampf** m competition; **~klausel** f restraint clause; **2los** without competition, unrival(l)ed; **~neid** m professional jealousy.

konkur'rieren compete (*mit* with; *um* for).

Konkurs [⌣'kurs] m (4) bankruptcy, failure; ~ **anmelden** file a bankruptcy petition; *in* ~ *gehen* go into bankruptcy; *in* ~ *geraten* go bankrupt; **~erklärung** f declaration of insolvency; **~masse** f bankrupt's estate; **~verfahren** n proceedings pl. in bankruptcy; **~verwalter** m trustee in bankruptcy, (official) receiver.

können ['kœnən] **1.** (30) be able; (*verstehen*) know, understand; *ich kann* I can; *er hätte es tun* ~ he could have done it; *es kann sein* it may be; *du kannst* (*darfst*) *hingehen* you may go (there); *er kann das* he knows how to do that; *er kann English* he knows English, he can speak English; *was kann ich dafür?* how can I help it?; s. dafür, umhin; **2.** **2** n (6) ability; skill, proficiency; (*Wissen*) knowledge; *nach bestem* ~ to the best of one's ability.

Könner ['kœnər] m (7) master, expert.

Konnossement [kɔnɔsə'mɛnt] n (3) bill of lading.

konnte ['kɔntə] pret. v. können.

konsequen|t [kɔnze'kvɛnt] consistent; **2z** [⌣ts] f (16) consistency; (*Folge*) consequence; *die* ~*en tragen* bear the consequences; *die* ~*en ziehen* draw the conclusions (*aus* from), *weitS.* act accordingly.

konservativ [⌣zɛrva'tiːf] conservative.

Konservatorium ♪ [⌣'toːrjum] n (9) conservatoire (*fr.*), academy of music, *Am.* conservatory.

Konserve [⌣'zɛrvə] f (15) preserve; **~n** pl. tinned (*bsd. Am.* canned)

food; **~nbüchse** f, **~ndose** f tin, *bsd. Am.* can; **~nfabrik** f canning factory, cannery; **~nmusik** F f canned music.

konservier|en [⌣'viːrən] preserve; **2ung** f preservation.

Konsist|enz [⌣zi'stɛnts] f (16) consistence; **~orium** [⌣'stoːrjum] n (9) consistory.

Konsol|e [⌣'zoːlə] f (15) console, bracket; **2i'dieren** consolidate.

Konsonant [kɔnzo'nant] m (12) consonant.

Konsort|e [⌣'zɔrtə] m (13) associate; (*Komplice*) a. accomplice; **~ium** [⌣tsjum] n (9) syndicate.

Konspir|ation [⌣spira'tsjoːn] f conspiracy; **2ieren** [⌣spi'riːrən] conspire, plot.

konstant [⌣'stant] constant; **2e** f constant (factor).

konstatieren [⌣sta'tiːrən] state; establish; 𝕤 diagnose.

Konstellation [⌣stɛla'tsjoːn] f constellation.

konsternieren [⌣stɛr'niːrən] dismay.

konstitu|ieren [⌣stitu'iːrən] constitute; *parl. sich* ~ *als* resolve itself into; **2tion** [⌣'tsjoːn] f constitution; **~tionell** [⌣tsjo'nɛl] constitutional.

konstruieren [⌣stru'iːrən] design, (*a. gr.*) construct.

Konstruk|teur [⌣k'tøːr] m (3¹) designer, design engineer; **~tion** [⌣'tsjoːn] f (16) design(ing), construction; **~ti'onsfehler** m constructional fault od. flaw; **2tiv** [⌣k-'tiːf] constructive.

Konsul ['kɔnzul] m (10) consul; **~ar...** [⌣zu'laːr] consular; **~at** [⌣-'laːt] n (3) consulate; **~ent** [⌣'lɛnt] m (12) legal adviser; **2'tieren** consult.

Konsum 1. [⌣'zuːm] m (3) consumption; **2.** ['⌣zuːm] s. **~geschäft**; **~ent** [⌣zu'mɛnt] m (12) consumer; **~genossenschaft** [⌣'zuːm-] f consumer co-operative; **~geschäft** n, **~laden** m co-operative store, F co-op; **~gesellschaft** f consumer society; **~güter** n/pl. consumer goods; **2ieren** [⌣zu'miːrən] consume; **~verein** [⌣'zuːm-] m co-operative society, F co-op; **~verhalten** n consumer behavio(u)r.

Kontakt [kɔn'takt] m (3) contact (*a. 𝓔*); ~ *aufnehmen* (*od. in* ~ *stehen*) *mit* *j-m* contact a p.; ~**abzug** *phot. m* contact print; ~**anzeige** *f* contact ad(vertisement); 2**freudig** sociable, being a good mixer; ~**gift** *n* contact poison; ~**linse** *f*, ~**schale** *f* contact lens; ~**person** *f bsd.* ⚓ contact.

Konter|admiral [ˈkɔntərʔatmiraːl] *m* rear-admiral; '~**bande** *f* contra-band; ~**fei** [~ˈfaɪ] *n* (11) portrait; '2**n** (29*) *Boxen u. fig.*: counter; ~**revolution** *f* counter-revolution.

Kontinent [ˈkɔntinɛnt] *m* (3) continent; 2**al** [~nɛnˈtaːl] continental.

Kontingent [~tiŋˈgɛnt] *n* (3) quota; ✕ contingent; 2**ieren** [~gɛnˈtiːrən] fix a quota on; ration.

kontinu·ierlich [~tinuˈʔiːrliç] continuous.

Konto [ˈkɔnto] *n* (9¹ *u.* 11) account; '~**auszug** *m* statement of account; '~**buch** *n* account-book; *Bank*: pass-book; ~**korrent** [~kɔˈrɛnt] *n* (3), ~**...** current account.

Kontor [kɔnˈtoːr] *n* (3¹) office; *fig. Schlag ins* ~ (bitter) blow; ~**ist** [~toˈrist] *m* (12) clerk; ~**istin** *f* (16¹) girl clerk.

kontra [ˈkɔntra] versus; *Kartenspiel:* 2 *geben* double; *s. Pro;* '2**baß** *m* double-bass; 2**hent** [~ˈhɛnt] *m* (12) 🖈 contracting party; *fig.* (*Gegner*) opponent.

Kontrakt [kɔnˈtrakt] *m* (3) contract; *s. Vertrag.*

'**Kontrapunkt** ♪ *m* counterpoint.

konträr [kɔnˈtrɛːr] contrary, opposite.

Kontrast [~ˈtrast] *m* (3²) contrast; 2**ieren** [~stiːrən] contrast; ~**mittel** ⚓ *n* contrast medium; 2**reich** *phot.* contrasty.

Kontroll·abschnitt [~ˈtrɔl-] *m* counterfoil, stub; ~**be·amte** *m*, ~**eur** [~ˈløːr] *m* controller; ~**e** *f* (15) control; (*Überwachung*) supervision; (*Prüfung*) check; *unter* ~ under control; *außer* ~ *geraten* get out of control; *die* ~ *verlieren über* (*acc.*) lose control of; 2**ieren** [~ˈliːrən] (*überwachen*) supervise; (*nachprüfen*) control, verify, check; (*beherrschen*) control; ~**kasse** *f* cash register; ~**lampe** *f* pilot lamp; ~**marke** *f* check; ~**nummer** *f* check number; ~**punkt** *m* check point; ~**schirm** *m* TV etc. monitor; ~**turm** *m* ✈ control tower; ~**uhr** *f* telltale (*od.* check-)clock.

Kontroverse [kɔntroˈvɛrzə] *f* (15) controversy.

Kontur [~ˈtuːr] *f* (16) contour, outline.

Konus [ˈkoːnus] *m* (14²) cone.

Konvention [kɔnvɛnˈtsjoːn] *f* (16) convention; ~**alstrafe** [~tsjoˈnaːl-] *f* penalty for non-fulfil(l)ment of a contract; 2**ell** [~ˈnɛl] conventional (*a.* ✕ *Waffe*).

Konversation [kɔnvɛrzaˈtsjoːn] *f* (16) conversation; ~**slexikon** *n* encyclop(a)edia.

konversieren [~ˈziːrən] converse.

konver|tierbar [kɔnvɛrˈtiːrbaːr] convertible; ~**tieren** convert.

konvex [~ˈvɛks] convex.

Konvoi [ˈkɔnvɔy] *m* (11) convoy.

Konzentr|at [~tsɛnˈtraːt] *n* (3) concentrate; ~**ation** [~traˈtsjoːn] *f* concentration; ~**ationslager** *n* concentration camp; 2**ieren** [~ˈtriːrən] concentrate; 2**isch** [~ˈtsɛntriʃ] concentric(ally *adv.*).

Konzept [kɔnˈtsɛpt] *n* (3) rough draft *od.* copy; *j-n aus dem* ~ *bringen* disconcert a p.; ~**ion** [~ˈtsjoːn] *f* (16) conception; ~**papier** *n* rough paper.

Konzern [~ˈtsɛrn] *m* (3¹) combine, group.

Konzert [~ˈtsɛrt] *n* (3) concert; (*Solovortrag*) recital; ~**flügel** *m* concert grand; 2**iert** [~tsɛrˈtiːrt]: ~**e** *Aktion* ♦, *pol.* concerted action; ~**saal** *m* concert-hall.

Konzession [kɔntsɛˈsjoːn] *f* (16) (*Zugeständnis*) concession; (*Genehmigung*) licen|ce, *Am.* -se; 2**ieren** [~joˈniːrən] license.

Konzil [kɔnˈtsiːl] *n* (3¹ *u.* 8²) council.

konziliant [~tsiliˈjant] conciliatory.

Kooperation [koˀopraˈtsjoːn] ♦ *f* co-operation.

Koordin|ate [koːʔɔrdiˈnaːtə] *f* (15) co-ordinate; 2**ieren** [~ˈniːrən] co-ordinate.

Köper [ˈkøːpər] *m* (7) twill.

Kopf [kɔpf] *m* (3⁸) head (*a. von Sachen*); (*oberer Teil*) top; (*Verstand*) brains *pl.*; (*Pfeifen*2) bowl; *ein fähiger* ~ *a clever fellow;* ~ *hoch!* cheer up!; *s. hängen, schlagen, setzen, zerbrechen, zusagen; e-n eigensinnigen* ~ *haben* be obstinate; *Tatsachen auf den* ~ *stellen* stand facts on their heads; *aus dem* ~ by heart; offhand; *mit bloßem* ~**e** bareheaded;

j-m über den ~ *wachsen* outgrow a p., *fig. Schwierigkeiten:* get beyond a p.; *von* ~ *bis Fuß* from head to foot; *j-n vor den* ~ *stoßen* offend; F *j-m (gehörig) den* ~ *waschen* give a p. a (good) dressing-down; '~-**arbeit** f brain-work; '~-**arbeiter** m brain-worker; '~**bahnhof** m terminus, terminal; rail head; '~**ball** m *Sport:* header; '~**bedeckung** f headgear, hat.

köpfen ['kœpfən] (25) behead, decapitate; *Fußball:* head.

'**Kopf**|-**ende** n head; '~**hörer** m headset, headphone; '~**hörer-anschluß** m headphone jack; '~**kissen** n pillow; '2**lastig** top-heavy; '2**los** headless; *fig.* panicky; *adv.* in panic; '~**nicken** n nod; '~**putz** m head--dress; '~**rechnen** n mental arithmetic; '~**salat** m (cabbage-)lettuce; '2**scheu** *Pferd:* restive, skittish; *P.:* nervous, alarmed; '~**schmerz** m *mst pl.* headache; ~**en haben** have a headache; '~**sprung** m header; '~**stand** m head-stand; '~**steinpflaster** n cobble-stone pavement; '~**steuer** f poll tax; '~**stimme** f head-voice, falsetto; '~**stütze** f headrest; *mot.* head restraint; '~**tuch** n head-scarf, kerchief; 2'-**über** head foremost, headlong; '~**zerbrechen** n: *j-m* ~ *machen* puzzle a p.

Kopie [ko'pi:] f (15) copy; *phot.* print; *(Zweitschrift)* duplicate.

Ko'pier|**buch** n copying-book; 2**en** copy (a. *fig.*); *phot.* print; ~**er** m (7), ~**gerät** n copier; ~**papier** *phot.* n printing-paper; ~**stift** m copying--pencil.

Kopilot ['ko:-] m copilot.

Koppel ['kɔpəl] **1.** f (15) (~ *Hunde*) leash; couple; (~ *Pferde*) string; *(Gehege)* enclosure, *(Pferde2)* paddock; **2.** ✗ n (7) belt; '2**n** (29) couple (a. ⊕, ♪); *Hunde:* leash; *Pferde:* string together; *Raumfahrt:* link up; '~**ung** f coupling; *Raumfahrt:* link-up.

Koproduktion ['ko:-] f joint production.

Koralle [ko'ralə] f (15) coral; ~**nbank** f coral-reef.

Koran [ko'rɑ:n] m (3¹) Koran.

Korb [kɔrp] m (3³) basket; *fig.* refusal; *fig. Hahn im* ~**e** cock of the walk; *e-n* ~ *bekommen* meet with a refusal; *j-m e-n* ~ *geben* give a p. a refusal; ~**ball** m netball; '~**flechter**

m, '~**macher** m basket-maker; '~**geflecht** n basket-work; '~**möbel** n/pl. wicker furniture; '~**wagen** m bassinet; '~**waren** f/pl. wickerwork sg.

Kord ['kɔrt] m (3 u. 11) corduroy.

Kordel ['kɔrdəl] f (15) cord.

Kordon [kɔr'dõ] m (11) cordon.

'**Kordsamt** m corduroy.

Korinth|**e** [ko'rintə] f (15) currant; ~**enkacker** F [~kakər] m (7) fusspot, *Am.* cookie pusher; ~**er** m, 2**isch** Corinthian.

Kork [kɔrk] m (3) cork; '2-**artig** corky; '~-**eiche** f cork-oak; '2**en** (25) cork; '~**(en)zieher** m cork--screw.

Korn [kɔrn] **1.** n (1² u. [= ~**arten**] 3) v. *Sand, Gold, Weizen usw.:* grain (a. *Getreide*); *am Gewehr:* front sight, bead; *der Münze:* standard, alloy; *aufs* ~ *nehmen* aim at (a. *fig.*); **2.** m (*Schnaps*) rye whisky; '~-**ähre** f ear of grain; '~**bau** m growing of grain; '~**blume** f corn-flower; '~**boden** m granary.

Körn|**chen** ['kœrnçən] n (6) grain (a. *fig. of truth, etc.*); '2**en** (25) granulate; *Leder:* grain; *in Zssgn* ...-**grained**.

'**Korn**|**feld** n grain-field; '~**kammer** f granary.

Körper ['kœrpər] m (7) body (a. v. *Farbe, Wein*); *phys.*, ♫ solid; '~**bau** m build, physique; '2**behindert** (*schwer* severely) disabled, handicapped; '~**chen** n (6) corpuscle, particle; '~**fülle** f corpulence; '~**geruch** m body odo(u)r; '~**größe** f height; '~**haltung** f bearing, posture; '~**kontakt** m physical contact; '~**kraft** f physical strength; '2**lich** bodily, physical; *(stofflich)* corporeal, material; '~**pflege** f care of the body, (personal) hygiene; '~**schaft** f corporation, corporate body; '~**teil** m part *(Glied:* member) of the body; '~**verletzung** f (r̃z *schwere* grievous) bodily harm; '~**wärme** f body heat.

Korporal ✗ [kɔrpo'rɑ:l] m (3¹) corporal; ~**schaft** ✗ f squad.

Korps [ko:r] n *inv.* corps; '~**geist** m esprit de corps (*fr.*).

Korpulenz [kɔrpu'lɛnts] f (16) corpulence, stoutness.

korrekt [kɔ'rɛkt] correct; 2**heit** f correctness; 2**or** [~ɔr] m (8¹) proof--reader.

Korrektur [~'tuːr] f (16) correction; typ. ~ lesen proof-read; **~bogen** typ. m page-proof; **~fahne** typ. f galley proof; **~zeichen** n proof-reader's mark.

Korrespon|dent [kɔrɛspɔn'dɛnt] m (12) correspondent; **~'dentenbericht** m correspondent's report; **~'denz** [~ts] f (16) correspondence; **2dieren** correspond.

Korridor ['kɔridoːr] m (3¹) corridor (a. pol.), passage(-way).

korrigieren [kɔri'giːrən] correct.

korrosionsfest ⊕ [kɔro'zjoːnsfɛst] corrosion-resistant.

kor|rumpieren [kɔrum'piːrən] corrupt; **~rupt** [~'rupt] corrupt; **2ruption** [~'tsjoːn] f (16) corruption.

Kors|e ['kɔrzə] m (12), **2isch** Corsican.

Korsett [kɔr'zɛt] n (3) corset.

Korvette ⚓ [kɔr'vɛtə] f (15) corvette; **~nkapitän** m lieutenant commander.

Koryphäe [kory'fɛːə] f (15) eminent authority, great expert.

kose|n ['koːzən] v/t. (27) caress, fondle; **2name** m pet name.

Kosmet|ik [kɔs'meːtik] f (16) cosmetics pl.; **~iker(in** f) m cosmetician; **2isch** cosmetic (a. 🐝).

kosm|isch ['kɔsmiʃ] cosmic(ally adv.); **2onaut** [~mo'naut] m (12) cosmonaut; **2opolit** [~mopo'liːt] m (13) cosmopolitan; **2os** ['~mɔs] (inv., o. pl.) cosmos.

Kost [kɔst] f (16) food; fare; (Ernährungsweise) diet; (Beköstigung) board; schmale ~ slender fare; 🐎 low diet; freie ~ free board; in ~ geben board out; in ~ sein bei board with; ~ und Logis board and lodging.

'kostbar costly, expensive; (wertvoll) precious; **'2keit** f expensiveness; preciousness; konkret: precious thing, pl. a. valuables.

'Kosten 1. pl. cost(s pl.), expenses; charges pl.; auf ~ (gen.) at the cost of, at a p.'s expense; auf seine ~ kommen get one's money's worth; **2.** 2 (26) Geld: cost; fig. a. take, require; **3.** 2 (schmecken) taste; **'~anschlag** m estimate; **'~anstieg** m rise (od. increase) in costs; **'~aufwand** m expenditure; **'2bewußt** cost-conscious; **'2deckend** cost--covering; **'~erstattung** f reimbursement of expenses; **'~frage** f question of cost (od. what it costs); **'2frei**, **'2los** free (of charge); **'2günstig** cost-effective; **'~-'Nutzen--Analyse** f cost-benefit analysis; **'2-pflichtig** with costs; **'~preis** m cost--price; **'~punkt** m (matter of) expense; **'~rechnung** f bill of costs; **'~senkung** f lowering of costs; **'~stelle** f cost cent|re, Am. -er; **'~voranschlag** m estimate.

Kost|gänger ['~gɛŋər] m (7) boarder; **'~geld** n board allowance; der Dienstbote: board-wages pl.

köstlich ['kœstliç] delicious; fig. exquisite; (lustig) delightful.

'Kost|probe f taste; fig. sample; **2spielig** ['~ʃpiːliç] expensive, costly.

Kostüm [kɔs'tyːm] n (3¹) costume, dress; (Jackenkleid) (two-piece) suit; **~ball** m, **~fest** n fancy-dress ball; **2ieren** [~ty'miːrən] (a. sich ~) dress up; **~probe** thea. f dress rehearsal.

Kot [koːt] m (3) (Schmutz) mud, mire; physiol. f(a)eces pl., excrement.

Kotelett [kɔt(ə)'lɛt] n (3¹) chop; **~en** pl. (Bart) side whiskers pl., Am. sideburns pl.

Köter ['køːtər] m (7) cur, tyke.

'Kotflügel mot. m mudguard, Am. fender.

'kotig muddy, miry.

kotzen P ['kɔtsən] (27) vomit, puke, spew; mot. splutter.

Krabbe ['krabə] f (15) shrimp; (Taschenkrebs) crab; fig. (Mädel) little monkey.

'krabbeln v/i. (29, sn) crawl; v/t. scratch softly.

Krach [krax] m (3) crash; (Lärm) row, din; (Streit) quarrel, F row; ⚡ crash, smash; ~ machen make (od. kick up) a row; **2en** (25) crash.

krächzen ['krɛçtsən] (27) croak.

Kraft [kraft] **1.** f (14¹) strength, (a. Natur2) force; (Macht; a. ⊕ od. fig.) power; (Energie) energy; (Rüstigkeit) vigo(u)r; (Wirksamkeit) efficacy; (Person) worker; aus eigner ~ by o.s.; in ~ sein (setzen, treten) be in (put into, come into) operation od. force, be (od. become) effective; außer ~ setzen annul, cancel, invalidate; außer ~ treten lapse, expire; s. best, vereinen; **2.** 2 (gen.) in (od. by) virtue of, on the strength of; **'~akt** m strong-man act; fig. feat; **'~anstrengung** f, **'~-**

aufwand *m* (strenuous) effort; '~-
ausdruck *m* swear-word, *pl.* strong
language; '~brühe *f* beef tea.
Kräfte|gleichgewicht ['krɛftə-] *n*
balance of power; '~verfall *m* loss of
strength.
'**Kraftfahr|er** *m* motorist, (car-)driv-
er; '~zeug *n* motor vehicle; '~zeug-
brief *m* (motor vehicle) registration
book; '~zeugsteuer *f* motor vehicle
tax.
'**Kraft|feld** *n* field of force; '~futter *n*
concentrated feed.
kräftig ['krɛftiç] strong, robust,
sturdy; (*mächtig*) powerful; (*tat~*)
vigorous, energetic; (*nahrhaft*) nourishing, substantial; *Farbton*: heavy,
deep; ~er *Fluch* round oath; ~en
['~igən] strengthen; *s. a.* stärken.
'**kraft|los** feeble, weak; ⚖ invalid;
'⚙**probe** *f* trial of strength; '⚙**rad** *n*
motor-cycle; '⚙**stoff** *m* fuel; '⚙**stoff-
anzeiger** *m* fuel gauge; '⚙**stoff-ein-
sparung** *f* fuel-saving; '⚙**stoff-ein-
spritzung** *f* fuel injection; '⚙**stoff-
verbrauch** *m* fuel consumption; '~-
strotzend vigorous; '⚙**verschwendung** *f* waste of energy; '~voll powerful, vigorous; '⚙**wagen** *m* (motor-)
car, *Am. a.* automobile; *allg.* motor
vehicle; '⚙**wagenpark** *m* fleet (of
motor vehicles); '⚙**werk** ⊕ *n* power
station *od.* plant; '⚙**wort** *n s.* Kraft-
ausdruck.
Kragen ['krɑːgən] *m* (6) collar; (*Umhang*) cape; *beim* ~ *packen* (seize by
the) collar; F *ihm platzte der* ~ he blew
his top; '~weite *f* collar size.
Kräh|e ['krɛːə] *f* (15) crow; '⚙**en**
(25) crow.
Krakeel F [kra'keːl] *m* (3¹) quarrel,
brawl; (*Lärm*) row; ⚙**en** (25) brawl;
make a row; '~er *m* brawler.
Kralle ['kralə] *f* (15) claw.
Kram [krɑːm] *m* (3³) (~waren) small
wares *pl.*; *weitS.* things *pl.*; *fig.*
stuff; (*Plunder*) rubbish; '⚙**en** (25)
rummage.
Krämer ['krɛːmər] *m* (7) shopkeeper.
'**Kramladen** *m* (small) shop.
Krampe ['krampə] *f* (15) cramp
(-iron), clamp; (*Draht*⚙) staple.
Krampf [krampf] *m* (3³) cramp,
spasm; *stärker*: convulsion; '~ader
f varicose vein; '⚙**haft** convulsive;
fig. frantic(ally *adv.*).
Kran [krɑːn] *m* (3³ *u.* 12) crane; '~-

führer *m* crane operator.
Kranich ['krɑːniç] *m* (3) crane.
krank [kraŋk] (18²) ill (*nur pred.*);
sonst sick; *stärker*: diseased (*bsd.
Körperteil*); ~ *schreiben* give *a p.* a
sick-certificate; *sich* ~ *melden* report (o.s.) sick; ~ *werden* fall ill *od.*
sick; '⚙**e** *m*, *f* (18) sick person,
patient.
kränkeln ['krɛŋkəln] (29) be sickly.
kranken ['kraŋkən] (25) suffer (*an
dat.* from).
kränken ['krɛŋkən] (25) hurt,
wound, offend.
'**Kranken|-anstalt** *f* hospital; '~-
auto *n* (motor) ambulance; '~bett *n*,
'~lager *n* sick-bed; '~geld *n* sick-
-benefit; '~gymnastik *f* remedial
gymnastics, physiotherapy; '~haus
n hospital; '~kasse *f* sick-fund;
'~kost *f* invalid diet; '~pflege *f*
nursing; '~pfleger *m* male nurse;
'~pflegerin *f*, '~schwester *f* nurse;
'~schein *m* (*Attest*) medical certificate; *der Krankenkasse*: medical
(card); '~stuhl *m* invalid-chair;
'~träger *m* stretcher-bearer; '~ver-
sicherung *f* health insurance; '~-
wagen *m* (motor) ambulance; '~-
wärter *m* male nurse; '~zimmer *n*
sick-room.
'**krankhaft** morbid; pathological.
'**Krankheit** *f* illness, sickness, disease; '~sbild *n* clinical picture; '~s-
erreger *m* pathogenic agent; '~s-er-
scheinung *f* symptom; '~sstoff *m*
morbid substance; '~s-überträger
(-in *f*) *m* carrier; '~s-urlaub *m* sick-
-leave.
'**kranklachen:** *sich* ~ split one's
sides with laughing.
'**kränklich** sickly; '⚙**keit** *f* sickli-
ness.
'**Kränkung** *f* insult, offen|ce, *Am.*
-se.
Kranz [krants] *m* (3² *u.* ³) garland,
wreath; △ cornice; *fig.* circle.
Kränz|chen ['krɛntsçən] *n* (6) small
wreath; *fig. bsd. v. Damen*: (ladies')
circle; '⚙**en** (27) wreathe, crown.
'**Kranz|gefäß** 🦴 *n* coronary artery;
'~niederlegung *f* laying of a wreath.
Krapfen ['krapfən] *m* (6) doughnut.
kraß [kras] crass, rank, gross.
Krater ['krɑːtər] *m* (7) crater.
'**Kratz|bürste** *f* scratch-brush; *fig.*
crosspatch; '⚙**bürstig** cross; '~e *f*
(15) scraper; (*Woll*⚙, *Hanf*⚙) card.

Krätze ['krɛtsə] f (15) itch, scabies.
'**Kratz-eisen** n scraper.
kratz|en ['kratsən] (27) scrape; (*schrammen*) scratch; '**2er** F m scratch.
Krätzer ['krɛtsər] m (7) rough wine.
krätzig ['krɛtsiç] itchy, scabious.
krau|en ['krauən] (25) tickle, scratch softly; '**~len** (25) v/t. = *krauen*; v/i. *Schwimmen*: crawl; '2**lschwimmen** n, '2**lstil** m crawl (-stroke).
kraus [kraus] frizzy, curly; *fig.* muddled; ~ *ziehen s.* krausen; 2**e** ['~zə] f (15) (*Rüsche*) frill, ruffle; (*Hals*2) ruff.
kräuseln ['krɔyzəln] v/t. u. refl. (29) curl, crimp; (*fälteln*) gather; *Wasser*: ripple, be ruffled; *Rauch*: curl up.
krausen ['krauzən] (27) *Stirn*: knit one's brow; *Nase*: wrinkle.
kraus|haarig ['kraus-] curly-haired; '2**kopf** m curly head.
Kraut [kraut] n (1²) herb; (*Pflanze*) plant; (*Kohl*) cabbage; *e-r Rübe*: top; F (*Tabak*) weed; *ins* ~ *schießen* run wild.
Kräuter|butter ['krɔytər-] f herb butter; '~**käse** m green cheese; '~**kunde** f herbal lore; '~**tee** m herb-tea.
Krawall [kra'val] m (3¹) riot, uproar; F rumpus; ~**macher** m rioter, rowdy.
Krawatte [kra'vatə] f (15) (neck-) tie; ~**nhalter** m tie clip.
kraxeln ['kraksəln] F (29, sn) climb.
kreat|iv [krea'ti:f] creative; 2**ivität** [~tivi'tɛːt] f (16) creativity; ~**ur** [~-'tuːr] f (16) creature.
Krebs [kreːps] m (4) crayfish, *Am.* crawfish; *ast.* Crab, Cancer; ⚕ cancer; '2-**artig** cancerous; '2-**erregend** ⚕ carcinogenic; '~**forschung** ⚕ f cancer research; '~**geschwulst** ⚕ f cancerous tumo(u)r; '2**krank** suffering from cancer; '~**schaden** m cancerous affection; *fig.* cancer; '~**schere** f crayfish claw; '~**vorsorge** ⚕ f cancer prevention; '~**vorsorge-untersuchung** ⚕ f cancer screening; '~**zelle** ⚕ f cancer(ous) cell.
kredenz|en [kre'dɛntsən] (27) present, serve.
Kredit 1. [kre'diːt] m (3) credit; *auf* ~ on credit; 2. ✝ ['kreːdit] n (11) credit; ~**bank** [kre'diːt-] f credit bank; ~**brief** m letter of credit; 2**fähig** cred-

it-worthy, sound; ~**geschäft** n credit-business (*od.* transaction); ~**gewerbe** n banking (business); ~**hai** F m loan shark.
kredi'tieren [~di-] v/t. *j-m et.*: credit a th. to a p.; v/i. (pass to the) credit.
Kre'dit|karte f credit card; ~**linie** f credit limit (*Am.* line); ~**markt** m loan market; ~**nachfrage** f credit demand; ~**seite** ['kreːdit-] f credit-side; 2**würdig** [kre'diːt-] s. kreditfähig.
Kreide ['kraɪdə] f (15) chalk; *bunte*: crayon; '2**n** chalk; '2'**weiß** as white as a sheet; '~**zeichnung** f crayon (*od.* chalk) drawing.
kreieren [kre'ʔiːrən] create.
Kreis [kraɪs] m (4) circle; (*Wirkungs*2) field, sphere; (*Ideen*2) range; *ast.* orbit; (*Gebiet*) district, *Am.* county; (*Personen*2) circle, *unterrichtete usw.* ~**e** quarters *pl.*; ⚡ circuit; *fig.* cycle; *s.* bewegen; '~-**abschnitt** m segment; '~-**ausschnitt** m sector; '~**bahn** f orbit; '~**bogen** m arc.
kreischen ['kraɪʃən] (27) scream; *stärker*: shriek (*a. Bremsen usw.*).
Kreisel ['kraɪzəl] m (7) (peg)top, whip(ping-)top; ⊕ gyroscope; '~**kompaß** m gyrocompass; '2**n** spin (the top); '~**pumpe** f rotary pump.
kreisen ['kraɪzən] (27) circle, revolve, rotate; *Blut, Geld usw.*: circulate.
kreis|förmig ['~s-] circular; '2**lauf** m circulation (*a.* ⚕); rotation; *der Jahreszeiten usw.*: succession; '2**lauf-störung** ⚕ f circulatory disturbance; '2**linie** f circular line; '~**rund** circular; '2**säge** f circular saw.
Kreißsaal ['kraɪs-] ⚕ m delivery room.
'**Kreis|stadt** f district town, *Am.* county seat; '~**verkehr** m roundabout (traffic), *Am.* traffic circle.
Krem [kreːm] f, F m (3) s. Creme.
Krematorium [krema'toːrjum] n (9) crematorium, *Am.* crematory.
Kreml ['krɛml] m the Kremlin.
Krempe ['krɛmpə] f (15) brim.
Krempel ['~pəl] m (7) stuff.
krepieren [kre'piːrən] (sn) *Tier*: perish; *Granate*: burst, explode.
Krepp [krɛp] m (11), '~**flor** m crêpe; *bsd. für Trauerkleidung*: crape; '~**gummi** m crêpe rubber; '~**papier** n crêpe paper; '~**sohle** f crêpe-rubber sole.

Kresse ♀ ['krɛsə] f (15) cress.
Kreuz [krɔyts] n (3²) cross; *Kartenspiel*: club(s *pl.*); ♪ sharp; *typ.* obelisk; *anat.* (small of the) back, loins *pl.*; *vom Pferd*: crupper, croup; *fig.* cross, affliction; *kreuz und quer* in all directions; *zu* ∼e *kriechen* truckle (*vor dat.* to); *über* ∼ crosswise; *s. schlagen*; '∼**band** n (postal) wrapper; *unter* ∼ *verschikken* send by book-post.
'**kreuzen** (27) v/t. cross; v/i. ⚓ cruise.
'**Kreuzer** m (7) kreutzer; ⚓ cruiser.
'**Kreuz|fahrer** m crusader; '∼**fahrt** f crusade; ⚓ cruise; '∼**feuer** n cross-fire; '♀**fi'del** as merry as a cricket; '∼**gang** m cloister; ♀igen ['∼igən] (25) crucify; '∼**igung** f crucifixion; '♀**lahm** broken-backed; *P.*: stiff-backed; '∼-**otter** f common viper; '∼**ritter** hist. m Knight of the Cross; '∼**schiff** n der Kirche: transept; '∼**schmerz** m lumbago; '∼**spinne** f cross (*od.* garden) spider; '∼**stich** m cross-stitch; '∼**ung** f crossing; v. Rassen: cross-breeding; (*Mischrasse*) cross-breed; '∼**verhör** n cross-examination; *ins* ∼ *nehmen* cross-examine; '∼**weg** m crossroads *pl.*; *eccl.* Way of the Cross; '♀**weise** crosswise; '∼**worträtsel** n crossword puzzle; '∼**zeichen** n sign of the cross; '∼**zug** m crusade.
'**kribb(e)lig** (*nervös*) fidgety, edgy.
kribbeln ['kribəln] (29) v/i. u. v/t. crawl; (*jucken*) itch.
Kricket ['krikət] n (11) cricket.
kriech|en ['kri:çən] (30, sn) creep (*a. ⚹*), crawl; *fig.* cringe (*vor dat.* to), fawn (on, upon); '♀**er** m (7), '♀**erin** f fig. toady, crawler; ♀**erei** [∼'raɪ] f (16) toadying; '∼**erisch** toadyish; '♀**pflanze** f creeper; '♀**spur** mot. f slow lane; '♀**tier** n reptile.
Krieg [kri:k] m (3) war; *im* ∼ at war; *s. führen, kalt.*
kriegen ['∼gən] F v/t. get.
'**Krieg|er** m (7) warrior; '∼**erdenkmal** n war memorial; '♀**erisch** (*kriegliebend*) warlike; (*zum Krieg gehörig*) martial; *fig.* belligerent; '∼**erwitwe** f war widow; ♀**führend** ['∼k-] belligerent.
Kriegs|-anleihe ['∼ks-] f war loan; '∼-**ausbruch** m outbreak of war; '∼**beil** n: fig. das ∼ begraben bury the hatchet; '∼**bericht-erstatter** m war correspondent; '♀**beschädigt** P.: war-disabled; '∼**beschädigte** m (18) war-disabled person; '∼**dienst** m war service; '∼**dienstverweigerer** m (7) conscientious objector; '∼-**erklärung** f declaration of war; '∼**flagge** f war-flag; '∼**flotte** f navy; '∼**freiwillige** m (18) war volunteer; '∼**führung** f warfare; '∼**fuß** m: mit j-m auf ∼ stehen be at daggers drawn with a p.; '∼**gebiet** n war zone; '∼**gefangene** m (18) prisoner of war, captive (*a. kriegsgefangen*); '∼**gefangenschaft** f (war) captivity; '∼**gericht** n court-martial; '∼**gewinnler** ['∼gəvinlər] m (7) war-profiteer; '∼**glück** n fortune of war; (*Erfolg*) military success; '∼**gott** m war-god; '∼**gräberfürsorge** f war-graves commission; '∼**hafen** m naval port; '∼**held** m war hero; '∼**hetze** f war-mongering; '∼**kamerad** m fellow soldier; '∼**kunst** f art of war; '∼**list** f stratagem; '∼**macht** f military power, forces *pl.*; '∼**marine** f navy; '∼-**opfer** n war victim; '∼-**pfad** m: auf (dem) ∼ on the warpath; '∼**rat** m council of war; '∼**recht** n martial law; '∼**schaden** m war damage; '∼**schauplatz** m theat|re (*Am.* -er) of war; '∼**schiff** n man-of-war, warship; '∼**schuld** f (*Verschulden*) war-guilt; (*Verschuldung*) war debt; '∼**teilnehmer** m combatant; *ehemaliger*: ex-serviceman, *Am.* veteran; '∼**treiber** m war-monger; '∼**verbrecher** m war criminal; '♀**versehrt** s. kriegsbeschädigt; '∼**zug** m expedition, campaign; '∼**zustand** m state of war.
Krimi ['kri:mi] F m (11) (crime) thriller.
Kriminal|be-amte [krimi'na:l-] m criminal investigator, detective; ∼**ist** [∼na'list] m (12) criminologist; *weitS.* detective; ♀**istisch** [∼na-'listiʃ] criminal investigation ...; *s. kriminell*; ∼**ität** [∼nali'tɛːt] f criminality, crime; ∼**kommissar** [∼-'na:l-] m detective superintendent; ∼**polizei** f criminal investigation police *od.* departemnt (*abbr.*C.I.D.); ∼**polizist** m s. Kriminalbeamte; ∼-**roman** m detective (*od.* crime) novel.
kriminell [∼'nɛl], ♀e m, f criminal.
krimpen ['krimpən] v/t. u. v/i. (sn) (25) ⊕ shrink.

Krimskrams ['krimskrams] *m inv.* junk, rubbish.

Kringel ['kriŋəl] *m* (7) curl; (*Gebäck*) cracknel.

Krinoline [krino'li:nə] *f* (15) crinoline.

Krippe ['kripə] *f* (15) crib, manger; (*Kinderheim*) crèche; (*Weihnachts*♀) (Christmas) crib.

Krise *f*, **Krisis** ['kri:zə, '♄zis] *f* (16²) crisis; **'kriseln:** *es kriselt* there is a crisis developing.

'**krisen|fest** stable; '♄**gebiet** *pol. n* crisis area (*od.* spot); '♄**herd** *pol. m* hot (*od.* trouble) spot; '♄**stab** *bsd. pol. m* crisis committee.

Kristall [kri'stal] *m* (3¹) crystal; ⚛ crystal(-glass); ♄i'**sieren** *v/t. u. v/i.* (25) crystallize.

Kriterium [kri'te:rium] *n* (9) criterion.

Kritik [kri'ti:k] *f* (16) criticism; (*Besprechung*) critique, review; *unter aller* ♄ beneath contempt; ♄ *üben an* (*dat.*) criticize.

Krit|iker ['kri:tikər] *m* (7) critic; ♄**iklos** [kri'ti:klo:s] uncritical, undiscriminating; ♄**isch** ['kri:tiʃ] critical (*gegenüber of*); (*entscheidend*) crucial; ♄**isieren** [kriti'zi:rən] criticize; (*besprechen*) review.

Krittel|ei [kritə'laɪ] *f* (16) fault-finding, cavil; '♄**n** (29) find fault (*an dat.* with), cavil (at).

'**Krittler** *m* (7), '♄**in** *f* fault-finder.

Kritzel|ei [kritsə'laɪ] *f* (16), '♄**n** (29) *v/i. u. v/t.* scribble, scrawl.

kroch [krɔx] *pret. v. kriechen.*

Krocket ['krɔket] *n* (11) croquet.

Krokant [kro'kant] *m* (6, *o. pl.*) croquant.

Krokodil [kroko'di:l] *n* (3) crocodile.

Krone ['kro:nə] *f* (15) crown (*a.* ♄, ⊕); (*Adels*♀) coronet.

krönen ['krø:nən] (25) crown (*zum König* king); *fig.* crown, top.

'**Kron|(en)korken** *m* crown cork; '♄**leuchter** *m* chandelier, light pendant; *mit Glasbehang*: lust|re, *Am.* -er; *elektrisch*: electrolier; '♄**prinz** *m* Crown Prince; *Brt.* Prince of Wales; '♄**prinzessin** *f* Crown Princess; *Brt.* Princess Royal.

'**Krönung** *f* coronation; *fig.* culmination.

'**Kronzeuge** *m* chief witness; *Brt.* Queen's (*Am.* state's) evidence.

Kropf [krɔpf] *m* (3³) crop; ♄

goit|re, *Am.* -er; '♄**ig** goitrous.

Kröte ['krø:tə] *f* (15) toad.

Krücke ['krykə] *f* (15) crutch; *des Croupiers*: rake.

'**Krückstock** *m* crutched stick.

Krug [kru:k] *m* (3³) jug; (*großer Ton*♀) pitcher; (*Trink*♀) mug; (*Bier-*♀) tankard; (*Wirtshaus*) inn.

Kruke ['kru:kə] *f* (15) stone jug.

Krüllschnitt ['kryl-] *m* (*Tabak*) crimp cut.

Krume ['kru:mə] *f* (15) crumb; (*Acker*♀) topsoil.

Krüm|chen ['kry:mçən] *n* (6), ♄**el** ['♄əl] *m* (7) small crumb; '♄**elig** crumbly; '♄**eln** *v/i.* (29) *u. v/t.* crumble.

krumm [krum] crooked (*a. contp. fig.*); bent; (*geschweift*) curved; ♄ *gehen* stoop; ♄ *sitzen* cower; ♄**beinig** ['♄baɪnıç] bow-legged.

krümm|en ['krymən] (*a. sich*) (25) crook, bend, curve; *sich* ♄ grow crooked; *fig.* cringe; *Fluß*: wind; *vor Schmerzen, Verlegenheit*: writhe with; *vor Lachen*: be doubled up with; '♄**er** ⊕ *m* bend, elbow.

'**krummnehmen:** *fig. et.* ♄ take a th. amiss.

'**Krümmung** *f* crookedness; curvature; *e-s Baches usw.*: bend, turn, winding.

Kruppe ['krupə] *f* (15) croup, crupper.

Krüppel ['krypəl] *m* (7) cripple; *zum* ♄ *machen* cripple; '♄**haft**, '♄**ig** crippled.

Kruste ['krustə] *f* (15) crust; '♄**n-tier** *n* crustacean.

'**krustig** crusty.

Kruzifix [kru:tsi'fıks] *n* (3²) crucifix.

Krypta ['krypta] *f* (16) crypt.

Kübel ['ky:bəl] *m* (7) bucket, pail.

Kubik|fuß [ku'bi:k-] *m* cubic foot; ♄**maß** *n* cubic measure; ♄**meter** *n, m* cubic met|re, *Am.* -er; ♄**wurzel** *f* cube (*od.* cubic) root.

kubisch ['ku:bıʃ] cubic.

Küche ['kyçə] *f* (15) kitchen; (*Kochart*) cuisine, cookery; *s. kalt.*

Kuchen ['ku:xən] *m* (6) cake; '♄**blech** *n* baking-tray.

'**Küchenchef** *m* chef (*fr.*).

'**Küchenform** *f* cake tin.

'**Küchen|gerät** *n*, '♄**geschirr** *n* kitchen utensils *pl.*; (*Töpferware*) crockery; '♄**herd** *m* (kitchen-)range, cooking stove; '♄**kräuter** *n/pl.* pot-herbs;

'**~meister** *m* headcook, chef (*fr.*); '**~personal** *n* kitchen staff; '**~schrank** *m* kitchen cabinet *od.* dresser; '**~wecker** *m* kitchen timer; '**~zettel** *m* menu.

Küchlein ['ky:çlaɪn] *n*, **Kü(c)ken** ['ky:kən] *n* (6) chick(en).

Kuckuck ['kukuk] *m* (3) cuckoo; F *zum* ~! damn it!

Kuddelmuddel F ['kudəl'mudəl] *m*, *n* muddle, jumble.

Kufe ['ku:fə] *f* (15) tub, vat; (*Schlitten*2) runner; ⚡ skid.

Küfer ['ky:fər] *m* (7) cooper; (*Kellermeister*) cellarman.

Kugel ['ku:gəl] *f* (15) ball; (*Gewehr*2) bullet; Å, *geogr.* sphere; *Sport*: weight, *Am.* shot; '**~abschnitt** *m* spherical segment; '2**fest**, '2**sicher** bullet-proof; '**~form** *f* spherical form; '2**förmig** globular, spherical; '**~gelenk** *n* anat. socket-joint; ⊕ ball-and-socket (joint); '**~kopf** *m* golf ball; '**~kopfschreibmaschine** *f* golf-ball typewriter; '**~lager** ⊕ *n* ball bearing; '2**n** *v/i.* (29, sn) roll (*a. v/t.*); *Spiel*: bowl; '2**rund** (as) round as a ball; '**~schreiber** *m* ball-point (pen), biro; '2**sicher** bullet-proof; '**~stoßen** *n* shot-put(ting).

Kuh [ku:] *f* (14[1]) cow; '**~-euter** *n* cow's udder; '**~fladen** *m* cow-pat; '**~handel** *m* fig. F contp. horse trading; '**~hirt** *m* cowherd.

kühl [ky:l] cool, fresh; fig. cool; *j-n* ~ *behandeln* give a p. the cold shoulder; '2**-anlage** *f* cold-storage plant; cooling plant; '2**-apparat** *m* refrigerator; '2**e** *f* (15) coolness; '**~en** *v/t. u. v/i.* (25) cool, chill.

'**Kühler** *m* (7) cooler; *mot.* radiator; '**~figur** *mot. f* radiator mascot; '**~haube** *mot. f* bonnet, *Am.* hood.

'**Kühl|haus** *n* cold-storage house; '**~mittel** *n* coolant, refrigerant; '**~raum** *m* cold-storage chamber; '**~schlange** *f* cooling pipe; '**~schrank** *m* refrigerator; '**~truhe** *f* (deep) freezer; '**~ung** *f* cooling; '**~wagen** *m* refrigerator truck; '**~wasser** *n* cooling water.

'**Kuh|milch** *f* cow's milk; '**~mist** *m* cow-dung.

kühn [ky:n] bold; (*keck*) daring, audacious; '2**heit** *f* boldness.

'**Kuh|pocken** *f/pl.* cow-pox; '**~stall** *m* cow-shed.

Küken ['ky:kən] *n* (6) chick (*a. fig.*).

kulan|t [ku'lant] obliging, fair; *Preis*: reasonable; 2**z** [~ts] *f* (16) fair dealing.

Kuli ['ku:li] *m* (11) coolie.

kulinarisch [kuli'na:rɪʃ] culinary.

Kulisse [ku'lisə] *f* (15) wing, scenery; fig. background; ⊕ link; *hinter den* ~n behind the scenes; **~nmaler** *m* scene-painter; **~nschieber** *m* scene-shifter.

kullern ['kulərn] *v/t. u. v/i.* (sn) (29) roll.

Kulmi|nations-punkt [kulmina-'tsjo:ns-] *m* culminating point; 2**nieren** culminate.

Kult [kult] *m* (3) cult.

kultivieren [kulti'vi:rən] cultivate.

Kultur [kul'tu:r] *f* (16) (*Anbau*) cultivation; fig. culture (*a.* 🐾), (**~gemeinschaft**, **~niveau**) *a.* civilization; **~beutel** *m* toilet bag; 2**ell** [~tu-'rɛl] cultural; **~film** [~'tu:r-] *m* educational film; **~geschichte** *f* history of civilization; **~land** *n bebautes*: cultivated (*od.* tilled) land; *weit S.* civilized nation; **~schande** *f* insult to good taste; **~seite** *f e-r Zeitung*: arts page; **~sprache** *f* civilized language; **~stufe** *f* stage of civilization; **~volk** *n* civilized race.

Kultus ['kultus] *m* (14[3]) cult, worship; '**~minister** *m* Minister of Education.

Kümmel ['kyməl] *m* (7) caraway (-seed); (*Likör*) kümmel; *echter* ~ ❀ cumin.

Kummer ['kumər] *m* (7, *o. pl.*) grief, (*Sorge*) worry; (*Unruhe*) trouble.

kümmer|lich ['kymərliç] miserable, wretched; (*wenig*) scant, meag|re, *Am.* -er; *sich* ~ *durchschlagen* eke out a miserable existence; '**~n** *v/t.* (29) (*angehen*) concern; *sich* ~ *um* mind, care about, concern o.s. about *od.* for; (*sorgen für*) see to; '2**nis** *f* (14[2]) affliction. '**kummervoll** sorrowful.

Kump|an [kum'pɑːn] *m* (3[1]) companion, fellow; **~el** ['~pəl] *m* (7) ⚒ pitman; F (*Freund*) chum, pal.

kund [kunt] known.

künd|bar ['kyntbɑːr] *Vertrag usw.*: terminable; *Anstellung*: subject to notice; *Kapital*: at call; *Anleihe*: redeemable; '**~en**: ~ *von* tell of.

Kund|e¹ ['kundə] *m* (13), '**~in** *f* (16[1])

customer (a. F fig.); '~e² f (15) news; (Kenntnis) knowledge; (Wissenschaft) science; '~enberatung f advisory service; '~endienst m service (to the customer); after--sales service; '~endienstberater (-in f) m (customer) service representative; '~enkreis m, '~enstamm m clientele, (regular) customers pl.; '~ennummer f client code.

'kund|geben make known; '2gebung f manifestation; (Erklärung) declaration; pol. meeting, rally; demonstration.

'kundig knowing, skil(l)ful; e-r S. ~ acquainted with, able to; (sachverständig) expert (gen. at, in).

kündig|en ['kyndigən] (25) v/i. give a p. notice od. warning (to quit); v/t. Kapital: call in; e-n Vertrag: give notice to terminate; die Wohnung ~ give notice to vacate; '2ung f (giving) notice; warning; (Entlassung) dismissal; '2ungsfrist f period of notice; vierteljährliche ~ three months' notice; '2ungsschutz m protection against unlawful dismissal; für Mieter: protection against unwarranted eviction.

kund|machen ['kunt-] make known; '2machung f publication.

'Kundschaft f clientele, custom(ers pl.); '2en (26) reconnoit|re, Am. -er; scout; '~er m (7) ✕ scout; (Spion) spy.

'kund|tun make known; '~werden (sn) become known.

künftig ['kynftiç] future, next week, year, etc.; in ~en Zeiten in times to come; adv. (a. '~hin) for the (od. in) future, henceforth.

Kunst [kunst] f (14¹) art; (Geschicklichkeit) skill; (Kniff) trick; s. bildend, frei, schön usw.; das ist keine ~! that's easy!; '~-akademie f academy of arts; '~-ausstellung f art exhibition; '~buch n art book; '~butter f (oleo)margarine; '~denkmal n monument of art; '~druck m art print(ing); '~druckpapier n art paper; '~dünger m artificial manure (od. fertilizer); '~-eisbahn f artificial ice-rink.

Künstelei [kynstə'laɪ] f (16) (Geziertheit) affectation.

'Kunst|fahrer(in f) m trick cyclist; '~faser f synthetic (od. man-made)

fib|re, Am. -er; '~fehler ♂ m malpractice; '2fertig skil(l)ful, skilled; '~fertigkeit f skill(fulness); '~flieger(in f) m stunt flyer; '~flug m aerobatics pl., stunt flying; '~flug... aerobatic; '~freund(in f) m lover of the fine arts; '~gärtner(in f) m horticulturist; landscape gardener; '~gegenstand m objet d'art (fr.); '2gemäß, '2gerecht expert, professional, workmanlike; '~geschichte f history of art; '2geschichtlich art--historical; '~gewerbe n arts and crafts pl.; applied art(s pl.); '~glied n artificial limb; '~griff m trick, knack, dodge; '~gummi n synthetic rubber; '~handel m trade in works of art; '~händler m art dealer; '~handlung f art dealer's shop; '~handwerk n s. Kunstgewerbe; '~harz n synthetic resin; '~herz n artificial heart; '~historiker m art historian; '~hochschule f art college; '~kenner(in f) m art connoisseur; '~lauf m Eissport: figure-skating; '~leder n imitation (od. artificial) leather.

Künstler ['kynstlər] m (7), '~in f (16¹) artist; ♪, thea. performer; '2isch artistic(ally adv.); '~name m stage--name; '~pech F n bad luck; '~viertel n Latin quarter.

'künstlich artificial; Fasern: synthetic, man-made; ~er Mond man--made moon.

'Kunst|liebhaber(in f) m art-lover; '2los artless; primitive; '~maler (-in f) m artist (painter); '~mappe f art folder; '~pause f dramatic pause; '2reich ingenious; '~reiter (-in f) m trick rider; '~sammlung f art collection; ~schätze ['~ʃɛtsə] m/pl. art treasures pl.; '~schule f school of arts; '~seide f artificial silk, rayon; '~sprache f artificial language; '~springen n fancy diving; '~sticke'rei f art needlework; '~stoff m plastic (material); '~stopfen n invisible mending; '~stück n trick, feat, bsd. Am. F stunt; (das ist kein) ~! anyone can do that!; '~tischler m cabinet--maker; '~turnen n gymnastics pl.; '~verlag m art publishers pl.; '2verständige m, f art expert; '2voll artistic, elaborate, ingenious; '~werk n work of art; '~wolle f artificial wool; '~wort n coined word.

kunterbunt ['kuntərbunt] *durcheinander*: higgledy-piggledy.
Kupfer ['kupfər] *n* (7) copper; *a.* =
~geld, ~stich; '~**barren** *m* copper
ingot; '~**blech** *n* sheet copper; '~
draht *m* copper wire; '~**druck** *m*
copperplate(-print[ing]); '~**geld** *n*
copper money; '2**haltig** containing
copper; '~**hütte** *f* copper-works *pl.*;
'2**ig** coppery; '~**münze** *f* copper
(coin); '2**n** of copper; copper ...;
'~**platte** *f* copperplate; '2**rot** copper-
-red; '~**schmied** *m* coppersmith; '~
stecher *m* copperplate engraver; '~
stich *m* copperplate (engraving); '~
vitriol *n* blue vitriol.
kupieren [ku'pi:rən] crop, dock.
Kupon [ku'põ] *m* (11) coupon; ✝
dividend-warrant.
Kuppe ['kupə] *f* (15) top; (*Nagel*2)
head.
Kuppel ['~l] *f* (15) cupola, dome;
~**ei** [~'laɪ] *f* (16) matchmaking; ♂
procuring; '2**n** (29) *v/t.* ⊕ couple;
v/i. mot. (de)clutch; (*Ehe vermitteln*)
match-make; *b.s.* pimp, procure.
Kuppler ['kuplər] *m* (7), '~**in** *f* (16[1])
matchmaker; *b.s.* procurer, *f* pro-
curess.
Kupplung ['kupluŋ] ⊕ *f* coupling;
mot. clutch; '~**spedal** *n* clutch
pedal; '~**sscheibe** *f* clutch disc.
Kur [ku:r] *f* (16) cure; e-e ~ *machen*
take a cure, take a course of
treatment.
Kür [ky:r] *f* (16) *Sport*: free exercise
(*swimming, etc.*).
Kurat|el [kura'tɛl] *f* (16) guardian-
ship; ~**or** [~'ra:tɔr] *m* (8[1]) guardian,
trustee; ~**orium** [~ra'to:rjum]. *n* (9)
board (of trustees).
Kurbel ['kurbəl] *f* (15) crank, handle; '~**gehäuse** ⊕ *n* crankcase; '2**n**
(29) crank; *Film*: shoot; '~**welle**
mot. f crankshaft.
Kürbis ['kyrbis] *m* (4[1]) gourd,
pumpkin; F (*Kopf*) nut.
küren ['ky:rən] (25) choose; elect.
Kur|fürst ['ku:r-] *m* elector; '~
fürstentum *n* (1[2]) electorate; '~
fürstin *f* (16[1]) electoress; '2**fürstlich** electoral; '~**gast** *m* visitor; '~
haus *n* kurhaus, spa house; '~
hotel *n* resort hotel.
Kurie ['ku:rjə] *f* (15) Curia.
Kurier [ku'ri:r] *m* (7) courier.
kurieren [ku'ri:rən] cure.
kurios [kur'jo:s] (18[1]) curious, odd.

Kuriosität [~jozi'tɛ:t] *f* (16) curiosity; (*Sammlungsstück*) curio(sity).
Kürlauf ['ky:rlauf] *m* (*Eislauf*) free
skating.
'**Kur|-ort** *m* health resort, spa; '~
park *m* spa gardens *pl.*; '~**pfuscher**
(-**in** *f*) *m* quack; '~**pfusche'rei** *f*
quackery.
Kurrentschrift [ku'rɛnt∫rift] *f* running hand.
Kurs [kurs] *m* (4) (*Umlauf*) currency;
(~*wert*) rate, price; (~*notierung*) quotation; ♏, ✈ *u. fig.* course; (*Lehrgang*) course; ♏ ~ *nehmen* (*a. fig.*)
head (*auf acc.* for); *außer* ~ *setzen*
withdraw from circulation; *in* ~ *setzen* circulate; *pol. harter* ~ hard line.
Kursaal ['ku:r-] *m* kursaal.
'**Kurs|-anstieg** *m* rise in rates (*od.*
prices); '~**bericht** *m* market report;
'~**buch** *n* railway (*Am.* railroad)
guide.
Kürschner ['kyr∫nər] *m* (7) furrier;
~**ei** [~'rai] *f* (16) furrier's trade;
(*Werkstatt*) furrier's shop; '~**ware** *f*
furs and skins *pl.*
'**Kursgewinn** *m* price gain.
kursieren [kur'zi:rən] *Geld*: circulate; *Gerücht*: *a.* go round.
Kursivschrift [~'zi:f∫rift] *f* italics *pl.*
'**Kurs|notierung** *f* quotation; '~
rückgang *m* fall in rates (*od.* prices);
'~**schwankung** *f* price fluctuation.
Kursus ['kurzus] *m* (14[3]) course.
'**Kurs|verlust** *m* loss on the ex-
change; '~**wechsel** *pol. m* change
of policy; '~**wert** *m* market-value;
'~**zettel** *m* exchange list.
Kurtaxe ['ku:r-] *f* visitors' tax.
Kür|turnen ['ky:r-] *n* free gymnas-
tics *pl.*; '~**übung** *f* free exercise.
Kurve ['kurvə] *f* (15) curve, bend;
'2**n** curve; ~ *um* drive round; '~**n-
bild** *n*, '~**nblatt** *n* graph; '2**nförmig** curved; '~**nlage** *f* cornering
(stability); '2**nreich** full of bends;
F curvaceous (*girl*); '~**nschreiber**
m plotter.
kurz [kurts] (18[2]) *Raum*: short; *Zeit,
Abfassung usw.*: short, brief; *adv.*
shortly; (*kurzum*) in short; ~ (*und
bündig*) concise(ly), brief(ly); ~ *angebunden sein* be curt; ~ *und gut*
in short, in a word; ~ *e Hose*
shorts *pl.*; ~ *vor* London short of
London; *binnen* ~*em* before long;
über ~ *oder lang* sooner or later;
seit ~*em* lately, recently; *vor* ~*em*

a little while ago; *mit ~en Worten* in a few words; *~ abweisen* be short with *a p.*; *um es ~ zu sagen* to cut a long story short; *s. abfertigen, binnen, fassen, über, Prozeß; zu ~ kommen* go short, come off a loser *od.* badly (*bei* in); *den kürzeren ziehen* get worsted; *~ und klein schlagen* smash to bits; '♀-**arbeit** *f* short time (work); '~-**arbeiten** be on short time; '♀-**arbeiter** *m* short--time worker; *~atmig* ['~ʔaːtmiç] asthmatic, short-winded.

Kürze ['kyrtsə] *f* (15) shortness; brevity; conciseness; *in ~* shortly, before long; *s. Würze*; '♀**en** (27) shorten; (*verringern*) cut; *s. a. abkürzen.*

Kürzel ['kyrtsəl] *n* (7) grammalogue.

'**kurz|er'hand** offhand; '♀**fassung** *f* abridged version; '♀**film** *m* short (film); '♀**form** *f* shortened form; '~**fristig** short-term; *adv.* at short notice; '♀**geschichte** *f* short story; '♀**haar**... short-hair; '~**halten**: *j-n ~* put a p. on short allowance; keep a p. short (*mit* of *money*); *~**lebig** ['~leːbiç] short-lived.

kürzlich ['kyrtsliç] recently, not long ago.

'**Kurz|meldung** *f*, '~**nachricht** *f* news flash, brief report; *pl.* news in brief; '♀**schließen** ≠ short-circuit; '~**schluß** ≠ *m* short circuit; *fig.* (*~handlung*) panic (action); '~**schrift** *f* shorthand(-writing), stenography; '♀**sichtig** short- (*Am.* near-)sighted; *fig.* short-sighted; '~**sichtigkeit** *f* short-sightedness (*a. fig.*); '~**streckenflug** *m* short--distance flight; '~**streckenläufer** *m* *Sport*: sprinter; '♀**treten** mark time (*a. fig.*); ♀'**um** in short.

'**Kürzung** *f* shortening; abridg(e)-ment; *v. Ausgaben*: cut.

'**Kurz|wahl** *teleph.* *f* abbreviated ad-

dress calling; '~**waren** *f/pl.* haberdashery *sg.*, *Am.* notions *pl.*; '~**warenhändler** *m* haberdasher; ♀**weg** ['~'vek] flatly; '~**weil** *f* (16, *o. pl.*) pastime, amusement; '♀**weilig** amusing, funny; '~**welle** ≠ *f* short wave; '~**wellen**... short-wave ...; '~-**zeitgedächtnis** *n* short-term memory; '~**zeitspeicher** *m* *Computer*: short-term storage.

kuschel|ig ['kuʃəliç] cosy, snug; '~**n** (29) *sich ~* snuggle up (*an acc.* to).

kuschen ['kuʃən] (27) *Hund*: lie down; *fig.* knuckle under.

Kusine [ku'ziːnə] *f* (15) (female) cousin.

Kuß [kus] *m* (4¹) kiss; '♀-**echt** kiss-proof.

küssen ['kysən] (28) kiss.

'**kuß|fest** kissproof; '♀**hand** *f*: *j-m eine ~ zuwerfen* blow a kiss to a p.; *fig. mit ~* with pleasure.

Küste ['kystə] *f* (15) coast, shore.

'**Küsten|gebiet** *n* coastal area; '~-**gewässer** *n* coastal waters *pl.*; '~-**handel** *m* coasting trade; '~**land** *n*, '~**strich** *m* coastland; '~**schiffahrt** *f* coastal shipping; '~**wache** *f* coast-guard.

Küster ['kystər] *m* (7) sexton; *~**ei** [~'raɪ] *f* (16) sexton's office.

Kutsch|e ['kutʃə] *f* (15) coach, carriage; *~**er** *m* (7) coachman, driver; ♀**ieren** [kut'ʃiːrən] *v/i.* (sn *u.* h.) drive (a coach); '~**pferd** *n* coach--horse.

Kutte ['kutə] *f* (15) cowl.

Kutteln ['kutəln] *f/pl.* tripe(s *pl.*) *sg.*

Kutter ⚓ ['kutər] *m* (7) cutter.

Kuvert [ku'vɛrt] *n* (3) envelope; (*Gedeck*) cover.

Kux ⚒ [kuks] *m* (3²) no-par (value) mining share.

Kybernetik [kybɛr'neːtik] *f* (16, *o. pl.*) cybernetics *sg.*

L

L [ɛl]., **l** *n inv.* L, l.

Lab [laːp] *n* (3) *zo.* rennet; *physiol.* (*Ferment*) rennin.

laben ['laːbən] (25) refresh; *fig. sich an e-m Anblick ~* feast one's eyes on.

labil [la'biːl] unstable (*a.* ⊕, ⚕); *phys.*, ⚗ labile; ♀**ität** [~bili'tɛːt] *f* (16) instability; *phys.*, ⚗ lability.

Labor [la'boːr] *F n* (11 *od.* 3¹) lab; *~**ant** [~bo'rant] *m* (12) laboratory

assistant; **~atorium** [~a'toːrjum] *n*
(9) laboratory; **⌀'ieren** ⚒ experiment; (*leiden*) ~ **an** (*dat.*) labo(u)r
under, suffer from.

Labsal ['laːpzaːl] *n* (3), **'Labung** *f*
refreshment; *fig.* comfort.

Labyrinth [laby'rint] *n* (3) labyrinth, maze.

Lache¹ F ['laxə] *f* (15) laugh(ter).

'Lache² *f* pool, puddle.

lächeln ['lɛçəln] **1.** *v/i.* (29) smile;
höhnisch ~ sneer (*beide: über acc.*
at); **2.** ⚢ *n* smile; *höhnisches* ~ sneer.

lachen ['laxən] **1.** *v/i.* (25) laugh
(*über acc.* at); *leise vor sich hin* ~
chuckle; *sich e-n Ast* ~ split one's
sides with laughing; *du hast gut*
~ F it's all very well for you to
laugh; *s. Fäustchen, biegen;* **2.** ⚢ *n*
(6) laugh, laughter; *das ist (nicht)*
zum ~ that's ridiculous (no laughing matter); *s. verbeißen, zumute.*

'Lacher *m* (7), **'~in** *f* (16¹) laugher;
die ~ *auf s-r Seite haben* have the
laugh on one's side.

lächerlich ['lɛçərliç] ridiculous,
laughable, absurd; (*unbedeutend*)
derisory; ~ *machen* ridicule; *sich* ~
machen make a fool (*od.* an ass)
of o.s.; **⌀keit** *f* ridiculousness.

lächern ['lɛçərn] (29): *es lächert*
mich it makes me laugh.

Lach|fältchen ['~fɛltçən] *n* (6)
laughter line; **'~gas** *n* laughing gas.

'lachhaft *s. lächerlich.*

'Lachkrampf *m* convulsive laughter, fit of laughter; *ich krieg 'nen* ~!
you'll have me in stitches!

Lachs [laks] *m* (4) salmon; **'~fang** *m*,
'~fischerei *f* salmon-fishing; **'⌀farben** salmon(-pink); **'~schinken** *m*
fillet of smoked ham.

Lack [lak] *m* (3) (gum-)lac; (*Firnis*)
varnish; (*gefärbter* ~) lacquer, enamel; *mot.* paintwork; **'~affe** F *m*
dandy; **'~arbeit(en** *pl.*) *f* lacquered
work; **'~farbe** *f* (*Klar⌀*) varnish;
(*Öl⌀*) paint; **'~firnis** *m* (lac) varnish;
⌀ieren [~'kiːrən] lacquer, varnish,
enamel; paint; F *fig.* dupe; **~ierer**
[~'kiːrər] *m* (7) varnisher; **'~leder** *n*
patent leather.

Lackmus ⚒ ['~mus] *m inv.* litmus.

'Lackschuh *m* patent (leather) shoe.

Lade ['laːdə] *f* (15) case; *für Wäsche*
usw.: press; (*Schub⌀*) drawer; **'~baum** *m* derrick; **'~fähigkeit** *f*
loading capacity; ⚓ tonnage; **'~-**

hemmung ✗ *f* jam, stoppage; **'~linie** ⚓ *f* loadline; **'~liste** *f* cargo
list; **'~meister** *m* chief-loader.

laden¹ ['laːdən] (30) load, lade;
Schußwaffe: load, (*a.* ⚡) charge; *als*
Fracht: freight; ⚖ cite, summon;
als Gast: invite, ask; *s. auf~.*

'Laden² *m* (6[¹]) ⚓ shop (*a.* F *fig.*),
store; (*Fenster⌀*) shutter; *s. schmeißen;* **~dieb** *m* shop-lifter; **~diebstahl** *m* shop-lifting; **'~gehilf|e** *m*,
-in *f* shop assistant, *Am.* sales-clerk; **'~geschäft** *n* shop, store;
'~hüter *m* drug in (*Am.* on) the
market, shelf warmer; **'~inhaber**
(**-in** *f*) *m* shopkeeper, *Am.* store-keeper; **'~kasse** *f* till; **'~kette** *f* chain
(of shops); **'~mädchen** *n* shop-girl;
'~preis *m* selling (*od.* retail) price;
'~schild *n* shop-sign; **'~schluß** *m*
closing time; **'~tisch** *m* counter.

'Lade|platz *m* loading-place; **'~rampe** *f* loading ramp *od.* platform;
'~raum *m* loading space; ⚓ hold;
Raumfähre: cargo bay; **'~schein** *m*
bill of lading.

lädieren [lɛ'diːrən] damage, injure.

'Ladung *f* (16) loading; *konkr.* load;
Güter: freight; ⚓ cargo; *e-r Schußwaffe od.* ⚡ charge; ⚖ summons.

Lafette [la'fɛtə] *f* (15) (gun) mount.

Laffe ['lafə] *m* (13) fop, puppy.

lag [laːk] *pret. v. liegen.*

Lage ['laːgə] *f* (15) position, (*a. fig.*)
situation; *e-s Hauses usw.:* site,
location; (*Zustand*) state, condition; *mißliche:* predicament, plight;
(*Haltung*) attitude; (*Schicht*) layer,
geol. a. stratum; *im Stapel:* tier; ⊕
ply; (*Runde Bier usw.*) round;
(*Papier⌀*) quire; ✗ (*Salve*) group,
volley; *nach* ~ *der Dinge* as matters
stand; *in der* ~ *sein zu tun* be in a
position to do; *j-n in die* ~ *versetzen,* et. *zu tun* enable a p. to do
a th.; **'~bericht** *m* situation report;
'~staffel *f Schwimmen:* medley relay; **'~plan** *m* site plan.

Lager ['laːgər] *n* (7) couch, bed; *geol.*
deposit; *e-s Wildes:* lair; ⊕ bearing;
(*Waren⌀*) stockroom, warehouse,
depot, (*Stapelplatz*) dump; (*Vorrat*)
stock(s *pl.*), store; ✗ *usw.* camp (*a.*
fig.); *auf* ~ ⚓ in stock, on hand, *fig.*
up one's sleeve; **'~arbeiter** *m* warehouseman, warehouser; **'~aufseher** *m* warehouseman; **'~bestellung**
f stock order; **'~bier** *n* lager (beer);

'~**buch** *n* stock-book; '~**fähigkeit** *f* shelf life; '~**feuer** *n* camp-fire; '~**gebühr** *f*, '~**geld** *n* storage, warehouse--rent; '~**haus** *n* warehouse; '⁀n *v/i.* (29, h., sn) lie down, rest (*a. sich* ~); ✗ (en)camp, be encamped; ✝ be stored; *v/t.* (h.) lay down; *Truppen:* (en)camp; *Waren:* store, warehouse; ⊕ mount in bearings, *Maschine:* seat; '~**platz** *m* ✝ depot, storage place; *s. Lagerstelle;* '~**raum** *m* store--room; '~**schein** *m* warehouse receipt; '~**stätte** *f*, '~**stelle** *f zum Ruhen:* resting-place; *zum Zelten:* camp site; *geol.* deposit; '~**ung** *f von Waren:* storage; *geol.* stratification; ⊕ (mounting in) bearings *pl.;* '~**verwalter** *m s. Lageraufseher;* '~**vorrat** *m* stock; '~**wirtschaft** *f* stockpiling.

'**Lageskizze** *f* sketch map.

Lagune [la'gu:nə] *f* (15) lagoon.

lahm [la:m] lame (*a. fig.*); '~**en** (25) be lame; limp.

lähmen ['lɛːmən] (25) lame, paralyse (*a. fig.*).

'**lahmlegen** *fig.* paralyse.

'**Lähmung** *f* laming, paralysing; *als Zustand:* paralysis.

Laib [laip] *m* (3) loaf.

Laich [laiç] *m* (3), '⁀en (25) spawn.

Laie ['laiə] *m* (13) layman (~*n pl.* laity); '~**nbruder** *m* lay brother; '⁀n**haft** amateurish, lay ...; '~**nmaler** *m* amateur painter; '~**npriester** *m* lay priest; '~**nschauspieler** *m* amateur actor.

Lakai [la'kai] *m* (12) lackey, footman; ⁀en**haft** [~ənhaft] servile.

Lake ['la:kə] *f* (15) brine, pickle.

Laken ['la:kən] *n* (6) sheet.

lakonisch [la'ko:niʃ] laconic(ally *adv.*).

Lakritze [la'kritsə] *f* (15) liquorice.

lallen ['lalən] (25) *v/i. u. v/t.* stammer.

Lamelle [la'mɛlə] *f* (15) lamella; ✗ lamina (*pl.* -ae), bar; ⊕ disc; *der Pilze:* gill.

lament|**ieren** [~'tiːrən] lament (*um* for; *über acc.* over); ⁀o [la'mento] *n* (11) lamentations *pl.*

Lametta [la'mɛta] *f inv. od. n* (9, *o. pl.*) silver tinsel.

Lamm [lam] *n* (1²) lamb; '~**braten** *m* roast lamb; '⁀en (25) lamb.

Lämm|**chen** ['lɛmçən] *n* (6) lambkin; ~**ergeier** ['lɛmər-] *m* lammergeier; '~**erwolke** *f* cirrus.

'**Lamm**|**fell** *n* lambskin; '~**fleisch**

n lamb; '⁀**fromm** (as) gentle as a lamb; meek.

Lampe ['lampə] *f* (15) lamp.

'**Lampen**|**fieber** *n* stage-fright; '~**licht** *n* lamplight; '~**schirm** *m* lamp-shade.

Lampion [lam'pjõ] *m* (11) Chinese lantern.

lancieren [lã'siːrən] launch (*a. fig.*).

Land [lant] *n* (1², *poet.* 3) (*Ggs. Wasser*) land; (*Ggs. Stadt*) country; (*Ackerboden*) land, ground, soil; (*Gebiet*) land, territory, country; (*Staat*) country; *pol. in Deutschland:* Land, Federal State; *ans* ~ ashore, on shore; *auf dem* ~e in the country; *außer* ~es abroad; *zu* ~e by land; '~**adel** *m* (landed) gentry; '~**arbeiter** *m* agricultural labo(u)rer, farm hand; ⁀**aus** ~ *landein* far and wide; '~**besitz** *m* landed property; '~**besitzer** *m* landed proprietor; '~**bewohner** *m* countryman.

Lande|-**anflug** ✈ ['landə-] *m* landing approach; '~**bahn** *f* runway, landing strip; '~**deck** *n* landing (*od.* flight) deck; '~-**erlaubnis** *f* landing permission; '~**feuer** *n* runway light.

land'-einwärts inland, up-country.

'**landen** *v/i.* (26, sn, h.) *u. v/t. allg.* land; (*ausschiffen*) *a.* disembark.

'**Land-enge** *f* neck of land, isthmus.

Landeplatz ['landə-] *m* quay, wharf; ✈ landing-ground *od.* -field.

Länderei [lɛndə'rai] *f* (16) landed property; *pl. a.* lands.

'**Länder**|**kampf** *m Sport:* international competition *od.* (*Spiel*) match; '~**kunde** *f* geography; '~**spiel** *n Sport:* international match.

'**Landes**|**beschreibung** *f* topography; '~**farben** *f/pl.* national colo(u)rs; '~**fürst** *m*, '~**herr** *m* sovereign; '~**grenze** *f* frontier, (national) boundary; '~**hoheit** *f* sovereignty; '~**kind** *n* native; '~**kirche** *f* national (*od.* regional) church; '~**meister** *m Sport:* national champion; '~**polizei** *f* state police; '~**regierung** *f* government; *in Deutschland:* Land government; '~**sprache** *f* language of a country, native (*od.* vernacular) language; '~**tracht** *f* national costume; '~**trauer** *f* public mourning; '⁀-**üblich** customary; '~**vater** *m* father of the people, sovereign; '~-**verrat** *m* treason; '~**verräter** *m* traitor to his country; '**~verteidigung** f national defen|ce, Am. -se; '**~verweisung** f expatriation; e-s Landfremden: deportation; '**⁀weit** nationwide.

'**Landeverbot** n landing prohibition.

'**Land|fahrzeug** n land vehicle; '**~flucht** f rural exodus; '**⁀flüchtig** fugitive; '**~friede(nsbruch)** m (breach of the) public peace; '**~gang** ⚓ m shore leave; '**~gemeinde** f rural community; '**~gericht** n district (od. superior) court; '**~gerichtsrat** m district court judge; '**⁀gestützt** ✗ Rakete: land-based; '**~gewinnung** f land reclamation; '**~gut** n country seat, estate; '**~haus** n country house; '**~jäger** m rural policeman; '**~junker** m (country) squire; '**~karte** f map; '**~kreis** m (rural) district; '**⁀läufig** current, common; '**~leben** n country life; '**~leute** pl. country-people.

ländlich ['lɛntliç] rural, country-like; (bäurisch) rustic.

'**Land|macht** f land power; '**~mann** m countryman, farmer; '**~messer** m surveyor; '**~partie** f outing, picnic; '**~pfarrer** m country parson; '**~plage** f public calamity; fig. (public) nuisance; '**~rat** m district president; '**~ratte** ⚓ f landlubber; '**~regen** m persistent rain; '**~rücken** m ridge of land.

'**Landschaft** f landscape (a. paint.), scenery; (Bezirk) region, district; '**⁀lich** provincial; Schönheit usw.: scenic; '**~sgärtner** m landscape gardener; '**~smaler(ei** f) m landscape-painter (-painting); '**~sschutz** m conservation.

Landser ✗ F ['lantsər] m (7) (common) soldier, Brt. Tommy (Atkins), Am. G.I. (Joe).

'**Landsitz** m country seat.

Lands|knecht ['~ts-] m mercenary; '**~mann** m fellow-countryman, compatriot; was für ein ~ sind Sie? what is your native country?; **~männin** ['~mɛnin] f fellow-countrywoman; '**~mannschaft** f expellee organization.

'**Land|spitze** f cape, promontory; '**~stadt** f country town; '**~straße** f highway; '**~streicher(in** f) m tramp; **~streiche'rei** f vagrancy; '**~streitkräfte** f/pl. land forces pl.; '**~strich** m tract of land, region; '**~tag** m diet.

Landung ['~duŋ] f (16) landing; ✈ a. touchdown; (Ausschiffung) disembarkation; '**~sbrücke** ⚓ f schwimmende: landing-stage; feste: jetty, pier.

'**Land-urlaub** ⚓ m shore leave.

'**Land|vermessung** f land surveying; '**~volk** n country-people; '**⁀wärts** landward; '**~wirt** m farmer; '**~wirtschaft** f agriculture, farming; (Anwesen) farm; '**⁀wirtschaftlich**, '**~wirtschafts...** agricultural; '**~zunge** f spit (of land).

lang [laŋ] (18²) long; P.: a. tall; F (entlang) along; drei Fuß ~ three feet long od. in length; e-e Woche ~ for a week; seit ~em for a long time (past); ~ und breit at (full od. great) length; die Zeit wird mir ~ time hangs heavy on my hands; ~ werden Tage: lengthen; er machte ein ~es Gesicht his face fell; ~ entbehrt (ersehnt) long missed (desired); s. lange, länger, Bank, Hand usw.; **~atmig** ['~ʔɑːtmiç] long-winded; '**~beinig** long-legged.

lange ['laŋə] adv. long, a long time; ~ her long ago; noch ~ nicht not for a long time yet, fig. not by a long way; es ist noch ~ nicht fertig it is not nearly ready; so ~ bis till, until.

Länge ['lɛŋə] f (15) length (a. zeitlich); (Größe) tallness; geogr., ast. longitude; fig. in e-m Buch usw.: tedious passage; auf die ~ in the long run; in die ~ ziehen draw out, protract, Erzählung: spin out; sich in die ~ ziehen drag on; der ~ nach (at) full length, lengthwise.

langen ['laŋən] (25) (genügen) suffice, be enough; ~ nach reach for; F j-m e-e ~ fetch a p. one; langt das? will that do?; damit lange ich e-e Woche this will last me a week.

'**Längen|(durch)schnitt** m longitudinal section; '**~grad** m degree of longitude; '**~kreis** m meridian; '**~maß** n long (od. linear) measure.

länger ['lɛŋər] longer; (ziemlich lang) prolonged; ~e Zeit (for) some time; nicht ~ not any longer.

'**Langeweile** f (15, o. pl., gen. u. dat. Lang[en]weile) tediousness, boredom, ennui (fr.); ~ haben be bored.

'**Lang|finger** F m thief; '**⁀fristig** [~'fristiç] long-term; ~ (gesehen) in the long run; '**⁀haarig** long-haired;

'⸞jährig of many years, of long standing; '⸞lauf m long-distance run(ning); (Schi⸞) cross-country skiing; '⸞läufer m (Schi⸞) cross-country skier; ⸞lebig ['⸞le:bɪç] long-lived; '⸞lebigkeit f longevity.
länglich ['lɛŋlɪç] longish, oblong; '⸞rund oval.
'Lang|mut f, ⸞mütigkeit ['⸞my:tɪç-kaɪt] f patience, forbearance; '⸞mütig patient, forbearing; ⸞ohrig ['⸞ʔo:rɪç] long-eared.
längs [lɛŋs] along; ⸞ der Küste along-shore; '⸞achse f longitudinal axis.
langsam ['laŋza:m] slow; '⸞keit f slowness.
Lang|schäfter ['⸞ʃɛftər] m/pl. (7) Wellingtons; '⸞schiff n e-r Kirche: nave; '⸞schläfer m late riser; '⸞spielplatte f long-play(ing) record.
Längs|schnitt ['lɛŋs-] m longitudinal section; ⸞seits ['⸞zaɪts] along-side.
längst [lɛŋst] long ago, long since; am ⸞en longest; ⸞ nicht so gut not nearly as good; '⸞ens at the latest.
'lang|stielig long-handled; Blume: long-stemmed; ⸞strecken... long-distance, ⚔ a. long-range; '⸞weile s. Langeweile; '⸞weilen bore; sich ⸞ feel bored; '⸞weilig tedious, boring, dull; ⸞e Person bore; '⸞welle f Radio: long wave; '⸞wellen... long-wave ...; ⸞wierig ['⸞vi:rɪç] protracted, lengthy; '⸞wierigkeit f lengthiness; '⸞zeitgedächtnis n long-term memory; '⸞zeitwirkung f long-range (od. long-term) effect.
Lanolin [lano'li:n] n lanolin.
Lanz|e ['lantsə] f (15) lance; fig. e-e ⸞ brechen für stand up for; ⸞ette [⸞'tsetə] f (15) lancet.
lapidar [lapi'da:r] lapidary.
Lappalie [la'pa:ljə] f (15) trifle.
Lappe ['lapə] m (13), 'Lappin f (16¹) Lapp; s. a. Lappländer.
Lappen ['lapən] m (6) anat., ⚕ lobe; (Flicken) patch; (Lumpen) rag; (Staub⸞) duster; s. Putz⸞, Wisch⸞.
läppern ['lɛpərn] (29): sich (zu-sammen)⸞ accumulate.
'lappig ragged; anat., ⚕ lobed; (schlaff) flabby.
läppisch ['lɛpɪʃ] foolish, silly.
Lappländer ['laplɛndər] m (7), '⸞in f (16¹) Laplander.
Lapsus ['lapsus] m (inv.) slip.

Lärche ⚕ ['lɛrçə] f (15) larch.
Lärm [lɛrm] m (3, o. pl.) noise; andauernder: din; ⸞ machen s. lär-men; ⸞ schlagen give the alarm; '⸞bekämpfung f noise abatement; '⸞en (25) make a noise; '⸞end noisy; '⸞pegel m noise level; '⸞schutz m noise prevention; '⸞schutzwall m noise barrier.
Larve ['larfə] f (15) mask; zo. larva.
las [la:s] pret. v. lesen.
lasch [laʃ] limp, lax; Getränk: insipid, (abgestanden) stale.
Lasche ['laʃə] f (15) ⊕ strap; am Schnürschuh: tongue.
Laser ['le:zər] m (7) laser; '⸞-abtast-strahl m laser scanner; '⸞drucker m typ. laser-printer; '⸞platte f laser-disc; '⸞plattenspieler m laser- (od. compact) disc player; '⸞strahl m laser beam; '⸞technik f laser tech-nology.
lassen ['lasən] (30) let; leave open, shut; (gestatten) allow, permit; (dulden) suffer; (veran⸞) make, cause to; (befehlen) order to; (ver-⸞, zurück⸞) leave; laßt uns gehen let us go; laß (das)! don't!; laß das Weinen! stop crying!; laß (es) gut sein! never mind!; ich kann es nicht ⸞ I cannot help (doing) it; sein Leben ⸞ für sacrifice (od. give) one's life for; von et. ⸞ desist from, give up; drucken ⸞ have ... printed; gehen ⸞ let ... go; von sich hören ⸞ send news; ich habe ihn dieses Buch lesen ⸞ I made him read this book; sich e-n Zahn ziehen ⸞ have a tooth drawn; das läßt sich denken I can imagine; es läßt sich nicht leugnen there is no denying (the fact); der Wein läßt sich trinken the wine is drinkable; s. Haar, hören, kommen, machen, Ruhe, sagen, übrig⸞, warten, Wasser, Zeit, zufrieden.
lässig ['lɛsɪç] lazy, indolent; (träge) sluggish; (nach⸞) negligent; (unbe-kümmert) nonchalant; '⸞keit f lazi-ness; negligence; nonchalance.
läßlich eccl. ['lɛslɪç] Sünde: venial.
Last [last] f (16) load, (Bürde) bur-den, (Gewicht) weight (alle a. fig.); (Tragfähigkeit) tonnage; (Fracht) cargo, freight; fig. weight, charge, trouble; 𝕤𝕥 ⸞ der Beweise weight of the evidence; ✝ zu ⸞en von to the debit of; zu ⸞en gehen von be chargeable to; j-m zur ⸞ fallen be

a burden to a p.; *j-m et. zur ~ legen* charge a p. with a th., blame a th. on a p.; '**~auto** *n s. Lastkraftwagen.* '**lasten** (26) *(auf dat.)* weigh (upon); '**♀-aufzug** *m* goods lift, *Am.* freight elevator; '**♀-ausgleich** *m* equalization of burdens; '**~frei** unencumbered; '**♀segler** ✈ *m* transport glider.

Laster[1] ['lastər] *n* (7) vice.

'**Laster**[2] *m* (7) *s. Lastkraftwagen.*

'**lasterhaft** depraved, wicked; '**♀ig-keit** *f* depravity.

'**Lasterhöhle** *f* den of vice.

läster|lich ['lεstər-] slanderous; *(gottes~)* blasphemous; F *(furchtbar)* F awful; '**♀maul** *n* slanderer, backbiter; '**~n** (29) *v/t. Gott:* blaspheme; *v/i. ~ über (acc.)* slander, defame; '**♀ung** *f* slander, calumny; blasphemy; '**♀zunge** *f* slanderous tongue; *s. Lästermaul.*

lästig ['lεstiç] troublesome, bothersome, annoying; *j-m ~ fallen (od. werden)* bother a p.; '**♀keit** *f* troublesomeness.

'**Last|kahn** *m* barge; '**~kraftwagen** *m* (motor) lorry, *Am.* truck; '**~pferd** *n* pack-horse; '**~schiff** *n* transport-ship; '**~schrift** ✝ *f (Anzeige)* debit note; *(Buchung)* debit item; '**~tier** *n* pack animal; '**~wagen** *m s. Lastkraftwagen;* '**~wagenfahrer** *m* lorry *(Am.* truck) driver; '**~zug** *m* truck trailer.

Lasur [la'zu:r] *f* glaze; ♀**blau** azure; **~lack** *m* transparent varnish; **~stein** *m* lapis lazuli.

Latein [la'taɪn] *n* (1, *o. pl.*) Latin; *fig. mit s-m ~ am Ende sein* be at one's wits' end; **~er** *m* (7) Latinist; ♀**isch** Latin.

latent [la'tεnt] latent.

Laterne [la'tεrnə] *f* (15) lantern, lamp; **~npfahl** *m* lamp-post.

Latinum [la'ti:num] *n* (9, *o. pl.*): *großes ~* A-level Latin; *kleines ~* O-level Latin.

Latrine [la'tri:nə] *f* (15) latrine.

Latsch|e ['la:tʃə] *f* (15) F *(Pantoffel)* slipper; ♀ dwarf pine; '**♀en** F (27, sn) shuffle (along); '**♀ig** shuffling, slouching; *fig.* slovenly.

Latte ['latə] *f* (15) lath; *Hochsprung, Fußball:* (cross-)bar; '**~nkiste** *f* crate; '**~nwerk** *n* lattice; '**~nzaun** *m* paling.

Lattich ['latiç] *m* (3) lettuce.

Latz [lats] *m* (3²) *(Brust♀)* bib; *(Hosen♀)* flap.

Lätzchen ['lεtsçən] *n* (6) *für Kinder:* bib.

'**Latzhose** *f* dungarees *pl.*

lau [lau] tepid, *(a. fig.)* lukewarm; *Luft, Wetter:* mild.

Laub [laup] *n* (3) foliage, leaves *pl.*; '**~baum** *m* deciduous tree.

Laube ['~bə] *f* (15) arbo(u)r; '**~ngang** *m* arcade; '**~nkolonie** *f* allotment gardens *pl.*

'**Laub|frosch** *m* tree-frog; '**~säge** *f* fretsaw; '**~säge-arbeit** *f* fretwork; '**~wald** *m* deciduous forest; '**~werk** *n* foliage.

Lauch ♀ [laux] *m* (3) leek.

Lauer ['lauər] *f* (15): *auf der ~ (liegen)* (lie) in wait; '**♀n** (29) lurk *(auf acc.* for); *~ auf e-e Gelegenheit:* watch for; *(j-m auflauern)* lie in wait for; '**♀nd** lurking; *Blick usw.:* lowering, *(argwöhnisch)* wary.

Lauf [lauf] *m* (3) run; *e-s Motors:* running; *(Strömung)* current; *(Fluß♀; Verlauf)* course; *(Wett♀)* race, *(Kurzstrecken♀)* dash; *(Gewehr♀)* barrel; *hunt.* leg; ♪ run; *s-n Gefühlen freien ~ lassen* give vent to one's feelings; *in vollem ~* in full career; *im ~e der Zeit* in course of time; *im ~e des Monats* in the course of; '**~bahn** *f* career; '**~bursche** *m* errand-boy.

'**laufen** (30, sn) run *(a.* ⊕); *(zu Fuß gehen)* walk; *(durch~)* Strecke: cover, do; *(fließen)* flow; *Zeit:* pass; *fig. (ab~)* go; *Gefäß:* leak, *(a. Nase)* run; *Film:* run, be on; *s. Gefahr, Geld, Schi, Sturm usw.; die Dinge ~ lassen* let things slide; '**~d** running; *Jahr, Preis, Ausgaben, Konto usw.:* current; *Wartung usw.:* regular; *Nummern:* consecutive, serial; *fig. (ständig)* continuous; ✝ *~en Monats* instant *(mst abbr.* inst.); *s. Band; auf dem ~en sein* be up to date, be fully informed; *j-n (sich) auf dem ~en halten* keep a p. (o.s.) informed *od.* F posted; '**~lassen** *j-n (straflos) ~* let a p. go.

Läufer ['lɔyfər] *m* (7) runner *(a.* '**~in** *f)*; *(Teppich)* runner *(a.* ♀); *(Treppen♀)* stair-carpet; *Schach:* bishop; *Fußball:* half(back); *s. Eis♀, Schi♀*; ⊕ *, a. e-r Turbine:* rotor.

Lauferei [laufə'raɪ] *f* running about. '**Lauf|feuer** *n fig.* wildfire; '**~fläche**

f e-s Radreifens: tread; '~**gewicht** *n* sliding weight.
'**läufig**, '**läufisch** in heat, ruttish.
'**Lauf|junge** *m s. Laufbursche*; '~**kran** ⊕ *m* travel(l)ing crane; '~**kunde** *m* chance customer; '~**masche** *f* ladder, *Am.* run; '~**paß** *m*: F j-m den ~ geben e-m Freund etc.: give a p. his marching orders; '~**planke** ⚓ *f* gangway, *Am. a.* gangplank; '~**ruhe** *f* ride quality; '~**schiene** *f* guide rail; '~**schritt** *m* jogtrot; ✕ double(quick) step; *im ~* at the double; ~**ställchen** ['~ʃtɛlçən] *n* (6) playpen; '~**steg** *m für Fußgänger*: foot-bridge; *s. Laufplanke*; '~**werk** ⊕ *n* drive mechanism; *Computer*: disk drive; '~**zeit** *f e-s Vertrags*: term; *e-s Wechsels*: currency; *e-s Films*: run; (*Brunftzeit*) rutting season; '~**zettel** *m* circular (letter); *für Akten*: interoffice slip.
Lauge ['laʊɡə] *f* (15) lye; ⊕ liquor; (*Salz*2) brine; (*Seifen*2) suds *pl.*
'**laugen** (25) ⚒ steep (in lye); '~**artig** alkaline; '2-**asche** *f* alkaline ashes *pl.*
'**Lauheit** *f* lukewarmness (*a. fig.*).
Laune ['laʊnə] *f* (15) humo(u)r; temper; mood; (*Grille*) caprice, fancy, whim; (*nicht*) *bei ~* in (out of) humo(u)r; *guter ~* in (high) spirits; (*nicht*) *in der ~ für* (not) in the mood for.
'**launenhaft** capricious, wayward; '2**igkeit** *f* capriciousness.
'**laun|ig** humorous; '~**isch** ill--humo(u)red; moody; *s. launenhaft.*
Laus [laʊs] *f* (14¹) louse (*pl.* lice); '~**bub(e)** *m s. Lausejunge*; '~**bubenstreich** *m* boy's prank; *fig.* mischievous trick.
Lausch-angriff ['laʊʃ-] *m* wiretapping (*od.* bugging) operation; '2**en** (27) listen (*dat. od. auf acc.* to); '~**er** *m* (7), '~**erin** *f* (16¹) listener; *b.s.* eavesdropper; '2**ig** snug, cosy; idyllic.
'**Lausejunge** *m* young scamp *od.* rascal.
lausen ['laʊzən] (27) louse.
lausig ['laʊziç] lousy (*a.* F *fig.*).
laut [laʊt] **1.** loud (*a. fig.*); (*lärmend*) noisy; (*hörbar*) audible; *so ~ man kann* at the top of one's voice; ~ *werden fig.* become public; **2.** *adv.* aloud, loud(ly); **3.** *prp.* according to; ✝ *as per*; **4.** 2 *m* (3) sound (*a. gr.*); *hunt.* ~ *geben* give tongue.

Laute ['laʊtə] *f* (15) lute.
'**lauten** (26) sound; *Inhalt, Worte*: run, read; ~ *auf* (*acc.*) *Paß usw.* be issued to, *Urteil*: be.
läuten ['lɔʏtən] (26) *v/i. u. v/t.* ring; *feierlich*: toll; *es läutet* the bell is ringing.
lauter ['laʊtər] (*rein*) pure (*a. fig.*); (*klar*) clear; *fig.* (*echt*) genuine; (*aufrichtig*) sincere; (*ehrlich*) honest; (*nichts als*) mere, nothing but; *aus ~ Neid* out of sheer envy; '2**keit** *f* purity; sincerity.
läuter|n ['lɔʏtərn] (29) purify; *Metall, Zucker*: refine; *Flüssigkeit*: clarify; *fig.* purify, chasten; '2**ung** *f* purification; refining; clarification; *fig.* chastening.
'**Läut(e)werk** *n* alarm.
'**Laut|gesetz** *n* phonetic law; '~**lehre** *f* phonetics *pl.*; phonology; '2**los** soundless, noiseless; (*still*) silent; (*stumm*) mute; *Stille*: hushed; '~**schrift** *f* phonetic transcription; '~**sprecher** *m* loudspeaker; '~**sprecher-anlage** *f*: *öffentliche ~* public-address system; '~**sprecherbox** *f* loudspeaker cabinet; '~**sprecherwagen** *m* loudspeaker van, *Am.* sound truck; '2**stark** vociferous, loud; '~**stärke** *f* sound intensity; loudness; *Radio*: sound-volume; ~**stärkeregler** ['~re:ɡlər] *m* volume control; '~**system** *n* phonetic system; '~**verschiebung** *f* shifting of consonants.
'**lauwarm** tepid, lukewarm (*a. fig.*).
Lava ['lɑːva] *f* (16²) lava.
Lavendel ⚘ [la'vɛndəl] *m* (7) lavender.
lavieren ⚓ [la'viːrən] (h., sn) tack; *fig.* manœuvre, *Am.* maneuver.
Lawine [la'viːnə] *f* (15) avalanche; 2**n-artig** like an avalanche; ~ *anwachsen* snowball; ~**ngefahr** *f* danger of avalanches; 2**nsicher** avalanche-proof.
lax [laks] lax, loose.
Lazarett [latsa'rɛt] *n* (3) (military) hospital; ~**schiff** *n* hospital ship.
leasen ['liːzən] (27) lease.
Leasing ['liːziŋ] *n* (11) leasing; '~**berater(in** *f*) *m* leasing consultant; '~**vertrag** *m* leasing contract.
Lebe'hoch *n* (11) cheer(s *pl.*).
'**Lebemann** *m* man about town; bon-vivant (*fr.*), playboy.
leben ['leːbən] **1.** (25) live (*a.* =

wohnen); (*am* ♀ *sein*) be alive; ~ *von e-r Nahrung, e-m Einkommen*: live (subsist) on, *von e-m Beruf*: make a living by; *j-n* (*hoch*)~ *lassen* cheer a p.; *bei Tisch*: drink a p.'s health; *s. wohl*; **2.** ♀ *n* (6) life; (*geschäftiges Treiben*) stir, activity, bustle; *Bild nach dem* ~ to the life; *am* ~ *bleiben* survive; *am* ~ *sein* be alive, live; *am* ~ *erhalten* keep alive; *ein neues* ~ *beginnen* turn over a new leaf; *ins* ~ *rufen* call into being, launch; F ~ *in die Bude bringen* jazz things up a bit; *mit dem* ~ *davonkommen* escape alive; *ums* ~ *kommen* lose one's life, be killed, perish; *sein* ~ *lang* all one's life; *s. lassen, schenken, Spiel*; '~**d** living (*a. Sprache*); live.

lebendig [le'bendiç] (*lebend*) living; *pred.* alive; (*flink*) quick; *fig. s. a.* **lebhaft**; *am* ~*em Leibe* alive; ♀**keit** *f s.* Lebhaftigkeit.

'**Lebens**|-**abend** *m* evening of life; '~-**ader** *fig. f* life-line; '~-**alter** *n* age; '~-**anschauung** *f* way of looking at life, outlook on life; '~-**arbeitszeit** *f* working life; '~-**art** *f* mode of living; (*Benehmen*) manners *pl.*, behavio(u)r; '~-**auffassung** *f* philosophy (of life); '~-**aufgabe** *f* mission (in life); *allg.* life-task; '~-**bedingungen** *f*|*pl.* living conditions; '♀**bedrohlich** life-threatening; '~**bedürfnisse** *n*|*pl.* necessaries of life; '~**bejahung** *f* acceptance of life; '~**beschreibung** *f* life, biography; '~**dauer** *f* duration of life; ⊕ (service) life; '~-**erfahrung** *f* experience of life; '~**erwartung** *f* life expectancy; '~**faden** *m* thread of life; '♀**fähig** ♂ *u. fig.* viable; '~**fähigkeit** *f* viability; '~**frage** *f* vital question; '♀**fremd** *s.* weltfremd; '~**freude** *f* joy of life, zest (for life); '~**gefahr** *f* danger to life; ~*!* danger of death!; *in* ~ *Kranker*: in a critical condition; *unter* ~ at the risk of one's life; '♀**gefährlich** dangerous (to life), perilous; '~**gefährt**|**e** *m*, ~**in** *f* life companion; '~**gemeinschaft** *f* community of life; '~**geschichte** *f* life-history, biography; '♀**groß** life-size(d); '~**größe** *f* life-size; *in* ~ life-sized, F *fig.* in the flesh; '~**haltung** *f* living (standard); '~**haltungskosten** *pl.* cost *sg.* of living; '~**interessen** *n*|*pl.* vital interests; '~**jahr** *n* year of

one's life; *im 20.* ~ at the age of twenty; '~**lang** vigo(u)r, vitality; '♀**länglich** for life (*a.* 🏴); lifelong; ~*e Rente* life annuity; '~**lauf** *m* course of life; *schriftlicher*: personal record, curriculum vitae; '~**licht** *n*: *j-m das* ~ *ausblasen* kill a p.; '♀**lustig** gay; '~**mittel** *n*|*pl.* food (-stuffs *pl.*), provisions *pl.*; '~**mittel-abteilung** *f* food department; '~**mittelgeschäft** *n* food shop (*bsd. Am.* store); '~**mittelvergiftung** *f* food poisoning; '♀**müde** weary (*od.* tired) of life; '♀**notwendig** vital, essential; '~**qualität** *f* quality of life; '~**raum** *m* living space; '~**regel** *f* rule of life; '~**retter** *m* life-saver; '~**standard** *m* standard of living, living standard; '~**stellung** *f* position in life, social status; *lebenslängliche*: permanent position; '~**stil** *m* life-style; '♀**treu** true to life; '♀-**überdrüssig** *s.* lebensmüde; '~**unterhalt** *m* livelihood, subsistence; *s-n* ~ *verdienen* earn one's living; '~**versicherung** *f* life insurance; '~**wandel** *m* life, conduct; '~**weise** *f* way of life; (*Gewohnheiten*) habits *pl.*; *gesunde* ~ regimen; '~**weisheit** *f* wordly wisdom; '~**werk** *n* life-work; '♀**wichtig** vital, essential; ~*e Organe pl.* vitals; '~**wille** *m* will to live; '~**zeichen** *n* sign of life; '~**zeit** *f* lifetime; *auf* ~ for life; '~**ziel** *n*, '~**zweck** *m* aim in life.

Leber ['le:bər] *f* (15) liver; *fig. frisch* (*od. frei*) *von der* ~ *weg* frankly, bluntly; '~**fleck** *m* mole; ~**käs** ['~kɛ:s] *m* liver loaf; '♀**krank**, '♀**leidend** suffering from a liver disease; '~**tran** *m* cod-liver oil; '~**wurst** *f* liver-sausage, *bsd. Am.* liverwurst.

'**Lebewesen** *n* living being, creature; *biol.* organism.

Lebe|'**wohl** *n* farewell.

leb|**haft** ['le:phaft] *allg.* lively (*a. fig. Nachfrage, Phantasie usw.*); (*munter*) vivacious; (*schwungvoll*) animated, active, brisk (*alle a.* ✝); *Farbe*: gay; *Erinnerung*: vivid; *Interesse*: keen; *Straße*: busy; '♀**haftigkeit** *f* liveliness; vivacity; vividness; briskness; '♀**kuchen** *m* gingerbread (cake); '~**los** lifeless; '♀**losigkeit** *f* lifelessness; '♀**tag** *m*: *mein*(*e*) ~(*e*) all my life; '♀**zeiten** *f*|*pl.*: *zu s-n* ~ in his lifetime.

lechzen ['lɛçtsən] (27) (*nach*) thirst, languish, yearn, pant (for).
Leck 1. *n* (3) leak; **2.** ⚥ leaky; ⚓ ~ **werden** spring a leak.
lecken[1] ['lɛkən] *v/t.* (25) lick; *Milch usw. auf*~: lap (up); '~[2] *v/i.* leak; *bsd.* ⚓ have (sprung) a leak.
lecker ['lɛkər] delicious; appetizing; '2**bissen** *m*, 2**ei** [~'raɪ] *f* (16) titbit (*a. fig.*), dainty; '2**maul** *n*, '2**mäulchen** *n*: *ein* ~ *sein* have a sweet tooth.
Leder ['le:dər] *n* (7) leather (*a. F Fußball*); *in* ~ *gebunden* calf-bound; '~**band** *m* (*Buch*) calf-binding; '~**fett** *n* dubbin(g); '~**handel** *m* leather trade; '~**händler** *m* dealer in leather; '~**hose** *f* leather trousers *pl.*; '2**n** leathern, (of) leather; *fig.* dull; '~**rücken** *m e-s Buches*: leather back; '~**waren** *f/pl.* leather goods *od.* articles; '~**zeug** *n* leathers *pl.*
ledig ['le:diç] (*unverheiratet*) single, unmarried; (*Kind*) illegitimate; (*unbesetzt*) vacant; *e-r S.*: free from, rid of; ~**lich** ['~dik-] solely, merely.
Lee ⚓ [le:] *f* (15, *o. pl.*) lee (side).
leer [le:r] *allg.* empty (*a. fig.*); (*unbesetzt*; *a. ausdruckslos*) vacant; (*eitel*) vain; (*unbeschrieben, unbespielt*) blank; ~*e Drohung* (~*es Versprechen*) empty threat (promise); ~*es Gerede* idle talk; *ins* 2*e gehen Schlag*: miss; *ins* 2*e starren* stare into vacancy; *mit* ~*en Händen* empty-handed; '2*e f* (15) void, emptiness (*a. fig.*); '~**en** (25) empty, clear; '2**formel** *f* empty phrase; '2**gut** ✝ *n* empties *pl.*; '2**kassette** *f* blank cassette; '2**lauf** *m* ✝ idling, idle motion; *mot.* (*Gang*) neutral (gear); *fig.* waste of energy; '~**laufen** ⊕ (run) idle; '~**stehend** *Wohnung*: unoccupied, vacant; '2**taste** *f Schreibmaschine*: space bar; '2**ung** *f* emptying; clearing; '2**zeile** *f* white line.
Lefzen ['lɛftsən] *f/pl.* flews *pl.*
legal [le'ga:l] legal; ~**isieren** [~gali'zi:rən] legalize; 2**ität** [~gali'tɛt] *f* (16, *o. pl.*) legality.
Legat [le'ga:t] **1.** *m* (12) legate; **2.** *n* (3) legacy.
Legation [lega'tsjo:n] *f* legation.
legen ['le:gən] (25) *v/t.* lay, place, put; *Eier, Fußboden, Teppich, Leitung usw.*: lay; *sich* (*hin*)~ lie down, *zu Bett*: *a.* go to bed; *Wind usw.*: calm down, abate; (*nachlassen*)

cease, fall; *sich auf e-e S.* ~ apply o.s. to, take up; *Karten* ~ tell fortunes by the cards; *s. Hand, Handwerk, Herz, Last, Mittel, Mund, Nachdruck, Wert 2., Zeug usw.*; *v/i. Huhn usw.*: lay (eggs).
legendär [legɛn'dɛ:r] legendary.
Legende [le'gɛndə] *f* (15) legend.
legier|en [le'gi:rən] alloy; *Kochkunst*: thicken; 2**ung** *f* alloy(ing).
Legion [le'gjo:n] *f* (16) legion; ~**är** [~gjo'nɛ:r] *m* (3[1]) legionary.
Legisla|tive [le:gisla'ti:və] *f* (15) legislative body *od.* power; ~**tur** [~'tu:r] *f* (16) legislature; ~**'turperiode** *f* legislative period.
legitim [legi'ti:m] legitimate; 2**ation** [~tima'tsjo:n] *f* (16) legitimation; 2**ati'onspapier** *n* paper of identification; ~**ieren** [~'mi:rən] legitimate; *sich* ~ prove one's identity; 2**ität** [~mi'tɛ:t] *f* (16) legitimacy.
Leh(e)n ['le:(ə)n] *n* (6) fief, fee; '~**smann** *m* (1[2], *pl. a.* Lehnsleute) vassal; '~**swesen** *n* feudalism.
Lehm [le:m] *m* (3) loam; (*Ton*) clay; (*Dreck*) mud; '~**boden** *m* loamy soil; '~**grube** *f* loam-pit; '2**ig** loamy (*schmutzig*) muddy.
Lehne ['le:nə] *f* (15) support; *e-s Stuhls*: arm, (*Rück*2) back; (*Abhang*) slope; '2**n** *v/t., v/i., v/refl.* (25) lean (*an acc.* against).
Lehns... *s.* Leh(e)n.
'**Lehn|sessel** *m*, '~**stuhl** *m* arm- (*od.* easy-)chair; '~**wort** *n* loan-word.
'**Lehr|-amt** *n* teachership; *höheres* ~ mastership; *univ.* professorship; '~**amts-anwärter** *m* trainee teacher; '~**anstalt** *f* educational establishment, school, academy; *höhere* ~ secondary school; '~**beruf** *m* teaching profession; '~**brief** *m* (apprentice's) indenture; '~**buch** *n* textbook.
Lehre ['le:rə] *f* **1.** (15) teaching, doctrine, theory; (*System*) system; (*Wissenschaft*) science; (*Richtschnur*) rule; (*moralische, Warnung*) lesson, warning; *e-r Fabel*: moral; (*Unterricht*) system of instruction; *des Lehrlings*: apprenticeship; *e-e* ~ *ziehen aus* take warning from; *in der* ~ *sein* be serving one's apprenticeship, *bei j-m* be apprenticed to a p.; *in die* ~ *geben od.* tun apprentice, article (*bei, zu* to); **2.** ⊕ ga(u)ge; (*Schablone*) pattern; ⚠

centering; '♀n (25) teach, instruct; (*dartun*) show.

Lehrer ['⁓rər] *m* (7) teacher, master, instructor; *s. Privat♀. Klassen♀, Hochschul♀*; '⁓**fortbildung** *f* in-service training of teachers; '⁓**in** *f* (16¹) (lady) teacher; '⁓**kollegium** *n*, '⁓**schaft** *f s.* Lehrkörper; '⁓**(innen)seminar** *n* teachers' training college; '⁓**verband** *m* teachers' professional association; '⁓**zimmer** *n* staff room.

'**Lehr|fach** *n* subject; *s.* Lehrberuf; '⁓**film** *m* instructional (*od.* training) film; '⁓**gang** *m* course (of instruction); '⁓**geld** *n* premium; *fig.* ⁓ zahlen pay dear for one's wisdom; '♀**haft** instructive; didactic; '⁓**herr** *m* master; '⁓**jahre** *n/pl.* (years *pl.* of) apprenticeship *sg.*; '⁓**junge** *m* apprentice; '⁓**körper** *m* teaching staff, (body of) teachers *pl.*; *univ.* professorate, *Am.* faculty; '⁓**kraft** *m* teacher; '⁓**ling** *m* (3¹) apprentice; '⁓**mädchen** *n* girl apprentice; '⁓**meister** *m* master; '⁓**methode** *f* teaching method; '⁓**mittel** *n/pl.* educational aids *pl. od.* material *sg.*; '⁓**plan** *m* (school) curriculum; '♀**reich** instructive; '⁓**saal** *m* lecture-room, class-room; '⁓**satz** *m* Å theorem; *eccl.* dogma; '⁓**stück** *thea. n* didactic play; '⁓**stuhl** *m* (professor's) chair, professorship; '⁓**vertrag** *m* articles *pl.* of apprenticeship; '⁓**werkstatt** *f* training workshop; '⁓**zeit** *f* apprenticeship.

Leib [laıp] *m* (1) body; (*Bauch*) belly; (*Mutter♀*) womb; (*Taille*) waist; *am ganzen* ⁓e all over; *mit* ⁓ *und Seele* (with) heart and soul; *zu* ⁓e *gehen od. rücken j-m*: attack, *e-r S.*: tackle; *sich j-n vom* ⁓e *halten* keep a p. at arm's length; ⁓ *und Leben* life and limb; *s. lebendig*; '⁓**arzt** *m* physician in ordinary (*j-s* to).

Leibchen ['⁓çən] *n* (6) bodice; (*Unter♀*) vest.

'**leib-eigen** in bondage; '♀e *m, f* serf, bond(wo)man; '♀**schaft** *f* serfdom, bondage.

Leibes|beschaffenheit ['laıbəs-] *f* constitution; (*Äußeres*) physique; '⁓**erbe(n** *pl.*) *m* issue; '⁓**frucht** *f* fetus; '⁓**kraft** *f* bodily strength; *aus Leibeskräften* with all one's might; '⁓**strafe** *f* corporal punishment; '⁓**übung** *f* physical exercise; *pl. a.* physical training; '⁓**visitation** *f* bodily search.

Leib|garde ['laıp-] *f* body-guard; '⁓**gericht** *n* favo(u)rite dish.

'**leibhaft**, '⁓**ig** corporeal, in person; (*wirklich*) real, true; *Ebenbild*: living (*image*); *der* ⁓e *Teufel* the devil incarnate.

leiblich ['laıp-] bodily (*a. adv.*), corporal; ⁓*es Wohl* physical well-being; ⁓*er Bruder* full brother; ⁓*er Vetter* cousin german; *ihr* ⁓*er Sohn* her own son.

'**Leib|rente** *f* life-annuity; '⁓**riemen** *m* belt; '⁓**schmerzen** *m/pl.* stomach-ache, colic; '⁓**speise** *f* favo(u)rite dish; '⁓**wache** *f* body-guard; '⁓**wäsche** *f* underwear.

Leiche ['laıçə] *f* (15) (dead) body, corpse; *über* ⁓n *gehen* stick at nothing.

'**Leichen|begängnis** *n* (4¹) funeral; '⁓**bestatter** *m* undertaker; '⁓**bittermiene** *f* woeful look *od.* countenance; '♀**blaß** deadly pale; '⁓**feier** *f* obsequies *pl.*; '⁓**frau** *f* layer-out; '⁓**geruch** *m* cadaverous smell; '⁓**gift** *n* ptomaine; '⁓**halle** *f* mortuary; '⁓**hemd** *n* shroud; '⁓**öffnung** *f* autopsy; '⁓**rede** *f* funeral oration; '⁓**schändung** *f* desecration of corpses; *sexuell*: necrophilia; '⁓**schau** *f* (coroner's) inquest; '⁓**schauhaus** *n* morgue; '⁓**starre** *f* rigor mortis; '⁓**stein** *m* tombstone; '⁓**träger** *m* (pall) bearer; '⁓**tuch** *n* shroud (*a. fig.*); '⁓**verbrennung** *f* cremation; '⁓**wagen** *m* hearse; '⁓**zug** *m* funeral procession.

Leichnam ['⁓nɑːm] *m* (3) (dead) body, corpse.

leicht [laıçt] light (*a. fig. Essen, Kleidung, Musik usw.*); ⊕ *a.* light-weight; (*nicht schwierig*) easy; (*gering*) slight; ☆ petty; *Tabak*: mild; *s. leichtfertig*; ⁓*er Sieg* walk-over; *s. Spiel*; ⁓ *entzündlich* highly inflammable; ⁓ *löslich* readily soluble; *et. auf die* ⁓e *Schulter nehmen* make light of a th.; ⁓*en Herzens* with a light heart; *es war ihm ein* ⁓es it was easy for him; *es ist* ⁓ *möglich* it is well possible; *das kann* ⁓ *passieren* it may easily happen; '♀**athlet** *m* (track and field) athlete; '♀**athletik** *f* (track and field) athletics *sg. u. pl.*, track and field sports *pl.*; '♀**bauweise** ⊕ *f* light-weight con-

struction; '⁓**beschwingt** jaunty; '⁓**blütig** sanguine.
'**Leichter** ⚓ m (7) lighter.
'**leicht|fertig** light, frivolous, flippant; (*unbedacht*) careless; '⁓**fertigkeit** f frivolity, flippancy, levity; carelessness; ⁓**füßig** ['⁓fy:sɪç] light--footed; '⁓**gewicht(ler** m) n *Boxen*: light-weight; '⁓**gläubig** credulous, gullible; '⁓**gläubigkeit** f credulity, gullibility; '⁓**hin** airily, casually; ⁓**igkeit** ['⁓ɪç-] f lightness; *fig. a.* easiness, ease, facility; *mit* ⁓ easily; ⁓**lebig** ['⁓le:bɪç] easy-going; '⁓**lohngruppe** f low-wage unskilled labo(u)r; '⁓**matrose** m ordinary seaman; '⁓**metall** n light metal; '⁓**nehmen:** es ⁓ take it easy; '⁓**sinn** m s.
leichtsinnig: light-mindedness, frivolity, levity; recklessness; carelessness; '⁓**sinnig** (*oberflächlich, gedankenlos*) light-minded, frivolous; (*unvorsichtig, fahrlässig*) reckless; (*sorglos*) careless; '⁓**verdaulich** easy to digest; '⁓**verderblich(e Waren** f/pl.) perishable(s pl.); '⁓**verständlich** easy to understand; '⁓**verwundet** lightly wounded.
leid [laɪt] **1.** es tut mir ⁓ (um) I am sorry (for), I regret; *du tust mir* ⁓ I am sorry for you; **2.** ♀ n (3, *o. pl.*) (*Schaden*) harm; (*Unrecht*) injury, wrong; (*Verletzung*) hurt; (*Betrübnis*) grief, sorrow; (*Unglück*) misfortune; *j-m ein* ⁓(s) *antun* harm a p., *sich*: lay hands upon o.s.; *j-m sein* ⁓ *klagen* pour out one's troubles to a p.
leiden ['laɪdən] **1.** (30) v/i. u. v/t. suffer (*an dat.* from); (*nicht*) ⁓ *mögen* (dis)like; **2.** ♀ n (6) suffering; ✠ complaint, disease; *das* ⁓ *Christi* The Passion; '⁓**d** suffering; *gr.* passive.
'**Leidenschaft** f passion; '♀**lich** passionate; (*glühend*) ardent; (*heftig*) vehement; '⁓**lichkeit** f passionateness; ardo(u)r; vehemence; '♀**slos** dispassionate.
'**Leidens|gefährte** m, '⁓**gefährtin** f fellow-sufferer; '⁓**geschichte** f tale of woe; *eccl.* Christ's Passion; '⁓**weg** m *eccl.* way of the cross; *fig.* (life of) suffering.
leid|er ['⁓dər] unfortunately; *int. alas!*; ⁓ *muß ich inf.* I'm (so) sorry to *inf.*; *ich muß* ⁓ *gehen* I am afraid I have to go; '⁓**ig** unpleasant; ⁓**lich**

['laɪt-] tolerable; (*halbwegs gut*) passable, fairly well; F (*a. adv.*) middling; '♀**tragende** m, f (18) mourner; *fig.* sufferer; '♀**wesen** n: zu meinem ⁓ to my regret.
Leier ['laɪər] f (15) lyre; *immer die alte* ⁓ always the same old story; '⁓**kasten** m barrel-organ; '⁓**(kasten)mann** m organ-grinder; '♀**n** (29) grind (out) a tune; *fig. s. herleiern*.
Leih|bibliothek ['laɪ-] f, '♀**en** (30) lend, Geld a. loan; (*entlehnen*) borrow (*von* from); s. *Ohr*; '⁓**gebühr** f lending fee(s *pl.*); '⁓**haus** n pawnshop; '⁓**wagen** m hired car; '♀**weise** as a loan.
Leim [laɪm] m (3) glue; *zum Steifen usw.*: size; (*Vogel♀*) bird-lime; F *aus dem* ⁓ *gehen* come apart; F *fig. auf den* ⁓ *gehen* fall into the trap; '♀**en** (25) glue; (*steifen*) size; '⁓**farbe** f glue-colo(u)r; (*Tempera*) distemper; '♀**ig** gluey, viscous.
Lein ♀ [laɪn] m (3) flax.
Leine ['laɪnə] f (15) line, cord; (*Hunde♀*) (dog-)lead, leash.
leinen ['⁓ən] **1.** linen; **2.** ♀ n (6) linen; '♀**band** m *Buchbinderei*: cloth binding; '♀**garn** n linen yarn; '♀**schuh** m canvas shoe; '♀**zeug** n linen (fabric).
'**Lein|kuchen** m linseed cake; '⁓**öl** n linseed-oil; '⁓**pfad** ⚓ m tow(ing)--path; '⁓**samen** m linseed; '⁓**wand** f linen (cloth); *paint.* canvas; *Film*: screen.
leise ['laɪzə] low, soft; (*sanft*) gentle; (*zart*) delicate; (*kaum merklich, gering*) slight, faint (*a. Ahnung, Zweifel usw.*); ⁓ *schlafen* be a light sleeper; *Radio*: ⁓ *stellen* tune down; '♀**treter** m (7) sneak, *Am. sl.* pussyfoot(er).
Leiste ['laɪstə] f (15) strip, ledge; ⚕ fillet; *anat.* groin.
'**leisten**[1] (26) do; (*verrichten*) perform (*a.* ⚙ *Vertrag*); (*erfüllen*) fulfil(l); (*vollbringen*) achieve; ⊕ do, perform; *Eid*: take; *Dienst*: render; *ich kann mir das* ⁓ I can afford it; *sich et.* ⁓ treat o.s. to a th.; *e-n Fehler usw.*: commit; s. *Beitrag, Bürgschaft, Folge, Gesellschaft, Verzicht, Vorschub, Widerstand usw.*
'**Leisten**[2] m (6) last; *nur zum Füllen*: shoe-tree; *alles über einen* ⁓ *schla-*

gen treat all alike; '**~bruch** ⚕ *m* inguinal hernia.

'**Leistung** *f allg.*, *a.* e-s *Künstlers od. Sportlers*, *a.* 🐎, ✈, ⊕: performance; (*Großtat*) achievement; (*Zahlung*) payment; (*Lieferung*) delivery; e-s *Arbeiters*: workmanship, *mengenmäßig*: output (*a.* e-r *Fabrik usw.*); ⚡ power, *aufgenommene*: input, *abgegebene*: output; piece of work; e-r *Fabrik usw.*: output; **~en** *pl.* e-s *Schülers*: achievements *pl.*; e-r *Versicherung*: benefit *sg.*; *erreichte* ~ result(s obtained); '**~sbewertung** *f* assessment and marking system; '**~sdruck** *m* pressure (to produce results); '⚙**sfähig** efficient; ⊕ *a.* powerful; *Fabrik usw.*: productive; '**~sfähigkeit** *f* efficiency, ⊕ *a.* power, capacity; '**~sgesellschaft** *f* performance-orientated society, Meritocracy; '**~slohn** *m* efficiency wage(s *pl.*); '⚙**s-orientiert** efficiency-oriented; '**~s-prinzip** *n* performance principle; '**~s-prüfung** *f* performance test; '**~sschwach** below average; weak (*a.* ✈); ⊕ low-performance; '⚙**sstark** above average; ⊕ powerful, high-performance; ✈ highly efficient; '⚙**ssteigernd** increasing efficiency (*od.* performance); '**~ssoll** *n* target; '**~ssport** *m* high-performance sport(s *pl.*); '**~s-wettbewerb** *m* efficiency contest; '**~szulage** *f* efficiency bonus.

'**Leit|artikel** *m* leading article, editorial; '**~bild** *n* model; ideal.

leiten ['laɪtən] (26) lead, guide, (*a. phys.*, ♪) conduct; ⊕ convey, pass, guide; (*anführen*) head (*a. Staat*); (*beaufsichtigen, verwalten*) direct, run, manage; *Sitzung usw.*: preside over; *Sport*: *das Spiel* ~ referee; *fig. sich von et.* ~ *lassen* be guided by; '**~d** leading; ✦ managerial, executive (*personnel, position*); *phys.* (*nicht*) ~ (non-)conductive.

'**Leiter**[1] *m* (7), '**~in** *f* (16[1]) leader, (*a. phys.*, ♪) conductor (*f* conductress), guide; e-r *Behörde, Abteilung*: head, chief; e-s *Unternehmens*: manager (*f* manageress); e-r *Schule*: head (master, *f* mistress), *bsd. Am.* principal; '**~**[2] *f* (16) ladder; '**~sprosse** *f* rung of a ladder; '**~wagen** *m* rack-wag(g)on.

'**Leit|faden** *m Buch*: textbook, manual, guide; '**~gedanke** *m* leading idea; '**~hammel** *m* bell-wether (*a. fig.*); '**~motiv** ♪ *n* leitmotiv; *fig.* key-note; '**~planke** *mot.* *f* guard rail; '**~satz** *m* thesis; '**~schiene** *f* guide rail; '**~spruch** *m* motto; '**~stern** *m* pole-star, lode-star (*a. fig.*); '**~strahl** *m* (guide) beam.

'**Leitung** *f* lead(ing), direction, guidance; (*Beaufsichtigung, Verwaltung*) management; *s.* An⚙; *phys.* conduction; *konkret*: ⚡ lead; *tel.* line; (*Gas-, Wasser-, Elektrizitäts⚙*) mains *pl.*; (*Rohr⚙*) pipeline; *unter s-r* ~ under his direction; *fig.* F e-e *lange* (*kurze*) ~ *haben* be slow (quick) in the uptake; '**~sdraht** *m* conducting wire; '**~srohr** *n* conduit-pipe; *für Gas, Wasser*: main; '**~svermögen** *n* conductivity; '**~swasser** *n* tap water.

'**Leit|währung** *f* reserve currency; '**~werk** ✈ *n* tail unit, control surfaces *pl.*, controls *pl.*

Lektion [lɛk'tsjoːn] *f* (16) lesson; (*a. fig.*) j-m e-e ~ *erteilen* teach a p. a lesson.

Lektor ['lɛktɔr] *m* (8[1]) lecturer; (*Verlags⚙*) editor; '**~at** [~to'raːt] *n* (3) editorial office.

Lektüre [lɛk'tyːrə] *f* (15) reading; (*Lesestoff*) reading matter.

Lende ['lɛndə] *f* (15) loin(s *pl.*); (*Hüfte*) haunch, hip.

'**Lenden|braten** *m* roast loin, *vom Rind*: sirloin, *Am.* porterhouse steak; '**~gegend** *f* lumbar region; '⚙**lahm** hip-shot; '**~schurz** *m* loincloth; '**~stück** *n* loin, *Am.* tenderloin.

lenk|bar ['lɛŋkbaːr] guidable; ⊕ man(o)euvrable; *fig. s.* **lenksam**; '**~es** *Luftschiff* dirigible (airship); '**~en** (25) direct, guide (*wenden*) turn; (*beherrschen*) rule; *Wagen*: drive, *mot. u.* ♣ *a.* steer; *Staat*: govern; *Aufmerksamkeit auf* (*acc.*) ~ *call ... to*; '⚙**er** *m* (7) ruler; e-s *Wagens*: driver; *s.* **Lenkstange**; '⚙**rad** *n* steering wheel; '**~sam** tractable, manageable; '⚙**samkeit** *f* docility, manageableness; '⚙**stange** *f Fahrrad*: handlebar; '⚙**ung** *mot. f* steering; '⚙**waffe** ✕ *f* guided missile.

Lenz [lɛnts] *m* (3[2]) spring; *fig.* prime (of life).

Leopard [leo'part] *m* (12) leopard.

Lepra ⚕ ['leːpra] *f inv.* leprosy.

Lerche ['lɛrçə] *f* (15) lark.

Lern|begierde [ˈlɛrn-] *f* desire to learn, studiousness; **ˈ2begierig** eager to learn, studious; **ˈ~computer** *m* educational computer; **ˈ2en** (25) learn; (*studieren*) study; *er lernt gut* he is an apt scholar; *s. gelernt*; **ˈ~er** *m* (7) learner; **ˈ~hilfe** *f* learning aid; **ˈ~maschine** *f* teaching machine; **ˈ~mittel** *n/pl.* teaching materials; **ˈ~mittelfreiheit** *f* free supply of teaching materials; **ˈ~prozeß** *psych. m* learning process; **ˈ~spiel** *n* educational game; **ˈ~ziel** *n* educational objective.

Lesart [ˈleːsˀɑːrt] *f* reading, version.

ˈlesbar legible; (*lesenswert*) readable.

Lesbe [ˈlɛsbə] F *f* (15), **Lesbierin** [ˈlɛsbiərin] *f* (16[1]) lesbian; *sl.* dike, dyke; **lesbisch** [ˈlɛsbiʃ] lesbian.

Lese [ˈleːzə] *f* (15) gathering; (*Ähren*2) gleaning; (*Wein*2) vintage; **ˈ~buch** *n* reading-book, reader; **ˈ~exemplar** *n* advance copy; **ˈ~gerät** *n für Mikrofilme*: viewer; **ˈ~halle** *f* public reading-room; **ˈ~lampe** *f* reading-lamp.

ˈlesen (30) **1.** read; *univ.* lecture (*über acc.* on); *die Messe ~* say mass; **2.** (*auflesen*) gather; ⚘ glean; (*aussuchen*) pick; **ˈ~swert** worth reading.

ˈLese|probe *thea. f* reading rehearsal; **ˈ~pult** *n* reading-desk.

ˈLeser *m* (7) reader.

ˈLese-ratte F *f* bookworm.

ˈLeser|brief *m* reader's letter; *Zeitungsrubrik*: *~e pl.* letters to the editor; **ˈ~kreis** *m*, **ˈ~schaft** *f* (circle of) readers *pl.*; **ˈ2lich** legible; **ˈ~zuschrift** *f s. Leserbrief.*

ˈLese|stoff *m* reading (matter); **ˈ~streifen** *m auf Warenpackung*: bar code; **ˈ~zeichen** *n* book-mark.

Lesung *parl.* [ˈleːzuŋ] *f*: *in dritter ~* on third reading.

Lethargie [letarˈgiː] *f* lethargy.

Lett|e [ˈlɛtə] *m* (13), **ˈ~in** *f* (16[1]), **ˈ2isch** Latvian.

Letter [ˈlɛtər] *f* (15) letter; *typ.* type.

letzt [lɛtst] last; (*endgültig*) final; ultimate; *der* (*die, das*) *~ere* (18) the latter; *das 2e* the end; *zu guter 2* last but not least, ultimately; *bis ins ~e prüfen* to the last detail; *bis zum ~en* to the last; *~e Nachrichten pl.* latest news; *~e Neuheit* latest novelty; *~en Endes* ultimately, after all; *~e Hand anlegen an* (*acc.*) put the finishing touches to; *s. Loch, Ölung, Schliff, Schrei*; **ˈ~ens, ˈ~hin** lately, the other day; **ˈ~willig** testamentary; *adv.* by will.

Leucht|boje [ˈlɔʏçt-] *f* light buoy; **ˈ~bombe** *f* flare (bomb); **ˈ~di·ode** *f* light-emitting diode; **ˈ~e** *f* (15) light, (*a. fig.*) lamp, (*a. fig., bsd. P.*) luminary; **ˈ2en[1]** (26) shine; (*strahlen*) *a.* beam; (*glänzen*) gleam, sparkle; *j-m ~* light a p.; **ˈ~en[2]** *n* (6) shining *etc.*; **ˈ2end** shining (*a. fig. Beispiel*), bright; *a. Uhrziffern usw.*: luminous; **ˈ~er** *m* (7) candlestick; *s. a. Kron2*; **ˈ~farbe** *f* luminous paint; **ˈ~feuer** *n* beacon; **ˈ~geschoß** *n* star shell; **ˈ~käfer** *m* glow-worm; **ˈ~kugel** *f* (signal) flare; **ˈ~mittel** *n* illuminant; **ˈ~patrone** *f* signal cartridge; **ˈ~pistole** ⚔ *f* Very pistol; **ˈ~rakete** *f* signal rocket; **ˈ~reklame** *f* luminous advertising; **ˈ~röhre** *f* fluorescent tube, luminous discharge lamp; **ˈ~schirm** *m* fluorescent screen; **ˈ~spurgeschoß** *n* tracer bullet; **ˈ~stoffröhre** *f* fluorescent tube; **ˈ~turm** *m* lighthouse; **ˈ~zifferblatt** *n* luminous dial.

leugnen [ˈlɔʏgnən] (26) deny; *nicht zu ~* undeniable.

Leukämie [lɔʏkɛˈmiː] *f* leuk(a)emia.

Leumund [ˈlɔʏmunt] *m* reputation; **ˈ~szeugnis** *n* certificate of good conduct.

Leute [ˈlɔʏtə] *pl.* (3) people *pl.*; *einzelne*: persons; ⚔ *u. pol.* men *pl.* (*a. Arbeiter*); *die ~ pl.* people *pl.*, the world *sg.*; *meine ~* (*Familie*) my people *pl.*, *Am.* my folks *pl.*; **ˈ~schinder** *m* martinet.

Leutnant [ˈlɔʏtnant] *m* (3[1] *u.* 11) ⚔ second lieutenant; ⚓ acting sublieutenant, *Am.* ensign; ✈ pilot officer, *Am.* second lieutenant.

leutselig [ˈ~zeːliç] affable; **ˈ2keit** *f* affability.

Levkoje ✿ [lɛfˈkoːjə] *f* (15) stock.

lexikalisch [lɛksiˈkɑːliʃ] lexical.

Lexikograph [~koˈgrɑːf] *m* (12) lexicographer; **~ie** [~graˈfiː] *f* (16) lexicography; **2isch** [~ˈgrɑːfiʃ] lexicographical.

Lexikon [ˈlɛksikɔn] *n* (9[1] *u.* [2]) dictionary; *s. a. Konversationslexikon.*

Libelle [liˈbɛlə] *f* (15) dragon-fly; ⊕ (water- *od.* spirit-)level.

liberal [libeˈrɑːl] liberal; **~isieren** [~raliˈziːrən] liberalize; **2ismus** [~raˈlismus] *m* (16, *o. pl.*) liberalism;

~**istisch** [~'listiʃ] liberalistic; 2**ität** [~li'tɛːt] f liberality.

Libretto [li'brɛto] ♪ n (11, pl. a. -tti) word-book.

Licht [liçt] **1.** n (1 u. 3) light; (leuchtender Körper) light; (Lampe) lamp; (Kerze) candle; hunt. ~er pl. eyes; fig. ans ~ bringen (kommen) bring (come) to light; bei ~e arbeiten usw. by lamp-light; j-m ein ~ aufstecken open a p.'s eyes (über acc. to); et. bei ~e besehen examine closely, als Redewendung: on closer inspection; das ~ der Welt erblicken be born; geh mir aus dem ~e! stand out of my light!; ~ machen strike a light, ⚡ put on the light; j-m (od. sich selbst) im ~e stehen stand in a p.'s (od. one's own) light; ein schlechtes ~ werfen auf (acc.) cast a reflection on; j-n hinter das ~ führen dupe a p.; jetzt geht mir ein ~ auf! now I see (daylight); s. Scheffel, schief; **2.** 2 light, bright; (durchsichtig) clear (a. ⊕ Höhe usw.); fig. lucid; ~er Augenblick bei Geisteskranken: lucid interval; ~er Tag broad daylight; ⊕ im 2en in the clear; '~anlage f lighting system; '~bad ♨ n solar bath, insolation; '2beständig fast to light; '~bild n photograph; '~bildervortrag m lantern-slide lecture; '2blau light blue; '~blick m bright spot; '~bogen ⚡ m arc; '2brechend opt. refractive; '~druck m phototype; '2durchlässig permeable to light, diaphanous; '2-echt fast to light; Stoff: non-fading; '2-empfindlich sensitive to light; phot. sensitive; ~ machen sensitize; '~empfindlichkeit f sensitivity; phot. speed.

'**lichten** (26) Wald: clear; Reihen, Haar: (a. sich) thin; s. Anker.

'**Lichter 1.** ⚓ m (7) lighter; **2.** pl. von Licht; 2**loh** [~'loː] blazing, in full blaze; ~ brennen be ablaze.

'**Licht|geschwindigkeit** f speed of light; '~griffel m Computer: light pen; '~hof m glass-roofed court; phot. halo; '~hupe mot. f headlamp flasher; '~jahr n light year; '~kegel m cone of light, beam (of light); '~maschine mot. f generator, dynamo; ~**meß** ['~mɛs] f Candlemas; '~-orgel f colo(u)r organ; ~**pausapparat** ['~paus-] m copying ap-

paratus; ~**pause** ['~pauzə] f photoprint; '~**pausverfahren** n photoprinting; '~**quelle** f light source; '~**reklame** f luminous advertising; '~**schacht** m light-well; '~**schalter** m light switch; '2**scheu** shunning the light; '~**schranke** f photoelectric barrier; '~**schutzfaktor** m protection factor; '~**seite** f fig. bright side; '~**spielhaus** n, '~**spieltheater** n cinema, Am. motion-picture theater; '~**stärke** f luminous intensity; phot. speed; '~**strahl** m ray, beam; '2**undurchlässig** opaque; '~**ung** f clearing.

Lid [liːt] n (1) eyelid; '~**schatten** m eye-shadow.

lieb [liːp] dear; (zärtlich geliebt) beloved; (nett) nice, kind; Kind: good; der ~e Gott the good God: es ist mir ~, daß I am glad that; das habe ich am ~sten I like that best of all; '~-äugeln ogle (mit j-m od. et. a p., a th.); flirt (with an idea); 2**chen** n (6) love, sweetheart.

Liebe ['liːbə] f (15) love (zu a. for); christliche ~ charity; aus ~ for love; aus ~ zu for the love of; 2**bedürftig** starved for love; ~**dienerei** [~diːnə'raɪ] f (16) obsequiousness, toadyism; ~**lei** [~'laɪ] f (16) flirtation.

liebeln ['liːbəln] (29) flirt, dally.

'**lieben** v/t. (25) love (a. v/i.); (gern mögen) be fond of, like; ~d gern gladly; 2**de** m, f (18) lover.

'**liebens|wert** lovable, amiable; '~**würdig** kind, obliging; s. a. liebenswert; '2**würdigkeit** f amiability; kindness.

'**lieber** dearer; adv. (eher) rather, sooner; ~ haben prefer, like better.

'**Liebes|-abenteuer** n, '~**affäre** f love-adventure, love-affair; '~**brief** m love-letter; '~**dienst** m favo(u)r, kindness; j-m e-n ~ erweisen do a p. a good turn; '~**-erklärung** f declaration of love; '~**-erlebnis** n romance; intimes: sex adventure; '~**gabe** f charitable gift; '~**gedicht** n love-poem; '~**geschichte** f love-story; '~**heirat** f love-match; '2**krank** love-sick; '~**kummer** m lover's grief; '~**leben** n love-life; '~**lied** n love-song; '~**paar** n (pair of) lovers pl., (courting) couple; '~**verhältnis** n love--affair; '~**werben** n wooing; '~**werk** n work of charity.

'**liebevoll** loving, affectionate.
lieb|gewinnen ['li:p-] get (od. grow) fond of, take a liking (od. fancy) to; '**~haben** love, be fond of; '**Ⴍhaber(in** f) m (7) lover; Kunst usw.: amateur; thea. erste ~ m leading man (od. f lady); thea. jugendliche ~ m juvenile lead; **Ⴍhaberei** [~'raɪ] f (16) (für) fondness (of), fancy (for, to); fig. (Steckenpferd) hobby; '**Ⴍhaberpreis** m fancy price; '**Ⴍhaberstück** n collector's item; '**Ⴍhabertheater** n private (od. amateur) theat|re, Am. -er; '**Ⴍhaberwert** m collector's value; '**~kosen** caress, fondle; '**Ⴍkosung** f caress.
lieblich ['li:plɪç] lovely, charming, sweet; Wein: mellow; '**Ⴍkeit** f loveliness.
Liebling ['li:plɪŋ] m (3¹) darling, favo(u)rite; bsd. Kind od. Tier: pet; bsd. als Anrede: darling; '**~s...** favo(u)rite.
'**lieb|los** unkind; weitS. careless; '**Ⴍlosigkeit** f unkindness; '**~reich** loving, tender; (freundlich) kind; '**Ⴍreiz** m charm, grace; '**~reizend** charming, sweet; '**Ⴍschaft** f (16) love(-affair); '**Ⴍste** m, f sweetheart, m a. lover, f a. love; Anrede: (my) darling.
Lied [li:t] n (1) song; (Weise) air, tune; geistliches ~ hymn; es ist das alte ~ it's always the same old story.
Lieder|-abend ['~dər-] m lieder recital; '**~buch** n song-book; '**~kranz** m choral society.
liederlich ['li:dərlɪç] loose, dissolute; (unordentlich) slovenly; '**Ⴍkeit** f dissoluteness; slovenliness.
'**Liedermacher** m (7) singer-song-writer.
lief [li:f] pret. v. laufen.
Lieferant [li:fə'rant] m (12) supplier; laut Vertrag: contractor; bsd. für Lebensmittel: caterer, purveyor.
Liefer|-auto ['li:fər-] n delivery-van, Am. delivery truck; '**Ⴍbar** deliverable; (vorrätig) available; '**~frist** f term of delivery; '**Ⴍn** (25) deliver; (beschaffen, a. fig.) furnish, supply; Ertrag: yield; Schlacht: give (battle); Kampf: put up (a fight); F ich bin geliefert sl. I am sunk; '**~schein** m delivery note.
'**Lieferung** f delivery, supply, Am.

mst shipment; (Buch) number; '**~s-bedingungen** f/pl. terms of delivery; '**~swerk** n serial.
'**Liefer|wagen** m s. Lieferauto; '**~zeit** f time (od. term) of delivery.
'**Liege** f (15) couch; '**~geld** ⚓ n demurrage; '**~kur** f rest-cure.
liegen ['li:gən] (30) lie; Stadt, Haus usw.: be (situated); das Zimmer liegt nach Süden faces south; es liegt mir daran, zu inf., mir ist daran gelegen, daß I am anxious to inf., I am concerned to inf. od. that; das (er) liegt mir nicht that (he) is not my cup of tea; es liegt mir nichts daran it does not matter, it is of no importance (to me); es liegt mir viel daran it matters a great deal to me; es liegt an (od. bei) ihm, zu inf. it is for him to inf.; ~ an (dat.; Ursache) be due to; es liegt daran, daß the reason is that; Schuld: an wem liegt es? whose fault is it?; das liegt im Blut (in der Familie) that runs in the blood (family); s. Anker, Bett, Luft, Sterben, zugrunde, Zunge usw.; '**~-bleiben** (sn) keep lying; im Bett: stay in bed; unterwegs, a. mot. usw.: break down; Arbeit: stand over; Brief usw.: be left unattended to; Ware: remain on hand; '**~lassen** let lie; (vergessen) leave behind; (nicht berühren) leave (od. let) alone; Arbeit: leave undone; j-n links ~ ignore (od. cut) a p.; '**Ⴍschaften** f/pl. real estate sg., (landed) property sg.
'**Liege|platz** m ⚓ berth; 🚍 couchette; '**~sitz** mot. m reclining seat; '**~stuhl** m deck-chair; '**~stütz** m Turnen: press-up; '**~wagen** 🚍 m couchette coach.
lieh [li:] pret. v. leihen.
ließ [li:s] pret. v. lassen.
Lift [lɪft] m (3) lift, elevator.
Liga ['li:ga] f (16²) league.
Liguster ⚘ [li'gustər] m (7) privet.
li-ieren [li'i:rən]: sich ~ mit team up with; liiert sein mit go with a girl.
Likör [li'kø:r] m (3¹) liqueur.
lila ['li:la] lilac.
Lilie ['li:ljə] f (15) lily.
Liliputaner [lilipu'ta:nər] m (7), **~in** f (16¹) Lilliputian.
Limonade [limo'na:də] f (15) fizzy drink, Am. soda pop.

Limousine *mot.* [limu'ziːnə] *f* (15) limousine, saloon car, *Am.* sedan.

lind [lint] soft, gentle; *(mild)* mild.

Linde ♀ ['lində] *f* (15) lime-tree, linden.

lindern ['lindərn] (29) *Übel:* mitigate; *(mildern)* soften; *(erleichtern)* alleviate, soothe; *Schmerzen:* allay.

'Linderung *f* alleviation, mitigation; **'~smittel** *n* lenitive, palliative.

Lindwurm ['lintvurm] *m* dragon.

Lineal [line'aːl] *n* (3¹) ruler.

linear [~'aːr] linear; ✝ *Lohnerhöhung etc.:* across the board.

Linguist [liŋ'guist] *m* (12) linguist.

Linie ['liːnjə] *f* (15) line *(a.* ⚓, ⚔, ✕ *u. fig.)*; *(Strecke)* route; *auf der ganzen ~* all along *(od.* down) the line; *auf gleicher ~ mit* on a level with; *in erster ~* in the first place.

'Linien|blatt *n* (sheet with) guide lines *pl.*; **'~flug** *m* scheduled flight; **'~maschine** ✈ *f* scheduled plane; **'~papier** *n* ruled paper; **'~richter** *m Sport:* linesman; **'~treu:** *~ sein* follow the party line; **'~treue** *m, f* (18) party liner.

lin(i)ieren [lin'jiːrən, lini'rən] rule.

link [liŋk] *(Ggs. recht)* left; **~e** *Seite* left(-hand) side, left; *v. Stoff:* reverse side; *mit dem ~en Fuß zuerst aufstehen* get out of bed on the wrong side; **'2e 1.** *f* (18) left hand; *pol. the* Left **2.** *m* (18) *Boxen:* left; **'~isch** awkward, clumsy.

links on *(od.* to) the left; *(nach ~)* (to the) left; *(verkehrt)* inside out; *(~händig)* left-handed; *pol.* leftist; *s. liegenlassen;* **'2...** *pol.* left-wing ...; **2'~außen** *m* (6) outside left; **'2~extremist(in** *f) m* left-wing extremist; **'~gerichtet** *pol.* leftist; **2'händer** ['~hɛndər] *m* (7) left-hander; **'2kurve** *f* left turn; **'2radikalismus** *pol. m* left-wing radicalism; **'2steuerung** *mot. f* left-hand drive; **'2verkehr** *mot. m:* *in England ist ~* in England people drive on the left.

Linoleum [li'noːleum] *n* (9) linoleum.

Linse ['linzə] *f* (15) lentil; *opt.* lens.

Lippe ['lipə] *f* (15) lip; **'~nbekenntnis** *n,* **'~ndienst** *m* lip-service; **'~nlaut** *m* labial; **'~nstift** *m* lipstick.

Liquid|ation [likvida'tsjoːn] *f* (16) liquidation, winding-up; *(Honorarforderung)* charge; **2ieren** [~'diːrən] liquidate *(a. pol.)*, wind up; charge;

~ität ✝ [~di'tɛːt] *f* (16, *o. pl.)* liquidity, solvency.

lispeln ['lispəln] *v/i. u. v/t.* (29) lisp; *(flüstern)* whisper.

List [list] *f* (16) ruse, trick; *(Schlauheit)* cunning.

Liste ['listə] *f* (15) list, roll; *s. schwarz;* **'~npreis** *m* list price.

'listig cunning, crafty, sly.

Litanei [lita'naɪ] *f* (16) litany.

Liter ['liːtər] *n, m* (7) lit|re, *Am.* -er.

literarisch [lita'raːriʃ] literary.

Literat [~'raːt] *m* (12) man of letters; *(Schriftsteller)* writer.

Literatur [~ra'tuːr] *f* (16) literature; **~geschichte** *f* history of literature; **~kritiker** *m* literary critic; **~preis** *m* literary prize; **~verzeichnis** *n* bibliography; **~wissenschaft** *f* literary studies *pl.*

Litfaßsäule ['litfaszɔylə] *f* advertising pillar.

Lithograph [lito'graːf] *m* (12) lithographer; **~ie** [~gra'fiː] *f* (16) lithography; **2ieren** [~'fiːrən] lithograph; **2isch** [~'graːfiʃ] lithographic.

litt [lit] *pret. v. leiden* 1.

Liturgie [litur'giː] *f* (16) liturgy.

liturgisch [li'turgiʃ] liturgical.

Litze ['litsə] *f* (15) cord, lace, braid; ⚡ strand(ed wire).

Livree [li'vreː] *f* (15) livery.

Lizenz [li'tsɛnts] *f* (16) licen|ce, *Am.* -se; *in ~ herstellen etc.:* under licence; **~geber** *m* licenser; **~gebühr** *f* royalty; **~inhaber** *m,* **~nehmer** *m* licensee; **~vertrag** *m* licensing *(od.* royalty) agreement.

Lob [loːp] *n* (3) praise; *zu seinem ~e* in his praise.

loben ['loːbən] (25) praise; F *da lobe ich mir ...* commend me to ...; **'~swert** laudable.

Lob|gesang ['loːp-] *m* hymn, song of praise; *fig.* eulogy; **~hude'lei** *f* (16) base flattery; **2hudeln** give *a p.* fulsome praise.

löblich ['løːpliç] commendable.

Lob|lied ['loːp-] *n: ein ~ auf j-n singen* sing a p.'s praises; **2preisen** praise, extol; **'~rede** *f* eulogy; **'~redner** *m* eulogist; **'~spruch** *m* eulogy.

Loch [lɔx] *n* (1²) hole *(a.* F *contp. Wohnung usw.)*; F *(Gefängnis) sl.* quod; F *auf dem letzten ~ pfeifen* be on one's last legs; **'~eisen** punch; **'2en** (25) perforate; *Fahr-*

karte, Lochkarte usw.: punch; '**~er** *m* (7) *für Papier, Lochkarten*: punch; (electronic) punch-card machine; *Person*: punch-card operator.

löcherig ['lœçəriç] full of holes.

'**Loch|karte** *f* punch(ed) card; '**~maschine** *f* punching machine; '**~säge** *f* keyhole-saw; '**~streifen** *m* punched tape; '**~ung** *f* perforation; punching; '**~zange** *f* (*eine* a pair of) punch pliers *pl.*; ⚙ ticket punch; '**~ziegel** *m* air-brick.

Locke ['lɔkə] *f* (15) curl, ringlet.

'**locken**[1] (25) (*a. sich*) curl; '**~**[2] bait, decoy, lure; *fig. a.* allure, attract, entice; tempt.

'**Locken|kopf** *m* curly head; '**~wickler** *m* curler.

locker ['lɔkər] loose (*a. fig. Sitten, Person*); (*schlaff*) slack; *Brot usw.*: spongy; *fig.* lax; *stärker*: dissolute; '**~heit** *f* looseness; sponginess; '**~lassen**: *fig. nicht* ~ stick to one's guns; '**~n** (29) loosen (*a. sich*); *Griff, a. Zwang usw.*: relax; '**~ung** *f* loosening; relaxation.

'**lockig** curly.

'**Lock|mittel** *n*, '**~speise** *f* bait, lure; '**~spitzel** *m* agent provocateur (*fr.*), *bsd. Am.* stool-pigeon; '**~ung** *f* lure, enticement; (*Versuchung*) temptation; '**~vogel** *fig. m* decoy.

Loden ['lo:dən] *m* (6) loden cloth, shag; '**~mantel** *m* lodenmantle.

lodern ['lo:dərn] (29) flame, blaze (*a. fig.*).

Löffel ['lœfəl] *m* (7) spoon; (*Schöpf*-♀) ladle; ⊕ scoop; *hunt.* ear; *s. barbieren*; '**♀n** (29) spoon (out); ladle (out); '**~stiel** *m* spoon-handle; '**~voll** *m* (3[1], *o. pl.*) spoonful.

log[1] [lo:k] *pret. v.* lügen.

Log[2] ⚓ [lɔk] *n* (3[1]) log.

Logarithmus [loga'ritmus] *m* (16[2]) logarithm.

Loge ['lo:ʒə] *f* (15) *thea.* box; (*Freimaurer*♀) lodge; '**~nbruder** *m* freemason; '**~nmeister** *m* master of a lodge.

logieren [lo'ʒi:rən] lodge; stay (*bei* with); *Am. a.* room.

Logik ['lo:gik] *f* (16) logic.

Logis [lo'ʒi:] *n inv.* lodging(s *pl.*).

logisch ['lo:giʃ] logical.

Logistik [lo'gistik] ✕ *f* (16, *o. pl.*) logistics *pl.*

logo *sl.* ['lo:go] sure.

Logopäd|e ⚚ [logo'pɛ:də] *m* (13) logop(a)edist, speech therapist; **~ie** [~pɛ'di:] *f* (16, *o. pl.*) logop(a)edics *sg.*, speech therapy.

Lohe[1] ['lo:ə] *f* (15) (*Flamme*) blaze, flame; '♀n[1] *v/i.* (25) blaze.

'**Lohe**[2] *f* (15) (*Gerber*♀) tan; '♀n[2] *v/t.* (25) treat with tan.

'**loh|farben** tawny; '♀**gerber** *m* tanner; '♀**gerbe'rei** *f* tannery.

Lohn [lo:n] *m* (3[3]) (*Arbeits*♀) wage(s *pl.*), pay(ment); (*Miet*♀) hire; *fig.* reward; '**~abbau** *m* wage cut(s *pl.*); '**~abkommen** *n* wage agreement; '**~arbeiter** *m*, '**~empfänger** *m* wage-earner, *Am. a.* wage-worker; '**~buchhalter** *m* pay-clerk.

'**lohnen** (25) reward (*j-m et.* a p. for); *Arbeiter*: pay; *sich* ~ pay (*für j-n* a p.), be worth while; '**~d** paying, profitable; worthwhile; *fig. a.* rewarding.

löhnen ['lø:nən] (25) pay.

'**Lohn|-erhöhung** *f* wage increase *od.* rise, *Am.* raise; '**~forderung** *f* wage claim; '**~gruppe** *f* pay bracket; '♀-**intensiv** wage-intensive; '**~kampf** *m* wage dispute; '**~kostenanteil** *m* wage factor in cost; '**~liste** *f* pay-roll; '**~skala** *f* wage scale; '**~steuer** *f* wages tax; '**~stopp** *m* pay freeze; '**~streifen** *m* pay (*od.* wage) slip; '**~tarif** *m* wage rate; '**~tüte** *f* pay (*od.* wage) packet.

'**Löhnung** *f* pay; '**~s-tag** *m* pay-day.

Loipe ['lɔʏpə] *f* (15) cross-country (skiing) course.

lokal [lo'ka:l] 1. local; 2. ♀ *n* (3) locality; (*Wirtshaus*) public house, restaurant; *s. a. Geschäfts*♀; '♀... local; **~isieren** [lokali'zi:rən] localize; ♀**-patriotismus** *m* sectional pride; ♀**-teil** *m e-r Zeitung*: local news *sg.*

Lokomotiv|e [lokomo'ti:və] *f* (15) engine, locomotive; **~führer** [~'ti:f-] *m* engine-driver, *Am.* engineer.

Lokus ['lo:kus] F *m* (14[2] *u. inv.*) *s.* Klo.

Lombardsatz [lɔm'bartzats] ✝ *m* lending rate.

Lorbeer ['lɔrbe:r] *m* (5[2]) laurel, bay; *fig. auf s-n* ~*en ausruhen* rest on one's laurels.

Lore ⊕ ['lo:rə] *f* (15) lorry.

Los[1] [lo:s] *n* (4) lot; (*Lotterie*♀) ticket; (*Schicksal*) fate, destiny; *s. groß*; *das* ~ *werfen* (*ziehen*) *s.* losen.

los[2] (18[1], *s. lose*) loose; (*frei*) *a.* free;

(ab) off; *was ist ~ (mit ihm)?* what's the matter (with him)?; *was ist heute abend ~?* what's on tonight?; *j-n, et. ~ sein* be rid of; *~!* go ahead!, *(schnell)* let's go!; *Sport: Achtung, fertig, ~!* are you ready? go!; *mit ihm ist nicht viel ~ sl.* he is no great shakes; F *er hat was ~ sl.* he is on the ball.

'los-**arbeiten** *v/t.*: *sich ~* extricate o.s., get loose; *v/i. (darauf ~)* work away *(auf acc. at).*

lösbar ['lø:sba:r] soluble.

'los|binden untie; '~brechen *v/t.* break off; *v/i. fig.* break out.

'Lösch|blatt *n*, '~papier *n* blotting--paper; '~eimer *m* fire-bucket.

löschen ['lœʃən] (27) *Feuer, Licht:* extinguish, put out; *Geschriebenes:* blot out, *a. Bandaufnahme:* erase; *(streichen)* cancel *(a. Schuld)*; *Durst:* quench; *Kalk:* slake; ♻ unload; *Computer:* delete.

'Löscher *m* (7) *s. Feuer♻, Tinten♻.*

'Lösch|kopf *m Bandgerät:* eraser head; '~mannschaft *f* fire-brigade; '~papier *n* blotting paper; '~taste *f Bandgerät:* erase button.

lose ['lo:zə] loose *(a. fig. Leben, Person, Zunge usw.); s. los².*

'Lösegeld *n* ransom.

losen ['lo:zən] (27) cast *(od. draw)* lots *(um for); mit Münze:* toss (for).

lösen ['lø:zən] (27) loosen; *(losbinden)* untie; *(wegmachen)* detach; *(lossprechen)* absolve; *(loskaufen)* redeem; *Fahrkarte:* book, take, buy; *Aufgabe, Rätsel, Zweifel usw.:* solve; *Verbindung, Verlobung:* break off; *Ehe:* dissolve *(a. ♻ u. sich); Vertrag:* terminate; *sich ~* get loose, *(sich befreien)* disengage o.s., *Schuß:* ring out, *Spannung, Muskeln, Griff:* relax; *fig. gelöst* relaxed.

'los|gehen (sn) *(sich lockern)* get loose, come off; *(davongehen)* *Schuß[waffe])* go off; *(anfangen)* begin, start; *auf j-n* fly at, go for, attack; *auf ein Ziel usw.* make for; '~haken unhook; '~kaufen buy off; *Gefangene:* ransom; '~ketten unchain; '~knüpfen untie; '~kommen (sn) get loose *od.* free; *fig. a.* get rid (*von* of); '~lachen laugh out; '~lassen let loose *od.* off *od.* go, release; *fig.* launch; '~legen let go *(mit* with), open up; *leg los!* fire away!; *~ gegen s. los-ziehen.*

löslich ♻ ['lø:sliç] soluble.

'los|lösen, '~machen *s. lösen*; '~reißen tear loose; *sich ~* break away, *fig.* tear o.s. away; *sich* '~sagen *von* dissociate o.s. from, break with; '~schießen *v/i. u. v/t.* fire (off); *(sich stürzen) auf (acc.)* rush at; F *schieß los!* fire away!, shoot!; '~schlagen *v/t.* knock off; *(verkaufen)* dispose of; *v/i.* open the attack, strike; *~ auf j-n* let fly at; '~schnallen unbuckle; '~schrauben unscrew; loosen; '~sprechen absolve; acquit (*von* of); release; '~springen, '~stürzen (sn) *auf (acc.)* pounce upon, fly at; '~steuern (sn) *auf (acc.)* make for; *fig. a.* be driving at; '~trennen detach; *Genähtes:* unstitch; *(a. fig.)* separate.

Losung ['lo:zuŋ] *f des Wildes:* dung; ✗ password, *(a. fig.)* watchword.

Lösung ['lø:zuŋ] *f* solution *(a. ♻, ♻)*; '~sheft *n* key; '~smittel *n* solvent.

'los|werden (sn) get rid of; '~ziehen (sn) set out, march away; *gegen j-n ~* inveigh against, let fly at.

Lot [lo:t] *n* (3) *(Blei♻)* lead, plummet; *(Lötmetall)* solder; ♻ perpendicular (line); *ein ~ errichten (fällen)* raise (drop) a perpendicular; *fig. im ~ sein* be in good order; *ins ~ bringen* set to rights; '♻en (26) *v/i. u. v/t.* plumb; ♻ sound.

löten ['lo:tən] (26) solder.

'Löt|kolben *m* soldering-iron; '~lampe *f* soldering-lamp, *Am.* blowtorch; '~metall *n* solder.

'lotrecht perpendicular.

'Lötrohr *n* blowpipe.

Lotse ♻ ['lo:tsə] *m* (13), '♻n (27) pilot; '~ndienst *m* pilotage service.

Lotterie [lɔtə'ri:] *f* (15) lottery; ~los *n* (lottery) ticket.

Lotterleben ['lɔtər-] *n* dissolute life.

Lotto ['lɔto] *n* (11) numbers pool.

Löwe ['lø:və] *m* (13) lion; *ast.* Leo.

'Löwen|-anteil *m* lion's share; '~bändiger(in *f*) *m* lion-tamer; '~grube *f* lion's den; '~maul ♀ *n* snapdragon; '~zahn ♀ *m* dandelion.

'Löwin *f* (16¹) lioness.

loyal [loa'ja:l] loyal; ♻ität [~jali'tɛt] *f* (16) loyalty.

Luchs [luks] *m* (4) lynx; ♻äugig ['~ʔɔʏgiç] lynx-eyed.

Lücke ['lykə] f (15) gap; (Riß, Bruch) breach; (offene Stelle) blank; (Mangel) deficiency; '**⁀nbüßer** m stopgap; '**⁀nhaft** defective, incomplete, fragmentary; '**⁀nlos** complete; Beweis: full, airtight.

Luder ['luːdər] n (7) (Aas) carrion; P fig. beast; (Dirne) hussy; armes ⁀ poor wretch.

Luft [luft] f (14¹) air; (Brise) breeze; frische ⁀ schöpfen draw breath, take the air; an die ⁀ gehen take an airing; fig. j-n wie ⁀ behandeln cut a p. dead; fig. et. aus der ⁀ greifen pull a th. out of thin air; (völlig) aus der ⁀ gegriffen totally unfounded; in freier ⁀ in the open air; fig. es liegt et. in der ⁀ there is something in the wind; in die ⁀ fliegen be blown up; in die ⁀ sprengen od. jagen blow up; F in die ⁀ gehen blow one's top; s-m Zorn usw. ⁀ machen give vent to; sich ⁀ machen P.: unbosom o.s., Gefühl: find vent; F j-n an die ⁀ setzen turn a p. out; s. rein 1; schnappen.

'**Luft|-abwehr** f air defen|ce, Am. -se; '**⁀alarm** m air-raid alarm; '**⁀angriff** m air-raid; '**⁀-aufklärung** f aerial reconnaissance; '**⁀ballon** m (air-)balloon; '**⁀bild** n aerial photo (-graph), aerial view; '**⁀bildvermessung** f aerial survey; '**⁀blase** f air bubble; '**⁀bremse** f air-brake; '**⁀brücke** ✠ f airlift.

Lüftchen ['lyftçən] n (6) gentle breeze, breath of air.

'**luft|dicht** airtight; '**⁀druck** m air (od. atmospheric) pressure; e-r Explosion: blast; '**⁀druckbremse** f air (od. pneumatic) brake; '**⁀durchlässig** permeable to air.

lüft|en ['lyftən] (26) air, ventilate; (heben) lift, raise; ein Geheimnis ⁀ disclose (od. reveal) a secret; '**⁀er** m (7) ventilator; ⊕ (Entⁿ) air exhauster.

'**Luft|fahrt** f aviation; '**⁀fahrtgesellschaft** f airline (company); '**⁀fahrzeug** n aircraft (a. pl.); '**⁀feuchtigkeit** f (atmospheric) humidity; air moisture; '**⁀flotte** f air force; '**⁀fracht** f air freight; '**⁀gekühlt** air-cooled; '**⁀gestützt** ✗ Rakete: air-launched; '**⁀gewehr** n air-gun; '**⁀hafen** m airport; '**⁀heizung** f hot-air heating; '**⁀herrschaft** f air supremacy; '**⁀hoheit** f air sovereignty; '**⁀ig**

airy; (windig) breezy; (dünn) flimsy; P.: flighty; '**⁀kampf** m aerial combat; '**⁀kissen** n air-cushion; '**⁀kissenfahrzeug** n air-cushion vehicle; '**⁀klappe** f air-valve; '**⁀korridor** m air corridor; '**⁀krank** air-sick; '**⁀krieg** m aerial warfare; '**⁀kühlung** f air cooling; '**⁀kur-ort** m climatic health-resort; '**⁀landetruppen** f|pl. airborne troops pl.; '**⁀leer** void of air, evacuated; ⁀er Raum vacuum; '**⁀linie** f air line (distance); s. a. Luftverkehrslinie; '**⁀loch** n airhole, vent; ✠ air-pocket; '**⁀matratze** f air mattress; '**⁀mine** ✗ f aerial mine; '**⁀pirat** m hijacker, skyjacker; '**⁀pistole** f air-pistol; '**⁀post** f air mail; '**⁀pumpe** f air-pump; '**⁀raum** m air space; '**⁀reifen** m pneumatic tyre (Am. tire); '**⁀reklame** f sky-line advertising; '**⁀rettung** f air rescue service; '**⁀röhre** f air-tube; anat. windpipe, trachea; '**⁀sack** mot. m airbag; '**⁀schacht** m airshaft; '**⁀schaukel** f swing-boat; '**⁀schiff** n airship; '**⁀schiffahrt** f aviation; '**⁀schiffer** m aeronaut, airman; '**⁀schlacht** f air battle; '**⁀schlauch** m air tube; Fahrrad, mot. inner tube; '**⁀schlösser** n|pl. castles in the air; '**⁀schraube** ✠ f air-screw, propeller; '**⁀schutz** m air-raid protection; civil air defence; '**⁀schutzkeller** m, '**⁀schutzraum** m air-raid shelter; '**⁀schutz-übung** f air-raid drill; '**⁀spiegelung** f mirage; '**⁀sprung** m caper; '**⁀streitkräfte** f|pl. air force(s pl.); '**⁀strom** m air-stream; '**⁀stützpunkt** ✗ m air base; '**⁀taxi** n air taxi; '**⁀tüchtig** ✠ air-worthy; '**⁀tüchtigkeit** f air-worthiness.

'**Lüftung** ['lyftuŋ] f airing; künstlich: ventilation; '**⁀s-anlage** f ventilating system.

'**Luft|ver-änderung** f change of air; '**⁀verkehrsgesellschaft** f air transport company, airline od. airways (company); '**⁀verkehrslinie** f airline, air-route, airway; '**⁀verpestung** f, '**⁀verschmutzung** f air pollution; '**⁀verteidigung** f air defen|ce, Am. -se; '**⁀waffe** f air force; '**⁀weg** m air-route; anat. respiratory tract; auf dem ⁀e by air; '**⁀zufuhr** f air supply; '**⁀zug** m draught (Am. draft) (of air).

Lug [luːk] m (3): ⁀ und Trug falsehood and deceit.

Lüge ['ly:gə] *f* (15) lie, falsehood; *j-n ~n strafen* give a p. the lie.

lugen ['lu:gən] (25) peer.

'**lügen 1.** *v/i.* (30) lie, tell a lie *od.* lies; **2.** ♀ *n* (6) lying; '♀**detektor** *m* lie detector; '**~haft** lying, deceitful, untrue.

Lügner ['ly:gnər] *m* (7), '**~in** *f* (16¹) liar; '♀**isch** deceitful, lying, false.

Luke ['lu:kə] *f* (15) (*Dachfenster*) dormer-window; ♣ *usw.* hatch.

lukrativ [lukra'ti:f] lucrative.

lukullisch [lu'kulif] sumptuous.

lullen ['lulən] (25): *in Schlaf ~* lull to sleep.

Lümmel ['lyməl] *m* (7), '♀**haft** loutish; '♀**n** (26) *v/i. u. v/refl.* loll.

Lump [lump] *m* (3 *u.* 12) scoundrel, blackguard, *sl.* louse; '**~en¹** *m* (6) rag; '♀**en²** (25): *sich nicht ~ lassen* come down handsomely.

'**Lumpen|gesindel** *n* riff-raff; (*Schurken*) scoundrels *pl.*; '**~händler** *m* ragman, *Am.* junkman; '**~hund** *m*, '**~kerl** *m s.* Lump; '**~pack** *n s.* Lumpengesindel; '**~papier** *n* rag paper; '**~sammler(in** *f*) *m* ragpicker; '**~wolle** *f* shoddy.

Lumperei [~'rai] *f* (16) shabby trick; (*Kleinigkeit*) trifle.

'**lumpig** ragged; *fig.* paltry (*sum*).

Lunge ['luŋə] *f* (15) lung(s *pl.*); *v. Schlachtvieh*: lights *pl.*; ♬ *eiserne ~* iron lung; '**~n...** ⚕ pulmonary ...

'**Lungen|-entzündung** *f* inflammation of the lungs, ⚕ pneumonia; '**~flügel** *m* lobe of the lungs; '**~heilstätte** *f* (tuberculosis) sanatorium; '♀**krank**, '**~kranke** *m*, *f* consumptive; '**~krankheit** *f* lung (*od.* pulmonary) disease; '**~krebs** *m* lung cancer; '**~schwindsucht** *f* pulmonary phthisis.

lungern ['luŋərn] (h. *u.* sn, 29) loiter (about); loll (about).

Lunte ['luntə] *f* (15) slow-match; *fig. ~ riechen* smell a rat.

Lupe ['lu:pə] *f* (15) magnifier; (*Taschen*♀) pocket-lens; *unter die ~ nehmen fig.* scrutinize closely.

Lupine ♀ [lu'pi:nə] *f* (15) lupine.

Lust [lust] *f* (14¹) pleasure (*a. psych.*), delight; (*Verlangen*) desire; *mit ~ und Liebe* with a will; *~ bekommen, ~ haben zu inf.* feel like ger.; *(gute) ~ haben zu* have a great (half a) mind to; *die ~ verlieren an* (*dat.*) lose all liking for; *hätten Sie*

~ zu inf.? would you like to *inf.?*; '**~barkeit** *f* diversion; *bsd. öffentliche:* entertainment.

Lüster ['lystər] *m* (7) lust|re, *Am.* -er; '**~klemme** ⚡ *f* strip connector.

lüstern ['lystərn] (*nach*) desirous (of), greedy (of, for); (*fleischlich*) lewd, lascivious; '♀**heit** *f* greediness; lewdness, lasciviousness.

'**Lust|garten** *m* pleasure garden; '**~gefühl** *n* pleasurable sensation; '**~gewinn** *psych. m* pleasure gain.

'**lustig** merry, gay; (*belustigend*) funny; *sich ~ machen über* (*acc.*) make fun of; *~ sein* (*sich festlich vergnügen*) make merry; '♀**keit** *f* gaiety; fun(niness).

Lüstling ['lystliŋ] *m* (3¹) libertine, rake, debauchee.

'**lust|los** listless, unenthusiastic(al); ✝ slack; '♀**mord** *m* sex murder; '♀**mörder** *m* sex maniac; '♀-**objekt** *n* sex object; '♀**prinzip** *psych. n* pleasure principle; '♀**schloß** *n* pleasure seat; '♀**seuche** *f* venereal disease, syphilis; '♀**spiel** *n* comedy; '**~wandeln** (sn) walk leisurely along, stroll about.

Lutheraner [lutə'rɑ:nər] *m* (7), **lutherisch** ['lutərif, lu'te:rif] Lutheran.

lutsch|en ['lutfən] (27) *v/i. u. v/t.* suck; '♀**er** *m für Säuglinge*: comforter, dummy; (*Bonbon*) lollipop.

Luv ♣ [lu:f] *f* (16, *o. pl.*) luff, weather side; ♀**en** ♣ ['~vən] (25) luff; **~seite** ['lu:f-] weather side.

luxuriös [luksu'rjø:s] (18¹) luxurious.

Luxus ['luksus] *m inv.* luxury (*a. fig.*); '**~...,** luxury ..., de luxe ...; '**~artikel** *m* luxury (article); '**~ausgabe** *f* (*Buch*) de luxe edition; '**~dampfer** *m* luxury liner; '**~kabine** ♣ *f* stateroom; '**~leben** *n* life of luxury; '**~wagen** *mot. m* de luxe model.

Lymph... ['lymf-] lymphatic; '**~drüse** *f* lymph(atic) gland; '**~e** *f* (15) lymph; (*Impfstoff*) vaccine.

lynch|en ['lynçən] (27) lynch; '♀**justiz** *f* lynch law; '♀**mord** *m* lynching.

Lyra ['ly:ra] *f* (16²) lyre.

Lyrik ['~rik] *f* (16) lyric poetry; '**~er** *m* (7) lyric poet.

'**lyrisch** lyric; *fig.* lyrical.

Lyzeum [ly'tse:um] *n* (9) secondary school for girls.

M

M [ɛm], **m** *n inv.* M, m.

Maat ♫ [maːt] *m* (3) mate; ✗ leading rating, *Am.* petty officer 3rd class.

Mach|-art ['max-] *f* make; '⌂**bar** feasible, practicable, possible; '⌄**e** *f* (15) *fig.* make-believe, F show; *et. in der* ⌄ *haben* have in hand; F *j-n in die* ⌄ *nehmen* work a p. over.

mach|en ['maxən] (25) (*herstellen*) make; (*tun*) do (*a.* F *thea.*); (*bewirken*) effect, produce; (*verursachen*) cause; (*schaffen*) create; (*erledigen*) deal with, handle, do; *Appetit, Freude usw.*: give; ⌄ *in et.* ✝ deal in, F *fig.* dabble in; *j-n zu et.* ⌄ make a p. a th.; *j-n glücklich usw.* ⌄ make (*od.* render) a p. happy, *etc.*; *was macht die Rechnung?, wieviel macht das?* how much is it?; *das macht 3 Mark* that will be (*od.* comes to) 3 marks; *was macht das (aus)?* what does it matter?; *das macht nichts!* never mind!; *es macht mir nichts (aus)* I don't mind; *nichts zu* ⌄*!* nothing doing!; *mach doch (zu)!* hurry up!; *mach, daß ...!* see (to it) that ...!; *mach's gut!* (*lebwohl*) take care of yourself!; *das macht sich gut* that looks well; *er macht sich jetzt* he is getting on now; *es wird sich* ⌄ it will come right; *dagegen kann man nichts* ⌄ that cannot be helped; *sich* ⌄ *an* (*acc.*) go (*od.* set) about; proceed to *inf.*; *sich an j-n* ⌄ approach a p.; *sich auf den Weg* ⌄ set out; *ich mache mir nichts daraus* I don't care about it; (*sich*) *et.* ⌄ *lassen* have a th. made, order a th.; *das läßt sich (schon)* ⌄ it can be arranged; *laß mich nur* ⌄*!* leave it to me!; *gemacht* made (*aus* of), (*unecht*) artificial; F *gemacht!* agreed!, *bsd. Am.* OK!, okay!; *ein gemachter Mann* a made man; *s. Angst, Anspruch, Arbeit, Ausflucht, bekannt, Besuch, Erfahrung, fertig, Feuer usw.*; '⌂**enschaften** *f/pl.* machinations; '⌂**er** F *m* (7) doer.

Macht [maxt] *f* (14¹) power (*a. Staat*), might (*beide a. Stärke*); (*Gewalt über acc.*) control (of), sway (over); *gesetzmäßige*: authority; *an der* ⌄ in power; *zur* ⌄ *gelangen* come into power; *mit aller* ⌄ with all one's might; *alles, was*

in m-r ⌄ *steht* everything within my power; '⌄**befugnis** *f* authority, power; '⌄**ergreifung** *f* s. *Macht-übernahme*; '⌄**haber** *m* (7) ruler; '⌂**haberisch** despotic.

mächtig ['mɛçtiç] powerful (*a. fig. Körper, Stimme, Schlag usw.*); mighty (*a.* F *adv.*); (*riesig*) huge; ✗ thick, wide; *e-r S.* ⌄ *sein* be master of, *e-r Sprache*: have command of.

'**Macht|kampf** *m* struggle for power; '⌂**los** powerless; helpless; '⌄**mißbrauch** *m* misuse of power; '⌄**politik** *f* power politics; '⌄**position** *f* position of power; '⌄**spruch** *m* authoritative decision; '⌄**übernahme** *f* assumption of power, takeover; '⌂**voll** powerful, mighty; '⌄**vollkommenheit** *f* absolute power; *aus eigener* ⌄ of one's own authority; '⌄**wechsel** *m* changeover of power; '⌄**wort** *n* (3): *ein* ⌄ *sprechen* put one's foot down; '⌄**zuwachs** *m* increase in power.

'**Machwerk** *n* concoction; *elendes* ⌄ miserable botch.

Macker F ['makər] *m* (7) fellow, guy; (*Freund*) boyfriend.

Mädchen ['mɛːtçən] *n* (6) girl; (*Jungfrau*) maid(en); (*Dienst*⌂) maid (-servant), servant(-girl); *in Zssgn* girl's ..., girls' ...; ⌄ *für alles* maid-of-all-work (*a. fig.*); '⌂**haft** girlish; maidenly; '⌄**handel** *m* white slavery; '⌄**name** *m* girl's name; *e-r Frau*: maiden name; '⌄**pensionat** *n* young ladies' boarding--school; '⌄**schule** *f* girls' school.

Made ['maːdə] *f* (15) maggot, mite; *in Obst*: worm; *wie die* ⌄ *im Speck sitzen* live in clover.

Mädel F ['mɛːdəl] *n* (7) girl, lass.

madig ['maːdiç] maggoty; worm--eaten; F ⌄ *machen sl.* knock.

Madonna [ma'dɔna] *f* (16²) Holy Virgin, Madonna.

Magazin [maga'tsiːn] *n* (3¹) store, warehouse; (✗; *am Gewehr usw.*; *a. Zeitschrift*) magazine.

Magd [maːkt] *f* (14¹) maid.

Magen ['maːgən] *m* (6, *a.* 6¹) stomach; *mit vollem* ⌄ on a full stomach; '⌄**beschwerden** *f/pl.* stomach (*od.* gastric) trouble, indigestion; '⌄**bitter** *m* bitters *pl.*; '⌄**geschwür** *n* gastric ulcer; '⌄**grube** *f* pit of the stomach; '⁓krampf m gastric spasm; '⚲krank suffering from a gastric complaint; '⁓krebs ⚸ m gastric cancer; '⁓leiden n gastric complaint; '⁓saft m gastric juice; '⁓säure f gastric acid; '⁓schleimhaut f stomach lining; '⁓schmerzen m/pl. stomach--ache; '⚲stärkend stomachic; '⁓verstimmung f indigestion.

mager ['mɑːgər] meag|re, Am. -er (a. fig.); lean (a. Fleisch, Treibstoff; fig. Jahre); (dürr) gaunt; Kost: slender (fare); Boden: poor; '⚲keit f meagreness; leanness; '⚲milch f skim milk; '⚲sucht ⚸ f anorexia nervosa.

Magie [ma'giː] f (15) magic.

Magier ['mɑːgjər] m (7) magician.

'**magisch** magic(al); Radio: ⁓es Auge magic eye. [master.⟩

Magister [ma'gistər] m (7) (school-)⟩

Magistrat [magi'strɑːt] m (3) municipal (od. town od. city) council; ⁓smitglied n town council(l)or.

Magnat [ma'gnɑːt] m (12) magnate, Am. a. tycoon.

Magnesi|a [ma'gneːzia] f inv. magnesia; ⁓um [⁓um] n (9, o. pl.) magnesium.

Magnet [ma'gneːt] m (3, sg. a. 12) magnet (a. fig.); ⁓feld n magnetic field; ⚲isch magnetic(ally adv.); ⁓iseur [⁓gneti'zøːr] m magnetizer; ⚲i'sieren magnetize; ⁓ismus [⁓'tismus] m magnetism; ⁓karte [⁓-'gneːt-] f magnetic (punch)card; ⁓nadel f magnetic needle.

Mahagoni [maha'goːni] n (11) (a. ⁓holz n) mahogany (wood).

Maharadscha [maha'rɑːdʒa] m (11) maharaja.

Mahd [mɑːt] f (7) mowing; (Schwaden) swath.

mähen[1] ['mɛːən] v/t. u. v/i. (25) mow (a. fig.), cut, reap.

'**mähen**[2] v/i. Schaf: bleat.

Mahl [mɑːl] n (3 u. 1²) meal, repast; festliches: feast, banquet.

'**mahlen** (25; p.p. ge⁓) grind.

'**Mahlzeit** f meal; F prost ⁓! good night!

'**Mähmaschine** f reaping-machine, reaper; für Rasen: mower.

'**Mahn|bescheid** ⚼ m default summons; '⁓brief m reminder, dunning letter.

Mähne ['mɛːnə] f (15) mane.

mahn|en ['mɑːnən] (25) remind, warn, admonish (alle: an acc. of);

j-n wegen e-r Schuld ⁓ press a p. for payment, dun a p.; zur Geduld usw. ⁓ urge to be patient etc.; '⚲er m (7) admonisher, um Zahlung: dun; '⚲ung f admonition, warning; um Zahlung: dunning; '⚲mal n (3, a. 1²) memorial; '⚲schreiben n s. ⚲-brief.

Mähre ['mɛːrə] f (15) mare.

Mai [mai] m (3 od. 14) May; der erste ⁓ the first of May, May Day; '⁓baum m maypole; '⁓blume f, '⁓glöckchen n lily of the valley.

Maid poet. [mait] f (16) maid(en).

'**Mai|feier** f (celebration of) May Day; '⁓käfer m cockchafer.

Mais [mais] m (4) maize, Indian corn, Am. corn; '⁓flocken f/pl. Am. cornflakes; '⁓kolben m (corn) cob.

Maisch|bottich ['maiʃ-] m mash--tub; '⁓e f (15), ⚲en mash.

Maisonettewohnung [mezo'nɛt-] f maisonette, Am. duplex apartment.

Majestät [maje'stɛːt] f (16) majesty; ⚲isch majestic; ⁓sbeleidigung f lese-majesty.

Major [ma'joːr] m (3¹) major.

Majoran ⚶ [⁓jo'rɑːn] m (3) marjoram.

Makel ['mɑːkəl] m (7) stain, blot, flaw (alle a. fig.); fig. blemish.

Mäkelei [mɛːkə'lai] f (16) fault--finding, carping; weitS. fastidiousness.

'**mäkelig** carping; fastidious, im Essen: squeamish.

'**makellos** spotless (a. fig.), immaculate (a. Schönheit); fig. a. impeccable.

mäkeln ['mɛːkəln] (29) find fault (an dat. with), carp (at).

Makkaroni [maka'roːni] pl. inv. macaroni.

Makler ['mɑːklər] m (7) broker; '⁓gebühr f brokerage; '⁓geschäft n broker's business.

'**Mäkler** m (7), ⁓in f fault-finder.

Makrele [ma'kreːlə] f (15) mackerel.

Makrone [ma'kroːnə] f (15) macaroon.

Makulatur [makula'tuːr] f (16) waste paper.

Mal [mɑːl] n (3) 1. (a. 1²) mark, sign; beim Spiel: (Ablauf⚲) start (-ing-point), (Ziel) home, base; (Fleck) spot, stain; (Mutter⚲) mole; s. Ehren⚲; 2. time; ⚼ times; dieses ⁓ this time; das nächste ⁓ next time;

zum ersten ∼e (for) the first time; *mit e-m* ∼e (*plötzlich*) all of a sudden; **3.** ⚥ *adv.* F = *einmal.*

Malaria [ma'laːria] *f* (16²) malaria.

malen ['maːlən] (25) paint; (*zeichnen*) draw; (*porträtieren*) portray; *fig.* paint, picture; *sich* ∼ *lassen* sit for one's portrait.

'**Maler** *m* (7), '∼**in** *f* (16¹) painter; *als Künstler oft*: artist; ∼**ei** [∼'raɪ] *f* (16) painting; '⚥**isch** picturesque; '∼**meister** *m* master (house-) painter.

Malheur [ma'løːr] *n* (3¹ *u.* 11) mishap; trouble.

maliziös [mali'tsjøːs] malicious.

'**Mal|kasten** *m* colo(u)r-box; '∼**kreide** *f* crayon.

'**Malkunst** *f* art of painting.

'**malnehmen 1.** multiply; **2.** ⚥ *n* (6) multiplication.

Malve ⚘ ['malvə] *f* (15) mallow; '⚥**nfarbig** mauve.

Malz [malts] *n* (3²) malt; '∼**bier** *n* malt liquor; '∼**bonbon** *m, n* cough-lozenge; '∼**darre** *f* malt-kiln.

Malzeichen ⚿ ['maːltsaɪçən] *n* multiplication mark.

Mälzer ['mɛltsər] *m* (7) maltster.

'**Malz|-extrakt** *m* malt extract; '∼**kaffee** *m* malt-coffee; '∼**zucker** *m* malt-sugar.

Mama [ma'ma, F'∼] *f* (11¹) mam(m)a, F ma, mum, *Am. a.* mom.

Mammographie ☤ [mamogra'fiː] *f* (15) mammography.

Mammon ['mamɔn] *m* (11) mammon, pelf, (filthy) lucre.

Mammut ['mamuːt] *n* (3 *u.* 11) mammoth; '⚥... *Baum, Firma, usw.*: mammoth; *fig. a.* giant ...

Mamsell [mam'zɛl] *f* (16) miss; (*Wirtschafterin*) housekeeper.

man [man] (*im dat. u. acc. durch einer ersetzt*) one; people, we, you, they; ∼ *sagte mir* I was told.

manag|en ['mɛnidʒən] manage (*a.* F); '⚥**er** *m* (7) manager; '⚥**erkrankheit** *f* stress disease.

manch [manç] (21) many a; '∼**e** *pl.* some, several; ∼**erlei** ['∼ərlaɪ] *inv.* all sorts of, of several sorts, various; '∼**mal** sometimes.

Mandant ⚖ [man'dant] *m* (12) client.

Mandarine [manda'riːnə] *f* (15) tangerine.

Mandat [∼'daːt] *n* (3) mandate;

authorization; ⚖ brief; *parl.* seat; ∼**sgebiet** mandate(d territory).

Mandel ['mandəl] *f* (15) almond; *anat.* tonsil; ⚕ shock; '∼**baum** *m* almond-tree; '∼**entzündung** *f* inflammation of the tonsils, tonsillitis; ⚥**förmig** ['∼fœrmiç] almond-shaped.

Mandoline ♪ [mando'liːnə] *f* (15) mandolin.

Manege [ma'nɛːʒə] *f* (15) (circus) ring.

Mangan [maŋ'gaːn] *n* (3¹) manganese; ∼**säure** *f* manganic acid.

Mange(l¹) ['maŋə(l)] *f* (15) mangle, calender.

'**Mangel²** *m* (7¹) want, lack, deficiency; (*Knappheit*) shortage (*an dat.* of); (*Armut*) penury; (*Fehler*) defect, shortcoming; (*Nachteil*) drawback; *aus* ∼ *an* for want of, *s. mangels*; ∼ *leiden an* (*dat.*) be short (*od.* in need) of; '∼**beruf** *m* critical occupation; '⚥**haft** (*fehlerhaft*) defective; (*unzulänglich*) deficient, inadequate; (*unbefriedigend*) unsatisfactory, poor; '∼**haftigkeit** *f* defectiveness; deficiency; '∼**krankheit** *f* deficiency disease; '⚥**n¹** (29) want; be wanting *od.* lacking *od.* deficient (*an dat.* in); *es mangelt mir an* (*dat.*) I am in want of, I want; '⚥**n²** mangle, calender; '⚥**s** (*gen.*) for lack (*od.* want) of, in the absence of; '∼**ware** *f* scarce commodities *pl.*; goods *pl.* in short supply.

Mangold ⚘ ['maŋɡɔlt] *m* (3) mangel (-wurzel), mangold.

Manie [ma'niː] *f* (15) mania.

Manier [∼'niːr] *f* (16) manner.

maniert [∼ni'riːrt] affected; *Kunst, Literatur*: mannered; ⚥**heit** *f* affectedness, mannerism.

ma'nierlich mannerly, polite; ⚥**keit** *f* mannerliness, politeness.

Manifest [mani'fɛst] *n* (3²) manifesto; ∼**ation** [∼fɛsta'tsjoːn] *f* manifestation; ∼**ieren** [∼fɛs'tiːrən] manifest.

Maniküre [∼'kyːrə] *f* (15) (*Handpflege*) manicure; (*Handpflegerin*) manicurist; ⚥**n** (25) manicure.

Manipul|ation [manipula'tsjoːn] *f* manipulation; ⚥**ieren** [∼pu'liːrən] manipulate.

manisch ['maːniʃ] manic; ∼-*depressiv* manic-depressive.

Manko ['maŋko] *n* (11) deficit; deficiency; *fig.* drawback.

Mann [man] *m* (1², *poet.* 5, ⚔ *u.* ⚓ *pl. inv.*) man (*pl.* men); ✖ enlisted man; (*Gatte*) husband; *der ~ auf der Straße* the man in the street; *~s genug sein für* be man enough for; *an den ~ bringen* dispose of; *fig.-s-n ~ stehen* stand one's ground; make a good job of it; *~ gegen ~* hand to hand; F *~* (*Gottes*)! man (alive)!; *s.* Wort.

'**mannbar** marriageable; *~ werden* reach (wo)manhood; '**Ωkeit** *f* (wo)manhood; *v. Mädchen a.* marriageable age.

Männchen ['mɛnçən] *n* (6) little man; *zo.* male; *bei Vögeln:* cock; *~ malen* doodle; *~ machen Tier:* sit up and beg.

Mannequin ['manəkɛ̃] *n*, *m* (11) mannequin, model.

Männer|gesangver·ein ['mɛnər-] *m* men's singing club; '**~welt** *f* male sex, men *pl.*

'**Mannes|·alter** *n* manhood; *im besten ~ in* the prime of life; '**~kraft** *f* virility.

'**mannhaft** manly, stout; '**Ωigkeit** *f* manliness; courage.

mannig|fach ['maniç-], '**~faltig** manifold, various; '**Ωfaltigkeit** *f* variety, diversity.

männlich ['mɛnliç] male (*a. zo.*, ⊕); masculine (*a. gr. u. fig.*); *fig.* manly; '**Ωkeit** *f* manhood; manliness; '**Ωkeitswahn** *m* male chauvinism.

'**Mannsbild** F *n* male, man.

'**Mannschaft** *f* (16) men *pl.*; ⚓, ✈, ✖ crew; *Sport u. fig.*: team; ✖ *die ~en pl.* the ranks; '**~sführer** *m*, '**~skapitän** *m Sport:* (team) captain; '**~sgeist** *m* team-spirit; '**~skamerad** *m* team mate.

'**manns|hoch** (as) tall as a man; '**Ωleute** *pl.* men(folk *sg.*); '**~toll** man-crazy.

'**Mannweib** *n* mannish woman, amazon.

Manometer [mano'me:tər] *n* (7) manometer.

Manö|ver [ma'nø:vər] *n* (7), Ωvrie-ren [~nø'vri:rən] manœuvre, *Am. mst* maneuver; Ω'**vrierfähig** manœuvrable, *Am. mst* maneuverable; Ω'**vrier·unfähig** disabled.

Mansarde [man'zardə] *f* (15) attic;

~nfenster n dormer-window.

mansch|en F ['manʃən] (27) dabble, splash; Ωe'**rei** *f* (16) dabbling, mess.

Manschette [man'ʃɛtə] *f* (15) cuff; ⊕ sleeve; F *~n haben vor* (*dat.*) be afraid of; *~nknopf m* cuff-link; *angenäht:* sleeve-button.

Mantel ['mantəl] *m* (7¹) (*HerrenΩ*) overcoat; (*DamenΩ*) coat; *bsd. leichter:* topcoat; *weiter, ärmelloser:* (*a. fig.*) cloak, *für Damen:* mantle (*a. fig.*); ⊕ case, jacket; *mot., Fahrrad:* cover; *fig. den ~ nach dem Winde hängen* trim one's sails to the wind; '**~tarif** *m* skeleton (*od.* basic tariff) agreement.

Manu|al ♪ [manu'ɑ:l] *n* (3¹) manual; Ωell [~'ɛl] manual.

Manufaktur [~fak'tu:r] *f* manufacture; (*Fabrik*) manufactory; *~wa-ren f/pl.* manufactured goods.

Manuskript [~'skript] *n* (3) manuscript (*abbr.* MS.); *typ.* copy.

Mappe ['mapə] *f* (15) portfolio, briefcase; (*Aktendeckel, Schnellhefter*) folder; *s. a. SammelΩ, SchreibΩ, SchulΩ.*

Mär(e) ['mɛ:rə] *f* (15) tale; (*Kunde*) tidings *pl.*

Märchen ['~çən] *n* (6) fairy-tale; *fig.* story; '**~buch** *n* book of fairy-tales; '**Ωhaft** fabulous.

Marder ['mardər] *m* (7) marten.

Margarine [marga'ri:nə] *f* (15) margarine.

Marien|bild [ma'ri:ən-] *n* image of the Virgin; *~fest n* Lady Day; *~käfer m* lady-bird, *Am. a.* ladybug; *~kult m* Mariolatry.

Marihuana [marihu'ɑ:na] *n* (11, *o. pl.*) marijuana, marihuana.

Marine [ma'ri:nə] *f* (15) marine; (*KriegsΩ*) navy; Ω**blau** navy-blue; *~flugzeug n* naval aircraft; *~-infanterie f*, *~truppen f/pl.* marines *pl.*; *~infanterist m* marine; *~-offizier m* naval officer.

marinieren [mari'ni:rən] pickle.

Marionette [mario'nɛtə] *f* (15) marionette, puppet (*a. fig.*); *~nregierung f* puppet government; *~n-theater n* puppet-show.

Mark¹ [mark] *n* (3) marrow; ♀ *u. fig.* pith; *fig. bis ins ~ to* the core; *j-m durch ~ und Bein gehen* set a p.'s teeth on edge; *~² f* boundary, border(-country); *die ~ Brandenburg* the March of Brandenburg;

~³ (16, *pl. nach Zahlen inv.*) *f* (*Münze*) mark.

markant [~'kant] marked; (*hervorragend*) salient, prominent (*a. fig.*).

Marke ['markə] *f* (15) mark; (*Brief-♀, Steuer♀*) stamp; (*Lebensmittel♀*) coupon; (*Fabrikat*) make; (*Waren♀*) brand; *s. Garderoben♀, Spiel♀*; '**~nartikel** *m* proprietary (*od.* patent *od.* branded) article; '**~nname** *m* trade mark, brand.

'**mark-erschütternd** blood-curdling.

Marketender [~'tɛndər] *m* (7), **~in** *f* (16¹) canteen-(wo)man, sutler.

'**Mark|graf** *m* margrave; '**~gräfin** *f* margravine.

mar'kier|en *v/t.* mark (*a. Sport: den Gegner*); (*vortäuschen*) sham, F put on; *v/i.* sham, F put it on; **♀ung** *f* mark(ing).

'**markig** marrowy; *fig.* pithy.

Markise [~'ki:zə] *f* (15) blind, (window) awning.

Mark|knochen *m* marrow-bone; '**~stein** *m* boundary-stone; *fig.* landmark, milestone.

Markt [markt] *m* (3³) market (*a. Absatz♀, Börse*); *s.* **~platz**; (*Jahr♀*) fair; *am ~* in the market; *auf den ~ bringen* (put on the) market; '**~analyse** *f* market analysis; '**~bericht** *m* market report; '**~bude** *f* booth, stall.

'**markten** (26) bargain (*um* for).

'**markt|fähig, ~gängig** ['~gɛŋiç] marketable; '**♀fähigkeit** *f*, '**♀gängigkeit** *f* marketability; '**♀flecken** *m* market town, borough; '**♀forscher** *m* market researcher; '**♀forschung** *f* market research; '**♀führer** *m* market leader; '**♀halle** *f* covered market; '**♀lage** *f* market condition(s *pl.*); '**♀lücke** *f* market gap, opening; '**♀platz** *m* market-place; '**♀schreier** *m* quack; (*Reklamemacher*) puffer; '**~schreierisch** ostentatious, loud; '**♀wert** *m* market value; '**♀wirtschaft** *f* market economy; *freie ~* free enterprise (economy); '**~wirtschaftlich** free-market, market-economy.

Marmelade [marmə'la:də] *f* (15) jam; *v. Apfelsinen:* marmalade.

Marmor ['marmɔr] *m* (3¹) marble; **♀ieren** [~mo'ri:rən] marble, vein; **♀n** ['~mɔrn] marble; '**~papier** *n* marbled paper; '**~platte** *f* marble slab.

marod|e [ma'ro:də] tired out; (*krank*) ill, sick; **♀eur** [~ro'dø:r] *m* (3¹) marauder.

Marone [ma'ro:nə] *f* (15) edible chestnut.

Marotte [ma'rɔtə] *f* (15) caprice, whim; (*Steckenpferd*) hobby, fad.

Mars¹ [mars] *m inv.* Mars; **~²** *m* (3²) ⚓ top.

Marsch¹ [marʃ] *m* (3² *u.* ³) march; (*sich*) *in ~ setzen* march off; *fig. F j-m den ~ blasen* give a p. a piece of one's mind; *~!* ✕ forward, march!, F (*schnell*) let's go!; **~²** *f* (16) marsh.

Marschall ['marʃal] *m* (3¹ *u.* ³) marshal; '**~stab** *m* marshal's baton.

'**Marsch|befehl** *m* marching orders *pl.*; '**♀bereit, ♀fertig** ready to march; '**~flugkörper** ✕ *m* cruise missile; **♀ieren** [~'ʃi:rən] (25, sn) march; '**♀ig** marshy; '**~kolonne** *f* route column; '**~land** *n* marshy country.

'**Mars|segel** ⚓ *n* topsail; **~stenge** ['~ʃtɛŋə] *f* (15) topmast.

Marstall ['marʃtal] *m* royal stables *pl.*

Marter ['martər] *f* (15) torture; '**~gerät** *n* instrument of torture; '**♀n** (29) torture, torment; '**~pfahl** *m* stake.

Märtyrer ['mɛrtyrər] *m* (7), '**~in** *f* martyr; '**~tod** *m* martyr's death; '**~tum** *n* (1, *o. pl.*) martyrdom.

Marx|ismus [mar'ksismus] *m* (16, *o. pl.*) Marxism; **~ist** [~'ksist] *m* (12), **♀istisch** [~'ksistiʃ] Marxian.

März [mɛrts] *m* (3² *od.* 14) March.

Marzipan [martsi'pa:n] *n*, *m* (3¹) marchpane, marzipan.

Masche ['maʃə] *f* mesh; (*Strick♀ usw.*) stitch; F *fig.* trick, line, play; (*leichte, einträgliche Sache*) soft thing; '**~ndraht** *m* wire-mesh; '**♀nfest** *Strumpf:* ladderproof, *Am.* runproof; '**~ngitter** *n* wire-netting; '**~ngitterzaun** *m* wire-netting fence.

'**maschig** meshy, meshed.

Maschine [ma'ʃi:nə] *f* (15) machine (*a. Schreib♀; a. weitS. Auto, Flugzeug usw.*); (*Dampf♀ usw.*) engine.

maschinell [maʃi'nɛl] mechanical; **~ bearbeiten** machine; **~ hergestellt** machine-made.

Ma'schinen|-antrieb *m* machine drive; *mit ~* machine-driven; **~bau** *m* mechanical engineering; **~garn** *n* machine-spun yarn; ⚲**geschrieben** typewritten; **~gewehr** ✗ *n* machine--gun; **~kode** *m* Computer: machine code; ⚲**mäßig** mechanical, automatic; **~pistole** *f* submachine gun; **~schaden** *m* engine trouble; **~schlosser** *m* engine (*od.* machine) fitter; **~schreiben** *n* typewriting, typing; **~schrift** *f*: *in* ~ typewritten; **~setzer** *typ. m* keyboard operator.

Maschin|erie [maʃinəˈriː] *f* (15) machinery (*a. fig.*); **~ist** [~ˈnist] *m* machinist, engine operator.

Maser [ˈmɑːzər] *f* (15) spot, speck (-le); *im Holz*: vein, streak; ⚲**ig** veined, streaky; **~n** ⚲ *pl.* measles; ⚲**n** (29) grain; **~ung** *f im Holz*: graining.

Maske [ˈmaskə] *f* (15) mask (*a. Schutz*⚲, *Fecht*⚲; *a. P.*); *fig. a.* guise; *thea.* make-up; **~nball** *m* fancy-dress ball; **~nbildner** *m* make-up artist; **~nkostüm** *n* fancy dress; **~rade** [~ˈrɑːdə] *f* (15) masquerade.

maskier|en [masˈkiːrən] (25), ⚲**ung** *f* mask, disguise.

Maskulinum [ˈmaskuliːnum] *n* (9²) masculine (word *od.* form).

Maß [mɑːs] **1.** *n* (3²) measure; (*Verhältnis*) proportion; (*Ausdehnung*) dimension; (*Grad*) degree; (*Mäßigung*) moderation; **~e** *pl.* *und Gewichte* weights and measures; *nach* ~ *gemacht* made to measure, *Am.* custom-made; *j-m* ~ *nehmen* measure a p. (*zu* for); *in hohem* ~*e* to a high degree, highly; *in dem* ~*e wie* in the same measure as; *mit* ~ *und Ziel* in reason; *ohne* ~ *und Ziel* excessively; *über alle* (*od. die*) ~*n* exceedingly; *das* ~ *ist voll!* that's the last straw!; **2.** *f* (14, *nach Zahlen inv.*) (~ *Bier*) quart; **3.** ⚲ *pret. v. messen.*

Massage [maˈsɑːʒə] *f* massage.

massakrieren [masaˈkriːrən] massacre.

'**Maß**-**anzug** *m* tailor-made suit, *Am.* custom(-made) suit; '**~arbeit** *f* bespoke work; *fig.* precision work.

Masse [ˈmasə] *f* (15) mass; (*klebrige usw.* ~) substance; (*Paste*) paste; (*Haupt*⚲) bulk; (*Volk*) multitude; (*Erbschafts*⚲, *Konkurs*⚲) estate; (*Erdung*) earth, *Am.* ground; F *e-e* ~ ... a lot (*od.* lots) of ...; *die breite* ~ the masses *pl.*; *in* ~*n herstellen*

mass-produce.

'**Maß**-**einheit** *f* unit of measurement.

'**Massekabel** ⚡ *n* ground cable.

'**Massen**|-**arbeitslosigkeit** *f* mass unemployment; '**~artikel** ✝ *m* wholesale article, mass-produced article; '**~entlassung** *f* mass dismissals *pl.*; '**~gesellschaft** *f* mass society; '**~grab** *n* common grave; '⚲**haft** plenty (of), abundant; *adv. a.* in coarse numbers; '**~karambolage** *f* pile-up; '**~kundgebung** *f* mass rally; '**~medium** *n* mass medium (*pl.* media); '**~mord** *m* wholesale (*od.* mass) murder; '**~produktion** *f* mass production; '**~psychose** *f* mass psychosis; '**~versammlung** *f* mass meeting, rally; '⚲**weise** in masses.

Masseu|r [maˈsøːr] *m* (3) masseur; **~se** [~ˈsøːzə] *f* masseuse.

'**Maß|gabe** *f* measure, proportion; *nach* ~ (*gen.*) according to; *mit der* ~, *daß* provided that; '⚲**gebend,** '⚲**geblich** authoritative, standard (*work etc.*); (*entscheidend*) decisive; (*zuständig*) competent; (*führend*) leading; ✝ ~*e Beteiligung* controlling interest; '⚲**geschneidert** made-to--measure; '⚲**halten** observe moderation.

mas'sieren¹ 🏥 massage; ~² ✗ mass.

'**massig** bulky, solid.

mäßig [ˈmɛːsiç] moderate; *im Genuß*: frugal; (*mittel*~) middling; (*ziemlich schlecht*) mediocre, poor; **~en** [ˈ~gən] (25) moderate; (*mildern*) mitigate; *Tempo*: slacken; *sich* ~ restrain o.s.; *s.* gemäßigt; '⚲**keit** *f* moderation; temperance; frugality; mediocre (*od.* poor) quality; '⚲**ung** *f* moderation; mitigation; restraint.

massiv [maˈsiːf] massive (*a. fig.*); ⚲ *geol. n* massif; ⚲**gold** *n* solid gold.

'**Maß|krug** *m* (beer) mug, stein; **~'lieb(chen)** ♀ *n* daisy; '⚲**los** (*unmäßig*) immoderate; (*übertrieben*) excessive; (*überspannt*) extravagant; '**~losigkeit** *f* immoderatness; excess; extravagance; '**~nahme** *f*, '**~regel** *f* measure; ~*n ergreifen od. treffen* take measures *od.* steps; '⚲**regeln** (29) reprimand, inflict disciplinary punishment on; '**~schneider** *m* bespoke tailor, *Am.* custom tailor; '**~stab** *m* measure; *auf Karten usw.*: scale; *fig.* standard; *in großem (kleinem)* ~ on a large (small) scale; e-n ~ *anlegen an (acc.)* apply a standard to; '~**voll** moderate.

Mast[1] [mast] *m* (3² *u.* 5¹), (⚓ *a.* '~**baum** *m*) mast; (*Trage*⚓) pylon; *tel.* pole.

Mast[2] *f* (16) mast, food; '~**darm** *m* rectum.

mästen ['mɛstən] (26) feed, fatten; *sich* ~ *an* (*dat.*) batten on.

'**Mast|korb** *m* top, masthead; '~-**ochse** *m* fattened ox; '~**vieh** *n* fattened cattle.

Mater *typ.* ['maːtər] *f* (15) matrix.

Material [mater'jaːl] *n* (8²) material (*a. fig.*); ~**disposition** *f* material management; ~**fehler** *m* fault in (the) material; ~**ismus** [~ja'lismus] *m* (16, *o. pl.*) materialism; ~**ist** [~'list] *m* (12) materialist; ⚓**istisch** [~'listiʃ] materialistic; ~**kosten** *pl.* cost *sg.* of materials; ~**lager** *n* stock of materials.

Mater|ie [~'teːrjə] *f* (15) matter; *fig. a.* subject; ⚓**iell** [~ter'jɛl] material; (*geldlich*) financial; (~ *eingestellt*) materialistic.

Mathe F ['matə] *f* (16, *o. pl.*) maths, *Am.* math; ~**matik** [matema'tiːk] *f* (16) mathematics *sg.*; ~**matiker** [~-'maːtikər] *m* (7) mathematician; ⚓-'**matisch** mathematical.

Matinee *thea.* [mati'neː] *f* (15) matinée, morning performance.

Matjeshering ['matjəsheːriŋ] *m* white herring, matie.

Matratze [ma'tratsə] *f* (15) mattress.

Mätresse [mɛ'trɛsə] *f* (15) (kept) mistress.

Matrikel [ma'triːkəl] *f* (15) register, roll.

Matrize [~'triːtsə] *f* (15) matrix, die; (*Schablone u. zum Maschinenschreiben*) stencil.

Matrone [~'troːnə] *f* (15) matron.

Matrose [~'troːzə] *m* (13) sailor, seaman; ~**n-anzug** *m* sailor suit.

Matsch [matʃ] *m* (3²) (*Brei*) pulp, squash; (*Schlamm*) mud, slush; '⚓**ig** pulpy; muddy, slushy.

matt [mat] weak, faint, feeble; (*schlaff*) limp; *Stimme*: faint; *Auge, Licht*: dim; *Farbe, Licht*, ✝ *Börse, Stil*: dull; *Gold*: dead; *bsd. phot.* mat(t); *Kugel*: spent; *Schach*: mate; ⚔ ~e *Birne* frosted bulb;

Schach: ~ *setzen* (check)mate.

Matte ['matə] *f* (15) mat; (*Wiese*) meadow.

'**Matt|glas** *n* ground (*od.* frosted) glass; '~**gold** *n* dead gold; '~**heit** *f* faintness; dul(l)ness; ⚓**ieren** [~'tiː-rən] mat; *Glas*: frost; '~**igkeit** *f* (16) exhaustion; '~**scheibe** *f phot.* ground glass; *TV* screen; F *fig.* ~ *haben* be in a daze.

Matur(um) [ma'tuːr(um)] *n* (3¹, *o. pl.*) *s. Abitur.*

Mätzchen ['mɛtsçən] F *n*/*pl.* (6) tricks; (*Unnötiges*) frills; ⊕ gimcracks; ~ *machen* play tricks.

Mauer ['mauər] *f* (15) wall; '~-**blümchen** *fig. n* wallflower; '⚓n (29) *v/i.* make a wall, lay bricks; *Sport*: stonewall; *v/t.* build (in stone *od.* brick); '~**segler** *orn. m* (common) swift; '~**stein** *m*, '~**ziegel** *m* brick; '~**werk** *n* masonry.

Mauke *vet.* ['maukə] *f* (15) malanders *pl.*

Maul [maul] *n* mouth; P *das* ~ *halten* hold one's tongue, shut up; *s. a. Mund*; '~-**affe** F *m* gaper; ~n *feilhalten* stand gaping; '~**beere** *f* mulberry.

Mäulchen ['mɔʏlçən] *n* (6) little mouth.

maulen ['maulən] (25) grumble.

'**Maul|-esel** *m* mule; '⚓**faul** F too lazy to speak; '~**held** *m* braggart; '~**korb** *m* muzzle; '~**schelle** *f* slap; '~**sperre** *f* lock-jaw; '~**tier** *n* mule; '~- **und** '**Klauenseuche** *vet. f* foot-and-mouth disease; '~**werk** F *n* (*gutes* ~ gift of the) gab; '~**wurf** *m* mole; '~**wurfs-haufen** *m* mole-hill.

Maurer ['maurər] *m* (7) bricklayer, mason; '~**kelle** *f* trowel; '~**meister** *m* master mason; '~**polier** *m* bricklayer's foreman.

'**maurisch** Moorish.

Maus [maus] *f* (14¹) mouse (*pl.* mice).

Mäus·chen ['mɔʏsçən] *n* (6) little mouse; F *fig.* (*Schatz*) darling, pet; '⚓'**still** stockstill; quite hushed.

mauscheln ['mauʃəln] (29) talk sheeny; *fig.* jabber.

'**Mausefalle** *f* mousetrap; *fig.* death-trap.

mausen ['mauzən] (27) *v/i.* catch mice; *v/t. u. v/i.* F filch, steal.

Mauser ['mauzər] *f* (15) mo(u)lt (-ing); '⚓n (29) (*a. sich*) mo(u)lt.

'**mausetot** quite dead, as dead as mutton. [put on airs.⟩
mausig F ['⁓ziç]: *sich* ⁓ *machen*⟩
Maut [maut] *f* (16), '⁓**gebühr** *f* toll (-charge); '⁓**stelle** *f* toll-gate; '⁓**straße** *f* toll-road, *Am.* turnpike.
maximal [maksi'mɑːl] maximum; *adv.* at the most; *s. a. Höchst…*; ♀**beschleunigung** *f* peak acceleration.
Maxime [ma'ksiːmə] *f* (15) maxim.
Maximum ['maksimum] *n* (9²) maximum.
Mayonnaise [majɔ'nɛːzə] *f* (15) mayonnaise.
Mäzen [mɛ'tseːn] *m* (3¹) patron, sponsor.
Mechanik [me'çɑːnik] *f* (16) mechanics *sg.*; (*Triebwerk*) mechanism; ⁓**er** *m* (7) mechanic(ian).
me'**chan|isch** mechanical (*a. fig.*); ⁓**isieren** [⁓çani'ziːrən] mechanize; ♀**ismus** [⁓'nismus] *m* (16¹) mechanism.
Mecker|er F ['mɛkərər] *m* (7) grumbler; ♀**n** (29) bleat; F *fig.* grumble, *sl.* grouse, *Am.* F gripe.
Medaill|e [me'daljə] *f* (15) medal; ⁓**on** [⁓'jõ] *n* (11) (⁓*bild usw.*) medallion; (*Schmuckstück*) locket.
Medien ['meːdiən] *n/pl.* (9) media; '⁓**technologie** *f* media technology; '⁓**verbund** *m* multi-media system.
Medikament [medika'mɛnt] *n* (3) medicament, medicine.
Mediothek [medio'teːk] *f* (16) media library.
Medium ['meːdium] *n* (9) medium.
Medizin [medi'tsiːn] *f* (16) *allg.* medicine; (*Arznei*) *a.* medicament; ⁓**er** *m* (7) medical student; (*Arzt*) doctor; ♀**isch** [⁓'tsiːniʃ] medical; (*arzneilich usw.*) medicinal; *Seife usw.*: medicated.
Meer [meːr] *n* (3) sea, ocean; '⁓**busen** *m* gulf, bay; '⁓**enge** *f* straits *pl.*; '⁓**esbiologe** *m* marine biologist; '⁓**esbiologie** *f* marine biology; '⁓**esfrüchte** *f/pl.* seafood *sg.*; '⁓**esgrund** *m* sea-bed; '⁓**eshöhe** *f*, '⁓**esspiegel** *m* sea level; '⁓**esstille** *f* calm (at sea); '⁓**esverschmutzung** *f* pollution of the sea; '⁓**grün** *n* sea-green; '⁓**katze** *f* green monkey; '⁓**rettich** *m* horse-radish; '⁓**schaum** *m* meerschaum; '⁓**schwein** *n* porpoise; '⁓**schweinchen** *n* guinea-pig; '⁓**ungeheuer** *n* sea-monster; '⁓**wasser** *n* sea-water;

'⁓**weib** *n* mermaid.
Mega|hertz [mega'hɛrts] *n inv.* megacycles *pl.* per second (*abbr.* Mc/s); ⁓**phon** [⁓'foːn] *n* (3¹) megaphone.
Mehl [meːl] *n* (3) flour; *grobes*: meal; (*Staub*) dust; '⁓**brei** *m* pap; '♀**ig** mealy, farinaceous; '⁓**kloß** *m* dumpling; '⁓**sack** *m* flour-bag; ⁓**schwitze** ['⁓ʃvitsə] *f* (15) roux; '⁓**speise** *f* farinaceous food; *süß*: sweet dish, pudding; '⁓**suppe** *f* gruel; '⁓**tau** *m* mildew, blight; '⁓**wurm** *m* meal-worm.
mehr [meːr] **1.** (*comp. v. viel*) more; *nicht* ⁓ no more, *zeitlich a.*: no (*od.* not any) longer; *nie* ⁓ never again; *s. immer*; ⁓ *als* more than, *ein gewisses Maß* in excess of; ⁓ *und* ⁓ more and more; ⁓ *oder weniger* more or less; *nicht* ⁓, *nicht minder* neither more nor less; *ich habe niemand* (*nichts*) ⁓ I have no one (nothing) left; *s. um*; **2.** *n* (*Zuwachs*) increase; (*Überschuß*) (sur)plus; '♀**arbeit** *f* extra work; *im Betrieb*: overtime; '♀**ausgabe** *f* additional expenditure; '♀**betrag** *m* surplus; (*Zuschlag*) extra charge; '⁓**deutig** ambiguous; '♀**einnahme** *f* additional receipts.
'**mehr|en** (25) (*a. sich*) augment, increase; '⁓**ere** several; ♀**eres** *n* several things *pl.*; sundries *pl.*; '⁓**erlei** various, diverse; '⁓**fach** manifold; (*wiederholt*) repeated; (*a.* ⊕, ∮) multiple; *adv.* repeatedly, several times; '♀**fachbelichtung** *f* multiple exposure; '♀**fachsprengkopf** *m* multiple warhead; '♀**fahrtenkarte** *f* carnet, multiple-trip ticket; '♀**farbendruck** *m* multicolo(u)r print(ing); '♀**gebot** *n* higher bid; '♀**gewicht** *n* excess weight; '♀**heit** *f* (*a. parl.*) majority; '♀**heitsbeschluß** *m*: *durch* ⁓ by a majority of votes, *Am.* by a plurality; '♀**kosten** *pl.* additional cost *sg.*; (*Zuschlag*) extra charges; ⁓**malig** ['⁓mɑːliç] repeated; ⁓**mals** ['⁓mɑːls] several times; ⁓**seitig** ['⁓zaitiç] ∡ polygonal; *pol.* multilateral; ⁓**silbig** ['⁓zilbiç] polysyllabic; ⁓**sprachig** ['⁓praːxiç] polyglot; ⁓**stimmig** ♪ ['⁓timiç] (arranged) for several voices; ⁓**er** *Gesang* part-song; ⁓**stöckig** ['⁓ʃtœkiç] multi-storey; ⁓**stufig** ['⁓ʃtuːfiç] *Rakete*: multi-stage; '♀**ung** *f* increase; ⁓**tägig** ['⁓tɛːgiç] of several days; '♀-

verbrauch *m* excess consumption; '2**wert** *m* surplus value; '2**wert-steuer** *f* value-added tax; '2**zahl** *f* majority; *gr.* plural (number); '2**zweck...** general-purpose, multi--purpose.

meiden ['maɪdən] (30) avoid, shun.

Meier ['maɪər] *m* (7) dairy-farmer; ~**ei** [~'raɪ] *f,* '~**hof** *m* dairy-farm.

Meile ['maɪlə] *f* (15) mile; '~**nstein** *m* milestone (*a. fig.*); '2**nweit** (extending) for miles; *fig.* very far.

Meiler ['maɪlər] *m* (7) charcoal-pile; (*Atom*2) (atomic) pile.

mein [maɪn] (20) my; *der, die, das* ~**e,** *meinige* mine; *das* 2 *und Dein* mine and thine; *die* 2*en pl.* my people *od.* family *sg.*

Mein·eid ['maɪn²aɪt] *m* (3) perjury; *e-n* ~ *leisten* commit perjury; 2**ig** ['~dɪç] perjured; ~ *werden* perjure o.s.

meinen ['maɪnən] (25) think, believe; (*beabsichtigen; sagen wollen*) mean; (*sagen*) say; ~ *Sie das ernst?* do you (really) mean it?; *es ehrlich* (*od. gut*) ~ mean well.

'**meiner** a) of me; b) mine; ~**seits** ['~zaɪts] for my part; *ganz* ~*!* F same here!

meinesgleichen ['~əs'glaɪçən] people like me, the like(s) of me.

meinet|halben ['~ət'halbən] for my sake, in (*od.* on) my behalf; '~**-'wegen** *s.* meinethalben; (*ich habe nichts dagegen*) I don't mind.

meinige ['~igə] (18b): *der, die, das* ~ mine; *die* 2*n pl.* my family *sg.*

'**Meinung** *f* opinion, view; *die öffentliche* ~ (the) public opinion; *meiner* ~ *nach* to my mind, in my opinion; *j-m* (*gehörig*) *die* ~ *sagen* give a p. a piece of one's mind; *mit j-m e-r* ~ *sein* agree with a p.; '~**s-äußerung** *f* expression of opinion; '~**s-austausch** *m* exchange of views; '~**sbefragung** *f,* '~**s-umfrage** *f* opinion poll; '2**sbildend** opinion-forming; '~**sbildner** *m* opinion leader (*od.* maker); '~**sforscher** *m* public opinion pollster; '~**sforschung** *f* opinion research; '~**sfreiheit** *f* freedom of thought; '~**sverschiedenheit** *f* difference (of opinion), disagreement.

Meise ['maɪzə] *f* (15) titmouse.

Meißel ['maɪsəl] *m* (7), '2**n** (29) chisel.

meist [maɪst] (18, *sup. v. viel*) most; *die* ~*en pl.* most people; *das* ~*e* the most, the greater (*od.* best) part; *am* ~*en* most; ~*enteils,* ~*ens* mostly, generally; (*gewöhnlich*) usually; '2**begünstigungs...** preferential; *most favo(u)red nation clause usw.*; '~**bietend** bidding highest; 2**bietende** ['~bi:təndə] *m* (18) highest bidder.

Meister ['maɪstər] *m* (7) master (*a. fig.*); *im Betrieb:* foreman; *Sport:* champion; '2**haft,** '2**lich** masterly; *adv.* brilliantly; '~**in** *f* mistress; master's wife; *Sport:* champion(ess); '~**leistung** *f* superb performance; '2**n** (29) master (*a. fig. Gefühle, Lage, Sprache usw.*); '~**prüfung** *f* trade examination; '~**schaft** *f* (16) mastery; *Sport:* championship; '~**schaftsspiel** *n* league match; '~**schütze** *m* crack shot; '~**stück** *n,* '~**werk** *n* masterpiece; '~**titel** *m Sport:* title.

'**Meistgebot** *n* highest bid.

Melanch|olie [melaŋko'li:] *f* (15), 2**olisch** [~'ko:lif] melancholy.

'**Melde|-amt** *n* registration office; '~**fahrer** *m* dispatch-rider; ~**gänger** ⚔ ['~gɛŋər] *m* messenger; '~**hund** *m* messenger dog; '~**liste** *f Sport:* list of entries; '2**n** (26) *v/t.* announce; (*berichten*) report; *j-m* et. ~ inform a p. of a th., *amtlich:* notify a th. to a p.; *dienstlich:* report a th. to a p.; *sich* ~ *dienstlich:* report (*bei* to; *zu* for); *teleph.* answer; *fig.* make itself felt; *sich* ~ *zu* apply for, *freiwillig:* volunteer for; *zum Examen usw.:* enter (one's name) for; *sich* ~ *lassen* send in one's name; *sich auf ein Inserat* ~ answer an ad(vertisement); *s. krank, Wort;* *v/i. Sport:* enter (*zu* for); 2**pflichtig** 📋 notifiable.

'**Meldung** *f* announcement; (*Nachricht*) advice, information, notification; (*dienstliche* ~, *Zeitungs*2) report; (*Funk*2 *usw.*) message; (*Bewerbung*) application; *Sport:* entry.

meliert [me'li:rt] mottled; *Haar:* greying.

Melisse ⚘ [me'lisə] *f* (15) balm-mint; ~**ngeist** *m* Carmelite water.

melk|en ['mɛlkən] (30) milk; '2**maschine** *f* milking machine.

Melod|ie [melo'di:] *f* (15) tune,

melody, air; ²isch [~ˈloːdiʃ] melodious.

Melone [meˈloːnə] *f* (15) melon; F (*steifer Hut*) bowler, *Am.* derby.

Meltau [ˈmeːltaʊ] *m* (3) mildew.

Membran(e) [mɛmˈbrɑːn(ə)] *f* (16) membrane; ⊕ diaphragm.

Memme [ˈmɛmə] *f* (15) coward.

Memoiren [memoˈɑːrən] *n/pl.* memoirs.

Memorandum [memoˈrandum] *n* (9[2]) memorandum; (*Notiz*) *mst* memo.

memorieren [memoˈriːrən] memorize.

Menagerie [menaʒəˈriː] *f* (15) menagerie.

Menge [ˈmɛŋə] *f* (15) quantity; amount; ♗ set; (*Vielheit*) multitude; (*Menschen*²) crowd; *in großer* ~ in abundance, *v. Menschen u. Tieren*: in crowds; *e-e* ~ *Geld* plenty (*od.* F lots) of money; *e-e* ~ *Bücher* a great many (F a lot of) books; ˈ²**n** (25) mingle, mix (*a. sich*; *unter acc.* with); *sich* ~ *in* (*acc.*) meddle with; ˈ~**nlehre** ♗ *f* set theory; ˈ²**nmäßig** quantitative(ly *adv.*); ˈ~**nrabatt** *m* quantity discount.

Mennig [ˈmɛniç] *m* (3), ˈ~**e** *f* minium, red lead.

Mensch [mɛnʃ] *m* (12) human being, (*a. der* ~ *als Gattung*) man; *einzelner*: person; (*Kerl*) fellow; *die* ~*en pl.* people *pl.*, the world *sg.*, *s.* ~*heit*; *kein* ~ nobody; F ~*!* man!, oh boy!

ˈ**Menschen|-affe** *m* anthropoid ape; ˈ~**-alter** *n* generation, age; ˈ~**feind** (**-in** *f*) *m* misanthropist; ˈ~**fresser** *m* (7) cannibal; ˈ~**freund(in** *f*) *m* philanthropist, humanitarian; ˈ²**freundlich** philanthropic, humanitarian; *seit* ˈ~**gedenken** *n* from time immemorial; within the memory of man; ˈ~**geschlecht** *n* human race, mankind; *in* ˈ~**gestalt** *f* in human shape; ˈ~**handel** *m* slave-trade; ˈ~**haß** *m* misanthropy; ˈ~**jagd** *f* manhunt; ˈ~**kenner(in** *f*) *m* judge of men; ˈ~**kenntnis** *f* knowledge of human nature; ˈ~**kunde** *f* anthropology; ˈ~**leben** *n* (human) life; ˈ²**leer** deserted; ˈ~**liebe** *f* philanthropy; ˈ~**material** *n* manpower, human stock; ˈ²**möglich** humanly possible; ˈ~**pflicht** *f* duty of (*od.* as) a human being; ˈ~**raub** *m* kidnap(p)ing; ˈ~**rechte** *n/pl.* human rights; ˈ~**rechtler(in** *f*) *m* human rights activist; ˈ~**rechtsbewegung** *f* human rights movement; ˈ²**scheu** shy, unsociable; ˈ~**schinder** *m* slave-driver; ˈ~**schlag** *m* race (of men); ˈ~**seele** *f* human soul; *keine* ~ not a living soul; ˈ~**sˈkind!** goodness!, good heavens!; ˈ~**sohn** *m* Son of Man; ˈ²ˈ**-unwürdig** degrading; ˈ~**verstand** *m*: *gesunder* ~ common sense; ˈ~**würde** *f* man's dignity.

ˈ**Menschheit** *f* mankind, humanity, human race.

ˈ**menschlich** human; (*human*) humane; ˈ²**keit** *f* human nature; (*Humanität*) humanity, humaneness.

Menschwerdung [ˈ~veːrduŋ] *f* incarnation.

Menstru|ation [mɛnstruaˈtsjoːn] *f* menstruation; ²**ieren** [~ˈiːrən] menstruate.

Mensur [mɛnˈzuːr] *f* (16) ⚗ measure; (*Studenten*²) students' duel.

Mentalität [mɛntaliˈtɛːt] *f* (16) mentality.

Menthol [mɛnˈtoːl] *n* (3[1]) menthol.

Menü [məˈnyː] *n* (11) set meal, *mittags*: set lunch.

Menuett [menuˈɛt] *n* (3) minuet.

Mergel [ˈmɛrgəl] *m* (7) marl.

Meridi|an [meriˈdjɑːn] *m* (3[1]) meridian; ²**onal** [~djoˈnɑːl] meridional.

Meringe [meˈriŋgə] *f* (15) meringue.

merk|bar [ˈmɛrkbɑːr] perceptible, noticeable; ˈ²**blatt** *n* (instructional) leaflet; ˈ²**buch** *n* note-book; ˈ~**en** (25) notice; (*spüren*) feel, sense; (*erkennen*) realize; (*gewahr sein, werden*) be(come) aware of; *sich et.* ~ retain (*od.* remember) a th.; *das werde ich mir* ~ I will bear that in mind; ~ *auf* (*acc.*) pay attention to; ~ *lassen* show, betray; *nichts* ~ *lassen* not to show one's feelings; ˈ~**lich** *s. merkbar*; (*beträchtlich*) considerable; (*deutlich*) marked; ˈ²**mal** *n* sign, mark; (*Eigentümlichkeit*) characteristic, feature; *besondere* ~*e pl.* peculiarities, *Am.* marks.

ˈ**merkwürdig** (*auffallend*) remarkable, noteworthy; (*seltsam*) odd, curious, strange; ~**erweise** [ˈ~igərˈvaɪzə] strange to say, oddly enough; ˈ²**keit** *f* remarkableness; (*Gegenstand*) curiosity; (*das Seltsame*) oddness.

'**Merk|zeichen** n mark; '**~zettel** m note, memo.

meschugge [me'ʃugə] F crazy, mad.

Mesner ['mɛsnər] m (7) sexton.

meßbar ['mɛsbɑːr] measurable.

'**Meß|becher** m measuring cup; ⚓ beaker; '**~buch** n missal; '**~diener** m acolyte.

Messe ['mɛsə] f (15) fair; eccl. mass; s. lesen; ✗, ⚓ mess (hall).

messen ['mɛsən] (30) measure (a. groß usw. sein; a. mit Blicken); sich ~ mit compete (od. grapple) with, geistig: match wits with; sich nicht ~ können mit P.: be no match for, S.: not to compare with.

Messer[1] ['mɛsər] n (7) knife; (Rasier2) razor; ⚕ scalpel; fig. bis aufs ~ to the knife; auf des ~s Schneide stehen be on a razor's edge; s. Kehle; **~**[2] m (7) (Gas2 usw.) meter; '**~held** m cut-throat; '**~klinge** f knife-blade; '**~rücken** m back of a knife; '2**scharf** razor-sharp (a. fig.); '**~schmied** m cutler; '**~schneide** f edge of a knife; **~stecherei** [~ʃtɛçə'raɪ] knife-battle; '**~stich** m thrust (od. stab) with a knife.

'**Meßgewand** n chasuble.

Messias [mɛ'siːas] m inv. Messiah.

Messing ['mɛsɪŋ] n (3¹) brass; '**~blech** n sheet-brass; '**~draht** m brass wire; '**~rohr** n brass tube.

'**Meß|-instrument** n measuring instrument; '**~latte** f surveyor's (od. stadia) rod; '**~opfer** n (sacrifice of the) mass; '**~rute** f surveyor's rod; '**~tisch** m plane table; '**~tischblatt** n topographic map.

Messung ['mɛsʊŋ] f (15) measurement; (Ablesung) reading.

Mestize [mɛ'stiːtsə] m (12) mestizo.

Met [meːt] m (3) mead.

Metall [me'tal] n (3¹) metal; **~arbeiter** m metal worker; **~baukasten** m meccano; 2en, 2isch metallic; **~geld** n specie, coins pl.; **~glanz** m metallic lustre; 2haltig metalliferous; 2ic(farben) [me'talik(-)] metallic; **~industrie** f metal industry; **~säge** f hacksaw; 2verarbeitend metal-working; **~verbindung** f metallic compound; **~vorrat** m der Bank: bullion reserve; **~waren** f/pl. hardware sg.

Metamorphose [metamɔr'foːzə] f (15) metamorphosis.

Metapher [me'tafər] f (15) metaphor.

Meta|phy'sik f metaphysics pl., oft sg.; 2¹**physisch** metaphysical.

Meteor [mete'oːr] n, m (3¹) meteor; **~-eisen** n meteoric iron; **~olog(e)** [~ʔoro'loːk, ~gə] m (12 [13]) meteorologist; **~ologie** [~lo'giː] f (15) meteorology; 2**ologisch** [~'loːgiʃ] meteorologic(al); **~stein** [~'ʔoːr-] m meteoric stone, meteorite.

Meter ['meːtər] n u. m (7) met|re, Am. -er; '**~maß** n metre rule; (Bandmaß) tape-measure; '**~ware** f goods pl. sold by the metre.

Method|e [me'toːdə] f (15) method; 2**isch** methodical; **~ist** [~to'dɪst] m (12) methodist.

Methan [me'taːn] n (3¹, o. pl.) methane.

Methyl-alkohol [me'tyːlʔalkohol] m methyl alcohol.

Metr|ik ['meːtrik] f (16) metrics pl., prosody; 2**isch** metrical.

Metronom [metro'noːm] n (3¹) metronome.

Metropole [metro'poːlə] f (15) metropolis.

Mette ['mɛtə] f (15) matins pl.

Mettwurst ['mɛtvʊrst] f Bologna sausage.

Metz|elei [mɛtsə'laɪ] f (16) slaughter; '2**eln** (29) slaughter, butcher; **~ger** ['~gər] m (7) butcher.

Meuchel|mord ['mɔʏçəl-] m assassination; '**~mörder(in** f) m assassin; '2n (29) assassinate.

meuch|lerisch ['~ləriʃ] treacherous; **~lings** ['~lɪŋs] treacherously.

Meute ['mɔʏtə] f (15) pack of hounds; fig. gang; **~rei** [~'raɪ] f (16) mutiny; '**~rer** m (7) mutineer; '2**rn** (29) mutiny; rebel (a. fig.); '2**rnd** mutinous.

Mexikan|er [mɛksi'kɑːnər] m (7), **~erin** f (16¹), 2**isch** Mexican.

miau [mi'aʊ], **~en** (25) mew.

mich [mɪç] (s. ich 19) me; ~ selbst myself.

mied [miːt] pret. v. meiden.

Mieder ['miːdər] n (7) bodice; '**~höschen** n panty girdle; '**~waren** f/pl. corsetry sg., Am. foundation garments.

Mief F [miːf] m (3, o. pl.) fug, pong; (Gestank) stink, stench; '2en F pong.

Miene ['miːnə] f (15) countenance, air; (Gesicht) face; ~ machen et. zu tun offer to do; e-e ernste ~ aufsetzen look stern; *keine* ~ *verziehen* not to flinch; *s. gut;* '~**nspiel** *n*, '~**nsprache** *f* play of features.

mies [miːs] F miserable, bad, F awful; ♀**macher** ['miːsmaxər] *m* alarmist; '♀**muschel** *f* mussel.

Miet|-auto ['miːt-] *n* hired car; '~**e¹** *f* (15) (*Wohnungs*♀) rent; *weitS.* hire; (*Mietsumme*) rental; *in* ~ *nehmen* hire, rent; *zur* ~ *wohnen* live in lodgings; ~**e²** ⚡ *f* (*Heu*♀, *Korn*♀) stack, shock, rick; (*Kartoffel*♀ *usw.*) clamp; '♀**en** (26) rent; *weitS.* hire; *Schiff usw.*: charter; '~**er** *m* (7), '~**erin** *f* tenant; (*Unter-*♀) lodger; ⚡ lessee; *v. Sachen*: hirer; '~**erschaft** *f* tenantry; '~**erschutz** *m* (legal) protection of tenants; '~**ertrag** *m* rental; '♀**frei** rent-free; '~**pferd** *n* hired horse; '~**shaus** *n* block of flats, *Am.* apartment house; '~**skaserne** *f* tenement house; '~**spiegel** *m* rent guidelines *pl.*; '~**verhältnis** *n* tenancy; '~**vertrag** *m* lease; '~**wagen** *m* hired car; '~**wagenverleih** *m* car-hire service; '♀**weise** on hire; '~**wert** *m* rental value; '~**wohnung** *f* rented flat, *Am.* rental apartment; '~**zins** *m* rent.

Miez(e) F ['miːts(ə)] *f* (15) puss, pussy (-cat).

Migräne [miˈgrɛːnə] *f* (15) migraine.

Mikrob|e [miˈkroːbə] *f* (15) microbe; ♀**isch** microbial.

Mikro|-elektronik ['miːkro-] *f* microelectronics *sg.*; '~**film** *m* microfilm.

Mikroko'pie [mikro-] *f* microcopy.

Mikrolaufwerk ['miːkro-] *n* *Computer*: micro drive.

Mikro'meter [mikro-] *n* micrometer.

Mikro-orga'nismus [mikro-] *m* micro-organism.

Mikrophon [mikroˈfoːn] *n* (3¹) microphone, F mike.

Mikroprozessor ['miːkroprotsɛsɔr] *m* (8¹) microprocessor.

Mikroskop [~ˈskoːp] *n* (3¹) microscope; ♀**isch** (*a.* ~ *klein*) microscopic(ally *adv.*).

Mikrowelle ['miːkro-] *f* microwave; '~**nherd** *m* microwave oven.

Milbe ['milbə] *f* (15) mite.

Milch [milç] *f* (16) milk; (*Fisch*♀) milt, soft roe; *Am.* (*Fisch*♀) milt, soft roe; '~**bar** *f* milk bar; '~**bart** *m* *fig.* milksop; '~**brot** *n*, '~**brötchen** *n* (French) roll; '~**bru-**

der *m* foster-brother; '~**drüse** *f* lacteal gland; '~**er** *m* (7) milter, soft-roe(d) fish; '~**geschäft** *n* dairy, creamery; '~**glas** *n* opalescent (*od.* frosted) glass; '♀**ig** milky; '~**kaffee** *m* coffee with milk; '~**kuh** *f* milch cow; '~**kur** *f* milk diet; '~**mädchen** *n* milkmaid; '~**mann** *m* milkman, dairyman; '~**mixgetränk** *n* milk shake; '~**ner** *m* *s. Milcher;* '~**pulver** *n* powdered milk; '~**reis** *m* rice-pudding; '~**säure** 🜊 *f* lactic acid; '~**schorf** ⚕ *m* milk crust; '~**speise** *f* milk-food; '~**straße** *ast.* *f* Milky Way, Galaxy; '~**suppe** *f* milk-soup; '~**vieh** *n* dairy cattle; '~**wirtschaft** *f* dairy(-farm); '~**zahn** *m* milk-tooth; '~**zucker** *m* milk sugar, lactose.

mild, ~**e¹** [milt, '~də] *allg.* mild; (*sanft*) gentle, soft; *Wein:* smooth; (*nachsichtig*) indulgent; *Stiftung:* charitable; *Strafe:* mild, lenient; ~**e** *gesagt* to put it mildly.

'**Milde²** *f* (15) mildness *usw.*, *s. mild;* ~ *walten lassen* be lenient.

milder|n ['~dərn] (29) soften, mitigate; *Schmerz:* soothe, alleviate; (*erleichtern*) relieve; 🜊 correct; *Ausdruck:* qualify; ~**de** *Umstände* *m/pl.* extenuating circumstances; '♀**ung** *f* 🜊 correction; '♀**ungsgrund** *m* mitigating cause.

'**mild|herzig**, '~**tätig** ['milt-] charitable; '♀**herzigkeit** *f* charitableness; '♀**tätigkeit** *f* charity.

Milieu [milˈjøː] *n* (11) environment, surroundings *pl.*, milieu (*fr.*); ♀**bedingt** environmental.

Militär [miliˈtɛːr] (11) **1.** *n* (*o. pl.*) *the* military, soldiery, army; **2.** *m* (11) military man, soldier; *in Zssgn* military; ~**arzt** *m* medical officer, army surgeon; ~**attaché** *m* military attaché; ~**bündnis** *n* military alliance; ~**dienst** *m* military service; ~**diktatur** *f* military dictatorship; ~**gericht** *n* military court; ♀**isch** military; *fig.* martial.

Militarismus [militaˈrismus] *m* *inv.* militarism.

Mili'tär|macht *f* military power; ~**musik** *f* military music; ~**regierung** *f* military government; ~**seelsorge** military religious welfare.

Miliz [miˈliːts] *f* (16) militia; ~**soldat** *m* militiaman.

Milliar|där [miljarˈdɛːr] *m* (3¹) multimillionaire; ~de [mil'jardə] f (15) billion; *in England* † thousand million.

Milli'meter [mili-] *n u. m* millimet|re, *Am.* -er; ~·**arbeit** f precision work; ~**papier** *n* graph paper.

Million [mil'joːn] f (16) million; ~**är** [~joˈnɛːr] *m* (3¹) millionaire; 2**ste(r, s)** [~'joːnstə] millionth.

Milz [milts] f (16) spleen, milt; '~**brand** ⚕ *m* anthrax; '~**krankheit** f splenopathy; '~**stechen** *n* splenalgia.

Mim|e ['miːmə] *m* (13) mime; '~**ik** f (16) mimic art, miming; '~**iker** *m* (7), '2**isch** mimic; ~**ikry** ['mimikri] f (11¹, *o. pl.*) mimicry.

Mimose [mi'moːzə] f (15) mimosa; 2**nhaft** *fig.* oversensitive.

minder ['mindər] (18, *s.* gering, wenig) *adv.* less; *adj.* less(er), smaller; *an Güte:* inferior; (*weniger bedeutend*) minor; *s.* mehr; '~**bemittelt** of moderate means; '2**betrag** *m* deficit, shortage; '2**-einnahme** f decrease of receipts; '2**-gewicht** *n* short weight; '2**heit** f minority; '2**heitsregierung** f minority government; '~**jährig** under age, minor; 2**jährige** ['~jɛːrigə] *m, f* (18) minor; 2**jährigkeit** ['~riçkaɪt] f minority; '~**n** (29) diminish, lessen; (*herabsetzen*) reduce; '2**ung** f diminution; reduction; '~**wertig** inferior; '2**wertigkeitsgefühl** *n* inferiority feeling; '2**wertigkeitskomplex** *m* inferiority complex; '2**zahl** f minority.

mindest ['mindəst] (18, *s.* minder) least; (*kleinst*) smallest; *adv.* ~(ens), zum ~en at least; *nicht im* ~en not in the least, by no means; '2... *mst* minimum; '2**-alter** *n* minimum age; '2**gebot** *n* lowest bid; '2**lohn** *m* minimum wage; '2**maß** *n* minimum; '2**preis** *m* minimum (*od.* bottom *od.* floor) price; '2**zinssatz** *m* minimum interest rate.

Mine ['miːnə] f (15) ✕ *u.* ⛏ mine; (*Bleistift*2) lead; (*Kugelschreiber*2) cartridge, refill; *auf e-e* ~ *laufen* hit a mine; *fig. alle* ~*n springen lassen* set all springs in motion; '~**nleger** ⚓ *m* (7) minelayer; '~**nräumboot** ⚓ *n* minesweeper; '~**nsperre** f mine barrier; '~**nsuchgerät** *n* mine detector.

Mineral [minə'raːl] *n* (3¹ *u.* 8²) mineral; 2**isch** mineral; ~**og(e)**

[~ra'loːk, ~gə] *m* (12 [13]) mineralogist; ~**ogie** [~lo'giː] f (15) mineralogy; ~**-öl** *n* mineral oil; ~**quelle** [~'raːl-] f mineral spring; ~**wasser** *n* mineral water, † *pl.* minerals.

Miniatur [minia'tuːr] f (16), ~**gemälde** *n* miniature; ~**malerei** f miniature(-painting).

Mini|golf ['miːni-] *n* miniature golf; '~**kleid** *n* mini-dress.

minimal [mini'maːl] minimal, minimum (*a. in Zssgn*); *fig.* negligible.

Minimum ['miːnimum] *n* (9²) minimum.

Minister [mi'nistər] *m* (7) minister, *Brt.* Secretary of State (*gen.* for), *Am.* Secretary; ~**ial...** [~ter'jaːl], 2**iell** [~ter'jɛl] ministerial; ~**ium** [~'teːrjum] *n* ministry, *Am.* department; ~**präsident** *m* Prime Minister; ~**rat** *m* Cabinet Council; *beim Europarat usw.:* Council of Ministers.

Ministrant [mini'strant] *m* (12) acolyte, F altar boy.

Minne *poet.* ['minə] f (15) love; '~**(ge)sang** *m* minnesong; '~**sänger** *m*, '~**singer** *m* minnesinger.

minor|enn [mino'rɛn] minor; 2**ität** [~i'tɛːt] f (16) minority.

minus ['miːnus] minus.

Minute [mi'nuːtə] f (15) minute; *auf die* ~ to the minute; *in der* ~ per minute; 2**nlang** lasting for minutes; *adv.* for (several) minutes; ~**nzeiger** *m* minute-hand.

minuziös [minu'tsjøːs] minute.

Minze ⚘ ['mintsə] f (15) mint.

mir [miːr] (*s.* ich, 19) me; to me; *refl.* (to) myself; *s.* aus, nichts, schlecht.

Mirabelle [mira'bɛlə] f (15) (small) yellow plum.

Misanthrop [mizan'troːp] *m* (12) misanthrope.

mischbar ['miʃbaːr] miscible; '2**keit** f miscibility.

Misch|becher *m* shaker; '~**ehe** ['miʃ-] f mixed marriage; '2**en** (27) mix, mingle; *verschiedene Sorten:* blend; *Karten:* shuffle; *metall.* alloy; *sich* ~ *in* (*acc.*) interfere with; *sich* ~ *unter* (*acc.*) mix with; join; '~**er** *m* (7) mixer; '~**gemüse** *n* mixed vegetables *pl.*; '~**ling** *m* (3¹) mongrel; (*Rassen*2) half-breed, half-caste; *zo.*, ⚘ hybrid; ~**masch** ['~maʃ] *m* (3²) medley, hodge-podge, jumble; '~-

pult *n* mixing console, (audio) mixer; '**.rasse** *f* cross(-breed); *von Menschen*: mixed race; '**.sprache** *f* hybrid language.

'**Mischung** *f* mixture; blend; *metall.* alloy; '**.sverhältnis** *n* mixture ratio.

'**Misch|volk** *n* mixed race; '**.wald** *m* mixed forest; '**.wolle** *f* blended wool.

miserabel [mizə'ra:bəl] miserable, *sl.* rotten, lousy.

Misere [mi'ze:rə] *f* (15) calamity.

Mispel ['mispəl] *f* (15) medlar(-tree).

miß|·'**achten** [mis-] despise; (*vernachlässigen*) disregard, ignore; '**2achtung** *f* disdain; disregard; '**.behagen**[1]: *j-m* ~ displease a p.; '**2behagen**[2] *n* uneasiness; displeasure; '**.bilden** misshape; '**2bildung** *f* deformity; ~'**billigen** disapprove (of); ~'**billigend** disapproving(ly *adv.*); '**2billigung** *f* disapproval; '**2brauch** *m* abuse; (*unrichtiger Gebrauch*) misuse; ~'**brauchen** abuse (*a. mißhandeln*); (*falsch gebrauchen*) misuse; **.bräuchlich** ['.brɔvçliç] improper; ~'**deuten** misinterpret; '**2deutung** *f* misinterpretation.

missen ['misən] (28) miss; (*entbehren*) do without.

'**Miß**|·**erfolg** *m* failure, fiasco; '**.ernte** *f* bad harvest, crop failure.

'**Misse|tat** *f* misdeed; (*Verbrechen*) crime; '**.täter(in** *f*) *m* evil-doer.

miß|'**fallen**[1]: *j-m* ~ displease a p.; '**2fallen**[2] *n* (6) displeasure, disgust; '**.fällig** displeasing; (*anstößig*) shocking; (*mißbilligend*) disparaging; '**2geburt** *f* monster, freak; '**.gelaunt** *s.* mißmutig; '**2geschick** *n* misfortune; (*Unfall*) misadventure, mishap; '**2gestalt** *f* deformity; (*Wesen*) monster; '**.gestalt(et)** misshapen, deformed; '**.gestimmt** *s.* mißmutig; ~'**glücken** (sn) fail, not to succeed; ~'**gönnen** envy, grudge (*j-m et. a p. a th.*); '**2griff** *m* mistake, blunder; '**2gunst** *f* ill-will, envy, jealousy; '**.günstig** envious, jealous; ~'**handeln** ill-treat, abuse; (*schlagen*) manhandle; **2-** '**handlung** *f* maltreatment, cruelty; '**2heirat** *f* misalliance; **.hellig** ['.heliç] discordant, dissentient; '**2helligkeit** *f* discord, dissension; unpleasant consequence.

Mission [mis'jo:n] *f* (16) mission

(*a. pol. u. fig.*); *Innere (Äußere)* ~ home (foreign) mission; **.ar** [.jo-'na:r] *m* (3) missionary.

'**Miß|klang** *m* dissonance; '**.kredit** *m* discredit (*a. in* ~ *bringen*).

mißlang [.'laŋ] *pret. v. mißlingen*[1].

'**mißlich** awkward; (*schwierig*) difficult; (*bedenklich*) critical; '**2keit** *f* awkwardness, inconvenience; difficulty.

miß|liebig ['.li:biç] not in favo(u)r; *sich bei j-m* ~ *machen* incur the displeasure of; **.lingen**[1] [.'liŋən] (sn) fail, miscarry, not to succeed; **2'lingen**[2] *n* (6) failure; '**2mut** *m* ill-humo(u)r; (*Unzufriedenheit*) discontent; '**.mutig** ill-humo(u)red, cross; (*unzufrieden*) discontented; ~'**raten** *s.* mißlingen; **.es Kind** wayward child; '**2stand** *m* (*Übelstand*) grievance, nuisance; (*Mißbrauch*) abuse; (*Mangel*) defect; '**2stimmung** *f* (*Uneinigkeit*) discord(ance), dissonance; *s.* Mißmut; '**2ton** *m* discord, dissonance (*a. fig.*); **.tönig** ['.tø:niç] dissonant; ~'**trauen**[1]: *j-m* ~ distrust a p.; '**2trauen**[2] *n* distrust, mistrust, suspicion; '**2trauens-antrag** *parl. m* motion of no-confidence; '**2trauensvotum** *parl. n* vote of no-confidence; '**.trauisch** distrustful, suspicious; '**2vergnügen** *n* displeasure; '**.vergnügt** displeased, discontented; *pol.* malcontent; '**2verhältnis** *n* disproportion, incongruity; '**2verständnis** *n* misunderstanding, mistake; (*leichter Streit*) disagreement, F tiff; '**.verstehen** misunderstand; '**2weisung** *f* (*magnetic*) declination; '**2-wirtschaft** *f* mismanagement.

Mist [mist] *m* (3²) dung, manure; (*Schmutz*) dirt; F *fig.* rubbish, rot; (*so ein*) ~! damn!; '**.beet** *n* hotbed.

Mistel ♀ ['mistəl] *f* (15) mistletoe.

misten ['mistən] (26) *Acker*: dung; *Stall*: clean; F *fig.* clear.

'**Mist|fink** F *m* pig; '**.gabel** *f* pitchfork; '**.haufen** *n* dung-hill; '**.käfer** *m* dung-beetle; '**.kerl** F *m sl.* bastard.

mit [mit] **1.** *prp. (dat.)* with; (*mittels*) *a.* by (means of); ~ 20 *Jahren* at the age of twenty; ~ *e-m Schlage* at a blow; ~ *Gewalt* by force; ~ 20 *zu* 11 *Stimmen beschließen* by 20 votes to 11; ~ *e-r Mehrheit* by a majority; ~ *der Bahn, Post usw.*: by; *s.* Mal,

Muße, Wort, Zeit usw.; **2.** *adv.* also, too; ~ *dabei sein* be (one) of the party, be there too, participate.

'**Mit|-angeklagte** *m*, *f* co-defendant; ♀'**-ansehen** witness; *fig.* tolerate.

'**Mit-arbeit** *f* co-operation, collaboration; '♀**en** collaborate, co-operate (*an dat.* in); contribute (to); *Zeitung usw.*: be on the staff (of); '~**er(in***f*) *m* co-worker; *wissenschaftlicher*: collaborator; (*Kollege*) colleague; (*Arbeitskamerad*) work-fellow; (*an dat.*) *e-r Zeitung*: contributor (to); *pl. e-s Werkes usw.*: staff (of); ~ *sein bei* be on the staff of; '~**erstab** *m* staff.

'**mitbekommen** be given (along), get; F (*verstehen*) catch, get.

'**mitbenutz|en** use *a th.* jointly; '♀**ung** *f* joint use.

'**Mitbesitz** *m* joint possession; '~**er** (**-in** *f*) *m* joint possessor.

'**Mitbestimmung**(**srecht** *n*)*f* (right of) co-determination.

mitbewerb|en ['~bəvɛrbən]: *sich um et.* ~ compete for a th.; '♀**er(in** *f*) *m* competitor.

'**Mitbewohner(in** *f*) *m* co-inhabitant; *e-s Hauses*: fellow-lodger.

'**mitbring|en** bring along (with one); ♀**sel** ['~zəl] *n* (7) little present.

'**Mitbürger(in** *f*) *m* fellow-citizen.

'**Mit-eigentümer(in** *f*) *m* joint owner.

mit-ei'nander together, jointly.

mit'-einbeziehen include.

'**mit-empfinden 1.** sympathize (*mit* with), feel (with); **2.** ♀ *n* (6) sympathy.

'**Mit-erb|e** *m*, '~**in** *f* coheir(ess *f*).

'**mit-erleben** *s.* erleben.

'**Mit-esser** ✄ *m* blackhead, comedo.

'**mitfahren** (sn) ride (*od.* go) with *a p.*; *j-n* ~ *lassen* give a p. a lift.

'**Mitfahrer(in** *f*) *m* (fellow-)passenger; *mot. s.* Beifahrer.

'**mitfühlen** *s.* mitempfinden; '~**d** sympathetic(ally *adv.*).

'**mitführen** carry along (with one).

'**mitgeben** give; *fig. Wissen usw.*: impart (to).

'**Mitgefangene** *m* fellow-prisoner.

'**Mitgefühl** *n* sympathy.

'**mitgehen** (sn) go along (*mit j-m* with a p.), accompany (*mit j-m* a p.); *fig. Publikum*: respond (to); F ~ *lassen* pinch.

'**Mitgift** *f* dowry; '~**jäger** *m* fortune-hunter.

'**Mitglied** *n* member; '~**erversammlung** *f* general meeting; '~**erzahl** *f* membership; '~**sbeitrag** *m* membership subscription, *Am.* dues *pl.*; '~**schaft** *f* membership; '~**skarte** *f* membership card; '~**staat** *m* member state.

'**mithalten** *v/i.* be one of the party; *ich halte mit* I'll join you; (*nicht*) ~ *können* be (not) equal to it.

'**Mit|helfer(in** *f*) *m* helper, assistant; '~**herausgeber** *m* co-editor; '~**hilfe** *f* assistance.

mit'hin consequently, therefore.

'**mithören** *teleph.*, *Radio*: listen in (*et.* to *od.* on); ⊕ monitor.

'**Mit-inhaber(in** *f*) *m* copartner.

'**mitkämpf|en** join in the fight; '♀**er** *m* (fellow-)combatant.

'**mitkommen** (sn) come along (*mit j-m* with a p.); *fig.* be able to follow; keep up (*od.* pace) (with).

'**mitkriegen** F (*verstehen*) get, catch.

'**Mitläufer** *pol. m* trimmer, hanger-on, fellow-travel(l)er.

'**Mitlaut** *m* (3) consonant.

'**Mitleid** *n* compassion, pity; ~ *haben mit* pity, be sorry for.

'**Mitleidenschaft** *f*: *in* ~ *ziehen* affect, involve; (*beschädigen*) damage.

'**mitleid|ig** compassionate(ly *adv.*); '~**los** pitiless.

'**mitmachen** *v/i.* make one of the party; *Zuhörer*: join in, respond; (*dem Beispiel folgen*) follow suit; *v/t.* take part in, join in; *Veranstaltungen*: go to; *die Mode*: follow; (*erleben*) go through; *ich mache* (*nicht*) *mit!* count me in (out)!

'**Mitmensch** *m* fellow(-man); '♀**lich** human, social.

'**Mitnahmepreis** *m* cash-and-carry price.

'**mitnehmen** take along (with one); *auf der Reise e-n Ort* ~ call at a place; *j-n* (*im Fahrzeug*) ~ give a p. a lift; *fig. j-n arg* ~ treat harshly; (*erschöpfen*) exhaust, wear (out), punish; *seelisch*: hit *a p.* hard; *S.*: (*beschädigen*) damage, batter; *Essen etc.*: *zum* ~ take-away *meal etc.*

mitnichten [~'niçtən] by no means, not at all, in no way.

'**mitrechnen** *v/t.* include (in the reckoning); *v/i.* count.

'**mitreden** join in the conversation; (*mitbestimmen*) have a say (*bei* in).

'**mitreisen** (*sn*) travel along (with a p.); '2**de** *m, f* (18) fellow-travel-(l)er.

'**mitreißen** (*h.*) drag along; *fig.* electrify, thrill.

mit'samt together with.

'**mit|schneiden** *auf Band*: record; '2**schnitt** *m* recording.

'**mitschreiben** take down; take notes.

'**Mitschuld** *f* complicity (*an dat.* in), joint guilt; 2**ig** ['~diç] accessary (to the crime); '~**ige** ['~digə] *m* (18) accomplice; '~**ner** *m* (7) joint debtor.

'**Mitschüler(in** *f*) *m* schoolmate.

'**mitsingen** join in the song.

'**mitspiel|en** join in the game, play; *fig. S.*: be involved; *j-m übel ~* use a p. ill, play a p. a nasty trick; '2**er(in** *f*) *m* partner.

'**Mitsprache(recht** *n*) *f* (right of) co-determination, *a* say (in the matter).

Mittag ['mita:k] *m* (3) midday, noon; (*Süden*) south; *s.* ~**essen**, *essen*; *des* ~**s**, 2**s** at noon.

'**Mittag|brot** *n*, '~-**essen** *n* lunch.

'**mittäglich** midday, noonday.

'**Mittags|kreis** *m*, '~**linie** *f* meridian; '~**pause** *f* lunch hour; '~**ruhe** *f*, '~**schläfchen** *n* (6) after-dinner nap, siesta; '~**sonne** *f* midday-sun; '~**stunde** *f* noon; (*Essensstunde*) lunch hour; '~**tisch** *m* dinner (-table); '~**zeit** *f* noon(tide); (*Essenszeit*) lunch hour.

'**mittanzen** join in the dance.

'**Mittäter** ‡‡ *m* accomplice.

Mitte ['mitə] *f* (15) middle; (~*lpunkt*) cent|re, *Am.* -er (*a. pol.*); Å mean; *fig. die goldene* ~ the happy mean; *aus unserer* ~ from our midst, from among us; ~ *Dreißig* in one's middle thirties; ~ *Juli* in the middle of July; *in die* ~ *nehmen* take between (*us, them*), *Sport*: sandwich in.

'**mitteil|bar** communicable; '~**en** communicate (*j-m* to a p.), *amtlich*: *a.* notify (a p.) of; *vertraulich*: intimate (to a p.); *Wissen usw.*: impart (to a p.); *j-m et.* ~ *od.* ~ *daß* ... inform a p. of a th. *od.* that ...; *ich werde es dir* ~ I shall let you know; *fig. sich* ~ *Freude, Erregung usw.*

communicate (*dat.* to); *die Bewegung teilt sich den Rädern mit* the motion is imparted to the wheels; '~**sam** communicative; '2**ung** *f* communication (*a. literarisch*); information; *amtliche*: notice, *für die Öffentlichkeit*: communiqué; bulletin; (*Nachricht*) message; (*Bericht*) report.

Mittel ['mitəl] **1.** *n* (7) means *sg. u. pl.*; (*Verfahren*) method; (*Maßnahme*) measure; (*Ausweg*) expedient; (*Heil*2) remedy (*für, gegen* for), drug; (*Geld*2) means *pl.*, funds *pl.*; *pl.* (*Reserven, a. geistige* ~) resources *pl.*; (*Durchschnitt*) average; Å mean; *phys.* medium; ~**m** agent; *im* ~ on an average; ~ *und Wege* ways and means; *mit allen* ~**n** by every possible means; *sich ins* ~ *legen* intervene, mediate; *s. Zweck*; **2.** 2 *adj.* (18; *comp.* *mittler, sup. mittelst*) middle, central; (*Zwischen...*) intermediate; (*durchschnittlich*) average, medium, Å, ⊕, *phys.* mean; (*mittelmäßig*) middling; *mittleren Alters* middle-aged; *von mittlerer Größe* medium-sized; **3.** ~..., 2... *s. mittel* 2; '~-**alter** *n* Middle Ages *pl.*; '2-**alterlich** medi(a)eval; '2**bar** mediate, indirect; '~**ding** *n* intermediate, cross (*zwischen between*); '~**feld** *n Sport*: midfield; '~**feldspieler** *m* midfield player; '~**finger** *m* middle finger; '2**fristig** medium-term; '~**gebirge** *n* hills, highlands *pl.*; '~**gewicht** (-ler *m*) *n Boxen*: middle-weight; '~**größe** *f* medium size; '2**hochdeutsch** Middle High German; '2**ländisch** midland; *engS.*: Mediterranean; '~**läufer** *m Sport*: cent|re (*Am.* -er) half; '2**los** without means, impecunious, destitute; '2-**mäßig** mediocre; (*leidlich*) middling, indifferent; (*durchschnittlich*) average; '~**mäßigkeit** *f* mediocrity; '~**meer** *n* Mediterranean (Sea); '~-**ohr-entzündung** *f* inflammation of the middle ear, ⨂ otitis (media); '~**punkt** *m* cent|re, *Am.* -er; *fig. a.* hub, (*Brennpunkt*) focus (*des Interesses* of attention); '~**scheitel** *m* centre parting, *Am.* center part; *e-n* ~ *tragen* part one's hair in the middle; '~**schiff** *n e-r Kirche*: nave; '~**schule** *f* lower-grade secondary school; '~**smann** *m*, '~**sperson** *f* mediator, go-between; ✝ middleman; '⸰motor *mot. m* midengine; '⸰s(t) (*gen.*) by means of, through; '⸰stand *m* middle classes *pl.*; '⸰streckenflug *m* medium-haul flight; '⸰streckenlauf *m Sport*: medium-distance race; '⸰streckenrakete *f* intermediate-range missile; '⸰streifen *mot. m* dividing (*Am.* median) strip; '⸰stürmer *m Fußball:* cent|re (*Am.* -er) forward; '⸰weg *m* (*goldener* golden) mean; middle road; e-n ⸰ *einschlagen* adopt a middle course; '⸰welle *f Radio:* medium wave; '⸰wert *m* mean (value); '⸰wort *gr. n* participle.

mitten ['mitən]: ⸰ *in* (*an, auf, unter dat.*) in the midst (*od.* middle) of, *im Gewühl:* in the thick of; ⸰ *aus* from amidst, *aus e-r Menge:* from among; ⸰ *entzwei* right in two; '⸰'drin right in the midst; '⸰(hin)'durch right through.

'**Mitter|nacht** *f* midnight; 2nächtig ['⸰nɛçtiç], 2nächtlich midnight; 2nachts at midnight.

Mittler ['mitlər] **1.** *m* (7), '⸰in *f* mediator; **2.** 2 *adj.* (18) *s. mittel* 2; '⸰-amt *n* mediatorship; 2'weile in the meantime, meanwhile.

'**mitt|schiffs** ⚓ (a)midships; '2sommer *m* midsummer; 2woch ['⸰vɔx] *m* (3) Wednesday.

mit'-unter now and then.

'**Mit|-unterschrift** *f* joint signature; '⸰-unterzeichner(in *f*) *m* co-signatory; '2verantwortlich jointly responsible; '⸰verschworene *m* fellow-conspirator; '⸰welt *f* our *etc.* contemporaries *pl.*

'**mitwirk|en** co-operate (*bei* in); *S.*: *a.* concur (with); '2ende *m, f thea.* actor, player (*a. ♪*); *pl. the* cast; *s. Mitarbeiter;* '2ung *f* co-operation; concurrence.

'**Mitwiss|en** *n* (joint) knowledge; *b.s.* connivance; *ohne j-s* ⸰ without a p.'s knowledge; '⸰er(in *f*) *m* person who is in the secret, confidant; ⚖ accessory.

'**mitzählen** *s. mitrechnen.*

mix|en ['miksən] (28) mix; '2becher *m* (cocktail- *etc.*) shaker; 2er ['miksər] *m* (7), '2gerät *n* mixer, liquidizer; '2getränk *n* mixed drink; 2tur [⸰'tu:r] *f* (15) mixture.

Möbel ['mø:bəl] *n* (7) piece of furniture; *pl.* furniture *sg.*; '⸰händler *m*

furniture-dealer; '⸰politur *f* furniture polish; '⸰spediteur *m* furniture-remover; '⸰stoff *m* furniture fabric; '⸰stück *n* piece of furniture; '⸰tischler *m* cabinet-maker; '⸰wagen *m* furniture(-removal) van, *Brt.* pantechnicon, *Am.* furniture truck.

mobil [mo'bi:l] (18) ✗ mobile; (*flink*) active; ⸰ *machen s.* ⸰isieren; 2iar [⸰bil'jɑ:r] *n* (3¹) furniture; 2ien [⸰'bi:ljən] *pl. inv.* movables; ⸰isieren [⸰bili'zi:rən] mobilize; 2ität [⸰bili'tɛ:t] *f* mobility.

Mobilmachung [mo'bi:lmaxuŋ] *f* mobilization; ⸰sbefehl *m* mobilization order.

möblieren [mø'bli:rən] furnish; *neu* ⸰ refurnish; *möbliertes Zimmer* furnished room, bed-sitter.

mochte ['mɔxtə] *pret. v. mögen.*

Modalität [modali'tɛ:t] *f* (16) modality.

Mode ['mo:də] *f* (15) fashion; (*Sitte*) vogue, mode; *contp. neue* ⸰n newfangled ideas; *in* ⸰ in fashion, in (vogue), fashionable; *aus der* ⸰ out (of fashion); ⸰ *sein* be the fashion; *die große* ⸰ *sein* be (all) the rage; *in* ⸰ *bringen* (*kommen*) bring (come) into fashion; *aus der* ⸰ *kommen* go out (of fashion); '⸰artikel *m* fancy article; *pl. a.* novelties *pl.*; '2bewußt fashion-conscious, trendy; '⸰farbe *f* fashionable colo(u)r; '⸰geschäft *n* fashion house.

Modell [mo'dɛl] *n* (3¹) model (*a. paint., Person*); (*Mode2*) model, mannequin; ⊕ (*Typ*) model, type; (*Muster*) pattern; ⸰ *stehen* serve as a model, pose (*j-m* for); ⸰eisenbahn *f* model railway; ⸰flugzeug *n* model aircraft; 2ieren [⸰'li:rən] model, mo(u)ld, fashion; ⸰iermasse [⸰'li:r-] *f* model(l)ing clay, plasticine; ⸰kleid [mo'dɛl-] *n* model (dress); ⸰macher *m*, ⸰tischler *m* patternmaker; ⸰studie *f* pilot study.

modeln ['mo:dəln] (29) *s. modellieren.*

'**Moden|haus** *n* fashion house; '⸰schau *f* fashion show; '⸰zeichner (-in *f*) *m* fashion designer; '⸰zeitung *f* fashion magazine.

Moder ['mo:dər] *m* (7) mo(u)ld; (*Fäulnis*) decay.

Moderator [mode'rɑ:tɔr] *Radio, TV m* (8¹) presenter.

'**Modergeruch** *m* musty smell.
moderieren [mode'ri:rən] *Radio,
TV Sendung*: present.
'**moder|ig** mo(u)ldy, musty; '**~n** (29)
(sn *u.* h.) mo(u)lder, rot.
modern [mo'dɛrn] modern; (*modisch*) fashionable, *a. weitS.* stylish;
(*auf dem laufenden*) up-to-date,
pred. up to date; *das ist ~* (*das
trägt man heute*) F that's quite the
go; ~**i'sieren** modernize, bring up
to date; **2i'sierung** *f* moderniza-
tion.
'**Mode|salon** *m* fashion house; '**~
schmuck** *m* costume jewel(le)ry;
'**~schöpfer** *m* fashion designer, cou-
turier (*fr.*); '**~schriftsteller(in** *f*) *m*
fashionable (*od.* popular) writer; '**~
waren** *f|pl.* fancy goods; '**~wort** *n*
vogue word; '**~zeichner** *s.* Moden-
zeichner.
modifizieren [modifi'tsi:rən] modify.
modisch ['mo:diʃ] fashionable,
stylish.
Modistin [mo'distin] *f* milliner.
modulieren [~du'li:rən] modulate.
Modus ['mo:dus] *m* (16, *pl. Modi*)
mode; method; *gr.* mood.
mogeln F ['mo:gəln] (29) cheat.
mögen ['mø:gən] (30) (*gewillt sein*)
be willing; (*wollen, wünschen*) want,
desire, wish; (*gern haben*) like;
v/aux. may, might; *ich möchte
wissen* I should like to know; *ich
mag nicht* I don't want (*od.* like,
care) to; *ich mag das nicht* I don't
like that; *lieber ~* like better; *ich
möchte lieber* I would rather; *was
ich auch (immer) tun mag* whatever
I may do; *wie dem auch sein mag*
be that as it may; *das mag sein
that may be (so); wo mag er sein?*
I wonder where he is; *möge es
ihm gelingen* may he succeed; *sie
mochte 30 Jahre alt sein* she looked
about 30 years old.
möglich ['mø:kliç] possible (*für j-n*
for); (*durchführbar*) practicable,
feasible; *alle ~en ... s.* allerhand;
nicht ~! you don't say so!; *es ~
machen, zu inf.* make it possible to
inf. (*s.* ermöglichen); ~**st viel usw.**
as much *etc.* as possible; *sein ~stes
tun* do one's utmost *od.* best; '**~en-
falls**, ~**er'weise** if possible, possibly; '**2keit** *f* possibility; (*Gelegenheit*) chance; (*Entwicklungs2*) po-

tentiality; ~**en** (*Vorteile*) *pl.* facili-
ties *pl.*
Mohair [mo'hɛ:r] *m* (3¹) mohair.
Mohammedan|er [mohame'da:-
nər] *m* (7), **2isch** Mohammedan.
Mohn ⚤ [mo:n] *m* (3) poppy.
Mohr [mo:r] *m* (12) Moor, negro.
Möhre ⚤ ['mø:rə] *f* (15) carrot.
'**Mohrrübe** ⚤ *f* carrot.
Moi|ré [moa're:] *m, n* (11) moire,
watered silk; **2'rieren** water.
mokieren [mɔ'ki:rən]: *sich über
(acc.) ~* laugh at.
Mokka ['mɔka] *m* (11) mocha
(coffee).
Molch [mɔlç] *m* (3) salamander.
Mole ⚓ ['mo:lə] *f* (15) mole, jetty.
Molekül [mole'ky:l] *n* (3¹) molecule.
Molekular... [moleku'lɑ:r-] molec-
ular ...
molk [mɔlk] *pret. v.* melken.
Molk|e(n) ['mɔlkə(n)] *f(/pl.*) (15)
whey *sg.*; ~**e'rei** *f* dairy; '**2ig**
wheyish.
Moll ♪ [mɔl] *n inv.* minor.
mollig F ['mɔliç] (*behaglich*) comfy,
snug; (*rundlich*) roly-poly.
Molotowcocktail ['mɔlotɔf-] *m*
Molotov cocktail, petrol bomb.
Moment [mo'mɛnt] **1.** *m* (3) moment; *s.* Augenblick; **2.** *n* ⊕ momentum; (*Antrieb*) impulse; impetus (*a. fig.*); *fig.* (*Anlaß*) motive;
(*Faktor*) fact(or), element; **2an** [~-
'ta:n] momentary; *adv.* at the moment, just now; ~**aufnahme** *f*
snapshot; (*Bewegungsaufnahme*) action shot.
Monarch [mo'narç] *m* (12), ~**in** *f*
monarch; ~**ie** [~'çi:] *f* (15) monarchy; **2isch** monarchic(al).
Monat ['mo:nat] *m* (3) month; '**2e-
lang** for months; '**2lich** monthly.
'**Monats|binde** *f* sanitary towel *od.*
napkin; '**~fluß** ⚕ *m* menses *pl.*,
period; '**~gehalt** *n* monthly salary;
'**~karte** *f* monthly season-ticket,
Am. commutation(-ticket); '**~
schrift** *f* monthly (magazine); '**~
tampon** *m* sanitary tampon.
'**monatweise** *adv.* by the month.
Mönch [mœnç] *m* (3) monk, friar;
'**2isch** monkish, monastic.
'**Mönchs|kloster** *n* monastery; '**~
kutte** *f* monk's frock; '**~orden** *m*
monastic order; '**~tum** *n* (1²) mon-
achism; '**~zelle** *f* friar's cell.
mondän [mɔn'dɛ:n] elegant.

Mond [moːnt] *m* (3) moon (*poet. a.* *Monat*); '~**aufgang** *m* moonrise; '~**finsternis** *f* lunar eclipse; '♀**hell** moonlit; '~**(lande)fähre** *f* lunar module; '~**landung** *f* landing on the moon; '~**schein** *m* moonlight; '~**scheintarif** F *teleph. m* cheap rate; '~**sichel** *f* crescent; '~**stein** *m* moonstone; '♀**süchtig** moonstruck; '~**wechsel** *m* change of the moon.

Moneten *sl.* [mo'neːtən] *pl.* dough *sg.*

Mongol|e [mɔŋ'goːlə] *m* (13), ~**in** *f* (16¹) Mongol; ♀**isch** Mongolian.

monieren [mo'niːrən] (*rügen*) censure, criticize; (*mahnen*) remind.

Monitor ['moːnitɔr] *m* (8¹) *TV usw.*: monitor.

Mono|gamie [monoga'miː] *f* (15, *o. pl.*) monogamy; ~**gramm** [mono'gram] *n* (3¹) monogram; *mit* ~ initial(l)ed; ~**graphie** [~gra'fiː] *f* (15) monography.

Monokel [mo'nɔkəl] *n* (7) monocle.

Mono|log [mono'loːk] *m* (3¹) (*innerer* ~ interior) monolog(ue); soliloquy; ~**pol** [~'poːl] *n* (3¹) monopoly (*auf acc.* of, *Am.* on); ♀**polisieren** [~poli'ziːrən] monopolize; ♀**ton** [~'toːn] monotonous; ~**tonie** [~to'niː] *f* monotony.

Monstranz [mɔn'strants] *f* (16) monstrance.

monströs [mɔn'strøːs] monstrous.

Monstrum ['mɔnstrum] *n* (9[²]) monster.

Monsun [mɔn'zuːn] *m* (3¹) monsoon.

Montag ['moːntaːk] *m* (3) Monday; *blauer* ~ blue (*od.* Saint) Monday; '♀s on Mondays.

Montage [mɔn'taːʒə] *f* (15) ⊕ mounting, fitting; erection; (*Zs.-bau*) assembly; *phot.* montage; ~**band** *n* assembly line; ~**halle** *f* assembly room *od.* shop.

Montan|-industrie [mɔn'taːn-] *f* coal, iron, and steel industries; ~**union** [~ʔu'nioːn] *f* Coal and Steel Community.

Mont|eur [mɔn'tøːr] *m* (3¹) fitter; assembly man; *bsd. mot. u.* 🔧 mechanic(ian); ~**eur-anzug** *m* overall; ♀**ieren** [~'tiːrən] mount, fit; (*aufstellen*) set up; erect; (*zs.-bauen*) assemble; *typ.* strip; ~**ierung** [~'tiːruŋ] *f s.* Montage; (*Ausrüstung*) equipment; ~**ur** [~'tuːr] *f* (16) ✕ uniform; *weit S.* overall.

Monument [monu'ment] *n* (3) monument; ♀**al** [~men'taːl] monumental.

Moor [moːr] *n* (3) fen, bog, swamp; '~**bad** *n* mud-bath; '♀**ig** marshy, boggy; '~**land** *n* marshy country; '~**packung** 🏥 *f* mud pack.

Moos [moːs] *n* (4) moss; *sl.* (*Geld*) dough; ♀**ig** ['~ziç] mossy.

Moped *mot.* ['moːpeːt] *n* (11) moped.

Mops [mɔps] *m* (4²) pug; ♀**en** F (*stehlen*) pinch; *sich* ~ be bored.

Moral [mo'raːl] *f* (16) (*Sittlichkeit*) morality; morals *pl.*; (*Lehre*) moral; (*Arbeits-, Kampf*♀ *usw.*) morale; ~**apostel** F *m* moralizer; ♀**isch** moral; ♀**isieren** [~rali'ziːrən] moralize; ~**i'tät** *f* (16) morality; ~**predigt** *f* lecture.

Moräne [mo'rɛːnə] *f* (15) moraine.

Morast [mo'rast] *m* (3³ *od.* 3²) marsh, slough; (*Schlamm*) mire, mud; ♀**ig** marshy, boggy; muddy.

Mord [mɔrt] *m* (3) murder (*an dat.* of); '~**anschlag** *m* assassination attempt; ♀**en** ['~dən] *v/t. u. v/i.* (26) murder.

Mörder ['mœrdər] *m* (7) murderer; '~**grube** *f*: *aus s-m Herzen keine* ~ *machen* speak one's mind, be frank (*od.* open); '~**in** *f* murderess; '♀**isch** murderous (*a. fig.*); '♀**lich** terrible, cruel.

'**Mord|gier** *f*, '♀**lust** *f* bloodthirstiness; '♀**gierig**, '♀**lustig** bloodthirsty; '~**kommando** *n* death squad; '~**kommission** *f* murder (*Am.* homicide) squad; '~**prozeß** *m* murder trial; '~**s...** F (*enorm*) terrific; '~**s-angst** F *f*: *e-e* ~ *haben* be scared stiff; '~**s'glück** *f* incredible luck; '~**s'kerl** *m* devil of a fellow; '♀**smäßig** awful, terrific; '~**sspektakel** *m* terrific noise; '~**tat** *f* murder; '~**verdacht** *m* suspicion of murder; '~**versuch** *m* attempt to murder.

Mores ['moːreːs]: *j-n* ~ *lehren* teach a p. manners.

Morgen ['mɔrgən] **1.** *m* (6) morning; (*Osten*) east; (*Landmaß*) acre; *des* ~s, ♀s, *am* ~ in the morning; *guten* ~ good morning; **2.** *n* the morrow, *the* future; **3.** ♀ *adv.* tomorrow; ~ *früh* tomorrow morning; ~ *abend* tomorrow evening *od.* night; *s. heute*; '~**ausgabe** *f* morning edition; '~**blatt** *n* morning paper; '~**dämmerung** *f* dawn; '~-

grauen *n*: im ~ at dawn, at day-break; '~**gymnastik** *f* morning gymnastics *pl.*; '~**land** *n* Orient, East; '2**ländisch** Oriental, Eastern; '~**luft** *f* morning air; *fig.* ~ *wittern* get hopeful; '~**rock** *m e-r Frau*: peignoir (*fr.*), dressing-gown; '~**rot** *n*, '~**röte** *f* dawn; '2**s** *s. Morgen*; '~**stern** *m* morning star; '~**stunde** *f* morning hour; ~ *hat Gold im Munde* the early bird catches the worm; *bis in die frühen* ~*n* until the small hours; '~**zeitung** *f* morning paper.

'**morgig** of tomorrow, tomorrow's.

Morphium ['mɔrfium] *n* (11) morphine; '~**sucht** *f* morphine addiction.

morsch [mɔrʃ] rotten, decayed; brittle; *fig.* shaky.

Morse|-alphabet ['mɔrzə-] *n*, '~**schrift** *f* Morse code; '2**n** morse; '~**zeichen** *n* Morse signal.

Mörser ['mœrzər] *m* (7) mortar (*a.* ⚔); '~**keule** *f* pestle.

Mörtel ['mœrtəl] *m* (7) mortar; (*Putz*) plaster; '~**kelle** *f* trowel.

Mosaik [moza'i:k] *n* (3^1) mosaic; ~**fußboden** *m* tesselated pavement.

Moschee [mɔ'ʃe:] *f* (15) mosque.

Moschus [mɔ'ʃus] *m inv.* musk.

Moskito [mɔs'ki:to] *m* (11) mosquito; ~**netz** *n* mosquito-net.

Moslem ['mɔslɛm] *m* (11) Muslim.

Most [mɔst] *m* (3^2) must; (*Apfel*2) cider.

Mostrich ['mɔstriç] *m* (3) mustard.

Motel [mo'tɛl] *n* (11) motel.

Motiv [mo'ti:f] *n* (3^1) motive; *paint.*, ♪ motif (*fr.*), theme; ~**forschung** *f* motivational research; 2**ieren** [~ti-'vi:rən] motivate; ~**ierung** *f* motivation.

Motor ['mo:tɔr] *m* (8^1) engine, *bsd.* ⚡ motor; '~**boot** *n* motor boat; '~**fahrzeug** *n* motor vehicle; '~**haube** *f* (engine) bonnet, *Am.* hood; 2**isieren** [motori'zi:rən] motorize; ⚔ mechanize; ~**i'sierung** *f* motorization; '~**rad** *n* motor-cycle; ~ *mit Beiwagen* motor-cycle combination; '~**radfahrer** *m* motor-cyclist; '~**roller** *m* motor-scooter; '~**säge** *f* power saw; '~**schaden** *m* engine trouble; '~**schlitten** *m* snowmobile; '~**sport** *m* motoring.

Motte ['mɔtə] *f* (14) moth; F *fig.* funny bird; '2**nfest** mothproof; '~**nfraß** *m* damage caused by moths;

'~**nkugel** *f* moth-ball; '2**nzerfressen** moth-eaten.

Motto ['mɔto] *n* (11) motto.

motzen F ['mɔtsən] (27) grumble, grouse.

moussieren [mu'si:rən] effervesce, sparkle; ~**d** sparkling.

Möwe ['mœ:və] *f* (15) (sea-)gull.

Mucke F ['mukə] *f* (15) whim, caprice; *fig.* ~*n haben P.*: have one's little moods, *S.*: have its snags, *Motor*: have got the bugs.

Mücke ['mykə] *f* (15) gnat, mosquito; *aus e-r* ~ *e-n Elefanten machen* make a mountain out of a molehill.

mucken ['mukən] (25) rebel.

'**Mückenstich** *m* gnat-bite.

Mucker ['mukər] *m* (7) bigot, hypocrite.

mucksen ['muksən] (27): *sich* ~ stir, budge.

müd|e ['my:də] tired, weary; *e-r S.* ~ *sein* be tired (*od.* weary *od.* sick) of; '~**igkeit** *f* tiredness, weariness, fatigue.

Muff [muf] *m* (3) **1.** muff; **2.** (*Geruch*) musty smell; '~**e** ⊕ *f* sleeve, socket; '~**el**[1] ⊕ *f* (15) muffle; '~**el**[2] F *fig. m* (7) sourpuss; '2**eln** (29) munch; (*undeutlich reden*) mumble; *a.* = '2**en** F (25) **1.** sulk, grumble; **2.** smell musty; '2**ig** grumbling; *Geruch usw.*: musty; *P.*: sulky, grumbling.

muh! [mu:] moo!; ~**en** ['mu:ən] (25) low.

Mühe ['my:ə] *f* (15) trouble, pains *pl.*; (*Anstrengung*) effort, exertion; (*nicht*) *der* ~ *wert* (not) worth--while; *j-m* ~ *machen* give a p. trouble; *sich* ~ *geben* mit et. take pains over (*od.* with) a th.; *sich die* ~ *machen zu inf.* bother to *inf.*; *mit* ~ *und Not* barely, with (great) difficulty; '2**los** effortless, easy; '2**n** (25): *sich* ~ struggle, toil; '2**voll** troublesome, hard; laborious; ~**waltung** ['~valtuŋ] *f* trouble; (*Sorgfalt*) care.

Mühle ['my:lə] *f* (15) mill; F (*Auto usw.*) bus; *s. Wasser.*

'**Mühl(en)|rad** *n* mill wheel; '~**stein** *m* millstone.

'**Müh|sal** *f* (14) toil, trouble; (*Ungemach*) hardship; (*Strapaze*) strain; '2**sam**, '2**selig** troublesome, difficult, hard; *adv.* with difficulty, laboriously; '**~seligkeit** *f* laboriousness; (great) difficulty.

Mulatt|e [mu'latə] *m* (13), **~in** *f* (16¹) mulatto.

Mulde ['muldə] *f* (15) trough; *geogr.* hollow; **2nförmig** ['~nfœrmiç] trough-shaped.

Mull [mul] *m* (3) mull, gauze; '**~binde** *f* gauze bandage.

Müll [myl] *m* (3) rubbish, refuse, *Am.* garbage; '**~-abfuhr** *f* removal of refuse, *Am.* garbage collection *od.* disposal; '**~beutel** *m* bin liner; '**~deponie** *f* rubbish tip (*od.* dump); '**~-eimer** *m* dustbin, *Am.* garbage pail; '**~-entsorgung** *f* waste disposal.

Müller ['mylər] *m* (7) miller.

'**Müll|fahrer** *m* dustman, *Am.* garbageman; '**~haufen** *m* dust-heap; '**~kasten** *m* dustbin, *Am.* garbage can; '**~schlucker** *m* waste disposal unit, rubbish chute; '**~tonne** *f* dustbin, *Am.* (tr)ashcan; '**~wagen** *m* dustcart, *Am.* garbage truck; '**~wolf** *m* garbage grinder.

mulmig ['mulmiç] mo(u)ldy; F *fig.* (*gefährlich*) ticklish.

multinational ['multi-] multinational.

Multipli|kation [multiplika'tsjo:n] *f* multiplication; **~kator** [~'ka:tər] *m* (8¹) multiplier; **2zieren** [~'tsi:rən] multiply (*mit* by).

Mumie ['mu:mjə] *f* (15) mummy.

Mumm [mum] F *m* (3¹, *o. pl.*) spunk, guts *pl.*

Mummelgreis ['muməl-] *m* F old fogey.

Mummenschanz ['mumənʃants] *m* (3²) masquerade, mummery.

Mumpitz ['mumpits] F *m* (3², *o.pl.*) rubbish, nonsense.

Mumps ⚕ [mumps] *m inv.* mumps.

Mund [munt] *m* (1², *rhet. a.* 3) mouth; *den ~ halten* hold one's tongue, F shut up; *reinen ~ halten über* (*acc.*) keep mum about *a th.*; *nicht auf den ~ gefallen sein* have a ready tongue; *j-m über den ~ fahren* cut a p. short; *j-m et. in den ~ legen* suggest a th. to a p.; *den ~ vollnehmen* talk big; *~ und Nase aufsperren* stand gaping, be dumbfounded; *s. Blatt, Hand, spitzen, verbrennen, wässerig usw.*; '**~-art** *f* dialect; '**2-artlich** dialectal.

Mündel ['myndəl] *m, f, n* (7) ward;

'**~gelder** *n/pl.* trust-money *sg.*; '**2-sicher: ~e** *Papiere pl.* gilt-edged securities.

munden ['mundən] (26) taste good; *es mundet mir* I like it.

münden ['myndən] (26): *~ in* (*acc.*) *Fluß*: flow into; *Straße*: run into.

Mund|fäule ['munt-] ⚕ *f* stomatitis; '**2gerecht** palatable; '**~geruch** *m* (*übler*) bad breath, halitosis; '**~harmonika** *f* mouth organ; '**~höhle** *f* cavity of the mouth.

mündig ['myndiç] (*werden come*) of age; *fig. a.* responsible; '**2keit** *f* majority.

mündlich ['myntliç] oral, verbal; *adv. a.* by word of mouth; '**2keit** ⚖ *f* oral proceedings *pl.*

'**Mund|pflege** *f* oral hygiene; '**~raub** ⚖ *m* theft of food (for immediate consumption); '**~schenk** *m* cup-bearer; '**~sperre** *f* lock-jaw; '**~stück** *n* mouthpiece; *e-r Zigarette*: tip; *mit Kork2* cork-tipped; '**2tot**: *j-n ~ machen* silence (*pol.* gag, muzzle) a p.

Mündung ['mynduŋ] *f* mouth; (*Gezeiten2*) estuary; *anat.* orifice; *e-r Feuerwaffe*: muzzle; '**~sfeuer** *n* muzzle flash.

'**Mund|voll** *m* mouthful; '**~vorrat** *m* provisions *pl.*, victuals *pl.*; '**~wasser** *n* mouth-wash, gargle; '**~werk** *n* mouth; *ein gutes ~ haben* have the gift of the gab; '**~winkel** *m* corner of the mouth; '**~zu-'Mund-Propaganda** *f* propaganda by word of mouth.

Munition [muni'tsjo:n] *f* ammunition; **~slager** *n* ammunition depot.

munkeln ['muŋkəln] (29) *v/i. u. v/t.* whisper, rumo(u)r; *man munkelt* it is rumo(u)red.

Münster ['mynstər] *n u. m* (7) cathedral, minster.

munter ['muntər] awake; (*lebhaft*) lively; (*fröhlich*) gay; *s. gesund*; '**2keit** *f* liveliness; merriness; '**2macher** F *m* pick-me-up.

Münz|e ['myntsə] *f* (15) coin; *kleine*: change; (*Denk2*) medal; (*Münzstätte*) mint; *klingende ~* hard cash; *fig. et. für bare ~ nehmen* take a th. for gospel truth; *j-m mit gleicher ~ heimzahlen* pay a p. back in his own coin; '**~-einheit** *f* unit *od.* standard of currency; '**2en** (27) coin; *gemünztes Geld* specie; F *das ist auf ihn gemünzt* that is meant for him; '**～er** m (7) coiner; '**～fern-sprecher** m coin(-box) telephone, public call-office; '**～fuß** m standard (of coinage); '**～kunde** f numismatics pl.; '**～sammlung** f numismatic collection; '**～wäscherei** f laundrette, Am. laundromat; '**～wesen** n monetary system.

mürbe ['myrbə] tender; (sehr reif) mellow; (gut durchgekocht) well-cooked; (knusperig, bröckelig) crisp, short; (brüchig) brittle; fig. weary; ～ machen wear out, ✗ soften up; ～ werden give in, wilt; '⚨kuchen m shortcake; '⚨teig m (short) pastry.

Murmel ['murməl] f (15) marble; '⚨n v/i. u. v/t. (29) murmur; '**～tier** n marmot, Am. woodchuck; schlafen wie im ～ sleep like a top.

murren ['murən] (25) grumble (über acc. at), Am. F grouch.

mürrisch ['myriʃ] surly, sullen.

Mus [muːs] n (4) pap; (Frucht⚨) stewed fruit, jam; F fig. j-n zu ～ schlagen beat to a pulp.

Muschel ['muʃəl] f (15) mussel; (～schale) shell; des Telephonhörers: ear-piece; s. Ohr⚨; ⚨förmig ['～fœrmiç] mussel-shaped; '**～kalk** m shell lime(stone).

Muse ['muːzə] f (15) Muse.

Muselman ['muːzəlman] m (12), '～n m (1²) Mussulman.

Museum [mu'zeːum] n (9) museum.

Musical ['mjuːzikəl] n (11) musical (comedy).

Musik [mu'ziːk] f (16) music; (Musikanten) (band of) musicians pl.; in ～ setzen set to music.

Musikalien [～zi'kaːljən] pl. inv. (pieces pl. of) music sg.; **～handlung** f music shop.

musik|alisch [muzi'kaːliʃ] musical; ⚨ant [～'kant] m (12), '⚨er ['muːzikər] m (7) musician; ⚨antenknochen [～'kant-] F m funny bone.

Mu'sik|-automat m, **～box** ['muːzikbɔks] f musical slot machine, Am. F juke-box; **～berieselung** [mu-'ziːk-] f piped music; **～hochschule** f conservatoire (fr.), Am. conservatory; **～instrument** n musical instrument; **～kapelle** f, **～korps** n band; **～lehrer** m music teacher; **～pavillon** m bandstand; **～stunde** f music lesson; **～truhe** f radiogram, Am. radio-phonograph console; **～unterricht** m music lessons pl.

Musikus ['muːzikus] m musician.

Mu'sikwissenschaft f musicology.

musisch ['muːziʃ] P.: artistically inclined; Fach usw.: fine-arts ...

musizieren [muzi'tsiːrən] make music, play; abends wurde musiziert they had music in the evening.

Muskat|(nuß f) [mus'kaːt-] m (3) nutmeg; **～blüte** f mace.

Muskateller [muska'tɛlər] m (7) (Wein) muscatel.

Muskel ['muskəl] m (10) muscle; '**～kater** m muscular ache, Am. F charley horse; '**～kraft** f muscular strength; '**～protz** F m muscle man; '**～riß** m torn muscle; '**～schwund** m muscular atrophy; '**～zerrung** f pulled muscle.

Musket|e [mus'keːtə] f (15) musket; **～ier** [～ke'tiːr] m (3¹) musketeer.

Muskulatur [muskula'tuːr] f (16) muscular system, muscles pl.

muskulös [～'løːs] muscular.

Muß [mus] n inv. necessity, must.

Muße ['muːsə] f (15) leisure; mit ～ at (one's) leisure.

Muß-ehe F ['mus-] f shotgun wedding.

Musselin [musə'liːn] m (3) muslin.

müssen ['mysən] (30): ich muß I must, I have to; (ich bin gezwungen) I am obliged (od. forced od. compelled) to; er muß verrückt sein he must be mad; das mußte (einfach) passieren that was bound to happen; ich mußte (einfach) lachen I could not help laughing.

Mußestunde ['muːsə-] f leisure-hour, spare hour.

müßig ['myːsiç] idle; (überflüssig) superfluous; ～es Geschwätz useless (od. idle) talk; '⚨gang m idleness; ⚨gänger ['～gɛŋər] m (7) idler.

mußte ['mustə] pret. v. müssen.

Muster ['mustər] n (7) model (⊕ a. Bautyp type); (Zeichnung usw.) pattern, design; (Probe) sample, specimen; (Richtschnur) standard; (Vorbild) model, example; s. wert 2.; '**～beispiel** n typical example (für of); '**～betrieb** m model factory od. farm; '**～exemplar** n sample copy; '**～gatte** m model husband; '⚨gültig, ⚨haft exemplary, perfect; (o. adv.) model; '**～karte** f show (od. sample) card; '**～knabe** m model boy, paragon; contp. prig; '**～koffer** m sample-bag; '**～kollektion** ✝ f range of samples; '♀n (29) (*prüfen, besehen*) examine, inspect; *neugierig*: eye; *abschätzend*: size *a p.* up; ✗ *Rekruten*: muster, *Truppe*: inspect; *Stoff*: figure, pattern; '~prozeß ⚥ *m* test case; '~schutz *m* trade-mark protection; copyright in designs; '~ung *f* examination, inspection; ✗ muster(ing); '~ungskommission ✗ *f* examination (*Am.* draft) board; '~zeichner(in *f*) *m* designer.

Mut [mu:t] *m* (3) courage; (*Verwegenheit*) daring; (*Schneid*) pluck; *s. gut;* ~ *fassen* summon up courage, take heart; *j-m* ~ *machen* encourage a p.; *j-m den* ~ *nehmen* discourage a p.; *den* ~ *sinken lassen* lose courage *od.* heart; *nur* ~*!* cheer up!; *s. zumute.*

Mut|ation [muta'tsjo:n] *f* mutation; ♀**ieren** [~'ti:rən] mutate.

Mütchen ['my:tçən] *n* (6, *o. pl.*): *sein* ~ *kühlen an* (*dat.*) take it out on.

mut|ig ['mu:tiç] courageous, brave; '~los discouraged; (*verzagt*) despondent; '♀losigkeit *f* discouragement; despondency; ~maßen ['~ma:sən] (27) guess, suppose, speculate; '~maßlich supposed; presumable; '♀maßung *f* conjecture, surmise, speculation.

Mutter ['mutər] *f* (14¹) mother; *s.* ~*tier;* ⊕ (*Schrauben♀*) (15) nut; *die* ~ *Gottes* the (Blessed *od.* Holy) Virgin; '~brust *f* mother's breast.

Mütter|beratungsstelle ['mytər-] *f* maternity cent|re, *Am.* -er; ~**chen** ['~çən] *n* (6) little mother; *altes*: good old woman, F granny.

Mutter|'gottesbild *n* image of the (Blessed *od.* Holy) Virgin; '~haus *n fig.* (*Stammhaus*) parent-house; '~instinkt *m* maternal instinct; '~komplex *m* mother fixation; '~korn *n* ergot; '~kuchen *physiol. m* placenta; '~land *n* mother country; '~leib *m* womb; *vom* ~*e an* from one's birth.

mütterlich ['mytərliç] motherly;

(*der Mutter eigen*) maternal; '~erseits on one's mother's side.

'Mutter|liebe *f* motherly love; '♀los motherless; '~mal *n* birthmark, mole; '~milch *f* mother's milk; '~pflicht *f* maternal duty; '~schaf *n* ewe; '~schaft *f* maternity; motherhood; '~schaftsgeld *n* maternity benefit; '~schafts-urlaub *m* maternity leave; '~schiff *n* mother ship; (*Begleitfahrzeug*) tender; '~schlüssel ⊕ *m* (nut) spanner, *Am.* wrench; '~schraube *f* female screw; '~schutz *m* legal protection for expectant mothers; '~schwein *n* sow; '♀seelen-al'lein utterly alone; ~**söhnchen** ['~zø:nçən] *n* (6) mother's darling, molly(-coddle), sissy; '~sprache *f* mother tongue, native language; ~**sprachler** ['~ʃpra:çlər] *m* (7) native speaker; '~tag *m* Mother's Day; '~tier *n* dam; '~trompete *anat. f* fallopian tube; '~witz *m* mother-wit, natural wit.

Mutti F ['muti] *f* (11¹) mum(my).

Mutung ⚒ ['mu:tuŋ] *f* claim.

'Mut|wille *m* frolicsomeness; mischievousness; *b.s.* wantonness; '♀willig (*ausgelassen*) frolicsome, playful; (*Streiche machend*) mischievous; *b.s.* (*frevlerisch*) wanton; (*bösartig*) malicious; (*vorsätzlich*) wil(l)-ful.

Mütze ['mytsə] *f* (15) cap; '~nschirm *m* peak.

Myriade [my:r'ja:də] *f* (15) myriad.

Myrrhe ['myrə] *f* (15) myrrh.

Myrte ['myrtə] *f* (15) myrtle.

mysteri|ös [myster'jø:s] mysterious; ♀**um** [~'ste:rjum] *n* (9) mystery.

Mystifi|kation [~stifika'tsjo:n] *f* mystification; ♀'**zieren** mystify.

Myst|ik ['mystik] *f* (16) mysticism; '♀isch mystical.

Myth|e ['my:tə] *f* (15) myth; '♀isch mythic; *bsd. fig.* mythical; ~**ologie** [mytolo'gi:] *f* (15) mythology; ♀**ologisch** [~'lo:giʃ] mythological; ~**os** ['my:tɔs], ~**us** ['~tus] *m* (16²) myth.

N

N [ɛn], **n** *n inv.* N, n.

na! [na] well!, why!, *Am. a.* hey!; ∼, ∼! come, come!; ∼ *also!* there you are!; ∼ *und?* so what?; ∼ *warte!* you just wait!

Nabe ['naːbə] *f* (15) hub, nave.

Nabel ['naːbəl] *m* (7¹) navel; '∼**binde** *f* umbilical band; '∼**bruch** *m* umbilical hernia; '∼**schau** F *f* narcissistic introspection; '∼**schnur** *f* umbilical cord.

nach [naːx] **1.** *prp.* (*dat.*) *Richtung, Streben:* (a. ∼ ... *hin*) to(wards), for; *Reihenfolge:* after; *Zeit:* after, past; *Art u. Weise, Maß, Vorbild:* according to, in accordance with; *der Zug* ∼ *London* the train for London; ∼ *dem Gewichte* by the weight; ∼ *deutschem Gelde* in German money; *einer* ∼ *dem andern* one by one; *fünf Minuten* ∼ *eins* five minutes past one; *s. Empfang, Haus, Reihe, schmecken usw.*; **2.** *adv.* after; ∼ *und* ∼ little by little, gradually; ∼ *wie vor* now as before, still; *mir* ∼! follow me!

'nach-äffen (25) *v/t.* ape, mimic; *s. a. nachahmen.*

nach-ahm|en ['∼ʔaːmən] (25) *v/t. u. v/i.* imitate, copy; ape; (*fälschen*) counterfeit; '∼**enswert** worth imitating, exemplary; '**2er** *m* (7), '**2erin** *f* imitator; '**2ung** *f* imitation; counterfeit; '**2ungs-trieb** *m* imitative instinct.

'nach-arbeiten *v/t.* (*nachahmen*) copy; (*ausbessern*) touch up; *v/i. zeitlich:* make up for lost time.

'nach-arten: *j-m* ∼ take after a p.

Nachbar ['naxbaːr] *m* (10 *u.* 13), '∼**in** *f* neighbo(u)r; '∼... neighbo(u)ring, adjacent; '**2lich** neighbo(u)rly; (*benachbart*) neighbo(u)ring; '∼**schaft** *f* neighbo(u)rhood (*a. fig.*); '∼**staat** *m* neighbo(u)ring state.

'Nachbau ⊕ *m* copying; reproduction.

Nachbehandlung ['naːx-] *f* 🟊 after-treatment; ⊕ subsequent treatment.

'nachbestell|en repeat one's order (et. *for a th.*); '**2ung** *f* repeat (-order).

'nachbet|en *v/i. u. v/t.* repeat mechanically, echo; '**2er** *m* (7), '**2erin** *f* (16¹) parrot.

'nachbezahl|en *v/t. u. v/i.* pay afterwards; *noch et.:* pay the rest (of); *s. a. nachzahlen*; '**2ung** *f* subsequent payment.

'nachbild|en copy, imitate; '**2ung** *f* copy, imitation; *genaue:* replica.

'nachbleiben (sn) remain (*od.* lag) behind; *Schule:* be kept in.

'nachblicken (*dat.*) look after.

'nachdatieren (*vorausdatieren*) postdate; (*zurückdatieren*) antedate.

nachdem [∼'deːm] *cj. zeitlich:* after, when; *Maß u. Grad: s. je.*

'nachdenk|en 1. think (*über acc.* over), reflect, meditate (on), *Am.* F mull (over); **2.** ♀ *n* (6) reflection, meditation; '∼**lich** thoughtful, reflecting, reflective; pensive.

'Nachdichtung *f* free version, adaptation.

'nachdrängen (sn; *dat.*) press (*od.* crowd) after; pursue closely.

'nachdringen (sn; *dat.*) pursue.

'Nachdruck *m* **1.** stress, emphasis; (*Tatkraft*) energy; *mit* ∼ emphatically, energetically; ∼ *legen auf* (*acc.*) stress, emphasize; **2.** *typ.* reprint; (*Raubdruck*) piracy; pirated edition; ∼ *verboten* all rights reserved; '**2en** reprint; *ungesetzlich:* pirate.

nachdrücklich ['∼dryklɪç] emphatic (-ally *adv.*); energetic(ally *adv.*), strong(ly *adv.*); ∼ *betonen* emphasize.

'Nachdrucks|recht *n* copyright; '**2voll** *s. nachdrücklich.*

'Nach-eifer|er *m* (7) emulator; '**2n** (*dat.*) emulate; '∼**ung** *f* emulation.

'nach-eilen (sn; *dat.*) hasten after.

'nach-ei'nander one after another, successively; *drei Tage* ∼ for three days running.

'nach-empfinden *s. nachfühlen.*

Nachen ['naxən] *m* (6) boat, skiff.

'Nach|-erbe *m* reversionary heir; '∼**ernte** *f* second crop; *von Heu:* aftermath (*a. fig.*).

'nach-erzähl|en (*wiederholen*) repeat; (*wiedererzählen*) retell; *dem Englischen nacherzählt* adapted from the English; '**2ung** *f* repetition; adaption; *Schule:* re-narration.

'Nachfahr *m* descendant; '**2en** (sn; *dat.*) follow (in a car, by train, *usw.*).

'**Nachfeier** *f* after-celebration.
'**Nachfolg|e** *f* succession; ~ *Christi* Imitation of Christ; '~ekonferenz *f* follow-up conference; '2en (sn; *dat.*) follow, succeed; '2end following; *im* ~en in the following; '~er(in *f*) *m* (7 [16¹]) successor.
'**nachforder|n** demand additionally (*od.* subsequently); '2ung *f* subsequent claim.
'**nachforsch|en** (*dat.*) investigate, make inquiries; inquire (*od.* search) for *a p.*, into *a th.*; '2ung *f* investigation, inquiry, search; ~en *anstellen s. nachforschen.*
'**Nachfrage** *f* inquiry; † demand (*nach* for); '2n ask, inquire.
'**nachfühlen:** *j-m et.* ~ (*können*) feel with *a p.* (for *a th.*).
'**nachfüllen** fill (*od.* top) up; refill.
'**nachgeben** (*dat.*) give way (to), *S.*: give; *fig.* give in, yield (to), come round.
'**nachgeboren** posthumous.
'**Nachgebühr** ℗ *f* surcharge.
'**Nachgeburt** *f* afterbirth.
'**nachgehen** (sn) *j-m:* follow; *Geschäften:* attend to; (*nachforschen*) trace, follow up; *Uhr:* be slow, lose.
nachgemacht ['~gəmaxt] (*gefälscht*) counterfeit; (*unecht*) fake, phon(e)y; (*künstlich*) artificial, (*nur vor su.*) imitation.
'**nachgenannt** under-mentioned.
nachge-ordnet ['~gə'ɔrdnət] subordinate(d).
'**nachgerade** by now; (*wirklich*) really; (*allmählich*) gradually.
'**Nachgeschmack** *m* aftertaste (*a. fig.*).
nachgiebig ['~giːbiç] yielding (*a.* ⊕ = elastic), compliant; (*nachsichtig*) indulgent; † *Kurse:* declining; '2keit *f* yieldingness; complaisance; indulgence.
'**nachgießen** add (more).
'**nachgrübeln** (*dat. od. über acc.*) ponder *od.* brood (over).
'**Nachhall** *m* (3¹, *o. pl.*) echo, resonance; '2en (re-)echo, resound.
nachhaltig ['~haltiç] lasting, enduring; (*wirksam*) effective; (*hartnäckig*) persistent.
'**nachhängen** (*dat.*) give o.s. up to *a th.*; *s-n Gedanken* ~ muse; *örtlich:* lag behind.
'**nachhelfen** (*dat.*) help.
nach'her afterwards; (*später*) later

(on); *bis* ~! see you later!, so long!; 2ig subsequent.
'**Nachhilfe** *f* assistance; *a.* = '~unterricht *m* repetitional lessons *pl.*, coaching.
'**nachhinken** lag behind.
'**Nachhol|bedarf** *m* backlog demand; '2en make up for; *Versäumtes* ~ make up leeway.
'**Nachhut** ⚔ *f* rear(-guard).
'**Nach-impfung** ✚ *f* re-vaccination.
'**nach-industriell** post-industrial.
'**nachjagen** (sn; *dat.*) pursue, chase.
'**Nachklang** *m* resonance; *fig.* reminiscence; (*Wirkung*) after-effect.
'**nachklingen** *s. nachhallen.*
Nachkomme ['~kɔmə] *m* (13) descendant, offspring; '2n (sn; *dat.*) come after, follow; (*Schritt halten*) keep pace (*dat.* with); *fig. e-m Befehl, Wunsch:* comply with; *s-n Verpflichtungen:* meet; *e-m Versprechen:* keep; '~nschaft *f* descendants *pl., bsd.* ⚖ issue.
'**Nachkriegs...** post-war.
'**Nachkur** *f* after-treatment.
Nachlaß ['~las] *m* (4[²]) *e-r Strafe usw.:* remission; *am Preis:* reduction; discount; *e-s Verstorbenen:* estate, assets *pl.*; *literarischer:* posthumous works *pl.*
'**nachlassen 1.** *v/t.* leave behind; *Geld:* allow; *et. vom Preise* ~ make a reduction in the price; (*lockern*) relax, let go; *v/i.* (*sich vermindern*) diminish, decrease; *Fieber, Schmerz, Regen, Sturm usw.:* abate; *Tätigkeit, Tempo usw.:* slacken; *Gesundheit,* † *Preise:* give way; *Interesse:* wane; *P.:* loosen one's grip; **2.** 2 *n* slackening; decrease; abatement.
'**nachlässig** careless, negligent; '2-keit *f* negligence, carelessness.
'**nachlaufen** (sn; *dat.*) run after.
'**nachleben**¹ (*dat.*) (*befolgen*) live up to, observe; '2² *n* after-life.
'**Nachlese** ✗ *f* gleaning(s *pl.*).
'**nachlesen** *im Buch usw.:* look up.
'**nachliefer|n** *Fehlendes:* deliver subsequently; (*nochmals liefern*) repeat delivery of; '2ung *f* subsequent delivery; repeat delivery.
'**nachlösen:** (*e-e Fahrkarte*) ~ take a supplementary ticket.
'**nachmachen** imitate (*j-m et. a p.* in *a th.*), copy; (*fälschen*) counterfeit, fake; *s. nachahmen.*
'**nachmalig** subsequent.

'**nachmals** afterwards.
'**nachmessen** check, measure again.
'**Nachmieter** m next (od. new) tenant.
'**Nachmittag** m afternoon; '2(s) in the afternoon; '~svorstellung *thea*. f matinée.
Nachnahme ['~nɑ:mǝ] f (15) cash (*Am*. collect) on delivery; gegen (od. per) ~ (schicken) (send a th.) C.O.D.
'**Nachname** m last name, surname.
'**nachplappern** parrot.
'**Nachporto** n surcharge.
'**nachprüf|en** check; *Richtigkeit*: a. verify; (nochmals prüfen) re-examine, ₻ review; '2ung f check (-ing).
'**nachrechnen** reckon over again; (prüfen) check.
'**Nachrede** ₻ f: üble ~ defamation, slander; '2n: j-m Übles ~ slander a p.
Nachricht ['~riçt] f (16) (e-e a piece of) news; (Bericht) report; (Zeitungs2) news (item); (Mitteilung) information, message, notice; ~en pl. Radio, TV: news(cast); j-m ~ geben let a p. know, inform a p., send a p. word (über acc., von of); '~en-agentur f news agency; '~endienst ✕ m intelligence service; *Radio*: news service; '~ensatellit m communication satellite; '~ensendung f newscast; '~ensperre f news blackout; '~ensprecher m newscaster; '~entechnik f (tele-) communication engineering; communications pl.; '~entruppe ✕ f signal corps; '~enwesen n communications pl.
'**nachrücken** (sn) move up.
'**Nachruf** m obituary (notice).
'**Nachruhm** m posthumous fame.
'**nachrühmen**: j-m et. ~ say (in praise) of a p.
'**nachrüst|en** ✕ rearm; '2ung f rearmament.
'**nachsagen** repeat; man sagt ihm nach, daß ... he is said to inf.
'**Nachsaison** f after-season.
'**Nachsatz** gr. m final clause.
'**nachschauen** have a look.
'**nachschicken**: j-m et. ~ send after a p.; *Brief*: forward.
'**Nachschlage|buch** n, '~werk n reference-book.
'**nachschlagen** in e-m Buch: refer

to, consult; *Wort usw.*: look up; *fig*. j-m ~ take after a p.
'**nachschleichen** (sn; dat.) steal after; (beschatten) shadow.
'**nachschleppen** drag after (one).
'**Nachschlüssel** m skeleton-key.
'**nachschreiben** write from dictation; (abschreiben) copy.
'**Nachschrift** f im Brief: postscript (abbr. P.S.).
'**Nachschub** m supply.
'**nachsehen** 1. v/i. u. v/t. j-m, e-r S.: look after; et. (prüfen) check; (schauen) have a look; examine; s. nachschlagen; j-m et. ~ (hingehen lassen) indulge a p. in a th., overlook (od. excuse) a p.'s mistake etc.; 2. 2 n (6): das ~ haben be the loser; *Sport*: dem Gegner das ~ geben dismiss one's opponent.
'**nachsenden** s. nachschicken.
'**nachsetzen** v/t. place behind; v/i. (sn; dat.) give chase (to).
'**Nachsicht** f indulgence; ~ üben stretch a point, mit j-m: have patience with; '2ig, '2svoll indulgent, lenient.
'**Nachsilbe** gr. f suffix.
'**nachsinnen** meditate, muse (dat. od. über acc. [up]on).
'**nachsitzen** *Schule*: be kept in; ~ lassen keep in, detain.
'**Nachsommer** m late (bsd. *Am*. Indian) summer.
'**Nachspeise** f s. Nachtisch.
'**Nachspiel** n thea. afterpiece; ♪ postlude; *fig*. sequel.
'**nachsprechen** repeat (j-m a p.'s words).
'**nachspüren** (dat.) track, trace; (nachspionieren) spy on a p.
nächst [ne:çst] 1. adj. (18, s. nahe) *Reihenfolge, Zeit*: next; *Entfernung, Beziehung, Verwandtschaft*: nearest; s. Angehörigen, Mal, Zeit; 2. prp. next to, next after; '~'best (just) any; '~dem soon; '2e m (18) fellow-creature, neighbo(u)r; jeder ist sich selbst der ~ charity begins at home.
'**nachstehen** (dat.) be second to; be inferior to; '~d (adv. in the) following.
'**nachstell|en** v/t. place behind od. after; *Uhr*: put back; *Stellschraube usw.*: readjust; v/i. j-m ~ persecute a p.; '2ung f persecution.
'**Nächst|enliebe** f charity; '2ens

nachziehen

shortly, (very) soon, before long; '⚲folgend next (in order); '⚲liegend nearest; *fig. das* ⚲e the obvious thing. [strive after.}
'nachstreben *j-m*: emulate; *e-r S.*:}
'nachsuch|en *v/t. u. v/i.* search (for *a th.*); *um et.* ⚲ apply for; '⚲ung *f* search, inquiry.
Nacht [naxt] *f* (14¹) night; *fig. a.* darkness; *bei* ⚲, *des* ⚲s *s. nachts; bei* ⚲ *und Nebel davongehen* under cover of the night; *bis in die* ⚲ *hinein arbeiten* burn the midnight oil; *mit einbrechender* ⚲ at nightfall; F *sich die* ⚲ *um die Ohren schlagen* make a night of it; *über* ⚲ overnight (*a. fig.*); *zu* ⚲ *essen* have supper; *s. heilig;* '⚲-**arbeit** *f* night-work; '⚲**blindheit** *f* night-blindness; '⚲-**dienst** *m* night-duty.
'**Nachteil** *m* disadvantage; (*Mangel*) *a.* drawback; (*Schaden*) detriment, *bsd.* ⚖ prejudice; *im* ⚲ *sein* be at a disadvantage, be handicapped; *zum* ⚲ (*gen.*) to the disadvantage *usw.* of; '⚲ig disadvantageous, detrimental, prejudicial; (*abträglich*) derogatory; *sich* ⚲ *auswirken* (*auf acc.*) affect adversely.
nächtelang ['nɛçtəlaŋ] *adv.* for nights (together), night after night.
'**Nacht|-essen** *n* supper; '⚲-**eule** *f* night-owl; '⚲**falter** *m* moth; '⚲-**frost** *m* night frost; '⚲**hemd** *n* (*Herren*⚲) night-shirt; (*Damen*⚲, *Kinder*⚲) night-dress, F nightie.
Nachtigall ['naxtigal] *f* (16) nightingale. [night.}
nächtigen ['nɛçtigən] (25) pass the}
'**Nachtisch** *m* dessert, F afters *pl.*; (*Süßspeise*) sweet.
'**Nacht|jäger** ✈ *m* night fighter; '⚲**klub** *m* night-club; '⚲**leben** night life.
nächtlich ['nɛçtliç] nightly, nocturnal; '⚲**er'weile** at night-time.
'**Nacht|lokal** *n* night-club; '⚲**mahl** *n* supper; '⚲**musik** *f* serenade; '⚲**portier** *m* night-porter; '⚲**quartier** *n* quarters *pl.* for the night.
Nachtrag ['naxtraːk] *m* (3³) supplement; *zu e-m Testament*: codicil; *s. Nachschrift; Nachträge pl. in e-m Buch*: addenda; '⚲en (*zufügen*) add; ✝ *Bücher*: post up; *Posten*: book; *j-m et.* ⚲ carry after a p.; *fig. j-m nichts* ⚲ bear a p. no grudge; '⚲end resentful.

nachträglich ['nachtreːkliç] (*ergänzend*) additional, supplementary; (*später*) subsequent.
'**Nachruhe** *f* night rest.
nachts [naxts] at (*od.* by) night.
'**Nacht|schatten** ♀ *m* nightshade; '⚲**schicht** *f* night-shift; '⚲**schlafend**: *zu* ⚲*er Zeit* in the middle of the night; '⚲**schwärmer(in** *f*) *m fig.* night-revel(l)er; '⚲**schwester** ⚕ *f* night-sister; '⚲**speicher-ofen** *m* night storage heater; '⚲**stuhl** ⚕ *m* night-stool; '⚲**tisch** *m* bedside table; '⚲**topf** *m* chamber(-pot).
'**nachtun**: *es j-m* ⚲ copy (*od.* imitate) a p.; *s. nachmachen.*
'**Nacht|wächter** *m* night-watchman; '⚲**wandeln** *usw. s. schlafwandeln usw.*; '⚲**zeug** *n* night--things *pl.*; '⚲**zug** ☒ *m* night-train.
'**Nach|-untersuchung** ⚕ *f* follow--up examination; '⚲**-urlaub** *m* extended leave.
'**nachwachsen** (sn) grow again.
'**Nachwahl** *parl. f* by-election, *Am.* special election.
'**Nachwehen** *f/pl.* after-pains; *fig.* painful consequences, aftermath *sg.*
'**nachweinen** (*dat.*) bewail.
Nachweis ['naːvaɪs] *m* (4) proof; *s. Arbeits*⚲; (*Verzeichnis*) record, list; *den* ⚲ *führen* (*od. erbringen*) prove, show; '⚲**bar**, '⚲**lich** demonstrable; traceable; *adv.* as can be proved; ⚲en ['naːzən] demonstrate; (*beweisen*) prove, show; (*feststellen*) establish; (*begründen*) substantiate; *j-m et.* ⚲ *e-e Schuld usw.*: prove that a p. has done a th., *et. Gewünschtes*: inform a p. about a th.
'**Nachwelt** *f* posterity.
'**Nachwinter** *m* second winter.
'**nachwirk|en** produce an after-effect; '⚲**ung** *f* after-effect; (*Folgen*) consequences *pl.*; ⚲*en des Krieges* aftermath of war.
'**Nachwort** *n* epilog(ue).
'**Nachwuchs** *m* after-growth; *fig. the* rising generation; '⚲... *junior* ...
'**nachzählen** count over, check.
'**nachzahl|en** *v/t. u. v/i.* pay extra *od.* in addition; '⚲**ung** *f* additional (*od.* extra) payment.
'**nachzeichnen** *v/t. u. v/i.* copy.
'**nachziehen** *v/t.* draw after (one); *den Fuß*: drag; *Strich usw.*: trace; *die Augenbrauen*: pencil; *Schraube usw.*: tighten; *v/i.* (sn; *dat.*) follow.

Nachzügler ['⸱tsy:glər] *m* (7), '⸱in
f (16¹) straggler, late-comer.
Nacken ['nakən] *m* (6) nape (of the
neck), neck; *s. steifen*; '⸱schlag *m*
rabbit-punch; *fig.* blow.
nackend ['nakənt], **nackt** [nakt]
naked, nude; *fig.* bare; *Wahrheit*:
naked, plain; *Tatsache*: hard.
'**Nackt|heit** *f* nakedness, nudity;
'⸱kultur *f* nudism.
Nadel ['nɑ:dəl] *f* (15) needle (*a.* ⊕);
(*Steck⸱, Haar⸱*) pin; *fig. wie auf
⸱n sitzen* be on pins and needles;
'⸱(holz)baum *m* conifer(ous tree);
⸱hölzer ['⸱hœltsər] *n/pl.* conifers;
'⸱kopf *m* pin-head; '⸱öhr *n* eye
of a needle; '⸱stich *m* prick of a
needle, stitch; *fig.* pin-prick; '⸱-
streifen *m/pl.* Stoffmuster: pin
stripes *pl.*; '⸱wald *m* conifer(ous)
wood.
Nagel ['nɑ:gəl] *m* (7¹) nail (*a. anat.*);
hölzerner: peg; (*Zier⸱*) stud; *langer*: spike; *fig. an den ⸱ hängen*
give up; *den ⸱ auf den Kopf treffen*
hit the nail on the head; *auf den
Nägeln brennen* be very urgent; '⸱-
bürste *f* nail-brush; '⸱feile *f* nail-
-file; '⸱geschwür *n* whitlow; '⸱haut
f cuticle; '⸱lack *m* nail-varnish; '⸱n
(29) nail (*an, auf acc.* to); '⸱neu
brand-new; '⸱pflege *f* manicure; '⸱-
probe *f*: *die ⸱ machen* thumb one's
glass; '⸱schere *f* (*eine ⸱* a pair of)
nail-scissors *pl.*
nagen ['nɑ:gən] (25) gnaw, nibble
(*an dat.* at); *an e-m Knochen ⸱* pick
a bone; *fig. ⸱ an* prey upon.
'**Nager** *m*, '**Nagetier** *n* rodent.
nah [nɑ:], **nahe** ['nɑ:ə] (18², *sup.*
nächst) near, close (*bei* to); *zeitlich*:
a. impending, forthcoming; *Verwandter*: near; *⸱ verwandt* closely
related; *Gefahr*: imminent; *s. näher,
nächst*; *nahe daran sein, et. zu tun*
be near doing a th.; *j-m zu nahe
treten* hurt a p.'s feelings; *von nah
und fern* from far and near.
'**Näh-arbeit** *f* needlework.
'**Nah-aufnahme** *f* Film: close-up.
Nähe ['nɛ:ə] *f* (15) nearness, proxim-
ity; *aus der ⸱* at close range; *in der
⸱* near at hand, close by; *in s-r ⸱*
near him; *in der ⸱ der Stadt* near
the town.
nahe'bei nearby, close by.
'**nahe|gehen** (sn; *dat.*) affect, grieve;
'⸱kommen (sn; *dat.*) (*a. fig.*) come

near, approach (to); '⸱legen suggest (*j-m et.* a th. to a p.); '⸱liegen
suggest itself, be obvious; '⸱lie-
gend near(by); *fig.* obvious.
nahen ['nɑ:ən] **1.** (25, sn; *a. sich ⸱*;
dat.) approach; **2.** ♀ *n* approach.
nähen ['nɛ:ən] *v/t. u. v/i.* (25) sew,
stitch; ♠ *a.* suture (up).
näher ['nɛ:ər] (18) nearer *usw.* (*s.
nahe*); *⸱e Einzelheiten* = '⸱e(s) *n*
(18) details *pl.*, (further) particulars
pl. [(*Nadelarbeit*) needlework.]
Näherei [nɛ:'raɪ] *f* (15) sewing;∫
'**Näherin** *f* (16¹) seamstress.
näher|n ['nɛ:ərn] (25) approach
(*sich j-m* a p.); *sich ⸱* draw near;
'⸱treten (*dat.*) *fig.* approach *a p.*,
a th.; '⸱ungswert *m* approximate
value. [(*dat.* with).]
'**nahestehend** closely connected∫
'**nahezu** *adv.* nearly, almost, next to.
'**Nähgarn** *n* sewing-thread.
'**Nahkampf** ✗ *m* close combat;
Boxen: infight(ing).
'**Näh|kästchen** *n* (lady's) work-box;
'⸱korb *m* work-basket; '⸱ma-
schine *f* sewing-machine; '⸱nadel
f (sewing-)needle.
nahm [nɑ:m] *pret. v. nehmen*.
'**Nährboden** *m* fertile soil (*a. fig.*);
für Bazillen: culture-medium; *des
Verbrechens usw.*: hotbed.
nähren ['nɛ:rən] (25) nourish (*a.
fig.*); *ein Kind*: nurse; *sich ⸱ von*
live (*od.* feed) on.
'**Nähr|flüssigkeit** *f* nutrient fluid;
'⸱gehalt *m* nutrient content.
nahrhaft ['nɑ:rhaft] nutritious,
nourishing, nutritive; *Speise*: substantial.
'**Nähr|hefe** *f* nutritive yeast; '⸱kraft *f*
nutritive power; '⸱krem *f* skin-
-food; '⸱lösung ♠ *f* nutrient solution; '⸱mittel *n*(*/pl.*) farinacious
products, cereal(s); '⸱salz *n* nutritive
salt(s *pl.*); '⸱stoff *m* nutrient.
'**Nahrung** *f* food (*a. fig.*), nourish-
ment; (*Kost*) diet; (*Futter*) feed;
(*Unterhalt*) support; '⸱smangel *m*
food shortage; '⸱smittel *n* (article
of) food, foodstuff, *pl.* foodstuffs;
'⸱smittelchemiker *m* food chemist; '⸱smittelvergiftung *f* food
poisoning; '⸱ssorgen *f/pl.* worries
about food; '⸱sstoff *m* nutrient.
'**Nährwert** *m* nutritive value.
'**Nähseide** *f* sewing-silk.
Naht [nɑ:t] *f* (14¹) seam; ♠, ♀ suture;

⚒ boundary; ⊕ seam, joint; '⊆los seamless (a. ⊕).

'**Nahverkehr** m local (od. suburban) traffic; mot. short-haul traffic; teleph. toll service; '~smittel n/pl. local transportation sg.; '~szug m commuter train.

'**Nähzeug** n sewing-kit.

'**Nahziel** n immediate objective.

naiv [na'ʔiːf] naive, ingenuous, simple; ⊆ität [~ʔiviˈtɛːt] f naïveté (fr.), ingenuousness, simplicity.

Name ['naːmə] m (13¹) name; fig. im ~n (gen.) on behalf of; (nur) dem ~n nach nominal, adv. in name only; j-n dem ~ nach kennen know a p. by name; ein Ding beim rechten ~n nennen call a spade a spade; darf ich um Ihren ~n bitten? may I ask your name?; sich e-n ~n machen make a name for o.s.; s. namens.

'**Namen|gebung** f naming; '~liste f, '~verzeichnis n list (od. register) of names; '⊆los nameless; fig. a. unspeakable.

'**namens** named, of the name of; (gen.) (in j-s Namen) in the name of, on behalf of.

'**Namens|-aktie** † f registered share; '~aufruf m roll-call; '~tag m fête-day, name-day; '~vetter m namesake; '~zug m signature, autograph.

'**namentlich** adj. nominal; adv. by name; (besonders) especially; parl. ~e Abstimmung roll-call vote.

namhaft ['naːmhaft] (berühmt) notable, renowned; (bedeutend) considerable, substantial; j-n ~ machen (mention by) name, weitS. identify.

nämlich ['nɛːmlɪç] 1. adj. the same; 2. adv. erläuternd: namely, that is (to say), (abbr. i.e. od. viz.); begründend: ..., you know.

nannte ['nantə] pret. v. nennen.

nanu! [na'nuː] I say!, Am. gee!

Napalm ⚔ ['naːpalm] n (11, o. pl.) napalm.

Napf [napf] m (3³) bowl; '~kuchen m pound-cake.

Naphtha ['nafta] n (11, o.pl.) naphtha; ~lin [~'liːn] n (11, o. pl.) naphthalene.

Narbe ['narbə] f (15) scar; ♈ cicatrice; (Leder⊆) grain; ♉ stigma; '⊆n (25) scar; cicatrize; Leder: grain.

'**narbig** scarred; Leder: grained.

Narko|se [nar'koːzə] f (15) narcosis;

~se-arzt m an(a)esthetist; ~tikum [~'koːtikum] n (9²), ⊆tisch narcotic; ⊆tisieren [~koti'ziːrən] an(a)esthetize.

Narr [nar] m (12) fool; e-n ~en an j-m gefressen haben dote (up)on a p., be infatuated with a p.; zum ~en haben od. halten, '⊆en make a fool of, dupe, fool.

'**Narren|freiheit** f fool's licen|ce, Am. -se; '~haus n madhouse; '~kappe f fool's cap; '~(s)posse(n pl.) f foolery sg.; '⊆sicher foolproof; '~streich m foolish trick.

Narretei [~'tai] f (16), '**Narrheit** f folly, tomfoolery.

Närrin ['nɛːrin] f fool(ish woman).

'**närrisch** foolish; (verrückt) mad, (F a. fig.) crazy; (sonderbar) odd.

Narzisse [nar'tsisə] f narcissus; gelbe ~ daffodil.

Narzißmus [~'tsismus] m (16, o.pl.) narcism.

nasal [na'zaːl] nasal; ⊆(laut) m nasal (sound).

naschen ['naʃən] v/i. u. v/t. (27) nibble (an dat. at); verstohlen: eat on the sly; gern ~ have a sweet tooth.

Nascher ['naʃər] m (7), '~in f (16¹) sweet-tooth; ~ei [~'rai] f (16) sweet(s pl.), titbit.

'**nasch|haft** fond of sweet things; '⊆katze f sweet-tooth; '⊆werk n sweets pl.; dainties pl.

Nase ['naːzə] f (15) nose; zo. a. snout; e-r Kanne usw.: spout; durch die ~ sprechen s. näseln; die ~ hoch tragen be stuck-up; j-m e-e lange ~ machen thumb one's nose at a p.; fig. e-e (gute od. feine) ~ haben für have a flair for; s. putzen, rümpfen; j-m auf der ~ herumtanzen play fast and loose with a p.; j-n an der ~ herumführen s. nasführen; j-m et. auf die ~ binden tell a p. a th.; s-e ~ in alles stecken poke one's nose into other people's business, be a busybody; immer der ~ nach! just follow your nose!; F j-m et. unter die ~ reiben bring a th. home to a p.; rub it in; die ~ voll haben von be fed up with, be sick of.

näseln ['nɛːzəln] 1. (29) speak through the nose, nasalize; 2. ⊆ n (6) nasal twang; '~d Sprache: nasal.

'**Nasen|bein** n nasal bone; '~bluten n nose-bleed(ing); '~flügel m side of the nose; '**~länge** f *Rennsport*: *um e-e ~* by a short head; '**~loch** n nostril; '**~schleim** m nasal mucus; '**~schleimhaut** f mucous membrane (of the nose); '**~spitze** f tip of the nose; '**~tropfen** m/pl. nose drops.

naseweis ['~vars] (18) pert, saucy; '**♀heit** f sauciness, pertness.

nasführen ['nɑ:sfy:rən] fool.

Nashorn ['nɑ:s-] n (1²) rhinoceros.

naß [nas] **1.** (18¹ [u. ²]) wet; (*feucht*) moist; **2.** ♀ n liquid; water.

Nassauer ['nasauər] F m (7) sponger; '♀n sponge (*bei j-m* on).

Nässe ['nɛsə] f (15) wet(ness); moisture; *vor ~ schützen!* keep dry!; '♀n (28) wet; moisten.

'**naß|forsch** F brash; '**~kalt** damp and cold; clammy.

Nation [na'tsjo:n] f (16) nation.

national [~jo'nɑ:l] national; ♀**flagge** f national flag; *die britische ~* the Union Jack; *die amerikanische ~* the Stars and Stripes *pl.*; ♀**hymne** f national anthem; **~i'sieren** [~nali-] nationalize; ♀**ismus** [~'lismus] m nationalism; ♀**ität** [~i'tɛ:t] f nationality; ♀**mannschaft** [~'nɑ:l-] f *Sport*: national team; ♀-**ökono'mie** f political economy; ♀**park** m national park; ♀**sozialismus** m National Socialism; ♀**spieler(in** f) m *Sport*: international player.

Natrium ['nɑ:trium] n (11) sodium.

Natron ['nɑ:trɔn] n (11) natron; (*doppelt*)*kohlensaures ~* (bi)carbonate of soda; '**~lauge** f soda lye.

Natter ['natər] f (15) adder, viper.

Natur [na'tu:r] f (16) nature; (*Leibesbeschaffenheit*) constitution; (*Gemütsanlage*) s. *Naturell*; *nach der ~ zeichnen* draw from nature; *von ~* by nature; *j-m zur zweiten ~ werden* become second nature with a p.; *in ~*, *in ♀a* in kind.

Naturalien [natu'rɑ:ljən] *pl. inv.* natural produce *sg.*; (*Naturalwert*) value in kind; **~kabinett** n, **~sammlung** f natural history collection.

natural|i'sieren [~rali-] naturalize; ♀**ismus** [~ra'lismus] m (16, *o. pl.*) naturalism; **~istisch** naturalistic(ally *adv.*).

Natural|leistung [~'rɑ:l-] f payment in kind; **~lohn** m wages *pl.* in kind.

Natur|-anlage [na'tu:r-] f disposition; **~arzt** m nature doctor; ♀**be-**

lassen natural; **~beschreibung** f description of nature; **~bursche** m child of nature.

Naturell [natu'rɛl] n (3¹) nature, disposition, temper(ament).

Na'tur|-ereignis n, **~-erscheinung** f phenomenon; **~forscher** m (natural) scientist; **~forschung** f natural science; **~gabe** f gift of nature, talent; ♀**gemäß** natural(ly *adv.*); **~geschichte** f natural history; ♀-**geschichtlich** of natural history; **~gesetz** n natural law; ♀**getreu** true to nature; life-like; full-scale; **~heilkunde** f naturopathy, nature cure; **~heilkundige** m naturopath; **~katastrophe** f natural disaster; **~kraft** f natural force; **~kunde** f *Schule*: nature study; **~lehre** f physics *sg.*; **~lehrpfad** m nature trail.

natürlich [na'ty:rliç] natural (*a.* ⚥, *Kind, Person, Tod*); (*echt*) genuine; (*ungekünstelt*) unaffected, artless; (*einfach*) simple; *adv.* of course, naturally; ♀**keit** f naturalness; simplicity.

Na'tur|mensch m man of nature; **~notwendigkeit** f physical necessity; **~recht** n natural right; **~reich** n kingdom of nature; **~schutz** m conservation; **~schützer** m (7) conservationist; **~schutzgebiet** n nature reserve; **~seide** f natural silk; **~trieb** m instinct; **~volk** n primitive race; **~wissenschaft** f (natural) science; **~wissenschaftler** m (natural) scientist; **~wunder** n prodigy.

Naut|ik ['nautik] f (16) nautical science, nautics *pl.*; '♀isch nautical.

Navigation [naviga'tsjo:n] f *inv.* navigation.

Nebel ['ne:bəl] m (7) fog; *weniger dicht*: mist; ✕ smoke(-screen); s. *Nacht*; **~bank** f fog-bank; '**~fleck** m nebula; '♀**haft** foggy; *fig. a.* nebulous, hazy; '**~horn** n fog-horn; '**~scheinwerfer** *mot.* m fog lamp; '**~schleier** m veil of mist; '**~schluß-leuchte** *mot.* f rear fog lamp; '**~wetter** n foggy weather.

neben ['ne:bən] beside, by the side of; (*unmittelbar ~*) next to; (*nahe bei*) close to, near; (*nebst*) apart from, beside; (*verglichen mit*) against, compared with.

'**Neben|-absicht** f secondary object; ♀'**-an** next door; in(to) the next room; '**~anschluß** *teleph.* m extension; '∼-**arbeit** f extra work; side-line; '∼-**ausgaben** f/pl. incidental expenses, extras; '∼-**ausgang** m side-door; '∼**bedeutung** f secondary meaning, connotation; '∼**begriff** m accessory notion; ♀'**bei** close by; (beiläufig) by the way, incidentally; (außerdem) besides; '∼**beruf** m, '∼**beschäftigung** f additional occupation, avocation, side-line; '♀**beruflich** avocational; nur attr. spare-time; side-line; '∼**buhler** m (7), '∼**buhlerin** f (16¹) rival; '∼**buhlerschaft** f rivalry; '∼-**einander** 1. n (7, o. pl.) coexistence; 2. ♀ side by side; (gleichzeitig) simultaneously; '∼-**ei'nanderschaltung** ⚡ f parallel connection; '∼-**ein'anderstellen** put side by side; fig. (vergleichen) compare; '∼-**eingang** m side-entrance; '∼-**einkünfte** f/pl., '∼-**einnahmen** f/pl. casual emoluments, perquisites pl.; '∼-**erscheinung** f accompaniment; side-effect; '∼**fach** n beim Studium: subsidiary subject, Am. minor; als ∼ studieren take as subsidiary subject, Am. minor in; '∼**fluß** m tributary; affluent; '∼**gasse** f by-lane; '∼**gebäude** n adjoining building; (Anbau) annex(e); '∼**gedanke** m secondary thought; s. Hintergedanke; '∼**geräusch** n Radio: atmospherics, strays pl.; '∼**gericht** n side-dish, entremets (fr.); '∼**geschmack** m smack (a. fig.); '∼**gewinn** m incidental profit; '∼**gleis** 🚂 n siding, bsd. Am. side-track; auf ein ∼ schieben side-track; '∼**handlung** f underplot, episode; '♀'**her**, '♀'**hin** by his (her) side; along with; s. nebenbei; '∼**höhle** anat. f sinus; '∼-**interesse** n private interest; '∼**kläger** ⚖ m accessory prosecutor; '∼**kosten** pl. extras; '∼**linie** f collateral line; ⚙ branch line; '∼**mann** m next man (a. ✗); '∼**mensch** m s. Mitmensch; '∼**niere** f adrenal gland; '∼**produkt** n by-product; der Raumforschung etc.: spin-off; '∼**rolle** f supporting part; '∼**sache** f matter of secondary importance, minor detail; '♀**sächlich** subordinate, incidental; (unwichtig) unimportant; (abwegig) irrelevant; '∼**saison** f off-season; '∼**satz** gr. m subordinate clause; '∼**sender** m Radio: relay (lokaler: regional) station; '♀**stehend** in the

margin; '∼**stehende** m, f by-stander; '∼**stelle** f branch(-office); teleph. extension; '∼**straße** f side-road (od. street); '∼**tisch** m next table; '∼**tür** f side-door; '∼-**umstand** m accessory circumstance; '∼**verdienst** m s. Nebeneinkünfte; ∼**weg** ['∼ve:k] m by-way; '∼**wirkung** f side-effect; '∼**zimmer** n adjoining room; '∼**zweck** m subordinate purpose.

'**neblig** foggy, misty.

nebst [ne:pst] (dat.) (together) with, besides; in addition to.

Necessaire [nesε'sε:r] n (11) necessaire (fr.); toiletry kit.

neck|en ['nεkən] (25) tease; ♀**erei** [∼ə'raı] f (16) banter; '∼**isch** (fond of) teasing; (mutwillig) playful; (drollig) droll, comical.

Neffe ['nεfə] m (16) nephew.

Negation [nega'tsjo:n] f negation.

negativ ['ne:gati:f, ∼'ti:f], ♀ n (3¹) Å, phys., phot. negative.

Neger ['ne:gər] m (7) negro; '∼**in** f (16¹) negress.

negieren [ne'gi:rən] answer in the negative; negate.

Negligé [negli'ʒe:] n (11) négligé (fr.).

nehmen ['ne:mən] (30) allg. take (a. an sich ∼; a. Beförderungsmittel, Hindernis, Kurve; a. ✗); (annehmen) a. accept; (weg∼) take away (a. fig. befreien von, rauben); (anstellen) take, engage; auf sich ∼ undertake, Amt, Bürde: assume, Verantwortung: accept, Folgen: bear; Speise zu sich ∼ have, take; (sich bedienen) help o.s. (von to); e-n Anfang (ein Ende) ∼ begin (end); j-n zu ∼ wissen have a way with; ich lasse es mir nicht ∼ I insist (zu inf. upon ger.); s. Angriff, Anspruch, Beispiel, ernst, Freiheit, genau, Partei, streng usw.; wie man's nimmt that depends!

Neid [naıt] m (3) envy; (Mißgunst) jealousy; aus ∼ out of envy; grün vor ∼ green with envy; das muß ihm der ∼ lassen you have to hand it to him; ♀**en** ['∼dən] (26) envy (j-m et. a. p. a th.); '∼**er** m (7) envier; ♀**isch** ['∼dıʃ] envious (auf acc. of); ♀**los** ['naıt-] free from envy, ungrudging; '∼**hammel** F m dog in the manger.

Neige ['naıgə] f (15) slope; a. fig. (Abnahme) decline; (Rest) im Fasse *usw.*: dregs *pl.*; *im Glas*: heel-tap; *zur* ~ *gehen* (be on the) decline, *Vorrat*: run low, *bsd.* ✝ run short; *zeitlich*: draw to an end; *bis zur* ~ *leeren* drain to the dregs; '2n (25) *v/t.* bend, incline; (*a. sich* ~) bow; (*kippen*) tilt; *Ebene*: slope; *sich* ~ *Tag usw.*: draw to a close; *s. geneigt*; *v/i.* ~ *zu et.* incline to, tend to, be liable (*od.* prone) to.

'**Neigung** *f allg.* inclination; (*Fläche*) slope, incline; ⚙, *Straße*: gradient; ⚓ dip (*a. der Magnetnadel, e-r Straße, e-s Schiffs*); (*Kipplage*) tilt; (*Hang, Vorliebe*) inclination, propensity, bent (*zu* to, for), tendency (*towards*); (*Zu2*) affection (for); (~ *zu Erkrankungen*) liability (to); '~**s-ehe** *f* love match; '~**swinkel** *m* angle of inclination.

nein [naɪn] no; '2**stimme** *parl. f* no (*pl.* noes), *Am.* nay.

Nektar ['nɛktɑ:r] *m* (3¹) nectar.

Nelke ['nɛlkə] *f* (15) carnation, pink; (*Gewürz2*) clove.

nennbar ['nɛnbɑ:r] mentionable.

nennen ['nɛnən] (30) name, call; (*bezeichnen*) a. term; *Kandidaten*: nominate; (*erwähnen*) mention; *Sport*: (*sich melden*) enter (*zu* for); *sich* ... ~ be called ...; '~**swert** worth mentioning; appreciable.

'**Nenn|er** ⚓ *m* (7) denominator; *s. bringen*; '~**form** *gr. f* infinitive; '~**geld** *n Sport*: entry-fee; '~**kurs** ✝ *m* par value; '~**leistung** ⊕ *f* rated output (*od.* power); '~**ung** *f* naming; *e-s Kandidaten*: nomination; *Sport*: entry; '~**wert** *m* nominal (*od.* face) value; *zum* ~ at par.

Neofaschismus *pol.* ['neo-] *m inv.* Neo-Fascism.

Neologismus [neolo'gɪsmus] *m* (16²) neologism.

Neon ⚛ ['ne:ɔn] *n* (9, *o. pl.*) neon; '~**licht** *n* neon light; '~**röhre** *f* neon tube.

Nerv [nɛrf] *m* (8 *u.* 12) nerve; *j-m auf die* ~*en fallen od. gehen* get on a p.'s nerves; *die* ~*en verlieren* lose one's head; '2**en** F (25) be a pain in the neck (*j-n* to a p.).

'**Nerven|-arzt** *m* neurologist; '2**aufreibend** nerve-racking; '~**bahn** *anat. f* nervous tract; '~**belastung** *f* nerve strain; '~**bündel** *n anat.* nerve bundle; *P.*: bundle of nerves; '~-

entzündung *f* neuritis; '~**gas** *n* nerve gas; '~**heil-anstalt** *f* mental hospital; '2**krank**, '2**leidend** neurotic; '~**krankheit** *f*, '~**leiden** *n* nervous disease; '~**krieg** *m* war of nerves; '~**sache** *f*: (*eine*) *reine* ~ a matter of nerves; '~**schmerz** *m* neuralgia; '~**schock** *m* nervous shock; '2**schwach** neurasthenic; '~**schwäche** *f* neurasthenia; *weitS.* bad nerves *pl.*; '2**stärkend** tonic; '~**system** *n* nervous system; '~**zelle** *f* nerve cell; '~**zentrum** *n* nerve cent|re, *Am.* -er; '~**zusammenbruch** *m* nervous breakdown.

nerv|ig ['nɛrvɪç] sinewy; '~**ös** [~'vø:s] nervous; ~ *machen* (*werden*) make (get) nervous; 2**osität** [~vozi'tɛ:t] *f* (16) nervousness.

Nerz *zo.* [nɛrts] *m* (3²) mink; '~**mantel** *m* mink coat.

Nessel ['nɛsəl] *f* (15) nettle; *fig. sich in die* ~*n setzen* get into hot water; '~**fieber** *n* nettle-rash; '~**tuch** *n* muslin.

Nest [nɛst] *n* (1¹) nest; *fig.* bed; (*Kleinstadt*) (*awful*) hole.

nesteln ['nɛstəln] (29): ~ *an* (*dat.*) fiddle (*od.* fuss) with.

'**Nest|häkchen** *n*, '~**küken** *n* nestling; *fig.* pet.

nett [nɛt] nice; ~ *von dir!* nice of you!; '2**igkeit** *f* niceness.

netto ['nɛto] net, clear; 2**betrag** *m* net amount; '2**-einkommen** *n* net income; '2**gewicht** *n* net weight; '2**gewinn** *m* net profit; '2**lohn** *m* take-home pay; '2**preis** *m* net price; '2**rendite** *f* net return.

Netz [nɛts] *n* (3²) net; (*Eisenbahn2, Fluß2*) network; ⚡ mains *pl.*; *Radio*: grid (*a. Kartengitter*), (*Sendebereich*) network; *ins* ~ *gehen fig.* walk into the trap; '~-**anschluß** *m* mains supply; '~(-**anschluß**)-**empfänger** *m* mains receiver; '~-**antenne** *f* mains aerial (*Am.* antenna); '~-**auge** *zo. n* compound eye; '~**ball** *m Tennis*: net; '~**betrieb** ⚡ *m*: *mit* ~ mains-operated; '2**en** (27) moisten; '~**haut** *f des Auges*: retina; '~**hemd** *n* string vest; '2**karte** 🚌 *f* area season ticket; '~**teil** *n e-s Batteriegeräts*: mains-adapter.

neu [nɔʏ] new; (*frisch*) fresh (*a. fig.*); (~*artig*) novel; (*kürzlich geschehen*) recent; (*neuzeitlich*) modern; *aufs* ~*e*, *von* ~*em* anew;

nicht

afresh; ~ere Sprachen f/pl. modern languages; ~e(re) Zeit modern times pl.; ~eren Datums of recent date; ~estens, in ~ester Zeit (quite) recently; ♀es something new; ~ste Nachrichten f/pl. latest news; was gibt es ♀es? what is the news?, Am. what is new?; das ist mir nichts ♀es that's no news to me; ~ beleben revive; '♀e m (18) new man; (Neuling) novice; s. Neuankömmling.

'Neu|-ankömmling m newcomer; '~-anschaffung f recent acquisition; '♀-artig novel; '~-auflage f, '~-ausgabe f new edition, republication; (Neudruck) reprint; '~bau m rebuilding; (Haus) new building; '♀be-arbeiten revise; '~be-arbeitung f revision; '~druck m reprint; '♀-entdeckt recently discovered.

neuer|dings ['~ordiŋs] of late, recently; '♀er m (7) innovator; '~lich adj. renewed, fresh; adv. lately.

'Neu-erscheinung typ. f new publication.

'Neuerung f innovation; '♀ssüchtig bent on innovation(s).

'neu|gebacken fresh; fig. newly-fledged; '~geboren new-born; sich wie ~ fühlen feel a (completely) different person; '~gestalten reorganize; bsd. ⊕ redesign; '♀gestaltung f reorganization; ♀gier(de) ['~gi:r (-də)] f curiosity, inquisitiveness; '~gierig curious (auf acc. about, of), inquisitive, F nosy; ich bin ~, ob I wonder whether od. if; '♀heit f newness, (a. Gegenstand) novelty; '~hochdeutsch Modern High German.

'Neuigkeit f (e-e a piece of) news; '~skrämer m newsmonger.

'Neu-inszenierung f new staging, new production.

'Neujahr n New Year('s Day); '~s-abend m New Year's Eve; '~s-wunsch m good wishes pl. for the New Year.

'Neu|land n: ~ erschließen break new ground (a. fig.); '♀lich adv. the other day, recently; '~ling m (3¹) novice, new hand, beginner; contp. greenhorn; '♀modisch fashionable; contp. new-fangled; '~mond m new moon.

neun [nɔyn] nine; alle ~(e) werfen throw all the ninepins; '♀-eck n (3¹) nonagon; ~erlei ['~ərlaɪ] of nine (different) sorts; '~fach, ~fältig ['~fɛltiç] ninefold; '~hundert nine hundred; '~jährig nine-year-old; '~mal nine times; '~malklug iro. over-smart; '♀malkluge m, f wiseacre, smart aleck; '~te ninth; '♀tel n (7) ninth (part); '~tens ninthly; '~zehn nineteen; '~zehnte nineteenth; ~zig ['~tsiç] ninety; '~zigste ninetieth.

'Neu-ordnung f reorganization, reform.

'Neuphilologe m student (od. teacher) of modern languages.

Neur|algie [nɔyral'gi:] f (15) neuralgia; ♀algisch [~'ralgiʃ] neuralgic; ~asthenie [~aste'ni:] f (15) neurasthenia; ~astheniker [~'ste:nikər] m (7), ♀asthenisch [~'ste:niʃ] neurasthenic.

'Neu|regelung f rearrangement, readjustment; '~reiche m (wealthy) parvenu (fr.); die ~n pl. the new rich.

Neuro|se ⚕ [nɔy'ro:zə] f (15) neurosis; ~tiker m, ♀tisch neurotic.

'Neu|schnee m new-fallen snow; '~silber n German silver; '~sprachler m s. Neuphilologe; '♀sprachlich modern language ...

neutral [nɔy'tra:l] neutral; ~ bleiben remain neutral; ~i'sieren [~trali-] neutralize; ♀ität [~'tɛ:t] f (16) neutrality.

Neutron phys. ['nɔytrɔn] n (8¹) neutron; ~enbombe [nɔy'tro:nən-] f neutron bomb.

Neutrum ['nɔytrum] n (9[²]) neuter (word).

'Neu|verfilmung f remake; '♀vermählt newly married; die ♀en pl. the newly-weds; '~wahl f new election; '♀wertig practically new; '~wort n neologism; '~zeit f modern times pl.; '♀zeitlich modern.

nicht [niçt] not; ~ besser no better; ~ abtrennbar non-detachable; ~ (doch)! don't!; er kam ~ he didn't come, he failed to appear; s. auch, gar usw.; ~ wahr? is it not so?, F isn't that so?; er ist krank, ~ wahr? he is ill, isn't he?; Sie tun es, ~ wahr? you will do it, won't you?; du kennst ihn nicht, ~ wahr? you don't know him, do you?

'**Nicht**|-**achtung** f disregard; want of respect; slight; '2-**amtlich** unofficial; '~-**angriffs-pakt** m non--aggression treaty; '~-**annahme** f non-acceptance; '~**be-achtung** f, '~**befolgung** f non-observance; '~**bezahlung** f non-payment.

Nichte ['niçtə] f (15) niece.

'**nicht**|-**ehelich** Kind: illegitimate; '2-**einhaltung** f non-observance; '2-**einmischung** f non-intervention; '2-**erfüllung** ṭ̣ f non-performance, default; '2-**erscheinen** n non-appearance; ṭ̣ a. default.

'**nichtig**: (null und) ~ (null and) void, invalid; (eitel) vain, futile; Vorwand: flimsy; für (null und) ~ erklären declare (null and) void, annul.

'**Nichtigkeit** f nullity, invalidity; vanity, nothingness; ~en pl. trifles; '~**sklage** ṭ̣ f nullity action.

'**Nicht**|**leiter** ⚡ m non-conductor; '~**mitglied** n non-member; '~**raucher** m non-smoker; '2**rostend** rustproof; Stahl: stainless.

nichts [niçts] **1.** nothing, naught, not anything; ~ als nothing but; ~ dergleichen no such thing; soviel wie ~ next to nothing; ~ weniger als anything but; um ~ for nothing; um ~ spielen play for love; mir ~, dir ~ quite cooly; s. ander, machen, weiter; **2.** 2 n inv. nothing(ness); (a. fig. P.) nonentity; (Leere) void; (Geringfügigkeit) trifle, a (mere) nothing; aus dem ~ from nowhere; vor dem ~ stehen be faced with utter ruin; '~**ahnend** unsuspecting.

'**Nichtschwimmer** m non-swimmer.

'**nichts**|**desto**'**weniger** nevertheless, none the less; '2**könner** m (7) incapable person, sl. washout; ~**nutzig** ['~nutsiç] good-for-nothing, useless; '~**sagend** meaningless; (leer) empty (a. Gesicht); (farblos) flat; Antwort: vague; 2**tuer** ['~tu:ər] m (7) do-nothing, idler; '2-**tun** n idleness; inaction; '~**wisser** m ignoramus; '~**würdig** base, infamous; '2**würdigkeit** f baseness, infamy.

'**Nicht**|**vorhandensein** n absence; lack; '~**wissen** n ignorance; '~**zu-treffendes** streichen delete which is inapplicable.

Nickel ['nikəl] n (7) nickel; '~**brille** f steel-rimmed spectacles pl.

nick|**en** ['nikən] (25) nod; '2**erchen** F n (6): ein ~ machen have a nap od. a snooze.

nie [ni:] never, at no time; fast ~ hardly ever; ~ wieder never again.

nieder ['ni:dər] **1.** adj. low (a. fig. gemein); Wert, Rang: inferior; der ~e Adel the gentry; **2.** adv. down (mit with); '~**brennen** v/t. u. v/i. (sn) burn down; '~**brüllen** boo; '~**deutsch** Low German; '2**druck** ⊕ m low pressure; '~**drücken** press down; fig. depress; '~**fallen** (sn) fall down; '2**frequenz** ⚡ f low frequency; '2**gang** m decline; '~**gehen** (sn) go down (a. 🛩); Gewitter: burst; Regen: fall; '~**geschlagen** fig. downcast (a. Augen), depressed, down-hearted; '2**geschlagenheit** f dejection, low spirits pl.; '~**halten** fig. suppress; '~**hauen** fell; '~**holen** Flagge: haul down, lower; '~**kämpfen** overpower; fig. overcome; '~**knien** kneel down; '~**knüppeln** bludgeon; '~**kommen** (sn) be confined; 2-**kunft** ['~kunft] f (14¹) confinement; '2**lage** f defeat; (Magazin) depot, warehouse; (Zweiggeschäft) branch; '~**lassen** let down; sich ~ sit down; Vogel: alight; (sich festsetzen) establish o.s., settle (down), Am. locate; geschäftlich: set o.s. up in business; '2**lassung** f establishment; (Siedlung) settlement; ✝ branch, agency; depot; '~**legen** lay down (a. die Waffen; a. fig. Regeln); Amt: resign; Krone: abdicate; sich ~ lie down (a. zu Bett); die Arbeit ~ (go on) strike, walk out; schriftlich ~ put down in writing; '2**legung** f laying down; resignation; abdication; '~**machen**, '~**metzeln** kill, slaughter; '~**reißen** pull down; '~**rheinisch** of the Lower Rhine; '~**schießen** v/t. u. v/i. shoot down; '2**schlag** m sediment; 🜂 deposit, precipitate; (atmosphärischer ~) precipitation; Boxen: knock-down, bis zehn: knock-out; s. radioaktiv; fig. s-n ~ finden in (dat.) be reflected in; '~**schlagen** knock down, fell; Augen: cast down; Kosten usw.: cancel; (unterdrücken) suppress; Revolte: put down, crush; Forderung: waive; ṭ̣

Verfahren: quash; ⚙ precipitate (*a.* sich); *fig.* cast down; *sich* ~ *in* (*dat.*) be reflected in; '⚥schlagung *f* cancellation; '~schmettern dash to the ground; *fig.* crush; '~-schmetternd *fig.* crushing, shattering; '~schreiben write down; '⚥schrift *f* record; (*Protokoll*) minutes *pl.*; '~setzen set (*od.* put) down; *sich* ~ sit down; '⚥spannung ⚡ *f* low tension; '~stechen stab down; '~strecken fell; '~-trächtig base, mean; '⚥trächtig-keit *f* baseness, meanness; '⚥ung *f* lowland; *im Gelände*: depression; '~werfen throw down; *Aufstand usw.*: put down, crush; '⚥wild *n* small game.

niedlich ['niːtliç] nice, sweet, *Am. a.* cute; (*drollig*) droll, funny.

Niednagel ['niːt-] *m* agnail.

niedrig ['niːdriç] low; *von Stand a.* lowly, humble; (*gemein*) mean, base; ~*er hängen fig.* debunk; '⚥keit *f* low(li)ness; humbleness; meanness; '⚥preis *m* low price; '⚥st-preis *m* lowest price; '⚥wasser *n* low water.

niemals ['~maːls] *s.* nie.

niemand ['~mant] nobody, no one, not ... anybody; '⚥sland *n* no man's land.

Niere ['niːrə] *f* (15) kidney; *künstliche* ~ kidney machine; '~nbank 🗡 *f* kidney transplant bank; '~nbecken *n* renal pelvis; '~nbraten *m*, '~n-stück *n* roast loin; '~n-entzündung *f* nephritis; '⚥nförmig kidney-shaped; '~nleiden *n* kidney trouble; '~nspender(in *f*) *m* kidney donor; '~nstein 🗡 *m* kidney stone.

nieseln ['niːzəln] (29) drizzle.

niesen ['niːzən] (27) sneeze.

Nießbrauch ['niːs-] *m* (3) usufruct; '~er(in *f*) *m* usufructuary.

Niet [niːt] *m* (3) rivet; '~e *f* (15) *in der Lotterie*: blank; *fig.* F *P. u. S.*: *sl.* flop, washout; '⚥en (26) rivet; '⚥- **und 'nagelfest** clinched and riveted.

Nihilismus [nihi'lismus] *m* (16, *o. pl.*) nihilism.

Nikolaus ['ni(ː)kolaus] *m* (11[1], *pl.* 3[3]) Santa Claus.

Nikotin [niko'tiːn] *n* (3[1]) nicotine; ⚥frei nicotine-free; ~vergiftung *f* nicotine-poisoning.

Nilpferd ['niːl-] *n* hippopotamus.

Nimbus ['nimbus] *m* (14[2]) nimbus; *fig.* prestige, aura.

nimmer ['nimər] never; '~mehr nevermore; (*ganz und gar nicht*) by no means; '~müde untiring; '~-satt[1] insatiable; '⚥satt[2] *m* glutton; '⚥'wiedersehen *n*: *auf* ~ never to meet again, for good.

Nippel ['nipəl] ⊕ *m* (7) nipple.

nippen ['nipən] (25) sip (*an dat.* at).

'Nippsachen *f/pl.* knick-knacks, bric-à-brac *sg.*

nirgend(s) ['nirgənt(s)] nowhere.

Nische ['niːʃə] *f* (15) niche, recess.

nisten ['nistən] (26) nest.

Nitrat ⚙ [ni'traːt] *n* (3) nitrate.

Nitroglyzerin ['niːtroglytsə'riːn] *n* nitroglycerine.

Niveau [ni'voː] *n* (11) level; *fig. a.* standard; *unter dem* ~ not up to standard.

nivellieren [nivɛ'liːrən] level, grade.

Nix *m* (3[2]), **Nixe** ['niks(ə)] *f* (15) water-sprite; *m a.* nix, merman; *f a.* nixie, mermaid, water-nymph.

nobel ['noːbəl] (*vornehm*) noble; (*großzügig*) generous; (*elegant*) elegant, fashionable.

Nobelpreis [no'bɛl-] *m* Nobel prize; ~träger *m* Nobel prize winner.

noch [nɔx] still; yet; ~ *immer* still; ~ *ein* another, one more; ~ *einmal* once more *od.* again; ~ *einmal so alt wie j.* double a p.'s age; ~ *etwas* something more; ~ *etwas?* anything else?; *was denn* ~ *alles?* what next?; ~ *nicht* not yet; ~ *nie* never before; ~ *gestern* only yesterday; ~ *heute* this very day; ~ *jetzt* even now; ~ *im 19. Jahrhundert* as late as the 19th century; ~ *so* ever so; *es wird* ~ *2 Jahre dauern* it will take two more (*od.* another two) years; ~ *und* ~ plenty (of); *s.* nur, weder *usw.*; ~malig repeated, second, new; ~mals ['~maːls] once more.

Nocke ⊕ ['nɔkə] *f* (15) cam; '~n-welle *f* camshaft.

Nomad|e [no'maːdə] *m* (13) nomad; ~en..., ⚥isch nomadic.

Nomin|alwert [nomi'naːlveːrt] *m* nominal value; ~ativ ['noːminatiːf] *m* (3[1]) nominative (case); ⚥ell [nomi'nɛl] nominal; ⚥ieren [~'niːrən] nominate.

Nonne ['nɔnə] *f* (15) nun; '~nkloster *n* nunnery, convent.

Noppe ['nɔpə] f (15), '⛫n burl, nap.
Nord [nɔrt] 1. north; 2. poet. m (3, o. pl.) north (wind); '~-at'lantikpakt m North Atlantic Treaty; ~en ['~ən] m (6, o. pl.) north; '~hang m north (-ern) slope; ⛫isch ['~diʃ] northern; (skandinavisch) Nordic; ~länder ['nɔrtlɛndər] m (7) inhabitant of the north, northerner.

nördlich ['nœrtliç] northern, northerly; ~ von (to the) north of.

'**Nord|licht** n northern lights pl., aurora borealis; ~'-ost(en) m northeast; ⛫'-östlich north-east(erly); '~pol m North Pole; '~po'larkreis m Arctic Circle; ~-'Süd-Konflikt m North-South conflict; '~see f North Sea; ⛫wärts ['~vɛrts] northward(s); '~west(en) m north-west; ⛫'-westlich north-west(erly); '~wind m north wind.

Nörg|elei [nœrgə'laɪ] f (16) faultfinding, carping; '⛫eln v/i. (29) nag, carp (an dat. at), Am. F gripe (od. kick) (about); ~ an (dat.) find fault with; ~ler ['~glər] m (7), '~lerin f faultfinder, grumbler.

Norm [nɔrm] f (16) norm, standard.
normal ['~maːl] normal; Maß, Gewicht: standard; ⛫benzin n regular (petrol, Am. gas); ⛫fall m normal case; im ~ normally; ⛫geschwindigkeit f normal speed; ⛫gewicht n standard weight; ~isieren [~mali-'ziːrən] normalize; sich ~ return to normal; ~spurig ⛫ [~'maːl-] standard-ga(u)ge; ⛫-uhr f standard clock; ⛫verbraucher co. m man in the street; geistiger ~ middlebrow; ⛫zeit f standard time; ⛫zustand m normal condition.

Normanne [nɔr'manə] m (13) Norman.

Nor|mblatt ['nɔrm-] n standard sheet; '⛫men (25), ⛫'mieren standardize; ~'mierung f standardization.

Norweg|er ['nɔrveːgər] m (7), '~e-rin f (16¹), '⛫isch Norwegian.

Not [noːt] f (14¹) (Mangel) need, want; (Notlage) necessity; (Bedrängtheit) difficulty, trouble; (Elend) misery; (Gefahr, Unglück) danger, (engS. ⛫) distress; zur ~ if need be, at a pinch; ~ leiden suffer want; ~ leiden an (dat.) be short of; in ~ bringen reduce to want; s. knapp; in Nöten sein be

in trouble; mir ist (od. tut) ⛫ I want; es tut ⛫, daß it is necessary that; ~ macht erfinderisch necessity is the mother of invention; s. Gebot, Teufel.

Notar [no'taːr] m (3¹) notary; ~iat [~tar'jaːt] n notary's office; ⛫iell [~'jɛl] notarial; attested by a notary.

'**Not|-arzt** m doctor on call; (beruflicher ~) emergency doctor; '~-aufnahme f Krankenhaus: emergency ward; '~-ausgang m emergency exit; '~behelf m makeshift, expedient, stopgap; '~beleuchtung f emergency lighting; '~bremse f emergency brake; ⛫ communication cord; '~brücke f emergency bridge; '~dienst m emergency service (od. duty); ~durft ['~durft] f (14¹): s-e ~ verrichten relieve nature; '⛫dürftig scanty; (bedürftig) needy; (behelfsmäßig) makeshift; improvised, rough(ly adv.).

Note ['noːtə] f (15) note (a. pol.); (Banknote) banknote, Am. bill; ♪ note, ~n pl. music; Schule, Sport: mark; fig. (Ton) tone; (Eigenart) character, feature; die persönliche ~ the personal touch; ♪ ganze ~ semibreve; halbe ~ minim; nach ~n singen sing at sight; F fig. nach ~ properly, thoroughly; '~n-austausch pol. m exchange of notes; '~nbank f bank of issue; '~nblatt n sheet of music; '~ndurchschnitt m average mark (Am. grade); '~n-pult n music-stand; '~nschlüssel ♪ m clef; '~nschrank m music cabinet; '~nständer m music-stand; '~nsystem n ♪ staff; Schule: marking (Am. grading) system; '~n-umlauf m circulation of (bank)notes.

'**Not|fall** m case of need, emergency; im ~, '⛫falls s. nötigenfalls; '~flagge f flag of distress; '⛫gedrungen compulsory, forced; adv. of necessity, needs; ~ mußte er he had no choice but; '~gemeinschaft f emergency pool; '~groschen m nest-egg; '~helfer(in f) m helper in need; '~hilfe f help in need; emergency aid; Technische ~ Technical Emergency Service.

notier|en [no'tiːrən] note (down), make a note of; take (od. jot) down; ♥ Preise: quote (zu at); ⛫ung ♥ f quotation.

nötig ['nøːtiç] necessary, required;

(*gebührend*) due (*respect etc.*); ~ **haben** want, need, stand in need of, require; *das* ~*e* what is necessary; ~**en** ['~gən] (25) force, compel; (*drängen*) urge; *e-n Gast*: press; *sich* ~ *lassen* stand upon ceremony; *sich genötigt sehen, zu inf.* find o.s. compelled to *inf.*; '~**en'falls** in case of need, in an emergency; if necessary, if need be; '2**ung** *f* coercion, compulsion; pressing (invitation); ⚕ duress, intimidation.

Notiz [no'ti:ts] *f* (16) note, F memo; (*Presse2*) notice, (news) item; ~ *nehmen von* note, take notice of; *keine* ~ *nehmen von* ignore; ~**block** *m* note block, memo pad; ~**buch** *n* notebook.

'**Not|lage** *f* distress, plight, predicament, emergency; '~**lager** *n* shakedown; '2**landen** ✈ (sn) make a forced landing, force-land; '~**landung** *f* forced landing; '2**leidend** needy; distressed; ✝ *Wechsel*: dishono(u)red; '~**lösung** *f* makeshift, expedient; '~**lüge** *f* white lie; '~**maßnahme** *f* emergency measure.

notorisch [no'to:riʃ] notorious.

'**Not|pfennig** *m* savings *pl.*, nest-egg; '~**ruf** *teleph. m* emergency call; (*Nummer*) emergency number; '~**rufsäule** *f* emergency telephone; '~**schlachtung** *f* forced slaughter; '~**schrei** *m* cry of distress; '~**signal** *n* distress signal, SOS; '~**sitz** *m* jump seat, *Am. a.* rumble seat; '~**stand** *m* state of distress, (state of) emergency; ⚕ necessity; '~**stands-gebiet** *n* distressed area; '~**stands-gesetz** *n* (national) emergency law; '~**standsmaßnahmen** *f/pl.* emergency measures; '~**strom-aggregat** *n* emergency generator; '~**treppe** *f* fire-escape; '~**unterkunft** *f* provisional accommodation; '~**verband** *m* emergency (*od.* first-aid) dressing; '~**ver-ordnung** *f* emergency decree; '~**wehr** *f* (*aus od. in* in) self-defen|ce, *Am.* -se; '2**wendig** necessary (*für* to, for; *daß* er for him to *inf.*); '~**wendigkeit** *f* necessity; '~**zeichen** *n* signal of distress; '~**zucht** *f*, '2**züchtigen** rape.

Nougat ['nu:gat] *m, n* (11) nougat.

Novelle [no'vɛlə] *f* (15) short novel; *parl.* amending law.

November [no'vɛmbər] *m* (7) November.

Novität [novi'tɛ:t] *f* (16) novelty.

Novize [no'vi:tsə] *m* (13), *f* (15) novice.

Novum ['no:vum] *n* (9²) something new.

Nu [nu:] *m inv.*: *im* ~ in no time, F in a trice *od.* jiffy *od.* flash.

Nuan|ce [ny'ɑ̃sə] *f* (15), 2'**cieren** shade.

nüchtern ['nyçtərn] with an empty stomach, not having eaten (anything); (*Ggs. betrunken*) sober (*a. fig. Urteil, Tatsache usw.*); (*ruhig denkend*) level-headed; (*leidenschaftslos*) cool, unemotional; (*alltäglich, unromantisch, trocken*) prosaic; (*sachlich*) matter-of-fact(*ly adv.*); (*mäßig*) temperate; (*besonnen*) calm; (*geistlos*) jejune; *auf* ~*en Magen* on an empty stomach; '2**heit** *f* sobriety; temperance; *fig.* prosiness.

Nudel ['nu:dəl] *f* (15) noodle; '2**n** (29) stuff.

Nugat ['nu:gat] *m, n* (11) *s. Nougat.*

nuklear [nukle'a:r] nuclear.

null [nul] **1.** null; nil (*bsd. bei Fehlanzeige*); *Tennis*: love; *s. nichtig*; **2.** 2 *f* (16) nought, cipher; *Skala*: zero; *fig. P.*: a mere cipher, nonentity; *s. a. Niete*; F *gleich* ~ next to nothing, nil; '2**lösung** *f* zero option; '2**menge** Å *f* null set; '2**punkt** *m* zero; ⊕, ⚡ neutral point; *auf dem* ~ (*a. fig.*) at zero; '2**tarif** *m*: *zum* ~ free of charge; '2**wachs-tum** ✝ *n* zero growth.

numerier|en [numə'ri:rən] number; *numerierter Platz* reserved seat; 2**ung** *f* numbering.

Nummer ['numər] *f* (15) number (*a. Programm2, Zirkus2*); *e-r Zeitung*: *a.* copy, issue; ✝ (*Größe*) size; *Sport*: event; F (*Kauz*) (quite a) character; '~**nkonto** *n* numbered account; '~**n-scheibe** *teleph. f* dial; '~**nschild** *mot. n* number-plate.

nun [nu:n] now, at present; *int.* well! ~*!* well?; *e-e Rede fortsetzend*: well, why; *cj.* ~ (*da*) now that; since; '~**mehr** now; '~**mehrig** present.

Nuntius ['nuntsjus] *m* (16²) nuncio.

nur [nu:r] only; solely; merely; (*nichts als*) (nothing) but; (*ausgenommen*) except, but; *nicht* ~ ... *sondern auch* ... not only ... but also ...; ~ *noch* still, only; ~ *zu!*,

~ *weiter!* go (*od.* carry) on!; *wenn* ~ *provided that*; *wer* ~ whoever; *wie* ~ how ... ever, how on earth; *das Stück ist* ~ *klein* the piece is but small; *alle,* ~ *er nicht* all except him; *du weißt* ~ *zu gut* you know well enough; *so schwierig es* ~ *sein könnte* as difficult as it could possibly be.

nuscheln F ['nuʃəln] slur, mumble.

Nuß [nus] f (14¹) nut (*a.* ⊕); (*Wal*♀) walnut; *fig.* e-e *harte* ~ a hard nut to crack, a tough job; '~**baum** m walnut-tree; '♀**braun** hazel; '~**kern** m kernel; '~**knacker** m (7) nut-cracker; '~**schale** f nut--shell.

Nüster ['nyːstər] f (15) nostril.

Nut(e) ['nuːtə] f (15) groove, *a.* slot.

nutz [nuts], **nütze** ['nytsə] useful; *zu nichts* ~ *sein* be good for nothing; *s. zunutze*; '♀-**anwendung** f practical application, utilization; (*Lehre*) moral.

'**nutzbar** useful; *sich et.* ~ *machen* utilize, turn to account; '♀**keit** f usefulness; '♀**machung** f utilization.

'**nutzbringend** profitable, useful; ~ *anwenden* turn to good account.

'**Nutz-effekt** m useful effect, (net) efficiency.

Nutzen ['nutsən] **1.** m (6) use; (*Gewinn*) profit; (*Vorteil*) advantage,

a. ⚖ benefit; *s. Nützlichkeit*; ~ *bringen* bring grist to the mill; ~ *ziehen aus* profit (*od.* benefit) from; *von* ~ *sein s.* 2.; **2.** ♀, **nützen** ['nytsən] v/i. (27): be of use *od.* useful (*zu et.* for; *j-m* for a p.); *j-m* ~ *a.* serve a p. (*vorteilhaft sein*) be of advantage (*j-m* to a p.); *es nützt nichts* it is (of) no use (*zu inf.* to); *was nützt* ...? what is the use of ...?; v/t. use, make use of.

'**Nutz**|**fahrzeug** n utility vehicle; '~**fläche** f useful area; '~**garten** m kitchen-garden; '~**holz** n timber; '~**last** f payload; '~**leistung** f effective capacity, (useful) efficiency; *mot.* brake horsepower.

nützlich ['nytslɪç] useful; '♀**keit** f usefulness, utility.

'**nutz**|**los** useless; '♀**losigkeit** f uselessness; ♀**nießer** ['~niːsər] m (7) usufructuary; *weitS.* beneficiary, *b.s.* profiteer; '♀**nießung** f usufruct.

'**Nutzung** f using; *s. Nutzbarmachung, Nutznießung*; (*Ausnutzung*) exploitation; (*Ertrag*) yield, produce; (*Einkommen*) revenue; '~**srecht** n right of usufruct, right to use; '~**swert** m economic value.

Nylon ['naɪlɔn] n (11) nylon; '~**strümpfe** m/pl. nylons.

Nymph|**e** ['nymfə] f (15) nymph; ~**omanie** [~foma'niː] f (15, *o. pl.*) nymphomania.

O

O [oː], **o** n inv. O, o.

o! int. oh!; ~ *weh!* alas!, oh dear!

Oase [o'⁹aːzə] f (15) oasis.

ob [ɔp] **1.** cj. whether, if; *als* ~ as if, as though; F (*na*) *und* ~! F rather!, Am. you bet!; ~ *er wohl kommt?* I wonder if he will come!; **2.** prp. **a)** gen. (*wegen*) on account of; (*über*) about; **b)** dat. (*oberhalb*) above.

Obacht ['oːbaxt] f (16): ~ *geben* (pay) heed, pay attention (*auf acc.* to), take care (of); ~! look out!, Am. watch out!

Obdach ['ɔpdax] n (1, *o.pl.*) shelter; (*Wohnstätte*) lodging; '♀**los** homeless; '~**lose** m, f casual (pauper).

Obduktion [ɔpduk'tsjoːn] f postmortem (examination), autopsy.

'**O-Beine** n/pl. bandy legs, bow legs; '**O-beinig** bandy-legged.

oben ['oːbən] above (*a. im Buch usw.*); (*an der Spitze*) at the top; *im Himmelsraum*: aloft, on high; *im Hause*: upstairs; *hoch* ~ high up; *nach* ~ upwards, *im Hause*: upstairs; *von* ~ from above; *von* ~ *bis unten* from top to bottom; *von* ~ *herab behandeln usw.* haughtily; ~ *ohne* topless; ~ *an* at the top *od.* head; ~'-**auf** on top, above; uppermost; on the surface; *fig.* F ~ *sein* be going strong; ~'**drein** over and above, into the bargain, on top of it (all); '~-**erwähnt** above(-mentioned); ~**'hin** superficially; *bemerken*: casually.

ober ['o:bər] **1.** (18, *nur attributiv*) upper, higher; *fig. a.* superior, senior, chief; *s.* **oberst** 1.; **2.** ♀ F *m* (7) (head) waiter.

'**Ober|-arm** *m* upper arm; '~-**arzt** *m* assistant medical director; '~-**aufseher** *m* chief inspector, superintendent; '~-**aufsicht** *f* superintendence; '~**bau** *m* (*pl. Oberbauten*) superstructure (*a. e-r Brücke*); *e-r Straße*: surface; 🏗 permanent way; '~**befehl** *m* supreme command; '~**befehlshaber** *m* commander-in-chief; '~**bekleidung** *f* outer wear; '~**bett** *n* coverlet; '~-**bürgermeister** *m* chief burgomaster; *Brt.* Lord Mayor; '~**deck** ⚓ *n* upper deck.

'**Obere** *eccl. m* (Father) Superior.

'**Ober|feldwebel**✕ *m* staff sergeant, *Am.* sergeant 1st cl. (= class); ✈ flight (*Am.* technical) sergeant; '~**fläche** *f* (*an der, die* ~ *on the*) surface; ♀**flächlich** ['~flɛçliç] superficial (*a. fig.*); *Bekanntschaft*: casual; '~**flächlichkeit** *f* superficiality; '~**förster** *m* head forester; '~**gefreite** *m*✕ lance corporal, *Am.* private 1st cl. (= class); ✈ leading aircraftman, *Am.* airman 2nd cl. (= class); ⚓ able rating, *Am.* seaman; '♀**halb** above; '~**hand** *f*: *die* ~ *gewinnen* get the upper hand, *über* (*acc.*) get the better of; '~**haupt** *n* head, chief; '~**haus** *n the* Upper House, *Brt. the* (House of) Lords; '~**haut** *f* epidermis; '~**hemd** *n* (day-)shirt; '~**herrschaft** *f* supremacy; '~**hoheit** *f* sovereignty; '~**in** *f eccl.* Mother Superior; 🏗 matron; '~**ingenieur** *m* chief engineer; '♀-**irdisch** overground; ✈ ~**e** *Leitung* overhead line; '~**kellner** *m* head waiter; '~**kiefer** *m* upper jaw; '~**klasse** *f* upper class(es *pl.*); *Schule*: *a.* higher form; '~**kleid** *n* upper garment; '~**kleidung** *s.* **Oberbekleidung**; '~**kommando** *n* high (*od.* supreme) command; '~**körper** *m* upper part of the body; '~**land** *n* upland; '~**landesgericht** *n* regional court of appeal; '♀**lastig** top-heavy; '~**lauf** *m e-s Flusses*: upper course; '~**leder** *n* uppers *pl.*;

'~**lehrer** *m* senior assistant master; '~**leitung** *f* supervision, direction; ⚡ *s.* oberirdisch(e Leitung); '~**leutnant** *m* ✕ (*Am.* first) lieutenant; ⚓ sublieutenant, *Am.* lieutenant (junior grade); ✈ flying officer; '~**licht** *n* skylight; '~**lippe** *f* upper lip; '~**prima** *f* top grade, *Brt.* Upper Sixth; '~**schenkel** *m* thigh; '~**schicht** *f* top layer; *der Bevölkerung*: upper class(es *pl.*); '~**schule** *f* secondary school; '~**schwester** *f* head nurse, sister; '~**seite** *f* upper side; top (side).

'**oberst 1.** uppermost, top(most); highest (*a. fig.*); *fig.* supreme, chief, principal; *s. kehren, zuoberst*; **2.** ♀ ✕ *m* (12) colonel.

'**Ober|'staats-anwalt** *m* Senior Public Prosecutor; '~**'stabs-arzt**✕ *m* major (medical); '~**steiger** ⚒ *m* foreman of the mine; '~**stimme** ♪ *f* treble, soprano.

'**Oberst'leutnant** *m* lieutenant--colonel.

'**Ober|stübchen** *n* garret, attic; *fig.* F *nicht richtig im* ~ *sein* not to be quite right in the upper stor(e)y; '~**'studiendirektor** *m* head master, *Am.* principal; '~**'studienrat** *m* senior assistant master; '~**tasse** *f* cup; '~**teil** *m, n* upper part, top; '~**wasser** *n e-r Schleuse*: upper water; *Mühle*: overshot water; *fig.* ~ *bekommen* (*od. haben*) get (*od.* have) the upper hand; '~**welt** *f* upper world.

obgleich [ɔp'glaiç] (al)though.

'**Obhut** *f inv.* care, guard; *in s-e* ~ *nehmen* take care (*od.* charge) of.

obig ['o:biç] above(-mentioned).

Objekt [ɔp'jɛkt] *n* (3) object; (*Vorhaben*) project; (*Vermögensgegenstand*) property.

objektiv [~'ti:f] **1.** objective; (*unparteiisch*) *a.* impartial, unbiassed; (*tatsächlich*) actual, practical; **2.** ♀ *opt. n* (3¹) objective, lens; ♀**ität** [~tivi'tɛ:t] *f* objectiveness; impartiality. [slide.↱

Ob'jektträger *m des Mikroskops*:↲

Oblate [o'bla:tə] *f* (15) wafer; *eccl.* host.

obliegen ['ɔp-] *e-r Arbeit usw.*: apply o.s. to; *j-m* ~ be incumbent on a p., be a p.'s duty; '♀**heit** *f* duty.

obligat [obli'ga:t] obligatory; (*unerläßlich*) indispensable; *iro.* (*un*-

vermeidlich) inevitable; ♀ion [~ga-'tsjo:n] ⚥ *f* bond, debenture; '~o-risch [~'to:riʃ] obligatory (*für* on), compulsory (for).

Obmann ['ɔpman] *m* (*Vorsitzender*) chairman; (*Schiedsmann*) umpire; (*Betriebs*♀) spokesman.

Obo|e [o'bo:ə] *f* (15) hautboy, oboe; '~ist [obo'ist] *m* (12) oboist.

Obrigkeit ['o:briçkaɪt] *f* authorities *pl*.; government; magistracy; '♀lich magisterial; *adv*. by authority; '~s-denken *n* (6) authoritarian mentality; '~sstaat *m* authoritarian state.

obschon [ɔp'ʃo:n] (al)though.

Observatorium [ɔpzɛrva'to:rjum] *n* (9) observatory.

'**obsiegen** be victorious; *weit S*. prevail; ⚖ ~de *Partei* successful party.

Obst [o:pst] *n* (3²) fruit; '~bau *m* fruit-growing; '~baum *m* fruit-tree; '~ernte *f* fruit-gathering; (*Ertrag*) fruit-crop; '~garten *m* orchard; '~händler(in *f*) *m* fruiterer, *Am*. fruit seller; '~handlung *f* fruiterer's (shop), *Am*. fruit store; '~konserven *f/pl*. tinned (*bsd*. *Am*. canned) fruit; '~messer *n* fruit-knife.

Obstruktion [ɔpstruk'tsjo:n] *f* obstruction; *Am. pol. a*. filibuster (*a*. *v/i*. ~ *treiben*); *im Betrieb*: ca'canny.

'**Obst|wein** *m* fruit-wine; '~zucht *f* s. *Obstbau*; '~züchter(in *f*) *m* fruit-grower, fruit-farmer.

obszön [ɔps'tsø:n] obscene; ♀ität [~tsøni'tɛ:t] *f* (16) obscenity.

Obus ['o:bus] *m* (4¹) trolley bus.

'**obwalten** exist; *Umstände*: prevail.

ob'wohl (al)though.

Ochse ['ɔksə] *m* (13) ox (*pl*. oxen); *engS*. bullock; F P.: oaf; F *fig. wie der Ochs vorm Berg* stupidly.

'**ochsen** F (27) cram, grind, swot.

'**Ochsen|fleisch** *n* beef; '~gespann *n* team of oxen; '~haut *f* ox-hide; '~schwanzsuppe *f* ox-tail soup.

Ocker ['ɔkər] *m* (7) och|re, *Am*. -er.

Ode ['o:də] *f* (15) ode.

öde ['ø:də] **1.** deserted, desolate; (*unbebaut*) waste; (*unschön, freudlos*) dreary; (*fad*) dull; **2.** ♀ *f* (15) desert, solitude.

Ödem ♪ [ø'de:m] *n* (3¹) edema.

oder ['o:dər] or; ~ *aber* or else; ~ *auch* or rather; (*sonst*) otherwise.

Ödipuskomplex ['ø:dipus-] *psych. m* Oedipus complex.

Ödland ['ø:tlant] *n* (5, *pl. Odlände-*'reien) waste (*od*. fallow) land.

Odyssee [ody'se:] *f* (15) Odyssey.

Ofen ['o:fən] *m* (6¹) stove; (*Back*♀) oven; (*Hoch*♀) furnace; (*Kalk*♀, *Dörr*♀) kiln; '~heizung *f* stove-heating; '~kachel *f* Dutch tile; '~rohr *n* stove-pipe; '~röhre *f* (heating-)oven; '~setzer *m* stove-fitter.

offen ['ɔfən] *allg*. open (*a. Geheimnis, Haß, Markt, Stadt usw.*; *a*. ♣ *u. gr*.); *Stelle*: a. vacant; (*aufrichtig, freimütig*) a. frank, sincere, outspoken; (*unentschieden*) open, undecided; ~er *Leib* open bowels *pl*.; ~e *Rechnung* open account; ~er *Wechsel* blank cheque (*Am*. check); ~ *gestanden* frankly speaking; *s. Handelsgesellschaft*; *s. a. offenlassen usw*.

offen'bar evident(ly *adv*.), obvious (-ly); (*anscheinend*) apparent(ly); ~en (25) disclose, manifest, reveal; ♀ung *f* manifestation, (*a. eccl. u. fig*.) revelation; ♀ungs-eid *m* affidavit of means.

'**Offenheit** *f* openness; frankness.

'**offen|herzig** open-hearted, candid, frank, sincere; '♀herzigkeit *f* candidness, frankness, sincerity; '~kundig well-known, public; *b.s*. notorious; *Lüge usw*.: patent, blatant; '~lassen leave open (*a. fig*.); '~'sichtlich evident(ly *adv*.), obvious(ly).

offensiv [ɔfɛn'zi:f], ♀e [~və] *f* (15) offensive; *die* ~ *ergreifen* take the offensive.

'**offenstehen** be open (*a. fig. j-m* to); *es steht ihm offen zu inf.* he is free to *inf*.; ~d ⚥ outstanding, open.

öffentlich ['œfəntliç] *allg*. public (*a. Dienst, Recht usw*.); ~e *Hand* public authorities, *the* Government, ⚖ *in* ~er *Sitzung* in open court; ~ *bekanntmachen* make public; publicise; ~ *beglaubigt* authenticated by a notary public; *s. Ärgernis, Betrieb, Fürsorge usw*.; '♀keit *f* publicity; (*das Volk*) the (general) public; *an die* ~ *treten* appear before the public; *in aller* ~ in public; *s. Ausschluß*; '♀keits-arbeit *f* public relations *pl*.; '~'rechtlich under public law.

offerieren [ɔfə'ri:rən] offer.

Offerte [ɔ'fɛrtə] *f* (15) offer; *auf e-e Ausschreibung:* tender, bid.

offiziell [ɔfi'tsjɛl] official.

Offizier [ʌ'tsiːr] *m* (3¹) (commissioned) officer; **ʌkorps** *n the* officers *pl.*; **ʌs-anwärter** *m* officer cadet; **ʌskasino** *n* officers' mess; **ʌs-patent** *n* commission.

offiziös [ʌ'tsjøːs] (18¹) semi-official.

öffn|en ['œfnən] (*a. sich*) (26) open; **'Ɂung** *f* opening, aperture.

oft [ɔft], **oftmals** ['ʌmaːls], **öfters** ['œftərs] often, frequently.

oh! [oː] oh!, o!

Oh(ei)m ['oː(haɪ)m] *m* (3) uncle.

ohne ['oːnə] without; but for; **ʌ** *daß*, **ʌ** *zu inf.* without *ger.*; F **ʌ** *mich!* count me out; F *nicht* **ʌ!** not bad!; *s.* **Frage,** *weiter usw.*; **'ʌdem,** **ʌ'dies,** **ʌ'hin** anyhow, anyway; **ʌ-** **'gleichen** unequal(l)ed, matchless.

'Ohn|macht *f* (*Machtlosigkeit*) impotence, powerlessness; **ꭇ** (*a.* **'ʌs-** **anfall** *m*) faint(ing fit), swoon, (*Bewußtlosigkeit*) unconsciousness; *in* **ʌ** *fallen* faint, swoon; **'Ɂmächtig** powerless, impotent; **ꭇ** unconscious; **ʌ** *werden* faint, swoon.

Ohr [oːr] *n* (5) ear; *ein* **ʌ** *haben für* have an ear for; *j-m sein* **ʌ** *leihen* listen to a p.; *j-m in den* **ʌen** *liegen* pester a p.; *sich aufs* **ʌ** *legen* take a nap; *sich et. hinter die* **ʌen** *schreiben* make a note of a th.; *j-n übers* **ʌ** *hauen* cheat (*od.* fleece) a p.; *die* **ʌen** *hängenlassen* be downcast; *j-m zu* **ʌen** *kommen* come to a p.'s ears; F *halte die* **ʌen** *steif!* keep a stiff upper lip!; *bis über die* **ʌen** *up to* the eyes; *s.* **faustdick, ganz, spitzen.**

Öhr [øːr] *n* (3) eye.

'Ohren|-arzt *m* ear-specialist; **'ʌ-** **beichte** *f* auricular confession; **'Ɂbetäubend** (ear-)deafening; **'ʌ-** **bläser(in** *f*) *m* talebearer; **'ʌ-ent-** **zündung** *f* otitis; **'ʌleiden** *n* ear complaint; **'ʌsausen** *n* buzzing in the ear; **'ʌschmalz** *n* ear-wax; **'ʌ-** **schmaus** *m* (musical) treat; **'ʌ-** **schmerzen** *m/pl.* ear-ache; **'ʌ-** **schützer** *m* earflap, *Am.* earmuff; **'Ɂzerreißend** ear-splitting; **'ʌ-** **zeuge** *m* ear-witness.

'Ohr|feige *f* slap (in the face; *a. fig.*); **'Ɂfeigen** (25) *j-n:* box a p.'s ears; **'ʌgehänge** *n* ear-drops *pl.*, pendants *pl.*; **'ʌhörer** *m* Radio: earphone; **ʌläppchen** ['ʌlɛpçən] *n* ear-

-lobe; **'ʌmuschel** *anat. f* external ear; **'ʌring** *m* ear-ring; **'ʌwurm** *m* ear-wig; F *fig.* catchy tune.

okkult [ɔ'kult] occult; **Ɂismus** [ɔkul-'tismus] *m* (16, *o. pl.*) occultism.

Ökolog|e [økø'loːgə] *m* (13) ecologist; **ʌie** [ʌlo'giː] *f* (15) ecology; **Ɂisch** [ʌ'loːgiʃ] ecological; **ʌes** *Gleichgewicht* ecological balance.

Ökonom [øko'noːm] *m* (12) economist; **ꭇ** farmer, agriculturist; (*Verwalter*) manager; **ʌie** [ʌno'miː] *f* (15) economy; agriculture; **Ɂisch** [ʌ'noː-miʃ] economical.

Ökosystem ['øːko-] *n* ecosystem.

Oktan(zahl *f*) [ɔk'taːn-] *n* (10, *o.pl.*) octane (number *od.* rating).

Oktav [ɔk'taːf] *n* (3¹) octavo; **ʌband** *m* octavo (volume); **ʌe** ♪ [ʌvə] *f* octave.

Oktober [ɔk'toːbər] *m* (7) October.

Okul|ar *opt.* [oku'laːr] *n* (3¹) eyepiece, ocular; **Ɂieren** ꭇ [ʌ'liːrən] inoculate, graft.

ökumenisch [øku'meːniʃ] *eccl.* (o)ecumenical.

Okzident ['ɔktsidɛnt] *m* (3) occident.

Öl [øːl] *n* (3) oil; *fig.* **ʌ** *ins Feuer gießen* add fuel to the flames; **ʌ** *auf die Wogen gießen* pour oil on troubled waters; **'ʌbaum** *m* olive--tree; **'ʌberg** *m* Mount of Olives; **'ʌbild** *n* oil-painting; **'ʌdruck** *m* (*Bild*) oleograph; ⊕ oil pressure; **'ʌdruckbremse** *f* hydraulic brake; **'ʌ-embargo** *n* oil embargo.

ölen ['øːlən] (25) oil, ⊕ *a.* lubricate; (*salben*) anoint; *wie ein geölter Blitz* like (a) greased lightning.

'Öl|farbe *f* oil colo(u)r, oil paint; **'ʌfläschchen** *n* oil-cruet; **'ʌge-** **mälde** *n* oil-painting; **'ʌgötze** F *m:* *wie ein* **ʌ** like a post; **'ʌheizung** *f* oil heating; **'Ɂig** oily (*a. fig.*); *fig.* (*salbungsvoll*) unctuous.

Olive [o'liːvə] *f* (15) olive; **ʌnbaum** *m* olive-tree; **ʌnfarbe** *f* olive--colo(u)r; **ʌn-öl** *n* olive oil.

o'livgrün olive-green, *Am. a.* olive drab.

'Öl|kanne *f* oil-can, oiler; **'ʌkata-** **strophe** *f* oil disaster; **'ʌkrise** *f* oil crisis; **'ʌleitung** ⊕ *f* oil-lead, oil--feed; *über Land:* pipeline; **'ʌmale-** **rei** *f* oil-painting; **'ʌmeßstab** *m* dipstick; **'ʌ-ofen** *m* oil-furnace; **'ʌpa-** **pier** *n* oil-paper; **'ʌpest** *f* oil pol-

Ölproduzent

lution; '**~produzent** m oil producer;
'**~quelle** f erbohrte: oil-well; natürliche: oil-spring, Am. gusher; '**~
stand** m oil level; '**~stand-anzeiger**
m oil ga(u)ge; '**~tank** m oil tank;
'**~teppich** m oil slick.

'**Ölung** f oiling, ⊕ a. lubrication;
(Salbung) anointment; eccl. letzte ~
extreme unction.

'**Ölwechsel** mot. m oil change.

Olymp|iade [olym'pjɑːdə] f a)
Olympiad; b) Sport: Olympic games
pl.; **♀isch** [o'lympiʃ] Olympian;
Sport: Olympic; ♀e Spiele s. Olympiade b).

'**Öl|zeug** n oilskins pl.; '**~zweig** m
olive-branch.

Oma ['oːma] F f (11¹) grandma.

Ombudsmann pol. ['ɔmbuts-] m
ombudsman.

Omelett [ɔm(ə)'lɛt] n (3), **~e** [~] f
(15) omelet(te).

Omen ['oːmən] n (6) omen.

ominös [omi'nøːs] ominous.

Omnibus ['ɔmnibus] m (4¹ od. inv.)
omnibus, F bus; (Überland♀) coach;
'**~haltestelle** f bus stop.

Onanie [ona'niː] f (15, o. pl.) mas-
turbation; **♀ren** masturbate.

ondulieren [ɔndu'liːrən] Haar:
wave.

Onkel ['ɔŋkəl] m (7) uncle.

Opa ['oːpa] F m (11) grandpa.

Opal [o'paːl] m (3¹) opal; **♀i'sieren**
[opali-] opalesce; **~d** opalescent.

Oper ['oːpər] f (15) opera.

Operateur [opəra'tøːr] m (3¹) operator; ⚕ operating surgeon.

Operation [~'tsjoːn] f operation;
~sbasis ✕ f base of operations;
♀sfähig ✕: (nicht) ~ (in)operable;
~snarbe f postoperative scar; **~s-
radius** ✕ m operating radius, range;
~ssaal m operating theatre, Am.
-er; **~sschwester** f theatre (Am.
-er) nurse.

operativ [~'tiːf] operative; ✕ operational.

Operette [opə'rɛtə] f (15) operetta,
comic opera.

operieren [~'riːrən] (25) v/i. u. v/t.
operate (an a p.); sich ~
lassen undergo an operation.

'**Opern|glas** n opera-glass(es pl.);
'**~haus** n opera-house; '**~musik** f
operatic music; '**~sänger(in** f) m
opera-singer, operatic singer; '**~text**
m libretto.

Opfer ['ɔpfər] n (7) sacrifice; (Gabe)
offering; (der, das Geopferte) victim; ein ~ bringen make a sacrifice;
zum ~ fallen fall a victim of, e-m
Betrüger usw.: be victimized by;
♀bereit s. opferwillig; '**~gabe** f
offering; '**~geld** n money-offering;
'**~lamm** n sacrificial lamb; eccl. the
Lamb (Jesus); fig. victim; '**~mut**
m spirit of sacrifice; '**♀n** v/t. u. v/i.
(29) sacrifice (a. Schach); '**~stock**
eccl. m poor-box; '**~tier** n victim;
'**~tod** m sacrifice of one's life; '**~ung** f
offering, sacrifice; '**♀willig** willing to
make sacrifices, self-sacrificing.

Opiat [op'jaːt] n (3) opiate.

Opium ['oːpjum] n (11) opium.

Oppon|ent [ɔpo'nɛnt] m (12) op-
ponent; **♀ieren** [ɔpo'niːrən] oppose
(gegen j-n a p.), resist.

Opportunist [ɔpɔrtu'nist] m (12)
time-server, opportunist.

Opposition [ɔpozi'tsjoːn] f opposition; **~sführer** m opposition leader.

optieren [ɔp'tiːrən] opt (für for).

Optik ['ɔptik] f (16) optics sg.; phot.
lens system; '**~er** m (7) optician.

optim|al [ɔpti'maːl] optimal; **~ieren**
[~'miːrən] optimize; **♀um** ['ɔpti-
mum] n (9²) optimum.

Optim|ismus [ɔpti'mismus] m (16,
o. pl.) optimism; **~ist** m (12), **~i-
stin** f optimist; **♀istisch** optimistic.

Option [ɔp'tsjoːn] f (16) option.

'**optisch** optical.

Opus ['oːpus] n (pl. Opera ['oːpəra])
work; ♪ ~ 12 usw. opus 12, etc.

Orakel [o'raːkəl] n (7), **~spruch** m
oracle; **♀haft** oracular; **♀n** (29)
speak (od. say) oracularly.

Orange [o'raŋʒə] f (15) orange;
♀farben orange(-colo[u]red); **~n-
baum** m orange-tree; **~'rie** f (16)
orangery.

Orang-Utan zo. ['oːraŋ'ʔuːtan] m
(11) orang-outang, orang-utan.

Oratorium [ora'toːrjum] n (9¹)
oratorio.

Orchester [ɔr'kɛstər] n (7) orchestra, als Musikkorps a. band;
~... orchestral; **~raum** thea. m
orchestra pit; **~sessel** thea. m stall,
Am. orchestra (seat).

orche'strieren orchestrate.

Orchidee [ɔrçi'deː] f (15) orchid.

Orden ['ɔrdən] m (6) order; (Ehren-
zeichen) order, decoration, medal.

'**Ordens|band** n ribbon (of an

order); '~**bruder** *m* member of an order; *eccl. a.* friar; '~**geistliche** *m* regular; '~**kleid** *n* monastic garb); '~**schnalle** *f* bar, clasp); '~**schwester** *f* sister, nun; '~**verleihung** *f* conferring (of) an order; '~**zeichen** *n* badge of an order.

ordentlich ['ordəntliç] tidy; (*methodisch geordnet*; *gesittet*) orderly (*a.* ⚖ *Gericht*); (*richtig*; *sorgfältig*) proper; (*regelrecht*) regular; (*achtbar*) respectable, of orderly habits; (*tüchtig*) good, sound; (*ziemlich gut*) quite good, decent; *adv.* properly; (*sehr*) fairly, thoroughly, downright; ~**er** *Professor* professor in ordinary, *Am.* full professor; '2-**keit** *f* orderliness; respectability.

Order ['ordər] *f* (15) order, command; ✝ *an die* ~ *von* to the order of.

ordin|är [ordi'nɛːr] common, ordinary; *b.s.* vulgar, low; 2**arius** [~'naːrjus] *m* (16²) *univ.* professor in ordinary; 2**ation** [~na'tsjoːn] *f* ordination; ~**ieren** [~'niːrən] ordain; *ordiniert in* (holy) orders; *ordiniert werden* take orders.

ordn|en ['ordnən] (26) order, arrange; *Angelegenheit:* arrange, settle, adjust; (*regeln*) regulate; '2**er** *m* (7) (*Fest2*, *Versammlungs2*) marshal, steward; *Schule:* monitor; *für Akten:* file; (*Brief2*) letter file.

'**Ordnung** *f* putting in order; (*Zustand*, *a. Reihenfolge*) order (*a.* ♀); (*Anordnung*) arrangement; (*Klasse*, *Stand*) class, rank; (*Vorschrift*) rules *pl.*, regulations *pl.*; *in* ~ *bringen* put in order, put (*od.* get) straight, *wieder:* repair, *Am.* fix, *fig.* straighten out (*matters*); ~ *schaffen* establish order; *in* ~ *halten* keep in order; *irgend etwas ist nicht in* ~ there is something wrong; *ist alles in* ~? is everything all right *od.* O.K. (= okay)?; '2**sgemäß** *s.* ordnungsmäßig; '~**sliebe** *f* love of order; '2**sliebend** orderly; '2**smäßig** orderly, regular; *pred.* in due order; *adv.* duly; '~**sruf** *parl. m* call to order; '~**sstrafe** ⚖ *f* fine; '2**swidrig** irregular; '~**szahl** *f* ordinal (number).

Ordonnanz ⚔ [ordo'nants] *f* (16) orderly; ~**offizier** *m* orderly officer.

Organ [or'gaːn] *n* (3¹) *anat.* organ (*weit S. a. Stimme, Zeitung usw.*;

Körperschaft); (*Behörde*) agency, authority, executive body; ~**isation** [organiza'tsjoːn] *f* organization; ~**isati'ons-talent** *n* organizing ability; ~**isator** [~'zaːtɔr] *m* (8¹) organizer; 2**isatorisch** [~za'toːriʃ] organisational, organizing; 2**isch** [or-'gaːniʃ] organic(ally *adv.*).

organi'sieren organize; ⚔ *sl.* (*sich beschaffen*) F commandeer; *organisiert(er Arbeiter)* unionist; *nicht organisiert(er Arbeiter)* non-union(ist).

Organ|ismus [~'nismus] *m* (16²) organism; ⚙ system; ~**ist** [~'nist] *m* (12) organist.

Or'gan-spende ⚙ *f* donation of an organ; ~**r(in** *f)* *m* organ donor.

Orgasmus [or'gasmus] *m* (16²) orgasm, climax.

Orgel ['orgəl] *f* (15) organ; '~**bauer** *m* organ-builder; '~**konzert** *n* organ-recital; '2**n** (29) play (on) an organ; *auf der Drehorgel:* grind a barrel-organ; '~**pfeife** *f* organ-pipe; '~**spieler** *m* organist; '~**stimme** *f* organ-stop, register.

Orgie ['orgjə] *f* (15) orgy (*a. fig.*); ~**n** *feiern* have orgies.

Orien|t... [ori'ent-], ~**tale** [~'taːlə] *m* (13), ~'**talin** *f* (16¹) oriental; 2'**talisch** oriental.

orientier|en [~'tiːrən] orient(ate); *fig. a.* (*in Kenntnis setzen*) inform (*über acc.* of); *sich* ~ orient o.s. (*a. fig.*), take one's bearings (*nach der Sonne usw.* from); *sich nicht (mehr)* ~ *können* have lost one's bearings; 2**ung** *f* orientation; *fig.* information; 2**ungspunkt** *m* landmark; 2**ungssinn** *m* sense of direction.

Origin|al [origi'naːl] *n* (3¹) (*Text*, *Person*) original; (*Film*, *Platte*) master copy; 2'**al** *adj.* original; ~**alität** [~nali'tɛːt] *f* (16) originality; ~**alsendung** [~'naːl-] *f* Radio, TV: live broadcast; ~**altreue** *f*: größte ~ high fidelity (*abbr.* hi-fi); 2**ell** [~'nɛl] original; (*spaßhaft*) *a.* funny.

Orkan [or'kaːn] *m* (3¹) hurricane; 2**-artig** *Sturm:* violent; *Beifall:* thunderous.

Ornament [orna'mɛnt] *n* (3) ornament.   [vestments *pl.*]

Ornat [or'naːt] *m* (3) robe(s *pl.*),

Ornithologe [ornito'loːgə] *m* (13) ornithologist.

Ort [ort] *m* (3 *u.* 1⁸) place; *s. Ortschaft*; (*Fleck, Stelle*) spot; (*Ört-*

lichkeit) locality; ~ *der Handlung* scene (of action); *fig. am ~ (angebracht)* appropriate; *an ~ und Stelle* on the spot; *höheren ~es* at high quarters; '2en ⚔ (26) locate, fix the position of.

ortho|dox [ɔrto'dɔks] orthodox; 2**do'xie** *f* orthodoxy; 2**graphie** [~gra'fiː] *f* orthography; **~graphisch** [~'graːfiʃ] orthographic(al); 2**päde** [~'pɛːdə] *m* (13) orthop(a)edist; 2**pädie** [~pɛ'diː] *f* orthop(a)edics *pl.*; **~pädisch** [~'pɛːdiʃ] orthop(a)edic.

örtlich ['œrtliç] local (*a.* 🎖); 2**keit** *f* locality.

'**Orts|-angabe** *f* statement of place; *auf Brief:* address; '2**-ansässig**, '~**-ansässige** *m*, *f* resident; '~**-behörde** *f* local authorities *pl.*

'**Ortschaft** *f* (16) place; (*Dorf*) village.

'**Orts|-empfang** *m Radio:* local reception; '2**fest** stationary; '2**-fremd** *sein* to be a stranger (to the locality); '~**gespräch** *teleph. n* local call; '~**gruppe** *f* local chapter; '~**kenntnis** *f* local knowledge; '~**krankenkasse** *f* local sick-fund; '2**kundig** familiar with the locality; '~**name** *m* place-name; '~**sender** *m* local transmitter; '~**sinn** *m* sense of locality; '~**statut** *n* by(e)-law, *Am.* city ordinance; '~**teil** *m* district; '2**-üblich** locally customary; '~**ver-änderung** *f* change of place; '~**verkehr** *m* local traffic; '~**zeit** *f* local time.

Ortung ['ɔrtuŋ] *f* location, position finding; '~**sgerät** *n* position finder.

Öse ['øːzə] *f* (15) eye, loop.

Ost [ɔst] 1. east; 2. *poet. m* (3, *o. pl.*) east (wind); '~**block** *pol. m* Eastern bloc; '~**en** [~ən] *m* (6, *o. pl.*) east; *geogr., pol.* East; *der Ferne (Nahe)* ~ the Far (Near) East.

ostentativ [ɔstɛnta'tiːf] ostentatious.

Oster|-ei ['oːstər-] *n* Easter egg; '~**fest** *n s.* Ostern; '~**glocke** ❀ *f* (yellow) daffodil; '~**hase** *m* Easter-bunny.

österlich ['øːstərliç] (of) Easter.

Ostern ['oːstərn] *n od. f/pl.* (*inv., mst ohne art.*) Easter.

Österreich|er ['øːstəraiçər] *m* (7), '~**erin** *f* (16[1]), '2**isch** Austrian.

östlich ['œstliç] eastern, easterly; ~ *von* east of.

'**Ost|hang** *m* east(ern) slope; '~**mark** *f* (*Geld*) East German mark.

Östrogen *biol.* [œstro'geːn] *n* (3) estrogen.

'**Ost|see** *f* Baltic (Sea); 2**wärts** ['~vɛrts] eastward; '~**wind** *m* east wind.

Otter ['ɔtər] 1. *f* (15) (*Schlange*) adder; 2. *m* (7) (*Fisch*2) otter.

Ouvertüre [uvɛr'tyːrə] *f* (15) overture.

oval [o'vaːl], 2 *n* (3) oval.

Ovation [ova'tsjoːn] *f* ovation.

Overall ['oːvərɔːl, 'ɔʊvərɔːl] *m* (11) (*Arbeitsanzug*) overalls *pl.*, boiler suit; *modischer:* catsuit, jumpsuit.

Oxyd [ɔ'ksyːt] *n* (3) oxide; **~ation** [~da'tsjoːn] *f* oxidation; 2**ieren** [~'diːrən] *v/t. u. v/i.* (sn) oxidize.

Ozean ['oːtseaːn] *m* (3[1]) ocean; '~**dampfer** *m* ocean liner; 2**isch** [~'aːniʃ] oceanic.

Ozon [o'tsoːn] *m, n* (3[1]) ozone; 2**haltig** [~haltiç] ozonic, ozoniferous; ~**schicht** *f* ozone layer.

P

P [peː], **p** *n inv.* P, p.

Paar [paːr] 1. *n* (3) pair; (*bsd. Mann u. Frau*) couple; *z. B. Rebhühner, Pistolen:* brace; 2. *ein* 2 a few, some, F a couple of; 3. 2 even; ~ *oder un*~ odd or even; '2**en** (25) pair, couple, *bsd. Vögel:* mate (*a. sich* ~); *Sport:* pair, match; *sich* ~ *fig.* join (*mit* with); '2**ig** in pairs,

paired; '~**laufen** *n Sport:* pair skating; '2**mal:** *ein* ~ several od. (a few) times; '~**ung** *f* pairing (*Sport: a.* matching); mating, copulation; '~**ungszeit** *f* mating season '2**weise** by pairs, in couples, two and two.

Pacht [paxt] *f* (16) lease, tenure; (~*geld*) rent; *in* ~ *geben (nehmen)*

let (take) on lease; '⁀**en** (26) (take on) lease, rent, farm; *fig.* monopolize.
Pächter ['pɛçtər] *m* (7), '~**in** *f* (16¹) (*Mieter*) lessee; *von Land*: tenant; *weitS.* farmer; ⚖ leaseholder.
'**Pacht|-ertrag** *m* rental; '⁀**frei** rent-free; '~**geld** *n* farm-rent; '~**gut** *n* farm; '~**ung** *f* taking on lease, farming; (*das Gepachtete*) leasehold; '~**vertrag** *m* lease; '⁀**weise** on lease.
Pack [pak] **1.** *m* (3³ *u.* 3) pack; (*Paket*) packet, parcel; (*Ballen*) bale; *s. Sack*; **2.** *n* (3, *o. pl.*) (*Lumpen*⁀) rabble.
Päckchen ['pɛkçən] *n* (6) small parcel; packet, package; *Zigaretten*: pack; F *fig.* burden, worries *pl.*
'**Pack-eis** *n* pack(-ice).
'**packen 1.** (25) pack (up); (*fassen*) seize, grasp, grip; *fig.* grip, thrill; *pack dich! sl.* beat it!; **2.** ⁀ *n* (6) packing; **3.** ⁀ *m* (6) pack; (*Ballen*) bale.
'**Packer** *m* (7), '~**in** *f* (16¹) packer.
'**Pack|-esel** *m* sumpter-mule; *fig.* drudge, fag; '~**leinwand** *f* pack-cloth; '~**material** *n* packing (material); '~**papier** *n* wrapping paper; *als Papiersorte*: brown paper; '~**pferd** *n* pack-horse; '~**sattel** *m* pack-saddle; '~**tasche** *f* pannier, saddlebag; '~**tier** *n* pack-animal; '~**ung** *f* (*Päckchen*) packet, pack (*a.* ⚕); F *fig.* awful beating; '~**wagen** *m* *Brt.* (luggage) van, *Am.* baggage car.
Pädagog|e [pɛːda'goːgə] *m* (13), ~**in** [~gin] *f* education(al)ist; ~**ik** [~gik] *f* pedagogics *pl.*; ⁀**isch** pedagogic(al).
Paddel ['padəl] *n* (7) paddle; '~**boot** *n* canoe; '⁀**n** (29, sn) paddle, canoe.
paff [paf] bang!, pop!; F *ganz ~ sein* be dumbfounded.
paffen ['pafən] (25) puff (*die Pfeife* at one's pipe).
Page ['pɑːʒə] *m* (13) page; *s. Hotel*⁀; '~**nkopf** *m* bob(bed hair).
Pagode [pa'goːdə] *f* (15) pagoda.
pah! [pɑː] pah!; pshaw!
Pak ⚔ [pak] *f* (*sg.* 16, *pl.* 11) anti-tank gun.
Paket [pa'keːt] *n* (3) parcel; *großes*: package (*a. fig. pol. usw.*); *kleines*: packet; ✝ *Wertpapiere*: block; ~-**annahme** *f* parcels receiving office; ~-**ausgabe** *f* parcel delivery; ~**bombe** *f* parcel bomb; ~**boot** *n* mail-boat; ~**karte** ☏ *f* parcel form; ~**post** *f* parcel post.
Pakt [pakt] *m* (3 *u.* 5) pact, agreement; ⁀**ieren** [~'tiːrən] make a deal (*mit* with).
Palast [pa'last] *m* (3² *u.* ³) palace; ⁀-**artig** palatial; ~**revolution** *fig. f* palace revolution.
Palästinenser [palɛsti'nɛnzər] *m* (7) Palestinian.
Palette [pa'lɛtə] *f* (15) palette.
Palisade [pali'zɑːdə] *f* (15) palisade; ~**nzaun** *m* stockade.
Palm|e ['palmə] *f* (15) palm(-tree); F *j-n auf die ~ bringen* put a p.'s monkey up; '~**kätzchen** *n* catkin; '~'**sonntag** *m* Palm Sunday.
Pampelmuse ⚘ [pampəl'muːzə] *f* (15) grapefruit.
Pamphlet [pam'fleːt] *n* (3) (*Flugblatt*) pamphlet; (*Schmähschrift*) lampoon; ~**ist** [~fle'tist] *m* (12) pamphleteer; lampoonist.
Paneel [pa'neːl] *n* (3¹) wainscot, panel.
Panier [pa'niːr] *n* (3¹) banner, standard.
pa'nier|en (25) *Kochkunst*: (bread-)crumb; ⁀**mehl** *n* breadcrumbs *pl.*
Pan|ik ['pɑːnik] *f* (16) panic, scare; '⁀**isch** panic.
Panne ['panə] *f* (15) break-down; (*Motor*⁀) engine failure; (*Reifen*⁀) puncture, blowout; *fig.* mishap, (*Fehler*) F slip-up; e-e ~ *haben* break down, have a break-down; '~**ndienst** *mot. m* break-down service.
Panoptikum [pa'nɔptikum] *n* (9¹) waxworks *pl.*
Panorama [pano'rɑːma] *n* (9¹) panorama, panoramic view; ~**scheibe** *mot. f* panoramic windscreen (*Am.* windshield).
panschen ['panʃən] (27) *s. pantschen.*
Panther ['pantər] *m* (7) panther.
Pantine [pan'tiːnə] *f* (15) clog.
Pantoffel [~'tɔfəl] *m* (10 *u.* 7) slipper, mule; *fig. unter dem ~ stehen* be henpecked; ~**held** *m* henpecked husband.
Pantomim|e [panto'miːmə] *f* (15) pantomime, dumb show; ⁀**isch** pantomimic.
pan(t)schen ['pan(t)ʃən] (27) splash (about); (*verfälschen*) adulterate.
Panzer ['pantsər] *m* (7) armo(u)r; (*Kampfwagen*) tank; ⚓ armo(u)r

(-plating); '~**abwehrgeschütz** *n* anti-tank gun; '~**abwehrrakete** *f* anti-tank rocket; '⁀**brechend** armo(u)r-piercing; '~**division** *f* armo(u)red division; '~**faust** ✕ *f* anti--tank grenade launcher; '~**glas** *n* bullet-proof glass; '~**handschuh** *m* gauntlet; '~**hemd** *n* coat of mail; '~**kreuzer** *m* armo(u)red cruiser; '⁀**n** (29) armo(u)r; *sich* ~ arm o.s.; *gepanzerte Faust* mailed fist; '~**platte** *f* armo(u)r-plate; '~**schrank** *m* safe; ~**spähwagen** ['~ʃpeː-] *m* armo(u)red (reconnaissance) car; '~**sperre** *f* anti-tank obstacle; '~**truppe** *f* tank force *od.* corps; '~**ung** ✕, ✝ *f* armo(u)r-plating; '~**wagen** *m* armo(u)red car; '~**zug** *m* 🚂 armo(u)red train; ✕ tank platoon.

Papa [pa'pa, F '~] *m* (11) papa, F dad(dy), *Am.* F pop.

Papagei [papa'gaɪ] *m* (3 *u.* 12) parrot; ~**enkrankheit** *f* psittacosis.

Papier [pa'piːr] *n* (3¹) paper; ~*e pl.* (*Ausweise*) (identity) papers *pl.*, ↓ (*Wertpapiere*) securities *pl.*, papers *pl.*; (*nur*) *auf dem* ~ on paper (only); *zu* ~ *bringen* commit to paper; ~**bogen** *m* sheet of paper; ⁀**en** (*of* paper; ~**fabrik** *f* paper-mill; ~**geld** *n* paper-money; ~**handlung** *f* stationer's (shop), *Am.* stationery (store); ~**handtuch** *n* paper towel; ~**korb** *m* waste-paper basket; ~**krieg** F *m* red tape, paper warfare; ~**maché** [papje:ma'ʃeː] *n* (11¹) papier mâché; ~**schlange** [pa'piːr-] *f* paper streamer; ~**schnitzel** *n*, ~**wisch** *m* scrap of paper; ~**taschentuch** *n* tissue; ~**währung** *f* paper-currency; ~**waren** *f/pl.* stationery; ~**warengeschäft** *n s. Papierhandlung.*

Papp [pap] *m* (3) (*Brei*) pap; (*Kleister*) paste; '~**band** *m* pasteboard binding; (book bound in) boards *pl.*; '~**becher** *m* paper cup; '~**deckel** *m* pasteboard.

Pappe ['papə] *f* (15) pasteboard; (*starke* ~) millboard; F *fig. nicht von* ~ quite something.

Pappel ['papəl] *f* (15) poplar.

päppeln ['pɛpəln] (29) feed (with pap); *fig.* coddle, pamper.

'**papp**|**en** *v/t.* paste; *v/i.* stick; '⁀**enstiel** F *fig. m* trifle; *für e-n* ~ for a song; ~**erlapapp!** [papɐla'pap] fiddlesticks!; '~**ig** sticky; '⁀**schachtel** *f* cardboard box; '⁀**schnee** *m*

sticky snow; '⁀**teller** *m* paper plate.

Paprika ['paprika] *m* (11) paprika; ♀ capsicum; '~**schote** *f* pepper.

Papst [paːpst] *m* (3² *u.* ³) pope.

päpstlich ['pɛːpstlɪç] papal.

'**Papsttum** *n* (1, *o. pl.*) papacy.

Parab|**el** [pa'raːbəl] *f* (15) (*Gleichnis*) parable; ♈ parabola; ⁀**olisch** [para'boːlɪʃ] parabolic(ally *adv.*).

Parade [pa'raːdə] *f* (15) parade; (*Prunk*) display; ✕ review; *fenc.* parry; *Fußball:* save; ~**anzug** ✕ *m* dress uniform, F full dress; ~**marsch** ✕ *m* march in review.

Paradentose 🦷 [paraden'toːzə] *f* (15) paradentosis.

Pa'radeplatz ✕ *m* parade-ground.

paradieren [para'diːrən] parade.

Paradies [~'diːs] *n* (4) paradise.

paradiesisch [~'diːzɪʃ] paradisiac (-al); *fig.* heavenly.

Para'diesvogel *m* bird of paradise.

paradox [~'dɔks] paradoxical.

Paraffin [para'fiːn] *n* (3¹) paraffin; ~**öl** *n* paraffin oil.

Paragraph [~'graːf] *m* (12) section, article; (*Absatz*) paragraph; (*das Zeichen* §) section-mark.

parallel [para'leːl] parallel (*mit* to, with); ⁀**e** *f* (15) parallel (line); ⁀**ogramm** [~lelo'gram] *n* (3¹) parallelogram; ⁀**schaltung** ⚡ *f* parallel connection.

Paraly|**se** [para'lyːzə] *f* (15) paralysis; ⁀'**sieren** [~ly-] paralyse; ⁀**tisch** [~'lyːtɪʃ] paralytic(ally *adv.*).

paranoi|**d** [parano'iːt] paranoid; ⁀**ker** [~'noːikɐr] *m* (7), ~**sch** [~'noːiʃ] paranoiac.

Paranuß ['paːra-] *f* Brazil-nut.

Parasit [para'ziːt] *m* (12) parasite; ⁀**isch** parasitic(al).

parat [pa'raːt] ready; ~ *haben Kenntnisse*: have at one's fingers' ends; *Antwort*: have pat.

Pärchen ['pɛːrçən] *n* (6) (courting) couple; *a. iro.* twosome.

Pardon [par'dõ] *m* (11) pardon; ✕ quarter.

Parenthese [parɛn'teːzə] *f* (15) parenthesis.

Parforcejagd [par'fɔrsjaːkt] *f* hunt (-ing) on horseback.

Parfüm [par'fyːm] *n* (3¹) perfume, scent; ~**e'rie** *f*, ~**e'rien** [~fymə'riː(n)] *pl.* perfumery; ~**fläschchen** (small) scent-bottle; ⁀**ieren** [~fy'miːrən] perfume, scent.

pari ✝ ['pɑːri] par; *al* ~ at par; *über* (*unter*) ~ above (below) par.

Paria ['pɑːrja] *m* (11) pariah.

parieren [pa'riːrən] *v*/*i.* (*dat.*) obey; *v*/*t. u. v*/*i. Pferd*: pull up, stop; *Stoß usw.*: parry (*a. fig.*).

Pariser [pa'riːzər] *m* (7) Parisian; F (*Kondom*) rubber.

Parität [pari'tɛːt] *f* (16) parity; 2isch proportional, pro rata.

Park [park] *m* (3) park; ✕ *a.* depot; *s. Wagen*2; '~**anlage** *f* park; '~**deck** *mot. n* parking level; '2en (25) park; 2 *verboten!* No parking!

Parkett [~'kɛt] *n* (3) parquet; *thea.* stalls *pl.*, *Am.* parquet; ~**fußboden** *m* parquet flooring.

'**Park|gebühr** *f* parking fee; '~**haus** *n* multi-storey car park; '~**licht** *n* parking light; '~**lücke** *f* parking space; '~**platz** *m* car park, *Am.* parking lot; (*einzelner Platz*) parking space; '~-**scheibe** *f* parking disc; '~**uhr** *f* parking meter; '~**verbot** *n*: *hier ist* ~ there's no parking here; '~**wächter** *mot. m* car park attendant.

Parlament [parla'mɛnt] *n* (3) parliament; ~**är** [~'tɛːr] *m* (3[1]) parlementaire (*fr.*); ~**arier** [~'tɑːrjər] *m* (7) parliamentarian; 2**arisch** [~'tɑːriʃ] parliamentary; 2**ieren** [~'tiːrən] parley; ~**s-ausschuß** *m* parliamentary committee.

Parmesan [parme'zɑːn] *m* (3, *o. pl.*), ~**käse** *m* Parmesan cheese.

Parodie [paro'diː] *f* (15) parody; 2**ren** parody.

Parole [pa'roːlə] *f* (15) ✕ password; *fig.* catchword, slogan.

Paroli [pa'roːli] *fig. n* (11): *j-m* ~ *bieten* stick up to a p.

Partei [par'taɪ] *f* (16) party (*a. pol. u. ⚖*); (*~sektion*) faction; *Sport*: side; *j-s* ~ *ergreifen,* ~ *nehmen für j-n* take the part of a p., side with a p.; *gegen j-n* ~ *ergreifen* take sides against a p.; ~**abzeichen** *n* party badge; ~**apparat** *m* party machine; ~**basis** *f* rank and file; ~**disziplin** *f* party discipline; *sich der* ~ *beugen* follow the party line; ~**führer** *m* party-leader; ~**gänger** *m* (7) partisan; ~**geist** *m* party spirit; ~**genosse** *m* party-member; 2**isch,** 2**lich** partial; ~**leitung** *f* party leadership; ~**lichkeit** *f* partiality; 2**los** impartial, neutral; *pol.* independent, non-party; ~**lose** *parl. m* (18) non-party

member; ~**losigkeit** *f* impartiality, neutrality; ~**mitglied** *n* party member; ~**nahme** [~nɑːmə] *f* (15) partisanship; ~**politik** *f* party politics; ~**programm** *n* party-programme; ~**sucht** *f* factious spirit; ~**tag** *m* party conference (*Am.* convention); ~**ung** *f* division into parties; ~**ver-anstaltung** *f* party function; ~**versammlung** *f* party meeting; ~**zugehörigkeit** *f* party affiliation.

Parterre [par'tɛr] *n* (11) ground floor, *Am.* first floor; *thea.* pit, *Am.* orchestra circle.

Partie [~'tiː] *f* (15) (*Teil*) part; ✝ (*Warenmenge*) lot, parcel; (*Gesellschaft*) party; (*Ausflug*) outing, excursion; *Sport*: match (*a. Heirat*), game; *mit von der* ~ *sein* make one of the party.

partiell [par'tsjɛl] partial.

Partik|el [~'tiːkəl] *f* (15) particle; ~**ularismus** [~tikula'rismus] *m* (16) particularism.

Partisan [parti'zɑːn] *m* (12) partisan, guerilla.

Partitur [~'tuːr] *f* (16) score.

Partizip *gr.* [~'tsiːp] *n* (8[2]) participle.

Partner ['partnər] *m* (7), '~**in** *f* (16[1]) partner; '~**schaft** *f* partnership; '~-**stadt** *f* twin town; '~**tausch** *m* wife-swapping.

Party ['pɑːti] *f* (11[1] *u. -ties*) party.

Parvenü [parvə'nyː] *m* (11) upstart, parvenu. [the Fates.]

Parze ['partsə] *f* (15): *die* ~*n pl.*

Parzel|le [par'tsɛlə] *f* (15) plot, allotment, *bsd. Am.* lot; 2'**lieren** divide into lots, parcel out.

Pasch [paʃ] *m* (3[2] *u.* [3]) *beim Würfeln*: doublets *pl.*

Pascha ['paʃa] *m* (11) pasha.

Paspel ['paspəl] *m* (7), *f* (15) piping.

Paß [pas] *m* (14[1] *u.* [2]) (*Gebirgs*2) pass; (*Reise*2) passport, *s. Paßgang*.

passabel [pa'sɑːbəl] passable, tolerable, fair(ly good).

Passage [pa'sɑːʒə] *f* (15) passage (*a. ♪*); △ arcade.

Passagier [pasa'ʒiːr] *m* (3[1]) passenger; *im Taxi*: fare; *s. blind*; ~**flugzeug** *n* passenger aircraft; ~**gut** *n* luggage, *Am.* baggage.

Passah ['pasa] *n* (11, *o. pl.*), *mst* '~**fest** *n* Passover.

'**Paß-amt** *n* pass-port office.

Passant [pa'sant] *m* (12), ~**in** *f* (16[1]) passer-by (*pl.* passers-by).

Passat [pa'saːt] *m* (3), **~wind** *m* trade-wind.

'Paßbild *n* passport photo(graph).

passen ['pasən] (28) fit (*j-m* a p.; *auf acc., für, zu* et. a th.); (*zusagen*) suit (*j-m* a p.); *Spiel*: pass; ~ (*warten*) *auf* (*acc.*) watch (*od.* wait) for; *nicht* ~ *für* be unfit for; ~ *zu e-m Kleid usw.*: go with, *bsd. in der Farbe*: match (with); *sie* ~ *zueinander* they are well matched; *sich* ~ be fit *od.* proper; *das paßt sich nicht* that is not good form; '**~d** fit; suitable; (*kleidsam*) becoming, *bsd. in der Farbe*: to match; (*gelegen*) convenient; *für* ~ *halten* think proper.

Passepartout [paspar'tuː] *n* (11) masterkey; (*Wechselrahmen*) mount.

'Paß|form *f* fit; '**~gang** *m* amble.

passier|bar [pa'siːrbaːr] passable, practicable; **~en** *v/i.* (sn) (*vorbeigehen*) pass; (*sich ereignen*) take place, happen, come to pass; *v/t.* pass (by); *Kochkunst*: strain; **2-schein** *m* pass (*bsd.* ✕); permit.

Passion [pa'sjoːn] *f* (16) passion; (*Liebhaberei*) hobby; **2iert** [~sjo-'niːrt] passionate; **~sspiel** [~-'sjoːns-] *n* Passion play.

passiv ['pasiːf] passive; **~er** *Widerstand* passive resistance; **~er** *Wortschatz* recognition vocabulary; '**2** *n* (9, *o. pl.*) *gr.* passive voice; **2a**, *a.* **2en** ✝ [~'siːva, ~vən] *pl.* liabilities; **~ieren** ✝ [~'viːren] enter on the liability side; **~ität** [~siviˈtɛːt] *f* (16) passiveness, passivity; **2posten** ✝ ['pasiːf-] *m* debit item; '**2seite** *f* liability side.

'Paß|kontrolle *f* passport control; '**~stelle** *f* passport office; '**~stück** *n*, '**~teil** ⊕ *n* fitting part.

Paste ['pastə] *f* (15) paste.

Pastell [pa'stɛl] **1.** *n* (3¹) (*Bild, Farbe, Malerei*) pastel; **2.** *m* (*Stift*) crayon; **~farbe** *f*, **~ton** *m* pastel shade; **~maler(in** *f*) *m* pastel(l)ist.

Pastete [pa'steːtə] *f* (15) pie.

pasteurisieren [pastøri'ziːrən] pasteurize.

Pastille [pa'stilə] *f* (15) lozenge.

Pastor ['pastɔr] *m* (8¹) pastor, vicar, minister.

Pate ['paːtə] *m* (13) godfather; *f* (15) godmother; *m*, *f* (= '**~nkind** *n*) godchild; ~ *stehen bei* stand godfather (*od.* godmother *od. fig.* sponsor) to; '**~nstelle** *f* sponsorship; ~ *vertreten bei s. Pate stehen bei.*

Patent [pa'tɛnt] **1.** *n* (3¹) patent; ✕ commission; *ein* ~ *anmelden* apply for a patent; (*zum*) ~ *angemeldet* patent pending; **2.** **2** F *adj.* clever; **~er** *Kerl* fine fellow; **~amt** *n* patent office; **~anmeldung** *f* patent application; **~anspruch** *m* patent claim; **~anwalt** *m* patent attorney; **~beschreibung** *f* patent specification; **2fähig** patentable; **~gebühr** *f* (patent-)fee; **2ieren** [~'tiːrən] patent; ~ *lassen* take out a patent for; **~inhaber** *m* patent-holder, patentee; **~lösung** *f* patent solution; **~recht** *n* patent law; *erworbenes*: patent right; **~schrift** *f* patent specification; **~schutz** *m* protection by patent; **~verletzung** *f* patent infringement; **~verschluß** *m* patent stopper, snap-fastener.

Pater ['paːtər] *m* (7, *pl.* **Patres** ['paːtreːs]) father.

Paternoster [paːter'nɔstər] *n* (7) paternoster; **~(-aufzug)** *m* paternoster lift; **~werk** ⊕ *n* chain-pump; *am Bagger*: (bucket-)elevator.

pathetisch [pa'teːtiʃ] emotional, lofty; *das* **2** *s. Pathos.*

Pathol|ogie [patolo'giː] *f* (16) pathology; **2ogisch** [~'loːgiʃ] pathological.

Pathos ['paːtɔs] *n* (*inv., o. pl.*) emotional (*od.* lofty) speech *od.* style.

Patience [pa'sjãːs] *f* (15) solitaire.

Patient [pa'tsjɛnt] *m* (12), **~in** *f* (16¹) patient.

Patin ['paːtin] *f* (16¹) godmother.

Patina ['paːtina] *f* (15, *o.pl.*) patina.

Patriarch [patri'arç] *m* (12) patriarch; **2alisch** [~'çaːliʃ] patriarchal.

Patriot [~tri'oːt] *m* (12), **~in** *f* (16¹) patriot; **2isch** patriotic(ally *adv.*); **~ismus** [~trio'tismus] *m* (16, *o.pl.*) patriotism.

Patriz|e ⊕ [~'triːtsə] *f* (15) punch (-eon), top die; **~ier** [~tsjər] *m* (7) patrician.

Patron [~'troːn] *m* (3¹) patron, protector; (*oft b.s.*) fellow; **~at** [~tro'naːt] *n* (3) patronage; **~e** [~'troːnə] *f* (15) cartridge; **~engurt** *m* cartridge belt; **~enhülse** *f* cartridge case; **~entasche** *f* cartridge pouch; **~in** *f* (16¹) patroness.

Patrouill|e ✕ [pa'truljə] f (15) patrol; **⊊ieren** ✕ [~'ji:rən] patrol.
Patsch|e F ['patʃə] f (15) **1.** (auch '**~hand** f) paw; **2.** in die ~ geraten get into a scrape (od. fix), get into hot water; in der ~ sitzen be in a scrape od. pickle od. in hot water; j-m aus der ~ helfen help a p. (out of a scrape); '⊊**en** (27, h. u. sn) im Wasser: splash; (schlagen) slap; '⊊'**naß** dripping (wet).
Patt [pat] n (11), ⊊ adj. Schach: stalemate.
patz|en ['patsən] F (27) muff (it); '⊊**er** F m (7) blunder; '**~ig** F snotty.
Pauke ['paukə] f (15) kettledrum; F fig. auf die ~ hauen go on the racket; mit ~n und Trompeten F gloriously, awfully; '⊊**n** v/i. (25) beat the kettledrum; F Schule: (a. v/t.) cram, swot, grind; '**~r** m (7) kettledrummer; F (Lehrer) crammer, schoolmaster.
pausbäckig ['pausbɛkiç] chubby (-faced).
pauschal [pau'ʃa:l] global, overall; adv. a. all included; fig. in the lump, wholesale; ⊊**-angebot** n package deal; ⊊**e** f, n (9) lump sum; im Hotel usw.: all-in price, Am. American plan; ⊊**gebühr** f flat rate; ⊊**reise** f package tour; ⊊**-urteil** n sweeping judg(e)ment; ⊊**zahlung** f lump-sum (als Ablösung: composition) payment.
Pause[1] ['pauzə] f (15) pause, stop, interval; Schule, a. Arbeit⊊: break, recess; thea. interval, Am. intermission; ♪ rest; (Nachlassen) lull.
'**Pause**[2] [~] f (15) (Pauszeichnung) tracing, blueprint; '⊊**n** (27) trace.
'**pausen|los** uninterrupted; '⊊**zeichen** n Radio: (station) identification signal.
pau'sieren pause.
Pauspapier ['paus-] n tracing--paper.
Pavian ['pɑ:viɑ:n] m (3[1]) baboon.
Pavillon ['paviljɔ] m (11) pavilion.
Pazifis|mus [patsi'fismus] m (16, o. pl.) pacifism; ~**st** m (12) pacifist; ⊊**stisch** pacifist(ic).
Pech [pɛç] n (3) pitch; fig. bad (Am. a. hard) luck; ~ haben be down on one's luck; '**~fackel** f torch; '**~kohle** f bituminous coal; '⊊**schwarz** jet-black; Nacht: pitch--dark; '**~strähne** f run of bad luck; '**~vogel** m unlucky fellow.
Pedal [pe'dɑ:l] n (3[1]) pedal.
Pedant [pe'dant] m (12) pedant, stickler; **~erie** [~ə'ri:] f (16) pedantry; ⊊**isch** [~'dantiʃ] pedantic (-ally adv.), punctilious.
Pegel ['pe:gəl] m (6) water-ga(u)ge; ⊕ level; '**~stand** m (water-)level.
Peil|-antenne ['pail-] f direction finder (abbr. D.F.) aerial; '⊊**en** (25) v/t. Tiefe: sound; Land: take the bearings of; v/i. take the bearings; '**~funk** m Radio: directional radio; '**~gerät** n radio direction finder; '**~ung** f sounding; bearing, direction finding.
Pein [pain] f (16) pain, torture.
peinig|en ['~igən] (25) torment; '⊊**er** m (7), '⊊**erin** f (16[1]) tormentor; '⊊**ung** f torment(ing), torture.
'**peinlich** painful (dat. for); (unangenehm) embarrassing, awkward; ‹‹ capital, penal; (sehr genau) precise, scrupulous (in dat. about); j-n ~ berühren distress a p.; '⊊**keit** f painfulness; awkwardness; preciseness, scrupulousness.
Peitsche ['paitʃə] f (15) whip; '⊊**n** (27) whip, lash; parl. s. durchpeitschen; '**~hieb** m (whip-)lash; '**~knall** m crack of a whip; '**~schnur** f lash.
pekuniär [pekun'jɛ:r] pecuniary.
Pelerine [pelə'ri:nə] f (15) pelerine, cape, (bsd. fur) tippet.
Pelikan ['pe:likɑ:n] m (3[1]) pelican.
Pelle ['pɛlə] f (15) skin, peel; '⊊**n** (25) skin, peel; s. Ei.
'**Pellkartoffeln** f/pl. potatoes in their jackets od. skin.
Pelz [pɛlts] m (3[2]) fur (als Kleidung mst pl.); (Fell) pelt; fig. skin, hide; '**~besatz** m fur trimming; '⊊**gefüttert** fur-lined; '**~handel** m fur--trade; '**~händler** m furrier; '**~handschuh** m furred glove; '⊊**ig** furry; ♂ Zunge: furred; Glied: numb; '**~kragen** m fur collar od. tippet; '**~mantel** m fur coat; '**~mütze** f fur cap; '**~tiere** n/pl. fur--bearing animals, furs; '**~tierfarm** f fur-farm; '**~werk** n furs pl.
Pendel ['pɛndəl] n (7) pendulum; '**~diplomatie** f shuttle diplomacy; '⊊**n** (29, h. u. sn) oscillate, swing; Zug usw.: shuttle, Am. commute; Person: commute; '**~tür** f swing door; '**~uhr** f pendulum clock; '**~**

verkehr 🚌 *m* shuttle service; **~zug** *m* shuttle (*Am.* commuter) train.

Pendler ['pɛndlər] *m* (7) commuter.

penetrant [pene'trant] penetrating.

penibel [pe'niːbəl] fussy, pernickety.

Penis ['peːnɪs] *m* (14²) penis.

Penizillin [penitsi'liːn] *n* (9, *o. pl.*) penicillin.

Pennäler [pɛ'nɛːlər] *m* (7) school-boy.

Pennbruder P ['pɛnbruːdər] *m* tramp, *Am. a.* hobo, *sl.* bum.

'Penne F *f* (15) (*Nachtasyl*) doss-house, *Am.* flophouse; (*Schule*) school; **²n** F (25) snooze.

Pension [pɑ̃'sjoːn] *f* (16) **a)** (old-age) pension; ✕ retired pay; *in ~ gehen* retire; **b)** (*Kostgeld*) board; (*Fremdenheim*) boarding-house; **~är** [~sjo'nɛːr] *m* (3) **a)** pensioner; **b)** boarder; **~at** [~'naːt] *n* (3) boarding-school; **²ieren** [~'niːrən] pension (off); ✕ put on half-pay; *sich ~ lassen* retire; **~iert** retired, in retirement; **~s-alter** *n* retiring age; **²sberechtigt** pensionable; **~sfonds** *m* superannuation fund.

Pensum ['pɛnzum] *n* (9²) task, lesson; *weitS.* work rate; *großes ~* a great deal of work.

per [pɛr] per, by; *Datum:* as of; *~ Adresse* care of (*abbr.* c/o); *~ Bahn* by train.

perfekt [pɛr'fɛkt] **1.** perfect; *Vertrag usw.:* settled, in the bag; **2.** ♀ *gr.* ['pɛrfɛkt] *n* (3) perfect (tense).

perforieren [~fo'riːrən] perforate.

Pergament [pɛrga'mɛnt] *n* (3) parchment; **~papier** *n* parchment (*od.* vellum) paper; *zum Einwickeln:* greaseproof paper.

Period|e [per'joːdə] *f* (15) period (*a. physiol. der Frau*); 𝆒 cycle; **²isch** periodic(al); **~er** *Dezimalbruch* recurring decimal.

Peripherie [perife'riː] *f* (16) circumference, periphery; *e-r Stadt:* outskirts *pl.*; **~gerät** *n* *Computer:* peripheral.

Periskop [peri'skoːp] *n* (3¹) periscope.

perkutan [pɛrku'taːn] 🐾 percutaneous.

Perle ['pɛrlə] *f* (15) pearl; (*Glas²* *usw.*) bead; *fig.* gem; *~n vor die Säue werfen* cast (one's) pearls before swine; **¹²n** (25) pearl (*a. Töne*); *Getränk:* sparkle; *Lachen:* ripple;

~nkette *f* string of pearls.

'perl|grau pearl-grey, *Am.* pearl-gray; **'²huhn** *n* guinea-fowl; **'²-muschel** *f* pearl-oyster; **²'mutter** *f* *inv.* mother-of-pearl, nacre; **'²-schrift** *typ. f* pearl.

permanen|t [pɛrma'nɛnt] permanent; **²z** [~ts] *f* (16) permanence.

Perpendikel [pɛrpɛn'diːkəl] *m*, *n* (7) **1.** pendulum; **2.** perpendicular (line).

perplex [~'plɛks] perplexed, bewildered.

Persenning [pɛr'zɛnɪŋ] *f* (14) tarpaulin.

Pers|er ['pɛrzər] *m* (7) Persian; **'~erteppich** *m* Persian carpet; **~ianer** [pɛr'zjaːnər] *m* (7) Persian lamb(skin); **²isch** Persian.

Person [pɛr'zoːn] *f* (16) person; *s. juristisch, natürlich; thea.* character; *in ~* in person, personally.

Personal [~zo'naːl] *n* (3¹) staff, personnel; **~abteilung** *f* staff department, *Am.* personnel division; **~angaben** *f/pl.* personal data; **~ausweis** *m* identity card; **~chef** *m* personnel manager; **~Computer** *m* personal computer; **~daten** *n/pl.* personal data; **~fragebogen** *m* application form; **~ien** [~jən] *pl.* particulars, personal data; **~pronomen** *gr. n* personal pronoun.

personell [~zo'nɛl] personal; (*Personal betreffend*) personnel.

Per'sonen|-aufzug *m* (passenger) lift, *bsd. Am.* elevator; **~beförderung** *f* conveyance of passengers; **~kraftwagen** *m* passenger car; **~kreis** *m* circle; **~kult** *m* personality cult; **~schaden** *m* personal injury; **~stand** *m* personal status; **~verzeichnis** *n* list of persons; *thea.* dramatis personae *pl.*; **~wagen** *m* 🚌 passenger-carriage, coach; *mot.* passenger car; **~zug** *m* passenger-train; (*Ggs. Schnellzug*) omnibus (*Am.* accommodation *od.* way) train.

personifizieren [pɛrzonifi'tsiːrən] personify.

persönlich [~'zøːnlɪç] personal; *adv.* personally, in person; **²keit** *f* personality; (*bedeutender Mensch*) personage.

Perspektiv|e [~spɛk'tiːvə] *f* (15) perspective; *fig. a.* prospect; **²isch** perspective; *Figuren ~ zeichnen* foreshorten.

Perücke [pɛ'rykə] f (15) wig.

pervers [pɛr'vɛrs] perverse; ⩗**ität** [⌣zi'tɛːt] f (16) perversity.

Pessar ✠ [pɛ'saːr] n (3¹) pessary.

Pessi|mismus [pɛsi'mismus] m (16, o. pl.) pessimism; '⌣**mist** m (12) pessimist; ⩗'**mistisch** pessimistic(ally adv.).

Pest [pɛst] f (16) pestilence, plague; fig. wie die ⌣ like poison; '⩗-**artig** pestilential; '⌣**beule** f plague-boil; fig. plague-spot; ⌣**ilenz** [⌣i'lɛnts] f (16) pestilence.   [parsley.⎱

Petersilie ♃ [petər'ziːljə] f (15)⎰

Petroleum [pe'troːleum] n (11) petroleum, Am. (mineral) oil; (Leucht⩗) paraffin, bsd. Am. kerosene; ⌣**lampe** f oil (Am. kerosene) lamp.

Petschaft ['pɛtʃaft] n (3) seal, signet.

petto ['pɛto]: et. in ⌣ haben have something up one's sleeve.

Petze F ['pɛtsə] f (15) telltale; Schul-sl. sneak; '⩗n F v/t. u. v/i. sl. peach (gegen j-n on); Schul-sl. sneak (against); ⌣'**rei** F f tale-telling.

Pfad [pfaːt] m (3) path, track; ⌣**finder** ['⌣findər] m Boy Scout; '⌣**finderin** f Girl Guide, Am. Girl Scout; '⩗**los** pathless.

Pfaffe contp. ['pfafə] m (13) priest, F parson; '⌣**ntum** n (1, o. pl.) clericalism; parsons pl.

Pfahl [pfaːl] m (3⁸) stake, pale, pile; (Pfosten) post; (Stange) pole; fig. ⌣ im Fleisch thorn in one's flesh; '⌣**bau** △ m pile-work; hist. lake-dwelling.

pfählen ['pfeːlən] (25) ✗ prop (up); als Strafe: impale.

'**Pfahlwurzel** f tap-root.

Pfalz [pfalts] f (16) imperial palace; geogr. the Palatinate.

Pfälzer ['pfɛltsər] m (7) inhabitant of the Palatinate.

Pfalzgraf ['pfaltsgraːf] m Count Palatine.

Pfand [pfant] n (1²) pledge; (Bürgschaft) security; im Spiel: forfeit; zum ⌣ geben od. setzen pawn, mortgage, fig. Ehre usw.: pledge, sein Leben: stake; '⌣**brief** m mortgage bond.

pfänd|bar ['pfɛntbaːr] distrainable; ⌣**en** ['⌣dən] (26) et.: seize; j-n od. et.: distrain (up)on, attach; '⩗**erspiel** n (game of) forfeits pl.

'**Pfand|gläubiger**   m mortgagee;

'⌣**haus** n, '⌣**leihe** f pawnshop; '⌣**leiher** m (7) pawnbroker; '⌣**recht** n lien; '⌣**schein** m pawn-ticket; '⌣**schuldner** m mortgagor.

'**Pfändung** f seizure, distraint; '⌣s**befehl** m distress-warrant; '⌣s**verfahren** n attachment proceedings pl.

Pfann|e ['pfanə] f (15) pan; anat. socket; '⌣**enstiel** m panhandle; '⌣**kuchen** m pancake; Berliner ⌣ doughnut.

Pfarr|amt ['pfar⁹amt] n (Pflichtbereich) incumbency; (Pfarrei) rectory; (Pastorat) pastorate; '⌣**bezirk** m parish; ⌣**e** f (15), ⌣**ei** [⌣'raɪ] f s. Pfarramt, -bezirk, -gemeinde,-haus, -stelle; '⌣**er** m (7) parson; der engl. Staatskirche: rector, vicar; bei Dissidenten: minister; '⌣**gemeinde** f parish; '⌣**haus** n parsonage; der engl. Staatskirche: rectory, vicarage; '⌣**kind** n parishioner; '⌣**kirche** f parish-church; '⌣**stelle** f benefice.

Pfau [pfau] m (5 u. 12) peacock; '⌣**en-auge** zo. n peacock-butterfly; '⌣**enfeder** f peacock's feather.

Pfeffer ['pfefər] m (7) pepper; fig. F j-n hinwünschen, wo der ⌣ wächst wish a p. in hell (first); s. Hase; '⌣**büchse** f pepper-box; '⌣**gurke** f gherkin; '⌣**kuchen** m gingerbread; '⌣**minze** ♃ f (15), '⌣**minzplätzchen** n peppermint; '⩗n (29) pepper; s. gepfeffert; '⌣**nuß** f ginger-nut, Am. -snap; '⌣**streuer** m (7) pepper pot.

Pfeife ['pfaɪfə] f (15) whistle; ⚓ (Bootsmanns⩗) pipe; (Orgel⩗) (organ-)pipe; (Quer⩗) fife; (Tabaks⩗) (tobacco-)pipe; nach j-s ⌣ tanzen dance to a p.'s tune; '⩗n (30) v/i. u. v/t. whistle; Schiedsrichter: blow the whistle; auf e-r Pfeife, a. Radio: pipe; F ⌣ auf (acc.) not to give a hoot about; s. Loch.

'**Pfeifen|kopf** m pipe-bowl; '⌣**reiniger** m pipe cleaner; '⌣**stiel** pipe-stem; '⌣**stopfer** pipe stopper.

'**Pfeif|kessel** m, '⌣**topf** m whistling kettle; '⌣**konzert** n (wild) booing.

Pfeil [pfaɪl] m (3) arrow (a. in Zeichnungen usw.); (Wurf⩗, Blas⩗) dart.

Pfeiler ['pfaɪlər] m (7) pillar (a. fig.); (Brücken⩗ usw.) pier; ⊕ standard.

'**pfeil|gerade** straight as an arrow; adv. straight; '⌣**schnell** as swift as an arrow; '⩗**schuß** m arrow-shot;

'**~zeichnung** ⊕ *f* functional diagram(me).
Pfennig ['pfeniç] *m* (3, *als Wertangabe im pl. inv.*) pfennig; *fig.* penny, farthing; '**~absatz** *m* stiletto heel; '**~fuchser** F *m* (7) pinchpenny.
Pferch [pfɛrç] *m* (3) fold, pen; '**Qen** (25) pen, fold; *fig.* cram.
Pferd [pfe:rt] *n* (3) horse; (*Turngerät*) vaulting-horse; *zu* ~e on horseback; *fig. das* ~ *beim Schwanze aufzäumen* put the cart before the horse; *s. a. Roß.*
Pferde|bremse *f*, **~fliege** ['pfe:rdə-] *f* horse-fly; '**~fleisch** *n* horse-flesh, horse-meat; '**~fuhrwerk** *f* horse-drawn vehicle; '**~fuß** *m fig.* cloven hoof; '**~futter** *n* horse's fodder; '**~geschirr** *n* harness; '**~händler** *m* horse-dealer; '**~knecht** *m* groom; *im Gasthaus*: (h)ostler; '**~koppel** *f* paddock; '**~kraft** *f s. Pferdestärke*; '**~länge** *f Sport*: um 3 ~en by 3 lengths; '**~rennen** *n* horse-race; '**~schwanz** *m* horse's tail; (*Frisur*) pony tail; '**~schwemme** *f* horse-pond; '**~stall** *m* stable; '**~stärke** *f* (*abbr.* PS) horse-power (*abbr.* h.p.); '**~wagen** *m* horse carriage; '**~zucht** *f* horse-breeding.
Pfiff [pfif] **1.** *m* (3) whistle; *fig.* trick; (*Schwung*) ginger; **2.** ♀ *pret. v. pfeifen*; **~erling** ['~ɔrlɪn] *m* (3¹) ♀ chanterelle; *fig.* trifle, straw; *keinen* ~ wert not worth a rush; '**Qig sly**; **~ikus** ['~ikus] *m* sly dog.
Pfingst|en ['pfɪnstən] *n od. f/pl.* (*inv.*, *mst ohne art.*), '**~fest** *n* Whitsuntide; '**~montag** *m* Whit Monday; '**~rose** *f* peony; '**~sonntag** *m* Whitsunday; '**~woche** *f* Whit(sun) week.
Pfirsich ['pfɪrzɪç] *m* (3) peach.
Pflanze ['pflantsə] *f* (15), '**Qn** (27) plant.
'**Pflanzen|faser** *f* vegetable fib|re, *Am.* -er; '**~fett** *n* vegetable fat; *Küche*: vegetable shortening; '**Qfressend** herbivorous; '**~kost** *f* vegetable diet; '**~kunde** *f* botany; '**~leben** *n* vegetable life; '**~öl** *n* vegetable oil; '**~reich** *n*, '**~welt** *f* vegetable kingdom, flora; '**~schutzmittel** *n* pesticide.
'**Pflanz|er** *m* (7), '**~erin** *f* (16¹) planter; '**~ung** *f* plantation.
Pflaster ['pflastər] *n* (7) **1.** (*Straßen*Q) pavement; *fig.* (*Ort*) place; **2.** ♂

(adhesive) plaster; *fig.* salve; '**~er** *m* (7) pavio(u)r, *Am.* paver; '**~maler** *m* pavement artist; '**Qn** (29) **1.** *Straße*: pave; **2.** ♂ plaster (*a.* F *fig. kleben*); '**~stein** *m* paving-stone.
Pflaume ['pflaumə] *f* (15) plum; (*Dörr*Q) prune; F silly ass; '**~nmus** *n* plum jam.
Pflege ['pfle:gə] *f* (15) (*Obhut*) care (*a. der Haut, Zähne usw.*); *e-s Kindes*: (child-)care; *e-s Kranken*: nursing, (medical) care; ⊕ maintenance; *e-s Gartens, der Künste, von Beziehungen*: cultivation; *Kind in* ~ *geben* put out to nurse; *in* ~ *nehmen* take charge of; '**~befohlene** ['~bəfo:lənə] *m* charge; '**~eltern** *pl.* foster-parents; '**~heim** *n* charitable home; ♂ nursing home; '**~kind** *n* foster-child; '**Qleicht** wash-and-wear; '**~mutter** *f* foster-mother.
pflegen ['pfle:gən] (25, *fig. a.* 30) *v/t.* care for; attend to; *sein Äußeres*: groom; *Kranke*: nurse; *Kranke, Maschine*: tend; (*instand halten*) maintain; *Garten, Künste, Beziehungen*: cultivate; *der Ruhe* ~ take rest; *s. gepflegt, Umgang*; *v/i. zu tun* ~ be accustomed (*od.* used *od.* wont) to, be in the habit of *ger.*; *nur im pret.* I *etc.* used to.
'**Pflegepersonal** ♂ *n* nursing staff.
'**Pfleger** *m* (7), '**~in** *f* (16¹) ♂ (*m male*) nurse; (*Denkmal*Q *usw.*) conservator; ⚖ guardian; *für Entmündigte*: curator, (*Verwalter*) *a.* trustee.
'**Pflege|sohn** *m* foster-son; '**~vater** *m* foster-father.
pfleg|lich ['~kliç] careful; *et.* ~ *behandeln* take good care of; '**Qling** *m* (3¹) foster-child; (*Pflegebefohlener*) charge; '**Qschaft** ⚖ *f* (16) guardianship.
Pflicht [pflɪçt] *f* (16) duty; (*Verpflichtung*) obligation; *Sport*: *s.* ~*übung*; '**Qbewußt** responsible; '**~bewußtsein** *n*, '**~gefühl** *n* sense of duty; '**Q-eifrig** zealous (in one's duties); '**~erfüllung** *f* performance of one's duty; '**~fach** *n* *Schule*, *univ.*: compulsory subject; '**~gefühl** *n s. Pflichtbewußtsein*; '**Qgemäß**, '**Qmäßig** dutiful, due; '**~lektüre** *f* required reading, set books *pl.*; '**Qschuldig** obligatory; *adv.* duly; '**~teil** *m* compulsory portion; '**Qtreu** dutiful, loyal; '**~treue** *f* dutifulness, loyalty; '**~-**

übung f compulsory (od. set) exercise; '⊆vergessen disloyal, undutiful; '⌣vergessenheit f dereliction of duty, disloyalty; '⌣versäumnis f neglect of duty; '⌣verteidiger m assigned counsel; '⊆widrig undutiful, contrary to (one's) duty.

Pflock [pflɔk] m (3³) plug, peg.

pflöcken ['pflœkən] (25) peg.

pflog ⌧ [pflo:k] pret. v. pflegen v/i.

pflücken ['pflykən] (25) pick, pluck, (einsammeln) gather.

Pflug [pflu:k] m (3³) plough, Am. plow; '⌣-eisen n co(u)lter.

pflüg|en ['pfly:gən] v/t. u. v/i. (25) plough, Am. plow; '⊆er m (7) ploughman, Am. plowman.

'**Pflugschar** f ploughshare.

Pförtchen ['pfœrtçən] n (6) little door od. gate. [⊈ port.⟩

Pforte ['pfɔrtə] f (15) gate, door;⟩

Pförtner ['pfœrtnər] m (7) doorkeeper, porter, Am. doorman, (Hausmeister) janitor; anat. pylorus.

Pfosten ['pfɔstən] m (6) post; upright; (Tür⊆, Fenster⊆) jamb.

Pfote ['pfo:tə] f (15) paw.

Pfriem [pfri:m] m (3) awl, bodkin.

Pfropf [pfrɔpf] (3), '⌣en¹ (6) m stopper; (Kork⊆) cork; weitS. plug; (Watte⊆) wad; s. Eiter⊆; '⊆en² (25) cork; (stopfen) cram; ✔ graft; '⌣messer n grafting-knife; '⌣reis ✔ n graft.

Pfründe ['pfryndə] f (15) eccl. prebend; (Pfarrstelle) benefice, living; fig. sinecure.

Pfuhl [pfu:l] m (3) pool, puddle.

Pfühl [pfy:l] m, n (3) pillow.

pfui [pfui] fie!, (for) shame!; Sport usw.: boo!; angeekelt: ugh!, phew!

Pfund [pfunt] n (3, als Mengenangabe im pl. inv.) pound; (Geld) ~ (Sterling) pound (Sterling); ⊆ig F ['⌣dɪç] great, swell, groovy.

Pfund|skerl F ['pfuntskerl] m brick, Am. great guy; '⊆weise by the pound.

Pfusch|arbeit ['pfuʃ⁹arbaɪt] f s. Pfuscherei; '⊆en v/i. u. v/t. (27) bungle, botch; j-m ins Handwerk ~ trespass on a p.'s preserves; '⌣er m (7) bungler; ⌣erei [⌣ə'raɪ] f (16) bungling; bungle.

Pfütze ['pfytsə] f (15) pool, puddle.

Phänomen [fɛno'me:n] n (3¹) phenomenon; ⊆al [⌣'na:l] phenomenal.

Phantasie [fanta'zi:] f (15) fancy; (schöpferische ⌣) imagination; (Traumbild) vision; ♪ fantasia; ⊆los unimaginative; ⌣preis m fancy price; ⊆reich imaginative; ⊆ren indulge in fancies, (day-)dream; ♪ rave (a. F fig.), be delirious; ♪ improvise.

Phantast [⌣'tast] m (12), ⌣in f (16¹) visionary; ⌣erei [⌣ə'raɪ] f (16) fantasy; ⊆isch [⌣'tastif] fantastic(ally adv.) (a. F fig.); (großartig) F great, terrific.

Phantom [⌣'to:m] n (3¹) phantom; ⌣bild n identikit.

Pharisä|er [fari'zɛ:ər] m (7) Pharisee; ⊆isch pharisaic(al).

Pharma-industrie ['farma-] f pharmaceutical industry.

Pharmakologie [farmako'gi:] f (15, o. pl.) pharmacology.

Pharmareferent ['farma-] m pharmaceutical consultant.

Pharmazeut [farma'tsɔʏt] m (12) pharmac(eut)ist; (Apotheker) a. pharmaceutical chemist, Am. druggist; ⌣ik f (16) pharmaceutics sg.; ⊆isch pharmaceutical.

Pharmazie [farma'tsi:] f (15) pharmacy.

Phase ['fɑ:zə] f (15) phase (a. ⚡).

Philanthrop [filan'tro:p] m (12), ⌣in f (16¹) philanthropist; ⊆isch philanthropic(ally adv.).

Philatel|ie [filate'li:] f (15, o. pl.) philately; ⌣ist [⌣'list] m (12) philatelist.

Philister [fi'listər] m (7), ⊆haft Philistine; ⌣haftigkeit f philistinism.

Philolog|e [filo'lo:gə] m (13), ⌣in f (16¹) philologist; ⌣ie [⌣lo'gi:] f philology; ⊆isch [⌣'lo:gif] philological.

Philosoph [⌣'zo:f] m (12) philosopher; ⌣ie [⌣zo'fi:] f (15) philosophy; ⊆ieren [⌣'fi:rən] philosophize; ⊆isch [⌣'zo:fif] philosophic (-al).

Phiole [fi'o:lə] f (15) phial, vial.

Phlegma ['flɛgma] n (11) phlegm.

Phlegmat|iker [⌣'mɑ:tikər] m (7) phlegmatic person; ⊆isch phlegmatic(ally adv.).

Phobie [fo'bi:] f (15) phobia.

Phonetik [fo'ne:tik] f (16) phonetics mst sg.; ⌣er m phonetician.

pho'netisch phonetic(ally adv.).

Phonotypistin [fonoty'pistin] f (16¹) audio typist.

Phosphat [fɔs'fɑ:t] n (3) phosphate.

Phosphor ['fɔsfɔr] *m* (3¹) phosphorus; '~.... phosphorous; **~eszenz** [~fɔrɛs'tsɛnts] *f* (16) phosphorescence; **♀eszieren** [~'tsi:rən] phosphoresce; **~d** phosphorescent; **♀ig** [~'fo:riç] phosphorous.

Photo ['fo:to] *n* (11) photo; '**~-apparat** *m* camera.

photogen [foto'ge:n] photogenic.

Photograph [foto'grɑ:f] *m* (12), **~in** *f* (16¹) photographer; **~ie** [~gra'fi:] *f* (15) *Bild*: photograph, F photo; *Kunst*: photography; **♀ieren** [~'fi:rən] *v/t. u. v/i.* photograph, take a picture (of); *sich ~ lassen* have one's photo(graph) taken; **♀isch** [~'grɑ:fiʃ] photographic(ally *adv*.).

Photo'kopie *f* photocopy; **♀ren** photocopy; **~rgerät** *n* photocopier.

'**Photo|montage** *f* (photo) montage, paste-up; '**~satz** *m typ.* photocomposition.

Photothek [foto'te:k] *f* (16) photo library.

'**Photozelle** *f* photo-electric cell, photocell.

Phrase ['frɑ:zə] *f* (15) phrase; *contp. a.* cliché, *pol.* catchphrase; '**~ndrescher** *m* phrasemonger; '**♀nhaft** empty, windy, rhetorical.

Physik [fy'zi:k] *f* (16) physics *sg.*, **♀alisch** [~'kɑ:liʃ] physical.

Physik|er ['fy:zikər] *m* (7) physicist, natural philosopher; '**~um** [~kum] *n* preliminary (medical) examination. [physiognomy.]

Physiognomie [fyzjogno'mi:] *f*

Physiolog|e [~'lo:gə] *m* (13) physiologist; **~ie** [~olo'gi:] *f* physiology; **♀isch** [~'lo:giʃ] physiological.

physisch ['fy:ziʃ] physical.

Pian|ino [pia'ni:no] *n* (11) cottage (*od.* upright) piano; **~ist** [~'nist] *m* (12), **~istin** [~'nistin] *f* (16¹) pianist.

Piano [pi'ɑ:no] *n*, **~forte** [piano-'fɔrtə] *n* (11) piano(forte).

picheln F ['piçəln] *v/i. u. v/t.* (29) tipple, F booze.

Picke ['pikə] *f* (15) pick(ax[e]).

Pickel ['pikəl] *m* (7) **1.** pimple; **2.** *s.* **Picke**, Eis♀; '**~haube** *f* spiked helmet.

'**pick(e)lig** pimpled, pimply.

picken ['pikən] *v/t. u. v/i.* (25) pick, peck.

Picknick ['~nik] *n* (11) picnic.

pieken F ['pi:kən] (25) prick.

piep|en ['pi:pən] (25) peep; *Maus*: squeak; F *zum* ♀ *a scream*; '**♀matz** F *m* dicky-bird.

pieps|en ['pi:psən] (25) *s.* piepen; '**♀er** F *m* (7) (*Funkrufempfänger*) bleeper.

Pier ⚓ [pi:r] *m* (3¹) jetty, pier.

piesacken F ['pi:zakən] pester, torment, persecute.

Pietät [pie'tɛ:t] *f* (16) piety, reverence; **♀los** irreverent; **♀voll** reverent.

Pigment [pi'gmɛnt] *n* (3) pigment.

Pik [pi:k] **1.** *m* (11) (*Berg*) peak; **2.** *n* (3¹, *o. pl.*) *Kartenspiel*: spade(s *pl.*); **3.** *m* (11) (*Groll*) grudge.

pikant [pi'kant] *a. fig.* piquant, spicy; *das* ♀e (the) piquancy; **♀erie** [~tə'ri:] *f* (15) piquant (*od.* spicy) story *od.* remark.

Pike ['pi:kə] *f* (15) pike; *von der ~ auf dienen* rise from the ranks.

pik'fein F tiptop, smart, slap-up.

pikiert [pi'ki:rt] piqued (*über acc.* about).

Pikkolo ['pikolo] *m* (11¹) boy waiter; '**~flöte** *f* piccolo.

Pilger ['pilgər] *m* (7), '**~in** *f* pilgrim; '**~fahrt** *f* pilgrimage; '♀**n** (29, sn) make (*od.* go on) a pilgrimage; *weitS.* wander; '**~schaft** *f* pilgrimage; '**~stätte** *f* place of pilgrimage.

Pille ['pilə] *f* (15) pill; F *die ~ nehmen* be on (*od.* take) the pill.

Pilot [pi'lo:t] *m* (12) pilot; **~film** *m* pilot (film); **~projekt** *n* pilot project; **~sendung** *f* pilot broadcast.

Pilz [pilts] *m* (3²) fungus; *eßbarer*: mushroom; *nicht eßbarer*: toadstool; *fig. wie ~e aus der Erde schießen* mushroom (up).

pingelig F ['piŋəliç] mean; pedantic, fussy.

Pinguin ['piŋgui:n] *m* (3) penguin.

Pinie ♣ ['pi:njə] *f* (15) stone-pine.

Pinke F ['piŋkə] *f* (*Geld*) *sl.* dough; '♀**ln** P (29) piddle, pee.

Pinscher ['pinʃər] *m* (7) pinscher.

Pinsel ['pinzəl] *m* (7) brush; *feiner*: pencil; *fig.* fool, ass; '**~ei** [~'lai] *f* (16) daub(ing); '♀**n** *v/i.* (29) paint; (*schmieren*) daub; '**~strich** *m* stroke of the brush.

Pinzette [pin'tsetə] *f* (15) (*eine a pair of*) tweezers *pl.*

Pionier [pio'ni:r] *m* (3¹) pioneer; ⚔ engineer; *Brt.* (*Dienstgrad*) sapper; **~arbeit** *f fig.* pioneering; **~truppe** *f* engineers *pl.*

Pipett|e [pi'pɛtə] ƒ (15), **⊆ieren** [~'tiːrən] pipette.

Pirat [pi'raːt] *m* (12) pirate; **~en-sender** *m Radio*: pirate station; **~e-rie** [~tə'riː] ƒ (15) piracy.

Pirsch [pirʃ] ƒ (16) deer-stalking, stalk, *Am.* still hunt; **'⊆en** (27) still--hunt, stalk (deer); **'~jagd** ƒ *s. Pirsch;* **'~jäger** *m* still-hunter.

Pisse P ['pisə] ƒ (15), **'⊆n** (28) piss.

Pistazie ♀ [pi'staːtsjə] ƒ (15) pistachio(-nut).

Piste ['pistə] ƒ (15) beaten track; *Rennsport:* course, *Sport:* a. ski--run; 🎿 runway.

Pistole [pi'stoːlə] ƒ (15) pistol; *mit vorgehaltener ~ at* pistol-point; *fig. j-m die ~ auf die Brust setzen* hold a pistol to a p.'s head; *wie aus der ~ geschossen* like a shot; **~nschuß** *m*, **~nschütze** *m* pistol-shot; **~n-tasche** ƒ (pistol) holster.

Pizz|a ['pitsa] ƒ (11¹ *u.* 16²) pizza; **~eria** [pitse'riːa] ƒ (16²) pizzeria.

placier|en [pla'(t)siːrən] place (*a. Sport,* ♥); *sich ~* be placed *second, etc.;* **~t** *Schuß:* well-placed.

plack|en ['plakən] (25) *s. plagen;* **⊆erei** [~'raɪ] ƒ (16) drudgery.

plä|dieren [plɛ'diːrən] plead (*auf acc. et.* a th.); **~** *für* et. advocate a th.; **⊆doyer** [plɛdoa'jeː] *n* (11) pleading.

Plage ['plaːgə] ƒ (15) trouble, vexation, bother, nuisance; *stärker:* torment; *mst biblisch* (*Seuche*): plague; **'~geist** *m* tormentor; **'⊆n** (25) trouble, bother, worry; torment, F plague; *mit Bitten od. Fragen:* pester; *sich ~* drudge, slave.

Plagiat [plag'jaːt] *n* (3) plagiarism; *ein ~ begehen* plagiarize; **~or** [~tɔr] *m* (8¹) plagiarist.

Plaid [plɛːt] *n* (11) plaid; (*Reisedecke*) travel(l)ing rug.

Plakat [pla'kaːt] *n* (3) poster, placard, bill; **~farbe** ƒ poster colo(u)r; **⊆ieren** [~ka'tiːrən] placard; *v/i.* stick bills; **~maler** *m* poster artist; **~säule** ƒ advertisement pillar; **~träger** *m* sandwich-man.

Plakette [~'kɛtə] ƒ (15) plaque; (*Abzeichen*) badge.

Plan [plaːn] **1.** *m* (3³) plan; (*Vorhaben*) *a.* project, scheme; *konkret:* plan; (*Karte*) map; *graphisch:* diagram; (*Blaupause*) blueprint; (*Anlage*) layout; (*Zeit⊆*) schedule; *s.*

Lehr⊆; fig. auf den ~ rufen call up; *auf den ~ treten* enter the lists, *weitS.* make an appearance; **2.** (*Ebene*) plain; **3.** ⊆ *adj.* plain, level; **'~e** ƒ (15) awning; *geteerte:* tarpaulin; **'⊆n** (25) plan, project; map out; *zeitlich:* time.

Pläne|macher *m*, **~schmied** ['plɛː-nə-] *m* schemer, projector.

Planet [pla'neːt] *m* (12) planet; **⊆arisch** [~ne'taːriʃ] planetary; **~a-rium** [~ne'taːrjum] *n* planetarium, orrery; **~en...** planetary.

planier|en ⊕ [pla'niːrən] level, *Gelände: a.* grade; **⊆maschine** ƒ, **⊆raupe** ƒ bulldozer, grader.

Planimetrie [planime'triː] ƒ (15) plane geometry, planimetry.

Planke ['plaŋkə] ƒ (15) plank, board.

Plänk|elei [plɛŋkə'laɪ] ƒ (16) skirmishing; **'⊆eln** (29) skirmish (*a.fig.*).

'plan|los aimless, haphazard, unsystematic(ally *adv.*); *adv.* (*aufs Geratewohl*) at random; **'⊆losigkeit** ƒ aimlessness; **'~mäßig** planned, systematic(ally *adv.*); *Beamtenstelle:* regular; *Verkehr:* scheduled; *adv.* according to plan *od.* (*zeitlich*) to schedule; **'⊆quadrat** *n* grid square.

Plansch|becken ['planʃ-] *n* paddlepond; **'⊆en** (27) splash.

'Planstelle ƒ permanent post (authorized in the budget).

Plantage [plan'taːʒə] ƒ (15) plantation.

Planung ['plaːnuŋ] ƒ planning; **'~s-amt** *n* planning board; **'~sstadium** *n*: *im ~* in the planning (*od.* blueprint) stage.

'planvoll methodical.

'Plan|wagen *m* covered wag(g)on; **'~wirtschaft** ƒ planned economy; **'~ziel** *n* target.

'Plapper|maul *n* chatterbox; **'⊆n** *v/t. u. v/i.* (29) babble, prattle.

plärren F ['plɛːrən] *v/i. u. v/t.* (25) blare; *singend:* bawl; (*weinen*) blubber, cry.

Plasma *phys.* ['plasma] *n* (16²) plasma; **'~physik** ƒ plasma physics *sg.*

Plasti|k ['plastik] **1.** ƒ (16) plastic art; (*Bildwerk*) sculpture; ✄ plastic surgery; **2.** *n* (11) plastic; **'~ktüte** ƒ polythene bag; **'⊆sch** plastic(ally *adv.*); *fig.* (*anschaulich*) graphic(ally *adv.*).

Platane [pla'taːnə] ƒ (15) plane-tree.

Plateau [pla'toː] *n* (11) plateau.

Platin   1054

Platin ['plɑːtiːn] *n* (11, *o. pl.*) platinum.

platonisch [pla'toːniʃ] Platonic(ally *adv.*).

plätschern ['plɛtʃərn] (29) dabble, splash; *Bach usw.*: ripple, murmur.

platt [plat] flat; (*eben*) level; (*nichtssagend*) trite, trivial, commonplace; F *vor Staunen*: dum(b)founded; ♀ *n s. Plattdeutsch.*

Plättbrett ['plɛt-] *n* ironing-board.

'plattdeutsch, ♀(e) *n* Low German.

Platte ['platə] *f* (15) plate (*a. phot., typ.*); (*Wand♀ usw.*) panel; *Metall, Glas*: sheet; (*Stein♀*) flag, slab; (*Kachel*) tile; (*Tisch♀*) top, *zum Einlegen*: leaf; (*Präsentierteller*) tray, salver; (*Speise*) dish; *s. kalt*; (*Schall♀*) disk, record; F *fig.* line; (*Glatze*) F bald pate, (*kahle Stelle*) bald patch; (*Gebiß♀*) dental plate.

Plätt|-**eisen** ['plɛt-] *n* flat-iron; '♀**en** (26) iron, press.

'Platten|sammlung *f* record collection; '♀**spieler** *m* record player; '♀**teller** *m* turn-table; ♀**wechsler** ['♀vɛkslər] *m* (7) (automatic) record changer.

platterdings ['platər'dɪŋs] absolutely, downright.

Plätterin ['plɛtərɪn] *f* (16¹) ironer.

'Platt|**form** *f* platform (*a. fig. pol.*); '♀**fuß** *m* flatfoot; *mot.* F flat; '♀**fußeinlage** *f* instep-raiser, arch-support; ♀**füßig** ['♀fyːsɪç] flat-footed; '♀**heit** *f* flatness; *fig.* triviality, banality, (*nichtssagende Bemerkung*) *a.* platitude; ♀**ieren** [♀'tiːrən] plate.

'Plättwäsche *f* linen to be ironed.

Platz [plats] *m* (3² *u.* ³) place; (*Raum*) space, room; *öffentlicher*: square, *runder*: circus; *zum Sitzen*: seat; *Sport*: field, pitch, *Tennis*: court; ~ *machen* (*dat.*) make way *od.* room (for); ~ *nehmen* take a seat; *fig.* (*nicht*) *am* ~*e sein* be in (out of) place; '♀**angst** *f* agoraphobia; F claustrophobia; '♀**anweiser(in** *f*) *m* usher(ette *f*).

Plätzchen ['plɛtscən] *n* (6) 1. little place; spot, patch; 2. (*Süßware*) pastille, drop; (*Gebäck*) biscuit, *Am.* cookie, *knusperig*: cracker.

Platzdeckchen ['♀dɛkçən] *n* (6) place mat.

platzen ['platsən] (27, sn) burst; (*Risse bekommen*) crack; *Luftreifen*: blow out; *Granate usw.*: burst, explode; F *Wechsel*: bounce; *ins Zimmer*: burst *into*; *fig.* vor *Neugier usw.* ~ burst with; F *Vorhaben*: not to come off; *fig.* ~ *lassen* explode; *s. Kragen.*

'Platz|**herren** *m/pl. Sport*: home team; '♀**karte** *f* ticket for a reserved seat; '♀**patrone** *f* blank cartridge; *mit* ~*n schießen* fire blank; '♀**raubend** bulky; '♀**regen** *m* cloudburst, downpour; ~**wart** ['♀vart] *m* (3) *Sport*: groundsman; '♀**wechsel** *m* change of place (*Sport*: of ends); ✝ local bill.

Plauder|**ei** [plaudə'raɪ] *f* (16) chat; (*small-*)talk; '♀**er** *m* (7), '♀**in** *f* (16¹) conversationalist, talker; '♀**n** (29) (have a) chat; (*aus*~) blab; *s. Schule*; '♀**tasche** F *f* chatterbox; '♀**ton** *m* conversational tone.

plausibel [plau'ziːbəl] plausible.

pla'zieren [pla'tsiːrən] *s. placieren.*

Plebej|**er** [ple'beːjər] *m* (6), ♀**erin** *f* (16¹), ♀**isch** plebeian, vulgar.

Plebiszit [plebis'tsiːt] *n* (3) plebiscite.

Plebs [plɛps] *f* (16) *od. m* (4) mob.

Pleite *sl.* ['plaɪtə] *f* (15) bankruptcy, *sl.* smash; *fig.* flop, washout; ~ *machen sl.* go smash (*Am.* bust); ♀ *sein* be broke; '♀**geier** F *m the wolves pl.*

Plenarsitzung [ple'nɑːrzitsuŋ] *f* plenary meeting.

Plenum *parl.* ['pleːnum] *n* (9, *o.pl.*) plenum.

Pleuelstange ['plɔyəl-] *f* connecting rod.

Plinse ['plɪnzə] *f* (15) pancake.

Pliss|**ee** [pli'seː] *n* (11, *o. pl.*) pleating; ~**eerock** *m* pleated skirt; ♀**ieren** [♀'siːrən] pleat.

Plomb|**e** ['plɔmbə] *f* (15) (lead) seal; (*Zahn♀*) stopping, filling, plug; ♀**ieren** [♀'biːrən] seal (with lead); *Zahn*: plug, stop, fill.

Plötze ['plœtsə] *f* (15) roach.

plötzlich ['plœtslɪç] sudden(ly *adv.*), abrupt(ly); *adv. a.* all of a sudden.

plump [plump] plump; (*unbeholfen*) clumsy; (*schwerfällig*) heavy; (*unfein*) coarse; *Lüge usw.*: gross; '♀**heit** *f* clumsiness; coarseness; ♀**s** *m* thud; ♀! plop!; ~**sen** ['♀sən] (27, *h. u. sn*) flop, plop, thud.

Plunder ['plundər] *m* (7) lumber, rubbish, trash, *bsd. Am.* junk.

Plünder|**er** ['plyndərər] *m* (7)

looter; '~n v/t. u. v/i. (29) plunder (a. weitS.), pillage, loot, sack; '~ung f plundering, pillage, looting, sacking.
Plural ['plu:ra:l] m (3¹) plural (number); **Qistisch** [plura'listiʃ] pluralistic.
plus [plus] plus; **Q** n (~zeichen) plus mark; (Überschuß) (sur)plus; fig. plus, asset.
Plüsch [ply:ʃ] m (3¹) plush.
Plusquamperfekt(um) gr. ['~kvamper'fɛkt(um)] n (3) pluperfect.
Pneumat|ik [pnɔy'ma:tik] m (11) pneumatic tire (bsd. Brt. tyre); **Qisch** pneumatic(ally adv.).
Po [po:] F m (11) s. Popo.
Pöbel ['pø:bəl] m (7) mob, populace, rabble; '**Qhaft** low, vulgar; '~haufen m mob; '~herrschaft f mobrule.
pochen ['pɔxən] v/i. (25) knock, rap; leise: tap; Herz: beat, throb; fig. auf (acc.) boast of; auf ein Recht insist on.
Pocke ['pɔkə] f (15) pock; ~n pl. smallpox; '~n-impfung f vaccination; '~nnarbe f pock-mark; 'Qnnarbig pock-marked.
Podagra ['po:dagra] n (11) gout.
Podest [po'dɛst] n, m (3²) pedestal (a. fig.); s. Podium.
Podium ['po:djum] n (9²) rostrum, platform; '~sdiskussion f, '~sgespräch n panel discussion.
Poesie [poe'zi:] f (15) poetry.
Poet [po'e:t] m (12) poet; ~ik f (16) poetics pl.; ~in f (16¹) poetess; **Qisch** poetic(al).
Point|e ['poɛ̃tə] f (15) point; **Qiert** [~ɛ̃'ti:rt] pointed.
Pokal [po'ka:l] m (3¹) goblet; (Sportpreis) cup; ~-endspiel n Sport: cup final; ~spiel n cup-tie.
Pökel ['pø:kəl] m (7) pickle; '~fleisch n salt meat; '~hering m pickled (od. red) herring; 'Qn (29) pickle, salt.
Pol [po:l] m (3¹) pole (a. ⚡); fig. der ruhende ~ the one constant factor.
Polar... [po'la:r-] polar.
polari|sieren phys. [polari'zi:rən] polarize; **Qtät** [~'tɛ:t] f (16) polarity.
Po'lar|kreis m: nördlicher ~ Arctic Circle; südlicher ~ Antarctic Circle; ~luft f polar current; ~stern m Pole star.

Pole ['po:lə] m (13), '**Polin** f Pole.
Polem|ik [po'le:mik] f (16) polemic(s pl.); ~iker m polemicist; **Qisch** polemic; **Qi'sieren** polemize.
polen ⚡ ['po:lən] pole.
Police [po'li:sə] f (15) policy.
Polier [po'li:r] m (3¹) foreman; **Qen** polish, burnish.
Poliklinik ['po:li-] f outpatient clinic od. department.
Politbüro [po'li:t-] n Politburo.
Politesse [poli'tɛsə] f (15) traffic warden, F meter maid.
Polit|ik [poli'ti:k] f (16) (Staats-, Weltklugheit; Taktik; politische Linie) policy; (Wissenschaft, Staatsangelegenheiten) politics pl.; ~iker [~'li:tikər] m (7) politician; führender: statesman; ~ikum [~'li:tikum] n (9²) political issue; **Qisch** [~'li:tiʃ] political; **Qisieren** [~liti'zi:rən] talk politics; v/t. politicise; ~ologe [~to'lo:gə] m (13) political scientist; ~ologie [~tolo'gi:] f political science.
Politur [poli'tu:r] f (16) polish.
Polizei [~'tsaɪ] f (16) police; ~-aktion f police operation; ~-aufsicht f: unter ~ under police supervision; ~beamte m police officer; ~dienststelle f police station; ~-eskorte f police escort; ~gewalt f police power; ~knüppel m truncheon, Am. club; ~kommissar m police inspector; **Qlich** (... der Polizei) (of the) police; (von der Polizei) by the police; ~präsident m Chief Constable, Am. Chief of the Police, Police Chief; ~präsidium n police headquarters; ~revier n police station, Am. station house; ~schüler m police cadet; ~spion m, ~spitzel m police spy; ~staat m police state; ~streife f police patrol; (Polizeitrupp) police squad; (Razzia) (police) raid; ~streifenwagen m s. Streifenwagen; ~streitkräfte f/pl. police force sg.; ~stunde f closing time (for public houses); ~ver-ordnung f police regulation(s pl.); ~wache f s. Polizeirevier; **Qwidrig** contrary to police regulations; F fig. infernally stupid.
Polizist [poli'tsist] m (12) policeman, constable; ~in f (16¹) policewoman.
Pollen ♀ ['pɔlən] m (6) pollen.
polnisch ['pɔlniʃ] Polish.
Polo ['po:lo] n (11) Sport: polo; '~hemd n Mode: polo shirt.
Polster ['pɔlstər] n (7) cushion; bsd. ⊕

bolster; (*Füllhaar*) stuffing; (*Wattierung*) pad(ding); '~**gruppe** *f* three-piece suite; '~**möbel** *n*/*pl.* upholstery *sg.*; '♀**n** (29) stuff, upholster; pad; wad; '~**sitz** *m* cushioned seat; '~**stuhl** *m* easy chair; '~**ung** *f* padding, stuffing.

Polter|-abend ['pɔltər-] *m* wedding-eve (party); '~**er** *m* (7) blustering (*od.* noisy) fellow; '~**geist** *m* poltergeist; '♀**n** (29) make a row; (*rumpeln*) rumble, lumber; (*schimpfen*) bluster.

Poly|äthylen ⚗ [polyɛty'leːn] *n* (3¹) polythene; ~**gamie** [~ga'miː] *f* (15, *o. pl.*) polygamy; ♀**mer** [~'meːr] polymeric.

Polyp [po'lyːp] *m* (12) *zo.* polyp; 𝄢 polypus; ~**en** *pl.* (*in der Nase*) adenoids *pl.*; F (*Polizist*) *sl.* bull, cop.

Polytechnikum [poly'tɛçnikum] *n* (9[²]) polytechnic (school).

Pomade [po'maːdə] *f* (15) pomade.

Pomeranze [pomə'rantsə] *f* (15) bitter orange.

Pommes frites (*fr.*) [pɔm'frit] *pl.* (potato) chips, *Am.* French-fried potatoes, French fries.

Pomp [pɔmp] *m* (3) pomp; '♀**haft**, ♀**ös** [~'pøːs] pompous.

Ponti|fikat [pɔntifi'kaːt] *n* (3) pontificate; ~**us** ['pɔntsjus]: *von* ~ *zu Pi'latus geschickt werden* F be driven from pillar to post, get the grand run-around.

Ponton [pɔ̃'tɔ̃, pɔn'tɔŋ] *m* (11) pontoon.

Pony ['pɔni] 1. *n* (11) pony; 2. *m* (*Frisur*) fringe, *Am.* bangs *pl.*

Popanz ['poːpants] *m* (3²) bugbear, *bsd. Am.* bugaboo.

Popelin(e *f*) [popə'liːn] *m* (3) poplin.

Pop|gruppe ['pɔp-] *f* pop group; '~**musik** *f* pop music.

Popo F [po'poː] *m* (11) bottom.

populär [popu'lɛːr] popular.

populari|sieren [~lari'ziːrən] popularize; ♀**tät** [~'tɛːt] *f* (16, *o. pl.*) popularity.

Por|e ['poːrə] *f* (15) pore; ♀**ös** [po'røːs] porous; ~**osität** [porozi'tɛːt] *f* (16) porosity.

Porno F ['pɔrno] *m* (11) (*Pornographie*) porn(o); *s.* Pornofilm; '~**film** *m* porno (film); ~**graphie** [~gra'fiː] *f* (15) pornography.

Portal [pɔr'taːl] *n* (3¹) portal.

Porte|feuille [pɔrt(ə)'fœj] *n* (11) portfolio (*a. parl.*); ~**monnaie**

[pɔrtmɔ'neː, ~'neː] *n* (11) purse.

Portepee [~ə'peː] *n* (11) sword-knot.

Portier [pɔr'tjeː] *m* (11) porter, door-keeper, *Am.* doorman, janitor.

Portion [~'tsjoːn] *f* portion; ✂, ⚓ ration; (*servierte* ~) helping, serving; *zwei* ~*en Kaffee* coffee for two; F *fig. halbe* ~ shrimp, *Am. sl.* punk; *e-e gehörige* ~ *Frechheit* a good dose of impudence.

Porto ['pɔrto] *n* (11, *pl. a.* -ti) postage; '♀**frei** post-free, prepaid, *bsd. Am.* postpaid; '~**gebühren** *f*/*pl.* postage *sg.*; postal rates; '~**kasse** ✝ *f* petty cash; '♀**pflichtig** liable to postage.

Porträt [pɔr'trɛː] *n* (11) portrait; ♀**ieren** [~trɛ'tiːrən] portray; ~**maler** [~'trɛː-] *m* portrait-painter, portraitist.

Portugies|e [pɔrtu'giːzə] *m* (13), ~**in** *f* (16¹), ♀**isch** Portuguese.

'**Portwein** *m* port(-wine).

Porzellan [pɔrtsə'laːn] *n* (3¹) china; *fig. unnötig* ~ *zerschlagen* do a lot of unnecessary damage; *s.* Elefant.

Posaune [po'zaunə] *f* (15) trombone; *fig.* trumpet; ♀**n** (25) *v*/*i.* play (on) the trombone; *v*/*t. fig.* trumpet (forth); ~**nbläser** *m*, **Posau'nist** *m* (12) trombonist.

Pose ['poːzə] *f* (15) (*Stellung*) pose, attitude; *fig. a.* air, act.

posieren [po'ziːrən] pose (*als* as).

Position [pozi'tsjoːn] position; *Buchhaltung usw.*: item; *fig.* ~ *beziehen* take one's stand; ~**slicht** *n* position light.

positiv ['poːziti:f, *a.* pozi'ti:f] positive (*a. phys., phot.,* ⚡); (*bejahend*) affirmative; (*günstig*) favo(u)rable.

Positur [pozi'tuːr] *f* (16) posture; *sich in* ~ *setzen* strike an attitude.

Posse ['pɔsə] *f* (15) drollery, antic(s *pl.*); *thea. u. fig.* farce; ~**n** *reißen* play the buffoon; ~**n** *treiben* play tricks (*mit* on).

'**Possen** *m* (6) trick, prank; *j-m e-n* ~ *spielen* play a trick on a p.; '♀**haft** droll, farcial; '~**reißer** *m* buffoon, clown; '~**spiel** *thea. n* farce.

pos'sierlich droll, funny.

Post [pɔst] *f* (16) post, *Am.* mail; (~*sachen*) letters *pl.*, mail; *s.* ~*amt*; *mit der ersten* ~ by the first delivery; *mit gewöhnlicher* ~ by surface mail; *mit umgehender* ~ by return of post; *zur* ~ *bringen od.*

geben, mit der ~ *schicken* post, *Am.* mail; Ձalisch [~'taːliʃ] postal.

Postament [pɔsta'mɛnt] *n* (3) pedestal, base.

'**Post|-amt** *n* post office; '~-**anweisung** *f* postal (*od.* money-)order; '~-**auftrag** *m* postal collection order; '~-**be-amte** *m* post-office clerk; '~**bote** *m* postman, *Am.* mailman.

Posten ['pɔstən] *m* (6) post, place; (*Anstellung*) post, situation, job; ✂ sentry, sentinel; *mst* ✝ *in e-r Aufstellung:* item, entry, sum; *Waren:* lot, parcel; *auf dem* ~ *sein* be on one's toes, *gesundheitlich:* be in good form; *s. verloren;* '~**jäger** *m* place hunter.

'**Post|fach** *n* post-office box (*abbr.* P.O.B.); '~**fachnummer** *f* box-number; '~**gebühr** *f* postage; '~**geheimnis** *n* sanctity of the mails.

posthum [pɔst'huːm] posthumous.

po'stieren post, place (*sich o.s.*).

Postillion ['pɔstiljoːn] *m* (3¹) postilion.

'**Post|karte** *f* post (*Am. a.* postal) card; '~**kutsche** *f* stage-coach; 'Ձ-**lagernd** to be (left till) called for, poste restante (*fr.*), *Am.* (in care of) general delivery; '~**leitzahl** *f* Brt. postcode, *Am.* zip code; '~**meister** *m* postmaster; '~**nachnahme** *f* *s. Nachnahme;* '~**paket** *n* postal parcel (*Am.* package); '~**sack** *m* mail-bag; '~**scheck** *m* postal cheque (*Am.* check); '~**scheck-amt** *n* postal cheque office; '~**scheckdienst** *m Brt. the* Giro; '~**scheckkonto** *n etwa:* postal cheque account; '~**schiff** *n* mail-boat; '~**schließfach** *n* post-office box; '~**sparbuch** *n* post-office savings book; '~**sparkasse** *f* postal savings bank; '~**station** *f* post station; '~**stempel** *m* postmark; „*Datum des* ~*s*" date as per postmark.

Postul|at [pɔstu'laːt] *n* (3), Ձieren [~'liːrən] postulate.

'**Post|versandhaus** *n* mail-order house; 'Ձ**wendend** by return (of post); *fig.* directly; '~**wertzeichen** *n* (postage) stamp; '~**wesen** *n* postal system; '~**wurfsendung** *f* mail circular.   [tate.)

Potentat [poten'taːt] *m* (12) potentate.

Potenti|al [poten'tsjaːl] *n* (3²), Ձell [~'tsjɛl] potential.

Potenz [po'tɛnts] *f* (16) (*a. sexual*)

potency; Ⱥ power; *zweite* ~ *a.* square; *dritte* ~ *a.* cube; Ձieren [~'tsiːrən] raise to a higher power; *fig.* magnify; ~**störung** *f* impaired potency.

Potpourri ♩ ['pɔtpuri] *n* (11) potpourri, (musical) selection, medley.

Pott-asche ['pɔt-] *f* potash.

poussieren F [pu'siːrən] flirt.

Präambel [prɛ'ʔambəl] *f* (15) preamble.

Pracht [praxt] *f* (16) splendo(u)r, magnificence; *verschwenderische:* luxury; *feierliche:* pomp; F *e-e wahre* ~ just great; '~**ausgabe** *f* édition de luxe (*fr.*); '~**exemplar** *n* splendid specimen, beauty.

prächtig ['prɛçtiç] *s. prachtvoll.*

'**Pracht|kerl** F *m* splendid fellow, F brick, *Am. sl.* great guy; '~**straße** *f* boulevard; '~**stück** *n s. Prachtexemplar;* 'Ձ**voll** magnificent, splendid (*a. fig.*); gorgeous; (*großartig*) grand, great.

Prädikat [predi'kaːt] *n* (3) predicate; *beim Namen:* title; (*Wertung*) attribute; *Schule:* mark; ~**snomen** *gr. n* [~'kaːtsnoːmən] complement.

präge|n ['prɛːgən] (25) stamp; *Münze, Wort:* coin; *fig. in das Gedächtnis:* engrave on; 'Ձ**stanze** *f*, 'Ձ**stempel** *m* (stamping) die; *auf Urkunden:* raised seal.

pragmatisch [pra'gmaːtiʃ] pragmatic(al).

prägnant [prɛ'gnant] pregnant; (*bündig*) terse, pithy.

'**Prägung** *f* stamping; coining, coinage; *fig.* stamp.

prähistorisch ['prɛːhis'toːriʃ] prehistoric.

prahlen ['praːlən] (25) brag, boast (*mit* of), talk big, bluster; (*angeben*) show off, parade (*mit et.* a th.).

'**Prahler** (*a.* **Prahlhans** ['~hans]) *m* (7), '~**in** *f* (16¹) boaster, braggart; ~**ei** [~'raɪ] *f* (16) boasting, big talk; (*Prunken*) ostentation; 'Ձ**isch** bragging, boastful; (*prunkend*) ostentatious.

Prahm ⚓ [praːm] *m* (3) barge.

Prakt|ik ['praktik] *f* (16) practice; *b.s.* ~*en pl.* (sharp) practices; ~**ikant** [~i'kant] *m* (12) probationer, pupil; ~**iker** ['~ikər] *m* (7) practical man; expert; ~**ikum** ['~ikum] *n* (9²) practical course; ~**ikus** ['~ikus] *m* (14²): *alter* ~ old stager *od.* hand;

'**~isch** practical; (*geschickt*) handy (*a. Gerät usw.*); (*tatsächlich*) virtual; **~er** Arzt general practitioner; **~izieren** [~i'tsi:rən] practise.
Prälat [prɛ'lɑ:t] *m* (12) prelate.
Praline [pra'li:nə] *f* (15), **Praliné** ['~line:] *n* (11) chocolate (cream).
prall [pral] **1.** (*straff*) tight, taut; (*feist*) plump (*a. Kissen*); *Backen*: chubby; *Sonne*: blazing; **2.** ♀ *m* (3) bound, shock, impact; '**~en** (25, sn) bounce (*auf acc.* against).
Präludium [prɛ'lu:djum] *n* (9) prelude.
Prämie ['prɛ:mjə] *f* (15) bsd. ♱ premium; (*Dividende, Leistungs♀*) bonus; *zur Förderung der Wirtschaft u.* ✕ bounty; (*Preis*) award, *bsd. Schule*: prize; (*Belohnung*) reward; '**~nschein** *m* premium-bond.
prämi'ieren award a prize to.
Prämisse [prɛ'misə] *f* (15) premise.
prang|en ['praŋən] (25) be resplendent, shine; '**♀er** *m* (7) pillory; *an den ~ stellen* (put in the) pillory.
Pranke ['praŋkə] *f* (15) claw, clutch.
Präpa|rat [prɛpa'rɑ:t] *n* (3) preparation; *Mikroskop*: slide preparation; *anat.* specimen; ♀'**rieren** prepare.
Präposition [~pozi'tsjo:n] *f* preposition; ♀**al** [~jo'nɑ:l] prepositional.
Prärie [prɛ:'ri:] *f* (15) prairie.
Präsens *gr.* ['prɛ:zɛns] *n inv.* present (tense).
Präsent [prɛ'zɛnt] *n* (3) present; ♀**ieren** [~'ti:rən] *v/t.* present; *v/i.* ✕ present arms; **~ierteller** [~'ti:r-] *m* tray, salver.
Präsenz [prɛ'zɛnts] *f* presence.
Präs|ident [prɛzi'dɛnt] *m* (12) president, chairman; *s. Polizei♀ usw.*; **~i'dentenwahl** *f* presidential election; ♀**i'dieren** preside (*dat. od. bei* over); **~idium** [~'zi:djum] *n* (9), **~i'dentschaft** *f* presidency, chair.
prasseln ['prasəln] (29) *Feuer*: crackle; *Regen*: patter; *Geschosse*: hail; *~der Beifall* thunderous applause.
prass|en ['prasən] (28) feast; *weitS.* live in luxury; '♀**er** *m* (7) reveller, spendthrift; ♀**erei** [~ə'raɪ] *f* (16) debauchery, luxury, dissipation.
Prätendent [prɛtɛn'dɛnt] *m* (12) pretender (*auf acc.* to).
Präteritum *gr.* [prɛ'te:ritum] *n* (9²)

preterite, past tense.
Pratze ['pratsə] *f* (15) paw.
Präventiv|... [prɛvɛn'tif...] preventive, ♱ *mst* prophylactic; **~angriff** ✕ *m*, **~schlag** ✕ *m* pre-emptive (first) strike; **~krieg** *m* preventive (*od.* pre-emptive) war; **~maßnahme** *f* preventive measure.
Praxis ['praksis] *f* (*sg. inv., pl. Praxen*) practice (*a.* ♱, ⚖); (*Raum*) consulting room; (*Erfahrung*) experience; *in der ~* in practice; *in die ~ umsetzen* put into practice.
Präzedenzfall [prɛtse'dɛntsfal] *m* precedent, ⚖ *a.* leading case.
präzis [prɛ'tsi:s] precise, exact; **~ieren** [~tsi'zi:rən] define, specify; ♀**ion** [~tsi'zjo:n] *f* precision; ♀**ions...** *in Zssgn* precision ...
predig|en ['pre:digən] *v/i. u. v/t.* (25) preach; '♀**er** *m* preacher; ♀**t** ['~diçt] *f* sermon (*a. fig.*).
Preis [praɪs] *m* (4) price; (*Kosten*) cost; (*Kurs; Satz*) rate; (*Fahr♀*) fare; *im Wettbewerb*: prize, award; (*Belohnung*) reward; (*Lob*) praise; *um jeden ~* at any price; *um keinen ~* not at any price; *der äußerste ~* the lowest (*od.* keenest) price; *den ~ davontragen* carry off the prize; *im ~ steigen* rise in price, go up; '**~abbau** *m* reduction of prices; '**~absprache** *f* prize agreement; '**~änderung** *f* change in price(s *pl.*); *~en pl.* vorbehalten subject to change; '**~angabe** *f* quotation (of prices); *ohne ~* not priced, not marked; '**~anstieg** *m* rise in prices; '**~aufgabe** *f* (subject for a) prize essay, competition; '**~aufschlag** *m* extra charge; '**~ausschreiben** *n* (prize) competition; '**~bildung** *f* price fixing; '**~boxer** *m* prize-fighter; '**~drücke'rei** *f* price-cutting.
Preiselbeere ['praɪzəlbe:rə] *f* red whortleberry, cranberry.
'**Preis-empfehlung** *f* recommended price.
preisen ['praɪzən] (30) praise; *sich glücklich ~* call o.s. happy.
'**Preis|-entwicklung** *f* trend of prices; '**~erhöhung** *f* price increase; '**~ermäßigung** *f* reduction in price(s); '**~festsetzung** *f* price fixing, pricing; '**~frage** *f s. Preisaufgabe*; '**~gabe** *f*, '**~gebung** *f* abandonment; (*Herausgabe*) surrender; *e-s Geheimnisses*: revelation; '♀**ge-**

ben abandon; (*herausgeben*) surrender; (*opfern*) sacrifice; *Geheimnis*: reveal; (*sich*) ~ (*dat.*) expose (o.s.) to; '♭gekrönt prize-winning; '♭gericht *n* jury; '♭gestaltung *f* s. *Preisbildung*; '♭grenze *f* price limit; '♭günstig *s. preiswert*; '♭klasse *f* price range; '♭lage *f* price level; *in jeder* ~ in all prices; '♭liste *f* price--list, list of prices; '♭nachlaß *m* discount; '♭politik *f* price policy; '♭rätsel *n* competition; '♭richter *m* judge; '♭schießen *n* rifle competition; '♭schild *n* price tag (*od.* ticket); '♭schwankung *f* price fluctuation; '♭senkung *f* price reduction *od.* cut; '♭spanne *f* price margin; '♭steigerung *f* rise in prices; ♭stopp ['♭ʃtɔp] *m* (11) price freeze; '♭sturz *m* sudden fall of price(s), slump; '♭träger (-*in f*) *m* prize-winner *od.* -holder; ♭treiberei ['♭'raɪ] *f* forcing up of prices; '♭wert, '♭würdig worth the money; (*billig*) low-priced; ♭es Angebot bargain; ~ *sein* be good value.

prekär [pre'kɛːr] precarious.

Prell|**bock** ['prɛlbɔk] *m* (3³) buffer--stop; '♭en (25) toss; ♣ contuse; *fig.* cheat (*um* of); ♭erei [♭ə'raɪ] *f* cheating; '♭stein *m* kerb-stone, *Am.* curbstone; '♭ung *f* contusion, bruise.

Premier|**e** *thea.* [prəm'jɛːrə] *f* (15) first night; ♭minister [prəm'jeː-ministər] *m* prime minister.

Presse ['prɛsə] *f* (15) ⊕, *typ.* press; *fig. the* Press; *Schule*: cramming--classes *pl.*; *e-e gute* ~ *haben* have a good press; '♭amt *n* public relations office; '♭bericht *m* press report, news item; '♭chef *m* chief press officer; '♭dienst *m* news service; '♭erklärung *f* press release; '♭feldzug *m* press campaign; '♭freiheit *f* freedom of the press; '♭konferenz *f* press conference; '♭meldung *f* news item; '♭mitteilung *f* press release; '♭n (28) press; (*formen*) mo(u)ld; '♭photograph *m* press-photographer; '♭spiegel *m* press review; '♭sprecher *m* press spokesman; '♭stimmen *f/pl.* commentaries of the press; '♭tribüne *f* press gallery; '♭verlautbarung *f* press release; '♭vertreter *m* reporter; '♭zar *m* press baron (*od.* lord).

'**Preß**|**glas** *n* mo(u)lded glass; '♭holz *n* laminar wood.

pressieren [prɛ'siːrən] be urgent; *es pressiert mir* I am in a hurry.

'**Preß**|**kohle** *f* briquette, compressed fuel; '♭luft *f* compressed air; '♭luftbohrer *m* pneumatic (*od.* air) drill; '♭lufthammer *m* pneumatic hammer; '♭stoff *m* plastic.

Prestige [prɛs'tiːʒ(ə)] *n* (11, *o. pl.*) prestige; ♭verlust *m* loss of prestige.

Preuß|**e** ['prɔysə] *m* (13), '♭in *f* (16¹) Prussian; '♭isch Prussian.

prickeln ['prikəln] (29) *v/i. u. v/t.* prick(le); *Glieder*: tingle; (*jucken*) itch.

Priem [priːm] *m* (3) quid, plug.

pries [priːs] *pret. v. preisen*.

Priester ['priːstər] *m* (7) priest; '♭-amt *n* priesthood; '♭in *f* (16¹) priestess; '♭lich priestly; clerical; '♭rock *m* cassock; '♭schaft *f*, '♭tum *n* priesthood; '♭weihe *f* ordination (of a priest).

prim|**a** ['priːma] **1.** first-class, first--rate, F A 1, A one; ✝ *a.* prime; F swell, super; **2.** ♀ *f* (16) top form; ♭aner [pri'maːnər] *m* (7), ♭anerin *f* (16¹) top-form boy (*f* girl); ♭är [♭'mɛːr] primary; ♭at [♭'maːt] *m*, *n* (3) primateship; ♭aten *biol. m/pl.* (12, *pl.*) primates.

Primel ['priːməl] *f* (15) primrose.

primitiv [primi'tiːf] primitive.

Primus ['priːmus] *m* (14²) head (*od.* top) boy.

Primzahl ['priːm-] *f* prime number.

Prinz [prints] *m* (12) prince; ♭essin [♭'tsɛsin] *f* (16¹) princess; '♭gemahl *m* Prince Consort.

Prinzip [prin'tsiːp] *n* (3¹ *u.* 8²) principle; *im* ~ in principle; *aus* ~ on principle; ♭al [♭tsi'paːl] *m* (3¹) principal, chief; (*Brotherr*) employer, F boss; ♭iell [♭tsi'pjɛl] *adv.* on principle; ♭ienreiter [♭'tsiː-pjən-] *m* stickler (for principles).

'**prinzlich** princely.

Prior ['priːɔr] *m* (8¹) prior; ♭in [pri'oːrin] *f* (16¹) prioress.

Priorität [♭ori'tɛːt] *f* (16) priority; ♭en setzen establish priorities; ♭s-aktie ✝ *f* preference share.

Prise ['priːzə] *f* (15) **1.** pinch of salt *etc.*; **2.** ⚓ prize.

Prism|**a** ['prisma] *n* (9¹) prism; ♭atisch [♭'maːtiʃ] prismatic(ally *adv.*).

Pritsche ['pritʃə] *f* (15) *des Harle-*

kins: slapstick; *allg.* bat; (*Lager-statt*) plank-bed.

privat [pri'vɑːt] private; personal.

Pri'vat|·adresse *f* home address; **~besitz** *m*, **~·eigentum** *n* private (*od.* personal) property; **~dozent** *m* unsalaried lecturer, *Am.* instructor; **~gespräch** *n* private conversation; *teleph.* private call; **~·initiative** *f* private venture; **~·interesse** *n* private interest; **~n verfolgen** *bsd. Am.* have an ax(e) to grind; **~leben** *n* private life; **~lehrer** *m* private tutor; **~mann** *m* private gentleman; **~recht** *n* private law; **~schule** *f* private school; **~sphäre** *f* privacy; **~stunde** *f* private lesson; **~·unterricht** *m* private tuition; **~wirtschaft** *f* private enterprise.

privi|legieren [privile'giːrən] privilege; **℔leg(ium)** [~'leːk, ~'leːgjum] *n* (8² [9]) privilege.

pro [proː] *prp.* per; ℔ *n* (11): **~ und Kontra** pro and con.

probat [pro'bɑːt] (ap)proved, tested, tried.

Probe ['proːbə] *f* (15) (*Versuch*) experiment; (*Erprobung*) trial, test, *Am.* F tryout; (*Bewährungs*℔) probation; (*Beweis*) proof; *iro.* (*Kost*℔) taste; *thea.* rehearsal; (*Erprobung e-r P.*) probation; (*Sprech- od. Gesangs*℔) audition; (*Prüfstück*) specimen; (*Waren*℔) sample; *metall.* assay; **auf ~** on probation, on trial; **Ehe auf ~** trial marriage; **auf die ~ stellen** put to the test; **auf e-e harte ~ stellen** tax, put to a severe test; **e-e ~ seines Mutes ablegen** give proof of one's courage; **'~abzug** *typ. m* proof-sheet; *phot.* test print; **'~·anwärter(in** *f*) *m* probationer; **'~·aufnahmen** *f/pl.* *Film*: screen test *sg.*; **'~auftrag** *m*, **'~bestellung** *f* trial order; **'~bogen** *m s.* Probeabzug; **'~·exemplar** *n* sample copy; **'~fahrt** *f mot.* test drive; **⚓** trial run (*od.* trip); **'℔haltig** proof; **'~jahr** *n* trial year; **'~lauf** *m e-r Maschine etc.*: test run; **'℔n** (25) *thea. u. weit S.* rehearse; **'~nummer** *f* specimen copy; **'~schuß** *m* trial shot; **'~sendung** *f* sample sent on approval; **'~start** 𝒦 *m* trial take-off; **'~stück** *n* sample, specimen, test piece; **'℔weise** on a trial basis; **'~zeit** *f* trial (*od.* probationary) period.

probier|en [pro'biːrən] try (*a.* =

es ~ mit), test; *metall.* assay; *Speise usw.*: taste; (*aus~*) sample; **℔nadel** *f* touchneedle; **℔stein** *m* touchstone.

Problem [pro'bleːm] *n* (3¹) problem; **~atik** [~ble'mɑːtik] *f* (16, *o. pl.*) problematic nature; problems *pl.*; **℔atisch** problematic(al); **~stück** *thea. n* thesis play.

Produkt [~'dukt] *n* (3) product (*a.* Å); *des Bodens usw.*: produce; **~·enhandel** *m* produce trade; **~·enmarkt** *m* produce market.

Produktion [~tsjoːn] *f* (16) production; (*Fabrikationsmenge*) output; **~s-anlage** *f* production plant(s *pl.*); **~sgüter** *n/pl.* producer goods; **~skosten** *pl.* production cost; **~sleiter** *m* production manager; *Film*: executive producer; **~s-planung** *f* production planning; **~sziel** *n* production target; **~szweig** *m* line of production.

produktiv [~'tiːf] productive; **℔ität** [~tivi'tɛːt] *f* (16) productivity.

Produz|ent [produ'tsent] *m* (12) producer; **℔ieren** [~'tsiːrən] produce; *contp. sich ~* show off.

profan [pro'fɑːn] *, ~ieren* [~fa'niːrən] profane.

Profession [~fɛ'sjoːn] *f* (16) profession; (*Handwerk*) trade; **℔ell** [~sjo'nɛl] professional.

Profess|or [~'fɛsɔr] *m* (8¹) professor; *s. ordentlich*; **~ur** [~'suːr] *f* (16) professorship.

Profi F ['proːfi] *m* (11) pro(fessional).

Profil [~'fiːl] *n* (3¹) profile; *mot. Reifen*: tread; **im ~** in profile; **℔ieren** [~fi'liːrən] profile; **℔iert** [~'liːrt] *fig. P.*: outstanding; **~neurose** *f* image neurosis.

Profit [~'fiːt] *m* (3) profit; **℔ieren** [~fi'tiːrən] *v/i. u. v/t.* profit (*von* by).

Proforma|rechnung [proː'fɔrma-] † *f* pro forma invoice; **~zahlung** *f* token payment.

profund [pro'funt] profound.

Prognose [pro'gnoːzə] *f* (15) forecast, *bsd.* 𝒦 prognosis.

Programm [~'gram] *n* (3¹) program(me) (*a. Computer*℔); *Rennsport usw.*: card; *Schule*: prospectus; *politisches ~* political programme, *Am.* platform; **~·ausstattung** *f Computer*: software; **℔gemäß** according to program(me) (*fig.* to plan); **℔ierbar** [~gra'miːr-] programmable; **℔ieren**

program(me); **~ierer** *m* programmer; **~musik** [~'gram-] *f* program(me) music; **~punkt** *m* item, *Am. pol.* plank; **~speicher** *m Computer*: program(me) memory; **~speicherplatz** *m Computer*: program(me) storage space; **~vorschau** *f* program(me) preview; *Film*: trailers *pl.*

progressiv [progrɛ'siːf] progressive.

Projekt [~'jɛkt] *n* (3) project; **2ieren** [~'tiːrən] project.

Projektion [~'tsjoːn] *f* (16) projection; **~s-apparat** *m* projector; **~sschirm** *m* screen.

projizieren [~ji'tsiːrən] project.

Proklam|ation [~klama'tsjoːn] *f* (16) proclamation; **2ieren** [~'miːrən] proclaim.

Pro-'Kopf-Einkommen *n* per capita income.

Prokur|a [pro'kuːra] *f inv.* procuration; *per ~* by proxy (*abbr.* per pro., p. p.); **~ist** [~ku'rist] *m* (12) confidential (*od.* signing) clerk.

Prolet *contp.* [~'leːt] *m* cad; **~ariat** [~leta'rjaːt] *n* (3) proletariat(e); **~arier** [~'taːrjər] *m* (7) proletarian; **2arisch** [~'taːriʃ] proletarian.

Prolog [pro'loːk] *m* (3¹) prolog(ue).

prolongier|en † [~lɔŋ'giːrən] renew, prolong; **2ung** *f* prolongation.

Promenade [~mə'naːdə] *f* (15) (*Straße u. Spaziergang*) promenade; **~ndeck** ⚓ *n* promenade deck.

prome'nieren promenade, (take a) stroll.

Promille [pro'milə] *n* (*inv.*) pars pro mille; F *mot.* blood-alcohol concentration; **~grenze** F *mot. f* (blood) alcohol limit.

prominen|t [~mi'nɛnt] prominent; **2te** *m, f* (18) prominent person, celebrity; **2z** [~ts] *f* (16, *o. pl.*) prominence; celebrities *pl.*

Promo|tion *univ.* [promo'tsjoːn] *f* (16) graduation; **2vieren** [~'viːrən] *v/t.* confer a degree on; *v/i.* graduate, take one's degree.

prompt [prɔmpt] prompt, quick.

Pronom|en [pro'noːmen] *n* (6, *pl.* -mina) pronoun; **2inal** [~nomi'naːl] pronominal.

Propa|ganda [propa'ganda] *f inv.* propaganda, publicity; **~gan'dist** *m*, **2gan'distisch** propagandist; **2'gieren** propagate.

Propeller [~'pɛlər] *m* (7) propeller.

Prophet [~'feːt] *m* (12) prophet; **~in** *f* (16¹) prophetess; **2isch** prophetic(ally *adv.*).

prophezei|en [~fe'tsaɪən] prophesy; **2ung** *f* prophecy.

prophylaktisch [profy'laktiʃ] ⚕ prophylactic(ally *adv.*).

Proportion [~pɔr'tsjoːn] *f* (16) proportion; **2al** [~tsjo'naːl] proportional; **2iert** [~'niːrt] proportionate.

Propst [proːpst] *m* (3² *u.* ³) provost.

Prosa ['proːza] *f inv.* prose.

Prosa|iker [pro'zaːikər] *m* (7) prose writer; **2isch** prosaic(ally *adv.*).

pros(i)t! ['proːzit, proːst] your health!, cheers!; *beim Niesen*: bless you!; ~ *Neujahr!* a happy New Year to you!

Prospekt [pro'spɛkt] *m* (3) (*Aussicht*) prospect; (*Preisliste*; *Werbeschrift*) prospectus; (*Handels2*) leaflet, brochure, *bsd. Am.* folder.

Prostata *anat.* ['prɔstata] *f* (16, *o. pl.*) prostate (gland).

prostitu|ieren [prostitu'iːrən] prostitute; **2'ierte** *f* (15) prostitute. **2tion** [~'tsjoːn] *f* (16) prostitution.

protegieren [prote'ʒiːrən] patronize.

Protektion [protɛk'tsjoːn] *f* (16) protection, patronage.

Protest [~'tɛst] *m* (3²) protest; *als ~ gegen* in protest against; ~ *einlegen* enter a protest.

Protestant [~tɛs'tant] *m* (12), **~in** *f* (16¹), **2isch** Protestant; **~ismus** [~'tismus] *m* (16, *o.pl.*) Protestantism.

protest|ieren [~tɛs'tiːrən] protest (*gegen* against, *Am. a. th.*); **2marsch** [~'tɛst-] *m* protest march; **2versammlung** *f* protest meeting.

Prothese [pro'teːzə] *f* (15) prosthesis, artificial limb; (*Gebiß*) denture.

Protokoll [proto'kɔl] *n* (3¹) record, minutes *pl.*; *diplomatisches*: protocol; ~ *führen* keep the minutes; *zu ~ geben* depose, state (in evidence); *zu ~ nehmen* take down; **2arisch** [~'laːriʃ] recorded, entered in the minutes; *adv.* by the minutes; **~führer** *m* secretary; **2ieren** [~'liːrən] record.

Protz [prɔts] *m* (12) ostentatious person; show-off; **'2en** (27) show off (*mit* [with] *a th.*); **'2ig** ostentatious, showy.

Proviant [pro'vjant] *m* (3) supplies, provisions, victuals *pl.*

Provinz [~'vints] f (16) province;
~ial... [~'tsjɑ:l], **2iell** [~'tsjɛl], **~ler**
m (7), **~lerin** f provincial.
Provis|ion [~vi'zjo:n] f (16) com-
mission, percentage; **~or** [~'vi:zɔr]
m (8¹) chemist's assistant, dispenser; **2orisch** [~vi'zo:riʃ] pro-
visional, temporary.
Provo|kation [provoka'tsjo:n] f (16)
provocation; **2'zieren** provoke; **~d**
provocative.
Prozedur [protse'du:r] f (16) procedure; iro. ritual.
Prozent [~'tsent] n (3) per cent;
(a. **~satz** m) percentage; **2ual**
[~u'a:l] percentage, percental; proportional; **~er Anteil** percentage.
Prozeß [~'tses] m (3) process; ⚖
lawsuit, action; (Rechtsfall) case;
(Rechtsgang) (legal) proceedings pl.;
e-n **~ anstrengen gegen** institute
(legal) proceedings against, bring an
action against; **kurzen ~ machen mit**
make short work of; **~akten** f/pl.
minutes pl. od. record (of a case);
~führer m litigant; (Anwalt) plaintiff's counsel; **~führung** f conduct
of a lawsuit; **~gegenstand** m matter in dispute.
prozes'sieren go to law (mit with);
carry on a lawsuit (with); litigate.
Prozession [~'jo:n] f (16) procession.
Pro'zeß|kosten pl. (law) costs; **~**
ordnung f rule(s pl.) of court; **~**
partei f party to the action; **~recht**
n adjective law; **~vollmacht** f
power of attorney.
prüde ['pry:də] prudish; **2rie** [pry-
də'ri:] f (15) prudery.
prüf|en ['pry:fən] (25) (erproben) try,
test; (nach~) check, verify; (examinieren; untersuchen) examine,
stärker: scrutinize; Sache: a. investigate, look into; (erwägen) consider; ✝ Bücher usw.: audit; (kosten) taste; (heimsuchen) afflict, try;
ein **~der Blick** a searching look; ge-
prüfter Masseur usw. licensed; '2er
m (7) examiner; tester; checker;
auditor; '2feld ⊕ n test bay; '2ling
m (3) examinee; '2stand ⊕ m test
stand (od. bed); '2stein m touchstone, test.
'**Prüfung** f (16) vgl. prüfen: trial,
test; check, verification; (mündliche
oral, schriftliche written) examination; scrutiny, investigation; ⚖ re-

view; (Über2, ⊕) inspection; ✝
(Buch2) audit; fig. affliction; **e-e ~**
machen go in for an examination;
'**~s-arbeit** f examination paper;
'**~s-ausschuß** m, '**~skommission** f
board of examiners.
Prügel ['pry:gəl] m (7) (Stock)
cudgel, stick; pl. fig. (a. Tracht ~)
beating, hiding; **~ei** [~'laɪ] f (16)
fight, brawl; '**~knabe** m whipping-
-boy; (Sündenbock) scapegoat; '2n
(29) beat (up), thrash; **sich ~** (have
a) fight; '**~strafe** f corporal punishment, flogging.
Prunk [pruŋk] m (3) pomp, splen-
do(u)r; b.s. ostentation; '2en (25)
make a show (mit of), show off (mit
et. a th.); '2end, '2haft ostentatious, showy; '2los unostentatious,
plain; '**~stück** F n show piece; '**~**
sucht f love of display, ostentation;
2süchtig ['~zʏçtiç] ostentatious;
'2voll splendid, gorgeous.
prusten ['pru:stən] (26) snort; burst
out (vor Lachen laughing).
Psalm [psalm] m (5²) psalm; **~ist**
[~'mist] m (12) psalmist.
Psalter ['psaltər] m (7) psalter.
Pseudo|... ['psɔydo-] in Zssgn pseu-
do...; **~nym** [~'ny:m] 1. n (3¹) as-
sumed name, pseudonym; e-s
Schriftstellers: pen-name; 2. 2 adj.
pseudonymous.
pst! [pst] hush!, stop!
Psyche ['psy:çe] f (15) psyche.
Psychiat|er [psyçi'a:tər] m (7) psy-
chiatrist, alienist; **~rie** [~a'tri:] f
psychiatry; (Krankenhausabteilung)
psychiatric ward.
psychisch ['psy:çiʃ] psychic(al).
Psycho-analy|se [psyço⁰ana'ly:zə] f
psychoanalysis; **~tiker** [~'ly:tikər] m
(7) psychoanalyst.
Psycholog|e [~o'lo:gə] m (13), **~in** f
(16¹) psychologist; **~ie** [~lo'gi:] f psychology; **2isch** [~'lo:giʃ] psycho-
logical.
Psychopath [~o'pa:t] m (12) psychopath; **2isch** psychopathic.
Psychopharmaka [~o'farmaka]
n/pl. (9²) psychiatric drugs.
Psychose [psy'ço:zə] f (15) psychosis.
psychosomatisch [~oso'mɑ:tiʃ] psy-
chosomatic.
Psychothera'pie f psychotherapy;
(Heilmethode) psychotherapeutics.
Pubertät [puber'tɛ:t] f (16) puberty.
publik [pu'bli:k]: **~ machen** make

public; ꬶation [ˌkaˈtsjoːn] *f* publication.
Publikum [ˈpuːblikum] *n* (9, *o.pl.*) public; (*Zuhörerschaft*) audience; (*Zuschauer*) spectators *pl.*; (*Leser*ꬶ) readers *pl.*; (9²) *univ.* (*öffentliche Vorlesung*) open lecture.
publiz|ieren [publiˈtsiːrən] publish; ꬶ**ist** [ˌˈtsist] *m* (12) writer.
Pudding [ˈpudiŋ] *m* (3¹) pudding.
Pudel [ˈpuːdəl] *m* (7) poodle; 'ꬶ**mütze** *f* fur-cap; 'ꬶ**naß** soaked, drenched, sopping (wet).
Puder [ˈpuːdər] *m* (7) powder; 'ꬶ**dose** *f* powder-box; *für die Handtasche*: vanity-case, compact; 'ꬶ**n** (29) powder; 'ꬶ**quaste** *f* powder-puff; 'ꬶ**zucker** *m* icing sugar.
Puff [puf] **1.** *m* (3[³]) (*Stoß*) cuff, thump, poke; *leichter*: F dig; (*Knall*) bang, pop; (*Bausch*) puff; P knocking-shop; **2.** *n* (ˌspiel) backgammon; **3.** ꬶ puff!, bang!; 'ꬶ**ärmel** *m* puffed sleeve; 'ꬶ**en** (25) *v/i.* puff; *v/t.* (*schlagen*) cuff, thump; *leicht*: nudge.
Puff|er [ˈˌər] *m* (7) 🔩 buffer; *s.* Kartoffelꬶ; 'ꬶ**erlösung** 🔩 *f* buffer solution; 'ꬶ**erstaat** *m* buffer state; 'ꬶ**mais** *m* popcorn.
Pulk [pulk] ✂ *m* (11) group.
Pulle [ˈpulə] F *f*(15) bottle; 'ꬶ**n** ⚓ (25) pull, row.
Pull|over [puˈloːvər] *m* (7) sweater, pullover; ꬶ**under** [ˌˈlundər] *m* (7) tank-top.
Puls [puls] *m* (4) pulse; *j-m den* ꬶ *fühlen* feel a p.'s pulse (*a. fig.*); 'ꬶ**ader** *f* artery; ꬶ**ieren** [ˌˈziːrən] pulsate; 'ꬶ**schlag** *m* pulsation; 'ꬶ**zahl** *f* pulse rate.
Pult [pult] *n* (3) desk (*a.* ⊕).
Pulver [ˈpulfər] *n* (7) powder; (*Schieß*ꬶ) gunpowder; F (*Geld*) *sl.* dough; *er hat das* ꬶ *nicht erfunden* he is no great light; *s.* Schuß; 'ꬶ**faß** *n* powder-keg; *fig.* volcano; 'ꬶ**ig** powdery; ꬶ**isieren** [ˌvəriˈziːrən] pulverize; 'ꬶ**schnee** *m* powdery snow.
Pump F *m* (3): *auf* ꬶ on tick; 'ꬶ**e** *f* (15) pump; 'ꬶ**en** *v/t. u. v/i.* (25) pump; F (*leihen*) lend, *bsd. Am.* loan; *sich et.* ꬶ borrow; ꬶ**ernickel** [ˌˈərnikəl] *m* (7) pumpernickel; 'ꬶ**hose** *f* (*eine* ꬶ a pair of) knickerbockers *pl.*, plus-fours *pl.*; 'ꬶ**werk** *n* pumping-work.

Punkt [puŋkt] *m* (3) point; (*Tüpfelchen*) dot; *typ.*, *gr.* full stop, period; (*Stelle*) spot; *fig.* (*Einzelheit*) point, head, item, detail; (*Gesprächsthema*) topic; *fig. in vielen* ꬶ**en** on many points; *nach* ꬶ**en siegen** *Boxen*: win on points; ꬶ *10 Uhr* on the stroke of ten, at 10 (o'clock) sharp; *s. tot, wund*; ꬶ**ieren** [ˌˈtiːrən] point, dot; *gr.* punctuate; ✂ puncture, tap; *Kunst*: stipple.
pünktlich [ˈpyŋktliç] punctual, F sharp; (*genau*) exact, accurate; *sei* ꬶ *be on time*; *sehr* ꬶ as punctual as clockwork; 'ꬶ**keit** *f* punctuality; (*Sorgfalt*) diligence.
'**Punkt|richter** *m Sport*: judge; 'ꬶ**sieg** *m Boxen*: win on points; *points decision*; 'ꬶ**um**: (*damit*) ꬶ! *that's flat!*; 'ꬶ**streik** *m* strike at selective sites; 'ꬶ**zahl** *f Sport*: score.
Punsch [punʃ] *m* (3) punch.
punzen [ˈpuntsən] (27) punch.
Pupille [puˈpilə] *f* (15) pupil.
Puppe [ˈpupə] *f* (15) doll (*a.* F *Mädchen*); (*Draht*ꬶ, *a. fig.*) puppet; *Schneiderei*: dummy; *zo.* chrysalis, pupa; *des Seidenspinners*: cocoon.
'**Puppen|gesicht** *n* doll's face; 'ꬶ**spiel** *n* puppet-show; 'ꬶ**stube** *f* doll's house; 'ꬶ**theater** *n* puppet-show; 'ꬶ**wagen** *m* doll's pram.
pur [puːr] pure; (*bloß*) *a.* sheer; *Whisky*: neat, *Am.* straight.
Püree [pyˈreː] *n* (11) purée (*fr.*), mash.
purgier|en [purˈgiːrən] *v/t. u. v/i.* purge; ꬶ**mittel** *n* purgative.
Puritaner [puriˈtaːnər] *m* (7), ꬶ**in** *f* Puritan; ꬶ**tum** *n* (1²) Puritanism.
puri'tanisch Puritan.
Purpur [ˈpurpur] *m* (11) purple; 'ꬶ**farben**, 'ꬶ**n**, 'ꬶ**rot** purple.
Purzel|baum [ˈpurtsəlbaum] *m* somersault; *Sport*: roll; *e-n* ꬶ *schlagen* turn a somersault; 'ꬶ**n** (29, sn) tumble.
Pustel [ˈpustəl] *f* (15) pustule.
puste|n [ˈpuːstən] *v/i. u. v/t.* (26) puff, (*a. = blasen*) blow; 'ꬶ**rohr** *n* pea-shooter.
Put|e [ˈpuːtə] *f* = 'ꬶ**henne** *f* (15) turkey-hen; *sl. fig.* dumme ꬶ silly goose; 'ꬶ**er** (7) *m*, 'ꬶ**hahn** *m* turkey-cock; 'ꬶ**er-rot** purple, crimson.
Putsch [putʃ] *m* (3²) putsch.
Putz [puts] *m* (3²) dressing, toilet;

(*feine Kleidung*) finery; (*Schmuck*) ornaments *pl.*; (*Mauer♀*) roughcast, plaster(ing); *s.* ~waren; '♀en (27) *Person*: dress, attire; (*schmükken*) adorn; (*reinigen*) clean; (*wischen*) wipe; (*glänzend machen*) polish; *Kerze*: snuff; *Lampe*: trim; *Pferd*: groom; *Schuhe*: polish, *Am.* shine; *Gemüse*: pick; *Zähne*: brush; *sich die Nase* ~ blow (*od.* wipe) one's nose; '~er ✗ *m* (7) batman; '~fimmel *m*: e-n ~ *haben* be very houseproud; '~frau *f* charwoman; '♀ig funny, droll; '~lappen *m* cloth; '~leder *n* chamois; ~macherei [~maxə'raɪ] *f* millinery; '~macherin *f* milliner; '♀süchtig fond of finery, dressy; '~waren *f/pl.* millinery *sg.*; '~wolle *f* (cotton) waste; '~zeug *n* cleaning things *pl.*

Pygmäe [pyg'mɛːə] *f* pygmy.

Pyjama [py'dʒaːma] *m* (11) (*ein* ~ a suit of) pyjamas, *Am.* pajamas *pl.*

Pyramide [pyra'miːdə] *f* (15) pyramid; ✗ (*Gewehr♀*) stack; ♀**nförmig** [~nfœrmiç] pyramidal.

Pyrotechnik [pyro'teçnik] *f* pyrotechnics *pl.*; ~er *m* pyrotechnist.

pythagoreisch [pytago're:iʃ] Pythagorean; ~er *Lehrsatz* Pythagorean proposition.

Q

Q [kuː], **q** *n inv.* Q, q.

quabbel|ig ['kvabəliç] flabby; '~n (29) wobble.

Quackelei [kvakə'laɪ] *f* foolish talk.

Quacksalber ['kvakzalbər] *m* (7) quack; ~ei [~'raɪ] *f* (16) quackery; '♀n (29) quack.

Quader ['kvaːdər] *m* (7), *f* (15), '~stein *m* square stone, ashlar.

Quadrant ⚹ [kva'drant] *m* (12) quadrant.

Quadrat [kva'draːt] *n* (3) square; 2 *Fuß im* ~ 2 feet square; ♀**isch** square; ⚹ quadratic; ~**meile** *f* square mile; ~**meter** *n* square met|re, *Am.* -er; ~**ur** [~dra'tuːr] *f* (16) quadrature, squaring; ~**wurzel** [~'draːt-] *f* square root.

qua'drieren square.

quadrophon [kvadro'foːn] quadrophonic.

quaken ['kvaːkən] (25) *Ente*: quack; *Frosch*: croak.

quäken ['kvɛːkən] (25) squeak.

Quäker ['kvɛːkər] *m* (7) Quaker.

Qual [kvaːl] *f* (16) pain; *stärker*: torture; *höchster Grad*: agony; *seelisch*: a. anguish; (*hartes Los, Nervenprobe*) ordeal; (*Mühsal*) drudgery.

quälen ['kvɛːlən] (25) torment; (*foltern*) torture; *stärker*: agonize; *fig. a.* worry, F bother; *mit Bitten*: pester; (*hänseln*) tease; (*betrüben*) afflict; *sich* ~ (*schwer arbeiten*) drudge.

'**Quäler** *m* (7) tormentor; ~**ei** [~'raɪ] *f* (16) tormenting; *fig.* vexation; '~**in** *f* (16¹) tormentress.

'**Quälgeist** *m* pest, tormentor.

Qualifikation [kvalifika'tsjoːn] *f* (16) qualification; ~**skampf** *m* *Sport*: qualifying contest, tie.

qualifizieren [~'tsiːrən] (*a. sich*) qualify (*für* for).

Qualität [~'tɛːt] *f* (16) quality.

qualitativ [~ta'tiːf] qualitative.

Quali'täts|-arbeit *f* work of (high) quality; ~**stahl** *m* high-grade steel; ~**ware** *f* high-quality article.

Qualle ['kvalə] *f* (15) jelly-fish.

Qualm [kvalm] *m* (3) smoke; '♀**en** (25) *v/i. u. v/t.* smoke; '♀**ig** smoky.

'**qualvoll** very painful, agonizing, excruciating.

Quant|enphysik ['kvantən-] *f* quantum physics *sg.*; '~**entheorie** *f* quantum theory; ~**ität** [~ti'tɛːt] *f* (16) quantity; ♀**itativ** [~ita'tiːf] quantitative; ~**um** ['~tum] *n* (9) quantum, quantity.

Quappe ['kvapə] *f* (*Fisch*) eel-pout; (*Kaul♀*) tadpole.

Quarantäne [karan'tɛːnə] *f* (15) quarantine (*a. v/t. in* ~ *legen*).

Quark [kvark] *m* (3, *o. pl.*) curds

pl.; *fig.* rubbish, tripe; '∼**käse** *m* cottage cheese.

Quart [kvart] **1.** *n* (3) quart; *Buch*: quarto; **2.** ∼ *f* (15) ♪ fourth; *fenc.* carte, quart(e); ∼**al** [∼'taːl] *n* (3¹) quarter (of a year); (*Schul*♀) term; '∼**band** *m* quarto volume; '∼**e** *f* *s. Quart* 2.; ∼**ett** ♪ [∼'tet] *n* (3) quartet(te).

Quartier [kvar'tiːr] *n* (3¹) lodging(s *pl.*); *bsd.* ⚔ quarters *pl.*, billets *pl.*; ∼ *beziehen* take up quarters; ∼ *machen* prepare quarters; ∼**ma-cher** ⚔ *m* billeting officer; ∼**mei-ster** ⚔ *m* quartermaster.

Quarz [kvaːrts] *m* (3²) quartz; '∼-**uhr** *f* quartz watch.

quasi ['kvaːzi] quasi, as it were.

quasseln F ['kvasəln] (29) *s. quat-schen.*

Quast [kvast] *m* (3¹) (*Pinsel*) brush; '∼**e** *f* (15) (*Troddel*) tassel; *s. Puder*♀.

Quatsch F [kvatʃ] *m* (3²) *sl.* rot, bilge, bunk, *Am.* baloney; '♀**en** F (27) *v/i.* talk rot, (*a. v/t.*) twaddle, blather; (*plaudern*) chat; '∼**kopf** F *m* twaddler; silly ass.

Quecksilb|er ['kvɛkzilbər] *n* quick-silver, mercury; '∼**ersäule** *f* mercury column; '♀**rig** mercurial; *fig. a.* lively.

Quell [kvɛl] *m* (3) *poet.* = '∼**e** *f* (15) source (*a. fig. Ursprung*), spring; (*Spring*♀) fountain(-head); (*Brun-nen*, *a. Öl*♀) well; *fig.* fount; *litera-risch*: authority; (*Gewährsmann*) informant; *aus sicherer* ∼ on good authority; '♀**en** *v/i.* (30, sn) spring, gush; (*fließen*) flow; (*anschwellen*) swell; *v/t.* (25) cause to swell; (*ein-weichen*) soak; '∼**en-angabe** *f* men-tion of sources used; '∼**enmaterial** *n* source material; '∼**enstudium** *n* original research; '∼**fluß** *m* source; '∼**gebiet** *n* *e-s Flusses*: headwaters *pl.*; '∼**wasser** *n* spring-water.

Quengel|ei [kvɛŋə'laɪ] *f* (16) nag-ging; '♀**ig** nagging, whining; '♀**n** (29) nag; whine.

Quentchen ['kvɛntçən] *n* (6) dram; *fig.* grain.

quer [kveːr] cross, transverse; diag-onal; (*seitlich*) lateral; *adv.* across, crosswise, athwart; ∼ *über* (*acc.*) across; ∼ *zu* at right angles to; *s. Kreuz.*

'**Quer...** *in Zssgn mst* cross-...; '∼-**achse** *f* lateral axis; '∼**balken** *m*

cross-beam; '∼**e** *f* (15): *der* ∼ *nach*, *in die* ∼ crosswise, across; *j-m in die* ∼ *kommen* cross a p.'s way *od.* (*fig. a.*) plans; '♀**en** *mount.* (25) traverse; '♀**feld'-ein** across coun-try; '∼**feld'-einlauf** *m* cross-coun-try run *od.* race; '∼**flöte** *f* German flute; '∼**format** *typ.* *n* oblong format; '∼**frage** *f* cross-question; '♀**gestreift** cross-striped; '∼**holz** *n* cross-bar; '∼**kopf** *m* wrong-headed fellow, crank; ♀**köpfig** ['∼kœpfiç] wrong-headed, cross-grained, cranky; '∼**pfeife** ♪ *f* fife; '∼**ruder** ✈ *n* aileron; '∼**schiff** ⚑ *n* transept; '∼**schläger** *m* ricochet; '∼**schnitt** *m* cross-section (*a. fig.*); '♀**schnitt(s)-gelähmt**, '∼**schnitt(s)gelähmte** *m*, *f* paraplegic; '∼**schnitt(s)lähmung** *f* paraplegia; '∼**schnittzeichnung** *f* sectional drawing; '∼**straße** *f* cross street; *zweite* ∼ *rechts* second turning to the right; '∼**streifen** *m* cross stripe; '∼**strich** *m* cross-line, bar, dash; '∼**summe** ✗ *f* sum of the digits, cross sum; '∼**treiber** *m* in-triguer; obstructionist; ∼**treiberei** [∼traɪbə'raɪ] *f* intriguing, obstruc-tion(ism).

Querulant [kveru'lant] *m* (12), ∼**in** *f* (16¹) grumbler, *Am. a.* griper.

'**Quer|verbindung** *f* cross connec-tion; '∼**weg** *m* cross road.

quetsch|en ['kvɛtʃən] (27) squeeze; (*kneifen*) pinch; (*zerquetschen*) crush; *Haut*: bruise, contuse; '♀-**kartoffeln** *f/pl.* mashed potatoes; '♀**kommode** F *f* (*Akkordeon*) squeeze-box; '♀**ung** *f* crushing; ✗ (*a.* = '♀**wunde** *f*) bruise, contusion.

quieken ['kviːkən] (25) squeak.

quietsch|en ['kviːtʃən] (27) squeal, squeak (*a. Tür usw.*); '∼**ver'gnügt** F cheerful(ly *adv.*).

Quint|(e) ♪ ['kvint(ə)] *f* (16 [15]) fifth; '∼**essenz** *f* (16) quintessence; ∼**ett** ♪ [∼'tet] *n* (3) quintet(te).

Quirl [kvirl] *m* (3) twirling-stick; ♀ whorl; '♀**en** (25) twirl; *Eier usw.*: whisk.

quitt [kvit] *pred.* quits, even; '♀**e** ♀ *f* (15) quince; ∼**ieren** [∼'tiːrən] re-ceipt; (*aufgeben*) quit, abandon; '♀**ung** *f* receipt.

quoll [kvɔl] *pret. v. quellen v/i.*

Quot|e ['kvoːtə] *f* (15) quota; share; rate; ∼**ient** [kvo'tsjent] *m* (12) quo-tient; ♀**ieren** ♥ [∼'tiːrən] quote.

R

R [ɛr], **r** *inv. n* R, r.

Rabatt [ra'bat] *m* (3) discount, rebate, allowance; **～e** *f* (15) border; **～marke** *f* discount stamp; **～satz** *m* discount rate.

Rabbiner [ra'biːnər] *m* (7) rabbi.

Rabe ['raːbə] *m* (13) raven; *fig.* weißer **～** rare bird.

'Raben|-eltern *pl.* unnatural parents; **'2'schwarz** jet-black; *Nacht:* pitch-dark.

rabiat [ra'bjaːt] rabid, furious; (*gefährlich*) desperate.

Rabulist [rabu'list] *m* (12) pettifogger; **2isch** pettifogging.

Rache ['raxə] *f* (15) revenge, vengeance; **～** brüten (schwören) brood (vow) vengeance; **～** nehmen *od.* üben take revenge (*an dat.* on); '**～akt** *m* act of revenge; '**～durst** *m s.* Rachgier.

Rachen ['raxən] *m* (6) throat; (*Tier2*) jaws *pl.* (*a. fig.*).

rächen ['rɛçən] (25) avenge, revenge (*an* [*dat.*] [up]on); *sich* **～** *an j-m* revenge o.s. (*od.* be revenged) on a p.; *fig.* es rächte sich (bitter), daß er ... he had to pay dearly for ger.

'Rachen|höhle *f* pharynx; '**～katarrh** *m* cold in the throat.

Rächer ['rɛçər] *m* (7), '**～in** *f* (16¹) avenger.

'Rach|gier *f*, '**～sucht** *f* thirst for revenge, revengefulness, vindictiveness; **2gierig**, **2süchtig** ['～zyçtiç] revengeful, vindictive.

Rachi|tis [ra'xiːtis] *f* (15, *o. pl.*) rickets (*sg. od. pl.*), **🜊** rachitis; **2tisch** rickety, **🜊** rachitic.

Racker F ['rakər] *m* (7) rascal, brat; (*Mädchen*) minx; '**2n** toil.

Rad [raːt] *n* (1²) wheel; (*Fahr2*) (bi)cycle, F bike; (*ein*) **～** schlagen *Pfau:* spread the tail, *Turnen: s.* radschlagen; unter die Räder kommen go to the dogs; *s.* fünfte; '**～achse** *f* axle-tree.

Radar [ra'daːr, 'raːdar] *m, n* (7, *o. pl.*) radar; **～anlage** *f* radar unit; **～falle** *f* speed trap; **～gerät** *n* radar set; **～schirm** *m* radar screen; **～suchgerät** *n* radar scanner.

Radau F [ra'dau] *m* (3¹) racket, row; **～** machen kick up a row, riot.

radebrechen ['raːdəbrɛçən] speak a language badly; französisch *usw.* **～** speak broken French *etc.*

radeln ['raːdəln] (29, sn) cycle, pedal, F bike.

Rädelsführer ['rɛːdəls-] *m* ringleader.

räder|n ['rɛːdərn] (29) *Verbrecher:* break (up)on the wheel; wie gerädert sein be all in; '**2werk** *n* wheelwork, gear(ing).

'rad|fahren (sn) cycle, (ride a) bicycle, F bike; '**2fahrer(in** *f*) *m* cyclist, *Am.* cycler; '**2fahrsport** *m* cycling; '**2fahrweg** *m* cycle track; '**2felge** *f* wheel rim.

radieren [ra'diːrən] erase, rub out; *Kunst:* etch.

Ra'dier|gummi *m* India rubber, *Am.* eraser; **～kunst** *f* (art of) etching; **～messer** *n* eraser, penknife; **～nadel** *f* etching-needle; **～ung** *f* etching.

Radies-chen 🜊 [ra'diːsçən] *n* (6) (red) radish.

radikal [radi'kaːl] radical; **2e** *pol.* *m* (18) radical; **～isieren** [～kali'ziːrən] radicalise; **2ismus** [～ka'lismus] *m* (16) radicalism; **2kur** *f* 🜊 drastic (*od.* radical) cure; *fig.* drastic measures *pl.*; (*Diät*) crash diet.

Radio ['raːdjo] *n* (11) radio, *Brt. a.* wireless; im **～** sprechen speak over the radio; *s. a.* Rundfunk; '**2-ak'tiv** radio-active; **～er** Niederschlag fall-out; '**～aktivi'tät** *f* radio-activity; '**～apparat** *m* radio (set), *Brt. a.* wireless set; **～loge** [～'loːgə] *m* (13) radiologist; **～logie** [～lo'giː] *f* (16, *o. pl.*) radiology; **2'logisch** radiological; **～recorder** ['～rekɔrdər] *m* (7) radio cassette recorder; '**～röhre** *f* radio valve (*Am.* tube); '**～sendung** *f*, '**～übertragung** *f* radio transmission; *Programm:* broadcast; '**～wecker** *m* clock radio.

Radium ['raːdjum] *n* (9) radium.

Radius ['raːdjus] *m* (16²) radius.

'Rad|kappe *f* hub cap; '**～kranz** *m* rim; '**～nabe** *f* hub, nave; '**～rennbahn** *f* cycling track; '**～rennen** *n* cycle race; '**～schaufel** *f* paddle (-board); '**2schlagen** *Turnen:* turn cartwheels (*Am.* handsprings); '**～speiche** *f* spoke; '**～sport** *m* cycling; '**～stand** *m* wheel-base; '**～tour** *f* cycle tour; '**～wandern** *n* cycling.

raff|en ['rafən] (25) snatch up; *Kleid*: gather up; *Näherei*: take up; '♀**gier** *f* greed.

Raffi|nade [rafi'nɑːdə] *f* (15) refined sugar; ~**nerie** [~nə'riː] *f* (16) refinery; ~**nesse** [~'nɛsə] *f* (15) cleverness, *a. künstlerisch usw.*: subtlety; ♀'**nieren** refine; ♀'**niert** refined; *fig.* clever, cunning; *a. künstlerisch usw.*: subtle; *Geschmack, Aufmachung*: sophisticated.

ragen ['rɑːgən] (25) tower, loom.

Ragout [ra'guː] *n* (11) ragout, stew, hash, (*a. fig.*) hotchpotch.

Rahe ⚓ ['rɑːə] *f* (15) yard.

Rahm [rɑːm] *m* (3) cream; **den ~ abschöpfen** (*a. fig.*) skim off the cream.

Rahmen ['rɑːmən] **1.** *m* (6) frame (*a.* ⊕, *mot.*); (*Gefüge*) framework; (*Bereich*) scope; *Roman*: (*Ort u. Handlung*) setting; *am Schuh*: welt; *fig. im ~ von* within the scope of; *im ~ des Festes* in the course of the festival; *in bescheidenem ~* on a modest scale; *in engem ~* within a close compass; *aus dem ~ fallen* go off the beaten track; *den ~ e-r S. sprengen* be beyond the scope of; **2.** ♀ (25) frame; '~-**abkommen** *n* skeleton agreement; '~-**erzählung** *f* 'link and frame' story; '~**gesetz** *n* skeleton law; '~**kampf** *m Boxen*: supporting bout; '~**ver-anstaltung** *f* fringe event.

'**rahmig** creamy.

Rahsegel ⚓ ['rɑː-] *n* square sail.

Rain [raɪn] *m* (3) ridge; (*ungepflügter Streifen*) balk.

räkeln ['rɛːkəln] *s. rekeln.*

Rakete [ra'keːtə] *f* (15) rocket; ~**n-abschußbasis** *f* rocket launching site; ~**n-abschußrampe** *f* rocket launcher; ~**n-antrieb** ✠ *m* rocket propulsion; *mit ~* rocket-propelled *od.* -powered; ~**nfeuer** *n* rocket fire; ~**nforschung** *f* rocketry; ~**ngeschoß** *n* rocket projectile; ~**npotential** *n* missile strength; ~**nspitze** *f* nose--cone; ~**nstart** *m* blast-off; *e-s Flugzeugs*: rocket-assisted take-off; ~**nstellung** *f* missile site; ~**nwerfer** *m* rocket launcher.

Rallye ['rali, 'rælɪ] *mot. f* (11¹) rally.

Ramm|bär *m,* ~**bock** ['ram-] *m* rammer, ram(-block); '~**e** *f* (15) rammer, pile-driver; (*Pflaster*♀)

beetle; '♀**en** (25) ram.

Rampe ['rampə] *f* (15) ramp; 🚋 platform; *thea.* apron; '~**nlicht** *n* footlights *pl.*; *fig. der Öffentlichkeit*: limelight.

ramponiert [rampo'niːrt] battered, damaged.

Ramsch [ramʃ] *m* (3²) job goods *pl.*; *contp.* junk, trash; '~**verkauf** *m* jumble-sale; '~**ware** *f* job lot.

ran! [ran] *F int.* let's go!; *in Zssgn s. heran*; *s. rangehen.*

Rand [rant] *m* (1²) edge; (*Saum*) border; *e-s Hutes*: brim; *e-s Tellers*: rim; *e-r Druckseite usw.*: margin; *e-r Wunde*: lip; *am ~e des Verderbens* on the verge of ruin; *außer ~ und Band* wild.

randalieren [randa'liːrən] riot.

'**Rand|-auslöser** *m der Schreibmaschine*: marginal release; '~**bemerkung** *f* marginal note.

ränd|eln ['rɛndəln], '~**ern** (29) rim; ⊕ knurl; *Münze*: mill.

'**Rand|gebiet** *n* borderland; *e-r Stadt*: outskirts *pl.*; '♀**los** *Brille*: rimless; '~**gruppe** *f* fringe group; '~**problem** *n* side-issue; '~**staat** *m* border state; '~**stein** *m* kerbstone, *Am.* curbstone; '~**steller** *m der Schreibmaschine*: margin stop; '♀**voll** brimful.

Rang¹ [raŋ] *m* (3³) rank; grade; (*Stand*) status; (*Stellung*) position; (*Würde*) dignity; *ersten ~es* first--class, first-rate; *thea. erster ~* dress-circle, *Am.* first balcony; *zweiter ~* upper circle, *Am.* second balcony; *j-m den ~ ablaufen* get the start of a p., *F* steal a march on a p.; *j-m od. e-r S. den ~ streitig machen* compete with; ♀² *pret. v. ringen*; '~**abzeichen** *n* badge of rank.

Range ['raŋə] *m* (13) young scamp, brat; *f* (15) romp, tomboy.

rangehen F ['ran-] *sl.* go it.

'**Rangfolge** *f* order.

Rangier|bahnhof [rɑ̃'ʒiːr-] *m* shunting-station; ♀**en** *v/t.* arrange; 🚋 shunt, *Am.* switch; *v/i. fig.* rank, be classed; 🚋 shunt; ~**gleis** *n* siding; ~**maschine** *f* shunting-engine.

'**Rang|liste** *f* ranking list; ✗ Army (*od.* Navy *od.* Air Force) List, *Am.* Army Register; '~**ordnung** *f* order (of precedence); '~**stufe** *f* rank, degree, order.

rank [raŋk] slender, slim.

Ranke ['raŋkə] f (15) tendril, runner; '**2n** (25, a. sich) climb, creep.

Ränke ['reŋkə] m/pl. (3⁸) tricks, intrigues; ~ schmieden plot and scheme; '**schmied** m intriguer, plotter, schemer; '**2voll** scheming.

rann [ran] pret. v. rinnen.

'rannte pret. v. rennen.

Ränzel ['rentsəl] n (7), **Ranzen** ['rantsən] m (6) knapsack; (Schulmappe) satchel; F s. Wanst.

ranzig ['rantsiç] rancid, rank.

rapid(e) [ra'piːt, -də] rapid.

Rapier [ra'piːr] n (3¹) rapier, foil.

Rappe ['rapə] m (13) black horse.

Rappel F ['rapəl] m (7) (fit of) madness; e-n ~ haben F be cracked; seinen ~ haben be in one's tantrums; '**2ig** nervy; cracked; '**2n** F v/i. (29) rattle; es rappelt bei ihm he is nuts.

Rapport [ra'pɔrt] m (3) report.

Raps ♀ [raps] m (4) rape(-seed).

rar [raːr] rare, scarce; sich ~ machen make o.s. scarce. [curiosity.]

Rarität [rari'tɛːt] f (16) rarity,⎰

rasan|t [ra'zant] Geschoßbahn: flat; fig. fast, rapid; **2z** f (15. o. pl.) flatness; fig. rapidity.

rasch [raʃ] quick, swift; (sofortig) prompt; (vorschnell) rash; (hastig) hasty; ~ machen be quick; '**eln** (29) rustle; '**2heit** f quickness, swiftness; haste.

rasen¹ ['raːzən] (27) vor Zorn: rage; vor Begeisterung: be frantic; (irre reden) rave; (sn) fig. (daher~) race, speed, tear; '**d** raging; raving; frantic; Tempo: tearing, breakneck; Hunger: ravenous; Schmerzen: agonizing; j-n ~ machen drive a p. mad; ~ werden go mad, wütend: see red.

Rasen² [~] m (6) grass; (~platz) lawn; (~decke) turf; '**mäher** m (7) lawn-mower; '**platz** m lawn, grass-plot; '**sprenger** m lawn-sprinkler.

Raser F ['raːzər] mot. m (7) speeder, reckless driver; **ei** [~'rai] f (16) mot. speeding, reckless driving; (Wut) fury; (Wahnsinn) frenzy, madness; in ~ geraten fly into a rage; zur ~ bringen drive a p. mad.

Rasier|-apparat [ra'ziːr-] m safety--razor; elektrischer: electric (od. dry-)shaver; **creme** f shaving cream; **2en** shave; sich ~ lassen get a shave, get shaved; **klinge** f

razor-blade; **messer** n razor; ~ **pinsel** m shaving-brush; **seife** f shaving soap; **wasser** n after--shave lotion; **zeug** n shaving things pl.

Räson [rɛ'zõ] f (16, o. pl.) reason; s. Einsicht, Vernunft; **2ieren** [~zɔ-'niːrən] argue.

Raspel ['raspəl] f (15) rasp; Küche: grater; '**2n** v/t. u. v/i. (29) rasp, grate; s. Süßholz.

Rasse ['rasə] f (15) race; bsd. v. Tieren: breed; '**hund** m pedigree dog.

Rassel ['rasəl] f (15) rattle; '**bande** F f (mischievous) gang; '**2n** (29, h. u. sn) rattle; F (im Examen durchfallen) be ploughed, Am. flunk; ~ lassen plough, Am. flunk.

'Rassen|diskriminierung f racial discrimination; '**frage** f race problem; '**gleichheit** f racial equality; '**haß** m racial hatred; '**hygiene** f eugenics pl.; '**kampf** m racial conflict; '**kreuzung** f v. Tieren: cross--breeding; '**merkmal** n racial characteristic; '**mischung** f mixture of races; (Tier) crossbreed; '**~politik** f racial policy; '**schranke** f colo(u)r bar; '**trennung** f (racial) segregation.

'Rasse|pferd n thoroughbred (horse); '**2rein** racially pure; Tier: pure-bred, thoroughbred.

'rass|ig racy; bsd. v. Tieren: thoroughbred; '**isch** racial.

Rassis|mus [ra'sismus] m (16²) racism; **t** m (12), **2tisch** racist.

Rast [rast] f (16) rest, repose; ✕ halt; (Station) stage; ⊕ notch, groove; stop; (e-e) ~ machen take a rest; '**e** ⊕ f stop; (Fuß2) foot-rest; '**2en** (26) rest; ✕ halt.

Raster ['rastər] m (7) phot., typ. screen; TV: raster.

'Rast|haus n road house; '**2los** restless; '**losigkeit** f restlessness; '**platz** m resting place; '**stätte** mot. f service area.

Rasur [ra'zuːr] f (16) shave.

Rat [raːt] m (3⁸, pl. mst ~schläge ['~ʃlɛːgə]) advice, counsel; (Kollegium) council, board; (Person) council(l)or; (Beratung) deliberation; (Ausweg) way (out), expedient; ~ schaffen find a way (out); ~ halten s. ratschlagen; ~ suchen (bei), sich (bei j-m) ~ holen ask a p. for advice; j-m e-n ~ erteilen give a p. a piece of advice; *e-n Arzt usw. zu ~e ziehen* consult; *j-s ~ befolgen* take a p.'s advice; *j-n um ~ fragen* ask a p.'s advice; *mit ~ und Tat* with word and deed; *(sich) keinen ~ wissen* be at one's wits' end; *da ist guter ~ teuer!* what are we to do?

Rate ['raːtə] *f* (15) instal(l)ment (*a.* ✝); (*Wachstums*Ϙ *usw.*) rate; *in ~n* by instal(l)ments.

raten ['raːtən] *v/t. u. v/i.* (30) advise, counsel (*j-m* [*zu* et.] a p. [to do a th.]); (*er~*) guess, divine; *Rätsel: a.* solve; *sich (von j-m) ~ lassen* take (a p.'s) advice; *F rate mal!* just guess!

'raten|weise by instal(l)ments; 'Ϙ**zahlung** *f* payment by instal(l)ments; *auf ~* on the hire-purchase (*Am.* instal[l]ment) plan.

'Rat|geber(in *f*) *m* adviser, counsel(l)or; '~**haus** *n* townhall, *Am.* city hall.

Ratifi|kation [ratifika'tsjoːn] *f* (16), ~'**zierung** *f* ratification; Ϙ'**zieren** ratify.

Ration. [ra'tsjoːn] *f* (16) ration, allowance; *s. eisern;* Ϙ**al** [~tsjo'naːl] rational; Ϙ**alisieren** [~nali'ziːrən] rationalize; ~**ali'sierung** *f* rationalization; ~**ali'sierungsfachmann** *m* efficiency expert, methods study man; ~**alismus** [~'lismus] *m* (16) rationalism; Ϙ**ell** [~'nɛl] rational; (*wirtschaftlich*) efficient, economical; Ϙ**ieren** [~'niːrən] ration; ~**ierung** [~'niːruŋ] *f* rationing.

rätlich ['rɛːtliç] *s. ratsam.*

'rat|los helpless, *pred.* at a loss; 'Ϙ**losigkeit** *f* helplessness.

'ratsam advisable; wise; Ϙ**keit** *f* advisability.

'Rat|schlag *m* (piece of) advice; 'Ϙ**schlagen** (25) deliberate, take counsel; '~**schluß** *m* decision; *Gottes ~* decree of God.

Rätsel ['rɛːtsəl] *n* (7) riddle, puzzle; (*Geheimnis*) *a.* enigma, mystery; *er* (*es*) *ist mir ein ~* he (it) puzzles me; 'Ϙ**haft** puzzling; (*geheimnisvoll*) mysterious, enigmatical; '~**raten** *n* solving riddles; *fig.* speculation.

'Rats|herr *m* council(l)or; senator; '~**keller** *m* townhall-cellar restaurant, *Am.* rathskeller.

Ratte ['ratə] *f* (15) rat; ~**nfänger** ['~nfɛŋər] *m* rat-catcher; (*Hund*)

ratter; *von Hameln, a. fig.*: Pied Piper; '~**ngift** *n* rat-poison.

rattern ['ratərn] (29) rattle; *Motoren:* roar.

Raub [raup] *m* (3) robbery; (*Beute*) loot; *zo. u. fig.* prey; '~**bau** *m* ✔ ruinous exploitation; *~ treiben* ✔ exhaust the soil, ✗ rob a mine, *mit s-r Gesundheit* undermine one's health; '~**druck** *m* (3) pirate edition.

rauben ['~bən] (25) *v/t.* rob; (*a. fig.*) *j-m* et. *~* rob (*od.* deprive) a p. of a th.; *v/i.* commit robberies.

Räuber ['rɔybər] *m* (7) robber; (*Straßen*Ϙ) highwayman, brigand; '~**bande** *f* gang of robbers, *Am.* holdup gang; ~**ei** [~'rai] *f* (16) robbery; '~**geschichte** F *fig. f* cock-and-bull story; '~**hauptmann** *m* captain of brigands; '~**höhle** *f* den of robbers; 'Ϙ**isch** rapacious; ~**er Überfall** holdup.

Raub|fisch ['raup-] *m* fish of prey; '~**gier** *f* rapacity; 'Ϙ**gierig** rapacious; '~**mord** *m* murder and robbery; '~**mörder** *m* murderer and robber; '~**ritter** *m* robber-knight; '~**tier** *n* beast of prey, predacious animal; '~**überfall** *m* robbery, holdup; '~**vogel** *m* bird of prey; '~**zug** *m* raid.

Rauch [raux] *m* (3) smoke; *s. aufgehen;* '~**bombe** ✗ *f* smoke-bomb; 'Ϙ**en** (25) smoke; Ϙ *verboten!* No smoking!

'Raucher *m* (7), '~**in** *f* (16¹) smoker; '~**abteil** *n* smoking compartment.

Räucher|-aal ['rɔyçər-] *m* smoked eel; '~**faß** *eccl. n* censer; '~**hering** *m* smoked (*od.* red) herring; '~**kammer** *f* smoking-chamber; '~**kerze** *f* fumigating candle; '~**lachs** *m* smoked salmon; 'Ϙ**n** (29) smoke (-dry); *desinfizierend:* fumigate; (*wohlriechend machen*) perfume; ⊕ *Eichenmöbel:* fume; ~**stäbchen** ['~ʃtɛːpçən] *n* (6) joss stick.

'Rauch|fahne *f* trail of smoke; '~**fang** *m* chimney(-hood), flue; '~**fleisch** *n* smoked meat; 'Ϙ**ig** smoky; 'Ϙ**los** smokeless; '~**säule** *f* column of smoke; '~**tabak** *m* smoking tobacco; '~**vergiftung** *f* smoke poisoning; '~**verzehrer** *m* smoke consumer; '~**vorhang** ✗ *m* smoke-screen; '~**waren** *f/pl.* (*Pelzwaren*) furs; (*Tabakwaren*) tobacco products; '~**warenhändler** *m* furrier;

tobacconist; '~wolke *f* cloud of smoke.

Räude ['rɔydə] *f* (15) mange.

'**räudig** mangy, scabby; ~es *Schaf fig.* black sheep.

rauf [rauf] F *adv. s.* herauf(...), hinauf(...).

Rauf|bold ['raufbɔlt] *m* (3) brawler, ruffian, rowdy; '~e *f* (15) rack; '2en (25) *v/t.* pluck, pull; *s. Haar; sich* ~ = *v/i.* fight, scuffle (*um* for); ~erei [~fə'rai] *f* scuffle, fight; '~handel *m* brawl; '2lustig pugnacious.

rauh [rau] *allg.* rough; *Hals:* sore; *Stimme:* hoarse; *Ton, Behandlung:* harsh; (*grob*) coarse, rude; *fig.* die ~e Wirklichkeit the hard facts *pl.*; F *in* ~en Mengen lots of; '2bein F *n* rough diamond, *Am.* F roughneck; '~beinig *f* rough; 2eit ['~hait] *f* roughness, hoarseness, harshness, rudeness; ~en ['rauən] (25) roughen; *Tuch:* tease, nap; '2futter *n* roughage; '~haarig rough-haired, shaggy; '2reif *m* hoar-frost.

Raum [raum] *m* (3¹) room, space; (*Platz*) place; (*Zimmer*) room; (*Bereich*) area, zone; (*Welt2*) space; (*Abteil, Koffer2*) compartment; *s.* ~inhalt; *fig.* scope; ~ geben e-m Gedanken: give way to, e-r Hoffnung *usw.*: indulge in, e-r Bitte: grant.

Räum|boot ['rɔym-] *n* mine sweeper; '2en (25) clear; (*verlassen*) leave, *bsd.* ⚔ evacuate; *Wohnung:* quit, vacate; ⚔ *Lager:* clear; ⚔ *Minen:* sweep; *s. Weg.*

'**Raum|-ersparnis** *f* space saving; *der* ~ *wegen* to save room *od.* space; '~fähre *f* space shuttle; '~fahrt *f* space travel (*od.* flight); astronautics *pl.*; '~fahrt-industrie *f* aerospace industry; '~fahrtzentrum *n* space cent|re, *Am.*-er; '~forschung *f* (aero)space research; '~inhalt *m* volume, capacity; '~kapsel *f* space capsule; '~kreuzer *m* space cruiser; '~kunst *f* interior decoration; '~labor *n* space laboratory; '~lehre *f* geometry.

'**räumlich** (of) space; (*Ggs. zeitlich*) spatial; *opt.* stereoscopic; '2keit *f* spatiality; (*Raum*) space, room; ~en *pl. e-s Hauses:* premises.

'**Raum|mangel** *m* lack of space; '~maß *n* measure of volume; '~meter *n, a. m* cubic met|re, *Am.* -er; '~

patrouille *f* space patrol; '~pflegerin *f* charwoman, cleaner.

'**Räumpflug** *m* bulldozer.

'**Raum|schiff** *n* space-ship; '~schiffahrt *f s. Raumfahrt*; '~sonde *f* space probe; '~station *f* space station.

'**Räumung** *f* (16) clearing; ✝ clearance; *e-r Stadt:* evacuation; *e-r Wohnung:* quitting, *zwangsweise:* eviction; '~sbefehl ⚖ *m* eviction order; '~sklage ⚖ *f* action for eviction; '~sverkauf *m* clearance sale.

raunen ['raunən] *v/i. u. v/t.* (25) whisper, murmur.

Raupe ['raupə] *f* (15) caterpillar; '~nfahrzeug *n* tracked vehicle; '~nkette ⊕ *f* track; '~nschlepper *m* crawler tractor.

raus [raus] F *s. heraus*(...), hinaus (-...); *int.* ~! get out!

Rausch [rauʃ] *m* (3² u. ³) intoxication, drunkenness; *fig.* transport, ecstasy; e-n ~ haben be drunk; s-n ~ ausschlafen sleep it off; '2-arm low-noise; '2en (27, h. u. sn) *Blätter, Seide, Wald:* rustle; *Wasser, Wind:* rush; *Brandung, Sturm:* roar; *Beifall:* thunder; *fig.* (*schwungvoll gehen*) sweep; es rauscht im Radio there's interference on the radio; '2end rustling *usw.*; *Fest:* grand; *Musik:* swelling; '~filter *m Radio:* noise filter; '~gift *n* narcotic (drug), F dope; '~giftdezernat *n* narcotics squad; '~gifthandel *m* drug traffic; '~giftring *m* drugs ring; '~giftschieber F *m* (dope) dealer; '~giftsucht *f* drug addiction; '2giftsüchtig addicted to drugs; '2giftsüchtige *m, f* drug-addict; '~gold *n* tinsel.

räuspern ['rɔyspərn] (29): sich ~ clear one's throat.

rausschmeiß|en P ['rausʃmaisən] kick *a p.* out; '2er P *m* chucker-out, *Am.* bouncer.

Raute ['rautə] *f* (15) lozenge; *bsd.* A rhomb; ♀ rue; 2nförmig ['~nfœrmiç] rhombic.

Razzia ['ratsja] *f* (11¹ u. 16²) (police) raid *od.* round-up.

Reagenz|glas [re⁹a'gɛnts-] *n* test tube; ~papier *n* test paper.

re-a'gieren react (*auf acc.* upon); *fig.* (*u.* ⊕) *a.* respond (to).

Reaktion [re⁹ak'tsjoːn] *f* (16) reaction (*a. pol.*); *fig. a.* response; 2är [~tsjoˈnɛːr] 1. reactionary; 2. 2 *m* (3¹), ~ärin *f* (16¹) reactionary; ~sfähig-

keit *f* responsiveness; ⁊ reactivity; ♀**sschnell**: ~ *sein* have fast reactions.

Reaktor *phys.* [reˈʔaktɔr] *m* (8¹) reactor.

real [reˈʔɑːl] real; ♀**gymnasium** *n*, ♀**schule** *f* non-classical secondary school; ♀**ien** [~jən] *pl.* real facts; **~isieren** [~ʔaliˈziːrən] realize; ♀**ismus** [~ˈlismus] *m* (16) realism; ♀**ist** *m* [~ˈlist] (12), ♀**istin** *f* realist; **~istisch** [~ˈlistiʃ] realistic(ally *adv.*); ♀**ität** [~iˈtɛːt] *f* (16) reality; ♀**lohn** *m* real wages *pl.*

Rebe [ˈreːbə] *f* (15) vine; (*Ranke*) tendril.

Rebell [reˈbɛl] *m* (12), **~in** *f* rebel; ♀**ieren** [~ˈliːrən] (*a. fig.*) rebel; **~ion** [~ˈjoːn] rebellion; ♀**isch** [~ˈbɛliʃ] rebellious.

ˈ**Rebensaft** *m* grape-juice, wine.

Reb|huhn [ˈrɛp-] *n* partridge; **~laus** [ˈreːp-] *f* vine-louse, Ⓠ phylloxera; ˈ**~stock** *m* vine.

Rechen [ˈrɛçən] *m* (6) rake; ♀ *v/i. u. v/t.* (25) rake.

ˈ**Rechen|-anlage** *f* computer; ˈ**~aufgabe** *f*, ˈ**~exempel** *n* (arithmetical) problem; ˈ**~buch** *n* arithmetic-book; ˈ**~fehler** *m* miscalculation, mistake; ˈ**~kunst** *f* arithmetic; ˈ**~künstler** *m* arithmetician; ˈ**~lehrer**(**in** *f*) *m* teacher of arithmetic; ˈ**~maschine** *f* calculator; computer; ˈ**~schaft** *f*: ~ *ablegen* give (*od.* render) (an) account (*über acc.* of); *zur* ~ *ziehen* call to account (*wegen* for); *j-m* ~ *schuldig sein* be accountable to; ˈ**~schaftsbericht** *m* statement (of accounts), report; ˈ**~schieber** *m* slide rule; ˈ**~tabelle** *f* ready reckoner; ˈ**~zentrum** *n* computer cent|re, *Am.* -er.

Recherche(**n** *pl.*) [rəˈʃɛrʃə(n)] *f* (15) investigation.

rechn|en¹ [ˈrɛçnən] *v/t. u. v/i.* (26) reckon; calculate; ~ *auf* (*acc.*) count *od.* rely (up)on, (*erwarten*) expect; ~ *mit et.* *Zukünftigem* reckon with; ~ *unter* (*acc.*) *od.* zu reckon (*od.* rank) among; (*v/i.*) ~ *zu* rank with; ˈ♀**en²** *n* arithmetic; calculation; ˈ♀**er** *m* (7), ˈ♀**erin** *f* calculator, computer (*beide a. Gerät*); *er ist ein guter* ~ he is good at figures; ˈ**~erisch** arithmetic(al).

ˈ**Rechnung** *f* calculation; (*Aufstellung*) bill, account; (*Waren♀*) invoice; *im Gasthaus*: bill, *Am.*

check; *auf* ~ on account; *laut* ~ as per account; *e-e* ~ *begleichen* balance (*od.* settle) an account; ~ *führen* keep accounts; *auf* ~ *kaufen* buy on credit; ~ *legen* render (an) account (*über acc.* of); *e-r Sache* ~ *tragen* take a th. into account (*bei* in); *es geht auf m-e* ~ it is my treat; *auf s-e* ~ *kommen bei* find one's account in; *j-m in* ~ *stellen* place to a p.'s account; *et. in* ~ *stellen od. ziehen fig.* take into account; *die* ~ *ohne den Wirt machen* reckon without one's host; *s. Strich*; ˈ**~s-abschluß** *m* closing of accounts; ˈ**~sführer** *m* book-keeper, accountant; ⚔ pay sergeant; ˈ**~sführung** *f* accountancy, *Am.* accounting; ˈ**~s-hof** *m* Audit Office; ˈ**~sjahr** *n* financial year; ˈ**~slegung** *f* rendering of the account; ˈ**~s-prüfer** *m* auditor; ˈ**~swesen** *n* accounting; accountancy.

recht¹ [rɛçt] (*Ggs. link*) right; (*der Regel, den Wünschen gemäß*) right; (*gerecht*) just; (*schuldig*) due; (*echt, wirklich*) true, real; (*gesetzmäßig*) legitimate; (*richtig*) right, correct; (*geeignet, schicklich*) right, proper; *adv.* right, well; (*sehr*) very; (*ziemlich*) rather; ~*e Hand* right hand; *ein* ~*er Narr* a regular fool; ~*er Winkel* right angle; *zur* ~*en Zeit* at the right moment; *ganz* ~! quite (so)!, exactly!; *erst* ~ all the more; *nun erst* ~ *nicht* now less than ever; *das ist* ~ that is right; *mir ist es* ~ I don't mind, it is all right with me; *mir ist alles* ~ I am pleased with anything; *j-m* ~ *geben* agree with a p.; *es geht nicht mit* ~*en Dingen zu* there is something funny about it; *es geschieht ihm* ~ it serves him right; ~ *haben* be right; *es j-m* ~ *machen* please a p.; ~ *daran tun, zu inf.* do right to *inf.*; *das kommt mir gerade* ~ that comes in handy; ~ *gut* not bad; ~ *schade* a great pity; *s. behalten*.

Recht² [~] *n* (3) right; (*Anspruch; auf acc.*) title (to), claim (on); (*Vor-* ♀) privilege; (*Vollmacht*) power; (*Gesetz*) law; (*Gerechtigkeit*) justice; ~ *sprechen* administer justice; *mit* ~ justly; *von* ~*s wegen* by rights; *das* ~ *auf s-r Seite haben* be within one's rights; ⚖ *für* ~ *erkennen* adjudge; *zu* ~ *bestehen* be valid *od.*

justified; (*wieder*) zu s-m ~ kommen come into one's own (again).

'**Rechte** 1. *f* (18) right hand; *pol.the* Right; *Boxen*: right; 2. *pol. m,f* (18) rightist, right-winger.

'**Recht-eck** *n* (3) rectangle; '₂**ig** rectangular.

'**rechten** (26) dispute, argue; ~s lawfully, by law; (*gültig*) valid.

'**recht|fertigen** justify; (*verteidigen*) defend; vindicate; '₂**fertigung** *f* justification, vindication; '~**gläubig** orthodox; '₂**gläubigkeit** *f* orthodoxy; '₂**haber(in** *f*) *m* dogmatist; ₂**haberei** [~ha:bə'raɪ] *f* dogmatism; '~**haberisch** dogmatic(ally *adv.*); (*stur*) pigheaded.

'**rechtlich** legal, lawful; (*gerichtlich*) juridical; (*gültig*) valid; *s. redlich*; '₂**keit** *f* legality, lawfulness; honesty.

recht|linig ['~li:niç] rectilinear; '~**los** having no rights; '~**mäßig** lawful, legitimate; ₂**mäßigkeit** *f* lawfulness, legitimacy.

rechts [rɛçts] on the right; (*nach* ~) (to the) right.

'**Rechts|-anspruch** *m* legal claim; '~**anwalt** *m* lawyer, solicitor; *vor Gericht plädierender*: counsel, *Brt.* barrister-at-law, *Am.* attorney-at-law; '~'-**außen(stürmer)** *m* (6 [7]) *Fußball*: outside right; '~**befugnis** *f* competence; '~**behelf** *m* legal remedy; '~**beistand** *m* legal adviser; '~**belehrung** 🏛 *f* legal instruction; '~**beratungsstelle** *f* legal advisory board; '~**beugung** *f* perversion of justice; '~**bruch** *m* breach of law.

'**rechtschaffen** honest, righteous; '₂**heit** *f* honesty, righteousness.

'**Rechtschreibung** *f* orthography.

'**Rechts|drall** ⊕ *m* right-hand twist; '~**extremist(in** *f*) *m* right-wing extremist; '₂**fähig** having legal capacity; '~**fall** *m* (law) case; '~**frage** 🏛 *f* question of law; '~**gelehrte** *m* jurist, lawyer; '~**geschäft** *n* legal transaction; '~**grund** *m* legal argument; '₂**gültig** legal(ly valid); ~ *machen* validate; '~**gültigkeit** *f* legality; '~**gut-achten** *n* legal opinion; '~**händer** ['~hɛndər] *m* (7) right-hander; '~**hilfe** *f* legal aid; '~**kraft** *f* legal force; ~ *erlangen* enter into effect; '₂**kräftig** legal(ly binding), valid; *Urteil*: final; *Gesetz*: effective; '~**lage** *f* legal position; '~**mittel** *n* legal

remedy; (right to) appeal; '~**nach-folger** *m* successor in interest; '₂**orientiert** *pol.* right-wing; '~**pflege** *f* administration of justice; '~**pfleger** *m* judicial officer, paralegal.

Rechtsprechung [~ʃprɛçuŋ] *f* jurisdiction, administration of justice.

'**Rechts|radikale** *m* rightist; '~**schutz** *m* legal protection; '~**schutz-versicherung** *f* legal costs insurance; '~**sprache** *f* legal terminology; '~**spruch** *m* legal decision; *in Zivilsachen*: judg(e)ment; *in Strafsachen*: sentence; '~**staat** *m* constitutional state; '₂**staatlich** constitutional; '~**staatlichkeit** *f* rule of law; '~**stellung** *f* legal status; '~**streit** *m* action, lawsuit; '~**titel** *m* legal title; '₂'**um!** right face!; '₂-**unfähig** (legally) disabled; '~-**unfähigkeit** *f* (legal) disability; '₂'-**unwirksam** (legally) ineffective; '~'-**unwirksamkeit** *f* ineffectiveness; '₂**verbindlich** (legally) binding (*für* on); '~**verdreher** *m* pettifogging lawyer; '~**verfahren** *n* legal procedure; (*Prozeß*) (legal) proceedings *pl.*; '~**verkehr** *m*: *in Frankreich ist* ~ in France they drive on the right; '~**verletzung** *f* infringement; '~**weg** *m* course of law; *den* ~ *beschreiten* go to law; '₂**widrig** illegal; '~**widrigkeit** *f* illegality; '₂-**wirksam** *s. rechtskräftig*; '~**wissenschaft** *f* jurisprudence.

'**recht|wink(e)lig** right-angled, ⬚ rectangular; '~**zeitig** opportune, timely, well-timed, seasonable; *adv.* in time.

Reck [rɛk] *n* (3) horizontal bar.

Recke ['rɛkə] *m* (13) hero, warrior.

recken ['~n] (25) stretch; *mit Geräten*: a. rack; *den Hals* (*nach etl.*) ~ crane one's neck (to see a th.).

Redakt|eur [redak'tø:r] *m* (3¹) editor; ~**ion** [~'tsjo:n] *f Tätigkeit*: editorship; *Personal*: editorial staff; *Büro*: editorial office; (*Fassung*) editing, draft(ing); ₂**ionell** [~tsjo-'nɛl] editorial.

Rede ['re:də] *f* (15) speech; (*Ansprache*) a. address; (*~weise*) language; (*Gespräch*) conversation, talk; *s. fallen*; *gr. direkte* ~ direct speech; *s. halten, schwingen*; ~ (*und Antwort*) *stehen* give an account (*über acc.* of), answer (for); *die in* ~ *stehende Person* the person in question; *j-n zur* ~ *stellen* call to account (*über acc.* for), take *a p.* to task (*wegen gen.* for); *wovon ist die* ~? what are you talking about?; *davon kann keine* ~ *sein!* that's out of the question; (*aber*) *keine* ~! by no means!; *es ist nicht der* ~ *wert* it is not worth speaking of, (*macht nichts*) never mind!; '~**freiheit** *f* freedom of speech; '~**gabe** *f*, '~**ge- wandtheit** *f* eloquence; '2**ge- wandt** eloquent; '~**kunst** *f* rheto- ric; '2**n** (26) speak, talk (*mit* to); *mit sich* ~ *lassen* listen to reason; *von sich* ~ *machen* cause a stir; *j-m ins Gewissen* ~ appeal to a p.'s con- science; *du hast gut* ~ it is easy for you to talk; *s. Wort.*

'**Redens-art** *f* phrase, expression; (*Spracheigenheit*) idiom; (*sprich- wörtliche* ~) saying.

'**Rede**|**schwall** *m* flood of words; '~**teil** *m* part of speech; '~**wendung** *f s.* Redensart.

redigieren [redi'giːrən] edit.

redlich ['reːtliç] honest, upright; '2**keit** *f* honesty, probity, integ- rity.

Redner ['reːdnər] *m* (7) speaker (*a.* '~**in** *f*); *bsd. geschickter*: orator; '~**bühne** *f* platform; '2**isch** rhet- orical; '~**pult** *n* speaker's desk.

redselig ['reːtzeːliç] talkative, gar- rulous; '2**keit** *f* talkativeness.

reduzieren [redu'tsiːrən] reduce (*auf acc.* to); *sich* ~ be reduced.

Redu'**zierstück** ⊕ *n* adapter, reduc- er.

Reede ⚓ ['reːdə] *f* (15) roads *pl.*, roadstead; '~**r** *m* (7) shipowner; ~'**rei** *f* shipping company.

reell [re'ʔɛl] real; *Firma*: solid, re- spectable; *Preis, Bedienung*: fair; ~ *bedienen* (*bedient werden*) give (get) good value for one's money.

Reep ⚓ [reːp] *n* (3) rope.

Refer|**at** [refe'raːt] *n* (3) report; *Schule*: essay; (*Dienststelle*) (depart- mental) section; *ein* ~ *halten* (*ver- lesen*) read a paper; ~**endar** [~ren- 'daːr] *m* (3¹) junior barrister *attend- ing the courts and thus qualifying for the title of 'Assessor'*; law clerk; ~**ent** [~'rɛnt] *m* (12) official in charge (of a departmental section); (*Berichterstatter*) reporter; *parl. usw.* referee; (*Sachverständiger*) ex- pert; ~**enz** [~'rɛnts] *f* (16) refer- ence; 2**ieren** [~'riːrən] *v/t. u. v/i.*

report (*über acc.* on); (*give a*) lec- ture (on).

reffen ⚓ ['rɛfən] (25) reef.

reflektieren [reflɛk'tiːrən] *v/t. u. v/i.* reflect; ~ *auf* (*acc.*) have *a th.* in view, want (*od.* wish) to have.

Reflektor [re'flɛktɔr] *m* (8¹) re- flector.

Reflex [re'flɛks] *m* (3²) reflex; ~**be- wegung** *f* reflex action; ~**ion** [~'ksjoːn] *f* (16) (*Widerschein*) re- flex; (*Spiegelbild*) reflection; 2**iv** *gr.* [~'ksiːf] reflexive.

Reform [re'fɔrm] *f* (16) reform; ~**ation** [~a'tsjoːn] *f* reformation; ~**ator** [~'maːtɔr] *m* (8¹) reformer; 2**bedürftig** in need of reform; ~**bestrebungen** *f/pl.* reformatory efforts; ~**haus** *n* health (food) shop (*Am.* store); 2**ieren** [~'miːrən] re- form; ~**ierte** [~'miːrtə] *m* (18) mem- ber of the Reformed Church, Cal- vinist; ~**kost** *f* health food(s *pl.*).

Refrain [rə'frɛ̃] *m* (11) refrain, bur- den.

Regal [re'gaːl] *n* (3¹) shelves *pl.*; ~**brett** *n* shelf.

Regatta [re'gata] *f* (16²) regatta, boat-race.

rege ['reːgə] active, brisk; lively; *fig.* ~ *werden* be stirred up, arise.

Regel ['reːgəl] *f* (15) rule; (*Vor- schrift*) regulation; ♂ menses *pl.*; *in der* ~ as a rule; '~**getriebe** ⊕ *n* (*stufenloses* ~ infinitely) variable speed transmission; '2**los** irregular; (*unordentlich*) disorderly; '~**losig- keit** *f* irregularity; '2**mäßig** regular; (~ *wiederkehrend*) periodical; '~**mäßigkeit** *f* regularity; '2**n** (29) reg- ulate, ⊕ *a.* control; (*ordnen*) arrange, settle; (*steuern*) control; '2'**recht** reg- ular; '~**ung** *f* regulation, ⊕ *a.* con- trol; arrangement, settlement; con- trol; '2**widrig** irregular; *Sport*: foul; '~**widrigkeit** *f* irregularity; *Sport*: foul. [stir.\

regen[1] ['reːgən] (25, *a. sich* ~) move,/

Regen[2] [~] *m* (6) rain; *fig. vom* ~ *in die Traufe kommen* jump out of the fry- ing-pan into the fire; *saurer* ~ acid rain; '2-**arm** with low rainfall; '~**bogen** *m* rainbow; '~**bogenfarben** *f/pl.* colo(u)rs of the rainbow; '~**bo- genhaut** *anat. f* iris; '2**dicht** rain- proof.

regenerier|**en** [regenə'riːrən] re- generate; 2**ung** *f* regeneration.

Regenguß

'**Regen|guß** m downpour; '**~haut** f plastic mac; '**~mantel** m raincoat; '**~menge** f rainfall; '**~pfeifer** m Vogel: plover; '**Qreich** rainy; '**~schauer** m shower of rain; '**~schirm** m umbrella.

Regent [re'gɛnt] m (12), **~in** f (16¹) regent; **~schaft** f regency.

'**Regen|tag** m rainy day; '**~tropfen** m raindrop; '**~wasser** n rain-water; '**~wetter** n rainy weather; '**~wolke** f rainy cloud; '**~wurm** m earthworm; '**~zeit** f rainy season.

Regie [re'ʒiː] f (15) (a. thea.) management, (a. Film) direction; (Staatsmonopol) state monopoly, régie (fr.); ~ führen (bei) direct; **~assistent** m assistant director; **~fehler** m mistake in the arrangements; **~kosten** pl. overhead (expenses); **~pult** n Radio: mixing desk; TV: control desk.

regieren [re'giːrən] v/t. govern (a. gr.), rule; (leiten) control, manage; v/i. rule, reign (a. fig.).

Re'gierung f government, Am. (Präsident u. Kabinett; deren Amtszeit) administration; (~szeit) e-s Fürsten: reign; unter der ~ des ... under (od. in) the reign of ...; **~s...** mst governmental; **~s-antritt** m accession (to the throne); **~sbe-amte** m government official; **~s-erklärung** f policy statement; **~s-form** f form of government, regime; **~sgewalt** f governmental power; **~s-lager** n government benches pl.; **~smannschaft** f cabinet; **~s-partei** f ruling party; **~ssprecher** m government spokesman; **~swechsel** m change of government.

Regime [re'ʒiːm] n (11) regime; **~kritiker** m dissident.

Regiment [regi'mɛnt] n (3) rule; (1) ✕ regiment; das ~ haben od. führen rule, command; **~s...** regimental.

Region [re'gjoːn] f (16) region; **Qal** [~gjo'naːl] regional; **~alverkehr** m regional transport.

Regisseur [reʒi'søːr] m (3¹) thea. stage-manager od. -director; Film: director.

'**Regist|er** [re'gistər] n (7) register (a. der Orgel), record; (Inhaltsverzeichnis) index; ein ~ ziehen pull a stop; **~rator** [~'straːtɔr] m (8¹) recorder, registrar; **~ratur** [~stra-'tuːr] f (16) registry.

registrier|en [regis'triːrən] register (a. fig.); a. ⊕ record; **Qkasse** f cash-register; **Qung** f registration, recording.

Reglement [reglə'mã] n (11) regulation(s pl.).

Regler ⊕ ['reːglər] m (7) regulator; governor, control(l)er.

reglos ['reːkloːs] motionless.

regne|n ['reːgnən] (26) rain; es regnet in Strömen it is pouring with rain; **~risch** rainy.

Regreß [re'grɛs] m (4) recourse; **Qpflichtig** liable to recourse.

regsam ['reːkzaːm] active, quick, live; **Qkeit** f activity.

regulär [regu'lɛːr] regular.

regulier|bar [~'liːrbaːr] adjustable; **~en** regulate, adjust; **Qung** f regulation, adjustment.

Regung ['reːguŋ] f motion; (Gefühlsq) emotion; (Anwandlung) impulse; **Qslos** motionless.

Reh [reː] n (3) roe, deer; weibliches: doe.

rehabilitier|en [rehabili'tiːrən] rehabilitate; **Qung** f rehabilitation.

'**Reh|bock** m roebuck; '**~braten** m roast venison; '**Qfarben** fawn--colo(u)red; '**~geiß** f doe; '**~kalb** n, '**~kitz** n fawn; '**~keule** f leg of venison; '**~posten** m/pl. buck-shot; '**~rücken** m saddle of venison.

Reibahle ['raɪpʔaːlə] f reamer.

Reibe ['raɪbə] f (15), **Reibeisen** ['raɪpʔaɪzən] n grater.

reib|en ['raɪbən] (30) rub; (zer~) grate; Farbe: grind; (klein od. fein ~) pulverize; sich an j-m ~ quarrel with a p.; s. Nase, wund; **Qerei** [~ə-'raɪ] f (constant) friction, squabbling; '**Qung** f friction (a. fig.); '**Qungsfläche** f friction surface; '**~ungslos** frictionless; fig. smooth.

reich¹ [raɪç] rich (an dat. in); (vermögend) wealthy; (~lich) copious, ample; '**Qe** m, f (18) rich man (woman); die ~n pl. the rich.

Reich² [~] n (3) empire; (König q, a. Pflanzenq, Tierq) kingdom; rhet. od. fig. realm; hist. das Deutsche Reich the (German) Reich.

reichen ['raɪçən] (25) v/t. reach; j-m et.: reach, hand, pass; s. Hand, Wasser; v/i. reach (bis to); (genügen) suffice, do, last; das reicht! that will do!

reichhaltig ['~haltiç] rich; (über-

reich) abundant, copious; '♀**keit** _f_ richness; abundance, copiousness.

'**reichlich** _adj._ ample; abundant, copious, plentiful; _vor su._ plenty of; _adv._ (_ziemlich_) rather, fairly, pretty, F plenty.

'**Reichtum** _m_ (1²) riches _pl._, wealth; (_Überfluß_) opulence, abundance, wealth (_an dat._ of).

'**Reichweite** _f_ (15) reach; ✕, ≼ range; _in_ ～ within reach.

reif¹ [raɪf] ripe, mature (_beide a. fig._).

Reif² [～] _m_ (3, _o. pl._) (_Frost_) hoar-frost, white frost.

Reif³ [～] _m_ (3) hoop; ring.

'**Reife** _f_ (15) ripeness, maturity.

'**reifen**¹ _v/i._ (25) ripen, mature (_beide a. fig._); '～² _zu Reif_²: _es reift_ there is a hoar-frost _od._ white frost.

'**Reifen**³ _m_ (6) hoop; ring; (_Rad♀_) tire, _Brt. a._ tyre; '～**panne** _f_, '～**schaden** _mot. m_ puncture, _Am._ blowout; '～**wechsel** _m_ change of tire(s _pl._).

'**Reife|prüfung** _f_ leaving-examination, matriculation (examination); '～**zeugnis** _n_ (school-)leaving certificate, _Brt._ "A" level G.C.E. (= General Certificate of Education).

'**reiflich** mature, careful; _nach_ ～_er Überlegung_ upon mature reflection.

'**Reifrock** _m_ crinoline.

Reigen ['raɪɡən] _m_ (6) round dance; _fig._ _den_ ～ _eröffnen_ open the ball.

Reihe ['raɪə] _f_ (15) row; (_Linie_) line; _hintereinander_: file; _nebeneinander_: rank; (_Sitz♀_) row (of seats), tier; (_Folge_) series, succession; _von Bergen usw._: range; (_Anzahl_) number; _nach der_ ～, _der_ ～ _nach_ in turn, by turns; _ich bin an der_ ～ it is my turn; _aus der_ ～ _tanzen_ have it one's own way; _in Reih' und Glied_ in rank and file; _an die_ ～ _kommen_ have one's turn; '♀**n** (25) range, rank; _Perlen usw._: string; '～**nfertigung** _f_ serial production; '～**nfolge** _f_ succession, sequence; _alphabetische_ ～ alphabetical order; '～**nhaus** _n_ terrace house, _Am._ row (_od._ attached) house; '～**nschaltung** ⚡ _f_ series connection; '～**n-untersuchung** ⚕ _f_ mass examination; '♀**nweise** in rows.

Reiher ['raɪər] _m_ (7) heron.

Reim [raɪm] _m_ (3) rhyme; '♀**en** _v/t._, _v/i._, _v/refl._ (25) rhyme (_auf acc._ to, with); _nur v/refl. fig._ agree

68*

(with); '♀**los** blank, rhymeless; '～**schmied** _m_ rhym(est)er.

rein¹ [raɪn] **1.** _adj._ pure (_a. fig._); (_sauber_) clean; (_klar_) clear (_a. Haut, Gewissen_); _Gewinn_: net; _Wahrheit_: plain; (_bloß_) mere, sheer; _fig. die Luft ist_ ～ the coast is clear; ～ _machen_ clean (up); _fig._ ～_en Tisch machen_ make a clean sweep of it; _fig. j-m_ ～_en Wein einschenken_ tell a p. the plain truth; _ins_ ～_e bringen_ clear up, settle; _mit j-m ins_ ～_e kommen_ come to terms with a p.; _ins_ ～_e schreiben_ make a fair copy of; _fig._ ～_waschen_ whitewash; _s._ Gewissen, Mund; **2.** _adv._ (_gänzlich_) quite; ～ _gar nichts_ nothing at all; ～ _unmöglich_ quite impossible.

rein² [raɪn] F _s. herein_(...), _hinein_(...).

Reineclaude [rɛnə'kloːdə] ♀ _f_ (15) greengage.

'**Rein|-ertrag** _m_ net proceeds _pl._; '～**fall** F _m_ F letdown; F frost, sell, washout; '～**gewicht** _n_ net weight; '～**gewinn** _m_ net (_od._ clear) profit; '～**heit** _f_ purity; cleanness.

'**reinig|en** (25) clean, cleanse (_von_ of); _a. fig._ purify; _metall._ refine; _Wolle_: scour; _s. chemisch_; '♀**ung** _f_ clean(s)ing; _a. fig._ purification; ～ _und Färberei_ cleaners and dyers _pl._; '♀**ungs-anstalt** _f_ (dry) cleaners _pl._; '♀**ungsmittel** _n_ detergent, cleansing agent.

'**Reinkultur** _f_ pure culture (_a. fig._); _fig. in_ ～ unadulterated.

'**reinlegen** _s. hereinlegen._

'**reinlich** _P._: cleanly; _S._: clean; '♀**keit** _f_ cleanliness; neatness.

'**Rein|machefrau** _f_ cleaning woman, charwoman; '♀**rassig** pedigree(d), purebred; _Pferd_: thoroughbred; '～**schrift** _f_ fair copy; '♀**seiden** all-silk; '♀**waschen** _fig._ whitewash, clear.

Reis¹ [raɪs] _m_ (4, _o. pl._) rice; ～² _n_ (2) twig, sprig; (_Pfropf♀_) scion; '～**-auflauf** _m_ rice pudding; '～**brei** _m_ rice boiled in milk.

Reise ['raɪzə] _f_ (15) journey; ⚓, ≼ voyage; (_längere, bsd. Auslands♀_) travel; (_Rund♀_) tour; _mst. kürzere_: trip; (_Überfahrt_) passage; '～**-apotheke** _f_ tourist's (_od._ portable) medicine-case; '～**bekanntschaft** _f_ travel(l)ing acquaintance; '～**büro** _n_ tourist(s') office, travel agency, _Am._ tourist(s') bureau; '～**diplomatie**

pol. f shuttle-diplomacy; '**⌣fertig** ready to start; '**⌣fieber** *n* travel fever; '**⌣führer** *m* guide; *(Buch)* guide (-book); '**⌣gefährte** *m*, '**⌣gefährtin** *f* fellow-travel(l)er; '**⌣gepäck** *n* luggage, *Am.* baggage; '**⌣geschwindigkeit** *f* cruising speed; '**⌣gesellschaft** *f* tourist party; '**⌣handbuch** *n* guide(-book); '**⌣koffer** *m* trunk; *kleiner:* suitcase; '**⌣kosten** *pl.* travel(l)ing expenses; '**⌣kostenzuschuß** *m* travel(ling) allowance; '**⌣leiter** *m* courier; '**⌣lustig** fond of travel(l)ing; **⌣mobil** ['⌣mobiːl] *n* (3¹) camper, *Am.* mobile home; '**⌣müde** travel-weary; '**⌣n** (27, sn) travel, journey; ⌣ *nach* go to; ⌣ *über (acc.)* go by way of, go via; *wir* ⌣ *morgen* we (shall) start tomorrow; *fig. auf et.* ⌣ trade on; ✝ ⌣ in *(dat.)* travel in; '**⌣nde** *m, f* (18) (✝ commercial) travel(l)er; *in der Bahn usw.:* passenger; *(Vergnügungs*⌣*)* tourist; '**⌣paß** *m* passport; '**⌣prospekt** *m* travel brochure; '**⌣route** *f* route, itinerary; '**⌣scheck** *m* traveller's cheque, *Am.* traveler's check; '**⌣schreibmaschine** *f* portable typewriter; '**⌣schriftsteller** *m* travel writer; '**⌣tasche** *f* travel(l)ing (*od.* overnight) bag, holdall; '**⌣unterlagen** *f/pl.* travel documents; '**⌣veranstalter** *m* tour operator; '**⌣verkehr** *m* tourist traffic; '**⌣wecker** *m* travel(l)ing alarm (clock); '**⌣zeit** *f* tourist season; '**⌣ziel** *n* destination.

Reisig ['raɪzɪç] *n* (3) brushwood; '**⌣besen** *m* birch-broom.

'**Reiß**|'**⌣aus** *m:* ⌣ *nehmen* take to one's heels; '**⌣brett** *n* drawing-board; '**⌣en** **1.** (30) *v/t.* tear; *(zer*⌣*)* *a.* rip; *(zerren)* tug; *(ziehen)* pull; *(weg*⌣*)* snatch; *an sich* ⌣ seize, *Macht usw.: a.* usurp; *entzwei*⌣ tear (*od.* rip) in two; *sich* ⌣ *(ritzen)* scratch o.s. *(an dat.* with); *sich* ⌣ *um* scramble for; *s. Possen, Witz, Zote; v/i.* (sn) tear, burst, split; *Faden usw.:* break, snap; ⌣ *an (dat.)* tear at; *die Geduld riß mir* I lost (all) patience; *es reißt mir in ...* (*dat.*) I have racking pains in ...; **2.** ⌣ *n* (6) bursting, rending; *des Fadens:* break(ing); *in Gliedern:* acute pains *pl.*, *engS.* rheumatism; *Sport:* snatch; '⌣**end** rapid; *Tier:* rapacious; *Schmerz:* acute, violent; *s. Absatz;* '**⌣er** *m* thriller; box-office success; '**⌣feder** *f* drawing-pen; '**⌣**

festigkeit *f* tensile strength; '**⌣leine** *f* rip cord; '**⌣nagel** *m* drawing-pin, *Am.* thumbtack; '**⌣schiene** *f* T--square; '**⌣verschluß** *m* zip fastener, *bsd. Am.* zip(per); '**⌣wolle** *f* reprocessed wool; '**⌣zahn** *m* fang, canine tooth; '**⌣zeug** *n* drawing instruments *pl.*; '**⌣zwecke** *f s. Reißnagel.*

Reit... *mst* riding-...; '**⌣-anzug** *m* riding-habit; '**⌣bahn** *f* riding--ground.

reiten ['raɪtən] (30, sn) ride, go on horseback; '**⌣d** on horseback.

'**Reiter** *m* (7) rider, horseman; *Polizei,* ✗ trooper; *Kartei:* tab; **⌣ei** [⌣'raɪ] *f* cavalry, horse; '**⌣in** *f* (16¹) horsewoman.

'**Reit**|**gerte** *f* riding-whip; '**⌣hose** *f* (riding-)breeches *pl.*; '**⌣knecht** *m* groom; '**⌣kunst** *f* horsemanship; '**⌣peitsche** *f* riding-whip; '**⌣pferd** *n* saddle-horse; '**⌣schule** *f* riding--school; '**⌣sport** *m* equestrian sport; '**⌣stiefel** *m/pl.* riding-boots; '**⌣weg** *m* bridle-path.

Reiz [raɪts] *m* (3²) charm, attraction; *(Verlockung)* allurement; *(Erregung)* thrill, *störend:* irritation; *physiol.* stimulus; '**⌣bar** irritable, touchy; '**⌣barkeit** *f* irritability; '**⌣en** (27) irritate (*a.* ⚕ *entzünden*); *(aufreizen)* provoke; *(ärgern)* nettle; *(lokken)* entice, attract, tempt; *(bezaubern)* charm; *Kartenspiel:* bid; ⚕ *(anregen)* stimulate; *s. a. an*⌣; '**⌣end** charming, lovely; '**⌣husten** *m* dry cough; '**⌣los** unattractive; '**⌣mittel** *n* stimulus, incentive; ⚕ stimulant, *störend:* irritant; '**⌣stoff** ⚗ *m* irritant; '**⌣ung** *f* irritation (*a.* ⚗); provocation; *(Anregung)* stimulation; '**⌣voll** charming, attractive; fascinating; '**⌣wäsche** *f* F flimsies *pl.*, *mit Spitzen:* frillies *pl.*; '**⌣wort** *n* (1²) emotive word.

rekapitulieren [rekapituˈliːrən] recapitulate.

rekeln ['reːkəln]: *sich* ⌣ loll, lounge.

Reklamation [reklamaˈtsjoːn] *f* complaint; protest, objection.

Reklame [reˈklaːmə] *f* (15) advertising; propaganda, publicity; *prahlerische:* puff; *(Schaufenster*⌣ *u. fig.)* window-dressing; ⌣ *machen* advertise, *lebhaft:* F boost (*beide: für et. a th.*); '**⌣artikel** *m* advertising article; '**⌣büro** *n* advertising agency; **⌣chef** *m* advertising manager; **⌣**

~fachmann *m* advertising expert; **~feldzug** *m s.* Werbefeldzug; **~film** *m* advertising film; **~fläche** *f* advertising space; **~rummel** *m sl.* ballyhoo; **~trick** *m* advertising stunt; *s. a.* Werbe...

rekla'mieren *v/t.* claim; *v/i.* complain (*wegen* about).

rekognoszieren [rekɔgnɔs'tsiːrən] reconnoit|re, *Am.* -er.

rekonstru'ieren reconstruct.

Rekonvaleszen|t [rekɔnvalesˈtsɛnt] *m* (18), **~tin** *f* (16¹) convalescent; **~z** *f* (16) convalescence.

Rekord [re'kɔrt] *m* (3¹) record; *s.* aufstellen; **~besuch** *m* record attendance; **~ernte** *f* bumper crop; **~halter** *m*, **~-inhaber** *m* record holder; **~lauf** *m* record run; **~versuch** *m* record attempt; **~zeit** *f* record time.

Rekrut ⚔ [re'kruːt] *m* (12) recruit; **2ieren** [~kruˈtiːrən] ⚔ recruit; *sich* **~** *aus* be recruited from; **~ierung** [~'tiːruŋ] *f* recruitment.

Rektor ['rɛktɔr] *m* (8¹) headmaster, *Am.* principal; *univ.* rector, vice--chancellor, *Am.* president; **~at** [~to'raːt] *n* (3) headmaster's *etc.* office; headmastership; rectorship.

Relais [rə'lɛː] *n inv.* relay.

relativ [rela'tiːf] relative; **2ität** [~tiviˈtɛːt] *f* (16) relativity; **2satz** *gr.* [~'tiːf-] *m* relative clause.

Releg|ation [relega'tsjoːn] *f* expulsion; **2ieren** [~'giːrən] expel, send down.

Relief [rel'jɛf] *n* (11) relief.

Religion [reliˈgjoːn] *f* (16) religion; **~sbekenntnis** *n* (religious) profession; **~sfreiheit** *f* freedom of worship, religious liberty; **~sgemeinschaft** *f* religious community; **2slos** irreligious; **~s-unterricht** *m* scripture.

religi|ös [~'gjøːs] religious; **2osität** [~gjoziˈtɛːt] *f* religiousness.

Reling ⚓ ['reːliŋ] *f* (16) rail.

Reliquie [re'liːkvjə] *f* (15) relic; **~nschrein** *m* reliquary.

Reminiszenz [reminisˈtsɛnts] *f* (16) reminiscence.

Remis [rə'miː] *n* (*inv. od.* 16) *Schach:* draw.

Remise [re'miːzə] *f* (15) coach-house.

Remit|tenden [remi'tɛndən] *pl.* returns; **2'tieren** return, remit.

Remoulade(nsoße) [remu'laːdə-] *f* remoulade.

rempeln ['rɛmpəln] (29) jostle, bump (into).

Ren [reːn] *n* (3) reindeer.

Renaissance [rənɛˈsãs] *f* (15) renaissance.

Rendezvous [rãdeˈvuː] *n inv.* rendezvous (*a.* ⚔), date.

Rendite [rɛnˈdiːtə] ✝ *f* (15) yield.

reniten|t [reniˈtɛnt] refractory; **2z** *f* (16) refractoriness.

Renn|bahn ['rɛn-] (race-)course, race track; *mot.* speedway; **~boot** *n* race-boat; **2en** (30) *v/i.* (sn) *u. v/t.* run; (*wett~*) race, (*rasen*) *a.* dash, rush; *Messer usw. durch den Leib* **~** run one's knife *etc.* through; *s.* Verderben; **'~en** *n* running; (*Wett2*) race; (*Einzel2*) heat; *totes* **~** dead heat; *das* **~** *machen* win the race; *fig.* make the running; **'~er** F *m* (*Erfolg*) hit; ✝ front-runner product; **'~fahrer** *m* racing-driver; **'~lenker** *m am Fahrrad:* dropped handlebars *pl.*; **'~pferd** *n* race-horse; **'~platz** *m s.* Rennbahn; **'~platzbesucher** *m* race-goer; **'~rad** *n* racing bicycle, racer; **'~schi** *m* race ski; **'~schuh** *m* spike(d shoe); **'~sport** *m* racing; *the* turf; **'~stall** *m* racing--stud; **'~strecke** *f* course, (race) track, circuit; **'~tier** *n s.* Ren; **'~wagen** *m* racing-car.

Renom|mee [renɔ'meː] *n* (11) reputation; **2'mieren** boast, brag (*mit* of); **2'miert** renowned; **~'mist** *m* (12) braggart, boaster.

renovier|en [reno'viːrən] do up, renovate; *Innenraum:* redecorate; **2ung** *f* renovation; redecoration.

rentab|el [rɛn'taːbəl] profitable, paying, lucrative; **2ilität** [~tabili-'tɛːt] *f* (16) profitability; **2ilitätsgrenze** *f* breakeven point.

Rent|e ['rɛntə] (15) (*Alters2*) (old-age) pension; *Versicherung u. Börse:* annuity; (*Zins2*, *Pacht2*) rent; **'~enalter** *n* retirement age; **'~enbrief** *m* annuity bond; **'~en-empfänger(in** *f*) *m s.* Rentner; **'~enversicherung** *f* pension scheme; **~ier** [~'tjeː] *m* (11) man of private means; **2ieren** [~'tiː-rən] *v/refl.* pay, be profitable; **'~ner** *m* (7) (old age) pensioner.

Reorganis|ation [reˀɔrganiza-'tsjoːn] *f* reorganization; **2ieren** [~'ziːrən] reorganize.

Reparation [repara'tsjoːn] *f* reparation; **~en** *leisten* make reparations; **~szahlungen** *f/pl.* reparation payments.

Reparatur [~'tuːr] *f* (16) repair; *in* ~ under repair; **2bedürftig** in need of repair; **2fähig** repairable; **~kosten** *pl.* cost of repairs; **~werkstatt** *f* repair-shop.

repa'rieren repair, *Am. a.* fix.

repatriier|en [repatri'?iːrən] repatriate; **2ung** *f* repatriation.

Repertoire *thea.* [reperto'aːr] *n* (11) repertoire, repertory; **~stück** *n* stock-piece.

repetier|en [repe'tiːrən] repeat; **2-gewehr** *n* magazine rifle, répeater; **2-uhr** *f* repeater.

Replik 🙰 [re'pliːk] *f* (16) reply.

Report [re'pɔrt] *m* (3) report; ✝ contango.

Reportage [repɔr'taːʒə] *f* (15) reporting; report, (running) commentary, *Am. a.* coverage.

Reporter [re'pɔrtər] *m* (7) reporter.

Repräsent|ant [reprezen'tant] *m* (12), **~antin** *f* (16¹) representative; **~ation** [~ta'tsjoːn] *f* representation; **2ieren** [~'tiːrən] represent.

Repressalie [repre'saːljə] *f* (15) reprisal; **~n** *ergreifen* make reprisal(s) (*gegen* on).

repressiv [repre'siːf] repressive.

Reprodu|ktion [reproduk'tsjoːn] *f* reproduction; **2'zieren** reproduce.

Reptil [rep'tiːl] *n* (3¹ *u.* 8²) reptile.

Republik [repu'bliːk] *f* (16) republic; **~aner** [~bli'kaːnər] *m* (7), **2a-nisch** [~'kaːniʃ] republican.

requirieren [rekvi'riːrən] requisition.

Requisit [~'ziːt] *n* (5) requisite; *thea.* **~en** *pl.* properties *pl.*, F props; **~ion** [~zi'tsjoːn] *f* (16) requisition.

Reservat [rezɛr'vaːt] *n* (3) reservation; (*Recht*) prerogative.

Reserve [re'zɛrvə] *f* (15) reserve; **~fonds** *m* reserve-fund; **~offizier** *m* reserve officer; **~rad** *mot. n* spare wheel; **~speicher** *m* *Computer*: reserve memory.

reserv|ieren [~'viːrən] reserve; ~ *lassen* book; **~iert** *adj.* reserved (*a. fig.*); **2ist** [~'vist] *m* (12) reservist; **2oir** [~vo'aːr] *n* (11) reservoir.

Resid|enz [rezi'dɛnts] *f* (16) residence; **2ieren** [~'diːrən] reside.

Resign|ation [rezigna'tsjoːn] *f* res-ignation; **2ieren** [~'gniːrən] resign.

resolut [rezo'luːt] resolute.

Resonanz [rezo'nants] *f* resonance (*a. fig.*); **~boden** *m* sounding-board.

resozialisier|en [rezotsjali'siːrən] rehabilitate; **2ung** *f* rehabilitation.

Respekt [re'spɛkt] *m* (3), **2ieren** [~'tiːrən] respect; *s. verschaffen;* **2abel** [~'taːbəl] respectable; **2los** irreverent; **~losigkeit** irreverence; **~s-person** *f* person held in respect; *angesehene:* notability; **2voll** respectful; **2widrig** disrespectful.

Ressentiment [resãti'mã] *n* (11) resentment, grudge; prejudice.

Ressort [re'soːr] *n* (11) department; *das fällt nicht in mein* ~ that is not in my province.

Rest [rest] *m* (3¹) rest; ✝ balance; (*Über2*) remnant; (*Restbestand*) remainder; *bsd.* 🙰, 🙰 residue; (*Speise2*) left-over; *sterbliche* **~e** *pl.* mortal remains; F *j-m den* ~ *geben* finish a p.

Restaur|ant [resto'rã] *n* (11) restaurant; **~ation** *f* [~taura'tsjoːn] restoration; [~tora'tsjoːn] (*Lokal*) restaurant; **2ieren** [~tau'riːrən] restore.

'Rest|bestand *m* remainder; 🙰 residue; **2lich** remaining, residual; **2-los** complete, total; *adv. fig. a.* entirely, perfectly; **~risiko** *n* final risk; **~zahlung** *f* payment of balance.

Resul|tat [rezul'taːt] *n* (3) result; *Sport:* score; **2'tieren** result (*aus* from).

Resüm|ee [rezy'meː] *n* (11) résumé (*fr.*), summary; **2ieren** [~'miːrən] recapitulate.

retirieren [reti'riːrən] retreat.

Retorte [re'tɔrtə] *f* (15) retort; **~n-baby** *n* test-tube baby.

Retour... [re'tuːr] return.

rett|en ['retən] (26) save, rescue (*aus, vor dat.* from); (*befreien*) deliver; *Güter:* salvage; *j-m das Leben* ~ save a p.'s life; *sich* ~ save o.s., escape; **'2er** *m* (7) saver, deliverer; (*Heiland*) Savio(u)r.

Rettich ['retiç] *m* (3¹) radish.

Rettung ['retuŋ] *f* rescue; deliverance; (*Entkommen*) escape; (*Bergung*) salvage; *eccl.* salvation; *er ist m-e einzige* ~ he is my only hope; **'~s-aktion** *f* rescue operation; **'~s-anker** *m* sheet-anchor; **'~sboje** *f* life-buoy; **'~sboot** *n* life-boat; **'~s-gerät** *n* life-saving equipment *od.*

device; '⁓**sgürtel** *m* life-belt; '⁓**s- leine** *f* life-line; '⁊**slos** past help, irremediable, irretrievable; '⁓**s- mannschaft** *f* rescue party; '⁓**s- medaille** *f* life-saving medal; '⁓**s- ring** *m* life-belt; '⁓**sversuch** *m* res- cue attempt.

retuschieren [retu'ʃiːrən] retouch.

Reu|e ['rɔʏə] *f* (15) repentance (*über acc.* of), remorse (at); '⁊**elos** re- morseless; '⁊**en** *v/t.* (25): *et. reut mich* I am sorry about (*od.* for) a th.; *vgl. be⁓*; '⁊**evoll**, '⁊(müt)**ig** repentant, remorseful.

Revanche [re'vãʃə] *f* (15) revenge; **⁓partie** *f* return match.

revan'chieren: sich ⁓ take one's revenge; reciprocate (*mit e-r Gegen- gabe* with); *sich für et. ⁓* return.

Reverenz [reve'rɛnts] *f* (16) rev- erence.

Revers [re'vɛrs] *m* (4) bond; (*Er- klärung*) declaration; *e-r Münze:* reverse; (*Rockaufschlag*) lapel.

revidieren [revi'diːrən] revise; ✝ audit, check.

Revier [re'viːr] *n* (3¹) district; ⚔ dispensary; *s. Jagd⁊*, **⁓stube** ⚔ *f* sick room.

Revision [revi'zjoːn] *f* revision, revisal; ✝ auditing; ⚖ appeal (on a question of law); ⚖ **⁓ einlegen** lodge an appeal.

Revisor [⁓'viːzɔr] *m* (8¹) reviser, ✝ auditor.

Revol|te [re'vɔltə] *f* (15), ⚥'**tieren** revolt.

Revolution [revolu'tsjoːn] *f* revo- lution; **⁓är** [⁓jo'nɛːr] *m* (3¹), ⚥ *adj.* revolutionary.

Revolver [re'vɔlvər] *m* (7) revolver, *Am. a.* gun.

Revue [rə'vyː] *f* (15) review; *thea.* revue, musical show; **⁓ passieren lassen** pass in review.

Rezen|sent [retsɛn'zɛnt] *m* (12) critic, reviewer; ⚥'**sieren** review; **⁓sion** [⁓'zjoːn] *f* review; **⁓si'ons- exemplar** *n* reviewer's copy.

Rezept [re'tsɛpt] *n* (3) ⚕ prescrip- tion; (*Koch⁊*) recipe (*a. fig.*); **⁓ge- bühr** *f* prescription charge.

Rezeption [retsɛp'tsjoːn] *f im Hotel:* reception, *Am.* check-in desk.

re'zeptpflichtig ⚕: **⁓e Medikamente** prescription drugs.

Rezession ✝ [retsɛs'joːn] *f* (16) re- cession.

reziprok [retsi'proːk] reciprocal.

Rezi|tator [retsi'taːtɔr] *m* (8¹) re- citer; ⚥'**tieren** *v/t. u. v/i.* recite.

Rhabarber [ra'barbər] *m* (7) rhubarb. [sody.⟩

Rhapsodie [rapso'diː] *f* (15) rhap-⟩

rhein|isch ['raɪniʃ] of the Rhine- land; '⁊**wein** *m* Rhine wine, hock.

Rhetor|ik [re'toːrik] *f* (16) rhetoric; ⚥**isch** rhetorical.

rheumat|isch [rɔʏ'maːtiʃ] rheu- matic(ally *adv.*); ⚥**ismus** [⁓ma'tis- mus] *m* (16) rheumatism.

Rhinozeros [ri'noːtsərɔs] *n* (4¹ *od.* 14²) rhinoceros. [rhomb(us).⟩

Rhombus ['rɔmbus] *m* (16²)⟩

rhythm|isch ['rʏtmiʃ] rhythmical; ⚥**us** ['⁓mus] *m* (16²) rhythm.

'**Richt|-antenne** *f* directional aerial (*Am.* antenna); '⁓**beil** *n* execu- tioner's ax(e); '⁓**blei** *n* plummet; '⁓**block** *m* executioner's block.

richten ['riçtən] *v/t.* (26) set right, arrange, adjust; *Zimmer:* put in order, tidy; *Segel:* trim; *Uhr:* set; (*zu-, vorbereiten*) prepare; (*zu⁓, a.* ⚔) dress; (*ausbessern*) repair, fix; *Richter:* judge (*a. v/i.*); *Henker:* execute; *s. zugrunde;* **⁓ auf** (*acc.*) *Waffe usw.:* level (*od.* point, aim) at, *Augen:* fix on, *Aufmerksamkeit, Bemühungen:* direct to, concentrate on; **⁓ an** (*acc.*) *Bitte, Brief usw.:* address to, *Frage:* put to; *in die Höhe ⁓* raise, lift up; *sich ⁓ nach* conform to, act according to, (*sich orientieren*) take one's bearings from, *gr.* agree with, (*abhängen von*) depend on, (*bestimmt werden von*) be determined (*od.* governed) by; *ich richte mich nach Ihnen* I leave it to you.

'**Richter** *m* (7), '⁓**in** *f* judge; '⁓**amt** *n* judgeship; '⚥**lich** judicial; '⁓**- spruch** *m* judgment, sentence; '⁓**- stand** *m* judicature, *bsd. Am.* judi- ciary; *the* bench; '⁓**stuhl** *m* tri- bunal.

'**Richt|funk** *m* radio relay system; '⁓**geschwindigkeit** *mot. f* recom- mended speed.

'**richtig** right; (*einwandfrei*) correct; (*genau*) accurate; (*gehörig*) proper; (*geeignet*) suitable; (*wirklich, echt*) real, true; (*regelrecht*) regular; (*ge- recht*) just, fair; **⁓e** *Abschrift* true copy; **⁓e** *Zeit* proper time; **⁓ gehen** *Uhr:* be (*od.* go) right; **⁓ rechnen** calculate correctly; ~er *gesagt* ... rather; *das ist das* 2e *für dich* that's the thing for you; *das ist nicht ganz das* 2e F that's not quite the ticket; ~! right (you are)! quite (so)!; F *nicht ganz* ~ (*im Kopf*) not quite right in the head; '~**gehend** F *fig.* regular, real;'2**keit** f correctness; accuracy; justness; '~**stellen** put right, rectify.

'**Richt|linien** f/pl. guidelines; '~**maß** n ga(u)ge, standard; '~**platz** m s. *Richtstätte*; '~**preis** m standard price; '~**scheit** n level, ruler; '~**schnur** f plumb-line; *fig.* guiding principle; '~**schwert** n executioner's sword; '~**stätte** f place of execution; '~**strahl** m (radio) beam; '~**strahlantenne** f beam aerial (*Am.* antenna); '~**strahler** m (7) beam transmitter; s. *Richtantenne*.

'**Richtung** f direction; (*Weg*, *Kurs*) course, way; *fig. a.* line, (*Entwicklung*) trend; *in der Wissenschaft usw.*: school of thought; *politische* ~ line of policy, (*Ansicht*) political views *pl.*; *in gerader* ~ in a straight line; '~**s-anzeiger** *mot.* m direction indicator; '2**weisend** guiding.

'**Richt|waage** f level; '~**wert** m standard value.

Ricke ['rikə] f (15) doe.

rieb [ri:p] *pret. v.* reiben.

riechen ['ri:çən] v/t. *u.* v/i. (30) smell(*nach* of; *an dat.* at); (*schnuppern*) sniff; *gut* (*übel*) ~ smell good (bad); F *ich kann ihn nicht* ~ I can't stand him; *s.* Braten, Lunte.

Ried [ri:t] n (3) reed; (*Moor*) marsh.

rief [ri:f] *pret. v.* rufen.

Riefe ['ri:fə] f (15) channel, chamfer; *bsd. an Säulen*: flute; 2**ln** ['~fəln] (29) channel, chamfer; flute.

Riege ['ri:gə] f (15) section, squad.

Riegel ['ri:gəl] m (7) bar, bolt; (*Kleider*2) (clothes-)rack; *Seife*, *Schokolade*: bar; *fig.* e-n ~ *vorschieben* (*dat.*) put a stop to; '2**n** (29) bar, bolt.

Riemen ['ri:mən] m (6) strap, thong; (*Leib*2; ⊕ *Treib*2) belt; (*Gewehr*2) sling; ⊕ oar; '~**antrieb** m belt drive; '~**scheibe** ⊕ f (belt-) pulley.

Ries [ri:s] n (4, *als Maß nach Zahlen inv.*) *Papiermaß*: ream.

Riese ['ri:zə] m (13) giant.

rieseln ['ri:zəln] (29, h. *u.* sn) purl,

ripple; (*tröpfeln*) trickle; *es rieselt* it drizzles.

'**Riesen|-erfolg** m enormous success; F smash (hit); '2**groß**, '2**haft** s. *riesig*; '~**rad** n Ferris wheel; '~**schlange** f boa constrictor; '~**schritt** m: *mit* ~*en* with giant strides; '~**schwung** m *Turnen*: giant circle; '~**slalom** m giant slalom.

'**riesig** gigantic(ally *adv.*), collossal, huge, enormous; F (*mst adv.*) *fig. a.* immense(ly), tremendous(ly).

'**Riesin** f giantess.

riet [ri:t] *pret. v.* raten.

Riff [rif] n (3) reef.

riffeln ['rifəln] (29) s. *riefeln*; *Flachs*: ripple.

Rille ['rilə] f (15) groove.

Rind [rint] n (1) ox, cow; *pl.* (horned) cattle *sg.*

Rinde ['rində] f (15) ♀ bark; (*Brot*2) crust; (*Käse*2) rind; (*Gehirn*2) cortex.

'**Rinder|braten** m roast beef; '~**pest** f cattle-plague; '~**zunge** f neat's (*od.* ox) tongue.

'**Rind|fleisch** n beef; '~(s)**leder** n neat's leather, cow-hide; '~**vieh** n horned cattle; P *fig.* idiot.

Ring [riŋ] m (3) ring (*a.* ♀ *u.* *Boxen*); (*Kreis*, *a. fig.*) circle; *e-r Kette*: link; ♦ pool, *Am.* combine; '~**bahn** f circular railway; '~**buch** n ring (*od.* loose-leaf) binder; '~**buch-einlage** f loose-leaf pages *pl.*

Ringel ['riŋəl] m (7) ringlet, curl; '~**haar** n curled hair; '~**locke** f ringlet; '2**n** (29, *a. sich*) curl; '~**natter** f grass snake; '~**reihen** m, '~**tanz** m round dance; '~**taube** f ring-dove.

ring|en¹ ['riŋən] (30) v/i. wrestle (*a. fig. mit sich*, *e-m Problem* with); *weitS.* struggle (*um*, *nach* for); *nach Atem* ~ gasp for breath; *s. Tod*; v/t. *die Hände*, *Wäsche*: wring; '2**en²** n wrestling; *fig.* struggle; '2**er** m (7) wrestler.

'**Ring|finger** m ring-finger; 2**förmig** ['~fœrmiç] ring-shaped, annular; '~**kampf** m wrestling (match); '~**kämpfer** m wrestler; '~**mauer** f circular wall; '~**richter** m *Boxen*: referee; '~**sendung** f *Radio*: hook-up.

rings [riŋs] (*a.* ~ *um prp.*) around; '~**he'rum**, ~'**um**, '~**um'her** round about; (*überall*) everywhere.

Rinn|e ['rinə] *f* (15) (*Rille*) groove; (*Dach♀*) gutter, eaves *pl.*; (*Leitungs♀*) conduit; (*Wasser♀*) gully; (*Kanal*) canal; '♀en (30): **a**) (sn) run, flow; (*tröpfeln*) drip, trickle; **b**) (h.) (*lecken*) leak; **∼sal** ['∼za:l] *n* streamlet, rill; '**∼stein** *m* gutter; *Küche*: sink.

'**Rippchen** *n* (6) rib of pork.

Rippe ['ripə] *f* (15) rib (*a.* ⚕, ♉); ⚕ groin; *mot.*, ♉ fin; *Schokolade*: bar; '♀n (25) rib.

'**Rippen|fell** *anat. n* pleura; '**∼fellentzündung** *f* pleurisy; '**∼stoß** *m* dig in the ribs; *heimlicher*: nudge.

'**Rippe(n)speer** *m* spare rib (of pork).

Rips [rips] *m* (4) *Stoff*: rep.

Risiko ['ri:ziko] *n* (11) risk; *auf eigenes ∼* at one's own risk; *ein ∼ eingehen* take (*od.* run) a risk; **∼zuschlag** *m* risk allowance.

risk|ant [ris'kant] risky; **∼ieren** [∼'ki:rən] risk.

Rispe ♉ ['rispə] *f* (15) panicle.

Riß [ris] **1.** *m* (4) rent, tear; (*Spalte*) crevice, fissure (*a.* ⊕); (*Sprung*) crack; (*Schramme*) scratch; (*Zeichnung*) draft, plan, sketch; *fig. in der Freundschaft usw.*: rupture; (*Spaltung*) split, schism; *Risse pl. in der Haut*: chaps; **2.** ♀ *pret. v. reißen* 1.

rissig ['risiç] cracked, fissured; *Haut, trockener Boden*: chappy; *∼ werden* crack.

Rist [rist] *m* (3²) *des Fußes*: instep; *der Hand*: wrist.

Ritt [rit] **1.** *m* (3) ride; **2.** ♀ *pret. v. reiten.*

'**Ritter** *m* (7) knight; (*Kämpe*) champion; *j-n zum ∼ schlagen* dub a p. a knight, knight a p.; *arme ∼ pl.* (*Speise*) fritters; '**∼burg** *f* knight's castle; '**∼gut** *n* manor; '♀**lich** knightly; *fig.* chivalrous; '**∼lichkeit** *f* gallantry, chivalry; '**∼orden** *m* knightly order; '**∼schaft** *f* knights *pl.*; (*Eigenschaft*) knighthood; '**∼schlag** *m* knighting, dubbing; '**∼sporn** ♉ *m* larkspur; '**∼tum** *n* (1, *o. pl.*) chivalry.

rittlings ['∼liŋs] astride (*auf dat. a th.*).

'**Rittmeister** *hist. m* captain of horse, (cavalry) captain.

Ritual [ritu'a:l] *n* (3¹), **rituell** [∼'εl] ritual.

Ritus ['ri:tus] *m* (16² *u. inv.*) rite.

Ritz [rits] *m* (3²), '**∼e** *f* (15) fissure, crevice, rift; (*Schramme*) scratch;

'♀en (27) scratch.

Rival|e [ri'va:lə] *m* (13), **∼in** *f* (16¹) rival; ♀i'**sieren** [∼vali-] rival; **∼ität** [∼i'tε:t] *f* (16) rivalry.

Rizinusöl ['ri:tsinus⁹ø:l] *n* castor oil.

Robbe ['rɔbə] *f* (15) seal; '♀n ✕ crawl; '**∼nfang** *m* sealing.

Robe ['ro:bə] *f* gown; (*Amts♀*) robe.

Roboter ['ro:bɔtər] *m* (7) robot; '**∼technik** *f* robot technology.

robust [ro'bust] robust, sturdy.

roch [rɔx] *pret. v. riechen.*

röcheln ['rœçəln] (29) gasp.

Roche(n) ['rɔxə(n)] *m* (6) ray.

rochieren [rɔ'ʃi:rən] *v/i. u. v/t. Schach*: castle (one's king); *v/i. Sport*: switch positions.

Rock [rɔk] *m* (3³) coat; (*Jacke*) jacket; (*Damen∼*) skirt; '**∼en** *m* (6) distaff.

Rodel|bahn ['ro:dəlba:n] *f* toboggan-slide; '♀n (29, *h. u.* sn), '**∼schlitten** *m* luge, toboggan.

rod|en ['ro:dən] (26) *Wurzeln*: root out, stub up; *Wald, Land*: clear, stub; '♀**ung** *f* clearing.

Rogen ['ro:gən] *m* (6) (hard) roe; '**∼er** *m* (*weiblicher Fisch*) spawner.

Roggen ['rɔgən] *m* (6) rye.

roh [ro:] (*unverarbeitet*) raw; *Diamant, Entwurf*: rough; *Öl, Metall* (*a. fig. primitiv*) crude; ✝ (*brutto*) gross; *fig.* rough, rude; brutal; *mit ∼er Gewalt* with brute force; '♀**bau** *m* carcass; outside finish; '♀**baumwolle** *f* raw cotton; '♀**bilanz** ✝ *f* trial balance; '♀-**eisen** *n* pig-iron.

Roheit ['∼hart] *f* rawness; (*Rauheit, a. fig.*) roughness; *fig.* rudeness, brutality.

'**Roh|-erzeugnis** *n* raw product; '**∼faser** *f* crude fib|re, *Am.* -er; '**∼fassung** *f* (*Entwurf*) rough draft; '**∼gewicht** *n* gross weight; '**∼gewinn** *m* gross profit; '**∼gummi** *m* crude rubber; '**∼kost** *f* raw diet, uncooked (vegetarian) food; '**∼köstler(in** *f*) *m* vegetarian, fruitarian; '**∼leder** *n* rawhide; '**∼ling** *m* (3¹) brute, ruffian; *metall.* slug; *Gießerei*: blank; '**∼material** *n* raw material; '**∼metall** *n* crude metal; '**∼öl** *n* crude oil; '**∼produkt** *n* raw product.

Rohr [ro:r] *n* (3) (*Schilf♀*) reed; (*Bambus♀*) cane; ⊕ (*Röhre*) tube, pipe; (*Kanal*) duct; ✕ barrel; '**∼bruch** *m* pipe burst.

Röhrchen ['rø:rçən] *n* (6) *für Alko-*

holtest: breathalyzer; *j-n ins ~ blasen lassen* give a p. a breathalyzer.

Röhre ['rø:rə] *f* (15) tube; (*nur Leitungs~*) pipe; ⊕ duct; *Radio usw.*: valve, *Am.* tube; (*Brat~*) oven; '2**n** *zo.* (25) *Hirsch*: bell; '2**nförmig** tubular; '~**nhosen** *f/pl.* F drainpipe trousers.

Rohr|krepierer ['~krepi:rər] *m* (7) ✕ barrel burst; *fig. Idee, Plan*: non--starter; '~**leger** *m* pipe-layer, plumber; '~**leitung** *f* conduit; *im Haus*: plumbing; (*Fernleitung*) pipeline; '~**post** *f* pneumatic post; '~**schelle** *f* pipe clamp; '~**schlange** ⊕ *f* spiral tube, coil; '~**spatz** *m* reed--bunting; F *schimpfen wie ein ~* rant and rave; '~**stock** *m* cane; '~**stuhl** *m* cane(-bottomed) chair; '~**zange** *f* pipe-wrench; '~**zucker** *m* cane--sugar.

'**Roh|seide** *f* raw silk; '~**stahl** *m* crude steel; '~**stoff** *m* raw material; '~**zucker** *m* unrefined sugar.

'**Rolladen** *m* roller blind.

'**Roll|bahn** ✈ *f* runway; '~**brett** *n* skateboard.

Rolle ['rɔlə] *f* (15) roll; (*Walze, Welle*) roller; (*Draht~, Tau~*) coil; (*Spule*) reel; *am Flaschenzuge*: pulley; *unter Möbeln*: cast|or, *Am.* -er; (*Wäsche~*) mangle; *~ Stoff* bolt of cloth; (*Liste*) list, register; *thea. u. fig.* part, rôle; *e-e ~ spielen* play a part (*a. fig. bei, in dat.* in), *fig. a.* figure (in); *das spielt keine ~* that makes no difference; *Geld spielt keine ~* money is no object; *fig. aus der ~ fallen* forget o.s., misbehave.

'**rollen** (25) *v/i.* (h. *u.* sn) *u. v/t.* roll; *auf Rädern*: wheel; ✈ taxi; 📷 *~des Material* rolling stock; *fig. ins* 2 *bringen* (*od. kommen*) get underway.

'**Rollen|besetzung** *thea. f* cast; '~**lager** *n* roller bearing; '~**spiel** *psych. n* role-playing; '~**tausch** *m fig.* exchange of roles.

'**Roller** *m* (7) motor-scooter; *für Kinder*: scooter; *Sport*: daisy-cutter; (*Vogel*) roller.

'**Roll|feld** ✈ *n* taxiway; runway; '~**film** *phot. m* roll-film; '~**kommando** *n* raiding squad; '~**kragen**(**pullover**) *m* turtle-neck, polo-neck; '~**mops** *m* collared herring; '~**schrank** *m* roll-fronted cabinet; '~**schuh** *m* roller-skate; '~**schuhbahn** *f* skating-rink; '~**schuhläufer** *m* rol-

ler-skater; '~**stuhl** *m* wheelchair; '~**treppe** *f* escalator; '~**wagen** *m* truck.

Roman [ro'mɑ:n] *m* (3[1]) novel, (work of) fiction; (*Ritter~ u. fig.*) romance; ~**dichter**(**in** *f*) *m* novelist; ~**en** *pl. the* Romanic peoples; 2**haft** romantic(ally *adv.*), fictitious; ~**held** *m* hero of a novel; 2**isch** Romanic; *von Sprachen oft*: Romance; ~**ist** [~ma'nist] *m* (12) Romance scholar *od.* student; ~**literatur** *f* fiction; ~**schriftsteller**(**in** *f*) *m* novelist.

Romant|ik [~'mantik] *f* (16) romanticism; ~**iker** *m* romanticist; 2**isch** romantic(ally *adv.*).

Romanze [~'mantsə] *f* (15) romance (*a. fig.*).

Röm|er ['rø:mər] *m* (7) Roman; (*Pokal*) rummer; '2**isch** Roman.

Rommé [rɔ'me:] *n* (11) rummy.

röntgen ['rœntgən] (25) 📷 X-ray; '2 *n* (*Einheit*) roentgen; '2**-apparat** *m* X-ray apparatus; '2**-assistent**(**in** *f*) *m* radiographer; '2**-aufnahme** *f*, '2**bild** *n* X-ray picture, radiograph; '2**bestrahlung** *f*, '2**behandlung** *f* X-ray treatment; 2**ologe** [~o'lo:gə] *m* (13) radiologist; 2**ologie** [~olo'gi:] *f* (15, *o. pl.*) radiology; '2**schirm** *m* (fluorescent) screen; '2**strahlen** *m/pl.* Roentgen (*od.* X-)rays *pl.*; '2**-untersuchung** *f* X-ray examination.

rosa ['ro:za] pink; *fig.* rose-col-o(u)red.

Rose ['ro:zə] *f* (15) rose; 🌿 *the* rose, 🔲 erysipelas; *s. Fenster~, Kompaß~*.

'**Rosen|busch** *m* rose-bush; '~**garten** *m* rosery; '~**kohl** *m* Brussels sprouts *pl.*; '~**kranz** *eccl. m* rosary; ~'**montag** *m* monday before Lent; '~**öl** *n* attar (of roses); '2**rot** rose--colo(u)red, rosy; '~**stock** *m* rose--tree.

Rosette [ro'zɛtə] *f* (15) rosette.

'**rosig** rosy (*a. fig.*).

Rosine [ro'zi:nə] *f* (15) raisin; *große ~* plum; *kleine ~* currant; F (*große*) *~n im Kopf haben* have high-flown ideas.

Rosmarin 🌿 [rɔsma'ri:n] *m* (3[1]) rosemary.

Roß [rɔs] *n* (4) horse; *rhet.* steed; *hoch zu ~* mounted on horseback; *fig. sich aufs hohe ~ setzen* mount the high horse; '~**arzt** *m* veterinarian.

Rösselsprung ['rœsəlʃpruŋ] *m Schach*: knight's move.

Roß|haar *n* horsehair; '**~kastanie** *f* horse-chestnut; '**~kur** *f* drastic cure.

Rost[1] [rɔst] *m* (3) rust; ~[2] (*Feuer*♀) grate; (*Brat*♀) gridiron, grill; '♀-**beständig** rust-resistant, rust-proof; '**~braten** *m* roast joint.

'**Röstbrot** *n* toast.

rosten ['rɔstən] (26, h. *u.* sn) rust; *nicht ~d Stahl usw.*: *s.* rostfrei.

rösten ['røːstən] (26) roast; *Brot*: toast.

'**rost|frei** rustless, rustproof; *bsd. Stahl*: stainless; '**~ig** rusty.

'**Röstkartoffeln** *f/pl.* fried potatoes.

'**Rost|schutzmittel** *n* anticorrosive agent; '**~umwandler** *m* (7) rust converter.

rot [roːt] **1.** *adj.* red (*a. pol.*); ♀es Kreuz Red Cross; F ~ *sehen* see red; (*wie*) *ein ~es Tuch für j-n* a red rag to a p.; ~ *werden im Gesicht*: redden, flush, *verlegen*: blush; **2.** ♀ *n* (3) red; (*Schminke*) rouge.

Rotation [rota'tsjoːn] *f* (16) rotation; **~sdruck** *typ. m* rotary printing; **~smaschine** *f* rotary press.

'**rot|blond** sandy; '**~braun** reddish brown; '♀**buche** ♀ *f* copper-beech; '♀**dorn** ♀ *m* pink hawthorn; '♀**e** *pol. m* Red.

Röt|e ['røːtə] *f* (15) redness, red colo(u)r; '**~el** *m* (7) red chalk; '**~eln** ⚘ *pl.* German measles; '♀**en** (26, *a. sich*) redden, flush.

'**Rot|fuchs** *m* (red) fox; (*Pferd*) bay (*od.* sorrel) horse; '♀**gelb** reddish yellow; '♀**glühend** red-hot; '**~glut** *f* red heat; '♀**haarig** red-haired; '**~haut** *f* redskin.

rotieren [ro'tiːrən] rotate.

Rot|käppchen ['~kɛpçən] *n* Red Riding Hood; **~kehlchen** ['~keːl-çən] *n* (6) robin (redbreast); '**~lauf** ⚘ *m* erysipelas; *vet.* red murrain.

rötlich ['røːtliç] reddish.

Rot|schwänzchen ['~ʃvɛntsçən] *n* (6) redstart; '**~stift** *m* red pencil; '**~tanne** *f* spruce.

Rotte ['rɔtə] *f* (15) gang (*a. b.s.*); '**~nführer** *m v. Arbeitern*: foreman.

'**Rot|wein** *m* red wine; *französischer*: claret; '**~welsch** *n* thieves' cant; '**~wild** *n* red deer.

Rotz [rɔts] *m* (3²) P snot; *vet.*

glanders *pl.*; '♀**ig** P snotty; *vet.* glandered; '**~nase** P *f* snot-nose (*a. als Schimpfwort*).

Rouge [ruːʒ] *n* (11) rouge, blusher.

Roulade [ru'laːdə] *f* (15) *Küche*: meat-roll, *Am.* roulade (*a. ♪*).

Rouleau [ru'loː] *n* (11) roller-blind.

Roulett(e *f*) [ru'lɛt] *n* (3 *od.* 11) roulette.

Route ['ruːtə] *f* (15) route.

Routin|e [ru'tiːnə] *f* (15), ♀**emäßig** *adj.* routine; ♀**iert** [~ti'niːrt] experienced.

Rübe ['ryːbə] *f* (15) rape; *weiße* ~ white beet, turnip; *rote* ~ red beet, beetroot; *gelbe* ~ carrot.

Rubel ['ruːbəl] *m* (7) rouble.

'**Rübenzucker** *m* beet sugar.

rüber F ['ryːbər] *s.* herüber(...), hinüber(...).

Rubin [ru'biːn] *m* (3¹) ruby.

Rubrik [ru'briːk] *f* (16) heading, rubric; (*Spalte*) column.

'**Rübsamen** *m* rape-seed.

ruch|bar ['ruːxbaːr]: ~ *werden* become known, get about *od.* abroad; '**~los** wicked, infamous, foul; '♀-**iosigkeit** *f* wickedness, profligacy.

Ruck [ruk] *m* (3) jerk, *Am.* F yank; (*Stoß*) shock, jolt (*a. fig.*); *auf 'ei-nen* ~ at one go; *sich e-n* ~ *geben* pull o.s. together; '♀-**artig** jerky; *adv.* (*plötzlich*) of a sudden.

'**Rück|-ansicht** *f* back view; '**~-an-spruch** *m* recourse; '**~-antwort** *f* reply; *Postkarte mit* ~ reply post-card; *Telegramm mit bezahlter* ~ reply-paid; ♀**bezüglich** *gr.* reflex-ive; '**~blende** *f*, '**~blendung** *f* *Film*: flashback; '♀**blenden** *Film*: cut back; '**~blick** *m* retrospect(ive view), glance back; '♀**datieren** backdate.

rücken[1] ['rykən] (25) *v/t.* move; (*schieben*) shift; *v/i.* (sn) move; (*Platz machen*) move over; *näher* ~ draw near, approach; *im Range höher* ~ rise; *an j-s Stelle* ~ take a p.'s place; *nicht von der Stelle* ~ not to budge (an inch); *s. Leib.*

Rücken[2] [~] *m* (6) back (*a. Buch*♀, *Hand*♀, *Messer*♀ *usw.*); (*Berg*♀) ridge; (*Nasen*♀) bridge; ⚘ rear; *hinter j-s* ~ behind a p.'s back; *j-m in den* ~ *fallen* attack a p. from the rear, *fig.* stab a p. in the back; *j-m den* ~ *stärken* stiffen a p.'s back; *s. kehren*; '**~deckung** *f* ⚔

rear cover; *fig.* backing; '~**flug** ✠ *m* inverted flight; '~**lage** *f* supine position; '~**lehne** *f* back(-rest); '~**mark** *n* spinal marrow *od.* cord; '~**schmerzen** *m/pl.* pain in the back, aching back *sg.*; '~**schwimmen** *n* back-stroke; '~**wind** *m* tail wind; '~**wirbel** *anat. m* dorsal vertebra.

'**Rück|-erstattung** *f* restitution; *v. Geld*: refund; *v. Kosten*: reimbursement; '~**fahrkarte** *f* return(-ticket), *Am.* round-trip ticket; '~**fahrt** *f* return (journey *od.* trip); '~**fall** *m* relapse; *e-s Verbrechers*: a. recidivism; '♀**fällig** relapsing; ⚕ *a.* recidivous; ~ **werden** (have a) relapse; '~**fenster** *n* rear window; '~**flug** ✠ *m* return flight; '~**fracht** *f* return freight; '~**frage** *f* further inquiry, check-back; '~**führung** *f in die Heimat*: repatriation; '~**gabe** *f* return; restitution; '~**gang** *m* (*Rückweg*) return; *fig.* decline, retrogression; ✝ *der Geschäfte*: recession; *der Produktion*: falling-off; ♀**gängig** ['~gɛŋɪç] retrograde; ✝ declining; ~ **machen** undo, *Auftrag usw.*: cancel; '~**gewinnung** *f* recovery; '~**grat** *n* spine, (*a. fig.*) backbone; '♀**gratlos** *fig.* spineless; '~**griff** *m* recourse (*auf acc.* to); '~**halt** *m* support; '♀**haltlos** unreserved, frank; '~**hand(schlag** *m*) *f Tennis*: backhand (stroke); '~**kampf** *m Sport*: return match; '~**kauf** *m* repurchase; (*Einlösung*) redemption; '~**kaufswert** *m* surrender value; '~**kehr** *f* (16), ~**kunft** ['~kunft] *f* (14¹) return; '~**kopplung** *f Radio*: feedback; '~**lage** *f* reserve(s *pl.*); '~**lauf** ⚒ *m* recoil; '♀**läufig** *s.* rückgängig; '~**licht** *mot. n* rear (*od.* tail) light; '♀**lings** backwards; (*von hinten*) from behind; '~**marsch** *m* march back *od.* home; (*Rückzug*) retreat; ~**nahme** ['~na:mə] *f* taking back; '~**paß** *m Sport*: back pass; '~**porto** *n* return postage; '~**prall** *m* rebound; '~**reise** *f* return journey; '~**ruf** *m* recall.

Rucksack ['rukzak] *m* rucksack, *Am.* backpack; '~**tourismus** *m* backpacking.

'**Rück|schau** *f s.* Rückblick; '~**schlag** *m* backstrike; *fig.* setback, reaction, reverse; *des Gewehrs*: kick; '~**schluß** *m* conclusion, inference; '~**schritt** *m* step back; *fig. a.* retrogression, regress; *pol.* reaction; '♀**schrittlich** reactionary; '~**seite** *f* back, reverse; *e-r Münze*: tail; '~**sendung** *f* return; '~**sicht** *f* respect, regard, consideration; ~ **nehmen** *auf* (*acc.*) have regard for *a p.*, to (*od.* for) *a th.*; (*in Betracht ziehen*) make allowance for; *ohne* ~ *auf* (*acc.*) without regard to *od.* for, without respect to, irrespective of; *mit* ~ *auf* (*acc.*) with regard to, considering; '~**sichtnahme** *f* considerateness, consideration (*auf acc.* of, for); '♀**sichtslos** regardless (*gegen* of), inconsiderate; (*unbekümmert*) reckless; (*unbarmherzig*) ruthless; '~**sichtslosigkeit** *f* lack of consideration, inconsiderateness; recklessness; '♀**sichtsvoll** regardful (*gegen* of, for); considerate; '~**sitz** *m* back-seat; '~**spiegel** *mot. m* rear-view mirror; '~**spiel** *n Sport*: return match; '~**sprache** *f* consultation; ~ **nehmen mit** consult with; *nach* ~ *mit* … on consultation with; '~**stand** *m* (*Zahlungs♀*) arrears *pl.*; (*Arbeits♀*) backlog; ⚕ residue; *im* ~ **sein mit** be behind with; '♀**ständig** in arrears (*mit* with); *Ansicht*: backward, antiquated; ~e *Miete* arrears *pl.* of rent; '~**ständigkeit** *f* backwardness; '~**stau** *mot. m* tailback; '~(**stell**)**taste** *f* back spacer; '~**stoß** *m* repulsion; *e-r Schußwaffe*: recoil, kick; '~**strahler** *mot. m* (7) rear reflector; '~**strom** ⚡ *m* reverse current; '~**taste** *f* back spacer; '~**tritt** *m* withdrawal, retreat; *vom Amt*: resignation; '~**trittbremse** *f Fahrrad*: backpedalling brake; *Am.* coaster brake; '~**trittsgebühr** *f* cancellation charge (*od.* fee); '~**trittsklausel** *f* cancellation clause; '~**übersetzung** *f* retranslation; '♀**vergüten** refund; '~**vergütung** *f* refund, reimbursement; '~**versicherung** *f* reinsurance; ♀**wärtig** ['~vɛrtɪç] rear(ward); '♀**wärts** back, backward(s); '~**wärtsgang** *mot. m* reverse (gear); '~**wechsel** ✝ *m* redraft; '~**weg** *m* way back, return.

'**ruckweise** by jerks, by fits and starts.

'**rück|wirkend** reacting; ⚕ retroactive; ~ *ab* backdated to; '♀**wirkung** *f* reaction; (*Auswirkung*) repercussion; '~**zahlbar** repayable;

rühren

'~zahlen repay; '2zahlung f repayment; '2zieher m Fußball: overhead kick; F fig. climbdown; e-n ~ machen back down; '2zoll m (customs-) drawback; '2zollgüter n/pl. debenture goods; '2zug m retreat; '2zugsgefecht n running fight.

Rüde[1] ['ry:də] m (13) large hound; male dog od. fox od. wolf; 2² rude.

Rudel ['ru:dəl] n (7) herd, troop; Wölfe, U-Boote: pack.

Ruder ['ru:dər] n (7) oar; (Steuer2) rudder, helm; ✗ control surface; fig. am ~ at the helm; ans ~ kommen come into power; '~boot n row (-ing)-boat; '~er m (7) rower, oarsman; '~fahrt f row; '~in f oarswoman; '~klub m rowing club; '2n (29) v/i. (h. u. sn) u. v/t. row; '~n n (6) rowing; '~pinne f tiller; '~regatta f boat race, regatta; '~sport m rowing (sport).

Ruf [ru:f] m (3) call; (Schrei) cry, shout; (Berufung) summons, univ. call; (Leumund) reputation, repute; ✝ standing, credit; (Ruhm) fame; in gutem (schlechtem) ~e stehen be well (ill) reputed; im ~e e-s ... stehen be reputed to be a ...; '2en v/t. u. v/i. (30) call; (schreien) cry, shout (alle: um, nach for); den Arzt: call (in); ~ lassen send for; es kommt mir wie gerufen that comes in handy. [rimand.}
Rüffel F ['ryfəl] m (7), '2n (29) rep-}
Ruf|mord m character assassination; '~name m Christian (od. first) name; '~nummer teleph. f call-number; '~weite f: in ~ within call od. earshot; '~zeichen n Radio usw.: call-sign(al).

Rüge ['ry:gə] f (15) reproof, censure, reprimand; '2n (25) reprove; censure, denounce.

Ruhe ['ru:ə] f (15) rest, repose; (Stille, Schweigen) quiet, silence; (Frieden) peace, innere: a. peace of mind; (Gelassenheit) calm(ness), composure; ~ und Ordnung peace (od. law) and order; ~ vor dem Sturm lull before the storm; ewige ~ eternal peace; in aller ~ very calmly, (gemütlich) leisurely; ~ bewahren keep quiet, nervlich: keep cool; sich zur ~ begeben go to rest; lassen Sie mich in ~! let me alone!; j-m keine ~ lassen give a p. no rest; sich zur ~ setzen retire; immer mit

der ~! take it easy!; ~! silence!, be quiet!; '2bedürftig in need of rest; '~bett n couch; '~gehalt n (retiring) pension; '~kissen n pillow; '~lage ⊕ f s. Ruhestellung; '2los restless; '~losigkeit f restlessness; '2n v/i. u. v/t. (25) rest, fig. a. sleep; (stillstehen) be at a standstill; ɫʰ̵ be in abeyance; ~ auf (dat.) a. fig. rest on (a. Blick), be based on; er ruhte nicht, bis he could not rest till; hier ruht here lies; er ruhe in Frieden! may he rest in peace!; laß die Vergangenheit ~! let bygones be bygones!; '~pause f break, breather; (ruhige Zeit) lull; '~platz m resting-place; '~punkt m rest; bsd. ♪ pause; ⊕ fulcrum; '~stand m retirement; in den ~ versetzen superannuate, retire, pension off; im ~ retired; vorzeitiger ~ early retirement; in den ~ treten retire; '~stätte f place of rest; letzte ~ fig. last resting-place; '~stellung f normal position, ⊕ a. neutral (od. idle) position; '~störer(in f) m disturber of the peace, peace--breaker, rioter; '~störung f disturbance, riot; '~strom ⚡ m closed--circuit current; '~tag m day of rest; '~zeit f time of rest.

ruhig ['ru:iç] quiet (a. Farbe, ✝ Markt); (still, schweigend) silent; (friedlich) peaceful, tranquil, calm (a. See); (nervlich ~) calm, cool; (beruhigt) reassured; (gemächlich) leisurely (a. adv.); adv. (ohne weiteres) easily, well; ⊕ ~er Gang smooth running; ~e Sache sl. soft job; ~ bleiben keep one's temper; tu das ~! go right ahead; ~ verlaufen be uneventful.

Ruhm [ru:m] m (3) glory; (Berühmtheit) fame; '2bedeckt covered with glory; '~begier(de) f thirst for glory.

rühmen ['ry:mən] (25) praise, extol; sich ~ boast (e-r Sache of a th.); sich e-r Sache ~ können (besitzen) boast a th.; '~swert praiseworthy.

'Ruhmesblatt n page of glory.

rühmlich ['ry:mliç] glorious; (löblich) laudable.

'ruhm|los inglorious; **~redig** ['~re:diç] boastful, vainglorious; '~voll glorious.

Ruhr [ru:r] f (16) dysentery.

Rührei ['ry:r'ʔaɪ] n scrambled eggs.

rühren ['ry:rən] (25, a. sich ~) stir,

move; *Kochkunst*: stir, *Eier*: beat; (*innerlich* ~, *ergreifen*) touch, move (*zu Tränen* to tears); ~ *an* (*acc.*) touch; (*her*)~ *von* come from; *fig.* *sich* ~ be active; *sich nicht* ~ not to budge, *fig.* make no move; *keinen Finger* ~, *keine Hand* ~ not to stir a finger; *das rührte ihn wenig* it left him cold; ✗ *rührt euch!* (stand) at ease!; *s.* *Donner, Trommel*; '~d touching, moving, affecting.

rührig ['ry:riç] active, busy; (*unternehmend*) enterprising; (*flink*) nimble; '♀keit *f* activity; enterprise; nimbleness.

'**Rühr|löffel** *m* (pot-)ladle; '♀selig sentimental; '~stück *thea.* *n* melodrama.

'**Rührung** *f* emotion.

Ruin [ru'i⁹i:n] *m* (3) ruin; (*Verfall*) decay; ~e *f* (15) ruin(s *pl.*); ♀ieren [~'ni:rən] *allg.* ruin (*sich o.s.*).

Rülps(er) ['rylps(ər)] *m* (4) belch. '**rülpsen** (27) belch.

Rum [rum] *m* (3¹ *u.* 11) rum.

rum F [rum] *s.* *herum*(...).

Rumän|e [ru'mɛ:nə] *m* (13), ~**in** *f* (16¹), ♀**isch** Ro(u)manian.

Rummel ['ruməl] *m* (7) (*Getöse, Tumult*) hurly-burly, racket; (*Geschäftigkeit*) bustle; (*Aufheben*) stir, F to-do; (*Reklame*♀) ballyhoo; *s.* ~**platz**; F *der ganze* ~ the whole bag of tricks; ✝ *im* ~ in the lump; F *den* ~ *kennen* know what's what; '~**platz** *m* amusement park.

rumoren [ru'mo:rən] (25) make a noise; *fig.* rumble.

Rumpel|kammer ['rumpəl-] *f* lumber-room; '♀n (29) rumble.

Rumpf [rumpf] *m* (3³) trunk, body; *e-r Statue u. fig.*: torso; (*Schiffs*♀) hull; ✈ body, fuselage.

rümpfen ['rympfən] (25): *die Nase* ~ turn up one's nose, sniff (*über acc.* at).

Rumpsteak ['rumpste:k] *n* (11) rumpsteak, *Am.* porterhouse steak.

rund [runt] *allg.* round (*a. fig.* *Summe usw.*); (*kreisförmig*) circular; (*kugelförmig*) spherical; *Absage usw.*: plain, flat; *adv.* (*etwa*) about, in round figures; ~ *um die Welt* round the world; '♀**bau** *m* circular building; '♀**blick** *m* view round, panorama; '♀**bogen** *m* round arch.

Runde ['rundə] *f* (15) *allg.* round (*a. Boxen*; *a. Bier usw.*); *Renn-,* *Luftsport*: lap; (*Gesellschaft*) party; *in der* (*od. die*) ~ (a)round; *die* ~ *machen Wächter*: make (*od.* go) one's rounds, *Neuigkeit usw.*: go the round; '♀n (26, *a. sich*) round; *fig.* round off.

'**Rund|-erlaß** *m* circular (notice); '♀**-erneuern** *Reifen*: retread; '~**fahrt** *f* drive round *a town etc.*; (circular) tour; '~**fahrt-auto** *n* sight-seeing car; '~**flug** ✈ *m* circuit; *um die Welt*: round-the-world flight; '~**frage** *f* inquiry (by questionnaire *od.* circular), poll.

'**Rundfunk** *m* broadcast(ing), radio; *als Einrichtung*: broadcasting system; *durch* ~ *verbreiten* broadcast; *im* (*od. durch*) ~ on (*od.* in) the radio, on (*od.* over) the air; *im* ~ *auftreten od. sprechen* speak over the radio, *Am.* be (*od.* go) on the air; '~**ansager** *m* (radio) announcer; '~**bericht** *m* radio report; '~**empfänger** *m*, '~**gerät** *n* (radio) receiver, radio set, *Brt. a.* wireless set; '~**gesellschaft** *f* broadcasting company, *Am.* radio corporation; '~**hörer(in** *f*) *m* listener; '~**programm** *n* radio program(me); '~**rechte** *n/pl.* broadcasting rights; '~**sender** *m* broadcast transmitter; *s. a.* *Rundfunkstation*; '~**sendung** *f* broadcast; program(me); '~**sprecher** *m* broadcaster; '~**station** *f* broadcasting (*od.* radio) station; '~**übertragung** *f* broadcasting, radio transmission; *einzelne*: broadcast.

'**Rund|gang** *m* circuit, tour; (*bsd.* ✗) round; '~**gesang** *m* roundelay, glee; '♀**he'raus** plainly, bluntly, point-blank; '♀**he'rum** round about; '~**holz** *n* round timber; '~**lauf** *m* (*Turngerät*) giant('s) stride; '♀**lich** round(ish); (*dicklich*) plump, F roly-poly; '~**reise** *f* circular tour *od.* trip, round trip; '~**reisekarte** *f* circular (tour) ticket, tourist ticket, *Am.* round-trip ticket; '~**schau** *f* panorama; (*Zeitung*) review; '~**schreiben** *n* circular (letter); '~**strecke** *f* circuit; ♀**um** all (a)round; '~**ung** *f* roundness; F curve; '♀**weg** flatly, plainly; '~**zange** *f* (*eine a pair of*) round-nose(d) pliers *pl.*

Rune ['ru:nə] *f* (15) runic letter, *pl.* runes; '~**nschrift** *f* runic characters *pl.*; '~**nstab** *m* runic wand.

Runge ['ruŋə] *f* (15) stake, stanchion.

Runkel ['ruŋkəl] *f* (15), '~rübe *f* beet(root).

Runzel ['runtsəl] *f* (15) wrinkle.

'**runz(e)lig** wrinkled.

'**runzeln** (29) wrinkle; *die Stirn* ~ knit one's brows, frown.

Rüpel ['ry:pəl] *m* (7) lout; '⌀haft loutish, rude.

rupfen ['rupfən] (25) *Huhn usw.*: pluck (*a. fig. j-n*); (*ausrupfen*) pull up; *fig. j-n*: fleece; *s. Hühnchen.*

ruppig ['rupiç] unkempt, ragged; (*schäbig*) shabby; *fig.* rude, gruff.

Rüsche ['ry:ʃə] *f* (15) ruche, frill, ruffle; '~nkragen *m* ruffle collar.

Ruß [ru:s] *m* (3²) soot.

Russ|e ['rusə] *m* (13), '~in *f* (16¹), '⌀isch Russian.

Rüssel ['rysəl] *m* (7) proboscis; *des Elefanten*: *a.* trunk; *des Schweins*: snout.

ruß|en ['ru:sən] (27) soot, blacken; *v/i.* smoke; '~ig sooty.

rüsten ['rystən] (26) *v/t.* prepare (*auf acc., zu* for); *bsd.* ⚔ arm; *s. aus~; v/i.* (*a. sich*) prepare, get ready (*zu* for).

Rüster ⚲ ['ry:stər] *f* (15) elm.

rüstig ['rystiç] vigorous, strong, well-preserved; *er ist (für sein Alter) noch recht* ~ he bears his years well; '⌀keit *f* vigo(u)r.

'**Rüstung** *f* preparation(s *pl.*); (*Bewaffnung*) arming, armament; (*Harnisch*) armo(u)r; '~s-**abbau** *m* arms reduction; '~s-**ausgaben** *f/pl.* defen|ce (*Am.* -se) expenditure *sg.*; '~s-**fabrik** *f* war (*od.* armament) factory; '~s-**industrie** *f* arms industry; '~s-**kontrolle** *f* arms control; '~sstopp *m* arms freeze; '~swettlauf *m* armament race.

'**Rüstzeug** *n* (set of) tools; *fig.* (*geistiges* mental) equipment.

Rute ['ru:tə] *f* (15) rod; (*Gerte*) switch; *zum Züchtigen*: rod, birch (rod); *anat.* penis; *hunt.* (*Schwanz, bsd. des Fuchses*) brush; *j-m die* ~ *geben* whip (*od.* flog) a p.

Rutengänger ['~ngɛŋər] *m* (7) dowser, diviner.

Rutsch [rutʃ] *m* (3²) slide, glide; '~bahn *f*, '~e *f* slide, (*a. Güter⌀, Wasser⌀*) chute; '⌀en (27, sn) glide, slide; (*aus~; entgleiten*) slip; *Fahrzeug*: skid; '⌀fest *Reifen*: anti-skid; *Sohle*: non-slip; '⌀ig slippery.

rütteln ['rytəln] *v/t. u. v/i.* (29) shake, jog; ⊕ vibrate; *Wagen*: jolt; ~ *an der Tür* rattle at, *fig.* assail, shake; *daran ist nicht zu* ~ that's a fact; *gerüttelt(es) Maß* good measure (of).

S

S [ɛs], **s** *n inv.* S, s.

Saal [zɑ:l] *m* (3³) hall.

Saat [zɑ:t] *f* (16) (*Säen*) sowing; (*Same*) seed; (*sprossende Pflanzen*) standing (*od.* growing) crops *pl.*; '~gut *n* seed (-grain); '~krähe *f* rook; '~zeit *f* seed-time.

Sabbat ['zabat] *m* (3) Sabbath; '~schändung *f* Sabbathbreaking.

sabbern ['zabərn] (29) drivel, slaver, *Am.* drool; (*schwatzen*) twaddle.

Säbel ['zɛ:bəl] *m* (7) sab|re, *Am.* -er; *fig. mit dem* ~ *rasseln* rattle the sabre; '~beine *n/pl.* bow-legs; '⌀beinig bow-legged; '~hieb *m* sword-cut; '⌀n (29) sab|re, *Am.* -er.

Sabot|age [zabo'tɑ:ʒə] *f* (15) sabotage; ~age-**akt** *m* act of sabotage; ~eur [~'tø:r] *m* (3¹) saboteur; ⌀ieren [~'ti:rən] sabotage.

Sacharin [zaxa'ri:n] *n* (3¹) saccharin(e).

'**Sach|be-arbeiter(in** *f*) *m* referee; *engS.* competent official; *in der Sozialpflege*: case worker; '~beschädigung *f* damage to property; '~beweis *m* material evidence; '⌀bezogen relevant, *pred.* to the point; '~bezüge *m/pl.* remuneration *sg.* in kind; '~bücher *n/pl.* non-fiction *sg.*; '~darstellung 🏛 *f* statement of facts; '⌀dienlich relevant, pertinent.

Sache ['zaxə] *f* (15) thing; (*Angelegenheit*) affair, matter, business, concern; (*Thema, Gebiet*) subject;

(*Punkt*) point; (*Streitfrage*) issue; (*Fall*) case; ⚖ case, (a. *weitS.*) cause; *s.* gemeinsam; (*nicht*) zur ~ (*gehörig*) (ir)relevant, *pred. a.* to (off) the point; *bei der* ~ *bleiben* stick to the point; *bei der* ~ *kommen* come to the point; *er versteht s-e* ~ he knows his job; *ganz. bei der* ~ *sn* be all attention; *nicht bei der* ~ *sn* be absent-minded; *s-r* ~ *sicher sein* be sure of one's ground; *das tut nichts zur* ~ that makes no difference; *es ist seine* ~ it is his business (*zu inf.* to *inf.*); *die* ~ *ist die, daß* ... the point is that ...; *s-e* ~ *gut* (*schlecht*) *machen* acquit o.s. well (ill); F *mit 100* ~*n mot.* with sixty (miles per hour); '~n *f/pl.* (*Waren, Gepäck usw.*) things, belongings, luggage, clothes, *etc.*

'Sach|frage *f* practical issue; '⚖fremd ⍩rrelevant; '~gebiet *n* subject, field; '~gemäß, '⚖gerecht proper(ly *adv.*), appropriate(ly); '~katalog *m* subject catalog(ue); '~kenner *m*, '~kundige ['~kundigə] *m* expert; '~kenntnis *f* special (*od.* expert) knowledge, experience; '⚖kundig *s.* sachverständig; '~lage *f* state of affairs, position; '~leistung *f* performance in kind.

'sachlich factual, real; (*zur Sache gehörig*) pertinent, relevant, *pred.* to the point; (*unparteiisch*) unbias(s)ed, impartial; *a.* 🜊 practical; (*Ggs. subjektiv*) objective; (*nüchtern*) matter-of-fact, businesslike, unemotional; *aus* ~*en Gründen* for technical reasons; ~ *richtig* factually correct.

sächlich ['zɛçlɪç] neuter.

'Sachlichkeit *f* objectivity; impartiality; matter-of-factness; realism.

'Sach|register *n* (subject) index; '~schaden *m* damage to property; *es entstand ein* ~ *von* ... the material damage amounted to ...

Sachse ['zaksə] *m* (13), Sächsin ['zɛksɪn] *f* (16[1]), 'sächsisch Saxon.

'Sachspende *f* gift in kind.

sacht(e) ['zaxt(ə)] soft, gentle; (*langsam*) slow; (*vorsichtig*) cautious, gentle; ~! gently!; F (*immer*) ~! take it easy!, come, come!

Sach|verhalt ['~fɛrhalt] *m* (3) facts *pl.* (of the case); *s. a. Sachlage*; '~vermögen *n* tangible property; '⚖verständig expert(ly *adv.*), com-

petent(ly); '~verständige *m*, *f* expert; '~verständigengut-achten *n* expert opinion; '~walter *m* advocate; (*Anwalt*) solicitor; (*Treuhänder*) trustee; (*Vertreter*) agent; '~wert *m* real value; *konkret:* ~*e pl.* material assets *pl.*

Sack [zak] *m* (3[3]) sack, bag; *anat., zo.* sac; *mit* ~ *und Pack* with bag and baggage; *s. Katze*.

Säckel ['zɛkəl] *m* (6) purse.

sacken ['zakən] (25) 1. *v/t.* sack, put into sacks; 2. *v/i.* (sn) (*sinken*) sink, give way, sag.

'Sack|gasse *f* blind alley; *fig.* impasse, deadlock; '~hüpfen *n*, '~laufen *n* sack-race; '~leinwand *f* sacking, burlap; '~pfeife *f* bagpipe; '~tuch *n* sacking; (*Taschentuch*) pocket-handkerchief.

Sadis|mus [za'dismus] *m inv.* sadism; ~t *m* (12) sadist; ⚖tisch sadistic.

säen ['zɛːən] *v/t. u. v/i.* (25) sow.

Safari [za'faːri] *f* (11[1]) safari; ~park *m* safari park, wildlife reserve.

Safe [seːf] *m*, *n* (11) safe; ~knacker ['~knakər] *m* (7) safe-breaker, *sl.* cracksman.

Saffian ['zafjaːn] *m* (3[1]) morocco (leather).

Safran ['zafraːn] *m* (3[1]) saffron; '⚖gelb saffron(-colo[u]red).

Saft [zaft] *m* (3) juice; *bot.* sap (a. *fig.*); *ohne* ~ *und Kraft* wishy-washy; '⚖ig juicy, succulent; (*kraftvoll*) sappy; *fig. Witz usw.*: juicy, spicy; *Niederlage:* crushing; *Ohrfeige:* resounding; '⚖los sapless; juiceless.

Sage ['zaːgə] *f* (15) legend, myth; (*Überlieferung*) tradition; *es geht die* ~ *the* story goes.

Säge ['zɛːgə] *f* (15) saw; '~blatt *n* saw-blade; '~bock *m* saw-horse, *Am. a.* sawbuck; '~fisch *m* sawfish; '⚖förmig sawlike, serrate(d); '~mehl *n* sawdust.

sagen ['zaːgən] (25) say; (*mitteilen*) tell; *j-m* ~ *lassen* send a p. word; *ich habe mir* ~ *lassen, daß* I have been told that; *ich muß schon* ~ I dare say; *sich* ~, *daß* ... tell o.s. that ...; *sich nichts* ~ *lassen* take no advice; *er läßt sich nichts* ~ he will not listen to reason; *das will* (*nicht*) ~ ... that is (not) to say ...; *es ist nicht gesagt, daß* ... that doesn't necessarily mean that ...;

unter uns (gesagt) between you and me (and the bedpost); das hat nichts zu ~ that doesn't matter; ~ wollen mit mean by; j-m gute Nacht ~ bid a p. good night; laß dir das gesagt sein let it be a warning to you; gesagt, getan no sooner said than done; etwas (nichts) zu ~ haben bei have a (no) say in; man sagt, er sei krank they say he is ill; schwer zu ~ hard to tell; sage und schreibe no less than; ~ wir (mal) say.

sägen ['zɛːɡən] v/t. u. v/i. (25) saw.

'sagen|haft legendary, mythical; F fig. fantastic, fabulous; '⦵kreis m legendary cycle.

Säge|späne ['~ʃpɛːnə] m/pl. sawdust sg.; '~werk n saw-mill.

Sago ['zɑːɡo] m (11) sago.

sah [zɑː] pret. v. sehen.

Sahne ['zɑːnə] f (15) cream; '~bonbon m, n toffee, toffy, Am. taffy; '~käse m cream cheese; '~quark m high-fat curd cheese; '~torte f layer cake.

sahnig ['zɑːniç] creamy.

Saison [sɛ'zɔ̃] f (11¹) season; ~arbeit(er m) f seasonal work(er); ~ausverkauf m seasonal sale; ⦵bedingt, ⦵mäßig seasonal; ~schwankungen f/pl. seasonal fluctuation sg.

Saite ['zaɪtə] f (15) string, chord; s. aufziehen; '~n-instrument n stringed instrument.

Sakko ['zako] m (11) lounge jacket; '~anzug m lounge suit.

sakral [za'krɑːl] sacral (a. anat.).

Sakrament [zakra'mɛnt] n (3) sacrament.

Sakrist|an [zakri'stɑːn] m (3¹ u. ³) sexton; ~ei [~'staɪ] f (16) vestry.

Säkular... [zɛːkuˈlɑːr-] secular; ⦵isieren [~lari'ziːrən] secularize.

Salamander [zala'mandər] m (7) salamander.

Salami [za'lɑːmi] f salami; ~taktik fig. f salami tactics sg.

Salat [za'lɑːt] m (3) salad;. (Pflanze) lettuce; ~besteck n salad servers pl.; ~öl n salad oil; ~schüssel f salad bowl; ~soße f salad dressing.

salbadern [zal'bɑːdərn] (29) twaddle.   [in Zssgn u. fig. salve.⟩

Salbe ['zalbə] f (15) ointment; mstʃ

Salbei ⚥ [zal'baɪ] m (3¹), f (16) sage.

salben ['zalbən] (25) rub with ointment; weitS. anoint (j-n zum König a p. king).

'Salbung f anointing, (a. fig.) unction; '⦵svoll unctuous.

saldieren ✝ [zal'diːrən] balance, settle; ~ mit set off a th. against.

Saldo ['~do] m (11; pl. a. -di) balance; den ~ ziehen strike the balance; '~vortrag m balance forward.

Saline [za'liːnə] f (15) salt-works.

Salm zo. [zalm] m (3) salmon.

Salmiak [zal'mjak] m (11) sal ammoniac; ~geist m liquid ammonia.

Salmonelle [zalmo'nɛlə] f (15) mst pl. salmonella; ~n-erkrankung ⚕ f salmonellosis.

Salon [za'lɔ̃] m (11) drawing-room, Am. parlor; ⚓ saloon; ⦵fähig fit for good society; ~held m, ~löwe m carpet-knight, ladies' man; ~wagen m saloon-car, Am. Pullman (od. parlor) car.

salopp [za'lɔp] sloppy; (lässig) nonchalant, casual.

Salpeter [zal'peːtər] m (7) saltpet|re, nit|re, Am. -er; ~erde f nitrous earth; ⦵ig nitrous; ~säure f nitric acid.

Salto ['zalto] m (11) somersault; ~ mortale [~ mɔr'tɑːle] m breakneck leap.

Salut [za'luːt] m (3) salute; ~ schießen fire a salute; ⦵ieren [~lu'tiːrən] v/t. u. v/i. salute.

Salve ['zalvə] f (15) (Gewehr⦵) volley; (Geschütz⦵) salvo; (Ehren-⦵) salute.

Salz [zalts] n (3²) salt; '~bergwerk n salt-mine; '⦵en (27) salt; s. gesalzen; '~faß n, '~fäßchen n auf dem Tische: salt-cellar; '~fleisch n salt meat; '~gurke f pickled cucumber; '~hering m pickled herring; '⦵ig salt(y); (salzhaltig) saline; '~kartoffeln f/pl. boiled potatoes; '~lake f, '~lauge f brine, pickle; '⦵los saltless; Diät: salt-free; '~rückstände m/pl. salt residue sg.; '~säule f Bibel: pillar of salt; fig. zur ~ erstarren freeze; '~säure f hydrochloric acid; '~see m salt-lake; '~siederei [~zi:də'raɪ] f salt-works, saltern; '~sole f brine; '~streuer m (7) salt shaker; '~wasser n salt-water; '~werk n salt-works.

Samariter [zama'riːtər] m (7) (barmherziger good) Samaritan.

Same [za:mə] m (13¹), '~n m (6) seed (a. fig.); physiol. sperm; '~nbehälter m, '~ngehäuse n seed-case, ⚘ pericarp; '~n-erguß m ejaculation; '~n-

faden *m* spermatozoon; '**~nflüssig-keit** *f* semen; '**~ngang** *m*, '**~nleiter** *m* seminal duct; '**~nkapsel** *f* (seed) capsule; '**~nkorn** *n* grain of seed; '**~nstaub** *m* pollen; '**~nstrang** *m* spermatic cord.

Sämischleder ['zɛ:miʃ-] *n* chamois (leather).

Sammel|**-album** ['zaməl-] *n* album; '**~band** *m* omnibus volume; '**~bek-ken** *n* reservoir; *geogr.* catchment basin; '**~behälter** *m* collecting tank; '**~bestellung** *f* collective order; '**~bezeichnung** *f* collective name; '**~büchse** *f* collecting-box; '**~güter** *n*/*pl.* miscellaneous goods *pl.*; '**~ladung** ⴲ *f* collective consignment; '**~lager** *n* assembly camp; '**~mappe** *f* file; '**~n** (29, *a.* sich) gather; *Brief-marken, Geld usw.*, *a.* ⊕: collect; (*anhäufen*) heap up, accumulate, amass; *Kunden, Stimmen*: canvass; (*vereinigen, a.* ✕) concentrate; (*ver~*) assemble, rally (*beide a.* sich); *fig.* sich (*s-e Gedanken*) ~ concentrate, (*sich fassen*) compose o.s.; ~ *für e-n Zweck* collect money for; '**~name** *gr.* *m* collective noun; '**~nummer** *f* collective number; '**~objekt** *n* collectible; '**~platz** *m* place of assembly; ✕ assembly (*od.* rallying) point; '**~stecker** ⚡ *m* universal adapter plug; **~surium** [~'zu:rjum] *n* jumble, omnium gatherum; '**~taxi** *n* shared taxi; '**~titel** *m* collective title; '**~werk** *n* collected edition; '**~wut** *f* collector's mania.

Sammler ['zamlər] *m* (7) collector (*a.* '**~in** *f* [16¹]); ⚡ accumulator; '**~batterie** ⚡ *f* storage battery.

'**Sammlung** *f* collection; *fig.* composure; concentration.

Sams·tag ['zamsta:k] *m* (3) Saturday; '**~s** on Saturdays.

samt¹ [zamt] together (*od.* along) with; ~ *und sonders* all of them (*etc.*).

Samt² [~] *m* (3) velvet; '**~-artig**, '**~ig** velvety; '**~handschuh** *m*: *j-n mit* ~*en anfassen* *fig.* handle a p. with kid-gloves.

sämtlich ['zɛmtliç] *adj.* all; (*voll-ständig*) complete; *adv.* all (to-gether *od.* of them).

Sanatorium [zana'to:rjum] *n* (9) sanatorium, *Am.* sanitarium.

Sand [zant] *m* (3) sand; *fig. im* ~*e verlaufen* come to nothing, peter

out; *j-m* ~ *in die Augen streuen* throw dust in a p.'s eyes; *zahllos wie* ~ *am Meer* numberless as the sand(s).

Sandale [zan'da:lə] *f* (15) sandal.

'**Sand**|**bahn** *f Rennsport:* dirt-track; '**~bank** *f* sandbank; '**~blattnagel-feile** *f* emery board; '**~boden** *m* sandy soil; '**~burg** *f* sandcastle; '**~dorn** ⚘ *m* sea buckthorn.

Sandelholz ['zandəl-] *n* sandalwood.

'**Sand**|**grube** *f* sand pit; '**~ig** ['~diç] sandy; '**~kasten** *m* sand-box; *für Kinder:* sand-pit; ✕ sand-table; '**~korn** *n* grain of sand; '**~mann** *m fig.* sandman; '**~papier** *n* sandpaper; '**~sack** *m* sandbag; *Boxen:* body bag; '**~stein** *m* sandstone; '**~strahlgeblä-se** ⊕ *n* sandblast unit; '**~sturm** *m* sandstorm.

sandte [zantə] *pret. v.* senden.

'**Sand**|**torte** *f* Madeira cake; '**~uhr** *f* sand-glass; '**~wüste** *f* sandy desert.

sanft [zanft] soft; (*leicht, zart*) *a.* gentle; (*milde*) gentle, mild; (*glatt*) smooth; *Abhang, Tod:* easy.

Sänfte ['zɛnftə] *f* (15) sedan (chair).

'**Sanft**|**heit** *f* softness; gentleness; mildness; '**~mut** *f* (16) gentleness; ♀**mütig** ['~my:tiç] gentle.

Sang [zaŋ] **1.** *m* (3⁸) song; singing; *ohne* ~ *und Klang*, ♀*- und klanglos fig.* unhono(u)red and unsung; **2.** ♀ *pret. v.* singen.

Sänger ['zɛŋər] *m* (7), '**~in** *f* (16¹) singer; vocalist; (*Dichter*) bard; '**~fest** *n* singing-festival.

Sanguin|**iker** [zaŋgu'i:nikər] *m* (7) sanguine person; ♀**isch** sanguine.

sanier|**en** [za'ni:rən] (*heilen*) cure; (*vorbeugen*) give prophylactic treat-ment; *Stadtviertel, Haus:* redevelop; ⴲ reorganize, (*stabilisieren*) stabilize, rehabilitate; ♀**ung** *f* redevelopment; stabilization; rehabilitation; ♀**ungs-gebiet** *n* redevelopment area.

sanitär [zani'tɛ:r] sanitary; ~*e Ein-richtung* sanitary facility.

Sanitäter [~'tɛ:tər] *m* (7) ambulance (*od.* first-aid) man; ✕ medical order-ly.

Sani|**täts**|**-artikel** *m*/*pl.*, ~**bedarf** *m* medical supplies *pl.*; ~**dienst** *m* medical service; ~**flugzeug** *n* air am-bulance; ~**kasten** *m* first-aid kit; ~**raum** *m* first-aid room; ~**truppe** *f* medical corps; ~**wesen** *n* sanitary

matters *pl.*, ✖ medical service.
sank [zaŋk] *pret. v. sinken.*
Sankt [zaŋkt], **St.** Saint, St.
Sanktion [zaŋk'tsjoːn] *f* sanction;
 Ձieren [˷tsjo'niːrən] sanction.
sann [zan] *pret. v. sinnen.*
Saphir ['zaːfir] *m* (3¹) sapphire.
Sard|elle [zar'dɛlə] *f* (15) anchovy;
 ˷**ellenpaste** *f* anchovy paste; ˷**ine**
 [˷'diːnə] *f* (15) sardine.
Sarg [zark] *m* (3³) coffin, *Am. a.*
 casket; '˷**deckel** *m* coffin-lid; '˷**trä-**
 ger *m* pallbearer.
Sark|asmus [zar'kasmus] *m* (16²)
 sarcasm; Ձ**astisch** [˷'kastiʃ] sar-
 castic(ally *adv.*).
Sarkophag [zarko'faːk] *m* (3¹) sar-
 cophagus.
saß [zaːs] *pret. v. sitzen.*
Satan ['zaːtan] *m* (3¹) Satan; Ձ**isch**
 [za'taːniʃ] satanic(ally *adv.*).
Satellit [zatɛ'liːt] *m* (12) satellite;
 ˷**en-abwehr** ✖ *f* satellite intelligence; ˷**enphoto** *n* satellite picture;
 ˷**enstaat** *pol. m* satellite state; ˷**en-**
 stadt *f* satellite town; ˷**en-über-**
 tragung *f* satellite transmission.
Satin [za'tɛ̃] *m* (11) (*Seidenatlas*)
 satin; (*Baumwoll*Ձ) sateen; Ձ**ieren**
 [zati'niːrən] satin, glaze; *Papier: a.*
 calender.
Satir|e [za'tiːrə] *f* (15) satire; ˷**iker**
 [˷rikər] *m* satirist; Ձ**isch** satiric(al).
Satisfaktion [zatisfak'tsjoːn] *f* satisfaction.
satt [zat] satisfied, satiate(d), full;
 Farbe: deep, saturated; *ich bin* ˷
 I have enough; *sich* ˷ *essen* eat
 one's fill; *et.* ˷ *bekommen* (*haben*)
 get (be) sick of, F get (be) fed up
 with.
Sattel ['zatəl] *m* (7¹) saddle (*a.* =
 *Gebirgs*Ձ); *der Nase:* bridge; *aus*
 dem ˷ *heben* unhorse, (*a. fig.*) un-
 seat; *fest im* ˷ firmly in the saddle
 (*a. fig.*); '˷**decke** *f* saddle-cloth;
 'Ձ**fest** saddle-fast; *fig.* quite firm
 (*in dat.* in); '˷**gurt** *m* girth; 'Ձ**n** *v/t. u.*
 v/i. (29) saddle; '˷**pferd** *n* saddle-
 -horse; '˷**platz** *m* paddock; '˷-
 schlepper *mot. m* articulated lorry;
 '˷**tasche** *f* saddle-bag; '˷**zeug** *n* saddle and harness.
'**Sattheit** *f* satiety; saturation; *von*
 Farben: richness.
sättig|en ['zɛtigən] (25) satiate,
 satisfy; *Essen:* be substantial; 🜛
 usw.: saturate; *j-n* (*sich*) ˷ appease

a p.'s (one's) hunger; 'Ձ**ung** *f*
 satiation; 🜛 saturation.
Sattler ['zatlər] *m* (7) saddler; ˷**ei**
 [˷'raɪ] *f* (16) saddlery.
'**sattsam** sufficiently; ˷ *bekannt a.*
 notorious.
saturieren [zatu'riːrən] saturate.
Satyr ['zaːtyr] *m* (10 *od.* 13) satyr.
Satz [zats] *m* (3² *u.* ³) sentence (*a.*
 gr.); *gr.* clause; proposition (*a. phls.*,
 Å); (*Boden*Ձ) sediment, dregs *pl.*;
 (*Kaffee*Ձ) grounds *pl.*; *typ.*, ♩ (*Ver-*
 tonung) composition; ♩ (*Teil e-s*
 Tonstücks) movement; (*zs.-gehörige*
 Dinge) set; ⊕ (*Schub*) batch;
 Tennis: set; (*Sprung*) leap, bound;
 (*bestimmtes Verhältnis; Preis*) rate;
 '˷**-aussage** *gr. f* predicate; '˷**ball**
 m Tennis: set point; '˷**bau** *m* construction; 'Ձ**fertig** *typ.* ready for
 composition; '˷**gefüge** *gr. n* complex
 sentence; '˷**gegenstand** *gr. m* subject; '˷**lehre** *gr. f* syntax; '˷**spiegel**
 typ. m type area; '˷**teil** *gr. m* part of
 sentence.
'**Satzung** *f* statute; *e-s Vereins usw.:*
 (statutes *pl.* and) articles *pl.*, by-
 -laws *pl.*; 'Ձ**smäßig** statutory.
'**Satzzeichen** *n* punctuation mark.
Sau [zaʊ] *f* (14¹) sow; V *fig.* (dirty)
 pig, (*Frau*) slut; F *unter aller* ˷
 lousy; F *zur* ˷ *machen* let a *p.* have
 it.
sauber ['zaʊbər] clean (*a. fig. mo-*
 ralisch); *a. fig. Äußeres, Arbeit,*
 Handschrift usw.: neat; *iro.* fine,
 nice; 'Ձ**keit** *f* cleanness, neatness;
 (*Ehrlichkeit*) integrity.
säuberlich ['zɔʏbərlɪç] *s. sauber;*
 fig. proper; (*sorgfältig*) careful.
saubermachen ['zaʊbər-], **säu-**
 bern ['zɔʏbərn] (29) clean, cleanse;
 Zimmer: clean up, tidy; (*frei ma-*
 chen) clear (*von* of); *fig. u. pol.*
 purge (of, from).
'**Säuber|ung** *f* cleaning, *etc.*; *pol.*
 = 'Ձ**ungs-aktion** *pol. f* purge.
'**Saubohne** *f* broad (*od.* horse) bean.
Sauce ['zoːsə] *f s. Soße.*
Sauciere [zo'sjɛːrə] *f* (15) sauce-boat.
'**sau'dumm** F *Person:* (as) thick as
 two short planks; *Sache:* really stupid.
sauer ['zaʊər] (18, *comp. saurer, sup.*
 ˷*st*) sour, acid (*a.* 🜛); *fig.* hard,
 painful; (*mürrisch*) cross, sour; *saure*
 Gurke pickled cucumber; 🜛 *saurer*
 Regen acid rain; ˷ *werden* turn sour,

69*

Milch: turn (sour); F *fig.* get cross; *in den sauren Apfel beißen müssen* have to swallow the bitter pill; *j-m das Leben* ~ *machen* make life miserable for a p.; ~ *reagieren auf et.* take *a th.* in bad part; *s. Drops.*

'**Sauer|-ampfer** *m* sorrel; '~**braten** *m* meat soaked in vinegar and stewed; '~**brunnen** *m* acidulous mineral water; ~**ei** [zauə'raɪ] F *s. Schweinerei;* '~**kirsche** *f* morello cherry; '~**klee** *m* wood-sorrel; '~**kohl** *m,* '~**kraut** *n* sauerkraut.

säuer|lich ['zɔyərliç] sourish; ⚕ acidulous; *fig.* wintry *(smile)*; '~**n** (29) make sour; ⚕ acidify, acidulate; *Teig:* leaven.

'**Sauer|milch** *f* curdled milk; '~**stoff** *m* oxygen; '~**stoff-apparat** *m* oxygen-respirator; '~**stoffflasche** *f* oxygen cylinder; '~**stoffmangel** ⚕ *m* oxygen deficiency; '~**stoffmaske** *f* oxygen mask; '~**stoffzelt** ⚕ *n* oxygen tent; '~**teig** *m* leaven; ⚕**töpfisch** ['~tœpfiʃ] peevish, sour.

saufen ['zaufən] *v/t. u. v/i.* (30) *Tier:* drink; *P.:* a. F booze, guzzle, soak.

Säufer F ['zɔyfər] *m* (7) drunkard, alcoholic, F boozer.

Sauferei F [zaufə'raɪ] *f* hard drinking; *a.* = '**Saufgelage** *n* drinking-bout, F booze, binge, soak.

saugen ['zaugən] **1.** *v/t. u. v/i.* (30) suck *(an et. [dat.]* a th.); **2.** ⚕ *n* sucking; *mst* ⊕ suction.

säugen ['zɔygən] (25) suckle, nurse.

Sauger ['zaugər] *m* (7) sucker; *e-r Flasche:* nipple.

'**Säugetier** *n* mammal.

saug|fähig ['zauk-] absorbent; '⚕**flasche** *f* feeding-bottle; '⚕**heber** *m* siphon.

Säugling ['zɔyklɪŋ] *m* (3¹) baby, infant, suckling; '~**s-ausstattung** *f* *(Wäsche)* layette; '~**sfürsorge** *f* infant welfare; '~**s-heim** *n* crèche *(fr.);* '~**spflege** *f* baby care; '~**sschwester** *f* baby nurse; '~**ssterblichkeit** *f* infant mortality.

Saug|papier ['zauk-] *n* absorbent paper; '~**pumpe** *f* suction pump; '~**rohr** *n* suction pipe; '~**wirkung** *f* suction effect.

Säule ['zɔylə] *f* (15) *allg.* (a. *fig.*) column; *(Pfeiler)* pillar (a. *fig.*); ⚡ pile.

'**Säulen|gang** *m* colonnade, arcade;

'~**schaft** *m* shaft of a column.

Saum [zaum] *m* (3³) seam, hem; *(Rand)* border, edge; *e-r Stadt:* outskirts *pl.*

'**saumäßig** F beastly, filthy, vile, awful, lousy.

säum|en ['zɔymən] (25) *v/t.* hem; (*a. fig.*) border; *fig. die Straßen* ~ line the streets; '~**en²** *v/i.* (*zögern, verweilen*) tarry; '~**ig** *s. saumselig.*

'**Saum|pfad** *m* mule-track; '~**pferd** *n* pack-horse; '~**sattel** *m* pack-saddle; '⚕**selig** tardy, slow; *(trödelnd)* dawdling; *(hinausschiebend)* dilatory; *(nachlässig)* negligent; '~**seligkeit** *f* tardiness; negligence; '~**tier** *n* sumpter-mule.

Sauna ['zauna] *f* (11¹) sauna.

Säure ['zɔyrə] *f* (15) sourness, *a.* ⚗ *des Magens:* acidity; ⚕ acid; '~**ballon** *m* carboy; ⚕**beständig,** ⚕**fest** acid-proof.

Saure|gurkenzeit *f* silly season.

'**säure|haltig** acidiferous; '~**löslich** acid-soluble.

Saurier ['zaurjər] *m* (7) saurian.

Saus [zaus] *m: in* ~ *und Braus leben* live on the fat of the land, revel and riot.

säuseln ['zɔyzəln] *v/i. u. v/t.* (29) whisper, rustle; *fig.* P.: purr.

sausen ['zauzən] (27, *h. u. sn*) rush, whiz, flit; *Wind, Geschoß:* whistle.

'**Saustall** *m* pigsty; F *fig. a.* awful mess.   [saxophone.]

Saxophon ♪ [zakso'foːn] *n* (3¹)⌡

Schabe ['ʃaːbə] *f* (15) cockroach; '~**fleisch** *n* scraped meat; '~**messer** *n* scraping-knife; ⚕**n** *v/t. u. v/i.* (25) scrape; *mit Reibeisen usw.:* grate, rasp; '~**r** *m* (7) scraper; ~**r-nack** ['~nak] *m* (3) practical joke, hoax, prank(s *pl.*); *j-m e-n* ~ *spielen* play a p. a trick.

schäbig ['ʃɛːbiç] shabby; *fig. a.* mean; ⚕**keit** *f* shabbiness; *fig. a.* meanness.

Schablone [ʃa'bloːnə] *f* (15) *(Modell)* model; *(Muster)* pattern; (~*nform, Mal*⚕) stencil; *fig. (mechanische Arbeit)* routine; *(Denkweise usw.)* stereotype; ⚕**nhaft,** ⚕**nmäßig** stereotyped; *(mechanisch)* mechanical, *nur attr.* routine.

Schach [ʃax] *n* (3) chess; ~ *(dem König)!* check!; ~ *und matt!* checkmate!; ~ *bieten* (give) check, *fig.* *j-m:* defy a p.; *in* ~ *halten* keep in

check (*a. fig.*), *mit e-r Waffe*: *a.*
cover; '~**brett** *n* chessboard; '♀-
brett-artig checkered; '~**computer**
m chess computer.

Schacher ['ʃaxər] *m* (7) haggling,
low trade; *bsd. pol.* jobbery; '♀**n**
(29) haggle (*um* about, over).

Schächer ['ʃɛçər] *m* (7) *biblisch*:
thief; (*Mörder*) murderer; *fig. armer*
~ poor wretch.

'**Schach|feld** *n* square; '~**figur** *f*
chessman; '♀'**matt** (check)mate;
fig. (*erschöpft*) all in; ~ setzen check-
mate (*a. fig.*); '~**partie** *f*, '~**spiel** *n*
game of chess; '~**spieler** *m* chess-
-player.

Schacht [ʃaxt] *m* (3[³]) shaft, ⚔ *a.*
pit; ⚒ (*Licht♀ usw.*) well; (*Mann-
loch*) manhole.

Schachtel ['ʃaxtəl] *f* (15) box; *für
Hüte, Putz usw.*: bandbox; *fig.* F
alte ~ old frump; '~**halm** ⚘ *m*
shave-grass; '~**satz** *m* involved
sentence.

'**Schach|turnier** *n* chess tourna-
ment; '~**zug** *m* move (*a. fig.*).

schade ['ʃaːdə] **1.** (*es ist* [*sehr*]) ~
it is a (great) pity (*um* for; *daß*
that), F it's too bad (*he couldn't
come*); *wie* ~! what a pity!; *zu* ~
für ihn too good for him; **2.** ♀ *m*
(13¹, *pl. Schäden*) *s. schaden 2.*

Schädel ['ʃɛːdəl] *m* (7) skull; '~**basis**
f base of the skull; '~**bruch** *m*
fracture of the skull, fractured
skull; '~**decke** *f* skullpan.

schaden ['ʃaːdən] **1.** (26) injure,
harm, hurt (*j-m* a p.); (*nachteilig
sein*) be prejudicial (to a p.); *das
schadet nichts* it will do no harm;
das schadet ihm gar nichts that
serves him right; *was schadet es?*
what does it matter?; *e-e Aussprache könnte nicht* ~ a discussion
might not be amiss; **2.** ♀ *m* (6²)
damage (*an dat.* to); (*Mangel*) defect; (*Beschädigung*) injury, harm;
(*a.* ⊕) defect; (*Nachteil*) detriment,
prejudice; (*Verlust*) loss; *zu meinem* ~ to my damage *od.* cost; *j-m*
~ *zufügen* do a p. harm; *mit* ~ *verkaufen* sell at a loss; ~ *erleiden od.
nehmen, zu* ~ *kommen* be damaged,
come to harm; *durch* ~ *wird man
klug* once bitten twice shy; '♀-**ersatz** *m* compensation, indemnification; (*Geldsumme*) damages *pl.*; ~
leisten pay damages (*für* for); *auf* ~

verklagen sue for damages; '♀-**er-
satzklage** *f* action for damages;
'~-**ersatzpflichtig** liable for dam-
age(s); '♀**freiheitsrabatt** *mot. m* no-
-claims bonus; '♀**freude** *f* malicious
joy, gloating; *voller* ~ gloatingly, ma-
liciously; '~**froh** malicious, gloating.

schadhaft ['ʃaːthaft] defective;
'♀**igkeit** *f* defectiveness.

schädig|en ['ʃɛːdigən] (25) damage,
impair; *j-n*: harm, wrong, prejudice; '♀**ung** *f* damage, prejudice
(*gen.* to).

schädlich ['ʃɛːtlɪç] harmful, in-
jurious, hurtful; (*nachteilig*) detrimental, prejudicial; (*gesundheits~*)
noxious, unwholesome (*alle*: *dat.
od. für* to); '♀**keit** *f* harmfulness,
injuriousness; noxiousness.

Schädling ['ʃɛːlɪŋ] *m* (3¹) pest; ~e *pl.*
🪲 *a.* vermin; '~**bekämpfung** *f*
pest control; '~**bekämpfungsmit-
tel** *n* pesticide.

schadlos ['ʃaːloːs]: ~ *halten* indemnify; '♀**haltung** *f* indemnification.

'**Schadstoff** *m* pollutant.

Schaf [ʃaːf] *n* (3) sheep; (*Mutter♀*)
ewe; *fig.* ninny; *schwarzes* ~ black
sheep; '~**bock** *m* ram.

Schäfchen ['ʃɛːfçən] *n* (6) little
sheep, lamb(kin); *pl.* (*Wolken*)
fleecy clouds; *fig. sein* ~ *ins trockene
bringen* feather one's nest.

Schäfer ['ʃɛːfər] *m* (7), '~**in** *f* shep-
herd(ess *f*); '~**hund** *m* shepherd('s)
dog; *deutscher* ~ German shepherd
(dog), Alsatian; '~**stündchen** *n*
lover's hour.

schaffen ['ʃafən]: **a)** *v/t.* (30) (*er*~)
create; (*hervorbringen*) *a.* produce
(*a. weitS. Situation usw.*); (*gründen*)
organize, set up; *er ist für diesen
Posten wie geschaffen* he is cut out
for this post; **b)** *v/t. u. v/i.* (25)
(*tun, arbeiten*) do, make, work;
(*fertig werden mit*) cope with,
manage; (*ver~*) provide; (*befördern*)
convey, (*weg~*) take, (*her~*) bring;
(*bewältigen*) manage, (*erreichen*) *a.*
reach, *Am.* make; F *e-e Strecke, e-e
Geschwindigkeit, Zeit*: do; F *es* ~
succeed, F make it; *viel* ~ get a great
deal done; *nichts zu* ~ *haben mit*
have nothing to do with; *j-m* (*viel*)
zu ~ *machen* give a p. (a great deal
of) trouble; *sich unbefugt zu* ~
machen an (*dat.*) tamper with; *sich
eifrig zu* ~ *machen mit et.* busy o.s.

(od. be busy) with a th.; F *er (es) schafft mich!* he (it) gets me (down)!; *s. Hals, Rat, Seite, Vergnügen, Weg, Welt.*

'**Schaffens|drang** *m* creative urge; '**~kraft** *f* creative power; *weitS.* vigo(u)r.

'**Schaf-fleisch** *n* mutton.

Schaffner ['ʃafnər] *m* (7) 🚌 guard, *Am.* conductor; *(Bus♀ usw.)* conductor; '**~in** *f* (16¹) 🚌 conductress.

Schaffung ['ʃafuŋ] *f* creation; provision; organizing.

'**Schaf|garbe** ♀ *f* yarrow; '**~herde** *f* flock of sheep; '**~hirt** *m* shepherd; '**~hürde** *f* sheep-pen, -fold; '**~leder** *n* sheepskin; '**~(s)kopf** *m fig.* idiot.

Schafott [ʃa'fɔt] *n* (3) scaffold.

'**Schaf|pelz** *m: Wolf im ~* wolf in sheep's clothing; '**~schur** *f* sheep-shearing; '**~smilch** *f* ewe's milk.

Schaft [ʃaft] *m* (3³) shaft; *(Gewehr♀)* stock; *e-s Werkzeugs, Ankers, Schlüssels:* shank; *(Griff)* handle; *(Stiefel♀)* leg.

schäften ['ʃeftən] (26) *Gewehr:* stock, mount; *Stiefel:* leg.

'**Schaftstiefel** *m* top boot.

'**Schaf|wolle** *f* sheep's wool; '**~zucht** *f* sheep-breeding.

Schah [ʃa:] *m* (11) Shah.

Schakal [ʃa'ka:l] *m* (3¹) jackal.

Schäker ['ʃɛːkər] *m* (7) rogue, wag; *(Hofmacher)* flirt; '**~ei** [~'raɪ] *f* (16) joking, badinage; *(Liebelei)* flirtation, dalliance; '**♀n** (29) joke, make fun; *(tändeln)* dally; *(liebeln)* flirt.

schal¹ [ʃa:l] stale *(a. fig.).*

Schal² [~] *m* (3¹ *u.* 11) scarf; *(Schultertuch e-r Frau)* shawl; *wollener:* comforter; '**~brett** *n* slab.

Schale ['ʃaːlə] *f* (15) bowl, basin; *für Früchte usw.:* dish; *(Tasse)* cup; *v. Pellkartoffeln, Obst:* skin; *(Hülse)* shell, husk; *(Schote)* pod; *(Obst♀)* peel; *(abgeschälte ~)* paring, *(bsd. Kartoffel♀)* peeling; *(Eier♀, Nuß♀)* shell; *(Muschel♀)* valve; *(Messer♀, Waag♀)* scale; *fig.* shell; F *sich in ~ werfen* spruce s. up.

schälen ['ʃeːlən] (25) peel, pare; *Hülsenfrüchte:* shell, husk; *Baum:* bark; *sich ~* peel off.

'**Schalheit** *f* staleness.

Schalk [ʃalk] *m* (3[³]) rogue; *(Spaßvogel)* wag; '**♀haft** arch, roguish; *(spaßend)* waggish; '**~haftigkeit** *f*

archness, roguery; waggishness.

Schall [ʃal] *m* (3[³]) sound; *schneller als der ~* supersonic; '**~boden** *m* sound(ing)-board; '**♀dämpfend** sound deadening; '**~dämpfer** *m* sound absorber; *mot.* silencer *(a. an Schußwaffen)*, *Am.* muffler; '**♀dicht** soundproof; '**♀en** (30, h. *u.* sn) sound, ring; *~des Gelächter* peal of laughter, guffaw; '**~geschwindigkeit** *f* speed of sound, sonic speed; '**~grenze** *f*, '**~mauer** *f* sound *(od.* sonic) barrier; '**~lehre** *f* acoustics; '**~messung** *f* sound ranging; '**~platte** *f* disc, record; '**~platten-aufnahme** *f* disc recording; '**~plattenmusik** *f* recorded music; '**~plattennadel** *f* stylus; '**♀schluckend** sound deadening; '**~schutz** *m* noise control; *(Isolierung)* sound insulation; '**~schutzfenster** *n* soundproof window; '**~trichter** *m* bell-mouth; *des Grammophons:* horn; '**~welle** *f* sound-wave.

Schalmei [ʃal'maɪ] *f* (16) shawm.

schalt [ʃalt] *pret. v. schelten.*

'**Schalt|anlage** *f* switch-gear; '**~bild** *n* wiring *(od.* circuit) diagram; '**~brett** *n* switchboard, control panel; *mot.,* 💺 instrument panel, dashboard.

schalten ['ʃaltən] (26) ⊕ *(auslösen)* actuate; *(bedienen)* operate; *(steuern)* control; ⚡ *(um~)* switch, *(verbinden)* connect, *(verdrahten)* wire; *mot.* change *(od.* shift) gears; *Kupplung:* engage; *auf den ersten Gang ~* shift *(od.* change) into the bottom gear; *~ und walten* manage, *(hantieren)* potter about; *mit et. ~* deal with; F *fig. (schnell) ~* do some quick thinking.

'**Schalter** *m* (7) 🚌 *usw.:* booking-office; 💰, *Bank:* counter, window, desk; ⚡ switch; ⊕, *mot.* controller; '**~be-amte** *m* counter-clerk; 🚌 *usw.:* booking-clerk; '**~dienst** *m* counter-service.

'**Schalt|getriebe** *n* control gear; *mot.* change-speed gear; '**~hebel** *m* control lever; *mot.* gear(shift) lever; ⚡ switch lever.

Schaltier ['ʃa:lti:r] *n* shellfish, crustacean.

'**Schalt|jahr** *n* leap-year; '**~knopf** *m* (control) button; '**~kreis** *m* circuit; '**~plan** *m*, '**~schema** *n s. Schaltbild*; '**~pult** *n* control desk; '**~tafel** *f* *s. Schaltbrett*; '**~tag** *m* intercalary day; '**~ung** *f* ⊕ control; ⚡ circuit; connection(s *pl.*); (*Verdrahtung*) wiring; (*Umschalten*) switching; *mot.* gear-change, changing, shifting.

Schalung ['ʃɑːluŋ] ⚠ *f* form.

Schaluppe ⚓ [ʃa'lupə] *f* (15) sloop.

Scham [ʃɑːm] *f* (16, *o. pl.*) shame; (*~haftigkeit*) modesty; *anat.* (*~teile*) private parts *pl.*, genitals *pl.*; (*weibliche*) ~ 🕮 vulva; '**~bein** *n* pubic bone.

schämen ['ʃɛːmən] (25): *sich* ~ be (*od.* feel) ashamed (*e-r S.* [*wegen*], *über acc.* of).

'**Scham|gefühl** *n* sense of shame; '**~gegend** *f* pubic region; '**~haare** *n/pl.* pubic hair *sg.*; '**♀haft** bashful, modest; '**~haftigkeit** *f* bashfulness, modesty; '**♀los** shameless; '**~losigkeit** *f* shamelessness.

Schamotte [ʃa'mɔtə] *f* (15) fire-clay; **~stein** *m* fire-brick.

'**scham|rot** blushing; ~ *werden* blush; ~ *machen* put to the blush; '**♀röte** *f* blush; '**♀teile** *m/pl.* private parts, genitals.

schandbar ['ʃantbɑːr] *s. schändlich.*

Schande ['ʃandə] *f* (15) shame, disgrace; *s. zuschanden.*

schänd|en ['ʃɛndən] (26) dishono(u)r, disgrace; (*entweihen*) desecrate, profane; (*verunstalten*) disfigure; *ein Mädchen*: ravish, rape; '**♀er** *m* (7) ravisher; violator.

Schandfleck ['ʃant-] *m* stain, blot; (*häßlicher Anblick*) eyesore.

schändlich ['ʃɛntliç] shameful, infamous; scandalous; '**♀keit** *f* infamy; baseness.

'**Schand|mal** *n* stigma, brand; '**~maul** *n* slanderer; '**~pfahl** *m* pillory; '**~tat** *f* infamous action; foul crime.

'**Schändung** *f s. schänden*: violation; desecration; disfigurement; ravishment, rape.

Schank|-erlaubnis ['ʃaŋk-] *f* publican's licence, *Am.* excise license; '**~stätte** *f* licensed premises *pl.*; '**~stube** *f* tap-room, *Am.* bar; '**~wirt** *m* publican, *Am.* saloonkeeper; '**~wirtschaft** *f s. Schenke.*

Schanze ['ʃantsə] *f* (15) entrenchment; ⚓ quarter-deck; *s. Sprungschanze*; *in die ~ schlagen* risk, hazard; '**♀n** (27) entrench; *fig.* (*schwer arbeiten*) drudge; '**~ntisch** *m Schisport*: ski-jumping platform.

Schar [ʃɑːr] *f* (16) **1.** troop, band, group; *v. Gänsen usw.*: flock; (*gedrängte Menge*) crowd; **2.** (*Pflug♀*) ploughshare, *Am.* plowshare; '**♀en** (25, *a. sich*) assemble, collect, flock (together); *um sich* ~ rally; *sich* ~ *um* (*acc.*) rally round; '**♀enweise** in crowds (*od.* droves).

scharf [ʃarf] *allg.* sharp (*a. fig. Blick, Gegensatz, Kurve, Stimme, Verstand, Zunge usw.*); *Schneide, a. fig. Verstand, Beobachter*: keen; (*beißend, brennend*) biting, burning; *Geruch*: pungent; *Pfeffer*: hot; *Brille*: strong; (*streng*) severe, strict; (*schroff*) abrupt, sharp; (*genau*) exact; *phot.* well-focus(s)ed; *Munition*: live; *Mine usw.*: armed; ✝ *Konkurrenz*: stiff; *ein ~es Ohr* a quick ear; *j-n ~ ansehen* look hard at a p.; ~ *aufpassen* give close attention; ~ *reiten* ride hard; ~ *schießen* shoot with live ammunition; ~ *sein auf* (*acc.*) be keen on; '**♀blick** *m* quick eye; *fig.* penetration.

Schärfe ['ʃɛrfə] *f* (15) sharpness; (*Schneide*) edge.

'**schärfen** (25) sharpen (*a. fig.*).

'**Schärfentiefe** *phot. f* depth of focus.

'**scharf|kantig**, **~randig** ['~randiç] sharp-edged; '**~machen** ⚔ arm, activate; *fig.* (*aufhetzen*) instigate; '**♀macher** *m fig.* agitator; '**♀richter** *m* executioner; '**♀schießen** *n* live shooting; '**♀schütze** *m* sharp-shooter, marksman; ⚔ sniper; **~sichtig** ['~ziçtiç] sharp-sighted; *fig. a.* penetrating; '**♀sinn** *m* sagacity, acumen; '**~sinnig** shrewd, sagacious, penetrating.

Scharlach ['ʃarlax] *m* (3¹) scarlet; ⚕ = '**~fieber** *n* scarlet fever; '**♀rot** scarlet(-red).

Scharlatan ['ʃarlatan] *m* (3¹) charlatan, quack, mountebank.

Scharm *m usw. s. Charme usw.*

Scharmützel [ʃar'mytsəl] *n* (7) skirmish; **♀n** (29) skirmish.

Scharnier [ʃar'niːr] *n* (3¹) hinge; joint; **~deckel** *m* hinged lid.

Schärpe ['ʃɛrpə] *f* (15) scarf, sash.

scharren ['ʃarən] *v/t. u. v/i.* (25) scrape, scratch; *Pferd*: paw.

Scharte ['ʃartə] *f* (15) notch; (*Riß*) fissure; (*Lücke*) gap; *s. Schieß♀*; *fig.*

die ~ *auswetzen* wipe out the disgrace, make up for it.

Scharteke [ʃar'teːkə] *f* (15) old (*od.* trashy) volume.

'**schartig** notchy, jagged.

scharwenzeln F [ʃar'ventsəln] (29) fawn (*um* [up]on).

Schatten ['ʃatən] *m* (6) (*Schattenbild*) shadow (*a. fig.*); (*Dunkel*) shade; *in den* ~ *stellen fig.* put in the shade, eclipse; *e-n* ~ *werfen auf* (*acc.*) *fig.* cast a shadow upon; '~**bild** *n* silhouette; *fig.* phantom; '~**boxen** *n* shadow-boxing; '~**dasein** *n*: *ein* ~ *führen* live in the shadow; '~**haft** shadowy; '~**kabinett** *pol. n* shadow cabinet; '~**könig** *m* mock king; '~**riß** *m* silhouette; '~**seite** *f* shady side; *fig.* seamy side; '~**spiel** *n* shadow play.

schattier|en [ʃa'tiːrən] shade, tint; (*schraffieren*) hatch; **♀ung** *f* shading; hatching; (*Farbton*) shade, tint.

'**schattig** shady.

Schatulle [ʃa'tulə] *f* (15) casket; *e-s Fürsten*: privy purse.

Schatz [ʃats] *m* (3² *u.* ³) treasure (*a. fig.*); *als Kosewort*: darling, F deary; F (*Geliebte*[*r*]) sweetheart; '~**amt** *n Brt.* Exchequer, *Am.* Treasury (Department); '~**anweisung** *f* Treasury bond (*Am.* certificate).

schätzbar ['ʃɛtsbaːr] estimable.

schätzen ['ʃɛtsən] (27) estimate; value, assess (*auf acc.* at); (*taxieren*) *a.* rate; (*hoch*~) esteem, *et.*: *a.* treasure; (*würdigen*) appreciate; *sich glücklich* ~, *zu inf.* be delighted to *inf.*; '~**swert** estimable.

Schätzer ['ʃɛtsər] *m* (7) valuer; *Versicherung*: appraiser.

'**Schatz|fund** *m* treasure-trove; '~**gräber** *m* treasure-seeker; '~**kammer** *f* treasury; '~**meister** *m* treasurer; '~**suche** *f* treasure hunt.

'**Schätzung** *f* estimate; (*Taxierung*) valuation; assessment; (*Ein♀*) rating; (*Würdigung*) estimation; (*Hoch♀*) esteem.

Schau [ʃau] *f* (16) (point of) view; (*Ausstellung*) show, exhibition; *zur* ~ *stellen* exhibit, display; *zur* ~ *tragen* display, sport, *Miene usw.*: wear; F *e-e* ~ *abziehen* put on a show; '~**bild** ⊕ *n* chart, graph; diagram; '~**bude** *f* show-booth; '~**budenbesitzer** *m* showman; '~**bühne** *f* stage.

Schauder ['ʃaudər] *m* (7) shudder (-ing), shiver; *fig.* horror; '♀**haft** horrible; '♀**n** (29, h. *u.* sn) shudder, shiver (*vor dat.* with; *bei* at).

schauen ['ʃauən] (25) *v/t.* see; (*betrachten*) view, behold; *v/i.* look; ~ *auf* (*acc.*) look at, *als Vorbild*: look upon.

Schauer ['ʃauər] *m* (7) (*Regen♀*, *Hagel♀ u. fig.*) shower; (*Schauder*) shudder, shiver; (*Anfall*) attack, fit; (*innere Erregung*) thrill; '~**drama** *n* thriller; '♀**lich** horrible, ghastly; '~**mann** ♣ *m* stevedore, docker, *bsd. Am.* longshoreman; '♀**n** (29) *s.* *schaudern*; *hageln*; '~**roman** *m* F thriller, shocker, *Am.* dime novel.

Schaufel ['ʃaufəl] *f* (15) shovel; *zum Schöpfen*: scoop; (*Rad♀*) paddle; (*Geweih♀*) palm; '~**geweih** *n* palmed antlers *pl.*; '♀**n** *v/t. u. v/i.* (29) shovel; '~**rad** *n* paddle-wheel.

'**Schaufenster** *n* shop-window, *Am.* store window; '~**auslage** *f* window display; '~**dekoration** *f* window-dressing; '~**reklame** *f* window-display advertising; '~**wettbewerb** *m* window-display competition.

'**Schau|fliegen** *n* stunt (flying), air display; '~**haus** *n* mortuary; '~**kampf** *m* exhibition bout; '~**kasten** *m* showcase, display case.

Schaukel ['ʃaukəl] *f* (15) swing; (*Wipp♀*) = '~**brett** *n* seesaw; '♀**n** *v/t. u. v/i.* (29) swing; *Wiege, Stuhl, Schiff*: rock; (*wippen*) seesaw; F (*zuwege bringen*) *sl.* swing, wangle; '~**pferd** *n* rocking-horse; '~**politik** *f* seesaw policy; '~**stuhl** *m* rocking-chair. [looker.)

'**schaulustig** curious; '♀**e** *m*, *f* on-)

Schaum [ʃaum] *m* (3³) foam, (*a. Bier♀*) froth; (*Seifen♀*) lather; (*Ab♀*) scum; *zu* ~ *schlagen* whip, beat up (*egg*); '~**bad** *n* bubble bath.

schäumen ['ʃɔymən] (25) foam, froth; *Wein usw.*: sparkle; *fig.* (*vor Wut* ~) foam (with rage).

'**Schaum|gebäck** *n* meringue(s *pl.*); '~**gummi** *m* foam rubber; '♀**ig** foamy, frothy; '~**löscher** *m* foam fire-extinguisher; '~**schläger** *m* (*Gerät*) whisk, egg-beater; *fig.* (*Prahler*) gas-bag; '~**schlägerei** [~ˈrai] *f fig.* humbug; '~**teppich** ✈ *m* foam carpet.

Scheiterhaufen

'**Schaumünze** *f* medal.
'**Schaumwein** *m* sparkling wine.
'**Schau|nummer** *f fig.* stunt; '**~platz** *m* scene; *s. Kriegs*♀; '**~prozeß** ⚥ *m* show trial.
schaurig ['ʃauriç] horrible, horrid.
'**Schau|spiel** *n* spectacle; *thea.* play; '**~spieler** *m* actor, player; *contp. fig.* play-actor; '**~spiele'rei** *f fig.* play--acting; '**~spielerin** *f* actress; '♀-**spielern** (29) *fig.* play-act, sham, F put it on; '**~spielhaus** *n* playhouse, theat|re, *Am.* -er; '**~spielkunst** *f* dramatic art; '**~spielschule** *f* drama school; '**~steller** *m* (7) exhibitor; *auf Jahrmärkten usw.*: showman; '**~stellung** *f* exhibition, show; '**~stück** *n* exhibit.
Scheck [ʃɛk] *m* (11) cheque, *Am.* check; '**~betrug** *m* cheque (*Am.* check) fraud; '**~betrüger(in** *f*) *m* person issuing bad cheques (*Am.* checks); '**~buch** *n*, '**~heft** *n* cheque--book, *Am.* checkbook.
Scheck|e ['ʃɛkə] *m* (13) piebald (*od.* dappled) horse; '♀**ig** piebald.
'**Scheckkarte** *f* cheque (*Am.* check) card.
scheel [ʃeːl] squint-eyed; *fig.* envious, jealous (*a.* '**~süchtig**); *j-n ~ ansehen* look askance at a p.
Scheffel ['ʃɛfəl] *m* (7) bushel; *sein Licht unter den ~ stellen* hide one's light under a bushel; '♀**n** *Geld*: amass, rake in.
Scheibe ['ʃaibə] *f* (15) disk (*a. der Sonne*); ⊕ *mst* disc, plate; (*Brot*♀ *usw.*) slice; (*Glas*♀) pane; (*Schieß*♀) target; (*Töpfer*♀) potter's wheel; *s. a. Töpfer*♀*, Riemen*♀*, Unterleg*♀.
'**Scheiben|bremse** *mot. f* disc brake; '**~honig** *m* honey in the comb; '**~schießen** *n* target practice; '**~stand** *m* butts *pl.*; '**~waschanlage** *mot. f* windscreen (*Am.* windshield) washers *pl.*; '**~wischer** *mot. m* wind-screen (*Am.* windshield) wiper.
Scheich [ʃaiç] *m* (3¹ *od.* 11) sheik(h).
Scheide ['ʃaidə] *f* (15) (*Säbel*♀) sheath, scabbard; *anat.* vagina; (*Grenze*) borderline; '**~linie** *f* separating line; '♀**n** (30) *v/t.* separate, divide; 🜂 analyse, refine, (*zerlegen*) decompose; *Eheleute*: divorce; *Ehe*: dissolve; *sich ~ lassen* (seek a) divorce; *v/i.* (sn) separate; (*weg-*

gehen) depart; (*sich trennen*) part; *aus dem Dienst ~* retire from service; *aus e-r Firma ~* leave a firm; *aus dem Leben ~* depart this life; '♀**nd** parting; *Jahr*: closing; '**~wand** *f* partition; *fig.* barrier; '**~wasser** 🜍 *n* aqua fortis; '**~weg** *m* cross-road; *fig. am ~e* at the cross--roads.
'**Scheidung** *f* separation; (*Ehe*♀) divorce; *die ~ einreichen* file a petition for divorce; '**~s-anwalt** *m* divorce lawyer; '**~sgrund** *m* ground for divorce; '**~sklage** *f* divorce-suit.
Schein [ʃain] *m* (3) shine, light; (*Schimmer*) gleam; (*Strahl*) flash; (*Feuer*♀) blaze; (*Bescheinigung*) certificate; (*Formular*) form; (*Zettel*) slip; (*Fahr*♀) ticket; (*Quittung*) receipt; (*Rechnung usw.*) bill; (*Geld*♀) bank-note, *Am.* bill; (*Ggs. Wirklichkeit*) appearance, *s. Anschein*; (*nur*) *zum ~* just for show; *der ~ trügt* appearances are deceptive; *den ~ wahren* keep up appearances; '**~angriff** *m* feint (attack); '♀**bar** apparent(ly *adv.*), seeming(ly); '**~blüte** 🜊 *f* specious prosperity; '**~-ehe** *f* fictitious marriage.
'**scheinen** (30) shine; *fig.* appear, seem; *wie es scheint* as it seems; *es scheint mir* it seems to me.
'**Schein|firma** *f* dummy firm; '**~friede** *m* hollow peace; '**~gefecht** *n* sham fight; '**~geschäft** 🜊 *n* fictitious transaction; '**~grund** *m* fictitious reason; (*Vorwand*) pretext; '♀**heilig** hypocritical; '**~heilige** *m* (18) hypocrite; '**~heiligkeit** *f* hypocrisy; '**~tod** *m* suspended animation; '♀**tot** seemingly dead; '**~werfer** *m* reflector, projector; ✂, ⚓ searchlight; *mot.* headlight; *thea.* (*a.* '**~werferlicht** *n*) spotlight.
Scheiß|dreck V ['ʃais-] *m* crap; (*ärgerliche Situation*) bloody nuisance; *sich um jeden ~ kümmern müssen* have to see to every bloody little thing; '**~e** V *f* (15) shit; '♀**en** V (30) shit; '**~kerl** V *m* bastard.
Scheit [ʃait] *n* (1 *u.* 3) log.
Scheitel ['ʃaitəl] *m* (7) crown of the head; *von Dingen*: vertex (*bsd.* 🜂); summit, top; (*Haar*♀) parting (of the hair); '♀**n** (29) part; '**~punkt** *m* vertex; *ast.* zenith (*a. fig.*); '**~winkel** *m* (vertically) opposite angle.
'**Scheiterhaufen** *m* (6) (funeral)

pile, pyre; *zur Hinrichtung*: stake.
scheitern ['ʃaɪtərn] (29, sn) (*a. fig.*)
be wrecked (*an dat.* on); *fig.* mis-
carry, fail; *zum* ♀ *bringen* wreck.
Schellack ['ʃɛlak] *m* (3) shellac.
Schelle ['ʃɛlə] *f* (15) (little) bell;
⊕ clamp, clip; *s. Maul*♀; *Kartenspiel*: ∼*n pl.* diamonds; '♀**n** (25)
s. klingeln.
'**Schellfisch** *m* haddock.
Schelm [ʃɛlm] *m* (3) rogue;
(*Schurke*) knave; *armer* ∼ poor
wretch; '∼**enroman** *m* picaresque
novel; '∼**enstreich** *m*, ∼**erei** [∼ə-
'raɪ] *f* (16) roguish trick; roguery;
'♀**isch** roguish, arch.
Schelt|e ['ʃɛltə] *f* (15) scolding; ∼
bekommen be scolded; '♀**en** (30)
v/t. scold, chide (*a. v/i.*); (*nennen*)
call; '∼**wort** *n* (3) abusive word.
Schema ['ʃeːma] *n* (11[²]) scheme;
⊕ *a.* diagram; (*Muster, Anordnung*)
pattern; *nach* ∼ F by rote; ♀**tisch**
[ʃeˈmaːtiʃ] schematic(ally *adv.*);
systematic(ally); ♀**tisieren** [∼mati-
'ziːrən] schematize, standardize.
Schemel ['ʃeːməl] *m* (7) (foot)stool.
Schemen ['ʃeːmən] *m* (6) phantom,
shadow; '♀**haft** shadowy.
Schenke ['ʃɛŋkə] *f* (15) inn, public
(-house), tavern.
Schenkel ['ʃɛŋkəl] *m* (7) (*Ober*♀)
thigh; (*Unter*♀) shank; (*Bein*) leg;
e-s Winkels: side; *e-s Dreiecks, e-r
Röhre*: leg; *e-s Zirkels*: foot; '∼**-
bruch** *m* thigh-bone fracture.
schenken ['ʃɛŋkən] (25) give, make
a present of; (*stiften*) donate; (*gewähren*) grant; *j-m et.* ∼ give *a* p.
a th., present *a* p. with *a* th.;
Schuld, Strafe: remit; *Getränke*:
retail, (*ein*∼) pour (out); *sich et.* ∼
(*weglassen, nicht tun*) skip; *j-m das
Leben* ∼ spare *a p.'s* life, *e-m Kinde*:
give birth to; *s. Aufmerksamkeit,
Freiheit, Gehör, Glauben usw.*
'**Schenkung** *f* donation; '∼**s-urkun-
de** *f* deed of gift.
scheppern ['ʃɛpərn] F (29) rattle.
Scherbe ['ʃɛrbə] *f* (15), '∼**n** *m* (6)
fragment, broken piece *od.* bit;
(*Topf*♀) potsherd.
Schere ['ʃeːrə] *f* (15) (*eine a pair of*)
scissors *pl.*; (*große* ∼) shears *pl.*;
(*Krebs*♀) claw; '♀**n** (30, *a.* 25) shear,
clip; *Haare*: cut; *Rasen*: mow; ⚓
warp, sheer; *sich* (*weg*)∼ F beat it;
sich nicht ∼ *um* not to bother about.

'**Scheren|fernrohr** ⚔ *n* scissor(s)-
-telescope; '∼**schleifer** *m* knife-
-grinder; '∼**schnitt** *m* silhouette.
Schererei [ʃeːrəˈraɪ] *f* (16) trouble.
Scherflein ['ʃɛrflaɪn] *n* (6) mite;
sein ∼ *beitragen* give one's mite,
weitS. do one's bit.
Scherge ['ʃɛrɡə] *m* (13) catchpole;
weitS. myrmidon.
Scherz [ʃɛrts] *m* (3²) jest, joke; ∼
treiben mit make fun of; *aus* ∼ in jest,
for fun; ∼ *beiseite* joking apart; '∼**-
artikel** *m* novelty; '♀**en** (27) joke,
make fun; *damit ist nicht zu* ∼ that's
not to be trifled with; '♀**haft** joking,
jocular; facetious; '∼**haftigkeit** *f*
facetiousness; '∼**wort** *n* (3) jocular
word; joke.
scheu [ʃɔy] **1.** shy; (*furchtsam*)
timid; *Pferd*: skittish; ∼ *machen*
frighten; **2.** ♀ *f* (16, *o. pl.*) shyness;
timidity; (*Ehrfurcht, Angst*) awe
(*vor dat.* of).
Scheuche ['ʃɔyçə] *f* (15) scarecrow;
'♀**n** (25) scare, frighten (*Vögel*:
shoo) away.
scheuen ['ʃɔyən] (25) *v/i.* shy *od.*
balk (*vor dat.* at); *v/t.* fear; *sich* ∼
vor (*dat.*) shy at, be afraid of; *sich*
∼ *zu inf.* be afraid to *inf.*, shrink
from *ger.*
Scheuer ['ʃɔyər] *f* (15) *s. Scheune*;
'∼**bürste** *f* scrubbing-brush; '∼**lappen** *m*, '∼**tuch** *n* scouring-cloth; '∼**-
leiste** *f* skirting-board; '♀**n** (29)
scour, scrub; *Haut*: chafe, rub.
'**Scheu|klappe** *f*, '∼**leder** *n* blinker
(*a. fig.*), *Am.* blinder.
Scheune ['ʃɔynə] *f* (15) barn, shed.
Scheusal ['ʃɔyzaːl] *n* (3) monster;
F (*Ekel*) beast; (*häßliche Person*) F
fright.
scheußlich ['ʃɔyslɪç] hideous, atrocious, abominable; '♀**keit** *f* hide-
ousness *usw.*; *konkret*: abomination,
horror; *Tat*: atrocity.
Schi [ʃiː] *m* (11, *pl.* '∼er) ski; ∼ *laufen*
ski; '∼**-abfahrt** *f* ski run; '∼**-anzug** *m*
ski suit.
Schicht [ʃɪçt] *f* (16) layer; *geol.* (*a.
Gesellschafts*♀) stratum, *pl.* strata;
Holz usw.: stack, pile; (*Reihe*) tier;
phot. emulsion; (*Arbeits*♀) shift (*a.
die Arbeiter*); (*Pause*) pause, rest;
(*Volks*♀) class; *breite* ∼*en der Bevölkerung* wide sections; ∼ *machen*
knock off (work); '∼**-arbeit(er** *m*)*f*
shift-work(er); '♀**en** (26) put in

layers; stack, pile up; stratify; *nach Klassen*: classify; F (*v/i.*) work in shifts; '~stoff *m* laminate(d plastic); '~ung *f* stratification; '~wechsel *m* change of shift; '2weise in layers; *bei der Arbeit*: in shifts; '~zuschlag *m* shift allowance.

Schick [ʃik] **1.** *m* (3, *o. pl.*) chic, stylishness, elegance; **2.** 2 chic, stylish; F swell.

schicken ['ʃikən] (25) send; *nach j-m od. et.* ~ send for; *sich* ~ hurry up; *sich* ~ *für j-n* be becoming to (*od.* befit) a p.; *sich* ~ *in* (*acc.*) put up with, resign o.s. to; *das schickt sich nicht* it isn't done; *s. April, Pontius.*

Schickeria [ʃikə'riːa] *f* (16, *o. pl.*): *die* ~ the trendies *pl.*

'**schicklich** proper, becoming; (*anständig*) decent; '2keit *f* propriety, decorum; decency; '2keitsgefühl *n* sense of propriety.

'**Schicksal** *n* (3) destiny, fate; *j-n s-m* ~ *überlassen* leave a p. to his fate; '2haft fateful; '~sfrage *f* vital question; '~sgefährte *m*, '~s- genosse *m* companion in misfortune; '~sglaube *m* fatalism; '~s- schlag *m* heavy blow.

'**Schickung** *f* providence, (divine) dispensation.

'**Schiebe|dach** *mot. n* sliding roof; '~fenster *n* sash-window.

schieben ['ʃiːbən] *v/t. u. v/i.* (30) push, shove; F *fig.* (*unredlich verfahren*) F wangle; *mit Lebensmitteln usw.*: profiteer, racketeer; *s. Bank, Kegel, Schuh.*

'**Schieber** *m* (7) ⊕ slide; (*Riegel*) bolt, (slide) bar; F *fig.* (*Betrüger*) profiteer, racketeer.

'**Schiebe|sitz** *mot. m* sliding seat; '~tür *f* sliding door; '~vorrichtung *f* slide, shifter.

'**Schiebung** F *f* swindle, F wangling; profiteering (job); racket; *a. Sport*: put-up job, rigging.

schied [ʃiːt] *pret. v. scheiden.*

Schieds|gericht ['ʃiːts-] *n* court of arbitration; *Sport usw.*: jury; *sich e-m* ~ *unterwerfen* submit to arbitration; '~richter *m* arbitrator; *bei Wettbewerben, Sport*: judge, *pl. a.* jury; *Tennis*: umpire; *Boxen, Fußball*: referee; '~richterball *m* throwdown; '2richterlich arbitral; *adv.* by arbitration; '~spruch *m*

(arbitral) award; '~verfahren *n* arbitration.

schief [ʃiːf] *adj.* (*schräg*) oblique (*a.* A), slanting; (*abfallend*) sloping, inclined; (*nach e-r Seite hängend*) lop-sided; *Mund, Gesicht*: wry; *fig.* (*falsch*) false, wrong; (*schlecht*) bad; (*verdreht*) distorted; *Urteil*: warped; ~e *Lage* false position; ~e *Ebene* inclined plane; *fig. auf die* ~e *Ebene geraten* go astray; *in ein* ~*es Licht setzen* place a p. in a bad light; *adv.* obliquely, aslant; at an angle; awry; *j-n* ~ *ansehen* look askance at a p.; '2e *f* (15) obliquity.

Schiefer ['ʃiːfər] *m* (7) slate; '~dach *n* slate roof; '2ig slaty; '~tafel *f* slate.

'**schief|gehen** go wrong; '~lachen *s. kranklachen*; '~wink(e)lig oblique- (-angled).

schielen ['ʃiːlən] **1.** (28) squint; ~ *nach* leer at, *fig. begehrlich*: ogle (at); **2.** 2 *n* squint(ing); '~d squint (-ing), cross-eyed.

schien [ʃiːn] *pret. v. scheinen.*

Schienbein ['ʃiːnbaɪn] *n* shin-bone.

Schiene ['ʃiːnə] *f* (15) rail; *am Rad*: iron band, rim; 🎗 splint; ⊕ bar, guide rail; '2n (25) 🎗 splint, put in splints.

'**Schienen|bus** *m* rail bus; '~fahr- zeug *n* rail vehicle; '~netz *n* railway (*Am.* railroad) system; '~strang *m* track, railway-line.

schier [ʃiːr] sheer, pure; *adv.* (*beinahe*) almost, nearly.

Schierling 🎗 ['ʃiːrlɪŋ] *m* (3[1]) hemlock.

'**Schieß|baumwolle** *f* gun-cotton; '~befehl *m* firing order; '~bude *f* shooting gallery.

schießen ['ʃiːsən] **1.** (30) *v/t.* shoot; (*feuern*) fire; ⚔ blast; *Fußball*: *ein Tor* ~ score (a goal); *sich mit j-m* ~ fight a pistol duel with a p.; *e-e S.* ~ *lassen* let fly *od.* go; F *schieß los!* fire away!; *s. Bock, Zügel*; *v/i.* (h.) shoot (*auf acc.* at); (*das Feuer eröffnen*) open fire; (sn) (*sich schnell bewegen*) shoot, dart, rush; *Wasser, Blut*: gush; *Pflanze usw.*: spring (up); *Gedanke*: flash (*durch den Kopf* through one's mind); *gut* ~ be a good shot; *weit* ~ carry far; *in Samen* ~ go (*od.* run) to seed; *s. Pilz, Kraut*; **2.** 2 *n* (6) shooting, firing;

F *er (es) ist zum* ~*!* he (it) is a scream!
Schießerei [~'raɪ] *f* (16) shoot-out; (*ständiges Schießen*) shooting.
'**Schieß|hund** *fig. m: aufpassen wie ein* ~ watch like a lynx; '~**krieg** *m* shooting war; '~**pulver** *n* gunpowder; '~**scharte** ⚔ *f* loop-hole, embrasure; '~**scheibe** *f* target; '~**stand** *m* shooting-range, ⚔ rifle-range, butts *pl.*; '⚩**wütig** trigger-happy.
Schiff [ʃif] *n* (3) ship, vessel, *kleineres:* boat, (*a.pl.*) craft; (*Kirchen*⚩) nave; *typ.* galley.
Schiffahrt *f* navigation.
schiff|bar navigable; '⚩**bau** *m* shipbuilding; '⚩**bruch** *m* shipwreck; ~ *erleiden* be shipwrecked, *fig.* be wrecked, fail; '~**brüchig** shipwrecked; '⚩**brücke** *f* pontoon-bridge; '⚩**chen** *n* (6) little ship; (*Weber*⚩) shuttle; ⚔ *sl.* forage cap; '~**en** *v/i.* (25, sn) navigate, sail; F (*harnen*; h.) piss; *v/t.* ship.
Schiffer ['ʃifər] *m* (7) sailor; (*Fluß*⚩) boatman; (*Schiffsführer*) navigator; (*Handelsschiffskapitän*) skipper; '~**klavier** F *n* accordion.
'**Schiffs-arzt** *m* ship's doctor.
'**Schiffschaukel** *f* swing-boat.
'**Schiffs|eigner** *m* shipowner; '~**fracht** *f* (ship's) freight; '~**frachtbrief** *m* bill of lading; '~**journal** *n* log-book; '~**junge** *m* cabin-boy; '~**kapitän** *m* (sea-)captain; '~**koch** *m* ship's cook; '~**kran** *m* ship's crane; '~**küche** *f* galley, caboose; '~**ladung** *f* shipload; (*Fracht*) cargo, freight; '~**mannschaft** *f* crew; '~**raum** *m* hold; (*Rauminhalt*) tonnage; '~**rumpf** *m* hull; '~**schraube** *f* screw; '~**verkehr** *m* shipping traffic; '~**werft** *f* dockyard; '~**zwieback** *m* ship's biscuit, hardtack.
'**Schi|gebiet** *n* skiing area; '~**hose** *f* ski pants *pl.*
Schikan|e [ʃi'kɑːnə] *f* (15) chicane (-ry), nasty trick; *pl. a.* persecution; *Rennsport:* hazard; F *fig. mit allen* ~*n* with all the trimmings; ⚩**ieren** [~ka'niːrən] persecute; ⚩**ös** [~'nøːs] vexatious, spiteful.
'**Schi|lauf(en** *n*) *m* skiing; '~**läufer** (-*in* *f*) *m* skier.
Schild [ʃilt] **1.** *m* (3) shield (*a.* ⊕); (*Wappen*⚩) (e)scutcheon, coat-of-arms; *im* ~*e führen* be up to *a th.*;

2. *n* (1) (*Laden*⚩) sign(-board), facia; (*Tür*⚩) door-plate; (*Namens-, Firmen-, Tür*⚩) name-plate; (*Wegweiser*) sign-post; (*Etikett*) label; (*Mützen*⚩) peak; '~**bürger** *m* Gothamite; '~**drüse** *f* thyroid gland.
Schilder|haus ['ʃildərhaus] *n* sentry-box; '⚩**n** (29) *v/t. fig.* describe, depict, *kurz:* outline; '~**ung** *f* description.
'**Schild|knappe** *m* shield-bearer, squire; '~**kröte** *f* (*Land*⚩) tortoise; (*See*⚩) turtle; '~**krötensuppe** *f* turtle-soup; ~**patt** ['~pat] *n* tortoise-shell; '~**wache** ⚔ *hist.* *f* sentry.
Schilf [ʃilf] *n* (3) reed; '⚩**ig** reedy; '~**matte** *f* rush-mat; '~**rohr** *n* reed.
'**Schilift** *m* ski-lift.
schillern ['ʃilərn] (29) play in different colo(u)rs; *in Regenbogenfarben:* iridesce; '~**d** *adj.* iridescent, opalescent; *fig. P.:* dazzling.
Schimär|e [ʃi'mɛːrə] *f* (15) chimera; ⚩**isch** chimerical.
Schimmel ['ʃiməl] *m* (7) **1.** white horse; **2.** (*Pilz*) mo(u)ld, mildew.
'**schimm(e)lig** mo(u)ldy, musty.
'**schimmeln** (29, h. *u.* sn) get mo(u)ldy.
'**Schimmelpilz** *m* mo(u)ld fungus.
Schimmer ['ʃimər] *m* (7) gleam (*a. fig. der Hoffnung*), glimmer; F *keinen* ~ *s.* Ahnung; '⚩**n** (29) gleam, glisten.
Schimpanse [ʃim'panzə] *m* (13) chimpanzee.
Schimpf [ʃimpf] *m* (3) insult; (*Schande*) disgrace; *mit* ~ *und Schande* ignominiously; '⚩**en** (25) *v/t.* abuse, revile; *v/i.* be abusive; *rail* (*über, auf acc.* at, against); '⚩**lich** ignominious, disgraceful (*für* to); '~**name** *m* abusive name; '~**wort** *n* invective.
Schindel ['ʃindəl] *f* (15) shingle; '~**dach** *n* shingle-roof.
schinden ['ʃindən] (30) flay, skin; (*bedrücken*) oppress, drive hard, *Arbeiter:* sweat; *sich* ~ work hard, slave; F *fig.* (*heraus*~) *sl.* wangle; *Eindruck* ~ show off; *Zeit* ~ play for time.
'**Schinder** *m* (7) knacker; *fig.* oppressor, martinet; sweater; ~**ei** [~'raɪ] *fig. f* oppression; sweating; (*schwere Arbeit*) grind, drudgery.

Schindluder F [ˈʃintluːdər] *n*: ~ *treiben mit* play fast and loose with.
Schinken [ˈʃiŋkən] *m* (6) ham; F *fig.* (*Bild*) daub; (*Buch*) old *od.* fat book; '~**wurst** *f* spiced ham.
Schipiste [ˈʃiː-] *f* ski run.
Schippe [ˈʃipə] *f* (15) shovel; *Kartenspiel*: ~*n pl.* spades; '♀**n** (25) shovel.
Schirm [ʃirm] *m* (3) (*Wand*♀, *Wind*♀, *Projektions*♀, *Bild*♀) screen; (*Lampen*♀) shade; (*Mützen*♀) peak; (*Regen*♀) umbrella; (*Schutz*♀) shield; *fig. a.* shelter, protection; '♀**en** (25) shield, protect; '~**herr(in** *f*) *m* protector, *f* protectress, patron(ess *f*); '~**herrschaft** *f* protectorate; *e-r Veranstaltung*: auspices *pl.*; '~**mütze** *f* peaked cap; '~**ständer** *m* umbrella-stand; '~**wand** *f* screen(ing wall).
Schispringen [ˈʃiː-] *n* ski-jumping.
Schiß V [ʃis] 1. *m* (4) shit(ting); *fig.* (*Angst*) funk; ~ *haben* be in a blue funk (*vor dat.* of); ~ *bekommen* get cold feet; 2. ♀ *pret. v.* scheißen.
'**Schi|stiefel** *m* ski boot; '~**stock** *m* ski stick (*Am.* pole); '~**träger** *mot. m* ski rack.
schizo|phren [ʃitsoˈfreːn] schizophrenic; ♀**phrenie** [~freˈniː] *f* (15) schizophrenia.
Schlacht [ʃlaxt] *f* (16) battle; *e-e* ~ *liefern* give battle (*dat.* to); '~**bank** *f* shambles *pl.*, oft *sg.*; '~**beil** *n* butcher's ax(e); '♀**en** (26) kill; slaughter (*a. fig.*); '~**enbummler** *m* camp-follower; *Sport*: fan.
Schlächter [ˈʃlɛçtər] *m* (7) butcher; ~**ei** [~təˈrai] *f* (16) butcher's shop; *fig.* slaughter.
'**Schlacht|feld** *n* battlefield; '~**getümmel** *n* mêlée (*fr.*); '~**haus** *n*, '~**hof** *m* slaughter-house, abattoir (*fr.*); '~**kreuzer** *m* battle-cruiser; '~**messer** *n* butcher's knife; '~**opfer** *n* victim; '~**ordnung** *f* order of battle; '~**plan** *m* plan of action (*a. fig.*); '~**reihe** *f* line of battle; '~**roß** *hist. n* charger; '~**ruf** *m* war-cry; '~**schiff** *n* battleship; '~**ung** *f* slaughter(ing); '~**vieh** *n* slaughter cattle.
Schlack|e [ˈʃlakə] *f* (15) *v. Kohle*: cinder; *metall.* dross, slag, scoria; ⚒ waste product; ~*n pl.* (*Diät*) roughage; '♀**en** (25) slag; '♀**(e)rig** F *Wetter*: slushy; '♀**ig** slaggy, drossy; '~**wurst** *f* *etwa*: German

sausage.
Schlaf [ʃlaːf] *m* (5, *o. pl.*) sleep; *im* ~ asleep; in one's sleep, *fig.* (*leicht*) blindfold; *e-n festen* (*leichten*) ~ *haben* be a sound (light) sleeper; *in* ~ *sinken* fall asleep; *in tiefem* ~ *liegen* be fast asleep; '~**abteil** *n* sleeping-compartment; '~**anzug** *m* pyjamas, *Am.* pajamas *pl.*; ~**couch** [ˈ~kautʃ] *f* (11¹, *pl.* -es) daybed.
Schläfchen [ˈʃlɛːfçən] *n* (6) doze, nap; F *ein* ~ *machen* take a nap.
'**Schlafcouch** *f* studio couch.
Schläfe [ˈʃlɛːfə] *f* (15) temple.
schlafen [ˈʃlaːfən] (30) sleep (*a. fig.*); be asleep; F (*unaufmerksam sein*) be napping; ~ *gehen*, *sich* ~ *legen* go to bed; *länger* ~ sleep late; ~ *Sie wohl!* good night!, sleep well!; '♀**szeit** *f* bedtime.
'**Schlaf-entzug** *m* sleep deprivation.
Schläfer [ˈʃlɛːfər] *m* (7), '~**in** *f* sleeper; '♀**n** (29): *mich schläfert* I feel (*od.* I am) sleepy.
schlaff [ʃlaf] slack, loose; (*kraftlos*) limp; *Fleisch*, *Haut*, *Charakter*: flabby; *fig. Grundsätze usw.*: lax; (*träge*) indolent; (*nachlässig*; *a.* ✝ *Börse*) slack; (*träge*) sluggish; '♀**heit** *f* slackness; limpness; flabbiness; laxity; indolence.
'**Schlaf|gast** *m* overnight guest; '~**gelegenheit** *f* sleeping accommodation; '~**gemach** *n* bedroom.
Schlafittchen [ʃlaˈfitçən] F *n*: *j-n beim* ~ *nehmen* (seize by the) collar.
'**Schlaf|krankheit** *f* sleeping-sickness; '~**lied** *n* lullaby; '♀**los** sleepless; '~**losigkeit** *f* sleeplessness, insomnia; '~**mittel** *n* soporific; '~**mütze** *f* nightcap; F *fig.* slowcoach, sleepyhead.
schläfrig [ˈʃlɛːfriç] sleepy, drowsy; '♀**keit** *f* drowsiness.
'**Schlaf|rock** *m* dressing-gown; '~**saal** *m* dormitory; '~**sack** *m* sleeping-bag; '~**sofa** *n* bed-couch; '~**stadt** *f* dormitory town; '~**sucht** *f* somnolence; '~**tablette** *f* sleeping-pill; '~**trunk** *m* F nightcap; '♀**trunken** drowsy; '~**wagen** 🚋 *m* sleeping-car, *bsd. Am.* sleeper; '♀**wandeln** walk in one's sleep; ~**wandler** [ˈ~vandlər] *m* sleep-walker; somnambulist; '♀**wandlerisch** somnambulistic; *mit* ~*er Sicherheit* with uncanny sureness, unerringly; '~**zimmer** *n* bedroom.

Schlag [ʃlaːk] *m* (3³) blow (*a. fig.*); *a. der Uhr, des Kolbens, beim Tennis od. Rudern*: stroke; *mit der flachen Hand*: slap; *Boxen* (*a. ~kraft*): punch; *Pferd, Gewehr*: kick; *mit der Peitsche*: lash; (*Aufprall*) impact; *⚡* shock; *lauter ~* bang; *dumpfer ~* thud; (*Krach*) crash; (*Schlagfluß*) apoplexy; (*Puls♀, Herz♀, Trommel♀*) beat; (*Donner♀*) clap (of thunder); (*Essen, Portion*) helping; (*Vogelsang*) warbling; (*Holz♀*) cut (in the wood); (*Wagen♀*) carriage-door; (*Art*) race, kind, sort, *bsd. vom Tier*: breed; *~ ins Gesicht* slap in the face (*a. fig.*); *s. Kontor, Wasser; Schläge bekommen* get a beating; *~ sechs Uhr* on the stroke of six; *mit 'einem ~ at a blow, s. a. schlagartig; *~ader** [ˈʃlak-] *f* artery; '**~anfall** *m* apoplectic fit, stroke; '**♀-artig** abrupt (*-ly adv.*); '**~ball** *m Spiel*: rounders *sg.*; '**~baum** *m* turnpike; '**~bolzen** *✕ m* firing-pin; '**~bohrer** *m* percussion drill.

schlagen [ˈʃlaːgən] (30) *v/t.* strike, knock, (*a. verprügeln*) beat; *mit der Faust*: punch, hit; (*besiegen*) defeat, (*a. = übertreffen*) beat; *Eier*: beat, whip; *Geld*: coin; *Holz*: fell, hew; *e-e Schlacht*: fight; *ans Kreuz ~* crucify; *ein Kreuz ~* make the sign of the cross; *auf den Preis ~* clap on; *in Papier ~* wrap up in paper; *s. Alarm, Blindheit, Brücke, Kapital usw.*; *sich ~* (have a) fight, (*duellieren*) fight a duel; *sich aus dem Kopf od. Sinn ~* put *a th.* out of one's mind; *sich ~ zu j-m* side with; *sich gut ~* stand one's ground; *sich geschlagen geben* give up, *fig. j-m*: bow to; *fig. geschlagen* (*erschöpft*) all in, (*überrascht*) dum(b)founded, (*entmutigt*) down and out; *e-e geschlagene Stunde* a full (F solid) hour; *v/i.* strike, beat; *Herz, Puls*: beat, *stärker*: throb; *Uhr*: strike; *Pferd, Gewehr usw.*: kick; *Vogel*: warble, sing; *das schlägt nicht in mein Fach* that is not in my line; *um sich ~* lay about one; *s. Art*; '**~d** *fig.* striking; *Argument, Beweis*: conclusive; *~e Wetter ✕ n/pl.* firedamp.

Schlager [ˈʃlaːgər] *m* (7) *♪* (song) hit; *thea.* draw, smash hit; *♣* drawcard, (sales) hit; *weitS.* hit.

Schläger [ˈʃlɛːgər] *m* (7) **a)** *Sport*: batsman; (*Raufbold*) rough, *Am.* tough, *sl.* bruiser; (*Pferd*) kicker; **b)** *Gerät, Kricket usw.*: bat; *Golf*: club; *Fechten*: rapier, sword; *Tennis*: racket; *Federball*: battledore; *Hockey*: stick; *Küche*: whisk, (egg-)beater.; **c)** (*Vogel*) warbler; **~ei** [~ˈraɪ] *f* (16) brawl, (free) fight, scuffle.

'**Schlager|festival** *n* song festival; '**~musik** *f* pop music; '**~sänger(in** *f*) *m* pop singer.

schlag|fertig [ˈʃlaːkfɛrtiç] *fig.* ready-witted, quick at repartee; *~e Antwort* repartee; '**♀fertigkeit** *f fig.* ready wit, quickness of repartee; '**♀fluß** *m* apoplexy; '**♀holz** *n Sport*: bat; '**♀-instrument** *♪ n* percussion instrument; '**♀kraft** *f Boxen u. fig.*: punch; *✕* combat effectiveness; '**~kräftig** powerful; *Beweis*: conclusive; '**♀licht** *n paint. u. fig.* strong light; '**♀loch** *n* pot-hole; '**♀mann** *m beim Rudern*: stroke; '**♀-obers** *n*, '**♀rahm** *m s. Schlagsahne*; '**♀ring** *m* brass knuckles; *♪* plectrum, quill; '**♀sahne** *f* whipped cream; '**♀schatten** *m* cast shadow; '**♀seite** *⚓ f* list; *~ haben ⚓* list; F (*betrunken sein*) be half-seas-over; '**♀stock** *m der Polizei*: truncheon, baton; '**♀-uhr** *f* striking clock; '**♀wechsel** *m Boxen*: exchange of blows; '**♀werk** *n* striking mechanism; '**♀wort** *n* catchword; *weitS.* slogan; '**♀wortregister** *n* subject index; '**♀zeile** *typ. f* headline; '**♀zeug** *♪ n* percussion instruments *pl.*, drums *pl.*; '**♀zeuger** *♪ m* drummer; *im Orchester*: percussionist.

schlaksig F [ˈʃlaːkziç] gangling.

Schlamassel [ʃlaˈmasəl] F *m, n* (7) mess.

Schlamm [ʃlam] *m* (3) mud, mire; '**~bad** *n* mud bath.

schlämmen ⊕ [ˈʃlɛmən] (25) wash.

'**schlammig** muddy, miry.

'**Schlammpackung** *f* mud pack.

Schlamp|e [ˈʃlampə] *f* (15) slut, slattern; '**♀en** (25) *v/i.* do a sloppy job; *a. v/t.* botch; '**~er** *m* slouch; **~erei** [~ˈraɪ] slovenliness; (*Nachlässigkeit*) slackness; *konkret*: mess, muddle; sloppy job; '**♀ig** slovenly; *Arbeit*: a. sloppy, slipshod.

schlang [ʃlaŋ] *pret. v. schlingen.*

Schlange [ˈʃlaŋə] *f* (15) snake, *bsd. rhet.* serpent; ⊕ coil; *fig.* (*Men-*

schen♀) queue, *Am.* line; *falsche ~*
snake in the grass; *~ stehen* F stand
in queue, queue up, *Am.* stand in
line, line up (*nach* for).

schlängeln ['ʃlɛŋəln] (29): *sich ~*
twist, wind; worm o.s. (*durch*
through *a crowd etc.*); *hin und her:*
wriggle; *bsd. Fluß u. Weg:* meander.

'**Schlangen|beschwörer** *m* snake-
-charmer; '*~biß* *m* snake-bite; '*~-*
gift *n* snake-poison; '*~linie* *f* sin-
uous line; '*~mensch* *m* contortion-
ist; '*~rohr* *n* spiral tube *od.* pipe.

schlank [ʃlaŋk] slender, slim, svelte;
die moderne ~e Linie the waistline;
'♀**heit** *f* slenderness; '♀**heitskur** *f*
reducing (*od.* slimming) cure; *e-e ~*
machen reduce, slim; *~weg* ['~'vɛk]
flatly.

schlapp [ʃlap]s. *schlaff*; '♀**e** *f* (15)
setback, reverse; (*Niederlage*) beating, defeat; '♀**hut** *m* slouch hat;
'*~machen* F let down; '♀**macher** *m*,
'♀**schwanz** F *m* slacker, F sissy,
softy; '♀**schuh** F *m* slipper.

Schlaraffen|land [ʃla'rafənlant] *n*
fool's paradise, (land of) Cockaigne;
~leben *n* idle and luxurious life.

schlau [ʃlau] sly, cunning, crafty,
wily; F *fig. ~er Posten* soft job;
F *ich werde nicht ~ daraus* I can't
make head or tail of it; ♀**berger**
['~bɛrgər] F *m* (7) slyboots *sg.*, F
smartie.

Schlauch [ʃlaux] *m* (3¹) tube, (*bieg-
samer:* flexible) pipe; *zum Spritzen:*
hose; (*Fahrrad♀, Auto♀*) inner tube;
(*Strapaze*) strain; (*Eselsbrücke*) F
crib, *Am.* pony; '*~boot* *n* (air *od.*
⚓ life) raft; (*Gummiboot*) rubber
dinghy; '♀**en** F *fig. v/t.* fag *a p.*
(out), tell on *a p.*; *seelisch:* go hard
with *a p.*; ✗ give *a p.* hell (*Am. sl.*
chicken).

Schläue ['ʃlɔʏə] *f* (15, *o. pl.*) *s.*
Schlauheit.

Schlaufe ['ʃlaufə] *f* (15) loop.

'**Schlau|heit** *f* slyness, cunning;
'*~kopf* *m*, '*~meier* F *m* (7) *s. Schlauberger.*

schlecht [ʃlɛçt] **1.** *adj. allg.* bad;
(*boshaft, verworfen*) *a.* wicked;
(*böse*) evil; (*gemein*) base, mean;
(*armselig, wertlos*) poor; *Ware:* inferior; *~ sein in et.* be poor at a th.;
~e Laune haben be in a bad temper;
~er Tag leistungsmäßig: off day; *~e*
Zeiten hard times; *mir ist ~* I

feel sick; *~ werden* go bad; *~er*
werden get worse, worsen; *s. gehen,*
stehen, Trost; **2.** *adv.* badly, ill; *~*
und recht after a fashion; *~erdings*
['~ər'diŋs] absolutely, downright;
'♀**erstellung** *f* discrimination (*gen.*
against); *~gelaunt* ['~gə'launt] ill-
-humo(u)red, in a bad temper;
'*~hin*, *~weg* ['~'vɛk] simply; in a
word; '♀**igkeit** *f* *s. schlecht:* bad-
ness; baseness; wickedness; '*~-*
machen: *j-n ~* run a p. down,
backbite a p.; '♀'**wetterfront** *f* bad
weather front; '♀'**wetterperiode** *f*
spell of bad weather.

schlecken ['ʃlɛkən] *usw. s.* lecken.

Schlegel ['ʃle:gəl] *m* (7) (*Trommel♀*)
drumstick; ⊕ mallet, beetle; *vom*
Kalb usw.: leg.

Schleh|dorn ♀ ['ʃle:dɔrn] *m* black-
thorn; '*~e* ✗ *f* (15) sloe, wild
plum.

Schlei(e *f*) ['ʃlaɪ(ə)] *m* (3 [15]) tench.

schleich|en ['ʃlaɪçən] (30, sn) sneak,
slink; (*kriechen, a. Zeit*) creep,
crawl; (*sich hinschleppen*) drag; *im*
Finstern ~ prowl in the dark; *~end*
sneaking; creeping; (*verstohlen*)
furtive; *Fieber, Gift usw.:* slow,
lingering; '♀**er** *m* (7) creeper; *fig.*
sneak; (*Leisetreter*) *Am.* F pussy-
foot(er); ♀**erei** [~ə'raɪ] *f* sneaking;
'♀**handel** *m* illicit trade; smuggling;
(*schwarzer Markt*) black market;
♀**weg** ['~ve:k] *m* secret path; *fig.*
underhand means *pl.*; *auf ~en* surreptitiously; '♀**werbung** *f* surrepti-
tious advertising, F plugging.

Schleier ['ʃlaɪər] *m* (7) veil (*a. fig.*);
(*Dunst♀, Nebel♀*) haze; *phot.* fog;
fig. unter dem ~ (*gen.*) under the
veil of; '*~eule* *f* barn-owl; '*~flor*
m crape; '♀**haft** *fig.* (*verschwommen*)
hazy; (*rätselhaft*) mysterious, inexplicable.

Schleif|bahn ['ʃlaɪfba:n] *f* slide;
'*~e* *f* (15) (*Schlinge; a.* ✗, ✈) loop;
(*gebundene ~*) slip-knot; (*Band♀*)
bow, knot; (*Kurve*) loop (*a.* ✗),
(*horseshoe*) bend; (*schlittenartiges*
Gestell) sled(ge), drag; *s. Schleif-
bahn;* '♀**en** **1.** (30) *a.* (*schärfen*)
grind; (*wetzen*) whet; (*glätten,*
schmirgeln) abrade, *feiner:* smooth,
polish (*a. fig.*); *Edelstein, Glas:* cut;
F ✗ drill hard, *s. a. schlauchen;*
2. *v/t. u. v/i.* (25) (*schleppen*) drag;
(*rutschen*) skid, slide; *Bauten:* raze,

demolish, ✗ a. dismantle; ♪ slur;
'**~er** m (7) grinder; polisher;
(Edelstein⌂) cutter; F ✗ martinet;
'**~lack** m body varnish; '**~ma-
schine** f grinding-machine; '**~
mittel** n abrasive; '**~papier** n
emery paper; '**~rad** n grinding-
-wheel; '**~ring** ⚡ m slip ring; '**~
stein** m whetstone, hone; *drehbarer*: grindstone.

Schleim [ʃlaɪm] m (3) slime; *physiol.*, ⚕ mucus, *bsd. in der Brust*:
phlegm; '**~absonderung** f mucous
secretion; '**~drüse** f mucous gland;
'**~haut** f mucous membrane; '⌂**ig**
slimy (a. fig. contp.); mucous; '⌂**-
lösend** expectorant; '**~suppe** f
gruel.

schlemm|en ['ʃlɛmən] (25) feast,
gorge, gormandize; *weitS.* revel, live
high; '⌂**er** m (7) (*Feinschmecker*)
gourmet; (*Fresser*) glutton; *weitS.*
reveller; ⌂**erei** [~'raɪ] f feasting, rev-
elry; gormandizing; '⌂**erlokal** n
gourmet restaurant.

schlen|dern ['ʃlɛndərn] (29, sn)
stroll, saunter; ⌂**drian** ['~drɪɑːn] m
(3) (old) jogtrot; (*Bummelei*) dawdling, muddling on.

schlenkern ['ʃlɛŋkərn] (29) dangle;
swing (*mit den Armen usw.* one's
arms *etc.*).

Schlepp|dampfer ['ʃlɛp-] m tug
(-boat); '**~e** f (15) *am Kleid*: train;
(*Schweif*) trail; '⌂**en** v/t. u. v/i. (25)
drag (*sich o.s.*), lug; (*schwer tragen*)
carry, *Am.* F tote; ⚓, ✈, *mot.*
tow, haul, ⚓ tug; ✈ (*Kunden werben*) tout; '⌂**end** dragging; (*langsam, a.* ✈) slow, sluggish; *Sprache*:
drawling; '**~er** m (7) ⚓ tug (-boat);
mot. tractor; ✈ (*Kundenwerber*)
tout; '**~kahn** m lighter, barge; '**~-
lift** m ski tow; '**~netz** n drag-net;
'**~netzfischer(boot** n) m trawler; '**~
schiff** n tug (-boat); '**~seil** n, '**~tau** n
tow-rope; *ins Schlepptau nehmen* take
in tow (a. fig.); '**~zug** m train of
barges; *mot.* truck train.

Schles|ier ['ʃleːzjər] m (7), '⌂**isch**
Silesian.

Schleuder ['ʃlɔʏdər] f (15) sling,
(a. ✗) catapult, *Am.* slingshot; ⊕
s. ~maschine; '**~artikel** ✝ m catchpenny article; '**~ball** m sling ball;
'**~honig** m strained honey; '**~-
maschine** f centrifuge; '⌂**n** (29)
v/t. fling, hurl; *mit e-r Schleuder*:

sling; ✗ catapult; ⊕ centrifuge;
Honig: strain; *Wäsche*: spin-dry;
v/i. *mot.* skid, side-slip; '**~preis** m
ruinous (*od.* give-away) price; '**~-
sitz** ✗ m ejector seat; '**~ware** f
catchpenny article.

schleunig ['ʃlɔʏnɪç] quick, speedy;
adv. (a. '**~st**) in all haste; (*sofort*)
immediately, forthwith.

Schleuse ['ʃlɔʏzə] f (15) sluice (a.
fig.); (*Kanal⌂*) lock; '⌂**n** lock; *fig.*
channel; *P.*: direct; *s. ein~*; '**~ntor**
n flood-gate.

Schlich[1] [ʃlɪç] m (3) trick, dodge;
j-m auf die ~ *e kommen* find a p. out.

schlich[2] *pret. v.* schleichen.

schlicht [ʃlɪçt] plain, simple; (*glatt*)
smooth, sleek; '**~en** (26) (*glätten*)
smooth; *Streit usw.*: settle, adjust;
'⌂**er** m (7), '⌂**erin** f mediator;
durch Schiedsspruch: arbitrator;
'⌂**feile** f smooth-cut file; '⌂**heit** f
plainness, simplicity; '⌂**ung** f settlement; (*Vermittlung*) mediation;
durch Schiedsspruch: arbitration;
'⌂**ungs-ausschuß** m arbitration
committee.

Schlick [ʃlɪk] m (3) mud, slime.

schlief [ʃliːf] *pret. v.* schlafen.

schließ|bar ['ʃliːsbaːr] lockable;
⌂**e** ['~sə] f (15) catch, latch; *am
Kleid, an der Handtasche usw.*:
clasp; '**~en** (30) v/t. shut, close
(*beide a.* sich; *a.* ⚡ *Stromkreis*);
mit Schlüssel: lock; *Betrieb*: shut
down; *Bündnis, Kreis*: form;
Freundschaft, Ehe: contract; *Handel*: strike, conclude; *Vertrag,
Brief, Rede*: conclude; *Frieden*:
conclude, make; (*beenden*) finish,
end; *parl. usw. Debatte, Sitzung*:
close, *auf Antrag*: closure; *sich* ~
Wunde: close; *sich* ~ *an* (acc.) follow (upon); *in die Arme* ~ clasp in
one's arms; *j-n ins Herz geschlossen
haben fig.* be very fond of a p.;
in sich ~ include, (*unausgesprochen*)
imply; *geschlossen für et. sein od.
stimmen* go (*od.* be) solid for; *ge-
schlossene Gesellschaft* private
party; v/i. shut, close; *Läden*: close;
Schule: break up; *bei e-r Rede usw.*:
close (*mit* with); *aus et.* ~ *auf* (acc.)
infer (*od.* conclude *od.* gather) a th.
from a th.; *auf et.* ~ *lassen* suggest
a th.; *dem Aussehen nach zu* ~ judging from the appearance; '⌂**er** m (7)
door-keeper; *im Gefängnis*: jailer,

turnkey; ♀**fach** n Bank: safe deposit box; (Bahnhofs♀) left-luggage locker; s. Postfach; '**⁓lich** final, last, eventual; adv. finally, at last; (am Ende) eventually; (⁓ doch, eigentlich) after all; '♀**muskel** m constrictor; '♀**ung** f closing (a. ⚟), conclusion; e-r Debatte: closure, Am. cloture; e-s Betriebes: shut-down, closure.

Schliff [ʃlif] **1.** m (3) polish (a. fig.); v. Edelstein, Glas: cut; fig. letzter ⁓ finishing touch(es); F ⚔ hard drill; **2.** ♀ pret. v. schleifen 1.

schlimm [ʃlim] allg. bad; (bedenklich) serious, grave; ⁓er worse; am ⁓sten, das ♀ste the worst; ⁓er machen (werden) s. verschlimmern; ⁓ daran sein be badly off; '**⁓sten-falls** at the worst.

Schling|e ['ʃliŋə] f (15) sling (a. ⚔), loop; sich zusammenziehende: noose (a. fig.); gebundene: (running) knot; Draht, Tau: coil; hunt. snare (a. fig.); fig. j-m in die ⁓ gehen walk into a p.'s trap; sich aus der ⁓ ziehen wriggle out of it; '**⁓el** m (7) rascal; '♀**en** (30) wind, twine; (gierig schlucken) gulp, gorge; sich ⁓ um wind (od. coil) round; '♀**ern** ⚓ (29) roll; '**⁓gewächs** n, '**⁓pflanze** f climbing plant, creeper, bsd. Am. climber.

Schlips [ʃlips] m (4) (neck)tie.

Schlitten ['ʃlitən] m (6) sledge, bsd. Am. sled; (bsd. Pferde♀) sleigh; (Rodel♀) toboggan; ⊕ sliding carriage; der Schreibmaschine: carriage; F (Auto) car, sl. heap; ⁓ fahren sledge, (rodeln) toboggan; F fig. mit j-m ⁓ fahren F wipe the floor with a p.; '**⁓bahn** f sledge-run; '**⁓fahrt** f sledge-ride; sleigh-ride.

schlittern ['ʃlitərn] (29, h. u. sn) slide (a. fig.), a. mot. skid.

'**Schlittschuh** m skate; ⁓ laufen skate; '**⁓laufen** n skating; '**⁓läufer(in** f) m skater.

Schlitz [ʃlits] m (3³) slit, im Kleid: slash; (Einwurf♀) slot; '**⁓-auge** n slit eye; '♀**-äugig** slit-eyed; '♀**en** v/t. u. v/i. (27, sn) slit, slash; ⊕ slot.

schlohweiß ['ʃloː'vais] snow-white.

Schloß[1] [ʃlɔs] n (2¹) castle; (Palast) palace; ⁓[2] (Tür♀, Schußwaffen♀ usw.) lock; (Gewehr♀) mst bolt; (Buch♀, Handtaschen♀ usw.) clasp;

(Gürtel♀, Koppel♀) buckle; hinter ⁓ und Riegel behind bars; ♀³ pret. v. schließen. [castle.\
Schlößchen ['ʃlœsçən] n (6) small\
Schloße ['ʃloːsə] f (15) sleet (a. pl.).\
Schlosser ['ʃlɔsər] m (7) locksmith; weitS. mechanic, fitter; **⁓ei** [⁓'rai] f (a. '**⁓werkstatt** f) locksmith's workshop; (a. '**⁓handwerk** n) locksmith's trade.

Schlot [ʃloːt] m (3[³]) chimney; ⛴, ⚓ funnel; F (Flegel) lout.

schlotter|ig ['ʃlɔtəriç] shaky; (lose) loose; fig. (schlampig) slovenly; '**⁓n** (29) flap; (zittern) shake, tremble; (wackeln) wobble.

Schlucht [ʃluxt] f (16) gorge; (Hohlweg) ravine, Am. a. gulch.

schluchzen ['ʃluxtsən] (27) sob; ♀ n (6) sobbing, sobs pl.

Schluck [ʃluk] m (3[³]) gulp; kleiner ⁓ = **Schlückchen** ['ʃlykçən] n (6) sip, F drop; '**⁓auf** m hiccup(s pl.); '♀**en**[1] (25) v/t. u. v/i. swallow (a. fig. Geld, Tadel usw.); gulp (down); '**⁓en**[2] m (6) hiccup(s pl.); '**⁓er** m (7) fig. armer ⁓ poor wretch; '**⁓-impfung** ⚔ f oral vaccine; '♀**weise** in (small) sips.

schluder|ig ['ʃluːdəriç] sloppy; '**⁓n** scamp.

schlug [ʃluːk] pret. v. schlagen.

Schlummer ['ʃlumər] m (7) slumber; '♀**n** (29) slumber; fig. lie dormant; '♀**nd** fig. dormant, latent.

Schlund [ʃlunt] m (3³) throat, gullet; ⚔ pharynx; (Speiseröhre) (o)esophagus; (Abgrund) abyss.

schlüpf|en ['ʃlypfən] (25, sn) slip, glide; '♀**er** m (7) (Unterziehhöschen) (ein a pair of ladies') knickers pl., F panties pl. od. briefs pl.

Schlupfloch ['ʃlupf-] n loop-hole; (Versteck) s. Schlupfwinkel.

'**schlüpfrig** slippery (a. fig.); fig. Witz usw.: risqué (fr.).

'**Schlupfwinkel** m hiding-place, Am. hideout; fig. recess.

schlurfen ['ʃlurfən] v/i. (25, sn) shuffle along, drag one's feet.

schlürfen ['ʃlyrfən] (25) v/t. sip.

Schluß [ʃlus] m (4¹) close, end; (Ab-♀; Folgerung) conclusion; parl. e-r Debatte: closing, auf Antrag: closure, Am. cloture; ⁓ (damit)! stop (it)!; ⁓ machen (die Arbeit beenden) call it a day; ⁓ machen mit put an end to a th., have done with a p.;

Schlußabrechnung

zu dem ~ *kommen, daß* decide that; *zum* ~ finally; '~-**abrechnung** *f* final account; '~-**akt** *thea. m* last act; '~**bemerkung** *f* final observation.

Schlüssel ['ʃlysəl] *m* (7) key (*zu* of; *fig.* to); ♪ *a.* clef; (*Chiffrier*⁐) code; (*Verteilungsquote*) formula; ⊕ spanner, wrench; '~**bein** *n* collar-bone; '~**blume** *f* cowslip; *blaßgelbe* ~ primrose; '~**bund** *m, n* bunch of keys; '⁐**fertig** ready for occupancy; ~*es Haus* turnkey house; '~-**industrie** *f* key industry; '~**kind** *n* latchkey child; '~**loch** *n* key-hole; '~**ring** *m* key-ring; '~**rolle** *f* key role; '~**roman** *m* roman à clef (*fr.*); '~**stellung** *f* key position (*a.* ✕); '~**wort** *n* key-word; code word.

'**Schluß**|**feier** *f Schule*: speech-day, *Am.* commencement; '~**folgerung** *f* conclusion, inference; '~**formel** *f im Brief*: complimentary close.

schlüssig ['ʃlysiç] resolved, determined; *Beweis*: conclusive; *sich* ~ *werden* make up one's mind.

'**Schluß**|**licht** *n* tail-light; F *fig.* tail-ender; *das* ~ *bilden* bring up the rear; '~**notierung** ✝ *f des Kurses*: closing quotation; '~**pfiff** *m Sport*: final whistle; '~**rechnung** *f* final account; '~**runde** *f Sport*: final; '~**runden-teilnehmer**(**in** *f*) *m Sport*: finalist; '~**satz** *m* conclusion; ♪ finale; '~**stein** *m* keystone; '~**strich** *m*: *fig.* e-n ~ *ziehen* draw the line, *unter* (*acc.*) put an end to; '~**szene** *f* final scene; '~**verkauf** *m* (end-of-season) sale; '~**wort** *n* (3) last word; (*Zusammenfassung*) summary.

Schmach [ʃmaːx] *f* (16) disgrace; (*Beleidigung*) insult.

schmachten ['ʃmaxtən] (26) languish; ~ *nach* yearn for.

schmächtig ['ʃmɛçtiç] slight, thin; ~*er Junge* slip of a boy.

schmachvoll ['ʃmaːx-] disgraceful.

schmackhaft ['ʃmakhaft] savo(u)ry, tasty; *fig. j-m et.* ~ *machen* make a th. palatable to a p.; '⁐**igkeit** *f* savo(u)riness.

schmäh|**en** ['ʃmɛːən] (25) (*schimpfen*) abuse, revile; (*verleumden*) calumniate; '~**lich** ignominious, disgraceful; *adv. fig.* outrageously; '⁐**rede** *f* abuse, invective; '⁐-**schrift** *f* libel, lampoon; '⁐**sucht** *f* slanderous disposition; '⁐**ung** *f* abuse, invective.

schmal [ʃmaːl] (18[²]) narrow; (*dünn*) thin; *fig.* small, poor; ~*e Kost f* short commons *pl.*

schmäler|**n** ['ʃmɛːlərn] (29) curtail, impair; *bsd. fig.* detract from; '⁐**ung** *f* curtailment, impairment.

'**Schmal**|**film** *m* cine film; '~**film-kamera** *f* cine camera; '~**spur** *f*, '⁐**spurig** narrow-gauge.

Schmalz [ʃmalts] *n* (3²) lard; '⁐**ig** greasy; F *fig.* sentimental, maudlin.

schmarotzen [ʃma'rɔtsən] (27) sponge (*bei* [up]on).

Schma'rotzer *m* (7), ~**in** *f* (*a. zo.*, ♀) parasite; *fig. a.* sponger; ⁐**isch** parasitic; sponging; ~**pflanze** *f* parasitic plant; ~**tum** *n* [~tuːm] *n* (1²) parasitism.

Schmarre ['ʃmarə] *f* (15) cut, slash; (*Narbe*) scar; '~**n** *m* (6) minced pancake; (*Schund*) trash, hokum.

Schmatz F [ʃmats] *m* (3²) smack; '⁐**en** (27) smack (*mit den Lippen* one's lips).

schmauchen ['ʃmauxən] *v/t. u. v/i.* (25) smoke.

Schmaus [ʃmaus] *m* (4²) feast, banquet; ⁐**en** ['~zən] (27) feast (*von* upon); eat heartily; ~**erei** [~'rai] *f* feasting; *s. Schmaus.*

schmecken ['ʃmɛkən] (25) *v/t.* taste; *v/i.* taste (*nach* of); ~ *nach a.* smack of (*a. fig.*); *dieser Wein schmeckt mir* I like (*od.* enjoy) this wine.

Schmeichel|**ei** [ʃmaiçə'lai] *f* (16) *vgl. schmeicheln*: flattery; (flattering) compliment; adulation; cajolery; '⁐**haft** flattering; '⁐**katze** *f fig.* cajoler; '~**n** (29) flatter (*j-m* a p.); *kriecherisch*: adulate; *bittend*: coax; *zärtlich*: cajole; (*kosen*) caress; *sich geschmeichelt fühlen* feel flattered; *geschmeichelt Bild*: flattering.

Schmeichler ['ʃmaiçlər] *m* (7), '~**in** *f* (16¹) flatterer; '⁐**isch** flattering.

schmeiß|**en** F ['ʃmaisən] (30) fling, hurl, chuck; *Tür*: slam, bang; F *die Sache* (*od. den Laden*) ~ run the show; '⁐**fliege** *f* blowfly, bluebottle.

Schmelz [ʃmɛlts] *m* (3²) enamel (*a. Zahn*⁐); *fig.* bloom; ♪ (melting) sweetness; '⁐**bar** fusible; '~**draht** *m* fuse wire; '~**e** *f* (15) *des Schnees*: melting; *s. Schmelzhütte;* '⁐**en** *v/t.* (27, *oft* 30) (*v/i.* [30, sn]) melt (*a. fig.*); *bsd. Metalle*: smelt, fuse;

'2end melting; *fig. a.* languishing; ♪ melodious, sweet (*a. Stimme*); ~erei [~tsə'raı] *f*, '~hütte *f* smelting-works *pl.*, *oft sg.*; foundry; '~käse *m* soft cheese; '~ofen *m* (s)melting furnace; '~punkt *m* melting-point; '~sicherung ⚡ *f* (safety) fuse; '~tiegel *m* melting-pot (*a. fig.*), crucible; '~wasser *n* melted snow (*od.* ice).

Schmerbauch ['ʃmeːr-] *m* paunch, big (*od.* pot-)belly.

Schmerz [ʃmɛrts] *m* (5¹) pain, ache; (*Kummer*) grief; (*Qual*) agony; ~en haben be in pain; '2en (27) *v/t. u. v/i.* pain, hurt, (*nur v/i.*) ache; *seelisch: a.* grieve.

'Schmerzens|geld *n* smart-money; '~lager *n* bed of suffering; '~schrei *m* cry of pain.

'schmerz|-erfüllt grieved; '~frei free of pain; '~haft, '~lich painful; *fig.* grievous; '~lindernd soothing; (*a. ~es Mittel*) anodyne, analgesic; '~los painless; '~stillend *s.* schmerzlindernd(es *Mittel*).

Schmetter|ball *m*, ~schlag ['ʃmɛtər-] *m* Tennis: smash; ~ling ['~lıŋ] *m* (3¹) butterfly; '~lingsstil *m* Schwimmen: butterfly (stroke); '2n (29) *v/t.* smash; F Lied: sing lustily; *v/i.* Stimme: ring (out); Trompete: blare; Vögel: warble.

Schmied [ʃmiːt] *m* (3) (black)smith; '2bar malleable.

Schmiede ['ʃmiːdə] *f* (15) forge, smithy; '~-eisen *n* wrought iron; '~hammer *m* sledge-hammer.

'schmieden *v/t. u. v/i.* (26) forge; *fig. a.* form, frame; *s.* Eisen, Ränke; Pläne: make, *b.s.* hatch.

schmiegen ['ʃmiːgən] (25, *a. sich*) nestle *od.* snuggle (*an acc.* to).

schmiegsam ['ʃmiːkzaːm] pliant, flexible, supple.

Schmier|büchse ['ʃmiːr-] *f* ⊕ grease-box; (*Kanne*) oil-can; '~e *f* (15) ooze; (*Fett*, *Öl*) grease; *thea.* troop of strolling players, *bsd. Am.* barnstormers *pl.*, (*schlechtes Theater*) F penny gaff; P ~e stehen be look-out man, *sl.* keep cave; '2en (25) smear; ⚔ anoint; ⊕ *mit Fett*: grease, *mit Öl*: oil, lubricate; Brot: butter; Butter usw.: spread; (*schlecht schreiben, kritzeln*) scrawl, scribble; *bsd. paint.* daub; F j-n ~ (*bestechen*) grease a p.'s palm; F

j-m eine ~ paste a p. one; wie geschmiert smoothly, without a hitch; '~enschauspieler(in *f*) *m* strolling player, *bsd. Am.* barnstormer, *contp. sl.* ham; '~er(in *f*) *m* greaser; (*Sudler*) scribbler; *bsd. paint.* dauber; ~erei [~'raı] *f* (16) *s.* schmieren: smearing; scrawl; daub; '~esteher P *m* (7) look-out man; '~fett ⊕ *n* grease; '~fink *m* dirty fellow; daub(st)er; '~geld(er *pl.*) F *n* slush fund; '2ig (*fettig*) greasy; (*schmutzig*) grimy; *fig.* sordid; '~käse *m* soft cheese; '~mittel ⊕ *n* lubricant; '~öl *n* lubricating oil; '~papier *n* scribbling-paper; '~plan ⊕ *m* lubricating chart; '~seife *f* soft soap; '~stoff *m* lubricant; '~ung ⊕ *f* lubrication.

Schmink|e ['ʃmıŋkə] *f* (15) (grease) paint, rote: rouge; weitS. make-up; '2en (25, *a. sich*) paint (one's face), make (o.s.) up; rot: rouge; Lippen: put on lipstick; *fig. Bericht:* colo(u)r; ~täsch-chen ['~tɛʃçən] *n* (6) make-up bag.

Schmirgel ['ʃmırgəl] *m* (7) emery; '2n (29) rub with emery, sand; '~papier *n* emery paper.

Schmiß¹ [ʃmıs] *m* (4) gash, cut; (*Narbe*) (duelling) scar; F *fig.* (*Schwung*) verve, go, F pep.

schmiß² *pret. v.* schmeißen.

'schmissig F racy, F full of pep.

Schmöker ['ʃmøːkər] *m* (7) old book; *s.* Schundroman; '2n (29) (*lesen*) browse.

schmoll|en ['ʃmɔlən] (25) pout; weitS. sulk; '2winkel *m* sulking- -corner.

schmolz [ʃmɔlts] *pret. v.* schmelzen.

Schmor|braten ['ʃmoːr-] *m* braised beef; '2en *v/t. u. v/i.* (25) stew (*a. fig.*); (*dünsten*) braise; ⚔ scorch.

Schmu F [ʃmuː] *m* (11) swindle, skullduggery.

Schmuck [ʃmuk] 1. *m* (3) ornament; (*Putz*) finery; (*Juwelen*) jewels *pl.*, jewel(le)ry; (*Ausschmückung*) decoration; 2. ♀ smart, trim, spruce; (*hübsch*) pretty; '~blattelegramm *n* de luxe telegram.

schmücken ['ʃmykən] (25) adorn (*a. fig.*), decorate; sich ~ dress up.

'Schmuck|kästchen *n* jewel-case; *fig.* gem; '2los unadorned, plain; '~sachen *f/pl.* jewels; '~stück *n*

ornament; *engS.* piece of jewel-
(le)ry; *fig.* gem; '**~waren** *f/pl.*
jewel(le)ry *sg.*

Schmuggel ['ʃmugəl] *m* (7), **~ei**
[ˌ~'laɪ] *f* smuggling; '**2n** *v/t. u. v/i.*
(29) smuggle; '**~ware(n** *pl.*) *f*
smuggled goods *pl.*, contraband.

Schmuggler ['ʃmuglər] *m* (7) smug-
gler.

schmunzeln ['ʃmuntsəln] (29)
smile, grin; 2 *n* (6*) (amused)
smile, grin.

Schmus F [ʃmuːs] *m* (4, *o. pl.*) soft
soap; 2**en** ['~zən] soft-soap; (*kosen*)
pet, F neck.

Schmutz [ʃmuts] *m* (3²) dirt, filth,
fig. b.s. a. smut; (*Kot, Schlamm*)
mud; ~ *und Schund* smut and
thrash, ȶ harmful publications;
'2**en** (27) soil, get dirty; '**~fink** F *m*
pig, mudlark; '**~fleck** *m* smudge;
'2**ig** dirty, filthy, *fig. b.s. a.* smutty;
(*beschmutzt*) soiled; *fig.* (*gemein*)
dirty, shabby; ~ *machen* dirty, soil;
'**~igkeit** *f* dirtiness *etc.*; '**~titel** *m e-s
Buches*: half title; '**~zulage** *f* dirty
work allowance.

Schnabel ['ʃnɑːbəl] *m* (7¹) bill,
beak; ⊕ nozzle; *e-r Kanne*: spout;
F *halt den* ~! shut up; '2**förmig**
bill-shaped; '**~tasse** *f* feeding cup;
'**~tier** *n* duck-bill, platypus.

schnäbeln ['ʃnɛːbəln] (29) *v/i. u.
sich* ~ bill and coo.

schnacken ['ʃnakən] *v/i. u. v/t.* (25)
chatter, chat.

Schnake ['ʃnɑːkə] *f* (15) crane-fly,
Brt. daddy-longlegs.

Schnalle ['ʃnalə] *f* (15), '2**n** (25)
buckle; '**~nschuh** *m* buckled shoe.

schnalzen ['ʃnaltsən] (27) smack;
mit der Zunge ~ click one's tongue;
mit den Fingern ~ snap one's fingers.

'**schnappen** (25) snap; *nach et.* ~
snap at, *a.* snatch at; F (*erwischen*)
catch; (*packen*) grab; nab; *nach
Luft* ~ gasp for breath; F *Luft* ~
(*gehen*) take an airing.

Schnäpper ['ʃnɛpər] *m* (7) ⊕ snap,
catch; (*Blut*2) ⚕ blood lancet.

'**Schnapp|feder** *f* catch-spring; '**~**
messer *n* clasp-knife; '**~schloß** *n*
spring-lock; '**~schuß** *m* snapshot.

Schnaps ['ʃnaps] *m* (4²) spirit(s
pl.), strong (*Am.* hard) liquor,
schnap(p)s; (*ein Glas* ~) dram; '**~**
brenne'rei *f* distillery; '**~flasche** *f*
brandy bottle; '**~idee** F *f* crazy

idea.

schnarch|en ['ʃnarçən] (25) snore;
'2**er** *m* (7) snorer.

Schnarre ['ʃnarə] *f* (15) rattle; '2**n**
(25) rattle; (*rauh tönen*) rasp.

schnattern ['ʃnatərn] (29) cackle;
bsd. fig. chatter; *nur fig.* gabble.

schnauben ['ʃnaubən] *v/i. u. v/t.*
(30) pant, puff; *Tier, a. P. verächtlich*: snort; *vor Wut* ~ foam with
rage; *Rache* ~ pant for revenge;
sich (die Nase) ~ blow one's nose.

schnauf|en ['ʃnaufən] (25) breathe
heavily, wheeze; (*keuchen*) pant;
'2**er** F *m* breath.

Schnauz|bart ['ʃnauts-] *m* (walrus)
moustache; '**~e** *f* (15) snout, muzzle; *e-r Kanne usw.*: spout; P *die* ~
halten shut up; '2**en** F (27) jaw,
bark; '**~er** *m* (*Hund*) schnauzer.

Schnecke ['ʃnɛkə] *f* (15) snail;
(*Nackt*2) slug; *fig.* scroll; *e-r Säule*:
a. volute; *der Uhr*: fusee; ⊕ worm;
(*Förder*2) screw conveyor.

schnecken|förmig ['~fœrmiç] spi-
ral, winding; '2**gang** *m* winding
alley; *s. Schneckentempo*; '2**getriebe** *n* worm gear(ing); '2**haus** *n*
snail's shell; '2**linie** *f* spiral line;
'2**post** *f*: *mit der* ~, *im* 2**tempo** *n*
at a snail's pace.

Schnee [ʃneː] *m* (3¹) snow; (*Ei*2)
whipped whites *pl.* of egg, froth;
'**~ball** *m* snowball (*a.* ⚘); '**~ball-
system** *n* snowball system; 2**bedeckt** ['~bədɛkt] snow-covered;
'**~besen** *m Küche*: (egg) whisk, egg-
-beater; '2**blind** snow-blind; '**~**
brille *f* (*eine a pair of*) snow-gog-
gles *pl.*; '**~fall** *m* snowfall; '**~flocke**
f snow-flake; '**~gestöber** *n* snow-
-flurry; '**~glöckchen** ⚘ *n* snow-
drop; '**~grenze** *f* snow-line; '**~**
huhn *n* white grouse; '**~hütte** *f*
igloo; '2**ig** snowy; '**~kette** *f* non-
-skid chain; '**~könig** F *m*: *sich
freuen wie ein* ~ be as pleased as
Punch; '**~mann** *m* snowman; '**~**
matsch *m* slush; '2**mobil** ['~mobiːl]
n (3¹) snowmobile; '**~pflug** *m* snow-
-plough, *Am.* snowplow; '**~schieber**
m snow pusher; '**~schläger** *m s.
Schneebesen*; '**~schmelze** *f* melting
of the snow; '**~schuh** *m* snow-shoe;
s. Schi; '**~sturm** *m* snowstorm; *heftiger*: blizzard; '**~treiben** *n* snow-
-flurry; '**~verwehung** *f*, '**~wehe** *f*
snow-drift; '2**weiß** snow-white; '**~**

wetter *n* snowy weather; **~wittchen** [~'vitçən] *n* (6) Snow-White.

Schneid F ['ʃnaɪt] *m*, *f* (3) pluck, gut(s); *j-m den ~ abkaufen* discourage a p.; **'~brenner** *m* cutting torch.

Schneide ['ʃnaɪdə] *f* (15) edge; *s. Messer;* **'~brett** *n* carving-board; **'2n** (30) *allg.* cut (*a. Sport: den Ball*); *Fingernägel:* a. pare; *Baum be~:* lop, prune; *Hecke:* trim; (*mähen*) mow; *sich ~ ⅋ Linien:* intersect; *fig.* be mistaken; *s. Grimasse, Haar;* **'2nd** cutting, sharp; *Kälte:* biting (*alle a. fig.*).

'Schneider *m* (7) tailor; **~ei** [~'raɪ] *f* (16) tailoring; **'~in** *f* (16¹) ladies' tailor, dressmaker; **'~kleid** *n* tailor-made dress; **'~kostüm** *n* tailor-made suit; **'~meister** *m* master tailor; **'2n** (29) *v/i.* do tailoring *od.* dressmaking; *v/t.* make; **'~puppe** *f* dress form, dummy.

'Schneide|tisch *m* Film: editing table; **'~werkzeuge** *n/pl.* cutting tools; **'~zahn** *m* incisor, cutter.

'schneidig *fig.* (*forsch*) dashing; (*entschlossen*) resolute; (*fesch*) smart; (*mutig*) plucky; *Rede usw.:* terse; **'2keit** *f* dash, smartness; pluck.

schneien ['ʃnaɪən] (25) snow.

Schneise ['ʃnaɪzə] *f* (15) (forest-) aisle, vista; ✈ flying lane.

schnell [ʃnɛl] quick, fast; *Handeln:* a. speedy, prompt (*a. Erwiderung*); (*~füßig, a. Vogel, Flug*) swift; *Strömung, Wuchs,* ✗ *Feuer:* rapid; *Rennbahn usw.:* fast; ✝ *Verkauf:* brisk; *Umsatz:* quick; (*plötzlich*) sudden; (*hastig*) hasty; **~!** be quick!; *mach ~!* be quick!, hurry up!, look sharp!; *nicht so ~!* gently!; **'2boot** *n* speedboat; ✗ motor torpedo boat; **'2bus** *m* express bus; **'~en** (25) *v/t.* jerk; *mit dem Finger:* flick; *v/i.* (sn) jerk, bound, flip; **'2feuer** *n* quick fire; **'2feuergeschütz** *n* quick-firer, automatic gun; **~füßig** ['~fyːsiç] swift(-footed); **'2gang** *mot. m* overdrive; **'2gaststätte** *f* fast-food restaurant; **'2gericht** *n* ⚖ summary court; (*Speise*) fast food; **'2hefter** *m* (7) (rapid) letter-file.

'Schnelligkeit *f* quickness, fastness; swiftness, rapidity; promptness; (*Tempo*) speed; ⊕ velocity; **'~s-rekord** *m* speed record.

'Schnell|-imbiß *m* snack; **'~-imbiß-**

stube *f* snack bar; **'~kochplatte** *f* high-speed plate; **'~kochtopf** *m* pressure cooker; **'~kraft** *f* elasticity; **'~(l)auf** *m* run, race; (*Eis2*) speed-skating; **'~(l)äufer(in** *f*) *m* sprinter; (*Eis2*) speed-skater; **2(l)ebig** ['~leːbiç] *Zeit:* fast-moving; **'~reinigung** *f* express dry-cleaning; **'~schuß** *m* (*rasch produziertes Produkt*) rush job; **'~segler** ⚓ *m* fast sailer; **~stahl** ⊕ *m* high-speed steel; **'~(ver-kehrs)straße** *f* express roadway, *Am.* speedway; **'~verfahren** *n* ⚖ summary jurisdiction; ⊕ rapid method, short cut; **'~waage** *f* steel-yard; **'~zug** *m* fast train, express.

Schnepfe ['ʃnɛpfə] *f* (15) snipe.

Schneppe ['ʃnɛpə] *f* (15) spout; *e-r Haube:* peak; **'~r** ⊕ *m* (7) snap.

schneuzen ['ʃnɔʏtsən] (27): *sich ~* blow one's nose.

schniegeln ['ʃniːgəln] (29) dress (*od.* spruce *od.* smarten) up.

Schnipp|chen ['ʃnɪpçən] *n* (6): *j-m ein ~ schlagen fig.* outwit (*od.* fool) a p.; **'~el** *m*, *n* (7) *s. Schnipsel;* **'2eln** *v/t. u. v/i.* (29) cut, snip; **'2en** *v/t. u. v/i.* (25) snip; (*mit den Fingern*) ~ snap one's fingers; **'2isch** pert, snappish, *Am.* F snippy.

Schnipsel ['~səl] *m*, *n* (7) scrap, shred, snip, cut.

Schnitt [ʃnɪt] **1.** *m* (3) (*Schneiden*) cutting; *ins Fleisch:* incision; (*Haar-2, Kleider2, ~wunde; a. Film*) cut; *am Buch:* edge; (*~muster*) pattern; (*Scheibe*) slice; ⅋ (inter)section; (*Längs2*) longitudinal section; (*Durch2*) average; *im ~* on an average; *s. golden;* F (*Gewinn*) profit; **2.** ♀ *pret. v. schneiden;* **'~blumen** *f/pl.* cut flowers; **'~bohnen** *f/pl.* sliced French beans; **'~e** *f* (15) cut, slice of bread *etc.*); *belegte:* sandwich; **'~er** *m* (7), **'~erin** *f* reaper, mower; **'2fest** *Tomaten:* firm; **'~fläche** *f* section(al plane); **'~holz** *n* sawed timber; **'2ig** stylish; *Auto usw.:* streamlined; **'~lauch** ♀ *m* chive; **'~muster** *n* pattern; **'~punkt** *m Linien:* (point of) intersection; *Winkel:* vertex; **'~stelle** *f* cut; *Computer:* interface; **'~wunde** *f* cut; **'~zeichnung** ⊕ *f* sectional drawing.

Schnitz [ʃnɪts] *m* (3²) cut, slice; **'~arbeit** *f* wood-carving.

Schnitzel[1] ['~əl] *m* (7) (*Fleisch*) escalope, cutlet; *Wiener* ~ (veal) cutlet, *Wiener* schnitzel.

Schnitzel² *n*, *m* (7) chip, snip; ⊕ ~ *pl.* (*Abfälle*) parings, shavings; (*Papier-*♀) scraps *pl.*; '~**jagd** *f* paper-chase; '♀**n** (29) whittle, chip.

'**schnitzen** (27) carve, cut.

'**Schnitzer** *m* (7) carver, cutter; (*Fehler*) blunder, slip(-up), *Am. sl.* boner; ~**ei** [~'rai] *f* (16) (wood-) carving; carved work.

'**Schnitz|kunst** *f* (art of) carving; '~**werk** *n* carved work.

schnob [ʃnoːp] *pret. v.* schnauben.

schnodd(e)rig F ['ʃnɔd(ə)riç] pert, flippant.

schnöde ['ʃnøːdə] (*verächtlich*) scornful; *Undank:* black, base; *Handlungsweise:* vile, shabby; *Profit:* filthy.

Schnorchel ['ʃnɔrçəl] ⚓ *m* (7) snort, snorkel; (~*maske, zum Schwimmen*) snorkel mask.

Schnörkel ['ʃnœrkəl] *m* (7) flourish, squiggle; ⚠ scroll; '♀**n** (29) *v/i.* make flourishes; *v/t.* ⚠ (adorn with) scroll(s); '♀**haft** full of flourishes.

schnorr|en F ['ʃnɔrən] (25) cadge; '♀**er** *m* (7) cadger.

schnüff|eln ['ʃnyfəln] (29) sniff (*an dat.* at), snuffle; nose (*an dat.* at; *nach* after, for); F *fig.* snoop (around); '♀**ler** F *fig. m* (7) sniffer; *fig.* spy, F snooper; (*Detektiv*) sleuth.

Schnuller ['ʃnʊlər] *m* (7) comforter, dummy, *Am.* pacifier.

Schnulze F ['ʃnʊltsə] *f* (15) *sl.* tearjerker.

Schnupf|en¹ ['ʃnʊpfən] *m* (6) cold (in the head), catarrh; *den* ~ *bekommen* catch (a) cold; '♀**en²** (25) take snuff; '~**en³** *n* (6) taking snuff; '~**tabak** *m* snuff; '~**tuch** *n* (pocket-)handkerchief.

Schnuppe ['ʃnʊpə] *f* (15) *am Licht:* snuff; (*Stern*♀) falling (*od.* shooting) star; F *das ist mir* ♀ F I don't care (a damn); '♀**rn** (29) *s.* schnüffeln.

Schnur [ʃnuːr] *f* cord; (*Bindfaden*) string; (*Leine*) line; *zum Schnüren:* lace; *fig. über die* ~ *hauen* kick over the traces, *beim Essen usw.:* overindulge.

Schnür|boden ['ʃnyːr-] *thea. m* gridiron; '~**chen** *n* (6): *das geht wie am* ~ it goes like clock-work; *et. wie am* ~ *können* have a th. at

one's finger-tips; '♀**en** (25) lace; (*zubinden*) cord, tie up; *sich* ~ *wear* stays.

'**schnurgerade** straight (as an arrow).

Schnurr|bart ['ʃnur-] *m* moustache; '~**e** *fig. f* (15) funny tale; '♀**en** (25) hum, buzz; *Rad:* whir(r); *Katze:* purr; F (*schnorren*) cadge.

'**Schnürriemen** *m* lace, strap.

'**schnurrig** droll, funny; (*wunderlich*) odd.

'**Schnür|senkel** *m* shoe-lace, *bsd. Am. a.* shoestring; '~**stiefel** *m* lace-boot.

'**schnurstracks** straight, directly, right away; ~ *zuwider* diametrically opposed; ~ *zugehen auf* (*acc.*) make a bee-line for.

Schnute ['ʃnuːtə] *f* (15) mouth; *e-e* ~ *ziehen* pout.

schob [ʃoːp] *pret. v.* schieben.

Schober ['ʃoːbər] *m* (7) stack, rick.

Schock¹ [ʃɔk] *n* (3; *nach Zahlen inv.*) threescore; ~² *m* (3¹) ✻ *u. fig.* shock; '~**farbe** *f* blaze colo(u)r; ♀**ieren** [~'kiːrən] shock, scandalize; '~**therapie** *f* shock therapy.

schofel ['ʃoːfəl] mean, shabby.

Schöffe ['ʃœfə] ⚖ *m* (13) lay assessor; '~**ngericht** *n* lay assessors court.

Schokolade [ʃokoˈlaːdə] *f* (15) chocolate; ~**ntafel** *f* bar of chocolate.

scholl [ʃɔl] *pret. v.* schallen.

Scholle ['ʃɔlə] *f* (15) clod; (*Eis*♀) floe; *Fisch:* plaice; *fig.* soil.

schon [ʃoːn] already; (*jetzt* ~) yet; (~ *einmal,* ~ *früher*) before; (*sogar*) even; (*natürlich*) of course; (*sicherlich*) sure enough; ~ *damals* even then; ~ *ganz* quite; ~ *deswegen* for that reason alone; ~ *weil* if only because; ~ *immer* all along; ~ *lange* long since, for a long time; ~ *wieder* again; ~ *gut!* all right!; *das ist* ~ *wahr, aber ...* that is very well (*od.* quite true), but ...; *wenn* ~ although; (*na*) *wenn* ~! so what?; ~ *der Gedanke* the very idea; *hast du* ~ (*ein*)*mal* ...? have you ever ...?; *er wird* ~ *kommen* don't worry, he will come; ~ *im 16. Jahrhundert* as early as the 16th century; ~ *um 8 Uhr* as early as 8 o'clock; ~ *seit 50 Jahren,* ~ *50 Jahre* as long as 50 years.

schön [ʃøːn] beautiful; *Frau: a.* fair;

bsd. Mann: handsome; (*gut, fein*) good, fine; (*großzügig, ansehnlich*) handsome; (*prächtig*) splendid; (*nett, lieb*) nice, kind (*von* of); *Wetter*: fair, fine; *das ~e Geschlecht* the fair sex; *die ~en Künste* the fine arts; *~e Literatur* polite letters *pl.*, belles-lettres *pl.*; *~en Dank!* many thanks!; *eines ~en Tages* one day; *~ warm* nice and warm; *es war sehr ~* (*auf dem Fest*) we had a good time; *das wäre noch ~er!* certainly not!; *~ wär's!* some hope!; *das sind mir ~e Sachen!* pretty doings indeed!; *et. ~ bleiben lassen* do nothing of the kind; *aufs ~ste* most beautifully; *~!* all right!, F *od. Am.* okay!; ⚲*e* (18) 1.*f* belle, beauty; 2. *das ~* the beautiful.

schonen ['ʃoːnən] (25) spare; (*schonend umgehen mit et.*) be careful with; (*erhalten*) preserve; (*nicht strapazieren*) be easy on; *Augen, Kräfte, Vorrat*: save; *sich ~* take care of o.s., (*a. weitS.*) take it easy; *sich nicht ~* exert (*od.* drive) o.s.; '*~d* careful; (*rücksichtsvoll*) considerate; (*nachsichtig*) indulgent; *s.* beibringen.

Schoner ['ʃoːnər] ⚓ *m* (7) schooner.
'**schön|färben** *fig.* gloss (over); '⚲**färber** *m fig.* optimist; '⚲**geist** *m* (a)esthete, bel esprit (*fr.*); '*~geistig* aesthetical; *Literatur*: belletristic.

'**Schönheit** *f allg.* beauty; '*~sfehler m* corporal defect; *e-s Gegenstandes*: flaw (*a. fig.*); '*~skonkurrenz f* beauty contest; '*~s-operation f* cosmetic operation; *~s-pfläster-chen* ['*~pflɛstərçən*] *n* (6) beauty spot; '*~s-pflege f* beauty culture; '*~ssalon m* beauty parlo(u)r; '*~s-wettbewerb m* beauty contest.
'**Schonkost** *f* light food.
'**Schön|redner** *m contp.* speechifier; (*Schmeichler*) flatterer; '⚲**tun** *j-m*: (*schmeicheln*) coax, cajole; (*schäkern*) flirt (with).
'**Schonung** *f* (*Gnade*) mercy; (*Nachsicht*) forbearance; (*pflegliche Behandlung*) careful treatment; (*Erhaltung, Schutz*) protection; (*Baumschule*) tree-nursery; '⚲**slos** pitiless, relentless.
'**Schonzeit** *hunt. f* close season, *Am.* closed season.
Schopf [ʃɔpf] *m* (3³) (*Haar⚲*) tuft; *voller*: mop (of hair); *der Vögel*:

tuft, crest.
Schöpf|-eimer ['ʃœpf-] *m* pail; '⚲**en** (25) *v/t.* scoop; draw *water etc.*; *mit e-m Löffel*: ladle; *Atem*: draw, take; *Mut*: take; *s. Hoffnung, Verdacht.*
'**Schöpfer** *m* (7) creator; (*Gott*) *the* Creator; '*~geist m* creative genius; '*~in f* (16¹) creatress; '⚲**isch** creative.
'**Schöpf|kelle** *f* scoop, ladle; '*~löffel m* ladle; '*~ung f* creation.
Schoppen ['ʃɔpən] *m* (6) pint.
schor [ʃoːr] *pret. v.* scheren.
Schorf [ʃɔrf] *m* (3) scurf; (*Wund⚲*) scab; '⚲**ig** scurfy, scabby.
Schornstein ['ʃɔrnʃtaɪn] *m* chimney; ⚓, 🚂 funnel; (*Fabrik⚲*) smokestack; *fig. s.* Kamin; '*~feger m* chimney-sweep.
schoß¹ [ʃɔs] *pret. v.* schießen.
Schoß² 🌿 [ʃɔs] *m* (3²) shoot, sprout.
Schoß³ [ʃoːs] *m* (4²) lap; (*Mutterleib*) womb; (*Rock⚲*) flap, tail, skirt; *der Kirche, Familie, Partei*: fold; *s. Hand*; '*~hund m* lap-dog; '*~kind n* darling, pet.
Schößling 🌿 ['ʃœslɪŋ] *m* (3¹) shoot.
Schote ['ʃoːtə] *f* (15) cod, pod, husk, shell; ⚓ sheet; *~n pl.* green peas.
Schott ⚓ [ʃɔt] *n* (3) bulkhead; '*~e m* (13) Scot, Scotsman, Scotchman; *die ~n pl.* the Scots *od.* Scotch; '*~er m* (7) metal, gravel; 🚂 ballast; (*Geröll*) rubble; '*~in f* (16¹) Scotswoman, Scotchwoman; '⚲**isch** Scottish, Scotch.
schraffier|en [ʃra'fiːrən] hatch; ⚲**ung** *f* hatching.
schräg [ʃrɛːk] oblique, slanting; (*~ abfallend*) sloping; (*~ verlaufend*) diagonal; (*~ gegenüber* across (*von* from); ⚲*e* ['*~gə*] *f* (15) obliquity, slope; ⚲**lage** ['*~'lɛː-k-*] *f* sloping position; ⚡ bank(ing); '⚲**strich** *m* oblique, *Am.* slash.
schrak [ʃraːk] *pret. v.* schrecken *v/i.*
Schramm|e ['ʃramə] *f* (15) scratch; (*Narbe*) scar; '⚲**en** (25) scratch, scar; *Haut*: *a.* graze; '⚲**ig** scarred.
Schrank [ʃraŋk] *m* (3³) cupboard, *bsd. Am.* closet; (*Kleider⚲*) wardrobe; (*Spind*) locker; *s. Bücher⚲, Wäsche⚲*; '*~bett n* fold-away bed.
Schranke ['ʃraŋkə] *f* (15) barrier (*a. fig.*); 🚂 bar; 🚪 gate; '*~n pl. des Turnierplatzes*: lists; *fig.* limits, bounds; *in die ~ fordern* challenge;

~n setzen (dat.) set bounds to; (sich) in ~ halten keep within bounds; j-n in s-e ~en weisen put a p. in his place.

schränken ['ʃrɛŋkən] (25) *Beine*: cross; *Arme*: fold; *Säge*: set.

'**schranken|los** boundless; '**2wärter** 🏠 *m* gate-keeper.

'**schrank|fertig** *Wäsche*: washed and ironed; '**2koffer** *m* wardrobe trunk; '**2wand** *f* wall unit. [cap.]

Schraubdeckel ['ʃraup-] *m* screw]

Schraube ['ʃraubə] *f* (15) screw (*a*. ⚓); ✈ air-screw, *Am*. propeller; ~ *und Mutter* bolt and nut; *fig*. F *bei ihm ist e-e* ~ *locker* he has a screw loose; '**2n** *v/t. u. v/i.* (30) screw; (*drehen*) twist, spiral; *fig*. *niedriger* ~ lower, scale down; *s*. *geschraubt*.

'**Schrauben|dampfer** ⚓ *m* screw steamer; **2förmig** ['~fœrmiç] screw-shaped, helical, spiral; '**~gang** *m*, '**~gewinde** *n* screw thread; '**~linie** *f* spiral line; '**~mutter** *f* female screw, nut; '**~schlüssel** *m* wrench, spanner; (*verstellbarer* ~) monkey-wrench; '**~spindel** *f* male screw; **~zieher** ['~tsiːər] *m* screw-driver.

Schraub|fassung ['ʃraup-] *f* screw fixture; '**~stock** *m* vice, *Am*. vise; '**~verschluß** *m* screw cap.

Schrebergarten ['ʃreːbərgartən] *m* allotment (garden).

Schreck [ʃrɛk] *m* (3), '**~en**[1] *m* (6) fright, terror; shock, panic; *die* ~*en des Krieges usw*. the horrors of; *in* ~*en versetzen* frighten, terrify; *mit dem* ~*en davonkommen* get off with a bad fright; '**2en**[2] (*v/t*. [25], *v/i*. 30, sn) = *ab~, auf~, er~*; '**2en-erregend** horrific.

'**Schreckens|botschaft** *f* alarming (*od*. terrible) news; '**~herrschaft** *f* reign of terror; '**~ruf** *m* cry of terror; '**~tat** *f* atrocious deed.

'**Schreck|gespenst** *fig. n* bugbear, nightmare; '**2haft** easily frightened, nervous; '**2lich** frightful, terrible, dreadful; F *fig. a.* awful(ly *adv*.); '**~nis** *n* (4[1]) horror; *s. Schrecken*; '**~schuß** *m* shot in the air; *fig*. false alarm; *e-n* ~ *abgeben* fire in the air; '**~schußpistole** *f* booby pistol; '**~sekunde** *f* reaction time.

Schrei [ʃraɪ] *m* (3) cry; shout; *gellender*: yell; *spitzer*: scream;

(*Brüllen; der Menge*) roar; *fig. der letzte* ~ the latest rage, the dernier cri (*fr*.).

Schreib|arbeit ['ʃraɪpˀarbaɪt] *f* clerical (*od*. desk) work; *bsd. contp*. paperwork; '**~block** *m* writing-pad; '**~büro** *n* writing office.

schreiben ['ʃraɪbən] **1.** *v/t. u. v/i.* (30) write (*j-m* to a p.; ✝, F a p.; *über ein Thema* on); (*orthographisch* ~) spell; (*mit der*) *Maschine* ~ type (-write); *sich* (*od. ea*.) ~ correspond; (*Bücher* ~) be a writer; *wie schreibt er sich?* how does he spell his name?; *s. Ohr, rein* 1, *Zeile*; **2.** **2** *n* (6) writing; (*Brief*) letter.

'**Schreiber** *m* (7), '**~in** *f* (16[1]) writer; (*Angestellter*) secretary, clerk; ⊕ *m* recorder; **~ei** [~'raɪ] *f* (endless) writing, scribbling; '**~ling** *contp. m* pen-pusher.

schreib|faul ['ʃraɪpfaul] lazy in writing; '**2feder** *f* pen; '**2fehler** *m* mistake in spelling *od*. writing, slip of the pen, clerical error; '**2gerät** *n* writing utensils *pl*.; ⊕ recorder; '**2heft** *n* copy- (*od*. exercise-)book; '**2kraft** *f* typist; '**2krampf** *m* writer's cramp; '**2kunst** *f* art of writing; '**2mappe** *f* writing-case; *mit Löschpapier*: blotting-case; '**2maschine** *f* typewriter; ~ *schreiben* type(write); *mit* ~ *geschrieben* typewritten; '**2maschinenpapier** *n* typing paper; '**2material** *n* writing material(s *pl*.), stationery; '**2papier** *n* writing-paper; '**2pult** *n* (writing-)desk; '**2schrift** *f* script; '**2stube** ✕ *f* orderly room, office; '**2tisch** *m* desk; writing-table; '**2ung** *f* spelling; '**~unkundig** unable to write; '**2unterlage** *f* writing-pad, blotting-pad; '**2waren** *f/pl*. stationery *sg*.; '**2warenhändler** *m* stationer; '**2warenhandlung** *f* stationer's shop; '**2weise** *f* style; *e-s Wortes*: spelling; '**2zentrale** *f* typing pool; '**2zeug** *n s. Schreibgerät*.

schrei|en ['ʃraɪən] *v/i. u. v/t.* (30) cry (*um, nach* for); *laut*: shout; *gellend*: yell; *spitz*: scream, shriek; (*brüllen*) roar; *nur v/i. Hirsch*: bell; F *zum* **2** (*komisch*) a scream; '**~end** *fig. Farbe*: loud; *Schande*: crying; *Unrecht*: flagrant; *Gegensatz*: glaring; '**2er** *m* (7), '**2erin** *f*, '**2hals** *m* bawler; (*Lärmmacher*) brawler; *kleiner Schreihals* cry-baby.

Schrein [ʃraın] *m* (3) chest; (*Sarg*) coffin; (*Reliquien♀*) shrine; '*er m* (7) joiner; (*Kunst♀*) cabinet-maker.
schreiten ['ʃraıtən] (30, sn) step, pace, stride; ~ *zu* proceed to.
schrie [ʃriː] *pret. v.* schreien.
schrieb [ʃriːp] *pret. v.* schreiben 1.
Schrift [ʃrıft] *f* (16) writing; (*Schreib♀*; ~*art*) script; *s. Hand♀, ln♀*; (~*zeichen*) letter, character; *typ.* typeface; (~*stück*) document, (*a. Abhandlung*) paper; (*Veröffentlichung*) publication; (*Werk*) work; (*Broschüre*) pamphlet; *die Heilige* ~ the Holy Scripture(s *pl.*); '~**art** *f* type; '~**bild** *n* face; '~**deutsch** *n* literary German; '~**enreihe** *f* serial publication; '~**führer(in** *f*) *m* secretary; '~**gelehrte** *m* scribe; '~**gießer** *typ. m* type-founder; '~**leiter** *m* editor; '~**leiterin** *f* editress; '~**leitung** *f* editorship; (*Personal*) editorial staff, editors *pl.*; '♀**lich** written, in writing; (*brieflich*) by letter; *et.* ~ *beantragen* apply for a th. in writing; *wegen e-r S.* ~ *anfragen* write for a th. (*bei j-m* to a p.); ~ *niederlegen* put *a th.* (down) in writing, (put *a th.* on) record; *jetzt haben wir es* ~ now we have it in black and white; '~**muster** *typ. n* type specimen; '~**rolle** *f* scroll; '~**satz** *tӡ̣ m* memorandum, letter(s *pl.*); '~**setzer** *m* compositor, type-setter; '~**sprache** *f* written (*od.* literary) language; '~**steller** *m* author, writer; ~**stellerei** [~'raı] *f* writing; '~**stellerin** *f* (16¹) author(ess), writer; '♀**stellerisch** literary; *adv.* as an author; '~**stellerverband** *m* authors' association; '~**stück** *n* document, paper, deed; '~**tum** *n* (1²) literature; '~**wechsel** *m* exchange of letters, correspondence; '~**zeichen** *n* letter, character; '~**zug** *m* character; (*Schnörkel*) flourish.
schrill [ʃrıl] shrill.
Schrippe ['ʃrıpə] *f* (15) (French) roll.
Schritt [ʃrıt] 1. *m* (3; *als Maß im pl. inv.*) step (*a. fig. u. pol.*); *s. als Maß*: pace; *langer*: stride; *diplomatischer*: démarche (*fr.*); (*Gangart*) gait, walk; *der Hose*: crotch; *hörbarer*: footstep; ~ *für* ~ step by step (*a.fig.*); ~ *fahren!* dead slow!, drive at walking speed!; ~ *halten* keep step, *fig. a.* keep abreast (*mit* of); *fig.* ~*e tun od. unternehmen* take steps; *auf* ~ *und Tritt* at every turn; *s. folgen*;

2. ♀ *pret. v.* schreiten; '~**macher** *m* *Rennsport*: pace-maker (*a. fig.*), pacer; ♂ (*Herz♀*) pace-maker; *fig. Mode*: trend-setter; '~**macherdienste** *m/pl.* pace-setting *sg.*; '♀**weise** *adj. fig.* gradual; *adv.* step by step (*a. fig.*).
schroff [ʃrɔf] *Berge*: rugged; (*steil*) steep; *fig.* gruff, harsh; (*plötzlich*) abrupt; '♀**heit** *f* steepness; gruffness; abruptness.
schröpfen ['ʃrœpfən] (25) cup, bleed; *fig.* fleece, milk (*um* for).
Schrot [ʃroːt] *m u. n* (3) *zum Schießen*: small shot; (*Korn*) bruised grain, grist; *fig. von echtem* ~ *und Korn* true; '~**brot** *n* whole-meal bread; '♀**en** (26, *p.p.* ~ *geschroten*) *Faß usw.*: shoot, lower; ⚓ parbuckle; *Korn*: rough-grind, bruise (*a. Malz*); '~**flinte** *f* shotgun; '~**korn** *n* (grain of) shot; '~**mehl** *n* coarse meal; '~**mühle** *f* bruising mill; '~**säge** *f* crosscut saw.
Schrott [ʃrɔt] *m* (7, *o. pl.*) scrap (iron); '~**händler** *m* scrap-dealer; '~**platz** *m* scrap yard; '♀**reif** ready for the scrap heap; '~**wert** *m* scrap value.
schrubb|en ['ʃrubən] *v/t. u. v/i.* (26) scrub; '♀**er** *m* (7) scrubber.
Schrulle ['ʃrulə] *f* (15) whim, crotchet; (*Frau*) old crone; ~*n haben* F have a kink; '♀**nhaft**, 'schrullig crotchety, cranky.
schrump(e)lig ['ʃrump(ə)lıç] shrivel(l)ed, wrinkled.
schrumpf|en ['ʃrumpfen] (25, sn) shrink (*a.* ⚒, ⊕ *u. fig.*); shrivel; '♀**ung** *f* shrinking, shrinkage.
Schrund|e ['ʃrundə] *f* (15) crack, chap; '♀**ig** cracked, chapped.
Schub [ʃuːp] *m* (3) push; *phys.,* ⊕ thrust; *von Broten usw., a. fig.*: batch; '~**fach** *n*, '~**kasten** *m*, '~**lade** *f* drawer; '~**karren** *m* wheel-barrow, *Am. a.* pushcart; '~**kraft** *f*, '~**leistung** ⊕ *f* thrust.
Schubs F [ʃups] *m* (3) push, shove; '♀**en** push, shove.
schüchtern ['ʃyçtərn] shy, bashful, timid; '♀**heit** *f* shyness, bashfulness, timidity.
schuf [ʃuːf] *pret. v.* schaffen.
Schuft [ʃuft] *m* (3) scoundrel, rascal; '♀**en** (26) drudge, slave; ~**erei** [~tə-'raı] *f* drudgery, F grind; '♀**ig** low, mean.

Schuh [ʃuː] *m* (3) shoe; (*hoher ~*) boot; *fig. j-m et. in die ~e schieben* put the blame for a th. on a p.; '**~anzieher** *m* (7) shoehorn; '**~band** *n* shoe-lace, *Am. a.* shoe-string; '**~bürste** *f* shoe-brush; '**~creme** *f s. Schuhwichse*; '**~geschäft** *n* shoe-shop; '**~größe** *f* size (of shoes); '**~macher** *m* shoemaker; **~plattler** ['~platlər] *m* (7) Bavarian folk dance; '**~putzer** *m* shoeblack; '**~riemen** *m*, '**~senkel** *m s. Schuhband*; '**~sohle** *f* sole; '**~spanner** *m* shoe-tree; '**~waren** *f/pl.*, '**~werk** *n* footwear, footgear; '**~wichse** *f* shoe-polish, *Am. a.* shoe-shine.

'**Schul|abgänger** *m* school-leaver; '**~amt** *n* (*Behörde*) school board, education authority; (*Haupt♀*) Board of Education; '**~arbeit** *f* a) *mst pl.* homework; **~en machen** do one's homework; **b)** = '**~aufgabe** test (in class), class exercise; '**~ausgabe** *f* school edition; '**~ausflug** *m* school outing; '**~bank** *f* desk; *die ~ drücken* go to school; '**~behörde** *f s. Schulamt*; '**~beispiel** *n* test-case, typical example; '**~besuch** *m* attendance at school; '**~bildung** *f* (*höhere* secondary) education; '**~buch** *n* school-book; '**~buchverlag** *m* educational publishers *pl.*

Schuld [ʃult] *f* (16) guilt; (*Veranlassung, Fehler*) fault; (*Ursache*) cause; (*Missetat*) wrong; (*Sünde*) sin; (*Geld♀*) debt; (*Verpflichtung*) obligation; **~en machen** incur debts; *in ~en geraten, sich in ~en stürzen* run into debts; *in j-s ~ sein* be indebted to a p.; *er ist* (*od. hat* ♀ (*daran*), *es ist s-e ~* it is his fault; *j-m* (*od. e-r Sache*) *die ~ geben* blame a p *od.* a th.; *die schlechten Zeiten sind* ♀ *daran* the bad times are to blame for it; *j-m die ~* (*an et.*) *zuschieben od. zuschreiben* lay (*od.* put) the blame (for a th.) on a p.; *die ~ auf sich nehmen* take the blame; *ohne m-e ~* through no fault of mine; '♀**beladen** laden with guilt, guilty; '♀**bewußt** conscious of one's guilt; '**~buch** *n* account-book, ledger.

schulden ['ʃuldən] (26): *j-m et. ~* (*a. fig.*) owe a p. a th.; *vgl. schuldig*; '**~frei** free from debt; *Grundbesitz*: unencumbered; '♀**last** *f* burden of debt; *v. Grundbesitz*:

encumbrance; '♀**tilgungsfonds** *m* sinking-fund.

'**Schuld|forderung** *f* (active) debt, claim; '**~frage** *f* question of guilt; '♀**haft** culpable.

schuldig ['ʃuldiç] (*strafbar*) guilty (*e-r S.* of a th.), culpable; *Zivilrecht*: responsible; *Geld*: owing, due; (*gebührend*) due; *j-m et. ~ sein od. bleiben* owe a p. a th. (*a. fig.*); *j-m et. ~ sein* be indebted to a p. for a th.; *j-m Dank ~ sein* owe gratitude to a p.; *j-m die Antwort ~ bleiben* make no reply; *♀ für ~ befinden* find guilty; *j-n ~ sprechen* pronounce a p. guilty; *s. bekennen*; *der, die* ♀ ['~gə] (18) the culprit; ♀**keit** ['~diçkaɪt] *f* duty, obligation.

'**Schuldirektor**(*in f*) *m* headmaster, *f* headmistress, *Am.* principal.

'**schuld|los** guiltless, innocent; '♀**losigkeit** *f* guiltlessness, innocence.

Schuldner ['ʃuldnər] *m* (7), '**~in** *f* (16¹) debtor.

'**Schuld|recht** ♀ *n* law of obligation; '**~schein** ['ʃultʃaɪn] *m*, '**~verschreibung** *f* promissory note; IOU (= I owe you); *öffentliche*: debenture, bond.

Schule ['ʃuːlə] *f* (15) school (*a. weitS.*); *höhere ~* secondary school, *Am.* high school; *fig. e-e harte ~* a severe school (*od.* test); *Hohe ~ Reiten*: haute école (*fr.*); *auf* (*od. in der*) *~* at school; *in die ~ gehen* go to school; *aus der ~ plaudern* tell tales out of school, blab; *fig. ~ machen* be imitated, spread; *s. schwänzen*; '♀**n** (25) school, train.

Schüler ['ʃyːlər] *m* (7) schoolboy; pupil; *höherer*: student; (*Jünger*) disciple; '**~austausch** *m* exchange of pupils; '♀**haft** schoolboy-like; '**~in** ['~rin] *f* (16¹) schoolgirl; '**~karte** *f* school season-ticket; '**~lotse** *m* lollipop man; '**~lotsin** *f* lollipop woman.

'**Schul|ferien** *pl.* holidays, *bsd. Am.* vacation(s *pl.*); '**~fernsehen** *n* educational television; '**~flugzeug** *n* training airplane; '♀**frei**: *~ haben* have a holiday; '**~freund**(**in** *f*) *m* schoolmate; '**~funk** *m* schools' radio; '**~gelände** *n* school-grounds *pl.*, *Am.* campus; '**~geld** *n* school fee(s *pl.*); '**~gelehrsamkeit** *f* book-learning; '**~haus** *n* school(-house), school building; '**~hof** *m* playground, schoolyard; '**~jahr** *n* school year; *~e* *pl.* school-days; '⁓**jugend** *f* school--children *pl.*; '⁓**junge** *m* schoolboy; '⁓**kamerad** *m* schoolmate; '⁓**kenntnisse** *f/pl.* school knowledge *sg.*; '⁓**lehrer** *m* schoolmaster, teacher; '⁓**lehrerin** *f* schoolmistress, (lady) teacher; '⁓**leiter** *m s. Schuldirektor;* '⁓**mann** *m* education(al)ist; '⁓**mappe** *f* school-bag; '⁓**meister** *contp. m* schoolmaster; '⁀**meisterlich** like a schoolmaster, pedantic; '⁀**meistern** (29) censure; '⁓**ordnung** *f* school regulations *pl.*; '⁓**pferd** *n* trained horse; '⁓**pflicht** *f* compulsory education *od.* school attendance; ⁀**pflichtig** ['⁓pfliçtiç] schoolable, of school age; ⁓es *Alter* school age; '⁓**prüfung** *f* school examination; '⁓**ranzen** *m* satchel; '⁓**rat** *m* supervisor; '⁓**raum** *m*, '⁓**stube** *f* schoolroom; '⁓**recht** *n* education law; '⁓**reiten** *n* schooling; '⁓**schiff** *n* school ship; '⁓**schluß** *m* break-up; '⁓**schwänzer** *m* truant; '⁓**speisung** *f* school lunch; '⁓**stunde** *f* lesson, period; '⁓**tasche** *f* school bag *od.* satchel.

Schulter ['ʃultər] *f*(15) shoulder;⁓ *an* ⁓ (*a. fig.*) shoulder to shoulder; *s. kalt, leicht;* '⁓**blatt** *n* shoulder-blade; '⁀**frei** *Kleid:* off-the-shoulder; (*trägerlos*) strapless; '⁓**klappe** *f*, '⁓**stück** ✕ *n* shoulder strap; '⁀**n** (29) shoulder; '⁓**sieg** *m Ringen:* win by fall.

Schulung ['ʃuːluŋ] *f* training.

'**Schul**|**unterricht** *m* school instruction, lessons *pl.*; '⁓**versuch** *m* education pilot scheme; '⁓**verwaltung** *f* school administration; '⁓**weg** *m* way to school; '⁓**weisheit** *f* book-learning; '⁓**wesen** *n* education(al system); *öffentliches* ⁓ state education (system); '⁓**zeit** *f* schooltime; *rückblickend:* school-days *pl.*; '⁓**zeugnis** *n* school record *od.* report; '⁓**zimmer** *n* schoolroom; '⁓**zwang** *m* compulsory school education.

schummel|**n** F ['ʃuməln] *v/i.* (29) cheat; '⁀**zettel** *m* crib.

schumm(e)rig ['ʃum(ə)riç] dusky.

schund¹ [ʃunt] *pret. v. schinden.*

Schund² [ʃunt] *m* (3) trash; ⚖ ⁓*und-Schmutzgesetz n Harmful Publications Act;* '⁓**literatur** *f* trashy literature; '⁓**roman** *m* penny dreadful, *Am.* dime novel.

Schupo F ['ʃuːpo] **1.** *f (inv. o. pl.) abbr. für (Schutz-)Polizei;* **2.** *m* (11)

abbr. für (Schutz-)Polizist: (police) officer, F bobby, *bsd. Am.* cop.

Schupp|**e** ['ʃupə] *f* (15) scale; *pl.* (*Kopf⁀n*) dandruff *sg.*; *es fiel mir wie* ⁓*n von den Augen* the scales fell from my eyes; '⁀**en¹** (25) scale; (*kratzen*) rub, scratch; *sich* ⁓ scale off; '⁓**en²** *m* (6) shed; *mot.* garage; ✕ hangar; '⁀**ig** scaly, squamous, flaky.

Schur [ʃuːr] *f* (16) shearing; (*Wolle*) fleece.

Schür|**eisen** ['ʃyːr⁹aɪzən] *n* poker; '⁀**en** (25) stir (up *fig.*), poke, rake; *fig.* fan (*the fire*), foment.

schürfen ['ʃyrfən] (25) *v/i. nach Erz:* prospect (*nach* for); *v/t. Haut:* scratch, graze.

schurigeln ['ʃuːriːɡəln] *v/t.* (29) torment, bully, F plague.

Schurk|**e** ['ʃurkə] *m* (13) scoundrel, villain, knave; '⁓**enstreich** *m*, ⁓**erei** [⁓'raɪ] *f* knavish trick, villainy; '⁀**isch** rascally, villainous, knavish.

Schurz [ʃurts] *m* (3² *u.* ³) apron.

Schürze ['ʃyrtsə] *f* (15) apron; '⁀**n** (27) tuck up; *Knoten:* tie; *Lippen:* purse; '⁓**nband** *n* apron-string; '⁓**njäger** *m* philanderer, Casanova; '⁓**nkleid** overall.

Schuß [ʃus] *m* (4²) shot (*a. Sport*); (*Knall*) report; (*Ladung*) charge; (*Munition*) round; *Weberei:* weft, woof; *s. Schußwunde;* (*schießende Bewegung*) rush, dash; *Schisport:* schuss; (*Emporschießen*) shooting; ⚘ (*Trieb*) shoot; *ein* ⁓ *Wein usw.* (*a. fig.*) a dash of ...; F *fig. gut in* (*od. im*) ⁓ in good order, *P.:* in good form; *in* ⁓ *bringen* get in order, get going; *in* ⁓ *kommen* get under way; *keinen* ⁓ *Pulver wert P.:* not worth powder and shot, *S.:* no good; '⁓**bereich** *s. Schußweite;* '⁀**bereit** *s.* ⁀**fertig.**

Schussel ['ʃusəl] F *m* (7) fidget; *s. Tolpatsch.*

Schüssel ['ʃysəl] *f*(15) bowl, basin; (*Eß⁀* *usw.*) dish.

'**Schuß**|**fahrt** *f Schisport:* schuss; '⁀**fertig** ready to fire; *Waffe:* a. cocked; '⁓**linie** *f* line of fire; *fig. in die* ⁓ *geraten* come under fire; '⁓**waffe** *f* fire-arm; '⁓**wechsel** *m* exchange of fire; '⁓**weite** *f* range; *in* (*außer*) ⁓ within (out of) range; '⁓**wunde** *f* gunshot wound, bullet wound.

Schuster ['ʃustər] *m* (7) shoemaker;

(*Flick♀*; *a. fig.*) cobbler; *auf ~s Rappen* on Shanks's mare *od.* pony; '♀n (29) cobble; F *fig.* (*pfuschen*) botch.

Schute ['ʃuːtə] *f* (15) ⚓ barge, lighter; (*Hut*) bonnet.

Schutt [ʃut] *m* (3) rubbish; (*Stein♀*) rubble; *in ~ und Asche legen* lay in ruins; '~**abladeplatz** *m* dump site.

Schüttel|frost ['ʃytəlfrɔst] *m* shivering fit, *the* shivers *pl.*, chill '♀n (29) shake; '~**reim** *m* spoonerism.

schütt|en ['ʃytən] (26) pour; *Korn:* shoot; *es schüttet* it is pouring (with rain).

'Schutt|halde *f geol.*, *mount.* scree, talus; '~**haufen** *m* dust-heap, dump; (*Steine*) heap of rubble (*a. fig.*).

Schutz [ʃuts] *m* (3²) protection; (*Verteidigung*) defen|ce, *Am.* -se (*beide: vor dat.* from, against); (*Obdach*) shelter; (*Geleit*; *a. fig. Sicherung*) safeguard; (*Deckung*) cover; (*Abschirmung*) screen, shield; *~ suchen* take shelter (*vor dat.* from), take refuge (*bei* with); *in ~ nehmen* defend; '~**anstrich** *m* protective coat(ing); *zur Tarnung:* ✗ camouflage paint(ing), ⚓ dazzle-paint (-ing).

Schütz [ʃyts] **1.** ⚡ *n* (3²) contactor; **2.** ⊕ *s. ~e* 2.

'Schutz|-anzug *m* overall; '~**befohlene** ['~bəfoːlənə] *m*, *f* charge, protégé(e *f*); '~**blech** *n* guard-plate; *mot.* mudguard, *Am.* fender; '~**brille** *f* (*eine a pair of*) (safety) goggles *pl.*; glasses *pl.*; '~**bündnis** *n* defensive alliance; '~**dach** *n* protective roof; shelter.

Schütze ['ʃytsə] **1.** *m* (13) marksman, shot; *ast.* Archer, Sagittarius; ✗ rifleman, (*Dienstgrad*) private; *Ballsport:* scorer; **2.** ⊕ *f* (15) *Wasserbau:* sluice-board; (*Weber♀*) shuttle.

'schützen (27) protect, guard; (*verteidigen*) defend (*gegen* against; *vor dat.* from); *gegen Wetter usw.:* shelter *od.* shield (from).

'Schützen|fest *n* shooting-match (*a. fig.*); '~**feuer** ✗ *n* rifle fire; (*selbständiges Schießen*) independent fire.

'Schutz-engel *m* guardian angel.

'Schützen|gilde *f* rifle-association; '~**graben** *m* trench; '~**hilfe** *fig. f:*

j-m ~ geben back a p. up; '~**kette** *f*, '~**linie** ✗ *f* riflemen extended; '~**könig** *m* champion shot; *Sport:* top scorer; '~**loch** ✗ *n* foxhole, rifle-pit; '~**panzer** ✗ *m* armo(u)red personnel carrier.

'Schutz|färbung *zo. f* protective colo(u)ring; '~**gebiet** *n* protectorate; *s. Natur♀*; '~**geländer** *n* guard rail; '~**geleit** *n* safe-conduct, (*a.* ✈) escort; '~**gitter** *n* guard, protective railing; *Radio:* screen grid; '~**haft** *f* preventive (*od.* protective) custody; '~**haube** *f* (protective) cover *od.* hood; '~**heilige** *m, f* patron saint; '~**helm** *m* safety helmet, *e-s Bauarbeiters: a.* F hard hat; '~**herr** *m* patron, protector; '~**herrin** *f* patroness, protectress; '~**herrschaft** *f* protectorate; '~**hülle** *f* protective covering; sheath; *s. Schutzumschlag*; '~**hütte** *f* (shelter) hut, refuge; '~**impfung** *f* protective inoculation; *gegen Pocken:* vaccination; '~**insel** *f* *Verkehr:* traffic island.

Schützling ['ʃytsliŋ] *m* (3¹) protégé(e *f*), charge.

'schutz|los defenceless, unprotected; '♀**mann** *m* constable, policeman; '♀**marke** *f* trade-mark; '♀**maske** *f* (protective) mask; '♀**maßregel** *f* protective measure, precaution; '♀**mittel** *n* preservative, preventive (*gegen* of); *vorbeugendes:* prophylactic; '♀**patron**(**in** *f*) *m* patron saint; '♀**polizei** *f* constabulary, police; '♀**polizist** *m* *s. Schutzmann*; '♀**raum** *m* shelter; '♀**rechte** *n/pl.* patent (*od.* trade-mark) rights; '♀**schild** *m* shield; *der Polizei:* riot shield; '♀**stoff** ⚕ *m* antibody, vaccine; '♀-**umschlag** *m* *e-s Buches:* (dust) jacket, wrapper; '♀**vorrichtung** *f* protective device; '♀**waffen** *f/pl.* defensive arms; '♀**zoll** *m* protective duty; '♀**zone** *f* protected area; *zur ~ erklären* declare a protected area.

schwabbel|ig ['ʃvabəliç] wobbly; '~**n** F *v/i. u. v/t.* (29) wobble; (*schwatzen*) babble; ⊕ (*polieren*) buff.

Schwabe ['ʃvaːbə] **1.** *m* (13) Swabian; **2.** *f* (15) *Insekt:* cockroach; '~**nstreich** *m* tomfoolery.

Schwäb|in ['ʃvɛːbin] *f* Swabian (woman); '♀**isch** Swabian.

schwach [ʃvax] (18²) *allg.* weak (*a.*

fig.); (*kraftlos*) feeble; (*schlecht*) poor; (*gering*) meag|re (*Am.* -er); *Ähnlichkeit*: remote; *Erinnerung, Hoffnung, Licht, Ton*: faint; ~es *Geschlecht the* weaker sex; ~e *Seite fig.* weak point; ~e *Stunde* scant hour; *fig. a* moment of weakness; ~ *werden* weaken.

Schwäche ['ʃvɛçə] *f* (15) weakness (*a. fig.*; *für* for); *des Charakters*: *a.* foible, weak point; (*Hinfälligkeit*) infirmity; *von Ton, Licht* (*a. ~zustand*) faintness; '~-**anfall** *m* (sudden) feeling of faintness; '2**n** (25) weaken (*a. fig.*); (*vermindern*) lessen, diminish; '~**zustand** *m* faintness; *allgemeiner*: debility.

'**Schwachheit** *f* weakness; *moralische*: *a.* frailty.

'**schwach|herzig** faint-hearted; '2-**kopf** *m* imbecile; ~**köpfig** ['~kœpfiç] brainless.

schwächlich ['ʃvɛçliç] feeble, weakly; (*empfindlich*) delicate; *fig.* weak (-kneed); '2**keit** *f* feebleness, weakliness; delicacy.

Schwächling ['~liŋ] *m* (3¹) weakling, F softy.

schwach|sichtig ['~ziçtiç] weak-sighted; '2**sinn** *m* feeble-mindedness; '~**sinnig** feeble-minded; '2-**sinnige** *m, f* (*a. contp.*) half-wit, moron; ⚥ mental defective; '2-**strom** ⚡ *m* weak (*od.* low-voltage) current.

'**Schwächung** *f* weakening.

Schwaden ['ʃvɑːdən] *m* (6) 1. 🗡 swath; 2. (*Rauch*2, *Gas*2) (smoke, gas) cloud; ⚒ fire-damp.

Schwadron [ʃvaˈdroːn] *f* (16) squadron; 2**ieren** [~droˈniːrən] swagger, brag.

schwafeln ['ʃvɑːfəln] F (29) twaddle.

Schwager ['ʃvɑːgər] *m* (7) brother--in-law.

Schwäger|in ['ʃvɛːgərin] *f* (16) sister-in-law; '~**schaft** *f* affinity by marriage; *konkret*: in-laws *pl.*

Schwalbe ['ʃvalbə] *f* (15) swallow; '~**nschwanz** *m Tischlerei*: dovetail; F *fig.* (*Frack*) swallow-tail.

Schwall [ʃval] *m* (3³) flood (*a. fig.*); *von Worten*: *a.* torrent.

schwamm¹ [ʃvam] *pret. v.* schwim-men.

Schwamm² *m* (3³) sponge; (*Pilz*) fungus, *eßbarer*: mushroom; (*Feuer*2) German tinder; (*Haus*2) dry

rot; ~ *drüber!* (let's) forget it!; '2**ig** spongy (*a. fig.*); (*gedunsen*) bloated; '~**taucher(in** *f*) *m* sponge diver.

Schwan [ʃvɑːn] *m* (3³) swan.

schwand [ʃvant] *pret. v.* schwinden.

schwanen ['ʃvɑːnən] (25): *es schwant mir* (et.) I have a presentiment (of a th.); *ihm schwante nichts Gutes* he had dark forebodings; '2**gesang** *fig. m* swan song.

schwang [ʃvaŋ] *pret. v.* schwingen.

Schwang [~] *m*: *im* ~(e) *sein* be a tradition *od.* (*Mode*) the fashion.

schwanger ['ʃvaŋər] pregnant, with child, *feiner*: expectant; '2**enfürsorge** *f* antenatal care.

schwänger|n ['ʃvɛŋərn] (29) get with child, (*a. fig.*) impregnate; '2**ung** *f* impregnation.

'**Schwangerschaft** *f* (16) pregnancy; '~**s-test** *m* pregnancy test; '~**s-unterbrechung** *f* induced abortion; '~**sverhütung** *f* contraception.

Schwank [ʃvaŋk] 1. *m* (3³) merry tale; (*Streich*) prank; *thea.* farce; 2. 2 flexible; (*wackelig*) shaky; '2**en**¹ (25) (*sich wiegen*) wave, swing; (*wanken*) totter, stagger; *Boden usw.*: shake, rock; *Baum usw.*: sway; *Magnetnadel usw.*: oscillate; *fig.* (*zaudern*) waver, falter, vacillate; (*sich ändern*) vary; ✝ *Kurse, Preise*: fluctuate; ~ *zwischen* ... *und P.*: waver between ... and, *S.*: vary (*od.* range) from ... to; ~d wavering *etc.*; (*unsicher*) unstable; vague; '~**en**² *n* (6), '~**ung** *f* waving, staggering *etc.*; ✝ fluctuation; *fig.* vacillation.

Schwanz [ʃvants] *m* (3² *u.* ³) tail.

schwänz|eln ['ʃvɛntsəln] (29) wag one's tail; *contp.* fawn (*um j-n* upon); '~**en** F *v/i. u. v/t.* (27) shirk, miss; (*die Schule*) ~ play truant (*Am. a.* hooky); *geschwänzt* tailed, caudate.

'**Schwanz|-ende** *n* tip of the tail; *fig.* (*a.* ⚓) tail end; '~**feder** *f* tail feather; '~**flosse** *f* tail fin.

schwappen ['ʃvapən] (25, *h. u.* sn) swash, slop.

Schwäre ['ʃvɛːrə] *f* (15) abscess, boil, festering wound; ulcer; '2**n** (25, *h. u.* sn) suppurate, fester (*a. fig.*).

Schwarm [ʃvarm] *m* (3³) *allg.* swarm; *Vögel*: *a.* flight (*a.* ⚓); *Fische*: shoal; (*Menschen*2) swarm,

crowd; *v. Damen, Mädchen*: bevy;
F *fig. P.*: idol; (*Angebetete*) flame;
S.: ideal, F craze.

schwärmen ['ʃvɛrmən] (25, h. *u.* sn)
swarm; ✕ (*aus*)~ (*lassen*) extend;
(*schwelgen*) revel; ~ *für* be enthusiastic (*od.* wild) about *a th.*, have
a crush on *a p.*; ~ *von* gush about
a p., a th.

'**Schwärmer** *m* (7), '~**in** *f* revel(l)er;
(*Begeisterter*) enthusiast, bsd. eccl.
fanatic; (*Träumer*) visionary; *Feuerwerk*: squib; (*Abendfalter*) hawk
moth; ~**ei** [~'raɪ] *f* (16) revel(l)ing;
(*für*) enthusiasm (for), bsd. eccl.
fanaticism, *contp.* gushing; '2isch
enthusiastic(ally *adv.*); fanatical;
(*verzückt*) ecstatic(ally *adv.*); (*überspannt*) eccentric.

Schwarte ['ʃvartə] *f* (15) rind, skin;
⊕ (*Schalbrett*) slab, plank; F (*Buch*)
old (*od.* trashy) volume.

schwarz [ʃvarts] **1.** (18²) black;
Teint: swarthy; *fig.* (*finster*) gloomy,
dark, black; (*ungesetzlich*) illicit;
2es Brett *für Anschläge* notice (*Am.*
bulletin) board; ~**er** *Erdteil* Black
Continent; ~**er** *Humor* sick hu-
mo(u)r, black comedy; ~**e** *Kunst* art
of printing, (*Zauberei*) black art;
~**er** *Mann* (*Schreckgespenst*) bog(e)y;
~**er** *Markt* black market; *s. Schaf*;
~ *auf weiß* in black and white; ~
sehen be pessimistic; *ich sehe* ~
(*für dich*) things look bad (for you);
auf die ~**e** *Liste setzen* blacklist;
2. 2 *n* black; *ins* ~**e** *treffen* hit the
bull's-eye (*a. fig.*).

'**Schwarz**|-**arbeit** *f* illicit work, F
moonlighting; '~**arbeiter** *m* F
moonlighter; '2**blau** very dark blue;
'~**blech** *n* black sheet-iron; '~**brot** *n*
(black) rye bread; '~**drossel** *f* blackbird.

'**Schwarze** *m, f* (18) (*Neger*) black.
Schwärze ['ʃvɛrtsə] *f* (15) black-
ness; (*Färbemittel*) blacking; ⊕ *typ.*
printer's ink; '2**n** (27) blacken.

'**Schwarz**|**fahrer** *m* mot. joy-rider;
(*der kein Fahrgeld zahlt*) fare
dodger; '~**fahrt** mot. *f* joy-ride;
'~**färber** *m fig.* pessimist; '~**handel**
m black-market(eering), illicit trade;
'~**händler** *m* black-marketeer; '~**
hörer** *m* (radio) licen|ce (*Am.* -se)
dodger.

schwärzlich ['ʃvɛrtslɪç] blackish.
'**Schwarz**|**markt** *m* black market; '~**

pulver *n* black powder; '~**schlach-
tung** *f* illicit slaughtering; '~**seher**
(-**in** *f*) *m* pessimist; *TV*: (television)
licen|ce (*Am.* -se) dodger; '~**sender**
m pirate station; '2**weiß** black and
white; '~**weiß...** *phot. usw.*: black-
-and-white ...; '~**wild** *n* wild boars
pl.; '~**wurzel** *f* comfrey.

Schwatz [ʃvats] F *m* (3²) chat; '~**
base** F *f s.* Schwätzer; '2**en** *v/i. u.
v/t.* (27) (*plaudern*) talk, chat;
(*schnatternd u. seicht daherreden*)
chatter, tattle; (*kindlich plappern*)
prattle; (*ausplaudern*) blab.

schwätzen ['ʃvɛtsən] (27) *s.* schwatzen.

Schwätzer ['ʃvɛtsər] *m* (7), '~**in** *f*
(16¹) chatterbox, babbler; (*Klatsch-
tante*) gossip; (*dummer* ~) blather-
skite.

'**schwatzhaft** talkative, garrulous;
'2**igkeit** *f* talkativeness.

Schwebe ['ʃve:bə] *f* (15): *in der* ~
in suspense, undecided; *zt* pending, in abeyance; '~**bahn** *f* suspension railway; '~**balken** *m* Sport:
balance beam; '2**n** (25, h. *u.* sn) be
suspended, float; *Vogel, Hubschrauber usw.*: hover; (*hoch*~) soar; (*unentschieden sein*) be undecided, *Prozeß usw.*: be pending; (*leicht gehen*)
glide, swim; *in Gefahr usw.* ~ be in
danger *etc.*; *vor Augen* ~ *s.* vorschweben; '2**nd** suspended (*a.* ⌂);
floating *etc.*; *Frage, Verfahren*:
pending.

'**Schwebung** *f Radio*: beat.
Schwed|**e** ['ʃve:də] *m* (13), '~**in** *f*
(16¹) Swede; '2**isch** Swedish.
Schwefel ['ʃve:fəl] *m* (7) sulphur;
'~**bad** *n* sulphur bath; (*Ort*) sulphur springs *pl.*; '~**blumen** *f/pl.*,
'~**blüte** *f* sulphur flowers; '2**farbig**, '2**gelb** brimstone-colo(u)red.
'**schwef(e)lig** sulphur(e)ous.
'**Schwefel**|**kies** *m* pyrite(s); '~**
kohlenstoff** *m* carbon disulphide;
'2**n** (29) sulphurate, sulphurize; '~**
säure** *f* sulphuric acid; '~**wasserstoff** *m* hydrogen sulphide.
Schweif [ʃvaɪf] *m* (3) tail (*a. ast.*);
fig. train; '2**en** (25) *v/i.* (h. *u.* sn)
rove, ramble; *v/t.* curve; '~**ung** *f*
curve, bend(ing); '2**wedeln** wag
one's tail; *fig.* fawn (*vor dat.* upon).
'**Schweige**|**geld** *n* hush-money; '~**
marsch** *m* silent protest march.
schweigen ['ʃvaɪgən] **1.** (30) be

silent (*a. fig. über acc.* on); say nothing, hold one's tongue; *ganz zu ~ von* ... to say nothing of, let alone; **2.** ♀ *n* (6) silence; *zum ~ bringen* silence (*a. ⚔*); *~ bewahren* keep silence; '*~d* silent; *sich ~ verhalten* keep silent, hold one's peace. '**Schweigepflicht** *f* secrecy, professional discretion.

schweigsam ['ʃvaɪkzaːm] silent; (*wortkarg*) taciturn; *s. verschwiegen*; '♀**keit** *f* taciturnity.

Schwein [ʃvaɪn] *n* (3) pig, *bsd. Am.* hog, *zo. u. pl.* swine (*alle a. contp. fig.*); (*~efleisch*) pork; F (*Glück*) luck; F *~ haben* be lucky; F *kein ~* nobody.

'**Schweine**|**braten** *m* roast pork; '*~fleisch* *n* pork; '*~hund* P *m contp.* swine, rat; *innerer ~* cowardice; *~rei* [~'raɪ] *f* (16) filthiness; (*Unordnung*) (awful) mess; (*Gemeinheit*) dirty trick; (*Zote*) smut(ty joke), obscenity; (*Schande*) crying shame; '*~stall* *m* pigsty (*a. fig.*); '*~zucht* *f* pig-breeding, *Am.* hog raising; '*~züchter* *m* pig-breeder, *Am.* hog raiser.

Schwein|**igel** ['ʃvaɪnˀiːgəl] F *m* filthy pig; *~igelei* [~'laɪ] *f* (16) smut(ty joke), obscenity; '♀**-igeln** F (29) talk smut; '♀**isch** swinish (*zotig*) smutty.

'**Schweins**|**kotelett** *n* pork chop; '*~leder* *n* pigskin.

Schweiß [ʃvaɪs] *m* (3²) sweat, perspiration; *Wolle:* yolk; *hunt.* blood; '*~blatt* *n* dress-shield; '*~brenner* *m* welding torch, blowpipe, oxyacetylene torch; '*~brille* *f* welding goggles *pl.*; '*~drüse* *f* perspiratory gland; '♀**en** (27) *v/t.* ⊕ weld; *v/i. hunt.* bleed; '*~er* *m* (7) welder; '*~fuchs* *m* sorrel horse; '*~fuß* *m* perspiring (*od.* sweaty) foot; '♀**gebadet** bathed in perspiration; '*~hund* *m* bloodhound; '♀**ig** sweaty, perspiring; *hunt.* bloody; '*~naht* ⊕ *f* welding seam; '*~perlen* *f/pl.* beads of perspiration; '*~stelle* ⊕ *f* (point of) weld; '♀**treibend(es Mittel)** sudorific; '♀**triefend** *s. schweißgebadet*; '*~tropfen* *m* drop of sweat.

Schweizer ['ʃvaɪtsər] **1.** *m* (7) Swiss (*a. '~in f*); (*Melker*) dairyman; **2.** *adj.* Swiss; *~ Käse* Swiss cheese; '♀**isch** Swiss.

schwelen ['ʃveːlən] (25) smo(u)lder.

schwelg|**en** ['ʃvɛlgən] (25) revel (*in dat.* in); '♀**er** *m* (7), '♀**erin** *f* revel(l)er; ♀**erei** [~'raɪ] *f* (16) revelry; (*Ausschweifung*) debauch(ery); '*~erisch* luxurious.

Schwell|**e** ['ʃvɛlə] *f* (15) doorstep; threshold (*a. fig.; a. ⚓, phys.*); 🚃 sleeper, *Am. a.* tie; '♀**en** *v/t.* swell; *v/i.* (sn) swell; *Wasser usw.:* rise; (*anwachsen*) increase; '*~körper anat. m* erectile tissue; '*~ung f* swelling; *des Bodens:* swell.

Schwemm|**e** ['ʃvɛmə] *f* (15) horse-pond; *für Vieh:* watering-place; *Bierlokal:* tap-room; ✝ glut (*an dat.* of); '♀**n** (25) *Vieh:* water; (*weg~*) wash; *Holz:* float; '*~land* *n* alluvial land.

Schwengel ['ʃvɛŋəl] *m* (7) (*Wagen*♀) swing-bar; (*Glocken*♀) clapper; (*Pumpen*♀) handle.

Schwenk [ʃvɛŋk] *m Film:* panning (shot); '*~arm* *m* swivel arm; '♀**bar** swivel(ling); '♀**en** *v/t.* (25) swing; *Stock usw.:* flourish, brandish; *Hut, Tuch usw.:* wave; *Film:* pan; ⊕ swivel; (*spülen*) rinse; *v/i.* turn; ⚔, *pol.* wheel (about); (*umkehren*) about-face; '*~kran* *m* slewing crane; '*~ung f* swinging *etc.*; ⚔ wheel, pivoting manoeuvre; *fig.* change of mind (about); ⊕ swivel, slew round.

schwer [ʃveːr] *Gewicht u. körperlich:* heavy (*a. ⚔ Angriff, Kreuzer usw.*); (*gewichtig*) weighty; (*~fällig*) heavy, ponderous; (*schwierig*) hard, difficult; *Fehler:* bad, gross; *Entscheidung, Kampf, Zeit:* hard; *Krankheit, Unfall, Wunde:* serious; *Strafe:* severe; *Verbrechen usw.:* grave; *Speise:* heavy, rich; *Wein, Zigarre:* strong; *Kleiderstoff:* heavy-weight; *~er Atem* short breath; F *~er Junge* criminal, crook; *~er* (*gehaltvoller*) *Kuchen* rich cake; *~ von Begriff* slow (in the uptake), dense; *zwei Pfund ~* weighing two pounds, two pounds in weight; *~ arbeiten* work hard; *~ zu sagen* hard to say; *~ enttäuscht* badly disappointed; '♀**-arbeit** *f* heavy work; '♀**-arbeiter** *m* heavy worker; '♀**-athlet** *m* heavy athlete; '♀**-athletik** *f* heavy athletics *sg. u. pl.*; '*~behindert* severely disabled; '*~beladen* heavily laden; '♀**beschädigte** *m* (18) seriously disabled person; '*~bewaffnet* heavily armed; '*~blütig* grave, heavy; '2e f (15) s. schwer: heaviness; weight; gravity (a. phys.); seriousness; severity; '∼elos weightless; '2elosigkeit f weightlessness; 2enöter ['∼ɔ'nøːtər] m (7) philanderer, gay Lothario; '∼er'ziehbar difficult to educate; recalcitrant; '∼fallen be difficult (dat. to); es fällt mir ∼ I find it hard; '∼fällig heavy, slow; (unhandlich) unwieldy, cumbersome; '2fälligkeit f heaviness, slowness, unwieldiness, cumbersomeness; '∼flüssig viscid, viscous; '2gewicht n Boxen: heavy-weight (a. '2gewichtler m); fig. chief importance, chief stress; '∼halten be difficult; '∼hörig hard of hearing; '2-industrie f heavy industry; '2kraft f (force of) gravity; '2'kriegsbeschädigte m (18) seriously disabled war veteran; '∼lich hardly, scarcely; '2mut f, ∼mütig ['∼myːtiç] melancholy; '2-öl n heavy oil; '2punkt m cent/re (Am. -er) of gravity; fig. focal point; (Nachdruck) (chief) stress; '2punktstreik m pinpoint strike; 2spat ['∼ʃpaːt] m barite, heavy spar.

Schwert [ʃveːrt] n (1) sword; '∼fisch m sword-fish; '∼lilie f iris.

'**Schwer|transport** m transport of heavy goods; '∼transporter m heavy goods vehicle; '∼verbrecher m dangerous criminal, ⚖ felon; '2verdaulich hard to digest, heavy; '2verständlich difficult to understand; abstruse; '2verwundet seriously wounded; '2wiegend weighty (a. fig.); fig. grave.

Schwester ['ʃvɛstər] f (15) sister; (Kranken2) (hospital) nurse; s. a. barmherzig; '∼firma † associated company; '∼kind n sister's child; '2lich sisterly; '∼liebe f sisterly love; '∼nhelferin f nursing auxiliary (Am. assistant); '∼n-orden m, '∼nschaft f sisterhood, sorority; '∼ntracht f uniform; '∼schiff n sister ship; '∼sohn m sister's son.

schwieg [ʃviːk] pret. v. schweigen 1.

Schwieger... ['ʃviːgər-] mst: ...-in-law, z.B. '∼eltern pl. parents-in-law; '∼sohn m son-in-law.

Schwiel|e ['ʃviːlə] f (15) callosity; (Strieme) weal; '2ig callous, horny; full of weals.

schwierig ['ʃviːriç] difficult (a. P.), hard; (verwickelt) complicated; '2keit f difficulty, trouble.

Schwimm|bad ['ʃvim-] n swimming bath, swimming pool; '∼blase f (Fisch2) air-bladder; '∼dock n floating dock; '2en (30, h. u. sn) swim; S.: float; fig. (unsicher sein; a. ins 2 kommen) flounder; im Geld ∼ be rolling in money; '∼er m (7) swimmer (a. '∼erin f); an Angel, Netz, ✂ u. ⊕: float; '∼flosse f fin; Sport: flipper; '∼flügel m/pl. water-wings; '∼fuß m web-foot; v. Robben usw.: flipper; '∼gürtel m swimming-belt; (Rettungsgürtel) life-belt; '∼haut f web; '∼lehrer m swimming-master; '∼panzer m amphibious tank; '∼sport m swimming; '∼vogel m web-footed bird; '∼wagen m amphibious car; '∼weste f life-jacket, Am. life-preserver (vest).

Schwindel ['ʃvindəl] m (7) ☞ vertigo, giddiness, dizziness; (Betrug) swindle, fraud, cheat, Am. F flimflam; F der ganze ∼ the whole bag of tricks; '∼anfall m fit of dizziness; '∼ei [∼'laɪ] f (16) swindling, cheat; '2-erregend dizzy, giddy; fig. a. staggering; '∼firma † f long firm, Am. wildcat (firm); '2frei free from giddiness; nicht ∼ high-shy; '∼gesellschaft † f bogus company.

'**schwind(e)lig** giddy, dizzy; fig. a. staggering; mir ist ∼ I am (od. feel) dizzy.

'**schwindeln** (29) v/i. (lügen, betrügen) cheat, swindle, humbug, Am. sl. chisel; mir schwindelt I am (od. feel) giddy, my head swims; ∼ machen fig. stagger; ∼de Höhe dizzy height.

schwinden ['ʃvindən] (30, sn) dwindle; (schrumpfen) shrink; Ton, Farbe, Licht: fade; (ver∼) disappear, vanish.

'**Schwindler** m (7), '∼in f swindler, cheat, crook; (Lügner) liar.

Schwind|sucht ['ʃvintzuxt] f consumption; '2süchtig consumptive.

Schwing|e ['ʃviŋə] f (15) wing; (Getreide2) fan; (Flachs2) swingle; '2en v/t. swing (sich o.s.); (handhaben) wield; Waffe usw.: brandish; Flachs: swingle; F e-e Rede ∼ make a speech; v/i. swing; ⊕ (hin und her ∼) oscillate; Saite, Ton usw.: vibrate; '∼er m (7) Boxen: swing; '∼ung f swinging; oscillation; vibration; '2ungsfrei

Seele

non-oscillating; '**⁀ungszahl** f frequency of oscillations.

Schwips F [ʃvips] m (7): e-n ⁀ haben be tipsy.

schwirren ['ʃvirən] (25, h. u. sn) whiz(z), whir(r); *Insekt usw.*: buzz.

Schwitz|bad ['ʃvits-] n Turkish bath; (*Dampfbad*) steam-bath; '2̥**en** v/i. u. v/t. sweat, *feiner*: perspire; *Fenster*: s. beschlagen; '**⁀kasten** m *Ringen*: headlock; '**⁀kur** f sweating-cure.

schwoll [ʃvɔl] *pret. v.* schwellen.

schwor [ʃvoːr] *pret. v.* schwören.

schwören ['ʃvøːrən] (30) v/i. u. v/t. swear (*bei* by), take an oath; *fig.* ⁀ auf (*acc.*) F swear by; s. Rache.

schwul F [ʃvuːl] queer.

schwül [ʃvyːl] sultry, close, oppressive; *fig.* sultry.

'**Schwule** F m (18) queer.

'**Schwüle** f (15) sultriness.

Schwulität [ʃvuliˈtɛːt] F f (16): ⁀en kommen get into trouble.

Schwulst [ʃvulst] m (3² u. ³) bombast.

schwülstig ['ʃvylstiç] bombastic (-ally *adv.*).

Schwund [ʃvunt] m (3) dwindling; (*Verlust*) loss; *durch Einlaufen*: shrinkage; *durch Aussickern*: leakage, wastage; ⁀ atrophy; *Film, Radio*: fading; s. a. Haar2; '**⁀ausgleich** m, '**⁀regelung** f *Radio*: automatic volume control.

Schwung [ʃvuŋ] m (3³) swing (*a. Turnen*); *Schisport*: turn; (*Tempo*) speed; *phys.* momentum; *fig.* impetus; (*Energie, Wucht*) energy, drive, F vim; (*Schmiß*) verve, F go, pep; *der Phantasie*: flight; *des Geistes*: buoyancy; (*Menge*) batch; v. Personen: F bunch; in ⁀ bringen set a th. going; (*richtig*) in ⁀ kommen get into one's stride; '**⁀feder** f pinion; '2̥**haft** *Geschäft, Handel*: brisk, roaring; '**⁀kraft** f centrifugal force; *fig.* buoyancy, verve; '2̥**los** spiritless, tired; '**⁀rad** n fly-wheel; '2̥**voll** full of verve *od.* F go, spirited; *Entwurf*: bold; *Melodie*: racy.

Schwur [ʃvuːr] m (3³) oath; (*Gelübde*) vow; '**⁀gericht** n jury court.

sechs [zɛks] **1.** six; **2.** 2̥ f (16³) six; '2̥**-eck** n hexagon; '**⁀-eckig** hexagonal; '**⁀fach**, ⁀**fältig** ['⁀fɛltiç] sixfold, sextuple; '**⁀jährig** six-year(s)-old, ▯ sexennial; '**⁀malig** six

times repeated; '**⁀monatig** lasting six months; '**⁀monatlich** six-monthly; *adv.* every six months; '**⁀seitig** hexagonal; ⁀**stündig** ['⁀-ʃtyndiç] of six hours; 2̥'**tagerennen** n six-day (cycling) race; ⁀**tägig** ['⁀teːɡiç] of (*od.* lasting) six days.

sechs|te ['⁀tə], '2̥**tel** n (7) sixth; '**⁀tens** sixthly, in the sixth place.

sechzehn ['zɛçtseːn] sixteen; '**⁀te** sixteenth; '2̥**tel** n (7) sixteenth (part); 2̥**telnote** ♪ f semiquaver; '**⁀tens** in the sixteenth place.

sechzig ['zɛçtsiç] sixty; 2̥er ['⁀ɡər] m (7), '2̥**erin** f (16¹) sexagenarian.

Sediment [zediˈmɛnt] n (3¹) sediment; 2̥**är** [⁀'tɛːr] sedimentary.

See [zeː] **1.** m (10) lake; **2.** f (15) sea; an die ⁀ gehen go to the seaside (*Am.* seashore); auf ⁀ at sea; in ⁀ gehen *od.* stechen put to sea; zur ⁀ gehen go to sea.

'**See|bad** n sea-bath; (*Ort*) seaside resort; '**⁀bär** m: *fig.* alter ⁀ F old salt; '**⁀dienst** m naval service; '2̥**fahrend** seafaring; '**⁀fahrer** m sailor; '**⁀fahrt** f seafaring; (*Seereise*) voyage, cruise; '2̥**fest** seaworthy; *P.*: (*nicht*) ⁀ sein be a good (bad) sailor; '**⁀fisch** m saltwater fish; '**⁀fracht** ✝ f sea-freight, *Am.* ocean freight; '**⁀gang** m: hoher ⁀ rough sea; schwerer ⁀ heavy sea; '**⁀gefecht** n naval action; '2̥**gestützt** ✕ sea--based; '**⁀gras** n seaweed; '**⁀hafen** m seaport; '**⁀handel** m maritime trade; '**⁀held** m naval hero; '**⁀herrschaft** f naval supremacy; '**⁀hund** m seal; '**⁀hundsfell** n sealskin; '**⁀-igel** m sea-urchin; '**⁀kadett** ⚓ m naval cadet; '**⁀karte** f (sea-)chart; '2̥**klar** ready to sail; '2̥**krank** seasick; *leicht* ⁀ werden be a bad sailor; '**⁀krankheit** f seasickness; '**⁀krieg(führung** f) m naval war(fare); '**⁀küste** f (sea-)coast, seashore; seaboard; '**⁀lachs** m coalfish, pollack.

Seele ['zeːlə] f (15) soul (*a. fig.*: *Lebenskraft*; *Kern*; *menschliches Wesen*); (*Geist*) mind; e-s *Herings*: bladder; e-r *Schußwaffe*: bore; e-s *Kabels*: core; e-e ⁀ von Mensch a good soul; *fig.* keine ⁀ not a soul; mit (*od. von*) ganzer ⁀ with all one's heart; er ist die ⁀ des Ganzen he is the life and soul of it all; du sprichst mir aus der ⁀ you express my sentiments exactly.

Seelen|-amt n office for the dead; '**~freund** m soul brother;'**~frieden** m peace of mind; '⁀**froh** heartily glad; '**~größe** f greatness of mind; '⁀**gut** kind-hearted, pred. a good soul; '**~heil** n salvation, spiritual welfare; '**~hirt** m pastor; '**~kunde** f psychology; '**~leben** n inner life; '**~leiden** n mental suffering; '⁀**los** soulless; '**~messe** f mass for the dead, requiem; '**~pein** f, '**~qual** f mental agony; '**~ruhe** f peace of mind; weitS. calmness; '⁀**ruhig** adv. cooly; '**~stärke** f fortitude; '⁀**vergnügt** (quite) cheerful; '⁀**verwandt** congenial; ~ sein be kindred souls; '**~verwandtschaft** f congeniality; '⁀**voll** soulful; '**~wanderung** f transmigration of souls, 🕮 metempsychosis.

'**Seeleute** pl. seamen, sailors.

'**seelisch** psychic(al), mental, spiritual.

'**Seelöwe** m sea-lion.

'**Seelsorge** f religious welfare, care of souls; '**~r** m (7) pastor, clergyman.

'**See|luft** f sea air; '**~macht** f naval (od. sea) power; '**~mann** m seaman, sailor; ⁀**männisch** ['~mɛnɪʃ] sailorlike, seamanlike; Fertigkeit usw.: nautical; '⁀**mäßig** Verpackung: seaworthy; '**~meile** f nautical mile; '**~mine** f sea-mine; '**~möwe** f sea-gull; '**~not** f distress at sea; '**~offizier** m naval officer; '**~pferdchen** n sea-horse; '**~räuber** m pirate; **~räuberei** [~'raɪ] f piracy; '**~recht** n maritime law; '**~reise** f voyage, cruise; '**~rose** f water-lily; '**~schaden** m sea-damage, average; '**~schiff** n sea-going vessel; '**~schlacht** f naval battle; '**~schwalbe** f tern; '**~sieg** m naval victory; '**~stadt** f seaside town; '**~stern** m starfish; '**~streitkräfte** f/pl. naval forces; '**~tier** n marine animal; '**~tang** m seaweed; '⁀**tüchtig** seaworthy; '**~ufer** n lakeside, shore; '**~verkehr** m ocean traffic; '**~volk** n maritime nation; '**~warte** f naval observatory; ⁀**wärts** ['~vɛrts] seawards; '**~wasser** n sea-water; '**~weg** m sea-route; auf dem ~ by sea; '**~wind** m sea-breeze; '**~zunge** f Fisch: sole.

Segel ['zeːgəl] n (7) sail; ~ setzen, unter ~ gehen set sail; ~ hissen make sail; die ~ streichen strike sail, fig.

give in; '**~boot** n sailing-boat, Am. sailboat; Sport: yacht; '⁀**fertig** ready to sail; '**~fliegen** n (6) gliding, soaring, sailplaning; '**~flieger** m glider pilot; s. Segelflugzeug; '**~flug** m glide; s. Segelfliegen; '**~flugzeug** n glider, sailplane; '⁀**klar** s. segelfertig; '**~klasse** f e-s Rennbootes: rating; '**~klub** m yachting club; '⁀**n** (29, h. u. sn) sail (a. fig.), sportlich: yacht; ⚓ glide, soar; '**~regatta** f yacht-race, regatta; '**~schiff** n sailing-ship; '**~schlitten** m ice-yacht; '**~sport** m yachting; '**~tuch** n sail-cloth, canvas; '**~werk** n sails pl.

Segen ['zeːgən] m (7) blessing (a. fig. Wohltat, Glück); (bsd. eccl.) benediction; fig. (Fülle) abundance; F der ganze ~ the whole lot; '⁀**sreich**, '⁀**svoll** beneficial, blessed; pred. a blessing; '**~swunsch** m benediction; pl. good wishes pl.

Segler ['zeːglər] m (7) yachtsman; (Schiff) sailing-vessel, good, fast etc. sailer; '**~in** f (16¹) yachtswoman.

segn|en ['zeːgnən] (26) bless; '⁀**ung** f blessing (a. fig. der Zivilisation usw.) (bsd. eccl.) benediction.

sehen ['zeːən] (30) v/t. see (a. v/i.); (wahrnehmen) perceive; (plötzlich ~) catch sight of; fig. (ein~) realize, see; v/i. (hin~) look; sieh nur! just look!; sieh(e) da! behold!; sieh mal look here; siehe oben see above; siehe Seite 14 see page 14; gut ~ have good eyes; auf et. (acc.) ~ look at, fig. (Wert legen auf) be particular about, s. a. achten; darauf ~, daß see to it that; nach et. ~ look for, (sorgen für) look (od. see) after; ~ lassen show; ich kenne ihn nur vom ⁀ I know him only by sight.

'**sehens|wert**, '**~würdig** worth seeing, remarkable; '⁀**würdigkeit** f object of interest, curiosity; pl. e-r Stadt: sights pl.

Seher ['zeːər] m (7) seer; '**~blick** m, '**~gabe** f prophetic eye od. gift; '**~in** f (16¹) prophetess.

'**Seh|fehler** m defective vision; '**~feld** n field of vision; '**~kraft** f (eye)sight, vision, visual power.

Sehne ['zeːnə] f (15) sinew, tendon; e-s Bogens: string; 🜨 chord.

sehnen ['zeːnən] **1.** (25) sich ~ nach long for; stärker: yearn for; **2.** ⁀ n (6) longing, yearning.

'**Sehnen|scheiden-entzündung** ✚ *f* tendovaginitis; '**~zerrung** ✚ *f* pulled tendon.

'**Sehnerv** *m* optic nerve.

'**sehnig** sinewy; *Fleisch:* stringy.

'**sehn|lich** eager, anxious; (*glühend*) ardent; (*leidenschaftlich*) passionate; '**⁀sucht** *f* longing, yearning (*nach* for); '**~süchtig** longing, yearning.

'**Sehprüfung** *f* sight test.

sehr [zeːr] *vor adj. u. adv.* very; *beim vb.* (very) much, greatly, highly; F pretty; ~ *vermissen* miss badly; *s. viel, so.*

'**Seh|rohr** *n* periscope; '**~schärfe** *f* visual acuity; '**~schlitz** ✖ *m* observation slit; '**~störung** *f* defective vision, dysopia; '**~test** *m s. Sehprüfung;* '**~vermögen** *n* (faculty of) vision, sight; '**~weite** *f* range of sight; *in (außer)* ~ (with)in (out of) sight *od.* eyeshot.

seicht [zaɪçt] shallow (*a. fig.*); '**⁀heit** *f* shallowness.

Seide ['zaɪdə] *f* (15) silk.

Seidel ['zaɪdəl] *n* (7) (*Maß*) pint; (*Trinkgefäß*) mug.

seiden ['zaɪdən] silk(en); '**~artig** silky; '**⁀bau** *m* sericulture, silk--culture; '**⁀faden** *m* silk thread; '**⁀flor** *m* silk gauze; '**⁀garn** *n* silk yarn; '**⁀glanz** *m* silky lustre; '**⁀papier** *n* tissue-paper; '**⁀raupe** *f* silkworm; '**⁀(raupen)zucht** *f* cultivation of silkworms; '**⁀spinne'rei** *f* silk-spinning mill; '**⁀stoff** *m* silk cloth *od.* fabric; '**⁀strümpfe** *m/pl.* silk stockings; '**~weich** (as) soft as silk, silky; '**⁀zucht** *f s. Seidenbau.*

'**seidig** silky.

Seife ['zaɪfə] *f* (15), '**⁀n** (25) soap.

'**Seifen|behälter** *m* soap-dish; '**~blase** *f* soap-bubble; '**~kistenrennen** *n* soap-box derby *od.* race; '**~lauge** *f* (soap-)suds *pl.*; '**~pulver** *n* soap--powder; '**~schale** *f* soap-dish; '**~schaum** *m* lather; '**~sieder** *m* soap--boiler; F *fig. ihm ging ein* ~ *auf* the scales fell from his eyes; '**~siede'rei** *f* soap-works; '**~wasser** *n* (soap-)suds *pl.*

'**seifig** soapy.

seih|en ['zaɪən] (25) strain, filter; '**⁀er** *m* strainer; filter.

Seil [zaɪl] *n* (3) rope; (*Tau*) cable; ~ *springen* skip; '**~bahn** *f* cable (*od.* funicular) railway; '**~er** *m* (7) rope--maker; '**~hüpfen** *n*, '**~springen** *n*

(rope-)skipping; '**~schaft** *mount. f* roped party; '**~schwebebahn** *f* suspension railway, (aerial) cable-way; '**~tänzer(in** *f*) *m* rope-dancer.

sein[1] [zaɪn] **1.** (30, sn) be; (*vorhanden* ~) *a.* exist; et. ~ *lassen* leave (*od.* let) a th. alone; *es sei denn, daß* ... unless; *sei es, daß* ... *oder daß* ... whether ... or ...; *wenn ich nicht gewesen wäre* ... *if it had not been for me* ...; **2.** ⚥ *n* (6) being; existence.

sein[2] (20) his; its; *s. seinige.*

seiner|seits ['~ərzaɪts] for his part; '**~zeit** in his (*od.* its) time; (*einst*) then, at that time.

seinesgleichen ['~əs'glaɪçən] his equal(s *pl.*); the likes of him; *nicht* ~ *haben* have no equal *od.* parallel, stand alone.

seinet|halben ['~əthalbən], '**~wegen,** (*um*) '**~willen** for his sake, on his account; (*durch seine Schuld usw.*) because of him.

seinige ['~igə] his; its; *das* ⚥ (*a. das Seine*) his own; his duty; *die* ⚥ his wife; *die* ⚥*n pl.* his family *sg.*

seismisch ['zaɪsmɪʃ] seismic.

Seismo|graph [zaɪsmo'graːf] *m* (12) seismograph; **~logie** [~lo'giː] *f* (15, *o. pl.*) seismology.

seit [zaɪt] *prp.* (*von* ... *an*) since; (*während*) for; ~ *1960* since 1960; ~ *drei Wochen* for (the last) three weeks; ~ *wann* (*welchem Zeitpunkt*)? since when?; ~ *wann* (*wie lange schon*) *sind Sie hier?* how long have you been here?; *s. kurz, lang; cj.* since; **~dem** [~'deːm] *adv.* (ever) since, since that time; *cj.* since.

Seite ['zaɪtə] *f* (15) side; (*Flanke, a.* ✖) flank; (*Richtung*) direction; *im Buch:* page; ⟨X⟩ ~ *e-r Gleichung:* member; *fig. e-r Angelegenheit:* side, aspect; *s. schwach, stark; an j-s* ~ at (*od.* by) a p.'s side; ~ *an* ~ side by side; *von der* ~ *ansehen* askance; *auf die* ~ *bringen od. schaffen* put aside; *heimlich od. j-n:* make away with; *auf j-s* ~ *sein od. treten od. sich stellen* side with a p.; *in die* ~ *gestemmt Arm:* akimbo; *von* ⚥*n j-s* on the part of a p., by *od.* from a p.; *j-m zur* ~ *stehen* stand by a p.

'**Seiten|angriff** *m* flank attack; '**~ansicht** *f* side-view; '**~blick** *m* side-glance; '**~eingang** *m* side--entrance; '**~flügel** ⌂ *m* wing; '**~**

gewehr ✂ *n* bayonet; *pl. a.* side-
-arms; '**~gleis** *n* siding; '**~hieb** *fig.*
m passing shot, cut (*gegen* at); '♀-
lang pages (and pages) of; '**~lehne**
f arm; '**~linie** *f* *e-r Familie:* col-
lateral line; ✚ branch-line; '**~nu-
merierung** *f* pagination; '♀s (*gen.*)
on the part of; by (*od.* from) *a p.*;
'**~schiff** ⚓ *n* aisle; '**~schwimmen** *n*
side-stroke; '**~sprung** *m* side-leap; F
fig. escapade; '**~stechen** *n* stitch in
the side; '**~straße** *f* side road (*od.*
street), by-street; '**~stück** *n* side-
-piece; (*Gegenstück*) counterpart (*zu*
of); '**~tasche** *f* side-pocket; '**~tür** *f*
side-door; '♀**verkehrt** the wrong
way round; '**~wagen** *mot. m* sidecar;
'**~wechsel** *m* *Sport:* change of ends;
'**~weg** *m* by-way; '**~wind** *m* cross-
wind; '**~zahl** *f* page-number; *insgesamt:* number of pages.

seither [~'he:r] since (that time).
'**seitlich** lateral, side-...
seitwärts ['~vɛrts] sideways, side-
wards; aside.
Sekante ⚹ [zeˈkantə] *f* (15) secant.
Sekret [zeˈkre:t] *n* (3), **~ion** [~kre-
ˈtsjoːn] *f* (16) secretion.
Sekret|är [zekreˈtɛ:r] *m* (3¹), **~ärin**
f (16¹) secretary; **~ariat** [~tariˈɑːt]
n (3¹) secretary's office, secretariate.
Sekt [zɛkt] *m* (3) sparkling wine.
Sekte ['zɛktə] *f* (15) sect.
'**Sektfrühstück** *n* champagne breakfast.
Sektierer [~'ti:rər] *m* (7) sectarian.
Sektion [zɛkˈtsjoːn] *f* section; *e-r
Leiche:* dissection, autopsy.
'**Sektkühler** *m* champagne bucket.
Sektor ['zɛktɔr] *m* (8¹) sector.
'**Sektquirl** *m* swizzle-stick.
Sekun|dant [zekunˈdant] *m* (12)
second; ♀**där** [~'dɛːr] secondary.
Se'kun|de *f* (15) second; *auf die* ~
(*pünktlich*) (punctual) to the second;
♀**denlang** for seconds; **~denzeiger**
m second-hand; ♀'**dieren** second
(*j-m a p.*).

selb|e ['zɛlbə], **~ig** [~iç] same; '**~er:**
ich ~ I myself.
selbst [zɛlpst] **1.** *pron.* himself (*f*
herself, *n* itself), *pl.* themselves;
(*ohne fremde Hilfe*) by oneself; *ich*
~ I myself; *er* ~ he himself; *wir* ~
we ourselves; *von* ~ *entstanden*
spontaneous; *von* ~ of one's own
accord, *S.* of itself, automatically,
spontaneously; **2.** *adv.* even; **3.** ♀ *n*

(one's own) self; '♀-**achtung** *f* self-
-respect.
selbständig ['zɛlpʃtɛndiç] *allg.* independent; *beruflich: a.* self-em-
ployed; *sich* ~ *machen* set up for
o.s.; '♀**keit** *f* independence.
'**Selbst|-anlasser** ⊕ *m* self-starter;
'**~anschluß** *teleph. m* automatic
telephone; dial system; '**~auslöser**
phot. m self-timer; '**~ausschal-
tung** ⚡ *f* automatic cut-out; '**~be-
dienung**(**sladen** *m*) *f* self-service
(shop); '**~befriedigung** *f* masturba-
tion; '**~behauptung** *f* self-assertion;
'**~beherrschung** *f* self-control; *die* ~
verlieren lose one's temper; '**~besin-
nung** *f* stocktaking of o.s.; '**~be-
stimmung**(**srecht** *n*) *f* (right of)
self-determination; '**~beteiligung** *f*
Versicherung: excess; '**~betrug** *m*
self-deception; '♀**bewußt** self-con-
fident; '**~bewußtsein** *n* self-confi-
dence; '**~biographie** *f* autobiography; '**~disziplin** *f* self-discipline;
'**~einschätzung** *f* self-assessment;
'**~entladung** ⚡ *f* self-discharge; '**~
entzündung** *f* spontaneous ignition; '**~erhaltung** *f* self-preservation; '**~erhaltungstrieb** *m* instinct
of self-preservation; '**~erkenntnis** *f*
self-knowledge; '**~erniedrigung** *f*
self-abasement; '**~fahrer** *m* (*Rollstuhl*) self-propelling chair; *mot.*
(*Person*) owner-driver; *Auto für* ~
self-drive car; '♀**gebacken** home-
-made; '♀**gefällig** (self-)compla-
cent; '**~gefälligkeit** *f* (self-)compla-
cency; '**~gefühl** *n* self-esteem,
amour-propre (*fr.*); ♀**gemacht** ['~
gəmaxt] home-made; '**~genügsam-
keit** *f* self-sufficiency; '♀**gerecht**
self-righteous; '**~gespräch** *n* mono-
logue, soliloquy; '♀**herrlich** high-
-handed; '**~herrscher** *m* autocrat;
'**~hilfe** *f* self-help; '♀**isch** selfish;
'♀**klebend** (self-)adhesive; '**~kon-
trolle** *f* self-control; '**~kosten**(**preis**
m) *pl.* prime cost, cost price; '**~kritik**
f self-criticism; '**~ladepistole** *f* automatic (pistol); '**~laut** *m* vowel;
'♀**los** unselfish; self-sacrificing; '**~
mitleid** *n* self-pity; '**~mord** *m*, '**~
mörder** *m* suicide; '♀**mörderisch**
suicidal; '**~mordkommando** *n* suicide squad; '**~porträt** *n* self-por-
trait; '♀**redend** *s.* selbstverständlich;
'**~regierung** *f* self-government; '♀
schmierend ⊕ self-lubricating; '**~**

schuß m spring-gun; '~**schutz** m self-protection; '2**sicher** self-confident; '~**sicherheit** f self-confidence, aplomb; '~**sucht** f selfishness; '2**süchtig** selfish; '2**tätig** automatic(ally adv.), ⊕ a. self-acting; '~**täuschung** f self-deception; '~**überschätzung** f overestimation of o.s.; '~**überwindung** f self-victory; '~**unterricht** m self-instruction; '~**verachtung** f self-contempt; '2**vergessen** lost to the world; '~**verlag** m: im ~ published by the author; '~**verleugnung** f self-denial; '~**vernichtung** f self-destruction; '~**verpflegung** f self-catering; '2**verschuldet** arising through one's own fault; ~**versorger** ['~fɛrzɔːrgər] m (7) self-supporter od. -supplier; '~**versorgung** f self-sufficiency; '2**verständlich** self-evident, obvious; pred. a matter of course; adv. of course; ~! a. by all means!; es ist ~, daß it goes without saying that ...; et. als ~ betrachten take a th. for granted; '~**verständlichkeit** f matter of course; '~**verteidigung** f self-defen|ce, Am. -se; '~**vertrauen** n self-confidence; '~**verwaltung** f self-government; '~**verwirklichung** f self-realization; '~**wählbetrieb** teleph. m long-distance dialling; '~**wert** m self-esteem; '~**zucht** f self-discipline; '2**zufrieden** self-satisfied, complacent; '~**zufriedenheit** f self-satisfaction, complacency; '~**zündung** f self-ignition; '~**zweck** m end in itself.

selchen ['zɛlçən] smoke.

Selen ⚗ [ze'leːn] n (11) selenium.

selig ['zeːliç] blessed; fig. a. blissful, happy; (verstorben) late; ·die 2en pl. the blessed; ~en Angedenkens of blessed memory; '2**keit** f happiness, bliss; '~**sprechen** beatify; '2**sprechung** f beatification.

Sellerie ['zɛləriː] m (11) u. f (15) celery; (Knolle) celeriac.

selten ['zɛltən] rare (a. weitS. Schönheit usw.); (knapp) scarce; adv. seldom, rarely; '2**heit** f rarity (a. konkret), scarcity; nur konkret: curiosity.

Selterswasser ['zɛltərsvasər] n seltzer (water), soda-water.

seltsam ['zɛltzaːm] strange, odd; '~**erweise** strange to say, oddly enough; '2**keit** f strangeness, oddness; konkret: oddity.

Semester [ze'mɛstər] univ. n (7) (half-year) term, semester; ~·**abschluß...** end-of-term; ~**ende** n, ~**schluß** m close of term; ~**ferien** pl. vacation (between terms).

Semikolon [zemi'koːlɔn] n (11, pl. a. -la) semicolon.

Seminar [~'naːr] n (3¹) univ. seminar; (Lehrer2) training-college; (Priester2) seminary; ~**ist** [~na'rist] m (12), ~**istin** f (16¹) pupil of a training-college; seminarist.

Semit [ze'miːt] m (12), ~**in** f Semite.

Semmel ['zɛməl] f (15) roll; wie warme ~ n weggehen go like hot cakes; geriebene ~ bread crumbs pl.

Senat [ze'naːt] m (3) senate; ~**or** [~tɔr] m (8¹) senator.

Sendbote ['zɛnt-] m emissary.

Sende|-anlage ['zɛndə-] transmitting station; '~**bereich** m transmission range; '~**folge** f program(me); '~**leiter** m producer, production director.

senden ['zɛndən] (30) send (nach j-m, et. for); tel., Radio: transmit, send, bsd. Am. radio; Radio usw.: broadcast, TV a. telecast; ein Stück wird gesendet Am. a show is on the air.

'**Sender** m (7) tel., Radio: transmitter; (Station) (broadcasting) station. '**Sende|raum** m studio; '~**reihe** f series.

'**Sender|gruppe** f, '~**netz** n Radio: network.

'**Sende|station** f, '~**stelle** f tel., Radio: transmitting station; '~**zeichen** n call-sign; '~**zeit** f transmission time; beste ~ prime time.

'**Sendschreiben** n missive, epistle; circular (letter).

'**Sendung** f sending; fig. mission; v. Waren: consignment, Am. shipment; tel., Radio: transmission, (Programmteil) broadcast.

Senf [zɛnf] m (3) mustard (a. ♥); '~**gas** n mustard gas; '~**gurke** f cucumber pickled with mustard seeds; '~**korn** n (grain of) mustard seed; '~**pflaster** n mustard plaster; '~**topf** m mustard-pot.

Senge ['zɛŋə] F f/pl.: ~ bekommen get a beating; '2**n** v/t. u. v/i. (25) singe, scorch; ~ und brennen lay waste (by fire); ~**de Hitze** parching heat.

senil [ze'niːl] senile; **2ität** [ˌ‿niliˈtɛːt] *f* senility.

senior ['zeːnjɔr], **2** *m* (8¹) senior; **2en** [zenˈjoːrən] *m/pl.* senior citizens; **2enheim** *n* old people's home.

Senkblei ['zɛŋk-] *n* **Δ** plummet, plumb bob; **⚓** sounding lead.

'Senke *geogr. f* (15) depression, hollow.

senk|en ['zɛŋkən] (25) sink (*a.* **✗**); let down, *a. Preis, Stimme*: lower; *Augen*: cast down; *Kopf*: bow; **↗** lay; *sich* ~ sink, drop, go down; *Mauer*: sag; *Boden(satz)*: settle; *Straße*: dip, fall; *Nacht, Stimmung*: descend; **'2er** **↗** *m* (7) layer.

'Senk|fuß **↗** *m* flat foot; **'‿fuß-einlage** *f* arch support, instep raiser; **'‿grube** *f* cesspool; **'2recht** vertical, *bsd.* **⅄** perpendicular (*beide a.* **'‿rechte** *f* [15¹]); **'‿rechtstarter** *m* **✈** vertical take-off plane; **F** *fig.* whizz-kid; **'‿ung** *f* sinking, *a. der Preise*: lowering; *e-r Mauer usw.*: sag; **↗** (*Blut2*) sedimentation; (*Vertiefung*) depression, hollow; **'‿waage** *f* aerometer.

Senn [zɛn] (3), **'‿er** (13) *m* Alpine herdsman; **‿erei** [ˌ‿ˈraɪ] *f* Alpine dairy; **'‿erin** *f* (16¹) Alpine dairy-maid; **'‿hütte** *f* chalet.

Sensation [zɛnzaˈtsjoːn] *f* sensation; **2ell** [ˌ‿tsjoˈnɛl], **‿s...** [‿ˈtsjoːns-] sensational; **‿slust** *f* sensationalism; **2slustig** sensationalist; **‿smeldung** *f* sensational report; **‿spresse** *f* yellow press.

Sense ['zɛnzə] *f* (15) scythe; **'‿nmann** *m* mower; *fig.* Death.

sensi|bel [zɛnˈziːbəl] sensitive; **2bilität** [ˌ‿zibiliˈtɛːt] *f* (16) sensitiveness, sensibility.

Sensor ['zɛnzɔr] *m* (8¹) sensor; **'‿bildschirm** *m* *Computer*: sensor screen.

Sentenz [zɛnˈtɛnts] *f* (16) maxim, aphorism; **2iös** [ˌ‿ˈtsjøːs] sententious.

sentimental [zɛntimɛnˈtɑːl] sentimental; **2ität** [ˌ‿taliˈtɛːt] *f* (16) sentimentality.

separat [zepaˈrɑːt] separate; **2ismus** [ˌ‿raˈtismus] *m* (16, *o. pl.*) separatism.

Sepia ['zeːpja] *f inv. zo.* cuttle-fish; (*Farbe*) sepia.

September [zɛpˈtɛmbər] *m* (7) September.

septisch ['zɛptiʃ] septic(ally *adv.*).

Serail [zeˈraɪl] *n* (11) seraglio.

Serb|e ['zɛrbə] *m* (13), **'‿in** *f* (16¹) Serb(ian); **'2isch** Serbian.

Serenade [zereˈnɑːdə] *f* (15) serenade.

Serie ['zeːrjə] *f* (15) series; (*Satz*) set; *Billard*: break; **↑** e-e ~ *von Waren* a range (*od.* line) of; **'‿n-ausstattung** *f* standard fittings *pl.*; **'‿nherstellung** *f*, **'‿produktion** *f* serial (*od.* mass) production; **'2n-mäßig** standard (type); *adv.* in series; ~ *herstellen* produce in series; **'2nreif** ready for production; **'‿n-schaltung** *f* series connection; **'‿n-wagen** *mot. m* stock car.

seriös [zeˈrjøːs] serious; (*vertrauenswürdig*) trustworthy.

Serpentine [zɛrpɛnˈtiːnə] *f* (15) serpentine (line); (*Straße*) serpentine (road); (*Kurve*) double bend.

Serum ['zeːrum] *n* (9²) serum; **'‿kunde** *f* serology.

Service [zɛrˈviːs] *n* (7) (*Geschirrsatz*) service, set; **↑**, *mot. etc.* ['zɔrvis] (*a. m*) (*Bedienung, Kundendienst*) service; **'2freundlich** *mot.* easy to service.

Servier|brett [zɛrˈviːr-] *n* tray; **2en** *v/t.* serve; *v/i.* wait (at table); **‿erin** *f* (16¹) waitress; **‿tisch** *m* side-table.

Serviette [zɛrˈvjɛtə] *f* (15) (table-)napkin; **‿nring** *m* napkin-ring.

servil [zɛrˈviːl] servile.

Servo|lenkung ['zɛrvo-] *mot. f* power steering; **'‿motor** **↯** *m* servo-motor.

Sessel ['zɛsəl] *m* (7) arm- (*od.* easy-)chair; **'‿lift** *m* chair-lift.

seßhaft ['zɛshaft] settled, established, stationary; (*irgendwo ansässig*) resident; **'2igkeit** *f* settledness, stationariness.

Set [sɛt] *n, m* (11) (*Platzdeckchen*) place mat.

'Setz-ei *n* fried egg.

setzen ['zɛtsən] (27) *v/t.* set, place, put; *typ.* set up in type, (*a.* **♪**) compose; (*pflanzen*) plant; *Denkmal*: erect, raise; *e-e Frist* ~ fix a term (*j-m* for a p.); *bei Wetten usw.*: stake (*auf acc.* on); *alles daran* ~ do one's utmost; *auf j-s Rechnung* ~ charge to a p.'s account; *es sich in den Kopf* ~, *daß ...* get it into one's head that; *in die Zeitung* ~

insert; *s-e Unterschrift* ~ *unter*
(*acc.*) put (*od.* affix) one's signature
to, sign; *sich* ~ sit down; *Vogel:*
perch; (*sinken*) sink; *Haus, Boden-*
satz: settle; *s. Druck, Fall, Freiheit,*
Gang[1], *Gefecht, Luft usw.; v/i.* (sn)
~ *über* (*acc.*) leap (over), clear; *e-n*
Strom: cross; (h.) *typ.* set type;
beim Wetten: ~ *auf* (*acc.*) bet on,
back.

'**Setzer** *m* (7) compositor, type-
setter; ~**ei** [~'raɪ] *f* (16) composing
room.

'**Setz|kasten** *typ. m* (letter-)case;
'~**ling** ♀ *m* (3[1]) slip, young plant;
'~**maschine** *typ. f* composing (*od.*
type-setting) machine; '~**reis** ♀ *n*
layer; '~**waage** *f* level.

Seuche ['zɔʏçə] *f* (15) epidemic;
'~**nbekämpfung** *f* control of epi-
demics; '~**nherd** *m* cent|re (*Am.*
-er) of an epidemic.

seufz|en ['zɔʏftsən] (27) sigh; '♀**er**
m (7) sigh.

Sex [sɛks] F *m* (3[2], *o. pl.*) sex; ~-
Appeal ['~ə'pi:l] *m* (3[1], *o. pl.*) sex
appeal.

Sextett ♪ [zɛks'tɛt] *n* (3) sextet.

sexual, ♀... [zɛksu'ɑ:l] sexual.

Sexualität [~ali'tɛ:t] *f* (16) sexuality.

Sexual|kunde [zɛksu'ɑ:l-] *f* sex edu-
cation; ~**verbrechen** *n* sex crime.

sexuell [zɛksu'ɛl] sexual.

Sexus ['zɛksus] *m* (11[1], *o. pl.*) sex.

Sezier|besteck [ze'tsi:r-] *n* dissecting
instruments *pl.*; ♀**en** dissect; ~**mes-**
ser *n* scalpel.

Showmaster ['ʃoːmɑːstər, 'ʃəu-] *m*
(11) *TV:* compère, host, F emcee.

Sibir|ier [zi'biːrjər] *m* (7), ♀**isch**
Siberian.

sich [ziç] *allg.:* oneself; *3. P. sg.*
himself, herself, itself, *pl.* themselves; *nach prp.* him, her, it, *pl.*
them; (*statt: einander*) each other,
one another.

Sichel ['ziçəl] *f* (15) sickle; (*Mond*♀)
crescent; ♀**förmig** ['~fœrmiç]
sickle-shaped.

sicher ['ziçər] secure, safe (*beide:*
vor dat. from); (*gewiß*) certain, sure;
(*bestimmt od. zuversichtlich*) positive; (*zuverlässig*) reliable; (*tüchtig*)
efficient; *Auge usw.:* sure; *Auftre-*
ten: self-assured; *Ort, Methode:*
safe; *Schütze:* sure, dead *shot*; *um*
~ *zu gehen s. sicherheitshalber; s-r*
S. ~ *sein* be quite positive; *sind Sie*

~? are you sure?; *adv. u. int. s.*
~*lich.*

'**Sicherheit** *f s. sicher;* security (*a.*
= *Pfand, Wertpapier*); safety; certainty; positiveness; *des Auftretens:*
assurance; *in* ~ *sein* be safe; *in* ~
bringen place in safety; *sich in* ~
bringen save one's bacon; ~ *leisten*
✝ furnish security; ⚖ ~ *stellen*
give (*od.* offer) bail, *Am. a.* post
bond; *s. wiegen*[2]; '~**s-abstand** *m* safe
distance; '~**sbe-amte** *m* security
agent; '~**sbindung** *f Schi:* safety
binding; '~**sfaktor** *m* factor of safety; '~**sglas** *n* safety glass; '~**sgurt** *m*
seat belt, *mot. a.* safety belt; '♀**shal-**
ber to be on the safe side, to make
sure; '~**s-interessen** *n/pl.* security
interests; '~**sklausel** *f* safeguard;
'~**skontrolle** *f am Flughafen:* security check; '~**smaßnahme** *f* safety
measure, precaution; '~**snadel** *f*
safety-pin; '~**s-polizei** *f* security
police; '~**srat** *m* Security Council;
'~**srisiko** *n a. Person:* security risk;
'~**sschloß** *n* safety-lock; '~**sventil** *n*
safety valve.

'**sicher|lich** surely, certainly; ~! *a.*
to be sure!, *Am.* F sure!; ~ *hat er*
recht I am sure he is right; ~ *wird*
er kommen he is sure to come; '~**n**
(29) secure (*a.* ⊕ *u.* ✝), (*schützen*)
a. (safe)guard (*beide: vor dat.,*
gegen against), protect (from); (*ge-*
währleisten) ensure; *Waffe:* put at
"safe"; *v/i. hunt.* scent; '~**stellen**
secure; '♀**ung** *f* securing; (*Maß-*
nahme) safeguard(ing); ⚡ fuse, cut-
-out; ⊕ safety device; *am Gewehr:*
safety(-catch); '♀**ungsverwahrung**
⚖ *f* preventive detention.

Sicht [ziçt] *f* (15) sight; (*Aus*♀) view
(*a. fig.*); (~*verhältnisse*) visibility;
✝ *auf* ~, *bei* ~ at sight; *60 Tage*
nach ~ 60 days after sight; *fig. auf*
weite (*od. lange*) ~ on a long-term
basis, (*auf die Dauer*) in the long
run; *aus seiner* ~ as he sees it; *in*
~ *kommen* come into sight; *in* ~
sein be in sight; '♀**bar** visible; (*auf-*
fallend) conspicuous; ~ *machen*
(*werden*) show; '~**barkeit** *f* visible-
ness; '~**beton** *m* fair-faced concrete; '♀**en** (26) (*erblicken*) sight;
(*sieben*) sift; *fig. a.* screen; (*ordnen*)
sort; '~**feld** *n* field of vision; '~**gerät**
n Computer: visual display terminal;
'♀**lich** visible; (*offenbar*) evident; '~-

tratte ✝ f, '**~wechsel** m sight-draft; '**~verhältnisse** n/pl. visibility sg.; '**~vermerk** m auf Reisepaß: visé, visa; auf Wechsel: endorsement; '**~weite** f range of sight; in (außer) ~ in (out of) sight.

sicker|n ['zikərn] (29, sn u. h.) trickle, ooze, leak, bsd. Am. seep; '**♀wasser** n water leakage.

sie [zi:] **1.** pron. sg. she; Sache: it; pl. they; acc. sg. her; it; acc. pl. them; Sie you; **2.** ♀ f she, female.

Sieb [zi:p] n (3) sieve; (grobes ~) riddle; (Kies♀ usw.) screen.

sieben[1] ['zi:bən] (25) sift, strain; fig. (auslesen) screen, sift.

sieben[2] [~] **1.** seven; **2.** ♀ f inv. seven; böse ~ vixen, shrew.

'**sieben|fach**, **~fältig** ['~fɛltiç] sevenfold; '**♀gebirge** n Seven Mountains pl.; '**♀gestirn** n Pleiades pl.; '**~jährig** seven-year(s)-old, of seven years; der ~e Krieg the Seven Years' War; '**~mal** seven times; '**~malig** seven times repeated; '**♀'meilenstiefel** m/pl. seven-league boots; '**♀sachen** f/pl. things, belongings; seine ~ packen pack up one's traps; '**♀schläfer** m/pl. the Seven Sleepers; sg. fig. = Langschläfer; zo. dormouse; **~tägig** ['~tɛ:giç] of (od. lasting) seven days.

siebent ['~t] seventh; '**♀el** n (7) seventh (part); '**~ens** seventhly.

siebzehn ['zi:ptse:n] seventeen; '**~t**, '**♀tel** n (7) seventeenth.

siebzig ['~tsiç] seventy; ♀**er** ['~gər] m (7), ♀**erin** f (16[1]) septuagenarian; '**~ste** seventieth.

siech [zi:ç] sickly, invalid; '**~en** (25) be ailing; languish (a. fig.); '**♀tum** n (1[2]) lingering illness, invalidism.

'**Siede|grad** m boiling-point; '**~hitze** f boiling heat; '**~kessel** m boiler.

siedeln ['zi:dəln] (29) settle.

siede|n ['zi:dən] (30) boil (a. fig.); gelind: simmer; nur fig. seethe; Zucker: refine; '**♀punkt** m boiling-point; '**♀r** m boiler, refiner.

Siedler ['zi:dlər] m (7) (An♀) settler; (Arbeiter♀) homecrofter, Am. homesteader.

'**Siedlung** f settlement; (Stadt♀) housing estate, suburban colony; '**~sgesellschaft** f land-settlement society.

Sieg [zi:k] m (3) victory, triumph

(über acc. over); Sport: win; den ~ davontragen od. erringen gain the victory (über acc. over), carry (od. win) the day.

Siegel ['zi:gəl] n (7) seal; unter dem ~ der Verschwiegenheit under the seal of secrecy; '**~lack** m sealing--wax; '**♀n** (29) seal; '**~ring** m signet-ring.

sieg|en ['zi:gən] (25) be victorious (über acc. over), conquer (a. p.); Sport: win; '**♀er** m (7), '**♀erin** f (16[1]) conqueror, rhet. victor; Sport: winner; '**♀er-ehrung** f Sport: presentation ceremony; '**♀ermächte** f/pl. victorious powers; '**♀er-urkunde** f (winner's) diploma.

'**Sieges|bogen** m triumphal arch; '**~denkmal** n victory monument; '**♀gewiß** sure of victory; '**~göttin** f Victory; '**♀trunken** flushed with victory; '**~zeichen** n trophy; '**~zug** m triumphal procession; fig. triumphant advance.

sieg|haft, **~reich** ['zi:k-] victorious, triumphant.

Siel [zi:l] n (3) (Deichschleuse) sluice (-way); (Abwasserleitung) culvert; '**~e** f (15) (Gurt) belt; e-s Pferdes: breast harness; fig. in den ~n sterben die in harness.

Sigel ['zi:gəl] n (7) Kurzschrift: grammalogue.

Signal [zig'na:l] n (3[1]) signal; **~ement** [~nal(ə)'mɑ̃] n (11) personal description; '**~flagge** [~'na:l-] f signal-flag; '**~horn** n signal horn, horn, bugle; ♀**i'sieren** v/t. u. v/i. signal.

Signatarmächte [zigna'ta:rmɛçtə] pol. f/pl. signatory powers (e-s Vertrages to a treaty).

Sign|atur [~'tu:r] f (16) signature; ✝ mark, brand; auf Landkarten: conventional sign; Bücherei: call number; ♀**ieren** [~'ni:rən] sign; mark, brand.

Silbe ['zilbə] f syllable; fig. keine ~ not a word; '**~ntrennung** f syllabification.

Silber ['zilbər] n (7, o. pl.) silver; '**~barren** m silver ingot; '**~bergwerk** n silver mine; '**~gehalt** m silver content; '**~geld** n silver money; '**~gerät** n, '**~geschirr** n silver (plate), Am. silverware; '**♀hell** silvery; '**~medaille** f Sport: silver medal; '**~münze** f silver coin; '**♀n** (of) silver; Farbe, Klang usw.: silvery; ~e Hoch-

zeit silver wedding; '⁓**papier** *n* tin foil; '⁓**pappel** ♀ *f* white poplar; '⁓**schmied** *m* silversmith; '⁓**stahl** *m* silver steel; '⁓**streifen** *m fig.*: ⁓ am Horizont silver lining; '⁓**währung** *f* silver standard; '⁓**waren** *f/pl.* silverware *sg.*; '⁓**zeug** *n s.* Silbergeschirr.

Silhouette [zilu'ɛtə] *f* (15) silhouette.

Silikat [zili'kɑːt] *n* (3) silicate.

Silikon [zili'koːn] *n* (3¹) silicon; ⁓**zelle** *f* silicon cell.

Silo ['ziːlo] *m* (11) silo; (*Getreide*⁀) (grain) elevator; '⁓**futter** *n* silage.

Silvester [zil'vɛstər] *m*, *n* (7), ⁓**abend** *m* New Year's Eve; ⁓**ball** *m* New Year's Eve ball.

simpel ['zimpəl] simple, plain; ♀ F *m* blockhead; '⁀**fransen** *f/pl.* fringe *sg.*, ponies.

Sims [zims] *m*, *n* (4) ledge; (*Fenster*⁀) sill; (*Wandbrett*) shelf; ⚠ mo(u)lding, cornice.

Simu|**lant** [zimu'lant] *m* (12), ⁓'**lantin** *f* (16¹) malingerer; ⁓**lator** [⁓- 'lɑːtər] ⊕, ✗ *m* (8¹) simulator; ♀- '**lieren** *v/t. u. v/i.* feign, sham; *nur v/t.*: simulate (*a.* ⊕,✗, *nachahmen*); *nur v/i.*: (*sich krank stellen*) sham ill, *bsd.* ✗ *u.* ⚓ malinger.

Simultan... [⁓'tɑːn] simultaneous; *eccl.*, *Schule*: undenominational; *tel.* composite(d); ⁓**dolmetschen** *n* simultaneous translation; ⁓**dolmetscher(in** *f)* *m* simultaneous translator.

Sinfonie [zinfo'niː] *f* (15) symphony; ⁓**orchester** *n* symphony orchestra.

Sing... [ziŋ-] *in Zssgn mst* singing...; '♀**bar** singable; '⁓**drossel** *f* song thrush; '♀**en** *v/i. u. v/t.* (30) sing; ⁓**sang** ['⁓zaŋ] *m* singsong; '⁓**spiel** *n* musical comedy; '⁓**stimme** *f* singing-voice; ♩ vocal part.

Singular ['ziŋgulɑːr] *m* (3¹) singular (number).

'**Singvogel** *m* singing bird, songbird, songster.

sinken ['ziŋkən] (30, sn) *allg.* sink; *a. Preise usw.*: drop, go down; *Sonne*: set, sink; *die Stimme* ⁓ *lassen* lower one's voice; *fig.* tief gesunken sunk very low; *in Ohnmacht* ⁓ faint, swoon; *s. Mut, Schlaf, Wert*.

Sinn [zin] *m* (3) sense (*für* of); (*Geist*, *Verstand*; *Meinung*) mind; (*Vorliebe*) taste (*für* for); (*Instinkt*) flair; (*Wunsch*) wish; (*Bedeutung*)

sense, meaning; (*Grundgedanke*) (basic) idea; (*Zweck*) purpose; ⁓ *für Humor* sense of humo(u)r; *der* ⁓ *der Sache* the point; ⁓ *haben für* have a taste for, (be able to) appreciate; *anderen* ⁓*es werden* change one's mind; *bei* (*von*) ⁓*en sein* be in (out of) one's senses; *im* ⁓*e des Gesetzes usw.* within the meaning of; *im* ⁓ *haben* have in mind; *in gewissem* ⁓*e* in a sense; *ohne* ⁓ *und Verstand* without rhyme or reason; *seine fünf* ⁓*e beisammen haben* have one's wits about one; *es kam mir in den* ⁓ it occurred to me (*zu inf.* to *inf.*); *das will mir nicht aus dem* ⁓ I can't get it out of my head; *das will mir nicht in den* ⁓ I just can't understand it; *es hat keinen* ⁓ it makes no sense; (*ist zwecklos*) it is no use; *s. schlagen*.

'**Sinnbild** *n* symbol, emblem; '♀**lich** symbolic(al); ⁓ *darstellen* symbolize; *Kunst*: allegorize.

sinnen ['zinən] (30) (*über dat.*) meditate, reflect (*beide*: [up]on), ponder (over); *mit Muße*: muse ([up]on); ⁓ *auf* (*acc.*) meditate, *b.s.* plot, scheme; '⁓**d** musing, pensive, thoughtful.

'**sinnen**|**freudig** sensuous; '♀**genuß** *m*, '♀**lust** *f* sensual pleasure, sensuality; '♀**rausch** *m*, '♀**taumel** *m* intoxication of the senses.

'**sinn-entstellend** garbling, distorting.

'**Sinnes**|**-änderung** *f* change of mind; '⁓**art** *f* temper, character; mentality; '⁓**organ** *n* sense organ; '⁓**täuschung** *f* illusion, hallucination; '⁓**wandel** *m* change of mind.

'**sinn**|**fällig** obvious, striking; '♀**gedicht** *n* epigram; '⁓**gemäß** analogous; *adv. a.* accordingly; '⁓**getreu** faithful; ⁓**ieren** [⁓'niːrən] ruminate; '⁓**ig** thoughtful; (*sinnreich*) ingenious; '⁓**lich** sensual; (*Ggs. geistig*) material, physical; '♀**lichkeit** *f* sensuality; material existence; '⁓**los** senseless; meaningless; (*unsinnig*) absurd; (*zwecklos*) useless, futile; ⁓ *betrunken* dead drunk; '♀**losigkeit** *f* senselessness; absurdity; futility; '⁓**reich** ingenious, clever; '♀**spruch** *m* device, motto; '⁓**verwandt** synonymous; '⁓**voll** wise; (*zweckvoll*) ingenious, efficient; '⁓**widrig** absurd.

Sinter ['zintər] *m* (7) 🗡 sinter; *metall.* dross of iron.

Sintflut ['zintfluːt] *f* (great) flood, deluge; *biblisch*: the Flood, *the* Deluge.

Sinus ⚕ ['ziːnus] *m* (*inv. u.* 14²) sine; **'∼kurve** *f* sine curve; **'∼leistung** *f* *Radio*: sine rating.

Siphon ['ziːfɔn] *m* (11) siphon.

Sipp|e ['zipə] *f* (15), **'∼schaft** *f* (16) kin, family, relations *pl.*; *a. zo.*, ⚕ tribe; *fig. iro.* clan, clique, gang, lot; **'∼enforschung** *f* genealogical research.

Sirene [zi'reːnə] *f* (15) *allg.* siren.

Sirup ['ziːrup] *m* (3¹) treacle, *Am.* molasses; (*bsd. Frucht*⚕) syrup, *Am.* sirup.

sistieren [zi'stiːrən] stay, stop; (*verhaften*) arrest.

Sitte ['zitə] *f* (15) custom; (*Gewohnheit*) habit; (*Brauch*) usage; **∼n** *pl.* manners, (*Moral*) morals.

'Sitten|bild *n*, **'∼gemälde** *n* picture of manners *od.* morals; **'∼gesetz** *n* moral code (*od.* law); **'∼lehre** *f* ethics *pl.*, moral philosophy; **'⚕los** immoral; **'∼losigkeit** *f* immorality; **'∼polizei** *f* Vice Squad; **'∼prediger** *m* moralizer; **'∼richter** *m* censor; **'⚕streng** austere, puritanical; **'∼strolch** F *m* sexual offender; **'∼verderbnis** *f* corruption of morals.

Sittich *zo.* ['zitiç] *m* (3) parakeet.

sittig ['∼] *s. sittsam*.

sittlich ['zitliç] moral, ethical; **'⚕keit** *f* morality; **'⚕keitsverbrechen** *n* sex crime; **'⚕keitsverbrecher** *m* sex offender.

'sittsam (*züchtig*) modest, demure; (*keusch*) chaste, virtuous; (*brav*) well-behaved; (*anständig*) decent; **'⚕keit** *f* modesty; good manners *pl.*; decency.

Situation [zitua'tsjoːn] *f* situation; *die* **∼** *retten* save the situation; **∼skomik** *f* comedy of situation, slapstick.

situiert [zitu'iːrt]: *gut* **∼** well-off, well-to-do, *Am.* F well-fixed.

Sitz [zits] *m* (3²) seat (*a. fig.*); (*Stuhl*) chair; (*Wohnort*) (place of) residence; *e-s Kleides*: fit; **'∼bad** *n* sitz-bath.

'sitzen (30) sit (*a. fig. tagen*); *Vogel u. fig.* (*hoch oben* ∼) be perched; *Firma usw.*: be, have its seat (*in dat.* at); *Kleid*: fit; F *im Gefängnis*: do time; *Hieb*: tell, hit home; F *einen* **∼** *haben* be drunk; ∼ *bleiben* remain sitting *od.* seated; *bleiben Sie* ∼*!* keep your seat!; **'∼bleiben** (sn) *beim Tanz*: be left without partners; *Mädchen*: (*nicht geheiratet werden*) get on the shelf; *in der Schule*: not to get one's remove; **'∼d:** ∼*e Lebensweise* sedentary life; **'∼lassen** *fig.* leave, desert, throw *a p.* over; (*im Stich lassen*) let *a p.* down; *e-n Schimpf auf sich* ∼ pocket an affront.

'Sitz|fleisch F *n* perseverance; **'∼gelegenheit** *f* seat; **'∼gruppe** *f* three--piece suite; **'∼ordnung** *f* seating arrangement(s *pl.*); **'∼platz** *m* seat; **'∼streik** *m* sit-down strike.

'Sitzung *f* sitting, ⚖ *a.* hearing; **'∼sbericht** *m* minutes *pl.* (of proceedings); **∼s-periode** *f* session; ⚖ term; **∼s-saal** *m* conference room; *parl.* chamber, *Am. a.* floor.

Sizilian|er [zitsil'jaːnər] *m* (7), **∼erin** *f* (16¹), **⚕isch** Sicilian.

Skala ['skaːla] *f* (16² *u.* 11¹) scale (*a. ♪*); *in Kreisform*: dial; *bewegliche* (*od. gleitende*) ∼ sliding scale.

'Skalenscheibe *f* *Radio usw.*: dial.

Skalp [skalp] *m* (3¹), **⚕ieren** [∼'piːrən] scalp.

Skandal [skan'daːl] *m* (3¹) scandal; (*Schande*) disgrace, shame; (*Lärm*) row; **∼blatt** *n* scandal-sheet; **⚕ös** [∼da'løːs] scandalous; **∼presse** [∼'daːl-] *f* gutter press.

skandieren [skan'diːrən] scan.

skandinavisch [skandi'naːviʃ] Scandinavian.

Skat [skaːt] *m* (3) skat.

Skelett [ske'lɛt] *n* (3) skeleton.

Skep|sis ['skepsis] *f* *inv.* scepticism; **∼tiker** ['∼tikər] *m* (7) sceptic; **⚕tisch** sceptical.

Sketch [skɛtʃ] *m* (3, *pl. a.*11) sketch.

Ski [ʃiː] *m* *usw. s.* **Schi**.

Skizze ['skitsə] *f* (15) sketch; **'∼nbuch** *n* sketch-book; **'⚕nhaft** sketchy, in rough outlines.

skiz'zieren *v/t. u. v/i.* sketch, outline.

Sklav|e ['sklaːvə] *m* (13), **'∼in** *f* slave; **'∼enhandel** *m* slave-trade; **'∼enhändler** *m* slave-trader; **'∼entreiber** *m a. fig.* slave-driver; **∼erei** [∼ə'raɪ] *f* (16) slavery; **'⚕isch** slavish (*a. fig.*), servile.

Skonto ✝ ['skɔnto] *m*, *n* (11) discount.

solid(e)

Skorbut [skɔr'buːt] *m* (3) scurvy.
Skorpion [skɔrp'joːn] *m* (3¹) scorpion; *ast.* Scorpio(n).
Skrof|eln ['skroːfəln] *f/pl.* (15) scrofula *sg.*; **ℒulös** [skrofu'løːs] scrofulous; **ℒulose** [ˌ'loːzə] *f* (16) scrofula.
Skrup|el ['skruːpəl] *m* (7) scruple; '**ℒellos** unscrupulous; **ℒulös** [skrupu'løːs] scrupulous.
Skulptur [skulp'tuːr] *f* (16) sculpture.
skurril [sku'riːl] ludicrous.
S-Kurve *mot.* ['ɛs-] *f* double hairpin bend.   [slalom.⟩
Slalom ['slaːlɔm] *m, n* (11) *Schi:*⟩
Slaw|e ['slaːvə] *m* (13), '**ℒin** *f*, '**ℒisch** Slav, Slavonian; *adj. a.* Slavic.
Slip [slip] *m* (11) briefs *pl.*; '**ℒ-einlage** *f* panty-liner.
Slowak|e [slo'vaːkə] *m* (13) Slovak; **ℒisch** Slovakian.
Smaragd [sma'rakt] *m* (3), **ℒen**, **ℒgrün** emerald.
Smoking ['smoːkiŋ] *m* (11) dinner--jacket, *Am.* tuxedo; '**ℒ-anzug** *m* dinner(-jacket) suit.
so [zoː] so, thus; *vergleichend:* as; *cj.* if; ℒ *daß* so that; ℒ *sehr, daß* so much that; ℒ *ein* such a; ℒ *etwas* such a thing; F *nein*, ℒ *etwas!* well, I never!; ℒ ... *denn* so; ℒ ... *wie od. als* as ... as; *nicht* ℒ ... *wie od. als* not so ... as; ℒ *oder* ℒ one way or another, *(ohnehin)* anyhow; *sie war* ℒ ... *zu inf.* she was ... enough to *inf.*; *wir machen es* ℒ we do it this way; ℒ *im Nachsatz nicht zu übersetzen, z.B.:* wenn du Zeit hast, ℒ schreibe mir if you have time, write to me; *s. ach, noch, um, soviel, weit;* **ℒbald** [zo'balt] *(als)* as soon as.
Söckchen ['zœkçən] *n* (6) anklet.
Socke ['zɔkə] *f* (15) sock; ℒ*n* ✝ *pl. a.* half-hose; '**ℒl** *m* (12) base, socle, pedestal; '**ℒnhalter** *m* suspender, *Am.* garter.
Soda ['zoːda] *f*, *n inv.* soda.
sodann [zo'dan] then.
'**Sodawasser** *n* soda-water.
Sodbrennen ['zoːt-] *n* heartburn.
soeben [zo'ʔeːbən] just (now).
Sofa ['zoːfa] *n* (11) sofa; '**ℒkissen** *n* sofa-cushion.
so'fern *cj.* so *(od.* as) far as, if; *(wenn nur)* provided that; ℒ *nicht* unless.
soff [zɔf] *pret. v. saufen.*
Soffitten *thea.* [zɔ'fitən] *f/pl.* (15) flies; **ℒlampe** *f* tubular lamp.

sofort [zo'fɔrt] *adv.* at once, directly, instantly, immediately, forthwith, straight *(bsd. Am.* right) away; ℒ ℒ **lieferbar** *od. zahlbar* spot; **ℒhilfe** *f* emergency (relief) aid; **ℒhilfeprogramm** *n* emergency aid program(me); **ℒig** immediate, prompt, instant; **ℒmaßnahme** *f* immediate action *(a. pl.)*, prompt measure.
Software ['zɔftwɛːər] *f Computer:* software.
Sog [zoːk] 1. *m* (3, *o. pl.*) suction; ⚓ *(Kielwasser)*, ⚓ *(Luftwirbel)* wake *(a. fig.)*; 2. ℒ *pret. v. saugen.*
so|gar [zo'gaːr] even; **ℒgenannt** ['zoːgənant] so-called; *(sich für et. ausgebend)* self-styled, would-be; **ℒgleich** [zo'glaiç] *s. sofort.*
Sohl|e [zoːlə] *f* (15) sole; *e-s Tals usw.:* bottom; ✖ floor; '**ℒ(en)leder** *n* sole-leather.
Sohn [zoːn] *m* (3³) son; *der verlorene* ℒ the prodigal son.
Soiree [soa'reː] *f* (15) evening party, soirée.
Sojabohne ['zoːja-] *f* soya-bean.
so'lange *(als)* so *(od.* as) long as.
Solar|batterie [zo'laːr-] ⚡ *f* solar battery; **ℒenergie** *f* solar energy.
Solarium [zo'laːrium] *n* (9) solarium.
So'larzelle *f* solar cell.
Solbad ['zoːlbaːt] *n* salt-water bath.
solch [zɔlç] (21) such; *als* ℒ*er* as such; '**ℒer-'art**, **ℒerlei** ['ℒərlai] of such a kind, such; '**ℒer'maßen**, '**ℒer'weise** in such a way.
Sold [zɔlt] *m* (3) pay; *fig.* wages *pl.*
Soldat [zɔl'daːt] *m* (12) soldier; serviceman; *aktiver* ℒ regular (soldier); *einfacher* ℒ private; *gedienter* ℒ ex-serviceman; *der Unbekannte* ℒ the Unknown Warrior; **ℒ(en)** *spielen* play at soldiers; **ℒeska** [ℒda-'tɛska] *f inv. the* soldiery; **ℒisch** [ℒ'daːtiʃ] soldierlike, military.
'**Soldbuch** ✖ *n* pay book.
Söld|ling ['zœltliŋ] *m* (3¹), **ℒner** ['ℒdnər] *m* (7) mercenary.
Sole ['zoːlə] *f* (15) brine.
solidar|isch [zoli'daːriʃ] solidary; ⚖ jointly responsible *od.* liable; *adv.* jointly and severally; *sich* ℒ *erklären mit* declare one's solidarity with; **ℒität** [ℒdari'tɛːt] *f* solidarity.
solid|(e) [zo'liːt, -də] solid *(a. fig.)*; *(kräftig)* robust, rugged; *Grundlage:* sound; *Preise:* reasonable; ✝

Firma: sound, solvent; *fig.* respectable; (*nicht ausschweifend*) steady; ⊇**ität** [‿di'tɛːt] *f* solidity; soundness; *fig.* respectability.

Solist [zo'list] *m* (12), ‿**in** *f* (16¹) soloist; solo singer; solo player.

Soll [zɔl] *n* (11 *u. inv.*) debit; (*Lieferungs*⊇) fixed quota; (*Produktionsziel*) target; ‿ *und Haben* debit and credit; '‿**bestand** *m* nominal stock; ✝ *a.* calculated assets *pl.*; ✕ *s. Sollstärke.*

'**sollen** (30) 2. *u.* 3. *P.* shall; *sonst*: be to; *angeblich*: be said to; *sollte* should, *stärker*: ought to.

Söller ['zœlɐr] *m* (7) balcony.

'**Soll|maß** *n* specified size; '‿**stärke** ✕ *f* authorized strength; '‿**wert** ⊕ *m* nominal (*od.* rated) value.

Solo ['zoːlo] *n* (11) solo; '‿**stimme** *f* solo part; '‿**tänzer(in** *f*) *m* dance soloist.

'**Solquelle** *f* salt-spring.

solven|t [zɔl'vɛnt] solvent; ⊇**z** *f* (16) solvency.

somit [zo'mit] consequently, thus.

Sommer ['zɔmɐr] *m* (7) summer; '‿**aufenthalt** *m* summer residence *od.* stay; '‿**fäden** *m/pl.* gossamer; '‿**frische** *f* summer resort; ‿**frischler** ['‿frɪʃlɐr] *m* (7) holiday-maker, *Am.* vacationer; '‿**kleidung** *f*, '‿**sachen** *f/pl.* summer clothes *pl.*, ✝ summer-wear; '⊇**lich** summer(l)y; '‿**reifen** *mot. m* normal tyre (*Am.* tire); '‿**sprosse** *f* freckle; '⊇**sprossig** freckled; '‿**zeit** *f* summer time, *zur Lichtersparnis*: *a.* daylight-saving time.

sonach [zo'naːx] consequently.

Sonate [zo'naːtə] *f* (15) sonata.

Sonde ['zɔndə] *f* (15) 🖈 sound, (*a. Mond*⊇ *usw.*) probe; ⚓ plummet; *Radar*: sonde.

sonder ['zɔndɐr] without.

'**Sonder|abdruck** *m* off-print, separate (print); '‿**anfertigung** *f* special design; '‿**angebot** *n* special (offer); '‿**auftrag** *m* special mission; '‿**ausbildung** *f* special training; '‿**ausgabe** *f* special edition; *geldlich*: extra; '‿**ausschuß** *m* special committee; '⊇**bar** strange, odd, peculiar; '⊇**barerweise** oddly enough; '‿**barkeit** *f* strangeness, oddity; '‿**be-auftragte** *m* special representative; '‿**beilage** *f e-r Zeitung*: inset, supplement; '‿**bericht-**

erstatter *m* special correspondent; '‿**bevollmächtigte** *m* plenipotentiary; '‿**druck** *m s. Sonderabdruck*; '‿**fall** *m* special (*od.* exceptional) case; '‿**frieden** *m* separate peace; ⊇'**gleichen** *adv.* (*im Englischen als adj.*) matchless, unprecedented; '‿**interesse** *n* private interest; '‿**klasse** *f* special class; *Segelsport*: *Am.* sonderclass; '‿**klausel** *f* special clause; '⊇**lich** special, peculiar, remarkable; *nicht* ‿ not particularly, not much (*od.* very); '‿**ling** *m* (3¹) queer fellow, crank; '‿**meldung** *f* special announcement; '⊇**n 1.** *cj.* but; 2. *v/t.* (29) separate, sever, segregate; '‿**nummer** *f e-r Zeitung usw.*: special edition; '‿**recht** *n* privilege; '‿**regelung** *f* separate treatment *od.* settlement; '‿**sitzung** *f* special session; '‿**stellung** *f* exceptional position; '‿**ung** *f* separation; '‿**urlaub** *m* special leave; '‿**zug** 🚂 *m* special (*od.* extra) train; '‿**zulage** *f* special bonus.

sondieren [zɔn'diːrən] *v/t. u. v/i.* 🖈 probe, (*a.* ⚓) sound (*beide a. fig.*); *fig.* (*v/i.*) explore the ground.

Sonett [zo'nɛt] *n* (3) sonnet.

Sonn|-abend ['zɔn-] *m* Saturday; '‿**e** *f* (15) sun; ⊇**en** (25) sun; *sich* ‿ sun o.s., bask in the sun.

'**Sonnen|-aufgang** *m* sunrise, *Am. a.* sunup; '‿**bad** *n* sun-bath; '‿**blende** *phot. f* lens shade; '‿**blume** *f* sunflower; '‿**brand** *m* sunburn; '‿**brille** *f* (*eine a pair of*) sun-glasses *pl.*; '‿**creme** *f* sun(tan) cream; '‿**dach** *n vor Fenstern*: sun-blind; *mot.* sunshine roof; '‿**energie** *f* solar energy; '‿**finsternis** *f* eclipse of the sun; '‿**fleck** *m* sun-spot; '‿**jahr** *n* solar year; '⊇**klar** as clear as daylight; (quite) obvious; '‿**kollektor** ['‿kɔlɛktor] *m* (8¹) solar panel; '‿**kraftwerk** *n* solar power farm; '‿**licht** *n* sunlight; '‿**öl** *n* suntan oil; '‿**schein** *m* sunshine; '‿**schirm** *m* sunshade; *für Damen*: parasol; '‿**schutzcreme** *f* sun(tan) cream; '‿**segel** *n* awning; '‿**seite** *f* sunny side; '‿**stich** *m* sunstroke; '‿**strahl** *m* sunbeam; '‿**system** *n* solar system; '‿**uhr** *f* sun-dial; '‿**untergang** *m* sunset, *Am. a.* sundown; '⊇**verbrannt** sunburnt, tanned; '‿**wende** *f* solstice; '‿**zelt** *n* awning.

sowjetisch

'**sonnig** sunny (*a. fig.*).

'**Sonntag** *m* Sunday; ♀s, *des* ⁓s on Sundays, every Sunday.

'**sonntäglich** Sunday; ⁓ *gekleidet* dressed in one's Sunday best.

'**Sonntags**|‑**anzug** *m* Sunday best; '⁓**ausflügler(in** *f*) *m* week-ender; '⁓**fahrer** *m* mot. contp. Sunday driver; '⁓**fahrkarte** *f* week-end ticket; '⁓**jäger** *m* would-be sportsman; '⁓**kind** *n* person born on a Sunday; *er ist ein* ⁓ he was born under a lucky star; '⁓**maler** *m* Sunday painter; '⁓**ruhe** *f* Sunday rest; '⁓**schule** *f* Sunday school; '⁓**staat** *m* Sunday best.

sonn|**verbrannt** ['zɔn-] sunburnt, tanned; ♀**wendfeier** *f* ['⁓vɛnt-] midsummer festival.

sonor [zo'noːr] sonorous.

sonst [zɔnst] else, otherwise; (*ehemals*) formerly; (*außerdem*) besides; (*für gewöhnlich*) as a rule; usually; *drohend*: or else!; ⁓ (*noch*) et. od. jemand? anything (*od.* anybody, anyone) else?; *wer* ⁓? who else?; *wie* ⁓ as usual; ⁓ *nichts* nothing else; ⁓ *nirgends* nowhere else; '⁓**ig** other; '⁓**wie** in some other way; '⁓**wo** elsewhere.

sooft [zo'⁹ɔft] whenever.

Sophist [zo'fist] *m* (12), ⁓**in** *f* sophist; ⁓**erei** [⁓ə'raɪ] *f* (16) sophistry; ♀**isch** [⁓'fistiʃ] sophistic(al).

Sopran [zo'praːn] *m* (3¹) soprano, treble; ⁓**ist** [⁓pra'nist] *m* (12), ⁓**istin** *f* (16¹) sopranist, soprano.

Sorge ['zɔrgə] *f* (15) care; (*Kummer*) sorrow; (*Unruhe*) uneasiness, anxiety; (*Angst*) alarm; ♏ care (and custody) (*für of*); ⁓ *tragen für* take care of, see to, (*verbürgen*) ensure; *dafür* ⁓ *tragen, daß* see to it (*od.* ensure) that; *j-m* ⁓*n machen* worry a p.; *sich* ⁓*n machen um* be anxious (*od.* worried) about; *sich* ⁓*e machen*, *daß* be concerned that; *sei ohne* ⁓, *mach dir keine* ⁓*n* don't worry; *lassen Sie das meine* ⁓ *sein* leave that to me; *ich habe andere* ⁓*n* F I have other fish to fry.

'**sorgen** (25): **a**) ⁓ *für care for*, look after (*a.* = *betreuen*), provide for; (*beschaffen*) provide; *für Lebensmittel usw.*: cater for; *für sich selbst* ⁓ provide for o.s.; *dafür* ⁓, *daß* ... take care (*od.* see to it) that; *dafür* ⁓, *daß et. geschieht* see a th. done;

b) (*in Sorge sein*) *mst sich* ⁓ be anxious, worry; *sich* ⁓ *um* be anxious (*od.* worried) about; '♀**falten** *f*|*pl.* worry-lines; '⁓**frei**, '⁓**los** free from care, carefree; '♀**kind** *n* problem child; F handful; '⁓**voll** full of cares; *P.*, *Miene*: anxious, worried.

'**Sorgerecht** *n* care and custody.

Sorg|**falt** ['zɔrkfalt] *f* (16) care, carefulness; '♀**fältig** careful; '♀**lich** careful, anxious; '♀**los** (*gedankenlos*) thoughtless; (*nachlässig*) negligent; (*unachtsam*) careless; (*gleichgültig*) unconcerned; (*sorgenfrei*) carefree; '⁓**losigkeit** *f* thoughtlessness; negligence; carelessness; unconcern; lightheartedness; '♀**sam** careful; (*vorsichtig*) cautious.

Sor|**te** ['zɔrtə] *f* (15) sort, kind, type; ♥ (*Qualität*) quality; ⁓*n pl.* (*Geld*) foreign notes and coins; ♀'**tieren** sort (out); assort; *nach Qualität*: grade.

Sortiment [⁓ti'mɛnt] *n* (3) assortment, range; *s.* ⁓**sbuchhandel**; ⁓**er** *m*, ⁓**sbuchhändler** *m* (retail) bookseller; ⁓**sbuchhandel** *m* (retail) book-trade.

Soße ['zoːsə] *f* (15) sauce; (*Bratensaft*) gravy; '⁓**nschüssel** *f* sauceboat.

Souffl|**é** [su'fle] *n* (11) soufflé (*fr.*); ⁓**eur** [⁓'fløːr] *m* (3¹), ⁓**euse** [⁓'fløː-zə] *f* (15) prompter; ⁓**eurkasten** [⁓'fløːr-] *m* prompt-box; ♀**ieren** [⁓'fliːrən] prompt (*j-m* a p.).

'**so-**⁓**ndso 1.** *adv.* ⁓ *viel* a certain amount; ⁓ *viele sl.* umpteen; ⁓ *oft* over and over again; **2.** ♀: *Herr* ⁓ Mr. What's his name; ♀**vielte** *m*, *f sl.* umpteenth.

Soutane [zu'taːnə] *f* (15) cassock.

Souterrain [zutə'rɛ̃] *n* (11) basement; ⁓**wohnung** *f* basement flat (*Am.* apartment).

Souverän [zuvə'rɛːn] *m* (3¹) sovereign; ♀ *adj.* sovereign; *fig.* superior; (*a. adv.*) in superior style; ⁓**ität** [⁓reni'tɛːt] *f* (16) sovereignty.

so'viel *adv.* so much; *noch einmal* ⁓ as much again, twice as much; *conj.* as much as; ⁓ *ich weiß* as far as I know, for aught I know.

so'weit *cj.* as (*od.* so) far as; ⁓ *ich unterrichtet bin* for aught I know.

sowie'so anyhow, in any case.

Sowjet [zɔv'jɛt] *m* (11), ♀**isch** Soviet.

so'wohl: ~ ... *als (auch)* ... as well as ..., both ... and ...

sozial [zo'tsja:l] social; ~e *Wohlfahrt* social welfare; ~e *Fürsorge* social welfare work; 2-**abgaben** *f/pl.* social contribution; 2-**amt** *n* social welfare cent|re, *Am.* -er; 2**beitrag** *m* social insurance contribution; 2**demokrat(in** *f*) *m* social democrat; 2**demokratie** *f* social democracy; ~**demokratisch** social-democratic; 2-**einrichtungen** *f/pl.* social services; 2**hilfe** *f* social security (*Am.* welfare); *von der* ~ *leben* be on welfare; ~**isieren** [~tsjali'zi:rən] socialize; 2**i'sierung** *f* socialization; ~**ismus** [~'lismus] *m* (16) socialism; 2**ist** [~'list] *m* (12), 2**istin** *f* socialist; ~**istisch** [~'listiʃ] socialistic(ally *adv.*); ~**kritisch** [~'tsja:l-] socio-critical; 2**lasten** *f/pl.* social charges; 2**leistung** *f* social contribution; 2**pädagogik** *f* social p(a)edagogics; 2**politik** *f* social policy; ~**politisch** socio-political; 2-**produkt** *n* (gross) national product; 2-**unterstützung** *f* poor (*od.* public) relief; 2**verhalten** *n* social behavio(u)r; 2**versicherung** *f* social insurance; 2**wissenschaft** *f* social science, sociology; 2**wissenschaftler** *m* sociologist; 2**wohnung** *f* council flat, *Am.* publicly financed apartment.

Soziolog|e [zotsjo'lo:gə] *m* (13) sociologist; ~**ie** [~lo'gi:] *f* (15) sociology; 2**isch** [~'lo:giʃ] sociological.

Sozius ['zo:tsjus] *m* (14²) partner; ~**fahrer(in** *f*) *m* pillion-rider; ~**sitz** *mot. m* pillion; *auf dem* ~ *mitfahren* ride pillion.

sozu'sagen so to speak, as it were.

Spachtel ['ʃpaxtəl] *m* (7) spatula; *a.* ◄~'**masse** *f* surfacer; ~'**messer** *n* putty knife; 2**n** ⊕ surface.

Spagat [ʃpa'ga:t] *m u. n* (3): ~ *machen* do the splits *pl.*

Spaghetti [ʃpa'gɛti] *pl.* (*inv.*) spaghetti.

spähen ['ʃpɛ:ən] (25) look out (*nach* for); (*blicken*) peer; (*spionieren*) spy; ✕ scout.

'Späher *m* (7), '~**in** *f* spy; ✕ scout. **'Späh|trupp** ✕ *m* reconnaissance patrol; '~**wagen** ✕ *m* reconnaissance (*od.* scout) car.

Spalier [ʃpa'li:r] *n* (3¹) espalier, trellis; *fig.* lane; ~ *bilden* form a lane; ~**baum** *m* espalier (tree); ~**obst** *n* espalier fruit; *engS.* wallfruit.

Spalt [ʃpalt] *m* (3), '~**e** *f* (15) crack, split, cleft, crevice, fissure; (*Lücke*) gap; *nur* ~e: *typ.* column; (*Gletscher*2) crevasse; '2**bar** cleavable; *phys.* fissile, fissionable; '2**en** (26; *p.p. mst ge*~; *a. sich*) split, cleave; chop; rend; (*teilen*) divide; ⟋⟍ decompose; '2**enlang** covering several columns; '~**pilz** *m* fission fungus, ▱ schizomycete; '~**ung** *f* splitting, cleavage; *biol., phys.* fission; *fig.* split; cleavage; *e-s Landes, der Meinungen usw.*: division; *eccl.* schism.

Span [ʃpa:n] *m* (3³) chip, shaving; (*Splitter*) splinter; '2-**abhebend** ⊕ metal-cutting; '~**ferkel** *n* sucking pig, porkling.

Spange ['ʃpaŋə] *f* (15) clasp; (*Schnalle*) buckle; (*Brosche*) clip; (*Arm*2) bracelet; (*Haar*2) slide; (*Ordens*2) bar; '~**nschuh** *m* strap shoe.

Span|ier ['ʃpa:njər] *m* (7), '~**ierin** *f* (16¹) Spaniard; 2**isch** Spanish. **'Span|korb** *m* chip basket; '2**los** ⊕ non-cutting.

spann[1] [ʃpan] *pret. v. spinnen.*

Spann[2] *m* (3) instep; '~**beton** *m* pre-stressed concrete; '~**bettuch** *n* fitted sheet; '~**draht** *m* tension wire; '~**e** *f* (15) span; *Zeit*: (short) space; ✝ (*Verdienst*2) margin; '2**en** stretch, strain; *Gewehr*: cock; *Bogen*: bend; *Feder, Schraube usw.*: tighten; *Muskeln*: flex; *Neugier usw.*: excite; *s. Folter*; *vor den Wagen* ~ put to the carriage; ⊕ *Werkstück*: clamp, chuck; (*v/i.*) *Kleid usw.*: be (too) tight; *s. a. gespannt*; '2**end** exciting, thrilling, gripping; '~**feder** *f* tension spring; '~**futter** *n* chuck; '~**kraft** *f* elasticity; *fig. a.* energy; '2**kräftig** elastic(ally *adv.*); '~**ung** *f allg.* tension; ⚡ *a.* voltage; ⊕ *verformende*: strain, *elastische*: stress; △ span; (*Aufmerksamkeit*) close attention; *nervliche*: tension (*a. pol. usw.*), tenseness; (*Ungewißheit*) suspense; *mit* (*od. voll*) ~ with bated breath, intently; *in* ~ *versetzen* thrill, excite; '2**ungsgeladen** *Film usw.*: exciting, gripping; '~**ungsprüfer** ⚡ *m* voltage detector; '~**ungsregler** ⚡ *m* voltage regulator; '~**ungsverhältnis** *n* tension, tense relationship; '**~weite** *f* spread; **⚠, ⚡** span; *fig.* range.

'**Spanplatte** *f* chipboard.

Spant [ʃpant] *n* (5) **⚓** rib; **⚡** frame.

Spar|brief ['ʃpaːrbriːf] *m* savings certificate; '**~buch** *n* savings account (pass-)book; '**~büchse** *f* money-box; '**~einlagen** *f/pl.* savings deposits; '**2en** *v/t. u. v/i.* (25) *allg.* save; *(sich einschränken)* economize, *(sparsam umgehen mit)* be sparing of *(a. fig.)*; '**~er** *m* (6) saver; *Bank:* depositor.

Spargel ['ʃpargəl] *m* (7) asparagus; '**~spitzen** *f/pl.* asparagus tips.

'**Spar|guthaben** *n* savings balance; *(Konto)* savings account; '**~haushalt** *m* austerity budget; '**~kasse** *f* savings-bank; '**~konto** *n* savings account.

spärlich ['ʃpɛːrliç] scant(y); *(zerstreut, dünn)* sparse; *(dürftig)* meag|re, *Am.* -er; '**2keit** *f* scantiness; sparseness.

'**Spar|maßnahmen** *f/pl.* austerity measures, economy drive *sg.*; '**~packung** *f* economy size; '**~programm** *n* austerity program(me); *e-r Waschmaschine:* energy-saving cycle.

Sparren ['ʃparən] *m* (6) spar, rafter; *fig.* e-n ~ zuviel haben be not quite right in the upper story.

sparsam ['ʃpaːrzaːm] saving, economical *(mit of)*; ~ umgehen mit use sparingly, *fig. mit Lob usw.*: *a.* be chary of; '**2keit** *f* economy, thrift; *(strengste Einfachheit)* austerity; *(Knauserigkeit)* parsimony.

spartanisch [ʃpar'taːniʃ] Spartan *(a. fig.)*.

Sparte ['ʃpartə] *f* (15) line.

'**Spar|vertrag** *m* savings agreement; '**~zulage** *f* (tax-free) savings bonus.

Spaß [ʃpaːs] *m* (3² *u.* ³) fun; *(Scherz)* joke, jest; *(Gaudi)* lark; *(Streich)* prank; *aus (od. im od. zum)* ~ for *(od.* in) fun; ~ machen amuse *(j-m* a p.), *(scherzen)* be joking; *s-n* ~ treiben mit make fun of; *das macht (keinen)* ~ that's (no) fun; ~ beiseite joking apart; *viel* ~! have a good time!; *s.* verstehen; '**2en** (27) joke, jest; '**2haft**, '**2ig** facetious, jocose; *(komisch)* funny; '**~macher** *m* wag, joker; *s. a. Hanswurst;* '**~verderber** *m* spoil-sport, kill-joy, F wet blanket; '**~vogel** *m* wag.

spast|isch **✻** ['ʃpastiʃ], **2iker** ['~ikər]

m (7), '**2ikerin** *f* (16¹) spastic.

Spat [ʃpaːt] *m* (3) *min.* spar; *vet.* spavin.

spät [ʃpɛːt] late; *zu* ~ kommen be late *(zu* for); *wie* ~ *ist es?* what time is it?, what is the time?

Spatel ['ʃpaːtəl] *m* (7), *f* (15) **✻** spatula; *löffelförmig:* scoop.

Spaten ['ʃpaːtən] *m* (6) spade.

'**spät|er** later; *(folgend)* subsequent, posterior *(als* to); *adv. a.* '**~erhin** later on; **~estens** ['~əstəns] at the latest; '**2folgen** **✻** *f/pl.* late sequelae; '**2herbst** *m* later part of autumn *od. bsd. Am.* fall, late autumn; '**2-obst** *n* late fruit; '**2sommer** *m* late *(od.* Indian) summer.

Spatz [ʃpats] *m* (12) sparrow; *das pfeifen die ~en von den Dächern* it is everybody's secret.

'**Spät|zünder** *m* F: *ein* ~ *sein* be slow on the uptake; '**~zündung** *mot. f* retarded ignition.

spazieren [ʃpa'tsiːrən] *(sn)* walk, stroll; **~fahren** *v/i.* *(sn)* take a drive; *v/t.* (h.) drive out; **~führen** take (out) for a walk; **~gehen** *(sn)* take *(od.* go for) a walk.

Spa'zier|fahrt *f* drive; *zu Wasser:* sail, row; **~gang** *m* walk, stroll; *fig. (leichter Sieg)* walkover; *e-n* ~ *machen* take a walk; **~gänger** [~gɛŋər] *m* (7) stroller, promenader; **~ritt** *m* ride; **~stock** *m* walking-stick; **~weg** *m* walk.

Specht [ʃpɛçt] *m* (3) woodpecker.

Speck [ʃpɛk] *m* (3) *(Schweine2)* bacon; *weitS.* fat; *s. Made;* '**~bauch** *m* paunch; '**2ig** fat(ty); *(schmierig)* greasy; '**~schnitte** *f* slice of bacon, rasher *(of bacon)*; '**~schwarte** *f* rind *(od.* skin) of bacon; '**~seite** *f* flitch of bacon; '**~stein** *m* soap-stone.

sped|ieren [ʃpe'diːrən] forward, haul; **⚓** *u. Am.* ship; **2iteur** [~di'tøːr] *m* (3¹) forwarding agent, carrier; *(Möbel2)* (furniture) remover.

Spedition [~di'tsjoːn] *f* forwarding, **⚓** *u. Am.* shipping; *a.* = **~sgeschäft** *n* forwarding trade; *(Firma)* forwarding agency, carriers *pl.*

Speer [ʃpeːr] *m* (3) spear; *(Wurf2)* javelin; '**~werfen** *n Sport:* javelin-throw(ing).

Speiche ['ʃpaɪçə] *f* (15) spoke; *anat.* radius.

Speichel ['ʃpaɪçəl] *m* (7) spittle,

saliva; (*Geifer*) slaver; '**~drüse** *f* salivary gland; '**~fluß** *m* salivation; '**~lecker** *m* toady, sycophant; **~lecke'rei** *f* toadyism.

Speicher ['ʃpaiçər] *m* (7) (*Getreide-* ♀) granary, *Am.* elevator, (*Möbel-*, *Waren*♀) warehouse, store; (*Wasser*♀) reservoir; (*Dachboden*) loft; *Computer*: store, memory; '**~chip** *m* *Computer*: memory chip; '**~kapazität** *f Computer*: memory (*od.* storage) capacity; '**~modul** *n Computer*: memory module; '♀**n** store (up); *Computer*, ⚡: store; '**~ung** *f a.* ⚡ *usw.* storage.

speien ['ʃpaiən] *v/i. u. v/t.* (30) spit; ([*sich*] *erbrechen*) vomit.

Speise ['ʃpaizə] *f* (15) food; (*Mahl*) meal; (*Kost*) fare; (*Gericht*) dish; *s. Süß*♀; '**~brei** ◻ *m* chyme; '**~eis** *n* ice-cream; '**~fett** *n* edible fat; '**~haus** *n* eating-house; '**~kammer** *f* larder, pantry; '**~karte** *f* menu, bill of fare; '**~leitung** ⊕ *f* feeder (line).

'**speisen** (27) *v/i.* eat, have a meal; *im Gasthaus*: take one's meals; (*zu Mittag* ~) lunch, dine; (*zu Abend* ~) have supper; *v/t.* feed (*a.* ⊕); '♀**-folge** *f* menu.

'**Speise|-öl** *n* salad-oil; '**~rohr** ⊕ *n* feed pipe; '**~röhre** *anat. f* gullet, ◻ (o)esophagus; '**~saal** *m* dining-hall; '**~saft** ◻ *m* chyle; '**~schrank** food-cupboard, (meat-)safe; '**~wagen** ◻ *m* dining-car, *bsd. Am.* diner; '**~zettel** *m s.* Speisekarte; '**~zimmer** *n* dining-room.

'**Speisung** *f* feeding.

Spektakel [ʃpɛk'taːkəl] *m* (7) noise, racket; *s. Lärm.*

Spektr|al-analyse [ʃpɛk'traːl-] *f* spectral (*od.* spectrum) analysis; **~um** ['~trum] *n* (9²) spectrum.

Speku|lant [ʃpeku'lant] *m* (12) speculator; **~lation** [~la'tsjoːn] *f* *allg.* speculation; **~lati'onsgeschäft** *n* speculative operation *od.* transaction; ♀'**lieren** *allg.* speculate (*auf acc.* on).

Spelunke [ʃpe'luŋkə] *f* (15) den; (*niedere Kneipe*) jerry-shop, *Am.* F dive, *sl.* joint.

Spelz ♀ [ʃpɛlts] *m* (3²) spelt; '**~e** ♀ *f* (15) beard, ◻ glume.

Spende ['ʃpɛndə] *f* (15) gift; (*Beitrag*) contribution; (*Almosen*) alms, charity; (*Stiftung*) donation; '♀**n**

(26) give; *bsd.* ✚ *Blut usw.*: donate; *Sakrament*: administer; (*austeilen*) deal out, dispense; (*beitragen*) contribute (*zu* to); '**~n-aktion** *f* collection campaign; '**~r** *m* (7), '**~rin** *f* (16¹) giver; (*bsd.* ✚ *Blut*♀, *Herz*♀ *usw.*) donor; contributor; (*Verteiler*) distributor, (*a. Automat*) dispenser; (*Wohltäter*) benefactor.

spen'dieren *v/t.* stand; *j-m et.* ~ treat a p. to a th., stand a p. a th.; *v/i.* stand treat.

Sperber ['ʃpɛrbər] *m* sparrow hawk.

Sperling ['ʃpɛrliŋ] *m* (3¹) sparrow.

Sperma ['ʃpɛrma] *biol. n* (9¹, *pl. a.* *-ta*) sperm.

'**sperr|-angel'weit** wide open; '♀**-ballon** ✈ *m* barrage balloon.

Sperr|e ['ʃpɛrə] *f* (15) shutting, closing; (*Versperrung*) block(ing); ⚓ embargo; (*Blockade*) blockade; (*Gesundheits*♀) quarantine; (*Eingang*) gate; ◻ barrier, *Am.* gate; (*Straßen*♀) barricade, road block; (*Sperrbaum*) bar; ⚒ barrage; ⊕ look, stop, detent; (*Verbot*) prohibition, ban; *Sport*: suspension; '♀**en** (25) (*auseinander*~) spread open; *die Beine*: straddle; *typ.* space (out); (*ver*~) bar, stop; (*schließen*) close, shut; ⊕ lock, stop, arrest; *Straße*: block, barricade, *amtlich*: close; ⚓, ⚒ *e-n Hafen*: lock; (*blockieren*) blockade; *Warenverkehr*: embargo; *Konto*, *Löhne*, *Zahlungen*: stop, freeze; *Gas usw.*: cut off; *Sport*: block, *unfair*: obstruct, *durch Spiel- od.* *Startverbot*: disqualify, suspend; *ins Gefängnis* ~ put in prison; *sich* ~ (*gegen et.*) oppose (a th.), struggle (against a th.); *gesperrt gedruckt* spaced out; '**~feuer** ⚒ *n* barrage, curtain-fire; '**~gebiet** *n s.* Sperrzone; '**~gut** *n* bulky goods *pl.*, *Am.* bulk freight; '**~hahn** *m* stopcock; '**~haken** *m* click, catch; '**~holz** ⊕ *n* plywood; '♀**ig** bulky; '**~kette** *f* drag-chain; '**~konto** *n* blocked account; '**~müll** *m* bulky refuse; '**~(r)ad** *n* ratchet-wheel; '**~sitz** *thea. m* stall, reserved seat, *Am.* orchestra (-seat); '**~ung** *f* barring; stoppage; blocking; ⚓ blockade; *s.* Sperre; '**~zoll** *m* prohibitive duty; '**~zone** *f* prohibited area.

Spesen ['ʃpeːzən] *f/pl. inv.* charges, (petty) expenses; '♀**frei** free of

charges; '**∼konto** *n* expense account; '**∼rechnung** *f* bill of expenses.
Spezi ['ʃpeːtsi] F *m* (11) crony, *Am.* buddy.
Spezial|-ausbildung [ʃpe'tsjɑːl-] *f* special training; **∼fach** *n* special(i)ty; **∼gebiet** *n* special field; **∼geschäft** *n* one-line shop; **⌀i'sieren** [∼tsjali-] (*a. sich*) specialize; **∼ist(in** *f*) [∼'list] *m* (12) specialist; **∼ität** [∼li'tɛːt] *f* (16) speciality; (*Sonderfach*) *bsd. Am.* specialty; **∼sprunglauf** [ʃpe'tsjɑːl-] *m* ski-jumping proper.
speziell [ʃpe'tsjɛl] special, specif-ic(ally *adv.*).
Spezies ['speːtsjɛs] *f inv.* species.
spezifisch [ʃpe'tsiːfiʃ] specific(ally *adv.*); **∼es** *Gewicht* specific gravity.
spezifizieren [ʃpetsifi'tsiːrən] speci-fy, *Am. a.* itemize.
Sphär|e ['sfɛːrə] *f* (15) sphere; '**⌀isch** spherical.
spicken ['ʃpikən] (25) lard; *fig. Rede usw.*: interlard; F (*abschreiben*) crib; *gespickt mit* bristling with.
spie [ʃpiː] *pret. v.* speien.
Spiegel ['ʃpiːɡəl] *m* (7) mirror, (look-ing-)glass; *phys.*, 🪖 speculum; ⚓ stern; (*Stand, Höhe, Niveau*) level; *s. Satz⌀, Meeres⌀, Wasser⌀*; '**∼bild** *n* mirror image; *fig.* reflection; '⌀-**blank** shining; '**∼-ei** *n* fried egg; **∼fechterei** ['∼fɛçtə'raɪ] *f* (16) *fig.* humbug, make-believe; '**∼glas** *n* plate-glass; '⌀**glatt** as smooth as a mirror, dead-smooth; '**⌀n** *v/i.* shine; *v/t.* mirror, reflect (*beide a. fig.*); *sich* **∼** be mirrored *od.* reflected; (*sich besehen*) look at o.s. in the glass; '**∼reflexkamera** *f* reflex camera; '**∼-scheibe** *f* (pane of) plate-glass; '**∼schrift** *f* mirror-writing; *typ.* re-flected face; '**∼teleskop** *n* reflector (telescope); '**∼ung** *f* reflection; (*Luft⌀*) mirage.
Spiel [ʃpiːl] *n* (3) play; (*Karten⌀, Schach⌀, Sport⌀ usw.*) game (*a. Tennis; a. fig. b.s.*); (*Wettkampf*) match; ♪, *thea.* playing, (*Vorfüh-rung*) performance, (*Stück*) play; *ein* **∼** *Karten* a pack (*Am.* deck) of cards; ⊕ play, clearance; (*gewagtes* **∼**, *Glücks⌀*) gamble; *leichtes* **∼** *haben* have little trouble; *gewonnenes* **∼** *haben* have made it; *im* **∼** *sein* (*bei et.*) be involved (in); *ins* **∼** *bringen* (*kommen*) bring (come) into play; *fig. das* **∼** *verloren geben* throw up

the sponge; *auf dem* **∼** *stehen* be at stake; *aufs* **∼** *setzen* stake, jeop-ardize, *a. sein Leben*: risk; *aus dem* **∼e** *lassen* leave out; *sein* **∼** *treiben mit* trifle with; *falsches* **∼** double--dealing; *ein falsches* **∼** *treiben mit* practise upon; *fig. das* **∼** *ist aus* the game is up; *s. gut, Hand*; '**∼-anzug** *m für Kinder*: rompers, play-suit; '**∼-art** ♀, *zo. fig. f* variety; '**∼-auto-mat** *m* slot machine; '**∼ball** *m* ball; *Tennis*: game ball; *fig.* sport, play-thing; *ein* **∼** *der Wellen sein* be at the mercy of the waves; '**∼bank** *f* gam-ing-table; *s. Spielkasino*; '**∼dose** *f* musical box; '⌀**n** *v/i. u. v/t.* (25) *allg.* play (*a. Muskeln, Lächeln usw.*); *Karten, Schach usw.*: play *cards, etc.*; *um Einsatz*: gamble; *thea.* play, act, perform, *e-e Rolle*: *a.* do; **∼** *mit* (*fingern*) toy with, *mit j-s Gefühlen a.* trifle with; *mit e-m Gedanken* **∼** toy (*od.* flirt) with an idea; (*vortäuschen*) feign; *den Höflichen* **∼** do the polite; *Sport*: *A. spielte gegen B. A.* played B.; *ins Blaue* **∼** have a bluish tint; *fig.* **∼** *lassen* bring into play; *s. Hand, Rolle, Theater*; '⌀**end** *fig.*: **∼** (*leicht*) easily, with effortless ease; **∼** *gewin-nen* win hands down; **∼** *leicht* sein be child's play (*od. Am. sl.* a cinch).
'**Spieler** *m* (7), '**∼-in** *f allg.* player; (*Glücks⌀*) gambler; **∼ei** [∼'raɪ] *f* (16) play, sport; *fig.* trifle; *s. Spielsachen*.
'**Spiel|-ergebnis** *n Sport*: score; '**∼-feld** *n Sport*: field, ground, pitch; *Tennis*: court; '**∼film** *m* feature (film); '**∼folge** *f* program(me); '**∼-führer** *m* (team) captain; '**∼gefährte** *m*, '**∼genosse** *m* playmate; '**∼geld** *n* play-money; (*Einsatz*) stake, pool; '**∼gewinn** *m* gambling profit; '**∼halle** *f* amusement arcade; '**∼hölle** *f* gam-bling-den; '**∼kamerad** *s. Spielgenos-se*; '**∼karte** *f* playing-card; '**∼kasino** *n* (gambling) casino; '**∼leiter** *m thea.* stage-manager; *Film*: director; '**∼-mann** *m hist.* minstrel; ✗ bands-man; '**∼marke** *f* counter, chip; '**∼-plan** *thea. m* program(me); (*Reper-toire*) repertory; '**∼platz** *m* play-ground; '**∼raum** *fig. m* free play, elbow-room; (*Frist*) margin, lati-tude; ⊕ play, clearance; *freien* **∼** *haben* have full scope; '**∼regel** *f* rule (of the game); '**∼sachen** *f/pl.* play-things, toys; '**∼schuld** *f* gambling--debt; '**∼schule** *f* pre-school, infant-

-school; '**～tisch** *m* card-table, gaming-table; '**～uhr** *f* musical clock; '**～verderber(in** *f)* *m* spoil-sport, kill-joy; '**～verlängerung** *f* *Sport:* extra time; '**～waren** *f/pl. s. Spielsachen;* '**～warenhändler(in** *f)* *m* toy-merchant, F toyman; '**～warenhandlung** *f* toy-shop; '**～wut** *f* passion for gambling; '**～zeit** *f thea., Sport:* season; *e-s Kampfes:* time of play; *e-s Films (Laufzeit):* run; '**～zeug** *n* toy(s *pl.),* plaything(s *pl.).*

Spieß [ʃpiːs] *m* (3²) spear, pike; *(Brat~)* spit; *typ.* work-up; *am ～ braten* barbecue; *den ～ umdrehen* turn the tables (gegen on); *schreien wie am ～* F cry blue murder; '**～bürger** *m* bourgeois, Philistine, *Am. a.* Babbitt, *sl.* square; '**②bürgerlich** bourgeois, Philistine, *sl.* square; '**～bürgertum** *n* philistinism, *Am. a.* babbittry; '**②en** (27) pierce; spear; spit; '**～er** *m* (7) *s. Spießbürger;* '**②ig** *s. spießbürgerlich;* '**～geselle** *m* accomplice; '**～ruten** *f/pl.:* ～ *laufen* run the ga(u)ntlet *(a. fig.).*

Spill ⚓ [ʃpil] *n* (3) capstan.

spinal [ʃpiˈnaːl] spinal; **～e** *Kinderlähmung* infantile paralysis, polio (-myelitis).

Spinat [ʃpiˈnaːt] *m* (3) spinach.

Spind [ʃpint] *n, a. m* (3) wardrobe, press; *bsd.* ✕ locker.

Spindel [ˈʃpindəl] *f* (7) spindle; *(Spinnrocken)* distaff; ⊕ *Presse:* screw; *(Dorn)* mandril; *(Leit②)* lead screw; '**②dürr** (as) lean as a rake, spindly.

Spinett [ʃpiˈnɛt] ♪ *n* (3) spinet.

Spinn|e [ˈʃpinə] *f* (15) spider; '**②e'feind:** *j-m ～ sein* hate a p. like poison; '**②en** (30) *v/t.* spin; *(ausdenken)* hatch; *v/i.* spin; *Katze:* purr; F *(verrückt sein)* be mad; '**～er** *m* (7), '**～erin** *f* spinner; F *(Narr)* crank; **～erei** [～ˈraɪ] *f* spinning; *(Fabrik)* spinning-mill; '**～gewebe** *n* cobweb; '**～maschine** *f* spinning-machine; '**～rad** *n* spinning-wheel; '**～rocken** *m* distaff; '**～webe** *f* cobweb. [*(über acc.* on).}

spintisieren [ʃpintiˈziːrən] muse}

Spion [ʃpiˈoːn] *m* (3¹), **～in** *f* spy; **～age** [～oˈnaːʒə] *f* (15) espionage, spying; **～age-abwehr** *f* counter-espionage, *Am.* counter-intelligence; **②ieren** [～ˈniːrən] spy.

Spiral|e [ʃpiˈraːlə] *f*(15) spiral (line);

⊕ worm, helix, coil; ✝ *(Preis② usw.)* spiral; ⚮ *zur Empfängnisverhütung:* coil; **～feder** *f* spiral spring; **②förmig**, **②ig** spiral; **～kabel** *n* spiral (spring) cord.

Spiritismus [ʃpiriˈtismus] *m* (16) spiritualism, spiritism.

Spiri'tist *m* (12), **～in** *f* spiritualist; **②isch** spiritualistic, spiritist.

Spirituosen [～tuˈoːzən] *pl.* spirits, spirituous liquors.

Spiritus [ˈʃpiːritus] *m* (*inv., pl. a.* 14²) spirit, alcohol; *gr.* breathing; '**～kocher** *m* spirit stove.

Spital [ʃpiˈtaːl] *n* (1²) hospital.

Spitz [ʃpits] 1. *m* (3²) Pomeranian (dog); 2. ② pointed; *fig. a.* biting; *(kränklich)* peaked; ⚕ acute; ～ *zulaufen* taper; '**～bart** *m* pointed beard; '**～bauch** *m* paunch; '**～bogen** *m* pointed arch; '**～bube** *m* thief; *weitS.* rogue, rascal; '**～bubenstreich** *m*, **～büberei** [～byːbə'raɪ] *f* roguery, rascality; **②bübisch** [ˈ～byːbiʃ] roguish.

Spitz|e [ˈʃpitsə] *f* (15) *allg.* point (*a. Kinn②, Schuh②*); *(Berg②)* top, summit, peak; *(Baum②)* top; *(Turm②)* spire; *(spitzes Ende, a. e-s Körperteils)* tip; *(～engewebe)* lace; ⊕ *Werkzeugmaschine:* cent|re, *Am.* -er; *(～ntempo)* top speed; *(Höchstmaß, -wert)* peak; *e-r Kolonne, e-s Unternehmens usw.:* head; ✕ *(Angriffs②)* (spear)head; *Sport:* leading group, *(Führung)* lead; *Fußball:* striker(s *pl.*); *(spitze Bemerkung)* pointed remark, cut; *die ～n der Gesellschaft* the cream of society; *j-m die ～ bieten* make head against, defy; *Sport: an der ～ liegen* be in the lead; *an der ～ (e-r S.) stehen* be at the head (of a th.); *auf die ～ treiben* carry to extremes; '**～el** *m* (7) police-spy, informer; *weitS.* spy; '**②en** (27) point, sharpen; *den Mund ～* purse (up) one's lips; *die Ohren ～* prick up one's ears; F *(sich) auf et. (acc.)* ～ be eager about a th.

'**Spitzen|belastung** ⚡ *f* peak load; '**～drehbank** *f* cent|re (*Am.* -er) lathe; '**～gehalt** *n* top salary; '**～geschwindigkeit** *f* top speed; '**～gruppe** *f* leading group; '**～kandidat** *m* top candidate, front-runner; '**～klasse** *f* champion class, top-rankers *pl.*; élite (*fr.*); '**～kleid** *n* lace dress; '**～leistung** *f allg.* peak performance, record; ⊕ peak output; '~**lohn** *m* peak wage(s *pl.*); '~**politiker(in** *f*) *m* top politician; '~**reiter** *m bsd. Sport:* front-runner, leader; '~**tanz** *m* toe-dancing; '~**technologie** *f* leading technology; '~**verdiener(in** *f*) *m* top earner; '~**zeit** *f Sport:* record time; ⚡ *in* ~en (*des Verbrauches*) at peak periods.

'**spitz|findig** subtle; hair-splitting; '2**findigkeit** *f* subtlety, subtleness, sophistry; '2**hacke** *f*, '2**haue** *f* pick (-ax[e]); '~**ig** *s. spitz*; '~**kriegen** F: et. ~ find a th. out; '2**maus** *f* shrew (-mouse); '2**name** *m* nickname; '~**wink(e)lig** Å: acute-angled.

Spleen [spli:n] *m* (3¹) crotchet, craze; '2**ig** crotchety, eccentric.

Splint ⊕ [ʃplint] *m* (3) cotter.

Splitt [ʃplit] *m* (3¹) stone chips *pl.*

Splitter ['ʃplitər] *m* (7) splinter; fragment; (*Span*) chip; *biblisch:* mote (*in another's eye*); '2**frei** splinter-proof; *Glas:* non-splintering; '~**gruppe** *pol. f* splinter group; '2**ig** splintery; '2**n** *v/t. u. v/i.* (29, *h. u.* sn) splinter; '2'**nackt** stark naked; '~**partei** *parl. f* splinter party.

Spoiler *mot.* ['spɔʏlər] *m* spoiler.

spontan [ʃpɔn'ta:n] spontaneous.

sporadisch [spo'ra:diʃ] sporadic (-ally *adv.*).

Spore ♀ ['ʃpo:rə] *f* (15) spore.

Sporen ['ʃpo:rən] *pl. v. Sporn.*

Sporn [ʃpɔrn] *m* (5³) spur; ✈ (tail) skid; *fig.* stimulus; *dem Pferd die Sporen geben* put spurs to; *sich die Sporen verdienen* win one's spurs; '2**en** (25) spur; ~**rädchen** ['~re:t-çən] *n* rowel; 2**streichs** ['~ʃtraiçs] post-haste, directly.

Sport [ʃpɔrt] *m* (3) sport; athletics *pl.*; *fig.* (*Steckenpferd*) hobby; ~ *treiben* go in for sports; '~-**anlage** *f* athletic ground(s *pl.*), sports facilities *pl.*; '~-**anzug** *m* sports suit; '~-**art** *f* (form of) sport; (*Disziplin*) event; '~-**artikel** *m/pl.* sports goods; '~**bericht** *m* sporting report; '~**be-richt-erstatter(in** *f*) *m* sports reporter.

Sporteln ['ʃpɔrtəln] **1.** *f/pl.* (15) perquisites, fees; **2.** 2 F (29) *v/i* go in for sports.

'**Sport|fest** *n* sports day; '~**flugzeug** *n* sporting plane; '~**freund(in** *f*) *m* sports enthusiast; '~**geschäft** *n*

sporting-goods shop; '~**halle** *f* gymnasium; '~**hemd** *n* sports shirt; '~**herz** 🞧 *n* athlete's heart; '~**hochschule** *f* physical education college; '~**hose** *f* shorts *pl.*; '~**jacke** *f* sports jacket; '~**kleidung** *f* sportswear; '~**klub** *m* sports club; '~**lehrer(in** *f*) *m* sports instructor, trainer; '~**lenkrad** *mot. n* sports steering wheel; '~**ler** *m* (7) sportsman; '~**lerin** *f* (16¹) sportswoman; '2**lich** sporting, athletic; (*fair*) sportsmanlike; '~**lichkeit** *f* sportsmanship; '~**nachrichten** *f/pl.* sporting news; '~**platz** *m* athletic (*od.* sports) ground *od.* field; '~**schuh** *m* sports shoe; '~**smann** *m* sportsman; '~**tauchen** *n* skin (*od.* scuba) diving; '2**treibend** sporting; '~**ver-anstaltung** *f* sport(ing) event; '~**wagen** *m mot.* sports car; *für Kinder:* pushchair; '~**waren** *f/pl.* sports articles; '~**zeitung** *f* sporting paper.

Spotmarkt ['spɔt-] *m für Erdöl:* spot market.

Spott [ʃpɔt] *m* (3) mockery; *lächerlich machend:* derision; *verächtlich:* scorn; *gutmütig:* banter; (*seinen*) ~ *treiben mit* make sport of; '~**bild** *n* caricature; '2'**billig** dirt-cheap.

Spöttel|ei [ʃpœtə'lai] *f* (16) mockery, raillery, sarcasm; '2**n** (29) mock, gibe (*über acc.* at).

spotten ['ʃpɔtən] (26) mock, scoff (*über acc.* at), jeer (at), deride; *fig.* (*gen.*) defy; *s. Beschreibung.*

Spötter ['ʃpœtər] *m* (7), '~**in** *f* (16¹) scoffer, mocker; cynic; ~**ei** [~'rai] *f* (16) mockery, derision.

'**Spott|gedicht** *n* squib, satirical poem; '~**gelächter** *n* derisive laugh(ter); '~**geld** *n s. Spottpreis; für ein* ~ for a mere song.

'**spöttisch** mocking; derisive; sarcastic; ironical.

'**Spott|lied** *n* satirical song; '~**lust** *f* mocking spirit; '~**name** *m* nickname; '~**preis** *m* ridiculous price, trifling sum; '~**schrift** *f* satire, lampoon.

sprach [ʃpra:x] *pret. v. sprechen.*

'**Sprache** *f* (15) (*Sprachfähigkeit*) speech; (~ *des Volkes*) language; *gewählter:* tongue; (*Landes2*) vernacular; (*Ausdrucksweise*) language, parlance; (*Mundart*) idiom; (*Stil*) diction; (*Aussprache*) articulation; *heraus mit der* ~! out with it!, speak out!; *nicht mit der* ~ *herauswollen* hem and haw; *et. zur* ~ *bringen* bring up; *zur* ~ kommen come up.

'**Sprach|-eigenheit** *f*, '**~-eigentümlichkeit** *f* idiomatic expression, idiom; '**~endienst** *m* translating service; '**~fehler** *m* grammatical mistake; ✿ speech defect; '**~forscher** *m* philologist; linguist; '**~forschung** *f* philology; linguistics; '**~führer** *m* phrase-book; '**~gebiet** *n* speech area; '**~gebrauch** *m* usage; '**~gefühl** *n* linguistic instinct; '**~gruppe** *f* speech community; '**~insel** *f* speech island; '**~kenner** *m* linguist; '2**kundig** versed in languages; '**~labor** *n* language laboratory; '**~lehre** *f* grammar; '**~lehrer(in** *f*) *m* teacher of languages, language-master; '2**lich** of language(s), lingual; (*grammatisch*) grammatical; '2**los** speechless; '**~mittler** *m* interpreter; '**~raum** *m* speech area; '**~regel** *f* rule of grammar; **~reiniger** ['~raɪnɪgər] *m* purifier of a language; *b.s.* purist; '**~rohr** *n* speaking-tube, megaphone; *fig.* mouthpiece; '**~schatz** *m* vocabulary; '**~störung** *f* speech disorder; '**~studium** *n* study of languages; '**~-unterricht** *m* instruction in languages; *englischer* ~ English lessons *pl.*; '**~werkzeug** *n* organ of speech; '2**widrig** incorrect, ungrammatical; '**~wissenschaft** *f* science of language, philology; *eng S.* linguistics *pl.*; '**~wissenschaftler** *m* philologist; linguist; '2**wissenschaftlich** philological; linguistic(ally *adv.*).

sprang [ʃpraŋ] *pret. v.* springen.

Spray [spre:; spreɪ] *n* (11) spray.

Sprech|-anlage ['ʃprɛç-] *f* intercom; *an der Haustür*: entryphone; '**~-art** *f* manner of speaking; '**~blase** *f* in *Comics*: balloon; '**~chor** *m* speaking chorus; '2**en** *v/i. u. v/t.* (30) speak (*mit* to; *über acc.*, *von* of, about); (*sich unterhalten*) talk (*mit* to, with; *über acc.*, *von* about, of, over); ~ *mit* (*konsultieren*) see; *über Politik* (*Geschäfte*) ~ talk politics (business); *er ist nicht zu* ~ he is engaged (*od.* busy); *zu* ~ *kommen auf* (*acc.*) come to speak of; ~ *für* speak for a *p.*, *vermittelnd*, *befürwortend*: plead for; *j-n zu* ~ *wünschen* wish to see a *p.*; *von et. anderem* ~ change the subject; *s. Recht*, schuldig, *Urteil*, *Tischgebet*; *das spricht für j-n od. et.* that speaks well for; *das spricht*

für sich selbst this tells its own tale; *laßt Blumen* ~! say it with flowers!; '2**end** *fig.* *Ähnlichkeit*: speaking; *Augen*, *Blick*: eloquent; '2**er** *m* (7), '2**erin** *f* speaker; (*Wortführer*) spokesman; *Radio*: (*Ansager*) announcer; '**~frequenz** ✿ *f* speech frequency; '**~funk** *m* radiotelephony, voice radio; '**~funkgerät** *n* radiotelephone; '**~platte** *f* speech record; '**~stunde** *f* ärztliche: consulting hour; *amtliche*: office hour; '**~stundenhilfe** *f* receptionist; assistant; '**~taste** *f* speaking key; '**~übung** *f* speech practice; '**~weise** *f s.* Sprechart; '**~zimmer** *n* office; *e-s* *Arztes*: consulting-room.

Spreiz|e ['ʃpraɪtsə] (15) (*Stütze*) stay, prop; (*Strebe*) strut; '2**en** (27) spread; *Beine*: a. straddle; *sich* ~ *fig.* swagger, strut; *gegen*: struggle against; *mit*: boast of; '**~fuß** ✿ *m* splayfoot.

Spreng|bombe ['ʃprɛŋ-] *f* demolition bomb, high-explosive (*od.* H.E.) bomb; '**~el** *eccl. m* (7) *e-s* *Bischofs*: diocese; *e-s* *Pfarrers*: parish; '2**en** (25) *v/t. Flüssigkeit*: sprinkle, spray; *Garten*, *Pflanze*: water; (*spray*~) burst (*od.* force) open; *Fesseln*, *Griff*: break; (*in die Luft* ~) blow up, blast; *Mine usw.*: spring; *Versammlung usw.*: break up, disperse; *Bank*: break; *v/i.* (sn) gallop, ride hard; '**~geschoß** *n* high-explosive (*od.* H.E.) shell; '**~kapsel** *f* detonator; '**~kommando** *n* demolition party; *zur Bombenentschärfung*: bomb disposal squad; '**~kopf** ✕ *m* warhead; '**~körper** *m*, '**~ladung** *f* explosive charge; '**~loch** *n* blast hole; '**~satz** *m* blasting composition; '**~schuß** *m* blast; '**~stoff** *m* explosive; '**~stoffpaket** *n* parcel bomb; '**~ung** *f* sprinkling; blowing-up, blasting; dispersion; breaking; '**~wirkung** *f* explosive effect; '**~wolke** *f* burst cloud; '**~zünder** *m* fuse, detonator.

sprenkeln ['ʃprɛŋkəln] (29) speckle, spot.

Spreu [ʃprɔɪ] *f* (16) chaff; *fig. die* ~ *vom Weizen sondern* sift the chaff from the wheat.

Sprich|wort ['ʃpriç-] *n* (1²) proverb, (proverbial) saying; '2**wörtlich** proverbial (*a. fig.*); ~ *sein wegen* be a byword for.

sprießen ['ʃpriːsən] (30, h. *u.* sn) sprout.

Spriet ⚓ [ʃpriːt] *n* (3) sprit.

Spring|brunnen ['ʃpriŋ-] *m* fountain; '⸝en (30, sn *u.* h.) jump; *weit*: leap; *lit.*, *a. v. Dingen*, *bsd. Wasser*, *Blut*: spring; *elastisch*, *bsd. Ball*: bound; *beim Schwimmen*: dive; (*zer-⸝*) burst, crack, break; *in die Augen* ⸝ strike the eye, be obvious; F *et.* ⸝ *lassen* stand; *e-e Mine* ⸝ *lassen* spring a mine; *der* ⸝*de Punkt* the crucial point; *s. Seil*; '⸝er *m* (7) jumper, leaper (*a.* '⸝erin *f*); *Schach*: knight; '⸝flut *f* spring tide; ⸝insfeld ['⸝ʔinsfelt] *m* (3) young whipper-snapper; '⸝quell *m* fountain, spring; '⸝seil *n* skipping-rope.

Sprinkler-anlage ['ʃpriŋklər-] *f* sprinkler system.

Sprint [ʃprint] *m* (3), '⸝en (26) sprint; '⸝er *m* (7) sprinter.

Sprit [ʃprit] *m* (3) spirit, alcohol; F *mot.* fuel, *sl.* juice, *Am.* gas.

Spritz|e ['ʃpritsə] *f* (15) syringe, sprayer; (*Feuer⸝*) fire-engine; ⚕ syringe, (*Einspritzung*) injection, F shot; *fig.* (*Hilfe*) shot-in-the-arm; '⸝en (27) *v/t.* squirt, syringe; (*be⸝*) splash; (*sprengen*) sprinkle; *Lack*, *Parfüm usw.*: spray; ⚕ inject; ⊕ injection-mo(u)ld; *Getränk*: mix with soda-water; *v/i.* throw water, splash; (*heraus⸝*) spurt; *Feder*: splutter; F (*eilen*) dash, rush; '⸝en-haus *n* fire-station; '⸝er *m* (7) splash; '⸝fahrt F *f* (pleasure-)trip, *mot.* F spin; ⸝flakon ['⸝flakõ] *n*, *m* (11) spray bottle; '⸝guß ⊕ *m* die-casting; *Kunststoff*: injection mo(u)lding; '⸝ig *Wein*: sparkling (*a. fig. geistreich*); *fig.* (*behend*) quick; (*lebhaft*) spirited, racy; '⸝-lackieren (paint-)spray; '⸝pistole *f* water-pistol; ⊕ spray gun; '⸝-tour *f s. Spritzfahrt*.

spröd|e ['ʃpröːdə] brittle (*a. Stimme*); *Haut*: chapped; (*hart*) hard; *fig.* reserved; *Mädchen*: coy, prudish; '⸝igkeit *f* brittleness; reserve; coyness, prudery.

Sproß [ʃprɔs] **1.** *m* (4) shoot, sprout, scion; *fig.* scion, offspring; **2.** ⸝ *pret. v. sprießen.*

Sprosse ['ʃprɔsə] *f* (15) (*Leiter⸝*) round, step, rung; *am Geweih*: tine, point; '⸝n (28, h. *u.* sn) sprout.

Sprößling ['ʃprœsliŋ] *m* (3¹) *s. Sproß*; F (*Sohn*) son, junior.

Sprotte ['ʃprɔtə] *f* (15) sprat.

Spruch [ʃprux] *m* (3³) (*Ausspruch*) saying, dictum; (*Weisheits⸝*) maxim, aphorism; *s. Bibel⸝, Schieds⸝, Urteil*; F (*große*) *Sprüche machen* talk big, brag; '⸝band *n* banner; '⸝reif ripe for decision.

Sprudel ['ʃpruːdəl] *m* (7) bubbling water; (*Mineralwasser*) mineral water; '⸝n (29, sn *u.* h.) bubble (*od.* gush) forth; *Getränk*: effervesce; (*hastig reden*) sputter; *fig.* ⸝ *vor* bubble with; *in* ⸝*der Laune* sparkling with humo(u)r.

Sprüh|dose ['ʃpryː-] *f* aerosol, spray (can); '⸝en (25) *v/i.* (sn *u.* h.) *u. v/t. Wasser usw.*: spray; *Funken*: emit, (*v/i.*) fly; *Feuer*: spit; *Regen*: drizzle; *fig. Augen*: flash (*vor Zorn* with anger); *vor Witz* ⸝ sparkle with wit; '⸝farbe *f* aerosol paint; '⸝regen *m* drizzling rain.

Sprung [ʃpruŋ] *m* (3³) jump, bound, leap; *Schwimmen*: dive; (*Riß*) crack, fissure; *auf dem* ⸝*e sein* be on the alert; *auf dem* ⸝*e stehen od. sein zu ...* be on the point of *ger.*; *auf e-n* ⸝ *vorbeikommen* drop in (for a minute); *j-m auf die Sprünge kommen* find a p. out; *j-m auf die Sprünge helfen* help a p. out; *er kann keine großen Sprünge machen* he cannot get far; '⸝bein *n* ankle-bone; '⸝brett *n Schwimmen*: diving-board; *a. Turnen*: spring-board; *fig.* stepping-stone; '⸝feder *f* (elastic) spring; '⸝federmatratze *f* spring mattress; '⸝haft erratic(ally *adv.*); (*plötzlich*) abrupt; ⸝ *steigen go up* by leaps and bounds; '⸝lauf *m* ski-jumping; '⸝schanze *f* ski-jump; '⸝stab *m* jumping-pole; '⸝tuch *n Feuerwehr*: jumping-sheet; '⸝turm *m* high-diving board; '⸝weise by leaps (and bounds).

Spuck|e ['ʃpukə] *f* (15) spittle, saliva; '⸝en (25) *v/i.* spit; *v/t.* spit out; '⸝napf *m* spittoon, *Am. a.* cuspidor.

Spuk [ʃpuːk] *m* (3) apparition, ghost, spect(re, *Am.* -er; *fig.* nightmare; '⸝en (25) *an e-m Ort* haunt a place; *es spukt in dem Hause* the house is haunted; '⸝geschichte *f* ghost-story; '⸝haft ghostly, weird.

Spule ['ʃpuːlə] *f* (15) spool, reel;

(*Spinn*♀) bobbin; (*Feder*♀) quill; *ϟ* coil.

Spüle ['ʃpyːlə] *f* (15) kitchen sink.

spulen ['ʃpuːlən] (25) reel, spool.

spül|en ['ʃpyːlən] (25) rinse; *Geschirr*: wash (up); *Abort*: flush; ⊕, *mot.* scavenge; *an Land* ~ wash ashore; '♀**icht** *n* (3) dish-water, dirty water; '♀**lappen** *m* dish-cloth; '♀**mittel** *n* washing-up liquid; '♀**ung** *f* rinsing; flushing; ⊕, *mot.* scavenging; *Abort*: water flush; '~**wasser** *n* rinsing water; *s. Spülicht.*

'**Spulwurm** *m* mawworm.

Spund [ʃpunt] *m* (3^3) bung, plug; *Tischlerei*: tongue; ♀**en** ['~dən] (26) bung; *Tischlerei*: tongue and groove; ~**loch** ['ʃpunt-] *n* bung-hole.

Spur [ʃpuːr] *f* (16) trace (*a.* ⚗, *Leucht*♀ *u. fig.*); (*Fährte, a. fig.*) trail, track; *hunt. a.* scent; (*Abdruck*) print; (*Fuß*♀) footprint; (*Wagen*♀) track, *tiefe*: rut; ⚓ wake; *s.* ~**weite**; (*Fleck, Narbe, Brems*♀, *fig. Merkmal*) mark; (*Anzeichen*) sign; (*Überrest, winzige* ~) vestige; *e-e* ~ *Salz usw.* a touch of salt *etc.*; *F keine* ~! not a bit; *fig. auf die (richtige)* ~ *bringen* give a *p.* a clue; *auf die Spur kommen* (*dat.*) trace, find out; *auf der falschen* ~ *sein* be on a wrong track.

spür|bar ['ʃpyːrbɑːr] sensible; *fig.* marked; ~ *sein* be felt; '~**en** (25) track, trace (*a. fig.*); (*empfinden*) feel; *nur innerlich*: sense; (*wahrnehmen*) perceive.

spuren ['ʃpuːrən] F (25) toe the line; '♀**-element** *n* trace element.

'**Spürhund** *m* trackhound; *fig.* (*Detektiv*) sleuth.

'**spurlos:** ~ *verschwinden* disappear without leaving a trace.

'**Spür|nase** *f* scent (*a. fig.*); '~**sinn** *m* flair.

Spurt [ʃpurt] *m* (3), '♀**en** (26) spurt.

'**Spurweite** *f* 🚂 ga(u)ge; *mot.* wheel-track; *Reifen*: tread.

sputen ['ʃpuːtən] (26): *sich* ~ make haste, hurry up.

St. *s. Sankt.*

Staat [ʃtaːt] *m* (5) (*Aufwand*) state, pomp; (*Putz*) finery; (*~swesen*) state; (*Regierung*) government; ~ *machen mit* make a show of, parade; '~**enbund** *m* confederation; '♀**en-los** stateless; '♀**lich** state-..., gov-

ernment ..., national, public; political.

'**Staats|-akt** *m* state ceremony; '~**aktion** F *f* great fuss; '~**angehörige** *m, f* national, *Brt.* subject, *Am.* citizen; '~**angehörigkeit** *f* nationality, national status, *Am. mst* citizenship; '~**angelegenheit** *f* state-affair; '~**anleihe** *f* government loan; '~**anwalt** *m* public prosecutor, *Am.* district attorney; ~**anzeiger** *m* official gazette; '~**archiv** *n* Public Record Office; '~**be-amte** *m* public (*od. Brt.* civil) servant, government official; '~**begräbnis** *n* state funeral; '~**besuch** *m* state visit; '~**bürger** *m* citizen; '~**bürgerkunde** *f* civics *pl.*; '♀**bürgerlich** civic(ally *adv.*); '~**bürgerschaft** *f* citizenship; '~**chef** *m* head of state; '~**dienst** *m* civil (*Am.* public) service; '♀**-eigen** state-owned; '~**-einkünfte** *f/pl.* public revenue(s *pl.*) *sg.*; '~**feind** *m* public enemy; '♀**feindlich** subversive; '~**form** *f* form of government, polity; '~**gebäude** *n* public building; '~**gefangene** *m* prisoner of state; '~**geheimnis** *n* state (*od. fig.* top) secret; ~**gelder** ['~ɡɛldər] *n/pl.* public money *sg.*; '~**gewalt** *f* supreme (*od.* executive) power; '~**haushalt** *m* national budget; '~**hoheit** *f* sovereignty; '~**kasse** *f* (public) treasury, *Brt.* exchequer; '~**kirche** *f* state church; *die englische*: Established Church, Church of England; '♀**klug** politic(ally *adv.*), diplomatic (-ally *adv.*); '~**körper** *m* body politic; *auf* '~**kosten** *pl.* at (the) public expense; '~**kunst** *f* statecraft, statesmanship; '~**mann** *m* statesman, politician; ♀**männisch** ['~menɪʃ] statesmanlike; ~**e** *Fähigkeiten od. Kunst* statesmanship; '~**minister** *m* Minister of State; '~**oberhaupt** *n* head of state; '~**papiere** *n/pl.* government securities *od.* stocks; '~**prozeß** *m* state-trial; ~**räson** ['~rɛːzɔ] *f* reason of State; '~**rat** *m* Privy Council; (*Person*) Privy Council(l)or; '~**recht** *n* constitutional law; '♀**rechtlich** relating to (*od.* under) constitutional law; '~**regierung** *f* government; '~**schatz** *m s.* ~**kasse**; '~**schuld** *f* national debt; '~**sekretär** *m* State Secretary; '~**sicherheitsdienst** *m* state security service; '~**streich** *m* coup d'état (*fr.*); '~**trauertag** *m* national day of mourning; '~**verbrechen** *n* political crime; '~**verfassung** *f* political constitution; '~**vertrag** *m* (international) treaty; '~**verwaltung** *f* (public) administration; '~**wesen** *n* political system, polity; state; '~**wissenschaft** *f* political science; '~**wohl** *n* public weal; '~**zuschuß** *m* government grant, state subsidy.

Stab [ʃtɑːp] *m* (3³) staff, stick; (*Gitter*♀, *Metall*♀) bar; (*Stange*) rod, pole (*a.* *Sport*: *Sprung*♀); *Sport*: (*Staffel*♀) baton (*a.* ♪ *Dirigenten*♀, ✗ *Marschall*♀); *s.* *Zauber*♀; *fig.* (*Mitarbeiter*♀, *a.* ✗) staff; ✗ (*Hauptquartier*) headquarters *pl.*; den ~ über j-n brechen condemn a p.; '~-**antenne** *f* rod aerial *od.* antenna; '~**batterie** *f* torch battery; '~-**eisen** *n* bar iron; '~**hochspringer** *m* pole-vaulter; '~**hochsprung** *m* pole-vault(ing).

stabil [sta'biːl] *allg.* stable; (*fest*, *robust*) sturdy, rugged; ~**i'sieren** [~bili-] stabilize; *sich* ~ become stabilized; ♀**i'sierung** *f* stabilization; ♀**ität** *f* [~'tɛːt] (16) stability.

'**Stabreim** *m* stave rhyme, *weitS.* alliteration.

'**Stabs**|-**arzt** ✗ *m* surgeon-major, *Am.* captain (Medical Corps); '~-**chef** *m* Chief of Staff; '~**feldwebel** *m* *Brt.* Warrant Officer Class II, *Am.* master sergeant; '~-**offizier** *m* (*Major bis Oberst*) field (grade) officer; (*Offizier beim Stabe*) staff officer; '~**quartier** *n* headquarters *pl.* *od.* *sg.*

stach [ʃtɑːx] *pret.* *v.* stechen.

Stachel ['ʃtaxəl] *m* (10) prick; ♀ *a.* spine (*a. des Igels*); (*Insekten*♀) sting; *am Zaun* *od.* *Rennschuh*: spike; *fig.* (*Verletzendes*) sting; (*Ansporn*) goad; '~**beere** *f* gooseberry; '~**draht** *m* barbed wire.

'**stach(e)lig** prickly, (*a. fig.*) thorny.

'**stacheln** (29) sting, prick; *fig.* *s.* an~; ♀**schwein** *n* porcupine.

Stadi|**on** ['ʃtɑːdjɔn] *n* (9¹) stadium; ~**um** ['~um] *n* (9¹) stage, phase.

Stadt [ʃtat] *f* (14¹) town; (*Groß*♀) city; '~-**amt** *n* municipal office; '~-**autobahn** *f* urban motorway; '~**bahn** *f* city-railway; '♀**bekannt** known all over the town, notorious; '~**bewoh-**

ner *m* *s.* Städter; '~**bild** *n* townscape. **Städt**|**chen** ['ʃtɛːt-] *n* (6) small town; '~**ebau** *m* town-planning; urban development; '~**ebauer** *m* town-planner; '~**er** *m* (7) townsman, *pl.* townspeople, city dwellers; '~**erin** *f* (16¹) townswoman; '~**ezug** *m* interurban (express) train.

'**Stadt**|**gebiet** *n* urban area; '~**gemeinde** *f* township; '~**gespräch** *n* *fig.* the talk of the town; ~**guerilla** ['~gerilja] *m* (16, *o. pl.*) urban guerilla.

städtisch ['ʃtɛːtiʃ] town(-)...; municipal; urban.

'**Stadt**|**kasse** *f* city treasury; '~**köfferchen** *n* attaché case; '~**kommandant** *m* town major; '~**leben** *n* town life, city life; '~**leute** *pl.* townspeople; '~**mauer** *f* town-wall; '~**parlament** *n* city parliament; '~**plan** *m* map of the city; '~**planung** *f* *s.* Städtebau; '~**rand** *m* outskirts *pl.* of the town *od.* city; '~**randsiedlung** *f* suburban settlement; '~**rat** *m* municipal council; (*Person*) town (*od.* city) council(l)or; '~**recht** *n* freedom of the city; '~**sanierung** *f* urban renewal (*od.* redevelopment); '~**staat** *m* city-state; '~**streicher**(**in** *f*) *m* city tramp; ~**streicherei** ['~ʃtraɪçəˈraɪ] *f* urban vagrancy; '~**teil** *m* quarter, district, ward; '~**tor** *n* town-gate; '~**väter** *m/pl.* city fathers; '~**verordnete** *m* (18) town (*od.* city) council(l)or; '~**ver-ordnetenversammlung** *f* town council; '~**verwaltung** *f* municipality; '~**viertel** *n* *s.* Stadtteil; '~**wappen** *n* city-arms *pl.*

Stafette [ʃtaˈfetə] *f* (15) (mounted) courier; *Sport*: relay; ~**nlauf** *m* relay race. [sories *pl.*]

Staffage [ʃtaˈfɑːʒə] *f* (15) acces-]

Staffel ['ʃtafəl] *f* (15) step; *fig.* degree; *Sport*: relay; (*Teilstrecke*) stage; (~**aufstellung**) echelon (formation); ✈, ✗ squadron; ~**ei** [~'laɪ] *f* (16) easel; ♀**förmig** ['~fœrmɪç] in echelons; '~**lauf** *m* relay race; '♀**n** (29) *Steuern usw.*: graduate, differentiate; *Arbeitszeit usw.*, *a.* ⊕, ✈, *Sport*: stagger; '~**ung** *f* graduation, differentiation; staggering.

Stagn|**ation** [stagnaˈtsjoːn] stagnation; ♀**ieren** [~ˈgniːrən] stagnate.

stahl[1] [ʃtɑːl] *pret.* *v.* stehlen.

Stahl[2] *m* (3⁸) steel; '~**bad** *n* chalybeate bath (od. Ort: spa); '~bau m steel construction; '~beton ⊕ m steel concrete; '♀blau steel-blue; '~blech n sheet-steel.

stähl|en [ˈʃtɛːlən] (25) temper; fig. steel; '~ern (of) steel; fig. steel(y).

'Stahl|feder f steel spring; zum Schreiben: steel nib; '~gürtelreifen mot. m belted-bias tyre (Am. tire); '~helm m steel helmet; '~kammer f strong-room, Am. steel-vault; '~(rohr)möbel n/pl. tubular (steel) furniture sg.; ~späne ['~ʃpɛːnə] m/pl., '~wolle f steel wool sg.; '~stich m steel engraving; '~werk n steel works.

stak [ʃtɑːk] pret. v. stecken².

Staken [ˈʃtɑːkən] **1.** m (6) stake; **2.** ♀ (25) pole, punt.

Staket [ʃtaˈkeːt] n (3) fence, palisade.

Stall [ʃtal] m (3³) (Pferde♀) stable (a. fig. Renn♀ usw.); (Kuh♀) cowshed; (Schaf♀) sheep-pen; s. Hundehütte, Hühner♀, Schweine♀; (Schuppen) shed, Am. a. barn; '~gefährte m Sport: stable companion (a. fig.); '~geld n stable-money, stallage; '~knecht m groom; '~meister m equerry; '~ung f stabling; ~en pl. stables.

Stamm [ʃtam] m (3³) ♀ stem (a. gr.); (Stengel) stalk; (Baum♀) trunk (a. anat.); (Volks♀ usw.) race; (Geschlecht) stock; (Familie, Haus) family, in Schottland: clan; (Eingeborenen♀) tribe; von Vieh: breed; biol. phylum; fig. (Bestand) stock; (Kern) core, nucleus; (Kader) cadre; s. Kunden♀, Stammpersonal; '~aktie f ordinary share, Am. common stock; '~baum m family (od. genealogical) tree; von Tieren: pedigree; '~buch n album; '~burg f ancestral castle; ~datei ['~datai] f Computer: master file; '♀eln v/i. u. v/t. (29) stammer; '~eltern pl. progenitors, first parents; '♀en (25, sn): ~ von P.: be descended from; (s-n Ursprung haben in) originate (Am. a. stem) from; zeitlich: date from; gr. be derived from; vgl. ab~, her~; '~esgeschichte f racial history; biol. phylogeny; '~form gr. f cardinal form; '~gast m habitué (fr.), regular guest; '~halter m son and heir; '~haus ✝ n parent house od. firm.

stämmig [ˈʃtɛmiç] fig. (stark) sturdy, stalwart, husky, F hefty; (untersetzt) stocky.

'Stamm|kapital n original capital; '~kunde m, '~kundin f regular customer; '~lokal n habitual haunt; '~personal n permanent staff; (Mindest♀) skeleton staff; (Kader) cadre personnel; '~rolle ✕, ♣ f personnel roster; '~silbe f root syllable; '~sitz m ancestral seat; '~tafel f genealogical table; '~tisch m (table reserved for) regular guests; '~vater m ancestor; '♀verwandt kindred, cognate; pred. of the same race; '~volk n aborigines pl., primitive people; '~wähler pol. m regular voter; '~wort n (1²) root word, stem.

Stampfe [ˈʃtampfə] f (15) tamper; (Ramme) rammer; (Stößel) pestle; '♀n v/t. u. v/i. (25) stamp; (hämmern) pound; Schiff: pitch; (zer~) crush; Kartoffeln usw.: mash.

Stand [ʃtant] **1.** m (3³) (Stehen) stand(ing), upright position; (Halt für den Fuß) footing; s. Standplatz; (Niveau) level; (Verkaufs♀, Pferde♀) stall; (Zu♀) state, condition; (Lage) position, state of affairs; (soziale Stellung) status, station, rank; (Klasse) class; (Beruf) profession; (Gewerbe) trade; des Thermometers usw.: reading; ast. position; Sport: (Spiel♀) score; pol. die Stände pl. the estates; Mann von ~e man of rank; Patentrecht: ~ der Technik prior art; j-n in den ~ setzen et. zu tun enable a p. to do a th.; Sprung aus dem ~ standing jump; e-n schweren ~ haben have a hard time (of it); auf den neuesten ~ bringen bring up to date, update; s. imstande, instand, zustande; **2.** ♀ pret. v. stehen.

Standard [ˈʃtandart] m (11) standard; ♀i'sieren [~di-] standardize; ~i'sierung f standardization; ~lösung ['~dart-] f standard solution; '~werk n standard work.

Standarte [~ˈdartə] f (15) standard.

Standbild [ˈʃtant-] n statue.

Ständchen [ˈʃtɛntçən] n (6) serenade; j-m ein ~ bringen serenade a p.

Stander [ˈʃtandər] m (7) pennant.

Ständer [ˈʃtɛndər] m (7) (Gestell) stand; (Gewehr♀, Pfeifen♀ usw.) rack; (Pfosten) post, pillar; ✻ stator.

Standes|amt [ˈʃtandəsˀamt] n registry office, Am. marriage license bureau; '℈-**amtlich:** ⁓e *Trauung* civil marriage; '⁓**be-amte** *m* registrar; '⁓**bewußtsein** *n* class-consciousness; '⁓**dünkel** *m* pride of position, snobbery; '⁓**ehre** *f* professional hono(u)r; '℈**gemäß**, '℈-**mäßig** in accordance with one's rank; '⁓**person** *f* person of rank *od.* quality; '⁓**unterschied** *m* social difference.

'**stand**|**fest** stable; '℈**geld** *n* stall--rent; '℈**gericht** ✕ *n* drumhead court-martial.

'**standhaft** steadfast, steady, firm; '℈**igkeit** *f* steadfastness.

'**standhalten** hold one's ground; *(aushalten)* stand; *j-m od.* e-r *S.* ⁓ resist a p. *od.* a th.

ständig ['ʃtɛndiç] permanent; *(fortwährend)* constant; *Einkommen:* fixed, regular; *Ausschuß:* standing; ⁓er *Begleiter* constant companion; et. ⁓ *tun* keep doing a th.

'**Stand**|**licht** *mot. n* parking light; '⁓**motor** *m* stationary engine; '⁓**ort** *m* (3) station, location, ⚓ *usw.* position (*a. fig.*); ✕ garrison, *Am.* post; '⁓**pauke** F *f* severe lecture, harangue; '⁓**platz** *m* stand(ing--place); '⁓**punkt** *m* point of view, view(point); den ⁓ *vertreten* take the view *(that)*; *j-m* den ⁓ *klarmachen* give a p. a piece of one's mind; *s. Standort*; '⁓**quartier** ✕ *n* fixed quarters *pl.*; '⁓**recht** ✕ *n* martial law; '℈**rechtlich** according to martial law; '⁓**spur** *mot. f* hard shoulder; '⁓**uhr** *f* grandfather's clock.

Stange ['ʃtaŋə] *f* (15) pole; *(Vogel℞)* perch; *(Metall℞)* bar, rod; *v. Siegellack usw.:* stick; *v. Zigaretten:* carton; F *(lange Person)* bean-pole; F e-e ⁓ *Geld* F quite a packet; *(Kleid) von der* ⁓ *(fertiggekauft)* F reach- *(Am.* hand-)me-down; *fig. j-m die* ⁓ *halten* stick up for a p.; F *bei der* ⁓ *bleiben* stick to it; '⁓**nbohne** *f* runner bean; '⁓**nspargel** *m* asparagus spears *pl.*

stank [ʃtaŋk] *pret. v.* stinken.

Stänker F ['ʃtɛŋkər] *m* (7) *fig.* squabbler; ⁓**ei** [⁓'raɪ] *f* (16) squabble; '℈**n** (29) *fig.* squabble

Stanniol [ʃta'njoːl] *n* (3¹) tinfoil.

Stanze¹ ['ʃtantsə] *f* (15) *(Strophe)* stanza.   [stamp.)

'**Stanze²** ⊕ *f* punch; '℈**n** punch,)

Stapel ['ʃtaːpəl] *m* (7) pile, stack; ⚓ slip(way); *der Wolle:* staple; *auf* ⁓

legen lay down; *vom* ⁓ *lassen* launch (*a. fig.*); *vom* ⁓ *laufen* be launched (*a. fig.*); '⁓**güter** *n*/*pl.* staple commodities; '⁓**lauf** *m* launch(ing); '℈**n** (20) stack, (*a. sich*) pile up; *(lagern)* store; '⁓**platz** *m* dump; *(Handelsplatz)* emporium.

stapfen ['ʃtapfən] (25) plod, trudge.

Star¹ [ʃtaːr] *m* (3¹) *zo.* starling; ⁓² *m* ♟ *grauer* ⁓ cataract, *grüner* ⁓ glaucoma, *schwarzer* ⁓ amaurosis; *j-m den* ⁓ *stechen fig.* open a p.'s eyes; ⁓³ [staːr] *m thea. etc.* star.

Star|**allüren** ['⁓'aly:rən] *f*/*pl.* airs and graces; '⁓-**anwalt** *m* top lawyer (*Am.* attorney).

starb [ʃtarp] *pret. v.* sterben.

'**Starbesetzung** *f thea. etc.* star cast.

stark [ʃtark] (18²) **1.** *allg.* strong (*a. Getränk usw., gr. u. fig.*); *P.*: *a.* sturdy; (*a. Maschine, Schlag usw.*) powerful; *(beleibt)* stout, corpulent; ⊕ *(dick)* thick; *(intensiv)* intense; *(heftig)* violent; *(beträchtlich)* large; *(schlimm)* bad; *Fieber:* high; *Frost:* hard; *Familie:* numerous; *Regen, Verkehr:* heavy; ⁓e *Auflage e-s Buches* large edition; ⁓er *Band* big volume; ⁓e *Erkältung* bad cold; ⁓er *Esser* hearty eater; ⁓er *Trinker* hard drinker; *pol.* ⁓er *Mann* strong man; ⁓e *Meile (Stunde)* good mile (hour); ⁓e *Seite fig.* strong point, forte; F *das ist (doch) zu* ⁓! that's a bit thick!; **2.** *adv.* very much; greatly, strongly; hard; badly.

Stärke ['ʃtɛrkə] *f* (15) **1.** *s. stark:* strength (*a. e-s Heeres usw.*); force; stoutness; power (*a.* ⊕ *Leistung*); ⊕ thickness; intensity; violence; largeness; *fig.* forte, strong point; **2.** ⚛ starch; '℈**haltig** starchy; '⁓**mehl** *n* starch-flour; '℈**n** (25) strengthen (*a. fig.*); *(beleben)* invigorate; *Wäsche:* starch; *sich* ⁓ *fig.* take some refreshment.

'**Starkstrom** ⚡ *m* power (*od.* high--voltage *od.* heavy) current; '⁓**leitung** *f* power line.

'**Stärkung** *f* strengthening; *(Erfrischung)* refreshment; '⁓**smittel** *n* restorative, tonic.

starr [ʃtar] rigid (*a. fig. u. Luftschiff*), stiff; *Blick:* staring, fixed; *(unbeugsam)* inflexible; *vor Schreck usw.:* paralysed (*with fear etc.*); *vor Staunen:* dum(b)founded; *vor Kälte:* numb; '⁓**en** (25) stare (*auf acc.*

at); *von Waffen usw.*: bristle with; *von Schmutz usw.*: be covered with; '**2heit** f stiffness, rigidity; numbness; **köpfig** ['kœpfiç], '**sinnig** stubborn, obstinate; '**2krampf** m tetanus; '**2sinn** m obstinacy, stubbornness; '**2sucht** f catalepsy.

Start [ʃtart] m (3) start (*a. fig.*); ✈ take-off; (*Raketen2*) lift-off; *Sport*: *fliegender* (*stehender*) ~ flying (standing) start; '**bahn** ✈ f runway; '**2bereit** ready to start; ✈ ready to take off; '**2en** (26, h. *u.* sn) start; *fig. a.* launch; ✈ take off; '**er** m (7) starter; '**erlaubnis** f permission to start; ✈ clearance for take-off; '**hilfekabel** *mot.* n jump leads *pl.*; '**kapital** n initial capital; '**2klar** s. startbereit; '**platz** m starting-place; '**schleuder** f catapult; '**schuß** m *Sport*: starting shot; '**verbot** n *Sport*: suspension; ✈ take-off restriction; ~ *erhalten* be grounded.

Statik ['ʃtaːtik] f (16) statics *sg.*; '**er** ⚠ m stress analyst.

Station [ʃtaˈtsjoːn] f *allg.* station; (*Kranken2*) ward; (*gegen*) *freie* ~ board and lodging (found); ~ *machen* stop (*in dat. at*); **2är** [~tsjoˈnɛːr] stationary; ⚕ in-patient; **2ieren** [~ˈniːrən] station; **ierungskosten** [~ˈniːruŋs-] *pl.* stationing costs; **s-arzt** [~ˈtsjoːns-] m ward physician; **s-schwester** f ward sister; **vorsteher** 🚉 m station-master, *Am.* station agent.

statisch ['ʃtaːtiʃ] static(ally *adv.*).

Statist [ʃtaˈtist] m (12), '**in** f (16[1]) *thea.* super(numerary); *Film*: extra; **ik** f (16) statistics *pl. u. sg.*; **iker** m (7) statistician; **2isch** statistical.

Stativ [ʃtaˈtiːf] n (3[1]) stand, support; *phot. usw.* tripod.

Statt [ʃtat] **1.** f (16, *o. pl.*) place, stead; *an Kindes* ~ *annehmen* adopt; *s. vonstatten, zustatten*; **2.** 2 *prp.* (*gen., zu mit inf.*) instead of, in lieu of.

Stätte ['ʃtɛtə] f (15) place, spot; *e-s Ereignisses*: scene; (*Wohnung*) abode; *keine bleibende* ~ *haben* have no fixed abode.

'**statt|finden**, '**haben** take place, happen; come off; *Veranstaltung*: be held; '**geben** (*dat.*) grant, allow; '**haft** admissible; (*gesetzlich* ~) legal.

'**Statthalter** m (7) governor; *rhet. b.s.* satrap.

'**stattlich** stately; (*ansehnlich*) handsome; (*würdevoll*) portly; (*beträchtlich*) considerable; '**2keit** f stateliness *etc.*

Statue ['ʃtaːtuə] f (15) statue; '**2n-haft** statuesque.

statuieren [ʃtatuˈiːrən] establish; *ein Exempel* ~ make an example (*an dat.* of).

Statur [ʃtaˈtuːr] f (16) stature, size.

Status ['ʃtaːtus] m (*inv.*) status (*a. fig. Prestige*); state, condition; '**symbol** n status symbol.

Statut [~ˈtuːt] n (5) statute, regulations *pl.*; **en** *pl.* e-r *Handelsgesellschaft usw.*: articles *pl.* of association; **2enmäßig** statutory.

Stau [ʃtau] m (3) s. Stauung.

Staub [ʃtaup] m (3) dust; (*Pulver*) powder; *sich aus dem* ~*e machen* make off, decamp; *s. aufwirbeln*; '**beutel** ⚘ m anther.

Stäubchen ['ʃtɔʏpçən] n (6) particle of dust, mote, atom.

staubdicht ['ʃtaupdiçt] dustproof.

Stau-becken ['ʃtau-] n reservoir.

stauben ['~bən] v/i. (25, h. *u.* sn) give off dust; *es staubt* it is dusty.

stäuben ['ʃtɔʏbən] v/t. dust (*a.* ⚘ *Pflanzen*); v/i. = stauben.

'**Staub|faden** ⚘ m filament; '**fänger** m dust-trap; '**flocke** f fluff; '**2frei** dust-free; '**gefäß** ⚘ n stamen; '**2haltig** dust-laden; ['~biç] dusty; '**korn** n dust-particle; '**lunge** ⚕ f pneumoconiosis; '**mantel** m dust-coat; '**sauger** m vacuum cleaner; '**tuch** n duster; '**wedel** m feather duster; '**wolke** f cloud of dust.

stauchen ['ʃtauxən] (25) jolt; *mit dem Fuß*: kick; ⊕ upset.

'**Staudamm** m dam.

Staude ['ʃtaudə] f (15) shrub, bush.

stauen ['ʃtauən] (25) *Wasser*: dam up; *Güter*: stow (away); *sich* ~ be banked up, *weitS.* accumulate.

'**Stauer** ⚓ m (7) stevedore.

staunen ['ʃtaunən] **1.** (25) be astonished *od.* amazed (*über acc.* at); **2.** 2 n (6) astonishment, amazement; *in* ~ *versetzen* amaze; '**swert** astonishing, amazing.

Staupe *vet.* ['ʃtaupə] f (15) distemper.

'**Stau|see** m storage-lake, reservoir; '**ung** f damming up; (*Stockung*)

stoppage; ⚡ (*a. Verkehrs*⚲) congestion; (*Verkehrs*⚲) *a.* bank-up; (*ge-
staute Masse*) jam; '⟋**werk** *n* barrage.
Stearin [ʃtea'riːn] *n* (3¹) stearin.
stechen ['ʃteçən] **1.** *v/t. u. v/i.* (30)
prick; *Insekt:* sting; *Floh, Mücke:*
bite; (*durch*⟋) pierce; *mit e-m Messer usw.*: stab; *Kartenspiel:* trump
(*od.* take) *a card; Sonne:* burn;
Rasen, Spargel, Torf: cut; ⊕ *in
Kupfer:* cut, engrave; *sich in den
Finger* ⟋ prick one's finger; *s. Auge,
See, Star²;* **2.** ⚺ *n* (*Schmerz*) stitches
pl.; Sport: jump *od.* shoot *od.* fence
etc. off; '⟋**d** *fig. Blick:* piercing; *Geruch, Geschmack:* acrid, pungent;
Schmerz: stabbing.
'**Stech|fliege** *f* stinging fly; (*Bremse*)
gadfly; '⟋**ginster** *m* furze, gorse;
'⟋**heber** *m* siphon, pipette; '⟋**karte** *f*
clocking-in card; '⟋**mücke** *f* gnat,
mosquito; '⟋**palme** *f* holly; '⟋**-
schritt** ✕ *m* goose-step; '⟋**uhr** *f*
time-clock; '⟋**zirkel** *m* dividers *pl.*
'**Steck|brief** *m* warrant of arrest,
"wanted" circular; '⚺**brieflich:**
j-n ⟋ *verfolgen* take out a warrant
against a p.; '⟋**dose** ⚡ *f* (wall)
socket.
Stecken¹ ['ʃtekən] *m* (6) stick, staff.
'**stecken²** **1.** *v/t.* stick; (*wohin
tun*) put; *bsd.* ⊕ insert (*in acc.* into),
Kabel usw.: plug (into); ⚘ set,
plant; (*fest*⟋) fix; *mit Nadeln:* pin;
fig. Geld in ein Geschäft: put into;
F *j-m et.* ⟋ tell a p. a th.; *s. Brand,
Decke, Nase, Tasche, Ziel, dahin-
ter*⟋; **2.** *v/i.* (*sich befinden*) be; (*festsitzen*) stick (fast); *in Schulden usw.*
⟋ be involved in; '⟋**bleiben** (sn)
stick fast, get (*od.* be) stuck, come
to a dead stop; *im Sumpf:* bog
down (*a. fig. Verhandlungen usw.*);
in e-r Rede: break down; *s. Kehle;*
'⟋**lassen** leave; '⚺**pferd** *n* hobby-
-horse; *fig.* hobby.
'**Steck|er** ⚡ *m* (7) plug; '⟋**kontakt** *m*
plug-contact; '⟋**ling** *m* (3¹), '⟋**reis**
n ⚘ layer, slip, cutting; '⟋**nadel** *f*
pin; *wie e-e* ⟋ *suchen* hunt for *a p.*
(high and low); '⟋**rübe** ⚘ *f* turnip;
'⟋**schlüssel** ⊕ *m* socket wrench;
'⟋**schuh** *phot. m* accessory shoe; '⟋**-
schuß** ✗ *m* retained missile.
Steg [ʃteːk] *m* (3) path; (*Brücke*) foot-
-bridge; *typ.* stick; (*Hosen*⚲) strap;
(*Brillen*⚲, *Geigen*⚲) bridge; '⟋**reif** *m:*

aus dem ⟋ extempore, off-hand, off
the cuff; *aus dem* ⟋ *sprechen usw.*
extemporize, *Am.* F ad-lib.
'**Steh|-auf(männchen** *n*) *m* skip-
jack, tumbler; '⟋**bierhalle** *f* bar.
stehen ['ʃteːən] **1.** (30, h. *u.* sn)
stand (up); (*sein, sich befinden*) be;
(*still*⟋) stand still, *Uhr usw.*: have
stopped; (*geschrieben* ⟋) be written;
(*kleiden*) suit, become (*j-m* a p.);
⟋ *bleiben* remain standing; *es steht
bei dir, zu inf.* it is for you to *inf.;*
⟋ *für* stand (*od.* answer) for; *fig.* ⟋
auf (*acc.*) *Aktien:* be at 75, *Barometer usw.*: point to, stand at; F (*begeistert sein von*) *sl.* dig; *gr. auf* ...
steht der Akkusativ ... answers the
accusative; *hinter j-m* ⟋ back a p.;
*fig. vor e-m Rätsel, dem Ruin, e-r
Schwierigkeit usw.* ⟋ be faced with;
sich gut (*schlecht*) ⟋ be well (badly)
off; (*sich*) *gut* (*schlecht*) ⟋ *mit j-m* be
on good (bad) terms with a p.; *es
steht schlecht mit ihm* he is in a bad
way; *zu j-m* ⟋ stand by a p.; *zu e-m
Versprechen usw.* ⟋ stand to; *teuer
zu* ⟋ *kommen* cost dear; *was steht
in dem Brief?* what does it say in the
letter?; *wie steht's mit* ...? what
about ...?; *Sport:* wie *steht das
Spiel?* what's the score?; *s. dahin-
stehen, Debatte, Mann, Modell, Pa-
te, Rede usw.*; **2.** ⚺ *n* standing; *Mahlzeit im* ⟋ stand-up meal; *zum* ⟋
bringen (*kommen*) bring (come) to
a stop; '⟋**bleiben** (sn) (*nicht weitergehen*) stand still; stop; *Fehler usw.*:
remain, be overlooked; *beim Lesen:*
leave off; '⟋**d** standing (*a. fig. Heer,
Regel, Redensart; Wasser*); *s. Fuß;* '⟋**-
lassen** leave (standing); (*vergessen*)
leave (behind); (*nicht anrühren*) let
(*od.* leave) *a th.* alone; *s. Bart.*
'**Steher** *m* (7) *Rennsport:* stayer.
'**Stehkragen** *m* stand-up collar.
'**Steh|lampe** *f* standard (lamp); *auf
dem Fußboden stehend:* floor-lamp;
'⟋**leiter** *f* stepladder.
stehlen ['ʃteːlən] *v/t. u. v/i.* (30) steal
(*j-m Geld usw.* a p.'s money *etc.*).
'**Steh|platz** *m* standing-place *od.*
-room; '⟋**pult** *n* standing-desk, high
desk; '⟋**vermögen** *n Sport usw.*:
staying power, stamina.
steif [ʃtaɪf] stiff (*a. fig.*); *bsd. phys.*
rigid; *vor Kälte:* numb, benumbed;
⟋*er Hut* bowler hat, *Am.* derby
(hat); *fig.* ⟋ *und fest* obstinately,

categorically; *s. Ohr*; '~**en** (25)
stiffen; *Wäsche*: starch; *j-m den*
Nacken ~ stiffen a p.'s back; '♀**heit**
f stiffness; '♀**leinwand** *f* buckram.
Steig [ʃtaɪk] *m* (3) path; '~**bügel** *m*
stirrup; ~**e** ['~ɡə] *f* (15) ladder;
(*Treppe*) steep stairs *pl.*; (*Zaun-*
übertritt) stile; (*steiler Pfad*) ascent;
(*Kiste*) crate; ~**eisen** ['~k-] *n*
climbing-iron; *mount.* crampon;
♀**en**[1] ['~ɡən] (30, sn) mount, go up;
(*klettern*) climb (up) (*a.* ⚔ *u. fig.*);
fig. (*zunehmen*) increase, *a. Wasser,*
Temperatur, Barometer, Preis usw.:
rise; *Pferd*: prance, rear; F (*statt-*
finden) come off, be staged; *auf e-n*
Baum ~ climb (up) a tree; *j-m in*
den Kopf ~ go to a p.'s head; *zu*
Pferde ~ mount (a horse); *vom*
Pferde ~ dismount; '~**en**[2] *n* rise;
increase; '♀**end** *fig.* rising; (*wach-*
send) growing; ~**er** ⚔ ['~ɡər] *m* (7)
pit-foreman; '♀**ern** (29) raise; (*ver-*
mehren) increase; (*verstärken*) en-
hance; *Produktion*: step up; (*hoch-*
treiben) force up; *gr.* compare; *sich*
~ increase, *Person*: improve, *in*
Wut: work o.s. up into a rage.
'**Steigerung** *f* raising; increase, rise;
enhancement; *gr.* comparison; '~**s-**
grad *gr. m* degree of comparison;
'~**srate** *f* rate of increase.
Steigfähigkeit ['~k-] *f* ⚔ climbing
power; *mot.* hill-climbing ability.
Steigung ['ʃtaɪɡuŋ] *f* rise, gradient,
Am. a. grade; (*Hang*) slope; (*Auf-*
stieg) ascent.
steil [ʃtaɪl] steep; '♀**feuer** ⚔ *n* high-
angle fire; '♀**hang** *m* precipice, steep
slope; '♀**heit** *f* steepness; '♀**paß** *m*
Fußball: through ball.
Stein [ʃtaɪn] *m* (3) stone (*a.* ♘, ♟ *u.*
Edel♀); (*Fels*) rock; *Uhr*: jewel;
Damespiel: man; *für Feuerzeuge*:
flint; *fig.* *den* ~ *ins Rollen bringen*
set the ball rolling; *e-n* ~ *im Brett*
haben bei j-m be in a p.'s good
books; *ein* ~ *fällt mir vom Herzen*
that takes a load off my mind; *s.*
Anstoß.
'**Stein|-adler** *m* golden eagle; '♀'-**alt**
very old; '~**bock** *m* ibex; *ast.* Cap-
ricorn; '~**bruch** *m* quarry; '~**butt**
m (3) turbot; '~**druck** *m* lithography; (*Bild*) lithograph; '~**drucker**
m lithographer; '~'-**eiche** ♀ *f* holm-
-oak; '♀**ern** stone-..., of stone; *fig.*
stony; '~**frucht** *f* stone(-)fruit; '~-

garten *m* rock garden; '~**gut** *n*
earthenware, stoneware; '♀'**hart**
(as) hard as stone.
'**steinig** full of stones, stony, rocky;
~**en** ['~iɡən] (25) stone; '♀**ung** *f*
stoning.
'**Stein|kohle** *f* mineral (*od.* hard)
coal, pit-coal; '~**kohlenbergwerk**
n colliery; '~**marder** *m* beech marten; '~**metz** *m* (12) stone-mason;
'~**obst** *n* stone-fruit; '~**pilz** *m*
(edible) boletus; '♀**reich** *fig.* im-
mensely rich; '~**salz** *n* rock-salt;
'~**schlag** *mount. m* rockfall; '~**wurf**
m stone's throw; '~**zeit** *f* Stone
Age.
Steiß [ʃtaɪs] *m* (3²) buttocks *pl.*,
rump; '~**bein** *anat. n* coccyx.
Stellage [ʃtɛ'lɑːʒ] *f* (15) frame,
rack, stand; ♱ *Börse*: put and call;
(~*ngeschäft*) dealing in futures.
Stelldichein ['ʃtɛldɪçˀaɪn] *n* (*inv.*
gen. a. ~s) rendezvous, *bsd. Am.* F
date.
Stelle ['ʃtɛlə] *f* (15) place; (*Fleck*)
spot; (*wo j. steht*) stand, position;
(*Arbeitsstelle*) employment, job, situation, place, post; (*Behörde, Dienst-*
stelle) agency, office; (*Buch*♀) passage; *e-r Zahl*: digit, (*Dezimal*♀)
place; *freie* ~ (*freier Arbeitsplatz*)
vacancy; *offene* ~ (*Öffnung*) opening; *an erster* ~ in the first place;
fig. an erster ~ *stehen* come first;
an ~ *von od. gen.* in place of, instead
of; *an deiner* ~ in your place; *an j-s*
~ *treten* take the place of a p.; *auf*
der ~ on the spot, immediately;
auf der ~ *treten* ⚔ *u. fig.* mark time;
nicht von der ~ *kommen* not to get
ahead; *zur* ~ *sein* be present *od.* at
hand.
'**stellen** (25) put; place, set; stand;
(*richtig ein*~) regulate, adjust;
Wecker, Aufgabe: set; (*aufhalten*)
stop; *Verbrecher, Wild*: bring to
(*od.* hold at) bay, hunt down; (*her-*
ausfordern) challenge; (*liefern*) furnish, supply; provide; *Zeugen*:
produce; *sich wohin* ~ place o.s.;
⚔ join up, enlist; (*sich einfinden*)
present o.s.; *dem Verfolger*: turn to
(*od.* stand at) bay (*a. fig.*); *e-m*
Gegner: face up to *an opponent*;
sich ~ *gegen et.* oppose; *sich der*
Polizei ~ give o.s. up to the police;
sich gut mit j-m ~ put o.s. on good
terms with a p.; *fig. sich krank usw.*

~ feign (*od.* pretend) to be ill *etc.*; *sich* ~, *als ob* ... feign (*od.* pretend) to *do*; *sich zum Kampf* ~ accept combat; *sich (im Preis)* ~ *auf* come to, cost; *der Preis stellt sich auf* ... the price is ...; *Bedingungen* ~ make conditions; *wie stellt er sich dazu?* what does he say (to it)?; *in Dienst* ~ engage, *Schiff*: put into commission; *s. Antrag, Bein, Falle, Frage, Rechnung usw.*; *gestellt Bild usw.*: posed; *gut gestellt sein* be well off; *auf sich selbst gestellt sein* be on one's own.

'**Stellen**|-**angebot** *n* position offered; ~*e pl. in der Zeitung*: vacancies; '~-**ausschreibung** *f* advertising of a post; '~**beschreibung** *f* job description; '~**gesuch** *n* application for a job; ~*e pl. in der Zeitung*: jobs wanted; '~**jäger** *m* job-hunter; '2**los** unemployed, jobless; '~**markt** *m* job market; '~**nachweis** *m*, '~**vermittlung(sbüro** *n)f* employment agency (*Am.* bureau); '2**weise** here and there, in places (*od.* spots); '~**wert** *m fig.* rank, rating.

'**Stell**|**macher** *m* wheelwright; '~**schraube** *f* adjusting screw.

'**Stellung** *f* position (*a.* ⚔ *u. fig.* *Einstellung*); (*Berufs*2) position, situation, employment, job, place; (*Rang*) (social) position, status, rank; (*Ansehen*) standing; (*Körperhaltung*) posture; (*das Stellen*) furnishing; ~ *beziehen*, ~ *nehmen* declare o.s., give one's opinion, comment (*alle: zu* on); *die* ~ *halten fig.* hold the fort; ~**nahme** ['~na:mǝ]*f* (15) opinion, comment, statement (*zu* on); '~**skrieg** stabilized (*od.* static) warfare; '2**slos** *s. stellenlos*; '~**sspiel** *n Sport*: positional play; '~**suchende** *m, f* applicant; '~**s-wechsel** *m* change of position.

'**stell**|**vertretend** vicarious; *amtlich*: acting, deputy; ~**er** *Vorsitzender* vice-chairman; '2**vertreter(in** *f*) *m* representative; *amtlich*: deputy; (*Bevollmächtigter*) proxy; (*Ersatzmann*) substitute; '2**vertretung** *f* representation; agency; substitution; '2**vorrichtung** *f* adjusting device; '2**werk** 🔩 *n* signal box.

Stelze ['ʃtɛltsǝ] *f* (15) stilt; '2**n** (27, sn) stalk.

Stemm|**bogen** ['ʃtɛm-] *m* stem turn; '~-**eisen** *n* crowbar; (*Meißel*) chisel.

stemmen ['ʃtɛmǝn] (25) prop, support; (*hochwuchten*) lever up; *Gewicht*: lift; *Loch*: chisel; *sich* ~ *gegen* press against, *fig.* resist *od.* oppose *a th.*; *die Füße* ~ *gegen* plant one's feet against.

Stempel ['ʃtɛmpǝl] *m* (7) stamp; ⊕ piston; (*Präge*2) die; (*Loch*2) punch; ♀ pistil; ✂ (*Stützholz*) prop; ⚓ brand, (*Echtheitszeichen*) hallmark; *fig.* den ~ *e-r S. tragen* bear the stamp of; '~**bogen** *m* stamped sheet of paper; '~**farbe** *f* stamping-ink; '~**gebühr** *f* stamp-duty; '~**kissen** *n* ink-pad; '~**marke** *f* (duty) stamp; '2**n** (29) stamp, mark; *fig.* ~ *zu* stamp (*od.* label) as; F ~ *gehen* be on the dole; '~-**uhr** *f* time-clock.

Stengel ['ʃtɛŋǝl] *m* (7) stalk, stem.

Stenogra|**mm** [ʃteno'gram] *n* (3) shorthand notes *pl.*; ~**ph** [~'graːf] *m* (12), ~**phin** *f* shorthand writer, stenographer; ~**phie** [~gra'fiː] *f* (15) shorthand, stenography; 2'**phieren** *v*/*t. u. v*/*i.* write (in) shorthand; 2**phisch** [~'graːfiʃ] (*adv.* in) shorthand.   [(16¹) shorthand typist.⟩
Stenotypist [~ty'pist] *m* (12), ~**in** *f*⟩
Stentorstimme ['ʃtɛntɔrʃtimǝ] *f* stentorian voice.

Stepp|**decke** ['ʃtɛpdɛkǝ] *f* (continental) quilt; '~**e** *f* (15) steppe; '2**en** (25) quilt; '~**naht** *f* quilting-seam.

Steptanz ['ʃtɛptants] *m* tap-dance.

Sterbe|**bett** ['ʃtɛrbǝbɛt] *n* death-bed; '~**fall** *m* (case of) death; '~**fallversicherung** *f* death insurance; '~**geld** *n* death grant; '~**hilfe** ⚕ *f* euthanasia; '~**kasse** *f* burial-fund; '2**n** 1. (30, sn) die (*an dat.* of); 2. 2 *n* dying, death; *im* ~ *liegen* be dying.

'**sterbens**|'**krank** dangerously ill; '~'**müde** dead tired; '2'**wort** *n*, '2-'**wörtchen** *n*: *kein* ~ not a (single) word.

'**Sterbe**|**sakramente** *n/pl.* last sacraments; '~**stunde** *f* dying-hour; '~-**urkunde** *f* death-certificate.

sterblich ['ʃtɛrpliç] mortal; ~ *verliebt* desperately in love (*in acc.* with); *gewöhnliche* 2**e** *pl.* ordinary mortals; '2**keit** *f* mortality; '2**keits-ziffer** *f* death-rate, mortality.

Stereo ['ste:reo] *n* stereo; '~-**anlage** *f* stereo set; '~-**aufnahme** *f* stereo recording; *phot.* stereoscopic photo (-graph); ~**metrie** [~me'triː] *f* (15) stereometry, solid geometry; 2‑**phon** [∿'foːn] stereophonic; **∿skop** [∿'skoːp] n (3¹) stereoscope; '**∿ton** m stereo sound.

stereotyp [∿'tyːp] stereotype; *fig.* stereotyped; 2e f (15) stereotype; 2ie [∿'piː] f (15) stereotype‑printing; **∿ieren** [∿'piːrən] stereotype.

steril [ste'riːl] *allg.* sterile; **∿isieren** [∿rili'ziːrən] sterilize; 2**isation** [∿iza'tsjoːn] f sterilization; 2**ität** [∿rili'tɛːt] f (16, *o. pl.*) sterility.

Stern [ʃtɛrn] m (3) star (*a. fig.*); (*un)glücklicher* ∿ (un)lucky star; *typ.* asterisk (*a.* '**∿chen** n [6]); '**∿bild** n constellation; '**∿deuter** m astrologer; '**∿deuterei** [∿'raɪ] f astrology; '**∿enbanner** n Star‑‑Spangled Banner, Stars and Stripes *pl.*; '**∿fahrt** *mot.* f motor rally; 2**förmig** ['∿fœrmiç] starlike, stellar; *a.* ⊕ radial; '2**hagelvoll** F dead drunk; '2**hell**, '2**klar** starli(gh)t, starry; '**∿himmel** m firmament, starry sky; '**∿kunde** f astronomy; '**∿licht** n starlight; '**∿motor** m radial engine; '**∿schaltung** ∮ f Y‑connection; '**∿schnuppe** f shooting star; '**∿stunde** f siderial hour; *fig.* fateful hour; '**∿warte** f observatory.

Sterz [ʃtɛrts] m (3²) tail; (*Pflug*2) plough‑tail, *Am.* plowtail.

stet [ʃteːt] steady, constant; *fig.* ∿er *Tropfen höhlt den Stein* little strokes fell big oaks.

'**stetig** continual, constant; (*unerschütterlich*) steady; '2**keit** f steadiness; continuity, constancy.

stets [ʃteːts] always, constantly.

Steuer ['ʃtɔyər] **1.** ⚓ n (7) rudder, helm; ✈ control(s *pl.*); *mot.* steering wheel; *am* ∿ at the helm (*a. fig.*), *mot.* at the wheel; **2.** ∿ f (15) tax, *bsd. indirekte*: duty; (*Kommunal*2) rate (*alle: auf acc. on*); *von der* ∿ *absetzbar* tax‑deductible; '**∿abzug** m tax deduction; '**∿aufkommen** n tax receipts *pl.*, inland (*Am.* internal) revenue; '2**bar** assessable, taxable; ⊕ *s.* lenkbar; '**∿be‑amte** m revenue‑officer; '**∿befreiung** f tax exemption; '**∿behörde** f inland‑revenue office; '**∿berater** m tax consultant; '**∿bescheid** m notice of assessment; '**∿bord** ⚓ n starboard; '**∿delikt** n tax offen|ce, *Am.* ‑se; '**∿‑einnahmen** f/pl. s. Steueraufkom‑

men; '**∿erklärung** f (income‑)tax return; '**∿‑erlaß** m remission of taxes; '**∿‑erleichterung** f, '**∿‑ermäßigung** f tax relief; '**∿flosse** ✈ f fin; '2**frei** tax‑free, tax‑exempt; '**∿freibetrag** m tax‑allowance; '**∿freiheit** f exemption from taxation; '**∿hinterzieher** m tax dodger; '**∿hinterziehung** f tax evasion; '**∿klasse** f tax bracket; '**∿knüppel** ✈ m control stick *od.* lever, joystick; '**∿last** f tax burden; '2**lich** tax ..., fiscal; '**∿mann** ⚓ m helmsman; (*Boots*2) coxswain; (*Titel*) mate; *ohne* ∿ (*Bootsrennen*) coxswainless; '**∿marke** f duty‑stamp; '**∿mittel** n/pl. tax money *sg.*

'**steuern** (h. *u.* sn) steer, *bsd.* ✈ pilot; *mot.* drive; ⊕ control; *e‑r S.* ∿ check a th., *vorbeugend*: obviate, *abhelfend*: remedy; *der Not* ∿ meet need.

'**Steuer**|**‑o‑ase** f, '**∿paradies** n tax haven; 2**pflichtig** ['∿pfliçtiç] taxable; *S.*: dutiable; '**∿politik** f fiscal policy; '**∿pult** ⊕ n control desk; '**∿rad** n ⚓, *mot.* steering wheel; ✈ control wheel; '2**rechtlich** fiscal; '**∿rück‑erstattung** f tax refund; '**∿ruder** n ⚓ rudder, helm; ✈ control surface; '**∿satz** m tax rate; '**∿senkung** f lowering of taxes; '**∿sünder** m tax‑dodger.

'**Steuerung** f steering; piloting; ⊕, ∮ control; (*Vorrichtung*) steering gear; ✈ controls *pl.*; (*Ventil*2) valve gear.

'**Steuer**|**ver‑anlagung** f assessment; '**∿zahler** m *Brt.* staatlich: taxpayer, *städtisch*: ratepayer; *Am. allg.* tax‑payer.

Steven ⚓ ['ʃteːvən] m (6) stem.

Steward ✈, ⚓ ['stjuːərt] m (11) steward; **∿eß** ['∿dɛs] f (16³) f stewardess, air hostess.

stibitzen F [ʃti'bitsən] (27) *sl.* filch.

Stich [ʃtiç] m (3) (*Nadel*2) prick; *e‑s Insekts*: sting; (*Dolch*2, *Messer*2) stab; (*Näh*2) stitch; (*Stoß*) thrust; *Karten*: trick; (*Kupfer*2) engraving; ✸ (*Schmerz*) stitch, twinge; stitch; ⚓ knot; *fig.* (*Seitenhieb*) cut, gibe; ∿ *halten* hold water; *im* ∿ *lassen* abandon, desert, *Gefährten*: *a.* forsake, let down, leave in the lurch; *e‑n* ∿ *haben Bier usw.*: be turning sour, *Fleisch*: be (a bit) high, F *P.*: be touched; *ein* ∿ *ins Blaue* a tinge of blue; *es gab ihm e‑n* ∿ it cut him to the quick.

Stichel ['ʃtiçəl] m (7) engraver's

tool; ~ei [~'laɪ] f (16), '~rede f taunt, sneer, gibe, needling; '2n (29) v/i. stitch; prick (beide a. v/t.); fig. taunt, sneer (gegen at), needle.

'stich|fest proof; '2flamme f blast flame, flash; '~haltig valid, sound; ~ sein hold water; '2haltigkeit f validity, soundness; '2ler m taunter; '2ling m (3¹) (Fisch) stickleback; '2probe f spot check; random sample; † sample test; '2-säge f compass saw; '2tag m fixed day, target-date; deadline; '2waffe f stabbing (od. thrusting) weapon; '2-wahl f second ballot; '2wort n catchword; im Wörterbuch: a. entry; bsd. thea. cue; '2wortkatalog m classified catalogue; '2wortverzeichnis n index; '2wunde f stab.

sticken ['ʃtɪkən] (25) embroider.

'Sticker m (7), '~in f embroiderer; ~ei [~'raɪ] f (16) embroidery.

'Stick|garn n embroidery silk; '2ig stifling, close, stuffy; '~luft f close (od. stuffy) air; ~oxyd ⌐ ['~'ɔksi:t] n nitric oxide; '~rahmen m tambour (-frame); '~stoff ⌐ m nitrogen; 2-stoffhaltig ['~haltiç] nitrogenous.

stieben ['ʃti:bən] (30, h. u. sn) fly about; Flüssigkeit: spray; Menge: scatter.

Stiefbruder ['ʃti:f-] m stepbrother.

Stiefel ['ʃti:fəl] m (7) boot, Am. a. shoe; F (Unsinn) sl. rot; '~hose f (eine a pair of) breeches pl.; '~-knecht m boot-jack; '2n F (29) march; '~putzer m im Hotel: boots; auf der Straße: shoeblack; '~schaft m leg (of a boot).

'Stief|geschwister pl. stepbrother(s) and stepsister(s); '~mutter f stepmother; b.s. cruel mother; '~-mütterchen ♀ n pansy; '2müt-terlich stepmotherly; fig. ~ behandeln neglect badly; '~schwester f stepsister; '~sohn m stepson; '~-tochter f stepdaughter; '~vater m stepfather.

stieg [ʃti:k] pret. v. steigen¹.

Stiege ['ʃti:gə] f (15) s. Steige.

Stieglitz ['ʃti:glits] m (3²) goldfinch.

Stiel [ʃti:l] m (3) handle; e-s Glases, e-r Pfeife: stem; (Besen2) stick; ♀ stalk.

Stier [ʃti:r] 1. m (3) bull; ast. Bull, Taurus; den ~ bei den Hörnern packen take the bull by the horns; 2. 2 adj. staring; '2en (25) stare

(auf acc., nach at); (glotzen) goggle (at); '~kampf m bull-fight; '~-kämpfer m bull-fighter; '2nackig bull-necked.

stieß [ʃti:s] pret. v. stoßen.

Stift¹ [ʃtift] m (3) pin; (Holz2) peg; (Zier2) stud; (Zwecke) tack; (Zeichen2) pencil, farbiger: crayon; F (Lehrling) youngster; ~² n (1 u. 3) (charitable) foundation; (Domka-pitel) chapter(-house); (Kloster) convent; (Altersheim) home for aged ladies; (Theologenschule) seminary; '2en (26) found; establish; (spenden) give, Am. donate; (verursachen) cause; Frieden: make; s. Unfriede; F ~ gehen bolt; '~er m (7), '~erin f (16¹) founder; donor; (Urheber) author.

'Stifts|dame f, '~fräulein n canoness; '~herr m canon, prebendary; '~kirche f collegiate church.

'Stiftung f (Schenkung) donation, grant; (Gründung; Anstalt) foundation; milde ~ charitable institution, charity; '~sfest n foundation-festival, founder's day.

'Stiftzahn m pivot tooth.

Stil [ʃti:l] m (3¹) allg. style (a. '~-art f); im großen ~ on a large scale, attr. large-scale; '~blüte F f howler; '2-echt s. stilgerecht; ~ett [sti'let] n (3) stiletto; ~gefühl ['ʃti:l-] n stilistic sense; '2gerecht stylish, true to style; adv. in (proper) style; 2i'sie-ren stylize; Text: compose, word, stylize; ~istik [~'listik] f (16) theory of style; 2istisch [~'listiʃ] stylistic (-ally adv.); ~kunde ['ʃti:l-] f style.

still [ʃtil] still, quiet; (schweigend) a. silent; (ruhig) calm; (bewegungslos) still, motionless; † dull, flat; (heimlich) secret (a. Hoffnung, Liebe, Reserven); ~! silence!, quiet!; ~es Gebet silent prayer; im ~en silently, (heimlich) secretly; 2er Freitag Good Friday; † ~er Gesellschafter od. Teilhaber sleeping (Am. silent) partner; der 2e Ozean the Pacific Ocean; s. Wasser; '2e f (15) stillness, quiet(ness), silence; calm; lull (vor dem Sturm before the storm); in der ~ quietly, (heimlich) secretly.

'Stilleben paint. n (6, bei Trennung: Still-leben) still life.

'stilleg|en (bei Trennung: still-legen) Betrieb: shut (od. close) down; Ver-

kehr: stop; '**2ung** *f* closure, shut-
-down; stoppage.
'**stillen** (25) *Schmerz*: still; *Zorn,
Hunger*: appease, stay; *Blut*: stop,
sta(u)nch; *Durst*: quench; *Kind*:
breast-feed, nurse; *Begierde*: gratify.
'**Stillhalte|-abkommen** *n* standstill
agreement; '**2n** *v/i.* keep still (*a.
v/t.*); *fig.* refrain from action; (*einhalten*) stop.
'**stilliegen** (*bei Trennung*: still-lie-
gen; 30) lie still; *fig.* lie dormant;
Betrieb: lie idle; *Handel usw.*: be
at a standstill; *Verkehr*: be suspended.
stillos ['ʃtiːloːs] without (*od.* in bad)
style.
'**still|schweigen** be silent (*zu*
about); '**2schweigen** *n* silence;
mit ~ übergehen pass (over) in
silence; '**~schweigend** silent; *fig.*
tacit, implied; '**2stand** *m* standstill,
stop(page); *v. Verhandlungen usw.*:
deadlock; *zum ~ bringen* (*kommen*)
bring (come) to a standstill; '**~ste-
hen** stand still; ✕ stand at attention; ⊕ be idle; *fig.* be at a standstill; ✕ *stillgestanden!* attention!;
der Verstand stand ihm still his
mind reeled (*bei* at); '**2ung** *f s.
stillen*; stilling; appeasing;
sta(u)nching; quenching; nursing,
suckling; gratification; '**~vergnügt**
cheerful(ly *adv.*).
'**Stil|möbel** *n/pl.* period furniture;
'**~übung** *f* stylistic exercise; '**2voll**
stylish.
'**Stimm|-abgabe** *f* voting; '**~auf-
wand** *m* vocal effort; '**~band** *n*
vocal c(h)ord; '**2berechtigt** entitled
to vote; '**~bezirk** *m* constituency,
electoral district; '**~bruch** *m* change
of voice.
Stimme ['ʃtimə] *f* (15) voice (*a.
fig.*); (*Wahl2*) vote; (*Presse2*) comment; ♪ (*Noten*) part; *entscheidende
~* casting vote; (*gut*) *bei ~* in (good)
voice; *seine ~ abgeben* (cast *od.*
give one's) vote; *mit lauter ~* in a
loud voice; '**2n** (25) *v/t.* tune; *fig.
günstig usw.*: dispose; *j-n gegen et.
~* prejudice a p. against; *glücklich ~*
make (feel) happy; *v/i.* (*zutreffen*)
be true; *Summe usw.*: be correct;
(*übereinstimmen*) agree, tally; *~ für*
(*gegen*) vote for (against); *für* (*das*)
stimmt (that's) right; *da stimmt et.
nicht* there is something wrong.

'**Stimmen|-einheit** *f* unanimity;
'**~fang** *m* vote-getting; '**~gleich-
heit** *f* parity of votes; *parl.* tie; '**~
mehrheit** *f* majority (of votes);
einfache ~ simple majority.
'**Stimm-enthaltung** *f* abstention
(from voting).
'**Stimmenzählung** *f* counting of
votes.
'**Stimmer** ♪ *m* (7) tuner.
'**stimm|fähig** entitled to vote; '**2-
gabel** *f* tuning-fork; '**~gewaltig**
loud-voiced; '**~haft** *gr.* voiced; '**2-
lage** *f* pitch; '**~lich** vocal; '**~los**
voiceless; *gr. a.* unvoiced; '**2recht**
n (right to) vote; *nur pol.* franchise,
suffrage; '**2ritze** *anat. f* glottis.
'**Stimmung** *f* ♪ tune; *fig.* mood (*a.
paint. usw.*), frame of mind; ✕ *der
Truppe*: morale; *der Öffentlichkeit*:
sentiment; *allgemeine*: atmosphere;
✝ *Börse*: tone, tendency; *in guter ~*
in good humo(u)r, in high spirits;
(*nicht*) *in der ~ zu ...* in the (in no)
mood for *a th. od.* to *inf.*; *~ machen
für* make propaganda for; '**~skano-
ne** *f* great joker, life of the party;
'**~smache** *f* boom(ing); '**~smensch**
m moody creature; '**~smusik** *f*
mood music; '**~s-umschwung** *m*
change of mood (*Börse*: of tone);
'**2svoll** atmospheric.
'**Stimm|wechsel** *m* change of
voice; '**~zettel** *m* ballot.
Stimul|ans ['stiːmulans] *n* (11[1], *pl.
-lantia od. -lanzien*) stimulant (*a.
fig.*); **2ieren** [stimuˈliːrən] stimulate.
Stink|bombe ['ʃtiŋk-] *f* stink-bomb;
'**2en** (30) stink (*nach* of; *a. fig.*);
'**2faul** F bone-lazy; '**2langweilig** F
deadly boring; '**~tier** *n* skunk; '**~wut**
F *f: e-e ~ haben* be furious (*auf* with).
Stipendi|at [stipenˈdjaːt] *m* (12)
scholar; **~um** [*~*ˈpɛndjum] *n* (9)
scholarship.
stipp|en F ['ʃtipən] (25) steep, dip;
'**2visite** F *f* flying visit.
Stirn [ʃtirn] *f* (16) forehead; *fig.* impudence, face; *j-m die ~ bieten*
defy; '**~band** *n*, '**~binde** *f* head-
-band, frontlet; '**~höhle** *f* frontal
cavity *od.* ᒐ sinus; '**~höhlenver-
eiterung** ᒐ *f* frontal sinusitis; '**~-
locke** *f* forelock; '**~rad** ⊕ *n* spur-
-gear; '**~runzeln** *n* frown(ing); '**~-
seite** *f* front (side), face; '**~wand** *f*
front wall.
stob [ʃtoːp] *pret. v.* **stieben**.

stöbern ['ʃtøːbərn] (29) hunt, rummage; es stöbert a fine snow (od. rain) is falling.

stochern ['ʃtɔxərn] v/i. (29) im Feuer: poke, stir; in den Zähnen: pick; im Essen: pick at.

Stock [ʃtɔk] m (3³) stick (a. Schi♀); (Rohr♀) cane; ♪ (Takt♀) baton; s. Bienen♀, Billard♀ usw.; ♀ stock; (~werk) (3, pl. inv.) stor(e)y, floor; im ersten ~ on the first (Am. second) floor; über ~ und Stein over hedge and ditch; '♀'blind stone-blind; '~degen m sword-cane; '♀-'dumm utterly stupid; '♀'dunkel pitch-dark. [-heeled shoe.]

Stöckelschuh ['ʃtœkəlʃuː] m high-♪

stocken ['ʃtɔkən] (25, h. u. sn) stop, come to a standshill; langsam: slacken; Flüssigkeit, a. fig.: stagnate; Herz: cease to beat; mot. stall; (zögern) hesitate; Stimme: falter; Verhandlungen usw.: reach a deadlock; (schimmeln) turn mo(u)ldy od. fusty; Zahn: decay, rot; ins ♀ geraten come to a standstill.

'**Stock**|'-engländer m thorough (od. true-born) Englishman; '~ente f mallard; '♀'finster pitch-dark; '~-fisch m stockfish, dried cod; fig. F stick; '~fleck m damp-stain; ~e pl. (a. ♀) mildew sg.; '♀fleckig foxed, foxy, (a. ♀) mildewy.

...**stöckig** [~ʃtœkiç] ...-storeyed, Am. ...-storied.

'**stock**|'konservativ ultra-conservative; '~'nüchtern stone-cold sober; '♀punkt m Öl: solidifying point; '♀schnupfen m chronic cold in the head; '~'steif (as) stiff as a poker; '~'still stock-still; '~'taub stone-deaf; '♀ung f s. stocken; stoppage; stagnation (a. ♪); flagging; standstill; hesitation; des Verkehrs: (traffic) jam, congestion (a. ♪ des Blutes); fig. deadlock; '♀werk n stor(e)y, floor; '♀zahn m molar.

Stoff [ʃtɔf] m (3) matter, substance; (Textil♀) material, fabric; (Tuch) cloth; (Wollzeug) stuff (a. F Schnaps usw.); (Wirk♀) agent; fig. subject (-matter); zu e-m Roman usw.: material (for); ~el ['~əl] m (7) yokel, boor; '♀lich material; with regard to the subject-matter; '~wechsel m metabolism; ~.... metabolic.

stöhnen ['ʃtøːnən] 1. (25) groan, moan; 2. ♀ n groaning, groans pl.

Stoiker ['ʃtoːʔikər] m (7) stoic.

'**sto-isch** stoical.

Stola ['stoːla] f (16²) stole.

Stolle ['ʃtɔlə] f (15) (Kuchen) fruit loaf; '~n m (6) (Pfosten) post; ♀ tunnel, adit, (a. ♀) gallery; am Huf-eisen; calk; s. Stolle.

stolper|n ['ʃtɔlpərn] (29, sn) stumble, trip (über acc. over; beide a. fig.); '♀stein m fig. stumbling block.

stolz [ʃtɔlts] 1. allg. proud (auf acc. of); (hochmütig) haughty; fig. (großartig) proud (day, ship, etc.); noble, stately; ~ sein auf (acc.) be proud of, take pride in; 2. ♀ m (3²) pride (a. fig. Person, Sache); s-n ~ setzen in pride o.s. on.

stol'zieren (sn) strut, swagger.

stopfen ['ʃtɔpfən] (25) v/t. (voll♀, hinein♀) stuff, cram; Pfeife, Loch: fill; (zu~) stop, plug; ♪ constipate; Strümpfe usw.: darn; ♀ (das Feuer) ~ cease firing; j-m den Mund ~ stop a p.'s mouth; gestopft voll crammed full; ♪ gestopfte Trompete muted trumpet; v/i. ♪ cause constipation.

'**Stopf**|garn n darning-cotton; '~-mittel ♪ n emplastic; '~nadel f darning-needle.

Stopp [ʃtɔp] m (11) stop; (Verbot) prohibition, ban.

Stoppel ['ʃtɔpəl] f (15) stubble; '~bart m stubbly beard; '~feld n stubble-field; '♀ig stubbly; '♀n v/t. u. v/i. (29) glean; fig. patch; '~werk n (literary) patchwork.

stopp|en ['ʃtɔpən] v/t. u. v/i. stop; mit Stoppuhr: time, clock; '♀licht mot. n stop light; '♀schild mot. n stop sign; '♀-uhr f stop watch.

Stöpsel ['ʃtœpsəl] m (7) stopper, cork, bsd. ♀ plug; F (kleiner Kerl) little man, Am. F shortie; '♀n (29) stopper, cork, bsd. ♀ plug.

Stör [ʃtøːr] m (3) sturgeon.

Storch [ʃtɔrç] m (3³) stork; '~-schnabel m stork's bill; ⊕ pantograph; bot. crane's bill.

Store [ʃtoːr] m (11) net curtain.

stören ['ʃtøːrən] (25) disturb, trouble; (durcheinanderbringen) upset, disarrange; (sich einmengen in) interfere with, Radio: a. jam; stört es Sie, wenn ich ...? do you mind if I ...?; nur v/i. be intruding; (im Wege sein) be in the way; das Gesamtbild: mar the picture; (unangenehm sein) be awkward; ♀fried

['~fri:t] *m* (3) intruder; trouble-
maker.
stornieren [stɔr'ni:rən] *Buchung*:
reverse; *Auftrag*: cancel.
störrig ['ʃtœriç], *a.* '**störrisch** stubborn, obstinate; (*stur*) mulish; *bsd.*
Pferd: restive; 'keit stubbornness,
obstinacy; restiveness.
'**Störsender** *m Radio*: jamming
station *od.* transmitter, jammer.
'**Störung** *f* disturbance, trouble
(*beide a.* ⚙); ⊕ trouble, *völlige*:
breakdown; (*Einmischung*) interference, *Radio*: a. jamming; (*Eindringen*) intrusion; (*Behinderung*)
obstruction; (*Unterbrechung*) interruption; *s.* atmosphärisch; *geistige* ~
mental disorder; 'sdienst *m*, 's-
stelle *teleph. f* fault section; 's-
frei undisturbed; ⊕ trouble-free.
Stoß [ʃto:s] *m* (3² *u.* ³) push, shove,
(*a. fenc.*; ⚔ *Vor*; *phys. Schub*)
thrust; (*Fuß*) kick; (*Schlag*) blow;
mit den Hörnern, dem Kopf: butt;
(*Rippen*) dig, nudge; (*Erschütterung*) shock, jolt; blow; (*Schwimm*)
stroke; *Kugelstoßen*: put; *des Gewehrs*: recoil; (*Anprall*) bump, *phys.
u. weitS.* impact; (*Explosions*,
Wind, *Trompeten*) blast; ⊕
(*Ende*) butt joint; (~ *Holz usw.*) pile,
stack; (*Brief*) batch; *fig.* e-n ~
versetzen (*dat.*) be a blow to; '-
dämpfer *mot. m* shock-absorber;
'degen *m* rapier, foil.
Stößel ['ʃtø:səl] *m* (7) *Mörser*:
pestle; (*Kolben*) plunger; (*Ventil*)
tappet.
stoßen ['ʃto:sən] (30) *v/t.* push,
shove; *stärker*: thrust; *mit dem
Fuß*: kick; *mit der Faust*: punch;
mit den Hörnern, dem Kopf: butt;
mit e-m Stock: poke; *schlagend*:
knock, strike; (*rammen*) ram; *Sport*:
die Kugel ~ put the shot; *Zucker
usw.*: pound; ~ *aus dem Hause*, e-m
Verein usw.: expel from, turn out
of; *j-n in die Rippen* ~ nudge a p.;
von sich ~ push away, reject; *s.
Kopf*; *sich* ~ *an* (*dat.*) strike (*od.*
knock *od.* run) against, *fig.* take
offen|ce (*Am.* -se) at, stick at, ob-
ject to; *v/i.* **a**) thrust; kick; butt (*a.
v/t.*; *alle*: *nach* at); *Gewehr*: recoil;
Wagen: jolt, bump; *an et.* (*acc.*) ~
(*grenzen*) adjoin, border (*od.* abut)
on; *ins Horn* ~ blow the horn;
b) (sn) ~ *auf* (*acc.*) (happen to)

meet, run into *a p.*, (*entdecken*)
come across, stumble on; *auf Ablehnung, Widerstand usw.*: meet
with, encounter; *zu j-m* ~ join (up
with); **c**) (h. *u.* sn) ~ *gegen od. an*
(*acc.*) knock (*od.* strike) against.
'**Stoß|fänger** *m s.* *Stoßdämpfer*;
'fest shockproof; 'gebet *n* fast
(*od.* ejaculatory) prayer; 'hobel
⊕ *m* (cooper's) jointer; 'kante *f*
hem, edge, lining; 'keil ⚔ *m*
spearhead; 'kraft *f* ⊕ impact
(force) *weitS.* impetus, force; '-
kugel *f Sport*: shot; 'seufzer *m*
deep sigh, groan; 'sicher shockproof; 'stange *f mot.* bumper; 🚗
buffer bar; 'trupp ⚔ *m* raiding
patrol, assault party; 'truppe ⚔ *f*
shock troops *pl.*; 'verkehr *m* rush-
-hour traffic; 'weise intermittently; in waves; 'zahn *m* tusk; 'zeit *f*
rush hour.
Stotter|er ['ʃtɔtərər] *m* (7) stutterer,
stammerer; 'n *v/i.* *v/t.* (29) stut-
ter, stammer; F *auf* kaufen buy on
the never-never.
stracks [ʃtraks] directly.
'**Straf|-anstalt** *f* penal institution,
prison; *Am.* (*Zuchthaus*) peniten-
tiary; '-antrag *m* private application (by the injured party); *des
Staatsanwaltes*: sentence demanded
by the public prosecutor; '-an-
zeige *f*: ~ *erstatten gegen* bring a
(criminal) charge against; '-arbeit
f Schule: imposition, F lines *pl.*
'**strafbar** punishable; *stärker*: criminal; (*schuldig*) culpable; *sich* ~
machen make o.s. liable to prosecution; 'keit *f* punishableness.
'**Strafbefehl** ⚖ *m* order of summary
punishment.
Strafe ['ʃtra:fə] *f* (15) punishment;
⚖, ✝, *Sport, fig.*: penalty; (*Geld*)
fine; (*Strafurteil*) sentence; *bei* ~
von on pain (*od.* penalty) of; ~ *zahlen* ⚖ pay a fine; 'n (25) punish;
bsd. Sport, a. fig. penalize; (*züchtigen*) chastise; *um Geld* ~ fine; *s.
Lüge, Verachtung*.
'**Straf|-entlassene** *m* (18) ex-con-
vict; '-erlaß *m* remission of (a)
punishment; *allgemeiner*: amnesty;
bedingter ~ conditional sentence;
'-expedition *f* punitive expedition.
straff [ʃtraf] tight; *Seil, Sehne,
Muskel*: taut; *Haltung*: erect; *fig.*

rigid, strict; *Stil*: concise; '2**heit** *f* tightness, *etc.*

'**straf|fällig** liable to prosecution; '~**frei** exempt from punishment; ~ *ausgehen* go unpunished; '2**gefangene** *m* convict; '2**gericht** *n* ṭⁿ̣ criminal court; *fig.* punishment; *göttliches*: judg(e)ment (of God); '2**gesetz** *n* penal law; '2**gesetzbuch** *n* penal code; '2**kammer** *f* criminal division.

sträf|lich ['ʃtrɛːfliç] punishable, criminal (*a. weit S.*); (*unverzeihlich*) unpardonable; *adv. fig.* badly; '2**ling** ['~liŋ] *m* (3¹) convict.

'**Straf|liste** *f* police record; '2**los** *s. straffrei*; '~**mandat** ṭⁿ̣ *n* penalty, *Am.* ticket; '~**maß** *n* degree of punishment; '2**mildernd** extenuating, mitigating; '~**mündigkeit** *f* criminal capacity; '~**porto** *n s. Nachgebühr*; '~**predigt** *f* (severe) lecture; '~**prozeß** *m* criminal case (*od.* proceedings *pl.*), trial; '~**prozeß-ordnung** *f* Code of Criminal Procedure; '~**punkt** *m Sport*: bad point, penalty; '~**raum** *m Fußball*: penalty area; '~**recht** *n* criminal law; '2**rechtlich** criminal, penal; ~ *verfolgen* prosecute; '~**register** *n* penal record; '~**sache** *f* criminal case; '~**stoß** *m Fußball*: penalty kick; '~**tat** *f* (criminal) offen|ce, *Am.* -se; '~**täter** *m* (criminal) offender; '~**verfahren** *n* criminal procedure (*konkret*: proceedings *pl.*); '2**verschärfend** aggravating; '2**versetzen** *v/t.*, '~**versetzung** *f* transfer for disciplinary reasons; '~**verteidiger** *m* trial lawyer; '~**vollstreckung** *f*, '~**vollzug** *m* execution of the sentence; '~**vollzugsbeamte** *m* prison officer; '2**würdig** *s. sträflich*; '~**zettel** *m für falsches Parken*: parking ticket.

Strahl [ʃtraːl] *m* (5) ray (*a. fig. of hope*); (*Licht*2) *a.* beam; (*Blitz*2) flash; (*Wasser*2, *Luft*2, *Gas*2) jet; ⚕ radius; '~**antrieb** ⚙ *m* jet propulsion; '2**en** (25) radiate; (*a. fig.*) beam, shine (*vor dat.* with).

'**Strahlen|behandlung** *f* radiotherapy; '2**brechend** refractive; '~**brechung** *f* refraction; '2**d** radiating; *a. fig.* radiant, beaming; 2-**förmig** ['~fœrmiç] radial; '~**forschung** *phys. f* radiology; '~**heilkunde** *f* radiotherapeutics *pl.*; '~**krone** *f* glory, halo, nimbus; '~-

schutz *m* radiation protection.

'**Strahler** *m* (7) *phys.* emitter; (*Wärme*2, *Heiz*2) radiator; (*Punktleuchte*) spotlight.

'**strahl|ig** radiate; '2-**ofen** *m* radiator; '2**rohr** ⚒ *n* jet pipe; '2**triebwerk** *n* jet (propulsion) engine; '2**turbine** *f* turbo-jet.

'**Strahlung** *f* radiation; '~**s-energie** *f* radiation energy; '~**sschäden** *m/pl.* radiation damage *sg.*; '2**ssicher** radiation-proof.

Strähn|e ['ʃtrɛːnə] *f* (15) strand; *Garnmaß*: hank, skein; *Haar*: lock; '2**ig** wispy.

stramm [ʃtram] (*straff*) tight; (*kräftig*) strapping, stalwart; (*scharf, streng*) strict, stiff; *Arbeit*: hard; *Soldat, Ehrenbezeigung usw.*: smart; F *adv.* (*schnell, tüchtig*) smartly, briskly; '~**stehen** stand at attention.

Strampel|hös-chen ['ʃtrampəl-] *n* rompers *pl.*; '2**n** (29) kick (about), fidget, struggle; F (*radfahren*) pedal (away); '~**sack** *m* baby's sleeping bag.

Strand [ʃtrant] *m* (3) (sea-)shore, (*a. Bade*2) beach; '~**anzug** *m* beach suit; '~**bad** *n* bathing-beach, lido; 2**en** ['~dən] (26, sn) be stranded; *nur* ⚓ run ashore; *fig.* fail, *Mädchen*: go to the bad; ~**gut** ['ʃtrant-] *n* stranded goods *pl.*, jetsam; *fig.* ~ *des Lebens* derelict(s *pl.*); '~**hotel** *n* seaside hotel; '~**korb** *m* (canopied) beach-chair; '~**promenade** *f* promenade, *Am.* boardwalk; '~**räuber** *m* wrecker; '~**schuhe** *m/pl.* beach-shoes; '~**wächter** *m* life-guard.

Strang [ʃtraŋ] *m* (3³) cord (*a. anat.*); (*Seil*) rope; *zum Anschirren*: trace; (*Garn*2) skein, hank; ⛓ (*Schienen*2) track; *fig. über die Stränge schlagen* kick over the traces; *an e-m* ~ *ziehen* pull together; *wenn alle Stränge reißen* as a last resort, if all else fails; '~**presse** ⊕ *f* extrusion press.

strangulieren [ʃtraŋgu'liːrən] strangle.

Strapaz|e [ʃtra'paːtsə] *f* (15) strain; 2**ieren** [~pa'tsiːrən] strain (*a. fig.*); exhaust; *sich* ~ exert o.s.; *Stoff*: wear hard, F punish; 2**ierfähig** [~'tsiːrfɛːiç] for hard wear; *nur attr.* hard-wearing; 2**iös** [~'tsjøːs] exhausting, trying.

Straße ['ʃtraːsə] f (15) road, high-way; e-r Stadt: street; (Meerenge) strait, bei Namen mst Straits pl.; ⊕ (Fertigungs♀ usw.) line; auf der ~ on the road; in Städten usw.: in (Am. on) the street; auf die ~ setzen turn out, sack; s. Mann.

'**Straßen|-anzug** m lounge suit, Am. business suit; '**~-arbeiten** f/pl. road works; '**~-arbeiter** m roadworker, Am. road laborer; '**~bahn** f tram; (~linie) tram(way), Am. trolley line; s. ~wagen; '**~bahnführer** m tram-driver, Am. motorman; '**~bahn-wagen** m tram(-car), Am. streetcar; '**~bau** m road construction; '**~belag** m road surfacing; '**~beleuchtung** f street-lighting; '**~café** n pavement (Am. sidewalk) café; '**~damm** m roadway; '**~dirne** f streetwalker; '**~graben** m (road) ditch; '**~händler** m street-vendor; '**~junge** m street urchin; '**~kampf** m street-fighting; '**~karte** f road map; '**~kehrer** m, a. '**~kehrmaschine** f street-sweeper; '**~kreuzer** mot. m road cruiser, Am. sl. heap; '**~kreuzung** f (street-)crossing; '**~lage** mot. f road-holding; '**~laterne** f streetlight, streetlamp; '**~mädchen** n streetwalker; '**~netz** n network of roads; '**~raub** m highway robbery; '**~räuber** m highwayman; '**~reinigung** f street-cleaning, scavenging; '**~rennen** n Sport: road race; '**~sammlung** f street collection; '**~schild** n street (od. road) sign; '**~sperre** f road block; '**~tunnel** m vehicular tunnel; '**~-überführung** f overpass; '**~-unterführung** f subway, underpass; '**~verkehr** m road (od. street) traffic; '**~verkehrs-ordnung** f Highway Code; '**~walze** f road-roller; '**~zustand** m road conditions pl.

Strateg|e [ʃtra'teːgə] m (13) strategist; '**~ie** [~teˈgiː] f (15, o. pl.) strategy; ♀**isch** [~ˈteːgiʃ] strategic(al).

Stratosphäre [strato'sfɛːrə] f (15) stratosphere; '**~nkreuzer** m stratocruiser, stratoliner.

sträuben ['ʃtrɔybən] 1. (25) ruffle; bristle; sich ~ Haar: stand on end, bristle (up); fig. struggle, strive (gegen against); 2. ♀ struggling, resistance.

Strauch [ʃtraux] m (1², pl. Sträucher ['ʃtrɔyçər]) shrub, bush; '**~dieb** m footpad.

straucheln ['ʃtrauxəln] (29, sn) (a. fig.) stumble, trip; fig. founder, come to grief.

'**Strauchwerk** n shrubs pl.

Strauß[1] [ʃtraus] m (3²) (Vogel) ostrich; ~² m (3² u. ³) (Streit) strife, struggle, (Zweikampf) duel, (Fehde) feud (a. fig.); ~³ m (Blumen♀) bunch (of flowers); bouquet; '**~enfeder** f ostrich-feather.

Strebe ⊕ ['ʃtreːbə] f (15) prop, stay, support; (Quer♀) crossbeam; ⊕, ⚒ usw. (△ a. '**~balken** m) strut.

'**streben** 1. (25) strive, aspire (nach after), struggle (for); (sich anstrengen) endeavo(u)r; F Schule: sl. swot; ~ nach (bezwecken) aim at, pursue; zu ... hin ~, nach e-r Richtung ~ tend to(wards), marschieren usw.: make for; 2. ♀ n (6) striving (nach after), aspiration (for, after); pursuit (of); (Anstrengung) effort, endeavo(u)r; (Ehrgeiz) ambition.

'**Strebepfeiler** m buttress.

'**Streber** m (7) pusher, careerist, Am. contp. place-hunter, gesell-schaftlicher: tuft-hunter, Am. F (social) climber; Schule: sl. swot; '**~tum** n (1¹, o. pl.) pushing.

strebsam ['ʃtreːpzaːm] assiduous; aspiring; ambitious; ♀**keit** f assi-duity; ambition.

'**streckbar** extensible; (dehnbar) ductile; (hämmerbar) malleable.

Strecke ['ʃtrekə] f (15) stretch; (Gegend) tract, extent; (Entfernung; a. Sport) distance; (Renn♀) course; ⚗ straight line; 🚌, ⚓, ⚒, teleph. line; ⚒ roadway; hunt. bag; zur ~ bringen shoot down, bag, fig. hunt down; auf der ~ bleiben break down, fig. a. fail, (sterben) perish; '♀**n** (25) stretch, extend; Speise, Vorrat: eke (od. spin) out; j-n zu Boden ~ fell; die Waffen ~ lay down one's arms; s. Decke, gestreckt.

'**Strecken|-arbeiter** 🚌 m plate-layer; '**~wärter** 🚌 m lineman, Am. trackman; '♀**weise** here and there.

'**Streck|muskel** anat. m extensor (muscle); '**~verband** ⚕ m exten-sion bandage; im ~ in high traction.

Streich [ʃtraiç] m (3) stroke, blow; fig. trick, prank; j-m e-n ~ spielen play a p. a trick; auf 'einen ~ at a blow.

streicheln ['ʃtraiçəln] (29) stroke, (a. fig.) caress.

'**streich|en** (30) *v/t.* stroke, rub
gently; *Butter, Pflaster*: spread;
(*glätten,* a. ⊕) sleek, smooth; *Messer*: whet; *Rasiermesser*: strop;
Zündhölzchen: strike (*an acc.*
against); (*an⌣*) paint, *a.* ⊕ coat;
s. frisch; (*aus⌣*) strike (*od.* cross)
out *od.* off, *bsd. fig.* cancel; *Flagge,
Segel*: strike, lower; *Sport: Meldung* ⌣ scratch; *Ziegel*: make;
Wolle: card; ♪ *Geige usw.*: play;
gestrichen voll brimful; *drei gestri-
chene Eßlöffel* three level table-
-spoons; *v/i.* **a)** (sn) (*sich erstrecken*)
extend, sweep, run; (*vorbei⌣*) pass
(*vorbei an j-m* a p.), move, rush
(past); (*über, durch, gegen et. hin⌣*)
sweep (over, through, towards (*a.
Vogel*); (*wandern*) roam, ramble;
Raubtier, Verbrecher: prowl; *s.
streifen*² ; **b)** (h.) *mit der Hand über
et.* ⌣ pass one's hand over a th.;
'**℗er** ♪ *m/pl. the* strings.
'**Streich|holz** *n,* ⌣**hölzchen** ['⌣-
hœltsçən] *n* match, *Am.* F match-
stick; '⌣**holzschachtel** *f* match-
-box; '⌣**instrument** ♪ *n* stringed
instrument; *die* ⌣*e in e-m Orchester*:
the strings; '⌣**käse** *m* cheese spread;
'⌣**orchester** ♪ *n* string orchestra;
'⌣**quartett** ♪ *n* string quartet(te);
⌣**riemen** *m* razor-strop; '⌣**ung** *f*
cancellation (*a. fig.*); *typ.* deletion;
(*Kürzung*) cut; '⌣**wurst** *f etwa* meat
paste.
Streif [ʃtraif] *m* (3), '⌣**en**¹ *m* (6)
stripe, streak; (*Gelände℗; Film℗*)
strip; (*Film*) film; '⌣**band** *n* (postal)
wrapper; *unter* ⌣ by book-post;
'⌣**blick** *m* (brief) glance; '⌣**e** *f* (15)
(*Polizei℗,* a. ✗) patrol; (*Razzia*)
raid; '℗**en**² (25) *v/t.* stripe, streak;
(*ab⌣*) strip off; (*berühren*) graze,
brush, *Thema*: touch; *v/i.* (sn)
(*wandern*) roam, range (*a. Blick*);
(h.) *fig.* ⌣ *an* (*acc.*) border on; '⌣**en-
polizist** *m bsd. Am.* patrolman;
'⌣**enwagen** *m der Polizei*: patrol
(*Am.* squad *od.* prowl, *Brt.* panda)
car; '℗**ig** striped; '⌣**licht** *n* side-light;
'⌣**schuß** *m* grazing shot; '⌣**zug** *m*
(roving) expedition, raid.
Streik [ʃtraik] *m* (3 *u.* 11) strike, *Am.*
F walkout; *in* (*den*) ⌣ *treten* go on
strike; '⌣**-aufruf** *m* strike call; '⌣-
brecher *m* strike-breaker, blackleg,
scab; '℗**en** (25) (be *od.* go on) strike,
Am. F walk out; F *fig.* (*sich weigern*)

rebel; *Gerät usw.*: refuse to work;
'⌣**ende** *m* (18) striker; '⌣**geld** *n*
strike-pay; '⌣**kasse** *f* strike-fund; '⌣-
posten *m* picket; ⌣ *stehen* picket;
'⌣**recht** *n* freedom to strike; '⌣**welle** *f*
series of strikes.
Streit [ʃtrait] *m* (3) quarrel; (*bsd.
Wort℗*) dispute, argument; *lauter,
handgreiflicher*: brawl, F row; (*Gezänk*) squabble; (*Kampf*) fight;
conflict, strife; (*Fehde*) feud; *in* ⌣
geraten mit (have a) quarrel with;
s. suchen; *e-n* ⌣ *vom Zaun brechen*
pick a quarrel; '⌣**-axt** *f* battle-ax(e);
'℗**bar** pugnacious; '℗**en** (30) (*a.
sich*) *s. Streit*: quarrel; dispute,
argue; fight; *darüber läßt sich* ⌣ that's
a moot point (*od.* open to argument);
'⌣**er** *m* (7), '⌣**erin** *f* quarrel(l)er;
combatant; fighter; (*Vorkämpfer*)
champion; '⌣**fall** *m* quarrel; controversy; '⌣**frage** *f* (point at) issue,
(point of) controversy; '⌣**gegenstand** ⚖ *m* matter in dispute; '℗**ig**
(*bestreitbar*) contestable, debatable,
disputable, controversial; (*umstritten*) contested, *pred.* in dispute, at
issue; *j-m et.* ⌣ *machen* dispute a p.'s
right to; *s. Rang*; '⌣**igkeit** *f s. Streit*;
'⌣**kräfte** *f/pl.* (armed) forces; '℗**lustig** belligerent; '⌣**punkt** *m s. Streitfrage*; '⌣**sache** *f s. Streitfall*; ⚖ case,
litigation; '⌣**schrift** *f* polemic pamphlet; '⌣**sucht** *f* quarrelsomeness;
℗**süchtig** ['⌣zyçtiç] quarrelsome; '⌣-
wert ⚖ *m* value in dispute.
streng [ʃtrɛŋ] (*Ggs. mild*) severe,
rigorous (*a. von der Kälte*), stern;
(*hart*) harsh (*a. Geschmack*); *Sitte,
Stil usw.*: austere; (*scharf, bestimmt*)
strict (*gegen j-n* with); ⌣ *geheim*
top secret; ⌣ *vertraulich* strictly
confidential; ⌣ *verboten* strictly forbidden; '℗**e** *f* (15) *s. streng*: severity, rigo(u)r; austerity; strictness;
harshness; '⌣**genommen** strictly
speaking; '⌣**gläubig** orthodox.
Streß [ʃtrɛs] ✺ *m* (3²) stress.
Streu [ʃtrɔy] *f* (15) litter; *für Menschen*: bed of straw; '⌣**büchse** *f für
Gewürz usw.*: castor; *für Mehl*:
dredger; '℗**en** (25) *v/t.* strew; (*um-
her⌣*) scatter; *v/i. Schußwaffe*:
scatter, ✗ *absichtlich*: sweep; ♂
stray; *dem Vieh*: litter (down) *the
cattle*; *s. Sand*.
streuen ['ʃtrɔynən] roam about,
rove, stray.

'**Streu|sand** *m* dry sand; *für Tinte*: writing sand; '**~zucker** *m* castor sugar.
Strich [ʃtriç] **1.** *m* (3) stroke; (*Linie*) line; (*Gedanken♀*, *Morse♀*) dash; (*Streif*) stripe; (*Land♀*) region, tract; (*Kompaß♀*) point; *der Vögel*: flight; ♪ (*Bogenführung*) bowing; (*Pinsel♀*) touch; *des Holzes usw.*: grain; F *j-n auf dem ~ haben* have it in for a p.; F *auf den ~ gehen* walk the streets; *j-m e-n ~ durch die Rechnung machen* cross a p.'s plans; F *fig. das ging mir gegen den ~* it rubbed me the wrong way; *e-n (dicken) ~ unter e-e S. machen* make a clean break with a th.; *nach ~ und Faden* thoroughly; **2.** ♀ *pret. v. streichen*; '**~ätzung** *f* line-plate; '**~einteilung** *f* graduation; **♀eln** (29) dot; (*schraffieren*) hatch; '**~junge** F *m* male prostitute; '**~mädchen** F *n* streetwalker; '**~punkt** *m* semicolon; '**~regen** *m* local shower; '**~vogel** *m* migratory bird, visitant; '**♀weise** by strokes; *s. streckenweise*; '**~zeichnung** *f* line drawing.
Strick [ʃtrik] *m* (3) cord, line; (*Seil*) rope; *s. Strang*; F *fig.* young rascal; *wenn alle ~e reißen* if all else fails; '**♀en** *v/t. u. v/i.* (25) knit; '**~er(in** *f*) *m* knitter; '**~garn** *n* knitting-yarn; '**~jacke** *f* cardigan; '**~leiter** *f* rope-ladder; '**~maschine** *f* knitting-machine; '**~nadel** *f* knitting-needle; '**~waren** *f/pl.* knit(ted) goods *pl.*; '**~weste** *f* cardigan (sweater); '**~wolle** *f* knitting wool; '**~zeug** *n* knitting (things *pl.*).
Striegel ['ʃtriːgəl] *m* (7) curry-comb; '**♀n** (29) curry.
Strieme ['ʃtriːmə] *f* (15), '**~en** *m* (6) stripe, streak; *in der Haut*: wale, weal; '**♀ig** streaked; *Haut*: covered with wales.
strikt [ʃtrikt] strict(ly *adv.*).
Strippe F ['ʃtripə] *f* (15) strap; (*Schnur*) string; F (tele)phone.
stritt [ʃtrit] *pret. v. streiten*.
strittig ['ʃtritiç] *s. streitig*; *der ~e Punkt* the point at issue.
Stroh [ʃtroː] *n* (3) straw; (*Dach♀*) thatch; *fig. leeres ~ dreschen* talk hot air; '**~dach** *n* thatch(ed roof); '**♀farben**, '**♀gelb** straw-colo(u)red; '**~feuer** *fig. n* short-lived passion; '**~halm** *m* (blade of) straw; *fig. nach e-m ~ greifen* catch at a straw; '**~hut** *m* straw hat; '**♀ig**

strawy; '**~kopf** *m* empty head; '**~mann** *m* man of straw; *fig. a.* dummy, front; '**~sack** *m* straw mattress, pallet; '**~matte** *f* straw mat; '**~witwe(r** *m*) *f* F grass-widow(er).
Strolch [ʃtrɔlç] *m* (3) tramp, *Am. sl.* bum; (*Lump*) *a.* blackguard, *Am.* F hoodlum; *a. co.* scamp; '**♀en** (h. *u.* sn) roam, ramble, loaf about.
Strom [ʃtroːm] *m* (3³) stream, (large) river; (*Strömung*) current (*a. ⚡ u. fig.*), (*a. Menschen♀*) stream; ⚡ *a.* power; (*Blut♀, Verkehrs♀*) flow; *v. Tränen, Worten*: flood; ⚡ *unter ~ live*; *gegen den ~ schwimmen* (*a.fig.*) swim against the current; *es regnet in Strömen* it is pouring with rain; '**~abnehmer** ⚡ *m* (current) collector; ♀'**~ab(wärts)** downstream; ♀'**~auf(wärts)** upstream; '**~ausfall** *m* power failure; '**~bedarf** *m* electricity requirement.
strömen ['ʃtrøːmən] (25, h. *u.* sn) stream, flow; *Regen*: pour; (*sich drängen*) flock, crowd.
Stromer ['ʃtroːmər] *m* (7) *s. Strolch*.
'**Strom|-ersparnis** *f* electricity saving; '**~erzeuger** ⚡ *m* dynamo, generator; (*E-Werk*) power station; '**~erzeugung** *f* power generation; '**♀führend** ⚡ live; '**~gebiet** *n* (river-)basin; '**~kreis** ⚡ *m* (electric) circuit; '**~leiter** ⚡ *m* current conductor; '**~linie(nform)** *f* streamline(d design); **♀linienförmig** ['~fœrmiç] streamline(d); '**~netz** *n* mains supply; '**~schiene** ⚡ *f* contact rail; '**~schnelle** *f* rapid; '**~spannung** ⚡ *f* voltage; '**♀sparend** electricity-saving; '**~sperre** *f* power cut; '**~stärke** ⚡ *f* current (intensity); amperage.
'**Strömung** *f* (16) current; *fig. a.* trend.
'**Strom|-unterbrecher** ⚡ *m* circuit-breaker; '**~verbrauch** *m* current consumption; '**~versorgung** ⚡ *f* power supply; '**~wandler** ⚡ *m* (7) current transformer; '**~wender** ⚡ *m* (7) commutator; '**~zähler** ⚡ *m* electric meter. [verse.)
Strophe ['ʃtroːfə] *f* (15) stanza,)
strotzen ['ʃtrɔtsən] (27) exuberate; *~ von, vor* (*dat.*) abound in; (*wimmeln von*) teem with; *vor Gesundheit usw.* burst with; '**~d** exuberant; *~ von, vor* (*dat.*) abundant in.
strubbelig F ['ʃtrubəliç] unkempt, dishevel(l)ed; shock-headed.

'**Strudel** *m* (7) **1.** swirl, whirlpool, vortex; **2.** (*Gebäck*) (pastry-)roll; '♀n (29, h. *u.* sn) swirl, whirl.

Struktur [ʃtruk'tuːr] *f* (16) structure; ♀ell [‿tu'rel] structural.

Strumpf [ʃtrumpf] *m* (3³) stocking; (*Glüh♀*) mantle; ✝ (*lange*) Strümpfe *pl.* hose; '♵band *n* garter; '♵halter *m* suspender, *Am.* garter; '♵haltergürtel *m* suspender (*Am.* garter) belt; '♵hose *f* tights *pl.*, pantyhose; '♵waren *f/pl.* hosiery.

Strunk [ʃtruŋk] *m* (3³) stalk; (*Baum♀*) stump, trunk.

struppig ['ʃtrupiç] *Haar:* rough; *Bart:* bristly; *Hund:* shaggy.

Struwwel|kopf ['ʃtruvəl-] *m* shock head; '♵peter *m* shock-headed Peter.

Strychnin [ʃtryç'niːn] *n* (11) strychnine.

Stube ['ʃtuːbə] *f* (15) room.

'**Stuben|-arrest** *m* confinement to one's room; ⚔ arrest in quarters; '♵fliege *f* common (house) fly; '♵gelehrsamkeit *f* book-learning, bookishness; '♵gelehrte *m* bookworm; '♵hocker *m*, '♵sitzer *m* stay-at-home; '♵kamerad *m* room-mate; '♵mädchen *n* parlo(u)r-maid; *Hotel:* chambermaid; '♀rein *Tier:* house-trained, *Am.* housebroken.

Stuck [ʃtuk] *m* (3) stucco.

Stück [ʃtyk] *n* (3; *als Maß nach Zahlen inv.*) piece (*a.* ♪, *paint. usw.*); (*Bißchen*) bit; (*Bissen*) morsel; (*Teil♀*) part; (*Bruch♀*) fragment; *Vieh:* head; *Zucker:* lump; *thea.* play; (~ *Land*) piece of land, plot; (~ *Weg*) stretch, distance; (*Text*) passage, part; (*Handlung*) act; F (*Person*) type; ~ *Arbeit* job; ~ *für* ~ piece by piece; *aus* e-m ~ all of a piece; *aus freien* ♵en of one's own free will; *in vielen* ♵en in many respects; *in* ♵e *gehen* go to pieces; *in* ♵e *schlagen* smash (to bits); *ein schönes* ♵ *Geld* a nice little sum; *große* ♵e *halten auf* (*acc.*) think highly of; *das ist ein starkes* ♵! that's a bit thick!; '♵arbeit *f* piece-work; '♵arbeiter(in *f*) *m* piece-worker; '♵chen *n* (6) small piece etc. (*s.* Stück); *fig.* (*Streich*) trick; (*Kunst♀*) stunt; '♀eln (29) *v.* zerstückeln; (*flicken*) piece (together); '♵fracht *f*, '♵gut *n* mixed cargo;

'♵kosten *pl.* unit cost *sg.*; '♵lohn *m* piece-wage(s *pl.*); '♵preis *m* price per unit; '♀weise piecemeal; ✝ *by the piece*; '♵werk *n* contp. patchwork; '♵zahl *f* number of pieces.

Student [ʃtu'dɛnt] *m* (12), ♵in *f* (16¹) (*f* woman) student, (*f* girl) undergraduate; ♵en-ausweis *m* student card; ♵enschaft *f* (body of) students *pl.*; ♵enverbindung *f* students' club, *Am.* fraternity; ♵enwohnheim *n* student hostel.

Studie ['ʃtuːdjə] *f* (15) *paint. usw.:* study; *e-s Schriftstellers:* sketch, essay; ♵n *pl. s.* Studium; '♵nberatung *f* student guidance (service); '♵nbewerber(in *f*) *m* university applicant; '♵ndirektor(in *f*) *m* headmaster (headmistress) of a secondary school, *Am.* high-school principal; '♵nfach *n* subject; '♵ngang *m*, '♵nplan *m* course of studies; curriculum; '♵njahr *n* academic year; ♵e *pl. s.* Studienzeit; '♵nplatz *m* university place; '♵nrat (♵rätin ['♵rɛːtin] *f* [16]) *m* (assistant) master (mistress) of a secondary school; '♵nreise *f* informative trip; '♵nzeit *f* years *pl.* of study; college days *pl.*

studier|en [ʃtu'diːrən] *v/i. u. v/t.* study (*a. weitS. lesen, betrachten usw.*); (*die Hochschule besuchen*) go to college; ~ *lassen* send to college; ♀te *m* (18) university man; ♀zimmer *n* study.

Studio ['ʃtuːdjo] *n* (11) studio.

Studium ['ʃtuːdjum] *n* (9) study; (*a. pl.* Studien) studies *pl.*

Stufe ['ʃtuːfə] *f* (15) step; *fig.* (*Entwicklungs♀ usw.*; *a.* ⊕, *e-r Rakete*) stage; (*Grad*) degree (*a. gr.*); (*Niveau*) level, standard; (*Rang*) rank; (*Farb♀*) shade; *auf gleicher* ~ *mit* on a par with.

'**stufen|-artig**, '♵förmig step-like; *fig.* graduated, graded; '♀barren *m Turnen:* asymmetrical bars *pl.*; '♀folge *f*, '♀gang *m* gradation, succession; '♀leiter *f* stepladder; *fig.* scale; '♵los: ⊕ ~ (*regelbar*) infinitely variable; '♵weise gradually, by degrees.

Stuhl [ʃtuːl] *m* (3³) chair; seat; (*Kirchen♀*) pew; (*Web♀*) loom; ✦ (*Kot*) stool, *s.* ♵gang; *eccl. der Heilige* ~ the Holy See; *fig. sich zwischen zwei Stühle setzen* fall between two stools; '♵bein *n* leg of a chair; '**~gang** ⚡ *m* motion, bowel movement; ~ *haben* go to stool, *regelmäßig*: have open bowels; '**~lehne** *f* back of chair.

Stulle F ['ʃtulə] *f* (15) slice of bread (and butter), sandwich.

Stulpe ['ʃtulpə] *f* (15) (*Stiefel*♀) top; (*Manschette*) cuff.

stülpen ['ʃtylpən] (25) turn (*hoch*: up); *Hut*: clap (*auf acc.* on), *schief*: cock.

'**Stulp(en)stiefel** *m* top-boot.

'**Stulp(en)handschuh** *m* gauntlet.

'**Stülpnase** *f* turn(ed)-up nose.

stumm [ʃtum] dumb, mute (*beide a. fig.*); (*still*) silent (*a. gr.*); (*sprachlos*) speechless (*vor dat.* with).

Stummel ['ʃtuməl] *m* (7) (*Arm*♀, *Baum*♀ *usw.*) stump; (*Zigaretten*♀) (fag) end, *Am.* butt, stub.

'**Stummfilm** *m* silent film.

Stümper ['ʃtympər] *m* (7), '**~in** *f* bungler; **~ei** [~'raɪ] *f* (16) bungling; '♀**haft** bungling, clumsy; '♀**n** *v/i. u. v/t.* (29) bungle, botch.

stumpf[1] [ʃtumpf] blunt; *Winkel*: obtuse; *Kegel*: truncate(d); *Geist, Auge usw.*: obtuse, dull; (*teilnahmslos*) apathetic (*ally adv.*).

Stumpf[2] *m* (3³) stump (*a. Arm*♀ *usw.*); *mit ~ und Stiel* root and branch; '**~heit** *f* bluntness; *fig.* dullness; '**~sinn** *m* stupidity, dullness; '♀**sinnig** stupid, dull; '♀**wink(e)lig** obtuse-angled.

Stunde ['ʃtundə] *f* (15) hour; (*Unterricht*) lesson, *Am.* (*Schul*♀) period; *fig. in letzter ~* at the eleventh hour; *zur ~* at this hour; *bis zur ~* as yet; *mot. 50 Meilen in der ~* 50 miles per hour; '♀**n** (26): (*j-m*) *e-e Zahlung ~* grant (a p.) delay (*od. a* respite) for payment.

'**Stunden|geschwindigkeit** *f* speed per hour; '**~glas** *n* hour-glass; '**~kilometer** *m/pl.* kilomet|res (*Am.* -ers) per hour; '♀**lang** *adv.* (*adj.* lasting) for hours; '**~lohn** *m* wage(s *pl.*) per hour; '**~plan** *m* time-table, curriculum, *Am.* schedule; '♀**weise** by the hour; '**~zeiger** *m* hour-hand.

Stünd|lein ['ʃtyntlaɪn] *n* (6): *letztes ~* last hour; '♀**lich** hourly, every hour, per hour.

'**Stundung** *f* respite, delay.

Stunk [ʃtuŋk] F *m* (3, *o. pl.*): ~ *machen sl.* raise a stink.

stupid(e) [ʃtu'piːt, -də] stupid, idiotic.

stups|en ['ʃtupsən] (27) nudge; '♀**nase** *f* snub nose; '**~nasig** snub-nosed.

stur [ʃtuːr] (*störrisch*) stubborn, mulish; (*stumpf*) stolid; (*geisttötend*) dull; *Blick*: fixed.

Sturm [ʃturm] *m* (3³) storm (*a.fig.*); ⚓ gale; ✗ assault; *Fußball*: forwards *pl.*; ~ *und Drang* storm and stress; ~ *auf* (*acc.*) ✝ rush for *goods*, run on *a bank*; ~ *der Entrüstung* outcry; ~ *laufen gegen* assault, assail (*beide a. fig.*); *im ~ erobern* take by storm (*a. fig.*); ~ *im Wasserglas* storm in a teacup; '**~boot** ✗ *n* assault boat.

stürm|en ['ʃtyrmən] (25) *v/t.* storm (*a. fig. u.* ✗); *v/i.* **a**) (h.) ✗ assault; *Wind*: rage, roar, storm (*alle a.fig. zürnen*); *es stürmt* it is stormy weather; **b**) (sn) (*rennen*) rush; '♀**er** *m* (7) *Fußball*: forward; '♀**erreihe** *f Fußball*: forward line.

'**Sturm|flut** *f* storm tide; '**~geschütz** ✗ *n* (self-propelled) assault gun; '**~glocke** *f* tocsin.

'**stürmisch** stormy; *fig.* (*ungestüm*) impetuous; (*lärmend, tosend*) tumultuous, uproarious; (*leidenschaftlich*) tempestuous; (*schnell*) rapid.

'**sturm|reif**: ~ *machen* soften up; '♀**schritt** *m*: ✗ *u. allg. im ~* at the double; '♀**spitze** *f Fußball*: spearhead; '♀**vogel** *m* (stormy) petrel; '♀**warnung** *f* gale warning; '♀**wind** *m* heavy gale; '♀**wolke** *f* storm cloud.

Sturz [ʃturts] *m* (3² *u.* ³) (sudden) fall, *tiefer*: plunge, *lauter*: crash; (*Untergang*) ruin, (down)fall; *e-r Regierung usw.*: overthrow; *Börse*: slump; (*Ungnade*) disgrace; *s.* **Temperatursturz**; '**~acker** *m* new-ploughed (*Am.* -plowed) field; '**~bach** *m* torrent.

stürzen ['ʃtyrtsən] (27) *v/i.* (sn) fall, tumble, *krachend*: crash, *tief, ins Wasser, a. Preise*: plunge; (*vorwärts~, eilen*) rush; *Abgrund*: descend precipitously; *v/t.* precipitate; (*tauchen*) plunge; (*werfen*) throw; *Regierung usw.*: overthrow; *nicht ~!* (*Aufschrift auf Kisten*) this side up!; *sich auf j-n ~* rush at, *e-e Arbeit usw.*: throw o.s. into, pounce (up)on; *ins Elend ~* ruin; *in e-n*

Krieg ~ plunge into a war; *sich in Unkosten* ~ put o.s. to expenses; *s. Schuld, Verderben.*

'**Sturz|flug** ✗ *m* (nose-)dive; e-n ~ machen dive; '**~helm** *m* ✗, *mot.* crash helmet; '**~kampfflugzeug** *n* dive-bomber; '**~see** ⚓ *f* heavy sea; '**~welle** ⚓ *f:* e-e ~ *bekommen* ship a sea.

Stuß [ʃtus] F *m* (3², *o. pl.*) *s. Quatsch.*

Stute ['ʃtuːtə] *f* (15) mare; '**~nfüllen** *n* filly.

Stütz [ʃtyts] *f* (3²) *Turnen:* straight-arm rest; '**~balken** *m* supporting beam.

Stütze ['ʃtytsə] *f* (15) (*a. fig.*) support; prop, stay; ~ *der Hausfrau* lady help.

stutzen ['ʃtutsən] **1.** (27) *v/t.* cut (short), curtail (*a. fig.*); *Ohren:* crop; *Flügel, Hecke:* clip; *Bart:* trim; *Schwanz:* dock; *Baum:* lop; *v/i.* (*stutzig werden*) stop short, be startled, start; be puzzled; (*argwöhnisch werden*) become suspicious; **2.** ⚲ *m* (6) short rifle, carbine; ⊕ (*Rohransatz*) connecting piece; (*Düse*) nozzle.

stützen ['ʃtytsən] (27) (*a. fig.*) support, uphold; prop, stay; *Behauptung usw.:* ~ *auf* (*acc.*) base (*od.* found) on; *sich* ~ *auf* (*acc.*) lean (*od.* rest) on, *fig.* rely (*od.* base o.s.) on, *Urteil usw.:* be based on.

Stutz|er ['ʃtutsər] *m* (7) fop, dandy, *Am. a.* dude; '**2erhaft** foppish; '**~flügel** ♪ *m* miniature grand; '**2ig** startled, taken aback, perplexed; ~ *machen* startle, puzzle, (*Argwohn wecken*) make suspicious; ~ *werden s. stutzen v/i.*

'**Stütz|kurs** *m für schwache Schüler:* remedial instruction; '**~pfeiler** *m* supporting pillar, buttress; '**~punkt** *m* point of support; *fig.* foothold, (*bsd.* ✕) base; *taktisch:* strong point; (*Hebelpunkt*) fulcrum.

'**Stutz-uhr** *f* mantelpiece clock.

Styropor [ʃtyro'poːr] *n* (3¹, *o. pl.*) polystyrene.

subaltern [zup'ʔal'tɛrn] subordinate; *bsd.* ✕ subaltern.

Subjekt [zup'jɛkt] *n* (3) *gr.* subject; F *contp.* (*Person*) fellow, type; **2iv** [~'tiːf] subjective; **~ivität** [~tivi'tɛːt] *f* (16) subjectivity.

Subkultur ['zupkultuːr] *f* subculture.

subkutan [zupku'taːn] subcutaneous, hypodermic(ally *adv.*).

Subli|mat [zubli'maːt] *n* (3) sublimate; **2mieren** sublimate.

Submission ✝, ⚖ [zupmi'sjoːn] *f* (contract by) tender.

subskribieren [~skri'biːrən] subscribe (*auf acc.* to).

Subskription [~skrip'tsjoːn] *f* subscription; **~s-preis** *m* prepublication (*od.* subscription) price.

substantiell [zupstan'tsjɛl] substantial.

Substantiv ['~stantiːf] *n* (3¹) substantive, noun; **2isch** [~'tiːviʃ] substantival.

Substanz [~'stants] *f* (16) substance.

subtil [zup'tiːl] subtle.

subtra|hieren [~tra'hiːrən] subtract; **2ktion** [~trak'tsjoːn] *f* subtraction.

subtropisch ['zup-] subtropical.

Subvention [~ven'tsjoːn] *f* subsidy; **2ieren** [~tsjo'niːrən] subsidize.

Such|-aktion ['zuːx-] *f* search; '**~anzeige** *f* want ad(vertisement); '**~dienst** *m* tracing service; '**~e** *f* (15) search, *stärker:* hunt (*nach* for); *auf der* ~ *nach* in search (*od.* quest) of, on the look-out for; '**2en** (25) *v/t.* (*u. v/i.* ~ *nach*) search for, *bsd. weitS.* seek (*advice, etc.*); *schauend u. weitS.:* look for; *aufgeregt:* hunt for; *Fehler, Vermißte:* trace; *nur v/t.* (*wünschen*) want; ~ *zu inf.* (*sich bemühen*) seek to, try to; *Streit* ~ pick a quarrel; *Sie haben hier nichts zu* ~ you have no business to be here; *s. Rat, Weite, gesucht;* '**~er** *m* (7) seeker (*a. weitS. of truth, etc.*), searcher (*a.* '**~erin** *f*); *opt.* finder; *phot.* view-finder; (*a.* '**~gerät** *n*) detector; '**~kartei** *f* tracing file; '**~mannschaft** *f* search party; '**~scheinwerfer** *m* searchlight.

Sucht [zuxt] *f* (16) mania (*nach* for), *a. Rauschgift usw.:* addiction (to); (*Krankheit*) sickness, disease; '**2-erzeugend** ✽ habit-forming, addictive.

süchtig ['zyçtiç] (*e-m Rauschgift usw. verfallen*) addicted, *z. B.* morphium~ addicted to morphine; (*gierend*) craving; (*besessen*) maniac(al); **2e** ['~igə] *m, f* (18) addict.

'**Suchtmittel** *n* addictive drug.

Suchtrupp ['zu:x-] *m* search party.
Sud [zu:t] *m* (3) decoction.
Süd [zy:t] **1.** south; **2.** *poet. m* (3, *o. pl.*) south (wind); '2**deutsch,**
'~**deutsche** *m*, *f* South German.
Sudel|arbeit ['zu:dəl⁹arbaɪt], ~**ei**
[~'laɪ] *f* (16) dirty (*od. schlampig:*
slovenly) work; *paint.* daub; *Ge-schriebenes:* scrawl, scribble; '2**ig**
slovenly, dirty; '2**n** (29) *v/i. u. v/t.*
malend: daub; *schreibend:* scribble;
(*manschen*) mess about; (*pfuschen*)
botch.
Süden ['zy:dən] *m* (6) south; *im* ~
in the south, *e-r Stadt usw.*: (to the)
south (*gen.* of); *nach* ~ south(ward).
Süd|früchte ['zy:tfryçtə] *f/pl.* trop-ical fruit(s); '~**hang** *m* south(ern)
slope; '~**länder** *m* (7), '~**länderin** *f*
southerner; '2**ländisch** southern.
Sudler(in *f*) ['zu:dlər] *m s. sudeln:*
dauber; scribbler; botcher.
süd|lich ['zy:t-] south (*a. adv.*),
southern, southerly; ~ *von* south of;
2'-**ost(en)** *m* south-east; ~'-**östlich**
south-east(ern); '2**pol** *m* South
Pole; '~**wärts** ['~verts] south-ward(s); '2**wein** *m* sweet wine; 2-
'**west(en)** *m* southwest; 2'**wester** *m*
(7) southwester; ~'**westlich** south--western; '2**wind** *m* south wind.
Suff [zuf] *m* (3, *o. pl.*) boozing.
süffig ['zyfiç] tasty. [*adv.*).}
süffisant [syfi'zant] sarcastic(ally)}
suggerieren [zuge'ri:rən] suggest.
Suggestion [zuges'tjo:n] *f* sugges-tion.
suggestiv [~'ti:f] suggestive; 2-
frage *f* leading question.
Suhle *hunt.* ['zu:lə] *f* (15), '2**n:**
sich ~ wallow.
Sühn|e ['zy:nə] *f* (15) expiation,
atonement; '2**en** (25) expiate, atone
for; '~**etermin** 🕱 *m* conciliation
hearing; '~**opfer** *n* expiatory sac-rifice; '~**ung** *f s.* Sühne.
Suite ['svi:tə] *f* (15) suite (*a. ♩*),
retinue.
sukzessiv [zuktse'si:f] successive;
~**e** [~'si:və] *adv.* gradually.
Sulfonamid *pharm.* [zulfona'mi:t] *n*
sulphonamide.
Sultan ['zultɑ:n] *m* (3¹) sultan; '~**in**
f sultana; ~**ine** [~ta'ni:nə] *f* (15)
(*Rosine*) sultana.
Sülze ['zyltsə] *f* (15) aspic; jellied
meat; '2**n** (27) jelly.
summarisch [zu'mɑ:riʃ] summary.

Summ|e ['zumə] *f* (15) sum (*a.fig.*);
(*Gesamt*2) (sum) total; (*Betrag*)
amount; '2**en** (25) *v/t.* hum; *v/i.*
buzz, hum; *Ohr:* tingle; '~**er** ⚥ *m*
(7) buzzer; 2**ieren** [~'mi:rən] sum
(*od.* add); *sich* ~ run up.
Sumpf [zumpf] *m* (3⁸) swamp, bog,
marsh; *fig.* morass; *mot.* sump; '~**boden** *m* marshy ground; '~**fieber**
n malaria; '~**huhn** *n* moorhen; *fig.*
rake; (*Säufer*) boozer; '2**ig** boggy,
marshy, swampy; '~**land** *n* marsh-land; '~**pflanze** *f* marsh plant; '~**vogel** *m* wader. [fuss.}
Sums [zums] F *m* (3², *o. pl.*) (great)}
Sund [zunt] *m* (3) sound, strait.
Sünde ['zyndə] *f* (15) sin; '~**nbock**
m scapegoat; '~**n-erlaß** *m* absolu-tion; '~**nfall** *m* fall of man; '~**ngeld**
n ill-gotten money; (*Riesensumme*)
enormous sum; '~**nregister** *n* list
of misdeeds.
'**Sünd|er** *m* (7), '~**erin** *f* (16¹) sin-ner; *armer* ~ criminal under sen-tence of death, *fig.* poor wretch.
sündhaft ['zynt-] sinful; F ~ *teuer*
awfully expensive.
sündig ['zyndiç] sinful; ~**en** ['~di-gən] (25) sin (*an dat., gegen* against).
Super ['zu:pər] *n* (7, *o. pl.*) *s. Super-benzin;* 2 F *adj.* super, smashing;
'~**benzin** *n* super, *Am.* premium gas;
'2**klug** overwise; ~**er** *Mensch* wise-acre.
Superlativ ['~lati:f] *m* (3¹) super-lative (*degree bsd. gr.*); 2**isch** [~'ti:-viʃ] superlative.
'**Super|macht** *f* superpower; '~**markt** *m* supermarket.
Suppe ['zupə] *f* (15) soup; *fig.* F *die*
~ *auslöffeln* face the music; F *j-m*
die ~ *versalzen* give a p. what for.
'**Suppen|fleisch** *n* stock-meat; '~**grün** *n* greens *pl.*; '~**kelle** *f* dipper;
'~**kraut** *n* pot-herb; '~**löffel** *m*
soup-ladle; *zum Essen:* soup-spoon;
'~**schüssel** *f* (soup-)tureen; '~**teller** *m* soup-plate; '~**würfel** *m* soup
cube.
Support [zu'pɔrt] ⊕ *m* (3) (slide)
rest; (*Schlitten*) carriage.
Surf|brett ['sœrf-] *n* surfboard; '~**er**
m (7) surfer.
surren ['zurən] (25) whiz(z); *Insekt*
usw.: buzz.
Surrogat [zuro'gɑ:t] *n* (3) sub-stitute, ersatz.
suspekt [zu'spɛkt] suspect.

suspendieren [zuspɛn'diːrən] suspend.

süß [zyːs] sweet (*a. allg. fig.*); '♀**e** *f* (15) sweetness; *als Kosewort*: sweetie; '♫**en** (25) sweeten; '♀**holz** *n* liquorice; F ~ *raspeln* flirt; '♀**igkeit** *f* sweetness; ~*en pl.* sweets, *Am.* candy *sg.*; '♫**lich** sweetish; *fig.* honeyed; (*kitschig*) mawkish, treacly; '♀**speise** *f* sweet, dessert; '♀**stoff** *m* sweetener; '♀**waren** *f/pl.* sweets, *Am.* candy *sg.*; '♀**warengeschäft** *n* sweet-shop, *Am.* candy store; '♀**wasser** *n* fresh water.

Sylphe ['zylfə] *f* (15) sylph.
Sylvester [zil'vɛstər] *s. Silvester.*
Symbol [zym'boːl] *n* (3[1]) symbol; ~**ik** *f* (16) symbolism; ♀**isch** symbolic(al); ♀**isieren** [~boli'ziːrən] symbolize.
Symmetr|ie [zyme'triː] *f* (15) symmetry; ♀**isch** [~'meːtriʃ] symmetrical.
Sympathie [zympa'tiː] *f* (15) sympathy; ~**streik** *m* sympathetic strike.
Sympath|isant [~pati'zant] *m* (12) sympathizer; ♀**isch** [~'paːtiʃ] sympathetic(ally *adv.*); (*gewinnend*) likable, engaging; *er ist mir* ~ I like him; ♀**i'sieren** sympathize.
Symphon|ie [zymfo'niː] *f* (15) symphony; ♀**isch** [~'foːniʃ] symphonic(ally *adv.*).
Symptom [zymp'toːm] *n* (3[1]) symptom; ♀**atisch** [~to'maːtiʃ] symptomatic (*für* of).

Synagoge [zyna'goːgə] *f* (15) synagogue.
synchron [zyn'kroːn] synchronous; ~/*nicht*~ F in/out of sync(h); ~**isieren** [~kroni'ziːrən] synchronize; *Film*: dub; ♀**getriebe** [~'kroːn-] *mot. n* synchromesh gear.
Syndikat [zyndi'kaːt] *n* (3) syndicate.
Syndikus ['zyndikus] *m* (14[2]) syndic, *Am.* corporation lawyer.
Synkop|e ♪ [zyn'koːpə] *f* (15) syncope; ♀**ieren** [~ko'piːrən] syncopate.
Synode [zy'noːdə] *f* (15) synod.
synonym [zyno'nyːm] **1.** *a.* ~**isch** synonymous; **2.** ♀ *n* (3[1]) synonym.
syntaktisch [zyn'taktiʃ] syntactic(al).
Syntax ['zyntaks] *f* (16) syntax.
Synthe|se [~'teːzə] *f* (15) synthesis; ♀**tisch** [~'teːtiʃ] synthetic(ally *adv.*).
Syphil|is ['zyːfilis] *f inv.* syphilis; ♀**itisch** [zyfi'liːtiʃ] syphilitic.
Syr|(i)er ['zyːr(j)ər] *m* (7), '~**(i)erin** *f*, '♀**isch** Syrian.
System [zy'steːm] *n* (3[1]) system; ~**atik** [~ste'maːtik] *f* system(atic manner); ♀**atisch** systematic(ally *adv.*); ~**kritiker(in** *f*) [~'steːm-] *m* dissident; ♀**los** unmethodical.
Szen|e ['stseːnə] *f* (15) scene (*a. fig.*); *Film*: sequence; *in* ~ *setzen* (put on the) stage, mount, (*sich*) show off; '~**enbild** *n thea, Film*: setting, scenery; ~**erie** [~'riː] *f* (15) scenery; '♀**isch** scenic(ally *adv.*).

T

T [teː], *t n inv.* T, t.
Tabak ['taːbak] *m* (3) tobacco; '~**bau** *m* tobacco growing; '~**händler** *m* tobacconist; '~**qualm** *m* tobacco-smoke; '~**sbeutel** *m* tobacco-pouch; '~**sdose** *f* snuff-box; '~**-waren** *f/pl.* tobacco goods, F smokes.
tabellar|isch [tabɛ'laːriʃ] tabulated, tabular; *adv.* in tabular form; ~**isieren** [~lari'ziːrən] tabulate.
Tabelle [ta'bɛlə] *f* (15) table.
Tabernakel [tabɛr'naːkəl] *n*, *m* (7) tabernacle.

Tablett [ta'blɛt] *n* (3) tray; *aus Metall*: salver; ~**e** *f* (15) tablet; ⚕ pill.
tabu [ta'buː] *adj.*, ♀ *n* (11) taboo; *ein* ♀ *brechen* break a taboo; *et. für* ~ *erklären* (put under a) taboo; ~**frei**: ~*e Gesellschaft* permissive society.
Tabulator [tabu'laːtɔr] *m* (8[1]) tabulator.
Tachometer ⊕ [taxo'meːtər] *n* (7) tachometer; *mot. a.* speedometer.
Tadel ['taːdəl] *m* (7) blame; (*Rüge*) censure; (*Mißbilligung*) reproof; (*Vorwurf*) reproach; (*Makel*) flaw; *ohne* ~ = '♀**los** faultless, blameless,

above reproach; F *fig.* splendid, first-class; '♀n (29) blame (*wegen* for), censure, criticize; '♀nswert blameworthy; '♀süchtig censorious, faultfinding.

Tadler ['tɑ:dlər] *m* (7) faultfinder, critic.

Tafel ['tɑ:fəl] *f* (15) table (*a. Liste usw.*); (*Platte, a. Bild♀ im Buch*) plate; (*Stein♀*) slab; *Schokolade usw.*: tablet, bar, cake; (*Schreib♀, a. Gedenk♀*) tablet; (*Schiefer♀*) slate; (*Wand♀*) blackboard; (*Täfelung*) panel; (*das Speisen*) dinner; '♀fertig ready to serve, instant; '**~land** *n* table-land, plateau; '♀n (29) dine, banquet.

täfeln ['tɛ:fəln] (29) *Fußboden:* inlay; *Wand:* wainscot, panel.

'**Tafel**|**obst** *n* dessert fruit; '**~runde** *f* (guests *pl.* at) table; '**~silber** *n* table-plate, *Am.* silverware.

Täfel|**ung** ['tɛ:fəluŋ] *f* inlaying; (*a.* '**~werk** *n*) wainscot([t]ing).

'**Tafel**|**wasser** *n* table-water; '**~wein** *m* table wine.

Taf(fe)t ['taf(ə)t] *m* (3) taffeta.

Tag [tɑ:k] *m* (3) day; *am* ~e by day; *am* ~e *nach* the day after; *bei* ~e by day, in the day-time; (*bei* ~*eslicht*) by daylight; *alle* ~e every day; *dieser* ~e (*demnächst*) one of these days, (*jüngst*) the other day; *eines* ~es some day; *zweimal des* ~es twice a day; *den ganzen* ~ all day long; *s. frei, heute, Abend*; ~ für day by day; *einen* ~ *um den andern* every other day; ⚒ *unter* ~e underground; *guten* ~*! allg.* how do you do?, *engS.*: good morning!, good afternoon!; F hallo!, *Am.* hello!; *bei Verabschiedung:* good day!, F so long!; *heller* ~ (~*eslicht*) broad daylight; *es wird* ~ it dawns; *an den* ~ *kommen* come to light; *an den* ~ *bringen, zu* ~e *fördern* bring to light; *an den* ~ *legen* exhibit, display; *in den* ~ *hinein leben usw.* from hand to mouth, at random; ♀'**~aus:** ~, *tag'ein* day in, day out; '**~(e)bau** ⚒ *m* open-cast working.

Tage|**blatt** ['tɑ:gə-] *n* daily (paper); '**~buch** *n* journal, diary; ✝ *a.* daybook; ⚓ logbook; '**~dieb** *m* idler, loafer; **~gelder** ['~gɛldər] *n*/*pl.* daily allowance *sg.*; ♀**lang** for days (together), day after day; '**~lohn** *m* day's (*od.* daily) wages *pl.*; '**~löhner**

m (7) day-labo(u)rer; '**~marsch** *m* day's march.

tagen ['tɑ:gən] (25) dawn; (*beraten*) meet, sit (in conference), ⚖ be in session.

'**Tagereise** *f* day's journey.

'**Tages**|**anbruch** *m* (*bei* ~ at) daybreak; '**~ausflug** *m* day's excursion; '**~befehl** *m* order of the day; '**~creme** *f* day cream; '**~geld** ✝ *n* call-money; '**~gespräch** *n* topic of the day; '**~heim** *n* day-care centre; '**~heimschule** *f* day school; '**~kasse** *f thea.* advance-booking office; ✝ receipts of the day; *für kleine Ausgaben:* petty cash; '**~kurs** *m* ✝ current rate; *e-r Fachschule:* day course; '**~leistung** *f* day's output; '**~licht** *n* daylight; *ans* ~ *bringen* (*kommen*) bring (come) to light; '**~mutter** *f* child- (*od.* baby-)minder; '**~ordnung** *f* order of the day, *e-r Versammlung:* agenda; *auf der (die)* ~ on the agenda; *zur* ~ *übergehen* proceed to the order of the day; *fig. das ist an der* ~ that is the order of the day; '**~preis** *m* current price; '**~presse** *f* daily press; '**~rückfahrkarte** *f* day return (ticket); '**~tour** *f* day trip; '**~zeit** *f* time of day; (*Ggs. Nachtzeit*) day-time; *zu jeder* ~ at any time of the day; '**~zeitung** *f* daily (paper).

'**tage**|**weise** by the day; '♀**werk** *n* day's work; (*Arbeitseinheit*) man- -day.

Tagfalter ['tɑ:k-] *m* buterfly.

...tägig [-tɛ:giç] of ... days.

täglich ['tɛ:kliç] daily; ✝ ~*es Geld* call-money.

tags: ~ *darauf* the day after; ~ *zuvor* the day before; '**~über** during the day, in the day-time.

'**tag**|'**täglich** every day; '♀**-und-** '**Nachtdienst** *m* day and night service; '♀**-und**'**nachtgleiche** *f* (15) equinox.

Tagung ['tɑ:guŋ] *f* meeting, conference, *Am. a.* convention; '**~sbericht** *m* proceedings *pl.*

Taifun [taɪ'fu:n] *m* (3¹) typhoon.

Taill|**e** ['taljə] *f* (15) waist; (*Mieder*) bodice; ♀**iert** [~'ji:rt] waisted.

Takel ⚓ ['tɑ:kəl] *n* (7) tackle; **~age** [~'lɑ:ʒə] *f* (15), '**~ung** *f*, '**~werk** *n* rigging, tackle; '♀n ⚓ (29) rig.

Takt [takt] *m* (3) ♪ time, measure; (~*strich*) bar; *weitS.* rhythm, cadence; *mot.* cycle; *fig.* tact, delicacy; ~ *halten* keep time; *den* ~ *schlagen* beat the time; *aus dem* ~ *kommen* lose the beat, *fig.* be put out; *aus dem* ~ *bringen fig.* put out; '**꒒fest** steady in keeping time; *fig.* firm; **꒒ieren** [꒦'tiːrən] beat the time; '**꒦ik** ✕ *u. fig. f* tactics *pl. u. sg.*; '**꒦iker** ✕ *m* tactician; '**꒒isch** tactical; '**꒒los** tactless; '**꒦losigkeit** *f* tactlessness, indiscretion; '**꒦stock** *m* baton; '**꒦strich** ♪ *m* bar; '**꒒voll** tactful.

Tal [taːl] *n* (1²; *poet. a.* 3) valley; *poet. u. fig.* vale; *zu* ~ = **꒒'abwärts** downhill.

Talar [ta'laːr] *m* (3¹) gown, robe.

Talent [ta'lɛnt] *n* (3) talent (*a. Person*; *zu* for); **꒒iert** [꒦'tiːrt] *s. talentvoll*; **꒦los** untalented; **꒦sucher** *m* talent scout; **꒒voll** talented, gifted.

Talg [talk] *m* (3) *roh*: suet; *ausgelassen*: tallow; '**꒦drüse** *f* sebaceous gland; **꒒ig** ['꒦giç] suety; tallowy; **꒦licht** ['talk-] *n* tallow-candle.

Talisman ['taːlisman] *m* (3¹) mascot, (good-luck) charm.

Talk [talk] *m* (3) talc; '**꒦erde** *f* magnesia; '**꒦um** *n* (7) talcum.

Talkessel ['tal-] *m s. Talmulde*.

Talk|master ['tɔːkmaːstər] *m* (7) *im Fernsehen*: host; **꒦show** ['꒦ʃoː; '꒦ʃəu] *f* chat show, *Am.* talk show.

Talmi ['talmi] *n* (11) pinchbeck.

Talmulde ['taːlmuldə] *f* basin (*od.* hollow) of the valley.

Talon ✝ [ta'lɔ̃] *m* (11) talon.

'**Tal|sohle** *f* bottom of the valley; *fig.* ✝ depression; '**꒦sperre** *f* dam.

Tamburin [tambu'riːn] *n* (3¹) tambourine. [pon.]

Tampon ['tampɔn] ♂ *m* (11) tam-

Tamtam ['tam'tam] *n inv.* tomtom; *fig.* noise, fuss; (*Reklame*) ballyhoo.

Tand [tant] *m* (3) trumpery, (worthless) trifles *pl.*; (*Flitter*) tinsel; (*Spielzeug*) bauble, gewgaw.

Tändel|ei [tɛndə'lai] *f* (16) trifling, dallying; *fig.* flirt(ing), flirtation; '**꒒n** (29) trifle, dally; flirt; (*trödeln*) dawdle.

Tandem ['tandɛm] *n* (11) tandem.

Tang ♀ [taŋ] *m* (3) seaweed.

Tang|ente ⚭ [taŋ'gɛntə] *f* (15) tangent; **꒒ieren** [꒦'giːrən] be tangent to; *fig.* touch, affect.

Tango ['taŋgoː] *m* (11) tango.

Tank [taŋk] *m* (3) tank (*a.* ✕; *s. Panzer*); '**꒒en** (25) (re)fuel, fill up,

take in petrol; '**꒦er** ⚓ *m* (7), '**꒦schiff** *n* tanker; '**꒦er-unglück** *n* (oil) tanker disaster; '**꒦stelle** *f* filling (*od.* petrol, *Am.* gas) station; '**꒦verschluß** *m* fuel cap; '**꒦wagen** *m* tank lorry (*Am.* truck); 🚃 tank car; '**꒦wart** *m* (3) filling-station attendant.

Tann *poet.* [tan] *m* forest; '**꒦e** *f*, '**꒦enbaum** *m* (15) fir(-tree); '**꒦enholz** *n* fir-wood, deal; '**꒦ennadel** *f* fir-needle; '**꒦enzapfen** *m* fir-cone.

Tantalusqualen ['tantalus-] *f/pl.* torments of Tantalus, *weitS. a.* agony, martyrdom.

Tante ['tantə] *f* (15) aunt; **꒦'Emma-Laden** F *m* corner shop, *Am.* mom-and-pop store.

Tantieme [tã'tjɛːmə] *f* (15) royalty, percentage, share in profits.

Tanz [tants] *m* (3² *u.* ³) dance; '**꒦abend** *m* dancing-party; '**꒦bär** *m* dancing bear; '**꒦bein** *n*: *das* ~ *schwingen* dance, do the light fantastic.

tänzeln ['tɛntsəln] (29, *h. u.* sn) trip, skip, frisk.

tanzen ['tantsən] *v/t. u. v/i.* (27, *h. u.* sn) dance (*a. fig.*); *s.* Reihe.

Tänzer ['tɛntsər] *m* (7), '**꒦in** *f* (16¹) dancer; *thea.* (ballet-)dancer, *f a.* danseuse; (*Mit*꒒) partner.

'**Tanz|fläche** *f* dance floor; '**꒦gesellschaft** *f* dancing-party; '**꒦kapelle** *f* dance band; '**꒦lehrer** *m* dancing-master; '**꒦lokal** *n* dance-hall; '**꒦musik** *f* dance music; '**꒦saal** *m* dance-hall, ball-room; '**꒦schritt** *m* (dancing-)step; '**꒦schule** *f* dancing-school; '**꒦stunde** *f* dancing-lesson; '**꒦turnier** *n* dancing contest.

Tapet [ta'peːt] *n* (3): *aufs* ~ *bringen* bring *a subject* up; **꒦e** *f* (15) wallpaper; **꒦enwechsel** F *m* change (of scenery).

Tapezier|er [tape'tsiːrər] *m* (7) paperhanger; (*Polsterer*) upholsterer; **꒒en** paper.

tapfer ['tapfər] brave, valiant; '꒒**keit** *f* bravery, valo(u)r.

tappen ['tapən] (25, *h. u.* sn) grope *od.* fumble (about).

täppisch ['tɛpiʃ] awkward, clumsy.

tapsen ['tapsən] walk clumsily.

Tara ✝ ['taːra] *f inv.* tare.

Tarantel *zo.* [ta'rantəl] *f* (15) tarantula; *fig. wie von der* ~ *gestochen* like a flash.

tarieren ✝ [ta'riːrən] tare.

Tarif [ta'riːf] *m* (3¹) *allg.* rate; (*Lohn*꒒)

(wage) scale; (*Zoll&*) tariff; **~-abschluß** *m* collective wage agreement; **~-aus·einandersetzungen** *f/pl.* pay disputes; **~autonomie** *f* free collective bargaining; **~gehalt** *n* agreed-scale salary; **~kündigung** *f* wage reopening; **&lich, &mäßig** standard, contractual, according to scale; **~lohn** *m* standard wage(s *pl.*); **~partner** *m* party to a wage agreement; **~runde** *f* pay round; **~verhandlungen** *f/pl.* collective bargaining, wage negotiations; **~vertrag** *m* (standard) wage agreement, industrial (*Am.* collective) agreement.

tarn|en ['tarnən] (25) ✕, ⚓, *fig.* camouflage; mask; screen; **'&farbe** *f* camouflage colo(u)r (*od.* paint); **'&kappe** *f* magic hood; **'&-organisation** *f* cover organisation; **'&ung** *f* camouflage.

Tasche ['taʃə] *f* (15) *in der Kleidung:* pocket; (*Hand&, Reise&* usw.) bag; (*Etui*) case; (*Beutel*) pouch (*a.* anat., zo.); *s.* Akten&, Schul&; *in die* ~ *stecken* (put into one's) pocket, F *j-n:* be head and shoulders above a p.; *j-m auf der* ~ *liegen* F live off a p.; *tief in die* ~ *greifen müssen* have to pay through one's nose; *wie s-e* ~ *kennen* know ... like the back of one's hand; F *ich habe es in der* ~ it's in the bag.

'Taschen|-ausgabe *f* pocket-edition; **'~buch** *n* pocket-book, paperback; **'~computer** *m* hand-held computer; **'~dieb** *m* pickpocket; **'~feuerzeug** *n* pocket-lighter; **'~flasche** *f* hip flask (*od.* bottle); **'~format** *n* pocket-size; **'~geld** *n* pocket-money, allowance; **'~kalender** *m* pocket diary; **'~lampe** *f* pocket lamp; (*Stab&*) (electric) torch, *bsd. Am.* flashlight; **'~messer** *n* pocket- (*od.* clasp-)knife, *Am. a.* jackknife; *kleines:* penknife; **'~rechner** *m* pocket calculator; **'~spieler** *m* juggler; **~spielerei** ['~ʃpiːlə'raɪ] *f* jugglery, sleight of hand; **'~tuch** *n* handkerchief; **'~uhr** *f* (pocket) watch; **'~wörterbuch** *n* pocket-dictionary.

Tasse ['tasə] *f* (15) cup.

Tastatur [tasta'tuːr] *f* (16) keyboard, keys *pl.*

Tast|e ['tastə] *f* (15) key (*a.* ⊕); **'&en** (26) touch, feel; (*tappen*) grope, fumble (*nach* for; *a. fig.*); *sich* ~ (*s-n Weg*

suchen) feel one's way; **'&end** *fig.* groping, tentative; **'~endruck** *m:* *auf* ~ at the press of a button; **'~en- (wahl)fernsprecher** *m*, **'~entelephon** *n* digital (*od.* push-button) telephone; **'~er** *m* ⊕, *𝄢* probe, feeler (*a. zo.*); (*Druckknopf*) push-button; *Zirkel:* cal(l)iper(s *pl.*); **'~sinn** *m* (sense of) touch.

Tat [taːt] **1.** *f* (16) deed, act, action; *große:* feat; ⚖ criminal act, offen|ce (*Am.* -se); *Mann der* ~ man of action; *in der* ~ indeed, in (point of) fact; *s.* frisch, umsetzen; **2.** ♀ *pret. v.* tun 1.

Tatar [ta'taːr] *m* (12) Tartar.

'Tat|bestand *m* state of affairs; ⚖ facts *pl.* of the case, factual findings *pl.*; **'~einheit** *f:* *in* ~ *mit* (in coincidence) with.

'Taten|drang *m* urge (*od.* zest) for action; **'&durstig** burning for action; enterprising; **'&los** inactive.

Täter ['tɛːtər] *m* (7), **'~in** *f* (16¹) doer; (*Übeltäter*) perpetrator (*a.* ⚖ = committer); culprit; (*Urheber*) author; **'~schaft** *f* guilt.

'tätig active (*a. gr.*); (*geschäftig*) busy; *bei e-r Firma usw.* ~ *sein* be in the employ of, work for; ~ *sein als* act (*od.* work *od.* function) as; **~en** ['~gən] (25) *bsd.* ♰ effect, transact; (*abschließen*) conclude; **'&keit** *f* activity; *berufliche:* occupation, business; *anat.,* ⊕ *usw.:* action; *in* ~ *setzen* put in action; *in voller* ~ in full swing; **'&keitsfeld** *n* field of activity; **'&keitsmerkmale** *n/pl.* job characteristics; **&ung** ['~gun] *f* transaction.

'Tat|kraft *f* energy; (*Unternehmungsgeist*) enterprise; **'&kräftig** energetic(ally *adv.*), active.

'tätlich violent; ~ *werden* resort to violence; ~ *werden gegen* assault; ⚖ *~e Beleidigung* assault and battery; **'&keit** *f* (*mst pl.*) (act of) violence; ⚖ assault (and battery).

'Tat-ort ⚖ *m* scene of crime.

tätowier|en [tɛto'viːrən] tattoo; **&ung** *f* tattoo(ing).

'Tat|sache *f* fact; *pl.* (*Unterlagen*) data; *j-n vor vollendete* ~*n stellen* confront a p. with a fait accompli; **'~sachenbericht** *m* factual (*od.* documentary) report; **'&sächlich** actual, factual, real; *adv.* actually, in fact (*a.* ⚖), as a matter of fact.

tätscheln ['tɛtʃəln] (29) pat.

'Tatwerkzeug n (murder) weapon.

Tatze ['tatsə] f (15) paw.

Tau[1] [tau] n (3) rope; *bsd.* ⚓ cable; ~[2] m (3[1], *o. pl.*) dew.

taub [taup] deaf (*fig. gegen, für* to); *Nuß:* deaf, empty; *Gestein:* dead; *Glieder:* numb; *fig. auf ~e Ohren stoßen Mahnungen etc.:* fall on deaf ears.

Taube ['taubə] f (15) pigeon; *rhet.* dove; **'2ngrau** dove-colo(u)red; **'~nschlag** m dovecot; **'~nzucht** f pigeon-breeding.

'Tauber m (7), **Täuberich** ['tɔybəriç] m (3) cock pigeon.

Taubheit ['tauphait] f deafness; numbness.

'Taubnessel ⚘ f dead-nettle.

'taubstumm deaf and dumb; **'2e** m, f (18) deaf-mute; **'2ensprache** f deaf-and-dumb language.

tauchen ['tauxən] (25) *v/t.* plunge, dip, duck; *v/i.* (h. u. sn) dive (*bsd. Schwimmer*), plunge, dip; *Unterseebot:* submerge.

'Taucher m (7) diver; **'~anzug** m diving-suit; **'~gerät** n, **'~lunge** f aqualung; **'~glocke** f diving-bell; **'~maske** f diving mask.

'Tauch|sieder m immersion heater; **'~sport** m skin-diving.

tauen ['tauən] (25) *v/i.* a) (h. u. sn) *Eis, Schnee:* thaw, melt; *es taut* it is thawing; b) *Tau:* (h.) *es taut* dew is falling.

Tauf|-akt ['tauf-] m (ceremony of) baptism; **'~becken** n baptismal font; **'~buch** n parish-register; **'~e** f (15) baptism, christening; *aus der ~ heben* stand godfather (*od.* godmother) to, *fig.* initiate; **'2en** (25) (*a. fig.*) baptize, christen.

Täuf|er ['tɔyfər] m (7): *Johannes der ~* John the Baptist; **'~ling** m (3[1]) child (*od.* person) to be baptized.

'Tauf|name m Christian name; **'~pate** m godfather, f (*a.* **'~patin**) godmother; **'~schein** m certificate of baptism; **'~stein** m baptismal font; **'~zeuge** m sponsor.

taugen ['taugən] (25) be of use, be good *od.* fit (*alle: zu* for); (*zu*) *nichts ~* be good for nothing.

'Taugenichts m (4; *sg. a. inv.*) good-for-nothing.

tauglich ['taukliç] fit, good; apt, useful (*für, zu* for; *to do*); (*fähig*)

able; ✕, ⚓ able-bodied; **'2keit** f fitness *etc.*; ability, usefulness.

Taum|el ['tauməl] m (7) giddiness; (*Überschwang*) rapture, ecstasy; **'2(e)lig** reeling; (*schwindlig*) giddy; **'2eln** (29, h. u. sn) reel, stagger; (*schwindlig sein*) be giddy.

'Taupunkt m dew-point.

Tausch [tauʃ] m (3[2]) exchange; (*~handel*) barter; **'2en** (27) *v/t. u. v/i.* exchange (*a. fig. Blicke, Schläge usw.*); (*ein~*) *a.* barter, F swop (*gegen* for); *ich möchte nicht mit ihm ~* I would not change places with him.

täuschen ['tɔyʃən] (27) *allg.* deceive (*j-n*; *a. Hoffnung*); (*narren*) fool, dupe; (*prellen*) cheat; *Sport:* deceive, *nur v/i.*: feint; *sich ~* deceive o.s., (*sich irren*) be mistaken; *sich ~ lassen* let o.s. be deceived; *in Hoffnungen usw. getäuscht werden* be disappointed in; **'~d** deceptive; *Ähnlichkeit:* striking; *~ nachahmen* mimic to perfection.

'Tausch|geschäft n, **'~handel** m barter; **'~mittel** n barter-medium; **'~objekt** n bartering object.

'Täuschung f deception; (*a. Selbst2*) delusion; 🏛 fraud, deceit; *optische ~* optical delusion; **'~smanöver** n feint, diversion; **'~sversuch** m attempted deception.

'Tauschwert m barter value.

tausend ['tauzənt] (a) thousand; *zu 2en* by thousands; *2undeine Nacht* Arabian Nights *pl.*; **~erlei** ['~dər-'lai] *adj.* of a thousand different kinds; *als su.* a thousand (different kinds) (of); **'~fach**, **~fältig** ['~zənt-feltiç] thousandfold; **'2fuß** m, **'2-füß(l)er** m millepede, *bsd. Am.* millipede; **'~jährig** of a thousand years; *2es Reich bibl.* millennium; **'2künstler** m wizard; Jack of all trades; **'~mal** a thousand times; *2sasa* ['~sasa] F m (11) devil of a fellow; **'2schön(chen)** ⚘ n (3[1] [6]) daisy.

'tausendst, **'2el** n (7) thousandth.

'Tau|tropfen m dew-drop; **'~werk** n ropes *pl.*; **'~wetter** n thaw; **'~-ziehen** n tug of war (*a. fig.*).

Taxameter [taksa'me:tər] m (7) (*Fahrpreisanzeiger*) clock, taximeter.

Taxator [ta'ksa:tɔr] m (8[1]) appraiser, taxer, valuer.

Taxe ['taksə] f (15) rate; (*Steuer*)

tax; (*Gebühr*) fee; (*Schätzung*) estimate, appraisal; (*Autodroschke*) s. *Taxi*.
Taxi ['taksi] n (11) taxi(cab), cab.
ta'xieren rate, estimate; *amtlich*: value, tax, appraise, assess.
'Taxi|fahrer m taxi-driver; '**~stand** m taxi-rank, *Am.* taxi stand.
Technik ['tɛçnik] f (16) ⊕ engineering; (*Wissenschaft*) technology; (*Verfahren*) technique (*a. Kunst, Sport*); (*Fertigkeit*) workmanship, skill; *in der Kunst*: technique; '**~er** m (7) (technical) engineer; (*Spezialist*; *a. weitS.*) technician; **~um** ['~um] n (9) technical school.
'technisch ⊕ *allg.* engineering (*department, journal, process, etc.*); (*bsd. betriebs~ u. weitS.*) technical; (*mechanisch*) mechanical; *Sport*: **~e** *Disziplin* field event; *Boxen*: **~er** K.o. technical knock-out; **~es** *Personal* technical staff; **~e** *Hochschule* technical college *od.* university; **~e** *Störung* breakdown.
Technisierung [tɛçni'ziːruŋ] f mechanization.
Technolog|ie [tɛçnolo'giː] f (15, *o. pl.*) technology; **2isch** [~'loːgiʃ] technological.
Techtelmechtel ['tɛçtəl'mɛçtəl] F n (7) (love) affair.
Teckel ['tɛkəl] m (7) dachshund.
Teddybär ['tɛdibɛːr] m Teddy bear.
Tee [teː] m (11) tea; '**~beutel** m teabag; '**~büchse** f tea-caddy; '**~-Ei** n tea infuser; '**~gebäck** n tea-cake; *weiches*: scone; *Am.* biscuit; '**~geschirr** n tea-service; '**~kanne** f teapot; '**~kessel** m tea-kettle; '**~löffel** m tea-spoon; '**~löffelvoll** m tea-spoonful; '**~maschine** f tea-urn; '**~mischung** f blend of tea; '**~pause** tea-break.
Teer [teːr] m (3) tar; **2en** (25) tar; **2ig** tarry.
'Teerpappe f tar-board.
'Tee|sieb n tea-strainer; '**~strauch** m tea-plant; '**~tasse** f teacup; '**~wagen** m tea wagon, teacart; '**~wärmer** ['~vɛrmər] m (7) tea-cosy.
Teich [taɪç] m (3) pond, pool; F *der große* ~ (*Ozean*) the Pond.
Teig [taɪk] m (3) dough, paste; **~ig** ['~gɪç] doughy, pasty; '**~waren** [taɪk-] f/pl. farinaceous products.
Teil [taɪl] m, n (3) part (*a.* ⊕); (*Anteil*) portion, share; (*Abschnitt*) sec-

tion; (*Bestandteil*) component; *edle* **~e** *pl. des Körpers* vital parts; *beide* **~e** *pl.* (*Parteien*) both parties; *ein ~ davon* part of it; *ein großer ~* a great deal; *der größte ~ der Menschen* the greater part (*od.* the majority) of mankind; *zum ~* partly, in part, to some extent; *zum großen ~* largely; *zum größten ~* mostly; *zu gleichen* **~en** share and share alike; *sein ~ beitragen* do one's share; *sich sein ~ denken* have one's own thoughts about it; *ich für mein ~* I for my part; '**~ansicht** f partial view; '**2bar** divisible; '**~barkeit** f divisibility; '**~chen** n (6) particle; '**2en** (25) divide; (*teilhaben an*) share; '**~er** m (7) divider; Ⅱ divisor; '**~erfolg** m partial success; '**2haben** participate, share (*beide: an dat.* in); **~haber(in** f [16¹]) m (7) participator; ✝ partner, associate; '**~haberschaft** f partnership; '**2haftig** partaking (*gen.* of); *e-r S.* ~ *werden* s. *teilhaben*.
...teilig consisting of ... parts, *two-piece ... etc.*
'Teil|kaskoversicherung f partial coverage insurance; **~nahme** ['~naːmə] f (15) participation (*an dat.* in); *fig.* interest (in); (*Mitgefühl*) sympathy (with); (*Beileid*) condolence(s *pl.*); '**2nahmeberechtigt** eligible; '**2nahmslos** (*gleichgültig*) indifferent; (*gefühllos*) impassible; (*untätig*) passive; *vor Schwäche*: apathetic(ally *adv.*); '**~nahmslosigkeit** f indifference; impassibility; passiveness; apathy; '**2nahmsvoll** sympathetic(ally *adv.*); '**2nehmen** *an* (*dat.*) take part (*od.* participate) in; *gemeinsam mit anderen*: join in; (*anwesend sn*) be present at, attend; *fig.* take an interest, in, *mitfühlend*: sympathize with; *an e-r Mahlzeit* ~ partake of a meal; '**2nehmend** s. *teilnahmsvoll*; '**~nehmer(in** f [16¹]) m (7) participant, participator; *Sport usw.*: competitor, entrant; *teleph.* subscriber; '**~nehmerverzeichnis** *teleph.* n telephone directory.
teils [taɪls] partly.
'Teil|strecke f section, fare stage; *weitS.* leg, stage; '**~strich** m graduation mark.
'Teilung f division; (*Ver2*) distribution; (*in Anteile*) sharing; (*Unterteilung*) graduation, scale; '**~s-**

artikel *gr. m* partitive article; '**~s-zahl** *f* dividend.

'**teil|weise** *adv.* partly, partially, in part; '**~zahlung** *f* part-payment, (payment by) instal(l)ment; *auf ~ kaufen* buy on the instal(l)ment-plan; '**~zeit-arbeit** *f* part-time employment; '**~zeit-Arbeitskraft** *f* part-time employee; '**~zeitbeschäftigung** *f* part-time job.

Teint [tɛ̃] *m* (11) complexion.

Tele'fon *usw. s. Telephon.*

Telegramm [tele'gram] *n* (3¹) telegram, wire; (*bsd. Übersee⌣*) cable; **~-anschrift** *f* cable address; **~formular** *n* telegraph form (*Am.* blank); **~gebühr** *f* telegram charge; **~stil** *m* telegraphic style, telegraphese.

Telegraph [~'gra:f] *m* (12) telegraph; **~en-amt** *n* telegraph office; **~enmast** *m* telegraph-pole; **~ie** [~gra'fi:] *f* (15) telegraphy; *drahtlose ~* wireless telegraphy; **⌣ieren** [~'fi:rən] *v/t. u. v/i.* telegraph, wire; *nach Übersee:* cable; **⌣isch** [~'gra:fiʃ] telegraphic(ally *adv.*), *adv. mst* by telegram, by wire, by cable; **~e** *Überweisung* cable transfer; **~ist** [~gra'fist] *m* (12), **~istin** *f* telegraphist, telegraph operator.

Telekommunikation ['te:lekɔmunikatsjo:n] *f* telecommunications *pl.*

Tele-objektiv *phot.* ['te:le-] *f* telephoto lens.

Telepath|ie [~pa'ti:] *f* telepathy; **⌣isch** [~'pa:tiʃ] telepathic(ally *adv.*).

Telephon [~'fo:n] *n* (3¹) telephone, F phone; *am ~* on the (tele)phone; *ans ~ gehen* (*wenn es klingelt*) answer the telephone; *~ haben* be on the telephone; **~-anruf** *m* (tele-) phone call; **~-anschluß** *m* telephone connection; *~ haben* be on the telephone *od.* F phone; **~-apparat** *m* telephone set; **~at** [~fo'na:t] *n* (3) *s. Telephongespräch;* **~-auskunft** [~'fo:n-] *f* directory enquiries *pl.* (*Am.* assistance); **~buch** *n* telephone directory; **~gebühren** *f/pl.* telephone charges; **~gespräch** *n* telephone call *od.* conversation; **~hörer** *m* receiver; **⌣ieren** [~fo'ni:rən] *v/t. u. v/i.* telephone, F phone; **⌣isch** [~'fo:niʃ] telephonic(ally *adv.*); *adv. mst* by telephone; **~ist** [~fo'nist] *m* (12), **~istin** *f* (16¹) telephonist, telephone operator; **~netz** [~'fo:n-] *n*

telephone network; **~nummer** *f* telephone number; **~verbindung** *f* telephone connection; **~vermittlung** *f*, **~zentrale** *f* (telephone) exchange *od.* (*Am.*) central office; **~zelle** *f* telephone (*od.* call) box.

Teleskop [tele'sko:p] *n* (3¹) telescope; **⌣isch** telescopic(ally *adv.*).

Television [televi'zjo:n] *f* (16, *o. pl.*) television.

Telex ['te:lɛks] *n* telex.

Teller ['tɛlər] *m* (7) plate; ⊕ disk, disc (*a. Schi⌣*); **~mütze** *f* flat cap; (*Baskenmütze*) beret.

Tempel ['tɛmpəl] *m* (7) temple; '**~herr** *m*, '**~ritter** *m* (Knight) Templar; '**~raub** *m*, '**~schändung** *f* sacrilege. [temper.⌣

Temperafarbe ['tɛmpera-] *f* dis-⌣

Temperament [tɛmpəra'mɛnt] *n* (3) temper(ament); (*Feuer*) mettle, spirits *pl.*, vivacity; **⌣los** spiritless; **⌣voll** vivacious, (high-)spirited, passionate.

Temperatur [~'tu:r] *f* (16) temperature; *~ haben* have (*od.* run) a temperature; *j-s ~ messen* take a p.'s temperature; **~schwankung** *f* variation of temperature.

tempe'rieren temper (*a. ♪*).

Tempo ['tɛmpo] *n* (11) ♪ time, (*a. weit S.*) tempo; (*Gangart*) pace; (*Geschwindigkeit*) speed, rate; *in langsamem ~* at a slow pace; *das ~ angeben* set the pace; **~limit** *mot.* ['~limit] *n* (11) speed limit; **⌣rär** [~'rɛ:r] temporary; *adv.* for the time being.

Tempus *gr.* ['tɛmpus] *n* (*sg. inv., pl. Tempora* ['~pora]) tense.

Tendenz [ten'dɛnts] *f* (16) tendency, trend; **⌣iös** [~'tsjø:s] tendentious; **~roman** *m* tendentious novel, purpose-novel; **~stück** *n* tendentious play, purpose-play.

Tender ['tɛndər] *m* (7) tender.

tendieren [tɛn'di:rən] tend (*nach, zu* to[wards]).

Tenne ['tɛnə] *f* (15) threshing-floor.

Tennis ['tɛnis] *n inv.* (lawn-)tennis; '**~ball** *m* tennis-ball; '**~platz** *m* tennis-court; '**~schläger** *m* tennis-racket; '**~spieler(in** *f*) *m* tennis-player; '**~turnier** *n* tennis-tournament. [substance.⌣

Tenor¹ ['te:nɔr] *bsd. ⌣it. m* tenor,⌣

Tenor² ♪ [te'no:r] *m* (3¹ *u.* ³) tenor; **~ist** [~no'rist] *m* (12) tenor(-singer).

Teppich ['tɛpiç] *m* (3¹) carpet, *Am. a.*

rug; '**~boden** m fitted carpet, wall-
-to-wall carpeting; '**~kehrmaschi-
ne** f carpet-sweeper; '**~schaum** m
carpet foam.

Termin [tɛrˈmiːn] m (3¹) (fixed) date
od. term, (appointed) time, target-
-date; (Frist) time-limit; äußerster ~
final date, bsd. Am. deadline; Sport:
fixture; ⚖ (Verhandlung) hearing;
(Besprechung, Treffen) appointment;
e-n ~ anberaumen od. stellen (absetzen) fix (rescind) a date.

Terminal [ˈtœrminəl] m, n (11) terminal; Computer: (video display)
terminal.

Terˈmin|geld ♣ n fixed deposit; ♀-
gemäß, ♀gerecht in due time, on
the due date; **~geschäft** ♣ n time-
-bargain, pl. futures; **~kalender** m
desk diary, appointments calendar;
⚖ cause-list, Am. calendar; **~ologie**
[~minoloˈgiː] f (15) terminology; **~
plan** m schedule.

Termite [tɛrˈmiːtə] f (15) termite,
white ant.

Terpentin [tɛrpənˈtiːn] n, m (3¹) turpentine, F turps.

Terrain [tɛˈrɛ̃] n (11) ground, terrain;
(Grundstück) plot of land; (Bauplatz) building site.

Terrasse [tɛˈrasə] f (15) terrace; ♀n-
förmig [~nfœrmiç] terraced; **~ntür**
f French window.

Terrine [tɛˈriːnə] f (15) tureen.

terri|torial [tɛritorˈjaːl] territorial; ♀-
torium [~ˈtoːrjum] n (9¹) territory.

Terror [ˈtɛrɔr] m (11, o. pl.) terror;
'**~akt** m act of terrorism; '**~an-
schlag** m terrorist attack; ♀**isieren**
[tɛroriˈziːrən] terrorize; **~ist** [~ˈrist]
m (12) terrorist.

Terz [tɛrts] f (16) ♪ third; fenc. tierce;
♪ kleine (große) ~ minor (major)
third; **~ett** ♪ [~ˈtsɛt] n (3) trio.

Test [tɛst] m (3 u. 11) test.

Testament [tɛstaˈmɛnt] n (3) (last)
will, ⚖ last will and testament; eccl.
Testament; sein ~ machen make a
will; ♀**arisch** [~ˈtaːriʃ] testamentary; adv. by will; **~s-er-öffnung** f
opening (od. probate) of the will;
~svollstrecker m executor; gerichtlich bestellter: administrator.

'**Test|bild** n Fernsehen: test card; '♀**en**
(26) test; '**~fall** m test case.

testieren [tɛsˈtiːrən] v/i. make a will;
v/t. (letztwillig anordnen) dispose by
will; (bezeugen) testify.

'**Test|person** f subject; '**~pilot** m test-
-pilot; '**~puppe** f dummy; '**~stopp-
abkommen** n test-ban treaty; '**~
strecke** mot. f test track.

teuer [ˈtɔyər] dear, costly, expensive;
fig. dear, beloved; **~e** Preise high
prices; wie ~ ist es? how much is it?,
what does it cost?; s. Rat, stehen;
'♀**ung** f dearness, high (od. rising)
prices, high cost of living; ♀**ungs-
rate** f rate of price increases;
'♀**ungszulage** f cost-of-living bonus.

Teufel [ˈtɔyfəl] m (7) devil; armer ~
poor devil (od. wretch); pfui ~! angeekelt: ugh!, entrüstet: for shame!,
disgusting!, wer zum ~? who the
devil (od. hell); wie der ~ like mad;
in (des) ~s Küche kommen get it in the
neck; man soll den ~ nicht an die
Wand malen talk of the devil (and he
will appear); j-n zum ~ jagen send
a p. packing; in der Not frißt der ~
Fliegen beggars can't be choosers;
der ~ ist los the fat is in the fire;
zum ~ gehen (Sache) go to pot; scher
dich zum ~ go to hell; **~ei** [~ˈlaɪ] f
(16) devilish trick, devil(t)ry; '**~s-
kerl** m devil of a fellow; '**~skreis** fig.
m vicious circle.

'**teuflisch** devilish, diabolic(al).

Text [tɛkst] m (3²) text; (Lied♀)
words pl.; (Opern♀) book, libretto;
j-m den ~ lesen lecture a p.; aus
dem ~ bringen (kommen) (be) put
out; '**~buch** n play book, libretto.

Textil... [teksˈtiːl] textile; **~ien**
[~jən] pl. inv. textiles pl.

'**textlich** textual.

'**Text|seite** f text page; '**~speicher** m
Computer: text memory; '**~ver-ar-
beitung** f Computer: word processing; '**~ver-arbeitungs-anlage** f
word processor.

Theater [teˈaːtər] n (7) theat|re,
Am. -er; (Bühne u. weitS.) stage;
fig. contp. farce; (Aufregung, Getue)
fuss; fig. ~ spielen play-act; zum ~
gehen go on the stage; **~besucher**
(-in f) m play-goer; **~karte** f
(theat|re, Am. -er) ticket; **~kasse** f
box office; **~kritiker** m drama
critic; **~stück** n (stage-)play; **~vor-
stellung** f theatrical performance;
~zettel m play-bill.

theatralisch [~aˈtraːliʃ] theatrical.

Theke [ˈteːkə] f (15) bar, Am. a.
counter.

Thema ['teːma] n (9², pl. a. ~ta) theme (a. ♪ usw.), subject; (nur Gesprächs≗) topic; beim ~ bleiben stick to the point.
Theolog [teo'loːk] m (12), ~e [~gə] (13) m theologian; ~ie [~lo'giː] f (15) theology; ≗isch [~'loːgiʃ] theological.
Theoret|iker [teo're:tikər] m (7) theorist; ≗isch theoretic(al); ≗i-'sieren theorize.
Theorie [teo'riː] f (15) theory.
Therap|eut [tera'pɔʏt] m (12) therapist; ~eutik [~'pɔʏtik] f (16, o. pl.) therapeutics sg.; ≗eutisch therapeutic(ally adv.); ~ie [~'piː] f (15) therapy.
Thermal|bad [tɛr'maː-l-] n thermal spa; ~quelle f s. Therme.
Therm|e ['tɛrmə] f (15) thermal spring; ≗isch thermal, thermic.
Thermo|dy'namik [tɛrmo-] f thermodynamics sg.; ~-element thermocouple.
Thermometer [tɛrmo'meːtər] n (7) thermometer; ~säule f thermometer column; ~stand m thermometer reading.
thermo'plastisch thermoplastic(ally adv.)
Thermos|flasche ['tɛrmɔs-] f vacuum (od. thermos) flask; ~kanne f vacuum jug.
Thermostat phys. [tɛrmo'staːt] m (3) thermostat.
These ['teːzə] f (15) thesis.
Thrombose ♫ [trɔm'boːzə] f (15) thrombosis.
Thron [troːn] m (3) throne; ~-anwärter m heir apparent; ~besteigung f accession to the throne; ~bewerber m pretender to the throne; ≗en (25) be enthroned; fig. sit, be placed; ~-erbe m heir to the throne; ~folge(r m [7]) f succession (successor) to the throne; ~himmel m canopy; ~räuber m usurper; ~rede f Brt. parl. Queen's (od. King's) Speech; ~wechsel m change of sovereign.
Thunfisch ['tuːnfiʃ] m tunny, tuna.
Thüring|er ['tyːriŋər] m (7), ~erin f (16¹), ≗isch Thuringian.
Thymian ['tyːmjaːn] m (3¹) thyme.
Tick [tik] m (3¹ od. 11) ♫ (mst Tic) tic; (Schrulle) fad, kink; ≗en (25) tick.
tief [tiːf] 1. allg. deep (a. fig.); Wis-

sen, Geheimnis usw.: profound; (niedrig: z.B. Tal) low; Farbe: dark; fig. (äußerst) utter, extreme; im ~sten Winter in the depth (od. dead) of winter; ~ in der Nacht in the dead of night; bis ~ in die Nacht far into the night; ~ enttäuscht badly disappointed; 2. ♀ n (6) (barometric) depression od. low.
'**Tief|-angriff** ≫ m low-level attack; '~atmung f deep breathing; '~bau ⊕ m (3) underground construction engineering; '≗be'trübt deeply grieved, very sad; '≗be-'wegt deeply moved; ≗blau deep blue; '~blick m keen insight, penetration; '≗blickend penetrating; '~decker ≫ m (7) low-wing monoplane; '~druck print. m intaglio (printing), roto(gravure); '~druck(-gebiet n) m low-pressure (area); '~e f (15) depth; fig. a. profoundness; profundity; '~ebene f (low) plain; ≗empfunden ['~ᵊɛm'pfundən] heart-felt; '~enpsychologie f depth psychology; '~enregler m Radio etc.: bass control; '~enschärfe phot. f depth of focus; '~enwirkung f depth effect; paint. plastic effect; '~flug m low-level flight; '~gang ⚓ m draught; '~garage f underground car park; ≗gebeugt ['~gə'bɔʏkt] fig. deeply afflicted; ≗gefroren deep--frozen; ≗gefühlt ['~gə'fyːlt] heart-felt; '≗gekühlt deep-freeze, (fresh-) frozen; '≗greifend far-reaching, thorough; radical; '~kühlfach n freezing compartment; '~kühlkost f, '~kühlware f frozen foods pl.; '~kühltruhe f deep-freeze, freezer; ~lader ['~laːdər] m (7) flat-bed car; '~land n lowland(s pl.); '≗liegend deep-seated; Augen: sunken; '~punkt fig. m low; '~schlag m Boxen: low hit, hit below the belt; '≗schür-fend fig. profound; '≗schwarz jet--black; '~see f deep-sea; '~seefor-schung f deep-sea research; '~sinn m profoundness; (Schwermut) melancholy; '≗sinnig profound; melancholy; '~stand m low level; fig. low.
Tiegel ['tiːgəl] m (7) saucepan, stew-pan; (Schmelz≗) crucible.
Tier [tiːr] n (3) animal; großes: beast; (Rohling) brute; F fig. großes (od. hohes) ~ bigwig, big shot; '~art f (animal) species; '~-arzt m veterinary (surgeon), bsd. Am. veterinar-

ian, F vet; '~**bändiger(in** f) m tamer
of wild beasts; '~**freund** m animal
lover; '~**garten** m zoological gardens
pl., zoo; '~**handlung** f pet shop;
'~**heilkunde** f veterinary science;
'~**heim** n animal home (Am. shelter); '2**isch** animal; fig. a. (roh) bestial, brutish; '~**kreis** ast. m zodiac;
'~**kunde** f zoology; '~**leben** n animal
life; '2**lieb** fond of animals; '~**park** m
s. Tiergarten; '~**pfleger(in** f) m zoo-
-keeper; ~**präparator** ['~prɛpa'rɑ:-
tor] m (8¹) taxidermist; '~**quälerei** f
cruelty to animals; '~**reich** n animal
kingdom; '~**schutzver-ein** m Society for the Prevention of Cruelty to
Animals; '~**versuch** m animal test;
'~**welt** f animal world; '~**zucht** f
animal (od. livestock) breeding.
Tiger ['ti:gər] m (7) tiger; '~**fell** n tiger
skin; '~**in** f (16¹) tigress; '2**n** (29)
speckle, spot.
tilgbar ['tilkbɑ:r] ✝ redeemable.
tilg|en ['tilgən] (25) extinguish;
(auswischen) efface, (a. fig. vernichten) wipe out; (streichen) blot out,
obliterate; (aufheben) annul, cancel;
Schuld: pay off, discharge; Anleihe,
Staatsschuld: redeem; (amortisieren) amortize; '2**ung** f s. tilgen:
extinction; cancel(l)ing; discharge,
payment; redemption; '2**ungs-
fonds** m sinking-fund.
Tinktur [tiŋk'tu:r] f (16) tincture.
Tinte ['tintə] f (15) ink; fig. F in der
~ sitzen be in a scrape.
'**Tinten|faß** n inkpot; eingelassenes:
ink-well; '~**fisch** zo. m cuttle-fish;
'~**fleck** m, '~**klecks** m ink-blot; '~-
löscher m (rocker) blotter; '~**stift**
m copying(-ink) pencil, indelible
(ink) pencil.
Tip [tip] m (11) tip.
tippeln F ['tipəln] (29) tramp.
tipp|en ['tipən] v/t. u. v/i. (25) tap,
tip; F (auf der Maschine schreiben)
type; F (wetten) bet; '2**fehler** m
typing error; 2**se** contp. F ['tipsə] f
(15) typist; '~**topp** tiptop, first-
-class; '2**zettel** m pools (od. lottery)
coupon.
Tirol|er [ti'ro:lər] m (7), ~**erin** f (16¹),
2**(er)isch** Tyrolese.
Tisch [tiʃ] m (3²) table; (Kost) board;
bei ~e at table; s. decken, grün, rein; zu
~ einladen invite to dinner; fig. unter
den ~ fallen (lassen) fall flat (drop);
'~**dame** f partner at table; '~**decke** f

table-cloth; '~**fußball** m table football; '~**gerät** n table set; '~**gast** m
guest; '~**gebet** n: das ~ sprechen say
grace; '~**gespräch** n table-talk; '~-
herr m partner at table; '~**karte** f
place card; '~**klopfen** n table-rap-
ping; '~**lampe** f table lamp;
(Schreib2) desk lamp.
Tischler ['tiʃlər] m (7) joiner; (Kunst-
2) cabinet-maker; ~**ei** [~'raɪ] f (16)
joinery; (Werkstatt) joiner's workshop; '~**leim** m solid glue; '2**n** (29)
v/i. do joiner's work; v/t. make.
'**Tisch|nachbar(in** f) m neighbo(u)r
at table; '~**platte** f table-top; zum
Ausziehen: leaf; '~**rechner** m desk
calculator; '~**rede** f toast, after-din-
ner speech; '~**rücken** n table-turn-
ing; '~**telephon** n desk-telephone;
'~**tennis** n table tennis; '~**tuch** n
table-cloth; '~**wein** m table-wine;
'~**zeit** f dinner-time.
Titan(e) [ti'tɑ:n(ə)] m (12) Titan; ~**in**
f (16¹) Titaness; 2**isch** titanic.
Titel ['ti:təl] m (7) allg. title; Sport:
e-n ~ innehaben hold a title; '~**bild** n
frontispiece; e-s Magazins usw.: cover (picture); '~**blatt** n title-page;
'~**geschichte** f cover story; '~**halter**
m Sport: title-holder; '~**kampf** m
Sport: title bout; '~**kopf** m heading;
'~**melodie** f Film: theme music; '~-
rolle f title-role; '~**seite** f front page;
'~**verteidiger** m Sport: title-holder;
'~**zeile** f headline.
Titten V ['titən] f/pl. (15) tits.
Titul|ar... [titu'lɑ:r] titulary, nomi-
nal; ~**atur** [~la'tu:r] f (16) titles pl.;
2**ieren** [~'li:rən] style, call.
Toast [to:st] m (3²) (Trinkspruch)
toast (a. Röstbrot); e-n ~ ausbringen
propose a toast; '2**en** (26) (rösten)
toast; '~**er** m (7) toaster.
toben ['to:bən] (25) rage (a. fig.);
Kinder: romp.
Tob|sucht ['to:pzuxt] f raving mad-
ness, frenzy; '2**süchtig** raving mad,
frantic; '~**suchts-anfall** m raving
fit; fig. tantrum.
Tochter ['toxtər] f (14¹) daughter;
'~**gesellschaft** ✝ f subsidiary
company.
Tod [to:t] m (3) death; feierlich od.
⚖ decease; des ~es sein be doomed;
den ~ finden be killed; sich den ~
holen (sich erkälten) catch one's
death (of cold); mit dem ~e ringen
be in the last agonies; zu ~e er-

schrecken, langweilen usw. to death; **für den** ~ **nicht leiden können** hate like poison; '♀**bringend** deadly, fatal; '♀'**-ernst** deadly serious.

Todes|-ahnung ['~dǝs-] *f* presentiment of death; '~**angst** *f* fear of death; *fig.* mortal dread; '~**anzeige** *f* obituary (notice); '~**art** *f* manner of death; '~**erklärung** *f* declaration of death; '~**fall** *m* (case of) death, decease; '~**gefahr** *f* deadly peril, peril (*od.* danger) of *one's* life; '~**jahr** *n* year of *a p.'s* death; '~**kampf** *m* death-struggle; '~**kandidat** *m* doomed man; '~**opfer** *n/pl.* victims *pl.*, casualities *pl.*; '~**stoß** *m* death-blow; '~**strafe** *f* death penalty, capital punishment; *bei* ~ on pain of death; '~**stunde** *f* hour of death; '~**tag** *m* day (*od.* anniversary) of *a p.'s* death; '~**ursache** *f* cause of *a p.'s* death; '~**urteil** *n* sentence of death; *fig.* death-warrant; '~**ver-achtung** *f* defiance of death; *mit* ~ recklessly; '~**wunde** *f* mortal wound; '~**wunsch** *m* death-wish; '~**zelle** *f* death cell; *pl. a.* death row *sg.*

'**Tod|feind** *m* deadly enemy; '♀**krank** dangerously ill; '♀'**langweilig** deadly boring.

tödlich ['tøːtliç] deadly, fatal, mortal, lethal.

'**tod|'müde** dead tired, dead-beat; '~'**schick** F dead smart; (*prima*) *a.* F fab(ulous), super; '~'**sicher** cocksure; '♀**sünde** *f* deadly (*od.* mortal) sin.

Tohuwabohu ['toːhuva'boːhu] *n* hubbub, wild confusion.

Toilette [toa'lɛtǝ] *f* (15) (*Ankleiden, Anzug*) toilet; (*Abort*) lavatory, *bsd. Am.* restroom; *s.* ~**ntisch**; ~ **machen** do one's toilet; ~**n-artikel** *m* toilet-article; ~**nbrille** *f* toilet seat; ~**nfrau** *f* toilet attendant; ~**ngarnitur** *f* toilet set; ~**npapier** *n* toilet-paper; ~**nseife** *f* toilet soap; ~**ntisch** dressing-table, *Am.* dresser.

tole|rant [tole'rant] tolerant (*gegen* of); ♀'**ranz** *f* (16) tolerance (*a.* ⊕, ⚡); ⊕ *a.* allowance; ~'**rieren** tolerate.

toll [tɔl] mad, crazy, wild (*alle a. fig.*); (*unglaublich*) fantastic; (*großartig*) *a.* F terrific; F *nicht so* ~ *sl.* not so hot; *wie* ~ like mad; ♀e F *f* (15) tuft; '~**en**[1] F (25) *Kinder usw.*: romp, frolic; '~**en**[2] (*fälteln*) crimp;

'♀**haus** *n* madhouse; *fig.* bedlam; '♀**heit** *f* madness; (*toller Streich*) mad trick; '♀**kirsche** ♀ *f* deadly nightshade; '~**kühn** foolhardy, dare-devil; '♀**kühnheit** *f* foolhardiness; '♀**wut** *f* rabies.

Tolpatsch ['tɔlpatʃ] *m* (3), **Tölpel** ['tœlpǝl] *m* (7) awkward (*od.* clumsy) fellow, booby.

Tölpel|ei [~'laɪ] *f* (16) clumsiness; '♀**haft** awkward, clumsy.

Tomate [to'maːtǝ] *f* (15) tomato; ~**n-mark** *n* tomato purée (*Am.* paste).

Tombola ['tɔmbola] *f* (16[1]) raffle.

Ton[1] [toːn] *m* (3³) sound; (*Klang, ~fall*) tone (*a. fig.*); ♩ tone, note, (~*art*) key; (*Betonung*) accent, stress; (*Farb♀*) tone (*a. phot.*), *heller:* tint, *dunkler:* shade; *guter* ~ good form; *den* ~ *angeben* give the key-note (*a. fig.*), *fig.* set the tone; *zum guten* ~ *gehören* be the fashion; *F große Töne reden* talk big; *in höchsten Tönen reden von* rave about; ~[2] *m* (3) (~*erde*) clay; '~**abnehmer** *m* pick-up; '♀**angebend** leading; '~**arm** *m* tone (*od.* pickup) arm; '~**art** ♩ *f* key; *fig.* e-e *andere* ~ *anschlagen* change one's tune; '~**aufnahme** *f* sound recording; '~**band** *n* (recording) tape; *auf* ~ *aufnehmen* tape-record; '~**bandgerät** *n* tape recorder; '~**dichtung** *f* symphonic poem.

'**tonen** *phot.* (25) tone.

tönen ['tøːnǝn] (25) *v/i.* sound; F *fig.* sound off; *v/t.* (*färben*) tint, tone; shade.

'**Ton-erde** *f* argillaceous earth; *essigsaure* ~ alumin(i)um acetate (solution).

tönern ['tøːnǝrn] (of) clay, earthen.

'**Ton|fall** *m* cadence; *beim Sprechen:* intonation, accent, tone; '~**film** *m* sound film; '~**frequenz** *f* audio frequency; '~**geschirr** *n* earthenware, pottery; '♀(**halt**)**ig** clayey; '~**höhe** *f* pitch.

Tonika ♩ ['toːnika] *f* (16[2]) tonic.

'**Ton-ingenieur** *m* sound engineer.

'**tonisch** ♩ *u.* ⚡ tonic(ally *adv.*).

'**Ton|kopf** *m von Tonbandgerät etc.:* recording head, *von Plattenspieler:* pick-up; '~**kunst** *f* musical art; '~**künstler(in** *f*) *m* musician; '~**lage** *f* pitch; '~**leiter** *f* scale, gamut; '♀**los** soundless; *gr.* unstressed; *fig.* toneless; '~**meister** *m* sound engineer.

Tonnage [tɔˈnaːʒə] f (15) tonnage.

Tonne [ˈtɔnə] f (15) barrel, cask, tun; ⚓, *Gewicht:* ton; '**~ngehalt** m tonnage; '**~ngewölbe** n barrel-vault; '**Qnweise** by (*od.* in) barrels.

'**Ton|pfeife** f clay pipe; '**~qualität** f sound quality; '**~regler** m tone control; '**~silbe** f accented syllable; '**~spur** f, '**~streifen** m *Film:* sound track.

Tonsur [tɔnˈzuːr] f (16) tonsure.

'**Ton|taube** f *Sport:* clay pigeon; '**~taubenschießen** n trap shooting; '**~techniker** m sound engineer; '**~träger** m sound carrier.

Tönung [ˈtøːnuŋ] f tint, tinge, shading; *phot.* tone.

'**Tonwaren** f/pl. s. Töpferware.

Topas [toˈpaːs] m (4) topaz.

Topf [tɔpf] m (3³) pot; *fig.* in e-n ~ werfen lump together; '**~deckel** m potlid.

Töpfer [ˈtœpfər] m (7) potter; (*Ofensetzer*) stove-fitter; **~ei** [~ˈraɪ] f (16) pottery; (*Werkstatt*) potter's shop; '**~scheibe** f potter's wheel; '**~ware** f earthenware, pottery.

'**Topf|lappen** m oven-cloth; '**~pflanze** f pot-plant, potted plant.

topographisch [topoˈgraːfɪʃ] topographic(al).

topp![1] [tɔp] done!, agreed!

Topp[2] ⚓ [~] m (3¹ u. 11) top, head; '**~mast** m topmast; '**~reep** n guy; '**~segel** n topsail.

Tor[1] [toːr] n (3) gate (*a. Slalom*♀); (*Einfahrt*) gateway (*a. fig.*); *Sport:* goal; s. schießen.

Tor[2] [~] m (12) fool.

Torf [tɔrf] m (3) peat; '**~boden** m peat-soil; '**~moor** n peat-bog; '**~mull** m peat-dust.

Torheit [ˈtoːrhaɪt] f folly.

'**Torhüter** m gate-keeper; *Sport:* (goal)keeper, F goalie.

töricht [ˈtøːrɪçt] foolish, silly.

Törin [ˈtøːrɪn] f fool(ish woman).

torkeln [ˈtɔrkəln] (29, h. u. sn) reel, stagger, totter.

Tor|latte [ˈtoːr-] f *Fußball:* crossbar; '**~lauf** m slalom; '**~linie** f *Sport:* goal-line; '**Qlos** *Sport:* scoreless.

Tornister [tɔrˈnɪstər] m (7) knapsack, ⚔ a. pack; (*Schul*♀) satchel.

torpedieren [tɔrpeˈdiːrən] torpedo.

Torpedo [tɔrˈpeːdo] m (11) torpedo; **~boot** n torpedo-boat.

'**Tor|pfosten** m *Sport:* goal-post; '**~raum** m *Fußball:* goal area; '**~schlußpanik** f last-minute panic; '**~schütze** m *Sport:* scorer; '**~steher** m *Sport:* goal-keeper.

Torso [ˈtɔrzo] m (11) torso.

Torte [ˈtɔrtə] f (15) gateau; (*Obst*♀) tart, *Am.* pie; '**~nheber** m (7) cake server.

Tortur [tɔrˈtuːr] f (16) torture.

'**Torwart** m (3) s. Torhüter.

tosen [ˈtoːzən] (27, h. u. sn) roar, rage, thunder.

tot [toːt] *allg.* dead (*a. fig.*); **~e** Zeit dull (*od.* dead) season; **~er** Gang ⊕ dead travel, lost motion, *e-s Gewindes:* backlash; **Qe** Hand mortmain; **~es** *Kapital* unemployed capital; **~er** Punkt ⊕ dead cent|re, *Am.* -er, *fig.* impasse, deadlock, (*Erschöpfung*) exhaustion; *fig.* auf dem **~en** Punkt ankommen reach a deadlock, *P.:* be exhausted; den **~en** Punkt überwinden break the deadlock, *bei Erschöpfung:* get one's second wind; **~er** Winkel blind spot; **~e** Zone *Radio:* blind spot *od.* area; s. *Geleise, Rennen.*

total [toˈtaːl] total, complete; (*umfassend*) all-out; **Q~ausfall** m total loss; **Q~ausverkauf** m clearance sale; **Q~isator** [totaliˈzaːtɔr] m (8¹) totalizator, totalizer.

totalitär [~ˈtɛːr] totalitarian.

To'talschaden *mot.* m write-off.

'**tot-arbeiten:** sich ~ work o.s. to death.

'**Tote** m, f (18) dead (person); s. *Leiche;* die **~n** pl. the dead.

töten [ˈtøːtən] (26) kill; *Nerv:* deaden.

'**Toten|bahre** f bier; '**~beschwörung** f calling up the dead; '**~bett** n death-bed; '**Q'blaß** deadly pale; '**~blässe** f deadly pallor; '**~feier** f obsequies pl.; '**~geläut** n, '**~glocke** f knell; '**~gräber** m (7) grave-digger; '**~hemd** n shroud; '**~kopf** m, '**~schädel** m death's-head (*a. zo. u. Symbol*), skull; '**~liste** f list of the dead; *bsd.* ⚔ death-roll; '**~maske** f death-mask; '**~messe** f mass for the dead, requiem; '**~reich** n realm of the dead; '**~schein** m death certificate; '**~starre** f rigor mortis; '**Q'still** as still as death; '**~stille** f dead(ly) silence; '**~tanz** m *Kunst:* danse macabre (*fr.*); '**~urne** f (funeral) urn; '**~wache** f wake.

'**tot|geboren** stillborn; *fig.* abortive; *fig.* ein ~es *Kind Idee, Plan:* a non--starter; '♀**geburt** *f* stillbirth; '~**lachen:** *sich* ~ nearly die with laughter; *zum* ♀ F a scream; '♀**lauf** ⊕ *m* dead travel; '~**laufen:** *sich* ~ *fig.* peter out.

Toto ['to:to] *m* (11) (*Totalisator*) tote; (*Fußball*♀) (football) pool; *im* ~ *spielen* bet on the pools.

'**tot|schießen** shoot dead; '♀**schlag** ɪ̯ɫ *m* second-degree murder; '~**schlagen** kill, slay; *die Zeit* ~ kill time; '♀**schläger** *m* homicide; (*Schlagstock*) life-preserver, *sl.* cosh, *Am.* blackjack; '~**schweigen** hush up; '~**stechen** stab to death; *sich* '~**stellen** feign death.

Tötung ['tø:tuŋ] *f* killing.

Toupet [tu'pe:] *n* (11) toupee.

Tour [tu:r] *f* (16) tour; (*Ausflug*) trip, excursion; ⊕ (*Umdrehung*) revolution, turn; F (*Trick*) dodge, ploy; *auf (der)* ~ on the road; *auf* ~en *bringen mot.* rev (up); *auf* ~en *kommen mot.* pick (od. rev) up, *fig.* get going; *fig. auf vollen* ~en *laufen* be in full swing; *in e-r* ~ at a stretch, (*dauernd*) incessantly; '~**enrad** *n* roadster; '~**enschi** *m* touring ski; '~**enwagen** *mot. m* touring car; tourer; '~**enzahl** *f* speed, revolutions *pl.* (per minute) (*abbr.* r.p.m.); '~**enzähler** *m* revolution counter.

Touris|mus [tu'rismus] *m* (16, *o. pl.*), ~**tik** *f* (16, *o. pl.*) tourism; ~**t** *m* (12), ~**tin** *f* (16¹) tourist; ~**tenattraktion** *f* tourist attraction; ~**tenklasse** *f* economy class.

Tournee [tur'ne:] *f* (16) tour.

Trab [tra:p] *m* (3) trot; *im* ~ at a trot, F *fig.* on the run; *fig. j-n auf (den)* ~ *bringen* make a p. get a move on.

Trabant [tra'bant] *m* (12) satellite; ~**enstadt** *f* satellite town.

traben ['tra:bən] (25, *h. u.* sn) trot.

'**Traber** *m* (7) trotter.

Trabrennen ['tra:p-] *n* trotting race.

Tracht [traxt] *f* (16) **1.** dress, attire, (*a.* traditional) costume; (*Schwestern*♀) uniform; (*Mode*) fashion; **2.** (*Last*) load; *der Bienen* (*Ertrag*) yield; *e-e* (*gehörige*) ~ *Prügel* a sound thrashing.

trachten ['traxtən] **1.** *v/i.* ~ *nach et.* endeavo(u)r after, strive for *od.* after, seek; (*danach*) ~, *zu inf.* en-

deavo(u)r (*od.* strive, seek, try) to *inf.*; *j-m nach dem Leben* ~ seek a p.'s life; **2.** ♀ *n* striving; pursuit (*nach of*).

trächtig ['treçtiç] (big) with young, pregnant; '♀**keit** *f* pregnancy.

Tradition [tradi'tsjo:n] *f* (16) tradition; ♀**ell** [~tsjo'nεl] traditional.

traf [tra:f] *pret. v. treffen 1.*

Trag|bahre ['tra:k-] *f* stretcher, litter; '~**balken** *m* (supporting) beam; (*Längsträger*) girder; (*Querträger*) transom; '♀**bar** portable; *Kleid:* wearable; *fig.* bearable; (*annehmbar*) acceptable.

Trage ['tra:gə] *f* (15) hand-barrow; *s. Tragbahre.*

träg(e) [trε:k, '~gə] lazy, indolent; (*langsam*) sluggish; *phys.* inert.

tragen ['tra:gən] (30) *v/t.* carry (*a. v/i. Gewehr, Stimme*); *Kosten, Namen, Verantwortung usw.:* bear; (*ertragen*) bear (*a. v/i. Eis*); (*stützen*) carry; (*hervorbringen*) bear, yield; (*am Körper* ~) wear; *bei sich* ~ have about one; *sich* ~ (*sich kleiden*) dress; *sich gut* ~ (*Stoff*) wear well; † *sich* (*selbst*) ~ pay its way; *fig. sich mit et.* ~ be thinking of; *von e-r Idee usw. getragen* inspired by, based on; *s. Absicht, Bedenken, Folge, Schau, Sorge, Verlangen, Zins, getragen.*

Träger ['trε:gər] *m* (7), '~**in** *f* (16¹) carrier (*a.* ⚕ *Krankheits*♀); (*Gepäck*♀) porter; (*Inhaber*) holder, bearer; *e-s Kleides:* wearer; *am Damenhemd usw.:* (shoulder) strap; (*Unterhalts*♀) providing body; ⊕ support; ⚔ girder; ⚡ carrier; ⚓ vehicle; '~**lohn** *m* porterage; '♀**los** *Kleid:* strapless; '~**rakete** *f* *Weltraumfahrt:* booster (rocket).

'**Tragetasche** *f* carrier bag.

tragfähig ['tra:k-] capable of carrying *od.* bearing; *fig.* sound; *e-e* ~e *Basis für* ... a working basis for ...; '♀**keit** *f* carrying (*od.* load) capacity; ⚓ tonnage.

Trag|fläche ⚓ ['tra:kflεçə] *f* wing; '~**flächenboot** *n*, '~**flügelboot** *n* hydrofoil (craft).

Trägheit ['trε:khait] *f* laziness, indolence, *a. phys.* inertia.

Tragik ['tra:gik] *f* (16, *o. pl.*) tragicalness; tragedy; '~**er** *m* (7) tragic poet, tragedian.

tragikom|isch [~gi'ko:miʃ] tragicomic(ally *adv.*); **Ωödie** [ˌko'møː-djə] *f* tragicomedy.

'**tragisch** tragic(al *fig.*); *ich nehme es nicht* ~ I don't take it hard.

Trag|korb ['trɑːk-] *m* (back-)basket; '**⸝kraft** *f s.* Tragfähigkeit.

Tragöd|e [tra'gøːdə] *m* (13) tragic actor, tragedian; **⸝ie** [ˌdjə] *f* (15) tragedy; **⸝in** *f* (16¹) tragedienne.

Trag|riemen ['trɑːkriːmən] *m* (carrying) strap; '**⸝schrauber** *m* gyroplane, autogiro; '**⸝tier** *n* pack animal; '**⸝tüte** *f* carrier bag; '**⸝weite** *f* range; *fig.* import(ance), consequences *pl.*, implications *pl.*; '**⸝werk** ⚙ *n* wing unit.

Train|er ['trɛːnər] *m* (7) trainer, coach; **Ωieren** [ˌ'niːrən] *v/t. u. v/i.* train, coach (*zu e-m Sport* for); **⸝ing** ['⸝niŋ] *n* (11, *o. pl.*) training; '**⸝ings-anzug** *m* training overall, track suit; '**⸝ingslager** *n* training camp.

Trakt|at [trak'tɑːt] *m*, *n* (3) (*Abhandlung*) treatise; *eccl.* tract; (*Vertrag*) treaty; **Ωieren** [ˌ'tiːrən] treat.

Traktor ⊕ ['traktor] *m* (8¹) tractor. **trällern** ['trɛlərn] (29) trill, hum. **trampel|n** ['trampəln] (29) trample; '**Ωpfad** *m* beaten path; '**Ωtier** *n* Bactrian camel.

Tran [trɑːn] *m* (3) train(-oil), whale-oil.

Trance [trãːns(ə)] *f* (15) trance.

Tranchier|besteck [trãˈʃiːr-] *n* (*ein a pair of*) carvers *pl.*; **⸝brett** *n* carving-board; **Ωen** carve, cut up; **⸝messer** *n* carving-knife.

Träne ['trɛːnə] *f* (15) tear; *den* ~*n nahe* on the verge of tears; *unter* ~*n* amid tears; *s.* ausbrechen.

'**tränen** (25) water, run with tears; '**Ωdrüse** *f* lachrymal gland; '**Ωgas** *n* tear-gas; '**Ωsack** *m* lachrymal sac.

'**tranig** smelling (*od.* tasting) of train-oil; F (*träg*) dull.

Trank [traŋk] 1. *m* (3³) drink, beverage; ✶ potion; 2. Ω *pret. v.* trinken.

Tränke ['trɛŋkə] *f* (15) watering-place; '**Ωn** (25) give *a p.* to drink; *Vieh, Boden*: water; (*durchtränken*) soak, steep, ⊕ *a.* impregnate.

trans|atlantisch [transˀat'lantiʃ] transatlantic; **Ωfer** ✶ [ˌ'feːr] *m* (11), **⸝ferieren** [ˌfeˈriːrən] transfer; **Ωformator** ⚡ [ˌfɔrˈmɑːtɔr] *m* transformer; **⸝formieren** [ˌfɔrˈmiːrən] transform.

Transfusion [ˌfuˈzjoːn] *f* transfusion.

Transistor [tranˈzistɔr] *m* transistor; **Ωisieren** [ˌtoriˈziːrən] transistorize.

Transit|handel [tranˈziːt-] *m* transit-trade; **Ωiv** ['ˌziːtiːf] transitive; **⸝weg** *m* transit route.

Transkription [transkripˈtsjoːn] *f* transcription.

Transmission ⊕ [transmiˈsjoːn] *f* transmission.

transparent [ˌpaˈrɛnt] 1. transparent; 2. Ω *n* (3) transparency; *bei Demonstrationen*: banner.

Transpi|ration [ˌpiraˈtsjoːn] *f* perspiration; **Ωrieren** perspire.

Transplant|ation ⚕ [transplantaˈtsjoːn] *f*, **Ωieren** [ˌ'tiːrən] transplant.

Transport [ˌ'pɔrt] *m* (3) transport (-ation), carriage, ⚓ *u. Am. allg.* shipment; (*Straßen*Ω) haulage; ✈ *während des* ~*s* in transit; **Ωabel** [ˌ'tɑːbəl] transportable; (*tragbar*) portable; (*beweglich*) mobile; **⸝arbeiter** [ˌ'pɔrt-] *m* transport worker; **⸝er** *m* (7) ⚓ transport; ✈ transport aircraft; *s.* Truppen Ω; **⸝eur** [ˌ'tøːr] *m* (3¹) transporter; ⚙ protractor; **Ωfähig** [ˌ'pɔrt-] transportable; *Kranke*: transferable; **⸝flugzeug** *n* transport aircraft *od.* airplane; **⸝gelegenheit** *f* transport(ation) (facility); **Ωieren** [ˌ'tiːrən] transport, carry, move, haul; **⸝mittel** [ˌ'pɔrt-] *n* (means of) transport(ation) *od.* conveyance; **⸝schiff** *n* transport; **⸝unternehmen** *n* carriers *pl.*, haulage contractors *pl.*; **⸝versicherung** *f* transport insurance.

Trapez [traˈpeːts] *n* (3²) ⚡ trapezoid; *mit zwei parallelen Seiten*: trapezium; *Turnen*: trapeze; **⸝künstler(in** *f*) *m* trapezist.

trappeln ['trapəln] (29, h. u. sn) *Pferd usw.*: clatter; *Kind usw.*: patter.

Tras|sant ✶ [traˈsant] *m* (12) drawer; **⸝sat** ✶ [ˌ'sɑːt] *m* (12) drawee; '**⸝se** ⊕ *f* (15) line; Ω'**sieren** ✶ draw; ⊕ lay out, trace (out).

trat [trɑːt] *pret. v.* treten.

Tratsch [trɑːtʃ] F *m* (3), '**Ωen** gossip.

Tratte ✶ ['tratə] *f* (15) draft.

'**Trau-altar** *m* marriage-altar.

Traube ['traubə] *f* (15) bunch of

grapes; (*Beere*) grape; *weitS.* cluster; '**~nlese** *f* vintage; '**~nsaft** *m* grape-juice; '**~nzucker** *m* glucose, dextrose.

trauen ['traʊən] **1.** *v/t.* marry; *sich (kirchlich) ~ lassen* get married (in church); **2.** *v/i.* trust (*j-m* a p.), have confidence (*dat.* in); *trau, schau, wem!* look before you leap!; *ich traute meinen Ohren nicht* I could not believe my ears; *sich ~ s. getrauen*; *Weg.*

Trauer ['traʊər] *f* (15) sorrow, affliction; (*Gram*) grief; (*um e-n Toten*; *~kleidung*, *~zeit*) mourning; '**~-anzeige** *f* obituary (notice); '**~fall** *m* death; '**~feier** *f* obsequies *pl.*; '**~flor** *m* mourning-crape; '**~geleit** *n* funeral train; '**~kleid** *n* mourning(-dress); '**~marsch** *m* funeral march; '**2n** (29) mourn (*um* for); *weitS.* grieve (about); (*äußerlich ~*) be in mourning; '**~rand** *m* mourning-edge; *Briefpapier mit ~* mourning-paper; '**~schleier** *m* mourning-veil, weeper; '**~spiel** *n* tragedy; '**~weide** ⚘ *f* weeping willow; '**~zug** *m* funeral procession.

Traufe ['traʊfə] *f* (15) eaves *pl.*; *s. Regen.*

träufeln ['trɔʏfəln] (29) drip, trickle.

traulich ['traʊliç] (*vertraut*) intimate; (*gemütlich*) cosy, snug; '**2keit** *f* intimacy; cosiness.

Traum [traʊm] *m* (3³) dream; *das fällt mir nicht im ~e ein* I would not dream of (doing) it; **~a** ['~ma] ⚕ *n* (9¹, *pl. a. ~ta*) (*seelisches ~* psychic) trauma; '**~bild** *n* vision; '**~deuter** *m* (7), '**~deuterin** *f* (16¹) interpreter of dreams.

träum|en ['trɔʏmən] *v/i. u. v/t.* (25) dream (*von* of); '**2er** *m* (7), '**2erin** *f* dreamer; **2erei** [~'raɪ] *f* (16) dreaming; *fig.* reverie, day-dream; '**~erisch** dreamy; (*sinnend*) musing.

'**Traum|fabrik** *f* (*Film*) dream factory; '**~frau** F *f* dream woman; '**~haus** F *n* dream house; '**~land** *n* dreamland; '**~welt** *f* world of dreams.

'**Traurede** *f* marriage sermon.

traurig ['traʊriç] sad (*über acc.* at), sorrowful; (*elend*) wretched; (*beklagenswert*) deplorable, sorry; '**2keit** *f* sadness.

'**Trau|ring** *m* wedding-ring; '**~schein** *m* marriage certificate *od.* lines *pl.*

traut [traʊt] beloved, dear; *s. a. traulich.*

'**Trau|ung** *f* wedding; '**~zeuge** *m* witness to a marriage.

Travestie [travɛ'stiː] *f* (15), **2ren** travesty.

Treber ['treːbər] *pl.* (7) husks of grapes; (*Bier2*) draff *sg.*

Treck [trɛk] *m* (3), '**2en** (25, sn) trek; '**~er** ⊕ *m* (7) tractor.

Treff¹ [trɛf] *n* (11) *Karten*: club(s *pl.*); **~²** *m* F (*Treffen*) rendezvous.

treffen ['trɛfən] **1.** (30) *v/t.* hit; (*befallen*) befall, affect; (*begegnen*) meet; *sich (mit j-m) ~* meet, (*sich versammeln*) *a.* gather, assemble; *sich ~* (*geschehen*) happen; *das trifft sich gut* that's lucky; F *es gut ~* be in luck; *paint.*, *phot.* *du bist gut getroffen* this is a good likeness of you; *fig. j-n (empfindlich) ~* hit hard, *Kränkung*: cut to the quick; *sich getroffen fühlen* feel hurt; *nicht ~* miss; *das Los traf ihn* the lot fell on him; *s. Anstalt, Blitz, Entscheidung, Maßnahme, Vorkehrung usw.*; *v/i.* hit, go home (*beide a. fig.*); *Boxen*: *a.* land; *nicht ~* miss; *jeder Schuß trifft* every shot tells; *~ auf (acc.)* meet with, *zufällig*: come across; *auf den Feind ~* encounter, fall in with; *s. schwarz 2.*; **2.** 2 *n* (6) meeting, *Am. a.* rally; *zwangloses*: gathering; ⚔ encounter; *Gründe ins ~ führen* put forward; '**~d** (*auffallend*) striking; (*angemessen*) appropriate, apt; *Bemerkung*: pertinent, *pred.* to the point.

'**Treffer** *m* (7) hit; *Fußball*: goal; *fig.* (lucky) hit, lucky strike; (*Gewinnlos*) prize.

'**treffgenau** accurate; '**2igkeit** *f* accuracy.

'**trefflich** excellent; '**2keit** *f* excellence.

'**Treff|punkt** *m* meeting point, rendezvous; '**2sicher** accurate; *a. fig. Urteil*: unerring.

Treibeis ['traɪpʔaɪs] *n* drift-ice.

treiben ['~bən] **1.** (30) *v/t. allg.* drive; ⊕ (*an~*) *a.* propel; *Maschine usw.*: *a.* work, operate; *fig.* (*an~*) drive, impel, *stärker*: press, urge; *j-n ~ zu inf.* prompt (*od.* drive) a p. to; (*betreiben*) practise; *Geschäft, Handel usw.*: carry on; *Beruf*: pursue, follow; *e-e Politik*: pursue;

Sprachen: study; *s. Sport;* ⅔ (*ver-üben*) commit, practise; (*tun*) do; es *toll* ~ carry on like mad; *Metall:* (en)chase, emboss; *Blätter usw.:* put forth; *Pflanze:* force; *die Preise* ~ force up the market; *s. Enge, Flucht, Spitze usw.;* *v/i.* (h. u. sn) drive; *im Wasser:* float; drift (*a. v. Schnee usw.;* in e-n *Krieg* into a war); (*keimen*) shoot forth, germinate; ⚓ vor *Anker* ~ drag the anchor; ~de *Kraft* moving power, (*a. fig.*) prime mover; *fig. die Dinge* ~ *lassen* let things drift; *sich* ~ *lassen* float, *fig.* let o.s. drift; **2.** ⚲ *n* (6) driving *etc.;* (*Tun*) doings, activities *pl.,* (*Vorgänge*) *a.* goings-on *pl.;* (*geschäftiges* ~) bustle, stir.

'**Treiber** *m* (7) driver; (*Vieh*⚲) drover; *hunt.* beater.

Treib|gas ['traɪp-] *n* fuel (*od.* propellent) gas; '**~haus** *n* hothouse; '**~hauspflanze** *f* hothouse plant; '**~holz** *n* drift-wood; '**~jagd** *f* battue; *fig.* hunt; '**~kraft** *f*, '**~rad** *n*, '**~sand** *m s. Trieb...;* '**~ladung** *f*, '**~satz** ⚔ *m* propelling charge; '**~mine** *f* floating mine; '**~mittel** ⊕ *n* propell|ant, -ent; '**~öl** *n* motor (*od.* fuel) oil; '**~riemen** *m* driving belt; '**~stoff** *m* fuel; *s. Benzin*(...).

treidel|n ⚓ ['traɪdəln] (29) tow; '⚲**pfad** *m* tow(ing)-path.

tremolieren [tremo'liːrən] ♪ quaver, sing with a tremolo.

Trend [trɛnd] *m* (11) trend, tendency (*zu* toward[s]).

'**trennbar** separable.

trenn|en ['trɛnən] (25) separate (*a.* ⊕, ⚲ₘ), sever; (*teilen*) divide; *Naht:* rip up; (*loslösen*) detach; (*isolieren*) isolate, segregate; *teleph.,* ⚡ cut off, disconnect; *sich* ~ separate (*von* from), part (*P.:* with; *S.:* from, with); '**~scharf** *Radio:* selective; '⚲**schärfe** *f Radio:* selectivity; '⚲**ung** *f* separation; parting; division (*a. Silben*⚲); segregation; disconnection; ⅔ *eheliche* ~ judicial separation; '⚲**ungslinie** *f* dividing (*od.* parting) line; '⚲**ungsstrich** *m* dash; '⚲(**ungs)wand** *f* partition wall.

Trense ['trɛnzə] *f* (15) snaffle.

treppauf [trɛp'¹⁹aʊf]: ~, *trepp'-ab* upstairs, downstairs.

Treppe ['trɛpə] *f* (15) staircase, (*eine* a flight of *od.* a pair of) stairs *pl.;* *außerhalb des Hauses:* (*eine* a flight of) steps *pl.;* 2 ~n *hoch* on the second floor; *die* ~ *hinauf* (*hinab*) upstairs (downstairs); '**~n-absatz** *m* landing; '**~nflucht** *f* flight of steps; '**~ngeländer** *n* banisters *pl.;* '**~nhaus** *n* staircase; '**~nläufer** *m* staircarpet; '**~nstufe** *f* stair, step.

Tresor [tre'zoːr] *m* (3¹) treasury; (*Stahlkammer*) strong-room, *bsd. Am.* vault; *eng S.* safe.

Tresse ['trɛsə] *f* (15) galloon, lace; ⚔ stripe.

Trester ['trɛstər] (7) *pl. s. Treber.*

treten ['treːtən] (30) *v/i.* (h. u. sn) tread; (*gehen*) step, walk; *Radfahrer usw.:* treadle, pedal; *ins Haus* ~ enter the house; ~ *Sie näher!* come in!; *j-m zu nahe* ~ offend; *j-m unter die Augen* ~ appear before; *über die Ufer* ~ overflow its banks; *s. Kraft, näher~, Verbindung; v/t.* tread; (*e-n Fußtritt geben*) kick; *mit Füßen* ~ (*a. fig.*) trample (up)on.

'**Tretmühle** *f* treadmill (*a. fig.*).

treu [trɔʏ] faithful, loyal, true (*dat.* to); *zu* ~*en Händen* in trust; *s. Glauben.*

'**Treu|bruch** *m* breach of faith (*od.* trust); disloyalty; '⚲**brüchig** faithless, disloyal; '**~e** *f* (15) fidelity, faith(fulness), loyalty; *j-m die* ~ *halten* remain loyal to; '**~eid** *m* oath of allegiance; **~händer** ['~hɛndər] *m* (7) trustee; ⚲**händerisch** ['~hɛndərɪʃ] fiduciary; *adv.* in trust; '**~händerschaft** *f* trusteeship; '**~handgesellschaft** *f* trust-company; '⚲**herzig** guileless; (*offen*) frank; (*naiv*) ingenuous; '⚲**lich** faithfully; (*wahrhaft, aufrichtig*) truly; '⚲**los** faithless, perfidious; '**~losigkeit** *f* faithlessness, perfidy.

Tribun [tri'buːn] *m* (3¹ *u.* 12) tribune; **~al** [~bu'naːl] *n* (3¹) tribunal.

Tribüne [tri'byːnə] *f* (15) (*Redner*⚲) platform, rostrum; (*Zuschauer*⚲) (grand-)stand.

Tribut [~'buːt] *m* (3) tribute; *fig. j-m s-n* ~ *zollen* pay tribute to; ⚲**pflichtig** [~pflɪçtɪç] tributary.

Trichine [tri'çiːnə] *f* (15) trichina.

Trichter ['trɪçtər] *m* (7) funnel; ⊕ (*Aufgabe*⚲) feeding hopper; (*Granat*⚲, *Minen*⚲) crater; *des Lautspre-*

chers usw.: horn; ◱**förmig** ['⌐fœr-miç] funnel-shaped.

Trick [trik] *m* (11) trick; '⌐**-aufnahme** *f* trick shot; *auf Tonband*: trick recording; *pl. phot.* trick photography *sg.*; '⌐**betrüger** *m* trickster; '⌐**film** *m* trick film; *gezeichneter*: animated cartoon (film).

Trieb [tri:p] **1.** *m* (3) ⚘ sprout, young shoot; (*Keimkraft*) germinating power; *fig.* (*treibende Kraft*) driving force; (*Antrieb*) impulse; (*Natur*◱) instinct; (*Drang*) urge; (*Geschlechts*◱) (sexual) urge; **2.** ◱ *pret. v.* treiben **1.**; '⌐**feder** *f* mainspring; *fig. a.* motive; '⌐**haft** instinctive; animal-like; (*sinnlich*) carnal; '⌐**kraft** *f* propelling (*od. a. fig.* motive) power, driving power (*od. a. fig.* force); '⌐**rad** *n* driving--wheel; '⌐**sand** *m* quicksand; '⌐**verbrecher** *m* sex maniac; '⌐**wagen** *m* 🚌 motor coach; *Straßenbahn*: prime mover; '⌐**werk** *n* drive (mechanism); power plant, ⚒ *a.* engine.

trief|äugig ['tri:f⁹ɔʏgiç] blear-eyed; '⌐**en** (30) drip (*von* with); *Auge*: run; *Kerze*: gutter; '⌐'**naß** dripping wet.

triezen F ['tri:tsən] *v/t.* (27) (*quälen*) persecute; (*necken*) tease.

Trift [trift] *f* (15) pasture (land); (*Holz*◱) floating; *geol.* drift.

'**triftig** valid; (*gewichtig*) weighty; (*einleuchtend*) conclusive, convincing; (*vernünftig*) sound.

Trigonometr|ie [trigonome'tri:] *f* (15) trigonometry; ◱**isch** [⌐'me:triʃ] trigonometrical.

Trikot [tri'ko:] **1.** *m, n* (11) (*Stoff*) tricot; **2.** *n* (11) *der Ballettänzer usw.*: leotard; *der Fußballer usw.*: shirt; ⌐**agen** [⌐ko'tɑ:ʒən] *pl.* hosiery *sg.*

Triller ['trilər] *m* (7) trill, shake; ♪ quaver; '◱**n** *v/i. u. v/t.* (29) trill, shake; ♪ quaver; *Vogel*: warble; '⌐**pfeife** *f* (alarm) whistle.

Trillion [tril'jo:n] *f* (16) trillion, *Am.* quadrillion.

Trilogie [trilo'gi:] *f* (15) trilogy.

trimm|en ['trimən] (25) *allg.* trim; '◱**pfad** *m* fitness trail.

trink|bar ['triŋkbɑ:r] drinkable; '◱**becher** *m* drinking-cup; '◱**branntwein** *m* potable spirit(s *pl.*); '⌐**en** (30) *v/t.* drink (*a. v/i.*); *Tee usw.*: take, have; *fig.* (*in sich auf-*

nehmen) imbibe; ⌐ *auf j-n od. et.* toast, drink to; '◱**er** *m* (7), '◱**erin** *f* drinker; *contp.* alcoholic, drunkard; '◱**erheil-anstalt** *f* institution for the cure of alcoholics; '⌐**fest** holding one's liquor well; '◱**gelage** *n* drinking-bout; '◱**geld** *n* gratuity, *mst* F tip; *j-m* (*ein*) ⌐ *geben* F tip a p.; '◱**glas** *n* drinking-glass; '◱**halle** *f im Kurort*: pump-room; *auf der Straße*: refreshment kiosk; '◱**kur** *f* mineral water cure; '◱**lied** *n* drinking-song; '◱**spruch** *m* toast; '◱**wasser** *n* drinking-water.

Trio ['tri:o] *n* (11) trio.

Triole ♪ [tri'o:lə] *f* (15) triplet.

trippeln ['tripəln] (29, *h. u.* sn) trip.

Tripper ⚕ ['tripər] *m* (7) gonorrh(o)ea, *sl.* clap.

trist [trist] dreary.

Tritt [trit] *m* (3) tread, step; (*Schritt*) pace; (⌐*spur*) footprint, footstep; (*Geräusch des* ⌐*es*) footfall; (*Fuß*◱) kick; (*Möbel*) stepstool; ⊕ treadle; *mount.* foothold; *s.* ⌐*brett*, ⌐*leiter*; *im* ⌐ in step; *in falschem* ⌐ out of step; ⌐ *fassen* fall in step; ⌐ *halten* keep step; *aus dem* ⌐ *geraten* break step; *s. Schritt*; '⌐**brett** *n* foot--board, *mot.* running-board; '⌐**leiter** *f* step-ladder.

Triumph [tri'umf] *m* (3) triumph; *in Zssgn mst* triumphal, *z.B.* ⌐**bogen** *m* triumphal arch; ◱**al** [⌐'fɑ:l] triumphant; ◱**ieren** [⌐'fi:rən] triumph (*fig.* ⌐ *über j-n* over a p.).

trivial [tri'vjɑ:l] trivial; ◱**literatur** *f* light fiction.

trocken ['trɔkən] dry (*a. weitS. Husten, Wein*; *fig. Humor usw.*); (*dürr*) arid; *fig.* dull; *im Trockenen* under cover, *fig. im trocknen* in safety; *auf dem trocknen sitzen* be in low water, be on the rocks; *s. Schäfchen.*

'**Trocken|batterie** ⚡ *f* dry (cell) battery; '⌐**boden** *m* drying-loft; '⌐**dock** *n* dry dock; '⌐**ei** *n* dried (whole) eggs *pl.*; '⌐**eis** *n* dry ice; '⌐**element** ⚡ *n* dry cell; '⌐**fäule** *f* dry rot; '⌐**gemüse** *n* dried (*od.* dehydrated) vegetables *pl.*; '⌐**gewicht** *n* dry weight; '⌐**haube** *f* drying hood; '⌐**hefe** *f* dry yeast; '⌐**heit** *f* dryness (*a. weitS. u. fig.*); (*Dürre*) drought, aridity; *fig.* dullness; '◱**legen** dry up; *Land*: drain; *Säugling*: change a baby's nappies (*Am.*

diapers); '⁓legung f drainage; '⁓maß n dry measure; '⁓milch f dried milk; '⁓rasierer m dry-shaver; '⁓reinigung f dry-cleaning.

trockn|en ['trɔknən] (26) v/i. (sn) u. v/t. dry (up); 'Ꞩer m drier.

Troddel ['trɔdəl] f (15) tassel.

Trödel ['trøːdəl] m (7) second-hand articles pl.; (Gerümpel) lumber, Am. junk; (Schund) rubbish, trash; ⁓ei [⁓'laɪ] f (16) dawdling; '⁓kram m s. Trödel; '⁓markt m rag-fair; 'Ꞩn (29) deal in second-hand goods; fig. dawdle.

Trödler ['trøːdlər] m (7) second-hand dealer; fig. dawdler.

troff [trɔf] pret. v. triefen.

Trog¹ [troːk] m (3³) trough.

trog² [⁓] pret. v. trügen.

Trojan|er [tro'jaːnər] m (7), ⁓erin f (16¹), Ꞩisch Trojan.

trollen ['trɔlən] (25, sn) toddle along; sich ⁓ toddle off.

Trommel ['trɔməl] f (15) drum; ⊕ a. cylinder; die ⁓ rühren beat the drum, fig. advertise; '⁓fell n drumskin; anat. eardrum, ☐ tympanic membrane; '⁓fell-entzündung ⚕ f tympanitis; '⁓feuer ✕ n drum fire, a. fig. barrage; 'Ꞩn v/i. (29) drum (a. v/t.), beat the drum; nervös mit den Fingern ⁓ beat the devil's tattoo; '⁓schlag m beat of the drum; '⁓schlegel m, '⁓stock m drumstick; '⁓wirbel m (drum) roll.

Trommler ['trɔmlər] m (7) drummer.

Trompete [trɔm'peːtə] f (15), Ꞩn (26) trumpet; ⁓r m (7) trumpeter.

Tropen ['troːpən] pl. tropics; 'Ꞩfest tropicalised; '⁓helm m sun- (od. pith-)helmet, topi; '⁓koller m tropical frenzy.

Tropf¹ [trɔpf] m (3³) simpleton; (Schelm) rogue; armer ⁓ poor wretch.

Tropf² ⚕ [⁓] m (3, o. pl.) drip; am ⁓ hängen be on the drip.

tröpfeln ['trœpfəln] v/i. (29, h. u. sn) drop (a. v/t.), drip, trickle; Wasserhahn: leak; Kerze: gutter.

tropfen ['trɔpfən] 1. (25) s. tröpfeln; 2. Ꞩ m (6) drop; (Schweiß⚕) a. bead; ⚕ pl. drops; guter ⁓ splendid wine; fig. ein ⁓ auf den heißen Stein a drop in the ocean; s. stet; ⁓förmig ⊕ ['⁓fœrmiç] drop-shaped; '⁓weise by drops.

'tropf|'naß dripping wet; 'Ꞩstein m stalactite, stehender: stalagmite.

Trophäe [tro'fɛːə] f (15) trophy.

tropisch ['troːpiʃ] tropical.

Troß ✕ [trɔs] m (4) train (a. fig.), supply lines pl., baggage.

Trosse ['trɔsə] f (15) cable, ⚓ hawser.

Trost [troːst] m (3²) comfort, consolation; ein schlechter ⁓ cold comfort; nicht (recht) bei ⁓e sein be out of one's mind.

tröst|en ['trøːstən] (26) console, comfort; sich ⁓ take comfort, console o.s.; 'Ꞩer m (7), 'Ꞩerin f comforter, consoler; '⁓lich s. trostreich.

'trost|los disconsolate, desolate; fig. cheerless; (öde) dreary, desolate; (jämmerlich) wretched; v. Dingen: a. hopeless; 'Ꞩlosigkeit f desolation; fig. dreariness; wretchedness; 'Ꞩpreis m consolation prize, F booby-prize; '⁓reich comforting.

Tröstung ['trøːstuŋ] f consolation.

Trott [trɔt] m (3) trot; fig. jog-trot, routine; '⁓el m (7) idiot, F nincompoop, sap; 'Ꞩen (26, h. u. sn) trot.

Trottoir [trɔto'aːr] n (3¹) pavement, Am. sidewalk.

trotz [trɔts] 1. in spite of, despite; ⁓ alledem for all that; 2. Ꞩ m (3²) defiance; (Störrigkeit) obstinacy; j-m ⁓ bieten defy; aus ⁓ out of spite; mir zum ⁓ to spite me; ⁓dem [⁓'deːm] adv. nevertheless, for all that, notwithstanding, still; cj. (al-)though; '⁓en (27) defy (j-m a p.); Gefahren: brave; (schmollen) sulk; (eigensinnig sein) be obstinate; '⁓ig, a. ⁓köpfig ['⁓kœpfiç] defiant; (widerspenstig) refractory; (schmollend) sulky; (eigensinnig) obstinate; 'Ꞩkopf m sulky child; weitS. pig-headed person; 'Ꞩre-aktion f act of defiance.

trüb [tryːp], ⁓e ['⁓bə] Flüssigkeit: muddy, turbid, cloudy; (glanzlos) unklar) dim, dull; Wetter: cloudy, a. fig.: gloomy, bleak, dreary; Erfahrung: sad; ⁓ gestimmt sein F have the blues; im ⁓en fischen fig. fish in troubled waters.

Trubel ['truːbəl] m (7) bustle.

trüben ['tryːbən] (25) s. trüb: make muddy etc.; (glanzlos, unklar machen); a. sich) dim; Spiegel usw.: tarnish; (dunkel machen; a. sich) darken; Freude usw.: spoil; Sicht, Sinn: blur; Beziehungen: upset, sich: become strained; der Himmel *trübt sich* the sky is getting over-cast.

Trüb|heit ['try:p-] *f s. trüb*: mud-diness, turbidity; dimness; *fig.* gloom, dreariness; '⁓**sal** *f* (14) af-fliction; (*Elend*) misery; (*Not*) dis-tress; ⁓ *blasen* F be in the dumps, mope; '⁰selig sad, gloomy, melan-choly; (*öde*) bleak, dreary; '⁓**selig-keit** *f* sadness, gloominess; '⁓**sinn** *m* melancholy, sadness, gloom, F *the* blues *pl.*; '⁰**sinnig** melancholy, sad; ⁓**ung** ['⁓buŋ] *f s. trüben*: mak-ing muddy; dimming *etc.*; *Zustand*: *s. Trübheit.*

trudeln ['tru:dəln] (29) *v/i.* (sn) ✈ (go into a) spin.

Trüffel ⚘ ['tryfəl] *f* (15) truffle.

Trug¹ [tru:k] *m* (3, *o. pl.*) deceit, fraud; *der Sinne*: delusion.

trug² [⁓] *pret. v. tragen.*

'**Trugbild** *n* phantom, illusion.

trüg|en ['try:gən] *v/t. u. v/i.* (30) deceive; '⁓**erisch** deceptive, delu-sive; (*unzuverlässig*) treacherous.

Trugschluß ['tru:k-] *m* fallacy.

Truhe ['tru:ə] *f* (15) chest.

Trümmer ['trymər] *n/pl.* (7) ruins *pl.*; (*Schutt*) rubble *sg.*, *grober*: debris *sg.*; (*Schiffs⁰*) wreckage *sg.*; *in* ⁓ *legen* lay in ruins; '⁓**feld** *n* shambles; '⁓**haufen** *m* heap of ruins *od.* rubble.

Trumpf [trumpf] *m* (3³) (*a. fig.*) trump(-card); ⁓ *sein a. fig.* be trumps (*bei in*); *alle Trümpfe in der Hand haben* hold all the trumps (*a. fig.*); '⁰**en** *v/i. u. v/t.* (25) trump.

Trunk [truŋk] *m* (3³) drink; (*Schluck*) draught; (*das Trinken*) drinking; *im* ⁓ when drunk *od.* intoxicated.

'**trunken** drunken; *pred.* drunk (*a. fig.*, *von* with); intoxicated; '⁰**bold** ['⁓bɔlt] *m* (3) drunkard, sot; '⁰**heit** *f* drunkenness; ⁓ *am Steuer* drunken driving.

'**Trunksucht** *f* dipsomania, alcohol-ism.

'**trunksüchtig** addicted to alcohol; '⁰**e** ['⁓gə] *m* (18) dipsomaniac.

Trupp [trup] *m* (11) troop, band, gang; ✗ detachment, detail, party.

'**Truppe** *f* (15) ✗ troop, body; (*Ein-heit*) unit; *thea.* company, troupe; ✗ ⁓*n pl.* forces, troops.

'**Truppen|-abzug** ✗ *m* withdrawal of troops, pull-out; '⁓**formation** *f* unit, formation; '⁓**gattung** *f* branch

(of service), arm; '⁓**schau** *f* military review; '⁓**teil** *m* unit; '⁓**transporter** *m* (7) ⚓ transport, troopship; ✗ troop-carrier; '⁓**übung** *f* (field) exercise; '⁓**übungs-platz** *m* train-ing area.

'**Trupp|führer** *m* squad leader; '⁰**weise** in troops.

Trust [trast] ✝ *m* (3³) trust.

Trut|hahn ['tru:tha:n] *m* turkey (-cock); '⁓**henne** *f* turkey-hen.

Trutz *poet.* [truts] *m* (3²) = *Trotz.*

Tschech|e ['tʃɛçə] *m* (13), '⁓**in** *f* (16¹), '⁰**isch** Czech.

tschüs! [tʃys] F bye-bye, so long.

Tube ['tu:bə] *f* (15) tube; F *auf die* ⁓ *drücken* F step on it.

Tuberk|el [tu'bɛrkəl] *f* (15) tu-bercle; ⁰**ulös** [⁓ku'lø:s] tubercular, tuberculous; ⁓**ulose** [⁓'lo:zə] *f* (15) tuberculosis.

Tuch [tu:x] *n*: **a)** (3) (*Stoff*) cloth; **b)** (1²) (*Kopf⁰*) kerchief; (*Umhän-ge⁰*) shawl; (*Hals⁰*) scarf, necker-chief; (*Wisch⁰*) rag; *s. rot*; '⁓**fabrik** *f* cloth factory; '⁓**fühlung** *f* close touch; ⁓ *haben mit fig.* be in close touch with; '⁓**handel** *m* cloth--trade, drapery; '⁓**händler** *m* drap-er; '⁓**handlung** *f* draper's shop; '⁓**macher** *m* clothmaker, clothier.

tüchtig ['tyçtiç] able, fit; (*fähig*) (cap)able, competent, clever; (*lei-stungsfähig*) efficient; (*erfahren*) ex-perienced; (*vortrefflich*) excellent; (*beträchtlich*) good; (*gründlich*) thor-ough; ⁓ *arbeiten* work hard; ⁓ *essen* eat heartily; '⁰**keit** *f* ability, fitness; cleverness; excellency; efficiency; prowess.

'**Tuchware(n** *pl.*) *f* drapery *sg.*

Tück|e ['tykə] *f* (15) malice; (*Streich*) trick; '⁰**isch** malicious, insidious; (*böse, gefährlich*) vicious; (*verräte-risch*; *a. Eis usw.*) treacherous.

Tuff [tuf] *m* (3¹), '⁓**stein** *m* tuff.

tüft|eln F ['tyftəln] (29) subtilize; ⁓ *an* (*dat.*) puzzle over; '⁰**ler(in** *f*) *m* tink-erer.

Tugend ['tu:gənt] *f* (16) virtue; '⁓**bold** *m*, '⁓**held** *m* paragon of vir-tue; '⁰**haft**, '⁰**reich**, '⁰**sam** vir-tuous; '⁓**richter(in** *f*) *m* moralist, censor.

Tüll [tyl] *m* (3¹) (*Stoff*) tulle; '⁓**e** *f* (15) socket; (*Gießröhre*) spout.

Tulpe ⚘ ['tulpə] *f* (15) tulip.

tummel|n ['tuməln] (29) put in

motion; *Pferd*: work; *sich* ~ disport o.s., bustle about, *(sich beeilen)* hurry, *(sich rühren, arbeiten)* bestir o.s.; *Kind*: romp; '♀**platz** *m* playground *(a. fig.)*.

Tumor ['tuːmɔr] ⚥ *m* (8¹) tumo(u)r.

Tümpel ['tympəl] *m* (7) pool.

Tumult [tu'mult] *m* (3) tumult; *(Aufruhr)* riot; **~uant** [~tu'ant] *m* (12) rioter; ♀**uarisch** [~tu'ɑːriʃ] tumultuous, riotous.

tun [tuːn] **1.** (30) do; *(ausführen)* perform, make; *Äußerung, Bitte*: make; *Schluck, Schritt, Sprung, Eid*: take; *(wohin ~)* put *(to school, into the bag, etc.)*; *so ~ als ob* make as if, pretend to *inf.*; *es tut nichts* it doesn't matter; *was tut's?* what does it matter?; *es tut nichts zur Sache* it is irrelevant; *es tut sich etwas* something is going on; *das tut man nicht!* that is not done!; *du tätest besser zu gehen* you had better go; *dazu ~ (beitragen)* contribute (*zu* to), *(bewirken)* do in the matter; *ich kann nichts dazu ~* I cannot help it; *es ist mir darum zu ~* I am anxious about (it), it is of (great) consequence to me; *ihm ist nur um das Geld zu ~* he is only interested in the money; *das tut gut!* that does one good!; *das tut nicht gut* no good can come of it; *j-m nicht gut ~ (Arznei usw.)* disagree with a p.; *was man zu ~ und zu lassen hat* do's and don'ts; *nichts zu ~ haben mit* have nothing to do with; *zu ~ haben (beschäftigt sein)* be busy; *mit den Augen usw. zu ~ haben* have trouble with one's eyes *etc.*; *es mit j-m zu ~ bekommen* have to deal with a p.; *was ist zu ~?* what is to be done?; *s. daran, Haus, leid, vornehm, weh usw.*; **2.** ♀ *n* (6) doing(s *pl.*), action; *(Verhalten)* conduct; *~ und Treiben* doings *pl.*, activities *pl.*

Tünche ['tynçə] *f* (15) whitewash; '♀**n** (25) whitewash.

Tunichtgut ['tuːniçtguːt] *m* (3 *u. inv.*) ne'er-do-well.

Tunke ['tuŋkə] *f* (15) sauce; '♀**n** (25) dip, steep.

tunlich ['tuːnliç] feasible, practicable; '~**st** if possible.

Tunnel ['tunəl] *m* (11) tunnel; *(Unterführung)* subway.

Tüpfel ['typfəl] *m, n* (7) dot, spot;

'♀**n** (29) dot, spot.

tupfen ['tupfən] **1.** (25) touch lightly, dab; *s. tüpfeln*; **2.** ♀ *m* (6) dot, spot.

Tupfer ['tupfər] *m* (7) ☞ tampon, pad, swab; *(Tüpfel)* dot, spot.

Tür [tyːr] *f* (16) door; *in der ~ in the doorway*; *fig. e-r S. ~ und Tor öffnen* open a door to; *fig. mit der ~ ins Haus fallen* blunder it out; *fig. vor der ~ stehen (bevorstehen)* be near at hand; *fig. zwischen ~ und Angel* while about to leave; '~-**angel** *f* (door-)hinge.

Turban ['turbɑːn] *m* (3¹) turban.

Turbine [tur'biːnə] *f* (15) turbine; **~n-antrieb** *m* turbine drive; **~n-dampfer** *m* turbine steamer; **~n-motor** *m* turbine engine; **~n-strahltriebwerk** *n* turbojet engine.

Turbolader ['turbo-] *mot. m* (7) turbo-charger.

'**Tür|flügel** *m* leaf of a door; '~**füllung** *f* door-panel; '~**griff** *m* door-handle.

Türk|e ['tyrkə] *m* (13) Turk; '~**in** *f* Turk(ish woman); **~is** [~'kiːs] *m* (4) turquoise; '♀**isch** Turkish; *~er Honig* Turkish delight; *~er Teppich* Turkey (*od.* Turkish) carpet; ♧ *~er Weizen* Indian corn.

'**Tür|klinke** *f* door-handle; '~**klopfer** *m* knocker.

Turm [turm] *m* (3³) tower; *(Kirch*♀*)* steeple; *Schach*: castle, rook; ⚔ *(Geschütz*♀*)* turret.

Türm|chen ['tyrmçən] *n* (6) turret; '♀**en** (25) *v/t.* heap up; *sich ~* tower (up), *weitS. a.* pile up; *v/i.* F *(sich davonmachen)* F bolt, skedaddle; '~**er** *m* (7) warder (on the tower).

'**Turm|falke** *m* kestrel; '♀**hoch:** *j-m ~ überlegen sein* be head and shoulders above a p.; '~**spitze** *f* spire; '~**springen** *n* high diving; '~-**uhr** *f* church-clock.

turn|en ['turnən] **1.** (25) practise *(od.* do) gymnastics; **2.** ♀ *n* (6) gymnastics *pl.*; '♀**er** *m* (7), '♀**erin** *f* gymnast; '~**erisch** gymnastic.

'**Turn|gerät(e** *pl.*) *n* gymnastic apparatus; '~**halle** *f* gym(nasium); '~**hose(n** *pl.*) *f* gym shorts *pl.*

Turnier [tur'niːr] *n* (3¹) tournament; *nur hist.* joust(ing); ♀**en** joust, tilt; ~**platz** *m* tiltyard.

'**Turn|lehrer(in** *f*) *m* gym instructor; '~**riege** *f* gym squad; '~**schuh** *m*

plimsoll, gym shoe; '⟋**stunde** f
Schule: gym lesson; '⟋-**unterricht** m
instruction in gymnastics.
Turnus ['turnus] m (14, *o. pl.*) rotation; *im* ⟋ in rotation, by turns;
'2**mäßig** regular(ly recurring); in
rotation.
'**Turnver-ein** m gymnastic club.
'**Tür**|-**öffner** m (7) *elektrischer*: buzz-
er; '⟋**pfosten** m door-post; '⟋**rahmen** m door-frame; '⟋**schild** n door-
-plate; '⟋**schließer** m (*Person*) door-
-keeper; (*Vorrichtung*) door catch.
Turteltaube ['turtəl-] f turtle-dove.
Tusch ♪ [tuʃ] m (3³) flourish; '⟋**e** f
(15) India(n) ink; *s. Tuschfarbe*;
'2**eln** v/i. u. v/t. (29) whisper; '2**en**
(29) wash; (*aquarellieren*) paint in
water-colo(u)rs; *mit schwarzer Tusche*: draw in India(n) ink; '⟋**farbe**
f water-colo(u)r; '⟋**kasten** m paint-
-box; '⟋**zeichnung** f India(n)-ink
drawing.
Tüte ['tyːtə] f (15) (paper-)bag; F
kommt nicht in die ⟋! nothing
doing!

tuten ['tuːtən] (26) toot(le); *mot.*
honk.   [dot; *fig.* jot.⟍
Tüttel ['tytəl] m (7), '⟋**chen** n (6)⟍
Twen [tven] F m (11) person in his
(*od.* her) twenties; *pl.* under-thirties.
Typ [tyːp] m (12), '⟋**e** f (15) type;
⊕ *a.* model; '⟋**endruck** m type
printing; '⟋**enhebel** m *der Schreibmaschine*: typebar; '⟋**enkopf** m
type; '⟋**ennummer** f model number; '⟋**enrad** n daisy wheel; '⟋**en-
schild** n name-plate; '⟋**ensetz-
maschine** f typesetting machine.
Typhus ♨ ['tyːfus] m *inv.* typhoid
(fever); '⟋**kranke** m, f typhoid
patient.
'**typisch** typical (*für* of); *das* '2**e** the
typical character.
typisieren [typi'ziːrən] typify.
Typograph [typo'graːf] m (12) ty-
pographer; 2**isch** typographic(al).
Typus ['tyːpus] m (16²) type.
Tyrann [ty'ran] m (12) tyrant; ⟋**ei**
[⟋'naɪ] f (16) tyranny; ⟋**in** f (female)
tyrant; 2**isch** tyrannical; 2**i'sieren**
tyrannize (over) *a p.*, bully *a p.*

U

U [uː], **u** n *inv.* U, u.
U-Bahn ['uː-] f *s. Untergrundbahn.*
übel ['yːbəl] **1.** evil, bad; *adv.* ill;
badly; *s. a. schlecht*; (*krank*) sick,
nur pred. ill; (*stinkend*) foul;
(*scheußlich*) vile, nasty; (*katastrophal*) disastrous; *nicht* ⟋ not bad;
mir ist ⟋ I feel sick; *mir wird* ⟋ I
am feeling sick; *dabei kann e-m* ⟋
werden it is enough to make one
sick; *sich in e-r üblen Lage befinden* be in a fix; *s. daran, mitspielen, wohl*; **2.** 2 n (6) evil; (*Unglück*)
mischief, harm; (*Krankheit*) complaint, malady; *s. Übelstand*; *das
kleinere* ⟋ the lesser evil; *vom* ⟋ no
good; '2**befinden** n indisposition;
⟋**gelaunt** ['⟋gəlaunt], '⟋**launig** ['⟋-
gəzint] ill-disposed (*dat.* towards);
'2**keit** f sickness, nausea; '⟋**nehmen**
take *a th.* ill *od.* amiss, take offen|ce
(*Am.* -se) at, resent *a th.*; es j-m ⟋
take it ill of a *p.*; '⟋**nehmend**, '⟋-

nehmerisch easily offended,
touchy, huffy; '⟋**riechend** evil-
-smelling, malodorous, F smelly;
Atem: foul, bad; '2**stand** m grievance, abuse, nuisance; (*Nachteil*)
drawback; '2**tat** f misdeed; '2**tä-
ter(in** f) m evil-doer, wrong-doer,
malefactor; '2**wollen**¹ n (6) ill-will,
malevolence; '⟋**wollen**² wish ill
(*dat.* to), bear *a p.* a grudge; '⟋**wollend** malevolent.
üben ['yːbən] v/t. u. v/i. (25) (*a.
sich* ⟋ *in dat.*) exercise, (*a.* ♪) practise; *bsd. Sport*: train; *Geduld* ⟋
have patience; *s. Nachsicht, Rache*;
geübt (*P.*) practised, experienced.
über ['yːbər] **1.** *prp.* (*wo?* dat.; *wohin?* acc.) over, above; *reisen, gehen
usw.* ⟋: across *a river, the sea*; by
way of, via *a town*; *sprechen usw.* ⟋:
about, of; *Vortrag, Buch usw.* ⟋:
on; *nachdenken* ⟋: think about, over;
reflect (up)on; *schreiben* ⟋: (up)on;
(*nicht*) ⟋ (not) exceeding; *Fehler* ⟋

Fehler fault upon fault; *s. heute*; ~*s Jahr* next year; ~ ... *(hinaus)* beyond, past; ~ *meine Kräfte* beyond my strength; *s. Maß*; ~ *Nacht* over night; ~ *dem Lesen* while reading; *zehn Minuten* ~ *zwölf* ten minutes past twelve; ~ *hundert* more than a hundred; ~ *kurz oder lang* sooner or later; **2.** *adv.*: ~ *und* ~ over and over, all over; *j-m in et.* *(dat.)* ~ *sein* surpass a p. in a th.; *ich habe es* ~ I am tired *(od.* sick) of it; F *s. übrig, vorüber.*

über'-all everywhere, *Am.* all over; *(in jeder Beziehung)* throughout; ~**'hin** everywhere.

überaltert [~'°altərt] superannuated.

'**Über**|**-angebot** *n* excessive supply; '**2-ängstlich** over-anxious.

über'-anstreng|**en** over-exert, overstrain; **2ung** *f* over-exertion, overstrain; ~ *der Augen* eyestrain.

über'-antworten deliver up, give over *(dat.* to).

über'-arbeit|**en** do over again, retouch; *Buch usw.*: revise; *sich* ~ overwork o.s.; ~**et** overworked, overwrought; **2ung** *f* revision; *(zuviel Arbeit)* overwork.

'**über'-aus** exceedingly, extremely.

'**Über**|**bau** *m* superstructure; '**2beanspruchen** ⊕ overload, overstress; *fig.* overtax; '~**bein** 𝔤 *n* node, 🝔 exostosis; '**2belasten**, '~**belastung** *f* overload; '**2belichten** *phot.* over-expose; '~**belichtung** *f* over-exposure; '~**beschäftigung** *f* overemployment; '**2besetzt** *Betrieb*: overstaffed; '**2betonen** overemphasize; '**2bewerten** overrate. *[fig.* surpass.)

über'bieten *bsd. Auktion*: outbid;)

Überbleibsel ['~blaIpsəl] *n* (7) remainder, remnant, *Am.* holdover; *pl.* remains *(a. fig.)*; *e-r Mahlzeit*: leavings, left-overs; *geschichtliches*: survival.

über'blend|**en** *Film, Radio*: fade over; **2ung** *f* fading.

'**Überblick** *m* survey *(a. fig. über acc.* of).

über|'**blicken** survey; ~'**bringen** deliver, convey; **2'bringer**(**in** *f*) *m* bearer; **2'bringung** *f* delivery; ~'**brücken** (25) bridge *(a. fig.)*, span; **2'brückungsbeihilfe** *f* stopgap relief; **2'brückungsgeld** *n* tide-over

allowance; ~**'buchen** *Flug, Hotel etc.*: overbook; ~**'bürden** (26) overburden; **2'bürdung** *f* overburdening; overpressure; ~**dachen** [~'daxən] (25) roof (over); ~**'dauern** outlast; ~**'decken** cover; '~**denken** think *a th.* over, reflect (up)on *a th.*; ~**'dies** besides, moreover.

über|**dimensional** ['~dimɛnzjonɑːl] outsize, huge; '**2dosis** *f* overdose.

über'drehen *Uhr*: overwind; *Gewinde*: strip.

'**Überdruck** *m* *(Umdruck)* transfer; ✆ surcharge, overprint; ⊕ overpressure; **2en** [~'drukən] overprint; '~**kabine** *f* pressurized cabin.

Überdruß ['~drus] *m* (4) disgust, *(bis zum* ~ to) satiety.

überdrüssig ['~drysiç] *(gen.)* disgusted with, tired *(od.* sick *od.* weary) of.

'**überdurchschnittlich** above the average, *attr.* above-average.

'**Über-eifer** *m* over-zeal; '**2-eifrig** over-zealous.

über'-eign|**en** transfer, assign *(dat.* to); **2ung** *f* transfer.

über'-eil|**en** precipitate *(die Sache* matters); *sich* ~ hurry too much; *übereilt* rash, precipitate, overhasty; **2ung** *f* precipitance; *nur keine* ~! take your time!

über-ei'nander one upon another; ~**schlagen** *Arme*: fold; *Beine*: cross.

über'-ein|**kommen**[1] (sn) agree; come to terms; **2kommen**[2] *n* (6), **2kunft** [~kunft] *f* (14[1]) agreement; ~**stimmen** *P.*: agree; *S.*: correspond, square, be in keeping *(alle: mit* with); ~**stimmend** corresponding; *(einstimmig)* unanimous; *adv.* in accordance; **2stimmung** *f* agreement; correspondence, conformity; *in* ~ *bringen* reconcile; *in* ~ *mit* in accordance *(od.* conformity) with.

'**über-empfindlich** oversensitive.

über'-essen: *sich* ~ overeat o.s.

'**überfahren 1.** *v/i.* (sn) pass over; **2.** über'**fahren** *v/t. Person, Hund usw.*: run over; *Signal*: overrun; F *fig. sl.* bulldoze *a p.*; *Sport*: trounce *a team*; *Fluß usw.*: traverse, cross.

'**Überfahrt** *f* passage; crossing *(über e-n Fluß usw.* a river, *etc.*).

'**Überfall** *m* sudden attack, surprise (attack), assault; *(Raub2)* hold-up; *(Einfall)* inroad, raid.

über'fallen attack suddenly, surprise, assault; (*einfallen in*) invade, raid; *räuberisch*: hold up; *Nacht, Krankheit usw.*: overtake.

'**überfällig** overdue.

'**Überfallkommando** *n der Polizei*: flying (*Am.* riot) squad.

überfeiner|n [~'faɪnərn] (29) over-refine; ℒ**erung** *f* over-refinement.

über'fliegen fly over; *mit den Augen*: glance over, skim; *den Ozean* ~ fly the ocean.

'**überfließen** (sn) flow over.

über'flügeln (29) ✕ outflank; *fig.* surpass, outstrip.

'**Überfluß** *m* abundance, plenty; (*unnötiger*) superfluity; (*Reichtum, Fülle*) wealth (*alle: an dat.* of); ~ haben an (*dat.*), im ~ haben abound in, have plenty of; *zum* ~ unnecessarily; '~**gesellschaft** *f* affluent society.

'**überflüssig** (*unnötig*) superfluous, unnecessary; (*überschüssig*) surplus, excess.

über'fluten overflow; inundate, flood (*a. fig. u. v. Licht*).

über'fordern *im Preis*: overcharge; *Leistungsfähigkeit usw.*: overtax.

'**Über|fracht** *f* overweight, excess freight; *Gepäck*: excess luggage; ℒ-'**frachten** overload; *fig.* überfrachtet top-heavy.

Überfremdung [~'frɛmduŋ] *f* foreign infiltration *od.* control.

'**überführ|en** 1. carry *a p.* over, transport; 2. über'führen (*befördern*) transport; (*als schuldig erweisen*) convict (*gen.* of); ℒ**ung** [~'fyːruŋ] *f* 1. transportation; *Straßenbau*, 🚊 road-bridge, fly-over, *Am.* overpass; 2. ⚖ conviction; ℒ**ungskosten** [~'fyː-ruŋs-] *pl.* transport costs.

'**Überfülle** *f* superabundance.

über'füll|en overfill, cram; *mit Menschen*: overcrowd; *Magen*: glut; *den Markt*: overstock, glut; ℒ**ung** *f* overfilling *etc.*; repletion; *Verkehr*: congestion.

'**Überfunktion** 🎬 *f* hyperfunction.

über'füttern overfeed.

'**Übergabe** *f* delivery; handing over; ✕, *a.* ⚖ surrender.

'**Übergang** *m* passage; 🚊 crossing; *fig.* transition, change; *zum Feind*: going over (to); ⚖ *v. Rechten*: devolution; '~**sbestimmungen** *f/pl.* transitional regulations; '~**slösung** *f*

temporary solution; '~**sregierung** *f* transitional government; '~**sstadium** *n* transition stage; '~**szeit** *f* transition(al) period.

über'geben deliver (up), give up; hand over; ✕ surrender (*a. sich* ~); *sich* ~ (*erbrechen*) vomit; *dem Verkehr* ~ open for traffic.

'**übergehen** 1. *v/i.* (sn) pass over (*zu* to); *auf Nachfolger, Stellvertreter* ~ (*Amt usw.*) devolve upon; ~ *in* (*acc.*) pass (*od.* change) into; *s. Fäulnis*; *zu et.* ~ proceed to, switch (over) to; *zu e-m anderen Punkt*: pass on to; *s. Angriff*; *in andre Hände* ~ change hands; 2. über'gehen *v/t.* (*übersehen*) pass over; ignore; (*auslassen*) omit, skip.

Über'gehung *f* passing over; omission.

'**übergenug** too much, more than enough.

'**überge-ordnet** higher, superior.

'**Übergewicht** *n* overweight; *fig.* preponderance; ~ *haben* be overweight; *das* ~ *bekommen* lose one's balance, *fig.* get the upper hand.

über'gießen pour over; *Braten*: baste; *mit Zuckerguß*: ice.

'**überglücklich** extremely happy.

'**übergreifen** overlap; *fig.* ~ *auf od. in* (*acc.*) encroach on; *Feuer, Panik usw.*: spread to.

'**Übergriff** *m* encroachment.

'**übergroß** outsize(d); (*riesenhaft*) colossal, immense, huge.

'**Übergröße** *f* outsize (*a.* ✝), oversize.

über'handnehmen *v/i.*, ℒ *n* increase, spread.

'**Überhang** *m* overhang; (*Geld* ℒ) surplus; (*Auftrags* ℒ *usw.*) backlog.

'**überhängen** *v/i.* (30) hang over, overhang; *v/t.* (25) hang over.

über'hastet overhasty, hurried.

über'häufen overwhelm (*od.* swamp) (*mit* with).

über'haupt generally, on the whole; (*eigentlich, tatsächlich*) actually; ~ *nicht* not at all; ~ *kein* ... no ... whatever; *wenn* ~ if at all.

über|'heben exempt (*e-r S.* from); *e-r Mühe usw.* ~ spare *a p.* a trouble *etc.*; *sich* ~ overstrain o.s. (by lifting); *fig.* be overbearing; ~**heblich** [~'heːplɪç] overbearing, arrogant; ℒ'**heblichkeit** *f* arrogance.

überhitzen [~'hɪtsən] (27) overheat

(a. fig.); ⊕ *bsd. Dampf:* superheat.
überhöht [~'høːt] *Kurve:* banked;
Preise: excessive.
über'hol|en 1. pass *(a. mot.)*, overtake; *(übertreffen)* outdistance, *(a. fig.)* outstrip; ⊕ *(nachsehen u. ausbessern)* overhaul, *bsd. Am.* service; überholt *(veraltet)* antiquated, outdated; superseded *(durch* by); **2.** 'überholen fetch *a p.* over; *v/i.* ⚓ *Schiff:* keel; ♀**manöver** *n* overtaking manœuvre, *Am.* passing maneuver; ♀**spur** *mot. f* passing lane.
über'hören not to hear; *Worte:* miss; *absichtlich:* ignore.
'**über-irdisch** supernatural.
'**Überkapazität** *f* overcapacity.
'**überkippen** tilt *(od.* tip) over.
über'kleben paste *a th.* over.
'**Überkleidung** *f (Ggs. Unterkleidung)* outer wear.
'**überklug** overwise; ~er *Mensch* wiseacre.
'**überkochen** (sn) boil over.
über'kommen *v/t.* receive; *Furcht usw.* überkam ihn he was overcome by fear *etc.*; *v/i.* (sn) *diese Sitte ist uns* ~ this custom has been handed down to us.
'**überkonfessionell** interdenominational.
über'krusten *(a. sich)* encrust.
'**Überkultur** *f* over-refinement.
über'laden 1. *v/t.* overload *(a. den Magen)*; ♀, *Bild usw.:* overcharge; *mit Arbeit:* overburden, swamp *with work*; **2.** *adj. Bild, Stil usw.:* florid, too profuse.
über'lager|n super(im)pose; ⊕ overlay; *Radio:* heterodyne; ♀**ung** *f* super(im)position; heterodyning.
Über'land|flug *m* cross-country flight; ~**leitung** ⚡ *f* long-distance line.
über'lass|en: *j-m et.* ~ let *a p.* have *a th.*; *(anheimstellen)* leave *a th.* to *a p.*; *(abtreten)* cede *a th.* to *a p.*; *(preisgeben)* abandon *a th.* to *a p.*; *sich e-m Gefühl usw.* ~ give o.s. up to; *j-n sich selbst* ~ leave *a p.* to himself; ♀**ung** *f* leaving; ⚖ cession.
'**Überlast** *f* overweight; overload.
über'last|en overload, overcharge; *fig.* overburden, overtax; ♀**ung** *f* overload; *fig.* overstress, overwork.
'**überlaufen 1.** *v/i.* (sn) run *(od.* flow) over; ✕ desert *(a. fig.)*, *weitS.* go over *(zu* to); **2.** *über'laufen v/t.*

overrun; *(belästigen)* annoy, pester; *Beruf, Gegend ist* ~ is overcrowded; *es überlief mich kalt* a cold shudder seized me.   [turncoat.]
'**Überläufer** *m* deserter; *pol. a.*ʃ
'**überlaut** too noisy, overloud.
über'leben survive; *das hat sich überlebt* that has had its day; *die Nacht usw.* ~ live the night *etc.* out; ♀**de** *m, f* (18) survivor; ♀**s...** survival ...; '~**sgroß** larger than life; ♀**swille** *m* will to survive.
überlebt [~'leːpt] *adj.* antiquated, outdated.
'**überleg|en 1.** lay over; **2.** *über'legen* a) *v/t.* consider, reflect (up)on; *ich will es mir* ~ I will think it over; *es sich wieder (od. anders)* ~ *(s-e Meinung ändern)* change one's mind; *wenn ich es mir recht überlege* on second thoughts; *s. zweimal*; **b)** *adj.* superior *(dat.* to; *an dat.* in); *allen anderen weit* ~ head and shoulders above the rest; ♀**enheit** [~'leːgənhaɪt] *f* superiority; ~**t** [~'leːkt] considered; *wohl* ~ deliberate; *(klug)* prudent; ♀**ung** *f* [~'leːgʊŋ] *f* consideration, reflection; *(reifliche* ~) deliberation; *s. reiflich*.
'**überleiten** *v/t.* lead over *(zu* to; *a. v/i.)*.
über'lesen read *(od.* run) *a th.* over, peruse; *(übersehen)* overlook.
über'liefer|n deliver; *der Nachwelt:* hand down (to); ♀**ung** *f* delivery; *fig.* tradition.
über'listen (26) outwit, fool.
über'machen make over *(dat.* to).
'**Übermacht** *f* superiority; *bsd.* ✕ supremacy *(a. fig.)*, superior force; *fig.* predominance.
'**übermächtig** overwhelming, too powerful.
'**übermalen 1.** paint over; **2.** *über-'malen* paint out *(a.* over).
über'mannen (25) overcome, overpower.
'**Über|maß** *n* excess; *im* ~ in excess; *bis zum* ~ to excess; '♀**mäßig** excessive; *adv. Am.* F overly.
'**Übermensch** *m* superman; '♀**lich** superhuman.
über'mitt|eln transmit; convey; ♀**(e)lung** *f* transmission.
'**übermodern** ultra-modern.
'**übermorgen** the day after tomorrow.

über'müd|et overtired; ℒ**ung** *f* overfatigue.

'**Über|mut** *m* wantonness; (*Ausgelassenheit*) high spirits *pl.*, frolicsomeness; (*Anmaßung*) insolence; ℒ**mütig** ['~myːtiç] wanton; frolicsome, rollicking; insolent.

'**übernächst** *the* next but one; ~e Woche the week after next.

über'nachten (26) pass (*od.* spend) the night, stay over night.

übernächtig ['~neçtiç] fatigued (from lack of sleep), blear-eyed.

Über'nachtung *f* passing the night; *im Hotel*: overnight stay; ~ *und Frühstück* bed and breakfast; ~**smöglichkeit** *f* overnight accommodation.

Übernahme ['~naːmə] *f* s. *übernehmen*: taking over; acceptance; undertaking; assumption; (*Inbesitznahme*) taking possession (*gen.* of).

'**übernational** supra-national.

'**übernatürlich** supernatural.

über'nehm|en 1. *allg.* take over (*a. v/i.*); *Arbeit, Verantwortung usw.*: undertake; *Amt, Befehl, Pflicht*: assume; *Last, Verantwortung*: take upon o.s.; *Befehl, Führung, Risiko*: take; *Verfahrensweise usw.*: adopt; *Anvertrautes*: take charge of; (*in Besitz nehmen*) take possession of; *Ware, Erbschaft*: accept; *s. Bürgschaft*; *sich* ~ undertake too much, in e-r *S.*: overdo *a th.*; *im Essen*: overeat; *fig.* overreach o.s.; **2.** '*übernehmen*: shoulder; *das Gewehr* ~ slope (*Am.* shoulder) arms.

'**über-ordnen** *j-n* (*od. et.*) *j-m* (*od. e-r S.*) ~ place (*od.* set) a *p.* (*od.* a th.) over a *p.* (*od.* a th.).

'**überparteilich** all-party.

'**Überproduktion** *f* over-production.

über'prüf|en check; ⊕ *a.* test; *genau*: scrutinize; *j-n* (*politisch usw.*): screen; (*bedenken*) (re)consider; (*untersuchen*) investigate, review; *s. nachprüfen*; ℒ**er(in** *f*) *m* revisor; ℒ**ung** *f* check(ing); scrutiny, review; consideration; investigation; test(ing).

'**überquellen** flow over.

überqueren [~'kveːrən] (25) cross.

über'ragen rise above *a th.*, tower above (*a. fig.*); *fig.* excel, surpass; ~**d** outstanding, excellent.

über'rasch|en (27) surprise; ~**end** surprising; (*unerwartet*) unexpected; ℒ**ung** *f* surprise; ℒ**ungs-an-**

griff *m* surprise attack; ℒ**ungsmoment** *n* surprise element.

'**überre-agieren** overreact (*auf acc.* to).

über'red|en persuade (*zu* [in]to); talk a *p.* into (doing) *a th.*; ℒ**ung** *f* persuasion; ℒ**ungskunst** *f* powers *pl.* of persuasion.

'**überregional** supraregional; *Zeitung*: national; *Sendung*: nationwide.

'**überreich** abounding (*an dat.* in); superabundant.

über'reichen hand *a th.* over, present, deliver (*alle: dat.* to); *schriftlich*: submit; *anliegend*: enclose.

'**überreichlich** superabundant.

Über'reichung *f* presentation.

'**überreif** overripe.

über'reizen over-excite.

über'rennen (*umrennen*) run over *od.* down, *bsd.* ✗ overrun.

'**Überrest** *m* rest, remainder; (*a.* ~e *pl.*) remains *pl.*; *a. fig.* remnant; (*Rückstand*) residue; *sterbliche* ~ mortal remains.

'**Überrollbügel** *mot. m* roll-bar.

über'rollen overrun.

über'rumpel|n surprise; ✗ take by surprise; ℒ**ung** *f* surprise.

über'runden *Sport*: outlap; *fig.* outstrip.

über'sät *fig.* dotted, studded.

'**übersatt** surfeited (*von* with).

über'sättig|en surfeit; ⌢ oversaturate; ℒ**ung** *f* surfeit; ⌢ oversaturation, supersaturation.

über'|säuert hyperacidic; ℒ'**säuerung** *f* hyperacidity.

'**Überschall...** *phys.* supersonic; '~**knall** *m* sonic boom.

über'schatten overshadow (*a. fig.*).

über'schätz|en overrate, overestimate; ℒ**ung** *f* overestimation.

über'schau|bar (*leicht verständlich*) easily comprehensible; (*in kleinem Rahmen*) of a manageable size; ~**en** overlook, survey.

'**überschäumen** foam over; *fig.* brim over (*vor Freude usw.* with); ~**d** *fig.* exuberant.

'**überschießend** *Ballast*: shifting; *Betrag*: surplus.

über'schlafen sleep on *a th.*

'**Überschlag** *m* *Turnen*: somersault; *Schneiderei*: facing; (*Schätzung*) (rough) estimate; ✄ flashover.

'**überschlagen 1.** *v/t. Beine*: cross;

2. *über'schlagen* (*weglassen*) omit, skip, miss *a page*; (*schätzen*) estimate; *sich* ~ go head over, *mot.* overturn, ⚓ capsize, ⚔ *beim Kunstflug*: loop, *beim Landen*: nose over; *Stimme*: crack, break; *Ereignisse*: follow hot on the heels of one another; **3.** *über'schlagen adj.* (*lauwarm*) lukewarm, tepid.

'überschnappen (sn) *Stimme*: squeak; F (*verrückt werden*) go crazy *od.* mad; *übergeschnappt* F cracked, *sl.* nuts.

über'schneid|en (*a. sich*) overlap (*a. fig.*); *Linien*: *sich* ~ intersect; ℒung *f* overlapping; intersection.

über'schreiben superscribe, entitle; (*übertragen*) transfer, ✝ carry over; (*bezeichnen*) label.

über'schreiten cross, pass over *a th.*, go across *a th.*; *fig.* transgress; *Gesetz*: infringe; *Maß, Termin*: exceed; *Kredit*: overdraw.

'Überschrift *f* heading, title.

'Überschuh *m* overshoe; (*Gummi*ℒ) galosh; ~e *pl. Am. a.* rubbers *pl.*

über'schuldet deeply involved in debt; *Grundstück usw.*: heavily encumbered.

'Überschuß *m* surplus.

überschüssig ['~ʃysiç] surplus, excess.

über'schütten cover; *fig.* overwhelm; *mit Geschenken*: shower with.

Überschwang ['~ʃvaŋ] *m* (3) exuberance.

über'schwemm|en flood, inundate; *fig.* flood (*od.* swamp) (*mit* with); ✝ *den Markt*: overstock, glut; ℒung *f* flood, inundation; ℒungsgebiet *n* flood area.

überschwenglich ['~ʃveŋliç] effusive, gushing; 'ℒkeit *f* effusiveness.

'Übersee: *in, nach usw.* ~ oversea(s); '~..., 'ℒisch transoceanic (*steamer*); transmarine (*cable*); oversea (*route, trade,* ⚔ *forces*); '~verkehr *m* oversea (*od.* transoceanic) traffic.

über'sehbar *s.* übersichtlich.

über'sehen survey; (*nicht bemerken*) overlook, miss; *absichtlich*: disregard, ignore; (*erkennen*) *Lage usw.*: realize, perceive; *s.* überblicken.

über'send|en send, transmit; ℒung *f* transmission; ✝ consignment.

über'setzbar translatable.

'übersetzen 1. *v/i.* (sn) pass over,

cross; *v/t.* carry *a p.* over; **2.** *über-'setzen* translate (*in acc.* into); ⊕ gear, transmit.

Über'setz|er *m* (7), ~erin *f* (16[1]) translator; ~ung *f* translation; ⊕ gear ratio, transmission; ~ungsbüro *n* translating agency; ~ungsrecht *n* right of translation.

'Übersicht *f* survey; *fig. a.* general view; (*Zusammenfassung*) summary, ⅏ synopsis; *die* ~ *verlieren* lose control; 'ℒlich easy to survey, clear(ly arranged); *Gelände*: open; (*klar gefaßt*) lucid; '~lichkeit *f* clearness; lucidity; '~skarte *f* general (*Am.* overview) map; '~s-tabelle *f* tabular summary.

'übersied|eln (29, sn) (re)move; (*auswandern*) emigrate; 'ℒ(e)lung *f* removal; emigration.

'übersinnlich transcendental; *Kräfte*: psychic(al).

über'spann|en *mit et.* cover *a th.* over with; (*zu stark spannen*) overstrain; *fig.* exaggerate; *s. Bogen*; ~t extravagant; eccentric; ℒt-heit *f* eccentricity, extravagance.

über'spielen *Sport*: *den Gegner*: outplay; *fig.* outmanœuvre, *Am.* outmaneuver; *Schallplatte usw.*: re-record.

über'spitz|en subtilize; (*übertreiben*) overdo; ~t over-subtle.

'überspringen 1. *v/i.* (sn) leap over; *Funke*: flash over; **2.** *v/t.* *über-'springen* jump (over *od.* across), clear; (*weglassen*) skip.

'übersprudeln (sn) bubble (*od.* gush) over (*fig. vor dat.* with).

'überstaatlich supernational.

'überstehen 1. *v/i.* jut out, project; **2.** *v/t. über'stehen* (*erdulden*) endure, stand; *Krankheit usw.*: get over; (*überleben*) survive.

'übersteigen 1. *v/i.* (sn) step over, climb over; **2.** *v/t. über'steigen* cross, pass; *fig.* overcome, surmount; (*hinausgehen über*) exceed, pass.

über'steigern force up; *fig.* overdo.

über'steuern *mot.* oversteer; *Verstärker etc.*: overmodulate.

über'stimmen outvote.

über'strahlen shine upon; (*verdunkeln*) outshine (*a. fig.*).

über'streichen paint *a th.* over.

'überstreifen slip *a th.* over.

'überströmen 1. *v/i.* (sn) overflow;

2. v/t. *über'strömen* s. *überschwem-*
men; '**∼d** *fig.* gushing.
'**Überstunde** f, '**∼n** pl. overtime
(hour); **∼n** *machen* work overtime.
über'stürz|en hurry, precipitate;
sich **∼** act rashly; *Ereignisse:* press
one another; **∼t** adj. precipitate;
2ung f precipitancy.
Über'tagebau ⚒ m surface mining.
übertölpeln [∼'tœlpəln] (29) dupe.
über'tönen drown (out) *a sound.*
Übertrag ✝ ['∼traːk] m (3⁸) *auf die*
andere Seite: carrying forward;
(Posten) carry-over.
über'trag|bar transferable; ✝ *(be-*
gebbar) negotiable; ✻ communica-
ble, catching, infectious, *durch Be-*
rührung: contagious; **∼en** [∼gən] ✝
carry over, bring forward; *(um-*
buchen) transfer; *Besitz:* transfer,
make over *(auf j-n* to); *(zedieren)*
assign (to); *Blut:* transfuse *(auf acc.*
to); *Vollmacht:* delegate *(auf acc.*
to); *Amt:* confer *(auf acc.* [up]on);
j-m (die Besorgung von) *et.* **∼** charge
(od. commission) *a* p. with; *sprach-*
lich: translate, render, do *(in acc.*
into); *Kurzschrift:* transcribe, extend; ⊕, *phys.,* ✻, *Radio:* transmit;
Radio: a. broadcast, relay; *TV* a.
televise; *sich* **∼** *Krankheit, Stim-*
mung usw. communicate itself *(auf*
acc. to); be infectious; **∼e** *Bedeu-*
tung figurative sense; **2ung** f transfer (a. ✝); assignment *(of rights,*
patents, etc.); v. *Blut:* transfusion;
⊕, *phys.,* ✻, *Radio:* transmission,
(Sendung) broadcast, *TV* telecast;
e-s Amtes: conferring; *(Überset-*
zung) translation; v. *Kurzschrift:*
transcription; **2ungsfehler** m *Radio,*
Computer: transfer error; **2ungswa-**
gen m *Radio:* outside broadcast
van; *Fernsehen:* mobile transmission
unit.
'**übertrainieren** overtrain.
über'treffen *P.:* excel, outdo; *P.*
u. S.: surpass, exceed, beat.
über'treib|en *Tätigkeit:* overdo;
carry *a th.* too far; *mit Worten:* exaggerate (a. v/i.), overstate; *thea.*
overact; *s.* *übertrieben;* **2ung** f ex-
aggeration.
'**übertreten 1.** v/i. (sn) pass *(od.*
step) over; *fig.* go over *(zu* to);
Fluß: overflow; *zu e-r andern Par-*
tei (Religion) **∼** change sides (one's
religion); *zum Katholizismus* **∼** turn

Roman Catholic; **2.** v/t. *über'treten*
Sport: overstep; *sich den Fuß* **∼**
sprain one's ankle; *fig.* trespass
against, infringe, violate.
Über'tret|er m (7), **∼erin** f trans-
gressor, trespasser, offender; **∼ung**
f transgression, trespass; ⚏ infrac-
tion, violation; *eng S.* petty offen|ce,
Am. -se.
übertrieben [∼'triːbən] exaggerat-
ed, excessive.
'**Übertritt** m going over *(zu* to);
eccl. conversion.
über'trumpfen overtrump; *fig.*
outdo.
über'tünchen whitewash (a. *fig.*);
fig. varnish, gloss over.
übervölker|n [∼'fœlkərn] (29) over-
populate; **2ung** f overpopulation.
'**übervoll** brimful; *Raum:* overcrowded.
über'vorteil|en (25) overreach; *beim*
Kauf: overcharge, *Brt.* F do
(down); *(betrügen)* cheat; **2ung** f
overreaching *etc.*
über'wach|en watch (over); *(be-*
aufsichtigen) supervise, superintend, control; *polizeilich:* keep
under surveillance, *(beschatten)*
shadow; **2ung** f supervision, control; *polizeiliche:* surveillance;
2ungs-anlage f monitoring system
(od. device); **2ungsnetz** n monitoring network.
überwältigen [∼'vɛltigən] (25) overcome, overpower, overwhelm *(alle a.*
fig.); **∼d** *fig.* overwhelming.
über'weis|en assign, transfer; *zur*
Entscheidung: refer *(dat. od. an acc.*
to); *Geld:* remit; **2ung** f assignment,
bsd. v. Besitz: transfer; *zur Entschei-*
dung: reference *(an acc.* to); *(Geld2)*
remittance.
'**überwerfen 1.** throw over; *Kleid*
usw.: fling on; **2.** *über'werfen: sich*
mit j-m **∼** fall out with a p.
über'wiegen 1. v/t. outweigh; v/i.
preponderate, prevail; *(vorherr-*
schen) predominate; **2.** 2 n (6) preponderance; **∼d** adj. preponderant,
prevailing; *Mehrheit:* overwhelming; **∼er** *Teil* majority; adv. pre-
dominantly, mainly.
über'wind|en overcome (a. *fig.*),
subdue; *(besiegen)* conquer; *Hinder-*
nis: surmount; *sich* **∼** *zu* bring o.s.
to *(do);* *ein überwundener Stand-*
punkt an antiquated view; **2er** m

(7) conqueror; **Ջung** f conquest, overcoming; s. Selbst♫; ~ kosten cost an effort.

überwintern [~'vintərn] (29) v/i. (pass the) winter; bsd. Tiere: hibernate; v/t. winter.

über'wölben arch (over).

über'wuchern overgrow, overrun.

'Überwurf m wrap, shawl; **'~mutter** ⊕ f screw cap.

'Überzahl f superior number(s) od. (nur ⚔) forces pl., numerical superiority, odds pl.

über'zahlen overpay.

über'zählen count money over.

'überzählig supernumerary, odd; (übrig) surplus, left over.

über'zeichn|en over-subscribe; **Ջung** f over-subscription.

über'zeug|en convince (von of); ⚖ satisfy (as to); weitS. Leistung, Spieler usw.: be convincing; sich ~ (von) make sure (of); **~end** convincing (a. fig.); **~t** convinced, positive; Sozialist usw.: ardent, strong; Sie dürfen ~ sein, daß you may rest assured that; **Ջung** f conviction; (fester Glaube) persuasion; (Gewißheit) assurance; der (festen) ~ sein, daß be (thoroughly) convinced that; **Ջungskraft** f persuasive power, bsd. fig. logic.

über'ziehen 1. cover; (bestreichen) coat; (verkleiden) line; Bett: put fresh linen on; ✝ Konto: overdraw; ein Land mit Krieg ~ invade a country with war; sich ~ Himmel: become overcast; 2. 'überziehen put (od. draw od. slip) over; Kleid usw.: put on.

'Überzieh|er m (7) overcoat; **'~hose** f (eine a pair of) overalls pl.

Über'ziehung ✝ f overdraft; **~skredit** m overdraft credit; **~szinsen** m/pl. interest sg. on overdrafts.

über'zuckern sugar (over).

'Überzug m cover, coat(ing); (Bett♫) case, tick; (Kissen♫) slip.

üblich ['y:pliç] usual, customary.

'U-Boot ⚓ n s. Unterseeboot; **'~Jäger** m submarine chaser.

übrig ['y:briç] left (over), remaining; die **~en** pl. the others, the rest; im **~en, ~ens** (as) for the rest, (beiläufig) by the way, (außerdem) besides; ~ behalten od. haben have a th. left; keine Zeit ~ haben have no time to spare; etwas (nichts) ~ ha-

ben für (not to) care for; ein **~es** tun make a special effort, go out of one's way (to do); das **~e** Geld the rest of the money; **'~bleiben** (sn) be left, remain; fig. es blieb ihm nichts anderes ~ (als) he had no choice (but); **'~lassen** leave; viel (wenig) zu wünschen ~ leave much (little) to be desired.

Übung ['y:buŋ] f exercise (a. Turnen u. ⚔), practice (a. praktische Anwendung); (Gewohnheit) practice, use; (Ausbildung) training; nicht mehr in (od. aus der) ~ sein be out of practice; **'~s-aufgabe** f exercise; **'~sbuch** n book of exercises; **'~shang** m Wintersport: nursery slope; **'~s-heft** n exercise-book, Am. composition book; **'~smunition** f practice ammunition; **'~s-platz** ⚔ m training area od. ground.

Ufer ['u:fər] n (7) (Meer♫, See♫) shore; (Strand) beach; (Fluß♫) bank; am (od. ans) ~ ashore; **'~damm** m e-s Flusses: embankment; **'♫los** fig. boundless; extravagant; ins **~e führen** lead nowhere; **'~promenade** f promenade.

Ufo ['u:fo] n (11) ufo, unidentified flying object.

Uhr [u:r] f (16) (Turm♫ usw.) clock; (Taschen♫, Armband♫) watch; (Stunde, Zeit) hour, time (of the day); wieviel ~ ist es? what time is it?, F what's the time?; es ist halb drei ~ it is half past two; nach meiner ~ ist es vier by my watch it is four o'clock (Am. a. four hours); um vier ~ at four o'clock; **'~armband** n watch bracelet; **'~kette** f watch-chain; **'~macher** m watch-maker, clock-maker; **'~werk** n clockwork; works pl.; **'~zeiger** m hand; **'~zeigersinn** m: im ~ clockwise; entgegen dem ~ anticlockwise; **'~zeit** f (clock) time.

Uhu ['u:hu:] m (3¹) eagle-owl.

Ukas ['u:kas] m (3²) ukase.

Ulk [ulk] m (3) fun, F spree, lark; ~ treiben lark, mit: make fun of; **'♫en** (25) joke, lark; **'♫ig** funny.

Ulme ['ulmə] f (15) elm.

Ulster ['ulstər] m (7) ulster.

Ultimatum [ulti'ma:tum] n (9) ultimatum; ein ~ stellen deliver an ultimatum (dat. to).

Ultimo ['ultimo] m (11) last day of the month; **'~...** monthly ...

'Ultra'**kurzwelle** ['ultra-] f Radio:

ultra high frequency; *phys.* ⚡ ultra-
-short wave; '∼'**kurzwellensender**
m ultra-short wave transmitter; '⚡-
ma'rin ultramarine; '⚡**rot** ultra-
-red, infra-red; '∼**schall** *phys. m* ul-
tra-sound; '∼**schall...** ultrasonic,
supersonic; ∼**schalldiagnostik** ['∼-
dia'gnɔstik] *f* (16) ultrasonic diagnosis; '∼**schallwelle** *f* ultrasonic *od.*
supersonic wave; '⚡**violett** ultra-
-violet.
um [um] **1.** *prp.* (*acc.*) about; *s. un-*
gefähr; (∼ ... *herum*) (a)round,
round about; *Lohn, Preis usw.*: for;
Maß: by; ∼ *vier* (*Uhr*) at four
(o'clock); ∼ *die Zeit* (*herum*) about
the time; *einer* ∼ *den andern* one by
one, (*abwechselnd*) alternately, by
turns; ∼ *so besser* so much the better;
∼ *so mehr* all the more, (so much) the
more (*als* as; *weil* because); ∼ *so*
weniger all the less; ∼ *e-r S. od. j-s*
willen for the sake (*od.* in behalf)
of; ∼ *Gottes willen!* for goodness'
sake!; *s. Entschuldigung, Leben,*
Preis, Rat, Tag, Wette, Wort; **2.** *cj.*
∼ *zu* (in order) to; **3.** *adv.* about; ∼
und ∼ round about; ∼ (*vorüber*) *sein*
be over (*od.* up).
'**um·adressieren** redirect.
'**um·ändern** alter, change.
'**um·arbeit|en** rework (*od.* do) over;
Kleid: make over; *Buch*: revise;
Schriftstück: rewrite; *für den Film*
usw.: readapt; *fig.* ∼ *zu et.* make
(*od.* turn) into; '⚡**ung** *f* making
over; revision; readaptation.
umarm|en [∼'⁹armən] (25) em-
brace, hug; ⚡**ung** *f* embrace, hug.
'**Umbau** *m* rebuilding; alteration(s
pl.); reconstruction; conversion;
reorganization; '⚡**en 1.** rebuild;
teilweise: alter; *Maschine usw.*: reconstruct; *zu e-m neuen Zweck, a.*
Wohnung: convert (*in acc.* into);
Verwaltung usw.: reorganize; **2.** *um-*
'*bauen*: build round; *umbauter*
Raum interior space.
'**umbetten** put into a fresh bed.
'**umbiegen** bend (over); *abwärts od.*
aufwärts: turn down *od.* up.
'**umbild|en** remodel, reconstruct,
transform; reorganize, *bessernd*: reform; *Regierung*: reshuffle; '⚡**ung**f
transformation, remodel(l)ing; reorganization; reshuffle.
'**umbinden** tie round; *Schürze usw.*:
put on.

'**umblättern** *v/t.* turn over (the leaf
v/i.).
'**umbrechen 1.** break down *od.* up;
2. *um*'*brechen typ.* make up (into
pages).
'**umbringen** kill.
'**Umbruch** *m typ.* make-up; *am Bild-*
schirm: page formatting; *fig., bsd.*
pol. upheaval; *parl.* landslide.
'**umbuchen** transfer (to another account); *Reise usw.*: book for another date.
'**umdenken** *v/t.* rethink; *v/i.* change
one's views.
'**umdirigieren** redirect.
'**umdisponieren** *v/t.* redispose,
rearrange; *v/i.* make new arrangements.
'**umdrehen** turn (round, *a. sich*);
j-s Worte, Arm: twist; *j-m den Hals*
∼ wring a p.'s neck; *s. Spieß.*
Um'drehung *f* turn(ing round);
phys. rotation, revolution; ∼**en** *pl.*
pro Minute revolutions per minute
(*abbr.* r.p.m.); ∼**sgeschwindigkeit** *f*
speed of rotation.
'**Umdruck** *m* transfer; '⚡**en** transfer.
'**um-ei'nander** round each other.
'**Um-erziehung** *f* re-education; '∼**s-**
lager *n* re-education centre.
'**umfahren** *v/t.* **1.** run down; **2.** *um-*
'*fahren* drive (*od.* sail) round *a th.*
'**umfallen** (sn) fall (down *od.* over);
vor Schwäche: collapse; *fig.* (*nach-*
geben) cave in; *zum* ⚡ *müde sein*
feel ready to drop.
'**Umfang** *m* circumference, circuit;
des Leibes, e-s Baumstammes usw.:
girth; *Schneiderei*: width; (*Ausdeh-*
nung, a. fig.) extent, size (*a. wissen-*
schaftl. Arbeiten); ♪ compass; (*Be-*
reich) range; (*Masse, Rauminhalt,*
Buch⚡, Tonfülle) volume; *10 Zoll*
im ∼ 10 inches round; *fig. in vollem*
∼**e** in its entirety.
um'fangen embrace; *fig.* surround.
'**umfangreich** extensive; (*dick*)
voluminous; (*geräumig*) wide.
um'fass|en embrace (*a. fig.*); (*in*
sich schließen) comprise, cover; ⚔
envelop, outflank; ∼**end** extensive,
comprehensive; (*vollständig*) complete; ⚡**ung** *f* embrace; ⚔ envel-
opment, outflanking; (*Einfriedi-*
gung) enclosure.
'**umfliegen** fly round *a th.*
umflort [um'flo:rt] *Augen*: dim.
um'fluten flow round *a th.*

'**umform|en** transform, remodel; *⚡* transform, convert; '**₂er** *⚡ m* converter, transformer.

'**Umfrage** *f* (general) inquiry; *s.* Meinungs₂; '**~-ergebnis** *n* survey results *pl.*

umfried(ig)|en [~'fri:d(ig)ən] enclose; **₂ung** *f* enclosure.

'**umfüllen** pour into other containers, *etc.*; *Wein:* decant.

'**umfunktionieren** convert (*in acc.* into).

'**Umgang** *m* (*Drehung*) rotation; (*Weg*) circular passage; (*Prozession*) procession; (*Verkehr*) (social) intercourse, relations *pl.*; (*Bekanntenkreis*) company, friends *pl.*; (*Art, umzugehen mit*) way how to deal with *a p.*; ~ *haben od.* pflegen mit associate with; *wenig* ~ *haben* not to see many people.

umgänglich ['~gɛŋliç] sociable.

'**Umgangs|formen** *f/pl.* (social) manners *pl.*; '**~sprache** *f* colloquial language; *englische* ~ colloquial English.   [ensnare.⟩

umgarnen [um'garnən] (25) *fig.*⟩

um'geb|en surround; ~ *von* surrounded with *od.* by; **₂ung** *f* environs *pl.*, *a.* e-r *P.*: surroundings *pl.*; e-r *P.* (*a. Milieu*): environment; (*Nachbarschaft*) neighbo(u)rhood, *weitS. a.* vicinity; (*Gesellschaft*) company.

'**Umgegend** *f* environs *pl.*, vicinity, neighbo(u)rhood.

'**umgehen 1.** *v/i.* (sn) go round; (*die Runde machen*) circulate; *Geist:* walk, ~ *an* (*od. in*) e-m Ort haunt a place; *mit j-m* ~ keep company with, (*behandeln, a.* e-e *Sache*) deal with, handle, ⊕ operate; (*vorhaben*) intend, plan, (*beschäftigt sein*) be occupied with; *mit dem Gedanken* (*od. Plan*) ~ *zu inf.* be thinking of *ger.*; *mit j-m hart* ~ treat a p. harshly; *er weiß mit Frauen* (*Pferden usw.*) *umzugehen* he has a way with women (horses, *etc.*); **2.** *v/t.* um'gehen go round (about); (*vermeiden*) avoid, evade, *geschickt:* by-pass (*a. Verkehr*), F dodge; ✗ outflank; '**~d** *allg.* immediate(ly *adv.*); ✝ *höflich:* at your earliest convenience; *mit* ~er *Post* by return of post.

Um'gehung *f* by-passing, *Am.* beltway; *fig. a.* evasion; *Verkehr: a.*

detour(ing); ✗ outflanking; **~sstra-ße** *f* bypass (road).

umgekehrt ['~gəke:rt] reverse, inverse; (*dasselbe* ~) vice versa, conversely; (*genauso, mit gleichem Recht usw.*) by the same token; (*entgegengesetzt*) opposite, contrary; (*genau*) ~! (just) the other way (round)!, quite the contrary!; *das* ₂e the reverse (*od.* opposite).

'**umgestalten** *s.* umbilden.

'**umgießen** (*umfüllen*) decant; *metall.* refound, recast.

'**umgraben** dig (*od.* turn) up.

um'grenzen bound; (*umschließen*) encircle; *fig.* circumscribe.

'**umgruppier|en** regroup; *pol.*, *Sport:* reshuffle; '**₂ung** *f* regrouping; reshuffling.

um'gürten gird; '**umgürten** gird on.

'**umhaben** have on.

'**umhacken** hoe up; *s.* umhauen.

um'halsen hug, embrace.

'**Umhang** *m* cape; wrap; (*Umschlagetuch*) shawl.

'**umhängen** *Mantel usw.*: put on, wrap about one; *Gewehr:* sling; *Bild:* rehang.

'**Umhängetasche** *f* shoulder-bag.

'**umhauen** fell, cut down; F *fig.* bowl over.

um'her about, (*Am.* a)round; *s.* herum(...); **~schweifen, ~streichen, ~streifen, ~ziehen** rove, roam (about), wander (about).

um'hin: *ich kann nicht* ~, *zu sagen* I cannot help saying.

um'hüll|en wrap up (*mit in*), envelop, cover (*a.* ⊕); ⊕ sheathe; **₂ung** *f* wrapping, wrap(per), cover (-ing).

Umkehr ['~ke:r] *f* (16) turning back, return (*zu* to; *a. fig.*); *fig.* (*Änderung*) change; (*Bekehrung*) conversion; '**₂en** *v/i.* (sn) turn back, return; *v/t.* turn round *od.* about *od.* the other way round; (*das Unterste zu oberst kehren*) turn upside down; (*umstoßen*) overturn; *Tasche usw.*: turn (inside) out; ♪, ♫, *gr.* invert; *⚡* reverse; *s.* umgekehrt; '**~ung** *f* reversal; inversion.

'**umkippen** *v/t.* tip over, upset; *v/i.* (sn) tilt over, be upset; *Fahrzeug: a.* overturn, ⚓ capsize; F *s.* zusammenklappen *v/i.*

um'klammer|n clasp, embrace; *Boxen:* clinch; ✗ envelop; **₂ung** *f* embrace; *Boxen*: clinch; ✕ envelopment.

'**umklappen** *v/t.* turn down; *e-n Sitz*: tip; *v/i.* F *s. zusammenklappen.*

'**umkleide|n 1.** *j-n (sich)* ~ change a p.'s (one's) dress; **2.** *um'kleiden* clothe, cover; '2raum *m* dressing--room.

'**umknicken** *v/t.* bend (down); snap (off); *v/i.* (sn) *mit dem Fuß* ~ sprain one's foot.

'**umkommen** (sn) perish, die; *(verderben)* spoil.

'**Umkreis** *m* circuit, circumference; *(Nähe)* vicinity; *im* ~ *von* within a radius of, for *three miles* round.

um'kreisen circle round *a th.*

'**umkrempeln** (29) turn up, tuck up; *völlig*: turn *a th.* inside out; *fig.* turn *a th.* upside down, change radically.

'**umladen** reload; *bsd.* ⚓ transship.

'**Umlage** *f* distribution of cost; *s. Abgabe.*

um'lagern surround, besiege.

'**Umland** *n* hinterland.

'**Umlauf** *m* circulation (*a. des Geldes*); *phys.* rotation, revolution; *(Zyklus)* cycle; *s.* ~*schreiben*; *in* (*od. im*) ~ in circulation; *ast.* in orbit; *in* ~ *bringen od. setzen od. sein* circulate; *außer* ~ *setzen* withdraw from circulation; '~**bahn** *ast. f* orbit; '2en *v/t.* run down; *v/i.* (sn) revolve; *Blut, Geld, Gerücht*: circulate; '~**geschwindigkeit** *f* rotational speed; *Raumfahrt*: orbital velocity; '~**schreiben** *n* circular (letter).

'**Umlaut** *m* vowel-mutation, umlaut; *Laut*: mutated (*od.* modified) vowel; '2en *v/t.* umlaut.

'**Umlege|kragen** *m* turn-down collar; '2n **1.** *Mantel usw.*: put on; *(umkniffen, umdrehen)* turn down; *(zum Liegen bringen)* lay (down); *(anders legen)* place differently, shift; *(kippen)* tilt; ⊕ *Hebel*: throw; *Verkehr*: divert; *fig. Kosten*: apportion; *sl. (töten)* bump off; **2.** *um'legen*: ~ *mit et.* lay *a th.* round with.

'**umleit|en** *Verkehr*: divert, bypass; '2ung *f* bypass, detour; '2ungs-schild *n* diversion (*Am.* detour) sign.

'**umlenken** turn round *od.* back.

'**umlernen** learn anew; *fig.* ~ *müssen* have to change one's views.

'**umliegend** surrounding; ~e *Gegend a.* environs *pl.*

'**ummodeln** change.

'**ummelden:** *(polizeilich)* ~ re-register (with the police).

um'nacht|et *fig.* clouded; *geistig* ~ mentally deranged; 2ung *f*: *geistige* ~ mental derangement.

um'nebeln (29) *fig.* (be)fog.

'**umnehmen** put on.

'**um-organisieren** reorganize.

'**umpacken** repack.

'**umpflanzen 1.** transplant; **2.** *um'pflanzen mit* plant *a th.* round with.

'**umpflügen** plough (*Am.* plow) up.

umpol|en ⚡ ['~po:lən] (25) change the polarity; '2ung *f* pole-changing.

'**umquartieren** remove to other quarters; ✕ rebillet.

um'rahmen frame.

umrand|en [~'randən] (26) edge, border; 2ung *f* edge, border.

um'ranken twine (itself) around *a th.*; ~ *mit et.* entwine with.

'**umräumen** *(umstellen)* move; *(neu ordnen)* rearrange.

'**umrechn|en** convert; '2ung *f* conversion; '2ungsfaktor *m* conversion factor; '2ungskurs *m Börse*: rate of exchange; '2ungs-tabelle *f* conversion table.

'**umreißen 1.** pull down; *(umstoßen)* knock down; **2.** *um'reißen* outline.

'**umrennen** run down.

um'ringen (25) surround.

'**Umriß** *m* (4) outline (*a. fig.*), contour; '~**zeichnung** *f* sketch.

'**umrühren** stir (up).

'**umsatteln** resaddle; *fig.* change one's occupation *od.* studies; *pol.* change sides; ~ *auf* (*acc.*) switch to.

'**Umsatz** ✝ *m* (3² *u.* ³) turnover; *(Absatz)* sales *pl.*; *(Einnahme)* returns *pl.*; '~**beteiligung** *f* commission; '~**steigerung** *f* increase in turnover; '~**steuer** *f* turnover tax.

um'säumen hem (round); *fig.* line.

'**umschalt|en** ⚡ switch (over); *mot.* change over (*auf acc.* into), change gears; '2er *m* ⚡ change-over switch, commutator; (*a.* 2taste *f*) *an der Schreibmaschine*: shift-key; '2ung *f* ⚡ switching, commutation.

'**Umschau** *f* look(ing) round; ~ *halten od. sich* 2en look round; *s. a. umsehen.*

'**umschicht|ig** *fig.* by (*od.* in) turns; '2ung *f* regrouping, shifting; *gesellschaftliche* ~ social upheaval.

um'schiff|en circumnavigate, sail

round; *ein Kap*: double; ♀**ung** *f* circumnavigation; doubling.

'**Umschlag** *m* (3³) (*Änderung*) (sudden) change; (*Brief* ♀) envelope; (*Hülle*) cover, wrapper; *bsd. e-s Buches od. Heftes*: jacket; *am Ärmel*: cuff; *an der Hose*: turn-up; ⚕ *feuchter*: compress, (*Brei* ♀) poultice, cataplasm; (*Umladung*) transfer, transshipment; '**∼bild** *n* cover picture; '♀**en** *v/i.* (sn) turn over, upset, fall down; ⚓ capsize; (*sich ändern*) turn, change; *Wind*: shift; *Stimme*: break; *v/t.* knock down; *Seite usw.*: turn over; *Saum*: turn up; *Kragen*: turn down; *Ärmel*: tuck up; *Waren*: transship; '**∼(e)-tuch** *n* shawl; '**∼hafen** *m* port of transshipment; '**∼platz** *m* reloading (*od.* transfer) point; *weitS.* emporium.

um'**schließen** surround, enclose; *fig.* encompass.

um'**schlingen** embrace, clasp.

'**umschmelzen** remelt, recast.

'**umschnallen** buckle on.

'**umschreib|en 1.** (*nochmals schreiben*) rewrite; (*abschreiben*) transcribe; *Besitz*: transfer (*auf acc.* to); **2.** um'**schreiben** *bsd.* ♉ circumscribe; *durch Worte*: paraphrase; '♀**ung** *f* **1.** transcription; transfer; **2.** *Um*'*schreibung* paraphrase.

'**Umschrift** *f e-r Münze*: legend; (*phonetische* ∼ *usw.*) transcription.

'**Umschuldungskredit** *m* conversion credit.

'**umschul|en** retrain; '♀**ungskurs** *m* course for retraining.

'**umschütt|eln** shake (up); '**∼en** pour out into another vessel; (*umstoßen*) spill.

um'**schwärmen** swarm round; *fig.* adore.

'**Umschweif** *m* digression; *ohne* ∼**e** point-blank; '♀**ig** roundabout.

'**umschwenken** (sn) wheel round; *fig.* veer round.

'**Umschwung** *m* (*Drehung*) revolution; (*Umkehrung*) reversal; (*Änderung*) change; *völliger*: about-face; *der Gefühle*: revulsion.

um'**segeln** *s.* umschiffen.

'**umsehen**: *sich* ∼ look round (*od.* back); *fig.* look out (*nach* for); *an, in e-m Ort usw.* have a look (a)round; *im* ♀ in a twinkling.

'**umseitig** overleaf.

'**umsetz|bar** ♉ realizable; sal(e)-able; '**∼en** transpose, shift; ♪ transplant; ♉ (*zu Geld machen*) realize, *Ware*: sell; *in die Tat, Musik usw.* ∼ translate into action, music, *etc.*; *sich* ∼ *in Eiweiß usw.* change into.

'**Umsichgreifen** *n* spread(ing).

'**Umsicht** *f* circumspection; '♀**ig** circumspect.

'**umsied|eln** resettle; '♀**ler** *m* resettler; '♀**lung** *f* resettlement.

'**umsinken** (sn) sink down.

um'**sonst** for nothing, gratis, gratuitously, free (of charge); (*vergebens*) in vain; (*zwecklos*) useless, to no purpose; *nicht* ∼ (*ohne Grund*) not for nothing.

'**umspann|en 1.** change horses; ⚡ transform; **2.** um'*spannen* span, encompass; *mit der Hand*: clasp; '♀**er** ⚡ *m* transformer.

um'**spinnen** spin (all) round; ⊕ *Draht*: cover.

'**umspringen** (sn) *Wind*: change, veer; ∼ *mit* treat, deal with.

'**umspulen** rewind.

'**Umstand** *m* circumstance; (*Tatsache*) fact; (*Einzelheit*) detail; *Umstände pl.* (*Lage*) conditions *pl.*, situation *sg.*; *unter Umständen* possibly, (*notfalls*) if need be; *unter allen Umständen* in any case, at all events; *unter keinen Umständen* on no account; *F in andern* (*od. gesegneten*) *Umständen* in the family way; *ohne Umstände* without ceremony; *unter diesen Umständen* in these circumstances, as matters stand; *Umstände machen S.*: cause inconvenience; *P.*: be formal *od.* ceremonious, (make a) fuss; *machen Sie sich keine Umstände* don't (go to) trouble.

umständ|**ehalber** [ˈumʃtɛndə-] owing to circumstances; **∼lich** [ˈ∼-ʃtɛntliç] *Erzählung usw.*: circumstantial; (*förmlich*) ceremonious; (*unnötig* ∼) fussy; (*verwickelt*) complicated; (*unbequem*) awkward; '♀**lichkeit** *f* circumstantiality; formality; fussiness; complicatedness.

'**Umstands|kleid** *n* maternity dress; '**∼krämer** *m* fusspot; '**∼wort** *n* adverb.

'**umstehend** *Seite*: next; *die* ♀**en** *pl.* the bystanders; (*wie* ∼ as stated) overleaf.

'**Umsteige|(fahr)karte** f tranfer-
-ticket; '♀n 🚋(sn) change (*nach* for).
'**umstell|en 1.** shift, transpose;
Möbel usw.: rearrange; *Betrieb,
Währung*: convert, shift (*auf acc.*
to), (*a. sich*) change over (*a.* ⊕);
auf andere Erzeugnisse usw. switch
to; *fig. sich ~* adapt o.s. (*auf acc.* to),
change one's attitude; **2.** *um'stellen*
surround, encircle; '♀ung f transposition; *e-s Betriebes, der Währung*: conversion, change-over; *fig.*
adaptation; change.
'**umsteuern** ⊕ reverse.
'**umstimmen** tune to another pitch;
fig. j-n ~ change a person's mind,
bring a p. round.
'**umstoßen** knock down *od.* over,
overthrow; *fig.* annul; *Urteil, Entscheid*: set aside, overturn; *Plan*:
upset.
um'stricken *fig.* ensnare.
umstritten [~'ʃtritən] contested;
(*strittig*) controversial.
umstrukturieren [~ʃtrukturiːrən]
restructure.　　　　　[upheaval.}
'**Umsturz** m overthrow, revolution;}
'**umstürz|en** v/t. upset, overturn;
fig. overthrow; v/i. (sn) fall down
od. over, overturn; '♀ler m (7),
'♀lerin f (16¹) revolutionist; '~-
lerisch subversive, revolutionary.
'**umtaufen** rebaptize, rename.
'**Umtausch** m exchange; v. *Wertpapiere, der Währung*: conversion;
'♀en exchange (*gegen* for); convert;
'~**frist** f exchange term; '~**recht** n
right to exchange.
'**umtreiben** *fig.* worry, be on *a p.'s*
mind.
Umtriebe ['~triːbə] m/pl. machina-
tions, intrigues, activities.
'**umtun** *Tuch usw.*: put on; *sich ~
nach* look about for.
'**umwälz|en** roll round; *fig.* revolu-
tionize; '~**end** revolutionary; '♀ung
f revolution, upheaval.
'**umwand|elbar** ✝ convertible;
'~**eln** change, (*a. phys.*) transform
(*in acc., zu* into); ✝ *Zinsfuß usw.*:
convert; ⚖ *Strafe*: commute (*into*); '♀lung f change, transformation; ✝ conversion; ⚖ commutation.
'**umwechs|eln**, '♀lung f (ex)change.
'**Umweg** m detour, roundabout way;
fig. auf ~en indirectly.
'**Umwelt** f environment; *weitS.* the

world around us; '♀**bedingt** environmental; '♀**bewußt** environment-
-conscious; '♀**feindlich** ecologically
harmful; '~**frage** f: *die ~* the environment issue; '♀**freundlich** non-pol-
luting; *Stoffe*: a. biodegradable; '~
katastrophe f environmental disaster, ecocatastrophe; '~**krise** f ecolog-
ical crisis, ecocrisis; '~**schutz** m pollution control; conservation; '~
schutzbewegung f ecology movement; '~**schützer** m (7) environ-
mentalist, conservationist; '~
schutz-experte m ecologist; '~**sünder** m polluter; '~**verschmutzung** f
pollution (of the environment); '~
zerstörung f ecocide.
'**umwenden** turn over; *sich ~* turn
round.
um'werben court, (*a. fig.*) woo;
umworben a. sought after.
'**umwerfen** overthrow, overturn,
upset; '~d *fig.* fabulous.
'**umwert|en** revalue; '♀ung f re-
valuation.
um'wickeln wrap up; *a.* ⊕ cover.
um'winden wind round, entwine.
'**Umwohner** m (7) neighbo(u)r.
umwölken [~'vœlkən] (25) (*a. sich*)
cloud (over), darken (*beide a. fig.*).
umzäun|en [~'tsɔynən] (25) fence
in, enclose; ♀ung f enclosure.
'**umziehen** v/i. (sn) (*Wohnung wechseln*) (re)move; v/t. *sich ~* change
(one's clothes).
umzingel|n [~'tsiŋəln] (29) sur-
round, encircle; ♀ung f encircle-
ment.
'**Umzug** m procession; *prächtiger*:
pageant; *pol.* demonstration march;
(*Wohnungswechsel*) move, removal;
Umzüge besorgen vom Spediteur:
remove furniture.
un-ab|änderlich ['unʔap'ʔɛndərliç]
unalterable, irrevocable; ~**dingbar**
[~'diŋbaːr] unalterable; *Rechte*: inalienable; ~**hängig** ['~hɛniç] independent (*von* of); ~ *von* (*ohne Rücksicht auf*) irrespective of; ♀**hängige**
pol. ['~igə] m (18) independent; '♀-
hängigkeit f independence; ~-
kömmlich ['~'kœmliç] indispensable; ✂ in reserved occupation;
(*momentan ~*) busy; '~'**lässig** incessant, unremitting; '~**sehbar** *fig.* not
to be foreseen; incalculable; (*ungeheuer*) immense; ~'**setzbar** irre-
movable; '~**sichtlich** unintention-

al; ~**weisbar**, ~**weislich** [~'vaɪs-] not to be refused; (*dringend*; *gebieterisch*) imperative, peremptory; ~**wendbar** [~'vɛntbɑːr] inevitable.

'**un-achtsam** inattentive; careless; '2**keit** *f* carelessness.

'**un-ähnlich** unlike, dissimilar; '2**keit** *f* unlikeness, dissimilarity.

'**un-an**|'**fechtbar** unimpeachable, unchallengeable, incontestable; ~**gebaut** ['~ʔaŋɡəbaʊt] uncultivated; '~**gebracht** out of place, inappropriate; (*ungelegen*) inopportune; ~**gefochten** ['~ɡəfɔxtən] undisputed; (*unbelästigt*) unmolested; ~**gemeldet** ['~ɡəmɛldət] unannounced; '~**gemessen** unsuitable; (*unschicklich*) improper; (*unangebracht*) inadequate; '~**genehm** disagreeable, unpleasant; (*mißlich*, *peinlich*) awkward; '~**getastet** untouched; '~**greifbar** impregnable (*a. fig.*); '~**nehmbar** unacceptable; '2**nehmlichkeit** *f* unpleasantness; difficulty; (*Übelstand*) inconvenience; trouble (*a.* ~*en pl.*); *s.* zuziehen; '~**sehnlich** (*unscheinbar*) plain; (*unbedeutend*) insignificant; '~**ständig** indecent (*a. weitS.*); (*unmanierlich*) unmannerly; '2**ständigkeit** *f* indecency; unmannerliness; '~**tastbar** unimpeachable; *Rechte*: inviolable.

'**un-appetitlich** unsavo(u)ry, nasty.

'**Un-art** *f* bad habit *od.* trick; (*Grobheit*) rudeness; ill-breeding; *e-s Kindes*: naughtiness (*a. weitS.*); *vom Pferd*: vice; '2**ig** rude, ill-bred; *Kind*: naughty.

'**un-artikuliert** inarticulate.

'**un-ästhetisch** un(a)esthetic(ally *adv.*), offensive; *pred.* not (a)esthetical, in bad taste.

'**un-auf**|**dringlich** unobtrusive; '~**fällig** inconspicuous; unobtrusive; ~**findbar** ['~'fɪntbɑːr] undiscoverable, *pred.* not to be found; ~**gefordert** ['~ɡəfɔrdərt] unasked; *adv.* spontaneously; ~'**haltsam** irresistible; ~'**hörlich** incessant; ~'**lösbar**, ~'**löslich** indissoluble; *a.* ꝑᴄ, ⚗ insoluble; ~'**merksam** inattentive; '2**merksamkeit** *f* inattention; '~**richtig** insincere; '2**richtigkeit** *f* insincerity; ~**schiebbar** ['~'ʃiːpbɑːr] not to be delayed; urgent.

un-aus|**bleiblich** ['~ʔaʊs'blaɪpliç] inevitable; '~'**führbar** impracti-

cable; '~**gefüllt** *Formular usw.*: blank; ~**geglichen** ['~ɡəɡliçən] unbalanced; '2**geglichenheit** *f* unbalance; '~**gesetzt** uninterrupted, incessant; '~'**rottbar** ineradicable; '~'**sprechlich** unspeakable, ineffable; '~'**stehlich** insupportable, insufferable, intolerable; (*widerlich*) detestable; '~'**weichlich** inevitable, unavoidable.

unbändig ['unbɛndiç] unruly; F (*ungeheuer*) tremendous.

'**unbarmherzig** unmerciful, pitiless, relentless; '2**keit** *f* unmercifulness, pitilessness, relentlessness.

'**un**|**be**'-**absichtigt** unintentional; '~**be-achtet** unnoticed; ~ *lassen* disregard; '~**be-anstandet** not objected to, unopposed; '~**be**'**antwortet** unanswered; '~**be-arbeitet** (*roh*) raw; ⊕ unfinished, unmachined; *Land*: uncultivated; '~**bebaut** ⚘ untilled; *Gelände*: undeveloped; '~**bedacht(sam)** thoughtless; (*unklug*) imprudent; (*voreilig*) rash; '~**bedenklich** *S.*: unobjectionable; harmless; *P.*: unhesitating; *adv.* without hesitation; '~**bedeutend** insignificant; (*geringfügig*) slight, negligible; '~**bedingt** unconditional, absolute; (*bestimmt*) positive; *Gehorsam*, *Vertrauen*: implicit; *adv.* absolutely; by all means; '~**bedruckt** blank; '~**befahrbar** impassable, impracticable; '~**befangen** (*unparteiisch*) impartial, (*a.* ⚖) unbias(s)ed; (*nicht verlegen*) uninhibited; (*natürlich*) unaffected; '2**befangenheit** *f* impartiality; unaffectedness; '~**befleckt** spotless (*a. fig.*); *fig.*, *a. eccl.* immaculate; '~**befriedigend** unsatisfactory; '~**befriedigt** unsatisfied; '~**befristet** unlimited; '~**befugt** unauthorized; 2*en ist der Eintritt untersagt* trespassing prohibited, no admittance except on business; '~**begabt** untalented, not gifted; '~**be**'**greiflich** inconceivable, incomprehensible; '2**be**'**greiflichkeit** *f* inconceivability; '~**begrenzt** unlimited; '~**begründet** unfounded, groundless; '2**behagen** *n* uneasiness; '~**behaglich** uncomfortable; *fig. a.* uneasy; *pred. a.* ill at ease; '~**behelligt** unmolested; '~**beherrscht** *fig.* lacking self-control; quick-tempered; '2**beherrschtheit** *f* lack of self-control; '**~behindert** unhindered, unhampered; **~behol- fen** ['~bəhɔlfən] clumsy, awkward; '2**beholfenheit** *f* clumsiness, awk- wardness; '**~be-irrbar** imperturba- ble, unwavering; **~be-irrt** ['~bə'ɪrt] unswerving, unperturbed; '**~be- kannt** unknown; *ich bin hier* ~ I am a stranger here; *die* 2e *A̸ f* (18) the unknown; ~e *Größe* unknown quan- tity; ⚖ *Anzeige gegen* 2 charge against a person or persons un- known; '**~bekehrbar** inconvertible; *weitS.* inveterate; '**~bekleidet** un- clothed, naked; '**~bekömmlich** dif- ficult to digest; '**~bekümmert** care- less (*um* of), unconcerned (about); '**~belastet** *P.*: carefree; *Grund*: un- encumbered; *pol.* with a clean rec- ord; ⚖ uncompromised; '**~belebt** inanimate; *Straße*: unfrequented; **~be'lehrbar** obstinate; ~ *sein* take no advice; '**~belichtet** *phot.* unexposed; '**~beliebt** disliked; unpopular (*bei* with); '2**beliebtheit** *f* unpopularity; '**~bemannt** unmanned; ✈ pilot- less; '**~bemerkbar** imperceptible; '**~bemerkt** unnoticed; '**~bemittelt** without means, impecunious; '**~be- nannt** unnamed; *A̸* abstract; '**~be- 'nommen**: *es ist* (*od. bleibt*) *Ihnen* ~ *zu* ... you are at liberty to ...; '**~be- nutzbar** unserviceable; '**~benutzt** unused; *Geld*: idle; '**~be-obachtet** unobserved; '**~bequem** inconven- ient, uncomfortable; (*unhandlich*) unwieldy; (*lästig*) troublesome; '2**- bequemlichkeit** *f* inconvenience; **~be'rechenbar** incalculable (*a. P.*); (*gefährlich*) dangerous; '**~berechtigt** unauthorized; (*unbillig*) unfair; (*un- gerechtfertigt*) unjustified; '**~er'weise** without authority; without reason *od.* justification; '**~bereinigt** unex- purgated; '**~berücksichtigt** not tak- en into account, disregarded; '**~be- rufen** *s. unbefugt*; ~*!* (*mst unbe'rufen*) touch wood!; '**~berühmt** obscure; '**~berührt** untouched; *fig.* ~ *bleiben von* not to be affected by; **~bescha- det** ['~bə'ʃɑːdət] (*gen.*) without prej- udice to; (*ungeachtet*) irrespective of, notwithstanding; '**~beschädigt** un- injured, (*a. ⚓*) undamaged; '**~be- schäftigt** unemployed, non-em- ployed; '**~bescheiden** immodest; *Preis usw.*: unreasonable; '2**beschei- denheit** *f* immodesty; '**~bescholten**

blameless, irreproachable; '2**be- scholtenheit** *f* blamelessness, integ- rity; '**~beschränkt** unrestricted; *Macht, Eigentum, Rechte*: absolute; **~beschreiblich** [~be'[raɪplɪç] inde- scribable; **~beschrieben** ['~bə[riː- bən] *Papier*: blank; *fig.* ~es *Blatt* unknown quantity; '**~beschwert** *fig.* light-hearted, carefree, free and easy; *Gewissen*: light, easy; '2**be- schwertheit** *f* detachment; '**~be- seelt** inanimate; '**~be'sehen** unseen; '**~besetzt** unoccupied; *Amt usw.*: vacant; **~besiegbar** [~bə'ziːkbɑːr] invincible; '**~besiegt** undefeated; '**~- besoldet** unsalaried; '**~besonnen** thoughtless, reckless, rash; '2**beson- nenheit** *f* thoughtlessness, rashness; '**~besorgt** easy, unconcerned; *seien Sie deswegen* ~*!* don't let it worry you!; '2**bestand** *m s. Unbeständig- keit*; '**~beständig** inconstant, unsta- ble; fickle; (*veränderlich*) changea- ble; '2**beständigkeit** *f* inconstancy, changeableness; '**~bestätigt** uncon- firmed; '**~be'stechlich** incorrupti- ble; *fig.* keen, unerring; 2**be'stech- lichkeit** *f* incorruptibility; '**~be- stellbar** ✉ undeliverable; *Brief*: dead; '**~bestimmt** (*undeutlich*) in- determinate; (*a. gr.*) indefinite; vague; (*unsicher*) uncertain; (*unent- schieden*) undecided; *auf* ~e *Zeit* for an indefinite time; '2**bestimmt- heit** *f* indetermination; indefinite- ness; vagueness; uncertainty; '**~be- straft** unpunished; '**~be'streitbar** incontestable; '**~be'stritten** uncon- tested; undisputed; '**~beteiligt** un- concerned, not interested; (*nicht verwickelt*) not involved; (*gleichgül- tig*) indifferent; '**~betont** unac- cented, unstressed; '**~beträchtlich** inconsiderable; '**~beugsam** *fig.* in- flexible; uncompromising, rigid; '**~- bewacht** unwatched; *fig.* unguard- ed; '**~bewaffnet** unarmed; *Auge*: naked; '**~bewandert** inexperi- enced, not versed (*in dat.* in); '**~be- weglich** immovable; (*bewegungslos*) motionless; ⊕ fixed, rigid; *s. Habe*; '2**beweglichkeit** *f* immovableness; **~beweibt** ['~bəvaɪpt] unmarried; '**~- beweint** unwept (for); '**~bewiesen** unproved; '**~bewohnbar** uninhab- itable; '**~bewohnt** uninhabited; *Haus, Raum*: unoccupied; '**~bewußt** unconscious; **~be'zahlbar** priceless

(*a. fig.*); '**bezahlt** unpaid; **be-**
'**zähmbar** untamable; *fig.* indomi-
table; **be'zwingbar** invincible.
'**un|biegsam** inflexible; '**bilden**
pl. der Witterung inclemency *sg.* of
the weather; '**bildung** *f* lack of
education, want of culture, illiter-
acy; **bill** ['bil] *f* (16) injury,
wrong; '**billig** unfair, unjust; '**-**
billigkeit *f* unfairness; '**blutig**
bloodless.
'**unbotmäßig** insubordinate, unruly;
'**keit** *f* insubordination.
'**unbrauchbar** useless; (*Abfall...*)
waste; ~ *machen* render useless;
'**keit** *f* uselessness.
'**unbrennbar** non-flammable.
'**unchristlich** unchristian.
und [unt] and; F *na* ~? so what? ~
wenn (*auch*) even if; ~ *so weiter* od.
fort and so on od. forth, et cetera
(*abbr.* etc., a.s.o.).
'**Undank** *m* ingratitude; ~ *ernten* F
get small thanks for it; '**bar** un-
grateful (*gegen* to); *Aufgabe usw.*:
thankless; '**barkeit** *f* ingratitude;
thanklessness.
'**un|datiert** undated; '**defi'nier-**
bar indefinable; '**denkbar** un-
thinkable; '**denklich**: seit ~en
Zeiten from times immemorial;
'**deutlich** indistinct; *Laut*: inarticulate; *Bild, Eindruck*: blurred;
fig. obscure, vague, hazy; '**-**
deutsch un-German; '**dicht** not
tight; leaky; '**ding** *n* absurdity;
'**diszipliniert** undisciplined.
'**unduldsam** intolerant; '**keit** *f* in-
tolerance.
undurch'dringlich impenetrable
(*für* to); *weitS.* impervious; *Ge-*
sicht: inscrutable.
undurch'führbar impracticable.
'**undurchlässig** impervious (*für* to),
impermeable; (*wasser~*) watertight,
waterproof.
'**undurchsichtig** non-transparent,
opaque; *fig.* impenetrable; '**keit** *f*
opacity; *fig.* impenetrability.
'**un·eben** uneven; *fig. nicht* ~ not
bad; '**heit** *f* unevenness.
'**un·echt** not genuine, spurious,
false; (*gefälscht*) counterfeit(ed),
fake(d); (*nachgemacht*) imitation
(*nur attr.*), artificial; *Farbe*: fading,
not fast; **Ą** improper.
'**un·ehelich** illegitimate.
'**Un·ehr|e** *f* dishono(u)r; '**enhaft**

dishono(u)rable; '**erbietig** disrespectful; '**erbietigkeit** *f* disre-
spect(fulness); '**lich** dishonest;
'**lichkeit** *f* dishonesty.
'**un|·eigennützig** disinterested, un-
selfish; '**eigentlich** not proper;
not literal; '**eingedenk** unmindful (*gen.* of); **eingelöst** ['~ʔaɪngə-
løːst] unredeemed; '**einge-**
schränkt unrestricted; '**einge-**
weiht P.: uninitiated; '**einge-**
weihte *m, f* outsider; *pl. the* uninitiated; '**einheitlich** non-uni-
form; '**einig** disagreeing; ~ *sein*
be at variance od. issue od. odds;
'**einigkeit** *f* disagreement; *stär-*
ker: dissension; **ein'nehmbar**
impregnable; '**eins**: ~ *sein* s. *un-*
einig; '**empfänglich** insuscepti-
ble (*für* to); '**empfindlich** insensible (*gegen* to); ~ *gegen Druck,*
Licht usw.: insensitive to; '**emp-**
findlichkeit *f* insensibility; **end-**
lich infinite (*a. fig.*); *phot. auf* ~
einstellen focus for infinity; *adv.fig.*
(*sehr*) enormously; ~ *viel* ... immense, no end of; **'endlichkeit** *f*
infinity; (*Raum*) infinite space; '**-**
englisch un-English; '**ent'behr-**
lich indispensable; **ent'geltlich**
gratuitous, free (of charge); *adv. u.*
adj. gratis.
'**un·enthaltsam** intemperate; *bsd.*
geschlechtlich: incontinent; '**ent-**
haltsamkeit *f* intemperance; in-
continence.
unentrinnbar [un ʔent'rinbɑːr] in-
escapable.
unentschieden ['un ʔentʃiːdən] undecided; *s. unentschlossen; Sport*:
drawn; **2** *n Sport*: draw; ~ *enden*
end in a draw; '**heit** *f* undecided-
ness; *s. Unentschlossenheit*.
'**un·entschlossen** irresolute; '**heit** *f*
irresolution, indecision.
'**un·entschuldbar** inexcusable.
unentwegt ['un ʔent've:kt] steadfast,
stalwart; *adv.* constantly; '**e** *pol. m*
(18) die-hard, stalwart, *Am.* F
standpat(ter); '**heit** *f* steadfastness; *pol.* die-hardism.
'**un·ent'wirrbar** inextricable.
un|·er'bittlich inexorable; '**er-**
fahren inexperienced; **erfind-**
lich ['~ʔer'fintliç] mysterious; '**er-**
forschlich inscrutable; '**er-**
forscht unexplored; '**erfreulich**
unpleasant; '**er'füllbar** unreal-

izable; '~**erfüllt** unfulfilled; '~**er-giebig** unproductive; ~**ergründlich** ['~ʔɛr'gryntliç] unfathomable; *fig. a.* inscrutable; '~**erheblich** inconsiderable, insignificant; *bsd.* ⚖ irrelevant *(für* to); '♀-**erheblichkeit** *f* inconsiderableness; irrelevance; '~**erhört 1.** not granted, unheard; **2.** uner'hört *(noch nie dagewesen)* unheard-of; *(empörend)* outrageous, scandalous; ~! F damned cheek!; F *(großartig)* terrific; '~**erkannt** unrecognized; '~**erkennbar** unrecognizable; '~**erklärlich** inexplicable; ~er'**läßlich** indispensable; '~**erlaubt** ['~ʔɛrlaupt] unauthorized; *(ungesetzlich)* illicit; ~e Entfernung von der Truppe ✖ absence without leave (A.W.O.L.); ⚖ ~e Handlung civil wrong; '~**erledigt** unsettled, not disposed of; '~**erlöst** unredeemed; ~er'**meßlich** immeasurable, immense; ♀-er'**meßlichkeit** *f* immeasurableness, immensity; ~er**müdlich** [~ʔɛr'my:tliç] *P.*: indefatigable; *Bemühen: a.* untiring, unremitting(ly); ♀-er'**müdlichkeit** *f* indefatigableness; '~**erörtert** undiscussed; '~**erquicklich** unpleasant; '~**erreichbar** unattainable; *pred.* out of reach; '~**erreicht** *fig.* unequal(l)ed; unrival(l)ed; ~er**sättlich** [~ʔɛr'zɛtliç] insatiable; '~**erschlossen** *Gelände, Markt usw.*: undeveloped; ~er'**schöpflich** inexhaustible; '~**erschrocken** undaunted; intrepid; '♀-**erschrockenheit** *f* intrepidity; ~er'**schütterlich** unshakable; *Sinn*: imperturbable, stolid; ~er'**schwinglich** unattainable; *Preis*: exorbitant; *für mich* ~ I can't afford it; ~er'**setzlich** irreplaceable; ~er'**sprießlich** unprofitable; unpleasant; ~er'**träglich** intolerable, unbearable; '~**erwähnt** unmentioned; '~**erwartet** unexpected; ~er'**weislich** indemonstrable; '~**erwidert** *Brief*: unanswered; *Liebe*: unrequited; '~**erwünscht** undesired, undesirable; '~**erzogen** uneducated; *b.s.* ill-bred.

'**unfähig** incapable *(gen., zu* of *a th.,* of *doing); (außerstande)* unable *(to do); (untauglich)* unfit (for), incompetent *(to inf.); (leistungs~)* inefficient; '♀**keit** *f* incapacity *(zu* for

[doing] a th., to *do);* inability (for); incompetence, unfitness; inefficiency.

'**unfahrplanmäßig** unscheduled.

'**unfair** unfair; *Sport: a.* foul.

'**Unfall** *m* accident; *Tod durch* ~ accidental death; '~**flucht** ⚖ *f* leaving the scene of an accident; '~**opfer** *n* casualty; '~**quote** *f* number of accidents; '~**station** *f* first-aid station; *im Krankenhaus*: casualty ward; '~**stelle** *f* scene of (the) accident; '~**tod** *m* accidental death; '~**verhütung** *f* prevention of accidents; '~**versicherung** *f* accident insurance.

un'**faßbar** incomprehensible.

un'**fehlbar** *(nie irrend)* infallible *(a. eccl.);* unerring *(a. Schuß, Schütze); (nie versagend)* unfailing; *adv. (bestimmt)* without fail; *(unvermeidlich)* inevitably; ♀**keit** *f* infallibility.

'**unfein** indelicate; *(unhöflich)* impolite; *(grob)* coarse; *pred.* not nice, bad form.

'**unfern** not far (off); *prp. (gen. od. von)* not far from.

'**unfertig** unfinished; *fig. P.*: immature.

Unflat ['unflɑ:t] *m* (3) dirt, filth.

unflätig ['~flɛ:tiç] dirty, filthy.

'**unfolgsam** disobedient; '♀**keit** *f* disobedience.

unförm|ig ['~fœrmiç] misshapen, monstrous; '♀**igkeit** *f* shapelessness; '~**lich** informal, unceremonious.

'**unfrankiert** not prepaid; *Brief*: unstamped.

'**unfrei** unfree, not free; '~**willig** involuntary; *Humor*: unconscious.

'**unfreundlich** unfriendly, unkind *(zu, gegen* to); *Klima, Wetter*: inclement; *Zimmer usw.*: cheerless; '♀**keit** *f* unfriendliness; inclemency.

'**Unfriede** *m* discord; ~ *stiften* sow discord.

'**unfruchtbar** *a. fig.* barren, sterile; '♀**keit** *f* barrenness, sterility.

Unfug ['unfu:k] *m* (3) mischief; nuisance; ⚖ *grober* ~ gross misdemeano(u)r; ~ *treiben* be up to mischief.

unfügsam intractable.

un'**fühlbar** intangible, impalpable.

'**ungangbar** impassable; *Münze*: not current; *Ware*: unsal(e)able.

Ungar ['uŋgɑ:r] *m* (13), '~**in** *f* (16[1]), '♀**isch** Hungarian.

'**ungastlich** inhospitable.
unge|achtet ['ɡəᵊaxtət] **1.** *adj.* not
esteemed; **2.** *prp.* (*gen.*) regardless
of, notwithstanding; '**⁓-ahndet** unpunished; '**⁓-ahnt** undreamt-of,
unthought-of; (*unerwartet*) unexpected; '**⁓bahnt** untrodden, un-
beaten; **⁓bärdig** ['⁓ɡəbɛːrdiç] unruly; '**⁓beten** uninvited, unbidden;
⁓er *Gast* intruder; '**⁓bildet** uneducated; *Benehmen*: ill-bred, unpol-
ished; '**⁓bräuchlich** unusual; '**⁓-
braucht** unused.
'**Ungebühr** *f* impropriety, indecency, unseemliness; '**⁓lich** improper,
indecent, unseemly; *adv.* (*mehr als
recht ist*) unduly; '**⁓lichkeit** *f s.*
Ungebühr.
'**ungebunden** unbound; *Buch*: in
sheets; *fig.* free, unrestrained; *b.s.*
licentious; **⁓e** *Rede* prose; '**⁓heit** *f*
freedom; *b.s.* licentiousness.
'**ungedeckt** *allg.* uncovered (*a.*
Scheck usw.); *Kredit*: unsecured;
Tisch: not yet laid.
'**ungedruckt** unprinted.
'**Ungeduld** *f* impatience; **⁓ig** ['⁓diç]
impatient.
'**unge-eignet** *S.*: unsuitable; *P.*:
unfit (*zu* for).
ungefähr ['ungəfɛːr] approximate,
rough; *adv. a.* about, *Am. a.*
around; *von* **⁓** by chance; '**⁓det** un-
endangered, safe(ly *adv.*), *nur pred.*
out of danger; '**⁓lich** harmless; not
dangerous.
'**ungefällig** disobliging, unkind; '**⁓-
keit** *f* unkindness.
unge|färbt ['⁓ɡəfɛrpt] undyed; '**⁓-
fragt** unasked; *adv.* without being
asked; '**⁓füge** unwieldy; '**⁓fügig**
unpliant, unyielding; '**⁓gerbt** un-
tanned; '**⁓halten** (*unwillig*) annoyed (*über acc.* at); '**⁓heilt** un-
cured; '**⁓heißen** unbidden; *adv.* of
one's own accord; '**⁓hemmt** un-
checked; *adv.* without restraint;
'**⁓heuchelt** unfeigned.
'**ungeheuer 1.** vast, huge, enormous, immense; monstrous; (*toll*)
F tremendous, terrific; **2.** ♀ *n* (7)
monster; '**⁓lich** monstrous, outrageous; '**⁓lichkeit** *f* monstrosity.
ungehobelt ['⁓ɡəhoːbəlt] *fig.* rude,
rough.
'**ungehörig** undue; (*unschicklich*)
improper; '**⁓keit** *f* impropriety.
'**ungehorsam 1.** disobedient; **2.** ♀

m (3) disobedience.
unge|hört ['⁓ɡəhøːrt] unheard; '**⁓-
klärt** unsettled; *Abwässer*: un-
treated, raw; '**⁓künstelt** unaffected,
unstudied; '**⁓kürzt** *Werk, Recht*
usw.: unabridged; '**⁓laden** *Gast*:
uninvited; *Waffe*: unloaded.
'**ungelegen** inopportune, inconvenient, untimely; *j-m* **⁓** kommen be
inconvenient to a p.; ♀**heit** *f* inconvenience; *einzelne*: trouble; *j-m*
⁓en machen give a p. trouble.
'**un|gelehrig** indocile; '**⁓gelehrt**
unlearned; '**⁓gelenk** awkward,
clumsy; '**⁓gelernt** *Arbeit(er)*: un-
skilled; '**⁓gelöscht** *Kalk*: unslaked;
'♀**gemach** *n* hardship, trouble;
'**⁓gemein** uncommon, extraordi-
nary; *adv.* exceedingly; '**⁓gemischt**
unmixed; '**⁓gemütlich** uncomfortable; *P.*: unpleasant, nasty; '**⁓-
genannt** unnamed; *P.*: anonymous; '**⁓genau** inaccurate, inexact;
'♀**genauigkeit** *f* inaccuracy; '**⁓ge-
niert** ['unʒeniːrt] free and easy,
nonchalant; (*ungestört*) undisturbed; '**⁓genießbar** *Speise*: un-
eatable, inedible; *Getränk*: un-
drinkable; (*unschmackhaft*; *a. fig.*)
unpalatable; F *P.*: in a foul temper.
'**ungenüg|end** insufficient; '**⁓sam**
['⁓ɡənyːkzaːm] insatiable; '♀**samkeit** *f* insatiability.
'**ungenützt** unused; **⁓** vorübergehen
lassen let slip.
'**unge|ordnet** unarranged, unset-
tled; *b.s.* disorderly; '**⁓pflastert**
unpaved; '**⁓pflegt** unkempt, neg-
lected; **⁓rächt** ['⁓ɡərɛçt] un-
avenged; **⁓rade** ['⁓raːdə] uneven;
Zahl: odd; '**⁓raten** *Kind*: spoilt,
undutiful; '**⁓rechnet** uncounted;
(*nicht einbegriffen*) not included.
'**ungerecht** unjust; '**⁓fertigt** un-
justified, unwarranted; '♀**igkeit** *f*
injustice (*gegen* to).
ungereimt ['⁓ɡəraɪmt] unrhymed;
fig. absurd; '♀**heit** *f* absurdity.
'**ungern** unwillingly; (*widerstrebend*)
reluctantly; **⁓** *tun a.* hate to do.
'**unge|röstet** unroasted; '**⁓rührt** *fig.*
unmoved, untouched, unaffected;
'**⁓sagt** unsaid; '**⁓salzen** unsalted;
'**⁓säumt**[1] *Stoff*: seamless; **⁓**[2] (*sofortig*) prompt; *adv. a.* without
delay; '**⁓schehen** undone; **⁓** *machen* undo; '**⁓schichtlich** unhis-
torical.

'**Ungeschick** *n*, '**⸚lichkeit** *f* awkwardness, clumsiness; '⸗t awkward, clumsy, maladroit.

unge|schlacht ['ungəʃlaxt] bulky; (*grob*) uncouth; '**⸚schliffen** unpolished; *Edelstein*: uncut; *fig.* rude, rough; '**⸚schmälert** uncurtailed; undiminished; '**⸚schminkt** unpainted; *fig.* unvarnished, plain; '**⸚schoren** unshorn; *fig.* unmolested; ⸚ *lassen* leave alone; '**⸚schrieben**: ⸚*es Gesetz* unwritten law; '**⸚schützt** unprotected; '**⸚schwächt** unweakened; ⸚*e Tatkraft* unimpaired energy; '**⸚sehen** unseen, unnoticed; '**⸚sellig** unsociable.

'**ungesetzlich** illegal, unlawful, illicit; '⸗keit *f* illegality.

'**unge|sittet** uncivilized; (*unmanierlich*) unmannerly; '**⸚stalt(et)** misshapen; '**⸚stört** undisturbed; '**⸚straft** unpunished; *adv.* with impunity; ⸚ *davonkommen* go scot-free.

ungestüm ['⸚gəʃtyːm] 1. impetuous, vehement; 2. ⸗ *m, n* (3, *o. pl.*) impetuosity, vehemence.

'**ungesund** *P.*: unhealthy; *S.: a.* unwholesome; *fig.* unsound.

'**unge|teilt** undivided; '**⸚trübt** unclouded, (*a. fig.*) untroubled; ⸗tüm ['⸚gətyːm] *n* (3) monster; '**⸚übt** ['⸚gəˀyːpt] untrained; '**⸚wandt** unskil(l)ful; awkward.

'**ungewiß** uncertain; *j-n im ungewissen lassen* keep a p. in suspense; '⸗heit *f* uncertainty; (*spannende* ⸚) suspense.

'**Ungewitter** *n* thunderstorm.

'**ungewöhnlich** unusual.

'**ungewohnt** *P.*: unaccustomed (*gen.* to); *S.*: unusual; '⸗heit *f* unwontedness.

ungezählt ['⸚gətsɛːlt] numberless, countless.

ungezähmt ['⸚gətsɛːmt] untamed.

Ungeziefer ['ungətsiːfər] *n* (7) vermin.

'**ungeziemend** improper.

ungezogen ['⸚gətsoːgən] ill-bred, rude, uncivil; *Kind*: naughty; '⸗heit *f* rudeness; naughtiness.

ungezügelt ['⸚gətsyːgəlt] unbridled; *adv.* unrestrainedly.

'**ungezwungen** un(con)strained; without constraint; (*natürlich*) unaffected, easy; '⸗heit *f* unconstraint; ease.

'**Unglaube** *m* unbelief.

'**ungläubig** incredulous; *eccl.* unbelieving; (*heidnisch*) infidel; '⸗e *m, f* (18) unbeliever; infidel.

unglaub|lich [⸚'glauplɪç] incredible; '**⸚würdig** untrustworthy; *S.*: incredible.

'**ungleich** 1. *adj.* unequal; (*uneben*) uneven; *Zahl*: odd; (*unähnlich*) unlike, dissimilar; 2. *adv.* (by) far, much (*vor Komparativ*); '**⸚artig** heterogeneous, diverse; '**⸚förmig** ['⸚fœrmɪç] unequal; (*unregelmäßig*) irregular; '⸗gewicht *n* imbalance; '⸗heit *f* inequality; irregularity; '**⸚mäßig** uneven, disproportionate, asymmetrical.

Unglimpf ['unglimpf] *m* (3) harshness; (*Schimpf*) insult.

'**Unglück** *n* (3, *pl.* -*fälle*) misfortune; (*Pech*) ill (*od.* bad) luck; (*Unfall*) accident; (*Katastrophe*) disaster, calamity; (*Elend*) misery; '⸗lich unfortunate, unlucky; (*a. = traurig*) unhappy; (*verhängnisvoll*) fatal; (*elend*) wretched, miserable; *Liebe*: unrequited; '⸗licher'weise unfortunately, unluckily; '**⸚bringer** *m* voodoo, *Am.* hoodoo, *Am. sl.* jinx; '⸗selig unfortunate; *S.*: disastrous.

'**Unglücks|fall** *m* misadventure; (*Unfall*) accident; '**⸚rabe** *fig. m* unlucky fellow *od.* bird; '**⸚tag** *m* black day.

'**Ungnade** *f* disgrace; *in* ⸚ *fallen* (*bei*) fall into disgrace (with), *bei j-m a.* incur the displeasure of.

'**ungnädig** ungracious, unkind.

'**ungültig** invalid, (null and) void; *Fahrkarte*: not available; *Münze*: not current; ⸚*e* (*Wahl*)*Stimme* spoilt vote; ⸚ *machen* cancel, *Scheck: usw.* invalidate; '⸗keit *f* invalidity.

'**Un|gunst** *f* disfavo(u)r; *des Wetters*: inclemency; *zu j-s* ⸚*en* in a p.'s disfavo(u)r; '⸗günstig unfavo(u)rable; (*nachteilig*) disadvantageous; '⸗gut bad; ⸚*es Gefühl* misgivings *pl.*; *nichts für* ⸚! no offen|ce, *Am.* -se!, no hard feelings!; '⸗haltbar untenable; '⸗handlich unwieldy; '⸗harmonisch inharmonious.

'**Unheil** *n* mischief, harm; (*Katastrophe*) disaster, calamity; ⸚ *anrichten* cause mischief, *Sturm usw.*: cause havoc; ⸗bar ['unhaɪlbɑːr] incurable; '⸗bringend fatal, baneful, unlucky; '~stifter(in) mischief-maker; 'Ⱦvoll disastrous, sinister, ominous.

'unheimlich uncanny, weird (*beide a. fig.*); (*unheilvoll*) sinister; F *fig.* tremendous, terrific; *adv. a.* awfully.

'unhöflich uncivil, impolite; 'Ⱦkeit *f* incivility, impoliteness.

'unhold 1. ungracious; (*abgeneigt*) ill-disposed; 2. Ⱦ *m* (3) monster.

'unhörbar inaudible.

'unhygienisch insanitary.

Uniform [uni'fɔrm] *f* (16), Ⱦ *adj.* uniform; [~'mɪːrt] uniformed.

Unikum ['uːnikum] *n* (11 *u.* 9²) unique (thing); F *P.*: original, character.

'un-interess|ant uninteresting; '~iert uninterested (*an dat.* in).

Union [u'njoːn] *f* union.

unisono [uni'zoːno] in unison.

universal [univɛr'zaːl] universal; Ⱦ... ⊕ general-purpose; Ⱦ-erbe *m* sole (*od.* universal) heir; Ⱦmittel *n* universal remedy, panacea; Ⱦschraubenschlüssel *m* monkey wrench.

Universität [univɛrzi'tɛːt] *f* (16) university; ~s-professor *m* university professor; ~szeit *f* college years *pl.*

Universum [uni'vɛrzum] *n* (9) universe.

Unke ['uŋkə] *f* (15) toad; 'Ⱦn F *fig.* (25) croak.

'unkennt|lich unrecognizable; 'Ⱦlichkeit *f*: bis zur ~ past recognition; 'Ⱦnis *f* ignorance; *in* ~ *sein über* (*acc.*) be unaware of; *j-n in* ~ *lassen* (*über acc.*) keep a p. in the dark (about).

'unkeusch unchaste; 'Ⱦheit *f* unchastity.

'unkindlich unchildlike; *gegen Eltern*: unfilial; (*altklug*) precocious.

'unklar not clear; (*trüb*) muddy; (*nebelig*) misty; *fig.* vague, obscure; (*verworren*) muddled; (*undeutlich*) indistinct; *im* ~ *sein fig.* be in the dark (*über acc.* about); 'Ⱦheit *f* want of clearness; vagueness, obscurity.

'unkleidsam unbecoming.

'unklug unwise, imprudent; 'Ⱦheit *f* imprudence.

unkollegial ['unkɔlegjaːl] uncooperative.

'unkompliziert uncomplicated.

unkontrollierbar ['~kɔntrɔliːrbɑːr] uncontrollable.

'unkörperlich incorporeal, immaterial.

'Unkosten *pl.* costs, expenses, charges; *allgemeine od. laufende* ~ overhead (*od.* running) expenses, † overhead; *s.* stürzen.

'Unkraut *n* weed(s *pl.*); *fig.* ~ *vergeht nicht* ill weeds grow apace; '~vertilgungsmittel *n* weed-killer.

'un|kultiviert uncultivated; *P.*: uncultured; '~kündbar *Kapital*: non-callable; *Staatspapier*: irredeemable; *Rente*: perpetual; *Stellung*: permanent; '~kundig ignorant (*gen.* of), not knowing (*a th. od. how to do a th.*); *des Englischen* ~ having no (command of) English; '~längst lately, recently; '~lauter impure; *Wettbewerb*: unfair; '~leidlich intolerable; '~lenksam unmanageable, unruly; '~leserlich illegible; ~leugbar [~'lɔykbɑːr] undeniable; '~lieb disagreeable; *es ist mir nicht* ~ I am rather glad about it; '~liebsam disagreeable; '~liniiert unruled; '~logisch illogical; '~lösbar unsolvable; ⌢ₘ = '~löslich insoluble.

'Unlust *f* listlessness; (*Abneigung*) dislike (*zu* for); 'Ⱦig listless; (*widerstrebend*) reluctant (*zu* to).

'unmanierlich unmannerly.

'unmännlich unmanly; 'Ⱦkeit *f* unmanliness.

'Unmasse F *f* enormous (*od.* vast) quantity *od.* number; *a.* host *od.* sea (*gen.* of), F lots (of).

'unmaßgeblich not authoritative; *nach meiner* ~*en Meinung* speaking under correction.

'unmäßig immoderate, excessive; inordinate; *bsd. im Trinken*: intemperate; 'Ⱦkeit *f* immoderateness, excess; intemperance.

'Unmenge *f s.* Unmasse.

'Unmensch *m* monster, brute; 'Ⱦlich inhuman; (*menschenunwürdig*) degrading; (*übermenschlich*) superhuman; F *fig.* awful; '~lichkeit *f* inhumanity, brutality.

un|merklich [~'mɛrkliç] imperceptible; '~methodisch unmethodical; '~militärisch unmilitary; '~mißverständlich unmistakable; *adv.* (*offen*) plainly, bluntly; '~mittelbar immediate, direct;

'**~möbliert** unfurnished; '**~modern** unfashionable, outmoded.
'**unmöglich** impossible; *adv.* not possibly; '**2keit** *f* impossibility.
'**unmoralisch** immoral.
unmotiviert ['~motiviːrt] unmotivated.
'**unmündig** under age, minor; 2e ['~digə] *m, f* minor; '**2keit** *f* minority.
'**unmusikalisch** unmusical.
'**Unmut** *m* ill humo(u)r, displeasure (*über acc.* about); '**2ig** annoyed.
un|**nachahmlich** ['~naːxˀaːmliç] inimitable; '**~nachgiebig** unyielding; '**~nachsichtig** strict, severe, inexorable; **~nahbar** [~'naːbaːr] inaccessible, unapproachable.
'**unnatürlich** unnatural; '**2keit** *f* unnaturalness; (*Ziererei*) affectation.
un|'**nennbar** inexpressible; '**~nötig** unnecessary, needless; **~nütz** ['~nyts] useless; **~es** Gerede idle talk; '**~ordentlich** disorderly; *Kleidung, Zimmer usw.*: untidy; '**2ordnung** *f* disorder, confusion, mess; *in* ~ in a mess; *in* ~ bringen mess up; '**~organisch** inorganic; '**~paar** Zahl: not even; Schuhe usw.: odd; '**~pädagogisch** unpedagogical.
'**unpartei|isch** impartial, unbias(s)ed; '**2ische** *m* (18) umpire, referee; '**2lichkeit** *f* impartiality.
'**unpassend** unsuitable; (*unangebracht*) inappropriate, misplaced; (*unschicklich*) improper.
'**unpassierbar** impassable.
unpäßlich ['~pesliç] indisposed, unwell, *pred.* poorly, F out of sorts; '**2keit** *f* indisposition.
'**un|patriotisch** unpatriotic(ally *adv.*); '**~persönlich** impersonal; '**~pfändbar** unseizable; '**~politisch** non-political; *fig.* impolitic; '**~praktisch** unpractical, *Am.* impractical; '**~produktiv** unproductive; '**~qualifiziert** unqualified; '**~pünktlich** unpunctual; '**2pünktlichkeit** *f* unpunctuality; '**~rasiert** unshaven; '**2rat** *m* (3, *o. pl.*) rubbish; (*Schmutz*) filth; ~ *wittern* F smell a rat; '**~rationell** inefficient, wasteful; '**~rätlich** ['~reːtliç], '**~ratsam** unadvisable.
'**unrecht 1.** wrong; (*ungerecht*) unjust; (*ungeeignet*) improper; (*zur* ~*en Zeit*) inopportune; *an den* 2*en*

kommen come to the wrong man, catch a Tartar; *fig. am* ~*en Orte sein* be out of place; *adv. a. zu* ~ wrongly; unjustly; **2.** 2 *n* (3, *o. pl.*) wrong; injustice; *j-m* ~ *tun* do a p. injustice, wrong a p.; *im* ~ *sein*, 2 *haben* be (in the) wrong; *j-m* ~ *geben* decide against a p.
'**unrechtmäßig** unlawful, illegal; '**2keit** *f* unlawfulness, illegality.
'**unredlich** dishonest; '**2keit** *f* dishonesty.
'**unre·ell** dishonest; (*unlauter*) unfair.
'**unregelmäßig** irregular; '**2keit** *f* irregularity (*a. Verfehlung*).
'**unreif** unripe; *fig.* immature; '**2e** *f* (15) unripeness; *fig.* immaturity.
'**unrein** impure (*a. fig.*), unclean; '**2heit** *f* impurity, uncleanness.
'**unreinlich** uncleanly.
unrentabel ['~rentaːbəl] unprofitable.
un|'**rettbar** irrecoverable, *pred.* past recovery; ~ *verloren* irretrievably lost; *P.*: past help.
'**unrichtig** incorrect, wrong; '**2keit** *f* incorrectness.
Unruh ['unruː] *f* (16) *der Uhr*: balance; '**~e** *f* (15) restlessness, (*a. fig. im Volk*) unrest; *fig.* uneasiness; (*Störung*) trouble; (*Besorgnis*) alarm, anxiety; (*Bewegung*) commotion, *stärker*: tumult; ~*n pl.* (*Aufruhr*) riots, disturbances; '**~estifter** *m* trouble-maker; '**2ig** restless; (*zappelig*) *a.* fidgety, nervous; *fig.* uneasy (*über acc.* about); (*besorgt*) worried, alarmed (at); (*lärmend*) turbulent; *Zeiten*: troubled.
'**unrühmlich** inglorious.
uns [uns] us; *nur dat.*: to us; *refl.* (to) ourselves; (*einander*) each other; *s. unter.*
'**un|sachgemäß** improper; inexpert, faulty; '**~sachlich** not objective; (*nicht zur S. gehörig*) irrelevant, not pertinent; *pred. od. adv.* off the point; '**~sagbar** [~'zaːkbaːr], **~säglich** [~'zeːkliç] unspeakable; ineffable; untold; '**~sanft** ungentle, harsh; '**~sauber** unclean, dirty; (*unlauter*) unfair; '**2sauberkeit** *f* uncleanliness; '**~schädlich** harmless; ~ *machen* render harmless, *Gift*: neutralize, *Verbrecher*: hunt down; '**~scharf** *Bild*: blurred; *opt.* ~ *eingestellt* dimly focus(s)ed, *pred.* out of focus; **~'schätzbar** in-

estimable, invaluable; '~scheinbar insignificant; (*schlicht*) plain, *bsd. Am.* homely; (*unauffällig*) inconspicuous.

'unschicklich unbecoming, unseemly, improper; (*unanständig*) indecent; '2keit *f* impropriety, unseemliness; indecency.

un'schlagbar unbeatable.

unschlüssig ['~ʃlysiç] irresolute; '2keit *f* irresolution.

'unschmackhaft unpalatable, unsavo(u)ry; insipid.

'unschön unlovely, unsightly; *fig.* unkind, not nice.

'Unschuld *f* innocence; (*Jungfernschaft*) virginity; F ~ *vom Lande* country cousin; *ich wasche m-e Hände in* ~ I am innocent; ~ig ['~diç] innocent (*an dat.* of); (*keusch*) *a.* chaste; *für* ~ *erklären* declare innocent; ⚖ *sich für* ~ *erklären* plead not guilty; *den* 2*en spielen* do the innocent.

'unschwer not difficult, easy; *adv.* without difficulty.

'Unsegen *m* (*Unglück*) adversity; (*Fluch*) curse.

'unselbständig dependent (on others); (*unbeholfen*) helpless, resourceless; (*angestellt*) employed; '2keit *f* dependence; helplessness.

'unselig unfortunate, fatal.

unser ['unzər] 1. *gen. v. wir*: of us; 2. *besitzanzeigend*: (20) our; *pred.* ours; *der* ~*e od.* uns(e)*rige* ['~igə] (18b) ours; *die Unsrigen pl.* our people; '~eins (such as) we; (*a.* ~esgleichen ['~əs'glaiçən]) the likes *pl.* of us.

unsert|halben ['~thalbən], '~wegen for our sake, on account of us.

'unsicher insecure; *Hand usw.*: unsteady, shaky; (*gefährlich*) unsafe; (*ungewiß*) uncertain, precarious; *Gegend* ~ *machen* haunt, *viele Leute*: infest; '2heit *f* insecurity; unsteadiness; unsafeness; uncertainty; '2heitsfaktor *m* element of uncertainty.

'unsichtbar invisible; '2keit *f* invisibility.

'Unsinn *m* (3, *o. pl.*) nonsense; *s. a. Quatsch*; ~ *machen od.* treiben fool about (*Am.* around); '2ig nonsensical; (*närrisch*) foolish; (*sinnlos, maßlos*) mad.

'Unsitt|e *f* bad habit; (*Mißbrauch*)

abuse; '2lich immoral; indecent; '~lichkeit *f* immorality.

'un|solid(e) not solid; ✝ unreliable; *Charakter, Lebensweise*: loose, dissipated; '~sozial unsocial; '~sportlich unsportsmanlike; unfair.

unsr(ig)e ['unzr(ig)ə] *s. unser* 2.

'unstatthaft inadmissible; *pred. a.* not permissible; (*ungesetzlich*) illicit.

'unsterblich immortal; F *adv.* awfully; 2keit [~'ʃtɛrp-] *f* immortality.

'Unstern *m* unlucky star; *fig.* bad luck, misfortune.

'unstet unsteady; (*wankelmütig*) inconstant; (*ruhelos*) restless; (*nicht seßhaft*) vagrant; '2igkeit *f* unsteadiness; inconstancy; restlessness; vagrancy.

un'stillbar unappeasable; *Durst*: unquenchable.

Unstimmigkeit ['unʃtimiçkaɪt] *f* discrepancy, inconsistency; (*Meinungsverschiedenheit*) dissension.

'unstreitig indisputable.

'Unsumme *f* vast sum.

'unsymmetrisch asymmetrical.

'unsympathisch disagreeable, unpleasant; *er* (*es*) *ist mir* ~ I don't like him (it).

'untadel|haft, '~ig blameless, irreproachable; (*einwandfrei*) flawless.

'Untat *f* (monstrous) crime, outrage.

'untätig inactive; (*müßig, träg*) idle; '2keit *f* inactivity; idleness.

'untauglich unfit (*a.* ✗); (*ungeeignet*) unsuitable; (*nutzlos*) useless; (*unfähig*) incompetent; ~ *machen* disqualify, (make) unfit; '2keit *f* unfitness; uselessness; disqualification.

un'teilbar indivisible.

unten ['untən] below; (*a. nach* ~) *im Hause*: downstairs; ~ *am Berge* at the foot of the hill; (*dort*) ~ *am See* down by the lake; ~ *an der Seite* at the bottom (*od.* foot) of the page; *siehe* ~! see below!; ~ *im Wasser, Faß* at the bottom of the water, of the cask; *von oben bis* ~ from top to bottom, from head to foot; F *er ist bei mir* ~ *durch* I am through with him; '~-erwähnt, '~genannt undermentioned.

unter ['untər] 1. *prp.* under, below; (*zwischen*) among; (*während*) during; ~ ... *hervor* from under ...; ~ *Null* below zero; ~ *21* (*Jahren*) under 21 (years of age); *einer* ~

hundert one in a hundred; ⁓ *anderem* among other things; ⁓ *uns gesagt* between you and me; *wir sind ganz* ⁓ *uns* we are quite alone; ⁓ *10 Mark* for less than 10 marks; ⁓ *seiner Regierung* under (*od.* in) his reign; ⁓ *dem 18. 1. 1984* under the date of ...; ⁓ *Tränen* with tears in one's eyes; ⁓ *sich haben* be in charge of; *s. Bedingung, Bezugnahme, Hand, Kritik, Tag, Umstand, verstehen, Vorbehalt, Vorwand, Würde usw.*; **2.** *adj.* (18, *sup.* ⁓*st*) ⁓(*e*) low(er), inferior; ⁓*ste* lowest; **3.** ⚋ *m* (7) *Karte*: knave.

'Unter|-abteilung *f* subdivision; **'⁓-arm** *m* forearm; **'⁓-art** *f* subspecies; **'⁓-ausschuß** *m* subcommittee; **'⁓bau** ⊕ *m* (3, *pl.* ⁓*ten*) foundation (*a. fig.*), substructure, base; **'⚋belichten** *phot.* under-expose; **'⁓belichtung** *f* under-exposure; **'⁓beschäftigung** *f* underemployment; **'⚋besetzt** understaffed; **'⚋bewerten** undervalue, understate; **'⚋bewußt** subconscious; **'⁓bewußtsein** *n* the subconscious; *im* ⁓ subconsciously.

unter'bieten underbid; ✝ *Preis*: undercut; ✝ *Konkurrenz*: undersell; *Rekord*: lower.

'Unterbilanz *f* adverse balance, deficit.

'unterbinden 1. tie underneath; **2.** *unter'binden* ⚒ tie up, ligature; *fig.* stop; (*verhindern*) forestall.

unter'bleiben (*sn*) remain undone; not to take place; (*aufhören*) cease; *das muß* ⁓ that must be stopped.

unter'brech|en interrupt; break; *Fahrt, Reise*: break, (*v/i.*) stop over; *⚡, teleph.* disconnect; *sich* ⁓ *P.*: pause; **⚋er** *⚡ m* interrupter, contact-breaker; **⚋ung** *f* interruption, break; *⚡, teleph.* disconnection; **⚅** ⁓ *der Fahrt* stop-over.

'unterbreiten 1. lay (*od.* spread) under; **2.** *unter'breiten*: *j-m* ⁓ lay before a p., submit to a p.

'unterbring|en place (*a p.*); *a.* ✝ *orders, loans, etc.*); (*beherbergen*) lodge, house, accommodate; (*lagern*) store; ✝ (*verkaufen*) sell; ⊕ install, fit (*in dat.* into); **'⚋ung** *f* placing; accommodation, housing; **'⚋ungsmöglichkeit(en** *pl.*) *f* accommodation.

'Unterdeck ⚓ *n* lower deck.

unterder'hand *adv.* secretly; ✝

privately.

unter|des [⁓'dɛs], **⁓dessen** [⁓'dɛsən] in the meantime, meanwhile.

'Unterdruck *m* low pressure.

unter'drück|en *allg.* suppress (*a. Veröffentlichung*); *Fluch, Lachen usw.*: *a.* stifle; (*bedrücken*) oppress; suppress; *Aufstand*: crush, put down, quell; **⚋er** *m* (7) oppressor; **⚋ung** *f* suppression; oppression.

'unter-einander 1. one beneath the other; **2.** *unterein'ander* one (with) another, among one another, mutually.

'unter-entwickelt underdeveloped (*a. phot.*); *Kind, Land usw.*: *a.* backward.

'unter-ernähr|t underfed, undernourished; **'⚋ung** *f* malnutrition.

unter'fangen: *sich e-r S.* (*gen.*) ⁓ attempt, (dare to) undertake *a th.*; *sich* ⁓ *zu inf.* presume to *inf.*; ⚋ *n* (6) (bold) attempt *od.* venture, risky enterprise, undertaking.

unter'fertig|en sign; **⚋te** *m, f the* undersigned.

Unter'führung *f* subway, *Am.* underpass.

'Untergang *m ast.* setting; *fig.* (*Sturz*) (down)fall, ruin; *der Welt*: end; (*Zerstörung*) destruction; ⚓ (ship)wreck.

'Untergattung *f* subspecies.

unter'geben: *j-m* ⁓ *sein* be under a p.'s authority *od.* control; **⚋e** *m, f* (18) inferior, subordinate.

'untergehen (*sn*) ⚓ go down *od.* under (*a. fig.*); sink; *ast.* set; *fig.* perish; be ruined; *im Lärm*: be lost in.

untergeordnet ['⁓gəˀɔrdnət], **⚋e** *m, f* (18) subordinate.

'Untergeschoß *n* (*Erdgeschoß*) ground-floor, *Am.* first floor.

'Untergestell *n* underframe; (*Sokkel*) base; *am Wagen*: undercarriage.

'Untergewicht *n* underweight.

unter'graben sap, undermine.

'Untergrund *m* subsoil; (*Fundament*) foundation; *paint.* ground; *pol. usw.*: underground; **'⁓bahn** *f* underground (railway), *in London mst* tube, *Am.* subway; **'⁓bewegung** *f* underground movement; **'⁓kämpfer** *m* underground fighter.

'unterhalb (*gen.*) below, under (-neath).

'Unterhalt *m* (3, *o. pl.*) support;

maintenance, upkeep; (*Lebens*♀) subsistence, livelihood, living.

unter'halt|en *allg.* maintain; (*unterstützen*) support; *Feuer:* feed; (*in Betrieb haben*) operate, have; *Briefwechsel:* keep up, have; (*die Zeit verkürzen*) entertain; (*vergnügen*) amuse; *sich* ~ (*ein Gespräch führen*) converse, talk, (*sich vergnügen*) amuse (*od.* enjoy) o.s.; **~end, ~sam** entertaining, amusing; ♀**er** *m* conversationalist; *thea.* entertainer; '♀**s-anspruch** *m* right (*od.* claim) to alimony; '♀**sbeihilfe** *f* subsistence allowance; '♀**skosten** *pl.* maintenance costs; *für Ehepartner u. Kinder:* alimony *sg.*; '♀**spflicht** *f* liability to maintain; '♀**szahlung** *f* alimony; ♀**ung** [~'haltuŋ] *f* (*Vergnügen*) entertainment; (*Gespräch*) conversation, talk; (*Aufrechterhaltung*) maintenance, upkeep; ♀**ungs-elektronik** *f* (*Computerspiele*) electronic games; (*Video, Stereo etc.*) video and audio systems *pl.*; ♀**ungsfilm** *m* feature film; ♀**ungs-industrie** *f* entertainment industry; ♀**ungskosten** *pl.* (cost of) upkeep *sg.*; ♀**ungslektüre** *f*, ♀**ungsliteratur** *f* light reading, fiction; ♀**ungsmusik** *f* light music; ♀**ungsprogramm** *n Radio:* light program(me).

unter'handeln negotiate; ✕ parley.

'**Unterhändler** *m* negotiator; ✝ agent; ✕ parlementaire (*fr.*).

Unter'handlung *f* negotiation; *in* ~ *stehen* (*treten*) *mit* negotiate (enter into negotiations) with.

'**Unterhaus** *parl. n* Lower House; *Brt.* House of Commons.

'**Unterhemd** *n* vest, *Am.* undershirt.

unter'höhlen undermine (*a. fig.*).

'**Unterholz** *n* underwood, undergrowth, *Am.* underbrush.

'**Unterhose(n** *pl.*) *f* drawers *pl.*; (*Männer*♀) underpants *pl.*; *lange* ~ F longjohns *pl.*; *s.* Schlüpfer.

'**unter-irdisch** subterranean, underground.

unterjoch|en [~'jɔxən] (25) subdue, subjugate; ♀**ung** *f* subjugation.

unter'kellern provide with a cellar.

'**Unter|kiefer** *m* lower jaw; '~**kleid** *n* undergarment; *mit Trägern:* slip; '~**kleidung** *f* underwear; '♀**kommen**[1] (sn) find accommodation *od.* (*Anstellung*) employment; '~**kom**-

men[2] *n* (6) *s.* Unterkunft; (*Anstellung*) place, situation; '♀**kriegen** F bring *a p.* down *od.* to heel; *er läßt sich nicht* ~ he won't give in; ~'**kühlung** *f* undercooling; ✗ hypothermia; ~**kunft** ['~kunft] *f* (15) accommodation, lodging(s *pl.*); ✕ quarters *pl.*; '~**lage** *f* foundation (*a. fig.*); ⊕ base, support; *geol.* substratum; (*Schreib*♀) writing- (*od.* blotting-) pad; (*Beleg*) voucher, proof; *fig.* ~**n** *pl.* (*Akten*) (supporting) documents, records, material *sg.*, (*Angaben*) data *pl.*; ~**lagscheibe** ⊕ ['~lɑ:k-] *f* washer; '~**land** *n* lowland, low country; ~**laß** ['~las] *m:* *ohne* ~ without intermission, incessantly.

unter'lass|en omit; (*versäumen*) fail (*to do*); *aus Schonung:* forbear; (*sich enthalten*) abstain from; (*aufhören mit*) stop; ♀**ung** *f* omission; ♀**ungssünde** *f* sin of omission, lapse; ♀**ungs-urteil** ⚖ *n* restraining order.

'**Unterlauf** *m* lower course.

unter'laufen 1. (sn) *Fehler usw.:* creep in; *mir ist ein Fehler* ~ I made a mistake; **2.** *p.p. u. adj. mit Blut* ~ bloodshot.

'**unterlegen 1.** lay (*od.* put) under; *e-n Sinn:* give; **2.** *unter'legen v/t.* underlay; *adj.* inferior (*dat.* to).

Unter'leg|e *m, f* (18[1]) loser; ~**heit** *f* inferiority. [washer.)

'**Unterlegscheibe** ⊕ ['~le:k-] *f*)

'**Unterleib** *m* abdomen, belly; '~**s...** abdominal; '~**skrebs** *m* cancer of the womb; '~**sschmerzen** *m/pl.* abdominal pains.

unter'liegen (sn) be defeated (*dat.* by; *a. Sport* = lose [to]); succumb; *fig.* be subject to; (*verpflichtet sein*) be liable to; (*zugrunde liegen*) underlie; *es unterliegt keinem Zweifel* there is no doubt about it.

'**Unterlippe** *f* lower lip.

unter'mal|en *musikalisch:* accompany; ♀**ung** *f musikalisch:* background music; *zur* ~ *dienen* act as a background.

unter'mauern underpin; *fig.* bolster, corroborate.

unter|'mengen, ~'**mischen** mix.

'**Untermensch** *m* subman, subhuman creature; *weitS.* brute.

'**Untermieter(in** *f*) *m* subtenant, lodger, *Am. a.* roomer.

untermi'nieren undermine (*a.fig.*).

unter'nehm|en 1. undertake; (*ver-*

suchen) attempt; *s.* Schritt; **2.** ♀ *n s.*
Unternehmung; *(Geschäft)* firm,
business, enterprise, company; ✂
operation; ~**end** enterprising; ♀**ens-
berater** *m* management consultant;
♀**ensführung** *f* management; ♀**er** *m*
(7) enterpreneur *(fr.)*; *vertraglicher*:
contractor; *(Arbeitgeber)* employer;
weitS. industrialist; ♀**ertum** *n* the
industrialists *pl.*, *the* employers *pl.*;
freies ~ free enterprise; ♀**ung** *f* enterprise, undertaking; venture; proj-
ect; ✂ operation; ♀**ungsgeist** *m*
(spirit of) enterprise; ~**ungslustig**
enterprising; *(verwegen)* adventurous.

'**Unter|-offizier** ‾ *m* non-commis-
sioned officer *(abbr.* NCO); *Dienstgrad*: corporal; '♀**-ordnen** subordinate; *sich* ~ *(dat.)* submit (to); '~**-
ordnung** *f* subordination; *biol.*
suborder; '~**pfand** *n* pledge.

unter'red|en: *sich* ~ converse, con-
fer; ♀**ung** *f* conversation; conference, talk; interview.

Unterricht ['~riçt] *m* (3) instruction; *(Stunden)* lessons *pl.*; *Schule*:
classes *pl.*; *(Einzel*♀*)* tuition.

unter'richten instruct, teach, give
lessons; *fig.* inform *(von, über acc.*
about).

'**Unterrichts|briefe** *m/pl.* corre-
spondence-lessons; *Lehrgang in* ~**n**
correspondence course; '~**fach** *n*,
'~**gegenstand** *m* subject of instruction; '~**film** *m* educational film;
'~**plan** *m* syllabus; '~**stunde** *f* lesson, *Am.* period.

Unter'richtung *f* information.

'**Unterrock** *m* *(mst Halbrock)* petti-
coat; *mit Trägern*: slip.

unter'sagen forbid (et. a th.; *j-m*
et. a p. to do a th.), prohibit (a th.;
a p. from doing a th.).

'**Untersatz** *m* support; *(Gestell)*
stand; ⵣ socle; *für Töpfe*: saucer.

'**Unterschall...** subsonic.

unter'schätz|en underestimate, un-
derrate; ♀**ung** *f* undervaluation;
underestimate.

unterscheid|bar [~'ʃaɪtbɑːr] dis-
tinguishable; discernible; ~**en** [~
dən] *v/t. u. v/i.* distinguish; *scharfsinnig*: discriminate; *(deutlich wahrnehmen)* discern; *sich* ~ differ;
♀**ung** *f* distinction; differentiation;
discrimination; ♀**ungsmerkmal** *n*
distinctive mark; *(a.* ⊕*)* character-

istic; ♀**ungsvermögen** *n* power of
distinction.

'**Unterschenkel** *m* shank, lower leg.

'**unterschieb|en 1.** push under; **2.**
a. unter'**schieben** *als Ersatz*: substitute; *fig.* attribute falsely *(dat.* to),
impute (to); '♀**ung** *f* [*a.* ~'ʃiːbuŋ] *f*
substitution.

Unterschied ['~ʃiːt] *m* (3) difference, distinction; *zum* ~ *von* ... unlike ..., in contrast to; *ohne* ~ in-
discriminately; '♀**lich** different;
(schwankend) varying; '♀**slos** in-
discriminate; undiscriminating.

'**unterschlagen** cross *one's arms.*

unter'schlag|en *Geld*: embezzle;
Brief: intercept; *Testament usw.*:
suppress; *fig. (verheimlichen)* hold
back; ♀**ung** *f* embezzlement; inter-
ception; suppression.

Unterschleif ['~ʃlaɪf] *m* (3) embezzlement.

Unterschlupf ['~ʃlupf] *m* (3³)
(Schlupfwinkel) hiding-place; *(Obdach)* shelter, refuge; *j-m* ~ *gewähren*
give a p. shelter, *e-m Verbrecher etc.*:
a. harbo(u)r a p.

unter'schreiben sign; subscribe *(fig.*
to).

unter'schreiten fall short of.

'**Unterschrift** *f* signature; *s.* setzen;
'~**enmappe** *f* signature blotting-
-book; '~**sstempel** *m* signature
stamp.

unterschwellig ['~ʃvɛlɪç] *psych.* sub-
liminal.

Unterseeboot ['~zeːboːt] *n* submarine (boat); *deutsches*: *a.* U-Boat;
'~**krieg** *m* submarine warfare.

unterseeisch ['~zeːɪʃ] submarine.

'**Unterseite** *f* underside, bottom side.

unter'setzen place *(od.* put) under.

unter'setzt stocky, squat.

'**untersinken** (sn) sink (under).

unter'spülen wash away, hollow
out (from below).

unterst ['untərst] lowest, under-
most, lowermost, bottommost.

'**Unterstand** *m* shelter; ✂ dug-out.

unter'stehen 1. *v/i.*: *j-m* ~ be subordinate to; *j-s Aufsicht (od. j-m)* ~
be under a p.'s control; *e-m Gesetz
usw.*: be subject to; **2.** *v/refl. sich* ~
(zu inf.) dare (to *inf.*); **3.** '**unterstehen** *v/i.* take shelter.

'**unterstell|en 1.** place *(od.* put)
under; *mot.* garage, park; *sich* ~
zum Schutz take shelter; **2.** *unter-*

'stellen (*zuschreiben*) impute (*dat.* to); (*vorläufig annehmen*) (pre)suppose, assume; *Truppen usw.*: j-m ∼ place under a p.'s command *od.* control; ♀ung f zu 2. imputation.

unter'streichen underline (*a. fig.*).

'Unterstufe f lower grade.

unter'|stützen prop, support; *fig.* support, back (up); *beistimmend:* a. second; (*helfen*) assist; *Arme:* relieve; ♀'stützung f support (*a.* ✕); *fig. a.* aid, assistance; (*Beihilfe durch Geld usw.*) relief; (*staatliche Geld*♀) subsidy; ∼'suchen inquire (*od.* look) into; (*prüfen*) examine (*a.* ✍); (*erforschen*) explore; *wissenschaftlich u.* 🔬: investigate; ⚗ u. *weitS.* analy|se, *Am.* -ze.

Unter'suchung f inquiry; examination (*a.* ✍); investigation (*a.* 🔬); ⚗ analysis (*a. weitS.*); ∼s-ausschuß m investigating (*od.* fact-finding) committee; ∼sgefangene m, f prisoner at the bar *od.* on trial *od.* on remand; ∼shaft f imprisonment on remand, detention pending trial; *die* ∼ *anrechnen* compensate the detention; *in* ∼ *sein* be on remand; ∼srichter m examining magistrate, investigating judge.

Untertagebau [∼'tɑːgə-] ✕ m underground mining.

Untertan ['∼tɑːn] m (8) subject; j-m ♀ *sein* be subject to a p.

unter'tänig [∼'tɛːnɪç] subject (*dat.* to); *fig.* submissive, humble; '♀-keit f *fig.* submission, humility.

'Untertasse f saucer.

'untertauchen v/i. (sn) dive, *U-Boot:* submerge, (*a. v/t.*) duck, dip, immerse; *fig. Verbrecher usw.:* go underground, go into hiding.

'Unterteil m, n lower part; base; ♀en [∼'taɪlən] subdivide; ∼ung [∼'taɪlʊŋ] f subdivision.

'Untertitel m e-s Buches: subtitle (*a. Film*); *Film, Zeitung:* caption.

'Unterton m undertone.

Unter'treibung f understatement.

unter'tunneln tunnel.

'untervermieten sublet.

unter'wander|n infiltrate; ♀ung f infiltration.

'Unterwäsche f underwear.

Unter'wasser... underwater (*camera, etc.*).

unterwegs [∼'veːks] on the way, en route (*fr.*) (*nach* for); ✦ in transit.

unter'weis|en instruct; ♀ung f instruction.

'Unterwelt f underworld (*a. fig. Verbrecherwelt*), lower world.

unter'werf|en subdue, subjugate; *e-r Herrschaft, e-m Verhör usw.:* subject (*dat.* to); *sich* ∼ submit (*dat.* to; *a. fig.*); ♀ung f subjugation, subjection; *fig.* submission (*unter acc.* to).

unterworfen [∼'vɔrfən]: *e-r Sache* ∼ *sein* be subject to.

unter'wühlen undermine.

unterwürfig [∼'vyrfɪç] submissive, servile; ♀keit f submissiveness.

unter'zeichn|en sign; ♀er m (7) signer; *e-r Anleihe, Resolution usw.:* subscriber; *e-s Staatsvertrags:* signatory; ♀ete m (18) undersigned; ♀ung f signing, signature; *pol.* ratification.

'Unterzeug n underwear.

'unterziehen¹ put on underneath.

unter'ziehen² v/t. (*dat.*) subject to; *sich e-r Operation usw.* ∼ undergo, *e-r Prüfung:* go in for, *e-r Mühe:* take *the trouble*.

'untief shallow; '♀e f shallow, shoal.

'Untier n monster.   [deemable.)

un'tilgbar indelible; *Anleihe:* irre-)

un'tragbar unbearable, intolerable.

un'trennbar inseparable.

'untreu unfaithful, disloyal, *bsd. in der Ehe:* untrue (*alle: dat.* to); '♀e f unfaithfulness; disloyalty; infidelity; 🔨 breach of trust.   [solate.)

un'tröstlich inconsolable, discon-)

untrüglich [∼'tryːklɪç] infallible, unfailing; ♀keit f infallibility.

'untüchtig unfit, incapable (*zu* for); incompetent, inefficient.

'Untugend f vice, bad habit.

un-über'|brückbar unbridgeable; ∼legt ['∼˟yːbɛrleːkt] ill-considered, unwise; (*übereilt*) rash; ∼'sehbar immense, vast, huge; *s. a. unabsehbar*; ∼'setzbar untranslatable; '∼sichtlich *Anordnung:* badly arranged; difficult to survey; (*verwickelt*) complex, involved; *Kurve:* blind; ∼steigbar [∼'ʃtaɪkbɑːr] insurmountable; ∼'trefflich unsurpassable, matchless; ∼windlich [∼'vɪntlɪç] invincible; *Schwierigkeit:* insurmountable, (*a. Abneigung*) insuperable.

un-um'|gänglich unavoidable; ∼ (*notwendig*) indispensable, absolutely necessary; **~schränkt** [~um'frɛŋkt] unlimited; *pol.* absolute; autocratic(ally *adv.*); **~stößlich** [~'ʃtøːsliç] irrefutable; (*unwiderruflich*) irrevocable; **~stritten** [~'ʃtritən] undisputed, indisputable; **~wunden** ['~vundən] frank(ly *adv.*), plain(ly).

ununterbrochen ['~ʔuntərbrɔxən] uninterrupted, unbroken; (*unaufhörlich*) incessant, continuous.

unver|änderlich [~fer'ʔɛndərliç] unchangeable, invariable; '**~ändert** unchanged; **~'-antwortlich** irresponsible; (*unentschuldbar*) inexcusable; **♀'-antwortlichkeit** *f* irresponsibility; **~'-äußerlich** inalienable; **~'besserlich** incorrigible; **~bindlich** ['~fɛrbintliç] not obligatory, *adv.* without obligation; (*zwanglos*) informal; (*unfreundlich*) disobliging; non-committal; **~blümt** [~'blyːmt] plain, blunt; '**~braucht** unused; unspent; (*frisch*) fresh; '**~brennbar** incombustible; **~brüchlich** [~'bryçliç] inviolable, absolute; *Treue usw.*: unswerving; **~bürgt** [~'byrkt] unwarranted; *Nachricht:* unconfirmed; '**~dächtig** unsuspected; **~daulich** ['~dauliç] indigestible (*a. fig.*); '**♀daulichkeit** *f* indigestibility; '**~daut** undigested; **~derbt** ['~dɛrpt], **~dorben** ['~dɔrbən] unspoilt (*a. fig.*); *bsd. fig.* uncorrupted; (*rein*) pure; '**~dient** undeserved; '**~dienter-'maßen** undeservedly; '**~drossen** indefatigable; (*geduldig*) patient; '**♀drossenheit** *f* indefatigability; '**~dünnt** undiluted; '**~-ehelicht** unmarried, single; '**~-eidigt** unsworn; **~'-einbar** incompatible; '**~fälscht** unadulterated, pure; *fig. a.* genuine; **~fänglich** ['~fɛŋliç] harmless; **~froren** ['~froːrən] brazen, impertinent; '**♀frorenheit** *f* impertinence, impudence, F cheek; **~gänglich** ['~gɛŋliç] everlasting; immortal; '**~gessen** unforgotten; **~geßlich** [~'gesliç] unforgettable; **~'gleichlich** incomparable; '**~hältnismäßig** disproportionate; '**~heiratet** unmarried, single; '**~hofft** unhoped-for, unexpected; '**~hohlen** unconcealed, open; '**~hüllt** unveiled (*a. fig.*); *fig. s. a.* unverhohlen; '**~jährbar** *Recht:* imprescriptible; *Tat:* not subject to

the statute of limitations; '**~käuflich** unsal(e)able; (*nicht feil*) not for sale; '**~kauft** unsold; **~'kennbar** unmistakable; '**~kürzt** uncurtailed; *Text:* unabridged; *adv.* in full; **~letzbar** [~'lɛtsbaːr] invulnerable, (*a. fig.*) inviolable; '**~letzt** uninjured, unhurt; **~'lierbar** *fig.* eternal; '**~mählt** unmarried, single; **~meidlich** [~'maitliç] inevitable, unavoidable; *sich ins* ♀ *fügen* bow to the inevitable; '**~mindert** undiminished; '**~mischt** unmixed; '**~mittelt** abrupt.

'**Unvermögen** *n* inability, incapacity; impotence; '**♀d** unable (*zu* to), incapable (*zu* of); (*kraftlos*) impotent; (*arm*) impecunious.

'**unvermutet** unexpected(ly *adv.*).

'**unvernehmlich** inaudible.

'**Unver|nunft** *f* lack of reason, unreasonableness; absurdity; '**♀nünftig** irrational, unreasonable; absurd.

'**unver-öffentlicht** unpublished.

'**unverrichtet** unperformed; '**~er-dinge**, '**~er'sache** without having achieved one's object, unsuccessfully.

'**unverschämt** impudent, impertinent, shameless; F *Preis, Forderung:* exorbitant; '**♀heit** *f* impudence, impertinence, insolence; *die* ~ *haben zu* ... have the face to ...

'**unver|schnitten** *Getränk:* unadulterated; '**~schuldet** undeserved; (*schuldenfrei*) not in debt; *Grundstück:* unencumbered; '**~sehens** unexpectedly, unawares; '**~sehrt** uninjured, intact; '**~sichert** uninsured; **~siegbar** [~'ziːkbaːr] inexhaustible; '**~siegelt** unsealed; '**~söhnlich** implacable, irreconcilable; *pol.* intransigent; '**♀söhnlichkeit** *f* implacability; *pol.* intransigence; **~sorgt** ['~zɔrkt] unprovided for.

'**Unverstand** *m* lack of judgment, injudiciousness; (*Torheit*) folly.

'**unver|ständig** injudicious, imprudent, foolish; '**~ständlich** unintelligible; **~sucht** ['~zuːxt] untried; *nichts* ~ *lassen* leave nothing undone, leave no stone unturned (*um zu* to); '**~träglich** quarrelsome; *fig.* ~ *mit* incompatible with; '**♀träglichkeit** *f* unsociableness; incompatibility; **~wandt** ['~vant] *Blick:* fixed, (*a. Bemühungen usw.*) steadfast; '**~wehrt:** *es ist Ihnen* ~ *zu*

you are at liberty to ...; ~**weilt**
['~vaɪlt] without delay; ~**welklich**
['~velkliç] unfading; '~**wendbar**
unusable; ~**wundbar** [~'vuntɑːr]
invulnerable; ~**wüstlich** [~'vyːst-
liç] indestructible; *fig. Humor usw.*:
irrepressible; ~**zagt** ['~tsɑːkt] intrepid, undaunted; ~**zeihlich** [~-
'tsaɪliç] unpardonable; '~**zichtbar**
Recht etc.: inalienable; ~**zinslich**
[~'tsinsliç] bearing no interest; ~e
Wertpapiere non-interest-bearing
securities; ~es *Darlehen* free loan;
~**züglich** [~'tsyːkliç] immediate;
adv. a. without delay.
'**unvoll-endet** unfinished.
'**unvollkommen** imperfect; '2**heit**f
imperfection. [*f* incompleteness.⟩
'**unvollständig** incomplete; '2**keit**⟨
'**unvorbereitet** unprepared; *adv. u.*
adj. Rede usw.: extempore.
unvordenklich ['~fɔːrdɛŋkliç]: *seit*
~*en Zeiten* from time immemorial.
'**unvor-eingenommen** unbias(s)ed,
unprejudiced.
'**unvorhergesehen** ['unfɔːrheːrgə-
zeːən] unforeseen.
'**unvorschriftsmäßig** *adj.*irregular;
(*a.* ⊕ *unsachgemäß*) improper; *adv.*
contrary to regulations.
'**unvorsichtig** incautious; (*unklug*)
imprudent; (*übereilt*) rash; (*sorglos*)
careless; '2**keit** *f* incautiousness;
imprudence; carelessness.
'**unvorteilhaft** unprofitable; *Kleid*
usw.: unbecoming.
un'wägbar imponderable.
'**unwahr** untrue; ~**haftig** untruth-
ful; '2**heit** *f* untruth.
'**unwahrscheinlich**improbable, un-
likely; F *fig.* incredible, fantastic;
'2**keit** *f* improbability.
un'wandelbar unchangeable.
unwegsam ['~veːkzaːm]impassable.
'**unweiblich** unwomanly.
unweigerlich [~'vaɪgərliç] unques-
tionable; *adv.* inevitably; *ich muß* ~
tun I cannot help doing.
'**unweise** unwise, imprudent.
'**unweit** *adv.* not far (off); *prp.* (*gen.*
od. von) not far from.
'**unwert 1.** unworthy (*gen.* of); **2.** 2
m unworthiness.
'**Unwesen** *n* nuisance; excesses *pl.*;
sein ~ *treiben* do one's foul work,
F be up to one's tricks; '2**tlich** un-
essential, immaterial (*für to*); unimportant (*a. = geringfügig* negligible).

'**Unwetter** *n* bad (*od.* stormy)
weather; (*Gewitter*) (thunder)storm.
'**unwichtig** unimportant, insignificant; 2**keit** *f* insignificance.
unwider'leg|bar, ~**lich** irrefutable;
2**barkeit** *f* irrefutability.
unwider'ruflich irrevocable, beyond recall.
unwider'stehlich irresistible; 2-
keit *f* irresistibility.
unwieder'bringlich irretrievable.
'**Unwill|e** *m s. unwillig*: indigna-
tion, displeasure, anger; unwilling-
ness; '2**ig** (*ungehalten*) indignant,
displeased; (*ärgerlich*) annoyed,
angry (*alle*: über *acc.* at); (*widerstrebend*) unwilling; '2**kommen**
unwelcome; '2**kürlich** involuntary; instinctive, automatic(ally
adv.).
'**unwirklich** unreal.
'**unwirksam** ineffective, inopera-
tive; ⚕ inactive; '2**keit** *f* inefficacy; inoperativeness; ⚕ inactivity.
unwirsch ['unvirʃ] cross, testy.
'**unwirt|lich**inhospitable; '~**schaft-
lich** uneconomic(al); unthrifty;
(*unrationell*) inefficient.
'**unwissen|d** ignorant; '2**heit** *f*
ignorance; ~**schaftlich** unscientif-
ic(ally *adv.*); '~**tlich** unwitting.
'**unwohl** unwell (*a. Frau*), indisposed; '2**sein** *n* (6, *o. pl.*) indisposition.
'**unwohnlich** uncomfortable.
'**unwürdig** unworthy (*gen.* of); *s.*
würdelos; '2**keit** *f* unworthiness.
'**Unzahl** *f* immense number.
unzählbar, **unzählig** [~'tsɛːlbaːr,
~'tsɛːliç] innumerable.
'**unzart** indelicate; (*rauh*) rough.
Unze ['untsə] *f* (15) ounce.
'**Unzeit** *f*: *zur* ~ at the wrong time,
inopportunely; '2**gemäß** unseason-
able; (*altmodisch*) old-fashioned;
'2**ig** untimely (*a. adv.*), unseason-
able; (*ungelegen*) ill-timed.
unzer|'brechlich unbreakable; ~-
'**reißbar** untearable; ~'**störbar**
indestructible; ~'**trennlich** inseparable. [seemly; indecent.⟩
'**unziemend**, '**unziemlich** un-⟨
'**unzivilisiert** uncivilized.
'**Unzucht** *f* lewdness; ⚖ sexual of-
fen|ce, *Am.* -se; (act of) indecency;
außereheliche: fornication; *gewerbsmäßige*: prostitution. [scene.⟩
'**unzüchtig** lewd; indecent; ob-⟩

'**unzufrieden** discontented, dissatisfied, displeased; '2heit *f* discontent, dissatisfaction.
'**unzugänglich** inaccessible.
'**unzulänglich** insufficient, inadequate; '2keit *f* insufficiency, inadequacy, deficiency, shortcoming.
'**unzulässig** inadmissible.
'**unzumutbar** unreasonable, unacceptable.
'**unzurechnungsfähig** irresponsible; (*geisteskrank*) insane, ᵼᵼ *a.* non compos (mentis); '2keit *f* irresponsibility; insanity.
'**unzureichend** insufficient.
'**unzusammenhängend** disconnected, incoherent.
'**unzuständig** incompetent, ᵼᵼ *a.* having no jurisdiction; '2keit *f* incompetence.
'**unzuträglich** disadvantageous, prejudicial (*dat.* to), not good (for); (*ungesund*) unwholesome; '2keit *f* unwholesomeness.
'**unzutreffend** incorrect; (*nicht anwendbar*) inapplicable.
'**unzuverlässig** unreliable; (*unsicher*) uncertain; *Eis, Gedächtnis, Wetter*: treacherous; '2keit *f* untrustworthiness; uncertainty; treacherousness.
'**unzweckmäßig** inexpedient, unsuitable; '2keit *f* inexpediency, unsuitableness. [ambiguous.)
'**unzweideutig** unequivocal, un-f
'**unzweifelhaft** undoubted, indubitable; *adv.* doubtless, without doubt.
üppig ['ypiç] luxurious; ♀, *Sprache, Gesundheit usw.*: luxuriant, exuberant; *Mahl*: opulent; *Gras, a. Figur, Frau usw.*: lush; (*sinnlich*) voluptuous; (*übermütig*) cocky; (*großzügig*) generous; '2keit *f* luxury; exuberance; opulence; voluptuousness; presumption.
Ur [u:r] *m* (3) aurochs.
Ur... ['u:r-] (*ursprünglich*) original; (*Kern...*) thorough; *als adv. bei adj., z.B.* urkomisch: extremely; '~abstimmung *f* strike ballot; '~ahn *m* great-grandfather; *weitS.* ancestor; '~ahne *f* great-grandmother; *weitS.* ancestress; '2-alt very old, ancient. F old as the hills; '~anfang *m* first beginning; '2anfänglich original, primeval; '~aufführung *f* first night *od.* performance; *Film*: (world) première.
Uran ⚛ [u'ra:n] *n* (3¹) uranium; ~brenner *m* uranium pile; 2haltig uraniferous.
urbar ['u:rba:r] arable, cultivated; ~ *machen* cultivate, reclaim; '2-machung *f* cultivation; reclamation.
'**Ur|bewohner**, '~einwohner *m/pl.* aborigines; '~bild *n* original, prototype; '2-eigen *one's* very own; innate; '~eltern *pl.* ancestors; '~enkel *m* great-grandson; '~enkelin *f* great-granddaughter; '~form *f* original form; '~gebirge *n* primitive mountains *od.* rocks *pl.*; '~geschichte *f* early history; '2geschichtlich prehistoric; '~großeltern *pl.* great-grandparents; '~großmutter *f* great-grandmother; '~großvater *m* great-grandfather.
'**Urheber** *m* author; '~recht *n* copyright; '~schaft *f* authorship.
Urin [u'ri:n] *m* (3¹) urine; 2ieren [~ri'ni:rən] urinate; ~-untersuchung *f* urinalysis.
'**Urknall** *phys. m* big bang.
'**ur|komisch** extremely funny.
'**Ur|kunde** *f* document, deed; (*Protokoll*2) record; (*Zeugnis*) diploma; '~kundenfälschung *f* forgery of documents; 2kundlich ['~kuntliç] documentary; (*verbürgt*) authentic (-ally *adv.*); ~ *belegt* documented; '~kundsbe-amte *m* Clerk of the Court, registrar; '~laub ['~laup] *m* (3) leave (of absence); (*Ferien*) vacation, holidays *pl.*; *bsd.* ⚔ furlough; *auf* ~ on vacation, (*a.* ⚔) on leave; '~lauber ['~laubər] *m* (7) ⚔ man on leave; *Zivilist*: holiday-maker, *Am.* vacationist; '~lauberverkehr *m* holiday traffic; '~laubsanspruch *m* leave entitlement, *Am.* leave credit; '~laubsgeld *n* holiday (*Am.* leave) pay; '~mensch *m* primitive man.
Urne ['urnə] *f* (11) urn; (*Wahl*2) ballot-box.
Ur|ochs ['u:r°ɔks] *m* aurochs; '2-plötzlich very sudden, abrupt; *adv.* all of a sudden; '~quell *m* primary source; '~sache *f* cause; (*Anlaß*) occasion; (*Grund*) reason; (*Beweggrund*) motive; keine ~! don't mention it!, (you are) welcome!; '2sächlich causal; '~schrift *f* original (text); '2schrift-

lich (*adv.* in the) original; '*~*-**sprache** *f* primitive language; *e-r Übersetzung*: original (language); '*~***sprung** *m* source; *fig.* origin; *s-n* *~* **haben** *in* (*dat.*) originate in *od.* from; ♀**sprünglich** ['*~*ʃpryŋliç] original (*a. fig.*); '*~***sprungsland** *n* country of origin; '*~***sprungszeugnis** *n* certificate of origin; '*~***stoff** *m* primary matter; ⚗ *usw.* element.

Urteil ['urtaɪl] *n* (3) judg(e)ment; (*Ansicht*) opinion; (*Entscheidung*) decision; ⚖ judg(e)ment, (*Strafmaß*) sentence; (*~ der Geschworenen*) verdict; (*Scheidungs*♀) decree; *meinem ~ nach* in my judg(e)ment; *sich ein ~ bilden über* (*acc.*) form (a) judg(e)ment of *od.* on; *das ~ sprechen* (*über acc.*) pronounce (*od.* pass) judg(e)ment (on); '♀**en** (25) judge (*über* [of] *a p. od. a th.*; *nach* by *od.* from); *anders darüber ~* take a different view (of it); *nach ... zu ~ judging* by ...

'**Urteils**|**-er-öffnung** *f* publication of the judg(e)ment; '♀**fähig** discerning, discriminating; '*~***kraft** *f* (power of) judg(e)ment; '*~***spruch** *m s.* Urteil; '*~***vollstreckung** *f* execution of the sentence.

Ur|**text** ['u:r-] *m* original (text); ♀**tümlich** ['*~*ty:mliç] original, native; '*~*-**urgroßvater** *m* great-great-grandfather; '*~***väterzeit** *f* olden times *pl.*; '*~***volk** *n* primitive people; *s. a.* Urbewohner; '*~***wald** *m* primeval (*od.* virgin) forest; jungle; '*~***welt** *f* primeval world; ♀**weltlich** primeval, antediluvian; ♀-**wüchsig** ['*~*vy:ksiç] original, native; *Humor, Person*: earthy; '*~***zeit** *f* primitive times *pl.*; *fig. vor ~en* ages ago; *seit ~en* for ages; '*~***zustand** *m* primitive state.

Usur|**pator** [uzur'pɑ:tɔr] *m* usurper; ♀**pieren** usurp.

Utensilien [utɛn'zi:ljən] *pl.* utensils.

Utop|**ie** [uto'pi:] *f* (16) Utopia(n idea), chimera; *~***ien** [u'to:pjən] *n* Utopia; ♀**isch**, *~***ist** *m* (12), *~***istin** [uto'pist(in)] *f* (16[1]) Utopian.

uzen F ['u:tsən] (27) tease, chaff.

V

V [fau], **v** *n inv.* V, v.

Vagabund [vaga'bunt] *m* (12) vagabond, vagrant, tramp; *Am.* F hobo, bum; ♀**ieren** [*~*'di:rən] tramp about, vagabondize; *⚥* stray.

vakan|**t** [va'kant] vacant; ♀**z** *f* (16) vacancy.

Vakuum *phys.* ['va:kuum] *n* (9[2]) vacuum; '*~***bremse** *f* vacuum brake; '*~***pumpe** *f* vacuum pump; '♀**verpackt** vacuum-packed.

Valuta [va'lu:ta] *f* (16[2]) (*Wert*) value; (*Währung*) currency; (*Devisen*) foreign exchange; (*Gelder*) monies *pl.*

Vampir ['vampi:r] *m* (3[1]) vampire.

Vandal|**e** [van'dɑ:lə] *m* (13), ♀**isch** *fig.* Vandal; *~***ismus** [*~*da'lismus] *m* (16) vandalism.

Vanille [va'niljə] *f* (15) vanilla.

varia|**bel** [vari'ɑ:bəl] variable; ♀**nte** [*~*'antə] *f* (15) variant; *weitS. a.* version; ♀**tion** [*~*a'tsjo:n] *f* (16) variation.

Varietät [varie'tɛ:t] *f* (16) variety.

Varieté [varie'te:] *n*, *~***theater** *n* variety theatre, music-hall, *Am.* vaudeville theater; *~***vorstellung** *f* variety show, *Am.* vaudeville.

variieren [vari'⁹i:rən] *v/i. u. v/t.* vary.

Vasall [va'zal] *m* (12) vassal; *~***enstaat** *m* satellite state.

Vase ['va:zə] *f* (15) vase.

Vater ['fɑ:tər] *m* (7[1]) father; *von Tieren*: sire; '*~***haus** *n* paternal house; '*~***land** *n* native (*od.* one's) country; ♀**ländisch** ['*~*lɛndiʃ] national; (*~ gesinnt*) patriotic(ally *adv.*); '*~***landsliebe** *f* patriotism.

väterlich ['fɛ:tərliç] fatherly; (*dem Vater eigen*) paternal; *~***erseits** ['*~*ərzaɪts] on one's father's side.

'**Vater**|**liebe** *f* paternal love; '♀**los** fatherless; '*~***mord** *m* patricide; '*~***mörder** *m* patricide (*a.* '*~***mörderin** *f*); (*hoher Kragen*) stand-up collar.

'**Vaterschaft** *f* paternity, fatherhood; '*~***sklage** *f* affiliation case.

'**Vater|stadt** *f* native town, home-town; **~'-unser** *n* (7) Lord's Prayer.
Vati F ['fɑːti] *m* (11¹) dad(dy).
Veget|arier [vege'tɑːrjər] *m* (7), **ℒarisch** [~'tɑːriʃ] vegetarian; **~a-tion** [~ta'tsjoːn] *f* (16) vegetation; **ℒativ** [~ta'tiːf] vegetative; **~es** *Nervensystem* autonomic nervous system; **ℒieren** [~'tiːrən] vegetate (*a. fig.*).
Vehikel [ve'hiːkəl] *n* (7) vehicle.
Veilchen ['faɪlçən] *n* (6) violet; '**ℒ-blau** violet.   [dance.]
Veitstanz ['faɪtstants] *m* St. Vitus's
Vene ['veːnə] *f* (15) vein; '**~n·ent-zündung** *f* phlebitis.
venerisch [ve'neːriʃ] venereal.
Venezian|er [vene'tsjɑːnər] *m* (12), **~erin** *f* (16¹), **ℒisch** Venetian.
Ventil [vɛn'tiːl] *n* (3¹) valve; *fig.* outlet; **~ation** [~tila'tsjoːn] *f* (16) ventilation; **~ator** [~'lɑːtɔr] *m* (8¹) ventilator, fan; **ℒieren** [~'liːrən] ventilate (*a. fig.*).
verabfolg|en [fɛr'ʔapfɔlgən] give, hand over (*j-m* to); *Speisen, Getränke:* provide, serve; **✠** administer; *j-m* et. ~ lassen let a p. have a th.; **ℒung** *f* delivery; provision; **✠** administration.
ver'-abred|en *et.* agree (up)on, arrange; *Zeit, Ort:* appoint, fix; *sich* ~ make an appointment; *als Stelldichein:* F (have) a date; *schon anderweitig verabredet sein* have a previous engagement; **ℒung** *f* agreement; appointment, F date.
ver'-abreichen *s.* verabfolgen.
ver'-absäumen neglect, omit.
ver'-abscheuen hate, abhor, detest; **~swert** detestable.
verabschied|en [fɛr'ʔapʃiːdən] dismiss; **✕** discharge; *Gesetz:* pass; *sich* ~ take leave (*von* of); bid farewell, say good-bye (to *a p.*); **ℒung** *f* dismissal; **✕** discharge; passing.
ver'-achten despise; (*verächtlich abtun; verschmähen*) scorn; *nicht zu* ~ F not to be sneezed at.
Verächt|er [fɛr'ʔɛçtər] *m* (7), **~erin** *f* (16¹) despiser; **ℒich** contemptuous; (*verachtenswert*) despicable, contemptible.
Ver'-achtung *f* contempt, disdain; *mit* ~ *strafen* ignore.
ver·allge'meiner|n (29) generalize; **ℒung** *f* generalization.
ver'-alte|n (26, sn) become obsolete

od. antiquated, go out (of date); **~t** antiquated, obsolete, out of date, dated; (*altmodisch*) outmoded.
Veranda [ve'randa] *f* (11¹ *u.* 16²) veranda(h).
veränder|lich [fɛr'ʔɛndərliç] changeable; (*a.* A) variable; **ℒich-keit** *f* changeableness; variability; **~n** (*a. sich*) alter, change; (*abwechseln*) vary; **ℒung** *f* change, alteration; variation.
verängstigt [~'ʔɛŋstiçt] frightened, scared.
ver'-anker|n ⚓ anchor (*a. fig.*); ⊕ stay; ⚠ tie; *fig. in e-m Gesetz usw.*: embody in; **ℒung** *f* ⚓ anchorage; ⊕ staying; ⚠ tying.
ver'-anlag|en (25) *steuerlich:* assess; **~t** *adj.* (*befähigt*) talented; **✠** predisposed; *methodisch* ~ *sein* have a methodical turn of mind, be methodical; **ℒung** *f* assessment; *fig.* disposition; (*Neigung*) bent, inclination; (*Begabung*) talent(s *pl.*); **✠** predisposition.
veranlass|en [~'ʔanlasən] (28) cause, occasion; (*anordnen*) arrange; *j-n zu et.* ~ (*a. S.*) induce a p. to do a th., make a p. do a th.; *nur P.:* prevail (up)on a p. to do a th.; **ℒung** *f* occasion, cause; *auf meine* ~ at my suggestion; *auf* ~ *von od. gen.* at the instance of; *zu et.* ~ *geben* give rise to; *zur (weiteren)* ~ *for further* action.
veranschaulich|en [~'ʔanʃauliçən] (25) illustrate; *sich et.* ~ visualize, picture; **ℒung** *f* illustration.
ver'-anschlag|en (25) rate, value, estimate (*auf acc.* at); **ℒung** *f* valuation, estimate.
ver'-anstalt|en (26) arrange, organize; stage (*a. fig. co.*); *Konzert usw.*: give; **ℒer(in** *f*) *m* (7) organizer; *Sport:* promoter; **ℒung** *f* arrangement, organizing; *konkret:* event; show; *Sport:* event, meeting; **ℒungskalender** *m* calendar of events.
ver'-antwort|en answer for; *sich* ~ justify (*od. entschuldigen*) o.s.; **~lich** responsible (*a. Stellung usw.*), answerable (*für* for); ~ *machen* hold responsible, *weitS.* blame a p. (*für* for); **ℒichkeit** *f* responsibility; **ℒung** *f* responsibility; (*Rechtfertigung*) justification; *auf seine* ~ on his own responsibility; *auf eigene* ~

at one's own risk; *j-m die ~ zu-schieben* offload the responsibility on a p.; *s. abwälzen; die ~ tragen* be responsible; *zur ~ ziehen* call to account; ~ungsbewußt responsible; ~ungsbewußtsein *n* sense of responsibility; ~ungslos irresponsible; ~ungsvoll responsible.

veräppeln *sl.* [~'Ɂɛpəln] *sl.* kid.

ver'-arbeit|en work up; ⊕ manufacture, process (*zu* into), *maschinell*: machine; *Speise, fig.*: digest; (*abnutzen*) wear (out); ~de *Industrie* manufacturing (*od.* finishing) industry; 2ung *f* working up; manufacturing, processing; digestion; (*Ausführung*) workmanship.

verargen [~'Ɂargən] (25): *j-m et. ~* blame a p. for a th.

ver'-ärgern annoy, anger.

verarm|en [~'Ɂarmən] (25, sn) become poor; ~t impoverished; 2ung *f* impoverishment, pauperization.

ver'-arzten doctor.

verästel|n [fɛr'Ɂɛstəln] (29, *a. sich*) ramify; 2ung *f* ramification.

ver'-ausgaben (25) spend, expend; *sich ~* spend (all) one's money; *fig.* spend o.s.

ver'-auslagen disburse, advance.

ver'-äußer|lich alienable; *Wertpapier*: negotiable; ~n alienate; (*verkaufen*) dispose of, sell; 2ung *f* alienation; disposal, sale; 2ungs-erlös *m* sales proceeds *pl.*

Verb [vɛrp] *n* (5²) verb; 2al [~'ba:l] verbal.

verballhornen [fɛr'balhɔrnən] (26) transmogrify.

Ver'band *m* (3³) ⊕ binding; ✚ dressing, bandage; (*Vereinigung*) federation, union; ✕ unit, task force, *bsd.* ⚓, ✈ formation; ~kasten *m* first-aid box; ~stoff *m*, ~zeug *n* bandaging material.

ver'bann|en banish, exile; 2ung *f* banishment, exile; 2te *m* (18) exile.

verbarrikadieren [~barika'di:rən] barricade.

ver'bauen build up; (*versperren*) obstruct; (*falsch bauen*) build badly; *Geld, Material*: spend in building; *fig. j-m (a. sich) den Weg ~* bar a p.'s (one's) way (*zu* to).

verbauern [~'bauərn] (29, sn) become countrified.

ver'beißen suppress; *sich das Lachen ~* stifle one's laughter; *fig. sich*

in et. ~ keep grimly at a th.

ver'bergen conceal, hide.

ver'besser|n (*a. sich*) improve; (*berichtigen*) correct; 2ung *f* improvement; correction; 2ungsvorschlag *m* suggestion for improvement.

ver'beug|en: *sich ~* bow (*vor dat.* to); 2ung *f* bow.

verbeulen [~'bɔʏlən] (25) dent, batter.

ver'biegen bend, twist, distort.

ver'bieten forbid (*j-m et. [zu tun]* a p. [to do] a th.), prohibit (a th.; a p. from doing a th.).

verbilligen [~'biligən] (25) reduce in price, cheapen.

ver'bind|en bind (up); (*vereinigen; a. sich*) join, unite, combine (*a.* 🧪) (*mit* with); connect (*a.* ⊕, *teleph.*) (with), link (to); ✚ bandage, dress (*j-n a p.'s wounds); ✝ sich ~ mit* associate with; *sich ehelich ~* (*mit*) marry; *j-m die Augen ~* blindfold; *fig.* (*eng*) *verbunden sein mit* be bound up with; *ich bin Ihnen sehr verbunden* I am greatly obliged to you; *teleph. falsch verbunden!* wrong number!; *mit Gefahr verbunden* dangerous, involving a risk; ~lich [~'bintliç] binding (*für j-n* upon), obligatory; (*höflich*) obliging; ~(*st*)*en Dank!* my best thanks!; 2lichkeit *f* obligation, liability; (*Höflichkeit*) obligingness, civility, readiness to oblige; (*Schmeichelei*) compliment; ✝ ~*en pl.* (*Passiva*) liabilities; *s-n ~en nachkommen* meet one's engagements.

Ver'bindung *f* union (*a. Ehe*); (*Zs.-schluß*; *Vereinigung mehrerer Eigenschaften*) combination; (*Zs.-hang*) connection (*a. teleph.*, 📞, ⚓, ⊕), junction; (*Personenvereinigung; a. Ideen* 2) association; *s. Studenten* 2; (*Beziehung*) relation; (*Verkehr*) communication; 🧪 compound; ✕ liaison, *taktisch*: contact; *in ~ bleiben (treten)* keep (get) in touch (*mit* with); *in ~ bringen mit* connect with; *sich in ~ setzen mit* get in touch with, contact; *in ~ stehen mit* communicate with, be in touch with, *fig.* be connected with; *teleph. ~ bekommen (haben)* get (be) through; *die ~ verlieren mit* lose touch with; ~sgang *m* connecting passage; ~s-mann *m* contact; ~s-offizier ✕ *m* liaison officer; ~srohr *n* connecting tube; **~sschlauch** *m* connecting hose; **~sstelle** *f* junction; ⊕ joint; (*Amt*) liaison office; **~sstraße** *f* feeder road; **~sstück** *n* connecting piece, coupling; *s. Bindeglied;* **~s-tür** *f* connecting door.

verbissen [fɛr'bisən] grim; (*zäh*) dogged; (*mürrisch*) crabbed; **2heit** *f* sourness of temper; doggedness.

ver'bitten: *sich ~* (beg to) decline; (*nicht dulden*) not to stand for; *das verbitte ich mir!* I won't have that!

verbitter|n [~'bitərn] (29) embitter; *verbittert a.* bitter; **2ung** *f* bitterness (of heart).

verblassen [~'blasən] (28, sn) *Stoff usw. u. fig.* fade; *fig.* ~ *gegenüber* (*dat.*) pale beside.

Verbleib [~'blaip] *m* (3, *o. pl.*) whereabouts; **2en** [~bən] (sn) to be left; remain; (*abmachen*) agree; ~ *bei s-r Meinung usw.* persist in.

ver'blend|en blind, delude; (*närrisch machen*) infatuate; ⊕ face; **2ung** *f* blindness; delusion; infatuation; ⊕ facing.

verblichen [~'bliçən] *Farbe usw.:* faded; **2e** *m, f* (18) deceased.

verblöden [~'blø:dən] (26, sn) become an idiot; F *fig.* go mad.

verblüff|en [~'blyfən] (25) amaze, perplex, puzzle; nonplus, flabbergast; *verblüfft* perplexed; taken aback; **2ung** *f* amazement, perplexity, stupefaction.

ver'blühen (25, sn) fade, wither.

verblümt [~'bly:mt] veiled.

ver'bluten (sn) (*a. sich* ~) bleed to⎫
ver'bocken F bungle;   [death.⎭

ver'bohr|en: *sich ~ in* (*acc.*) bend o.s. to, *stärker:* go mad about; **~t** *adj.* cranky; (*stur*) pigheaded.

ver'borgen[1] *v/t.* lend (out).

ver'borgen[2] *adj.* hidden; (*geheim*) secret; *im ~en* secretly; **2heit** *f* concealment; secrecy; (*Zurückgezogenheit*) retirement.

Verbot [fɛr'bo:t] *n* (3) prohibition; *e-r Sache a.* ban (on); **~sschild** *n* prohibitive sign.

verbrämen [~'brɛ:mən] (25) border, trim; *fig.* garnish, gloss over.

Verbrauch [~'braux] *m* (3, *o. pl.*) consumption; **2en** consume, use up; (*abnutzen*) wear out; (*ausgeben*) spend; (*vergeuden*) waste; *verbraucht Luft:* stale, *P.:* worn out; **~er** *m* (7) consumer; **~ermarkt** *m* hypermar-

ket; **~er-umfrage** *f* consumer survey; **~erverband** *m* consumer association; **~erverhalten** *n* consumer behavio(u)r; **~erwaren** *f/pl.,* **~sgüter** *n/pl.* commodities, consumer goods, articles of consumption; **~ssteuer** *f* excise (duty).

ver'brech|en 1. (*a.* F *e-n Witz usw.*) perpetrate; *was hat er verbrochen?* what is his offen|ce, *Am.* -se?, what has he done?; 2. **2** *n* (6) crime; $\frac{t}{t}$ *a.* major offen|ce, *Am.* -se; **2er** *m* (7) criminal (*a.* **2erin** *f* [16¹]); **2er-album** *n* rogues' gallery; **~erisch** criminal; **2ertum** *n* (1²) criminality; (*a.* **2erwelt** *f*) underworld; **2ervisage** F *f* criminal face.

ver'breiten (*a. sich*) spread (*a. Gerücht usw.*); *Licht, Wärme usw.:* *a.* diffuse; *Lehre usw.:* disseminate; *Licht, Frieden:* shed; *sich ~* spread; *sich ~ über ein Thema* enlarge (up)on, hold forth on; (*weit*) *verbreitet* wide-spread.

verbreitern [~'braitərn] (29, *a. sich*) widen, broaden.

Ver'breitung *f* spread(ing); dissemination.

ver'brenn|bar combustible; **~en** *v/t. u. v/i.* (sn) burn; *nur v/i. lebend:* be burnt to death; *Leiche:* cremate; (*versengen*) scorch; *fig. sich den Mund* ~ put one's foot in it; *s. Finger.*

Ver'brennung *f* burning, combustion; (*Leichen*2) cremation; (*Brandwunde*) burn; **~smaschine** *f,* **~smotor** *m* (internal) combustion engine; **~s-ofen** *m* incinerator.

verbriefen [fɛr'bri:fən] (25) confirm by documents; *verbrieftes Recht* vested right.

ver'bringen spend, pass.

verbrüder|n [~'bry:dərn] (29): *sich* ~ fraternize; **2ung** *f* fraternization.

ver'brüh|en scald; **2ung** *f* scald.

ver'buchen book; *fig.* secure.

Verbum ['vɛrbum] *n* (9²) verb.

ver'bummeln [fɛr-] *v/t. Geld:* squander, *sl.* blue; *Zeit:* idle away; F (*versäumen*) neglect, forget; (*verlieren*) lose; *v/i.* (sn) go to seed.

Verbund... [~'bunt-] ⊕, *⚡* compound ...; ✝ co-operative, co-ordinate ...; **~bauweise** *f* composite construction.

verbünden [~'byndən] (26) ally (*mit* to); *sich ~ a.* form an alliance (with).

Verbundenheit [~'bundənhaɪt] *f* solidarity; bond(s *pl.*), ties *pl.*
Ver'bündete *m, f* (18) ally.
verbürg|en [fɛr'byrgən] guarantee; *sich ~ für* vouch for; **~t** established, authentic (*fact*).
ver'büßen: *seine Strafe ~* complete one's sentence, serve one's time.
verchromt [~'kro:mt] chromium--plated.
Verdacht [~'daxt] *m* (3) suspicion; *in ~ haben* suspect; *~ schöpfen* become suspicious, F smell a rat.
verdächtig [~'dɛçtɪç] *P.*: suspected, *pred.* suspect (*gen.* of); *P. u. S.*: suspicious; **~en** [~'dɛçtɪgən] (25) cast suspicion on, suspect (*gen.* of); **2ung** [~tɪguŋ] *f* accusation; suspicion. [*fact*; **~person** *f* suspect.)
Ver'dachts|moment *n* suspicious)
verdamm|en [~'damən] (25) condemn, *a. eccl.* damn; **~enswert**, **~lich** damnable; **2nis** *f* (14²) damnation; **~t** damned; **~!** damn (it)!; *dazu ~ zu inf. fig.* doomed (*od.* condemned) *to inf.*; **2ung** *f* condemnation; damnation.
ver'dampf|en (sn) evaporate; **2ung** *f* evaporation.
ver'danken: *j-m et. ~* owe a th. to a p., be indebted to a p. for a th.; *es ist diesem Umstand zu ~* it is owing to
verdarb [~'darp] *pret v.* verderben¹.
verdattert F [~'datərt] flabbergasted.
verdau|en [~'dauən] (25) digest (*a. fig.*); **~lich** digestible; **2lichkeit** *f* digestibility; **2ung** *f* digestion.
Ver'dauungs... digestive (*canal, troubles, etc.*); **~apparat** *m* digestive system; **~spaziergang** *m* constitutional; **~störung** *f* indigestion.
Ver'deck *n* (3) covering; ⚓ deck; *mot.* roof, top; **2en** cover; (*verbergen*) conceal, hide.
ver'denken *s. verargen.*
Verderb [fɛr'dɛrp] *m* (3) ruin; *von Nahrung usw.*: waste; **2en¹** [~bən] *v/i.* (30, 25, sn) get spoiled, go bad; (*verfaulen*) rot; (*zugrunde gehen*) perish; *es mit j-m ~* get into a p.'s bad books; *v/t.* spoil; *sittlich:* corrupt; (*zugrunde richten*; *a. weitS. Bild, Augen usw.*) ruin; (*verpfuschen*) make a mess of; *sich den Magen ~* upset one's stomach; **~en²** *n* (6) corruption; destruction; ruin; *j-n ins ~ stürzen* ruin a p.; *ins ~ rennen* rush (headlong) into de-

struction; **2lich** [~'dɛrp-] pernicious, fatal; *Ware:* perishable; **~lichkeit** *f* perniciousness; perishableness; **~nis** *f* (14²) corruption, depravity; **2t** corrupted, depraved; **~t-heit** *f* corruptness, depravity.
verdeutlichen [~'dɔytlɪçən] (25) make plain, elucidate.
verdeutschen [~'dɔytʃən] (25) translate into German.
ver'dicht|en (*a. sich*) condense; **2ung** *f* condensation.
verdicken [fɛr'dikən] (25, *a. sich*) thicken; 🛠 inspissate.
ver'dienen deserve, merit; *Geld:* earn, gain, make; *gut ~* be doing well; *sich verdient machen um* deserve well of.
Ver'dienst 1. *m* (3²) earnings *pl.*; (*Lohn*) wages *pl.*; (*Gehalt*) salary; (*Gewinn*) gain, profit; 2. *fig. n* merit; *es ist sein ~, daß* it is owing to him that; *s. erwerben;* **~ausfall** loss of earnings; **2lich**, **2voll** meritorious, deserving; **~spanne** 🞥 *f* profit margin.
ver'dient *P.*: deserving; *S., a. Strafe:* well-deserved; **~ermaßen** [~ər'ma:sən] deservedly.
ver'dingen (30, 25) *s. vermieten; sich ~* go into service (*bei* with).
ver'dolmetschen (27) interpret, translate. [demn.)
ver'donnern F (*verurteilen*) con-)
verdoppel|n [fɛr'dɔpəln] (29) double; **2ung** *f* doubling.
verdorben [~'dɔrbən] 1. *p.p. v.* verderben¹; 2. *adj.* spoiled; *Luft:* foul; *sittlich:* corrupt, depraved; *Magen:* disordered.
ver'dorren (25, sn) dry up.
ver'drahten 🗲 wire.
ver'dräng|en push away, thrust aside; *phys. u. fig.* displace; ⚒ dislodge; *fig. a.* supersede, *bsd. durch List:* supplant; *psych.* repress; **2ung** *f* displacement; supersession; repression.
ver'dreh|en distort, twist (*beide a. fig.*); *Glied:* sprain; *Augen:* roll; *Recht:* pervert; *fig. j-m den Kopf ~* turn a p.'s head; **~t** distorted; (*verrückt*) crazy; **2t-heit** *f* craziness; **2ung** *f* distortion, twist(ing).
ver'dreifachen (25) treble.
ver'dreschen F thrash.
verdrieß|en [~'dri:sən] (30) vex, annoy; *sich et. nicht ~ lassen* not

to be discouraged by, not to shrink from; **~lich** vexed, annoyed (*über et. acc.* at); (*schlecht gelaunt*) ill--humo(u)red, peevish, morose; *S.*: annoying, irksome; **2lichkeit** *f* peevishness; *konkret*: vexation, annoyance.

verdroß [~'drɔs] *pret. v. verdrießen*.

verdrossen [~'drɔsən] **1.** *p.p. v. verdrießen*; **2.** *adj.* peevish, sulky; (*unlustig*) listless.

ver'drucken *typ.* misprint.

ver'drücken F (*essen*) polish off; *sich heimlich* ~ slip away.

Verdruß [~'drus] *m* (2) annoyance, vexation; *j-m* ~ *bereiten* vex (*od.* annoy) a p.

ver'duften (sn) F *fig. sl.* beat it.

verdummen [~'dumən] *v/t.* (25) make (*od.* [*v/i.*; sn] become) stupid.

ver'dunkel|n darken (*a. sich*), obscure (*a. fig.*); *durch Wolken, a. fig.* cloud; *Luftschutz*: black out; *ast., fig.* eclipse; **2ung** *f* darkening; obscuration; *Luftschutz*: blackout; *ast.* eclipse; **2ungsgefahr** ⚖ *f* danger of collusion.

verdünn|en [fɛr'dynən] (25) thin; *Gas*: rarefy; *Flüssiges*: dilute; *sich* ~ (*Luft*) thin out; **2ung** *f* thinning; rarefaction; dilution.

verdunst|en [~'dunstən] (26, sn) evaporate; **2er** *m* (7) humidifier; **2ung** *f* evaporation.

verdursten [~'durstən] (24, sn) die with thirst.

verdüstern [~'dy:stərn] (29, *a. sich*) darken.

verdutzen [~'dutsən] (27) startle, nonplus, bewilder.

verebben [~'ʔɛbən] (25), sn) ebb.

veredel|n [~'ʔeːdəln] (29) ennoble; (*verfeinern*) refine; *Güter*: finish; *Boden, Pflanze, Tier*: improve; *Rohstoff*: process, finish; **2ung** *f* refinement; improvement; processing, finishing; **2ungs-industrie** *f* finishing industry.

verehelichen [~'ʔeːəliçən] (25, *sich*) marry.

ver'ehr|en revere, venerate; (*anbeten*) worship, *fig.* adore; *j-m et.* ~ make a p. a present of a th.; *verehrte Anwesende!* Ladies and Gentlemen!; **2er** *m* (7[1]), **2erin** (16[1]) worship(p)er; (*Bewunderer, Liebhaber*) admirer; *e-s Stars*: fan; **~lich** hono(u)red, estimable (*a.* **~t**

adj.); **2ung** *f* reverence, veneration; worship, (*a. fig.*) adoration; **~ungs-würdig** venerable.

vereid|(ig)en [fɛr'ʔaɪd(ig)ən] (26 [25]) swear *a p.* (in *bei Amtsantritt*), administer an oath to *a p.*; **~igt** *adj.* sworn; **2igung** *f* swearing in.

Verein [fɛr'ʔaɪn] *m* (3) union; *im* ~ *mit* together with; *konkret*: society, association; *geselliger*: club.

ver'-einbar compatible, consistent; **~en** (25) agree (upon *a th.*), arrange; **2keit** *f* compatibility; **2ung** *f* agreement, arrangement.

ver'einen *s. vereinigen*; *Vereinte Nationen* United Nations; *mit vereinten Kräften* with a combined effort, jointly.

vereinfach|en [~'ʔaɪnfaxən] (25) simplify; **2ung** *f* simplification.

vereinheitlich|en [~'ʔaɪnhaɪtliçən] (25) make uniform, standardize; **2ung** *f* standardization.

ver'-einig|en (25) join, unite (*a. sich*); combine (*a. sich u. in sich* ~); (*vergesellschaften*) associate (*a. sich*); (*versammeln*) assemble (*a. sich*); (*in Einklang bringen*) reconcile; *Vereinigte Staaten m/pl.* (*von Amerika*) United States (of America), U.S.(A.); **2ung** *f* union; combination; *s. Verein*.

ver'-einnahmen (25) receive.

vereinsamen [fɛr'ʔaɪnza:mən] (25, sn) become lonely *od.* isolated.

Ver'-eins|mitglied *n* club member; **'~wesen** *n* clubs and associations *pl.*, club activities *pl.*

ver'-einzel|n isolate; **~t** *adj.* isolated; single; (*verstreut*) sporadic (-ally *adv.*), scattered (*a. Regenschauer*).

vereis|en [fɛr'ʔaɪzən] *v/t. u. v/i.* (27, sn) freeze (*a.* ⚙); *mot.*, 🛬 ice (up); **~t** [~'ʔaɪst] ice-coated, iced (over); *geol.* glaciated; **2ung** [~'ʔaɪzuŋ] *f* freezing; icing; 🛬 icing-up; *geol.* glaciation.

vereitel|n [~'ʔaɪtəln] (29) thwart, foil, frustrate; defeat; *Hoffnung*: shatter; **2ung** *f* frustration.

ver'-eiter|n (sn) suppurate; **2ung** *f* suppuration.

ver'-ekeln (29): *j-m et.* ~ disgust a p. with a th.

verelend|en [~'ʔeːlɛndən] (26, sn) be reduced to misery; **2ung** *f* reduction to misery, pauperization.

ver'·enden (sn) perish.

vereng|e(r)n [~'ᵊɛŋə(r)n] (25[29]) narrow; (zs.-ziehen) contract; ♀(er)ung f narrowing; contraction.

ver'·erb|en leave (dat. to); biol. transmit (to); Brauch usw.: hand down; sich ~ be hereditary; sich ~ auf (acc.) descend (up)on; ~t biol. [~pt] hereditary; ♀ung [~buŋ] f leaving, etc.; biol. (hereditary) transmission, heredity; ♀ungsgesetz n Mendelian law; ♀ungslehre f genetics sg.

verewig|en [fɛr'ᵊe:vigən] (25) perpetuate; (unsterblich machen) immortalize; ~t [~viçt] (verstorben) deceased, late.

ver'fahren 1. v/i. (sn u. h.) proceed, act (nach on); mit ... ~ deal with; v/t. Geld: spend on travelling about; sich ~ lose one's way, fig. blunder; **2.** adj. (verpfuscht) bungled, muddled; ~ sein be in a bad tangle; **3.** ♀ n (6) (~sweise) procedure (a. ⚖); ⚖ konkret: proceedings pl.; a. ⊕ process, method; (Schema, Plan) system; ♀s... procedural; ♀s-technik ⊕ f process engineering; ♀sweise f s. Verfahren.

Ver'fall m (3, o. pl.) decay, ruin, (a. ♣) decline; e-s Hauses: dilapidation; ⚖ forfeiture; (Fristablauf) expiration; e-s Wechsels: maturity; bei ~ when due, at maturity; in ~ geraten s. verfallen; ♀en **1.** (sn) (fall into) decay; ⊕, Haus: dilapidate, fall into disrepair; (ablaufen) expire; Pfand: become forfeited; Recht: lapse; Wechsel: fall due; Kranker: waste away; j-m ~ become a slave to a p., e-m Laster: become addicted to; Karte ~ lassen let go to waste; ~ auf (acc.) hit upon an idea, etc.; ~ in (acc.) fall (od. run) into; in Strafe ~ incur; in e-e Krankheit ~ fall ill; **2.** adj. decayed; Gebäude: dilapidated; Gesichtszüge: wasted, worn; ⚖ forfeited, lapsed; Fahrschein usw.: expired; e-m Laster: addicted to; ~tag m, ~zeit f day of payment; due date.

ver'fälsch|en falsify; Wein usw.: adulterate; ♀er m (7) falsifier; v. Wein usw.: adulterator; ♀ung f falsification; adulteration.

ver'fangen (Erfolg haben) tell (bei on); das verfängt bei mir nicht that won't take with me; sich ~ become entangled, be caught.

verfänglich [fɛr'fɛŋliç] Frage: captious, insidious; Lage: risky; (unangenehm) embarrassing.

ver'färben discolo(u)r; sich ~ change colo(u)r.

ver'fass|en compose, write; ♀er m (7) author; ♀erin f (16¹) authoress.

Ver'fassung f state, condition; (Staats♀) constitution; (Gemüts♀) disposition, frame of mind; in guter (körperlicher) ~ in good form (od. shape); ~s-änderung f amendment of the constitution; ~sfeind m enemy of the constitution; ♀sfeindlich anticonstitutional; Aktivitäten: directed against the constitution; ~sgericht n Constitutional Court; ♀smäßig, ♀srechtlich constitutional; ~srecht n constitutional law; ~sschutz m: Bundesamt für ~ Office for the Protection of the Constitution; ♀swidrig unconstitutional.

ver'faulen (sn) rot, decay.

ver'fecht|en fight for, defend, advocate; ♀er m (7) advocate.

ver'fehl|en allg. miss; nicht ~ zu ... not to fail to; s. Wirkung; ~t wrong, false; (erfolglos) abortive; ♀ung f (Vergehen) offen|ce, Am. -se.

verfeind|en [fɛr'faɪndən] (26, a. sich) make an enemy (mit of); ~et hostile; on bad terms.

verfeiner|n [~'faɪnərn] (29, a. sich) refine; ♀ung f refinement.

verfemen [~'fe:mən] (25) outlaw; gesellschaftlich: ostracize; et. ~ ban a th.

ver'fertig|en make, manufacture; ♀er m (7¹) maker, manufacturer; ♀ung f making, manufacture.

Verfettung [~'fɛtuŋ] f fatty degeneration, ⚕ adiposis.

ver'feuern use up for fuel; Munition: fire, use up.

ver'film|en film, screen; ♀ung f screening; konkret: film-version.

verfilzen [~'filtsən] (27) felt; Haare: mat. [dunkeln.\]

verfinstern [~'finstərn] (29) s. ver-∫

verflachen [~'flaxən] (25) v/t. flatten; v/i. (sn) (a. sich ~) flatten, grow flat, (become) shallow (a. fig.).

ver'flecht|en interlace; fig. ~ in (acc.) entangle in, involve in; ♀ung f entanglement; † interlocking.

ver'fliegen (sn) fig. vanish; Zeit: fly; (sich verflüchtigen) evaporate,

⚛ volatilize; *sich ~ Vogel*: stray, 🦋 lose one's bearings.

ver'**fließen** (sn) flow away; *Zeit*: elapse.

ver**flixt** F [~'flɪkst] blasted, darned.

ver'**flossen** *adj. Zeit*: past; *Freund, Minister usw.*: late, ex-...

ver'**fluchen** curse; *verflucht s.* ver**dammt**.

ver**flüchtigen** [~'flʏçtigən] (25) volatilize; *sich ~* evaporate (*a. fig.*).

ver**flüssigen** [fɛr'flʏsigən] (25) (*a. sich*) liquefy.

Verfolg [~'fɔlk] *m* (3, *o. pl.*) course, progress; *im ~* (*gen.*) in pursuance of, (*im Verlauf*) in course of; 2**en** [~gən] pursue (*a. fig. Laufbahn, Politik usw.*); *ungerecht, grausam*: persecute; (*beschatten*) shadow, trail; *Spur*: trace: *fig. e-e Sache*: follow up; *v. Gedanken, Träumen*: haunt; *e-n Vorgang*: follow, observe; *gerichtlich ~* prosecute; ~**er** *m* (7), ~**erin** *f* (16¹) pursuer; *grausamer*: persecutor; ~**ung** *f* pursuit; persecution; (*Fortführung*) pursuance; *gerichtliche ~* prosecution; ~**te** [~ktə] *m, f: politisch ~* political persecutee; ~**ungswahn** [~guŋs-] *m* persecution mania.

ver**form|en** ⊕ [~'fɔrmən] (de)form, work, shape; 2**ung** *f* shaping; *b.s.* deformation.

ver**fracht|en** [~'fraxtən] (26) *Schiff*: charter; *Ware usw.*: freight, *Am. od.* 🚢 ship; 2**er** *m* freighter.

ver**franzen** 🛩 *sl.* [~'frantsən]: *sich ~* get lost, lose one's bearings.

Ver'**fremdung** *f* alienation.

ver**froren** [~'froːrən] sensitive to cold; (*durchkältet*) chilled through.

ver**früht** [~'fryːt] premature.

ver**füg|bar** [~'fyːkbaːr] available; 2**barkeit** *f* availability; ~**en** [~gən] *v/t.* decree, order; *Gesetz*: enact; *sich ~* betake o.s. (*nach usw.* to); *v/i. ~ über* (*acc.*) have at one's disposal, dispose of, *S.*: have, be equipped with; 2**ung** *f* decree, order; (~*srecht*) disposal; *j-m zur ~ stehen* be at a p.'s disposal *od.* command; et. *zur ~ haben* have at one's disposal *od.* command; *j-m et. zur ~ stellen* make a th. available to a p., place a th. at a p.'s disposal; 2**ungsfreiheit** *f* discretion; 2**ungsrecht** *n* right of disposal.

ver'**führ|en** seduce; 2**er** *m* (7), 2**e-**

rin *f* (16¹) seducer; ~**erisch** seductive; 2**ung** *f* seduction.

ver'**fünffachen** (25) quintuple.

ver'**füttern** *Hafer usw.*: feed.

Vergabe [~'gaːbə] *f* (15) placing of an order, award of a contract.

ver'**gaffen**: *sich ~* fall in love (*in acc.* with).

ver**gällen** [fɛr'gɛlən] (25) embitter; *Spiritus*: methylate, denature.

ver'**gammeln** F (29, sn) rot; *fig. a. P.*: go to seed.

ver**gangen** [~'gaŋən] gone, past; *im ~en Jahr* last year; 2**heit** *f* past; *gr.* past tense; (*Vorleben*) past, antecedents *pl.*; *politische ~* political background; *s. ruhen*; 2**heitsbewältigung** *f* coming to terms with the past.

ver**gänglich** [~'gɛŋliç] transient; fugitive; 2**keit** *f* transitoriness.

ver**gas|en** [~'gaːzən] (25) gasify; *mot.* carburet; (*durch Gas töten od. vergiften*) gas; 2**er** *mot. m* (7) carburet(t)or; 2**ung** *f* gasifying; *mot.* carburetion; gassing.

ver**gaß** [~'gaːs] *pret. v.* vergessen 1.

ver'**geb|en** give away (*an j-n* to); (*übertragen*) confer, bestow (on); † *Auftrag*: place (with); (*verteilen*) give out; *Chance*: let slip, miss; *Karten*: misdeal; (*verzeihen*) forgive; *sich et. ~* compromise o.s.; ~**ens** in vain, vainly; (*nutzlos*) to no purpose; ~**lich** [~'geːpliç] fruitless, futile, vain; *adv.* in vain; 2**lichkeit** *f* futility; 2**ung** *f* [~buŋ] *f* giving (away); bestowal, conferment (*an acc.* on); (*Verzeihung*) forgiveness, pardon(ing); *~ der Sünden* remission of. sins; *s.* Vergabe.

ver**gegenwärtigen** [fɛrge:gən'vɛrtigən] (25) represent; *sich et. ~* picture *od.* visualize a th.

ver'**gehen** 1. (sn) pass (away); *allmählich*: fade (away); *fig. vor et. ~* die of; *ihm verging Hören und Sehen* he was quite stunned; *der Appetit ist mir vergangen* I have lost my appetite; *sich ~* commit an offen|ce, *Am.* -se; *sich ~ an j-m tätlich*: assault, *unsittlich*: violate; *sich gegen das Gesetz usw. ~* violate, offend against; **2.** 2 *n* (6) ⚖ minor offen|ce, *Am.* -se.

ver**geistig|en** [~'gaɪstigən] (25) spiritualize; 2**ung** *f* spiritualization.

ver'**gelt|en** repay (*dat.* to), return;

(belohnen) reward *(j-m et. a p. for a th.)*; *b.s.* retaliate, pay back; ⚲ung *f* requital, return; *b.s.* retribution, retaliation, reprisal; ~ *üben* retaliate *(an dat.* on); ⚲ungs... *a.* ✕ retaliatory...; ⚲ungsmaßnahme *f* reprisal; ⚲ungsschlag ✕ *m* retaliatory strike.

verge'sellschaft|en (26) socialize; ✝ convert into a company; ⚓ associate; ⚲ung *f* socialization; ✝ conversion into a company; ⚓ association.

vergessen [~'gɛsən] (30) **1.** forget; *(liegenlassen)* leave; *(übersehen)* overlook; *sich* ~ forget o.s., lose one's head; **2.** *p.p. v.* ~ 1; ⚲heit *f* oblivion; *in* ~ *geraten* fall *(od.* sink) into oblivion.

vergeßlich [~'gɛsliç] forgetful; ⚲keit *f* forgetfulness.

vergeud|en [fɛr'gɔʏdən] (26) *Geld, Vermögen*: dissipate, squander; *weitS.* waste; ⚲er *m* (7), ⚲erin *f* (16¹) squanderer; waster; ⚲ung *f* dissipation; waste.

vergewaltig|en [~gə'valtigən] (25) violate, do violence to; *Frau:* violate, rape, ravish; ⚲ung *f* violation; rape; *fig.* outrage *(gen.* upon).

vergewissern [~gə'visərn] (29): *sich* ~ make sure *(e-r S.* of a th.), ascertain *(a th.)*.

ver'gießen spill; *Blut, Tränen:* shed.

vergift|en [~'giftən] (25) poison; *(verseuchen)* contaminate; ⚲ung *f* poisoning; contamination.

vergilbt [~'gilpt] yellowed.

Vergißmeinnicht ⚘ [fɛr'gismaɪnniçt] *n* (3) forget-me-not.

vergittern [~'gitərn] (29) bar up, grate; *mit Holz:* lattice.

verglasen [~'glɑːzən] (27) glaze.

Vergleich [~'glaɪç] *m* (3) comparison; *gütlicher:* arrangement, settlement; *mit Gläubigern:* composition; *s. abschließen:* im ~ *zu* compared to, in comparison with; *s. ziehen;* ⚲bar comparable; ⚲en compare *(mit* with; = *gleichstellen:* to); *sich* ~ come to terms, settle *(mit* with), *mit Gläubigern:* compound (with); *verglichen mit* as against, compared to; ~smaßstab *m* standard of comparison; ⚲sweise comparatively, in comparison; ~ung *f s. Vergleich.*

ver'glimmen (sn) die away.

vergnüg|en [fɛr'gnyːgən] **1.** (25) amuse; *sich* ~ amuse *(od.* enjoy *od.* divert) o.s.; **2.** ⚲ *n* (16) pleasure, enjoyment; *(Spaß)* fun; *konkret:* entertainment; *mit* ~ with pleasure, gladly; *viel* ~*!* have a good time!; ~ *finden an, sein* ~ *haben an (dat.)* take pleasure in; *j-m* ~ *bereiten od.* *schaffen* afford a p. pleasure, amuse a p.; ~lich [~'gnyːkliç] amusing, pleasant; ~t *(über acc.)* pleased (with), delighted (at); *(froh)* gay, merry, cheerful.

Ver'gnügung [~guŋ] *f* pleasure, amusement; entertainment; ~**spark** *m* amusement park, *bsd. Brt.* fun fair; ~**sreise** *f* pleasure-trip; ~**sreisende** *m, f* (18) tourist; ~**ssteuer** *f* entertainment *(Am.* admission) tax; ~**ssucht** *f* (inordinate) love of pleasure; ⚲**ssüchtig** pleasure-seeking; ~**sviertel** *n* entertainment cent|re, *Am.* -er.

vergold|en [~'gɔldən] (26) gild; ⚲er *m* (7) gilder; ⚲ung *f* gilding.

ver'gönnen grant, allow.

vergötter|n [~'gœtərn] (29) deify; *fig.* idolize, adore; ⚲ung *f* deification; *fig.* adoration.

ver'graben hide in the ground; *(a. fig.)* bury.

ver'gräm|en *hunt.* frighten away; ~t care-worn, grief-stricken.

vergraulen F [~'graulən] (25) scare off.

ver'greifen: *sich* ~ be mistaken; ♪ touch the wrong note; *sich* ~ *an j-m:* assault *od. (a. geschlechtlich)* violate a p., *an Eigentum:* steal.

vergreis|en [~'graɪzən] (27, sn) become senile; ⚲ung *f* senescence.

vergriffen [~'grifən] *Ware:* sold out; *Buch:* out(-)of(-)print.

vergrößer|n [fɛr'grøːsərn] (29, *a. sich)* enlarge *(a. phot.)*; *Lupe:* magnify *(a. fig.)*; *(ausdehnen; a. sich)* expand, extend; *(vermehren)* increase, add to; ⚲ung *f* enlargement; magnification; expansion; increase; *phot.* blow-up, enlargement; ⚲ungs-apparat *phot. m* enlarger; ⚲ungsglas *n* magnifying-glass.

Vergünstigung [~'gynstiguŋ] *f* privilege, favo(u)r; benefit.

vergüt|en [~'gyːtən] (26) compensate *(j-m et. a. p. for a th.)*; *Auslagen:* reimburse; *Verlust:* compensate for, make good, indemnify for; ⊕ improve, *Stahl*: temper; 2*ung* *f* compensation; reimbursement; (*Honorar*) fee; ⊕ improvement; tempering.

verhaft|en arrest, apprehend; 2*ung* *f* arrest, apprehension.

ver'hallen (sn) die away.

ver'halten 1. keep back, retain; *den Atem*: hold in; *Lachen usw.*: suppress; *Pferd*: rope; *sich ~ P.*: behave, conduct o.s., act, *S.*: be; *sich ruhig ~* keep quiet; *wenn es sich so verhält* if that is the case; **2.** *p.p. v.* **1.** *u. adj.* restrained; *Atem*: bated; *Stimme*: low; *Gefühle, Zorn*: pent-up; *Lachen*: suppressed; **3.** 2 *n* (6) behavio(u)r (*a. zo. usw.*), conduct; (*Haltung*) attitude; ⊕ characteristics *pl.*; 2s... behavio(u)ral; 2**sforschung** *f* behavio(u)ral research; *~s*-**gestört** maladjusted; 2s-**psychologie** *f* behavio(u)ral psychology.

Verhältnis [fɛr'hɛltnis] *n* (4¹) relation; *a.* ⅋ proportion, ratio; *pl.* (*Umstände*) conditions, circumstances *pl.*; (*Mittel*) means *pl.*; (*Beziehung*) relation(s *pl.*) (*zu* with); (*Liebes*2) liaison, love-affair; (*Geliebte*) mistress; außer jedem *~* stehen be out of all proportion; *im ~ zu* in proportion to, compared with; *im ~ von 4 : 1* in the ratio of four to one; *im umgekehrten ~* (*zu*) at an inverse ratio (to); *in freundschaftlichem ~ mit* on friendly terms with; *über s-e Verhältnisse leben* live beyond one's means; 2-**mäßig** proportional; comparative; *adv.* in proportion; comparatively (speaking); relatively; *~wahl parl. f* proportional representation; 2**wid-rig** disproportionate; *~wort gr. n* (1²) preposition.

Ver'haltungsmaßregeln *f/pl.* instructions.

ver'hand|eln *v/i. u. v/t.* negotiate, treat (*über acc., wegen* for); ⅋⅋ try ([*über*] et. a th.; *gegen j-n* a p.); (*verkaufen*) sell; (*erörtern*) discuss; 2**lung** *f* negotiation; ⅋⅋ hearing, proceedings *pl.*, *Strafrecht*: trial; discussion; 2**lungs-partner** *m* negotiating party; opposite number; 2**lungsrunde** *f* round of negotiations; 2**lungs-tisch** *m* negotiating table.

ver'häng|en (25) cover, hang (*mit*

with); *Strafe*: impose; inflict (*über acc.* [*up*]on), *a. Sport*: award; 2**nis** *n* (4¹) fate, doom; (*Katastrophe*) disaster; *j-m zum ~ werden* be a p's undoing; *~nisvoll* fateful, fatal; (*unselig*) disastrous; 2**ung** *f* infliction.

ver'harmlosen (27) play down.

verhärmt [~'hɛrmt] care-worn.

ver'harren (h. *u.* sn) persevere; (*auf, bei, in dat.*) persist (in), abide (by), F stick (to).

verharschen [~'harʃən] *v/i.* (27, sn) *Schnee*: crust; *Wunde a.*: close.

ver'härt|en (*a. sich*) harden; 2**ung** *f* hardening; *fig. a.* induration.

ver'haspeln (29, *a. sich*) tangle; *sich ~ fig.* get muddled.

verhaßt [~'hast] hated; *S.*: hateful.

ver'hätscheln coddle, pamper.

Verhau [~'hau] *m* (3) abatis; F mess; 2**en** thrash; *fig. sl.* muff; *sich ~* (make a) blunder.

verheddern F [~'hɛdərn] (*a. sich*) get entangled; *fig.* get muddled.

verheer|en [~'he:rən] (25) devastate, lay waste; *~end fig.* disastrous; 2**ung** *f* devastation, havoc.

ver'hehl|en, 2**ung** *f* s. verheimlichen.

ver'heilen heal (up).

verheimlich|en [fɛr'haimliçən] (25) hide, conceal (*dat.* from), keep *a th.* a secret (from); *s.* vertuschen; 2**ung** *f* concealment.

ver'heirat|en marry (*mit, an acc.* to); *sich ~ a.* get married; 2**ung** *f* marriage.

ver'heiß|en, 2**ung** *f* promise; *~ungsvoll* promising.

ver'helfen: *j-m ~ zu* help a p. to.

verherrlich|en [~'hɛrliçən] (25) glorify; 2**ung** *f* glorification.

ver'hetz|en instigate; fanaticize; 2**ung** *f* instigation.

ver'hexen bewitch.

verhimmeln [~'himəln] worship.

ver'hinder|n prevent (*j-n an dat.* a p. from); 2**ung** *f* prevention.

ver'höhn|en deride, jeer, taunt; 2**ung** *f* derision, mockery.

Verhör ⅋⅋ [~'hø:r] *n* (3) interrogation, examination; *weitS.* trial, hearing; *j-n ins ~ nehmen =* 2**en** examine; try, hear; *sich ~* hear wrong.

ver'hüll|en cover, veil; *~t fig.* veiled; 2**ung** *f* veil, disguise, cover.

verhundertfachen [ˌ'hundərt-faxən] (25) centuple.

ver'hungern (sn) die of hunger, starve; ~ *lassen* starve to death.

verhunzen [fer'huntsən] (27) ruin, *sl.* louse up; *Sprache:* murder.

ver'hüten prevent, avert, obviate.

verhütt|en ⚒ [ˌ'hytən] (26) *Erz:* smelt; ℒ**ung** *f* smelting.

Ver'hütung *f* prevention; ~**smaßnahme** *f* preventive measure; ~s**mittel** *n* ⚕ prophylactic; (*Empfängnis*ℒ) contraceptive.

verhutzelt [ˌ'hutsəlt] shrivel(l)ed; *P., Gesicht:* wizened.

verinnerlich|en [ˌ'ʔinərliçən] (25) spiritualize; ℒ**ung** *f* spiritualization.

ver'-irr|en (*sich*) lose one's way, go astray; ~**t** *Kugel, Tier:* stray; ℒ**ung** *f fig.* aberration, error.

ver'jagen drive (*od.* chase) away.

verjähr|bar [ˌ'jɛːrbaːr] prescriptible; ~**en** (25, sn) become prescriptive; *bsd. Straftat:* come under the statute of limitations; ~**t** ⚖ prescriptive, superannuated (*a. fig.*); statute-barred; ℒ**ung** *f* limitation (by lapse of time); (negative) prescription; ℒ**ungsfrist** *f* limitation period.

ver'jubeln F squander, F blue.

verjüng|en [ˌ'jyŋən] (25) make (*sich* ~ grow) young again, (*a. sich*) rejuvenate; *Maßstab:* reduce; *sich* ~ (*spitz zulaufen*) taper (off); ℒ**ung** *f* rejuvenescence; tapering; reduction; ℒ**ungskur** *f* rejuvenating cure; ℒ**ungsmittel** *n* rejuvenation tonic.

verkalk|en [ˌ'kalkən] (26) (*a. sich* ~) ⚕, *physiol.* calcify; ~**t** ⚕ sclerotic, F fossilated; ℒ**ung** *f* calcification; (arterio)sclerosis.

verkalku'lieren: *sich* ~ miscalculate, make a mistake.

ver'kappt disguised, ... in disguise; crypto- *communist, etc.*

verkapsel|n [ˌ'kapsəln] (25): *sich* ~ encyst; ℒ**ung** *f* encystment.

Ver'kauf *m* (3³) sale; ℒ**en** sell (*a. sich*); *zu* ~(*d*) for sale.

Ver'käuf|er(in *f*) *m* seller; *im kleinen:* retailer; ⚖ vendor (*a. Straßen*-ℒ, *Zeitungs*ℒ); (*Ladengehilfe*) shop-assistant, *Am.* (sales-)clerk (*m u. f*), *m* salesman, *f* saleswoman, shopgirl, *Am. a.* salesgirl; ℒ**lich** sal(e)-able, marketable; *pred.* for sale; ~-

lichkeit *f* sal(e)ableness.

Ver'kaufs|-automat *m* vending machine, vendomat; ~**bedingungen** *f/pl.* terms of sale; ~**förderung** *f* sales promotion; ~**leiter** *m* sales manager; ~**organisation** *f* sales organization; ~**personal** *n* sales staff; ~**preis** *m* selling-price; ~**schlager** *m s. Schlager*; ~**sständer** *m* display stand.

Verkehr [ˌ'keːr] *m* (3, *o. pl.*) traffic; (*Beförderung v. Gütern u. Personen*) transport(ation *Am.*); (*Verbindung*) communication; 🕿, 🚍, 🚋 (~s**dienst**) service; (*Handel*) commerce, trade; *freundschaftlich od. geschlechtlich:* intercourse; *aus dem* ~ *ziehen* withdraw from service (*Geld:* from circulation); ℒ**en** *v/t.* reverse; (*verwandeln*) turn, convert (*beide:* in *acc.* into); *fig.* pervert; *v/i. Fahrzeug:* run, be operated; (*regelmäßig hin- u. zurückfahren*) ply *od.* run (*zwischen between*); (*Handel treiben*) traffic, trade; ~ *bei j-m* visit (*od.* go to) a p.'s house; ~ *in e-m Lokal usw.* frequent; *mit j-m* ~ associate (*od.* keep company) with, see a great deal of, *mit e-r Gruppe* ~ *a.* mix with, *geschlechtlich:* have (sexual) intercourse with; *sich* ~ *in* (*acc.*) be changed into.

Ver'kehrs|-ader *f* arterial road; ~**ampel** *f* traffic lights *pl.*; ~**an-drang** *m* rush (of traffic); ~**aufkommen** *n* volume of traffic; ~**behinderung** *f* obstruction of traffic; ~**betrieb** *m s. Verkehrsunternehmen*; ~**dichte** *f* density of traffic; ~**disziplin** *f* road discipline; ~**flugzeug** *n* commercial aircraft, air-liner; ~**hindernis** *n* traffic block; ~**insel** *f* refuge; ~**knotenpunkt** *m* traffic junction; ~**kontrolle** *f* traffic (spot-)check; ~**meldungen** *f/pl.* traffic news *sg.*; ~**minister** *m* Minister of Transport; ~**mittel** *n Fahrzeuge:* (*öffentliches* public) conveyance, transport(ation *Am.*); ~**netz** *n* network of communication; ~**opfer** *n* road casualty; ~**ordnung** *f* traffic regulations *pl.*; ~**polizei** traffic police; ~**polizist** *m s. Verkehrsschutzmann*; ~**regelung** *f* (*durch Ampeln:* automatic) traffic control; ℒ**reich** frequented, busy, congested; ~**schild** *n* traffic sign; ~**schutzmann** *m stehender:* traffic constable, pointsman; *motorisierter*: mobile policeman, *bsd. Am.* F speed cop; ⚥-**schwach:** ～e Zeit off-peak hours *pl.*; ⚥**sicher** *Auto*: roadworthy; **～sicherheit** *f* roadworthiness; ⚥**stark:** ～e Zeit rush (*od.* peak) hours *pl.*; **～stauung** *f*, **～stockung** *f* traffic jam *od.* congestion *od.* bank-up; **～störung** *f* interruption of traffic; 🐂 *usw.* breakdown; **～straße** *f* thoroughfare; **～sünder** *m* traffic-offender; **～tafel** *f* traffic sign; **～teilnehmer** *m* road user; **～-überwachung** *f* traffic monitoring; **～-unfall** *m* traffic accident; **～-unternehmen** *n* transport(ation) service (*od.* company), public carrier; **～ver-ein** *m* (tourist) information cent|re, *Am.* -er; **～verhältnisse** *n/pl.* traffic conditions; **～vorschrift** *f* traffic regulation; **～wert** ✝ *m* market value; **～wesen** *n* traffic; (system of) communications *pl.*; transport(ation *Am.*); **～zählung** *f* traffic census; **～zeichen** *n* traffic sign.

verkehrt [fɛr'keːrt] inverted, reversed; upside down; inside out; (*falsch*) wrong; (*unsinnig*) absurd; ⚥**heit** *f* wrongness; folly, absurdity.

ver'kennen *P.*: mistake; *S.*: misunderstand, misjudge; (*unterschätzen*) underestimate; *e-e Sache nicht* ～ be fully aware of; *nicht zu* ～ unmistakable; *verkanntes Genie* unappreciated genius.

ver'kett|en (26) chain up; *fig.* link together, concatenate; *bsd.* ⚡ interconnect; ⚥**ung** *f fig.* concatenation.

verketzern [～'kɛtsərn] (29) brand as a heretic.

verkitten cement (*a. fig.*), putty.

ver'klagen accuse, inform against; 🖋 sue (*auf acc., wegen* for); *s. ver-petzen.*   [transfiguration.⟩

ver'klär|en transfigure; ⚥**ung** *f*⟩

verklausulieren [～klauzuˈliːrən] safeguard (*od.* hedge) by clauses.

ver'kleben paste *a th.* over *od.* up.

ver'kleid|en disguise; ⚡ line, *außen*: (en)case, *a.* 🛡 face; (*täfeln*) wainscot; ✂ *s. tarnen;* ⚥**ung** *f* disguise; ⚡ lining, facing; wainscot(t)ing.

verkleiner|n [～'klaɪnərn] (29) make smaller, reduce (in size); *Maßstab,* ⚕ reduce; (*vermindern*) diminish; *fig.* belittle, minimize; detract from; ⚥**ung** *f* reduction; diminution; *fig.* belittling, detraction;

⚥**ungswort** *n* (1²) diminutive.

ver'kleistern glue, paste up.

ver'klemmt *fig. P.*: repressed, inhibited.

ver'klingen (sn) die away.

ver'knacken F *s. verurteilen.*

ver'knallen F: *sich* ～ (*in j-n*) fall violently in love with; *verknallt sein in j-n* F be gone on, *Am.* have a crush on.

verknapp|en [～'knapən] *v/i.* (25, sn) run short, become scarce; ⚥**ung** *f* shortage, scarcity.

ver'kneifen F: *sich et.* ～ deny o.s. a th.; *er konnte sich nicht* ～ *zu sagen* he couldn't help saying.

verknöcher|n [～'knœçərn] *v/t. u. v/i.* (29, sn) ossify; *fig. a.* fossilize; ⚥**ung** *f* ossification; fossilization.

ver'knoten knot, tie (up).

ver'knüpf|en knot *od.* tie (together); *fig.* connect, combine; **～t** *fig.*: ～ *mit* involving, entailing; ⚥**ung** *f* connection.

ver'kohlen (25) *v/t.* (sn) carbonize, char; *v/t.* F (*zum besten haben*) kid.

ver'kommen 1. (sn) decay, go to ruin; *P.*: come down in the world, go to seed; **2. adj.** decayed; *sittlich*: depraved; ⚥**heit** *f* depravity.

ver'koppeln (29) couple.

ver'korken (25) cork (up).

verkorksen [～'kɔrksən] F (27) *s. verpatzen; sich den Magen* ～ upset one's stomach.

verkörper|n [～'kœrpərn] (29) personify, embody; *bsd. thea.* impersonate; ⚥**ung** *f* personification, embodiment; impersonation.

verköstigen [～'kœstigən] (25) feed, board.

ver'krachen F: *sich* ～ fall out (*mit* with).

verkraften [～'kraftən] (26) cope with, handle, bear.

ver'krampft cramped.

ver'kriechen: *sich* ～ hide.

ver'krümeln F: *sich* ～ F beat it, make off.

ver'krümm|en crook, curve, bend; **～t** crooked; ⚥**ung** *f*: ～ *der Wirbelsäule* curvature of the spine.

verkrüppeln [fɛr'krypəln] (29) *v/t.* cripple; (*verkümmern*) stunt; *v/i.* (sn) become crippled; become stunted (*od.* deformed).

ver'krusten (en)crust.

ver'kühlen: *sich* ～ catch (a) cold.

verkümmern

ver'kümmer|n *v/i.* (sn) become stunted, ⫿ atrophy; *(dahinsiechen)* waste away, pine (away); *aus Mangel an Nahrung:* starve; *v/t. Recht:* curtail; **~t** stunted.

ver'künd(ig)|en (26 [25]) announce; *öffentlich:* publish, proclaim; *Urteil:* pronounce; **2ung** *f* announcement; proclamation; pronouncement; *Mariä* ~ Annunciation, Lady Day.

verkupfern [~'kupfərn] (29) copper.

ver'kuppeln pander, sell, procure; ⊕ couple.

ver'kürz|en shorten; *(abkürzen)* abridge; *(beschränken)* curtail; *Zeit:* beguile; *verkürzte Arbeitszeit* short time; **2ung** *f* shortening; abridg(e)ment.

ver'lachen laugh at, deride.

Ver'lade|bahnhof *m* loading station; **~kran** *m* loading crane.

ver'lad|en load, ship; ✗ entrain, *in Schiffe:* embark, *in Flugzeuge:* emplane, *in Lastwagen:* entruck; **2e-rampe** *f* loading platform; **2ung** *f* loading, shipping; entraining *etc.*

Verlag [fɛr'laːk] *m* (3) *Tätigkeit:* publication; *Firma:* the publishers *pl.*; *s. Verlagsbuchhandlung; im ~ von* published by.

ver'lager|n *v/t. allg.* (a. sich) shift; *(überführen)* transfer; *(evakuieren)* evacuate; **2ung** *f* shifting; transfer; evacuation; *fig.* shift.

Ver'lags|-anstalt *f* publishing house; **~buchhandel** *m* publishing trade; **~buchhändler** *m* publisher; **~buchhandlung** *f*, **~haus** *n* publishing house; **~katalog** *m* publisher's list; **~leiter(in** *f) m* general manager; **~recht** *n* copyright; **~werk** *n* publication.

ver'langen 1. (25) *v/t.* demand, ask for; *(erfordern)* require, call for; *(beanspruchen)* claim; *(wünschen)* desire; *viel ~ an Leistungen* set a high standard; *es verlangt mich zu inf.* I am anxious to *inf.*; *das ist zuviel verlangt* that's asking too much; *was ~ Sie von ihm?* what do you want of him?; *v/i. ~ nach* ask *od.* (*sich sehnen*) long for; **2.** **2** *n* (6) desire; *(Sehnsucht)* longing *(nach* for), *Am.* F yen; *(Forderung)* demand, request; *auf ~* by request, ✝ on demand; *auf ~ von* at the request of; *~ tragen nach* have a longing for.

verlänger|n [~'lɛŋərn] (29) lengthen; *Frist usw.:* prolong, extend; **2ung** *f* lengthening; prolongation, extension; *Sport:* *(Spiel2)* extra time; *(Vorsprung)* projection; **2ungsschnur** *⨎* *f* extension flex *od. Am.* cord.

verlangsamen [fɛr'laŋzaːmən] (25) (a. sich) slow down, slacken; *(verzögern)* retard.

Verlaß [~'las] *m* (4) reliance; *es ist kein ~ auf ihn* there is no relying on him, he is unreliable.

ver'lassen 1. leave, *gänzlich a.* quit; *(im Stich lassen)* forsake, abandon, desert; *sich ~ auf* (acc.) rely *(od.* count *od.* depend) on; *Sie können sich darauf ~* you may rely on it, you may rest assured!; **2.** *adj.* forsaken, abandoned; deserted *(a. = öde)*; *(einsam)* lonely, isolated; **2-heit** *f* abandonment; loneliness; isolation.

verläßlich [~'lɛslɪç] reliable.

ver'lästern malign, slander, defame.

Verlaub [fɛr'laup] *m* (3): *mit ~* with your permission.

Ver'lauf *m* (3, *o. pl.) der Zeit:* lapse, course; *e-s Vorgangs:* progress, course, development; *(Tendenz)* trend; *weiterer ~* sequel; *e-n schlimmen ~ nehmen* take a bad turn; **2en 1.** *v/i.* (sn) *Zeit:* pass, elapse; *Vorgang:* take a ... course, come off, go *well, etc.*; *Grenze, Weg usw.:* run, extend; *Farben:* run, bleed; *sich ~* go astray, lose one's way; *Volksmenge:* scatter, disperse; *s. Sand;* **2.** *adj. Tier:* stray; *Kind:* lost.

verlaust [~'laust] lousy.

verlaut|baren [~'lautbaːrən] (25) *v/t.* make known, disclose; *v/i.* (h., *a.* sn) = **~en** (26) be reported *od.* disclosed, transpire; *~ lassen* give to understand, hint; *wie verlautet* as reported.

ver'leb|en spend, pass; **~t** [~'leːpt] worn out; *(hinfällig)* decrepit.

ver'leg|en 1. *v/t.* misplace; *anderswohin:* transfer *(a. Truppen)*, shift; remove; *Verlagswerk:* publish; ⊕ *Kabel usw.:* lay; *Straße,* 🚆 relocate; *Weg (versperren):* bar, cut off; *zeitlich:* put off, postpone *(auf acc.* to); *sich ~ auf* (acc.) apply *(od.* devote).

o.s. to, take to, *aufs Bitten, Leugnen usw.*: resort to; **2.** *adj.* embarrassed, confused; self-conscious; ~ *um* at a loss for; 2**enheit** *f* embarrassment; (*Klemme*) difficulty; (*mißliche Lage*) predicament; *in* ~ *sein* be at a loss (*um* for); *in* ~ *bringen* embarrass; *in* ~ *kommen* get embarrassed; 2**enheitslösung** *f* stop-gap solution; 2**enheits-pause** *f* awkward silence; 2**er** *m* (7) publisher; ~**erisch** editorial, publishing; 2**ung** *f* transfer, removal; ⊕ laying; *zeitlich*: postponement.

ver'**leiden** (26): *j-m et.* ~ disgust a p. with a th.; spoil a th. for a p.

Ver'leih *m* hire service; *Film*: distribution, (*Gesellschaft*) distributors *pl.*; 2**en** lend (out), *Am.* loan; *gegen Miete*: hire out, let out; (*gewähren*) *Titel, Recht usw.*: bestow, confer (*j-m* on a p.); *Gunst*: grant; *Auszeichnung, Preis*: award; *e-n Reiz*: give; ~**er** *m* (7), ~**erin** *f* (16¹) lender; bestower; ~**ung** *f* lending out; grant; bestowal; award; ~**ungs-urkunde** *f* diploma.

ver'**leit**|**en** mislead, lead astray; (*verführen*) seduce; (*veranlassen*) induce, lead (to *inf.*); *sich* ~ *lassen zu inf.* be induced to *inf.*, be carried away into *ger.*; 2**ung** *f* misleading; seduction.

ver'**lernen** unlearn, forget.

ver'**lesen** read out; *Namen usw.*: call over; *Erbsen usw.*: pick; *sich* ~ make a mistake (in reading).

verletz|**bar** [fer'letsbɑːr], ~**lich** damageable; (*verwundbar*) vulnerable; (*leicht gekränkt*) sensitive, touchy; ~**en** (27) hurt, injure; *fig.* *Gefühl*: hurt; (*kränken*) offend; *Eid, Recht usw.*: violate; *Gesetz*: infringe; ~**end** offensive; 2**te** *m*, *f* (18) injured person; 2**ung** *f* hurt, (*a.* = *Wunde*) injury; violation; infraction, infringement.

ver'**leugn**|**en** deny; *Freund, Kind*: disown; *Grundsatz*: renounce, disclaim; *sich* ~ *lassen* have o.s. denied, not to be at home (*vor j-m* to); 2**ung** *f* denial; disavowal; renunciation.

verleumd|**en** [~'lɔymdən] (26) calumniate, defame; *a.* ⚖ slander, *schriftlich*: libel; 2**er** *m* (7), 2**erin** (16¹) calumniator, slanderer; ~**erisch** defamatory; slanderous; libel(l)ous; 2**ung** *f* calumny, defa-

mation; slander, libel; 2**ungskampagne** *f* smear campaign; 2**ungs-klage** *f* libel suit.

ver'**lieb**|**en**: *sich* ~ *in* (*acc.*) fall in love with; ~**t** [~pt] (*in acc.*) in love (with), enamo(u)red (of); *a. Blick usw.*: amorous; (*liebeskrank*) love-sick; 2**t-heit** *f* amorousness.

verlier|**en** [~'liːrən] (30) *v/t.* lose (*a. v/i.*); *Blätter, Haar usw.*: shed; *sich* ~ lose o.s., (*verschwinden*) disappear, *Volksmenge*: disperse, *Farbe*: fade, *Schmerz*: subside; *s. Nerv, Geduld, Verstand*; 2**er** *m* (7) loser; *ein schlechter* ~ a bad loser; 2**erseite** *f*: *auf der* ~ *sein* be on the losing side.

Ver'lies *n* (4) dungeon, keep.

ver'**loben**: *sich* ~ become engaged *od.* betrothed (*mit* to).

Verlöbnis [~'løːpnis] *n* (4¹) engagement, betrothal.

Verlob|**te** [~'loːptə] *m*, *f* (18): *ihr* ~**r** her fiancé *od.* intended (husband); *s-e* ~ his fiancée *od.* intended (wife); *die* ~**n** *pl.* the engaged couple *sg.*, the betrothed *pl.*

Verlobung [~'loːbuŋ] *f* engagement, betrothal; ~**s-anzeige** *f* announcement of an engagement; ~**s-ring** *m* engagement ring.

ver'**lock**|**en** allure, entice; (*versuchen*) tempt; (*verführen*) seduce; ~**end** *adj.* tempting; 2**ung** *f* allurement, enticement; temptation.

verlogen [fer'loːgən] (given to) lying, mendacious; 2**heit** *f* untruthfulness, mendacity.

ver'**lohnen** *v/refl. s.* (sich) lohnen.

verlor [~'loːr] *pret. v.* verlieren.

ver'**loren** *p.p. v.* verlieren *u. adj.* lost; (*einsam, hilflos*) forlorn; ~**e** *Eier* poached eggs; ~**er Haufen** forlorn hope; ~**e** *Partie* losing game; *s. Sohn*; ~ *geben* give up for lost; *auf* ~**em** *Posten stehen* fight a losing battle; *das Spiel* ~ *geben* throw up the game, *fig.* give in; ~**gehen** (sn) get (*od.* be) lost.

ver'**löschen** *v/t.* extinguish; *Schrift*: efface; *v/i.* (sn) *s.* erlöschen.

ver'**los**|**en** dispose of by lot, raffle (off); 2**ung** *f* lottery, raffle.

ver'**löten** solder (up).

verlotter|**n** [~'lɔtərn] (29) go to seed; ~**t** *P.*: dissolute, rackety; *S.*: ruined.

Verlust [~'lust] *m* (3²) loss; ~**e** *pl.* ✕ casualties; *im Spiel*: losings; *bei*

~ *von* under pain of, with forfeiture of; *in* ~ *geraten* get lost; *mit* ~ *arbeiten, verkaufen usw.* at a loss, at a sacrifice; **~anzeige** *f* notice of (a) loss; **2bringend** involving (a) loss, losing *business;* **2ig** (*gen.*): *j-n* e-r S. *für* ~ *erklären* declare a p. to have forfeited a th.; e-r S. ~ *gehen* forfeit a th.; **~liste** ✕ *f* casualty list.

ver'machen bequeath *od.* leave (*dat.* to).

Vermächtnis [~'mɛçtnis] *n* (4¹) (last) will; (*das Vermachte*) bequest; *von Geld:* legacy (*a. fig.*); *von Grundeigentum:* devise.

vermähl|en [~'mɛːlən] (25) (*a. sich*) wed, marry (*mit* to); **2ung** *f* wedding, marriage.

ver'mahnen *s.* ermahnen.

ver'manschen F mess up.

vermarkt|en [~'marktən] (26) commercialize; **2ung** *f* commercialization.

vermasseln F [~'masəln] (29) *s.* verpatzen.

Vermassung [~'masuŋ] *f* de-personalization.

ver'mauern wall up (*od.* in).

ver'mehr|en (*a. sich*) increase (*um* by), augment, *an Zahl: a.* multiply; ([*sich*] *fortpflanzen*) propagate, breed; (*beitragen zu*) add to; **2ung** *f* increase; addition (*gen.* to).

ver'meid|en avoid; **~lich** [~'maɪt-] avoidable; **2ung** [~duŋ] *f* avoidance.

ver'mein|en think, suppose; **~tlich** [~'maɪntlɪç] supposed, pretended.

ver'melden announce, report.

ver'mengen mix (up), mingle; (*verwechseln*) confound, mix up.

ver'menschlichen (25) humanize.

Vermerk [fer'mɛrk] *m* (3) note, entry; **2en** note (down), record; (*eintragen*) enter; *geistig:* observe, make a (mental) note of; *übel* ~ *take amiss*.

ver'mess|en 1. *v/t.* measure; *Land:* survey; *sich* ~ measure wrong; (*sich erdreisten*) dare; **2.** *adj.* daring; impudent; **2enheit** *f* presumption; **2ung** *f* measurement; *des Landes:* survey; **2ungs-amt** *n* survey-office; **2ungs-ingenieur** *m* land surveyor.

vermiet|bar [~'miːtbɑːr] rentable; **~en** let, *bsd. Am.* rent; hire (out); 🏛 lease; *Haus zu* ~ house to (be)

let; *Möbel usw. zu* ~ furniture *etc.* on hire; **2er** *m* (7) letter, 🏛 lessor; hirer (out); **2ung** *f* letting; leasing; hiring (out).

ver'minder|n (*a. sich*) diminish, decrease, lessen; (*beeinträchtigen*) impair; (*beschränken*) reduce; **2ung** *f* diminution, decrease, lessening; impairment; reduction.

verminen [~'miːnən] (25) mine.

ver'misch|en mix (up), mingle; *Tee usw.:* blend; *sich* ~ mix; ~t *adj.* mixed; *Nachrichten usw.:* miscellaneous; **2ung** *f* mixing, mixture.

ver'missen miss; (*beklagen*) regret; ~ *lassen* lack; *vermißt* missing.

Ver'mißte *m* (18) missing person.

vermitt|eln [~'mɪtəln] (29) *v/t.* mediate; (*zustande bringen*) arrange; *Frieden, Anleihe:* negotiate; (*beschaffen*) procure; *Eindruck, Vorstellung:* give, convey; *Wissen:* impart (*j-m* to); *v/i.* mediate (*bei* in); intercede, interpose (*zwischen between*); **~els(t)** (*gen.*) by means (*od.* dint) of; **2ler** *m* (7), **2lerin** *f* (16¹) mediator (*f a.* mediatrix); (*oft b.s.*) go-between; ✝ middleman; agent; **2lung** *f* mediation; arrangement; intercession; procuring; conveying; imparting; *teleph.* switchboard, (*Amt*) exchange, (*Person*) operator; *durch* (*gütige*) ~ *des Herrn X* by the (good) offices of Mr. X.; **2lungs-amt** *teleph. n* exchange; **2lungsgebühr** *f* commission.

vermöbeln F [~'møːbəln] (29) *s.* verprügeln.

ver'modern (sn) mo(u)lder, rot.

ver'mögen 1. (*können*) be able to do; ~ *zu inf.* be able to; et. ~ *bei j-m* have influence with a p.; **2.** 2 *n* (6) ability, power; (*Geld2*) fortune; (*Besitz*) property; ✝ (*Aktiva*) assets *pl.;* **~d** wealthy, well-to-do; *pred.* well to do, well off; **2s-abgabe** *f* capital levy; **2s-anlage** *f* (productive) investment; **2sbildung** *f* wealth formation; **~srechtlich** proprietary; **2ssteuer** *f* property tax; **2sverhältnisse** *n/pl.* pecuniary circumstances; **2swerte** *m/pl.* assets *pl.*

vermumm|en [fer'mumən] (25) disguise, mask; **2ung** *f* disguise.

vermut|en [~'muːtən] suppose, presume, *Am. a.* guess; (*argwöhnen*) suspect; **~lich** presumable; probable; *adv. oft* I suppose; 2ung *f* supposition, presumption; *Am. a.* guess; (*Schluß*) conjecture; (*Gedanke*) idea; (*Mutmaßung*) speculation (*a. pl.*).

vernachlässig|en [~'nɑːxlɛsigən] (25) neglect; 2ung *f* neglect(ing).

ver'nagel|n nail (up); *mit Brettern* ~ board up; **~t** F: *er war wie* ~ *his mind was a complete blank.*

ver'nähen sew up.

vernarben [~'narbən] (25, sn) (*a. sich*) cicatrice, scar (over).

vernarr|en [~'narən] (25): *sich* ~ *in* (*acc.*) become infatuated with; **~t** *in* infatuated with, F gone on.

ver'naschen spend on sweets; F *fig.* have it away with.

vernebel|n [~'neːbəln] (29) ✗ screen; *fig.* obscure; 2ung *f* smoke-screen (*a. fig.*).

vernehm|bar [~'neːmbaːr] audible; **~en**[1] *v/t.* perceive, hear; (*erfahren*) learn, hear; (*verhören*) interrogate, question, 🔱 *a.* examine; ~ *lassen* declare; *sich* ~ *lassen* make o.s. heard; 2en[2] *n* (6): *dem* ~ *nach according to report, from what I* (*od. we*) *hear*; **~lich** audible, distinct; 2ung *f* interrogation.

ver'neig|en (*sich*) 2ung *f* bow (*vor dat. to*).

vernein|en [~'naɪnən] (25) say no, answer in the negative (*eine Frage to a question*); (*leugnen*) deny; **~end** negative; 2ung *f* negation; denial; *gr.* negative.

vernicht|en [~'niçtən] (26) annihilate; (*zerstören*) destroy; *Hoffnung*: dash; (*ausrotten*) exterminate; **~end** *Blick, Kritik*: scathing; *Antwort, Schlag, Niederlage*: crushing; 2ung *f* annihilation; destruction; 2ungslager *n* extermination camp; 2ungskrieg *m* war of annihilation.

ver'nickeln (29) nickel(-plate).

verniedlichen [~'niːtliçən] (25) play down.

ver'nieten rivet.

Vernunft [~'nunft] *f* (16) reason; ~ *annehmen* listen to reason; *j-n zur* ~ *bringen* bring a p. to his senses; *wieder zur* ~ *kommen* come back to one's senses; **~ehe** *f* marriage of convenience.

vernünftig [~'nynftiç] (*vernunft-begabt*) rational; (*verständig*; *ver-*

nunftgemäß, angemessen) reasonable; (*verständig*) sensible, level-headed; ~ *reden* talk sense.

ver'nunft|los senseless, unreasonable; **~mäßig** rational; **~widrig** irrational, unreasonable.

veröd|en [~'ʔøːdən] (26) *v/t.* make desolate; (*verheeren*) lay waste, devastate; *v/i.* (sn) become desolate; 2ung *f* desolation; devastation.

veröffentlich|en [fɛr'ʔœfəntliçən] (25) publish; 2ung *f* publication.

ver'-ordn|en *gesetzlich*: ordain, decree; (*a.* ⚕) order, ⚕ prescribe (*j-m for a p.*); 2ung *f* order, ordinance, decree; ⚕ prescription.

ver'pachten lease (*dat. to*).

Ver'pächter *m* (7), **~in** *f* (16[1]) lessor.

Ver'pachtung *f* leasing.

ver'pack|en pack (up); ✝ *einzelne Artikel*: *a.* package; (*einwickeln*) wrap up; 2ung *f* packing; packaging; (*Packmaterial*) packing (material); (*Hülle*) wrapping; 2ungs-material *n* packaging.

ver'passen let slip; *bsd. Zug usw.*: miss, lose; F *j-m e-n Hieb usw.*: give; ✗ *Uniform usw.*: fit (on).

verpatzen F [~'patsən] bungle, *bsd. Sport*: muff, *sl.* foozle.

verpesten [~'pɛstən] (26) pollute (*the air*); *weitS. die Luft* ~ raise a stench.

ver'petzen inform against, F peach (up)on; *bsd. Schule*: sneak against.

ver'pfänd|en pawn, (*a. fig.*) pledge; mortgage; 2ung *f* pledging; pawning; mortgaging.

ver'pfeifen F squeal on.

ver'pflanz|en transplant; 2ung *f* transplanting; ⚕ transplantation.

ver'pfleg|en (25) feed, board; (*mit Lebensmitteln beliefern*) cater for; *im Großen*: provision, victual; 2ung *f* boarding; catering; *konkret*: food, board; provisions *pl.*, ✗ rations *pl.*

verpflicht|en [~'pfliçtən] (26) oblige; engage; *sich zu et.* ~ bind (*od.* engage) o.s. to do a th.; *zu Dank* ~ lay *a p.* under an obligation; *gesetzlich verpflichtet sein* be liable; *j-m zu Dank verpflichtet sein* be obliged to a p.; 2ung *f* obligation, duty; liability; *übernommene*: engagement, commitment.

ver'pfuschen bungle, botch; *se Leben*: ruin.

ver'**plappern** (29), ver'**plaudern** (29) prattle away (*time*); *sich verplappern* blab out a secret.

ver**plempern** F [ˌ∼'plɛmpərn] (29) fritter away, squander; *sich ∼* fritter away one's energies.   [spised.⟩

ver**pönt** [∼'pøːnt] taboo(ed), de-⟩

ver'**prassen** dissipate, squander.

ver**provian'tieren** supply with food *od.* ⚔ rations; provision.

ver'**prügeln** thrash, beat up.

ver'**puffen** (sn) detonate, explode; *fig.* fizzle out.   [F blue.⟩

ver**pulvern** F [ˌ∼'pulfərn] (29) *Brt.*⟩

ver'**pumpen** F lend.

ver**puppen** [∼'pupən] (25) (*sich*) change into a chrysalis.

ver'**pusten** F (*sich*) recover breath.

Ver'putz △ *m* roughcast, plaster; **⊇en** △ roughcast, plaster; F (*ganz aufessen*) polish off.

ver'**qualmen** fill with smoke.

ver**quicken** [fɛr'kvikən] (25) mix up.

ver**quollen** [∼'kvɔlən] *Holz*: warped; *Gesicht*: bloated.

ver'**rammeln** (29) bar(ricade).

ver**ramschen** F [∼'ramʃən] sell for a mere song; *Bücher*: remainder.

ver**rannt** [∼'rant]: *fig. ∼ sein in* (*acc.*) be stuck in.

Verrat [∼'raːt] *m* (3) ⚖ treason (*an dat.* to); betrayal (of); (*Treulosigkeit*) treachery (to); **⊇en** betray (*sich o.s.*); F give *a p.*, *a secret* away; *fig.* (*offenbaren*) show, reveal, betray.

Verräter [∼'rɛːtər] *m* (7) traitor (*an dat.* to); *weitS.* betrayer; **∼ei** [∼'raɪ] *f* treachery; **∼in** *f* (16¹) traitress; **⊇isch** treacherous; ⚖ treasonable, traitorous; *fig. Blick, Spur usw.*: telltale.

ver'**rauchen** *v/i.* (sn) go off in smoke; *Zorn*: pass away; *v/t.* spend on smoking.

ver'**räucher|n** fill with smoke; **∼t** *adj.* smoky.

ver'**rechn|en** charge (to account); (*gegeneinander aufrechnen*) set off (*mit* against); (*ausgleichen*) balance; *sich ∼* miscalculate, *a. fig.* make a mistake; *sich verrechnet haben* be out in one's reckoning, *fig.* be mistaken; **⊇ung** *f* charging (to account); offset; *im Verrechnungsverkehr*: clearing; *nur zur ∼* only for account.

Ver'rechnungs|scheck *m* crossed (*od.* not negotiable) cheque (*Am.* check); **∼stelle** *f* clearing-house;

∼verkehr *m* clearing (system).

ver'**recken** (sn) *Tier*: perish, die; V *Mensch*: *sl.* peg out, croak.

ver'**reg|nen** spoil by rain(ing); **∼net** rainy.

ver'**reisen** *v/i.* (sn) go on a journey; *verreist oft*: out of town, away.

ver'**reißen** F *fig.* pull to pieces.

ver**renk|en** [∼'rɛŋkən] (25) contort; ⚕ wrench, sprain; (*ausrenken*) dislocate; **⊇ung** *f* contortion; dislocation.

ver'**rennen**: *fig. sich in e-e Idee ∼* get stuck in.

ver'**richt|en** do, perform; (*ausführen*) execute; *s-e Andacht od. sein Gebet ∼* say one's prayer; *s. Notdurft*; **⊇ung** *f* performance; (*Arbeit*) work; (*Pflicht*) duty; (*Geschäft*) business.

ver'**riegel|n** (29) bolt, bar.

ver**ringer|n** [∼'riŋərn] (29), **⊇ung** *f* *s. vermindern usw.*

ver'**rinnen** (sn) run off *od.* away; *Zeit*: elapse, fly, pass.

ver**roh|en** [∼'roːən] (25, sn) become brutalized; **⊇ung** *f* brutalization.

ver'**rosten** (sn) rust.

ver**rotten** [∼'rɔtən] (26, sn) rot.

ver**rucht** [∼'ruːxt] wicked, villainous; **⊇heit** *f* wickedness, villainy.

ver'**rück|en** displace, (re)move; **∼t** mad (*fig. nach dat., auf acc.* on), crazy (for, about), *sl.* nuts (on); *j-n ∼ machen* drive a p. mad *od. sl.* nuts; **∼e** *Idee* crazy idea; *∼ spielen* F act up; *sl. ich werd' ∼!* I'll be damned!; *wie ∼* like mad; **⊇te** *m, f* (18) lunatic, *m* madman, *f* madwoman; **⊇theit** *f* madness; (*Handlung*) *a.* folly; (*Modenarrheit*) craze.

Ver'ruf *m* (3): *in ∼ bringen* (*kommen*) bring (get) into discredit; *in ∼ sein* be notorious, *weitS.* be under a cloud; *in ∼ tun* boycott; **⊇en 1.** *v/t.* decry; **2.** *adj.* ill-reputed, ill-famed, notorious.

ver'**rutschen** slip, get out of place.

Vers [fɛrs] *m* (4) verse; (*Strophe*) stanza; *fig. er kann sich keinen ∼ darauf machen* he can't make head or tail of it.

ver'**sachlichen** (25) *Diskussion etc.*: de-emotionalize.

ver'**sag|en 1.** *v/t.* refuse, deny; *den Dienst ∼* fail; *versagt sein* (*verpflichtet sein*) be engaged; *sich et. ∼* deny o.s. a th., forgo a th.; *v/i.* fail (*a.*

j-m, Stimme usw.), ⊕ *a.* break down; *Gewehr*: fail to go off, miss fire; **2.** ♀ *n* failure; **2er** *m* (7) *beim Schießen*: misfire; *fig.* failure, F flop; **2ung** *f* refusal, denial.   [*Suppe.*⟩

ver'salzen oversalt; *fig.* spoil; *s.*⟩

ver'samm|eln assemble; (*einberufen*) convoke, convene; *sich* ~ assemble, meet; **2lung** *f* assembly, meeting; **2lungsfreiheit** *f* freedom of assembly.

Versand [fɛr'zant] *m* (3) dispatch; (*Auslieferung*) delivery; ♱ *od. Am.* shipment; *durch Post*: mailing; ~**abteilung** *f* forwarding department; ~**anweisungen** *f/pl.* shipping instructions; ~**anzeige** *f* advice of dispatch; ~**bereit** ready for delivery; ~**buchhändler** *m* mail-order bookseller.

versanden [~'zandən] (26, sn) silt up; *fig.* bog down.

Versand|geschäft [~'zant-] *n* mail--order business; (*a.* ~**haus** *n*) mail--order house; ~**hauskatalog** *m* mail-order catalog(ue); ~**kosten** *pl.* forwarding costs; ~**papiere** *n/pl.* shipping papers *pl.*

versauen F [~'zauən] (25) ruin, *sl.* louse up.

versauern [~'zauərn] (29, sn) *fig.* go stale (*od.* sour).

ver'saufen P waste on drink.

ver'säumen *Pflicht usw.*: neglect; *Gelegenheit, Schule, Zug usw.*: miss; ~ *zu tun* fail to do.

Versäumnis [~'zɔʏmnis] *f* (14²), *n* (4¹) neglect, omission, failure; (*Zeit-* ♀) loss of time; ~**urteil** *n* judg(e)ment by default.

'Versbau *m* (3) versification.

ver'schachern barter away, job off.

ver'schaffen (25) procure, get (*j-m for* a p.; *a* p. *a th.*), provide, furnish, supply (a p. with *a th.*); *sich* ~ obtain, get, secure; *sich Respekt* ~ make o.s. respected; *s. Gewißheit.*

verschal|en [~'ʃaːlən] (25) plank; ♠ board; **2ung** *f* planking; boarding.   [*f* bashfulness.⟩

verschämt [~'ʃɛːmt] bashful; **2heit**⟩

verschandeln [~'ʃandəln] (29) disfigure, spoil, deface, ruin.

ver'schanzen entrench, fortify; *fig. sich* ~ *hinter* (*dat.*) shelter behind.

ver'schärf|en add to, (*a. sich*) intensify; (*verschlimmern; a. sich*) aggravate; **2ung** *f* intensification; ag-

gravation.

ver'scharren bury (hurriedly).

ver'scheiden 1. (sn) pass away; **2.** ♀ *n* (6) decease.

ver'schenken give away (*a. fig.*).

ver'scherzen forfeit, throw away.

ver'scheuchen scare (*bsd. Vögel*: shoo) away; *fig.* banish.

ver'schick|en send away, dispatch; *Sträfling*: deport; **2ung** *f* sending away, dispatch(ing); deportation.

Ver'schieb|ebahnhof *m* marshalling yard; **2en** shift, displace; 🚃 shunt; (*in Unordnung bringen*) disarrange; *zeitlich*: defer, put off, postpone; ♱ sell underhand, job away; *sich* ~ shift, get out of place; ~**ung** *f* shifting; postponement; ♱ illicit sale.

verschieden [fɛr'ʃiːdən] different, distinct (*von* from); ~e *pl.* various, several, diverse; **2es** various things *pl.*, *bsd.* ♱ *n* sundries *pl.*; ~**artig** of a different kind, different, various; ~**erlei** of various kinds, various, diverse; ~**farbig** of different colo(u)rs, varicolo(u)red; **2heit** *f* difference; (*Mannigfaltigkeit*) diversity, variety; ~**tlich** repeated(ly *adv.*); *adv.* now and then.

ver'schießen *v/t.* (*verbrauchen*) use up; *v/i.* (sn) *Farbe*: fade.

ver'schiff|en ship; **2ung** *f* shipment.

ver'schimmeln (sn) get mo(u)ldy.

ver'schlacken (25, sn) turn into dross, slag, scorify.

ver'schlafen 1. *v/t.* miss (*od.* lose *od.* neglect) by sleeping; *Zeit*: sleep away; (*die Zeit* ~, *sich* ~) oversleep (o.s.); **2.** *adj.* sleepy, drowsy; **2heit** *f* sleepiness.

Ver'schlag *m* partition; (*Bretterbude*) shed; (*Lattenkiste*) crate; **2en** [~gən] **1.** *v/t.*: *mit Brettern* ~ board (up); *e-n Ball*: lose; *e-e Buchseite* ~ lose one's place (in a book); ~ *werden* ♱ be driven out of one's course; *in e-e Stadt usw.* ~ *werden* be driven to, find o.s. in; *es verschlägt mir die Sprache* it makes me speechless, it dum(b)founds me; *es verschlägt nichts* it does not matter; **2.** *adj.* cunning, crafty, wily; *Wasser*: lukewarm; ~**enheit** *f* cunning, craftiness.

verschlammen [~'ʃlamən] (25, sn) silt up; become muddy.

ver'schlampen v/t. lose; v/i. get slovenly.

verschlechter|n [~'ʃlɛçtərn] (29) deteriorate, make worse; *sich ~* deteriorate, get worse, worsen; **♀ung** f deterioration, worsening; change for the worse.

verschleier|n [~'ʃlaɪərn] (29) veil (*a. fig.* = mask, disguise); ✕ screen; ✈ b.s. cook, doctor; **♀ung** f veiling; *in der Bilanz:* window-dressing.

ver'schleifen *Silben usw.:* slur.

ver'schleimen (25, sn) get obstructed with phlegm.

Verschleiß [~'ʃlaɪs] m (3²) ⊕ wear (and tear); **♀en** wear out (*a. sich*); **♀fest** wear-resistant.

ver'schlepp|en *Menschen:* carry off, *pol.* displace; (*entführen*) abduct; (*verlegen*) misplace; (*in die Länge ziehen*) delay, protract; ⚕ *Ansteckungsstoff:* spread; *Krankheit:* protract, neglect; **♀te** m, f (18) displaced person; **♀ung** f abduction; delay(ing); protraction (*a.* ⚕); **♀ungs-taktik** f obstructionism.

ver'schleudern dissipate, waste; ✈ sell at a loss *od.* dirt-cheap.

ver'schließ|bar lockable; **~en** shut, close; *mit e-m Schlüssel:* lock (up); *e-n Brief:* seal; *sich e-r Sache ~* close one's mind to.

verschlimmer|n [fɛr'ʃlɪmərn] (29) make worse; *fig. a.* aggravate; *sich ~* get worse (*od.* grow) worse; **♀ung** f aggravation, change for the worse.

ver'schlingen devour, (*a. fig. mit den Augen od. Ohren*) swallow (up *fig.*); *gierig:* gobble (up), wolf; (*inea.schlingen*; *a. sich*) intertwine, interlace, entangle; *verschlungen fig.* intricate; *Pfad:* tortuous.

verschlossen [~'ʃlɔsən] closed, shut; locked; *fig.* reserved, taciturn; **♀heit** f reserve.

ver'schlucken swallow; *sich ~* swallow the wrong way.

Ver'schluß m (~mittel) fastener, fastening; (*Schloß*) lock; (*Schnapp-♀*) catch; *an Taschen usw.:* clasp; ⊕ (*Dichtung, Plombe*) seal; *phot.* shutter; *e-r Flasche:* stopper; *e-s Geschützes:* breech (mechanism); *Ware in ~ legen* bond; *unter ~* under lock and key; **~laut** *gr. m* explosive.

ver'schlüssel|n (en)code; **♀ung** f (en)coding.

ver'schmachten (sn) languish, pine away; die (*od.* be dying) of thirst.

ver'schmähen disdain, scorn.

ver'schmelz|en v/t. u. v/i. (sn) melt into one another; (*a. fig.*) fuse; ✒ amalgamate (*a. fig.* = merge) (*zu, mit* in[to]); *Farben usw.:* blend; **♀ung** f fusion, amalgamation, ✈ a. merger.

ver'schmerzen get over (the loss of).

ver'schmieren smear (over).

verschmitzt [~'ʃmɪtst] sly; arch(ly *adv.*); **♀heit** f slyness.

ver'schmutz|en v/t. soil; *Luft, Wasser:* pollute; v/i. (sn) get dirty, soil; **♀ung** f pollution.

ver'schnappen: F *sich ~* let the cat out of the bag, blurt it out.

ver'schnauf|en (*a. sich*) have a breather; **♀pause** f breather.

ver'schneiden cut (up); *Stoff usw.:* cut wrong; *Wein usw.:* blend; (*kastrieren*) geld, castrate.

verschneit [~'ʃnaɪt] covered with snow, snow-covered, snowed up.

Ver'schnitt m blend.

verschnörkelt [fɛr'ʃnœrkəlt] ornate (*a. fig.*).

ver'schnupfen *fig.* nettle, pique; ⚕ *verschnupft sein* have a cold.

ver'schnüren tie up, cord (up); (*a. mit Schnüren zieren*) lace.

verschollen [~'ʃɔlən] not heard of (again); missing; ⚖ presumed dead.

ver'schonen spare; *j-n mit et. ~* spare a p. a th.; *von Steuern usw. verschont* exempt(ed) from.

verschöne|(r)n [~'ʃøː:nə(r)n] (29) embellish, beautify; (*verbessern; a. sich*) improve; **♀rung** f embellishment.

verschossen [~'ʃɔsən] *Farbe:* faded; *fig.* F *~ in* (*acc.*) madly in love with.

verschränken [~'ʃrɛŋkən] (25) *Arme:* cross.

ver'schrauben screw (up).

ver'schreib|en use (in writing); ⚕ prescribe (*j-m* for a p.); ⚖ assign, make over (to); (*falsch schreiben*) write incorrectly; *sich ~* make a slip of the pen; *fig. sich e-r S. ~* devote (*od. b.s.* sell) o.s. to a th.; **♀ung** f order; prescription; bond, assignment; **~ungs-pflichtig** → *rezept-pflichtig.*   [ous.]

verschrien [~'ʃriː(ə)n] *adj.* notori-⎰

verschroben [~'ʃroːbən] eccentric, odd, cranky; **♀heit** f eccentricity.

verschrotten [ʌˈʃrɔtən] (26) scrap, *Auto*: a. junk.

ver'schrump|fen, ~eln v/t. u. v/i. (sn) shrink, shrivel (up).

ver'schüchtern intimidate.

ver'schuld|en 1. encumber with debts; (*schuld sein an*) be guilty of, be to blame for; *fig.* be the cause of; **2.** ⓢ *n* (6) wrong, fault; (*Schuld*) guilt; ~et indebted; involved in debts; *Sache*: encumbered; ⓢung *f* indebtedness.

ver'schütten *Flüssigkeit*: spill; (*versperren*) block (up); *j-n*: bury alive.

verschwägert [ʌˈʃvɛːgərt] related by marriage

ver'schweig|en keep secret, conceal (*j-m* from a p.); ⓢ *n* (6) *u.* ⓢung *f* concealment.

verschwend|en [ʌˈʃvɛndən] (26) waste, lavish, squander; ⓢer *m* (7), ⓢerin *f* (16¹) spendthrift, prodigal; ~erisch prodigal, lavish (*mit* of); extravagant; wasteful; ⓢung *f* waste, extravagance; ⓢungssucht *f* prodigality, squandermania.

verschwiegen [fɛrˈʃviːgən] discreet; *Ort*: secret, secluded; ⓢheit *f* discretion, secrecy.

ver'schwimmen (sn) become indistinct od. blurred; *fig.* fade (away).

ver'schwinden 1. (sn) disappear, vanish; *j-n* (*od. et.*) *spurlos* ~ *lassen* spirit a p. (*od.* a th.) away; F *verschwinde!* make yourself scarce!, beat it!; ~d *klein* infinitely small; **2.** ⓢ *n* (6) disappearance.

verschwistert [ʌˈʃvistərt] brother and sister; *fig.* closely united.

ver'schwitzen soak with sweat; F *fig.* forget (completely).

verschwollen [ʌˈʃvɔlən] swollen.

verschwommen [ʌˈʃvɔmən] vague, indistinct, hazy; *fig.* a. foggy; *Bild*: blurred; ⓢheit *f* indistinctness, vagueness.

ver'schwör|en: *sich* ~ conspire, plot (*zu* et. a th.); ⓢer *m* (7) conspirator; ⓢerin *f* (16¹) conspiratress; ⓢung *f* conspiracy, plot.

ver'sehen: *Pflichten usw.*: perform, discharge; *Amt*: a. hold, administer; *Stellung*: fill; *Haushalt*: look after *the house*, keep *house*; (*übersehen*) overlook; *sich* ~ make a mistake; *sich e-r S.* ~ expect a th., be aware of a th.; *mit et.* ~ furnish (*od.* supply *od.* provide *od.* equip) with;

2. ⓢ *n* (6) oversight; mistake; slip; ~tlich by (a) mistake, inadvertently.

versehr|en [ʌˈzeːrən] (25) injure, disable; ⓢte *m* (18) disabled person.

ver'send|en send, dispatch, forward; *auf dem Wasser-, Am. a. Landwege*: ship; *ins Ausland* ~ export; ⓢung *f* dispatch, shipment, forwarding; transport.

ver'sengen singe, burn, scorch.

ver'senk|en sink; *Schraubenkopf usw.*: countersink; *sich* ~ *in* (acc.) immerse o.s. into, *fig.* become absorbed in; ⓢung *f* sinking; *thea.* trap-door.

versessen [ʌˈzɛsən]: ~ *auf* (acc.) bent (*od. sl.* nuts) on, mad after.

ver'setz|en v/t. displace, a. *Schüler*: remove; *bsd. Am. Schüler*: promote; *Baum*: transplant; (*staffeln*; a. ⊕) stagger; (*mit-ea. vertauschen*) transpose; *Beamte*: transfer; ⚒ post; (*verpfänden*) pawn, pledge; F (*vergebens warten lassen*) let a p. down, *Liebhaber usw.*: stand a p. up; (*vermischen*) mix, *metall.* alloy; *Schlag*: give, deal; *in e-e Lage, e-n Zustand* ~ put into; *in Schwingungen* ~ set vibrating; *s. Angst, Ruhestand usw.*; v/i. (*antworten*) reply, retort; ⓢung *f* removal; transplanting; transposition; transfer; *Schule*: remove, *bsd. Am.* promotion; pledging; alloy; ⓢungszeugnis *n* end-of-year report.

verseuch|en [fɛrˈzɔʏçən] (25) infect; contaminate; ⓢung *f* infection, contamination.

'Versfuß *m* (metrical) foot.

Versicher|er [fɛrˈziçərər] *m* (7) insurer; ⓢn assure, affirm; *Eigentum usw.*: insure; *j-n e-r Sache* ~ assure a p. of; *sich e-r Sache* ~ make sure of, ascertain; *seien Sie dessen versichert* you may rest assured of it; ~te *m, f* (18) insurant, *the* insured.

Ver'sicherung *f* affirmation; (*Eigentums*ⓢ *usw.*) insurance; ~sbetrug *m* insurance fraud; ~sgesellschaft *f* insurance-company; ~snehmer *m* insurant, *the* insured; ~s-pflicht *f* compulsory insurance; ⓢs-pflichtig subject to obligatory insurance; ~s-police *f*, ~sschein *m* insurance policy; ~s-prämie *f* insurance premium; ~sschutz *m* insurance coverage; ~ssumme *f* sum insured; ~s-träger *m* underwriter.

versickern [ʌˈzikərn] ooze away.

ver'sieben F s. verpatzen.
ver'siegeln seal.
ver'siegen (sn) dry up.
versiert [vɛr'ziːrt] versed (in dat. in), experienced.
versilbern [fɛr'zilbərn] (29) silver (a. fig.); ⊕ silver-plate; fig. (zu Geld machen) convert into cash, sell.
ver'sinken (sn) sink; fig. lapse (in acc. into); s. versunken.
ver'sinnbildlich|en (25) symbolize; 2ung f symbolization.
Version [vɛr'sjoːn] f version.
versippt [~'zipt] related (mit to).
versklaven [fɛr'sklaːvən] enslave.
'Vers|kunst f versification; **'~maß** n metre, Am. meter.
ver'soffen P boozy.
versohlen F [~'zoːlən] fig. (25) thrash (soundly); bsd. Kind: spank.
versöhn|en [~'zøːnən] (25) reconcile (mit j-m to, with; mit e-m Schicksal usw. to); sich (wieder) ~ be(come) reconciled, make it up; **~lich** conciliatory; ~ stimmen conciliate, placate; 2ung f reconciliation.
versonnen [~'zɔnən] pensive.
ver'sorg|en provide, supply (mit with); Familie: provide for; (betreuen) take care of, look after; Wunde: tend, dress; 2er m (7), 2erin f (16¹) provider; 2ung f providing, supplying (with); providing (for); (a. ⚔) supply, provision; (Betreuung) care; (Existenz) subsistence, living; 2ungsbetrieb m public supply service, public utility; 2ungs-empfänger(in f) m pensioner; 2ungsgüter f/pl. supplies; 2ungsleitung f supply line; 2ungsnetz n supply system; 2ungsschwierigkeiten f/pl. difficulties of supply.
ver'spannen ⊕ brace, stay, guy.
verspät|en [~'ʃpɛːtən] (26): sich ~ be (od. com~ too) late; **~et** belated; 2ung f lateness, delay; Zug usw.: (20 Minuten) ~ haben be (20 minutes) late od. overdue; mit 2 Stunden ~ 2 hours behind schedule; ~ aufholen make up lost time.
ver'speisen eat up.
verspeku'lieren: sich ~ make a bad speculation, ruin ó.s. by speculation; fig. make a mistake.
ver'sperren bar, block up, barricade; a. Aussicht: obstruct.

ver'spiel|en v/t. lose (at play), gamble away; v/i. lose (the game); fig. bei j-m ~ get into a p.'s bad books; **~t** adj. playful.
versponnen [~'ʃpɔnən] meditative; ~ in (dat., acc.) wrapt (up) in.
ver'spott|en scoff at, mock, deride; 2ung f derision, scoffing.
ver'sprech|en 1. promise (a. fig.); sich ~ make a slip (of the tongue); s. sich verloben; sich etwas ~ von expect much of; **2.** 2 n (6), 2ung f promise.
ver'sprengen disperse, scatter.
ver'spritzen squirt (away), spray; (verschütten) spill; sein Blut: shed.
ver'sprühen spray.
ver'spüren feel, perceive, sense.
verstaatlich|en [fɛr'ʃtaːtliçən] (25) nationalize; 2ung f nationalization.
verstädter|n [~'ʃtɛːtərn] v/t. (29) urbanize; 2ung f urbanization.
verstadtlichen [~'ʃtatliçən] (25) municipalize.
Verstand [~'ʃtant] m (3) (Denkkraft) understanding, intelligence, intellect, brains pl.; (Vernunft) reason; (Urteilsfähigkeit) judg(e)ment; (praktischer ~) sense; gesunder ~ common sense; klarer ~ clear head; den ~ verlieren lose one's mind; j-n um den ~ bringen drive a p. mad; s-n ~ zusammennehmen keep one's wits about one; das geht über m-n ~ that's beyond me.
Verstandes|kraft [~'ʃtandəs-] f intellectual power od. faculty; 2mäßig rational; **~mensch** m matter--of-fact person; **~schärfe** f sagacity.
verständ|ig [~'ʃtɛndiç] intelligent; (vernünftig denkend od. gedacht) reasonable, sensible; (richtig urteilend) judicious; **~igen** [~gən] inform, notify (von of); sich ~ mit j-m in e-r fremden Sprache: make o.s. understood to a p.; (übereinkommen) come to an understanding with a p.; 2igung f information; (Übereinkunft) understanding, agreement; teleph. usw. communication; (Hörbarkeit) audibility; 2igungsschwierigkeiten f/pl. communication difficulties; **~lich** [~'ʃtɛnt-] intelligible; (deutlich) distinct, clear; fig. understandable; j-m et. ~ machen make a th. clear to a p.; sich ~ machen make o.s. understood (j-m by a p.).
Verständnis [~'ʃtɛntnis] n (4¹) (Ver-

Verstrebung

stehen) comprehension, *a. weitS.* understanding; *(Einsicht)* insight; *(Würdigung)* appreciation *(für* of); *(Mitfühlen)* sympathy; ~ *haben für* appreciate, understand; **♀-innig** knowing; **♀los** uncomprehending; *Blick, Gesicht:* blank; *(nicht würdigend)* unappreciative; **~losigkeit** *f* lack of understanding; unappreciativeness; **♀voll** intelligent; *weitS.* understanding; *(würdigend)* appreciative; *Blick:* knowing.

ver'stärk|en strengthen, *(a. ✕ u. ⊕)* reinforce; *⚡* boost; *Radio:* amplify; *(steigern)* intensify, strengthen, increase *(alle a. sich)*; **♀er** *m* (7) *Radio:* amplifier; **♀erröhre** amplifier valve *(Am.* tube); **♀ung** *f* strengthening, *(a. ✕)* reinforcement; amplification; intensification.

ver'staub|en get dusty; **~t** *fig.* antiquated.

ver'stauch|en (25) sprain; **♀ung** *f* sprain(ing).

ver'stauen stow away.

Versteck [fɛr'ʃtɛk] *n* (3) hiding-place; ~ *spielen* play hide-and-seek; **♀en¹** *v/t. (a.* versteckt halten) hide *(a. sich)*, conceal; **~en²** *n od.* **~spiel** *n* hide-and-seek *(a. fig.)*; **♀t** hidden *(a. fig.)*.

ver'stehen understand, F get; *(einsehen)* see; *(begreifen)* comprehend, grasp, catch; *(erkennen)* realize; *(deuten)* read; *(können) Sprache usw.:* know; *es ~ zu inf.* manage to, know how to *inf.*; *sich* ~ *auf (acc.)* know well; *sich mit j-m gut* ~ get on *(od.* along) well with a p.; *sich ~ zu (sich entschließen)* bring o.s. to *do*, *(einwilligen)* agree to; *(j-m) zu ~ geben* intimate (to a p.), give (a p.) to understand; *Spaß* ~ take *(od.* see) a joke; ~ *Sie?* (do) you see?; *ich verstehe!* I see!; *verstanden?* do you understand *(od.* F get) me?; *falsch ~* misunderstand; *verstehe mich recht!* don't misunderstand me!; *(das) versteht sich!* that's understood!; *was ~ Sie unter (dat.) ...?* what do you mean *(od.* understand) by ...?; *er versteht etwas davon* he knows a thing or two about it; *er versteht gar nichts davon* he doesn't know the first thing about it; *es versteht sich von selbst* it goes without saying.

ver'steif|en ⊕ strut, prop; *(a. sich* ~) stiffen; *fig. sich ~ auf (acc.)* keep

doggedly at; insist on; **♀ung** *f* ⊕ strut(ting) *etc.*

ver'steigen: *sich* ~ lose one's way (in the mountains); *fig. sich ~ zu ...* go so far as to.

ver'steiger|n sell by auction; **♀ung** *f* (sale by [*Am.* at]) auction, public sale.

versteiner|n [~'ʃtaɪnərn] *v/t. u. v/i.* (29, sn) *(a. fig.)* turn (in)to stone, *(a. fig.)* petrify; **♀ung** *f* petrifaction, fossil.

verstell|bar [~'ʃtɛlbaːr] adjustable; **~en** *(falsch stellen)* misplace; *(versperren)* block; *Handschrift, Stimme usw.:* disguise, dissemble; ⊕ shift, adjust; *sich* ~ play-act, feign, dissemble; **♀ung** *f* dissimulation; disguise.

ver'steuer|n pay duty *(od.* tax) on; *zu ~* taxable; **♀ung** *f* payment of duty (e-r *S.* on a th.).

verstiegen [~'ʃtiːɡən] *adj. fig.* high-flown, eccentric(ally *adv.*); **♀heit** *f* eccentricity.

ver'stimm|en put out of tune; *Radio:* detune; *fig.* put out (of humo[u]r), annoy; **~t** out of tune; *fig.* cross *(über acc.* with); **♀ung** *f* ill-humo(u)r; *zwischen zweien:* disagreement, tiff, resentment, ill-feeling.

verstockt [~'ʃtɔkt] hardened, callous; impenitent; **♀heit** *f* obduracy; *(a. eccl.)* impenitence.

verstohlen [~'ʃtoːlən] furtive, stealthy; *adv. a.* by stealth; ~ *lachen* laugh in one's sleeve.

ver'stopf|en stop (up); *(versperren)* clog, obstruct; *Straße:* jam; *⚕* constipate; **♀ung** *f* stopping; obstruction; *Verkehr:* jam; *⚕* constipation.

verstorben [fɛr'ʃtɔrbən] late, deceased, defunct; **♀e** *m, f* deceased.

verstört [~'ʃtøːrt] distracted; consternated, wild; **♀heit** *f* distraction, consternation.

Ver'stoß *m* (3² *u.* ³) offen|ce, *Am.* -se *(gegen* against); *(Zuwiderhandlung) a.* contravention, violation (of); *(Übertretung)* infringement (of); *(Fehler)* blunder, mistake; **♀en** *v/t.* *(austreiben)* expel *(aus* from); cast off *(od.* out); *Kind usw.:* reject; *v/i.* ~ *gegen* offend against, violate, contravene; **~ung** *f* expulsion; rejection. [*f* strut(ting), bracing.]

ver'streb|en ⊕ strut, brace; **♀ung**

ver'streichen *v/i.* (sn) *Zeit*: pass (away), slip by; *Frist*: expire; *v/t. Fuge*: stop up; *Butter, Salbe*: spread.

ver'streuen disperse, scatter; *fig. a.* dot (about); *über e-e Fläche verstreut sein* dot *a country etc.*

ver'stricken entangle, ensnare; *verstrickt in e-e S.* involved in.

verstümmel|n [ˌ-ˈʃtyməln] (29) mutilate; ℒung *f* mutilation.

verstummen [ˌ-ˈtumən] (25, sn) grow dumb *od.* silent.

Versuch [-ˈzuːx] *m* (3) attempt, trial (*a.* ⊕), F try; *phys. usw.* experiment; (*Probe, a.* ⊕) test; (*Bemühung*) effort; *e-n ∼ machen mit* give *a p. od. a th.* a trial; *try a p. od. a th.*, F have a go at *a th.*; ℒen try, attempt; (*kosten*) taste; *j-n*: tempt; *es ∼ mit s. Versuch (machen)*; **∼er** *m* (7), **∼erin** *f* (16¹) tempter, *f a.* temptress.

Ver'suchs|-anlage *f* experimental (*od.* pilot) plant; **∼-anstalt** *f* research institute; **∼ballon** *m* trial balloon; *fig. a.* ballon d'essai (*fr.*), kite; **∼bohrung** *f* trial drilling; **∼gelände** *n* testing ground; **∼-ingenieur** *m* research engineer; **∼kaninchen** *n fig.* guinea-pig; **∼projekt** *n* pilot project; **∼reihe** ✻, ⊕ *f* series of tests; **∼stadium** *n* experimental stage; **∼tier** *n* experimental animal; ℒ**weise** by way of trial *od.* (an) experiment; tentatively; **∼zwecke** *m/pl.*: *zu ∼n for* experimental purposes.

Ver'suchung *f* temptation; *in ∼ bringen* tempt; *in ∼ sein* (*od.* *kommen*) be tempted.

versumpf|en [ˌ-ˈzumpfən] (25, sn) become marshy; F *fig.* get bogged down; **∼t** swampy, boggy.

ver'sündig|en: *sich ∼ sin* (*an dat.* against); ℒung *f* sin.

versunken [ˌ-ˈzuŋkən] *fig. ∼ in* (*acc.*) absorbed (*od.* lost) in; ℒheit *f fig.* absorption.

ver'süßen sweeten (*a. fig.*).

ver'tag|en (*a. sich*) adjourn (*auf* till); ℒung *f* adjournment.

vertändeln trifle away.

vertäuen ⊕ [ˌ-ˈtɔyən] moor.

ver'tausch|en exchange (*gegen* for); *die Rollen*: reverse; *s. verwechseln*; ℒung *f* exchange.

verteidig|en [ˌ-ˈtaɪdigən] (25) defend; ℒer *m* (7), ℒerin *f* (16¹) defender; *fig. a.* advocate; ḿ ∼ *des Angeklagten*: counsel for the defence, *Am.* defense counsel; *Fußball*: back; ℒung *f* defen|ce, *Am.* -se; ℒ**ungs-ausgaben** *f/pl.* defen|ce (*Am.* -se) expenditure *sg.*; ℒ**ungsbündnis** *n* defensive alliance; ℒ**ungsfall** *m*: *im ∼e* in case of defen|ce, *Am.* -se; ℒ**ungskrieg** *m* defensive war; ℒ**ungsminister** *m* Minister of Defence, *Am.* Secretary of Defense; ℒ**ungsministerium** *n* Ministry of Defence, *Am.* Department of Defense; ℒ**ungs-politik** *f* defen|ce (*Am.* -se) policy; ℒ**ungsrede** *f* speech for the defen|ce, *Am.* -se; *weit S.* apology.

ver'teil|en distribute (*auf acc., unter acc.* among); (*teilen*) divide; (*unter sich ∼*) share; *s. zuteilen; Farbe usw., a. fig.*: spread; *Geschwulst, Nebel*: (*a. sich*) disperse; ℒer *m* (7) distributor (*a.* ⊕ *u.* ✝); (*Einzelhändler*) retailer; ℒ**erkasten** ⨍ *m* distributor box; ℒung *f* distribution.

verteuern [fɛrˈtɔyərn] (29) raise (*od.* increase) the price of.

verteufel|n [ˌ-ˈtɔyfəln] (29) demonise; **∼t** F devilish, fiendish, hellish.

vertief|en [ˌ-ˈtiːfən] (25) (*a. sich*) deepen (*a. fig.*); (*aushöhlen*) hollow out; *sich ∼ in* (*acc.*) plunge into, *in Gedanken*: become absorbed in; ℒung *f* deepening (*a. fig.*); (*Höhlung*) hollow, cavity; (*Aussparung*) recess; *fig.* absorption.

vertiert [fɛrˈtiːrt] brutish.

vertikal [vɛrtiˈkaːl] vertical; ℒe *f* (15) vertical line.

vertilg|en [fɛrˈtilgən] exterminate; *Vorrat*, F *Speise*: consume; ℒung *f* extermination.

ver'tippen type wrong; *sich ∼ make* a typing error.

verton|en ♩ [ˌ-ˈtoːnən] (25) set to music; ℒung *f* setting to music.

vertrackt F [ˌ-ˈtrakt] confounded.

Vertrag [ˌ-ˈtraːk] *m* (3³) agreement, contract; *pol.* treaty; (*Pakt*) pact; *e-n ∼ schließen* make (*od.* enter into) an agreement; ℒen (ˌ-gən) (*aushalten*) endure, (*a. j-n, Widerspruch, Alkohol usw.*) stand; (*dulden, zulassen*) bear (*a. v. Sachen*); tolerate; *diese Speise kann ich nicht ∼* this food does not agree with me; *sich ∼ Sachen*: be compatible, *Farben* *usw.*, *a. Personen*: agree; *sich wieder* ~ be reconciled (*mit* with *a p.*), make it up (with); *sich* (*gut*, *schlecht*) *mit-ea.* ~ get on *od.* along (well, ill) together; 2lich [~'traːk-] contractual, (*adv.* as) stipulated; *adv.* by contract; *sich* ~ *verpflichten* contract (*zu* to).

verträglich [fer'trɛːkliç] sociable, peaceable; *Nahrung usw.*: (easily) digestible; 2keit *f* sociability; digestibility.

Ver'trags|bedingungen *f/pl.* terms of the contract; **~bruch** *m* breach of contract; 2brüchig defaulting; ~ *werden* commit a breach of contract.

ver'tragschließend contracting.

Ver'trags|-entwurf *m* draft agreement; 2gemäß, 2mäßig (*adv.* as) stipulated; **~gegenstand** *m* object of the agreement; **~händler** *m* authorized retailer; **~partei** *f*, **~partner** *m* party to an agreement; **~strafe** *f* (conventional) penalty; **~verhältnis** *n* contractual relationship; 2widrig contrary to an agreement.

ver'trauen 1. *v/t. s. an~*; *v/i.* trust (*j-m* a p.); ~ *auf* (*acc.*) trust in, rely (up)on; 2. 2 *n* (6) confidence, trust (*auf acc.* in); *im* ~ confidentially; *ganz im* ~ F between you and me; *im* ~ *auf* (*acc.*) trusting to, relying on; ~ *haben zu* have confidence in, trust; *j-m sein* ~ *schenken*, ~ *in j-n setzen* place confidence in a p.; *j-n ins* ~ *ziehen* confide in a p.; **~erweckend** inspiring trust *od.* confidence.

Ver'trauens|basis *f* basis of mutual trust; **~bruch** *m* breach (*od.* betrayal) of trust; **~frage** *f* matter of trust; *pol. die* ~ *stellen* propose a vote of confidence; **~mann** *m*, **~person** *f* confidant(e *f*); (*Sprecher*) spokesman; **~sache** *f* confidential matter; 2selig (too) confiding; gullible; ~**seligkeit** *f* blind confidence; **~stellung** *f* position of trust; 2voll trustful, trusting; **~votum** *n* vote of confidence; 2würdig trustworthy, reliable.

ver'trauern pass in mourning.

ver'traulich confidential; *Verkehr*: intimate, familiar; *s. streng*; 2keit *f* confidence; intimacy, familiarity.

ver'träum|en dream away; **~t** dreamy.

ver'traut intimate, familiar; ~ *mit*

78*

well acquainted with, well versed in; (*sich*) ~ *machen mit* acquaint *od.* familiarize (o.s.) with; 2e *m*, *f* (18) intimate friend, confidant(e *f*); 2heit *f* familiarity (*mit* with); intimate knowledge (of).

ver'treib|en drive away; (*ausstoßen*) expel (*aus* from); *Ware*: sell, distribute; *Sorgen usw.*: banish; *Krankheit*: cure; (*sich*) *die Zeit* ~ while away; 2ung *f* expulsion.

ver'tret|bar justifiable; *Standpunkt*: tenable; **~en** *j-n*, *Firma usw.*: represent; *im Amt*: act (*od.* substitute *od.* deputize) for; (*für j-n auftreten*, *a.* ⫶) appear (*od.* plead) for *a p.*; ⫶ *u. fig. j-s Sache* ~ plead a p.'s cause, hold a brief for a p.; *j-s Interesse*: attend to, look after; *Ansicht*: hold, take; *als Fürsprecher*: advocate; *parl. Bezirk*: sit for; (*verantworten*) answer for *a th.*; ~ *sein* (*zugegen od. vorhanden sn*) be present; *sich den Fuß* ~ sprain one's foot; *sich die Beine* ~ stretch one's legs; *j-m den Weg* ~ stop a p.; 2er *m* (7), 2erin *f* (16¹) representative; ♱ *a.* agent; (*Reise*2) commercial travel(l)er, *Am.* traveling salesmann; (*Bevollmächtigte*) agent, proxy; *im Amt*: substitute, deputy; (*Fürsprecher*) advocate; (*hervorragender od. typischer* ~) exponent; 2ung *f* representation; ♱ agency; *im Amt*: substitution; *in* ~ by proxy, acting for, (signed) for; *in* ~ *j-s* as representative of a p.; *j-s* ~ *übernehmen* deputize for a p.

Vertrieb [fer'triːp] *m* (3) sale, distribution, marketing; **~ene** [~'triː-bənə] *m*, *f* (18) expellee; **~s-abteilung** *f* sales department; **~skosten** *pl.* marketing costs; **~sleiter(in** *f*) *m* sales manager; **~s-organisation** *f* marketing organization; **~srecht** *n* right of sale; (*Konzession*) licen|ce, *Am.* -se.

ver'trinken spend on drink.

ver'trocknen (*sn*) dry (up).

ver'trödeln dawdle away.

ver'trösten feed with hopes (*auf acc.* of); (*hinhalten*) put off.

ver'tun waste, squander; *sich* ~ make a mistake.

ver'tusch|en hush up; 2ung(**sma-növer** *n*) *f* cover-up.

ver'-übeln (26) *et.*: take amiss; *j-m et.* ~ blame a p. for a th.; *ich hoffe*,

Sie werden mir die Frage nicht ~ I hope you won't mind the question.

ver'-üb|en commit, perpetrate; **ℒung** *f* committing, perpetration.

ver'-ulken F (25) make fun of, F pull *a p.*'s leg, kid.

ver'-un|glimpfen [~glimpfən] (25) disparage, calumniate; **~glücken** [~glYkən] (sn) have (*tödlich:* die in) an accident; *S.:* fail, go wrong; **ℒglückte** *m, f* (18) casualty.

ver'-unreinig|en soil; dirty (*a. Wunde*); *Luft, Wasser usw.:* pollute; *fig.* defile; **ℒung** *f* soiling; pollution; defilement.

ver'-unsichern F rattle.

ver'-unstalten [~ʃtaltən] (26) deform, disfigure, deface.

ver'-untreuen [~trɔYən] (25) embezzle; **ℒung** *f* embezzlement.

ver'-unzieren disfigure, mar.

verursachen [~'⁹uːrzaxən] (25) cause, occasion; give rise to, produce; (*nach sich ziehen*) entail.

ver'-urteil|en sentence; condemn (*a. fig.*); **ℒung** *f* condemnation.

vervielfältig|en [~'fiːlfɛltigən] (25) (*a. sich*) multiply; (*nachbilden, a. Schriftsatz*) duplicate; *Text, Bild:* copy; (*hektographieren*) mimeograph; **ℒung** *f* multiplication; duplication, copying; *konkret:* duplicate; **ℒungs-apparat** *m* duplicator, copying machine.

vervollkommn|en [~'fɔlkɔmnən] (26) perfect; **ℒung** *f* perfection.

vervollständig|en [~'fɔlʃtɛndigən] (25) complete; **ℒung** *f* completion.

ver'wachs|en 1. (sn) grow together; 𝕱 *Knochen:* unite; *Wunde:* heal up; (*überwachsen*) become overgrown; **2.** *adj.* (*verkrüppelt*) deformed; (*bucklig*) hunchbacked; *fig.* ~ *mit* bound up with; (deeply) rooted in.

ver'wackeln *phot.* blur.

ver'wahren keep; *fig. sich* ~ protest (*gegen* against).

verwahrlos|en [~'vaːrloːzən] *v/t.* neglect; *v/i.* (sn) be neglected, *P.:* be demoralized, go to the bad; **~t** [~st] uncared-for, neglected; *P.:* a. unkempt, *sittlich:* demoralized, wayward; **ℒung** [~zuŋ] *f* neglect; demoralization.

Ver'wahrung *f* keeping; (*Obhut*) charge, custody; *fig.* protest; *zur* ~ *in* trust; (*j-m*) *in* ~ *geben* deposit (with a p.), give into (a p.'s) charge;

in ~ *nehmen* take charge of; *gegen et.* ~ *einlegen* enter a protest against.

verwaisen [~'vaɪzən] (sn) be orphaned; *fig.* be deserted.

ver'walt|en administer, manage; (*führen*) conduct; *Amt:* hold; **ℒer** *m* (7) administrator, manager; (*Treuhänder*) trustee, custodian; (*Guts*ℒ) steward; (*Haus*ℒ) caretaker; **ℒerin** *f* (16¹) manageress.

Ver'waltung *f* administration (*a. = Staats*ℒ), management; **~(sbehörde)** *f* administrative authority; **~s-apparat** *m* administrative machinery; **~sbe-amte** *m* Civil Servant; **~sbezirk** *m* administrative district; **~sdienst** *m* Civil Service; **~skosten** *pl.* administrative expenses; **~s-personal** *n* administrative staff; **~srat** *m* managing board; **~szweig** *m* administrative department.

ver'wand|eln change (*a. sich*); (*umwandeln*) turn, convert; (*umformen*) transform (*alle: in acc.* into); *Strafe:* commute; *Fußball:* score; *sich* ~ be transformed, *etc.*; **ℒlung** *f* change; conversion; transformation; **ℒlungskünstler** *m* quick-change artist.

verwandt [fɛr'vant] related (*mit* to); *fig. a.* kindred, (*bsd. Wörter*) cognate (to, with); *pred.* (*a. fig.*) (a)kin (to); **~e** *Seele* congenial (*od.* kindred) soul; **ℒe** *m, f* (18) relative, relation; **ℒschaft** *f* relationship (*a. fig.*), kinship; (*die Verwandten*) relations *pl.*; *fig.* congeniality; *bsd. durch Heirat od.* 🝧 affinity; **~schaftlich** as (among) relatives; **~e** *Beziehungen* relations; **ℒschaftsgrad** *m* degree of relationship *od.* affinity.

verwanzt [~'vantst] buggy.

ver'warn|en warn (off), admonish; *strafend:* caution (*a. Sport*); **ℒung** *f* warning, admonition; caution.

ver'waschen 1. *v/t.* use up in washing; **2.** *adj.* washed out, faded; *fig. a.* vapid, wishy-washy.

ver'wässern water (down *a. fig.*).

ver'weben interweave.

ver'wechs|eln change by mistake, exchange; (*durch-ea.-bringen*) confound (*mit* with), mix up (with); *j-n mit e-m andern* ~ (mis)take a p. for another; **ℒlung** *f* mistake; confusion.

verwegen [~'veːgən] audacious, daring, bold; 2**heit** f audacity, boldness, daredevilry.

ver'**weh**|**en** (sn) blow away; *Stimme usw.*: trail away; 2**ung** f drift.

ver'**wehren** *et.*: bar; *j-m et.*: keep (*od.* debar) a p. from.

verweichlich|en [~'vaiçliçən] (25) v/t. render effeminate (*od.* soft); v/i. (sn) grow effeminate (*od.* soft); ~t *adj.* effeminate, soft, coddled.

ver'**weiger**|**n** deny, refuse; 2**ung** f denial, refusal.

ver'**weilen** stay, linger; *fig.* ~ *bei et.* dwell on.

verweint [~'vaint] tear-stained *face*; *eyes* red with tears.

Verweis [~'vais] m (4) reprimand, reproof, rebuke; (*Hinweis*) reference; 2**en** [~zən] (*verbannen*) banish, exile; *Schüler*: expel; *Sport*: warn (*des Feldes* off the field); *j-m et.* ~ reprimand a p. for; ~ *auf od. an* (*acc.*) refer to; ~**ung** f banishment; expulsion; reference (*auf, an acc.* to); ~**ungszeichen** n mark of reference.

ver'**welken** (sn) fade, wither.

verweltlich|en [fɛr'vɛltliçən] (25) secularize; 2**ung** f secularization.

verwend|bar [fɛr'vɛntbaːr] applicable, usable; 2**barkeit** f usability, applicability; ~**en** [~dən] apply (*auf acc., für* to), employ, use (in, for); (*nützlich*) ~ utilize; (*aufwenden*) spend, expend; *Mühe, Sorgfalt* ~ *auf* bestow on; *Zeit* ~ *auf* devote to; *sich bei j-m* ~ *für* intercede with a p. for; 2**ung** f application, use, employment; intercession; *keine* ~ *haben für* have no use for; ~**ungsfähig** s. verwendbar; 2**ungszweck** m use, purpose.

ver'**werf**|**en** reject; ⚖ dismiss (*a. weitS.*); *sich* ~ *Holz*: warp; *geol.* fault; ~**lich** objectionable, blamable, reprehensible; 2**ung** f rejection; ⚖ dismissal; warping; *geol.* fault.

verwert|bar [~'veːrtbaːr] usable; ✝ realizable; ~**en** turn to account, utilize, use; (*zu Geld machen*) realize; *geschäftlich*: commercialize; *Patent*: exploit; 2**ung** f utilization; realization; commercialization; exploitation.

verwes|en [~'veːzən] (27) v/i. (sn) rot, putrefy; (*sich zersetzen*) decay, decompose; v/t. (*verwalten*) admin-

ister; 2**er** m (7) administrator; ~**lich** [~'veːsliç] putrefiable; 2**ung** [~zuŋ] f decay, putrefaction, decomposition; (*Verwaltung*) administration.

ver'**wetten** bet, stake (*für* on); (*verlieren*) lose by betting.

ver'**wickel**|**n** entangle (*in acc.* in); *fig. a.* engage (in), involve (in); *Angelegenheit*: complicate; ~t *fig.* complicated, intricate; 2**ung** f entanglement; complication.

ver'**wildern** ⚘ *u. fig.* (29, sn) run wild.

ver'**wind**|**en** get over a *th.*; ⊕ distort, twist; 2**ung** f ⊕ distortion.

ver'**wirken** forfeit; *Strafe*: incur.

ver'**wirklich**|**en** (25) realize; *sich* ~ be realized, come true; 2**ung** f realization.

Ver'**wirkung** f forfeiture.

verwirr|en [~'virən] (25) entangle; *fig. j-n*: confound, bewilder, perplex, *a. et.*: confuse; (*verlegen machen*) embarrass; *sich* ~ get entangled; 2**ung** f entanglement; *fig.* confusion, perplexity; *in* ~ *geraten od. sein* get into (*od.* be in) confusion.

ver'**wirtschaften** squander away.

ver'**wischen** wipe (*od.* blot) out; (*a. fig.*) efface; (*undeutlich machen*) blur.

ver'**witter**|**n** (sn) weather; ~t *adj.* weather-beaten, weather-worn.

verwitwet [~'vitvət] widowed.

verwöhn|en [fɛr'vøːnən] (25) spoil; (*verhätscheln*) coddle, pamper; ~t *adj.* pampered; *Kind*: a. spoilt; *Gaumen, Geschmack*: fastidious; 2**ung** f spoiling; pampering.

verworfen [~'vɔrfən[depraved; 2**heit** f depravity.

verworren [~'vɔrən] confused, muddled; 2**heit** f confusion.

verwund|bar [~'vuntbaːr] vulnerable; ~**en** [~dən] (26) wound.

ver'**wunder**|**lich** astonishing, odd, strange; ~**n** astonish; *sich* ~ wonder, be astonished (*über acc.* at); *verwundert* amazed; 2**ung** f astonishment, amazement.

Ver'**wund**|**ete** m (18) wounded person; ✗ casualty; ~**ung** f wound.

ver'**wünsch**|**en** curse, execrate; *verwünscht!* confound it!; 2**ung** f curse.

verwurschteln F [~'vurʃtəln] mess up.

ver'**wurzelt** deeply rooted.

verwüst|en [~'vy:stən] (26) devastate, (a. *fig.*) ravage; Ωung *f* devastation, ravage(s *pl.*).

ver'zag|en despair (*an dat.* of); ~t [~'tsɑ:kt] despondent, disheartened; Ωt-heit *f* despondency.

ver'zählen: *sich* ~ miscount.

verzahnen [~'tsɑ:nən] *Rad*: tooth, gear, cog; *Balken usw.*: indent; (*mit-ea.*) ~ *fig.* dovetail, mesh.

ver'zapfen *Bier usw.*: sell on draught; ⊕ tenon, mortise; F *fig.* dish out; *Unsinn* ~ talk nonsense.

verzärtel|n [fɛr'tsɛ:rtəln] (29) coddle, pamper; Ωung *f* pampering; softness.

ver'zaubern bewitch, enchant, charm; ~ *in* (*acc.*) transform into.

verzehnfachen [~'tse:nfaxən] (25) increase tenfold, decuple.

Ver'zehr *m* (3, *o. pl.*) consumption; Ωen consume (*a. fig.*), eat (up); *fig. sich* ~ *vor* (*dat.*) be consumed with.

ver'zeich|nen note down, register; *in e-r Liste*: list; *amtlich*: record; (*schlecht zeichnen*) draw incorrectly; *opt. u. fig.* distort; *fig.* (*erzielen*) register, secure; ~net *adj. paint.* out of drawing; Ωnis *n* (4¹) list; catalog(ue); *amtliches*: register; *v. Möbeln usw.*: inventory; *im Buch*: index; (*Tabelle*) table, schedule.

ver'zeih|en pardon, forgive (*beide*: *j-m* [*et.*] a *p.* [a th.]); *bsd.* ⚖ condone; ~ *Sie!* pardon me!, excuse me!; (so) sorry!; ~lich pardonable; Ωung *f* pardon; *j-n um* ~ *bitten* beg a p.'s pardon; ~! (I beg your) pardon!; (so) sorry!

ver'zerr|en distort (*a. fig.*); Ωung *f* distortion; *körperlich*: contortion.

verzetteln [~'tsɛtəln] (29) card-index; *fig.* fritter away; *sich* ~ squander one's strength.

Verzicht [fɛr'tsɪçt] *m* (a. ~leistung *f*) renunciation (*auf acc.* of); (*Opfer*) sacrifice; ⚖ waiver; ~ *leisten* = Ωen (26) (*auf acc.*) renounce; dispense with; *auf Vergnügen usw.*: for(e)go; ⚖ waive; *ich kann darauf* ~ I can do without it.

ver'ziehen *v/i.* (sn) (re)move; (*zögern*) linger; *v/t. Kind*: spoil; (*verzerren*) distort; *Mund*: screw up; *das Gesicht* ~ (make a) grimace; *s. Miene*; *sich* ~ *Holz*: warp; (*verschwinden, sich entfernen*) disappear, vanish, F beat it; *Volksmenge, Wol-*

ken: disperse.

ver'zier|en adorn, decorate; Ωung *f* decoration; (*Schmuck*) ornament.

verzinken [~'tsɪŋkən] (25) zinc.

verzinnen [~'tsɪnən] (25) tin.

verzins|en [~'tsɪnzən] (27) pay interest foɪ; *e-e Summe zu* 3⁰/₀ ~ pay 3 per cent on a sum; *sich* ~ yield interest; ~lich [~'tsɪns-] interest-bearing; ~ *mit* 4⁰/₀ bearing interest at 4 per cent; ~ *anlegen* put out at interest; Ωung *f* (~zuŋ) *f* (payment of) interest; (*Zinssatz*) interest rate; (*Zinsertrag*) interest return.

ver'zöger|n delay, retard; slow down (*a. sich*); *sich* ~ be delayed; Ωung *f* delay, retardation; *phys.* lag; Ωungs-taktik *f* delaying tactics *pl.*

ver'zoll|en pay duty on; ⚓ clear; *haben Sie et. zu* ~? have you anything to declare?; Ωung *f* payment of duty; ⚓ clearance.

ver'zück|en ecstasize, enrapture; ~t ecstatic(ally *adv*); Ωung *f* ecstasy, rapture; *in* ~ *geraten* go into ecstasies.

ver'zuckern (29) sugar (*a. fig.*).

Ver'zug *m* (3) delay; *es ist Gefahr im* ~ there is imminent danger; ⚖ *in* ~ *geraten* come in default; *im* ~ *sein* default (*mit* with); ~s-tage *m/pl.* days of grace; ~szinsen *m/pl.* interest *sg.* on arrears.

ver'zweif|eln (h. *u.* sn) despair (*an dat.* of); *es ist zum* Ω *it* is enough to drive one to despair; ~elt *adj.* despairing; (*aussichtslos; rücksichtslos*) desperate; Ωlung *f* despair; *zur* ~ *bringen od. treiben* drive to despair.

verzweig|en [fɛr'tsvaɪgən] (25) (a. *sich*) branch out, ramify; Ωung *f* ramification, branching.

verzwickt [~'tsvɪkt] intricate, complicated, tricky.

Vesper *eccl.* ['fɛspər] *f* (15) vespers *pl.*; ~brot *n* snack; Ωn (29) have a snack. [hall.]

Vestibül [vɛsti'by:l] *n* (3) vestibule,

Veteran [vete'rɑ:n] *m* (12) *bsd. Brt.* ex-serviceman, *Am. od. fig.* veteran.

Veterinär [veteri'nɛ:r] *m* (3) veterinary surgeon, veterinarian; ~klinik *f* veterinary hospital.

Veto ['ve:to] *n* (11) veto; *ein* ~ *einlegen gegen* put a veto on, veto *a th.*; ~recht *n* power of veto.

Vettel ['fɛtəl] *f* (16): *alte* ~ old hag.

Vetter ['fɛtər] m (10) cousin; '⁓n-wirtschaft f nepotism, F cronyism.

Vexier|bild [vɛ'ksiːrbilt] n picture-puzzle; ⁀en vex, tease; ⁓spiegel m distorting mirror.

Viadukt [via'dukt] m (3) viaduct.

Vibration [vibra'tsjoːn] f vibration.

vibrieren [vi'briːrən] vibrate.

Video|-aufnahme ['viːdeo-] f video-recording; '⁓band n video tape; '⁓film m video film; '⁓gerät n video recorder; '⁓kamera f video camera; '⁓kassette f video cassette; ⁓recorder ['⁓rekɔrdər] m (7) video recorder; '⁓spiel n video game; '⁓system n video system; '⁓text m tele-text; ⁓thek [video'teːk] f (15) video-tape library; '⁓überwachung f closed-circuit television monitoring.

Vieh [fiː] (3, o. pl.) (Tier) animal; agr. cattle, livestock; weitS., a. fig. brute, beast; '⁓-ausstellung f cattle-show; '⁓bestand m livestock; '⁓bremse f gadfly; '⁓futter n fodder; '⁓händler m cattle-dealer; '⁓hof m stockyard.

'**viehisch** bestial, beastly, brutal.

'**Vieh|markt** m cattle-market; '⁓seuche f cattle-plague, rinderpest; '⁓wagen 🚋 m cattle van; '⁓weide f pasturage; '⁓zucht f stock-farming, cattle-breeding; '⁓züchter m stock-farmer, cattle-breeder.

viel [fiːl] (comp. mehr, sup. meist) much, pl. many; sehr ⁓ a great deal; sehr ⁓e pl. a great many; ⁓ besser much better; ziemlich ⁓ a good deal (of); ziemlich ⁓e pl. a good many; viel Platz, Zeit usw. F plenty of room, time, etc.; das ⁓e Geld all that money; seine ⁓en Geschäfte his numerous affairs; s. Spaß; '⁓beschäftigt very busy; ⁓deutig ['⁓dɔytiç] ambiguous; '⁀eck n (3) polygon; ⁓erlei ['⁓ər'laɪ] adj. of many kinds, many kinds of, multifarious; ⁓erorts ['⁓ər'ʔɔrts] in many places, widely; '⁓fach multiple; adv. in many cases; frequently; ⁀falt ['⁓falt] f (16, o. pl.) (great) variety, diversity; ⁓fältig ['⁓fɛltiç] manifold, multifarious; '⁀fältigkeit f s. Vielfalt; '⁓farbig many-colo(u)red; ⁀fraß ['⁓fraːs] m glutton (a. zo.); '⁓geliebt well beloved; ⁓geprüft ['⁓gəpryːft] much tried; ⁓gereist ['⁓gəraɪst] (much) travel(l)ed; ⁓gestaltig ['⁓gəʃtaltiç]

multiform; ⁀götterei ['⁓gœtə'raɪ] f polytheism; '⁀heit f multiplicity, variety; (Menge) multitude; '⁓jährig of many years, many years of ...; ⁓'leicht perhaps, bsd. Am. maybe; ⁓ haben Sie recht you may be right; ⁓malig ['⁓maːliç] often repeated, frequent; ⁓mals ['⁓maːls] many times, frequently; ich danke Ihnen ⁓ many thanks; '⁓mehr rather; '⁓sagend significant; Blick: a. knowing; '⁓seitig many-sided; P. a.: all-round, versatile; ⁓ verwendbar multi-purpose, versatile; '⁓silbig polysyllabic; '⁓stimmig many-voiced, polyphonic; '⁓verheißend, '⁓versprechend (very) promising, of great promise; nicht ⁓ unpromising; ⁀völker... multi-racial; ⁀weiberei ['⁓vaɪbə'raɪ] f polygamy; '⁀zahl f multitude.

vier [fiːr] four; unter ⁓ Augen confidentially; auf allen ⁓en on all fours; ⁓beinig ['⁓baɪniç] four-legged; ⁓blätt(e)rig ['⁓blet(ə)riç] four-leaved; ⁓dimensional ['⁓dimenzjonaːl] four-dimensional; '⁀eck n square, quadrangle; '⁓eckig square, quadrangular.

'**Vierer** m (7) Rudern: four; '⁀lei adj. of four different sorts; als su. four different things; ⁓(spiel n) m Golf: foursome; Bridge: four.

'**vier|fach, ⁓fältig** ['⁓fɛltiç] fourfold; quadruple; ⁓füßig ['⁓fyːsiç] four-footed; zo. quadruped; ⁀füß(l)er ['⁓fyːs(l)ər] m (7) quadruped; '⁀ganggetriebe n four-speed gearbox; '⁀gespann n four-in-hand, carriage-and-four; ⁓händig ['⁓hendiç] zo. quadrumanous; ♪ four-handed; ⁓ spielen play a duet; '⁓hundert four hundred; '⁓jährig four years old, attr. four-year-old; Dauer: four-year; '⁓kantig square; '⁀linge pl. quadruplets, F quads; ⁀mächtebesprechung [⁓'mɛçtə-] f four-power talk; '⁓mal four times; '⁓malig four times repeated; ⁓motorig ['⁓motoːriç] four-engined; ⁓räd(e)rig ['⁓rɛːd(ə)riç] four-wheeled; ⁓schrötig ['⁓ʃrøːtiç] square-built, thick-set; '⁓seitig four-sided; ♤ quadrilateral; '⁓silbig of four syllables, ⬜ tetrasyllabic; '⁀sitzer m (7), '⁓sitzig four-seater; ⁀spänner ['⁓ʃpɛnər] m (7) carriage-and-four, (a. '⁓spännig) four-in-

-hand; '~spurig *mot.* four-lane; '~stellig *Zahl:* of four digits; ~stöckig ['~ʃtøkiç] four-storied; ~tägig ['~tɛːgiç] of four days, four-day; 'Ꝗ-taktmotor *mot. m* four-stroke (*od.* -cycle) engine; '~te fourth; '~teilen quarter.

Viertel ['firtəl] *n* (7) fourth (part); (*Maß; Stadt*Ꝗ; *Mond*Ꝗ) quarter; (*ein*) ~ *fünf*, (*ein*) ~ *nach vier* a quarter past four; *drei* ~ *vier*, (*ein*) ~ *vor vier* a quarter to (*Am.* of) four; '~finale *n Sport:* quarter-finals *pl.*; ~'jahr *n* three months, quarter (of a year); ~'jahres... quarterly ...; 'Ꝗjährig of three months; 'Ꝗjährlich three months'; quarterly (*a. adv.*); *adv.* every three months; '~note *f* crotchet; '~pause *♩ f* crotchet-rest; '~pfund *n* quarter of a pound; ~'stunde *f* quarter of an hour; 'Ꝗstündlich every quarter of an hour.

viertens ['fiːrtəns] fourthly.

Vier|'vierteltakt *♩ m* common time; 'Ꝗzehn fourteen; ~ *Tage* a fortnight, *Am.* fourteen days; 'Ꝗzehntägig fortnightly, two-week; 'Ꝗzehnte fourteenth; '~zehntel *n* (7) fourteenth (part); '~zeiler *m* four-lined stanza.

vierzig ['firtsiç] forty; Ꝗer ['~gər] *m* (7), 'Ꝗerin *f* (16¹) quadragenarian; *in den Vierzigern* in one's forties; F on the wrong side of forty; '~ste fortieth.

Vignette [vin'jɛtə] *f* (15) vignette.

Vikar [vi'kaːr] *m* (3¹) curate.

Viktualien [viktu'aːljən] *n/pl.* victuals, provisions, eatables.

Vill|a ['vila] *f* (9¹) villa; '~enviertel *n* residential district.

Viola *♩* [vi'oːla] *f* (16²) viola.

violett [vio'let] violet.

Violin|e *♩* [~'liːnə] *f* (15) violin; ~ist *♩* [~li'nist] *m* (12), ~istin *f* (16¹) violinist; ~schlüssel [~'liːn-] *m* G (*od.* treble) clef.

Violoncell(o) [violɔn'tʃɛl(o)] *n* (11, *pl. a.* -celli) violoncello.

Viper *zo.* ['viːpər] *f* (15) viper.

virtuo|s [virtu'oːs] masterly, virtuoso; Ꝗse [~'oːzə] *m* (13), Ꝗsin *f* (16¹) virtuo|so, *pl.* -si; Ꝗsität [~ozi'tɛːt] *f* (16) virtuosity, artistic perfection.

virulent [viru'lent] virulent.

Virus *♣* ['viːrus] *n, m* (16²) virus; '~-infektion *f* virus (*od.* viral) in-

fection; '~krankheit *f* virus disease.

Visage F [vi'zaːʒə] *f* (15) mug.

Visier [vi'ziːr] *n* (3¹) *am Helm:* visor; *am Gewehr:* sight; Ꝗen *v/t.* ⊕ adjust; (*eichen*) ga(u)ge; *Paß:* visa; *v/i.* (take) aim *od.* sight; ~kimme *f* rear sight notch; ~korn *n* foresight; ~linie *f* sighting-line.

Vision [vi'zjoːn] *f* vision; Ꝗär [~zjo'nɛːr] visionary.

Visi|tation [vizita'tsjoːn] *f* (*Durchsuchung*) search; (*Besichtigung*) inspection; ~te [vi'ziːtə] *f* (15) visit (*a. ♣*), (social) call; ~tenkarte *f* visiting-card, *Am.* calling card; Ꝗ-'tieren search; (*besichtigen*) inspect.

visuell [vizu'⁹ɛl] visual.

Visum ['viːzum] *n* (9² *u.* 11) visa.

vital [vi'taːl] vigorous; Ꝗität [vitali'tɛːt] *f* vitality.

Vitamin [vita'miːn] *n* (3¹) vitamin(e); *mit* ~(*en*) *anreichern s.* Ꝗisieren; Ꝗ-arm poor in vitamins; Ꝗhaltig vitamin-containing; Ꝗ-sieren [~mini'ziːrən] vitaminize; ~mangel [~'miːn-] *m* vitamin deficiency; Ꝗreich rich in vitamins.

Vitrine [vi'triːnə] *f* (15) glass cupboard; ✝ show-case.

Vitriol [vitri'oːl] *n, m* (3¹) vitriol.

vivat ['viːvat] 1. long live ...!; three cheers for ...!; 2. Ꝗ *n* (11) cheer.

Vize... ['fiːtsə, 'viːtsə] *mst* vice..., *z. B.* '~admiral *m* vice-admiral; '~kanzler *m* vice-chancellor; '~könig *m* viceroy; '~konsul *m* vice-counsel.

Vlies [fliːs] *n* (4) fleece.

Vogel ['foːgəl] *m* (7¹) bird; F *fig.* e-n ~ *haben* have a bee in one's bonnet, *sl.* be nuts; *fig.* den ~ *abschießen* steal the show, *sl.* take the cake; *loser* ~ wag; '~bauer *n* bird-cage; '~beerbaum *m* mountain ash, rowan(-tree); '~beere *f* rowan-berry; '~fänger ['~fɛŋər] *m* (7) bird-catcher; '~flinte *f* fowling-piece; 'Ꝗfrei outlawed; '~futter *n* bird-seed; '~haus *n* aviary; '~kunde *f* ornithology; '~mist *m* bird-dung.

vögeln V ['føːgəln] (29) fuck, screw.

'Vogel|nest *n* bird's nest; '~perspektive *f*, '~schau *f* bird's-eye view; '~scheuche *f* scarecrow (*a. fig.*); '~schutzgebiet *n* bird sanctuary; '~steller *m* (7) bird-catcher; ~-'Strauß-Politik *f* ostrich policy;

'~**warte** f ornithological station; '~**zug** m migration of birds.

Vöglein ['fø:glaɪn] n (6) little bird.

Vogt [fo:kt] m (3³) overseer; (*Amtmann*) bailiff; (*Statthalter*) governor; e-s Gutes: steward.

Vokab|el [vo'ka:bəl] f (15) word; ~**el-heft** n vocabulary book; ~**ular** [vokabu'la:r] n (3¹) vocabulary.

Vokal [vo'ka:l] m (3¹) vowel; ~**musik** f vocal music.

Volant [vo'lɑ̃] m (11) *Schneiderei:* flounce; *mot.* steering-wheel.

Volk [fɔlk] n (1²) people; (*Leute*) people pl.; (*Nation*) nation; (*Rasse, Schlag*) race; (*Masse*) populace; contp. (*Pöbel*) mob, rabble; (*Bienen-* ⚥) swarm; *hunt.* (*Rebhühner* ⚥) covey; der Mann aus dem ~e the man in the street.

Völker|bund ['fœlkər-] m (von 1919) League of Nations; '~**kunde** f ethnology; '~**mord** m genocide; '~**recht** n law of nations, international law; '⚥**rechtlich** relating to (adv. under) international law; '~**schaft** f people; (*Stamm*) tribe; '~**schlacht** f battle of (the) nations; '~**verständigung** f agreement between nations; '~**wanderung** f migration of nations.

'**volkreich** populous.

'**Volks|-abstimmung** f plebiscite; '~**-aufstand** m (popular) uprising, revolt; '~**ausgabe** f popular edition; '~**begehren** n (popular) initiative; '~**bibliothek** f public library; '~**bildung** f national education; '~**charakter** m national character; '~**deutsche** m, f ethnic German; '~**dichter** m popular (od. national) poet; '~**entscheid** m (popular) referendum; '~**feind** m public enemy; '~**fest** n public festival; '~**gunst** f popularity; '~**haufe(n)** m crowd; (die große Masse) populace, mob; '~**herrschaft** f democracy; '~**hochschule** f University Extension; in Deutschland: adult college; '~**justiz** f lynch law; '~**kunde** f folklore; '~**lied** n folk-song; '~**menge** f crowd (of people), multitude, b.s. mob; '~**partei** f people's party; '~**redner** m popular speaker; (*Agitator*) mob (Am. stump) orator, '~**sage** f folk-tale; '~**schicht** f class of (the) people, social stratum; '~**schule** f

elementary (od. primary, Am. a. grade) school; '~**schullehrer** m elementary (Am. grade) teacher; '~**sprache** f popular (od. vulgar) tongue; (*Landessprache*) vernacular (language); '~**stamm** m tribe, race; '~**stimme** f voice of the people; '~**stimmung** f public feeling; '~**stück** n folk-play; '~**tanz** m folk-dance; '~**tracht** f national costume; '~**tum** n (1²) nationality; '⚥**tümlich** national; (einfach od. beliebt) popular; '~**tümlichkeit** f popularity; '~**versammlung** f public meeting; '~**vertreter** m representative of the people; '~**vertretung** f representation of the people; '~**wirt** m (political) economist; '~**wirtschaft** f praktische: political economics pl.; '~**wirtschaftslehre** f political economy; '~**zählung** f census.

voll [fɔl] allg. full; (gefüllt) filled; F (betrunken) drunk; (ganz) whole, complete, entire (a. Betrag); (füllig, prall) full, round; ⊕ (massiv) solid; mit ~em Recht with perfect right; e-e ~e Stunde a full (od. solid) hour; ein ~es Jahr a whole year; ~e Beschäftigung full (ganztägige: full--time) employment; aus ~er Brust heartily; s. Hals, Nase; aus ~em Herzen from the bottom of one's heart; im ~(st)en Sinne des Wortes in the fullest sense of the word; j-n für ~ nehmen take a p. seriously; ~(er) Knospen full of; aus dem ~en schöpfen draw on plentiful resources; adv. ~ (und ganz) fully, entirely; '~-**auf** abundantly, amply, perfectly; '~-**automatisch** fully automatic; '⚥**bad** n full bath; '⚥**bart** m full beard; '~**berechtigt** fully qualified; '~**beschäftigt** fully employed; '⚥**beschäftigung** f full employment; '~**besetzt** Theater usw.: packed; '⚥**besitz** m full possession; '⚥**blut(pferd)** n thoroughbred (horse); '~**blütig** ['~bly:tiç] full-blooded; ~'**bringen** accomplish, achieve; ⚥'**bringung** f accomplishment, achievement; ~**busig** ['~bu:ziç] fullbosomed; '⚥**dampf** m (mit at) full steam; fig. mit ~ at full blast; '~-**elektronisch** fully electronic (od. automatic); ~**enden** (beenden) finish; (vervollständigen) complete; (vervollkommnen)

perfect, accomplish; ~'**endet** *adj.*
perfect, accomplished; *s. Tatsache.*
vollends ['fɔlɛnts] entirely, wholly,
altogether; ~ *da* especially since.
Voll'-endung *f* finishing; completion; (*Zustand*) perfection.
Völlerei [fœlə'raɪ] *f* (16) gluttony.
voll'führen execute, carry out;
Lärm: make; '~**füllen** fill (up);
'2**gas** *mot. n* (*mit at*) full throttle;
~ *geben* open the throttle, F step
on it; '2**gefühl** *n: im* ~ (*gen.*) fully
conscious of; '2**genuß** *m* full enjoyment; '~**gepfropft** crammed
(full), F packed; '~**gießen** fill (up);
'~**gültig** of full value, valid; '2-
gummi *m* solid rubber.
völlig ['fœlɪç] **1.** *adj.* (*ganz*) full,
entire; (*vollständig*) complete; total;
(*vollkommen*) perfect; (*gründlich*)
thorough; **2.** *adv.* fully, entirely,
etc.; quite.
'**voll'jährig** of (full) age; '2**jährigkeit**
f full age, majority; '2**kaskoversicherung** *f* comprehensive insurance; ~'**kommen** perfect; (*völlig
ausgebildet*) accomplished; *Macht,
Recht usw.*: absolute; *s. völlig*; 2-
'**kommenheit** *f* perfection; '2**korn-
brot** *n* whole-meal bread; '2**kraft** *f*
full vigo(u)r; *in der* ~ *des Lebens* in
the prime of life; '~**machen** fill (up); *fig.*
complete; *um das Unglück vollzu-
machen* to make things worse; (*beschmutzen*) dirty; '2**macht** *f* full
power(s *pl.*), authority; (*Urkunde*)
proxy, ⚖ power of attorney; *j-m* ~
erteilen give a p. authority; ~ *haben* be
authorized; '2**matrose** *m* able-bodied seaman; '2**milch** *f* whole (*od.*
unskimmed) milk; '2**mond** *m* full
moon; ~**mundig** ['~mundɪç] *Wein:*
full-bodied; '2**narkose** *f* general an-
(a)esthetic; '~**packen** fill (up); '2-
pension *f* full board (and lodging);
'~**pfropfen** stuff, cram; '~**schenken**
fill (up); '~**schlank** full-figured;
Frau: a. matronly; '2**sitzung** *f* plenary session; ~**spurig** ['~ʃpuːrɪç],
'2**spur...** 🚋 standard-ga(u)ge; '~-
ständig complete, full; whole, entire, total; *s. völlig*; '2**ständigkeit** *f*
completeness; entirety; '~**stopfen**
stuff, cram; '~**streckbar** enforce-
able; '~**strecken** execute, ⚖ *a.* enforce; *Fußball:* score; 2'**strecker(in**
f) *m* executor, *f a.* executrix; 2'**strek-
kung** *f* execution; 2'**streckungs-**

be-amte ⚖ *m* executory officer;
2'**streckungsbefehl** *m* writ of execution; '~**synthetisch:** ~*e Chemie-
faser* synthetic fib|re, *Am.* -er; '~-
tanken fill up; '2**treffer** *m* direct
hit; *fig.* bull's-eye; '2**versammlung**
f plenary assembly; '~**wertig** full, of
full value; ~**zählig** ['~tsɛːlɪç] complete; '2**zähligkeit** *f* completeness;
'2**zeit...** full-time; '2**zeit-Arbeits-
kraft** *f* full-time employee; ~'**ziehen**
execute, perform; (*ausführen*) effect;
kirchliche Handlung: solemnize; *die*
~*de Gewalt* the executive; *sich* ~ take
place; 2'**ziehung** *f*, 2'**zug** *m* execution; 2'**zugs-anstalt** *f* penal institution.
Volontär [vɔlɔ̃'tɛːr] *m* (3¹) improver,
trainee, unsalaried clerk.
Volt ⚡ [vɔlt] *n* (3 *u. inv.*) volt; '~**meter**
n (7) voltmeter; '~**zahl** *f* voltage.
Volumen [vo'luːmən] *n* (6; *pl. mst
Volumina*) volume (*a. fig.*).
vom [fɔm] = *von dem; s. von.*
von [fɔn] *räumlich u. zeitlich:* from;
für den Genitiv: of; *beim Passiv:* by;
(*über*) about, of; *s. a.* **an** 2.; *Stoff:*
~ *Holz* (made) of wood; 2 ~ 3 *Kindern*
2 in (*od.* out of) 3 children; *ein Gedicht* ~ *Schiller* a poem by Schiller;
Kinder haben ~ have children by;
~ *selbst*, ~ *sich aus* of oneself; ~
mir aus I don't mind (if); *s. Anfang,
früh, Kindheit, vornherein usw.*: ~-
nöten [~'nøːtən] necessary; ~**stat-
ten** [~'ʃtatən]: ~ *gehen* proceed,
pass off.
vor [foːr] *räumlich u. zeitlich:* before; *räumlich:* in front of; (~ *soundso langer Zeit*) ago; (*früher als*) prior
to; (*schützen, verstecken, warnen
usw.* ~) from, against; (*zittern* ~
Freude, Kälte usw.) with; *vor* ... (*in
Gegenwart von*) in the presence of;
s. all; ~ *e-m Hintergrund* against a
background; ~ *Hunger sterben* die
of hunger; *sich fürchten* ~ be afraid
of, fear; (*heute*) ~ *acht Tagen* a
week ago (today); ~ *Zeiten* formerly; 5 *Minuten* ~ 9 five minutes to
(*Am.* of) 9; ~ *allen Dingen* above
all; ~ *der Tür sein* be at the door;
~ *sich gehen* take place, happen,
pass off, proceed; *et.* ~ *sich haben*
be in for a th.
vor'ab in advance; beforehand.
'**Vor-abend** *m* eve; *am* ~ (*gen.*) on
the eve of.

'**vor-ahn**|**en** have a presentiment of; '**ung** f presentiment, foreboding.
voran [fo'ran] before, at the head (dat. of); nur ~! go on!, go ahead!; **~gehen** (sn) räumlich: lead the way; (a. fig.) take the lead; zeitlich u. räumlich, a. im Rang: precede (j-m usw. a p. etc.); Arbeit: gut ~ = **~kommen** make headway (od. progress), get ahead.
'**Vor-ankündigung** f announcement.
'**Vor-anmeldung** f: teleph. Gespräch mit ~ person-to-person call.
'**Vor-anschlag** m estimate.
'**Vor-anzeige** f previous notice.
'**Vor-arbeit** f preparatory work, preparations pl.; '**en** v/t. prepare, do a th. in advance; v/i. prepare work; j-m ~ pave the way for a p.; '**~er** m foreman; '**~erin** f (16¹) forewoman.
vorauf [fo'rauf] s. voran.
voraus [~'raus] in front, ahead (dat. of); im ~, zum ~ (mst 'voraus) in advance, beforehand; danken: in anticipation; Kopf ~ head foremost; s-m Alter ~ sein be forward (for one's age); **2-abteilung** ✕ f advance guard, vanguard; **~bedingen** stipulate beforehand; **~bestellen** s. vorbestellen; **~bestimmen** predetermine; **~bezahlen** pay in advance, prepay; **2bezahlung** f advance payment; **~denken** look ahead; **~eilen** (sn) hurry on ahead (dat. of); **2-exemplar** n advance copy; **~gehen** (sn) walk ahead (dat. of); s. a. vorangehen; **~gesetzt**: ~, daß provided (that); **~haben**: j-m et. ~ have an advantage over a p.; **2planung** f forward planning; **2sage, 2sagung** f prediction; (Prophezeiung) prophecy; (Wetter2) forecast (a. fig. ✝); (Renntip usw.) tip; **~sagen** foretell, predict; forecast; **2schau** f forecast; **~schauend** far-sighted; long-range; **~schicken** send on in advance; fig. mention before; **~sehen** foresee, anticipate; **~setzen** presuppose, require; (annehmen) assume; s. vorausgesetzt; **2setzung** f (pre)supposition, assumption; s. Vorbedingung; unter der ~, daß on condition that; zur ~ haben presuppose; die ~en erfüllen meet the requirements, qualify; **2sicht** f foresight; aller ~

nach in all probability; **~sichtlich** prospective, probable, presumable; expected; adv. probably; er kommt ~ a. he is likely (od. expected) to come; **2zahlung** f advance payment.
'**Vorbau** m front building; projecting part of a building; '**2en** v/t. (vorspringend bauen) build out; v/i. e-r S.: guard against.
'**Vorbedacht 1.** m: mit ~ deliberately, on purpose; 2. 2 premeditated.
'**vorbedeut**|**en** presage; '**2ung** f foreboding, omen.
'**Vorbedingung** f precondition, prerequisite, (basic) requirement.
Vorbehalt ['~bəhalt] m (3) reservation, reserve, proviso; mit dem ~, daß ... on the proviso that; ohne ~ without reservation; unconditionally; unter ~ with reservations; unter ~ aller Rechte all rights reserved; '**2en**: sich ~ reserve to o.s.; j-m ~ sein be reserved for a p.; Änderungen ~ subject to change (without notice); es bleibt der Zukunft ~ it remains for the future (to show, etc.); '**2lich** with reservation (gen. as to); ~ gen. subject to; '**2los** unreserved(ly adv.).
'**Vorbehandlung** f preliminary treatment.
vorbei [for'baɪ] along, by, past (alle a.: ~ an dat.); zeitlich: over, past, gone; **~fahren** drive past; **~gehen** (sn) pass by (an j-m a p.); (aufhören) pass; (fehlgehen) miss the mark; im 2 in passing; **~kommen** pass by; an e-m Hindernis usw.: get past; F (besuchen) drop in; **~lassen** let pass; **2marsch** m march(ing) past; **~marschieren** (sn) march past (an j-m a p.); **~müssen** have to pass (an dat. by); **~reden**: an-ea. ~ be at cross purposes; **~schießen** miss (an e-r S. a th.).
'**Vorbemerkung** f preliminary remark od. note; preamble.
vorbenannt ['~bənant] (afore)said, aforementioned.
'**vorbereit**|**en** (a. sich ~) prepare (für, auf acc. for); e-e vorbereitete Rede a set speech; '**~end** adj. preparatory; '**2ung** f preparation (für, auf acc. for); '**2ungs...** preparatory.
'**Vorbericht** m preliminary report.
'**vorberuflich** prevocational.
'**Vorbesprechung** f preliminary discussion.

'**vorbestell|en** order in advance; *Platz, Zimmer usw.*: book, *Am. a.* make a reservation for; '**2ung** *f* advance order; booking, *Am. a.* reservation, billing.

'**vorbestraft** previously convicted; ∼ sein have a police record.

'**vorbeten** *v/t.*: *j-m et.* ∼ repeat a th. to a p.

'**Vorbeugehaft** *f* preventive detention.

'**vorbeug|en** *v/i.* (*dat.*) prevent, obviate, guard against; *v/t.* (*a. sich*) bend forward; '**∼end** *adj.* preventive, ⟨♏⟩, ✗ prophylactic; '**2ung** *f* prevention; '**2ungsmaßnahme** *f* preventive measure; '**2ungsmittel** *n* preventive, ⟨♏⟩, ✗ prophylactic.

'**Vorbild** *n* model *v*; (*Beispiel*) *a.* example; (*Urbild*) prototype; '**2lich** exemplary, *attr. a.* model; (*vollkommen*) ideal; (*kennzeichnend*) typical (*für of*); '**∼ung** *f* preparatory training; educational background.

'**Vorbote** *m* forerunner (*a. ✗*); *fig.* harbinger, precursor; early sign.

'**vorbringen** bring forward, *a.* ⚖ *Beweise*: produce; *Meinung, Entschuldigung*: advance; ⚖ *Klage*: prefer, *als Einwand*: plead; (*behaupten, sagen*) state, say.

'**vorbuchstabieren** spell out (*j-m*)
'**Vorbühne** *f* apron. [to a p.).⟩

'**vordatieren** (= *zurückdatieren*) antedate; (= *vorausdatieren*) postdate.

vordem ['fo:rde:m] formerly.

vorder ['fɔrdər] front, fore.

'**Vorder|-achse** *mot. f* front axle; '**∼ansicht** *f* front view; '**∼arm** *m* forearm; '**∼bein** *n* foreleg; '**∼deck** *n* foredeck; '**∼fuß** *m* forefoot; '**∼gebäude**, **∼haus** *n* front building; '**∼grund** *m* foreground; *fig. im* ∼ *stehen* (*in den* ∼ *rücken*) be in the (place into the) foreground; *in den* ∼ *treten* come to the fore; **2gründig** ['∼gryndiç] *fig.* (*adv.* in the) foreground; '**∼hand**[1] *f des Pferdes*: forehand.

vorderhand[2] ['fo:rdər'hant] for the present, for the time being.

'**Vorder|lader** *m* (7) muzzle-loader; '**2lastig** ⚓ nose-heavy; '**∼lauf** *hunt. m* foreleg; '**∼mann** *m* man in front (*of a p.*); ✝ *bei Wechsel usw.*: prior endorser, *bei Papieren*: previous holder; F *j-n auf* ∼ *bringen* make a p.

toe the line; '**∼rad** *n* front wheel; '**∼rad-antrieb** *m* front-wheel drive; '**∼radbremse** *f* front-wheel brake; '**∼reihe** *f* front rank (*od.* row); '**∼schinken** *m* shoulder ham; '**∼seite** *f* front (side); ⌂, ⊕ *a.* face; '**∼sitz** *m* front seat.

'**vorderst** foremost.

'**Vorder|steven** ⚓ *m* stem; '**∼teil** *m*, *n* front (part); ⚓ prow; '**∼tür** *f* front door; '**∼zahn** *m* front tooth.

'**vordrängen** (*a. sich*) press (*od.* push) forward.

'**vordring|en** (sn) push (*od.* press) forward, advance; '**∼lich** urgent, priority ...

'**Vordruck** *m* form, *Am.* blank.

'**vor-ehelich** premarital.

'**vor-eilig** hasty, rash, precipitate; ∼*e Schlüsse ziehen* jump to conclusions; '**2keit** *f* rashness.

'**vor-eingenommen** prejudiced, bias(s)ed; '**2heit** *f* prejudice, bias.

'**Vor-eltern** *pl.* forefathers, ancestors, progenitors.

'**vor-enthalt|en** keep back, withhold (*j-m from a p.*); '**2ung** *f* withholding.

'**Vor-entscheidung** *f* preliminary decision.

'**vor-erst** for the time being.

vorerwähnt ['fo:r²ɛrvɛːnt] aforesaid, before- (*od.* afore)mentioned.

'**Vor-examen** *n s.* Vorprüfung.

Vorfahr ['∼fɑːr] *m* (12) ancestor.

'**vorfahr|en** (sn) drive up; (*vorbeifahren*) pass; *den Wagen* ∼ *lassen* order; '**2t**(**recht** *n*) *f* right of way; '**2tszeichen** *n* give way (*Am.* yield) sign.

'**Vorfall** *m* incident, occurrence; event; ✗ prolapsus; '**2en** (sn) happen, occur; ✗ prolapse.

'**Vor|feier** *f* preliminary celebration; '**∼feld** *n* ✗ forefield; '**∼fertigung** *f* prefabrication; '**∼film** *m* program(me) picture.

'**vorfinden** find.

'**Vorfrage** *f* preliminary question.

'**Vorfreude** *f* anticipated joy.

'**Vorfrühling** *m* early spring.

'**vorfühlen** put out one's feelers; *bei j-m*: sound out.

'**Vorführ|dame** *f* mannequin; '**2en** bring forward, produce; ⊕ demonstrate; (*zeigen*) show, display; '**∼er** *m* (7) demonstrator; *Kino*: projectionist, operator; '**∼raum** *m* projection room; '**~ung** f production; demonstration; showing; (Aufführung) performance, F show; '**~wagen** m demonstration car.

'**Vorgabe** f Spiel, Sport: points (od. odds) pl. given, handicap.

'**Vorgang** m s. Vorfall; (Hergang) proceedings pl.; bsd. ⊕ process; (Akte) file, reference.

Vorgänger ['~gɛŋər] m (7), '**~in** f (16¹) predecessor.

'**Vorgarten** m front garden, Am. frontyard.

'**vorgeben 1.** v/t. Sport: give, owe; (behaupten) allege, pretend; v/i. give odds (j-m to a p.); **2.** ⚲ n (6) preten|ce, Am. -se, pretext.

'**Vorgebirge** n promontory, cape; (Vorberge) foot-hills pl.

vorgeblich ['~ge:pliç] pretended, ostensible, alleged.

vorgefaßt ['~gəfast] preconceived.

'**Vorgefühl** n presentiment, premonition.

'**vorgehen 1.** (sn) advance; Uhr: be fast, gain (fünf Minuten five minutes); im Range: take precedence (dat. of); be more important (than); (handeln) take action, act; (verfahren) proceed (a. gerichtlich; gegen against); (sich ereignen) go on, happen, occur; **2.** ⚲ n (6) advance; (Handlungsweise) action, proceeding.

'**vorgenannt** s. vorerwähnt.

'**Vorgericht** n entree, s. a. Vorspeise.

'**Vorgeschicht|e** f prehistory; e-r S.: previous (od. past) history; e-r P.: antecedents pl.; ✄ case history; '⚲**lich** prehistoric(ally adv.).

'**Vorgeschmack** m foretaste.

Vorgesetzte ['fo:rgəzɛtstə] m, f (18) superior; (Chef) bsd. Am. F boss.

'**Vorgespräche** n/pl. preliminary talks.

'**vorgest|ern** the day before yesterday; '**~rig** of the day before yesterday.

'**vorgreifen** anticipate (j-m, e-r S. a p., a th.).

'**Vorgriff** m anticipation.

'**vorgucken** F Unterkleid usw.: show.

'**vorhaben 1.** Schürze usw.: have a th. on; (beabsichtigen) intend, purpose, mean; (beschäftigt sein mit) be busy with; haben Sie heute abend etwas vor? are you doing anything tonight?; **2.** ⚲ n (6) intention; plan,

scheme; (Projekt) project.

'**Vorhalle** f vestibule, (entrance-) hall; parl. lobby; thea., Hotel: a. lounge.

'**Vorhalt** m ✕ lead; ♩ suspension; ⚭ query; '⚲**en** v/t. j-m et. ~ hold a th. before a p.; fig. reproach a p. with a th.; v/i. (dauern) last; beim Schießen: apply a lead; '**~ung** f remonstrance, representation; j-m ~en machen remonstrate with a p.

'**Vorhand** f Kartenspiel u. fig.: lead.

vorhanden [fo:r'handən] present, at hand; (verfügbar) available; ✝ a. on hand, in stock; (bestehend) extant, existing; ~ sein be at hand etc.; ~ exist; ⚲**sein** n presence, existence. [hand (stroke).⚭

'**Vorhandschlag** m Tennis: fore-⅃

'**Vorhang** m curtain (a. thea.), Am. a. shade; pol. Eiserner ~ Iron Curtain.

'**Vorhängeschloß** n padlock.

'**Vorhaut** f foreskin, prepuce.

vorher ['fo:rhe:r] before, previously; (voraus) in advance, before (-hand).

vorher|bestimmen [~'he:r-] determine beforehand; eccl. predestine; ⚲**bestimmung** f predetermination; eccl. predestination; **~gehen** (sn; dat.) precede (a. th.); **~gehend** foregoing, preceding.

vor'herig preceding, previous.

'**Vorherr|schaft** f predominance; '⚲**schen** predominate, prevail; '⚲**schend** adj. predominant, prevalent, prevailing.

Vor'her|sage f, **~sagung** f, ⚲**sagen** s. Voraussage usw.; ⚲**sehen** foresee; ⚲**wissen** foreknow.

vor'hin a little while ago, just now.

'**Vorhof** m vestibule, front-court.

'**Vorhut** ✕ f vanguard.

vorig ['fo:riç] former, previous; (letztvergangen) last.

'**vor-industriell** pre-industrial.

'**Vor|jahr** n previous year; last year; '⚲**jährig** of last year.

'**Vorkämpfer(in** f) m champion.

'**vorkauen** j-m: chew a th. for; fig. F spoon-feed a th. to.

'**Vorkauf** m pre-emption; '**~srecht** n right of pre-emption, option right; das ~ haben a. have the refusal.

'**Vorkehrung** f precaution; **~en** treffen take precautions od. measures; make arrangements.

ˈVorkenntnis *f* (*a.* ~se *pl.*) previous (*od.* basic) knowledge (von of); (er *hat gute*) ~se *pl. in* (*dat.*) (he is well grounded in the) elements of ...

ˈvorknöpfen: F *sich j-n* ~ take a p. to task.

ˈvorkomm|en¹ (sn) be found, be met (with), occur; (*sich ereignen*) occur, happen; *es kommt mir vor* it seems to me; *so etwas ist mir noch nicht vorgekommen!* F well, I never!; *das kommt dir nur so vor* you are just imagining that; *sich dumm usw.* ~ feel silly, *etc.*; *sich klug* ~ fancy o.s. clever; *er kommt mir bekannt vor* he looks familiar; *es kommt mir merkwürdig vor* I think it (rather) strange; **ˈ2en²** *n* (6) occurrence; *min. a.* deposit; **ˈ2nis** *n* (4¹) occurrence, incidence.

ˈVorkosten *pl.* preliminary cost *sg.*

ˈVorkriegs... pre-war.

ˈvorlad|en summon, cite; **ˈ2ung** *f* summons *sg.*, citation.

ˈVorlage *f* (*Schreib2, Zeichen2*) copy; (*Muster*) pattern, model; (*Unterbreitung*) submission, presentation; *parl.* bill; *Fußball*: pass; *Ski*: vorlage, forward lean.

ˈvorlass|en let *a p.* pass in front *od.* before; (*zulassen*) admit; **ˈ2ung** *f* admission, admittance.

ˈVorlauf *m Sport*: eliminating heat.

Vorläuf|er [ˈfoːrlɔʏfər] *m*, **ˈ~erin** *f* (16¹) forerunner, precursor; **ˈ2ig** preliminary; provisional, temporary; *adv.* provisionally, *etc.*; (*fürs erste*) for the time being.

ˈvorlaut forward, pert; ~es *Wesen* pertness.

ˈVorleben *n* former life, past, antecedents *pl.*

ˈVorlege|besteck *n* (*ein* a pair of) carvers *pl.*; **ˈ~gabel** *f* carving-fork; **ˈ~messer** *n* carving-knife.

ˈvorlegen *et.*: put forward; (*vorbringen*) produce; *Plan usw.*: propose; *Schloß*: put on; *Rechnung*: present; *j-m et.* ~ lay (*od.* place *od.* put) a th. before a p.; *bei Tische*: help a p. to a th.; *zur Prüfung usw.*: submit (*od.* present) a th. to a p.; *sich* ~ lean forward.

ˈVorlege|r *m* (7) (*Bett2 usw.*) rug; **ˈ~schloß** *n* padlock.

ˈvorles|en read (*j-m* to a p.); **ˈ2er** (**-in** *f*) *m* reader; (*Vortragender*) lecturer; **ˈ2ung** *f* lecture (*über acc.* on; *vor dat.* to); *e-e* ~ *halten* (give a) lecture; **ˈ2ungsverzeichnis** *n* (university) calendar, *Am.* catalog(ue).

vorletzt [ˈ~lɛtst] last but one, *Am.* next to the last.

ˈVorliebe *f* predilection, preference, special liking (*für* for).

vorliebnehmen [forˈliːpneːmən]: ~ *mit* put up with; *beim Essen*: (~ *mit dem, was da ist*) take potluck.

ˈvorliegen: *j-m* ~ lie before a p.; *fig. Antrag usw.*: be in hand, be submitted, (*behandelt werden*) be under consideration; *weitS. Grund, Irrtum usw.*: be, exist; *es liegt heute nichts vor* there is nothing to be discussed (*od.* on) today; *was liegt gegen ihn vor?* what is the charge against him?; **ˈ~d** *adj.* present, in hand; in question, under consideration.

ˈvorlügen: *j-m et.* ~ tell a p. lies.

ˈvormachen *Brett usw.*: put before; *j-m et.* ~ show a p. how to do a th., (*täuschen*) humbug a p.; *sich* (*selbst*) *et.* ~ fool o.s.

ˈVormacht(stellung) *f* supremacy; hegemony.

vormal|ig [ˈfoːrmaːliç] former; **ˈ~s** formerly.

ˈVormarsch *m* advance.

ˈvormerken make a note of; (*reservieren*) reserve; (*bestellen*) book; *für e-n Zweck*: earmark.

ˈVormieter(in *f*) *m* previous tenant; *s-e* ~ the tenants before him.

ˈvormilitärisch: ~*e Ausbildung* pre-military training.

ˈVormittag *m* morning, forenoon; **ˈ2s** in the morning (*abbr.* a.m.).

ˈVormund *m* guardian; **ˈ~schaft** *f* guardianship; **ˈ2schaftlich** of (*adv.* as) a guardian, tutelary; **ˈ~schaftsgericht** *n* guardianship court.

vorn [fɔrn] in front, before, ahead; *ganz* ~ right in the front; *nach* ~ forward; *nach* ~ *heraus wohnen* live in the front; *nach* ~ *heraus liegen* face the front; *von* ~ from the front; *ich sah sie von* ~ I saw her face; *von* ~ *anfangen* begin at the beginning, (*von neuem*) begin anew *od.* afresh; *von* ~ *bis hinten* from front to back, from first to last; *noch einmal von* ~ all over again.

Vornahme [ˈfoːrnaːmə] *f* (15) effecting, undertaking.

ˈVorname *m* Christian name, first name.

vornehm ['ˌneːm] distinguished, refined; aristocratic; (*elegant*) fashionable; (*edel*) noble; (*erstklassig*) high-class; ˌe *Gesinnung* high mind; ˌes *Äußere*, ˌer *Anstrich* distinguished air *od.* appearance; *die* ˌe *Welt* the rank and fashion, high society; ˌ *tun* give o.s. airs; ˌste *Pflicht usw.* principal; 'ˌen take before one; *Schürze*: put on; (*beginnen*) undertake; (*behandeln*) deal with, occupy o.s. with; (*durchführen*) effect; *Änderung usw.*: make; *sich j-n* ˌ take a p. to task; *sich et.* ˌ resolve (*od.* decide) to do a th.; *sich vorgenommen haben* intend, purpose; 'ˌheit *f* rank, distinction; refinement; high-mindedness; distinguished appearance; 'ˌlich especially, chiefly.

'**vornherein:** *von* ˌ from the first.

'**vornotieren** *s.* vormerken.

vorn'-über forward; (*Kopf voraus*) head foremost.

'**Vor-ort** *m* suburb; 'ˌ(s)... *in Zssgn* suburban; 'ˌbahn *f* suburban (*od.* local) railway; 'ˌzug *m* suburban train.

'**Vorposten** ✂ *m* outpost.

'**vorprogrammieren** (pre)program(me); *fig.* vorprogrammiert preprogram(m)ed, predetermined.

'**Vorprüfung** *f* preliminary examination.

'**vorragen** project, protrude.

'**Vorrang** *m* pre-eminence, precedence; priority; *den* ˌ *haben vor* (*dat.*) take precedence of, *S.: a.* have priority over; ˌig (having) priority.

Vorrat ['foːraːt] *m* (3³) store, stock, supply, provision (*an dat.* of); reserve; *heimlicher:* hoard; *an Material: bsd. Am.* stockpile.

vorrätig ['ˌrɛːtiç] available, on hand, in stock, in store; *nicht* (*mehr*) ˌ out of stock.

'**Vorratskammer** *f* store-room; (*Speisekammer*) pantry.

'**Vorraum** *m* anteroom.

'**vorrechnen** reckon up (*j-m* to a p.).

'**Vorrecht** *n* privilege, prerogative.

'**Vorred|e** *f* preface; 'ˌen *j-m et.*: tell a p. tales (*über acc.* about); 'ˌner *m* previous speaker.

'**vorricht|en** prepare; 'ˌung *f* preparation; (*Gerät usw.*) device, contrivance, appliance; mechanism.

'**vorrücken** *v/t. Stuhl usw.*: move forward, advance; *Uhr:* put on; *v/i.* (sn) advance; *in vorgerücktem Alter* in an advanced age; *zu e-r vorgerückten Stunde* at a late hour.

'**vorrufen** call forth. [round.)

'**Vorrunde** *f Sport:* preliminary)

'**Vorsaal** *m* anteroom.

'**vorsagen** *v/t. j-m et.:* tell a p. a th.; *v/i.* (*zuflüstern*) *j-m:* prompt a p.

'**Vorsaison** *f* early season.

'**Vorsänger(in** *f*) *eccl. m* precentor.

'**Vorsatz** *m* intention, resolution, design, purpose; ⚖ (criminal) intent; *mit* ˌ designedly, on purpose; ⚖ wil(l)fully; ˌblatt *typ. n* fly-leaf.

'**vorsätzlich** intentional, deliberate; ⚖ wil(l)ful, premeditated.

'**Vorsatzlinse** *phot. f* ancillary lens.

'**Vorschau** *f* preview (*auf acc.* of); (*Wetter⚥, Finanz⚥ usw.*) forecast; *s. Film⚥.*

'**Vorschein** *m: zum* ˌ *bringen* bring forward *od.* to light, produce; *zum* ˌ *kommen* come forward *od.* to light, appear, show.

'**vorschieben** push forward *od.* on, advance; *Riegel:* shoot; *als Entschuldigung, Grund usw.:* plead, pretend; *j-n:* use as a front.

'**vorschießen** *Summe:* advance.

'**Vorschlag** *m* proposal; (*Empfehlung*) recommendation; (*Anregung*) suggestion; (*Anerbieten*) offer; *parl.* motion; *e-s Kandidaten:* nomination; ♪ grace(-note); ⚥en propose; offer; suggest; nominate.

'**Vorschluß|runde** *f Sport:* semifinal.

'**Vorschneide|messer** *n* carving-knife; ⚥n carve.

'**vorschnell** hasty, rash, precipitate.

'**vorschreiben** set a copy of *a th. to a p.*; (*anordnen*) prescribe, order.

'**vorschreiten** (sn) advance.

'**Vorschrift** *f* (*bsd.* ⚕) prescription; (*Anweisung*) direction, instruction; (*Befehl*) order; (*Dienst⚥*) regulation(s *pl.*); *streng nach* ˌ *arbeiten* work to rule; '⚥smäßig regulation (*nur attr.*); *according to* regulations; *in due form*, duly; '⚥swidrig *adj., adv.* contrary to regulations.

'**Vorschub** *m* assistance; ⊕ feed; ˌ *leisten* (*dat.*) pander to, encourage, abet; ⚖ aid and abet.

'**Vorschul|-alter** *n* pre-school age; 'ˌe *f* pre-school, nursery school; 'ˌ-erziehung *f* pre-school education.

'**Vorschuß** *m* advance (*auf acc.* against); (*Gehalts*♀, *Lohn*♀) advance (on salary, on wages).

'**vorschützen** plead.

'**vorschweben:** *mir schwebt et. vor* I have a th. in mind.

'**vorschwindeln:** *j-m et.* ~ humbug a p. about a th., tell a p. lies.

'**vorseh|en:** ~ *für e-n Zweck* assign (*od.* earmark) for; (*planen*) schedule for; *sich* ~ take care, be on one's guard; *sich* ~ *vor* (*dat.*) guard against, look out for *a th.*; '♀**ung** *f* Providence.

'**vorsetzen** put forward; (*dat.*) place (*od.* put *od.* set) before; (*auftischen*) serve; *gr. Silbe*: prefix; *fig. j-m* ~ (*überordnen*) set over a p.

Vorsicht ['fo:rzɪçt] *f* caution; (*Behutsamkeit*) care; *als Aufschrift*: caution!, beware!; *auf Kisten*: (handle) with care!; *mit* ~ cautiously; ~, *Stufe!* mind the step!; *s. a. Achtung*; '♀**ig** cautious, chary (*in dat.* of); (*behutsam*) careful; *Schätzung usw.*: conservative; ~*!* careful!, look (*Am.* watch) out!; ♀**s-halber** ['~shalbər] as a precaution; '~**smaßnahme,** '~**smaßregel** *f* precaution(ary measure).

'**Vorsilbe** *gr. f* prefix.

'**vorsingen** *v/t. j-m et.* ~ sing a th. to a p.; *v/i.* lead (the choir).

'**vorsintflutlich** antediluvian (*a. fig.*).

'**Vorsitz** *m* presidency, chair(man-ship); *den* ~ *haben od. führen* be in the chair, preside (*bei* over); *unter* ~ *von* ... with ... in the chair; ~**ende** ['~ǝndǝ] *m, f* (18) chairman, president; *f* chairwoman; *des Gerichts*: presiding judge.

'**Vorsorg|e** *f* provision, providence; (*Vorsicht*) precaution; ~ *treffen* take precautions, provide (*gegen* against); '♀**en** provide (*für* for; against); provide for the future; '~**e-untersuchung** ✍ *f* (preventive) medical check-up; ♀**lich** ['~zɔrklɪç] provident, precautionary; *adv.* as a precaution.

'**Vorspann** *m Film*: cast and credits *pl.*, credit titles *pl.*; introduction; '♀**en** put horses *etc.* to the cart *etc.*

'**Vorspeise** *f* hors d'œuvre, appetizer.

'**vorspiegel|n** pretend, feign; *j-m et.* ~ deceive a p. with a th., delude a p. (with false hopes); '♀**ung** *f* preten|ce, *Am.* -se; (*unter*) ~ *fal-*

scher Tatsachen (under) false pretences *pl.*

'**Vorspiel** *n* ♪ prelude (*a. fig.*; *zu* to); *thea.* curtain-raiser (*a. fig.*), introductory piece; *sexuelles*: foreplay; '♀**en** *j-m*: play *a th.* to.

'**vorsprechen** *v/t. j-m*: pronounce to a p.; *v/i.* (*Besuch machen*) call (*bei on a p.*; at *an office*).

'**vorspringen** (sn) jump (*od.* leap) forward; (*hervortreten*) project, jut (out); '~**d** *adj. Winkel*: salient.

'**Vorsprung** *m* △ projection; (*Sims, a. Fels*♀) ledge; (*Abstand*) (head) start, lead, advantage (*vor dat.* of); *mit großem* ~ by a wide margin.

'**Vorstadt** *f* suburb.

'**Vorstädt|er(in** *f*) *m* (7 [16¹]) suburban resident; '♀**isch** suburban.

'**Vorstand** *m* board of directors, managing (*od.* executive) board; *P.*: head, principal; '~**s-etage** *f* executive suite; '~**smitglied** *n* member of the managing board.

'**vorstecken** put before; *mit e-r Nadel usw.*: pin before; *den Kopf*: stick out; *vorgestecktes Ziel* object, target.

'**vorsteh|en** (*hervorragen*) project, protrude, jut out; *e-r Sache usw.*: direct, be at the head (*od.* in charge) of, manage; ~**d** (*vorhergehend*) foregoing, preceding, above; *wie* ~**d** as above; '♀**er** *m* (7), '♀**erin** *f* (16¹) principal, director, manager(ess *f*), superintendent, head; '♀**erdrüse** *f* prostate gland; '♀**hund** *m* pointer; *langhaarig*: setter.

'**vorstell|bar** imaginable; '~**en** put forward *od.* in front; *Uhr*: put on; *j-n j-m*: introduce, seltener: present *a p. to a p.*; (*bedeuten*) mean, stand for; (*darstellen*) represent; *j-m et.* ~ (*hinweisen auf*) point out a th. to a p., *mahnend*: remonstrate with a p. about a th.; *sich* ~ stand in front, (*sich bekannt machen*) introduce o.s., *bei*: present o.s. at; *sich et.* ~ imagine, fancy, (*abwägend*) envisage, (*sich ein Bild machen von*) visualize, picture; *ich stelle Ihnen hier Herrn X. vor* allow me to introduce Mr. X. to you, *Am.* meet Mr. X.; F *stell dir (nur) vor!* just fancy!; '~**ig:** ~ *werden bei der Behörde* apply to (*protestierend*: lodge a complaint with) the authorities (*wegen* for); '♀**ung** *f* introduction, presentation;

thea. performance; *s. Film*♀; (*Begriff*) idea, conception; *sich e-e* ~ *machen von* form (*od.* get) an idea of; (*Mahnung*) remonstrance, representation; '♀**ungsgespräch** *n* interview; '♀**ungsvermögen** *n* imagination.

Vorstoß *m* ✕ thrust, drive (*a. fig.*); *Sport:* rush; '♀**en** thrust (*Sport:* rush) forward, advance.

'**Vorstrafe** *f* previous conviction; '~**n(register** *n) pl.* police record.

'**vorstrecken** stretch out; *den Kopf:* stick out; *Geld:* advance.

'**Vorstufe** *f* first step (*od.* stage); *e-s Lehrgangs:* primary course; (*Anfangsgründe*) (first) elements *pl.*

'**vorstürmen** rush forward.

'**vortanzen** lead the dance; *j-m:* dance (...) before a p.

'**vortasten** (*sich*) grope one's way (*bis zu* to).

'**vortäuschen** feign, simulate, sham, pretend, fake.

'**Vorteil** *m* (3) advantage; (*Gewinn*) profit, benefit; *Tennis:* (ad)vantage; *die Vor- und Nachteile e-r S.* the pros and cons; *auf s-n* ~ *bedacht sein* have an ax(e) to grind; *sich im* ~ *befinden gegenüber* (*dat.*) have an advantage over; ~ *ziehen aus* profit by; '♀**haft** advantageous, profitable (*für* to); ~ *aussehen* look one's best.

Vortrag ['foːrtraːk] *m* (3³) performance; (~*sweise*) delivery, *rhet.* elocution; *e-s Gedichtes:* recitation; ♩ (*Solo*♀) recital; (~*stechnik*) execution; (*Abhandlung, Vorlesung*) lecture; (*Bericht*) report; ✝ balance carried forward; (*einen*) ~ *halten* read a paper, (*über acc.* on); ♀**en** ['~gən] carry forward; (*berichten*) report (*über acc.* on, *j-m* to); (*hersagen*) recite; (*Vortrag halten*) lecture (on); *Rede:* deliver; *Gedicht:* recite; ♩ perform; *Ansichten:* state; (*vorschlagen*) propose, submit; ✝ *den Saldo* ~ carry forward the balance; '~**ende** *m, f* (18) (*Künstler*) performer; (*Dozent*) lecturer.

'**Vortrags|kunst** *f* art of reciting *od.* lecturing *od.* delivery; '~**künstler(in** *f) m* rhet. elocutionist; ♩ executant, performer; '~**reihe** *f* series of lectures; '~**reise** *f* lecture tour.

vor'**trefflich** excellent; ♀**keit** *f* excellence.

'**vortreten** (sn) step (*od.* come) forward; (*vorragen*) project, protrude.

'**Vortritt** *m* precedence; *j-m den* ~ *lassen* give precedence to a p.

vor**über** [foˈryːbər] along, by, past; *zeitlich:* gone (by), over, past; ~**gehen** (sn) pass; *nur räumlich:* pass (*od.* go) by; ~**gehend** *adj.* passing, transitory; (*zeitweilig*) temporary; ♀**gehende** *m* (18) passer-by (*pl.* passers-by); ~**ziehen** march past, pass by; *Gewitter:* pass.

'**Vor-übung** *f* preliminary exercise (*od.* practice).

'**Vor-untersuchung** *f* preliminary examination (*od. a.* ⚖ investigation).

'**Vor-urteil** *n* prejudice; '♀**sfrei,** '♀**slos** unprejudiced, unbias(s)ed.

Vorväter ['~fɛːtər] *m/pl.* ancestors.

'**Vorvergangenheit** *gr. f* past perfect, pluperfect.

'**Vorverkauf** *m* advance sale; *thea.* advance booking; '~**skasse** *f,* '~**sstelle** *f* ticket agency, (advance) booking office.

'**vorverlegen** advance.

'**Vorverstärker** *m Radio:* pre-amplifier.

'**vorvorgestern** three days ago *od.* since.

'**vorvorig** last but one.

'**Vorwahl** *f* preliminary election; ✂ preselection; *teleph.* dialling (*Am.* area) code.

'**vorwaltend** prevailing.

Vorwand ['~vant] *m* (3³) pretext, preten|ce, *Am.* -se, excuse; *unter dem* ~ *von od. daß* on the pretext (*od.* plea) of *od.* that.

'**vorwärmen** preheat.

'**vorwarn|en** warn in advance; '♀**ung** *f* (advance) warning.

vor**wärts** ['fɔrverts] forward, onward, on; ~*!* go ahead!; '~**drängen** press on; '♀**gang** *mot. m* forward gear; '~**gehen** go ahead, advance, *fig. a.* progress; '~**kommen** (sn) get on, make headway; *fig. a. im Leben:* get on (in the world), make one's way; '♀**verteidigung** ✕ *f* forward defen|ce (*Am.* -se).

'**Vorwäsche** *f Waschmaschine:* pre-wash.

vor**weg** [forˈvɛk] beforehand; ♀**nahme** *f* anticipation; ~**nehmen** anticipate.

'**Vorweihnachtszeit** *f* Advent (season).

'**vorweisen** produce, show.

'**Vorwelt** *f* prehistoric world.

'**vorwerfen** (*dat.*) throw before; *fig.* *j-m et.* ~ reproach a p. with a th.

'**vorwiegen** preponderate; '~**d** preponderant, predominant; *adv. a.* mainly, chiefly, mostly.

'**Vorwissen** *n* (previous) knowledge; *ohne mein* ~ unknown to me.

'**Vorwitz** *m* inquisitiveness; (*vorlaute Art*) forwardness, pertness; '⚥**ig** inquisitive; (*vorlaut*) forward, pert.

'**Vorwort** *n* (3) *des Autors*: preface; *bsd. v. e-m andern*: foreword.

'**Vorwurf** *m* reproach; *eines Dramas usw.*: subject; *e-n* ~ *od.* Vorwürfe machen s. vorwerfen; '⚥**frei** irreproachable; '⚥**svoll** reproachful.

'**vorzählen** enumerate, count out.

'**Vorzeichen** *n* omen; ♪ signature, (*Versetzungszeichen*) accidental; ♭ sign; ⚕ preliminary symptom; *fig. mit umgekehrten* ~ with reversed premises.

'**vorzeichnen** trace out; *j-m et.* ~ show a p. how to draw a th.; *als Richtschnur*: mark (out) *od.* indicate a th. to a p.

'**vorzeig|en** produce, show; *Wechsel*: present; (*darlegen*) exhibit; '~**bar** presentable; '⚥**ung** *f* producing, showing; exhibition.

'**Vorzeit** *f* (remote) antiquity; *in Erzählungen*: olden times *pl.*

vor'**zeiten** in olden times.

'**vorzeitig** premature.

'**Vorzensur** *f* precensorship; *e-r* ~ *unterwerfen* pre-censor.

'**vorziehen** draw forth; *Truppen*: move up; *fig.* prefer (*et. e-r anderen S. a th. to another th.*); *es* ~ *zu inf. a.* choose to *inf.*

'**Vorzimmer** *n* antechamber, anteroom; *e-s Büros*: outer office; '~**dame** *f* receptionist.

'**Vorzug** *m* preference; (*Vorteil*) advantage; (*gute Eigenschaft*) merit, virtue; (*Vorrang*) priority (*vor dat.* to); (*Vorrecht*) privilege; *den* ~ *geben s.* vorziehen; *den* ~ *haben zu...* have the distinction of *ger.*

vor'**züglich** [~'tsy:kliç] excellent, superior, exquisite, first-rate; *adv.* (*vornehmlich*) expecially; ⚥**keit** *f* excellence, superiority.

'**Vorzugs|-aktien** *f/pl.* preference shares, *Am.* preferred stock *sg.*; '~**preis** *m* special price, preferential rate; '⚥**weise** preferably, by preference; '~**zoll** *m* preferential tariff.

votieren [vo'ti:rən] vote.

Votiv|bild [vo'ti:fbilt] *n* votive picture; ~**tafel** *f* votive tablet.

Votum ['vo:tum] *n* (9¹ *u.* ²) vote.

vulgär [vul'gɛ:r] vulgar.

Vulkan [vul'ka:n] *m* (3¹) volcano; ~**ausbruch** *m* volcanic eruption; ⚥**isch** volcanic(ally *adv.*); ⚥**isieren** [~kani'zi:rən] vulcanize; *Autoreifen*: *a.* recap.

W

W [ve:], **w** *n inv.* W, w.

Waage ['va:gə] *f* (15) balance, (pair of) scales *pl.*; (~ *mit Laufgewicht*) steelyard; (*automatische Abfüll*⚥) weigher; (*Brücken-, Tafel*⚥) weighing-machine; *für Wagenlasten*: weighbridge; (*Wasser*⚥) spirit-level; *ast.* Balance, Libra; *die* ~ *halten* (*dat.*) counterbalance; *in der* ~ *halten* hold in equilibrium; '~**balken** *m* (scale-)beam; '⚥**recht** horizontal, level.

Waagschale ['va:k-] *f* scale; *fig. in die* ~ *fallen* be of weight; *in die* ~

werfen throw into the scale(s).

wabbelig ['vabəliç] flabby.

Wabe ['va:bə] *f* (15) honeycomb; '~**nhonig** *m* comb honey.

wach [vax] *pred.* awake; *ganz* ~ wide awake; ~ *werden* awake; *attr.* wakeful *state*; *fig.* alert *mind*; wide--awake *person*; '⚥**dienst** *m* guard--duty.

Wache ['vaxə] *f* (15) watch, guard; (*Wachlokal*) guardhouse, guardroom; (*Polizeidienststelle*) police--station; (*Posten*) guard, ⚔ *a.* sentry, sentinel; *auf* ~ on guard; ~

Wagen

halten keep guard; ~ *stehen* stand sentry; *auf* ~ *ziehen* mount guard; '2n be awake; (*achtgeben*) watch (*über acc.* over), guard; *bei j-m* ~ sit up with a p.

'Wach|habende *m* guard commander; '~haus *n* guardhouse; '~-hund *m* watchdog; '~lokal *n* guardroom; '~mannschaft *f* guard detail, sentry squad.

Wacholder [va'xɔldər] *m* (7) juniper; ~beere *f* juniper berry; ~branntwein *m* gin.

'Wach|posten *m* guard, ✕ *a.* sentry; '2rufen call forth, rouse; *Erinnerung: a.* evoke; '2rütteln rouse (*a. fig.*).

Wachs [vaks] *n* (4) wax; '~-abdruck *m* impression in wax.

'wach|sam watchful, vigilant; ~ *sein* be on the alert; '2samkeit *f* vigilance; '2schiff *n* guard-ship.

wachsen[1] ['vaksən] *v/i.* (30, sn) grow; *fig. a.* increase (*an dat.* in); *s. gewachsen, Bart.*

'wachsen[2] *v/t.* (27) wax.

wächsern ['vɛksərn] wax; *fig.* waxen, waxy.

'Wachs|figur *f* wax figure, *pl. a.* waxwork *sg.*; '~figurenkabinett *n* waxworks (*mst sg.*); '~kerze *f*, '~-licht *n* wax candle; '~leinwand *f* oilcloth; '~matrize *f* stencil; '~-puppe *f* wax doll; '~streichholz *n* (wax) vesta; '~tuch *n* oilcloth.

'Wachs-tum *n* (1, *o. pl.*) growth; *fig. a.* increase; *im* ~ *hindern* stunt; '2s-hemmend growth-retarding; '~s-industrie *f* growth industry; '~s-potential *n* growth potential; '~s-rate *f* rate of (economic) growth; '~sstörung *f* disturbance of growth.

Wacht(...) [vaxt] *f* (16) *s. Wache, Wach...*

Wächte mount. ['vɛçtə] *f* cornice.

Wachtel ['vaxtəl] *f* (15) quail; '~-hund *m* spaniel.

Wächter ['vɛçtər] *m* (7) watcher (*a.* '~-in *f*); guard(ian); (*bsd. Nacht*2) watchman; (*Parkplatz*2) attendant.

'Wachtmeister *m* sergeant.

'Wachtraum *m* day-dream.

'Wachturm *m* watch-tower.

'wack(e)lig shaky (*a. fig.*), tottery; *alte Möbel usw.*: rickety; *Zahn:* loose; (*baufällig*) ramshackle.

'Wackelkontakt ⚡ *m* loose contact.

wackeln ['vakəln] (29) shake;

(*wanken*) rock, wobble; (*taumeln, a.* ~d *gehen*) totter; (*locker sein*) be loose; ~ *mit* wag *a th.*

wacker ['vakər] (*bieder*) honest, worthy (*a. iro.*); (*tapfer*) brave; *adv.* (*tüchtig*) heartily, lustily.

Wade ['va:də] *f* (15) calf (of the leg); '~nkrampf *m* cramp in the leg; '~nstrumpf *m* half-stocking.

Waffe ['vafə] *f* (15) weapon (*a. fig.*); *mst im pl.* arm; *s.* greifen, strecken; *j-n mit s-n eigenen* ~n *schlagen* beat a p. at his own game; *unter den* ~n *stehen* be under arms.

Waffel ['vafəl] *f* (15) waffle, wafer; '~-eisen *n* waffle-iron.

'Waffen|-appell *m* arms inspection; '~-arsenal *n* arsenal; '~bruder *m* brother in arms; '~brüderschaft *f* brotherhood in arms; '~dienst *m* military service; '~fabrik *f* arms factory; '~fabrikant *m* manufacturer of arms; '2fähig fit to bear arms; '~-gang *m* passage of (*od.* at) arms; '~gattung *f* arm, branch (of the service); '~gewalt *f* force of arms, armed force; '~handel *m* arms trade; '~kammer *f* armo(u)ry; '~lager *n* ordnance depot; '~lieferungen *f/pl.* arms supplies; '2los weaponless, unarmed; '~meister *m* armo(u)rer; '~-rock ✕ *m* service coat; '~ruhe *f* truce; *kurze:* suspension of hostilities, cease-fire; '~schein *m* firearm certificate; *Am.* gun license; '~-schmied *m* armo(u)rer; '~schmuggel *m* gun-running; '~stillstand *m* armistice, (*a. fig.*) truce; '~still-standslinie *f* ceasefire-line; '~sy-stem *n* weapons system; '~-übung *f* military exercise.

waffnen ['vafnən] (26) arm.

wägbar ['vɛ:kba:r] weighable; *fig. a.* ponderable.

Wage|hals ['va:gəhals] *m* (4²) daredevil; 2halsig ['~halziç] foolhardy, daring, *nur attr.* daredevil, breakneck; '~halsigkeit *f* foolhardiness, daredevilry; '~mut *m* daring.

wagen[1] ['va:gən] (25) venture (*a. sich*); *et. Gefährliches:* risk, hazard; (*sich getrauen*) *a. sich erdreisten*) dare; *es* ~ take the plunge; *es* ~ *mit* try *a th.*; *wer nicht wagt, der nicht gewinnt* nothing venture nothing have; *s. gewagt.*

Wagen[2] [~] *m* (6) carriage (*a.* 🚃,

Am. car); (*Fahrzeug*) vehicle; (*Kutsche*) coach; *für schwere Fracht:* wag(g)on; (*Karren*) cart; (*Kraft*2̩) car; (*Last*2̩) lorry, *Am.* truck; (*Möbel*2̩) van; *der Schreibmaschine:* carriage; *ast. der Große* ~ Charles's Wain, the Plough, *Am.* the Plow, the Big Dipper.

wägen ['vɛːɡən] (30) weigh (*nur noch fig.*).

'**Wagen|-abteil** 🚃 *n* compartment; '~**heber** *m* (lifting-)jack; '~**kolonne** *f* line of cars; '~**ladung** *f* carload, wag(g)on-load; '~**park** *m* fleet (of cars); '~**pflege** *f* maintenance (of a car; (*Kundendienst*) servicing; '~**rad** *n* wheel; '~**runge** *f* stanchion; '~**schlag** *m* car(riage) door; '~**schmiere** *f* cart-grease; '~**spur** *f* wheel--track, rut; '~**winde** *f* screw-jack.

'**Wag(e)stück** *n* daring deed.

Waggon [va'ɡɔ̃] *m* (11) railway carriage, wag(g)on, *Am.* (railroad) car.

Wagnis ['vaːknɪs] *n* (4¹) hazard(ous enterprise), venture, risk.

Wahl [vaːl] *f* (16) choice; (*freie* ~) option; (~ *zwischen zwei Dingen*) alternative; (*Auslese*) selection; *pol.* election; ✝ **erste** (*zweite*) ~ choice (second rate) quality; *pol.* ~**en abhalten** hold elections; *fig.* **die** ~ **haben** have one's choice; *fig.* **keine** ~ **haben** have no alternative (*als* but); *ich habe keine* (*andere*) ~ I have no choice; *in die engere* ~ *kommen* be on the short list; *s-e* ~ *treffen* make one's choice; *e-e gute* ~ *treffen* choose well; '~-**akt** *m* polling, voting; '~-**alter** *n* voting age.

'**wählbar** eligible; '2̩**keit** *f* eligibility.

'**wahl|berechtigt** entitled to vote; '2̩**bericht** *m* election return; '2̩**beteiligung** *f* voting, turnout; '2̩**bezirk** *m* electoral district; *städtischer:* ward.

wählen ['vɛːlən] (25) choose; (*auslesen*) select; *pol.* elect; (*Stimme abgeben*) vote; *teleph.* dial; ~ *gehen pol.* go to the polls.

'**Wähler** *m* (7) voter.

'**Wahl-ergebnis** *n* election result *od.* return.

'**Wähler|in** *f* (16¹) (female) voter; '~**initiative** *f* electors' initiative; '2̩**isch** particular, nice (*in dat.* about), choosy; *im Essen:* dainty, *a. weitS.* fastidious; '~**liste** *f* register of voters; '~**schaft** *f* constituency; *weitS.* vot-

ing population; '~**scheibe** *teleph. f* dial.

'**Wahl|fach** *n Schule, univ.:* optional subject, *Am.* elective; '2̩**fähig** *aktiv:* having a vote; *passiv:* eligible; '~**fähigkeit** *f s.* Wahlrecht; '~**feldzug** *m* election campaign; '2̩**frei** *Schule, univ.:* optional, *Am.* elective; '~**gang** *m* ballot; '~**geschenk** *n* pre-election promise; '~**heimat** *f* adopted country; '~**helfer(in** *f)* *m* polling officer; '~**jahr** *n* election year; '~**kabine** *f* polling booth; '~**kampf** *m* election campaign; '~**kreis** *m s.* Wahlbezirk; '~**lokal** *n* polling-station; '2̩**los** indiscriminate; '~**mann** *m* (1²) delegate, constituent, *Am.* elector; '~**plakat** *n* election poster; '~**prüfer** *m* scrutineer; '~**prüfung** *f* scrutiny; '~**recht** *n aktives:* franchise; *passives:* eligibility; *allgemeines* ~ universal suffrage; '~**rede** *f* election speech; '~**schlacht** *f* election campaign, electoral battle; '~**spruch** *m* device, motto; (*Schlagwort*) slogan; '~**stimme** *f* vote; '~**tag** *m* election-day; '~-**urne** *f* ballot-box; *zur* ~ *schreiten* go to the polls; '~**versammlung** *f* election meeting; '~**versprechen** campaign promise; '~**verwandtschaft** *f* elective affinity; *fig. a.* congeniality; '~**vorschlag** *m* election proposal; '2̩**weise** alternatively; '~**zelle** *f* polling-booth; '~**zettel** *m* voting-paper, ballot.

Wahn [vaːn] *m* (3) delusion; *s. a.* Wahnsinn; '~**bild** *n* chimera, phantom.

wähnen ['vɛːnən] (25) fancy, imagine; believe, think.

'**Wahn|sinn**, '~**witz** *m* insanity, (*a. fig.*) madness; '2̩**sinnig**, '2̩**witzig** insane, (*a. fig.*) mad (*vor dat.* with); *fig.* frantic(ally *adv.*); *Angst, Schmerzen usw.:* horrible, dreadful; *F* (*toll*) terrific; *s. a.* verrückt; '~**sinnige** (18) *m* madman; *f* madwoman; lunatic; '~**vorstellung** *f* delusion; hallucination.

wahr [vaːr] true; (*wirklich*) *a.* real; (*echt*) genuine; (*eigentlich*) proper; (*aufrichtig*) sincere; *ein* ~*er Künstler* a true artist; *es ist eine* ~*e Wohltat* quite a comfort; *so* ~ *ich lebe!* as sure as I live!; *so* ~ *mir Gott helfe!* so help me God!; *et.* ~ *machen* go ahead with a th., make a th. come true; ~ *werden* come true;

sein ~es Gesicht zeigen show the cloven hoof; *das ist nicht das* ♀e that's not the real McCoy; '**~en** (25) preserve (*vor dat.* from), (*a. ein Geheimnis*) keep; *Interessen*: safeguard, protect; *s. Form, Schein.*

währen ['vɛːrən] (25) continue, last; '**~d 1.** *prp.* (*gen.*) during; ⚷ pending; **2.** *cj.* while, whilst; *Gegensatz*: whereas, while.

'**wahrhaben**: *er will es nicht ~* he will not admit it.

'**wahrhaft, ~ig** [~'haftiç] true; (*wahrheitsliebend, wahrheitsgemäß*) truthful, veracious; (*wirklich*) true, real; *adv.* truly, really; ♀**igkeit** [~'haft-] *f* veracity.

'**Wahrheit** *f* truth; *in ~* in truth; F *j-m die ~ sagen* (*schelten*) give a p. a piece of one's mind; *um die ~ zu sagen* to tell the truth, truth to tell; '**~sbeweis** *m*: *den ~ antreten* prove one's case; '♀**sgemäß**, '♀**s-getreu** truthful, true; '**~sliebe** *f* veracity; '♀**sliebend** truthful, veracious; '♀**swidrig** contrary to the truth.

'**wahrlich** truly; *Bibel*: verily.

'**wahr|nehmbar** perceptible, noticeable; '**~nehmen** perceive, notice; *Gelegenheit*: make use of, seize; *Interesse*: look after, protect; *Amt*: exercise the functions of ...; *Termin*: observe; ♀**nehmung** ['~neːmuŋ] *f* perception; observation; (*Sorge für s*) care (*gen.* of); *der Interessen*: safeguarding; ♀**nehmungsvermögen** *n* perceptive faculty; '**~sagen** prophesy; *aus Karten usw.*: tell fortunes; *sich ~ lassen* have one's fortune told; '♀**sager(in** *f*) *m* soothsayer; *aus Karten usw.*: fortune-teller; ♀**sagerei** [~'raɪ] *f* (16) fortune-telling; **~'scheinlich** probable, likely; *er wird ~* (*nicht*) *kommen* he is (not) likely to come; ♀'**scheinlichkeit** *f* probability, likelihood; *aller ~ nach* in all probability; ♀'**scheinlichkeitsgrad** *m* degree of probability; ♀'**scheinlichkeitsrechnung** *f* theory of probabilities; '♀**spruch** *m* verdict.

'**Wahrung** *f* maintenance; *von Interessen*: safeguarding, protection.

Währung ['vɛːruŋ] *f* currency; (*Gold♀ usw.*) standard; '**~s-ausgleichsfonds** *m* exchange equaliza-

tion fund; '**~sbank** *f* bank of issue; '**~s-einheit** *f* currency unit; '**~s-fonds** *m*: *Internationaler ~* International Monetary Fund; '**~skrise** *f* monetary crisis; '**~s-politik** *f* monetary policy; '**~sreform** *f* monetary (*od.* currency) reform.

'**Wahrzeichen** *n* distinctive sign *od.* mark, token; *e-r Stadt usw.*: landmark.

'**Waidmann** *m s. Weidmann.*

Waise ['vaɪzə] *f* (15) orphan; '**~n-haus** *n* orphanage; '**~nkind** *n*, '**~n-knabe** *m* orphan; *fig. ein Waisen-knabe gegen j-n sein* not to be a patch on a p.

Wal [vaːl] *m* (3) whale.

Wald [valt] *m* (1²) wood, (*a. fig.*) forest; *er sieht den ~ vor Bäumen nicht* he does not see the wood for trees; '♀**-arm** sparsely wooded; '**~bestand** *m* forest cover; '**~brand** *m* forest-fire; '**~-erdbeere** *f* wood strawberry; '**~frevel** *m* offen|ce (*Am.* -se) against the forest laws; '**~gebirge** *n* woody mountains *pl.*; '**~gegend** *f* woodland; '**~horn** ♩ *n* French horn; '**~hüter** *m* forest-keeper, ranger.

waldig ['~diç] woody, wooded.

'**Wald|land** *n* woodland; '**~lauf** *m* cross-country race; '**~meister** ♀ *m* woodruff; '**~nymphe** *f* wood-nymph; '**~rand** *m* edge of the forest; '♀**reich** rich in forests; '**~sterben** *n* dying(-off) of forests.

Waldung ['~duŋ] *f* wood, forest, woodland.

'**Wald|weg** *m* wood-path; '**~wiese** *f* (forest-)glade.

Wall|fänger ['vaːl-] *m* (*Schiff u. Mensch*) whaler; '**~fisch** *m* whale; '**~-öl** *n*, '**~tran** *m* train-oil.

walk|en ['valkən] (25) full, mill; '♀**er** *m* (7) fuller; '♀**mühle** *f* fulling-mill.

Walküre [val'kyːrə] *f* (15) Valkyrie.

Wall [val] *m* (3⁸) ✕ rampart; (*Damm*) dam, dike; (*Erdaufschüttung als Schutz*) mound; *fig.* bulwark, dam.

Wallach ['valax] *m* (3 *od.* 12) gelding.

wallen ['valən] (25, sn *u.* h.) wave; *Haar, Gewand usw.*: flow; (*sieden*) simmer; (*brodeln*; *a. fig. v. Blut*) boil; *s. a. wallfahren.*

'**wall|fahren** (25, sn) (go on a) pilgrimage; '♀**fahrer** *m* (7) pilgrim; '♀**fahrt** *f* pilgrimage; '♀**fahrts-ort** *m* place of pilgrimage.

'**Wallung** f ebullition (a. fig.); ♨ (Blut♀) congestion; (Hitze) flush; fig. in ~ bringen enrage a p.; in ~ kommen boil (with rage).

Walnuß ['val-] f (Am. English) walnut; '**~baum** m walnut-tree.

Walroß ['val-] n walrus.

Walstatt ['val-] f battle-field.

walten ['valtən] **1.** v/i. u. v/t. (26) govern, rule; (wirken) be at work; s. schalten; seines Amtes ~ do one's duty; Gnade ~ lassen show mercy; Sorgfalt ~ lassen exercise proper care; das walte Gott! God grant it!; **2.** ⦶ n (6) rule; working; the hand of God, etc.

'**Walzblech** n rolled plate.

Walze ['valtsə] f (15) roller (a. typ. u. Straßen♀ usw.), cylinder (a. typ.); ⊕ a. roll; der Schreibmaschine: platen; der Drehorgel usw.: barrel; F fig. auf der ~ on the tramp.

'**walzen** (27) **1.** v/t. ⊕ roll; **2.** v/i. (Walzer tanzen) waltz.

wälzen ['veltsən] (27) (a. sich) roll; sich ~ im Wasser usw.: wallow; in s-m Blute: welter; fig. von sich ~ off-load a th.; sich vor Lachen ~ be convulsed with laughter; die Schuld auf j-n ~ lay the blame on a p.

walzenförmig ['~fœrmiç] cylindrical.

Walzer ♪ ['valtsər] m (7) waltz.

Wälzer ['veltsər] m (7) bulky volume, huge tome.

'**Walzgold** n rolled gold.

'**Wälzlager** ⊕ n roller bearing.

'**Walz|straße** ⊕ f rolling (od. mill) train; '**~werk** n rolling-mill.

Wamme ['vamə] f (15) (Kehlfalte) dewlap; F (dicker Bauch) paunch.

Wams [vams] n (2¹) jacket; hist. doublet.

wand¹ [vant] pret. v. winden.

Wand² [~] f (14¹) wall; (Scheide♀) partition; e-s Gefäßes: side; fig. an die ~ gedrückt werden go to the wall; j-n an die ~ stellen execute; '**~-arm** m (wall-)bracket; '**~behang** m wall hanging.

Wandel ['vandəl] m (7) change; (Lebenswandel) way of living; (Betragen) behavio(u)r, conduct; Handel und ~ trade, commerce; ~ schaffen bring about a change; '♀-**bar** changeable, variable; '**~bar- keit** f changeableness; '**~gang** m, '**~halle** f parl., thea. lobby; '♀n

(29) v/i. (sn) poet. walk; (wandern) wander, travel; v/t. change (a. sich); sich ~ in (acc.) turn into; '**~obliga- tion** ♥ f convertible bond.

Wander|-ausstellung ['vandər-] f itinerant (od. flying) exhibition; '**~bühne** f travelling theatre, Am. touring company; '**~bursche** m travel(l)ing journeyman; '**~düne** f shifting sand dune; '**~er** m (7), '**~in** f (16¹) wanderer, travel(l)er; bsd. sportlich: hiker; '**~gewerbe** n itinerant trade; '**~heuschrecke** f migratory locust; '**~jahre** n/pl. (journeyman's) years of travel; '**~ karte** f trail map; '**~leben** n vagrant life; '♀n (29, sn) wander (a. Blick, Gedanken), travel; (umherstreifen) ramble; (zu Fuß gehen) walk; bsd. sportlich: hike; Vögel, Völker usw.: migrate; Düne: shift; F fig. go; '**~ niere** f floating kidney; '**~pokal** m challenge cup; '**~prediger** m itiner- ant preacher; '**~preis** m challenge trophy; '**~ratte** f brown (od. Nor- way) rat; '**~schaft** f wanderings pl., travel(l)ing, travels pl.; auf der ~ on the tramp; auf die ~ gehen take to the road; '**~smann** m (1, pl. 'Wanders- leute) s. Wanderer; '**~stab** m (walk- ing-)stick; den ~ ergreifen set out on one's travels; '**~trieb** m roving spirit; zo. migratory instinct; '**~truppe** f s. Wanderbühne; '**~ung** f walking-tour; vgl. wandern: ramble; hike; migra- tion; '**~ver-ein** m rambling club; '**~vogel** m bird of passage; '**~zirkus** m travel(l)ing circus.

'**Wand|gemälde** n mural (painting); '**~halter** m (7) wall bracket; '**~ka- lender** m tear-off calendar; '**~karte** f wall-map; '**~leuchter** m bracket (-lamp), sconce.

Wandlung ['vandluŋ] f change, (a. ⚡) transformation; eccl. transsub- stantiation; ⚖ redhibition.

'**Wand|male'rei** f mural painting; '**~pfeiler** m pilaster; '**~schirm** m folding-screen; '**~schrank** m closet, wallchest; '**~spiegel** m pier-glass; '**~tafel** f blackboard; '**~teppich** m tapestry; '**~-uhr** f wall-clock.

wandte ['vantə] pret. v. wenden.

Wange ['vaŋə] f (15) cheek (a. ⊕). **...wangig** [...vaniç] ...-cheeked.

Wankelmotor ['vaŋkəl-] m Wan- kel engine, rotary piston engine.

Wankel|mut ['vaŋkəlmu:t] m fickleness, inconstancy; ⚲**mütig** ['⌣my:-tiç] fickle, inconstant.

wanken ['vaŋkən] (25, h. *u.* sn) totter, stagger; *Boden, Haus:* rock; *fig.* waver, falter; *ins* ⚲ *bringen od. kommen* shake.

wann [van] when; *s. dann; seit* ⌣? how long?, since what time?

Wanne ['vanə] f (15) tub; (*Bade*⚲) bath; '⌣**nbad** n tub-bath.

Wanst [vanst] m (3² u. ³) paunch.

Want ⚓ [vant] f (16, *mst pl.*) shroud.

Wanz|e ['vantsə] f (15) bug, *Am.* bedbug; F (*Abhörgerät*) bug; '⚲**ig** buggy.

Wappen ['vapən] n (6) (coat of) arms *pl.*; '⌣**bild** n heraldic figure; '⌣**kunde** f heraldry; '⌣**schild** m escutcheon, blazon; '⌣**spruch** m heraldic motto.

wappnen ['vapnən] (26) arm; *fig. gewappnet* forearmed.

war [vɑːr] *pret. v. sein*[1] 1.

warb [varp] *pret. v. werben.*

Ware ['vɑːrə] f (15) *allg. u. in Zssgn* ware (*z. B.* earthenware); article (of commerce), commodity; *als Sammelwort:* ⌣ *od.* ⌣n *pl.* merchandise *sg.*; ⌣n *pl. a.* goods *pl.*

wäre ['vɛːrə] *s. sein; wie* ⌣ *es mit* ...? how about ...?; *wie* ⌣ *es, wenn* ...? what if ...?

Waren|-angebot n range of items (for sale); '⌣**aufzug** m hoist, *Am.* (freight-)elevator; '⌣**ausfuhr** f export(ation of goods); '⌣**bestand** m stock (on hand); '⌣**börse** f Commodity Exchange; '⌣**haus** n department store; '⌣**konto** n goods account; '⌣**kredit** m goods credit; '⌣**lager** n (*Vorrat*) stock-in-trade; (*Raum*) warehouse, *Am.* stockroom; '⌣**probe** f sample; *v. Stoff usw.:* pattern; '⌣**rechnung** f invoice; '⌣**umsatz** m goods turnover; '⌣**zeichen** n trade-mark.

warf [varf] *pret. v. werfen.*

warm [varm] warm (*a. fig.*); *stärker* (*a. Speisen u.* ⊕): hot; *mir ist* ⌣ I am (*od.* feel) warm; ⌣ *halten* keep warm; ⌣ *werden* warm up (*a. fig.*); ⌣ *empfehlen* recommend warmly; '⚲**bad** n warm bath; (*Quelle*) thermal springs *pl.*; ⚲**blüter** ['⌣bly:tər] (7) warm-blooded animal.

Wärme ['vɛrmə] f (15, *o. pl.*) warmth (*a. fig.*); *phys.* heat; '⌣**be-**

handlung ⚕ f heat treatment; '⚲**beständig** heat-resistant; '⌣**dämmung** f heat insulation; '⌣**einheit** f thermal unit, calorie; '⌣**energie** f thermal energy; '⌣**grad** m degree of heat; '⌣**kraftwerk** n thermo-electric power plant; '⌣**lehre** f theory of heat; '⌣**leiter** m conductor of heat; '⌣**messer** m thermometer; *nach Kalorien:* calorimeter; '⚲**n** (25) warm; heat; '⌣**pumpe** f heat pump; '⌣**technik** f heat engineering; '⌣**verlust** m heat loss.

'**Wärmflasche** f hot-water bottle.

'**warm|halten** *fig.:* sich j-n ⌣ keep in with a p.; '⚲**halteplatte** f hot plate; '⌣**herzig** warmhearted; '⚲**luft** f warm air; '⚲**miete** F f rent including heating.

Warm'wasser|bereiter m electric water heater; ⌣**heizung** f hot-water heating; ⌣**speicher** m hot-water tank; ⌣**versorgung** f hot-water supply.

Warn|blink-anlage *mot.* ['varn-] f warning flashers *pl.*; '⌣**drei-eck** *mot.* n warning triangle; '⚲**en** (25) (*vor dat.*) warn (of, against), caution (against); *vor Dieben usw. wird gewarnt!* beware of ...!; *davor* ⌣, *zu inf.* warn against *doing a th.*; *Sie sollten gewarnt sein durch* you should take warning from; '⌣**er** m (7) warner; '⌣**lampe** f warning lamp; '⌣**schuß** m warning shot; '⌣**signal** n danger-signal; '⌣**streik** m token strike; '⌣**tafel** f danger notice; '⌣**ung** f warning; *laß dir das zur* ⌣ *dienen* let that be a warning (od. lesson) to you.

Warte ['vartə] f (15) watch-tower, look-out; *fig.* level; standpoint; '⌣**frau** f *s.* Wärterin; '⌣**geld** n half-pay; '⌣**liste** f waiting list.

warten ['vartən] (26) v/i. wait; (*bleiben*) stay; ⌣ *auf* (*acc.*) wait for, (*bevorstehen*) be in store for *a p.*; (*nicht lange*) *auf sich* ⌣ *lassen* (not to) be long in coming; *j-n* ⌣ *lassen* keep a p. waiting; *s. na*; v/t. *allg.* tend; (*pflegen*) nurse; *weitS.* attend to, look after; ⊕ service, maintain.

Wärter ['vɛrtər] m (7) attendant; (*bsd. Irren*⚲) keeper; (*Pfleger*) (male) nurse; (*Wächter*) guard; 🚒 signalman; '⌣**in** f (16¹) (female) attendant; (*Pflegerin*) nurse.

Warte|raum m, '⌣**saal** m, '⌣**zim-**

mer *n* waiting-room; '**~zeit** *f* waiting period.
'**Wartung** *f* attendance; tending; (*Pflege*) nursing; ⊕ maintenance, servicing; '⌂**s-arm** ⊕ low-maintenance; '⌂**sfrei** ⊕ maintenance-free.
warum [va'rum] why, for what reason.
Warze ['vartsə] *f* (15) wart; (*Brust⌂*) nipple; ⊕ lug, stud; '**~enschwein** *n* warthog; '⌂**ig** warty.
was [vas] **1.** (24) *interr. pron.* what; *rel. pron.* (= *das, was*) what, *a.* that which; *den Inhalt des vorhergehenden Satzes aufnehmend*: which; ~ *auch immer*, ~ *nur* what(so)ever; ~ *für* (*ein*) ...? what ...? what sort (*od.* kind) of ...?; ~ *für* (*ein*) ...! what (a) ...!; *was nun?* F so what?; **2.** F = *etwas*; F *ich will dir* ~ *sagen* I'll tell you what; **3.** = *wieviel*: ~ *kostet das Buch?* how much is?
'**Wasch|-anlage** ['vaʃ-] *f* car-wash; '**~automat** *m* washing-machine; '⌂**bar** washable; '**~bär** *m* rac(c)oon, *Am.* F coon; '**~becken** *n* wash- (*od.* hand-)basin; '**~beutel** *m* sponge bag; '**~blau** *n* washing-blue; '**~brett** *n* wash-board.
Wäsche ['vɛʃə] *f* (15) (*Waschen*) wash; (*Waschen; Zeug während des Waschens*) washing; (*schmutzige* ~) laundry; (*Leib⌂, Tisch⌂, Bett⌂*) linen; (*Unter⌂*) underwear; ♀ (*Damenunter⌂*) lingerie; *schmutzige* ~ *soiled* (*fig.* dirty) linen; *in die* ~ *geben* get *a th.* washed, send *a th.* to the laundry; *in der* ~ *sein* be at the wash; '**~beutel** *m* laundry bag.
'**wasch-echt** laundry-proof, fast; *fig.* genuine, true-blue.
'**Wäsche|geschäft** *n* lingerie store; '**~klammer** *f* clothes-peg; '**~korb** *m* linen (*od.* laundry) basket; '**~leine** *f* clothes-line.
waschen ['vaʃən] *v/t., v/i., v/refl.* (30) wash; *Wäsche:* a. launder; *Haar:* shampoo; *sich gut* ~ *lassen* wash well; ♀ *und Legen* shampoo and set; *s. Kopf.*
'**Wäschepuff** *m* linen (*od.* laundry) basket.
Wäscher ['vɛʃər] *m* (7) washer; *in e-r Wäscherei:* laundryman; **~ei** [~'raɪ] *f* (16) laundry; '**~in** *f* (16¹) wash(er)woman, laundress.
'**Wäsche|schleuder** *f* spin drier; '**~schrank** *m* linen-press, clothes-press; '**~ständer** *m* clothes horse;

'**~tinte** *f* marking-ink; '**~trockner** ⚡ *m* tumble-drier; '**~zeichen** *n* laundry-mark.
'**Wasch|frau** *f s.* Wäscherin; '**~gelegenheit** *f* washing facility; '**~kessel** *m* wash-boiler; '**~korb** *m* clothes-basket; '**~küche** *f* washhouse; F (*Nebel*) *sl.* pea-soup; '**~lappen** *m fürs Gesicht:* face cloth, *Am.* washrag; *für Geschirr:* dishcloth; F (*Weichling*) *sl.* sissy; '**~lauge** *f* lye; '**~leder** *n*, '⌂**ledern** wash-leather, chamois, shammy; '**~maschine** *f* washing-machine, washer; '⌂**maschinenfest** machine-washable; '**~mittel** *n* washing agent, detergent; '**~pulver** *n* washing powder; '**~raum** *m* lavatory, *Am. a.* washroom; '**~schüssel** *f* wash bowl; '**~seide** *f* washing silk; '**~seife** *f* washing- (*od.* laundry) soap; '**~tag** *m* washing day; '**~tisch** *m*, '**~toilette** *f* wash-stand; '**~trog** *m* washing trough; '**~ung** *f* washing; *bsd.* ♂, *eccl.* ablution; '**~weib** *contp. n* old gossip; '**~wasser** *n* washwater; '**~zettel** *m* (*Buchanpreisung*) blurb.
Wasser ['vasər] *n* (7) water; *fig. ein stilles* ~ (*Person*) a deep one; *Schlag ins* ~ *sl.* flop; *zu* ~ *und zu Lande* by sea and land; ~ *lassen* pass water; *unter* ~ *setzen* flood, submerge; *ins* ~ *fallen fig.* not to come off; *zu* ~ *werden fig.* come to naught, end in smoke; *das ist* ~ *auf seine Mühle* that is grist to his mill; *er kann ihm nicht das* ~ *reichen* he is not fit to hold a candle to her; *er ist mit allen* ~*n gewaschen* he knows all the tricks; *mir läuft das* ~ *im Munde zusammen* my mouth waters; *fig. sich mühsam über* ~ *halten* keep one's head barely above water; *s. abgraben*; '⌂**-abstoßend** water-repellent; '⌂**-arm** ill supplied with water, arid; '**~ball** *m* beach-ball; *s. Wasserballspiel*; '**~ballspiel** *n Sport:* water polo; '**~bau** *m* hydraulic engineering; '**~behälter** *m* reservoir; ⊕ cistern, tank; '**~bett** *n* water bed; '**~blase** *f* bubble; *auf der Haut:* blister; vesicle; '**~bombe** *f* depth charge; '**~bruch** ♂ *m* hydrocele.
Wässerchen ['vɛsər-] *n* (6): *fig. er sah aus, als könne er kein* ~ *trüben* he looked as though butter would not melt in his mouth.
'**Wasser|dampf** *m* water vapo(u)r,

steam; '2**dicht** waterproof; ⚓ water-
-tight; ~ *sein a.* hold water; '~-**eimer**
m pail, bucket; '~-**enthärter** *m* water
softener; '~**fahrzeug** *n* watercraft,
vessel; '~**fall** *m* waterfall; *kleiner od.*
künstlicher: cascade; *großer:* cataract; '~**farbe** *f* water-colo(u)r; '~-
fläche *f* (*Oberfläche*) surface of (the)
water; (*weite Strecke*) sheet of water;
'~**flasche** *f* water-bottle; '~**floh** *m*
water-flea; '~**flugzeug** *n* seaplane,
hydroplane; '~**flut** *f* flood; '~**fracht** *f*
waterfreight; '~**glas** *n* water-glass (*a.*
⚗); (*Trinkglas ohne Fuß*) tumbler; *s.*
Sturm; '~**graben** *m* drain; ⚔ moat;
'~**hahn** *m* (water-)tap, *Am. a.* faucet;
'2**haltig** containing water; 🜄 hy-
drated; '~**haushalt** *m* water economy; ⚗ water equilibrium; '~**heil**-
kunde *f* hydrotherapy; '~**hose** *f*
waterspout; '~**huhn** *n* coot.

wässerig ['vɛsəriç] watery; 🜄 *Lö-*
sung: aqueous; ⚗ serous; *fig.*
washy; *j-m den Mund* ~ *machen*
make a p.'s mouth water.

'**Wasser**|**kasten** *m* water tank; '~-
kessel *m* kettle; ⊕ boiler; '~**klo**-
sett *n* water-closet (*abbr.* W.C.);
'~**kopf** *m* ⚗ hydrocephalus; '~-
kraft *f* waterpower; '~**kraftwerk**
n hydroelectric power plant; '~-
krug *m* water-jug, pitcher; '~**küh**-
lung ⊕ *f* water-cooling (system);
mit ~ water-cooled; '~**kunst** *f* artificial fountain; '~**kur** *f* water-cure;
'~**lauf** *m* watercourse; '~**leiche** *f*
drowned corpse; '~**leitung** *f* water
pipes *pl.*, (water-)main; aqueduct;
'~**leitungsrohr** *n* water-pipe; '~**lilie**
f water-lily; '~**linie** ⚓ *f* water-line;
'2**löslich** water-soluble; '~**mangel**
m water famine (*od.* shortage); '~-
mann *ast. m* Watercarrier, Aquar-
ius, *Am. a.* Water Bearer; '~**mantel**
⊕ *m* water jacket; '~**melone** *f* water-
-melon; '~**messer** *m* hydrometer,
waterga(u)ge; '~**mühle** *f* water-mill.

wassern ≋ ['vasərn] (29) alight on
water.

wässern ['vɛsərn] (29) (*be~*; *ver~*)
water; (*be~*) irrigate; (*einweichen*)
water-soak; *phot.* wash.

'**Wasser**|**nymphe** *f* water-nymph,
naiad; '~**pflanze** *f* aquatic plant;
'~**pistole** *f* water pistol; '~**pocken**
f|*pl.* chicken-pox; '~**polizei** *f* river
police; '~**rad** *n* water-wheel; '~-
ratte *f* water-rat; F *fig.* enthusiastic

swimmer; '2**reich** abounding in
water; '~**reservoir** *n* reservoir,
(water) tank; '~**rohr** *n* water-pipe;
'~**rutschbahn** *f* water-chute; '~-
säule *f* water column; '~**schaden**
m damage caused by water; '~-
scheide *f* watershed, *Am. a.* divide;
'2**scheu**[1] afraid of water; '~**scheu**[2]
f dread of water, F water-funk; '~-
schi *m* water-ski; ~ *fahren* go (*od.*
do) water-skiing; '~**schlange** *f*
water-snake; '~**schlauch** *m* water-
-hose; '~**schutzpolizei** *f* river police; '~**speier** *m* (7) gargoyle; '~**spie**-
gel *m* surface of the water; (*Wasser*-
stand) water level; '~**sport** *m* aquatic
sports *pl.*, aquatics *pl.*; '~**spülung** *f*
water flushing; '~**stand** *m* water
level; '~**stands-anzeiger** *m* water-
-level ga(u)ge; '~**stiefel** *m*|*pl.* water-
proof boots, waders *pl.*; '~**stoff** 🜄 *m*
hydrogen; '~**stoffbombe** *f* hydrogen bomb, hydrobomb, H-bomb;
'2**stoffhaltig** hydrogenous; ~**stoff**-
superoxyd ['~'zu:pər'ɔksy:t] *n* hydrogen peroxide; '~**strahl** *m* jet of
water; '~**straße** *f* waterway; '~**sucht**
f dropsy; '2**süchtig** dropsical; '~-
suppe *f* water-gruel; F *fig.* slops *pl.*;
'~**tank** *m* water tank; '~**tier** *n* aquatic
animal; '~**turm** *m* water-tower; '~-
uhr *f* water meter.

Wässerung ['vɛsəruŋ] *f vgl. wässern:*
watering; irrigation; soaking, steep-
ing; *phot.* washing.

'**Wasser**|**verbrauch** *m* water con-
sumption; '~**verdrängung** *f* dis-
placement (of water); '~**ver**-
schmutzung *f* water pollution; '~-
versorgung *f* water supply; '~**vogel**
m aquatic bird, *pl. a.* water-fowl;
'~**waage** *f* spirit-level; '~**weg** *m* wa-
ter-way; *auf dem* ~ by water; '~**welle**
f (*Frisur*) water-wave; '~**werfer** *m*
water cannon; '~**werk**(**e** *pl.*) *n* water
works; '~**zähler** *m* water meter; '~-
zeichen *n* watermark.

wäßrig ['vɛsriç] *s. wässerig*.

waten ['vɑːtən] (26, sn) wade.

watschel|**ig** ['vɑːtʃəliç] waddling; '~**n**
(29, h. *u.* sn) waddle.

Watt[1] [vat] *m* 2) *geogr.* banks *pl.* of
sand, flats *pl.*; ~[2] (11, *im pl. mst inv.*)
⚡ watt; '~**e** *f* (15) cotton (wool); (*zum*
Ausstopfen) wadding; '~**ebausch** *m*
(cotton) swab *od.* pad; '~**epfropf** *m*
cotton plug; '~**e-stäbchen** ['~ʃtɛːp-
çən] *n* (6) cotton-wool tip; 2**ieren**

[ˌ'tiːrən] pad, wad; '⁓leistung ⚡ f wattage.

Watvogel ['vɑːt-] m wader.

wauwau ['vau'vau] 1. bow-wow!; 2. ♀ m (11) *Kindersprache*: bow-wow.

WC ['veː'tseː] n (11) lavatory, *Am.* restroom; **⁓-Reiniger** m toilet cleaner.

weben ['veːbən] (30) weave.

'**Weber** m (7) weaver; '⁓baum m loom-beam; ⁓ei [ˌ'rai] f (16) weaving; (*Gebäude*) weaving-mill; '⁓knecht zo. m harvestman, *Am.* daddy-longlegs; '⁓schiffchen n shuttle.

Web|fehler ['veː-p-] m (weaving) flaw; '⁓stuhl m loom; '⁓waren f/pl. textiles, woven goods.

Wechsel ['veksəl] m (7) change; (*Aufeinanderfolge*) succession; (*regelmäßiger Personalaustausch*) a. ⚡ *Saat*♀) rotation; (*Tausch*) exchange; *v. Geldsorten*: a. change; ♱ bill (of exchange); (*monatliche Geldzuwendung*) allowance; *hunt.* runway, *Am.* trace; *Sport*: (*Stab*♀) (baton) change, (*Seiten*♀) change of ends; ⁓ *auf Sicht* bill payable at sight; *eigener* (*od. trockener*) ⁓ promissory note; *gezogener* (*od. trassierter*) ⁓ draft (*auf zwei Monate* at two months); *offener* ⁓ letter of credit; ⁓ *zum Inkasso* bill for collection; ⁓ *zum Verkauf* bill for negotiation; '⁓-agio n bill discount; '⁓-akzept n acceptance of a bill; '⁓-aussteller m drawer of a bill; '⁓bad ♣ n contrast bath; '⁓balg m changeling; '⁓bank f discount-house; '⁓beziehung f correlation; '⁓brief m bill of exchange; '⁓bürgschaft f guarantee for a bill of exchange; ⁓fälle ['ˌfɛlə] m/pl. vicissitudes, ups and downs of *life etc.*; '⁓fieber n intermittent fever; '⁓folge f alternation, rotation; '⁓frist f days pl. of grace; '⁓geld n change; '⁓gesang m antiphony, glee; '⁓gespräch n dialog(ue); '⁓getriebe ⊕ n change-gear, variable gear; '⁓gläubiger m, '⁓inhaber m holder of a bill of exchange, bill creditor; '♀haft changeable; '⁓jahre physiol. n/pl. climacteric (period) sg., menopause sg., change sg. of life; '⁓kurs m rate of exchange.

wechseln ['veksəln] v/t. u. v/i. (29) change; (*verschieden sein, ab⁓*) vary; (*austauschen, a. Briefe, Blicke,*

Schläge, Worte usw.) exchange; *Szene*: shift; (*ab⁓* [*lassen*]) alternate; *hunt.* pass; *die Kleider* ⁓ change (one's clothes); ⁓ *mit den Speisen usw.* vary.

'**Wechsel|nehmer** m (7) taker of a bill; '⁓protest m bill protest; '⁓recht n law of exchange; '⁓schuld f bill debt; '♀seitig mutual, reciprocal; '⁓seitigkeit f reciprocity; '⁓strom ⚡ m alternating current (*abbr.* AC, a-c); '⁓stube f exchange-office; '♀voll changeable; eventful; '⁓wähler m/pl. floating voters; '♀weise alternately, by turns; (*gegenseitig*) mutually; '⁓winkel m/pl. alternate angles; '⁓wirkung f reciprocal action od. effect, interaction.

Weck [vɛk] m (3), '⁓e f (15), '⁓en¹ m (6) roll; '♀en² (25) (a)wake, waken (a. fig.); F call; (*aufstören*) rouse (a. fig.); '⁓er m (7) (a)wakener; (*Uhr*) alarm-clock; '⁓ruf m reveille.

Wedel ['veːdəl] m (7) (*Fächer*) fan; (*Staub*⁓) duster; ♀ frond; '♀n v/t. u. v/i. (29) fan; wag (*mit dem Schwanz* the tail). [... nor.⟩

weder ['veːdər]: ⁓ ... *noch* neither⟨

Weg¹ [veːk] m (3) way; (*Pfad*) path; (*Straße*) road; (*Reise*♀) route; (*Gang*) walk; (*Durchgang*) passage; (*Strecke*) distance (a. *phys.*); ⊕ travel; *fig.* (*Art und Weise*; *Methode*) way; *fig.* (⁓ *zum Ziel*) course; *e-e Meile* ⁓es a distance of a mile; *am* ⁓e by the wayside; *auf gütlichem* ⁓e amicably; *fig. auf dem richtigen* ⁓ *sein* be on the right track; *er steht mir im* ⁓e he is in my way; *s-r* ⁓e (*od. s-s* ⁓es) *gehen* go one's way(s); *aus dem* ⁓e *gehen* get out of the way, stand aside; *fig.* (*dat.*) (*vermeiden*) avoid, steer clear of; *j-m weit aus dem* ⁓e *gehen* give a p. a wide berth; *aus dem* ⁓e *räumen od. schaffen* remove (a. *fig. j-n*); *et. in die* ⁓e *leiten* set on foot, initiate, (*vorbereiten*) prepare; *ich traue ihm nicht über den* ⁓ I don't trust him round the corner; s. *ebnen, machen, halb.*

weg² [vɛk] away, off; (⁓*gegangen usw.*) gone; (*verloren*) gone, lost; ⁓ *da*! be off!; ⁓ *damit*! off with it!, take it away!; *Hände* ⁓! hands off!; F *ich muß* ⁓ I must be off; F *völlig od. ganz* ⁓ (*von Sinnen*) (clean) gone, (*erstaunt*) flabbergasted.

'**wegbekommen** get off; (*verstehen*) get the knack of; *e-e Krankheit:* catch.

Wegbereiter ['ve:k-] *m* pioneer.

weg|blasen ['vɛk-] blow away; *fig. wie weggeblasen* clean gone; '**~bleiben** (sn) stay away; (*ausgelassen werden*) be omitted; '**~blicken** look away; '**~bringen** take away; *Sache, Fleck: a.* remove.

Wege|lagerer ['ve:gəla:gərər] *m* (7) highwayman; '**~meister** *m* road-surveyor.

wegen ['ve:gən] (*gen. od. dat.*) because of, on account of, by reason of; (*um ... willen*) for the sake of, for; *von Amts* ~ ex officio, officially; *von Rechts* ~ by right; ɪ̯̃ ~ *Diebstahls* for larceny; F *von* ~! that's what you think!

'**Wegerecht** *n* right of way.

Wegerich ♀ ['ve:gəriç] *m* (3) plantain.

weg|fahren ['vɛk-] *v/t.* remove; *v/i.* leave; *im Wagen:* drive away; '**2-fall** *m* (*Auslassung*) omission; (*Aufhören*) cessation; (*Abschaffung*) *a. weitS. v. Gründen, Hindernissen*) removal; *in* ~ *kommen* = '**~fallen** (sn) fall away; (*ausgelassen werden*) be omitted *od.* dropped; (*nicht in Frage kommen*) be inapplicable; (*aufhören*) cease; (*abgeschafft werden*) be abolished; (*ausfallen*) not to take place; ~ *lassen* drop, leave out; '**~fangen,** F '**~fischen** snatch away (*j-m et. a th.* from under a p.'s nose); '**~fegen** sweep away (*a. fig.*); '**~führen** lead (*od.* take) away; '**2gang** *m* departure; '**~geben** give away; '**~gehen** (sn) go away *od.* off; *Ware:* sell; ~ *über* (*acc.*) pass over (*a. fig.*); '**~haben** have got *one's* share; *fig.* (*gut verstehen*) have got the hang of; '**~helfen** (*dat.*) help *a p.* to get away; '**~holen** take away; '**~jagen** drive (*od.* chase) away; '**~kommen** (sn) get away *od.* off; (*abhanden kommen*) be lost; *fig. gut usw.* ~ come off well *etc.*, get a good *etc.* deal; '**~lassen** let go; *Sache:* leave out, omit; '**2-lassung** *f* omission; '**~laufen** run away; '**~legen** lay (*od.* put) aside; '**~machen** take away, remove; *Fleck:* take out; *sich* ~ make off; '**~müssen: ich muß weg** I must go; *der Hund usw. muß weg* (*abgeschafft werden*) must go; **2nahme** ['~na:-mə] *f* (15) taking (away) (*a.* ɪ̯̃ɪ̯̃); (*Beschlagnahme*) seizure; ⚔, ⚓ capture; '**~nehmen** take away (*j-m* from a p.); (*beschlagnahmen*) seize; *Raum, Zeit usw.:* take up, occupy; ⚔, ⚓ capture; '**~packen** pack away; *sich* ~ pack off; '**~putzen** wipe away; F (*abschießen*) pick off; F (*essen*) polish off; '**~raffen** carry off; '**~räumen** clear away, remove; '**~reisen** (sn) depart, leave; *s. verreisen*; '**~reißen** tear (*od.* snatch) away (*j-m* from a p.); *durch Sturm usw.:* sweep (*od.* carry) away; '**~rücken** move away (*a. v/i.*); '**~schaffen** clear away, remove, do away with; ⚕ eliminate; *sich* '**~scheren** be off; '**~schicken** send away *od.* off, dispatch; (*sich*) '**~schleichen** steal away; '**~schleppen** drag off; '**~schließen** lock up (*od.* away); '**~schmeißen** F throw away; '**~schnappen** snatch away (*j-m et. a th.* from a p.).

Wegschnecke ['ve:k-] *f* slug.

weg|sehen ['vɛk-] look away; ~ *über* (*acc.*) shut one's eyes to a th.; '**~sein** be away *od.* absent; (*weggegangen usw.*); *a. verloren sein*; F *verzückt sein*) be gone; ~ *über* (*acc.*) have got over *a th.*; '**~setzen** *v/t.* put away; *sich* ~ *über* (*acc.*) *fig.* disregard; *v/i.* (sn) ~ *über* (*acc.*) jump (over) *a th.*, clear *a th.*; '**~streben** *von* tend from.

Wegstrecke ['ve:k-] *f* stretch (of road); *zurückgelegte:* distance covered, mileage.

weg|streichen ['vɛk-] strike out, cancel; '**~treten** (sn) step aside; ⚔ break the ranks; '**~tun** put away *od.* aside, remove; (*tu die*) *Hände weg!* (take your) hands off!

Wegweiser ['ve:k-] *m* (7) signpost, guidepost; *im Gebäude:* directory; (*Person, Buch*) guide.

weg|wenden ['vɛk-] (*a. sich*) turn away *od.* off; *bsd. Gesicht:* avert; '**~werfen** throw away; *fig. sich* ~ throw o.s. away (*an j-n* on a p.), degrade o.s.; '**~werfend** disparaging; '**2werfflasche** *f* non-returnable bottle; '**2werfgesellschaft** *f* throw--away society; '**2werfpackung** *f* throw-away pack; '**~wischen** wipe off; '**~zaubern** spirit away.

Wegzehrung ['ve:k-] *f* provisions

pl. for the journey; *eccl. letzte:* viaticum.

wegziehen ['vɛk-] *v/t.* pull (*od.* draw) away; *v/i.* (sn) *aus der Wohnung:* (re)move; ✗ march away.

weh [ve:] **1.** sore, aching; ⸯ*! woe!;* ⸯ *mir! woe is me!;* ⸯe *dir usw.! woe* be to you *etc.!, allg.* just you wait!; ⸯ *tun* ache; *j-m:* pain (*od.* hurt) a p., cause a p. pain; *seelisch:* a. grieve a p.; *sich* ⸯ *tun* hurt o.s.; **2.** ⸰ *n* (3, *o. pl.*) pain; *seelisch:* a. grief; *s. wohl* **2.**

Wehe[1] ['ve:ə] *f* (15) (*Schnee*⸰, *Sand*⸰) drift; ⸯ**[2]:** ⸯn *pl.* labo(u)r (-pains); *fig.* travail; ⸰n *v/i. u. v/t.* (25) blow; (*fort*ⸯ) drift, waft; (*flattern*) flutter, wave; *fig. Geist:* live.

'**Weh|geschrei** *n* woeful cries *pl.*, wail; 'ⸯ**klage** *f* lament(ation); '⸰**klagen** lament (*um* for; *über acc.* over); '⸰**leidig** snivel(l)ing; 'ⸯ**mut** *f inv.* melancholy, sadness; *über Vergangenes:* nostalgia; ⸰**mütig** ['ⸯmy:tiç] sad, melancholy; nostalgic.

Wehr[1] [ve:r] *f* (16) (*Ab*⸰) defen|ce, *Am.* -se, resistance; (*Waffe*) weapon; (*Panzer*) armo(u)r; (*Schutz*⸰) bulwark; *sich zur* ⸯ *setzen* show (*od.* put up a) fight, *gegen:* struggle against, oppose; *s. a.* (*sich*) wehren; ⸯ**[2]** *n* (3) weir; 'ⸯ**beauftragte** *m* ombudsman (for the Armed Forces); 'ⸯ**bereich** *m* military district; 'ⸯ**bereichskommando** *n* military district headquarters *od.* command; 'ⸯ**dienst** ✗ *m* military service; 'ⸯ**dienstbeschädigung** *f* disability incurred in line of duty; '⸰**diensttauglich** fit for military service; '⸰**dienst-untauglich** unfit for military service; 'ⸯ**dienstverweigerer** *m* conscientious objector; '⸰**en** (25) (*dat.*) restrain, check; *dem Feuer* ⸯ arrest (*od.* check) the spread of fire; *sich* ⸯ defend o.s., offer resistance; 'ⸯ**ersatzdienst** *m* alternative service (for conscientious objectors); 'ⸯ**fähig** fit for military service, able-bodied; '⸰**los** defen|celess, *Am.* -seless; (*waffenlos*) unarmed; (*hilflos*) helpless; ⸯ *machen* disarm; 'ⸯ**losigkeit** *f* defen|celessness, *Am.* -selessness; 'ⸯ**pflicht** *f:* (*allgemeine*) ⸯ (universal) compulsory military service, (universal) conscription; '⸰**pflichtig** liable to military service;

'ⸯ**sold** *m* (service) pay; 'ⸯ**stammrolle** *f* service roster; 'ⸯ**technik** *f* defen|ce (*Am.* -se) technology.

Weib †, P [vaɪp] *n* (1) woman; (*Gattin*) wife; 'ⸯ**chen** *n* (6) little woman *od.* wife; *v. Tieren:* female.

Weiber... ['ⸯbər] *mst* women's; 'ⸯ**art** *f* women's way(s *pl.*); 'ⸯ**feind** *m* woman-hater, misogynist; 'ⸯ**geschwätz** *n* female gossip; 'ⸯ**held** *m* lady-killer, lady's man; 'ⸯ**herrschaft** *f,* 'ⸯ**regiment** *n* petticoat-government; 'ⸯ**volk** F *n* women(folk *sg.*) *pl.*

weib|isch ['ⸯbiʃ] womanish, effeminate; ⸯ**lich** ['vaɪp-] *Geschlecht:* female, *gr.* feminine; *Wesensart:* womanly, feminine; *das ewig* ⸰e the Eternal Woman; '⸰**lichkeit** *f* womanliness; *die holde* ⸯ the fair sex.

'**Weibsbild** *n* female, *sl.* broad.

weich [vaɪç] soft (*a. fig.*); (*zart*) tender (*a. Fleisch*); (*schwach*) weak; *s.* weichherzig; ⸯ *werden* soften; *fig.* (*nachgeben*) yield; (*milder werden*) soften, relent; (*gerührt werden*) be moved (*bei* at); '⸰**bild** *n* precincts *pl.*, municipal area; (*Außenbezirke*) outskirts *pl.*; '⸰**e**[1] *f* (15) *anat.* flank, side; (*Leiste*) groin; '⸰**e**[2] *f* 🚋 switch, *Brt. a.* points *pl.*; ⸯn *stellen* throw the switch, *fig.* set a new course; 'ⸯ**en**[1] *v/i.* (30, sn) give way, yield; ✗ retreat; *Preise:* decline, fall; *von j-m* ⸯ leave, abandon; *j-m nicht von der Seite* ⸯ not to budge from a p.'s side; 'ⸯ**en**[2] (25) *s.* aufweichen.

'**Weichensteller** 🚋 *m* (7) pointsman. *bsd. Am.* switchman.

'**weichgekocht:** ⸯe *Eier* soft-boiled eggs.

'**Weichheit** *f s.* weich: softness; tenderness; weakness.

'**weichherzig** tender-hearted; '⸰**keit** *f* tender-heartedness.

'**weich|lich** soft, tender; *Nahrung, Empfinden:* sloppy; *fig.* weak, effeminate; soft; '⸰**lichkeit** *f* tenderness; sloppiness; effeminacy, softness; '⸰**ling** *m* (3[1]) weakling, mollycoddle, F softie; '⸰**macher** ⊕ *m* softener, softening agent.

Weichsel|kirsche ['vaɪksəl-] *f* mahaleb-cherry; 'ⸯ**rohr** *n* cherrywood tube.

Weich|spüler ['ⸯʃpy:lər] *m* (7) soft-

ener; *für Haare*: conditioner; '⌄teile
anat. m/pl. soft parts; '⌄tier *n* mollusc.

Weide[1] ♀ ['vaɪdə] *f* (15) willow;
(*Korb*♀) osier; '⌄[2] ✔ *f* pasture; *auf
der* ⌄ *at grass; auf die* ⌄ *gehen*
(*schicken*) go (send) to grass; '⌄land *n*
pasture-land *od.* -ground.

weiden ['vaɪdən] *v/i. u. v/t.* (26)
graze, pasture; *Vieh* ⌄ (*lassen*) put
to pasture *od.* grass; *s-e Augen* (*a.
sich*) ⌄ *an* (*dat.*) feast one's eyes on,
b.s. gloat over *a th.*

'**Weiden|baum** *m* willow-tree; '⌄-
kätzchen ♀ *n* willow-catkin; '⌄-
korb *m* wicker-basket.

'**Weideplatz** *m* pasture-ground.

weid|gerecht ['vaɪt-] sportsman-
like; '⌄lich *adv.* thoroughly, greatly.

'**Weid|mann** *m* (1²) huntsman,
sportsman; ♀**männisch** ['⌄menɪʃ]
sportsmanlike; ⌄**manns'heil** *n*: ⌄!
good sport!; '⌄**werk** *n the* chase,
hunting.

weiger|n ['vaɪgərn] (29) (*sich*) re-
fuse; '♀**ung** *f* refusal.

Weih [vaɪ] *m* (12) (*Vogel*) kite.

'**Weihbischof** *m* suffragan (bishop).

Weihe[1] ['vaɪə] *f* (15) consecration;
(*Einweihung*) inauguration; *e-s Prie-
sters*: ordination; '⌄[2] *f s. Weih*; '♀n
(25) consecrate; *Priester*: ordain;
(*widmen*) devote, dedicate (*dat.* to);
dem Tode usw. **geweiht** doomed to
death *etc.*

Weiher ['vaɪər] *m* (7) (fish-)pond.

'**weihevoll** solemn.

Weihnacht|en ['vaɪnaxtən] *n* (6) *od.
f/pl.* (*inv., mst ohne art.*) Christmas,
verkürzt: Xmas; *Fröhliche* ⌄! Merry
Christmas!; ♀**lich** Christmas(sy).

'**Weihnachts|-abend** *m* Christmas
Eve; '⌄**baum** *m* Christmas-tree;
'⌄**bescherung** *f* (giving) Christmas
presents *pl.*; '⌄**(feier)tag** *m* Christmas Day; '⌄**fest** *n* Christmas;
'⌄**geld** *n s. Weihnachtsgratifikation*;
'⌄**geschäft** *n* Christmas business;
'⌄**geschenk** *n* Christmas present; '⌄-
gratifikation *f* Christmas bonus;
'⌄**lied** *n* Christmas carol; '⌄**mann** *m*
Father Christmas, Santa Claus; '⌄-
markt *m* Christmas fair; '⌄**zeit** *f*
Christmas-tide, Yuletide.

'**Weih|rauch** *m* incense; '⌄**rauch-
faß** *n* censer; '⌄**wasser** *n* holy
water; '⌄**wasserbecken** *n* (holy-
-water) font.

weil [vaɪl] because, since.

weiland † ['⌄lant] formerly, erst-
while, *bsd. Am.* onetime.

Weil|chen ['vaɪlçən] *n* (6): *ein* ⌄ a
little while; F a spell; *warte ein* ⌄
wait a bit; '⌄**e** *f* (15) a while, a
(space of) time; (*Muße*) leisure;
damit hat es gute ⌄ there is no
hurry (about it); *s. eilen*; '♀**en** (25)
stay; *zu lange*: tarry, linger.

Weiler ['vaɪlər] *m* (7) hamlet.

Wein [vaɪn] *m* (3) wine; (⌄*stock*)
vine; *wilder* ⌄ Virginia creeper;
s. rein 1; '⌄**bau** *m* wine-growing,
⫿ viticulture; '⌄**baugebiet** *n* wine-
-growing region; '⌄**bauer** *m* wine-
-grower; '⌄**beere** *f* grape; '⌄**berg** *m*
vineyard; '⌄**bergschnecke** *f* edible
snail; '⌄**blatt** *n* vine leaf; '⌄**brand** *m*
brandy.

wein|en ['vaɪnən] (25) weep (*um*;
vor dat. for); *laut*: cry; *dem* ♀ *nahe*
on the verge of tears; '⌄**erlich**
tearful; *Stimme, Ton*: whining,
lachrymose.

'**Wein|-ernte** *f* vintage; '⌄**-essig** *m*
wine-vinegar; '⌄**faß** *n* wine-cask;
'⌄**flasche** *f* wine-bottle; '⌄**garten**
m vineyard; '⌄**gärtner** *m* vine-
-dresser; wine-grower; '⌄**geist** *m*
spirit(s *pl.*) of wine; '⌄**glas** *n* wine-
glass; '⌄**händler** *m* wine-merchant;
'⌄**handlung** *f* wine shop; '⌄**jahr** *n*:
ein gutes (*schlechtes*) ⌄ a good (bad)
wine year (*od.* year for wine); '⌄-
karte *f* wine-list; '⌄**keller** *m* wine-
-cellar; '⌄**kellerei** *f* winery; '⌄**kelter**
f winepress; '⌄**kenner** *m* connoisseur of wine; '⌄**krampf** *m* crying fit;
'⌄**krug** *m* wine jug; '⌄**laub** *n* vine
leaves *pl.*; '⌄**laube** *f* vine arbo(u)r;
'⌄**lese** *f* vintage; '⌄**leser(in** *f*) *m* vintager; '⌄**most** *m* must; '⌄**presse** *f*
winepress; '⌄**probe** *f* wine-tasting;
'⌄**rebe** *f* (grape-)vine; '♀**rot** ruby
(-colo[u]red); '⌄**säure** *f* acidity of
wine; ⫿ tartaric acid; '⌄**schenke** *f*,
'⌄**stube** *f* wine tavern; '⌄**sorte** *f* sort
of wine; '⌄**stein** *m* tartar; '⌄**stock** *m*
vine; '⌄**traube** *f* bunch of grapes;
(*Beere*) grape; '⌄**trester** *pl.* skins (*od.*
husks) *pl.* of pressed grapes.

weise[1] ['vaɪzə] 1. wise; 2. ♀ *m* (18)
wise man, sage; *die* ⌄*n aus dem
Morgenland* the (three) Magi; *Stein
der* ⌄*n* philosophers' stone.

Weise[2] [⌄] *f* (15) manner, way; ♪
melody, tune; *auf diese* ⌄ in this

way; *auf jede* ~ in every way; *in keiner* ~ in no way; *in der* ~, *daß* in such a way that, so that; *in Zssgn mst durch adv. z.B. natürlicherweise* naturally; '♀n (30) *v/t.* point out, show; ~ *an* (*acc.*) refer to; *j-n* ~ *nach* direct to; *von sich* ~ refuse, reject; *aus dem Lande* ~ banish, exile; *j-m die Tür* ~ show a p. the door; *das wird sich* ~ we shall see; *v/i.* ~ *auf* (*acc.*) point at *od.* to.

'**Weiser** *m* (7) pointer; indicator; *s. Weg♀.*

Weis|heit ['vaɪshaɪt] *f* wisdom; *mit s-r* ~ *zu Ende sein* be at one's wit's end; '**~heitszahn** *m* wisdom-tooth; '♀**lich** wisely, prudently; '♀**machen:** *j-m et.* ~ make a p. believe a th., tell a p. a yarn; *laß dir nichts* ~! don't be fooled!; *mach das anderen weis!* tell that to the marines!

weiß [vaɪs] white; *gebrochen* ~ off--white; *das* ♀*e Haus* (*in Washington*) the White House; *der* ♀*e Sonntag* the Low Sunday; *das* ♀*e im Auge, im Ei* the white; *s. schwarz.*

'**weis|sagen** foretell, predict, prophesy; '♀**sager**(**in** *f*) *m* prophet(ess *f*); '♀**sagung** *f* prophecy, prediction.

'**Weiß|bier** *n* wheat beer; '**~blech** *n* tinplate; '**~brot** *n* white bread; '**~buch** *pol. n* white paper, *Am.* white book; '**~buche** ♀ *f* white beech; '**~dorn** ♀ *m* whitethorn; '**~e** (18) *m* white man; *f* white woman; '♀**en** (27) whiten; (*tünchen*) whitewash; '**~fisch** *m* whiting, dace; *kleinerer:* whitebait; '♀**gelb** pale yellow; '**~gerber** *m* tawer; '♀**glühend** white-hot; '**~glut** *f* white heat; '♀**haarig** white--haired; '**~käse** *m* curds *pl.*; '**~kohl** ♀ *m* (white-heart) cabbage; '♀**lich** whitish; '**~metall** *n* white metal; '**~näherei** *f* plain (needle-)work; '**~näherin** *f* plain seamstress; '**~tanne** ♀ *f* white fir; '**~waren** *f/pl.* linen goods *pl.*; '**~waschen:** *j-n* ~ white-wash a p.; '**~wein** *m* white wine; hock; '**~zeug** *n* (household-)linen.

Weisung ['vaɪzuŋ] *f* direction, directive; instruction, order; '**~sbefugnis** *f* authority to issue directives; '♀**sgebunden** subject to directions; '♀**sgemäß** as instructed.

weit [vaɪt] *adj.* (*Ggs. nah*) distant,

far; (*ausgedehnt*) extensive; (*breit*) broad; *bsd.* ⊕ wide; (*Ggs. eng*) wide, (*lose*) loose (*a.* ⊕); (*geräumig*) large; *adv.* far; wide(ly); *ein* ~*er Weg* a long way; ~ *entfernt* far away, *fig.* far from it; ~ *und breit* far and wide; ~*es Gewissen* elastic conscience; 5 *Meter* ~ (a distance of) five met|res (*Am.* -ers); *e-e Meile* ~ (*entfernt*) a mile off; *bei* ~*em vor comp. od. sup.* by far; *bei* ~*em nicht so gut* not nearly so good; *von* ~*em* from afar, from a distance; *im* ~*esten Sinne* in the broadest sense; *ich bin so* ~ I am ready; *es ist noch nicht so* ~ things have not come to that point yet; *es ist nicht* ~ *her mit ... ...* is (are) not worth much, *sl.* ... is (are) not so hot; *fig. zu* ~ *gehen* go too far; *s. bringen, fehlen, herholen, Weite, weiter;* '~'**ab** far away (*von* from); '**~aus** (by) far; '♀**blick** *m* far-sightedness; '**~blickend** far-sighted.

'**Weite** 1. *f* (15) wideness, width; largeness; (*Ferne*) distance; 2. *das* ~ *suchen* decamp; '♀**n** (26) (*a. sich*) widen, enlarge, expand, *fig. a.* broaden; *Schuhe:* stretch.

'**weiter** wider; (*entfernter*) more distant, farther, (*bsd. fig.*) further; ~! go on!; *nichts* ~ nothing more *od.* else; *und so* ~ and so forth *od.* on, et cetera (*abbr.* etc., &c.); *das* ♀*e* the rest; ♀*es* (*Genaueres*) further details; more; *bis auf* ~*es* until further notice; *ohne* ~*es* without further ado, (*mühelos*) easily, (*sofort*) readily, off-hand; '**~befördern** forward, send on; '**~beschäftigen** continue to employ; '♀**beschäftigung** *f* continued employment; '**~bestand** *m* continued existence, survial; '**~bestehen** continue to exist, survive; '**~bilden** develop; *sich* ~ continue one's studies, develop one's knowledge; '**~bringen** help on; *es* ~ (*im Leben*) get on; *das bringt mich nicht weiter* that's not much help; '♀**e** *n s. weiter;* '**~erzählen** tell others, repeat; '**~führen** carry on; '**~geben** pass on; '**~gehen** (*sn*) go on, walk on, pass on; (*fortfahren*) continue; *das kann so nicht* ~! things cannot go on like this!; '**~hin** in future, further on; (*ferner*) further(more); ~ *tun* continue to do, keep doing; '**~kommen** (*sn*) get on; *fig. a.* (make) progress, advance; '⟋**können** be able to go on; '⟋**leben 1.** live on, survive (*a. fig.*); **2.** ⚦ *n* survial; '⟋**leiten** *Brief usw.*: forward, transmit; *Antrag usw.*: refer (*an acc.* to); '⟋**lesen** *v/i. u. v/t.* go on (reading), continue reading; '⟋**machen** carry on, continue; '⟋**sagen** tell others; '⚦**ungen** *f/pl.* complications, (unpleasant) consequences; '⚦**ver-arbeitung** *f* processing, finishing; '⟋**verbreiten** spread, retail.

'**weit|gehend** extensive, large, far-reaching; *Behauptung*: sweeping; *Vollmacht*: wide; *adv.* largely; '⟋**her:** *von* ⟋ from afar; '⟋**herzig** broad-minded; '⟋**hin** far off; '⟋**läufig** (*ausgedehnt*) extensive, vast; (*geräumig*) spacious; (*ausführlich*) detailed; *s. weitschweifig; Dorf usw.*: straggling; *Verwandter*: distant; *adv.* at great length; ⟋ *verwandt* distantly related; '⚦**läufigkeit** *f* vast extent; *s. Weitschweifigkeit; pl. s. Weiterungen*; '⟋**maschig** wide-meshed; '⟋**reichend** far-reaching; '⟋**schweifig** diffuse, lengthy, long-winded; '⚦**schweifigkeit** *f* diffuseness, lengthiness, prolixity; '⟋**sichtig** long-sighted, (*a. fig.*) far-sighted; '⚦**sichtigkeit** *f* long-sightedness; '⚦**sprung** *m* long (*Am.* broad) jump; '⟋**tragend** long-range; *fig.* far-reaching; '⟋**verbreitet** *Ansicht usw.*: widespread; '⟋**verzweigt** widely ramified; '⚦**winkel-objektiv** *opt. n* wide-angle lens.

Weizen ['vaɪtsən] *m* (6) wheat; *fig. sein* ⟋ *blüht* he is in clover; '⟋**mehl** *n* wheat(en) flour.

welch [vɛlç] (21¹) *interr. pron.* what; *auswählend*: which; *rel. pron.* who, which, that; ⟋**er** (*auch*) *immer* who(so)ever; ⟋ *ein Mann!* what a man!; *unbestimmtes Fürwort*: some, any, *z.B. haben Sie Geld? ja, ich habe* ⟋**es** yes, I have some; *brauchen Sie* ⟋**es?** do you want any?; ⟋**erlei** ['⟋ərlaɪ] *Art usw.* of what kind *etc.*

welk [vɛlk] withered, faded (*a. fig. Reize, Schönheit*); (*schlaff*) flabby; '⟋**en** (25, sn) fade, wither.

Wellblech ['vɛlblɛç] *n* corrugated sheet iron; '⟋**baracke** *f* tin hut, *Am.* ✕ Quonset hut.

Welle ['vɛlə] *f* (15) **1.** wave (*a. im Haar*, ⚡, ✕ *Angriffs*⚦, *fig. der Begeisterung usw.*); *stärkere*: billow;

(*Sturz*⚦) breaker; *Radio*: wave (-length); *mot. grüne* ⟋ progressive signal system; **2.** ⊕ shaft, axle; '⚦**n** (25) *Haar*: (*a. sich*) wave.

'**Wellen|band** *n Radio*: (wave-) band; '⟋**bereich** *m Radio*: wave-range; '⟋**bewegung** *f* undulation; '⟋**brecher** ⚓ *m* breakwater; ⚦**förmig** ['⟋fœrmiç] undulatory, wavy; '⟋**gang** *m* swell; '⟋**länge** *f Radio*: wave-length; '⟋**linie** *f* wavy line; '⟋**reiten** *n* surfing; '⟋**schlag** *m* wash (*od.* dashing) of the waves; '⟋**sittich** *m* budgerigar, Australian grass parakeet, love-bird; '⟋**tal** *n* wave trough; '⟋**theorie** *f* wave theory.

wellig ['vɛliç] wavy.

'**Wellpappe** *f* corrugated board.

Welpe ['vɛlpə] *m* (13) whelp, puppy.

welsch [vɛlʃ] Roman, Latin, southern (*Italian, French, etc.*).

Welt [vɛlt] *f* (16) world (*a. fig. der Kunst usw.*); *alle* ⟋ all the world; *die ganze* ⟋ the whole world; *auf der* ⟋ in the world; *auf der ganzen* ⟋ *bekannt* known all over the world; *was in aller* ⟋ *...?* what in the world (*od.* on earth) *...?*; *um alles in der* ⟋*!* for goodness sake!; *in die* ⟋ *setzen* put into the world; *zur* ⟋ *bringen* give birth to; *zur* ⟋ *kommen* be born; *aus der* ⟋ *schaffen* get rid of, remove.

'**welt|'-abgeschieden** secluded (from the world); '⟋'-**abgewandt** detached from the world; '⚦-**all** *n* universe; '⚦-**alter** *n* age; '⟋**-anschaulich** ideological; '⚦-**anschauung** *f* Weltanschauung, philosophy (of life), world-outlook; (*Ideologie*) ideology; '⚦-**atlas** *m* world atlas; '⚦-**ausstellung** *f* World Fair; '⚦-**bank** *f* World Bank; '⟋**bekannt,** '⟋**berühmt** world-renowned, world-famed; universally known; '⚦**best...** world-best; '⚦**bewegend:** *nicht* ⟋ *iro. sl.* not so hot; '⚦**bild** *n* view of life; '⚦**bürger** *m* citizen of the world, cosmopolite; '⚦**en-bummler** *m* globe-trotter; '⚦-**ereignis** *n* event of world-wide importance; '⟋**-erfahren** experienced in the ways of the world, worldly wise; '⚦-**erfahrung** *f* experience in the ways of the world.

Weltergewicht(ler *m*) *n* ['vɛltər-] *Boxen*: welter-weight.

'**welt|-erschütternd** world-shaking; '⁀firma f world-renowned firm; '⁀fremd ignorant of the world; unrealistic; (idealistisch) starry-eyed; Gelehrter usw.: ivory-towered; '⁀friede(n) m universal peace; '⁀gefüge n cosmic system; '⁀geltung f international reputation; '⁀gericht n last judg(e)ment; '⁀geschichte f universal history; '⁀gewandt versed in the ways of the world; '⁀gewandtheit f savoir faire (fr.); '⁀ge'werkschaftsbund m World Federation of Trade Unions; '⁀handel m international trade; '⁀herrschaft f world supremacy; '⁀karte f map of the world; '⁀kenntnis f knowledge of the world; '⁀kind n worldling, child of this world; '⁀klug worldly-wise, politic(ally adv.); '⁀klugheit f worldly wisdom; '⁀krieg m world war; der Erste (Zweite) ⁀ World War I (World War II); '⁀kugel f globe; '⁀lage f international situation; '⁀lauf m course of the world.

'weltlich worldly; (Ggs. geistlich) secular, temporal; ⁀e Schule secular school; ⁀ gesinnt worldly-minded.

'Welt|literatur f universal literature; '⁀macht f world power; '⁀machtpolitik f imperialist policy, imperialism; '⁀mann m man of the world; '⁀männisch gentlemanly, man-of-the-world; '⁀markt m world market; '⁀meer n ocean; '⁀meister(in f) m world champion; '⁀meisterschaft f world championship; '⁀öffentlichkeit f world public; '⁀ordnung f system of the world; '⁀politik f international (od. world-)politics pl.; '⁀postver-ein m (Universal) Postal Union.

'Weltraum m (outer) space; (für Zssgn s. Raum...).

'Welt|reich n world empire; '⁀reise f journey round the world, world tour; '⁀reisende m, f globe-trotter; '⁀rekord m world('s) record; ⁀rekordler ['⁀rekɔrtlər] m, '⁀rekordmann m world-record holder; '⁀ruf m world-wide renown; '⁀schmerz m world-weariness, Weltschmerz; '⁀'sicherheitsrat m U.N. Security Council; '⁀sprache f universal language; '⁀stadt f metropolis; '⁀teil m part of the world, continent; '⁀umfassend world-wide, global; '⁀umsegler m circum-

navigator (of the globe); '⁀um-spannend world-wide; '⁀untergang m end of the world; '⁀weise m philosopher; '⁀weis-heit f philosophy; '⁀weit world-wide; '⁀wirtschaft f world (od. international) economy; '⁀wirtschaftskrise f world-wide economic crisis; '⁀wunder n wonder of the world, prodigy.

wem [ve:m] to whom; von ⁀ of whom; by whom.

wen [ve:n] whom; F (jemand) somebody.

Wend|e¹ ['vɛndə] m (13), '⁀in f (16¹) Wend; ⁀² f (15) turn(ing); (Wendepunkt) turning-point (a. fig.). '**Wendekreis** m geogr. tropic; ⁀ des Krebses Tropic of Cancer; mot. turning circle.

'**Wendel** ⊕ f helix; '⁀treppe f (eine a flight of) winding stairs pl., spiral staircase.

wend|en ['vɛndən] v/t. u. v/i. (30) (a. sich) turn (about od. round); Buchseite usw.: turn over; Geld usw. ⁀ an (acc.) spend on; Mühe, Zeit usw.: devote to; bitte ⁀! please turn over! (abbr. p.t.o.); mit ⁀der Post by return of post; sich ⁀ an j-n (ansprechen) address (o.s. to) to a p., um Auskunft, Erlaubnis usw.: apply to a p. (um for), um Rat: consult (od. see) a p., um Hilfe: turn (od. appeal) to a p.; sich ⁀ gegen turn against od. on; '⁀epunkt m turning-point (a. fig.); '⁀ig (behend) nimble, agile (a. Geist); fig. flexible; P.: versatile; Auto usw.: manœuvrable, Am. a. maneuverable; '⁀ung f turn (-ing); ✗ facing, turn; fig. turn, change (zum Besseren for the better); (Wort⁀) s. Redensart.

wenig ['ve:niç] little; pl. few; ⁀er less, A a. minus; pl. fewer; das ⁀ste the least; am ⁀sten least; mit ⁀en Worten in a few words; (noch) ein ⁀ a little (more); nicht ⁀er als no less than, pl. no(t) fewer than; nichts ⁀er als anything but; '⁀keit f small quantity; (Kleinigkeit) little, trifle; meine ⁀ my humble self; '⁀stens at least; wenn ⁀ ... if only.

wenn [vɛn] zeitlich: when; bedingend: if; ⁀ nicht if not, unless; s. außer; (vorausgesetzt) provided (that); ⁀ nur if only; ⁀ auch (al-)though, even if od. though; ⁀ auch *noch so* ... however ...; ~ ... *nicht gewesen wäre* but for ...; *und* ~ *nun* ...?, *was macht es,* ~ ...? what if ...?; F (*na,*) ~ *schon!* so what?; ~ *man von* ... *spricht* speaking of ...; *wie wäre es,* ~ *wir jetzt heimgingen?* how about going home now?; *ohne* ♀ *und Aber* with no "ifs" or "buts"; ~'**gleich,** ~'**schon** although, though.

wer [veːr] (24) *rel. pron.* who, he who; *interr. pron.* who?; *auswählend*: which?; ~ *auch* (*immer*) who(so)ever; ✗ ~ *da?* who goes there?; F *indef. pron.* (*jemand*) somebody, anybody.

Werbe... ['vɛrbə-] propaganda, *bsd.* ✝ advertising, publicity; '~**abteilung** *f* advertising (*od.* publicity) department; '~**agentur** *f* advertising agency; '~**aktion** *f s.* Werbefeldzug; '~**assistent(in** *f*) *m* advertising assistant; '~**berater** *m* advertising consultant; '~**büro** *n* advertising agency; '~**etat** *m* advertising budget; '~**fachmann** *m* advertising agent; '~**feldzug** *m* publicity campaign, (advertising) drive; '~**fernsehen** *n* television commercials *pl.*; '~**film** *m* advertising film; '~**funk** *m* radio commercials *pl.*; '~**graphik** *f* commercial art; '~**graphiker** *m* commercial artist; '~**kampagne** *f s.* Werbefeldzug; '~**kosten** *pl.* advertising costs; '~**leiter** *m* advertising (*od.* publicity) manager; '~**mittel** *n* advertising medium (*pl.* media).

werb|en ['vɛrbən] (30) *v/t.* ✗ enlist, recruit; *Mitglieder usw.*: enlist; *Kunden, Stimmen*: canvass; *j-n für e-e Sache* ~ win a p. over to a cause; *v/i.* make propaganda (*für* for); ✝ advertise (*a th.*); ~ *um* (*acc.*) sue for, *liebend*: court, *rhet.* woo (*beide a. fig.*); '♀**er** *m* (7) suitor; ✝ canvasser; ✗ recruiting officer; '♀**eschrift** *f* advertising pamphlet (*od.* brochure), leaflet; '♀**espruch** *m* (advertising) slogan; '♀**etext** *m* advertisement copy; '♀**etexter** *m* advertising copywriter; '♀**etrommel** *f*: *die* ~ *rühren fig.* make propaganda, advertise; '~**ewirksam** effective; '♀**ung** *f* recruiting; courting, courtship; ✝ advertising, publicity, canvassing; *weitS.* propaganda; '♀**ungskosten** *pl. steuerlich*: professional expenses *pl.*

'**Werdegang** *m* (3) development;

e-r Person, Partei usw.: career; ⊕ process of production.

werden ['veːrdən] **1.** (30) *v/i.* (sn) become, get; *allmählich*: grow; *plötzlich*: turn *pale, sour, etc.*; (*entstehen*) come into existence, arise; (*ausfallen*) turn out, prove; *Arzt* ~ become a doctor; *böse* ~ grow angry; *Mohammedaner usw.* ~ turn Mohammedan *etc.*; *es wird kalt usw.* it is getting cold *etc.*; *was soll aus ihm* (*od. daraus*) ~? what will become of him (*od.* of it)?; *was will er* ~? what is he going to be?; *was soll nun* ~? what are we going to do now?; *es ist nichts daraus geworden* it has come to nothing; *es wird schon* ~ it will be all right; ~*de Mutter* expectant mother; **2.** *v/aux. ich werde fahren* I shall drive; *geliebt* ~ be loved; *sie wird gleich weinen* she is going to cry; **3.** ♀ *n* (6) growing, development; (*Fortschreiten*) progress; *noch im* ~ *sein* be in process of development, be in the making; *große Dinge sind im* ~ great things are preparing.

werf|en ['vɛrfən] (30) *v/t.* throw (*a. v/i.*; *nach* at); (*schleudern*) fling; *a. Anker, Blick, Licht, Schatten*: cast; *Brief in den Kasten, Bomben, Anker*: drop; *Junge*: bring forth, produce; *Falten* ~ raise folds; *sich* ~ *Holz*: warp; *sich auf e-e Tätigkeit* ~ throw o.s. into; *um sich* ~ *mit Geld usw.* be lavish with; *aufs Papier* ~ jot down; (*sich*) *hin und her* ~ toss (about); *s. Brust, Hals usw.*; '♀**er** *m Kricket*: bowler; *Baseball*: pitcher; ✗ (*Granat*♀) mortar; (*Raketen*♀) launcher.

Werft [vɛrft] *f* (16) shipyard, dockyard; '~**arbeiter** *m* docker.

Werg [vɛrk] *n* (3) tow (*gezupftes Tauwerk*) oakum.

Werk [~] *n* (3) work (*a. künstlerisch usw.*); (*Tat*) act, deed; (*Erzeugnis*) work, production; (*Getriebe*) mechanism, works *pl.*; ✗ work(s *pl.*); (*Fabrik*) works *mst sg.*, factory, plant; (*Unternehmung*) undertaking, enterprise; *ein gutes* ~ *tun* do an act of kindness (*an dat.* to); *ans* ~*!* let us begin!; *am* ~ *sein* be at work; *im* ~*e sein* be on foot, be in the wind; *ins* ~ *setzen* set on foot, bring about; *ans* ~ *gehen* set to work; *b.s. es war sein* ~ it was

his doing; '∼**bank** f (work-)
bench; '∼**meister** m foreman; '∼**schutz** m factory security officers
pl.; '∼**spionage** f industrial espionage; '∼**statt** f, '∼**stätte** f workshop,
shop; (Auto♀) garage; '∼**stoff** m material; (Kunstharz-Preßstoff) plastic
(material); '∼**stück** n workpiece,
work; '∼**student** m working student;
'∼**swohnung** f company flat (Am.
apartment); '∼**tag** m (Wochentag)
workday, weekday; (tägliche Arbeitszeit) working-day; '♀**tags** on weekdays; '♀**tätig** working; die ♀en the
working population; '∼**tisch** m work-
-table; '∼**vertrag** m work contract;
'∼**unterricht** m handicrafts pl.; '∼**zeichnung** f workshop drawing; '∼**zeug** n tool (a. fig.); feines: instrument; (Gerät) implement; physiol.
organ; '∼**zeugkasten** m tool box (od.
kit); '∼**zeugmacher** m toolmaker;
'∼**zeugmaschine** f machine tool; '∼**zeugtasche** f tool-bag.

Wermut ['ve:rmu:t] m (3) ♀ wormwood; (Wein) verm(o)uth; '∼**bruder**
F m wino; '∼**s-tropfen** fig. m shadow,
sorrow.

wert [ve:rt] **1.** worth (e-e S. a th.);
(würdig) worthy (gen. of); (lieb)
dear; (∼geschätzt) esteemed; nicht
viel ∼ not up to much; nichts ∼
worth nothing, worthless; s. Mühe,
Rede; Ihr ∼es Schreiben your letter;
2. ♀ m (3²) value (a. phys., ♀ usw.);
worth; (Gegenwert) equivalent;
(Vermögens♀) asset; phys., ⊕ factor,
coefficient; ∼e pl. phys., ⊕ data;
(Nutzen) value; künstlerischer
merit; value; im ∼e von ... of the
value of; von gleichem ∼ tantamount
(wie to); ♀ (als) Muster ohne ∼ by
pattern-post; (großen) ∼ legen auf
(acc.) set great store by; im ∼ sinken
depreciate.

'**Wert**|-**angabe** f declaration of
value; '∼-**arbeit** f high-class workmanship; '♀**beständig** of fixed
value; (Währung): stable; '∼-**beständigkeit** f fixed value; stability; '∼**brief** m insured letter; '♀**en**
(26) (bewerten) value; (schätzen) appraise; (beurteilen) judge; bsd.
Sport, Schule: rate (nach Leistungen
on performance), (gelten lassen)
allow; (auswerten) evaluate; '∼-**gegenstand** m article of value; pl.
valuables; '♀**geschätzt** esteemed;

'♀**ig** ♠: 2-∼ bivalent, divalent; 3-∼
trivalent; '∼**igkeit** ♠ f valence;
'♀**los** worthless (a. P.); valueless;
(nutzlos) useless; '∼**maßstab** m,
'∼**messer** m standard (of value);
'∼**minderung** f depreciation; '∼**paket** n insured parcel; '∼**papiere**
n/pl. securities; '∼**sachen** f/pl. valuables pl.; '♀**schätzen** esteem
highly; '∼**schätzung** f esteem;
'∼**steigerung** f increase in value;
'∼**ung** f s. werten: valuation; appraisal; judging; rating; evaluation; '∼**urteil** n value judgement; '∼**verlust**
m loss of value; '∼**verringerung** f
depreciation; '♀**voll** valuable; '∼**zeichen** ♀ n (postage) stamp; '∼**zuwachs(steuer** f) m increment-value
(tax).

Wesen ['ve:zən] n (6) (Lebe♀) being,
creature; (inneres Sein, Kern) essence; (Natur) nature, character;
(Betragen) manners pl., way, air;
(größeres Ganze) organization; in
Zssgn: system, z.B. Sparkassen♀
savings bank system; (Getue) fuss,
ado; '∼**heit** f (Wesenskern) essence;
(Wirklichkeit) substantiality; '♀**los**
unsubstantial; unreal; '∼-**art** f
nature, character; '♀**sfremd** foreign to one's nature; '♀**sgleich**
identical in character; '∼**szug** m
characteristic (feature od. trait);
'♀**tlich** essential, (a. beträchtlich)
substantial; (wichtig) material (für
to); (grundlegend) fundamental;
adv. ∼ verschieden very (od. vastly)
different; das ♀e the essential; im
∼en essentially, in the main.

weshalb [ves'halp] **1.** interr. pron.
why; **2.** cj. and so, and that's why.

Wespe ['vespə] f (15) wasp; '∼-**nest** n wasps' nest; fig. in ein ∼
stechen stir up a hornet's nest; '∼-**nstich** m wasp's sting; '∼**ntaille** f
wasp-waist.

wessen ['vesən] whose.

West [vest] **1.** west; **2.** poet. m (3²,
o. pl.) west(wind); '∼**en** (6) m west;
(Land) West, (Abendland a.) Occident.

Weste ['vestə] f (15) waistcoat, ♀
u. Am. vest; e-e reine ∼ haben fig.
have a clean slate; '∼**ntasche** f
vest-pocket; ∼ wie s-e ∼ kennen
know a p. or th. inside out; im '∼**ntaschenformat** n pocket-size car,
etc.

West|fale [vɛst'fɑːlə] m (13), 2**fä-
lisch** [~'fɛːliʃ] Westphalian.
'**Westhang** m west(ern) slope.
'**westlich** west(ern); westerly; ~ von
(to the) west of.
'**West|mächte** f/pl. Western powers;
'~**mark** f (Geld) Western mark;
2**wärts** ['~vɛrts] westward; '~**wind**
m west(erly) wind.
weswegen ['vɛs've:gən] s. weshalb.
wett [vɛt] even, equal, F quits;
'2**bewerb** m competition; Sport:
a. (Einzel2) event; in ~ treten mit
enter into competition with; '2**be-
werber(in** f) m competitor; '~**be-
werbsfähig** competitive; '2**büro** n
betting office.
Wette ['vɛtə] f (15) bet, wager; e-e
~ eingehen make a bet; was gilt
die ~? what do (od. will) you bet?;
et. um die ~ tun vie with each other
in doing a th.; um die ~ laufen
race each other.
'**Wett-eifer** m rivalry; '2n vie (mit
j-m with; in e-r Eigenschaft in);
compete (with; in e-r Tätigkeit in;
um et. for); mit j-m ~ a. emulate
(od. rival) a p.
wetten ['vɛtən] v/i. u. v/t. (26) bet,
wager (mit j-m a p.; um et. a th.);
Rennsport: ~ auf (acc.) back; '2**de**
m, f (18) s. Wetter².
Wetter¹ ['vɛtər] n (7) weather;
(Un2) storm; (Gewitter) thunderstorm; ⚒ böses ~ damp; schlagende
~ pl. firedamp sg.; alle ~! dear
me!; '~² m (7) ('~in f [16¹]) better,
backer; '~-**aussichten** f/pl. weather
outlook; '~**bedingungen** f/pl.
weather conditions; '~**be-obach-
tung** f meteorological observation;
'2**bericht** m weather report; '2**beständig** weather-proof; '~**dienst** m
weather service; '~**fahne** f (weath-
er-)vane; '2**fest** weather-proof; '~-
frosch F m weatherman; '2**fühlig**
sensitive to changes in the weather;
'~**hahn** m weathercock; '2**hart**
weather-beaten; '~**häus-chen** n
weather house; '~**karte** f weather
chart (od. map); '~**kunde** f meteorology; '~**lage** f weather conditions
pl.; '~**leuchten** n (6) sheet lightning;
'~**mantel** m trench-coat; '~**meldung** f weather report; '2n (29) be
stormy; fig. storm, thunder; '~**prophet** m weather-prophet; '~**satellit**
m weather satellite; '~**schacht** ⚒ m

air-shaft; '~**schaden** m damage
caused by the weather; '~**seite** f
weather-side; '~**station** f weather
station; '~**sturz** m sudden fall of
temperature; '~**verhältnisse** n/pl.
weather conditions; '~**voraussage** f
weather-forecast; '~**warte** f weath-
er-station; '~**wechsel** m change in
the weather; '2**wendisch** changeable, fickle; '~**wolke** f thunder-cloud.
'**Wett|fahrt** f race; '~**fliegen** n, '~**flug**
m air-race; '~**gesang** m singing-
-match; '~**kampf** m contest, match,
competition; '~**kämpfer(in** f) m
competitor; '~**lauf** m (foot)race; fig.
~ mit der Zeit race against time;
'~**läufer(in** f) m runner; '2**machen**
make up for, make good; '~**rennen** n
race; '~**rudern** n boat-race; '~**rüsten** n arms race; '~**schwimmen** n
swimming match; '~**segeln** n regatta; '~**spiel** n match, Am. game;
'~**streit** m contest, match; '~**zettel** m
betting-slip.
wetzen ['vɛtsən] (27) whet, sharpen.
'**Wetz|stahl** m whet steel; '~**stein**
m whetstone, hone.
Whisky ['wiski] m whisk(e)y.
wich [viç] pret. v. weichen 1.
Wichs [viks] m (4) gala; in vollem ~
in full dress, F in full fig; '~**bürste**
f blacking (od. polishing) brush.
Wichse ['viksə] f (15) blacking,
polish; F (Prügel) thrashing; '2n
(27) black, polish, shine; F (prügeln) thrash, lick.
Wicht [viçt] m (3) wight, creature;
armer ~ poor wretch; kleiner ~
whipper-snapper, (Kind) urchin,
brat.
wichtig ['viçtiç] important (für to);
~ tun give o.s. airs; 2**keit** f importance; von ~ of importance; 2**tuer**
['~tu:ər] m (7) pompous fellow; 2-
tuerei [~'raɪ] f pomposity.
Wicke 🌿 ['vikə] f (15) vetch.
Wickel ['vikəl] m (7) roll(er); ⚕
(Umschlag) pack; heißer ~ fomen-
tation; (Haar2) hair-)curler; '~**gamasche** f puttee; '~**kind** n child
in swaddling-clothes, baby (in
arms); '~**kommode** f baby's changing unit; '2n (29) wind, roll, coil (alle
a. sich); Haar: curl; (ein~) wrap up;
Säugling: swathe, swaddle; j-n um
den (kleinen) Finger ~ fig. twist s.o.
round one's (little) finger; '~**rock** m
wrap-around skirt.

Wick(e)lung ['vik(ə)luŋ] *f* bandaging; *≠* coil.
Widder ['vidər] *m* (7) ram; *ast.* Ram, Aries.
wider ['vi:dər] (*acc.*) against, contrary to; versus; *s. für, Wille*; '~**borstig** stubborn, cross-grained; ~'**fahren** (sn) *j-m*: befall a p., happen to a p.; *s. Gerechtigkeit*; '~**haarig** refractory; '2**haken** *m* barbed hook; *an Pfeil, Angel usw.*: barb; *mit* ~ (*versehen*) barbed; '2**hall** *m* echo, reverberation, resonance (*alle a. fig.*); *fig. keinen* ~ *finden* meet with no response; '~**hallen** (re-)echo, resound (*von* with); '2**lager** *n* △ abutment; (*Gegenpfeiler*) counterfort; ⊕ support; ~**legbar** [~'le:k-] refutable; ~'**legen** refute, disprove; 2'**legung** *f* refutation.
widerlich ['vi:dərliç] repulsive, repugnant; (*ekelhaft*) disgusting, loathsome, sickening; '2**keit** *f* repulsiveness.
'**wider|natürlich** unnatural; perverse; '2**part** *m* opponent; ~ *halten* (*dat.*) oppose; ~'**raten** *j-m et.*: dissuade a p. from; '~**rechtlich** illegal, unlawful; *≠₂* ~ *betreten* trespass (up)on; '2**rede** *f* contradiction; '2**ruf** *m* revocation; *e-r Erklärung*: recantation, retractation; (*Rückgängigmachen*) cancel(l)ation; (*Abbestellung*) countermand; *gültig bis auf* ~ until recalled, unless countermanded; ~'**rufen** revoke; *Aussage*: retract; *Gesetz*: repeal; *Auftrag, Befehl, Vertrag*: cancel, countermand; ~'**ruflich** revocable; 2**sacher** ['~zaxər] *m* (7), '2**sacherin** *f* (16¹) adversary; (*der Teufel*) the Foe; '2**schein** *m* reflection; *sich* ~'**setzen** (*dat.*) oppose, resist, struggle against; *e-m Befehl*: disobey; ~'**setzlich** refractory; *bsd. im Dienst*: insubordinate; 2'**setzlichkeit** *f* refractoriness; insubordination; '2**sinn** *m* nonsense, absurdity; '~**sinnig** absurd, paradoxical, preposterous; ~**spenstig** ['~ʃpenstiç] refractory, rebellious; obstinate; '2**spenstigkeit** *f* refractoriness, obstinacy; '~**spiegeln** reflect; *sich* ~ be reflected (*in dat.* by); ~'**sprechen** (*dat.*) contradict (*sich o.s.*); *e-m Vorschlag*: oppose; *sich od. einander* ~ *Meinungen usw.*: be

contradictory; ~'**sprechend** contradictory; '2**spruch** *m* contradiction (*in sich selbst* in terms); *gegen e-n Vorschlag*: opposition to; *im* ~ *zu* in contradiction to; '~**sprüchlich** contradictory, inconsistent; '2**spruchsgeist** *m* spirit of contradiction; '~**spruchslos** uncontradicted; *adv.* without contradiction; (*demütig*) meekly; '~**spruchsvoll** *s. widersprüchlich*; '2**stand** *m* resistance, opposition (*gegen* to); *≠* resistance, (*Gerät*) resistor; ~ *leisten* offer resistance; *den* ~ *aufgeben* give in; '2**standsbewegung** *f* resistance movement; '~**standsfähig** resistant, robust; '2**standsfähigkeit** *f* (capability of) resistance; '2**standskämpfer** *pol. m* member of the Resistance; '2**standskraft** *f* power of resistance; ⊕ strength; '~**standslos** unresisting; ~'**stehen** (*dat.*) resist, withstand; (*zuwider sein*) be repugnant to; ~'**streben** **1.** (*dat.*) oppose, resist; (*zuwider sein*) be repugnant to; **2.** 2 *n* resistance; (*Unwilligkeit*) reluctance; *mit* ~ = ~'**strebend** *adv.* reluctantly; '2**streit** *m* opposition; *fig.* conflict, clash; ~'**streiten** (*dat.*) conflict (*od.* clash) with, be contrary to; ~**wärtig** ['~vertiç] unpleasant, disagreeable; (*scheußlich*) repulsive; (*ekelhaft*) disgusting, loathsome; (*verhaßt*) hateful, odious; '2**wärtigkeit** *f* unpleasantness, disagreeableness; repulsiveness; (*widriger Zufall*) adversity; '2**wille** *m* aversion (*gegen* to), dislike (for); (*Ekel*) disgust (for); (*Unwilligkeit*) reluctance; '~**willig** unwilling, reluctant.
widm|en ['vitmən] (26) (*zueignen*) dedicate, (*weihen, a. Zeit, Aufmerksamkeit*) devote (*dat.* to); *sich e-r S.* ~ devote o.s. (*od.* apply o.s.) to a th.; '2**ung** *f* dedication; '2**ungsexemplar** *n* presentation copy.
widrig ['vi:driç] adverse, untoward; ~**enfalls** ['~gən-] failing which, in default of which; '2**keit** *f* contrariety; (*widriger Zufall*) adversity.
wie [vi:] *in Frage u. Ausruf*: how; *im Vergleich*: as; (*gleich e-m ...*) like; *zeitlich*: as; ~ *auch* (*immer*) however; ~ *bitte?* (I beg your) pardon?; *s. heißen*; ~ *ist* (*od. war*) *es mit ...?* what about ...?; ~ *wäre es mit ...?* how about ...?; ~ *dem auch sei*

be that as it may; ～ *du mir, so ich dir* tit for tat; F *und* ～*!* and how!
Wiedehopf ['viːdəhɔpf] *m* (3) hoopoe.

wieder ['viːdər] again, anew; (*zurück*) back; (*als Vergeltung*) in return; *in Zssgn allg.* re-..., re-...; *s. hin, immer*; '₂-**abdruck** *m* reprint; '₂-**anfang** *m s.* Wiederbeginn; ～'-**anknüpfen** *fig.* renew; ～'-**anstellen** reappoint, reinstall; ₂'-**anstellung** *f* reappointment; ₂'-**aufbau** *m* reconstruction (*a. wirtschaftlicher usw.*); rebuilding; ～'-**aufbauen** rebuild, reconstruct; ～'-**aufbereiten** reprocess; ₂'-**aufbereitungs-anlage** *f* reprocessing plant; ～'-**aufblühen** (sn) *s. wiederaufleben*; ～'-**auf-erstehen** (sn) rise from the dead; ₂'-**auf-erstehung** *f* resurrection; '₂-**aufführung** *thea. f* revival; ～'-**aufkommen 1.** (sn) *Mode usw.*: revive, come into fashion again; *Kranker*: recover; **2.** ₂ *n e-s Kranken*: recovery; ～'-**aufleben 1.** (sn) revive; **2.** ₂ *n* revival; ₂'-**aufnahme** *f* resumption; ⚖ reopening; ₂'**aufnahmeverfahren** ⚖ *n* new hearing; *Strafrecht*: retrial; ～'-**aufnehmen** resume; ₂'-**aufrüstung** *f* rearmament; ₂'-**auftreten** *n* reappearance; '₂**beginn** *m* recommencement; *Schule usw.*: reopening; '～**bekommen** get back, recover; '～**beleben** resuscitate; *fig.* revive, reanimate; '₂**belebung** *f* resuscitation; *fig.* revival; '₂**belebungsversuch** *m* attempt at resuscitation; '～**bewaffnen** rearm; '～**bringen** bring back; (*zurückgeben*) restore (*dat.* to); ～'**einbringen** make good, recover; *sich* ～'**einfinden** turn up again; ～'**einführen** reintroduce; *Gebrauch usw.*: re-establish; ✝ re-import; ₂'**einführung** *f* reintroduction; re--establishment; ₂'-**eingliederung** *f* reintegration; ～'-**einlösen** redeem; ₂'-**einlösung** *f* redemption; ₂'-**einnahme** *f* recapture; ～'-**einnehmen** recapture; *e-n Platz*: resume; ₂'**einschiffung** *f* re-embarkation; ～'-**einsetzen** replace; *in ein Amt usw.*: reinstate (*in acc.* in), restore (to); ₂'-**einsetzung** *f* reinstatement, restoration; ～'-**einstellen** *Arbeiter usw.*: re-engage; ✕ re-enlist; *sich* ～ turn up again; ₂'-**einstellung** *f* re--engagement; re-enlistment; ₂'-**ein**

tritt *m*: ～ *in die Erdatmosphäre* re--entry; '～**ergreifen** *Flüchtling*, '₂**ergreifung** *f* recapture; '～**erkennen** recognize; *nicht wiederzuerkennen* totally changed, (*verstümmelt usw.*) past recognition; '₂-**erkennung** *f* recognition; '～**erlangen** recover; '₂-**erlangung** *f* recovery; '₂-**er-öffnung** *f* reopening; '～**erstatten** restore, return; *Kosten*: refund, reimburse; '₂-**erstattung** *f* restitution; *der Kosten*: refund, reimbursement; '～**erstehen** rise again; be rebuilt; *fig.* (*a.* ～ *lassen*) revive; '～**erzählen** retell; '～**finden** find again; '₂**gabe** *f* restitution, return; *im Bilde usw.*: reproduction; *e-s Textes od. Musikstücks*: rendering; '₂**gabequalität** *f* reproduction quality; '～**geben** give back, return; *Ehre, Gesundheit*: restore; (*übersetzen usw.*) render; (*nachbilden*; *a. Ton usw.*) reproduce; *Musikstück, Rolle*: interpret; (*zitieren*) quote; '₂**geburt** *f* rebirth; '～**genesen** (sn) recover; '₂**genesung** *f* recovery; '～**gewinnen** regain; ⊕ reclaim; ～'**gutmachen** make good, repair; ₂'**gutmachung** *f* reparation; ～'**herstellen** restore; ₂-'**herstellung** *f* restoration; rehabilitation; *e-s Kranken*: recovery; ～'**holen** repeat; (*öfter sagen od. tun*) reiterate; '**wiederholen** fetch back; (*zurücknehmen*) take back; ～'**holt** repeated(ly *adv.*); ₂'**holung** *f* repetition; reiteration; *TV*: repeat, rerun, *e-r Szene*: replay; ₂'**holungsfall** *m*: *im* ～*e* in case of recurrence; ₂'**holungsspiel** *n Sport*: replay; ～'**instandsetzen** repair; ₂-'**instandsetzung** *f* repair; ～'**käuen** ['～kɔyən] (25) ruminate; *fig.* rehash; '₂**käuer** *m* (7) ruminant; '₂**kauf** *m* repurchase; ₂-**kehr** ['～keːr] *f* (16, *no pl.*) return; *periodische*: recurrence; '～**kehren** (sn) return; recur; '～**kehrend** recurrent; '～**kommen** (sn) come again; (*zurückkommen*) come back, return; ₂**kunft** ['～kunft] *f* (14¹) return; '～**sagen** repeat; '～**sehen 1.** (*a. sich*) see (*od.* meet) again; **2.** ₂ *n* (6) meeting again, reunion; *auf* ～*!* good-by(e)!, (hope to) see you again!, F so long!; '₂**taufe** *f* rebaptism; '₂**täufer** *m* anabaptist; '～**tun** do again, repeat; '～**um** again, anew; ～'-**umkehren** (sn) turn back, retrace one's steps; '～**ver-einigen** (*a. sich*) reunite; '₂-

ver-einigung f reunion; a. pol. re-unification; '~**vergelten** b.s. pay back, requite; '2**vergeltung** f re-quital, retaliation; '~**verheiraten** (a. sich) remarry; '2**verheiratung** f re-marriage; '2**verkäufer** m reseller; (Einzelhändler) retailer, retail deal-er; '2**verkaufspreis** m trade price; '2**verwendung** f re-use; '2**verwer-tung** f recycling; '2**wahl** f re-elec-tion; '~**wählbar** re-eligible; '~**wäh-len** re-elect; ~'**zulassen** readmit; 2'**zulassung** f readmission; ~'**zu-stellen**, 2'**zustellung** f return.

Wiege ['vi:gə] f (15) cradle; '~**messer** n mincing-knife.

wiegen¹ ['vi:gən] v/t. u. v/i. (30) weigh.

'**wiegen**² v/t. (25) **1.** (schaukeln) rock; sich ~ sway; fig. (sich) in Sicherheit ~ lull (o.s.) into security; **2.** (zerklei-nern) mince.

'**Wiegen|fest** n birthday; '~**lied** n lullaby.

wiehern ['vi:ərn] **1.** (29) neigh; vor Lachen: guffaw; ~des Gelächter horse-laugh; **2.** 2 n (6) neighing.

Wiener ['vi:nər] m (7), '~**in** f (16¹), '2**isch** Viennese.

wies [vi:s] pret. v. weisen.

Wiese ['vi:zə] f (15) meadow.

Wiesel zo. ['vi:zəl] n (7) weasel.

'**Wiesenland** n meadow-land.

wie'so? why?

wie'viel how much; pl. how many; ~**mal** how many times?

wievielte [~'fi:ltə] m, f, n which; den 2n haben wir? what day of the month is it?

wie'wohl though, although.

wild [vilt] **1.** allg. wild; (unzivilisiert) savage; (grausam) ferocious; (grim-mig) fierce; (wütend) furious; Kind: unruly; Stier: fig. Hast: mad; ~e Ehe concubinage; ~er Streik unoffi-cial (bsd. Am. wildcat) strike; s. Wein: ~ machen infuriate, Tier: frighten; fig. ~ sein auf (acc.) be mad for od. about; ~ wachsen grow wild; ~ werden turn wild, fig. see red; **2.** 2 n (1, o. pl.) game; (Reh) deer; s. Wildbret.

'**Wild|bach** m torrent; '~**bad** n thermal baths pl., hot springs pl.; '~**bahn** f hunting-ground; '~**bra-ten** m roast venison; ~**bret** ['~brɛt] n (11) game; v. Hochwild: venison; '~**dieb** m poacher; ~**diebe'rei** f

poaching; '~**ente** f wild duck.

Wilde ['vildə] m, f (18) savage; F wie ein ~r like mad.

Wilder|er ['~rər] m (7) poacher; '2**n** (29) poach.

'**Wild|fang** m madcap; Mädchen: a. romp, tomboy; '2'**fremd** quite strange; ~er Mensch complete stranger; '~**heit** f s. wild **1**: wild-ness; savageness; fierceness; '~**hü-ter** m gamekeeper; '~**leder** n, '2-**ledern** buckskin; bsd. Handschuh: doeskin, chamois (leather); suède; '~**lederschuhe** m/pl. suède shoes pl.; '~**ling** m (3¹) ♣ wild stock od. tree, wild(l)ing; s. Wildfang; '~**nis** f (14²) wilderness; '~**park** m (game-)preserve, deer-park; '~**sau** f wild sow; '~**schaden** m damage caused by game; '~**schütz(e)** m poacher; '~**schwein** n wild boar; '~**stand** m stock of game; '2**wachs-end** (growing) wild; '~**wasser** n torrent; '~**wechsel** m game pass; ~'**west...**, ~'**westfilm** m Western.

Wille ['vilə] (13¹), '~**n** m (6) will; (Absicht) intention; aus freiem ~n of one's own free will; guter ~ good intention; Letzter ~ (last) will; s. um; wider ~n unwillingly; 2ns sein be willing, be ready; j-m s-n ~n lassen let a p. have his own way; j-m zu ~n sein comply with a p.'s wishes; ich kann es beim besten ~n nicht tun I cannot do it, much as I should like to; es geht beim besten ~n nicht it just can't be done.

'**willen|los** lacking will-power; (unentschlossen) irresolute; (weich) spineless; '2**losigkeit** f lack of will-power.

'**Willens|-akt** m act of volition; '~-**erklärung** ⚖ f declaratory act; '~**freiheit** f free will; '~**kraft** f will-power; '2**schwach** weak--willed; '~**schwäche** f weak will; '2**stark** strong-willed; '~**stärke** f will-power, strong will.

willfahren [~'fa:rən] (25) (dat.) comply with, grant; j-m ~ humour a p.

willfährig ['~fɛ:riç] compliant, com-plaisant; j-s ~es Werkzeug sein be at a p.'s beck and call; '2**keit** f compliance, complaisance.

'**willig** willing, ready; '2**keit** f willingness, readiness.

'**Will|komm** m (3¹), ~'**kommen**¹ n, m (6), ♀'**kommen**² adj. welcome; s. heißen; ~**kür** ['~ky:r] f (16) arbitrariness; a. = '~**kür-akt** m arbitrary act; '♀**kürlich** arbitrary, high-handed; '~**kürlichkeit** f s. Will-kür.

wimmeln ['viməln] (29) (a. fig.) swarm od. teem (von with).

wimmern ['vimərn] (29) whimper.

Wimpel ['vimpəl] m (7) pennant.

Wimper ['vimpər] f (15) eyelash; ohne mit der ~ zu zucken without turning a hair, without wincing; '~**ntusche** f mascara.

Wind [vint] m (3) wind; (Blähung) flatulence, wind; guter ~ fair wind; sanfter ~ gentle breeze; fig. ~ bekommen von get wind of; fig. ~ machen boast, brag (mit of); bei ~ und Wetter in storm and rain; fig. in den ~ reden waste one's breath; in den ~ schlagen ignore, disregard; fig. j-m den ~ aus den Segeln nehmen take the wind out of a p.'s sails; den Mantel nach dem ~ hängen trim one's sails to the wind; in alle ~e zerstreuen scatter to the four winds; gegen den Wind into the wind; wie der ~ rapidly; '~**beutel** m cream puff; F fig. windbag.

Winde ['vində] f (15) ⊕ windlass, winch, hoist; (Anker♀) capstan; (Garn♀) reel; ♀ bindweed.

'**Wind-ei** n wind-egg.

Windel ['vindəl] f (15) diaper, napkin; pl. ~n mst swaddling-clothes pl. (a. fig.); '♀**n** (29) (wickeln) swaddle, swathe; '♀'**weich:** ~ schlagen beat to a jelly.

winden ['vindən] (30) wind; (hoch♀) hoist; Garn usw.: reel; Kranz: make, bind; j-m et. aus den Händen ~ wrest a th. out of a p.'s hands; sich ~ wind; vor Schmerz: writhe; Fluß: meander.

'**Windes-eile** f: mit ~ at lightning speed.

'**Wind|fahne** f (weather) vane; '♀**geschützt** protected against the wind; '~**harfe** f Aeolian harp; '~**hose** f whirlwind; '~**hund** m greyhound; fig. fly-by-night.

windig ['~diç] windy; fig. Person: giddy; Sache: precarious; Ausrede: thin, lame.

'**Wind|jacke** f windcheater; '~**kanal** m wind tunnel; '~**messer** m ane-

mometer; '~**mühle** f windmill; fig. gegen ~n kämpfen fight windmills; '~**pocken** f/pl. chicken-pox; '~**richtung** f direction of the wind; ~**röschen** ♀ ['~rø:sçən] n anemone; '~**rose** ⚓ f compass card; '♀**schief** (a)skew; fig. awry, sl. cockeyed; '♀**schlüpfig**, '♀**schnittig** streamlined; '~**schutzscheibe** ⚔, mot. f windscreen, Am. windshield; '~**spiel** n whippet; '~**stärke** f wind force od. velocity; '♀**still** calm; '~**stille** f calm; '~**stoß** m blast of wind, gust; '~**surfen** n wind-surfing.

Windung ['vinduŋ] f winding, turn, convolution; e-s Weges, Stromes: bend; e-r Taurolle, Schlange: coil; e-r Spirale, Muschel: whorl.

Wink [viŋk] m (3) sign; mit der Hand: wave; mit den Augen: wink; durch Nicken: nod; fig. hint, tip, F pointer; j-m e-n ~ geben give (od. drop) a p. a hint; s. Zaunpfahl.

Winkel ['viŋkəl] m (7) ⅄ angle; weitS. (Ecke) corner, nook; ⚒ (Abzeichen am Ärmel) chevron; ⊕ square; '~**advokat** m pettifogger, hedge-lawyer; Am. F shyster; '~**eisen** n angle iron; ♀**förmig** ['~fœrmiç] angular; '~**haken** typ. m composing-stick.

'**wink(e)lig** angular; in Zssgn, bsd. ⅄ ...-angled; Straße: crooked.

'**Winkel|maß** ⊕ n square; '~**messer** m ⅄ protractor; surv. goniometer; '~**zug** m dodge, subterfuge, trick; (Ausflucht) evasion; Winkelzüge machen dodge, shuffle, prevaricate.

wink|en ['viŋkən] (25) make a sign, signal (dat. to); mit der Hand: wave, (her~) beckon; mit den Augen: wink; ⚔ signal, flag, mit Winkflagge: semaphore; fig. Belohnung usw.: be in store (dat. for); mit der Hand od. dem Taschentuch ~ wave one's hand od. handkerchief; '♀**er** m (7) mot. direction indicator; ⚔ flag-man, signalman; '♀**spruch** ⚔ m semaphore message.

winseln ['vinzəln] (29) whimper, whine.

Winter ['vintər] m (7) winter; '♀**fest** wintertight; ♀ hardy; ~ machen winterize; '~**frucht** f, '~**getreide** n, '~**korn** n winter grain; '~**garten** m winter garden; '~**halbjahr** n winter half-year; '♀**lich** wintry; '~**mantel** m

winter overcoat; '~-**olympiade** f, '~-
spiele n/pl. Olympic Winter Games;
'~**reifen** m winter tyre (Am. tire);
'~**saat** f winter corn; '~**schlaf** m
hibernation; ~ halten hibernate; '~-
'**schlußverkauf** m winter clearance
sale; '~**sport** m winter sport(s pl.);
'~**sport-ort** m winter resort; '~(s)-
zeit f winter time; '~**vorrat** m winter
stock.

Winzer ['vintsər] m (7) vine-dresser;
(Traubenleser) vintager; (Weinzüch-
ter) wine-grower.

winzig ['vintsiç] tiny, minute.

Wipfel ['vipfəl] m (7) (tree-)top.

Wippe ['vipə] f (15) seesaw; '~**n** (25)
seesaw, rock; ~ mit wag a th.

wir [viːr] we; ~ alle all of us; ~ drei
we three, the three of us.

Wirbel ['virbəl] m (7) (Drehung)
whirl (a. fig.); (Knochen♀) vertebra;
(Haar♀) crown (of the head);
(Trommel♀) roll; (Violin♀) peg;
(Wind♀) whirlwind; (Wasser♀) eddy, größerer: whirlpool, vortex; v.
Rauch usw.: wreath, eddy; v.
Schnee, Staub, Hieben: flurry; ⊕
(Drehring) swivel; F e-n ~ machen
(Aufhebens) make a big fuss; '♀**ig**
whirling; fig. giddy; '~**knochen** m
vertebra; '♀**los** invertebrate; '♀**n**
(20) v/t. whirl; eddy; Trommel:
roll; Lerche usw.: warble (a. v/t.);
mir wirbelt der Kopf my head
swims; '~**säule** f vertebral column,
spine; '~**sturm** m cyclone, tornado;
'~**tier** n vertebrate; '~**wind** m
whirlwind (a. fig.).

wirk|en ['virkən] **1.** (25) v/t. work,
cause; Strümpfe usw.: knit, weave;
Teig: knead; v/i. (be at) work;
operate; take (effect) (a. 🗲); (treffen) tell (alle: auf acc. [up]on); ~
als act as, function as (a. ⊕); beruhigend usw. ~ have a soothing etc.
effect; auf die Sinne ~ affect the
senses; dahin ~, daß … see that …;
er wirkt viel jünger he looks (od.
seems to be) much younger; **2.** ♀ n
work; effect; functioning; activity;
'♀**er** ⊕ m knitter; '~**lich** real,
actual; (echt) true; (wesentlich) substantial; ~? really?, indeed?; ~**e**
Leistung ⊕ effective output, actual
power; '♀**lichkeit** f reality; '~**lichkeitsfremd** unrealistic; '~**lich-
keitsnah** realistic; '~**sam** effective,
efficacious; efficient; operative;

Hieb usw.: telling; ~ werden take
effect (a. Gesetz); '♀**samkeit** f efficacy, effectiveness; '♀**stoff** 🝁 m
active substance.

'**Wirkung** f effect; (Tätigkeit) operation, action; (Erfolg) result;
(Eindruck) impression; (starke ~)
impact; mit ~ vom … as from …;
mit sofortiger ~ effective immediately; ~ haben take (od. be of) effect;
s-e ~ verfehlen fail to work, prove
ineffectual; '~**sbereich** m sphere
(⚔ radius) of action; Gesetz: operation; '~**sgrad** ⊕ m efficiency; '~**s-
kraft** f efficacy; '~**skreis** m sphere
(od. field) of activity, province, domain; '♀**slos** inefficacious, ineffectual; '~**slosigkeit** f inefficacy; '♀**s-
voll** s. wirksam; '~**sweise** f (mode
of) operation, working; functioning.

'**Wirkwaren** f/pl. knit(ted) goods.

wirr [vir] confused; Haar: di-
shevel(l)ed.

'**Wirren** f/pl. disorders, troubles.

'**Wirr|kopf** m fig. muddle-headed
fellow, scatter-brain; '~**nis** f (14²),
'~**sal** n (3) chaos, confusion; ~**warr**
['~var] m (3¹) confusion, chaos,
jumble, muddle, mess.

Wirsing(kohl) ['virziŋ(-)] m savoy.

Wirt [virt] m (3) host (a. biol.);
(Haus♀, Gast♀) landlord; (Gast♀)
innkeeper; s. Rechnung; '~**in** f
hostess; (Haus♀, Gast♀) landlady;
'♀**lich** hospitable.

'**Wirtschaft** f (Haushaltung) housekeeping; † e-s Gemeinwesens: economy; (gewerbliche ~) business, trade
and industry; freie ~ free enterprise; (Hauswesen) household;
(Bauernhof) farm; (Treiben) goings-
-on pl.; (Durcheinander) mess; s.
Wirtshaus; '♀**en** (26) keep house;
gut ~ economize, manage well,
schlecht ~ mismanage; (geräuschvoll
hantieren) bustle (od. potter) about;
'~**er** m (7) manager; (Gutsverwalter)
steward; '~**erin** f (16¹) manageress;
im Haushalt: housekeeper; '~**ler** m
economist; '♀**lich** economic(ally
adv.); † a. business…, commercial;
financial; (haushälterisch) economical; (rationell) efficient; (ertragreich) profitable; '~**lichkeit** f economy; efficiency; '~**s-abkommen** n
trade agreement; '~**sberater** m
business consultant; '~**sbeziehun-
gen** f/pl. trade relations; '~**sgebäude**

n/pl. farm-buildings, outhouses; '~s-**geld** *n* housekeeping money; '~sge-**meinschaft** *f: Europäische* ~ European Economic Community; '~s-**geographie** *f* economic geography; '~sgipfel *m* economic summit; '~s-**gymnasium** *n* commercial high school; '~shilfe *f* economic aid; '~s-**jahr** *n* financial year; '~skriminali-**tät** *f* white-collar crime; '~skrise *f* economic crisis; '~sminister *m* Minister of Economics; '~sministe-**rium** *n* Ministry of Economics; '~s-**politik** *f* economic policy; '2s-**poli-tisch** economic(ally *adv.*), pertaining to economic policy; '~s-**prüfer** *m* chartered accountant, *Am.* certified public accountant; '~sverband *m* trade association; '~swachstum *n* economic growth; '~swissenschaft *f* economics; '~swissenschaftler *m* economist; '~swunder *n* economic miracle; '~szweig *m* sector of the economy, branch of trade.

'**Wirts|haus** *n* public house, F pub, *Am.* saloon; *mst ländlich:* inn; '~-**leute** *pl.* host and hostess.

Wisch [viʃ] *m* (3^2) wisp *of straw etc.*; *contp.* (*Papier*2) scrap of paper; '2en (27) wipe; '~er *m* (7) wiper (*a. mot.*); *zum Zeichnen:* stump; '~erblatt *mot. n* wiper blade; '~lappen *m für Ge-schirr:* dish-cloth; *für den Fußboden:* floor-cloth; (*Staubtuch*) duster.

Wisent ['viːzɛnt] *m* (3) bison, aur-ochs. [whisper.]

wispern ['vɪspərn] *v/i. u. v/t.* (29)}

Wiß|begierde ['vis-] *f* thirst for knowledge; (*Neugier*) curiosity; '2-**begierig** eager for knowledge *od.* to learn; *weitS.* curious, inquisitive.

wissen ['visən] **1.** (30) know (et. a th.; *um, von* about of); ~ *von a.* be aware of; ~ *zu inf.* know how to *inf.*; *j-n etwas* ~ *lassen* let a p. know a th.; *ich möchte (gern)* ~, *ob ..., wie ... usw.* I should like to know (*od.* I wonder) whether *od.* if, how ... *etc.*; *man kann nie* ~ you never know *od.* can tell; *nicht daß ich wüßte!* not that I know of!; *weißt du noch?* do you remember?; F *ich will von ihr nichts mehr* ~ I am through with her; *s. aus* 2., *Be-scheid, bestimmt usw.*; **2.** 2 *n* (6) knowledge; (*Bildung*) learning; *ohne mein* ~ without my knowledge; *meines* ~*s* to my knowledge, as far

as I know; *wider besseres* ~ despite one's better knowledge; *nach be-stem* ~ *und Gewissen* to the best of a p.'s knowledge and belief.

'**Wissenschaft** *f* science; (*Wissen*) knowledge; '~ler *m* (7) scholar; (*bsd. Natur*2) scientist, scientific man; '2lich scientific(ally *adv.*); ~ *gebildet* academically trained.

'**Wissens|drang**, '~**durst**, '~**trieb** *m* urge (*od.* thirst) for knowledge; '~**gebiet** *n*, '~**zweig** *m* field of knowledge; '2**wert** worth know-ing, interesting; '~**schatz** *m* store of knowledge.

'**wissentlich** knowing, conscious; (*absichtlich*) wil(l)ful.

wittern ['vitərn] (29) scent, smell; *Gefahr* ~ smell a rat.

'**Witterung** *f* weather; (*Geruch*) scent; *bei günstiger* ~ weather per-mitting; '2**sbeständig** weather--resisting; '~s-**einflüsse** *m/pl.* in-fluence *sg.* of the weather; '~s-**um-schlag** *m* sudden change of the weather; '~s-**verhältnisse** *n/pl.* atmospheric (*od.* meteorological) conditions.

Witwe ['vitvə] *f* (15) widow; (~ *von Stande*) dowager, *z.B. Königin*2 Queen dowager; '~**ngeld** *n* widow's allowance; '~**nkleidung** *f* widow's weeds *pl.*; '~**nrente** *f* widow's pen-sion; '~**nstand** *m* widowhood.

'**Witwer** *m* (7) widower.

Witz [vits] *m* (3^2) (*Geist*) wit; (*Scherz, Spaß*) joke; (*witzige Be-merkung*) quip, gag; *alter* ~ stale joke, F chestnut; ~*e reißen* crack jokes; F *das ist der* ~ *an der Sache* that's where the fun comes in, *weitS.* that's the point (of it); '~**blatt** *n* comic paper; ~**bold** ['~bɔlt] *m* (3) wag, witty fellow, *Am.* F wisecracker; ~**elei** [~ə'laɪ] *f* (16) witticism(s *pl.*); '2**eln** (29) quip, F wisecrack; '~**figur** *f* ridiculous fig-ure; '2**ig** witty; (*spaßig*) funny; '~**ig-keit** *f* wittiness.

wo [voː] where; ~ *nicht* if not, unless; ~ *auch*, ~ *nur* wherever; F (*irgend*~) somewhere; *zeitlich:* when; ~'-**an-ders** elsewhere, somewhere else.

wob [voːp] *pret. v.* **weben**.

wobei [voˈbaɪ] *interr. adv.* at what?; *rel. adv.* at which; in doing so, in the course of which; (*wodurch*) whereby, through which.

Woche ['vɔxə] f (15) week; in e-r ~ in a week; heute über (od. vor) drei ~n this day three weeks; dreimal die (od. in der) ~ three times a week; in den ~n sein be lying in; in die ~n kommen be confined, mit e-m Kind: be delivered of.

'**Wochen|-arbeitszeit** f working week; '~**bett** n childbed, confinement; '~**blatt** n weekly (paper); ~**end...** ['~ʔɛnt-], '~**ende** n week-end; '♀**lang** for weeks; nach ~em Warten after many weeks of waiting; '~**lohn** m weekly pay sg. od. wages pl.; '~**markt** m weekly market; '~**schau** f Film: news-reel; '~**tag** m week-day; bestimmter: day of the week; '♀**tags** on week-days.

wöchentlich ['vœçəntliç] weekly; adv. every week, weekly; einmal ~ once a week.

'**wochenweise** by the week.

Wöchnerin ['vœçnərin] f (16¹) woman in childbed; ~**nen-abteilung** f maternity ward; ~**nenheim** n maternity home.

wo|'**durch** interr. adv. by what?, whereby?, how?; rel. adv. by which, whereby; ~'**fern** provided that, if; ~ nicht unless; ~'**für** interr. adv. for what?, what (...) for?; rel. adv. for which.

wog [vo:k] pret. v. wägen u. wiegen¹.

Woge ['vo:gə] f (15) wave (a. fig.); fig. die ~n glätten pour oil on troubled waters.

wo'**gegen** interr. adv. against what?; rel. adv. against which; tauschend: in exchange for what? od. which; conj. whereas.

wogen ['vo:gən] (25) surge (a. fig.), billow; Getreide: a. wave; schwellend: heave; hin u. her: fluctuate, Kampf: seesaw.

wo|'**her** from where; ~ kommt er? where does he come from?; ~ wissen Sie das? how do you know?; ~'**hin** interr. u. rel. adv. where (... to); indef. adv. somewhere; ~**hin**-'**gegen** whereas.

wohl [vo:l] **1. a)** well, Am. F good; er ist ~ he is well; ihm ist ~ he is feeling fine; ~ oder übel willy-nilly; leben Sie ~! good-by(e)!, farewell!; ich habe mich nie so ~ gefühlt I never felt better; es sich ~ sein lassen enjoy o.s.; ~ dem, der ... happy he who ...; s. bekommen, ~-

tun; **b)** vermutend, einräumend: I presume (od. suppose, think); er wird ~ reich sein he is rich, I suppose; **c)** fragend: ob sie ~ ...? I wonder whether (od. if) she ...; **2.** ♀ n (3) welfare; (Gedeihen) well--being, prosperity; (Nutzen, Vorteil) benefit, good; das gemeine ~ the common weal; sein ~ und Weh his weal and woe; auf Ihr ~! your health!, here's to you!

wohl|'**an** well then!; '~**ange**-**bracht** (very) apt; '~**anständig** decent; ~'**auf** well, in good health; int. well!, cheer up!; '~**bedacht** well-considered; '♀**befinden** n well-being; good health; '~**begründet** well-founded; '♀**behagen** n comfort, pleasure; '~**behalten** safe (and sound); '~**bekannt** well--known; '~**beleibt** corpulent; '♀-**er-gehen** n (6) well-being, welfare, prosperity; '~**erwogen** well-considered; ~**erworben** ['~ʔɛrvɔrbən] duly acquired; ~e Rechte n/pl. vested (od. well established) rights; ~**er-zogen** ['~ʔɛrtso:gən] well-bred; '♀**fahrt** f (16, o. pl.) welfare; (öffentliche) ~ a. (public) relief; public assistance; '♀**fahrtsamt** n welfare cen|tre, Am. -er; '♀**fahrts-einrichtung** f welfare institution; '♀**fahrtspflege** f welfare work; '♀**fahrtsstaat** m welfare state; '♀**fahrts-unterstützung** f public relief; '~**feil** cheap; '♀**gefallen** n pleasure, satisfaction; sein ~ haben an (dat.) take pleasure in; sich in ~ auflösen co. end in smoke, (verschwinden) vanish (into thin air); '~**gefällig** pleasant, agreeable; (selbstzufrieden) complacent; '♀**gefühl** n pleasant sensation; allgemeines: sense of well-being; '~**gemeint** well-meant; '~**gemerkt!** mark you!, mind you!, remember!; '~**gemut** cheerful; '~**genährt** well--fed; '~**geraten** Kind: good; '♀**geruch** m fragrance, perfume; '♀**geschmack** m pleasant taste od. flavo(u)r; '~**gesinnt** well-meaning; j-m ~ well-disposed towards a p.; '~**gesittet** well-mannered; '~**gestaltet** well-shaped, shapely; '~**habend** well-to-do, wealthy, prosperous, well-off (pred. well off); '♀**haben**-**heit** f s. Wohlstand.

'**wohlig** comfortable.

'**Wohl**|**klang** m, '~**laut** m melodious

sound, harmony, euphony; '♀klin-
gend harmonious, melodious; '♀-
leben *n* life of pleasure, good living,
luxury; '♀meinend well-meaning;
'♀riechend fragrant, sweet-scent-
ed; '♀schmeckend savo(u)ry, tasty;
'~sein *n s. Wohlbefinden; '~stand
m prosperity, affluence, wealth;
'~standsgesellschaft *f* affluent
society; '~tat *f* good deed, kindness; *(a. ⚖)* benefit; *fig.* boon,
comfort; *s. wahr;* '~täter *m* benefactor; '~täterin *f* (16¹) benefac-
tress; '♀tätig beneficent; *(mild-
tätig)* charitable; '~tätigkeit *f*
charity; '~tätigkeitsbasar *m* charity bazaar; '~tätigkeitsver-anstal-
tung *f* charity performance; '~-
tätigkeitsver-ein *m* charitable society; ♀tuend ['~tuːənt] pleasant,
beneficial; '♀tun: *(j-m)* ~ do (a p.)
good; *das tut e-m wohl* it does one
good; '♀-überlegt well-consid-
ered; '♀-unterrichtet well-informed; '♀verdient well-deserved;
'♀verstanden well-understood; ~!
mind you!; '♀weislich very wisely,
prudently; '~wollen¹ *n* (6) goodwill, benevolence; '♀wollen² *f.*
wish a p. well; '♀wollend kind,
benevolent; *(günstig)* favo(u)rable.
'Wohn|-anhänger *m s. Wohnwagen;*
'~anlage *f* housing estate *(Am.*
development); '~bezirk *m* residential area; '~block *m* block of flats;
'~einheit *f* dwelling unit.
wohnen ['voːnən] (25) live *(bei j-m*
with); *feiner:* dwell, reside *(alle a.
fig.); amtlich:* reside *(in dat.* at);
vorübergehend: stay *(bei* with); *als
Mieter:* lodge, *Am. a.* room *(in dat.
at, bei* with).
'Wohn|gebäude *n* dwelling-house;
(Etagenhaus) block of flats, *Am.*
apartment house; '~gebiet *n,* '~ge-
gend *f* residential area; '~geld *n*
housing subsidy; '~gelegenheit *f*
living accommodation; '~gemein-
schaft *f* flat-sharing community; '♀-
haft living, resident *(in dat.* at);
'~haus *n s. Wohngebäude;* '~heim *n*
hostel; '~küche *f* kitchen-living-
-room; '♀lich comfortable; *(traulich)*
cosy; ~mobil ['~mobiːl] *n* (3¹) mobile home, camper; '♀ort *m* (place
of) residence, ⚖ *a.* domicile; '~-
raum *m* housing space; '~recht *n*
right of residence; '~schlafzimmer

n bed-sitting-room; '~sitz *m s.
Wohnort;* '~stube *f s. Wohnzimmer.*
'Wohnung *f* dwelling, home; *eng S.*
lodgings, rooms, apartments *pl.; im
Stockwerk:* flat, *Am.* apartment; '~s-
amt *n* Housing Office; '~sbau *m*
housing construction; '~sbaupro-
jekt *n* housing scheme; '~s-inhaber
m occupant, tenant; '~smangel *m,*
'~snot *f* housing shortage; '~ssuche *f*
house-hunting; '~s-tür *f* front-door;
'~swechsel *m* change of residence.
'Wohn|viertel *n* residential quarter
(Am. section); '~wagen *m* caravan,
Am. trailer; '~zimmer *n* sitting-
-room, *bsd. Am.* living room.
wölb|en ['vœlbən] (25) vault; *(a.
sich)* arch; '♀ung *f* vault; *(gewölbte
Form)* curvature; ⊕ camber.
Wolf [vɔlf] *m* (3³) wolf; *Spinnerei:*
willow; *metall.* devil; *(Fleischhack-
maschine)* mincer; ♨ chafe, gall;
fig. man muß mit den Wölfen heulen
when (you are) in Rome do as the
Romans do; *s. Schafpelz.*
Wölfin ['vœlfin] *f* (16¹) she-wolf.
Wolfram ♒ ['vɔlfram] *n* (6, *o. pl.*)
tungsten.
'Wolfs|hund *m* wolf-hound, wolf
dog; '~hunger *m* ravenous hunger;
'~milch ♀ *f* spurge.
Wolke ['vɔlkə] *f* (15) cloud *(a. fig.);
fig. aus allen ~n fallen* be thunder-
struck.
'Wolken|bruch *m* cloud-burst; '~-
decke *f* cloud cover; '~himmel *m*
clouded sky; '~kratzer *m* skyscraper; ~'kuckucks-heim *n* Cloud-
-Cuckoo-Land; '♀los cloudless;
'~schicht *f* cloud layer; ♀verhangen
['~fɛrhaŋən] overcast.
'wolkig cloudy; *Himmel:* clouded.
'Woll|decke ['vɔl-] *f* (wool) blanket;
'~e *f* (15) wool; *fig. in der ~ sitzen*
live in clover; *sich in die ~ geraten*
F have a row; '♀en¹ *adj.* wool(l)en;
Strumpf: a. worsted.
'wollen² 1. (30) wish; *(verlangen)*
want; *(bereit sein)* be willing; *(beabsichtigen)* intend; *(im Begriff sein
zu ...)* be going to, be about to;
lieber ~ prefer; *nicht ~* refuse; *so
Gott will!* please God!; *ich will es
(nicht) tun* I will (won't) do it; *ich
wollte, ich hätte es getan* I wish I
had done it; *was ~ Sie (von mir)?*
what do you want (of me)?; *was ~
Sie damit sagen?* what do you mean

by it?; **er mag** ~ **oder nicht** willy-
-nilly, whether he likes it or not;
ich will (*od.* **wollte**) **lieber** I would
(*od.* had) rather, I should prefer;
das will ich meinen I should think
so; **das will überlegt sein** that requires some thinking; **dem sei wie
ihm wolle** be that as it may; **er weiß,
was er will** he knows his own mind;
mach was du willst! do what you
want!, *ärgerlich:* do your worst!;
wir ~ **gehen** let us go; **wie du willst**
as you like; **2.** ♀ *n* (6, *o. pl.*) will;
phls. volition.

'**Woll|fett** *n* wool-grease, yolk; '~-
garn *n* wool(l)en yarn, worsted;
'~**handel** *m* wool-trade; '♀**ig**
wool(l)y; '~**jacke** *f* cardigan; '~-
schur *f* sheep-shearing; '~**spinnerei** *f* wool-spinning (mill *Fabrik*);
'~**stoff** *m* wool(l)en (fabric).

Wol|lust ['vɔlʊst] *f* (14¹) voluptu-
ousness, lust; ♀**lüstig** ['~lʏstɪç] voluptuous; *s. a.* **lüstern**; '~**lüstling** *m*
(3¹) libertine, debauchee.

'**Wollwaren** *f/pl.* wool(l)en goods,
wool(l)ens; '~**händler** *m* wool(l)en-
draper.

wo|'mit with what?; what ... with?;
rel. adv. with which; *s.* **dienen**;
~'**möglich** possibly; ~'**nach** after
what?; *rel. adv.* after which,
whereupon; (*gemäß*) according to
which.

Wonne ['vɔnə] *f* (15) delight, bliss;
F **mit** ~ with relish; '~**monat** *m*, '~-
mond *m* month of delight (*od.* of
May); ♀**trunken** blissful, enrap-
tured; *pred.* in raptures.

'**wonnig** delightful, blissful; (*herzig*)
lovely, sweet.

wo|ran [vo:'ran] at what?; *rel. adv.*
at (*od.* by) which; ~ **denken Sie?**
what are you thinking of?; **ich weiß
nicht,** ~ **ich bin** I don't know where
I stand; ~ **liegt es, daß ...?** how is
it that ...?; ~ **erkennt man ...?** how
(*od.* by what) do you see ...?; ~'**rauf**
on what?; ~ **warten Sie?** what are
you waiting for?; *rel. adv.* on which;
(*und danach*) whereupon; ~'**raus**
out of (*od.* from) what?; **~ ist das
gemacht?** what is it made of?; *rel.
adv.* out of (*od.* from) which,
whence; ~'**rein** into what?; *rel. adv.*
into which.

worfeln 🗲 ['vɔrfəln] (29) winnow.
worin [vo:'rin] in what?; *rel. adv.*
in which, wherein.

Wort [vɔrt] *n* (3, *einzeln:* 1²) word;
(*Ausdruck*) term, expression; (*Ausspruch*) saying; (*Ehren*♀) word (of
hono[u]r); **das** ~ **Gottes** the Gospel;
bei Zahlenangaben: in ~**en ... in**
letters ...; **ein Mann von** ~ **sein** be as
good as one's word; **ein Mann, ein
~!** word of hono(u)r!, hono(u)r
bright!; **auf ein** ~**!** a word with
you!; **aufs** ~ **gehorchen** obey to the
letter; **j-m ins** ~ **fallen, j-m das** ~
abschneiden cut a p. short; **mit
andern** ~**en** in other words; **mit e-m**
~ **in a word; ums** ~ **bitten, sich zu**
~ **melden** ask permission to speak;
zu ~**e kommen** get a hearing; **nicht
zu** ~ **kommen** not to get a word in
edgewise; **das** ~ **ergreifen** (begin to)
speak, *parl.* rise to speak, address
the House, *bsd. Am.* take the floor;
j-m das ~ **erteilen** give a p. permission to speak; *parl.* **j-m das** ~ **entziehen** rule a p. out of order; **das** ~
erhalten be allowed to speak, *parl.*
catch the Speaker's eye, *bsd. Am.*
get the floor; **das** ~ **führen** be the
spokesman; **das große** ~ **führen** talk
big; (*tonangebend sein*) lay down the
law; ~ **halten** keep one's word; *parl.*
das ~ **haben** have the ear of the
House, *bsd. Am.* have the floor; **ein**
~ **gab das andere** one word led another; **kein** ~ **mehr!** not another
word!; **j-n beim** ~**e nehmen** take a
p. at his (*od.* her) word; **mit j-m
ein** ~ **reden** have a word with a p.;
e-r S. das ~ **reden** hold a brief for;
s. **einlegen, geben, Geld, Kehle, kurz,
zurücknehmen.**

'**Wort|-akzent** *m* word-stress; '♀-
arm poor in words; '~**armut** *f*
poverty of words; '~**art** *gr. f* part
of speech, class of word; '~**bedeu-
tungslehre** *f* semantics; '~**bildung**
f word-formation; '~**bruch** *m* breach
of one's word *od.* of faith; '♀**brüchig**
false to one's word; ~ **werden** break
one's word.

'**Wortemacher(in** *f*) *m* big talker.

Wörter|buch ['vœrtər-] *n* diction-
ary; '~**verzeichnis** *n* list of words,
vocabulary, word-index.

'**Wort|folge** *f* word-order; '~**fü-
gung** *f* construction; (*a.* '~**fügungs-
lehre** *f*) syntax; '~**führer(in** *f*) *m*
speaker; *nur m* spokesman; '~**fülle**
f verbosity; '~**gefecht** *n* dispute;

'₂getreu literal; '₂gewandt eloquent, glib; '₂karg taciturn, silent;
'‿kargheit f taciturnity; '‿klasse
gr. f s. Wortart; '‿klauber m (7)
quibbler, word-splitter; ‿klaube-
rei ['‿raɪ] f (16) word-splitting;
'‿laut m wording; (Inhalt) text; ₨
(genauer ‿) tenor; der Brief usw.
hat folgenden ‿ runs as follows.
wörtlich ['vœrt-] literal.
'wort|los wordless(ly adv.); '‿reich
abundant in words; contp. verbose;
'₂schatz m stock of words, vocabulary; '₂schwall m flood of words,
verbiage; '₂sinn m literal sense;
'₂spiel n play on words, pun; '₂-
stamm m stem, root; '₂stellung f
word-order; '₂streit m dispute;
'₂verdreher(in f) m distorter of
words; '₂verdrehung f distortion
of words; '₂wechsel m dispute,
altercation; e-n ‿ haben have words.
wo|rüber [vo:'ry:bər] over (od.
upon) what?, what ... about?; rel.
adv. over (od. upon, about) which;
vgl. a. Zeitwörter wie z.B. lachen;
‿'rum about what?, what ...
about?; rel. adv. about which; vgl.
a. Zeitwörter wie z.B. trauern; ‿
'runter under (od. among) what?;
rel. adv. under (od. among) which.
wo|'selbst where; ‿'von of (od.
from) what?; what are you talking
about?; rel. adv. of (od. from)
which; vgl. a. Zeitwörter wie z.B.
leben; ‿'vor before what?; rel.
adv. before which; vgl. a. Zeitwörter wie z.B. sich fürchten; ‿'zu
for what?, F what for?; rel. adv. for
which; (warum) why; ‿ noch kommt,
daß to which must be added that.
Wrack ⚓ [vrak] n (3) wreck (a.fig.);
'‿gut n wreckage.
wrang [vraŋ] pret. v. wringen.
wringen ['vrɪŋən] (30) wring.
Wucher ['vu:xər] m (7) usury;
(Waren₂) profiteering; ‿ treiben s.
wuchern; '‿er m (7) usurer; (Waren₂) profiteer; '₂haft, '₂isch
usurious; mit Waren: profiteering;
'‿handel m usurious trade, profiteering; '‿miete f rack-rent; '₂n
(29) ⚘ grow exuberantly, proliferate;
(Wucher treiben) practise usury; mit
Waren: profiteer; '‿ung ⚘ f excres-
cence, growth; bsd. in Nase u. Rachen: vegetation; '‿zins m, '‿zinsen
pl. usurious interest.

Wuchs¹ [vu:ks] m (4²) growth;
(Gestalt) figure, stature, build.
wuchs² pret. v. wachsen¹.
Wucht [vuxt] f (16) weight; (Gewalt) force; (Schwung) impetus;
(Anprall) impact (a. fig.); F 'ne
Wucht! (tolle Sache) sl. a wow!;
mit voller ‿ gegen ... rennen cannon
against; '₂en (26) v/i. weigh heavy;
v/t. lever up, heave; '₂ig weighty,
heavy; Schlag, Gestalt, a. fig. Stil
usw.: powerful.
Wühl|-arbeit ['vy:l-] f fig. subver-
sive activity; '₂en (25) dig; Tier:
burrow; Schwein: root; (wild um-
hersuchen) rummage; fig. mst pol.
agitate; im Gelde ‿ fig. wallow (od.
be rolling) in money; '‿er m (7)
fig. agitator; '₂erisch subversive;
'‿maus f vole; '‿tisch F m im Warenhaus: rummage counter.
Wulst [vulst] m (3² u. ³) roll; zum
Ausstopfen: pad; (Ausbauchung)
bulge; (Reifen₂) bead (of a tyre);
'₂ig stuffed, padded; (bauchig)
bulging; (aufgedunsen) puffed up;
Lippen: protruding, thick.
wund [vunt] (offen) sore; (verwundet) wounded; ‿e Stelle sore; fig.
‿er Punkt tender spot; sich die Füße
‿ laufen become footsore; ‿ reiben
gall, chafe; '₂brand m gangrene;
'₂e ['vundə] f (15) wound; die Zeit
heilt alle ‿n time is a great healer;
fig. alte ‿n wieder aufreißen open
old sores.
Wunder ['vundər] n (7) miracle;
(a. Sache, Vorgang, Person) wonder,
marvel, prodigy; ‿ der Technik
engineering marvel; ‿ tun (od. vollbringen, wirken) do (od. work)
wonders, perform miracles; (es ist)
kein ‿, daß ... small wonder that
...; es geschehen Zeichen und ‿
wonders will never cease; sein
blaues ‿ erleben get the shock of
one's life; ⚦ was halten von think a
world of; '₂bar wonderful, mar-
vel(l)ous; (übernatürlich; a. fig.)
miraculous; '‿bild n miraculous
image; '‿ding n prodigy; ‿e pl.
vollbringen perform miracles; '‿-
doktor m quack; '‿droge f miracle
drug; '‿glaube m belief in miracles; '₂hübsch lovely; '‿kind n
infant prodigy; '‿knabe m boy-
-wonder; '‿kur f miraculous cure;
'‿land n Fairyland, wonderland;

'**Ջlich** queer, odd, strange; (*launisch*) whimsical; '**Ջlichkeit** *f* queerness, oddity, strangeness; '**Ջn** (29): *sich ~ wonder* (*über acc.* at), be surprised (at); *be surprised to see etc.* (*a. th.*); *es wundert mich* I am surprised *od.* astonished; (*ich frage mich*) I wonder (*wo usw.* where *etc.*); *es sollte mich nicht ~* I shouldn't wonder; '**Ջnehmen:** *es nimmt mich wunder, daß* I am astonished that; '**Ջsam** wondrous; '**Ջ'schön** very beautiful, of breathtaking beauty; '**Ջtat** *f* miracle; '**Ջtäter(in** *f)* *m* miracle-worker; '**Ջtätig** wonder-working, miraculous; '**Ջtier** *n* monster; *fig.* prodigy; '**Ջvoll** wonderful, marvel(l)ous; '**Ջwelt** *f* world of wonders; '**Ջwerk** *n* miracle; *fig. a.* wonder; '**Ջzeichen** *n* miraculous sign.

'**Wund|fieber** *n* wound-fever; *sich* '**Ջlaufen** get footsore; *sich* '**Ջliegen** get bedsore; '**Ջmal** *n* scar; *~e pl. eccl.* stigmata; '**Ջsalbe** *f* healing ointment; '**Ջstarrkrampf** *m* tetanus.

Wunsch [vunʃ] *m* (3² *u.* ³) wish, desire; *auf ~* on request; *auf j-s ~* at a p.'s desire *od.* request; (*je*) *nach ~* as desired; *mit den besten Wünschen zum Fest* with the compliments of the season; '**Ջbild** *n* ideal; '**Ջdenken** *n* wishful thinking.

Wünschelrute ['vynʃəl-] *f* divining-rod; **~ngänger** ['Ջgɛŋər] *m* (7) diviner, dowser.

wünschen ['vynʃən] (27) wish, want, desire; *s. Glück; viel zu ~ übrig lassen* leave much to be desired; *wie Sie ~* as you wish; *was ~ Sie?* may I help you?; '**Ջswert** desirable.

'**wunsch|gemäß** as desired; '**Ջkind** *n* planned child; '**Ջkonzert** *n* (musical) request program(me); '**Ջlos:** *~ glücklich* perfectly happy; '**Ջtraum** *m* wishdream, wishful thinking, *Am.* F pipe dream; '**Ջzettel** *m* list of things desired.

wurde ['vurdə] *pret. v.* werden 1 *u.* 2.

Würde ['vyrdə] *f* (15) dignity (*a. weitS.*); (*Ehre*) hono(u)r; (*Titel*) title; *akademische:* degree; *unter j-s ~* beneath one's dignity; *unter aller ~* beneath contempt; '**Ջlos** undignified; '**Ջnträger** *m* digni-

tary; '**Ջvoll** dignified; (*feierlich*) solemn, grave.

würdig ['Ջdiç] worthy (*gen.* of); (*verdient*) deserving (of); *s.* **würdevoll**; **~en** ['Ջgən] (25) appreciate, value; (*erwähnen*) mention hono(u)rably, laud; *j-n e-s Blickes* (*Wortes*) *~* deign to look at (speak to) a p.; **Ջkeit** ['Ջdiç-] *f* worthiness; (*Verdienst*) merit; (*würdiges Äußere*) dignified appearance; **Ջung** ['Ջguŋ] *f* appreciation; assessment (*a. ⚖*).

Wurf [vurf] *m* (3³) throw; (*~ Junge*) brood, litter; *fig.* großer *~* great success; *alles auf einen ~* setzen stake all on a single card.

Würfel ['vyrfəl] *m* (7) die; ᛉ cube (*a. Eis⚹ usw.*); *die ~ sind gefallen* the die is cast; '**Ջbecher** *m* dice-box; **Ջförmig** ['Ջfœrmiç] cubic (-al); **Ջig** cubical; *Muster:* chequered, *bsd. Am.* check(er)ed; '**Ջn** (29) *v/i.* play (at) dice; *~ um* throw dice for; *v/t. Stoff:* chequer, *bsd. Am.* check(er); '**Ջspiel** *n* game of dice; '**Ջzucker** *m* lump sugar.

'**Wurf|geschoß** *n* missile; '**Ջkreis** *m Sport:* (throwing) circle; '**Ջpfeil** *m* dart; '**Ջscheibe** *f* quoit; (*Diskus*) discus; '**Ջspeer** *m*, '**Ջspieß** *m* javelin, dart; '**Ջtaube** *f Schießsport:* clay pigeon.

würg|en ['vyrgən] (25) *v/t.* throttle, choke (*beide a.* ⊕); *poet.* (*töten*) slay; *v/i.* choke; *beim Erbrechen:* retch; *beim Essen:* gag on one's food; *fig. an e-r Arbeit:* struggle hard at; **Ջengel** ['vyrk-] *m* destroying angel; **Ջer** ['Ջgər] *m* (7) slayer, murderer (*a.* '**Ջerin** *f*); (*Vogel*) butcher-bird.

Wurm [vurm] *m* (1²) worm (*a. fig.*); (*Made*) maggot, grub; ⚕ *am Finger:* whitlow; F *n* (*bsd. Kind*) little mite; F *j-m die Würmer aus der Nase ziehen* draw a p. out.

Würmchen ['vyrmçən] *n* (6) little worm; *fig.* tiny mite.

wurmen ['vurmən] (25) gall, vex.

wurm|förmig ['Ջfœrmiç] worm-shaped, vermiform; '**Ջfortsatz** *anat. m* appendix; '**Ջig** wormy; maggoty; '**Ջkrank** suffering from worms; '**Ջmittel** *n* vermifuge; '**Ջstich** *m*, '**Ջloch** *n* worm-hole; '**Ջstichig** worm-eaten; *fig.* unsound, rotten.

Wurst [vurst] *f* (14¹) sausage; F *~*

wider ~ tit for tat; F *jetzt geht's um die* ~! it's do or die now!; F *es ist mir* ~ I don't care (a rap); '~blatt F *n* (*Zeitung*) (lousy) rag.

Würstchen ['vyrstçən] *n* (6): *warme* ~ *pl.* hot sausages, *Am.* hot dogs; F *fig. armes* ~ poor thing.

Wurstel|ei F [vurstə'laɪ] *f* (16) muddling, muddle; '~n F (29) muddle. **wurst|ig** *sl.* absolutely indifferent; '2vergiftung *f* sausage-poisoning, ⚕ botulism; '2waren *f/pl.* sausages.

Würze ['vyrtsə] *f* (15) (*Gewürz*) spice, condiment; (*Aroma*) seasoning, flavo(u)r; ⊕ (*Bier*2) wort; *fig.* zest, flavo(u)r; *in der Kürze liegt die* ~ brevity is the soul of wit.

Wurzel ['vurtsəl] *f* (16) root (*a. gr.*, ⅄, *Zahn*2 *u. fig.*); ~ *fassen od. schlagen* (*a. fig.*) take (*od.* strike) root; '~behandlung ⚕ *f* root-treatment; '~größe ⅄ *f* radical quantity; '~knolle *f* tuber, bulb.

'**wurzeln** (29, h. *u.* sn) (take) root; ~ *in* (*dat.*) be rooted in; '~d rooted.

'**Wurzel|schößling** *m* sucker, runner; '~stock *m* root-stock; '~werk *n* roots *pl.*; '~wort *n* radical word, root; '~zeichen ⅄ *n* radical sign;

'~ziehen ⅄ *n* evolution, root extraction.

würz|en ['vyrtsən] (27) season, flavo(u)r, spice; '~ig spicy; aromatic; '2mischung *f* mixed herbs *pl.*

wusch [vu:ʃ] *pret. v.* waschen.

wußte ['vustə] *pret. v.* wissen 1.

Wust [vu:st] *m* (3) tangled mass; (*Kram*) trash; (*Durcheinander*) mess, jumble.

wüst [vy:st] desert, waste; (*wirr*) confused; (*liederlich*) depraved; (*roh*) rude; (*gemein*) vile; F (*arg*) awful; 2e['~ə] *f*, 2enei [~'naɪ] *f* (15) desert, waste; '2ensand *m* desert sand; '2ling *m* (3¹) libertine, rake, lecher.

Wut [vu:t] *f* (16, *o. pl.*) rage, fury; *in* ~ in a rage; *j-n in* ~ *bringen* enrage (*od.* infuriate) a p.; *in* ~ *geraten* fly into a rage; '~anfall *m*, '~ausbruch *m* fit (*od.* outburst) of rage.

wüten ['vy:tən] (26) *allg.* rage; '~d furious (*a. fig. heftig*); F *bsd. Am.* mad (*beide: auf, über acc.* at; *with a p.*).

'**wut-entbrannt** enraged.

'**wutschäumend** foaming with rage.

'**wutschnaubend** furious.

X, Y

X [iks], **x** *n inv.* X, x; *j-m ein X für ein U vormachen* throw dust in a p.'s eyes.
'**X-Achse** ⅄ *f* axis of x.
Xanthippe [ksan'tipə] *f* (15) *fig.* Xanthippe, termagant.
'**X-Beine** *n/pl.* turned-in legs, knock-knees; '**X-beinig** knock-kneed.
x-be'liebig any (... you please); *jede(r, s)* ~e ... any (given) ...
'**x-mal** F (ever so) many times, F umpteen times.

x-te ['ikstə]: F *zum* ~*n Male* for the umpteenth (*od.* nth) time.
Xylograph [ksylo'grɑːf] *m* (12) xylographer; 2isch xylographic(al).
Xylophon ♪ [~'foːn] *n* (3¹) xylophone.

Y ['ypsilɔn], **y** *n inv.* Y, y.
'**Y-Achse** ⅄ *f* axis of y.
Yacht [jaxt] *f* (16) *s.* Jacht.
Yankee ['jɛŋki] *m* (11) Yankee.
Ysop ♀ ['yːzɔp] *m* (3¹) hyssop.
Yucca ♀ ['juka] *f* (11¹) yucca.

Z

Z [tset], z *n inv.* Z, z; *s.* A.

Zacke ['tsakə] *f* (15), '~n¹ *m* (6) (sharp) point; (*Zinke*) prong; (*Auszackung*) indent(ation); (*Eisenspitze*) spike; (*Fels*♀) jag.

'**zacken²** (25) indent; (*zähnen*) tooth; *ungleichmäßig:* jag; *Kleid:* scallop.

'**zackig** indented, notched; *Felsen, Glas usw.:* jagged; ♣ *Blatt:* crenate; *fig. sl.* (*schneidig*) smart.

zag [tsaːk] *s.* zaghaft; ~en ['tsaːgən] **1.** (25) quail; (*zurückschrecken*) shrink, flinch; **2.** ♀ *n* (6) quailing; shrinking, flinching; ~haft ['tsaːkhaft] timid; '♀**haftigkeit** *f* timidity.

zäh|(**e**) ['tsɛː(ə)] tough, *fig. a.* tenacious; *Energie:* grim, dogged; *Flüssigkeit:* ropy, viscous; *ein* ~*es Leben haben* be tenacious of life; '~**flüssig** viscous, sticky; *Verkehr:* slow-moving; '♀**igkeit** *f* toughness, tenacity; ropiness, viscosity.

Zahl [tsaːl] *f* (16) number; (*Ziffer*) figure (*a.* = *Betrag, Wert*), numeral; (*arabische Ziffer*) cipher; (*Stelle*) digit.

'**zahlbar** payable (*bei* at, with; *an acc.* to); ~ *sein od.* werden fall due, be(come) payable; ~ *machen od. stellen* make payable, *Wechsel:* domiciliate; ~ *bei Lieferung* cash on delivery.

'**zählbar** countable, computable.

zählebig ['~leːbiç] tenacious of life.

zahlen ['tsaːlən] *v/t. u. v/i.* (25) pay; *im Gasthaus:* ~, *bitte!* the bill (*Am.* the check), please!

zählen ['tsɛːlən] *v/t. u. v/i.* (25) count, (*a.* = *sich belaufen auf*) number; *fig.* (*haben*) have, number; ~ *auf* (*acc.*) count on; *unter* (*acc.*) ... ~, *zu* ... ~ number among, rank with; *er* (*es*) *zählt nicht* he (it) does not count; *s.* drei.

'**Zahlen**|**lotto** *n s.* Lotto; '♀**mäßig** numerical; *j-m* ~ *überlegen sein* outnumber; '~**material** *n* numerical data *pl.*, figures *pl.*; '~**schloß** *n* combination lock; '~**verhältnis** *n* numerical proportion.

'**Zahler** *m* (7), '~**in** *f* (16¹) payer.

'**Zähler** *m* (7) ⊕ counter; *für Gasverbrauch usw.:* meter; ♣ numera-

tor; '~**ablesung** *f* reading.

'**Zahl**|**grenze** *f* fare stage; '~**karte** *f* paying-in form.

'**zahl**|**los** numberless, countless; '♀**meister** *m* ✗ paymaster; ⚓ purser; '~**reich** numerous; '♀**stelle** *f* paying-office; '♀**tag** *m* pay-day.

'**Zahlung** *f* payment; ~ *leisten* make payment; *et. in* ~ *nehmen* accept a th. in part payment (*od.* part exchange).

'**Zählung** *f* counting; (*a. als Ergebnis, z.B. Blutkörperchen*♀) count; (*Volks*♀ *usw.*) census.

'**Zahlungs**|-**abkommen** *n* payments agreement; '~**anweisung** *f* order to pay; (*Überweisung*) money order; '~**aufforderung** *f* demand for payment; '~**aufschub** *m* respite; '~**auftrag** *m e-s Bankkunden:* banker's order; '~**bedingungen** *f/pl.* terms of payment; *zu erleichterten* ~ on easy terms; '~**befehl** ⚖ *m s.* Mahnbescheid; '~**bilanz** *f* balance of payments; '~**einstellung** *f* suspension of payment; '~**empfänger** *m* payee; '~**erleichterung**(**en** *pl.*) *f* facilities (of payment), easy terms *pl.*; '♀**fähig** solvent; '~**fähigkeit** *f* solvency; '~**frist** *f* term of payment; *s.* Zahlungsaufschub; '~**mittel** *n* currency; *gesetzliches* ~ legal tender; '~**ort** *m* place of payment; '~**schwierigkeiten** *f/pl.* financial difficulties *pl.*; '~**termin** *m* date of payment; '♀-**unfähig** insolvent; '~**unfähigkeit** *f* insolvency.

'**Zählwerk** *n* counter.

'**Zahl**|**wort** *gr. n* numeral; '~**zeichen** *n* figure, cipher.

zahm [tsaːm] tame (*a. fig.*), domestic(ated); (*gefügig*) tractable.

zähm|**bar** ['tsɛːm-] tamable; '~**en** (25) tame (*a. fig.*), domesticate; *Pferd:* break in; *fig.* restrain.

'**Zahmheit** *f* tameness.

'**Zähmung** *f* taming.

Zahn [tsaːn] *m* (3³) tooth (*pl.* teeth); ⊕ *am* ~*rad:* tooth, cog; *fig.* F (*Tempo*) speed; *sl.* (*Mädel*) doll, chick; *der* ~ *der Zeit* the ravages *pl.* of time; *die Zähne zeigen* show one's teeth (*a. fig. j-m* to a p.); *j-m auf den* ~ *fühlen* sound a p.; *bis an die Zähne bewaffnet* armed to the teeth; *s.* Haar, zusammenbeißen;

'~**arzt** *m* dentist, dental surgeon; '♀-**ärztlich** dental; '~**behandlung** *f* dental treatment; '~**belag** *m* (dental) plaque; '~**bürste** *f* tooth-brush; '~**creme** *f* tooth-paste.

Zähne|fletschen ['tsɛ:nə-] *n* bared teeth *pl.*; '~**klappern** *n* (6) chattering of teeth; '~**knirschen** *n*, '♀-**knirschend** (6) gritting one's teeth. **zahnen** ['tsɑ:nən] (25) *v/i.* teethe, cut one's teeth; *v/t.* ⊕ tooth. **zähnen** ['tsɛ:nən] (25) *v/t.* indent, notch.

'**Zahn|-ersatz** *m* (artificial) denture; ~**fäule** ['~fɔrlə] *f* (dental) caries, tooth decay; '~**fistel** *f* fistula in the gums; '~**fleisch** *n* gums *pl.*; '~**fleischbluten** *n* bleeding of the gums; '~**füllung** *f* filling, stopping; '~**geschwür** *n* gumboil; '~**heilkunde** *f* dentistry; '~**krone** *f* crown; '~**labor** *n* dental laboratory; '~**laut** *m* dental (sound); '♀**los** toothless; '~**lücke** *f* gap between two teeth; '~**medizin** *f* dentistry; '~**nerv** *m* nerve of a tooth; '~**pasta** *f* tooth-paste; '~**pflege** *f* oral hygiene; '~**prothese** *f* dental prosthesis, denture; '~**pulver** *n* tooth-powder; '~**rad** ⊕ *n* gear (wheel), cog-wheel, toothed wheel; '~**rad-antrieb** *m* gear drive; '~**radbahn** 🚋 *f* rack-railway; '~**radgetriebe** *n* toothed gear; '~**schmelz** *m* (tooth) enamel; '~**schmerz** *m* toothache; '~**seide** *f* dental floss; '~**stein** *m* tartar, scale; '~**stocher** *m* (7) toothpick; '~**techniker** *m* dental technician; '~**wechsel** *m* second dentition; '~**weh** *n* toothache; '~**werk** ⊕ *n* rack-work; '~**wurzel** *f* root (of a tooth); '~**zange** *f* dental forceps.

Zähre ['tsɛ:rə] *poet. f* (15) tear.

Zange ['tsaŋə] *f* (15) (*eine a pair of*) tongs *pl.*; (*Kneif♀*) nippers *pl.*; (*Rund♀, Flach♀*) pliers *pl.*; (*Pinzette*) tweezers *pl.*; ✽, *zo.* forceps; *kleinere:* pincers *pl.*; *fig. j-n in die* ~ *nehmen* press a p. hard; '~**ngeburt** ✚ *f* forceps delivery.

Zank [tsaŋk] *m* (3) quarrel; '~**apfel** *m* apple of discord, bone of contention; '♀**en** (25) scold; (*a. sich*) quarrel, squabble; *lärmend:* brawl; *sich* ~ *mit* have words (*od.* a row) with '♀**haft**, **zänkisch** ['tsɛŋkiʃ] quarrelsome, nagging; '~**sucht** *f* quarrelsomeness; '♀**süchtig** quar-

relsome, contentious.

Zäpfchen ['tsɛpfçən] *n* (6) little peg; *anat.* uvula; 🏥 (*Einführ♀*) suppository; '~... *anat.*, *gr.* uvular.

Zapfen ['tsapfən] **1.** *m* (6) plug; (*Pflock*) peg, pin; (*Verbindungs♀*) tenon; (*Faß♀*) tap, bung; (*Dreh♀*) pivot; ♣ cone; **2.** ♀ (25) tap; '~**bohrer** *m* tap-borer; '~**lager** *n* pivot (*od.* trunnion) bearing; '~**loch** *n* tap-hole; *Tischlerei:* mortise; '~**streich** ✕ *m* tattoo, taps *pl.* '**Zapf|hahn** *m* tap, *Am.* faucet; '~**pistole** *f* (petrol) gun, nozzle; '~**säule** *f* petrol pump.

zappel|ig ['tsapəliç] fidgety; '~**n** (29) flounder; *vor Unruhe:* fidget; *sich windend:* wriggle; *kämpfend:* struggle; *fig. j-n* ~ *lassen* keep a p. in suspense, tantalize a p.; ♀**philipp** F ['~fi:lip] *m* fidget.

zappenduster F [tsapən'du:stər] pitch-dark; *fig. dann wird's* ~ things will look pretty grim.

Zar [tsɑ:r] *m* (12) czar, tsar.

Zarge ['tsargə] *f* (15) ⊕ border, edge; (*Rahmen*) frame, case; (*Seitenstück der Geige usw.*) side.

Zarin ['tsɑ:rin] *f* (16[^1]) czarina.

zart [tsɑːrt] tender; *Haut*, *Farbe*, *Ton usw.:* soft; *Gesundheit usw.:* delicate; (*sanft*) gentle; '~**besaitet** *fig.* (very) sensitive; '~**fühlend** delicate; '♀**gefühl** *n* delicacy of feeling, tactfulness; '♀**heit** *f* tenderness; softness; delicacy; gentleness.

zärtlich ['tsɛ:rtliç] tender; '♀**keit** *f* tenderness; (*Liebkosung*) caress.

Zaster F ['tsastər] *m* (7) (*Geld*) *sl.* dough.

Zauber ['tsaubər] *m* (7) spell, charm, magic (*alle a. fig.*); *s. Zauberei*; (*Bezauberung*) enchantment; (~*glanz*) glamo(u)r; *s. faul*; ~**ei** [~'rai] *f* (16) magic, sorcery; '~**er** *m* (7) sorcerer, magician; *s.* ~*künstler*; *fig.* enchanter; '~**flöte** *f* magic flute; '~**formel** *f* magic formula; '♀**haft**, '♀**isch** magical, enchanting, glamorous; '~**in** *f* sorceress; *fig.* enchantress; '~**kraft** *f* magic power; '~**kunst** *f* magic (art); '~**künstler** *m* illusionist, conjurer; *fig.* wizard; '~**kunststück** *n* conjuring trick; '~**land** *n* enchanted land, Fairyland; '♀**n** (29) *v/i.* practise magic; *weitS.* do conjuring tricks; *fig.* do wonders; *v/t.* conjure (up); '~**spie-**

Zauberspruch

gel *m* magic mirror; '**~spruch** *m* (magic) spell; '**~stab** *m* (magic) wand; '**~trank** *m* magic potion, philt|re, *Am.* -er; '**~wort** *n* magic word.

Zauder|er ['tsaʊdərər] *m* (7) lingerer; (*Zögernder*) waverer; '**~n**[1] (29) linger, delay; (*zögern*) waver, hesitate; '**~n**[2] *n* (6) lingering; hesitation.

Zaum [tsaʊm] *m* (3³) bridle; *im* ~ *halten* keep in check, bridle.

zäumen ['tsɔymən] (25) bridle.

'**Zaumzeug** *n* headgear, bridle.

Zaun [tsaʊn] *m* (3³) fence; *fig. vom* ~ *brechen e-n Streit*: pick *a* quarrel, *e-n Krieg*: start; '**~gast** *m* deadhead; '**~könig** *zo. m* wren; '**~pfahl** *m* pale; *ein Wink mit dem* ~ a broad hint.

zausen ['tsaʊzən] (27) pull about.

Zebra *zo.* ['tse:bra] *n* (11) zebra; '**~streifen** *m für Fußgänger*: zebra crossing.

Zech|bruder ['tseç-] *m* tippler, toper; '**~e** *f* (15) bill, score; ⚒ mine; (*Kohlen*⚒) coal-pit, colliery; (*Bergwerksgesellschaft*) mining company; *die* ~ *bezahlen* foot the bill, F pay the piper; '⚒**en** (25) carouse, tipple; '**~er** *m* (7) (hard) drinker, tippler, toper; '**~gelage** *n* carouse; '**~kumpan** *m* boon-companion; '**~preller** *m* (7) bilk(er); **~prellerei** [~'raɪ] *f* (16) hotel fraud, bilking.

Zecke ['tsɛkə] *f* (15) tick.

Zeder ♀ ['tse:dər] *f* (15) cedar.

zedieren rt̬ [tse'di:rən] cede, transfer, assign (*dat.* to).

Zeh [tse:] *m* (3 u. 12), '**~e** *f* (15) toe; '**~enspitze** *f* point (*od.* tip) of the toe; *auf* (*den*) ~*n* on tiptoe.

zehn [tse:n] **1.** ten; **2.** ♀ *f* (16) (number) ten; '⚒**-eck** *n* (3¹) decagon; '⚒**-ender** *m* (7) ten-point stag.

Zehner ⚹ ['tse:nər] *m* (7) ten; '⚒**lei** *adj.* ... of ten sorts *od.* kinds; *als su.* ten different things *pl.*

'**zehn|fach**, '**~fältig** ['~fɛltɪç] tenfold; ⚒'**fingersystem** *n* touch system; '**~jährig** ten-year(s)-old; of ten years, ten-year; '⚒**kampf** *m* decathlon; '**~mal** ten times; '**~malig** ten (times repeated); **~tägig** ['~tɛ:gɪç] of (*od.* lasting) ten days, ten-day; '**~tausend** ten thousand; *die oberen* ♀ the upper ten (*od.* crust); **~e von** *Exemplaren* tens of

thousands of copies.

zehnte ['tse:ntə] **1.** (18) tenth; **2.** ♀ *m* (13) tenth; (*Abgabe*) tithe; '⚒**l** *n* (7) tenth (part); '**~ns** tenthly.

zehr|en ['tse:rən] (25) *am Körper*: make thin; *fig.* (*nagen*) gnaw (*an dat.* at); ~ *von* live on; live off (*a. e-m Kapital*); *von e-r Erinnerung* ~ feed on; '**~end** ⚕ *adj.* consumptive; '⚒**ung** *f* (expenses *pl.* of) living; (*Weg*⚒) provisions *pl.*; (*Schwinden*) waste; *eccl. letzte* ~ viaticum.

Zeichen ['tsaɪçən] *n* (6) sign (*a. ast., typ.,* ♪, *Wunder*⚒), token; (*Merk*⚒, *Satz*⚒) mark; (*An*⚒) indication, sign, *a.* ⚒ symptom; (*Signal*) signal; (*Vor*⚒) omen; ✝ (*Waren*⚒) trade-mark, brand; ✝ *unser* ~ our reference (*abbr.* Ref.); *ein* ~ *geben* make a sign (*dat.* to); *s-s* ~*s ein Bäcker* a baker by trade; *zum* ~ (*gen.*) in (*od.* as a) sign of; *zum* ~, *daß* as a proof that; *s. Wunder*; '**~block** *m* sketch-block; '**~brett** *n* drawing-board; '**~drei-eck** ⚹ *n* set-square; '**~erklärung** *f* signs and symbols *pl.*; '**~feder** *f* drawing-pen; '**~heft** *n* sketch-book; '**~kunst** *f* (art of) drawing; '**~lehrer** *m* art master; '**~papier** *n* drawing-paper; '**~saal** *m* drawing-office; *Schule*: art room; '**~schule** *f* school of drawing; '**~setzung** *gr. f* punctuation; '**~sprache** *f* sign language; '**~stift** *m* crayon; '**~trickfilm** *m* animated cartoon; '**~unterricht** *m* drawing lessons *pl.*; *Schule*: art.

zeichn|en ['tsaɪçnən] (26) *v/t.* (*a. v/i.*) *paint.* draw (*nach* from); (*entwerfen*) design, *flüchtig* (*a. fig.*): sketch; (*be~, kenn~*) mark; (*unter~*) sign; *Spende usw.*: subscribe (*für e-n Fonds* to); *Anleihe, Aktien*: subscribe (for); *Brief*: *ich zeichne hochachtungsvoll* I remain yours truly; '⚒**er** *m* (7) draughtsman, *bsd. Am.* draftsman, (*a.* ⚒**erin** *f*) designer; *e-r Spende, Anleihe usw.*: subscriber (*gen.* to; for); ⚒**erin** *f* (16¹) draughtswoman, *bsd. Am.* draftswoman; '**~erisch** drawing; *Darstellung*: graphic; '⚒**ung** *f* drawing (*a.* ⊕), sketch, design; illustration; (*erläuternde Figur*) diagram; (*Kenn*⚒) marking; (*Muster*) pattern; subscription (to; for); '**~ungsberechtigt** authorized to sign.

'**Zeigefinger** *m* forefinger, index.

              Zeitspanne

zeigen ['tsaɪgən] (25) show; (*deuten auf*) point out; ~ *auf* (*acc.*) point at; (*an*~) indicate; *erklärend:* demonstrate; (*zur Schau stellen, a. fig.*) display, exhibit; (*vorführen*) present, show; *sich* ~ appear, show up, *plötzlich:* turn up, *Sache:* show, (*herausstellen*) turn out, prove; *sich prahlend* ~ *wollen, sich* ~ *mit* show off.

'**Zeige|r** *m* (7) (*Uhr*♀:) *großer* long, *kleiner* short) hand; *des Barometers usw.:* pointer; '**~stock** *m* pointer.

zeihen ['tsaɪən] (30) accuse (*gen.* of).

Zeile ['tsaɪlə] *f* (15) (*gedruckte* ~ *usw.*) line; (*Reihe*) row; *TV* (scanning) line; *j-m eine* ~ *od. ein paar* ~*n schreiben* drop a p. a line; '**~n-honorar** *n* linage, *Am.* F space rates *pl.*; '**~nraster** *TV m* line-scanning pattern; '**~nschalter** *m* *Schreibmaschine:* line space lever; '♀**nweise** by the line.

Zeisig ['tsaɪzɪç] *m* (3) *zo.* siskin; *fig. lockerer* ~ loose fish.

Zeit [tsaɪt] *f* (16) time; (*~raum*) period, space (of time); (*~alter*) age, era; *gr.* tense; (*Jahres*♀:, *Saison*, *a. geeignete* ~:) season; *freie* ~ spare time; *s. ganz* 1.; ♀ *meines Lebens* all my life; *schlimme* ~*en* hard times; *der beste Spieler usw. aller* ~*en* of all time; *die ganze* ~ (*über*) all along; ♱ *auf* ~ on account, on credit; *mit der* ~ in the course of time, with time; *von* ~ *zu* ~ from time to time; *vor der* ~ prematurely; *vor* ~*en* in former times; *vor langer* ~ long ago, a long time ago; *zur* ~ (*gen.*) in the time of; (*jetzt*) (*abbr. z. Z.*) at present; *zu* ~*en* (*gen.*) in the time of; *zu meiner* ~ in my time; *zu s-r* ~ in due course (of time); *s. recht*¹; *das hat* ~ there is plenty of time for that; *es ist* ~ *anzufangen* it is about time to begin; *es ist die höchste* ~ it is high time; *wenn* (*als*) *es an der* ~ *ist* (*war*) in the fullness of time; *mit der* ~ *gehen* keep pace (*od. go*) with the times; *j-m* ~ *lassen* give a p. time; *laß* (*od. nimm*) *dir* ~! take your time!; *die* ~ *nützen* make the most of one's time; *s. vertreiben.*

'**Zeit|·abschnitt** *m* epoch, *a. engS.* period; '**~abstand** *m* interval; '**~alter** *n* age; '**~angabe** *f* date; exact time; '**~ansage** *f* time-check;

'**~·arbeit** *f* temp work; '**~aufnahme** *phot. f* time exposure; '**~·aufwand** *m* time spent (*für* on); '♀**bedingt** entailed by the times; '**~bombe** *f* time bomb; '**~dauer** *f* space of time, period, duration, term; '**~enfolge** *gr. f* sequence of tenses; '**~faktor** *m* time element; '**~folge** *f* chronological order; '**~form** *gr. f* tense; '**~funk** *m* topical talk(s *pl.*); '**~geist** *m* spirit of the age, zeitgeist; '♀**gemäß** seasonable, opportune, timely; (*zur Zeit üblich*) modern, up-to-date; '**~genosse** *m*, '**~genossin** *f*, ♀**genössisch** ['~gənœsɪʃ] contemporary; '♀**gerecht** timely; *adv.* on time; '**~geschichte** *f* contemporary history; '**~gewinn** *m* time gained; '**~guthaben** *n bei gleitender Arbeitszeit:* time credit.

'**zeitig** early; (*reif*) mature; **~en** ['~ɪgən] (25) mature, ripen; (*hervorbringen*) produce, call forth.

'**Zeit|karte** *f* season-ticket, *Am.* commuter's ticket; *auf* ~ *fahren* travel by season-ticket, *Am.* commute; '♀**kritisch** topical; '**~lang** *f: eine* ~ for some time, for a while; '**~lauf** *m* course of time, period; *Zeitläuf(t)e pl.* times; ♀**lebens** for life, during life; all one's life; '♀**lich** temporal; time (*factor, etc.*); *das* ♀*e segnen* depart this life; *adv.* as to time; ~ *abstimmen od. berechnen* time; '**~lichkeit** *f* temporality; '♀**los** timeless; '**~lupe** *f* Film: slow-motion camera; '**~lupen-aufnahme** *f* slow-motion picture; *im* '**~lupentempo** *n* in slow motion; *fig.* at a snail's pace; '**~mangel** *m* lack of time; '**~maß** *n* measure of time; *poet.* quantity; ♪ *time*; '**~messer** *m* chronometer; '♀**nah** up-to-date, topical, current; '**~nehmer** *m* (7) *Sport:* time-keeper; '**~plan** *m* time-table, schedule; '**~punkt** *m* (point of) time; moment; date; '**~raffer** *m* (7) Film: time-lapse (*od. quick-motion*) camera; '**~raffer-aufnahme** *f* quick-motion picture; '♀**raubend** taking up much time, time-consuming; '**~raum** *m* space (of time), period; '**~rechnung** *f* chronology; *christliche* ~ Christian era; '**~schalter** ⚡ *m* time switch; (*electronic*) timer; '**~schrift** *f* journal, periodical, magazine; *literarische:* review; '**~spanne** *f* space (of time); '2**sparend** time-saving; '~**studie** *f* time-and-motion study; '~**studienbeamte** ✝ *m* time-study man; '~**tafel** *f* chronological table; '~-**umstände** *m/pl.* circumstances of the time(s).

'**Zeitung** *f* (news)paper, journal.

'**Zeitungs**|-**abonnement** *n* subscription to a paper; '~-**artikel** *m* newspaper article; '~-**ausschnitt** *m* newspaper cutting; '~**beilage** *f* supplement (of *od.* to a newspaper); '~-**ente** *f* hoax, canard; '~**händler** *m* news-agent, *Am.* newsdealer; '~-**inserat** *n* (newspaper) advertisement, F ad; '~**junge** *m* news-boy; '~**kiosk** *m* news-stall, *bsd. Am.* newsstand; '~**meldung**, '~**notiz** *f* press item; '~**papier** *n* newsprint; '~**redakteur** *m* newspaper editor; '~**schreiber**(**in** *f*) *m* journalist; '~**sprache** *f*, '~**stil** *m* journalese; '~**stand** *m* newsstand; '~**verkäufer**(**in** *f*) *m auf der Straße*: news-vendor, news-man; '~**verleger** *m* newspaper publisher; '~**wesen** *n* journalism, *the* (daily) press; '~**wissenschaft** *f* journalism.

'**Zeit**|**verlust** *m* loss of time; '~**verschiebung** *f* time difference; '~**verschwendung** *f* waste of time; ~**vertreib** ['~fɛrtraɪp] *m* pastime, diversion, amusement; *zum* ~ to pass the time; 2**weilig** ['~vaɪlɪç] temporary; *adv.* = '2**weise** (*eine Zeitlang*) for a time; (*von Zeit zu Zeit*) from time to time, at times; '~**wort** *n* (1^2) verb; '~**zeichen** *n Radio*: time-signal; '~**zünder** *m* time fuse.

zelebrieren [tsele'bri:rən] solemnize.

Zelle ['tsɛlə] *f* (15) *allg.* cell; ✈ air-frame; *teleph.* booth; '2**nförmig** cellular.

'**Zell**|**gewebe** *n* cell tissue; '~**glas** *n* cellophane; '2**ig** cellular; '~**kern** *m* nucleus.

Zellophan [tsɛlo'fa:n] *n* cellophane.

'**Zellstoff** *m* cellulose; *Papier*: pulp; '2**haltig** cellulosic; '~**watte** *f* cellu-cotton.

'**Zellteilung** *biol. f* cell division.

Zellu|**loid** [tsɛlulo'ʔi:t, ~'lɔʏt] *n* (3) celluloid; ~'**lose** *f* (15) cellulose.

'**Zell**|**wand** *anat. f* cell wall; '~**wolle** *f* staple fib|re, *Am.* -er.

Zelt [tsɛlt] *n* (3) tent; '~**bahn** *f* tent square; '~**dach** *n* tent-roof; '2**en** *v/i.* (26) camp; go camping; '~**lager** *n* (tent) camp; '~**leine** *f* guy line; '~**pflock** *m* tent-peg; '~**platz** *m* camping site; '~**stadt** *f* tent city; '~**stange** *f* tent-pole.

Zement [tse'mɛnt] *m* (3) cement; 2**ieren** [~'ti:rən] cement (*a. fig.*); ~**ierung** [~'ti:ruŋ] *f* cementation.

Zenit [tse'ni:t] *m* (3) (*im* at the) zenith.

zensieren [tsɛn'zi:rən] *Buch usw.*: censor; *Schule*: mark, *Am.* grade.

Zensor ['tsɛnzɔr] *m* (8^1) censor.

Zensur [~'zu:r] *f* (16) censorship; (*Zeugnis*) certificate, marks *pl.*; *für Schüler*: (term's) report, *Am. a.* credit, grade; *für eine Leistung*: mark, *Am.* point; *gute* ~ good mark.

Zenti|'**gramm** [tsɛnti-] *n* centigram(me); ~'**meter** *n*, *m* centimetre, *Am.* centimeter.

Zentner ['tsɛntnər] *m* (7) (metric) hundredweight (*abbr.* cwt.); '~**last** *f fig.* heavy burden; '2**schwer** very heavy.

zentral [tsɛn'tra:l] central; 2**e** *f* (15) central office *od.* ⚡ station; headquarters *pl.*; ⊕ control room; (telephone) exchange; 2**heizung** *f* central heating; ~**i'sieren** [~trali-] centralize; 2**i'sierung** *f* centralization; 2'**nervensystem** [~'tra:l-] *n* central nervous system; 2**verriegelung** *mot. f* central locking (system).

zentrifugal [tsɛntrifu'ga:l] centrifugal; 2**kraft** *f* centrifugal force.

Zentri|'**fuge** *f* centrifuge; 2**petal** [~pe'ta:l] centripetal.

'**zentrisch** centric(al).

Zentrum ['tsɛntrum] *n* (9) cent|re, *Am.* -er; *ins* ~ *treffen* hit the bull's-eye.

Zeppelin [tsɛpə'li:n] *m* (3^1) (*Luftschiff*) Zeppelin, F Zepp.

Zepter ['tsɛptər] *n* (7) sceptre, *Am.* scepter.

zer'beißen [tsɛr-] bite to pieces, crunch.

zer'bersten (sn) burst asunder.

zerbombt [~'bɔmt] bomb-wrecked.

zer'brech|**en** *v/t. u. v/i.* (sn) (*a. fig.*) break (to pieces), crack; *sich den Kopf* ~ rack one's brains (*über acc.* over); ~**lich** breakable, *a. P., Figur*: fragile; (*spröde*) brittle; 2**lichkeit** *f* fragility, brittleness.

zer'bröckeln *v/t. u. v/i.* (sn) crumble.

zer'drücken crush; *Kleid*: crease.

Zeremon|**ie** [tseremo'ni:] *f* (15) ceremony; 2**iell** [~'njɛl], ~**iell** *n*

(3¹) ceremonial; ⁓ienmeister [⁓-'moːnjən-] *m* master of ceremonies; ℒiös [⁓moˈnjøːs] ceremonious.

zer'fahren 1. ruin (by driving over); **2.** *adj. Weg*: rutted; *P.*: (*faselig*) flighty, harum-scarum; (*konfus*) scatter-brained; *Antwort usw.*: inconsistent; (*zerstreut*) absent-minded; ℒ**heit** *f* flightiness; absent-mindedness.

Zer'fall *m* ruin, decay; 🜊 decomposition; *phys.* disintegration; ℒ**en** (sn) fall to pieces *od.* into ruin, decay; collapse, crumble; *in s-e Bestandteile* ⁓ disintegrate (*a. phys.*); ⁓ *in mehrere Teile* fall (*od.* divide) into; *fig.* ⁓ *mit* fall out with; ⁓ *sein mit* be at variance with; ⁓**s-produkt** *n* disintegration product.

zer'fetzen tear in (*od.* to) pieces, rend; *schlitzend*: slash; *in Stückchen*: shred; *s.* zerfleischen.

zerfleischen [⁓ˈflaɪʃən] (27) mangle; (*zerreißen*) lacerate; *in Stücke* ⁓ tear to pieces.

zer'fließen (sn) dissolve, melt (*fig. in Tränen* in tears); *Farbe, Tinte*: run; *Hoffnung usw.*: melt away.

zer'fressen eat away; 🜊 *usw.* corrode.

zer'gehen (sn) dissolve, melt.

zer'glieder|n dismember; *anat.* dissect; *fig.* analy|se, *Am.* -ze; ℒ**ung** *f* dismemberment; dissection; analysis.

zer'hacken cut (in)to pieces; *Holz*: chop (up); *ganz fein*: mince.

zer'hauen cut asunder *od.* to pieces.

zer'kauen chew.

zerkleinern [⁓ˈklaɪnɐn] (29) reduce to small pieces; *Holz*: chop (up); *Steine*: crush.

zerklüftet [⁓ˈklyftət] cleft, rugged.

zerknirsch|t [⁓ˈknɪrʃt] contrite; ℒ**ung** *f* contrition.

zer'knittern, zer'knüllen (c)rumple, wrinkle, crease.

zer'kochen *v/t. u. v/i.* (sn) cook to rags.

zer'kratzen scratch.

zer'lassen melt.

zer'leg|en take apart; ⊕ *a.* dismantle; 🜊 dissect; *Braten*: carve; *fig.* analy|se, *Am.* -ze; 🜊 decompose; *in zwei Teile* ⁓ divide in two; ℒ**ung** *f* taking to pieces; carving; analysis; dissection; dismantling; decomposition.

zer'lesen *adj.* well-thumbed.

zerlumpt [tsɛrˈlumpt] ragged, tattered.

zer'mahlen grind.

zermalmen [⁓ˈmalmən] crush.

zer'martern torment; *sich den Kopf* ⁓ rack one's brain.

zermürb|en [⁓ˈmyrbən] wear down *od.* out; ⁓**end** gruelling, punishing; ℒ**ung** *f* wearing down, attrition; ℒ**ungskrieg** *m* war of attrition.

zer'nagen gnaw (asunder); 🜊 *usw.* corrode.

zer'pflücken pluck (*od. fig.* pull) to pieces.

zer'platzen (sn) burst.

zer'quetschen crush, bruise, squash; *bsd. Kartoffeln*: mash.

Zerrbild [ˈtsɛr-] *n* caricature; *fig. a.* distorted picture.

zer'reiben grind (*od.* rub) to powder, pulverize.

zerreiß|bar [tsɛrˈraɪs-] capable of being torn, tearable; ⁓**en** *v/t.* tear (*a. v/i.*; sn), rend (*in Stücke* to pieces); (*trennen*) disconnect, disrupt; (*zerstückeln*) dismember; (*zerfleischen*) lacerate; *nur v/i.* Faden, Nebel, Wolken: break; ℒ**festigkeit** *f* tensile strength; ℒ**probe** *f fig.* gruel(l)ing test; ℒ**ung** *f* rending, tearing, dismemberment; 🜊 rupture; laceration.

zerren [ˈtsɛrən] (25) tug, pull (*an dat.* at); (*schleppen*) drag; *Muskel, Sehne*: strain.

zer'rinnen (sn) melt away; *fig. a.* vanish, dissolve.

zerrissen [tsɛrˈrɪsən] torn (*a. fig.*); ℒ**heit** *f* (*Zerlumptheit*) raggedness; (*a. fig.*) disruption; *seelische*: inner strife.

'Zerrspiegel *m* distorting mirror.

'Zerrung 🜊 *f* strain.

zerrütt|en [tsɛrˈrytən] (26) disrupt; *e-e Einrichtung*: disorganize; (*ruinieren*) ruin, *Gesundheit, Nerven*: a. shatter; *den Geist*: unhinge, derange; *e-e Ehe*: wreck, break down; ℒ**ung** *f* disruption; ruin; derangement; breakdown.

zer'sägen saw up, saw to pieces.

zer'schellen (25) *v/t.* smash (to pieces), shatter; *v/i.* (sn) be smashed, ⚓ be wrecked; ✈ crash.

zer'schießen shoot to pieces, batter.

zer'schlagen 1. *v/t.* smash (to pieces); *fig.* smash; *sich* ⁓ *fig.* come

to nothing; **2.** *adj.* battered; (*erschöpft*) knocked up.
zer'schmelzen melt (away).
zer'schmettern smash, shatter.
zer'schneiden cut to pieces.
zer'schrammen scratch.
zer'setz|en (*a. sich*) decompose, disintegrate (*a. fig.*); *fig.* undermine, demoralize; **♀ung** *f* decomposition, disintegration; (*Zerfall*) decay; *pol.* subversion.
zer'spalten cleave, split.
zerspanen ⊕ [tsɛr'ʃpɑːnən] cut.
zer'splittern *v/t.* split (up), splinter (*alle a. v/i.*; sn); *Truppen*: disperse; *Zeit, Kraft*: fritter away (*sich one's powers*).
zer'sprengen break, burst open; *Menge*: scatter, disperse, ✗ rout.
zer'springen (sn) burst; *Glas*: crack; *fig. Kopf*: split.
zer'stampfen crush; *im Mörser*: pound; (*zertreten*) trample down.
zer'stäub|en pulverize; *Flüssigkeit*: spray; *fig.* disperse; **♀er** *m* (7) für *Flüssigkeit*: sprayer, *bsd.* 🗲 atomizer; *für Parfüm*: scent-spray.
zer'stechen prick *od.* sting (all over); *v. Ungeziefer*: bite.
zer'stieben (sn) be scattered.
zerstör|bar [tsɛr'ʃtøːr-] destructible; **∼en** destroy ruin, wreck (*alle a. fig.*); **♀er** *m* (7) destroyer (*a.* ⚓), ✗ pursuit interceptor; **♀ung** *f* destruction; **♀ungs-trieb** *m* impulse to destroy; **♀ungswut** *f* vandalism.
zer'stoßen bruise, break; *im Mörser*: pound; *zu Pulver*: powder.
zer'streu|en disperse, scatter (*beide a. sich*); *Bedenken*: dispel, dissipate; (*belustigen*) divert; **∼t** scattered, dispersed; *Licht*: diffuse(d); *fig.* absent(-minded); **♀t-heit** *f* absent-mindedness; **♀ung** *f* dispersion; (*Erholung*) diversion; *s.* Zerstreutheit.
zerstückel|n [∼'ʃtykəln] (29) cut up; *Körper*: dismember, *Land a.* (*parzellieren*) parcel out; **♀ung** *f* dismemberment.
zer'teil|en (*a. sich*) divide (*in acc.* into); (*zerstreuen*) disperse; ⚕, ∼ resolve; **♀ung** *f* division; dispersion; 🗲, ⚕ resolution.
zer'trampeln trample down, crush underfoot.
zer'treten tread down; *Feuer, a. fig.* tread out; (*zermalmen*) crush.

zertrümmer|n [∼'trymərn] (29) wreck, demolish, smash; **♀ung** *f* demolition; smashing.
Zervelatwurst [tsɛrvə'lɑːt-] *f* saveloy.
zer'wühlen *Erdboden*: root up; *Haar*: dishevel; *a. Bett*: rumple.
Zerwürfnis [∼'vyrfnɪs] *n* (4¹) discord, disunion, quarrel.
zer'zaus|en rumple, tousle; *j-n*: pull about; **∼t** *adj.* untidy; *Haar*: tousled.
Zession [tsɛ'sjoːn] *f* (16) assignment, transfer.
Zeter ['tseːtər] *n* (7, *o. pl.*): ∼ *schreien* cry murder, raise a hue and cry; **'∼geschrei** *n*, **∼mordio** [∼'mɔrdjo] *n* (11, *o. pl.*) loud outcry, clamo(u)r; **'♀n** (29) (*lärmen*) clamo(u)r; (*schelten*) scold, nag.
Zettel ['tsetəl] *m* (7) slip (of paper); (*mit Notiz od. kurzer Mitteilung*) note; (*angeklebter od. angehängter ∼ mit Angabe der Adresse, des Inhalts usw.*) ticket, label, (*Kleb♀*) adhesive label, *Am.* sticker, (*Anhänge♀*) tag; *zum Anschlagen*: placard, bill, poster; (*Hand♀*) leaflet; **'∼kasten**, **∼katalog** *m* card-index.
Zeug [tsɔyk] *n* (3) stuff (*a.* F *Alkohol usw.*), material; (*Tuch*) cloth; (*Handwerks♀*) tools *pl.*; (*Sachen*) things *pl.*; (*schlechtes ∼*) trash, (*a. dummes ∼*) stuff, rubbish; *er hat das ∼ zum Arzt* he has the makings of a doctor; F *was das ∼ hält* hell for leather; *sich ins ∼ legen* put one's back into it; *scharf ins ∼ gehen* not to pull one's punches; *s. flicken*.
Zeuge ['tsɔygə] *m* (13) witness; **♀n¹** (25) *v/i.* ⚖ give evidence; *für* (*od. gegen od. von*) et. ∼ testify for (*od. against od. of*) a th.; **'♀n²** beget, procreate; *fig.* generate, produce.
'Zeugen|-aussage *f* testimony (of a witness), evidence; **'∼bank** *f* witness-box, *Am.* witness stand; **'∼beweis** *m* evidence; **'∼eid** *m* oath of a witness; **'∼verhör** *n*, **'∼vernehmung** *f* hearing of witnesses.
'Zeughaus ✗ *n* arsenal. [ness.∖
Zeugin ['∼gɪn] *f* (16¹) (female) wit-∫
Zeugnis ['tsɔyknɪs] *n* (4¹) ⚖ testimony, evidence; (*Bescheinigung*) certificate, testimonial; (*Schul♀*) (*term's*) report; *zum ∼* (*gen.*) in witness of; *∼ ablegen od. geben* bear witness (*für* to; *von* of), testify (to).

Zeugung ['ˏɡuŋ] f generation, pro-creation; '**ˏs-akt** m reproductive act; '**ˏsfähig** capable of begetting; '**ˏs-kraft** f procreative capacity; '**ˏs-organe** n/pl. genital (od. reproductive) organs; '**ˏs-unfähig** sterile, impotent.

Zichorie [tsi'çoːrjə] f (15) chicory.

Zick|e ['tsikə] f (15) s. Ziege; '**ˏen** F pl.: mach keine ˏ stop being awk-ward; **ˏig** F bitchy; '**ˏlein** n kid.

Zickzack ['tsiktsak] m (3) zigzag; '**ˏkurs** m zigzag course; '**ˏschere** f pinking shears pl.

Ziege ['tsiːɡə] f (15) goat; engS. she-goat, nanny-goat; F bitch.

Ziegel ['tsiːɡəl] m (7) brick; (Dachˏ) tile; **ˏbrennerei** [ˏ'raɪ]f, **ˏei** [ˏ'laɪ]f (16) brickworks, brickyard; '**ˏdach** n tiled roof; '**ˏ-ofen** m brick-kiln; '**ˏrot** brick-red; '**ˏstein** m brick.

'**Ziegen|bart** m goat's beard; v. Menschen: goatee; '**ˏbock** m he-goat; '**ˏfell** n goatskin; '**ˏhirt** m goatherd; '**ˏkäse** m goat-cheese; '**ˏleder** n kid(-leather); '**ˏmilch** f goat's milk; '**ˏpeter** m mumps sg.

zieh [tsiː] pret. v. zeihen.

'**Zieh|bank** ⊕ f draw-bench; '**ˏbrunnen** m draw-well.

ziehen ['tsiːən] (30) **1.** v/t. pull, draw; Linie, Los, Folgerung, Schluß, Waffe usw.: draw (a. ✝ Wechsel auf j-n on); ⊕ draw; (zerren) drag; (züchten) 🌱 cultivate, grow, zo. breed; beim Schach usw.: move; Gewehrlauf: rifle; Hut: take off (vor j-m to); Mauer: build, erect; Graben: dig; Zahn: draw, pull, ex-tract; Schiff: tow; auf Draht ˏ wire; auf Fäden ˏ thread; auf Flaschen ˏ bottle; Blasen ˏ raise blisters; Wasser ˏ leak; e-n Vergleich ˏ draw (od. make) a comparison; j-n an den Haaren usw. ˏ pull a p.'s hair etc.; an sich ˏ draw to one, fig. take hold of; Aufmerksamkeit usw. auf sich ˏ attract; die Wurzel aus e-r Zahl ˏ extract the root of a num-ber; et. nach sich ˏ entail, involve; s. Affäre, Bilanz, Erwägung, Fell Gesicht, kurz, Länge, Nutzen, Rat, Rechenschaft usw.; **2.** v/i. (h. u. sn) pull (an dat. at); (sich bewegen) move, go; (marschieren) march; (durch ein Dorf usw.) ˏ pass (through a village, etc.); (Wohnung wechseln) (re)move; Vögel: migrate; Ofen,

Pfeife usw.: draw; Schmerz: twinge, ache; an der Zigarette usw.: (have a) drag (at); Tee: infuse, draw; Theaterstück: catch on, draw (large audiences); Ware: draw (custom), take; dieser Grund zieht bei mir nicht this reason does not weigh with me; das (dieses Verhalten usw.) zieht bei mir nicht sl. that cuts no ice with me; es zieht (im Zimmer) there is a draught; **3.** v/refl. sich ˏ extend, stretch; Holz: warp; sich in die Länge ˏ drag on; **4.** ♀ n (6) drawing (a. ⊕); cultivation; breed-ing; (Wandern, bsd. der Vögel) mi-gration; (Schmerz) twinge(s pl.).

'**Zieh|harmonika** f accordion; '**ˏkind** n foster-child; '**ˏung** f draw-ing (a. ✝).

Ziel [tsiːl] n (3) aim; fig. a. end, ob-ject, target; ✕ taktisches: objective; (ˏpunkt) mark; der Reise: destina-tion; Sport: finish(ing line); (ˏschei-be) target; des Spottes: butt; (Termin) term, ✝ credit; Sport: durchs ˏ gehen finish od. come in (als erster first); fig. sein ˏ erreichen gain one's end(s); sich das ˏ setzen od. stecken zu (inf.) aim at (ger. od. to inf.); über das ˏ hinausschießen overshoot the mark; zum ˏ führen succeed; '**ˏband** n Sport: tape; '**ˏbewußt** purpose-ful, single-minded; systematic(ally adv.); '**ˏen** (25) (take) aim od. level (auf acc. at); fig. ˏ auf (acc.) aim at; (tendieren) tend to; fig. gezielt Maß-nahme: specific, carefully directed; '**ˏfernrohr** n telescopic sight; '**ˏgerade** f Sport: home stretch; '**ˏgruppe** f target group; '**ˏkamera** f Sport: photo-finish camera; '**ˏlinie** f finishing line; '**ˏlos** aimless; '**ˏpunkt** m aiming point; Sport u. fig. goal; '**ˏrichter** m Sport: judge; '**ˏscheibe** f target; ˏ des Spottes butt of derision, laughing-stock; '**ˏsetzung** f object, target; '**ˏsicher** unerring; '**ˏsprache** f target language; ♀**stre-big** ['ˏʃtreːbiç] s. zielbewußt; '**ˏstre-bigkeit** f single-mindedness.

ziemen ['tsiːmən] (25) (a. sich) s. geziemen.

Ziemer ['tsiːmər] m (7) (Wild-rücken) saddle (of venison); (Peit-sche) whip.

'**ziemlich 1.** adj. (leidlich) passable, tolerable; e-e ˏe Anzahl a fair (od. good) number; e-e ˏe Strecke a

considerable distance, rather a long way; **2.** *adv.* pretty, fairly, tolerably, rather; (*ungefähr*) about; ~ **spät** rather late; so ~ *alles* practically everything; so ~ *dasselbe* pretty much (*od.* rather) the same thing.
Zier [tsiːr] *f* (16), **Zierat** ['tsiːraːt] *m* (3) ornament, decoration.
'**Zier|de** *f* (15) ornament; *fig. a.* hono(u)r, credit (*für* to); '**2en** (25) adorn, grace; (*verschönern*) embellish; (*schmücken*) decorate; *sich* ~ *fig.* be affected, *bsd. Frau:* be coy, (*Umstände machen*) stand on ceremony; (*sich sträuben*) refuse; **~erei** [~rəˈraɪ] *f* (16) affectation; '**~fisch** *m* toy fish; '**~garten** *m* flower garden; '**~leiste** *f* mo(u)lding (*a. mot.*); '**2lich** (*zart*) dainty, delicate; (*dünn*) slight; (*anmutig*) graceful; '**~lichkeit** *f* daintiness, delicacy; gracefulness; '**~pflanze** *f* ornamental plant.
Ziffer ['tsifər] *f* (15) figure, numeral; (*Schriftzeichen*) cipher; '**~blatt** *n* dial(-plate), face.
zig F [tsiç] (*sehr viele*) umpteen.
Zigarette [tsigaˈrɛtə] *f* (15) cigarette, *Am. a.* cigaret; **~n-anzünder** *mot. m* (7) cigarette lighter; **~n-automat** *m* cigarette slot-machine; **~n-etui** *n* cigarette-case; **~npapier** *n* cigarette paper; **~nschachtel** *f* cigarette packet; **~nspitze** *f* cigarette-holder; **~n-stummel** *m* cigarette-end, stub.
Zigarillo [~ˈrilo] *m* (11) cigarillo, small cigar.
Zigarre [tsiˈgarə] *f* (15) cigar; **~n-abschneider** *m* cigar-cutter; **~n-händler** *m* tobacconist; **~nkiste** *f* cigar-box; **~nladen** *m* tobacconist's (shop), *Am.* cigar store; **~nspitze** *f* cigar-holder; (*spitzes Ende e-r Zigarre*) cigar-tip; **~nstummel** *m* cigar-end, butt.
Zigeuner [tsiˈgɔynər] *m* (7), **~in** *f* (16¹) gipsy, *bsd. Am.* gypsy.
Zikade [tsiˈkaːdə] *f* (15) cicada.
Zimmer ['tsimər] *n* (7) room; '**~antenne** *f Radio:* indoor aerial (*Am.* antenna); '**~einrichtung** *f* furnishing; (*Möbel*) furniture; (*Innenausstattung*) interior (decoration); '**~flucht** *f* suite of rooms; '**~genosse** *m* room-mate; '**~handwerk** *n* carpenter's trade, carpentry.
...**zimmerig** ...-roomed.
'**Zimmer|mädchen** *n im Hotel:* chamber-maid; '**~mann** *m* car-

penter; '**~meister** *m* master carpenter; '**2n** (29) *v/t.* make *od.* build (of wood); *beruflich:* carpenter (*a. v/i.*); *fig.* frame; '**~nachweis** *m* accommodation bureau; '**~pflanze** *f* indoor plant; '**~reservierung** *f* room reservation(s *pl.*); '**~service** *m im Hotel:* room service; '**~temperatur** *f* room temperature; '**~theater** *n* little thea|tre, *Am.* -er; '**~vermittlung** *f s. Zimmernachweis.*
zimperlich ['tsimpərliç] prim; (*prüde*) prudish; (*geziert*) affected; (*heikel, bsd. beim Essen*) squeamish; (*empfindlich*) (super-)sensitive, soft; (*allzu sanft, vorsichtig*) dainty; '**2-keit** *f* primness; prudery; affectation; squeamishness; sensitiveness; daintiness. [*s. Quatsch.*]
Zimt [tsimt] *m* (3) cinnamon; F *fig.*]
Zink [tsiŋk] *n* (3) zinc; '**~blech** *n* sheet zinc; *grobes:* zinc-plate.
Zinke ['tsiŋkə] *f* (15) prong, tine; *e-s Kammes:* tooth; '**~n** *m* (6) *s. Zinke;* F *co.* (*Nase*) beak, snozzle.
...zinkig ...-pronged.
Zinn [tsin] *n* (3) tin; (*Material für Hausgerät*) pewter.
Zinne ['tsinə] *f* (15) △ pinnacle; ✗ (*Mauer2*) battlement.
'**zinne(r)n** tin; pewter.
'**Zinngeschirr** *n* pewter.
Zinnober [tsiˈnoːbər] *m* (7) cinnabar; F *s. Quatsch.* 2**rot** vermilion.
Zins [tsins] *m* (5¹ *u.* ³; *Mieten* 4) (*Miete, Pacht*) rent; (*Abgabe*) tribute; (*Geld2, mst* **~en** ['~zən] *pl.*) interest; **~en tragen** yield (*od.* bear) interest; 2**bar**, 2**bringend** bearing interest, interest-bearing; ~ *anlegen* put out at interest; '**~erhöhung** *f* increase in interest rates; **~eszins** ['~zəs-] *m* compound interest; '**~fuß** *m* rate of interest; '2**los** interest-free; 2**pflichtig** tributary; '**~rechnung** *f* calculation of interest; *konkret:* interest-account; '**~satz** *m* rate of interest; '**~schein** *m* coupon; *für Aktien:* dividend-warrant; '**~senkung** *f* lowering of interest rates.
Zionis|mus [tsioˈnismus] *m* (16, *o. pl.*) Zionism; **~t** *m* (12), **~tin** *f* (16¹), 2**tisch** Zionist.
Zipfel ['tsipfəl] *m* (7) tip, point; (*Taschentuch2 usw.*) corner; (*Rock2*) lappet; '**~mütze** *f* pointed cap.
zirka ['tsirka] about, approximately; '2**preis** *m* tentative price.

Zirkel ['tsirkəl] *m* (7) (*Kreis*) circle (*a. fig.*); (*Gerät*) (*ein* a pair of) compasses *pl.*, (*Stech⸲*) dividers *pl.*; '⸲n (29) measure with compasses.

Zirku|lar [tsirku'lɑːr] *n* (3¹) circular; **⸗lation** [⸗la'tsjoːn] *f* (16) circulation; ⸲'**lieren** circulate (*a.* ⸗ *lassen*).

Zirkumflex [tsirkum'flɛks] *m* (3²) circumflex.

Zirkus ['tsirkus] *m* (*inv., pl. a.* 4¹) circus; '⸗**reiter**(**in** *f*) *m* circusrider.

zirpen ['⸗pən] *v/i. u. v/t.* (25) chirp.

zisch|eln¹ ['tsiʃəln] *v/i. u. v/t.* (29) hiss, whisper; '⸲**eln²** *n* hiss(ing), whisper(ing); '⸗**en** (27) hiss; (*schwirren*) whiz(z); '⸲**laut** *m* hissing sound; *gr.* sibilant.

Ziselier|·arbeit [tsize'liːr-]*f* chased work; ⸲**en** chase.

Zisterne [tsi'stɛrnə] *f* (15) cistern.

Zitadelle [tsita'dɛlə] *f* (15) citadel.

Zitat [tsi'tɑːt] *n* (3) quotation.

Zither ♪ ['tsitər] *f* (15) zither.

zitieren [tsi'tiːrən] cite, quote; (*vorladen*) summon, cite.

Zitronat [tsitro'nɑːt] *n* (3) candied (lemon-)peel.

Zitrone [⸗'troːnə] *f* (15) lemon; ⸗**nfalter** *m* brimstone; ⸗**nlimonade** *f* lemonade; *mit Sodawasser:* lemon soda; ⸗**npresse** *f* lemon-squeezer; ⸗**nsaft** *m* lemon juice; ⸗**nsäure** *f* citric acid; ⸗**nschale** *f* lemon-peel; ⸗**nwasser** *n s. Zitronenlimonade.*

zitt(e)rig ['tsit(ə)riç] shaky.

zitter|n ['tsitərn] (29) tremble, shake (*vor* [*dat.*] *Kälte, Furcht, Erregung usw.* with); *Laub, Stimme usw.:* quiver; (*schaudern*) shiver; (*vibrieren*) vibrate; '⸲**pappel** *f* (quaking) aspen, trembling poplar.

Zitze ['tsitsə] *f* (15) teat, dug.

zivil [tsi'viːl] **1.** civil; (*Ggs. militärisch*) civilian; *Preise:* moderate, reasonable; **2.** ⸲ *n* (3¹, *o. pl.*) (*Ggs. Militär*) civilians *pl.*; (*Ggs. Uniform*) civilian (*od.* plain) clothes *pl., sl.* mufti, civ(v)ies *pl.*; ⸲**bevölkerung** *f* civilian population, civilians *pl.*; ⸲**courage** *f* (15) courage of one's opinions, moral courage; ⸲**dienst** *m* community service; ⸲**ehe** *f* civil marriage; ⸲**fahnder** *m* (7) *der Polizei:* plainclothes policeman; ⸲**gericht** *n* civil court; ⸲**isation** [⸗viliza'tsjoːn] *f* civilization; ⸗**isatorisch**

[⸗'toːriʃ] civilizing; ⸗i'**sieren** civilize; ⸲**ist** [⸗'list] *m* (12) civilian; ⸲**kleidung** [⸗'viːl-] *f* civilian (*od.* plain) clothes *pl.*; ⸲**luftfahrt** *f* civil aviation; ⸲**prozeß** ɪ͡ɪ *m* civil action *od.* suit *od.* case; ⸲**prozeß-ordnung** *f* Code of Civil Procedure; ⸲**recht** *n* civil law; ⸗**rechtlich** civil law ...; *adv.* under (*od.* according to) civil law; ⸲**regierung** *f* civilian government.

Zobel ['tsoːbəl] *m* (7) *zo.* sable; *a.* = '⸗**fell** *n* sable-skin; '⸗**pelz** *m* sable-fur.

Zofe ['tsoːfə] *f* (15) lady's maid.

zog [tsoːk] *pret. v. ziehen* 1., 2., 3.

zöger|n¹ ['tsøːgərn] (29) hesitate; (*sich aufhalten*) linger; (*Zeit verlieren*) delay; ⸗ mit defer, delay; '⸲n² *n* (6), '⸲ung *f* hesitation; (*Verzögerung*) delay; '⸗nd hesitating; (*langsam*) slow.

Zögling ['tsøːkliŋ] *m* (3¹) pupil.

Zölibat [tsøli'bɑːt] *m, n* (3) celibacy.

Zoll [tsɔl] *m* **1.** (*als Maß im pl. nach Zahlen inv.*) inch; **2.** (*Abgabe*) customs *pl.*, duty; *a.* = ⸗**behörde**; (*Brückenzoll usw.*) toll; (*Zins; a. fig.*) tribute; '⸗**abfertigung** *f* customs clearance; '⸗**amt** *n* custom-house; '⸗**be-amte** *m* customs officer; '⸗**behörde** *f* Customs *pl.*, customs authorities *pl.*; '⸲**en** (25) *fig.* give, pay; '⸗**erklärung** *f* customs declaration; '⸗**fahnder**(**in** *f*) *m* customs investigator; '⸲**frei** duty-free; '⸗**gebühren** *f/pl.* customs duties; ⸗**grenzbezirk** *m* customs control area; '⸗**grenze** *f* customs frontier; '⸗**haus** *n* custom-house; '⸗**hinterziehung** *f* evasion of customs duties; ...**zöllig** [-tsœliç] ...-inch.

'**Zoll|kontrolle** *f* customs examination; '⸗**krieg** *m* tariff war.

Zöllner ['tsœlnər] *m* (7) customs collector; *Bibel:* publican.

'**zoll|pflichtig** dutiable; '⸲**plombe** *f* custòms seal; '⸲**schein** *m* customs receipt, (bill of) clearance; '⸲**schranke** *f* customs barrier; '⸲**speicher** *m* bonded warehouse; '⸲**stock** *m* foot-rule, folding rule, yard-stick; '⸲**tarif** *m* customs tariff; ⸲-**union** ['⸗unjoːn] *f* customs (*od.* tariff) union; '⸲**verschluß** *m* customs seal, bond; *unter* ⸗ bonded; *unter* ⸗ *lassen* leave in bond; '⸲**vorschriften** *f/pl.* customs regulations.

Zone ['tso:nə] f (15) allg. zone; '**~n-grenze** f zonal border.
Zoo [tso:] m (inv. abbr. für Zoologischer Garten) Zoo, abbr. für Zoological Gardens.
Zoolog|e [tsoˀoˈlo:gə] m (13) zoologist; **~ie** [~loˈgi:] f (15) zoology; **2isch** [~ˈlo:giʃ] zoological.
Zopf [tsɔpf] m (3³) plait (of hair), tress; der Männer: pigtail; fig. (alter) ~ antiquated custom; sie trägt Zöpfe she wears her hair plaited od. in plaits; '**2ig** fig. pedantic(ally adv.); (altmodisch) old-fashioned; '**~muster** n cable stitch.
Zorn [tsɔrn] m (3) anger, rhet. wrath; (Wut) rage; in ~ geraten fly into a passion; '**2-entbrannt** boiling with rage, furious; '**2ig** angry (auf et. at, j-n with); furious (at).
Zote ['tso:tə] f (15) smutty joke, obscenity; ~n reißen talk smut; '**2n-haft**, '**zotig** obscene, smutty; '**~n-reißer** m obscene talker.
Zott|e ['tsɔtə] f, '**~el** f (15) tuft (of hair); '**2eln** v/i. toddle; '**2ig** shaggy.
zu [tsu:] **1.** prp. Bewegung: to; towards; (bis ~) up to; Ruhe: at; in; on; hinzufügend, -tretend: in addition to; (zusammen mit) along with; (neben) beside, next to; Zweckangabe: for; ~ Berlin in (amtlich: at) Berlin; ~ Beginn at the beginning od. outset; ~ meinem Erstaunen usw. to my astonishment etc.; ~ e-m ... Preise at a ... price; Sport: mit 2 ~ 3 by 2 points to 3; zum Schluß möchte ich ... in conclusion I should like to ...; der Schlüssel zum Schrank the key of the cupboard; j-n ~m Präsidenten wählen elect a p. President; sich ~ j-m setzen sit down by a p.'s side; ~ Weihnachten usw. at Christmas etc.; ~ zweien usw. by twos etc.; s. Beispiel, Bett, Hand usw.; **2.** adv. **a)** vor adj. u. adv.: too; ~ sehr too much; gar ~ far too; **b)** Richtung bezeichnend: towards, to; nach Norden ~ towards the north; **c)** (Ggs. offen) closed; Tür ~! shut the door!; die Tür ist ~ is to od. shut; **d)** immer (od. nur) ~! go on!
zualler|erst [~ˀaləˀˀeːrst] first of all; **~ˀletzt** last of all.
zubauen build (od. wall) up od. in; (versperren, a. Aussicht) block.
Zubehör ['~bəhøːr] n, a. m (3) appurtenances (a. ⚖⚖), fittings, Am. F

fixings, bsd. ⊕ accessories (alle pl.); Sechszimmerwohnung mit ~ six-roomed flat (Am. apartment) with all conveniences; '**~teil** n accessory (part).
'**zubeißen** bite; Hund: snap (at).
'**zubekommen** get in addition; Tür usw.: get a th. shut.
Zuber ['tsu:bər] m (7) tub.
'**zubereit|en** allg. prepare; Medizin: dispense; ⊕, Salat usw. dress; Speise a. cook; '**2ung** f preparation.
'**zubilligen** grant, concede, allow; (zusprechen) award (dat. to).
'**zubinden** tie (od. bind) up; j-m die Augen ~ blindfold.
'**zubleiben** (sn) remain closed od. shut.
'**zublinzeln** j-m: wink at a p.
'**zubring|en** Zeit: pass, spend; ⊕ Material usw.: feed; '**2er** ⊕ m (7) feeder; '**2erbus** m shuttle bus; '**2er-straße** f feeder road.
Zucchini [tsuˈki:ni] f (11¹, p. -i) courgette.
Zucht [tsuxt] f (16) (Tätigkeit) breeding, rearing, farming; von Kleinwesen (Bienen usw.): culture; von Pflanzen: cultivation; (Rasse) breed, race; (gezüchtete Bakterien) culture; (Erziehung) education, training; (harte ~) drill; (Manneszucht usw.) discipline; (Züchtigkeit) propriety, modesty; '**~buch** n stud-book; '**~bulle** m s. Zuchtstier.
zücht|en ['tsyçtən] (26) Tiere: breed; Pflanzen: grow, cultivate; Bakterien, Perlen: culture; '**2er** m (7), '**2erin** f (16¹) von Vieh: breeder; von Bienen: keeper; von Pflanzen: grower.
'**Zucht|haus** n penitentiary; (~strafe) penal servitude; **~häusler** ['~hɔyslər] m (7) convict; '**~hengst** m stud-horse, stallion.
züchtig ['tsyçtiç] chaste, modest; **~en** ['~gən] (25) correct, punish; körperlich: cane, flog, rhet. chastise; '**2keit** f chastity, modesty; '**2ung** f correction, punishment; flogging.
'**zucht|los** undisciplined, without discipline; (liederlich) disorderly; '**2losigkeit** f want of discipline; disorderly ways pl.; '**2meister** m task-master; '**2mittel** n disciplinary measure; '**2perle** f culture pearl; '**2rute** f rod of correction; '**2sau** f brood-sow; '**2schaf** n ewe

(for breeding); '♀**stier** *m* bull (for breeding); '♀**stute** *f* stock mare.

'**Züchtung** *f von Tieren:* breeding; *von Pflanzen:* growing, cultivation.

'**Zucht**|**vieh** *n* cattle for breeding; '**~wahl** *f* (natural) selection.

zucken ['tsukən] (25) jerk; *krampfhaft:* move convulsively *od.* suddenly, twitch *(alle: mit et. a th.)*; *vor Schmerzen:* wince; *Blitz:* flash; *s. Achsel, Wimper.*

zücken ['tsykən] (25) draw.

Zucker ['tsukər] *m* (7) sugar; ♂ *er hat ~* he is suffering from diabetes; '**~bäcker** *m* confectioner; '**~büchse,** '**~dose** *f* sugar-basin, *Am.* -bowl; '**~erbse** ♀ *f* green pea; '**~fabrik** *f* sugar factory; '**~guß** *m* (sugar-)icing, frosting, sugar-coating; '**~hut** *m* sugar-loaf; '♀**ig** sugary; '♀**krank,** '**~kranke** *m, f* diabetic; '**~krankheit** *f* diabetes; '♀**n** (29) sugar; '**~rohr** *n* sugar-cane; '**~rübe** *f* sugar-beet; '**~schale** *f s. Zuckerbüchse*; '**~sirup** *m* molasses *pl.,* treacle; '♀'**süß** (as) sweet as sugar; *fig.* honeyed; '**~wasser** *n* sugared water; '**~watte** *f* candy floss; '**~werk** *n* confectionery, sweetmeats *pl., Am.* candy; '**~würfel** *m* sugar lump; '**~zange** *f* (*eine* a pair of) sugar-tongs *pl.*

'**Zuckung** *f* convulsion, spasm.

'**zudämmen** dam up.

'**zudecken** cover (up).

zudem [tsu'de:m] besides, moreover.

'**zudenken**: *j-m et. ~* intend a th. *as a present etc.* for a p.

'**zudiktieren** *Strafe:* impose, inflict *(j-m* [up]on a p.).

'**Zudrang** *m* rush; run (*zu* on).

'**zudrehen** *Wasserhahn usw.:* turn off; *j-m den Rücken ~* turn one's back on a p.

'**zudringlich** importunate, obtrusive; '♀**keit** *f* importunity, obtrusiveness.

'**zudrücken** close, shut; *s. Auge.*

zueign|**en** ['~ʔaignən] *Buch:* dedicate *(dat.* to); '♀**ung** *f* dedication.

'**zu-eilen** (sn; *dat.; auf acc.*) hasten to *od.* towards, run up to.

'**zu-erkenn**|**en** award, adjudge *(dat.* to); '♀**ung** *f* award.

zu'**erst** [tsu-] *(als erste*[*r, s*]; *zunächst*) first; *(anfangs)* at first; *fig. wer ~ kommt, mahlt ~* first come first served.

'**zu-erteilen** *s. zuteilen, zuerkennen.*

'**zufahr**|**en** (sn) drive on; *auf et. ~* drive to(wards).

'**Zufahrt** *f* approach, access; '**~straße** *f* approach (road).

'**Zufall** *m* chance, accident; *(Zs.-treffen)* coincidence; *glücklicher ~* lucky chance, fluke; *unglücklicher ~* unfortunate accident; *durch ~ s. zufällig (adv.)*; '♀**en** (sn) *Augen:* be closing; *Tür:* slam shut; *j-m ~ fall* to a p.('s share), *Aufgabe:* fall to a p., *a. Erbe:* devolve upon a p.

'**zufällig** accidental; *nur attr.* chance; fortuitous; *(gelegentlich)* casual; *adv.* accidentally, by chance; *er war ~(erweise) zu Hause* he happened to be at home; '♀**keit** *f* accidentalness; casualness; fortuitousness; contingency.

'**Zufalls**|**bekanntschaft** *f* chance acquaintance; '**~treffer** *m* fluke; *Sport:* chance goal.

'**zufassen** (make a) grab; *Hund:* snap; *helfend* (*mit*) *~ lend* (*od.* give) a hand; *fig.* (*die Gelegenheit wahrnehmen*) seize the opportunity.

'**zufliegen** (sn; *dat.; auf acc.*) fly to(wards); *Tür:* slam (shut), bang.

'**zufließen** (sn; *dat.*) flow to(wards); *fig. j-m:* come to; *j-m ~ lassen* grant (to), let *a p.* have.

'**Zuflucht** *f* refuge, shelter, resort; *s-e ~ zu et. nehmen* take refuge to, have recourse to, resort to; '**~s-ort** *m* place of refuge, asylum.

'**Zufluß** *m* afflux; *(Einströmen)* influx *(a. fig. Kapital usw.)*; *(Nebenfluß)* affluent; ✝ supply.

'**zuflüstern** *j-m:* whisper to.

zu'**folge** [tsu-] *(gen. u. dat.)* as a result of, owing to; *(kraft)* on the strength of; *(gemäß, laut)* according to.

zu'**frieden** content(ed), satisfied, pleased; *j-n ~ lassen* let a p. alone; *sich ~geben* (*mit*) content o.s. (with); ♀**heit** *f* contentment, satisfaction; **~stellen** satisfy; **~stellend** satisfactory; ♀**stellung** *f* satisfaction.

'**zufrieren** (sn) freeze up *od.* over.

'**zufügen** add; *(antun)* do, cause; *Böses, Verluste: a.* inflict *(j-m* [up]on a p.).

Zufuhr ['~fu:r] *f* (16) *allg.* supply; *(Versorgungsgüter)* supplies *pl.; s. a. Zuführung.*

'**zuführ**|**en** carry, convey, lead,

bring; ⊕ feed; *Versorgungsgüter, Ware, a.* ⊕: supply; *(liefern)* deliver; *⚡ Draht:* lead in; '⚤**ung** *f* conveyance; ⊕ feeding, *(Maschinenteil)* feed; *a.* ⚓ supply, delivery; *⚡ (Drahtleitung)* lead.

'**zufüllen** add; *Loch usw.:* fill up.

Zug [tsu:k] *m* (3³) draw(ing); *a. allg. Sport:* pull; *(Ruck)* jerk; ⊕ traction, *(Spannung)* tension; *(Fisch⚤)* draught; *(Marsch)* march; *(Fest⚤, Um⚤)* procession; *(Berg⚤)* range; *(Eisenbahn⚤)* train; *(Feder⚤)* stroke, dash; *(Feld⚤)* expedition *(a. Forschungs⚤)*, campaign; *(Kolonne)* column; *(Gesichts⚤)* feature; *(Wesens⚤)* trait, feature, characteristic; *(Neigung, Hang)* bent, tendency, trend; ⚔ platoon; *(Zugluft, a. im Ofen)* draught, *Am. a.* draft; *(Kamin, Heizrohr)* flue; *(Orgel⚤)* stop, register; *(Schach⚤ usw.)* move; *beim Trinken:* draught; *beim Rauchen:* drag, puff; *der Vögel:* passage, flight, migration; *im Gewehr:* groove, *pl.* Züge rifling; ~ *der Zeit* trend of the times; ~ *des Herzens* promptings *pl.* of one's heart; *auf einen* ~ *beim Trinken:* at one draught; *im* ~*e (im Gang)* in train, in progress; *im* ~*e der Neugestaltung usw.* in the course of the reorganization etc.; *im besten* ~ in full swing, *P.:* going strong; *in einem* ~*e* at a stretch; *in kurzen Zügen* in brief outlines; *in den letzten Zügen liegen* be breathing one's last, *fig. S.:* be fizzling out; *in vollen Zügen genießen* enjoy thoroughly; *fig. er kam nicht zum* ~*e* he did not get a chance.

'**Zugabe** *f* addition; extra; *zum Gewicht:* makeweight; *thea.* encore; *als* ~ into the bargain.

'**Zugang** *m* access *(a. fig.)*; *(Tor)* gate(way *a. fig.*); *(Weg)* approach; *(Eingang)* entrance, entry; *(Zunahme)* increase (zu of); ⚓ *(Einnahmen)* receipts *pl.*; *(Ware)* arrivals *pl.*; *v. Büchern, Personal usw.:* accession(s *pl.*).

zugänglich ['~gɛnliç] accessible *(für to; a. fig. für Gründe usw.)*; *fig. a.* amenable (to); *fig. (umgänglich)* approachable, get-at-able.

'**Zugbrücke** *f* drawbridge.

'**zugeben** add; ⚓ give into the bargain; *(zulassen)* tolerate; *(eingestehen)* confess; *(einräumen)* concede, admit, grant, allow; *zugegeben* granted; ♪ *ein Lied* ~ give a song as an extra (treat.)

zu'gegen [tsu-] present *(bei* at*)*.

'**zugehen** (sn) *(sich schließen)* close, shut; *(weiter- od. schneller gehen)* move on, walk faster; *(geschehen)* happen; *auf j-n* ~ go up to, go *od.* walk towards; *Brief, Ware usw.: j-m* ~ come to a p.'s hand, reach a p.; *j-m e-e Sendung* ~ *lassen* forward to a p.; *wie geht es zu, daß ...?* how is it that ...?; *s. hergehen, Ding.*

'**zugehören** *(dat.)* belong to.

'**zugehörig** *(dat.)* belonging to *a p. od. a th.*; appertaining to *a th.*; '⚤**keit** *f* membership *(zu e-m Verein* of*)*; belonging (to); affiliation (to).

Zügel ['tsy:gəl] *m* (7) rein; *bsd. des Reitpferdes:* bridle; *fig.* bridle, rein, curb; *fig. die* ~ *schießen lassen (dat.)* give the rein(s) to; '⚤**los** *(unbridled), fig. a.* unrestrained; *(ausschweifend)* licentious; '~**losigkeit** *f* licentiousness; '⚤**n** (29) rein, pull up; *fig.* rein, curb, check.

'**zugesellen** *(a. sich)* associate *(dat.* with*)*, join *a p.*

'**Zuge**|**ständnis** *n* concession, admission; '⚤**stehen** concede, admit.

'**zugetan** *(dat.)* attached to, devoted to; fond of.

'**Zug**|**festigkeit** *f* tensile strength; '~**führer** *m* ⚓ chief guard, *Am.* conductor; ⚔ platoon-leader.

'**zugießen** add.

zugig ['tsu:giç] draughty, *Am.* drafty.

'**Zug**|**kraft** *f* tractive power, tensile force; *fig.* attraction, draw; '⚤**kräftig** *fig.* attractive; ~ *sein* be a draw.

zu'gleich at the same time; together.

'**Zug**|**luft** *f* draught, *Am. a.* draft; '~**maschine** *f* prime mover; tractor; '~**mittel** *n fig.* draw, attraction; '~**nummer** *thea. f* drawing card; '~**personal** *n* train staff; '~**pferd** *n* draught- *(Am.* draft*)* horse; '~-**pflaster** *n* blistering plaster.

'**zugreifen** *s. zufassen; bei Tisch:* help o.s.; *fig.* seize the opportunity; *(stramm arbeiten)* put one's back into it.

'**Zugriff** *m* grip *(a. fig.)*; *Computer:* access; '~**szeit** *f Computer:* access time.

zugrunde [tsu'grundə]: ~ *gehen fig.*

go to ruin, perish; ~ *legen* take as a basis (*dat.* for); e-r *Sache* ~ *liegen* underlie a th., be at the bottom of a th.; ~*liegend* underlying; ~ *richten* ruin, destroy, wreck.

'**Zug|schalter** *m* pull switch; '~**seil** *n* towing-line; traction-rope; '~**stück** *n* draw, *Am.* hit; '~**tier** *n* draught (*Am.* draft) animal.

'**zugucken** F (25) *s.* zuschauen.

'**Zug-unglück** *n* train accident.

zugunsten [tsu'gunstən] (*gen.*) in favo(u)r of, for the benefit of.

zu'gute: *j-m et.* ~ *halten* give a p. credit for a th., (*verzeihen*) pardon a p. a th.; *j-m sein Alter* ~ *halten* make allowance for a p.'s age; ~ *kommen* (*dat.*) be an advantage to, stand *a p.* in good stead; *j-m et.* ~ *kommen lassen* give a p. the benefit of a th.; *sich et.* ~ *tun auf* e-e *S.* pride (*od.* preen) o.s. on a th.

zuguter'letzt in the end; (*endlich*) at long last.

'**Zug|verkehr** *m* train service; railway traffic; '~**vieh** *n* draught- (*Am.* draft) cattle; '~**vogel** *m* bird of passage, migrant (bird); '~**wind** *m* s. Zugluft.

'**zuhaben** keep (*od.* have) … shut *od.* closed *od.* (*Kleid*) buttoned up.

'**zuhalten** *v/t.* keep … shut; *Ohren:* stop; *v/i. auf et.* (*acc.*) ~ make for a th.

Zuhälter ['~hɛltər] *m* (7) souteneur (*fr.*), *sl.* pimp.

'**zuhängen** hang (*od.* cover) with curtains *etc.*

'**zuhauen** *v/i.* strike; *v/t.* (*behauen*) rough-hew; dress, trim.

Zuhause [tsu'hauzə] *n* (10, *o. pl.*) home.

zuheften ['tsu:-] stitch up.

'**zuheilen** (sn) heal up.

Zuhilfenahme [tsu'hilfənɑːmə] *f:* *unter* ~ *von* by (*od.* with) the aid of.

zu'hinterst last of all, at the end.

zuhören ['tsu:-] (*dat.*) listen (to).

'**Zuhörer** *m*, '~**in** *f* listener, hearer; '~**raum** *m* auditorium; '~**schaft** *f* audience.

'**zujauchzen**, '**zujubeln** (*dat.*) shout to, cheer; *a. fig.* hail.

'**zukaufen** buy in addition.

'**zukehren** (*dat.*) turn to(wards); *j-m den Rücken* ~ *s.* zudrehen.

'**zuklappen** shut; close with a snap.

'**zukleben** paste (*od.* glue) up.

'**zuklinken** (25) latch.

'**zuknallen** *Tür usw.*: bang, slam (to).

'**zuknöpfen** button (up); *fig.* er ist sehr zugeknöpft he is very reserved.

'**zuknüpfen** tie (up).

'**zukommen** (sn) *auf j-n*: come up to a p.; *j-m* ~ (*Brief usw.*) reach a p., (*zuteil werden*) fall to a p.'s share, (*gebühren*) be due to a p.; *das kommt ihm nicht zu* he has no right to (do) that; *j-m et.* ~ *lassen* let a p. have a th.; send a p. a th.

'**zukorken** (25) cork (up).

Zukunft ['tsu:kunft] *f* (16, *o. pl.*) future, *a.* time to come; *gr.* future (tense); *in* ~ in future; *was die* ~ *j-m bringt* what the future has in store for a p.; *der Mann der* ~ the coming man.

'**zukünftig** future; *meine* Qe, *mein* Qer my intended; *adv.* in future.

'**Zukunfts|forscher** *m* futurologist; '~**forschung** *f* futurology; '~**musik** *f fig.* dreams *pl.* of the future; 'Q**-orientiert** future-oriented; '~**pläne** *m/pl.* plans for the future; 'Q**reich** with a great future; promising; '~**roman** *m* science fiction novel.

'**zulächeln** (*dat.*) smile at *od.* (up)on.

'**Zulage** *f* additional allowance; extra pay; (*Gehaltserhöhung*) rise, *Am.* raise.

zulande [tsu'landə]: *bei uns* ~ in my *od.* our country.

'**zulangen** *v/i. bei Tisch*: help o.s.; (*genügen*) be enough *od.* sufficient.

zulänglich ['tsu:lɛŋliç] sufficient, adequate; 'Q**keit** *f* sufficiency.

'**zulassen** *Tür usw.*: leave shut; *j-n*: admit; *behördlich*: license; (*geschehen lassen*) allow, suffer; *Deutung, Zweifel*: admit of.

'**zulässig** admissible, permissible, allowable; *das ist* (*nicht*) ~ that is (not) allowed; 'Q**keit** *f* admissibility.

'**Zulassung** *f* admission; permission; *amtliche*: licen|ce, *Am.* -se; '~**s-nummer** *mot. f* registration number; '~**s-papiere** *n/pl.* registration papers.

'**Zulauf** *m* (*Andrang*) rush (of people); ⊕ feed, supply, intake; *großen* ~ *haben* be much sought after, *Theaterstück*: be very popular, draw large crowds; 'Qen (sn) (*weiter od. schneller laufen*) run on *od.* faster; *j-m in Massen*: crowd (*od.* flock) to; *Hund usw.*: stray (to);

auf j-n ~ run up to; *s. spitz*; *zu-gelaufener Hund* stray dog.

'zulegen add (*dat.* to); *e-m Gehalt et.* ~ increase a salary by; *sich et.* ~ get (o.s.), (*kaufen*) buy.

zuleide [tsu'laɪdə]: *j-m et.* ~ *tun do a p.* harm, harm (*od.* hurt) *a p.*; *was hat er Ihnen* ~ *getan?* what (harm) has he done you?

zuleit|en ['tsu:-] ⊕ supply, feed; (*dat.*) conduct (*od.* lead *od.* direct) to; (*weitergeben*) pass (*od.* forward, transmit) to *a p.*; '♀**ung** *f* supply; transmittal; ∉ lead; '♀**ungsrohr** *n* supply (*od.* feed) pipe.

zu'letzt [tsu-] finally, at last; (*als letzter*) last; *bis* ~ *bleiben* sit it out.

zu'liebe: *j-m* ~ for a p.'s sake.

'Zuliefer|ant *m*, '♀**er** *m* (7) supplier.

zulöten ['tsu:-] solder up.

zum [tsum] = *zu dem*; *s. zu, Teil.*

'zumachen *v/t.* shut, close; *Loch:* stop up; *Jacke:* button (up), do up; (*fest* ~) fasten; *v/i.* F *mach zu!* hurry up!

zumal [tsu'ma:l] *cj.* ~ (*da od. weil*) *negativ:* the less so since; *positiv:* especially since.

zumauern ['tsu:-] wall up.

zumeist [tsu'maɪst] mostly.

zumessen ['tsu:-] *j-m s-n Teil, e-e Zeit:* apportion, allot.

zumindest [tsu'mɪndəst] at least.

zu'mute: *mir ist gut od. schlecht od. eigentümlich* ~ I feel well *od.* ill *od.* queer; *mir ist nicht danach* (*nach Lachen*) ~ I am not in the mood for it (for laughing), I don't feel like it (like laughing).

zumut|en ['tsu:mu:tən] (26): *j-m et.* ~ expect a th. of a p.; *sich zuviel* ~ overtask o.s.; '♀**ung** *f* unreasonable demand; (*Unverschämtheit*) impudence; *eine* (*starke*) ~ a bit strong.

zu'nächst [tsu-] *prp.* (*dat.*) next to; *adv.* (*vor allem*) first of all; (*vorläufig*) for the present, for the time being; (*erstens*) to begin with.

zunageln ['tsu:na:gəln] nail up.

'zunähen sew up.

Zunahme ['∼na:mə] *f* (15) increase, growth.

'Zuname *m* surname, last name.

Zünd|-anlage ['tsynt-] *f* ignition system; '♀**en** ['tsyndən] (26) *v/i.* catch fire; *fig.* arouse enthusiasm; electrify; *v/t. u. v/i.* kindle; *bsd.*

mot. ignite; ✗ fire; *Sprengung:* detonate.

Zunder ['tsundər] *m* (7) tinder, touchwood.

'Zünder ✗ *u.* ✗ *m* (7) fuse.

'Zünd|holz *n*, **∼hölzchen** ['tsynt-hœltsçən] (6) *n* match; **∼hütchen** ⊕ ['∼hy:tçən] *n* (6) percussion cap; '**∼kapsel** *f* detonator; '**∼kerze** *mot. f* spark(ing) plug, *Am.* spark plug; '**∼punkt** *m* ignition point; '**∼satz** *m* primer; '**∼schlüssel** *mot. m* ignition key; '**∼schnur** *f* (safety) fuse, slow match; '**∼stein** *m* flint; '**∼stoff** *m* inflammable matter; *fig.* dynamite.

Zündung *mot.* ['tsyndun] *f* ignition.

'zunehmen increase (*an dat.* in); (*anwachsen*) grow (larger, bigger, longer, stronger, stout[er]); *an Gewicht:* put on weight; **∼d** increasing, growing; *Mond:* waxing; *mit* ∼*em Alter* with advancing years; *in* ∼*em Maße* increasingly; *der* ∼*e Mond* the waxing (*od.* crescent) moon.

'zuneig|en (*a. sich*) (*dat.*) incline to(wards); *sich dem Ende* ~ draw to a close; '♀**ung** *f* affection (*für, zu* for); ~ *zu j-m fassen* take a liking to a p.

Zunft [tsunft] *f* (14¹) guild, corporation; *b.s.* clique, gang.

zünftig ['tsynftiç] belonging to a guild; *fig.* (*kunstgerecht*) expert, competent; *bsd. Sport:* scientific, sportsmanlike; F (*tüchtig*) thorough (-ly *adv.*).

Zunge ['tsuŋə] *f* (15) tongue (*a.* = *Sprache*); (*Fisch*) sole; ♪ reed; *e-e lose* (*spitze*) ~ *haben* have a loose (sharp) tongue; *es lag mir auf der* ~ I had it on the tip of my tongue.

züngeln ['tsyŋəln] (29) play with the tongue; *Flamme:* lick.

'Zungen|brecher *m* tongue-twister, crack-jaw; '♀**fertig** glib, voluble; '**∼fertigkeit** *f* volubility; '♀**förmig** tongue-shaped; '**∼kuß** *m* French kiss; '**∼laut** *gr. m* lingual (sound); '**∼spitze** *f* tip of the tongue.

Zünglein ['tsyŋlaın] *n* (6) little tongue; *fig. das* ~ *an der Waage bilden* tip the scales.

zunichte [tsu'niçtə]: ~ *machen* bring to nothing; destroy, ruin; *Plan usw.:* frustrate, defeat; ~ *werden* come to nothing, be frustrated.

zunicken ['tsu:-] (*dat.*) nod to.

zunutze [tsu'nutsə]: *sich et.* ~ *machen* turn a th. to account, utilize a th.

zu'-oberst (quite) at the top, uppermost.

'**zu-ordnen** (*dat.*) attach (to); class (with).

'**zupacken** *s.* zugreifen.

zu'paß [tsu-]: ~ *kommen* come at the right time, come in handy; *j-m*: suit *a p.* (admirably).

zupf|en ['tsupfən] (25) *v/t.* pull, pluck, twitch, tug (*alle a. v/i.*; *an dat.* at); *Wolle*: pick; *j-n am Ärmel usw.* ~ pull a p. by the ...; '2-**instrument** ♪ *n* plucking instrument.

zupfropfen ['tsu:-] (25) cork (up).

zur [tsu:r] = zu der; *s. zu.*

'**zuraten** *j-m*: advise a p. (to do) a th.; *auf sein* 2 on his advice.

'**zurechn|en** add; *zu e-r Klasse usw.*: number among, class with; *fig. j-m*: ascribe to, *Schlechtes*: *a.* impute to; '2**ung** *f* addition; inclusion; attribution; imputation; '**~ungsfähig** sane, of sound mind, ♈ *a.* responsible; '2**ungsfähigkeit** *f* sanity, soundness of mind; ♈ *a.* (penal) responsibility.

zu'recht [tsu-] (a)right, in order; ~**basteln** rig up; ~**bringen** put to rights, set right; (*bewerkstelligen*) bring about; manage; ~**finden**: *sich* ~ find (*fig.* see) one's way; ~**kommen** (sn) arrive in time; *fig.* get on well (*mit* with), *mit et.*: *a.* manage; ~**legen** put out; (*a. fig.*) arrange; *sich e-e S.* ~ (*erklären*) explain a th. to o.s.; (*vorher überlegen*) prepare (*od.* figure out) a th.; ~**machen** get ready, prepare, *Am.* F fix; *für e-n Zweck*: adapt to *od.* for; *sich* ~ get ready, *Dame*: make (o.s.) up; ~**setzen** set right; *j-m den Kopf* ~ bring a p. to his senses; ~**stellen** set up; put in the right place; ~**stutzen** trim (to size); ~**weisen** *v/t.*, 2**weisung** *f* rebuke, reprimand.

zureden ['tsu:-] **1.** *j-m* ~ try to persuade a p.; (*drängen*) urge a p.; (*ermutigen*) encourage a p.; **2.** 2 *n* (6) persuasion; encouragement; (*Bitte*) entreaty, urgent request.

'**zureichen** *v/t.* hand (over), pass (*dat.* to); *v/i.* be sufficient.

'**zureit|en** *v/t.* break in; *v/i.* (sn)

(*weiter od. schneller reiten*) ride on *od.* faster; ~ *auf* (*acc.*) ride up to; '2**er** *m* breaker-in, trainer.

'**zurichten** prepare; *bsd.* ⊕ dress, fit; *Holz*, *Steine*: cut, trim; *typ.* get (*od.* make) ready; *übel* ~ *j-n*: use badly, (*verletzen*) maul, *a. et.*: batter.

'**zuriegeln** (29) bolt.

zürnen ['tsyrnən] (25) be angry (*j-m* with a p.; *über acc.* at, about).

Zur'schaustellung *f* exhibition, display; *fig. a.* parading.

zurück [tsu'ryk] back; (*rückwärts*) backward(s); (*hinten*) behind; (*im Rückstand*) in arrears, behindhanded; ~! stand back!; ~ *an den Absender* returned to writer; ~**begeben**: *sich* ~ return; ~**begleiten** conduct back; ~**behalten** keep back, retain; ~**bekommen** get back; ~**berufen** call back; ~**bezahlen** pay back; ~**bleiben** (sn) remain (*od.* stay) behind; be left behind (*a.* = *überleben*); *fig.* fall (*od.* lag) behind; *Sport*: drop back; *als Rest*: be left over (over); *in der Entwicklung*, *geistig*: be backward, be retarded; ~ *hinter Erwartungen usw.* fall short of; *geistig zurückgeblieben* backward, (mentally) retarded; ~**blicken** look back; ~**bringen** bring (*od.* take) back; ♈ reduce (*auf acc.* to); ~**datieren** backdate; ~**denken** think back; ~ *an* (*acc.*) recall *a th.* to memory; *sich* ~ cast one's mind back; ~**drängen** push back; *fig.* repress; ~**dürfen** be allowed to return; ~**eilen** (sn) hasten back; ~**erbitten** ask back; ~**erobern** reconquer; ~**erstatten** restore; *Ausgaben*, *Kosten*: refund, reimburse; ~**fahren** *v/t. u. v/i.* (sn) drive back; *v/i. plötzlich*: start back; ~**fallen** (sn) fall back; (*zurückbleiben*) fall (*od.* drop) behind; (*rückfällig werden*) relapse (*in acc.* into); ♈ (*heimfallen*) ~ *an* (*acc.*) revert to; *sich* ~**finden** find one's way back; ~**fordern** demand back, reclaim; ~**führen** lead back; *in die Heimat*: repatriate; *fig.* ~ *auf e-n Nenner*, *e-e Regel*, *ein Minimum usw.* reduce to; ~ *auf e-e Ursache usw.* trace (back) to, attribute to; 2**gabe** *f* giving back, return, restitution; ~**geben** give back, return; *Fußball*: pass back; *in der Rede*: retort; ~-

gehen (sn) go back, return; ✗ retreat; *fig.* (*sich vermindern*) diminish, decrease, drop; ✝ *Preis*: fall, drop, go down; *Geschäfte*: fall off; (*nicht zustande kommen*) be broken off; *auf e-e Quelle* ~ trace back to, have its origin in; be due to; *Sendung* ~ *lassen* return; **~geleiten** escort back; **~gezogen** retired, secluded; **2gezogenheit** *f* retirement, seclusion; **~greifen:** *fig. auf Reserven usw.* ~ fall back (up)on; *weiter* ~ *in der Erzählung usw.* begin (*od.* go) farther back; **~halten** hold back; *Tränen, Gefühl usw.*: restrain; ~ *mit hold* (*od.* keep) back; *sich* ~ be reserved, keep to o.s., *im Zorn usw.*: restrain o.s.; **~haltend** reserved (*a.* ✝ *Börse*); (*vorsichtig*) guarded, cautious; **2haltung** *f* retention; *fig.* reserve; **~holen** fetch back; *j-n* (*a. fig.*): call back; **~kaufen** buy back; **~kehren** (sn) return; **~kommen** (sn) come back, return; *mit der Arbeit usw.* ~ get behind with; *auf e-e Sache* ~ return (*od.* revert) to *a th.*, refer to *a letter*; **~können** be able to return *od.* go back; **2kunft** [~kunft] *f* (16) return; **~lassen** leave (behind *a. Angehörige*); (*überholen*) outstrip, leave (far) behind; (*Rückkehr erlauben*) allow to return; **~legen** *Geld, Ware*: lay aside; *e-m Käufer*: put aside (for); *Geld* (*sparen*): put by; *Jahre*: complete; *Weg*: cover; *sich* ~ lie back; **~liegen** *zeitlich*: date back; **~melden:** *sich* ~ report back; **~müssen** be obliged to return; *das Buch muß zurück* has to be returned; *der Tisch muß zurück* must be moved back; **2nahme** [~na:mə] *f*(15) *s.* zurücknehmen: taking back; withdrawal; retraction; revocation; **~nehmen** take back (*a. fig. Wort*); *Truppen*: withdraw; *Angebot, Behauptung, Klage, Versprechen usw.*: withdraw, retract; (*widerrufen*) revoke, *Auftrag*: countermand, cancel; **~prallen** (sn) rebound; *vor Schreck*: recoil, start back; **~rechnen** count back; **~reisen** (sn) travel back, return; **~rufen** call back; *ins Gedächtnis* ~ recall to mind; **~schaffen** take back; **~schaudern** (h. *u.* sn) shrink (back) (*vor dat.* from); **~schauen** look back; **~scheuen** shrink (back) (*vor*

dat. from); *vor nichts* ~ stick at nothing; **~schicken** send back; **~schlagen** *v/t.* strike back; *Feind, Angriff*: repel, repulse; *Decke*: fold back; *Mantel*: throw open; *Tennisball*: return; *v/i. Flamme*: flash back; **~schrecken** *v/t.* (25) frighten away; *v/i.* (30, sn) shrink (back) (*von, vor dat.* from); **~schreiben** write back; **~sehnen:** *sich* ~ long to return; **~sein** (sn) be back, have come back; *fig.* be behind(handed) (*mit* with); *in Kenntnissen, in der Entwicklung usw.*: be backward; *sehr* ~ (*rückständig sein*) be very much behind the times; **~setzen** place back; *fig.* slight, neglect; *Preis*: reduce, cut (down); **2setzung** *f* slight, neglect; **~spulen** *Tonband, Film*: rewind; **~stecken** *fig.* ~ *müssen* have to climb down; **~stehen** (h. *u.* sn) stand back; *fig.* be inferior (*hinter dat.* to); ~ (*müssen*) (have to) take a back seat; **~stellen** put back (*a. Uhr*), replace; (*aufschieben*) defer; (*hintansetzen*) postpone; ✗ defer; **2stellung** *f* putting back, replacement; deferment; **~stoßen** *v/t.* push back; *fig.* (*abstoßen*) repel; *v/i.* (sn *u.* h.) *mot.* reverse, back up; **~strahlen** *v/t.* reflect; *v/i.* be reflected; **~streifen** *Ärmel*: turn up; **~stufen** (25) *Person*: demote; *Sache*: downgrade; **2stufung** *f* demotion; downgrading; **~treiben** drive back; **~treten** (sn) step (*od.* stand) back; *fig.* recede (*von* from); *vom Amt*: resign; (*von*) *e-m Unternehmen usw.*: withdraw (from), *von e-m Vertrag*: *a.* terminate; *fig.* take a back seat; **~übersetzen** translate back (*ins Englische* into); **~verfolgen** *Weg*: retrace; *fig.* trace back (*zu* to); **~verlangen** reclaim, demand back; **~versetzen** restore (*to a former state*); *Schüler*: send back to a lower form, *Am.* demote; *sich in eine frühere Zeit* ~ turn one's mind back to a former period; **~verwandeln** retransform (*in acc.* into); (*a. sich*) change back (into); **~verweisen** refer back (*an acc.* to); **~weichen** (sn) fall back, retreat; (*a. fig.*) recede; (*nachgeben*) yield; **~weisen** *v/t.* turn back; (*ablehnen*) refuse, decline, reject; *Angriff*: repulse; *als unberechtigt* ~ repudiate; (*a. v/i.*) *auf e-e Anmerkung usw.*: refer to; **2weisung** *f* refusal, rejection; repulse; repudiation; ~**werfen** throw back; *Feind: a.* repulse; *den Kopf: toss; fig. wirtschaftlich usw.:* set back; *phys. Lichtstrahlen usw.:* reflect, reverberate; ~**wirken** react *(auf acc.* upon); ~**wünschen** wish back; ~**zahlen** pay back, repay *(beide a. fig.)*; *Auslagen:* refund; ♀**zahlung** *f* repayment; refund; ~**ziehen** *v/t.* draw back; ✗ *Truppen, a. fig.* withdraw, retire *(beide a. sich)*; *sich* ~✗ *a.* retreat; *sich auf et. (acc.)* ~ fall back (up)on; *sich* ~ *von* retire from, give up; *v/i.* move *(od.* march) back; ♀**ziehung** *f* withdrawal.

'**Zuruf** *m* call; *(Beifalls*♀*)* acclamation; *durch* ~ by acclamation; '♀**en** *v/i. u. v/t. j-m:* call (out) to; *laut:* shout to; *beifällig:* acclaim.

'**zurüst|en** prepare; *(ausrüsten)* fit out, equip; '♀**ung** *f* preparation; fitting-out, equipment.

'**Zusage** *f* (15) promise; *(Zustimmung)* assent; '♀**n** *v/t.* promise; *j-m et. auf den Kopf* ~ tell a p. a th. to his face; *v/i.* promise to come; *j-m* ~ *Speise, Klima usw.:* agree with a p.; *(Einladung annehmen)* accept a p.'s invitation; *(gefallen)* suit *od.* please a p.; ~*de Antwort* acceptance.

zusammen [tsu'zamən] together; *(gemeinschaftlich) a.* jointly; *(gleichzeitig)* at the same time; ~ *mit* along with; ~ *betragen* amount to, total; *alle (pl.)* ~ all in a body; *alles* ~ all in all; *wir haben* ~ *5 Mark* we have 5 marks between us; ♀-**arbeit** *f* co-operation; *bsd. mit dem Feind* collaboration; *e-r Gemeinschaft:* team-work; ~•**arbeiten** work together; co-operate, collaborate; ~**ballen** *(a. sich)* form into a ball, conglomerate; gather; *a.* ✗ concentrate, mass; ♀**ballung** *f* concentration, conglomeration; ♀**bau** ⊕ *m* assembly; ~**bauen** ⊕ assemble; *die Zähne* ~**beißen** clench one's teeth; ~**bekommen** get together; *Geld:* raise; ~**berufen** convoke, call together; ~**binden** bind *(od.* tie) together; ~**brauen** concoct *(a. fig.); fig. sich* ~ be brewing; ~**brechen** (sn) break down, collapse; ~**bringen** bring together; *(sammeln)* collect, gather; *Geld:* raise; ♀**bruch** *m* breakdown, collapse; ~**drängen** press together;

Menschen, Tiere: (a. sich) crowd *(od.* huddle) together; *(verdichten)* compress; *(kürzen)* condense; ~**drücken** compress; ~**fahren** (sn) *(aufea.-fahren, -stoßen)* collide *(mit* with); *fig.* start *(bei e-m Anblick usw.* at; *vor Schreck usw.* with); *schmerzhaft:* wince; ~**fallen** fall in, collapse; *zeitlich:* coincide; ~**falten** fold (up); ~**fassen** *(in sich fassen)* comprise; *(sammeln)* collect; *(mitea. verbinden)* combine; *a.* ✗ concentrate; *(gedrängt darstellen)* summarize, sum up; *Schriftwerk:* condense; ♀**fassung** *f e-s Inhalts:* summary, résumé; synopsis; ~**finden:** *sich* ~ meet; ~**flicken** patch up; ~**fließen** (sn) flow together, meet; ♀**fluß** *m* confluence; ~**fügen** join (together), unite *(a. sich);* ~**gehen** (sn) go together *(a. fig.); (schrumpfen)* shrink; ~**gehören** belong together; *Schuhe usw.: a.* be fellows; ~**gehörig** belonging together; *fig. a.* related, allied; ♀**gehörigkeit** *f* unity; ♀**gehörigkeitsgefühl** *n* solidarity; *inniges:* togetherness; ~**geraten** (sn) *fig.* clash; ~**gesetzt** composed *(aus* of); *bsd.* ♩~, *gr., Arznei, Speise:* compound; *(verwickelt)* complex; *gr.* ~*er Satz* complex *(od.* compound) sentence; ~*es Wort* compound (word); ~**gewürfelt** motley, *bsd. Mannschaft:* scratch; ♀**halt** *m* holding together; *v. Freunden:* unity; ~**halten** *v/i.* hold together *(a. v/t.); Freunde:* stick together; ♀**hang** *m* coherence, connection; *des Textes:* context; *(Fortlaufendes)* continuity; *in diesem* ~ in this connection; *aus dem* ~ *reißen* divorce from its context; *in* ~ *bringen mit* connect with; *im* ~ *stehen mit* be connected with; ~**hängen** hang together *(a. fig.),* cohere; *fig.* be connected; ~**hängend** coherent; *(in Beziehung stehend)* connected; *(verwandt)* related; ~**hang(s)los** incoherent; ~**hauen** smash to pieces; F *j-n:* beat up; ~**häufen** heap up, accumulate; ~**heften** stitch together; *Schneiderei:* tack; ~**heilen** (sn) heal up *od.* over; ~**holen** fetch from all sides; ~**kaufen** buy up; ~**kitten** cement; ♀**klang** *m* accord, harmony; ~**klappbar** folding, collapsible; ~**klappen** v/t. fold up; *Messer:* shut; v/i. *P.:* break down; ~**kleben** v/t. glue (*od.* paste) together; v/i. stick together; ~**knüllen** (25) crumple; ~**kommen** (sn) come together, meet, assemble; 2**kunft** f (14¹) meeting; *sich* ~**läppern** F [~lɛpərn] (29) add up; ~**laufen** (sn) run (*od.* crowd) together; ∱ converge; (*gerinnen*) curdle; *s. Wasser;* ~**leben** live together; *mit j-m:* live with; 2**leben** n living together; *mit j-m:* life with; ~**legen** lay together; *Brief, Wäsche usw.:* fold up; *Geld:* club (together), pool; (*vereinigen*) combine, consolidate, fuse, merge (into one); 2**legung** f consolidation, merger; ~**nehmen** gather (up); *Gedanken:* collect; *sich* ~ collect o.s., *im Benehmen:* be on one's good behavio(u)r, *a. bei Anstrengung:* pull o.s. together; ~**packen** pack up; ~**passen** v/t. adjust, match; v/i. be (well) matched, harmonize, go well together; ~**pferchen** crowd together; 2**prall** m (3) collision, clash (*beide a. fig.*); ~**prallen** collide, clash; ~**raffen** snatch up; *Vermögen:* amass; *sich* ~ pull o.s. together; ~**rechnen** add up, sum up, total; ~**reimen** *fig.* make out; *sich* ~ add up; *es sich* ~ put two and two together; *sich* ~ put two and two together; ~**reißen** pull o.s. together; ~**rollen** coil up; *sich* ~ *a.* roll o.s. up; *sich* ~**rotten** (26) gang (*od.* throng) together; *Aufrührer:* riot; 2**rottung** f riot (-ing), *konkret:* riotous mob (*od.* 🏛 assembly); ~**rücken** v/t. move together (*od. Stühle usw.:* closer); v/i. (sn) move up; ~**rufen** call together, convoke; *sich* ~**scharen** flock together, rally; ~**schießen** shoot down; *mit Kanonen:* batter; *Geld:* club together; ~**schlagen** v/t. beat (*od.* strike) together; (*zerschlagen*) smash to pieces; *j-n:* beat up; *die Hände* ~ clap one's hands (together); v/i. (sn) ~ *über* (*dat.*) close over; (*sich*) ~**schließen** join (closely); (*vereinigen*) unite; consolidate; (*gemeinschaftliche Sache machen*) combine; 2**schluß** m union; consolidation; (*Bündnis*) alliance; ~**schmelzen** (sn) melt away (*a. fig.*); v/t. melt down; ~**schnüren** cord up; ~**schreiben** *Rechtschreibung:* write in one word; (*aus Bü-*

chern usw. zs.-stellen) compile; *contp.* scribble; ~**schrumpfen** (sn) shrivel, shrink (up); ~**schweißen** (*a. fig.*) weld together (*zu into*); 2**sein** n meeting, gathering; ~**setzen** put together; *zu e-m Ganzen:* compose; 📐 *Arznei, Wort:* compound; ⊕ assemble; *sich* ~ sit down together; *sich* ~ *aus* (*bestehen aus*) consist of; *s. zusammengesetzt;* 2**setzung** f composition; *gr.,* 📐 compound; ⊕ assembly; (*Bestandteile*) ingredients *pl.*; ~**sinken** (sn) sink down; 2**spiel** n *Sport, thea.* team-work; ~**stecken** v/t. put together; v/i. *fig.* be very thick (*mit with a friend*); ~**stehen** stand (*od. fig.* hold *od.* stick) together; ~**stellen** put together; *aus Einzelteilen, z. B. Liste, Medizin, Radiosendung, Wörterbuch usw.:* a. compile; (*zusammenfassend vereinigen*) combine; *in e-r Liste:* list; 2**stellung** f putting together; combination; compilation; list; (*Übersicht*) synopsis; ~**stoppeln** (29) patch up; 2**stoß** m collision (*a. fig.* = clash, conflict); *mot. usw. a.* crash; ⚔ encounter; ~**stoßen** v/t. strike (*od.* knock) together; *Gläser:* touch, clink; v/i. (sn) collide (*a. fig.* = clash); (*anea.-grenzen*) adjoin, meet; ~ *mit a.* run into, crash with; ~**streichen** cut down; ~**strömen** (sn) flow together; *Menschen:* flock together; ~**stürzen** (sn) collapse; ~**suchen** gather; *zu e-r Sammlung:* collect; ~**tragen** carry together; gather (*a. fig.*); *Notizen usw.:* compile; ~**treffen**¹ (sn) meet; (*gleichzeitig geschehen*) coincide; 2**treffen**² n (6) meeting; *feindliches:* encounter; *von Umständen:* coincidence; ~**treten** (sn) meet; *parl. a.* assemble, convene; 2**tritt** m meeting; ~**trommeln** call together; *weitS.* drum up; ~**tun** put together; *sich* ~ combine, join forces, team up (*mit with*); ~**wachsen** (sn) grow together; ~**werfen** throw together; (*verwechseln*) mix up; *unterschiedslos:* lump together; ~**wirken**¹ cooperate; *S.:* combine; 2**wirken**² n (6) co-operation; interaction; ~**zählen** add up, sum up; ~**ziehen** draw together (*a. sich*); (*verengern*) contract (*a. sich*); *Truppen:* gather, concentrate (*a. sich*); *sich* ~ *Gewit-*

ter: be gathering; ♀*ziehung f* contraction; ⚒ concentration.

'**Zusatz** *m* (3² *u.* ³) addition; *zu Nahrungsmitteln:* additive; (*Beimischung*) admixture, *zu Metallen:* alloy; (*Anhang*) appendix; (*Ergänzung*) supplement; (*Nachschrift*) postscript; *zu e-m Testament:* codicil; '⁓**antrag** *parl. m* supplementary motion; '⁓**ausbildung** *f* additional training; '⁓**frage** *f* additional question; '⁓**gerät** *n* accessory unit; attachment.

'**zusätzlich** additional, supplementary; *adv.* in addition (*zu* to), besides.

'**Zusatz|ver·einbarung** *f* supplementary agreement; '⁓**versicherung** *f* additional insurance.

zuschanden [tsu'ʃandən]: ⁓ *hauen* knock to pieces; ⁓ *machen* ruin, (*a. Hoffnungen*) destroy; *Plan:* frustrate, thwart; ⁓ *werden* be ruined *etc.*

'**zuschanzen:** *j-m et.* ⁓ put a p. in the way of a th.

'**zuscharren** cover (*od.* fill) up.

'**zuschau|en** look on (*e-r S.* at a th.), watch (a th.); *j-m* ⁓ watch a p. (*bei et.* doing a th.); '♀**er** *m* (7), '♀**erin** *f* (16¹) spectator, looker-on, onlooker; '♀**erraum** *thea. m* auditorium; '♀**tribüne** *f s. Tribüne.*

'**zuschicken** send, forward (*dat.* to); *mit der Post:* a. mail (to).

'**zuschieben** close; *j-m:* push towards a p.; *fig. b.s.* impute to a p.; *s. Schuld, Verantwortung.*

'**zuschießen** *v/t.* (*beitragen*) contribute; *ergänzend:* add, supply; *v/i.* (sn) ⁓ *auf* (*acc.*) rush up to.

'**Zuschlag** *m* addition; (*Preis♀*) extra charge; *zum Fahrpreis:* excess fare; (*Steuer♀*) surtax; *Auktion:* knocking down; ✝ *bei Ausschreibung:* award (of contract); *metall.* flux; ♀**en** ['⁓gən] *v/i.* (sn) strike; *v/t. Tür usw.:* bang, (*a. v/i.*) slam; *Auktion:* knock down; '♀(**s)frei** without surcharge; '⁓(**s)karte** *f* extra ticket.

'**zuschließen** lock (up).

'**zuschmeißen** F *Tür usw.:* bang, slam; *j-m et.:* throw (*od.* fling) to.

'**zuschmieren** smear over.

'**zuschnallen** buckle (up), strap up.

'**zuschnappen** (h.) snap; (sn) *Schloß usw.:* snap to, close with a snap.

'**zuschneid|en** cut up; *Anzug, a. fig.* cut (to size); '♀**er** (*in f*) *m* cutter.

'**Zuschnitt** *m* cut; *weitS.* style.

'**zuschnüren** lace up; *Ballen:* cord up; *j-m den Hals od. die Kehle* ⁓ strangle (*od.* choke) a p.

'**zuschrauben** screw down *od.* tight.

'**zuschreiben** *v/t. j-m od. e-r S. et.* ⁓ (*beimessen*) ascribe (*od.* attribute *od.* put down) to; *es ist dem Umstand zuzuschreiben, daß* it is due to the fact that; *das hast du dir selbst zuzuschreiben* that's your own doing.

'**zuschreien** *v/t. u. v/i. j-m:* shout (*od.* call out) to a p.

'**Zuschrift** *f* letter.

zu'schulden [tsu-]: *sich et.* ⁓ *kommen lassen* do something wrong.

Zuschuß ['tsu:-] *m* (4²) contribution; *staatlicher:* subsidy, grant; '⁓**betrieb** *m* subsidized undertaking.

'**zuschütten** (*hinzutun*) add; *Graben usw.:* fill up.

'**zusehen** *s. zuschauen;* (*sorgen*) ⁓, *daß* see (to it) that; *da müssen Sie selber* ⁓ you must see to it yourself; ⁓**ds** ['⁓ts] visibly, noticeably.

'**zusenden** send *od.* forward (*dat.* to).

'**zusetzen** *v/t.* (*hinzufügen*) add; *Geld, Zeit usw.:* lose; *v/i.* (*Geld einbüßen*) lose (money); *j-m* ⁓ press a p. hard, give a p. a hard time, (*in j-n dringen*) urge a p., *mit Fragen, Gründen:* ply a p. with, (*belästigen*) pester a p. with, *weitS. Hitze, Mühsal usw.:* be hard on a p., tell on a p.

'**zusicher|n** *j-m et.:* assure a p. of a th., guarantee a p. a th.; (*versprechen*) promise a p. a th.; '♀**ung** *f* promise, assurance, guarantee; pledge.

'**zusiegeln** seal (up).

Zu'spätkommende *m, f* (18) latecomer.

'**zuspielen** *j-m:* play *a th.* into a p.'s hands; (*a. v/i.*) *Sport:* pass to a p.

'**zuspitzen** point; *sich* ⁓ taper (off); *fig.* come to a point *od.* head.

'**zusprechen** *v/t. j-m Trost* ⁓ comfort a p.; *j-m Mut* ⁓ cheer a p. up; (*zubilligen*) adjudge, award (to); *v/i. e-r Speise wacker* ⁓ eat heartily of; *Getränken:* drink copiously.

'**zuspringen** (sn) *auf j-n:* leap towards, rush at; *Schloß:* snap to.

'**Zuspruch** *m von Mut:* encouragement; *von Trost:* consolation; *von Kunden:* run; (*Kundschaft*) custom.

'**Zustand** *m* condition; state; *in*

gutem ~ in good condition; *Haus usw.*: in good repair; *in betrunkenem* ~ drunk; F *Zustände bekommen* have a fit; *contp. hier herrscht Zustände!* what a mess!

zustande [tsu'ʃtandə]: ~ *bringen* bring about, manage, achieve; realize; ~ *kommen* come about; be realized; *Vertrag:* be reached (*od.* signed); *die Reise wird* ~ *kommen* will take place; *das Gesetz kommt* ~ will pass; *nicht* ~ *kommen* fail, not to come off, come to naught; ♀-**kommen** *n* realization.

zuständig ['tsu:ʃtendiç] (*befugt*) competent; (*verantwortlich*) responsible; (*maßgeblich*) proper; ♃ having jurisdiction (*für* over); '♀**keit** *f* competence; responsibility; jurisdiction; '♀**keitsbereich** *m* (sphere of) responsibility, scope; jurisdiction.

zustatten [tsu'ʃtatən]: ~ *kommen* come in handy, *j-m* be useful to a p., stand a p. in good stead.

zustecken ['tsu:-] pin (up); *j-m et.* ~ slip a th. into a p.'s hand.

'zustehen (*dat.*) *rechtlich:* be due to, belong to; *es* (*das Besitztum, das Recht*) *steht ihm zu* he is entitled to it; *es steht ihm* (*nicht*) *zu, zu ... he* has a (no) right to ...

'zustell|en deliver (*dat.* to); ♃ *j-m:* serve *a writ* on a p.; '♀**gebühr** *f* delivery charge; '♀**ung** *f* delivery; ♃ service, ~*en pl.* (service of) legal process; '♀**ungsgebühr** *f s.* Zustellgebühr.

'zustimm|en (*dat.*) agree (to *a th.*; with *a p.*); consent (to *a th.*), approve (of *a th.*); F *a.* okay; '~**end** affirmative; ~ *nicken* nod one's approval; '♀**ung** *f* consent, agreement.

'zustopfen stop up, plug; *Loch im Strumpf usw.*: mend, darn.

'zustöpseln stopper, plug (up).

'zustoßen *v/t.* push ... to; *v/i. fenc.* lunge, thrust; (*sn*) *j-m* ~ happen to a p., befall a p.; *ihm ist ein Unfall zugestoßen* he has had (*od.* met with) an accident.

'Zustrom *m von Personen:* concourse, throng, stream; *v. Dingen:* influx.

'zuströmen (*sn*; *dat.*) stream towards; *Personen:* throng to(wards).

'zustürzen (*sn*) *auf* (*acc.*) rush up to.

'zustutzen trim; (*passend machen*)

fit (up), cut to size (*a. fig.*); *Stück für die Bühne, Text für den Unterricht:* adapt (for).

zutage [tsu'ta:gə]: ~ *fördern od. bringen* bring to light; ~ *liegen* be evident; ~ *treten od.* kommen come to light; *geol.* outcrop.

Zutaten ['tsu:ta:tən] *f/pl.* (16) *e-r Speise:* ingredients *pl.*; *e-s Kleides:* trimmings *pl.*; (*Stoff*♀) material *sg.*

zu'teil [tsu-]: *j-m* ~ *werden* fall to a p.'s share (*fig. a.* lot); *j-m et.* ~ *werden lassen* allot (*od.* grant) a th. to a p., bestow a th. on a p.; *ihm wurde eine freundliche Aufnahme* ~ he met with a kind reception.

'zuteil|en allot (*a.* ♰ *Aktien usw.*), allocate, apportion; (*genehmigen*) grant, allow; (*ausgeben*) issue (*dat.* to); ⚔ *od. pol.* attach (to); '♀**ung** *f* allotment, allocation, apportionment; attachment; (*zugeteilte Ration*) ration; (*Kontingent*) quota.

zu'tiefst deeply.

'zutragen carry (*dat.* to; *a. fig.*); *Gerücht:* report; *sich* ~ happen, take place, occur.

'Zuträger|(in *f*) *m* talebearer, telltale; ~**ei** [~'raɪ] *f* (16) talebearing.

zuträglich ['~trɛ:k-] conducive, beneficial (*dat. od. für* to); *Klima:* salubrious; *Nahrung:* wholesome; *j-m* (*nicht*) ~ *sein* (dis)agree with a p.; '♀**keit** *f* conduciveness; salubrity; wholesomeness.

'zutrau|en 1. *j-m et.* ~ believe a p. capable of a th.; *j-m nicht viel* ~ have no high opinion of a p.; *sich zuviel* ~ overrate o.s., (*sich übernehmen*) take too much on o.s.; *ich traue es mir zu* I think I can do it; *iro. ich traue es ihm glatt zu* I would not put it past him; 2. ♀ *n* (6) confidence (*zu* in); '~**lich** trusting; *Tier:* friendly, tame; '♀**lichkeit** *f* confidingness; tameness.

'zutreffen (*sn*) be right *od.* true, hold true; ~ *auf* (*acc.*) be true of, (*a.* ~ *für*) apply to; '~**d** right, true; (*anwendbar*) applicable; '~**denfalls** if so; *in Formularen:* where applicable.

'zutrinken *j-m:* drink to a p.

'Zutritt *m* access; (*Einlaß*) admission; ~ *verboten!* no admittance!, no entry!

'zutun 1. (*schließen*) close; (*hinzufügen*) add; *s.* Auge, zugetan; 2. ♀ *n*

(6): *ohne sein* ⌄ without his help, *(ohne s-e Schuld)* through no fault of his.

zu¹-ungunsten [tsu-] *(gen.)* to the disadvantage of.

zu¹-unterst right at the bottom.

zuverlässig ['tsu:fɛrlɛsiç] reliable *(a.* ⊕*); nur P.*: dependable, trustworthy; *(sicher)* safe *(a.* ✝, ⊕*); Nachricht*: sure, certain; *aus* ⌄*er Quelle* from a reliable source; *von* ⌄*er Seite erfahren (haben), daß …* have it on good authority that …; '2**keit** *f* reliability; trustworthiness; certainty; '2**keits-prüfung** *mot. f* reliability test; '2**keits-überprüfung** *pol. f des Personals*: security clearance, screening.

Zuversicht ['⌄fɛrziçt] *f* (16) confidence; '2**lich** confident; '⌄**lichkeit** *f* confidence; assurance.

zu¹viel 1. too much; *einer usw.* ⌄ one *etc.* too many; **2.** 2 *n* excess.

zu¹vor before, previously.

zu¹vor|kommen (sn) *j-m*: anticipate, forestall, F beat *a p.* to it; *e-r S.*: obviate, anticipate; ⌄**kommend** obliging; 2**kommenheit** *f* obligingness; ⌄**tun:** *es j-m* ⌄ surpass *(od.* outdo*)* *a p.*

Zuwachs ['tsu:-] *m* (4) *(Vermehrung)* increase, increment; *s. Familien*2; *auf* ⌄ *geschneidert* made so as to allow for growing; '2**en** (sn) become overgrown; 𝄢 heal up, close; *j-m* ⌄ accrue to a p. '⌄**rate** *f* rate of increase, growth rate.

'**zuwandern** (sn) immigrate.

'**zuwarten** wait (and see).

zuwege [tsu've:gə]: ⌄ *bringen* bring about, accomplish.

zuwehen ['tsu:-] *(dat.)* blow to *od.* towards; *mit Schnee, Sand*: cover.

zu¹weilen sometimes, occasionally.

zuweis|en ['tsu:-] assign, allocate; '2**ung** *f* assignment, allocation.

'**zuwend|en** *(dat.)* turn to(wards); *fig. j-m e-e Gabe usw.* ⌄ let a p. have, present a p. with, give a p. *a th.*; *Gefühl usw.*: bestow on a p.; *Aufmerksamkeit, Bemühungen*: devote to; *sich e-r Tätigkeit* ⌄ proceed to *do*, apply o.s. to; *sich e-m Beruf* ⌄ devote o.s. to; '2**ung** *f* allowance, grant, gift; *(Schenkung)* donation; *(Vermächtnis)* bequest; *(Liebe)* love, (loving) care.

zuwenig [tsu've:niç] too little.

zuwerfen ['tsu:-] *Grube*: fill up; *Tür*: slam; *j-m*: throw to a p., *e-n Blick*: cast to a p.

zuwider [tsu'vi:dər] *(dat.)* contrary to, against; *(verhaßt)* repugnant, distasteful (to); *er (es) ist mir* ⌄ I loathe him (it); ⌄**handeln** *(dat.)* act contrary to, *bsd.* 𝈓 contravene, violate; 2**handelnde** *m* (18) offender; 2**handlung** 𝈓 *f* contravention, violation; ⌄**laufen** (sn; *dat.)* run counter *(od.* be contrary*)* to. *[weitS.* make a sign to.*]*

zuwinken ['tsu:-] *(dat.)* wave to;∫

'**zuzahlen** pay extra.

'**zuzählen** add *(dat. od. zu* to).

zuzeiten [tsu'tsaitən] at times.

zuzieh|en ['tsu:-] *v/t. Knoten*: draw together; *Schlinge, Schleife*: *(a. sich)* tighten; *Vorhang*: draw; *Arzt, Berater usw.*: consult, call in; *sich e-e Strafe, Tadel usw.* ⌄ incur; *Krankheit*: contract, catch; *sich Unannehmlichkeiten* ⌄ get into trouble; *j-n als Zeugen* ⌄ call a p. as witness; *v/i.* (sn) *Mieter*: move in; *(sich niederlassen)* settle; '2**ung** *f* consultation, calling in.

'**Zuzug** *m* moving in; arrival, immigration; '⌄**sgenehmigung** *f* residence permit.

zuzüglich ['⌄tsy:kliç] plus; *(einschließlich)* including.

Zwang¹ [tsvaŋ] *m* (3, *o. pl.)* compulsion, coercion; *moralischer*: constraint, restraint; *(Druck)* pressure *(a.* 𝈓*); (Gewalt)* force; *bsd.* 𝈓 duress; *sich* ⌄ *antun od. auferlegen* restrain o.s.; *unter* ⌄ *stehen (od. handeln)* be *(od.* act*)* under coercion.

zwang² *pret. v.* zwingen.

zwängen ['tsvɛŋən] (25) press, force.

'**zwanglos** unconstrained; *fig. a.* free and easy, unceremonious, informal; '2**igkeit** *f* ease, informality.

'**Zwangs|-anleihe** *f* forced loan; '⌄**arbeit** *f* hard labo(u)r; '2**bewirtschaftet** under economic control, control(l)ed; '⌄**ent-eignung** *f* compulsory expropriation; '2**-ernähren** force-feed; '⌄**ernährung** *f* forcible feeding; '⌄**haft** *f* coercive detention; '⌄**handlung** *f* compulsive act; '⌄**herrschaft** *f* despotism; '⌄**idee** *f* compulsive idea; '⌄**jacke** *f* strait-jacket *(a. fig.)*; '⌄**lage** *f* quandary, embarrassing situation; '2**läu-**

fig ⊕ guided, geared; *mot.* positive; *fig.* necessary; *adv.* inevitably; '~**maßnahme** *f* coercive measure; *zu* ~n *greifen* resort to coercion; '~**mittel** *n* means of coercion; '~**neurose** ⚕ *f* compulsion neurosis; '~**räumung** *f* compulsory evacuation; '~**verkauf** *m* forced sale; '⚩**verpflichtet** conscript; '~**versteigerung** *f* forced sale; '~**verwaltung** *f* forced administration, sequestration; '~**vollstreckung** *f* execution; '~**vorstellung** ⚕ *f* compulsive idea, obsession; '⚩**weise** compulsorily, by force; '~**wirtschaft** *f* Government control; *die* ~ *für ein Gewerbe usw.* *aufheben* decontrol; *Aufhebung der* ~ decontrol.

zwanzig ['tsvantsiç] twenty; ⚩**er** ['~gər] *m* (7) person of twenty; *in den* ~n *sein* be between twenty and thirty; '~**er**'lei *adj.* of twenty kinds; *als su.* twenty different things *pl.*; '~**fach**, '~**fältig** twentyfold; '~**st** twentieth; '⚩**stel** *n* (7) twentieth (part); '~**stens** in the twentieth place.

zwar [tsva:r] indeed, (it is) true, of course, to be sure; *und* ~ and that, *(nämlich)* that is; *er kam* ~, *aber* ... he did come, but ..., (al-) though he came, the ...

Zweck [tsvɛk] *m* (3) purpose; *(Ziel)* object (*a.* ✝); aim, end; *(Absicht)* intent; *(Verwendung)* use, application; *ein Mittel zum* ~ a means to an end; *e-n* ~ *verfolgen* pursue an object, be after something; *keinen* ~ *haben* be useless; *s-n* ~ *erfüllen*, *dem* ~ *entsprechen* answer (*od.* serve) the purpose; *zu dem* ~ (*gen. od. zu inf.*) for the purpose of; *zu welchem* ~? to what purpose?, what ... for?; F *das ist der* ~ *der Übung!* that's the idea!; *der* ~ *heiligt die Mittel* the end justifies the means; '~**bau** ⬠ *m* functional building; '⚩**bestimmt** functional; '⚩**dienlich** serviceable, expedient, useful; *(einschlägig)* pertinent; '~**dienlichkeit** *f* serviceableness, expediency, usefulness.

Zwecke ['tsvɛkə] *f* (15) tack; *s. Reißnagel.*

'**zweck**|-**entfremdet** alienated (from its purpose); '~-**entsprechend** answering the purpose; proper, appropriate; '~**gebunden** *Gelder*: ear-

marked, appropriated; '~**los** aimless, purposeless; *(unnütz)* useless, pointless, *pred.* of no use; '⚩**losigkeit** *f* aimlessness; uselessness, futility; '~**mäßig** expedient, suitable, proper; *(ratsam)* advisable; '⚩**mäßigkeit** *f* expediency, suitableness; '⚩**pessimismus** *m* calculated pessimism.

zwecks (*gen.*) for the purpose of.

'**Zweck**|**verband** *m* local administrative union; '⚩**widrig** inexpedient, inappropriate, unsuitable.

zwei [tsvaɪ] (*gen.* ~*er*, *dat.* ~*en*) two; *zu* ~*en* in twos.

zwei|**armig** ['~'armiç] two-armed; '~**bändig** two-volume (*attr.*); ~-**beinig** ['~baɪniç] two-legged; '⚩-**bettzimmer** *n* twin-bedded room; '⚩**decker** ⚔ *m* (7) biplane; ~**deutig** ['⚩dɔʏtiç] ambiguous, equivocal; *b.s.* suggestive, *Witz usw.*: risqué (*fr.*), *Am.* off-color; '⚩**deutigkeit** *f* ambiguity, equivocality; *b.s.* risqué joke; '~**dimensional** two-dimensional; ⚩'**drittelmehrheit** *f* two-thirds majority; ~-**eiig** *biol.* ['~-ʔaɪç] dizygotic; ~*e Zwillinge a.* non-identical twins; '⚩**er** *m* (7) (figure) two; *Rudern*: pair, two; ~**erlei** ['~ər-'laɪ] *adj.* of two kinds; *als su.* two different things *pl.*; '~**fach**, '~**fältig** double, two-fold; '⚩**familienhaus** *n* two-family house, *Am.* duplex house; '~**farbig** two-colo(u)red.

Zweifel ['tsvaɪfəl] *m* (7) doubt; *ohne* ~ without doubt; *im* ~ *sein* be doubtful (*über acc.* about); *in* ~ *ziehen* call in question; '⚩**haft** doubtful, *stärker*: dubious; '⚩**los** undoubted; (*a. adv.*) doubtless; '⚩**n** (29) doubt (*an e-r S.* [of] a th., *an j-m* a p.); '~**sfall** *m* (*im* ~ in) case of doubt; '⚩**s'-ohne** doubtless, without doubt; '~**sucht** *f* scepticism, *Am.* skepticism.

'**Zweifler** *m* (7), '~**in** *f* (16¹) doubter, sceptic, *Am.* skeptic; '⚩**isch** doubting, sceptical, *Am.* skeptical.

Zweig [tsvaɪk] *m* (3) branch (*a. fig.*); bough; *kleiner* ~ twig; *s. grün*; '~**bahn** *f* branch-line.

'**Zwei**|**spann** *n* carriage-and-pair; *fig.* twosome, duo; '⚩**geteilt** divided.

'**Zweig**|**geschäft** *n*, '~**niederlassung** *f* branch(-establishment); '~**stelle** *f* branch(-office).

zwei|**gleisig** ['~glaɪziç] double-

-track(ed); **～händig** ['～hɛndɪç]
two-handed; ♪ for two hands; '♀-
hufer m (7) cloven-footed animal;
'**～jährig** two-year(s)-old; *Dauer*:
of two years, two-year; *bsd.* ♀
biennial; '**～jährlich** (happening)
every two years, biennial; '♀**kampf**
m duel; ✗ single combat; '**～mal**
twice; *es sich ～ überlegen* think
twice (before doing it); *es sich nicht
～ sagen lassen* not to wait to be
told twice; '**～malig** done twice,
twice (repeated); '♀**master** ⚓ m
(7) two-master; **～motorig** ['～mo-
toːrɪç] twin– (*od.* two-)engined;
'♀**par'teiensystem** n two-party
system; '♀**rad** n bicycle, F bike;
～räd(e)rig ['～rɛːd(ə)rɪç] two-
-wheeled; **～reihig** ['～raɪç] having
two rows; *Jacke usw.*: double-
-breasted; '**～schläf(e)rig** *Bett*:
double; '**～schneidig** double-edged
(*a. fig.*); *fig. ～ sein a.* cut both ways;
～seitig ['～zaɪtɪç] two-sided; *Vertrag usw.*: bilateral; *Stoff*: reversible; **～silbig** ['～zɪlbɪç] dissyllabic;
～es *Wort* dissyllable; '♀**sitzer** m (7)
two-seater; '**～sitzig** two-seated;
♀**spänner** ['～ʃpɛnər] m (7) carriage-
-and-pair; '**～sprachig** ['～ʃpraːxɪç]
in two languages, bilingual; '♀**stär-
kenbrille** f bifocals *pl.*; '**～stellig**: **～e**
Zahl two-digit (*od.* two-place) number; '**～stimmig** for (*Gesang*: in) two
voices; **～stöckig** ['～ʃtœkɪç] two-
-stor|eyed, *Am.* -ied; **～strahlig** ['～-
ʃtraːlɪç] *Triebwerk*: twin-jet; '**～stu-
fig** *Rakete*: two-stage; **～stündig** ['～-
ʃtyndɪç] of two hours, two-hour;
'**～stündlich** every two hours.
zweit [tsvaɪt] (18) second; *in Zssgn*
... but one (*s. zweitjüngst*); *ein ～er*
m, *eine ～e* f, *ein ～es* n another;
Sport: ♀e m, f runner-up, second;
ein ～er Churchill another Churchill;
s. Gesicht; aus ～er Hand second-hand
(*a. adv.*); *zu ～* (*paarweise*) by twos;
wir sind zu ～ we are two of us; *zum
～en, ～ens* secondly, in the second
place; *fig. die ～e Geige spielen* play
second fiddle.
'**zwei|tägig** of two days, two-day;
'♀**taktmotor** m two-stroke (*od.*
two-cycle) engine.
'**zweit|-'älteste** second eldest; '♀-
ausfertigung f duplicate; '**～'best**
second-best.
'**zweiteilig** two-part; *Anzug usw.*:

two-piece; ♀, ⚏ bipartite.
'**zweit|'größt** second largest; '**～-
jüngst** youngest but one; '**～klassig**
second-class *od.* -rate; '**～'letzt** last
but one, *Am.* next to the last; '**～ran-
gig** secondary; '♀**schrift** f second
copy, duplicate; '♀**wagen** m second
car; '♀**wohnung** f second home.
'**Zwei|-und'dreißigstelnote** f demi-
semiquaver; **～'vierteltakt** m two-
-four time; '♀**wöchentlich** biweek-
ly; '♀**zackig** two-pronged; '**～zeiler**
m couplet; '♀**zeilig** of two lines;
～'zimmerwohnung f two-room
flat (*Am.* apartment).
Zwerchfell ['tsvɛrç-] n diaphragm;
'♀-**erschütternd** side-splitting.
Zwerg [tsvɛrk] m (3), **～in** ['gɪn] f (16¹)
dwarf, gnome; ♀**enhaft** ['～g-] dwarf-
ish; '**～huhn** n bantam; '**～kiefer** f
dwarf pine; '**～mensch** m pygmy;
'**～schule** f one-room school; '**～staat**
m mini-state.
Zwetsch(g)e ['tsvɛt∫(g)ə] f (15) plum.
Zwick|el ['tsvɪkəl] m (7) am *Strumpf*:
clock; *Schneiderei*: gore, gusset; ⊕
wedge; '♀**en¹** (25) pinch, tweak;
'**～en²** n (6) (*Schmerz*) twinge; '**～er** m
(7) (*Augenglas*) pince-nez (*fr.*); '**～-
mühle** f *fig.* dilemma, fix, tight
squeeze.
Zwieback ['tsviːbak] m (3³) rusk,
zwieback.
Zwiebel ['tsviːbəl] f (15) onion; (*Blumen*♀) bulb; '♀**förmig** bulb-shaped,
bulbous; '**～gewächs** n bulbous
plant; '**～haube** f onion dome; '**～-
kuchen** m onion tart; '♀**n** F (29) *give
a p.* hell, make it hot for *a p.*;
'**～schale** f onion-skin; '**～turm** m
onion tower.
zwie|fach ['tsviː-], **～fältig** ['～fɛltɪç]
double, twofold; '♀**gespräch** n
dialog(ue); colloquy; ♀**licht** n twilight; '**～lichtig** dusky; *fig.* shady.
'**Zwie|spalt** m (*Uneinigkeit*) discord;
(*innerer ～* inner) conflict; (*Abweichung*) discrepancy; *im ～ sein mit*
be at variance with; ♀**spältig** ['～-
ʃpɛltɪç] disunited; discrepant; *Gefühle*: conflicting; '**～tracht** f (16,
o. pl.) discord; (*Fehde*) feud;
(*Kampf*) strife; *～ säen* sow the
seeds of discord; '♀**trächtig** dis-
cordant, hostile; *nur pred.* at variance.
Zwil(li)ch ['tsvɪl(i)ç] m (3) tick(ing).
Zwilling ['tsvɪlɪŋ] m (3¹) twin; '**～e**

pl. ast. Gemini, Twins; '**~sbruder** *m* twin brother; '**~s-paar** *n* pair of twins; '**~sschwester** *f* twin sister.

Zwing|burg ['tsviŋ-] *f* (tyrant's) strong castle; '**~e** *f* (15) (*Stock*²) ferrule; ⊕ clamp; '²**en** (30) compel (*j-n* et. *zu* tun a p. to do a th.), make (a p. do a th.), *bsd. mit Gewalt*: force; (*verpflichten*) oblige; (*fertigwerden mit*) manage, finish; *sich zu et.* ~ force o.s. to a *th.* *od.* to *do* (a *th.*); *s.* bezwingen, gezwungen; '²**end** *adj.* compelling; *Grund*: cogent; *Notwendigkeit*: imperative; *Beweis*: conclusive; '**~er** *m* (7) tower, dungeon; (*Hof*) outer court--yard; (*Hunde*²) kennel; (*Bären*²) bear-pit; '**~herr** *m* tyrant, despot; '**~herrschaft** *f* despotism, tyranny.

zwinkern ['tsviŋkərn] (29) blink; *lustig, schlau*: wink.

Zwirn [tsvirn] *m* (3) (twisted) thread; *Spinnerei*: twine, twisted yarn; '²**en** 1. *adj.* thread; 2. *v/t.* (25) twist; '**~sfaden** *m* thread.

zwischen ['tsviʃən] *zweien*: between; *mehreren*: among.

'**Zwischen|·akt** *m* entr'acte (*fr.*); *im* ~ between the two acts; '**~bemerkung** *f* incidental remark; interruption; '**~bescheid** *m* intermediate reply; '**~bilanz** *f* interim financial statement; '**~deck** ⚓ *n* between-decks *pl.*; '**~ding** *n* mixture, cross; ²'**durch** through; (*inmitten*) in the midst; *zeitlich*: at intervals, occasionally; (*eingeschoben*) in between; '**~ergebnis** *n* Sport: provisional result; '**~erzeugnis** *n* intermediate (product); '**~fall** *m* incident; '**~frage** *f* interpolated question; '**~gericht** *n* entremets *pl.* (*fr.*); '**~handel** *m* intermediate trade; (*Durchfuhrhandel*) transit trade; (*Großhandel*) wholesale trade; '**~händler** *m* middleman, intermediary; commission agent; '**~handlung** *f* episode; '**~kredit** *m* interim credit; '**~landung** ✈ *f* intermediate landing, stop (-over *Am.*); *Flug ohne* ~ non-stop flight; '²**liegend** intermediate; '**~lösung** *f* interim solution; *s. Notbehelf*; '²**menschlich**: ~*e Beziehungen* human relations; '**~pause** *f* interval, intermission; '**~produkt** *n* intermediate product; '**~prüfung** *f* intermediate examination; '**~raum**

m space, (*a. zeitlich*) interval; (*Entfernung*) distance (between); (*Lücke*) interstice; (*Zeilenabstand*) spacing; '**~raumtaste** *f der Schreibmaschine*: space-bar; '**~ruf** *m* (loud) interruption; *mißbilligend*: boo; '**~rufer** *m* interrupter; '**~runde** *f* Sport: semi--final; '**~satz** *m* parenthesis; '**~spiel** *n* intermezzo, interlude; '²**staatlich** international, *Am.* inter-state; '**~stadium** *n* intermediate stage; '**~station** *f* intermediate stop, stopover; ~ *machen* stop (over *od.* off) (*in* at); '**~stecker** *m* ⚡, Radio: adapter; '**~stock** *m* entresol (*fr.*), intermediate stor|ey, *Am.* -y; '**~stück** *n* intermediate piece; connection; ⚡ adapter; *thea.* interlude, entr'acte (*fr.*); '**~stufe** *f* intermediate stage; '**~träger(in** *f*) *m s.* Zuträger; '**~urteil** ⚖ *n* interlocutory decree; '**~verkauf** ✝ *m*: ~ *vorbehalten* subject to prior sale; '**~vorhang** *m* drop-scene; '**~wand** *f* partition (wall); '**~zeit** *f* interval; *in der* ~ (*a.* '²**zeitlich**) in the meantime.

Zwist [tsvist] *m* (3²) (*Zwietracht*) discord; (*Uneinigkeit*) disunion; (*Streit*) quarrel; '²**ig** *s.* zwieträchtig; '**~igkeit** *f s.* Zwist.

zwitschern ['tsvitʃərn] (29) twitter, chirp.

Zwitter ['tsvitər] *m* (7) hermaphrodite; (*Mischling*) hybrid (*a.* ♀); '²**haft** hermaphrodite; hybrid.

zwo [tsvo:] *s.* zwei.

zwölf [tsvœlf] twelve; *um* ~ *Uhr* at twelve (o'clock), *mittags*: *a.* at noon, *nachts*: *a.* at midnight; '²**-eck** *n* dodecagon; '**~eckig** dodecagonal; '²**-ender** *m* twelve-point stag; '**~er'lei** *adj.* of twelve different kinds *od.* sorts; *als su.* twelve different things *pl.*; '**~fach** twelvefold; ²'**fingerdarm** *m* duodenum; '**~jährig** *Kind*: twelve-year(s)-old; *allg.*: of twelve years; **~stündig** ['~ʃtyndiç] of twelve hours, twelve--hour; **~t** twelfth; **~tägig** ['~tɛːgiç] of twelve days; '²**tel** *n* (7) twelfth (part); '**~tens** in the twelfth place; '²**tonmusik** *f* twelve-tone music.

Zyankali [tsyan'ka:li] *n* cyanide of potassium.

zyklisch ['tsy:kliʃ] cyclic(al).

Zyklon [tsy'klo:n] *m* (3¹), **~e** *f* (15) cyclone.

Zyklop [~'klo:p] *m* (12) Cyclops, *pl.* Cyclopes; ²**isch** Cyclopean.

Zyklotron [~klo'troːn] *n* (3) *Atom-wissenschaft*: cyclotron.

Zyklus ['tsyːklus] *m* (16²) cycle; *v. Vorlesungen usw.*: course, set.

Zylinder [tsy'lindər] *m* (7) ⚗, ⊕ cylinder; (*Lampen*⚑) chimney; *Hut*: silk hat, top-hat; ~**block** ⊕ *m* cylinder block; ~**bohrung** ⊕ *f* cylinder bore; ~**kopf** ⊕ *m* cylinder head; ~**kopfdichtung** *f* cylinder head gasket.

zylindrisch [~'lindriʃ] cylindrical.

Zyn|iker ['tsyːnikər] *m* (7) cynic; '⚑**isch** cynical; ~**ismus** [tsy'nismus] *m* cynicism.

Zypresse [tsy'prɛsə] *f* (15) cypress (-tree).

Zyste ⚕ ['tsystə] *f* (15) cyst.

Proper Names

Eigennamen

(For declension of proper names see page 1331)

A

Aachen [ˈɑːxən] n Aachen, Fr. Aix--la-Chapelle.

Aargau [ˈɑːrgaʊ] m Argovia (Swiss canton).

Adenauer [ˈɑːdənaʊər] first chancellor of the Federal Republic of Germany.

Adler [ˈɑːdlər] Austrian psychologist.

Adorno [aˈdɔrno] German philosopher.

Adria [ˈɑːdria] f, **Adriatische(s) Meer** [adriˈɑːtiʃə(s)] n Adriatic Sea.

Afghanistan [afˈgɑːnistɑːn] n Afghanistan.

Afrika [ˈɑːfrika] n Africa.

Ägäis [ɛˈgɛːis] f, **Ägäische(s) Meer** [ɛˈgɛːiʃə(s)] n Aegean Sea.

Ägypten [ɛˈgyptən] n Egypt.

Albanien [alˈbɑːniən] n Albania.

Albert [ˈalbɛrt], **Albrecht** [ˈalbrɛçt] m Albert.

Albertus Magnus [alˈbɛrtus ˈmagnus] German philosopher.

Alexander [alɛˈksandər] m Alexander.

Alfons [ˈalfɔns] m German Christian name.

Algerien [alˈgeːriən] n Algeria.

Algier [ˈalʒiːr] n Algiers.

Allgäu [ˈalgɔy] n Al(l)gäu (region of Bavaria).

Alpen [ˈalpən] pl. Alps pl.

Altdorfer [ˈaltdɔrfər] German painter.

Amazonas [amaˈtsoːnas] m Amazon (river in Brazil).

Amerika [aˈmeːrika] n America.

Anden [ˈandən] pl. Andes pl.

Andorra [anˈdɔra] n Andorra.

Andrea [anˈdreːa] f, **Andreas** [anˈdreːas] m Andrea, Andrew.

Angola [aŋˈgoːla] n Angola.

Anna [ˈana], **Anne** [ˈanə] f Anna.

Antarktis [antˈʔarktis] f Antarctic.

Antillen [anˈtilən] pl. Antilles pl.

Anton [ˈantoːn] m Anthony.

Antwerpen [antˈvɛrpən] n Antwerp.

Apenninen [apɛˈniːnən] pl. Apennines pl.

Appenzell [apənˈtsɛl] n Swiss canton.

Arabien [aˈrɑːbiən] n Arabia.

Argentinien [argɛnˈtiːniən] n Argentina.

Ärmelkanal [ˈɛrməlkanɑːl] m English Channel.

Armenien [arˈmeːniən] n Armenia.

Art(h)ur [ˈartur] m Arthur.

Asien [ˈɑːziən] n Asia.

Athen [aˈteːn] n Athens.

Äthiopien [ɛtiˈoːpiən] n Ethiopia.

Atlantik [atˈlantik], **Atlantische(r) Ozean** [atˈlantiʃə(r)] m Atlantic, Atlantic Ocean.

Ätna [ˈɛːtna] m Etna.

Augsburg [ˈaʊksburk] n town in Bavaria.

Australien [aʊsˈtrɑːliən] n Australia.

Azoren [aˈtsoːrən] pl. Azores pl.

B

Bach [bax] German composer.

Baden-Württemberg [ˈbɑːdən-ˈvyrtəmbɛrk] n Land of the Federal Republic of Germany.

Bahrain [baˈraɪn] n Bahrein.

Balearen [baleˈɑːrən] pl. Balearic Islands pl.

Balkan [ˈbalkɑːn] m Balkan Peninsula.

Baltikum [ˈbaltikum] n the three former Baltic Provinces of Russia.

Banglades(c)h [baŋglaˈdɛʃ] n Bangladesh.

Barbarossa [barbaˈrɔsa] hist. appellation of the German emperor Friedrich I.

Barlach [ˈbarlax] German sculptor.

Basel ['bɑːzəl] *n* Basel, Basle, *Fr.* Bâle (*Swiss town and canton*).

Baskenland ['baskənlant] *n*, **Baskische(n) Provinzen** ['baskiʃə(n)] *f/pl.* Basque Provinces *pl.*

Baumeister ['baʊmaɪstər] *German painter.*

Bayern ['baɪərn] *n* Bavaria (*Land of the Federal Republic of Germany*).

Bayerische(r) Wald ['baɪəriʃə(r)] *m* Bavarian Forest.

Bebel ['beːbəl] *German socialist.*

Beckmann ['bɛkman] *German painter.*

Beethoven ['beːthoːfən] *German composer.*

Belgien ['bɛlgiən] *n* Belgium.

Belgrad ['bɛlgrɑːt] *n* Belgrade.

Benn [bɛn] *German writer.*

Beringstraße ['beːrinʃtrɑːsə] *f* Bering Strait.

Berlin [bɛr'liːn] *n* Berlin.

Bermuda-Inseln [bɛr'muːda-] *f/pl.* Bermudas *pl.*

Bern [bɛrn] *n* Bern, *Fr.* Berne (*capital and canton of Switzerland*).

Bernhard ['bɛrnhart] *m* Bernard.

Birma ['birma] *n* Burma.

Biskaya [bis'kɑːja] *f* Biscay, **Golf von ~** *m* Bay of Biscay.

Bloch [blɔx] *German philosopher.*

Bodensee ['boːdənzeː] *m* Lake Constance.

Böhmen ['bøːmən] *n* Bohemia, **Böhmer Wald** *m* Bohemian Forest.

Bolivien [bo'liːviən] *n* Bolivia.

Böll [bœl] *German author.*

Bonn [bɔn] *n* capital of the Federal Republic of Germany.

Borneo ['bɔrneo] *n* Borneo.

Bosporus ['bɔsporus] *m* Bosporus.

Botswana [bɔts'vɑːna] *n* Botswana.

Brahms [brɑːms] *German composer.*

Brandt [brant] *fourth chancellor of the Federal Republic of Germany.*

Brasilien [bra'ziːliən] *n* Brazil.

Brecht [brɛçt] *German dramatist.*

Bremen ['breːmən] *n* Land of the Federal Republic of Germany.

Brigitte [bri'gitə] *f* Bridget.

Bruckner ['bruknər] *Austrian composer.*

Brüssel ['brysəl] *n* Brussels.

Buber ['buːbər] *German philosopher.*

Büchner ['byːçnər] *German dramatist.*

Bukarest ['buːkarɛst] *n* Bucharest.

Bulgarien [bul'gɑːriən] *n* Bulgaria.

Bundesrepublik Deutschland ['bundəsrepubliːk 'dɔytʃlant] *f* Federal Republic of Germany.

Bunsen ['bunzən] *German chemist.*

Burgenland ['burgənlant] *n* province of Austria.

Burgund [bur'gunt] *n* Burgundy.

Burma ['burma] *n* → *Birma.*

Busch [buʃ] *German satirist.*

Butenandt ['buːtənant] *German chemist.*

C

Calais [ka'lɛː] *n*: **Straße von ~** *f* Straits of Dover.

Calvin [kal'viːn] *Swiss Protestant reformer.*

Carstens ['karstəns] *fifth president of the Federal Republic of Germany.*

Ceylon ['tsaɪlɔn] *n* Ceylon (*heute* → *Sri Lanka*).

Chile ['tʃiːle] *n* Chile.

China ['çiːna] *n* China.

Christoph ['kristɔf] *m* Christopher.

Christus ['kristus] *m* Christ.

D

Daimler ['daɪmlər] *German inventor.*

Dänemark ['dɛːnəmark] *n* Denmark.

Den Haag [den'hɑːk] *n* The Hague.

Delhi ['deːli] *n* Delhi.

Deutsche Demokratische Republik ['dɔytʃə demo'krɑːtiʃə repu'bliːk] *f* German Democratic Republic.

Deutschland ['dɔytʃlant] *n* Germany.

Diesel ['diːzəl] *German inventor.*

Döblin ['døːbliːn] *German novelist.*

Dolomiten [dolo'miːtən] *pl.* Dolomites *pl.*

Dominikanische Republik [domini'kɑːniʃə repu'bliːk] *f* Dominican Republic.

Donau ['doːnaʊ] *f* Danube.

Dresden ['dreːsdən] *n* town and district in the German Democratic Republic.

Droste-Hülshoff ['drɔstə 'hylshɔf] *German poetess.*

Dünkirchen ['dyːnkirçən] *n* Dunkirk.

Dürer ['dyːrər] *German painter and engraver.*

Dürrenmatt ['dyrənmat] *Swiss dramatist.*
Düsseldorf ['dysəldɔrf] *n capital of North Rhine-Westphalia.*

E

Ebert ['e:bərt] *first president of the Weimar Republic.*
Ecuador [ekua'do:r] *n Ecuador.*
Egk [ɛk] *German composer.*
Eichendorff ['aıçəndɔrf] *German poet.*
Einstein ['aınʃtaın] *German physicist.*
Eismeer ['aısme:r] *n Nördliches ~ Arctic Ocean, Südliches ~ Antarctic Ocean.*
Elbe ['ɛlbə] *f German river.*
Elfenbeinküste ['ɛlfənbaınkystə] *f Ivory Coast.*
El Salvador [ɛl zalva'do:r] *n El Salvador.*
Elsaß ['ɛlzas] *n Alsace.*
Emil ['e:mi:l] *m German Christian name.*
Engadin ['ɛngadi:n] *n Engadine.*
Engels ['ɛŋəls] *German socialist philosopher.*
England ['ɛŋlant] *n England.*
Erhardt ['e:rhart] *second chancellor of the Federal Republic of Germany.*
Eritrea [eri'tre:a] *n Eritrea.*
Estland ['e:stlant] *n Estonia.*
Euphrat ['ɔyfrat] *m Euphrates.*
Eurasien [ɔy'ra:ziən] *n Eurasia.*
Europa [ɔy'ro:pa] *n Europe.*
Eva ['e:fa, 'e:va] *f Eve.*

F

Feuerbach ['fɔyərbax] *German philosopher.*
Fichte ['fıxtə] *German philosopher.*
Finnland ['fınlant] *n Finland.*
Florenz [flo'rɛnts] *n Florence.*
Fontane [fɔn'ta:nə] *German author.*
Franken ['fraŋkən] *n Franconia.*
Frankfurt (am Main) ['fraŋkfurt] *n Frankfurt (on the Main).*
Frankfurt an der Oder ['fraŋkfurt] *n Frankfurt on the Oder (town and district in the German Democratic Republic).*
Frankreich ['fraŋkraıç] *n France.*
Freiburg ['fraıburk] *n Fr. Fribourg (Swiss town and canton).*
Freiburg im Breisgau ['fraıburk im 'braısgaʊ] *n town in West Germany.*
Freud [frɔyt] *Austrian psychologist.*
Friedrich ['fri:driç] 1. *German painter;* 2. ~ der Große *Frederik the Great (king of Prussia).*
Friedrich ['fri:driç] *m Frederick.*
Friesische(n) Inseln ['fri:ziʃə(n)] *f/pl.* Frisian Islands *pl.*
Frisch [friʃ] *Swiss author.*
Fritz [frits] *m shortened form of →* Friedrich.
Fudschijama [fudʒi'ja:ma] *m* Mount Fuji.

G

Gabun [ga'bu:n] *n Gabon.*
Gambia ['gambia] *n the Gambia.*
Ganges ['gaŋgɛs] *m Ganges.*
Garmisch ['garmiʃ] *n health resort in Bavaria.*
Gauss [gaʊs] *German mathematician.*
Genf [gɛnf] *n Geneva (Swiss town and canton).*
Genua ['ge:nua] *n Genoa.*
Georg [ge'ɔrk, 'ge:ɔrk] *m George.*
Gera ['ge:ra] *n town and district in the German Democratic Republic.*
Ghana ['ga:na] *n Ghana.*
Gibraltar [gi'braltar] *n Gibraltar.*
Goethe ['gø:tə] *German writer.*
Goldküste ['gɔltkystə] *f Gold Coast.*
Grass [gras] *German writer.*
Graubünden [grau'byndən] *n Fr. Grisons (Swiss canton).*
Grenada [gre'na:da] *n Grenada.*
Griechenland ['gri:çənlant] *n Greece.*
Grimm [grim]: Gebrüder ~ *German philologists.*
Grönland ['grø:nlant] *n Greenland.*
Großbritannien [gro:sbri'taniən] *n Great Britain.*
Grünewald ['gry:nəvalt] *German painter.*
Guinea [gi'ne:a] *n Guinea.*
Guyana [gu'ja:na] *n Guyana.*

H

Hahn [ha:n] *German chemist.*
Haiti [ha'i:ti] *n Haiti.*
Hamburg ['hamburk] *n seaport and Land of the Federal Republic of Germany.*

Händel ['hɛndəl] Handel (*German composer*).

Hannover [ha'noːfər] *n* Hanover (*capital of Lower Saxony*).

Hauptmann ['haʊptman] *German dramatist.*

Haydn ['haɪdən] *Austrian composer.*

Hebriden [he'briːdən] *pl.* Hebrides *pl.*

Hegel ['heːgəl] *German philosopher.*

Heidegger ['haɪdɛgər] *German philosopher.*

Heidelberg ['haɪdəlbɛrk] *n town in West Germany.*

Heine ['haɪnə] *German writer.*

Heinemann ['haɪnəman] *third president of the Federal Republic of Germany.*

Heisenberg ['haɪzənbɛrk] *German physicist.*

Helena ['heːlena], **Helene** [he'leːnə] *f* Helen.

Helgoland ['hɛlgolant] *n* Heligoland.

Hermann der Cherusker ['hɛrman der çe'ruskər] *hist.* Arminius.

Hesse ['hɛsə] *German writer.*

Hessen ['hɛsən] *n* Hesse (*Land of the Federal Republic of Germany*).

Hertz [hɛrts] *German physicist.*

Heuss [hɔys] *first president of the Federal Republic of Germany.*

Himalaja [hi'maːlaja] *m the* Himalayas *pl.*

Hindemith ['hindəmit] *German composer.*

Hiros(c)hima [hiro'ʃiːma] *n* Hiroshima.

Hoffmann ['hɔfman] *German writer.*

Holbein ['hɔlbaɪn] *German painters.*

Hölderlin ['hœldərlin] *German poet.*

Holland ['hɔlant] *n* Holland.

I

Indien ['indiən] *n* India.

Indische(r) Ozean ['indiʃə(r)] *m* Indian Ocean.

Indochina ['indo'çiːna] *n* Indochina.

Indonesien [indo'neːziən] *n* Indonesia.

Innerasien ['inɛrˀ'ᵊaːziən] *n* Central Asia.

Innsbruck ['insbruk] *n town in Austria.*

Irak [i'raːk] *m* Iraq.

Iran [i'raːn] *m* Iran.

Irische Republik ['iːriʃə] *f* Republic of Ireland, Eire.

Irische See ['iːriʃə] *f* Irish Sea.

Irland ['irlant] *n* Ireland.

Island ['iːslant] *n* Iceland.

Israel ['israɛl] *n* Israel.

Italien [i'taːliən] *n* Italy.

J

Jalta ['jalta] *n* Yalta.

Jamaika [ja'maɪka] *n* Jamaica.

Japan ['jaːpan] *n* Japan.

Jaspers ['jaspərs] *German philosopher.*

Java ['jaːva] *n* Java.

Jean Paul [ʒã 'paʊl] *German writer.*

Jemen ['jeːmən] *m* Yemen.

Jerusalem [je'ruːzalɛm] *n* Jerusalem.

Jesus ['jeːzus] *m* Jesus.

Johann(es) [jo'hanəs, 'joːhan] *m* John.

Jordanien [jɔr'daːniən] *n* Jordan.

Jugoslawien [jugo'slaːviən] *n* Yugoslavia.

Julia ['juːlia], **Julie** ['juːliə] *f* Julia.

K

Kafka ['kafka] *German writer.*

Kairo ['kaɪro] *n* Cairo.

Kalifornien [kali'fɔrniən] *n* California.

Kambodscha [kam'bɔdʒa] *n* Kampuchea.

Kamerun [kamə'ruːn] *n* Cameroon.

Kanada ['kanada] *n* Canada.

Kanalinseln [ka'naːlinzəln] *f/pl.* Channel Islands *pl.*

Kanarische(n) Inseln [ka'naːriʃə(n)] *f/pl.* Canary Islands *pl.*, Canaries *pl.*

Kanton ['kantɔn] *n* Canton.

Kap der Guten Hoffnung *n* Cape of Good Hope.

Kapstadt ['kapʃtat] *n* Cape Town.

Karibik [ka'riːbik] *f* Caribbean.

Karin ['kaːriːn; -in] *f* Karen.

Karl der Große *hist.* Charlemagne (*Holy Roman emperor*).

Karl-Marx-Stadt [karl'marksʃtat] *n* (*formerly Chemnitz*) *town and district in the German Democratic Republic.*

Kärnten ['kɛrntən] *n* Carinthia (*province of Austria*).

Karpaten [kar'paːtən] *pl.* Carpathian Mountains *pl.*

Kaschmir ['kaʃmir] *n* Kashmir.
Kaspische(s) Meer ['kaspiʃə(s)] *n* Caspian Sea.
Katharina [kata'riːna] *f* Catherine.
Kaukasus ['kaukazus] *m* Caucasus Mountains *pl.*
Kenia ['keːnia] *n* Kenya.
Kiesinger ['kiːziŋər] *third chancellor of the Federal Republic of Germany.*
Kiew ['kiːɛf] *n* Kiev.
Kilimandscharo [kiliman'dʒaːro] *m* Mount Kilimanjaro.
Kleinasien [klaɪn'ʔaːziən] *n* Asia Minor.
Kohl [koːl] *sixth chancellor of the Federal Republic of Germany.*
Köln [kœln] *n* Cologne.
Kolumbien [ko'lumbiən] *n* Columbia.
Kongo ['kɔŋgo] *m* Congo.
Konstanz ['kɔnstants] *n* Constance; → *Bodensee.*
Kopenhagen [kopən'haːgən] *n* Copenhagen.
Korea → *Nordkorea, Südkorea.*
Korfu ['kɔrfu] *n* Corfu.
Korsika ['kɔrzika] *n* Corsica.
Kreml ['kreːməl] *m* Kremlin.
Kreta ['kreːta] *n* Crete.
Krim [krim] *f* Crimea.
Kuba ['kuːba] *n* Cuba.
Kuwait [ku'vaɪt] *n* Kuwait.

L

Lappland ['laplant] *n* Lapland.
Lateinamerika [la'taɪnameːrika] *n* Latin America.
Leipzig ['laɪptsiç] *n town and district in the German Democratic Republic.*
Lenz [lɛnts] *German writer.*
Leonhard ['leːɔnhart] *m* Leonard.
Lessing ['lɛsiŋ] *German dramatist.*
Lettland ['lɛtlant] *n* Latvia.
Libanon ['liːbanɔn] *m* Lebanon.
Liberia [li'beːria] *n* Liberia.
Libyen ['liːbyən] *n* Libya.
Liebig ['liːbiç] *German chemist.*
Liebknecht ['liːpknɛçt] *German socialist.*
Liechtenstein ['liçtənʃtaɪn] *n* Liechtenstein.
Lissabon ['lisabɔn] *n* Lisbon.
Litauen ['liːtauən] *n* Lithuania.
London ['lɔndɔn] *n* London.
Lothringen ['loːtriŋən] *n Fr.* Lorraine.

Lübeck ['lyːbɛk] *n town in West Germany.*
Lübke ['lypkə] *second president of the Federal Republic of Germany.*
Ludwig ['luːtviç] *m* Louis.
Luise [lu'iːzə] *f* Louisa.
Lüneburg ['lyːnəburk] *n town in West Germany,* ∼*er Heide f* Lüneburg Heath.
Luxemburg ['luksəmburk] **1.** *n* Luxemb(o)urg; **2.** *German female socialist.*
Luzern [lu'tsɛrn] *n Fr.* Lucerne (*Swiss town and canton*).

M

Maas [maːs] *f* Maas, *Fr.* Meuse.
Madagaskar [mada'gaskar] *n* Madagascar.
Madeira [ma'deːra] *n* Madeira.
Madrid [ma'drit] *n* Madrid.
Magdeburg ['makdəburk] *n town and district in the German Democratic Republic.*
Mailand ['maɪlant] *n* Milan.
Mainz [maɪnts] *n capital of Rhineland-Palatinate.*
Malaysia [ma'laɪzia] *n* Malaysia.
Malediven [male'diːven] *pl.* Maldives *pl.*
Mali ['maːli] *n* Mali.
Mallorca [ma'lɔrka] *n* Majorca.
Malta ['malta] *n* Malta.
Mandschurei [mandʒu'raɪ] *f* Manchuria.
Mann [man] *German writers.*
Marcuse [mar'kuːzə] *German sociologist.*
Marokko [ma'rɔko] *n* Morocco.
Marx [marks] *German socialist philosopher.*
Mathilde [ma'tildə] *f* Mat(h)ilda.
Matthias [ma'tiːas] *m* Matthias.
Mauretanien [maure'taːniən] *n* Mauritania.
Mauritius [mau'riːtsiʊs] *n* Mauritius.
Max(imilian) [maks(i'miːliaːn)] *m* Max(imilian).
Mazedonien [matsə'doːniən] *n* Macedonia.
Mekka ['mɛka] *n* Mecca.
Memel ['meːməl] *f* Niemen (River).
Mexiko ['mɛksiko] *n* Mexico.
Metternich ['mɛtərniç] *Austrian statesman.*

Michael ['miçaɛl], **Michel** ['miçəl] *m* Michael.

Mittelamerika ['mitəla'meːrika] *n* Central America.

Mitteldeutschland ['mitəldɔytʃlant] *n* Central Germany.

Mitteleuropa ['mitəlɔy'roːpa] *n* Central Europe.

Mittelmeer ['mitəlmeːr] *n* Mediterranean (Sea).

Mittlere(r) Osten *m* Middle East.

Moldau ['mɔldaʊ] *f* Moldavia.

Mongolei [mɔŋɡo'laɪ] *f*: *die Innere* ~ Inner Mongolia; *die Äußere* ~ Outer Mongolia.

Monika ['moːnika] *f* Monica.

Mörike ['møːrikə] *German poet.*

Moritz ['moːrits] *m* Maurice.

Mosel ['moːzəl] *f Fr.* Moselle.

Moskau ['mɔskaʊ] *n* Moscow.

Mozambique [mozam'bik] *n* Mozambique.

Mozart ['moːtsart] *Austrian composer.*

München ['mynçən] *n* Munich (*capital of Bavaria*).

N

Nahe(r) Osten ['naːə(r) 'ɔstən] *m* Near East.

Namibia [na'miːbia] *n* Namibia.

Neapel [ne'aːpəl] *n* Naples.

Nepal ['neːpal] *n* Nepal.

Neufundland [nɔy'funtlant] *n* Newfoundland.

Neuguinea [nɔygi'neːa] *n* New Guinea.

Neuseeland [nɔy'zeːlant] *n* New Zealand.

Niederlande ['niːdərlandə] *pl.* Netherlands *pl.*

Niedersachsen [niːdərzaksən] *n* Lower Saxony (*Land of the Federal Republic of Germany*).

Nigeria [ni'ɡeːria] *n* Nigeria.

Nikaragua [nika'raːgua] *n* Nicaragua.

Nikolaus ['niːkolaʊs] *m* Nicholas.

Nil [niːl] *m* Nile.

Nizza ['nitsa] *n Fr.* Nice.

Nordamerika ['nɔrta'meːrika] *n* North America.

Nordirland ['nɔrt'ʔirlant] *n* Northern Ireland.

Nordkap ['nɔrtkap] *n* North Cape.

Nordkorea ['nɔrtko'reːa] *n* North Korea.

Nordrhein-Westfalen ['nɔrtraɪn-vɛst'faːlən] *n* North Rhine-Westphalia (*Land of the Federal Republic of Germany*).

Nordsee ['nɔrtzeː] *f* North Sea.

Norwegen ['nɔrveːɡən] *n* Norway.

Nubien ['nuːbiən] *n* Nubia.

Nürnberg ['nyrnbɛrk] *n* Nuremberg.

O

Obervolta [oːbər'vɔlta] *n* Upper Volta.

Odenwald ['oːdənvalt] *m* mountainous region in Hesse.

Oder ['oːdər] *f German river.*

Oslo ['ɔslo] *n* Oslo.

Osnabrück [ɔsna'bryk] *n town in West Germany.*

Ossietzky [ɔsi'ɛtski] *German writer and pacifist.*

Ostasien ['ɔst'ʔaːziən] *n* Eastern Asia.

Ost-Berlin ['ɔstbɛrliːn] *n* East Berlin (*town and district in the German Democratic Republic*).

Ostende [ɔst'ʔɛndə] *n* Ostend.

Osterinsel ['oːstər'ʔinzəl] *f* Easter Island.

Österreich ['øːstəraɪç] *n* Austria.

Ostsee ['ɔstzeː] *f* Baltic (Sea).

Otto der Große *hist.* Otto the Great (*Holy Roman emperor*).

Ozeanien [otse'aːniən] *n* Oceania, South Sea Islands *pl.*

P

Pakistan ['paːkista(ː)n] *n* Pakistan.

Paraguay [paragu'aːi] *n* Paraguay.

Paris [pa'riːs] *n* Paris.

Paul [paʊl] *m*, **Paula** ['paʊla] *f* Paul, Paula.

Pazifik [pa'tsiːfik], **Pazifische(r) Ozean** [pa'tsiːfiʃə(r)] *m* Pacific (Ocean).

Peking ['peːkiŋ] *n* Peking.

Persien ['pɛrziən] *n* Persia (*heute → Iran*).

Persische(r) Golf ['pɛrziʃə(r) 'ɡɔlf] *m* Persian Gulf.

Peru [pe'ruː] *n* Peru.

Peter ['peːtər] *m* Peter.

Pfalz [pfalts] *f → Rheinland-Pfalz.*

Philipp ['fiːlip] *m* Philip.

Philippinen [fili'piːnən] *pl.* Philippine Islands, Philippines *pl.*

Polen ['po:lən] *n* Poland.
Polynesien [poly'ne:ziən] *n* Polynesia.
Pommern ['pɔmərn] *n* Pomerania.
Portugal ['pɔrtugal] *n* Portugal.
Prag [prɑːk] *n* Prague.
Preußen ['prɔysən] *n hist.* Prussia.
Puerto Rico [pu'ɛrto 'riːko] *n* Puerto Rico.
Pyrenäen [pyre'nɛːən] *pl.* Pyrenees *pl.*

Q

Qatar ['katar] *n* Qatar.

R

Rhein [raɪn] *m* Rhine.
Rheinland-Pfalz ['raɪnlant'pfalts] *n* Rhineland-Palatinate (*Land of the Federal Republic of Germany*).
Rhodesien [ro'deːziən] *n* Rhodesia (*heute → Simbabwe*).
Rhodos ['roː(ː)dɔs] *n* Rhodes.
Rom [roːm] *n* Rome.
Rosemarie ['roːzəmariː] *f* Rosemary.
Rostock ['rɔstɔk] *n town and district in the German Democratic Republic.*
Rote(s) Meer *n* Red Sea.
Ruhr [ruːr] *f German river;* ~**gebiet** *n industrial centre of West Germany.*
Rumänien [ru'mɛːniən] *n* Ro(u)mania.
Rußland ['ruslant] *n* Russia.

S

Saale ['zaːlə] *f German river.*
Saar [zaːr] *f affluent of the Moselle;* ~**brücken** [~'brykən] *n capital of the Saar;* ~**land** ['~lant] *n* Saar (*Land of the Federal Republic of Germany*).
Sachsen ['zaksən] *n* Saxony.
Sahara ['zaːhara, za'hɑːra] *f* Sahara.
Salzburg ['zaltsburk] *n town and province of Austria.*
Sambia ['zambia] *n* Zambia.
Sardinien [zar'diːniən] *n* Sardinia.
Saudi-Arabien [zaʊdia'rɑːbiən] *n* Saudi Arabia.
Scheel [ʃeːl] *fourth president of the Federal Republic of Germany.*
Schiller ['ʃilər] *German poet and dramatist.*
Schlesien ['ʃleːziən] *n* Silesia.

Schleswig-Holstein ['ʃleːsviç'hɔlʃtaɪn] *n Land of the Federal Republic of Germany.*
Schmidt [ʃmit] *fifth chancellor of the Federal Republic of Germany.*
Schopenhauer ['ʃoːpənhaʊər] *German philosopher.*
Schottland ['ʃɔtlant] *n* Scotland.
Schubert ['ʃuːbərt] *Austrian composer.*
Schwaben ['ʃvaːbən] *n* Swabia.
Schwarze(s) Meer *n* Black Sea.
Schwarzwald ['ʃvartsvalt] *m* Black Forest.
Schweden ['ʃveːdən] *n* Sweden.
Schweiz [ʃvaɪts] *f:* die ~ Switzerland.
Schwyz [ʃviːts] *n Swiss town and canton.*
Senegal ['zeːnegal] *n* Senegal.
Serbien ['zɛrbiən] *n* Serbia.
Seychellen [ze'ʃɛlən] *pl.* Seychelles *pl.*
Shetland-Inseln ['ʃɛtlantinzəln] *f/pl.* Shetland Islands *pl.*
Sibirien [zi'biːriən] *n* Siberia.
Siebengebirge ['ziːbəngəbirgə] *n mountain range along the Rhine.*
Simbabwe [zim'baːbve] *n* Zimbabwe.
Sinai ['ziːnai] *m* Sinai.
Singapur ['zingapuːr] *n* Singapore.
Sizilien [zi'tsiːliən] *n* Sicily.
Skandinavien [skandi'naːviən] *n* Scandinavia.
Slowakei [slova'kaɪ] *f:* die ~ Slovakia.
Somalia [zo'maːlia] *n* Somalia.
Sophie [zo'fiː] *f* Sophia.
Sowjetunion [zɔ'vjɛtunioːn] *f* Soviet Union.
Spanien ['ʃpaːniən] *n* Spain.
Spengler ['ʃpɛŋlər] *German philosopher.*
Spitzbergen ['ʃpitsbɛrgən] *n* Spitsbergen.
Spitzweg ['ʃpitsveːk] *German painter.*
Sri Lanka ['sriː 'laŋka] *n* Sri Lanka.
Stefan, Stephan ['ʃtɛfan] *m* Stephen.
Steiermark ['ʃtaɪərmark] *f* Styria (*province of Austria*).
Stille(r) Ozean *m* → Pazifik.
Stockholm ['ʃtɔkhɔlm] *n* Stockholm.
Straßburg ['ʃtraːsburk] *n Fr.* Strasbourg.

Strauss [ʃtraʊs]: *Richard ~ German composer.*
Strauss [ʃtraʊs]: *Johann ~ Austrian composer.*
Stresemann [ˈʃtreːzəman] *German statesman.*
Stuttgart [ˈʃtutgart] *n capital of Baden-Württemberg.*
Südafrika [ˈzyːtˈʔɑːfrika] *n* South Africa.
Südamerika [ˈzyːtaˈmeːrika] *n* South America.
Sudan [zuˈdaːn] *m* Sudan.
Sudeten [zuˈdeːtən] *pl.* Sudetes, Sudeten Mountains *pl.*
Südjemen [ˈzyːtjeːmen] *m* Southern Yemen.
Südkorea [ˈzyːtkoˈreːa] *n* South Korea.
Südsee [ˈzyːtzeː] *f* South Pacific.
Südwestafrika [zyːtˈvɛstɑːfrika] *n* South West Africa (*heute → Namibia*).
Sueskanal [ˈzuːɛskanɑːl] *m* Suez Canal.
Sumatra [zuˈmɑːtra; ˈzuːmatra] *n* Sumatra.
Susanne [zuˈzanə] *f* Susan.
Swasiland [ˈsvaːzilant] *n* Swaziland.
Syrien [ˈzyːriən] *n* Syria.

T

Taipeh [taɪˈpeː] *n* Taipei.
Taiwan [taɪˈvan; taɪˈvɑːn] *n* Taiwan.
Tanganjika [taŋganˈjiːka] *n* Tanganyika.
Tansania [tanzaˈniːa] *n* Tanzania.
Tasmanien [tasˈmɑːniən] *n* Tasmania.
Tessin [tɛˈsiːn] *n* Ticino (*Swiss canton*).
Thailand [ˈtaɪlant] *n* Thailand.
Themse [ˈtɛmzə] *f* Thames.
Theodor [ˈteːodoːr] *m* Theodore.
Thüringen [ˈtyːriŋən] *n* Thuringia.
Tibet [ˈtiːbɛt] *n* Tibet.
Tigris [ˈtiːgris] *m* Tigris.
Tirol [tiˈroːl] *n* Tyrol (*province of Austria*).
Tokio [ˈtoːkio] *n* Tokyo.
Toskana [tɔsˈkaːna] *f* Tuscany.
Tote(s) Meer *n* Dead Sea.
Trier [triːr] *n* Trier, *Fr.* Trèves.
Tschad [tʃat; tʃɑːt] *n* Chad.
Tschechoslowakei [tʃɛçoslovaˈkaɪ] *f*: *die ~* Czechoslovakia.
Tunesien [tuˈneːziən] *n* Tunisia.

Tunis [ˈtuːnis] *n* Tunis.
Türkei [tyrˈkaɪ] *f*: *die ~* Turkey.

U

Uganda [uˈganda] *n* Uganda.
Ukraine [ukraˈiːnə, uˈkraɪnə] *f* Ukraine.
Ungarn [ˈuŋgarn] *n* Hungary.
Union der Sozialistischen Sowjetrepubliken *f* Union of Soviet Socialist Republics.
Ural [uˈrɑːl] *m* Ural, Ural Mountains *pl.*
Uruguay [uruguˈɑːi] *n* Uruguay.

V

Vatikan [vatiˈkaːn] *m* Vatican.
Venedig [veˈneːdiç] *n* Venice.
Venezuela [venetsuˈeːla] *n* Venezuela.
Vereinigte(s) Königreich (von Großbritannien und Nordirland) *n* United Kingdom (of Great Britain and Northern Ireland).
Vereinigte(n) Staaten (von Amerika) *pl.* United States (of America).
Vesuv [veˈzuːf] *m* Vesuvius.
Vietnam [viɛtˈnam] *n* Vietnam, Viet Nam.
Vogesen [voˈgeːzən] *pl. Fr.* Vosges *pl.*
Volksrepublik China [ˈçiːna] *f* People's Republic of China.
Vorderasien [ˈfɔrdərˈʔaːziən] *n* Near East.

W

Wagner [ˈvaːgnər] *German composer.*
Walther von der Vogelweide [ˈvaltər fɔn der ˈfoːgəlvaɪdə] *medieval German poet.*
Warschau [ˈvarʃaʊ] *n* Warsaw.
Weichsel [ˈvaɪksəl] *f* Vistula.
Weiße(s) Meer *n* White Sea.
Weißrußland [ˈvaɪsruslant] *n* White Russia, Byelorussia.
Weizsäcker [ˈvaɪtsɛkər]: *Richard von ~ sixth president of the Federal Republic of Germany.*
Weizsäcker [ˈvaɪtsɛkər]: *Carl Friedrich von ~ German physicist.*
Werfel [ˈvɛrfəl] *Austrian writer.*

Westfalen [vɛst'fɑːlən] *n* Westphalia.
Westindische(n) Inseln ['vɛst'ʔin-diʃə(n) 'inzəln] *f/pl.* West Indies *pl.*
Wien [viːn] *n* Vienna (*capital and province of Austria*).
Wiesbaden ['viːsbɑːdən] *n* capital of Hesse.
Wilhelm ['vilhɛlm] *m* William.
Wolfram von Eschenbach ['vɔlfram fɔn 'ʔɛʃənbax] *medieval German poet.*
Württemberg ['vyrtəmbɛrk] *n* → Baden-Württemberg.
Würzburg ['vyrtsburk] *n* town in West Germany.

Z

Zaire [zaˈiːr] *n* Zaïre.
Zentralafrikanische Republik [tsɛn'trɑːlafrikɑːniʃə repuˈbliːk] *f* Central African Republic.
Zuckmayer ['tsukmaɪər] German dramatist.
Zugspitze ['tsuːkʃpitsə] *f* highest mountain of Germany.
Zürich ['tsyːriç] *n* Zurich (Swiss town and canton).
Zypern ['tsyːpərn] *n* Cyprus.

Current German Abbreviations
Gebräuchliche deutsche Abkürzungen

A

AA *Auswärtiges Amt* Foreign Office.
Abb. *Abbildung* illustration, *abbr.* fig. (= figure).
Abf. *Abfahrt* departure.
Abk. *Abkürzung* abbreviation.
Abo *Abonnement* subscription.
Abs. *Absatz* paragraph; *Absender* sender.
Abschn. *Abschnitt* paragraph, chapter.
Abt. *Abteilung* department.
a. D. *außer Dienst* retired; *an der Donau* on the Danube.
ADAC *Allgemeiner Deutscher Automobil-Club* German automobile association.
ADN *Allgemeiner Deutscher Nachrichtendienst* General German News Service (*in the → DDR*).
AG *Aktiengesellschaft* (public) limited company, *Am.* (stock) corporation.
allg. *allgemein* general.
a. M. *am Main* on the Main.
amtl. *amtlich* official.
Ank. *Ankunft* arrival.
Anm. *Anmerkung* note.
AOK *Allgemeine Ortskrankenkasse* general health insurance scheme.
ao. Prof., a. o. Prof. *außerordentlicher Professor etwa* associate professor.
APO *Außerparlamentarische Opposition* extra-parliamentary opposition.
ARD *Arbeitsgemeinschaft der öffentlich-rechtlichen Rundfunkanstalten der Bundesrepublik Deutschland* Association of the Broadcasting Corporations of the Federal Republic of Germany.
a. Rh. *am Rhein* on the Rhine.
Art. *Artikel* article.
Aufl. *Auflage* edition.
Az *Aktenzeichen* file number.

B

b. *bei* at; with; *place*: near; *address*: care of.
Bd. *Band* volume.
beil. *beiliegend* enclosed.
Bem. *Bemerkung* note, comment, observation.
BENELUX *Belgien, Niederlande, Luxemburg* Belgium, Netherlands, Luxemb(o)urg.
bes. *besonders* especially.
Best.Nr. *Bestellnummer* order number.
Betr. *Betreff, betrifft at head of letter*: subject, re.
betr. *betreffend, betrifft, betreffs* concerning, regarding.
bez. *bezahlt* paid; *bezüglich* with reference to.
BFH *Bundesfinanzhof* Federal Finance Court.
BGB *Bürgerliches Gesetzbuch* (German) Civil Code.
BGH *Bundesgerichtshof* Federal Supreme Court.
BGS *Bundesgrenzschutz* Federal Border Police.
Bhf. *Bahnhof* station.
BLZ *Bankleitzahl* bank code number.
BND *Bundesnachrichtendienst* Federal Intelligence Service.
BP *Bundespost* Federal Postal Administration.
BRD *Bundesrepublik Deutschland* Federal Republic of Germany.
BRT *Brutto-Register-Tonnen* gross register tons.
Bw *Bundeswehr* Federal Armed Forces.
b. w. *bitte wenden* please turn over.
bzgl. *bezüglich* with reference to.
bzw. *beziehungsweise* respectively.

C

C *Celsius* Celsius, centigrade.
ca. *circa, ungefähr, etwa* about, approximately.

cand. *candidatus, Kandidat* candidate.

CDU *Christlich-Demokratische Union* Christian Democratic Union.

Co. *Kompagnon* partner; *Kompanie* Company.

CSU *Christlich-Soziale Union* Christian Social Union.

c. t. *cum tempore, mit akademischem Viertel* with a quarter of an hour's allowance.

D

d. Ä. *der Ältere* the Elder.

DAG *Deutsche Angestellten-Gewerkschaft* Trade Union of German Employees.

DB *Deutsche Bundesbahn* German Federal Railway; *Deutsche Bundesbank* German Federal Bank.

DDR *Deutsche Demokratische Republik* German Democratic Republic, *abbr.* G.D.R.

DFB *Deutscher Fußballbund* German Football Association.

DGB *Deutscher Gewerkschaftsbund* Federation of German Trade Unions.

d. Gr. *der Große* the Great.

d. h. *das heißt* that is, *abbr.* i.e.

d. i. *das ist* that is, *abbr.* i.e.

DIN *Deutsche Industrie-Norm(en)* German Industrial Standard(s).

Dipl. *Diplom*(... holding a) diploma.

d. J. *dieses Jahres* of this year; *der Jüngere* the Younger.

DKP *Deutsche Kommunistische Partei* German Communist Party.

DM *Deutsche Mark* German Mark.

d. M. *dieses Monats* instant.

DNA *Deutscher Normenausschuß* German Committee of Standards.

do. *dito* ditto.

d. O. *der (die, das) Obige* the above-mentioned.

Doz. *Dozent* university lecturer.

dpa *Deutsche Presse-Agentur* German Press Agency.

Dr. *Doktor* Doctor; ~ **jur.** *Doktor der Rechte* Doctor of Laws (LL.D.); ~ **med.** *Doktor der Medizin* Doctor of Medicine (M.D.); ~ **phil.** *Doktor der Philosophie* Doctor of Philosophy (Ph.D., D.Phil.); ~ **theol.** (*evangelisch* **D. theol.**) *Doktor der Theologie* Doctor of Divinity (D.D.).

dt(sch.) *deutsch* German.

Dtschld. *Deutschland* Germany.

E

ebd. *ebenda* ibidem, ib(id).

Ed. *Edition, Ausgabe* edition.

EDV *elektronische Datenverarbeitung* electronic data processing.

EG *Europäische Gemeinschaft* European Community.

e.h. *ehrenhalber of degree*: honorary.

ehem., ehm. *ehemals* formerly.

eig., eigtl. *eigentlich* really, strictly speaking.

einschl. *einschließlich* inclusive(ly), including.

EKD *Evangelische Kirche in Deutschland* Protestant Church in Germany.

EKG *Elektrokardiogramm* electrocardiogram.

entspr. *entsprechend* corresponding.

erg. *ergänze* supply, add.

Erl. *Erläuterung* explanation, (explanatory) note.

Euratom *Europäische Atomgemeinschaft* European Atomic Community.

ev. *evangelisch* Protestant.

e. V. *eingetragener Verein* registered society *or* association.

evtl. *eventuell* perhaps, possibly.

exkl. *exklusive* except(ed), not included.

Expl. *Exemplar* sample, copy.

F

F *Fahrenheit* Fahrenheit.

Fa. *Firma* firm; *in letters*: Messrs.

Fam. *Familie* family.

FDGB *Freier Deutscher Gewerkschaftsbund* Free Federation of German Trade Unions (*of the* → *DDR*).

FDP *Freie Demokratische Partei* Liberal Democratic Party.

fig. *figürlich, bildlich* figurative.

fortl. *fortlaufend* running, successive.

Forts. *Fortsetzung* continuation.

Fr. *Frau* Mrs., Ms.

frdl. *freundlich* kind.

Frl. *Fräulein* Miss.

FU *Freie Universität* (*Berlin*) Free University of Berlin.

G

g *Gramm* gram(me).
geb. *geboren* born; *geborene* ... née; *gebunden* bound.
Gebr. *Gebrüder* Brothers.
gegr. *gegründet* founded.
gek. *gekürzt* abbreviated.
Ges. *Gesellschaft* association, company; society; *Gesetz* law.
ges. gesch. *gesetzlich geschützt* registered.
gest. *gestorben* deceased.
gez. *gezeichnet* (*in front of signatures*) signed.
GG *Grundgesetz* Basic Constitutional Law.
GmbH, G.m.b.H. *Gesellschaft mit beschränkter Haftung* limited liability company.

H

Hbf. *Hauptbahnhof* central (*or* main) station.
h. c. *honoris causa, ehrenhalber* (*of univ. degree*) honorary.
HG *Handelsgesellschaft* trading company.
HGB *Handelsgesetzbuch* Commercial Code.
höfl. *höflich(st)* (most) kindly.
hpts. *hauptsächlich* principally, mainly.
Hr., Hrn. *Herr(n)* Mr.

I

i. *im, in* in.
i. A. *im Auftrag* for, by order, under instruction.
i. allg. *im allgemeinen* in general, generally speaking.
i. b. *im besonderen* in particular.
i. D. *im Durchschnitt* on average.
IG *Industriegewerkschaft* industrial union.
Ing. *Ingenieur* engineer.
Inh. *Inhaber* proprietor; *Inhalt* contents.
inkl. *inklusive, einschließlich* inclusive(ly), including.
Interpol *Internationale Kriminalpolizei-Kommission* International Criminal Police Commission.

i. R. *im Ruhestand* retired, *esp. univ.*: emeritus.
IRK *Internationales Rotes Kreuz* International Red Cross.
i. V. *in Vertretung* by proxy, by order, on behalf of.

J

jhrl. *jährlich* annual.
jr., jun. *junior* junior.
jur. *juristisch* legal.

K

Kap. *Kapitel* chapter.
kath. *katholisch* Catholic.
Kfm. *Kaufmann* merchant.
kfm. *kaufmännisch* commercial.
Kfz. *Kraftfahrzeug* motor vehicle.
KG *Kommanditgesellschaft* limited partnership.
Kl. *Klasse* class.
KP *Kommunistische Partei* Communist Party.
KPdSU *Kommunistische Partei der Sowjetunion* Communist Party of the Soviet Union.
Kripo *Kriminalpolizei* Criminal Investigation Department.
Kto. *Konto* account.
KZ *Konzentrationslager* concentration camp.

L

led. *ledig* unmarried.
lfd. *laufend* current, running.
lfd. Nr. *laufende Nummer* current issue.
Lfg., Lfrg. *Lieferung* delivery; instal(l)ment.
LG *Landgericht* District Court.
Lkw, LKW *Lastkraftwagen* lorry, truck.
Lok *Lokomotive* engine, locomotive.
lt. *laut* according to.
ltd. *leitend* managing.
Ltg. *Leitung* direction, management.
luth. *lutherisch* Lutheran.

M

M *Mark* Mark (*in the* → *DDR*).
MAD *Militärischer Abschirmdienst*

German Counter-Intelligence Service.

max. *maximum* maximum.

m. b. H. *mit beschränkter Haftung* with limited liability.

MdB, M. d. B. *Mitglied des Bundestages* Member of the "Bundestag".

MdL, M. d. L. *Mitglied des Landtages* Member of the "Landtag".

mdl. *mündlich* verbal.

m. E. *meines Erachtens* in my opinion.

MEZ *mitteleuropäische Zeit* Central European Time.

MG *Maschinengewehr* machine-gun.

Mill. *Million(en)* million(s).

Min., min. *Minute(n)* minute(s).

min. *minimal* minimum.

möbl. *möbliert* furnished.

mod. *modern* modern.

MP *Militärpolizei* Military Police; *Maschinenpistole* submachine gun.

Mrd. *Milliarde* billion, *Brt. a.* thousand million.

mtl. *monatlich* monthly.

m. W. *meines Wissens* as far as I know.

MWSt *Mehrwertsteuer* value-added tax.

N

N *Norden* north; *Leistung* power.

Nachf. *Nachfolger* successor.

nachm. *nachmittags* in the afternoon, *abbr.* p.m.

N. B. *notabene* note carefully.

n. Chr. *nach Christus* after Christ, *abbr.* A.D.

N.N. *nescio nomen, Name unbekannt* name unknown.

NO *Nordosten* north-east.

NPD *National-Demokratische Partei Deutschlands* National-Democratic Party of Germany.

Nr. *Numero, Nummer* number.

NW *Nordwesten* north-west.

O

O *Osten* east.

o. *oben* above; *oder* or; *ohne* without.

o. ä. *oder ähnlich* or the like.

OB *Oberbürgermeister* Chief Burgomaster.

o. B. ♣ *ohne Befund* results negative.

Obb. *Oberbayern* Upper Bavaria.

od. *oder* or.

OEZ *osteuropäische Zeit* East European Time.

öff., öffentl. *öffentlich* public.

offiz. *offiziell* official.

OHG *Offene Handelsgesellschaft* general partnership.

OLG *Oberlandesgericht* Higher Regional Court.

o. Prof. *ordentlicher Professor* (full) professor.

Orig. *Original* original.

orth. *orthodox* orthodox.

P

p. A(dr). *per Adresse* care of.

Pf *Pfennig* (*German coin*) pfennig.

Pfd. *Pfund* (*weight*) German pound.

PH *Pädagogische Hochschule* teachers' college.

Pkw, PKW *Personenkraftwagen* (motor) car.

Pl. *Platz* square.

p.p., p.pa., ppa. *per procura* per proxy.

Prof. *Professor* professor.

PS *Pferdestärke(n)* horse-power; *postscriptum, Nachschrift* postscript.

Q

qkm *Quadratkilometer* square kilometre.

qm *Quadratmeter* square metre.

R

R *Réaumur* Réaumur *abbr.* R.

rd. *rund* roughly.

Reg.Bez. *Regierungsbezirk* administrative district.

Rel. *Religion* religion.

Rep. *Republik* republic.

resp. *respektive* respectively.

RIAS *Rundfunk im amerikanischen Sektor* (*von Berlin*) Radio in the American Sector (of Berlin).

rk. *römisch-katholisch* Roman Catholic.

röm. *römisch* Roman.

S

S *Süden* south.
S. *Seite* page.
s. *siehe* see, *abbr.* v. (= vide).
S-Bahn *Schnellbahn* city-railway.
sec *Sekunde* second.
SED *Sozialistische Einheitspartei Deutschlands* United Socialist Party of Germany (*of the* → *DDR*).
sen. *senior* senior.
SO *Südosten* south-east.
s. o. *siehe oben* see above.
sog. *sogenannt* so-called.
SOS *internationales Notsignal* international signal of distress.
SPD *Sozialdemokratische Partei Deutschlands* Social Democratic Party of Germany.
SS *Sommersemester* summer term.
St. *Stück* piece; *Sankt* Saint.
Std., Stde. *Stunde* hour.
stdl. *stündlich* every hour.
stellv. *stellvertretend* assistant.
StGB *Strafgesetzbuch* Penal Code.
StPO *Strafprozeßordnung* Code of Criminal Procedure.
Str. *Straße* street, road.
stud. *studiosus, Student* student.
StVO *Straßenverkehrsordnung* Traffic Regulations.
s. t. *sine tempore, ohne akademisches Viertel* sharp, on time.
s. u. *siehe unten* see below.
SW *Südwesten* south-west.
s. Z. *seinerzeit* at that time.

T

tägl. *täglich* daily, per day.
Tel. *Telephon* telephone; *Telegramm* wire, cable.
TH *Technische Hochschule* technical university *or* college.
TU *Technische Universität* technical university.
TÜV *Technischer Überwachungsverein* Association for Technical Inspection.

U

u. *und* and.
u. a. *und andere(s)* and others; *unter anderem or anderen* among other things, inter alia.
u. ä. *und ähnliche(s)* and the like.
U. A. w. g. *Um Antwort wird gebeten* an answer is requested.
u. dgl. (m.) *und dergleichen (mehr)* and the like.
u. d. M. *unter dem Meeresspiegel* below sea level; **ü. d. M.** *über dem Meeresspiegel* above sea level.
UdSSR *Union der Sozialistischen Sowjetrepubliken* Union of Soviet Socialist Republics.
UKW *Ultrakurzwelle* ultra-short wave, very high frequency.
U/min. *Umdrehungen in der Minute* revolutions per minute.
urspr. *ursprünglich* original(ly).
US(A) *Vereinigte Staaten (von Amerika)* United States (of America).
usw. *und so weiter* and so on, *abbr.* etc.
u. U. *unter Umständen* circumstances permitting.
UV *ultraviolett* ultra-violet.
u. v. a. (m.) *und viele(s) andere (mehr)* and many others.
u. zw. *und zwar* that is, namely.

V

v. *von, vom* of; from; by.
V *Volt* volt; *Volumen* volume.
V. *Vers* line, verse.
VB *Verhandlungsbasis* or near(est) offer, *abbr.* o.n.o.
v. Chr. *vor Christus* before Christ, *abbr.* B.C.
VEB *Volkseigener Betrieb* People's Enterprise (*in the* → *DDR*).
Verf., Vf. *Verfasser* author.
verh. *verheiratet* married.
Verl. *Verlag* publishing firm; *Verleger* publisher.
vgl. *vergleiche* compare, *abbr.* cf., cp.
v. g. u. *vorgelesen, genehmigt, unterschrieben* read, approved and signed.
v. H. *vom Hundert* per cent.
v. J. *vorigen Jahres* of last year.
v. M. *vorigen Monats* of last month.
vorm. *vormittags* in the morning, *abbr.* a.m.; *vormals* formerly.
Vors. *Vorsitzender* chairman.
VR *Volksrepublik* People's Republic.
v. T. *vom Tausend* per thousand.
v. u. *von unten* from below.

W

W *Westen* west; *Watt* watt(s).
WE *Wärmeeinheit* thermal unit.
WEU *Westeuropäische Union* Western European Union.
WEZ *westeuropäische Zeit* Western European Time (Greenwich Mean Time).
WGB *Weltgewerkschaftsbund* World Federation of Trade Unions.
WS *Wintersemester* winter term.
Wz. *Warenzeichen* registered trade-mark.

Z

Z. *Zahl* number; *Zeile* line.

z. *zu, zum, zur* at; to.
z. B. *zum Beispiel* for instance, *abbr.* e.g.
ZDF *Zweites Deutsches Fernsehen* Second Channel of German Television Broadcasting.
z. H(d). *zu Händen* attention of, to be delivered to.
ZPO *Zivilprozeßordnung* Code of Civil Procedure.
z. T. *zum Teil* partly.
Ztg. *Zeitung* newspaper.
Ztschr. *Zeitschrift* periodical.
zus. *zusammen* together.
zw. *zwischen* between; among.
z. Z(t). *zur Zeit* at the time; at present, for the time being.

Numerals — Zahlwörter

Cardinal Numbers — Grundzahlen

0	null *nought, zero, cipher*	41	einundvierzig *forty-one*
1	eins *one*	50	fünfzig *fifty*
2	zwei *two*	51	einundfünfzig *fifty-one*
3	drei *three*	60	sechzig *sixty*
4	vier *four*	61	einundsechzig *sixty-one*
5	fünf *five*	70	siebzig *seventy*
6	sechs *six*	71	einundsiebzig *seventy-one*
7	sieben *seven*	80	achtzig *eighty*
8	acht *eight*	81	einundachtzig *eighty-one*
9	neun *nine*	90	neunzig *ninety*
10	zehn *ten*	91	einundneunzig *ninety-one*
11	elf *eleven*	100	hundert *a (od. one) hundred*
12	zwölf *twelve*	101	hundert(und)eins *hundred and one*
13	dreizehn *thirteen*		
14	vierzehn *fourteen*	200	zweihundert *two hundred*
15	fünfzehn *fifteen*	300	dreihundert *three hundred*
16	sechzehn *sixteen*	572	fünfhundert(und)zweiund-
17	siebzehn *seventeen*		siebzig *five hundred and seventy-two*
18	achtzehn *eighteen*		
19	neunzehn *nineteen*	1000	tausend *a (od. one) thousand*
20	zwanzig *twenty*	2000	zweitausend *two thousand*
21	einundzwanzig *twenty-one*	1 000 000	eine Million *a (od. one) million*
22	zweiundzwanzig *twenty-two*		
23	dreiundzwanzig *twenty-three*	2 000 000	zwei Millionen *two million*
30	dreißig *thirty*		
31	einunddreißig *thirty-one*	1 000 000 000	eine Milliarde *a billion, Brt. a. a thousand million*
40	vierzig *forty*		

Ordinal Numbers — Ordnungszahlen

1.	erste *first*	16.	sechzehnte *sixteenth*
2.	zweite *second*	17.	siebzehnte *seventeenth*
3.	dritte *third*	18.	achtzehnte *eighteenth*
4.	vierte *fourth*	19.	neunzehnte *nineteenth*
5.	fünfte *fifth*	20.	zwanzigste *twentieth*
6.	sechste *sixth*	21.	einundzwanzigste *twenty-first*
7.	siebente *seventh*	22.	zweiundzwanzigste *twenty-second*
8.	achte *eighth*		
9.	neunte *ninth*	23.	dreiundzwanzigste *twenty-third*
10.	zehnte *tenth*		
11.	elfte *eleventh*	30.	dreißigste *thirtieth*
12.	zwölfte *twelfth*	31.	einunddreißigste *thirty-first*
13.	dreizehnte *thirteenth*	40.	vierzigste *fortieth*
14.	vierzehnte *fourteenth*	41.	einundvierzigste *forty-first*
15.	fünfzehnte *fifteenth*	50.	fünfzigste *fiftieth*

51. einundfünfzigste *fifty-first*
60. sechzigste *sixtieth*
61. einundsechzigste *sixty-first*
70. siebzigste *seventieth*
71. einundsiebzigste *seventy-first*
80. achtzigste *eightieth*
81. einundachtzigste *eighty-first*
90. neunzigste *ninetieth*
100. hundertste *(one) hundredth*
101. hundertunderste *hundred and first*

200. zweihundertste *two hundredth*
300. dreihundertste *three hundredth*
572. fünfhundert(und)zweiundsiebzigste *five hundred and seventy-second*
1000. tausendste *(one) thousandth*
2000. zweitausendste *two thousandth*
1 000 000. millionste *millionth*
2 000 000. zweimillionste *two millionth*

Fractions and other Numerical Values

Bruchzahlen und andere Zahlenwerte

$^1/_2$ ein halb *one (od. a) half*
$1^1/_2$ anderthalb *one and a half*
$2^1/_2$ zweieinhalb *two and a half*
$^1/_2$ Meile *half a mile*
$^1/_3$ ein Drittel *one (od. a) third*
$^2/_3$ zwei Drittel *two thirds*
$^1/_4$ ein Viertel *one (od. a) fourth, one (od. a) quarter*
$^3/_4$ drei Viertel *three fourths, three quarters*
$1^1/_4$ ein und eine Viertelstunde *one hour and a quarter*
$^1/_5$ ein Fünftel *one (od. a) fifth*
$3^4/_5$ drei vier Fünftel *three and four fifths*
0,4 Null Komma vier *point four (.4)*
2,5 zwei Komma fünf *two point five (2.5)*

Einfach *single*
zweifach *double*
dreifach *treble, triple, threefold*
vierfach *fourfold, quadruple*
fünffach *fivefold usw.*

Einmal *once*
zweimal *twice*
drei-, vier-, fünfmal *usw. three, four, five times*
zweimal soviel(e) *twice as much (many)*
noch einmal *once more*

Erstens, zweitens, drittens *usw. firstly, secondly, thirdly, in the first (second, third) place*

$2 \times 3 = 6$ zweimal drei ist *(od. macht) sechs twice three are (od. make) six*

$7 + 8 = 15$ sieben und *(od. plus)* acht ist fünfzehn *seven and eight are fifteen*

$10 - 3 = 7$ zehn weniger *(od. minus)* drei ist sieben *ten less three are seven*

$20 : 5 = 4$ zwanzig geteilt *(od. dividiert)* durch fünf ist vier *twenty divided by five make four*

German Weights and Measures
Deutsche Maße und Gewichte

I. Linear Measures

1 mm   *Millimeter* millimetre
- = $^1/_{1000}$ metre
- = 0.001 093 6 yard
- = 0.003 280 9 foot
- = 0.039 370 79 inch

1 cm   *Zentimeter* centimetre
- = $^1/_{100}$ metre
- = 0.3937 inch

1 dm   *Dezimeter* decimetre
- = $^1/_{10}$ metre
- = 3.9370 inches

1 m   *Meter* metre
- = 1.0936 yard
- = 3.2809 feet
- = 39.37079 inches

1 km   *Kilometer* kilometre
- = 1000 metres
- = 1093.637 yards
- = 3280.8692 feet
- = 39370.79 inches
- = 0.621 38 British or Statute Mile

1 sm   *Seemeile* nautical mile
- = 1852 metres

II. Surface or Square Measures

1 qmm   *Quadratmillimeter* square millimetre
- = $^1/_{1\,000\,000}$ square metre
- = 0.000001196 square yard
- = 0.0000107641 square foot
- = 0.00 155 square inch

1 qcm   *Quadratzentimeter* square centimetre
- = $^1/_{10\,000}$ square metre

1 qdm   *Quadratdezimeter* square decimetre
- = $^1/_{100}$ square metre

1 qm   *Quadratmeter* square metre
- = 1×1 metre
- = 1.19599 square yard
- = 10.7641 square feet
- = 1550 square inches

1 a   *Ar* are
- = 100 square metres
- = 119.5993 square yards
- = 1076.4103 square feet

1 ha   *Hektar* hectare
- = 100 ares
- = 10000 square metres
- = 11959.90 square yards
- = 107641.03 square feet
- = 2.4711 acres

1 qkm   *Quadratkilometer* square kilometre
- = 100 hectares
- = 1 000 000 square metres
- = 247.11 acres
- = 0.3861 square mile

1 Morgen
- = 25.5322 ares
- = about $^2/_3$ acre

III. Cubic or Solid Measures

1 ccm   *Kubikzentimeter* cubic centimetre
- = 1000 cubic millimetres
- = 0.061 cubic inch

1 cdm   *Kubikdezimeter* cubic decimetre
- = 1000 cubic centimetres
- = 61.0253 cubic inches

1 cbm   *Kubikmeter*
1 rm   *Raummeter* } cubic metre
1 fm   *Festmeter*
- = 1000 cubic decimetres
- = 1.3079 cubic yard
- = 35.3156 cubic feet

1 RT   *Registertonne* register ton
- = 2.832 cbm
- = 100 cubic feet

IV. Measures of Capacity

1 l *Liter* litre
= 10 decilitres
= 1.7607 pint (Brit.)
= 7.0431 gills (Brit.)
= 0.8804 quart (Brit.)
= 0.2201 gallon (Brit.)
= 2.1134 pints (U.S.)
= 8.4534 gills (U.S.)
= 1.0567 quart (U.S.)
= 0.2642 gallon (U.S.)

1 hl *Hektoliter* hectolitre
= 100 litres
= 22.009 gallons (Brit.)
= 2.751 bushels (Brit.)
= 26.418 gallons (U.S.)
= 2.84 bushels (U.S.)

V. Weights

1 mg *Milligramm* milligramme
= 1/1000 gramme
= 0.0154 grain (troy)

1 g *Gramm* gramme
= 1/1000 kilogramme
= 15.4324 grains (troy)

1 Pfd *Pfund* pound (German)
= 1/2 kilogramme
= 500 grammes
= 1.1023 pound (avdp.)
= 1.3396 pound (troy)

1 kg *Kilogramm, Kilo* kilogramme
= 1000 grammes
= 2.2046 pounds (avdp.)
= 2.6792 pounds (troy)

1 Ztr. *Zentner* centner
= 100 pounds (German)
= 50 kilogrammes
= 110.23 pounds (avdp.)
= 0.9842 British hundredweight
= 1.1023 U.S. hundredweight

1 dz *Doppelzentner*
= 100 kilogrammes
= 1.9684 British hundredweight
= 2.2046 U.S. hundredweights

1 t *Tonne* ton
= 1000 kilogrammes
= 0.984 British ton
= 1.1023 U.S. ton

Temperature Conversion Tables

Temperatur-Umrechnungstabellen

1. FROM −273 °C TO + 1000 °C
1. VON −273 °C BIS + 1000 °C

Celsius °C	Kelvin K	Fahrenheit °F	Réaumur °R
1000	1273	1832	800
950	1223	1742	760
900	1173	1652	720
850	1123	1562	680
800	1073	1472	640
750	1023	1382	600
700	973	1292	560
650	923	1202	520
600	873	1112	480
550	823	1022	440
500	773	932	400
450	723	842	360
400	673	752	320
350	623	662	280
300	573	572	240
250	523	482	200
200	473	392	160
150	423	302	120
100	373	212	80
95	368	203	76
90	363	194	72
85	358	185	68
80	353	176	64
75	348	167	60
70	343	158	56
65	338	149	52
60	333	140	48
55	328	131	44
50	323	122	40
45	318	113	36
40	313	104	32
35	308	95	28
30	303	86	24
25	298	77	20
20	293	68	16
15	288	59	12
10	283	50	8
+ 5	278	41	+ 4
0	273.15	32	0
− 5.	268	23	− 4
− 10	263	14	− 8

Celsius °C	Kelvin K	Fahrenheit °F	Réaumur °R
— 15	258	+ 5	— 12
— 17.8	255.4	0	— 14.2
— 20	253	— 4	— 16
— 25	248	— 13	— 20
— 30	243	— 22	— 24
— 35	238	— 31	— 28
— 40	233	— 40	— 32
— 45	228	— 49	— 36
— 50	223	— 58	— 40
— 100	173	— 148	— 80
— 150	123	— 238	— 120
— 200	73	— 328	— 160
— 250	23	— 418	— 200
— 273.15	0	— 459.4	— 218.4

2. CLINICAL THERMOMETER
2. FIEBERTHERMOMETER

Celsius °C	Fahrenheit °F	Réaumur °R
42.0	107.6	33.6
41.8	107.2	33.4
41.6	106.9	33.3
41.4	106.5	33.1
41.2	106.2	33.0
41.0	105.8	32.8
40.8	105.4	32.6
40.6	105.1	32.5
40.4	104.7	32.3
40.2	104.4	32.2
40.0	104.0	32.0
39.8	103.6	31.8
39.6	103.3	31.7
39.4	102.9	31.5
39.2	102.6	31.4
39.0	102.2	31.2
38.8	101.8	31.0
38.6	101.5	30.9
38.4	101.1	30.7
38.2	100.8	30.6
38.0	100.4	30.4
37.8	100.0	30.2
37.6	99.7	30.1
37.4	99.3	29.9
37.2	99.0	29.8
37.0	98.6	29.6
36.8	98.2	29.4
36.6	97.9	29.3

3. RULES FOR CONVERTING TEMPERATURES
3. UMRECHNUNGSREGELN

	Celsius	*Kelvin*
x °C	—	$= x + 273.15$ K
x K	$= x - 273.15$ °C	—
x °F	$= \dfrac{5}{9}(x-32)$ °C	$= \dfrac{5}{9}(x-32) + 273.15$ K
x °R	$= \dfrac{5}{4}x$ °C	$= \left(\dfrac{5}{4}x\right) + 273.15$ K
	Fahrenheit	*Réaumur*
x °C	$= \dfrac{9}{5}x + 32$ °F	$= \left(\dfrac{4}{5}x\right)$ °R
x K	$= \dfrac{9}{5}(x-273.15) + 32$ °F	$= \dfrac{4}{5}(x-273.15)$ °R
x °F	—	$= \dfrac{4}{9}(x-32)$ °R
x°R	$= \left(\dfrac{9}{4}x\right) + 32$ °F	—

Examples of German Declension
and Conjugation

Muster für die deutsche Deklination und Konjugation

A. Declension

Order of cases: *nom., gen., dat., acc., sg.* and *pl.* – Compound nouns and adjectives (e.g. *Eisbär, Ausgang, abfällig* etc.) inflect like their last elements (*Bär, Gang, fällig*). The letters in parentheses may be omitted.

I. Nouns

1
Bild   ~(e)s[1]   ~(e)   ~
Bilder[2]   ~   ~n   ~

[1] **es** *only:* Geist, Geistes.
[2] **a, o, u > ä, ö, ü:** Rand, Ränder; Haupt, Häupter; Dorf, Dörfer; Wurm, Würmer.

2
Reis*   ~es ['~zəs]   ~(e)   ~
Reiser[1] ['~zər] ~   ~n   ~

[1] **a, o > ä, ö:** Glas, Gläser ['glɛ:-zər]; Haus, Häuser ['hɔyzər]; Faß, Fässer; Schloß, Schlösser.
* **ß > ss:** Faß, Fasse(s).

3
Arm   ~(e)s[1],[2]   ~(e)[1]   ~
Arme[3]   ~   ~n   ~

[1] *without* **e:** Billard, Billard(s).
[2] **es** *only:* Maß, Maßes.
[3] **a, o, u > ä, ö, ü:** Gang, Gänge; Saal, Säle; Gebrauch, Gebräuche [gə-'brɔyçə]; Sohn, Söhne; Hut, Hüte.

4
Greis[1]*   ~es ['~zəs]   ~(e)   ~
Greise[2] ['~zə] ~   ~n   ~

[1] **s > ss:** Kürbis, Kürbisse(s).
[2] **a, o, u > ä, ö, ü:** Hals, Hälse; Baß, Bässe; Schoß, Schöße; Fuchs, Füchse; Schuß, Schüsse.
* **ß > ss:** Roß, Rosse(s).

5
Strahl   ~(e)s[1],[2]   ~(e)[2]   ~
Strahlen[3] ~   ~   ~

[1] **es** *only:* Schmerz, Schmerzes.
[2] *without* **e:** Juwel, Juwel(s).
[3] Sporn, Sporen.

6
Lappen   ~s   ~   ~*
Lappen[1] ~   ~   ~

[1] **a, o > ä, ö:** Graben, Gräben; Boden, Böden.
* *Infinitives used as nouns have no* pl.: Geschehen, Befinden etc.

7
Maler   ~s   ~   ~
Maler[1]   ~   ~n   ~

[1] **a, o, u > ä, ö, ü:** Vater, Väter; Kloster, Klöster; Bruder, Brüder.

8
Untertan   ~s   ~   ~
Untertanen[1],[2] ~   ~   ~

[1] *with change of accent:* Pro'fessor, Profes'soren [~'so:rən]; 'Dämon ['dɛ:mɔn], Dä'monen [dɛ'mo:nən].
[2] *pl.* **ien** [~jən]: Kolleg, Kollegien [~'le:gjən]; Mineral, Mineralien [~'le:gjən].

9 Studium   ~s   ~   ~
Studien[1],[2] ['~djən] ~ ~ ~
[1] a and o(n) > en: Drama, Dramen; Stadion, Stadien.
[2] on and um > a: Lexikon, Lexika; Faktum, Fakta.

10 Auge   ~s   ~   ~
Augen ~   ~   ~

11 Genie   ~s[1]*   ~   ~
Genies[2]* ~   ~   ~
[1] without inflexion: Bouillon etc.
[2] pl. s or ta: Komma, Kommas or Kommata; but: 'Klima, Klimate [kli'maːtə] (3).
* s is pronounced: [ʒe'niːs].

12 Bär[1]*   ~en[2]   ~en[2]   ~en[2]
Bären ~   ~   ~
[1] ß > ss: Genoß, Genossen.
[2] Herr, sg. mst Herrn; Herz, gen. Herzens, acc. Herz.
* ...'log as well as ...'loge (13), e. g. Biolog(e).

13 Knabe   ~n[1]   ~n   ~n
Knaben ~   ~   ~
[1] ns: Name, Namens.

14 Trübsal   ~   ~   ~
Trübsale[1],[2],[3], ~   ~n   ~
[1] a, o, u > ä, ö, ü: Hand, Hände; Braut, Bräute; Not, Nöte; Luft, Lüfte; without e: Tochter, Töchter; Mutter, Mütter; ß > ss: Nuß, Nüsse.
[2] s > ss: Kenntnis, Kenntnisse; Nimbus, Nimbusse.
[3] is or us > e: Kultus, Kulte; with change of accent: Di'akonus, Dia'kone [~'koːnə].

15 Blume   ~   ~   ~
Blumen ~   ~   ~
...ee: eː, pl. eːən, e. g. I'dee, I'deen.
...ie { stressed syllable: iː, pl. iːən, e. g. Batte'rie(n).
{ unstressed syllable: jə, pl. jən, e. g. Ar'terie(n).

16 Frau   ~   ~   ~
Frauen[1],[2],[3] ~   ~   ~
[1] in > innen: Freundin, Freundinnen.
[2] a, is, os and us > en: Firma, Firmen; Krisis, Krisen; Epos, Epen; Genius, Genien; with change of accent: 'Heros, He'roen [he'roːən]; Di'akonus, Dia'konen [~'koːnən].
[3] s and ß > ss: Kirmes, Kirmessen.

II. Proper nouns

17 *In general proper nouns have no pl. The following form the gen. sg. with s:*
1. *Proper nouns without a definite article:* Friedrichs, Paulas, (Friedrich von) Schillers, Deutschlands, Berlins;
2. *Proper nouns, masculine and neuter (except the names of countries) with a definite article and an adjective:* des braven Friedrichs Bruder, des jungen Deutschlands (Söhne).

After s, sch, ß, tz, x, *and* z *the gen. sg. ends in* -ens *or* ' *(instead of* ' *it is more advisable to use the definite article or* von*), e. g.* die Werke des [or von] Sokrates, Voß or Sokrates', Voß' [not Sokratessens, seldom Vossens] Werke; *but:* die Umgebung von Mainz.

Feminine names ending in a consonant or the vowel e *form the gen. sg. with* (en)s *or* (n)s; *in the dat. and acc. sg. such names may end in* (e)n *(pl. = a).*

If a proper noun is followed by a title, only the following forms are inflected:
1. *the title when used* with *a definite article:*
der Kaiser Karl (der Große)
des   ~s ~   (des   ~n) etc.;
2. *the (last) name when used* without *an article:*
Kaiser Karl (der Große)
~   ~s (des   ~n) etc.
(*but:* Herrn Lehmanns Brief).

III. Adjectives und participles
(also used as nouns*), pronouns etc.

18

	m	f	n	pl.	
a) gut	er[1,2]	‿e	‿es	‿e°	without article, after prepositions, personal pronouns, and invariables
	en**	‿er	‿en**	‿er	
	em	‿er	‿em	‿en	
	en	‿e	‿es	‿e	

	m	f	n	pl.	
b) gut	e[1,2]	‿e	‿e	‿en	with definite article (22) or with pronoun (21)
	en	‿en	‿en	‿en	
	en	‿en	‿en	‿en	
	en	‿e	‿e	‿en	

	m	f	n	pl.	
c) gut	er[1,2]	‿e	‿es	‿en	with indefinite article or with pronoun (20)
	en	‿en	‿en	‿en	
	en	‿en	‿en	‿en	
	en	‿e	‿es	‿en	

[1] ß = ss: kraß, krasse(r, ‿s, ‿st etc.).
[2] a, o, u > ä, ö. ü when forming the *comp.* and *sup.*: alt, älter(e, ‿es etc.), ältest (der ‿e, am ‿en); grob, gröber(e, ‿es etc.), gröbst (der ‿e, am ‿en); kurz, kürzer(e, ‿es etc.), kürzest (der ‿e, am ‿en).

* e. g. Böse(r) *su.*: der (die, eine) Böse, ein Böser; Böse(s) *n*: das Böse,

without article Böses; *in the same way* Abgesandte(r) *su.*, Angestellte(r) *su.* etc.; *in some cases the use varies.*
** *Sometimes the gen. sg. ends in* ‿es *instead of* ‿en: gutes (*or* guten) Mutes sein.
° *In* böse, böse(r, ‿s, ‿st etc.) *one* e *is dropped.*

The Grades of Comparison

The endings of the *comparative* and *superlative* are:

	reich	schön	
comp.	reicher	schöner	*inflected according to* (18[2]).
sup.	reichst	schönst	

After vowels (except e [18°]) *and after* d, s, sch, ß, st, t, tz x, y, z *the* sup. *ends in* ‿est, *but in unstressed syllables after* d, sch *and* t *generally in* ‿st: blau, 'blauest; rund, 'rundest; rasch, 'raschest etc.; *but:* 'dringend, 'dringendst; 'närrisch, 'närrischst; ge'eignet, ge'eignetst.

Note. — The adjectives ending in ‿el, ‿en (*except* ‿nen) *and* ‿er (*e. g.* dunkel, eben, heiter), *and also the possessive adjectives* unser *and* euer *generally drop* e (*in this case* ss *changes to* ß: angemessen, angemeßner).

Inflexion:	‿e	‿em	‿en	‿er	‿es, *and*
‿el >	‿le	‿lem*	‿len*	‿ler	‿les
‿en >	‿(e)ne	‿(e)nem	‿(e)nen	‿(e)ner°	‿(e)nes
‿er >	‿(e)re	‿rem*	‿ren*	‿(e)rer°	‿(e)res

* *or* ‿elm, ‿eln, ‿erm, ‿ern; *e. g.* **dunk|el:** ‿le, ‿lem (*or* ‿elm), ‿len (*or* ‿eln), ‿ler, ‿les; **eb|en:** ‿(e)ne, ‿(e)nem etc.; **heit|er:** ‿(e)re, ‿rem (*or* ‿erm) etc.

° *The inflected* comp. *ends in* ‿ner *and* ‿rer *only:* eben, ebnere(r, ‿s etc.); heiter, heitrere(r, ‿s etc.); *but* sup. ebenst, heiterst.

19

	1st pers.	2nd pers.	3rd pers.		
	m, f, n	*m, f, n*	*m*	*f*	*n*
	ich	du	er	sie	es
sg.	meiner*	deiner*	seiner*	ihrer	seiner*
	mir	dir	ihm	ihr	ihm°
	mich	dich	ihn	sie	es°
	wir	ihr	sie		(Sie)
pl.	unser	euer	ihrer		(Ihrer)
	uns	euch	ihnen		(Ihnen)°
	uns	euch	sie		(Sie)°

* *In poetry sometimes without inflexion:* gedenke mein!; *also* es *instead of* seiner *n* (= e-r S.): ich bin es überdrüssig.

° *Reflexive form:* sich.

20

	m	*f*	*n*	*pl.*
mein		~e	~	~e*
dein	es	~er	~es	~er
sein	em	~er	~em	~en
(k)ein	en	~e	~	~e

* *The indefinite article* ein *has no pl.* — *In poetry* mein, dein, *and* sein *may stand behind the su. without inflexion:* die Mutter (Kinder) mein, *or as predicate:* der Hut [die Tasche, das Buch] ist mein; *without su.:* meiner *m*, meine *f*, mein(e)s *n*, meine *pl.* etc.: wem gehört der Hut [die Tasche, das Buch]? es ist meiner (meine, mein[e]s); *or with definite article:* der (die, das) meine, *pl.* die meinen (18b). *Regarding* unser *and* euer *see note* (18), *p.* 1332.

21

	m	*f*	*n*	*pl.*
dies	er	~e	~es*	~e***
jen	es	~er	~es	~er[1]
manch	em	~er	~em	~en[1]
welch	en	~e	~es*	~e

[1] welche(r, s) *as rel. pron.: gen. sg.* dessen, deren, *gen. pl.* deren, *dat. pl.* denen (23).

* *Used as su.,* dies *is preferable to* dieses.

** manch, solch, welch *frequently are uninflected:*

---

manch | guter (ein guter) Mann
solch | ~en (~es ~en) ~es
welch | ~em (~em ~en) ~e

Similarly all: etc. (18)

all der (dieser, mein) Schmerz
~ des (~es, ~es) ~es

22

m	*f*	*n*	*pl.*	
der	die	das	die[1]	
des	der	des	der	definite
dem	der	dem	den	article
den	die	das	die	

[1] derjenige, derselbe—desjenigen, demjenigen, desselben, demselben etc. (18b).

---

23 Relative pronoun

m	*f*	*n*	*pl.*
der	die	das	die
dessen*	deren	dessen*	deren[1]
dem	der	dem	denen
den	die	das	die

[1] *also* derer, *when used as dem. pron.*

* *also* des.

24

wer	was	jemand, niemand
wessen*	wessen	~(e)s
wem	—	~(em°)
wen	was	~(en°)

* *also* wes.

° *preferably without inflexion.*

B. Conjugation

General remarks. — In the conjugation tables (25—30) only the simple verbs may be found; in the alphabetic list [p. 1335—1341] compound verbs are only included when no simple verb exists (e. g. be-ginnen; *ginnen* does not exist). In order to find the conjugation of any compound verb (with separable or inseparable prefix, regular or irregular) look up the respective simple verb.

Verbs with separable and stressed prefixes such as **'ab-**, **'an-**, **'auf-**, **'aus-**, **'bei-**, **be'vor-**, **'dar-**, **'ein-**, **em'por-**, **ent'gegen-**, **'fort-**, **'her-**, **he'rab-** etc. and also **'klar-[legen]**, **'los-[schießen]**, **'sitzen-[bleiben]**, **über-'hand-[nehmen]** etc. (but not the verbs derived from compound nouns as **be'antragen** or **be'ratschlagen** from *Antrag* and *Ratschlag* etc.) take the preposition **zu** (in the *inf.* and the *p.pr.*) and the syllable **ge** (in the *p.p.* and in the passive voice) between the stressed prefix and their root.

Verbs with inseparable and unstressed prefixes such as **be-**, **emp-**, **ent-**, **er-**, **ge-**, **ver-**, **zer-** and generally **miß-** (in spite of its being stressed) take the preposition **zu** before the prefix and drop the syllable **ge** in the *p.p.* and in the passive voice. The prefixes **durch-**, **hinter-**, **über-**, **um-**, **unter-**, **voll-**, **wi(e)der-** are separable when stressed and inseparable when unstressed, e. g.

geben: *zu geben, zu gebend*; *gegeben*; *ich gebe, du gibst* etc.;
'abgeben: *'abzugeben*, *'abzugebend*; *'abgegeben*; *ich gebe (du gibst* etc.*) ab*;
ver'geben: *zu ver'geben, zu ver'gebend*; *ver'geben*; *ich ver'gebe, du ver'gibst* etc.;
'umgehen: *'umzugehen*, *'umzugehend*; *'umgegangen*; *ich gehe (du gehst* etc.*) um*;
um'gehen: *zu um'gehen, zu um'gehend*; *um'gangen*; *ich um'gehe, du um'gehst* etc.

The same rules apply to verbs with two prefixes, e. g.
zu'rückbehalten [see *halten*]: *zu-'rückzubehalten*, *zu'rückzubehaltend*; *zu'rückbehalten*; *ich behalte (du behältst* etc.*) zurück*;
wieder'aufheben [see *heben*]: *wie-der'aufzuheben*, *wieder'aufzuhebend*; *wieder'aufgehoben*; *ich hebe (du hebst* etc.*) wieder auf*.

The forms in parentheses ( ) follow the same rules.

a) 'Weak' Conjugation

25 **loben**

prs. ind.	lobe	lobst	lobt
	loben	lobt	loben
prs. subj.	lobe	lobest	lobe
	loben	lobet	loben
pret. ind.	lobte	lobtest	lobte
and *subj.*	lobten	lobtet	lobten

imp.sg. lob(e), *pl.* lob(e)t, loben Sie;
inf.prs. loben; *inf.perf.* gelobt haben;
p.pr. lobend; *p.p.* gelobt (18; 29**).

26 **reden**

prs. ind.	rede	redest	redet
	reden	redet	reden
prs. subj.	rede	redest	rede
	reden	redet	reden
pret. ind.	redete	redetest	redete
and *subj.*	redeten	redetet	redeten

imp.sg. rede, *pl.* redet, reden Sie;
inf.prs. reden; *inf.perf.* geredet haben; *p.pr.* redend; *p.p.* geredet (18; 29**).

27 **reisen**

prs. ind.	reise	rei(se)st*	reist
	reisen	reist	reisen
prs. subj.	reise	reisest	reise
	reisen	reiset	reisen
pret. ind.	reiste	reistest	reisten
and *subj.*	reisten	reistet	reisten

imp.sg. reise, *pl.* reist, reisen Sie;
inf.prs. reisen; *inf.perf.* gereist sein *od. now rare* haben; *p.pr.* reisend; *p.p.* gereist (18; 29**).

* **sch**: naschen, nasch(e)st; **ß**: spaßen, spaßt (spaßest); **tz**: ritzen, ritzt (ritzest); **x**: hexen, hext (hexest); **z**: reizen, reizt (reizest); faulenzen, faulenzt (faulenzest).

28 **fassen**

prs. ind.	fasse	faßt (fassest)	faßt
	fassen	faßt	fassen
prs. subj.	fasse	fassest	fasse
	fassen	fasset	fassen
pret. ind.	faßte	faßtest	faßte
and *subj.*	faßten	faßtet	faßten

imp.sg. fasse (faß), *pl.* faßt, fassen Sie; *inf.prs.* fassen; *inf.perf.* gefaßt haben; *p.pr.* fassend; *p.p.* gefaßt (18; 29**).

29   handeln

prs. ind.

handle*	handelst	handelt
handeln	handelt	handeln

prs. subj.

handle*	handelst	handle*
handeln	handelt	handeln

pret. ind. and subj.

handelte	handeltest	handelte
handelten	handeltet	handelten

imp.sg. handle, *pl.* handelt, handeln
Sie; *inf.prs.* handeln; *inf. perf.* gehandelt haben; *p.pr.* handelnd; *p.p.*
gehandelt (18).

* Also handele; wandern,
wand(e)re; bessern, bessere (béßre);
donnern, donnere.

** *Without* **ge**, *when the first syllable
is unstressed, e. g.* be'grüßen, be-
'grüßt; ent'stehen, ent'standen; stu-
'dieren, stu'diert (*not* gestudiert);
trom'peten, trom'petet (*also when pre-
ceded by a stressed prefix:* 'austrom-
peten, 'austrompetet, *not* 'ausgetrom-
petet). *In some weak verbs the p.p. ends
in* **en** *instead of* **t**, *e. g.* mahlen —
gemahlen. *With the verbs* brauchen,
dürfen, heißen, helfen, hören, können, lassen, lehren, lernen, machen,
mögen, müssen, sehen, sollen, wollen
the p.p. is replaced by inf. (*without* ge),
*when used in connection with another
inf., e. g.* ich habe ihn singen hören,
du hättest es tun können, er hat
gehen müssen, ich hätte ihn laufen
lassen sollen.

30   b) 'Strong' Conjugation

fahren

prs. ind.	fahre	fährst	fährt
	fahren	fahrt	fahren
prs. subj.	fahre	fahrest	fahre
	fahren	fahret	fahren
pret. ind.	fuhr	fuhr(e)st*	fuhr
	fuhren	fuhrt	fuhren
pret. subj.	führe	führest	führe*
	führen	führet	führen

imp.sg. fahr(e), *pl.* fahr(e)t, fahren
Sie; *inf.prs.* fahren; *inf.perf.* gefahren haben *or* sein; *p.pr.* fahrend;
p.p. gefahren (18; 29**).
* In the following alphabetical
list the 2nd person of the *pret.
ind.* is only mentioned when there
are doubts as to its formation.

Alphabetical List
of Strong and Irregular Verbs

Abbreviations see p. 683 and 684; *subj.* = *subjunctive pret.*

backen *prs.* backe, bäckst, bäckt;
pret. backte (buk, buk[e]st);
subj. büke; *imp.* back(e); *p.p.*
gebacken.
befehlen *prs.* befehle, befiehlst, be-
fiehlt; *pret.* befahl; *subj.* beföhle
(befähle); *imp.* befiehl; *p.p.* befohlen.
beginnen *prs.* beginne, beginnst,
beginnt; *pret.* begann; *subj.* be-
gönne (begänne); *imp.* beginn(e);
p.p. begonnen.
beißen *prs.* beiße, beißt, beißt;
pret. biß, bissest; *subj.* bisse;
imp. beiß(e); *p.p.* gebissen.
bergen *prs.* berge, birgst, birgt;

pret. barg; *subj.* bärge; *imp.* birg;
p.p. geborgen.
bersten *prs.* berste, birst (*rarely:*
berstest), birst (*rarely:* berstet);
pret. barst, barstest; *subj.* bärste;
imp. birst; *p. p.* geborsten.
bewegen *prs.* bewege, bewegst, bewegt; *pret.* bewegte (*fig.* bewog);
subj. bewegte(*fig.* bewöge);*imp.* be-
weg(e);*p.p.* bewegt(*fig.* bewogen).
biegen *prs.* biege, biegst, biegt;
pret. bog; *subj.* böge; *imp.* bieg(e);
p.p. gebogen.
bieten *prs.* biete, biet(e)st, bietet;
pret. bot, bot(e)st; *subj.* böte;
imp. biet(e); *p.p.* geboten.

binden *prs.* binde, bindest, bindet; *pret.* band, band(e)st; *subj.* bände; *imp.* bind(e); *p.p.* gebunden.

bitten *prs.* bitte, bittest, bittet; *pret.* bat, bat(e)st; *subj.* bäte; *imp.* bitte (bitt'); *p.p.* gebeten.

blasen *prs.* blase, bläst, bläst; *pret.* blies, bliesest; *subj.* bliese; *imp.* blas(e); *p.p.* geblasen.

bleiben *prs.* bleibe, bleibst, bleibt; *pret.* blieb, bliebst; *subj.* blieb *imp.* bleib(e); *p.p.* geblieben.

braten *prs.* brate, brätst, brät; *pret.* briet, briet(e)st; *subj.* briete; *imp.* brat(e); *p.p.* gebraten.

brechen *prs.* breche, brichst, bricht; *pret.* brach; *subj.* bräche; *imp.* brich; *p.p.* gebrochen*).

brennen *prs.* brenne, brennst, brennt; *pret.* brannte; *subj.* brennte; *imp.* brenne; *p.p.* gebrannt.

bringen *prs.* bringe, bringst, bringt; *pret.* brachte; *subj.* brächte; *imp.* bring(e); *p.p.* gebracht.

denken *prs.* denke, denkst, denkt; *pret.* dachte; *subj.* dächte; *imp.* denk(e); *p.p.* gedacht.

dingen *prs.* dinge, dingst, dingt; *pret.* dingte (dang); *subj.* dingte (dänge); *imp.* dinge; *p.p.* gedungen (*rarely:* gedingt).

dreschen *prs.* dresche, drischst, drischt; *pret.* drosch, drosch(e)st; *subj.* drösche; *imp.* drisch; *p.p.* gedroschen.

dringen *prs.* dringe, dringst, dringt; *pret.* drang, drangst; *subj.* dränge; *imp.* dring(e); *p.p.* gedrungen.

dünken *prs.* mich dünkt (deucht); *pret.* dünkte (deuchte); *subj.* —; *imp.* —; *p.p.* gedünkt (gedeucht).

dürfen *prs.* darf, darfst, darf; wir dürfen etc.; *pret.* durfte; *subj.* dürfte; *imp.* —; *p.p.* gedurft (*auxiliary verb:* dürfen).

empfehlen *prs.* empfehle, empfiehlst, empfiehlt; *pret.* empfahl; *subj.* empföhle (empfähle); *imp.* empfiehl; *p.p.* empfohlen.

erbleichen *prs.* erbleiche, erbleichst, erbleicht; *pret.* erbleichte (erblich); *subj.* erbliche (erbleichte); *imp.* erbleiche; *p.p.* erbleicht (erblichen = gestorben).

erkiesen *poet. prs.* erkiese, erkie(se)st, erkiest; *pret.* erkor (erkieste); *subj.* erköre; *imp.* erkies(e); *p.p.* erkoren.

erlöschen *pres.* erlösche, erlischst, erlischt; *pret.* erlosch, erloschest; *subj.* erlösche; *imp.* erlisch; *p.p.* erloschen.

essen *prs.* esse, ißt, ißt; *pret.* aß, aßest; *subj.* äße; *imp.* iß; *p.p.* gegessen.

fahren *prs.* fahre, fährst, fährt; *pret.* fuhr, fuhrst; *subj.* führe; *imp.* fahr(e); *p.p.* gefahren.

fallen *prs.* falle, fällst, fällt; *pret.* fiel; *subj.* fiele; *imp.* fall(e); *p.p.* gefallen.

fangen *prs.* fange, fängst, fängt; *pret.* fing; *subj.* finge; *imp.* fang(e); *p.p.* gefangen.

fechten *prs.* fechte, fichtst, ficht; *pret.* focht, fochtest; *subj.* föchte; *imp.* ficht; *p.p.* gefochten.

finden *pres.* finde, findest, findet; *pret.* fand, fand(e)st; *subj.* fände; *imp.* find(e); *p.p.* gefunden.

flechten *prs.* flechte, flichtst, flicht; *pret.* flocht, flochtest; *subj.* flöchte; *imp.* flicht; *p.p.* geflochten.

fliegen *prs.* fliege, fliegst, fliegt; *pret.* flog, flogst; *subj.* flöge; *imp.* flieg(e); *p.p.* geflogen.

flieh(e)n *prs.* fliehe, fliehst, flieht; *pret.* floh, flohst; *subj.* flöhe; *imp.* flieh(e); *p.p.* geflohen.

fließen *prs.* fließe, fließt, fließt; *pret.* floß, flossest; *subj.* flösse; *imp.* fließ(e); *p.p.* geflossen.

fressen *prs.* fresse, frißt, frißt; *pret.* fraß, fraßest; *subj.* fräße; *imp.* friß; *p.p.* gefressen.

frieren *prs.* friere, frierst, friert; *pret.* fror; *subj.* fröre; *imp.* frier(e); *p.p.* gefroren.

gären *prs.* gäre, gärst, gärt; *pret.* gor (*bsd. fig.* gärte); *subj.* göre (gärte); *imp.* gäre; *p.p.* gegoren (gegärt).

gebären *prs.* gebäre, gebierst, gebiert; *pret.* gebar; *subj.* gebäre; *imp.* gebier; *p.p.* geboren.

geben *prs.* gebe, gibst, gibt; *pret.* gab; *subj.* gäbe; *imp.* gib; *p.p.* gegeben.

gedeihen *prs.* gedeihe, gedeihst, gedeiht; *pret.* gedieh; *subj.* gediehe; *imp.* gedeih(e); *p.p.* gediehen.

---

*) ehebrechen: daß sie ehebrechen (ehebrachen), but: er bricht (brach) die Ehe, er hat die Ehe gebrochen.

gehen *prs.* gehe, gehst, geht; *pret.* ging; *subj.* ginge, gingest; *imp.* geh(e); *p.p.* gegangen.

gelingen *prs.* es gelingt; *pret.* es gelang; *subj.* es gelänge; *imp.* geling(e); *p.p.* gelungen.

gelten *prs.* gelte, giltst, gilt; *pret.* galt, galt(e)st; *subj.* gölte (gälte); *imp.* gilt; *p.p.* gegolten.

genesen *prs.* genese, genest, genest; *pret.* genas, genasest; *subj.* genäse; *imp.* genese; *p.p.* genesen.

genießen *prs.* genieße, genießt, genießt; *pret.* genoß, genossest; *subj.* genösse; *imp.* genieß(e); *p.p.* genossen.

geschehen *prs.* es geschieht; *pret.* es geschah; *subj.* es geschähe; *imp.* —; *p.p.* geschehen.

gewinnen *prs.* gewinne, gewinnst, gewinnt; *pret.* gewann, gewannst; *subj.* gewönne (gewänne); *imp.* gewinn(e); *p.p.* gewonnen.

gießen *prs.* gieße, gießt, gießt; *pret.* goß, gossest; *subj.* gösse; *imp.* gieß(e); *p.p.* gegossen.

gleichen *pres.* gleiche, gleichst, gleicht; *pret.* glich, glichst; *subj.* gliche; *imp.* gleich(e); *p.p.* geglichen.

gleiten *prs.* gleite, gleitest, gleitet; *pret.* glitt (*rarely:* gleitete), glitt(e)st; *subj.* glitte, glitt(e)st (*rarely:* gleitetest); *imp.* gleit(e); *p.p.* geglitten (*rarely:* gegleitet).

glimmen *prs.* glimme, glimmst, glimmt; *pret.* glomm (*rarely:* glimmte); *subj.* glömme, glömmest (*rarely:* glimmte, glimmtest); *imp.* glimm(e); *p.p.* geglimmt (*rarely:* geglommen).

graben *prs.* grabe, gräbst, gräbt; *pret.* grub, grubst; *subj.* grübe; *imp.* grab(e); *p.p.* gegraben.

greifen *prs.* greife, greifst, greift; *pret.* griff, griffst; *subj.* griffe; *imp.* greif(e); *p.p.* gegriffen.

haben *prs.* habe, hast, hat; *pret.* hatte; *subj.* hätte; *imp.* hab(e); *p.p.* gehabt.

halten *prs.* halte, hältst, hält; *pret.* hielt, hielt(e)st; *subj.* hielte; *imp.* halt(e); *p.p.* gehalten.

hangen, *now usually* **hängen** *v/i.:* *prs.* hänge, hängst, hängt; *pret.* hing, hingst; *subj.* hinge; *imp.* häng(e); *p.p.* gehangen.

hauen *prs.* haue, haust, haut; *pret.* hieb, hiebst; *subj.* hiebe; *imp.* hau(e); *p.p.* gehauen.

heben *prs.* hebe, hebst, hebt; *pret.* hob, hobst; *subj.* höbe; *imp.* heb(e); *p.p.* gehoben.

heißen *prs.* heiße, heißt, heißt; *pret.* hieß, hießest; *subj.* hieße; *imp.* heiß(e); *p.p.* geheißen.

helfen *prs.* helfe, hilfst, hilft; *pret.* half, halfst; *subj.* hülfe (hälfe); *imp.* hilf; *p.p.* geholfen.

kennen *prs.* kenne, kennst, kennt; *pret.* kannte; *subj.* kennte; *imp.* kenne; *p.p.* gekannt.

klimmen *prs.* klimme, klimmst, klimmt; *pret.* klomm (klimmte), klommst (klimmtest); *subj.* klömme (klimmte); *imp.* klimm(e); *p.p.* geklommen (geklimmt).

klingen *prs.* klinge, klingst, klingt; *pret.* klang, klangst; *subj.* klänge; *imp.* kling(e); *p.p.* geklungen.

kneifen *prs.* kneife, kneifst, kneift; *pret.* kniff, kniffst; *subj.* kniffe; *imp.* kneif(e); *p.p.* gekniffen.

kommen *prs.* komme, kommst, kommt; *pret.* kam; *subj.* käme; *imp.* komm(e); *p.p.* gekommen.

können *prs.* kann, kannst, kann; *wir* können etc.; *pret.* konnte; *subj.* könnte; *imp.* —; *p.p.* gekonnt (*auxiliary verb:* können).

kriechen *prs.* krieche, kriechst, kriecht; *pret.* kroch; *subj.* kröche; *imp.* kriech(e); *p.p.* gekrochen.

laden *prs.* lade, lädst (F *fig.* ladest), lädt (F *fig.* ladet); *pret.* lud, lud(e)st; *subj.* lüde; *imp.* lad(e); *p.p.* geladen.

lassen *prs.* lasse, läßt, läßt; *pret.* ließ, ließest; *subj.* ließe; *imp.* laß; *p.p.* gelassen (*auxiliary verb:* lassen).

laufen *prs.* laufe, läufst, läuft; *pret.* lief, liefst; *subj.* liefe; *imp.* lauf(e); *p.p.* gelaufen.

leiden *prs.* leide, leidest, leidet; *pret.* litt, litt(e)st; *subj.* litte; *imp.* leid(e); *p.p.* gelitten.

leihen *prs.* leihe, leihst, leiht; *pret.* lieh, liest; *subj.* liehe; *imp.* leih(e); *p.p.* geliehen.

lesen *prs.* lese, liest, liest; *pret.* las, lasest; *subj.* läse; *imp.* lies; *p.p.* gelesen.

liegen *prs.* liege, liegst, liegt; *pret.* lag; *subj.* läge; *imp.* lieg(e); *p.p.* gelegen.

lügen *prs.* lüge, lügst, lügt; *pret.* log, logst; *subj.* löge; *imp.* lüg(e); *p.p.* gelogen.

meiden *prs.* meide, meidest, meidet; *pret.* mied, mied(e)st; *subj.* miede; *imp.* meid(e); *p.p.* gemieden.

melken *prs.* melke, melkst (milkst), melkt (milkt); *pret.* melkte (molk); *subj.* mölke; *imp.* melk(e); *p.p.* gemolken (gemelkt).

messen *prs.* messe, mißt, mißt; *pret.* maß, maßest; *subj.* mäße; *imp.* miß; *p.p.* gemessen.

mißlingen *prs.* es mißlingt; *pret.* es mißlang; *subj.* es mißlänge; *imp.* —; *p.p.* mißlungen.

mögen *prs.* mag, magst, mag; *wir* mögen etc.; *pret.* mochte; *subj.* möchte; *imp.* —; *p.p.* gemocht (*auxiliary verb*: mögen).

müssen *prs.* muß, mußt, muß; *pl.* müssen, müßt, müssen; *pret.* mußte; *subj.* müßte; *imp.* —; *p.p.* gemußt (*auxiliary verb*: müssen).

nehmen *prs.* nehme, nimmst, nimmt; *pret.* nahm, nahmst; *subj.* nähme; *imp.* nimm; *p.p.* genommen.

nennen *prs.* nenne, nennst, nennt; *pret.* nannte; *subj.* nennte; *imp.* nenn(e); *p.p.* genannt.

pfeifen *prs.* pfeife, pfeifst, pfeift; *pret.* pfiff, pfiffst; *subj.* pfiffe; *imp.* pfeif(e); *p.p.* gepfiffen.

pflegen *prs.* pflege, pflegst, pflegt; *pret.* pflegte (*fig. rarely*: pflog, pflog[e]st); *subj.* pflegte (*fig. rarely*: pflöge); *imp.* pfleg(e); *p.p.* gepflegt (*fig. rarely*: gepflogen).

preisen *prs.* preise, preist, preist; *pret.* pries, priesest; *subj.* priese; *imp.* preis(e); *p.p.* gepriesen.

quellen (*v/i.*) *prs.* quelle, quillst, quillt; *pret.* quoll; *subj.* quölle; *imp.* quill; *p.p.* gequollen.

raten *prs.* rate, rätst, rät; *pret.* riet, riet(e)st; *subj.* riete; *imp.* rat(e); *p.p.* geraten.

reiben *prs.* reibe, reibst, reibt; *pret.* rieb, riebst; *subj.* riebe; *imp.* reib(e); *p.p.* gerieben.

reißen *prs.* reiße, reißt, reißt; *pret.* riß, rissest; *subj.* risse; *imp.* reiß(e); *p.p.* gerissen.

reiten *prs.* reite, reit(e)st, reitet; *pret.* ritt, ritt(e)st; *subj.* ritte; *imp.* reit(e); *p.p.* geritten.

rennen *prs.* renne, rennst, rennt; *pret.* rannte; *subj.* rennte; *imp.* renn(e); *p.p.* gerannt.

riechen *prs.* rieche, riechst, riecht; *pret.* roch; *subj.* röche; *imp.* riech(e); *p.p.* gerochen.

ringen *prs.* ringe, ringst, ringt; *pret.* rang; *subj.* ränge; *imp.* ring(e); *p.p.* gerungen.

rinnen *prs.* rinne, rinnst, rinnt; *pret.* rann, rannst; *subj.* ränne; *imp.* rinn(e); *p.p.* geronnen.

rufen *prs.* rufe, rufst, ruft; *pret.* rief, riefst; *subj.* riefe; *imp.* ruf(e); *p.p.* gerufen.

saufen *prs.* saufe, säufst, säuft; *pret.* soff, soffst; *subj.* söffe; *imp.* sauf(e); *p.p.* gesoffen.

saugen *prs.* sauge, saugst, saugt; *pret.* sog (saugte); *subj.* söge; *imp.* saug(e); *p.p.* gesogen (gesaugt).

schaffen (*schöpferisch hervorbringen*) *prs.* schaffe, schaffst, schafft; *pret.* schuf, schufst; *subj.* schüfe; *imp.* schaff(e); *p.p.* geschaffen.

schallen *prs.* schalle, schallst, schallt; *pret.* schallte (scholl); *subj.* schölle; *imp.* schall(e); *p.p.* geschallt.

scheiden *prs.* scheide, scheidest, scheidet; *pret.* schied, schied(e)st; *subj.* schiede; *imp.* scheid(e); *p.p.* geschieden.

scheinen *prs.* scheine, scheinst, scheint; *pret.* schien, schienst; *subj.* schiene; *imp.* schein(e); *p.p.* geschienen.

scheißen V *prs.* scheiße, scheißt, scheißt; *pret.* schiß; *subj.* schisse; *imp.* scheiß(e); *p.p.* geschissen.

schelten *prs.* schelte, schiltst, schilt; *pret.* schalt, schalt(e)st; *subj.* schölte; *imp.* schilt; *p.p.* gescholten.

scheren (*abschneiden*) *prs.* schere, scherst, schert; *pret.* schor (*refl.* scherte), schor(e)st (*refl.* schertest); *subj.* schöre (*refl.* scherte); *imp.* scher(e); *p.p.* geschoren (*refl.* geschert).

schieben *prs.* schiebe, schiebst, schiebt; *pret.* schob, schobst; *subj.* schöbe; *imp.* schieb(e); *p.p.* geschoben.

schießen *prs.* schieße, schießt, schießt; *pret.* schoß, schossest; *subj.* schösse; *imp.* schieß(e); *p.p.* geschossen.

schinden *prs.* schinde, schindest, schindet; *pret.* schund, schund(e)st; *subj.* schünde; *imp.* schind(e); *p.p.* geschunden.

schlafen *prs.* schlafe, schläfst, schläft; *pret.* schlief, schliefst; *subj.* schliefe; *imp.* schlaf(e); *p.p.* geschlafen.

schlagen *prs.* schlage, schlägst, schlägt; *pret.* schlug, schlugst; *subj.* schlüge; *imp.* schlag(e); *p.p.* geschlagen.

schleichen *prs.* schleiche, schleichst, schleicht; *pret.* schlich, schlichst; *subj.* schliche; *imp.* schleich(e); *p.p.* geschlichen.

schleifen (*schärfen*; *glätten*) *prs.* schleife, schleifst, schleift; *pret.* schliff, schliffst; *subj.* schliffe; *imp.* schleif(e); *p.p.* geschliffen.

schleißen *prs.* schleiße, schleißt, schleißt; *pret.* schliß (schleißte), schlissest (schleißtest); *subj.* schlisse; *imp.* schleiß(e); *p.p.* geschlissen (geschleißt).

schließen *prs.* schließe, schließt (schließest), schließt; *pret.* schloß, schlossest; *subj.* schlösse; *imp.* schließ(e); *p.p.* geschlossen.

schlingen *prs.* schlinge, schlingst, schlingt; *pret.* schlang, schlangst; *subj.* schlänge; *imp.* schling(e); *p.p.* geschlungen.

schmeißen F *prs.* schmeiße, schmeißt, schmeißt; *pret.* schmiß, schmissest; *subj.* schmisse; *imp.* schmeiß(e); *p.p.* geschmissen.

schmelzen *prs.* schmelze, schmilzt, schmilzt; *pret.* schmolz, schmolzest; *subj.* schmölze; *imp.* schmilz; *p.p.* geschmolzen.

schnauben *prs.* schnaube, schnaubst, schnaubt; *pret.* schnaubte (*älter*: schnob); *subj.* schnaubte (*älter*: schnöbe); *imp.* schnaub(e); *p.p.* geschnaubt (*älter*: geschnoben).

schneiden *prs.* schneide, schneidest, schneidet; *pret.* schnitt, schnitt(e)st; *subj.* schnitte; *imp.* schneid(e); *p.p.* geschnitten.

schrecken (*v/i.* = er⁓) *prs.* schrecke, schrickst, schrickt; *pret.* schrak, schrakst; *subj.* schräke; *imp.* schrick; *p.p.* erschrocken.

schreiben *prs.* schreibe, schreibst, schreibt; *pret.* schrieb, schriebst; *subj.* schriebe; *imp.* schreib(e); *p.p.* geschrieben.

schreien *prs.* schreie, schreist, schreit; *pret.* schrie; *subj.* schriee; *imp.* schrei(e); *p.p.* geschrie(e)n.

schreiten *prs.* schreite, schreitest, schreitet; *pret.* schritt, schritt(e)st; *subj.* schritte; *imp.* schreit(e); *p.p.* geschritten.

schweigen *prs.* schweige, schweigst, schweigt; *pret.* schwieg, schwiegst; *subj.* schwiege; *imp.* schweig(e); *p.p.* geschwiegen.

schwellen (*v/i.*) *prs.* schwelle, schwillst, schwillt; *pret.* schwoll, schwollst; *subj.* schwölle, schwöllest; *imp.* schwill; *p.p.* geschwollen.

schwimmen *prs.* schwimme, schwimmst, schwimmt; *pret.* schwamm, schwammst; *subj.* schwömme (schwämme); *imp.* schwimm(e); *p.p.* geschwommen.

schwinden *prs.* schwinde, schwindest, schwindet; *pret.* schwand, schwand(e)st; *subj.* schwände; *imp.* schwind(e); *p.p.* geschwunden.

schwingen *prs.* schwinge, schwingst, schwingt; *pret.* schwang, schwangst; *subj.* schwänge; *imp.* schwing(e); *p.p.* geschwungen.

schwören *prs.* schwöre, schwörst, schwört; *pret.* schwor (schwur), schwor(e)st (schwur[e]st); *subj.* schwüre; *imp.* schwör(e); *p.p.* geschworen.

sehen *prs.* sehe, siehst, sieht; *pret.* sah; *subj.* sähe; *imp.* sieh(e); *p.p.* gesehen.

sein *prs.* bin, bist, ist; sind, seid, sind; *subj.* prs. sei, sei(e)st, sei; seien, seiet, seien; *pret.* war, warst, war; waren; *subj. pret.* wäre; *imp.* sei; seid; *p.p.* gewesen.

senden *prs.* sende, sendest, sendet; *pret.* sandte (*bsd. Radio*: sendete); *subj.* sendete; *imp.* send(e); *p.p.* gesandt (*bsd. Radio*: gesendet).

sieden *prs.* siede, siedest, siedet; *pret.* sott (siedete), sottest; *subj.* sötte (siedete); *imp.* sied(e); *p.p.* gesotten (gesiedet).

singen *prs.* singe, singst, singt; *pret.* sang, sangst; *subj.* sänge; *imp.* sing(e); *p.p.* gesungen.

sinken *prs.* sinke, sinkst, sinkt; *pret.* sank, sankst; *subj.* sänke; *imp.* sink(e); *p.p.* gesunken.

sinnen *prs.* sinne, sinnst, sinnt;

pret. sann, sannst; *subj.* sänne; *imp.* sinn(e); *p.p.* gesonnen.

sitzen *prs.* sitze, sitzt, sitzt; *pret.* saß, saßest; *subj.* säße; *imp.* sitz(e); *p.p.* gesessen.

sollen *prs.* soll, sollst, soll; *pret.* sollte; *subj.* sollte; *imp.* —; *p.p.* gesollt (*auxiliary verb:* sollen).

speien *prs.* speie, speist, speit; *pret.* spie; *subj.* spiee; *imp.* spei(e); *p.p.* gespie(e)n.

spinnen *prs.* spinne, spinnst, spinnt; *pret.* spann, spannst; *subj.* spönne (spänne); *imp.* spinn(e); *p.p.* gesponnen.

sprechen *prs.* spreche, sprichst, spricht; *pret.* sprach, sprachst; *subj.* spräche; *imp.* sprich; *p.p.* gesprochen.

sprießen *prs.* sprieße, sprießt, sprießt; *pret.* sproß, sprossest; *subj.* sprösse; *imp.* sprieß(e); *p.p.* gesprossen.

springen *prs.* springe, springst, springt; *pret.* sprang, sprangst; *subj.* spränge; *imp.* spring(e); *p.p.* gesprungen.

stechen *prs.* steche, stichst, sticht; *pret.* stach, stachst; *subj.* stäche; *imp.* stich; *p.p.* gestochen.

stecken (*v/i.*) *prs.* stecke, steckst, steckt; *pret.* stak (steckte); *subj.* stäke (steckte); *imp.* steck(e); *p.p.* gesteckt.

stehen *prs.* stehe, stehst, steht; *pret.* stand, standst; *subj.* stände (stünde); *imp.* steh(e); *p.p.* gestanden.

stehlen *prs.* stehle, stiehlst, stiehlt; *pret.* stahl, stahlst; *subj.* stähle; *imp.* stiehl; *p.p.* gestohlen.

steigen *prs.* steige, steigst, steigt; *pret.* stieg, stiegst; *subj.* stiege; *imp.* steig(e); *p.p.* gestiegen.

sterben *prs.* sterbe, stirbst, stirbt; *pret.* starb; *subj.* stürbe; *imp.* stirb; *p.p.* gestorben.

stieben *prs.* stiebe, stiebst, stiebt; *pret.* stob (stiebte), stobst; *subj.* stöbe (*rarely:* stiebte); *imp.* stieb(e); *p.p.* gestoben (gestiebt).

stinken *prs.* stinke, stinkst, stinkt; *pret.* stank, stankst; *subj.* stänke; *imp.* stink(e); *p.p.* gestunken.

stoßen *prs.* stoße, stößt, stößt; *pret.* stieß, stießest; *subj.* stieße; *imp.* stoß(e); *p.p.* gestoßen.

streichen *prs.* streiche, streichst, streicht; *pret.* strich, strichst; *subj.* striche; *imp.* streich(e); *p.p.* gestrichen.

streiten *prs.* streite, streitest, streitet; *pret.* stritt, stritt(e)st; *subj.* stritte; *imp.* streit(e); *p.p.* gestritten.

tragen *prs.* trage, trägst, trägt; *pret.* trug; *subj.* trüge; *imp.* trag(e); *p.p.* getragen.

treffen *prs.* treffe, triffst, trifft; *pret.* traf, trafst; *subj.* träfe; *imp.* triff; *p.p.* getroffen.

treiben *prs.* treibe, treibst, treibt; *pret.* trieb; *subj.* triebe; *imp.* treib(e); *p.p.* getrieben.

treten *prs.* trete, trittst, tritt; *pret.* trat, trat(e)st; *subj.* träte; *imp.* tritt; *p.p.* getreten.

triefen *prs.* triefe, triefst, trieft; *pret.* triefte (troff), trieftest (troffst); *subj.* triefte (tröffe) *imp.* trief(e); *p.p.* getrieft.

trinken *prs.* trinke, trinkst, trinkt; *pret.* trank, trankst; *subj.* tränke; *imp.* trink(e); *p.p.* getrunken.

trügen *prs.* trüge, trügst, trügt; *pret.* trog, trogst; *subj.* tröge; *imp.* trüg(e); *p.p.* getrogen.

tun *prs.* tue, tust, tut; *wir* tun etc.; *pret.* tat, tat(e)st; *subj.* täte; *imp.* tu(e); *p.p.* getan.

verderben *prs.* verderbe, verdirbst, verdirbt; *pret.* verdarb; *subj.* verdürbe; *imp.* verdirb; *p.p.* verdorben.

verdrießen *prs.* verdrieße, verdrießt, verdrießt; *pret.* verdroß, verdrossest; *subj.* verdrösse; *imp.* verdrieß(e); *p.p.* verdrossen.

vergessen *prs.* vergesse, vergißt, vergißt; *pret.* vergaß, vergaßest; *subj.* vergäße; *imp.* vergiß; *p.p.* vergessen.

verlieren *prs.* verliere, verlierst, verliert; *pret.* verlor; *subj.* verlöre; *imp.* verlier(e); *p.p.* verloren.

wachsen *prs.* wachse, wächst, wächst; *pret.* wuchs, wuchsest; *subj.* wüchse; *imp.* wachs(e); *p.p.* gewachsen.

wägen (er~) *prs.* wäge, wägst, wägt; *pret.* wog; *subj.* wöge; *imp.* wäg(e); *p.p.* gewogen.

waschen *prs.* wasche, wäschst, wäscht; *pret.* wusch, wuschest; *subj.* wüsche; *imp.* wasch(e); *p.p.* gewaschen.

weben *prs.* webe, webst, webt; *pret.*
webte (wob), webtest (wobst);
subj. webte (wöbe); *imp.* web(e);
p.p. gewebt (gewoben).

weichen *prs.* weiche, weichst, weicht;
pret. wich, wichst; *subj.* wiche;
imp. weich(e); *p.p.* gewichen.

weisen *prs.* weise, weist, weist;
pret. wies, wiesest; *subj.* wiese;
imp. weis(e); *p.p.* gewiesen.

wenden *prs.* wende, wendest, wen-
det; *pret.* wandte (wendete); *subj.*
wendete; *imp.* wende; *p.p.* gewandt (gewendet).

werben *prs.* werbe, wirbst, wirbt;
pret. warb; *subj.* würbe; *imp.*
wirb; *p.p.* geworben.

werden *prs.* werde, wirst, wird;
pret. wurde (*poet.* ward); *subj.*
würde; *imp.* werde; *p.p.* geworden
(worden)*).

werfen *prs.* werfe, wirfst, wirft;
pret. warf, warfst; *subj.* würfe;
imp. wirf; *p.p.* geworfen.

wiegen *prs.* wiege, wiegst, wiegt;
pret. wog; *subj.* wöge; *imp.*
wieg(e); *p.p.* gewogen.

winden *prs.* winde, windest, windet;
pret. wand, wandest; *subj.* wände;
imp. winde; *p.p.* gewunden.

wissen *prs.* weiß, weißt, weiß; *pl.*
wissen, wißt, wissen; *pret.* wußte;
subj. wüßte; *imp.* wisse; *p.p.* gewußt.

wollen *prs.* will, willst, will; *pl.*
wollen, wollt, wollen; *pret.*
wollte; *subj.* wollte; *imp.* wolle;
p.p. gewollt (*auxiliary verb:* wollen).

wringen *s.* ringen.

zeihen *prs.* zeihe, zeihst, zeiht;
pret. zieh, ziehst; *subj.* ziehe;
imp. zeih(e); *p.p.* geziehen.

ziehen *prs.* ziehe, ziehst, zieht; *pret.*
zog, zogst; *subj.* zöge; *imp.* zieh(e);
p.p. gezogen.

zwingen *prs.* zwinge, zwingst,
zwingt; *pret.* zwang, zwangst;
subj. zwänge; *imp.* zwing(e); *p.p.*
gezwungen.

*) only in connection with the *p.p.* of other verbs, e.g. er ist gesehen
worden.

Phonetic Alphabets

Buchstabieralphabete

	German	British English	American English	International	ICAO
A	Anton	Andrew	Abel	Amsterdam	Alfa
Ä	Ärger	—	—	—	—
B	Berta	Benjamin	Baker	Baltimore	Bravo
C	Cäsar	Charlie	Charlie	Casablanca	Charlie
CH	Charlotte	—	—	—	—
D	Dora	David	Dog	Danemark	Delta
E	Emil	Edward	Easy	Edison	Echo
F	Friedrich	Frederick	Fox	Florida	Foxtrot
G	Gustav	George	George	Gallipoli	Golf
H	Heinrich	Harry	How	Havana	Hotel
I	Ida	Isaac	Item	Italia	India
J	Julius	Jack	Jig	Jérusalem	Juliett
K	Kaufmann	King	King	Kilogramme	Kilo
L	Ludwig	Lucy	Love	Liverpool	Lima
M	Martha	Mary	Mike	Madagaskar	Mike
N	Nordpol	Nellie	Nan	New York	November
O	Otto	Oliver	Oboe	Oslo	Oscar
Ö	Ökonom	—	—	—	—
P	Paula	Peter	Peter	Paris	Papa
Q	Quelle	Queenie	Queen	Québec	Quebec
R	Richard	Robert	Roger	Roma	Romeo
S	Samuel	Sugar	Sugar	Santiago	Sierra
Sch	Schule	—	—	—	—
T	Theodor	Tommy	Tare	Tripoli	Tango
U	Ulrich	Uncle	Uncle	Upsala	Uniform
Ü	Übermut	—	—	—	—
V	Viktor	Victor	Victor	Valencia	Victor
W	Wilhelm	William	William	Washington	Whiskey
X	Xanthippe	Xmas	X	Xanthippe	X-Ray
Y	Ypsilon	Yellow	Yoke	Yokohama	Yankee
Z	Zacharias	Zebra	Zebra	Zürich	Zulu